SCOTT®

# 2019 STANDARD POSTAGE STAMP CATALOGUE

**ONE HUNDRED AND SEVENTY-FIFTH EDITION IN SIX VOLUMES**

## VOLUME 5A

### N-PHIL



Released August 2018
Includes New Stamp Listings through the June 2018 *Linn's Stamp News Monthly* Catalogue Update



AMOS MEDIA

911 Vandemark Road, Sidney, OH 45365-4129
Publishers of *Linn's Stamp News, Linn's Stamp News Monthly, Coin World* and *Coin World Monthly.*

# Table of Contents



See the following volumes for other country listings:
Volume 1A: United States, United Nations, Abu Dhabi-Australia; Volume 1B: Austria-B
Volume 2A: C-Cur; Volume 2B: Cyp-F
Volume 3A: G; Volume 3B: H-I
Volume 4A: J-L; Volume 4B: M
Volume 5B: Pit-Sam
Volume 6A: San-Tete; Volume 6B: Thai-Z

**Scott Catalogue Mission Statement**

The Scott Catalogue Team exists to serve the recreational, educational and commercial hobby needs of stamp collectors and dealers.

We strive to set the industry standard for philatelic information and products by developing and providing goods that help collectors identify, value, organize and present their collections.

Quality customer service is, and will continue to be, our highest priority. We aspire toward achieving total customer satisfaction.



ISBN 978-0-89487-552-6

Library of Congress Card No. 2-3301

# Vols. 5A-5B Number Additions, Deletions & Changes

### Natal

| Number in 2018 Catalogue | Number in 2019 Catalogue |
|---|---|
| new | 72b |

### Nepal

| Number in 2018 Catalogue | Number in 2019 Catalogue |
|---|---|
| new | 12B |

### Netherlands

| Number in 2018 Catalogue | Number in 2019 Catalogue |
|---|---|
| new | 243Cs |
| new | 243Et |
| new | 243Hu |
| new | 599a |
| new | 608a |
| new | 844b |
| new | 845b |
| new | 845c |
| new | 974a |
| new | 975a |
| new | 990a |
| new | B683a |
| new | B684a |
| new | B685b |

### Netherlands Antilles

| Number in 2018 Catalogue | Number in 2019 Catalogue |
|---|---|
| new | 746a |
| new | 749a |
| new | 1193a |

### Netherlands Indies

| Number in 2018 Catalogue | Number in 2019 Catalogue |
|---|---|
| new | 21a |
| new | 47a |
| new | 58a |
| new | 79b |
| new | 79c |
| new | 79d |
| new | 131c |
| new | 146a |
| new | 151c |
| new | 152c |
| new | 301b |
| new | 318a |
| new | 319a |
| new | 320a |
| new | 322a |
| new | 323a |
| new | 325a |
| new | 326a |

### New Zealand

| Number in 2018 Catalogue | Number in 2019 Catalogue |
|---|---|
| new | 37c |
| new | 39a |
| new | 39b |
| new | 44c |
| new | 44d |
| new | 46a |
| new | 51c |
| new | 51fg |
| new | 51i |
| new | 52 |
| new | 52c |
| new | 52fg |
| new | 52fh |
| new | 52i |
| new | 53fg |
| new | 54fg |
| new | 54i |
| new | 55fg |
| new | 55i |
| new | 56fg |
| new | 56i |
| new | 67d |
| new | 91b |
| new | 99Bc |
| new | 99Bd |
| new | 99Be |
| new | 99Bf |
| new | 99Bg |
| new | 100c |
| new | 100d |
| new | 100e |
| new | 100f |
| new | 100g |
| new | 101c |
| new | 102a |
| new | 102c |
| new | 102d |
| new | 102e |
| new | 102f |
| new | 103b |
| new | 103c |
| new | 103d |
| new | 103e |
| new | 103f |

### New Zealand

| Number in 2018 Catalogue | Number in 2019 Catalogue |
|---|---|
| new | 104a |
| new | 104b |
| new | 104c |
| new | 104d |
| new | 105b |
| new | 105c |
| new | 105d |
| new | 107e |
| new | 107i |
| new | 107j |
| new | 107k |
| new | 108k |
| new | 108l |
| new | 108m |
| new | 108o |
| new | 109i |
| new | 109k |
| new | 110i |
| new | 110k |
| new | 111e |
| new | 112a |
| new | 112e |
| new | 112i |
| new | 112k |
| new | 113b |
| new | 113e |
| new | 113f |
| new | 113i |
| new | 113k |
| new | 114e |
| new | 114i |
| new | 114k |
| new | 115e |
| new | 115h |
| new | 115i |
| new | 115k |
| new | 116e |
| new | 116g |
| new | 116h |
| new | 116i |
| new | 116k |
| new | 117e |
| new | 117i |
| new | 117k |
| new | 118e |
| new | 119e |
| new | 119k |
| new | 120e |
| new | 120i |
| new | 120k |
| new | 121b |
| new | 126a |
| new | 126b |
| new | 127a |
| new | 127b |
| new | 128a |
| new | 133a |
| new | 133b |
| new | 133c |
| new | 134a |
| new | 136a |
| new | 136b |
| new | 136c |
| new | 137a |
| new | 137b |
| new | 137c |
| new | 138a |
| new | 138b |
| new | 138c |
| new | 139a |
| new | 145a |
| new | 145b |
| new | 146a |
| new | 146b |
| new | 147a |
| new | 147b |
| new | 148b |
| new | 149b |
| new | 150b |
| new | 151a |
| new | 151b |
| new | 152a |
| new | 152b |
| new | 153b |
| new | 153c |
| new | 154b |
| new | 154c |
| new | 155a |
| new | 155b |
| new | 156a |
| new | 156b |

### New Zealand

| Number in 2018 Catalogue | Number in 2019 Catalogue |
|---|---|
| new | 158b |
| new | 158c |
| new | 159b |
| new | 159c |
| new | 162a |
| new | 163a |
| new | 164a |
| new | 184c |
| new | 186c |
| new | 187a |
| new | 189a |
| new | 192a |
| new | 197a |
| new | 198a |
| new | 207a |
| new | 207b |
| new | 209b |
| new | 209c |
| new | 210b |
| new | 211b |
| new | 212b |
| new | 215c |
| new | 216b |

### Nicaragua

| Number in 2018 Catalogue | Number in 2019 Catalogue |
|---|---|
| new | 365Dg |
| new | 1102 |
| new | 1102A-1102E |
| mew | 1102f-1102k |

### Philippines

| Number in 2018 Catalogue | Number in 2019 Catalogue |
|---|---|
| new | 1050a |
| new | 1531a |
| new | 1532a |
| new | 1544a |
| new | 1546a |
| new | 1577a |
| new | 1579a |
| new | 1580a |
| newe | 1583a |
| new | 1587a |
| new | 1588a |
| new | 1589a |
| new | 1590a |
| new | 1591a |
| new | 1592a |
| new | 1593a |
| new | 1594a |
| new | 1595a |
| new | 1599a |
| new | 1599c |
| new | 1600c-1600e |
| new | 1601a |
| new | 1603a |
| new | 1604a |
| new | 1605A |
| new | 1608a |
| new | 1609a |
| new | 1610a |
| new | 1611a |
| new | 1612a |
| new | 1618a |
| new | 1619a-1619b |
| new | 1622a |
| new | 1624a |
| new | 1625a-1625b |
| new | 1626a-1626b |
| new | 1627a-1627b |
| new | 1628a-1628b |
| new | 1629a-1629b |
| new | 1630a |
| new | 1631a |
| new | 1632a |
| new | 1633a-1633c |
| new | 1636a |
| new | 1637a |
| new | 1638a |
| new | 1639a |
| new | 1640a |
| new | 1641a |
| new | 1642a |
| 1643a | 1643b |
| new | 1643a-1643o |
| new | 1646g |
| new | 1646h-l |
| new | 1647a |
| new | 1648a |
| new | 1649a |
| new | 1650a |
| new | 1653f |
| new | 1653g-k |

### Philippines

| Number in 2018 Catalogue | Number in 2019 Catalogue |
|---|---|
| new | 1654a |
| new | 1661a-1661b |
| new | 1662a |
| new | 1663a |
| new | 1664a-1664b |
| new | 1665a-1665c |
| new | 1666b |
| new | 1669a |
| new | 1675a-1675c |
| new | 1680a |
| new | 1681a-1681b |
| new | 1682a |
| new | 1683a-1683b |
| new | 1686a |
| new | 1690C |
| new | 1690Ca-d |
| new | 1713a |
| new | 1734k |
| new | 1734l-p |
| new | 1734q-u |
| new | 1740a |
| new | 1741a |
| new | 1742a |
| new | 1743a |
| new | 1744a-1744c |
| new | 1745a |
| new | 1749a |
| new | 1754a |
| new | 1767a |
| new | 1776a |
| new | 1777a |
| new | 1780a |
| new | 1781a |
| new | 1783e |
| new | 1783f-j |
| new | 1784e |
| new | 1784f-j |
| new | 1785c |
| new | 1785d-e |
| new | 1786a |
| new | 1787a |
| new | 1788a |
| new | 1789a |
| new | 1790a |
| new | 1791a |
| new | 1793a |
| new | 1794a |
| new | 1795a |
| new | 1796a |
| new | 1797a |
| new | 1798a |
| new | 1799a |
| new | 1906a |
| new | 1910a |
| new | 1911a |
| new | 1912a |
| new | 1922a |
| new | 1923a |
| new | B8a |
| new | B9a |
| new | B12b |
| new | B13a |

### Portugal

| Number in 2018 Catalogue | Number in 2019 Catalogue |
|---|---|
| new | 1124a-1124d |
| new | 1125a-1125d |
| new | 1126a-1126c |
| new | 1127a-1127b |
| new | 1128a-1128b |
| new | 1129a-1129b |
| new | 1130a-1130b |
| new | 1131a-1131c |
| new | 1132a-1132c |
| new | 1133a-1133c |
| new | 1134a |
| new | 1209a-1209c |
| new | 1212a-1212b |
| new | 1213a |
| new | 1214a |
| new | J14a |
| new | J15a |
| new | J17a |
| new | J18a |
| new | J19a |

### St. Kitts-Nevis

| Number in 2018 Catalogue | Number in 2019 Catalogue |
|---|---|
| new | 100b |

### Samoa

| Number in 2018 Catalogue | Number in 2019 Catalogue |
|---|---|
| 1275-1284 | 1278-1287 |

# Acknowledgments

Our appreciation and gratitude go to the following individuals who have assisted us in preparing information included in this year's Scott Catalogues. Some helpers prefer anonymity. These individuals have generously shared their stamp knowledge with others through the medium of the Scott Catalogue.

Those who follow provided information that is in addition to the hundreds of dealer price lists and advertisements and scores of auction catalogues and realizations that were used in producing the catalogue values. It is from those noted here that we have been able to obtain information on items not normally seen in published lists and advertisements. Support from these people goes beyond data leading to catalogue values, for they also are key to editorial changes.

A special acknowledgment to Liane and Sergio Sismondo of The Classic Collector for their assistance and knowledge sharing that have aided in the preparation of this year's Standard and Classic Specialized Catalogues.

Roland Austin
Jim Bardo (Bardo Stamps)
William Barclay (South Sudan Philatelic Society)
John Birkinbine II
Helmut Blaschczyk
Roger S. Brody
Tina & John Carlson (JET Stamps)
Henry Chlanda
Bob Coale
David & Julia Crawford
Tony L. Crumbley (Carolina Coin & Stamp, Inc.)
Chris de Haer
Christopher Dahle
Tony Davis
Ubaldo Del Toro
Leon Djerahian
Bob & Rita Dumaine (Sam Houston Duck Co.)
Sister Theresa Durand
Paul G. Eckman
George Epstein (Allkor Stamp Co.)
Robert A. Fisher
Jeffrey M. Forster
Richard Frajola
Robert S. Freeman
Ernest E. Fricks
Michael Fuchs
Bob Genisol (Sultan Stamp Center)
Stan Goldfarb
Allen Grant (Rushstamps (Retail) Ltd.)
Daniel E. Grau
Robin Harris
Bruce Hecht (Bruce L. Hecht Co.)
Peter Hoffman
John Hotchner
Armen Hovsepian (Armenstamp)
Doug Iams
Eric Jackson
John Jamieson (Saskatoon Stamp and Coin)
Peter Jeannopoulos
William A. Jones
Allan Katz (Ventura Stamp Co.)
Lewis Kaufman (The Philatelic Foundation)
Patricia Kaufmann (Confederate Stamp Alliance)
Jon Kawaguchi (Ryukyu Philatelic Specialist Society)
Roland Kretschmer
William V. Kriebel (Brazil Philatelic Association)
Frederick P. Lawrence
John R. Lewis (The William Henry Stamp Co.)
Ulf Lindahl
Ignacio Llach (Filatelia Llach S.L.)
Marilyn R. Mattke
William K. McDaniel
Mauricio Mejia
Gary Morris (Pacific Midwest Co.)
Peter Mosiondz, Jr.
Bruce M. Moyer (Moyer Stamps & Collectibles)
Richard H. Muller
Scott Murphy (Professional Stamp Experts)
Leonard Nadybal
Dr. Tiong Tak Ngo
Gerald Nylander
Nik & Lisa Oquist
Dr. Everett Parker
Don Peterson (International Philippine Philatelic Society)
Stanley M. Piller (Stanley M. Piller & Associates)
Virgil Pirvulescu
Todor Drumev Popov
Peter W. W. Powell
Bob Prager (Gary Posner, Inc.)
Siddique Mahmudur Rahman
Ghassan D. Riachi
Mehrdad Sadri (Persiphila)
Sabah Jawad Salih
Theodosios Sampson PhD
Alexander Schauss (Schauss Philatelics)
Michael Schreiber
Jeff Siddiqui
Sergio & Liane Sismondo (The Classic Collector)
Jay Smith
Kenneth Thompson
Peter Thy
Scott R. Trepel (Robert A. Siegel Auction Galleries, Inc.)
Dan Undersander (United Postal Stationery Society)
Herbert R. Volin
Philip T. Wall
Giana Wayman
Don White (Dunedin Stamp Centre)
Ralph Yorio
Val Zabijaka
Michal Zika

SCOTT

# What's new for 2019 Scott Standard Volume 5A?

Greetings, Fellow Scott Catalog User:

This year celebrates another milestone in the 150-year history of the Scott catalogs. The 2019 volumes are the 175th edition of the Scott *Standard Postage Stamp Catalogue*. Vol. 5A includes listings for countries of the world N through the Philippines. Listings for countries of the world Pitcairn Islands through Samoa can be found in Vol. 5B.

Many value changes were made in Vol. 5A for the stamps issued by the Netherlands and its colonies. Most of these changes resulted in increases in values. A thorough review of the **Netherlands** resulted in more than 2,750 value changes. The booklet pane of six of the 1941 2½¢ dark green Gull stamp (Scott 243Ab) climbs from $10 mint never-hinged to $15. The 1926 Arms set with syncopated perforations (type A), Scott B12a-B15a, rose in value, from $40 both unused and used to $45 unused. The used value slid downward slightly, to $38.75. The 1931 36¢ orange-red and dark blue Queen Wilhelmina airmail stamp (C9) jumps from $10 unused to $13, and from 60¢ used to 75¢.

The Netherlands 1931 36¢ orange-red and dark blue Queen Wilhelmina airmail stamp (Scott C9) jumps from $10 unused to $13, and from 60¢ used to 75¢.

**Netherlands Antilles** also received a complete review, resulting in more than 3,100 value changes, the majority of which are increases. The set values for the 1873-79 first-issue King William II stamps (Scott 1-7) increase substantially, from $214.25 unused to $267, and from $197 used to $213.40. The 1996 Capex 96 souvenir sheet of two (768a) rises from $4.75 mint to $7.50, and from $4.75 used to $5.75.

A complete review of **Netherlands Indies** resulted in more than 1,060 value changes. The 1902 2.50-gulden on 2½g brown lilac surcharged in black (Scott 37) dramatically increases in value, from $45 unused to $70, and from $11 used to $20. The normal stamp is perforated gauge 11½ by 11. The perforated gauge 11 variety (37a) climbs upward in value, from $50 unused to $72.50, and from $12.50 used to $24. The 1948 set of 10 overprinted "INDONESIA" (294-303) increases in value, from $166.45 mint to $223.60, and from $73.95 used to $90.15. The 1949 2½g red orange with the same overprint (304) more than doubles in value for a mint example, from $20 to $52.50. The value for used examples jumps from $7.25 to 9.75. The values for the 1931 1g blue and brown airmail stamp (C13) increase from $11 both unused and used, to $16 unused and $18 used.

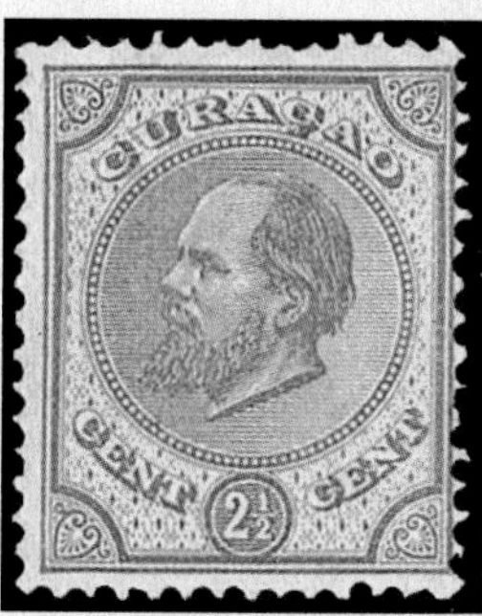

Set values for the Netherlands Antilles 1873-79 first-issue King William II stamps (Scott 1-7) increase substantially, from $214.25 unused to $267, and from $197 used to $213.40.

**Netherlands New Guinea** also received a line-by-line overview, resulting in more than 100 value changes; most are increases, with scattered decreases throughout. The 1953 5¢-on-5¢ ultramarine semipostal stamp (Scott B1) moves upward, from $10 unused to $12, and from $8 used to $9.50.

Values for classic **Nepal** increase significantly. The 1881 1-anna ultramarine stamp (Scott 1) soars in value, from $300 unused to $575, and from $475 used to $650. The value for the 1881 4a green (3) moves upward, from $500 unused to $650, and from $650 used to $2,500. A footnote states that "No. 3 postally used is probably unique." The value is in italics, to designate that this stamp seldom trades and is difficult to value.

Nepal's 1881 1-anna ultramarine stamp (Scott 1) soars in value, from $300 unused to $575, and from $475 used to $650.

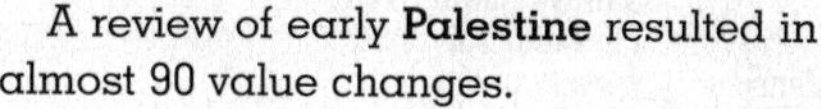

A review of early **Palestine** resulted in almost 90 value changes.

***Editorial enhancements for Vol. 5A***

**Nepal:** The 1898 ½-anna black with blurry impressions was added as major number 12B.

**Netherlands:** Several footnotes within the Netherlands listings were expanded and updated. Particularly noteworthy are newly added footnotes for coil stamps that were made from sheet stamps.

**Netherlands Antilles:** Two new minor listings were added to Netherlands Antilles. Scott 746a and 749a are assigned to the 1995 Flags issue with the colors in the flag of St. Martin reversed. The flag varieties show the blue on top, red on bottom. A new explanatory footnote states: "Both were quickly withdrawn from sale after the error was discovered. ..." Also new among the Netherlands Antilles listings is the 2008 Shells 106¢ stamp without the country name. This variety has been assigned minor number 1193a.

**Netherlands Indies:** Numerous perforation varieties were added to the islands now known as Indonesia.

**Nicaragua:** For many years, the Scott editors have reserved numbers for a set of six stamps overprinted in red or silver for the Year of Liberation and the 1980 Olympic Games. The stamps with the red overprint are now listed as Scott 1102 and 1102A-1102E. The stamps with silver overprints are assigned minor numbers 1102f-1102k. Nos. 1102f-1102k were not issued without the overprints.

**Philippines:** Many editorial changes have been installed, including minor number listings for a watermark variety that has been added to the catalog.

As always, we encourage you to pay special attention to the Number Additions, Deletions & Changes found on page 3A in this volume. We also suggest reading the catalog introduction, which includes an abundance of useful information.

Set time aside each day to enjoy this wonderful hobby!

Donna Houseman

Donna Houseman/Catalogue Editor

# Addresses, Telephone Numbers, Web Sites, E-Mail Addresses of General & Specialized Philatelic Societies

Collectors can contact the following groups for information about the philately of the areas within the scope of these societies, or inquire about membership in these groups. Aside from the general societies, we limit this list to groups that specialize in particular fields of philately, particular areas covered by the Scott Standard Postage Stamp Catalogue, and topical groups. Many more specialized philatelic society exist than those listed below. These addresses are updated yearly, and they are, to the best of our knowledge, correct and current. Groups should inform the editors of address changes whenever they occur. The editors also want to hear from other such specialized groups not listed. Unless otherwise noted all website addresses begin with http://

**American Philatelic Society**
100 Match Factory Place
Bellefonte PA 16823-1367
Ph: (814) 933-3803
www.stamps.org
E-mail: apsinfo@stamps.org

**American Stamp Dealers Association, Inc.**
P.O. Box 692
Leesport PA 19553
Ph: (800) 369-8207
www.americanstampdealer.com
E-mail: asda@americanstampdealer.com

**National Stamp Dealers Association**
Richard Kostka, President
3643 Private Road 18
Pinckneyville IL 62274-3426
Ph: (800) 875-6633 or (618) 357-5497
www.nsdainc.org
E-mail: nsda@nsdainc.org

**International Society of Worldwide Stamp Collectors**
Joanne Berkowitz, MD
P.O. Box 19006
Sacramento CA 95819
www.iswsc.org
E-mail: executivedirector@iswsc.org

**Royal Philatelic Society**
41 Devonshire Place
London, W1G 6JY
UNITED KINGDOM
www.rpsl.org.uk
E-mail: secretary@rpsl.org.uk

**Royal Philatelic Society of Canada**
P.O. Box 69080
St. Clair Post Office
Toronto, ON, M4T 3A1
CANADA
Ph: (888) 285-4143
www.rpsc.org
E-mail: info@rpsc.org

**Young Stamp Collectors of America**
Janet Houser
100 Match Factory Place
Bellefonte PA 16823-1367
Ph: (814) 933-3820
www.stamps.org/ysca/intro.htm
E-mail: ysca@stamps.org

## Philatelic Research Resources

(The Scott editors encourage any additional research organizations to submit data for inclusion in this listing category.)

**American Philatelic Research Library**
Scott Tiffney
100 Match Factory Place
Bellefonte PA 16823
Ph: (814) 933-3803
www.stamplibrary.org
E-mail: library@stamps.org

**Institute for Analytical Philately, Inc.**
P.O. Box 8035
Holland MI 49422-8035
Ph: (616) 399-9299
www.analyticalphilately.org
E-mail: info@analyticalphilately.org

**The Western Philatelic Library**
P.O. Box 2219
1500 Partridge Ave.
Sunnyvale CA 94087
Ph: (408) 733-0336
www.fwpf.org

## Groups focusing on fields or aspects found in worldwide philately (some might cover U.S. area only)

**American Air Mail Society**
Stephen Reinhard
P.O. Box 110
Mineola NY 11501
www.americanairmailsociety.org
E-mail: sreinhard1@optonline.net

**American First Day Cover Society**
Douglas Kelsey
P.O. Box 16277
Tucson AZ 85732-6277
Ph: (520) 321-0880
www.afdcs.org
E-mail: afdcs@afdcs.org

**American Revenue Association**
Eric Jackson
P.O. Box 728
Leesport PA 19533-0728
Ph: (610) 926-6200
www.revenuer.org
E-mail: eric@revenuer.com

**American Topical Association**
Vera Felts
P.O. Box 8
Carterville IL 62918-0008
Ph: (618) 985-5100
www.americantopicalassn.org
E-mail: americantopical@msn.com

**Christmas Seal & Charity Stamp Society**
John Denune
234 E. Broadway
Granville OH 43023
Ph: (740) 587-0276
www.seal-society.org
E-mail: john@christmasseals.net

**Errors, Freaks and Oddities Collectors Club**
Scott Shaulis
P.O. Box 549
Murrysville PA 15668-0549
Ph: (724) 733-4134
www.efocc.org
E-mail: Scott@shaulisstamps.com

**First Issues Collectors Club**
Kurt Streepy, Secretary
3128 E. Mattatha Drive
Bloomington IN 47401
www.firstissues.org
E-mail: secretary@firstissues.org

**International Society of Reply Coupon Collectors**
Peter Robin
P.O. Box 353
Bala Cynwyd PA 19004
E-mail: peterrobin@verizon.net

**The Joint Stamp Issues Society**
Richard Zimmermann
29A Rue Des Eviats
Lalaye F-67220
FRANCE
www.philarz.net
E-mail: richard.zimmermann@club-internet.fr

**National Duck Stamp Collectors Society**
Anthony J. Monico
P.O. Box 43
Harleysville PA 19438-0043
www.ndscs.org
E-mail: ndscs@ndscs.org

**No Value Identified Club**
Albert Sauvanet
Le Clos Royal B, Boulevard des Pas Enchantes
St. Sebastien-sur Loire, 44230
FRANCE
E-mail: alain.vailly@irin.univ nantes.fr

**The Perfins Club**
Ken Masters
111 NW 94th Street Apt. 102
Kansas City MO 64155-2993
Ph: (816) 835-5907
www.perfins.org
E-mail: kmasters@aol.com

**Postage Due Mail Study Group**
John Rawlins
13, Longacre
Chelmsford, CM1 3BJ
UNITED KINGDOM
E-mail: john.rawlins2@ukonline.co.uk

**Post Mark Collectors Club**
Bob Milligan
7014 Woodland Oaks
Magnolia TX 77354
Ph: (281) 259-2735
www.postmarks.org
E-mail: bob.milligan@gmail.net

**Postal History Society**
Gary Wayne Loew
P.O. Box 468101
Atlanta GA 31146-8101
www.postalhistorysociety.org
E-mail: garywloew@gmail.com

**Precancel Stamp Society**
Dick Kalmbach
2658 Iron Works Drive
Buford GA 30519
Ph: (610) 248-8844
www.precancels.com
E-mail: promo@precancels.com

**United Postal Stationery Society**
Stuart Leven
1659 Branham Lane Suite F-307
San Jose CA 95118-2291
www.upss.org
E-mail: poststat@gmail.com

**United States Possessions Philatelic Society**
Daniel F. Ring
P.O. Box 113
Woodstock IL 60098
www.uspps.net
E-mail: danielfring@hotmail.com

## Groups focusing on U.S. area philately as covered in the Standard Catalogue

**Canal Zone Study Group**
Tom Brougham
737 Neilson St.
Berkeley CA 94707
www.CanalZoneStudyGroup.com
E-mail: czsgsecretary@gmail.com

**Carriers and Locals Society**
Martin Richardson
P.O. Box 74
Grosse Ile MI 48138
www.pennypost.org
E-mail: martinr362@aol.com

**Confederate Stamp Alliance**
Patricia A. Kaufmann
10194 N. Old State Road
Lincoln DE 19960
Ph. (302) 422-2656
www.csalliance.org
E-mail: trishkauf@comcast.net

**Hawaiian Philatelic Society**
Gawwon Sugimura
P.O. Box 10115
Honolulu HI 96816-0115
E-mail: hiphilsoc@gmail.com

**Plate Number Coil Collectors Club**
Gene Trinks
16415 W. Desert Wren Court
Surprise AZ 85374
Ph: (623) 322-4619
www.pnc3.org
E-mail: gctrinks@cox.net

**Ryukyu Philatelic Specialist Society**
Laura Edmonds, Secy.
P.O. Box 240177
Charlotte NC 28224-0177
Ph: (336) 509-3739
www.ryukyustamps.org
E-mail: secretary@ryukyustamps.org

**United Nations Philatelists**
Blanton Clement, Jr.
P.O. Box 146
Morrisville PA 19067-0146
www.unpi.com
E-mail: bclemjunior@gmail.com

**United States Stamp Society**
Executive Secretary
Larry Ballantyne
P.O. Box 6634
Katy TX 77491-6634
www.usstamps.org

**U.S. Cancellation Club**
Roger Curran
20 University Avenue
Lewisburg PA 17837
E-mail: rcurran@dejazzd.com

**U.S. Philatelic Classics Society**
Rob Lund
2913 Fulton St.
Everett WA 98201-3733
www.uspcs.org
E-mail: membershipchairman@uspcs.org

## Groups focusing on philately of foreign countries or regions

**Aden & Somaliland Study Group**
Gary Brown
P.O. Box 106
Briar Hill, Victoria, 3088
AUSTRALIA
E-mail: garyjohn951@optushome.com.au

**American Society of Polar Philatelists (Antarctic areas)**
Alan Warren
P.O. Box 39
Exton PA 19341-0039
www.polarphilatelists.org

**Andorran Philatelic Study Circle**
D. Hope
17 Hawthorn Drive
Stalybridge, Cheshire, SK15 1UE
UNITED KINGDOM
www.andorranpsc.org.uk
E-mail: andorranpsc@btinternet.com

**Australian States Study Circle of The Royal Sydney Philatelic Club**
Ben Palmer
GPO 1751
Sydney, N.S.W., 2001
AUSTRALIA
www.philas.org.au/states

**Austria Philatelic Society**
Ralph Schneider
P.O. Box 23049
Belleville IL 62223
Ph: (618) 277-6152
www.austriaphilatelicsociety.com
E-mail: rschneiderstamps@att.net

**Bechuanalands and Botswana Society**
Neville Midwood
69 Porlock Lane
Furzton, Milton Keynes, MK4 1JY
UNITED KINGDOM
www.nevsoft.com
E-mail: bbsoc@nevsoft.com

**Bermuda Collectors Society**
John Pare
405 Perimeter Road
Mount Horeb WI 53572
www.bermudacollectorssociety.com
E-mail: pare16@mhtc.net

**Brazil Philatelic Association**
William V. Kriebel
1923 Manning St.
Philadelphia PA 19103-5728
www.brazilphilatelic.org
E-mail: info@brazilphilatelic.org

**British Caribbean Philatelic Study Group**
Duane Larson
2 Forest Blvd.
Park Forest IL 60466
www.bcpsg.com
E-mail: dlarson283@aol.com

**The King George VI Collectors Society (British Commonwealth)**
Brian Livingstone
21 York Mansions, Prince of Wales Drive
London, SW11 4DL
UNITED KINGDOM
www.kg6.info
E-mail: livingstone484@btinternet.com

**British North America Philatelic Society (Canada & Provinces)**
Andy Ellwood
10 Doris Avenue
Gloucester, ON, KIT 3W8
CANADA
www.bnaps.org
E-mail: secretary@bnaps.org

**British West Indies Study Circle**
John Seidl
4324 Granby Way
Marietta GA 30062
Ph: (404) 229-6863
www.bwisc.org
E-mail: john.seidl@gmail.com

**Burma Philatelic Study Circle**
Michael Whittaker
1, Ecton Leys, Hillside
Rugby, Warwickshire, CV22 5SL
UNITED KINGDOM
www.burmastamps.homecall.co.uk
E-mail: manningham8@mypostoffice.co.uk

**Cape and Natal Study Circle**
Dr. Guy Dillaway
P.O. Box 181
Weston MA 02493
www.nzsc.demon.co.uk

**Ceylon Study Circle**
R. W. P. Frost
42 Lonsdale Road, Cannington
Bridgwater, Somerset, TA5 2JS
UNITED KINGDOM
www.ceylonsc.org
E-mail: rodney.frost@tiscali.co.uk

**Channel Islands Specialists Society**
Richard Flemming
64, Falconers Green, Burbage
Hinckley, Leicestershire, LE10 2SX
UNITED KINGDOM
www.ciss1950.org.uk
E-mail: secretary@ciss1950.org.uk

**China Stamp Society**
H. James Maxwell
1050 West Blue Ridge Blvd.
Kansas City MO 64145-1216
www.chinastampsociety.org
E-mail: president@chinastampsociety.org

**Colombia/Panama Philatelic Study Group (COPAPHIL)**
Thomas P. Myers
P.O. Box 522
Gordonsville VA 22942
www.copaphil.org
E-mail: tpmphil@hotmail.com

**Association Filatelic de Costa Rica**
Giana Wayman (McCarty)
SJO 4935, P.O. Box 025723
Miami FL 33102-5723
E-mail: scotland@racsa.co.cr

**Society for Costa Rica Collectors**
Dr. Hector R. Mena
P.O. Box 14831
Baton Rouge LA 70808
www.socorico.org
E-mail: hrmena@aol.com

**International Cuban Philatelic Society**
Ernesto Cuesta
P.O. Box 34434
Bethesda MD 20827
www.cubafil.org
E-mail: ecuesta@philat.com

**Cuban Philatelic Society of America ®**
P.O. Box 141656
Coral Gables FL 33114-1656
www.cubapsa.com
E-mail: cpsa.usa@gmail.com

**Cyprus Study Circle**
Colin Dear
10 Marne Close, Wem
Shropshire, SY4 5YE
UNITED KINGDOM
www.cyprusstudycircle.org/index.htm
E-mail: colindear@talktalk.net

**Society for Czechoslovak Philately**
Tom Cossaboom
P.O. Box 4124
Prescott AZ 86302
Ph: (928) 771-9097
www.csphilately.org
E-mail: klfckl@aol.com

**Danish West Indies Study Unit of the Scandinavian Collectors Club**
Arnold Sorensen
7666 Edgedale Drive
Newburgh IN 47630
Ph: (812) 480-6532
www.scc-online.org
E-mail: valbydwi@hotmail.com

**East Africa Study Circle**
Michael Vesey-Fitzgerald
Gambles Cottage, 18 Clarence Road
Lyndhurst, SO43 7AL
UNITED KINGDOM
www.easc.org.uk
E-mail: secretary@easc.org.uk

**Egypt Study Circle**
Mike Murphy
109 Chadwick Road
London, SE15 4PY
UNITED KINGDOM
Trent Ruebush: North American Agent
E-mail: tkruebrush@gmail.com
www.egyptstudycircle.org.uk
E-mail: egyptstudycircle@hotmail.com

**Estonian Philatelic Society**
Juri Kirsimagi
29 Clifford Ave.
Pelham NY 10803
Ph: (914) 738-3713

**Ethiopian Philatelic Society**
Ulf Lindahl
21 Westview Place
Riverside CT 06878
Ph: (203) 722-0769
http://ethiopianphilatelicsociety.weebly.com
E-mail: ulindahl@optonline.net

**Falkland Islands Philatelic Study Group**
Carl J. Faulkner
615 Taconic Trail
Williamstown MA 01267-2745
Ph: (413) 458-4421
www.fipsg.org.uk
E-mail: cfaulkner@taconicwilliamstown.com

**Faroe Islands Study Circle**
Norman Hudson
40 Queen's Road, Vicar's Cross
Chester, CH3 5HB
UNITED KINGDOM
www.faroeislandssc.org
E-mail: jntropics@hotmail.com

**Former French Colonies Specialist Society**
COLFRA
BP 628
75367 Paris, Cedex 08
FRANCE
www.colfra.org
E-mail: secretaire@colfra.org

**France & Colonies Philatelic Society**
Edward Grabowski
111 Prospect St., 4C
Westfield NJ 07090
www.franceandcolps.org
E-mail: edjjg@alum.mit.edu

**Gibraltar Study Circle**
Susan Dare
22, Byways Park, Strode Road,
Clevedon, North Somerset, BS21 6UR
UNITED KINGDOM
www.gibraltarstudycircle.wordpress.com
E-mail: smldare@yahoo.co.uk

**Germany Philatelic Society**
P.O. Box 6547
Chesterfield MO 63006
www.germanyphilatelicusa.org

**Plebiscite-Memel-Saar Study Group of the German Philatelic Society**
Clayton Wallace
100 Lark Court
Alamo CA 94507
E-mail: claytonwallace@comcast.net

**Great Britain Collectors Club**
Steve McGill
10309 Brookhollow Circle
Highlands Ranch CO 80129
www.gbstamps.com/gbcc
E-mail: steve.mcgill@comcast.net

**International Society of Guatemala Collectors**
Jaime Marckwordt
449 St. Francis Blvd.
Daly City CA 94015-2136
www.guatemalastamps.com
E-mail:
membership@guatamalastamps.com

**Haiti Philatelic Society**
Ubaldo Del Toro
5709 Marble Archway
Alexandria VA 22315
www.haitiphilately.org
E-mail: u007ubi@aol.com

**Federacion Filatelica de la Republica de Honduras (Honduran Philatelic Federation, FFRH)**
Mauricio Mejia
Apartado postal 1465
Tegucigalpa
HONDURAS

**Hong Kong Stamp Society**
Ming W. Tsang
P.O. Box 206
Glenside PA 19038
www.hkss.org
E-mail: hkstamps@yahoo.com

**Society for Hungarian Philately**
Alan Bauer
P.O. Box 3024
Andover MA 01810
Ph: (978) 682-0242
www.hungarianphilately.org
E-mail: alan@hungarianstamps.com

**India Study Circle**
John Warren
P.O. Box 7326
Washington DC 20044
Ph: (202) 488-7443
www.indiastudycircle.org
E-mail: jw-kbw@earthlink.net

**Indian Ocean Study Circle**
E. S. Hutton
29 Patermoster Close
Waltham Abby, Essex, EN9 3JU
UNITED KINGDOM
www.indianoceanstudycircle.com
E-mail: secretary@
indianoceanstudycircle.com

**Society of Indo-China Philatelists**
Ron Bentley
2600 N. 24th St.
Arlington VA 22207
www.sicp-online.org
E-mail: ron.bentley@verizon.net

**Iran Philatelic Study Circle**
Mehdi Esmaili
P.O. Box 750096
Forest Hills NY 11375
www.iranphilatelic.org
E-mail: m.esmaili@earthlink.net

**Eire Philatelic Association (Ireland)**
David J. Brennan
P.O. Box 704
Bernardsville NJ 07924
www.eirephilatelicassoc.org
E-mail: brennan704@aol.com

**Society of Israel Philatelists**
Jacqueline Baca
100 Match Factory Place
Bellefonte PA 16823-1367
Ph: (814) 933-3803 ext. 212
www.israelstamps.com
E-mail: israelstamps@gmail.com

**Italy and Colonies Study Circle**
Richard Harlow
7 Duncombe House, 8 Manor Road
Teddington, TW11 8BE
UNITED KINGDOM
www.icsc.pwp.blueyonder.co.uk
E-mail: richardharlow@outlook.com

**International Society for Japanese Philately**
William Eisenhauer
P.O. Box 230462
Tigard OR 97281
www.isjp.org
E-mail: secretary@isjp.org

**Korea Stamp Society**
John Talmage
P.O. Box 6889
Oak Ridge TN 37831
www.koreastampsociety.org
E-mail: jtalmage@usit.net

**Latin American Philatelic Society**
Jules K. Beck
30½ St. #209
St. Louis Park MN 55426-3551

**Liberian Philatelic Society**
William Thomas Lockard
P.O. Box 106
Wellston OH 45692
Ph: (740) 384-2020
E-mail: tlockard@zoomnet.net

**Liechtenstudy USA (Liechtenstein)**
Paul Tremaine
410 SW Ninth St.
Dundee OR 97115
Ph: (503) 538-4500
www.liechtenstudy.org
E-mail: editor@liechtenstudy.org

**Lithuania Philatelic Society**
John Variakojis
8472 Carlisle Court
Burr Ridge IL 60527
Ph: (630) 974-6525
www.lithuanianphilately.com/lps
E-mail: variakojis@sbcglobal.net

**Luxembourg Collectors Club**
Gary B. Little
7319 Beau Road
Sechelt, BC, V0N 3A8
CANADA
lcc.luxcentral.com
E-mail: gary@luxcentral.com

**Malaya Study Group**
David Tett
4 Amenbury Court
Harpenden Herts,
Wheathampstead Herts AL5 2BU
UNITED KINGDOM
www.m-s-g.org.uk
E-mail: davidtett@aol.com

**Malta Study Circle**
Rodger Evans
Ravensbourne, Hook Heath Road
Woking, Surrey, GU22 0LB
UNITED KINGDOM
www.maltastudycircle.org.uk
E-mail: carge@hotmail.co.uk

**Mexico-Elmhurst Philatelic Society International**
Eric Stovner
P.O. Box 10097
Santa Ana CA 92711-0097
www.mepsi.org
E-mail: treasurer@mepsi.org

**Asociacion Mexicana de Filatelia AMEXFIL**
Alejando Grossman
Jose Maria Rico, 129, Col. Del Valle
Mexico City DF, 03100
MEXICO
www.amexfil.mx
E-mail: amexfil@gmail.com

**Society for Moroccan and Tunisian Philately S.P.L.M.**
206, bld Pereire
Paris 75017
FRANCE
splm-philatelie.org
E-mail: splm206@aol.com

**Nepal & Tibet Philatelic Study Group**
Ken Goss
2643 Wagner Place
EL Dorado Hills CA 95762
Ph: (510) 207-5369
www.fuchs-online.com/ntpsc/
E-mail: kfgoss@comcast.net

**American Society for Netherlands Philately**
Hans Kremer
50 Rockport Court
Danville CA 94526
Ph: (925) 820-5841
www.asnp1975.com
E-mail: hkremer@usa.net

**New Zealand Society of Great Britain**
Michael Wilkinson
121 London Road
Sevenoaks, Kent, TN13 1BH
UNITED KINGDOM
www.nzsgb.org.uk
E-mail: mwilkin799@aol.com

**Nicaragua Study Group**
Erick Rodriguez
11817 SW 11th St.
Miami FL 33184-2501
clubs.yahoo.com/clubs/
nicaraguastudygroup
E-mail: nsgsec@yahoo.com

**Society of Australasian Specialists/Oceania**
David McNamee
P.O. Box 37
Alamo CA 94507
www.sasoceania.org
E-mail: treasurer@sasoceania.org

**Orange Free State Study Circle**
J. R. Stroud
24 Hooper Close
Burnham-on-sea, Somerset, TA8 1JQ
UNITED KINGDOM
orangefreestatephilately.org.uk
E-mail: richard@richardstroud.plus.com

**Pacific Islands Study Circle**
John Ray
24 Woodvale Ave.
London, SE25 4AE
UNITED KINGDOM
www.pisc.org.uk
E-mail: secretary@pisc.org.uk

**Pakistan Philatelic Study Circle**
Jeff Siddiqui
P.O. Box 7002
Lynnwood WA 98046
E-mail: jeffsiddiqui@msn.com

**Asociacion Filatelica de Panama (ASOFILPA)**
Edward D. Vianna
Apartado Postal 0819-03400
El Dorado, Panama
PANAMA
www.asociacionfilatelicadepanama.
blogspot.com
E-mail: asofilpa@gmail.com

**Papuan Philatelic Society**
Steven Zirinsky
P.O. Box 49, Ansonia Station
New York NY 10023
Ph: (718) 706-0616
www.communigate.co.uk/york/pps
E-mail: szirinsky@cs.com

**International Philippine Philatelic Society**
Donald J. Peterson
P.O. Box 122
Brunswick MD 21716
Ph: (301) 834-6419
www.theipps.info
E-mail: dpeterson4526@gmail.com

**Pitcairn Islands Study Group**
Dr. Everett L. Parker
117 Cedar Breeze South
Glenburn ME 04401-1734
Ph: (207) 573-1686
www.pisg.net
E-mail: eparker@hughes.net

**Polonus Philatelic Society (Poland)**
Daniel Lubelski
P.O. Box 2212
Benicia CA 94510
Ph: (419) 410-9115
www.polonus.org
E-mail: info@polonus.org

**International Society for Portuguese Philately**
Clyde Homen
1491 Bonnie View Road
Hollister CA 95023-5117
www.portugalstamps.com
E-mail: ispp1962@sbcglobal.net

**Rhodesian Study Circle**
William R. Wallace
P.O. Box 16381
San Francisco CA 94116
www.rhodesianstudycircle.org.uk
E-mail: bwall8rscr@earthlink.net

**Rossica Society of Russian Philately**
Alexander Kolchinsky
1506 Country Lake Drive
Champaign IL 6821-6428
www.rossica.org
E-mail: alexander.kolchinsky@rossica.org

**St. Helena, Ascension & Tristan Da Cunha Philatelic Society**
Dr. Everett L. Parker
117 Cedar Breeze South
Glenburn ME 04401-1734
Ph: (207) 573-1686
www.shatps.org
E-mail: eparker@hughes.net

**St. Pierre & Miquelon Philatelic Society**
James R. (Jim) Taylor
2335 Paliswood Road SW
Calgary, AB, T2V 3P6
CANADA
www.stamps.org/spm

**Asociacion Filatelica Salvadorena**
Joseph D. Hahn
301 Rolling Ridge Drive, Apt. 111
State College PA 16801-6149
www.elsalvadorphilately.org
E-mail: joehahn100@hotmail.com

**Fellowship of Samoa Specialists**
Donald Mee
23 Leo St.
Christchurch, 8051
NEW ZEALAND
www.samoaexpress.org
E-mail: donanm@xtra.co.nz

**Sarawak Specialists' Society**
Stephen Schumann
2417 Cabrillo Drive
Hayward CA 94545
Ph: (510) 785-4794
www.britborneostamps.org.uk
E-mail: stephen.schumann@att.net

**Scandinavian Collectors Club**
Steve Lund
P.O. Box 16213
St. Paul MN 55116
www.scc-online.org
E-mail: steve88h@aol.com

**Slovakia Stamp Society**
Jack Benchik
P.O. Box 555
Notre Dame IN 46556

**Philatelic Society for Greater Southern Africa**
Alan Hanks
34 Seaton Drive
Aurora, ON, L4G 2K1
CANADA
www.psgsa.thestampweb.com

**South Sudan Philatelic Society**
William Barclay
1370 Spring Hill Road
South Londonderry VT 05155
E-mail: barclayphilatelics@gmail.com

**Spanish Philatelic Society**
Robert H. Penn
1108 Walnut Drive
Danielsville PA 18038
Ph: (610) 844-8963
E-mail: roberthpenn43@gmail.com

**Sudan Study Group**
David Sher
5 Ellis Park Road
Toronto, ON, M6S2V1
CANADA
www.sudanstamps.org
e-mail: sh3603@hotmail.com

**American Helvetia Philatelic Society (Switzerland, Liechtenstein)**
Richard T. Hall
P.O. Box 15053
Asheville NC 28813-0053
www.swiss-stamps.org
E-mail: secretary2@swiss-stamps.org

**Tannu Tuva Collectors Society**
Ken R. Simon
P.O. Box 385
Lake Worth FL 33460-0385
Ph: (561) 588-5954
www.tuva.tk
E-mail: yurttuva@yahoo.com

**Society for Thai Philately**
H. R. Blakeney
P.O. Box 25644
Oklahoma City OK 73125
E-mail: HRBlakeney@aol.com

**Transvaal Study Circle**
Chris Board
36 Wakefield Gardens
London, SE19 2NR
UNITED KINGDOM
www.transvaalstamps.org.uk
E-mail: c.board@macace.net

**Ottoman and Near East Philatelic Society (Turkey and related areas)**
Bob Stuchell
193 Valley Stream Lane
Wayne PA 19087
www.oneps.org
E-mail: rstuchell@msn.com

**Ukrainian Philatelic & Numismatic Society**
Martin B. Tatuch
5117 8th Road N.
Arlington VA 22205-1201
www.upns.org
E-mail: treasurer@upns.org

**Vatican Philatelic Society**
Sal Quinonez
1 Aldersgate, Apt. 1002
Riverhead NY 11901-1830
Ph: (516) 727-6426
www.vaticanphilately.org

**British Virgin Islands Philatelic Society**
Giorgio Migliavacca
P.O. Box 7007
St. Thomas VI 00801-0007
www.islandsun.com/category/collectables/
E-mail: issun@candwbvi.net

**West Africa Study Circle**
Martin Bratzel
1233 Virginia Ave.
Windsor, ON, N8S 2Z1
CANADA
www.wasc.org.uk
E-mail: marty_bratzel@yahoo.ca

**Western Australia Study Group**
Brian Pope
P.O. Box 423
Claremont, Western Australia, 6910
AUSTRALIA
www.wastudygroup.com
E-mail: black5swan@yahoo.com.au

**Yugoslavia Study Group of the Croatian Philatelic Society**
Michael Lenard
1514 N. Third Ave.
Wausau WI 54401
Ph: (715) 675-2833
E-mail: mjlenard@aol.com

## Topical Groups

**Americana Unit**
Dennis Dengel
17 Peckham Road
Poughkeepsie NY 12603-2018
www.americanaunit.org
E-mail: ddengel@americanaunit.org

**Astronomy Study Unit**
John Budd
728 Sugar Camp Way
Brooksville FL 34604
Ph: (352) 345-4799
www.astronomystudyunit.net
E-mail: jwgbudd@gmail.com

**Bicycle Stamps Club**
Steve Andreasen
2000 Alaskan Way, Unit 157
Seattle WA 98121
E-mail: steven.w.andreasen@gmail.com

**Biology Unit**
Alan Hanks
34 Seaton Drive
Aurora, ON, L4G 2K1
CANADA
Ph: (905) 727-6993

**Bird Stamp Society**
S. A. H. (Tony) Statham
Ashlyns Lodge, Chesham Road,
Berkhamsted, Hertfordshire HP4 2ST
UNITED KINGDOM
www.bird-stamps.org/bss
E-mail: tony.statham@sky.com

**Captain Cook Society**
Jerry Yucht
8427 Leale Ave.
Stockton CA 95212
www.captaincooksociety.com
E-mail: US@captaincooksociety.com

**The CartoPhilatelic Society**
Marybeth Sulkowski
2885 Sanford Ave, SW, #32361
Grandville MI 49418-1342
www.mapsonstamps.org
E-mail: secretary@mapsonstamps.org

**Casey Jones Railroad Unit**
Jeff Lough
2612 Redbud Lane, Apt. C
Lawrence KS 66046
www.uqp.de/cjr/index.htm
E-mail: jeffydplaugh@gmail.com

**Cats on Stamps Study Unit**
Robert D. Jarvis
2731 Teton Lane
Fairfield CA 94533
www.catstamps.info
E-mail: bobmarci@aol.com

**Chemistry & Physics on Stamps Study Unit**
Dr. Roland Hirsch
20458 Water Point Lane
Germantown MD 20874
www.cpossu.org
E-mail: rfhirsch@cpossu.org

**Chess on Stamps Study Unit**
Ray C. Alexis
608 Emery St.
Longmont CO 80501
E-mail: chessstuff911459@aol.com

**Christmas Philatelic Club**
Jim Balog
P.O. Box 744
Geneva OH 44041
www.christmasphilatelicclub.org
E-mail: jpb4stamps@windstream.net

**Cricket Philatelic Society**
A. Melville-Brown, President
11 Weppons, Ravens Road
Shoreham-by-Sea
West Sussex, BN43 5AW
UNITED KINGDOM
www.cricketstamp.net
E-mail: mel.cricket.100@googlemail.com

**Dogs on Stamps Study Unit**
Morris Raskin
202A Newport Road
Monroe Township NJ 08831
Ph: (609) 655-7411
www.dossu.org
E-mail: mraskin@cellurian.com

**Earth's Physical Features Study Group**
Fred Klein
515 Magdalena Ave.
Los Altos CA 94024
epfsu.jeffhayward.com

**Ebony Society of Philatelic Events and Reflections, Inc. (African-American topicals)**
Manuel Gilyard
800 Riverside Drive, Suite 4H
New York NY 10032-7412
www.esperstamps.org
E-mail: gilyardmani@aol.com

**Europa Study Unit**
Tonny E. Van Loij
3002 S. Xanthia St.
Denver CO 80231-4237
Ph: (303) 752-0189
www.europastudyunit.org
E-mail: tvanloij@gmail.com

**Fine & Performing Arts**
Deborah L. Washington
6922 S. Jeffery Blvd., #7 - North
Chicago IL 60649
E-mail: brasslady@comcast.net

**Fire Service in Philately**
John Zaranek
81 Hillpine Road
Cheektowaga NY 14227-2259
Ph: (716) 668-3352
E-mail: jczaranek@roadrunner.com

**Gay & Lesbian History on Stamps Club**
Joe Petronie
P.O. Box 190842
Dallas TX 75219-0842
www.facebook.com/glhsc
E-mail: glhsc@aol.com

**Gems, Minerals & Jewelry Study Unit**
Mrs. Gilberte Proteau
138 Lafontaine
Beloeil QC J3G 2G7
CANADA
Ph: (978) 851-8283
E-mail: gilberte.ferland@sympatico.ca

**Graphics Philately Association**
Mark H. Winnegrad
P.O. Box 380
Bronx NY 10462-0380
www.graphics-stamps.org
E-mail: indybruce1@yahoo.com

**Journalists, Authors & Poets on Stamps**
Clete Delvaux
800 East River Drive
De Pere WI 54115
E-mail: cdelvaux@msn.com

**Lighthouse Stamp Society**
Dalene Thomas
1805 S Balsam St., #106
Lakewood CO 80232
Ph: (303) 986-6620
www.lighthousestampsociety.org
E-mail: dalene@lighthousestampsociety.org

**Lions International Stamp Club**
John Bargus
108-2777 Barry Road RR 2
Mill Bay, BC, V0R 2P2
CANADA
Ph: (250) 743-5782

**Mahatma Gandhi On Stamps Study Circle**
Pramod Shivagunde
Pratik Clinic, Akluj
Solapur, Maharashtra, 413101
INDIA
E-mail: drnanda@bom6.vsnl.net.in

**Masonic Study Unit**
Gene Fricks
25 Murray Way
Blackwood NJ 08012-4400
E-mail: genefricks@comcast.net

**Mathematical Study Unit**
Monty Strauss
4209 88th St.
Lubbock TX 79423-2941
www.mathstamps.org
E-mail: montystrauss@gmail.com

**Medical Subjects Unit**
Dr. Frederick C. Skvara
P.O. Box 6228
Bridgewater NJ 08807
E-mail: fcskvara@optonline.net

**Military Postal History Society**
Ed Dubin
1 S. Wacker Drive, Suite 3500
Chicago IL 60606
www.militaryPHS.org
E-mail: dubine@comcast.net

**Mourning Stamps and Covers Club**
James Camak, Jr.
3801 Acapulco Ct.
Irving TX 75062
www.mscc.ms
E-mail: jamescamak7@gmail.com

**Napoleonic Age Philatelists**
Ken Berry
4117 NW 146th St.
Oklahoma City OK 73134-1746
Ph: (405) 748-8646
www.nap-stamps.org
E-mail: krb4117@att.net

**Old World Archeological Study Unit**
Caroline Scannell
11 Dawn Drive
Smithtown NY 11787-1761
www.owasu.org
E-mail: editor@owasu.org

**Petroleum Philatelic Society International**
Feitze Papa
922 Meander Dr.
Walnut Creek CA 94598-4239
E-mail: oildad@astound.net

**Rotary on Stamps Unit**
Gerald L. Fitzsimmons
105 Calle Ricardo
Victoria TX 77904
rotaryonstamps.org
E-mail: glfitz@suddenlink.net

**Scouts on Stamps Society International**
Woodrow (Woody) Brooks
498 Baldwin Road
Akron OH 44312
Ph: (330) 612-1294
www.sossi.org
E-mail: rfrank@sossi.org

**Ships on Stamps Unit**
Les Smith
302 Conklin Ave.
Penticton, BC, V2A 2T4
CANADA
Ph: (250) 493-7486
www.shipsonstamps.org
E-mail: lessmith440@shaw.ca

**Space Unit**
David Blog
P.O. Box 174
Bergenfield NJ 07621
www.space-unit.com
E-mail: davidblognj@gmail.com

**Sports Philatelists International**
Mark Maestrone
2824 Curie Place
San Diego CA 92122-4110
www.sportstamps.org
Email: president@sportstamps.org

**Stamps on Stamps Collectors Club**
Alf Jordan
156 W. Elm St.
Yarmouth ME 04096
www.stampsonstamps.org
E-mail: ajordan1@maine.rr.com

**Windmill Study Unit**
Walter J. Hollien
607 N. Porter St.
Watkins Glenn NY 14891-1345
Ph: (607) 229-3541
www.windmillworld.com
E-mail: whollien@earthlink.net

**Wine On Stamps Study Unit**
David Wolfersberger
768 Chain Ridge Road
St. Louis MO 63122-3259
Ph: (314) 961-5032
www.wine-on-stamps.org
E-mail: dewolf2@swbell.net

**Women on Stamps Study Unit**
Hugh Gottfried
2232 26th St.
Santa Monica CA 90405-1902
E-mail: hgottfried@adelphia.net

# Expertizing Services

The following organizations will, for a fee, provide expert opinions about stamps submitted to them. Collectors should contact these organizations to find out about their fees and requirements before submiting philatelic material to them. The listing of these groups here is not intended as an endorsement by Amos Media Co.

## General Expertizing Services

**American Philatelic Expertizing Service (a service of the American Philatelic Society)**
100 Match Factory Place
Bellefonte PA 16823-1367
Ph: (814) 237-3803
Fax: (814) 237-6128
www.stamps.org
E-mail: twhorn@stamps.org
Areas of Expertise: Worldwide

**B. P. A. Expertising, Ltd.**
P.O. Box 1141
Guildford, Surrey, GU5 0WR
UNITED KINGDOM
www.bpaexpertising.com
E-mail: sec@bpaexpertising.org
Areas of Expertise: British Commonwealth, Great Britain, Classics of Europe, South America and the Far East

**Philatelic Foundation**
22 E. 35th St., 4th Floor
New York NY 10016
Ph: (212) 221-6555
Fax: (212) 221-6208
www.philatelicfoundation.org
E-mail: philatelicfoundation@verizon.net
Areas of Expertise: U.S. & Worldwide

**Philatelic Stamp Authentication and Grading, Inc.**
P.O. Box 41-0880
Melbourne FL 32941-0880
Customer Service: (305) 345-9864
www.psaginc.com
E-mail: info@psaginc.com
Areas of Expertise: U.S., Canal Zone, Hawaii, Philippines, Canada & Provinces

**Professional Stamp Experts**
P.O. Box 539309
Henderson NV 89053-9309
Ph: (702) 776-6522
www.gradingmatters.com
www.psestamp.com
E-mail: info@gradingmatters.com
Areas of Expertise: Stamps and covers of U.S., U.S. Possessions, British Commonwealth

**Royal Philatelic Society Expert Committee**
41 Devonshire Place
London, W1N 1PE
UNITED KINGDOM
www.rpsl.org.uk/experts.html
E-mail: experts@rpsl.org.uk
Areas of Expertise: Worldwide

## Expertizing Services Covering Specific Fields or Countries

**China Stamp Society Expertizing Service**
1050 W. Blue Ridge Blvd.
Kansas City MO 64145
Ph: (816) 942-6300
E-mail: hjmesq@aol.com
Areas of Expertise: China

**Confederate Stamp Alliance Authentication Service**
Gen. Frank Crown, Jr.
P.O. Box 278
Capshaw AL 35742-0396
Ph: (302) 422-2656
Fax: (302) 424-1990
www.csalliance.org
E-mail: csaas@knology.net
Areas of Expertise: Confederate stamps and postal history

**Errors, Freaks and Oddities Collectors Club Expertizing Service**
138 East Lakemont Drive
Kingsland GA 31548
Ph: (912) 729-1573
Areas of Expertise: U.S. errors, freaks and oddities

**Estonian Philatelic Society Expertizing Service**
39 Clafford Lane
Melville NY 11747
Ph: (516) 421-2078
E-mail: esto4@aol.com
Areas of Expertise: Estonia

**Hawaiian Philatelic Society Expertizing Service**
P.O. Box 10115
Honolulu HI 96816-0115
Areas of Expertise: Hawaii

**Hong Kong Stamp Society Expertizing Service**
P.O. Box 206
Glenside PA 19038
Fax: (215) 576-6850
Areas of Expertise: Hong Kong

**International Association of Philatelic Experts United States Associate members:**

Paul Buchsbayew
119 W. 57th St.
New York NY 10019
Ph: (212) 977-7734
Fax: (212) 977-8653
Areas of Expertise: Russia, Soviet Union

William T. Crowe
P.O. Box 2090
Danbury CT 06813-2090
E-mail: wtcrowe@aol.com
Areas of Expertise: United States

John Lievsay
(see American Philatelic Expertizing Service and Philatelic Foundation)
Areas of Expertise: France

Robert W. Lyman
P.O. Box 348
Irvington on Hudson NY 10533
Ph and Fax: (914) 591-6937
Areas of Expertise: British North America, New Zealand

Robert Odenweller
P.O. Box 401
Bernardsville NJ 07924-0401
Ph and Fax: (908) 766-5460
Areas of Expertise: New Zealand, Samoa to 1900

Sergio Sismondo
The Regency Tower, Suite 1109
770 James Street
Syracuse NY 13203
Ph: (315) 422-2331
Fax: (315) 422-2956
Areas of Expertise: British East Africa, Camerouns, Cape of Good Hope, Canada, British North America

**International Society for Japanese Philately Expertizing Committee**
132 North Pine Terrace
Staten Island NY 10312-4052
Ph: (718) 227-5229
Areas of Expertise: Japan and related areas, except WWII Japanese Occupation issues

**International Society for Portuguese Philately Expertizing Service**
P.O. Box 43146
Philadelphia PA 19129-3146
Ph and Fax: (215) 843-2106
E-mail: s.s.washburne@worldnet.att.net
Areas of Expertise: Portugal and Colonies

**Mexico-Elmhurst Philatelic Society International Expert Committee**
Expert Committee Administrator
Marc E. Gonzales
P.O. Box 29040
Denver CO 80229-0040
www.mepsi.org/expertization
Areas of Expertise: Mexico

**Ukrainian Philatelic & Numismatic Society Expertizing Service**
30552 Dell Lane
Warren MI 48092-1862
Areas of Expertise: Ukraine, Western Ukraine

**V. G. Greene Philatelic Research Foundation**
P.O. Box 204, Station Q
Toronto, ON, M4T 2M1
CANADA
Ph: (416) 921-2073
Fax: (416) 921-1282
www.greenefoundation.ca
E-mail: vggfoundation@on.aibn.com
Areas of Expertise: British North America

# Information on Catalogue Values, Grade and Condition

## Catalogue Value

The Scott Catalogue value is a retail value; that is, an amount you could expect to pay for a stamp in the grade of Very Fine with no faults. Any exceptions to the grade valued will be noted in the text. The general introduction on the following pages and the individual section introductions further explain the type of material that is valued. The value listed for any given stamp is a reference that reflects recent actual dealer selling prices for that item.

Dealer retail price lists, public auction results, published prices in advertising and individual solicitation of retail prices from dealers, collectors and specialty organizations have been used in establishing the values found in this catalogue. Amos Media Co. values stamps, but Amos Media is not a company engaged in the business of buying and selling stamps as a dealer.

Use this catalogue as a guide for buying and selling. The actual price you pay for a stamp may be higher or lower than the catalogue value because of many different factors, including the amount of personal service a dealer offers, or increased or decreased interest in the country or topic represented by a stamp or set. An item may occasionally be offered at a lower price as a "loss leader," or as part of a special sale. You also may obtain an item inexpensively at public auction because of little interest at that time or as part of a large lot.

Stamps that are of a lesser grade than Very Fine, or those with condition problems, generally trade at lower prices than those given in this catalogue. Stamps of exceptional quality in both grade and condition often command higher prices than those listed.

Values for pre-1900 unused issues are for stamps with approximately half or more of their original gum. Stamps with most or all of their original gum may be expected to sell for more, and stamps with less than half of their original gum may be expected to sell for somewhat less than the values listed. On rarer stamps, it may be expected that the original gum will be somewhat more disturbed than it will be on more common issues. Post-1900 unused issues are assumed to have full original gum. From breakpoints in most countries' listings, stamps are valued as never hinged, due to the wide availability of stamps in that condition. These notations are prominently placed in the listings and in the country information preceding the listings. Some countries also feature listings with dual values for hinged and never-hinged stamps.

## Grade

A stamp's grade and condition are crucial to its value. The accompanying illustrations show examples of Very Fine stamps from different time periods, along with examples of stamps in Fine to Very Fine and Extremely Fine grades as points of reference. When a stamp seller offers a stamp in any grade from fine to superb without further qualifying statements, that stamp should not only have the centering grade as defined, but it also should be free of faults or other condition problems.

**FINE** stamps (illustrations not shown) have designs that are quite off center, with the perforations on one or two sides very close to the design but not quite touching it. There is white space between the perforations and the design that is minimal but evident to the unaided eye. Imperforate stamps may have small margins, and earlier issues may show the design just touching one edge of the stamp design. Very early perforated issues normally will have the perforations slightly cutting into the design. Used stamps may have heavier than usual cancellations.

**FINE-VERY FINE** stamps will be somewhat off center on one side, or slightly off center on two sides. Imperforate stamps will have two margins of at least normal size, and the design will not touch any edge. For perforated stamps, the perfs are well clear of the design, but are still noticeably off center. *However, early issues of a country may be printed in such a way that the design naturally is very close to the edges. In these cases, the perforations may cut into the design very slightly.* Used stamps will not have a cancellation that detracts from the design.

**VERY FINE** stamps will be just slightly off center on one or two sides, but the design will be well clear of the edge. The stamp will present a nice, balanced appearance. Imperforate stamps will be well centered within normal-sized margins. *However, early issues of many countries may be printed in such a way that the perforations may touch the design on one or more sides. Where this is the case, a boxed note will be found defining the centering and margins of the stamps being valued.* Used stamps will have light or otherwise neat cancellations. This is the grade used to establish Scott Catalogue values.

**EXTREMELY FINE** stamps are close to being perfectly centered. Imperforate stamps will have even margins that are slightly larger than normal. Even the earliest perforated issues will have perforations clear of the design on all sides.

**Amos Media Co. recognizes that there is no formally enforced grading scheme for postage stamps, and that the final price you pay or obtain for a stamp will be determined by individual agreement at the time of transaction.**

## Condition

*Grade* addresses only centering and (for used stamps) cancellation. *Condition* refers to factors other than grade that affect a stamp's desirability.

Factors that can increase the value of a stamp include exceptionally wide margins, particularly fresh color, the presence of selvage, and plate or die varieties. Unusual cancels on used stamps (particularly those of the 19th century) can greatly enhance their value as well.

Factors other than faults that decrease the value of a stamp include loss of original gum, regumming, a hinge remnant or foreign object adhering to the gum, natural inclusions, straight edges, and markings or notations applied by collectors or dealers.

Faults include missing pieces, tears, pin or other holes, surface scuffs, thin spots, creases, toning, short or pulled perforations, clipped perforations, oxidation or other forms of color changelings, soiling, stains, and such man-made changes as reperforations or the chemical removal or lightening of a cancellation.

## Grading Illustrations

On the following two pages are illustrations of various stamps from countries appearing in this volume. These stamps are arranged by country, and they represent early or important issues that are often found in widely different grades in the marketplace. The editors believe the illustrations will prove useful in showing the margin size and centering that will be seen on the various issues.

In addition to the matters of margin size and centering, collectors are reminded that the very fine stamps valued in the Scott catalogues also will possess fresh color and intact perforations, and they will be free from defects.

Examples shown are computer-manipulated images made from single digitized master illustrations.

## Stamp Illustrations Used in the Catalogue

It is important to note that the stamp images used for identification purposes in this catlaogue may not be indicative of the grade of stamp being valued. Refer to the written discussion of grades on this page and to the grading illustrations on the following two pages for grading information.

Fine-Very Fine →

SCOTT CATALOGUES VALUE STAMPS IN THIS GRADE

Very Fine →

Extremely Fine →

Fine-Very Fine →

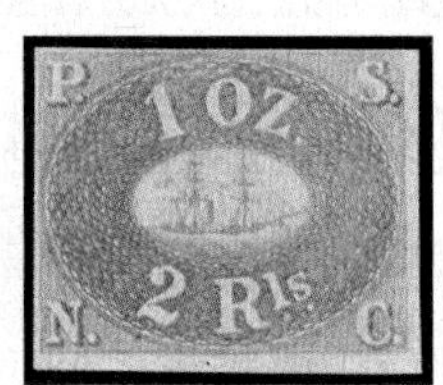

SCOTT CATALOGUES VALUE STAMPS IN THIS GRADE

Very Fine →

Extremely Fine →

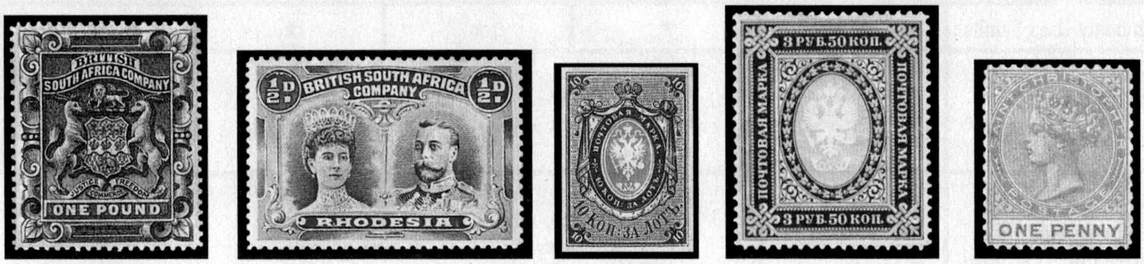

Fine-Very Fine

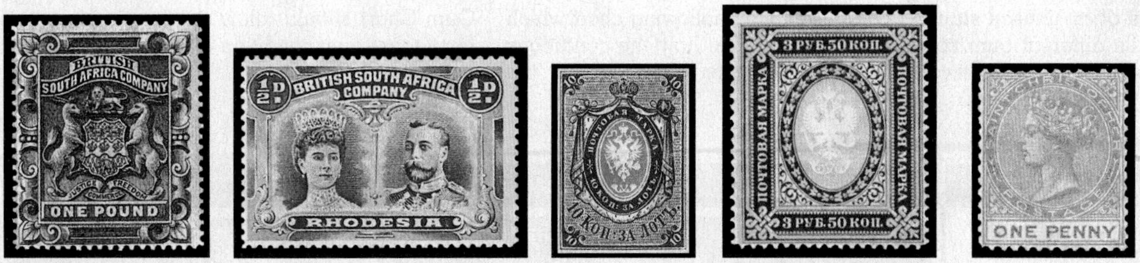

SCOTT CATALOGUES VALUE STAMPS IN THIS GRADE

Very Fine

Extremely Fine

Fine-Very Fine

SCOTT CATALOGUES VALUE STAMPS IN THIS GRADE

Very Fine

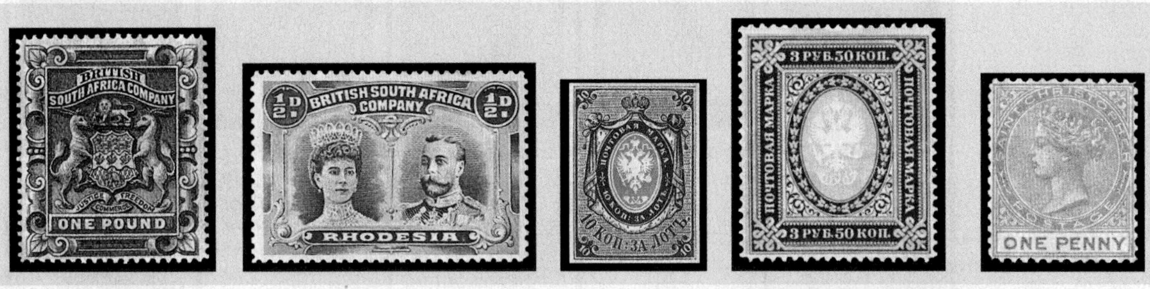

Extremely Fine

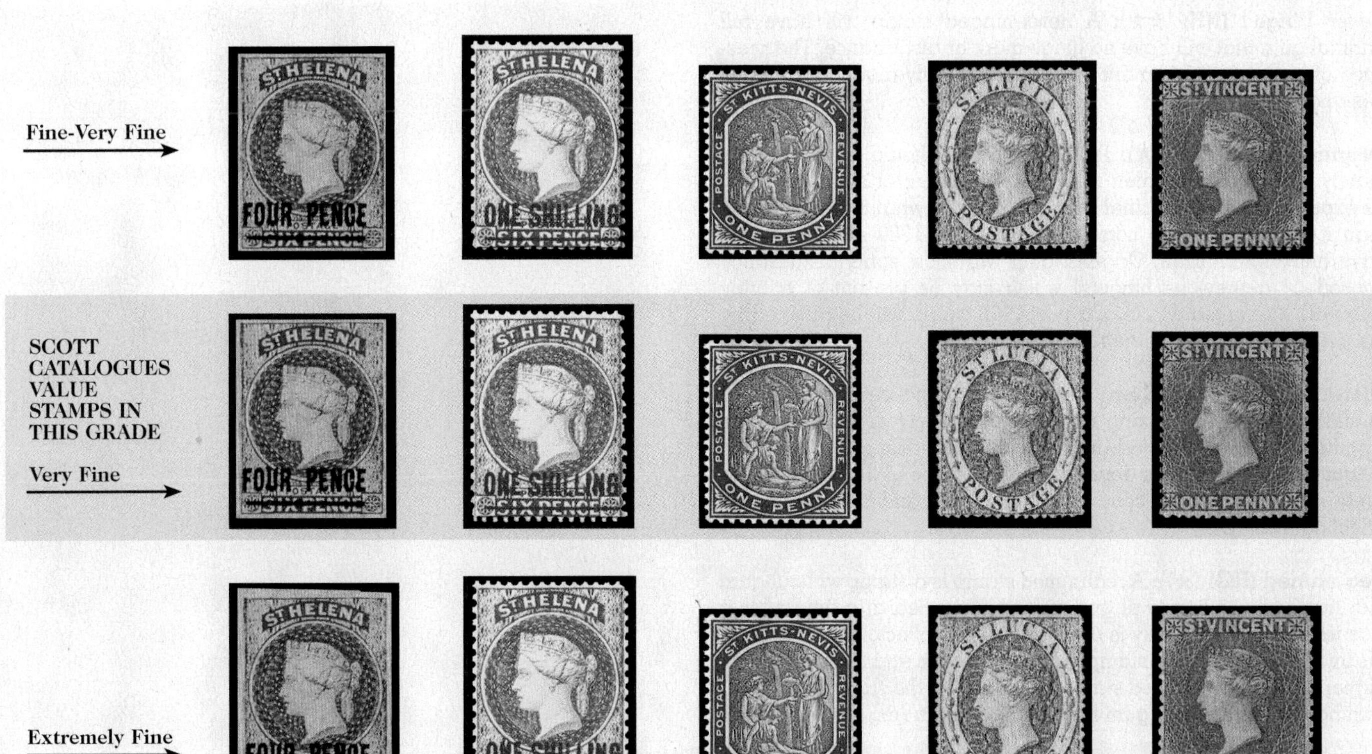

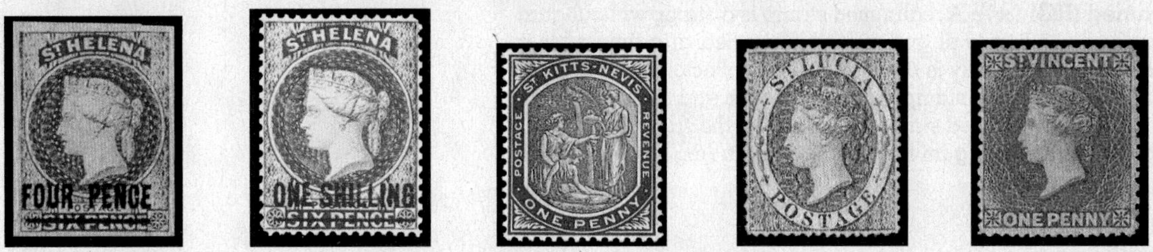

For purposes of helping to determine the gum condition and value of an unused stamp, Scott presents the following chart which details different gum conditions and indicates how the conditions correlate with the Scott values for unused stamps. Used together, the Illustrated Grading Chart on the previous pages and this Illustrated Gum Chart should allow catalogue users to better understand the grade and gum condition of stamps valued in the Scott catalogues.

| Gum Categories: | MINT N.H. | ORIGINAL GUM (O.G.) | | | | NO GUM |
|---|---|---|---|---|---|---|
| |  **Mint Never Hinged** *Free from any disturbance* |  **Lightly Hinged** *Faint impression of a removed hinge over a small area* |  **Hinge Mark or Remnant** *Prominent hinged spot with part or all of the hinge remaining* |  **Large part o.g.** *Approximately half or more of the gum intact* |  **Small part o.g.** *Approximately less than half of the gum intact* | **No gum** *Only if issued with gum* |
| Commonly Used Symbol: | ★★ | ★ | ★ | ★ | ★ | (★) |
| Pre-1900 Issues (Pre-1881 for U.S.) | *Very fine pre-1900 stamps in these categories trade at a premium over Scott value* | | | Scott Value for "Unused" | | Scott "No Gum" listings for selected unused classic stamps |
| From 1900 to breakpoints for listings of never-hinged stamps | Scott "Never Hinged" listings for selected unused stamps | Scott Value for "Unused" (Actual value will be affected by the degree of hinging of the full o.g.) | | | | |
| From breakpoints noted for many countries | Scott Value for "Unused" | | | | | |

**Never Hinged (NH; ★★):** A never-hinged stamp will have full original gum that will have no hinge mark or disturbance. The presence of an expertizer's mark does not disqualify a stamp from this designation.

**Original Gum (OG; ★):** Pre-1900 stamps should have approximately half or more of their original gum. On rarer stamps, it may be expected that the original gum will be somewhat more disturbed than it will be on more common issues. Post-1900 stamps should have full original gum. Original gum will show some disturbance caused by a previous hinge(s) which may be present or entirely removed. The actual value of a post-1900 stamp will be affected by the degree of hinging of the full original gum.

**Disturbed Original Gum:** Gum showing noticeable effects of humidity, climate or hinging over more than half of the gum. The significance of gum disturbance in valuing a stamp in any of the Original Gum categories depends on the degree of disturbance, the rarity and normal gum condition of the issue and other variables affecting quality.

**Regummed (RG; (★)):** A regummed stamp is a stamp without gum that has had some type of gum privately applied at a time after it was issued. This normally is done to deceive collectors and/or dealers into thinking that the stamp has original gum and therefore has a higher value. A regummed stamp is considered the same as a stamp with none of its original gum for purposes of grading.

# Catalogue Listing Policy

It is the intent of Amos Media Co. to list all postage stamps of the world in the *Scott Standard Postage Stamp Catalogue*. The only strict criteria for listing is that stamps be decreed legal for postage by the issuing country and that the issuing country actually have an operating postal system. Whether the primary intent of issuing a given stamp or set was for sale to postal patrons or to stamp collectors is not part of our listing criteria. Scott's role is to provide basic comprehensive postage stamp information. It is up to each stamp collector to choose which items to include in a collection.

It is Scott's objective to seek reasons why a stamp should be listed, rather than why it should not. Nevertheless, there are certain types of items that will not be listed. These include the following:

1. Unissued items that are not officially distributed or released by the issuing postal authority. If such items are officially issued at a later date by the country, they will be listed. Unissued items consist of those that have been printed and then held from sale for reasons such as change in government, errors found on stamps or something deemed objectionable about a stamp subject or design.

2. Stamps "issued" by non-existent postal entities or fantasy countries, such as Nagaland, Occusi-Ambeno, Staffa, Sedang, Torres Straits and others. Also, stamps "issued" in the names of legitimate, stamp-issuing countries that are not authorized by those countries.

3. Semi-official or unofficial items not required for postage. Examples include items issued by private agencies for their own express services. When such items are required for delivery, or are valid as prepayment of postage, they are listed.

4. Local stamps issued for local use only. Postage stamps issued by governments specifically for "domestic" use, such as Haiti Scott 219-228, or the United States non-denominated stamps, are not considered to be locals, since they are valid for postage throughout the country of origin.

5. Items not valid for postal use. For example, a few countries have issued souvenir sheets that are not valid for postage. This area also includes a number of worldwide charity labels (some denominated) that do not pay postage.

6. Egregiously exploitative issues such as stamps sold for far more than face value, stamps purposefully issued in artificially small quantities or only against advance orders, stamps awarded only to a selected audience such as a philatelic bureau's standing order customers, or stamps sold only in conjunction with other products. All of these kinds of items are usually controlled issues and/or are intended for speculation. These items normally will be included in a footnote.

7. Items distributed by the issuing government only to a limited group, club, philatelic exhibition or a single stamp dealer or other private company. These items normally will be included in a footnote.

8. Stamps not available to collectors. These generally are rare items, all of which are held by public institutions such as museums. The existence of such items often will be cited in footnotes.

The fact that a stamp has been used successfully as postage, even on international mail, is not in itself sufficient proof that it was legitimately issued. Numerous examples of so-called stamps from non-existent countries are known to have been used to post letters that have successfully passed through the international mail system.

There are certain items that are subject to interpretation. When a stamp falls outside our specifications, it may be listed along with a cautionary footnote.

A number of factors are considered in our approach to analyzing how a stamp is listed. The following list of factors is presented to share with you, the catalogue user, the complexity of the listing process.

**Additional printings** — "Additional printings" of a previously issued stamp may range from an item that is totally different to cases where it is impossible to differentiate from the original. At least a minor number (a small-letter suffix) is assigned if there is a distinct change in stamp shade, noticeably redrawn design, or a significantly different perforation measurement. A major number (numeral or numeral and capital-letter combination) is assigned if the editors feel the "additional printing" is sufficiently different from the original that it constitutes a different issue.

**Commemoratives** — Where practical, commemoratives with the same theme are placed in a set. For example, the U.S. Civil War Centennial set of 1961-65 and the Constitution Bicentennial series of 1989-90 appear as sets. Countries such as Japan and Korea issue such material on a regular basis, with an announced, or at least predictable, number of stamps known in advance. Occasionally, however, stamp sets that were released over a period of years have been separated. Appropriately placed footnotes will guide you to each set's continuation.

**Definitive sets** — Blocks of numbers generally have been reserved for definitive sets, based on previous experience with any given country. If a few more stamps were issued in a set than originally expected, they often have been inserted into the original set with a capital-letter suffix, such as U.S. Scott 1059A. If it appears that many more stamps than the originally allotted block will be released before the set is completed, a new block of numbers will be reserved, with the original one being closed off. In some cases, such as the U.S. Transportation and Great Americans series, several blocks of numbers exist. Appropriately placed footnotes will guide you to each set's continuation.

**New country** — Membership in the Universal Postal Union is not a consideration for listing status or order of placement within the catalogue. The index will tell you in what volume or page number the listings begin.

**"No release date" items** — The amount of information available for any given stamp issue varies greatly from country to country and even from time to time. Extremely comprehensive information about new stamps is available from some countries well before the stamps are released. By contrast some countries do not provide information about stamps or release dates. Most countries, however, fall between these extremes. A country may provide denominations or subjects of stamps from upcoming issues that are not issued as planned. Sometimes, philatelic agencies, those private firms hired to represent countries, add these later-issued items to sets well after the formal release date. This time period can range from weeks to years. If these items were officially released by the country, they will be added to the appropriate spot in the set. In many cases, the specific release date of a stamp or set of stamps may never be known.

**Overprints** — The color of an overprint is always noted if it is other than black. Where more than one color of ink has been used on overprints of a single set, the color used is noted. Early overprint and surcharge illustrations were altered to prevent their use by forgers.

**Personalized Stamps** — Since 1999, the special service of personalizing stamp vignettes, or labels attached to stamps, has been offered to customers by postal administrations of many countries. Sheets of these stamps are sold, singly or in quantity, only through special orders made by mail, in person, or through a sale on a computer website with the postal administrations or their agents for which an extra fee is charged, though some countries offer to collectors at face value personalized stamps having generic images in the vignettes or on the attached labels. It is impossible for any catalogue to know what images have been chosen by customers. Images can be 1) owned or created by the customer, 2) a generic image, or 3) an image pulled from a library of stock images on the stamp creation website. It is also impossible to know the quantity printed for any stamp having a particular image. So from a valuing standpoint, any image is equivalent to any other image for any personalized stamp having the same catalogue number. Illustrations of personalized stamps in the catalogue are not always those of stamps having generic images.

Personalized items are listed with some exceptions. These include:
1. Stamps or sheets that have attached labels that the customer cannot personalize, but which are nonetheless marketed as "personalized," and are sold for far more than the franking value.
2. Stamps or sheets that can be personalized by the customer, but where a portion of the print run must be ceded to the issuing country for sale to other customers.
3. Stamps or sheets that are created exclusively for a particular commercial client, or clients, including stamps that differ from any similar stamp that has been made available to the public.
4. Stamps or sheets that are deliberately conceived by the issuing authority that have been, or are likely to be, created with an excessive number of different face values, sizes, or other features that are changeable.
5. Stamps or sheets that are created by postal administrations using the same system of stamp personalization that has been put in place for use by the public that are printed in limited quantities and sold above face value.
6. Stamps or sheets that are created by licensees not directly affiliated or controlled by a postal administration.

Excluded items may or may not be footnoted.

**Se-tenants** — Connected stamps of differing features (se-tenants) will be listed in the format most commonly collected. This includes pairs, blocks or larger multiples. Se-tenant units are not always symmetrical. An example is Australia Scott 508, which is a block of seven stamps. If the stamps are primarily collected as a unit, the major number may be assigned to the multiple, with minors going to each component stamp. In cases where continuous-design or other unit se-tenants will receive significant postal use, each stamp is given a major Scott number listing. This includes issues from the United States, Canada, Germany and Great Britain, for example.

# Understanding the Listings

On the opposite page is an enlarged "typical" listing from this catalogue. Below are detailed explanations of each of the highlighted parts of the listing.

**1 Scott number** — Scott catalogue numbers are used to identify specific items when buying, selling or trading stamps. Each listed postage stamp from every country has a unique Scott catalogue number. Therefore, Germany Scott 99, for example, can only refer to a single stamp. Although the Scott catalogue usually lists stamps in chronological order by date of issue, there are exceptions. When a country has issued a set of stamps over a period of time, those stamps within the set are kept together without regard to date of issue. This follows the normal collecting approach of keeping stamps in their natural sets.

When a country issues a set of stamps over a period of time, a group of consecutive catalogue numbers is reserved for the stamps in that set, as issued. If that group of numbers proves to be too few, capital-letter suffixes, such as "A" or "B," may be added to existing numbers to create enough catalogue numbers to cover all items in the set. A capital-letter suffix indicates a major Scott catalogue number listing. Scott generally uses a suffix letter only once. Therefore, a catalogue number listing with a capital-letter suffix will seldom be found with the same letter (lower case) used as a minor-letter listing. If there is a Scott 16A in a set, for example, there will seldom be a Scott 16a. However, a minor-letter "a" listing may be added to a major number containing an "A" suffix (Scott 16Aa, for example).

Suffix letters are cumulative. A minor "b" variety of Scott 16A would be Scott 16Ab, not Scott 16b.

There are times when a reserved block of Scott catalogue numbers is too large for a set, leaving some numbers unused. Such gaps in the numbering sequence also occur when the catalogue editors move an item's listing elsewhere or have removed it entirely from the catalogue. Scott does not attempt to account for every possible number, but rather attempts to assure that each stamp is assigned its own number.

Scott numbers designating regular postage normally are only numerals. Scott numbers for other types of stamps, such as air post, semi-postal, postal tax, postage due, occupation and others have a prefix consisting of one or more capital letters or a combination of numerals and capital letters.

**2 Illustration number** — Illustration or design-type numbers are used to identify each catalogue illustration. For most sets, the lowest face-value stamp is shown. It then serves as an example of the basic design approach for other stamps not illustrated. Where more than one stamp use the same illustration number, but have differences in design, the design paragraph or the description line clearly indicates the design on each stamp not illustrated. Where there are both vertical and horizontal designs in a set, a single illustration may be used, with the exceptions noted in the design paragraph or description line.

When an illustration is followed by a lower-case letter in parentheses, such as "A2(b)," the trailing letter indicates which overprint or surcharge illustration applies.

Illustrations normally are 70 percent of the original size of the stamp. Oversized stamps, blocks and souvenir sheets are reduced even more. Overprints and surcharges are shown at 100 percent of their original size if shown alone, but are 70 percent of original size if shown on stamps. In some cases, the illustration will be placed above the set, between listings or omitted completely. Overprint and surcharge illustrations are not placed in this catalogue for purposes of expertizing stamps.

**3 Paper color** — The color of a stamp's paper is noted in italic type when the paper used is not white.

**4 Listing styles** — There are two principal types of catalogue listings: major and minor.

Major listings are in a larger type style than minor listings. The catalogue number is a numeral that can be found with or without a capital-letter suffix, and with or without a prefix.

Minor listings are in a smaller type style and have a small-letter suffix or (if the listing immediately follows that of the major number) may show only the letter. These listings identify a variety of the major item. Examples include perforation and shade differences, multiples (some souvenir sheets, booklet panes and se-tenant combinations), and singles of multiples.

Examples of major number listings include 16, 28A, B97, C13A, 10N5, and 10N6A. Examples of minor numbers are 16a and C13Ab.

**5 Basic information about a stamp or set** — Introducing each stamp issue is a small section (usually a line listing) of basic information about a stamp or set. This section normally includes the date of issue, method of printing, perforation, watermark and, sometimes, some additional information of note. *Printing method, perforation and watermark apply to the following sets until a change is noted.* Stamps created by overprinting or surcharging previous issues are assumed to have the same perforation, watermark, printing method and other production characteristics as the original. Dates of issue are as precise as Scott is able to confirm and often reflect the dates on first-day covers, rather than the actual date of release.

**6 Denomination** — This normally refers to the face value of the stamp; that is, the cost of the unused stamp at the post office at the time of issue. When a denomination is shown in parentheses, it does not appear on the stamp. This includes the non-denominated stamps of the United States, Brazil and Great Britain, for example.

**7 Color or other description** — This area provides information to solidify identification of a stamp. In many recent cases, a description of the stamp design appears in this space, rather than a listing of colors.

**8 Year of issue** — In stamp sets that have been released in a period that spans more than a year, the number shown in parentheses is the year that stamp first appeared. Stamps without a date appeared during the first year of the issue. Dates are not always given for minor varieties.

**9 Value unused and Value used** — The Scott catalogue values are based on stamps that are in a grade of Very Fine unless stated otherwise. Unused values refer to items that have not seen postal, revenue or any other duty for which they were intended. Pre-1900 unused stamps that were issued with gum must have at least most of their original gum. Later issues are assumed to have full original gum. From breakpoints specified in most countries' listings, stamps are valued as never hinged. Stamps issued without gum are noted. Modern issues with PVA or other synthetic adhesives may appear ungummed. Unused self-adhesive stamps are valued as appearing undisturbed on their original backing paper. Values for used self-adhesive stamps are for examples either on piece or off piece. For a more detailed explanation of these values, please see the "Catalogue Value," "Condition" and "Understanding Valuing Notations" sections elsewhere in this introduction.

In some cases, where used stamps are more valuable than unused stamps, the value is for an example with a contemporaneous cancel, rather than a modern cancel or a smudge or other unclear marking. For those stamps that were released for postal and fiscal purposes, the used value represents a postally used stamp. Stamps with revenue cancels generally sell for less.

Stamps separated from a complete se-tenant multiple usually will be worth less than a pro-rated portion of the se-tenant multiple, and stamps lacking the attached labels that are noted in the listings will be worth less than the values shown.

**10 Changes in basic set information** — Bold type is used to show any changes in the basic data given for a set of stamps. These basic data categories include perforation gauge measurement, paper type, printing method and watermark.

**11 Total value of a set** — The total value of sets of three or more stamps issued after 1900 are shown. The set line also notes the range of Scott numbers and total number of stamps included in the grouping. The actual value of a set consisting predominantly of stamps having the minimum value of 25 cents may be less than the total value shown. Similarly, the actual value or catalogue value of se-tenant pairs or of blocks consisting of stamps having the minimum value of 25 cents may be less than the catalogue values of the component parts.

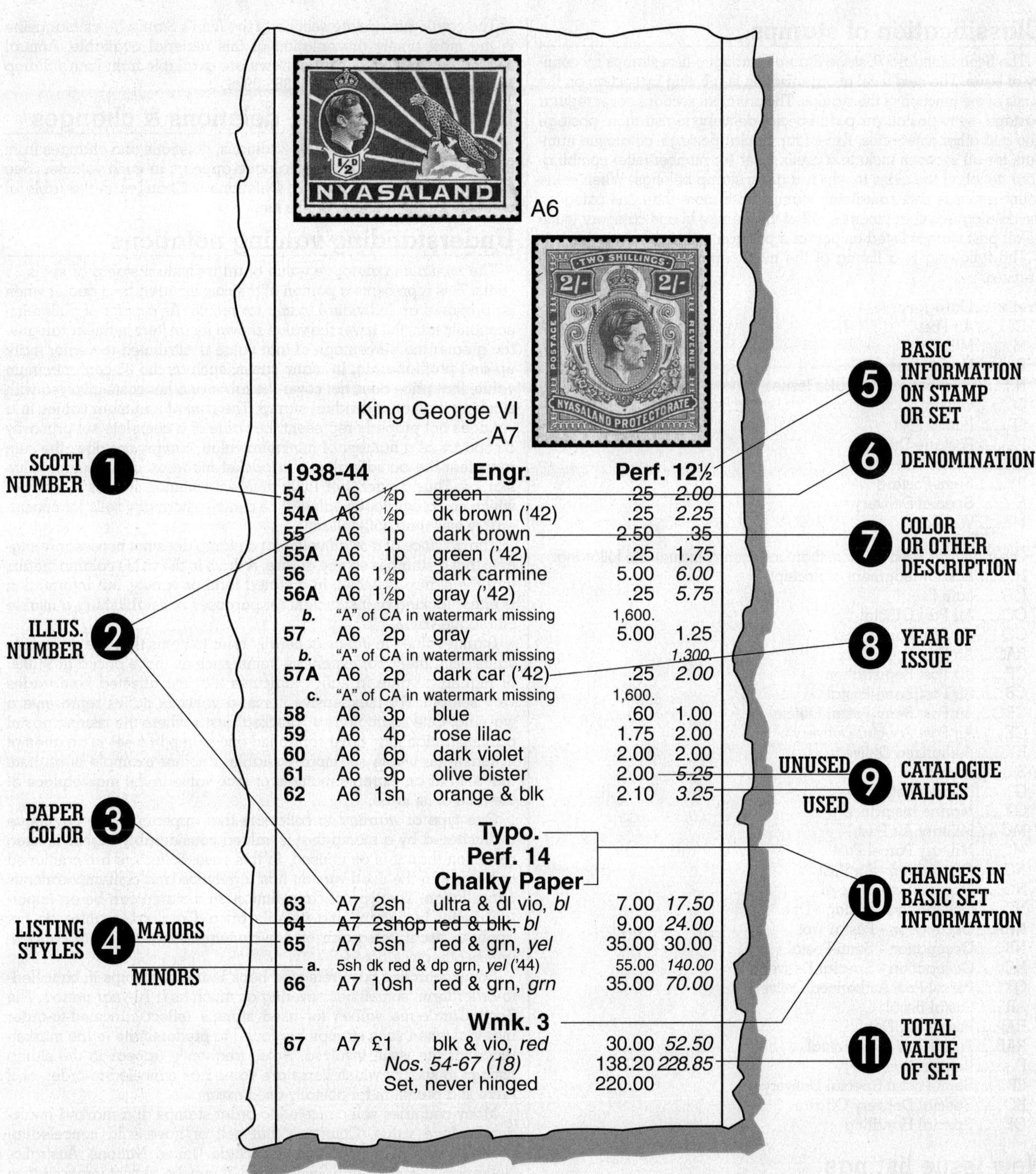


**1938-44 Engr. Perf. 12½**

| | | | | | |
|---|---|---|---|---|---|
| **54** | A6 | ½p | green | .25 | *2.00* |
| **54A** | A6 | ½p | dk brown ('42) | .25 | *2.25* |
| **55** | A6 | 1p | dark brown | 2.50 | .35 |
| **55A** | A6 | 1p | green ('42) | .25 | *1.75* |
| **56** | A6 | 1½p | dark carmine | 5.00 | *6.00* |
| **56A** | A6 | 1½p | gray ('42) | .25 | *5.75* |
| *b.* | "A" of CA in watermark missing | | | 1,600. | |
| **57** | A6 | 2p | gray | 5.00 | 1.25 |
| *b.* | "A" of CA in watermark missing | | | | *1,300.* |
| **57A** | A6 | 2p | dark car ('42) | .25 | *2.00* |
| *c.* | "A" of CA in watermark missing | | | 1,600. | |
| **58** | A6 | 3p | blue | .60 | 1.00 |
| **59** | A6 | 4p | rose lilac | 1.75 | 2.00 |
| **60** | A6 | 6p | dark violet | 2.00 | 2.00 |
| **61** | A6 | 9p | olive bister | 2.00 | *5.25* |
| **62** | A6 | 1sh | orange & blk | 2.10 | *3.25* |

**Typo.**
**Perf. 14**
**Chalky Paper**

| | | | | | |
|---|---|---|---|---|---|
| **63** | A7 | 2sh | ultra & dl vio, *bl* | 7.00 | *17.50* |
| **64** | A7 | 2sh6p | red & blk, *bl* | 9.00 | *24.00* |
| **65** | A7 | 5sh | red & grn, *yel* | 35.00 | 30.00 |
| **a.** | 5sh dk red & dp grn, *yel* ('44) | | | 55.00 | *140.00* |
| **66** | A7 | 10sh | red & grn, *grn* | 35.00 | *70.00* |

**Wmk. 3**

| | | | | | |
|---|---|---|---|---|---|
| **67** | A7 | £1 | blk & vio, *red* | 30.00 | *52.50* |
| | *Nos. 54-67 (18)* | | | 138.20 | *228.85* |
| | Set, never hinged | | | 220.00 | |

# Special Notices

## Classification of stamps

The *Scott Standard Postage Stamp Catalogue* lists stamps by country of issue. The next level of organization is a listing by section on the basis of the function of the stamps. The principal sections cover regular postage, semi-postal, air post, special delivery, registration, postage due and other categories. Except for regular postage, catalogue numbers for all sections include a prefix letter (or number-letter combination) denoting the class to which a given stamp belongs. When some countries issue sets containing stamps from more than one category, the catalogue will at times list all of the stamps in one category (such as air post stamps listed as part of a postage set).

The following is a listing of the most commonly used catalogue prefixes.

**Prefix .... Category**
C......... Air Post
M........ Military
P......... Newspaper
N......... Occupation - Regular Issues
O........ Official
Q........ Parcel Post
J.......... Postage Due
RA...... Postal Tax
B......... Semi-Postal
E......... Special Delivery
MR...... War Tax

Other prefixes used by more than one country include the following:
H......... Acknowledgment of Receipt
I.......... Late Fee
CO...... Air Post Official
CQ...... Air Post Parcel Post
RAC.... Air Post Postal Tax
CF...... Air Post Registration
CB...... Air Post Semi-Postal
CBO... Air Post Semi-Postal Official
CE...... Air Post Special Delivery
EY....... Authorized Delivery
S......... Franchise
G........ Insured Letter
GY...... Marine Insurance
MC..... Military Air Post
MQ..... Military Parcel Post
NC...... Occupation - Air Post
NO...... Occupation - Official
NJ........ Occupation - Postage Due
NRA.... Occupation - Postal Tax
NB...... Occupation - Semi-Postal
NE...... Occupation - Special Delivery
QY...... Parcel Post Authorized Delivery
AR...... Postal-fiscal
RAJ..... Postal Tax Due
RAB.... Postal Tax Semi-Postal
F......... Registration
EB....... Semi-Postal Special Delivery
EO...... Special Delivery Official
QE...... Special Handling

## New issue listings

Updates to this catalogue appear each month in the *Linn's Stamp News* monthly magazine. Included in this update are additions to the listings of countries found in the *Scott Standard Postage Stamp Catalogue* and the *Specialized Catalogue of United States Stamps and Covers*, as well as corrections and updates to current editions of this catalogue.

From time to time there will be changes in the final listings of stamps from the *Linn's Stamp News* magazine to the next edition of the catalogue. This occurs as more information about certain stamps or sets becomes available.

The catalogue update section of the *Linn's Stamp News* magazine is the most timely presentation of this material available. Annual subscriptions to *Linn's Stamp News* are available from Linn's Stamp News, Box 926, Sidney, OH 45365-0926.

## Number additions, deletions & changes

A listing of catalogue number additions, deletions and changes from the previous edition of the catalogue appears in each volume. See Catalogue Number Additions, Deletions & Changes in the table of contents for the location of this list.

## Understanding valuing notations

The *minimum catalogue value* of an individual stamp or set is 25 cents. This represents a portion of the cost incurred by a dealer when he prepares an individual stamp for resale. As a point of philatelic-economic fact, the lower the value shown for an item in this catalogue, the greater the percentage of that value is attributed to dealer mark up and profit margin. In many cases, such as the 25-cent minimum value, that price does not cover the labor or other costs involved with stocking it as an individual stamp. The sum of minimum values in a set does not properly represent the value of a complete set primarily composed of a number of minimum-value stamps, nor does the sum represent the actual value of a packet made up of minimum-value stamps. Thus a packet of 1,000 different common stamps — each of which has a catalogue value of 25 cents — normally sells for considerably less than 250 dollars!

The *absence of a retail value* for a stamp does not necessarily suggest that a stamp is scarce or rare. A dash in the value column means that the stamp is known in a stated form or variety, but information is either lacking or insufficient for purposes of establishing a usable catalogue value.

Stamp values in *italics* generally refer to items that are difficult to value accurately. For expensive items, such as those priced at $1,000 or higher, a value in italics indicates that the affected item trades very seldom. For inexpensive items, a value in italics represents a warning. One example is a "blocked" issue where the issuing postal administration may have controlled one stamp in a set in an attempt to make the whole set more valuable. Another example is an item that sold at an extreme multiple of face value in the marketplace at the time of its issue.

One type of warning to collectors that appears in the catalogue is illustrated by a stamp that is valued considerably higher in used condition than it is as unused. In this case, collectors are cautioned to be certain the used version has a genuine and contemporaneous cancellation. The type of cancellation on a stamp can be an important factor in determining its sale price. Catalogue values do not apply to fiscal, telegraph or non-contemporaneous postal cancels, unless otherwise noted.

Some countries have released back issues of stamps in canceled-to-order form, sometimes covering as much as a 10-year period. The Scott Catalogue values for used stamps reflect canceled-to-order material when such stamps are found to predominate in the marketplace for the issue involved. Notes frequently appear in the stamp listings to specify which items are valued as canceled-to-order, or if there is a premium for postally used examples.

Many countries sell canceled-to-order stamps at a marked reduction of face value. Countries that sell or have sold canceled-to-order stamps at *full* face value include United Nations, Australia, Netherlands, France and Switzerland. It may be almost impossible to identify such stamps if the gum has been removed, because official government canceling devices are used. Postally used examples of these items on cover, however, are usually worth more than the canceled-to-order stamps with original gum.

## Abbreviations

Scott uses a consistent set of abbreviations throughout this catalogue to conserve space, while still providing necessary information.

## COLOR ABBREVIATIONS

| | | |
|---|---|---|
| amb. amber | crim.. crimson | ol .... olive |
| anil.. aniline | cr ..... cream | olvn . olivine |
| ap.... apple | dk .... dark | org... orange |
| aqua aquamarine | dl ..... dull | pck .. peacock |
| az .... azure | dp .... deep | pnksh pinkish |
| bis ... bister | db .... drab | Prus . Prussian |
| bl ..... blue | emer emerald | pur... purple |
| bld... blood | gldn. golden | redsh reddish |
| blk ... black | gryshgrayish | res ... reseda |
| bril... brilliant | grn... green | ros ... rosine |
| brn... brown | grnsh greenish | ryl .... royal |
| brnsh brownish | hel ... heliotrope | sal .... salmon |
| brnz. bronze | hn.... henna | saph sapphire |
| brt.... bright | ind... indigo | scar . scarlet |
| brnt . burnt | int .... intense | sep .. sepia |
| car... carmine | lav ... lavender | sien . sienna |
| cer ... cerise | lem .. lemon | sil..... silver |
| chlky chalky | lil ..... lilac | sl...... slate |
| chamchamois | lt ..... light | stl .... steel |
| chnt . chestnut | mag. magenta | turq.. turquoise |
| choc chocolate | man. manila | ultra ultramarine |
| chr ... chrome | mar.. maroon | Ven .. Venetian |
| cit ... citron | mv ... mauve | ver ... vermilion |
| cl...... claret | multi multicolored | vio ... violet |
| cob .. cobalt | mlky milky | yel ... yellow |
| cop .. copper | myr .. myrtle | yelsh yellowish |

When no color is given for an overprint or surcharge, black is the color used. Abbreviations for colors used for overprints and surcharges include: "(B)" or "(Blk)," black; "(Bl)," blue; "(R)," red; and "(G)," green.

Additional abbreviations in this catalogue are shown below:

Adm. ............Administration
AFL...............American Federation of Labor
Anniv. ............Anniversary
APS ...............American Philatelic Society
Assoc. ...........Association
ASSR. ............Autonomous Soviet Socialist Republic
b. ..................Born
BEP...............Bureau of Engraving and Printing
Bicent. ...........Bicentennial
Bklt................Booklet
Brit.................British
btwn. .............Between
Bur.................Bureau
c. or ca...........Circa
Cat.................Catalogue
Cent. ..............Centennial, century, centenary
CIO ................Congress of Industrial Organizations
Conf. ..............Conference
Cong. .............Congress
Cpl. ................Corporal
CTO ...............Canceled to order
d. ...................Died
Dbl. ................Double
EDU...............Earliest documented use
Engr. ..............Engraved
Exhib..............Exhibition
Expo...............Exposition
Fed. ................Federation
GB .................Great Britain
Gen. ...............General
GPO ...............General post office
Horiz. .............Horizontal
Imperf. ...........Imperforate
Impt................Imprint
Intl. ...............International
Invtd. .............Inverted
L .....................Left
Lieut., lt. ........Lieutenant
Litho. .............Lithographed
LL ...................Lower left
LR....................Lower right
mm..................Millimeter
Ms. ..................Manuscript
Natl. ...............National
No. ..................Number
NY ...................New York
NYC .................New York City
Ovpt. ...............Overprint
Ovptd. .............Overprinted
P.......................Plate number
Perf. .................Perforated, perforation
Phil. .................Philatelic
Photo................Photogravure
PO ....................Post office
Pr. ....................Pair
P.R. ..................Puerto Rico
Prec. .................Precancel, precanceled
Pres. .................President
PTT ...................Post, Telephone and Telegraph
R........................Right
Rio.....................Rio de Janeiro
Sgt.....................Sergeant
Soc. ...................Society
Souv. .................Souvenir
SSR....................Soviet Socialist Republic, see ASSR
St.......................Saint, street
Surch. ................Surcharge
Typo. .................Typographed
UL.......................Upper left
Unwmkd. ...........Unwatermarked
UPU ....................Universal Postal Union
UR ......................Upper Right
US .......................United States
USPOD ...............United States Post Office Department
USSR ..................Union of Soviet Socialist Republics
Vert.....................Vertical
VP.......................Vice president
Wmk. ..................Watermark
Wmkd. ................Watermarked
WWI....................World War I
WWII...................World War II

## Examination

Amos Media Co. will not comment upon the genuineness, grade or condition of stamps, because of the time and responsibility involved. Rather, there are several expertizing groups that undertake this work for both collectors and dealers. Neither will Amos Media Co. appraise or identify philatelic material. The company cannot take responsibility for unsolicited stamps or covers sent by individuals.

All letters, E-mails, etc. are read attentively, but they are not always answered due to time considerations.

## How to order from your dealer

When ordering stamps from a dealer, it is not necessary to write the full description of a stamp as listed in this catalogue. All you need is the name of the country, the Scott catalogue number and whether the desired item is unused or used. For example, "Japan Scott 422 unused" is sufficient to identify the unused stamp of Japan listed as "422 A206 5y brown."

# Basic Stamp Information

A stamp collector's knowledge of the combined elements that make a given stamp issue unique determines his or her ability to identify stamps. These elements include paper, watermark, method of separation, printing, design and gum. On the following pages each of these important areas is briefly described.

## Paper

Paper is an organic material composed of a compacted weave of cellulose fibers and generally formed into sheets. Paper used to print stamps may be manufactured in sheets, or it may have been part of a large roll (called a web) before being cut to size. The fibers most often used to create paper on which stamps are printed include bark, wood, straw and certain grasses. In many cases, linen or cotton rags have been added for greater strength and durability. Grinding, bleaching, cooking and rinsing these raw fibers reduces them to a slushy pulp, referred to by paper makers as "stuff." Sizing and, sometimes, coloring matter is added to the pulp to make different types of finished paper.

After the stuff is prepared, it is poured onto sieve-like frames that allow the water to run off, while retaining the matted pulp. As fibers fall onto the screen and are held by gravity, they form a natural weave that will later hold the paper together. If the screen has metal bits that are formed into letters or images attached, it leaves slightly thinned areas on the paper. These are called watermarks.

When the stuff is almost dry, it is passed under pressure through smooth or engraved rollers - dandy rolls - or placed between cloth in a press to be flattened and dried.

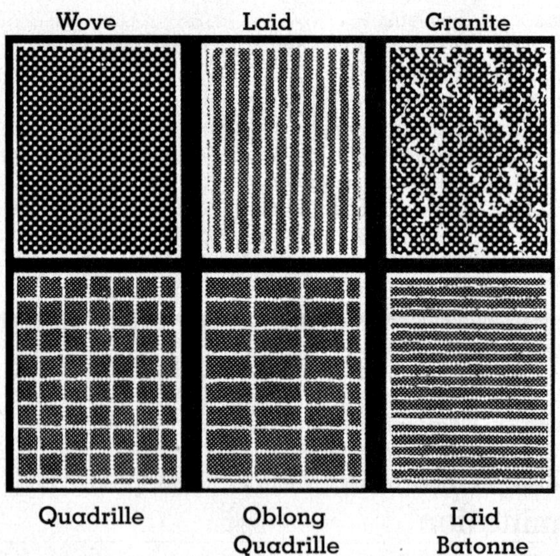


Stamp paper falls broadly into two types: wove and laid. The nature of the surface of the frame onto which the pulp is first deposited causes the differences in appearance between the two. If the surface is smooth and even, the paper will be of fairly uniform texture throughout. This is known as *wove paper*. Early papermaking machines poured the pulp onto a continuously circulating web of felt, but modern machines feed the pulp onto a cloth-like screen made of closely interwoven fine wires. This paper, when held to a light, will show little dots or points very close together. The proper name for this is "wire wove," but the type is still considered wove. Any U.S. or British stamp printed after 1880 will serve as an example of wire wove paper.

Closely spaced parallel wires, with cross wires at wider intervals, make up the frames used for what is known as *laid paper*. A greater thickness of the pulp will settle between the wires. The paper, when held to a light, will show alternate light and dark lines. The spacing and the thickness of the lines may vary, but on any one sheet of paper they are all alike. See Russia Scott 31-38 for examples of laid paper.

*Batonne*, from the French word meaning "a staff," is a term used if the lines in the paper are spaced quite far apart, like the printed ruling on a writing tablet. Batonne paper may be either wove or laid. If laid, fine laid lines can be seen between the batons.

*Quadrille* is the term used when the lines in the paper form little squares. *Oblong quadrille* is the term used when rectangles, rather than squares, are formed. Grid patterns vary from distinct to extremely faint. See Mexico-Guadalajara Scott 35-37 for examples of oblong quadrille paper.

Paper also is classified as thick or thin, hard or soft, and by color. Such colors may include yellowish, greenish, bluish and reddish.

Brief explanations of other types of paper used for printing stamps, as well as examples, follow.

**Colored** — Colored paper is created by the addition of dye in the paper-making process. Such colors may include shades of yellow, green, blue and red. *Surface-colored papers*, most commonly used for British colonial issues in 1913-14, are created when coloring is added only to the surface during the finishing process. Stamps printed on surface-colored paper have white or uncolored backs, while true colored papers are colored through. See Jamaica Scott 71-73.

**Pelure** — Pelure paper is a very thin, hard and often brittle paper that is sometimes bluish or grayish in appearance. See Serbia Scott 169-170.

**Native** — This is a term applied to handmade papers used to produce some of the early stamps of the Indian states. Stamps printed on native paper may be expected to display various natural inclusions that are normal and do not negatively affect value. Japanese paper, originally made of mulberry fibers and rice flour, is part of this group. See Japan Scott 1-18.

**Manila** — This type of paper is often used to make stamped envelopes and wrappers. It is a coarse-textured stock, usually smooth on one side and rough on the other. A variety of colors of manila paper exist, but the most common range is yellowish-brown.

**Silk** — Introduced by the British in 1847 as a safeguard against counterfeiting, silk paper contains bits of colored silk thread scattered throughout. The density of these fibers varies greatly and can include as few as one fiber per stamp or hundreds. U.S. revenue Scott R152 is a good example of an easy-to-identify silk paper stamp.

Silk-thread paper has uninterrupted threads of colored silk arranged so that one or more threads run through the stamp or postal stationery. See Great Britain Scott 5-6 and Switzerland Scott 14-19.

**Granite** — Filled with minute cloth or colored paper fibers of various colors and lengths, granite paper should not be confused with either type of silk paper. Austria Scott 172-175 and a number of Swiss stamps are examples of granite paper.

**Chalky** — A chalk-like substance coats the surface of chalky paper to discourage the cleaning and reuse of canceled stamps, as well as to provide a smoother, more acceptable printing surface. Because the designs of stamps printed on chalky paper are imprinted on what is often a water-soluble coating, any attempt to remove a cancellation will destroy the stamp. *Do not soak these stamps in any fluid.* To remove a stamp printed on chalky paper from an envelope, wet the paper from underneath the stamp until the gum dissolves enough to release the stamp from the paper. See St. Kitts-Nevis Scott 89-90 for examples of stamps printed on this type of chalky paper.

**India** — Another name for this paper, originally introduced from China about 1750, is "China Paper." It is a thin, opaque paper often used for plate and die proofs by many countries.

**Double** — In philately, the term double paper has two distinct meanings. The first is a two-ply paper, usually a combination of a thick and a thin sheet, joined during manufacture. This type was used experimentally as a means to discourage the reuse of stamps.

The design is printed on the thin paper. Any attempt to remove a cancellation would destroy the design. U.S. Scott 158 and other Banknote-era stamps exist on this form of double paper.

The second type of double paper occurs on a rotary press, when the end of one paper roll, or web, is affixed to the next roll to save time feeding the paper through the press. Stamp designs are printed over the joined paper and, if overlooked by inspectors, may get into post office stocks.

**Goldbeater's Skin** — This type of paper was used for the 1866 issue of Prussia, and was a tough, translucent paper. The design was printed in reverse on the back of the stamp, and the gum applied over the printing. It is impossible to remove stamps printed on this type of paper from the paper to which they are affixed without destroying the design.

**Ribbed** — Ribbed paper has an uneven, corrugated surface made by passing the paper through ridged rollers. This type exists on some copies of U.S. Scott 156-165.

Various other substances, or substrates, have been used for stamp manufacture, including wood, aluminum, copper, silver and gold foil, plastic, and silk and cotton fabrics.

## Watermarks

Watermarks are an integral part of some papers. They are formed in the process of paper manufacture. Watermarks consist of small designs, formed of wire or cut from metal and soldered to the surface of the mold or, sometimes, on the dandy roll. The designs may be in the form of crowns, stars, anchors, letters or other characters or symbols. These pieces of metal - known in the paper-making industry as "bits" - impress a design into the paper. The design sometimes may be seen by holding the stamp to the light. Some are more easily seen with a watermark detector. This important tool is a small black tray into which a stamp is placed face down and dampened with a fast-evaporating watermark detection fluid that brings up the watermark image in the form of dark lines against a lighter background. These dark lines are the thinner areas of the paper known as the watermark. Some watermarks are extremely difficult to locate, due to either a faint impression, watermark location or the color of the stamp. There also are electric watermark detectors that come with plastic filter disks of various colors. The disks neutralize the color of the stamp, permitting the watermark to be seen more easily.

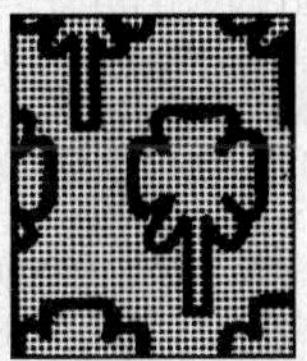

**Multiple watermarks of Crown Agents and Burma**

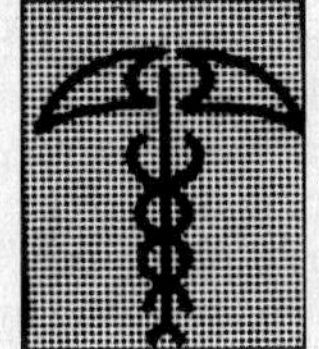

**Watermarks of Uruguay, Vatican City and Jamaica**

**WARNING: Some inks used in the photogravure process dissolve in watermark fluids (Please see the section on Soluble Printing Inks).** Also, see "chalky paper."

Watermarks may be found normal, reversed, inverted, reversed and inverted, sideways or diagonal, as seen from the back of the stamp. The relationship of watermark to stamp design depends on the position of the printing plates or how paper is fed through the press. On machine-made paper, watermarks normally are read from right to left. The design is repeated closely throughout the sheet in a "multiple-watermark design." In a "sheet watermark," the design appears only once on the sheet, but extends over many stamps. Individual stamps may carry only a small fraction or none of the watermark.

"Marginal watermarks" occur in the margins of sheets or panes of stamps. They occur on the outside border of paper (ostensibly outside the area where stamps are to be printed). A large row of letters may spell the name of the country or the manufacturer of the paper, or a border of lines may appear. Careless press feeding may cause parts of these letters and/or lines to show on stamps of the outer row of a pane.

## Soluble Printing Inks

**WARNING:** Most stamp colors are permanent; that is, they are not seriously affected by short-term exposure to light or water. Many colors, especially of modern inks, fade from excessive exposure to light. There are stamps printed with inks that dissolve easily in water or in fluids used to detect watermarks. Use of these inks was intentional to prevent the removal of cancellations. Water affects all aniline inks, those on so-called safety paper and some photogravure printings - all such inks are known as fugitive colors. *Removal from paper of such stamps requires care and alternatives to traditional soaking.*

## Separation

"Separation" is the general term used to describe methods used to separate stamps. The three standard forms currently in use are perforating, rouletting and die-cutting. These methods are done during the stamp production process, after printing. Sometimes these methods are done on-press or sometimes as a separate step. The earliest issues, such as the 1840 Penny Black of Great Britain (Scott 1), did not have any means provided for separation. It was expected the stamps would be cut apart with scissors or folded and torn. These are examples of imperforate stamps. Many stamps were first issued in imperforate formats and were later issued with perforations. Therefore, care must be observed in buying single imperforate stamps to be certain they were issued imperforate and are not perforated copies that have been altered by having the perforations trimmed away. Stamps issued imperforate usually are valued as singles. However, imperforate varieties of normally perforated stamps should be collected in pairs or larger pieces as indisputable evidence of their imperforate character.

### PERFORATION

The chief style of separation of stamps, and the one that is in almost universal use today, is perforating. By this process, paper between the stamps is cut away in a line of holes, usually round, leaving little bridges of paper between the stamps to hold them together. Some types of perforation, such as hyphen-hole perfs, can be confused with roulettes, but a close visual inspection reveals that paper has been removed. The little perforation bridges, which project from the stamp when it is torn from the pane, are called the teeth of the perforation.

As the size of the perforation is sometimes the only way to differentiate between two otherwise identical stamps, it is necessary to be able to accurately measure and describe them. This is done with a perforation gauge, usually a ruler-like device that has dots or graduated lines to show how many perforations may be counted in the space of two centimeters. Two centimeters is the space universally adopted in which to measure perforations.

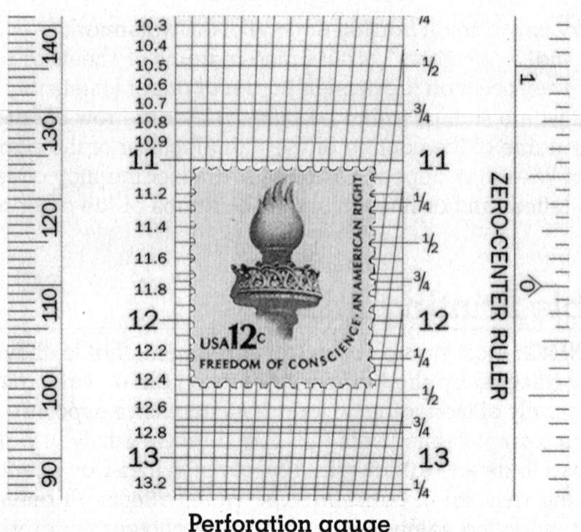

**Perforation gauge**

To measure a stamp, run it along the gauge until the dots on it fit exactly into the perforations of the stamp. If you are using a graduated-line perforation gauge, simply slide the stamp along the surface until the lines on the gauge perfectly project from the center of the bridges or holes. The number to the side of the line of dots or lines that fit the stamp's perforation is the measurement. For example, an "11" means that 11 perforations fit between two centimeters. The description of the stamp therefore is "perf. 11." If the gauge of the perforations on the top and bottom of a stamp differs from that on the sides, the result is what is known as *compound perforations.* In measuring compound perforations, the gauge at top and bottom is always given first, then the sides. Thus, a stamp that measures 11 at top and bottom and 10½ at the sides is "perf. 11 x 10½." See U.S. Scott 632-642 for examples of compound perforations.

Stamps also are known with perforations different on three or all four sides. Descriptions of such items are clockwise, beginning with the top of the stamp.

A perforation with small holes and teeth close together is a "fine perforation." One with large holes and teeth far apart is a "coarse perforation." Holes that are jagged, rather than clean-cut, are "rough perforations." *Blind perforations* are the slight impressions left by the perforating pins if they fail to puncture the paper. Multiples of stamps showing blind perforations may command a slight premium over normally perforated stamps.

The term *syncopated perfs* describes intentional irregularities in the perforations. The earliest form was used by the Netherlands from 1925-33, where holes were omitted to create distinctive patterns. Beginning in 1992, Great Britain has used an oval perforation to help prevent counterfeiting. Several other countries have started using the oval perfs or other syncopated perf patterns.

A new type of perforation, still primarily used for postal stationery, is known as microperfs. Microperfs are tiny perforations (in some cases hundreds of holes per two centimeters) that allows items to be intentionally separated very easily, while not accidentally breaking apart as easily as standard perforations. These are not currently measured or differentiated by size, as are standard perforations.

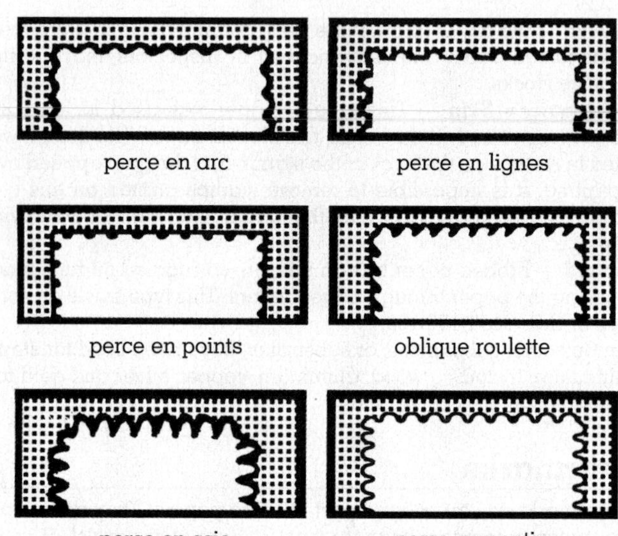


## ROULETTING

In rouletting, the stamp paper is cut partly or wholly through, with no paper removed. In perforating, some paper is removed. Rouletting derives its name from the French roulette, a spur-like wheel. As the wheel is rolled over the paper, each point makes a small cut. The number of cuts made in a two-centimeter space determines the gauge of the roulette, just as the number of perforations in two centimeters determines the gauge of the perforation.

The shape and arrangement of the teeth on the wheels varies. Various roulette types generally carry French names:

*Perce en lignes* - rouletted in lines. The paper receives short, straight cuts in lines. This is the most common type of rouletting. See Mexico Scott 500.

*Perce en points* - pin-rouletted or pin-perfed. This differs from a small perforation because no paper is removed, although round, equidistant holes are pricked through the paper. See Mexico Scott 242-256.

*Perce en arc* and *perce en scie* - pierced in an arc or saw-toothed designs, forming half circles or small triangles. See Hanover (German States) Scott 25-29.

*Perce en serpentin* - serpentine roulettes. The cuts form a serpentine or wavy line. See Brunswick (German States) Scott 13-18.

Once again, no paper is removed by these processes, leaving the stamps easily separated, but closely attached.

## DIE-CUTTING

The third major form of stamp separation is die-cutting. This is a method where a die in the pattern of separation is created that later cuts the stamp paper in a stroke motion. Although some standard stamps bear die-cut perforations, this process is primarily used for self-adhesive postage stamps. Die-cutting can appear in straight lines, such as U.S. Scott 2522, shapes, such as U.S. Scott 1551, or imitating the appearance of perforations, such as New Zealand Scott 935A and 935B.

# Printing Processes

## ENGRAVING (Intaglio, Line-engraving, Etching)

**Master die** — The initial operation in the process of line engraving is making the master die. The die is a small, flat block of softened steel upon which the stamp design is recess engraved in reverse.

Master die

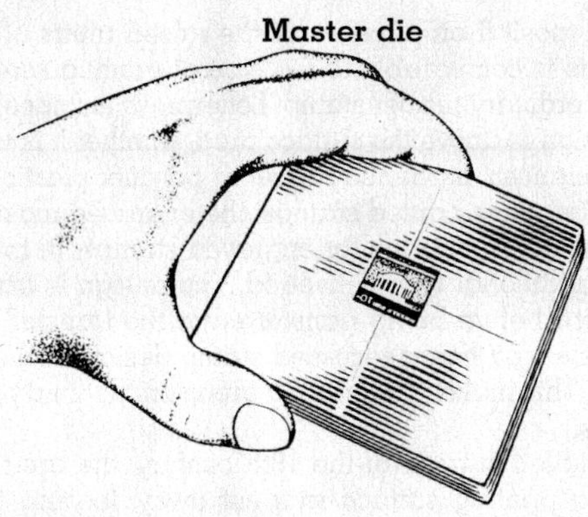

Photographic reduction of the original art is made to the appropriate size. It then serves as a tracing guide for the initial outline of the design. The engraver lightly traces the design on the steel with his graver, then slowly works the design until it is completed. At various points during the engraving process, the engraver hand-inks the die and makes an impression to check his progress. These are known as progressive die proofs. After completion of the engraving, the die is hardened to withstand the stress and pressures of later transfer operations.

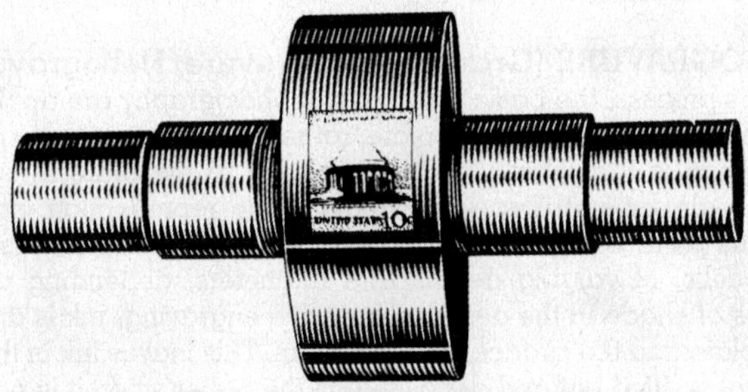

Transfer roll

**Transfer roll** — Next is production of the transfer roll that, as the name implies, is the medium used to transfer the subject from the master die to the printing plate. A blank roll of soft steel, mounted on a mandrel, is placed under the bearers of the transfer press to allow it to roll freely on its axis. The hardened die is placed on the bed of the press and the face of the transfer roll is applied to the die, under pressure. The bed or the roll is then rocked back and forth under increasing pressure, until the soft steel of the roll is forced into every engraved line of the die. The resulting impression on the roll is known as a "relief" or a "relief transfer." The engraved image is now positive in appearance and stands out from the steel. After the required number of reliefs are "rocked in," the soft steel transfer roll is hardened.

Different flaws may occur during the relief process. A defective relief may occur during the rocking in process because of a minute piece of foreign material lodging on the die, or some other cause. Imperfections in the steel of the transfer roll may result in a breaking away of parts of the design. This is known as a relief break, which will show up on finished stamps as small, unprinted areas. If a damaged relief remains in use, it will transfer a repeating defect to the plate. Deliberate alterations of reliefs sometimes occur. "Altered reliefs" designate these changed conditions.

**Plate** — The final step in pre-printing production is the making of the printing plate. A flat piece of soft steel replaces the die on the bed of the transfer press. One of the reliefs on the transfer roll is positioned over this soft steel. Position, or layout, dots determine the correct position on the plate. The dots have been lightly marked on the plate in advance. After the correct position of the relief is determined, the design is rocked in by following the same method used in making the transfer roll. The difference is that this time the image is being transferred from the transfer roll, rather than to it. Once the design is entered on the plate, it appears in reverse and is recessed. There are as many transfers entered on the plate as there are subjects printed on the sheet of stamps. It is during this process that double and shifted transfers occur, as well as re-entries. These are the result of improperly entered images that have not been properly burnished out prior to rocking in a new image.

Modern siderography processes, such as those used by the U.S. Bureau of Engraving and Printing, involve an automated form of rocking designs in on preformed cylindrical printing sleeves. The same process also allows for easier removal and re-entry of worn images right on the sleeve.

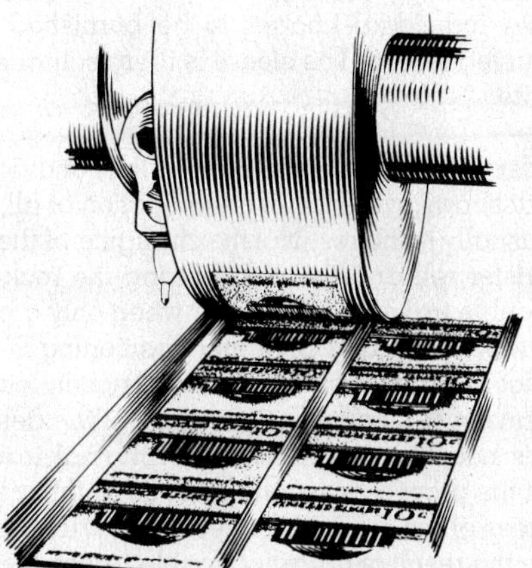

Transferring the design to the plate

Following the entering of the required transfers on the plate, the position dots, layout dots and lines, scratches and other markings generally are burnished out. Added at this time by the siderographer are any required *guide lines, plate numbers* or other *marginal markings*. The plate is then hand-inked and a proof impression is taken. This is known as a plate proof. If the impression is approved, the plate is machined for fitting onto the press, is hardened and sent to the plate vault ready for use.

On press, the plate is inked and the surface is automatically wiped clean, leaving ink only in the recessed lines. Paper is then forced under pressure into the engraved recessed lines, thereby receiving the ink. Thus, the ink lines on engraved stamps are slightly raised, and slight depressions (debossing) occur on the back of the stamp. Prior to the advent of modern high-speed presses and more advanced ink formulations, paper had to be dampened before receiving the ink. This sometimes led to uneven shrinkage by the time the stamps were perforated, resulting in improperly perforated stamps, or misperfs. Newer presses use drier paper, thus both *wet* and *dry printings* exist on some stamps.

**Rotary Press** — Until 1914, only flat plates were used to print engraved stamps. Rotary press printing was introduced in 1914, and slowly spread. Some countries still use flat-plate printing.

After approval of the plate proof, older *rotary press plates* require additional machining. They are curved to fit the press cylinder. "Gripper slots" are cut into the back of each plate to receive the "grippers," which hold the plate securely on the press. The plate is then hardened. Stamps printed from these bent rotary press plates are longer or wider than the same stamps printed from flat-plate presses. The stretching of the plate during the curving process is what causes this distortion.

**Re-entry** — To execute a re-entry on a flat plate, the transfer roll is re-applied to the plate, often at some time after its first use on the press. Worn-out designs can be resharpened by carefully burnishing out the original image and re-entering it from the transfer roll. If the original impression has not been sufficiently removed and the transfer roll is not precisely in line with the remaining impression, the resulting double transfer will make the re-entry obvious. If the registration is true, a re-entry may be difficult or impossible to distinguish. Sometimes a stamp printed from a successful re-entry is identified by having a much sharper and clearer impression than its neighbors. With the advent of rotary presses, post-press re-entries were not possible. After a plate was curved for the rotary press, it was impossible to make a re-entry. This is because the plate had already been bent once (with the design distorted).

However, with the introduction of the previously mentioned modern-style siderography machines, entries are made to the preformed cylindrical printing sleeve. Such sleeves are dechromed and softened. This allows individual images to be burnished out and re-entered on the curved sleeve. The sleeve is then rechromed, resulting in longer press life.

**Double Transfer** — This is a description of the condition of a transfer on a plate that shows evidence of a duplication of all, or a portion of the design. It usually is the result of the changing of the registration between the transfer roll and the plate during the rocking in of the original entry. Double transfers also occur when only a portion of the design has been rocked in and improper positioning is noted. If the worker elected not to burnish out the partial or completed design, a strong double transfer will occur for part or all of the design.

It sometimes is necessary to remove the original transfer from a plate and repeat the process a second time. If the finished re-worked image shows traces of the original impression, attributable to incomplete burnishing, the result is a partial double transfer.

With the modern automatic machines mentioned previously, double transfers are all but impossible to create. Those partially doubled images on stamps printed from such sleeves are more than likely re-entries, rather than true double transfers.

**Re-engraved** — Alterations to a stamp design are sometimes necessary after some stamps have been printed. In some cases, either the original die or the actual printing plate may have its "temper" drawn (softened), and the design will be re-cut. The resulting impressions from such a re-engraved die or plate may differ slightly from the original issue, and are known as "re-engraved." If the alteration was made to the master die, all future printings will be consistently different from the original. If alterations were made to the printing plate, each altered stamp on the plate will be slightly different from each other, allowing specialists to reconstruct a complete printing plate.

**Dropped Transfers** — If an impression from the transfer roll has not been properly placed, a dropped transfer may occur. The final stamp image will appear obviously out of line with its neighbors.

**Short Transfer** — Sometimes a transfer roll is not rocked its entire length when entering a transfer onto a plate. As a result, the finished transfer on the plate fails to show the complete design, and the finished stamp will have an incomplete design printed. This is known as a "short transfer." U.S. Scott No. 8 is a good example of a short transfer.

## TYPOGRAPHY (Letterpress, Surface Printing, Flexography, Dry Offset, High Etch)

Although the word "Typography" is obsolete as a term describing a printing method, it was the accepted term throughout the first century of postage stamps. Therefore, appropriate Scott listings in this catalogue refer to typographed stamps. The current term for this form of printing, however, is "letterpress."

As it relates to the production of postage stamps, letterpress printing is the reverse of engraving. Rather than having recessed areas trap the ink and deposit it on paper, only the raised areas of the design are inked. This is comparable to the type of printing seen by inking and using an ordinary rubber stamp. Letterpress includes all printing where the design is above the surface area, whether it is wood, metal or, in some instances, hardened rubber or polymer plastic.

For most letterpress-printed stamps, the engraved master is made in much the same manner as for engraved stamps. In this instance, however, an additional step is needed. The design is transferred to another surface before being transferred to the transfer roll. In this way, the transfer roll has a recessed stamp design, rather than one done in relief. This makes the printing areas on the final plate raised, or relief areas.

For less-detailed stamps of the 19th century, the area on the die not used as a printing surface was cut away, leaving the surface area raised. The original die was then reproduced by stereotyping or electrotyping. The resulting electrotypes were assembled in the required number and format of the desired sheet of stamps. The plate used in printing the stamps was an electroplate of these assembled electrotypes.

Once the final letterpress plates are created, ink is applied to the raised surface and the pressure of the press transfers the ink impression to the paper. In contrast to engraving, the fine lines of letterpress are impressed on the surface of the stamp, leaving a debossed surface. When viewed from the back (as on a typewritten page), the corresponding line work on the stamp will be raised slightly (embossed) above the surface.

## PHOTOGRAVURE (Gravure, Rotogravure, Heliogravure)

In this process, the basic principles of photography are applied to a chemically sensitized metal plate, rather than photographic paper. The design is transferred photographically to the plate through a halftone, or dot-matrix screen, breaking the reproduction into tiny dots. The plate is treated chemically and the dots form depressions, called cells, of varying depths and diameters, depending on the degrees of shade in the design. Then, like engraving, ink is applied to the plate and the surface is wiped clean. This leaves ink in the tiny cells that is lifted out and deposited on the paper when it is pressed against the plate.

Gravure is most often used for multicolored stamps, generally using the three primary colors (red, yellow and blue) and black. By varying the dot matrix pattern and density of these colors, virtually any color can be reproduced. A typical full-color gravure stamp will be created from four printing cylinders (one for each color). The original multicolored image will have been photographically separated into its component colors.

Modern gravure printing may use computer-generated dot-matrix screens, and modern plates may be of various types including metal-coated plastic. The catalogue designation of Photogravure (or "Photo") covers any of these older and more modern gravure methods of printing.

For examples of the first photogravure stamps printed (1914), see Bavaria Scott 94-114.

## LITHOGRAPHY (Offset Lithography, Stone Lithography, Dilitho, Planography, Collotype)

The principle that oil and water do not mix is the basis for lithography. The stamp design is drawn by hand or transferred from engraving to the surface of a lithographic stone or metal plate in a greasy (oily) substance. This oily substance holds the ink, which will later be transferred to the paper. The stone (or plate) is wet with an acid fluid, causing it to repel the printing ink in all areas not covered by the greasy substance.

Transfer paper is used to transfer the design from the original stone or plate. A series of duplicate transfers are grouped and, in turn, transferred to the final printing plate.

**Photolithography** — The application of photographic processes to lithography. This process allows greater flexibility of design, related to use of halftone screens combined with line work. Unlike photogravure or engraving, this process can allow large, solid areas to be printed.

**Offset** — A refinement of the lithographic process. A rubber-covered blanket cylinder takes the impression from the inked lithographic plate. From the "blanket" the impression is *offset* or transferred to the paper. Greater flexibility and speed are the principal reasons offset printing has largely displaced lithography. The term "lithography" covers both processes, and results are almost identical.

### EMBOSSED (Relief) Printing

Embossing, not considered one of the four main printing types, is a method in which the design first is sunk into the metal of the die. Printing is done against a yielding platen, such as leather or linoleum. The platen is forced into the depression of the die, thus forming the design on the paper in relief. This process is often used for metallic inks.

Embossing may be done without color (see Sardinia Scott 4-6); with color printed around the embossed area (see Great Britain Scott 5 and most U.S. envelopes); and with color in exact registration with the embossed subject (see Canada Scott 656-657).

### HOLOGRAMS

For objects to appear as holograms on stamps, a model exactly the same size as it is to appear on the hologram must be created. Rather than using photographic film to capture the image, holography records an image on a photoresist material. In processing, chemicals eat away at certain exposed areas, leaving a pattern of constructive and destructive interference. When the photoresist is developed, the result is a pattern of uneven ridges that acts as a mold. This mold is then coated with metal, and the resulting form is used to press copies in much the same way phonograph records are produced.

A typical reflective hologram used for stamps consists of a reproduction of the uneven patterns on a plastic film that is applied to a reflective background, usually a silver or gold foil. Light is reflected off the background through the film, making the pattern present on the film visible. Because of the uneven pattern of the film, the viewer will perceive the objects in their proper three-dimensional relationships with appropriate brightness.

The first hologram on a stamp was produced by Austria in 1988 (Scott 1441).

### FOIL APPLICATION

A modern technique of applying color to stamps involves the application of metallic foil to the stamp paper. A pattern of foil is applied to the stamp paper by use of a stamping die. The foil usually is flat, but it may be textured. Canada Scott 1735 has three different foil applications in pearl, bronze and gold. The gold foil was textured using a chemical-etch copper embossing die. The printing of this stamp also involved two-color offset lithography plus embossing.

### THERMOGRAPHY

In the 1990s stamps began to be enhanced with thermographic printing. In this process, a powdered polymer is applied over a sheet that has just been printed. The powder adheres to ink that lacks drying or hardening agents and does not adhere to areas where the ink has these agents. The excess powder is removed and the sheet is briefly heated to melt the powder. The melted powder solidifies after cooling, producing a raised, shiny effect on the stamps. See Scott New Caledonia C239-C240.

### COMBINATION PRINTINGS

Sometimes two or even three printing methods are combined in producing stamps. In these cases, such as Austria Scott 933 or Canada 1735 (described in the preceding paragraph), the multiple-printing technique can be determined by studying the individual characteristics of each printing type. A few stamps, such as Singapore Scott 684-684A, combine as many as three of the four major printing types (lithography, engraving and typography). When this is done it often indicates the incorporation of security devices against counterfeiting.

### INK COLORS

Inks or colored papers used in stamp printing often are of mineral origin, although there are numerous examples of organic-based pigments. As a general rule, organic-based pigments are far more subject to varieties and change than those of mineral-based origin.

The appearance of any given color on a stamp may be affected by many aspects, including printing variations, light, color of paper, aging and chemical alterations.

Numerous printing variations may be observed. Heavier pressure or inking will cause a more intense color, while slight interruptions in the ink feed or lighter impressions will cause a lighter appearance. Stamps printed in the same color by water-based and solvent-based inks can differ significantly in appearance. This affects several stamps in the U.S. Prominent Americans series. Hand-mixed ink formulas (primarily from the 19th century) produced under different conditions (humidity and temperature) account for notable color variations in early printings of the same stamp (see U.S. Scott 248-250, 279B, for example). Different sources of pigment can also result in significant differences in color.

Light exposure and aging are closely related in the way they affect stamp color. Both eventually break down the ink and fade colors, so that a carefully kept stamp may differ significantly in color from an identical copy that has been exposed to light. If stamps are exposed to light either intentionally or accidentally, their colors can be faded or completely changed in some cases.

Papers of different quality and consistency used for the same stamp printing may affect color appearance. Most pelure papers, for example, show a richer color when compared with wove or laid papers. See Russia Scott 181a, for an example of this effect.

The very nature of the printing processes can cause a variety of differences in shades or hues of the same stamp. Some of these shades are scarcer than others, and are of particular interest to the advanced collector.

## Luminescence

All forms of tagged stamps fall under the general category of luminescence. Within this broad category is fluorescence, dealing with forms of tagging visible under longwave ultraviolet light, and phosphorescence, which deals with tagging visible only under shortwave light. Phosphorescence leaves an afterglow and fluorescence does not. These treated stamps show up in a range of different colors when exposed to UV light. The differing wavelengths of the light activates the tagging material, making it glow in various colors that usually serve different mail processing purposes.

Intentional tagging is a post-World War II phenomenon, brought about by the increased literacy rate and rapidly growing mail volume. It was one of several answers to the problem of the need for more automated mail processes. Early tagged stamps served the purpose of triggering machines to separate different types of mail. A natural outgrowth was to also use the signal to trigger machines that faced all envelopes the same way and canceled them.

Tagged stamps come in many different forms. Some tagged stamps have luminescent shapes or images imprinted on them as a form of security device. Others have blocks (United States), stripes, frames (South Africa and Canada), overall coatings (United States), bars (Great Britain and Canada) and many other types. Some types of tagging are even mixed in with the pigmented printing ink (Australia Scott 366, Netherlands Scott 478 and U.S. Scott 1359 and 2443).

The means of applying taggant to stamps differs as much as the intended purposes for the stamps. The most common form of tagging is a coating applied to the surface of the printed stamp. Since the taggant ink is frequently invisible except under UV light, it does not interfere with the appearance of the stamp. Another common application is the use of phosphored papers. In this case the paper itself either has a coating of taggant applied before the stamp is printed, has taggant applied during the papermaking process (incorporating it into the fibers), or has the taggant mixed into the coating of the paper. The latter method, among others, is currently in use in the United States.

Many countries now use tagging in various forms to either expedite mail handling or to serve as a printing security device against counterfeiting. Following the introduction of tagged stamps for public use in 1959 by Great Britain, other countries have steadily joined the parade. Among those are Germany (1961); Canada and Denmark (1962); United States, Australia, France and Switzerland (1963); Belgium and Japan (1966); Sweden and Norway (1967); Italy (1968); and Russia (1969). Since then, many other countries have begun using forms of tagging, including Brazil, China, Czechoslovakia, Hong Kong, Guatemala, Indonesia, Israel, Lithuania, Luxembourg, Netherlands, Penrhyn Islands, Portugal, St. Vincent, Singapore, South Africa, Spain and Sweden to name a few.

In some cases, including United States, Canada, Great Britain and Switzerland, stamps were released both with and without tagging. Many of these were released during each country's experimental period. Tagged and untagged versions are listed for the aforementioned countries and are noted in some other countries' listings. For at least a few stamps, the experimentally tagged version is worth far more than its untagged counterpart, such as the 1963 experimental tagged version of France Scott 1024.

In some cases, luminescent varieties of stamps were inadvertently created. Several Russian stamps, for example, sport highly fluorescent ink that was not intended as a form of tagging. Older stamps, such as early U.S. postage dues, can be positively identified by the use of UV light, since the organic ink used has become slightly fluorescent over time. Other stamps, such as Austria Scott 70a-82a (varnish bars) and Obock Scott 46-64 (printed quadrille lines), have become fluorescent over time.

Various fluorescent substances have been added to paper to make it appear brighter. These optical brightners, as they are known, greatly affect the appearance of the stamp under UV light. The brightest of these is known as Hi-Brite paper. These paper varieties are beyond the scope of the Scott Catalogue.

Shortwave UV light also is used extensively in expertizing, since each form of paper has its own fluorescent characteristics that are impossible to perfectly match. It is therefore a simple matter to detect filled thins, added perforation teeth and other alterations that involve the addition of paper. UV light also is used to examine stamps that have had cancels chemically removed and for other purposes as well.

## Gum

The Illustrated Gum Chart in the first part of this introduction shows and defines various types of gum condition. Because gum condition has an important impact on the value of unused stamps, we recommend studying this chart and the accompanying text carefully.

The gum on the back of a stamp may be shiny, dull, smooth, rough, dark, white, colored or tinted. Most stamp gumming adhesives use gum arabic or dextrine as a base. Certain polymers such as polyvinyl alcohol (PVA) have been used extensively since World War II.

The *Scott Standard Postage Stamp Catalogue* does not list items by types of gum. The *Scott Specialized Catalogue of United States Stamps and Covers* does differentiate among some types of gum for certain issues.

Reprints of stamps may have gum differing from the original issues. In addition, some countries have used different gum formulas for different seasons. These adhesives have different properties that may become more apparent over time.

Many stamps have been issued without gum, and the catalogue will note this fact. See, for example, United States Scott 40-47. Sometimes, gum may have been removed to preserve the stamp. Germany Scott B68, for example, has a highly acidic gum that eventually destroys the stamps. This item is valued in the catalogue with gum removed.

## Reprints and Reissues

These are impressions of stamps (usually obsolete) made from the original plates or stones. If they are valid for postage and reproduce obsolete issues (such as U.S. Scott 102-111), the stamps are *reissues*. If they are from current issues, they are designated as *second, third,* etc., *printing*. If designated for a particular purpose, they are called *special printings*.

When special printings are not valid for postage, but are made from original dies and plates by authorized persons, they are *official reprints. Private reprints* are made from the original plates and dies by private hands. An example of a private reprint is that of the 1871-1932 reprints made from the original die of the 1845 New Haven, Conn., postmaster's provisional. *Official reproductions* or imitations are made from new dies and plates by government authorization. Scott will list those reissues that are valid for postage if they differ significantly from the original printing.

The U.S. government made special printings of its first postage stamps in 1875. Produced were official imitations of the first two stamps (listed as Scott 3-4), reprints of the demonetized pre-1861 issues (Scott 40-47) and reissues of the 1861 stamps, the 1869 stamps and the then-current 1875 denominations. Even though the official imitations and the reprints were not valid for postage, Scott lists all of these U.S. special printings.

Most reprints or reissues differ slightly from the original stamp in some characteristic, such as gum, paper, perforation, color or watermark. Sometimes the details are followed so meticulously that only a student of that specific stamp is able to distinguish the reprint or reissue from the original.

## Remainders and Canceled to Order

Some countries sell their stock of old stamps when a new issue replaces them. To avoid postal use, the *remainders* usually are canceled with a punch hole, a heavy line or bar, or a more-or-less regular-looking cancellation. The most famous merchant of remainders was Nicholas F. Seebeck. In the 1880s and 1890s, he arranged printing contracts between the Hamilton Bank Note Co., of which he was a director, and several Central and South American countries. The contracts provided that the plates and all remainders of the yearly issues became the property of Hamilton. Seebeck saw to it that ample stock remained. The "Seebecks," both remainders and reprints, were standard packet fillers for decades.

Some countries also issue stamps *canceled-to-order (CTO),* either in sheets with original gum or stuck onto pieces of paper or envelopes and canceled. Such CTO items generally are worth less than postally used stamps. In cases where the CTO material is far more prevalent in the marketplace than postally used examples, the catalogue value relates to the CTO examples, with postally used examples noted as premium items. Most CTOs can be detected by the presence of gum. However, as the CTO practice goes back at least to 1885, the gum inevitably has been soaked off some stamps so they could pass as postally used. The normally applied postmarks usually differ slightly from standard postmarks, and specialists are able to tell the difference. When applied individually to envelopes by philatelically minded persons, CTO material is known as *favor canceled* and generally sells at large discounts.

## Cinderellas and Facsimiles

*Cinderella* is a catch-all term used by stamp collectors to describe phantoms, fantasies, bogus items, municipal issues, exhibition seals, local revenues, transportation stamps, labels, poster stamps and many other types of items. Some cinderella collectors include in their collections local postage issues, telegraph stamps, essays and proofs, forgeries and counterfeits.

A *fantasy* is an adhesive created for a nonexistent stamp-issuing authority. Fantasy items range from imaginary countries (Occusi-Ambeno, Kingdom of Sedang, Principality of Trinidad or Torres Straits), to non-existent locals (Winans City Post), or nonexistent transportation lines (McRobish & Co.'s Acapulco-San Francisco Line).

On the other hand, if the entity exists and could have issued stamps (but did not) or was known to have issued other stamps, the items are considered *bogus* stamps. These would include the Mormon postage stamps of Utah, S. Allan Taylor's Guatemala and Paraguay inventions, the propaganda issues for the South Moluccas and the adhesives of the Page & Keyes local post of Boston.

*Phantoms* is another term for both fantasy and bogus issues.

*Facsimiles* are copies or imitations made to represent original stamps, but which do not pretend to be originals. A catalogue illustration is such a facsimile. Illustrations from the Moens catalogue of the last century were occasionally colored and passed off as stamps. Since the beginning of stamp collecting, facsimiles have been made for collectors as space fillers or for reference. They often carry the word "facsimile," "falsch" (German), "sanko" or "mozo" (Japanese), or "faux" (French) overprinted on the face or stamped on the back. Unfortunately, over the years a number of these items have had fake cancels applied over the facsimile notation and have been passed off as genuine.

## Forgeries and Counterfeits

Forgeries and counterfeits have been with philately virtually from the beginning of stamp production. Over time, the terminology for the two has been used interchangeably. Although both forgeries and counterfeits are reproductions of stamps, the purposes behind their creation differ considerably.

Among specialists there is an increasing movement to more specifically define such items. Although there is no universally accepted terminology, we feel the following definitions most closely mirror the items and their purposes as they are currently defined.

*Forgeries* (also often referred to as *Counterfeits*) are reproductions of genuine stamps that have been created to defraud collectors. Such spurious items first appeared on the market around 1860, and most old-time collections contain one or more. Many are crude and easily spotted, but some can deceive experts.

An important supplier of these early philatelic forgeries was the Hamburg printer Gebruder Spiro. Many others with reputations in this craft included S. Allan Taylor, George Hussey, James Chute, George Forune, Benjamin & Sarpy, Julius Goldner, E. Oneglia and L.H. Mercier. Among the noted 20th-century forgers were Francois Fournier, Jean Sperati and the prolific Raoul DeThuin.

Forgeries may be complete replications, or they may be genuine stamps altered to resemble a scarcer (and more valuable) type. Most forgeries, particularly those of rare stamps, are worth only a small fraction of the value of a genuine example, but a few types, created by some of the most notable forgers, such as Sperati, can be worth as much or more than the genuine. Fraudulently produced copies are known of most classic rarities and many medium-priced stamps.

In addition to rare stamps, large numbers of common 19th- and early 20th-century stamps were forged to supply stamps to the early packet trade. Many can still be easily found. Few new philatelic forgeries have appeared in recent decades. Successful imitation of well-engraved work is virtually impossible. It has proven far easier to produce a fake by altering a genuine stamp than to duplicate a stamp completely.

*Counterfeit* (also often referred to as *Postal Counterfeit* or *Postal Forgery*) is the term generally applied to reproductions of stamps that have been created to defraud the government of revenue. Such items usually are created at the time a stamp is current and, in some cases, are hard to detect. Because most counterfeits are seized when the perpetrator is captured, postal counterfeits, particularly used on cover, are usually worth much more than a genuine example to specialists. The first postal counterfeit was of Spain's 4-cuarto carmine of 1854 (the real one is Scott 25). Apparently, the counterfeiters were not satisfied with their first version, which is now very scarce, and they soon created an engraved counterfeit, which is common. Postal counterfeits quickly followed in Austria, Naples, Sardinia and the Roman States. They have since been created in many other countries as well, including the United States.

An infamous counterfeit to defraud the government is the 1-shilling Great Britain "Stock Exchange" forgery of 1872, used on telegraph forms at the exchange that year. The stamp escaped detection until a stamp dealer noticed it in 1898.

## Fakes

*Fakes* are genuine stamps altered in some way to make them more desirable. One student of this part of stamp collecting has estimated that by the 1950s more than 30,000 varieties of fakes were known. That number has grown greatly since then. The widespread existence of fakes makes it important for stamp collectors to study their philatelic holdings and use relevant literature. Likewise, collectors should buy from reputable dealers who guarantee their stamps and make full and prompt refunds should a purchased item be declared faked or altered by some mutually agreed-upon authority. Because fakes always have some genuine characteristics, it is not always possible to obtain unanimous agreement among experts regarding specific items. These students may change their opinions as philatelic knowledge increases. More than 80 percent of all fakes on the philatelic market today are regummed, reperforated (or perforated for the first time), or bear forged overprints, surcharges or cancellations.

Stamps can be chemically treated to alter or eliminate colors. For example, a pale rose stamp can be re-colored to resemble a blue shade of high market value. In other cases, treated stamps can be made to resemble missing color varieties. Designs may be changed by painting, or a stroke or a dot added or bleached out to turn an ordinary variety into a seemingly scarcer stamp. Part of a stamp can be bleached and reprinted in a different version, achieving an inverted center or frame. Margins can be added or repairs done so deceptively that the stamps move from the "repaired" into the "fake" category.

Fakers have not left the backs of the stamps untouched either. They may create false watermarks, add fake grills or press out genuine grills. A thin India paper proof may be glued onto a thicker backing to create the appearance an issued stamp, or a proof printed on cardboard may be shaved down and perforated to resemble a stamp. Silk threads are impressed into paper and stamps have been split so that a rare paper variety is added to an otherwise inexpensive stamp. The most common treatment to the back of a stamp, however, is regumming.

Some in the business of faking stamps have openly advertised fool-proof application of "original gum" to stamps that lack it, although most publications now ban such ads from their pages. It is believed that very few early stamps have survived without being hinged. The large number of never-hinged examples of such earlier material offered for sale thus suggests the widespread extent of regumming activity. Regumming also may be used to hide repairs or thin spots. Dipping the stamp into watermark fluid, or examining it under longwave ultraviolet light often will reveal these flaws.

Fakers also tamper with separations. Ingenious ways to add margins are known. Perforated wide-margin stamps may be falsely represented as imperforate when trimmed. Reperforating is commonly done to create scarce coil or perforation varieties, and to eliminate the naturally occurring straight-edge stamps found in sheet margin positions of many earlier issues. Custom has made straight-edged stamps less desirable. Fakers have obliged by perforating straight-edged stamps so that many are now uncommon, if not rare.

Another fertile field for the faker is that of overprints, surcharges and cancellations. The forging of rare surcharges or overprints began in the 1880s or 1890s. These forgeries are sometimes difficult to detect, but experts have identified almost all. Occasionally, overprints or cancellations are removed to create non-overprinted stamps or seemingly unused items. This is most commonly done by removing a manuscript cancel to make a stamp resemble an unused example. "SPECIMEN" overprints may be removed by scraping and repainting to create non-overprinted varieties. Fakers use inexpensive revenues or pen-canceled stamps to generate unused stamps for further faking by adding other markings. The quartz lamp or UV lamp and a high-powered magnifying glass help to easily detect removed cancellations.

The bigger problem, however, is the addition of overprints, surcharges or cancellations - many with such precision that they are very difficult to ascertain. Plating of the stamps or the overprint can be an important method of detection.

Fake postmarks may range from many spurious fancy cancellations to a host of markings applied to transatlantic covers, to adding normally appearing postmarks to definitives of some countries with stamps that are valued far higher used than unused. With the increased popularity of cover collecting, and the widespread interest in postal history, a fertile new field for fakers has come about. Some have tried to create entire covers. Others specialize in adding stamps, tied by fake cancellations, to genuine stampless covers, or replacing less expensive or damaged stamps with more valuable ones. Detailed study of postal rates in effect at the time a cover in question was mailed, including the analysis of each handstamp used during the period, ink analysis and similar techniques, usually will unmask the fraud.

## Restoration and Repairs

Scott bases its catalogue values on stamps that are free of defects and otherwise meet the standards set forth earlier in this introduction. Most stamp collectors desire to have the finest copy of an item possible. Even within given grading categories there are variances. This leads to a controversial practice that is not defined in any universal manner: stamp *restoration.*

There are broad differences of opinion about what is permissible when it comes to restoration. Carefully applying a soft eraser to a stamp or cover to remove light soiling is one form of restoration, as is washing a stamp in mild soap and water to clean it. These are fairly accepted forms of restoration. More severe forms of restoration include pressing out creases or removing stains caused by tape. To what degree each of these is acceptable is dependent upon the individual situation. Further along the spectrum is the freshening of a stamp's color by removing oxide build-up or the effects of wax paper left next to stamps shipped to the tropics.

At some point in this spectrum the concept of *repair* replaces that of restoration. Repairs include filling thin spots, mending tears by reweaving or adding a missing perforation tooth. Regumming stamps may have been acceptable as a restoration or repair technique many decades ago, but today it is considered a form of fakery.

Restored stamps may or may not sell at a discount, and it is possible that the value of individual restored items may be enhanced over that of their pre-restoration state. Specific situations dictate the resultant value of such an item. Repaired stamps sell at substantial discounts from the value of sound stamps.

# Terminology

**Booklets** — Many countries have issued stamps in small booklets for the convenience of users. This idea continues to become increasingly popular in many countries. Booklets have been issued in many sizes and forms, often with advertising on the covers, the panes of stamps or on the interleaving.

The panes used in booklets may be printed from special plates or made from regular sheets. All panes from booklets issued by the United States and many from those of other countries contain stamps that are straight edged on the sides, but perforated between. Others are distinguished by orientation of watermark or other identifying features. Any stamp-like unit in the pane, either printed or blank, that is not a postage stamp, is considered to be a *label* in the catalogue listings.

Scott lists and values booklet panes. Modern complete booklets also are listed and valued. Individual booklet panes are listed only when they are not fashioned from existing sheet stamps and, therefore, are identifiable from their sheet stamp counterparts.

Panes usually do not have a used value assigned to them because there is little market activity for used booklet panes, even though many exist used and there is some demand for them.

**Cancellations** — The marks or obliterations put on stamps by postal authorities to show that they have performed service and to prevent their reuse are known as cancellations. If the marking is made with a pen, it is considered a "pen cancel." When the location of the post office appears in the marking, it is a "town cancellation." A "postmark" is technically any postal marking, but in practice the term generally is applied to a town cancellation with a date. When calling attention to a cause or celebration, the marking is known as a "slogan cancellation." Many other types and styles of cancellations exist, such as duplex, numerals, targets, fancy and others. See also "precancels," below.

**Coil Stamps** — These are stamps that are issued in rolls for use in dispensers, affixing and vending machines. Those coils of the United States, Canada, Sweden and some other countries are perforated horizontally or vertically only, with the outer edges imperforate. Coil stamps of some countries, such as Great Britain and Germany, are perforated on all four sides and may in some cases be distinguished from their sheet stamp counterparts by watermarks, counting numbers on the reverse or other means.

**Covers** — Entire envelopes, with or without adhesive postage stamps, that have passed through the mail and bear postal or other markings of philatelic interest are known as covers. Before the introduction of envelopes in about 1840, people folded letters and wrote the address on the outside. Some people covered their letters with an extra sheet of paper on the outside for the address, producing the term "cover." Used airletter sheets, stamped envelopes and other items of postal stationery also are considered covers.

**Errors** — Stamps that have some major, consistent, unintentional deviation from the normal are considered errors. Errors include, but are not limited to, missing or wrong colors, wrong paper, wrong watermarks, inverted centers or frames on multicolor printing, inverted or missing surcharges or overprints, double impressions, missing perforations, unintentionally omitted tagging and others. Factually wrong or misspelled information, if it appears on all examples of a stamp, are not considered errors in the true sense of the word. They are errors of design. Inconsistent or randomly appearing items, such as misperfs or color shifts, are classified as freaks.

**Color-Omitted Errors** — This term refers to stamps where a missing color is caused by the complete failure of the printing plate to deliver ink to the stamp paper or any other paper. Generally, this is caused by the printing plate not being engaged on the press or the ink station running dry of ink during printing.

**Color-Missing Errors** — This term refers to stamps where a color or colors were printed somewhere but do not appear on the finished stamp. There are four different classes of color-missing errors, and the catalog indicates with a two-letter code appended to each such listing what caused the color to be missing. These codes are used only for the United States' color-missing error listings.

**FO** = A *foldover* of the stamp sheet during printing may block ink from appearing on a stamp. Instead, the color will appear on the back of the foldover (where it might fall on the back of the selvage or perhaps on the back of the stamp or another stamp). FO also will be used in the case of foldunders, where the paper may fold underneath the other stamp paper and the color will print on the platen.

**EP** = A piece of *extraneous paper* falling across the plate or stamp paper will receive the printed ink. When the extraneous paper is removed, an unprinted portion of stamp paper remains and shows partially or totally missing colors.

**CM** = A misregistration of the printing plates during printing will result in a *color misregistration*, and such a misregistraion may result in a color not appearing on the finished stamp.

**PS** = *A perforation shift* after printing may remove a color from the finished stamp. Normally, this will occur on a row of stamps at the edge of the stamp pane.

**Measurements** - When measurements are given in the Scott catalogues for stamp size, grill size or any other reason, the first measurement given is always for the top and bottom dimension, while the second measurement will be for the sides (just as perforation gauges are measured). Thus, a stamp size of 15mm x 21mm will indicate a vertically oriented stamp 15mm wide at top and bottom, and 21mm tall at the sides. The same principle holds for measuring or counting items such as U.S. grills. A grill count of 22x18 points (B grill) indicates that there are 22 grill points across by 18 grill points down.

**Overprints and Surcharges** — Overprinting involves applying wording or design elements over an already existing stamp. Overprints can be used to alter the place of use (such as "Canal Zone" on U.S. stamps), to adapt them for a special purpose ("Porto" on Denmark's 1913-20 regular issues for use as postage due stamps, Scott J1-J7) or to commemorate a special occasion (United States Scott 647-648).

A *surcharge* is a form of overprint that changes or restates the face value of a stamp or piece of postal stationery.

Surcharges and overprints may be handstamped, typeset or, occasionally, lithographed or engraved. A few hand-written overprints and surcharges are known.

**Personalized Stamps** — In 1999, Australia issued stamps with se-tenant labels that could be personalized with pictures of the customer's choice. Other countries quickly followed suit, with some offering to print the selected picture on the stamp itself within a frame that was used exclusively for personalized issues. As the picture used on these stamps or labels vary, listings for such stamps are for any picture within the common frame (or any picture on a se-tenant label), be it a "generic" image or one produced especially for a customer, almost invariably at a premium price.

**Precancels** — Stamps that are canceled before they are placed in the mail are known as precancels. Precanceling usually is done to expedite the handling of large mailings and generally allow the affected mail pieces to skip certain phases of mail handling.

In the United States, precancellations generally identified the point of origin; that is, the city and state. This information appeared across the face of the stamp, usually centered between parallel lines. More recently, bureau precancels retained the parallel lines, but the city and state designations were dropped. Recent coils have a service inscription that is present on the original printing plate. These show the mail service paid for by the stamp. Since these stamps are not intended to receive further cancellations when used as intended, they are considered precancels. Such items often do not have parallel lines as part of the precancellation.

In France, the abbreviation *Affranchts* in a semicircle together with the word *Postes* is the general form of precancel in use. Belgian precancellations usually appear in a box in which the name of the city appears. Netherlands precancels have the name of the city enclosed between concentric circles, sometimes called a "lifesaver." Precancellations of other countries usually follow these patterns, but may be any arrangement of bars, boxes and city names.

Precancels are listed in the Scott catalogues only if the precancel changes the denomination (Belgium Scott 477-478); if the precanceled stamp is different from the non-precanceled version (such as untagged U.S. precancels); or if the stamp exists only precanceled (France Scott 1096-1099, U.S. Scott 2265).

**Proofs and Essays** — Proofs are impressions taken from an approved die, plate or stone in which the design and color are the same as the stamp issued to the public. Trial color proofs are impressions taken from approved dies, plates or stones in colors that vary from the final version. An essay is the impression of a design that differs in some way from the issued stamp. "Progressive die proofs" generally are considered to be essays.

**Provisionals** — These are stamps that are issued on short notice and intended for temporary use pending the arrival of regular issues. They usually are issued to meet such contingencies as changes in government or currency, shortage of necessary postage values or military occupation.

During the 1840s, postmasters in certain American cities issued stamps that were valid only at specific post offices. In 1861, postmasters of the Confederate States also issued stamps with limited validity. Both of these examples are known as "postmaster's provisionals."

**Se-tenant** — This term refers to an unsevered pair, strip or block of stamps that differ in design, denomination or overprint.

Unless the se-tenant item has a continuous design (see U.S. Scott 1451a, 1694a) the stamps do not have to be in the same order as shown in the catalogue (see U.S. Scott 2158a).

**Specimens** — The Universal Postal Union required member nations to send samples of all stamps they released into service to the International Bureau in Switzerland. Member nations of the UPU received these specimens as samples of what stamps were valid for postage. Many are overprinted, handstamped or initial-perforated "Specimen," "Canceled" or "Muestra." Some are marked with bars across the denominations (China-Taiwan), punched holes (Czechoslovakia) or back inscriptions (Mongolia).

Stamps distributed to government officials or for publicity purposes, and stamps submitted by private security printers for official approval, also may receive such defacements.

The previously described defacement markings prevent postal use, and all such items generally are known as "specimens."

**Tete Beche** — This term describes a pair of stamps in which one is upside down in relation to the other. Some of these are the result of intentional sheet arrangements, such as Morocco Scott B10-B11. Others occurred when one or more electrotypes accidentally were placed upside down on the plate, such as Colombia Scott 57a. Separation of the tete-beche stamps, of course, destroys the tete beche variety.

# Pronunciation Symbols

ə .... banana, collide, abut

ˈə, ˌə .... humdrum, abut

ə .... immediately preceding \l\, \n\, \m\, \ŋ\, as in battle, mitten, eaten, and sometimes open \ˈō-pᵊm\, lock and key \-ᵊŋ-\; immediately following \l\, \m\, \r\, as often in French table, prisme, titre

ər .... further, merger, bird

ˈər- / ˈə-r .... as in two different pronunciations of hurry \ˈhər-ē, ˈhə-rē\

a .... mat, map, mad, gag, snap, patch

ā .... day, fade, date, aorta, drape, cape

ä .... bother, cot, and, with most American speakers, father, cart

ȧ .... father as pronounced by speakers who do not rhyme it with *bother*; French patte

au̇ .... now, loud, out

b .... baby, rib

ch .... chin, nature \ˈnā-chər\

d .... did, adder

e .... bet, bed, peck

ˈē, ˌē .... beat, nosebleed, evenly, easy

ē .... easy, mealy

f .... fifty, cuff

g .... go, big, gift

h .... hat, ahead

hw .... whale as pronounced by those who do not have the same pronunciation for both *whale* and *wail*

i .... tip, banish, active

ī .... site, side, buy, tripe

j .... job, gem, edge, join, judge

k .... kin, cook, ache

k̲ .... German ich, Buch; one pronunciation of loch

l .... lily, pool

m .... murmur, dim, nymph

n .... no, own

ⁿ .... indicates that a preceding vowel or diphthong is pronounced with the nasal passages open, as in French *un bon vin blanc* \œⁿ -bōⁿ -vaⁿ -bläⁿ\

ŋ .... sing \ˈsiŋ\, singer \ˈsiŋ-ər\, finger \ˈfiŋ-gər\, ink \ˈiŋk \

ō .... bone, know, beau

ȯ .... saw, all, gnaw, caught

œ .... French boeuf, German Hölle

œ̄ .... French feu, German Höhle

ȯi .... coin, destroy

p .... pepper, lip

r .... red, car, rarity

s .... source, less

sh .... as in shy, mission, machine, special (actually, this is a single sound, not two); with a hyphen between, two sounds as in *grasshopper* \ˈgras-ˌhä-pər\

t .... tie, attack, late, later, latter

th .... as in thin, ether (actually, this is a single sound, not two); with a hyphen between, two sounds as in *knighthood* \ˈnīt-ˌhu̇d\

t̲h̲ .... then, either, this (actually, this is a single sound, not two)

ü .... rule, youth, union \ˈyün-yən\, few \ˈfyü\

u̇ .... pull, wood, book, curable \ˈkyu̇r-ə-bəl\, fury \ˈfyu̇r-ē\

ue .... German füllen, hübsch

ue̅ .... French rue, German fühlen

v .... vivid, give

w .... we, away

y .... yard, young, cue \ˈkyü\, mute \ˈmyüt\, union \ˈyün-yən\

ʸ .... indicates that during the articulation of the sound represented by the preceding character the front of the tongue has substantially the position it has for the articulation of the first sound of *yard*, as in French *digne* \dēnʸ\

z .... zone, raise

zh .... as in vision, azure \ˈa-zhər\ (actually, this is a single sound, not two); with a hyphen between, two sounds as in *hogshead* \ˈhȯgz-ˌhed, ˈhägz-\

\ .... slant line used in pairs to mark the beginning and end of a transcription: \ˈpen\

ˈ .... mark preceding a syllable with primary (strongest) stress: \ˈpen-mən-ˌship\

ˌ .... mark preceding a syllable with secondary (medium) stress: \ˈpen-mən-ˌship\

- .... mark of syllable division

( ) .... indicate that what is symbolized between is present in some utterances but not in others: *factory* \ˈfak-t(ə-)rē\

÷ .... indicates that many regard as unacceptable the pronunciation variant immediately following: *cupola* \ˈkyü-pə-lə, ÷-ˌlō\

# Currency Conversion

| Country | Dollar | Pound | S Franc | Yen | HK $ | Euro | Cdn $ | Aus $ |
|---|---|---|---|---|---|---|---|---|
| Australia | 1.3031 | 1.8318 | 1.3669 | 0.0122 | 0.1660 | 1.6074 | 1.0120 | — |
| Canada | 1.2877 | 1.8101 | 1.3508 | 0.0121 | 0.1641 | 1.5884 | — | 0.9882 |
| European Union | 0.8107 | 1.1396 | 0.8504 | 0.0076 | 0.1033 | — | 0.6296 | 0.6221 |
| Hong Kong | 7.8480 | 11.032 | 8.2325 | 0.0737 | — | 9.6805 | 6.0946 | 6.0226 |
| Japan | 106.42 | 149.59 | 111.63 | — | 13.560 | 131.27 | 82.643 | 81.667 |
| Switzerland | 0.9533 | 1.3401 | — | 0.0090 | 0.1215 | 1.1759 | 0.7403 | 0.7316 |
| United Kingdom | 0.7114 | — | 0.7462 | 0.0067 | 0.0906 | 0.8775 | 0.5524 | 0.5459 |
| United States | — | 1.4057 | 1.0490 | 0.0094 | 0.1274 | 1.2335 | 0.7766 | 0.7674 |

| Country | Currency | U.S. $ Equiv. |
|---|---|---|
| Namibia | dollar | .0846 |
| Nauru | Australian dollar | .7674 |
| Nepal | rupee | .0096 |
| Netherlands | euro | 1.2335 |
| Nevis | East Caribbean dollar | .3704 |
| New Caledonia | Community of French Pacific (CFP) franc | .0103 |
| New Zealand | dollar | .7235 |
| Nicaragua | cordoba | .0320 |
| Niger | CFA franc | .0019 |
| Nigeria | naira | .0028 |
| Niue | New Zealand dollar | .7235 |
| Norfolk Island | Australian dollar | .7674 |
| Norway | krone | .1274 |
| Oman | rial | 2.6008 |
| Pakistan | rupee | .0087 |
| Palau | U.S. dollar | 1.0000 |
| Palestinian Authority | Jordanian dinar | 1.4104 |
| Panama | balboa | 1.0000 |
| Papua New Guinea | kina | .3093 |
| Paraguay | guarani | .0002 |
| Penrhyn Island | New Zealand dollar | .7235 |
| Peru | new sol | .3096 |
| Philippines | peso | .0192 |

*Source:* ***xe.com*** *Apr. 2, 2018. Figures reflect values as of Apr. 2, 2018.*

# COMMON DESIGN TYPES

Pictured in this section are issues where one illustration has been used for a number of countries in the Catalogue. Not included in this section are overprinted stamps or those issues which are illustrated in each country. Because the location of Never Hinged breakpoints varies from country to country, some of the values in the listings below will be for unused stamps that were previously hinged.

## EUROPA

### Europa, 1956

The design symbolizing the cooperation among the six countries comprising the Coal and Steel Community is illustrated in each country.

| Country | Nos. |
|---|---|
| *Belgium* | *496-497* |
| *France* | *805-806* |
| *Germany* | *748-749* |
| *Italy* | *715-716* |
| *Luxembourg* | *318-320* |
| *Netherlands* | *368-369* |

| | | |
|---|---|---|
| *Nos. 496-497 (2)* | 9.00 | .70 |
| *Nos. 805-806 (2)* | 5.25 | 1.00 |
| *Nos. 748-749 (2)* | 7.30 | 1.20 |
| *Nos. 715-716 (2)* | 9.25 | 1.25 |
| *Nos. 318-320 (3)* | 65.50 | 42.00 |
| *Nos. 368-369 (2)* | 25.75 | 1.50 |
| *Set total (13) Stamps* | 122.05 | 47.65 |

### Europa, 1958

"E" and Dove — CD1

European Postal Union at the service of European integration.

**1958, Sept. 13**

| Country | Nos. |
|---|---|
| Belgium | 527-528 |
| France | 889-890 |
| Germany | 790-791 |
| Italy | 750-751 |
| Luxembourg | 341-343 |
| Netherlands | 375-376 |
| Saar | 317-318 |

| | | |
|---|---|---|
| *Nos. 527-528 (2)* | 4.25 | .60 |
| *Nos. 889-890 (2)* | 1.65 | .55 |
| *Nos. 790-791 (2)* | 3.65 | .65 |
| *Nos. 750-751 (2)* | 1.05 | .60 |
| *Nos. 341-343 (3)* | 1.35 | .90 |
| *Nos. 375-376 (2)* | 1.25 | .75 |
| *Nos. 317-318 (2)* | 1.05 | 2.30 |
| *Set total (15) Stamps* | 14.25 | 6.35 |

### Europa, 1959

6-Link Enless Chain — CD2

**1959, Sept. 19**

| Country | Nos. |
|---|---|
| Belgium | 536-537 |
| France | 929-930 |
| Germany | 805-806 |
| Italy | 791-792 |
| Luxembourg | 354-355 |
| Netherlands | 379-380 |

| | | |
|---|---|---|
| *Nos. 536-537 (2)* | 1.55 | .60 |
| *Nos. 929-930 (2)* | 1.40 | .80 |
| *Nos. 805-806 (2)* | 1.55 | .65 |
| *Nos. 791-792 (2)* | .80 | .50 |
| *Nos. 354-355 (2)* | 2.65 | 1.00 |
| *Nos. 379-380 (2)* | 2.10 | 1.85 |
| *Set total (12) Stamps* | 10.05 | 5.40 |

### Europa, 1960

19-Spoke Wheel CD3

First anniversary of the establishment of C.E.P.T. (Conference Europeenne des Administrations des Postes et des Telecommunications.) The spokes symbolize the 19 founding members of the Conference.

**1960, Sept.**

| Country | Nos. |
|---|---|
| Belgium | 553-554 |
| Denmark | 379 |
| Finland | 376-377 |
| France | 970-971 |
| Germany | 818-820 |
| Great Britain | 377-378 |
| Greece | 688 |
| Iceland | 327-328 |
| Ireland | 175-176 |
| Italy | 809-810 |
| Luxembourg | 374-375 |
| Netherlands | 385-386 |
| Norway | 387 |
| Portugal | 866-867 |
| Spain | 941-942 |
| Sweden | 562-563 |
| Switzerland | 400-401 |
| Turkey | 1493-1494 |

| | | |
|---|---|---|
| *Nos. 553-554 (2)* | 1.25 | .55 |
| *No. 379 (1)* | .55 | .50 |
| *Nos. 376-377 (2)* | 1.70 | 1.80 |
| *Nos. 970-971 (2)* | .50 | .50 |
| *Nos. 818-820 (3)* | 2.25 | 1.50 |
| *Nos. 377-378 (2)* | 8.00 | 5.00 |
| *No. 688 (1)* | 5.00 | 2.00 |
| *Nos. 327-328 (2)* | 1.30 | 1.85 |
| *Nos. 175-176 (2)* | 47.50 | 27.50 |
| *Nos. 809-810 (2)* | .50 | .50 |
| *Nos. 374-375 (2)* | 1.00 | .80 |
| *Nos. 385-386 (2)* | 2.00 | 2.00 |
| *No. 387 (1)* | 1.25 | 1.25 |
| *Nos. 866-867 (2)* | 3.00 | 1.75 |
| *Nos. 941-942 (2)* | 1.50 | .75 |
| *Nos. 562-563 (2)* | 1.05 | .55 |
| *Nos. 400-401 (2)* | 1.25 | .65 |
| *Nos. 1493-1494 (2)* | 2.10 | 1.35 |
| *Set total (34) Stamps* | 81.70 | 50.80 |

### Europa, 1961

19 Doves Flying as One — CD4

The 19 doves represent the 19 members of the Conference of European Postal and Telecommunications Administrations C.E.P.T.

**1961-62**

| Country | Nos. |
|---|---|
| Belgium | 572-573 |
| Cyprus | 201-203 |
| France | 1005-1006 |
| Germany | 844-845 |
| Great Britain | 382-384 |
| Greece | 718-719 |
| Iceland | 340-341 |
| Italy | 845-846 |
| Luxembourg | 382-383 |
| Netherlands | 387-388 |
| Spain | 1010-1011 |
| Switzerland | 410-411 |
| Turkey | 1518-1520 |

| | | |
|---|---|---|
| *Nos. 572-573 (2)* | .75 | .50 |
| *Nos. 201-203 (3)* | *2.10* | *1.20* |
| *Nos. 1005-1006 (2)* | .50 | .50 |
| *Nos. 844-845 (2)* | .60 | .75 |
| *Nos. 382-384 (3)* | .75 | .75 |
| *Nos. 718-719 (2)* | .80 | .50 |
| *Nos. 340-341 (2)* | 1.10 | 1.60 |
| *Nos. 845-846 (2)* | .50 | .50 |
| *Nos. 382-383 (2)* | .55 | .55 |
| *Nos. 387-388 (2)* | .50 | .50 |
| *Nos. 1010-1011 (2)* | .70 | .55 |
| *Nos. 410-411 (2)* | 1.25 | .60 |
| *Nos. 1518-1520 (3)* | 2.45 | 1.30 |
| *Set total (29) Stamps* | 12.55 | 9.80 |

### Europa, 1962

Young Tree with 19 Leaves CD5

The 19 leaves represent the 19 original members of C.E.P.T.

**1962-63**

| Country | Nos. |
|---|---|
| Belgium | 582-583 |
| Cyprus | 219-221 |
| France | 1045-1046 |
| Germany | 852-853 |
| Greece | 739-740 |
| Iceland | 348-349 |
| Ireland | 184-185 |
| Italy | 860-861 |
| Luxembourg | 386-387 |
| Netherlands | 394-395 |
| Norway | 414-415 |
| Switzerland | 416-417 |
| Turkey | 1553-1555 |

| | | |
|---|---|---|
| *Nos. 582-583 (2)* | .65 | .65 |
| *Nos. 219-221 (3)* | *76.25* | *6.75* |
| *Nos. 1045-1046 (2)* | .60 | .50 |
| *Nos. 852-853 (2)* | .70 | .80 |
| *Nos. 739-740 (2)* | 2.25 | 1.15 |
| *Nos. 348-349 (2)* | .85 | .85 |
| *Nos. 184-185 (2)* | 2.00 | .50 |
| *Nos. 860-861 (2)* | 1.00 | .55 |
| *Nos. 386-387 (2)* | .75 | .55 |
| *Nos. 394-395 (2)* | 1.35 | .90 |
| *Nos. 414-415 (2)* | 2.25 | 2.25 |
| *Nos. 416-417 (2)* | 1.65 | 1.00 |
| *Nos. 1553-1555 (3)* | *3.00* | 1.55 |
| *Set total (28) Stamps* | 93.30 | 18.00 |

### Europa, 1963

Stylized Links, Symbolizing Unity — CD6

**1963, Sept.**

| Country | Nos. |
|---|---|
| Belgium | 598-599 |
| Cyprus | 229-231 |
| Finland | 419 |
| France | 1074-1075 |
| Germany | 867-868 |
| Greece | 768-769 |
| Iceland | 357-358 |
| Ireland | 188-189 |
| Italy | 880-881 |
| Luxembourg | 403-404 |
| Netherlands | 416-417 |
| Norway | 441-442 |
| Switzerland | 429 |
| Turkey | 1602-1603 |

| | | |
|---|---|---|
| *Nos. 598-599 (2)* | 1.60 | .55 |
| *Nos. 229-231 (3)* | *64.00* | *9.40* |
| *No. 419 (1)* | 1.25 | .55 |
| *Nos. 1074-1075 (2)* | .60 | .50 |
| *Nos. 867-868 (2)* | .50 | .55 |
| *Nos. 768-769 (2)* | 5.25 | 1.90 |
| *Nos. 357-358 (2)* | 1.20 | 1.20 |
| *Nos. 188-189 (2)* | 4.75 | 3.25 |
| *Nos. 880-881 (2)* | .50 | .50 |
| *Nos. 403-404 (2)* | .75 | .55 |
| *Nos. 416-417 (2)* | 1.30 | 1.00 |
| *Nos. 441-442 (2)* | 4.75 | 3.00 |
| *No. 429 (1)* | .90 | .60 |
| *Nos. 1602-1603 (2)* | 1.40 | .60 |
| *Set total (27) Stamps* | 88.75 | 24.15 |

### Europa, 1964

Symbolic Daisy — CD7

5th anniversary of the establishment of C.E.P.T. The 22 petals of the flower symbolize the 22 members of the Conference.

**1964, Sept.**

| Country | Nos. |
|---|---|
| Austria | 738 |
| Belgium | 614-615 |
| Cyprus | 244-246 |
| France | 1109-1110 |
| Germany | 897-898 |
| Greece | 801-802 |
| Iceland | 367-368 |
| Ireland | 196-197 |
| Italy | 894-895 |
| Luxembourg | 411-412 |
| Monaco | 590-591 |
| Netherlands | 428-429 |
| Norway | 458 |
| Portugal | 931-933 |
| Spain | 1262-1263 |
| Switzerland | 438-439 |
| Turkey | 1628-1629 |

| | | |
|---|---|---|
| *No. 738 (1)* | 1.20 | .80 |
| *Nos. 614-615 (2)* | 1.40 | .60 |
| *Nos. 244-246 (3)* | *32.25* | *5.10* |
| *Nos. 1109-1110 (2)* | .50 | .50 |
| *Nos. 897-898 (2)* | .50 | .50 |
| *Nos. 801-802 (2)* | 5.00 | 1.90 |
| *Nos. 367-368 (2)* | 1.40 | 1.15 |
| *Nos. 196-197 (2)* | 17.00 | 4.25 |
| *Nos. 894-895 (2)* | .50 | .50 |
| *Nos. 411-412 (2)* | .75 | .55 |
| *Nos. 590-591 (2)* | 2.50 | .70 |
| *Nos. 428-429 (2)* | .75 | .60 |
| *No. 458 (1)* | 4.50 | 4.50 |
| *Nos. 931-933 (3)* | *10.00* | *2.00* |
| *Nos. 1262-1263 (2)* | 1.30 | .80 |
| *Nos. 438-439 (2)* | 1.60 | .50 |
| *Nos. 1628-1629 (2)* | 2.65 | 1.35 |
| *Set total (34) Stamps* | 83.80 | 26.30 |

### Europa, 1965

Leaves and "Fruit" CD8

**1965**

| Country | Nos. |
|---|---|
| Belgium | 636-637 |
| Cyprus | 262-264 |
| Finland | 437 |
| France | 1131-1132 |
| Germany | 934-935 |
| Greece | 833-834 |
| Iceland | 375-376 |
| Ireland | 204-205 |
| Italy | 915-916 |
| Luxembourg | 432-433 |
| Monaco | 616-617 |
| Netherlands | 438-439 |
| Norway | 475-476 |
| Portugal | 958-960 |
| Switzerland | 469 |
| Turkey | 1665-1666 |

| | | |
|---|---|---|
| *Nos. 636-637 (2)* | .50 | .50 |
| *Nos. 262-264 (3)* | *25.35* | *6.00* |
| *No. 437 (1)* | 1.25 | .55 |
| *Nos. 1131-1132 (2)* | .70 | .55 |
| *Nos. 934-935 (2)* | .50 | .50 |
| *Nos. 833-834 (2)* | 2.25 | 1.15 |
| *Nos. 375-376 (2)* | 2.50 | 1.75 |
| *Nos. 204-205 (2)* | 16.00 | 3.35 |
| *Nos. 915-916 (2)* | .50 | .50 |
| *Nos. 432-433 (2)* | .75 | .55 |
| *Nos. 616-617 (2)* | 3.25 | 1.65 |
| *Nos. 438-439 (2)* | .55 | .50 |
| *Nos. 475-476 (2)* | 4.00 | 3.10 |
| *Nos. 958-960 (3)* | *10.00* | *2.75* |
| *No. 469 (1)* | 1.15 | .25 |
| *Nos. 1665-1666 (2)* | 3.50 | 2.10 |
| *Set total (32) Stamps* | 72.75 | 25.75 |

### Europa, 1966

Symbolic Sailboat — CD9

**1966, Sept.**

| Country | Nos. |
|---|---|
| Andorra, French | 172 |
| Belgium | 675-676 |
| Cyprus | 275-277 |
| France | 1163-1164 |
| Germany | 963-964 |

Greece ....................862-863
Iceland ....................384-385
Ireland ....................216-217
Italy ....................942-943
Liechtenstein ....................415
Luxembourg ....................440-441
Monaco ....................639-640
Netherlands ....................441-442
Norway ....................496-497
Portugal ....................980-982
Switzerland ....................477-478
Turkey ....................1718-1719

*No. 172 (1)* 3.00 3.00
*Nos. 675-676 (2)* .80 .50
*Nos. 275-277 (3)* *4.75* *2.75*
*Nos. 1163-1164 (2)* .55 .50
*Nos. 963-964 (2)* .50 .55
*Nos. 862-863 (2)* 2.25 1.05
*Nos. 384-385 (2)* 4.50 3.50
*Nos. 216-217 (2)* 6.75 2.00
*Nos. 942-943 (2)* .50 .50
*No. 415 (1)* .40 .35
*Nos. 440-441 (2)* .70 .55
*Nos. 639-640 (2)* 2.00 .65
*Nos. 441-442 (2)* .85 .50
*Nos. 496-497 (2)* 5.00 3.00
*Nos. 980-982 (3)* *9.75* 2.25
*Nos. 477-478 (2)* 1.60 .60
*Nos. 1718-1719 (2)* 3.35 1.75
*Set total (34) Stamps* 47.25 24.00

## Europa, 1967

Cogwheels
CD10

### 1967

Andorra, French ....................174-175
Belgium ....................688-689
Cyprus ....................297-299
France ....................1178-1179
Germany ....................969-970
Greece ....................891-892
Iceland ....................389-390
Ireland ....................232-233
Italy ....................951-952
Liechtenstein ....................420
Luxembourg ....................449-450
Monaco ....................669-670
Netherlands ....................444-447
Norway ....................504-505
Portugal ....................994-996
Spain ....................1465-1466
Switzerland ....................482
Turkey ....................B120-B121

*Nos. 174-175 (2)* 10.75 6.25
*Nos. 688-689 (2)* 1.05 .55
*Nos. 297-299 (3)* *4.25* *2.50*
*Nos. 1178-1179 (2)* .55 .50
*Nos. 969-970 (2)* .55 .55
*Nos. 891-892 (2)* 3.75 1.00
*Nos. 389-390 (2)* 3.00 2.00
*Nos. 232-233 (2)* 5.90 2.30
*Nos. 951-952 (2)* .60 .50
*No. 420 (1)* .45 .40
*Nos. 449-450 (2)* 1.00 .70
*Nos. 669-670 (2)* 2.75 .70
*Nos. 444-447 (4)* 2.70 2.05
*Nos. 504-505 (2)* 3.25 2.75
*Nos. 994-996 (3)* *9.50* 1.85
*Nos. 1465-1466 (2)* .50 .50
*No. 482 (1)* .70 .25
*Nos. B120-B121 (2)* 3.50 2.75
*Set total (38) Stamps* 54.75 28.10

## Europa, 1968

Golden Key
with
C.E.P.T.
Emblem
CD11

### 1968

Andorra, French ....................182-183
Belgium ....................705-706
Cyprus ....................314-316
France ....................1209-1210
Germany ....................983-984
Greece ....................916-917
Iceland ....................395-396
Ireland ....................242-243
Italy ....................979-980
Liechtenstein ....................442
Luxembourg ....................466-467
Monaco ....................689-691
Netherlands ....................452-453
Portugal ....................1019-1021
San Marino ....................687
Spain ....................1526
Switzerland ....................488
Turkey ....................1775-1776

*Nos. 182-183 (2)* 16.50 10.00
*Nos. 705-706 (2)* 1.25 .50
*Nos. 314-316 (3)* *2.90* *2.50*
*Nos. 1209-1210 (2)* .85 .55
*Nos. 983-984 (2)* .50 .55
*Nos. 916-917 (2)* 3.75 1.65
*Nos. 395-396 (2)* 3.00 2.20
*Nos. 242-243 (2)* 3.30 2.25
*Nos. 979-980 (2)* .50 .50
*No. 442 (1)* .45 .40
*Nos. 466-467 (2)* .80 .70
*Nos. 689-691 (3)* *5.40* .95
*Nos. 452-453 (2)* 1.05 .70
*Nos. 1019-1021 (3)* *9.75* 2.10
*No. 687 (1)* .55 .35
*No. 1526 (1)* .25 .25
*No. 488 (1)* .45 .25
*Nos. 1775-1776 (2)* 5.00 2.00
*Set total (35) Stamps* 56.25 28.40

## Europa, 1969

"EUROPA"
and "CEPT"
CD12

Tenth anniversary of C.E.P.T.

### 1969

Andorra, French ....................188-189
Austria ....................837
Belgium ....................718-719
Cyprus ....................326-328
Denmark ....................458
Finland ....................483
France ....................1245-1246
Germany ....................996-997
Great Britain ....................585
Greece ....................947-948
Iceland ....................406-407
Ireland ....................270-271
Italy ....................1000-1001
Liechtenstein ....................453
Luxembourg ....................475-476
Monaco ....................722-724
Netherlands ....................475-476
Norway ....................533-534
Portugal ....................1038-1040
San Marino ....................701-702
Spain ....................1567
Sweden ....................814-816
Switzerland ....................500-501
Turkey ....................1799-1800
Vatican ....................470-472
Yugoslavia ....................1003-1004

*Nos. 188-189 (2)* 18.50 12.00
*No. 837 (1)* .65 .30
*Nos. 718-719 (2)* .75 .50
*Nos. 326-328 (3)* *3.00* *2.25*
*No. 458 (1)* .75 .75
*No. 483 (1)* 3.50 .75
*Nos. 1245-1246 (2)* .55 .50
*Nos. 996-997 (2)* .80 .50
*No. 585 (1)* .25 .25
*Nos. 947-948 (2)* 5.00 1.50
*Nos. 406-407 (2)* 4.20 2.40
*Nos. 270-271 (2)* 3.50 2.00
*Nos. 1000-1001 (2)* .50 .50
*No. 453 (1)* .45 .45
*Nos. 475-476 (2)* .95 .50
*Nos. 722-724 (3)* *10.50* 2.00
*Nos. 475-476 (2)* 1.35 1.00
*Nos. 533-534 (2)* 3.75 2.35
*Nos. 1038-1040 (3)* 17.75 2.40
*Nos. 701-702 (2)* .90 .90
*No. 1567 (1)* .25 .25
*Nos. 814-816 (3)* 4.00 2.85
*Nos. 500-501 (2)* 1.85 .60
*Nos. 1799-1800 (2)* 3.85 2.25
*Nos. 470-472 (3)* .75 .75
*Nos. 1003-1004 (2)* 4.00 4.00
*Set total (51) Stamps* 92.30 44.50

## Europa, 1970

Interwoven
Threads
CD13

### 1970

Andorra, French ....................196-197
Belgium ....................741-742
Cyprus ....................340-342
France ....................1271-1272
Germany ....................1018-1019
Greece ....................985, 987
Iceland ....................420-421
Ireland ....................279-281
Italy ....................1013-1014
Liechtenstein ....................470
Luxembourg ....................489-490
Monaco ....................768-770
Netherlands ....................483-484
Portugal ....................1060-1062
San Marino ....................729-730
Spain ....................1607
Switzerland ....................515-516
Turkey ....................1848-1849
Yugoslavia ....................1024-1025

*Nos. 196-197 (2)* 20.00 8.50
*Nos. 741-742 (2)* 1.10 .55
*Nos. 340-342 (3)* *2.70* *2.75*
*Nos. 1271-1272 (2)* .65 .50
*Nos. 1018-1019 (2)* .60 .50
*Nos. 985,987 (2)* 7.75 2.00
*Nos. 420-421 (2)* 6.00 4.00
*Nos. 279-281 (3)* 7.50 2.50
*Nos. 1013-1014 (2)* .50 .50
*No. 470 (1)* .45 .45
*Nos. 489-490 (2)* .80 .55
*Nos. 768-770 (3)* *6.35* 2.10
*Nos. 483-484 (2)* 1.30 1.15
*Nos. 1060-1062 (3)* *9.75* 2.35
*Nos. 729-730 (2)* .90 .55
*No. 1607 (1)* .25 .25
*Nos. 515-516 (2)* 1.85 .60
*Nos. 1848-1849 (2)* 5.00 2.25
*Nos. 1024-1025 (2)* .80 .80
*Set total (40) Stamps* 74.25 32.85

## Europa, 1971

"Fraternity,
Cooperation,
Common
Effort"
CD14

### 1971

Andorra, French ....................205-206
Belgium ....................803-804
Cyprus ....................365-367
Finland ....................504
France ....................1304
Germany ....................1064-1065
Greece ....................1029-1030
Iceland ....................429-430
Ireland ....................305-306
Italy ....................1038-1039
Liechtenstein ....................485
Luxembourg ....................500-501
Malta ....................425-427
Monaco ....................797-799
Netherlands ....................488-489
Portugal ....................1094-1096
San Marino ....................749-750
Spain ....................1675-1676
Switzerland ....................531-532
Turkey ....................1876-1877
Yugoslavia ....................1052-1053

*Nos. 205-206 (2)* 20.00 7.75
*Nos. 803-804 (2)* 1.30 .55
*Nos. 365-367 (3)* *2.60* *3.25*
*No. 504 (1)* 5.00 .75
*No. 1304 (1)* .45 .40
*Nos. 1064-1065 (2)* .60 .50
*Nos. 1029-1030 (2)* 4.00 1.80
*Nos. 429-430 (2)* 5.00 3.75
*Nos. 305-306 (2)* 4.50 1.50
*Nos. 1038-1039 (2)* .65 .50
*No. 485 (1)* .45 .45
*Nos. 500-501 (2)* 1.00 .65
*Nos. 425-427 (3)* *.80* *.80*
*Nos. 797-799 (3)* *15.00* 2.80
*Nos. 488-489 (2)* 1.20 .95
*Nos. 1094-1096 (3)* *9.75* 1.75
*Nos. 749-750 (2)* .65 .55
*Nos. 1675-1676 (2)* .75 .55
*Nos. 531-532 (2)* 1.85 .65
*Nos. 1876-1877 (2)* 5.60 2.50
*Nos. 1052-1053 (2)* .50 .50
*Set total (43) Stamps* 81.65 32.90

## Europa, 1972

Sparkles, Symbolic
of Communications
CD15

### 1972

Andorra, French ....................210-211
Andorra, Spanish ....................62
Belgium ....................825-826
Cyprus ....................380-382
Finland ....................512-513
France ....................1341
Germany ....................1089-1090
Greece ....................1049-1050
Iceland ....................439-440
Ireland ....................316-317
Italy ....................1065-1066
Liechtenstein ....................504
Luxembourg ....................512-513
Malta ....................450-453
Monaco ....................831-832
Netherlands ....................494-495
Portugal ....................1141-1143
San Marino ....................771-772
Spain ....................1718
Switzerland ....................544-545
Turkey ....................1907-1908
Yugoslavia ....................1100-1101

*Nos. 210-211 (2)* 21.00 7.00
*No. 62 (1)* 45.00 45.00
*Nos. 825-826 (2)* .95 .55
*Nos. 380-382 (3)* *5.95* *4.25*
*Nos. 512-513 (2)* 7.00 1.40
*No. 1341 (1)* .50 .35
*Nos. 1089-1090 (2)* 1.30 .50
*Nos. 1049-1050 (2)* 2.00 1.55
*Nos. 439-440 (2)* 2.90 2.65
*Nos. 316-317 (2)* 13.00 4.50
*Nos. 1065-1066 (2)* .55 .50
*No. 504 (1)* .45 .45
*Nos. 512-513 (2)* .95 .65
*Nos. 450-453 (4)* 1.05 1.40
*Nos. 831-832 (2)* 5.00 1.40
*Nos. 494-495 (2)* 1.20 .90
*Nos. 1141-1143 (3)* *9.75* 1.50
*Nos. 771-772 (2)* .70 .50
*No. 1718 (1)* .50 .40
*Nos. 544-545 (2)* 1.65 .60
*Nos. 1907-1908 (2)* 7.50 3.00
*Nos. 1100-1101 (2)* 1.20 1.20
*Set total (44) Stamps* 130.10 80.25

## Europa, 1973

Post Horn
and Arrows
CD16

### 1973

Andorra, French ....................219-220
Andorra, Spanish ....................76
Belgium ....................839-840
Cyprus ....................396-398
Finland ....................526
France ....................1367
Germany ....................1114-1115
Greece ....................1090-1092
Iceland ....................447-448
Ireland ....................329-330
Italy ....................1108-1109
Liechtenstein ....................528-529
Luxembourg ....................523-524
Malta ....................469-471
Monaco ....................866-867
Netherlands ....................504-505
Norway ....................604-605
Portugal ....................1170-1172
San Marino ....................802-803
Spain ....................1753
Switzerland ....................580-581
Turkey ....................1935-1936
Yugoslavia ....................1138-1139

*Nos. 219-220 (2)* 20.00 11.00
*No. 76 (1)* .65 .55
*Nos. 839-840 (2)* 1.00 .65
*Nos. 396-398 (3)* *4.25* *3.85*
*No. 526 (1)* 1.25 .55
*No. 1367 (1)* 1.25 .75
*Nos. 1114-1115 (2)* .90 .50
*Nos. 1090-1092 (3)* 2.10 1.40
*Nos. 447-448 (2)* 6.65 3.35

| | | |
|---|---|---|
| *Nos. 329-330 (2)* | 5.25 | 2.00 |
| *Nos. 1108-1109 (2)* | .50 | .50 |
| *Nos. 528-529 (2)* | .60 | .60 |
| *Nos. 523-524 (2)* | .90 | .75 |
| *Nos. 469-471 (3)* | .90 | 1.20 |
| *Nos. 866-867 (2)* | 15.00 | 2.40 |
| *Nos. 504-505 (2)* | 1.20 | .95 |
| *Nos. 604-605 (2)* | 6.25 | 2.40 |
| *Nos. 1170-1172 (3)* | 13.00 | 2.15 |
| *Nos. 802-803 (2)* | 1.00 | .60 |
| *No. 1753 (1)* | .35 | .25 |
| *Nos. 580-581 (2)* | 1.55 | .60 |
| *Nos. 1935-1936 (2)* | 10.00 | 4.50 |
| *Nos. 1138-1139 (2)* | 1.15 | 1.10 |
| *Set total (46) Stamps* | 95.70 | 42.60 |

### Europa, 2000

CD17

**2000**

Albania ....2621-2622
Andorra, French ....522
Andorra, Spanish ....262
Armenia ....610-611
Austria ....1814
Azerbaijan ....698-699
Belarus ....350
Belgium ....1818
Bosnia & Herzegovina (Moslem) ....358
Bosnia & Herzegovina (Serb) ....111-112
Croatia ....428-429
Cyprus ....959
Czech Republic ....3120
Denmark ....1189
Estonia ....394
Faroe Islands ....376
Finland ....1129
Aland Islands ....166
France ....2771
Georgia ....228-229
Germany ....2086-2087
Gibraltar ....837-840
Great Britain (Jersey) ....935-936
Great Britain (Isle of Man) ....883
Greece ....1959
Greenland ....363
Hungary ....3699-3700
Iceland ....910
Ireland ....1230-1231
Italy ....2349
Latvia ....504
Liechtenstein ....1178
Lithuania ....668
Luxembourg ....1035
Macedonia ....187
Malta ....1011-1012
Moldova ....355
Monaco ....2161-2162
Poland ....3519
Portugal ....2358
Portugal (Azores) ....455
Portugal (Madeira) ....208
Romania ....4370
Russia ....6589
San Marino ....1480
Slovakia ....355
Slovenia ....424
Spain ....3036
Sweden ....2394
Switzerland ....1074
Turkey ....2762
Turkish Rep. of Northern Cyprus ....500
Ukraine ....379
Vatican City ....1152

| | | |
|---|---|---|
| *Nos. 2621-2622 (2)* | 11.00 | 11.00 |
| *No. 522 (1)* | 2.00 | 1.00 |
| *No. 262 (1)* | 1.60 | .70 |
| *Nos. 610-611 (2)* | 4.75 | 4.75 |
| *No. 1814 (1)* | 1.40 | 1.40 |
| *Nos. 698-699 (2)* | 6.00 | 6.00 |
| *No. 350 (1)* | 1.75 | 1.75 |
| *No. 1818 (1)* | 1.40 | .60 |
| *No. 358 (1)* | 4.75 | 4.75 |
| *Nos. 111-112 (2)* | 110.00 | 110.00 |
| *Nos. 428-429 (2)* | 6.25 | 6.25 |
| *No. 959 (1)* | 2.10 | 1.40 |
| *No. 3120 (1)* | 1.20 | .40 |
| *No. 1189 (1)* | 3.50 | 2.25 |
| *No. 394 (1)* | 1.25 | 1.25 |
| *No. 376 (1)* | 2.40 | 2.40 |
| *No. 1129 (1)* | 2.00 | .60 |
| *No. 166 (1)* | 2.00 | 1.10 |
| *No. 2771 (1)* | 1.25 | .40 |
| *Nos. 228-229 (2)* | 9.00 | 9.00 |
| *Nos. 2086-2087 (2)* | 4.15 | 1.90 |
| *Nos. 837-840 (4)* | 5.50 | 5.30 |
| *Nos. 935-936 (2)* | 2.40 | 2.40 |
| *No. 883 (1)* | 1.75 | 1.75 |
| *No. 363 (1)* | 1.90 | 1.90 |
| *Nos. 3699-3700 (2)* | 6.50 | 2.50 |
| *No. 910 (1)* | 1.60 | 1.60 |
| *Nos. 1230-1231 (2)* | 4.35 | 4.35 |
| *No. 2349 (1)* | 1.50 | .40 |
| *No. 504 (1)* | 5.00 | 2.40 |
| *No. 1178 (1)* | 2.25 | 1.75 |
| *No. 668 (1)* | 1.50 | 1.50 |
| *No. 1035 (1)* | 1.40 | .85 |
| *No. 187 (1)* | 3.00 | 3.00 |
| *Nos. 1011-1012 (2)* | 4.35 | 4.35 |
| *No. 355 (1)* | 3.50 | 3.50 |
| *Nos. 2161-2162 (2)* | 2.80 | 1.40 |
| *No. 3519 (1)* | 1.25 | .75 |
| *No. 2358 (1)* | 1.25 | .65 |
| *No. 455 (1)* | 1.25 | .50 |
| *No. 208 (1)* | 1.25 | .50 |
| *No. 4370 (1)* | 2.50 | 1.25 |
| *No. 6589 (1)* | 2.00 | .85 |
| *No. 1480 (1)* | 1.00 | 1.00 |
| *No. 355 (1)* | 1.25 | .55 |
| *No. 424 (1)* | 3.25 | 3.25 |
| *No. 3036 (1)* | .75 | .40 |
| *No. 2394 (1)* | 3.00 | 2.25 |
| *No. 1074 (1)* | 2.10 | .75 |
| *No. 2762 (1)* | 2.00 | 2.00 |
| *No. 500 (1)* | 2.50 | 2.50 |
| *No. 379 (1)* | 4.50 | 3.00 |
| *No. 1152 (1)* | 1.25 | 1.25 |
| *Set total (68) Stamps* | 260.15 | 229.30 |

The Gibraltar stamps are similar to the stamp illustrated, but none have the design shown above. All other sets listed above include at least one stamp with the design shown, but some include stamps with entirely different designs. Bulgaria Nos. 4131-4132, Guernsey Nos. 802-803 and Yugoslavia Nos. 2485-2486 are Europa stamps with completely different designs.

### PORTUGAL & COLONIES
### Vasco da Gama

Fleet Departing CD20

Fleet Arriving at Calicut — CD21

Embarking at Rastello CD22

Muse of History CD23

San Gabriel, da Gama and Camoens CD24

Archangel Gabriel, the Patron Saint CD25

Flagship San Gabriel — CD26

Vasco da Gama — CD27

Fourth centenary of Vasco da Gama's discovery of the route to India.

**1898**

Azores ....93-100
Macao ....67-74
Madeira ....37-44
Portugal ....147-154
Port. Africa ....1-8
Port. Congo ....75-98
Port. India ....189-196
St. Thomas & Prince Islands ....170-193
Timor ....45-52

| | | |
|---|---|---|
| *Nos. 93-100 (8)* | 122.00 | 76.25 |
| *Nos. 67-74 (8)* | 136.00 | 96.75 |
| *Nos. 37-44 (8)* | 44.55 | 34.00 |
| *Nos. 147-154 (8)* | 155.00 | 50.25 |
| *Nos. 1-8 (8)* | 27.00 | 17.75 |
| *Nos. 75-98 (24)* | 41.50 | 34.45 |
| *Nos. 189-196 (8)* | 20.25 | 12.95 |
| *Nos. 170-193 (24)* | 38.75 | 34.30 |
| *Nos. 45-52 (8)* | 19.50 | 8.75 |
| *Set total (104) Stamps* | 604.55 | 365.45 |

### Pombal
### POSTAL TAX
### POSTAL TAX DUES

Marquis de Pombal — CD28

Planning Reconstruction of Lisbon, 1755 — CD29

Pombal Monument, Lisbon — CD30

Sebastiao Jose de Carvalho e Mello, Marquis de Pombal (1699-1782), statesman, rebuilt Lisbon after earthquake of 1755. Tax was for the erection of Pombal monument. Obligatory on all mail on certain days throughout the year. Postal Tax Dues are inscribed "Multa."

**1925**

Angola ....RA1-RA3, RAJ1-RAJ3
Azores ....RA9-RA11, RAJ2-RAJ4
Cape Verde ....RA1-RA3, RAJ1-RAJ3
Macao ....RA1-RA3, RAJ1-RAJ3
Madeira ....RA1-RA3, RAJ1-RAJ3
Mozambique ....RA1-RA3, RAJ1-RAJ3
Nyassa ....RA1-RA3, RAJ1-RAJ3
Portugal ....RA11-RA13, RAJ2-RAJ4
Port. Guinea ....RA1-RA3, RAJ1-RAJ3
Port. India ....RA1-RA3, RAJ1-RAJ3
St. Thomas & Prince Islands ....RA1-RA3, RAJ1-RAJ3
Timor ....RA1-RA3, RAJ1-RAJ3

| | | |
|---|---|---|
| *Nos. RA1-RA3,RAJ1-RAJ3 (6)* | 6.60 | 6.60 |
| *Nos. RA9-RA11,RAJ2-RAJ4 (6)* | 6.60 | 9.30 |
| *Nos. RA1-RA3,RAJ1-RAJ3 (6)* | 6.00 | 5.40 |
| *Nos. RA1-RA3,RAJ1-RAJ3 (6)* | 18.50 | 10.50 |
| *Nos. RA1-RA3,RAJ1-RAJ3 (6)* | 4.35 | 12.45 |
| *Nos. RA1-RA3,RAJ1-RAJ3 (6)* | 2.40 | 2.55 |
| *Nos. RA1-RA3,RAJ1-RAJ3 (6)* | 52.50 | 38.25 |
| *Nos. RA11-RA13,RAJ2-RAJ4 (6)* | 5.95 | 5.20 |
| *Nos. RA1-RA3,RAJ1-RAJ3 (6)* | 3.30 | 2.70 |
| *Nos. RA1-RA3,RAJ1-RAJ3 (6)* | 3.45 | 3.45 |
| *Nos. RA1-RA3,RAJ1-RAJ3 (6)* | 3.60 | 3.60 |
| *Nos. RA1-RA3,RAJ1-RAJ3 (6)* | 2.10 | 3.90 |
| *Set total (72) Stamps* | 115.35 | 103.90 |

Vasco da Gama CD34

Mousinho de Albuquerque CD35

Dam CD36

Prince Henry the Navigator CD37

Affonso de Albuquerque CD38

Plane over Globe CD39

**1938-39**

Angola ....274-291, C1-C9
Cape Verde ....234-251, C1-C9
Macao ....289-305, C7-C15
Mozambique ....270-287, C1-C9
Port. Guinea ....233-250. C1-C9
Port. India ....439-453, C1-C8
St. Thomas & Prince Islands ... 302-319, 323-340, C1-C18
Timor ....223-239, C1-C9

| | | |
|---|---|---|
| *Nos. 274-291,C1-C9 (27)* | 132.90 | 22.85 |
| *Nos. 234-251,C1-C9 (27)* | 100.00 | 31.20 |
| *Nos. 289-305,C7-C15 (26)* | 701.70 | 135.60 |
| *Nos. 270-287,C1-C9 (27)* | 63.45 | 11.20 |
| *Nos. 233-250,C1-C9 (27)* | 88.05 | 30.70 |
| *Nos. 439-453,C1-C8 (23)* | 74.75 | 25.50 |
| *Nos. 302-319,323-340,C1-C18 (54)* | 319.25 | 190.35 |
| *Nos. 223-239,C1-C9 (26)* | 149.25 | 73.15 |
| *Set total (237) Stamps* | 1,629. | 520.55 |

### Lady of Fatima

Our Lady of the Rosary, Fatima, Portugal — CD40

**1948-49**

Angola ....315-318
Cape Verde ....266
Macao ....336
Mozambique ....325-328
Port. Guinea ....271
Port. India ....480
St. Thomas & Prince Islands ....351
Timor ....254

| | | |
|---|---|---|
| *Nos. 315-318 (4)* | 68.00 | 17.25 |
| *No. 266 (1)* | 8.50 | 4.50 |
| *No. 336 (1)* | 40.00 | 12.00 |
| *Nos. 325-328 (4)* | 73.25 | 16.85 |
| *No. 271 (1)* | 3.25 | 3.00 |
| *No. 480 (1)* | 2.50 | 2.25 |
| *No. 351 (1)* | 7.25 | 6.50 |
| *No. 254 (1)* | 2.75 | 2.75 |
| *Set total (14) Stamps* | 205.50 | 65.10 |

A souvenir sheet of 9 stamps was issued in 1951 to mark the extension of the 1950 Holy Year. The sheet contains: Angola No. 316, Cape Verde No. 266, Macao No. 336, Mozambique No. 325, Portuguese Guinea No. 271, Portuguese India Nos. 480, 485, St. Thomas & Prince Islands No. 351, Timor No. 254. The sheet also contains a portrait of Pope Pius XII and is inscribed "Encerramento do

Ano Santo, Fatima 1951." It was sold for 11 escudos.

### Holy Year

Church Bells and Dove CD41

Angel Holding Candelabra CD42

Holy Year, 1950.

**1950-51**

| | |
|---|---|
| Angola | 331-332 |
| Cape Verde | 268-269 |
| Macao | 339-340 |
| Mozambique | 330-331 |
| Port. Guinea | 273-274 |
| Port. India | 490-491, 496-503 |
| St. Thomas & Prince Islands | 353-354 |
| Timor | 258-259 |

| | | |
|---|---|---|
| *Nos. 331-332 (2)* | 7.60 | 1.35 |
| *Nos. 268-269 (2)* | 4.75 | 2.20 |
| *Nos. 339-340 (2)* | 55.00 | 12.50 |
| *Nos. 330-331 (2)* | 3.00 | 1.10 |
| *Nos. 273-274 (2)* | 3.50 | 2.60 |
| *Nos. 490-491,496-503 (10)* | 12.80 | 5.40 |
| *Nos. 353-354 (2)* | 7.50 | 4.40 |
| *Nos. 258-259 (2)* | 3.75 | 3.25 |
| *Set total (24) Stamps* | 97.90 | 32.80 |

A souvenir sheet of 8 stamps was issued in 1951 to mark the extension of the Holy Year. The sheet contains: Angola No. 331, Cape Verde No. 269, Macao No. 340, Mozambique No. 331, Portuguese Guinea No. 275, Portuguese India No. 490, St. Thomas & Prince Islands No. 354, Timor No. 258, some with colors changed. The sheet contains doves and is inscribed 'Encerramento do Ano Santo, Fatima 1951.' It was sold for 17 escudos.

### Holy Year Conclusion

Our Lady of Fatima — CD43

Conclusion of Holy Year. Sheets contain alternate vertical rows of stamps and labels bearing quotation from Pope Pius XII, different for each colony.

**1951**

| | |
|---|---|
| Angola | 357 |
| Cape Verde | 270 |
| Macao | 352 |
| Mozambique | 356 |
| Port. Guinea | 275 |
| Port. India | 506 |
| St. Thomas & Prince Islands | 355 |
| Timor | 270 |

| | | |
|---|---|---|
| *No. 357 (1)* | 5.25 | 1.50 |
| *No. 270 (1)* | 1.50 | 1.25 |
| *No. 352 (1)* | 37.50 | 10.00 |
| *No. 356 (1)* | 2.25 | 1.00 |
| *No. 275 (1)* | 1.00 | .65 |
| *No. 506 (1)* | 1.60 | 1.00 |
| *No. 355 (1)* | 2.50 | 2.00 |
| *No. 270 (1)* | 2.00 | 1.75 |
| *Set total (8) Stamps* | 53.60 | 19.15 |

### Medical Congress

CD44

First National Congress of Tropical Medicine, Lisbon, 1952. Each stamp has a different design.

**1952**

| | |
|---|---|
| Angola | 358 |
| Cape Verde | 287 |
| Macao | 364 |
| Mozambique | 359 |
| Port. Guinea | 276 |
| Port. India | 516 |
| St. Thomas & Prince Islands | 356 |
| Timor | 271 |

| | | |
|---|---|---|
| *No. 358 (1)* | 1.50 | .50 |
| *No. 287 (1)* | .70 | .50 |
| *No. 364 (1)* | 9.75 | 4.25 |
| *No. 359 (1)* | 1.25 | .55 |
| *No. 276 (1)* | .45 | .35 |
| *No. 516 (1)* | 4.75 | 2.00 |
| *No. 356 (1)* | .30 | .30 |
| *No. 271 (1)* | 1.00 | 1.00 |
| *Set total (8) Stamps* | 19.70 | 9.45 |

### Postage Due Stamps

CD45

**1952**

| | |
|---|---|
| Angola | J37-J42 |
| Cape Verde | J31-J36 |
| Macao | J53-J58 |
| Mozambique | J51-J56 |
| Port. Guinea | J40-J45 |
| Port. India | J47-J52 |
| St. Thomas & Prince Islands | J52-J57 |
| Timor | J31-J36 |

| | | |
|---|---|---|
| *Nos. J37-J42 (6)* | 4.05 | 3.15 |
| *Nos. J31-J36 (6)* | 2.80 | 2.30 |
| *Nos. J53-J58 (6)* | 17.45 | 6.85 |
| *Nos. J51-J56 (6)* | 1.80 | 1.55 |
| *Nos. J40-J45 (6)* | 2.55 | 2.55 |
| *Nos. J47-J52 (6)* | 6.10 | 6.10 |
| *Nos. J52-J57 (6)* | 4.15 | 4.15 |
| *Nos. J31-J36 (6)* | 6.20 | 3.50 |
| *Set total (48) Stamps* | 45.10 | 30.15 |

### Sao Paulo

Father Manuel da Nobrega and View of Sao Paulo — CD46

Founding of Sao Paulo, Brazil, 400th anniv.

**1954**

| | |
|---|---|
| Angola | 385 |
| Cape Verde | 297 |
| Macao | 382 |
| Mozambique | 395 |
| Port. Guinea | 291 |
| Port. India | 530 |
| St. Thomas & Prince Islands | 369 |
| Timor | 279 |

| | | |
|---|---|---|
| *No. 385 (1)* | .80 | .50 |
| *No. 297 (1)* | .70 | .60 |
| *No. 382 (1)* | 14.00 | 3.00 |
| *No. 395 (1)* | .40 | .30 |
| *No. 291 (1)* | .35 | .25 |
| *No. 530 (1)* | .80 | .40 |
| *No. 369 (1)* | .80 | .60 |
| *No. 279 (1)* | .85 | .70 |
| *Set total (8) Stamps* | 18.70 | 6.35 |

### Tropical Medicine Congress

CD47

Sixth International Congress for Tropical Medicine and Malaria, Lisbon, Sept. 1958. Each stamp shows a different plant.

**1958**

| | |
|---|---|
| Angola | 409 |
| Cape Verde | 303 |
| Macao | 392 |
| Mozambique | 404 |
| Port. Guinea | 295 |
| Port. India | 569 |
| St. Thomas & Prince Islands | 371 |
| Timor | 289 |

| | | |
|---|---|---|
| *No. 409 (1)* | 3.50 | 1.10 |
| *No. 303 (1)* | 5.50 | 2.10 |
| *No. 392 (1)* | 8.00 | 3.00 |
| *No. 404 (1)* | 2.50 | .85 |
| *No. 295 (1)* | 2.75 | 1.10 |
| *No. 569 (1)* | 1.75 | .75 |
| *No. 371 (1)* | 2.75 | 2.25 |
| *No. 289 (1)* | 3.00 | 2.75 |
| *Set total (8) Stamps* | 29.75 | 13.90 |

### Sports

CD48

Each stamp shows a different sport.

**1962**

| | |
|---|---|
| Angola | 433-438 |
| Cape Verde | 320-325 |
| Macao | 394-399 |
| Mozambique | 424-429 |
| Port. Guinea | 299-304 |
| St. Thomas & Prince Islands | 374-379 |
| Timor | 313-318 |

| | | |
|---|---|---|
| *Nos. 433-438 (6)* | 5.50 | 3.20 |
| *Nos. 320-325 (6)* | 15.25 | 5.20 |
| *Nos. 394-399 (6)* | 74.00 | 14.60 |
| *Nos. 424-429 (6)* | 5.70 | 2.45 |
| *Nos. 299-304 (6)* | 4.95 | 2.15 |
| *Nos. 374-379 (6)* | 6.75 | 3.20 |
| *Nos. 313-318 (6)* | 6.40 | 3.70 |
| *Set total (42) Stamps* | 118.55 | 34.50 |

### Anti-Malaria

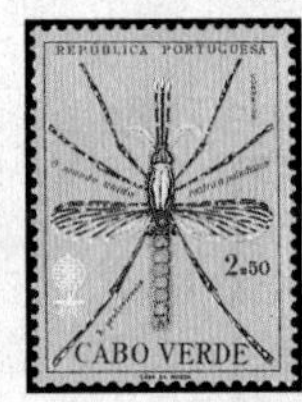

Anopheles Funestus and Malaria Eradication Symbol — CD49

World Health Organization drive to eradicate malaria.

**1962**

| | |
|---|---|
| Angola | 439 |
| Cape Verde | 326 |
| Macao | 400 |
| Mozambique | 430 |
| Port. Guinea | 305 |
| St. Thomas & Prince Islands | 380 |
| Timor | 319 |

| | | |
|---|---|---|
| *No. 439 (1)* | 1.75 | .90 |
| *No. 326 (1)* | 1.40 | .90 |
| *No. 400 (1)* | 6.50 | 2.00 |
| *No. 430 (1)* | 1.40 | .40 |
| *No. 305 (1)* | 1.25 | .45 |
| *No. 380 (1)* | 2.00 | 1.50 |
| *No. 319 (1)* | .75 | .60 |
| *Set total (7) Stamps* | 15.05 | 6.75 |

### Airline Anniversary

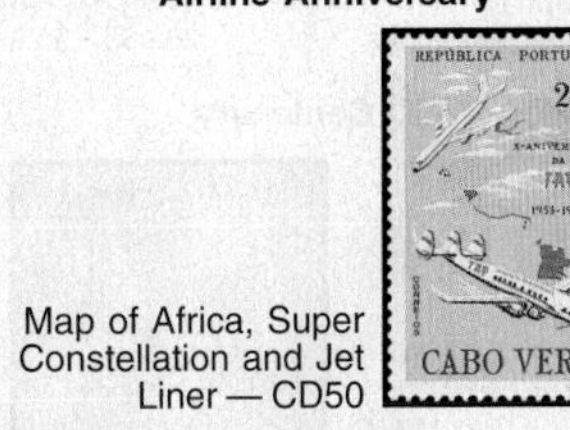

Map of Africa, Super Constellation and Jet Liner — CD50

Tenth anniversary of Transportes Aereos Portugueses (TAP).

**1963**

| | |
|---|---|
| Angola | 490 |
| Cape Verde | 327 |
| Mozambique | 434 |
| Port. Guinea | 318 |
| St. Thomas & Prince Islands | 381 |

| | | |
|---|---|---|
| *No. 490 (1)* | 1.00 | .35 |
| *No. 327 (1)* | 1.10 | .70 |
| *No. 434 (1)* | .40 | .25 |
| *No. 318 (1)* | .65 | .35 |
| *No. 381 (1)* | .70 | .60 |
| *Set total (5) Stamps* | 3.85 | 2.25 |

### National Overseas Bank

Antonio Teixeira de Sousa — CD51

Centenary of the National Overseas Bank of Portugal.

**1964, May 16**

| | |
|---|---|
| Angola | 509 |
| Cape Verde | 328 |
| Port. Guinea | 319 |
| St. Thomas & Prince Islands | 382 |
| Timor | 320 |

| | | |
|---|---|---|
| *No. 509 (1)* | .90 | .30 |
| *No. 328 (1)* | 1.10 | .75 |
| *No. 319 (1)* | .65 | .40 |
| *No. 382 (1)* | .70 | .50 |
| *No. 320 (1)* | .75 | .60 |
| *Set total (5) Stamps* | 4.10 | 2.55 |

### ITU

ITU Emblem and the Archangel Gabriel — CD52

International Communications Union, Cent.

**1965, May 17**

| | |
|---|---|
| Angola | 511 |
| Cape Verde | 329 |
| Macao | 402 |
| Mozambique | 464 |
| Port. Guinea | 320 |
| St. Thomas & Prince Islands | 383 |
| Timor | 321 |

| | | |
|---|---|---|
| *No. 511 (1)* | 1.25 | .65 |
| *No. 329 (1)* | 2.10 | 1.40 |
| *No. 402 (1)* | 5.00 | 2.00 |
| *No. 464 (1)* | .45 | .25 |
| *No. 320 (1)* | 1.90 | .75 |
| *No. 383 (1)* | 1.50 | 1.00 |
| *No. 321 (1)* | 1.50 | .90 |
| *Set total (7) Stamps* | 13.70 | 6.95 |

### National Revolution

CD53

40th anniv. of the National Revolution. Different buildings on each stamp.

**1966, May 28**

| | |
|---|---|
| Angola | 525 |
| Cape Verde | 338 |
| Macao | 403 |
| Mozambique | 465 |
| Port. Guinea | 329 |
| St. Thomas & Prince Islands | 392 |
| Timor | 322 |

| | | |
|---|---|---|
| *No. 525 (1)* | .50 | .25 |
| *No. 338 (1)* | .60 | .45 |
| *No. 403 (1)* | 5.00 | 2.00 |
| *No. 465 (1)* | .50 | .30 |
| *No. 329 (1)* | .55 | .35 |
| *No. 392 (1)* | .75 | .50 |
| *No. 322 (1)* | 1.50 | .90 |
| *Set total (7) Stamps* | 9.40 | 4.75 |

### Navy Club

CD54

Centenary of Portugal's Navy Club. Each stamp has a different design.

**1967, Jan. 31**

Angola ....................527-528
Cape Verde ....................339-340
Macao ....................412-413
Mozambique ....................478-479
Port. Guinea ....................330-331
St. Thomas & Prince Islands ...393-394
Timor ....................323-324

| | | |
|---|---|---|
| *Nos. 527-528 (2)* | 1.75 | .75 |
| *Nos. 339-340 (2)* | 2.00 | 1.40 |
| *Nos. 412-413 (2)* | 9.50 | 3.75 |
| *Nos. 478-479 (2)* | 1.40 | .65 |
| *Nos. 330-331 (2)* | 1.20 | .90 |
| *Nos. 393-394 (2)* | 3.20 | 1.25 |
| *Nos. 323-324 (2)* | 4.00 | 2.00 |
| *Set total (14) Stamps* | 23.05 | 10.70 |

### Admiral Coutinho

CD55

Centenary of the birth of Admiral Carlos Viegas Gago Coutinho (1869-1959), explorer and aviation pioneer. Each stamp has a different design.

**1969, Feb. 17**

Angola ....................547
Cape Verde ....................355
Macao ....................417
Mozambique ....................484
Port. Guinea ....................335
St. Thomas & Prince Islands ..........397
Timor ....................335

| | | |
|---|---|---|
| *No. 547 (1)* | .85 | .35 |
| *No. 355 (1)* | .35 | .25 |
| *No. 417 (1)* | 3.75 | 1.50 |
| *No. 484 (1)* | .25 | .25 |
| *No. 335 (1)* | .35 | .25 |
| *No. 397 (1)* | .50 | .35 |
| *No. 335 (1)* | 1.10 | .85 |
| *Set total (7) Stamps* | 7.15 | 3.80 |

### Administration Reform

Luiz Augusto Rebello da Silva — CD56

Centenary of the administration reforms of the overseas territories.

**1969, Sept. 25**

Angola ....................549
Cape Verde ....................357
Macao ....................419
Mozambique ....................491
Port. Guinea ....................337
St. Thomas & Prince Islands ..........399
Timor ....................338

| | | |
|---|---|---|
| *No. 549 (1)* | .35 | .25 |
| *No. 357 (1)* | .35 | .25 |
| *No. 419 (1)* | 5.00 | 1.00 |
| *No. 491 (1)* | .25 | .25 |
| *No. 337 (1)* | .25 | .25 |
| *No. 399 (1)* | .45 | .45 |
| *No. 338 (1)* | .40 | .25 |
| *Set total (7) Stamps* | 7.05 | 2.70 |

### Marshal Carmona

CD57

Birth centenary of Marshal Antonio Oscar Carmona de Fragoso (1869-1951), President of Portugal. Each stamp has a different design.

**1970, Nov. 15**

Angola ....................563
Cape Verde ....................359
Macao ....................422
Mozambique ....................493
Port. Guinea ....................340
St. Thomas & Prince Islands ..........403
Timor ....................341

| | | |
|---|---|---|
| *No. 563 (1)* | .45 | .25 |
| *No. 359 (1)* | .55 | .35 |
| *No. 422 (1)* | 2.25 | 1.25 |
| *No. 493 (1)* | .40 | .25 |
| *No. 340 (1)* | .35 | .25 |
| *No. 403 (1)* | .75 | .45 |
| *No. 341 (1)* | .25 | .25 |
| *Set total (7) Stamps* | 5.00 | 3.05 |

### Olympic Games

CD59

20th Olympic Games, Munich, Aug. 26-Sept. 11. Each stamp shows a different sport.

**1972, June 20**

Angola ....................569
Cape Verde ....................361
Macao ....................426
Mozambique ....................504
Port. Guinea ....................342
St. Thomas & Prince Islands ..........408
Timor ....................343

| | | |
|---|---|---|
| *No. 569 (1)* | .65 | .25 |
| *No. 361 (1)* | .65 | .30 |
| *No. 426 (1)* | 3.25 | 1.00 |
| *No. 504 (1)* | .30 | .25 |
| *No. 342 (1)* | .45 | .25 |
| *No. 408 (1)* | .35 | .25 |
| *No. 343 (1)* | .50 | .50 |
| *Set total (7) Stamps* | 6.15 | 2.80 |

### Lisbon-Rio de Janeiro Flight

CD60

50th anniversary of the Lisbon to Rio de Janeiro flight by Arturo de Sacadura and Coutinho, March 30-June 5, 1922. Each stamp shows a different stage of the flight.

**1972, Sept. 20**

Angola ....................570
Cape Verde ....................362
Macao ....................427
Mozambique ....................505
Port. Guinea ....................343
St. Thomas & Prince Islands ..........409
Timor ....................344

| | | |
|---|---|---|
| *No. 570 (1)* | .35 | .25 |
| *No. 362 (1)* | 1.50 | .30 |
| *No. 427 (1)* | 22.50 | 7.50 |
| *No. 505 (1)* | .25 | .25 |
| *No. 343 (1)* | .25 | .25 |
| *No. 409 (1)* | .35 | .25 |
| *No. 344 (1)* | .25 | .40 |
| *Set total (7) Stamps* | 25.45 | 9.20 |

### WMO Centenary

WMO Emblem — CD61

Centenary of international meterological cooperation.

**1973, Dec. 15**

Angola ....................571
Cape Verde ....................363
Macao ....................429
Mozambique ....................509
Port. Guinea ....................344
St. Thomas & Prince Islands ..........410
Timor ....................345

| | | |
|---|---|---|
| *No. 571 (1)* | .45 | .25 |
| *No. 363 (1)* | .65 | .30 |
| *No. 429 (1)* | 6.25 | 1.75 |
| *No. 509 (1)* | .30 | .25 |
| *No. 344 (1)* | .45 | .35 |
| *No. 410 (1)* | .60 | .50 |
| *No. 345 (1)* | 1.75 | 2.00 |
| *Set total (7) Stamps* | 10.45 | 5.40 |

## FRENCH COMMUNITY

**Upper Volta can be found under Burkina Faso in Vol. 1**
**Madagascar can be found under Malagasy in Vol. 3**

### Colonial Exposition

People of French Empire CD70

Women's Heads CD71

France Showing Way to Civilization CD72

"Colonial Commerce" CD73

International Colonial Exposition, Paris.

**1931**

Cameroun ....................213-216
Chad ....................60-63
Dahomey ....................97-100
Fr. Guiana ....................152-155
Fr. Guinea ....................116-119
Fr. India ....................100-103
Fr. Polynesia ....................76-79
Fr. Sudan ....................102-105
Gabon ....................120-123
Guadeloupe ....................138-141
Indo-China ....................140-142
Ivory Coast ....................92-95
Madagascar ....................169-172
Martinique ....................129-132
Mauritania ....................65-68
Middle Congo ....................61-64
New Caledonia ....................176-179
Niger ....................73-76
Reunion ....................122-125
St. Pierre & Miquelon ....................132-135
Senegal ....................138-141
Somali Coast ....................135-138
Togo ....................254-257
Ubangi-Shari ....................82-85
Upper Volta ....................66-69
Wallis & Futuna Isls. ....................85-88

| | | |
|---|---|---|
| *Nos. 213-216 (4)* | 23.00 | 18.25 |
| *Nos. 60-63 (4)* | 22.00 | 22.00 |
| *Nos. 97-100 (4)* | 26.00 | 26.00 |
| *Nos. 152-155 (4)* | 22.00 | 22.00 |
| *Nos. 116-119 (4)* | 19.75 | 19.75 |
| *Nos. 100-103 (4)* | 18.00 | 18.00 |
| *Nos. 76-79 (4)* | 30.00 | 30.00 |
| *Nos. 102-105 (4)* | 19.00 | 19.00 |
| *Nos. 120-123 (4)* | 17.50 | 17.50 |
| *Nos. 138-141 (4)* | 19.00 | 19.00 |
| *Nos. 140-142 (3)* | 12.00 | 11.50 |
| *Nos. 92-95 (4)* | 22.50 | 22.50 |
| *Nos. 169-172 (4)* | 7.90 | 5.00 |
| *Nos. 129-132 (4)* | 21.00 | 21.00 |
| *Nos. 65-68 (4)* | 22.00 | 22.00 |
| *Nos. 61-64 (4)* | 20.00 | 18.50 |
| *Nos. 176-179 (4)* | 24.00 | 24.00 |
| *Nos. 73-76 (4)* | 21.50 | 21.50 |
| *Nos. 122-125 (4)* | 22.00 | 22.00 |
| *Nos. 132-135 (4)* | 24.00 | 24.00 |
| *Nos. 138-141 (4)* | 20.00 | 20.00 |
| *Nos. 135-138 (4)* | 22.00 | 22.00 |
| *Nos. 254-257 (4)* | 22.00 | 22.00 |
| *Nos. 82-85 (4)* | 21.00 | 21.00 |
| *Nos. 66-69 (4)* | 19.00 | 19.00 |
| *Nos. 85-88 (4)* | 31.00 | 35.00 |
| *Set total (103) Stamps* | 548.15 | 542.50 |

### Paris International Exposition Colonial Arts Exposition

"Colonial Resources" CD74 CD77

Overseas Commerce CD75

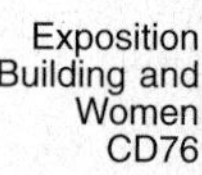
Exposition Building and Women CD76

"France and the Empire" CD78

Cultural Treasures of the Colonies CD79

Souvenir sheets contain one imperf. stamp.

**1937**

Cameroun ....................217-222A
Dahomey ....................101-107
Fr. Equatorial Africa ....................27-32, 73
Fr. Guiana ....................162-168
Fr. Guinea ....................120-126
Fr. India ....................104-110
Fr. Polynesia ....................117-123
Fr. Sudan ....................106-112
Guadeloupe ....................148-154
Indo-China ....................193-199
Inini ....................41
Ivory Coast ....................152-158
Kwangchowan ....................132
Madagascar ....................191-197
Martinique ....................179-185
Mauritania ....................69-75
New Caledonia ....................208-214
Niger ....................77-83
Reunion ....................167-173
St. Pierre & Miquelon ....................165-171
Senegal ....................172-178
Somali Coast ....................139-145
Togo ....................258-264
Wallis & Futuna Isls. ....................89

| | | |
|---|---|---|
| *Nos. 217-222A (7)* | 18.80 | 20.30 |
| *Nos. 101-107 (7)* | 23.60 | 27.60 |
| *Nos. 27-32, 73 (7)* | 28.10 | 32.10 |
| *Nos. 162-168 (7)* | 22.50 | 24.50 |
| *Nos. 120-126 (7)* | 24.00 | 28.00 |
| *Nos. 104-110 (7)* | 21.15 | 36.50 |
| *Nos. 117-123 (7)* | 58.50 | 75.00 |
| *Nos. 106-112 (7)* | 23.60 | 27.60 |
| *Nos. 148-154 (7)* | 19.55 | 21.05 |
| *Nos. 193-199 (7)* | 17.70 | 19.70 |
| *No. 41 (1)* | 21.00 | 27.50 |
| *Nos. 152-158 (7)* | 22.20 | 26.20 |
| *No. 132 (1)* | 9.25 | 11.00 |
| *Nos. 191-197 (7)* | 19.25 | 21.75 |
| *Nos. 179-185 (7)* | 19.95 | 21.70 |
| *Nos. 69-75 (7)* | 20.50 | 24.50 |
| *Nos. 208-214 (7)* | 39.00 | 50.50 |
| *Nos. 73-83 (11)* | 42.70 | 46.70 |
| *Nos. 167-173 (7)* | 21.70 | 23.20 |
| *Nos. 165-171 (7)* | 49.60 | 64.00 |
| *Nos. 172-178 (7)* | 21.00 | 23.80 |
| *Nos. 139-145 (7)* | 25.60 | 32.60 |
| *Nos. 258-264 (7)* | 20.40 | 20.40 |
| *No. 89 (1)* | 19.00 | 37.50 |
| *Set total (154) Stamps* | 608.65 | 743.70 |

### Curie

Pierre and Marie Curie CD80

40th anniversary of the discovery of radium. The surtax was for the benefit of the Intl. Union for the Control of Cancer.

**1938**

| | |
|---|---|
| Cameroun | B1 |
| Cuba | B1-B2 |
| Dahomey | B2 |
| France | B76 |
| Fr. Equatorial Africa | B1 |
| Fr. Guiana | B3 |
| Fr. Guinea | B2 |
| Fr. India | B6 |
| Fr. Polynesia | B5 |
| Fr. Sudan | B1 |
| Guadeloupe | B3 |
| Indo-China | B14 |
| Ivory Coast | B2 |
| Madagascar | B2 |
| Martinique | B2 |
| Mauritania | B3 |
| New Caledonia | B4 |
| Niger | B1 |
| Reunion | B4 |
| St. Pierre & Miquelon | B3 |
| Senegal | B3 |
| Somali Coast | B2 |
| Togo | B1 |

| | | |
|---|---|---|
| *No. B1 (1)* | 10.00 | 10.00 |
| *Nos. B1-B2 (2)* | 12.00 | 3.35 |
| *No. B2 (1)* | 9.50 | 9.50 |
| *No. B76 (1)* | 21.00 | 12.50 |
| *No. B1 (1)* | 24.00 | 24.00 |
| *No. B3 (1)* | 13.50 | 13.50 |
| *No. B2 (1)* | 8.75 | 8.75 |
| *No. B6 (1)* | 10.00 | 10.00 |
| *No. B5 (1)* | 20.00 | 20.00 |
| *No. B1 (1)* | 12.50 | 12.50 |
| *No. B3 (1)* | 11.00 | 10.50 |
| *No. B14 (1)* | 12.00 | 12.00 |
| *No. B2 (1)* | 11.00 | 7.50 |
| *No. B2 (1)* | 11.00 | 11.00 |
| *No. B2 (1)* | 13.00 | 13.00 |
| *No. B3 (1)* | 7.75 | 7.75 |
| *No. B4 (1)* | 16.50 | 17.50 |
| *No. B1 (1)* | 15.00 | 15.00 |
| *No. B4 (1)* | 14.00 | 14.00 |
| *No. B3 (1)* | 21.00 | 22.50 |
| *No. B3 (1)* | 10.50 | 10.50 |
| *No. B2 (1)* | 7.75 | 7.75 |
| *No. B1 (1)* | 20.00 | 20.00 |
| *Set total (24) Stamps* | 311.75 | 293.10 |

### Caillie

Rene Caillie and Map of Northwestern Africa — CD81

Death centenary of Rene Caillie (1799-1838), French explorer. All three denominations exist with colony name omitted.

**1939**

| | |
|---|---|
| Dahomey | 108-110 |
| Fr. Guinea | 161-163 |
| Fr. Sudan | 113-115 |
| Ivory Coast | 160-162 |
| Mauritania | 109-111 |
| Niger | 84-86 |
| Senegal | 188-190 |
| Togo | 265-267 |

| | | |
|---|---|---|
| *Nos. 108-110 (3)* | 1.20 | 3.60 |
| *Nos. 161-163 (3)* | 1.20 | 3.20 |
| *Nos. 113-115 (3)* | 1.20 | 3.20 |
| *Nos. 160-162 (3)* | 1.05 | 2.55 |
| *Nos. 109-111 (3)* | 1.05 | 3.80 |
| *Nos. 84-86 (3)* | 1.05 | 2.35 |
| *Nos. 188-190 (3)* | 1.05 | 2.90 |
| *Nos. 265-267 (3)* | 1.05 | 3.30 |
| *Set total (24) Stamps* | 8.85 | 24.90 |

### New York World's Fair

Natives and New York Skyline CD82

**1939**

| | |
|---|---|
| Cameroun | 223-224 |
| Dahomey | 111-112 |
| Fr. Equatorial Africa | 78-79 |
| Fr. Guiana | 169-170 |
| Fr. Guinea | 164-165 |
| Fr. India | 111-112 |
| Fr. Polynesia | 124-125 |
| Fr. Sudan | 116-117 |
| Guadeloupe | 155-156 |
| Indo-China | 203-204 |
| Inini | 42-43 |
| Ivory Coast | 163-164 |
| Kwangchowan | 133-134 |
| Madagascar | 209-210 |
| Martinique | 186-187 |
| Mauritania | 112-113 |
| New Caledonia | 215-216 |
| Niger | 87-88 |
| Reunion | 174-175 |
| St. Pierre & Miquelon | 205-206 |
| Senegal | 191-192 |
| Somali Coast | 179-180 |
| Togo | 268-269 |
| Wallis & Futuna Isls. | 90-91 |

| | | |
|---|---|---|
| *Nos. 223-224 (2)* | 2.80 | 2.40 |
| *Nos. 111-112 (2)* | 1.60 | 3.20 |
| *Nos. 78-79 (2)* | 1.60 | 3.20 |
| *Nos. 169-170 (2)* | 2.60 | 2.60 |
| *Nos. 164-165 (2)* | 1.60 | 3.20 |
| *Nos. 111-112 (2)* | 3.00 | *8.00* |
| *Nos. 124-125 (2)* | 4.80 | 4.80 |
| *Nos. 116-117 (2)* | 1.60 | 3.20 |
| *Nos. 155-156 (2)* | 2.50 | 2.50 |
| *Nos. 203-204 (2)* | 2.05 | 2.05 |
| *Nos. 42-43 (2)* | 7.50 | 9.00 |
| *Nos. 163-164 (2)* | 1.50 | 3.00 |
| *Nos. 133-134 (2)* | 2.50 | 2.50 |
| *Nos. 209-210 (2)* | 1.50 | 2.50 |
| *Nos. 186-187 (2)* | 2.35 | 2.35 |
| *Nos. 112-113 (2)* | 1.40 | 2.80 |
| *Nos. 215-216 (2)* | 3.35 | 3.35 |
| *Nos. 87-88 (2)* | 1.40 | 2.80 |
| *Nos. 174-175 (2)* | 2.80 | 2.80 |
| *Nos. 205-206 (2)* | 4.80 | 6.00 |
| *Nos. 191-192 (2)* | 1.40 | 2.80 |
| *Nos. 179-180 (2)* | 1.40 | 2.80 |
| *Nos. 268-269 (2)* | 1.40 | 2.80 |
| *Nos. 90-91 (2)* | 5.00 | 6.00 |
| *Set total (48) Stamps* | 62.45 | 86.65 |

### French Revolution

Storming of the Bastille CD83

French Revolution, 150th anniv. The surtax was for the defense of the colonies.

**1939**

| | |
|---|---|
| Cameroun | B2-B6 |
| Dahomey | B3-B7 |
| Fr. Equatorial Africa | B4-B8, CB1 |
| Fr. Guiana | B4-B8, CB1 |
| Fr. Guinea | B3-B7 |
| Fr. India | B7-B11 |
| Fr. Polynesia | B6-B10, CB1 |
| Fr. Sudan | B2-B6 |
| Guadeloupe | B4-B8 |
| Indo-China | B15-B19, CB1 |
| Inini | B1-B5 |
| Ivory Coast | B3-B7 |
| Kwangchowan | B1-B5 |
| Madagascar | B3-B7, CB1 |
| Martinique | B3-B7 |
| Mauritania | B4-B8 |
| New Caledonia | B5-B9, CB1 |
| Niger | B2-B6 |
| Reunion | B5-B9, CB1 |
| St. Pierre & Miquelon | B4-B8 |
| Senegal | B4-B8, CB1 |
| Somali Coast | B3-B7 |
| Togo | B2-B6 |
| Wallis & Futuna Isls. | B1-B5 |

| | | |
|---|---|---|
| *Nos. B2-B6 (5)* | 60.00 | 60.00 |
| *Nos. B3-B7 (5)* | 47.50 | 47.50 |
| *Nos. B4-B8,CB1 (6)* | 120.00 | 120.00 |
| *Nos. B4-B8,CB1 (6)* | 79.50 | 79.50 |
| *Nos. B3-B7 (5)* | 47.50 | 47.50 |
| *Nos. B7-B11 (5)* | 28.75 | *32.50* |
| *Nos. B6-B10,CB1 (6)* | 122.50 | 122.50 |
| *Nos. B2-B6 (5)* | 50.00 | 50.00 |
| *Nos. B4-B8 (5)* | 50.00 | 50.00 |
| *Nos. B15-B19,CB1 (6)* | 85.00 | 85.00 |
| *Nos. B1-B5 (5)* | 80.00 | 100.00 |
| *Nos. B3-B7 (5)* | 43.75 | 43.75 |
| *Nos. B1-B5 (5)* | 46.25 | 46.25 |
| *Nos. B3-B7,CB1 (6)* | 65.50 | 65.50 |
| *Nos. B3-B7 (5)* | 52.50 | 52.50 |
| *Nos. B4-B8 (5)* | 42.50 | 42.50 |
| *Nos. B5-B9,CB1 (6)* | 101.50 | 101.50 |
| *Nos. B2-B6 (5)* | 60.00 | 60.00 |
| *Nos. B5-B9,CB1 (6)* | 87.50 | 87.50 |
| *Nos. B4-B8 (5)* | 67.50 | 72.50 |
| *Nos. B4-B8,CB1 (6)* | 56.50 | 56.50 |
| *Nos. B3-B7 (5)* | 45.00 | 45.00 |
| *Nos. B2-B6 (5)* | 42.50 | 42.50 |
| *Nos. B1-B5 (5)* | 80.00 | 110.00 |
| *Set total (128) Stamps* | 1,562. | 1,621. |

Plane over Coastal Area CD85

All five denominations exist with colony name omitted.

**1940**

| | |
|---|---|
| Dahomey | C1-C5 |
| Fr. Guinea | C1-C5 |
| Fr. Sudan | C1-C5 |
| Ivory Coast | C1-C5 |
| Mauritania | C1-C5 |
| Niger | C1-C5 |
| Senegal | C12-C16 |
| Togo | C1-C5 |

| | | |
|---|---|---|
| *Nos. C1-C5 (5)* | 4.00 | 4.00 |
| *Nos. C1-C5 (5)* | 4.00 | 4.00 |
| *Nos. C1-C5 (5)* | 4.00 | 4.00 |
| *Nos. C1-C5 (5)* | 3.80 | 3.80 |
| *Nos. C1-C5 (5)* | 3.50 | 3.50 |
| *Nos. C1-C5 (5)* | 3.50 | 3.50 |
| *Nos. C12-C16 (5)* | 3.50 | 3.50 |
| *Nos. C1-C5 (5)* | 3.15 | 3.15 |
| *Set total (40) Stamps* | 29.45 | 29.45 |

### Defense of the Empire

Colonial Infantryman — CD86

**1941**

| | |
|---|---|
| Cameroun | B13B |
| Dahomey | B13 |
| Fr. Equatorial Africa | B8B |
| Fr. Guiana | B10 |
| Fr. Guinea | B13 |
| Fr. India | B13 |
| Fr. Polynesia | B12 |
| Fr. Sudan | B12 |
| Guadeloupe | B10 |
| Indo-China | B19B |
| Inini | B7 |
| Ivory Coast | B13 |
| Kwangchowan | B7 |
| Madagascar | B9 |
| Martinique | B9 |
| Mauritania | B14 |
| New Caledonia | B11 |
| Niger | B12 |
| Reunion | B11 |
| St. Pierre & Miquelon | B8B |
| Senegal | B14 |
| Somali Coast | B9 |
| Togo | B10B |
| Wallis & Futuna Isls. | B7 |

| | |
|---|---|
| *No. B13B (1)* | 1.60 |
| *No. B13 (1)* | 1.20 |
| *No. B8B (1)* | 3.50 |
| *No. B10 (1)* | 1.40 |
| *No. B13 (1)* | 1.40 |
| *No. B13 (1)* | 1.25 |
| *No. B12 (1)* | 3.50 |
| *No. B12 (1)* | 1.40 |
| *No. B10 (1)* | 1.00 |
| *No. B19B (1)* | 1.60 |
| *No. B7 (1)* | 1.75 |
| *No. B13 (1)* | 1.25 |
| *No. B7 (1)* | .85 |
| *No. B9 (1)* | 1.50 |
| *No. B9 (1)* | 1.40 |
| *No. B14 (1)* | .95 |
| *No. B12 (1)* | 1.40 |
| *No. B11 (1)* | 1.60 |
| *No. B8B (1)* | 4.50 |
| *No. B14 (1)* | 1.25 |
| *No. B9 (1)* | 1.60 |
| *No. B10B (1)* | 1.10 |
| *No. B7 (1)* | 1.75 |
| *Set total (23) Stamps* | 38.75 |

Each of the CD86 stamps listed above is part of a set of three stamps. The designs of the other two stamps in the set vary from country to country. Only the values of the Common Design stamps are listed here.

### Colonial Education Fund

CD86a

**1942**

| | |
|---|---|
| Cameroun | CB3 |
| Dahomey | CB4 |
| Fr. Equatorial Africa | CB5 |
| Fr. Guiana | CB4 |
| Fr. Guinea | CB4 |
| Fr. India | CB3 |
| Fr. Polynesia | CB4 |
| Fr. Sudan | CB4 |
| Guadeloupe | CB3 |
| Indo-China | CB5 |
| Inini | CB3 |
| Ivory Coast | CB4 |
| Kwangchowan | CB4 |
| Malagasy | CB5 |
| Martinique | CB3 |
| Mauritania | CB4 |
| New Caledonia | CB4 |
| Niger | CB4 |
| Reunion | CB4 |
| St. Pierre & Miquelon | CB3 |
| Senegal | CB5 |
| Somali Coast | CB3 |
| Togo | CB3 |
| Wallis & Futuna | CB3 |

| | | |
|---|---|---|
| *No. CB3 (1)* | 1.10 | |
| *No. CB4 (1)* | .80 | 5.50 |
| *No. CB5 (1)* | .80 | |
| *No. CB4 (1)* | 1.10 | |
| *No. CB4 (1)* | .40 | 5.50 |
| *No. CB3 (1)* | .90 | |
| *No. CB4 (1)* | 2.00 | |
| *No. CB4 (1)* | .40 | 5.50 |
| *No. CB3 (1)* | 1.10 | |
| *No. CB5 (1)* | 1.10 | |
| *No. CB3 (1)* | 1.25 | |
| *No. CB4 (1)* | 1.00 | 5.50 |
| *No. CB4 (1)* | 1.00 | |
| *No. CB5 (1)* | .65 | |
| *No. CB3 (1)* | 1.00 | |
| *No. CB4 (1)* | .80 | |
| *No. CB4 (1)* | 2.25 | |
| *No. CB4 (1)* | .35 | |
| *No. CB4 (1)* | .90 | |
| *No. CB3 (1)* | 7.00 | |
| *No. CB5 (1)* | .80 | 6.50 |
| *No. CB3 (1)* | .70 | |
| *No. CB3 (1)* | .35 | |
| *No. CB3 (1)* | 2.00 | |
| *Set total (24) Stamps* | 29.75 | 28.50 |

Cross of Lorraine & Four-motor Plane CD87

**1941-5**

| | |
|---|---|
| Cameroun | C1-C7 |
| Fr. Equatorial Africa | C17-C23 |
| Fr. Guiana | C9-C10 |
| Fr. India | C1-C6 |
| Fr. Polynesia | C3-C9 |
| Fr. West Africa | C1-C3 |
| Guadeloupe | C1-C2 |
| Madagascar | C37-C43 |

| | |
|---|---|
| Martinique | C1-C2 |
| New Caledonia | C7-C13 |
| Reunion | C18-C24 |
| St. Pierre & Miquelon | C1-C7 |
| Somali Coast | C1-C7 |

| | | |
|---|---|---|
| *Nos. C1-C7 (7)* | 6.30 | 6.30 |
| *Nos. C17-C23 (7)* | 10.40 | 6.35 |
| *Nos. C9-C10 (2)* | 3.80 | 3.10 |
| *Nos. C1-C6 (6)* | 9.30 | *15.00* |
| *Nos. C3-C9 (7)* | 13.75 | 10.00 |
| *Nos. C1-C3 (3)* | 9.50 | 3.90 |
| *Nos. C1-C2 (2)* | 3.75 | 2.50 |
| *Nos. C37-C43 (7)* | 5.60 | 3.80 |
| *Nos. C1-C2 (2)* | 3.00 | 1.60 |
| *Nos. C7-C13 (7)* | 8.85 | 7.30 |
| *Nos. C18-C24 (7)* | 7.05 | 5.00 |
| *Nos. C1-C7 (7)* | 11.60 | 9.40 |
| *Nos. C1-C7 (7)* | 13.95 | 11.10 |
| *Set total (71) Stamps* | 106.85 | 85.35 |

Somali Coast stamps are inscribed "Djibouti".

Transport Plane CD88

Caravan and Plane CD89

### 1942

| | |
|---|---|
| Dahomey | C6-C13 |
| Fr. Guinea | C6-C13 |
| Fr. Sudan | C6-C13 |
| Ivory Coast | C6-C13 |
| Mauritania | C6-C13 |
| Niger | C6-C13 |
| Senegal | C17-C25 |
| Togo | C6-C13 |

| | |
|---|---|
| *Nos. C6-C13 (8)* | 7.15 |
| *Nos. C6-C13 (8)* | 5.75 |
| *Nos. C6-C13 (8)* | 8.00 |
| *Nos. C6-C13 (8)* | 11.15 |
| *Nos. C6-C13 (8)* | 9.75 |
| *Nos. C6-C13 (8)* | 6.90 |
| *Nos. C17-C25 (9)* | 9.45 |
| *Nos. C6-C13 (8)* | 6.75 |
| *Set total (65) Stamps* | 64.90 |

## Red Cross

Marianne CD90

The surtax was for the French Red Cross and national relief.

### 1944

| | |
|---|---|
| Cameroun | B28 |
| Fr. Equatorial Africa | B38 |
| Fr. Guiana | B12 |
| Fr. India | B14 |
| Fr. Polynesia | B13 |
| Fr. West Africa | B1 |
| Guadeloupe | B12 |
| Madagascar | B15 |
| Martinique | B11 |
| New Caledonia | B13 |
| Reunion | B15 |
| St. Pierre & Miquelon | B13 |
| Somali Coast | B13 |
| Wallis & Futuna Isls. | B9 |

| | | |
|---|---|---|
| *No. B28 (1)* | 2.00 | 1.60 |
| *No. B38 (1)* | 1.60 | 1.20 |
| *No. B12 (1)* | 1.75 | 1.25 |
| *No. B14 (1)* | 1.50 | 1.25 |
| *No. B13 (1)* | 2.00 | 1.60 |
| *No. B1 (1)* | 6.50 | 4.75 |
| *No. B12 (1)* | 1.40 | 1.00 |
| *No. B15 (1)* | .90 | .90 |
| *No. B11 (1)* | 1.20 | 1.20 |
| *No. B13 (1)* | 1.50 | 1.50 |
| *No. B15 (1)* | 1.60 | 1.10 |
| *No. B13 (1)* | 2.60 | 2.60 |
| *No. B13 (1)* | 1.75 | 2.00 |
| *No. B9 (1)* | 3.00 | 3.00 |
| *Set total (14) Stamps* | 29.30 | 24.95 |

## Eboue

CD91

Felix Eboue, first French colonial administrator to proclaim resistance to Germany after French surrender in World War II.

### 1945

| | |
|---|---|
| Cameroun | 296-297 |
| Fr. Equatorial Africa | 156-157 |
| Fr. Guiana | 171-172 |
| Fr. India | 210-211 |
| Fr. Polynesia | 150-151 |
| Fr. West Africa | 15-16 |
| Guadeloupe | 187-188 |
| Madagascar | 259-260 |
| Martinique | 196-197 |
| New Caledonia | 274-275 |
| Reunion | 238-239 |
| St. Pierre & Miquelon | 322-323 |
| Somali Coast | 238-239 |

| | | |
|---|---|---|
| *Nos. 296-297 (2)* | 2.40 | 1.95 |
| *Nos. 156-157 (2)* | 2.55 | 2.00 |
| *Nos. 171-172 (2)* | 2.45 | 2.00 |
| *Nos. 210-211 (2)* | 2.20 | 1.95 |
| *Nos. 150-151 (2)* | 3.60 | 2.85 |
| *Nos. 15-16 (2)* | 2.40 | 2.40 |
| *Nos. 187-188 (2)* | 2.05 | 1.60 |
| *Nos. 259-260 (2)* | 2.00 | 1.45 |
| *Nos. 196-197 (2)* | 2.05 | 1.55 |
| *Nos. 274-275 (2)* | 3.40 | 3.00 |
| *Nos. 238-239 (2)* | 2.40 | 2.00 |
| *Nos. 322-323 (2)* | 4.40 | 3.45 |
| *Nos. 238-239 (2)* | 2.45 | 2.10 |
| *Set total (26) Stamps* | 34.35 | 28.30 |

## Victory

Victory — CD92

European victory of the Allied Nations in World War II.

### 1946, May 8

| | |
|---|---|
| Cameroun | C8 |
| Fr. Equatorial Africa | C24 |
| Fr. Guiana | C11 |
| Fr. India | C7 |
| Fr. Polynesia | C10 |
| Fr. West Africa | C4 |
| Guadeloupe | C3 |
| Indo-China | C19 |
| Madagascar | C44 |
| Martinique | C3 |
| New Caledonia | C14 |
| Reunion | C25 |
| St. Pierre & Miquelon | C8 |
| Somali Coast | C8 |
| Wallis & Futuna Isls. | C1 |

| | | |
|---|---|---|
| *No. C8 (1)* | 1.60 | 1.20 |
| *No. C24 (1)* | 1.60 | 1.25 |
| *No. C11 (1)* | 1.75 | 1.25 |
| *No. C7 (1)* | 1.00 | 4.00 |
| *No. C10 (1)* | 2.75 | 2.00 |
| *No. C4 (1)* | 1.60 | 1.20 |
| *No. C3 (1)* | 1.25 | 1.00 |
| *No. C19 (1)* | 1.00 | .55 |
| *No. C44 (1)* | 1.00 | .35 |
| *No. C3 (1)* | 1.30 | 1.00 |
| *No. C14 (1)* | 1.50 | 1.25 |
| *No. C25 (1)* | 1.10 | .90 |
| *No. C8 (1)* | 2.10 | 2.10 |
| *No. C8 (1)* | 1.75 | 1.40 |
| *No. C1 (1)* | 2.25 | 1.90 |
| *Set total (15) Stamps* | 23.55 | 21.35 |

## Chad to Rhine

Leclerc's Departure from Chad — CD93

Battle at Cufra Oasis — CD94

Tanks in Action, Mareth — CD95

Normandy Invasion — CD96

Entering Paris — CD97

Liberation of Strasbourg — CD98

"Chad to the Rhine" march, 1942-44, by Gen. Jacques Leclerc's column, later French 2nd Armored Division.

### 1946, June 6

| | |
|---|---|
| Cameroun | C9-C14 |
| Fr. Equatorial Africa | C25-C30 |
| Fr. Guiana | C12-C17 |
| Fr. India | C8-C13 |
| Fr. Polynesia | C11-C16 |
| Fr. West Africa | C5-C10 |
| Guadeloupe | C4-C9 |
| Indo-China | C20-C25 |
| Madagascar | C45-C50 |
| Martinique | C4-C9 |
| New Caledonia | C15-C20 |
| Reunion | C26-C31 |
| St. Pierre & Miquelon | C9-C14 |
| Somali Coast | C9-C14 |
| Wallis & Futuna Isls. | C2-C7 |

| | | |
|---|---|---|
| *Nos. C9-C14 (6)* | 12.05 | 9.70 |
| *Nos. C25-C30 (6)* | 14.70 | 10.80 |
| *Nos. C12-C17 (6)* | 12.65 | 10.35 |
| *Nos. C8-C13 (6)* | 12.80 | *15.00* |
| *Nos. C11-C16 (6)* | 17.55 | 13.40 |
| *Nos. C5-C10 (6)* | 16.05 | 11.95 |
| *Nos. C4-C9 (6)* | 12.00 | 9.60 |
| *Nos. C20-C25 (6)* | 6.40 | 6.40 |
| *Nos. C45-C50 (6)* | 10.30 | 8.40 |
| *Nos. C4-C9 (6)* | 8.85 | 7.30 |
| *Nos. C15-C20 (6)* | 13.40 | 11.90 |
| *Nos. C26-C31 (6)* | 10.25 | 6.55 |
| *Nos. C9-C14 (6)* | 17.30 | 14.35 |
| *Nos. C9-C14 (6)* | 18.10 | 12.65 |
| *Nos. C2-C7 (6)* | 13.75 | 10.45 |
| *Set total (90) Stamps* | 196.15 | 158.80 |

## UPU

French Colonials, Globe and Plane — CD99

Universal Postal Union, 75th anniv.

### 1949, July 4

| | |
|---|---|
| Cameroun | C29 |
| Fr. Equatorial Africa | C34 |
| Fr. India | C17 |
| Fr. Polynesia | C20 |
| Fr. West Africa | C15 |
| Indo-China | C26 |
| Madagascar | C55 |
| New Caledonia | C24 |
| St. Pierre & Miquelon | C18 |
| Somali Coast | C18 |
| Togo | C18 |
| Wallis & Futuna Isls. | C10 |

| | | |
|---|---|---|
| *No. C29 (1)* | 8.00 | 4.75 |
| *No. C34 (1)* | 16.00 | 12.00 |
| *No. C17 (1)* | 11.50 | 8.75 |
| *No. C20 (1)* | 20.00 | 15.00 |
| *No. C15 (1)* | 12.00 | 8.75 |
| *No. C26 (1)* | 4.75 | 4.00 |
| *No. C55 (1)* | 4.00 | 2.75 |
| *No. C24 (1)* | 7.50 | 5.00 |
| *No. C18 (1)* | 20.00 | 12.00 |
| *No. C18 (1)* | 14.00 | 10.50 |
| *No. C18 (1)* | 8.50 | 7.00 |
| *No. C10 (1)* | 11.00 | 8.25 |
| *Set total (12) Stamps* | 137.25 | 98.75 |

## Tropical Medicine

Doctor Treating Infant CD100

The surtax was for charitable work.

### 1950

| | |
|---|---|
| Cameroun | B29 |
| Fr. Equatorial Africa | B39 |
| Fr. India | B15 |
| Fr. Polynesia | B14 |
| Fr. West Africa | B3 |
| Madagascar | B17 |
| New Caledonia | B14 |
| St. Pierre & Miquelon | B14 |
| Somali Coast | B14 |
| Togo | B11 |

| | | |
|---|---|---|
| *No. B29 (1)* | 7.25 | 5.50 |
| *No. B39 (1)* | 7.25 | 5.50 |
| *No. B15 (1)* | 6.00 | 4.00 |
| *No. B14 (1)* | 10.50 | 8.00 |
| *No. B3 (1)* | 9.50 | 7.25 |
| *No. B17 (1)* | 5.50 | 5.50 |
| *No. B14 (1)* | 6.75 | 5.25 |
| *No. B14 (1)* | 16.00 | 15.00 |
| *No. B14 (1)* | 7.75 | 6.25 |
| *No. B11 (1)* | 5.00 | 3.50 |
| *Set total (10) Stamps* | 81.50 | 65.75 |

## Military Medal

Medal, Early Marine and Colonial Soldier — CD101

Centenary of the creation of the French Military Medal.

### 1952

| | |
|---|---|
| Cameroun | 322 |
| Comoro Isls. | 39 |
| Fr. Equatorial Africa | 186 |

Fr. India ....233
Fr. Polynesia ....179
Fr. West Africa ....57
Madagascar ....286
New Caledonia ....295
St. Pierre & Miquelon ....345
Somali Coast ....267
Togo ....327
Wallis & Futuna Isls. ....149

| | | |
|---|---|---|
| *No. 322 (1)* | 7.25 | 3.25 |
| *No. 39 (1)* | 50.00 | 40.00 |
| *No. 186 (1)* | 8.00 | 5.50 |
| *No. 233 (1)* | 5.50 | 7.00 |
| *No. 179 (1)* | 13.50 | 10.00 |
| *No. 57 (1)* | 8.75 | 6.50 |
| *No. 286 (1)* | 3.75 | 2.50 |
| *No. 295 (1)* | 6.50 | 6.00 |
| *No. 345 (1)* | 16.00 | 15.00 |
| *No. 267 (1)* | 9.00 | 8.00 |
| *No. 327 (1)* | 5.50 | 4.75 |
| *No. 149 (1)* | 7.25 | 7.25 |
| *Set total (12) Stamps* | 141.00 | 115.75 |

### Liberation

Allied Landing, Victory Sign and Cross of Lorraine — CD102

Liberation of France, 10th anniv.

**1954, June 6**

Cameroun ....C32
Comoro Isls. ....C4
Fr. Equatorial Africa ....C38
Fr. India ....C18
Fr. Polynesia ....C22
Fr. West Africa ....C17
Madagascar ....C57
New Caledonia ....C25
St. Pierre & Miquelon ....C19
Somali Coast ....C19
Togo ....C19
Wallis & Futuna Isls. ....C11

| | | |
|---|---|---|
| *No. C32 (1)* | 7.25 | 4.75 |
| *No. C4 (1)* | 35.00 | 20.00 |
| *No. C38 (1)* | 12.00 | 8.00 |
| *No. C18 (1)* | 11.00 | 8.00 |
| *No. C22 (1)* | 10.00 | 8.00 |
| *No. C17 (1)* | 12.00 | 5.50 |
| *No. C57 (1)* | 3.25 | 2.00 |
| *No. C25 (1)* | 7.50 | 5.00 |
| *No. C19 (1)* | 19.00 | 12.00 |
| *No. C19 (1)* | 10.50 | 8.50 |
| *No. C19 (1)* | 7.00 | 5.50 |
| *No. C11 (1)* | 11.00 | 8.25 |
| *Set total (12) Stamps* | 145.50 | 95.50 |

### FIDES

Plowmen CD103

Efforts of FIDES, the Economic and Social Development Fund for Overseas Possessions (Fonds d' Investissement pour le Developpement Economique et Social). Each stamp has a different design.

**1956**

Cameroun ....326-329
Comoro Isls. ....43
Fr. Equatorial Africa ....189-192
Fr. Polynesia ....181
Fr. West Africa ....65-72
Madagascar ....292-295
New Caledonia ....303
St. Pierre & Miquelon ....350
Somali Coast ....268-269
Togo ....331

| | | |
|---|---|---|
| *Nos. 326-329 (4)* | 6.90 | 3.20 |
| *No. 43 (1)* | 2.25 | 1.60 |
| *Nos. 189-192 (4)* | 3.20 | 1.65 |
| *No. 181 (1)* | 4.00 | 2.00 |
| *Nos. 65-72 (8)* | 16.00 | 6.35 |
| *Nos. 292-295 (4)* | 2.25 | 1.20 |
| *No. 303 (1)* | 1.90 | 1.10 |
| *No. 350 (1)* | 6.00 | 4.00 |
| *Nos. 268-269 (2)* | 5.35 | 3.15 |
| *No. 331 (1)* | 4.25 | 2.10 |
| *Set total (27) Stamps* | 52.10 | 26.35 |

### Flower

CD104

Each stamp shows a different flower.

**1958-9**

Cameroun ....333
Comoro Isls. ....45
Fr. Equatorial Africa ....200-201
Fr. Polynesia ....192
Fr. So. & Antarctic Terr. ....11
Fr. West Africa ....79-83
Madagascar ....301-302
New Caledonia ....304-305
St. Pierre & Miquelon ....357
Somali Coast ....270
Togo ....348-349
Wallis & Futuna Isls. ....152

| | | |
|---|---|---|
| *No. 333 (1)* | 1.60 | .80 |
| *No. 45 (1)* | 5.50 | 4.50 |
| *Nos. 200-201 (2)* | 3.60 | 1.60 |
| *No. 192 (1)* | 6.50 | 4.00 |
| *No. 11 (1)* | 8.75 | 7.50 |
| *Nos. 79-83 (5)* | 10.45 | 5.60 |
| *Nos. 301-302 (2)* | 1.60 | .60 |
| *Nos. 304-305 (2)* | 8.00 | 3.00 |
| *No. 357 (1)* | 4.50 | 2.25 |
| *No. 270 (1)* | 4.25 | 1.40 |
| *Nos. 348-349 (2)* | 1.10 | .50 |
| *No. 152 (1)* | 3.25 | 3.25 |
| *Set total (20) Stamps* | 59.10 | 35.00 |

### Human Rights

Sun, Dove and U.N. Emblem CD105

10th anniversary of the signing of the Universal Declaration of Human Rights.

**1958**

Comoro Isls. ....44
Fr. Equatorial Africa ....202
Fr. Polynesia ....191
Fr. West Africa ....85
Madagascar ....300
New Caledonia ....306
St. Pierre & Miquelon ....356
Somali Coast ....274
Wallis & Futuna Isls. ....153

| | | |
|---|---|---|
| *No. 44 (1)* | 11.00 | 11.00 |
| *No. 202 (1)* | 2.40 | 1.25 |
| *No. 191 (1)* | 13.00 | 8.75 |
| *No. 85 (1)* | 2.40 | 2.00 |
| *No. 300 (1)* | .80 | .40 |
| *No. 306 (1)* | 2.00 | 1.50 |
| *No. 356 (1)* | 3.50 | 2.50 |
| *No. 274 (1)* | 3.50 | 2.10 |
| *No. 153 (1)* | 4.50 | 4.50 |
| *Set total (9) Stamps* | 43.10 | 34.00 |

### C.C.T.A.

CD106

Commission for Technical Cooperation in Africa south of the Sahara, 10th anniv.

**1960**

Cameroun ....339
Cent. Africa ....3
Chad ....66
Congo, P.R. ....90
Dahomey ....138
Gabon ....150
Ivory Coast ....180
Madagascar ....317
Mali ....9
Mauritania ....117
Niger ....104
Upper Volta ....89

| | | |
|---|---|---|
| *No. 339 (1)* | 1.60 | .75 |
| *No. 3 (1)* | 1.90 | .65 |
| *No. 66 (1)* | 1.90 | .50 |
| *No. 90 (1)* | 1.00 | 1.00 |
| *No. 138 (1)* | .50 | .25 |
| *No. 150 (1)* | 1.40 | 1.10 |
| *No. 180 (1)* | 1.10 | .50 |
| *No. 317 (1)* | .60 | .30 |
| *No. 9 (1)* | 1.20 | .50 |
| *No. 117 (1)* | .75 | .40 |
| *No. 104 (1)* | .85 | .45 |
| *No. 89 (1)* | .65 | .40 |
| *Set total (12) Stamps* | 13.45 | 6.80 |

### Air Afrique, 1961

Modern and Ancient Africa, Map and Planes — CD107

Founding of Air Afrique (African Airlines).

**1961-62**

Cameroun ....C37
Cent. Africa ....C5
Chad ....C7
Congo, P.R. ....C5
Dahomey ....C17
Gabon ....C5
Ivory Coast ....C18
Mauritania ....C17
Niger ....C22
Senegal ....C31
Upper Volta ....C4

| | | |
|---|---|---|
| *No. C37 (1)* | 1.00 | .50 |
| *No. C5 (1)* | 1.00 | .55 |
| *No. C7 (1)* | 1.00 | .25 |
| *No. C5 (1)* | 1.75 | .90 |
| *No. C17 (1)* | .80 | .40 |
| *No. C5 (1)* | 11.00 | 6.00 |
| *No. C18 (1)* | 2.00 | 1.25 |
| *No. C17 (1)* | 2.50 | 1.25 |
| *No. C22 (1)* | 1.75 | .90 |
| *No. C31 (1)* | .80 | .30 |
| *No. C4 (1)* | 3.50 | 1.75 |
| *Set total (11) Stamps* | 27.10 | 14.05 |

### Anti-Malaria

CD108

World Health Organization drive to eradicate malaria.

**1962, Apr. 7**

Cameroun ....B36
Cent. Africa ....B1
Chad ....B1
Comoro Isls. ....B1
Congo, P.R. ....B3
Dahomey ....B15
Gabon ....B4
Ivory Coast ....B15
Madagascar ....B19
Mali ....B1
Mauritania ....B16
Niger ....B14
Senegal ....B16
Somali Coast ....B15
Upper Volta ....B1

| | | |
|---|---|---|
| *No. B36 (1)* | 1.00 | .45 |
| *No. B1 (1)* | 1.40 | 1.40 |
| *No. B1 (1)* | 1.25 | .50 |
| *No. B1 (1)* | 4.00 | 4.00 |
| *No. B3 (1)* | 1.40 | 1.00 |
| *No. B15 (1)* | .75 | .75 |
| *No. B4 (1)* | 1.00 | 1.00 |
| *No. B15 (1)* | 1.25 | 1.25 |
| *No. B19 (1)* | .75 | .50 |
| *No. B1 (1)* | 1.25 | .60 |
| *No. B16 (1)* | .80 | .80 |
| *No. B14 (1)* | .60 | .60 |
| *No. B16 (1)* | 1.10 | .65 |
| *No. B15 (1)* | 7.00 | 7.00 |
| *No. B1 (1)* | .75 | .70 |
| *Set total (15) Stamps* | 24.30 | 21.20 |

### Abidjan Games

CD109

Abidjan Games, Ivory Coast, Dec. 24-31, 1961. Each stamp shows a different sport.

**1962**

Cent. Africa ....19-20, C6
Chad ....83-84, C8
Congo, P.R. ....103-104, C7
Gabon ....163-164, C6
Niger ....109-111
Upper Volta ....103-105

| | | |
|---|---|---|
| *Nos. 19-20,C6 (3)* | 3.90 | 2.60 |
| *Nos. 83-84,C8 (3)* | 6.30 | 1.55 |
| *Nos. 103-104,C7 (3)* | 3.85 | 1.80 |
| *Nos. 163-164,C6 (3)* | 5.00 | 3.00 |
| *Nos. 109-111 (3)* | 2.60 | 1.10 |
| *Nos. 103-105 (3)* | 2.80 | 1.75 |
| *Set total (18) Stamps* | 24.45 | 11.80 |

### African and Malagasy Union

Flag of Union CD110

First anniversary of the Union.

**1962, Sept. 8**

Cameroun ....373
Cent. Africa ....21
Chad ....85
Congo, P.R. ....105
Dahomey ....155
Gabon ....165
Ivory Coast ....198
Madagascar ....332
Mauritania ....170
Niger ....112
Senegal ....211
Upper Volta ....106

| | | |
|---|---|---|
| *No. 373 (1)* | 2.00 | .75 |
| *No. 21 (1)* | 1.25 | .60 |
| *No. 85 (1)* | 1.25 | .25 |
| *No. 105 (1)* | 1.50 | .50 |
| *No. 155 (1)* | 1.25 | .90 |
| *No. 165 (1)* | 1.60 | 1.25 |
| *No. 198 (1)* | 2.10 | .75 |
| *No. 332 (1)* | .80 | .80 |
| *No. 170 (1)* | .75 | .50 |
| *No. 112 (1)* | .80 | .40 |
| *No. 211 (1)* | .80 | .50 |
| *No. 106 (1)* | 1.10 | .75 |
| *Set total (12) Stamps* | 15.20 | 7.95 |

### Telstar

Telstar and Globe Showing Andover and Pleumeur-Bodou — CD111

First television connection of the United States and Europe through the Telstar satellite, July 11-12, 1962.

**1962-63**

Andorra, French ....154
Comoro Isls. ....C7
Fr. Polynesia ....C29
Fr. So. & Antarctic Terr. ....C5
New Caledonia ....C33
St. Pierre & Miquelon ....C26
Somali Coast ....C31
Wallis & Futuna Isls. ....C17

| | | |
|---|---|---|
| *No. 154 (1)* | 2.00 | 1.60 |
| *No. C7 (1)* | 5.00 | 3.00 |
| *No. C29 (1)* | 11.50 | 8.00 |

| | | |
|---|---|---|
| *No. C5 (1)* | 29.00 | 21.00 |
| *No. C33 (1)* | 25.00 | 18.50 |
| *No. C26 (1)* | 7.25 | 4.50 |
| *No. C31 (1)* | 1.00 | 1.00 |
| *No. C17 (1)* | 3.75 | 3.75 |
| *Set total (8) Stamps* | 84.50 | 61.35 |

### Freedom From Hunger

World Map and Wheat Emblem CD112

U.N. Food and Agriculture Organization's "Freedom from Hunger" campaign.

**1963, Mar. 21**

Cameroun ........ B37-B38
Cent. Africa ........ B2
Chad ........ B2
Congo, P.R. ........ B4
Dahomey ........ B16
Gabon ........ B5
Ivory Coast ........ B16
Madagascar ........ B21
Mauritania ........ B17
Niger ........ B15
Senegal ........ B17
Upper Volta ........ B2

| | | |
|---|---|---|
| *Nos. B37-B38 (2)* | 2.25 | .75 |
| *No. B2 (1)* | 1.25 | 1.25 |
| *No. B2 (1)* | 2.00 | .50 |
| *No. B4 (1)* | 1.40 | 1.00 |
| *No. B16 (1)* | .80 | .80 |
| *No. B5 (1)* | 1.00 | 1.00 |
| *No. B16 (1)* | 1.50 | 1.50 |
| *No. B21 (1)* | .60 | .45 |
| *No. B17 (1)* | .80 | .80 |
| *No. B15 (1)* | .60 | .60 |
| *No. B17 (1)* | .80 | .50 |
| *No. B2 (1)* | .75 | .70 |
| *Set total (13) Stamps* | 13.75 | 9.85 |

### Red Cross Centenary

CD113

Centenary of the International Red Cross.

**1963, Sept. 2**

Comoro Isls. ........ 55
Fr. Polynesia ........ 205
New Caledonia ........ 328
St. Pierre & Miquelon ........ 367
Somali Coast ........ 297
Wallis & Futuna Isls. ........ 165

| | | |
|---|---|---|
| *No. 55 (1)* | 9.50 | 7.00 |
| *No. 205 (1)* | 15.00 | 12.00 |
| *No. 328 (1)* | 8.00 | 6.75 |
| *No. 367 (1)* | 12.00 | 5.50 |
| *No. 297 (1)* | 6.25 | 6.25 |
| *No. 165 (1)* | 4.00 | 4.00 |
| *Set total (6) Stamps* | 54.75 | 41.50 |

### African Postal Union, 1963

UAMPT Emblem, Radio Masts, Plane and Mail CD114

Establishment of the African and Malagasy Posts and Telecommunications Union.

**1963, Sept. 8**

Cameroun ........ C47
Cent. Africa ........ C10
Chad ........ C9
Congo, P.R. ........ C13
Dahomey ........ C19
Gabon ........ C13
Ivory Coast ........ C25
Madagascar ........ C75
Mauritania ........ C22
Niger ........ C27
Rwanda ........ 36
Senegal ........ C32
Upper Volta ........ C9

| | | |
|---|---|---|
| *No. C47 (1)* | 2.25 | 1.00 |
| *No. C10 (1)* | 1.90 | .85 |
| *No. C9 (1)* | 2.40 | .60 |
| *No. C13 (1)* | 1.40 | .75 |
| *No. C19 (1)* | .75 | .25 |
| *No. C13 (1)* | 1.90 | .80 |
| *No. C25 (1)* | 2.50 | 1.50 |
| *No. C75 (1)* | 1.25 | .80 |
| *No. C22 (1)* | 1.50 | .60 |
| *No. C27 (1)* | 1.25 | .60 |
| *No. 36 (1)* | 1.00 | .75 |
| *No. C32 (1)* | 1.75 | .50 |
| *No. C9 (1)* | 1.50 | .75 |
| *Set total (13) Stamps* | 21.35 | 9.75 |

### Air Afrique, 1963

Symbols of Flight — CD115

First anniversary of Air Afrique and inauguration of DC-8 service.

**1963, Nov. 19**

Cameroun ........ C48
Chad ........ C10
Congo, P.R. ........ C14
Gabon ........ C18
Ivory Coast ........ C26
Mauritania ........ C26
Niger ........ C35
Senegal ........ C33

| | | |
|---|---|---|
| *No. C48 (1)* | 1.25 | .40 |
| *No. C10 (1)* | 2.40 | .60 |
| *No. C14 (1)* | 1.60 | .60 |
| *No. C18 (1)* | 1.40 | .65 |
| *No. C26 (1)* | 1.00 | .50 |
| *No. C26 (1)* | .70 | .25 |
| *No. C35 (1)* | .90 | .50 |
| *No. C33 (1)* | 2.00 | .65 |
| *Set total (8) Stamps* | 11.25 | 4.15 |

### Europafrica

Europe and Africa Linked — CD116

Signing of an economic agreement between the European Economic Community and the African and Malagasy Union, Yaounde, Cameroun, July 20, 1963.

**1963-64**

Cameroun ........ 402
Cent. Africa ........ C12
Chad ........ C11
Congo, P.R. ........ C16
Gabon ........ C19
Ivory Coast ........ 217
Niger ........ C43
Upper Volta ........ C11

| | | |
|---|---|---|
| *No. 402 (1)* | 2.25 | .60 |
| *No. C12 (1)* | 2.50 | 1.75 |
| *No. C11 (1)* | 2.00 | .50 |
| *No. C16 (1)* | 1.60 | 1.00 |
| *No. C19 (1)* | 1.40 | .75 |
| *No. 217 (1)* | 1.10 | .35 |
| *No. C43 (1)* | .85 | .50 |
| *No. C11 (1)* | 1.50 | .80 |
| *Set total (8) Stamps* | 13.20 | 6.25 |

### Human Rights

Scales of Justice and Globe CD117

15th anniversary of the Universal Declaration of Human Rights.

**1963, Dec. 10**

Comoro Isls. ........ 56
Fr. Polynesia ........ 206
New Caledonia ........ 329
St. Pierre & Miquelon ........ 368
Somali Coast ........ 300
Wallis & Futuna Isls. ........ 166

| | | |
|---|---|---|
| *No. 56 (1)* | 9.50 | 7.50 |
| *No. 205 (1)* | 15.00 | 12.00 |
| *No. 329 (1)* | 7.00 | 6.00 |
| *No. 368 (1)* | 7.00 | 3.50 |
| *No. 300 (1)* | 8.50 | 8.50 |
| *No. 166 (1)* | 7.00 | 7.00 |
| *Set total (6) Stamps* | 54.00 | 44.50 |

### PHILATEC

Stamp Album, Champs Elysees Palace and Horses of Marly CD118

Intl. Philatelic and Postal Techniques Exhibition, Paris, June 5-21, 1964.

**1963-64**

Comoro Isls. ........ 60
France ........ 1078
Fr. Polynesia ........ 207
New Caledonia ........ 341
St. Pierre & Miquelon ........ 369
Somali Coast ........ 301
Wallis & Futuna Isls. ........ 167

| | | |
|---|---|---|
| *No. 60 (1)* | 4.50 | 4.00 |
| *No. 1078 (1)* | .25 | .25 |
| *No. 206 (1)* | 15.00 | 10.00 |
| *No. 341 (1)* | 6.50 | 6.50 |
| *No. 369 (1)* | 11.00 | 8.00 |
| *No. 301 (1)* | 7.75 | 7.75 |
| *No. 167 (1)* | 3.00 | 3.00 |
| *Set total (7) Stamps* | 48.00 | 39.50 |

### Cooperation

CD119

Cooperation between France and the French-speaking countries of Africa and Madagascar.

**1964**

Cameroun ........ 409-410
Cent. Africa ........ 39
Chad ........ 103
Congo, P.R. ........ 121
Dahomey ........ 193
France ........ 1111
Gabon ........ 175
Ivory Coast ........ 221
Madagascar ........ 360
Mauritania ........ 181
Niger ........ 143
Senegal ........ 236
Togo ........ 495

| | | |
|---|---|---|
| *Nos. 409-410 (2)* | 2.50 | .50 |
| *No. 39 (1)* | 1.00 | .55 |
| *No. 103 (1)* | 1.00 | .25 |
| *No. 121 (1)* | .80 | .35 |
| *No. 193 (1)* | .80 | .35 |
| *No. 1111 (1)* | .25 | .25 |
| *No. 175 (1)* | .90 | .60 |
| *No. 221 (1)* | 1.10 | .35 |
| *No. 360 (1)* | .60 | .25 |
| *No. 181 (1)* | .60 | .35 |
| *No. 143 (1)* | .80 | .40 |
| *No. 236 (1)* | 1.60 | .85 |
| *No. 495 (1)* | .70 | .25 |
| *Set total (14) Stamps* | 12.65 | 5.30 |

### ITU

Telegraph, Syncom Satellite and ITU Emblem CD120

Intl. Telecommunication Union, Cent.

**1965, May 17**

Comoro Isls. ........ C14
Fr. Polynesia ........ C33
Fr. So. & Antarctic Terr. ........ C8
New Caledonia ........ C40
New Hebrides ........ 124-125
St. Pierre & Miquelon ........ C29
Somali Coast ........ C36
Wallis & Futuna Isls. ........ C20

| | | |
|---|---|---|
| *No. C14 (1)* | 20.00 | 10.00 |
| *No. C33 (1)* | 80.00 | 52.50 |
| *No. C8 (1)* | 200.00 | 160.00 |
| *No. C40 (1)* | 10.00 | 8.00 |
| *Nos. 124-125 (2)* | 40.50 | 34.00 |
| *No. C29 (1)* | 24.00 | 11.50 |
| *No. C36 (1)* | 15.00 | 9.00 |
| *No. C20 (1)* | 16.00 | 16.00 |
| *Set total (9) Stamps* | 405.50 | 301.00 |

### French Satellite A-1

Diamant Rocket and Launching Installation — CD121

Launching of France's first satellite, Nov. 26, 1965.

**1965-66**

Comoro Isls. ........ C16a
France ........ 1138a
Reunion ........ 359a
Fr. Polynesia ........ C41a
Fr. So. & Antarctic Terr. ........ C10a
New Caledonia ........ C45a
St. Pierre & Miquelon ........ C31a
Somali Coast ........ C40a
Wallis & Futuna Isls. ........ C23a

| | | |
|---|---|---|
| *No. C16a (1)* | 11.00 | 11.00 |
| *No. 1138a (1)* | .65 | .65 |
| *No. 359a (1)* | 3.50 | 3.00 |
| *No. C41a (1)* | 14.00 | 14.00 |
| *No. C10a (1)* | 29.00 | 24.00 |
| *No. C45a (1)* | 7.00 | 7.00 |
| *No. C31a (1)* | 14.50 | 14.50 |
| *No. C40a (1)* | 7.00 | 7.00 |
| *No. C23a (1)* | 8.50 | 8.50 |
| *Set total (9) Stamps* | 95.15 | 89.65 |

### French Satellite D-1

D-1 Satellite in Orbit — CD122

Launching of the D-1 satellite at Hammaguir, Algeria, Feb. 17, 1966.

**1966**

Comoro Isls. ........ C17
France ........ 1148

| | |
|---|---|
| Fr. Polynesia | C42 |
| Fr. So. & Antarctic Terr. | C11 |
| New Caledonia | C46 |
| St. Pierre & Miquelon | C32 |
| Somali Coast | C49 |
| Wallis & Futuna Isls. | C24 |

| | | |
|---|---|---|
| *No. C17 (1)* | 4.00 | 4.00 |
| *No. 1148 (1)* | .25 | .25 |
| *No. C42 (1)* | 7.00 | 4.75 |
| *No. C11 (1)* | 57.50 | 40.00 |
| *No. C46 (1)* | 2.25 | 2.00 |
| *No. C32 (1)* | 9.00 | 6.00 |
| *No. C49 (1)* | 4.25 | 2.75 |
| *No. C24 (1)* | 3.50 | 3.50 |
| *Set total (8) Stamps* | 87.75 | 63.25 |

### Air Afrique, 1966

Planes and Air Afrique Emblem — CD123

Introduction of DC-8F planes by Air Afrique.

**1966**

| | |
|---|---|
| Cameroun | C79 |
| Cent. Africa | C35 |
| Chad | C26 |
| Congo, P.R. | C42 |
| Dahomey | C42 |
| Gabon | C47 |
| Ivory Coast | C32 |
| Mauritania | C57 |
| Niger | C63 |
| Senegal | C47 |
| Togo | C54 |
| Upper Volta | C31 |

| | | |
|---|---|---|
| *No. C79 (1)* | .80 | .25 |
| *No. C35 (1)* | 1.00 | .40 |
| *No. C26 (1)* | 1.00 | .25 |
| *No. C42 (1)* | 1.00 | .25 |
| *No. C42 (1)* | .75 | .25 |
| *No. C47 (1)* | .90 | .35 |
| *No. C32 (1)* | 1.00 | .60 |
| *No. C57 (1)* | .80 | .30 |
| *No. C63 (1)* | .65 | .35 |
| *No. C47 (1)* | .80 | .30 |
| *No. C54 (1)* | .80 | .25 |
| *No. C31 (1)* | .75 | .50 |
| *Set total (12) Stamps* | 10.25 | 4.05 |

### African Postal Union, 1967

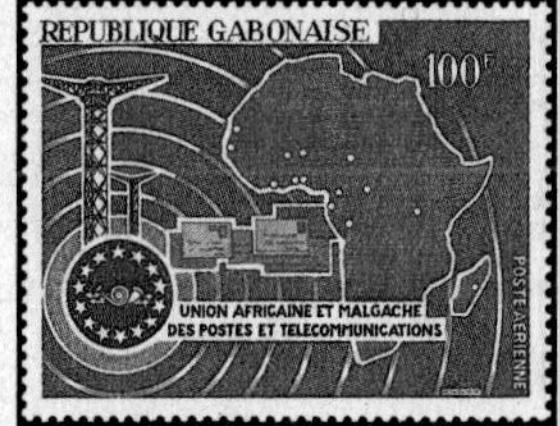


Telecommunications Symbols and Map of Africa — CD124

Fifth anniversary of the establishment of the African and Malagasy Union of Posts and Telecommunications, UAMPT.

**1967**

| | |
|---|---|
| Cameroun | C90 |
| Cent. Africa | C46 |
| Chad | C37 |
| Congo, P.R. | C57 |
| Dahomey | C61 |
| Gabon | C58 |
| Ivory Coast | C34 |
| Madagascar | C85 |
| Mauritania | C65 |
| Niger | C75 |
| Rwanda | C1-C3 |
| Senegal | C60 |
| Togo | C81 |
| Upper Volta | C50 |

| | | |
|---|---|---|
| *No. C90 (1)* | 2.40 | .65 |
| *No. C46 (1)* | 2.25 | .85 |
| *No. C37 (1)* | 2.00 | .60 |
| *No. C57 (1)* | 1.60 | .60 |
| *No. C61 (1)* | 1.75 | .95 |
| *No. C58 (1)* | 2.25 | .95 |
| *No. C34 (1)* | 3.50 | 1.50 |
| *No. C85 (1)* | 1.25 | .60 |
| *No. C65 (1)* | 1.25 | .60 |
| *No. C75 (1)* | 1.40 | .60 |
| *Nos. C1-C3 (3)* | 2.30 | 1.25 |
| *No. C60 (1)* | 1.75 | .50 |
| *No. C81 (1)* | 1.90 | .30 |
| *No. C50 (1)* | 1.80 | .70 |
| *Set total (16) Stamps* | 27.40 | 10.65 |

### Monetary Union

Gold Token of the Ashantis, 17-18th Centuries — CD125

West African Monetary Union, 5th anniv.

**1967, Nov. 4**

| | |
|---|---|
| Dahomey | 244 |
| Ivory Coast | 259 |
| Mauritania | 238 |
| Niger | 204 |
| Senegal | 294 |
| Togo | 623 |
| Upper Volta | 181 |

| | | |
|---|---|---|
| *No. 244 (1)* | .65 | .65 |
| *No. 259 (1)* | .85 | .40 |
| *No. 238 (1)* | .45 | .25 |
| *No. 204 (1)* | .45 | .25 |
| *No. 294 (1)* | .60 | .25 |
| *No. 623 (1)* | .60 | .25 |
| *No. 181 (1)* | .65 | .35 |
| *Set total (7) Stamps* | 4.25 | 2.40 |

### WHO Anniversary

Sun, Flowers and WHO Emblem CD126

World Health Organization, 20th anniv.

**1968, May 4**

| | |
|---|---|
| Afars & Issas | 317 |
| Comoro Isls. | 73 |
| Fr. Polynesia | 241-242 |
| Fr. So. & Antarctic Terr. | 31 |
| New Caledonia | 367 |
| St. Pierre & Miquelon | 377 |
| Wallis & Futuna Isls. | 169 |

| | | |
|---|---|---|
| *No. 317 (1)* | 3.00 | 3.00 |
| *No. 73 (1)* | 2.75 | 2.00 |
| *Nos. 241-242 (2)* | 22.00 | 12.75 |
| *No. 31 (1)* | 62.50 | 47.50 |
| *No. 367 (1)* | 4.00 | 2.25 |
| *No. 377 (1)* | 12.00 | 9.00 |
| *No. 169 (1)* | 5.75 | 5.75 |
| *Set total (8) Stamps* | 112.00 | 82.25 |

### Human Rights Year

Human Rights Flame — CD127

**1968, Aug. 10**

| | |
|---|---|
| Afars & Issas | 322-323 |
| Comoro Isls. | 76 |
| Fr. Polynesia | 243-244 |
| Fr. So. & Antarctic Terr. | 32 |
| New Caledonia | 369 |
| St. Pierre & Miquelon | 382 |
| Wallis & Futuna Isls. | 170 |

| | | |
|---|---|---|
| *Nos. 322-323 (2)* | 6.75 | 4.00 |
| *No. 76 (1)* | 3.50 | 3.50 |
| *Nos. 243-244 (2)* | 24.00 | 14.00 |
| *No. 32 (1)* | 55.00 | 47.50 |
| *No. 369 (1)* | 2.75 | 1.50 |
| *No. 382 (1)* | 8.00 | 5.50 |
| *No. 170 (1)* | 3.25 | 3.25 |
| *Set total (9) Stamps* | 103.25 | 79.25 |

### 2nd PHILEXAFRIQUE

CD128

Opening of PHILEXAFRIQUE, Abidjan, Feb. 14. Each stamp shows a local scene and stamp.

**1969, Feb. 14**

| | |
|---|---|
| Cameroun | C118 |
| Cent. Africa | C65 |
| Chad | C48 |
| Congo, P.R. | C77 |
| Dahomey | C94 |
| Gabon | C82 |
| Ivory Coast | C38-C40 |
| Madagascar | C92 |
| Mali | C65 |
| Mauritania | C80 |
| Niger | C104 |
| Senegal | C68 |
| Togo | C104 |
| Upper Volta | C62 |

| | | |
|---|---|---|
| *No. C118 (1)* | 3.25 | 1.25 |
| *No. C65 (1)* | 1.90 | 1.90 |
| *No. C48 (1)* | 2.40 | 1.00 |
| *No. C77 (1)* | 2.00 | 1.75 |
| *No. C94 (1)* | 2.25 | 2.25 |
| *No. C82 (1)* | 2.25 | 2.25 |
| *Nos. C38-C40 (3)* | 14.50 | 14.50 |
| *No. C92 (1)* | 1.75 | .85 |
| *No. C65 (1)* | 1.75 | 1.00 |
| *No. C80 (1)* | 1.90 | .75 |
| *No. C104 (1)* | 2.75 | 1.90 |
| *No. C68 (1)* | 2.00 | 1.40 |
| *No. C104 (1)* | 2.25 | .45 |
| *No. C62 (1)* | 4.00 | 3.25 |
| *Set total (16) Stamps* | 44.95 | 34.50 |

### Concorde

Concorde in Flight CD129

First flight of the prototype Concorde supersonic plane at Toulouse, Mar. 1, 1969.

**1969**

| | |
|---|---|
| Afars & Issas | C56 |
| Comoro Isls. | C29 |
| France | C42 |
| Fr. Polynesia | C50 |
| Fr. So. & Antarctic Terr. | C18 |
| New Caledonia | C63 |
| St. Pierre & Miquelon | C40 |
| Wallis & Futuna Isls. | C30 |

| | | |
|---|---|---|
| *No. C56 (1)* | 26.00 | 16.00 |
| *No. C29 (1)* | 24.00 | 16.00 |
| *No. C42 (1)* | .75 | .35 |
| *No. C50 (1)* | 55.00 | 35.00 |
| *No. C18 (1)* | 55.00 | 37.50 |
| *No. C63 (1)* | 27.50 | 20.00 |
| *No. C40 (1)* | 32.50 | 11.00 |
| *No. C30 (1)* | 15.00 | 10.00 |
| *Set total (8) Stamps* | 235.75 | 145.85 |

### Development Bank

Bank Emblem — CD130

African Development Bank, fifth anniv.

**1969**

| | |
|---|---|
| Cameroun | 499 |
| Chad | 217 |
| Congo, P.R. | 181-182 |
| Ivory Coast | 281 |
| Mali | 127-128 |
| Mauritania | 267 |
| Niger | 220 |
| Senegal | 317-318 |
| Upper Volta | 201 |

| | | |
|---|---|---|
| *No. 499 (1)* | .80 | .25 |
| *No. 217 (1)* | .70 | .25 |
| *Nos. 181-182 (2)* | .80 | .50 |
| *No. 281 (1)* | .70 | .40 |
| *Nos. 127-128 (2)* | 1.00 | .50 |
| *No. 267 (1)* | .60 | .25 |
| *No. 220 (1)* | .60 | .30 |
| *Nos. 317-318 (2)* | 1.55 | .50 |
| *No. 201 (1)* | .65 | .30 |
| *Set total (12) Stamps* | 7.40 | 3.25 |

### ILO

ILO Headquarters, Geneva, and Emblem — CD131

Intl. Labor Organization, 50th anniv.

**1969-70**

| | |
|---|---|
| Afars & Issas | 337 |
| Comoro Isls. | 83 |
| Fr. Polynesia | 251-252 |
| Fr. So. & Antarctic Terr. | 35 |
| New Caledonia | 379 |
| St. Pierre & Miquelon | 396 |
| Wallis & Futuna Isls. | 172 |

| | | |
|---|---|---|
| *No. 337 (1)* | 2.75 | 2.00 |
| *No. 83 (1)* | 1.25 | .75 |
| *Nos. 251-252 (2)* | 24.00 | 12.50 |
| *No. 35 (1)* | 15.00 | 10.00 |
| *No. 379 (1)* | 2.25 | 1.10 |
| *No. 396 (1)* | 10.00 | 5.50 |
| *No. 172 (1)* | 2.75 | 2.75 |
| *Set total (8) Stamps* | 58.00 | 34.60 |

### ASECNA

Map of Africa, Plane and Airport CD132

10th anniversary of the Agency for the Security of Aerial Navigation in Africa and Madagascar (ASECNA, Agence pour la Securite de la Navigation Aerienne en Afrique et a Madagascar).

**1969-70**

| | |
|---|---|
| Cameroun | 500 |
| Cent. Africa | 119 |
| Chad | 222 |
| Congo, P.R. | 197 |
| Dahomey | 269 |
| Gabon | 260 |
| Ivory Coast | 287 |
| Mali | 130 |
| Niger | 221 |
| Senegal | 321 |
| Upper Volta | 204 |

| | | |
|---|---|---|
| *No. 500 (1)* | 2.00 | .60 |
| *No. 119 (1)* | 2.25 | .80 |
| *No. 222 (1)* | 1.00 | .25 |
| *No. 197 (1)* | 2.00 | .40 |
| *No. 269 (1)* | .90 | .55 |
| *No. 260 (1)* | 1.75 | .75 |
| *No. 287 (1)* | .90 | .40 |
| *No. 130 (1)* | .90 | .40 |
| *No. 221 (1)* | 1.25 | .70 |
| *No. 321 (1)* | 1.60 | .50 |
| *No. 204 (1)* | 1.75 | 1.00 |
| *Set total (11) Stamps* | 16.30 | 6.35 |

### U.P.U. Headquarters

CD133

New Universal Postal Union headquarters, Bern, Switzerland.

**1970**

Afars & Issas....342
Algeria....443
Cameroun....503-504
Cent. Africa....125
Chad....225
Comoro Isls.....84
Congo, P.R.....216
Fr. Polynesia....261-262
Fr. So. & Antarctic Terr.....36
Gabon....258
Ivory Coast....295
Madagascar....444
Mali....134-135
Mauritania....283
New Caledonia....382
Niger....231-232
St. Pierre & Miquelon....397-398
Senegal....328-329
Tunisia....535
Wallis & Futuna Isls.....173

| | | |
|---|---|---|
| *No. 342 (1)* | 2.50 | 1.40 |
| *No. 443 (1)* | 1.10 | .40 |
| *Nos. 503-504 (2)* | 2.60 | .55 |
| *No. 125 (1)* | 1.90 | .70 |
| *No. 225 (1)* | 1.00 | .25 |
| *No. 84 (1)* | 5.50 | 2.00 |
| *No. 216 (1)* | .80 | .25 |
| *Nos. 261-262 (2)* | 20.00 | 10.00 |
| *No. 36 (1)* | 40.00 | 27.50 |
| *No. 258 (1)* | .90 | .55 |
| *No. 295 (1)* | 1.10 | .50 |
| *No. 444 (1)* | .55 | .25 |
| *Nos. 134-135 (2)* | 1.05 | .50 |
| *No. 283 (1)* | .60 | .30 |
| *No. 382 (1)* | 3.00 | 1.50 |
| *Nos. 231-232 (2)* | 1.20 | .60 |
| *Nos. 397-398 (2)* | 34.00 | 16.25 |
| *Nos. 328-329 (2)* | 1.55 | .55 |
| *No. 535 (1)* | .60 | .25 |
| *No. 173 (1)* | 3.25 | 3.25 |
| *Set total (26) Stamps* | 123.20 | 67.55 |

### De Gaulle

CD134

First anniversary of the death of Charles de Gaulle, (1890-1970), President of France.

**1971-72**

Afars & Issas....356-357
Comoro Isls.....104-105
France....1325a
Fr. Polynesia....270-271
Fr. So. & Antarctic Terr.....52-53
New Caledonia....393-394
Reunion....380a
St. Pierre & Miquelon....417-418
Wallis & Futuna Isls.....177-178

| | | |
|---|---|---|
| *Nos. 356-357 (2)* | 12.50 | 7.50 |
| *Nos. 104-105 (2)* | 9.00 | 5.75 |
| *No. 1325a (1)* | 3.00 | 2.50 |
| *Nos. 270-271 (2)* | 51.50 | 29.50 |
| *Nos. 52-53 (2)* | 40.00 | 29.50 |
| *Nos. 393-394 (2)* | 23.00 | 11.75 |
| *No. 380a (1)* | 9.25 | 8.00 |
| *Nos. 417-418 (2)* | 56.50 | 31.00 |
| *Nos. 177-178 (2)* | 20.00 | 16.25 |
| *Set total (16) Stamps* | 224.75 | 141.75 |

### African Postal Union, 1971

UAMPT Building, Brazzaville, Congo — CD135

10th anniversary of the establishment of the African and Malagasy Posts and Telecommunications Union, UAMPT. Each stamp has a different native design.

**1971, Nov. 13**

Cameroun....C177
Cent. Africa....C89
Chad....C94
Congo, P.R.....C136
Dahomey....C146
Gabon....C120
Ivory Coast....C47
Mauritania....C113
Niger....C164
Rwanda....C8
Senegal....C105
Togo....C166
Upper Volta....C97

| | | |
|---|---|---|
| *No. C177 (1)* | 2.00 | .50 |
| *No. C89 (1)* | 2.25 | .85 |
| *No. C94 (1)* | 1.50 | .50 |
| *No. C136 (1)* | 1.60 | .75 |
| *No. C146 (1)* | 1.75 | .80 |
| *No. C120 (1)* | 1.75 | .70 |
| *No. C47 (1)* | 2.00 | 1.00 |
| *No. C113 (1)* | 1.20 | .65 |
| *No. C164 (1)* | 1.25 | .60 |
| *No. C8 (1)* | 2.75 | 2.50 |
| *No. C105 (1)* | 1.60 | .50 |
| *No. C166 (1)* | 1.25 | .40 |
| *No. C97 (1)* | 1.50 | .70 |
| *Set total (13) Stamps* | 22.40 | 10.45 |

### West African Monetary Union

African Couple, City, Village and Commemorative Coin — CD136

West African Monetary Union, 10th anniv.

**1972, Nov. 2**

Dahomey....300
Ivory Coast....331
Mauritania....299
Niger....258
Senegal....374
Togo....825
Upper Volta....280

| | | |
|---|---|---|
| *No. 300 (1)* | .65 | .25 |
| *No. 331 (1)* | 1.00 | .50 |
| *No. 299 (1)* | .75 | .25 |
| *No. 258 (1)* | .55 | .30 |
| *No. 374 (1)* | .50 | .30 |
| *No. 825 (1)* | .60 | .25 |
| *No. 280 (1)* | .60 | .25 |
| *Set total (7) Stamps* | 4.65 | 2.10 |

### African Postal Union, 1973

Telecommunications Symbols and Map of Africa — CD137

11th anniversary of the African and Malagasy Posts and Telecommunications Union (UAMPT).

**1973, Sept. 12**

Cameroun....574
Cent. Africa....194
Chad....294
Congo, P.R.....289
Dahomey....311
Gabon....320
Ivory Coast....361
Madagascar....500
Mauritania....304
Niger....287
Rwanda....540
Senegal....393
Togo....849
Upper Volta....297

| | | |
|---|---|---|
| *No. 574 (1)* | 1.75 | .40 |
| *No. 194 (1)* | 1.25 | .75 |
| *No. 294 (1)* | 1.75 | .40 |
| *No. 289 (1)* | 1.60 | .50 |
| *No. 311 (1)* | 1.25 | .55 |
| *No. 320 (1)* | 1.40 | .75 |
| *No. 361 (1)* | 2.50 | 1.00 |
| *No. 500 (1)* | 1.10 | .35 |
| *No. 304 (1)* | 1.10 | .40 |
| *No. 287 (1)* | .90 | .60 |
| *No. 540 (1)* | 4.00 | 2.00 |
| *No. 393 (1)* | 1.60 | .50 |
| *No. 849 (1)* | 1.00 | .35 |
| *No. 297 (1)* | 1.25 | .70 |
| *Set total (14) Stamps* | 22.45 | 9.25 |

### Philexafrique II — Essen

CD138

CD139

Designs: Indigenous fauna, local and German stamps. Types CD138-CD139 printed horizontally and vertically se-tenant in sheets of 10 (2x5). Label between horizontal pairs alternately commemoratives Philexafrique II, Libreville, Gabon, June 1978, and 2nd International Stamp Fair, Essen, Germany, Nov. 1-5.

**1978-1979**

Benin....C286a
Central Africa....C201a
Chad....C239a
Congo Republic....C246a
Djibouti....C122a
Gabon....C216a
Ivory Coast....C65a
Mali....C357a
Mauritania....C186a
Niger....C292a
Rwanda....C13a
Senegal....C147a
Togo....C364a

| | | |
|---|---|---|
| *No. C286a (1)* | 9.00 | 8.50 |
| *No. C201a (1)* | 7.50 | 7.50 |
| *No. C239a (1)* | 8.00 | 4.00 |
| *No. C246a (1)* | 7.00 | 7.00 |
| *No. C122a (1)* | 8.50 | 8.50 |
| *No. C216a (1)* | 6.50 | 4.00 |
| *No. C65a (1)* | 9.00 | 9.00 |
| *No. C357a (1)* | 5.00 | 3.00 |
| *No. C186a (1)* | 4.50 | 4.00 |
| *No. C292a (1)* | 6.00 | 5.00 |
| *No. C13a (1)* | 4.00 | 4.00 |
| *No. C147a (1)* | 10.00 | 4.00 |
| *No. C364a (1)* | 3.00 | 1.50 |
| *Set total (13) Stamps* | 88.00 | 70.00 |

---

## BRITISH COMMONWEALTH OF NATIONS

The listings follow established trade practices when these issues are offered as units by dealers. The Peace issue, for example, includes only one stamp from the Indian state of Hyderabad. The U.P.U. issue includes the Egypt set. Pairs are included for those varieties issued with bilingual designs se-tenant.

### Silver Jubilee

Windsor Castle and King George V CD301

Reign of King George V, 25th anniv.

**1935**

Antigua....77-80
Ascension....33-36
Bahamas....92-95
Barbados....186-189
Basutoland....11-14
Bechuanaland Protectorate....117-120
Bermuda....100-103
British Guiana....223-226
British Honduras....108-111
Cayman Islands....81-84
Ceylon....260-263
Cyprus....136-139
Dominica....90-93
Falkland Islands....77-80
Fiji....110-113
Gambia....125-128
Gibraltar....100-103
Gilbert & Ellice Islands....33-36
Gold Coast....108-111
Grenada....124-127
Hong Kong....147-150
Jamaica....109-112
Kenya, Uganda, Tanzania....42-45
Leeward Islands....96-99
Malta....184-187
Mauritius....204-207
Montserrat....85-88
Newfoundland....226-229
Nigeria....34-37
Northern Rhodesia....18-21
Nyasaland Protectorate....47-50
St. Helena....111-114
St. Kitts-Nevis....72-75
St. Lucia....91-94
St. Vincent....134-137
Seychelles....118-121
Sierra Leone....166-169
Solomon Islands....60-63
Somaliland Protectorate....77-80
Straits Settlements....213-216
Swaziland....20-23
Trinidad & Tobago....43-46
Turks & Caicos Islands....71-74
Virgin Islands....69-72

The following have different designs but are included in the omnibus set:

Great Britain....226-229
Offices in Morocco (Sp. Curr.)....67-70
Offices in Morocco (Br. Curr.)....226-229
Offices in Morocco (Fr. Curr.)....422-425
Offices in Morocco (Tangier)....508-510
Australia....152-154
Canada....211-216
Cook Islands....98-100
India....142-148
Nauru....31-34
New Guinea....46-47
New Zealand....199-201
Niue....67-69
Papua....114-117
Samoa....163-165
South Africa....68-71
Southern Rhodesia....33-36
South-West Africa....121-124

| | | |
|---|---|---|
| *Nos. 77-80 (4)* | 20.25 | 23.25 |
| *Nos. 33-36 (4)* | 58.50 | 127.50 |
| *Nos. 92-95 (4)* | 25.00 | 46.00 |
| *Nos. 186-189 (4)* | 30.00 | 46.80 |
| *Nos. 11-14 (4)* | 11.60 | 21.25 |
| *Nos. 117-120 (4)* | 15.75 | 36.00 |
| *Nos. 100-103 (4)* | 16.80 | 58.50 |
| *Nos. 223-226 (4)* | 18.35 | 35.50 |
| *Nos. 108-111 (4)* | 15.25 | 16.35 |
| *Nos. 81-84 (4)* | 21.60 | 24.50 |
| *Nos. 260-263 (4)* | 10.40 | 21.60 |
| *Nos. 136-139 (4)* | 39.75 | 34.40 |
| *Nos. 90-93 (4)* | 18.85 | 19.85 |
| *Nos. 77-80 (4)* | 55.00 | 14.75 |
| *Nos. 110-113 (4)* | 15.25 | 27.90 |
| *Nos. 125-128 (4)* | 12.20 | 25.25 |
| *Nos. 100-103 (4)* | 28.75 | 42.75 |
| *Nos. 33-36 (4)* | 36.80 | 67.00 |
| *Nos. 108-111 (4)* | 25.75 | 78.10 |
| *Nos. 124-127 (4)* | 16.70 | 40.60 |
| *Nos. 147-150 (4)* | 59.00 | 18.75 |
| *Nos. 109-112 (4)* | 17.00 | 39.00 |
| *Nos. 42-45 (4)* | 8.75 | 11.00 |
| *Nos. 96-99 (4)* | 35.75 | 49.60 |
| *Nos. 184-187 (4)* | 22.00 | 33.70 |
| *Nos. 204-207 (4)* | 47.60 | 58.25 |
| *Nos. 85-88 (4)* | 10.25 | 30.25 |
| *Nos. 226-229 (4)* | 17.50 | 12.05 |
| *Nos. 34-37 (4)* | 17.50 | 70.00 |
| *Nos. 18-21 (4)* | 17.00 | 15.00 |
| *Nos. 47-50 (4)* | 39.75 | 80.25 |
| *Nos. 111-114 (4)* | 31.15 | 33.25 |
| *Nos. 72-75 (4)* | 10.80 | 18.65 |
| *Nos. 91-94 (4)* | 16.00 | 20.80 |
| *Nos. 134-137 (4)* | 9.45 | 21.25 |
| *Nos. 118-121 (4)* | 17.50 | 32.50 |
| *Nos. 166-169 (4)* | 24.25 | 56.00 |
| *Nos. 60-63 (4)* | 27.25 | 38.00 |
| *Nos. 77-80 (4)* | 17.00 | 48.25 |
| *Nos. 213-216 (4)* | 15.00 | 25.10 |
| *Nos. 20-23 (4)* | 6.80 | 18.25 |
| *Nos. 43-46 (4)* | 14.05 | 27.75 |
| *Nos. 71-74 (4)* | 8.40 | 14.50 |
| *Nos. 69-72 (4)* | 25.00 | 55.25 |
| *Nos. 226-229 (4)* | 5.15 | 4.40 |

| | | |
|---|---|---|
| Nos. 67-70 (4) | 14.35 | 26.10 |
| Nos. 226-229 (4) | 8.20 | 28.90 |
| Nos. 422-425 (4) | 3.90 | 2.00 |
| Nos. 508-510 (3) | 18.80 | 23.85 |
| Nos. 152-154 (3) | 45.75 | 60.35 |
| Nos. 211-216 (6) | 24.85 | 13.35 |
| Nos. 98-100 (3) | 9.65 | 12.00 |
| Nos. 142-148 (7) | 28.85 | 14.00 |
| Nos. 31-34 (4) | 9.90 | 9.90 |
| Nos. 46-47 (2) | 4.35 | 1.70 |
| Nos. 199-201 (3) | 21.75 | 31.75 |
| Nos. 67-69 (3) | 11.80 | 26.50 |
| Nos. 114-117 (4) | 9.20 | 17.00 |
| Nos. 163-165 (3) | 4.40 | 5.50 |
| Nos. 68-71 (4) | 57.00 | 155.00 |
| Nos. 33-36 (4) | 27.75 | 45.25 |
| Nos. 121-124 (4) | 13.00 | 36.10 |
| Set total (245) Stamps | 1,326. | 2,149. |

## Coronation

Queen Elizabeth and King George VI CD302

### 1937

Aden.........13-15
Antigua.........81-83
Ascension.........37-39
Bahamas.........97-99
Barbados.........190-192
Basutoland.........15-17
Bechuanaland Protectorate.........121-123
Bermuda.........115-117
British Guiana.........227-229
British Honduras.........112-114
Cayman Islands.........97-99
Ceylon.........275-277
Cyprus.........140-142
Dominica.........94-96
Falkland Islands.........81-83
Fiji.........114-116
Gambia.........129-131
Gibraltar.........104-106
Gilbert & Ellice Islands.........37-39
Gold Coast.........112-114
Grenada.........128-130
Hong Kong.........151-153
Jamaica.........113-115
Kenya, Uganda, Tanzania.........60-62
Leeward Islands.........100-102
Malta.........188-190
Mauritius.........208-210
Montserrat.........89-91
Newfoundland.........230-232
Nigeria.........50-52
Northern Rhodesia.........22-24
Nyasaland Protectorate.........51-53
St. Helena.........115-117
St. Kitts-Nevis.........76-78
St. Lucia.........107-109
St. Vincent.........138-140
Seychelles.........122-124
Sierra Leone.........170-172
Solomon Islands.........64-66
Somaliland Protectorate.........81-83
Straits Settlements.........235-237
Swaziland.........24-26
Trinidad & Tobago.........47-49
Turks & Caicos Islands.........75-77
Virgin Islands.........73-75

The following have different designs but are included in the omnibus set:

Great Britain.........234
Offices in Morocco (Sp. Curr.).........82
Offices in Morocco (Fr. Curr.).........439
Offices in Morocco (Tangier).........514
Canada.........237
Cook Islands.........109-111
Nauru.........35-38
Newfoundland.........233-243
New Guinea.........48-51
New Zealand.........223-225
Niue.........70-72
Papua.........118-121
South Africa.........74-78
Southern Rhodesia.........38-41
South-West Africa.........125-132

| | | |
|---|---|---|
| Nos. 13-15 (3) | 2.70 | 5.65 |
| Nos. 81-83 (3) | 1.85 | 8.00 |
| Nos. 37-39 (3) | 2.75 | 2.75 |
| Nos. 97-99 (3) | 1.05 | 3.05 |
| Nos. 190-192 (3) | 1.10 | 1.95 |
| Nos. 15-17 (3) | 1.15 | 3.00 |
| Nos. 121-123 (3) | .95 | 3.35 |
| Nos. 115-117 (3) | 1.25 | 5.00 |
| Nos. 227-229 (3) | 1.45 | 3.05 |
| Nos. 112-114 (3) | 1.20 | 2.40 |
| Nos. 97-99 (3) | 1.10 | 2.70 |
| Nos. 275-277 (3) | 8.25 | 10.35 |
| Nos. 140-142 (3) | 3.75 | 6.50 |
| Nos. 94-96 (3) | .85 | 2.40 |
| Nos. 81-83 (3) | 2.90 | 2.30 |
| Nos. 114-116 (3) | 1.50 | 5.75 |
| Nos. 129-131 (3) | .95 | 3.95 |
| Nos. 104-106 (3) | 2.25 | 6.45 |
| Nos. 37-39 (3) | .85 | 2.15 |
| Nos. 112-114 (3) | 3.10 | 10.00 |
| Nos. 128-130 (3) | 1.00 | .85 |
| Nos. 151-153 (3) | 23.00 | 12.50 |
| Nos. 113-115 (3) | 1.25 | 1.25 |
| Nos. 60-62 (3) | 1.00 | 2.35 |
| Nos. 100-102 (3) | 1.55 | 4.00 |
| Nos. 188-190 (3) | 1.25 | 1.60 |
| Nos. 208-210 (3) | 2.05 | 3.75 |
| Nos. 89-91 (3) | 1.00 | 3.35 |
| Nos. 230-232 (3) | 7.00 | 2.80 |
| Nos. 50-52 (3) | 3.25 | 8.50 |
| Nos. 22-24 (3) | .95 | 2.25 |
| Nos. 51-53 (3) | 1.05 | 1.30 |
| Nos. 115-117 (3) | 1.45 | 2.05 |
| Nos. 76-78 (3) | .95 | 2.15 |
| Nos. 107-109 (3) | 1.05 | 2.05 |
| Nos. 138-140 (3) | .80 | 4.75 |
| Nos. 122-124 (3) | 1.20 | 1.90 |
| Nos. 170-172 (3) | 1.95 | 5.65 |
| Nos. 64-66 (3) | .90 | 2.00 |
| Nos. 81-83 (3) | 1.10 | 3.40 |
| Nos. 235-237 (3) | 3.25 | 1.60 |
| Nos. 24-26 (3) | 1.05 | 1.75 |
| Nos. 47-49 (3) | 1.00 | 1.00 |
| Nos. 75-77 (3) | 1.30 | 1.15 |
| Nos. 73-75 (3) | 2.20 | 6.90 |
| No. 234 (1) | .25 | .25 |
| No. 82 (1) | .80 | .80 |
| No. 439 (1) | .35 | .25 |
| No. 514 (1) | .55 | .55 |
| No. 237 (1) | .35 | .25 |
| Nos. 109-111 (3) | .85 | .80 |
| Nos. 35-38 (4) | 1.10 | 5.50 |
| Nos. 233-243 (11) | 41.90 | 30.40 |
| Nos. 48-51 (4) | 1.40 | 7.90 |
| Nos. 223-225 (3) | 1.40 | 2.75 |
| Nos. 70-72 (3) | .80 | 2.05 |
| Nos. 118-121 (4) | 1.60 | 5.25 |
| Nos. 74-78 (5) | 9.25 | 10.80 |
| Nos. 38-41 (4) | 3.55 | 15.50 |
| Nos. 125-132 (8) | 5.00 | 8.40 |
| Set total (189) Stamps | 172.65 | 263.05 |

## Peace

King George VI and Parliament Buildings, London CD303

Return to peace at the close of World War II.

### 1945-46

Aden.........28-29
Antigua.........96-97
Ascension.........50-51
Bahamas.........130-131
Barbados.........207-208
Bermuda.........131-132
British Guiana.........242-243
British Honduras.........127-128
Cayman Islands.........112-113
Ceylon.........293-294
Cyprus.........156-157
Dominica.........112-113
Falkland Islands.........97-98
Falkland Islands Dep.........1L9-1L10
Fiji.........137-138
Gambia.........144-145
Gibraltar.........119-120
Gilbert & Ellice Islands.........52-53
Gold Coast.........128-129
Grenada.........143-144
Jamaica.........136-137
Kenya, Uganda, Tanzania.........90-91
Leeward Islands.........116-117
Malta.........206-207
Mauritius.........223-224
Montserrat.........104-105
Nigeria.........71-72
Northern Rhodesia.........46-47
Nyasaland Protectorate.........82-83
Pitcairn Islands.........9-10
St. Helena.........128-129
St. Kitts-Nevis.........91-92
St. Lucia.........127-128
St. Vincent.........152-153
Seychelles.........149-150
Sierra Leone.........186-187
Solomon Islands.........80-81
Somaliland Protectorate.........108-109
Trinidad & Tobago.........62-63
Turks & Caicos Islands.........90-91
Virgin Islands.........88-89

The following have different designs but are included in the omnibus set:

Great Britain.........264-265
Offices in Morocco (Tangier).........523-524
Aden
  Kathiri State of Seiyun.........12-13
  Qu'aiti State of Shihr and Mukalla.........12-13
Australia.........200-202
Basutoland.........29-31
Bechuanaland Protectorate.........137-139
Burma.........66-69
Cook Islands.........127-130
Hong Kong.........174-175
India.........195-198
  Hyderabad.........51-53
New Zealand.........247-257
Niue.........90-93
Pakistan-Bahawalpur.........O16
Samoa.........191-194
South Africa.........100-102
Southern Rhodesia.........67-70
South-West Africa.........153-155
Swaziland.........38-40
Zanzibar.........222-223

| | | |
|---|---|---|
| Nos. 28-29 (2) | .95 | 2.50 |
| Nos. 96-97 (2) | .50 | .80 |
| Nos. 50-51 (2) | .80 | 2.00 |
| Nos. 130-131 (2) | .50 | 1.40 |
| Nos. 207-208 (2) | .50 | 1.10 |
| Nos. 131-132 (2) | .55 | .55 |
| Nos. 242-243 (2) | 1.05 | 1.40 |
| Nos. 127-128 (2) | .50 | .50 |
| Nos. 112-113 (2) | .80 | .80 |
| Nos. 293-294 (2) | .60 | 2.10 |
| Nos. 156-157 (2) | .90 | .70 |
| Nos. 112-113 (2) | .50 | .50 |
| Nos. 97-98 (2) | .90 | 1.35 |
| Nos. 1L9-1L10 (2) | 1.30 | 1.00 |
| Nos. 137-138 (2) | .50 | 1.75 |
| Nos. 144-145 (2) | .50 | .95 |
| Nos. 119-120 (2) | .75 | 1.00 |
| Nos. 52-53 (2) | .50 | 1.10 |
| Nos. 128-129 (2) | 1.85 | 3.75 |
| Nos. 143-144 (2) | .50 | .95 |
| Nos. 136-137 (2) | .80 | 12.50 |
| Nos. 90-91 (2) | .65 | .65 |
| Nos. 116-117 (2) | .50 | 1.50 |
| Nos. 206-207 (2) | .65 | 2.00 |
| Nos. 223-224 (2) | .50 | 1.05 |
| Nos. 104-105 (2) | .50 | .50 |
| Nos. 71-72 (2) | .70 | 2.75 |
| Nos. 46-47 (2) | 1.25 | 2.00 |
| Nos. 82-83 (2) | .50 | .50 |
| Nos. 9-10 (2) | 1.40 | 1.40 |
| Nos. 128-129 (2) | .65 | .70 |
| Nos. 91-92 (2) | .50 | .50 |
| Nos. 127-128 (2) | .50 | .60 |
| Nos. 152-153 (2) | .50 | .50 |
| Nos. 149-150 (2) | .55 | .50 |
| Nos. 186-187 (2) | .50 | .50 |
| Nos. 80-81 (2) | .50 | 1.50 |
| Nos. 108-109 (2) | .70 | .50 |
| Nos. 62-63 (2) | .50 | .50 |
| Nos. 90-91 (2) | .50 | .50 |
| Nos. 88-89 (2) | .50 | .50 |
| Nos. 264-265 (2) | .50 | .50 |
| Nos. 523-524 (2) | 1.50 | 3.00 |
| Nos. 12-13 (2) | .50 | .90 |
| Nos. 12-13 (2) | .50 | 1.25 |
| Nos. 200-202 (3) | 1.60 | 3.00 |
| Nos. 29-31 (3) | 2.10 | 2.60 |
| Nos. 137-139 (3) | 2.05 | 4.75 |
| Nos. 66-69 (4) | 1.60 | 1.30 |
| Nos. 127-130 (4) | 2.00 | 1.85 |
| Nos. 174-175 (2) | 6.75 | 3.15 |
| Nos. 195-198 (4) | 5.60 | 5.50 |
| Nos. 51-53 (3) | 1.50 | 1.70 |
| Nos. 247-257 (11) | 3.85 | 3.80 |
| Nos. 90-93 (4) | 1.70 | 2.20 |
| No. O16 (1) | 5.50 | 7.00 |
| Nos. 191-194 (4) | 2.05 | 1.00 |
| Nos. 100-102 (3) | 1.20 | 4.00 |
| Nos. 67-70 (4) | 1.40 | 1.75 |
| Nos. 153-155 (3) | 1.85 | 3.25 |
| Nos. 38-40 (3) | 2.40 | 5.50 |
| Nos. 222-223 (2) | .65 | 1.00 |
| Set total (151) Stamps | 75.10 | 116.85 |

## Silver Wedding

King George VI and Queen Elizabeth

CD304 CD305

### 1948-49

Aden.........30-31
  Kathiri State of Seiyun.........14-15
  Qu'aiti State of Shihr and Mukalla.........14-15
Antigua.........98-99
Ascension.........52-53
Bahamas.........148-149
Barbados.........210-211
Basutoland.........39-40
Bechuanaland Protectorate.........147-148
Bermuda.........133-134
British Guiana.........244-245
British Honduras.........129-130
Cayman Islands.........116-117
Cyprus.........158-159
Dominica.........114-115
Falkland Islands.........99-100
Falkland Islands Dep.........1L11-1L12
Fiji.........139-140
Gambia.........146-147
Gibraltar.........121-122
Gilbert & Ellice Islands.........54-55
Gold Coast.........142-143
Grenada.........145-146
Hong Kong.........178-179
Jamaica.........138-139
Kenya, Uganda, Tanzania.........92-93
Leeward Islands.........118-119
Malaya
  Johore.........128-129
  Kedah.........55-56
  Kelantan.........44-45
  Malacca.........1-2
  Negri Sembilan.........36-37
  Pahang.........44-45
  Penang.........1-2
  Perak.........99-100
  Perlis.........1-2
  Selangor.........74-75
  Trengganu.........47-48
Malta.........223-224
Mauritius.........229-230
Montserrat.........106-107
Nigeria.........73-74
North Borneo.........238-239
Northern Rhodesia.........48-49
Nyasaland Protectorate.........85-86
Pitcairn Islands.........11-12
St. Helena.........130-131
St. Kitts-Nevis.........93-94
St. Lucia.........129-130
St. Vincent.........154-155
Sarawak.........174-175
Seychelles.........151-152
Sierra Leone.........188-189
Singapore.........21-22
Solomon Islands.........82-83
Somaliland Protectorate.........110-111
Swaziland.........48-49
Trinidad & Tobago.........64-65
Turks & Caicos Islands.........92-93
Virgin Islands.........90-91
Zanzibar.........224-225

The following have different designs but are included in the omnibus set:

Great Britain.........267-268
  Offices in Morocco (Sp. Curr.).........93-94
  Offices in Morocco (Tangier).........525-526
Bahrain.........62-63
Kuwait.........82-83
Oman.........25-26
South Africa.........106
South-West Africa.........159

| | | |
|---|---|---|
| Nos. 30-31 (2) | 40.40 | 47.25 |
| Nos. 14-15 (2) | 17.85 | 16.00 |
| Nos. 14-15 (2) | 18.55 | 12.50 |
| Nos. 98-99 (2) | 13.55 | 15.75 |
| Nos. 52-53 (2) | 55.55 | 50.45 |
| Nos. 148-149 (2) | 45.25 | 40.30 |
| Nos. 210-211 (2) | 18.35 | 13.05 |
| Nos. 39-40 (2) | 52.80 | 55.25 |
| Nos. 147-148 (2) | 42.85 | 47.75 |
| Nos. 133-134 (2) | 47.75 | 55.25 |
| Nos. 244-245 (2) | 24.25 | 28.45 |
| Nos. 129-130 (2) | 25.25 | 53.20 |
| Nos. 116-117 (2) | 25.25 | 33.50 |
| Nos. 158-159 (2) | 58.50 | 78.05 |
| Nos. 114-115 (2) | 25.25 | 32.75 |
| Nos. 99-100 (2) | 112.10 | 76.10 |
| Nos. 1L11-1L12 (2) | 4.25 | 6.00 |
| Nos. 139-140 (2) | 17.00 | 11.50 |
| Nos. 146-147 (2) | 21.25 | 21.25 |
| Nos. 121-122 (2) | 61.00 | 78.00 |
| Nos. 54-55 (2) | 14.25 | 26.25 |
| Nos. 142-143 (2) | 35.25 | 48.20 |
| Nos. 145-146 (2) | 21.75 | 21.75 |
| Nos. 178-179 (2) | 283.50 | 96.50 |
| Nos. 138-139 (2) | 27.85 | 60.25 |
| Nos. 92-93 (2) | 50.25 | 67.75 |
| Nos. 118-119 (2) | 7.00 | 8.25 |
| Nos. 128-129 (2) | 29.25 | 53.25 |
| Nos. 55-56 (2) | 35.25 | 50.25 |
| Nos. 44-45 (2) | 35.75 | 62.75 |
| Nos. 1-2 (2) | 35.40 | 49.75 |
| Nos. 36-37 (2) | 28.10 | 38.20 |
| Nos. 44-45 (2) | 28.00 | 38.05 |
| Nos. 1-2 (2) | 40.50 | 37.80 |

Nos. 99-100 (2) 27.80 37.75
Nos. 1-2 (2) 33.50 58.00
Nos. 74-75 (2) 30.25 25.30
Nos. 47-48 (2) 35.25 62.75
Nos. 223-224 (2) 40.55 45.25
Nos. 229-230 (2) 17.75 45.25
Nos. 106-107 (2) 9.25 18.25
Nos. 73-74 (2) 17.85 22.80
Nos. 238-239 (2) 35.30 45.75
Nos. 48-49 (2) 100.30 90.25
Nos. 85-86 (2) 18.25 30.25
Nos. 11-12 (2) 44.75 48.50
Nos. 130-131 (2) 32.80 42.80
Nos. 93-94 (2) 11.25 10.50
Nos. 129-130 (2) 22.25 45.25
Nos. 154-155 (2) 27.75 30.25
Nos. 174-175 (2) 50.40 52.90
Nos. 151-152 (2) 16.25 45.75
Nos. 188-189 (2) 24.75 26.25
Nos. 21-22 (2) 116.00 45.40
Nos. 82-83 (2) 13.40 13.40
Nos. 110-111 (2) 8.40 8.75
Nos. 48-49 (2) 40.30 47.75
Nos. 64-65 (2) 32.75 38.25
Nos. 92-93 (2) 11.25 16.25
Nos. 90-91 (2) 16.25 22.25
Nos. 224-225 (2) 29.60 38.00

Nos. 267-268 (2) 30.40 25.25
Nos. 93-94 (2) 20.10 25.35
Nos. 525-526 (2) 23.10 29.25
Nos. 62-63 (2) 38.50 57.75
Nos. 82-83 (2) 45.50 45.50
Nos. 25-26 (2) 46.00 47.50
No. 106 (1) .90 1.25
No. 159 (1) 1.10 .35
Set total (136) Stamps 2,353. 2,793.

### U.P.U.

Mercury and Symbols of Communications — CD306

Plane, Ship and Hemispheres — CD307

Mercury Scattering Letters over Globe CD308

U.P.U. Monument, Bern CD309

Universal Postal Union, 75th anniversary.

**1949**

Aden....................32-35
Kathiri State of Seiyun....................16-19
Qu'aiti State of Shihr and Mukalla ....................16-19
Antigua....................100-103
Ascension....................57-60
Bahamas....................150-153
Barbados....................212-215
Basutoland....................41-44
Bechuanaland Protectorate....................149-152
Bermuda....................138-141
British Guiana....................246-249
British Honduras....................137-140
Brunei....................79-82
Cayman Islands....................118-121
Cyprus....................160-163
Dominica....................116-119
Falkland Islands....................103-106
Falkland Islands Dep....................1L14-1L17
Fiji....................141-144
Gambia....................148-151
Gibraltar....................123-126
Gilbert & Ellice Islands....................56-59
Gold Coast....................144-147
Grenada....................147-150
Hong Kong....................180-183
Jamaica....................142-145
Kenya, Uganda, Tanzania....................94-97
Leeward Islands....................126-129
Malaya
Johore....................151-154
Kedah....................57-60
Kelantan....................46-49
Malacca....................18-21
Negri Sembilan....................59-62
Pahang....................46-49
Penang....................23-26
Perak....................101-104
Perlis....................3-6
Selangor....................76-79
Trengganu....................49-52
Malta....................225-228
Mauritius....................231-234
Montserrat....................108-111
New Hebrides, British....................62-65
New Hebrides, French....................79-82
Nigeria....................75-78
North Borneo....................240-243
Northern Rhodesia....................50-53
Nyasaland Protectorate....................87-90
Pitcairn Islands....................13-16
St. Helena....................132-135
St. Kitts-Nevis....................95-98
St. Lucia....................131-134
St. Vincent....................170-173
Sarawak....................176-179
Seychelles....................153-156
Sierra Leone....................190-193
Singapore....................23-26
Solomon Islands....................84-87
Somaliland Protectorate....................112-115
Southern Rhodesia....................71-72
Swaziland....................50-53
Tonga....................87-90
Trinidad & Tobago....................66-69
Turks & Caicos Islands....................101-104
Virgin Islands....................92-95
Zanzibar....................226-229

The following have different designs but are included in the omnibus set:

Great Britain....................276-279
Offices in Morocco (Tangier)....................546-549
Australia....................223
Bahrain....................68-71
Burma....................116-121
Ceylon....................304-306
Egypt....................281-283
India....................223-226
Kuwait....................89-92
Oman....................31-34
Pakistan-Bahawalpur 26-29, O25-O28
South Africa....................109-111
South-West Africa....................160-162

Nos. 32-35 (4) 5.85 8.45
Nos. 16-19 (4) 2.75 5.50
Nos. 16-19 (4) 2.60 4.20
Nos. 100-103 (4) 3.60 7.70
Nos. 57-60 (4) 11.10 9.00
Nos. 150-153 (4) 5.35 9.30
Nos. 212-215 (4) 4.40 14.15
Nos. 41-44 (4) 4.75 10.00
Nos. 149-152 (4) 3.35 7.25
Nos. 138-141 (4) 4.75 6.15
Nos. 246-249 (4) 2.75 4.20
Nos. 137-140 (4) 3.30 6.35
Nos. 79-82 (4) 9.50 8.45
Nos. 118-121 (4) 3.60 7.25
Nos. 160-163 (4) 4.60 10.70
Nos. 116-119 (4) 2.30 5.65
Nos. 103-106 (4) 14.00 17.10
Nos. 1L14-1L17 (4) 14.60 14.50
Nos. 141-144 (4) 3.35 14.75
Nos. 148-151 (4) 3.10 7.10
Nos. 123-126 (4) 5.90 8.75
Nos. 56-59 (4) 4.30 13.00
Nos. 144-147 (4) 2.55 10.35
Nos. 147-150 (4) 2.15 3.55
Nos. 180-183 (4) 57.25 18.25
Nos. 142-145 (4) 2.25 2.45
Nos. 94-97 (4) 2.90 3.40
Nos. 126-129 (4) 3.05 9.60
Nos. 151-154 (4) 4.70 8.90
Nos. 57-60 (4) 4.80 12.00
Nos. 46-49 (4) 4.25 12.65
Nos. 18-21 (4) 4.25 17.30
Nos. 59-62 (4) 3.50 10.75
Nos. 46-49 (4) 3.00 7.25
Nos. 23-26 (4) 5.10 11.75
Nos. 101-104 (4) 3.65 10.75
Nos. 3-6 (4) 3.95 14.25
Nos. 76-79 (4) 4.90 12.30
Nos. 49-52 (4) 4.95 9.75
Nos. 225-228 (4) 4.50 4.85
Nos. 231-234 (4) 4.35 6.70
Nos. 108-111 (4) 3.40 3.85
Nos. 62-65 (4) 1.60 4.25
Nos. 79-82 (4) 24.25 24.25
Nos. 75-78 (4) 2.80 9.25
Nos. 240-243 (4) 7.15 6.50
Nos. 50-53 (4) 5.00 6.50
Nos. 87-90 (4) 4.05 4.05
Nos. 13-16 (4) 18.50 16.50
Nos. 132-135 (4) 4.85 7.10
Nos. 95-98 (4) 3.35 5.55
Nos. 131-134 (4) 2.55 3.85
Nos. 170-173 (4) 2.20 5.05
Nos. 176-179 (4) 8.15 10.85
Nos. 153-156 (4) 3.25 4.10
Nos. 190-193 (4) 3.00 5.10
Nos. 23-26 (4) 5.10 11.75
Nos. 84-87 (4) 4.05 4.90
Nos. 112-115 (4) 3.95 8.70
Nos. 71-72 (2) 1.95 2.25
Nos. 50-53 (4) 2.80 4.65
Nos. 87-90 (4) 3.00 5.25
Nos. 66-69 (4) 3.15 3.15
Nos. 101-104 (4) 2.70 4.10
Nos. 92-95 (4) 2.60 5.90
Nos. 226-229 (4) 5.45 13.50

Nos. 276-279 (4) 1.35 1.00
Nos. 546-549 (4) 3.20 10.15
No. 223 (1) .60 .55
Nos. 68-71 (4) 4.75 16.50
Nos. 116-121 (6) 7.30 5.35
Nos. 304-306 (3) 3.35 4.25
Nos. 281-283 (3) 5.75 2.70
Nos. 223-226 (4) 27.25 10.50
Nos. 89-92 (4) 6.10 10.25
Nos. 31-34 (4) 5.55 15.75
Nos. 26-29,O25-O28 (8) 2.00 42.00
Nos. 109-111 (3) 2.20 3.00
Nos. 160-162 (3) 3.00 5.50
Set total (313) Stamps 447.10 694.70

### University

Arms of University College CD310

Alice, Princess of Athlone CD311

1948 opening of University College of the West Indies at Jamaica.

**1951**

Antigua....................104-105
Barbados....................228-229
British Guiana....................250-251
British Honduras....................141-142
Dominica....................120-121
Grenada....................164-165
Jamaica....................146-147
Leeward Islands....................130-131
Montserrat....................112-113
St. Kitts-Nevis....................105-106
St. Lucia....................149-150
St. Vincent....................174-175
Trinidad & Tobago....................70-71
Virgin Islands....................96-97

Nos. 104-105 (2) 1.35 3.75
Nos. 228-229 (2) 1.85 1.55
Nos. 250-251 (2) 1.10 1.25
Nos. 141-142 (2) 1.40 2.20
Nos. 120-121 (2) 1.40 1.75
Nos. 164-165 (2) 1.20 1.60
Nos. 146-147 (2) .90 .70
Nos. 130-131 (2) 1.35 4.00
Nos. 112-113 (2) .85 1.50
Nos. 105-106 (2) .90 2.25
Nos. 149-150 (2) 1.40 1.50
Nos. 174-175 (2) 1.00 2.15
Nos. 70-71 (2) .75 .75
Nos. 96-97 (2) 1.50 3.75
Set total (28) Stamps 16.95 28.70

### Coronation

Queen Elizabeth II — CD312

**1953**

Aden....................47
Kathiri State of Seiyun....................28
Qu'aiti State of Shihr and Mukalla....................28
Antigua....................106
Ascension....................61
Bahamas....................157
Barbados....................234
Basutoland....................45
Bechuanaland Protectorate....................153
Bermuda....................142
British Guiana....................252
British Honduras....................143
Cayman Islands....................150
Cyprus....................167
Dominica....................141
Falkland Islands....................121
Falkland Islands Dependencies....................1L18
Fiji....................145
Gambia....................152
Gibraltar....................131
Gilbert & Ellice Islands....................60
Gold Coast....................160
Grenada....................170
Hong Kong....................184
Jamaica....................153
Kenya, Uganda, Tanzania....................101
Leeward Islands....................132
Malaya
Johore....................155
Kedah....................82
Kelantan....................71
Malacca....................27
Negri Sembilan....................63
Pahang....................71
Penang....................27
Perak....................126
Perlis....................28
Selangor....................101
Trengganu....................74
Malta....................241
Mauritius....................250
Montserrat....................127
New Hebrides, British....................77
Nigeria....................79
North Borneo....................260
Northern Rhodesia....................60
Nyasaland Protectorate....................96
Pitcairn Islands....................19
St. Helena....................139
St. Kitts-Nevis....................119
St. Lucia....................156
St. Vincent....................185
Sarawak....................196
Seychelles....................172
Sierra Leone....................194
Singapore....................27
Solomon Islands....................88
Somaliland Protectorate....................127
Swaziland....................54
Trinidad & Tobago....................84
Tristan da Cunha....................13
Turks & Caicos Islands....................118
Virgin Islands....................114

The following have different designs but are included in the omnibus set:

Great Britain....................313-316
Offices in Morocco (Tangier)....................579-582
Australia....................259-261
Bahrain....................92-95
Canada....................330
Ceylon....................317
Cook Islands....................145-146
Kuwait....................113-116
New Zealand....................280-284
Niue....................104-105
Oman....................52-55
Samoa....................214-215
South Africa....................192
Southern Rhodesia....................80
South-West Africa....................244-248
Tokelau Islands....................4

No. 47 (1) 1.25 1.25
No. 28 (1) .75 1.50
No. 28 (1) 1.10 .60
No. 106 (1) .40 .75
No. 61 (1) 1.25 2.75
No. 157 (1) 1.40 .75
No. 234 (1) 1.00 .25
No. 45 (1) .50 .60
No. 153 (1) .75 .35
No. 142 (1) .85 .50
No. 252 (1) .45 .25
No. 143 (1) .60 .40
No. 150 (1) .40 1.75
No. 167 (1) 1.60 .75
No. 141 (1) .40 .40
No. 121 (1) .90 1.50
No. 1L18 (1) 1.80 1.40
No. 145 (1) 1.00 .60
No. 152 (1) .50 .50
No. 131 (1) .50 .50
No. 60 (1) .65 2.25
No. 160 (1) 1.00 .25

| | | |
|---|---|---|
| *No. 170 (1)* | .30 | .25 |
| *No. 184 (1)* | 6.00 | .35 |
| *No. 153 (1)* | .70 | .25 |
| *No. 101 (1)* | .40 | .25 |
| *No. 132 (1)* | 1.00 | *2.25* |
| *No. 155 (1)* | 1.40 | .30 |
| *No. 82 (1)* | 2.25 | .60 |
| *No. 71 (1)* | 1.60 | 1.60 |
| *No. 27 (1)* | 1.10 | *1.50* |
| *No. 63 (1)* | 1.40 | .65 |
| *No. 71 (1)* | 2.25 | .25 |
| *No. 27 (1)* | 1.75 | .30 |
| *No. 126 (1)* | 1.60 | .25 |
| *No. 28 (1)* | 1.75 | *4.00* |
| *No. 101 (1)* | 1.75 | .25 |
| *No. 74 (1)* | 1.50 | 1.00 |
| *No. 241 (1)* | .50 | .25 |
| *No. 250 (1)* | 1.00 | .25 |
| *No. 127 (1)* | .65 | .50 |
| *No. 77 (1)* | .75 | .60 |
| *No. 79 (1)* | .45 | .25 |
| *No. 260 (1)* | 2.00 | 1.00 |
| *No. 60 (1)* | .70 | .25 |
| *No. 96 (1)* | .75 | .75 |
| *No. 19 (1)* | 2.25 | 2.25 |
| *No. 139 (1)* | 1.25 | 1.25 |
| *No. 119 (1)* | .35 | .25 |
| *No. 156 (1)* | .70 | .35 |
| *No. 185 (1)* | .50 | .30 |
| *No. 196 (1)* | 2.00 | *1.75* |
| *No. 172 (1)* | .80 | .80 |
| *No. 194 (1)* | .40 | .40 |
| *No. 27 (1)* | 2.50 | .40 |
| *No. 88 (1)* | 1.00 | 1.00 |
| *No. 127 (1)* | .40 | .25 |
| *No. 54 (1)* | .30 | .25 |
| *No. 84 (1)* | .25 | .25 |
| *No. 13 (1)* | 1.00 | 1.75 |
| *No. 118 (1)* | .40 | *1.10* |
| *No. 114 (1)* | .40 | *1.00* |
| *Nos. 313-316 (4)* | 16.35 | 5.95 |
| *Nos. 579-582 (4)* | 7.40 | 5.20 |
| *Nos. 259-261 (3)* | 4.60 | 3.25 |
| *Nos. 92-95 (4)* | 15.25 | 12.75 |
| *No. 330 (1)* | .25 | .25 |
| *No. 317 (1)* | 1.50 | .25 |
| *Nos. 145-146 (2)* | 2.65 | 2.65 |
| *Nos. 113-116 (4)* | 16.00 | 8.50 |
| *Nos. 280-284 (5)* | 5.75 | 5.60 |
| *Nos. 104-105 (2)* | 1.60 | 1.60 |
| *Nos. 52-55 (4)* | 15.25 | 6.50 |
| *Nos. 214-215 (2)* | 2.10 | 1.00 |
| *No. 192 (1)* | .30 | .25 |
| *No. 80 (1)* | 7.25 | 7.25 |
| *Nos. 244-248 (5)* | 3.00 | 2.35 |
| *No. 4 (1)* | 2.75 | 2.75 |
| *Set total (106) Stamps* | 169.10 | 117.20 |

Separate designs for each country for the visit of Queen Elizabeth II and the Duke of Edinburgh.

## Royal Visit 1953

**1953**

Aden ........................................62
Australia ................................267-269
Bermuda ....................................163
Ceylon .......................................318
Fiji ............................................146
Gibraltar ...................................146
Jamaica .....................................154
Kenya, Uganda, Tanzania ..............102
Malta .........................................242
New Zealand ...........................286-287

| | | |
|---|---|---|
| *No. 62 (1)* | .65 | 1.25 |
| *Nos. 267-269 (3)* | 2.35 | 1.90 |
| *No. 163 (1)* | .50 | .25 |
| *No. 318 (1)* | 1.25 | .25 |
| *No. 146 (1)* | .65 | .35 |
| *No. 146 (1)* | .50 | .30 |
| *No. 154 (1)* | .50 | .25 |
| *No. 102 (1)* | .50 | .25 |
| *No. 242 (1)* | .35 | .25 |
| *Nos. 286-287 (2)* | .50 | .50 |
| *Set total (13) Stamps* | 7.75 | 5.55 |

## West Indies Federation

Map of the Caribbean
CD313

Federation of the West Indies, April 22, 1958.

**1958**

Antigua ..................................122-124
Barbados .................................248-250
Dominica .................................161-163
Grenada ...................................184-186
Jamaica ....................................175-177
Montserrat ...............................143-145
St. Kitts-Nevis ..........................136-138
St. Lucia ..................................170-172
St. Vincent ...............................198-200
Trinidad & Tobago .......................86-88

| | | |
|---|---|---|
| *Nos. 122-124 (3)* | 5.80 | 3.80 |
| *Nos. 248-250 (3)* | 1.60 | *2.90* |
| *Nos. 161-163 (3)* | 1.95 | 1.85 |
| *Nos. 184-186 (3)* | 1.50 | 1.20 |
| *Nos. 175-177 (3)* | 2.65 | 3.45 |
| *Nos. 143-145 (3)* | 2.35 | 1.35 |
| *Nos. 136-138 (3)* | 3.00 | 3.10 |
| *Nos. 170-172 (3)* | 2.05 | 2.80 |
| *Nos. 198-200 (3)* | 1.50 | 1.75 |
| *Nos. 86-88 (3)* | .75 | .90 |
| *Set total (30) Stamps* | 23.15 | 23.10 |

## Freedom from Hunger

Protein Food
CD314

U.N. Food and Agricultural Organization's "Freedom from Hunger" campaign.

**1963**

Aden .............................................65
Antigua ........................................133
Ascension .......................................89
Bahamas .......................................180
Basutoland ......................................83
Bechuanaland Protectorate ............194
Bermuda .......................................192
British Guiana ...............................271
British Honduras ............................179
Brunei ..........................................100
Cayman Islands .............................168
Dominica ......................................181
Falkland Islands .............................146
Fiji ...............................................198
Gambia .........................................172
Gibraltar .......................................161
Gilbert & Ellice Islands ....................76
Grenada ........................................190
Hong Kong ....................................218
Malta ............................................291
Mauritius ......................................270
Montserrat ....................................150
New Hebrides, British .....................93
North Borneo ................................296
Pitcairn Islands ...............................35
St. Helena .....................................173
St. Lucia .......................................179
St. Vincent ....................................201
Sarawak ........................................212
Seychelles .....................................213
Solomon Islands .............................109
Swaziland ......................................108
Tonga ...........................................127
Tristan da Cunha .............................68
Turks & Caicos Islands ...................138
Virgin Islands ................................140
Zanzibar ........................................280

| | | |
|---|---|---|
| *No. 65 (1)* | 1.50 | 1.75 |
| *No. 133 (1)* | .35 | .35 |
| *No. 89 (1)* | 1.00 | .50 |
| *No. 180 (1)* | .65 | .65 |
| *No. 83 (1)* | .50 | .25 |
| *No. 194 (1)* | .50 | .50 |
| *No. 192 (1)* | 1.00 | .50 |
| *No. 271 (1)* | .45 | .25 |
| *No. 179 (1)* | .60 | .25 |
| *No. 100 (1)* | 3.25 | 2.25 |
| *No. 168 (1)* | .55 | .30 |
| *No. 181 (1)* | .30 | .30 |
| *No. 146 (1)* | 10.50 | 2.50 |
| *No. 198 (1)* | 3.50 | 2.25 |
| *No. 172 (1)* | .50 | .25 |
| *No. 161 (1)* | 4.00 | 2.25 |
| *No. 76 (1)* | 1.40 | .40 |
| *No. 190 (1)* | .30 | .25 |
| *No. 218 (1)* | 47.50 | 7.50 |
| *No. 291 (1)* | 2.00 | 2.00 |
| *No. 270 (1)* | .50 | .50 |
| *No. 150 (1)* | .55 | .45 |
| *No. 93 (1)* | .60 | .25 |
| *No. 296 (1)* | 1.90 | .75 |
| *No. 35 (1)* | 10.00 | 4.50 |
| *No. 173 (1)* | 2.25 | 1.10 |
| *No. 179 (1)* | .40 | .40 |
| *No. 201 (1)* | .90 | .50 |
| *No. 212 (1)* | 1.60 | *1.75* |
| *No. 213 (1)* | .85 | .35 |
| *No. 109 (1)* | 3.00 | .85 |
| *No. 108 (1)* | .50 | .50 |
| *No. 127 (1)* | .60 | .35 |
| *No. 68 (1)* | .75 | .35 |
| *No. 138 (1)* | .50 | .25 |
| *No. 140 (1)* | .50 | .50 |
| *No. 280 (1)* | 1.50 | .80 |
| *Set total (37) Stamps* | 107.25 | 39.40 |

## Red Cross Centenary

Red Cross and Elizabeth II
CD315

**1963**

Antigua ...................................134-135
Ascension ....................................90-91
Bahamas ..................................183-184
Basutoland ...................................84-85
Bechuanaland Protectorate ......195-196
Bermuda ..................................193-194
British Guiana ...........................272-273
British Honduras .......................180-181
Cayman Islands .........................169-170
Dominica ..................................182-183
Falkland Islands ........................147-148
Fiji ..........................................203-204
Gambia ....................................173-174
Gibraltar ..................................162-163
Gilbert & Ellice Islands ................77-78
Grenada ...................................191-192
Hong Kong ...............................219-220
Jamaica ...................................203-204
Malta .......................................292-293
Mauritius .................................271-272
Montserrat ...............................151-152
New Hebrides, British ..................94-95
Pitcairn Islands ............................36-37
St. Helena ................................174-175
St. Kitts-Nevis ..........................143-144
St. Lucia ..................................180-181
St. Vincent ...............................202-203
Seychelles ................................214-215
Solomon Islands ........................110-111
South Arabia ....................................1-2
Swaziland .................................109-110
Tonga ......................................134-135
Tristan da Cunha ..........................69-70
Turks & Caicos Islands ..............139-140
Virgin Islands ...........................141-142

| | | |
|---|---|---|
| *Nos. 134-135 (2)* | 1.00 | *2.00* |
| *Nos. 90-91 (2)* | 6.75 | 3.35 |
| *Nos. 183-184 (2)* | 2.30 | 2.80 |
| *Nos. 84-85 (2)* | 1.20 | .90 |
| *Nos. 195-196 (2)* | .95 | .85 |
| *Nos. 193-194 (2)* | 3.00 | 2.80 |
| *Nos. 272-273 (2)* | 1.05 | .80 |
| *Nos. 180-181 (2)* | 1.00 | 2.50 |
| *Nos. 169-170 (2)* | 1.10 | *3.00* |
| *Nos. 182-183 (2)* | .70 | *1.05* |
| *Nos. 147-148 (2)* | 18.00 | 5.50 |
| *Nos. 203-204 (2)* | 3.25 | 2.80 |
| *Nos. 173-174 (2)* | .75 | 1.00 |
| *Nos. 162-163 (2)* | 6.25 | 5.40 |
| *Nos. 77-78 (2)* | 2.00 | *3.50* |
| *Nos. 191-192 (2)* | .80 | .50 |
| *Nos. 219-220 (2)* | 35.00 | 7.35 |
| *Nos. 203-204 (2)* | .75 | *1.65* |
| *Nos. 292-293 (2)* | 2.50 | 4.75 |
| *Nos. 271-272 (2)* | .90 | .90 |
| *Nos. 151-152 (2)* | 1.00 | .80 |
| *Nos. 94-95 (2)* | 1.00 | .50 |
| *Nos. 36-37 (2)* | 6.50 | 5.50 |
| *Nos. 174-175 (2)* | 1.70 | 2.30 |
| *Nos. 143-144 (2)* | .90 | .90 |
| *Nos. 180-181 (2)* | 1.25 | 1.25 |
| *Nos. 202-203 (2)* | .90 | .90 |
| *Nos. 214-215 (2)* | 1.10 | .90 |
| *Nos. 110-111 (2)* | 1.25 | 1.15 |
| *Nos. 1-2 (2)* | 1.25 | 1.25 |
| *Nos. 109-110 (2)* | 1.10 | 1.10 |
| *Nos. 134-135 (2)* | 1.00 | 1.25 |
| *Nos. 69-70 (2)* | 1.15 | .80 |
| *Nos. 139-140 (2)* | .85 | .75 |
| *Nos. 141-142 (2)* | .80 | 1.25 |
| *Set total (70) Stamps* | 111.00 | 74.00 |

## Shakespeare

Shakespeare Memorial Theatre, Stratford-on-Avon — CD316

400th anniversary of the birth of William Shakespeare.

**1964**

Antigua .........................................151
Bahamas ........................................201
Bechuanaland Protectorate ..............197
Cayman Islands ..............................171
Dominica ......................................184
Falkland Islands .............................149
Gambia .........................................192
Gibraltar .......................................164
Montserrat ....................................153
St. Lucia .......................................196
Turks & Caicos Islands ...................141
Virgin Islands ................................143

| | | |
|---|---|---|
| *No. 151 (1)* | .35 | .25 |
| *No. 201 (1)* | .60 | .35 |
| *No. 197 (1)* | .35 | .35 |
| *No. 171 (1)* | .35 | .30 |
| *No. 184 (1)* | .35 | .35 |
| *No. 149 (1)* | 1.60 | .50 |
| *No. 192 (1)* | .35 | .25 |
| *No. 164 (1)* | .65 | .55 |
| *No. 153 (1)* | .35 | .25 |
| *No. 196 (1)* | .45 | .25 |
| *No. 141 (1)* | .40 | .25 |
| *No. 143 (1)* | .45 | .45 |
| *Set total (12) Stamps* | 6.25 | 4.10 |

## ITU

ITU Emblem
CD317

Intl. Telecommunication Union, cent.

**1965**

Antigua ...................................153-154
Ascension ....................................92-93
Bahamas ..................................219-220
Barbados ..................................265-266
Basutoland ...............................101-102
Bechuanaland Protectorate ......202-203
Bermuda ..................................196-197
British Guiana ..........................293-294
British Honduras .......................187-188
Brunei .....................................116-117
Cayman Islands ........................172-173
Dominica .................................185-186
Falkland Islands .......................154-155
Fiji ..........................................211-212
Gibraltar ..................................167-168
Gilbert & Ellice Islands ................87-88
Grenada ...................................205-206
Hong Kong ...............................221-222
Mauritius .................................291-292
Montserrat ...............................157-158
New Hebrides, British ...............108-109
Pitcairn Islands ............................52-53
St. Helena ................................180-181
St. Kitts-Nevis ..........................163-164
St. Lucia ..................................197-198
St. Vincent ...............................224-225
Seychelles ................................218-219
Solomon Islands ........................126-127
Swaziland .................................115-116
Tristan da Cunha ..........................85-86
Turks & Caicos Islands ..............142-143
Virgin Islands ...........................159-160

| | | |
|---|---|---|
| *Nos. 153-154 (2)* | 1.45 | 1.35 |
| *Nos. 92-93 (2)* | 1.90 | 1.30 |
| *Nos. 219-220 (2)* | 1.35 | 1.50 |
| *Nos. 265-266 (2)* | 1.50 | 1.25 |
| *Nos. 101-102 (2)* | .85 | .65 |
| *Nos. 202-203 (2)* | 1.10 | .75 |
| *Nos. 196-197 (2)* | 2.15 | *2.25* |
| *Nos. 293-294 (2)* | .60 | .55 |
| *Nos. 187-188 (2)* | .75 | .75 |
| *Nos. 116-117 (2)* | 1.75 | 1.75 |
| *Nos. 172-173 (2)* | 1.00 | .85 |
| *Nos. 185-186 (2)* | .55 | .55 |
| *Nos. 154-155 (2)* | 6.75 | 3.15 |
| *Nos. 211-212 (2)* | 2.00 | 1.05 |
| *Nos. 167-168 (2)* | 9.00 | 5.95 |
| *Nos. 87-88 (2)* | .85 | .60 |
| *Nos. 205-206 (2)* | .50 | .50 |
| *Nos. 221-222 (2)* | 24.50 | 3.80 |
| *Nos. 291-292 (2)* | 1.20 | .65 |
| *Nos. 157-158 (2)* | 1.25 | 1.15 |
| *Nos. 108-109 (2)* | .65 | .50 |
| *Nos. 52-53 (2)* | 6.25 | 4.30 |
| *Nos. 180-181 (2)* | .80 | .60 |
| *Nos. 163-164 (2)* | .60 | .60 |
| *Nos. 197-198 (2)* | 1.25 | 1.25 |
| *Nos. 224-225 (2)* | .80 | .90 |
| *Nos. 218-219 (2)* | .90 | .60 |
| *Nos. 126-127 (2)* | .70 | .55 |
| *Nos. 115-116 (2)* | .75 | .75 |
| *Nos. 85-86 (2)* | 1.00 | .65 |
| *Nos. 142-143 (2)* | .75 | .50 |
| *Nos. 159-160 (2)* | .85 | .85 |
| *Set total (64) Stamps* | 76.30 | 42.40 |

### Intl. Cooperation Year

ICY Emblem
CD318

**1965**

| | |
|---|---|
| Antigua | 155-156 |
| Ascension | 94-95 |
| Bahamas | 222-223 |
| Basutoland | 103-104 |
| Bechuanaland Protectorate | 204-205 |
| Bermuda | 199-200 |
| British Guiana | 295-296 |
| British Honduras | 189-190 |
| Brunei | 118-119 |
| Cayman Islands | 174-175 |
| Dominica | 187-188 |
| Falkland Islands | 156-157 |
| Fiji | 213-214 |
| Gibraltar | 169-170 |
| Gilbert & Ellice Islands | 104-105 |
| Grenada | 207-208 |
| Hong Kong | 223-224 |
| Mauritius | 293-294 |
| Montserrat | 176-177 |
| New Hebrides, British | 110-111 |
| New Hebrides, French | 126-127 |
| Pitcairn Islands | 54-55 |
| St. Helena | 182-183 |
| St. Kitts-Nevis | 165-166 |
| St. Lucia | 199-200 |
| Seychelles | 220-221 |
| Solomon Islands | 143-144 |
| South Arabia | 17-18 |
| Swaziland | 117-118 |
| Tristan da Cunha | 87-88 |
| Turks & Caicos Islands | 144-145 |
| Virgin Islands | 161-162 |

| | | |
|---|---|---|
| *Nos. 155-156 (2)* | .55 | .50 |
| *Nos. 94-95 (2)* | 1.30 | 1.40 |
| *Nos. 222-223 (2)* | .65 | 1.90 |
| *Nos. 103-104 (2)* | .75 | .85 |
| *Nos. 204-205 (2)* | .85 | 1.00 |
| *Nos. 199-200 (2)* | 2.05 | 1.25 |
| *Nos. 295-296 (2)* | .65 | .60 |
| *Nos. 189-190 (2)* | .60 | .55 |
| *Nos. 118-119 (2)* | .85 | .85 |
| *Nos. 174-175 (2)* | 1.00 | .75 |
| *Nos. 187-188 (2)* | .55 | .55 |
| *Nos. 156-157 (2)* | 6.00 | 1.65 |
| *Nos. 213-214 (2)* | 1.95 | 1.25 |
| *Nos. 169-170 (2)* | 1.25 | *2.75* |
| *Nos. 104-105 (2)* | .85 | .60 |
| *Nos. 207-208 (2)* | .50 | .50 |
| *Nos. 223-224 (2)* | 22.00 | 3.10 |
| *Nos. 293-294 (2)* | .70 | .70 |
| *Nos. 176-177 (2)* | .80 | .65 |
| *Nos. 110-111 (2)* | .50 | .50 |
| *Nos. 126-127 (2)* | 12.00 | 12.00 |
| *Nos. 54-55 (2)* | 6.35 | 4.50 |
| *Nos. 182-183 (2)* | .95 | .50 |
| *Nos. 165-166 (2)* | .80 | .60 |
| *Nos. 199-200 (2)* | .55 | .55 |
| *Nos. 220-221 (2)* | .90 | .65 |
| *Nos. 143-144 (2)* | .70 | .60 |
| *Nos. 17-18 (2)* | 1.20 | .50 |
| *Nos. 117-118 (2)* | .75 | .75 |
| *Nos. 87-88 (2)* | 1.05 | .65 |
| *Nos. 144-145 (2)* | .65 | .50 |
| *Nos. 161-162 (2)* | .65 | .50 |
| *Set total (64) Stamps* | 70.90 | 44.20 |

### Churchill Memorial

Winston Churchill and St. Paul's, London, During Air Attack
CD319

**1966**

| | |
|---|---|
| Antigua | 157-160 |
| Ascension | 96-99 |
| Bahamas | 224-227 |
| Barbados | 281-284 |
| Basutoland | 105-108 |
| Bechuanaland Protectorate | 206-209 |
| Bermuda | 201-204 |
| British Antarctic Territory | 16-19 |
| British Honduras | 191-194 |
| Brunei | 120-123 |
| Cayman Islands | 176-179 |
| Dominica | 189-192 |
| Falkland Islands | 158-161 |
| Fiji | 215-218 |
| Gibraltar | 171-174 |
| Gilbert & Ellice Islands | 106-109 |
| Grenada | 209-212 |
| Hong Kong | 225-228 |
| Mauritius | 295-298 |
| Montserrat | 178-181 |
| New Hebrides, British | 112-115 |
| New Hebrides, French | 128-131 |
| Pitcairn Islands | 56-59 |
| St. Helena | 184-187 |
| St. Kitts-Nevis | 167-170 |
| St. Lucia | 201-204 |
| St. Vincent | 241-244 |
| Seychelles | 222-225 |
| Solomon Islands | 145-148 |
| South Arabia | 19-22 |
| Swaziland | 119-122 |
| Tristan da Cunha | 89-92 |
| Turks & Caicos Islands | 146-149 |
| Virgin Islands | 163-166 |

| | | |
|---|---|---|
| *Nos. 157-160 (4)* | 3.05 | 3.05 |
| *Nos. 96-99 (4)* | 10.00 | 6.40 |
| *Nos. 224-227 (4)* | 2.30 | *3.20* |
| *Nos. 281-284 (4)* | 3.00 | 4.45 |
| *Nos. 105-108 (4)* | 2.80 | 3.25 |
| *Nos. 206-209 (4)* | 2.50 | 2.50 |
| *Nos. 201-204 (4)* | 4.00 | *4.75* |
| *Nos. 16-19 (4)* | 37.85 | 18.00 |
| *Nos. 191-194 (4)* | 2.45 | 1.30 |
| *Nos. 120-123 (4)* | 7.65 | 6.55 |
| *Nos. 176-179 (4)* | 3.10 | 3.65 |
| *Nos. 189-192 (4)* | 1.15 | 1.15 |
| *Nos. 158-161 (4)* | 12.75 | 9.55 |
| *Nos. 215-218 (4)* | 4.40 | 3.00 |
| *Nos. 171-174 (4)* | 3.05 | 5.30 |
| *Nos. 106-109 (4)* | 1.50 | 1.30 |
| *Nos. 209-212 (4)* | 1.10 | 1.10 |
| *Nos. 225-228 (4)* | 52.50 | 11.40 |
| *Nos. 295-298 (4)* | 4.05 | 4.05 |
| *Nos. 178-181 (4)* | 1.60 | 1.55 |
| *Nos. 112-115 (4)* | 2.30 | 1.00 |
| *Nos. 128-131 (4)* | 10.25 | 10.25 |
| *Nos. 56-59 (4)* | 11.00 | 6.75 |
| *Nos. 184-187 (4)* | 1.85 | 1.95 |
| *Nos. 167-170 (4)* | 1.50 | 1.70 |
| *Nos. 201-204 (4)* | 1.50 | 1.50 |
| *Nos. 241-244 (4)* | 1.50 | 1.75 |
| *Nos. 222-225 (4)* | 3.20 | 3.60 |
| *Nos. 145-148 (4)* | 1.50 | 1.60 |
| *Nos. 19-22 (4)* | 2.95 | 2.20 |
| *Nos. 119-122 (4)* | 1.70 | 2.55 |
| *Nos. 89-92 (4)* | 5.95 | 2.70 |
| *Nos. 146-149 (4)* | 1.60 | 1.75 |
| *Nos. 163-166 (4)* | 1.90 | 1.90 |
| *Set total (136) Stamps* | 209.50 | 136.70 |

### Royal Visit, 1966

Queen Elizabeth II and Prince Philip
CD320

Caribbean visit, Feb. 4 - Mar. 6, 1966.

**1966**

| | |
|---|---|
| Antigua | 161-162 |
| Bahamas | 228-229 |
| Barbados | 285-286 |
| British Guiana | 299-300 |
| Cayman Islands | 180-181 |
| Dominica | 193-194 |
| Grenada | 213-214 |
| Montserrat | 182-183 |
| St. Kitts-Nevis | 171-172 |
| St. Lucia | 205-206 |
| St. Vincent | 245-246 |
| Turks & Caicos Islands | 150-151 |
| Virgin Islands | 167-168 |

| | | |
|---|---|---|
| *Nos. 161-162 (2)* | 3.50 | 2.60 |
| *Nos. 228-229 (2)* | 3.05 | 3.05 |
| *Nos. 285-286 (2)* | 3.00 | 2.00 |
| *Nos. 299-300 (2)* | 3.35 | 1.60 |
| *Nos. 180-181 (2)* | 3.45 | 1.80 |
| *Nos. 193-194 (2)* | 3.00 | .60 |
| *Nos. 213-214 (2)* | .80 | .50 |
| *Nos. 182-183 (2)* | 1.70 | 1.00 |
| *Nos. 171-172 (2)* | .90 | .75 |
| *Nos. 205-206 (2)* | 1.50 | 1.35 |
| *Nos. 245-246 (2)* | 2.75 | 1.35 |
| *Nos. 150-151 (2)* | 1.20 | .55 |
| *Nos. 167-168 (2)* | 1.75 | 1.75 |
| *Set total (26) Stamps* | 29.95 | 18.90 |

### World Cup Soccer

Soccer Player and Jules Rimet Cup
CD321

World Cup Soccer Championship, Wembley, England, July 11-30.

**1966**

| | |
|---|---|
| Antigua | 163-164 |
| Ascension | 100-101 |
| Bahamas | 245-246 |
| Bermuda | 205-206 |
| Brunei | 124-125 |
| Cayman Islands | 182-183 |
| Dominica | 195-196 |
| Fiji | 219-220 |
| Gibraltar | 175-176 |
| Gilbert & Ellice Islands | 125-126 |
| Grenada | 230-231 |
| New Hebrides, British | 116-117 |
| New Hebrides, French | 132-133 |
| Pitcairn Islands | 60-61 |
| St. Helena | 188-189 |
| St. Kitts-Nevis | 173-174 |
| St. Lucia | 207-208 |
| Seychelles | 226-227 |
| Solomon Islands | 167-168 |
| South Arabia | 23-24 |
| Tristan da Cunha | 93-94 |

| | | |
|---|---|---|
| *Nos. 163-164 (2)* | .80 | .85 |
| *Nos. 100-101 (2)* | 2.50 | 2.00 |
| *Nos. 245-246 (2)* | .65 | .65 |
| *Nos. 205-206 (2)* | 1.75 | 1.75 |
| *Nos. 124-125 (2)* | 1.30 | 1.25 |
| *Nos. 182-183 (2)* | .75 | .65 |
| *Nos. 195-196 (2)* | 1.20 | .75 |
| *Nos. 219-220 (2)* | 1.70 | .60 |
| *Nos. 175-176 (2)* | 1.85 | 1.75 |
| *Nos. 125-126 (2)* | .70 | .60 |
| *Nos. 230-231 (2)* | .65 | *.95* |
| *Nos. 116-117 (2)* | 1.00 | 1.00 |
| *Nos. 132-133 (2)* | 7.00 | 7.00 |
| *Nos. 60-61 (2)* | 5.50 | 5.00 |
| *Nos. 188-189 (2)* | 1.25 | .60 |
| *Nos. 173-174 (2)* | .85 | .80 |
| *Nos. 207-208 (2)* | 1.15 | .90 |
| *Nos. 226-227 (2)* | .85 | .85 |
| *Nos. 167-168 (2)* | 1.10 | 1.10 |
| *Nos. 23-24 (2)* | 1.90 | .55 |
| *Nos. 93-94 (2)* | 1.25 | .80 |
| *Set total (42) Stamps* | 35.70 | 30.40 |

### WHO Headquarters

World Health Organization Headquarters, Geneva — CD322

**1966**

| | |
|---|---|
| Antigua | 165-166 |
| Ascension | 102-103 |
| Bahamas | 247-248 |
| Brunei | 126-127 |
| Cayman Islands | 184-185 |
| Dominica | 197-198 |
| Fiji | 224-225 |
| Gibraltar | 180-181 |
| Gilbert & Ellice Islands | 127-128 |
| Grenada | 232-233 |
| Hong Kong | 229-230 |
| Montserrat | 184-185 |
| New Hebrides, British | 118-119 |
| New Hebrides, French | 134-135 |
| Pitcairn Islands | 62-63 |
| St. Helena | 190-191 |
| St. Kitts-Nevis | 177-178 |
| St. Lucia | 209-210 |
| St. Vincent | 247-248 |
| Seychelles | 228-229 |
| Solomon Islands | 169-170 |
| South Arabia | 25-26 |
| Tristan da Cunha | 99-100 |

| | | |
|---|---|---|
| *Nos. 165-166 (2)* | 1.15 | .55 |
| *Nos. 102-103 (2)* | 6.60 | 3.35 |
| *Nos. 247-248 (2)* | .80 | .80 |
| *Nos. 126-127 (2)* | 1.35 | 1.35 |
| *Nos. 184-185 (2)* | 2.25 | 1.20 |
| *Nos. 197-198 (2)* | .75 | .75 |
| *Nos. 224-225 (2)* | 4.70 | 3.30 |
| *Nos. 180-181 (2)* | 6.50 | 4.50 |
| *Nos. 127-128 (2)* | .80 | .70 |
| *Nos. 232-233 (2)* | .80 | .50 |
| *Nos. 229-230 (2)* | 11.25 | 2.30 |
| *Nos. 184-185 (2)* | 1.00 | 1.00 |
| *Nos. 118-119 (2)* | .75 | .50 |
| *Nos. 134-135 (2)* | 8.75 | 8.75 |
| *Nos. 62-63 (2)* | 7.25 | 6.50 |
| *Nos. 190-191 (2)* | 3.50 | 1.50 |
| *Nos. 177-178 (2)* | .60 | .60 |
| *Nos. 209-210 (2)* | .80 | .80 |
| *Nos. 247-248 (2)* | 1.15 | 1.05 |
| *Nos. 228-229 (2)* | 1.25 | .75 |
| *Nos. 169-170 (2)* | .95 | .80 |
| *Nos. 25-26 (2)* | 2.10 | .70 |
| *Nos. 99-100 (2)* | 1.90 | 1.25 |
| *Set total (46) Stamps* | 66.95 | 43.50 |

### UNESCO Anniversary

"Education" — CD323

"Science" (Wheat ears & flask enclosing globe). "Culture" (lyre & columns). 20th anniversary of the UNESCO.

**1966-67**

| | |
|---|---|
| Antigua | 183-185 |
| Ascension | 108-110 |
| Bahamas | 249-251 |
| Barbados | 287-289 |
| Bermuda | 207-209 |
| Brunei | 128-130 |
| Cayman Islands | 186-188 |
| Dominica | 199-201 |
| Gibraltar | 183-185 |
| Gilbert & Ellice Islands | 129-131 |
| Grenada | 234-236 |
| Hong Kong | 231-233 |
| Mauritius | 299-301 |
| Montserrat | 186-188 |
| New Hebrides, British | 120-122 |
| New Hebrides, French | 136-138 |
| Pitcairn Islands | 64-66 |
| St. Helena | 192-194 |
| St. Kitts-Nevis | 179-181 |
| St. Lucia | 211-213 |
| St. Vincent | 249-251 |
| Seychelles | 230-232 |
| Solomon Islands | 171-173 |
| South Arabia | 27-29 |
| Swaziland | 123-125 |
| Tristan da Cunha | 101-103 |
| Turks & Caicos Islands | 155-157 |
| Virgin Islands | 176-178 |

| | | |
|---|---|---|
| *Nos. 183-185 (3)* | 1.90 | *2.50* |
| *Nos. 108-110 (3)* | 11.00 | 5.80 |
| *Nos. 249-251 (3)* | 2.35 | 2.35 |
| *Nos. 287-289 (3)* | 2.50 | 2.15 |
| *Nos. 207-209 (3)* | 3.80 | *3.90* |
| *Nos. 128-130 (3)* | 4.65 | 5.40 |
| *Nos. 186-188 (3)* | 2.50 | 1.50 |
| *Nos. 199-201 (3)* | 1.60 | .75 |
| *Nos. 183-185 (3)* | 6.50 | 3.25 |
| *Nos. 129-131 (3)* | 2.50 | *2.45* |
| *Nos. 234-236 (3)* | 1.10 | 1.20 |
| *Nos. 231-233 (3)* | 69.50 | 17.50 |
| *Nos. 299-301 (3)* | 2.10 | 1.50 |
| *Nos. 186-188 (3)* | 2.40 | 2.40 |
| *Nos. 120-122 (3)* | 1.90 | 1.90 |
| *Nos. 136-138 (3)* | 7.75 | 7.75 |
| *Nos. 64-66 (3)* | 7.10 | 4.75 |
| *Nos. 192-194 (3)* | 5.25 | 3.65 |
| *Nos. 179-181 (3)* | .90 | .90 |
| *Nos. 211-213 (3)* | 1.15 | 1.15 |
| *Nos. 249-251 (3)* | 2.30 | 1.35 |
| *Nos. 230-232 (3)* | 2.40 | 2.40 |
| *Nos. 171-173 (3)* | 2.00 | 1.50 |
| *Nos. 27-29 (3)* | 5.50 | 5.50 |
| *Nos. 123-125 (3)* | 1.45 | 1.45 |
| *Nos. 101-103 (3)* | 2.00 | 1.40 |
| *Nos. 155-157 (3)* | 1.05 | .90 |
| *Nos. 176-178 (3)* | 1.40 | 1.30 |
| *Set total (84) Stamps* | 156.55 | 88.55 |

### Silver Wedding, 1972

Queen Elizabeth II and Prince Philip — CD324

Designs: borders differ for each country.

**1972**

| | |
|---|---|
| Anguilla | 161-162 |
| Antigua | 295-296 |
| Ascension | 164-165 |
| Bahamas | 344-345 |
| Bermuda | 296-297 |
| British Antarctic Territory | 43-44 |
| British Honduras | 306-307 |
| British Indian Ocean Territory | 48-49 |

Brunei 186-187
Cayman Islands 304-305
Dominica 352-353
Falkland Islands 223-224
Fiji 328-329
Gibraltar 292-293
Gilbert & Ellice Islands 206-207
Grenada 466-467
Hong Kong 271-272
Montserrat 286-287
New Hebrides, British 169-170
New Hebrides, French 188-189
Pitcairn Islands 127-128
St. Helena 271-272
St. Kitts-Nevis 257-258
St. Lucia 328-329
St.Vincent 344-345
Seychelles 309-310
Solomon Islands 248-249
South Georgia 35-36
Tristan da Cunha 178-179
Turks & Caicos Islands 257-258
Virgin Islands 241-242

| | | |
|---|---|---|
| *Nos. 161-162 (2)* | 1.30 | *1.50* |
| *Nos. 295-296 (2)* | .50 | .50 |
| *Nos. 164-165 (2)* | .70 | .70 |
| *Nos. 344-345 (2)* | .60 | .60 |
| *Nos. 296-297 (2)* | .50 | *.65* |
| *Nos. 43-44 (2)* | 7.75 | 6.10 |
| *Nos. 306-307 (2)* | .80 | .80 |
| *Nos. 48-49 (2)* | 2.00 | 1.00 |
| *Nos. 186-187 (2)* | .70 | .70 |
| *Nos. 304-305 (2)* | .75 | .75 |
| *Nos. 352-353 (2)* | .65 | .65 |
| *Nos. 223-224 (2)* | 1.00 | 1.15 |
| *Nos. 328-329 (2)* | .70 | .70 |
| *Nos. 292-293 (2)* | .50 | .50 |
| *Nos. 206-207 (2)* | .50 | .50 |
| *Nos. 466-467 (2)* | .70 | .70 |
| *Nos. 271-272 (2)* | 1.70 | 1.50 |
| *Nos. 286-287 (2)* | .55 | .55 |
| *Nos. 169-170 (2)* | .50 | .50 |
| *Nos. 188-189 (2)* | 1.05 | 1.05 |
| *Nos. 127-128 (2)* | .90 | .85 |
| *Nos. 271-272 (2)* | .70 | 1.20 |
| *Nos. 257-258 (2)* | .65 | .50 |
| *Nos. 328-329 (2)* | .75 | .75 |
| *Nos. 344-345 (2)* | .55 | .55 |
| *Nos. 309-310 (2)* | .95 | .95 |
| *Nos. 248-249 (2)* | .50 | .50 |
| *Nos. 35-36 (2)* | 1.40 | 1.40 |
| *Nos. 178-179 (2)* | .70 | .70 |
| *Nos. 257-258 (2)* | .50 | .50 |
| *Nos. 241-242 (2)* | .50 | .50 |
| *Set total (62) Stamps* | 31.55 | 29.50 |

### Princess Anne's Wedding

Princess Anne and Mark Phillips — CD325

Wedding of Princess Anne and Mark Phillips, Nov. 14, 1973.

**1973**

Anguilla 179-180
Ascension 177-178
Belize 325-326
Bermuda 302-303
British Antarctic Territory 60-61
Cayman Islands 320-321
Falkland Islands 225-226
Gibraltar 305-306
Gilbert & Ellice Islands 216-217
Hong Kong 289-290
Montserrat 300-301
Pitcairn Islands 135-136
St. Helena 277-278
St. Kitts-Nevis 274-275
St. Lucia 349-350
St. Vincent 358-359
St. Vincent Grenadines 1-2
Seychelles 311-312
Solomon Islands 259-260
South Georgia 37-38
Tristan da Cunha 189-190
Turks & Caicos Islands 286-287
Virgin Islands 260-261

| | | |
|---|---|---|
| *Nos. 179-180 (2)* | .55 | .55 |
| *Nos. 177-178 (2)* | .60 | .60 |
| *Nos. 325-326 (2)* | .50 | .50 |
| *Nos. 302-303 (2)* | .50 | .50 |
| *Nos. 60-61 (2)* | 1.10 | 1.10 |
| *Nos. 320-321 (2)* | .50 | .50 |
| *Nos. 225-226 (2)* | .70 | .60 |
| *Nos. 305-306 (2)* | .55 | .55 |
| *Nos. 216-217 (2)* | .50 | .50 |
| *Nos. 289-290 (2)* | 2.65 | 2.00 |
| *Nos. 300-301 (2)* | .65 | .65 |
| *Nos. 135-136 (2)* | .70 | .60 |
| *Nos. 277-278 (2)* | .50 | .50 |
| *Nos. 274-275 (2)* | .50 | .50 |
| *Nos. 349-350 (2)* | .50 | .50 |
| *Nos. 358-359 (2)* | .50 | .50 |
| *Nos. 1-2 (2)* | .50 | .50 |
| *Nos. 311-312 (2)* | .70 | .70 |
| *Nos. 259-260 (2)* | .70 | .70 |
| *Nos. 37-38 (2)* | .75 | .75 |
| *Nos. 189-190 (2)* | .50 | .50 |
| *Nos. 286-287 (2)* | .50 | .50 |
| *Nos. 260-261 (2)* | .50 | .50 |
| *Set total (46) Stamps* | 15.65 | 14.80 |

### Elizabeth II Coronation Anniv.

CD326

CD327

CD328

Designs: Royal and local beasts in heraldic form and simulated stonework. Portrait of Elizabeth II by Peter Grugeon. 25th anniversary of coronation of Queen Elizabeth II.

**1978**

Ascension 229
Barbados 474
Belize 397
British Antarctic Territory 71
Cayman Islands 404
Christmas Island 87
Falkland Islands 275
Fiji 384
Gambia 380
Gilbert Islands 312
Mauritius 464
New Hebrides, British 258
New Hebrides, French 278
St. Helena 317
St. Kitts-Nevis 354
Samoa 472
Solomon Islands 368
South Georgia 51
Swaziland 302
Tristan da Cunha 238
Virgin Islands 337

| | | |
|---|---|---|
| *No. 229 (1)* | 2.00 | 2.00 |
| *No. 474 (1)* | 1.35 | 1.35 |
| *No. 397 (1)* | 1.40 | 1.75 |
| *No. 71 (1)* | 6.00 | 6.00 |
| *No. 404 (1)* | 2.00 | 2.00 |
| *No. 87 (1)* | 3.50 | *4.00* |
| *No. 275 (1)* | 4.00 | 5.50 |
| *No. 384 (1)* | 1.75 | 1.75 |
| *No. 380 (1)* | 1.50 | 1.50 |
| *No. 312 (1)* | 1.25 | 1.25 |
| *No. 464 (1)* | 2.75 | 2.75 |
| *No. 258 (1)* | 1.75 | 1.75 |
| *No. 278 (1)* | 3.50 | 3.50 |
| *No. 317 (1)* | 1.75 | 1.75 |
| *No. 354 (1)* | 1.00 | 1.00 |
| *No. 472 (1)* | 2.00 | 2.00 |
| *No. 368 (1)* | 2.50 | 2.50 |
| *No. 51 (1)* | 3.00 | 3.00 |
| *No. 302 (1)* | 1.75 | 1.75 |
| *No. 238 (1)* | 1.50 | 1.50 |
| *No. 337 (1)* | 1.80 | 1.80 |
| *Set total (21) Stamps* | 48.05 | 50.40 |

### Queen Mother Elizabeth's 80th Birthday

CD330

Designs: Photographs of Queen Mother Elizabeth. Falkland Islands issued in sheets of 50; others in sheets of 9.

**1980**

Ascension 261
Bermuda 401
Cayman Islands 443
Falkland Islands 305
Gambia 412
Gibraltar 393
Hong Kong 364
Pitcairn Islands 193
St. Helena 341
Samoa 532
Solomon Islands 426
Tristan da Cunha 277

| | | |
|---|---|---|
| *No. 261 (1)* | .40 | .40 |
| *No. 401 (1)* | .45 | .75 |
| *No. 443 (1)* | .40 | .40 |
| *No. 305 (1)* | .40 | .40 |
| *No. 412 (1)* | .40 | .50 |
| *No. 393 (1)* | .35 | .35 |
| *No. 364 (1)* | 1.10 | 1.25 |
| *No. 193 (1)* | .60 | .60 |
| *No. 341 (1)* | .50 | .50 |
| *No. 532 (1)* | .55 | .55 |
| *No. 426 (1)* | .50 | .50 |
| *No. 277 (1)* | .45 | .45 |
| *Set total (12) Stamps* | 6.10 | 6.65 |

### Royal Wedding, 1981

Prince Charles and Lady Diana — CD331

CD331a

Wedding of Charles, Prince of Wales, and Lady Diana Spencer, St. Paul's Cathedral, London, July 29, 1981.

**1981**

Antigua 623-627
Ascension 294-296
Barbados 547-549
Barbuda 497-501
Bermuda 412-414
Brunei 268-270
Cayman Islands 471-473
Dominica 701-705
Falkland Islands 324-326
Falkland Islands Dep. 1L59-1L61
Fiji 442-444
Gambia 426-428
Ghana 759-764
Grenada 1051-1055
Grenada Grenadines 440-443
Hong Kong 373-375
Jamaica 500-503
Lesotho 335-337
Maldive Islands 906-909
Mauritius 520-522
Norfolk Island 280-282
Pitcairn Islands 206-208
St. Helena 353-355
St. Lucia 543-549
Samoa 558-560
Sierra Leone 509-518
Solomon Islands 450-452
Swaziland 382-384
Tristan da Cunha 294-296
Turks & Caicos Islands 486-489
Caicos Island 8-11
Uganda 314-317
Vanuatu 308-310
Virgin Islands 406-408

| | | |
|---|---|---|
| *Nos. 623-627 (5)* | 6.55 | 2.55 |
| *Nos. 294-296 (3)* | 1.00 | 1.00 |
| *Nos. 547-549 (3)* | .90 | .90 |
| *Nos. 497-501 (5)* | 10.95 | 10.95 |
| *Nos. 412-414 (3)* | 2.00 | 2.00 |
| *Nos. 268-270 (3)* | 2.15 | *4.50* |
| *Nos. 471-473 (3)* | 1.20 | 1.30 |
| *Nos. 701-705 (5)* | 8.35 | 2.35 |
| *Nos. 324-326 (3)* | 1.65 | 1.70 |
| *Nos. 1L59-1L61 (3)* | 1.45 | 1.45 |
| *Nos. 442-444 (3)* | 1.35 | 1.35 |
| *Nos. 426-428 (3)* | .80 | .80 |
| *Nos. 759-764 (9)* | 6.20 | 6.20 |
| *Nos. 1051-1055 (5)* | 9.85 | 1.85 |
| *Nos. 440-443 (4)* | 2.35 | 2.35 |
| *Nos. 373-375 (3)* | 3.05 | 2.85 |
| *Nos. 500-503 (4)* | 1.45 | 1.35 |
| *Nos. 335-337 (3)* | .90 | .90 |
| *Nos. 906-909 (4)* | 1.55 | 1.55 |
| *Nos. 520-522 (3)* | 2.75 | 2.75 |
| *Nos. 280-282 (3)* | 1.35 | 1.35 |
| *Nos. 206-208 (3)* | 1.10 | 1.10 |
| *Nos. 353-355 (3)* | .85 | .85 |
| *Nos. 543-549 (5)* | 8.50 | 8.50 |
| *Nos. 558-560 (3)* | .85 | .85 |
| *Nos. 509-518 (10)* | 15.50 | 15.50 |
| *Nos. 450-452 (3)* | 1.25 | 1.25 |
| *Nos. 382-384 (3)* | 1.30 | 1.25 |
| *Nos. 294-296 (3)* | .90 | .90 |
| *Nos. 486-489 (4)* | 2.20 | 2.20 |
| *Nos. 8-11 (4)* | 5.00 | 5.00 |
| *Nos. 314-317 (4)* | 3.30 | 3.00 |
| *Nos. 308-310 (3)* | 1.15 | 1.15 |
| *Nos. 406-408 (3)* | 1.10 | 1.10 |
| *Set total (131) Stamps* | 110.80 | 94.65 |

### Princess Diana

CD332

CD333

Designs: Photographs and portrait of Princess Diana, wedding or honeymoon photographs, royal residences, arms of issuing country. Portrait photograph by Clive Friend. Souvenir sheet margins show family tree, various people related to the princess. 21st birthday of Princess Diana of Wales, July 1.

**1982**

Antigua 663-666
Ascension 313-316
Bahamas 510-513
Barbados 585-588
Barbuda 544-547
British Antarctic Territory 92-95
Cayman Islands 486-489
Dominica 773-776
Falkland Islands 348-351
Falkland Islands Dep. 1L72-1L75
Fiji 470-473
Gambia 447-450
Grenada 1101A-1105
Grenada Grenadines 485-491
Lesotho 372-375
Maldive Islands 952-955
Mauritius 548-551
Pitcairn Islands 213-216
St. Helena 372-375
St. Lucia 591-594
Sierra Leone 531-534
Solomon Islands 471-474
Swaziland 406-409
Tristan da Cunha 310-313
Turks and Caicos Islands 531-534
Virgin Islands 430-433

| | | |
|---|---|---|
| *Nos. 663-666 (4)* | 8.25 | 7.35 |
| *Nos. 313-316 (4)* | 3.50 | 3.50 |
| *Nos. 510-513 (4)* | 6.00 | 3.85 |
| *Nos. 585-588 (4)* | 3.40 | 3.25 |
| *Nos. 544-547 (4)* | 9.75 | 7.70 |
| *Nos. 92-95 (4)* | 5.30 | 3.45 |
| *Nos. 486-489 (4)* | *4.75* | *2.70* |
| *Nos. 773-776 (4)* | 7.05 | 7.05 |
| *Nos. 348-351 (4)* | 2.95 | 2.95 |
| *Nos. 1L72-1L75 (4)* | 2.50 | 2.60 |
| *Nos. 470-473 (4)* | 3.25 | 2.95 |
| *Nos. 447-450 (4)* | 2.85 | 2.85 |
| *Nos. 1101A-1105 (7)* | 16.05 | 15.55 |

*Nos. 485-491 (7)* 17.65 17.65
*Nos. 372-375 (4)* 4.00 4.00
*Nos. 952-955 (4)* 5.50 3.90
*Nos. 548-551 (4)* 5.50 5.50
*Nos. 213-216 (4)* 2.15 2.15
*Nos. 372-375 (4)* 2.95 2.95
*Nos. 591-594 (4)* 9.90 9.90
*Nos. 531-534 (4)* 7.20 7.20
*Nos. 471-474 (4)* 2.90 2.90
*Nos. 406-409 (4)* 3.85 2.25
*Nos. 310-313 (4)* 3.65 1.45
*Nos. 486-489 (4)* 2.20 2.20
*Nos. 430-433 (4)* 3.00 3.00
*Set total (110) Stamps* 146.05 130.80

**250th anniv. of first edition of Lloyd's List (shipping news publication) & of Lloyd's marine insurance.**

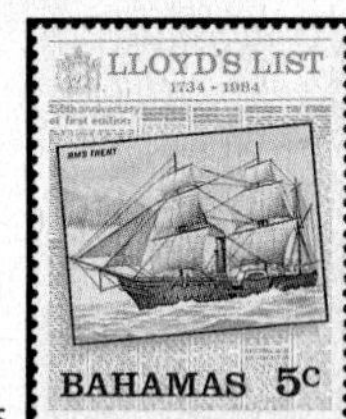

CD335

Designs: First page of early edition of the list; historical ships, modern transportation or harbor scenes.

**1984**

Ascension ....................351-354
Bahamas ....................555-558
Barbados ....................627-630
Cayes of Belize ....................10-13
Cayman Islands ....................522-526
Falkland Islands ....................404-407
Fiji ....................509-512
Gambia ....................519-522
Mauritius ....................587-590
Nauru ....................280-283
St. Helena ....................412-415
Samoa ....................624-627
Seychelles ....................538-541
Solomon Islands ....................521-524
Vanuatu ....................368-371
Virgin Islands ....................466-469

*Nos. 351-354 (4)* 2.90 2.55
*Nos. 555-558 (4)* 4.15 2.95
*Nos. 627-630 (4)* 6.10 5.15
*Nos. 10-13 (4)* 2.65 2.65
*Nos. 522-526 (5)* 9.30 8.45
*Nos. 404-407 (4)* 3.50 3.65
*Nos. 509-512 (4)* 5.30 4.90
*Nos. 519-522 (4)* 4.20 4.30
*Nos. 587-590 (4)* 8.95 8.95
*Nos. 280-283 (4)* 2.40 2.35
*Nos. 412-415 (4)* 2.40 2.40
*Nos. 624-627 (4)* 2.75 2.55
*Nos. 538-541 (4)* 5.25 5.25
*Nos. 521-524 (4)* 4.65 3.95
*Nos. 368-371 (4)* 2.40 2.40
*Nos. 466-469 (4)* 4.25 4.25
*Set total (65) Stamps* 71.15 66.70

**Queen Mother 85th Birthday**

CD336

Designs: Photographs tracing the life of the Queen Mother, Elizabeth. The high value in each set pictures the same photograph taken of the Queen Mother holding the infant Prince Henry.

**1985**

Ascension ....................372-376
Bahamas ....................580-584
Barbados ....................660-664
Bermuda ....................469-473
Falkland Islands ....................420-424
Falkland Islands Dep ....................1L92-1L96
Fiji ....................531-535
Hong Kong ....................447-450
Jamaica ....................599-603
Mauritius ....................604-608
Norfolk Island ....................364-368
Pitcairn Islands ....................253-257
St. Helena ....................428-432
Samoa ....................649-653
Seychelles ....................567-571
Zil Elwannyen Sesel ....................101-105
Solomon Islands ....................543-547
Swaziland ....................476-480
Tristan da Cunha ....................372-376
Vanuatu ....................392-396

*Nos. 372-376 (5)* 4.65 4.65
*Nos. 580-584 (5)* 7.70 6.45
*Nos. 660-664 (5)* 8.00 6.70
*Nos. 469-473 (5)* 9.40 9.40
*Nos. 420-424 (5)* 7.35 6.65
*Nos. 1L92-1L96 (5)* 8.00 8.00
*Nos. 531-535 (5)* 6.15 6.15
*Nos. 447-450 (4)* 9.50 8.50
*Nos. 599-603 (5)* 6.15 7.00
*Nos. 604-608 (5)* 11.80 11.80
*Nos. 364-368 (5)* 5.05 5.05
*Nos. 253-257 (5)* 5.25 5.95
*Nos. 428-432 (5)* 5.25 5.25
*Nos. 649-653 (5)* 8.65 7.80
*Nos. 567-571 (5)* 8.70 8.70
*Nos. 101-105 (5)* 7.15 7.15
*Nos. 543-547 (5)* 3.95 3.95
*Nos. 476-480 (5)* 8.00 7.50
*Nos. 372-376 (5)* 5.40 5.40
*Nos. 392-396 (5)* 5.25 5.25
*Set total (99) Stamps* 141.35 137.30

**Queen Elizabeth II, 60th Birthday**

CD337

**1986, April 21**

Ascension ....................389-393
Bahamas ....................592-596
Barbados ....................675-679
Bermuda ....................499-503
Cayman Islands ....................555-559
Falkland Islands ....................441-445
Fiji ....................544-548
Hong Kong ....................465-469
Jamaica ....................620-624
Kiribati ....................470-474
Mauritius ....................629-633
Papua New Guinea ....................640-644
Pitcairn Islands ....................270-274
St. Helena ....................451-455
Samoa ....................670-674
Seychelles ....................592-596
Zil Elwannyen Sesel ....................114-118
Solomon Islands ....................562-566
South Georgia ....................101-105
Swaziland ....................490-494
Tristan da Cunha ....................388-392
Vanuatu ....................414-418
Zambia ....................343-347

*Nos. 389-393 (5)* 2.80 3.30
*Nos. 592-596 (5)* 2.75 *3.70*
*Nos. 675-679 (5)* 3.35 3.20
*Nos. 499-503 (5)* 4.65 *5.15*
*Nos. 555-559 (5)* 4.55 5.60
*Nos. 441-445 (5)* 3.95 *4.95*
*Nos. 544-548 (5)* 3.00 3.00
*Nos. 465-469 (5)* 8.75 6.75
*Nos. 620-624 (5)* 2.75 2.70
*Nos. 470-474 (5)* 2.10 2.10
*Nos. 629-633 (5)* 3.70 3.70
*Nos. 640-644 (5)* 4.50 4.50
*Nos. 270-274 (5)* 2.70 2.70
*Nos. 451-455 (5)* 3.05 3.05
*Nos. 670-674 (5)* 2.90 2.90
*Nos. 592-596 (5)* 2.70 2.70
*Nos. 114-118 (5)* 2.25 2.25
*Nos. 562-566 (5)* 2.90 2.90
*Nos. 101-105 (5)* 3.30 3.65
*Nos. 490-494 (5)* 2.30 2.30
*Nos. 388-392 (5)* 3.00 3.00
*Nos. 414-418 (5)* 3.10 3.10
*Nos. 343-347 (5)* 1.75 1.75
*Set total (115) Stamps* 76.80 78.95

**Royal Wedding**

Marriage of Prince Andrew and Sarah Ferguson CD338

**1986, July 23**

Ascension ....................399-400
Bahamas ....................602-603
Barbados ....................687-688
Cayman Islands ....................560-561
Jamaica ....................629-630
Pitcairn Islands ....................275-276
St. Helena ....................460-461
St. Kitts ....................181-182
Seychelles ....................602-603
Zil Elwannyen Sesel ....................119-120
Solomon Islands ....................567-568
Tristan da Cunha ....................397-398
Zambia ....................348-349

*Nos. 399-400 (2)* 1.60 1.60
*Nos. 602-603 (2)* 2.75 2.75
*Nos. 687-688 (2)* 2.25 1.25
*Nos. 560-561 (2)* 1.70 *2.35*
*Nos. 629-630 (2)* 1.35 1.35
*Nos. 275-276 (2)* 2.40 2.40
*Nos. 460-461 (2)* 1.05 1.05
*Nos. 181-182 (2)* 1.50 2.25
*Nos. 602-603 (2)* 2.50 2.50
*Nos. 119-120 (2)* 2.30 2.30
*Nos. 567-568 (2)* 1.00 1.00
*Nos. 397-398 (2)* 1.40 1.40
*Nos. 348-349 (2)* 1.10 1.30
*Set total (26) Stamps* 22.90 23.50

**Queen Elizabeth II, 60th Birthday**

Queen Elizabeth II & Prince Philip, 1947 Wedding Portrait — CD339

Designs: Photographs tracing the life of Queen Elizabeth II.

**1986**

Anguilla ....................674-677
Antigua ....................925-928
Barbuda ....................783-786
Dominica ....................950-953
Gambia ....................611-614
Grenada ....................1371-1374
Grenada Grenadines ....................749-752
Lesotho ....................531-534
Maldive Islands ....................1172-1175
Sierra Leone ....................760-763
Uganda ....................495-498

*Nos. 674-677 (4)* 8.00 8.00
*Nos. 925-928 (4)* 5.50 6.20
*Nos. 783-786 (4)* 23.15 23.15
*Nos. 950-953 (4)* 7.25 7.25
*Nos. 611-614 (4)* 8.25 7.90
*Nos. 1371-1374 (4)* 6.80 6.80
*Nos. 749-752 (4)* 6.75 6.75
*Nos. 531-534 (4)* 5.25 5.25
*Nos. 1172-1175 (4)* 6.25 6.25
*Nos. 760-763 (4)* 6.30 6.30
*Nos. 495-498 (4)* 8.50 8.50
*Set total (44) Stamps* 92.00 92.35

**Royal Wedding, 1986**

CD340

Designs: Photographs of Prince Andrew and Sarah Ferguson during courtship, engagement and marriage.

**1986**

Antigua ....................939-942
Barbuda ....................809-812
Dominica ....................970-973
Gambia ....................635-638
Grenada ....................1385-1388
Grenada Grenadines ....................758-761
Lesotho ....................545-548
Maldive Islands ....................1181-1184
Sierra Leone ....................769-772
Uganda ....................510-513

*Nos. 939-942 (4)* 7.00 *8.75*
*Nos. 809-812 (4)* 14.55 14.55
*Nos. 970-973 (4)* 7.25 7.25
*Nos. 635-638 (4)* 8.55 8.55
*Nos. 1385-1388 (4)* 8.30 8.30
*Nos. 758-761 (4)* 9.00 9.00
*Nos. 545-548 (4)* 7.45 7.45
*Nos. 1181-1184 (4)* 8.45 8.45
*Nos. 769-772 (4)* 5.35 5.35
*Nos. 510-513 (4)* 9.25 10.00
*Set total (40) Stamps* 85.15 87.65

**Lloyds of London, 300th Anniv.**

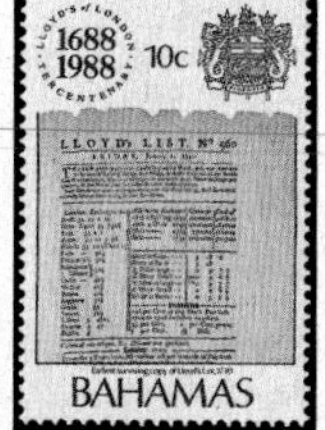

CD341

Designs: 17th century aspects of Lloyds, representations of each country's individual connections with Lloyds and publicized disasters insured by the organization.

**1986**

Ascension ....................454-457
Bahamas ....................655-658
Barbados ....................731-734
Bermuda ....................541-544
Falkland Islands ....................481-484
Liberia ....................1101-1104
Malawi ....................534-537
Nevis ....................571-574
St. Helena ....................501-504
St. Lucia ....................923-926
Seychelles ....................649-652
Zil Elwannyen Sesel ....................146-149
Solomon Islands ....................627-630
South Georgia ....................131-134
Trinidad & Tobago ....................484-487
Tristan da Cunha ....................439-442
Vanuatu ....................485-488

*Nos. 454-457 (4)* 5.00 5.00
*Nos. 655-658 (4)* 8.90 4.95
*Nos. 731-734 (4)* 12.50 8.35
*Nos. 541-544 (4)* 8.00 *6.60*
*Nos. 481-484 (4)* 5.45 3.85
*Nos. 1101-1104 (4)* 4.25 4.25
*Nos. 534-537 (4)* 11.00 7.85
*Nos. 571-574 (4)* 8.35 8.35
*Nos. 501-504 (4)* 8.70 7.15
*Nos. 923-926 (4)* 9.40 9.40
*Nos. 649-652 (4)* 13.10 13.10
*Nos. 146-149 (4)* 11.25 11.25
*Nos. 627-630 (4)* 7.00 4.45
*Nos. 131-134 (4)* 6.30 3.70
*Nos. 484-487 (4)* 10.25 6.35
*Nos. 439-442 (4)* 7.60 7.60
*Nos. 485-488 (4)* 5.90 5.90
*Set total (68) Stamps* 142.95 118.10

**Moon Landing, 20th Anniv.**

CD342

Designs: Equipment, crew photographs, spacecraft, official emblems and report profiles created for the Apollo Missions. Two stamps in each set are square in format rather than like the stamp shown; see individual country listings for more information.

**1989**

Ascension ....................468-472
Bahamas ....................674-678
Belize ....................916-920
Kiribati ....................517-521
Liberia ....................1125-1129
Nevis ....................586-590
St. Kitts ....................248-252
Samoa ....................760-764
Seychelles ....................676-680
Zil Elwannyen Sesel ....................154-158
Solomon Islands ....................643-647
Vanuatu ....................507-511

*Nos. 468-472 (5)* 9.40 8.60
*Nos. 674-678 (5)* 23.00 19.70
*Nos. 916-920 (5)* 22.85 18.10
*Nos. 517-521 (5)* 12.50 12.50
*Nos. 1125-1129 (5)* 8.50 8.50
*Nos. 586-590 (5)* 7.50 7.50

| | | |
|---|---|---|
| *Nos. 248-252 (5)* | 8.00 | 8.25 |
| *Nos. 760-764 (5)* | 9.60 | 9.05 |
| *Nos. 676-680 (5)* | 16.05 | 16.05 |
| *Nos. 154-158 (5)* | 26.85 | 26.85 |
| *Nos. 643-647 (5)* | 9.00 | 6.75 |
| *Nos. 507-511 (5)* | 9.90 | 9.90 |
| *Set total (60) Stamps* | 163.15 | 151.75 |

### Queen Mother, 90th Birthday

CD343

CD344

Designs: Portraits of Queen Elizabeth, the Queen Mother. See individual country listings for more information.

**1990**

Ascension ....................491-492
Bahamas ....................698-699
Barbados ....................782-783
British Antarctic Territory ..........170-171
British Indian Ocean Territory ........106-107
Cayman Islands ....................622-623
Falkland Islands ....................524-525
Kenya ....................527-528
Kiribati ....................555-556
Liberia ....................1145-1146
Pitcairn Islands ....................336-337
St. Helena ....................532-533
St. Lucia ....................969-970
Seychelles ....................710-711
Zil Elwannyen Sesel ....................171-172
Solomon Islands ....................671-672
South Georgia ....................143-144
Swaziland ....................565-566
Tristan da Cunha ....................480-481

| | | |
|---|---|---|
| *Nos. 491-492 (2)* | 4.75 | 4.75 |
| *Nos. 698-699 (2)* | 5.25 | 5.25 |
| *Nos. 782-783 (2)* | 4.00 | 3.70 |
| *Nos. 170-171 (2)* | 6.75 | 6.75 |
| *Nos. 106-107 (2)* | 18.00 | 18.50 |
| *Nos. 622-623 (2)* | 4.00 | *5.50* |
| *Nos. 524-525 (2)* | 4.75 | 4.75 |
| *Nos. 527-528 (2)* | 7.00 | 7.00 |
| *Nos. 555-556 (2)* | 4.75 | 4.75 |
| *Nos. 1145-1146 (2)* | 3.25 | 3.25 |
| *Nos. 336-337 (2)* | 4.25 | 4.25 |
| *Nos. 532-533 (2)* | 5.25 | 5.25 |
| *Nos. 969-970 (2)* | 5.25 | 5.25 |
| *Nos. 710-711 (2)* | 6.60 | 6.60 |
| *Nos. 171-172 (2)* | 8.25 | 8.25 |
| *Nos. 671-672 (2)* | 5.00 | *5.30* |
| *Nos. 143-144 (2)* | 5.50 | 6.50 |
| *Nos. 565-566 (2)* | 4.35 | 4.35 |
| *Nos. 480-481 (2)* | 5.60 | 5.60 |
| *Set total (38) Stamps* | 112.55 | 115.55 |

### Queen Elizabeth II, 65th Birthday, and Prince Philip, 70th Birthday

CD345

CD346

Designs: Portraits of Queen Elizabeth II and Prince Philip differ for each country. Printed in sheets of 10 + 5 labels (3 different) between. Stamps alternate, producing 5 different triptychs.

**1991**

Ascension ....................506a
Bahamas ....................731a
Belize ....................970a
Bermuda ....................618a
Kiribati ....................572a
Mauritius ....................734a
Pitcairn Islands ....................349a
St. Helena ....................555a
St. Kitts ....................319a
Samoa ....................791a
Seychelles ....................724a
Zil Elwannyen Sesel ....................178a
Solomon Islands ....................689a
South Georgia ....................150a
Swaziland ....................587a
Vanuatu ....................541a

| | | |
|---|---|---|
| *No. 506a (1)* | 3.50 | 3.75 |
| *No. 731a (1)* | 4.00 | 4.00 |
| *No. 970a (1)* | 3.75 | 3.75 |
| *No. 618a (1)* | 3.50 | *4.00* |
| *No. 572a (1)* | 4.00 | 4.00 |
| *No. 734a (1)* | 3.75 | 3.75 |
| *No. 349a (1)* | 3.25 | 3.25 |
| *No. 555a (1)* | 2.75 | 2.75 |
| *No. 319a (1)* | 3.00 | 3.00 |
| *No. 791a (1)* | 4.25 | 4.25 |
| *No. 724a (1)* | 5.00 | 5.00 |
| *No. 178a (1)* | 6.50 | 6.50 |
| *No. 689a (1)* | 3.75 | 3.75 |
| *No. 150a (1)* | 4.75 | 7.00 |
| *No. 587a (1)* | 4.25 | 4.25 |
| *No. 541a (1)* | 2.50 | 2.50 |
| *Set total (16) Stamps* | 62.50 | 65.50 |

### Royal Family Birthday, Anniversary

CD347

Queen Elizabeth II, 65th birthday, Charles and Diana, 10th wedding anniversary: Various photographs of Queen Elizabeth II, Prince Philip, Prince Charles, Princess Diana and their sons William and Henry.

**1991**

Antigua ....................1446-1455
Barbuda ....................1229-1238
Dominica ....................1328-1337
Gambia ....................1080-1089
Grenada ....................2006-2015
Grenada Grenadines ....................1331-1340
Guyana ....................2440-2451
Lesotho ....................871-875
Maldive Islands ....................1533-1542
Nevis ....................666-675
St. Vincent ....................1485-1494
St. Vincent Grenadines ....................769-778
Sierra Leone ....................1387-1396
Turks & Caicos Islands ....................913-922
Uganda ....................918-927

| | | |
|---|---|---|
| *Nos. 1446-1455 (10)* | 21.70 | 20.05 |
| *Nos. 1229-1238 (10)* | 125.00 | 119.50 |
| *Nos. 1328-1337 (10)* | 30.20 | 30.20 |
| *Nos. 1080-1089 (10)* | 24.65 | 24.40 |
| *Nos. 2006-2015 (10)* | 25.45 | 22.10 |
| *Nos. 1331-1340 (10)* | 23.85 | 23.35 |
| *Nos. 2440-2451 (12)* | 21.40 | 21.15 |
| *Nos. 871-875 (5)* | 13.55 | 13.55 |
| *Nos. 1533-1542 (10)* | 28.10 | 28.10 |
| *Nos. 666-675 (10)* | 25.65 | 25.65 |
| *Nos. 1485-1494 (10)* | 26.75 | 25.90 |
| *Nos. 769-778 (10)* | 25.40 | 25.40 |
| *Nos. 1387-1396 (10)* | 26.55 | 26.55 |
| *Nos. 913-922 (10)* | 27.50 | 25.30 |
| *Nos. 918-927 (10)* | 26.60 | 26.60 |
| *Set total (147) Stamps* | 472.35 | 457.80 |

### Queen Elizabeth II's Accession to the Throne, 40th Anniv.

CD348

Various photographs of Queen Elizabeth II with local Scenes.

**1992**

Antigua ....................1513-1518
Barbuda ....................1306-1311
Dominica ....................1414-1419
Gambia ....................1172-1177
Grenada ....................2047-2052
Grenada Grenadines ....................1368-1373
Lesotho ....................881-885
Maldive Islands ....................1637-1642
Nevis ....................702-707
St. Vincent ....................1582-1587
St. Vincent Grenadines ....................829-834
Sierra Leone ....................1482-1487
Turks and Caicos Islands ....................978-987
Uganda ....................990-995
Virgin Islands ....................742-746

| | | |
|---|---|---|
| *Nos. 1513-1518 (6)* | 15.00 | *15.10* |
| *Nos. 1306-1311 (6)* | 125.25 | 83.65 |
| *Nos. 1414-1419 (6)* | 12.50 | 12.50 |
| *Nos. 1172-1177 (6)* | 16.60 | 16.35 |
| *Nos. 2047-2052 (6)* | 15.95 | 15.95 |
| *Nos. 1368-1373 (6)* | 17.00 | 15.35 |
| *Nos. 881-885 (5)* | 11.90 | 11.90 |
| *Nos. 1637-1642 (6)* | 17.55 | 17.55 |
| *Nos. 702-707 (6)* | 13.80 | 13.80 |
| *Nos. 1582-1587 (6)* | 14.40 | 14.40 |
| *Nos. 829-834 (6)* | 19.65 | 19.65 |
| *Nos. 1482-1487 (6)* | 22.50 | 22.50 |
| *Nos. 913-922 (10)* | 27.50 | 25.30 |
| *Nos. 990-995 (6)* | 19.50 | 19.50 |
| *Nos. 742-746 (5)* | 15.50 | 15.50 |
| *Set total (92) Stamps* | 364.60 | 319.00 |

CD349

**1992**

Ascension ....................531-535
Bahamas ....................744-748
Bermuda ....................623-627
British Indian Ocean Territory ........119-123
Cayman Islands ....................648-652
Falkland Islands ....................549-553
Gibraltar ....................605-609
Hong Kong ....................619-623
Kenya ....................563-567
Kiribati ....................582-586
Pitcairn Islands ....................362-366
St. Helena ....................570-574
St. Kitts ....................332-336
Samoa ....................805-809
Seychelles ....................734-738
Zil Elwannyen Sesel ....................183-187
Solomon Islands ....................708-712
South Georgia ....................157-161
Tristan da Cunha ....................508-512
Vanuatu ....................555-559
Zambia ....................561-565

| | | |
|---|---|---|
| *Nos. 531-535 (5)* | 6.10 | 6.10 |
| *Nos. 744-748 (5)* | 6.90 | 4.70 |
| *Nos. 623-627 (5)* | 7.40 | *7.55* |
| *Nos. 119-123 (5)* | 22.75 | 19.25 |
| *Nos. 648-652 (5)* | 7.60 | 6.60 |
| *Nos. 549-553 (5)* | 5.95 | 5.90 |
| *Nos. 605-609 (5)* | 5.15 | *5.50* |
| *Nos. 619-623 (5)* | 5.10 | 5.25 |
| *Nos. 563-567 (5)* | 9.10 | 9.10 |
| *Nos. 582-586 (5)* | 3.85 | 3.85 |
| *Nos. 362-366 (5)* | 5.35 | 5.35 |
| *Nos. 570-574 (5)* | 5.70 | 5.70 |
| *Nos. 332-336 (5)* | 6.60 | 5.50 |
| *Nos. 805-809 (5)* | 8.10 | 6.15 |
| *Nos. 734-738 (5)* | 10.80 | 10.80 |
| *Nos. 183-187 (5)* | 9.40 | 9.40 |
| *Nos. 708-712 (5)* | 5.00 | 5.30 |
| *Nos. 157-161 (5)* | 5.60 | 5.90 |
| *Nos. 508-512 (5)* | 8.75 | 8.30 |
| *Nos. 555-559 (5)* | 3.65 | 3.65 |
| *Nos. 561-565 (5)* | 5.60 | 5.60 |
| *Set total (105) Stamps* | 154.45 | 145.45 |

### Royal Air Force, 75th Anniversary

CD350

**1993**

Ascension ....................557-561
Bahamas ....................771-775
Barbados ....................842-846
Belize ....................1003-1008
Bermuda ....................648-651
British Indian Ocean Territory ........136-140
Falkland Is. ....................573-577
Fiji ....................687-691
Montserrat ....................830-834
St. Kitts ....................351-355

| | | |
|---|---|---|
| *Nos. 557-561 (5)* | 15.60 | 14.60 |
| *Nos. 771-775 (5)* | 24.65 | 21.45 |
| *Nos. 842-846 (5)* | 13.65 | 12.35 |
| *Nos. 1003-1008 (6)* | 16.55 | 16.50 |
| *Nos. 648-651 (4)* | 9.65 | *10.45* |
| *Nos. 136-140 (5)* | 16.10 | 16.10 |
| *Nos. 573-577 (5)* | 10.85 | 10.85 |
| *Nos. 687-691 (5)* | 17.75 | 17.40 |
| *Nos. 830-834 (5)* | 14.35 | 14.35 |
| *Nos. 351-355 (5)* | 22.80 | 23.55 |
| *Set total (50) Stamps* | 161.95 | 157.60 |

### Royal Air Force, 80th Anniv.

Design CD350 Re-inscribed

**1998**

Ascension ....................697-701
Bahamas ....................907-911
British Indian Ocean Terr ....................198-202
Cayman Islands ....................754-758
Fiji ....................814-818
Gibraltar ....................755-759
Samoa ....................957-961
Turks & Caicos Islands ....................1258-1265
Tuvalu ....................763-767
Virgin Islands ....................879-883

| | | |
|---|---|---|
| *Nos. 697-701 (5)* | 16.10 | 16.10 |
| *Nos. 907-911 (5)* | 13.60 | 12.65 |
| *Nos. 136-140 (5)* | 16.10 | 16.10 |
| *Nos. 754-758 (5)* | 15.25 | 15.25 |
| *Nos. 814-818 (5)* | 14.00 | 12.75 |
| *Nos. 755-759 (5)* | 9.70 | 9.70 |
| *Nos. 957-961 (5)* | 16.70 | 15.90 |
| *Nos. 1258-1265 (2)* | 27.50 | 27.50 |
| *Nos. 763-767 (5)* | 9.75 | 9.75 |
| *Nos. 879-883 (5)* | 15.00 | 15.00 |
| *Set total (47) Stamps* | 153.70 | 150.70 |

### End of World War II, 50th Anniv.

CD351

CD352

**1995**

Ascension ....................613-617
Bahamas ....................824-828
Barbados ....................891-895
Belize ....................1047-1050
British Indian Ocean Territory ........163-167
Cayman Islands ....................704-708
Falkland Islands ....................634-638
Fiji ....................720-724
Kiribati ....................662-668
Liberia ....................1175-1179
Mauritius ....................803-805
St. Helena ....................646-654
St. Kitts ....................389-393
St. Lucia ....................1018-1022
Samoa ....................890-894
Solomon Islands ....................799-803
South Georgia ....................198-200
Tristan da Cunha ....................562-566

| | | |
|---|---|---|
| *Nos. 613-617 (5)* | 21.50 | 21.50 |

| | | |
|---|---|---|
| *Nos. 824-828 (5)* | 22.00 | 18.70 |
| *Nos. 891-895 (5)* | 14.20 | 11.90 |
| *Nos. 1047-1050 (4)* | 6.05 | 5.90 |
| *Nos. 163-167 (5)* | 16.25 | 16.25 |
| *Nos. 704-708 (5)* | 17.65 | 13.95 |
| *Nos. 634-638 (5)* | 18.65 | 17.15 |
| *Nos. 720-724 (5)* | 17.50 | 14.50 |
| *Nos. 662-668 (7)* | 16.30 | 16.30 |
| *Nos. 1175-1179 (5)* | 15.25 | 11.15 |
| *Nos. 803-805 (3)* | 7.50 | 7.50 |
| *Nos. 646-654 (9)* | 26.10 | 26.10 |
| *Nos. 389-393 (5)* | 16.40 | 16.40 |
| *Nos. 1018-1022 (5)* | 14.25 | 11.15 |
| *Nos. 890-894 (5)* | 14.25 | 13.50 |
| *Nos. 799-803 (5)* | 14.75 | 14.75 |
| *Nos. 198-200 (3)* | 14.50 | 15.50 |
| *Nos. 562-566 (5)* | 20.10 | 20.10 |
| *Set total (91) Stamps* | 293.20 | 272.30 |

**UN, 50th Anniv.**

CD353

**1995**

Bahamas ....................839-842
Barbados ....................901-904
Belize ....................1055-1058
Jamaica ....................847-851
Liberia ....................1187-1190
Mauritius ....................813-816
Pitcairn Islands ....................436-439
St. Kitts ....................398-401
St. Lucia ....................1023-1026
Samoa ....................900-903
Tristan da Cunha ....................568-571
Virgin Islands ....................807-810

| | | |
|---|---|---|
| *Nos. 839-842 (4)* | 7.15 | 6.40 |
| *Nos. 901-904 (4)* | 7.00 | 5.75 |
| *Nos. 1055-1058 (4)* | 4.70 | 4.70 |
| *Nos. 847-851 (5)* | 5.40 | 5.45 |
| *Nos. 1187-1190 (4)* | 9.65 | 9.65 |
| *Nos. 813-816 (4)* | 3.90 | 3.90 |
| *Nos. 436-439 (4)* | 8.15 | 8.15 |
| *Nos. 398-401 (4)* | 6.15 | 7.15 |
| *Nos. 1023-1026 (4)* | 7.50 | 7.25 |
| *Nos. 900-903 (4)* | 9.35 | 8.20 |
| *Nos. 568-571 (4)* | 13.50 | 13.50 |
| *Nos. 807-810 (4)* | 7.45 | 7.45 |
| *Set total (49) Stamps* | 89.90 | 87.55 |

**Queen Elizabeth, 70th Birthday**

CD354

**1996**

Ascension ....................632-635
British Antarctic Territory ....................240-243
British Indian Ocean Territory ....................176-180
Falkland Islands ....................653-657
Pitcairn Islands ....................446-449
St. Helena ....................672-676
Samoa ....................912-916
Tokelau ....................223-227
Tristan da Cunha ....................576-579
Virgin Islands ....................824-828

| | | |
|---|---|---|
| *Nos. 632-635 (4)* | 5.30 | 5.30 |
| *Nos. 240-243 (4)* | 10.50 | 8.90 |
| *Nos. 176-180 (5)* | 11.50 | 11.50 |
| *Nos. 653-657 (5)* | 13.55 | 11.20 |
| *Nos. 446-449 (4)* | 8.60 | 8.60 |
| *Nos. 672-676 (5)* | 12.70 | 12.70 |
| *Nos. 912-916 (5)* | 11.50 | 11.50 |
| *Nos. 223-227 (5)* | 10.50 | 10.50 |
| *Nos. 576-579 (4)* | 8.35 | 8.35 |
| *Nos. 824-828 (5)* | 11.30 | 11.30 |
| *Set total (46) Stamps* | 103.80 | 99.85 |

**Diana, Princess of Wales (1961-97)**

CD355

**1998**

Ascension ....................696
Bahamas ....................901A-902
Barbados ....................950
Belize ....................1091
Bermuda ....................753
Botswana ....................659-663
British Antarctic Territory ....................258
British Indian Ocean Terr. ....................197
Cayman Islands ....................752A-753
Falkland Islands ....................694
Fiji ....................819-820
Gibraltar ....................754
Kiribati ....................719A-720
Namibia ....................909
Niue ....................706
Norfolk Island ....................644-645
Papua New Guinea ....................937
Pitcairn Islands ....................487
St. Helena ....................711
St. Kitts ....................437A-438
Samoa ....................955A-956
Seycelles ....................802
Solomon Islands ....................866-867
South Georgia ....................220
Tokelau ....................252B-253
Tonga ....................980
Niuafo'ou ....................201
Tristan da Cunha ....................618
Tuvalu ....................762
Vanuatu ....................718A-719
Virgin Islands ....................878

| | | |
|---|---|---|
| *No. 696 (1)* | 5.25 | 5.25 |
| *Nos. 901A-902 (2)* | 5.30 | 5.30 |
| *No. 950 (1)* | 5.00 | 5.00 |
| *No. 1091 (1)* | 5.00 | 5.00 |
| *No. 753 (1)* | 5.00 | 5.00 |
| *Nos. 659-663 (5)* | 8.25 | 8.80 |
| *No. 258 (1)* | 6.25 | 6.25 |
| *No. 197 (1)* | 5.50 | 5.50 |
| *Nos. 752A-753 (3)* | 7.40 | 7.40 |
| *No. 694 (1)* | 5.00 | 5.00 |
| *Nos. 819-820 (2)* | 5.25 | 5.25 |
| *No. 754 (1)* | 4.75 | 4.75 |
| *Nos. 719A-720 (2)* | 4.85 | 4.85 |
| *No. 909 (1)* | 1.75 | 1.75 |
| *No. 706 (1)* | 5.50 | 5.50 |
| *Nos. 644-645 (2)* | 5.25 | 5.25 |
| *No. 937 (1)* | 6.50 | 6.50 |
| *No. 487 (1)* | 4.75 | 4.75 |
| *No. 711 (1)* | 4.25 | 4.25 |
| *Nos. 437A-438 (2)* | 5.15 | 5.15 |
| *Nos. 955A-956 (2)* | 7.00 | 7.00 |
| *No. 802 (1)* | 6.25 | 6.25 |
| *Nos. 866-867 (2)* | 5.40 | 5.40 |
| *No. 220 (1)* | 4.50 | 5.00 |
| *Nos. 252B-253 (2)* | 5.50 | 5.50 |
| *No. 980 (1)* | 5.75 | 5.75 |
| *No. 201 (1)* | 6.50 | 6.50 |
| *No. 618 (1)* | 5.00 | 5.00 |
| *No. 762 (1)* | 4.00 | 4.00 |
| *Nos. 718A-719 (2)* | 8.00 | 8.00 |
| *No. 878 (1)* | 4.50 | 4.50 |
| *Set total (46) Stamps* | 168.35 | 169.40 |

**Wedding of Prince Edward and Sophie Rhys-Jones**

CD356

**1999**

Ascension ....................729-730
Cayman Islands ....................775-776
Falkland Islands ....................729-730
Pitcairn Islands ....................505-506
St. Helena ....................733-734
Samoa ....................971-972
Tristan da Cunha ....................636-637
Virgin Islands ....................908-909

| | | |
|---|---|---|
| *Nos. 729-730 (2)* | 4.50 | 4.50 |
| *Nos. 775-776 (2)* | 4.95 | 4.95 |
| *Nos. 729-730 (2)* | 14.00 | 14.00 |
| *Nos. 505-506 (2)* | 7.00 | 7.00 |
| *Nos. 733-734 (2)* | 5.00 | 5.00 |
| *Nos. 971-972 (2)* | 5.00 | 5.00 |
| *Nos. 636-637 (2)* | 7.50 | 7.50 |
| *Nos. 908-909 (2)* | 7.50 | 7.50 |
| *Set total (16) Stamps* | 55.45 | 55.45 |

**1st Manned Moon Landing, 30th Anniv.**

CD357

**1999**

Ascension ....................731-735
Bahamas ....................942-946
Barbados ....................967-971
Bermuda ....................778
Cayman Islands ....................777-781
Fiji ....................853-857
Jamaica ....................889-893
Kirbati ....................746-750
Nauru ....................465-469
St. Kitts ....................460-464
Samoa ....................973-977
Solomon Islands ....................875-879
Tuvalu ....................800-804
Virgin Islands ....................910-914

| | | |
|---|---|---|
| *Nos. 731-735 (5)* | 12.80 | 12.80 |
| *Nos. 942-946 (5)* | 14.10 | 14.10 |
| *Nos. 967-971 (5)* | 8.65 | 7.75 |
| *No. 778 (1)* | 9.00 | 9.00 |
| *Nos. 777-781 (5)* | 9.25 | 9.25 |
| *Nos. 853-857 (5)* | 9.25 | 8.45 |
| *Nos. 889-893 (5)* | 8.30 | 7.18 |
| *Nos. 746-750 (5)* | 8.85 | 8.85 |
| *Nos. 465-469 (5)* | 9.25 | 8.00 |
| *Nos. 460-464 (5)* | 11.35 | 11.65 |
| *Nos. 973-977 (5)* | 13.45 | 13.30 |
| *Nos. 875-879 (5)* | 7.50 | 7.50 |
| *Nos. 800-804 (5)* | 7.45 | 7.45 |
| *Nos. 910-914 (5)* | 11.75 | 11.75 |
| *Set total (66) Stamps* | 140.95 | 137.03 |

**Queen Mother's Century**

CD358

**1999**

Ascension ....................736-740
Bahamas ....................951-955
Cayman Islands ....................782-786
Falkland Islands ....................734-738
Fiji ....................858-862
Norfolk Island ....................688-692
St. Helena ....................740-744
Samoa ....................978-982
Solomon Islands ....................880-884
South Georgia ....................231-235
Tristan da Cunha ....................638-642
Tuvalu ....................805-809

| | | |
|---|---|---|
| *Nos. 736-740 (5)* | 15.50 | 15.50 |
| *Nos. 951-955 (5)* | 13.75 | 12.65 |
| *Nos. 782-786 (5)* | 8.35 | 8.35 |
| *Nos. 734-738 (5)* | 30.00 | 28.25 |
| *Nos. 858-862 (5)* | 12.80 | 13.25 |
| *Nos. 688-692 (5)* | 10.30 | 10.30 |
| *Nos. 740-744 (5)* | 16.15 | 16.15 |
| *Nos. 978-982 (5)* | 12.50 | 12.10 |
| *Nos. 880-884 (5)* | 7.50 | 7.00 |
| *Nos. 231-235 (5)* | 29.75 | 30.00 |
| *Nos. 638-642 (5)* | 18.00 | 18.00 |
| *Nos. 805-809 (5)* | 8.65 | 8.65 |
| *Set total (60) Stamps* | 183.25 | 180.20 |

**Prince William, 18th Birthday**

CD359

**2000**

Ascension ....................755-759
Cayman Islands ....................797-801
Falkland Islands ....................762-766
Fiji ....................889-893
South Georgia ....................257-261
Tristan da Cunha ....................664-668
Virgin Islands ....................925-929

| | | |
|---|---|---|
| *Nos. 755-759 (5)* | 15.50 | 15.50 |
| *Nos. 797-801 (5)* | 11.15 | 10.90 |
| *Nos. 762-766 (5)* | 24.60 | 22.50 |
| *Nos. 889-893 (5)* | 12.90 | 12.90 |
| *Nos. 257-261 (5)* | 29.00 | 28.75 |
| *Nos. 664-668 (5)* | 21.50 | 21.50 |
| *Nos. 925-929 (5)* | 14.50 | 14.50 |
| *Set total (35) Stamps* | 129.15 | 126.55 |

**Reign of Queen Elizabeth II, 50th Anniv.**

CD360

**2002**

Ascension ....................790-794
Bahamas ....................1033-1037
Barbados ....................1019-1023
Belize ....................1152-1156
Bermuda ....................822-826
British Antarctic Territory ....................307-311
British Indian Ocean Territory ....................239-243
Cayman Islands ....................844-848
Falkland Islands ....................804-808
Gibraltar ....................896-900
Jamaica ....................952-956
Nauru ....................491-495
Norfolk Island ....................758-762
Papua New Guinea ....................1019-1023
Pitcairn Islands ....................552
St. Helena ....................788-792
St. Lucia ....................1146-1150
Solomon Islands ....................931-935
South Georgia ....................274-278
Swaziland ....................706-710
Tokelau ....................302-306
Tonga ....................1059
Niuafo'ou ....................239
Tristan da Cunha ....................706-710
Virgin Islands ....................967-971

| | | |
|---|---|---|
| *Nos. 790-794 (5)* | 14.10 | 14.10 |
| *Nos. 1033-1037 (5)* | 15.25 | 15.25 |
| *Nos. 1019-1023 (5)* | 13.15 | 13.15 |
| *Nos. 1152-1156 (5)* | 12.65 | 12.25 |
| *Nos. 822-826 (5)* | 18.00 | 18.00 |
| *Nos. 307-311 (5)* | 25.00 | 25.00 |
| *Nos. 239-243 (5)* | 19.40 | 19.40 |
| *Nos. 844-848 (5)* | 13.25 | 13.25 |
| *Nos. 804-808 (5)* | 23.00 | 22.00 |
| *Nos. 896-900 (5)* | 6.65 | 6.65 |
| *Nos. 952-956 (5)* | 16.65 | 16.65 |
| *Nos. 491-495 (5)* | 17.75 | 17.75 |
| *Nos. 758-762 (5)* | 19.50 | 19.50 |
| *Nos. 1019-1023 (5)* | 14.50 | 14.50 |
| *No. 552 (1)* | 9.25 | 9.25 |
| *Nos. 788-792 (5)* | 19.75 | 19.75 |
| *Nos. 1146-1150 (5)* | 12.25 | 12.25 |
| *Nos. 931-935 (5)* | 12.40 | 12.40 |
| *Nos. 274-278 (5)* | 28.00 | 28.50 |
| *Nos. 706-710 (5)* | 12.75 | 12.75 |
| *Nos. 302-306 (5)* | 14.50 | 14.50 |
| *No. 1059 (1)* | 8.50 | 8.50 |
| *No. 239 (1)* | 8.75 | 8.75 |
| *Nos. 706-710 (5)* | 18.50 | 18.50 |
| *Nos. 967-971 (5)* | 16.50 | 16.50 |
| *Set total (113) Stamps* | 390.00 | 389.10 |

**Queen Mother Elizabeth (1900-2002)**

CD361

**2002**

Ascension ....................................799-801
Bahamas .................................1044-1046
Bermuda......................................834-836
British Antarctic Territory..........312-314
British Indian Ocean Territory........245-247
Cayman Islands..........................857-861
Falkland Islands .........................812-816
Nauru..........................................499-501
Pitcairn Islands..........................561-565
St. Helena ..................................808-812
St. Lucia .................................1155-1159
Seychelles .........................................830
Solomon Islands.........................945-947
South Georgia .............................281-285
Tokelau .......................................312-314
Tristan da Cunha.........................715-717
Virgin Islands..............................979-983

| | | |
|---|---|---|
| *Nos. 799-801 (3)* | 8.85 | 8.85 |
| *Nos. 1044-1046 (3)* | 9.10 | 9.10 |
| *Nos. 834-836 (3)* | 12.25 | 12.25 |
| *Nos. 312-314 (3)* | 19.25 | 19.25 |
| *Nos. 245-247 (3)* | 17.35 | 17.35 |
| *Nos. 857-861 (5)* | 15.00 | 15.00 |
| *Nos. 812-816 (5)* | 28.50 | 28.50 |
| *Nos. 499-501 (3)* | 14.00 | 14.00 |
| *Nos. 561-565 (5)* | 15.25 | 15.25 |
| *Nos. 808-812 (5)* | 12.00 | 12.00 |
| *Nos. 1155-1159 (5)* | 13.00 | 13.00 |
| *No. 830 (1)* | 6.50 | 6.50 |
| *Nos. 945-947 (3)* | 9.25 | 9.25 |
| *Nos. 281-285 (5)* | 19.50 | 19.50 |
| *Nos. 312-314 (3)* | 11.85 | 11.85 |
| *Nos. 715-717 (3)* | 16.25 | 16.25 |
| *Nos. 979-983 (5)* | 23.50 | 23.50 |
| *Set total (63) Stamps* | 251.40 | 251.40 |

**Head of Queen Elizabeth II**

CD362

**2003**

Ascension .............................................822
Bermuda................................................865
British Antarctic Territory.................322
British Indian Ocean Territory .........261
Cayman Islands....................................878
Falkland Islands ..................................828
St. Helena ............................................820
South Georgia ......................................294
Tristan da Cunha..................................731
Virgin Islands.....................................1003

| | | |
|---|---|---|
| *No. 822 (1)* | 12.50 | 12.50 |
| *No. 865 (1)* | 50.00 | 50.00 |
| *No. 322 (1)* | 10.00 | 10.00 |
| *No. 261 (1)* | 11.00 | 11.00 |
| *No. 878 (1)* | 14.00 | 14.00 |
| *No. 828 (1)* | 9.00 | 9.00 |
| *No. 820 (1)* | 9.00 | 9.00 |
| *No. 294 (1)* | 8.50 | 8.50 |
| *No. 731 (1)* | 10.00 | 10.00 |
| *No. 1003 (1)* | 10.00 | 10.00 |
| *Set total (10) Stamps* | 144.00 | 144.00 |

**Coronation of Queen Elizabeth II, 50th Anniv.**

CD363

**2003**

Ascension ....................................823-825
Bahamas ..................................1073-1075
Bermuda......................................866-868
British Antarctic Territory..........323-325
British Indian Ocean Territory........262-264
Cayman Islands..........................879-881
Jamaica .......................................970-972
Kiribati ........................................825-827
Pitcairn Islands..........................577-581
St. Helena ...................................821-823
St. Lucia .................................1171-1173
Tokelau .......................................320-322
Tristan da Cunha.........................732-734
Virgin Islands............................1004-1006

| | | |
|---|---|---|
| *Nos. 823-825 (3)* | 12.50 | 12.50 |
| *Nos. 1073-1075 (3)* | 13.00 | 13.00 |
| *Nos. 866-868 (2)* | 14.25 | 14.25 |
| *Nos. 323-325 (3)* | 26.00 | 26.00 |
| *Nos. 262-264 (3)* | 28.00 | 28.00 |
| *Nos. 879-881 (3)* | 19.25 | 19.25 |
| *Nos. 970-972 (3)* | 10.00 | 10.00 |
| *Nos. 825-827 (3)* | 13.50 | 13.50 |
| *Nos. 577-581 (5)* | 14.40 | 14.40 |
| *Nos. 821-823 (3)* | 7.25 | 7.25 |
| *Nos. 1171-1173 (3)* | 8.75 | 8.75 |
| *Nos. 320-322 (3)* | 17.25 | 17.25 |
| *Nos. 732-734 (3)* | 16.75 | 16.75 |
| *Nos. 1004-1006 (3)* | 25.00 | 25.00 |
| *Set total (43) Stamps* | 225.90 | 225.90 |

**Prince William, 21st Birthday**

CD364

**2003**

Ascension ...............................................826
British Indian Ocean Territory .........265
Cayman Islands...........................882-884
Falkland Islands ...................................829
South Georgia .......................................295
Tokelau ..................................................323
Tristan da Cunha...................................735
Virgin Islands...............................1007-1009

| | | |
|---|---|---|
| *No. 826 (1)* | 7.25 | 7.25 |
| *No. 265 (1)* | 8.00 | 8.00 |
| *Nos. 882-884 (3)* | 6.95 | 6.95 |
| *No. 829 (1)* | 13.50 | 13.50 |
| *No. 295 (1)* | 8.50 | 8.50 |
| *No. 323 (1)* | 7.25 | 7.25 |
| *No. 735 (1)* | 6.00 | 6.00 |
| *Nos. 1007-1009 (3)* | 10.00 | 10.00 |
| *Set total (12) Stamps* | 67.45 | 67.45 |

# British Commonwealth of Nations

## Dominions, Colonies, Territories, Offices and Independent Members

Comprising stamps of the British Commonwealth and associated nations.

A strict observance of technicalities would bar some or all of the stamps listed under Burma, Ireland, Kuwait, Nepal, New Republic, Orange Free State, Samoa, South Africa, South-West Africa, Stellaland, Sudan, Swaziland, the two Transvaal Republics and others but these are included for the convenience of collectors.

## 1. Great Britain

Great Britain: Including England, Scotland, Wales and Northern Ireland.

## 2. The Dominions, Present and Past

### AUSTRALIA

The Commonwealth of Australia was proclaimed on January 1, 1901. It consists of six former colonies as follows:

New South Wales
Queensland
South Australia
Victoria
Tasmania
Western Australia

The following islands and territories are, or have been, administered by Australia: Australian Antarctic Territory, Christmas Island, Cocos (Keeling) Islands, Nauru, New Guinea, Norfolk Island, Papua.

### CANADA

The Dominion of Canada was created by the British North America Act in 1867. The following provinces were former sepa- rate colonies and issued postage stamps:

British Columbia and Vancouver Island
New Brunswick
Newfoundland
Nova Scotia
Prince Edward Island

### FIJI

The colony of Fiji became an independent nation with dominion status on Oct. 10, 1970.

### GHANA

This state came into existence Mar. 6, 1957, with dominion status. It consists of the former colony of the Gold Coast and the Trusteeship Territory of Togoland. Ghana became a republic July 1, 1960.

### INDIA

The Republic of India was inaugurated on January 26, 1950. It succeeded the Dominion of India which was proclaimed August 15, 1947, when the former Empire of India was divided into Pakistan and the Union of India. The Republic is composed of about 40 predominantly Hindu states of three classes: governor's provinces, chief commissioner's provinces and princely states. India also has various territories, such as the Andaman and Nicobar Islands.

The old Empire of India was a federation of British India and the native states. The more important princely states were autonomous. Of the more than 700 Indian states, these 43 are familiar names to philatelists because of their postage stamps.

### CONVENTION STATES

Chamba
Faridkot
Gwalior
Jhind
Nabha
Patiala

### FEUDATORY STATES

Alwar
Bahawalpur
Bamra
Barwani
Bhopal
Bhor
Bijawar
Bundi
Bussahir
Charkhari
Cochin
Dhar
Dungarpur
Duttia
Faridkot (1879-85)
Hyderabad
Idar
Indore
Jaipur
Jammu
Jammu and Kashmir
Jasdan
Jhalawar
Jhind (1875-76)
Kashmir
Kishangarh
Kotah
Las Bela
Morvi
Nandgaon
Nowanuggur
Orchha
Poonch
Rajasthan
Rajpeepla
Sirmur
Soruth
Tonk
Travancore
Wadhwan

### NEW ZEALAND

Became a dominion on September 26, 1907. The following islands and territories are, or have been, administered by New Zealand:

Aitutaki
Cook Islands (Rarotonga)
Niue
Penrhyn
Ross Dependency
Samoa (Western Samoa)
Tokelau Islands

### PAKISTAN

The Republic of Pakistan was proclaimed March 23, 1956. It succeeded the Dominion which was proclaimed August 15, 1947. It is made up of all or part of several Moslem provinces and various districts of the former Empire of India, including Bahawalpur and Las Bela. Pakistan withdrew from the Commonwealth in 1972.

### SOUTH AFRICA

Under the terms of the South African Act (1909) the self-governing colonies of Cape of Good Hope, Natal, Orange River Colony and Transvaal united on May 31, 1910, to form the Union of South Africa. It became an independent republic May 3, 1961.

Under the terms of the Treaty of Versailles, South-West Africa, formerly German South-West Africa, was mandated to the Union of South Africa.

### SRI LANKA (CEYLON)

The Dominion of Ceylon was proclaimed February 4, 1948. The island had been a Crown Colony from 1802 until then. On May 22, 1972, Ceylon became the Republic of Sri Lanka.

## 3. Colonies, Past and Present; Controlled Territory and Independent Members of the Commonwealth

Aden
Aitutaki
Anguilla
Antigua
Ascension
Bahamas
Bahrain
Bangladesh
Barbados
Barbuda
Basutoland
Batum
Bechuanaland
Bechuanaland Prot.
Belize
Bermuda
Botswana
British Antarctic Territory
British Central Africa
British Columbia and Vancouver Island
British East Africa
British Guiana

British Honduras
British Indian Ocean Territory
British New Guinea
British Solomon Islands
British Somaliland
Brunei
Burma
Bushire
Cameroons
Cape of Good Hope
Cayman Islands
Christmas Island
Cocos (Keeling) Islands
Cook Islands
Crete,
British Administration
Cyprus
Dominica
East Africa & Uganda
Protectorates
Egypt
Falkland Islands
Fiji
Gambia
German East Africa
Gibraltar
Gilbert Islands
Gilbert & Ellice Islands
Gold Coast
Grenada
Griqualand West
Guernsey
Guyana
Heligoland
Hong Kong
Indian Native States
(see India)
Ionian Islands
Jamaica
Jersey
Kenya
Kenya, Uganda & Tanzania
Kuwait
Labuan
Lagos
Leeward Islands
Lesotho
Madagascar
Malawi
Malaya
Federated Malay States
Johore
Kedah
Kelantan
Malacca
Negri Sembilan
Pahang
Penang
Perak
Perlis
Selangor
Singapore
Sungei Ujong
Trengganu
Malaysia
Maldive Islands
Malta
Man, Isle of
Mauritius
Mesopotamia
Montserrat
Muscat
Namibia
Natal
Nauru
Nevis
New Britain
New Brunswick
Newfoundland
New Guinea
New Hebrides
New Republic
New South Wales
Niger Coast Protectorate
Nigeria
Niue
Norfolk Island
North Borneo
Northern Nigeria
Northern Rhodesia
North West Pacific Islands
Nova Scotia
Nyasaland Protectorate
Oman
Orange River Colony
Palestine
Papua New Guinea
Penrhyn Island
Pitcairn Islands
Prince Edward Island
Queensland
Rhodesia
Rhodesia & Nyasaland
Ross Dependency
Sabah
St. Christopher
St. Helena
St. Kitts
St. Kitts-Nevis-Anguilla
St. Lucia
St. Vincent
Samoa
Sarawak
Seychelles
Sierra Leone
Solomon Islands
Somaliland Protectorate
South Arabia
South Australia
South Georgia
Southern Nigeria
Southern Rhodesia
South-West Africa
Stellaland
Straits Settlements
Sudan
Swaziland
Tanganyika
Tanzania
Tasmania
Tobago
Togo
Tokelau Islands
Tonga
Transvaal
Trinidad
Trinidad and Tobago
Tristan da Cunha
Trucial States
Turks and Caicos
Turks Islands
Tuvalu
Uganda
United Arab Emirates
Victoria
Virgin Islands
Western Australia
Zambia
Zanzibar
Zululand

**POST OFFICES IN FOREIGN COUNTRIES**

Africa
East Africa Forces
Middle East Forces
Bangkok
China
Morocco
Turkish Empire

# Colonies, Former Colonies, Offices, Territories Controlled by Parent States

## Belgium

Belgian Congo
Ruanda-Urundi

## Denmark

Danish West Indies
Faroe Islands
Greenland
Iceland

## Finland

Aland Islands

## France

### COLONIES PAST AND PRESENT, CONTROLLED TERRITORIES

Afars & Issas, Territory of
Alaouites
Alexandretta
Algeria
Alsace & Lorraine
Anjouan
Annam & Tonkin
Benin
Cambodia (Khmer)
Cameroun
Castellorizo
Chad
Cilicia
Cochin China
Comoro Islands
Dahomey
Diego Suarez
Djibouti (Somali Coast)
Fezzan
French Congo
French Equatorial Africa
French Guiana
French Guinea
French India
French Morocco
French Polynesia (Oceania)
French Southern & Antarctic Territories
French Sudan
French West Africa
Gabon
Germany
Ghadames
Grand Comoro
Guadeloupe
Indo-China
Inini
Ivory Coast
Laos
Latakia
Lebanon
Madagascar
Martinique
Mauritania
Mayotte
Memel
Middle Congo
Moheli
New Caledonia
New Hebrides
Niger Territory
Nossi-Be
Obock
Reunion
Rouad, Ile
Ste.-Marie de Madagascar
St. Pierre & Miquelon
Senegal
Senegambia & Niger
Somali Coast
Syria
Tahiti
Togo
Tunisia
Ubangi-Shari
Upper Senegal & Niger
Upper Volta
Viet Nam
Wallis & Futuna Islands

### POST OFFICES IN FOREIGN COUNTRIES

China
Crete
Egypt
Turkish Empire
Zanzibar

## Germany

### EARLY STATES

Baden
Bavaria
Bergedorf
Bremen
Brunswick
Hamburg
Hanover
Lubeck
Mecklenburg-Schwerin
Mecklenburg-Strelitz
Oldenburg
Prussia
Saxony
Schleswig-Holstein
Wurttemberg

### FORMER COLONIES

Cameroun (Kamerun)
Caroline Islands
German East Africa
German New Guinea
German South-West Africa
Kiauchau
Mariana Islands
Marshall Islands
Samoa
Togo

## Italy

### EARLY STATES

Modena
Parma
Romagna
Roman States
Sardinia
Tuscany
Two Sicilies
  Naples
  Neapolitan Provinces
  Sicily

### FORMER COLONIES, CONTROLLED TERRITORIES, OCCUPATION AREAS

Aegean Islands
  Calimno (Calino)
  Caso
  Cos (Coo)
  Karki (Carchi)
  Leros (Lero)
  Lipso
  Nisiros (Nisiro)
  Patmos (Patmo)
  Piscopi
  Rodi (Rhodes)
  Scarpanto
  Simi
  Stampalia
Castellorizo
Corfu
Cyrenaica
Eritrea
Ethiopia (Abyssinia)
Fiume
Ionian Islands
  Cephalonia
  Ithaca
  Paxos
Italian East Africa
Libya
Oltre Giuba
Saseno
Somalia (Italian Somaliland)
Tripolitania

### POST OFFICES IN FOREIGN COUNTRIES

"ESTERO"*
Austria
China
  Peking
  Tientsin
Crete
Tripoli
Turkish Empire
  Constantinople
  Durazzo
  Janina
Jerusalem
Salonika
Scutari
Smyrna
Valona

*Stamps overprinted "ESTERO" were used in various parts of the world.

## Netherlands

Aruba
Caribbean Netherlands
Curacao
Netherlands Antilles (Curacao)
Netherlands Indies
Netherlands New Guinea
St. Martin
Surinam (Dutch Guiana)

## Portugal

### COLONIES PAST AND PRESENT, CONTROLLED TERRITORIES

Angola
Angra
Azores
Cape Verde
Funchal
Horta
Inhambane
Kionga
Lourenco Marques
Macao
Madeira
Mozambique
Mozambique Co.
Nyassa
Ponta Delgada
Portuguese Africa
Portuguese Congo
Portuguese Guinea
Portuguese India
Quelimane
St. Thomas & Prince Islands
Tete
Timor
Zambezia

## Russia

### ALLIED TERRITORIES AND REPUBLICS, OCCUPATION AREAS

Armenia
Aunus (Olonets)
Azerbaijan
Batum
Estonia
Far Eastern Republic
Georgia
Karelia
Latvia
Lithuania
North Ingermanland
Ostland
Russian Turkestan
Siberia
South Russia
Tannu Tuva
Transcaucasian Fed. Republics
Ukraine
Wenden (Livonia)
Western Ukraine

## Spain

### COLONIES PAST AND PRESENT, CONTROLLED TERRITORIES

Aguera, La
Cape Juby
Cuba
Elobey, Annobon & Corisco
Fernando Po
Ifni
Mariana Islands
Philippines
Puerto Rico
Rio de Oro
Rio Muni
Spanish Guinea
Spanish Morocco
Spanish Sahara
Spanish West Africa

### POST OFFICES IN FOREIGN COUNTRIES

Morocco
Tangier
Tetuan

# Dies of British Colonial Stamps

**DIE A:**

**1.** The lines in the groundwork vary in thickness and are not uniformly straight.

**2.** The seventh and eighth lines from the top, in the groundwork, converge where they meet the head.

**3.** There is a small dash in the upper part of the second jewel in the band of the crown.

**4.** The vertical color line in front of the throat stops at the sixth line of shading on the neck.

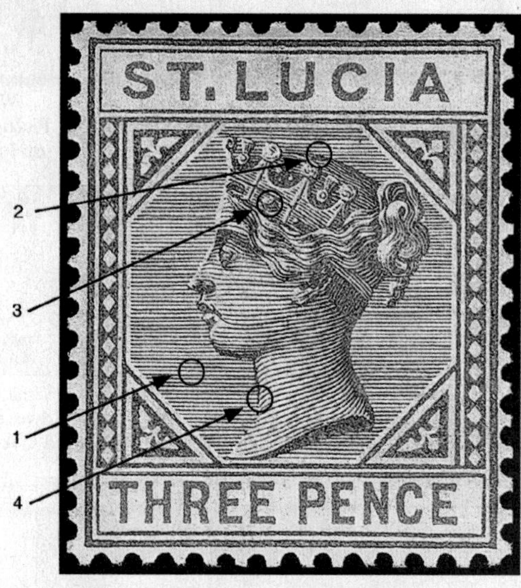


**DIE B:**

**1.** The lines in the groundwork are all thin and straight.

**2.** All the lines of the background are parallel.

**3.** There is no dash in the upper part of the second jewel in the band of the crown.

**4.** The vertical color line in front of the throat stops at the eighth line of shading on the neck.

**DIE I:**

**1.** The base of the crown is well below the level of the inner white line around the vignette.

**2.** The labels inscribed "POSTAGE" and "REVENUE" are cut square at the top.

**3.** There is a white "bud" on the outer side of the main stem of the curved ornaments in each lower corner.

**4.** The second (thick) line below the country name has the ends next to the crown cut diagonally.

| DIE Ia. | DIE Ib. |
|---|---|
| 1 as die II. | 1 and 3 as die II. |
| 2 and 3 as die I. | 2 as die I. |

**DIE II:**

**1.** The base of the crown is aligned with the underside of the white line around the vignette.

**2.** The labels curve inward at the top inner corners.

**3.** The "bud" has been removed from the outer curve of the ornaments in each corner.

**4.** The second line below the country name has the ends next to the crown cut vertically.

# British Colonial and Crown Agents Watermarks

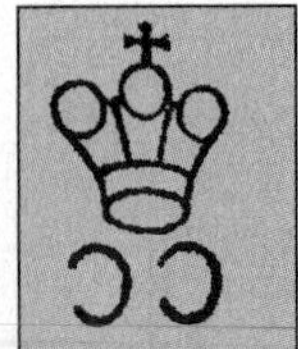
Wmk. 1
Crown and C C

Wmk. 2
Crown and C A

Wmk. 3
Multiple Crown and C A

Wmk. 4
Multiple Crown and Script C A

Wmk. 4a

Wmk. 46

Wmk. 314
St. Edward's Crown and C A Multiple

Wmk. 373

Wmk. 384

Wmk. 406

Watermarks 1 to 4, 314, 373, 384 and 406, common to many British territories, are illustrated here to avoid duplication.

The letters "CC" of Wmk. 1 identify the paper as having been made for the use of the Crown Colonies, while the letters "CA" of the others stand for "Crown Agents." Both Wmks. 1 and 2 were used on stamps printed by De La Rue & Co.

Wmk. 3 was adopted in 1904; Wmk. 4 in 1921; Wmk. 46 in 1879; Wmk. 314 in 1957; Wmk. 373 in 1974; Wmk. 384 in 1985; Wmk 406 in 2008.

In Wmk. 4a, a non-matching crown of the general St. Edwards type (bulging on both sides at top) was substituted for one of the Wmk. 4 crowns which fell off the dandy roll. The non-matching crown occurs in 1950-52 printings in a horizontal row of crowns on certain regular stamps of Johore and Seychelles, and on various postage due stamps of Barbados, Basutoland, British Guiana, Gold Coast, Grenada, Northern Rhodesia, St. Lucia, Swaziland and Trinidad and Tobago. A variation of Wmk. 4a, with the non-matching crown in a horizontal row of crown-CA-crown, occurs on regular stamps of Bahamas, St. Kitts-Nevis and Singapore.

Wmk. 314 was intentionally used sideways, starting in 1966. When a stamp was issued with Wmk. 314 both upright and sideways, the sideways varieties usually are listed also – with minor numbers. In many of the later issues, Wmk. 314 is slightly visible.

Wmk. 373 is usually only faintly visible.

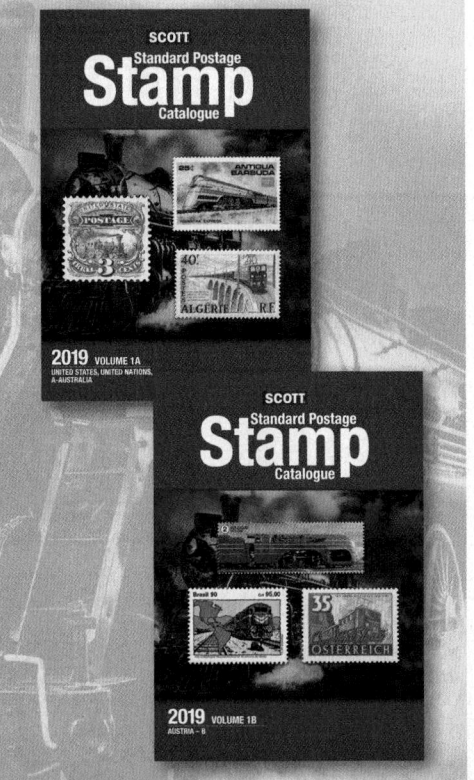

# NAMIBIA

nə-ˈmi-bē-ə

LOCATION — In southwestern Africa between Angola and South Africa, bordering on the Atlantic Ocean
GOVT. — Republic
AREA — 318,261 sq. mi.
POP. — 1,648,270 (1999 est.)
CAPITAL — Windhoek

Formerly South West Africa.

100 Cents = 1 Rand
100 Cents = 1 Dollar (1993)

**Catalogue values for unused stamps in this country are for Never Hinged items.**

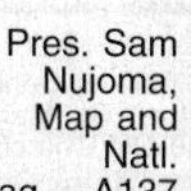

Pres. Sam Nujoma, Map and Natl. Flag — A137

Designs: 45c, Dove, map, hands unchained, vert. 60c, Flag, map.

***Perf. 14½x14, 14x14½***

**1990, Mar. 21** **Litho.** **Unwmk.**

| No. | Type | Description | Unused | Used |
|---|---|---|---|---|
| **659** | A137 | 18c shown | .30 | .25 |
| **660** | A137 | 45c multicolored | .60 | .60 |
| **661** | A137 | 60c multicolored | 1.40 | 1.40 |
| | | *Nos. 659-661 (3)* | 2.30 | 2.25 |

Independence from South Africa.

Sights of Namibia A138

Designs: 18c, Fish River Canyon. 35c, Quiver-tree Forest. 45c, Tsaris Mountains. 60c, Dolerite Hills.

**1990, Apr. 26** ***Perf. 14½x14***

| No. | Type | Description | Unused | Used |
|---|---|---|---|---|
| **662** | A138 | 18c multicolored | .35 | .30 |
| **663** | A138 | 35c multicolored | .55 | .50 |
| **664** | A138 | 45c multicolored | .75 | .60 |
| **665** | A138 | 60c multicolored | 1.00 | .90 |
| *a.* | | Souvenir sheet of 1 | 4.25 | 4.25 |
| | | *Nos. 662-665 (4)* | 2.65 | 2.30 |

No. 665a publicizes the 150th anniv. of the Penny Black. Sold for 1.50r.

Architectural Development of Windhoek A139

Designs: 18c, Early central business area. 35c, Modern central business area. 45c, First municipal building. 60c, Current municipal building.

**1990, July 26** ***Perf. 14½x14***

| No. | Type | Description | Unused | Used |
|---|---|---|---|---|
| **666** | A139 | 18c multicolored | .30 | .30 |
| **667** | A139 | 35c multicolored | .45 | .45 |
| **668** | A139 | 45c multicolored | .55 | .55 |
| **669** | A139 | 60c multicolored | .85 | .85 |
| | | *Nos. 666-669 (4)* | 2.15 | 2.15 |

Farming and Ranching A140

**1990, Oct. 11** ***Perf. 14½x14***

| No. | Type | Description | Unused | Used |
|---|---|---|---|---|
| **670** | A140 | 20c Cornfields | .25 | .25 |
| **671** | A140 | 35c Sanga cattle | .40 | .40 |
| **672** | A140 | 50c Damara sheep | .60 | .55 |
| **673** | A140 | 65c Irrigation | .90 | .95 |
| | | *Nos. 670-673 (4)* | 2.15 | 2.15 |

Gypsum — A141

Oranjemund Alluvial Diamond Mine A142

2c, Fluorite. 5c, Mimetite. 10c, Azurite. 20c, Dioptase. 30c, Tsumeb mine. 35c, Rosh Pinah mine. 40c, Diamond. 50c, Uis mine. 65c, Boltwoodite. 1r, Rossing mine. 1.50r, Wulfenite. 2r, Gold. 5r, Willemite.

**1991, Jan. 2** ***Perf. 14½x14***

| No. | Type | Description | Unused | Used |
|---|---|---|---|---|
| **674** | A141 | 1c shown | .25 | .30 |
| **675** | A141 | 2c multi | .25 | .30 |
| **676** | A141 | 5c multi | .30 | .30 |
| **677** | A141 | 10c multi | .40 | .30 |
| **679** | A141 | 20c multi | .45 | .25 |
| **680** | A142 | 25c shown | .45 | .30 |
| **681** | A142 | 30c multi | .60 | .35 |
| **682** | A142 | 35c multi | .70 | .40 |
| **683** | A141 | 40c multi | .90 | .30 |
| **684** | A142 | 50c multi | .90 | .35 |
| **685** | A141 | 65c multi | .85 | .35 |
| **686** | A142 | 1r multi | 1.10 | .50 |
| **687** | A141 | 1.50r multi | 1.40 | .75 |
| **688** | A141 | 2r multi | 2.00 | 1.25 |
| **689** | A141 | 5r multi | 3.25 | 2.75 |
| | | *Nos. 674-689 (15)* | 13.80 | 8.75 |

Nos. 676, 677 were reprinted in 1992 on phosphorescent paper.

Namibian Weather Service, Cent. A143

20c, Weather balloon. 35c, Sunshine recorder. 50c, Measuring equipment. 65c, Gobabeb weather station.

**1991, Feb. 2** ***Perf. 14½x14***

| No. | Type | Description | Unused | Used |
|---|---|---|---|---|
| **690** | A143 | 20c multicolored | .25 | .25 |
| **691** | A143 | 35c multicolored | .40 | .40 |
| **692** | A143 | 50c multicolored | .55 | .50 |
| **693** | A143 | 65c multicolored | .65 | .60 |
| | | *Nos. 690-693 (4)* | 1.85 | 1.75 |

Mountain Zebra A144

20c, Four zebras. 25c, Mother suckling foal. 45c, Three zebras. 60c, Two zebras.

**1991, Apr. 18** ***Perf. 14½x14***

| No. | Type | Description | Unused | Used |
|---|---|---|---|---|
| **694** | A144 | 20c multi | *1.00* | *.65* |
| **695** | A144 | 25c multi | *1.10* | *.70* |
| **696** | A144 | 45c multi | *1.50* | *1.75* |
| **697** | A144 | 60c multi | *2.10* | *2.50* |
| | | *Nos. 694-697 (4)* | *5.70* | *5.60* |

A souvenir sheet of 1 #696 was sold for 1.50r by the Philatelic Foundation of South Africa. Value $7.

Mountains A145

**1991, July 18** ***Perf. 14½x14***

| No. | Type | Description | Unused | Used |
|---|---|---|---|---|
| **698** | A145 | 20c Karas | .30 | .30 |
| **699** | A145 | 25c Gamsberg | .40 | .40 |
| **700** | A145 | 45c Brukkaros | .55 | .55 |
| **701** | A145 | 60c Erongo | .70 | .70 |
| | | *Nos. 698-701 (4)* | 1.95 | 1.95 |

Tourist Camps A146

Designs: 20c, Bernabe De la Bat Tourist Camp, Waterberg. 25c, Von Bach Recreation Resort. 45c, Gross Barmen Hot Springs. 60c, Namutoni Rest Camp.

**1991, Oct. 24** ***Perf. 14½x14***

| No. | Type | Description | Unused | Used |
|---|---|---|---|---|
| **702** | A146 | 20c multicolored | .35 | .25 |
| **703** | A146 | 25c multicolored | .45 | .30 |
| **704** | A146 | 45c multicolored | .75 | .60 |
| **705** | A146 | 60c multicolored | 1.15 | .95 |
| | | *Nos. 702-705 (4)* | 2.70 | 2.10 |

Windhoek Conservatoir, 21st Anniv. — A147

Designs: 20c, Artist's palette, brushes. 25c, French horn, neck of violin. 45c, Pan pipes, masks of Comedy and Tragedy, lyre. 60c, Ballet pas de deux.

**1992, Jan. 30** ***Perf. 14x14½***

| No. | Type | Description | Unused | Used |
|---|---|---|---|---|
| **706** | A147 | 20c multicolored | .25 | .25 |
| **707** | A147 | 25c multicolored | .30 | .25 |
| **708** | A147 | 45c multicolored | .60 | .55 |
| **709** | A147 | 60c multicolored | .75 | .75 |
| | | *Nos. 706-709 (4)* | 1.90 | 1.80 |

Freshwater Fish — A148

**1992, Apr. 16** ***Perf. 14½x14***

| No. | Type | Description | Unused | Used |
|---|---|---|---|---|
| **710** | A148 | 20c Blue kurper | .35 | .25 |
| **711** | A148 | 25c Yellow fish | .50 | .25 |
| **712** | A148 | 45c Carp | .80 | .50 |
| **713** | A148 | 60c Catfish | .95 | .65 |
| | | *Nos. 710-713 (4)* | 2.60 | 1.65 |

A souvenir sheet of 1 No. 712 was sold by the Philatelic Foundation of South Africa. Value, $5.75.

Views of Swakopmund — A149

20c, Jetty. 25c, Swimming pool. 45c, State House, lighthouse. 60c, Palm beach.

**1992, July 2** ***Perf. 14½x14***

| No. | Type | Description | Unused | Used |
|---|---|---|---|---|
| **714** | A149 | 20c multi | .25 | .25 |
| **715** | A149 | 25c multi | .35 | .25 |
| **716** | A149 | 45c multi | .70 | .55 |
| **717** | A149 | 60c multi | .95 | .70 |
| *a.* | | Souvenir sheet of 4, #714-717 | .95 | .70 |
| | | *Nos. 714-717 (4)* | 2.25 | 1.75 |

1992 Summer Olympics, Barcelona A150

**1992, July 24** ***Perf. 14½x14***

| No. | Type | Description | Unused | Used |
|---|---|---|---|---|
| **718** | A150 | 20c Runners | .30 | .25 |
| **719** | A150 | 25c Flag, emblem | .35 | .30 |
| **720** | A150 | 45c Swimmers | .65 | .55 |
| **721** | A150 | 60c Olympic stadium | .75 | .65 |
| *a.* | | Souvenir sheet of 4, #718-721 | 2.75 | 2.75 |
| | | *Nos. 718-721 (4)* | 2.05 | 1.75 |

No. 721a sold for 2r.

Disabled Workers — A151

Designs: 20c, Wrapping cucumbers. 25c, Finishing a woven mat. 45c, At a spinning wheel. 60c, Cleaning potted plants.

**1992, Sept. 10** ***Perf. 14x14½***

| No. | Type | Description | Unused | Used |
|---|---|---|---|---|
| **722** | A151 | 20c multicolored | .25 | .25 |
| **723** | A151 | 25c multicolored | .30 | .25 |
| **724** | A151 | 45c multicolored | .40 | .40 |
| **725** | A151 | 60c multicolored | .55 | .50 |
| | | *Nos. 722-725 (4)* | 1.50 | 1.40 |

Endangered Animals A152

Designs: 20c, Loxodonta africana. 25c, Tragelaphus spekei. 45c, Diceros bicornis. 60c, Lycaon pictus.

**1993, Feb. 25** ***Perf. 14½x14***

| No. | Type | Description | Unused | Used |
|---|---|---|---|---|
| **726** | A152 | 20c multicolored | .50 | .25 |
| **727** | A152 | 25c multicolored | .50 | .30 |
| **728** | A152 | 45c multicolored | 1.00 | .50 |
| **729** | A152 | 60c multicolored | 1.25 | .60 |
| *a.* | | Souvenir sheet of 4, #726-729 | 4.50 | 4.50 |
| | | *Nos. 726-729 (4)* | 3.25 | 1.65 |

Namibia Nature Foundation. No. 729a sold for 2.10r.

Arrival of Simmentaler Cattle in Namibia, Cent. A153

20c, Cows and calves. 25c, Cow and calf. 45c, Head of stud bull. 60c, Arrival on boat, 1893.

**1993, Apr. 16** ***Perf. 14½x14***

| No. | Type | Description | Unused | Used |
|---|---|---|---|---|
| **730** | A153 | 20c multi | .25 | .25 |
| **731** | A153 | 25c multi | .30 | .25 |
| **732** | A153 | 45c multi | .50 | .40 |
| **733** | A153 | 60c multi | .80 | .60 |
| | | *Nos. 730-733 (4)* | 1.85 | 1.50 |

A souvenir sheet of one No. 732 has inscription for National Philatelic Exhibition. Sold for 3r. Value, $3.75.

Namib Desert A154

**1993, June 4** ***Perf. 14½x14***

| No. | Type | Description | Unused | Used |
|---|---|---|---|---|
| **734** | A154 | 30c Sossusvlei | .25 | .25 |
| **735** | A154 | 40c Blutkuppe | .35 | .30 |
| **736** | A154 | 65c Homeb | .60 | .60 |
| **737** | A154 | 85c Moon landscape | .75 | .80 |
| | | *Nos. 734-737 (4)* | 1.95 | 1.95 |

SOS Children's Village A155

**1993, Aug. 6 Litho. *Perf. 14***

**738** A155 30c Happiness .25 .25
**739** A155 40c A loving family .30 .25
**740** A155 65c Home sweet home .60 .55
**741** A155 85c My village .75 .75
*Nos. 738-741 (4)* 1.90 1.80

A156

Butterflies: 5c, Charaxes jasius saturnus. 10c, Acraea anemosa. 20c, Papilio nireus lyaeus. 30c, Junonia octavia sesamus. (35c), Graphium antheus. 40c, Hypolimnas misippus. 50c, Physcaeneura panda. 65c, Charaxes candiope. 85c, Junonia hierta cebrene. 90c, Colotis celimene pholoe. $1, Cacyreus dicksoni. $2, Charaxes bohemani. $2.50, Stugeta bowkeri tearei. $5, Byblia anvatara acheloia.

**1993-94 *Perf. 14x14½***

**742** A156 5c multicolored .25 .25
**743** A156 10c multicolored .25 .25
**744** A156 20c multicolored .25 .25
**745** A156 30c multicolored .25 .25
**745A** A156 (35c) multicolored .55 .25
**746** A156 40c multicolored .25 .25
**747** A156 50c multicolored .30 .30
**748** A156 65c multicolored .40 .35
**749** A156 85c multicolored .50 .40
**750** A156 90c multicolored .50 .40
**751** A156 $1 multicolored .55 .40
**752** A156 $2 multicolored 1.00 1.00
**753** A156 $2.50 multicolored 1.25 1.25
**754** A156 $5 multicolored 1.75 1.75
*Nos. 742-754 (14)* 8.05 7.35

No. 745A is inscribed "STANDARDISED MAIL" and sold for 35c when issued.
Issued: No. 745A, 4/8/94; others, 10/1/93.

***Perf. 14½x15 Syncopated Type A***

**1997**

*742a* A156 5c multicolored .35 .35
*747a* A156 50c multicolored 1.25 1.00

Issued: Nos. 742a, 747a, 3/3/97.

Coastal Angling A157

**1994, Feb. 4 Litho. *Perf. 14***

**755** A157 30c Blacktail .25 .25
**756** A157 40c Kob .30 .25
**757** A157 65c Steenbras .50 .50
**758** A157 85c Galjoen .75 .70
*a.* Souvenir sheet of 4, #755-758 2.75 2.75
*Nos. 755-758 (4)* 1.80 1.70

Incorporation of Walvis Bay into Namibia A158

**1994, Mar. 1**

**759** A158 30c Quay .45 .40
**760** A158 65c Aerial view .65 .65
**761** A158 85c Map of Namibia 1.00 1.00
*Nos. 759-761 (3)* 2.10 2.05

A159

Flowers: 35c, Adenolobus pechuelii. 40c, Hibiscus elliottiae. 65c, Pelargonium cortusifolium. 85c, Hoodia macrantha.

**1994, Apr. 8 Litho. *Perf. 14***

**762** A159 35c multicolored .25 .25
**763** A159 40c multicolored .30 .25
**764** A159 65c multicolored .50 .40
**765** A159 85c multicolored .70 .60
*Nos. 762-765 (4)* 1.75 1.50

Storks of Etosha — A160

**1994, June 3 Litho. *Perf. 14***

**766** A160 35c Yellowbilled .50 .30
**767** A160 40c Abdim's .55 .40
**768** A160 80c Openbilled .60 .60
**769** A160 $1.10 White .80 .80
*Nos. 766-769 (4)* 2.45 2.10

Trains A161

**1994, Aug. 5 Litho. *Perf. 13½x14***

**770** A161 35c Steam railcar .50 .35
**771** A161 70c Class Krauss .70 .50
**772** A161 80c Class 24 .75 .55
**773** A161 $1.10 Class 7C 1.00 .85
*Nos. 770-773 (4)* 2.95 2.25

A souvenir sheet of 1 #772 was sold for 3r by the Philatelic Foundation of South Africa. Value $2.75.

Railways in Namibia, Cent. A162

Locomotives: 35c, Prince Edward, 1st in service. 70c, Ex-German SWA 2-8-0 tank. 80c, Class 8. $1.10, Class 33 400 diesel electric.

**1995, Mar. 8 Litho. *Perf. 14***

**774** A162 35c multicolored .45 .25
**775** A162 70c multicolored .70 .40
**776** A162 80c multicolored .75 .55
**777** A162 $1.10 multicolored 1.10 .85
*a.* Souvenir sheet of 4, #774-777 3.25 3.25
*Nos. 774-777 (4)* 3.00 2.05

No. 777a sold for $3.50.
No. 777a exists inscribed "Reprint November 1996." Value $4.75.

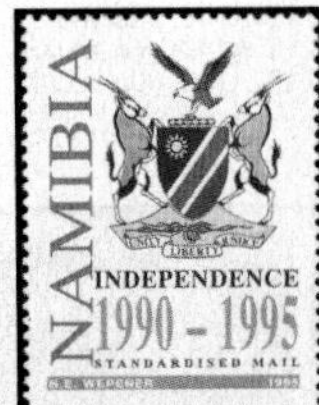

A163

**1995, Mar. 21 Litho. *Perf. 14***

**778** A163 (35c) multicolored .50 .50

Independence, 5th anniv. No. 778 is inscribed "STANDARDISED MAIL" and sold for 35c on day of issue.

A164

Fossils: 40c, Geochelone stromeri. 80c, Diamantornis wardi. 90c, Prohyrax hendeyi. $1.20, Crocodylus lloydi.

**1995, May 24 Litho. *Perf. 14***

**779** A164 40c multicolored .55 .30
**780** A164 80c multicolored .90 .55
**781** A164 90c multicolored 1.00 .60
**782** A164 $1.20 multicolored 1.25 1.25
*Nos. 779-782 (4)* 3.70 2.70

A souvenir sheet of 1 #780 was sold for 3r by the Philatelic Foundation of South Africa. Value $3.

Finnish Mission, 125th Anniv. A165

Designs: 40c, Mission church, Martti Rautanen (1845-1926). 80c, Albin Savola (1867-1934), Oniipa printing press. 90c, Oxwagon, Karl Emanuel August Weikkolin (1842-91). $1.20, Dr. Selma Raino (1873-1939), Onandjokwe Hospital.

**1995, July 10 Litho. *Perf. 14***

**783** A165 40c multicolored .30 .25
**784** A165 80c multicolored .50 .50
**785** A165 90c multicolored .60 .65
**786** A165 $1.20 multicolored .75 .75
*Nos. 783-786 (4)* 2.15 2.15

Traditional Adornments — A166

**1995, Aug. 16 Litho. *Perf. 14½x14***

**787** A166 40c Ivory buttons .30 .25
**788** A166 80c Conus shell .45 .40
**789** A166 90c Cowrie shells .55 .50
**790** A166 $1.20 Shell button .80 .80
*Nos. 787-790 (4)* 2.10 1.95

Souvenir Sheet

Singapore '95 — A167

$1.20, Phacochoerus aethiopicus.

**1995, Sept. 10 Litho. *Perf. 14***

**791** A167 $1.20 multi 1.60 1.60

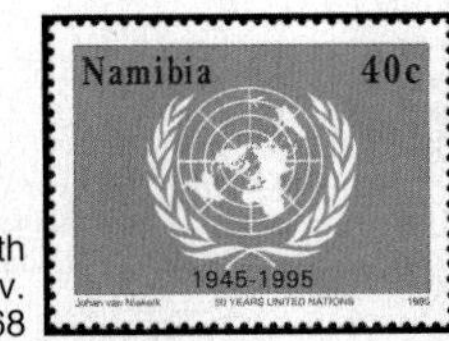

UN, 50th Anniv. A168

**1995, Oct. 24**

**792** A168 40c blue & black .45 .45

Tourism A169

**1996, Apr. 1 Litho. *Perf. 15x14***

**793** A169 (45c) Bogenfels Arch .25 .25
**794** A169 90c Ruacana Falls .30 .30
**795** A169 $1 Epupa Falls .35 .30
**796** A169 $1.30 Wild horses .50 .50
*Nos. 793-796 (4)* 1.40 1.35

No. 793 is inscribed "Standardised Mail" and sold for 45c on day of issue.

Catholic Missions in Namibia A170

50c, Döbra Education and Training Centre. 95c, Heirachabis. $1, Windhoek St. Mary's Cathedral. $1.30, Ovamboland Old Church & School.

**1996, May 27 Litho. *Perf. 15x14***

**797** A170 50c multicolored .25 .25
**798** A170 95c multicolored .35 .35
**799** A170 $1 multicolored .40 .40
**800** A170 $1.30 multicolored .55 .55
*Nos. 797-800 (4)* 1.55 1.55

Souvenir Sheet

CAPEX 96 — A171

**1996, June 8 Litho. *Perf. 14½x14***

**801** A171 $1.30 African lynx 1.50 1.50

UNICEF, 50th Anniv. A172

Designs: (45c), Children have rights. $1.30, Educate the girl.

**1996, June 14 Litho. *Perf. 15x14***

**802** A172 (45c) multicolored .25 .25
**803** A172 $1.30 multicolored .60 .60

No. 802 is inscribed "Standard Postage" and sold for 45c on day of issue.

1996 Summer Olympic Games, Atlanta A173

**1996, June 27**

**804** A173 (45c) Boxing .25 .25
**805** A173 90c Cycling .50 .40
**806** A173 $1 Swimming .30 .50
**807** A173 $1.30 Running .40 .40
*Nos. 804-807 (4)* 1.45 1.55

No. 804 is inscribed "Standard Postage" and sold for 45c on day of issue.

Constellations — A174

Designs: (45c), Scorpio. 90c, Sagittarius. $1, Southern Cross. $1.30, Orion.

**1996, Sept. 12 Litho. *Perf. 15x14***

**808** A174 (45c) multicolored .25 .25
**809** A174 90c multicolored .30 .30
**810** A174 $1 multicolored .35 .35
*a.* Souvenir sheet of 1 2.00 2.00
**811** A174 $1.30 multicolored .50 .50
*Nos. 808-811 (4)* 1.40 1.40

No. 808 is inscribed "Standard Postage" and sold for 45c on day of issue.

No. 810a sold for $3.50. No. 810a exists inscribed "Reprint February 17, 1997. Sold in aid of organized philately N$3.50."

Early Pastoral Pottery — A175

Designs: (45c), Urn-shaped storage vessel. 90c, Bag-shaped cooking vessel. $1, Reconstructed pot. $1.30, Large storage vessel.

**1996, Oct. 17 *Perf. 14x15***

**812** A175 (45c) multicolored .25 .25
**813** A175 90c multicolored .35 .35
**814** A175 $1 multicolored .40 .40
**815** A175 $1.30 multicolored .45 .45
*Nos. 812-815 (4)* 1.45 1.45

No. 812 is inscribed "Standard Postage" and sold for 45c on day of issue.

Ancient //Khauxa!nas Ruins, near Karasburg — A176

Various views of stone wall.

**1997, Feb. 6 Litho. *Perf. 15x14***

**816** A176 (50c) multicolored .30 .25
**817** A176 $1 multicolored .65 .50
**818** A176 $1.10 multicolored .75 .65
**819** A176 $1.50 multicolored 1.25 1.25
*Nos. 816-819 (4)* 2.95 2.65

No. 816 is inscribed "Standard Postage" and sold for 45c on day of issue.

Souvenir Sheet

Hong Kong '97, Intl. Stamp Exhibition — A176a

**1997, Feb. 12 Litho. *Perf. 14½x14***

**819A** A176a $1.30 Sanga bull *2.00 2.00*

No. 819A sold for $3.50. An inscription, "REPRINT 1 APRIL 1997," was added to a later printing of this sheet. Value $3.

A177

**1997, Apr. 8 Litho. *Perf. 14x14½***

**820** A177 $2 multicolored .85 .85

Heinrich von Stephan (1831-97), founder of UPU.

Jackass Penguins — A178

**1997, May 15 Litho. *Perf. 14x14½***

**821** A178 (50c) shown .30 .30
**822** A178 $1 Nesting .50 .35
**823** A178 $1.10 With young .60 .40
**824** A178 $1.50 Swimming .75 .60
*Nos. 821-824 (4)* 2.15 1.65

**Souvenir Sheet**

**824A** A178 Sheet of 4, #b.-e. 2.75 2.75

World Wildlife Fund. No. 821 is inscribed "Standard Postage" and sold for 45c on day of issue.

Nos. 824Ab-824Ae are like Nos. 821-824 but do not have the WWF emblem. No. 824A sold for $5.

Wild Cats A179

**1997, June 12 Litho. *Perf. 14½x14***

**825** A179 (45c) Felis caracal .25 .25
**826** A179 $1 Felis lybica .40 .40
**827** A179 $1.10 Felis serval .50 .50
**828** A179 $1.50 Felis nigripes .60 .60
*Nos. 825-828 (4)* 1.75 1.75

No. 825 is inscribed "Standard Postage" and sold for 45c on day of issue. A souvenir sheet containing a $5 stamp like #828 exists. Value $2.25.

See Nos. 878-881.

Helmeted Guineafowl A180

**1997, June 5 *Perf. 14½x14***

**829** A180 $1.20 multicolored .90 .90

A181

Baskets: 50c, Collecting bag. 90c, Powder basket. $1.20, Fruit basket. $2, Grain basket.

**1997, July 8 Litho. *Perf. 14x14½***

**830** A181 50c multicolored .25 .25
**831** A181 90c multicolored .30 .30
**832** A181 $1.20 multicolored .40 .35
**833** A181 $2 multicolored .70 .70
*Nos. 830-833 (4)* 1.65 1.60

Cinderella Waxbill — A182

60c, Blackchecked waxbill.

***Perf. 14x14½ Syncopated Type A***

**1997, May 5 Booklet Stamps**

**834** A182 50c shown .45 .45
**835** A182 60c multicolored .55 .55
*a.* Booklet pane, 5 each #834-835 6.00
Complete booklet, #835a 6.00

A183

Greetings Stamps A184

Flowers: No. 836, Catophractes alexandri. No. 837, Crinun paludosum. No. 838, Gloriosa superba. No. 839, Tribulus zeyheri. No. 840, Aptosimum pubescens.

Helmeted guineafowl: No. 841, In bed. No. 842, Holding flowers. No. 843, As music conductor. No. 844, Prepared to travel. No. 845, Wearing heart necklace.

**1997, July 11 Litho. *Perf. 14x13½***

**Booklet Stamps**

**836** A183 (50c) multicolored .40 .40
**837** A183 (50c) multicolored .40 .40
**838** A183 (50c) multicolored .40 .40
**839** A183 (50c) multicolored .40 .40
**840** A183 (50c) multicolored .40 .40
*a.* Booklet pane, 2 each #836-840 + 10 labels 4.50
Complete booklet, #840a 4.50
**841** A184 50c multicolored .40 .40
**842** A184 50c multicolored .40 .40
**843** A184 50c multicolored .40 .40
**844** A184 $1 multicolored .80 .80
**845** A184 $1 multicolored .80 .80
*a.* Booklet pane, 2 each #841-845 + 10 labels 6.25
Complete booklet, #845a 6.25

Nos. 836-840 are inscribed "Standard Postage" and sold for 45c on day of issued.

Namibian Veterinary Assoc., 50th Anniv. — A185

**1997, Sept. 12 *Perf. 14***

**846** A185 $1.50 multicolored .60 .60

Souvenir Sheet

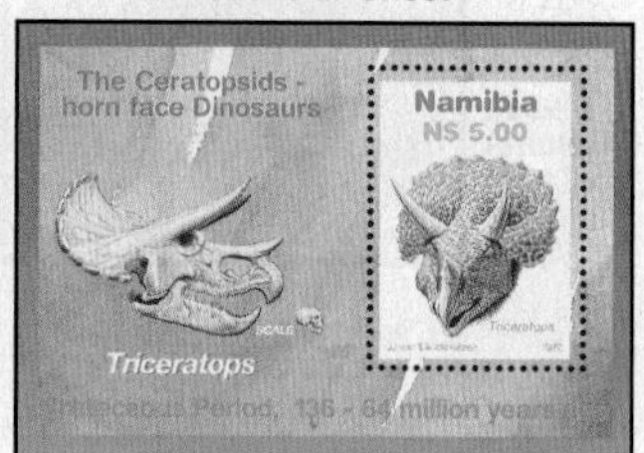


Triceratops — A186

**1997, Sept. 27 Litho. *Perf. 13***

**847** A186 $5 multicolored 2.00 2.00

World Post Day — A187

**1997, Oct. 9 Litho. *Perf. 14x15***

**848** A187 (45c) multicolored .50 .35

No. 848 is inscribed "Standard Postage" and sold for 45c on day of issue.

Trees — A188

Designs: (50c), False mopane. $1, Ana tree. $1.10, Shepherd's tree. $1.50, Kiaat.

**1997, Oct. 10**

**849** A188 (50c) multi .25 .25
**850** A188 $1 multi .30 .30
**851** A188 $1.10 multi .35 .35
**852** A188 $1.50 multi .55 *.70*
*Nos. 849-852 (4)* 1.45 1.60

No. 849 is inscribed "Standard Postage" and sold for 45c on day of issue.

Fauna and Flora — A189

5c, Flame lily. 10c, Bushman poison. 20c, Camel's foot. 30c, Western rhigozum. 40c, Bluecheeked bee-eater. (50c), Rosyfaced lovebird. 50c, Laughing dove. 60c, Lappetfaced vulture. 90c, Yellowbilled hornbill. $1, Lilacbreasted roller. $1.10, Hippopotamus. ($1.20), Leopard. $1.20, Giraffe. $1.50, Elephant. $2, Lion. $4, Buffalo. $5, Black rhinoceros. $10, Cheetah.

**1997, Nov. 3 Litho. *Perf. 13½***

**853** A189 5c multi .25 .40
**854** A189 10c multi .25 .40
**855** A189 20c multi .25 .25
**856** A189 30c multi .25 .25
**857** A189 40c multi .25 .25
**858** A189 (50c) multi .25 .25
*a.* Booklet pane of 10, perf 14x13½ 2.50
Complete booklet, #858a 2.50
**859** A189 50c multi .25 .25
**860** A189 60c multi .30 .25
**861** A189 90c multi .35 .30
**862** A189 $1 multi .40 .35
**863** A189 $1.10 multi .45 .40
**864** A189 ($1.20) multi .50 .60
*a.* Booklet pane of 10, perf 14x13½ 5.50
Complete booklet, #864a 5.50
**865** A189 $1.20 multi .40 .40
**866** A189 $1.50 multi .45 .45
**867** A189 $2 multi .60 .45
**868** A189 $4 multi .90 .80
**869** A189 $5 multi 1.25 1.00
**870** A189 $10 multi 2.25 2.00
*a.* Bklt. pane, 1 ea #853-870, perf 14x13½ 10.00
Complete booklet, #870a 10.00
*Nos. 853-870 (18)* 9.60 9.05

**Self-Adhesive**

***Die Cut Perf. 12x12½***

**870B** A189 (45c) like #858 .25 .25
**870C** A189 $1 like #862 .50 .40
**870D** A189 ($1.20) like #864 .65 .55
*Nos. 870B-870D (3)* 1.40 1.20

No. 858 is inscribed "Standard Postage" and sold for 50c on day issue. No. 864 is inscribed "Postcard Rate" and sold for $1.20 on day of issue. Nos. 853-854, 857, 860, 864, 866-867 and maybe others, exist imperf. Value: $100-$125 each pair.

For surcharges see #959-962, 1060-1063, 1071-1080, 1132-1040.

Christmas A190

Various pictures of a helmeted guineafowl.

**1997, Nov. 3** *Perf. 13x12½*

**871** A190 (50c) multicolored .25 .25
**872** A190 $1 multicolored .40 .30
**873** A190 $1.10 multicolored .45 .35
**874** A190 $1.50 multicolored .55 .55
*Nos. 871-874 (4)* 1.65 1.45

**Souvenir Sheet**

**875** A190 $5 multi, vert. 2.25 2.25

No. 871 is inscribed "Standard Postage" and sold for 50c on day of issue.

A191

**1997, Nov. 27** *Perf. 14x15*

**876** A191 (50c) multicolored .45 .45

John Muafangejo (1943-87), artist. No. 876 is inscribed "Standard Postage" and sold for 50c on day of issue.

A192

**1998, Jan. 15**

**877** A192 (50c) brown & gray .35 .35

Gabriel B. Taapopi (1911-85). No. 877 is inscribed "Standard Postage" and sold for 50c on day of issue.

**Wild Cats Type of 1997**

Designs: $1.20, Panthera pardus. $1.90, Panthera leo, female carrying young. $2, Panthera leo, male. $2.50, Acinonyx jubatus.

**1998, Jan. 26** *Perf. 13x12½*

**878** A179 $1.20 multicolored .60 .40
**879** A179 $1.90 multicolored .70 .60
**880** A179 $2 multicolored .75 .75
**881** A179 $2.50 multicolored .90 .90
*a.* Souvenir sheet, #878-881 3.50 3.50
*Nos. 878-881 (4)* 2.95 2.65

Narra Plant — A194

**1998, Feb. 9** *Perf. 12½x13*

**882** A194 $2.40 multicolored .65 .65

Water Awareness A195

**1998, Mar. 23** **Litho.** *Perf. 14x15*

**883** A195 (50c) multicolored .35 .35

No. 883 is inscribed "Standard Postage" and sold for 50c on date of issue.

---

Nos. 885-895 were initially not available in Namibia. They were issued Nov. 23, 1997, at a Shanghai, China, stamp exhibition by a Chinese stamp dealer acting for the Namibia Post Office. There is some question whether they were sold in Namibia, but if they were, it was not until early 1998.

---

A197

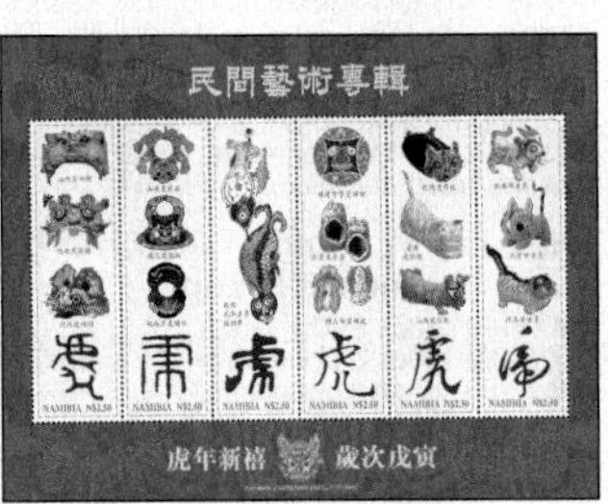
Lunar New Year — A198

Chinese inscriptions, wood cut images of a tiger, stylized drawings of tiger in — #885: a, orange. b, light green. c, yellow. d, blue. e, dark green. f, lilac.

No. 886: Various tiger figures, Chinese inscriptions.

No. 887, Chinese inscriptions, stylized tigers.

*Perf. 13½x12½*

**1997, Nov. 23** **Litho.**

**885** A197 $2.50 Sheet of 6, #a.-f. 6.00 6.00

*Perf. 14x13½*

**886** A198 $2.50 Sheet of 6, #a.-f. 6.00 6.00

**Souvenir Sheets**

*Perf. 12½*

**887** A197 $6 multicolored 2.75 2.75
**888** A198 $6 multicolored 2.75 2.75

Nos. 887-888 each contain one 69x38mm stamp.

Macau Returns to China in 1999 A199

Designs: No. 890, Flag, building. No. 892, Flag, Deng Xiaoping, building.

**1997, Nov. 23** *Perf. 13½*

**889** A199 $4.50 multicolored 2.50 2.50

**Size: 59x27mm**

*Perf. 13½x13*

**890** A199 $4.50 multicolored 3.25 3.25

**Souvenir Sheets**

*Perf. 13½x12½*

**891** A199 $6 multicolored 3.00 3.00

*Perf. 12½*

**892** A199 $6 multicolored 3.00 3.00

Nos. 889-890 issued in sheets of 3. No. 891 contains one 62x33mm stamp, No. 892 one 69x33mm stamp.

Return of Hong Kong to China — A200

Chinese landmarks — #892A: b, Beijing, Natl. Capital of China. c, Return of Hong Kong, 1997. d, Return of Macao, 1999. e, The Taiwan Region.

**1997, Nov. 17** **Litho.** *Perf. 14x13½*

**892A** A200 $3.50 Sheet of 4, #b.-e. 6.25 6.25

**Souvenir Sheet**

*Perf. 12½*

**893** A200 $6 Chinese landmarks 2.50 2.50

No. 893 contains one 72x41mm stamp.

Shanghai Communique, 25th Anniv. — A201

No. 894: a, Pres. Nixon, Mao Zedong, 1972. b, Pres. Carter, Deng Xiaoping, 1979. c, Pres. Reagan, Deng Xiaoping, 1984. d, Pres. Bush, Deng Xiaoping, 1989.

$6, Nixon, Zhou Enlai, 1972.

**1997, Nov. 17** *Perf. 13½x12½*

**894** A201 $3.50 Sheet of 4, #a.-d. 5.00 5.00

**Souvenir Sheet**

*Perf. 14x13½*

**895** A201 $6 multicolored 2.75 2.75

No. 895 contains one 67x33mm stamp.

Owls — A204

No. 898, Rat (prey). No. 899, Whitefaced owl. No. 900, Barred owl. No. 901, Spotted eagle owl. No. 902, Barn owl.

**1998, Apr. 1** **Litho.** *Perf. 13½x13*

**Booklet Stamps**

**898** A204 55c multi .40 .40

**Size: 38x23mm**

**899** A204 $1.50 multi .70 .70
**900** A204 $1.50 multi .70 .70
**901** A204 $1.90 multi .90 .90

**Size: 61x21mm**

**902** A204 $1.90 multi .90 .90
*a.* Booklet pane, #898-902 3.75
Complete booklet, #902a 3.75

See No. 950.

Shells A205

Designs: (55c), Patella granatina. $1.10, Cymatium cutaceum africanum. $1.50, Conus mozambicus. $6, Venus verrucosa.

**1998, May 14** **Litho.** *Perf. 12½*

**903** A205 (55c) multicolored .30 .25
**904** A205 $1.10 multicolored .45 .30
**905** A205 $1.50 multicolored .60 .60
**906** A205 $6 multicolored 2.25 2.25
*a.* Souvenir sheet, #903-906 4.25 4.25
*Nos. 903-906 (4)* 3.60 3.40

No. 903 inscribed "Standard Postage."

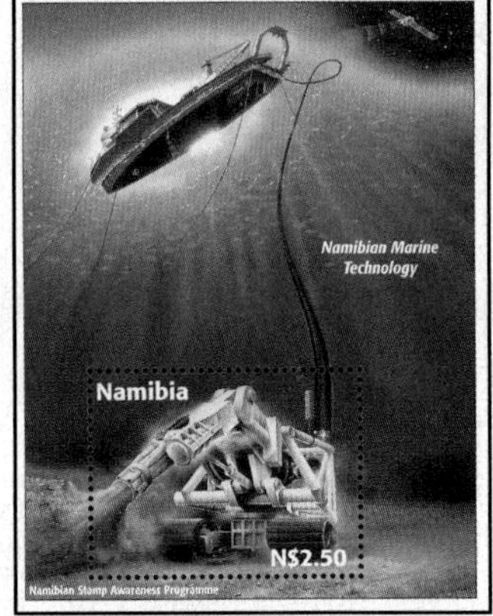
Namibian Marine Technology — A206

**1998, May 18** **Litho.** *Perf. 14½x14*

**908** A206 $2.50 multicolored 2.00 2.00

**Diana, Princess of Wales (1961-97)**

Common Design Type

Working for removal of land mines: a, Wearing face shield. b, Wearing Red Cross shirt. c, In white blouse. d, With child.

**1998, May 18** **Litho.** *Perf. 14½x14*

**909** CD355 $1 Sheet of 4, #a.-d. 1.75 1.75

World Environment Day — A207

(55c), Namibian coast. $1.10, Okavango sunset. $1.50, Sossusvlei. $1.90, African moringo.

**1998, June 5** **Litho.** *Perf. 13x13½*

**910** A207 (55c) multicolored .30 .25
**911** A207 $1.10 multicolored .45 .30
**912** A207 $1.50 multicolored .50 .45
**913** A207 $1.90 multicolored .55 .55
*Nos. 910-913 (4)* 1.80 1.55

No. 910 is inscribed "Standard Postage."

Souvenir Sheet

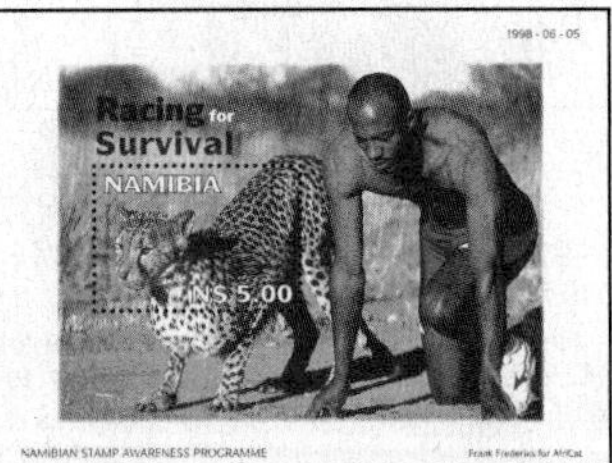
Racing for Survival — A208

**1998, June 5** *Perf. 13*

**914** A208 $5 Acinonyx jubatus 2.25 2.25

Animals and Their Young — A209

a, Chacma baboon. b, Blue wildebeest. c, Suricate. d, Elephant. e, Burchell's zebra.

**1998, June 18** ***Perf. 13½x13***
**915** A209 $1.50 Sheet of 5, #a.-e. 3.00 3.00

Souvenir Sheet

1998 World Cup Soccer Championships, France — A210

**1998, July 1** **Litho.** ***Perf. 14***
**916** A210 $5 multicolored 2.00 2.00

Flora and Fauna of the Caprivi Strip — A211

Designs: a, Carmine bee-eater. b, Sable antelope. c, Lechwe. d, Woodland waterberry. e, Nile monitor. f, African jacana. g, African fish eagle. h, Woodland kingfisher. i, Nile crocodile. j, Black mamba.

**1998, Sept. 26** **Litho.** ***Perf. 12½***
**917** A211 60c Sheet of 10, #a.-j. *10.00 10.00*

#917b-917c, 917e are 40x40mm, #917i is 54x30mm, #917j is 32x30mm.

Souvenir Sheet

Black Rhinoceros — A212

**1998, Oct. 20** **Litho.** ***Perf. 13***
**918** A212 $5 multicolored 2.00 2.00

Ilsapex '98, Intl. Philatelic Exhibition, Johannesburg.

Souvenir Sheet

Whales — A213

**1998, Oct. 9** **Litho.** ***Perf. 13½x14***
**919** A213 $5 multicolored 2.25 2.25

See Norfolk Island No. 665, South Africa No. 1095.

Damara Dik Dik — A214

Striped Tree Squirrel — A215

**1999, Jan. 18** **Litho.** ***Perf. 13½***
**920** A214 $1.80 multi 2.50 1.50
**921** A215 $2.65 multi 4.25 4.25

"Yoka" the Snake — A216

"Yoka" the Snake A217

Cartoon pictures of Yoka: No. 922, Turning head. No. 923, Wrapped around tree branch. No. 924, Tail wrapped around branch and female snake. No. 925, With female snake and mouse. No. 926, In love. No. 927, Yoka tied up in knots. No. 928, Smashed with footprint. No. 929, Female snake's tail, Yoka's head. No. 930, Female snake singing to dazed Yoka. No. 931, Lying with tail over nose.

***Serpentine Die Cut***

**1999, Feb. 1** **Self-Adhesive** **Litho.**

**Booklet Stamps**

**922** A216 $1.60 multicolored .50 .50
**923** A217 $1.60 multicolored .50 .50
**924** A216 $1.60 multicolored .50 .50
**925** A217 $1.60 multicolored .50 .50
**926** A216 $1.60 multicolored .50 .50
**927** A217 $1.60 multicolored .50 .50
**928** A216 $1.60 multicolored .50 .50
**929** A216 $1.60 multicolored .50 .50
**930** A216 $1.60 multicolored .50 .50
**931** A217 $1.60 multicolored .50 .50
*a.* Bklt. pane of 10, #922-931 5.00

The peelable paper backing serves as a booklet cover.

Souvenir Sheet

Passenger Liner "Windhuk" — A218

**1999, Mar. 18** ***Perf. 14***
**932** A218 $5.50 multicolored 2.00 2.00

Gliders A219

**1999, Apr. 13** **Litho.** ***Perf. 13***
**933** A219 $1.60 Zögling, 1928 .80 .80
**934** A219 $1.80 Schleicher, 1998 1.00 1.00

Souvenir Sheet

IBRA '99, Nuremberg, Germany — A220

**1999, Apr. 27** **Litho.** ***Perf. 14x14¼***
**935** A220 $5.50 multi 2.00 2.00

Falcons — A221

60c, Greater kestrel. $1.60, Rock kestrel. $1.80, Red-necked falcon. $2.65, Lanner falcon.

**1999, May 18** **Litho.** ***Perf. 13¼x13½***
**936** A221 60c multicolored .70 .40
**937** A221 $1.60 multicolored 1.00 .90
**938** A221 $1.80 multicolored 1.10 1.00
**939** A221 $2.65 multicolored 1.75 2.00
*Nos. 936-939 (4)* 4.55 4.30

Souvenir Sheet

Termitomyces Schimperi — A222

**1999, June 19** **Litho.** ***Perf. 13¾***
**940** A222 $5.50 multicolored 2.10 2.10

PhilexFrance '99 World Philatelic Exhibition.

Wetland Birds A223

Designs: $1.60, Wattled crane. $1.80, Burchell's sand grouse. $1.90, Rock pratincole. $2.65, Eastern white pelican.

**1999, June 28** ***Perf. 12¾***
**941** A223 $1.60 multicolored .75 .60
**942** A223 $1.80 multicolored .90 .75
**943** A223 $1.90 multicolored 1.20 1.00
**944** A223 $2.65 multicolored 1.60 1.60
*Nos. 941-944 (4)* 4.45 3.95

Orchids A224

Designs: $1.60, Eulophia hereroensis. $1.80, Ansellia africana. $2.65, Eulophia leachii. $3.90, Eulophia speciosa. $5.50, Eulophia walleri.

**Litho. & Embossed**

**1999, Aug. 21** ***Perf. 12¾***
**945** A224 $1.60 multicolored .65 .55
**946** A224 $1.80 multicolored .75 .65
**947** A224 $2.65 multicolored 1.25 1.25
**948** A224 $3.90 multicolored 1.60 1.60
*Nos. 945-948 (4)* 4.25 4.05

**Souvenir Sheet**

**949** A224 $5.50 multicolored 2.50 2.50

Embossing is found only on the margin of No. 949. China 1999 World Philatelic Exhibition (No. 949).

**Owl Type of 1998**
**Souvenir Sheet**

***Perf. 13½x12¾***

**1999, Sept. 30** **Litho.**
**950** A204 $11 Like #902 5.75 5.75

Selection of stamp design as "most beautiful," 5th Stamp World Cup.

Urieta Kazahendike (Johanna Gertze) (1836-1935) A225

**1999, Oct. 1** **Litho.** ***Perf. 12¾***
**951** A225 $20 multicolored 5.50 5.50

Souvenir Sheet

Turn of the Millennium — A226

***Perf. 13¾x13¼***

**1999, Dec. 31** **Litho.**
**952** A226 $9 multi 4.00 4.00

No. 952 has a holographic image. Soaking in water may affect the hologram.

Sunset Over Namibia — A227

**1999-2000** ***Perf. 13¼x13¾***
**953** A227 $2.20 shown 1.25 1.25
**954** A227 $2.40 Sunrise 1.40 1.40

Issued: $2.20, 12/31; $2.40, 1/1/00.

Ducks A228

Designs: $2, South African shelduck. $2.40, Whitefaced duck. $3, Knobbilled duck. $7, Cape shoveller.

**2000, Feb. 18** **Litho.** ***Perf. 13***
**955** A228 $2 multi 1.10 1.10
**956** A228 $2.40 multi 1.25 1.25
**957** A228 $3 multi 1.50 1.50
**958** A228 $7 multi 3.25 3.25
*Nos. 955-958 (4)* 7.10 7.10

Nos. 853-856 Surcharged

**2000, Mar. 1 Litho. *Perf. 13½***

**959** A189 (65c) on 5c multi .40 .40
**960** A189 $1.80 on 30c multi .90 .90
**961** A189 $3 on 10c multi 1.50 1.50
**962** A189 $6 on 20c multi 3.00 3.00
*Nos. 959-962 (4)* 5.80 5.80

See No. 1000.

Independence, 10th Anniv. — A229

**2000, Mar. 21 *Perf. 13¼x13¾***

**963** A229 65c Children .75 .40
**964** A229 $3 Flag 2.00 2.00

Passion Play — A230

Designs: $2.10, Jesus with crown of thorns. $2.40, Carrying cross.

**2000, Apr. 1 *Perf. 13¾***

**965** A230 $2.10 multi .75 .75
**966** A230 $2.40 multi .85 .85

Fauna of the Namib Desert — A231

Designs: a, $2, Tenebrionid beetle. b, $2 Brown hyena. c, $2, Namib golden mole. d, $2, Shovel-snouted lizard. e, $2, Dune lark. f, $6, Namib side-winding adder.

**2000, May 22 *Perf. 14½***

**967** A231 Sheet of 6, #a-f 9.00 9.00

The Stamp Show 2000, London.

Sizes of stamps: Nos. 967a-967c, 30x25mm; No. 967d, 30x50mm; Nos. 967e-967f, 26x37mm. Portions of the design were applied by a thermographic process, producing a shiny raised effect.

Welwitschia Mirabilis — A232

Various views of Welwitschia plants. Denominations: (65c), $2.20, $3, $4.

**2000, June 21 Litho. *Perf. 13¾***

**968-971** A232 Set of 4 4.50 4.50

No. 968 is inscribed "Standard inland mail."

Souvenir Sheet

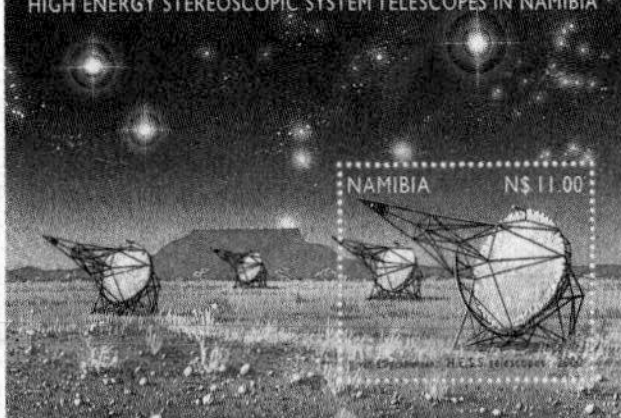

High Energy Stereoscopic Sytem Telescopes — A233

**2000, July 7 *Perf. 13¼x13¾***

**972** A233 $11 multi 6.25 6.25

Fruit Trees — A234

Designs: (65c), Jackalberry. $2, Sycamore fig. $2.20, Bird plum. $7, Marula.

**2000, Aug. 16 Litho. *Perf. 13¼x14***

**973-976** A234 Set of 4 6.25 6.25

No. 973 is inscribed "Standard inland mail."

Souvenir Sheet

Yoka in Etosha — A235

**2000, Sept. 1 *Perf. 13¼x13***

**977** A235 $11 multi 5.50 5.50

Coelenterates A236

Designs: ($1), Anthothoe stimpsoni. $2.45, Bundosoma capensis. $3.50, Anthopleura stephensoni. $6.60, Pseudactinia flagellifera.

**2001, Apr. 18 Litho. *Perf. 13¾***

**978-981** A236 Set of 4 5.50 5.50

No. 978 is inscribed "Standard inland mail."

Civil Aviation A237

Designs: ($1), Cessna 210 Turbo. $2.20, Douglas DC-6B. $2.50, Pitts 52A. $13.20, Bell 407 helicopter.

**2001, May 9 *Perf. 13¼x13¾***

**982-985** A237 Set of 4 10.00 10.00

No. 982 is inscribed "Standard inland mail."

Renewable Energy Resources — A238

No. 986: a, Wood efficient stove. b, Biogas digester. c, Solar cooker. d, Repair, reuse, recycle. e, Solar water pump. f, Solar home system. g, Solar street light. h, Solar water heater. i, Solar telecommunication. j, Wind water pump.

**2001, Aug. 15 *Perf. 13½x14***

**986** A238 Sheet of 10 10.00 10.00
*a.-e.* ($1) Any single .40 .40
*f.-j.* $3.50 Any single 1.10 1.10

Nos. 986a-986e are inscribed "Standard Mail."

Central Highlands Flora and Fauna — A239

No. 987: a, ($1.00), Ruppell's parrot (31x29mm). b, $3.50, Camel thorn (54x29mm). c, ($1.00), Flap-necked chameleon (39x29mm). d, ($1.00), Klipspringer (39x29mm). e, $3.50, Berg aloe (39x29mm). f, $3.50, Kudu (39x39mm). g, ($1.00), Rockrunner (39x29mm). h, $3.50, Namibian rock agama (39x39mm). i, ($1.00), Pangolin (39x39mm). j, $3.50, Armored ground cricket (39x29mm).

**2001, Sept. 5 *Perf. 12½x12¾***

**987** A239 Sheet of 10, #a-j 12.50 12.50

Nos. 987a, 987c, 987d, 987g, 987i are inscribed "Standard Mail."

Tribal Women — A240

No. 988, ($1.30): a, Mbalantu. b, Damara. c, Herero (leather headdress). d, San. e, Mafue. f, Baster.

No. 989, ($1.30): a, Mbukushu. b, Herero (flowered headdress). c, Himba. d, Kwanyama. e, Nama. f, Ngandjera/Kwaluudhi.

**2002, Apr. 20 Litho. *Perf. 13¼x13***
**Sheets of 6, #a-f**

**988-989** A240 Set of 2 9.00 9.00
*988g* Sheet of 6 with incorrect back inscriptions 10.00 10.00
*989g* Sheet of 6 with incorrect back inscriptions 15.00 15.00

Stamps are inscribed "Standard Mail."

The back inscriptions on Nos. 988g and 989g are placed incorrectly so that the inscriptions for the stamps on the left side of the sheet have the back inscriptions of the stamps on the right side of the sheet, and vice versa.

The Mbukushu stamp on No. 989g reads "Standard Maiil."

Birds — A241

Designs: ($1.30), African hoopoe. $2.20, Paradise flycatchers. $2.60, Swallowtailed bee-eaters. $2.80, Malachite kingfisher.

**2002, May 15 *Perf. 13¾x13¼***

**990-993** A241 Set of 4 6.50 6.50

No. 990 is inscribed "Standard Mail."

Ephemeral Rivers A242

Designs: ($1.30), Kuiseb River floods halting movement of sand dunes, vert. (36x48mm). $2.20, Bird flying over lake of Tsauchab River flood water. $2.60, Elephants in dry bed of Hoarusib River (86x22mm). $2.80, Birds near Nossob River flood water. $3.50, Birds near Fish River, vert. (55x21mm).

**2002, July 1 *Perf. 13x13¼,13¼x13***

**994-998** A242 Set of 5 7.50 7.50

See No. 1023.

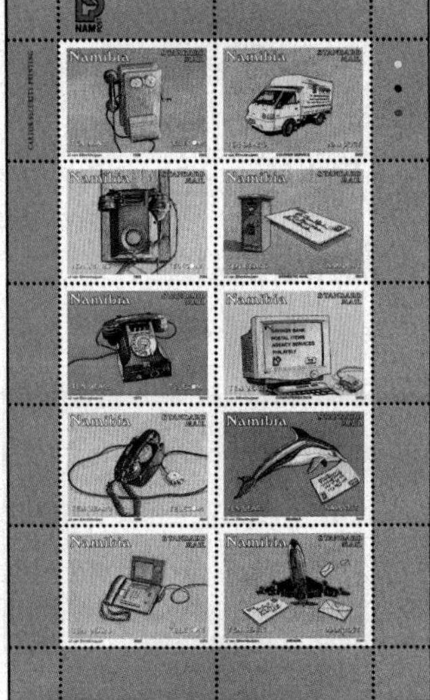

Namibia Post and Telecommunications, 10th Anniv. — A243

No. 999: a, Telephone, blue background. b, Telephone, yellow background. c, Telephone, green background. d, Telephone, lilac background. e, Telephone, brown background. f, Mail van. g, Pillar box and letter. h, Computer. i, Dolphin with letter. j, Airplane and letters.

**2002, Aug. 1 Litho. *Perf. 13¼x13***

**999** A243 ($1.30) Sheet of 10, #a-j 6.00 6.00
*k.* Sheet of 10, 2 each #a-e 6.00 6.00
*l.* Sheet of 10, 2 each #f-j 6.00 6.00

Stamps are inscribed "Standard Mail."

Nos. 853-854 Surcharged

**2002, Oct. 21 Litho. *Perf. 13½***

**1000** A189 ($1.45) on 5c #853 .75 .75
**1001** A189 ($1.45) on 10c #854 .75 .75

Surcharge on No. 1000 has letters that lean more to the right than those on No. 959. The two "d's" have tops that curve to the right on No. 1000, but have serifs that point left on No. 959. The cross line of the "t's" are lower on No. 1000 than on No. 959.

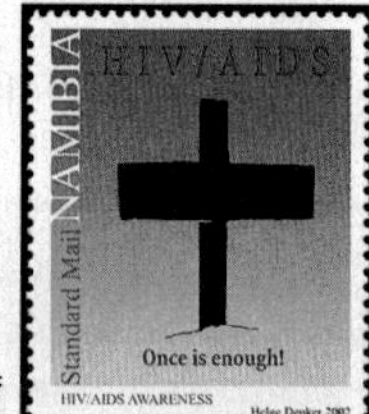


Prevention of AIDS — A244

Designs: ($1.45), Cross. $2.45, Condom. $2.85, Man and hand. $11.50, Test tubes.

**2002, Dec. 1 *Perf. 13½x13***

**1002-1005** A244 Set of 4 7.00 7.00

No. 1002 is inscribed "Standard Mail."

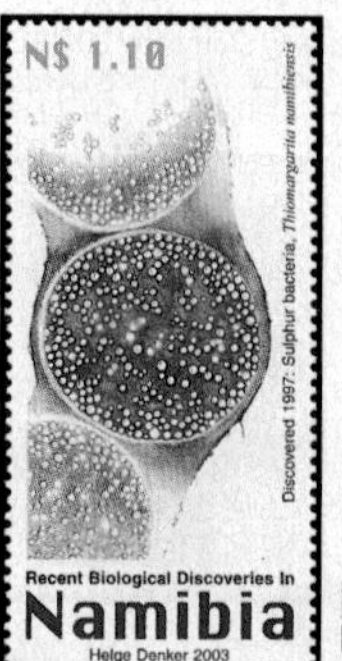


Recent Biological Discoveries A245

Designs: $1.10, Sulphur bacteria. $2.45, Whiteheadia etesionamibensis. $2.85, Cunene flathead (catfish), horiz. $3.85, Zebra racer, horiz. $20, Gladiator (insect).

***Perf. 13¾x13¼, 13¼x13¾***

**2003, Feb. 24**

**1006-1010** A245 Set of 5 8.25 8.25

Rural Development — A246

Designs: $1.45, Water and electricity supply. ($2.75), Conservancy formation and land use diversification. $4.40, Education and health services. ($11.50), Communication and road infrastructure.

**2003, Apr. 17 Litho. *Perf. 13¼x13¾***

**1011-1014** A246 Set of 4 6.00 6.00

No. 1012 is inscribed "Postcard Rate" and No. 1014 is inscribed "Registered Mail."

Wetlands — A247

Designs: $1.10, Women and cattle near oshana. $2.85, Birds at Omadhiya Lakes. ($3.85), Cuvelai Drainage.

**2003, June 6**

**1015-1017** A247 Set of 3 5.75 5.75

No. 1017 is inscribed "Non-Standard Mail."

Heroes Acre Monuments — A248

Various monuments with inscriprions: ($1.45), Standard Mail. ($2.75), Postcard Rate. ($3.85), Non-Standard Mail.

**2003, Aug. 27 *Perf. 13¼***

**1018-1020** A248 Set of 3 4.25 4.25

Souvenir Sheet

Geological Surveying in Namibia, Cent. — A249

**2003, Sept. 10 *Perf. 13¼x13¾***

**1021** A249 $10 multi 8.25 8.25

Souvenir Sheet

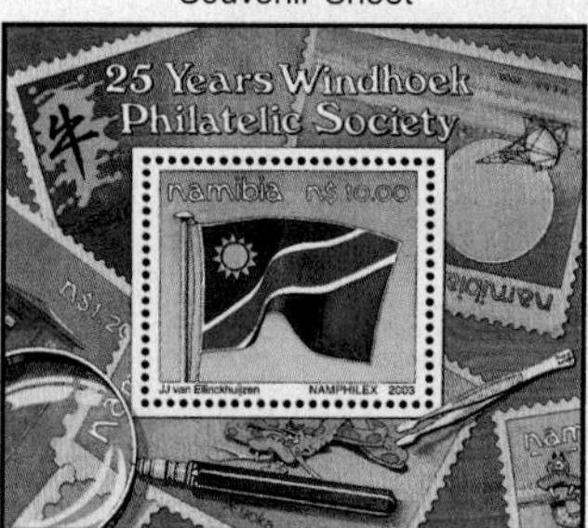


Windhoek Philatelic Society, 25th Anniv. — A250

**2003, Sept. 10**

**1022** A250 $10 multi 7.25 7.25

**Ephemeral Rivers Type of 2002**

Souvenir Sheet

**2003, Dec. 8 *Perf. 13¼x13***

**1023** A242 $3.15 Like #996 4.00 4.00

Design voted "most beautiful stamp" at 8th Stamp World Cup, Paris.

Vervet Monkeys — A251

Designs: $1.60, Adult holding fruit. $3.15, Two monkeys on tree branches. $3.40, Adult and young. ($14.25), Adult chewing on twig. $4.85, Like #1024.

**2004, Jan. 30 *Perf. 13***

**1024-1027** A251 Set of 4 8.75 8.75

**Souvenir Sheet**

**1028** A251 $4.85 multi 3.00 3.00

No. 1027 is inscribed "Inland Registered Mail Paid." 2004 Hong Kong Stamp Expo (#1028).

Honeybees on Flowers A252

Honeybees on: ($1.60), Sickle bush. $2.70, Daisy. ($3.05), Aloe. $3.15, Cat's claw. ($14.25), Edging senecio. $4.85, Pretty lady.

**2004, Feb. 2 *Perf. 13x13¼***

**1029-1033** A252 Set of 5 7.75 7.75

**Souvenir Sheet**

**1034** A252 $4.85 multi 2.75 2.75

No. 1029 is inscribed "Standard mail;" No. 1031, "Post card rate;" No. 1033, "Inland registered mail paid."

Anti-Colonial Resistance, Cent. — A253

**2004, Mar. 23 Litho. *Perf. 13¼***

**1035** A253 ($1.60) multi 1.40 1.40

**Souvenir Sheet**

**1036** A253 $5 multi 2.25 2.25

No. 1035 is inscribed "Standard Mail."

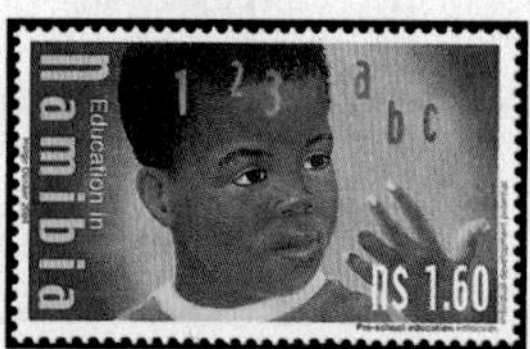


Education in Namibia — A254

Designs: $1.60, Pre-school education enhances individual development potential. $2.75, Primary and secondary school education for all lays the foundation for equal opportunity. $4.40, Advanced learning and vocational training provide career options. ($12.65), Lifelong learning encourages personal growth and the capacity for leadership.

**2004, Apr. 19 *Perf. 13¼x13¾***

**1037-1040** A254 Set of 4 6.75 6.75

No. 1040 is inscribed "Registered Mail."

Fishing Industry — A255

Fish and: $1.60, Ship and dockworkers. $2.75, Ship. $4.85, Workers at processing plant.

***Perf. 13¼x13¾***

**2004, June 22 Litho.**

**1041-1043** A255 Set of 3 6.00 6.00

Historic Buildings in Bethanie A256

Designs: ($1.60), Joseph Ferdericks House. ($3.05), Schmelen House. ($4.40), Rhenish Mission Church. ($12.65), Stone Church.

**2004, July 7 *Perf. 14x13½***

**1044-1047** A256 Set of 4 8.25 8.25

No. 1044 is inscribed "Standard Mail;" No. 1045, "Postcard rate;" No. 1046, "Non-Standard Mail," No. 1047, "Registered Mail."

2004 Summer Olympics, Athens A257

Designs: ($1.60), Wrestling. $2.90, Boxing, vert. $3.40, Pistol shooting. $3.70, Mountain biking, vert.

***Perf. 14x13¼, 13¼x14***

**2004, Aug. 3 Litho.**

**1048-1051** A257 Set of 4 8.75 8.75
*1051a* Inscribed "XXVIII Olympiad" 5.00 5.00

No. 1048 is inscribed "Standard Mail."

No. 1051 has incorrect inscription "XVIII Olympiad."

No. 1051a issued 9/14.

Miniature Sheet

Birds — A258

No. 1052: a, African fish eagles, national bird of Namibia. b, African fish eagles, national bird of Zimbabwe. c, Peregrine falcons, national bird of Angola. d, Cattle egrets, national bird of Botswana. e, Purple-crested louries, national bird of Swaziland. f, Blue cranes, national bird of South Africa. g, Bat-tailed trogons. h, African fish eagles, national bird of Zambia.

**2004, Oct. 11 Litho. *Perf. 14***

**1052** A258 $3.40 Sheet of 8, #a-h 17.00 17.00

See Botswana Nos. 792-793, South Africa No. 1342, Swaziland Nos. 727-735, Zambia No. 1033, and Zimbabwe No. 975.

Rotary International, Cent. — A259

**2005, Feb. 23 Litho. *Perf. 13x13¼***

**1053** A259 $3.70 multi 2.75 2.75

Pres. Hifikepunye Pohamba A260

**2005, Mar. 21 *Perf. 13¼x14***

**1054** A260 ($1.70) multi 2.25 2.25

Inscribed "Standard Mail."

Sunbirds
A261

Designs: $2.90, Marico sunbird. $3.40, Dusky sunbird. ($4.80), White-bellied sunbird. ($15.40), Scarlet-chested sunbird.
$10, Amethyst sunbird, horiz.

**2005, Apr. 14 Litho. *Perf. 13¼x14***
**1055-1058** A261 Set of 4 11.50 11.50

**Souvenir Sheet**
***Perf. 14x13¼***
**1059** A261 $10 multi 5.00 5.00

No. 1057 is inscribed "Non-Standard Mail"; No. 1058, "Registered Inland Postage Paid." Nos. 1055-1058 exists imperf. Value, each pair $40.

**Nos. 855, 859, 861 and 868 Surcharged**

a

b

c

**2005, June 7 Litho. *Perf. 13½***
**1060** A189(a) ($1.70) on 50c #859 1.00 1.00
**1061** A189(b) $2.90 on 20c #855 5.00 2.00
**1062** A189(c) ($4.80) on $4 #868 3.50 1.75
**1063** A189(b) $5.20 on 90c #861 2.50 1.75
*Nos. 1060-1063 (4)* 12.00 6.50

Medicinal Plants
A262

Designs: ($1.70), Nara. $2.90, Devil's claw. ($3.10), Hoodia. ($4.80), Tsamma.

**2005, July 22 *Perf. 14x13¼***
**1064-1067** A262 Set of 4 6.00 6.00

No. 1064 is inscribed "Standard Mail"; No. 1066, "Postcard Rate"; No. 1067, "Non-Standard Mail".

Crops — A263

Designs: $2.90, Vegetables. $3.40, Pearl millet. ($13.70), Corn.

**2005, Aug. 2 *Perf. 13¼x13¾***
**1068-1070** A263 Set of 3 8.50 8.50

No. 1070 is inscribed "Registered Mail."

**Nos. 855, 861, 862, 866, 868-870 Surcharged Type "b" and**

d

e

f

g

**2005, Aug. 10 Litho. *Perf. 13½***
**1070A** A189(a) ($1.70) on 10c #854 *200.00 75.00*
**1071** A189(d) ($1.70) on 20c #855 1.75 1.50
**1072** A189(d) ($1.70) on 90c #861 1.90 .75
**1073** A189(d) ($1.70) on $1 #862 1.50 1.25
**1074** A189(b) $2.90 on 90c #861 2.00 2.00
**1075** A189(e) ($4.80) on $1.50 #866 2.00 2.00
**1076** A189(b) $5.20 on 20c #855 4.00 4.00
**1077** A189(f) ($15.40) on $4 #868 4.75 4.75
**1078** A189(g) ($18.50) on $10 #870 8.00 8.00
**1079** A189(b) $25 on $5 #869 10.00 10.00
**1080** A189(b) $50 on $10 #870 17.50 17.50
*Nos. 1070A-1080 (11)* 253.40 126.75

Gulls
A264

Designs: $3.10, Cape gulls. $4, Hartlaub's gulls. $5.50, Sabine's gull. ($16.20), Gray-headed gulls.

**2006, Feb. 28 Litho. *Perf. 14x13¼***
**1081-1084** A264 Set of 4 11.50 11.50

No. 1084 is inscribed "Inland Registered Mail Paid."

Nos. 1003, 1030, 1042 Surcharged

**Methods and Perfs As Before**
**2006, Apr. 13**
**1085** A244 $3.10 on $2.45 #1003 1.60 1.25
**1086** A252 $3.10 on $2.70 #1030 1.60 1.25
**1087** A255 $3.10 on $2.75 #1042 1.60 1.25
*Nos. 1085-1087 (3)* 4.80 3.75

Size, location and fonts of surcharges differ.

Dolphins
A265

Designs: ($1.80), Risso's dolphin. $3.10, Southern right-whale dolphins, vert. $3.70, Benguela dolphin. $4, Common dolphins. $5.50, Bottlenose dolphins, vert.

***Perf. 13x13¼, 13¼x13***
**2006, Apr. 26 Litho.**
**1088-1092** A265 Set of 5 8.25 8.25

No. 1088 is inscribed "Standard Mail."

Miniature Sheets

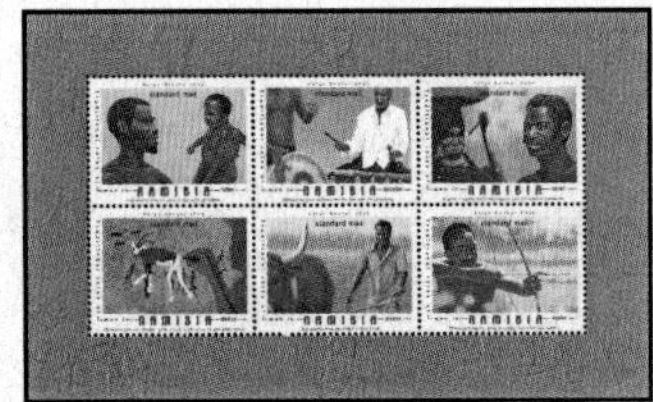
Traditional Roles of Men — A266

No. 1093, ($1.80): a, Father. b, Musician. c, Carver. d, Shaman. e, Planter. f, Hunter.
No. 1094, ($1.80): a, Leader. b, Blacksmith. c, Protector. d, Pastoralist. e, Trader. f, Storyteller.

**2006, May 24 *Perf. 13x13¼***
**Sheets of 6, #a-f**
**1093-1094** A266 Set of 2 6.75 6.75

Nos. 862, 865 Surcharged

**2006, June 20 Litho. *Perf. 13½***
**1095** A189 ($3.30) on $1 #862 2.25 1.60
**1096** A189 ($3.30) on $1.20 #865 2.25 1.60

Nos. 1095-1096 are inscribed "Postcard Rate." Location of surcharges differs.

Perennial Rivers
A267

Designs: $3.10, Orange River. $5.50, Kumene River, vert. (21x55mm). ($19.90), Zambezi River (87x22mm).

***Perf. 14x13¼, 13½ ($5.50)***
**2006, July 24**
**1097-1099** A267 Set of 3 11.50 11.50

No. 1099 is inscribed "Registered Non Standard Mail."

A268

Designs: $3.10, Construction of the rail line. $3.70, Henschel Class NG15 locomotive No. 41. $5.50, Narrow gauge Class Jung tank locomotive No. 9.

**2006, Aug. 9 *Perf. 14¾x14***
**1100-1102** A268 Set of 3 7.00 7.00

Otavi Mines and Railway Company (OMEG) Rail Line, Cent.

Otjiwarongo, Cent. — A269

**2006, Nov. 17 *Perf. 14***
**1103** A269 $1.90 multi 1.40 1.40

Printed in sheets of 10.

Flora and Fauna
A270

Named species: 5c, Bullfrog. 10c, Mesemb. 30c, Solifuge. 40c, Jewel beetle. 60c, Compass jellyfish. ($1.90), Web-footed gecko. $2, Otjikoto tilapia. No. 1111, $6, Milkbush. No. 1112, ($6), African hawk eagle. $10, Black-faced impala. $25, Lichens. $50, Baobab tree.

**2007, Feb. 15 Litho. *Perf. 14x13¼***
**1104** A270 5c multi .25 .25
**1105** A270 10c multi .25 .25
**1106** A270 30c multi .25 .25
**1107** A270 40c multi .25 .25
**1108** A270 60c multi .25 .25
**1109** A270 ($1.90) multi .65 .35
*a.* Perf. 14 .80 .80
**1110** A270 $2 multi .75 .50
**1111** A270 $6 multi 2.00 1.00
**1112** A270 ($6) multi 2.00 1.00
**1113** A270 $10 multi 3.25 1.75
**1114** A270 $25 multi 7.00 7.00
**1115** A270 $50 multi 14.00 14.00
*Nos. 1104-1115 (12)* 30.90 26.85

No. 1109 is inscribed "Standard Mail." No. 1112 is inscribed "Non-standard Mail."
See Nos. 1165-1168.

A271

Etosha National Park, Cent. — A272

Designs: ($1.90), Otjovasandu Wilderness Area. $3.40, Okaukuejo Waterhole. ($17.20), Scientist conducting anthrax research.

No. 1119: a, Gabar goshawk (30x30mm). b, Umbrella thorn tree (50x30mm). c, Red-billed queleas (40x30mm). d, Burchell's zebras (40x30mm). e, Elephant (40x30mm). f, Blue wildebeest (40x30mm). g, Mustard tree (40x30mm). h, Black emperor dragonfly (40x40mm). i, Springbok (40x40mm). j, Ground agama (40x40mm).

**Litho. With Foil Application**

**2007, Mar. 22** ***Perf. 14x13¼***

**1116-1118** A271 Set of 3 11.50 11.50

**Miniature Sheet**

**Litho.**

**1119** A272 ($2.25) Sheet of 10, #a-j 12.50 12.50

No. 1116 is inscribed "Standard Mail"; No. 1118, "Inland Registered Mail Paid"; Nos. 1119a-1119j, "Postcard Rate."

Dragonflies A273

Designs: ($1.90), Blue emperor dragonfly. $3.90, Rock dropwing dragonfly. $4.40, Red-veined dropwing dragonfly. ($6), Jaunty dropwing dragonfly.

$6, Blue basker dragonfly.

**2007, Apr. 16 Litho.** ***Perf. 12¾x14***

**1120-1123** A273 Set of 4 7.00 7.00

**Souvenir Sheet**

***Perf. 14x13¼***

**1124** A273 $6 multi 3.00 3.00

No. 1120 is inscribed "Standard Mail"; No. 1123, "Non Standard Mail Paid."

Trees A274

Designs: ($1.90), Commiphora kraeuseliana. $3.40, Commiphora wildii. $3.90, Commiphora glaucescens. ($6), Commiphora dinteri.

**2007, July 20 Litho.** ***Perf. 13¼x13¾***

**1125-1128** A274 Set of 4 6.75 6.75

No. 1125 is inscribed "Standard Mail"; No. 1128, "Non-standard Mail."

Flowers — A275

Designs: ($1.90), Cheiridopsis caroli-schmidtii. ($6), Namibia ponderosa. ($17.20), Fenestraria rhopalophylla.

**2007, Aug. 31**

**1129-1131** A275 Set of 3 10.00 10.00

No. 1129 is inscribed "Standard Mail"; No. 1130, "Non-standard Mail"; No. 1131, "Inland Registered Mail Paid."

Nos. 1129-1131 were each printed in sheets of 10 + 5 labels.

**Nos. 861, 865, 866 and 868 Surcharged**

h

i

j

k

**2007, Oct. 1 Litho.** ***Perf. 13½***

**1132** A189(h) ($2) on 90c #861 1.00 .65

**1133** A189(h) ($2) on $1.20 #865 1.00 .65

**1134** A189(h) ($2) on $1.50 #866 1.00 .65

**1135** A189(h) ($2) on $4 #868 1.00 .65

**1136** A189(i) $3.70 on $1.20 #865 1.25 1.10

**1137** A189(i) $4.20 on $1.20 #865 1.40 1.25

**1138** A189(i) $4.85 on $1.20 #865 1.60 1.50

**1139** A189(j) ($6.50) on $1.20 #865 2.25 2.00

**1140** A189(k) ($16.45) on $1.20 #865 7.00 *8.00*

*Nos. 1132-1140 (9)* 17.50 16.45

Location of surcharge varies.

Miniature Sheets

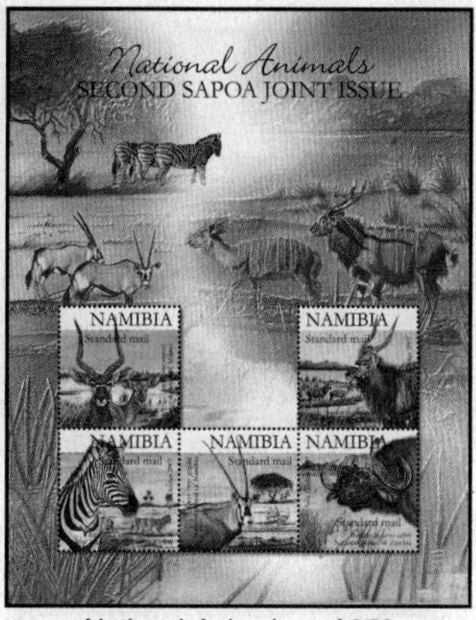


National Animals — A276

Nos. 1141 and 1142: a, Nyala (Malawi). b, Nyala (Zimbabwe). c, Burchell's zebra (Botswana). d, Oryx (Namibia). e, Buffalo (Zambia).

**2007, Oct. 9 Litho.** ***Perf. 13¾***

**Granite Paper (#1141)**

**Country Name in Black**

**1141** A276 ($2) Sheet of 5, #a-e 4.50 4.50

**Litho. With Foil Application**

**Country Name in Silver**

**1142** A276 ($2) Sheet of 5, #a-e 5.00 5.00

Nos. 1141a-1141e, 1142a-1142e are inscribed "Standard mail."

See No. 1193A, Botswana No. 838, Malawi No. 752, Zambia Nos. 1097-1101, Zimbabwe Nos. 1064-1068.

Weaver Birds — A277

Designs: ($2), Southern masked weaver. $3.70, Red-headed weaver. ($3.90), White-browed sparrow weaver. $4.20, Sociable weaver. ($18.45), Thick-billed weaver.

**2008, Feb. 28 Litho.** ***Perf. 13½x14***

**1143-1147** A277 Set of 5 11.00 11.00

No. 1143 is inscribed "Standard Mail"; No. 1145, "Postcard Rate"; No. 1147, "Inland Registered Mail Paid."

Euphorbia Flowers — A278

Designs: ($3.90), Euphorbia virosa. $6.45, Euphorbia dregeana. ($22.95), Euphorbia damarana.

$6.45 — Type I: "E" over "I" in Latin inscription. Type II: Corrected version, no "I".

**2008**

**1148** A278 ($3.90) multi 1.10 .60

**1149** A278 $6.45 multi, Type I 1.50 1.50

*a.* Type II 2.25 2.25

**1150** A278 ($22.95) multi 5.75 5.75

*Nos. 1148-1150 (3)* 8.35 7.85

Issued: Nos. 1148-1150, 3/3; No. 1149a, 5/27. No. 1148 inscribed "Postcard Rate"; No. 1150, "Registered Non-Standard Mail."

Miniature Sheet

Discovery of Diamonds in Namibia, Cent. — A279

No. 1151: a, Uncut diamonds. b, Land mining. c, Marine mining. d, Diamond jewelry.

**Litho. With Foil Application**

**2008, Apr. 15** ***Perf. 14x13½***

**1151** A279 $2 Sheet of 4, #a-d 4.75 4.75

Miniature Sheet

Traditional Houses — A280

No. 1152: a, Herero. b, Kavango. c, Owambo. d, Nama. e, Caprivi. f, San.

**2008, May 27** **Litho.**

**1152** A280 ($2.20) Sheet of 6, #a-f 4.00 4.00

Nos. 1152a-1152f are each inscribed "Standard Mail."

Twyfelfontein UNESCO World Heritage Site — A281

Rock drawings: No. 1153, ($7.20), No. 1156a ($2.20), Lion man. No. 1154, ($7.20), No. 1156b ($2.20), Giraffe, Dancing kudu. No. 1155, ($7.20), No. 1156c ($2.20), Elephant.

**2008, June 27** ***Perf. 13½x13¾***

**1153-1155** A281 Set of 3 6.75 6.75

**Souvenir Sheet**

**1156** A281 ($2.20) Sheet of 3, #a-c 2.75 2.75

Nos. 1153-1155 are each inscribed "Non-Standard Mail"; Nos. 1156a-1156c, "Standard Mail."

Ediacaran Fossils — A282

Designs: ($2), Rangea. ($3.90), Swartpuntia. ($18.45), Pteridinium. ($22.95), Ernietta.

**Litho. & Embossed**

**2008, Aug. 8** ***Perf. 13¼x14***

**1157-1160** A282 Set of 4 12.50 12.50

No. 1157 is inscribed "Standard Mail"; No. 1158, "Postcard Rate"; No. 1159, "Registered Non-standard Mail"; No. 1160, "Registered Inland Mail Paid."

2008 Summer Olympics, Beijing — A283

Designs: $2, Female runner, sun and Earth. $3.70, Athlete with arms raised. $3.90, Athlete at finish line. $4.20, Female runner with arms extended.

**2008, Aug. 15 Litho. *Perf. 13¼x13***
**1161-1164** A283 Set of 4 3.75 3.75

**Flora and Fauna Type of 2007**

Designs: $4.10, Thimble grass. $4.60, Bronze whaler shark. $5.30, Deep sea red crab. ($18.20), False ink cap mushroom.

**2008, Oct. 1 Litho. *Perf. 14x13¼***
**1165** A270 $4.10 multi 1.00 .80
**1166** A270 $4.60 multi 1.10 .90
**1167** A270 $5.30 multi 1.40 1.25
**1168** A270 ($18.20) multi 4.75 4.00
*Nos. 1165-1168 (4)* 8.25 6.95

No. 1168 is inscribed "Registered Mail."

Eagles — A284

Designs: $4.10, Martial eagle. ($4.30), Bataleur eagle. $4.60, Verreaux's eagle. ($25.40), Tawny eagle.

**2009, Feb. 2 Litho. *Perf. 13¼x13¾***
**1169-1172** A284 Set of 4 12.00 12.00

No. 1170 is inscribed "Postcard Rate"; No. 1172, "Registered Non-Standard Mail." Nos. 1169-1172 exists imperf. Value, each $90.

New Year 2009 (Year of the Ox) A285

**Litho. With Foil Application**

**2009, Apr. 10 *Perf. 14x13¼***
**1173** A285 $2.20 multi 1.25 1.25

Miniature Sheet

Flora and Fauna of the Brandberg — A286

No. 1174: a, Augur buzzard (30x30mm). b, Numasfels Peak (50x30mm). c, Quiver tree (40x30mm). d, CMR beetle (40x30mm). e, Leopard (40x30mm). f, Kobas (40x30mm). g, Bokmakiri (40x30mm). h, Jameson's red rock rabbit (40x40mm). i, Brandberg halfmens (40x40mm). j, Jordan's girdled lizard (40x40mm).

**2009, Apr. 10 Litho. *Perf. 14x13¼***
**1174** A286 ($4.30) Sheet of 10, #a-j 8.50 8.50

Nos. 1174a-1174j are each inscribed "Postcard Rate."

Souvenir Sheet

First Crossing of Africa by Automobile, Cent. — A287

**2009, May 1 *Perf. 13¾x14¼***
**1175** A287 $7.10 multi 2.50 2.50

Wild Horses — A288

Designs: $5.30, Two horses. $8, Three horses. ($20.40), Four horses.

**2009, July 3 *Perf. 13¾x14***
**1176-1178** A288 Set of 3 9.50 9.50

No. 1178 is inscribed "Inland Registered Mail Paid." See Nos. 1185, 1340-1342.

Souvenir Sheet

German Higher Private School, Cent. — A289

**2009, Aug. 21 Litho. *Perf. 13½***
**1179** A289 $4.60 multi 2.00 2.00

Geckos A290

Designs: $4.40, Festive gecko. $5, Koch's barking gecko. $6, Giant ground gecko. $7.70, Velvety thick-toed gecko. ($18.20), Bradfield's Namib day gecko.

**2009, Sept. 30 *Perf. 13¾***
**1180-1184** A290 Set of 5 11.00 11.00

No. 1184 is inscribed "Registered Mail."

**Horses Type of 2009**

Design: Four horses in desert.

**2009, Nov. 2 *Perf. 13¾x14***
**1185** A288 ($4.60) multi 1.50 1.50

No. 1185 is inscribed "Postcard Rate."

Miniature Sheet

Endangered Species — A291

No. 1186: a, Wattled crane. b, Gazania thermalis. c, Leatherback turtle. d, Giant quiver tree. e, Cape vulture. f, White Namib toktokkie. g, Cheetah. h, Hook-lipped rhinoceros. i, wild dog. j, Nama-padloper tortoise.

**2010, Feb. 8 *Perf. 13¼x13***
**1186** A291 ($4.60) Sheet of 10, #a-j 11.00 11.00

Nos. 1186a-1186j are inscribed "Postcard Rate."

Independence, 20th Anniv. — A292

***Perf. 13¼x13¾***

**2010, Mar. 21 Litho.**
**1187** A292 ($2.50) multi .80 .80

No. 1187 is inscribed "Standard mail."

Miniature Sheet

2010 World Cup Soccer Championships, South Africa — A293

No. 1188 — Soccer players, ball, 2010 World Cup mascot and flag of: a, Namibia. b, South Africa. c, Zimbabwe. d, Malawi. e, Swaziland. f, Botswana. g, Mauritius. h, Lesotho. i, Zambia.

**2010, Apr. 9 Litho. *Perf. 13½***
**1188** A293 ($4.60) Sheet of 9, #a-i 11.00 11.00

Nos. 1188a-1188i are inscribed "Postcard rate." A miniature sheet containing No. 1188a and stamps from South Africa, Zimbabwe, Malawi, Swaziland, Botswana, Mauritius, Lesotho and Zambia was sold by Namibia Post for $40. The sheet apparently was not sold by any other country. See Botswana Nos. 896-905, Lesotho No. , Malawi No. 753, Mauritius No. 1086, South Africa No. 1403, Swaziland Nos. 794-803, Zambia Nos. 1115-1118, and Zimbabwe Nos. 1112-1121.

Miniature Sheet

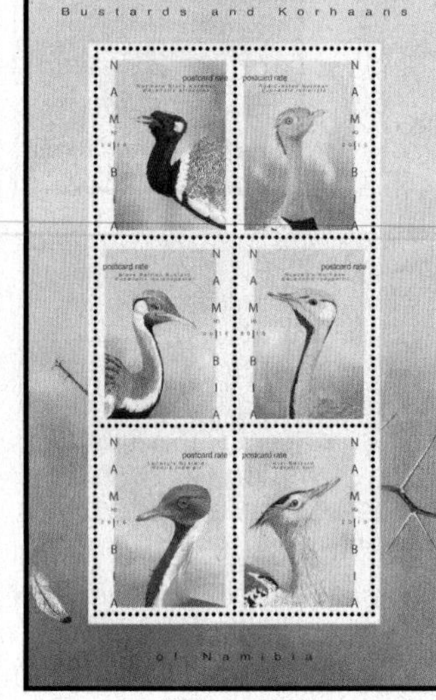

Birds — A294

No. 1189: a, Northern black korhaan. b, Red-crested korhaan. c, Black-bellied bustard. d, Rüppell's korhaan. e, Ludwig's bustard. f, Kori bustard.

**2010, Apr. 14 *Perf. 13½x14***
**1189** A294 ($4.60) Sheet of 6, #a-f 9.00 9.00

Nos. 1189a-1189f are inscribed "Postcard rate."

Lighthouses A295

Designs: $4.40, Swakopmund Lighthouse. ($9.50), Diaz Point Lighthouse, Lüderitzbucht. ($18.20), Pelican Point Lighthouse, Walvis Bay.

**2010, June 18 *Perf. 13½x13¾***
**1190-1192** A295 Set of 3 8.00 8.00

No. 1191 is inscribed "Non-standard mail." No. 1192 is inscribed "Registered Mail."

Souvenir Sheet

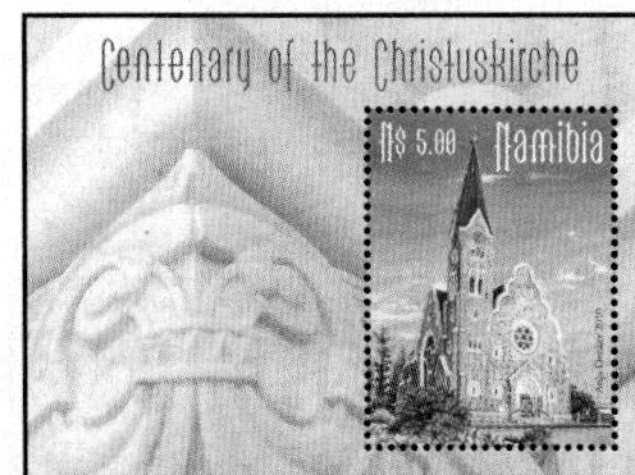

Christuskirche, Windhoek, Cent. — A296

**2010, Aug. 6 *Perf. 14***
**1193** A296 $5 multi 1.75 1.75

Oryx — A296a

**2010, Sept. 18** ***Perf. 13¾***
**1193A** A296a ($2.50) multi *4.00 4.00*

No. 1193A was printed in sheets of 5 that sold for $25. The lower half of the stamp, as shown, is a generic image that could be personalized.

See No. 1141d for similarity.

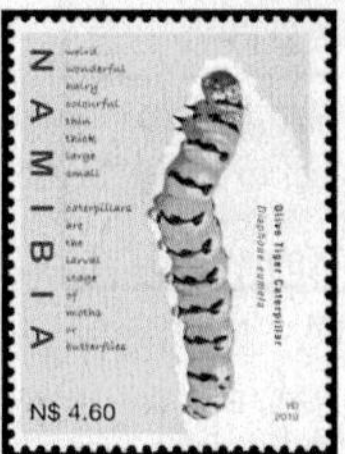


Caterpillars
A297

Designs: $4.60, Olive tiger caterpillar. $5.30, African armyworm. $6.40, Wild silk caterpillar. ($29.40), Mopane caterpillar.

**2010, Oct. 1** **Litho.**
**1194-1197** A297 Set of 4 13.50 13.50

Souvenir Sheet

World Standards Day — A298

**2010, Oct. 18** ***Perf. 14x13½***
**1198** A298 $5.30 multi 1.40 1.40

Wildlife
A299

Designs: $4.60, Leopard. ($5), African elephant, vert. $5.30, Black rhinoceros. $6.40, African buffalo. ($8.50), Lion, vert.

**2011, Jan. 28** ***Perf. 14x13¼, 13¼x14***
**1199-1203** A299 Set of 5 7.50 7.50

No. 1200 is inscribed "Postcard Rate." No. 1203 is inscribed "Non-standard Mail." Nos. 1199-1203 exists imperf. Value, each $65.

Miniature Sheet

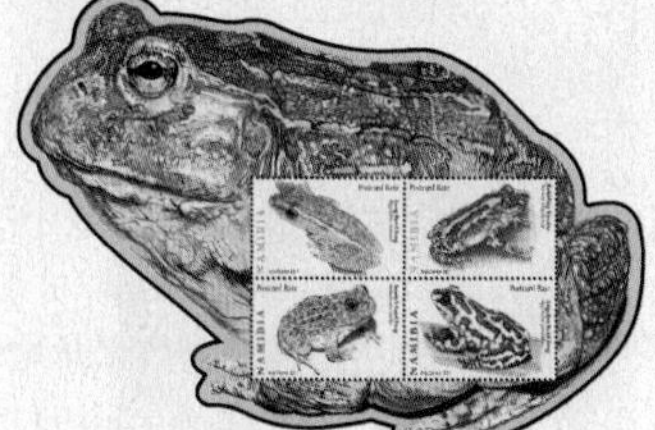

Frogs — A300

No. 1204: a, Long reed frog. b, Bubbling kassina. c, Tandy's sand frog. d, Angolan reed frog.

**2011, Mar. 23** ***Perf. 13¼x14***
**1204** A300 ($5) Sheet of 4, #a-d 6.75 6.75

Nos. 1204a-1204d each were inscribed "Postcard Rate."

Souvenir Sheet

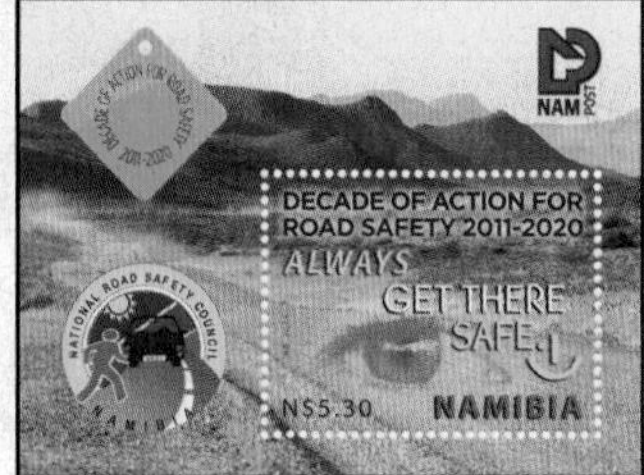


Road Safety Campaign — A301

**2011, May 11** ***Perf. 13x13¼***
**1205** A301 $5.30 multi 1.50 1.50

Miniature Sheet

Endangered Marine Life — A302

No. 1206: a, Cape gannet (30x30mm). b, Atlantic yellow-nosed albatross (50x30mm). c, African penguin (40x30mm). d, Southern right whale (40x30mm). e, Bank cormorant (40x30mm). f, West coast steenbras (40x30mm). g, Split-fan kelp (40x40mm). h, Cape rock lobster (40x40mm).

**2011, May 16** ***Perf. 14x13¼***
**1206** A302 $4.60 Sheet of 8, #a-h 12.00 12.00

Exists imperf. Value, $220.

Personalized Stamps — A303

Designs: No. 1207, Oryx. elephant and leopard, Etosha National Park. No. 1208, Lizard and rock paintings, Twyfelfontein UNESCO World Heritage Site. No. 1209, Bird over Fish River Canyon. No. 1210, Antelope, Sossusvlei Region. No. 1211, Rhinoceros in Community Conservation Area.

**2011, June 7** ***Perf. 13¼x13***
**1207** A303 ($5) multi + label 2.50 2.50
**1208** A303 ($5) multi + label 2.50 2.50
**1209** A303 ($5) multi + label 2.50 2.50
**1210** A303 ($5) multi + label 2.50 2.50
**1211** A303 ($5) multi + label 2.50 2.50
*a.* Sheet of 5, #1207-1211, + 5 labels 12.50 12.50
*Nos. 1207-1211 (5)* 12.50 12.50

Nos. 1207-1211, each inscribed "Postcard rate," were printed in sheets of 5 stamps + 5 labels that could be personalized. Label shown is a generic image. Sheets of 5, including No. 1211a, each sold for $35.

Aloes — A304

Designs: ($5), Aloe gariepensis. ($8.50), Aloe variegata. ($20.90), Aloe striata ssp. karasbergensis.

**2011, June 21** ***Perf. 13¼x14***
**1212-1214** A304 Set of 3 10.00 10.00

No. 1212 is inscribed "Postcard Rate." No. 1213 is inscribed "Non Standard Mail." No. 1214 is inscribed "Registered Mail."

Grebes — A305

Designs: No. 1215, ($2.70), Little grebe. No. 1216, ($2.70), Great crested grebe. ($23.60), Black-necked grebe, horiz.

**2011, July 18** ***Perf. 13¼x14, 14x13¼***
**1215-1217** A305 Set of 3 8.50 8.50

Nos. 1215-1216 are each inscribed "Standard Mail." No. 1217 is inscribed "Inland Registered Mail." Nos. 1215-1217 exists imperf. Value, each $90.

Grasses — A306

Designs: ($2.70), Natal red top. $4.80, Feather-top chloris. $5.40, Urochloa brachyura. $6.50, Nine-awned grass. ($8.50), Foxtail buffalo grass.

**2011, Sept. 30** **Litho.** ***Perf. 13½x14***
**1218-1222** A306 Set of 5 8.00 8.00

No. 1218 is inscribed "Standard mail"; No. 1222, "Non-standard mail."

Birds — A308

Designs: 5c, Carp's tit. 10c, Hartlaub's spurfowl. 20c, Herero chat.30c, Rüppell's parrot. 50c, Rüppell's korhaan. ($2.90), White-tailed shrike. $5, Rockrunner. ($5.30), Dune lark. ($8.90), Damara hornbill. $20, Damara tern. ($21.90), Violet wood hoopoe. $100, Bare-cheeked babbler.

**2012, Feb. 15** **Litho.** ***Perf. 13¼***
**1224** A308 5c multi .25 .25
**1225** A308 10c multi .25 .25
**1226** A308 20c multi .25 .25
**1227** A308 30c multi .25 .25
**1228** A308 50c multi .25 .25
**1229** A308 ($2.90) multi .80 .80
**1230** A308 $5 multi 1.50 1.50
**1231** A308 ($5.30) multi 1.75 1.75
**1232** A308 ($8.90) multi 3.00 3.00
**1233** A308 $20 multi 5.00 5.00
**1234** A308 ($21.90) multi 5.75 5.75
**1235** A308 $100 multi 25.00 25.00
*Nos. 1224-1235 (12)* 44.05 44.05

No. 1229 is inscribed "Standard mail"; No. 1231, "Postcard rate"; No. 1232, "Non-standard mail"; No. 1234, "Registered mail." No. 1235 exists imperf. Vlaue, $105.

See Nos. 1254-1258.

Bats
A309

Designs: No. 1236, ($5.30), Straw-colored fruit bats. No. 1237, ($5.30), Egyptian slit-faced bats. No. 1238, ($5.30), Angolan epauletted fruit bats.

**2012, Apr. 9** ***Perf. 13¼***
**Stamps + Labels**
**1236-1238** A309 Set of 3 5.00 5.00

Nos. 1236-1238 are inscribed "Postcard rate."

2012 Summer Olympics and Paralympics, London — A310

Designs: $2.90, Shooting. $4.80, Running, vert. $5.40, Cycling. $6.50, Wheelchair racer, vert.

**2012, Apr. 16** ***Perf. 13x13¼, 13¼x13***
**1239-1242** A310 Set of 4 5.75 5.75

Scorpions — A311

Designs: $4.80, Parabuthus villosus. ($5.30), Parabuthus namibensis. $5.40, Opistophthalmus carinatus. $6.50, Hottentotta arenaceus.

**2012, June 11** ***Perf. 14x13¾***
**1243-1246** A311 Set of 4 6.50 6.50

Souvenir Sheets

Telecom Namibia, 20th Anniv. — A312

Nampost, 20th Anniv. — A313

No. 1247: a, Satellite dishes. b, Fiber-optic cable strands.
No. 1248: a, Postman in bush. b, Mail truck.

**2012, July 31** ***Perf. 12½***
**1247** A312 $2.90 Sheet of 2, #a-b 1.80 1.80
**1248** A313 $2.90 Sheet of 2, #a-b 1.80 1.80

Souvenir Sheet

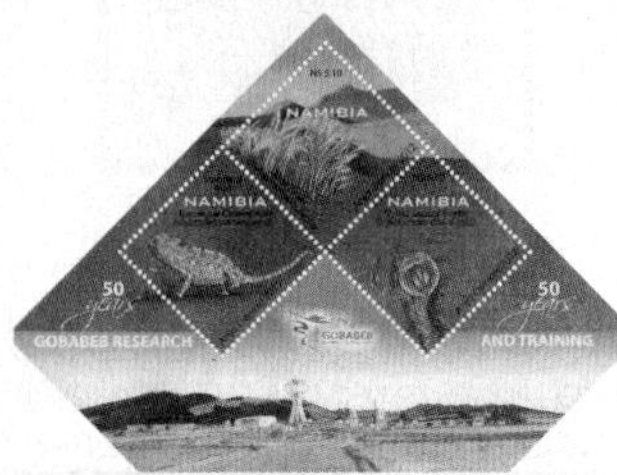

Gobabeb Research and Training Center, 50th Anniv. — A314

No. 1249: a, ($3.10), Namaqua chameleon. b, $5.10, Dune grass. c, $5.80, Flying saucer beetle.

**2012, Sept. 22** ***Perf. 13¼x14***
**1249** A314 Sheet of 3, #a-c 4.50 4.50

No. 1249a is inscribed "Standard Mail."

Mongooses A315

Designs: $5.10, Black mongoose. ($5.60), Yellow mongoose, vert. $5.80, Banded mongoose. $6.90, Dwarf mongoose.

***Perf. 14¾x14¼, 14¼x14¾***
**2012, Oct. 1**
**1250-1253** A315 Set of 4 6.00 6.00

No. 1251 is inscribed "Postcard Rate."

**Birds Type of 2012**

Designs: 90c, Benguela long-billed lark. $1, Barlow's lark. $3, Rosy-faced lovebirds. $10, Gray's larks. $12, Monteiro's hornbill.

**2013, Mar. 1** ***Perf. 13¼***
**1254** A308 90c multi .30 .30
**1255** A308 $1 multi .30 .30
**1256** A308 $3 multi 1.10 1.10
**1257** A308 $10 multi 3.25 3.25
**1258** A308 $12 multi 3.75 3.75
*Nos. 1254-1258 (5)* 6.15 6.15

Beetles A316

Designs: ($3.10), Glittering jewel beetle. $5.10, Red-spotted lily weevil. $5.50, Garden fruit chafer. $6.90, Lunate ladybird. ($26.50), Two-spotted ground beetle.

**2013, Apr. 5**
**1259-1263** A316 Set of 5 12.00 12.00

No. 1259 is inscribed "Standard mail;" No. 1263, "Inland registered mail."

Miniature Sheets

Children — A317

No. 1264, ($3.10) — Inscriptions: a, Right to family, shelter & a healthy environment. b, Faith & joy. c, Right to health, nutrition & safety. d, Freedom from neglect, fear, abuse & violence. e, Love & trust. f, Freedom of identity, traditions & beliefs.
No. 1265, ($3.10) — Inscriptions: a, Right to early development support, education & information. b, Aspirations & dreams. c, Right to special care & support. d, Freedom of expression, association & participation. e, Play & creativity. f, Freedom from discrimination & exploitation.

**2013, June 17 Litho.** ***Perf. 13x13¼***
**Sheets of 6, #a-f**
**1264-1265** A317 Set of 2 11.00 11.00

Nos. 1264a-1264f and 1265a-1265f are each inscribed "Standard mail."

Souvenir Sheet

Environmental Education — A318

**2013, June 20 Litho.** ***Perf. 13¼x13***
**1266** A318 $5.10 multi 1.75 1.75

Souvenir Sheet

Man and Woman Riding in Donkey Cart — A319

**2013, July 12 Litho.** ***Perf. 13x13¼***
**1267** A319 $5.80 multi 1.75 1.75

Johanna Benson, Gold Medalist at 2012 Paralympics A320

**2013, Aug. 21 Litho.** ***Perf. 13¼x13***
**1268** A320 ($3.10) multi 1.00 1.00
**1269** A320 ($6) multi + label 2.75 2.75

No. 1268 is inscribed "Standard mail" and was printed in sheets of 10.
No. 1269 is inscribed "Postcard rate" and was printed in sheets that sold for $40 containing 5 stamps + 5 labels that could be personalized.

Antelopes — A321

Designs: $5.40, Elands. No. 1271, ($6), Greater kudus. No. 1272, ($6), Gemsboks. $6.20, Sables. $7.30, Blue wildebeests.

**2013, Sept. 30 Litho.** ***Perf. 12½***
**1270-1274** A321 Set of 5 6.75 6.75

Nos. 1271 and 1272 are both inscribed "Postcard Rate."

Wooden Vessels A322

Designs: ($3.30), HaMbukushu. $5.40, BaSubiya. ($6), Naman. $6.20, AaWambo. $7.30, OvaHerero.

**2014, Feb. 10 Litho.** ***Perf. 14x13¼***
**1275-1279** A322 Set of 5 5.25 5.25

No. 1275 is inscribed "Standard Mail;" No. 1277; "Postcard Rate."

Miniature Sheet

Nocturnal Animals — A323

No. 1280: a, Southern lesser galago. b, Cape porcupine. c, Small-spotted genet. d, Ground pangolin. e, Aardvark. f, Aardwolf.

**2014, Mar. 14 Litho.** ***Perf. 13¼***
**1280** A323 ($3.30) Sheet of 6, #a-f, + label 4.50 4.50

Nos. 1280a-1280f are each inscribed "Standard Mail."

Namibian Flag on Map of Namibia A324

**2014, May 21 Litho.** ***Perf. 14x13¼***
**1281** A324 ($3.30) multi .85 .85

**Souvenir Sheet**

**1282** A324 ($27.20) multi 4.75 4.75

No. 1281 is inscribed "Standard Mail;" No. 1282, "Inland Registered Mail."

Antelopes — A325

Designs: No. 1283, ($6), Red lechwes. No. 1284, ($6), Bushbucks. No. 1285, ($6), Red hartebeests. No. 1286, ($6), Springboks.

**2014, May 27 Litho.** ***Perf. 13¼x13½***
**1283-1286** A325 Set of 4 4.50 4.50

Nos. 1283-1286 are each inscribed "Postcard Rate."

Snakes A326

Designs: $5.40, Black mamba. ($6), Boomslang. $6.20, Puff adder. $7.30, Zebra snake.

**2014, June 4 Litho.** ***Perf. 13¾***
**1287-1290** A326 Set of 4 4.50 4.50

No. 1288 is inscribed "Postcard Rate."

First Visit of Chinese Navy to Namibia A327

Designs: No. 1291, $3.30, Taihu. No. 1292, $3.30, Yancheng.

**2014, June 11 Litho.** ***Perf. 13x13¼***
**1291-1292** A327 Set of 2 1.50 1.50

A souvenir sheet containing two $3.30 stamps depicting Walvis Bay harbor and the Luoyang sold for $15. Value, $2.50.

Miniature Sheet

Flora and Fauna of the Kalahari Desert — A328

No. 1293: a, Peregrine falcon (30x30mm). b, Cape turtle doves (50x30mm). c, Shepherd's tree (40x30mm). d, Giraffe (40x30mm). e, African monarch butterfly (40x30mm). f, Cheetah (40x30mm). g, Gemsbok cucumbers (40x30mm). h, Suricates (40x40mm). i, Trumpet-thorn (40x40mm). j, Spotted sandveld lizard (40x40mm).

**2014, July 28 Litho. *Perf. 14x13½***
**1293** A328 ($6) Sheet of 10, #a-j 11.50 11.50

Nos. 1293a-1293j are each inscribed "Postcard Rate."

In 2014 and 2015, Namibia postal officials declared as "illegal" souvenir sheets with a $5 denomination depicting various dogs and other wildlife, and a stamp inscribed "Postage Paid" depicting a dog and cat.

Kingfishers — A329

Designs: ($5.70), Pied kingfishers. ($6.40), Half-collared kingfishers. ($6.60), Woodland kingfishers. ($7.70), Malachite kingfishers. ($28.30), Giant kingfishers.

**2014, Oct. 1 Litho. *Perf. 13¼x14***
**1294-1298** A329 Set of 5 10.00 10.00

No. 1294 is inscribed "Zone A;" No. 1295, "Postcard Rate;" No. 1296, "Zone B;" No. 1297, "Zone C;" No. 1298, "Inland Registered Mail." Nos. 1294-1298 exists imperf. Vlaue, each $60.

Souvenir Sheet

Namib Sand Sea UNESCO World Heritage Site — A330

No. 1299: a, Sossusvlei/Deadvlei. b, Comicus spp. c, Sandwich Harbor.

**2015, Feb. 6 Litho. *Perf. 13¼***
**1299** A330 ($6.40) Sheet of 3, #a-c 3.25 3.25

Nos. 1299a-1299c are each inscribed "Postcard Rate."

Presidents of Namibia — A331

Designs: ($3.50), Pres. Hage Geingob. $30, Presidents Sam Nujoma, Hifikepunye Pohamba, Hage Geingob, map and flag of Namibia, horiz.

**Litho. With Foil Application**

**2015, Mar. 21 *Perf. 13¼x13¾***
**1300** A331 ($3.50) multi .80 .80

**Litho., Sheet Margin Litho. With Foil Application**

**Souvenir Sheet**

***Perf. 14½x14***

**1301** A331 $30 multi 4.25 4.25

Inauguration of Pres. Geingob, Independence, 25th anniv. (No. 1301). No. 1301 contains one 75x26mm stamp.

Bee-Eaters A332

Designs: ($3.50), White-fronted bee-eater. $5.70, Southern carmine bee-eater, horiz. $6.60, Swallow-tailed bee-eater, horiz. $7.70, Little bee-eaters, horiz. ($28.30), European bee-eater.

***Perf. 14x14¼, 14¼x14***

**2015, May 15 Litho.**
**1302-1306** A332 Set of 5 7.50 7.50

No. 1302 is inscribed "Standard Mail;" No. 1306, "Inland Registered Mail." Nos. 1300-1306 exists imperf. Value, each $65.

Antelopes — A333

Designs: No. 1307, ($6.40), Steenbok. No. 1308, ($6.40), Common duiker. No. 1309, ($6.40), Klipspringer. No. 1310, ($6.40), Damara dik-dik.

**2015, June 22 Litho. *Perf. 14¼***
**1307-1310** A333 Set of 4 4.25 4.25

Nos. 1307-1310 are each inscribed "Postcard Rate."

Juvenile Big Game Animals A334

Designs: ($3.50), Leopard. $5.70, African elephant. $6.60, Black rhinoceros. $7.70, African buffalo. ($35.50), Lion.

**2015, July 6 Litho. *Perf. 14¾x14½***
**1311-1315** A334 Set of 5 9.50 9.50

No. 1311 is inscribed "Standard mail;" No. 1315, "Non-standard registered mail."

Sharks — A335

Designs: $5.70, Bronze whaler shark. ($6.40), Broadnose sevengill shark. $6.60, Great white shark. $7.70, Smooth hammerhead shark.

**2015, Aug. 19 Litho. *Perf. 14½x14***
**1316-1319** A335 Set of 4 5.25 5.25

No. 1317 is inscribed "Postcard Rate."

Coursers — A336

Designs: ($6.05), Burchell's courser. ($6.80), Three-banded courser. ($7), Double-banded courser. ($8.20), Bronze-winged courser.

**2015, Oct. 1 Litho. *Perf. 13½***
**1320-1323** A336 Set of 4 5.00 5.00

No. 1320 is inscribed "Zone A;" No. 1321, "Postcard Rate:" No. 1322, "Zone B;" No. 1323, "Zone C." Nos. 1320-1323 exists imperf. Value, each $60.

Souvenir Sheet

Hong Kong 2015 Intl. Stamp Exhibition — A337

No. 1324: a, Two rhinoceroses. b, Earth. c, Three elephants.

**2015, Nov. 22 Litho. *Perf. 13¾***
**1324** A337 ($6.80) Sheet of 3, #a-c 3.00 3.00

Nos. 1324a-1324c are each inscribed "Postcard rate."

Allgemeine Zeitung Newspaper, Cent. A338

Newspaper masthead dated: ($3.70), July 22, 2016. ($6.80), Aug. 1, 1919.

**2016 Litho. *Perf. 13***
**1325-1326** A338 Set of 2 1.40 1.40
*1326a* Souvenir sheet of 2, #1325-1326 1.50 1.50

Issued: Nos. 1325-1326, 3/4; No. 1326a, 7/22/16.

No. 1325 is inscribed "Standard mail;" No. 1326, "Postcard rate."

Whydahs — A339

Designs: $6.05, Shaft-tailed whydah. $7, Long-tailed paradise whydah, vert. ($30), Pin-tailed whydah, vert.

**2016, Mar. 18 Litho. *Perf. 13¼***
**1327-1329** A339 Set of 3 5.75 5.75

No. 1329 is inscribed "Inland registered mail."

Miniature Sheet

Tortoises — A340

No. 1330: a, Speke's hinged tortoise. b, Namaqualand tent tortoise. c, Nama padloper. d, Angulate tortoise.

**2016, May 11 Litho. *Perf. 14***
**1330** A340 ($3.70) Sheet of 4, #a-d 1.90 1.90

Nos. 1330a-1330d are each inscribed "Standard mail."

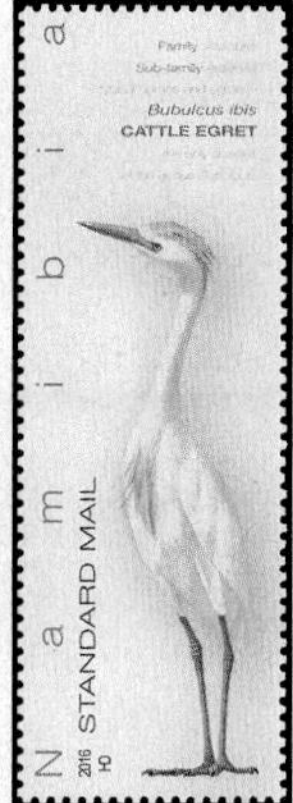

Birds — A341

Designs: ($3.70), Cattle egret. $6.05, Green-backed heron, horiz. ($6.80), Goliath heron, horiz. $7, Squacco heron, horiz. $8.20, Black heron, horiz.

***Perf. 13¼x12¾, 12¾x13¼***

**2016, July 7 Litho.**
**1331-1335** A341 Set of 5 4.75 4.75

No. 1331 is inscribed "Standard mail;" No. 1333, "Post card rate."

Souvenir Sheet

Forestry — A342

No. 1336: a, Forestry resources used in commercial buildings and housing, arts and crafts and household utensils. b, Elephant and trees, vert. c, Fruit, soap and oils.

**2016, Aug. 11 Litho. *Perf. 14x13¼***
**1336** A342 ($6.80) Sheet of 3, #a-c 2.75 2.75

Nos. 1336a-1336c are each inscribed "Postcard rate."

Mammals — A343

Designs: ($6.60), African wild dogs. ($7.50), Spotted hyenas. ($8.80), Brown hyena.

**2016, Sept. 30 Litho. *Perf. 12½x13***
**1337-1339** A343 Set of 3 3.50 3.50

No. 1337 is inscribed "Zone A;" No. 1338, "Zone B;" No. 1339, "Zone C."

**Wild Horses Type of 2009**

Designs: No. 1340, ($7.30), Two horses (like #1176). No. 1341, ($7.30), Three horses (like #1177). No. 1342, ($7.30), Four horses (like #1178).

**2016, Nov. 15 Litho. *Perf. 12½x13***
**1340-1342** A288 Set of 3 3.25 3.25

Nos. 1340-1342 are each inscribed "Postcard rate."

Souvenir Sheet

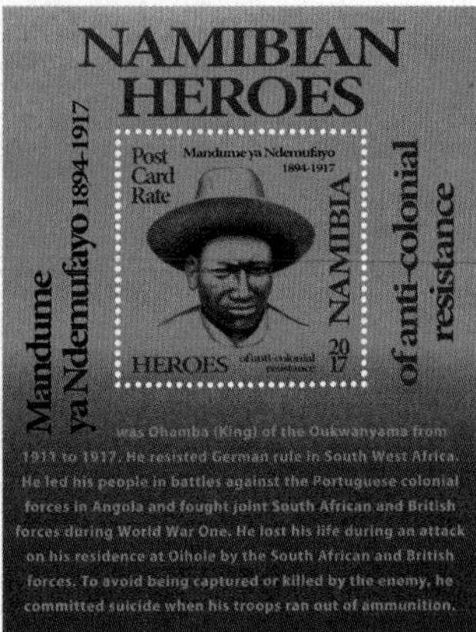


Mandume ya Ndemufayo (1894-1917), Last King of the Oukwanyama and Anti-Colonial Resistance Leader — A344

**2017, Feb. 6 Litho. *Perf. 13¼***
**1343** A344 ($7.30) multi 1.10 1.10

No. 1343 is inscribed "Post card rate."

Souvenir Sheet

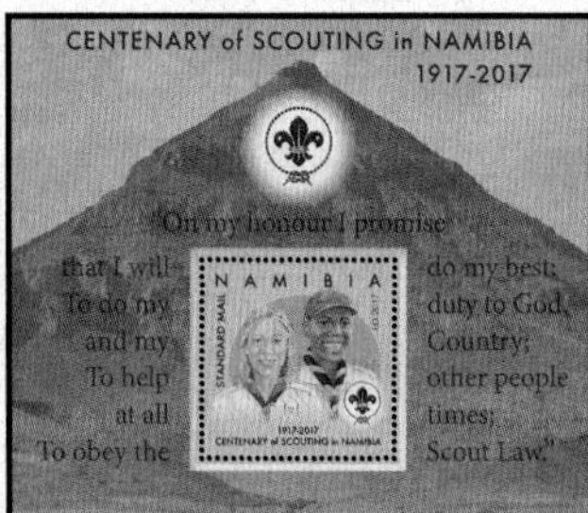


Scouting in Namibia, Cent. — A345

**2017, Feb. 17 Litho. *Perf. 13¼***
**1344** A345 ($4) multi .65 .65

No. 1344 is inscribed "Standard mail."

Barbets — A346

Designs: ($6.60), Black-collared barbets. ($7.50), Crested barbets, horiz. ($8.80), Acacia pied barbets.

***Perf. 13¼x13, 13x13¼***
**2017, Mar. 9 Litho.**
**1345-1347** A346 Set of 3 3.50 3.50

No. 1345 is inscribed "Zone A;" No. 1346, "Zone B;" No. 1347, "Zone C."

Hares and Rabbits — A347

No. 1348: a, Jameson's red rabbit. b, Scrub hare.

**2017, Apr. 15 Litho. *Perf. 12½x13***
**1348** A347 ($7.30) Horiz. pair, #a-b 2.25 2.25

No. 1348 is inscribed "postcard rate."

Souvenir Sheet

Protestant Reformation, 500th Anniv. — A348

**2017, May 12 Litho. *Perf. 13½***
**1349** A348 ($7.30) multi 1.10 1.10

No. 1349 is inscribed "Postcard Rate."

Flame Lilies — A349

Designs: ($6.60), Limestone lily. ($7.50), Flame lily. ($8.80), Namib lily, vert.

***Perf. 13¼x12¾, 12¾x13¼***
**2017, June 15 Litho.**
**1350-1352** A349 Set of 3 3.50 3.50

No. 1350 is inscribed "ZONE A." No. 1351 is inscribed "ZONE B." No. 1352 is inscribed "ZONE C."

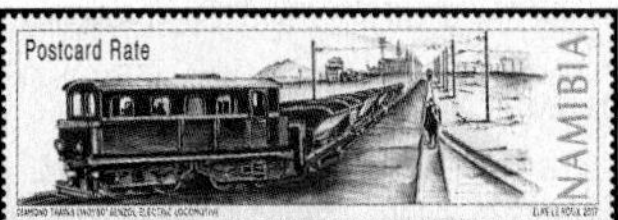


Diamond Trains — A350

Designs: No. 1353, ($7.30), (1AO) Bo Benzol-electric locomotive. No. 1354, ($7.30), Bo-Bo electric locomotive K.B.G. No. 1355, ($7.30), Bo-Bo Benzol-electric locomotive C.D.M. No. 40. No. 1356, ($7.30), Railcar No. 3 Kolmanskop.

**Litho. with Foil Application**
**2017, July 18 *Perf. 14¼x14***
**1353-1356** A350 Set of 4 4.50 4.50

Nos. 1353-1356 are inscribed "Postcard Rate."

Rollers A351

Designs: No. 1357, ($7.30), Lilac-breasted roller. No. 1358, ($7.30), Purple roller. No. 1359, ($7.30), Racket-tailed roller. No. 1360, ($7.30), Broad-billed roller. No. 1361, ($7.30), European roller.

**2017, Aug. 1 Litho. *Perf. 13¼***
**1357-1361** A351 Set of 5 5.50 5.50

Nos. 1357-1361 are inscribed "Postcard Rate."

Small Canines — A352

Designs: ($4.00), Bat-eared fox. ($6.60), Black-backed jackal. ($7.50), Side-striped jackal. ($8.80), Aardwolf. ($32.10), Cape fox.

**2017, Sept. 29 Litho. *Perf. 12½x13***
**1362-1366** A352 Set of 5 8.75 8.75

No. 1362 is inscribed "Standard Mail." No. 1363 is inscribed "Zone A." No. 1364 is inscribed "Zone B." No. 1365 is inscribed "Zone C." No. 1366 is inscribed "Inland Registered Mail."

## NATAL

nə-'tal

LOCATION — Southern coast of Africa, bordering on the Indian Ocean
GOVT. — British Crown Colony
AREA — 35,284 sq. mi.
POP. — 1,206,386 (1908)
CAPITAL — Pietermaritzburg

Natal united with Cape of Good Hope, Orange Free State and the Transvaal in 1910 to form the Union of South Africa.

12 Pence = 1 Shilling
20 Shillings = 1 Pound

Values for Nos. 1-7 are for examples with complete margins and free from damage. Unused values for No. 8 on are for stamps with original gum as defined in the catalogue introduction. Very fine examples of Nos. 8-49, 61-63 and 79 will have perforations touching the design on one or more sides due to the narrow spacing of the stamps on the plates. Stamps with perfs clear of the design on all four sides are scarce and will command higher prices.

**Watermark**

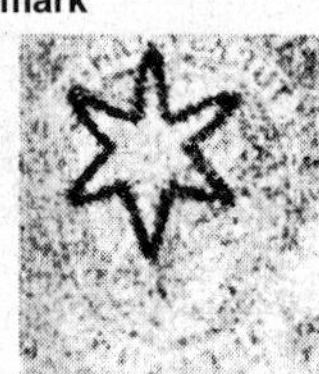

Wmk. 5 — Small Star

Crown and V R (Victoria Regina) — A1

Crown and V R (Victoria Regina) — A2

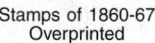

Crown and Laurel — A3

A4

A5

**Colorless Embossing**

**1857 Unwmk. *Imperf.***
**1** A1 3p *rose* 725.
*a.* Tete beche pair *55,000.*
**2** A2 6p *green* 2,000.
*a.* Diagonal half used as 3p on cover *16,500.*
**3** A3 9p *blue* 65,000. *13,000.*
**4** A4 1sh *buff* *10,500.*

**1858**
**5** A5 1p *blue* 1,400.
**6** A5 1p *rose* 2,200.
*a.* No. 1 embossed over No. 6 —
**7** A5 1p *buff* 1,450.

*Reprints: The paper is slightly glazed, the embossing sharper and the colors as follows: 1p pale blue, deep blue, carmine rose or yellow; 3p pale rose or carmine rose; 6p bright green or yellow green; 1sh pale buff or pale yellow. Bogus cancellations are found on the reprints.*

The stamps printed on surface-colored paper are revenue stamps with trimmed perforations.

Listings of shades will be found in the *Scott Classic Specialized Catalogue.*

Queen Victoria — A6

**1860 Engr. *Perf. 14***
**8** A6 1p rose 190.00 95.00
**9** A6 3p blue 225.00 60.00
*a.* Vert. pair, imperf betwn. *13,000.*

**1863 *Perf. 13***
**10** A6 1p red 130.00 35.00

**1861 *Clean-cut Perf. 14 to 16***
**11** A6 3p blue 350.00 82.50

**1862 *Rough Perf. 14 to 16***
**12** A6 3p blue 175.00 45.00
*a.* Imperf., pair *4,500.*
*b.* Horiz. or vert. pair, imperf. between *6,500.*
**13** A6 6p gray 275.00 75.00

**1862 Wmk. 5**
**14** A6 1p rose 180.00 82.50

Imperforate stamps of the 1p and 3p on paper watermarked small star are proofs.

**1864 Wmk. 1 *Perf. 12½***
**15** A6 1p carmine red 140.00 50.00
**16** A6 6p violet 90.00 37.50

No. 15 imperf is a proof.

Queen Victoria — A7

**1867 Typo. *Perf. 14***
**17** A7 1sh green 275.00 52.50

For types A6 and A7 overprinted or surcharged see Nos. 18-50, 61-63, 76, 79.

Stamps of 1860-67 Overprinted

**1869 Overprint 12¾mm**

**18** A6 1p carmine red (#15) 525.00 100.00
*b.* Double overprint — —
**19** A6 3p blue (#12) 700.00 110.00
**19A** A6 3p blue (#9) — 725.00
**19B** A6 3p blue (#11) 1,050. 325.00
**20** A6 6p violet (#16) 650.00 110.00
**21** A7 1sh green (#17) *30,000.* 2,100.

**Same Overprint 13¾mm**

**22** A6 1p rose (#15b) 1,200. 325.00
**23** A6 3p blue (#12) 2,800. 550.00
*a.* Inverted overprint
**23B** A6 3p blue (#9) — —
**23C** A6 3p blue (#11) — 1,100.
**24** A6 6p violet (#16) 2,750. 225.00
**25** A7 1sh green (#17) *35,000. 3,250.*

**Same Overprint 14½ to 15½mm**

**26** A6 1p rose (#15b) 1,050. 250.00
**27** A6 3p blue (#12) — 450.00
**27A** A6 3p blue (#11) — 775.00
**27B** A6 3p blue (#9) — —
**28** A6 6p violet (#16) 2,100. 140.00
**29** A7 1sh green (#17) *32,000. 2,750.*

Overprinted

**30** A6 1p rose (#15b) 150.00 55.00
*b.* Inverted overprint
**31** A6 3p blue (#12) 250.00 55.00
*a.* Double overprint *1,800.*
**31B** A6 3p blue (#11) 225.00 62.50
**31C** A6 3p blue (#9) 400.00 95.00
**32** A6 6p violet (#16) 210.00 77.50
**33** A7 1sh green (#17) 350.00 87.50

Overprinted

**34** A6 1p rose (#15b) 650.00 120.00
**35** A6 3p blue (#12) 825.00 120.00
**35A** A6 3p blue (#11) 1,200. 375.00
**35B** A6 3p blue (#9) *4,250. 925.00*
**36** A6 6p violet (#16) 825.00 120.00
*b.* Inverted overprint
**37** A7 1sh green (#17) *37,500. 2,000.*

Overprinted in Black or Red

**1870-73 Wmk. 1 *Perf. 12½***

**38** A6 1p red 120.00 16.50
**39** A6 3p ultra (R) ('72) 130.00 16.50
**40** A6 6p lilac ('73) 250.00 45.00
*Nos. 38-40 (3)* 500.00 78.00

Overprinted in Red, Black or Green — g

**1870 *Perf. 14***

**41** A7 1sh green (R) — *9,500.*
**42** A7 1sh green (Bk) — *1,750.*
*a.* Double overprint *3,900.*
**43** A7 1sh green (G) 150.00 13.00

See No. 76.

Type of 1867 Overprinted

**1873**

**44** A7 1sh brown lilac 425.00 37.50

No. 44 without overprint is a revenue.

Type of 1864 Overprinted

**1874 *Perf. 12½***

**45** A6 1p rose red 400.00 95.00
*a.* Double overprint

Overprinted

**1875**

**46** A6 1p rose red 185.00 70.00
*b.* Double overprint 1,900. 650.00

Overprinted

**1875 Overprint 14½mm *Perf. 12½***

**47** A6 1p yellow 100.00 100.00
*a.* Double overprint, one albino 275.00 —
**48** A6 1p rose red 140.00 87.50
*a.* Inverted overprint 2,250. 575.00
**49** A6 6p violet 95.00 10.00
*a.* Inverted overprint 900.00 190.00
*b.* Double overprint 1,050.

***Perf. 14***

**50** A7 1sh green 140.00 9.00
*a.* Double overprint 425.00
*Nos. 47-50 (4)* 475.00 206.50

The 1p yellow without overprint is a revenue.

A8

A9

A10

A11

Queen Victoria — A12

**1874-78 Typo. Wmk. 1 *Perf. 14***

**51** A8 1p dull rose 60.00 8.50
**52** A9 3p ultramarine 190.00 45.00
*a.* Perf. 14x12½ 2,500. 1,100.
**53** A10 4p brown ('78) 210.00 20.00
**54** A11 6p violet 110.00 9.00

***Perf. 15½x15***

**55** A12 5sh claret 525.00 120.00

***Perf. 14***

**56** A12 5sh claret ('78) 450.00 120.00
**57** A12 5sh carmine 120.00 42.50

***Perf. 12½***

**58** A10 4p brown ('78) 400.00 82.50

See Nos. 65-71. For types A8-A10 surcharged see Nos. 59-60, 72-73, 77, 80.

**Surcharged in Black**

n

No. 60

o

**1877 *Perf. 14***

**59** A8(n) ½p on 1p rose 45.00 *82.50*
*a.* Double surcharge "1/2"
**60** A8(n) ½p on 1p rose 110.00 —

Surcharge "n" exists in 3 or more types each of the large "1/2" (No. 59) and the small "1/2" (No. 60).

"HALF" and "½" were overprinted separately; "½" may be above, below or overlapping.

***Perf. 12½***

**61** A6(o) ½p on 1p yel 13.00 *25.00*
*a.* Double surcharge 400.00 230.00
*b.* Inverted surcharge 400.00 240.00
*c.* Pair, one without surcharge 4,750. 3,000.
*d.* "POTAGE" 350.00 250.00
*e.* "POSAGE" 350.00 325.00
*f.* "POSTAGE" omitted 2,500. —
**62** A6(o) 1p on 6p vio 82.50 13.00
*a.* "POSTAGE" omitted
*b.* "POTAGE" 650.00 190.00
**63** A6(o) 1p on 6p rose 150.00 60.00
*a.* Inverted surcharge 1,750. 600.00
*b.* Double surcharge — 350.00
*c.* Dbl. srch., one inverted 400.00 250.00
*d.* Triple srch., one invtd.
*e.* Quadruple surcharge 550.00 300.00
*f.* "POTAGE" 1,000. 390.00
*Nos. 61-63 (3)* 245.50 98.00

No. 63 without overprint is a revenue.

A14

**1880 Typo. *Perf. 14***

**64** A14 ½p blue green 30.00 40.00
*a.* Vertical pair, imperf. between

**1882-89 Wmk. Crown and CA (2)**

**65** A14 ½p blue green ('84) 120.00 22.50
**66** A14 ½p gray green ('84) 6.00 1.40
**67** A8 1p rose ('84) 8.50 .30
**68** A9 3p ultra ('84) 170.00 22.00
**69** A9 3p gray ('89) 12.50 5.75
**70** A10 4p brown 17.50 1.90
**71** A11 6p violet 14.50 2.75
*Nos. 65-71 (7)* 349.00 56.60

**Surcharged in Black**

p

q

**1885-86**

**72** A8(p) ½p on 1p rose 24.00 14.00
*b.* Inverted surcharge *1,000.*
**73** A9(q) 2p on 3p gray ('86) 40.00 7.00

A17

**1887**

**74** A17 2p olive green, die B ('89) 6.00 1.75
*a.* Die A 60.00 3.00

For explanation of dies A and B see "Dies of British Colonial Stamps" in the catalogue introduction.

Type of 1867 Overprinted Type "g" in Red

**1888**

**76** A7 1sh orange 13.50 2.00
*a.* Double overprint *3,250.*

Surcharged in Black

**1891**

**77** A10 2½p on 4p brown 17.50 17.50
*a.* "PENGE" 77.50
*b.* "PENN" 325.00 275.00
*c.* Double surcharge 400.00 350.00
*d.* As "c," in vert. pair with normal stamp 650.00 *750.00*
*e.* Inverted surcharge 550.00 475.00
*f.* Vert. pair, surcharge tete-beche 2,250. *3,000.*

A20

**1891, June**

**78** A20 2½p ultramarine 12.50 1.60

**Surcharged in Red or Black**

No. 79

No. 80

**1895, Mar. Wmk. 1 *Perf. 12½***

**79** A6 ½p on 6p vio (R) 3.00 *10.00*
*a.* "Ealf" 27.50 *75.00*
*b.* "Penny" 27.50 *75.00*
*c.* Double surcharge, one vertical 350.00
*d.* Double surcharge 350.00

Stamps with fancy "P," "T" or "A" in surcharge sell for twice as much.

**Wmk. 2 *Perf. 14***

**80** A8 ½p on 1p rose (Bk) 3.50 2.50
*a.* Double surcharge 525.00 550.00
*b.* Pair, one without surcharge and the other with double surcharge —

A23

King Edward VII — A24

**1902-03 Typo. Wmk. 2 *Perf. 14***

**81** A23 ½p blue green 7.50 .55
**82** A23 1p rose 13.00 .25
**83** A23 1½p blk & blue grn 4.50 *6.00*
**84** A23 2p ol grn & scar 7.00 .45
**85** A23 2½p ultramarine 2.25 *6.00*
**86** A23 3p gray & red vio 1.60 *2.75*
**87** A23 4p brown & scar 14.00 *27.50*
**88** A23 5p org & black 5.00 4.00
**89** A23 6p mar & bl grn 5.00 5.00
**90** A23 1sh pale bl & dp rose 6.50 5.25
**91** A23 2sh vio & bl grn 62.50 11.50
**92** A23 2sh6p red violet 50.00 15.00

93 A23 4sh yel & dp rose 95.00 95.00

**Wmk. 1**

94 A24 5sh car lake & dk blue 67.50 14.00
95 A24 10sh brn & dp rose 130.00 45.00
96 A24 £1 ultra & blk 350.00 85.00
97 A24 £1 10sh vio & bl grn 600.00 140.00
Revenue cancel 15.00
98 A24 £5 blk & vio *5,500.* *1,400.*
Revenue cancel 110.00
99 A24 £10 org & grn *14,000.* *6,500.*
Revenue cancel 180.00
100 A24 £20 grn & car *28,000.* *19,000.*
Revenue cancel 325.00
*Nos. 81-96 (16)* 821.35 323.25

**1904-08 Wmk. 3**

101 A23 ½p blue green 12.00 .25
102 A23 1p rose 12.00 .25
a. Booklet pane of 6 600.00
b. Booklet pane of 5 + 1 label 500.00
103 A23 2p ol grn & scar 18.50 4.00
104 A23 4p brn & scar 3.50 1.60
105 A23 5p org & blk ('08) 6.50 5.00
106 A23 1sh pale bl & dp rose 90.00 9.00
107 A23 2sh vio & bl grn 75.00 55.00
108 A23 2sh6p red violet 70.00 55.00
109 A24 £1 10sh vio & org brn, chalky paper 1,900. *5,000.*
Revenue cancel 55.00
*Nos. 101-108 (8)* 287.50 130.10

A25

A26

**1908-09**

110 A25 6p red violet 5.75 3.50
111 A25 1sh blk, *grn* 7.75 3.25
112 A25 2sh bl & vio, *bl* 19.00 3.75
113 A25 2sh6p red & blk, *bl* 32.00 5.50
114 A26 5sh red & grn, *yell* 30.00 *52.50*
115 A26 10sh red & grn, *grn* 135.00 135.00
116 A26 £1 blk & vio, *red* 450.00 400.00
*Nos. 110-116 (7)* 679.50 603.50

### OFFICIAL STAMPS

Nos. 101-103, 106 and Type A23 Overprinted

**1904 Wmk. 3 *Perf. 14***

O1 A23 ½p blue green 3.75 .45
O2 A23 1p rose 16.00 1.25
O3 A23 2p ol grn & scar 45.00 22.50
O4 A23 3p gray & red vio 27.50 *5.50*
O5 A23 6p mar & bl grn 87.50 82.50
O6 A23 1sh pale bl & dp rose 250.00 *275.00*
*Nos. O1-O6 (6)* 429.75 *387.20*

Stamps of Natal were replaced by those of the Union of South Africa.

## NAURU

nä-'ü-ˌrü

LOCATION — An island on the Equator in the west central Pacific Ocean, midway between the Marshall and Solomon Islands.
GOVT. — Republic
AREA — 8½ sq. mi.
POP. — 10,605 (1999 est.)
CAPITAL — None. Parliament House is in Yaren District.

The island, a German possession, was captured by Australian forces in 1914 and, following World War I, was mandated to the British Empire. It was administered jointly by Great Britain, Australia and New Zealand.

In 1947 Nauru was placed under United Nations trusteeship, administered by Australia. On January 31, 1968, Nauru became a republic.

See North West Pacific Islands.

12 Pence = 1 Shilling
100 Cents = 1 Dollar (1966)

**Catalogue values for unused stamps in this country are for Never Hinged items, beginning with Scott 39.**

**Watermarks**

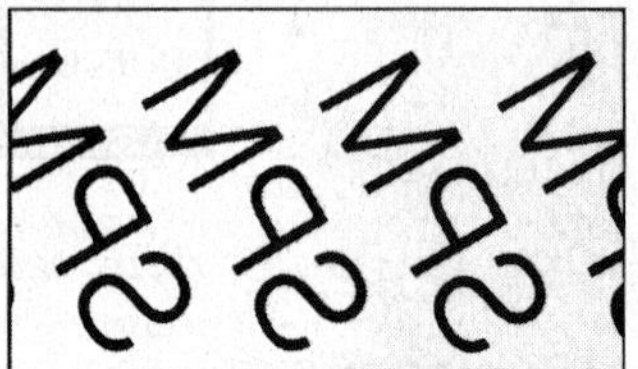
Wmk. 388 — Multiple "SPM"

Great Britain Stamps of 1912-13 Overprinted at Bottom of Stamp

**1916-23 Wmk. 33 *Perf. 14½x14***

1 A82 ½p green 3.50 *12.50*
2 A83 1p scarlet 2.50 *14.50*
3 A84 1½p red brn ('23) 57.50 *85.00*
4 A85 2p org (die I) 3.00 *15.00*
c. 2p deep orange (die II) ('23) 75.00 *110.00*
6 A86 2½p ultra 3.00 *7.50*
7 A87 3p violet 2.50 *6.50*
8 A88 4p slate green 2.50 *9.00*
a. Double ovpt 260.00
9 A89 5p yel brown 2.75 *14.00*
10 A89 6p dull violet 8.50 *11.00*
11 A90 9p blk brn 10.00 *24.00*
12 A90 1sh bister 8.50 *20.00*
*Nos. 1-12 (11)* 104.25 *219.00*

**Great Britain Stamps of 1915 Overprinted**

**Wmk. 34 *Perf. 11x12***

13 A91 2sh6p lt brn 80.00 *125.00*
a. 2sh6p black brown 625.00 *1,600.*
14 A91 5sh carmine 125.00 *175.00*
b. 5sh rose carmine 3,000. 2,750.
15 A91 10sh lt blue (R) 275.00 *375.00*
c. 10sh indigo blue *12,500.* *6,000.*

**Same Ovpt. on Great Britain No. 179a and 179b**

**1920**

16 A91 2sh6p gray brown 85.00 *200.00*
*Nos. 13-16 (4)* 565.00 *875.00*
*Nos. 1-16 (15)* 669.25 *1,094.*

Double and triple overprints, with one overprint albino, exist for most of the 1-16 overprints. Additional color shades exist for No. 13-16, and values given are for the most common varieties. For detailed listings, see *Scott Classic Specialized Catalogue.*

**1923 Overprint Centered**

*1b* A82 ½p 5.00 *55.00*
*2c* A83 1p 20.00 *45.00*
*3a* A84 1½p 30.00 *57.50*
*4d* A85 2p As No. 4a 32.50 *80.00*
*Nos. 1b-4d (4)* 87.50 *237.50*

On Nos. 1-12 "NAURU" is usually 12¾mm wide and at the foot of the stamp. In 1923 four values were overprinted with the word 13½mm wide and across the middle of the stamp.

Forged overprints exist.

Freighter — A1

**1924-48 Unwmk. Engr. *Perf. 11***

17 A1 ½p orange brown 2.75 *3.00*
b. Perf. 14 ('47) 1.75 *10.00*
18a A1 1p green 2.50 *4.00*
19a A1 1½p red 1.10 *2.00*
20a A1 2p orange 4.50 *8.00*
21a A1 2½p blue ('48) 4.00 *4.00*
c. Horiz. pair, imperf between *17,000.* *20,000.*
d. Vert. pair, imperf between *17,000.* *20,000.*
22a A1 3p grnsh gray ('47) 7.00 *23.00*
23a A1 4p olive green 7.00 *15.00*
24 A1 5p dk brown 4.50 *7.50*
25 A1 6p dark violet 5.25 *21.00*
26 A1 9p brown olive 11.00 *21.00*
27a A1 1sh brown red 14.00 3.25
28a A1 2sh6p slate green 34.00 *37.50*
29a A1 5sh claret 40.00 *55.00*
30a A1 10sh yellow 85.00 *110.00*
*Nos. 17-30a (14)* 222.60 314.25

Two printings were made of Nos. 17-30, the first (1924-34) on unsurfaced, grayish paper (Nos. 17-30), the second (1937-48) on glazed surfaced white paper (Nos. 17a-30a). Values are for the most common type. For detailed listings, see *Scott Classic Specialized Catalogue.*

Stamps of Type A1 Overprinted in Black

**1935, July 12 *Perf. 11***

**Glazed Paper**

31 A1 1½p red .90 *.90*
32 A1 2p orange 1.50 *3.75*
33 A1 2½p blue 1.50 *1.75*
34 A1 1sh brown red 6.00 *3.50*
*Nos. 31-34 (4)* 9.90 *9.90*
Set, never hinged 16.00

25th anniv. of the reign of George V.

George VI — A2

**1937, May 10 Engr.**

35 A2 1½p salmon rose .25 *1.00*
36 A2 2p dull orange .25 *2.00*
37 A2 2½p blue .25 *1.25*
38 A2 1sh brown violet .35 *1.25*
*Nos. 35-38 (4)* 1.10 *5.50*
Set, never hinged 1.75

Coronation of George VI & Elizabeth.

**Catalogue values for unused stamps in this section, from this point to the end of the section, are for Never Hinged items.**

Casting Throw-net — A3

Anibare Bay — A4

3½p, Loading phosphate. 4p, Frigate bird. 6p, Nauruan canoe. 9p, Meeting house (domaneab). 1sh, Palms. 2sh6p, Buada lagoon. 5sh, Map.

**1954, Feb. 6 *Perf. 14½x14, 14x14½***

39 A3 ½p purple .25 .50
40 A4 1p green .25 .30
41 A3 3½p red 1.50 .60
42 A3 4p deep blue 2.00 1.75
43 A3 6p orange .60 .25
44 A3 9p brown lake .55 .25
45 A4 1sh dk rose violet .45 .30
46 A3 2sh6p dk gray green 2.50 .80
47 A4 5sh lilac rose 7.00 2.00
*Nos. 39-47 (9)* 15.10 6.75

See Nos. 58-71.

Balsam — A5

Black Lizard — A6

Capparis — A7

Coral Pinnacles — A8

White Tern — A9

2p, Micronesian pigeon, vert. 3p, Poison nut flower. 3sh3p, Nightingale reed warbler.

***Perf. 13½, Perf. 14½x13½ (10p), Perf. 14½ (2sh3p)***

**Photo.; Engraved (10p, 2sh3p)**

**1963-65 Unwmk.**

49 A9 2p multi ('65) .75 1.50
50 A6 3p red org, sl grn & yel ('64) .40 .30
51 A5 5p gray, bl grn & yellow .40 .50
52 A6 8p green & black 1.75 .65
53 A7 10p black ('64) .60 .40
54 A9 1sh3p ap grn, blk & Prus bl ('65) 1.25 *3.50*
55 A8 2sh3p vio blue ('64) 2.25 .55
56 A6 3sh3p lt yel, bl, brn & blk ('65) 1.50 3.25
*Nos. 49-56 (8)* 8.90 10.65

Issue dates: 5p, Apr. 22. 8p, July 1. 3p, 10p, 2sh3p, Apr. 16. 2p, 1sh3p, 3sh3p, May 3.

"Simpson and His Donkey" by Wallace Anderson — A9a

***Perf. 13½x13***

**1965, Apr. 14 Photo. Unwmk.**

57 A9a 5p brt green, sepia & blk .30 .35

See note after Australia No. 387.

**Types of 1954-65 Values in Cents and Dollars**

Designs: 1c, Anibare Bay. 2c, Casting throw-net. 3c, Loading phosphate. 4c, Balsam. 5c, Palms. 7c, Black lizard. 8c, Capparis. 10c, Frigate bird. 15c, White tern. 25c, Coral pinnacles. 30c, Poison nut flower. 35c, Reed warbler. 50c, Micronesian pigeon, vert. $1, Map.

**Engr.; Photo. (4c, 7c, 15c, 30c-50c)**

**1966 *Perf. 14½x14, 14x14½***

58 A4 1c dark blue .25 .25
59 A3 2c claret .25 .50
60 A3 3c green .30 *1.50*
61 A5 4c lilac, grn & yel .25 .25
62 A4 5c violet blue .25 .75
63 A6 7c fawn & black .35 .25
64 A7 8c olive green .25 .25
65 A3 10c dark red .40 .25

| | | | | |
|---|---|---|---|---|
| 66 | A9 | 15c ap grn, blk & Prus blue | .55 | *2.75* |
| 67 | A3 | 25c sepia | .30 | *1.25* |
| 68 | A6 | 30c brick red, sl grn, & yellow | .45 | .35 |
| 69 | A6 | 35c lt yel, bl, brn & black | .70 | .40 |
| 70 | A9 | 50c yel, bluish blk & brown | 1.25 | .75 |
| 71 | A4 | $1 claret | 1.00 | 1.00 |
| | | *Nos. 58-71 (14)* | 6.55 | 10.50 |

The engraved stamps are luminescent.

Issued: 2c, 3c, 5c, 15c, 25c, 35c, 5/25; others, 2/14.

## Republic

Nos. 58-71 Overprinted in Red, Black or Orange "REPUBLIC / OF / NAURU"

**1968**

| | | | | |
|---|---|---|---|---|
| 72 | A4 | 1c dark blue (R) | .25 | .35 |
| 73 | A3 | 2c claret | .25 | .25 |
| 74 | A3 | 3c green | .25 | .25 |
| 75 | A5 | 4c lilac, grn & yel | .25 | .25 |
| 76 | A4 | 5c violet blue (O) | .25 | .25 |
| 77 | A6 | 7c fawn & blk (R) | .25 | .25 |
| 78 | A7 | 8c olive green (R) | .25 | .25 |
| 79 | A3 | 10c dark red | .60 | .30 |
| 80 | A9 | 15c ap grn, blk & Prus blue | 1.25 | *3.25* |
| 81 | A3 | 25c sepia (R) | .40 | .30 |
| 82 | A6 | 30c brick red, sl grn & yellow | .55 | .30 |
| 83 | A6 | 35c multicolored | 1.40 | .45 |
| 84 | A9 | 50c yel, bluish blk & brown | 1.25 | .50 |
| 85 | A4 | $1 claret | 1.00 | .80 |
| | | *Nos. 72-85 (14)* | 8.20 | 7.75 |

Issued: 4c, 7c, 30c, 35c, 5/15; others, 1/31.

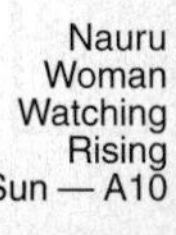

Nauru Woman Watching Rising Sun — A10

Planting Seedling and Map of Nauru — A11

*Perf. 13x13½*

**1968, Sept. 11 Photo. Unwmk.**

| | | | | |
|---|---|---|---|---|
| 86 | A10 | 5c multicolored | .30 | .25 |
| 87 | A11 | 10c brt blue, blk & green | .30 | .25 |

Independence of Nauru.

Flag of Nauru — A12

**1969, Jan. 31 Litho.** ***Perf. 13½***

| | | | | |
|---|---|---|---|---|
| 88 | A12 | 15c dk vio blue, yel & org | .50 | .45 |

For overprint see No. 90.

Commission Emblem and Nauru A13

**1972, Feb. 7 Litho.** ***Perf. 14½x14***

| | | | | |
|---|---|---|---|---|
| 89 | A13 | 25c blue, yellow & black | .55 | .50 |

South Pacific Commission, 25th anniv.

No. 88 Ovptd. in Gold

**1973, Jan. 31** ***Perf. 13½***

| | | | | |
|---|---|---|---|---|
| 90 | A12 | 15c multicolored | .35 | .35 |

Fifth anniversary of independence.

Lotus (Ekwenababae) A14

Map of Nauru, Artifacts A15

Catching Flyingfish A16

Designs: 2c, Kauwe iud. 3c, Rimone. 4c, Denea. 5c, Beach morning-glory. 7c, Golden butterflyfish. 10c, Nauruan ball game (itsibweb). 15c, Nauruan wrestling. 20c, Snaring frigate birds. 25c, Nauruan girl with flower garland. 30c, Men catching noddies. 50c, Frigate birds.

**1973 Litho.** ***Perf. 13½x14***

| | | | | |
|---|---|---|---|---|
| 91 | A14 | 1c pale yellow & multi | .30 | .25 |
| 92 | A14 | 2c pale ocher & multi | .35 | .25 |
| 93 | A14 | 3c pale violet & multi | .35 | .25 |
| 94 | A14 | 4c pale green & multi | .35 | .35 |
| 95 | A14 | 5c pale blue & multi | .35 | .35 |

***Perf. 14½x14, 14x14½***

| | | | | |
|---|---|---|---|---|
| 96 | A16 | 7c blue & multi | .50 | *.90* |
| 97 | A16 | 8c black & multi | .30 | .25 |
| 98 | A16 | 10c multicolored | .30 | .25 |
| 99 | A15 | 15c green & multi | .35 | .25 |
| 100 | A15 | 20c blue & multi | .60 | *.90* |
| 101 | A15 | 25c yellow & multi | .45 | .45 |
| 102 | A16 | 30c multicolored | .55 | .50 |
| 103 | A16 | 50c multicolored | .80 | .75 |
| 104 | A15 | $1 blue & multi | 1.00 | .75 |
| | | *Nos. 91-104 (14)* | 6.55 | 6.45 |

Issue dates: Nos. 97-100, May 23; Nos. 96, 101-103, July 25; others Mar. 28, 1973.

Cooperative Store — A17

Eigigu, the Girl in the Moon — A18

Design: 25c, Timothy Detudamo and cooperative store emblem.

**1973, Dec. 20 Litho.** ***Perf. 14½x14***

| | | | | |
|---|---|---|---|---|
| 105 | A17 | 5c multicolored | .50 | .50 |
| 106 | A17 | 25c multicolored | .50 | .50 |
| 107 | A18 | 50c multicolored | 1.00 | *1.25* |
| | | *Nos. 105-107 (3)* | 2.00 | 2.25 |

50th anniversary of Nauru Cooperative Society, founded by Timothy Detudamo.

"Eigamoiya" — A19

10c, Phosphate mining. 15c, "Nauru Chief" plane over Nauru. 25c, Nauru chieftain with frigate-bird headdress. 35c, Capt. J. Fearn, sailing ship "Hunter" & map of Nauru. 50c, "Hunter" off Nauru.

***Perf. 13x13½, 13½x13***

**1974, May 21 Litho.**

**Sizes: 70x22mm (7c, 35c, 50c); 33x20mm (10c, 15c, 25c)**

| | | | | |
|---|---|---|---|---|
| 108 | A19 | 7c multicolored | .70 | *.95* |
| 109 | A19 | 10c multicolored | .55 | .25 |
| 110 | A19 | 15c multicolored | .70 | .35 |
| 111 | A19 | 25c multicolored | .60 | .40 |
| 112 | A19 | 35c multicolored | 3.50 | 3.50 |
| 113 | A19 | 50c multicolored | 2.00 | *2.25* |
| | | *Nos. 108-113 (6)* | 8.05 | 7.70 |

175th anniversary of Nauru's first contact with the outside world.

Map of Nauru — A20

Post Office — A21

UPU Emblem and: 20c, Mailman on motorcycle. $1, Flag of Nauru and UPU Building, Bern, vert.

**1974, July 23 Litho.** ***Perf. 14***

| | | | | |
|---|---|---|---|---|
| 114 | A20 | 5c multicolored | .25 | .25 |

***Perf. 13½x13, 13x13½***

| | | | | |
|---|---|---|---|---|
| 115 | A21 | 8c multicolored | .25 | .25 |
| 116 | A21 | 20c multicolored | .25 | .25 |
| 117 | A21 | $1 multicolored | 1.25 | 1.25 |
| *a.* | | Souv. sheet of 4, #114-117, imperf. | 3.00 | 3.00 |
| | | *Nos. 114-117 (4)* | 2.00 | 2.00 |

Cent. of the UPU.

Rev. P. A. Delaporte — A22

**1974, Dec. 10 Litho.** ***Perf. 14½***

| | | | | |
|---|---|---|---|---|
| 118 | A22 | 15c brt pink & multi | .30 | .30 |
| 119 | A22 | 20c blue & multi | .50 | .50 |

Christmas 1974. Delaporte, a German-born American missionary, took Christianity to Nauru and translated the New Testament into Nauruan.

Nauru, Grain, Albert Ellis, Phosphate Rock — A23

Designs: 7c, Phosphate mining and coolie carrying load. 15c, Electric freight train, tugs and ship. 25c, Excavator, cantilever and truck.

**1975, July 23 Litho.** ***Perf. 14½x14***

| | | | | |
|---|---|---|---|---|
| 120 | A23 | 5c multicolored | .30 | .30 |
| 121 | A23 | 7c multicolored | .40 | .40 |
| 122 | A23 | 15c multicolored | 1.10 | 1.10 |
| 123 | A23 | 25c multicolored | 1.40 | 1.40 |
| | | *Nos. 120-123 (4)* | 3.20 | 3.20 |

75th anniv. of discovery of phosphate (5c); 70th anniv. of Pacific Phosphate Co. Mining Agreement (7c); 50th anniv. of British Phosphate Commissioners (15c); 5th anniv. of Nauru Phosphate Corp. (25c).

Melanesian Outrigger and Map of SPC's Area — A24

No. 124, Micronesian outrigger. No. 125, Polynesian double hull. No. 127, Polynesian outrigger.

**1975, Sept. 1 Litho.** ***Perf. 14x14½***

| | | | | |
|---|---|---|---|---|
| 124 | A24 | 20c multicolored | .60 | .60 |
| 125 | A24 | 20c multicolored | .60 | .60 |
| 126 | A24 | 20c shown | .60 | .60 |
| 127 | A24 | 20c multicolored | .60 | .60 |
| *a.* | | Block of 4, #124-127 | 3.25 | 3.25 |
| | | *Nos. 124-127 (4)* | 2.40 | 2.40 |

South Pacific Commission Conference, Nauru, Sept. 29-Oct. 10.

Nos. 124-127 exist imperf. Value, block of four *$50.*

New Civic Center A25

Design: 50c, "Domaneab" (meeting house) and flags of participating nations.

**1975, Sept. 29 Litho.** ***Perf. 14½***

| | | | | |
|---|---|---|---|---|
| 128 | A25 | 30c multicolored | .25 | .25 |
| 129 | A25 | 50c multicolored | .45 | .45 |

South Pacific Commission Conference, Nauru, Sept. 29-Oct. 10.

Nos. 128-129 exist imperf. Value, set $12.

Virgin Mary, Stained-glass Window — A26

Christmas: 7c, 15c, "Suffer little children to come unto me," stained-glass window, Orro Protestant Church. 25c, like 5c, Yaren Catholic Church.

**1975, Nov. 7 Litho.** ***Perf. 14½***

| | | | | |
|---|---|---|---|---|
| 130 | A26 | 5c gray blue & multi | .25 | .25 |
| 131 | A26 | 7c green & multi | .25 | .25 |
| 132 | A26 | 15c brown & multi | .25 | .50 |
| 133 | A26 | 25c lilac & multi | .25 | .70 |
| | | *Nos. 130-133 (4)* | 1.00 | 1.70 |

Frangipani Forming Lei Around Nauru — A27

14c, Hand crowning Nauru with lei. 25c, Reed warbler, birds flying from Truk to Nauru. 40c, Reunion of islanders in Boar Harbor.

**1976, Jan. 31 Litho.** ***Perf. 14½***

| | | | | |
|---|---|---|---|---|
| 134 | A27 | 10c green & multi | .25 | .25 |
| 135 | A27 | 14c violet & multi | .25 | .25 |
| 136 | A27 | 25c red & multi | .25 | .25 |
| 137 | A27 | 40c blue & multi | .30 | .25 |
| | | *Nos. 134-137 (4)* | 1.05 | 1.00 |

30th anniversary of the return of the islanders from Japanese internment on Truk.

Nos. 134-137 exist imperf. Value, set $20.

Nauru Nos. 7 and 11 A28

15c, Nauru Nos. 10, 12. 25c, Nauru No. 13. 50c, Nauru No. 14, "Specimen."

**1976, May 6 Litho. *Perf. 13½x14***

**138** A28 10c multicolored .25 .25
**139** A28 15c multicolored .25 .25
**140** A28 25c multicolored .25 .25
**141** A28 50c multicolored .40 .40
*Nos. 138-141 (4)* 1.15 1.15

60th anniv. of Nauru's 1st postage stamps.
Nos. 138-141 exist imperf. Value, set $17.50.

Nauru Shipping and Pandanus — A29

Designs: 20c, Air Nauru Boeing 737 and Fokker F28, and tournefortia argentea. 30c, Earth satellite station and thespesia populnea. 40c, Area produce and cordia subcordata.

**1976, July 26 Litho. *Perf. 13½x14***

**142** A29 10c multicolored .25 .25
**143** A29 20c multicolored .25 .25
**144** A29 30c multicolored .25 .25
**145** A29 40c multicolored .45 .45
*Nos. 142-145 (4)* 1.20 1.20

7th South Pacific Forum, Nauru, July 1976.
Nos. 142-145 exist imperf. Value, set $35.

Nauruan Children's Choir — A30

20c, Angels. Nos. 146, 148, denominations at lower right. Nos. 147, 149, denominations at lower left.

**1976, Nov. Litho. *Perf. 14x13½***

**146** 15c multicolored .25 .25
**147** 15c multicolored .25 .25
*a.* A30 Pair, #146-147 .55 .55
**148** 20c multicolored .25 .25
**149** 20c multicolored .25 .25
*a.* A30 Pair, #148-149 .55 .55
*Nos. 146-149 (4)* 1.00 1.00

Christmas.
Nos. 146-149 exist imperf. Value, set of two se-tenant pairs $65.

Nauru House, Melbourne, and Coral Pinnacles — A32

30c, Nauru House and Melbourne skyline.

**1977, Apr. 14 Photo. *Perf. 14½***

**150** A32 15c multicolored .25 .25
**151** A32 30c multicolored .40 .40

Opening of Nauru House in Melbourne, Australia.
For surcharges see Nos. 161-164.

Cable-laying Ship Anglia, 1902 — A33

Designs: 15c, Nauru radar station. 20c, Stern of Anglia. 25c, Radar antenna.

**1977, Sept. 7 Photo. *Perf. 14½***

**152** A33 7c multicolored .25 .25
**153** A33 15c multicolored .25 .25
**154** A33 20c multicolored .30 .30
**155** A33 25c multicolored .40 .40
*Nos. 152-155 (4)* 1.20 1.20

1st transpacific cable, 75th anniv., and 1st artificial earth satellite, 20th anniv.

Catholic Church, Yaren, and Father Kayser — A34

Designs: 25c, Congregational Church, Orro. 30c, Catholic Church, Arubo.

**1977, Oct. Photo. *Perf. 14½***

**156** A34 15c multicolored .25 .25
**157** A34 25c multicolored .25 .25
**158** A34 30c multicolored .25 .25
*Nos. 156-158 (3)* .75 .75

Christmas, and 55th anniversary of first Roman Catholic Church on Nauru.

Coat of Arms of Nauru — A35

**1978, Jan. 31 Litho. *Perf. 14½***

**159** A35 15c blue & multi .25 .25
**160** A35 60c emerald & multi .35 .35

10th anniversary of independence. Exists imperf, value $14.

**Nos. 150-151 Surcharged with New Value and Two Bars**

**1978, Apr. Photo. *Perf. 14½***

**161** A32 4c on 15c multi 2.50 2.50
**162** A32 5c on 15c multi 2.50 2.50
**163** A32 8c on 30c multi 2.50 2.50
**164** A32 10c on 30c multi 2.50 2.50
*Nos. 161-164 (4)* 10.00 10.00

Girls Catching Fish in Buada Lagoon A36

Designs: 1c, Fisherman and family collecting shellfish. 2c, Pigs foraging near coral reef. 3c, Gnarled tree and birds. 4c, Girl catching fish with hands. 5c, Bird catching fish. 10c, Ijuw Lagoon. 15c, Young girl and coral formation. 20c, Reef pinnacles, Anibare Bay. 25c, Pinnacles, Meneng shore. 30c, Frigate bird. 32c, Coconut palm and noddies. 40c, Iwiyi, wading bird. 50c, Frigate birds. $1, Pinnacles, Topside. $2, Newly uncovered pinnacles, Topside. $5, Old pinnacles, Topside.

**1978-79 Photo. *Perf. 14½***

**165** A36 1c multicolored .35 .25
**166** A36 2c multicolored .35 .25
**167** A36 3c multicolored .85 .75
**168** A36 4c multicolored .40 .25
**169** A36 5c multicolored .85 .75
**170** A36 7c multicolored .25 *1.00*
**171** A36 10c multicolored .25 .25
**172** A36 15c multicolored .25 .25
**173** A36 20c multicolored .25 .30
**174** A36 25c multicolored .25 .30
**175** A36 30c multicolored 1.00 .45
**176** A36 32c multicolored 1.40 1.00
**177** A36 40c multicolored 1.00 1.50
**178** A36 50c multicolored 1.00 1.10
**179** A36 $1 multicolored .70 .80
**180** A36 $2 multicolored .90 .90
**181** A36 $5 multicolored 1.65 1.75
*Nos. 165-181 (17)* 11.70 11.85

Issued: #166-169, 6/6/79; others, 5/1978.
Nos. 179-181 exists on an "official black print without franking validity" numbered souvenir sheet of 3. Value, $15.

"APU" — A37

**1978, Aug. 28 Litho. *Perf. 13½***

**182** A37 15c multicolored .40 .90
**183** A37 20c gold, blk & dk blue .60 1.10

14th General Assembly of Asian Parliamentary Union, Nauru, Aug. 28-Sept. 1. On sale during conference only.

Mother and Child — A38

Christmas: 15c, 20c, Angel over the Pacific, horiz. 30c, like 7c.

**1978, Nov. 1 Litho. *Perf. 14***

**184** A38 7c multicolored .25 .25
**185** A38 15c multicolored .25 .25
**186** A38 20c multicolored .25 .25
**187** A38 30c multicolored .25 .25
*Nos. 184-187 (4)* 1.00 1.00

Lord Baden-Powell and Cub Scout — A39

30c, Boy Scout. 50c, Explorer.

**1978, Dec. 1 Litho. *Perf. 14***

**188** A39 20c multicolored .25 .25
**189** A39 30c multicolored .25 .25
**190** A39 50c multicolored .35 .35
*Nos. 188-190 (3)* .85 .85

70th anniversary of 1st Scout Troop.

Flyer A over Nauru Airfield A40

Designs: No. 192, "Southern Cross" and Boeing 727. No. 193, "Southern Cross" and Boeing 737. 30c, Wright Flyer over Nauru.

**1979, Jan. *Perf. 14½***

**191** A40 10c multicolored .30 .30
**192** A40 15c multicolored .35 .35
**193** A40 15c multicolored .35 .35
*a.* Pair, #192-193 .90 .90
**194** A40 30c multicolored .60 .60
*Nos. 191-194 (4)* 1.60 1.60

1st powered flight, 75th anniv. and Kingsford Smith's US-Australia and Australia-New Zealand flights, 50th anniv.
Nos. 192-193 printed checkerwise.
Nos. 191-194 exist imperf. Value, set of two singles (Nos. 191, 194) and pair (193a), $65.

Rowland Hill, Marshall Islands No. 15 with Nauru Cancel A41

**1979, Feb. 27 Litho. *Perf. 14½***

**195** A41 5c shown .25 .25
**196** A41 15c Nauru No. 15 .25 .25
**197** A41 60c Nauru No. 160 .40 .60
*a.* Souvenir sheet of 3, #195-197 1.00 1.25
*Nos. 195-197 (3)* .90 1.10

Sir Rowland Hill (1795-1879), originator of penny postage.

Dish Antenna, Earth Station, ITU Emblem — A42

ITU Emblem and: 32c, Woman operating Telex machine. 40c, Radio beacon operator.

**1979, Aug. Litho. *Perf. 14½***

**198** A42 7c multicolored .25 .25
**199** A42 32c multicolored .30 .30
**200** A42 40c multicolored .35 .35
*Nos. 198-200 (3)* .90 .90

Intl. Radio Consultative Committee (CCIR) of the ITU, 50th anniv.
Nos. 198-200 exist imperf. Value, set $20.

Nauruan Girl — A43

IYC Emblem, Nauruan Children: 15c, Boy. 25c, 32c, 50c, Girls, diff.

**1979, Oct. 3 Litho. *Perf. 14½***

**201** A43 8c multicolored .25 .25
**202** A43 15c multicolored .25 .25
**203** A43 25c multicolored .25 .25
**204** A43 32c multicolored .25 .25
**205** A43 50c multicolored .25 .25
*a.* Strip of 5, #201-205 1.25 1.25

International Year of the Child.

Star, Scroll, Ekwenababa Flower — A44

Star and Flowers: 15c, Milos. 20c, Denea. 30c, Morning glories.

**1979, Nov. 14 Litho. *Perf. 14½***

**206** A44 7c multicolored .25 .25
**207** A44 15c multicolored .25 .25
**208** A44 20c multicolored .25 .25
**209** A44 30c multicolored .25 .25
*Nos. 206-209 (4)* 1.00 1.00

Christmas.
Nos. 206-209 exist imperf. Value, set $65.

Nauruan Plane over Melbourne — A45

Air Nauru, 10th Anniversary (Plane Over): 20c, Tarawa. 25c, Hong Kong. 30c, Auckland.

**1980, Feb. 28 Litho. *Perf. 14½***

**210** A45 15c multicolored .35 .25
**211** A45 20c multicolored .35 .25
**212** A45 25c multicolored .45 .30
**213** A45 30c multicolored .55 .40
*Nos. 210-213 (4)* 1.70 1.20

Early Steam Locomotive — A46

32c, Electric locomotive. 60c, Clyde diesel-hydraulic locomotive.

**1980, May 6 Litho. *Perf. 15***

**214** A46 8c shown .25 .25
**215** A46 32c multicolored .30 .30
**216** A46 60c multicolored .45 .45
*a.* Souvenir sheet of 3, #214-216 1.50 1.75
*Nos. 214-216 (3)* 1.00 1.00

Nauru Phosphate Corp., 10th anniv. No. 216a also for London 1980 Intl. Stamp Exhibition, May 6-14; Penny Black, 140th anniv.

Christmas 1980 — A47

Designs: 30c, "Glory to God in the Highest . . ." in English and Nauruan.

**1980, Sept. 24 Litho. *Perf. 15***

**217** 20c English .25 .25
**218** 20c Nauruese .25 .25
*a.* A47 Pair, #217-218 .55 .55
**219** 30c English .25 .25
**220** 30c Nauruese .25 .25
*a.* A47 Pair, #219-220 .55 .55
*Nos. 217-220 (4)* 1.00 1.00

See Nos. 236-239.

Flags of Nauru, Australia, Gt. Britain and New Zealand, UN Emblem — A49

30c, UN Trusteeship Council. 50c, 1968 independence ceremony.

**1980, Dec. 20 Litho. *Perf. 14½***

**221** A49 25c shown .25 .25

**Size: 72x22mm**

***Perf. 14***

**222** A49 30c multicolored .30 .30
**223** A49 50c multicolored .40 .40
*Nos. 221-223 (3)* .95 .95

UN de-colonization declaration, 20th anniv.

No. 222 printed se-tenant with label showing flags of UN and Nauru, issued Feb. 11, 1981.

Timothy Detudamo (Former Head Chief), Domaneab (Meeting House) — A50

**1981, Feb. Litho. *Perf. 14½***

**224** A50 20c shown .25 .25
**225** A50 30c Raymond Gadabu .30 .25
**226** A50 50c Hammer DeRoburt .45 .35
*Nos. 224-226 (3)* 1.00 .85

Legislative Council, 30th anniversary.

Casting Net by Hand — A51

**1981 Litho. *Perf. 12***

**227** A51 8c shown .25 .25
**228** A51 20c Ancient canoe .25 .25
**229** A51 32c Powered boat .25 .25
**230** A51 40c Fishing vessel .25 .25
*a.* Souvenir sheet of 4, #230 1.75 1.75
*Nos. 227-230 (4)* 1.00 1.00

Bank of Nauru, 5th Anniv. — A52

**1981, July 21 Litho. *Perf. 14x14½***

**231** A52 $1 multicolored 1.00 1.00

ESCAP Secy. Maramis Delivering Inaugural Speech — A53

20c, Maramis, Pres. de Robert. 25c, Plaque. 30c, Raising UN flag.

**1981, Oct. 24 Litho. *Perf. 14½***

**232** A53 15c shown .25 .25
**233** A53 20c multicolored .25 .25
**234** A53 25c multicolored .25 .25
**235** A53 30c multicolored .25 .25
*Nos. 232-235 (4)* 1.00 1.00

UN Day and first anniv. of Economic and Social Commission for Asia and Pacific (ESCAP) liaison office in Nauru.

**Christmas Type of 1980**

Christmas (Biblical Scriptures in English and Nauruan): 20c, "His Name Shall Be Called Emmanuel." 30c, "To You is Born This Day . . ."

**1981, Nov. 14 Litho. *Perf. 14½***

**236** A47 20c multicolored .25 .25
**237** A48 20c multicolored .25 .25
*a.* Pair, #236-237 .50 .50
**238** A47 30c multicolored .25 .25
**239** A48 30c multicolored .25 .25
*a.* Pair, #238-239 .50 .50
*Nos. 236-239 (4)* 1.00 1.00

10th Anniv. of South Pacific Forum A54

**1981, Dec. 9 Litho. *Perf. 13½x14***

**240** A54 10c Globe, dish antenna .25 .25
**241** A54 20c Ship .25 .25
**242** A54 30c Jet .35 .35
**243** A54 40c Produce .40 .40
*Nos. 240-243 (4)* 1.25 1.25

Scouting Year — A55

7c, Carrying packages. 8c, Scouts, life preserver, vert. 15c, Pottery making, vert. 20c, Inspection. 25c, Scout, cub. 40c, Troop.

**1982, Feb. 23 Litho. *Perf. 14***

**244** A55 7c multicolored .25 .25
**245** A55 8c multicolored .25 .25
**246** A55 15c multicolored .25 .25
**247** A55 20c multicolored .25 .25
**248** A55 25c multicolored .30 .30
**249** A55 40c multicolored .45 .45
*a.* Souv. sheet of 6, #244-249, imperf. 1.75 1.75
*Nos. 244-249 (6)* 1.75 1.75

A56

Ocean Thermal Energy Conversion — A57

Designs: No. 250, Plant under construction. No. 251, Completed plant.

**1982, June 10 Litho. *Perf. 13½***

**250** Pair + 2 labels 1.00 1.00
*a.-b.* A56 25c any single .45 .45
**251** Pair + 2 labels 1.50 1.50
*a.-b.* A57 40c any single .70 .70

75th Anniv. of Phosphate Industry A58

5c, Freighter Fido, 1907. 10c, Locomotive Nellie, 1907. 30c, Modern Clyde diesel train, 1982. 60c, Flagship Eigamoiya, 1969.
$1, Freighters.

**1982, Oct. 11 Litho. *Perf. 14***

**252** A58 5c multicolored .30 .25
**253** A58 10c multicolored .50 .30
**254** A58 30c multicolored .90 .60
**255** A58 60c multicolored 1.30 1.10
*Nos. 252-255 (4)* 3.00 2.25

**Souvenir Sheet**

**256** A58 $1 multicolored 1.75 1.75

ANPEX '82 Natl. Stamp Exhibition, Brisbane, Australia, Nos. 252-255 se-tenant with labels describing stamp. No. 256 contains one 68x27mm stamp.

Visit of Queen Elizabeth II and Prince Philip — A59

**1982, Oct. 21 *Perf. 14½***

**257** A59 20c Elizabeth, vert. .25 .25
**258** A59 50c Philip, vert. .65 .55
**259** A59 $1 Couple 1.10 1.00
*Nos. 257-259 (3)* 2.00 1.80

Christmas — A60

Clergymen: 20c, Father Bernard Lahn, Catholic Mission Church. 30c, Rev. Itubwa Amram, Orro Central Church. 40c, Pastor James Aingimea, Tsiminita Memorial Church, Denigomodu. 50c, Bishop Paul Mea, Diocese of Tarawa-Nauru-Tuvalu.

**1982, Nov. 17**

**260** A60 20c multicolored .25 .30
**261** A60 30c multicolored .30 .40
**262** A60 40c multicolored .40 .60
**263** A60 50c multicolored .55 .80
*Nos. 260-263 (4)* 1.50 2.10

15th Anniv. of Independence — A61

15c, Speaker of Parliament, vert. 20c, People's Court, vert. 30c, Law Courts. 50c, Parliament.

**1983, Mar. 23 Wmk. 373 *Perf. 14½***

**264** A61 15c multicolored .25 .25
**265** A61 20c multicolored .25 .25
**266** A61 30c multicolored .30 .30
**267** A61 50c multicolored .50 .50
*Nos. 264-267 (4)* 1.30 1.30

World Communications Year — A62

5c, Earth Satellite Staion NZ. 10c, Omnidirectional Range Installation. 20c, Fixed-station ambulance driver. 25c, Radio Nauru broadcaster. 40c, Air mail service.

**1983, May. 11 Litho. *Perf. 14***

**268** A62 5c multicolored .25 .25
**269** A62 10c multicolored .25 .25
**270** A62 20c multicolored .30 .30
**271** A62 25c multicolored .40 .40
**272** A62 40c multicolored .60 .60
*Nos. 268-272 (5)* 1.80 1.80

Angam Day (Homecoming) — A63

***Perf. 14x13½***

**1983, Sept. 14 Litho. Wmk. 373**

**273** A63 15c MV Trinza arriving .25 .25

**Size: 25x40mm**

***Perf. 14***

**274** A63 20c Elsie Agio in exile .25 .25
**275** A63 30c Baby on scale .35 .35
**276** A63 40c Children .40 .40
*Nos. 273-276 (4)* 1.25 1.25

Christmas A64

Designs: 5c, The Holy Virgin, the Holy Child and St. John, School of Raphael. 15c, The Mystical Betrothal of St. Catherine with Jesus, School of Paolo Veronese. 50c, Madonna on the Throne Surrounded by Angels, School of Seville.

***Perf. 14½x14, 14x14½***

**1983, Nov. 16 Litho. Wmk. 373**

**277** A64 5c multi, vert. .25 .25
**278** A64 15c multi, vert. .25 .25
**279** A64 50c multicolored .50 .50
*Nos. 277-279 (3)* 1.00 1.00

Common Design Types pictured following the introduction.

**Lloyd's List Issue**

Common Design Type

20c, Ocean Queen. 25c, Enna G. 30c, Baron Minto loading phosphate. 40c, Triadic, 1940.

**1984, May 23 Litho. *Perf. 14½x14***

**280** CD335 20c multicolored .40 .35
**281** CD335 25c multicolored .50 .50
**282** CD335 30c multicolored .70 .70
**283** CD335 40c multicolored .80 .80
*Nos. 280-283 (4)* 2.40 2.35

1984 UPU Congress — A65

**1984, June 4 Wmk. 373 *Perf. 14***

**284** A65 $1 No. 117 1.10 1.40

Coastal Scene A66

3c, Woman, vert. 5c, Fishing vessel. 10c, Golfer. 15c, Phosphate excavation, vert. 20c, Surveyor, vert. 25c, Air Nauru jet. 30c, Elderly man, vert. 40c, Social service. 50c, Fishing, vert. $1, Tennis, vert. $2, Lagoon Anabar.

***Perf. 13½x14, 14x13½***

**1984, Sept. 21**

**285** A66 1c shown .30 *.60*
**286** A66 3c multi .30 .30
**287** A66 5c multi .40 .40
**288** A66 10c multi .90 .60
**289** A66 15c multi .90 .60
**290** A66 20c multi .65 .50
**291** A66 25c multi .90 .50
**292** A66 30c multi .60 .50
**293** A66 40c multi 1.00 1.00
**294** A66 50c multi 1.25 1.25
**295** A66 $1 multi 2.50 2.50
**296** A66 $2 multi 3.25 3.25
*Nos. 285-296 (12)* 12.95 12.00

For surcharges see Nos. 425-427.

Local Butterflies A67

25c, Common eggfly (female). 30c, Common eggfly (male). 50c, Wanderer (female).

**1984, July 24 *Perf. 14***

**297** A67 25c multicolored .50 .50
**298** A67 30c multicolored .60 .60
**299** A67 50c multicolored .90 .90
*Nos. 297-299 (3)* 2.00 2.00

Christmas A68

30c, Buada Chapel, vert. 40c, Detudamo Memorial Church, vert. 50c, Candle-light service.

**1984, Nov. 14**

**300** A68 30c multicolored .45 .45
**301** A68 40c multicolored .55 .55
**302** A68 50c multicolored .75 .75
*Nos. 300-302 (3)* 1.75 1.75

Air Nauru, 15th Anniv. A69

20c, Jet. 30c, Crew, vert. 40c, Fokker F28 over Nauru. 50c, Cargo handling, vert.

**1985, Feb. 26 Wmk. 373 *Perf. 14***

**303** A69 20c multicolored .50 .40
**304** A69 30c multicolored .70 .60
**305** A69 40c multicolored .90 .90
**306** A69 50c multicolored 1.25 1.25
*Nos. 303-306 (4)* 3.35 3.15

Nauru Phosphate Corp., 15th Anniv. — A70

20c, Open-cut mining. 25c, Rail transport. 30c, Phosphate drying plant. 50c, Early steam engine.

**1985, July 31**

**307** A70 20c multicolored .80 .60
**308** A70 25c multicolored 1.65 .90
**309** A70 30c multicolored 1.40 .90
**310** A70 50c multicolored 2.40 1.50
*Nos. 307-310 (4)* 6.25 3.90

Christmas — A71

**1985, Oct.**

**311** 50c Canoe 1.25 1.25
**312** 50c Mother and child 1.25 1.25
*a.* A71 Pair, #311-312 2.50 2.50

No. 312a has a continuous design.

Audubon Birth Bicentenary A72

Illustrations of the brown noddy by John J. Audubon.

**1985, Dec. 31**

**313** A72 10c Adult and young .40 .40
**314** A72 20c Flying .60 .60
**315** A72 30c Two adults .75 .75
**316** A72 50c Adult 1.10 1.10
*Nos. 313-316 (4)* 2.85 2.85

Early Transportation — A73

15c, Douglas motorcycle. 20c, Truck. 30c, German steam locomotive, 1910. 40c, Baby Austin.

**1986, Mar. 5 Wmk. 384**

**317** A73 15c multicolored 1.00 .80
**318** A73 20c multicolored 1.25 .90
**319** A73 30c multicolored 1.50 1.50
**320** A73 40c multicolored 1.90 1.90
*Nos. 317-320 (4)* 5.65 5.10

Bank of Nauru, 10th Anniv. A74

Winning drawings of children's competition.

**1986, July 21 Litho. *Perf. 14***

**321** A74 20c multicolored .25 .25
**322** A74 25c multicolored .30 .30
**323** A74 30c multicolored .35 .35
**324** A74 40c multicolored .45 .45
*Nos. 321-324 (4)* 1.35 1.35

Flowers A75

20c, Plumeria rubra. 25c, Tristellateia australis. 30c, Bougainvillea cultivar. 40c, Delonix regia.

**1986, Sept. 30 Wmk. 384**

**325** A75 20c multicolored .40 .40
**326** A75 25c multicolored .60 .60
**327** A75 30c multicolored .75 .75
**328** A75 40c multicolored 1.10 1.10
*Nos. 325-328 (4)* 2.85 2.85

Christmas A76

**1986, Dec. 8 Wmk. 373**

**329** A76 20c Men caroling .60 .50
**330** A76 $1 Carolers, invalid 2.25 2.25

Tribal Dances A77

**1987, Jan. 31**

**331** A77 20c Girls .75 .75
**332** A77 30c Men and women 1.00 1.00
**333** A77 50c Boy, vert. 2.00 2.00
*Nos. 331-333 (3)* 3.75 3.75

Artifacts A78

25c, Hibiscus-fiber skirt. 30c, Headband, necklaces. 45c, Necklaces. 60c, Pandanus-leaf fan.

**1987, July 30 *Perf. 14***

**334** A78 25c multicolored .70 .70
**335** A78 30c multicolored .80 .80
**336** A78 45c multicolored 1.10 1.10
**337** A78 60c multicolored 1.65 1.65
*Nos. 334-337 (4)* 4.25 4.25

World Post Day — A79

40c, UPU emblem, airmail label.

***Perf. 14½x14***

**1987, Oct. 9 Litho. Wmk. 384**

**338** A79 40c multicolored 1.75 1.75

**Souvenir Sheet**

**1987, Oct. 20 *Imperf.***

**339** A79 $1 Emblem, vert. 4.00 4.00

Nauru Congregational Church, Cent. — A80

***Perf. 13x13½***

**1987, Nov. 5 Wmk. 373**

**340** A80 40c multicolored 1.50 1.50

Island Christmas Celebration — A81

**1987, Nov. 27 Wmk. 384 *Perf. 14***

**341** A81 20c shown .75 .50
**342** A81 $1 Sign on building 3.00 3.00

A82

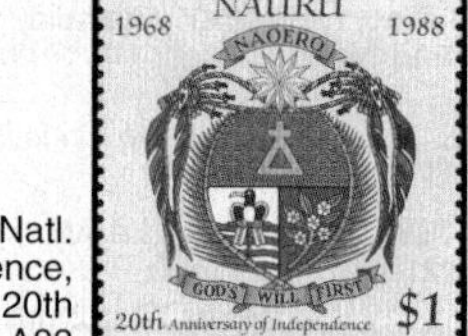

Natl. Independence, 20th Anniv. — A83

Heraldic elements independent of or as part of the natl. arms: 25c, Phosphate mining and shipping. 40c, Tomano flower, vert. 55c, Frigate bird, vert. $1, Natl. arms.

*Perf. 13½x14, 14x13½*

**1988, May 16 Unwmk.**

**343** A82 25c multicolored 1.25 1.25
**344** A82 40c multicolored 1.50 1.50
**345** A82 55c multicolored 2.25 2.25

*Perf. 13*

**346** A83 $1 multicolored 3.75 3.75
*Nos. 343-346 (4)* 8.75 8.75

Nauru Post Office, 80th Anniv. A84

30c, Nauru highlighted on German map of the Marshall Islands, & canceled Marshall Islands #25. 50c, Letter mailed from Nauru to Dresden & post office, 1908. 70c, Post office, 1988, & Nauru #348 canceled on airmail cover.

**1988, July 14 Wmk. 384 *Perf. 14***

**347** A84 30c multicolored .75 .75
**348** A84 50c multicolored 1.10 1.10
**349** A84 70c multicolored 1.75 1.75
*Nos. 347-349 (3)* 3.60 3.60

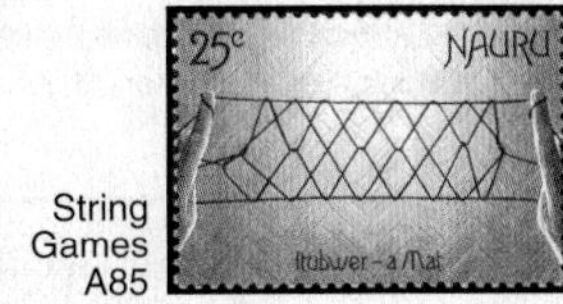

String Games A85

**1988, Aug. 1 Unwmk. *Perf. 13½x14***

**350** A85 25c Mat .35 .35
**351** A85 40c The Pursuer .55 .55
**352** A85 55c Holding Up the Sky .85 .85
**353** A85 80c Manujie's Sword 1.25 1.25
*Nos. 350-353 (4)* 3.00 3.00

UPU, Cent. — A86

**1988, Oct. 1 *Perf. 13½x14***

**354** A86 $1 multicolored 1.50 1.50

Hark! The Herald Angels Sing, by Charles Wesley (1703-91) A87

**1988, Nov. 28 *Perf. 13½***

**355** A87 20c "Hark..." .65 .65
**356** A87 60c "Glory to..." 1.50 1.50
**357** A87 $1 "Peace on Earth" 2.25 2.25
*Nos. 355-357 (3)* 4.40 4.40

A88

15c, NIC emblem. 50c, APT, ITU emblems. $1, Mounted photograph. $2, UPU emblem, US Capitol.

**1989, Nov. 19 *Perf. 14x15***

**358** A88 15c multicolored .50 .50
**359** A88 50c multicolored 1.00 1.00
**360** A88 $1 multicolored 2.25 2.25
**361** A88 $2 multicolored 3.50 3.50
*Nos. 358-361 (4)* 7.25 7.25

Annivs. and events: Nauru Insurance Corp., 15th Anniv. (15c). World Telecommunications Day and 10th anniv of the Asia-Pacific Telecommunity (50c); Photography 150th anniv. ($1); and 20th UPU Congress, Washington, DC ($2).

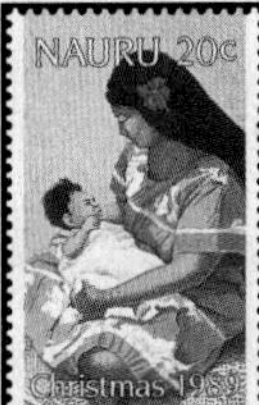

Christmas — A89

$1, Children opening gifts.

**1989, Dec. 15 Litho. *Perf. 14x15***

**362** A89 20c shown .60 .60
**363** A89 $1 multicolored 2.50 2.50

A90

Legend of Eigigu, The Girl in the Moon: 25c, Eigigu works while sisters play, rocket lift-off. 30c, Eigigu climbing tree, capsule in lunar orbit. 50c, Eigigu stealing from blind woman, lunar module on moon. $1, Eigigu with husband, Maramen (the moon), astronaut stepping on moon.

**1989, Dec. 22 Litho. *Perf. 14x15***

**364** A90 25c multicolored *3.50 3.50*
**365** A90 30c multicolored *3.75 3.75*
**366** A90 50c multicolored *7.00 7.00*
**367** A90 $1 multicolored *11.00 9.00*
*Nos. 364-367 (4) 25.25 23.25*

Limited supplies of Nos. 364-367 were available through agent.

A91

50c, Mining by hand. $1, Mechanized extraction.

**1990, July 3 Litho. *Perf. 14x15***

**368** A91 50c multicolored 1.00 1.00
**369** A91 $1 multicolored 1.50 1.50

Nauru Phosphate Corp., 20th anniv.

Christmas — A92

No. 370, Children. No. 371, Telling Christmas story.

**1990, Nov. 26 Litho. *Perf. 14***

**370** 25c multicolored 1.40 1.40
**371** 25c multicolored 1.40 1.40
*a.* A92 Pair, #370-371 3.25 3.25

Legend of Eoiyepiang, Daughter of Thunder and Lightning — A93

**1990, Dec. 24 Litho. *Perf. 14x15***

**372** A93 25c Woman with baby 1.25 1.00
**373** A93 30c Weaving flowers 1.50 1.00
**374** A93 50c Listening to storm 2.00 2.25
**375** A93 $1 Couple 3.00 3.25
*Nos. 372-375 (4)* 7.75 7.50

Flowers A94

**1991, July 15 Litho. *Perf. 14½***

**380** A94 15c Oleander .25 .25
**381** A94 20c Lily .25 .25
**382** A94 25c Passion Flower .30 .30
**383** A94 30c Lily, diff. .40 .40
**384** A94 35c Caesalpinia .45 .45
**385** A94 40c Clerodendron .50 .50
**387** A94 45c Bauhina pinnata .55 .55
**388** A94 50c Hibiscus, vert. .60 .60
**389** A94 75c Apocynaceae .85 .85
**390** A94 $1 Bindweed, vert. 1.10 1.10
**391** A94 $2 Tristellateia, vert. 2.25 2.25
**392** A94 $3 Impala lily, vert. 3.00 *4.00*
*Nos. 380-392 (12)* 10.50 11.50

Souvenir Sheet

Christmas — A95

$2, Stained glass window.

**1991, Dec. 12 Litho. *Perf. 14***

**395** A95 $2 multicolored 5.50 5.50

Asian Development Bank, 25th Meeting A96

**1992, May 4 Litho. *Perf. 14x14½***

**396** A96 $1.50 multicolored 2.75 2.75

Christmas A97

Children's drawings: 45c, Christmas trees, flags and balloons. 60c, Santa in sleigh, reindeer on flag.

**1992, Nov. 23 Litho. *Perf. 14½x14***

**397** A97 45c multicolored 1.00 1.00
**398** A97 60c multicolored 1.40 1.40

Hammer DeRoburt (1922-1992) A98

**1993, Jan. 31 Litho. *Perf. 14x14½***

**399** A98 $1 multicolored 2.50 2.50

Independence, 25th anniv.

Constitution Day, 15th Anniv. — A99

70c, Runners. 80c, Declaration of Republic.

**1993, May 17 Litho. *Perf. 14x14½***

**400** A99 70c multi 1.20 1.20
**401** A99 80c multi 1.30 1.30

24th South Pacific Forum — A100

**1993, Aug. 9 Litho. *Perf. 14½x14***

**402** A100 60c Seabirds 1.60 1.60
**403** A100 60c Birds, dolphin 1.60 1.60
**404** A100 60c Coral, fish 1.60 1.60
**405** A100 60c Fish, coral, diff. 1.60 1.60
*a.* Block of 4, #402-405 8.00 8.00
*b.* Souvenir sheet of 4, #402-405 8.00 8.00

No. 405a is a continuous design.

No. 405b exists with SINGPEX '93 overprint, sold at the exhibition. Value, unused or used, $10.

Christmas — A101

Designs: 55c, "Peace on earth..." 65c, "Hark the Herald Angels Sing."

**1993, Nov. 29 Litho. *Perf. 14½x14***

**406** A101 55c multicolored 1.00 1.00
**407** A101 65c multicolored 1.25 1.25

Child's Best Friend — A102

**1994, Feb. 10 Litho. *Perf. 14***
**408** $1 Girls, dogs 2.00 2.00
**409** $1 Boys, dogs 2.00 2.00
*a.* A102 Pair, #408-409 5.00 5.00
*b.* Souvenir sheet of 2, #408-409 5.25 5.25
*c.* As "b," ovptd. in sheet margin 6.00 6.00
*d.* As "b," ovptd. in sheet margin 6.50 6.50

No. 409c ovptd. with Hong Kong '94 emblem. No. 409d ovptd. with SINGPEX '94 emblem in gold.
Issued: #409c, 2/18/94; #409d, 8/31/94.

15th Commonwealth Games, Victoria — A103

**1994, Sept. 8 Litho. *Perf. 14x14½***
**410** A103 $1.50 Weight lifting 2.25 2.25

ICAO, 50th Anniv. A104

55c, Emblems. 65c, Nauru Intl. Airport. 80c, DVOR navigational aid. $1, Airport fire engines.

**1994, Dec. 14**
**411** A104 55c multicolored .65 .65
**412** A104 65c multicolored .75 .75
**413** A104 80c multicolored .95 .95
**414** A104 $1 multicolored 1.25 1.25
*a.* Souvenir sheet of 4, #411-414 6.00 6.00
*Nos. 411-414 (4)* 3.60 3.60

United Nations, 50th Anniv. A105

No. 415, National flag. No. 416, National coat of arms. No. 417, Canoe, UN emblem. No. 418, Jet, ship, UN emblem.

**1995, Jan. 1 *Perf. 14x14½***
**415** A105 75c multicolored 1.50 1.50
**416** A105 75c multicolored 1.50 1.50
**417** A105 75c multicolored 1.50 1.50
**418** A105 75c multicolored 1.50 1.50
*a.* Block of 4, #415-418 6.75 6.75
*b.* Souvenir sheet of 4, #415-418 7.00 7.00

Nos. 417-418 are a continuous design.

Christmas — A106

75c, Star over Bethlehem.

**1994, Nov. 20 Litho. *Perf. 14½x14***
**419** A106 65c shown 1.25 1.10
**420** A106 75c multicolored 1.40 1.30

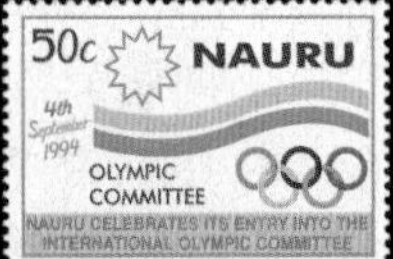


Membership in Intl. Olympic Committee A107

**1994, Dec. 27 *Perf. 14x14½***
**421** A107 50c multicolored .60 .60

Nauru Phosphate Corporation, 25th Anniv. A108

Designs: No. 422, Signing of Phosphate Agreement, June 15, 1967. No. 423, Nauru Pres. Bernard Dowiyogo, Australian Prime Minister Paul Keating at signing Nauru-Australia Compact of Settlement. $2, Mining phosphate.

**1995, July 1 Litho. *Perf. 14x15***
**422** A108 60c multicolored 1.40 1.40
**423** A108 60c multicolored 1.40 1.40
*a.* Pair, #422-423 3.75 3.75

**Souvenir Sheet**

**424** A108 $2 multicolored 4.00 4.00

**No. 291 Surcharged & Overprinted**

**1995, Aug. 19 Litho. *Perf. 13½x14***
**425** A66 50c on 25c "at Beijing" 1.75 1.75
**426** A66 $1 on 25c "at Singapore" 2.25 2.25
**427** A66 $1 on 25c "at Jakarta" 2.25 2.25
*a.* Strip of 3, #425-427 8.50 8.50

UN, 50th Anniv. A109

Designs: 75c, Nauru coastline. $1.50, UN headquarters, US, aerial view of Nauru.

**1995, Oct. 24 Litho. *Perf. 14***
**428** A109 75c multicolored 1.40 1.40
**429** A109 $1.50 multicolored 2.75 2.75

Christmas — A110

**1995, Dec. 7 Litho. *Perf. 14***
**430** 60c Seeking the Way 1.00 1.00
**431** 70c Finding the Way 1.10 1.10
*a.* A110 Pair, #430-431 2.60 2.60

Return From Truk, 50th Anniv. A111

**1996, Jan. 31 *Perf. 12***
**432** A111 75c multicolored 1.20 1.20
**433** A111 $1.25 multicolored 2.30 2.30
*a.* Souvenir sheet of 2, #432-433 4.00 4.00

**Souvenir Sheet**

Nanjing Stone Carving, Keeping off the Evils — A112

**1996, Mar. 20 Litho. *Perf. 12***
**434** A112 45c multicolored 1.40 1.40

CHINA '96, 9th Asian Intl. Philatelic Exhibition.

End of World War II, 50th Anniv. — A113

Designs: 75c, Children playing on old cannon. $1.50, Girls making flower leis in front of pillbox.

**1995, Sept. 13 Litho. *Perf. 14x13½***
**435** A113 75c multicolored 1.75 1.75
**436** A113 $1.50 multicolored 3.25 3.25
*a.* Pair, Nos. 435-436 + label 7.50 7.50
*b.* As "a," ovptd. in gold on label 10.00 10.00
*c.* As "a," ovptd. in gold on label 10.00 10.00

No. 436a exists with two different labels: one showing a war memorial, the other a dove. Gold overprint on memorial label is Hongpex '96 Exhibition emblem (No. 436b); on dove label, a silhouette of a rat (No. 436c). Nos. 436a and 436b-436c may be collected as blocks of four.
Issued: Nos. 436b, 436c, 1996.

1996 Summer Olympic Games, Atlanta A114

Discobolus and: 40c, Running pictograph, vert. 50c, Weight lifting pictograph, vert. 60c, Weight lifter. $1, Runner.

***Perf. 13½x14, 14x13½***
**1996, July 21 Litho.**
**437** A114 40c multicolored 1.00 1.00
**438** A114 50c multicolored 1.25 1.25
**439** A114 60c multicolored 1.50 1.50
**440** A114 $1 multicolored 1.75 1.75
*Nos. 437-440 (4)* 5.50 5.50

Christmas A115

Designs: 50c, Candles, angel with trumpet, nativity. 70c, Angel, candles, map, fauna.

**1996, Dec. 16 Litho. *Perf. 14***
**441** A115 50c multicolored 1.00 1.00
**442** A115 70c multicolored 1.25 1.25

World Wildlife Fund A116

Fish: a, 20c, Dolphinfish. b, 30c, Wahoo. c, 40c, Pacific sailfish. d, 50c, Yellowfin tuna.

**1997, Feb. 12 Litho. *Perf. 11½***
**443** A116 Strip of 4, #a.-d. 4.75 4.75

A117

Giant Buddha (various statues): a, 1c. b, 2c. c, 5c. d, 10c. e, 12c. f, 15c. g, 25c.

**1997, Feb. 12 *Perf. 14***
**444** A117 Sheet of 7, #a.-g. 3.00 3.00

Hong Kong '97, Hong Kong's return to China. No. 444g is 60x80mm.

A118

Designs: 80c, Engagement portrait. $1.20, 50th Wedding anniversary portrait.

**1997, July 15 Litho. *Perf. 13½***
**445** A118 80c multicolored 1.40 1.50
**446** A118 $1.20 multicolored 2.00 2.25
*a.* Souvenir sheet, #445-446 4.25 4.25

Queen Elizabeth II and Prince Philip, 50th wedding anniv.

Christmas A119

**1997, Nov. 5 Litho. *Perf. 13½***
**447** A119 60c Monument .80 .55
**448** A119 80c Church 1.30 1.30

Nauru Congregational Church, 110th anniv.

**Souvenir Sheet**

Commonwealth, Oceania and South Pacific Weight Lifting Championships — A120

Various contestants lifting weights: a, 40c. b, 60c. c, 80c. d, $1.20.

**1998, Mar. 25 Litho. *Perf. 14***
**449** A120 Sheet of 4, #a.-d. 4.00 4.00

A121

Design: Visit of Juan Antonio Samaranch, Pres. of Intl. Olympic Committee.

**1998, May 4** *Perf. 13½*
**450** A121 $2 multicolored 2.75 2.75

Souvenir Sheet

28th Parliamentary Conference — A122

**1997, July 24** **Litho.** *Perf. 14*
**451** A122 $2 multicolored 3.25 3.25

A123

Diana, Princess of Wales (1961-97): a, In yellow. b, White blouse. c, Wearing tiara. d, White & black outfit. e, Pink hat. f, White dress.

**1998, Aug. 31**
**452** A123 70c Sheet of 6, #a.-f. 5.25 5.25

A125

1998 Commonwealth Games, Kuala Lumpur: 40c, Gymnast on pommel horse. 60c, Throwing discus. 70c, Runner. 80c, Weight lifter.

**1998, Sept. 11** **Litho.** *Perf. 13½x14*
**454** A125 40c multicolored .60 .60
**455** A125 60c multicolored .90 .90
**456** A125 70c multicolored 1.00 1.00
**457** A125 80c multicolored 1.10 1.10
*a.* Souvenir sheet, #454-457 3.75 3.75
*Nos. 454-457 (4)* 3.60 3.60

Independence, 30th Anniv. — A126

Squadron Leader L.H. Hicks and: $1, Band. $2, National anthem.

**1998, Oct. 26** **Litho.** *Perf. 14*
**458** A126 $1 multicolored .90 .90
**459** A126 $2 multicolored 3.00 3.00
*a.* Souvenir sheet, #458-459 4.25 4.25

Christmas A127

Star, island scene and: 85c, Fish, candle, flowers. 95c, Flowers, fruits, Christmas present.

**1998** *Perf. 13½x12½*
**460** A127 85c multicolored 1.25 1.25
**461** A127 95c multicolored 1.40 1.40

First Contact with Island, Bicent. — A128

Designs: No. 462, Sailing ship Snow Hunter. No. 463, Capt. John Fearn.

**1998, Dec. 1** *Perf. 12*
**462** A128 $1.50 multicolored 2.00 2.00
**463** A128 $1.50 multicolored 2.00 2.00
*a.* Pair, #462-463 4.75 4.75
*b.* Souvenir sheet, #463a 5.25 5.25

Ships — A129

Designs: a, 70c, HMAS Melbourne. b, 80c, HMAS D'Amantina. c, $1.10, Traditional Nauruan canoe. d, 90c, Alcyone. e, $1, MV Rosie D.

**1999, Mar. 19** **Litho.** *Perf. 12*
**464** A129 Sheet of 5, #a.-e. 6.75 6.75

Australia '99, World Stamp Expo. No. 464c is 80x30mm.

### 1st Manned Moon Landing, 30th Anniv.

Common Design Type

Designs: 70c, Neil Armstrong. 80c, Service module and lunar module fire towards moon. 90c, Aldrin deploying EASEP. $1, Command module enters earth atmosphere.
$2, Earth as seen from moon.

*Perf. 14x13¾*
**1999, July 20** **Litho.** **Wmk. 384**
**465** CD357 70c multicolored .80 .80
**466** CD357 80c multicolored 1.15 1.15
**467** CD357 90c multicolored 1.40 1.40
**468** CD357 $1 multicolored 2.90 *1.65*
*Nos. 465-468 (4)* 6.25 5.00

**Souvenir Sheet**

*Perf. 14*
**469** CD357 $2 multicolored 3.00 3.00

No. 469 contains one circular stamp 40mm in diameter.

China 1999 World Philatelic Exhibition — A130

a, Tursiops truncatus. b, Xiphias gladius.

*Perf. 12¾x12½*
**1999, Aug. 21** **Litho.** **Unwmk.**
**470** A130 50c Sheet of 2, #a.-b. 3.75 3.75

UPU, 125th Anniv. A131

**1999, Aug. 23** **Litho.** *Perf. 11¾*
**471** A131 $1 multicolored 1.75 1.75

Christmas — A132

Designs: 65c, Native woman. 70c, Christmas tree and candle.

*Perf. 13½x13¾*
**1999, Nov. 10** **Litho.** **Wmk. 388**
**472** A132 65c multi 1.10 1.10
**473** A132 70c multi 1.25 1.25

Millennium A133

70c, Woman in native costume, fishermen on beach. $1.10, Satellite dish, runner, cross, airplane, crane, jeep and boat. $1.20, Man on computer, woman holding globe.

*Perf. 11¾x12*
**2000, Jan. 1** **Litho.** **Wmk. 388**
**474** A133 70c multi 1.75 2.00
**475** A133 $1.10 multi 2.75 3.25
**476** A133 $1.20 multi 3.25 3.50
*a.* Souvenir sheet of 3, #474-476 8.00 8.00
*Nos. 474-476 (3)* 7.75 8.75

Nauru Phosphate Corp. 30th Anniv. A134

Designs: $1.20, Power plant. $1.80, Phosphate train. $2, Albert Ellis.

**2000, May 27** **Litho.** *Perf. 12½x12¾*
**477-479** A134 Set of 3 7.75 7.75
*479a* Souv. sheet, #477-479, perf 12 7.50 7.50

No. 479a exists imperf. Value, $12.

Queen Mother, 100th Birthday A135

Designs: $1, Dark blue hat. $1.10, Lilac hat. $1.20, Waving, light blue hat. $1.40, Blue hat.

**2000, Aug. 4** *Perf. 14¼*
**480-483** A135 Set of 4 8.25 8.25
*483a* Souvenir sheet, #480-483, perf. 13¾x13½ 7.75 7.75

2000 Summer Olympics, Sydney — A136

Olympic rings, map of Australia, Sydney Opera House and: 90c, Running. $1, Basketball. $1.10, Weight lifting. $1.20, Olympic torch and runner.

**2000** **Photo.** *Perf. 11¾*
**484-487** A136 Set of 4 8.75 8.75

Christmas A137

Designs: 65c, Flower, girl decorating Christmas tree, star, decorated Christmas tree. 75c, Ornament, child on toy train, palm tree, gift.

**2000** **Litho.** *Perf. 13¾x13½*
**488-489** A137 Set of 2 3.00 3.00
*489a* Souvenir sheet, #488-489 3.25 3.25

Stamps from No. 489a are perf. 14¼x14¼x13¾x14¼.

32nd Pacific Islands Forum — A138

No. 490 — Island and: a, 90c, Yellow flowers, bird flying to right. b, $1, Red flowers, bird flying to left. c, $1.10, Yellow flowers, birds facing right. d, $2, Red flowers, bird facing left.

*Perf. 14½x14*
**2001, Aug. 14** **Litho.** **Unwmk.**
**490** A138 Block of 4, #a-d 11.00 11.00
*e.* Souvenir sheet, #490 12.00 12.00

### Reign Of Queen Elizabeth II, 50th Anniv. Issue

Common Design Type

Designs: Nos. 491, 495a, 70c, Princess Elizabeth in uniform, 1946. Nos. 492, 495b, 80c, Wearing patterned hat. Nos. 493, 495c, 90c, Wearing hat, 1951. Nos. 494, 495d, $1, In 1997. No. 495e, $4, 1955 portrait by Annigoni (38x50mm).

*Perf. 14¼x14½, 13¾ (#495e)*
**2002, Feb. 6** **Litho.** **Wmk. 373**

**With Gold Frames**

**491** CD360 70c multicolored 1.50 1.50
**492** CD360 80c multicolored 1.75 1.75
**493** CD360 90c multicolored 1.85 1.85
**494** CD360 $1 multicolored 2.15 2.15
*Nos. 491-494 (4)* 7.25 7.25

**Souvenir Sheet**

**Without Gold Frames**

**495** CD360 Sheet of 5, #a-e 10.50 10.50

Miniature Sheet

In Remembrance of Sept. 11, 2001 Terrorist Attacks — A139

No. 496: a, 90c. b, $1. c, $1.10. d, $2.

**Wmk. 373**

**2002, May 17 Litho. *Perf. 13¾***

**496** A139 Sheet of 4, #a-d 8.75 8.75

Butterflies — A140

No. 497: a, Parthenos sylvia. b, Delias madetes. c, Danaus philene. d, Arhopala hercules. e, Papilio canopus. f, Danaus schenkii. g, Parthenos figrina. h, Mycalesis phidon. i, Vindula sapor.

$2, Graphium agamemnon.

**2002, June 28 *Perf. 13¾x14¼***

**497** A140 50c Sheet of 9, #a-i 12.00 12.00

**Souvenir Sheet**

**498** A140 $2 multi 4.50 4.50

**Queen Mother Elizabeth (1900-2002)**

Common Design Type

Designs: Nos. 499, 501a, $1.50, Wearing hat (black and white photograph). Nos. 500, 501b, $1.50, Wearing blue hat.

***Perf. 13¾x4¼***

**2002, Aug. 5 Litho. Wmk. 373**

**With Purple Frames**

**499** CD361 $1.50 multicolored 3.00 3.00
**500** CD361 $1.50 multicolored 3.00 3.00

**Souvenir Sheet**

**Without Purple Frames**

***Perf. 14½x14¼***

**501** CD361 Sheet of 2, #a-b 8.00 8.00

Fire Fighting A141

Designs: 20c, Building fire. 50c, Blaze at sea. 90c, Forest fire. $1, New and old fire helmets. $1.10, Modern ladder truck, old pump engine. $2, Modern and late 19th cent. firefighters.

$5, Modern fire engine and rescue vehicle.

***Perf. 14x14¼***

**2002, Aug. 31 Litho. Wmk. 373**

**502-507** A141 Set of 6 11.00 11.00

**Souvenir Sheet**

**508** A141 $5 multi 14.00 14.00

Roman Catholic Church in Nauru, Cent. — A142

No. 509: a, First church building, Arubo. b, Father Friedrich Gründl, first missionary. c, Sister Stanisla, first sister. d, Second church building, Ibwenape. e, Brother Kalixtus Bader, first lay brother. f, Father Alois Kayser, missionary.

**Wmk. 373**

**2002, Dec. 8 Litho. *Perf. 13¾***

**509** A142 $1.50 Sheet of 6, #a-f 17.00 17.00

Christmas — A143

Designs: 15c, The Holy Family with Dancing Angels, by Sir Anthony Van Dyck. $1, The Holy Virgin with the Child, by Luca Cangiasus. $1.20, The Holy Family with the Cat, by Rembrandt. $3, The Holy Family with St. John, by Raphael.

**2002, Dec. 8**

**510-513** A143 Set of 4 10.00 10.00

Worldwide Fund For Nature (WWF) A144

Designs: 15c, Red-and-black anemone fish, Bubble tentacle sea anemone. $1, Orange-fin anemone fish, Leathery sea anemone. $1.20, Pink anemone fish, Magnificent sea anemone. $3, Clark's anemone fish, Merten's sea anemone.

**Wmk. 373**

**2003, Apr. 29 Litho. *Perf. 14***

**514-517** A144 Set of 4 10.00 10.00
*517a* Miniature sheet, 4 each #514-517 40.00 40.00

Powered Flight, Cent. — A145

No. 518: a, Santos-Dumont wins the Deutsch Prize, Oct. 1901. b, USS Shenandoah at Lakehurst, NJ. c, R101 at Cardington Mast, U.K., Oct. 1929. d, R34 crossing Atlantic, July 1919. e, Zeppelin No. 1, 1900. f, USS Los Angeles moored to the USS Patoka. g, Goodyear C-71 airship. h, LZ-130 Graf Zeppelin II at Friedrichshafen, Germany. i, Zeppelin NT.

No. 519 — LZ-127 Graf Zeppelin: a, Over Mt. Fuji. b, Over San Francisco. c, Exchanging mail with Russian ice breaker, Franz Josef Land.

**2003, Oct. 26**

**518** A145 50c Sheet of 9, #a-i 11.00 11.00
**519** A145 $2 Sheet of 3, #a-c 13.00 13.00

Bird Life International A146

Nauru reed warbler: No. 520, Bird on reed. No. 521, Bird on branch with insect in beak, vert. No. 522a, Close-up of head. No. 522b, Bird with open beak, vert. No. 522c, Nest with chicks.

**2003, Nov. 10 *Perf. 14¼x13¾***

**520** A146 $1.50 multi 4.75 4.75
*a.* Perf. 14¼x14½ 4.75 4.75

***Perf. 13¾x14¼***

**521** A146 $1.50 multi 4.75 4.75
*a.* Perf. 14½x14¼ 4.75 4.75

**Souvenir Sheet**

***Perf. 14¼x14½, 14½x14¼ (#522b)***

**522** Sheet, #520a, 521a, 522a-522c 15.00 15.00
*a.-c.* A146 $1.50 Any single 3.50 3.50

Battle of Trafalgar, Bicent. — A147

Designs: 25c, Aigle in action against HMS Defiance. 50c, French "Eprouvette." 75c, Santissima Trinidad in action against HMS Africa. $1, Emperor Napoleon Bonaparte, vert. $1.50, HMS Victory. No. 528, $2.50, Vice-Admiral Sir Horatio Nelson, vert.

No. 529, $2.50, vert.: a, Admiral Pierre Villeneuve. b, Formidable.

**2005, Mar. 29 Litho. *Perf. 13¼***

**523-528** A147 Set of 6 11.50 11.50

**Souvenir Sheet**

**529** A147 $2.50 Sheet of 2, #a-b 10.50 10.50

No. 527 has particles of wood from the HMS Victory embedded in the areas covered by a thermographic process that produces a shiny, raised effect.

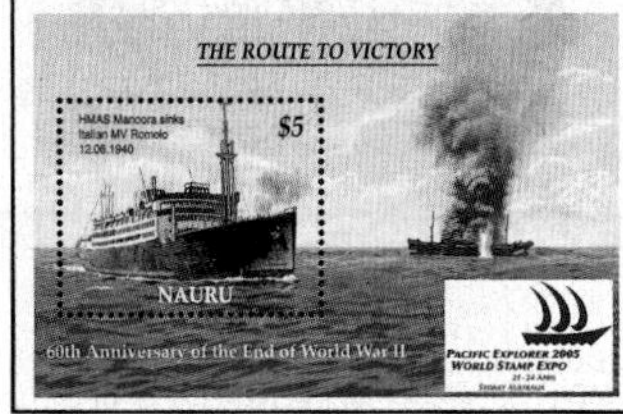


End of World War II, 60th Anniv. — A148

No. 530: a, German raider Komet shells Nauru, 1940. b, French warship Le Triomphant assists in evacuation of civilians, 1942. c, Japanese forces occupy Nauru, 1942. d, US Air Force B-24 Liberator aircraft bombing missions, 1943. e, USS Paddle stationed off Nauru, 1943. f, B-25G Mitchell "Coral Princess" shot down over Nauru, 1944. g, Spitfires, Battle of Britain, 1940. h, HMAS Diamantine arrives at Nauru, 1945. i, D-Day landings, 1944. j, Union Jack is hoisted again, 1945.

$5, HMAS Manoora sinks Italian MV Romolo, 1940.

**2005, Apr. 21 *Perf. 13¾***

**530** A148 75c Sheet of 10, #a-j 13.00 13.00

**Souvenir Sheet**

**531** A148 $5 multi 9.00 9.00

Pacific Explorer 2005 World Stamp Expo, Sydney (No. 531).

Pope John Paul II (1920-2005) A149

**2005, Aug. 18 Litho. *Perf. 14x14¼***

**532** A149 $1 multi 2.00 2.00

Rotary International, Cent. — A150

**2005, Sept. 12 *Perf. 14½x14¼***

**533** A150 $2.50 multi 4.75 4.75

BirdLife International — A151

No. 534, 25c: a, Rota bridled white-eye. b, Faichuk white-eye. c, Samoan white-eye. d, Bridled white-eye. e, Long-billed white-eye. f, Golden white-eye.

No. 535, 50c: a, Kuhl's lorikeet. b, Masked shining parrot. c, Crimson shining parrot. d, Blue lorikeet. e, Henderson lorikeet. f, Ultramarine lorikeet.

No. 536, $1: a, Atoll fruit dove. b, Henderson fruit dove. c, Cook Islands fruit dove. d, Rapa fruit dove. e, Whistling dove. f, Mariana fruit dove.

***Perf. 14¼x14½***

**2005, Sept. 12 Litho.**

**Sheets of 6, #a-f**

**534-536** A151 Set of 3 28.00 28.00

Christmas — A152

Stories by Hans Christian Andersen (1805-75): 25c, The Little Fir Tree. 50c, The Wild Swans. 75c, The Farmyard Cock and the Weather Cock. $1, The Storks. $2.50, The Toad. $5, The Ice Maiden.

**2005, Oct. 10 *Perf. 14***

**537-542** A152 Set of 6 16.50 16.50

Battle of Trafalgar, Bicent. — A153

Designs: 50c, HMS Victory. $1, Ships in battle, horiz. $5, Admiral Horatio Nelson.

**2005, Oct. 18** ***Perf. 13½***
**543-545** A153 Set of 3 13.00 13.00

Anniversaries — A154

No. 546, 25c: a, Wolfgang Amadeus Mozart. b, Piano and violin.
No. 547, 50c: a, Isambard Kingdom Brunel. b, Chain and pulley.
No. 548, 75c: a, Edmond Halley. b, Halley's quadrant.
No. 549, $1: a, Charles Darwin. b, Early microscope.
No. 550, $1.25: a, Thomas Alva Edison. b, Light bulb.
No. 551, $1.50: a, Christopher Columbus. b, Astrolabe.

**2006, May 27 Litho.** ***Perf. 13¼x12½***
**Horiz. Pairs, #a-b**
**546-551** A154 Set of 6 22.00 22.00

Birth of Mozart, 250th anniv., Birth of Brunel, bicent., Birth of Halley, 350th anniv., Darwin's voyage on the Beagle, 175th anniv., Death of Edison, 75th anniv., Death of Columbus, 500th anniv.

2006 World Cup Soccer Championships, Germany — A155

Scenes from championship matches won by: $1, Uruguay, 1950. $1.50, Argentina, 1978. $2, Italy, 1982. $3, Brazil, 2002.

**2006, June 9** ***Perf. 14***
**552-555** A155 Set of 4 15.00 15.00

Dinosaurs A156

Designs: 10c, Parasaurolophus. 25c, Quetzalcoatlus. 50c, Spinosaurus. 75c, Triceratops. $1, Tyrannosaurus rex. $1.50, Euoplocephalus. $2, Velociraptor. $2.50, Protoceratops.

**2006, Aug. 14** ***Perf. 13¼x13½***
**556-563** A156 Set of 8 16.00 16.00

Miniature Sheet

Victoria Cross, 150th Anniv. — A157

No. 564: a, Lt. Gerald Graham carrying wounded man. b, Pvt. Mac Gregor shooting rifle. c, Pvt. Alexander Wright repelling a sortie. d, Cpl. John Ross viewing evacuation of the Redan. e, Sgt. McWheeney digging with bayonet. f, Brevet Maj. G. L. Goodlake surprising enemy. Descriptions of vignettes are on labels below each stamp.

**2006, Sept. 12** ***Perf. 13¼x12½***
**564** A157 $1.50 Sheet of 6, #a-f, + 6 labels 18.00 18.00

Miniature Sheet

Inaugural Flight of the Concorde, 30th Anniv. — A158

No. 565: a, British Airways Concorde G-BOAF on ground. b, First flight of Concorde 002, 1969. c, Concorde landing. d, Queen's Golden Jubilee flypast, 2002. e, 50th anniv. of Battle of Britain, 1990. f, Concorde at 60,000 feet. g, Extreme condition testing. h, Concorde on runway. i, First commercial flight, 1976. j, Concorde above Earth. k, British Airways Concorde G-BOAF in flight. l, Two Concordes on ground.

**2006, Oct. 10** ***Perf. 14¼x13¾***
**565** A158 $1 Sheet of 12, #a-l, + 3 labels 26.00 26.00

Miniature Sheet

Year of Three Kings, 70th Anniv. — A159

No. 566: a, Queen Elizabeth II. b, King George V and Princess Elizabeth. c, King Edward VIII and Princess Elizabeth. d, King George VI and Princess Elizabeth.

**2006, Oct. 17**
**566** A159 $1.50 Sheet of 4, #a-d 13.00 13.00

Wedding of Queen Elizabeth II and Prince Philip, 60th Anniv. — A160

Designs: $1, Couple. $1.50, Couple in coach. $2, At wedding ceremony. $3, Couple walking.
$5, Queen Elizabeth II in bridal gown.

**2007, Jan. 31 Litho.** ***Perf. 13¾***
**567-570** A160 Set of 4 13.00 13.00

**Souvenir Sheet**
***Perf. 14¼***
**571** A160 $5 multi 10.00 10.00

No. 571 contains one 43x57mm stamp.

A161

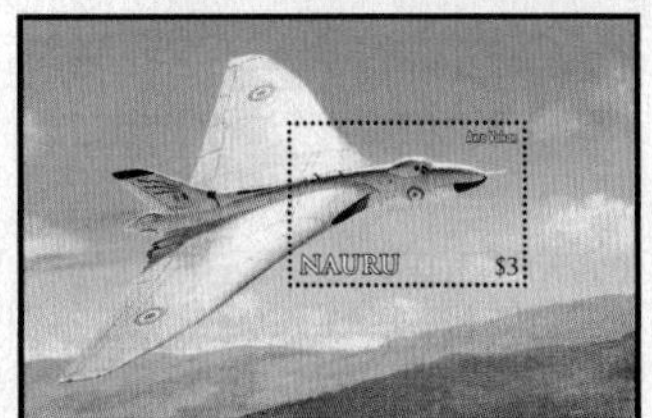


Royal Air Force, 90th Anniv. — A162

Aviation pioneers: No. 572, 70c, Sir Douglas Bader (1910-82), World War II fighter ace. No. 573, 70c, R. J. Mitchell (1895-1937), designer of Spitfire airplane. No. 574, 70c, Sir Frank Whittle (1907-96), inventor of jet engine. No. 575, 70c, Sir Sydney Camm (1893-1966), designer of Hawker Hurricane airplane. No. 576, 70c, Air Vice Marshal James E. "Johnnie" Johnson (1915-2001), World War II fighter ace.
$3, Avro Vulcan.

**Wmk. 373**
**2008, May 19 Litho.** ***Perf. 14***
**572-576** A161 Set of 5 8.50 8.50

**Souvenir Sheet**
**577** A162 $3 multi 7.00 7.00

Nos. 572-576 were each printed in sheets of 8 + central label.

2008 Summer Olympics, Beijing A163

Designs: 15c, Bamboo, badminton. 25c, Dragon, archery. 75c, Lanterns, weight lifting. $1, Fish, diving.

***Perf. 13¼***
**2008, Aug. 8 Litho. Unwmk.**
**578-581** A163 Set of 4 5.50 5.50

A164

End of World War I, 90th Anniv. — A165

World War I recruitment posters inscribed: No. 582, $1, "A Happy New Year to our Gallant Soldiers." No. 583, $1, "The Empire Needs Men." No. 584, $1, "South Australians." No. 585, $1, "Your King and Country Need You." No. 586, $1, "Britons." No. 587, $1, "An Appeal to You."
$2, Queen's Wreath of Remembrance.

**Wmk. 406**
**2008, Sept. 16 Litho.** ***Perf. 14***
**582-587** A164 Set of 6 13.00 13.00

**Souvenir Sheet**
**588** A165 $2 multi 4.50 4.50

Worldwide Fund for Nature (WWF) A166

Greater frigate bird: 25c, Adult and chick. 75c, Two in flight. $1, Landing. $2, One in flight.

***Perf. 13¼x13***
**2008, Oct. 14 Unwmk.**
**589-592** A166 Set of 4 8.25 8.25
*592a* Sheet, 4 each #589-592, perf. 13 30.00 30.00

NAURU
$1.50
Avro 504C

Naval Aviation, Cent. A167

Designs: No. 593, $1.50, Avro 504C. No. 594, $1.50, Fairey Flycatcher. No. 595, $1.50, Short Folder. No. 596, $1.50, De Havilland Sea Vixen.
$3, Grumman Avenger in Operation Meridian, 1945.

**Wmk. 406**
**2009, Sept. 3 Litho.** ***Perf. 14***
**593-596** A167 Set of 4 12.00 12.00

**Souvenir Sheet**
**597** A167 $3 multi 6.00 6.00

Nos. 593-596 each were printed in sheets of 8 + central label.

Russian Space Program — A168

Flags of Russia and Nauru and: No. 598, 60c, Sputnik satellite, 1957. No. 599, 60c, Yuri Gagarin, first man in space, 1961. $1.20, Nauru Island from space. $2.25, Vostok 1. $3, International Space Station.

*Perf. 14½x14*

**2011, Apr. 12** **Unwmk.**

| No. | Type | Description | Unused | Used |
|---|---|---|---|---|
| 598-602 | A168 | Set of 5 | 14.50 | 14.50 |

Souvenir Sheet

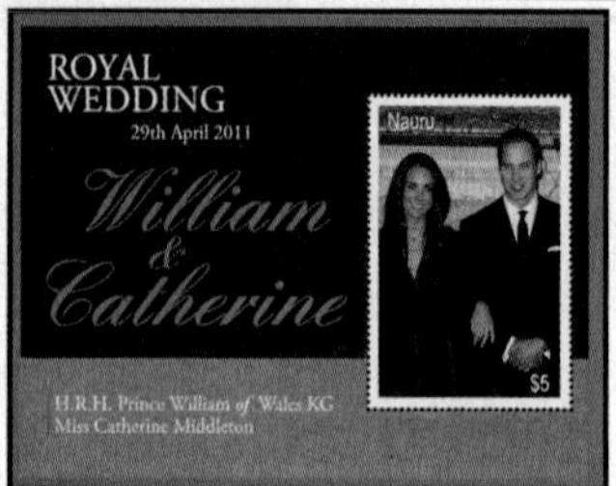


Wedding of Prince William and Catherine Middleton — A169

*Perf. 14¾x14¼*

**2011, Apr. 29** **Wmk. 406**

| No. | Type | Description | Unused | Used |
|---|---|---|---|---|
| 603 | A169 | $5 multi | 11.00 | 11.00 |

Port Development Project — A170

**Wmk. 406**

**2018, Jan. 31** **Litho.** ***Perf. 14¼***

| No. | Type | Description | Unused | Used |
|---|---|---|---|---|
| 604 | A170 | 50c multi | .75 | .75 |

Republic of Nauru, 50th anniv.

### SEMI-POSTAL STAMP

Miniature Sheet of 4

1996 Summer Olympics, Atlanta — SP1

Designs: a, Birds, denomination UR. b. Birds, denomination UL. c, 4 dolphins. d, 2 dolphins.

**1995, Sept. 1** **Litho.** ***Perf. 12***

| No. | Type | Description | Unused | Used |
|---|---|---|---|---|
| B1 | SP1 | 60c +15c, #a.-d. | 7.00 | 6.50 |

Surcharge for sports development in Nauru.

## NEPAL

nə-'pol

LOCATION — In the Himalaya Mountains between India and Tibet
GOVT. — Republic
AREA — 56,136 sq. mi.
POP. — 24,302,653 (1999 est.)
CAPITAL — Kathmandu

Nepal stamps were valid only in Nepal and India until April 1959, when they became valid to all parts of the world.

4 Pice = 1 Anna
64 Pice = 16 Annas = 1 Rupee
100 Paisa = 1 Rupee (1958)

**Catalogue values for unused stamps in this country are for Never Hinged items, beginning with Scott 103 in the regular postage section, Scott C1 in the air post section and Scott O1 in the officials section.**

Nos. 1-24, 29A were issued without gum.

Sripech and Crossed Khukris — A1

**1881** **Typo.** **Unwmk.** ***Pin-perf.***

**European Wove Paper**

| No. | Type | Description | Unused | Used |
|---|---|---|---|---|
| 1 | A1 | 1a ultramarine | 575.00 | *650.00* |
| 2 | A1 | 2a purple | 1,000. | 1,500. |
| *a.* | | Tete beche pair | | — |
| 3 | A1 | 4a green | 650.00 | *2,500.* |
| | | ***Imperf*** | | |
| 4 | A1 | 1a blue | 225.00 | 150.00 |
| 5 | A1 | 2a purple | 225.00 | *500.00* |
| *a.* | | Tete beche pair | *15,000.* | — |
| 6 | A1 | 4a green | 325.00 | *750.00* |

No. 3 postally used is probably unique. Only 2 No. 5a are known unused. No. 5a is only known to exist used in a strip of three.

**1886** **Native Wove Paper** ***Imperf.***

| No. | Type | Description | Unused | Used |
|---|---|---|---|---|
| 7 | A1 | 1a ultramarine | 50.00 | *50.00* |
| *a.* | | Tete beche pair | *500.00* | *500.00* |
| 8 | A1 | 2a violet | 60.00 | 60.00 |
| *a.* | | Tete beche pair | *275.00* | *500.00* |
| 9 | A1 | 4a green | 70.00 | 70.00 |
| *a.* | | Tete beche pair | *300.00* | *250.00* |
| | | *Nos. 7-9 (3)* | 180.00 | 180.00 |

Nos. 7-10 are clear to mostly clear designs on good quality native paper. European wove paper is of substantially higher quality, white, and lacks the wood fibers of the native paper.

Used values for Nos. 10-49 are for telegraph cancels.

Siva's Bow and Two Khukris — A2

**1899-1917** ***Imperf.***

**Native Wove Paper**

| No. | Type | Description | Unused | Used |
|---|---|---|---|---|
| 10 | A2 | ½a black, clear impression | 20.00 | 13.50 |
| *a.* | | Tete beche pair | *100.00* | 55.00 |
| 11 | A2 | ½a red orange ('17) | *1,750.* | 500.00 |
| *a.* | | Tete beche pair | | *2,000.* |
| | | ***Pin-perf.*** | | |
| 12 | A2 | ½a black | 30.00 | 17.50 |
| *a.* | | Tete beche pair | *225.00* | 55.00 |

No. 11 is known postally used on six covers.

No. 11a unused is only known in larger blocks, no unused pairs currently exist.

**Type of 1881**

**1898-1917** ***Imperf.***

| No. | Type | Description | Unused | Used |
|---|---|---|---|---|
| 12B | A2 | ½a black | 35.00 | 35.00 |
| 13 | A1 | 1a pale blue | 60.00 | 60.00 |
| *a.* | | 1a bluish green | *75.00* | *75.00* |
| *b.* | | Tete beche pair | *150.00* | *150.00* |
| *c.* | | As "a," tete beche pair | *300.00* | *300.00* |
| 14 | A1 | 2a gray violet | 60.00 | 60.00 |
| *a.* | | Tete beche pair | *140.00* | *140.00* |
| 15 | A1 | 2a claret ('17) | *100.00* | 32.50 |
| *a.* | | Tete beche pair | *225.00* | *100.00* |
| 16 | A1 | 2a brown ('17) | 25.00 | 12.00 |
| *a.* | | Tete beche pair | 55.00 | 42.50 |
| 17 | A1 | 4a dull green | 70.00 | 70.00 |
| *a.* | | Tete beche pair | 350.00 | *350.00* |
| *b.* | | Cliche of 1a in plate of 4a ('04) | *500.00* | *400.00* |
| *c.* | | As "b," pair | — | — |
| | | *Nos. 12B-17 (6)* | 350.00 | 269.50 |

No. 13-17 are blurry impressions on poor quality native paper.

#17b has the recut frame of the 1904 issue. #17b probably was used only on telegraph/telephone forms.

***Pin-perf.***

| No. | Type | Description | Unused | Used |
|---|---|---|---|---|
| 18 | A1 | 1a pale blue | 17.50 | 10.00 |
| *a.* | | Tete beche pair | *325.00* | — |
| 19 | A1 | 2a gray violet | 90.00 | 90.00 |
| *a.* | | Tete beche pair | *300.00* | *300.00* |
| 20 | A1 | 2a claret ('17) | 90.00 | 45.00 |
| *a.* | | Tete beche pair | 250.00 | — |
| 21 | A1 | 2a brown ('17) | 90.00 | 45.00 |
| *a.* | | Tete beche pair | 250.00 | — |
| 22 | A1 | 4a dull green | 150.00 | 150.00 |
| *a.* | | Tete beche pair | *900.00* | *900.00* |

**Frame Recut on All Cliches, Fewer Lines**

**1903-04** **Native Wove Paper** ***Imperf.***

| No. | Type | Description | Unused | Used |
|---|---|---|---|---|
| 23 | A1 | 1a bright blue | 20.00 | 13.00 |
| *a.* | | Tete beche pair | 60.00 | 42.50 |
| | | ***Pin-perf.*** | | |
| 24 | A1 | 1a bright blue | 30.00 | |
| *a.* | | Tete beche pair | *120.00* | |
| | | **European Wove Paper** | | |
| *23b* | A1 | 1a blue | *1,500.* | *1,000.* |
| *23c* | | Tete beche pair | *2,500.* | |
| | | ***Pin-perf.*** | | |
| *24b* | A1 | 1a blue | *1,500.* | *2,000.* |
| *24c* | | Tete beche pair | *3,500.* | |

No. 23 exists in emerald on native wove paper. All known examples are used with telegraph cancels.

Siva Mahadeva — A3

**1907** **Engr.** ***Perf. 13½***

**European Wove Paper**

| No. | Type | Description | Unused | Used |
|---|---|---|---|---|
| 26 | A3 | 2p brown | 9.00 | 2.50 |
| 27 | A3 | 4p green | 10.00 | 2.50 |
| 28 | A3 | 8p carmine | 14.00 | 2.50 |
| 29 | A3 | 16p violet | 27.50 | 6.00 |
| | | *Nos. 26-29 (4)* | 60.50 | 13.50 |

Type A3 has five characters in bottom panel, reading "Gurkha Sirkar." Date divided in lower corners is "1964." Outer side panels carry denomination (also on A5).

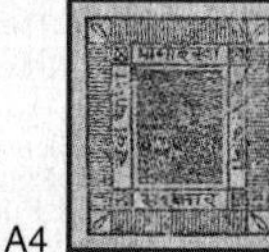

A4

**1917-18** ***Imperf.***

| No. | Type | Description | Unused | Used |
|---|---|---|---|---|
| 29A | A4 | 1a bright blue | 12.00 | 5.00 |
| *b.* | | 1a indigo | 12.00 | 6.00 |
| *c.* | | Pin-perf. | 17.50 | 15.00 |

No. 29A may not have been used postally.

In 1917 a telephone and telegraph system was started and remainder stocks and further printings of designs A1 and A2 were used to pay telegrams fees. Design A4 was designed for telegraph use but was valid for postal use. After 1929 design A3 was used for telegrams. The usual telegraph cancellation is crescent-shaped.

**Type of 1907 Redrawn**

A5

**Nine characters in bottom panel reading "Nepal Sirkar"**

**1930** ***Perf. 14, 14½***

**Size: 24¾x18¾mm**

| No. | Type | Description | Unused | Used |
|---|---|---|---|---|
| 30 | A5 | 2p dark brown | 12.00 | 1.00 |
| 31 | A5 | 4p green | 12.00 | 1.25 |
| 32 | A5 | 8p deep red | 45.00 | 3.00 |
| 33 | A5 | 16p dark red vio | 32.50 | 3.00 |
| 34 | A5 | 24p orange yellow | 27.50 | 4.00 |
| 35 | A5 | 32p dark ultra | 32.50 | 4.00 |
| | | **Size: 26x19½mm** | | |
| 36 | A5 | 1r orange red | 40.00 | 9.00 |
| | | **Size: 28x21mm** | | |
| 37 | A5 | 5r brown & black | 47.50 | *30.00* |
| | | *Nos. 30-37 (8)* | 249.00 | *55.25* |

On Nos. 30-37 the date divided in lower corners is "1986."

**Type of 1929 Redrawn**

**Date characters in Lower Corners read "1992"**

**1935** **Unwmk.** **Engr.** ***Perf. 14***

| No. | Type | Description | Unused | Used |
|---|---|---|---|---|
| 38 | A5 | 2p dark brown | 6.00 | 1.50 |
| 39 | A5 | 4p green | 6.00 | 2.00 |
| 40 | A5 | 8p bright red | 150.00 | 10.00 |
| 41 | A5 | 16p dk red violet | 15.00 | 3.00 |
| 42 | A5 | 24p orange yellow | 15.00 | 4.50 |
| 43 | A5 | 32p dark ultra | 16.00 | 5.00 |
| | | *Nos. 38-43 (6)* | 208.00 | 26.00 |

**Redrawn Type of 1935**

***Perf. 11, 11x11½, 12x11½***

**1941-46** **Typo.**

| No. | Type | Description | Unused | Used |
|---|---|---|---|---|
| 44 | A5 | 2p black brown | 1.25 | .70 |
| *a.* | | 2p green (error) | 13.00 | |
| 45 | A5 | 4p bright green | 2.50 | 1.25 |
| 46 | A5 | 8p rose red | 3.75 | 1.00 |
| 47 | A5 | 16p chocolate ('42) | 22.50 | 4.25 |
| 48 | A5 | 24p orange ('46) | 18.00 | 3.50 |
| 49 | A5 | 32p deep blue ('46) | 24.00 | 6.25 |
| | | **Size: 29x19½mm** | | |
| 50 | A5 | 1r henna brown ('46) | 47.50 | 30.00 |
| | | *Nos. 44-50 (7)* | 119.50 | 46.95 |
| | | Set, never hinged | 250.00 | |

Exist imperf. vert. or horiz. Full imperf. examples were not regularly issued.

Swayambhunath Stupa — A6

Temple of Krishna — A7

View of Kathmandu A8

Pashupati (Siva Mahadeva) A9

Designs: 4p, Temple of Pashupati. 6p, Tri-Chundra College. 8p, Mahabuddha Temple. 24p, Guheswori Temple, Patan. 32p, The 22 Fountains, Balaju.

*Perf. 13½x14, 13½, 14*

**1949, Oct. 1 Litho. Unwmk.**

| | | | | |
|---|---|---|---|---|
| 51 | A6 | 2p brown | 1.50 | 1.25 |
| 52 | A6 | 4p green | 1.50 | 1.25 |
| 53 | A6 | 6p rose pink | 2.75 | 1.25 |
| 54 | A6 | 8p vermilion | 3.00 | 2.00 |
| 55 | A7 | 16p rose lake | 3.00 | 2.00 |
| 56 | A8 | 20p blue | 6.25 | 3.25 |
| 57 | A8 | 24p carmine | 5.50 | 2.00 |
| 58 | A8 | 32p ultramarine | 10.00 | 3.25 |
| 59 | A9 | 1r red orange | 47.50 | 30.00 |
| | | *Nos. 51-59 (9)* | 81.00 | 46.25 |
| | | Set, never hinged | 150.00 | |

King Tribhuvana Bir Bikram — A10

**1954, Apr. 15 Unwmk. *Perf. 14***

**Size: 18x22mm**

| | | | | |
|---|---|---|---|---|
| 60 | A10 | 2p chocolate | 1.25 | .65 |
| 61 | A10 | 4p green | 4.50 | 2.00 |
| 62 | A10 | 6p rose | 1.00 | .65 |
| 63 | A10 | 8p violet | .80 | .65 |
| 64 | A10 | 12p red orange | 8.00 | 3.25 |

**Size: 25½x29½mm**

| | | | | |
|---|---|---|---|---|
| 65 | A10 | 16p red brown | 1.00 | .65 |
| 66 | A10 | 20p car rose | 2.25 | 2.00 |
| 67 | A10 | 24p rose lake | 1.75 | 2.00 |
| 68 | A10 | 32p ultramarine | 2.50 | 2.00 |
| 69 | A10 | 50p rose pink | 22.50 | 9.00 |
| 70 | A10 | 1r vermilion | 27.50 | 15.00 |
| 71 | A10 | 2r orange | 25.00 | 12.00 |
| | | *Nos. 60-71 (12)* | 98.05 | 49.85 |
| | | Set, never hinged | 225.00 | |

Map of Nepal A11

**1954, Apr. 15 Size: 29½x17½mm**

| | | | | |
|---|---|---|---|---|
| 72 | A11 | 2p chocolate | 1.25 | 1.25 |
| 73 | A11 | 4p green | 4.50 | 2.00 |
| 74 | A11 | 6p rose | 12.50 | 3.25 |
| 75 | A11 | 8p violet | .75 | .40 |
| 76 | A11 | 12p red orange | 19.00 | 1.00 |

**Size: 38x21½mm**

| | | | | |
|---|---|---|---|---|
| 77 | A11 | 16p red brown | 1.00 | .45 |
| 78 | A11 | 20p car rose | 1.50 | .45 |
| 79 | A11 | 24p rose lake | 1.50 | .45 |
| 80 | A11 | 32p ultramarine | 2.00 | .80 |
| 81 | A11 | 50p rose pink | 20.00 | 3.00 |
| 82 | A11 | 1r vermilion | 25.00 | 3.50 |
| 83 | A11 | 2r orange | 17.50 | 3.50 |
| | | *Nos. 72-83 (12)* | 106.50 | 20.05 |
| | | Set, never hinged | 235.00 | |

Planting Rice — A12

Throne — A13

Hanuman Gate — A14

King Mahendra Bir Bikram and Queen Ratna — A15

Design: 8p, Ceremonial arch and elephant.

*Perf. 13½x14, 11½, 13½, 14*

**Litho., Photo. (6p)**

**1956 Granite Paper Unwmk.**

| | | | | |
|---|---|---|---|---|
| 84 | A12 | 4p green | 4.50 | *9.00* |
| 85 | A13 | 6p crimson & org | 2.75 | *5.00* |
| 86 | A12 | 8p light violet | 2.25 | *2.50* |
| 87 | A14 | 24p carmine rose | 4.75 | *9.00* |
| 88 | A15 | 1r brown red | 100.00 | *110.00* |
| | | *Nos. 84-88 (5)* | 114.25 | *135.50* |
| | | Set, never hinged | 180.00 | |

Coronation of King Mahendra Bir Bikram and Queen Ratna Rajya Lakshmi.

Mountain Village and UN Emblem — A16

**1956, Dec. 14 Litho. *Perf. 13½***

| | | | | |
|---|---|---|---|---|
| 89 | A16 | 12p ultra & orange | 3.75 | *6.00* |
| | | Never hinged | 7.50 | |

1st anniv. of Nepal's admission to the UN.

Crown of Nepal — A17

*Perf. 13½x14*

**1957, June 22 Unwmk.**

**Size: 18x22mm**

| | | | | |
|---|---|---|---|---|
| 90 | A17 | 2p dull red brown | .50 | *1.00* |
| 91 | A17 | 4p light green | .70 | *1.00* |
| 92 | A17 | 6p pink | .50 | *1.00* |
| 93 | A17 | 8p light violet | .50 | *1.00* |
| 94 | A17 | 12p orange vermilion | 2.75 | *1.75* |

**Size: 25½x30mm**

| | | | | |
|---|---|---|---|---|
| 95 | A17 | 16p red brown | 4.00 | 2.75 |
| 96 | A17 | 20p deep pink | 6.00 | 3.75 |
| 97 | A17 | 24p brt car rose | 4.00 | 3.50 |
| 98 | A17 | 32p ultramarine | 5.50 | 3.75 |
| 99 | A17 | 50p rose red | 12.00 | 8.00 |
| 100 | A17 | 1r brown orange | 15.00 | 15.00 |
| 101 | A17 | 2r orange | 10.00 | *11.00* |
| | | *Nos. 90-101 (12)* | 61.45 | *53.50* |
| | | Set, never hinged | 110.00 | |

Lumbini Temple — A18

**1958, Dec. 10 Typo. *Perf. 11***

**Without Gum**

| | | | | |
|---|---|---|---|---|
| 102 | A18 | 6p yellow | 2.00 | 2.00 |

10th anniversary of Universal Declaration of Human Rights. Exists imperf.

**Catalogue values for unused stamps in this section, from this point to the end of the section, are for Never Hinged items.**

Map and Flag — A19

**1959, Feb. 18 Engr. *Perf. 14½***

| | | | | |
|---|---|---|---|---|
| 103 | A19 | 6p carmine & light green | .85 | .50 |

First general elections in Nepal.

Statue of Vishnu, Changu Narayan A20

Krishna Conquering Black Serpent A21

Designs: 4p, Nepalese glacier. 6p, Golden Gate, Bhaktapur. 8p, Nepalese musk deer. 12p, Rhinoceros. 16p, 20p, 24p, 32p, 50p, Nyatapola Temple, Bhatgaon. 1r, 2r, Himalayan impeyan pheasant. 5r, Satyr tragopan.

*Perf. 13½x14, 14x13½*

**1959-60 Litho. Unwmk.**

**Size: 18x22mm**

| | | | | |
|---|---|---|---|---|
| 104 | A20 | 1p chocolate | .25 | .25 |
| 105 | A21 | 2p gray violet | .25 | .25 |
| 106 | A20 | 4p light ultra | .55 | .40 |
| 107 | A20 | 6p vermilion | .55 | .25 |
| 108 | A21 | 8p sepia | .40 | .25 |
| 109 | A21 | 12p greenish gray | .55 | .25 |

**Size: 25½x30mm**

| | | | | |
|---|---|---|---|---|
| 110 | A20 | 16p brown & lt vio | .55 | .25 |
| 111 | A20 | 20p blue & dull rose | 2.00 | 1.00 |
| 112 | A20 | 24p green & pink | 2.00 | 1.00 |
| 113 | A20 | 32p brt vio & ultra | 1.20 | 1.00 |
| 114 | A20 | 50p rose red & grn | 2.00 | 1.00 |
| 115 | A20 | 1r redsh brn & bl | 24.00 | 8.50 |
| 116 | A20 | 2r rose lil & ultra | 16.00 | 9.00 |
| 117 | A20 | 5r vio & rose red ('60) | 100.00 | 80.00 |
| | | *Nos. 104-117 (14)* | 150.30 | 103.40 |

Nepal's admission to the UPU.

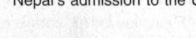

Spinning Wheel — A22

**1959, Apr. 10 Typo. *Perf. 11***

| | | | | |
|---|---|---|---|---|
| 118 | A22 | 2p dark red brown | .55 | .35 |

Issued to promote development of cottage industries.

Exists imperf. Value $26.

King Mahendra — A23

**1959, Apr. 14**

| | | | | |
|---|---|---|---|---|
| 119 | A23 | 12p bluish black | .65 | .50 |

Nepal's admission to UPU. Exists imperf. and ungummed. Value $200.

No. 119 exists with paper maker's watermark "LOVELY BOND / MADE IN SWEDEN". Value, unused or used, $12.

King Mahendra Opening Parliament — A24

**1959, July 1 Unwmk. *Perf. 10½***

| | | | | |
|---|---|---|---|---|
| 120 | A24 | 6p deep carmine | 1.20 | 1.20 |

First session of Parliament. Exists imperf. Value, pair $45.

Sri Pashupati Nath — A25

**1959, Nov. 19 *Perf. 11***

**Size: 18x24½mm**

| | | | | |
|---|---|---|---|---|
| 121 | A25 | 4p dp yellow green | .80 | .80 |

**Size: 20½x28mm**

| | | | | |
|---|---|---|---|---|
| 122 | A25 | 8p carmine | 1.60 | 1.00 |

**Size: 24½x33mm**

| | | | | |
|---|---|---|---|---|
| 123 | A25 | 1r light blue | 11.00 | 8.00 |
| | | *Nos. 121-123 (3)* | 13.40 | 9.80 |

Renovation of Sri Pashupati Temple. Nos. 121-123 exist imperf. between.

King Mahendra — A26

**1960, June 11 Photo. *Perf. 14***

**Size: 25x30mm**

| | | | | |
|---|---|---|---|---|
| 124 | A26 | 1r red lilac | 2.40 | 1.40 |

King Mahendra's 40th birthday. See Nos. 147-151A. For overprint see No. O15.

Children, Temple and Mt. Everest — A27

**1960 Typo. *Perf. 11***

| | | | | |
|---|---|---|---|---|
| 125 | A27 | 6p dark blue | 27.50 | 14.00 |

1st Children's Day, Mar. 1, 1960. Printed in sheets of four. Exists imperf.; value $45 unused.

Mount Everest — A28

Himalaya mountain peaks: 5p, Machha Puchhre. 40p, Mansalu.

**1960-61 Photo. *Perf. 14***

| | | | | |
|---|---|---|---|---|
| 126 | A28 | 5p claret & brown ('61) | .50 | .25 |
| 127 | A28 | 10p ultra & rose lilac | .70 | .25 |
| 128 | A28 | 40p vio & red brn ('61) | 1.50 | .85 |
| | | *Nos. 126-128 (3)* | 2.70 | 1.35 |

King Tribhuvana — A29

**1961, Feb. 18** *Perf. 13x13½*

**129** A29 10p red brown & orange .75 .25

Tenth Democracy Day.

King Mahendra — A30

**1961, June 11** *Perf. 14x14½*

**130** A30 6p emerald .50 .50
**131** A30 12p ultramarine .65 .65
**132** A30 50p carmine rose .90 .90
**133** A30 1r brown 2.25 2.25
*Nos. 130-133 (4)* 4.30 4.30

King Mahendra's 41st birthday.

Prince Gyanendra Canceling Stamps — A31

**1961 Typo.** *Perf. 11*

**134** A31 12p orange *40.00 40.00*

Children's Day, Mar. 1, 1961.
Exists imperf. Value, $75.

Malaria Eradication Emblem and Temple — A32

Design: 1r, Emblem and Nepalese flag.

**1962, Apr. 7 Litho.** *Perf. 13x13½*

**135** A32 12p blue & lt blue .55 .50
**136** A32 1r magenta & orange 1.75 1.50

WHO drive to eradicate malaria.

King Mahendra A33

**1962, June 11 Unwmk.** *Perf. 13*

**137** A33 10p slate blue .30 .25
**138** A33 15p brown .50 .40
**139** A33 45p dull red brown .75 .75
**140** A33 1r olive gray 1.40 1.10
*Nos. 137-140 (4)* 2.95 2.50

King Mahendra's 42nd birthday.

Bhanu Bhakta Acharya — A34

10p, Moti Ram Bhatta. 40p, Shambu Prasad.

**1962 Photo.** *Perf. 14x14½*

**141** A34 5p orange brown .45 .45
**142** A34 10p deep aqua .55 .45
**143** A34 40p olive bister .70 .55
*Nos. 141-143 (3)* 1.70 1.45

Issued to honor Nepalese poets.

**Mahendra Type of 1960 and**

King Mahendra — A35

**1962-66** *Perf. 14½x14*

**144** A35 1p car rose .25 .25
**145** A35 2p brt blue .25 .25
**145A** A35 3p gray ('66) .80 .40
**146** A35 5p golden brown .25 .25

*Perf. 14x14½*

**Size: 21½x38mm**

**147** A26 10p rose claret .25 .25
**148** A26 40p brown .55 .55
**149** A26 75p blue green 15.00 13.00

*Perf. 14*

**Size: 25x30mm**

**150** A26 2r red orange 2.00 1.50
**151** A26 5r gray green 4.00 3.00
**151A** A26 10r violet ('66) 13.00 10.00
*Nos. 144-151A (10)* 36.35 29.45

See No. 199. For overprints see Nos. O12-O14.

Blackboard, Book and UN Emblem — A36

**1963, Jan. 6** *Perf. 14½x14*

**152** A36 10p dark gray .50 .25
**153** A36 15p brown .70 .45
**154** A36 50p violet blue 1.50 .75
*Nos. 152-154 (3)* 2.70 1.45

UNESCO "Education for All" campaign.

Five-pointed Star and Hands Holding Lamps — A37

**Unwmk.**

**1963, Feb. 19 Photo.** *Perf. 13*

**155** A37 5p blue .45 .25
**156** A37 10p reddish brown .50 .25
**157** A37 50p rose lilac 1.50 .25
**158** A37 1r blue green 2.50 .25
*Nos. 155-158 (4)* 4.95 1.00

Panchayat System and National Day.

Man, Tractor and Wheat — A38

**1963, Mar. 21** *Perf. 14x14½*

**159** A38 10p orange .55 .25
**160** A38 15p dark ultra 1.00 .40
**161** A38 50p green 1.75 .80
**162** A38 1r brown 4.00 .90
*Nos. 159-162 (4)* 7.30 2.35

FAO "Freedom from Hunger" campaign.

Map of Nepal and Hand A39

**1963, Apr. 14 Unwmk.** *Perf. 13*

**163** A39 10p green .50 .25
**164** A39 15p claret 1.00 .40
**165** A39 50p slate 1.75 .55
**166** A39 1r violet blue 4.00 .90
*Nos. 163-166 (4)* 7.25 2.10

Rastriya Panchayat system.

King Mahendra — A40

**1963, June 11** *Perf. 13*

**167** A40 5p violet .35 .25
**168** A40 10p brown orange .60 .25
**169** A40 15p dull green .80 .50
*Nos. 167-169 (3)* 1.75 1.00

King Mahendra's 43rd birthday.

East-West Highway on Map of Nepal and King Mahendra A41

**1964, Feb. 19 Photo.** *Perf. 13*

**170** A41 10p blue & dp orange .40 .25
**171** A41 15p dk blue & dp org .60 .25
**172** A41 50p dk grn & redsh brn 1.25 .40
*Nos. 170-172 (3)* 2.25 .90

Issued to publicize the East-West Highway as "The Prosperity of the Country."

King Mahendra Speaking Before Microphone — A42

**1964, June 11** *Perf. 14*

**173** A42 1p brown olive .40 .25
**174** A42 2p gray .40 .25
**175** A42 2r golden brown 2.00 1.20
*Nos. 173-175 (3)* 2.80 1.70

King Mahendra's 44th birthday.

Crown Prince Birendra — A43

*Perf. 14x14½*

**1964, Dec. 28 Photo. Unwmk.**

**176** A43 10p dark green 1.50 .95
**177** A43 15p brown 1.40 .95

19th birthday (coming of age) of Crown Prince Birendra Bir Bikram Shah Deva.

Nepalese Flag and Swords, Olympic Emblem A44

**1964, Dec. 31 Litho.** *Perf. 13x13½*

**178** A44 10p red & ultra 1.75 .80

18th Olympic Games, Tokyo, Oct. 10-25.

Farmer Plowing — A45

Family — A46

Designs: 5p, Grain. 10p, Chemical plant.

**1965 Photo.** *Perf. 13½*

**179** A45 2p brt green & black .40 .40
**180** A45 5p pale yel green & brn .50 .40
**181** A45 10p gray & purple .65 .40
**182** A46 15p yellow & brown 1.00 .90
*Nos. 179-182 (4)* 2.55 2.10

Issued to publicize land reform.
The 2p also exists on light green paper.
Issue dates: 15p, Feb. 10; others, Dec. 16.

Mail Circling Globe A47

**1965, Apr. 13** *Perf. 14½x14*

**183** A47 15p rose lilac .55 .40

Issued for Nepalese New Year.

King Mahendra — A48

*Perf. 14x14½*

**1965, June 11 Photo. Unwmk.**

**184** A48 50p rose violet 1.25 .75

King Mahendra's 45th birthday.

Victims of Revolution, 1939-40 — A49

**1965, June 11** *Perf. 13*
**185** A49 15p bright green .65 .40

The men executed by the Rana Government 1939-40 were: Shukra Raj Shastri, Dasharath Chand, Dharma Bhakta and Ganga Lal Shresta.

ITU Emblem — A50

**1965, Sept. 15 Photo.** *Perf. 13*
**186** A50 15p deep plum & black .70 .50

Cent. of the ITU.

Devkota — A51

**1965, Oct. 14** *Perf. 14x14½*
**187** A51 15p red brown .55 .40

Lakshmi Prasad Devkota (1908-1959), poet.

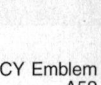

ICY Emblem A52

**Engr. and Litho.**

**1965, Oct. 24** *Perf. 11½x12*
**188** A52 1r multicolored 1.40 1.00

International Cooperation Year.

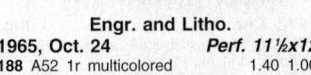

Nepalese Flag and King A53

**1966, Feb. 18 Photo.** *Perf. 14½x14*
**189** A53 15p deep blue & red 1.25 .60

Issued for Democracy Day.

Siva, Parvati and Pashupati Temple — A54

**1966, Feb. 18** *Perf. 14*
**190** A54 15p violet .65 .55

Hindu festival Maha Sivaratri.

Emblem — A55

*Perf. 14½x14*

**1966, June 10 Photo. Unwmk.**
**191** A55 15p dk green & orange .80 .50

National Philatelic Exhib., June 10-16.

King Mahendra — A56

**1966, June 11** *Perf. 13x13½*
**192** A56 15p yellow & vio brown .45 .30

Issued for King Mahendra's 46th birthday.

Kanti Rajya Lakshmi — A57

**1966, July 5 Photo.** *Perf. 14x14½*
**193** A57 15p golden brown .60 .45

60th birthday of Queen Mother Kanti Rajya Lakshmi.

Queen Ratna Rajya Lakshmi Devi Shah — A58

**1966, Aug. 19 Photo.** *Perf. 13*
**194** A58 15p yellow & brown .65 .50

Issued for Children's Day.

Krishna with Consort Radha and Flute — A59

**1966, Sept. 7**
**195** A59 15p dk purple & yellow .70 .50

Krishnastami 2023, the birthday of Krishna.

King Mahendra A60

**1966, Oct. 1 Photo.** *Perf. 14½x14*
**196** A60 50p slate grn & dp car 5.50 2.00

Issued to commemorate the official recognition of the Nepalese Red Cross.

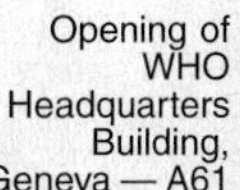

Opening of WHO Headquarters Building, Geneva — A61

**1966, Nov. 11 Photo.** *Perf. 14*
**197** A61 1r purple 3.00 1.75

Lekhnath Paudyal — A62

**1966, Dec. 29 Photo.** *Perf. 14*
**198** A62 15p dull violet blue .60 .50

Lekhnath Paudyal (1884-1966), poet.

**King Type of 1962**

**1967, Feb. 10 Photo.** *Perf. 14½x14*
**199** A35 75p blue green 1.60 .80

Rama and Sita — A63

**1967, Apr. 18 Litho.** *Perf. 14*
**200** A63 15p brown & yellow .75 .60

Rama Navami 2024, the birthday of Rama.

Buddha — A64

**1967, May 23 Photo.** *Perf. 13½x13*
**201** A64 75p orange & purple 1.40 1.10

2,511th birthday of Buddha.

King Mahendra Addressing Crowd and Himalayas — A65

**1967, June 11** *Perf. 13*
**202** A65 15p dk brown & lt blue .70 .45

King Mahendra's 47th birthday.

Queen Ratna among Children A66

**1967, Aug. 20 Photo.** *Perf. 13*
**203** A66 15p pale yel & dp brown .60 .45

Issued for Children's Day on the birthday of Queen Ratna Rajya Lakshmi Devi Shah.

Durbar Square, Bhaktapur A67

5p, Ama Dablam Mountain, ITY emblem.

**1967, Oct. 24** *Perf. 13½x14*

**Size: 29½x21mm**

**204** A67 5p violet .55 .45

*Perf. 14½x14*

**Size: 37½x19½mm**

**205** A67 65p brown 1.00 .85

Intl. Tourist Year, 1967. See No. C2.

Official Reading Proclamation — A68

**1967, Dec. 16 Litho.** *Perf. 13*
**206** A68 15p multicolored .75 .50

"Back to the Villages" campaign.

Crown Prince Birendra, Boy Scouts and Scout Emblem — A69

**1967, Dec. 29 Photo.** *Perf. 14½x14*
**207** A69 15p ultramarine 1.25 .70

60th anniv. of Boy Scouts.

Prithvi Narayan — A70

**1968, Jan. 11** *Perf. 14x14½*
**208** A70 15p blue & rose 1.25 .70

Rajah Prithvi Narayan (1779-1839), founder of modern Nepal.

Arms of Nepal — A71

**1968, Feb. 19 Photo.** *Perf. 14x14½*
**209** A71 15p crimson & dk blue 1.10 .70

Issued for National Day.

WHO Emblem and Flag of Nepal A72

**1968, Apr. 7** *Perf. 13*
**210** A72 1.20r dull yel, red & ultra 4.50 2.50

World Health Day (UN WHO).

Goddess Sita and Shrine A73

**1968, May 6 Photo.** ***Perf. 14½x14***
**211** A73 15p violet & org brown .80 .50

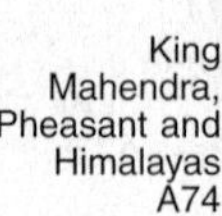

King Mahendra, Pheasant and Himalayas A74

**1968, June 11 Photo.** ***Perf. 13½***
**212** A74 15p multicolored 4.50 .40

King Mahendra's 48th birthday.

Flag, Children and Queen Ratna — A75

**1968, Aug. 19 Litho.** ***Perf. 13x13½***
**213** A75 5p blue grn, yel & ver .50 .30

Fourth National Children's Day.

Buddha and Human Rights Flame A76

**1968, Dec. 10 Photo.** ***Perf. 14½x14***
**214** A76 1r dk green & red 4.50 2.75

International Human Rights Year.

Young People Dancing Around Flag A77

**1968, Dec. 28 Photo.** ***Perf. 14½x14***
**215** A77 25p violet blue 1.25 .65

23rd birthday of Crown Prince Birendra, which is celebrated as Youth Festival.

UN Building, Nepalese and UN Flags — A78

**1969, Jan. 1** ***Perf. 13½x13***
**216** A78 1r multicolored 1.75 1.25

Issued to commemorate Nepal's admission to the UN Security Council for 1969-1970.

Amsu Varma — A79

Portraits: 25p, Ram Shah. 50p, Bhimsen Thapa.

**1969, Apr. 13 Photo.** ***Perf. 14x14½***
**217** A79 15p green & purple .70 .60
**218** A79 25p blue green .95 .75
**219** A79 50p orange brown 1.25 1.75
*Nos. 217-219 (3)* 2.90 3.10

Amsu Varma, 7th cent. ruler and reformer; Ram Shah, 17th cent. ruler and reformer, and Bhimsen Thapa, 18-19th cent. administrator and reformer.

ILO Emblem A80

**1969, May 1 Photo.** ***Perf. 14½x14***
**220** A80 1r car rose, blk & lt brown 7.00 4.00

50th anniv. of the ILO.

King Mahendra — A81

**1969, June 20** ***Perf. 13½x13***
**221** A81 25p gold & multi .75 .50

King Mahendra's 49th birthday (50th by Oriental count). Issuance delayed from June 11 to 20.

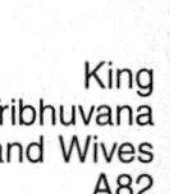

King Tribhuvana and Wives A82

**1969, July 1** ***Perf. 14½x14***
**222** A82 25p yellow & ol gray .75 .45

64th anniv. of the birth of King Tribhuvana.

Queen Ratna & Child Playing — A83

**1969, Aug. 20 Photo.** ***Perf. 14x14½***
**223** A83 25p gray & rose car .70 .50

5th Natl. Children's Day and to for the 41st birthday of Queen Ratna Rajya Lakshmi Devi Shah.

Rhododendron & Himalayas — A84

Flowers: No. 225, Narcissus. No. 226, Marigold. No. 227, Poinsettia.

**1969, Sept. 17 Photo.** ***Perf. 13½***
**224** A84 25p lt blue & multi 1.00 .65
**225** A84 25p brown red & multi 1.00 .65
**226** A84 25p black & multi 1.00 .65
**227** A84 25p multicolored 1.00 .65
***a.*** Block of 4, #224-227 4.50 4.50

Durga, Goddess of Victory — A85

**1969, Oct. 17 Photo.** ***Perf. 14x14½***
**228** A85 15p black & orange .50 .40
**229** A85 50p black, bis brn & vio 1.25 1.00

Issued to celebrate the Dasain Festival.

Crown Prince Birendra and Princess Aishwarya A86

**1970, Feb. 27 Photo.** ***Perf. 13½***
**230** A86 25p multicolored .70 .40

Wedding of Crown Prince Birendra Bir Bikram Shah Deva and Crown Princess Aishwarya Rajya Lakshmi Devi Rana, Feb. 27-28.

Agricultural Products, Cow, Fish — A87

**1970, Mar. 21 Litho.** ***Perf. 12½***
**231** A87 25p multicolored .70 .50

Issued to publicize the Agricultural Year.

Bal Bhadra Kunwar A88

**1970, Apr. 13 Photo.** ***Perf. 14½x14***
**232** A88 1r ol bister & red lilac 1.75 1.00

Bal Bhadra Kunwar, leader in the 1814 battle of Kalanga against British forces.

King Mahendra, Mountain Peak and Crown — A89

**1970, June 11 Litho.** ***Perf. 11½***
**233** A89 50p gold & multi 1.25 .65

King Mahendra's 50th birthday.

Gosainkund A90

Lakes: 25p, Phewa Tal. 1r, Rara Daha.

**1970, June 11 Photo.** ***Perf. 13½***
**234** A90 5p dull yellow & multi .50 .40
**235** A90 25p gray & multi .75 .60
**236** A90 1r pink & multi 1.25 1.10
*Nos. 234-236 (3)* 2.50 2.10

A.P.Y. Emblem A91

**1970, July 1** ***Perf. 14½x14***
**237** A91 1r dark blue & blue 1.25 .90

Asian Productivity Year 1970.

Bal Mandir Building and Queen Ratna A92

**1970, Aug. 20 Photo.** ***Perf. 14½x14***
**238** A92 25p gray & bister brn .70 .40

Issued for Children's Day. The Bal Mandir Building in Taulihawa is the headquarters of the National Children's Organization.

New UPU Headquarters, Bern — A93

**1970, Oct. 9 Photo.** ***Perf. 14½x14***
**239** A93 2.50r ocher & sepia 2.50 1.75

UN Flag A94

**1970, Oct. 24 Photo.** ***Perf. 14½x14***
**240** A94 25p blue & brown .70 .50

25th anniversary of the United Nations.

Royal Palace and Square, Patan A95

25p, Bodhnath stupa, near Kathmandu, vert. 1r, Gauri Shankar, holy mountain.

***Perf. 11x11½, 11½x11***
**1970, Dec. 28 Litho.**
**241** A95 15p multicolored .50 .25
**242** A95 25p multicolored .75 .50
**243** A95 1r multicolored 1.25 .80
*Nos. 241-243 (3)* 2.50 1.55

Crown Prince Birendra's 25th birthday.

Statue of Harihar (Vishnu-Siva) — A96

**1971, Jan. 26 Photo.** ***Perf. 14x14½***
**244** A96 25p bister brn & black .70 .45

Torch and Target A97

**1971, Mar. 21 Photo.** ***Perf. 13½x13***
**245** A97 1r bluish gray & dp org 1.75 1.00

Intl. year against racial discrimination.

King Mahendra and Subjects A98

**1971, June 11 Photo.** ***Perf. 14½x14***
**246** A98 25p dull purple & blue .70 .30

King Mahendra's 51st birthday.

Sweta Bhairab (Siva) — A99

Sculptures of Siva: 25p, Manhankal Bhairab. 50p, Kal Bhairab.

**1971, July 11** ***Perf. 13x13½***
**247** A99 15p org brn & blk .50 .40
**248** A99 25p lt green & black .60 .50
**249** A99 50p blue & black 1.25 .85
*Nos. 247-249 (3)* 2.35 1.75

Queen Ratna Receiving Garland A100

**1971, Aug. 20 Photo.** ***Perf. 11½***
**Granite Paper**
**250** A100 25p gray & multi .70 .35

Children's Day, Queen Ratna's birthday.

Map and Flag of Iran, Flag of Nepal A101

**1971, Oct. 14** **Granite Paper**
**251** A101 1r pink & multi 1.75 .75

2500th anniversary of the founding of the Persian empire by Cyrus the Great.

UNICEF Emblem, Mother and Child A102

**1971, Dec. 11** ***Perf. 14½x14***
**252** A102 1r gray blue 1.75 1.00

25th anniversary of UNICEF.

Everest A103

Himalayan Peaks: 1r, Kangchenjunga. 1.80r, Annapurna I.

**1971, Dec. 28** ***Perf. 13½x13***
**253** A103 25p blue & brown .50 .30
**254** A103 1r dp blue & brown 2.00 .70
**255** A103 1.80r blue & yel brown 2.25 1.25
*Nos. 253-255 (3)* 4.75 2.25

"Visit Nepal."

Royal Standard — A104

**1972, Feb. 19 Photo.** ***Perf. 13***
**256** A104 25p dark red & black .70 .35

National Day.

Araniko and White Dagoba, Peking — A105

**1972, Apr. 13 Litho.** ***Perf. 13***
**257** A105 15p lt blue & ol gray .40 .30

Araniko, a 14th century Nepalese architect, who built the White Dagoba at the Miaoying Monastery, Peking, 1348.

Book Year Emblem, Ancient Book A106

**1972, Sept. 8 Photo.** ***Perf. 14½x14***
**258** A106 2p ocher & brown .25 .25
**259** A106 5p tan & black .30 .25
**260** A106 1r blue & black 1.40 .90
*Nos. 258-260 (3)* 1.95 1.40

International Book Year.

Heart and WHO Emblem — A107

**1972, Nov. 6 Photo.** ***Perf. 13x13½***
**261** A107 25p dull grn & claret .75 .40

"Your heart is your health," World Health Month.

King Mahendra (1920-1972) A108

**1972, Dec. 15 Photo.** ***Perf. 13½x13***
**262** A108 25p brown & black .70 .35

King Birendra — A109

**1972, Dec. 28 Photo.** ***Perf. 13x13½***
**263** A109 50p ocher & purple .75 .50

King Birendra's 27th birthday.

Northern Border Costume A110

Nepalese Costumes: 50p, Hill dwellers. 75p, Kathmandu Valley couple. 1r, Inner Terai couple.

**1973, Feb. 18 Photo.** ***Perf. 13***
**264** A110 25p dull lilac & multi .50 .25
**265** A110 50p lemon & multi .70 .40
**266** A110 75p multicolored 1.00 .65
**267** A110 1r multicolored 1.50 .95
*a.* Block of 4, #264-267 4.25 4.25

National Day.

Babu Ram Acharya (1888-1972), Historian — A111

**1973, Mar. 12 Photo.** ***Perf. 13***
**268** A111 25p olive gray & car .60 .30

Nepalese Family and Home A112

**1973, Apr. 7 Photo.** ***Perf. 14½x14***
**269** A112 1r Prus blue & ocher 1.25 .85

25th anniv. of the WHO.

Lumbini Garden, Birthplace of Buddha — A113

**1973, May 17 Photo.** ***Perf. 13x13½***
**270** A113 25p shown .50 .25
**271** A113 75p Mt. Makalu .75 .50
**272** A113 1r Gorkha Village 1.25 .95
*Nos. 270-272 (3)* 2.50 1.70

FAO Emblem, Women Farmers A114

**1973, June 29 Photo.** ***Perf. 14½x14***
**273** A114 10p dark gray & violet .50 .25

World food program, 10th anniversary.

INTERPOL Headquarters and Emblem — A115

**1973, Sept. 3**
**274** A115 25p bister & blue .60 .30

50th anniversary of the International Criminal Police Organization (INTERPOL).

Shom Nath Sigdyal (1884-1972), Scholar — A116

**1973, Oct. 5 Photo.** ***Perf. 13x13½***
**275** A116 1.25r violet blue 1.25 .85

Cow A117

**1973, Oct. 25 Photo.** ***Perf. 13½x13***
**276** A117 2p shown .30 .25
**277** A117 3.25r Yak 2.25 1.50

Festival of Lights (Tihar).

King Birendra — A118

***Perf. 13, 13½x14, 15x14½***
**1973-74** **Photo.**
**278** A118 5p dark brown .25 .25
**279** A118 15p ol brn & dk brn ('74) .30 .25
**280** A118 1r reddish brn & dk brn ('74) 1.25 .70
*Nos. 278-280 (3)* 1.80 1.20

King Birendra's 28th birthday.

National Anthem A119

Natl. Day: 1r, Score of national anthem.

**1974, Feb. 18 Photo.** ***Perf. 13½x13***
**281** A119 25p rose carmine .50 .25
**282** A119 1r deep green .80 .65

King Janak on Throne — A120

**1974, Apr. 14 Litho.** ***Perf. 13½***
**283** A120 2.50r multicolored 2.00 1.75

Children's Village and SOS Emblem — A121

**1974, May 20 Litho. *Perf. 13½x13***

**284** A121 25p ultra & red .65 .45

25th anniv. of SOS Children's Village Intl.

Baghchal A122

**1974, July 1 Litho. *Perf. 13***

**285** A122 2p Soccer .25 .25
**286** A122 2.75r shown 1.50 1.10

Popular Nepalese games.

WPY Emblem — A123

**1974, Aug. 19 Litho. *Perf. 13***

**287** A123 5p ocher & blue .50 .25

World Population Year.

UPU Monument, Bern — A124

**1974, Oct. 9 Litho. *Perf. 13***

**288** A124 1r olive & black 1.25 .60

Centenary of Universal Postal Union.

Butterfly A125

Designs: Nepalese butterflies.

**1974, Oct. 16**

**289** A125 10p lt brown & multi .25 .25
**290** A125 15p lt blue & multi .45 .30
**291** A125 1.25r multicolored 1.75 1.00
**292** A125 1.75r buff & multi 2.50 1.10
*Nos. 289-292 (4)* 4.95 2.65

King Birendra — A126

**1974, Dec. 28 Litho. *Perf. 13½x13***

**293** A126 25p gray green & black .40 .25

King Birendra's 29th birthday.

Muktinath — A127

Peacock Window A128

**1974, Dec. 31 *Perf. 13x13½, 13½x13***

**294** A127 25p multicolored .50 .25
**295** A128 1r multicolored 1.10 .70

Tourist publicity.

Guheswari Temple — A129

Rara A130

Pashupati Temple — A131

King Birendra and Queen Aishwarya — A132

Designs: 1r, Throne. 1.25r, Royal Palace.

**1975, Feb. 24 Litho. *Perf. 13x13½***

**296** A129 25p multicolored .40 .25

**Photo.**

***Perf. 14½x14***

**297** A130 50p multicolored .60 .25

**Granite Paper**

***Perf. 11½, 11 (A131)***

**298** A132 1r olive & multi .75 .70
**299** A132 1.25r multicolored 1.50 .75
**300** A131 1.75r multicolored 1.00 .95
**301** A132 2.75r gold & multi 1.75 1.25
*a.* Souvenir sheet of 3 6.75 6.75
*Nos. 296-301 (6)* 6.00 4.15

Coronation of King Birendra, Feb. 24, 1975. No. 301a contains 3 imperf. stamps similar to Nos. 298-299, 301 and label with inscription.

Tourist Year Emblem A133

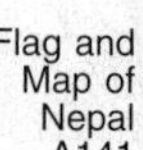

Swayambhunath Stupa, Kathmandu — A134

***Perf. 12½x13½, 13½x12½***

**1975, May 25 Litho.**

**302** A133 2p yellow & multi .25 .25
**303** A134 25p violet & black .50 .45

South Asia Tourism Year.

Tiger A135

**1975, July 17 Litho. *Perf. 13***

**304** A135 2p shown .50 .45
**305** A135 5p Deer, vert. .50 .55
**306** A135 1r Panda 1.25 1.10
*Nos. 304-306 (3)* 2.25 2.10

Wildlife conservation.

Queen Aishwarya and IWY Emblem — A136

**1975, Nov. 8 Litho. *Perf. 13***

**307** A136 1r lt blue & multi .80 .40

International Women's Year.

Ganesh Peak — A137

Rupse Falls — A138

Kumari, Living Goddess of Nepal — A139

**1975, Dec. 16 Litho. *Perf. 13½***

**308** A137 2p multicolored .25 .25
**309** A138 25p multicolored .35 .30
**310** A139 50p multicolored 1.00 .50
*Nos. 308-310 (3)* 1.60 1.05

Tourist publicity.

King Birendra — A140

**1975, Dec. 28 Photo. *Perf. 13***

**311** A140 25p rose lil & red lil .45 .25

King Birendra's 30th birthday.

Flag and Map of Nepal A141

**1976, Feb. 19 Litho. *Perf. 13***

**312** A141 2.50r dark blue & red 1.25 1.00

National or Democracy Day.

Rice Cultivation — A142

**1976, Apr. 11 Litho. *Perf. 13***

**313** A142 25p multicolored .40 .25

Agricultural development.

Flags of Nepal and Colombo Plan — A143

**1976, July 1 Photo. *Perf. 13x13½***

**314** A143 1r multicolored .80 .50

Colombo Plan, 25th anniversary.

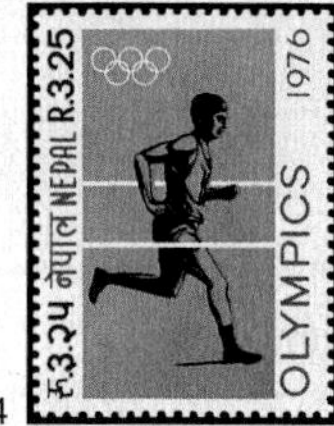

Runner — A144

**1976, July 31 Photo. *Perf. 13x13½***

**315** A144 3.25r black & ultra 2.25 1.25

21st Olympic Games, Montreal, Canada, July 17-Aug. 1.

Dove and Map of South East Asia — A145

**1976, Aug. 17 Litho. *Perf. 13½***

**316** A145 5r bister, black & ultra 2.75 1.50

5th Summit Conference of Non-aligned Countries, Colombo, Sri Lanka, Aug. 9-19.

Folk Dances A146

**1976, Sept. 27 Litho. *Perf. 13½x13***

**317** A146 10p Lakha mask .25 .25
**318** A146 15p Maruni .30 .25
**319** A146 30p Jhangad .50 .25
**320** A146 1r Sebru 1.00 .40
*Nos. 317-320 (4)* 2.05 1.15

Nepalese Lily — A147

Flowers: No. 322, Meconopsis grandis. No. 323, Cardiocrinum giganteum, horiz. No. 324, Megacodon stylophorus, horiz.

**1976-77 Litho. *Perf. 13***

**321** A147 30p lt ultra & multi .80 .25
**322** A147 30p brown & multi .80 .25
**323** A147 30p violet & multi .80 .25
**324** A147 30p violet & multi .80 .25
*Nos. 321-324 (4)* 3.20 1.00

Issue dates: Nov. 7, 1976, Jan. 24, 1977.

King Birendra — A148

**1976, Dec. 28 Photo. *Perf. 14***

**325** A148 5p green .25 .25
**326** A148 30p multicolored .45 .25

King Birendra's 31st birthday.

Bell and American Bicentennial Emblem — A149

**1976, Dec. 31 Litho. *Perf. 13½***

**327** A149 10r multicolored 4.00 3.00

American Bicentennial.

Warrior Kazi Amar Singh Thapa, Natl. Hero A150

**1977, Feb. 18 Photo. *Perf. 13x13½***

**328** A150 10p multicolored .50 .25

Terracotta Figurine, Kapilavastu Excavations — A151

Asoka Pillar, Lumbini A152

**1977, May 3 Photo. *Perf. 14½x14***

**329** A151 30p dark violet .30 .25
**330** A152 5r green & brown 2.00 1.50

Tourist publicity.

Cheer Pheasant A153

Birds of Nepal: 5p, Great pied hornbill, vert. 1r, Green magpie. 2.30r, Nepalese laughing thrush, vert.

**1977, Sept. 17 Photo. *Perf. 13***

**331** A153 5p multicolored .75 .30
**332** A153 15p multicolored 1.25 .30
**333** A153 1r multicolored 2.25 .65
**334** A153 2.30r multicolored 3.75 1.25
*Nos. 331-334 (4)* 8.00 2.50

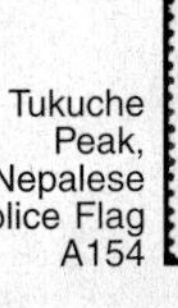

Tukuche Peak, Nepalese Police Flag A154

**1977, Oct. 2**

**335** A154 1.25r multicolored .85 .50

Ascent of Tukuche, Himalaya Mountains, by Nepalese police team, first anniversary.

Scout Emblem, Map of Nepal — A155

**1977, Nov. 7 Litho. *Perf. 13½***

**336** A155 3.50r multicolored 1.75 .85

Boy Scouts of Nepal, 25th anniversary.

Dhanwantari, Health Goddess — A156

**1977, Nov. 9 Photo. *Perf. 13***

**337** A156 30p bluish green .50 .25

Health Day.

Flags, Map of Nepal — A157

**1977, Dec. 5 Photo. *Perf. 13½***

**338** A157 1r multicolored .60 .30

Colombo Plan, 26th Consultative Meeting, Kathmandu, Nov. 29-Dec. 7.

King Birendra — A158

**1977, Dec. 28**

**339** A158 5p olive .25 .25
**340** A158 1r red brown .65 .50

King Birendra's 32nd birthday.

Post Office Seal, New Post Office A159

75p, Post Office date stamp & new Post Office.

**1978, Apr. 14 Photo. *Perf. 14½x14***

**341** A159 25p org brn & blk .25 .25
**342** A159 75p bister & black .50 .40

Centenary of Nepalese postal service.

Mt. Everest A160

Design: 4r, Mt. Everest, different view.

**1978, May 29 Photo. *Perf. 13½x13***

**343** A160 2.30r red brn & slate 1.25 .75
**344** A160 4r grn & vio blue 2.25 1.75

1st ascent of Mt. Everest, 25th anniv.

Mountains, Trees, Environmental Emblem — A161

**1978, June 5**

**345** A161 1r blue green & orange .70 .30

World Environment Day, June 5.

Queen Mother Ratna — A162

**1978, Aug. 20 Photo. *Perf. 14***

**346** A162 2.30r olive gray 1.25 .60

Queen Mother Ratna, 50th birthday.

Trisula River Rapids A163

Tourist Publicity: 50p, Nepalese window. 1r, Dancer, Mahakali dance, vert.

**1978, Sept. 15 Litho. *Perf. 14***

**347** A163 10p multicolored .30 .25
**348** A163 50p multicolored .50 .35
**349** A163 1r multicolored 1.00 .55
*Nos. 347-349 (3)* 1.80 1.15

Human Rights Emblem — A164

**1978, Oct. 10 Litho. *Perf. 13½***

**350** A164 25p red brown & red .30 .25
**351** A164 1r dark blue & red .70 .30

Universal Declaration of Human Rights, 30th anniversary.

Choerospondias Axillaris — A165

Designs: 1r, Castanopsis indica, vert. 1.25r, Elaeocarpus sphaericus.

**1978, Oct. 31 Photo. *Perf. 13***

**352** A165 5p multicolored .40 .25
**353** A165 1r multicolored .60 .50
**354** A165 1.25r multicolored 1.25 .60
*Nos. 352-354 (3)* 2.25 1.35

King Birendra — A166

**1978, Dec. 17 *Perf. 13½x14***

**355** A166 30p brown & indigo .30 .25
**356** A166 2r violet & black .80 .65

King Birendra's 33rd birthday.

Kamroop and Patan Temples and Deity A167

Red Machhindra Chariot — A168

***Perf. 14½x14, 13½***

**1979 Photo., Litho.**

**357** A167 75p claret & olive .60 .30
**358** A168 1.25r multicolored .70 .50

Red Machhindra Nath Festival, Lalitpur (Patan).

Issue dates: 75p, Apr. 27; 1.25r, July 25.

Bas-relief — A169

**1979, May 12 Photo. *Perf. 13***
**359** A169 1r yellow & brown .60 .30

Lumbini Year.

Tree Planting — A170

**1979, June 29 Photo. *Perf. 13x13½***
**360** A170 2.30r multicolored 1.50 .85

Afforestation campaign.

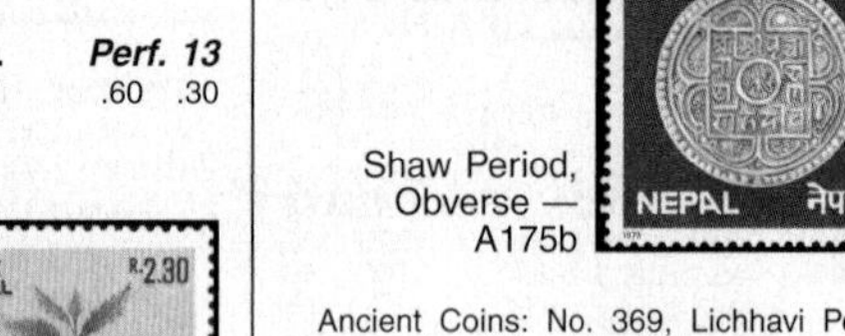
Children with Flag, IYC Emblem — A172

**1979, Aug. 20 *Perf. 13½***
**362** A172 1r light brown .75 .45

Intl. Year of the Child; Natl. Children's Day.

Mount Pabil A173

Tourism: 50p, Swargadwari Temple. 1.25r, Altar with statues of Shiva and Parbati.

**1979, Sept. 26 Photo. *Perf. 13½x13***
**363** A173 30p dk blue green .30 .25
**364** A173 50p multicolored .35 .25
**365** A173 1.25r multicolored .65 .55
*Nos. 363-365 (3)* 1.30 1.05

Northern Shrike — A174

Design: 10r, Aethopyga ignicauda.

***Perf. 14½x13½***
**1979, Nov. 22 Photo.**
**366** A174 10p shown .45 .25
**367** A174 10r multicolored 7.50 4.75

Intl. World Pheasant Assoc. Symposium, Kathmandu, Nov. 21-23. See No. C7.

Coin, Lichhavi Period, Obverse — A175

Malla Period, Obverse — A175a

Shaw Period, Obverse — A175b

Ancient Coins: No. 369, Lichhavi Period, reverse. No. 371, Malla Period, reverse. No. 373, Shah Period, reverse.

**1979, Dec. 16 Photo. *Perf. 15***
**368** A175 5p brn & brn org .25 .25
**369** A175 5p brn & brn org .25 .25
*a.* Pair, #368-369 .55 .55
**370** A175a 15p dark blue .30 .25
**371** A175a 15p dark blue .30 .25
*a.* Pair, #370-371 .65 .65
**372** A175b 1r slate blue .75 .50
**373** A175b 1r slate blue .75 .50
*a.* Pair, #372-373 1.75 1.75
*Nos. 368-373 (6)* 2.60 2.00

King Birendra — A176

Ban-Ganga Dam — A177

**1979, Dec. 28 Litho. *Perf. 14***
**374** A176 25p multicolored .25 .25
**375** A177 2.30r multicolored 1.00 .65

King Birendra's 34th birthday.

Samyak Pooja Festival A178

**1980, Jan. 15 *Perf. 13½***
**376** A178 30p vio brn & gray .50 .25

Holy Basil — A179

30p, Himalayan valerian. 1r, Nepalese pepper. 2.30r, Himalayan rhubarb.

**1980, Mar. 24 Photo. *Perf. 14x14½***
**377** A179 5p shown .25 .25
**378** A179 30p multicolored .30 .25
**379** A179 1r multicolored .60 .30
**380** A179 2.30r multicolored 1.25 .65
*Nos. 377-380 (4)* 2.40 1.45

Gyandil Das A180

Nepalese Writers: 30p, Shddhi Das Amatya. 1r, Pahal Man Singh Snwar. 2.30r, Jay Prithibi Bahadur Singh.

**1980, Apr. 13 *Perf. 13½x13***
**381** A180 5p bister & rose lilac .25 .25
**382** A180 30p vio brn & lt red brn .30 .25
**383** A180 1r blue & olive gray .50 .30
**384** A180 2.30r ol grn & dk blue 1.00 .65
*Nos. 381-384 (4)* 2.05 1.45

Jwalaji Dailekh (Temple), Holy Flame — A181

**1980, Sept. 14 Litho. *Perf. 14½***
**385** A181 10p shown .25 .25
**386** A181 1r Godavari Pond .50 .30
**387** A181 5r Mt. Dhaulagiri 2.25 1.25
*Nos. 385-387 (3)* 3.00 1.80

Temple Statue — A182

**1980, Oct. 29 *Perf. 14x13½***
**388** A182 25r multicolored 8.50 5.00

World Tourism Conf., Manila, Sept. 27.

King Birendra's 35th Birthday — A183

**1980, Dec. 28 Litho. *Perf. 14***
**389** A183 1r multicolored .60 .25

International Year of the Disabled A184

**1981, Jan. 1**
**390** A184 5r multicolored 2.25 1.40

Nepal Rastra Bank, 25th Anniv. A185

**1981, Apr. 26 Litho. *Perf. 14***
**391** A185 1.75r multicolored .80 .50

Nepalese Stamp Cent. — A186

**1981, July 16**
**392** A186 10p No. 1 .25 .25
**393** A186 40p No. 2 .30 .25
**394** A186 3.40r No. 3 1.75 1.25
*a.* Souvenir sheet of 3, #392-394 3.00 3.00
*Nos. 392-394 (3)* 2.30 1.75

A187

**1981, Oct. 30 Litho. *Perf. 14***
**395** A187 1.75r multicolored .50 .40

Intl. Hotel Assoc., 70th council meeting, Kathmandu.

Stamp Centenary — A188

**1981, Dec. 27 Litho. *Perf. 14***
**396** A188 40p multicolored .60 .25

Nepal '81 Stamp Exhibition, Kathmandu, Dec. 27-31.

King Birendra's 36th Birthday — A189

**1981, Dec. 28**
**397** A189 1r multicolored .55 .30

Hrishikesh, Buddhist Stone Carving, Ridi — A190

25p, Tripurasundari Pavilion, Baitadi. 2r, Mt. Langtang Lirung.

**1981, Dec. 30**
**398** A190 5p shown .25 .25
**399** A190 25p multicolored .30 .25
**400** A190 2r multicolored .75 .50
*Nos. 398-400 (3)* 1.30 1.00

Royal Nepal Academy, 25th Anniv. A191

**1982, June 23 Litho. *Perf. 14***
**401** A191 40p multicolored .40 .25

Balakrishna Sama — A192

**1982, July 21** *Perf. 13½*
**402** A192 1r multicolored .50 .30

Dish Antenna, Satellite — A193

**1982, Nov. 7 Litho.** *Perf. 14*
**403** A193 5r multicolored 2.00 1.25

Mt. Nuptse — A194

Intl. Union of Alpinists Assoc., 50th Anniv. (Himalaya Peaks): b, Mt. Lhotse (31x31mm). c, Mt. Everest (40x31mm). Continuous design.

**1982, Nov. 18** *Perf. 13½*
**404** A194 Strip of 3 3.50 3.50
*a.* 25p multicolored .25 .25
*b.* 2r multicolored .75 .50
*c.* 3r multicolored 1.75 .90

9th Asian Games — A195

**1982, Nov. 19** *Perf. 14*
**405** A195 3.40r multicolored 1.50 1.00

Kulekhani Hydro-electric Plant — A196

**1982, Dec. 2** *Perf. 13½*
**406** A196 2r Lake, dam 1.00 .50

King Birendra's 37th Birthday — A197

**1982, Dec. 28** *Perf. 12½*
**407** A197 5p multicolored .40 .25

A198

**1983, June 15 Litho.** *Perf. 14*
**408** A198 50p multicolored .50 .25

25th anniv. of Nepal Industrial Development Co.

25th Anniv. of Royal Nepal Airlines A199

**1983, Aug. 1** *Perf. 13½*
**409** A199 1r multicolored .90 .30

World Communications Year — A200

**1983, Oct. 30 Litho.** *Perf. 12*
**410** A200 10p multicolored .60 .25

Musical Instruments A201

**1983, Nov. 3**
**411** A201 5p Sarangi .25 .25
**412** A201 10p Kwota .30 .25
**413** A201 50p Narashinga .35 .25
**414** A201 1r Murchunga .65 .50
*Nos. 411-414 (4)* 1.55 1.25

A202

**1983, Dec. 20**
**415** A202 4.50r multicolored 1.75 1.00

Chakrapani Chalise (1883-1957), national anthem composer and poet.

King Birendra's 38th Birthday A203

**1983, Dec. 28** *Perf. 14*
**416** A203 5r multicolored 2.00 1.00

Temple, Barahkshetra A204

2.20r, Triveni pilgrimage site. 6r, Mt. Cho-oyu.

**1983, Dec. 30** *Perf. 14*
**417** A204 1r shown .30 .25
**418** A204 2.20r multicolored .80 .50
**419** A204 6r multicolored 2.25 1.50
*Nos. 417-419 (3)* 3.35 2.25

Auditor General, 25th Anniv. A204a

**1984, June 28 Litho.** *Perf. 14*
**419A** A204a 25p Open ledger .80 .60

A205

**1984, July 1 Litho.** *Perf. 14*
**420** A205 5r Transmission tower 2.00 1.25

Asia-Pacific Broadcasting Union, 20th anniv.

A206

**1984, July 8**
**421** A206 50p University emblem .45 .25

Tribhuvan University, 25th anniv.

A207

**1984, Aug. 5**
**422** A207 10r Boxing 3.75 2.10

1984 Summer Olympic Games, Los Angeles.

A208

**1984, Sept. 18**
**423** A208 1r multicolored .45 .25

Family Planning Assoc., 25th anniv.

Social Services Day — A209

**1984, Sept. 24**
**424** A209 5p multicolored .40 .25

Wildlife A210

10p, Gavialis gangeticus. 25p, Panthera uncia. 50p, Antilope cervicapra.

**1984, Nov. 30**
**425** A210 10p multicolored .40 .30
**426** A210 25p multicolored .60 .35
**427** A210 50p multicolored 1.00 .45
*Nos. 425-427 (3)* 2.00 1.10

Chhinna Masta Bhagvati Temple and Goddess Sakhandeshwari Devi, Statue — A211

Designs: 10p, Lord Vishu the Giant, Yajna Ceremony on Bali, bas-relief, A. D. 467, vert. 5r, Mt. Api, Himalayas, vert.

**1984, Dec. 21**
**428** A211 10p multicolored .25 .25
**429** A211 1r multicolored .30 .30
**430** A211 5r multicolored 2.00 1.25
*Nos. 428-430 (3)* 2.55 1.80

King Birendra, 39th Birthday A212

**1984, Dec. 28**
**431** A212 1r multicolored .45 .25

Sagarmatha Natl. Park — A213

**1985, May 6**
**432** A213 10r Mt. Everest, wildlife 6.00 2.25

King Mahendra Trust Congress for Nature Conservation, May 6-11.

Illustration from Shiva Dharma Purana, 13th Cent. Book — A214

Design: Maheshware, Lord Shiva, with brahma and vishnu. #433b, left person sitting on wall. #433d, left person on throne.

**1985, May 30**
**433** Strip of 5 3.50 2.50
*a.-e.* A214 50p any single .40 .25
*f.* Strip of 5, imperf within 4.50

#433 has a continuous design. Sizes: #433a, 433e, 26x22mm; #433b, 433d, 24x22mm; #433c, 17x22mm.

UN, 40th Anniv. — A215

**1985, Oct. 24 Litho. *Perf. 13½x14***

**434** A215 5r multicolored 1.75 1.00

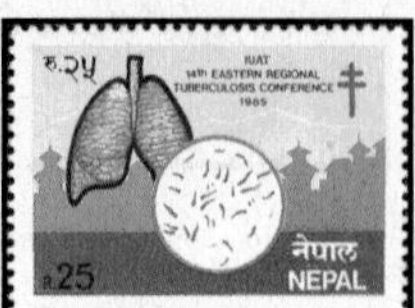

14th Eastern Regional Tuberculosis Conference A216

**1985, Nov. 25**

**435** A216 25r multicolored 7.50 5.50

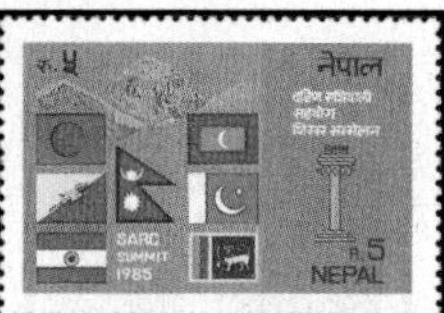

First South Asian Regional Cooperation Summit — A217

**1985, Dec. 8 *Perf. 14***

**436** A217 5r Flags 1.75 .75

Temple of Jaleshwar, Mohottary Underwater Project — A218

1r, Temple of Shaileshwari, Doti. 2r, Lake Phoksundo, Dolpa.

**1985, Dec. 15 Litho. *Perf. 14x13½***

**437** A218 10p shown .25 .25
**438** A218 1r multicolored .45 .30
**439** A218 2r multicolored .80 .40
*Nos. 437-439 (3)* 1.50 .95

Intl. Youth Year — A219

**1985, Dec. 21 *Perf. 14***

**440** A219 1r multicolored .45 .25

Devi Ghat Hydro-electric Dam Project A220

**1985, Dec. 28 Litho. *Perf. 14***

**441** A220 2r multicolored .80 .60

King Birendra, 40th Birthday — A221

**1985, Dec. 28**

**442** A221 50p Portrait .45 .25

Panchayat System, 25th Anniv. — A222

**1986, Apr. 10 *Perf. 13½***

**443** A222 4r multicolored 1.50 1.00

Pharping Hydroelectric Station, 75th Anniv. — A223

**1986, Oct. 9 Litho. *Perf. 14x13½***

**444** A223 15p multicolored .50 .25

Architecture, Artifacts — A224

5p, Pashupati Temple. 10p, Lumbini Fort. 1r, Crown of Nepal.

**1986, Oct. 9 Photo. *Perf. 13x13½***

**445** A224 5p multicolored .25 .25
**446** A224 10p multicolored .30 .25
**446A** A224 50p like 5p ('87) .40 .25
**447** A224 1r multicolored .50 .25
*Nos. 445-447 (4)* 1.45 1.00

No. 446A issued Apr. 14.

Asian Productivity Org., 25th Anniv. A225

**1986, Oct. 26 Litho. *Perf. 13½x14***

**448** A225 1r multicolored .50 .25

Reclining Buddha, Kathmandu Valley — A226

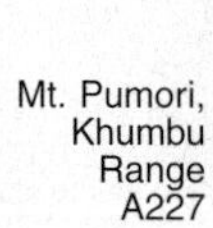

Mt. Pumori, Khumbu Range A227

***Perf. 14, 13½x13***

**1986, Oct. 26 Litho.**

**449** A226 60p multicolored .30 .25
**450** A227 8r multicolored 2.75 1.25

King Birendra, 41st Birthday — A228

**1986, Dec. 28 Litho. *Perf. 13x13½***

**451** A228 1r multicolored .45 .25

Intl. Peace Year — A229

**1986, Dec. 28 *Perf. 14***

**452** A229 10r multicolored 2.50 1.75

Social Service Natl. Coordination Council, 10th Anniv. — A230

**1987, Sept. 22 Litho. *Perf. 13½***

**453** A230 1r Natl. flag, emblem .45 .25

Birth of Buddha A231

Design: Asoka Pillar, enlargement of commemorative text and bas-relief of birth.

**1987, Oct. 28 *Perf. 14***

**454** A231 4r multicolored 1.25 .75

First Natl. Boy Scout Jamboree, Kathmandu — A232

**1987, Oct. 28 Litho. *Perf. 14***

**455** A232 1r multicolored .85 .40

A233

**1987, Nov. 2**

**456** A233 60p gold & lake .30 .25

3rd SAARC (Southeast Asian Assoc. for Regional Cooperation) Summit Conference, Kathmandu.

A234

**1987, Nov. 10**

**457** A234 4r multicolored 1.10 .75

Rastriya Samachar Samiti (Natl. news agency), 25th anniv.

Intl. Year of Shelter for the Homeless A235

**1987, Dec. 21 Litho. *Perf. 14***

**458** A235 5r multicolored 1.75 1.00

Kashthamandap Temple, Kathmandu A236

**1987, Dec. 21 Photo. *Perf. 13½x13***

**459** A236 25p multicolored .40 .25

Surya Bikram Gyawali (b. 1898), Historian — A237

**1987, Dec. 21 *Perf. 13x13½***

**460** A237 60p multicolored .50 .25

King Birendra, 42nd Birthday — A238

***Perf. 14½x13½***

**1987, Dec. 28 Litho.**

**461** A238 25p multicolored .50 .25

Mount Kanjiroba A239

**1987, Dec. 30 *Perf. 14***

**462** A239 10r multicolored 3.00 1.75

Crown Prince Dipendra's 18th Birthday — A240

**1988, Mar. 28 Litho. *Perf. 14***
**463** A240 1r multicolored .50 .25

Nepal Bank, Ltd., 50th Anniv. — A241

**1988, Apr. 8**
**464** A241 2r multicolored .50 .25

Kanti Childrens' Hospital, 25th Anniv. A242

**1988, Apr. 8**
**465** A242 60p multicolored .50 .25

Royal Shuklaphanta Wildlife Reserve A243

**1988, Apr. 8**
**466** A243 60p Swamp deer 1.25 .25

A244

**1988, Aug. 20 Litho. *Perf. 14x13½***
**467** A244 5r multicolored 1.75 1.25

Queen Mother Ratna Rajya Laxmi Devi Shah, 60th birthday.

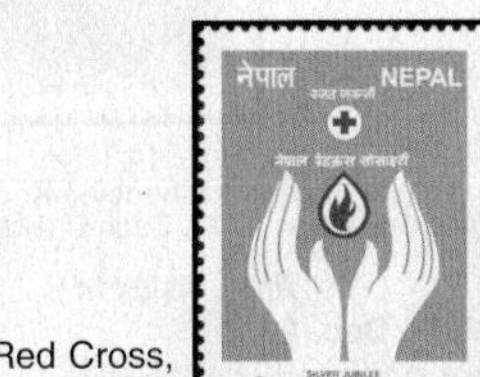

Nepal Red Cross, 25th Anniv. — A245

**1988, Sept. 12 Litho. *Perf. 14x13½***
**468** A245 1r dull fawn & dark red .50 .25

Bindhyabasini, Pokhara — A246

**1988, Oct. 16 Litho. *Perf. 14½***
**469** A246 15p multicolored .50 .25

King Birendra, 43rd Birthday — A247

**1988, Dec. 28 Litho. *Perf. 14***
**470** A247 4r multicolored 1.25 .60

A248

**1989, Mar. 3 Litho. *Perf. 13½x14***
**471** A248 1r Temple .50 .25

Pashupati Area Development Trust.

SAARC Year — A249

**1989, Dec. 8 *Perf. 13x13½***
**472** A249 60p multicolored .50 .25

Combating Drug Abuse & Trafficking.

A250

**1989, Oct. 5 *Perf. 14***
**473** A250 4r vio, brt grn & blk .85 .45

Asia-Pacific Telecommunity, 10th anniv.

King Birendra, 44th Birthday A251

***Perf. 13½x14½***
**1989, Dec. 28 Litho.**
**474** A251 2r multicolored .70 .25

Child Survival — A252

Design: Oral rehydration therapy, immunization, breast-feeding and growth monitoring.

**1989, Dec. 31 *Perf. 13½***
**475** A252 1r multicolored .50 .25

Rara Natl. Park — A253

**1989, Dec. 31 *Perf. 14½x15***
**476** A253 4r multicolored 1.00 .30

Mt. Ama Dablam A254

**1989, Dec. 31 *Perf. 14***
**477** A254 5r multicolored 1.25 .60

A255

**1990, Jan. 3**
**478** A255 1r multicolored .50 .25

Crown Prince Dipendra investiture, Jan. 3.

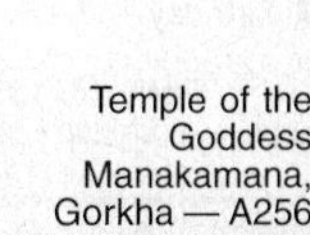

Temple of the Goddess Manakamana, Gorkha — A256

**1990, Apr. 12 Litho. *Perf. 14½***
**479** A256 60p deep blue & black .65 .25

A257

**1990, Aug. 20 Litho. *Perf. 14***
**480** A257 1r multicolored .50 .25

Nepal Children's Organization, 25th anniv.

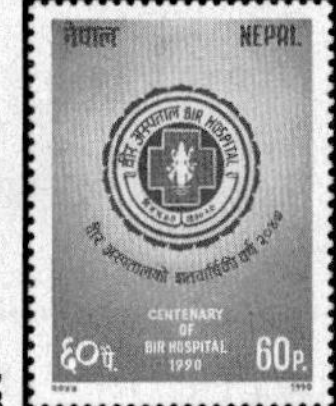

Bir Hospital, Cent. — A258

**1990, Sept. 13 Litho. *Perf. 14x13½***
**481** A258 60p orange, blue & red .50 .25

A259

**1990, Oct. 9 *Perf. 14½***
**482** A259 4r multicolored .80 .50

Asian-Pacific Postal Training Center, 20th anniv.

SAARC Year of the Girl Child A260

**1990, Dec. 24 Litho. *Perf. 14½***
**483** A260 4.60r multicolored 1.25 .65

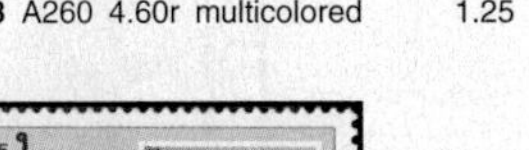

Bageshwori Temple, Nepalganj A261

Mt. Saipal A262

**1990, Dec. 24 *Perf. 13½***
**484** A261 1r multicolored .50 .25
**485** A262 5r multicolored .75 .40

B.P. Koirala (1914-82) — A263

**1990, Dec. 31 *Perf. 14***
**486** A263 60p red, org brn & blk .50 .25

King Birendra, 45th Birthday A264

**1990, Dec. 28**
**487** A264 2r multicolored .50 .25

Royal Chitwan Natl. Park A265

**1991, Feb. 10 Litho. *Perf. 14½***

**488** A265 4r multicolored 1.50 .65

Restoration of Multiparty Democracy, 1st Anniv. — A266

**1991, Apr. 9 Litho. *Perf. 14***

**489** A266 1r multicolored .50 .25

Natl. Census — A267

**1991, May 3 *Perf. 14x13½***

**490** A267 60p multicolored .50 .25

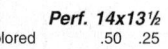

A268

**1991, Aug. 15 *Perf. 14½x13½***

**491** A268 3r multicolored .50 .25

Federation of Nepalese Chambers of Commerce and Industry, 25th anniv.

A269

**1991, Sept. 4 Litho. *Perf. 14***

**492** A269 60p gray & red .50 .25

Nepal Junior Red Cross, 25th anniv.

Re-establishment of Parliament, 1st Session — A270

**1991, Sept. 10 *Perf. 14½***

**493** A270 1r multicolored .50 .25

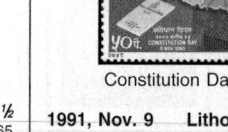

Constitution Day — A271

**1991, Nov. 9 Litho. *Perf. 15x14***

**494** A271 50p multicolored .65 .25

Mt. Kumbhakarna — A272

**1991, Oct. Litho. *Perf. 13½x14***

**495** A272 4.60r multicolored .75 .30

Vivaha Mandap — A274

**1991, Dec. 11 *Perf. 11½***

**497** A274 1r multicolored .50 .25

SAARC Year of Shelter — A275

**1991, Dec. 28 *Perf. 13½x14***

**498** A275 9r multicolored 2.00 1.00

King Birendra, 46th Birthday — A276

**1991, Dec. 28 *Perf. 14x13½***

**499** A276 8r multicolored 1.00 .60

Nepal Philatelic Society, 25th Anniv. — A277

**1992, July 11 Litho. *Perf. 13***

**500** A277 4r multicolored .60 .30

Protect the Environment A278

**1992, Oct. 24 Litho. *Perf. 12½x13***

**501** A278 60p multicolored .65 .25

Rights of the Child A279

**1992, Oct. 24 *Perf. 13½x13***

**502** A279 1r multicolored .50 .25

Temples A280

75p, Thakurdwara. 1r, Namo Buddha. 2r, Narijhowa. 11r, Dantakali.

**1992, Nov. 10 *Perf. 14***

**503** A280 75p multicolored .30 .25
**504** A280 1r multicolored .35 .25
**505** A280 2r multicolored .45 .25
**506** A280 11r multicolored 2.25 1.00
*Nos. 503-506 (4)* 3.35 1.75

No. 506 is airmail.

A281

**1992, Dec. 20 Photo. *Perf. 13x13½***

**507** A281 40p brown & green .50 .25

Agricultural Development Bank, 25th anniv.

Birds — A282

1r, Pin-tailed green pigeon. 3r, Bohemian waxwing. 25r, Rufous-tailed finch lark.

**1992, Dec. 20 Litho. *Perf. 11½***

**508** A282 1r multicolored .30 .25
**509** A282 3r multicolored .60 .30
**510** A282 25r multicolored 4.75 2.50
*Nos. 508-510 (3)* 5.65 3.05

King Birendra, 47th Birthday A283

**1992, Dec. 28 *Perf. 12½x13***

**511** A283 7r multicolored 1.10 .45

Poets — A284

Designs: No. 512, Pandit Kulchandra Gautam. No. 513, Chittadhar Hridaya. No. 514, Vidyapati. No. 515, Teongsi Sirijunga.

**1992, Dec. 31 *Perf. 11½***

**512** A284 1r blue & multi *.80* .25
**513** A284 1r brown & multi *.80* .25
**514** A284 1r tan & multi *.80* .25
**515** A284 1r gray & multi *.80* .25
*Nos. 512-515 (4)* *3.20* 1.00

1992 Summer Olympics, Barcelona — A285

**1992, Dec. 31**

**516** A285 25r multicolored 4.50 2.50

Fish — A286

Designs: 25p, Tor putitora. 1r, Schizothorax plagiostomus. 5r, Anguilla bengalensis, temple of Chhabdi Barahi. 10r, Psilorhynchus pseudecheneis.

**1993, Aug. 6 Litho. *Perf. 11½***

**Granite Paper**

**517** A286 25p multicolored .50 .25
**518** A286 1r multicolored .55 .40
**519** A286 5r multicolored 1.25 .90
**520** A286 10r multicolored 2.25 1.00
*a.* Souvenir sheet of 4, #517-520 7.00 7.00
*Nos. 517-520 (4)* 4.55 2.55

World AIDS Day — A287

**1993, Dec. 1 Litho. *Perf. 13½x14½***

**521** A287 1r multicolored .50 .25

Tanka Prasad Acharya — A288

1r, Sungdare Sherpa. 7r, Siddhi Charan Shrestha. 15r, Falgunand.

**1993, Dec. 2 *Perf. 13½***

**522** A288 25p shown .25 .25
**523** A288 1r multicolored .30 .25
**524** A288 7r multicolored 1.00 .40
**525** A288 15r multicolored 2.00 1.25
*Nos. 522-525 (4)* 3.55 2.15

Holy Places A289

1.50r, Halesi Mahadev, Khotang. 5r, Devghat, Tanahun. 8r, Bagh Bhairab, Kirtipur.

***Perf. 13½x14½***

**1993, Dec. 28 Litho.**

**526** A289 1.50r multicolored .25 .25
**527** A289 5r multicolored .75 .50
**528** A289 8r multicolored 1.25 .80
*Nos. 526-528 (3)* 2.25 1.55

Tourism A290

Designs: 5r, Tushahiti Sundari Chowk, Patan. 8r, White water rafting.

**1993, Dec. 28**

**529** A290 5r multicolored .75 .40
**530** A290 8r multicolored 1.25 .65

King Birendra, 48th Birthday — A291

**1993, Dec. 28** ***Perf. 14***

**531** A291 10r multicolored 1.25 .75

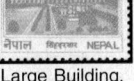

Large Building, Courtyard A293

Pagoda, Courtyard A293a

Monument A294

Arms A295

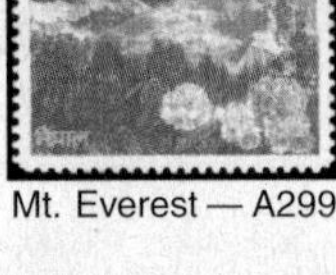

Fort — A296

Mt. Everest — A299

Pagoda (Nyata Pola) — A300

Map of Nepal — A301

Design: 50p, Pagoda, vert.

***Perf. 14½, 12, (#533A, 538, 540), 14¼x14***
**Photo., Litho. (#533A, 535A, 538, 540)**

**1994-96**

**533** A293 10p green .45 .25
**533A** A293a 10p claret & black .45 .25
**534** A294 20p violet brown .45 .25
**535** A295 25p carmine, 21x23mm .45 .25
**535A** A295 25p carmine, 21x26mm .75 .25
**536** A296 30p slate .45 .25
**537** A293 50p dark blue .45 .25
**538** A293a 50p black & claret .45 .25
**539** A299 1r multicolored 1.00 .25
**539A** A300 1r blue & claret .75 .25

***Perf. 14½x13½***

**540** A301 5r multicolored .75 .35
*Nos. 533-540 (11)* 6.40 2.85

Issued: 20p, No. 535, 30p, 5/17/94; No. 539, 7/6/94; 5r, 9/22/94; Nos. 533, 537, 1995; No. 535A, 8/2/96. Nos. 533A, 538, 539A, 10/9/96.

Pasang Lhamu Sherpa (1960-1993) A304

**1994, Sept 2** **Litho.** ***Perf. 14***

**544** A304 10r multicolored 1.50 .75

Stop Smoking Campaign A305

**1994, Sept. 26** ***Perf. 13½x14***

**545** A305 1r multicolored .75 .25

Mail Transport — A306

**1994, Oct. 9** ***Perf. 13x13½***

**546** A306 1.50r multicolored .80 .25

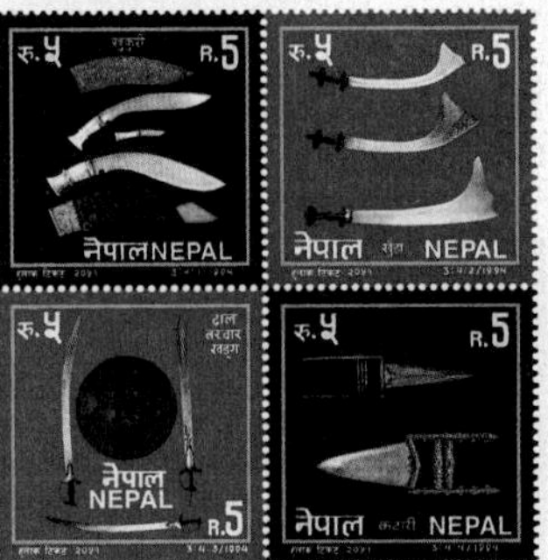

Traditional Weapons — A307

No. 547: a, Daggers, scabbards. b, Yataghans. c, Sabers, shield. d, Carved stone daggers.

**1994, Oct. 9** ***Perf. 14***

**547** A307 5r Block of 4, #a.-d. 3.25 3.25

ILO, 75th Anniv. A308

**1994, Oct. 9** ***Perf. 13***

**548** A308 15r blue & gold 2.00 1.25

World Food Day — A309

**1994, Oct. 23** ***Perf. 14***

**549** A309 25r multicolored 3.00 2.00

Orchids — A310

a, Dendrobium densiflorum. b, Coelogyne flaccida. c, Cymbidium devonianum. d, Coelogyne corymbosa.

**1994, Nov. 7** ***Perf. 14x13½***

**550** A310 10r Block of 4, #a.-d. 6.00 6.00

Intl. Year of the Family — A311

**1994, Dec. 5** ***Perf. 12½x13***

**551** A311 9r green & red 1.25 .75

ICAO, 50th Anniv. — A312

**1994, Dec. 7**

**552** A312 11r blue & gold 1.25 .80

Mushrooms — A313

**1994, Dec. 20** ***Perf. 14***

**553** A313 7r Cordyceps sinensis 1.10 .50
**554** A313 7r Morchella conica 1.10 .50
**555** A313 7r Amanita caesarea 1.10 .50
**556** A313 7r Russula nepalensis 1.10 .50
*Nos. 553-556 (4)* 4.40 2.00

Famous Men — A314

Designs: 1r, Dharanidhar Koirala, poet. 2r, Narayan Gopal Guruwacharya, singer. 6r, Bahadur Shah, military leader, vert. 7r, Balaguru Shadananda, religious leader.

**1994, Dec. 23** ***Perf. 13½x14, 14x13½***

**557** A314 1r multicolored .35 .25
**558** A314 2r multicolored .35 .25
**559** A314 6r multicolored .90 .50
**560** A314 7r multicolored 1.00 .55
*Nos. 557-560 (4)* 2.60 1.55

King Birendra, 49th Birthday A315

**1994, Dec. 28** ***Perf. 14***

**561** A315 9r multicolored 1.00 .70

Tilicho Lake, Manang A316

11r, Taleju Temple, Katmandou, vert.

**1994, Dec. 28** ***Perf. 13½x14, 14x13½***

**562** A316 9r multicolored .90 .70
**563** A316 11r multicolored 1.10 .80

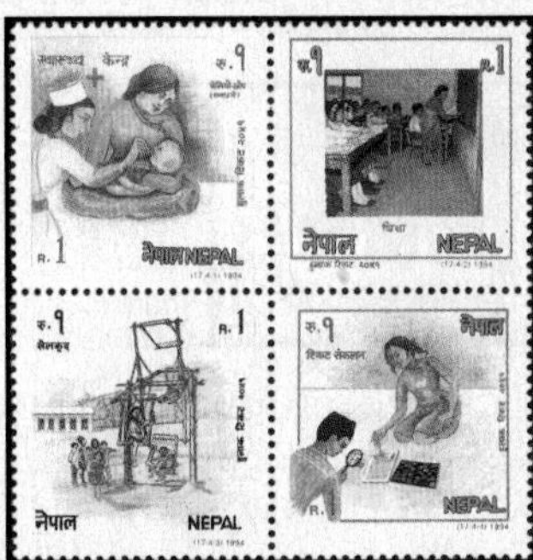

Care of Children — A317

No. 564: a, Vaccination. b, Education. c, Playground activities. d, Stamp collecting.

**1994, Dec. 30** ***Perf. 14***

**564** A317 1r Block of 4, #a.-d. .80 .80

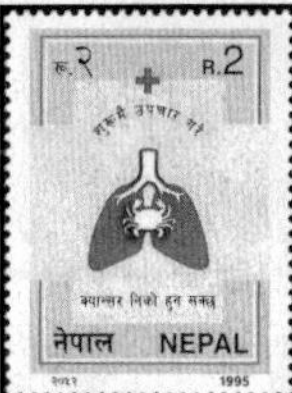

Fight Against Cancer — A318

**1995, June 23** **Litho.** ***Perf. 14x13½***

**565** A318 2r red & black .50 .25

A319

Famous People: a, Bhim Nidhi Tiwari, writer. b, Yuddha Prasad Mishra, writer. c, Chandra Man Singh Maskey, artist. d, Parijat, writer.

**1995, July 11** ***Perf. 14***

**566** A319 3r Block of 4, #a.-d. 2.00 2.00

A320

Famous Men: 15p, Bhakti Thapa, warrior. 1r, Madan Bhandari, politician. 4r, Prakash Raj Kaphley, human rights activist.

**1995, Sept. 1 Litho. *Perf. 14x13½***

| | | | | |
|---|---|---|---|---|
| **567** | A320 | 15p multicolored | .25 | .25 |
| **568** | A320 | 1r multicolored | .25 | .25 |
| **569** | A320 | 4r multicolored | .40 | .30 |
| | | *Nos. 567-569 (3)* | .90 | .80 |

Animals A321

Designs: a, Bos gaurus. b, Felis lynx. c, Macaca assamensis. d, Hyaena hyaena.

**1995, Sept. 1 Litho. *Perf. 12***

**570** A321 10p Block of 4, #a.-d. 6.00 6.00

Tourism A322

1r, Bhimeshwor Temple, Dolakha, vert. 5r, Ugra Tara Temple, Dadeldhura. 7r, Mt. Nampa. 18r, Thanka art, Nrity Aswora, vert.

***Perf. 14x13½, 13½x14***

**1995, Nov. 8 Litho.**

| | | | | |
|---|---|---|---|---|
| **574** | A322 | 1r multicolored | .25 | .25 |
| **575** | A322 | 5r multicolored | .60 | .35 |
| **576** | A322 | 7r multicolored | 1.00 | .50 |

**Size: 26x39mm**

| | | | | |
|---|---|---|---|---|
| **577** | A322 | 18r multicolored | 2.50 | 1.25 |
| | | *Nos. 574-577 (4)* | 4.35 | 2.35 |

FAO, 50th Anniv. A323

**1995, Oct. 16 Litho. *Perf. 13½x14***

**578** A323 7r multicolored .90 .45

UN, 50th Anniv. A324

**1995, Oct. 22 Litho. *Perf. 11½***

**Granite Paper**

**579** A324 50r multicolored 6.00 3.50

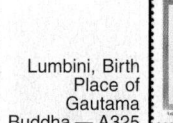

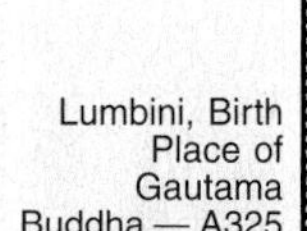
Lumbini, Birth Place of Gautama Buddha — A325

**1995, Dec. 23 Litho. *Perf. 14***

**580** A325 20r multicolored 3.00 1.50

King Birendra, 50th Birthday
A326 A327

**1995, Dec. 28 *Perf. 12***

**Granite Paper (No. 581)**

**581** A326 1r multicolored .50 .25

***Perf. 13x13½***

**582** A327 12r multicolored 1.50 .95

SAARC, 10th Anniv. A328

**1995, Dec. 28 *Perf. 13½***

**583** A328 10r multicolored 1.50 .70

Karnali Bridge — A329

**1996, May 13 Litho. *Perf. 14***

**584** A329 7r multicolored 1.00 .50

1996 Summer Olympic Games, Atlanta — A330

**1996, Oct. 9 Photo. *Perf. 12***

**Granite Paper**

**585** A330 7r multicolored 1.00 .45

Kaji Kalu Pande A331

Hem Raj Sharma, Grammarian A332

#587, Pushpa Lal Shrestha. #589, Padma Prasad Bhattarai, scholar, philosopher. #590, Suvarna Shamsher Rana. #591, Bhawani Bhikshu, novelist, writer.

***Perf. 13½x14, 14x13½***

**1996, Aug. 6 Litho.**

| | | | | |
|---|---|---|---|---|
| **586** | A331 | 75p multicolored | .35 | .25 |
| **587** | A331 | 1r multicolored | .35 | .25 |
| **588** | A332 | 1r multicolored | .35 | .25 |
| **589** | A332 | 3r multicolored | .35 | .25 |
| **590** | A331 | 5r multicolored | .60 | .30 |
| **591** | A332 | 5r multicolored | .60 | .30 |
| | | *Nos. 586-591 (6)* | 2.60 | 1.60 |

See Nos. 614-615.

Asoka Pillar, Lumbini — A333

**1996, Dec. 1 Litho. *Perf. 11½***

**592** A333 12r multicolored 2.00 1.00

Tourism A334

Designs: 1r, Arjun Dhara, Jhapa. 2r, Palace of Nuwakot. 8r, Traditional Gaijatra, Bhaktapur. 10r, Begnash Lake, Kaski.

**1996, Nov. 20 Litho. *Perf. 14***

| | | | | |
|---|---|---|---|---|
| **593** | A334 | 1r multicolored | .35 | .25 |
| **594** | A334 | 2r multicolored | .35 | .25 |
| **595** | A334 | 8r multicolored | 1.25 | .60 |
| **596** | A334 | 10r multicolored | 1.50 | .90 |
| | | *Nos. 593-596 (4)* | 3.45 | 2.00 |

Butterflies and Birds — A335

Designs: a, Krishna pea-cock butterfly. b, Great Himalayan barbet. c, Sarus crane. d, Northern junglequeen butterfly.

**1996, Nov. 20 Litho. *Perf. 14***

**597** A335 5r Block of 4, #a.-d. 4.25 4.25

Annapurna Mountain Range — A336

Designs: a, Annapurna South, Annapurna I. b, Machhapuchhre, Annapurna III. c, Annapurna IV, Annapurna II.

**1996, Dec. 28 Litho. *Perf. 14***

**601** A336 18r Strip of 3, #a.-c. 7.00 7.00

King Birendra, 51st Birthday — A337

**1996, Dec. 28 Photo. *Perf. 12***

**Granite Paper**

**602** A337 10r multicolored 1.00 .65

Accession of King Birendra to Throne, 25th Anniv. A338

**1997, Feb. 1 Litho. *Perf. 14***

**603** A338 2r multicolored 1.00 .25

Nepal Postal Service — A339

**1997, Apr. 12 Litho. *Perf. 14***

**604** A339 2r brown & red .60 .25

Nepalese-Japanese Diplomatic Relations, 40th Anniv. — A340

**1997, Apr. 6 Photo. *Perf. 12***

**605** A340 18r multicolored 2.50 1.25

Visit Nepal '98 — A341

2r, Emblem. 10r, Upper Mustang. 18r, Rafting Sunkoshi. 20r, Changunarayan (Bhaktapur), vert.

**1997, July 6 Litho. *Perf. 14***

| | | | | |
|---|---|---|---|---|
| **606** | A341 | 2r multicolored | .25 | .25 |
| **607** | A341 | 10r multicolored | 1.10 | .75 |
| **608** | A341 | 18r multicolored | 2.00 | 1.25 |
| **609** | A341 | 20r multicolored | 2.25 | 1.40 |
| | | *Nos. 606-609 (4)* | 5.60 | 3.65 |

A342

Traditional costumes.

**1997, Sept. 30 Litho. *Perf. 14***

| | | | | |
|---|---|---|---|---|
| **610** | A342 | 5r Rana Tharu | .50 | .30 |
| **611** | A342 | 5r Gurung | .50 | .30 |
| **612** | A342 | 5r Chepang | .50 | .30 |
| | | *Nos. 610-612 (3)* | 1.50 | .90 |

A343

**1997, Sept. 30 *Perf. 11½***

**613** A343 20r multicolored 2.25 1.50

Diplomatic relations between Nepal and US, 50th anniv.

### Personality Type of 1996

Designs: No. 614, Riddhi Bahadur Malla, writer. No. 615, Dr. K.I. Singh, political leader.

**1997, Nov. 6 Litho.** ***Perf. 11½***

| | | | | |
|---|---|---|---|---|
| **614** | A332 | 2r multicolored | .45 | .25 |
| **615** | A332 | 2r multicolored | .45 | .25 |

A344

Traditional Technology A345

#616, Janto (grinder), horiz. #617, Dhiki, horiz. #618, Okhal. #619, Kol (oil mill).

**1997, Dec. 29 Litho.** ***Perf. 14***

| | | | | |
|---|---|---|---|---|
| **616** | A344 | 5r multicolored | .60 | .35 |
| **617** | A344 | 5r multicolored | .60 | .35 |
| **618** | A344 | 5r multicolored | .60 | .35 |
| **619** | A345 | 5r multicolored | .60 | .35 |
| | | *Nos. 616-619 (4)* | 2.40 | 1.40 |

Flowers A346

40p, Jasminum gracile. 1r, Callistephus chinensis. 2r, Manglietia insignis. 15r, Luculia gratissima.

**1997, Dec. 11**

| | | | | |
|---|---|---|---|---|
| **620** | A346 | 40p multicolored | .25 | .25 |
| **621** | A346 | 1r multicolored | .25 | .25 |
| **622** | A346 | 2r multicolored | .35 | .25 |
| **623** | A346 | 15r multicolored | 2.00 | .90 |
| | | *Nos. 620-623 (4)* | 2.85 | 1.65 |

King Birendra, 52nd Birthday — A347

**1997, Dec. 29 Photo.** ***Perf. 11½***

| | | | | |
|---|---|---|---|---|
| **624** | A347 | 10r multicolored | 1.10 | .75 |

Visit Nepal '98 — A348

Designs: 2r, Sunrise, Shree Antudanda, Ilam. 10r, Maitidevi Temple, Kathmandu. 18r, Great Reunification Gate, Kapilavastu. 20r, Mt. Cholatse, Solukhumbu, vert.

**1998, May 8 Photo.** ***Perf. 11½***

| | | | | |
|---|---|---|---|---|
| **625** | A348 | 2r multicolored | .25 | .25 |
| **626** | A348 | 10r multicolored | 1.10 | .65 |
| **627** | A348 | 18r multicolored | 2.00 | 1.25 |
| **628** | A348 | 20r multicolored | 2.25 | 1.40 |
| | | *Nos. 625-628 (4)* | 5.60 | 3.55 |

Famous People — A349

Designs: 75p, Ram Prasad Rai, freedom fighter. 1r, Imansingh Chemjong, philologist. No. 631, Tulsi Meher Shrestha, social worker. No. 632, Dadhi Ram Marasini, Sanskrit expert. 5.40r, Mahananda Sapkota, linguist.

**1998, June 26 Litho.** ***Perf. 14x13½***

| | | | | |
|---|---|---|---|---|
| **629** | A349 | 75p brown & black | .25 | .25 |
| **630** | A349 | 1r rose lilac & black | .25 | .25 |
| **631** | A349 | 2r blue & black | .30 | .25 |
| **632** | A349 | 2r olive & black | .30 | .25 |
| **633** | A349 | 5.40r red & black | .65 | .30 |
| | | *Nos. 629-633 (5)* | 1.75 | 1.30 |

1998 World Cup Soccer Championships, France — A350

**1998, June 26** ***Perf. 14***

| | | | | |
|---|---|---|---|---|
| **634** | A350 | 12r multicolored | 1.50 | .85 |

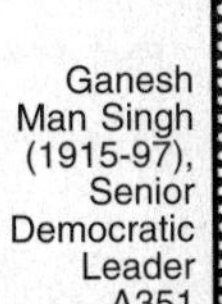

Ganesh Man Singh (1915-97), Senior Democratic Leader A351

**1998, Sept. 18 Photo.** ***Perf. 11½***

| | | | | |
|---|---|---|---|---|
| **635** | A351 | 5r multicolored | .60 | .35 |

A352

**1998, Oct. 9 Litho.** ***Perf. 13½x13***

| | | | | |
|---|---|---|---|---|
| **636** | A352 | 10r multicolored | 1.25 | .70 |

Peace Keeping Mission of the Royal Nepalese Army, 40th Anniv.

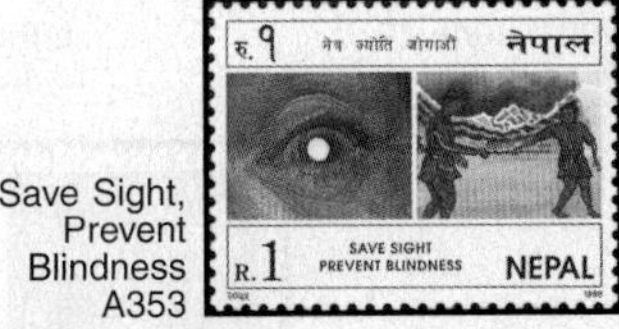


Save Sight, Prevent Blindness A353

**1998, Nov. 29 Photo.** ***Perf. 12***

**Granite Paper**

| | | | | |
|---|---|---|---|---|
| **637** | A353 | 1r multicolored | .40 | .25 |

Snakes A354

1.70r, King cobra. 2r, Golden tree snake. 5r, Asiatic rock python. 10r, Karan's pit viper.

**1998, Nov. 29 Litho.** ***Perf. 14***

| | | | | |
|---|---|---|---|---|
| **638** | A354 | 1.70r multicolored | .30 | .25 |
| **639** | A354 | 2r multicolored | .35 | .25 |
| **640** | A354 | 5r multicolored | .90 | .30 |
| **641** | A354 | 10r multicolored | 1.75 | .75 |
| | | *Nos. 638-641 (4)* | 3.30 | 1.55 |

Universal Declaration of Human Rights, 50th Anniv. A355

**1998, Dec. 10 Litho.** ***Perf. 14***

| | | | | |
|---|---|---|---|---|
| **642** | A355 | 10r multicolored | 1.10 | .65 |

A356

**1998, Dec. 27** ***Perf. 14x13½***

| | | | | |
|---|---|---|---|---|
| **643** | A356 | 10r multicolored | 1.10 | .60 |

Asian and Pacific Decade of Disabled Persons, 1993-2002.

A357

**1998, Dec. 29** ***Perf. 13x13½***

| | | | | |
|---|---|---|---|---|
| **644** | A357 | 2r multicolored | .40 | .25 |

King Birendra, 53rd birthday.

Marsyangdi Dam and Hydro-Electric Power Station — A358

**1998, Dec. 29** ***Perf. 11½***

**Granite Paper**

| | | | | |
|---|---|---|---|---|
| **645** | A358 | 12r multicolored | 1.35 | .85 |

Nepal Eye Hospital, 25th Anniv. A359

**1999, Apr. 8 Litho.** ***Perf. 14***

| | | | | |
|---|---|---|---|---|
| **646** | A359 | 2r multicolored | .50 | .40 |

Tourism A360

Designs: No. 647, Kalika Bhagawati Temple, Baglung. No. 648, Chandan Nath Temple, vert. 12r, Bajra Yogini Temple, Sankhu, vert. No. 650, Mt. Everest. No. 651, Lumbini Pillar Script translated into English.

**1999, June 7** ***Perf. 13½x13, 13x13½***

| | | | | |
|---|---|---|---|---|
| **647** | A360 | 2r multicolored | .35 | .25 |
| **648** | A360 | 2r multicolored | .35 | .25 |
| **649** | A360 | 12r multicolored | 1.75 | 1.10 |
| **650** | A360 | 15r multicolored | 2.00 | 1.25 |
| **651** | A360 | 15r multicolored | 2.00 | 1.25 |
| | | *Nos. 647-651 (5)* | 6.45 | 4.10 |

Tetracerus Quadricornis A361

No. 653, Ovis ammon hodgsonii.

**Granite Paper**

**1999, June 7 Photo.** ***Perf. 11¾***

| | | | | |
|---|---|---|---|---|
| **652** | A361 | 10r shown | 1.40 | .85 |
| **653** | A361 | 10r multicolored | 1.40 | .85 |

8th SAF Games, Kathmandu A362

***Perf. 13½x14¼***

**1999, Sept. 30 Litho.**

| | | | | |
|---|---|---|---|---|
| **654** | A362 | 10r multicolored | 1.40 | .85 |

UPU, 125th Anniv. — A363

**1999, Oct. 9** ***Perf. 13½***

| | | | | |
|---|---|---|---|---|
| **655** | A363 | 15r multicolored | 1.60 | 1.60 |

Famous People A364

Designs: No. 656, Ram Narayan Mishra (1922-67), freedom fighter. No. 657, Bhupi Sherchan (1935-89), poet. No. 658, Master Mitrasen (1895-1946), writer. No. 659, Rudra Raj Pandey (1901-87), writer. No. 660, Gopal Prasad Rimal (1917-73), writer. No. 661, Mangaladevi Singh (1924-96), politician.

**1999, Nov. 20 Litho.** ***Perf. 13¾***

| | | | | |
|---|---|---|---|---|
| **656** | A364 | 1r multicolored | .30 | .25 |
| **657** | A364 | 1r multicolored | .30 | .25 |
| **658** | A364 | 1r multicolored | .30 | .25 |
| **659** | A364 | 2r multicolored | .35 | .25 |
| **660** | A364 | 2r multicolored | .35 | .25 |
| **661** | A364 | 2r multicolored | .35 | .25 |
| | | *Nos. 656-661 (6)* | 1.95 | 1.50 |

Dances A365

**1999, Dec. 26 Litho.** ***Perf. 11¾x12***

| | | | | |
|---|---|---|---|---|
| **662** | A365 | 5r Sorathi | .75 | .45 |
| **663** | A365 | 5r Bhairav | .75 | .45 |
| **664** | A365 | 5r Jhijhiya | .75 | .45 |
| | | *Nos. 662-664 (3)* | 2.25 | 1.35 |

Intl. Labor Organization's Campaign Against Child Labor — A366

**1999, Dec. 29** ***Perf. 13½x14¼***
**665** A366 12r multi 1.60 1.00

A367

**1999, Dec. 29** ***Perf. 14¼x13½***
**666** A367 5r multi .70 .50

King Birendra's 54th birthday.

A368

**2000, Apr. 2 Photo.** ***Perf. 12x11¾***
**Granite Paper**
**667** A368 15r multi 2.00 1.75

Queen Aishwarya Rajya Laxmi Devi Shah, 50th birthday (in 1999).

Radio Nepal, 50th Anniv. A369

**2000, Apr. 2 Litho.** ***Perf. 13½x14¼***
**668** A369 2r multi .45 .25

Gorkhapatra Newspaper, Cent. — A370

**2000, May 5** ***Perf. 14***
**669** A370 10r multi 1.25 1.25

Tourism A371

Designs: 12r, Tchorolpa Glacial Lake, Dolakha. 15r, Dakshinkali Temple, Kathmandu. 18r, Annapurna.

**2000, June 30 Litho.** ***Perf. 13¾x14***
**670-672** A371 Set of 3 5.75 5.75

First ascent of Annapurna, 50th anniv. (No. 672).

Rani Pokhari and Temple, Kathmandu A372

Frame color: 50p, Orange. 1r, Blue. 2r, Brown.

**2000, July 7 Photo.** ***Perf. 11½***
**673-675** A372 Set of 3 .70 .70

Geneva Conventions, 50th Anniv. A373

**2000, Sept. 7 Litho.** ***Perf. 13½x14¼***
**676** A373 5r multi .75 .70

2000 Summer Olympics, Sydney A374

**2000, Sept. 7 Photo.** ***Perf. 11¾x12***
**Granite Paper**
**677** A374 25r multi 3.75 3.25

Famous People — A375

Designs: No. 678, 2r, Hridayachandra Singh Pradhan, writer (olive green frame). No. 679, 2r, Thir Bam Malla, revolutionary (brown frame). No. 680, 5r, Krishna Prasad Koirala, social reformer (indigo frame). No. 681, 5r, Manamohan Adhikari, politician (red frame).

**2000, Sept. 7 Litho.** ***Perf. 14***
**678-681** A375 Set of 4 1.70 1.70

Worldwide Fund for Nature (WWF) A376

#682, Bengal florican. #683, Lesser adjutant stork. #684, Female greater one-horned rhinoceros and calf. #685, Male greater one-horned rhinoceros.

**2000, Nov. 14 Photo.** ***Perf. 11¾***
**Granite Paper**
**682-685** A376 10r Set of 4 5.75 5.25

King Birendra's 55th Birthday — A377

**2000, Dec. 28 Photo.** ***Perf. 12x11¾***
**Granite Paper**
**686** A377 5r multi .80 .65

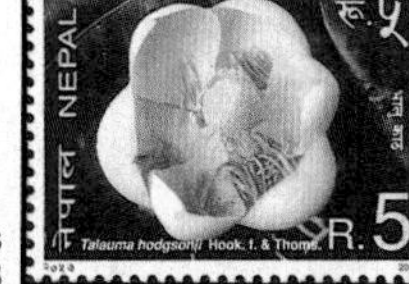

Flowers A378

Designs: No. 687, Talauma hodgsonii. No. 688, Mahonia napaulensis. No. 689, Dactylorhiza hatagirea, vert.

**2000, Dec. 28** ***Perf. 11¾x12, 12x11¾***
**Granite Paper**
**687-689** A378 5r Set of 3 2.60 2.10

Establishment of Democracy, 50th Anniv. A379

***Perf. 11¾x11½***
**2001, Feb. 16 Photo.**
**Granite Paper**
**690** A379 5r King Tribhuvan .80 .65

2001 Census A380

**2001, Apr. 17 Photo.** ***Perf. 11¾***
**Granite Paper**
**691** A380 2r multi .50 .25

Famous Nepalese — A381

Designs: No. 692, 2r, Khaptad Baba (bright pink background, white Nepalese numeral at UR), ascetic. No. 693, 2r, Bhikkhu Pragyananada Mahathera (red violet background), religious teacher. No. 694, 2r, Guru Prasad Mainali (pink background, red Nepalese numeral at UR), writer. No. 695, 2r, Tulsi Lal Amatya (brown violet background), politician. No. 696, 2r, Madan Lal Agrawal (light blue background), industrialist.

***Perf. 14¼x13½***
**2001, June 29 Litho.**
**692-696** A381 Set of 5 1.25 1.25

Ficus Religiosa — A382

**2001, Nov. 2 Litho.** ***Perf. 14¼x13½***
**697** A382 10r multi 1.40 1.40

UN High Commissioner for Refugees, 50th Anniv. — A383

**2001, Nov. 2** ***Perf. 14***
**698** A383 20r multi 2.75 2.50

Herbs — A384

Designs: 5r, Water pennywort. 15r, Rockfoil. 30r, Himalayan yew.

**2001, Nov. 2** ***Perf. 13¾***
**699-701** A384 Set of 3 7.50 7.50

Nepalese Flag — A385

**2001, Nov. 28** ***Perf. 14***
**702** A385 10r multi .50 .40

King Birendra (1945-2001) A386

**2001, Dec. 28** ***Perf. 14¼x13½***
**703** A386 15r multi 2.25 1.75

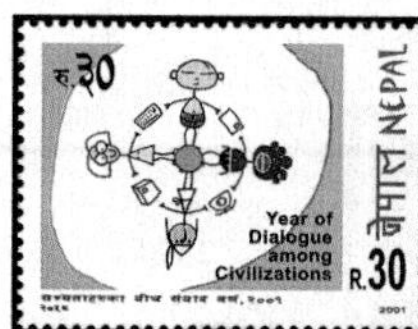

Year of Dialogue Among Civilizations A387

**2001, Dec. 28** ***Perf. 14***
**704** A387 30r multi 4.00 3.75

Tourism A388

Designs: 2r, Amargadi Fort. 5r, Hiranyavarna Mahavihar, vert. 15r, Jugal Mountain Range.

***Perf. 13½x14¼, 14¼x13½***
**2001, Dec. 28**
**705-707** A388 Set of 3 3.00 3.00

Nepal Scouts, 50th Anniv. — A389

**2002, Apr. 9 Litho.** ***Perf. 14¼x13½***
**708** A389 2r red brn & olive .50 .35

2002 World Cup Soccer Championships, Japan and Korea — A390

**2002, May 31 Litho.** ***Perf. 13½x12¾***
**709** A390 15r multi 2.10 2.10

King Gyanendra's Accession to Throne, 1st Anniv. — A391

**2002, June 5** ***Perf. 13¾***
**710** A391 5r multi .70 .70

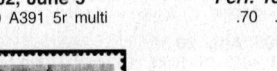

King Birendra (1945-2001) and Queen Aishwarya (1949-2001) A392

**2002, June 5** ***Perf. 14***
**711** A392 10r multi .80 .80

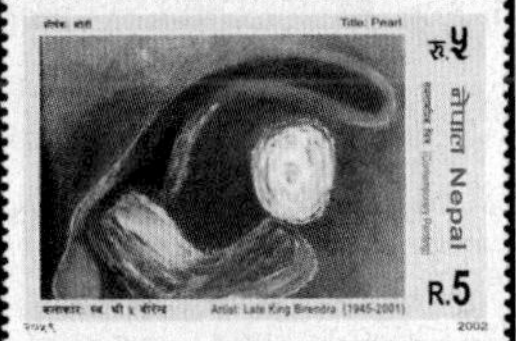
Paintings — A393

Designs: No. 712, 5r, Pearl, by King Birendra. No. 713, 5r, Aryabalokiteshwor, by Siddhimuni Shakya, vert.

***Perf. 13½x13¾, 13¾x13½***
**2002, July 29**
**712-713** A393 Set of 2 1.40 1.40

Insects — A394

Designs: 3r, Leaf beetle. 5r, Locust.

**2002, Sept. 6** ***Perf. 14***
**714-715** A394 Set of 2 1.25 1.25

Societal Messages A395

Designs: 1r, Untouchable family behind barbed wire (untouchables should not be discriminated against). 2r, Children and parents waving (female children should not be discriminated against).

**2002, Sept. 6** ***Perf. 14¼x14***
**716-717** A395 Set of 2 .70 .70

Intl. Year of Mountains — A396

**2002, Oct. 9 Litho.** ***Perf. 14***
**718** A396 5r multi .80 .65

Tourism A397

Designs: No. 719, 5r, Mt. Nilgiri, Mustang. No. 720, 5r, Pathibhara Devisthan, Taplejung. No. 721, 5r, Ramgram Stupa, Hawalparasi. No. 722, 5r, Galeshwor Mahadevsthan, Myagdi.

**2002, Oct. 9**
**719-722** A397 Set of 4 3.25 2.75

South Asian Association for Regional Cooperation Charter Day — A398

**2002, Dec. 8** ***Perf. 13½x12¾***
**723** A398 15r multi 2.00 1.60

Famous Men — A399

Designs: 2r, Dava Bir Singh Kansakar, social worker. 25r, Rev, Ekai Kawaguchi (1866-1945), Buddhist scholar.

**2002, Dec. 8** ***Perf. 13x13½***
**724-725** A399 Set of 2 3.00 3.00

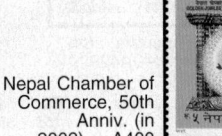

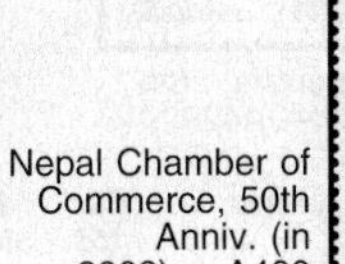
Nepal Chamber of Commerce, 50th Anniv. (in 2002) — A400

**2003, Apr. 10 Litho.** ***Perf. 14***
**726** A400 5r multi .60 .60

Industry and Commerce Day — A401

**2003, Apr. 11** ***Perf. 13½x12¾***
**727** A401 5r multi .60 .60

First Ascent of Mt. Everest, 50th Anniv. A402

**2003, May 29 Litho.** ***Perf. 13½x14¼***
**728** A402 25r multi 3.25 3.25

Babu Chiri Sherpa (1965-2001), Mountaineer — A403

**2003, June 27** ***Perf. 14***
**729** A403 5r multi .75 .60

King Gyanendra, 56th Birthday A404

**2003, July 7** ***Perf. 13½x14¼***
**730** A404 5r multi .75 .65

Tea Garden, Eastern Nepal A405

**2003, July 7** ***Perf. 14***
**731** A405 25r multi 3.00 3.00

Dr. Dilli Raman Regmi (1913-2001), Politician and Historian — A406

**2003, Aug. 31**
**732** A406 5r brown & blk .60 .60

Gopal Das Shrestha (1930-98), Journalist A407

**2003, Sept. 23 Litho.** ***Perf. 14***
**733** A407 5r multi .60 .60

Export Year 2003 — A408

**2003, Oct. 9** ***Perf. 13½x14***
**734** A408 25r multi 3.00 3.00

Sankhadhar Sakhwaa, Initiator of Nepalese Calendar A409

**2003, Oct. 26** ***Perf. 13½x12¾***
**735** A409 5r multi .60 .60

Flowers — A410

No. 736: a, Lotus. b, Picrorhiza. c, Himalayan rhubarb. d, Night jasmine.

***Perf. 14¼x13½***
**2003, Dec. 23 Litho.**
**736** A410 10r Block of 4, #a-d 4.25 4.25

Tourism A411

Designs: No. 737, 5r, Kali Gandaki "A" hydroelectric dam site. No. 738, 5r, Ganesh idol, Kageshwar, vert. 30r, Buddha icon, Swayambhunath.

**2003, Dec. 23** ***Perf. 14***
**737-739** A411 Set of 3 4.50 4.50

Social Services of United Mission to Nepal, 50th Anniv. — A412

**2004, Mar. 5 Litho.** ***Perf. 14***
**740** A412 5r multi .60 .60

National Society of Comprehensive Eye Care, 25th Anniv. — A413

**2004, Mar. 25**
**741** A413 5r multi .65 .65

Marwadi Sewa Samiti, 50th Anniv. A414

**2004, Apr. 9**
**742** A414 5r multi .65 .65

King Gyanendra, 57th Birthday — A415

**2004, July 7** **Litho.** ***Perf. 14***
**743** A415 5r multi .65 .65

Management Education, 50th Anniv. — A416

**2004, Sept. 24** **Litho.** ***Perf. 14***
**744** A416 5r multi .60 .60

Asia-Pacific Telecommunity, 25th Anniv. — A417

**2004, Sept. 24**
**745** A417 5r multi .65 .65

FIFA (Fédération Internationale de Football Association), Cent. — A418

**2004, Sept. 24**
**746** A418 20r multi 2.00 2.00

Mountains — A419

No. 747: a, Mt. Everest. b, Mt. Kanchenjunga Main. c, Mt. Lhotse. d, Mt. Makalu I. e, Mt. Cho Oyu. f, Mt. Dhaulagiri. g, Mt. Manasalu. h, Mt. Annapurna I.

**2004, Oct. 19** **Litho.** ***Perf. 14***
**747** A419 Block of 8 8.00 8.00
***a.-h.*** 10r Any single 1.00 1.00

Famous Men — A420

Designs: No. 748, 5r, Nayaraj Panta (1913-2002), historian. No. 749, 5r, Narahari Nath (1914-2003), yogi.

**2004, Nov. 3**
**748-749** A420 Set of 2 1.20 1.20

Flora and Fauna — A421

No. 750: a, Rufous piculet woodpecker. b, Giant atlas moth. c, Serma guru. d, High altitude rice.

**2004, Nov. 3**
**750** A421 10r Block of 4, #a-d 4.00 4.00

Mayadevi Temple, Lumbini A422

Gadhimai Temples, Bara A423

**2004, Nov. 30** ***Perf. 13½x13***
**751** A422 10r multi 1.40 1.00
**752** A423 10r multi 1.40 1.00

Madan Puraskar Trust, 50th Anniv. — A424

**2004, Dec. 13** ***Perf. 14***
**753** A424 5r multi .55 .55

Sculptures — A425

No. 754: a, Jayavarma. b, Umamaheshwar. c, Vishwarupa. d, Banshagopal.

**2004, Dec. 27** ***Perf. 13½***
**754** A425 10r Block of 4, #a-d 3.75 3.75

Nepal Rastra Bank, 50th Anniv. (in 2006) A426

**2005, Apr. 27** **Litho.** ***Perf. 14***
**755** A426 2r multi .60 .60

First Ascent of Mt. Makalu, 50th Anniv. — A427

**2005, May 15**
**756** A427 10r multi 1.00 1.00

First Ascent of Mt. Kanchanjunga, 50th Anniv. — A428

**2005, May 25**
**757** A428 12r multi 1.10 1.10

King Gyanendra, 58th Birthday — A429

**2005, July 7** **Litho.** ***Perf. 14***
**758** A429 5r multi .55 .55

Life of Buddha A430

No. 759: a, Birth at Lumbini. b, Enlightenment at Bodhagaya. c, First Sermon at Sarnath. d, Mahaparinirvana at Kushinagar.

**2005, July 21**
**759** Horiz. strip of 4, any background color 4.00 4.00
***a.-d.*** A430 10r Any single, any background color 1.00 1.00
Sheet of 4 horiz. strips 16.00 —

The sheet has four horizontal strips with background colors of yellow, green, red and purple.

Queen Mother Ratna Rajya Laxmi Devi Shah A431

**2005, Aug. 20**
**760** A431 20r multi 2.00 2.00

Fruits and Nuts — A432

No. 761: a, Indian gooseberry. b, Walnut. c, Wood apple. d, Golden evergreen raspberry.

**2005, Aug. 20**
**761** A432 10r Block of 4, #a-d 4.00 4.00

Mammals A433

No. 762: a, Gangetic dolphin. b, Indian pangolin. c, Asiatic wild elephant. d, Clouded leopard.

**2005, Aug. 31** **Litho.** ***Perf. 14***
**762** Horiz. strip of 4, any background color 4.00 4.00
***a.-d.*** A433 10r Any single, any background color 1.00 1.00
Sheet of 4 horiz. strips 16.00 —

The sheet has four horizontal strips with background colors of yellow, green, red and purple.

Late Bhupalmansingh Karki, Social Worker — A434

**2005, Sept. 24**
**763** A434 2r multi .60 .60

Tourism — A435

No. 764: a, Ghodaghodi Lake, Kailali. b, Budhasubba, Sunasari. c, Kalinchok Bhagawati, Dolakha. d, Panauti City, Kabhrepalanchok.

**2005, Oct. 9**
**764** A435 5r Block of 4, #a-d 2.00 2.00

Diplomatic Relations Between Nepal and People's Republic of China, 50th Anniv. — A436

**2005, Dec. 26**
**765** A436 30r multi 3.25 3.25

Admission to United Nations, 50th Anniv. A437

**2005, Dec. 26**
**766** A437 50r multi 5.50 5.50

Tribal Ornaments — A438

No. 767 — Ornaments of: a, Limbu tribes. b, Tharu tribes. c, Newar tribes. d, Sherpa tribes.

**2005, Dec. 26**
**767** A438 25r Block of 4, #a-d 11.00 11.00

King Tribhuvan (1906-55) A439

**2006, Feb. 17 Litho. *Perf. 13¼x13***
**768** A439 5r multi .55 .55

Democracy Day.

Queen Komal Rajya Laxmi Devi Shah — A440

**2006, Mar. 8**
**769** A440 5r multi .55 .55

Intl. Women's Day.

World Hindu Federation, 25th Anniv. — A441

**2006, Apr. 6 *Perf. 12¾***
**770** A441 2r multi .35 .35

First Ascent of Mt. Lhotse, 50th Anniv. A442

First Ascent of Mt. Manaslu, 50th Anniv. A443

**2006, May 9 *Perf. 13x13¼***
**771** A442 25r multi 2.50 2.50
**772** A443 25r multi 2.50 2.50

Supreme Court, 50th Anniv. A444

**2006, May 21**
**773** A444 5r multi .65 .65

Fauna, Flora and Mushrooms A445

Designs: No. 774, Imperial butterfly. No. 774A, Nepalese primrose. No., 774B, Chaffer beetle. No. 774C, Beautiful stream frog. No. 774D, White pine mushroom.

**2006, June 12 *Perf. 12¾***
**774-774D** Set of 5 5.50 5.50
*e.* Horiz. strip of 5, #774-774D 7.00 7.00

Nos. 774-774D were printed in sheets of 50 stamps, containing ten of each stamp, but containing only two horizontal strips of the stamps.

Diplomatic Relations Between Nepal and Russia, 50th Anniv. — A446

**2006, Aug. 22 *Perf. 13¼x13***
**775** A446 30r multi 1.75 1.75

Diplomatic Relations Between Nepal and Japan, 50th Anniv. A447

**2006, Sept. 1 *Perf. 13x13¼***
**776** A447 30r multi 1.75 1.75

Mt. Everest — A448

Stag Beetle — A449

**2006, Sept. 19 *Perf. 14¼x14***
**777** A448 1r blk & bl grn .25 .25
**778** A449 2r black .35 .35

***Perf. 14x13¾***
**Size: 29x25mm**

**779** A448 5r blk, pink & blue .55 .35
*Nos. 777-779 (3)* 1.15 .95

Membership in UPU, 50th Anniv. — A450

**2006, Oct. 9 *Perf. 13x13¼***
**780** A450 15r multi 1.00 1.00

Nepalese Postage Stamps, 125th Anniv. — A451

Designs: 5r, #1. 20r, #2. 100r, #3. 125r, #1-3.

**2006, Oct. 9 *Perf. 13¼***
**781-783** A451 Set of 3 7.50 7.50

**Size: 91x75mm**
***Imperf***

**784** A451 125r multi 7.50 7.50

No. 784 contains a perforated label that is not valid for postage showing Nepal #1-3.

Birth of Buddha, 2550th Anniv. — A452

**2006, Dec. 20 *Perf. 13¼x13***
**785** A452 30r multi 1.50 1.50

Chhatrapati Free Clinic, 50th Anniv. — A453

**2007, Feb. 6 Litho. *Perf. 13x13¼***
**786** A453 2r multi .55 .55

Mt. Everest A454

**2007, Mar. 14**
**787** A454 5r multi .80 .80

Miniature Sheet

Orchids — A455

No. 788: a, Satyrium nepalense. b, Dendrobium heterocarpum. c, Pelantheria insectifera. d, Coelogyne ovalis. e, Coelogyne cristata. f, Dendrobium chrysanthum. g, Phalaenopsis mannii. h, Dendrobium densiflorum. i, Esmeralda clarkei. j, Acampe rigida. k, Bulbophyllum leopardinum. l, Dendrobium fimbriatum. m, Arundina graminifolia. n, Dendrobium moschatum. o, Rhynchostylis retusa. p, Cymbidium devonianum.

**2007, Apr. 12**
**788** A455 10r Sheet of 16, #a-p 10.00 10.00

Sports A456

Designs: No. 789, 5r, Taekwondo. No. 790, 5r, Cricket.

**2007 *Perf. 13x13¼***
**789-790** A456 Set of 2 .90 .90

Issued: No. 789, 4/25; No. 790, 4/28.

Miniature Sheet

Martyrs of the Democratic Movement — A457

No. 791: a, Setu B. K. b, Tulasi Chhetri. c, Anil Lama. d, Umesh Chandra Thapa. e, Chakraraj Joshi. f, Chandra Bayalkoti. g, Devilal Poudel. h, Govindanath Sharma. i, Prof. Hari Raj Adhikari. j, Horilal Rana Tharu. k, Lal Bahadur Bista. l, Mohamad Jahangir. m, Pradhumna Khadka. n, Rajan Giri. o, Suraj Bishwas. p, Sagun Tamrakar. q, Bhimsen Dahal. r, Shivahari Kunwar. s, Basudev Ghimire. t, Bishnu Prasad Panday. u, Yamlal Lamichhane. v, Deepak Kami. w, Darshanial Yadab. x, Tahir Hussain Ansari. y, Hiralal Gautam.

**2007, June 4** ***Perf. 12½***
**791** A457 2r Sheet of 25, #a-y 5.00 5.00

Diplomatic Relations Between Nepal and Sri Lanka, 50th Anniv. A458

**2007, July 1** ***Perf. 13x13¼***
**792** A458 5r multi .50 .50

Diplomatic Relations Between Nepal and Egypt, 50th Anniv. A459

**2007, July 24**
**793** A459 5r multi .50 .50

Scouting, Cent. A460

**2007, Sept. 4**
**794** A460 2r multi .55 .55

Nepal Cancer Relief Society, 25th Anniv. A461

**2007, Sept. 17**
**795** A461 1r multi .45 .45

Nepalese Parliament Building and Documents — A462

No. 796, 1r: a, Reinstatement of the House of Representatives. b, Proclamation of the House of Representatives.

No. 797, 1r: a, Constitution of Legislature-Parliament. b, Interim Constitution of Nepal.

**2007, Dec. 28** **Litho.** ***Perf. 13x13¼***
**Horiz. Pairs, #a-b**
**796-797** A462 Set of 2 .90 .90

Chhaya Devi Parajuli (1918-2006), Politician — A463

**2007, Dec. 30**
**798** A463 2r multi .50 .50

Famous People — A464

No. 799, 5r: a, Shivapuri Baba (1862-1963), religious leader. b, Mahesh Chandra Regmi (1929-2003), writer.

No. 800, 5r: a, Princess Bhrikuti (617-49). b, Pundit Udayananda Arjyal, writer.

No. 801, 5r: a, Ganesh Lal Shrestha, musician. b, Tara Devi (1945-2006), singer.

**2007, Dec. 30** **Litho.**
**Horiz. Pairs, #a-b**
**799-801** A464 Set of 3 3.00 3.00

Tourism A465

No. 802: a, Mt. Abi. b, Shree Bhageshwor Temple, Dadeldhura. c, Shree Shaillya Malikarjun Temple, Darchula. d, Shiddakali Temple, Bhojpur. e, Buddha's Victory over the Mara.

**2007, Dec. 30**
**802** Vert. strip of 5 2.00 2.00
*a.-e.* A465 5r Any single .35 .35

Diplomatic Relations Between Nepal and Germany, 50th Anniv. A466

**2008, Apr. 2** **Litho.** ***Perf. 13x13¼***
**803** A466 25r multi 1.50 1.50

Nativity of Buddha — A467

**2008, July 18** ***Perf. 13¼x13***
**804** A467 2r multi 1.00 1.00

Nepal Coat of Arms — A468

**2008, Aug. 21**
**805** A468 1r multi .50 .50

2008 Summer Olympics, Beijing — A469

**2008, Aug. 21** ***Perf. 12¾***
**806** A469 15r multi 1.00 1.00

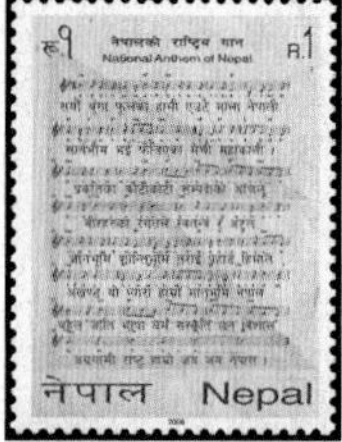

National Anthem and Flag of Nepal — A470

**2008, Nov. 13** **Litho.** ***Perf. 13¼x13***
**807** A470 1r multi .60 .60

Kaiser Library, Cent. A471

**2008, Nov. 13** ***Perf. 13x13¼***
**808** A471 5r multi .50 .50

Dr. Harka Gurung (1935-2006), Minister of Tourism, and Dr. Harka Gurung Peak — A472

**2008, Dec. 24** **Litho.**
**Granite Paper**
**809** A472 5r multi .60 .60

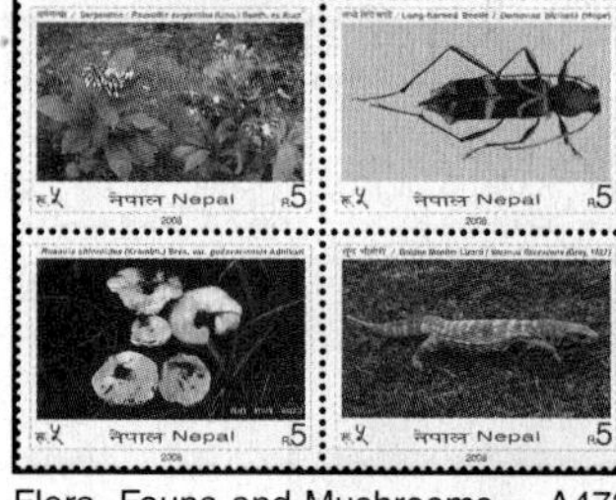

Flora, Fauna and Mushrooms — A473

No. 810: a, Serpentine. b, Long-horned beetle. c, Russula chloroides. d, Golden monitor lizard.

**2008, Dec. 24** ***Perf. 13x13¼***
**Granite Paper**
**810** A473 Block or horiz. strip of 4, #a-d 9.00 9.00
*a.-d.* 5r Any single .50 .50

Tourism A474

No. 811: a, Mustang village, Mustang District. b, Syarpu Lake, Rukum District. c, Jaljala Hill, Rolpa District. d, Pindeswor Babadham, Dharan. e, Shree Kumair Chariot Festival, Kathmandu.

**2008, Dec. 24** **Litho.**
**Granite Paper**
**811** Vert. strip of 5 3.25 3.25
*a.-e.* A474 5r Any single .45 .45

Family Planning Association of Nepal, 50th Anniv. A475

**2009, Sept. 14** **Litho.** ***Perf. 13x13¼***
**Granite Paper**
**812** A475 1r multi .35 .35

Office of Auditor General, 50th Anniv. A476

**2009, Sept. 14** ***Perf. 13x13¼***
**Granite Paper**
**813** A476 5r multi .60 .60

Tribhuvan University, 50th Anniv. A477

**2009, Sept. 14** **Litho.**
**Granite Paper**
**814** A477 5r multi .60 .60

Birthplace of Buddha UNESCO World Heritage Site, Lumbini A478

No. 815: a, Nativity sculpture and marker stone. b, Holy Pond. c, Asoka pillar. d, Excavated stupas. e, Mayadevi Temple.

**2009, Sept. 14** ***Perf. 13x13¼***
**Granite Paper**
**815** Horiz. strip of 5 4.50 4.50
*a.-e.* A478 10r Any single .50 .50

Establishment of Federal Democratic Republic — A479

**2009, Oct. 8** **Granite Paper** **Litho.**
**816** A479 2r multi 1.00 1.00

Miniature Sheet

Butterflies — A480

No. 817: a, Common Apollo. b, Striped blue crow. c, Common yellow swallowtail. d, Swinhoe's nawab. e, Great satyr. f, Large cabbage white. g, Common tiger. h, Common brimstone. i, Yellow orange tip. j, Glassy blue bottle. k, Banded Apollo. l, Blue admiral. m, Lime swallowtail. n, Red Helen. o, Spot swordtail. p, Green sapphire.

**2009, Oct. 8** ***Perf. 13x13¼***
**Granite Paper**

**817** A480 10p Sheet of 16, #a-p 11.00 11.00

Govinda Biyogi (1929-2006), Journalist A481

**2009, Nov. 2** ***Perf. 13¾x13½***
**Granite Paper**

**818** A481 5r multi .60 .60

Guruji Mangal Das (1896-1985), Religious Leader — A482

**2009, Nov. 9** **Granite Paper** **Litho.**

**819** A482 5r multi .50 .50

Art — A483

No. 820: a, Tej Bahadur Chitrakar (1898-1971), painter. b, Tribute to the Forefathers, painting by Chitrakar.

**2009, Dec. 5** ***Perf. 13½x13¼***
**Granite Paper**

**820** A483 5r Horiz. pair, #a-b .90 .90

Ramesh Vikal (1928-2008), Writer — A484

**2009, Dec. 27** ***Perf. 13¼x13½***
**Granite Paper**

**821** A484 2r multi .60 .60

Krishna Sen Ichhuk (1956-2002), Journalist A485

**2009, Dec. 27** ***Perf. 13½x13¼***
**Granite Paper**

**822** A485 5r multi .50 .50

Laxmi Prasad Devkota (1909-59), Poet A486

**2009, Dec. 31** ***Perf. 13¼x13½***
**Granite Paper**

**823** A486 1r multi .60 .60

Chhath Festival A487

**2009, Dec. 31** **Litho.**
**Granite Paper**

**824** A487 5r multi .60 .60

Lahurya Folk Dance A488

**2009, Dec. 31** ***Perf. 13¼x13½***
**Granite Paper**

**825** A488 5r multi .65 .65

Kayaking A489

**2009, Dec. 31**

**826** A489 10r multi .80 .80

Mountain Biking A490

**2009, Dec. 31**

**827** A490 10r multi .80 .80

Nepal Television, 25th Anniv. — A491

**2010, Jan. 31** ***Perf. 13½x13¼***

**828** A491 2r multi .50 .50

Worldwide Fund for Nature (WWF) — A492

***Perf. 13¼x13½***

**2010, Sept. 14** **Litho.**

**829** A492 5r multi .75 .75

New Year 2010 (Year of the Tiger).

First Ascent of Mt. Dhaulagiri, 50th Anniv. — A493

**2010, Sept. 26**

**830** A493 25r multi 1.75 1.75

Pemba Doma Sherpa (1970-2007), Mountaineer — A494

**2010, Sept. 26**

**831** A494 25r multi 1.75 1.75

Kankalini Mai Temple A495

**2010, Dec. 1** **Litho.**

**832** A495 2r multi .55 .55

Maru Ganesh Temple A496

**2010, Dec. 1**

**833** A496 2r multi .50 .50

Bhairab Aryal (1936-76), Writer A497

**2010, Dec. 1**

**834** A497 5r multi .50 .50

Natikaji Shrestha (1925-2003), Musician — A498

**2010, Dec. 1** ***Perf. 13½x13¼***

**835** A498 5r multi .50 .50

Jibraj Ashrit (1944-93), Politician A499

**2010, Dec. 1** ***Perf. 13¼x13½***

**836** A499 5r multi .50 .50

Bhagat Sarbajit Bishwokarma (1893-1955), Social Reformer A500

**2010, Dec. 5** ***Perf. 13½x13¼***

**837** A500 5r multi .50 .50

Mahasthabir Bhikshu Amritandanda (1918-90), Religious Leader — A501

**2010, Dec. 7** ***Perf. 13¼x13½***

**838** A501 5r multi .50 .50

Sadhana Adhikari (1925-2005), Politician — A502

**2010, Dec. 9** **Litho.**

**839** A502 5r multi .50 .50

Mai Pokhari Lake A503

**2010, Dec. 12**

**840** A503 2r multi .60 .60

Global Handwashing Day — A504

**2010, Dec. 30**
**841** A504 2r multi .50 .50

Nepal Tourism Year (in 2011) A505

**2010, Dec. 30**
**842** A505 5r multi .55 .55

Stamps and Postmarks — A506

Designs: No. 843, 1r, Nepal #1, 1881 Kathmandu postmark. No. 844, 1r, Nepal #27, 1910 Birganj postmark. No. 845, 2r, Nepal #26, 1915 Bethari postmark. No. 846, 2r, Nepal postal stationery indicia, 1934 Kanchanpur postmark. 3r, Nepal #53, 1952 Tamghas / Gulmi postmark.

**2011, June 13** ***Perf. 13¼x13½***
**843-847** A506 Set of 5 1.00 1.00

Turtles A507

No. 848: a, Ganges softshell turtle. b, Tricarinate Hill turtle. c, Elongated tortoise. d, Common roofed turtle.

**2011, Aug. 28** ***Perf. 13¾x13½***
**Granite Paper**
**848** Horiz. strip or block of 4 2.00 2.00
***a.-d.*** A507 10r Any single .40 .40

Mohan Gopal Khetan (1947-2007), Industrialist — A508

**2011, Nov. 22** **Litho.**
**Granite Paper**
**849** A508 5r multi .50 .50

Yagyaraj Sharma Aryjal (1903-89), Musician — A509

**2011, Nov. 23** ***Perf. 13¾x13½***
**Granite Paper**
**850** A509 10r multi .60 .60

Shankar Lamichhane (1928-76), Writer — A510

**2011, Nov. 23** ***Perf. 13½x13¾***
**Granite Paper**
**851** A510 10r multi .60 .60

Ekdev Aale (1923-68), Politician A511

**2011, Nov. 23** **Litho.**
**Granite Paper**
**852** A511 10r multi .60 .60

Motidevi Shrestha (1913-97), Politician A512

**2011, Nov. 23** ***Perf. 13½x13¾***
**Granite Paper**
**853** A512 10r multi .60 .60

Rishikesh Shaha (1925-2002), Human Rights Activist — A513

**2011, Dec. 9** **Granite Paper**
**854** A513 5r multi .60 .60

Religious Sites A514

Designs: 1r, Badimalika, Bajura. No. 856, 2r, Tansen Bhagawati, Palpa. No. 857, 2r, Siddha Ratannath Temple, Dang. No. 858, 2r, Deuti Bajai, Surkhet. No. 859, 2r, Bhat Bhateni Mai, Kathmandu. No. 860, 5r, Shree Baidhyanath Temple, Achham. No. 861, 5r, Gajurmukhi Dham, Ilam. 25r, Yetser Jangchubling Monastery, Upper Dolpa.

No. 863, 2r, vert.: a, Shree Aryavalokiteswora Seto Machhindranath, Kathmandu. b, Shree Aryavalokiteswora Seto Machhindranath Rath, Kathmandu.

**2011, Dec. 30** ***Perf. 13¾x13½***
**Granite Paper**
**855-862** A514 Set of 8 4.00 4.00
***Perf. 13½x13¾***
**863** A514 2r Horiz. pair, #a-b .70 .70

Nepalese Landscapes — A515

Designs: No. 864, 10r, Panch Pokhari, Sindhupalchok. No. 865, 10r, Mt. Mera Peak. No. 866, 10r, Badaiya Taal, Bardiya.

**2011, Dec. 30** ***Perf. 13¾x13½***
**Granite Paper**
**864-866** A515 Set of 3 1.50 1.50

A516

A517

A518

Cave Murals, Upper Mustang A519

**2011, Dec. 30** **Litho.**
**Granite Paper**
**867** Horiz. strip of 4 2.00 2.00
***a.*** A516 10r multi .40 .30
***b.*** A517 10r multi .40 .30
***c.*** A518 10r multi .40 .30
***d.*** A519 10r multi .40 .30

Ramesh Kumar Mahato, Martyr — A520

**2012, Jan. 19** ***Perf. 13½x13¾***
**Granite Paper**
**868** A520 10r multi .50 .50
Dated 2011.

Gajendra Narayan Singh (1929-2002), Politician A521

**2012, Jan. 19** **Litho.**
**Granite Paper**
**869** A521 10r multi .50 .50
Dated 2011.

Girija Prasad Koirala (1924-2010), Prime Minister — A522

**2012, Feb. 11** ***Perf. 13¾x13½***
**Granite Paper**
**870** A522 10r multi .50 .50
Dated 2011.

Nepalese National News Agency, 50th Anniv. — A523

**2012, Feb. 19** ***Perf. 13½x13¾***
**Granite Paper**
**871** A523 10r multi .60 .60

Nepali Shikshya Parishad (Organization Promoting Nepalese Language Education), 60th Anniv. — A524

**2012, July 29** **Granite Paper**
**872** A524 5r multi .60 .60

Biodiversity — A525

No. 873: a, Delphinium himalayai. b, Dendrobium eriiflorum. c, Podophyllum hexandrum. d, Ganodermna lucidum. e, Prinia burnesii nepalicola. f, Gyps bengalensis. g, Caprolagus hispidus. h, Cyrtopodion markuscombaii.

**2012, July 29** **Granite Paper**
**873** A525 10r Block of 8, #a-h 4.50 4.50

Dead Sea, Mt. Everest, Flags of Israel and Nepal — A526

**2012, Sept. 4** ***Perf. 13½x13¾***
**Granite Paper**
**874** A526 35r multi 2.00 2.00
**Souvenir Sheet**
**875** A526 50r multi 4.50 4.50

See Israel No. 1944.

B.P. Koirala Museum, Kathmandu, 8th Anniv. — A527

**2012, Sept. 10** ***Perf. 13¾x13½***
**Granite Paper**
**876** A527 10r multi .70 .70

Lions International Blindness Prevention Campaign — A528

**2012, Sept. 25** **Litho.**
**Granite Paper**
**877** A528 5r multi .50 .50

World AIDS Day — A529

**2012, Dec. 13** ***Perf. 13½x13¾***
**Granite Paper**
**878** A529 5r multi .45 .45

Mt. Everest A530

**2012, Dec. 13** ***Perf. 13¾x13½***
**Granite Paper**
**879** A530 10r multi .75 .75

Asian-Pacific Postal Union, 50th Anniv. — A531

**2012, Dec. 13** **Granite Paper**
**880** A531 35r multi 2.00 2.00

Intl. Year of Cooperatives — A532

**2012, Dec. 24** **Litho.**
**Granite Paper**
**881** A532 20r multi 1.25 1.25

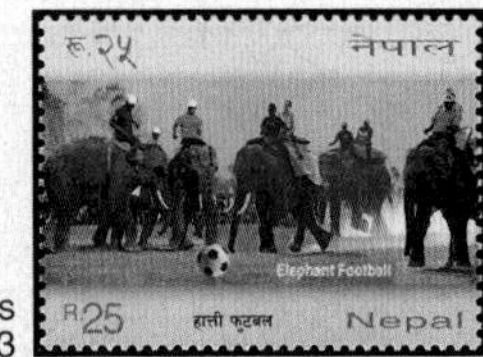

Sports A533

Designs: No. 882, 25r, Elephant soccer. No. 883, 25r, Bungee jumping, vert.

***Perf. 13¾x13½, 13½x13¾***
**2012, Dec. 28** **Granite Paper**
**882-883** A533 Set of 2 2.50 2.50

Krishna Prasad Bhattarai (1924-2011), Prime Minister — A534

**2012, Dec. 23** ***Perf. 13¾x13½***
**884** A534 10r multi .60 .60

Bhikshu Sudarshan (1938-2002), Monk — A535

***Perf. 13¾x13½***
**2012, Dec. 31** **Litho.**
**885** A535 5r multi .50 .50

Basudev Luintel, Writer A536

***Perf. 13¾x13½***
**2012, Dec. 31** **Litho.**
**886** A536 5r black .50 .50

Ali Miyan, Poet A537

***Perf. 13¾x13½***
**2012, Dec. 31** **Litho.**
**Granite Paper**
**887** A537 10r multi .50 .50

Ramniwas Pandeya, Educator — A538

***Perf. 13¾x13½***
**2012, Dec. 31** **Litho.**
**Granite Paper**
**888** A538 10r multi .50 .50

Bhuvaneswor Patheya, Writer — A539

***Perf. 13¾x13½***
**2012, Dec. 31** **Litho.**
**Granite Paper**
**889** A539 10r multi .50 .50

Khagendra Bahadur Basnet, Activist for Rights of the Disabled — A540

***Perf. 13¾x13½***
**2012, Dec. 31** **Litho.**
**Granite Paper**
**890** A540 10r multi .50 .50

Kishore and Kumar Narsingh Rama, Architects A541

***Perf. 13¾x13½***
**2012, Dec. 31** **Litho.**
**Granite Paper**
**891** A541 10r multi .50 .50

Karuna (1920-2008) and Lupau Ratna Tuladhar (1918-93), Operators of First Public Bus Service in Nepal — A542

***Perf. 13¾x13½***
**2012, Dec. 31** **Litho.**
**Granite Paper**
**892** A542 10r multi .50 .50

Visit Lumbini Year A543

***Perf. 13¾x13½***
**2012, Dec. 31** **Litho.**
**Granite Paper**
**893** A543 20r multi 1.00 1.00

Rajmansingh Chitrakar (1797-1865), Painter — A544

No. 894 — Chitrakar and his paintings of: a, Tibetan antelopes. b, Birds.

***Perf. 13¾x13½***
**2012, Dec. 31** **Litho.**
**Granite Paper**
**894** A544 10r Horiz. pair, #a-b 1.00 1.00

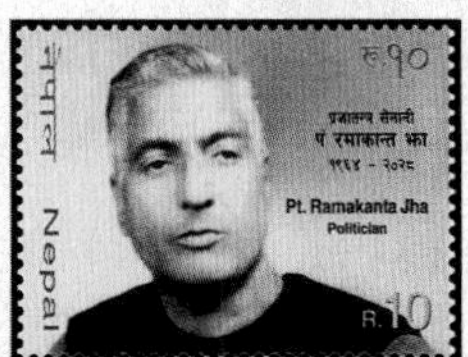

Pandit Ramakanta Jha, Politician — A545

**2013, Jan. 18** **Litho.** ***Perf. 13¾x13½***
**895** A545 10r multi .55 .55

Nepalese Partnership With World Bank Group, 50th Anniv. — A546

***Perf. 13¾x13½***
**2013, Mar. 18** **Litho.**
**Granite Paper**
**896** A546 10r multi .60 .60

Melwa Devi Gurung (1898-1955), Singer — A547

***Perf. 13¾x13½***
**2013, June 10** **Litho.**
**Granite Paper**
**897** A547 5r multi .50 .50

Lake Salpa A548

Lomanthang Durbar — A549

Salhes Garden, Lok Nayak Raja Salhes A550

Sahashra Dhara Jatra Festival — A551

***Perf. 13¾x13½***

**2013, June 10** **Litho.**

**Granite Paper**

| | | | | |
|---|---|---|---|---|
| **898** | A548 | 10r multi | .60 | .60 |
| **899** | A549 | 10r multi | .60 | .60 |
| **900** | A550 | 10r multi | .60 | .60 |

***Perf. 13½x13¾***

| | | | | |
|---|---|---|---|---|
| **901** | A551 | 10r multi | .60 | .60 |
| | | *Nos. 898-901 (4)* | 2.40 | 2.40 |

Ramraja Prasad Singh (1935-2012), Politician — A552

Moti Kaji Shakya (1913-97), Sculptor A553

Bhimbahadur Tamang (1933-2012), Politician — A554

Basudev Prasad Dhungana (1933-2012), Advocate for Senior Citizens — A555

Harihar Gautam (1901-65), Social Worker — A556

Gopal Pande (1913-78), Writer — A557

**2013, Oct. 9** **Litho.** ***Perf. 13¾x13½***

**Granite Paper**

| | | | | |
|---|---|---|---|---|
| **902** | A552 | 10r multi | .55 | .55 |
| **903** | A553 | 10r multi | .55 | .55 |
| **904** | A554 | 10r multi | .55 | .55 |
| **905** | A555 | 10r multi | .55 | .55 |

***Perf. 13½x13¾***

| | | | | |
|---|---|---|---|---|
| **906** | A556 | 10r multi | .55 | .55 |
| **907** | A557 | 10r multi | .55 | .55 |
| | | *Nos. 902-907 (6)* | 3.30 | 3.30 |

Nepal Red Cross Society, 50th Anniv. A558

**2013, Oct. 9** **Litho.** ***Perf. 13¾x13½***

**Granite Paper**

| | | | | |
|---|---|---|---|---|
| **908** | A558 | 50r multi | 2.25 | 2.25 |

Batsaladevi Bhagawali, Dhadhing — A559

**2013, Oct. 30** **Litho.** ***Perf. 13¾x13½***

| | | | | |
|---|---|---|---|---|
| **909** | A559 | 1r multi | .65 | .65 |

Rupchandra Bista (1933-99), Politician — A560

Kewalpure Kisan (1926-2011), Poet — A561

Rupak Raj Sharma (1954-92), Soccer Player A562

Ram Sharan Darnal (1937-2011), Music Researcher — A563

Diamond Shumsher Rana (1919-2011), Writer — A564

**2013, Oct. 30** **Litho.** ***Perf. 13¾x13½***

| | | | | |
|---|---|---|---|---|
| **910** | A560 | 5r multi | .40 | .40 |

**Granite Paper**

| | | | | |
|---|---|---|---|---|
| **911** | A561 | 5r multi | .40 | .40 |
| **912** | A562 | 10r multi | .65 | .65 |
| **913** | A563 | 10r multi | .65 | .65 |
| **914** | A564 | 20r multi | 1.25 | 1.25 |
| | | *Nos. 910-914 (5)* | 3.35 | 3.35 |

Bagalamukhi Devi, Lalitpur — A565

Rajdevi Temple, Saptari A566

Ivory Window, Hanumandhoka Palace, Kathmandu — A567

Kakre Bihar, Surkhet A568

Argha Bhagawati, Arghakhanchi — A569

**2013, Dec. 31** **Litho.** ***Perf. 13¼***

**Granite Paper**

| | | | | |
|---|---|---|---|---|
| **915** | A565 | 1r multi | .50 | .50 |
| **916** | A566 | 1r multi | .50 | .50 |
| **917** | A567 | 5r multi | .50 | .50 |
| **918** | A568 | 5r multi | .50 | .50 |
| **919** | A569 | 5r multi | .50 | .50 |
| | | *Nos. 915-919 (5)* | 2.50 | 2.50 |

Shankar Koirala (1930-97), Writer — A570

Ramhari Sharma (1916-2012), Politician A571

Bhanubhakta Acharya (1814-68), Poet — A572

Dr. Dilliraman Regmi (1913-2001), Historian — A573

**2013, Dec. 31** **Litho.** ***Perf. 13¼***

**Granite Paper**

| | | | | |
|---|---|---|---|---|
| **920** | A570 | 3r multi | .50 | .50 |
| **921** | A571 | 3r multi | .50 | .50 |
| **922** | A572 | 10r multi | .60 | .60 |
| **923** | A573 | 10r multi | .60 | .60 |
| | | *Nos. 920-923 (4)* | 2.20 | 2.20 |

Museums A574

Designs: No. 924, 20r, National Art Museum, Bhaktapur. No. 925, 20r, International Mountain Museum, Kaski. No. 926, 20r, Patan Museum, Patan. 35r, National Museum, Chhauni.

**2013, Dec. 31** **Litho.** ***Perf. 13¼***

**Granite Paper**

| | | | | |
|---|---|---|---|---|
| **924-927** | A574 | Set of 4 | 5.25 | 5.25 |

Kathmandu Valley World Heritage Property — A575

Designs: No. 928, 25r, Bhaktapur Durbar Square Monument Zone. No. 929, 25r, Baud-dhanath Monument Zone. No. 930, 25r, Changu Narayan Monument Zone. No. 931, 30r, Swayambhu Monument Zone. No. 932, 30r, Hanumandhoka Durbar Square Monument Zone. No. 933, 30r, Pashupati Monument Zone. No. 934, 30r, Patan Durbar Square Monument Zone.

**2013, Dec. 31 Litho. *Perf. 13¼***
**Granite Paper**

**928-934** A575 Set of 7 10.00 10.00

Rara Lake, Mugu A576

**2013, Dec. 31 Litho. *Perf. 13¼***
**Granite Paper**

**935** A576 40r multi 2.25 2.25

Flora A577

Designs: No. 936, 40r, Wild asparagus. No. 937, 40r, Chireta. No. 938, 40r, Long pepper. No. 939, 40r, Fragrant wintergreen.

**2013, Dec. 31 Litho. *Perf. 13¼***
**Granite Paper**

**936-939** A577 Set of 4 9.00 9.00

Extinct Animals and Their Fossils A578

Designs: No. 940, 50r, Giraffa punjabensis and fossil molar teeth. No. 941, 50r, Ramapithecus sivalensis and fossil molar teeth. No. 942, 50r, Hexaprotodon sivalensis and fossil skull. No. 943, 50r, Archidiskidon planifrons and fossil skull.

**2013, Dec. 31 *Perf. 13¼***
**Granite Paper**

**940-943** A578 Set of 4 10.00 10.00

Ascent of Mt. Everest, 60th Anniv, A579

**2013, Dec. 31 Litho. *Perf. 13¼***
**Granite Paper**

**944** A579 100r multi 5.50 5.50

Rishikesh Temple, Ridi A580

**2014, Oct. 9 Litho. *Perf. 13¼***
**Granite Paper**

**945** A580 5r multi .50 .50

Narayanhiti Palace Museum, Kathmandu — A581

**2014, Oct. 9 Litho. *Perf. 13¼***
**Granite Paper**

**946** A581 20r multi 1.00 1.00

Scouting in Nepal, 60th Anniv. — A582

**2014, Oct. 9 Litho. *Perf. 13¼***
**Granite Paper**

**947** A582 30r multi 2.00 2.00

Ascent of Mt. Cho-Oyu, 60th Anniv. A583

**2014, Oct. 9 Litho. *Perf. 13¼***
**Granite Paper**

**948** A583 100r multi 5.50 5.50

Manakamana Cable Car — A584

**2014, Oct. 30 Litho. *Perf. 13¼***
**Granite Paper**

**949** A584 50r multi 3.00 3.00

Junior Chamber International of Nepal, 50th Anniv. — A585

**2014, Nov. 11 Litho. *Perf. 13¼***
**Granite Paper**

**950** A585 10r multi .50 .50

Kathmandu Buildings A586

Designs: 1r, Shivaparbati Temple. 2r, Kumari Ghar.

**2014, Dec. 9 Litho. *Perf. 13¼***
**Granite Paper**

**951-952** A586 Set of 2 .80 .80

Natural History Museum, Kathmandu A587

**2014, Dec. 9 Litho. *Perf. 13¼***
**Granite Paper**

**953** A587 1r multi .35 .35

Aadeshwor Mahadev, Kathmandu A588

**2014, Dec. 9 Litho. *Perf. 13¼***
**Granite Paper**

**954** A588 1r multi .35 .35

2014 International Cricket Council World Twenty 20 Competition, Bangladesh A589

**2014, Dec. 9 Litho. *Perf. 13¼***
**Granite Paper**

**955** A589 2r multi .35 .35

Female Community Health Volunteers Program, 25th Anniv. (in 2013) — A590

**2014, Dec. 9 Litho. *Perf. 13¼***
**Granite Paper**

**956** A590 3r multi .35 .35

Koteshwor Mahadev, Kathmandu A591

**2014, Dec. 9 Litho. *Perf. 13¼***
**Granite Paper**

**957** A591 4r multi .45 .45

Prem Bahadur Kansakar (1917-91), Social Worker — A592

**2014, Dec. 9 Litho. *Perf. 13¼***
**Granite Paper**

**958** A592 5r multi .50 .50

Paragliding, Kaski — A593

**2014, Dec. 9 Litho. *Perf. 13¼***
**Granite Paper**

**959** A593 10r multi .55 .55

Miniature Sheets

Moths — A594

No. 960, 10r: a, Acherontia lachesis. b, Asota producta. c, Argina argus. d, Biston contectaria.

No. 961, 10r: a, Brahmaea wallichii. b, Campylotes histrionicus. c, Dermaleipa (Lagoptera) juno. d, Episteme adulatrix.

No. 962, 10r: a, Erasmia pulchella. b, Eterusia aedea edocla. c, Eudocima salaminia. d, Gynautocera papilionaria.

**2014, Dec. 9 Litho. *Perf. 13¼***
**Granite Paper**
**Sheets of 4, #a-d**

**960-962** A594 Set of 3 6.75 6.75

Miniature Sheet

Birthplace of Buddha — A595

No. 963: a, Birthplace of Lord Buddha, Lumbini. b, Ashoka Pillar, Lumbini. c, Ramagrama, Nawalparasi. d, Tilaurakot, Kapilavastu.

**2014, Dec. 9 Litho. *Perf. 13¼***
**Granite Paper**

**963** A595 20r Sheet of 4, #a-d 4.00 4.00

2014 Winter Olympics, Sochi, Russia — A596

**2014, Dec. 10 Litho. *Perf. 13¼***
**Granite Paper**

**964** A596 2r multi .50 .50

Tenzing-Hillary Everest Marathon A597

**2014, Dec. 19 Litho. *Perf. 13¼***
**Granite Paper**

**965** A597 3r multi .40 .40

B. P. Koirala (1914-82), Prime Minister — A598

**2014, Dec. 31 Litho. *Perf. 13¼***
**Granite Paper**

**966** A598 10r multi .40 .40

Dwarika Bhakta Mathema (1902-68), Musician — A599

**2015, July 1 Litho. *Perf. 13¼***
**Granite Paper**

**967** A599 1r multi .25 .25

Chandeshwori Temple, Banepa — A600

Makwanpur Gadhi, Makwanpur — A601

Lamjung Durbar, Lamjung A602

Siddha Pokhari, Bhaktapur A603

Doleshwor Mahadev, Bhaktapur — A604

Sindhuli Gadhi, Sindhuli A605

Kaliyadaman, Sundari Chowk, Hanumandhoka — A606

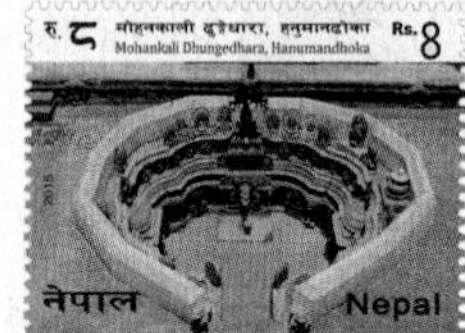

Mohankali Dhungedhara, Hanumandhoka — A607

Taleju Temple, Nuwakot A608

Bulbule Lake, Surkhet A609

**2015, July 1 Litho. *Perf. 13¼***
**Granite Paper**

| | | | | |
|---|---|---|---|---|
| **968** | A600 | 1r multi | .25 | .25 |
| **969** | A601 | 1r multi | .25 | .25 |
| **970** | A602 | 2r multi | .25 | .25 |
| **971** | A603 | 2r multi | .25 | .25 |
| **972** | A604 | 5r multi | .25 | .25 |
| **973** | A605 | 5r multi | .25 | .25 |
| **974** | A606 | 5r multi | .25 | .25 |
| **975** | A607 | 8r multi | .25 | .25 |
| **976** | A608 | 10r multi | .25 | .25 |
| **977** | A609 | 10r multi | .25 | .25 |
| | | *Nos. 968-977 (10)* | 2.50 | 2.50 |

Fewa Lake and Machhapuchchhre, Kaski — A610

***Serpentine Die Cut 12¼***
**2015, July 1 Litho.**
**Self-Adhesive**

**978** A610 60r multi 1.25 1.25

A611

A612

A613

B.P. Koirala Highway, Flags of Nepal and Japan A614

**2015, July 1 Litho. *Perf. 13¼***
**Granite Paper**

| | | | | |
|---|---|---|---|---|
| **979** | | Strip of 4 | 1.00 | 1.00 |
| *a.* | A611 | 10r multi | .25 | .25 |
| *b.* | A612 | 10r multi | .25 | .25 |
| *c.* | A613 | 10r multi | .25 | .25 |
| *d.* | A614 | 10r multi | .25 | .25 |

Nepal-Japan cooperation.

Prehistoric Elephants — A615

Emblem of Tribhuvan University Natural History Museum and: No. 980, 10r, Deinotherium indicum. No. 981, 10r, Elephas hysudricus. No. 982, 10r, Elephas namadicus. No. 983, 10r, Gomphotherium sp. No. 984, 10r, Stegodon bombifrons. No. 985, 10r, Stegodon ganesa.

**2015, July 7 Litho. *Perf. 13¼***
**Granite Paper**

**980-985** A615 Set of 6 1.25 1.25

A616

**2015, Aug. 1 Litho. *Perf. 13¼***
**Granite Paper**

**986** A616 20r multi .40 .40

Diplomatic Relations Between Nepal and People's Republic of China, 60th Anniv.

Narasimha, Hanumandhoka A617

Nautale Durbar, Hanumandhoka — A618

Rani Mahal, Palpa A619

Gaddi Baithak, Hanumandhoka — A620

**2015, Aug. 11 Litho. *Perf. 14x13½***
**Granite Paper**

**987** A617 10r multi .25 .25

***Perf. 13½x14***

| | | | | |
|---|---|---|---|---|
| **988** | A618 | 10r multi | .25 | .25 |
| **989** | A619 | 25r multi | .50 | .50 |
| **990** | A620 | 35r multi | .70 | .70 |
| | | *Nos. 987-990 (4)* | 1.70 | 1.70 |

Miniature Sheet

Ascent of Mounts Kanchenjunga and Makalu, 60th Anniv. — A621

No. 991: a, Mt. Kanchenjunga. b, Mt. Makalu. c, Airplane over mountains. d, Unnamed mountains. e, Hillary Peak. f, Tenzing Peak.

***Perf. 13½x13¼***
**2015, Aug. 11 Litho.**
**Granite Paper**

**991** A621 10r Sheet of 6, #a-f 1.25 1.25

Non-Violence, Harmony, Morality and Freedom From Addiction A622

**2015, Aug. 16 Litho. *Perf. 13¼***
**Granite Paper**

**992** A622 25r multi .50 .50

Wildlife Reserves and National Parks A623

Designs: 1r, Koshi Tappu Wildlife Reserve. No. 994, 2r, Sagarmatha National Park. No. 995, 2r, Chitwan National Park. No. 996, 5r, Shuklaphanta Wildlife Reserve. No. 997, 5r, Lamtang National Park.

**2015, Oct. 2 Litho. *Perf. 13¼***
**Granite Paper**

**993-997** A623 Set of 5 .30 .30

Flora A624

Designs: No. 998, 10r, Abies spectabilis. No. 999, 10r, Gentiana robusta. No. 1000, 10r, Lilium nepalense. No. 1001, 10r, Maharanga emodi. No. 1002, 10r, Paris polyphylla. No. 1003, 10r, Saussurea gossipiphora.

**2015, Oct. 2 Litho. *Perf. 13¼***
**Granite Paper**

**998-1003** A624 Set of 6 1.25 1.25

Sarbeshwor Mahadev, Lalitpur — A625

**2015, Oct. 9 Litho. *Perf. 13¼***
**Granite Paper**

**1004** A625 3r multi .25 .25

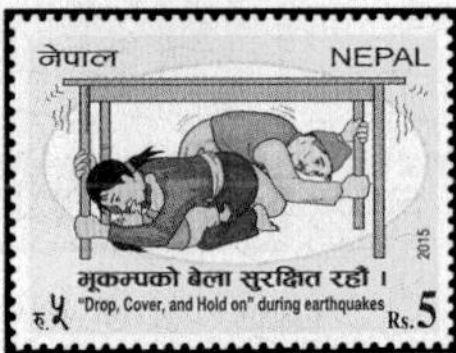

Earthquake Survival Techniques — A626

**2015, Oct. 9 Litho. *Perf. 13¼***
**Granite Paper**

**1005** A626 5r multi .25 .25

18th South Asian Association for Regional Cooperation Summit, Kathmandu, 1st Anniv. — A627

**2015, Oct. 9 Litho. *Perf. 13¼***
**Granite Paper**

**1006** A627 10r multi .25 .25

Famous Men A628

Designs: No. 1007, 8r, Deviprasad Uprety (1912-92), social worker. No. 1008, 8r, Nagendra Prasad Rijal (1927-94), politician. No. 1009, 8r, Yadav Prasad Pant (1915-2007), economist. No. 1010, 8r, Shreeprasad Parajuli (1911-62), martyr. No. 1011, 8r, Ganeshman Singh (1915-97), politician. No. 1012, 8r, Siddhi Charan Shrestha (1912-92), poet, vert.

**2015, Dec. 31 Litho. *Perf. 13¼***
**Granite Paper**

**1007-1012** A628 Set of 6 .95 .95

Diplomatic Relations Between Nepal and Japan, 60th Anniv. — A630

**2016, Nov. 3 Litho. *Perf. 12½***
**Granite Paper**

**1014** A630 10r multi .25 .25

Nepal Philatelic Society, 50th Anniv. — A631

***Serpentine Die Cut 11***
**2016, Nov. 3 Litho.**
**Self-Adhesive**
**Granite Paper**

**1015** A631 10r multi .25 .25

Federation of Nepal Chambers of Commerce and Industry, 50th Anniv. — A632

***Serpentine Die Cut 11***
**2016, Nov. 3 Litho.**
**Self-Adhesive**
**Granite Paper**

**1016** A632 10r multi .25 .25

Bal Bahadur Rai (1921-2010), Politician — A633

Lakhan Thapa Magar (1834-77), Revolutionist and First Martyr of Nepal — A634

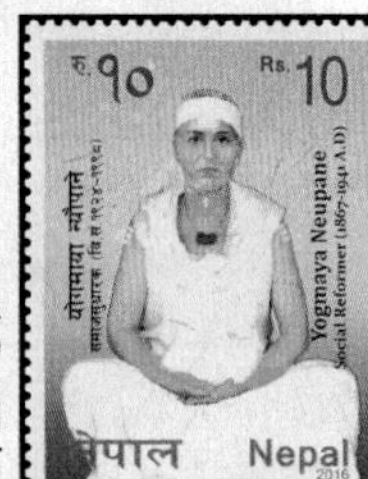

Mahendra Narayan Nidhi (1922-99), Politician — A635

Yogmaya Neupane (1867-1941), Social Reformer A636

Dev S. J. B. Rana (1862-1914), Social Reformer A637

Ratna Kumar Bantawa (1952-79), Politician and Martyr — A638

**2016 Litho. *Perf. 12½***
**Granite Paper**

| | | | | |
|---|---|---|---|---|
| **1017** | A633 | 10r multi | .25 | .25 |
| **1018** | A634 | 10r multi | .25 | .25 |
| **1019** | A635 | 10r multi | .25 | .25 |
| **1020** | A636 | 10r multi | .25 | .25 |
| **1021** | A637 | 10r multi | .25 | .25 |
| **1022** | A638 | 10r multi | .25 | .25 |
| | | *Nos. 1017-1022 (6)* | 1.50 | 1.50 |

Aadilinga Kusheshwor Mahadev, Sindhuli A639

Chandanbharateshwor Mahadev, Kathmandu — A640

Shree Parroha Parmeshwor Shiva Jyotirlinga, Rupandehi A641

Siddhakali Temple, Bhojpur A642

Matsyanarayan Temple, Kathmandu — A643

Hatuwaghadi, Capital of Majh Kirat, Bhojpur — A644

**2016 Litho. *Perf. 12½***
**Granite Paper**

| | | | | |
|---|---|---|---|---|
| **1023** | A639 | 1r multi | .25 | .25 |
| **1024** | A640 | 5r multi | .25 | .25 |
| **1025** | A641 | 5r multi | .25 | .25 |
| **1026** | A642 | 10r multi | .25 | .25 |
| **1027** | A643 | 10r multi | .25 | .25 |
| **1028** | A644 | 10r multi | .25 | .25 |
| | | *Nos. 1023-1028 (6)* | 1.50 | 1.50 |

Bhringareshwor Mahadev, Lalitpur — A645

**2016 Litho. *Serpentine Die Cut 11***
**Self-Adhesive**
**Granite Paper**

**1029** A645 2r multi .25 .25

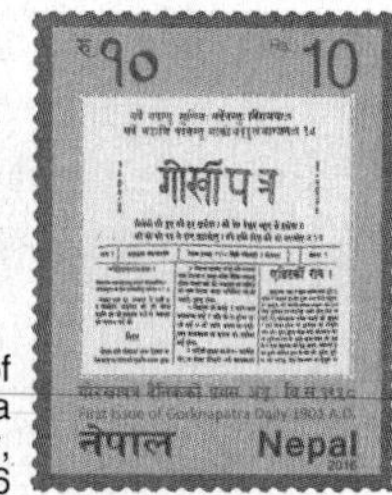

First Issue of Gorkhapatra Daily, 1901 — A646

**2016 Litho. *Serpentine Die Cut 11***
**Self-Adhesive**
**Granite Paper**

**1030** A646 10r multi .25 .25

Relations Between Nepal and Great Britain, 200th Anniv. — A647

**2016 Litho. *Serpentine Die Cut 11***
**Self-Adhesive**
**Granite Paper**

**1031** A647 10r multi .25 .25

Constitution of Nepal — A648

**2016 Litho. *Serpentine Die Cut 11***
**Self-Adhesive**
**Granite Paper**

**1032** A648 10r multi .25 .25

Francolinus Francolinus — A649

**2016 Litho. *Serpentine Die Cut 11***
**Self-Adhesive**
**Granite Paper**

**1033** A649 25r multi .45 .45

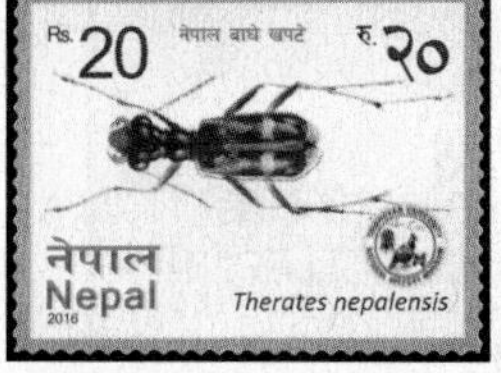

Beetles A650

Designs: No. 1034, 20r, Therates nepalensis. No. 1035, 20r, Mylabris phalerata. No. 1036, 20r, Dorcus nepalensis. No. 1037, 20r, Odontolabis (Calcodes) cuvera.

**2016 Litho. *Serpentine Die Cut 11***
**Self-Adhesive**
**Granite Paper**

**1034-1037** A650 Set of 4 1.50 1.50

Rhododendrons — A651

Designs: No. 1038, 20r, Rhododendron ciliatum. No. 1039, 20r, Rhododendron dalhousiae. No. 1040, 20r, Rhododendron fulgens. No. 1041, 20r, Rhododendron glaucophyllum.

**2016 Litho. *Serpentine Die Cut 11***
**Self-Adhesive**
**Granite Paper**

**1038-1041** A651 Set of 4 1.50 1.50

Mountains — A652

Designs: 35r, Mt. Manaslu. 100r, Mt. Lhotse.

**2016 Litho. *Serpentine Die Cut 11***
**Self-Adhesive**
**Granite Paper**

**1042-1043** A652 Set of 2 2.50 2.50

Prehistoric Mammals — A653

Designs: No. 1044, 10r, Dorcatherium. No. 1045, 10r, Hipparion. No. 1046, 10r, Pachyportax. No. 1047, 10r, Hemibos acuticornis. 100r, Brachypotherium perimense. 200r, Giraffokeryx punjabiensis.

***Serpentine Die Cut 11***
**2017, Sept. 22 Litho.**
**Self-Adhesive**
**Granite Paper**

**1044-1049** A653 Set of 6 6.50 6.50

Mammals — A654

Designs: No. 1050, 10r, Marbled cat. No. 1051, 10r, Large Indian civet. No. 1052, 10r, Pygmy hog. No. 1053, 10r, Black giant squirrel. No. 1054, 20r, Crested porcupine. No. 1055, 20r, Roylei's pika.

***Serpentine Die Cut 11***
**2017, Sept. 22 Litho.**
**Self-Adhesive**
**Granite Paper**

**1050-1055** A654 Set of 6 1.60 1.60

Flora — A655

Designs: No. 1056, 1r, Dryopteris cochleata. No. 1057, 1r, Lycopodium japonicum. No. 1058, 2r, Cyathea spinulosa. No. 1059, 2r, Drynaria propinqua. No. 1060, 3r, Nephrolepis cordifolia. No. 1061, 3r, Tectaria coadunate.

**2017 Litho. *Perf. 12½***
**Granite Paper**

**1056-1061** A655 Set of 6 .25 .25

Containers A656

Designs: 3r, Theki Madani. 8r, Karuwa.

**2017 Litho. *Perf. 12½***
**Granite Paper**

**1062-1063** A656 Set of 2 .25 .25

Famous Men A657

Designs: No. 1064, 10r, Janakabi Keshari Dharmaraj Thapa (1924-2014), folk singer. No. 1065, 10r, Saroj Prasad Koirala (1929-73), politician.

**2017 Litho. *Perf. 12½***
**Granite Paper**

**1064-1065** A657 Set of 2 .40 .40

Pokali Waterfall A658

**2017 Litho. *Perf. 12½***
**Granite Paper**

**1066** A658 1r multi .25 .25

Ugratara Temple, Dadeldhura — A659

**2017 Litho. *Perf. 12½***
**Granite Paper**

**1067** A659 1r multi .25 .25

Shreeantu — A660

**2017 Litho. *Perf. 12½***
**Granite Paper**

**1068** A660 2r multi .25 .25

Rauta Pokhari A661

**2017 Litho. *Perf. 12½***
**Granite Paper**

**1069** A661 2r multi .25 .25

Tansen Bhairav, Palpa — A662

**2017 Litho. *Perf. 12½***
**Granite Paper**

**1070** A662 2r multi .25 .25

Junge Mahadev Statue, Banke — A663

**2017 Litho. *Perf. 12½***
**Granite Paper**

**1071** A663 2r multi .25 .25

Flag of Nepal — A664

**2017 Litho. *Perf. 12½***
**Granite Paper**

**1072** A664 5r multi .25 .25

Pandit Amrit Nath Mishra (1920-2015), Srimadbhagwat Savant — A665

**2017 Litho. *Perf. 12½***
**Granite Paper**

| | | | | |
|---|---|---|---|---|
| **1073** | A665 | 10r multi | .25 | .25 |

Nepal Election Commission, 50th Anniv. — A666

**2017 Litho. *Perf. 12½***
**Granite Paper**

| | | | | |
|---|---|---|---|---|
| **1074** | A666 | 10r multi | .25 | .25 |

Foods — A667

No. 1075: a, Yomari. b, Sel. c, Anarasa. d, Lakhamari.

**2017 Litho. *Perf. 12½***
**Granite Paper**

| | | | | |
|---|---|---|---|---|
| **1075** | A667 | 1r Block of 4, #a-d | .25 | .25 |

Jewelry — A668

No. 1076: a, Bulaki. b, Hasuli. c, Tilhari. d, Kalli.

**2017 Litho. *Perf. 12½***
**Granite Paper**

| | | | | |
|---|---|---|---|---|
| **1076** | A668 | 500r Block of 4, #a-d | 40.00 | 40.00 |

## AIR POST STAMPS

**Catalogue values for unused stamps in this section are for Never Hinged items.**

Bird over Kathmandu AP1

***Rough Perf 11½***
**1958, Oct. 16 Typo. Unwmk.**
**Without Gum**

| | | | | |
|---|---|---|---|---|
| **C1** | AP1 | 10p dark blue | 2.40 | 2.00 |

Plane over Kathmandu AP2

**1967, Oct. 24 Photo. *Perf. 13½x13***

| | | | | |
|---|---|---|---|---|
| **C2** | AP2 | 1.80r multicolored | 2.00 | 1.50 |

International Tourist Year.

God Akash Bhairab and Nepal Airlines Emblem AP3

Map of Nepal with Airlines Network AP4

Design: 2.50r, Plane over Himalayas.

***Perf. 14½x14, 13 (65p)***
**1968, July 1 Photo.**

| | | | | |
|---|---|---|---|---|
| **C3** | AP3 | 15p blue & bis brn | .50 | .50 |
| **C4** | AP4 | 65p violet blue | 1.25 | 1.00 |
| **C5** | AP3 | 2.50r dp blue & scar | 3.75 | 2.75 |
| | | *Nos. C3-C5 (3)* | 5.50 | 4.25 |

10th anniv. of the Royal Nepal Airlines Corp.

Flyer and Jet — AP5

**1978, Dec. 12 Photo. *Perf. 13***

| | | | | |
|---|---|---|---|---|
| **C6** | AP5 | 2.30r blue & ocher | 1.40 | .80 |

75th anniversary of 1st powered flight.

**Pheasant Type of 1979**

3.50r, Impeyan pheasant, horiz.

**1979, Nov. 22 Photo. *Perf. 14½x14***

| | | | | |
|---|---|---|---|---|
| **C7** | A174 | 3.50r multicolored | 3.25 | 2.00 |

## OFFICIAL STAMPS

**Catalogue values for unused stamps in this section are for Never Hinged items.**

Soldiers and Arms of Nepal — O1

***Perf. 13½***
**1959, Nov. 1 Litho. Unwmk.**
**Size: 29x17½mm**

| | | | | |
|---|---|---|---|---|
| **O1** | O1 | 2p reddish brown | .25 | .25 |
| **O2** | O1 | 4p yel green | .25 | .25 |
| **O3** | O1 | 6p salmon pink | .25 | .25 |
| **O4** | O1 | 8p brt violet | .30 | .25 |
| **O5** | O1 | 12p red orange | .35 | .25 |
| | | **Size: 37½x21½mm** | | |
| **O6** | O1 | 16p red brown | .50 | .35 |
| **O7** | O1 | 24p carmine | .60 | .50 |
| **O8** | O1 | 32p rose car | 1.00 | .70 |
| **O9** | O1 | 50p ultramarine | 1.75 | 1.25 |
| **O10** | O1 | 1r rose red | 3.25 | 2.25 |
| **O11** | O1 | 2r orange | 6.50 | 5.00 |
| | | *Nos. O1-O11 (11)* | 15.00 | 11.30 |

Nos. 144-146 and 124 Overprinted in Black

**1960-62 Photo. *Perf. 14½x14***
**Overprint 12½mm Long**

| | | | | |
|---|---|---|---|---|
| **O12** | A35 | 1p carmine rose ('62) | .25 | .25 |
| **O13** | A35 | 2p bright blue ('62) | .25 | .25 |
| **O14** | A35 | 5p golden brown ('62) | .35 | .35 |
| | | *Nos. O12-O14 (3)* | .85 | .85 |

***Perf. 14***
**Overprint 14½mm Long**

| | | | | |
|---|---|---|---|---|
| **O15** | A26 | 1r red lilac | 1.50 | 1.50 |

The overprint, "Kaj Sarkari" in Devanagari characters means "Service." Five other denominations, 10p, 40p, 75p, 2r and 5r, were similarly overprinted but not issued. Value, 5 values $3. A few exist on 1960 first day covers.

In 1983 substantial quantities of the set of nine values were sold as remainders by the Post Office at face value (under $1 for the set).

The existence of covers from 1985-86 indicate that some of these may have been used as regular postage stamps.

# NETHERLANDS

'ne-th̲ər-lən,dz

(Holland)

LOCATION — Northwestern Europe, bordering on the North Sea
GOVT. — Kingdom
AREA — 16,029 sq. mi.
POP. — 15,807,641 (1999 est.)
CAPITAL — Amsterdam

100 Cents = 1 Gulden (Guilder or Florin)
100 Cents = 1 Euro (2002)

**Catalogue values for unused stamps in this country are for Never Hinged items, beginning with Scott 216 in the regular postage section, Scott B123 in the semi-postal section, Scott C13 in the airpost section, Scott J80 in the postage due section, and Scott O44 in the official section.**

Values for unused stamps are for examples with original gum as defined in the catalogue introduction. Very fine examples of Nos. 4-12 will have perforations touching the frameline on one or more sides due to the narrow spacing of the stamps on the plates. Stamps with perfs clear on all four sides are very scarce and command higher prices.

**Watermarks**

Wmk. 158

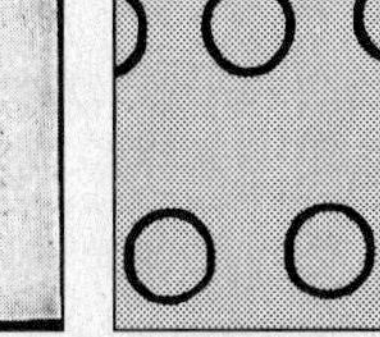

Wmk. 202 — Circles

King William III — A1

**Wmk. 158**
**1852, Jan. 1 Engr. *Imperf.***

| | | | | |
|---|---|---|---|---|
| **1** | A1 | 5c blue | 400.00 | 35.00 |
| *a.* | | 5c light blue | 450.00 | 40.00 |
| *b.* | | 5c steel blue | 750.00 | 100.00 |
| *c.* | | 5c dark blue | 450.00 | 35.00 |
| **2** | A1 | 10c lake | 450.00 | 27.50 |
| **3** | A1 | 15c orange yellow | 775.00 | 130.00 |

In 1895 the 10c was privately reprinted in several colors on unwatermarked paper by Joh. A. Moesman, whose name appears on the back.

King William III — A2

**1864 Unwmk. *Perf. 12½x12***

| | | | | |
|---|---|---|---|---|
| **4** | A2 | 5c blue | 300.00 | 16.00 |
| **5** | A2 | 10c lake | 425.00 | 8.00 |
| **6** | A2 | 15c orange | 1,050. | 100.00 |
| *a.* | | 15c yellow | 1,350. | 115.00 |

The paper varies considerably in thickness. It is sometimes slightly bluish, also vertically ribbed.

William III — A3

**1867 *Perf. 12¾x11¾***

| | | | | |
|---|---|---|---|---|
| **7** | A3 | 5c ultra | 115.00 | 2.75 |
| **8** | A3 | 10c lake | 225.00 | 4.75 |
| **9** | A3 | 15c orange brn | 640.00 | 35.00 |

**10** A3 20c dk green 625.00 24.00
**11** A3 25c dk violet 2,100. 110.00
**12** A3 50c gold 2,500. 160.00

The paper of Nos. 7-22 sometimes has an accidental bluish tinge of varying strength. During its manufacture a chemical whitener (bluing agent) was added in varying quantities. No particular printing was made on bluish paper.

Two varieties of numerals in each value, differing chiefly in the thickness.

Oxidized copies of the 50c are worth much less.

Imperforate varieties of Nos. 7-12 are proofs.

See the *Scott Specialized Catalogue* for listings by perforations.

**1869**

***Perf. 10½x10***

*7c* A3 5c ultra 225.00 11.50
*8c* A3 10c lake 230.00 7.75
*9c* A3 15c orange brown 2,700. 1,150.
*10c* A3 20c dark green 1,550. 155.00

Coat of Arms — A4

**1869-71 Typo. *Perf. 13¼, 14***

**17** A4 ½c red brown ('71) 24.00 3.75
*c.* Perf. 14 *2,300.* 875.00
**18** A4 1c black 210.00 70.00
**19** A4 1c green 15.50 2.25
*c.* Perf. 14 27.50 5.50
**20** A4 1½c rose 150.00 77.50
*b.* Perf. 14 175.00 97.50
**21** A4 2c buff 60.00 15.00
*c.* Perf. 14 55.00 14.00
**22** A4 2½c violet ('70) 475.00 70.00
*c.* Perf. 14 775.00 425.00

Imperforate varieties are proofs.

A5 A6

***Perf. 12½, 13, 13½, 13x14, 14, 12½x12 and 11½x12***

**1872-88**

**23** A5 5c blue 11.50 .30
*a.* 5c ultra 14.00 1.25
**24** A5 7½c red brn ('88) 35.00 18.00
**25** A5 10c rose 57.50 1.60
**26** A5 12½c gray ('75) 62.50 2.40
**27** A5 15c brn org 350.00 5.25
**28** A5 20c green 425.00 5.00
**29** A5 22½c dk grn ('88) 77.50 42.50
**30** A5 25c dull vio 525.00 4.00
**31** A5 50c bister 650.00 11.00
**32** A5 1g gray vio ('88) 480.00 40.00
**33** A6 2g50c rose & ultra 900.00 105.00

Imperforate varieties are proofs.

Numeral of Value — A7

HALF CENT:
Type I — Fraction bar 8 to 8½mm long.
Type II — Fraction bar 9mm long and thinner.

***Perf. 12½, 13½, 14, 12½x12, 11½x12***

**1876-94**

**34** A7 ½c rose (II) 11.50 .30
*a.* ½c rose (I) 15.00 .50
*c.* Laid paper 60.00
*d.* Perf. 14 (I) 1,950. 575.00
**35** A7 1c emer grn ('94) 2.75 .25
*b.* As "c," laid paper 70.00 7.25
*c.* 1c green 8.00 .25
**36** A7 2c olive yel ('94) 32.50 2.75
*a.* 2c yellow 65.00 3.50
**37** A7 2½c violet ('94) 14.00 .30
*b.* 2½c dark violet ('94) 17.50 .45
*c.* 2½c lilac 100.00 .80
*d.* Laid paper — —
*Nos. 34-37 (4)* 60.75 3.60

Imperforate varieties are proofs.

Princess Wilhelmina — A8

**1891-94 *Perf. 12½***

**40** A8 3c orange ('94) 8.00 2.30
*a.* 3c orange yellow ('92) 11.50 2.75
**41** A8 5c lt ultra ('94) 4.00 .25
*a.* 5c dull blue 5.00 .25
**42** A8 7½c brown ('94) 15.00 6.25
*a.* 7½c red brown 27.50 6.25
**43** A8 10c brt rose ('94) 23.50 1.60
*a.* 10c brick red 45.00 2.40
**44** A8 12½c bluish gray ('94) 23.50 1.60
*a.* 12½c gray 40.00 1.75
**45** A8 15c yel brn ('94) 60.00 5.00
*a.* 15c orange brown 80.00 5.50
**46** A8 20c green ('94) 70.00 3.00
*a.* 20c yellow green 80.00 3.00
**47** A8 22½c dk grn ('94) 32.50 13.50
*a.* 22½c deep blue green 55.00 13.50
**48** A8 25c dl vio ('94) 110.00 6.00
*a.* 25c dark violet 110.00 6.00
**49** A8 50c yel brn ('94) 550.00 20.00
*a.* 50c bister 575.00 27.50
**50** A8 1g gray vio 625.00 77.50

The paper used in 1891-93 was white, rough and somewhat opaque. In 1894, a thinner, smooth and sometimes transparent paper was introduced.

The 5c orange was privately produced.

Princess Wilhelmina — A9

**1893-96 *Perf. 11½x11***

**51** A9 50c emer & yel brn ('96) 80.00 15.00
*a.* Perf. 11 *2,500.* 200.00
**52** A9 1g brn & ol grn ('96) 200.00 22.50
*a.* Perf. 11 225.00 60.00
**53** A9 2g 50c brt rose & ultra 400.00 130.00
*a.* 2g 50c lil rose & ultra, perf. 11 475.00 130.00
*b.* Perf. 11½ 500.00 140.00

***Perf. 11***

**54** A9 5g brnz grn & red brn ('96) 700.00 425.00

A10

Queen Wilhelmina — A11

***Perf. 12½ (#70, 73, 75-77, 81-82), 11½, 11½x11, 11x11½***

**1898-1924**

**55** A10 ½c violet .45 .25
**56** A10 1c red .90 .25
*b.* Imperf., pair *2,000.* —
**57** A10 1½c ultra ('08) 6.00 .85
**58** A10 1½c dp blue ('13) 3.00 .35
**59** A10 2c yellow brn 3.75 .25
**60** A10 2½c deep green 3.25 .25
*b.* Imperf., pair *6,250.*
**61** A11 3c orange 16.50 3.25
**62** A11 3c pale ol grn ('01) 1.10 .25
**63** A11 4c claret ('21) 1.60 1.10
**64** A11 4½c violet ('19) 3.75 3.75
**65** A11 5c car rose 1.60 .25
**66** A11 7½c brown .75 .25
*a.* Tête bêche pair ('24) 80.00 72.50
**67** A11 10c gray lilac 6.25 .25
**68** A11 12½c blue 3.25 .30
**69** A11 15c yellow brn 100.00 3.25
**70** A11 15c bl & car ('08) 6.25 .25
**71** A11 17½c vio ('06) 50.00 12.00
**73** A11 17½c ultra & brn ('10) 15.00 .90
**74** A11 20c yellow green 150.00 .75
**75** A11 20c ol grn & gray ('08) 10.00 .50
**76** A11 22½c brn & ol grn 9.25 .60
**77** A11 25c car & blue 9.25 .45
**78** A11 30c lil & vio brn ('17) 24.00 .50
**79** A11 40c grn & org ('20) 34.00 1.10
**80** A11 50c brnz grn & red brn 110.00 1.10
**81** A11 50c gray & vio ('14) 70.00 1.10
*a.* Perf 11½x11 70.00 16.50
**82** A11 60c ol grn & grn ('20) 34.00 1.10
*a.* Perf 11½ 200.00 20.00
*Nos. 55-82 (27)* 673.90 35.20
Set, never hinged 3,000.

See Nos. 107-112. For overprints and surcharges see Nos. 102-103, 106, 117-123, 135-136, O1-O8.

A12 I II

Type I — The figure "1" is 3¾mm high and 2¾mm wide.

Type II — The figure "1" is 3½mm high and 2½mm wide, it is also thinner than in type I.

***Perf. 11, 11x11½, 11½, 11½x11***

**1898-1905 Engr.**

**83** A12 1g dk grn, II ('99) 52.50 .75
*a.* 1g dark green, I ('98) 190.00 110.00
**84** A12 2½g brn lil ('99) 100.00 3.25
**85** A12 5g claret ('99) 225.00 6.00
**86** A12 10g orange ('05) 775.00 675.00
Set, never hinged 2,975.

For surcharge see No. 104.

Admiral M. A. de Ruyter and Fleet — A13

**1907, Mar. 23 Typo. *Perf. 12x12½***

**87** A13 ½c blue 2.00 1.25
**88** A13 1c claret 3.50 2.25
**89** A13 2½c vermilion 6.00 2.25
*Nos. 87-89 (3)* 11.50 5.75
Set, never hinged 37.00

De Ruyter (1607-1676), naval hero.
For surcharges see Nos. J29-J41.

King William I — A14

Designs: 2½c, 12½c, 1g, King William I. 3c, 20c, 2½g, King William II. 5c, 25c, 5g, King William III. 10c, 50c, 10g, Queen Wilhelmina.

***Perf. 11½x11, 11½ (#97, 100-101)***

**1913, Nov. 29 Engr.**

**90** A14 2½c green, *grn* .80 .80
**91** A14 3c buff, *straw* 1.80 1.50
**92** A14 5c rose red, *sal* 1.25 .90
**93** A14 10c gray blk 4.25 2.40
**94** A14 12½c dp blue, *bl* 3.00 1.90
**95** A14 20c orange brn 13.00 11.00
**96** A14 25c pale blue 15.00 8.75
**97** A14 50c yel grn 32.50 27.50
**98** A14 1g claret 47.50 20.00
*a.* Perf. 11½ 60.00 20.00
**99** A14 2½g dull violet 120.00 50.00
**100** A14 5g yel, *straw* 225.00 40.00
**101** A14 10g red, *straw* 800.00 725.00
*Nos. 90-101 (12)* 1,264. 889.75
Set, never hinged 2,285.

Centenary of Dutch independence.
For surcharge see No. 105.

**No. 78 Surcharged in Red or Black**

a

b

**1919, Dec. 1 *Perf. 12½***

**102** A11 (a) 40c on 30c (R) 25.00 4.50
**103** A11 (b) 60c on 30c (Bk) 25.00 4.50
Set, never hinged 210.00

Nos. 86 and 101 Surcharged in Black

**1920, Aug. 17 *Perf. 11, 11½***

**104** A12 2.50g on 10g 145.00 80.00
Never hinged 350.00
**105** A14 2.50g on 10g 160.00 100.00
Never hinged 400.00
Set, never hinged 750.00

No. 64 Surcharged in Red

**1921, Mar. 1 Typo. *Perf. 12½***

**106** A11 4c on 4½c vio 3.75 1.40
Never hinged 7.00

A17

**1921-22 Typo. *Perf. 12½***

**107** A17 5c green ('22) 13.00 .25
**108** A17 12½c vermilion ('22) 19.00 1.75
**109** A17 20c blue 31.00 .25
*Nos. 107-109 (3)* 63.00 2.25
Set, never hinged 215.00

**Queen Type of 1898-99, 10c Redrawn**

**1922 *Perf. 12½***

**110** A11 10c gray 27.50 .25
Never hinged 85.00

***Imperf***

**111** A11 5c car rose 7.00 7.00
Never hinged 13.00
**112** A11 10c gray 7.00 7.00
Never hinged 13.00
*Nos. 110-112 (3)* 41.50 14.25

In redrawn 10c the horizontal lines behind the Queen's head are wider apart.

Orange Tree and Lion of Brabant A18

Post Horn and Lion A19

Numeral of Value — A20

**1923, Mar. 9 *Perf. 12½***

**113** A18 1c dark violet .55 .50
Never hinged 2.00
**114** A18 2c orange 5.00 .25
Never hinged 10.00
**115** A19 2½c bluish green 1.50 .65
Never hinged 4.00

116 A20 4c deep blue 1.25 .60
Never hinged 3.25
*Nos. 113-116 (4)* 8.30 2.00
Set, never hinged 19.50

**Nos. 56, 58, 62, 65, 68, 73, 76 Surcharged in Various Colors**

c

d

**1923, July** ***Perf. 12½***
117 A10(c) 2c on 1c (Bl) .45 .25
Never hinged 1.00
118 A10(c) 2c on 1½c (Bk) .45 .25
Never hinged 1.00
119 A11(d) 10c on 3c (Br) 4.00 .25
Never hinged 13.00
120 A11(d) 10c on 5c (Bk) 8.00 .50
Never hinged 22.50
121 A11(d) 10c on 12½c (R) 6.50 .75
Never hinged 24.00

***Perf. 11½x11***
122 A11(d) 10c on 17½c (R) 2.75 2.60
Never hinged 8.25
*a.* Perf. 11½ *1,600.* *800.00*
*b.* Perf. 12½ 4.00 4.00
Never hinged 8.00
123 A11(d) 10c on 22½c (R) 2.75 2.60
Never hinged 8.25
*a.* Perf. 11½ 3.00 3.50
Never hinged 6.50
*b.* Perf. 12½ 4.00 4.00
Never hinged 8.00
*Nos. 117-123 (7)* 24.90 7.20
Set, never hinged 78.00

Queen Wilhelmina
A21 A22

***Perf. 11½x12½, 11½x12 (5c)***
**1923, Oct.** **Engr.**
124 A22 2c myrtle green .25 .25
Never hinged 1.10
*a.* Vert. pair, imperf. between *2,400.*
125 A21 5c green .40 .25
Never hinged 1.10
*a.* Vert. pair, imperf. between *1,800.*
126 A22 7½c carmine .50 .25
Never hinged 2.25
127 A22 10c vermilion .40 .25
Never hinged 1.60
*a.* Vert. pair, imperf. between *550.00* *575.00*
128 A22 20c ultra 3.75 1.00
Never hinged 9.00
129 A22 25c yellow 5.00 1.10
Never hinged 15.00

***Perf. 11½***
130 A22 35c orange 5.00 3.00
Never hinged 15.00
131 A22 50c black 15.00 1.00
Never hinged 45.00
132 A21 1g red 30.00 7.25
Never hinged 65.00
133 A21 2½g black 190.00 200.00
Never hinged 450.00
134 A21 5g dark blue 175.00 175.00
Never hinged 360.00
*Nos. 124-134 (11)* 425.30 389.35
Set, never hinged 975.00

25th anniv. of the assumption as monarch of the Netherlands by Queen Wilhelmina at the age of 18.

No. 119 Overprinted in Red

No. 73 With Additional Surcharge in Blue

**1923** **Typo.** ***Perf. 12½***
135 A11 10c on 3c 1.10 1.00
Never hinged 8.00
136 A11 1g on 17½c 62.50 15.00
Never hinged 190.00
*a.* Perf. 11½ 95.00 40.00
*b.* Perf. 11½x11 80.00 30.00

Stamps with red surcharge were prepared for use as Officials but were not issued.

Queen Wilhelmina — A23

**1924, Sept. 6** **Photo.** ***Perf. 12½***
137 A23 10c slate green 32.50 32.50
Never hinged 65.00
138 A23 15c gray black 40.00 40.00
Never hinged 70.00
139 A23 35c brown orange 32.50 32.50
Never hinged 65.00
*Nos. 137-139 (3)* 105.00 105.00
Set, never hinged 200.00

These stamps were available solely to visitors to the International Philatelic Exhibition at The Hague and were not obtainable at regular post offices. Set of three on international philatelic exhibition cover dataed Sept. 6-12, 15-17, 1924, value, $110. Set of three on Netherland Philatelic Exhibition cover dated Sept. 13-14, value, $150.

See Nos. 147-160, 172-193. For overprints and surcharge see Nos. 194, O11, O13-O15.

Ship in Distress — A23a

Lifeboat — A23b

**1924, Sept. 15** **Litho.** ***Perf. 11½***
140 A23a 2c black brn 3.25 2.25
Never hinged 7.25
141 A23b 10c orange brn 5.50 1.75
Never hinged 13.00

Centenary of Royal Dutch Lifeboat Society.

**Type A23 and**

Gull — A24

**1924-26** **Unwmk.** ***Perf. 12½***
142 A24 1c deep red .75 .90
Never hinged 1.50
143 A24 2c red orange 2.60 .35
Never hinged 9.00
144 A24 2½c deep green 3.00 1.10
Never hinged 6.00
145 A24 3c yel grn ('25) 16.50 1.50
Never hinged 50.00
146 A24 4c dp ultra 3.25 .95
Never hinged 15.00

**Photo.**
147 A23 5c dull green 3.50 .75
Never hinged 8.00
148 A23 6c org brn ('25) .75 .50
Never hinged 1.40
149 A23 7½c orange ('25) .35 .25
Never hinged 1.10
150 A23 9c org red & blk ('26) 1.50 1.25
Never hinged 3.00
151 A23 10c red, *shades* 1.50 .25
Never hinged 5.50
152 A23 12½c deep rose 1.60 .35
Never hinged 4.50
153 A23 15c ultra 6.00 .45
Never hinged 15.00
154 A23 20c dp blue ('25) 10.00 .60
Never hinged 22.00
155 A23 25c olive bis ('25) 22.50 .85
Never hinged 40.00
156 A23 30c violet 13.00 .65
Never hinged 40.00
157 A23 35c olive brn ('25) 30.00 6.00
Never hinged 80.00
158 A23 40c dp brown 35.00 .75
Never hinged 200.00
159 A23 50c blue grn ('25) 60.00 .60
Never hinged 275.00
160 A23 60c dk violet ('25) 27.50 .80
Never hinged 100.00
*Nos. 142-160 (19)* 239.30 18.85
Set, never hinged 725.00

See Nos. 164-171, 243A-243Q. For overprints and surcharges see Nos. 226-243, O9-O10.

**Syncopated Perforations**

Type A

Type B

Type C

These special "syncopated" or "interrupted" perforations, devised for coil stamps, are found on Nos. 142-156, 158-160, 164-166, 168-185, 187-193 and certain semipostals of 1925-33, between Nos. B9 and B69. There are four types:

A (1st stamp is #142a). On two shorter sides, groups of four holes separated by blank spaces equal in width to two or three holes.

B (1st stamp is #164a). As "A," but on all four sides.

C (1st stamp is #164b). On two shorter sides, end holes are omitted.

D (1st stamp is #174c). Four-hole sequence on horiz. sides, three-hole on vert. sides.

***Syncopated, Type A (2 Sides)***
**1925-26**
*142a* A24 1c deep red .75 .80
Never hinged 1.60
*143a* A24 2c red orange 2.60 2.60
Never hinged 4.50
*144a* A24 2½c deep green 2.60 1.60
Never hinged 4.50
*145a* A24 3c yellow green 17.50 17.50
Never hinged 42.50
*146a* A24 4c deep ultra 2.25 2.25
Never hinged 7.50
*147a* A23 5c dull green 5.50 3.00
Never hinged 9.75
*148a* A23 6c orange brown 110.00 100.00
Never hinged 170.00
*149a* A23 7½c orange 1.10 1.10
Never hinged 1.60
*150a* A23 9c org red & blk 1.90 1.60
Never hinged 2.50
*151a* A23 10c red 9.25 3.00
Never hinged 16.50
*152a* A23 12½c deep rose 1.75 1.75
Never hinged 3.25
*153a* A23 15c ultra 90.00 6.25
Never hinged 225.00
*154a* A23 20c deep blue 11.00 4.75
Never hinged 20.00
*155a* A23 25c olive bister 40.00 40.00
Never hinged 105.00
*156a* A23 30c violet 15.00 11.50
Never hinged 30.00
*158a* A23 40c deep brown 55.00 47.50
Never hinged 210.00
*159a* A23 50c blue green 60.00 23.00
Never hinged 240.00
*160a* A23 60c dark violet 30.00 11.50
Never hinged 75.00
*Nos. 142a-160a (18)* 456.20 279.70
Set, never hinged 1,070.

A25

**1925-30** **Engr.** ***Perf. 11½***
161 A25 1g ultra 8.00 .65
Never hinged 25.00
162 A25 2½g car ('27) 90.00 3.00
Never hinged 175.00
163 A25 5g gray blk 160.00 2.50
Never hinged 300.00
*Nos. 161-163 (3)* 258.00 6.15

**Types of 1924-26 Issue**
***Perf. 12½, 13½x12½, 12½x13½***
**1926-39** **Wmk. 202** **Litho.**
164 A24 ½c gray ('28) .90 1.00
165 A24 1c dp red ('27) .25 .25
166 A24 1½c red vio ('28) 1.10 .25
*c.* "CEN" for "CENT" 165.00 275.00
*d.* "GENT" for "CENT" 120.00 115.00
167 A24 1½c gray ('35) .25 .25
*a.* 1½c dark gray .25 .25
168 A24 2c dp org .25 .25
*a.* 2c red orange .25 .25
169 A24 2½c green ('27) 2.75 .25
170 A24 3c yel grn ('27) .25 .25
171 A24 4c dp ultra ('27) .25 .25

**Photo.**
172 A23 5c dp green .25 .25
173 A23 6c org brn ('27) .25 .25
174 A23 7½c dk vio ('27) 3.25 .25
175 A23 7½c red ('28) .35 .25
176 A23 9c org red & blk ('28) 11.00 12.00
*b.* Value omitted *14,500.*
177 A23 10c red 1.30 .25
178 A23 10c dl vio ('29) 2.50 .25
179 A23 12½c dp rose ('27) 42.50 4.50
180 A23 12½c ultra ('28) .25 .25
181 A23 15c ultra 7.25 .25
182 A23 15c orange ('29) 1.30 .25
183 A23 20c dp blue ('28) 7.25 .25
184 A23 21c ol brn ('31) 25.00 .90
185 A23 22½c ol brn ('27) 7.25 3.00
186 A23 22½c dp org ('39) 15.50 16.00
187 A23 25c ol bis ('27) 4.50 .25
188 A23 27½c gray ('28) 4.50 .90
189 A23 30c violet 5.00 .25
190 A23 35c olive brn 62.50 12.50
191 A23 40c dp brown 9.00 .25
192 A23 50c blue grn 5.00 .25
193 A23 60c black ('29) 57.50 .90
*Nos. 164-193 (30)* 279.20 56.95
Set, never hinged 640.00

***Syncopated, Type A (2 Sides), 12½***
**1926-27**
*168b* A24 2c deep orange .40 .40
*170a* A24 3c yellow green .60 .60
*171a* A24 4c deep ultra .60 .60
*172a* A23 5c deep green .70 .60
*173a* A23 6c orange brown .40 .45
*174a* A23 7½c dark violet 4.50 2.00
*177a* A23 10c red 1.00 .85
*181a* A23 15c ultra 7.00 3.00
*185a* A23 22½c olive brown 7.00 2.50
*187a* A23 25c olive bister 20.00 18.00
*189a* A23 30c violet 19.00 12.00
*190a* A23 35c olive brown 77.50 22.50
*191a* A23 40c deep brown 50.00 40.00
*Nos. 168b-191a (13)* 188.70 103.50
Set, never hinged 360.00

**1928** ***Syncopated, Type B (4 Sides)***
*164a* A24 ½c gray .50 .50
*165a* A24 1c deep red .50 .30
*166a* A24 1½c red violet .50 .30
*168c* A24 2c deep orange .80 .80
*169a* A24 2½c green 2.00 .35
*170b* A24 3c yellow green .75 .75
*171b* A24 4c deep ultra .75 .75
*172b* A23 5c deep green 1.00 .75
*173b* A23 6c orange brown .70 .75
*174b* A23 7½c dark violet 3.50 2.00
*175a* A23 7½c red .35 .35
*176a* A23 9c org red & blk 9.00 10.00
*178a* A23 10c dull violet 4.50 3.50
*179a* A23 12½c deep rose 80.00 85.00
*180a* A23 12½c ultra 1.50 .75
*181b* A23 15c ultra 7.00 2.00
*182a* A23 15c orange 1.00 .75
*183a* A23 20c deep blue 6.50 3.50
*187b* A23 25c olive bister 17.00 10.00
*188a* A23 27½c gray 5.00 2.00
*189b* A23 30c violet 15.00 8.00
*191b* A23 40c deep brown 34.00 25.00
*192a* A23 50c blue green 50.00 45.00
*193a* A23 60c black 36.00 25.00
*Nos. 164a-193a (24)* 277.85 228.10
Set, never hinged 525.00

***Syncopated, Type C (2 Sides, Corners Only)***
**1930**
*164b* A24 ½c gray 1.00 .70
*165b* A24 1c deep red 1.00 .40
*166b* A24 1½c red violet .90 .25
*168d* A24 2c deep orange .80 .70
*169b* A24 2½c green 2.75 .25
*170c* A24 3c yellow green 1.10 .50
*171c* A24 4c deep ultra .50 .25
*172c* A23 5c deep green .70 .70
*173c* A23 6c orange brown .70 .70
*178b* A23 10c dull violet 8.00 7.00
*183b* A23 20c deep blue 7.75 3.75
*184a* A23 21c olive brown 25.00 9.00
*189c* A23 30c violet 12.00 7.00
*192b* A23 50c blue green 45.00 45.00
*Nos. 164b-192b (14)* 107.20 76.20
Set, never hinged 225.00

***Syncopated, Type D (3 Holes Vert., 4 Holes Horiz.)***
**1927**
*174c* A23 7½c dark violet *2,750.* *2,100.*
Never hinged *3,750.*

No. 185 Surcharged in Red

**1929, Nov. 11** ***Perf. 12½***
194 A23 21c on 22½c ol brn 19.00 1.40
Never hinged 47.50

Queen Wilhelmina — A26

**1931, Oct. Photo. *Perf. 12½***

| | | | | |
|---|---|---|---|---|
| **195** | A26 | 70c dk bl & red | 29.00 | .75 |
| | | Never hinged | 110.00 | |
| *a.* | | Perf. 14½x13½ ('39) | 50.00 | 11.00 |
| | | Never hinged | 190.00 | |

See No. 201.

Arms of the House of Orange — A27

William I — A28

Designs: 5c, William I, Portrait by Goltzius. 6c, Portrait of William I by Van Key. 12½c, Portrait attributed to Moro.

**1933, Apr. 1 Unwmk. Engr.**

| | | | | |
|---|---|---|---|---|
| **196** | A27 | 1½c black | .55 | .40 |
| **197** | A28 | 5c dark green | 1.75 | .40 |
| **198** | A28 | 6c dull violet | 2.75 | .30 |
| **199** | A28 | 12½c deep blue | 17.00 | 3.50 |
| | | *Nos. 196-199 (4)* | 22.05 | 4.60 |
| | | Set, never hinged | 55.00 | |

400th anniv. of the birth of William I, Count of Nassau and Prince of Orange, frequently referred to as William the Silent.

Star, Dove and Sword — A31

**1933, May 18 Photo. Wmk. 202**

| | | | | |
|---|---|---|---|---|
| **200** | A31 | 12½c dp ultra | 8.00 | .75 |
| | | Never hinged | 26.50 | |

For overprint see No. O12.

**Queen Wilhelmina Design of 1931**

Queen Wilhelmina and ships.

***Perf. 14½x13½***

**1933, July 26 Wmk. 202**

| | | | | |
|---|---|---|---|---|
| **201** | A26 | 80c Prus bl & red | 100.00 | 2.90 |
| | | Never hinged | 320.00 | |

Willemstad Harbor — A33

Van Walbeeck's Ship — A34

***Perf. 14x12½***

**1934, July 2 Engr. Unwmk.**

| | | | | |
|---|---|---|---|---|
| **202** | A33 | 6c violet blk | 3.50 | .25 |
| **203** | A34 | 12½c dull blue | 20.00 | 3.00 |
| | | Set, never hinged | 70.00 | |

Tercentenary of Curacao.

Minerva — A35

Design: 12½c, Gisbertus Voetius.

**Wmk. 202**

**1936, May 15 Photo. *Perf. 12½***

| | | | | |
|---|---|---|---|---|
| **204** | A35 | 6c brown lake | 2.50 | .25 |
| **205** | A35 | 12½c indigo | 4.50 | 4.50 |
| | | Set, never hinged | 16.00 | |

300th anniversary of the founding of the University at Utrecht.

Boy Scout Emblem A37

"Assembly" A38

Mercury — A39

**1937, Apr. 1 *Perf. 14½x13½***

| | | | | |
|---|---|---|---|---|
| **206** | A37 | 1½c multicolored | .40 | .25 |
| **207** | A38 | 6c multicolored | 1.25 | .25 |
| **208** | A39 | 12½c multicolored | 4.00 | 1.40 |
| | | *Nos. 206-208 (3)* | 5.65 | 1.90 |
| | | Set, never hinged | 12.00 | |

Fifth Boy Scout World Jamboree, Vogelenzang, Netherlands, 7/31-8/13/37.

Wilhelmina — A40

**1938, Aug. 27 *Perf. 12½x12***

| | | | | |
|---|---|---|---|---|
| **209** | A40 | 1½c black | .25 | .25 |
| **210** | A40 | 5c red orange | .30 | .25 |
| **211** | A40 | 12½c royal blue | 4.00 | 1.60 |
| | | *Nos. 209-211 (3)* | 4.55 | 2.10 |
| | | Set, never hinged | 13.50 | |

Reign of Queen Wilhelmina, 40th anniv.

St. Willibrord — A41

Design: 12½c, St. Willibrord as older man.

***Perf. 12½x14***

**1939, June 15 Engr. Unwmk.**

| | | | | |
|---|---|---|---|---|
| **212** | A41 | 5c dk slate grn | .75 | .25 |
| **213** | A41 | 12½c slate blue | 5.00 | 2.75 |
| | | Set, never hinged | 14.00 | |

12th centenary of the death of St. Willibrord.

Woodburning Engine — A43

Design: 12½c, Streamlined electric car.

***Perf. 14½x13½***

**1939, Sept. 1 Photo. Wmk. 202**

| | | | | |
|---|---|---|---|---|
| **214** | A43 | 5c dk slate grn | .80 | .25 |
| **215** | A43 | 12½c dark blue | 8.00 | 4.00 |
| | | Set, never hinged | 22.50 | |

Centenary of Dutch Railroads.

**Catalogue values for unused stamps in this section, from this point to the end of the section, are for Never Hinged items.**

Queen Wilhelmina — A45

**1940-47 *Perf. 13½x12½***

| | | | | |
|---|---|---|---|---|
| **216** | A45 | 5c dk green | .25 | .25 |
| **216B** | A45 | 6c hn brn ('47) | .50 | .25 |
| **217** | A45 | 7½c brt red | .25 | .25 |
| **218** | A45 | 10c brt red vio | .25 | .25 |
| **219** | A45 | 12½c sapphire | .25 | .25 |
| **220** | A45 | 15c light blue | .25 | .25 |
| **220B** | A45 | 17½c slate bl ('46) | 1.10 | .65 |
| **221** | A45 | 20c purple | .55 | .25 |
| **222** | A45 | 22½c olive grn | 1.75 | 1.60 |
| **223** | A45 | 25c rose brn | .45 | .25 |
| **224** | A45 | 30c bister | .95 | .35 |
| **225** | A45 | 40c brt green | 1.60 | .65 |
| **225A** | A45 | 50c orange ('46) | 6.75 | .65 |
| **225B** | A45 | 60c pur brn ('46) | 6.75 | 1.90 |
| | | *Nos. 216-225B (14)* | 21.65 | 7.80 |

Imperf. examples of Nos. 216, 218-220 were released through philatelic channels during the German occupation, but were never issued at any post office. Value, set, $1.

For overprints see Nos. O16-O24.

Type of 1924-26 Surcharged in Black or Blue

***Perf. 12½x13½***

**1940, Oct. Photo. Wmk. 202**

| | | | | |
|---|---|---|---|---|
| **226** | A24 | 2½c on 3c ver | 4.00 | .25 |
| **227** | A24 | 5c on 3c lt grn | .25 | .25 |
| **228** | A24 | 7½c on 3c ver | .25 | .25 |
| *a.* | | Pair, #226, 228 | 5.00 | 1.50 |
| **229** | A24 | 10c on 3c lt grn | .25 | .25 |
| **230** | A24 | 12½c on 3c lt bl (Bl) | .35 | .35 |
| **231** | A24 | 17½c on 3c lt grn | 1.00 | .55 |
| **232** | A24 | 20c on 3c lt grn | .70 | .25 |
| **233** | A24 | 22½c on 3c lt grn | 2.75 | 3.75 |
| **234** | A24 | 25c on 3c lt grn | 1.25 | .35 |
| **235** | A24 | 30c on 3c lt grn | 1.10 | .40 |
| **236** | A24 | 40c on 3c lt grn | 2.00 | 1.75 |
| **237** | A24 | 50c on 3c lt grn | 1.25 | .55 |
| **238** | A24 | 60c on 3c lt grn | 1.35 | 1.00 |
| **239** | A24 | 70c on 3c lt grn | 7.25 | 7.25 |
| **240** | A24 | 80c on 3c lt grn | 9.25 | 8.50 |
| **241** | A24 | 1g on 3c lt grn | 29.00 | 25.00 |
| **242** | A24 | 2.50g on 3c lt grn | 32.00 | 32.00 |
| **243** | A24 | 5g on 3c lt grn | 32.00 | 29.00 |
| | | *Nos. 226-243 (18)* | 126.00 | 111.70 |
| | | Set, hinged | 80.00 | |

No. 228a is from coils.

**Gull Type of 1924-26**

**1941**

| | | | | |
|---|---|---|---|---|
| **243A** | A24 | 2½c dk green | 1.00 | .25 |
| *b.* | | Booklet pane of 6 | 15.00 | |
| **243C** | A24 | 5c brt green | .25 | .25 |
| *s.* | | Booklet pane of 6 | 15.00 | |
| **243E** | A24 | 7½c henna | .25 | .25 |
| *r.* | | Pair, #243A, 243E | 2.50 | 2.50 |
| *t.* | | Booklet pane of 6 | 15.00 | |
| **243G** | A24 | 10c brt violet | .60 | .25 |
| **243H** | A24 | 12½c ultra | .35 | .25 |
| *u.* | | Booklet pane of 6 | 15.00 | |
| **243J** | A24 | 15c lt blue | .60 | .30 |
| **243K** | A24 | 17½c red org | .25 | .25 |
| **243L** | A24 | 20c lt violet | .85 | .25 |
| **243M** | A24 | 22½c dk ol grn | .25 | .30 |
| **243N** | A24 | 25c lake | .35 | .25 |
| **243O** | A24 | 30c olive | 2.25 | .25 |
| **243P** | A24 | 40c emerald | .25 | .25 |
| **243Q** | A24 | 50c orange brn | .25 | .25 |
| | | *Nos. 243A-243Q (13)* | 7.50 | 3.35 |

No. 243Er is from coils.

Stamps from coils have designs that are 21½mm wide instead of 22¼mm width of the sheet stamps. Stamps are Nos. 496-498, 663-664, 681-682, 705-706, 708-772, 719, 721, 736, 749, 794, 797, 800, 809, 982.

Post Horn and Lion — A46

**Gold Surcharge**

**1943, Jan. 15 Photo. *Perf. 12½x12***

| | | | | |
|---|---|---|---|---|
| **244** | A46 | 10c on 2½c yel | .25 | .25 |
| *a.* | | Surcharge omitted | *6,000.* | *6,500.* |

Founding of the European Union of Posts and Telegraphs at Vienna, Oct. 19, 1942.

Sea Horse — A47

Triple-crown Tree — A48

Admiral M. A. de Ruyter — A54

Designs: 2c, Swans. 2½c, Tree of Life. 3c, Tree with snake roots. 4c, Man on horseback. 5c, Rearing white horses. 10c, Johan Evertsen. 12½c, Martin Tromp. 15c, Piet Hein. 17½c, Willem van Ghent. 20c, Witte de With. 22½c, Cornelis Evertsen. 25c, Tjerk de Vries. 30c, Cornelis Tromp. 40c, Cornelis Evertsen De Jongste.

***Perf. 12x12½, 12½x12***

**1943-44 Photo. Wmk. 202**

| | | | | |
|---|---|---|---|---|
| **245** | A47 | 1c black | .25 | .25 |
| **246** | A48 | 1½c rose lake | .25 | .25 |
| **247** | A47 | 2c dk blue | .25 | .25 |
| **248** | A48 | 2½c dk blue grn | .25 | .25 |
| **249** | A47 | 3c copper red | .25 | .25 |
| **250** | A48 | 4c black brown | .25 | .25 |
| **251** | A47 | 5c dull yel grn | .25 | .25 |

**Unwmk.**

| | | | | |
|---|---|---|---|---|
| **252** | A54 | 7½c henna brn | .25 | .25 |
| *a.* | | Thinner numerals and letters ('44) | .25 | .25 |
| **253** | A54 | 10c dk green | .25 | .25 |
| **254** | A54 | 12½c blue | .25 | .25 |
| **255** | A54 | 15c dull lilac | .25 | .25 |
| **256** | A54 | 17½c slate ('44) | .25 | .25 |
| **257** | A54 | 20c dull brown | .25 | .25 |
| **258** | A54 | 22½c org red | .25 | .25 |
| **259** | A54 | 25c vio rose ('44) | .35 | .55 |
| **260** | A54 | 30c cobalt bl ('44) | .25 | .25 |

**Engr.**

| | | | | |
|---|---|---|---|---|
| **261** | A54 | 40c bluish blk | .25 | .25 |
| | | *Nos. 245-261 (17)* | 4.35 | 4.55 |

In 1944, 200,000 examples of No. 247 were privately punched with a cross and printed on the back with a number and the words "Prijs 15 Cent toeslag ten bate Ned. Roode Kruis." These were sold at an exhibition, the surtax going to the Red Cross. The Dutch post office tolerated these stamps.

Soldier — A64

S. S. "Nieuw Amsterdam" — A65

Pilot — A66

Cruiser "De Ruyter" — A67

Queen Wilhelmina — A68

*Perf. 12, 12½*

**1944-46 Unwmk. Engr.**

| | | | | |
|---|---|---|---|---|
| **262** | A64 | 1½c black | .25 | .25 |
| **263** | A65 | 2½c yellow grn | .25 | .25 |
| **264** | A66 | 3c dull red brn | .25 | .25 |
| **265** | A67 | 5c dk blue | .25 | .25 |
| **266** | A68 | 7½c vermilion | .25 | .25 |
| **267** | A68 | 10c yellow org | .25 | .25 |
| **268** | A68 | 12½c ultra | .25 | .25 |
| **269** | A68 | 15c dl red brn ('46) | 1.30 | 1.25 |
| **270** | A68 | 17½c gray grn ('46) | .75 | .85 |
| **271** | A68 | 20c violet | .35 | .25 |
| **272** | A68 | 22½c rose red ('46) | .90 | 1.00 |
| **273** | A68 | 25c brn org ('46) | 1.00 | 1.10 |
| **274** | A68 | 30c blue grn | .25 | .25 |
| **275** | A68 | 40c dk vio brn ('46) | 2.00 | 2.10 |
| **276** | A68 | 50c red vio ('46) | 1.10 | .85 |
| | | *Nos. 262-276 (15)* | 9.40 | 9.40 |

These stamps were used on board Dutch war and merchant ships until Netherlands' liberation.

Lion and Dragon — A69

**1945, July 14** *Perf. 12½x14*

| | | | | |
|---|---|---|---|---|
| **277** | A69 | 7½c red orange | .25 | .25 |

Netherlands' liberation or "rising again."

Queen Wilhelmina — A70

**1946 Engr.** *Perf. 13½x14*

| | | | | |
|---|---|---|---|---|
| **278** | A70 | 1g dark blue | 2.50 | .60 |
| **279** | A70 | 2½g brick red | 125.00 | 8.00 |
| **280** | A70 | 5g dk olive grn | 125.00 | 22.00 |
| **281** | A70 | 10g dk purple | 125.00 | 22.00 |
| | | *Nos. 278-281 (4)* | 377.50 | 52.60 |
| | | Set, hinged | 200.00 | |

A71

*Perf. 12½x13½*

**1946-47 Wmk. 202 Photo.**

| | | | | |
|---|---|---|---|---|
| **282** | A71 | 1c dark red | .25 | .25 |
| **283** | A71 | 2c ultra | .25 | .25 |
| **284** | A71 | 2½c dp orange ('47) | 3.50 | 1.00 |
| **285** | A71 | 4c olive green | .30 | .25 |
| | | *Nos. 282-285 (4)* | 4.30 | 1.75 |

The 1c was reissued in 1969 on phosphorescent paper in booklet pane No. 345b. The 4c was reissued on fluorescent paper in 1962.

The 2c was issued in coils in 1972. Every fifth stamp has black control number on back.

See Nos. 340-343A, 404-406.

Queen Wilhelmina
A72 A73

**1947-48** *Perf. 13½x12½*

| | | | | |
|---|---|---|---|---|
| **286** | A72 | 5c olive grn ('48) | 1.00 | .25 |
| **287** | A72 | 6c brown black | .30 | .25 |
| **288** | A72 | 7½c dp red brn ('48) | .40 | .25 |
| **289** | A72 | 10c brt red vio | .75 | .25 |
| **290** | A72 | 12½c scarlet ('48) | .75 | .35 |
| **291** | A72 | 15c purple | 7.00 | .25 |
| **292** | A72 | 20c deep blue | 7.00 | .25 |
| **293** | A72 | 22½c ol brn ('48) | .75 | .65 |
| **294** | A72 | 25c ultra | 14.00 | .25 |
| **295** | A72 | 30c dp orange | 14.00 | .25 |
| **296** | A72 | 35c dk blue grn | 14.00 | .45 |
| **297** | A72 | 40c henna brown | 15.50 | .45 |

**Engr.**

| | | | | |
|---|---|---|---|---|
| **298** | A73 | 45c dp bl ('48) | 16.50 | 8.50 |
| **299** | A73 | 50c brown ('48) | 11.50 | .35 |
| **300** | A73 | 60c red ('48) | 14.50 | 1.90 |
| | | *Nos. 286-300 (15)* | 117.95 | 14.65 |
| | | Set, hinged | 60.00 | |

For surcharge see No. 330.

**Type of 1947**

**1948 Photo.**

| | | | | |
|---|---|---|---|---|
| **301** | A72 | 6c gray blue | .50 | .25 |

Queen Wilhelmina — A74

*Perf. 12½x14*

**1948, Aug. 30 Engr. Unwmk.**

| | | | | |
|---|---|---|---|---|
| **302** | A74 | 10c vermilion | .25 | .25 |
| **303** | A74 | 20c deep blue | 1.25 | 1.00 |

Reign of Queen Wilhelmina, 50th anniv.

Queen Juliana — A75

*Perf. 14x13*

**1948, Sept. 7 Photo. Wmk. 202**

| | | | | |
|---|---|---|---|---|
| **304** | A75 | 10c dark brown | 1.10 | .25 |
| **305** | A75 | 20c ultra | 1.40 | .45 |

Investiture of Queen Juliana, Sept. 6, 1948.

Queen Juliana — A76

**1949** *Perf. 13½x12½*

| | | | | |
|---|---|---|---|---|
| **306** | A76 | 5c olive green | .65 | .25 |
| **307** | A76 | 6c gray blue | .35 | .25 |
| **308** | A76 | 10c deep orange | .35 | .25 |
| **309** | A76 | 12c orange red | 1.90 | 1.75 |
| **310** | A76 | 15c olive brown | 3.75 | .25 |
| **311** | A76 | 20c brt blue | 3.25 | .25 |
| **312** | A76 | 25c orange brn | 8.75 | .25 |
| **313** | A76 | 30c violet | 6.25 | .25 |
| **314** | A76 | 35c gray | 21.00 | .25 |
| **315** | A76 | 40c red violet | 35.00 | .25 |
| **316** | A76 | 45c red orange | 1.30 | .70 |
| **317** | A76 | 50c blue green | 8.75 | .25 |
| **318** | A76 | 60c red brown | 12.50 | .25 |
| | | *Nos. 306-318 (13)* | 103.80 | 5.20 |

See No. 325-327. For surcharge see No. B248.

Queen Juliana — A77

**1949 Unwmk. Engr.** *Perf. 12½x12*

| | | | | |
|---|---|---|---|---|
| **319** | A77 | 1g rose red | 3.25 | .25 |
| **320** | A77 | 2½g black brn | 200.00 | 2.25 |
| **321** | A77 | 5g orange brn | 360.00 | 3.50 |
| **322** | A77 | 10g dk vio brn | 250.00 | 11.50 |
| | | *Nos. 319-322 (4)* | 813.25 | 17.50 |
| | | Set, hinged | 350.00 | |

Two types exist of No. 321.

Post Horns Entwined — A78

*Perf. 11½x12½*

**1949, Oct. 1 Photo. Wmk. 202**

| | | | | |
|---|---|---|---|---|
| **323** | A78 | 10c brown red | .60 | .25 |
| **324** | A78 | 20c dull blue | 4.50 | 1.75 |

75th anniversary of the UPU.

**Juliana Type of 1949**

**1950-51** *Perf. 13½x12½*

| | | | | |
|---|---|---|---|---|
| **325** | A76 | 12c scarlet ('51) | 5.00 | 1.00 |
| **326** | A76 | 45c violet brn | 40.00 | .45 |
| **327** | A76 | 75c car rose ('51) | 60.00 | 1.50 |
| | | *Nos. 325-327 (3)* | 105.00 | 2.95 |

Janus Dousa — A79

Design: 20c, Jan van Hout.

**1950, Oct. 3** *Perf. 11½x13*

| | | | | |
|---|---|---|---|---|
| **328** | A79 | 10c olive brown | 2.60 | .25 |
| **329** | A79 | 20c deep blue | 2.60 | 1.10 |

375th anniversary of the founding of the University of Leyden.

No. 288 Surcharged in Black

**1950, May** *Perf. 13½x12½*

| | | | | |
|---|---|---|---|---|
| **330** | A72 | 6c on 7½c dp red brn | 1.10 | .25 |

Miner — A80

*Perf. 12x12½*

**1952, Apr. 16 Engr. Unwmk.**

| | | | | |
|---|---|---|---|---|
| **331** | A80 | 10c dark blue | 1.30 | .25 |

50th anniversary of the founding of Netherlands' mining and chemical industry.

Telegraph Poles and Train of 1852 — A81

Designs: 6c, Radio towers. 10c, Mail Delivery 1852. 20c, Modern postman.

**1952, June 28** *Perf. 13x14*

| | | | | |
|---|---|---|---|---|
| **332** | A81 | 2c gray violet | .40 | .25 |
| **333** | A81 | 6c vermilion | .50 | .25 |
| **334** | A81 | 10c green | .50 | .25 |
| **335** | A81 | 20c gray blue | 4.00 | 1.60 |
| | | *Nos. 332-335 (4)* | 5.40 | 2.35 |

Centenary of Dutch postage stamps and of the telegraph service.

**1952, June 28**

| | | | | |
|---|---|---|---|---|
| **336** | A81 | 2c chocolate | 14.00 | 10.00 |
| **337** | A81 | 6c dk bluish grn | 14.00 | 10.00 |
| **338** | A81 | 10c brown carmine | 14.00 | 10.00 |
| **339** | A81 | 20c violet blue | 14.00 | 10.00 |
| | | *Nos. 336-339 (4)* | 56.00 | 40.00 |

Nos. 336 to 339 sold for 1.38g, which included the price of admission to the International Postage Stamp Centenary Exhibition, Utrecht.

**Numeral Type of 1946-47**

*Perf. 12½x13½*

**1953-57 Wmk. 202 Photo.**

| | | | | |
|---|---|---|---|---|
| **340** | A71 | 3c dp org brn | .30 | .25 |
| **341** | A71 | 5c orange | .25 | .25 |
| **342** | A71 | 6c gray ('54) | .30 | .25 |
| **343** | A71 | 7c red org | .25 | .25 |
| **343A** | A71 | 8c brt lilac ('57) | .25 | .25 |
| | | *Nos. 340-343A (5)* | 1.35 | 1.25 |

The 5c and 7c perf. on 3 sides, and with watermark vertical, are from booklet panes Nos. 346a-346b. The 5c perf. on 3 sides, with wmk. horiz., is from No. 349a.

In 1972 the 5c was printed on phosphorescent paper.

A82

**1953-71 Wmk. 202** *Perf. 13½x12½*

| | | | | |
|---|---|---|---|---|
| **344** | A82 | 10c dk red brn | .25 | .25 |
| *a.* | | Bklt. pane of 6 (1 #344 + 5 #346C)('65) | 5.00 | |
| **345** | A82 | 12c dk Prus grn ('54) | .25 | .25 |
| *a.* | | Bklt. pane of 7 + label (5 #345 + 2 #347)('67) | 5.50 | |
| *b.* | | Bklt. pane, 4 #282 + 8 #345 ('69) | 12.50 | |
| **346** | A82 | 15c dp carmine | .25 | .25 |
| *a.* | | Bklt. pane of 8 (2 #341 in vert. pair + 6 #346)('64) | 17.00 | |
| *b.* | | Bklt. pane of 12 (10 #343 + 2 #346)('64) | 12.50 | |
| *e.* | | Bklt. pane of 8 (2 #341 in horiz. pair + 6 #346)('70) | 9.00 | |
| **346C** | A82 | 18c dull bl ('65) | .25 | .25 |
| *d.* | | Bklt. pane of 10 (8 #343A + 2 #346C)('65) | 4.50 | |
| **347** | A82 | 20c dk gray | .25 | .25 |
| *b.* | | Bklt. pane of 5 + label ('66) | 4.00 | |
| **347A** | A82 | 24c olive ('63) | .30 | .25 |
| **348** | A82 | 25c deep blue | .95 | .25 |
| **349** | A82 | 30c deep orange | .35 | .25 |
| *a.* | | Bklt. pane of 5 + label (2 #341 + 3 #349)('71) | 22.50 | |
| **350** | A82 | 35c dk ol brn ('54) | .70 | .25 |
| **351** | A82 | 37c aqua ('58) | .35 | .25 |
| **352** | A82 | 40c dk slate | .35 | .25 |
| **353** | A82 | 45c scarlet | .30 | .25 |
| **354** | A82 | 50c dk bl grn | .55 | .25 |
| **355** | A82 | 60c brown bister | .70 | .25 |
| **356** | A82 | 62c dl red lil ('58) | .80 | .80 |
| **357** | A82 | 70c blue ('57) | .70 | .25 |
| **358** | A82 | 75c deep plum | .70 | .25 |
| **359** | A82 | 80c brt vio ('58) | .70 | .25 |
| **360** | A82 | 85c brt bl grn ('56) | .85 | .25 |
| **360A** | A82 | 95c org brn ('67) | .85 | .35 |
| | | *Nos. 344-360A (20)* | 10.40 | 5.65 |

Coils of the 12, 15, 20, 25, 30, 40, 45, 50, 60, 70, 75 and 80c were issued in 1972. Black control number on back of every fifth stamp.

Watermark is vertical on some stamps from booklet panes.

Some booklet panes, Nos. 344a, 347b, 349a, etc., have a large selvage the size of four or six stamps, with printed inscription and sometimes illustration.

Phosphorescent paper was introduced in 1967 for the 12, 15, 20 and 45c; in 1969 for the 25c, and in 1971 for the 30, 40, 50, 60, 70, 75 and 80c.

Of the booklet panes, Nos. 345a, 345b, 346d, 346e and 347b were issued on both ordinary and phosphorescent paper, and No. 349a only on phosphorescent paper.

See No. 407. For surcharge see No. 374.

Queen Juliana — A83

*Perf. 12½x12*

**1954-57 Unwmk. Engr.**

**361** A83 1g vermilion 1.00 .25
**362** A83 2½g dk green ('55) 4.25 .25
**363** A83 5g black ('55) 2.60 .35
**364** A83 10g vio bl ('57) 8.25 1.60
*Nos. 361-364 (4)* 16.10 2.45

St. Boniface — A84

**1954, June 16**

**365** A84 10c blue 1.25 .25

1200th anniv. of the death of St. Boniface.

Queen Juliana — A84a

**Wmk. 202**

**1954, Dec. 15 Photo. *Perf. 13½***

**366** A84a 10c scarlet .75 .25

Issued to publicize the Charter of the Kingdom, adopted December 15, 1954.

See Netherlands Antilles No. 232, Surinam No. 264.

Flaming Sword — A85

**1955, May 4 *Perf. 12½x12***

**367** A85 10c crimson .80 .25

10th anniv. of Netherlands' liberation.

"Rebuilding Europe" — A86

**1956, Sept. 15 Unwmk. *Perf. 13x14***

**368** A86 10c rose brn & blk *1.75* .25
**369** A86 25c brt bl & blk *24.00 1.25*

Europa. Issued to symbolize the cooperation among the six countries comprising the Coal and Steel Community.

Admiral M. A. de Ruyter — A87

30c, Flagship "De Zeven Provincien."

**1957, July 2 Engr. *Perf. 12½x12***

**370** A87 10c orange .35 .25
**371** A87 30c dk blue 2.60 1.10

Adm. M. A. de Ruyter (1607-1676).

"United Europe" — A88

**1957, Sept. 16 Photo. *Perf. 13x14***

**372** A88 10c blk, gray & ultra *.70* .25
**373** A88 30c dull grn & ultra *3.25 1.25*

United Europe for peace and prosperity.

**No. 344 Surcharged in Silver with New Value and Bars**

***Perf. 13½x12½***

**1958, May 16 Photo. Wmk. 202**

**374** A82 12c on 10c .80 .25
*a.* Double surcharge 400.00 400.00
*b.* Inverted surcharge 400.00 400.00

Common Design Types pictured following the introduction.

**Europa Issue, 1958**

Common Design Type

***Perf. 13x14***

**1958, Sept. 13 Litho. Unwmk.**

**Size: 22x33mm**

**375** CD1 12c org ver & blue *.25* .25
**376** CD1 30c blue & red *1.00* .50

NATO Emblem — A89

**1959, Apr. 3 *Perf. 12½x12***

**377** A89 12c yel org & blue .25 .25
**378** A89 30c red & blue .50 .40

10th anniversary of NATO.

**Europa Issue, 1959.**

Common Design Type

**1959, Sept. 19 *Perf. 13x14***

**Size: 22x33mm**

**379** CD2 12c crimson *.50* .25
**380** CD2 30c yellow grn *1.60 1.60*

Douglas DC-8 and World Map — A90

Design: 30c, Douglas DC-8 in flight.

**1959, Oct. 5 Engr. *Perf. 14x13***

**381** A90 12c carmine & ultra .25 .25
**382** A90 30c dp blue & dp grn .90 .90

40th anniversary of the founding of KLM, Royal Dutch Airlines.

J. C. Schroeder van der Kolk — A91

Design: 30c, Johannes Wier.

***Perf. 12½x12***

**1960, July 18 Unwmk.**

**383** A91 12c red .55 .40
**384** A91 30c dark blue 2.75 2.00

Issued to publicize Mental Health Year and to honor Schroeder van der Kolk and Johannes Wier, pioneers of mental health.

**Europa Issue, 1960**

Common Design Type

**1960, Sept. 19 Photo. *Perf. 12x12½***

**Size: 27x21mm**

**385** CD3 12c car rose & org *.40 .40*
**386** CD3 30c dk blue & yel *1.60 1.60*

1st anniv. of CEPT. Spokes symbolize 19 founding members of Conference.

**Europa Issue, 1961**

Common Design Type

**1961, Sept. 18 *Perf. 14x13***

**Size: 32½x21½mm**

**387** CD4 12c golden brown .25 .25
**388** CD4 30c Prus blue .25 .25

Queen Juliana and Prince Bernhard A92

***Perf. 14x13***

**1962, Jan. 5 Unwmk. Photo.**

**389** A92 12c dk red .25 .25
**390** A92 30c dk green 1.00 .65

Silver wedding anniversary of Queen Juliana and Prince Bernhard.

Telephone Dial — A93

Designs: 12c, Map showing telephone network. 30c, Arch and dial, horiz.

**1962, May 22 *Perf. 13x14, 14x13***

**391** A93 4c brown red & blk .25 .30
**392** A93 12c brown ol & blk .50 .30
**393** A93 30c black, bis & Prus bl 1.40 1.40
*Nos. 391-393 (3)* 2.15 2.00

Completion of the automation of the Netherlands telephone network.

**Europa Issue, 1962**

Common Design Type

**1962, Sept. 17 *Perf. 14x13***

**Size: 33x22mm**

**394** CD5 12c lemon, yel & blk *.25* .25
**395** CD5 30c blue, yel & blk *1.10* .65

Polder with Canals and Windmills — A94

Design: 4c, Cooling towers, Limburg State Coal Mines. 10c, Dredging in Delta.

***Perf. 12½x13½***

**1962-66 Wmk. 202 Photo.**

**399** A94 4c dk blue ('63) .25 .25
**401** A94 6c grn & dk grn .40 .25
**403** A94 10c dp claret ('63) .25 .25
*a.* Booklet pane of 10 ('66) 3.50
*Nos. 399-403 (3)* .90 .75

The 10c was issued in coils in 1972. Every fifth stamp has black control number on back.

No. 403a was reissued in 1972 on phosphored paper. Value, $100 booklet pane of 10.

See No. 461Ab.

**Types of 1946 and 1953**

**1962-73 Unwmk.**

**Phosphorescent Paper**

**404** A71 4c olive green 1.30 1.30
**405** A71 5c orange ('73) 1.30 1.30
**406** A71 8c bright lilac 6.00 8.50
**407** A82 12c dk Prus green 1.30 1.30
*Nos. 404-407 (4)* 9.90 12.40

The 5c is from booklets and has the phosphor on the front only.

Issue dates: 5c, Jan. 12; others Aug. 27.

See Nos. 460d, 461c, 461d and 463a.

Wheat Emblem and Globe — A95

**1963, Mar. 21 Photo. *Perf. 14x13***

**413** A95 12c dl bl, dk bl & yel .25 .25
**414** A95 30c dl car, rose & yel .80 .80

FAO "Freedom from Hunger" campaign.

Inscription in Circle — A96

***Perf. 13x14***

**1963, May 7 Unwmk. Litho.**

**415** A96 30c brt blue, blk & grn 1.00 1.00

1st Intl. Postal Conf., Paris, cent.

**Europa Issue, 1963**

Common Design Type

**1963, Sept. 16 Photo. *Perf. 14x13***

**Size: 33x22mm**

**416** CD6 12c red brown & yel *.30* .25
**417** CD6 30c Prus green & yel *1.00 .75*

Prince William of Orange Landing at Scheveningen A97

Designs: 12c, G. K. van Hogendorp, A. F. J. A. Graaf van der Duyn van Maasdam and L. Graaf van Limburg Stirum, Dutch leaders, 1813. 30c, Prince William taking oath of allegiance.

**1963, Nov. 18 Photo. *Perf. 12x12½***

**Size: 27½x27½mm**

**418** A97 4c dull bl, blk & brn .25 .25
**419** A97 5c dk grn, blk & red .25 .25
**420** A97 12c olive & blk .25 .25
**421** A97 30c maroon & blk .50 .50
*Nos. 418-421 (4)* 1.25 1.25

150th anniversary of the founding of the Kingdom of the Netherlands.

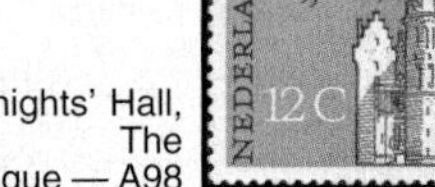

Knights' Hall, The Hague — A98

**1964, Jan. 9 *Perf. 14x13***

**422** A98 12c olive & blk .25 .25

500th anniversary of the meeting of the States-General (Parliament).

Arms of Groningen University — A99

Design: 30c, Initials "AG" and crown.

**1964, June 16 Engr. *Perf. 12½x12***
**423** A99 12c slate .25 .25
**424** A99 30c yellow brown .25 .25

350th anniv. of the University of Groningen.

Railroad Light Signal A100

Design: 40c, Electric locomotive.

**1964, July 28 Photo. *Perf. 14x13***
**425** A100 15c black & brt grn .25 .25
**426** A100 40c black & yellow .65 .55

125th anniv. of the Netherlands railroads.

Bible, Chrismon and Dove — A101

**1964, Aug. 25 Unwmk.**
**427** A101 15c brown red .25 .25

150th anniversary of the founding of the Netherlands Bible Society.

### Europa Issue, 1964
Common Design Type

**1964, Sept. 14 Photo. *Perf. 13x14***
**Size: 22x33mm**
**428** CD7 15c dp olive grn *.25* .25
**429** CD7 20c yellow brown *.50* *.35*

### Benelux Issue

King Baudouin, Queen Juliana and Grand Duchess Charlotte A101a

**1964, Oct. 12 *Perf. 14x13***
**Size: 33x22mm**
**430** A101a 15c purple & buff .25 .25

20th anniversary of the signing of the customs union of Belgium, Netherlands and Luxembourg.

Queen Juliana — A102

**1964, Dec. 15 Photo. *Perf. 13x14***
**431** A102 15c green .25 .25

10th anniversary of the Charter of the Kingdom of the Netherlands.

"Killed in Action" and "Destroyed Town" — A103

Statues: 15c, "Docker" Amsterdam, and "Killed in Action" Waalwijk. 40c, "Destroyed Town" Rotterdam, and "Docker" Amsterdam.

**1965, Apr. 6 Photo. *Perf. 12x12½***
**432** A103 7c black & dk red .25 .25
**433** A103 15c black & dk olive .25 .25
**434** A103 40c black & dk red .70 .60
*Nos. 432-434 (3)* 1.20 1.10

Resistance movement of World War II.

Knight Class IV, Order of William — A104

**1965, Apr. 29 *Perf. 13x14***
**435** A104 1g gray .75 .50

150th anniversary of the establishment of the Military Order of William.

ITU Emblem A105

**1965, May 17 Litho. *Perf. 14x13***
**436** A105 20c dull bl & tan .25 .25
**437** A105 40c tan & dull bl .30 .30

Centenary of the International Telecommunication Union.

### Europa Issue, 1965
Common Design Type

**1965, Sept. 27 Photo.**
**Size: 33x22mm**
**438** CD8 18c org brn, dk red & blk .25 .25
**439** CD8 20c sapphire, brn & blk .30 .25

Marines of 1665 and 1965 — A106

**1965, Dec. 10 Engr. *Perf. 13x14***
**440** A106 18c dk vio bl & car .25 .25

Netherlands Marine Corps, 300th anniv.

### Europa Issue, 1966
Common Design Type

**1966, Sept. 26 Photo. *Perf. 13x14***
**Size: 22x33mm**
**441** CD9 20c citron .25 .25
**442** CD9 40c dull blue .60 .25

Assembly Hall, Delft University A107

**1967, Jan. 5 Litho. *Perf. 14x13***
**443** A107 20c dl sage grn & sepia .25 .25

125th anniversary of the founding of the Delft University of Technology.

### Europa Issue, 1967
Common Design Type

***Perf. 13x14***
**1967, May 2 Unwmk. Photo.**
**Ordinary Paper**
**Size: 22x32½mm**
**444** CD10 20c dull blue *.35* .25
**445** CD10 45c dull vio brn *.75* *.60*

**Wmk. 202**
**446** CD10 20c dull blue *.65* *.30*
**447** CD10 45c dull vio brn *.95* *.90*
*Nos. 444-447 (4)* 2.70 2.05

Nos. 446-447 are on phosphorescent paper.

Stamp of 1852, #1 — A108

**1967, May 8 Engr. Unwmk.**
**448** A108 20c shown 1.75 1.75
**449** A108 25c No. 5 1.75 1.75
**450** A108 75c No. 10 1.75 1.75
*Nos. 448-450 (3)* 5.25 5.25

AMPHILEX 67, Amsterdam, May 11-21. Sold only in complete sets together with a 2.50g admission ticket to Amsterdam Philatelic Exhibition. Issued in sheets of 10 (5x2).

Coins and Punched Card — A109

**1968, Jan. 16 Photo. *Perf. 14x13***
**451** A109 20c ver, blk & dl yel .25 .25

50th anniversary of the postal checking service.

---

Luminescence

All commemorative issues from No. 451 to No. 511 are printed on phosphorescent paper except No. 478 which is printed with phosphorescent ink, and Nos. 490-492. Some later issues are tagged.

---

### Europa Issue, 1968
Common Design Type

**1968, Apr. 29 Photo. *Perf. 14x13***
**Size: 32½x22mm**
**452** CD11 20c deep blue .30 .25
**453** CD11 45c crimson .75 *.45*

National Anthem — A110

**1968, Aug. 27 Litho. *Perf. 13x14***
**454** A110 20c gray, org, car & dk bl .25 .25

400th anniversary of the national anthem "Wilhelmus van Nassouwe."

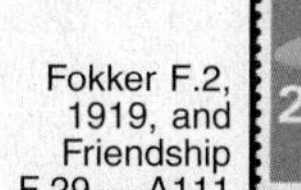

Fokker F.2, 1919, and Friendship F.29 — A111

Planes: 12c, Wright A, 1909, and Cessna sports plane. 45c, De Havilland DH-9, 1919, and Douglas DC-9.

**1968, Oct. 1 Photo. *Perf. 14x13***
**455** A111 12c crim, pink & blk .25 .25
**456** A111 20c brt grn, bl grn & blk .25 .25
**457** A111 45c brt bl, lt grn & blk 1.00 1.00
*Nos. 455-457 (3)* 1.50 1.50

50th anniv. of the founding in 1919 of Royal Dutch Airlines and the Royal Netherlands Aircraft Factories Fokker, and the 60th anniv. in 1967 of the Royal Netherlands Aeronautical Assoc.

"iao" — A112

Design is made up of 28 minute lines, each reading "1919 internationale arbeids-organisatie 1969".

**1969, Feb. 25 Engr. *Perf. 14x13***
**458** A112 25c brick red & blk .35 .25
**459** A112 45c ultra & blue .75 .65

International Labor Organization, 50th anniv.

A113

Queen Juliana — A114

***Perf. 13½ horiz. x 12½ on one vert. side***

**1969-75 Photo.**
**460** A113 25c orange ver .80 .25
*a.* Bklt. pane of 4 + 2 labels 10.00
**460B** A113 25c dull red ('73) 1.00 .25
*c.* Booklet pane of 6 (#460B + 5 #461A) 15.00
*d.* Booklet pane of 12 (5 #405 + 7 #460B) 14.00

***Perf. 13x12½***
**461** A113 30c choc ('72) .25 .25
*d.* Bklt. pane of 10 (4 #405 + 6 #461 + 2 labels)('74) 2.75
Complete booklet, #461d 2.75
**461A** A113 35c grnsh bl ('72) .25 .25
*b.* Bklt. pane of 5 (3 #403, 2 #461A + label)('72) 11.00
*c.* Bklt. pane of 10 (5 #405 + 5 #461A + 2 labels)('75) 3.00
Complete booklet, #461c 3.00
**462** A113 40c car rose ('72) .35 .25
*a.* Bklt. pane of 5 + label ('73) 5.50
**463** A113 45c ultra ('72) .35 .25
*a.* Bklt. pane of 8 (4 #405 + 4 #463) ('74) 2.00
Complete booklet, #463a 2.00
**464** A113 50c lilac ('72) .40 .25
*a.* Bklt. pane of 4 + 2 labels ('75) 2.00
Complete booklet, #464a 2.00
**465** A113 60c slate bl ('72) .50 .25
*a.* Bklt. pane of 5 + label ('80) 3.00
**466** A113 70c bister ('72) .60 .25
**467** A113 75c green ('72) .60 .25
**468** A113 80c red org ('72) .65 .25
**468A** A113 90c gray ('75) .65 .25

***Perf. 13x14***
**469** A114 1g yel green .65 .25
**470** A114 1.25g maroon .80 .25
**471** A114 1.50g yel bis ('71) 1.00 .25
**471A** A114 2g dp rose lil ('72) 1.10 .25
**472** A114 2.50g grnsh bl 1.40 .25
**473** A114 5g gray ('70) 2.75 .25
**474** A114 10g vio bl ('70) 5.50 .85
*Nos. 460-474 (19)* 19.60 5.35

Both 25c stamps issued only in booklets.

Printings were both ordinary and phosphorescent paper for Nos. 460, 460a, 469, 471-474.

Coil printings were issued later for Nos. 461, 462-472. Black control number on back of every fifth stamp.

Booklet panes have a large selvage the size of 4 or 6 stamps, with printed inscription.

See No. 542.

### Europa Issue, 1969
Common Design Type

**1969, Apr. 28 Photo. *Perf. 14x13***
**Size: 33½x22mm**
**475** CD12 25c dark blue *.25* .25
**476** CD12 45c red *1.10* *.75*

A114a

Möbius strip in Benelux colors.

**1969, Sept. 8 Photo. *Perf. 13x14***
**477** A114a 25c multicolored .25 .25

25th anniversary of the signing of the customs union of Belgium, Netherlands and Luxembourg.

A115

**Photo. & Engr.**
**1969, Sept. 30 *Perf. 13x14***
**478** A115 25c yellow grn & maroon .25 .25

Desiderius Erasmus (1469-1536), scholar.

Queen Juliana and Rising Sun — A116

**1969, Dec. 15 Photo. *Perf. 14x13***
**479** A116 25c blue & multi .25 .25

15th anniversary of the Charter of the Kingdom of the Netherlands.

Prof. E. M. Meijers A117

**1970, Jan. 13 Photo. *Perf. 14x13***
**480** A117 25c blue, vio bl & grn .25 .25

Issued to publicize the new Civil Code and to honor Prof. Meijers, who prepared it.

Dutch Pavilion, EXPO '70 — A118

**1970, Mar. 10 Photo. *Perf. 14x13***
**481** A118 25c multicolored .25 .25

EXPO '70 International Exposition, Osaka, Japan, Mar. 15-Sept. 13.

"V" for Victory — A119

**1970, Apr. 21 Photo. *Perf. 13x14***
**482** A119 12c red, ultra, brn ol & lt bl .25 .25

25th anniv. of liberation from the Germans.

**Europa Issue, 1970**
Common Design Type
**1970, May 4 Photo. *Perf. 14x13***
**Size: 32½x21½mm**
**483** CD13 25c carmine *.30 .25*
**484** CD13 45c dk blue *1.00 .90*

Panels — A120

Globe — A121

**1970, June 23 Photo. *Perf. 13x14***
**485** A120 25c gray, blk & brt yel grn .30 .25
**486** A121 45c ultra, blk & pur .60 .50

#485 publicizes the meeting of the interparliamentary Union; #486 the UN 25th anniv.

Punch Cards — A122

**1971, Feb. 16 Photo. *Perf. 14x13***
**487** A122 15c dp rose lilac .25 .25

14th national census, 1971.

**Europa Issue, 1971**
Common Design Type
**1971, May 3 Photo. *Perf. 14x13***
**Size: 33x22mm**
**488** CD14 25c lil rose, yel & blk *.40 .25*
**489** CD14 45c ultra, yel & blk *.80 .70*

No. 488 was issued in coils and sheets. In the coils every fifth stamp has a black control number on the back.

Prince Bernhard, Fokker F27, Boeing 747 B — A123

Designs: 15c, Stylized carnation (Prince Bernhard Fund). 20c, Giant Panda (World Wildlife Fund). 15c, 20c horiz.

**Photo., Litho. (20c)**
**1971, June 29 *Perf. 13x14***
**490** A123 15c black & yellow .30 .25
**491** A123 20c multicolored .75 .30
**492** A123 25c multicolored .30 .25
*Nos. 490-492,B475 (4)* 2.95 2.40

60th birthday of Prince Bernhard. See No. B475.

Map of Delta — A124

**1972, Feb. 15 Photo. *Perf. 14x13***
**493** A124 20c bl, grn, blk & red .25 .25

Publicity for the Delta plan, a project to shorten the coastline and to build roads.

**Europa Issue 1972**
Common Design Type
**1972, May 5 Photo. *Perf. 13x14***
**Size: 22x33mm**
**494** CD15 30c blue & bis *.40 .25*
**495** CD15 45c orange & bis *.80 .65*

No. 494 was issued in coils and sheets. In the coils every fifth stamp has a black control number on the back.

Thorbecke Quotation A126

**1972, June 2 Photo. *Perf. 14x13***
**496** A126 30c lt ultra & blk .40 .25

Jan Rudolf Thorbecke (1798-1872), statesman, who said: "There is more to be done in the world than ever before."

Dutch Flag — A127

**1972 *Perf. 13x14***
**497** A127 20c blue & multi .30 .25
**498** A127 25c blue & multi .60 .25

400th anniversary of the Dutch flag.
Issue dates: 20c, July 4; 25c, Nov. 1.

Woman Hurdler A128

30c, Woman swimmer. 45c, Bicycling.

**1972, July 11 *Perf. 14x13***
**499** A128 20c multicolored .25 .25
**500** A128 30c crimson & multi .30 .25
**501** A128 45c violet & multi .60 .60
*Nos. 499-501 (3)* 1.15 1.10

20th Olympic Games, Munich, 8/26-9/11.

Red Cross — A129

**1972, Aug. 15 Photo. *Perf. 13x14***
**502** A129 5c red .25 .25
*Nos. 502,B485-B488 (5)* 2.90 2.75

Netherlands Red Cross.

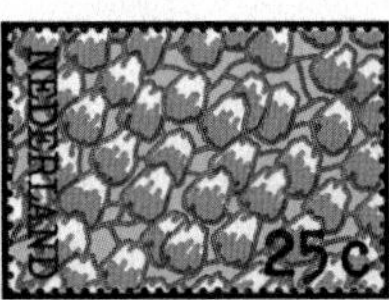
Tulips — A130

**1973, Mar. 20 Photo. *Perf. 14x13***
**503** A130 25c rose, brt grn & blk .40 .25

Dutch flower and bulb exports.

**Europa Issue 1973**
Common Design Type
**1973, May 1 Photo. *Perf. 14x13***
**Size: 32½x22mm**
**504** CD16 35c bright blue *.40 .25*
**505** CD16 50c purple *.80 .70*

Hockey A132

Woman Gymnast A133

Antenna, Burum A134

Rainbow, Measures A135

**Photo. (25c, 35c); Litho. (30c, 50c)**
**1973, July 31 *Perf. 13x14, 14x13***
**506** A132 25c black & green .35 .25
**507** A133 30c gray & multi .80 .50
**508** A134 35c blue & multi .50 .30
**509** A135 50c blue & multi .80 .70
*Nos. 506-509 (4)* 2.45 1.75

Netherlands Hockey Assoc., 75th anniv. (25c); Rhythmical Gymnastics World Championship, Rotterdam (30c); inauguration of satellite ground station at Burum (35c); cent. of intl. meteorological cooperation (50c).

Queen Juliana, Dutch and House of Orange Colors A136

**Engr. & Photo.**
**1973, Sept. 4 *Perf. 13x12***
**510** A136 40c silver & multi .40 .25

25th anniversary of reign of Queen Juliana.

Chain with Open Link — A137

**1973, Oct. 16 Photo. *Perf. 13x14***
**511** A137 40c grn, blk, gold & sil .40 .25

Development Corporation.

Nature and Environment — A138

**1974, Feb. 19 Photo. *Perf. 13x14***
**512** A138 Strip of 3 1.75 1.75
*a.* 25c Bird of prey .55 .35
*b.* 25c Tree .55 .35
*c.* 25c Fisherman in boat and frog .55 .35

75th anniv. of the Netherlands Assoc. for the Protection of Birds and of the State Forestry Service.

Soccer Ball — A139

Tennis Ball — A140

***Perf. 14x13, 13x14***

**1974, June 5** **Photo.**

**513** A139 25c multicolored .40 .25
**514** A140 40c multicolored .40 .25

World Cup Soccer Championship, Munich, June 13-July 7 (25c) and 75th anniversary of the Royal Dutch Lawn Tennis Association (40c).

Cattle — A141

Pierced Crab under Lens — A142

Shipwreck Seen Through Binoculars — A143

**1974, July 30** ***Perf. 13x14***

**515** A141 25c multicolored 1.20 1.20
**516** A142 25c sal pink & multi .90 .30
**517** A143 40c dk violet & multi .90 .30
*Nos. 515-517 (3)* 3.00 1.80

Cent. of the Netherlands Cattle Herdbook Soc. (#515); 25th anniv. of Queen Wilhelmina Fund (for cancer research) (#516); sesquicentennial of Royal Dutch Lifeboat Soc. (#517).

### BENELUX Issue

"BENELUX" A143a

**1974, Sept. 10** **Photo.** ***Perf. 14x13***

**518** A143a 30c bl grn, dk grn & lt bl .35 .25

30th anniv. of the signing of the customs union of Belgium, Netherlands and Luxembourg.

Council of Europe Emblem A144

NATO Emblem and Sea Gull A145

**1974, Sept. 10** ***Perf. 13x14***

**519** A144 45c black, bl & yel .40 .25
**520** A145 45c dk blue & silver .40 .25

25th anniv. of Council of Europe (No. 519) and of North Atlantic Treaty Organization (No. 520).

Letters and Hands, Papier-maché Sculpture — A146

**1974, Oct. 9**

**521** A146 60c purple & multi .35 .25

Centenary of Universal Postal Union.

People and Map of Dam Square A147

Brain with Window Symbolizing Free Thought A148

Design: No. 523, Portuguese Synagogue and map of Mr. Visser Square. 35c, No. 526, like No. 522.

**1975** **Photo.** ***Perf. 13x14***

**522** A147 30c multicolored .35 .25
**523** A147 30c multicolored .35 .25
**524** A147 35c multicolored .40 .25
**525** A148 45c dp blue & multi .30 .25
*Nos. 522-525 (4)* 1.40 1.00

### Coil Stamps

***Perf. 13 Horiz.***

**526** A147 30c multicolored .35 .25
**527** A147 35c multicolored .40 .25

700th anniv. of Amsterdam (No. 522); 300th anniv. of the Portuguese Synagogue in Amsterdam (No. 523) and 400th anniv. of the founding of the University of Leyden and the beginning of higher education in the Netherlands (No. 525).

Issue dates: Nos. 522-523, 525-526, Feb. 26; Nos. 524, 527, Apr. 1.

Eye Looking over Barbed Wire — A149

**1975, Apr. 29** **Photo.** ***Perf. 13x14***

**528** A149 35c black & carmine .40 .25

Liberation of the Netherlands from Nazi occupation, 30th anniversary.

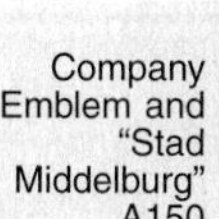

Company Emblem and "Stad Middelburg" A150

**1975, May 21** **Photo.** ***Perf. 14x13***

**529** A150 35c multicolored .50 .25

Zeeland Steamship Company, centenary.

Albert Schweitzer in Boat — A151

**1975, May 21**

**530** A151 50c multicolored .50 .25

Albert Schweitzer (1875-1965), medical missionary.

Symbolic Metric Scale — A152

**1975, July 29** **Litho.** ***Perf. 14x13***

**531** A152 50c multicolored .50 .25

Cent. of Intl. Meter Convention, Paris, 1875.

Playing Card with Woman, Man, Pigeons, Pens — A153

**1975, July 29** ***Perf. 13x14***

**532** A153 35c multicolored .50 .25

International Women's Year 1975.

Fingers Reading Braille — A154

**1975, Oct. 7** **Photo.** ***Perf. 13x14***

**533** A154 35c multicolored .50 .25

Sesquicentennial of the invention of Braille system of writing for the blind by Louis Braille (1809-1852).

Rubbings of 25¢ Coins A155

**1975, Oct. 7** ***Perf. 14x13***

**534** A155 50c green, blk & bl .50 .25

To publicize the importance of saving.

Lottery Ticket, 18th Century A156

**1976, Feb. 3** **Photo.** ***Perf. 14x13***

**535** A156 35c multicolored .40 .25

250th anniversary of National Lottery.

### Queen Type of 1969 and

A157

**1976-86** **Photo.** ***Perf. 12½x13½***

**536** A157 5c gray .25 .25
Booklet Panes
*a.* (3 #536, 2 #537, 3 #542) 3.00
Complete booklet, #536a 3.00
*b.* (4 #536, 2 #537, 4 #539 + 2 labels) 2.00
Complete booklet, #536b 2.00
*c.* (#536, 2 #537, 5 #542) 3.00
Complete booklet, #536c 3.00
*d.* (4 #536, 7 #539 + label) 3.00
Complete booklet, #536d 3.00
*e.* (2 #536, 2 #540, 4 #541) 3.00
*f.* (5 #536, 2 #537, 2 #540, 3 #542) + 2 labels 4.00
Complete booklet, #536f 4.00
*g.* (1 #536, 2 #537, 5 #543) ('86) 3.00
Complete booklet, #536g 3.00
**537** A157 10c ultra .25 .25
**538** A157 25c violet .25 .25
**539** A157 40c sepia .40 .25
**540** A157 45c brt blue .40 .25
**541** A157 50c lil rose ('80) .40 .25
*a.* Bklt. pane, 5 each #537, 541 + 2 labels 2.75
Complete booklet, #541a 2.75
**542** A113 55c carmine .60 .25
**543** A157 55c brt grn ('81) .55 .25
**544** A157 60c apple grn ('81) .65 .25
**545** A157 65c dk red brn ('86) .95 .25
*Nos. 536-545 (10)* 4.70 2.50

Compare No. 544 with No. 791. No. 542 also issued in coils with control number on the back of every 5th stamp.

See Nos. 903-905.

### Coil Stamps

**1976-86** ***Perf. 13½ Vert.***

**546** A157 5c slate gray .25 .25
**547** A157 10c ultra .25 .25
**548** A157 25c violet .30 .25
**549** A157 40c sepia ('77) .50 .25
**550** A157 45c brt blue .50 .25
**551** A157 50c brt rose ('79) .75 .25
**552** A157 55c brt grn ('81) .75 .25
**553** A157 60c apple grn ('81) .85 .25
**554** A157 65c dk red brn ('86) .95 .25
*Nos. 546-554 (9)* 5.10 2.25

See Nos. 772, 774, 786, 788, 791.

De Ruyter Statue, Flushing A158

**1976, Apr. 22** **Photo.** ***Perf. 14x13***

**555** A158 55c multicolored .50 .25

Adm. Michiel Adriaenszon de Ruyter (1607-1676), Dutch naval hero, 300th death anniversary.

Van Prinsterer and Page — A159

**1976, May 19** **Photo.** ***Perf. 14x13***

**556** A159 55c multicolored .40 .25

Guillaume Groen van Prinsterer (1801-1876), statesman and historian.

Women Waving American Flags — A160

Design is from a 220-year old permanent wooden calendar from Ameland Island.

**1976, May 25** **Litho.**

**557** A160 75c multicolored .60 .25

American Bicentennial.

Marchers A161

**1976, June 15** **Photo.** ***Perf. 14x13***

**558** A161 40c multicolored .50 .25

Nijmegen 4-day march, 60th anniversary.

A number of stamps issued from 1970 on appear to have parts of the designs misregistered, blurry, or look off-center. These stamps are deliberately designed that way. Most prominent examples are Nos. 559, 582, 602, 656, 711-712, 721, B638-B640, B662-B667.

Runners A162

**1976, June 15 Litho. Tagged**
**559** A162 55c multicolored .55 .25

Royal Dutch Athletic Soc., 75th anniv.

Printing: One Communicating with Many — A163

**1976, Sept. 2 Photo. *Perf. 13x14***
**560** A163 45c blue & red .50 .25

Netherlands Printers Organization, 75th anniv.

Sailing Ship and City — A164

Design: 75c, Sea gull over coast.

**1976, Sept. 2 Litho. *Perf. 14x13***
**Tagged**
**561** A164 40c bister, red & bl .50 .25
**562** A164 75c ultra, yel & red .70 .45

Zuider Zee Project, the conversion of water areas into land.

Radiation of Heat and Light — A165

Ballot and Pencil A166

***Perf. 13x14, 14x13***
**1977, Jan. 25 Photo.**
**563** A165 40c multicolored .45 .25
**564** A166 45c black, red & ocher .45 .25

**Coil Stamps**
***Perf. 13 Horiz.***
**565** A165 40c multicolored .35 .25
***Perf. 13 Vert.***
**566** A166 45c multicolored .35 .25

Publicity for wise use of energy (40c) and forthcoming elections (45c). Nos. 565-566 have black control number on back of every 5th stamp.

For overprint see No. 569.

Spinoza — A167

**1977, Feb. 21 Photo. *Perf. 13x14***
**567** A167 75c multicolored .80 .25

Baruch Spinoza (1632-1677), philosopher, 300th death anniversary.

Delft Bible Text, Old Type, Electronic "a" — A168

**1977, Mar. 8 *Perf. 14x13***
**568** A168 55c ocher & black .50 .25

Delft Bible (Old Testament), oldest book printed in Dutch, 500th anniversary. Printed in sheets of 50 se-tenant with label inscribed with description of stamp design and purpose.

No. 564 Overprinted in Blue

**1977, Apr. 15 Photo. *Perf. 14x13***
**569** A166 45c multicolored .40 .25

Elections of May 25.

Kaleidoscope of Activities — A169

**1977, June 9 Litho. *Perf. 13x14***
**570** A169 55c multicolored .45 .25

Netherlands Society for Industry and Commerce, bicentenary.

Man in Wheelchair Looking at Obstacles A170

Engineer's Diagram of Water Currents A171

Teeth, Dentist's Mirror — A172

**1977, Sept. 6 Photo. *Perf. 14x13***
**571** A170 40c multicolored .45 .25
**Litho.**
**572** A171 45c multicolored .45 .25

***Perf. 13x14***
**573** A172 55c multicolored .45 .25
*Nos. 571-573 (3)* 1.35 .75

50th anniversaries of AVO (Actio vincit omnia), an organization to help the handicapped (40c), and of Delft Hydraulic Laboratory (45c); centenary of Dentists' Training in the Netherlands (55c).

"Postcode" A173

**1978, Mar. 14 Photo. *Perf. 14x13***
**574** A173 40c dk blue & red .45 .25
**575** A173 45c red, dk & lt bl .50 .25

Introduction of new postal code.

European Human Rights Treaty — A174

**1978, May 2 Photo. *Perf. 13x14***
**576** A174 45c gray, blue & blk .50 .25

European Treaty of Human Rights, 25th anniv.

**Europa Issue**

Haarlem City Hall — A175

**1978, May 2**
**577** A175 55c multicolored *.80* .25

Chess Board and Move Diagram A176

Man Pointing to his Kidney — A178

Heart, Torch, Gauge and Clouds — A179

Korfball A177

**1978, June 1 Photo. *Perf. 13x14***
**578** A176 40c multicolored .40 .25
**Litho.**
**579** A177 45c red & vio bl .50 .25

18th IBM Chess Tournament, Amsterdam, July 12, and 75th anniversary of korfball in the Netherlands.

**1978, Aug. 22 Photo. *Perf. 13x13½***
**580** A178 40c multicolored .45 .25
***Perf. 13x14***
**581** A179 45c multicolored .45 .25

Importance of kidney transplants and drive against hypertension.

Epaulettes, Military Academy — A180

**1978, Sept. 12 Photo. *Perf. 13x14***
**582** A180 55c multicolored .50 .25

Royal Military Academy, sesquicentennial. Printed in continuous design in sheets of 100 (10x10).

Verkade as Hamlet A181

**1978, Oct. 17 Photo. *Perf. 14x13***
**583** A181 45c multicolored .50 .25

Eduard Rutger Verkade (1878-1961), actor and producer.

Clasped Hands and Arrows — A182

**1979, Jan. 23 Engr. *Perf. 13x14***
**584** A182 55c blue .60 .25

Union of Utrecht, 400th anniversary.

European Parliament A183

**1979, Feb. 20 Litho. *Perf. 13½x13***
**585** A183 45c blue, blk & red .50 .25

European Parliament, first direct elections, June 7-10.

Queen Juliana A184

**1979, Mar. 13 Photo. *Perf. 13½x14***
**586** A184 55c multicolored .60 .25

70th birthday of Queen Juliana.

A185

Europa: 55c, Dutch Stamps and magnifying glass. 75c, Hand on Morse key, and ship at sea.

**1979, May 2 Litho. *Perf. 13x13½***
**587** A185 55c multicolored *.50 .25*
**588** A185 75c multicolored *1.00 .30*

A186

Map of Netherlands with chamber locations.

**1979, June 5 Litho. *Perf. 13x14***
**589** A186 45c multicolored .50 .25

Netherlands Chambers of Commerce and 175th anniversary of Maastricht Chamber.

Soccer A187

**1979, Aug. 28 Litho. *Perf. 14x13***
**590** A187 45c multicolored .50 .25

Centenary of soccer in the Netherlands.

Suffragettes — A188

**1979, Aug. 28 Photo. *Perf. 13x14***
**591** A188 55c multicolored .60 .25

Voting right for women, 60th anniversary.

Inscribed Tympanum and Architrave A189

**1979, Oct. 2 Photo. *Perf. 14x13***
**592** A189 40c multicolored .45 .25

Joost van den Vondel (1587-1679), Dutch poet and dramatist.

"Gay Company," Tile Floor — A190

**1979, Oct. 2**
**593** A190 45c multicolored .50 .25

Jan Steen (1626-1679), Dutch painter.

Alexander de Savornin Lohman (1837-1924) — A191

Politicians: 50c, Pieter Jelles Troelstra (1860-1930), Social Democratic Workmen's Party leader. 60c, Pieter Jacobus Oud (1886-1968), mayor of Rotterdam.

**1980, Mar. 4 Photo. *Perf. 13x13½***
**594** A191 45c multicolored .40 .25
**595** A191 50c multicolored .45 .25
**596** A191 60c multicolored .55 .25
*Nos. 594-596 (3)* 1.40 .75

British Bomber Dropping Food, Dutch Flag — A192

Anne Frank — A193

***Perf. 13x14, 14x13***
**1980, Apr. 25 Photo.**
**597** A192 45c multicolored .55 .25
**598** A193 60c multicolored .60 .25

35th anniv. of liberation from the Germans.

Queen Beatrix, Palace — A194

**1980, Apr. 30 *Perf. 13x14, 13x13½***
**599** A194 60c multicolored .60 .25
*a.* Perf. 12¾x13¼ 2.00 1.00

Installation of Queen Beatrix. See No. 608.

Boy and Girl Inspecting Stamp — A195

**1980, May 1 *Perf. 14x13***
**600** A195 50c multicolored .50 .25

Youth philately; NVPH Stamp Show, s'Gravenhagen, May 1-3 and JUPOSTEX Stamp Exhibition, Eindhoven, May 23-27. No. 600 printed se-tenant with label.

Bridge Players, "Netherlands" Hand — A196

**1980, June 3 Litho. *Perf. 13x14***
**601** A196 50c multicolored .55 .25

6th Bridge Olympiad, Valkenburg, 9/27-10/11.

Truck Transport A197

60c, Two-axle railway hopper truck. 80c, Inland navigation barge.

**1980, Aug. 26 Photo. *Perf. 13½x13***
**602** A197 50c shown .45 .25
**603** A197 60c multicolored .55 .25
**604** A197 80c multicolored .75 .25
*Nos. 602-604 (3)* 1.75 .75

Queen Wilhelmina, Excerpt from Speech, Netherlands Flag — A198

80c, Winston Churchill, British flag.

**1980, Sept. 23 Litho. *Perf. 13½x13***
**605** A198 60c shown *.50 .25*
**606** A198 80c multicolored *1.00 .30*

Europa.

Abraham Kuyper, University Emblem, "100" — A199

**1980, Oct. 14 Litho. *Perf. 13½x13***
**607** A199 50c multicolored .55 .25

Free University centennial (founded by Kuyper).

**Queen Beatrix Type of 1980**

**1981, Jan. 6 Photo. *Perf. 12¾x13¼***
**608** A194 65c multicolored .70 .25
*a.* Perf. 12¾x14 2.50 1.00

Parcel A200

Designs: 55c, Dish antenna and telephone. 65c, Bank books.

**1981, May 19 Litho. *Perf. 13½x13***
**609** A200 45c multicolored .50 .25
**610** A200 55c multicolored .50 .25
**611** A200 65c multicolored .50 .25
*a.* Souvenir sheet of 3, #609-611 1.35 1.00

Centenaries: Parcel Post Service (45c); Public telephone service (55c); National Savings Bank (65c).

Huis ten Bosch (Royal Palace), The Hague A201

**1981, June 16 Litho. *Perf. 13½x13***
**612** A201 55c multicolored .60 .25

**Europa Issue**

Carillon A202

**1981, Sept. 1 Litho. *Perf. 13½x13***
**613** A202 45c shown *.50 .25*
**614** A202 65c Barrel organ *.65 .25*

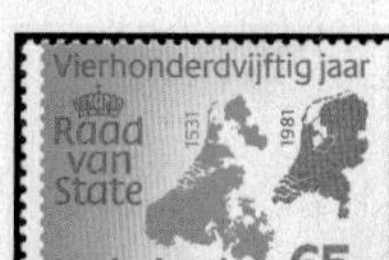

450th Anniv. of Council of State — A203

**1981, Oct. 1 Photo. *Perf. 13½x13***
**615** A203 65c multi .70 .25

Excavator and Ship's Screw (Exports) A204

55c, Cast iron component, scale. 60c, Tomato, lettuce. 65c, Egg, cheese.

**1981, Oct. 20 Photo. *Perf. 13½x13***
**616** A204 45c shown .45 .25
**617** A204 55c multi .50 .25
**618** A204 60c multi .60 .25
**619** A204 65c multi .65 .25
*Nos. 616-619 (4)* 2.20 1.00

Queen Beatrix — A205

**Black Vignette**

**1981-86 Photo. *Perf. 13½x12½***
**620** A205 65c tan .55 .25
**621** A205 70c lt vio ('82) .70 .25
*a.* Bklt. pane, 4 #536, 4 #621 3.00
Complete booklet, #621a 3.00
**622** A205 75c pale pink ('82) .70 .25
*a.* Bklt. pane of 4 ('86) 3.00
**623** A205 90c lt grn('82) .70 .25
**624** A205 1g lt vio('82) .70 .25
**625** A205 1.40g pale grn('82) 1.15 .25
**626** A205 2g lem ('82) 1.40 .25
**627** A205 3g pale vio ('82) 2.10 .25
**628** A205 4g brt yel grn ('82) 2.60 .25
**629** A205 5g lt grnsh bl ('82) 3.00 .25
**630** A205 6.50g lt lil rose ('82) 3.75 .30
**631** A205 7g pale bl ('86) 4.50 .40
*Nos. 620-631 (12)* 21.85 3.20

**Coil Stamps**
***Perf. 13½ Horiz.***
**632** A205 70c lt vio ('82) .80 .25
**633** A205 75c pale pink ('86) .80 .25
**634** A205 1g lt vio ('82) .80 .25
**635** A205 2g lem ('82) 1.60 .25
**636** A205 6.50g lt lil rose ('82) 5.50 .55
**637** A205 7g pale bl ('86) 6.50 .75
*Nos. 632-637 (6)* 16.00 2.30

See Nos. 685-699.

University of Amsterdam, 350th Anniv. A206

**1982, Jan. 14 Litho. *Perf. 13½x13***
**638** A206 65c multi .60 .25

Royal Dutch Skating Assoc. Centenary — A207

**1982, Feb. 26 Litho. *Perf. 13x13½***
**639** A207 45c multi .50 .25

Bicentenary of US-Netherlands Diplomatic Relations — A208

**1982, Apr. 20 Photo. *Perf. 13½x13***
**640** A208 50c multi .50 .25
**641** A208 65c multi .70 .25

See US No. 2003.

Sandwich Tern and Eider Duck, Waddenzee A209

**1982, June 8 Litho. *Perf. 13½x13***

**642** A209 50c shown .55 .25
**643** A209 70c Barnacle geese .75 .25

Dutch Road Safety Assoc, 50th Anniv. — A210

**1982, Aug. 24 Photo. *Perf. 13x14***

**644** A210 60c multi .50 .25

Europa 1982 — A211

Fortification Layouts.

**1982, Sept. 16 Litho. *Perf. 13x13½***

**645** A211 50c Enkhuizen, 1590 *.60 .25*
**646** A211 70c Coevorden, 1680 *.75 .25*

Royal Palace, Dam Square, Amsterdam — A212

50c, Facade, cross-section. 60c, Aerial view.

**1982, Oct. 5 Litho. *Perf. 13x13½***

**647** A212 50c multi .50 .25
**648** A212 60c multi .55 .25

Royal Dutch Touring Club Centenary A213

**1983, Mar. 1 Litho. *Perf. 13½x13***

**649** A213 70c multi .70 .25

A214

Europa: 50c, Netherlands Newspaper Publishers Assoc., 75th anniv. 70c, Launching of European Telecommunication Satellite Org. ECS F-1 rocket, June 3.

**1983, May 17 Litho. *Perf. 13x13½***

**650** A214 50c multi *.50 .25*
**651** A214 70c multi *.70 .25*

A215

De Stijl ("The Style") Modern Art Movement, 1917-31: 50c, Composition 1922, by P. Mondriaan. 65c, Maison Particuliere contra Construction, by C. van Eesteren and T. van Doesburg.

**1983, June 21 Litho. *Perf. 13x13½***

**652** A215 50c multi .50 .25
**653** A215 65c multi .65 .25

Symbolic Separation of Church — A216

**1983, Oct. 11 Litho. *Perf. 13x13½***

**654** A216 70c multi .70 .25

Martin Luther (1483-1546).

2nd European Parliament Election, June 14 — A217

**1984, Mar. 13 Litho. *Perf. 13½x13***

**655** A217 70c multicolored .70 .25

St. Servatius (d. 384) — A218

**1984, May 8 Photo. *Perf. 13x14***

**656** A218 60c Statue, 1732 .60 .25

Europa (1959-84) A219

**1984, May 22 *Perf. 13½x13***

**657** A219 50c blue *.50 .25*
*a.* Perf. 14x13 *3.00 2.50*
**658** A219 70c yellow green *.70 .30*
*a.* Perf. 14x13 *3.00 2.50*

Perf. 14x13 stamps are coils. Every fifth stamp has a control number on the back.

William of Orange (1533-84) A220

**1984, July 10 Photo. *Perf. 14x13***

**659** A220 70c multicolored .70 .25

World Wildlife Fund — A221

**1984, Sept. 18 Litho. *Perf. 14x13***

**660** A221 70c Pandas, globe 1.00 .25

11th Intl. Small Business Congress, Amsterdam, Oct. 24-26 — A222

**1984, Oct. 23 Litho. *Perf. 13x13½***

**661** A222 60c Graph, leaf .60 .25

Guide Dog Fund — A223

60c, Sunny, first guide dog.

**Photogravure and Engraved**

**1985, Jan. 22 *Perf. 14x13***

**662** A223 60c multi .60 .25

A224

Tourism A224a

**1985, Feb. 26 Photo.**

**663** A224 50c multicolored .50 .25
**664** A224a 70c multicolored .70 .25

Cent. of the Tourist office "Geuldal," and 50th anniv. of the Natl. Park "De Hoge Veluwe."

Liberation from German Forces, 40th Anniv. A225

Designs: 50c, Jewish star, mastheads of underground newspapers, resistance fighter. 60c, Allied supply air drop, masthead of The Flying Dutchman, Polish soldier at Arnhem. 65c, Liberation Day in Amsterdam, masthead, first edition of Het Parool (underground newspaper), American cemetery at Margraten. 70c, Dutch women in Japanese prison camp, Japanese occupation currency, building of the Burma Railway.

**1985, May 5 Photo. *Perf. 14x13***

**665** A225 50c blk, buff & red .55 .25
**666** A225 60c blk, buff & brt bl .65 .25
**667** A225 65c blk, buff & org .70 .50
**668** A225 70c blk, buff & brt grn .75 .25
*Nos. 665-668 (4)* 2.65 1.25

WWII resistance effort (1940-1945) and liberation of Europe, 1945.

Europa '85 — A226

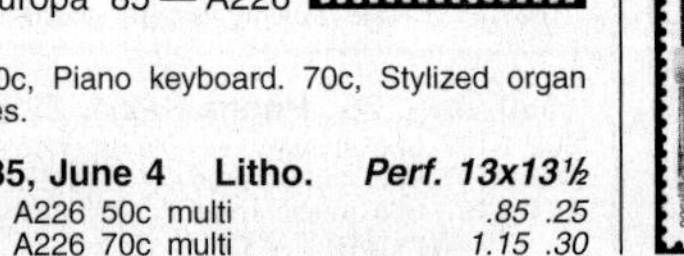

50c, Piano keyboard. 70c, Stylized organ pipes.

**1985, June 4 Litho. *Perf. 13x13½***

**669** A226 50c multi *.85 .25*
**670** A226 70c multi *1.15 .30*

Natl. Museum of Fine Arts, Amsterdam, Cent. — A227

Anniversaries and events: 50c, Museum in 1885, 1985. 60c, Nautical College, Amsterdam, bicent.: Students training. 70c, SAIL-85, Amsterdam: Sailboat rigging.

**1985, July 2 Photo. *Perf. 13½x13***

**671** A227 50c multicolored .50 .25
**672** A227 60c multicolored .60 .25

***Perf. 14x13***

**673** A227 70c multicolored .70 .25
*Nos. 671-673 (3)* 1.80 .75

Wildlife Conservation A228

Designs: 50c, Porpoise, statistical graph. 70c, Seal, molecular structure models.

**1985, Sept. 10 Litho. *Perf. 13½x13***

**674** A228 50c multicolored .55 .30
**675** A228 70c multicolored .75 .30

Penal Code, Cent. — A229

Amsterdam Datum Ordinance, 300th Anniv. A230

**Lithographed, Photogravure (60c)**

**1986, Jan. 21 *Perf. 14x13***

**676** A229 50c Text .55 .30
**677** A230 60c Elevation gauge .65 .25

Sexbierum Windmill Test Station Inauguration A231

**1986, Mar. 4 Litho. *Perf. 14x13***

**678** A231 70c multicolored .75 .25

Het Loo Palace Gardens, Apeldorn — A232

**1986, May 13 Litho. *Perf. 13x14***

**679** A232 50c shown *.60 .30*

**Photo.**

**680** A232 70c Air and soil pollution *.80 .25*

Europa 1986.

Utrecht Cathedral — A233

60c, German House, c.1350. 70c, Utrecht University charter, horiz.

**1986, June 10 Photo. *Perf. 13x14***

**681** A233 50c shown .55 .30
**682** A233 60c multicolored .65 .30

***Perf. 14x13***

**683** A233 70c multicolored .75 .30
*Nos. 681-683 (3)* 1.95 .90

Cathedral restoration, 1986. Heemschut Conservation. Soc., 75th anniv. Utrecht University, 350th anniv.

Willem Drees (1886-1988), Statesman — A234

**1986, July 1 Litho. *Perf. 13x13½***

**684** A234 55c multicolored .60 .25

**Queen Type of 1981**

**1986-90 Photo. *Perf. 13½x12½***

**685** A205 1.20g citron & blk .90 .25
**686** A205 1.50g lt rose vio & blk .85 .25
**688** A205 2.50g tan & blk 1.35 .25
**694** A205 7.50g lt grn & blk 5.00 1.00
*Nos. 685-694 (4)* 8.10 1.75

**Coil Stamps**

***Perf. 13½ Horiz.***

**697** A205 1.50g lt rose vio & blk 1.25 .25
**699** A205 2.50g tan & blk 2.00 .25

Issue dates: Nos. 685, 688, 699, 9/23. Nos. 686, 697, 8/19. 7.50g, 5/29/90.

Billiards A235

***Perf. 14x13, 13x14***

**1986, Sept. 9 Photo.**

**705** A235 75c shown .80 .30
**706** A235 75c Checkers, vert. .80 .25

Royal Dutch Billiards Assoc., Checkers Association, 75th annivs.

Delta Project Completion A236

65c, Storm-surge barrier. 75c, Barrier withstanding flood.

**1986, Oct. 7 Photo. *Perf. 14x13***

**708** A236 65c multicolored .70 .30
**709** A236 75c multicolored .80 .25

Princess Juliana and Prince Bernhard, 50th Wedding Anniv. — A237

**1987, Jan. 6 Photo. *Perf. 13x14***

**710** A237 75c multicolored .85 .25

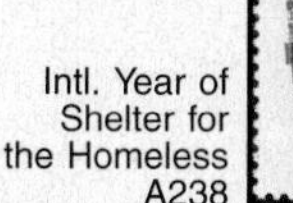

Intl. Year of Shelter for the Homeless A238

Designs: 75c, Salvation Army, cent.

**1987, Feb. 10 Photo. *Perf. 14x13***

**711** A238 65c multicolored .95 .30
**712** A238 75c multicolored 1.05 .25

Dutch Literature A239

Authors: 55c, Eduard Douwes Dekker (1820-1887) and De Harmonie Club, Batavia. 75c, Constantijn Huygens (1596-1687) and Scheveningseweg, The Hague.

**1987, Mar. 10 Litho. *Perf. 13½x13***

**713** A239 55c multicolored .60 .25
**714** A239 75c multicolored .80 .25

Europa 1987 — A240

Modern architecture: 55c, Scheveningen Dance Theater, designed by Rem Koolhaas. 75c, Montessori School, Amsterdam, designed by Herman Hertzberger.

**1987, May 12 Litho. *Perf. 14x13***

**715** A240 55c multicolored *.95* .25
**716** A240 75c multicolored *1.05* .25

Produce Auction at Broeck op Langedijk, 1887 — A241

Designs: 65c, Field in Groningen Province, signatures of society founders. 75c, Auction, bidding, price indicator, 1987.

**1987, June 16 Photo. *Perf. 14x13***

**717** A241 55c shown .55 .25
**718** A241 65c multicolored .65 .25
**719** A241 75c multicolored .75 .25
*Nos. 717-719 (3)* 1.95 .75

Sale of produce by auction in the Netherlands, cent., and Groningen Agricultural Society, 150th anniv. (No. 718).

Union of the Netherlands Municipalities, 75th Anniv. — A242

**1987, Oct. 6 Litho. *Perf. 13x14***

**720** A242 75c multicolored .80 .25

Noordeinde Palace, The Hague A243

**1987, Oct. 27 Photo. *Perf. 14x13***

**721** A243 65c multicolored .70 .25

A244

**Booklet Stamps**

***Perf. 13½x13 on 3 Sides***

**1987, Dec. 1 Photo.**

**722** A244 50c dk ultra, emer & dk red .50 .25
**723** A244 50c dk red, dk ultra & yel .50 .25
**724** A244 50c dk ultra, yel & dk red .50 .25
**725** A244 50c dk red, emer & yel .50 .25
**726** A244 50c emer, dk red & dk ultra .50 .25
*a.* Bklt. pane, 4 each #722-726 10.00 13.00
Complete booklet #726a 10.00
*Nos. 722-726 (5)* 2.50 1.25

Netherlands Cancer Institute, 75th Anniv. A246

**1988, Apr. 19 Litho. *Perf. 13½x13***

**728** A246 75c multicolored .80 .25

Europa 1988 — A247

Modern transportation meeting ecological requirements: 55c, Cyclist, rural scenery, chemical formulas, vert. 75c, Cyclists seen through car-door mirror.

**1988, May 17 Litho. *Perf. 13x13½***

**729** A247 55c multicolored *.95* .25

***Perf. 13½x13***

**730** A247 75c multicolored *1.05* .25

A248

Designs: 65c, Prism splitting light as discovered by Sir Isaac Newton, planet Saturn as observed by Christian Huygens, and pendulum clock, c. 1688. 75c, William of Orange (1650-1702) and Mary II (1662-1694).

**1988, June 14 *Perf. 14x13***

**731** A248 65c multicolored .70 .25
**732** A248 75c multicolored .80 .25

No. 731, Coronation of William III and Mary Stuart, King and Queen of England, 300th anniv. (in 1989). No. 732, Arrival of Dutch William in England, 300th anniv.

Modern Art — A249

Paintings by artists belonging to Cobra: 55c, *Cobra Cat,* 1950, by Appel. 65c, *Stag Beetle,* 1948, by Corneille. 75c, *Fallen Horse,* 1950, by Constant.

**1988, July 5 Litho. *Perf. 13½x13***

**733** A249 55c multicolored .70 .50
**734** A249 65c multicolored .80 .50
**735** A249 75c multicolored .90 .30
*Nos. 733-735 (3)* 2.40 1.30

Each stamp printed se-tenant with label picturing the featured artist's signature.

Cobra, an intl. organization established in 1948 by expressionist artists from Copenhagen, Brussels and Amsterdam.

Australia Bicentennial — A250

**1988, Aug. 30 Photo. *Perf. 13x14***

**736** A250 75c multicolored .80 .25

A251 A252

**1988, Sept. 27 Litho. *Perf. 13x13½***

**737** A251 75c dk green & green .80 .25
**738** A252 75c bright violet .80 .25

Erasmus University, Rotterdam, 75th anniv. (#737), Amsterdam Concertgebouw & Orchestra, cent. (#738).

Holiday Greetings — A253

**1988, Dec. 1 Photo. *Perf. 13½x12½***

**739** A253 50c multicolored .55 .25

"Holland," etc.

Stamps inscribed "Holland," "Stadspost," etc., are private issues. In some cases overprints or surcharges on Netherlands stamps may be created.

Privatization of the Netherlands Postal Service — A254

Mailbox, sorting machine, mailbag, mailman, telephone key pad, fiber optics cable, microwave transmitter & telephone handset.

**Litho. & Engr.**

**1989, Jan. 3 *Perf. 13x13½***

**740** A254 75c multicolored .85 .25

Dutch Trade Unions — A255

**1989, Feb. 7 Litho. *Perf. 13x13½***

**741** A255 55c shown .60 .25

**Photo.**

***Perf. 13x14***

**742** A255 75c Hands, mouths .80 .25

NATO, 40th Anniv. A256

**1989, Mar. 14 Litho. *Perf. 14x13***

**743** A256 75c multicolored .80 .25

Europa 1989 — A257

Children's games (string telephone): 55c, Boy. 75c Girl.

**1989, May 9 Litho. *Perf. 13½x13***

**744** A257 55c multicolored .95 *.25*
**745** A257 75c multicolored 1.05 *.25*

Dutch Railways, 150th Anniv. A258

**1989, June 20 Litho. *Perf. 13½x13***

**746** A258 55c Rails .55 .25
**747** A258 65c Trains .65 .25

***Perf. 14x13***

**748** A258 75c Passengers .75 .25
*Nos. 746-748 (3)* 1.95 .75

Royal Dutch Soccer Assoc., Cent. — A259

**1989, Sept. 5 Photo. *Perf. 13x14***

**749** A259 75c multicolored .75 .25

Treaty of London, 150th Anniv. — A260

Map of Limburg Provinces

**1989, Oct. 2 Litho. *Perf. 13x14***

**750** A260 75c multicolored .75 .25

See Belgium No. 1327.

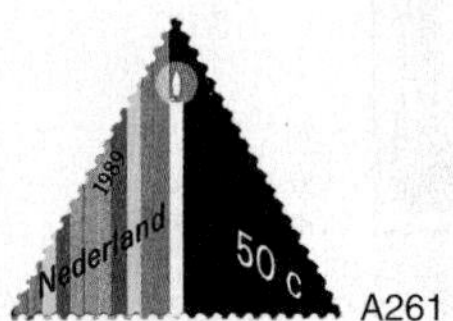


A261

***Perf. 13x13x13½***

**1989, Nov. 30 Photo.**

**751** A261 50c multicolored .55 .25

Sold only in sheets of 20.

Anniversaries A262

Designs: 65c, Leiden coat of arms (tulip), and layout of the Hortus Botanicus in 1601. 75c, Assessing work conditions (clock, sky, wooden floor), horiz.

**1990, Feb. 6 Litho. *Perf. 13x13½***

**752** A262 65c multicolored .70 .25

***Perf. 13½x13***

**753** A262 75c multicolored .80 .25

Hortus Botanicus, Leiden, 400th anniv. (65c); Labor Inspectorate, cent. (75c).

Vincent van Gogh (1853-1890) — A263

Details of works by van Gogh: 55c, *Self-portrait,* pencil sketch, 1886-87. 75c, *The Green Vineyard,* painting, 1888.

**1990, Mar. 6 *Perf. 13x13½***

**754** A263 55c multicolored .65 .25
**755** A263 75c multicolored .85 .25

Rotterdam Reconstruction — A264

**1990, May 8 Litho. *Perf. 13½x13***

**756** A264 55c shown .55 .25
**757** A264 65c Diagram .65 .25
**758** A264 75c Modern bldgs. .75 .25
*Nos. 756-758 (3)* 1.95 .75

Europa A264a

Post offices.

**1990, June 12**

**759** A264a 55c Veere *.95 .25*
**760** A264a 75c Groningen *1.05 .25*

Dutch East India Co. Ships — A265

Sail '90 — A266

**1990, July 3 *Perf. 13x13½***

**761** A265 65c multicolored .65 .25
**762** A266 75c multicolored .75 .25

Queens of the House of Orange A267

**1990, Sept. 5 Litho. *Perf. 13½***

**763** A267 150c multicolored 1.50 .90

Century of rule by Queens Emma, Wilhelmina, Juliana and Beatrix.

A268

**1990, Oct. 9 Photo. *Perf. 13x14***

**764** A268 65c multicolored .70 .30

Natl. emergency phone number.

A269

**1990, Nov. 29 Photo. *Perf. 14***

**765** A269 50c multicolored .55 .25
*a.* Tete-beche pair 1.10 .30

All pairs in sheet are tete-beche.

Threats to the Environment A270

**1991, Jan. 30 Litho. *Perf. 13½x13***

**766** A270 55c Air pollution .55 .25
**767** A270 65c Water pollution .65 .25
**768** A270 75c Soil pollution .75 .25
*Nos. 766-768 (3)* 1.95 .75

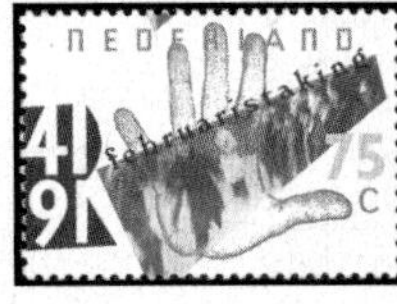


General Strike, 50th Anniv. A271

**1991, Feb. 25 Photo. *Perf. 14x13***

**769** A271 75c multicolored .80 .25

Queen Beatrix and Prince Claus, 25th Wedding Anniv. — A272

**1991, Mar. 11 Litho. *Perf. 13½x13***

**770** 75c shown .80 .30
**771** 75c Riding horses .80 .30
*a.* A272 Pair, #770-771 1.60 1.20

**Numeral Type of 1976 and**

Queen Beatrix — A273

***Perf. 12½x13½, 13½x12½***

**1991-94 Photo.**

**772** A157 70c gray violet .75 .25
*a.* Booklet pane, 5 each #537, 772 5.00
**773** A273 75c green 1.00 .25
*a.* Bklt. pane of 4 + 2 labels 4.00 2.00
Complete booklet, #773a 4.00
**774** A157 80c red lilac 1.00 .25
**774A** A273 80c red brown 1.00 .25
*b.* Booklet pane of 5 + label 4.00 2.00
Complete booklet, #774Ab 4.00
**775** A273 90c blue 1.00 1.25
**776** A273 1g purple 1.00 .40
**777** A273 1.30g gray blue 1.10 .25
**778** A273 1.40g gray olive 1.10 .25
**779** A273 1.60g magenta 1.40 .25
**780** A273 2g yel brown 1.75 .80
**781** A273 2.50g red lilac 2.25 1.20
**782** A273 3g blue 2.50 1.20
**783** A273 5g brown red 4.25 1.15

***Perf. 14x13, Syncopated***

**784** A273 7.50g purple 8.00 2.75
**785** A273 10g green 5.00 1.00
*Nos. 772-785 (15)* 33.10 11.50

**Coil Stamps**

***Perf. 13½ Vert. (A157), Horiz. (A273)***

**786** A157 70c gray violet .75 .25
**787** A273 75c green .95 .50
**788** A157 80c red lilac .90 .25
**789** A273 80c red brown .90 .25
**790** A273 1.60g magenta 1.75 .50
*Nos. 786-790 (5)* 5.25 1.75

**Booklet Stamp**

***Perf. 12½x13½***

**791** A157 60c lemon .65 .25
*a.* Bklt. pane, 2 #791, 4 #772 4.50

Issued: 75c, 3/14/91; 60c, 70c, #774, 1.60g, 6/25/91; #774A, 789, 1.30g, 1.40g, 9/3/91; 1g, 2g, 3g, 5g, 11/11/92; 90c, 2/2/93; 2.50g, 9/7/93; 10g, 11/29/93; 7.50g, 11/28/94.

See #902, 906-913, 1091-1104, 1216, 1218-1221, 1223.

A274

A275

Designs: 55c, Gerard Philips, carbon filament experiments, 1890. 65c, Electrical wiring. 75c, Laser video disk experiment.

***Perf. 13x14, 14x13***

**1991, May 15 Photo.**

**792** A274 55c multicolored .55 .25
**793** A275 65c multicolored .65 .25
**794** A274 75c multicolored .75 .25
*Nos. 792-794 (3)* 1.95 .75

Philips Electronics, cent. (Nos. 792, 794). Netherlands Normalization Institute, 75th anniv. (No. 793).

A276

Europa: 75c, Ladders to another world.

**1991, June 11 Litho. *Perf. 13x13½***

**795** A276 55c multicolored *.95 .30*
**796** A276 75c multicolored *1.05 .25*

Nijmegen Four Days Marches, 75th Anniv. A277

**1991, July 9 Photo. *Perf. 14x13***
**797** A277 80c multicolored .90 .25

Dutch Nobel Prize Winners A278

Designs: 60c, Jacobus H. Van't Hoff, chemistry, 1901. 70c, Pieter Zeeman, physics, 1902. 80c, Tobias M. C. Asser, peace, 1911.

**1991, Sept. 3 *Perf. 14x13***
**798** A278 60c multicolored .65 .25
**799** A278 70c multicolored .70 .25
**800** A278 80c multicolored .80 .25
*Nos. 798-800 (3)* 2.15 .75

Public Libraries, Cent. — A279

**1991, Oct. 1 Litho. *Perf. 13½x13***
**801** A279 70c Children reading .75 .25
**802** A279 80c Books .85 .25

A280

**1991, Nov. 28 Photo. *Perf. 14***
**803** A280 55c multicolored .50 .25

Delft University of Technology, Sesquicent. A281

New Civil Code — A282

**1992, Jan. 7 Litho. *Perf. 13½x13***
**804** A281 60c multicolored .65 .25
**805** A282 80c multicolored .85 .25

Souvenir Sheet

A283

1992 Olympics, Albertville and Barcelona: No. 806a, Volleyball, rowing. b, Shotput, rowing. c, Speedskating, rowing. d, Field hockey.

**1992, Feb. 4 Litho. *Perf. 13x14***
**806** A283 80c Sheet of 4, #a.-d. 3.00 3.00

Tulips — A284 Map — A284a

**1992, Feb. 25 Litho. *Perf. 13x12½***
**807** A284 70c multicolored .75 .25

**Photo.**
***Perf. 13x14***
**808** A284a 80c multicolored .85 .25

Expo '92, Seville.

Discovery of New Zealand and Tasmania by Abel Tasman, 350th Anniv. A285

**1992, Mar. 12 Photo. *Perf. 14x13***
**809** A285 70c multicolored .75 .25

A286 A287

**1992, Apr. 28 Litho. *Perf. 13x13½***
**810** A286 60c multicolored .65 .25
**811** A287 80c multicolored .85 .25

Royal Assoc. of Netherlands Architects, 150th Anniv. (#810). Opening of Building for Lower House of States General (#811).

Discovery of America, 500th Anniv. A288

***Perf. 13½x13, 13x13½***
**1992, May 12 Litho.**
**812** A288 60c Globe, Columbus *.60* .30
**813** A288 80c Sailing ship, vert. *.75* *.25*

Europa. On normally centered stamps the white border appears at the left side of No. 813.

Royal Netherlands Numismatics Society, Cent. — A289

**1992, May 19 Photo. *Perf. 13x14***
**814** A289 70c multicolored .75 .25

Netherlands Pediatrics Society, Cent. — A290

**1992, June 16 Litho. *Perf. 13½x13***
**815** A290 80c multicolored .90 .25

First Deportation Train from Westerbork Concentration Camp, 50th Anniv. — A291

**1992, Aug. 25 *Perf. 13x13½***
**816** A291 70c multicolored .75 .25

Single European Market A292

**1992, Oct. 6 *Perf. 13½x13***
**817** A292 80c multicolored .80 .25

Queen Beatrix, 12½Years Since Investiture — A293

**1992, Oct. 30 *Perf. 13x13½***
**818** A293 80c multicolored .80 .25

Christmas Rose — A294

**1992, Nov. 30 Photo. *Perf. 14***
**819** 55c Red flower .60 .25
**820** 55c Silver flower .60 .25
*a.* A294 Pair, #819-820 1.25 .25

Netherlands Cycle and Motor Industry Assoc. (RAI), Cent. — A295

Designs: 70c, Couple riding bicycle. 80c, Early automobile.

**1993, Jan. 5 Litho. *Perf. 13½x13***
**821** A295 70c multicolored .80 .25
**822** A295 80c black & yellow .90 .25

A296

Greeting Stamps — A296a

Geometric shapes.

**1993, Feb. 2 Photo. *Perf. 14x13½***
**823** A296 70c multi .70 .25
**824** A296a 70c multi, diff. .70 .25
*a.* Tete-beche pair, #823-824 1.40 .40

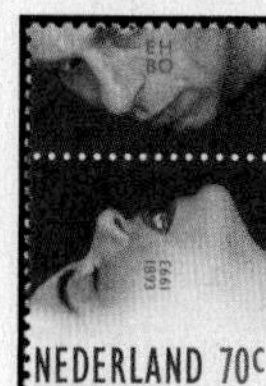

Mouth-to-mouth Resuscitation A297 Royal Horse Artillery Lead Driver, Horses A298

Leaf, Insect Pests — A299

**1993, Feb. 16 Litho. *Perf. 13x13½***
**825** A297 70c multicolored .85 .25
**826** A298 80c multicolored .85 .25
**827** A299 80c multicolored .85 .25
*Nos. 825-827 (3)* 2.55 .75

Royal Netherlands First Aid Assoc., cent. (#825). Royal Horse Artillery, bicent. (#826). University of Agriculture, 75th anniv. (#827).
On No. 826, normally centered stamps show design extending to top and right sides only.

Royal Dutch Notaries' Assoc., 150th Anniv. — A300

**Litho. & Engr.**
**1993, Mar. 2 *Perf. 14x13***
**828** 80c Top half of emblem .90 .25
**829** 80c Bottom half of emblem .90 .25
*a.* A300 Pair, #828-829 1.80 .40

No. 829a has continuous design.

Butterflies A301

Designs: 70c, Pearl-bordered fritillary (Zilvervlek). 80c, Large tortoiseshell (Grote vos). 90c, Large white (Koolwitje). 160c, Polyommatus icarus.

**1993, Mar. 23 Photo.**
**830** A301 70c black & multi .80 .50
**831** A301 80c yellow & multi .80 .30
**832** A301 90c green & multi .80 .80
*Nos. 830-832 (3)* 2.40 1.60

**Souvenir Sheet**
**833** A301 160c red & multi 2.40 2.40

On normally centered stamps the white border appears at the right side.

Radio Orange — A302

Designs: No. 834, Woman broadcasting. No. 835, Man listening.

**1993, May 5 Photo. *Perf. 14x13***
**834** 80c orange red & purple .85 .25
**835** 80c purple & orange red .85 .25
*a.* A302 Pair, #834-835 1.90 .40

European Youth Olympic Days — A303

Symbols of Olympic sports.

**1993, June 1** ***Perf. 13x14***

**836** A303 70c blue & multi .70 .25
**837** A303 80c yellow & multi .80 .25

Europa A304

Contemporary sculpture by: 70c, Wessel Couzijn. 80c, Per Kirkeby. 160c, Naum Gabo, vert.

***Perf. 13½x13, 13x13½***

**1993, July 6** **Litho.**

**838** A304 70c blk, blue & grn .85 *.40*
**839** A304 80c black, red & yel .85 *.30*
**840** A304 160c black, blue & pur 1.60 *1.40*
*Nos. 838-840 (3)* 3.30 2.10

Dutch Nobel Prize Winners — A305

Designs: 70c, J.D. van der Waals, physics, 1910. 80c, Willem Einthoven, medicine, 1924. 90c, Christiaan Eijkman, medicine, 1929.

**1993, Sept. 7** **Litho.** ***Perf. 13x13½***

**841** A305 70c multicolored .60 .35
**842** A305 80c multicolored .70 .25
**843** A305 90c multicolored .80 .80
*Nos. 841-843 (3)* 2.10 1.40

Letter Writing Day — A306

**1993, Sept. 14** **Photo.** ***Perf. 14x13***

**844** 80c Pencils, pen .75 .25
*b.* Perf. 14x13½ ('94) 2.50 .25
**845** 80c Envelope, contents .75 .25
*a.* A306 Pair, #844-845 1.60 .45
*b.* Perf. 14x13½ ('94) 2.50 .25
*c.* Pair, #844b-845b ('94) 5.00 1.00

Stamp Day — A307

80c, Dove with envelope.

**1993, Oct. 8** **Litho.** ***Perf. 13½x13***

**846** A307 70c shown .70 .30
**847** A307 80c multicolored .80 .30

December Stamps — A308

Clock hand pointing to "12:" and: No. 848, Star, candle, Christmas tree. No. 849, Fireworks.

**1993, Nov. 29** **Photo.** ***Perf. 12***

**848** A308 55c blue & multi .60 .25
**849** A308 55c red & multi .60 .25
*a.* Pair, #848-849 1.25 .25

Issued in sheets of 20, 10 each #848-849 + label. Each stamp contains perforations placed within the design to resemble snowflakes.

Piet Mondrian (1872-1944), Painter A309

Details from paintings: 70c, The Red Mill. 80c, Rhomboid with Yellow Lines. 90c, Broadway Boogie Woogie.

**1994, Feb. 1** **Litho.** ***Perf. 13½x13***

**850** A309 70c multicolored .70 .45
**851** A309 80c multicolored .75 .40
**852** A309 90c multicolored .85 .85
*Nos. 850-852 (3)* 2.30 1.70

Wild Flowers A310

70c, Downy rose. 80c, Daisy. 90c, Woods forget-me-not.
160c, Fire lily croceum.

**1994, Mar. 15** **Photo.** ***Perf. 14]x13***

**853** A310 70c multi .70 .40
**854** A310 80c multi .80 .30
**855** A310 90c multi .90 .90
*Nos. 853-855 (3)* 2.40 1.60

**Souvenir Sheet**

**856** A310 160c multi 2.50 2.50

Dutch Aviation, 75th Anniv. A311

**1994, Apr. 6** **Litho.** ***Perf. 13½x13***

**857** A311 80c KLM .85 .25
**858** A311 80c Fokker .85 .25
**859** A311 80c NLR .85 .25
*Nos. 857-859 (3)* 2.55 .75

Planetarium, Designed by Eise Eisinga — A312

Design: 90c, Television image of moon landing, footprint on moon.

**1994, May 5** **Photo.** ***Perf. 13x14***

**860** A312 80c multicolored .80 .25
**861** A312 90c multicolored 1.00 .80

First manned moon landing, 25th anniv. (#861).

1994 World Cup Soccer Championships, U.S. — A313

**1994, June 1**

**862** A313 80c multicolored .90 .60

No. 862 printed with se-tenant label.

Stock Exchange Floor, Initials KPN A314

**1994, June 13** **Litho.** ***Perf. 13½***

**863** A314 80c multicolored .90 .25

Offering of shares in Royal PTT Netherlands NV (KPN).

Bicycle, Car, Road Sign — A315

80c, Silhouettes of horses, riders, carriage.

**1994, June 14** **Photo.** ***Perf. 14x13***

**864** A315 70c multicolored .75 .25

**Litho.**

***Perf. 13½x13***

**865** A315 80c multicolored .85 .25

First road signs placed by Dutch motoring assoc. (ANWB), cent. (#864). World Equestrian Games, The Hague (#865).

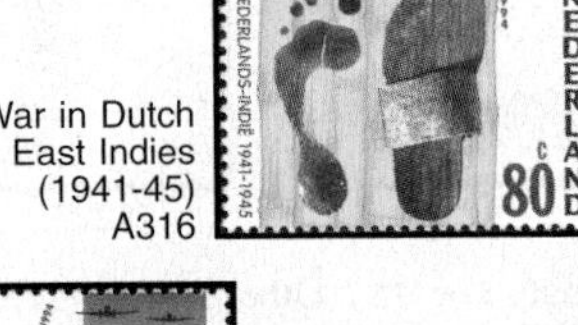


War in Dutch East Indies (1941-45) A316

Operation Market Garden (1944) — A316a

***Perf. 14x13, 13x14***

**1994, Aug. 15** **Photo.**

**866** A316 80c multicolored .75 .25
**867** A316a 90c multicolored .95 .75

Lighthouses A317

Designs: 70c, Brandaris, Terschelling Island. 80c, Ameland Island, vert. 90c, Vlieland Island, vert.

***Perf. 13½x13, 13x13½***

**1994, Sept. 13** **Litho.**

**868** A317 70c multicolored 1.00 .50
**869** A317 80c multicolored 1.00 .25
**870** A317 90c multicolored 1.00 .90
*Nos. 868-870 (3)* 3.00 1.65

December Stamps — A318

**1994, Nov. 28** **Photo.** ***Perf. 13½***

**871** A318 55c Snowflake, tree .55 .25
**872** A318 55c Candle, star .55 .25
*a.* Pair, #871-872 1.10 .25
*b.* Min. sheet, 10 #872a + label 11.00 8.00

One stamp in #872a is rotated 90 degrees to the other stamp.

Cow, Dutch Products A319

**1995, Jan 2** **Photo.** ***Perf. 14x13½***

**873** A319 100c multicolored 1.25 .30

Hendrik Nicolaas Werkman (1882-1945), Printer — A320

Mesdag Museum Restoration A321

Mauritius No. 2 — A322

**1995, Jan. 17** **Litho.** ***Perf. 14x13½***

**874** A320 80c multicolored 1.00 .35
**875** A321 80c multicolored 1.00 .35

**Litho. & Engr.**

***Perf. 13½x14***

**876** A322 80c multicolored 1.00 .35
*Nos. 874-876 (3)* 3.00 1.05

Acquisition of Mauritius No. 2 by Netherlands PTT Museum (#876).

Motion Pictures, Cent. — A323

70c, Joris Iven, documentary film maker. 80c, Scene from film, "Turkish Delight," 1972.

**1995, Feb. 28** **Photo.** ***Perf. 14x13***

**877** A323 70c multicolored .70 .25
**878** A323 80c multicolored .80 .25

Mahler Festival A324

Design: 80c, Gustav Mahler, (1860-1911), composer, 7th Symphony score.

**1995, Mar. 21** **Litho.** ***Perf. 13½x13***

**879** A324 80c blue & black .90 .25

Institute of Registered Accountants, Cent. — A325

Assoc. of Building Contractors, Cent. — A326

**1995, Mar. 28**

| | | | | |
|---|---|---|---|---|
| **880** | A325 | 80c multicolored | .80 | .30 |
| **881** | A326 | 80c multicolored | .80 | .30 |

50th Anniversaries A327

Designs: No. 882, End of World War II, "45, 95" No. 883, Liberation of the Netherlands, "40, 45." No. 884, Founding of the UN, "50."

**1995, May 3 Litho. *Perf. 13x13½***

| | | | | |
|---|---|---|---|---|
| **882** | A327 | 80c multicolored | .80 | .30 |
| **883** | A327 | 80c multicolored | .80 | .30 |
| **884** | A327 | 80c multicolored | .80 | .30 |
| | | *Nos. 882-884 (3)* | 2.40 | .90 |

Signs of the Zodiac, Birthday Cake — A328

**1995, May 22 Photo. *Perf. 14x13½***

| | | | | |
|---|---|---|---|---|
| **885** | A328 | 70c multicolored | 1.10 | .30 |

18th World Boy Scout Jamboree — A329

Sail Amsterdam '95 — A330

***Perf. 13x13½, 13½x13***

**1995, June 6 Litho.**

| | | | | |
|---|---|---|---|---|
| **886** | A329 | 70c multicolored | .70 | .35 |
| **887** | A330 | 80c multicolored | .80 | .25 |

Birds of Prey A330a

***Perf. 13x14, 14x13***

**1995, Sept. 5 Photo.**

| | | | | |
|---|---|---|---|---|
| **888** | A330a | 70c Kestrel, vert. | .80 | .25 |
| **889** | A330a | 80c Hen harrier | .80 | .25 |
| **890** | A330a | 100c Red kite | 1.00 | 1.00 |
| | | *Nos. 888-890 (3)* | 2.60 | 1.50 |

**Souvenir Sheet**

| | | | | |
|---|---|---|---|---|
| **891** | A330a | 160c Honey buzzard | 2.75 | 2.75 |

Nobel Prize Winners A331

No. 892, F. Zernike, physics, 1953. No. 893, P.J.W. Debye, chemistry, 1936. No. 894, J. Tinbergen, economics, 1969.

**1995, Sept. 26 Litho. *Perf. 13½x13***

| | | | | |
|---|---|---|---|---|
| **892** | A331 | 80c green & multi | .80 | .25 |
| **893** | A331 | 80c blue & multi | .80 | .25 |
| **894** | A331 | 80c red & multi | .80 | .25 |
| | | *Nos. 892-894 (3)* | 2.40 | .75 |

Dutch Cabaret, Cent. A332

Designs: 70c, Eduard Jacobs (1868-1914), Jean-Louis Pisuisse (1880-1927). 80c, Wim Kan (1911-83), Freek de Jonge (b. 1944).

**1995, Oct. 17 Litho. *Perf. 13½x14***

| | | | | |
|---|---|---|---|---|
| **895** | A332 | 70c multicolored | .70 | .25 |
| **896** | A332 | 80c multicolored | .80 | .25 |

**Numeral Type of 1976 and Queen Type of 1991**

**1995-2001 Photo. *Perf. 13½x12½***

| | | | | |
|---|---|---|---|---|
| **902** | A273 | 1.50g green | 1.50 | .40 |

**Self-Adhesive (Nos. 903-911)**

**Booklet Stamps**

***Die Cut Perf. 14¼***

| | | | | |
|---|---|---|---|---|
| **903** | A157 | 5c gray | .25 | .25 |
| *a.* | | Double-sided pane of 10 | .45 | |
| **904** | A157 | 10c ultramarine | .25 | .25 |
| *a.* | | Double-sided pane of 10 | .85 | |
| **905** | A157 | 25c violet | .30 | .25 |
| *a.* | | Double sided pane of 10 | 3.00 | |
| **906** | A273 | 85c blue green | .95 | .25 |
| *a.* | | Booklet pane of 5 | 5.00 | |
| **907** | A273 | 1g purple | 1.10 | .25 |
| *a.* | | Booklet pane of 5 | 5.50 | |
| **908** | A273 | 1.10g blue | 1.25 | .25 |
| *a.* | | Booklet pane of 5 | 6.25 | |
| **909** | A273 | 1.45g green | 1.60 | .30 |
| *a.* | | Booklet pane of 5 | 8.00 | |
| **910** | A273 | 2.50g red lilac | 2.75 | .55 |
| *a.* | | Booklet pane of 5 | 14.00 | |
| **911** | A273 | 5g brown red | 5.50 | 1.10 |
| *a.* | | Booklet pane of 5 | 27.50 | |
| | | *Nos. 903-911 (9)* | 13.95 | 3.45 |

**Coil Stamps**

***Perf. 13½ Horiz.***

| | | | | |
|---|---|---|---|---|
| **912** | A273 | 1g gray violet | 1.10 | .25 |
| **913** | A273 | 1.10g blue | 1.25 | .25 |

Issued: No. 912, 10/5; 1.50g, 3/17/98, No. 913, 8/1/00; 5c, 10c, 25c, 6/18/01; 85c, 1.45g, 7/2/01; Nos. 907, 908, 2.50g, 5g, 9/3/01. 85c has added euro denomination.

December Stamps — A333

***Serpentine Die Cut 12½x13***

**1995, Nov. 27 Self-Adhesive**

| | | | | |
|---|---|---|---|---|
| **916** | A333 | 55c Children, star | .70 | .25 |
| **917** | A333 | 55c Children, stars | .70 | .25 |
| *a.* | | Pair, Nos. 916-917 | 1.25 | |

Issued in sheets of 20, checkerboard style.

Nos. 916-917 exist imperf. Value, $62.50 for pair.

Paintings by Johannes Vermeer (1632-75) — A334

Entire paintings or details: 70c, A Lady Writing a Letter, with Her Maid. 80c, The Love Letter. 100c, A Woman in Blue Reading a Letter.

**1996, Feb. 27 Litho. *Perf. 13x13½***

| | | | | |
|---|---|---|---|---|
| **918** | A334 | 70c multicolored | .85 | .45 |
| **919** | A334 | 80c multicolored | .90 | .30 |
| **920** | A334 | 100c multicolored | 1.10 | 1.00 |
| *a.* | | Souvenir sheet, Nos. 918-920 | 3.25 | 3.25 |
| | | *Nos. 918-920 (3)* | 2.85 | 1.75 |

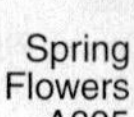

Spring Flowers A335

Designs: 70c, Daffodil bulb, garden tools. 80c, Closeup of woman, tulip. 100c, Snake's head (fritillaria). 160c, Crocuses.

**1996, Mar. 21 Litho. *Perf. 13½x13***

| | | | | |
|---|---|---|---|---|
| **921** | A335 | 70c multicolored | .85 | .40 |
| **922** | A335 | 80c multicolored | .90 | .30 |
| **923** | A335 | 100c multicolored | 1.10 | 1.00 |
| | | *Nos. 921-923 (3)* | 2.85 | 1.70 |

**Souvenir Sheet**

| | | | | |
|---|---|---|---|---|
| **924** | A335 | 160c multicolored | 2.10 | 1.90 |

A336

**1996, Apr. 1 *Perf. 13x13½***

| | | | | |
|---|---|---|---|---|
| **925** | A336 | 70c Moving stamp | .85 | .40 |

No. 925 was sold in sheets of 20. See #951.

Comic Strips, Cent. — A337

Mr. Olivier B. Bommel, by Marten Toonder: a, O.B. Bommel goes on holiday. b, O.B. Bommel receives letter.

**1996, May 14 Litho. *Perf. 13½x13***

| | | | | |
|---|---|---|---|---|
| **926** | | Sheet of 2 + 2 labels | 2.60 | 2.60 |
| *a.* | | A337 70c multicolored | 1.25 | 1.00 |
| *b.* | | A337 80c multicolored | 1.25 | 1.00 |

Vacations A338

Scene, flower: No. 927, Beach, sunflower. No. 928, Cyclists, gerbera. 80c, Gables in Amsterdam, cornflower. 100c, Windmills at "Zaanse Schans"' open air museum, anemone.

**1996, May 31**

| | | | | |
|---|---|---|---|---|
| **927** | A338 | 70c multicolored | .85 | .25 |
| **928** | A338 | 70c multicolored | .85 | .45 |
| **929** | A338 | 80c multicolored | .85 | .25 |
| **930** | A338 | 100c multicolored | .85 | .45 |
| | | *Nos. 927-930 (4)* | 3.40 | 1.40 |

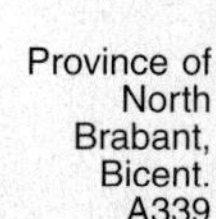

Province of North Brabant, Bicent. A339

**1996, June 13 Litho. *Perf. 13½x13***

| | | | | |
|---|---|---|---|---|
| **931** | A339 | 80c multicolored | .90 | .25 |

Sporting Events A340

Designs: 70c, Lighting the Olympic Torch, 1996 Summer Olympic Games, Atlanta. 80c, Tour de France cycling race. 100c, Euro '96 Soccer Championships, Wembley Stadium, England. 160c, Olympic rings, track sports, Atlanta stadium.

**1996, June 25**

| | | | | |
|---|---|---|---|---|
| **932** | A340 | 70c multicolored | .80 | .25 |
| **933** | A340 | 80c multicolored | .80 | .25 |
| **934** | A340 | 100c multicolored | 1.00 | .75 |
| **935** | A340 | 160c multicolored | 1.50 | .80 |
| | | *Nos. 932-935 (4)* | 4.10 | 2.05 |

Erasmus Bridge, Rotterdam — A341

Designs: No. 936, Martinus Nijhoff Bridge over Waal River, horiz. No. 938, Wijker Tunnel under North Sea Canal, horiz.

**1996, Aug. 6 *Perf. 13½x13, 13x13½***

| | | | | |
|---|---|---|---|---|
| **936** | A341 | 80c multicolored | .85 | .25 |
| **937** | A341 | 80c shown | .85 | .25 |
| **938** | A341 | 80c multicolored | .85 | .25 |
| | | *Nos. 936-938 (3)* | 2.55 | .75 |

UNICEF, 50th Anniv. — A342

Designs: 70c, School children from Ghana. 80c, Girl from Ghana with tray on head.

**1996, Sept. 3 *Perf. 13x13½***

| | | | | |
|---|---|---|---|---|
| **939** | A342 | 70c multicolored | .80 | .25 |
| **940** | A342 | 80c multicolored | .80 | .25 |

Sesame Street in Netherlands, 20th Anniv. A343

70c, Bert & Ernie. 80c, Pino, Ieiemienie & Tommie.

**1996, Sept. 3 *Perf. 13½x13***

| | | | | |
|---|---|---|---|---|
| **941** | A343 | 70c multicolored | .80 | .25 |
| **942** | A343 | 80c multicolored | .75 | .25 |

Nos. 941-942 were issued in sheets of 100 and sheets of 10. On Jan. 1, 1997, No. 942 was reprinted reading "Tien voor je post" instead of "Tien voor je brief" in the top selvage.

Voyages of Discovery A344

Voyages of: 70c, Petrus Plancius (1552-1622), cartographer. #944, Willem Barents (d. 1597). #945, Cornelis de Houtman (1540-99). 100c, Mahu en De Cordes (1598-1600).

**1996, Oct. 1**

| | | | | |
|---|---|---|---|---|
| **943** | A344 | 70c multicolored | .75 | .40 |
| **944** | A344 | 80c multicolored | .75 | .30 |
| **945** | A344 | 80c multicolored | .75 | .30 |
| **946** | A344 | 100c multicolored | 1.15 | 1.15 |
| | | *Nos. 943-946 (4)* | 3.40 | 2.15 |

December Stamps — A345

Collage of faces, hands: No. 947, Wing, ear, hands. No. 948, Mouth, two faces. No. 949, Woman with eyes closed, hand. No. 950, Eyes, face with mouth open.

***Serpentine Die Cut 9 Horiz.***

**1996, Nov. 26** **Self-Adhesive**

**947** A345 55c multicolored .50 .25
**948** A345 55c multicolored .50 .25
**949** A345 55c red violet & multi .50 .25
**950** A345 55c blue & multi .50 .25
*a.* Block or strip of 4, #947-950 2.00

Issued in sheets of 20.

**Moving Stamp Type of 1996**

***Die Cut Perf. 13***

**1997, Jan. 2** **Photo.**

**Self-Adhesive**

**951** A336 80c like No. 925 .90 .25

No. 951 sold in panes of 20.

Business Stamps A346

Geometric designs.

**Coil Stamps**

***Sawtooth Die Cut 13½, Syncopated (on 1 Side)***

**1997, Jan. 2** **Self-Adhesive**

**952** A346 80c pink & multi .75 .25
**953** A346 160c green & multi 1.40 .25

Cross-Country Skating Championships — A347

**1997, Jan. 4** **Photo.** ***Perf. 14x13***

**954** A347 80c multicolored .90 .25

Surprise Stamps A348

Inscriptions beneath scratch-off heart-shaped panels: b, Schrijf me. c, Groetjes. d, Ik hou van je. e, Tot gauw. f, Ik denk aan je. g, XXX-jes. h, Ik mis je. i, Geintje. j, Zomaar. k, Wanneer?

**1997, Jan. 21** ***Perf. 14x13½***

**955** Sheet of 10 7.50 6.50
*a.* A348 80c Any single, unscratched heart .75 .65
*b.-k.* A348 80c Any single, scratched heart .25

Unused value for #955a is with attached selvage. Inscriptions are shown in selvage beside each stamp.

Nature and Environment A349

**1997, Feb. 25** **Litho.** ***Perf. 13½x13***

**956** A349 80c Pony .90 .30
**957** A349 100c Sheep 1.10 1.00

**Souvenir Sheet**

**958** A349 160c Sheep, diff. 2.10 2.10

Suske & Wiske Comic Strip Characters A350

#959, Suske, Wiske, Tante Sidonia, & Lambik. #960a, Jerome making exclamation.

***Perf. 13½x12½***

**1997, Mar. 18** **Litho.**

**959** A350 80c multicolored .85 .25

**Souvenir Sheet**

**960** Sheet of 2, #959, 960a 2.60 2.10
*a.* A350 80c violet & red 1.25 .90

A351

Greetings Stamps A352

#961, Birthday cake. #962, Amaryllis surrounded by cup of coffee, two glasses of wine, hand writing card, candlelight.

**1997, May 6** **Photo.** ***Perf. 14x13½***

**961** A351 80c multicolored .80 .25
**962** A352 80c multicolored .80 .25

See No. 1035.

Marshall Plan, 50th Anniv. — A353

Designs: No. 963, Map of Europe. No. 964, Flag, quotation from George C. Marshall.

**1997, May 27** **Litho.** ***Perf. 13½x13***

**963** 80c multicolored .85 .30
**964** 80c multicolored .85 .30
*a.* A353 Pair, #963-964 1.75 1.75

Court of Audit, 550th Anniv. A354

**1997, May 27** ***Perf. 13½x13***

**965** A354 80c multicolored .85 .30

European Council of Ministers Meeting, Amsterdam A355

**1997, June 17** **Litho.** ***Perf. 13½***

**966** A355 100c multicolored 1.40 1.10

Water Recreation A356

80c, Swimming, row boat. 1g, Sailboats.

**1997, July 1** ***Perf. 13½x13***

**967** A356 80c multicolored .85 .25
**968** A356 1g multicolored 1.00 .55

Royal Institute of Engineers, 150th Anniv. A357

**1997, Aug. 5**

**969** A357 80c multicolored .90 .25

Netherlands Asthma Center, Cent. — A358

**1997, Aug. 5**

**970** A358 80c multicolored .90 .25

Horticultural Education at Florens College, Aalsmeer, Cent. — A359

**1997, Aug. 5**

**971** A359 80c multicolored .90 .25

Franz Schubert (1797-1828), Composer A360

**1997, Aug. 5**

**972** A360 80c multicolored .90 .25

A361

Youth Stamps A362

**1997, Sept. 2**

**973** A361 80c multicolored .75 .25
*a.* Bklt. pane of 5 + 2 labels 5.00
Complete booklet, #973a 5.00
**974** A362 80c multicolored .75 .25
*a.* Perf. 14x13 50.00 50.00

Issued: No. 973a, 7/6/99.

Booklet stamps differ from sheet stamps: the year date is closer to the edge.

Birth Announcement Stamp — A363

***Die Cut Perf. 13½x13***

**1997, Oct. 7** **Photo.**

**Self-Adhesive**

**975** A363 80c multicolored .80 .25
*a.* Litho. ('99) 1.25 1.25

See Nos. 1033, 1071, 1109, 1260.

A364

December Stamps: Stylized people head to head showing either a star or heart in the center.

***Serpentine Die Cut***

**1997, Nov. 25** **Photo.**

**Self-Adhesive**

**Background Colors**

**976** A364 55c yellow .55 .25
**977** A364 55c blue .55 .25
**978** A364 55c orange .55 .25
**979** A364 55c red .55 .25
**980** A364 55c yellow green .55 .25
**981** A364 55c green .55 .25
*a.* Sheet, 3 ea #976, 978-979, 981, 4 ea #977, 980 11.00 11.00

A365

**1998, Jan. 2** **Litho.** ***Perf. 13½***

**982** A365 80c gray blue .80 .25

Death announcement stamp.

See Nos. 1059, 1072, 1110, 1261

Delftware A366

100c, Cow, tiles with pictures of sailing ships. 160c, Tiles, one picturing boy standing on head.

**1998, Jan. 2** **Photo.** ***Die Cut***

**Self-Adhesive**

**983** A366 100c multicolored .95 .50
**984** A366 160c multicolored 1.50 1.00

Issued in both coil strips and sheets with priority labels.

A368

Growing Fruit in the Four Seasons: No. 986, Orchard in bloom, spring. No. 987, Strawberries, summer. No. 988, Harvesting, autumn. No. 989, Pruning, winter.

**1998, Feb. 17** **Litho.** ***Perf. 13x13½***

**Booklet Stamps**

**986** A368 80c multicolored .95 .80
**987** A368 80c multicolored .95 .80
**988** A368 80c multicolored .95 .80
**989** A368 80c multicolored .95 .80
*a.* Booklet pane, #986-989 4.00
Complete booklet, #989a 4.00

A369

***Die Cut Perf. 13½***

**1998, Mar. 17** **Photo.**

**Self-Adhesive**

**990** A369 80c multicolored .80 .25
*a.* Litho. ('99) 4.00 4.00

Marriage and wedding anniversaries. No. 990 was issued in sheets of 10.

See No. 1034.

Anniversaries A370

#991, Men shaking hands, Treaty of Munster, 350th anniv. #992, Statue of John Rudolf Thorbecke, Dutch constitution, 150th anniv. #993, Child on swing, Universal Declaration of Human Rights, 50th anniv.

**1998, Mar. 17 Litho. *Perf. 13½x13***

**991** A370 80c multicolored .85 .25
**992** A370 80c multicolored .85 .25
**993** A370 80c multicolored .85 .25
*a.* Strip of 3, #991-993 2.60 2.60

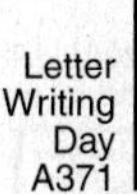

Letter Writing Day A371

**1998, May 8 Litho. *Perf. 13½***

**994** A371 80c multicolored .85 .25

1998 World Cup Soccer Championships, France — A372

**1998, May 19 Litho. *Perf. 13½***

**995** A372 80c multicolored .90 .25

Rabo Bank, Cent. — A373

**1998, May 19 *Perf. 13½x13***

**996** A373 80c multicolored .85 .25

Royal Netherlands Field Hockey Federation, Cent. — A374

**1998, May 19**

**997** A374 80c multicolored .85 .25

Central Administration in Friesland, 500th Anniv. A375

**1998, June 9 Litho. *Perf. 13½x13***

**998** A375 80c multicolored .85 .25

Water Management A375a

**1998, June 9**

**999** A375a 80c shown .80 .25
**1000** A375a 1g Aerial view 1.00 .75

Split of Royal Netherlands PTT — A376

#1001, TNT Post Groep. #1002, KPN NV.

**1998, June 29**

**1001** 80c red, black & blue .85 .25
**1002** 80c blue, blk & grn .85 .25
*a.* A376 Vert. pair, #1001-1002 1.75 1.75

No. 1002a is a continuous design.

Natl. Library of the Netherlands, Bicent. A377

**1998, July 7**

**1003** A377 80c multicolored .85 .25

A378

No. 1004, Maurits Cornelis Escher (1898-1972), Graphic Artist. No. 1005, Simon Vestdijk (1898-1971), writer.

**1998, July 7 *Perf. 13x13½***

**1004** A378 80c multicolored .85 .40
**1005** A378 80c multicolored .85 .40
*a.* Pair, #1004-1005 1.75 1.75

Souvenir Sheet

A379

Inauguration of Queen Wilhelmina, Cent.: a, Queen Wilhelmina. b, Gilded Coach.

**1998, Sept. 1 Litho. *Perf. 13x13½***

**1006** A379 80c Sheet of 2, #a.-b. 2.60 2.60

Greetings Stamps A380

Colors of stamp edges, clockwise from side adjacent to "Neder:" No. 1007: a, yellow, orange, red, red. b, red, orange, pink, yellow orange. c, red, orange, rose, orange. d, orange, red, light orange, yellow orange. e, yellow, orange, pink, red.

***Serpentine Die Cut Perf. 13½x13***

**1998, Sept. 1 Litho.**

**Self-Adhesive**

**1007** 80c Sheet of 10, 2 each #a.-e. 8.00
*a.-e.* A380 any single 1.00 .50

Each side of No. 1007 contains a pane of 1 each #1007a-1007e and 10 different self-adhesive labels.

Nos. 1008-1011 are unassigned.

Pets — A381

**1998, Sept. 22 *Perf. 13½x13***

**1012** A381 80c Dog .80 .30
*a.* Bklt. pane of 5 + 2 labels 4.75
Complete booklet, #1012a 4.75
**1013** A381 80c Kittens .80 .40
**1014** A381 80c Rabbits 1.00 .80
*Nos. 1012-1014 (3)* 2.60 1.50

Issued: No. 1012a, 7/6/99.

Jan, Jans en de Kinderen Comic Strip, by Jan Kruis — A382

Characters: No. 1015, Writing letters. No. 1016, In automobile, mailing letter.

**1998, Oct. 6 Litho. *Perf. 13½x13***

**1015** A382 80c multicolored .85 .25
*a.* Booklet pane, 10 #1015 + 20 labels 8.50
Complete booklet, #1015a 8.50
**1016** A382 80c multicolored 1.50 .25
*a.* Sheet of 2, #1015-1016 + 3 labels 2.60 2.50

December Stamps — A383

25c, Stylized tree, house on top of earth. No. 1018:
Silhouetted against moon: a, Rabbit. b, House. c, Bird. d, Tree. e, Deer.
Silhouetted against horizon: f, Rabbit. g, House. h, Bird. i, Tree. j, Deer.
House with: k, Rabbit. l, Heart. m. Bird. n, Tree. o, Deer.
Tree with: p, Rabbit. q, House. r, Bird. s, Heart. t, Deer.

**1998-99 Litho. *Perf. 13***

**1017** A383 25c multicolored .30 .25

**Self-Adhesive**

***Die Cut Perf. 9***

**1018** A383 55c Sheet of 20, #a.-t. 10.00 3.25

Issued: #1018, 11/24; #1017, 1/5/99.

Introduction of the Euro — A384

**1999, Jan. 5 Litho. *Perf. 13x12½***

**1019** A384 80c multicolored .85 .25

Netherlands Postal Services, Bicent. — A385

**1999, Jan. 15 Litho. *Perf. 13½x14***

**1020** A385 80c multi + label .90 .80

See No. 1039

A386

**1999, Feb. 2 Litho. *Perf. 12¾x13¼***

**1021** A386 80c Spoonbill .85 .25
**1022** A386 80c Globe, tern .85 .25

Protection of birds and migrating waterfowl. Netherlands Society for Protection of Birds, cent (#1021). African-Eurasian Waterbird Agreement (#1022).

A387

**1999, Feb. 2 *Perf. 12¾x13¼***

**Booklet Stamp**

**1023** A387 80c multicolored .85 .25
*a.* Booklet pane of 4 3.50
Complete booklet, #1023a 3.50

Royal Dutch Lawn Tennis Assoc., cent.

Views During the Four Seasons A388

Designs: a, Haarlemmerhout in fall. b, Sonsbeek in winter. c, Weerribben in spring. d, Keukenhof in summer.

**1999, Mar. 2 Litho. *Perf. 13¼x12¾***

**1024** Booklet pane of 4, #a.-d. 4.00 4.00
*a.-d.* A388 80c Any single .90 .80
Complete booklet, #1024 4.25

I Love Stamps A389

**1999, May 6 Litho. *Perf. 13¼x12¾***

**1025** A389 80c I Love Stamps .80 .40
**1026** A389 80c Stamps Love Me 1.00 .75
*a.* Booklet pane, 3 #1025, 2 #1026 + 2 labels 4.50
Complete booklet, #1026a 4.50

Nos. 1025-1026 each contain a hologram. Soaking may affect the hologram.

Maritime Anniversaries A390

**1999, May 6 Litho. *Perf. 12¾x13¼***

**1027** A390 80c Freighters .80 .25
**1028** A390 80c Lifeboats .80 .25

Schuttevaer Ship Masters Assoc., 150th anniv. (#1027). Netherlands Lifeboat Assoc., 175th anniv. (#1028).

Paintings A391

No. 1029: a, The Goldfinch, by Carel Fabritius. b, Self-portrait, by Rembrandt. c, Self-portrait, by Judith Leyster. d, St. Sebastian, by Hendrick Ter Brugghen. e, Beware of Luxury, by Jan Steen. f, The Sick Child, by Gabriel Metsu. g, Gooseberries, by Adriaen Coorte. h, View of Haarlem, by Jacob van Ruisdael. i, Mariaplaats Utrecht, by Pieter Saenredam. j, Danae, by Rembrandt.
1g, The Jewish Bride, by Rembrandt.

**1999, June 8 Litho. *Perf. 13¼x13¾***

**1029** Sheet of 10, #a.-j. 9.00 9.00
*a.-j.* A391 80c any single .85 .85

**Self-Adhesive**

***Die Cut Syncopated***

**1030** A391 1g multicolored 1.25 .95

No. 1030 issued in sheets of 5 stamps and blue priority mail etiquettes.

A392

**1999, July 6 Litho. *Perf. 13¼x12¾***

**1031** A392 80c multicolored .90 .25

**Self-Adhesive**

***Die Cut 13½ Syncopated***

**1032** A392 80c multicolored .90 .25

**Birth Announcement Type of 1997 and Marriage Type of 1998**

**1999, July 6 Litho. *Perf. 13¼x12¾***

**Booklet Stamps**

**1033** A363 80c multicolored .90 .25
*a.* Booklet pane of 5 + 2 labels 4.50
Complete booklet, #1033a 4.50

***Perf. 13¼***

**1034** A369 80c multicolored .90 .25
*a.* Booklet pane of 5 + 2 labels 4.50
Complete booklet, #1034a 4.50

**Greetings Type of 1997**

***Die Cut 13½ Syncopated***

**1999, July 6 Litho.**

**Self-Adhesive**

**1035** A352 80c multicolored 1.25 .50

VNO-NCW Employer Organization, Cent. A392a

**1999, Sept. 7 Litho. *Perf. 13¼x12¾***

**1036** A392a 80c multicolored .85 .25

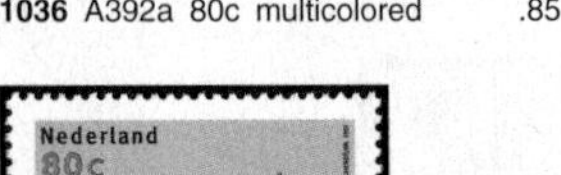

Tintin — A393

#1037, Tintin, Snowy in space suits. #1038a, Tintin, Snowy, Capt. Haddock in spacecraft.

**1999, Oct. 8 *Perf. 13¼x12¾***

**1037** A393 80c multicolored 1.25 .25
*a.* Booklet pane of 5 + 2 labels 7.75
Complete booklet, #1037a 8.00

**Souvenir Sheet**

**1038** Sheet of 2, #1037, 1038a 3.25 2.75
*a.* A393 80c multicolored 1.50 1.25

**Postal Service Bicentennial Type**

Souvenir Sheet

**1999, Oct. 15 Litho. *Perf. 13¼x13¾***

**1039** A385 5g multicolored 5.00 5.00

The numeral in the denomination is made up of perforations.

Millennium A394

Highlights of the 20th Century: a, Construction of barrier dam, 1932. b, Satellite. c, Amsterdam Bourse, 1903, designed by H. P. Berlage. d, Empty highway, 1973-74 oil crisis. e, Prime Minister Willem Drees's social welfare programs, 1947. f, Flood control projects 1953-97. g, European soccer champions, 1988. h, Liberation, 1945. i, Woman suffrage. j, Eleven-city skating race.

**1999, Oct. 25 Litho. *Perf. 13¼x12¾***

**1040** Sheet of 10 8.00 8.00
*a.-j.* A394 80c any single .80 .80

December Stamps — A395

Designs: a, Santa's head. b, Angel, musical notes, vert. c, Ornaments in box. d, Crescent-shaped Santa's head, vert. e, Santa, four trees. f, Clock, vert. g, Skater. h, Tree of people holding candles, vert. i, Man and woman. j, Woman, tree, star, vert. k, Angel, musical score. l, Hand, vert. m, Tree. n, Cat with crown, vert. o, Bird, house. p, Baby as angel, vert. q, Dog with cap. r, Angel with halo, vert. s, Family in house. t, Tree with presents, vert.

***Serpentine Die Cut 7***

**1999, Nov. 30 Photo.**

**Self-Adhesive**

**1041** A395 Sheet of 20, #a-t 10.00
*a.-t.* 55c any single .50 .25

A396

**2000, Jan. 4 Litho. *Perf. 13x12¾***

**1042** A396 25c multi .30 .25

Souvenir Sheet

Holy Roman Emperor Charles V (1500-58) — A397

Designs: a, Gulden coin, Charles' aunt and guardian, Margaret of Austria, Charles V on Horseback in Bologna, by Juan de la Corte. b, Map of the Netherlands, Charles V on Horseback at the Battle of Mühlberg, by Titian, Charles' daughter, Margaret of Parma.

**2000, Jan. 4 *Perf. 13¼***

**1043** A397 Sheet of 2 + label 2.25 2.00
*a.-b.* 80c Any single 1.00 1.00

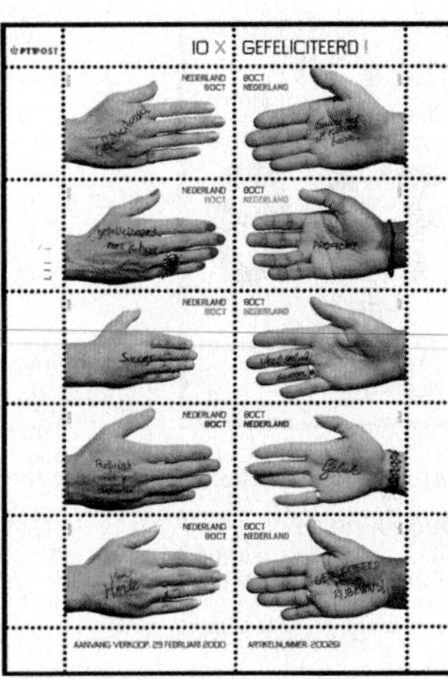

Greetings — A398

Color of denomination or country name and hands (back or palm) with written messages: a, Pink, back. b, Pink, palm. c, Orange, back. d, Orange, palm. e, Green, back. f, Green, palm. g, Blue, back. h, Blue, palm. i, Red, back. j, Red, palm.

***Perf. 13¼x13¾***

**2000, Feb. 29 Litho.**

**1044** A398 Sheet of 10, #a-j 8.00 8.00
*a.-j.* 80c any single .75 .75

European Soccer Championships, Netherlands and Belgium — A399

**2000, Mar. 25 *Perf. 12¾x13¼***

**Booklet Stamps**

**1045** A399 80c Crowd, players .75 .25
**1046** A399 80c Crowd, ball 1.10 .75
*a.* Booklet pane, 3 #1045, 2 #1046 + 2 labels 4.50
Booklet, #1046a 4.50

See Belgium No. 1796.

Items in Rijksmuseum — A400

a, Feigned Sorrow (woman wiping eye), by Cornelis Troost. b, Harlequin and Colombine, Meissen porcelain piece, by J. J. Kändler. c, Kabuki Actor Ebizo Ichikawa IV, by Sharaku. d, Apsara from India. e, Carved head of St. Vitus. f, Woman in Turkish Costume, by Jean Etienne Liotard. g, J. van Speyk (man with epaulet), by J. Schoemaker Doyer. h, Engraving of King Saul, by Lucas van Leyden. i, Statue, L'Amour Menacant, by E. M. Falconet. j, Photograph of two men, by C. Ariens.
100c, The Night Watch, by Rembrandt.

**2000, Apr. 14 *Perf. 13¼x13¾***

**1047** A400 Sheet of 10, #a-j 11.00 11.00
*a.-j.* 80c any single 1.00 1.00

***Die Cut Syncopated***

**Self-Adhesive**

**1048** A400 100c multi 1.10 .90

#1048 issued in sheets of 5 + 5 priority mail etiquettes.

See Nos. 1051, 1053.

Doe Maar, Popular Musical Group A401

**2000, May 2 Litho. *Perf. 13¼x12¾***

**1049** A401 80c Song titles 1.00 .75
**1050** A401 80c Album cover .75 .35
*a.* Booklet pane, 2 #1049, 3 #1050, + 2 labels 4.25
Booklet, #1050a 4.25

**Rijksmuseum Type of 2000 with Priority Mail Emblem Added and**

Dutch Landscape, by Jeroen Krabbé — A402

Designs: Nos. 1051, 1053, The Night Watch, by Rembrandt.
Die cut perf. 4 on right side and right parts of top and bottom sides.

***Die Cut Similar to Sync.***

**2000, Aug. 1 Litho.**

**Self-Adhesive**

**1051** A400 110c pur & multi 1.25 .60

***Die Cut Sync.***

**1052** A402 110c multi 1.25 .60

**Coil Stamp**

***Die Cut Similar to Sync.***

**1053** A400 110c blue & multi 3.25 1.60
*Nos. 1051-1053 (3)* 5.75 2.80

Nos. 1051-1052 issued in sheets of 5. No. 1051 lacks die cut "holes" on left side and at upper left. No. 1053 lacks die cut "holes" on left side, but has only two at upper left.

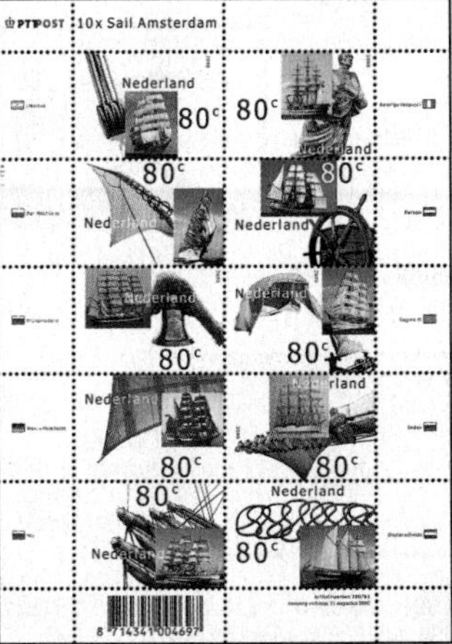

Sail 2000, Amsterdam Harbor — A403

No. 1054: a, Block and Libertad, Argentina. b, Figurehead and Amerigo Vespucci, Italy. c, Unfurled white sail, Dar Mlodziezy, Poland. d, Ship's wheel, Europa, Netherlands. e, Bell, Kruzenshtern, Russia. f, Deckhand adjusting sail, Sagres II, Portugal. g, Green sail, Alexander von Humboldt, Germany. h, Crewmen on bowsprit, Sedov, Russia. i. Spreaders, furled sails and ropes, Mir, Russia. j, Rope, Oosterschelde, Netherlands.

***Perf. 13¼x12¾***

**2000, Aug. 21 Litho.**

**1054** A403 Sheet of 10 9.25 9.25
*a.-j.* 80c Any single .90 .45

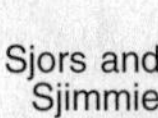

Sjors and Sjimmie
A404

Comic strip characters: No. 1055, Rollerblading. No. 1056, In go-kart. No. 1057, Wearing headphones. No. 1058, Hanging on rope.

**2000, Sept. 23**

**1055** A404 80c multi 1.25 .60
**1056** A404 80c multi 1.25 .60
*a.* Pair, #1055-1056 2.50 1.25
**1057** A404 80c multi .90 .45
*a.* Souvenir sheet, #1056-1057 3.00 3.00

**Booklet Stamp**

**1058** A404 80c multi 1.25 .60
*a.* Booklet pane, 3 #1057, 2 #1058 + 2 labels 5.25
Booklet, #1058a 5.25
*Nos. 1055-1058 (4)* 4.65 2.25

**Death Announcement Type of 1998**

***Die Cut Perf. 13¼***

**2000, Oct. 10** **Photo.**

**1059** A365 80c gray blue .90 .50

Endangered Species
A405

Designs: No. 1060, Aeshna viridis (Groene glazenmaker). No. 1061, Misgurnus fossilis (Grote modderkruiper).

**2000, Oct. 10 Litho.** ***Perf. 13¼x12¾***

**Booklet Stamps**

**1060** A405 80c multi .90 .50
**1061** A405 80c multi 1.10 .50
*a.* Booklet pane, 3 #1060, 2 #1061 + 2 labels 5.00
Booklet, #1061a 5.00

Souvenir Sheet

Amphilex 2002 Intl. Stamp Show, Amsterdam — A406

No. 1062: a, Boat. b, Carriage.

**2000, Oct. 10**

**1062** A406 Sheet of 2 2.10 2.10
*a.-b.* 80c Any single .90 .50

Christmas — A407

No. 1063: a, Woman, man with tree on shoulder. b, Woman, child decorating tree. c, Couple dancing. d, Tuba player. e, Man carrying hat and tree. f, Man with child on shoulder. g, Woman reading. h, Couple kissing. i, Piano player. j, Woman at window. k, Woman in chair. l, Santa by fire. m, Snowman. n, Couple in front of house. o, Violin player. p, Children on sled. q, Man writing letter. r, Woman with food tray. s, Four people. t, Woman asleep.

***Serpentine Die Cut 14½x15***

**2000, Nov. 28** **Photo.**

**Self-Adhesive**

**1063** A407 Sheet of 20 11.00
*a.-t.* 60c Any single .55 .25

A408

**2001, Jan. 2 Litho.** ***Perf. 12¾x13¼***

**1064** A408 20c multi .25 .25

Royal Dutch Nature Society, Cent. — A409

No. 1065: a, Whinchat thrush. b, People in rowboat. c, Fox. d, People with binoculars. e, Scotch rose and June beetles.

**2001, Jan. 26 Litho.** ***Perf. 13½x12¾***

**1065** Booklet pane of 5, #a-e, +2 labels 5.25 5.25
*a.-e.* A409 80c Any single 1.00 .75
Booklet, #1065 6.00

Rotterdam, 2001 European Cultural Capital — A410

***Die Cut Similar to Sync.***

**2001, Mar. 14** **Litho.**

**Self- Adhesive**

**1066** A410 110c multi 1.50 .90

Printed in sheets of 5. Die cutting has no "holes" at left, but has "holes" at top and bottom at the thin vertical line.

Book Week — A411

No. 1067: a, Quote by Edgar du Perron. b, Photograph by Ulay. c, Quote by Hafid Bouazza. d, Photograph by Ed van der Elsken. e, Quote by Adriaan van Dis. f, Photograph by Anton Corbijn. g, Quote by Kader Abdolah. h, Photographs by Celine van Balen. i, Quote by Ellen Ombre. j, Photograph by Cas Oorthuys.

**2001, Mar. 14** ***Perf. 13¼x13¾***

**1067** A411 Sheet of 10 7.25 7.25
*a.-j.* 80c Any single .90 .25

Souvenir Sheet

Max Euwe (1901-81), Chess Champion — A412

No. 1068: a, Chessboard. b, Euwe, chess pieces.

**2001, Apr. 3** ***Perf. 13¼x12¾***

**1068** A412 Sheet of 2 2.25 2.25
*a.-b.* 80c Any single 1.00 .90

Souvenir Sheet

Intl. Volunteers Year — A413

No. 1069: a, Rescue workers. b, People with animal cages.

**2001, Apr. 3**

**1069** A413 Sheet of 2 2.25 2.25
*a.-b.* 80c Any single 1.00 .75

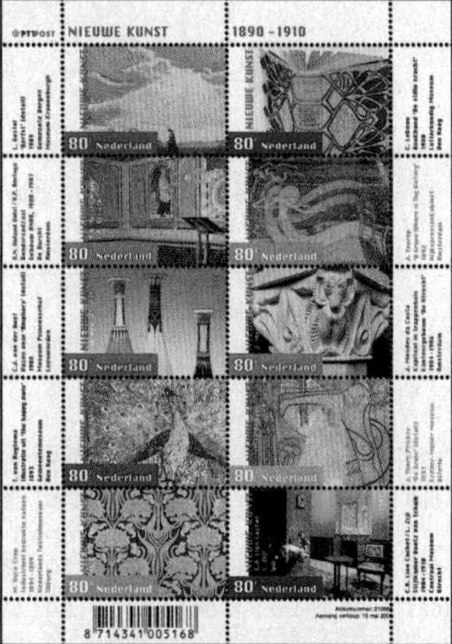

Art of 1892-1910 — A414

Art: a, "Autumn," L. Gestel. b, Book cover for "De Stille Kracht," C. Lebeau. c, Burcht Federal Council Hall, R. N. Roland Holst and H. P. Berlage. d, "O grave, where is thy victory?," J. Toorop. e, Vases from "Amphoras," C. J. van der Hoef. f, De Utrecht office building capital, J. Mendes da Costa. g, Illustration from "The Happy Owls," T. van Hoytema. h, "The Bride," J. Thorn Prikker. i, Printed fabric, M. Duco Crop. j, Dentz van Schaik period room, Central Museum, Utrecht, C. A. Lion Cachet and L. Zijl.

**2001, May 15** ***Perf. 14¾***

**1070** A414 Sheet of 10 7.25 7.25
*a.-j.* 80c Any single .70 .50

**Birth Announcement Type of 1997 with Added Euro Denomination**

***Die Cut Perf. 13¼x12¾***

**2001, July 2** **Litho.**

**Booklet Stamp**

**Self-Adhesive**

**1071** A363 85c multi 1.10 .80
*a.* Booklet pane of 5 6.00

**Death Announcement Type of 1998 with Added Euro Denomination**

***Die Cut Perf. 13¼***

**2001, July 2** **Litho.**

**Self-Adhesive**

**1072** A365 85c gray blue 1.25 1.00

Wedding Stamp — A415

***Die Cut Perf. 13¼x12¾***

**2001, July 2** **Photo.**

**Booklet Stamp**

**Self-Adhesive**

**1073** A415 85c multi 1.10 .25
*a.* Booklet pane of 5 5.50

See No. 1111.

A416

**2001, July 2** **Booklet Stamp**

**Self-Adhesive**

**1074** A416 85c multi 1.10 .50
*a.* Booklet pane of 10 11.00

See No. 1112.

Arrows
A417

***Serpentine Die Cut 14x13½***

**2001, July 2** **Coil Stamp** **Photo.**

**Self-Adhesive**

**1075** A417 85c pur & silver 1.00 .50

See Nos. 1105-1106.

Change of Address Stamp — A418

***Die Cut Perf. 14½x14***

**2001, July 2** **Photo.**

**Self-Adhesive**

**1076** A418 85c orange & blk 1.25 .80

See No. 1113.

Polder — A419

Coast at Zandvoort — A420

Design: 1.65g, Cyclists on Java Island, Amsterdam.

**2001, July 2** ***Die Cut Perf. 13¼x12¾***

**Booklet Stamps**

**Self-Adhesive**

**1077** A419 85c multi 1.25 .50
*a.* Booklet pane of 5 6.25

***Serpentine Die Cut 12¾ Syncopated***

**1078** A420 1.20g multi 1.50 1.10
*a.* Booklet pane of 5 7.50
**1079** A420 1.65g multi 2.00 1.75
*a.* Booklet pane of 5 10.00

Nos. 1078 and 1079 have rouletting between stamp and etiquette.

See Nos. 1114-1116.

Cartoon Network Cartoons — A421

No. 1080: a, Tom and Jerry. b, The Flintstones. c, Johnny Bravo. d, Dexter's Laboratory. e, The Powerpuff Girls.

*Perf. 13½x12¾*

**2001, Aug. 28** **Litho.**

**1080** A421 Booklet pane of 5, #a-e, + 2 labels 5.00 3.75
*a.-e.* 85c Any single .95 .60
Booklet, #1080 6.00

Greetings — A422

No. 1081: a, Veel Geluk (9 times). b, Gefeliciteerd! (11 times). c, Veel Geluk (4 times), horiz. d, Gefeliciteerd! (5 times), horiz. e, Proficiat (7 times). f, Succes! (7 times). g, Van Harte. . . (9 times). h, Proficiat (3 times), horiz. i, Succes! (3 times), horiz. j, Van Harte. . . (4 times), horiz.

*Die Cut Perf. 13x13¼, 13¼x13*

**2001, Sept. 3** **Photo.**

**Self-Adhesive**

**1081** Booklet of 10 10.50
*a.-j.* A422 85c Any single .95 .75

See No. 1117.

Change From Guilder to Euro Currency — A423

**Etched on Silver Foil**

**2001, Sept. 25** *Die Cut Perf. 12¾*

**Self-Adhesive**

**1082** A423 12.75g Guilder coins *9.50 6.50*

Cancels can be easily removed from these stamps.

Souvenir Sheet

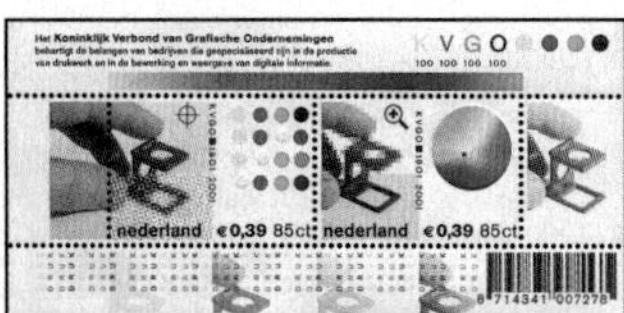

Royal Dutch Association of Printers, Cent. — A424

No. 1083 — Magnifying glass and: a, Color dots. b, Spectrum.

**Photo. & Embossed**

**2001, Oct. 12** *Perf. 14x13½*

**1083** A424 Sheet of 2 2.00 1.75
*a.-b.* 85c Any single .95 .75

Souvenir Sheet

Dutch Stamps, 150th Anniv. (in 2002) — A425

No. 1084: a, Waigaat Canal and ramparts, Williamstad, Curacao. b, Pangka sugar refinery, Java Island, Netherlands Indies.

**2001, Oct. 12** **Photo.** *Perf. 14x13½*

**1084** A425 Sheet of 2 2.00 2.00
*a.-b.* 85c Any single .95 .25

Amphilex 2002 Intl. Stamp Show, Amsterdam.

December Stamps — A426

No. 1085: a, Clock, grapes. b, Grapes, stars, doughnut balls. c, Doughnut balls, spire of church tower. d, Cherub. e, Champagne bottle. f, Wreath, roof. g, Windows of church tower. h, Ornament on Christmas tree. i, Christmas tree on sign. j, Cake in window. k, Christmas tree with ornaments, church tower. l, Santa Claus. m, Mug of hot chocolate on sign, snowman's head. n, Candles in window. o, Church tower, decorated market stalls. p, Reindeer. q, Snowman. r, Wrapped gift. s, Bonfire. t, Children on sled.

*Serpentine Die Cut 13¼x13*

**2001, Nov. 27** **Photo.**

**Self-Adhesive**

**1085** Sheet of 20 10.50
*a.-t.* A426 60c Any single .50 .25

100 Cents = 1 Euro (€)

**Queen Type of 1991, Arrows Type of 2001 With Euro Denominations Only and**

A427

*Die Cut Perf. 14¼, Serpentine Die Cut 14 (#1086, 12c), Serpentine Die Cut 14¼ (55c, 57c 70c, 72c), Perf 14¼x13½ (#1087, 5c, 10c)*

**Photo, Litho (5c, 12c)**

**2002-05** **Self-Adhesive**

**1086** A427 2c red .25 .25
*a.* Booklet pane of 5 .25

**Water-Activated Gum**

**1087** A427 2c red .25 .25
**1088** A427 5c red violet .25 .25
**1089** A427 10c blue .25 .25

**Self-Adhesive Booklet Stamps**

**1090** A427 12c green .30 .25
*a.* Booklet pane of 5 1.50
**1091** A273 25c brn & dk grn .60 .25
*a.* Booklet pane of 5 3.00
**1092** A273 39c bl grn & red .95 .25
*a.* Booklet pane of 5 4.75
*b.* Booklet pane of 10 9.50
**1093** A273 40c bl & brn .95 .25
*a.* Booklet pane of 5 4.75
**1094** A273 50c fawn & emer 1.25 .25
*a.* Booklet pane of 5 6.25
**1095** A273 55c lilac & brown 1.40 .25
*a.* Booklet pane of 5 7.00
**1096** A273 57c brn & blue grn 1.50 .30
*a.* Booklet pane of 5 7.50
**1097** A273 61c pur & red brn 1.60 .30
*a.* Booklet pane of 5 8.00
**1098** A273 65c grn & pur 1.60 .30
*a.* Booklet pane of 5 8.00
**1099** A273 70c ol grn & bl grn 1.75 .30
*a.* Booklet pane of 5 8.75
**1100** A273 72c blue & brt vio 1.90 .30
*a.* Booklet pane of 5 9.50
**1101** A273 76c olive & grn 2.00 .30
*a.* Booklet pane of 5 10.00
**1102** A273 78c bl & ol brn 1.90 .30
*a.* Booklet pane of 5 9.50
**1103** A273 €1 grn & blue 2.40 .40
*a.* Booklet pane of 5 12.00
**1104** A273 €3 red vio & grn 7.25 1.25
*a.* Booklet pane of 5 37.50
*Nos. 1086-1104 (19)* 28.35 6.25

**Coil Stamps**

**Self-Adhesive**

*Serpentine Die Cut Perf. 14x13½*

**1105** A417 39c pur & silver .95 .25
**1106** A417 78c blue & gold 1.90 .30

Issued: 12c, 25c, 39c, 40c, 50c, 65c, 78c, €1, €3, 1/2/02; 2c (#1086), 1/28/02; 2c (#1087), 9/2/02; 10c, 11/26/02; 5c, 55c, 70c, 1/2/03; 57c, 72c, 1/2/04; 61c, 76c, 1/3/05.

See No. 1259.

Souvenir Sheet

Wedding of Prince Willem-Alexander and Máxima Zorreguieta — A428

No. 1108: a, Portraits. b, Names.

**2002, Jan. 10** **Photo.** *Perf. 14*

**1108** A428 Sheet of 2 2.00 2.00
*a.-b.* 39c Either single .95 .50

**Types of 1998-2001 With Euro Denominations Only**

*Die Cut Perf. 13¼x12¾*

**Photo., Litho. (#1110)**

**2002, Jan. 28** **Self-Adhesive**

**1109** A363 39c multi .95 .50
*a.* Booklet pane of 5 4.75

*Die Cut Perf. 13¼*

**1110** A365 39c gray blue .95 .50

*Die Cut Perf. 13¼x12¾*

**1111** A415 39c multi .95 .50
*a.* Booklet pane of 5 4.75
**1112** A416 39c multi .95 .50
*a.* Booklet pane of 10 9.50

*Die Cut Perf. 14½x14*

**1113** A418 39c orange & blk 1.00 .50

*Die Cut Perf. 13¼x12¾*

**1114** A419 39c multi .95 .50
*a.* Booklet pane of 5 4.75

*Serpentine Die Cut 12¾ Syncopated*

**1115** A420 54c Like #1078 1.25 .50
*a.* Booklet pane of 5 6.25
**1116** A420 75c Like #1079 1.75 .50
*a.* Booklet pane of 5 8.75
*Nos. 1109-1116 (8)* 8.75 4.00

Nos. 1115-1116 have rouletting between stamp and etiquette.

**Greetings Type of 2001 with Euro Denominations Only**

No. 1117: a, Veel Geluk (9 times). b, Gefeliciteerd! (11 times). c, Veel Geluk (4 times), horiz. d, Gefeliciteerd! (5 times), horiz. e, Proficiat (7 times). f, Succes! (7 times). g, Van Harte. . . (9 times). h, Proficiat (3 times), horiz. i, Succes! (3 times), horiz. j, Van Harte. . . (4 times), horiz.

*Die Cut Perf. 13x13¼, 13¼x13*

**2002, Jan. 28** **Photo.**

**Self-Adhesive**

**1117** Booklet of 10 10.00
*a.-j.* A422 39c Any single .95 .70

Provinces A429

**2002** **Litho.** *Perf. 14½x14¾*

**1118** A429 39c Friesland .95 .95
**1119** A429 39c Drenthe .95 .95
**1120** A429 39c Noord-Holland .95 .95
**1121** A429 39c Gelderland .95 .95
**1122** A429 39c Noord-Brabant .95 .95
**1123** A429 39c Groningen .95 .95
**1124** A429 39c Zuid-Holland .95 .95
**1125** A429 39c Utrecht .95 .95
**1126** A429 39c Limburg .95 .95
**1127** A429 39c Overijssel .95 .95
**1128** A429 39c Zeeland .95 .95
**1129** A429 39c Flevoland .95 .95
*a.* Souvenir sheet of 12, #1118-1129 11.40
*Nos. 1118-1129 (12)* 11.40 11.40

Nos. 1118-1129 each were issued in sheets of 12 + 6 labels.

Issued: No. 1118, 3/12; No. 1119, 3/26; No. 1120, 4/9; No. 1121, 4/23. No. 1122, 5/7; No. 1123, 5/21. No. 1124, 6/4; No. 1125, 6/18; No. 1126, 7/2. No. 1127, 7/16; No. 1128, 7/30; No. 1129, 8/13.

Efteling Theme Park, 50th Anniv. A430

Characters: a, Bald man. b, Jester. c, Fairy. d, Man with thumb extended. e, Man with mouth open.

*Serpentine Die Cut 13¼x12¾*

**2002, May 14** **Photo.**

**Self-Adhesive**

**1130** Booklet pane of 5 4.75
*a.-e.* A430 39c Any single .95 .25

Europa A431

Designs: No. 1131, Lions and circus tent. No. 1132, Acrobats, juggler, animal acts.

*Perf. 14½x14¾*

**2002, June 11** **Litho.**

**1131** A431 54c multi 1.50 .75
**1132** A431 54c multi 1.50 .75
*a.* Tete-beche pair, #1131-1132 3.50 3.25

Landscape Paintings — A432

No. 1133: a, West Indian Landscape, by Jan Mostaert. b, Landscape with Cows, by Aelbert Cuyp. c, Grain Field, by Jacob van Ruisdael. d, Path in Middelharnis, by Meindert Hobbema. e, Italian Landscape, by Hendrik Vogel. f, Normandy Landscape, by Andreas Schelfhout. g, Landscape with Canal, by Jan Toorop. h, Landscape, by Jan Sluijters. i, Kismet, by Michael Raedecker. j, Untitled painting, by Robert Zandvliet. Names of artwork and artist are on sheet margins adjacent to stamps.

**2002, June 11** **Photo.** *Perf. 14½*

**1133** A432 Sheet of 10 9.25 6.25
*a.-j.* 39c Any single .90 .50

A433

*Die Cut Perf. 14¼*

**2002, July** **Coil Stamps** **Photo.**

**1134** A433 39c blue & red .95 .50
**1135** A433 78c green & red 1.90 .75

See Nos. 1157, 1173.

Souvenir Sheet

Amphilex 2002 Intl. Stamp Exhibition, Amsterdam — A434

No. 1136: a, One ship. b, Two ships.

**2002, Aug. 30 Litho. *Perf. 14x13½***
**1136** A434 Sheet of 2 1.90 1.90
*a.-b.* 39c Either single .95 .25

Dutch stamps, 150th anniv.; Dutch East India Company, 400th anniv.

Industrial Heritage — A435

No. 1137: a, Spakenberg shipyard, 1696. b, Dedemsvaart lime kilns, 1820. c, Cruquius steam pumping station, 1849. d, Heerlen coal mine shaft, 1898. e, Hengelo salt pumping tower, 1918. f, Weidum windmotor, 1920. g, Zevenaar brick oven, 1925. h, Breda brewery, 1926. i, Water works, Tilburg, 1927. j, Schoonebeck oil well pump, 1947.

**2002, Sept. 24 *Perf. 14½x14¾***
**1137** A435 Sheet of 10 9.50 9.50
*a.-j.* 39c Any single .95 .25

December Stamps — A436

No. 1138: a, Person, child, fence and trees. b, Man seated, trees. c, Head facing left. d, Red tree, person in black. e, Woman with white hair, tree. f, Person standing in grass. g, Man standing with legs crossed. h, Woman, windmill. i, Man on stool. j, Face with black lips. k, Man standing near tree, with bent knee. l, Man standing near trees, both hands in pockets. m, Two people seated. n, Person with black hair. o, Man with child on shoulders. p, Face, with black hair and eye looking right. q, Person with gold lips looking left. r, Head of person near shore. s, Person with sunglasses standing near shore. t, Woman with arms extended.

***Serpentine Die Cut 13***
**2002, Nov. 26 Photo.**
**Self-Adhesive**
**1138** A436 Sheet of 20 12.00
*a.-t.* 29c Any single .60 .25

Paintings by Vincent Van Gogh — A437

Designs: 39c, Self-portrait, 1886. 59c, Sunflowers, 1887. 75c, The Sower, 1888.

***Die Cut Perf. 14¼***
**2003, Jan. 2 Photo.**
**Booklet Stamps**
**Self-Adhesive**
**1139** A437 39c multi .95 .50
*a.* Booklet pane of 10 9.50

***Serpentine Die Cut 13¼ Syncopated***
**1140** A437 59c multi + etiquette 1.40 1.10
*a.* Booklet pane of 5+5 etiquettes 7.00
**1141** A437 75c multi + etiquette 1.75 1.50
*a.* Booklet pane of 5+5 etiquettes 8.75

A row of rouletting separates stamps from the etiquettes.

Paintings by Vincent Van Gogh — A438

No. 1142: a, Autumn Landscape with Four Trees, 1885. b, The Potato Eaters, 1885. c, Four Cut Sunflowers, 1887. d, Self-portrait with Gray Felt Hat, 1887-88. e, The Zouave, 1888. f, The Cafe Terrace on the Place du Forum, at Night, 1888. g, Pine Trees and Dandelions in the Garden of Saint-Paul Hospital, 1890. h, Blossoming Almond Tree, 1890. i, View of Auvers, 1890. j, Wheat Field with Crows, 1890.

**2003, Jan. 2 Litho. *Perf. 14½***
**1142** A438 Sheet of 10 10.00 10.00
*a.-j.* 39c Any single .95 .60

Water Control — A439

No. 1143: a, North Pier, Ijmuiden, 1869. b, Hansweert Lock, 1865. c, Damming of the Wieringermeer, 1929. d, Ijsselmeer Dam (no date). e, Water breaching dike at Willemstad, 1953. f, Repairing dike at Stavenisse, 1953. g, Damming of the Zandkreek, 1960. h, Damming of the Grevelingen, 1964. i, Oosterschelde flood barrier, 1995. j, High water in Roermond, 1993.

**2003, Feb. 1 Photo.**
**1143** A439 Sheet of 10 8.75 8.75
*a.-j.* 39c Any single .85 .60

Johann Enschedé and Sons, Printers, 300th Anniv. — A440

No. 1144: a, Binary code, mathematics symbols. b, Fleischman's musical notation symbols.

**Litho. & Embossed**
**2003, Mar. 4 *Perf. 14x12¾***
**1144** A440 Horiz. pair 1.60 1.00
*a.-b.* 39c Either single .80 .50

No. 1144a has photogravure back printing that can be seen through blank triangle on face of stamp.

Souvenir Sheets

Island Fauna — A441

No. 1145: a, Eurasian oyster catcher and pilings. b, Spoonbill, horiz. c, Eider. d, Harbor seal, horiz.

No. 1146: a, Sea gull. b, Stone curlew, horiz. c, Gull and seals. d, Crab, horiz.

**2003, May 6 Litho. *Perf. 14½***
**1145** A441 Sheet of 4 4.25 4.25
*a.-d.* 39c Any single .90 .60
**1146** A441 Sheet of 4 5.25 5.25
*a.-d.* 59c Any single 1.25 .80

A442

Personalized Stamps — A443

No. 1147: a, Flowers. b, Flag. c, Gift. d, Martini glass. e, Medal. f, Guitar. g, Balloons. h, Paper cut-outs. i, Cake. j, Party hat.

No. 1148 — Numeral color: a, Bright blue. b, Dull green. c, Lilac. d, Red violet. e, Dull orange. f, Yellow green. g, Olive. h, Dull blue. i, Red. j, Orange brown.

***Perf. 13½x12¾***
**2003, May 20 Photo.**
**1147** A442 Sheet of 10 + 10 labels 9.00 9.00
*a.-j.* 39c Any single .90 .25
**1148** A443 Sheet of 10 + 10 labels 9.00 9.00
*a.-j.* 39c Any single .90 .25

Labels could be personalized for an additional fee.

Douwe Egberts Co., 250th Anniv. — A444

**2003, June 3 Litho. *Perf. 14½x14¾***
**1149** 39c Spotted cup .95 .45
**1150** 39c White cup .95 .45
*a.* A444 Horiz. pair, #1149-1150 1.90 1.60

Land, Air and Water — A445

**2003, June 24**
**1151** A445 39c Airplate at UL .95 .45
**1152** A445 39c Fish at LR .95 .45
*a.* Horiz. pair, #1151-1152 1.90 .90

Nelson Mandela, 85th Birthday, and Nelson Mandela Children's Fund — A446

**2003, July 18**
**1153** A446 39c Mandela .95 .45
**1154** A446 39c Children's Fund .95 .45
*a.* Horiz. pair, #1153-1154 1.90 .90

"From Me to You" — A447

***Die Cut Perf. 14¼x14½***
**2003, Sept. 1 Photo.**
**Booklet Stamp**
**Self-Adhesive**
**1155** A447 39c multi .90 .50
*a.* Booklet pane of 5 4.50

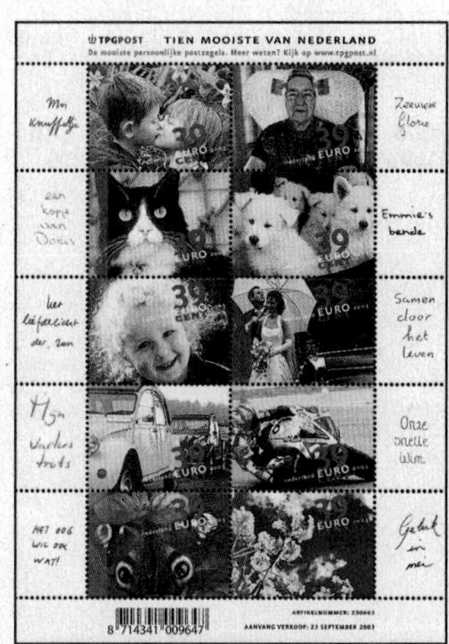

Photographs — A448

No. 1156: a, Children kissing. b, Woman. c, Cat. d, Puppies. e, Girl. f, Bride and groom. g,

Automobiles. h, Motorcycle race. i, Butterfly. j, Flowers and sky.

*Perf. 14½x14¾*

**2003, Sept. 23 Litho.**

**1156** A448 Sheet of 10 9.50 9.50
*a.-j.* 39c Any single .90 .65

**Numeral Type of 2002**

***Die Cut Perf. 13½***

**2003, Oct. 2 Photo.**

**Self-Adhesive**

**Stamp + Label**

**1157** A433 39c Prus bl & red 1.15 .75

No. 1157 has "2003" year date and was printed in sheets of 50 stamps + 50 labels. Labels could be personalized for an additional fee.

Stamp Collecting A449

**2003, Oct. 20 Litho. *Perf. 14½x14¾***

**1158** A449 39c multi .95 .50

A booklet containing 2 booklet panes of 4 #1158 and three different imperf incomplete progressive proofs of these panes sold for €9.95.

A450

December Stamps — A451

Designs: No. 1159, Five-pointed star.

No. 1160: a, Family. b, Open gift box. c, Cat and dog. d, Christmas tree. e, Toast. f, Bell. g, Hand with pencil. h, Head of reindeer. i, Hand with flower. j, Holly leaf and berries. k, Candle. l, Eight-pointed star. m, Man and woman. n, Snowman. o, Fireplace. p, Angel. q, Man and woman dancing. r, Round Christmas ornament. s, Mother and child. t, Treetop ornament.

*Perf. 13½x12¾*

**2003, Nov. 25 Litho.**

**1159** A450 29c multi + label .75 .75

**Photo.**

**Self-Adhesive**

***Serpentine Die Cut 13***

**1160** A451 Sheet of 20 15.00
*a.-t.* 29c Any single .60 .25

No. 1159 was printed in sheets of 10 stamps + 10 labels. Labels could be personalized. No. 1160 is printed with panel of thermochromic ink which reveals a message when warmed.

Queen Beatrix and Family — A452

No. 1161: a, Princess Beatrix as infant with Queen Juliana and Prince Bernhard, 1938. b, Princess Beatrix playing on swings with Princess Irene, 1943. c, Princess Beatrix with horse, 1951. d, Princess Beatrix reading book, 1964. e, Princess Beatrix talking with Prince Claus, 1965. f, Princess Beatrix, Prince Claus and infant Prince Willem-Alexander, 1967. g, Princess Beatrix, Prince Claus and three young sons, 1975. h, Queen Beatrix and Prince Claus dancing, 1998. i, Royal Family, 1999. j, Queen at art exhibition, 2000.

**2003, Dec. 9 Photo. *Perf. 14¼***

**1161** A452 Sheet of 10 9.50 9.50
*a.-j.* 39c Any single .95 .60

A booklet containing five panes each with two horizontally adjacent stamps from Nos. 1161a-1161j, in perf 13½x13¾, sold for €9.95.

Souvenir Sheet

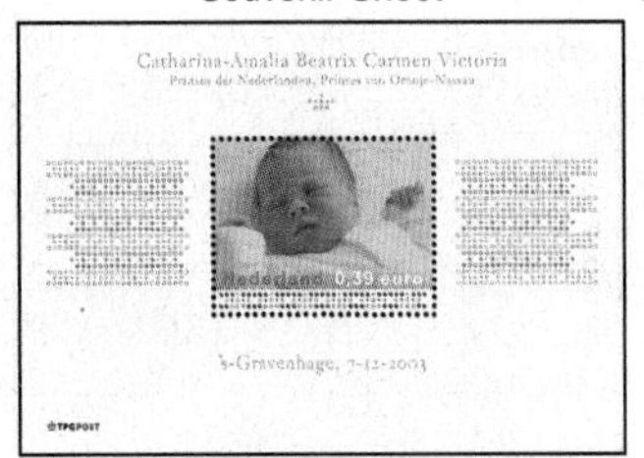

Birth of Princess Catharina-Amalia — A453

**2003, Dec. 16 Litho. *Perf. 13¾***

**1162** A453 39c multi 1.00 .75

See footnote below No. 1174.

Paintings — A454

Designs: 61c, Woman Reading a Letter, by Gabriel Metsu. 77c, The Letter, by Jan Vermeer.

***Serpentine Die Cut 13 Horiz. Syncopated***

**2004, Jan. 2 Photo.**

**Booklet Stamps**

**Stamp + Detachable Etiquette**

**1163** A454 61c multi 1.20 .50
*a.* Booklet pane of 5 6.00
**1164** A454 77c multi 1.45 .65
*a.* Booklet pane of 5 7.25

Royal Netherlands Meteorological Institute, 150th Anniv. — A455

Designs: No. 1165, Rain (rainbow at left. No. 1166, Sun (rainbow at right).

**2004, Jan. 31 Litho. *Perf. 14½x14¾***

**1165** 39c multi .80 .60
**1166** 39c multi .80 .60
*a.* A455 Horiz. pair, #1165-1166 2.00 .50

Retangles — A456

***Die Cut Perf. 14¼***

**2004, Mar. 2 Photo.**

**Self-Adhesive**

**1167** A456 39c red & multi .90 .60
**1168** A456 78c green & multi 1.75 1.00

See Nos. 1263-1264.

Spyker Automobiles — A457

Designs: No. 1169, 1922 Spyker. No. 1170, 2003 Spyker C8 Double 12 R.

**2004, May 10 Litho. *Perf. 14½***

**1169** 39c multi .90 .65
**1170** 39c multi .90 .65
*a.* A457 Horiz. pair, #1169-1170 1.80 1.80

A booklet containing four panes of perf 13¼x13 stamps (one pane of two No. 1169, one pane of two No. 1170, two panes containing two each of Nos. 1169-1170) sold for €9.95.

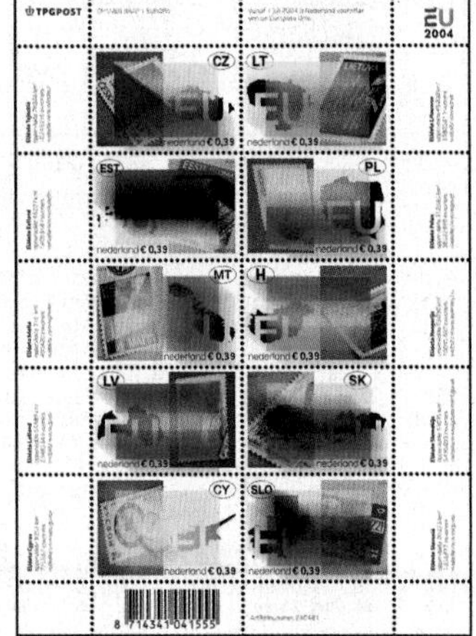

Expansion of European Union — A458

No. 1171 — Map, flag and stamps of new European Union members: a, Czech Republic. b, Lithuania. c, Estonia. d, Poland. e, Malta. f, Hungary. g, Latvia. h, Slovakia. i, Cyprus. j, Slovenia.

**2004, May 10 *Perf. 14½***

**1171** A458 Sheet of 10 10.00 10.00
*a.-j.* 39c Any single .95 .75

Numeral — A459

*Perf. 13½x12¾*

**2004, June 1 Photo.**

**1172** A459 39c multi + label .95 .70

Labels could be personalized.

**Numeral Type of 2002**

**2004, June 23 *Die Cut Perf. 13½***

**Self-Adhesive**

**Stamp + Label**

**1173** A433 39c org red & blue 1.10 1.10

No. 1173 has "2004" year date and has Olympic Torch Relay label.

Miniature Sheet

Prince Willem-Alexander, Princess Máxima and Princess Catharina-Amalia — A460

No. 1174: a, Prince Willem-Alexander and Princess Máxima announcing engagement. b, Princess Máxima showing engagement ring. c, Prince Willem-Alexander (without hat) and Princess Máxima looking at each other at wedding ceremony. d, Prince Willem-Alexander and Princess Máxima looking ahead at wedding ceremony. e, Prince Willem-Alexander and Princess Máxima kissing. f, Prince Willem-Alexander (with hat) looking at Princess Máxima. g, Prince Willem-Alexander and Princess Máxima looking at Princess Catharina-Amalia. h, Prince Willem-Alexander and Princess Máxima looking at book, Princess Máxima holding Princess Catharina-Amalia. i, Baptism of Princess Catharina-Amalia. j, Clergyman holding ceremony notes and touching head of Princess Catharina-Amalia at baptism.

**2004, June 23 Litho. *Perf. 13¾***

**1174** A460 Sheet of 10 9.50 9.50
*a.-j.* 39c Any single .90 .65

A booklet containing five panes, each with two horizontally adjacent stamps of Nos. 1174a-1174j, and a booklet pane of No. 1162, sold for €9.95.

Veluwe Nature Park — A461

No. 1175: a, Rabbit. b, Bird. c, Doe. d, Boar.
No. 1176: a, Fox. b, Woodpecker. c, Buck. d, Ram.

**2004, July 6 Photo. *Perf. 13¼x12¾***

**1175** A461 Sheet of 4 4.50 4.50
*a.-d.* 39c Any single 1.00 .40
**1176** A461 Sheet of 4 + 4 etiquettes 5.50 5.50
*a.-d.* 61c Any single 1.25 .50

Souvenir Sheet

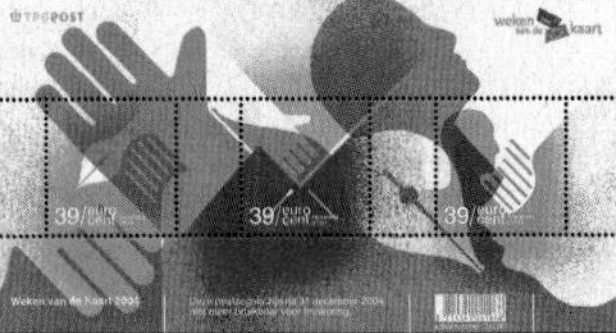

Greeting Card Week — A462

No. 1177: a, Pen nib. b, Hand. c, Head.

*Perf. 13¼x13¾*

**2004, Sept. 1 Photo.**

**1177** A462 Sheet of 3 + 2 labels 2.50 2.50
*a.-c.* 39c Any single .80 .60

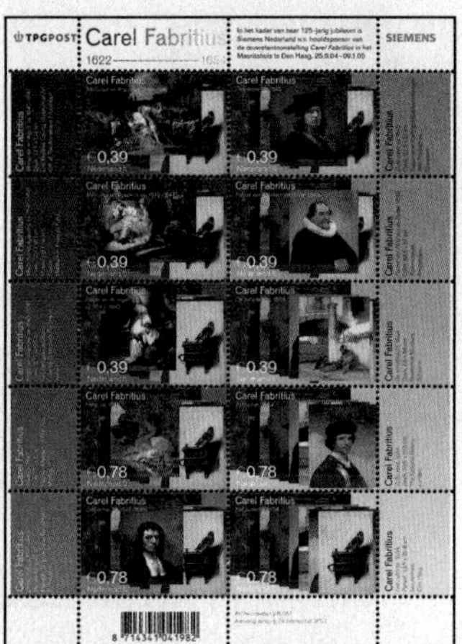

Paintings by Carel Fabritius (1622-54) — A463

No. 1178: a, Mercurius en Argus, c. 1645-47. b, Self-portrait, c. 1645. c, Mercurius en Aglauros, c. 1645-47. d, Abraham de Potter, 1649. e, Hagar en de Engel, c. 1643-45. f, De Schildwacht, c. 1654. g, Hera, c. 1643. h, Self-portrait, 1654. i, Self-portrait, c. 1647-48. j, Het Puttertje, 1654.

**2004, Sept. 24 Litho. *Perf. 14½***

**1178** A463 Sheet of 10 12.00 12.00
*a.-f.* 39c Any single .90 .70
*g.-j.* 78c Any single 1.60 1.25

Snowman — A464

December Stamps — A465

No. 1180: a, Shadows. b, People with gifts. c, Girl and dog. d, Children. e, Sheep. f, Polar bears. g, Children making snowman. h, People dragging Christmas tree. i, Man and woman in water. j, People around Christmas tree.

***Perf. 13½x12¾***

**2004, Nov. 25 Litho.**

**1179** A464 29c multi + label .85 .85

**Photo.**

**Self-Adhesive**

***Serpentine Die Cut 12¾x13¼***

**1180** Block of 10 8.00
*a.-j.* A465 29c Any single .80 .25

Hearts — A466

***Serpentine Die Cut 14¼***

**2005, Jan. 3 Photo.**

**Self-Adhesive**

**1181** A466 39c multi 1.00 .25
*a.* Booklet pane of 10 10.00

See No. 1262.

Building Silhouettes — A467

Designs: 39c, Windmill and field. 65c, House and brick wall. 81c, Greenhouse and field.

***Serpentine Die Cut 14¼***

**2005, Jan. 3 Self-Adhesive**

**1182** A467 39c multi 1.00 .25
*a.* Booklet pane of 10 10.00

***Serpentine Die Cut 13¼ Horiz. Syncopated***

**1183** A467 65c multi + etiquette 1.75 .45
*a.* Booklet pane of 5 8.75
**1184** A467 81c multi + etiquette 2.10 .50
*a.* Booklet pane of 5 10.50
*Nos. 1182-1184 (3)* 4.85 1.20

On Nos. 1183 and 1184 a row of rouletting separates stamp from etiquette.

Netherlands Views — A468

**2005 Litho. *Perf. 14¼***

| No. | Type | Value | Description | Unused | Used |
|---|---|---|---|---|---|
| **1185** | A468 | 39c | shown | 1.00 | .25 |
| **1186** | A468 | 39c | Nijmegen | 1.00 | .25 |
| **1187** | A468 | 39c | Rotterdam | 1.00 | .25 |
| **1188** | A468 | 39c | Weesp | 1.00 | .25 |
| **1189** | A468 | 39c | Monnickendam | .95 | .25 |
| **1190** | A468 | 39c | Goes | .95 | .25 |
| **1191** | A468 | 39c | Boalsert | 1.00 | .25 |
| **1192** | A468 | 39c | Amsterdam | 1.00 | .25 |
| **1193** | A468 | 39c | Roermond | .95 | .25 |
| *a.* | | | Souvenir sheet, #1186, 1187, 1190, 1192, 1193 | 5.00 | 5.00 |
| **1194** | A468 | 39c | Papendrecht | .95 | .25 |
| *a.* | | | Souvenir sheet, #1185, 1188, 1189, 1191, 1194 | 5.00 | 5.00 |
| | | | *Nos. 1185-1194 (10)* | 9.80 | 2.50 |

Issued: Nos. 1185-1186, 2/8; Nos. 1187-1188, 4/12; Nos. 1189-1190, 6/14. Nos. 1191-1192, 8/9; Nos. 1193-1194, 1193a, 1194a, 10/14.

A booklet containing five panes, each with the two stamps issued on the same day with perf. 13½x12¾, sold for €9.95.

Art — A469

No. 1195: a, Trying, by Liza May Post. b, Emilie, by Sidi El Karchi. c, ZT, by Koen Vermeule. d, Het Bedrijf, by Lieshout Studio. e, Me Kissing Vinoodh (Passionately), by Inez van Lamsweerde. f, Lena, by Carla van de Puttelaar. g, Nr. 13, by Tom Claasen. h, Untitled, by Pieter Kusters. i, Witte Roos, by Ed van der Kooy. j, Portrait of a Boy (Grand Prix), bu Tiong Ang.

**2005, Feb. 25 Litho. *Perf. 14½***

**1195** A469 Sheet of 10 10.00 10.00
*a.-j.* 39c Any single 1.00 .50

Business Symbols — A470

***Die Cut Perf. 14¼***

**2005, Mar. 22 Litho.**

**Self-Adhesive**

**1196** A470 39c multi 1.00 .25

Souvenir Sheets

Natuurmonumenten, Cent. — A471

No. 1197: a, Cormorant. b, Dragonfly. c, Water lily. d, Fish.

No. 1198: a, Bird. b, Butterfly. c, Lizard. d, Sheep.

**2005, Mar. 22 Photo. *Perf. 13¼x13***

**1197** A471 Sheet of 4 4.00 4.00
*a.-d.* 39c Any single 1.00 .25
**1198** A471 Sheet of 4 + 4 etiquettes 6.75 6.75
*a.-d.* 65c Any single 1.60 .40

A booklet containing four panes, each with two litho., perf 14x13¾ stamps like Nos. 1197a-1197d and 1198a-1198d, sold for €9.95.

Souvenir Sheet

Queen Beatrix, 25th Anniv. of Reign — A472

Photos: a, Coronation, 1980. b, Giving speech, 1991. c, With Nelson Mandela, 1999. d, Visiting colonies, 1999. e, At European Parliament, 2004.

**2005, Apr. 30 Litho. *Perf. 13¼x13¾***

| | | | |
|---|---|---|---|
| **1199** | A472 Sheet of 5 | 16.00 | 16.00 |
| *a.* | 39c multi | 1.00 | .25 |
| *b.* | 78c multi | 2.00 | .50 |
| *c.* | 117c multi | 3.00 | .75 |
| *d.* | 156c multi | 4.00 | 1.00 |
| *e.* | 225c multi | 6.00 | 1.50 |
| *f.* | Booklet pane of 1, #1199a | 1.75 | — |
| *g.* | Booklet pane of 1, #1199b | 3.25 | — |
| *h.* | Booklet pane of 1, #1199c | 5.00 | — |
| *i.* | Booklet pane of 1, #1199d | 6.50 | — |
| *j.* | Booklet pane of 1, #1199e | 9.50 | — |
| | Complete booklet, #1199f-1199j | 26.00 | |

Complete booklet sold for €9.95.

Numerals — A473

***Die Cut Perf. 14¼***

**2005, May 24 Photo.**

**Coil Stamps**

**Self-Adhesive**

**1200** A473 39c bronze .95 .25
**1201** A473 78c silver 1.90 .50

Souvenir Sheet

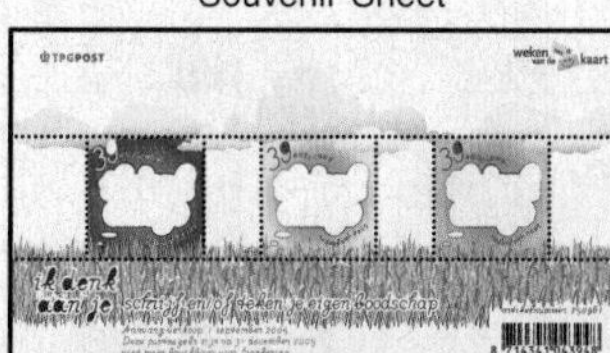

Greeting Card Week — A474

No. 1202: a, Red background, denomination in white. b, Yellow background, denomination in red. c, Blue background, denomination in red.

**2005, Sept. 1 Litho. *Perf. 13½x13¾***

**1202** A474 Sheet of 3 + 2 labels 3.00 3.00
*a.-c.* 39c Any single 1.00 .25

Farm Technology — A475

Sheep and: No. 1203, Dutch windmills. No. 1204, Chinese water wheel.

**2005, Sept. 22 Litho. *Perf. 14½***

**1203** 81c multi 2.00 .50
**1204** 81c multi 2.00 .50
*a.* A475 Horiz. pair, #1203-1204 4.00 1.00

See People's Republic of China Nos. 3452-3453.

World Press Photo, 50th Anniv. — A476

No. 1205 — Silver Camera award-winning news photographs by: a, Douglas Martin, 1957. b, Héctor Rondón Lovera, 1962. c, Co Rentmeester, 1967. d, Hanns-Jörg Anders, 1969. e, Ovie Carter, 1974. f, David Burnett, 1979. g, Anthony Suau, 1987. h, Georges Merillon, 1990. i, Claus Bjorn Larsen, 1999. j, Arko Datta, 2004.

**2005, Oct. 8 Litho.**

**1205** A476 Sheet of 10 9.50 9.50
*a.-j.* 39c Any single .95 .25

Trains — A477

Designs: No. 1206, Blue Angel. No. 1207, Locomotive 3737. No. 1208, ICE. No. 1209, Koploper.

**2005, Oct. 14 Litho.**

**1206** A477 39c blue & multi .95 .25
**1207** A477 39c green & multi .95 .25
**1208** A477 39c red & multi .95 .25
**1209** A477 39c yel & multi .95 .25
*a.* Block of 4, #1206-1209 3.80 1.00

A478

December Stamps — A479

No. 1211: a, Flames and hearts. b, Gifts. c, Comets. d, Bells. e, Doves. f, Snowmen. g, Ornaments. h, Ice skates. i, Christmas trees. j, Champagne flutes.

***Perf. 13½x12¾***

**2005, Nov. 24 Litho.**

**1210** A478 29c multi + label .70 .25

**Photo.**

**1211** A479 Sheet of 10 7.00 7.00
*a.-j.* 29c Any single .70 .25

Labels on No. 1210 could be personalized for a fee.

Modern Art — A480

No. 1212: a, Koe in de Optrekkende Avondmist, by Ed van der Elsken. b, Double Dutch, by Berend Strik. c, Hollandse Velden, by Hans van der Meer. d, Tomorrow, by Marijke van Warmerdam. e, A Day in Holland/Holland in a Day, by Barbara Visser. f, Composite mit Rode Ruit, by Daan van Golden. g, Untitled work, by J. C. J. Vanderhayden. h, De Groene Kathedraal, by Mariana Boozem. i, Hollandpan, by John Körmerling. j, Drijfbeeld, by Atelier Van Lieshout.

No. 1213: a, Study for Horizon, by Sigurdur Gudmundsson. b, Lost Luggage Depot, by Jeff Wall. c, 11,000 Tulipes, by Daniel Buren. d, Flets & Stal, by FAT. e, Double Sunset, by Olafur Eliasson.

No. 1214: a, Untitled, by Dustin Larson. b, Working Progress, by Tadashi Kawamata. c, Boerderijgezichten, by Sean Snyder. d, Toc Toc, by Amalia Pica. e, Freude, by Rosemarie Trockel.

***Serpentine Die Cut 14¼***

**2006, Jan. 2 Litho.**

**Self-Adhesive**

**1212** Booklet pane of 10 9.50
*a.-j.* A480 39c Any single .95 .25

***Serpentine Die Cut 13 Vert. Syncopated***

**1213** Booklet pane of 5 + 5 etiquettes 8.50
*a.-e.* A480 69c Any single + etiquette 1.60 .40
**1214** Booklet pane of 5 + 5 etiquettes 10.50
*a.-e.* A480 85c Any single + etiquette 2.00 .50

On Nos. 1213 and 1214, a row of microrouletting separates stamps from etiquettes.

**Queen Type of 1991**

***Die Cut Perf. 14¼ Syncopated***

**2006-09 Photo.**

**Self-Adhesive**

**Booklet Stamps**

**1216** A273 44c rose & ol grn 1.25 .25
*a.* Booklet pane of 10 12.50

***Die Cut Perf. 14¼***

**1218** A273 44c rose & ol grn 1.25 .25
*a.* Booklet pane of 10 12.50
**1219** A273 67c bl grn & blue 1.75 .30
*a.* Booklet pane of 5 8.75
**1220** A273 74c gray grn & pur 2.10 .50
*a.* Booklet pane of 5 10.50
**1221** A273 80c blue & red vio 2.00 .50
*a.* Booklet pane of 5 10.00
**1223** A273 88c lilac & gray grn 2.40 .40
*a.* Booklet pane of 5 12.00
*Nos. 1216-1223 (6)* 10.75 2.20

Issued: 80c, 1/2; 44c, 67c, 88c, 12/11; 74c, 1/2/09.

Netherlands Tourism Areas — A481

**2006 Litho. *Perf. 14½x14¼***

**1240** A481 39c Leiden .95 .25
**1241** A481 39c Sittard .95 .25
**1242** A481 39c Vlieland 1.00 .25
**1243** A481 39c Woudrichem 1.00 .25
**1244** A481 39c Enkhuizen 1.00 .25
*a.* Souvenir sheet, #1240-1244 5.00 5.00
**1245** A481 39c Schoonhoven 1.00 .25
**1246** A481 39c Zutphen 1.00 .25
**1247** A481 39c Deventer 1.00 .25
**1248** A481 39c Zwolle 1.00 .25
**1249** A481 39c Kampen 1.00 .25
*a.* Souvenir sheet, #1245-1249 5.00 5.00
*Nos. 1240-1249 (10)* 9.90 2.50

Issued: No. 1240, 2/1; No. 1241, 2/3; No. 1242, 4/28; No. 1243, 5/24; Nos. 1244-1245, 6/2; Nos. 1246-1247, 8/4; Nos. 1248-1249, 9/1. Nos. 1244a, 1249a, 10/10.

A booklet containing five panes of one each of Nos. 1240-1241, 1242-1243, 1244-1245, 1246-1247, and 1248-1249 sold for €9.95.

Souvenir Sheet

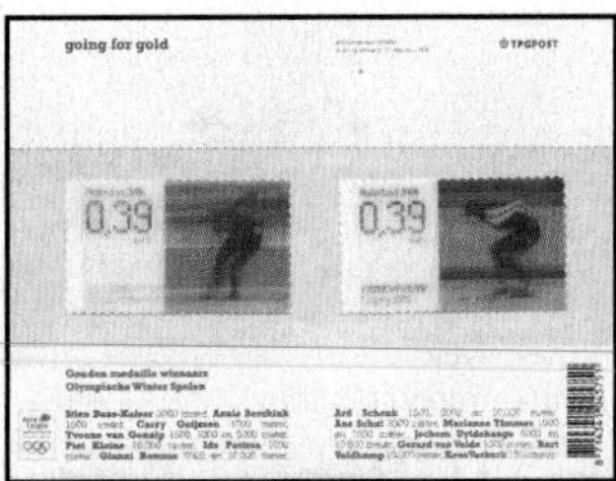

Dutch Speed Skating Gold Medalists in the Winter Olympics — A482

No. 1250: a, Ard Schenk. b, Yvonne van Gennip.

**Litho. With Three-Dimensional Plastic**

**2006, Feb. 10 *Serpentine Die Cut 9***

**Self-Adhesive**

**1250** A482 Sheet of 2 1.90
*a.-b.* 39c Either single .95 .50

The two stamps and a top and bottom sheet margin are affixed to a sheet of backing paper. A booklet containing five examples of No. 1250 sold for €9.95.

Personalized Stamp — A483

**2006, May 1 Litho. *Perf. 13½x14***

**1251** A483 39c multi 1.00 .25

No. 1251, showing Dutch soccer player Dirk Kuyt, sold for face value to the public and is the generic image for this stamp. Stamps depicting twenty other Dutch soccer players (Edwin van der Sar, Arjen Robben, Mark van Bommel, Ron Vlaar, Giovanni van Bronckhorst, Khalid Boulahrouz, Romeo Castelen, Jan Vennegoor of Hesselink, Urby Emanuelson, Ruud van Nistelrooy, Henk Timmer, Rafael van der Vaart, Hedwiges Maduro, Wesley Sneijder, Robin van Persie, Nigel de Jong, Barry Opdam, Joris Mathijsen, Denny Landzaat, and Phillip Cocu) were produced by postal authorities to sell as a special set for €12.95 per sheet of 10 different players. Examples of No. 1251 with other images are personalized stamps that sold for €12.95 per sheet of 10 stamps.

Miniature Sheet

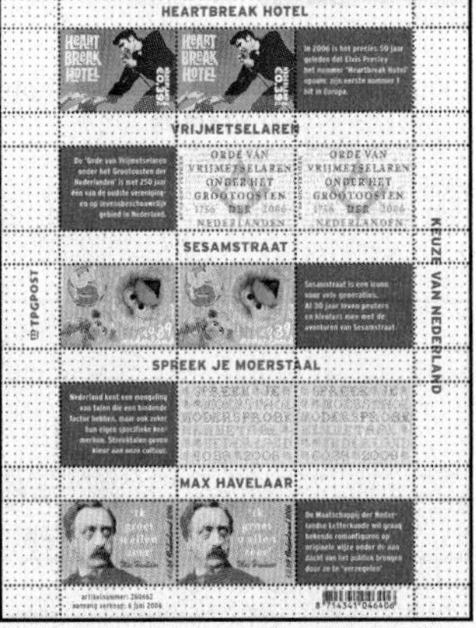

Stamps Chosen By the Public — A484

No. 1252: a, Elvis Presley. b, Masonic emblem. c, Muppets Purk and Pino. d, Needlepoint design of sayings in languages used in Twente, Limburg and Friesland. e, Max Havelaar, fictional character.

**2006, June 10 *Perf. 14½***

**1252** A484 Sheet of 10, 2 each #a-e, + 17 labels 10.00 10.00
*a.-e.* 39c Any single 1.00 .25

Heartbreak Hotel, by Presley, 50th anniv., Dutch Grand Masonic Lodge, 250th anniv.; Dutch version of Sesame Street. 30th anniv.

Rembrandt (1606-69), Painter — A485

No. 1253: a, Bearded Man in Oriental Cape and Robe. b, Old Woman Seated at a Table. c, Saskia van Uylenburgh. d, Rembrandt's Son, Titus. e, Portrait of a Woman at the Window. €6.45, Self-portrait with Saskia.

**2006, June 15 Litho. *Perf. 13¾***

**1253** A485 Block of 5 + label 5.00 5.00
*a.-e.* 39c Any single 1.00 .25

**Souvenir Sheet**

**Litho. & Engr.**

**On Thin Card**

**1254** A485 €6.45 tan & black 17.00 17.00

See Germany No. 2387. A booklet containing two panes, each containing Nos. 1253a, 1253b, and 1253d, one pane of No. 1253c and Germany No. 2387, and one pane containing two No. 1253e, sold for €9.95. The booklet was withdrawn from sale after it was discovered that the German stamp in the booklet was printed with perforations and tagging without the authorization of German postal authorities, but most of the booklets produced had already been distributed. Value, $80.

Drawing by Karel Appel (1921-2006) A486

**2006, Sept. 1 Litho. *Perf. 13¼x14***

**1255** A486 39c multi 1.00 .25

A booklet containing five panes of 2 No. 1255 sold for €9.95.

Miniature Sheet

Endangered Animals — A487

No. 1256: a, Giraffe. b, Butterfly. c, Manchurian crane. d, Francois' leaf monkey. e, Blue poison dart frog. f, Red panda. g, Lowland gorilla. h, Sumatran tiger. i, Asian lion. j, Indian rhinoceros. k, Asian elephant. l, Pygmy hippopotamus.

**2006, Oct. 4 *Perf. 13¾***

**1256** A487 Sheet of 12 12.00 12.00
*a.-l.* 39c Any single 1.00 .25

A booklet containing one pane each of Nos. 1256a-1256c, 1256d-1256f, 1256g-1256i, and 1256j-1256l sold for €9.95.

Renaming of Postal Corporation as TNT Post — A488

**2006, Oct. 16 Litho. *Perf. 14½***

**1257** A488 39c multi 1.00 .25

Snowflakes — A489

No. 1258: a, Small blue green, large dark blue flakes. b, Large pink, small red flakes. c, Small pink, large brown flakes. d, Large blue, small red flakes. e, Small blue green, large brown flakes. f, Small blue, large red flakes. g, Large green, small brown flakes. h, Small blue, large pink flakes. i, Large red, small brown flakes. j, Small pink, large blue green flakes.

***Serpentine Die Cut 12¾x13¼***

**2006, Nov. 23 Photo.**

**Self-Adhesive**

**1258** Block of 10 7.75
*a.-j.* A489 29c Any single .75 .25

**Numeral and "NL" Type of 2002**

***Perf. 14¼x13½***

**2006, Dec. 11 Photo.**

**1259** A427 3c brown .25 .25

**Birth Announcement Type of 1997**

***Serpentine Die Cut 13¼x12¾***

**2006, Dec. 11 Photo.**

**Self-Adhesive**

**1260** A363 44c multi 1.25 .30

**Death Announcement Type of 1997**

***Serpentine Die Cut 13¼***

**2006, Dec. 11 Photo.**

**Self-Adhesive**

**1261** A365 44c multi 1.25 .30

**Hearts Type of 2005**

***Serpentine Die Cut 14½x14¼***

**2006, Dec. 11 Litho.**

**Self-Adhesive**

**1262** A466 44c multi 1.25 .30
*a.* Booklet pane of 10 12.50

**Rectangles Type of 2004**

***Die Cut Perf. 14¼x14½***

**2006, Dec. 11 Photo.**

**Self-Adhesive**

**1263** A456 44c multi 1.25 .30
**1264** A456 88c multi 2.40 .40

Dutch Products — A490

No. 1265: a, Glide glass goblet. b, Revolt chair. c, Heineken beer bottle. d, Bugaboo stroller. e, Lapin kettle. f, Milk bottle lamp. g, Carrier bicycle. h, Fluorescent screw-bottom lightbulb. i, Unox smoked sausage. j, Tulip.

72c, Clap skates. 89c, Cheese slicer.

***Die Cut Perf. 14¼***

**2006, Dec. 11 Photo.**

**Self-Adhesive**

**1265** Booklet pane of 10 12.50
*a.-j.* A490 44c Any single 1.25 .25

***Serpentine Die Cut 11***

**1266** A490 72c multi + etiquette 1.90 .30
*a.* Booklet pane of 5 + 5 etiquettes 9.50
**1267** A490 89c multi + etiquette 2.40 .40
*a.* Booklet pane of 5 + 5 etiquettes 12.00

On Nos. 1266-1267, a row of microrouletting separates stamps from etiquettes.

Numerals — A491

**2007, Jan. 2** ***Die Cut Perf. 14¼x14½***

**Self-Adhesive**

**1268** A491 44c multi 1.25 .30
*a.* Serpentine die cut 13½ + label 1.25 .30
**1269** A491 88c multi, vert. 2.40 .40

The generic label on No. 1268a depicts a mailbox. These labels could be personalized for an additional fee.

A492

Personalized Stamps — A493

**2007** **Litho.** ***Perf. 14x13½***

**1270** A492 44c multi 1.25 .30

**Self-Adhesive**

***Serpentine Die Cut 13¼x13***

**1271** A493 44c multi 1.25 .30

Issued: No. 1270, 1/2; No. 1271, 9/21. The generic vignettes of Nos. 1270 (Royal Dutch Mint), and 1271 (Mathematician L. E. J. Brouwer), which sold for face value, are shown. These stamps, printed in sheets of 10, could be personalized with horizontal or vertical images for an additional fee.

Netherlands Tourism Areas — A494

**2007** **Litho.** ***Perf. 14½x14¼***

**1272** A494 44c Gouda 1.25 .30
**1273** A494 44c Groningen 1.25 .30
**1274** A494 44c Vlissingen 1.25 .30
**1275** A494 44c Hoorn 1.25 .30
**1276** A494 44c Leerdam 1.25 .30
**1277** A494 44c Den Helder 1.25 .30
**1278** A494 44c Lelystad 1.25 .30
**1279** A494 44c Den Haag (The Hague) 1.25 .30
*a.* Souvenir sheet, #1274-1275, 1277-1279 6.25 6.25
**1280** A494 44c Utrecht 1.25 .30
**1281** A494 44c Edam 1.25 .30
*a.* Souvenir sheet, #1272-1273, 1276, 1280-1281 6.25 6.25
*Nos. 1272-1281 (10)* 12.50 3.00

Issued: Nos. 1272-1273, 2/7; No. 1274, 3/23; No. 1275, 3/26; No. 1276, 4/13; No. 1277, 7/24; No. 1278, 8/8; No. 1279, 8/15. Nos. 1279a, 1281a, 10/17; No. 1280, 10/3; No. 1281, 10/10. A booklet containing five panes of one each of Nos. 1272-1273, 1274-1275, 1276-1277, 1278-1279, and 1280-1281 in perf. 13½x12½ sold for €9.95.

Trees in Spring — A495

Trees in Summer — A496

Trees in Autumn — A497

Trees in Winter — A498

Designs: No. 1282, Lime tree. No. 1283, Horse chestnut bud. No. 1284, Bark of plane tree. No. 1285, Oak tree. No. 1286, Maple samaras. No. 1287, Trunk and branches of beech tree. No. 1288, Black alder tree. No. 1289, White willow tree in water.

**2007** **Litho.** ***Perf. 14½***

**1282** 44c multi 1.25 .30
**1283** 44c multi 1.25 .30
*a.* A495 Horiz. pair, #1282-1283 2.50 .60
**1284** 44c multi 1.25 .30
**1285** 44c multi 1.25 .30
*a.* A496 Horiz. pair, #1284-1285 2.50 .60
**1286** 44c multi 1.25 .30
**1287** 44c multi 1.25 .30
*a.* A497 Horiz. pair, #1286-1287 2.50 .60
**1288** 44c multi 1.25 .30
**1289** 44c multi 1.25 .30
*a.* A498 Horiz. pair, #1288-1289 2.50 .60
*Nos. 1282-1289 (8)* 10.00 2.40

Issued: Nos. 1282-1283, 3/23; Nos. 1284-1285, 6/21; Nos. 1286-1287, 9/21; Nos. 1288-1289, 11/12.

Miniature Sheet

Flowers — A499

No. 1290: a, Yellow and white toadflax at L, blue lobelia at R, red pinks at LR. b, Blue lobelias and white petunia. c, Yellow and white toadflax at UL, red pinks at UR and LL, sky at LR. d, Red snapdragon at UL, blue lobelia at top, white petunias at UR, red and white petunias at bottom, sky at LL. e, Red pinks at top, white toadflax at UL and LL, sky at R. f, Red and white petunias at R, sky at left. g, White toadflax at L, pink snapdragons at LR, sky at UR. h, Red and white petunia at top, pink snapdragons at LL, red violet toadflax at LR, sky at UL. i, White toadflax at UL, red and white snapdragons at UR, white and red pinks at LL. j, Red violet toadflax.

**Litho & Embossed**

**2007, May 1** ***Perf. 13½***

**1290** A499 Sheet of 10 12.50 12.50
*a.-j.* 44c Any single 1.25 .30

Flower seeds are sealed under a round piece of adhesive tape in the embossed circle in the center of the stamps. The left and right sheet selvage contains instructions on planting the stamps and seeds. A booklet containing five panes, each containing one of the five horizontal pairs of stamps from the sheet and the adjacent selvage, sold for €9.95.

Europa — A500

**2007, July 26** **Litho.** ***Perf. 13½***

**1291** 72c Moon 2.00 .50
**1292** 72c Sun 2.00 .50
*a.* A500 Pair, #1291-1292 4.00 1.00

Scouting, cent. Printed in sheets of 10. Sheet margins inscribed "Priority" serve as etiquettes. A booklet containing three different panes, each containing a horizontal pair and two etiquettes, sold for €9.95.

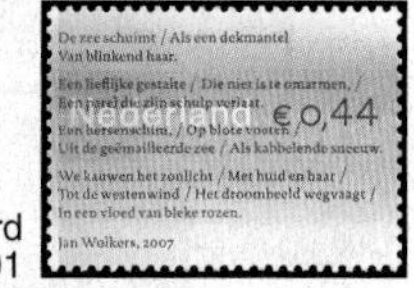


Greeting Card Weeks — A501

**2007, Sept. 3** ***Perf. 13¾***

**1293** A501 44c multi 1.25 .30

Printed in sheets of 3.

Kingdom of the Netherlands, Bicent. A502

**Litho. & Embossed**

**2007, Sept. 11** ***Perf. 13¼***

**Booklet Stamp**

**1294** A502 €6.45 multi 29.00 15.00
Complete booklet 29.00

No. 1294 was sold only in a booklet pane of one stamp in a booklet containing one pane, which sold for €9.95.

A503 A504

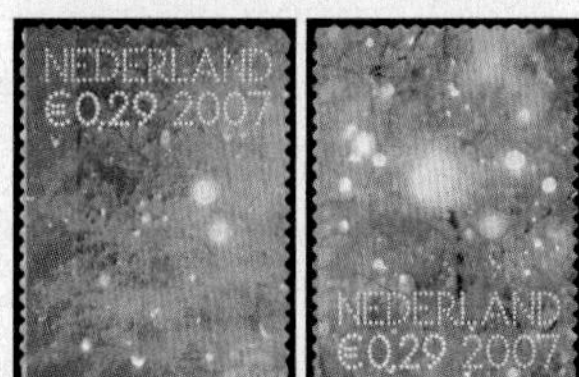


A505 A506

A507 A508

A509 A510

Snowflakes and Trees

A511 A512

A513 A514

A515 A516

A517 A518

A519 A520

Fireworks

A521 A522

***Serpentine Die Cut 12¾x13¼***

**2007, Nov. 22** **Photo.**

**Self-Adhesive**

**1295** Block of 10 8.50
*a.* A503 29c multi .85 .25
*b.* A504 29c multi .85 .25
*c.* A505 29c multi .85 .25
*d.* A506 29c multi .85 .25
*e.* A507 29c multi .85 .25
*f.* A508 29c multi .85 .25
*g.* A509 29c multi .85 .25
*h.* A510 29c multi .85 .25
*i.* A511 29c multi .85 .25
*j.* A512 29c multi .85 .25

**Litho.**

***Serpentine Die Cut 12¾***

**1296** Block of 10 13.00
*a.* A513 29c multi, unscratched panel 1.25 .30
*b.* A514 29c multi, unscratched panel 1.25 .30
*c.* A515 29c multi, unscratched panel 1.25 .30
*d.* A516 29c multi, unscratched panel 1.25 .30
*e.* A517 29c multi, unscratched panel 1.25 .30
*f.* A518 29c multi, unscratched panel 1.25 .30
*g.* A519 29c multi, unscratched panel 1.25 .30
*h.* A520 29c multi, unscratched panel 1.25 .30
*i.* A521 29c multi, unscratched panel 1.25 .30

| | | | |
|---|---|---|---|
| *j.* | A522 29c multi, unscratched panel | 1.25 | .30 |
| *k.-t.* | As #1296a-1296j, any single, scratched panel | | .30 |

No. 1296 sold for €4.40, with €1.50 of the total going towards lottery prizes awarded to the sender of and mail recipient of stamps with prizes found under the scratch-off panel at the bottom of the stamps. Scratch-off panels are separated from the stamps by a row of rouletting.

Ecology — A523

No. 1297: a, Hybrid vehicle with electric plug. b, House and sun (solar energy). c, Cow with electric plug (biofuels). d, Wind generators. e, Trees. f, Flowers, carpoolers in automobile. g, "Groen" with electric plug. h, Truck (soot filters). i, Birds and envelope (green mail). j, Insulated house.

75c, Bicycle with globe hemispheres as wheels. 92c, Heart-shaped globe.

***Die Cut Perf. 14¼***

**2008, Jan. 2** **Litho.**

**Self-Adhesive**

| | | | |
|---|---|---|---|
| **1297** | Booklet pane of 10 | 13.00 | |
| *a.-j.* | A523 44c Any single | 1.25 | .30 |

**Photo.**

***Serpentine Die Cut 11***

| | | | |
|---|---|---|---|
| **1298** | A523 75c multi + etiquette | 2.25 | .55 |
| **1299** | A523 92c multi + etiquette | 2.75 | .70 |

On Nos. 1298-1299 a row of microrouletting separates stamps from etiquettes.

See Nos. 1324-1325.

A524

A525

A526

A527

A528

A529

Personalized Stamps — A530

**2008** **Litho.** ***Perf. 14x13½***

| | | | |
|---|---|---|---|
| **1300** | A524 44c multi | 1.25 | .30 |

***Perf. 13½x14***

| | | | |
|---|---|---|---|
| **1301** | A525 44c multi | 1.25 | .30 |

***Perf. 13½x13, 13x13½***

| | | | |
|---|---|---|---|
| **1302** | Horiz. strip of 5 | 6.50 | 3.25 |
| *a.* | A526 44c multi | 1.25 | .30 |
| *b.* | A527 44c multi | 1.25 | .30 |
| *c.* | A528 44c multi | 1.25 | .30 |
| *d.* | A529 44c multi | 1.25 | .30 |
| *e.* | A530 44c multi | 1.25 | .30 |

Issued: Nos. 1300-1301, 1/2; No. 1302, 3/18. The generic vignettes of Nos. 1300 (Netherlands Federation of Philatelic Associations, cent.), 1301 (Netherlands Association of Stamp Dealers, 80th anniv.), and 1302 (winning art for personalized stamp design contest), which sold for face value, are shown. These stamps, printed in sheets of 10, could be personalized for an additional fee. A booklet containing 5 panes of Nos. 1300-1301, each with different pane margins, sold for € 9.95. Other booklets containing panes of Nos. 1300 or 1301 with different vignettes exist. These booklets usually sold for €9.95, and may contain fewer than ten stamps.

Netherlands Tourism Areas — A531

**2008** **Litho.** ***Perf. 14½x14¼***

| | | | |
|---|---|---|---|
| **1303** | A531 44c Sneek | 1.40 | .35 |
| **1304** | A531 44c Coevorden | 1.40 | .35 |
| **1305** | A531 44c Heusden | 1.40 | .35 |
| **1306** | A531 44c Amersfoort | 1.40 | .35 |
| **1307** | A531 44c Zoetermeer | 1.40 | .35 |
| *a.* | Souvenir sheet of 5, #1303-1307 | 7.00 | 3.50 |
| | *Nos. 1303-1307 (5)* | 7.00 | 1.75 |

Issued: Nos. 1303-1304, 3/25; Nos. 1305-1306, 4/22; No. 1307, 6/3; No. 1307a, 6/12. A booklet containing five panes, with each pane containing two perf. 13½x12¾ examples of each stamp, sold for €9.95.

Europa A532

**2008, May 20** **Litho.** ***Perf. 13½x12¾***

| | | | |
|---|---|---|---|
| **1308** | A532 75c multi | 2.40 | .60 |
| *a.* | Tete-beche pair | 4.80 | 1.25 |

Sheet margins, inscribed "Priority," served as etiquettes.

Royal Netherlands Academy of Arts and Sciences, 200th Anniv. A533

European Central Bank, 10th Anniv. A534

AEX Stock Index, 25th Anniv. A535

Bruna Bookshop Chain, 140th Anniv. A536

Royal Dutch Tourist Board, 125th Anniv. A537

**2008, May 20** ***Perf. 13¼x12¾***

| | | | |
|---|---|---|---|
| **1309** | Vert. strip of 5 | 7.00 | 3.50 |
| *a.* | A533 44c multi | 1.40 | .35 |
| *b.* | A534 44c multi | 1.40 | .35 |
| *c.* | A535 44c multi | 1.40 | .35 |
| *d.* | A536 44c multi | 1.40 | .35 |
| *e.* | A537 44c multi | 1.40 | .35 |

Souvenir Sheet

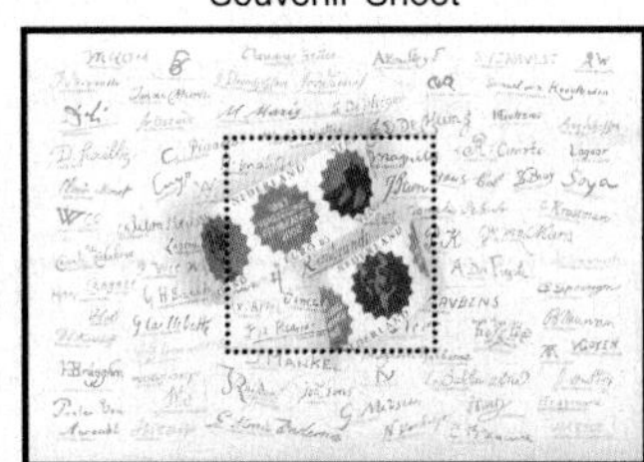

Rembrandt Association, 125th Anniv. — A538

**2008, June 12** ***Perf. 13¾***

| | | | |
|---|---|---|---|
| **1310** | A538 €6.65 multi | 21.00 | 10.50 |

Dutch Food Products A539

Designs: No. 1311, Container of adobo seasoning mix, Madame Jeannette peppers, Edam cheese. No. 1312, Peas, can of condensed milk, papaya, vert. No. 1313, Ham, plantain, bottle of Ponche Pistachio liqueur, vert.

**2008, July 8** ***Perf. 13¾***

| | | | |
|---|---|---|---|
| **1311** | A539 92c multi | 3.00 | .75 |
| **1312** | A539 92c multi | 3.00 | .75 |
| **1313** | A539 92c multi | 3.00 | .75 |
| *a.* | Souvenir sheet of 5, #1311-1313, Aruba #330, Netherlands Antilles #1187, + 3 etiquettes, 144x75mm | 9.00 | 4.50 |
| *b.* | Booklet pane, as "a," 150x102mm | 15.50 | — |
| | Complete booklet, 2 #1313b | 31.00 | |
| | *Nos. 1311-1313 (3)* | 9.00 | 2.25 |

No. 1313a sold for €2.76. Complete booklet sold for €9.95. Nos. 1312-1313 were available only in Nos. 1313a and 1313b. No. 1311 was available in Nos. 1313a, 1313b, Aruba No. 332a, and Netherlands Antilles No. 1189a.

Miniature Sheet

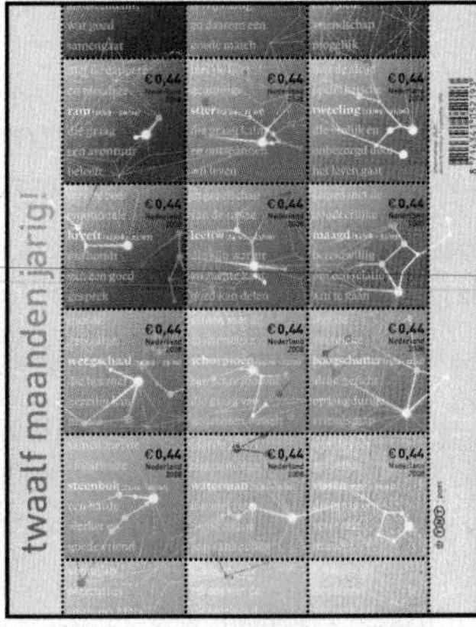


Zodiac Constellations — A540

No. 1314: a, Ram (Aries). b, Stier (Taurus). c, Tweeling (Gemini). d, Kreeft (Cancer). e, Leeuw (Leo). f, Maagd (Virgo). g, Weegschaal (Libra). h, Schorpioen (Scorpio). i, Boogschutter (Sagittarius). j, Steenbok (Capricorn). k, Waterman (Aquarius). l, Vissen (Pisces).

**2008, Sept. 1** **Litho.** ***Perf. 13¾***

| | | | |
|---|---|---|---|
| **1314** | A540 Sheet of 12 | 15.00 | 15.00 |
| *a.-l.* | 44c Any single | 1.25 | .30 |

Greeting Card Weeks A541

**2008, Sept. 1** ***Perf. 14½***

| | | | |
|---|---|---|---|
| **1315** | A541 44c multi | 1.25 | .30 |

Printed in sheets of 3.

Gnomes A542

Designs: No. 1316, Pinkeltje. No. 1317, Wipneus en Pim. No. 1318, Piggelmee. No. 1319, Paulus de boskabouter. No. 1320, De Kabouter.

**2008, Oct. 1** ***Perf. 13½x12¾***

| | | | |
|---|---|---|---|
| **1316** | A542 75c multi | 2.10 | .50 |
| **1317** | A542 75c multi | 2.10 | .50 |
| **1318** | A542 75c multi | 2.10 | .50 |
| **1319** | A542 75c multi | 2.10 | .50 |
| **1320** | A542 75c multi | 2.10 | .50 |
| *a.* | Vert. strip of 5, #1316-1320 | 10.50 | 2.50 |

Nos. 1316-1320 were printed in sheets of 10, containing two of each stamp. The other strip in the sheet is in a different stamp order and the two strips in the sheet are tete-beche.

Miniature Sheet

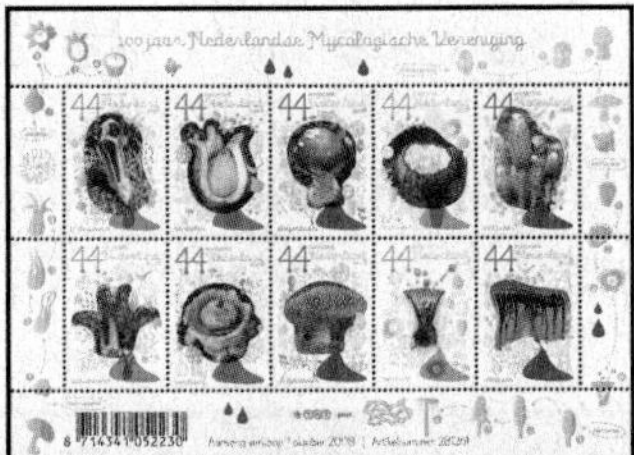

Mushrooms — A543

No. 1321 — Early and late stages of mushroom's life: a, Inktviszwam (early). b, Aardater (early). c, Vliegenzwam (early). d, Nestzwam (early). e, Inktzwam (early). f, Inktviszwam (late). g, Aardater (late). h, Vliegenzwam (late). i, Nestzwam (late). j, Inktzwam (late).

**2008, Oct. 1** ***Perf. 14½***

| | | | |
|---|---|---|---|
| **1321** | A543 Sheet of 10 | 12.50 | 12.50 |
| *a.-j.* | 44c Any single | 1.25 | .30 |

A booklet containing 5 panes, each showing a vertical pair from the sheet (same mushroom in different stages), sold for €9.95.

A544

December Stamps — A545

No. 1323: a, Building with large clock face and gift. b, Three dark envelopes, left half of Christmas tree. c, Right half of Christmas tree, top of ladder. d, Bell, Christmas tree. e, Building, gifts. f, Christmas tree, building with people on roof. g, Building, knife, fork and candle. h, House, bottom of ladder. i, Postcard, left side of fireplace. j, Right side of fireplace, fork and spoon.

***Serpentine Die Cut 12***

**2008, Nov. 18 Self-Adhesive**

**1322** A544 34c multi .90 .25
**1323** A545 Block of 10 9.00
*a.-j.* 34c Any single .90 .25

The vignette of No. 1322 could be personalized for a fee.

**Ecology Types of 2008**

Designs: 77c, Bicycle with globe hemispheres as wheels. 95c, Heart-shaped globe.

***Serpentine Die Cut 11***

**2009, Jan. 2 Photo.**

**Booklet Stamps**

**Self-Adhesive**

**1324** A523 77c multi + etiquette 2.25 .55
*a.* Booklet pane of 5 11.50
**1325** A523 95c multi + etiquette 2.75 .70
*a.* Booklet pane of 5 14.00

On Nos. 1324-1325 a row of microrouletting separates stamps from etiquettes.

Miniature Sheet

Braille Alphabet, 180th Anniv. — A546

No. 1326 — Letters (on front and back), and in Braille: a, Hulde roem mythe. b, Adres komst thuis. c, Uniek zelfs dank. d, Super zodra adieu. e, Hevig dwars naief. f, Moed extra kans. g, Begin marge exact. h, Afijn bekaf kus. i, Geluk wens bravo. j, Fabel credo liefs. k, Quasi niets ophef. l, Brief vurig hart.

**Litho., Photo & Embossed**

**2009, Jan. 10 *Perf. 13¾***

**1326** A546 Sheet of 12 14.00 14.00
*a.-l.* 44c Any single 1.10 .30
*m.* Booklet pane of 3, #1326a-1326c 6.50 —
*n.* Booklet pane of 3, #1326d-1326f 6.50 —
*o.* Booklet pane of 3, #1326g-1326i 6.50 —
*p.* Booklet pane of 3, #1326j-1326l 6.50 —
Complete booklet, #1326m-1326p 26.00

Louis Braille (1809-52), educator of the blind. Complete booklet sold for €9.95.

A547

Personalized Stamps — A548

***Serpentine Die Cut 12***

**2009, Mar. 10 Litho.**

**Self-Adhesive**

**1327** A547 44c multi 1.25 .30
**1328** A548 44c multi 1.25 .30

The generic vignettes of Nos. 1327 (Dutch Golf Federation) and 1328 (Dutch Stamp Collectors' Association), which sold at face value, are shown. These stamps, printed in sheets of 10, could be personalized for an additional fee. See Nos. 1300-1301 for perforated stamps having these frames.

Netherlands Tourism Areas — A549

**2009 Litho. *Perf. 14½x14¼***

**1329** A549 44c Assen 1.25 .30
**1330** A549 44c Tilburg 1.25 .30
**1331** A549 44c Oosterhout 1.25 .30
**1332** A549 44c Roosendaal 1.25 .30
**1333** A549 44c Delfzijl 1.25 .30
*a.* Souvenir sheet of 5, #1329-1333 6.25 3.25
*Nos. 1329-1333 (5)* 6.25 1.50

Issued: Nos. 1329-1330, 3/10; Nos. 1331-1332, 4/28; No. 1333, 6/16; No. 1333a, 6/12. A booklet containing five panes, with each pane containing two perf. 13½x12¾ examples of each stamp, sold for €9.95.

Europa — A550

Designs: No. 1334, Map of low frequency array radio telescopes superimposed on map of Europe. No. 1335, Sketch of Saturn and Titan, telescope lens of Christiaan Huygens.

**2009, Apr. 7 Litho. *Perf. 13¼x12¾***

**1334** 77c multi 2.10 .50
**1335** 77c multi 2.10 .50
*a.* A550 Horiz. pair, #1334-1335 4.20 1.00

Intl. Year of Astronomy. Sheet margins serve as etiquettes. No. 1335 is upside-down in relation to No. 1334.

Souvenir Sheet

Queens Wilhelmina, Juliana and Beatrix — A551

**Litho. & Engr.**

**2009, Apr. 28 *Perf. 13¾***

**1336** A551 €7 multi 19.00 9.50
*a.* Booklet pane of 1 27.00 —
Complete booklet, #1336a 27.00

Size of No. 1336a: 145x102mm. Complete booklet sold for €9.95.

Flasks, Artist's Mannequin, Party Streamer A552

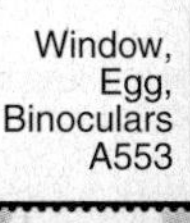

Window, Egg, Binoculars A553

Atlas Sheltering Figurines A554

Coffee Service A555

Blocks, Pictures of Children A556

**2009, May 12 Photo. *Perf. 14½***

**1337** Vert. strip of 5 6.25 3.25
*a.* A552 44c multi 1.25 .30
*b.* A553 44c multi 1.25 .30
*c.* A554 44c multi 1.25 .30
*d.* A555 44c multi 1.25 .30
*e.* A556 44c multi 1.25 .30

Dutch Cancer Society, 60th anniv. (No. 1337a); Netherlands Bird Protection Society, 110th anniv. (No. 1337b); Cordaid Mensen in Nood (Men in Need), 95th anniv. (No. 1337c); National Sunflower Society, 60th anniv. (No. 1337d); SOS Children's Village, 60th anniv. (No. 1337e).

Music — A557

No. 1338: a, Tuba, trumpet and saxophone players. b, "When you sing you begin with Do Re Mi." c, Baton twirlers. d, "Jauchzet, frohlockt." e, Sousaphone players. f, "Para bailar la bamba."

**2009, July 14 Litho. *Perf. 13½***

**1338** A557 Block of 6 13.50 6.75
*a.-f.* 77c Any single 2.25 .60

World Music Contest, Kerkrade and Europa Cantat, Utrecht. Printed in sheets of 10 containing Nos. 1338e, 1338f, and 2 each Nos. 1338a-1338d. Sheet margins served as etiquettes. Stamps showing text are upside-down in relation to stamps showing people.

Miniature Sheet

Dutch Connections With Brazil — A558

No. 1339: a, Tarairu Tribe War Dance, painting by Albert Eckhout, man standing on one hand. b, Capoeira performers, Tarairu tribesman. c, Passion fruit, and scientific book picturing passion fruit blossom. d, Cashews and scientific book picturing cashew tree. e, Sugar Plantation, painting by Frans Post; farmer looking at livestock. f, Church, Olinda, painting by Post; rose bush.

**2009, Aug. 4 *Perf. 13½x12¾***

**1339** A558 Sheet of 6 16.50 8.25
*a.-f.* 95c Any single 2.75 .70

No. 1339 was printed with three different illustrations in the bottom sheet margin, with each sheet having a different arrangement of stamps. Sheet margins at left and right served as etiquettes.

Athletes and Their Mentors A559

No. 1340: a, Anthony van Assche, gymnast, and mentor Jochem Uytdehaage. b, Leon Commandeur, cyclist, and mentor Johan Kenkhuis. c, Mike Marissen, swimmer, and mentor Bas van de Goor. d, Maureen Groefsema, judoist, and mentor Lobke Berkhout. e, Aniek van Koot, wheelchair tennis player, and mentor Marko Koers.

**2009, Aug. 25 Photo. *Perf. 14½***

**1340** Vert. strip of 5 6.25 3.25
*a.-e.* A559 44c Any single 1.25 .30

Stichting Sporttop, Olympic athlete development organization.

Greeting Card Week — A560

**2009, Sept. 7 Litho. *Perf. 14½***

**1341** A560 44c multi 1.40 .35

Miniature Sheets

Birthday Greetings — A561

"88" and: Nos. 1342a, 1343e, "Gefeliciteerd!" Nos. 1342b, 1343b, "Hoera!" Nos. 1342c, 1343c, "Proficiat!" Nos. 1342d, 1343d, "Nog Vele Jaren!" Nos. 1342e, 1343a, "Van Harte!"

**2009, Sept. 22 Litho. *Perf. 13½***

**1342** A561 Sheet of 5 7.00 3.50
*a.-e.* 44c Any single 1.40 .35

**Self-Adhesive**

***Serpentine Die Cut 13¼x13***

**Stamp Size: 20x25mm**

**1343** A561 Sheet of 5 7.00
*a.-e.* 44c Any single 1.40 .35

Lines in the "88" on each stamp could be colored in to create all ten digits. Unused values are for stamps without any such alterations. Used values are for stamps with or without alterations.

A562

Personalized Stamps A563

**2009-10** ***Perf. 13¼***
**1344** A562 44c multi 1.40 .35

**Self-Adhesive**

***Serpentine Die Cut 12½***

**1345** A563 44c multi 1.25 .30

Issued: No. 1344, 10/1; No. 1345, 1/12/10. The generic vignettes for Nos. 1344 (Stamp Day) and 1345 (Wadden Sea Society), which sold at face value, are shown. These stamps, printed in sheets of 10, could be personalized for an additional fee. A booklet containing five panes, each with two examples of No. 1344 with the Stamp Day vignette sold for €9.95.

Miniature Sheet

Powered Flight in the Netherlands, Cent. — A564

No. 1346: a, Medical helicopter. b, Boeing 747. c, Apache helicopter. d, Terminal B, Schiphol Airport. e, Fokker F-27. f, Lockheed Super Constellation. g, Fokker F-18 "Pelikaan." h, Douglas DC-2 "Uiver" in Melbourne race. i, Wright Flyer. j, Fokker Spin, piloted by Anthony Fokker.

**2009, Oct. 1** ***Perf. 13½***
**1346** A564 Sheet of 10 14.00 7.00
*a.-j.* 44c Any single 1.40 .35

A booklet containing five panes, each with a different horizontal pair from No. 1346, sold for €9.95.

December Stamps — A565

No. 1347: a, Green gift, pink ribbon, red background. b, Candelabra on yellow gift, blue background. c, Christmas tree on light blue gift, bright yellow green background. d, Light pink gift, red ribbon, gray background. e, Woman holding glass on yellow gift, pink background. f, Man holding glass on yellow gift, gray background. g, Christmas tree on blue gift, pink background. h, Red violet gift, red ribbon, carmine background. i, Christmas tree on yellow gift, blue background. j, Christmas tree on blue gift, red background.

***Serpentine Die Cut 12¾x13¼***

**2009, Nov. 19** **Self-Adhesive**
**1347** Block of 10 10.00
*a.-j.* A565 34c Any single 1.00 .25

Netherlands Tourism Areas — A566

**2010** **Litho.** ***Perf. 14½x14¼***
**1348** A566 44c Haarlem 1.25 .35
**1349** A566 44c Middelburg 1.25 .35
**1350** A566 44c Maastricht 1.25 .35
**1351** A566 44c Arnhem 1.25 .35
**1352** A566 44c Leeuwarden 1.10 .30
*a.* Souvenir sheet of 5, #1348-1352 6.25 3.25

Issued: Nos. 1348-1349, 1/12. Nos. 1350-1351, 3/29; Nos. 1352, 1352a, 6/22. A booklet containing five panes, with each pane containing two perf. 13½x12¾ examples of each stamp, sold for €9.95.

Miniature Sheet

Dutch Patent Act, Cent. — A567

No. 1353: a, Submarine invented by Cornelis Drebbel, 1620. b, Light-emitting diode lighting invented by Philips, 2007. c, Artificial kidney invented by Willem Kolff, 1943. d, VacuVin vacuum sealer for wine bottles invented by Bernd Schneider. e, Milking robot invented by Van der Lely, 1987. f, Bicycle chain case invented by Wilhelmine J. van der Woerd. g, Automated handwriting recognition invented by TNT Post, 1980. h, Solar-powered vehicle invented by Solar Team Twente. i, Dyneema fiber invented by DSM, 1979. j, Telescope invented by Hans Lipperhey, 1608.

**2010, Feb. 9** **Litho.** ***Perf. 13¼x12¾***
**1353** A567 Sheet of 10 12.50 6.25
*a.-j.* 44c Any single 1.25 .35

A booklet containing five panes, with each pane containing a horizontal pair from the sheet, sold for €9.95.

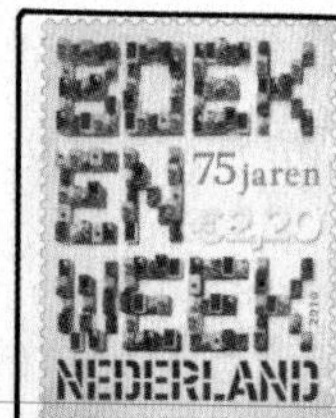

75th Book Week — A568

**2010, Mar. 9** **Litho.** ***Imperf.***
**1354** A568 €2.20 multi 6.00 3.00

No. 1354 is printed as a miniature book made up of two pieces of paper of different sizes. Both pieces of paper are printed on both sides, and are glued together. The cover of the book is the longer of the two pieces of paper, and is folded into three parts. The stamp, the front cover of the book, is the middle part of this piece of paper. The gum, applied to the left of the stamp, becomes the book's back cover when the longer piece of paper is folded. A photograph of a man holding a book, is to the right of the stamp, and is the book's first page. Text appears on the reverse of this picture and the stamp, and another picture depicting a man reading a book is printed on the back of the gum. The second piece of paper, folded in half to constitute four pages of the book, has text only, and is glued to the back of longer sheet where the fold between the stamp and the photo is found. Values are for the complete item.

VVV, Dutch Tourist Information Office, 125th Anniv. A569

Royal Tropical Institute, Cent. A570

Duinrell Amusement Park, Wassenaar, 75th Anniv. A571

Euromast Tower, Rotterdam, 50th Anniv. A572

Djoser Travel, 25th Anniv. A573

**2010, Mar. 23** **Photo.** ***Perf. 14½***
**1355** Vert. strip of 5 6.25 3.25
*a.* A569 44c multi 1.25 .35
*b.* A570 44c multi 1.25 .35
*c.* A571 44c multi 1.25 .35
*d.* A572 44c multi 1.25 .35
*e.* A573 44c multi 1.25 .35

Greeting Card Weeks A574

**2010, Mar. 29** **Litho.**
**1356** A574 44c multi 1.25 .35

Printed in sheets of 3.

Souvenir Sheet

Breskens Lighthouse — A575

**2010, Apr. 27** ***Perf. 13¾***
**1357** A575 €7 multi 19.00 9.50

Personalized Stamp — A576

**2010, July 1** **Litho.** ***Perf. 13½x14***
**1358** A576 1 gray & black 1.10 .30

The generic vignette of No. 1358, which sold for the franking value of 44c, and was printed in sheets of 10, is shown. The vignette part of the stamp could be personalized for an additional fee. Booklets containing stamps showing different vignettes that could not be personalized sold for €9.95.

Rectangles — A577

**2010, July 1** ***Die Cut Perf. 14¼***

**Self-Adhesive**

**1359** A577 1 multi 1.10 .30

Sold for 44c on day of issue. Compare with type A456.

Birth Announcement Stamp — A578

**2010, July 1** ***Die Cut Perf. 14¼***

**Self-Adhesive**

**1360** A578 1 multi 1.10 .30

Sold for 44c on day of issue.

Hearts — A579

**2010, July 1** ***Die Cut Perf. 14¼***

**Self-Adhesive**

**1361** A579 1 multi 1.10 .30
*a.* Booklet pane of 10 11.00

Sold for 44c on day of issue. Compare with type A466.

Death Announcement Stamp — A580

*Serpentine Die Cut 11¾*

**2010, July 1 Photo.**

**Self-Adhesive**

**1362** A580 1 multi 1.10 .30

Sold for 44c on day of issue. Compare with type A365.

Numerals

A581 A582

*Serpentine Die Cut 13½*

**2010, July 1 Litho.**

**Self-Adhesive**

**1363** A581 1 multi + label 1.10 .30

**Coil Stamps**

**Photo.**

*Die Cut Perf. 14¼*

**1364** A581 1 multi 1.10 .30
**1365** A582 2 multi 2.25 .60

On day of issue Nos. 1363-1364 each sold for 44c, and No. 1365 sold for 88c. Label on No. 1363 could be personalized. Compare with type A491.

Queen Beatrix With Large Numeral — A583

*Die Cut Perf. 14¼ Syncopated*

**2010, July 1 Photo.**

**Booklet Stamps**

**Self-Adhesive**

**1366** A583 1 metallic blue & lil 1.10 .30
*a.* Booklet pane of 10 11.00

*Die Cut Perf. 14¼*

**1367** A583 2 gold & metallic grn 2.25 .60
*a.* Booklet pane of 5 11.50

On day of issue, No. 1366 sold for 44c and No. 1367 sold for 88c. Compare with Type A273.

A584 A585

Ecology — A586

No. 1368: a, Hybrid vehicle with electric plug. b, House and sun (solar energy). c, Cow with electric plug (biofuels). d, Wind generators. e, Trees. f, Flowers, carpoolers in automobile. g, "Groen" with electric plug. h, Truck (soot filters). i, Birds and envelope (green mail). j, Insulated house.

*Die Cut Perf. 14¼*

**2010, July 1 Litho.**

**Booklet Stamps**

**Self-Adhesive**

**1368** Booklet pane of 10 11.00
*a.-j.* A584 1 Any single 1.10 .30

**Photo.**

*Serpentine Die Cut 11*

**1369** A585 1 Europa multi + etiquette 2.00 .50
*a.* Booklet pane of 5 + 5 etiquettes 10.00

**1370** A586 1 Wereld multi + etiquette 2.40 .60
*a.* Booklet pane of 5 + 5 etiquettes 12.00

On Nos. 1369-1370 a row of microrouletting separates stamps from etiquettes. On day of issue, Nos. 1368a-1368j each sold for 44c; No. 1369, for 77c; No. 1370, for 95c. Compare with type A523.

Miniature Sheet

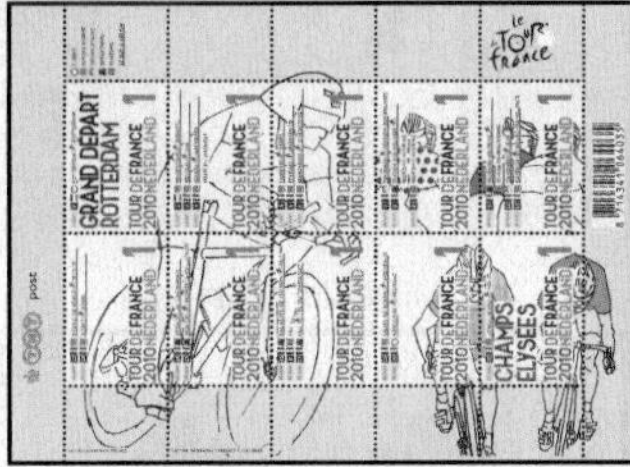

Start of 2010 Tour de France in Rotterdam — A587

No. 1371 — Dates and stages of the Tour de France: a, July 3 (preliminary stage). b, July 4-6 (stages 1-3). c, July 7-9 (stages 4-6). d, July 10-12 (stages 7-8). e, July 13-15 (stages 9-11). f, July 16-17 (stages 12-13). g, July 18-19 (stages 14-15). h, July 20-22 (stages 16-17). i, July 23-24 (stages 18-19). j, July 25 (stage 20).

**2010, July 1 Photo. *Perf. 14½***

**1371** A587 Sheet of 10 11.00 5.50
*a.-j.* 1 Any single 1.10 .30

On day of issue, Nos. 1371a-1371j each sold for 44c.

Miniature Sheet

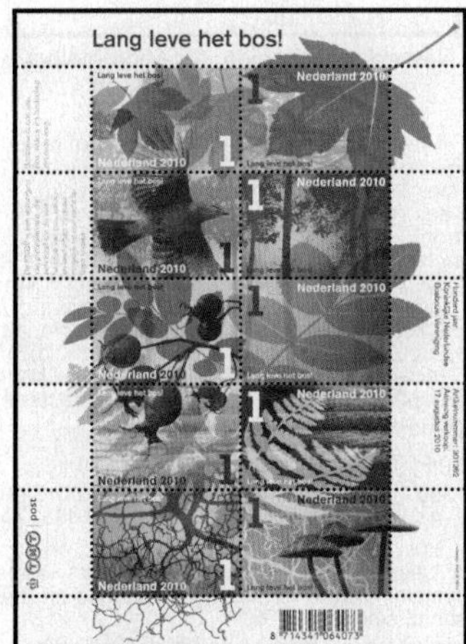


Royal Dutch Forestry Association, Cent. — A588

No. 1372: a, Maple leaves, forest canopy, tip of jay's wing, "1" in white at LR. b, Maple leaves, forest canopy, "1" in brown at UL. c, Jay, forest canopy, "1" in brown at LR. d, Forest canopy, rose leaves, "1" in white at UL. e, Rose hips and leaves, "1" in white at LR. f, Rose leaves, tree trunks, "1" in brown at UL. g, Rose hips, logs, bracken leaves, "1" in brown at LR. h, Bracken leaves, logs, "1" in white at UL. i, Tree roots, moss, "1" in white at LR. j, Tree roots, mushrooms, "1" in brown at UL.

*Perf. 13¼x12¾*

**2010, Aug. 17 Litho.**

**1372** A588 Sheet of 10 12.50 6.25
*a.-j.* 1 Any single 1.25 .35

On day of issue, Nos. 1372a-1372j each sold for 44c. A booklet containing five panes, each showing a horizontal pair from the sheet, sold for €9.95.

Miniature Sheet

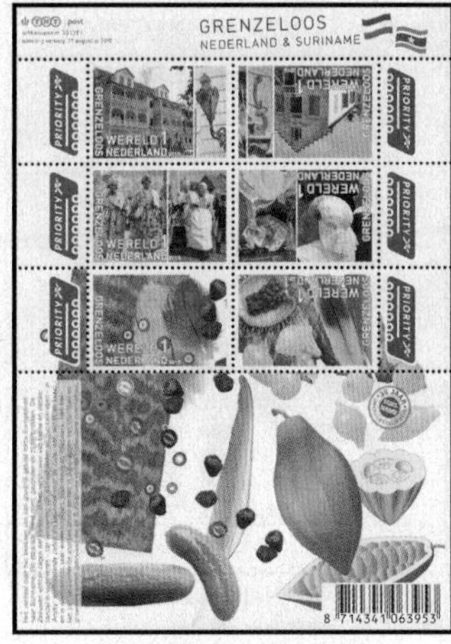


Dutch Connections With Surinam — A589

No. 1373: a, Building with balconies and dormers, lamp. b, Building with stairway, hand rail. c, Women in native dress. d, Two women, one upside-down. e, Wood, feathers, achiote seeds. f, Onions, achiote fruit, tobacco.

**2010, Aug. 17 Litho. *Perf. 13½x13***

**1373** A589 Sheet of 6 15.00 7.50
*a.-f.* 1 Wereld Any single 2.50 .65

No. 1373 was printed with three different illustrations in the bottom sheet margin, with each sheet having a different arrangement of stamps. Sheet margins at left and right served as etiquettes. On day of issue Nos. 1373a-1373f each sold for 95c.

Personalized Stamp — A590

**2010, Sept. 14 Litho. *Perf. 13½x14***

**1374** A590 1 multi 1.25 .35

The generic vignette shown on this stamp, commemorating Stamp Day, sold for 44c on day of issue. This stamp, printed in sheets of 10, could be personalized for an additional fee. A booklet containing five panes, each with two examples of No. 1374 with the generic vignette, sold for €9.95.

Woman and Windmill — A591

**Litho. With 3-Dimensional Plastic Affixed**

*Serpentine Die Cut 9x8¾*

**2010, Sept. 29 Self-Adhesive**

**1375** A591 5 multi 6.25 1.60

Sold for €2.20 on day of issue.

Stop AIDS Campaign — A592

No. 1376: a, African woman with "Stop AIDS Now!" poster on head. b, African woman, ribbon. c, Hand holding pill, ribbon. d, African woman pointing to ribbon. e, Ribbon, heads of African man and woman. f, African woman wearing headdress.

**2010, Oct. 12 Litho. *Perf. 14½***

**1376** A592 Block of 6 7.50 3.75
*a.-f.* 1 Any single 1.25 .35

Nos. 1376a-1376f each sold for 44c on day of issue.

Personalized Stamp — A593

**2010, Nov. 23 Litho. *Perf. 13½x14***

**1377** A593 (34c) multi .95 .25

The generic vignette shown on this stamp depicts Snoopy. This stamp, printed in sheets of 10, could be personalized for an additional fee.

December Stamps — A594

No. 1378: a, Santa Claus carrying tree. b, Bell and ribbon. c, Rocking horse and flowers. d, Embroidered heart. e, Deer, flower and candle on Christmas card. f, Deer and ribbon. g, Santa Claus. h, Handshake and flowers on Christmas card. i, Angel with flowers. j, Gingerbread house.

*Serpentine Die Cut 12¾*

**2010, Nov. 23 Self-Adhesive**

**1378** Block of 10 9.50
*a.-j.* A594 (34c) Any single .95 .25
*k.* Booklet pane of 10, #1378a-1378j 13.50
Complete booklet, 2 #1378k 27.00

Complete booklet sold for €9.95.

Personalized Stamp — A595

*Die Cut Perf. 13x13¼*

**2011, Jan. 10 Litho.**

**Self-Adhesive**

**1379** A595 1 black 1.25 .35

The generic vignette of No. 1379 depicting St. John's Cathedral, 's Hertogenbosch, which sold for the franking value of 46c and printed in sheets of 10, is shown. The vignette part of the stamp could be personalized for an additional fee.

Netherlands Tourism Areas — A596

**2011** *Perf. 14½x14¼*

| | | | | |
|---|---|---|---|---|
| **1380** | A596 1 Almere | | 1.25 | .35 |
| **1381** | A596 1 Eindhoven | | 1.25 | .35 |
| **1382** | A596 1 Apeldoorn | | 1.40 | .45 |
| **1383** | A596 1 Breda | | 1.40 | .45 |
| **1384** | A596 1 Enschede | | 1.40 | .45 |
| *a.* | Souvenir sheet of 5, #1380-1384 | | 6.75 | 3.50 |
| | *Nos. 1380-1384 (5)* | | 6.70 | 2.05 |

Issued: Nos. 1380-1381, 1/10; Nos. 1382-1383, 4/11; Nos. 1384, 1384a, 5/23. On day of issue, Nos, 1380-1384 each sold for 46c. A booklet containing five panes, with each pane containing two perf. 13½x12¾ examples of each stamp, sold for €9.95.

Personalized Stamp A597

**2011, Jan. 31** *Perf. 13¾*

**1385** A597 1 multi 1.25 .35

The generic vignette of No. 1385 depicting a great tit, which sold for the franking value of 46c and printed in sheets of 10, is shown. The vignette part of the stamp could be personalized for an additional fee. Numerous stamps depicting different birds in the vignette were created after Jan. 31 by postal authorities. An electronic audio pen which sold for €39.95 would play the song of the bird when placed near the stamp. Numerous stamps depicting recording artists in the vignette began appearing in 2012.

Miniature Sheet

Utrecht University, 375th Anniv. — A598

No. 1386 — Various anniversaries at Utrecht University: a, 90th anniv. of psychology studies (brain). b, 100th anniv. of Unitas Student Society (owl). c, 65th birthday of Gerard t'Hooft. 1999 Nobel Physics laureate (t'Hooft). d, 125th anniv. of Utrecht University Foundation (globe). e, 50th anniv. of Utrecht Science Park de Uithof (aerial view of park). f, 190th anniv. of veterinary medicine program (horse). g, 45th anniv. of Institute of Theater Studies (theater spotlight). h, 250th anniv. of death of Petrus van Musschenbroek, professor of mathematics and philosophy (van Musschenbroek). i, 25th anniv. of Mebiose Student Association for the Biological Sciences (stylized DNA molecule). j, 325th anniv. of Senaatzaal Portrait Gallery (Senaatzaal).

**2011, Mar. 28** *Perf. 13¼x12¾*

| | | | |
|---|---|---|---|
| **1386** | A598 Sheet of 10 | 14.00 | 7.00 |
| *a.-j.* | 1 Any single | 1.40 | .45 |

Nos. 1386a-1386j each sold for 46c on day of issue. A booklet containing 5 panes, each containing a horizontal pair of stamps on the sheet, sold for €9.95.

Miniature Sheet

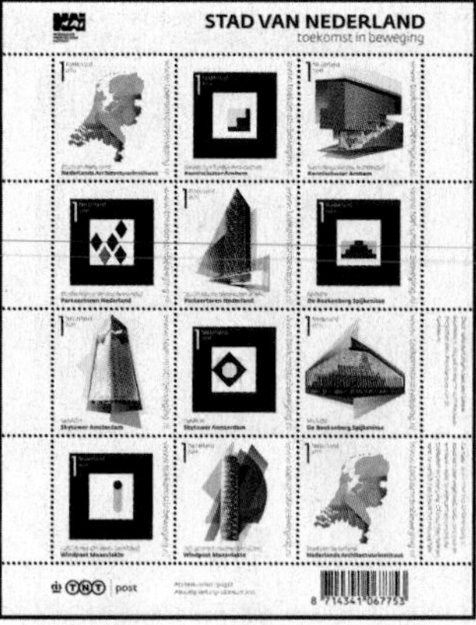

City of the Netherlands — A599

No. 1387 — Inscriptions in bold type: a, Kenniscluster, Arnhem (black-framed code box). b, Kenniscluster, Arnhem (building). c, Parkeertoren Nederland (black-framed code box). d, Parkeertoren Nederland (building). e, De Boekenberg, Spijkenisse (black-framed code box). f, Skytower, Amsterdam (building). g, Skytower, Amsterdam (black-framed code box). h, De Boekenberg, Spijkenisse (building). i, Windpost, Maasvlakte (black-framed code box). j, Windpost, Maasvlakte (building). k, Map of the Netherlands.

**2011, Mar. 28** *Perf. 13¼*

**1387** A599 Sheet of 12, #1387a-1387j, 2 #1387k 17.00 8.50

On day of issue, Nos. 1387a-1387k each sold for 46c. The code boxes activate an augmented reality application when scanned by a webcam when visting the www.toekomstinbeweging.nl website.

Greeting Card Week A600

**2011, Apr. 18** *Perf. 14½*

**1388** A600 1 multi 1.40 .45

No. 1388 sold for 46c on day of issue. Printed in sheets of 3.

Organization for Economic Cooperation and Development, 50th Anniv. — A601

Royal Dutch Billiards Federation, Cent. A602

Royal Dutch Checkers Federation, Cent. A603

Loevenstein Castle, 650th Anniv. A604

Association of Dutch Composers, Cent. A605

**2011, May 2** *Perf. 13¼x12¾*

| | | | |
|---|---|---|---|
| **1389** | Vert. strip of 5 | 7.00 | 3.50 |
| *a.* | A601 1 multi | 1.40 | .45 |
| *b.* | A602 1 multi | 1.40 | .45 |
| *c.* | A603 1 multi | 1.40 | .45 |
| *d.* | A604 1 multi | 1.40 | .45 |
| *e.* | A605 1 multi | 1.40 | .45 |

Nos. 1389a-1389e each sold for 46c on day of issue.

Miniature Sheet

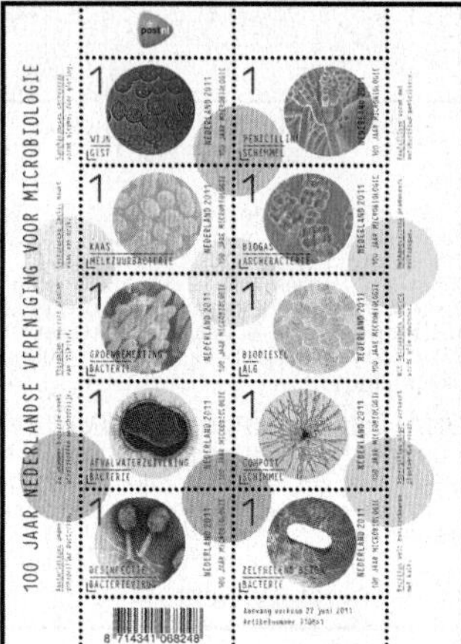

Netherlands Society for Microbiology, Cent. — A606

No. 1390 — Various microorganisms and inscription: a, Wijn / Gist (wine / yeast). b, Penicilline / Schimmel (penicillin / mold). c, Kaas / Melkzuurbacterie (cheese / lactic bacteria). d, Biogas / Archebacterie (biogas / archaea). e, Groenbemesting / Bacterie (green manure / bacteria). f, Biodiesel / Alg. (biodiesel / algae). g, Afvalwaterzuivering / Bacterie (waste water purification / bacteria). h, Compost / Schimmel (compost / mold). i, Desinfectie / Bacterievirus (disinfectant / bacteriophage). j, Zelfhelend beton / bacterie (self-curing concrete / bacteria).

**2011, May 27**

| | | | |
|---|---|---|---|
| **1390** | A606 Sheet of 10 | 14.00 | 7.00 |
| *a.-j.* | 1 Any single | 1.40 | .45 |

Nos. 1390a-1390j each sold for 46c on day of issue. A booklet containing 5 panes, each containing a horizontal pair of stamps on the sheet, sold for €9.95.

Initial Public Offering of Royal Post NL Stock A607

**2011, May 31** **Litho.**

**1391** A607 1 multi 1.40 .45

No. 1391 sold for 46c on day of issue.

Miniature Sheet

Dutch Connections With South Africa — A608

No. 1392: a, Dutch-style South African houses in elephant (olifant). b, Poem by Ingrid Jonker in leopard (luipaard). c, Grapes in buffalo (buffel). d, South African house in rhinoceros (neushoorn). e, Painting of Jan van Riebeeck arriving at Cape of Good Hope in lion (leeuw). f, Dutch East India Company pottery in penguin (pinguin).

**2011, July 25** *Perf. 13¼x12¾*

| | | | |
|---|---|---|---|
| **1392** | A608 Sheet of 6 | 16.50 | 8.25 |
| *a.-f.* | 1 Wereld Any single | 2.75 | .85 |

No. 1392 was printed with three different illustrations in the bottom sheet margin, with each sheet having a different arrangement of stamps. Sheet margins at left and right served as etiquettes. On day of issue Nos. 1392a-1392f each sold for 95c.

De Bond Heemschut Historical Preservation Society, Cent. — A609

No. 1393: a, American Embassy, The Hague. b, Amerongen Castle. c, Tricot factory, Winterswijk. d, Noord-Zuid-Hollands Coffee House, Amsterdam. e, St. Servatius Bridge, Maastricht. f, Synagogue, Groningen.

**2011, Aug. 22** *Perf. 13¼x12¾*

| | | | |
|---|---|---|---|
| **1393** | A609 Block of 6 | 7.50 | 3.75 |
| *a.-f.* | 1 Any single | 1.25 | .35 |

Nos. 1393a-1393f each sold for 46c on day of issue.

A610

A611

Ecology — A612

No. 1394: a, Shirt on clothesline. b, Stylized plant. c, Bird. d, Hen. e, Kites. f, House. g, Laptop computer. h, Suitcase and leaf, horiz. i,

Butterfly, horiz. j, Electric vehicle and plug, horiz.

***Die Cut Perf. 14¼***

**2011, Sept. 1** **Litho.**

**Booklet Stamps**
**Self-Adhesive**

**1394** Booklet pane of 10 12.50
*a.-j.* A610 1 Any single 1.25 .35

**Photo.**

***Serpentine Die Cut 11***

**1395** A611 1 Europa multi + etiquette 2.25 .60
*a.* Booklet pane of 5 11.50
**1396** A612 1 Wereld multi + etiquette 2.60 .80
*a.* Booklet pane of 5 13.00

On Nos. 1395-1396 a row of microrouletting separates stamps from etiquettes. On day of issue, Nos. 1394a-1394j each sold for 46c,; No. 139, for 79c; No. 1396, for 95c.

Miniature Sheet

Herman Renz Circus, Cent. — A613

No. 1397: a, Fire eater. b, Snake handler. c, Clown. d, Trained horse. e, Man balancing hat on nose. f, Tumbling act. g, Lion. h, Acrobat lifting another acrobat. i, Elephant. j, Unicyclist on tightrope.

***Perf. 12¾x13¼***

**2011, Sept. 19** **Litho.**

**1397** A613 Sheet of 10 12.50 6.25
*a.-j.* A613 1 Any single 1.25 .30

On day of issue, Nos. 1397a-1397j each sold for 46c.

Queen Wilhelmina (1880-1962) A614

**2011, Oct. 14** ***Perf. 13¼x13½***

**1398** A614 1 multi 1.25 .30

Stamp Day. No. 1398 sold for 46c on day of issue. A booklet containing five panes, each containing two No. 1398, sold for €9.95.

Postcrossing.com — A615

No. 1399 — Postcards depicting: a, Sunset, man and woman kissing under umbrella, donkey and house, puppies, nesting dolls, Eiffel Tower, Asian woman, beach in Rio. b, Baby surrounded by sunflower petals, sheep, beach, bull fight, Sphinx and Pyramid, Cuban car, building in Finland. c, Bridge, fish and coral, building in Antwerp, Belgium, Taj Mahal, Asian woman, soccer players, tower and Arabic text. d, Flamingo in Miami, beach in Rio, Petronas Towers, Kuala Lumpur, Acropolis, buildings in Warsaw, Big Ben and statue, London, woman, and China Central Television Building, Beijing. e, Boat and building in Finland, Prague and Hradcany Castle, tulips, chimpanzee wearing cowboy hat, Hong Kong skyline, Asian woman, bird, comic strip. f, Cat, windmill and tulips, Netherlands, Cliffs of Moher, Ireland, Calgary skyline, churches, St. Petersburg, Russia, Great Wall of China, woman praying, two boys.

**2011, Oct. 14** ***Perf. 13¼x12¾***

**1399** A615 Block of 6 + 6 etiquettes 15.00 7.50
*a.-c.* 1 Europa Any single 2.25 .60
*d.-f.* 1 Wereld Any single 2.60 .80

On day of issue Nos. 1399a-1399c each sold for 79c, and Nos. 1399d-1399f each sold for 95c.

December Stamps — A616

No. 1400: a, Candle. b, Reindeer, bird and fir trees. c, Bird on heart. d, Three Christmas ornaments. e, Church and houses. f, Reindeer with Christmas ornament, birds and candles on antlers. g, Angel with candles. h, Bird, holding Christmas ornament on fir branch. i, Snowman. j, Squirrel and Christmas ornament.

***Serpentine Die Cut 12½***

**2011, Nov. 22** **Litho.**

**Self-Adhesive**

**1400** Block of 10 10.00
*a.-j.* A616 (36c) Any single 1.00 .30

Personalized Stamp — A617

**2011, Nov. 22** ***Die Cut Perf. 13x13¼***

**Self-Adhesive**

**1401** A617 (36c) multi 1.00 .30

The generic vignette shown on this stamp depicts two birds under mistletoe. This stamp could be personalized for an additional fee.

A618

Personalized Stamps — A619

**2012, Jan. 2** **Litho.** ***Perf. 13½x14***

**1402** A618 1 Europa black 2.25 .55
**1403** A619 1 Wereld black 2.50 .65

The generic vignettes of Nos. 1402 and 1403, which are shown, sold for the franking value of 85c and 95c, respectively. Nos. 1402 and 1403 each were printed in sheets of 10. The vignette parts of the stamp could be personalized for an additional fee.

Country Houses — A620

Country houses in: No. 1404, Mattemburgh. No. 1405, Amstenrade. No. 1406, Trompenburgh. No. 1407, Vollenhoven. No. 1408, Middachten.

**2012** ***Perf. 14½x14¼***

**1404** A620 1 multi 1.40 .35
*a.* Perf. 13½x12¾ 2.50 2.50
*b.* Booklet pane of 2 #1404a 5.00 5.00
**1405** A620 1 multi 1.40 .35
*a.* Perf. 13½x12¾ 2.50 2.50
*b.* Booklet pane of 2 #1405a 5.00 5.00
**1406** A620 1 multi 1.40 .35
*a.* Perf. 13½x12¾ 2.50 2.50
*b.* Booklet pane of 2 #1406a 5.00 5.00
**1407** A620 1 multi 1.40 .35
*a.* Perf. 13½x12¾ 2.50 2.50
*b.* Booklet pane of 2 #1407a 5.00 5.00
**1408** A620 1 multi 1.25 .35
*a.* Perf. 13½x12¾ 2.50 2.50
*b.* Booklet pane of 2 #1408a 5.00 5.00
Complete booklet, #1404b, 1405b, 1406b, 1407b, 1408b 25.00
*c.* Souvenir sheet of 5, #1404-1408 7.00 3.50
*Nos. 1404-1408 (5)* 6.85 1.75

Issued: Nos. 1404-1405, 1/30; Nos. 1406-1407, 2/27; Nos. 1404a, 1404b, 1405a, 1405b, 1406a, 1406b, 1407a, 1407b, 1408, 1408a, 1408b, 1408c, 5/21. Nos. 1404-1408 each sold for 50c on day of issue. Complete booklet sold for €9.95 on day of issue.

Dutch Salvation Army, 125th Anniv. A621

**2012, Feb. 27** ***Perf. 13¼x13½***

**1409** A621 1 multi 1.40 .35

No. 1409 sold for 50c on day of issue.

Albert Heijn Grocery Stores, 125th Anniv. — A622

Designs: No. 1410, Original store, employee with first delivery bicycle. No. 1411, Coffee beans, coffee plant workers. No. 1412, Hamster, shoppers in grocery store. No. 1413, Shopper with child in shopping cart, store employees.

***Serpentine Die Cut 13¼x13***

**2012, Feb. 27** **Self-Adhesive**

**1410** A622 1 multi 1.40 .35
**1411** A622 1 multi 1.40 .35
**1412** A622 1 multi 1.40 .35
**1413** A622 1 multi 1.40 .35
*Nos. 1410-1413 (4)* 5.60 1.40

Nos. 1410-1413 each sold for 50c on day of issue.

Greeting Card Week — A623

**2012, Mar. 26** ***Perf. 13¼x13½***

**1414** A623 1 multi 1.40 .35

No. 1414 sold for 50c on day of issue. Printed in sheets of 3.

A624

Tourism — A625

No. 1415: a, National Maritime Museum, Dutch East Indiaman "The Amsterdam," country name in white. b, Muziekgebouw Concert Hall, cruise ship "MSC Lirica," country name in gold.

No. 1416: a, The Bend in the Herengracht Canal, painting by Gerrit Berckheyde, country name in white. b, Skinny Bridge over Amstel River, country name in gold.

**2012, Mar. 26** **Litho.**

**1415** A624 Horiz. pair 2.80 1.40
*a.-b.* 1 Either single 1.40 .35
**1416** A625 Pair 4.50 2.25
*a.-b.* 1 Europa Either single 2.25 .60

Europa (#1416b). On day of issue, Nos. 1415a-1415b each sold for 50c and Nos. 1416a-1416b each sold for 85c.

Netherlands Open Air Museum, Cent. — A626

Historical photographs: Nos. 1417a, 1417k, Women cleaning (green, at left), Marketplace (black, at right). Nos. 1417b, 1417l, Marketplace (black, at left). Woman sewing (purple, at right). Nos. 1417c, 1417m, Children with smartphone (rose, at left), Children crossing street (blue, at right). Nos. 1417d, 1417n, Children crossing street (blue, at left), Children playing (black, at right). Nos. 1417e, 1417o, Cots and worker at migrant worker's lodging (blue, at left), Sod hut (purple at right). Nos. 1417f, 1417p, Sod hut (purple, at left), Children watching television (rose, at right). Nos. 1417g, 1417q, Campers and van (purple, at left), Children with tablet and camp light (green, at right). Nos. 1417h, 1417r, Children with tablet and camp light (green, at left), Hockey players at Netherlands Open Air Museum (blue, at right). Nos. 1417i, 1417s, People boarding airplane at Schiphol Airport (black, at left), Car at gas station (rose, at right). Nos. 1417j, 1417t, Car at gas station (rose, at left), Hay cart (green, at right).

**2012, Apr. 23** ***Perf. 13¼x12¾***

**1417** A626 Sheet of 10 14.00 7.00
*a.-j.* 1 Any single 1.40 .35
*k.-t.* Any single, perf. 14½ 2.60 2.60
*u.* Booklet pane of 2, #1417k-1417l 5.25 —
*v.* Booklet pane of 2, #1417m-1417n 5.25 —
*w.* Booklet pane of 2, #1417o-1417p 5.25 —
*x.* Booklet pane of 2, #1417q-1417r 5.25 —
*y.* Booklet pane of 2, #1417s-1417t 5.25 —
Complete booklet, #1417u, 1417v, 1417w, 1417x, 1417y 26.50

Nos. 1417a-1417t each sold for 50c on day of issue.

Miniature Sheet

Madurodam Miniature Park, 60th Anniv. — A627

No. 1418 — Miniatures of: a, Dutch East India ship. b, Windmills and building. c, Cheese market (crowd in plaza in front of building). d, Port of Rotterdam and tanker ships. e, Field of flowers. f, Rijksmuseum. g, Schiphol Airport. h, Delta Works (people near white conneted pipes). i, Maasvlakte 2 port project (dredger). j, Binnenhof, horses and carriages.

**2012, May 21** ***Perf. 13¼x13½***

| | | | |
|---|---|---|---|
| **1418** A627 Sheet of 10 | 12.50 | 6.25 |
| *a.-j.* 1 Any single | 1.25 | .35 |

Nos. 1418a-1418j each sold for 50c on day of issue.

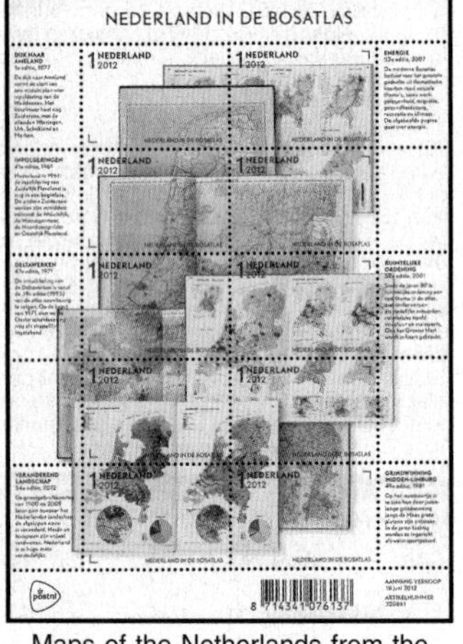

Maps of the Netherlands from the Bosatlas — A628

Designs: Nos. 1419a, 1419k, Upper left section of map from 1877 atlas, upper part of page 62 from 2007 atlas. Nos. 1419b, 1419l, Upper right section of map from 1877 atlas, upper sections of pages 62 and 63 from 2007 atlas. Nos. 1419c, 1419m, Section of map from 1877 atlas, upper left section of page 60 from 1961 atlas. Nos. 1419d, 1419n, Section of map from 1877 atlas, lower section of page 63 from 2007 atlas, upper right section of page 61 from 1961 atlas. Nos. 1419e, 1419o, Section of map from page 60 of 1961 atlas, sections of pages depicting South Netherlands (Zuid-Nederland) from 1971 atlas, upper left section of page 60 from 2001 atlas. Nos. 1419f, 1419p, Section of page 61 from 1961 atlas, upper right section of pages 60 and upper left section of 61 from 2001 atlas. Nos. 1419g, 1419q, Lower section of South Netherlands map from 1971 atlas, lower section of page 60 from 2001 atlas, upper sections of pages 39 from 2012 atlas. Nos. 1419h, 1419r, Lower sections of pages 60 and 61 from 2001 atlas, upper right section of page 39 from 2012 atlas, section of page from 1981 atlas. Nos. 1419i, 1419s, Lower sections of pages 38 and 39 from 2012 atlas. Nos. 1419j, 1419t, Lower right section of page 39 from 2012 atlas, lower right section of page from 1981 atlas.

**2012, June 18** ***Perf. 13¼x12¾***

| | | |
|---|---|---|
| **1419** A628 Sheet of 10 | 12.50 | 6.25 |
| *a.-j.* 1 Any single | 1.25 | .35 |
| *k.-t.* Any single, perf. 14½ | 2.50 | 2.50 |
| *u.* Booklet pane of 2, #1419k-1419l | 5.00 | — |
| *v.* Booklet pane of 2, #1419m-1419n | 5.00 | — |
| *w.* Booklet pane of 2, #1419o-1419p | 5.00 | — |
| *x.* Booklet pane of 2, #1419q-1419r | 5.00 | — |
| *y.* Booklet pane of 2, #1419s-1419t | 5.00 | — |
| Complete booklet, #1419u, 1419v, 1419w, 1419x, 1419y | 25.00 | |

Nos. 1419a-1419j each sold for 50c on day of issue. Complete booklet sold for €9.95.

Miniature Sheet

Netherlands Olympic Committee and Netherlands Sports Federation, Cent. — A629

No. 1420 — Athletes: a, Sjoukje Dijkstra, figure skater. b, Anton Geesink, judoka. c, Nico Rienks, rower. d, Ellen van Langen, runner. e, Field hockey player. f, Leontien Zijlaard-van Moorsel, cyclist. g, Esther Vergeer, Paralympian tennis player. h, Maarten van der Weijden, swimmer. i, Anky van Grunsven, dressage. j, Nicolien Sauerbreij, snowboarder.

**2012, July 4** ***Perf. 13¼x13½***

| | | |
|---|---|---|
| **1420** A629 Sheet of 10 | 12.50 | 6.25 |
| *a.-j.* 1 Any single | 1.25 | .35 |

Nos. 1420a-1420j each sold for 50c on day of issue.

Miniature Sheet

Seasons Magazine, 20th Anniv. — A630

No. 1422 — Photography from magazine with inscription at LR: a, Esdoorn (maple leaves). b, IJsbloem (frost flower). c, Peul (snow peas). d, Dahlia. e, Kievitsbloem (fritillaries). f, Lijsterbes (rowanberries). g, Rode zonnehoed (Purple coneflower). h, Rimpelroos, Rozenbottel, Rozengeranium (Rugosa rose, rose hips, rose geranium). i, Tulp (tulips). j, Blauwe bes (blueberries).

**2012, July 16** ***Perf. 13½x13¼***

| | | |
|---|---|---|
| **1421** A630 Sheet of 10 | 12.50 | 6.25 |
| *a.-j.* 1 Any single | 1.25 | .35 |

Nos. 1421a-1421j each sold for 50c on day of issue.

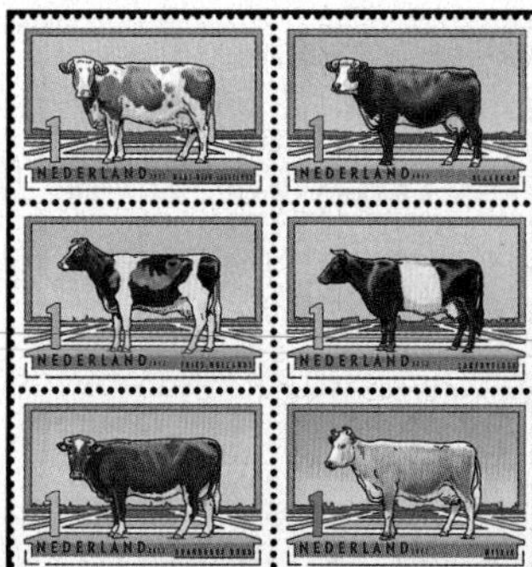

Cattle Breeds — A631

Designs: Nos. 1422a, 1422g, Maas-Rijn-Ijsselvee (Meuse-Rhine-Issel). Nos. 1422b, 1422h, Blaarkop. Nos. 1422c, 1422i, Fries-Hollands (Dutch Friesian). Nos. 1422d, 1422j, Lakenvelder (Dutch Belted). Nos. 1422e, 1422k, Brandrode Rund. Nos. 1422f, 1422l, Witrik.

**2012, Aug. 13** ***Perf. 13¼x12¾***

| | | |
|---|---|---|
| **1422** A631 Block of 6 | 8.50 | 4.25 |
| *a.-f.* 1 Any single | 1.40 | .35 |
| *g.-l.* 1 Any single, perf. 14½ | 2.60 | 2.60 |
| *m.* Booklet pane of 2 #1422g | 5.25 | — |
| *n.* Booklet pane of 2 #1422h | 5.25 | — |
| *o.* Booklet pane of 2 #1422i | 5.25 | — |
| *p.* Booklet pane of 2 #1422j | 5.25 | — |
| *q.* Booklet pane of 2, #1422k, 1422l | 5.25 | — |
| Complete booklet, #1422m, 1422n, 1422o, 1422p, 1422q | 26.50 | |

Nos. 1422a-1422f each sold for 50c on day of issue. Complete booklet sold for €9.95 on day of issue.

Miniature Sheet

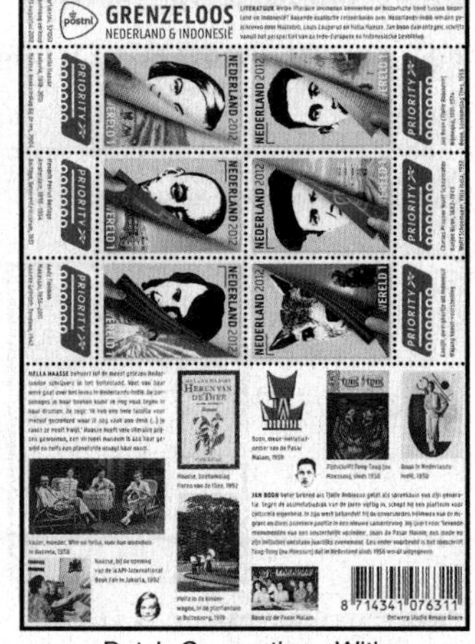

Dutch Connections With Indonesia — A632

No. 1423: a, Hella Haasse (1918-2011), writer, cattle and tea planters. b, Tjalie Robinson (1911-74), writer, dog on chain. c, Hendrik Petrus Berlage (1856-1934), architect, Gemeentemuseum, The Hague. d, Charles Prosper Wolff Schoemaker (1882-1949), architect, (wearing hat), Villa Isola, Bandung, Indonesia. e, Andy Tielman (1936-2011), musician, Anneke Grönloh, singer. f, Chevrotain, Indonesian shadow puppet.

**2012, Aug. 13** ***Perf. 13½x13¼***

| | | |
|---|---|---|
| **1423** A632 Sheet of 6 | 15.00 | 7.50 |
| *a.-f.* 1 Wereld Any single | 2.50 | .65 |

No. 1423 was printed with three different illustrations in the bottom sheet margin, with each sheet having a different arrangement of stamps. Sheet margins at left and right served as etiquettes. On day of issue, Nos. 1423a-1423f each sold for 95c.

Royal Carré Theater, Amsterdam, 125th Anniv. — A633

No. 1424: a, Theater. b, Toon Hermans, microphone, balloons. c, Oscar Carré's circus horses. d, Two male ballet dancers. e, Guitarist and lights. f, Two dancers from *Cats*. g, Tightrope artist with unicycle. h, Ballerina. i, Circus elephants. j, Chandeliers and "125.".

**2012, Sept. 10** ***Perf. 12¾x13¼***

| | | |
|---|---|---|
| **1424** A633 Sheet of 10 | 14.00 | 7.00 |
| *a.-j.* 1 Any single | 1.40 | .35 |
| *k.* Booklet pane of 2, #1424a, 1424c | 5.25 | — |
| *l.* Booklet pane of 2, #1424b, 1424j | 5.25 | — |
| *m.* Booklet pane of 2, #1424e, 1424f | 5.25 | — |
| *n.* Booklet pane of 2, #1424d, 1424h | 5.25 | — |
| *o.* Booklet pane of 2, #1424g, 1424i | 5.25 | — |
| Complete booklet, #1424k, 1424l, 1424m, 1424n, 1424o | 26.50 | |

On day of issue, Nos. 1424a-1424j each sold for 50c and complete booklet sold for €9.95.

Miniature Sheet

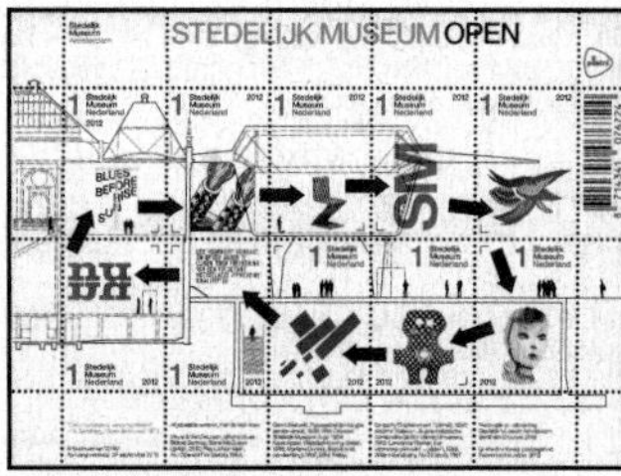

Reopening of Stedelijk Museum, Amsterdam — A634

No. 1425 — Arrows and: a, Blues Before Sunrise poster, by Mevis & Van Deursen. b, As I Opened Fire, by Roy Lichtenstein (cannons). c, Zig-zag chair prototype, by Gerrit Rietveld. d, Musuem logo (SM), by Wim Crouwel. e, Mural, by Karel Appel. f, Now 2, by Willem Sandberg (nu). g, An Object Made. . ., by Lawrence Weiner (text, man on staircase). h, Suprematist Composition (Eight Red Rectangles), by Kazimir Malevich. i, Empathy Displacement 7, by Mike Kelley (polka-dotted object). j, Barbie (With Pearl Necklace), by Marlene Dumas (doll's head).

**2012, Sept. 24** ***Perf. 13½x13¼***

| | | |
|---|---|---|
| **1425** A634 Sheet of 10 | 14.00 | 7.00 |
| *a.-j.* 1 Any single | 1.40 | .35 |

Nos. 1425a-1425j each sold for 50c on day of issue.

Souvenir Sheet

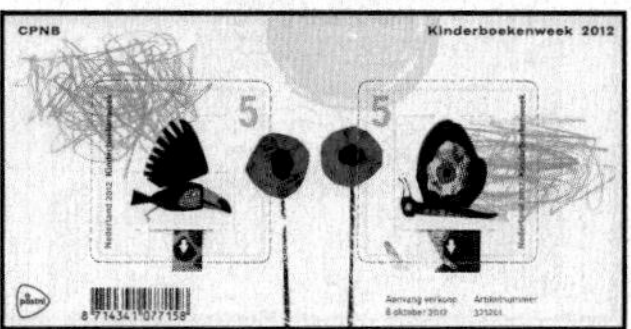

Children's Book Week — A635

No. 1426: a, Bird. b, Butterfly.

**2012, Oct. 8** ***Rouletted***

**On Cardboard**

| | | |
|---|---|---|
| **1426** A635 Sheet of 2 | 13.00 | 6.50 |
| *a.-b.* 5 Either single | 6.50 | 3.25 |

Nos. 1426a-1426b each sold for €2.50. Parts of the stamps pop up when the cardboard slide on each stamp is pulled out.

Queen Juliana — A636

**2012, Oct. 19** ***Perf. 13¼x14***

**1427** A636 1 multi 1.25 .35
*a.* Booklet pane of 2 5.00 —
Complete booket, 5 #1427a 25.00

Stamp Day. No. 1427 sold for 50c on day of issue. Complete booklet sold for €9.95 and contains five examples of No. 1427a, each with a different pane margin.

December Stamps — A637

No. 1428 — Christmas knitting patterns featuring: a, Christmas trees and red violet hearts. b, Candles. c, Christmas trees and green hearts. d, Reindeer. e, Snowmen. f, Angels with horns. g, Red reindeer and heart. h, Poinsettias. i, Christmas ornaments and poinsettias. j, Angels and musical notes.

***Serpentine Die Cut 12¾x12½***

**2012, Nov. 20** **Self-Adhesive**

**1428** A637 Block of 10 11.00
*a.-j.* (40c) Any single 1.10 .30

A638

Personalized Stamps — A639

**2013, Jan. 2** **Litho.** ***Perf. 13¼x14***

**1429** A638 1 multi 1.50 1.50

**Self-Adhesive**

**1430** A639 1 multi 1.50 1.50

Nos. 1429-1430 each sold for 54c on day of issue. Vignettes shown are the generic images available on the day of issue. Vignettes could be personalized for a fee.

Traditional Women's Head Coverings — A640

Head covering from: No. 1431, Bunschoten-Spakenburg. No. 1432, Staphorst. No. 1433, Marken. No. 1434, Walcheren. No. 1435, Noordwest-Veluwe.

**2013** **Litho.** ***Perf. 14½x14¼***

**1431** A640 1 multi 1.50 1.50
*a.* Perf. 13½x12½ 2.75 2.75
*b.* Booklet pane of 2 #1431a 5.50 —
**1432** A640 1 multi 1.50 1.50
*a.* Perf. 13½x12½ 2.75 2.75
*b.* Booklet pane of 2 #1432a 5.50 —
**1433** A640 1 multi 1.40 1.40
*a.* Perf. 13½x12½ 2.75 2.75
*b.* Booklet pane of 2 #1433a 5.50 —
**1434** A640 1 multi 1.40 1.40
*a.* Perf. 13½x12½ 2.75 2.75
*b.* Booklet pane of 2 #1434a 5.50 —
**1435** A640 1 multi 1.50 1.50
*a.* Perf. 13½x12½ 2.75 2.75
*b.* Booklet pane of 2 #1435a 5.50 —
Complete booklet, #1431b, 1432b, 1433b, 1434b, 1435b 27.50
*c.* Souvenir sheet of 5, #1431-1435 7.50 7.50
*Nos. 1431-1435 (5)* 7.30 7.30

Issued: Nos. 1431-1432, 1/2; Nos. 1433-1434, 2/25; Nos. 1431a-1431b, 1432a-1432b, 1433a-1433b, 1434a-1434b, 1435-1435c, 5/21. Nos. 1431-1435 each sold for 54c on day of issue. Complete booklet sold for €9.95.

Miniature Sheet

Netherlands Land Development Society, 125th Anniv. — A641

No. 1436 — Construction projects developed by Arcadis and KNHM: a, Millau Viaduct, France. b, Train under Zanderij Crailoo Wildlife Crossing Bridge. c, Lighthouse, flags and grass-covered dunes. d, Floriade (terraced garden), Venlo. e, Olympic Stadium, London. f, Storm barrier, New Orleans, Louisiana. g, Garden on Meuse River, Rotterdam. h, Water, trees and tower in distance (Kern met Pit Contest). i, Amsterdam Bijlmer ArenA railway station. j, Model constructed for Artcadia children's art and technology contest.

**2013, Jan. 28** **Litho.** ***Perf. 13¼x13½***

**1436** A641 Sheet of 10 15.00 15.00
*a.-j.* 1 Any single 1.50 1.50

Nos. 1436a-1436j each sold for 54c on day of issue.

Miniature Sheet

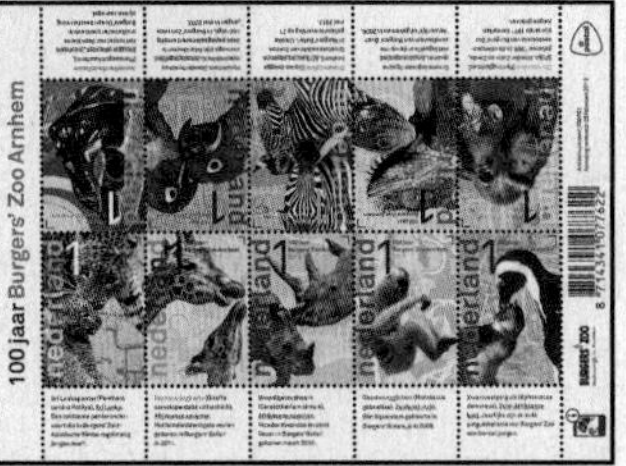


Animals in Burgers' Zoo, Arnhem — A642

No. 1437: a, Panthera pardus kotiya (Sri Lankan leopards). b, Pterapogon kauderni (Banggai cardinalfish) witheggs in mouth. c, Giraffa camelopardalis rothschildi (giraffes). d, Anodorhynchus hyacinthinus (hyacinth macaws). e, Ceratotherium simum (white rhinoceroses). f, Equus quagga boehmi (Grant's zebras). g, Nomascus gabriellae (yellow-cheeked gibbons). h, Iguana iguana (green iguanas). i, Spheniscus demersus (jackass penguins). j, Pan troglodytes (chimpanzees).

***Perf. 13¼x12¾***

**2013, Feb. 25** **Litho.**

**1437** A642 Sheet of 10 14.00 14.00
*a.-j.* 1 Any single 1.40 1.40
*k.* Booklet pane of 2, #1437a-1437b 5.25 —
*l.* Booklet pane of 2, #1437c-1437d 5.25 —
*m.* Booklet pane of 2, #1437e-1437f 5.25 —
*n.* Booklet pane of 2, #1437g-1437h 5.25 —
*o.* Booklet pane of 2, #1437i-1437j 5.25 —
Complete booklet, #1437k, 1437l, 1437m, 1437n, 1437o 26.50

Nos. 1437a-1437j each sold for 54c on day of issue. Complete booklet sold for €9.95.

Famous Women — A643

No. 1438: a, Alexandrine Tinne (1835-69), explorer of Sahara region. b, Belle van Zuylen (1740-1805), writer. c, Trijn van Leemput (c. 1530-1607), heroine in Eighty Years' War. d, Maria van Oosterwijck (1630-93), painter. e, Mary, Duchess of Burgundy (1457-82). f, Anna Zernike (1887-1972), theologian, first female minister in Netherlands.

***Perf. 13¼x12¾***

**2013, Mar. 25** **Litho.**

**1438** A643 Block of 6 8.50 8.50
*a.-f.* 1 Any single 1.40 1.40

Nos. 1438a-1438f each sold for 54c on day of issue.

Miniature Sheet

Reopening of Main Building of Rijksmuseum — A644

No. 1439: a, Right part of *The Gallant Conversation,* by Gerard ter Borch, left part of *Interior of the Church of St. Odulphus in Assendelft,* by Pieter Jansz. b, Right part of *Interior of the Church of St. Odolphus in Assendelft, Mary Magdalene,* by Jan van Scorel. c, *Still Life of Fruits and Flowers,* by Balthasar van der Ast, left part of *Still Life with Flowers,* by Hans Bollongier. d, Right part of *Still Life with Flowers,* left part of *Vivi in a Red Dress in a Forest,* by Jacob Olie, Jr. e, Right edge of *Sheet with Five Butterflies a Wasp and Two Flies,* by Pieter Withoos, Bunya no Yasuhide from *Modern Parody on the Six Poets and Six Flowers,* by Kunisada Utagawa, left edge of *Italian Landscape with Stone Pines,* by Hendrik Voogd. f, Right part of *Italian Landscape with Stone Pines,* left part of *The Threatened Swan,* by Jan Asselijn. g, Right part of *Still Life with Gilded Cup,* by Willem Claesz, *The Milkmaid,* by Johannes Vermeer. h, *Still Life with Cheeses,* by Floris Claesz van Dijck, left part of tile from Sommelsdijk Orphanage. i, Right part of *Gerard Andriesz Bicker,* by Bartholomeus van der Helst, left part of *Portrait of Giuliano da Sangallo,* by Piero di Cosomo. j, Right part of *Portrait of Giuliano da Sangallo,* left part of *The Night Watch,* by Rembrandt.

***Perf. 13¼x12¾***

**2013, Mar. 25** **Litho.**

**1439** A644 Sheet of 10 14.00 14.00
*a.-j.* 1 Any single 1.40 1.40

Nos. 1439a-1439j each sold for 54c on day of issue.

Abdication of Queen Beatrix A645

**2013, Mar. 25** **Litho.** ***Perf. 14x13½***

**1440** A645 1 blue & blk 1.40 1.40

No. 1440 sold for 54c on day of issue.

Europa — A646

No. 1441: a and c, Modern mail vans (2013 Renault Kangoo, 1976 Simca 1100 VF, 2010 Fiat Fiorino, 1974 Daf 33). b and d, Old mail vans (1960 Bedford CA, 1936, Opel P4, 1956 Opel Blitz, 1918 GMC).

**2013, Apr. 22** **Litho.** ***Perf. 13¼x12¾***

**1441** A646 Pair 4.80 4.80
*a.-b.* 1 Europa Either single 2.40 2.40
*c.-d.* 1 Europa Either single, perf. 14½ 4.25 4.25
*e.* Booklet pane of 2, #1441c-1441d 8.75 —
Complete booklet, 3 #1441e 26.50

Nos. 1441a-1441b each sold for 90c on day of issue. Complete booklet sold for €9.95, and contains three panes of No. 1441e with different orientations of the stamps.

Ascension to Throne of King Willem-Alexander A647

***Perf. 14¼x14 Syncopated***

**2013, Apr. 30** **Litho.**

**Booklet Stamps**
**Self-Adhesive**

**1442** A647 1 blk, red & bl 1.40 1.40
*a.* Booklet pane of 10 14.00
**1443** A647 2 blk, bl & grn 3.00 3.00
*a.* Booklet pane of 5 15.00

On day of issue, No. 1442 sold for 54c and No. 1443 sold for €1.08.

King Willem-Alexander — A648

**2013, May 21** **Litho.** ***Perf. 14x13½***

**1444** A648 1 red & blk 1.50 1.50

No. 1444 sold for 54c on day of issue.

Writers — A649

No. 1445: a, Simon Carmiggelt (1913-87). b, Gerrit Kouwenaar. c, Louis Couperus (1863-1923). d, Adriaan Roland Holst (1888-1976). e, Godfried Bomans (1913-71).

**2013, May 21 Litho. *Perf. 14½***

**1445** Horiz. strip of 5 7.50 7.50
***a.-e.*** A649 1 Any single 1.50 1.50

Nos. 1445a-1445e each sold for 54c on day of issue. Printed in sheets containing 2 each of Nos. 1445a-1445e + 5 central labels.

World Blood Donor Day — A650

No. 1446: a, Queen, "1" in red. b, King, "1" in white.

**2013, June 17 Litho. *Perf. 14½***

**1446** A650 Pair 3.00 3.00
***a.-b.*** 1 Either single 1.50 1.50

On day of issue Nos. 1446a-1446b each sold for 54c.

Miniature Sheet

Windmills — A651

No. 1447 — Various windmill types located in: a and k, Schermer. b and l, Burgwerd. c and m, Heeswijk-Dinther. d and n, Hoornaar. e and o, Zaandam. f and p, Wijk bij Duurstede. g and q, Klein Genhout. h and r, Zeddam. i and s, Nieuw- en Sint Joosland. j and t, Roderwolde.

**2013, June 17 Litho. *Perf. 14½***

**1447** A651 Sheet of 10 15.00 15.00
***a.-j.*** 1 Any single 1.50 1.50
***k.-t.*** 1 Any single, perf. 12¾x13¼ 2.75 2.75
***u.*** Booklet pane of 2, #1447k, 1447p 5.50 —
***v.*** Booklet pane of 2, #1447l, 1447q 5.50 —
***w.*** Booklet pane of 2, #1447m, 1447r 5.50 —
***x.*** Booklet pane of 2, #1447n, 1447s 5.50 —
***y.*** Booklet pane of 2, #1447o, 1447t 5.50 —
Complete booklet, #1447u, 1447v, 1447w, 1447x, 1447y 27.50

Nos. 1447a-1447j each sold for 54c on day of issue. Complete booklet sold for €9.95.

Miniature Sheet

Royal Dutch Swimming Association, 125th Anniv. — A652

No. 1448: a, People standing at edge of pool. b, Two synchronized divers. c, Water polo player. d, Diver about to enter water. e, People standing at edge of pool, people lined up on diving platform. f, Two synchronized swimmers. g, Swimmer and lane barriers. h, Teacher and children learning how to swim. i, Swimmer's head near edge of pool. j, Swimmer bent over ready to start race.

**2013, Aug. 12 Litho. *Perf. 14½***

**1448** A652 Sheet of 10 16.00 16.00
***a.-j.*** 1 Any single 1.60 1.60

Nos. 1448a-1448j each sold for 60c on day of issue.

Miniature Sheet

Dutch Connections With Belgium — A653

No. 1449: a, Museum aan de Stroom, Antwerp, Belgium, designed by Neutelings Riedijk Architectural Agency. b, Design for Hoenderloo Museum, by Henry van de Velde. c, Twelve books, country name at left. d, Thirteen books, country name at right. e, Après-midi à Amsterdam, by Rik Wouters. f, De Vlakte, by Jakob Smits.

***Perf. 13¼x12¾***

**2013, Aug. 12 Litho.**

**1449** A653 Sheet of 6 16.50 16.50
***a.-f.*** 1 Wereld Any single 2.75 2.75

Nos. 1449a-1449f each sold for €1 on day of issue. No. 1449 was printed with three different illustrations in the bottom sheet margin, with each sheet having a different arrangement of stamps. Sheet margins at left and right served as etiquettes.

Greeting Card Week — A654

**2013, Sept. 9 Litho. *Perf. 14½***

**1450** A654 1 multi 1.60 1.60

No. 1450 sold for 60c on day of issue and was printed in sheets of 3.

Miniature Sheet

Peace Palace, The Hague, Cent. — A655

No. 1451 — Details of architectural or artistic items of the Peace Palace in circle at left, word at top in inner ring of words in circle at right: a and k, Detail of wall tile, Artes. b and l, Bronze medallion on entrance gates, Amicitia. c and m, Stained-glass window in Central Hall, Iustitia. d and n, Portrait of Hugo de Groot, by Michiel Jansz.van Mierevelt, Mercatura. e and o, Marble floor in Entrance Hall, Scientia. f and p, Relief sculpture by Toon Dupuis, Veritas. g and q, Prestudy for unmade tapestry, Concordia. h and r, Tile panel, Securitas. i and s, Peace Goddess with Child, by Herman Rosse, Prosperitas. j and t, Stained-glass window depicting locomotive, Industria.

**2013, Sept. 9 Litho. *Perf. 13¼x12¾***

**1451** A655 Sheet of 10 16.00 16.00
***a.-j.*** 1 Any single 1.60 1.60
***k.-t.*** 1 Any single, perf. 14½ 2.75 2.75
***u.*** Booklet pane of 2, #1451k-1451l 5.50 —
***v.*** Booklet pane of 2, #1451m-1451n 5.50 —
***w.*** Booklet pane of 2, #1451o-1451p 5.50 —
***x.*** Booklet pane of 2, #1451q-1451r 5.50 —
***y.*** Booklet pane of 2, #1451s-1451t 5.50 —
Complete booklet, #1451u, 1451v, 1451w, 1451x, 1451y 27.50

Nos. 1451a-1451j each sold for 60c on day of issue. Complete booklet sold for €9.95.

Airplanes and Queen Wilhelmina From Type AP5 A656

**2013, Oct. 18 Litho. *Perf. 14x13½***

**1452** A656 1 multi 1.60 1.60
***a.*** Booklet pane of 2 5.50 —
Complete booklet, 5 #1452a 27.50

Stamp Day. No. 1452 sold for 60c on day of issue. Complete booklet sold for €9.95.

Legend of St. Nicholas (Santa Claus) — A657

No. 1453: a, St. Nicholas on horse, Black Peter, and Moon. b, Black Peter with gift. c, Moon, tree and house. d, St. Nicholas with crozier. e, Shoe filled with gifts.

**2013, Nov. 4 Litho. *Perf. 13¾x13¼***

**1453** Horiz. strip of 5 8.00 8.00
***a.-e.*** A657 1 Any single 1.60 1.60

Nos. 1453a-1453e sold for 60c on day of issue and emit a spice scent when scratched.

Miniature Sheet

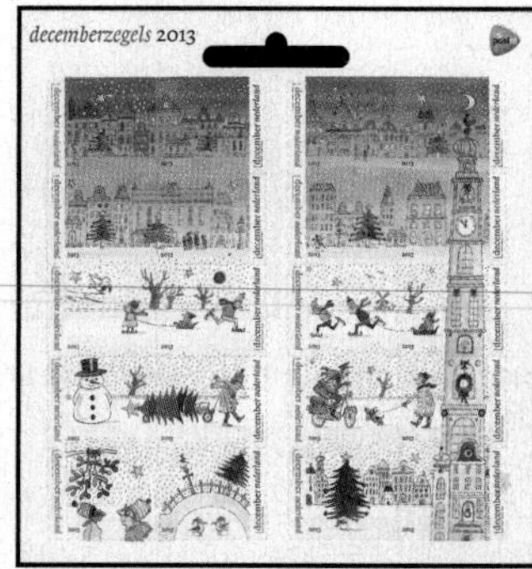


December Stamps — A658

No. 1454: a, Buildings at night, comet in sky over Christmas tree. b, Buildings at night, Christmas tree. c, Buildings at night, people viewing fireworks. d, Buildings at night, Christmas tree, large star at left, Moon over top of tower. e, Buildings at night, large star at left, Christmas trees. f, Buildings at night, people viewing large star at right. g, Buildings at night, Christmas tree, man running. h, Buildings at night, clock on tower at right. i, Girl on ice skates looking at bird in tree. j, Boy in sled on ice, man ice skating. k, Two ice skaters, windmill. l, Boy in sled on ice, tower at right. m, Snowman, star and top of Christmas tree. n, Man pulling Christmas tree on cart. o, Dog looking at postman on bicycle. p, Woman holding dog's leash, tower at right. q, Man and woman under mistletoe. r, Birds under bridge, Christmas tree. s, Buildings in day, Christmas tree. t, Buidlings in day, tower at right.

***Serpentine Die Cut 12½x12¼***

**2013, Nov. 19 Litho.**

**Self-Adhesive**

**1454** A658 Sheet of 20 30.00
***a.-t.*** (55c) Any single 1.50 1.50

Kingdom of the Netherlands, 200th Anniv. — A659

No. 1455: a, Landing of Willem I, 1813, King Willem I, flag of the Netherlands. b, List of monarchs.

**2013, Nov. 30 Litho. *Perf. 14½***

**1455** A659 Pair, #a-b 7.00 7.00
***a.-b.*** 2 Either single 3.50 3.50

On day of issue Nos. 1455a-1455b both sold for €1.28.

King Willem-Alexander
A660 A661

***Die Cut Perf. 14¼ Syncopated***

**2013, Nov. 30 Photo.**

**Booklet Stamps**

**Self-Adhesive**

**1456** A660 1 blue & blk 1.75 1.75
***a.*** Booklet pane of 10 17.50
***b.*** Dated "2014" — —
***d.*** Dated "2015" 1.60 1.60
***e.*** Booklet pane of 10 #1456d 16.00

***Serpentine Die Cut 11¼***

**1457** A661 1 Internationaal gray & blk 3.00 3.00
***a.*** Booklet pane of 5 15.00
***b.*** Dated "2014" — —

*d.* Dated "2015" 2.60 2.60
*e.* Booklet pane of 5 #1457d 13.00

***Die Cut Perf. 14¼***

**1458** A660 2 ver & blk 3.50 3.50
*a.* Booklet pane of 5 17.50
*b.* Dated "2014" — —
*d.* Dated "2015" 3.25 3.25
*e.* Booklet pane of 5 #1458d 16.50
*Nos. 1456-1458 (3)* 8.25 8.25

On day of issue, No. 1456 sold for 64c; No. 1457, for €1.05; No. 1458, for €1.28.

Issued: Nos. 1456b, 1457b, 1458b, 10/23/14; Nos. 1456d, 1456e, 1457d, 1457e, 1458d, 1458e, 1/5/15. On day of issues, No. 1456b sold for 64c; No. 1456d, 69c; No. 1457b, €1.05; No. 1457d, €1.15; No. 1458b, €1.28;No. 1458d, €1.38.

Numerals
A662 A663

***Die Cut Perf. 13½ Syncopated***

**2014, Jan. 2 Coil Stamps Litho.**
**Self-Adhesive**

**1459** A662 1 multi 1.75 1.75
**1460** A663 2 multi 3.50 3.50

On day of issue, No. 1459 sold for 64c; No. 1460, for €1.28.

A664

Dutch Items — A665

Designs: No. 1461a, Frisian flat-bottomed boat. Nos. 1461b, 1462a, Windmill. No. 1461c, Wedge of Gouda cheese. Nos. 1461d, 1462d, House with step-gable roof. No. 1461e, Boy and girl in Dutch costumes kissing. Nos. 1461f, 1462b, Bicycle. Nos. 1461g, 1462c, Holstein-Frisian cow. Nos. 1461h, 1462e, Tulip. No. 1461i, Ice skate. No. 1461j, Wooden shoe.

***Die Cut Perf. 14¼***

**2014, Jan. 2 Litho.**
**Self-Adhesive**

**1461** A664 Booklet pane of 10 17.50
*a.-j.* 1 Any single 1.75 1.75

***Serpentine Die Cut 11¼***

**1462** A665 Booklet pane of 5 15.00
*a.-e.* 1 Internationaal Any single 3.00 3.00

On day of issue, Nos. 1461a-1461j each sold for 64c; Nos. 1462a-1462 each sold for €1.05.

Miniature Sheet

Automobiles in Louwman Museum Collection — A666

No. 1463: a, 1887 De Dion-Bouton & Trépardoux. b, 1910 Brooke Swan Car. c, 1912 Eysink. d, 1912 Spyker. e, 1932, Bugatti. f, 1935 Duesenberg. g, 1936 Toyota. h, 1960 Porsce race car. i, 1964 Aston Martin. j, 1965 Ferrari.

**2014, Jan. 27 Litho. *Perf. 13¼x13½***

**1463** A666 Sheet of 10 17.50 17.50
*a.-j.* 1 Any single 1.75 1.75
*k.* Booklet pane of 2, #1463a-1463b 6.75 —
*l.* Booklet pane of 2, #1463c-1463d 6.75 —
*m.* Booklet pane of 2, #1463e-1463f 6.75 —
*n.* Booklet pane of 2, #1463g-1463h 6.75 —
*o.* Booklet pane of 2, #1463i-1463j 6.75 —
Complete booklet, #1463k-1463o 34.00

On day of issue, Nos. 1463a-1463j each sold for 64c. Complete booklet sold for €12.45.

Ceramics — A667

Ceramics from: No. 1464, Loosdrecht. No. 1465, Tegelen. No. 1466, Harlingen. No. 1467, Makkum. No. 1468, Delft.

**2014 Litho. *Perf. 14½x14¼***

**1464** A667 1 multi 1.75 1.75
*a.* Perf. 13½x12½ 3.25 3.25
*b.* Booklet pane of 2 #1464a 6.75 —
**1465** A667 1 multi 1.75 1.75
*a.* Perf. 13½x12½ 3.25 3.25
*b.* Booklet pane of 2 #1465a 6.75 —
**1466** A667 1 multi 1.75 1.75
*a.* Perf. 13½x12½ 3.25 3.25
*b.* Booklet pane of 2 #1466a 6.75 —
**1467** A667 1 multi 1.75 1.75
*a.* Perf. 13½x12½ 3.25 3.25
*b.* Booklet pane of 2 #1467a 6.75 —
**1468** A667 1 multi 1.75 1.75
*a.* Perf. 13½x12½ 3.25 3.25
*b.* Booklet pane of 2 #1468a 6.75
Complete booklet, #1464b, 1465b, 1466b, 1467b, 1468b 34.00
*c.* Souvenir sheet of 5, #1464-1468 8.75 8.75

Issued: Nos. 1464, 1465, 1/27; Nos. 1466, 1467, 2/24; Nos. 1464a, 1464b, 1465a, 1465b, 1466a, 1466b, 1467a, 1467b, 1468, 1468a, 1468b, 1468c, 5/19. On day of issue, Nos. 1464-1468 each sold for 64c. Complete booklet sold for €12.45.

Youth Philately Day — A668

No. 1469: a, Carrier pigeon (duif). b, Hedgehog (egel).

**2014, Mar. 24 Litho. *Die Cut***
**Self-Adhesive**

**1469** A668 Pair, #a-b 3.50
*a.-b.* 1 Either single 1.75 1.75

Printed in sheets of 10 containing five each Nos. 1469a-1469b, with adjacent stamps at different distances from each other. On day of issue, Nos. 1469a-1469b each sold for 64c.

Constitution of the Kingdom of the Netherlands, 200th Anniv. — A669

No. 1470: a, King Willem-Alexander, text from coronation oath, blue panel. b, Statue of King Willem I, text from oath to the Constitution, red panel.

***Perf. 13½x13¼***

**2014, Mar. 29 Litho.**

**1470** A669 Pair, #a-b 7.00 7.00
*a.-b.* 2 Either single 3.50 3.50

On day of issue, Nos. 1470a-1470b each sold for €1.28.

Europa — A670

No. 1471 — Drie Pruiken Barrel Organ: a, Internal machinery. b, Front of organ with figurines and builder's name.

**2014, Apr. 22 Litho. *Perf. 13¼x13½***

**1471** A670 Horiz. pair 6.00 6.00
*a.-b.* 1 Internationaal Either single 3.00 3.00

On day of issue, Nos. 1471a-1471b each sold for €1.05.

Miniature Sheet

Orchids — A671

No. 1472: a, Gymnadenia conopsea. b, Orchis militaris. c, Orchis anthropophora. d, Anacamptis pyramidalis. e, Dactylorhiza maculata. f, Orchis purpurea. g, Platanthera bifolia. h, Orchis mascula. i, Coeloglossum viride. j, Orchis simia.

**2014, Apr. 22 Litho. *Perf. 13½x13¼***

**1472** A671 Sheet of 10 17.50 17.50
*a.-j.* 1 Any single 1.75 1.75
*k.* Booklet pane of 2, #1472a, 1472f 7.00 —
*l.* Booklet pane of 2, #1472b, 1472g 7.00 —
*m.* Booklet pane of 2, #1472c, 1472h 7.00 —
*n.* Booklet pane of 2, #1472d, 1472i 7.00 —
*o.* Booklet pane of 2, #1472e, 1472j 7.00 —
Complete booklet, #1472k-1472o 35.00

On day of issue, Nos. 1472a-1472j each sold for 64c. Complete booklet sold for €12.45.

Miniature Sheet

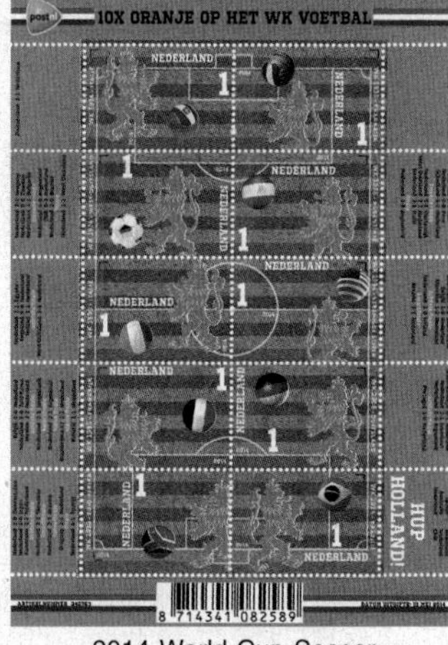


2014 World Cup Soccer Championships, Brazil — A672

No. 1473 — Dutch lion, soccer ball with host county flag and year: a, Italy, 1934. b, France, 1938. c, West Germany, 1974. d, Argentina, 1978. e, Italy, 1990. f, United States, 1994. g, France, 1998. h, Germany, 2006. i, South Africa, 2010, j, Brazil, 2014.

**2014, May 19 Litho. *Perf. 13¼x13½***

**1473** A672 Sheet of 10 17.50 17.50
*a.-j.* 1 Any single 1.75 1.75

On day of issue, Nos. 1473a-1473j each sold for 64c.

Personalized Stamp — A673

**2014, July 1 Litho. *Perf. 13½x14***

**1474** A673 1 Internationaal multi 3.00 3.00

No. 1474 sold for €1.05 on day of issue. The vignette shown is the generic image available on the day of issue. Vignettes could be personalized for a fee.

Miniature Sheet

Dutch Connections With Japan — A674

No. 1475: a, Gentaku Otsuki (1757-1827), Japanese expert on the Dutch ("1" at UL). b, Philipp Franz von Siebold (1796-1866), physician in Japan ("1" at UR). c, The Courtesan, by Vincent van Gogh ("1" at UL). d, The Red

Kimono, by George Hendrik Breitner ("1" at UR). e, Dutch ship Liefde ("1" at UL). f, Dejima Island, detail of painting by Keiga Kawahara ("1" at UR).

**2014, July 14 Litho.** ***Perf. 13¼x13½***

**1475** A674 Sheet of 6 18.00 18.00
*a.-f.* 1 Internationaal Any single 3.00 3.00

Nos. 1475a-1475f each sold for €1.05 on day of issue. No. 1475 was printed with three different illustrations in the bottom sheet margin, with each sheet having a different arrangement of stamps. Sheet margins at left and right served as etiquettes.

Royal Family Riding Bicycles — A675

King Willem-Alexander and Queen Máxima at 2014 Winter Olympics — A676

King Willem-Alexander and Queen Máxima — A677

2001 Announcement of Engagement — A678

Royal Family in New York City — A679

**2014, Aug. 2 Litho.** ***Perf. 13¼x13½***

**1476** Vert. strip of 5 8.75 8.75
*a.* A675 1 multi 1.75 1.75
*b.* A676 1 multi 1.75 1.75
*c.* A677 1 multi 1.75 1.75
*d.* A678 1 multi 1.75 1.75
*e.* A679 1 multi 1.75 1.75

12½ year anniv. of marriage of King Willem-Alexander and Queen Máxima. Printed in sheets containing two vertical strips. Nos. 1476a-1476e each sold for 64c on day of sale.

Miniature Sheet

UNESCO World Heritage Sites in the Netherlands — A680

No. 1477: a, Beemster Polder, 1999. b, Wadden Sea, 2009. c, Schokland and Surroundings, 1995. d, Windmill Network at Kinderdijk-Elshout, 1997. e, Rietveld Schröder House, 2000. f, D.F. Wouda Steam Pumping Station, 1998. g, Canal Ring of Amsterdam, 2010. h, Willemstad, Curaçao, 1997. i, Fort near Spijkerboor, Defense Ring of Amsterdam, 1996. j, Pampus Island Fort, Defense Ring of Amsterdam, 1996.

***Perf. 13¼x13½***

**2014, Aug. 11 Litho.**

**1477** A680 Sheet of 10 17.50 17.50
*a.-j.* 1 Any single 1.75 1.75
*k.* Booklet pane of 2, #1477a-1477b 6.75 —
*l.* Booklet pane of 2, #1477c-1477d 6.75 —
*m.* Booklet pane of 2, #1477e-1477f 6.75 —
*n.* Booklet pane of 2, #1477g-1477h 6.75 —
*o.* Booklet pane of 2, #1477i-1477j 6.75 —
Complete booklet, #1477k-1477o 34.00

On day of issue, Nos. 1477a-1477j each sold for 64c. Complete booklet sold for €12.45.

Miniature Sheet

Railways in the Netherlands, 175th Anniv. — A681

No. 1478: a, Locomotives and electric cable towers. b, Locomotive, clock with second hand, Arnhem train station stairway and escalator. c, Tile work and Haarlem station. d, Electric locomotive and map of railway line stations. e, Vertical lift railway bridge, green track signal. f, Emblem for Tienertoer reduced rate program, winged wheel emblem. g, Locomotive and red track signal. h, Clock without second hand, Rotterdam train station. i, New and old symbols for Netherlands Railways, track network. j, Locomotive, Netherlands #215.

**2014, Sept. 8 Litho.** ***Perf. 13¼x13½***

**1478** A681 Sheet of 10 16.00 16.00
*a.-j.* 1 Any single 1.60 1.60
*k.* Booklet pane of 2, #1478a-1478b 6.50 —
*l.* Booklet pane of 2, #1478c-1478d 6.50 —
*m.* Booklet pane of 2, #1478e-1478f 6.50 —
*n.* Booklet pane of 2, #1478g-1478h 6.50 —
*o.* Booklet pane of 2, #1478i-1478j 6.50 —
Complete booklet, #1478k-1478o 32.50

On day of issue, Nos. 1478a-1478j each sold for 64c. Complete booklet sold for €12.45.

Hardwell, Disk Jockey — A682

Tiesto, Disk Jockey — A683

Afrojack, Disk Jockey — A684

Dash Berlin, Disk Jockey — A685

Armin Van Buuren, Disk Jockey — A686

**2014, Oct. 6 Litho.** ***Perf. 13½x13¼***

**1479** Horiz. strip of 5 8.00 8.00
*a.* A682 1 multi 1.60 1.60
*b.* A683 1 multi 1.60 1.60
*c.* A684 1 multi 1.60 1.60
*d.* A685 1 multi 1.60 1.60
*e.* A686 1 multi 1.60 1.60

Printed in sheets containing two strips. On day of issue, Nos. 1479a-1479e each sold for 64c.

Stamp Day A687

**2014, Oct. 17 Litho.** ***Perf. 13x13¼***

**1480** A687 1 multi 1.60 1.60
*a.* Booklet pane of 2 6.25 —
Complete booklet, 5 #1480a 31.50

On day of issue No. 1480 sold for 64c. Complete booklet sold for €12.45. The five examples of No. 1480a in the complete booklet have different margins.

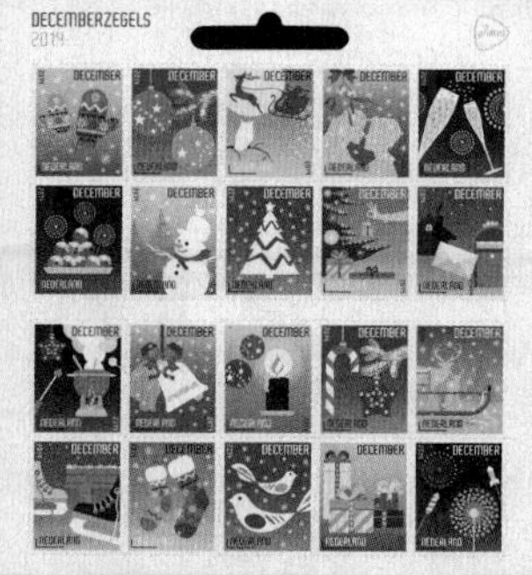


December Stamps — A688

No. 1481: a, Mittens. b, Two round Christmas ornaments. c, Owl, Santa's sleigh in flight. d, People kissing under mistletoe. e, Champagne flutes. f, Plate of Christmas pastries. g, Snowman. h, Christmas tree. i, Hand placing ornament on Christmas tree. j, House, envelope, mailbox. k, Fondue pot and Christmas ornament. l, Bells. m, Candle. n, Candy cane and Christmas ornament. o, Reindeer and sleigh. p, Ice skates. q, Stockings. r, Birds. s, Wrapped gifts. t, Rockets and fireworks.

***Serpentine Die Cut 12½***

**2014, Nov. 17 Photo.**

**Self-Adhesive**

**1481** A688 Booklet pane of 20 30.00
*a.-t.* (59c) Any single 1.50 1.50

Miniature Sheet

Dutch Top 40 Music Rankings, 50th Anniv. — A689

No. 1482: a, "Radar Love," by Golden Earring. b, "One Way Wind," by The Cats. c, "Willempie," by André van Duin. d, "Mon Amour," by BZN. e, "No Limit," by 2 Unlimited. f, "Vlieg Met Me Mee," by Paul de Leeuw. g, "Dromen Zijn Bedrog," by Marco Borsato. h, "We're Going to Ibiza!" by Vengaboys. i, "Cupido," by Jan Smit. j, "Birds," by Anouk.

**2015, Jan. 5 Litho.** ***Perf. 13½x13¼***

**1482** A689 Sheet of 10 16.00 16.00
*a.-j.* 1 Any single 1.60 1.60

On day of issue, Nos. 1482a-1482j each sold for 69c.

Fortified Towns — A690

Fortifications of: No. 1483, Bourtange. No. 1484, Elburg. No. 1485, Naarden. No. 1486, Willemstad. No. 1487, Hulst.

**2015 Litho.** ***Perf. 14½x14¼***

**1483** A690 1 multi 1.60 1.60
*a.* Perf. 13½x12¾ 2.75 2.75
*b.* Booklet pane of 2 #1483a 5.50 —
**1484** A690 1 multi 1.60 1.60
*a.* Perf. 13½x12¾ 2.75 2.75
*b.* Booklet pane of 2 #1484a 5.50 —
**1485** A690 1 multi 1.60 1.60
*a.* Perf. 13½x12¾ 2.75 2.75
*b.* Booklet pane of 2 #1485a 5.50 —
**1486** A690 1 multi 1.60 1.60
*a.* Perf. 13½x12¾ 2.75 2.75
*b.* Booklet pane of 2 #1486a 5.50 —
**1487** A690 1 multi 1.60 1.60
*a.* Perf. 13½x12¾ 2.75 2.75
*b.* Booklet pane of 2 #1487a 5.50 —
Complete booklet, #1483b, 1484b, 1485b, 1486b, 1487b 27.50
*c.* Souvenir sheet of 5, #1483-1487 8.00 8.00
*Nos. 1483-1487 (5)* 8.00 8.00

Issued: Nos. 1483, 1484, 1485, 2/2/15. Nos. 1483a, 1484a, 1485a, 1486, 1486a, 1487, 1487b, 1487c, 5/26/15. Nos. 1483-1487 each sold for 69c on day of issue. Complete booklet sold for €12.45.

Baby Carriage, Baby Bottle, Rocking Horse and Baby Toys — A691

***Die Cut Perf. 14¼x14½***

**2015, Mar. 2 Photo.**

**Self-Adhesive**

**1488** A691 1 multi 1.60 1.60

No. 1488 sold for 69c on day of issue.

Map of Netherlands and Royal Items — A692

No. 1489 — Map and: a, Royal arms, inscription "Koning Willem-Alexander / 2013." b, Signature of King William I. inscription "Koning Willem I / 1815."

**2015, Mar. 2 Litho. *Perf. 13½x13¼***

| | | | | |
|---|---|---|---|---|
| 1489 | A692 | Pair, #a-b | 6.50 | 6.50 |
| *a.-b.* | | 2 Either single | 3.25 | 3.25 |

On day of issue, Nos. 1489a and 1489b each sold for €1.38.

Bridges — A693

No. 1490: a and k, High speed railroad Bridge, Moerdijk, 2006. b and l, Ehzer Bridge, Almen, 1946. c and m, Kolenhaven Bridge, Delft, 2004. d and n, Cable-stayed bridge, Heusden, 1989. e and o, Zouthaven Bridge, Amsterdam, 2005. f and p, Jan Waaijer Bridge, Zoetermeer, 2013. g and q, De Oversteek Bridge, Nijmegen, 2013. h and r, Zeeland Bridge, Oosterschelde, 1965. i and s, Hanzeboog Bridge, Zwolle, 2011. j and t, Nescio Bridge, Amsterdam, 2006.

***Perf. 13½x12¾***

**2015, Mar. 30 Litho.**

| | | | | |
|---|---|---|---|---|
| 1490 | A693 | Sheet of 10 | 16.00 | 16.00 |
| *a.-j.* | | 1 Any single | 1.60 | 1.60 |
| *k.-t.* | | 1 Any single, perf. 14½x14¼ | 2.75 | 2.75 |
| *u.* | | Booklet pane of 2, #1490k-1490l | 5.50 | — |
| *v.* | | Booklet pane of 2, #1490m-1490n | 5.50 | — |
| *w.* | | Booklet pane of 2, #1490o-1490p | 5.50 | — |
| *x.* | | Booklet pane of 2, #1490q-1490r | 5.50 | — |
| *y.* | | Booklet pane of 2, #1490s-1490t | 5.50 | — |
| | | Complete booklet, #1490u, 1490v, 1490w, 1490x, 1490y | 27.50 | |

On day of issue, Nos. 1490a-1490j each sold for 69c. Complete booklet sold for €12.45. Descriptions of the bridges shown are found on the adjacent sheet selvage.

Hearts and Dots — A694

***Die Cut Perf. 14¼x14½***

**2015, Apr. 28 Photo.**

**Booklet Stamp Self-Adhesive**

| | | | | |
|---|---|---|---|---|
| 1491 | A694 | 1 multi | 1.60 | 1.60 |
| *a.* | | Booklet pane of 10 | 16.00 | |

No. 1491 sold for 69c on day of issue.

Toys and Games — A695

No. 1492: a, Video game equipment. b, Rubik's cube.

No. 1493: a, Robot and wind-up key. b, Board game.

**2015, Apr. 28 Litho. *Perf. 13¼x13½***

| | | | | |
|---|---|---|---|---|
| 1492 | A695 | Horiz. pair | 3.25 | 3.25 |
| *a.-b.* | | 1 Either single | 1.60 | 1.60 |
| 1493 | A695 | Horiz. pair | 5.25 | 5.25 |
| *a.-b.* | | 1 Internationaal Either single | 2.60 | 2.60 |

Europa (No. 1493). On day of issue, Nos. 1492a-1492b each sold for 69c; Nos. 1493a-1493b, €1.15.

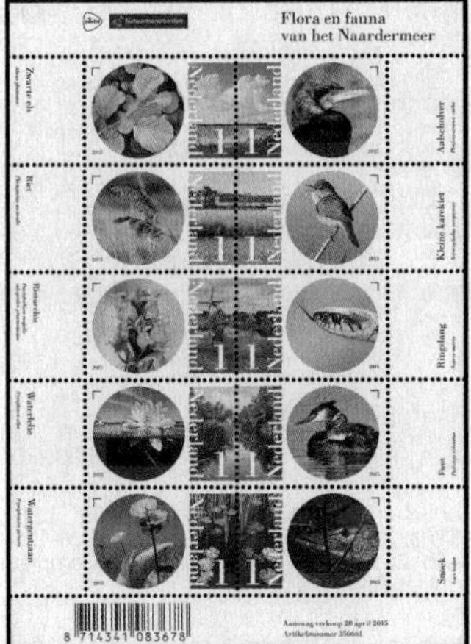


Flora and Fauna — A696

No. 1494: a and k, Alnus glutinosa. b and l, Phalacrocorax carbo. c and m, Phragmites australis. d and n, Acrocephalus scirpaceus. e and o, Dactylorhiza majalis subspecies praetermissa. f and p, Natrix natrix. g and q, Nymphaea alba. h and r, Podiceps cristatus. i and s, Nymphoides peltata. j and t, Esox lucius.

**2015, Apr. 28 Litho. *Perf. 13¼x12¾***

| | | | | |
|---|---|---|---|---|
| 1494 | A696 | Sheet of 10 | 16.00 | 16.00 |
| *a.-j.* | | 1 Any single | 1.60 | 1.60 |
| *k.-t.* | | 1 Any single, perf. 14½x14¼ | 2.75 | 2.75 |
| *u.* | | Booklet pane of 2, #1494s-1494t | 5.50 | — |
| *v.* | | Booklet pane of 2, #1494q-1494r | 5.50 | — |
| *w.* | | Booklet pane of 2, #1494o-1494p | 5.50 | — |
| *x.* | | Booklet pane of 2, #1494m-1494n | 5.50 | — |
| *y.* | | Booklet pane of 2, #1494k-1494l | 5.50 | — |
| | | Complete booklet, #1494u, 1494v, 1494w, 1494x, 1494y | 27.50 | |

On day of issue, Nos. 1494a-1494j each sold for 69c. Complete booklet sold for €12.45.

Volvo Ocean Race — A697

No. 1495: a, Three crewmembers on boat. b, Wave crashing against sailboat with Volvo Ocean Race emblem on bow. c, Sailboats in harbor. d, Four crewmembers in protective gear. e, View from mast of crew on deck. f, Boat with sail inscribed "Vestas."

**2015, May 26 Litho. *Perf. 13¼x13¾***

| | | | | |
|---|---|---|---|---|
| 1495 | A697 | Block of 6 | 9.75 | 9.75 |
| *a.-f.* | | 1 Any single | 1.60 | 1.60 |

On day of issue, Nos. 1495a-1495f each sold for 69c.

King William II (1792-1849) — A698

***Perf. 13½x13¼***

**2015, June 22 Litho.**

| | | | | |
|---|---|---|---|---|
| 1496 | A698 | 1 Internationaal multi | 2.60 | 2.60 |

Battle of Waterloo, 200th anniv. No. 1496 sold for €1.15 on day of issue.

Simple Science Experiments — A699

No. 1497: a, Match under egg passing through neck of bottle. b, Water in heated balloon. c, Battery made of lemons. d, Optical illusion of pencil behind glass of water. e, Lightbulb and positively and negatively charged balloons.

**2015, July 20 Litho. *Perf. 13½x13¼***

| | | | | |
|---|---|---|---|---|
| 1497 | | Horiz. strip of 5 | 7.50 | 7.50 |
| *a.-e.* | A699 | 1 Any single | 1.50 | 1.50 |

On day of issue, Nos. 1497a-1497e each sold for 69c.

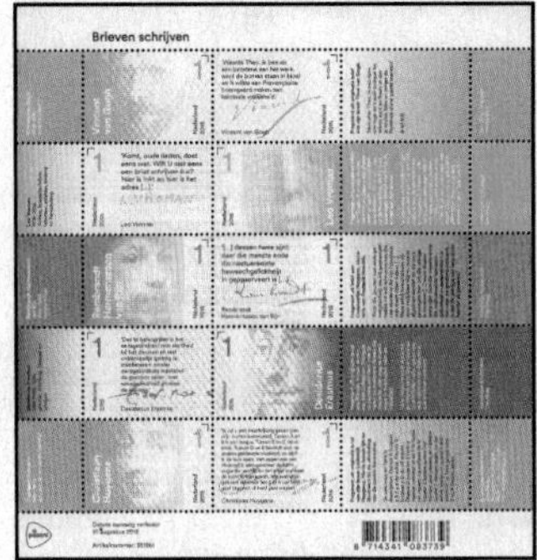


Famous Men and Excerpts From Their Letters — A700

No. 1498: a and k, Vincent van Gogh (1853-90), painter. b and l, Signature and excerpt from letter by van Gogh. c and m, Signature and excerpt from letter by Leo Vroman (1915-2014), poet. d and n, Vroman. e and o, Rembrandt van Rijn (1606-69), painter. f and p, Signature and excerpt from letter by Rembrandt. g and q, Signature and excerpt from letter by Desiderius Erasmus (1466-1536), theologian. h and r, Erasmus. i and s, Christiaan Huygens (1629-95), scientist. j and t, Signature and excerpt of letter by Huygens.

***Perf. 13½x12¾***

**2015, Aug. 17 Litho.**

| | | | | |
|---|---|---|---|---|
| 1498 | A700 | Sheet of 10 + 5 labels | 16.00 | 16.00 |
| *a.-j.* | | 1 Any single | 1.60 | 1.60 |
| *k.-t.* | | 1 Any single, perf. 14½ | 2.75 | 2.75 |
| *u.* | | Booklet pane of 2, #1498k-1498l | 5.50 | — |
| *v.* | | Booklet pane of 2, #1498m-1498n | 5.50 | — |
| *w.* | | Booklet pane of 2, #1498o-1498p | 5.50 | — |
| *x.* | | Booklet pane of 2, #1498q-1498r | 5.50 | — |
| *y.* | | Booklet pane of 2, #1498s-1498t | 5.50 | — |
| | | Complete booklet, #1498u, 1498v, 1498w, 1498x, 1498y | 27.50 | |

On day of issue, Nos. 1498a-1498j each sold for 69c. Complete booklet sold for €12.45.

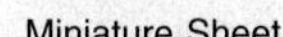

Miniature Sheet

Photographs of Animals by Charlotte Dumas — A701

No. 1499 — Title of photograph: a, Retrieved (retriever named Guinness and trailer in background), 2011. b, Day is Done, 2004 (horse named Isolde, white wall behind horse), 2004. c, Reverie (wolf named Taza sleeping), 2005. d, Tiger Tiger (tiger named Zeus), 2007. e, Heart Shaped Hole (dog named Tom Tom standing next to wall), 2008. f, Retrieved (dog named Moxie sitting on dock), 2011. g, Randagi (street dog laying on step), 2006. h, Anima (horse named Ringo in darkened stall), 2012. i, The Widest Prairies (horse named Rocky Road standing in field), 2013. j, Casa Voyageurs (cat named Kat), 2012.

***Perf. 13¼x13½***

**2015, Sept. 14 Litho.**

| | | | | |
|---|---|---|---|---|
| 1499 | A701 | Sheet of 10 | 16.00 | 16.00 |
| *a.-j.* | | 1 Any single | 1.60 | 1.60 |

On day of issue Nos. 1499a-1499j each sold for 69c. Titles of photographs are in sheet selvage adjacent to each stamp.

Miniature Sheet

Dutch Connections With the United States of America — A702

No. 1500: a, "Jan Kees" on pinstriped uniform in script of New York Yankees emblem. b, New York City subway signs using Dutch spellings of Harlem and Brooklyn. c, City Hall, The Hague, designed by Richard Meier. d, High Line Linear Park, New York City. e, Hotdog USA, by Jan Cremer. f, Photograph of breakedancer Kid Freeze holding boom box, by Jamel Shabazz.

***Perf. 13¼x13½***

**2015, Sept. 14 Litho.**

| | | | | |
|---|---|---|---|---|
| 1500 | A702 | Sheet of 6 | 16.00 | 16.00 |
| *a.-f.* | | 1 Internationaal Any single | 2.60 | 2.60 |

Nos. 1500a-1500f each sold for €1.15 on day of issue. No. 1500 was printed with three different illustrations in the bottom sheet margin, with each sheet having a different arrangement of stamps. Sheet margins at left and right served as etiquettes.

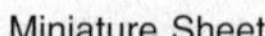

Miniature Sheet

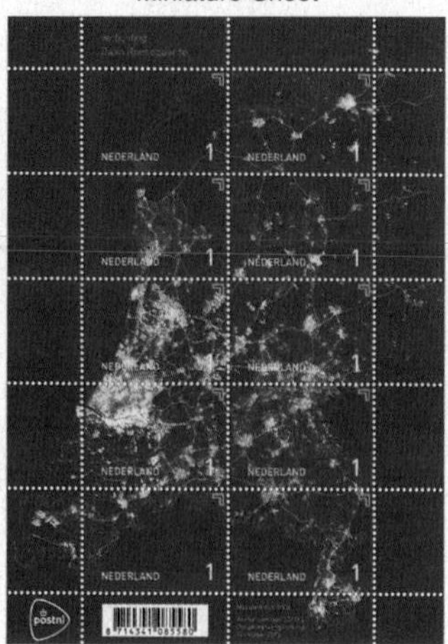

Netherlands at Night as Seen From Space — A703

No. 1501: a, West Frisian Islands. b, Northern Netherlands (area around Groningen and Leeuwarden). c, North Holland Province (area around Alkmaar). d, Drenthe and Overijssel Provinces (area around Hoogeveen and Meppel). e, Area around Amsterdam and Utrecht. f, Flevoland Province (area around Deventer and Apeldoorn). g, Area around Rotterdam. h, Area around Nijmegen and 's Hertogenbosch. i, Zeeland Province and North Brabant Province area north of Belgian border. j, Southeastern Netherlands (area around Eindhoven and Echt).

**2015, Oct. 12 Litho. *Perf. 13¼x13½***

**1501** A703 Sheet of 10 16.00 16.00
*a.-j.* 1 Any single 1.60 1.60

On day of issue Nos. 1501a-1501j each sold for 69c.

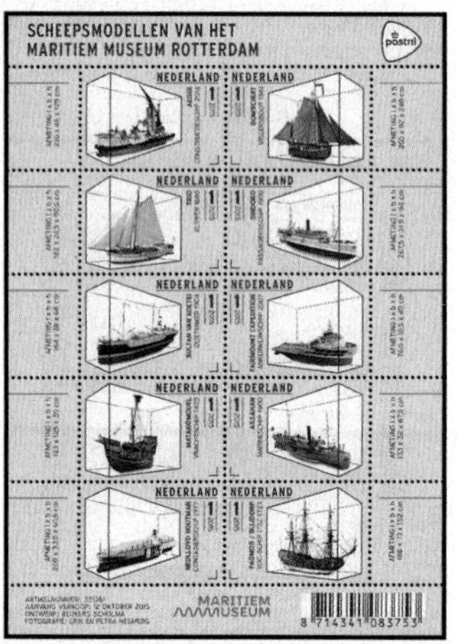

Ship Models at Rotterdam Maritime Museum — A704

No. 1502: a and k, Aegir. b and l, Bomschuit. c and m, Trio. d and n, Sindoro. e and o, Sultan van Koetei. f and p, Fairmount Expedition. g and q, Mataró. h and r, Assahan. i and s, Nedlloyd Houtman. j and t, Padmos/Blijdorp.

**2015, Oct. 12 Litho. *Perf. 13½x12¾***

**1502** A704 Sheet of 10 16.00 16.00
*a.-j.* 1 Any single 1.60 1.60
*k.-t.* 1 Any single, perf. 14½ 2.75 2.75
*u.* Booklet pane of 2, #1502q, 1502t 5.50 —
*v.* Booklet pane of 2, #1502l, 1502m 5.50 —
*w.* Booklet pane of 2, #1502n, 1502o 5.50 —
*x.* Booklet pane of 2, #1502r, 1502s 5.50 —
*y.* Booklet pane of 2, #1502k, 1502p 5.50 —
Complete booklet, #1502u, 1502v, 1502w, 1502x, 1502y 27.50

On day of issue Nos. 1502a-1502j each sold for 69c. Complete booklet sold for €12.45.

Netherlands No. 266 — A705

**2015, Oct. 16 Litho. *Perf. 13½x14***

**1503** A705 1 multi 1.60 1.60
*a.* Booklet pane of 2 5.50 —
Complete booklet, 5 #1503a 27.50

No. 1503 sold for 69c on day of issue. Complete booklet sold for €12.45. The five examples of No. 1503a in the complete booklet have different margins.

December Stamps — A706

No. 1504 — Snowflakes and: a, Fox in den, deer and bird. b, Woman and deer. c, Bird on woman's hand. d, Swans. e, Polar bear and bird. f, Rabbits. g, Squirrels. h, Birds in flight. i, Woman and dog. j, Rabbit, bird, fawn, and deer.

***Serpentine Die Cut 12½x12¾***

**2015, Nov. 24 Photo.**

**Self-Adhesive**

**1504** A706 Block of 10 14.00
*a.-j.* (64c) Any single 1.40 1.40

The Hay Wagon, by Hieronymus Bosch (c. 1450-1516) — A707

No. 1505 — Painting details: a and k, Man holding stick, woman holding infant. b and l, Wagon wheel, woman holding stick. c and m, Man in blue with lifted arms at side of wagon. d and n, Man in red looking at wagon wheel from behind. e and o, People with heads of animals. f and p, Man holding stick and carrying infant on back, child. g and q, Bird roasting on a spit. h and r, Man looking in woman's mouth. i and s, Bagpipe player and nun holding hay. j and t, Woman reaching in bag of hay, monk holding glass.

**2016, Jan. 4 Litho. *Perf. 13½x13¼***

**1505** A707 Sheet of 10 16.00 16.00
*a.-j.* 1 Any single 1.60 1.60
*k.* Booklet pane of 2, #1505a, 1505f 5.50 —
*l.* Booklet pane of 2, #1505b, 1505g 5.50 —
*m.* Booklet pane of 2, #1505c, 1505h 5.50 —
*n.* Booklet pane of 2, #1505d, 1505i 5.50 —
*o.* Booklet pane of 2, #1505e, 1505j 5.50 —
Complete booklet, #1505k, 1505l, 1505m, 1505n, 1505o 27.50

On day of issue, Nos. 1505a-1505j each sold for 73c. Complete booklet sold for €12.45.

Fishing Communities — A708

Designs: No. 1506, Urk. No. 1507, Zoutkamp. No. 1508, Volendam. No. 1509, Arnemuiden. No. 1510, Scheveningen.

**2016 Litho. *Perf. 14½x14¼***

**1506** A708 1 multi 1.60 1.60
*a.* Perf. 13½x12¾ 2.75 2.75
*b.* Booklet pane of 2 #1506a 5.50 —
**1507** A708 1 multi 1.60 1.60
*a.* Perf. 13½x12¾ 2.75 2.75
*b.* Booklet pane of 2 #1507a 5.50 —
**1508** A708 1 multi 1.60 1.60
*a.* Perf. 13½x12¾ 2.75 2.75
*b.* Booklet pane of 2 #1508a 5.50 —
**1509** A708 1 multi 1.60 1.60
*a.* Perf. 13½x12¾ 2.75 2.75
*b.* Booklet pane of 2 #1509a 5.50 —
**1510** A708 1 multi 1.60 1.60
*a.* Perf. 13½x12¾ 2.75 2.75
*b.* Booklet pane of 2 #1510a 5.50 —
Complete booklet, #1506b, 1507b, 1508b, 1509b, 1510b 27.50
*c.* Souvenir sheet of 5, #1506-1510 8.00 8.00
*Nos. 1506-1510 (5)* 8.00 8.00

Issued: Nos. 1506, 1507, 1508, 2/1. Nos. 1506a, 1507a, 1508a, 1509, 1509a, 1510, 1510a, 1510b, 1510c, 5/23. Nos. 1506-1510 each sold for 73c on day of issue. Complete booklet sold for €12.45.

Miniature Sheet

Postcrossing — A709

No. 1511 — Inscriptions: a, Deltawerken (Delta works). b, De Waddeneiland (Wadden Island). c, De Hoge Veluwe (Hoge Veluwe National Park). d, Het Binnenhof (Binnenhof, The Hague) e, Alkmaar Kaasmarkt (Alkmaar Cheese Market). f, Bollenvelden (Flower fields). g, Giethoorn. h, Marken. i, Zaanse Schans. j, Nacht Wacht (Night Watch).

***Perf. 13¼x13½***

**2016, Mar. 29 Litho.**

**1511** A709 Sheet of 10 30.00 30.00
*a.-j.* 1 Internationaal Any single 3.00 3.00

On day of issue Nos. 1511a-1511j each sold for €1.25. Sheet margins at left and right served as etiquettes.

Europa — A710

No. 1512: a, Painter with roller, buildings, wind generators, bicyclist. b, Bicycle.

**2016, Apr. 25 Litho. *Perf. 13¼x13½***

**1512** A710 Pair 6.00 6.00
*a.-b.* 1 Internationaal Either single 3.00 3.00

Think Green Issue.

On day of issue, Nos. 1512a-1512b each sold for €1.25.

Miniature Sheet

Birds From Griend in the Wadden Islands — A711

No. 1513: a, Thalasseus sandvicensis in flight. b, Two Haematopus ostralegus in flight. c, Tadorna tadorna with bill in water. d, Limosa lapponica with beak in water. e, Two Calidris alpina on land. f, Pluvialis squatarola walking. g, Charadrius hiaticula on nest. h, Sterna hirundo on nest. i, Head of Calidris canutus. j, Head of Somateria mollissima.

**2016, Apr. 25 Litho. *Perf. 13¼x13½***

**1513** A711 Sheet of 10 17.50 17.50
*a.-j.* 1 Any single 1.75 1.75
*k.* Booklet pane of 2, #1513a-1513b 6.00 —
*l.* Booklet pane of 2, #1513c-1513d 6.00 —
*m.* Booklet pane of 2, #1513e-1513f 6.00 —
*n.* Booklet pane of 2, #1513g-1513h 6.00 —
*o.* Booklet pane of 2, #1513i-1513j 6.00 —
Complete booklet, #1513k, 1513l, 1513m, 1513n, 1513o 30.00

Latin names of birds are on the selvage to left or right of the stamps. On day of issue Nos. 1513a-1513j each sold for 73c. Complete booklet sold for €12.45.

Wolfgang Amadeus Mozart in the Netherlands — A712

No. 1514: a, Musical score at left, Mozart at right. b, Mozart at left, Müller Organ, Church of St. Bavo, Haarlem.

**2016, May 23 Litho. *Perf. 13¼x13½***

**1514** A712 Horiz. pair 3.25 3.25
*a.-b.* 1 Either single 1.60 1.60

On day of issue, Nos. 1514a-1514b each sold for 73c.

Photographs by Ed van der Elsken (1925-90) — A713

No. 1501: a, Women crossing street, women standing on street corner. b, People lying on grass, woman and girls. c, Man lighting cigarette near car, woman and child wearing helmets on bicycle. d, People kissing. e, Women standing near track lanes, men on motorcycles. f, Man with tattoos on cobblestone street, man, woman holding child and cigarette. g, Man and woman holding gardening tools, man, woman pushing baby carriage. h, Man and woman walking past older woman at street corner, woman adjusting shoe near fence. i, Young woman standing in field, man, woman and child standing on vehicle rails. j, Man and woman on crowded street, seated woman.

**2016, May 23 Litho. *Perf. 13¼x13½***

| | | | | |
|---|---|---|---|---|
| **1515** | A713 | Sheet of 10 | 16.00 | 16.00 |
| *a.-j.* | | 1 Any single | 1.60 | 1.60 |

On day of issue Nos. 1515a-1515j each sold for 73c.

Comic Book Characters by Marten Toonder — A714

No. 1516: a, Tom Poes. b, Olivier B. Bommel.

**2016, June 3 Litho. *Perf. 13½x13¼***

| | | | | |
|---|---|---|---|---|
| **1516** | A714 | Pair | 3.25 | 3.25 |
| *a.-b.* | | 1 Either single | 1.60 | 1.60 |

Tom Poes, 75th anniv. On day of issue, Nos. 1516a-1516b each sold for 73c.

Europride Amsterdam 2016 Gay Pride Festival — A715

No. 1517: a, Woman, stars at top of circle. b, Man, stars at bottom of circle.

**2016, July 18 Litho. *Perf. 13½x13¼***

| | | | | |
|---|---|---|---|---|
| **1517** | A715 | Pair | 3.25 | 3.25 |
| *a.-b.* | | 1 Either single | 1.60 | 1.60 |

On day of issue, Nos. 1517a-1517b each sold for 73c.

Souvenir Sheet

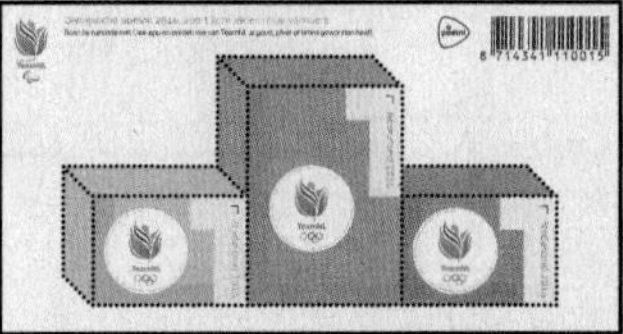

2016 Summer Olympics, Rio de Janeiro — A716

No. 1518 — Netherlands team emblem on winner's platform in: a, Gold (36x50mm). b, Silver (36x25mm). c, Bronze (36x25mm).

**2016, July 18 Litho. *Perf. 14½***

| | | | | |
|---|---|---|---|---|
| **1518** | A716 | Sheet of 3 | 5.00 | 5.00 |
| *a.-c.* | | 1 Any single | 1.60 | 1.60 |

On day of issue, Nos. 1518a-1518c each sold for 73c.

Miniature Sheet

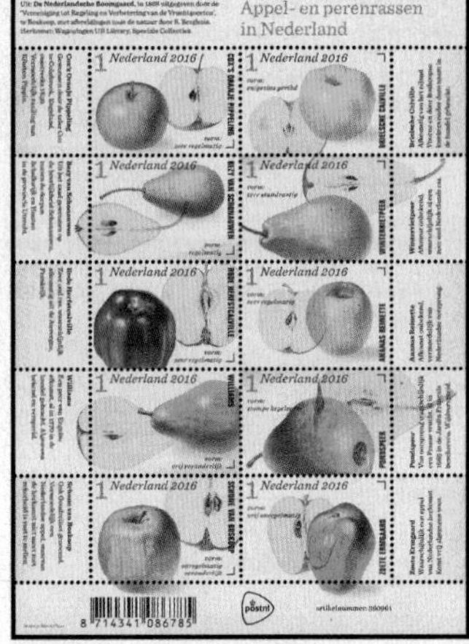


Apple and Pear Varieties — A717

No. 1513: a, Cox's orange pippeling apples. b, Brielsche Calville apples. c, Bezy van Schonauwen pears. d, Winterriet pears. e, Rode Herftscalville apples. f, Ananas Reinette apples. g, Williams pears. h, Ponds pears. i, Schone van Boskoop apples. j, Zoete Ermgaard apples.

***Perf. 13¼x13½***

**2016, Aug. 15 Litho.**

| | | | | |
|---|---|---|---|---|
| **1519** | A717 | Sheet of 10 | 17.50 | 17.50 |
| *a.-j.* | | 1 Any single | 1.75 | 1.75 |
| *k.* | | Booklet pane of 2, #1519a-1519b | 6.00 | — |
| *l.* | | Booklet pane of 2, #1519c-1519d | 6.00 | — |
| *m.* | | Booklet pane of 2, #1519e-1519f | 6.00 | — |
| *n.* | | Booklet pane of 2, #1519g-1519h | 6.00 | — |
| *o.* | | Booklet pane of 2, #1519i-1519j | 6.00 | — |
| | | Complete booklet, #1519k, 1519l, 1519m, 1519n, 1519o | 30.00 | |

On day of issue Nos. 1519a-1519j each sold for 73c. Complete booklet sold for €12.45.

Miniature Sheet

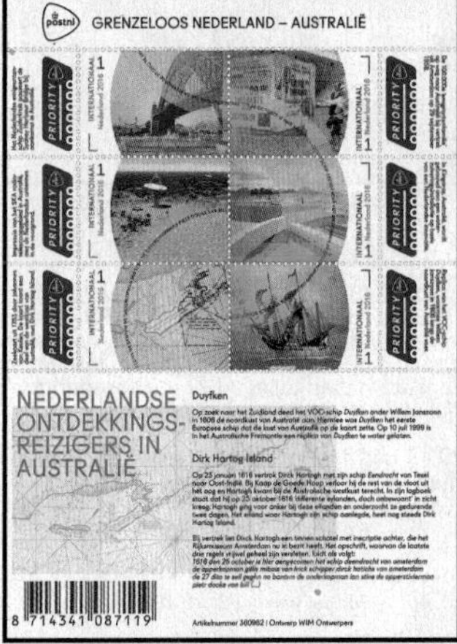


Dutch Connections With Australia — A718

No. 1520: a, Sydney Harbour Bridge. b, Moving crate of 100,000th Dutch emigrant to Australia on dock. c, Radio telescope in Australian desert. d, Water purification plant. e, Nautical chart showing Dirk Hartog's Island. f, Dutch East India Company ship Duyfken.

***Perf. 13¼x13½***

**2016, Aug. 15 Litho.**

| | | | | |
|---|---|---|---|---|
| **1520** | A718 | Sheet of 6 | 18.00 | 18.00 |
| *a.-f.* | | 1 Internationaal Any single | 3.00 | 3.00 |

Nos. 1520a-1520f each sold for €1.25 on day of issue. No. 1520 was printed with three different illustrations in the bottom sheet margin, with each sheet having a different arrangement of stamps. Sheet margins at left and right served as etiquettes.

Schiphol Airport, Cent. — A719

No. 1521: a, Airplanes, terminal and control tower. b, Airport check-in area. c, Sign to Gates B21-B33. d, Airplane and portable boarding stairway. e, Old KLM ticket counter and waiting room.

***Perf. 13¼x13½***

**2016, Sept. 12 Litho.**

| | | | | |
|---|---|---|---|---|
| **1521** | | Vert. strip of 5 | 8.00 | 8.00 |
| *a.-e.* | A719 | 1 Any single | 1.60 | 1.60 |

On day of issue, Nos. 1521a-1521c each sold for 73c.

Photographs of Model Doutzen Kroes by Anton Corbijn — A720

No. 1522 — Kroes: a, With arms raised, no blue violet circle. b, Wearing white panties, blue violet circle over lower back. c, With two blue violet circles over eyes. d, Wearing black swimsuit, blue violet circle at UR. e, Facing left, wearing swimsuit with white straps, large blue violet circle at UR. f, With large blue violet circle over back of ear, jaw and neck. g, Wearing white swimsuit, blue violet circle over legs. h, Topless, with arms crossed, blue violet circle at UR. i, Wearing white swimsuit, looking at hands, small blue violet circle above fingers. j, Wearing black swimsuit, blue violet circle over fingertips.

***Perf. 13½x13¼***

**2016, Sept. 12 Litho.**

| | | | | |
|---|---|---|---|---|
| **1522** | A720 | Sheet of 10 | 16.00 | 16.00 |
| *a.-j.* | | 1 Any single | 1.60 | 1.60 |

On day of issue Nos. 1522a-1522j each sold for 73c.

Miniature Sheet

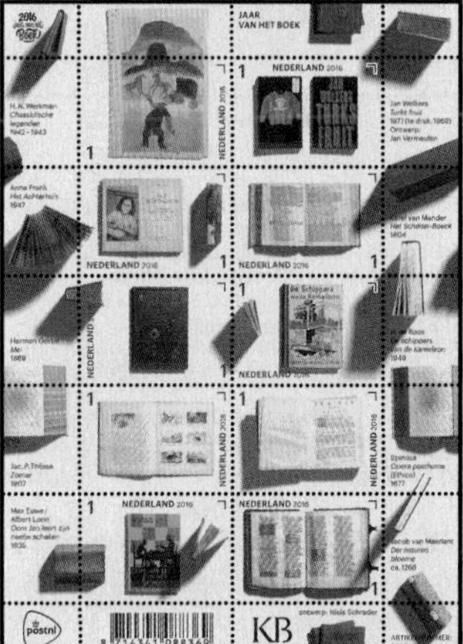


Book Year — A721

No. 1523: a, Illustration from *Chassidische Legenden,* by H. N. Werkman. b, Cover of *Turks Fruit,* by Jan Wolkers. c, Photograph and title page of the *Het Achterhuis* (*Diary of Anne Frank*). d, Pages from *Het Schilder-Boeke,* by Karel van Mander. e, *Mei,* by Herman Gorter. f, Cover of *De Schippers van de Kameleon,* by H. de Roos. g, Pages and illustrations of insects from *Zomer,* by Jac. P. Thijsse. h, Title page from *Opera Postuma / Ethica,* by Spinoza. i, Cover of *Oom Jan Leert Zijn Neefje Schaken,* by Max Euwe and Alber Loon. j, Pages with illustrations from *Der Naturen Bloeme,* by Jacob van Maerlant.

***Perf. 13¼x13½***

**2016, Sept. 12 Litho.**

| | | | | |
|---|---|---|---|---|
| **1523** | A721 | Sheet of 10 | 16.00 | 16.00 |
| *a.-j.* | | 1 Any single | 1.60 | 1.60 |
| *k.* | | Booklet pane of 2, #1523a-1523b | 5.50 | — |
| *l.* | | Booklet pane of 2, #1523c-1523d | 5.50 | — |
| *m.* | | Booklet pane of 2, #1523e-1523f | 5.50 | — |
| *n.* | | Booklet pane of 2, #1523g-1523h | 5.50 | — |
| *o.* | | Booklet pane of 2, #1523i-1523j | 5.50 | — |
| | | Complete booklet, #1523k, 1523l, 1523m, 1523n, 1523o | 27.50 | |

Titles and authors are on the selvage to left or right of the stamps. On day of issue Nos. 1523a-1523j each sold for 73c. Complete booklet sold for €12.45.

Kings William I, William II, William III, Queen Wilhelmina — A722

**2016, Oct. 14 Litho. *Perf. 13¼x13***

| | | | | |
|---|---|---|---|---|
| **1524** | A722 | 1 multi | 1.60 | 1.60 |
| *a.* | | Booklet pane of 2 | 5.50 | — |
| | | Complete booklet, 5 #1524a | 27.50 | |

No. 1524 sold for 73c on day of issue. Complete booklet sold for €12.45. The five examples of No. 1524a in the complete booklet have different margins.

December Stamps — A723

Designs: No. 1525, Fingers of people making five-pointed star. No. 1526, Gifts on sled. No. 1527, Ice skate. No. 1528, Snow sphere with snowman. No. 1529, Squirrels. No. 1530, Snowflake, Christmas tree and Star of Bethlehem ornaments. No. 1531, Bicycle carrying Christmas tree. No. 1532, Two Christmas ornaments and drink mug. No. 1533, Two champagne glasses. No. 1534, Silhouette of person wearing stocking cap and scarf, Dutch building. No. 1535, Bells, record on turntable.

***Serpentine Die Cut 12½***

**2016, Nov. 14 Litho.**

**Self-Adhesive**

| | | | | |
|---|---|---|---|---|
| **1525** | A723 | (65c) multi | 1.40 | 1.40 |
| **1526** | A723 | (65c) multi | 1.40 | 1.40 |
| **1527** | A723 | (65c) multi | 1.40 | 1.40 |
| **1528** | A723 | (65c) multi | 1.40 | 1.40 |
| **1529** | A723 | (65c) multi | 1.40 | 1.40 |
| **1530** | A723 | (65c) multi | 1.40 | 1.40 |
| **1531** | A723 | (65c) multi | 1.40 | 1.40 |
| **1532** | A723 | (65c) multi | 1.40 | 1.40 |
| **1533** | A723 | (65c) multi | 1.40 | 1.40 |
| **1534** | A723 | (65c) multi | 1.40 | 1.40 |
| **1535** | A723 | (65c) multi | 1.40 | 1.40 |
| *a.* | | Block of 11, #1525-1535 | 15.50 | |
| | | *Nos. 1525-1535 (11)* | 15.40 | 15.40 |

Nos. 1525-1535 are each inscribed "December" at UR, and were printed in sheets of 21, containing No. 1525 and two each Nos. 1526-1535.

Miniature Sheet

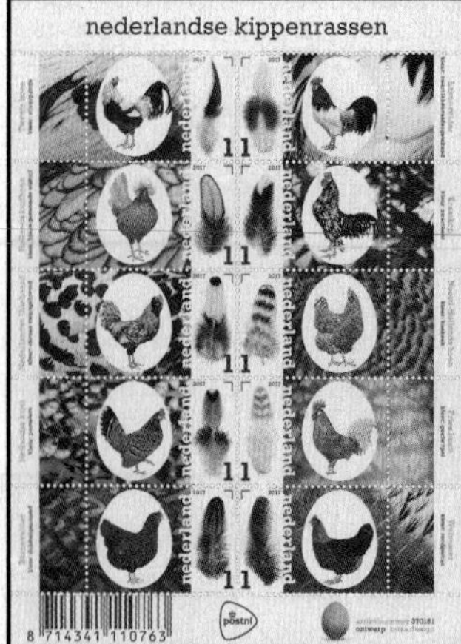


Dutch Chicken Breeds — A724

No. 1536: a, Twents hoen. b, Lakenvelder. c, Hollands kuifhoen. d, Kraaikop. e, Nederlandse Uilebaard. f, Noord-Hollands hoen. g, Hollandse kriel. h, Fries hoen. i, Barnevelder. j, Welsumer.

**2017, Jan. 2 Litho. *Perf. 13¼x12¾***

**1536** A724 Sheet of 10 16.00 16.00
*a.-j.* 1 Any single 1.60 1.60
*k.-t.* 1 As #1536a-1536j, any single, perf. 14¼x14½ 1.60 1.60
*u.* Booklet pane of 2, #1536k-1536l 5.25 —
*v.* Booklet pane of 2, #1536m-1536n 5.25 —
*w.* Booklet pane of 2, #1536o-1536p 5.25 —
*x.* Booklet pane of 2, #1536q-1536r 5.25 —
*y.* Booklet pane of 2, #1536s-1536t 5.25 —
Complete booklet, #1536u, 1536v, 1536w, 1536x, 1536y 26.50

Breed are on the selvage to left or right of the stamps. On day of issue Nos. 1536a-1536j each sold for 78c. Complete booklet sold for €12.45.

Silver-Studded Blue Butterflies — A725

Tulips — A726

***Die Cut Perf. 14½***

**2017, Jan. 30 Litho.**

**Self-Adhesive Coil Stamps**

**1537** A725 1 multi 1.75 1.75
**1538** A726 1 Internationaal multi 3.00 3.00

On day of issue, No. 1537 sold for 78c; No. 1538, €1.33. Country name, "1," "Internationaal" and codes were printed on the labels by the vending machine at the time of sale. Stamps with other denominations could not be printed.

River Valley Communities — A727

Designs: No. 1539, Church, Oud-Avereest, map of Reest River. No. 1540, Saxon Farm, map of Drentsche Aa River. No. 1541, Fort Asperen, map of Linge River. No. 1542, Vaantje Ferryhouse, map of Dommel River. No. 1543, Wooden house, map of Geul River.

**2017 Litho. *Perf. 14¼***

**1539** A727 1 multi 1.75 1.75
*a.* Perf. 13½x12¾ 2.75 2.75
*b.* Booklet pane of 2 #1539a 5.50 —
**1540** A727 1 multi 1.75 1.75
*a.* Perf. 13½x12¾ 2.75 2.75
*b.* Booklet pane of 2 #1540a 5.50 —
**1541** A727 1 multi 1.75 1.75
*a.* Perf. 13½x12¾ 2.75 2.75
*b.* Booklet pane of 2 #1541a 5.50 —
**1542** A727 1 multi 1.75 1.75
*a.* Perf. 13½x12¾ 2.75 2.75
*b.* Booklet pane of 2 #1542a 5.50 —
**1543** A727 1 multi 1.75 1.75
*a.* Perf. 13½x12¾ 2.75 2.75
*b.* Booklet pane of 2 #1543a 5.50 —
Complete booklet, #1539b, 1540b, 1541b, 1542b, 1543b 27.50
*c.* Souvenir sheet of 5, #1539-1543 8.75 8.75
*Nos. 1539-1543 (5)* 8.75 8.75

Issued: Nos. 1539, 1540, 1541, 1/30. Nos. 1539a, 1540a, 1541a, 1542, 1542a, 1543, 1543a, 1543c, 5/22. Nos. 1539-1543 each sold for 78c on day of issue. Complete booklet sold for €12.45.

Europa — A728

No. 1544: a, Doornenburg Castle, three coats of arms at left. b, Ammersoyen Castle, coat of arms at right.

***Perf. 13½x12¾***

**2017, Feb. 20 Litho.**

**1544** A728 Horiz. pair 5.75 5.75
*a.-b.* 1 Internationaal Either single 2.75 2.75

On day of issue, Nos. 1544a-1544b each sold for €1.33.

Miniature Sheet

Special Moments — A729

No. 1545 — Inscription: a, Gefeliciteerd (31x27mm heart-shaped stamp). b, Liefs (31x27mm heart-shaped stamp). c, Veel geluk (31x27mm heart-shaped stamp). d, Sterkte (28x29mm). e, Succes (28x29mm). f, Hoera (28x29mm). g, Fijne dag (28x29mm). h, Procifiat (31x27mm heart-shaped stamp). i, Voor jou (31x27mm heart-shaped stamp). j, Beterschap (31x27mm heart-shaped stamp).

***Die Cut (heart-shaped stamps), Serpentine Die Cut 14¼***

**2017, Mar. 27 Litho.**

**Self-Adhesive**

**1545** A729 Sheet of 10 + 7 stickers 17.50
*a.-j.* 1 Any single 1.75 1.75

On day of issue, Nos. 1545a-1545j each sold for 78c.

Miniature Sheet

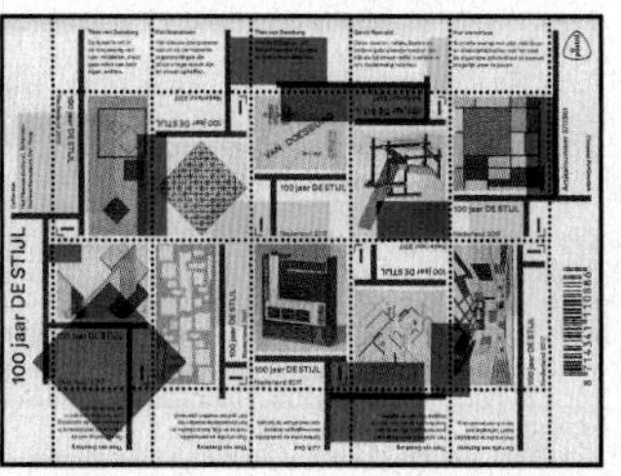


De Stijl Art Movement, Cent. — A730

No. 1546: a, Drawing by Theo van Doesburg (1883-1931), red and blue panels, "1" under red panel. b, Drawing by van Doesburg, yellow and blue panels. c, Drawing by van Doesburg, red and yellow panels. d, Painting of diamond with horizontal and vertical lines by Piet Mondriaan (1872-1944), blue and yellow panels. e, Model of restaurant, by J.J. P. Oud (1890-1963), red and yellow panels, vert. f, De Stijl magazine cover by van Doesburg, yellow and red panels. g, Drawing by van Doesburg, red and blue panels, "1" not under colored panel. h, Chair by Gerrit Rietveld (1888-1964), red and blue panels, vert. i, Architectural drawing by Cornelis van Eesteren (1897-1988), blue and yellow panels. j, Painting of rectangles and squares by Mondrian, yellow and blue panels.

***Perf. 13¼x12¾***

**2017, Mar. 27 Litho.**

**1546** A730 Sheet of 10 17.50 17.50
*a.-j.* 1 Any single 1.75 1.75

On day of issue, Nos. 1546a-1546j each sold for 78c.

Miniature Sheet

King Willem-Alexander, 50th Birthday — A731

No. 1547 — Photograph of King Willem-Alexander: a, Reading book as teenager. b, Standing on stairway. c, Standing in boat near bridge. d, Standing in front of building, wearing winter jacket. e, Wearing blue suit and tie. f, With Queen Máxima.

**2017, Apr. 24 Litho. *Perf. 14½***

**1547** A731 Sheet of 6 10.50 10.50
*a.-f.* 1 Any single 1.75 1.75

On day of issue, Nos. 1547a-1547f each sold for 78c.

Plants in Dutch Botanical Gardens — A732

No. 1548: a, Echinacea purpurea. b, Metasequoia glyptostroboides. c, Pyrostegia venusta. d, Sarracenia flava. e, Veratrum nigrum. f, Ginkgo biloba. g, Arum italicum. h, Vanilla planifolia. i, Clerodendrum trichotomum. j, Atropa belladonna.

**2017, Apr. 24 Litho. *Perf. 12¾x13¼***

**1548** A732 Sheet of 10 17.50 17.50
*a.-j.* 1 Any single 1.75 1.75
*k.* Booklet pane of 2, #1548a, 1548f 5.50 —
*l.* Booklet pane of 2, #1548b, 1548g 5.50 —
*m.* Booklet pane of 2, #1548c, 1548h 5.50 —
*n.* Booklet pane of 2, #1548d, 1548i 5.50 —
*o.* Booklet pane of 2, #1548e, 1548j 5.50 —
Complete booklet, #1548k, 1548l, 1548m, 1548n, 1548o 27.50

On day of issue, Nos. 1548a-1548j each sold for 78c. Complete booklet sold for €12.45.

Netherlands Red Cross, 150th Anniv. — A733

No. 1549: a, Red Cross worker comforting elderly woman. b, Child and Red Cross banner. c, Red Cross worker examining woman's arm.

**2017, May 22 Litho. *Perf. 14½***

**1549** Vert. strip of 3 5.25 5.25
*a.-c.* A733 1 Any single 1.75 1.75

On day of issue, Nos. 1549a-1549c each sold for 78c.

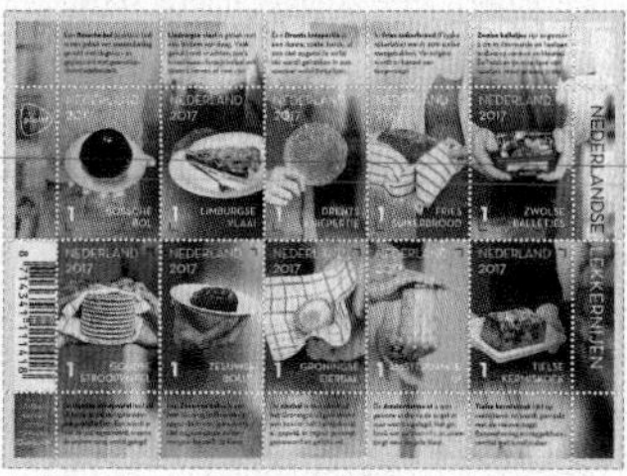


Foods — A734

Designs: Nos. 1550a, 1550k, Bossche bol. Nos. 1550b, 1550l, Limburgse vlaai. Nos. 1550c, 1550m, Drents kniepertie. Nos. 1550d, 1550n, Fries suikerbrood. Nos. 1550e, 1550o, Zwolse balletjes. Nos. 1550f, 1550p, Goudse stroopwafel. Nos. 1550g, 1550q, Zeeuwse bolus. Nos. 1550h, 1550r, Groningse eierbal. Nos. 1550i, 1550s, Amsterdamse ui. Nos. 1550j, 1550t, Tielse kermiskoek.

**2017, June 19 Litho. *Perf. 14½***

**1550** A734 Sheet of 10 17.50 17.50
*a.-j.* 1 Any single 1.75 1.75
*k.-t.* 1 Any single, perf. 12¾x13¼ 3.00 3.00
*u.* Booklet pane of 2, #1550k, 1550p 6.00 —
*v.* Booklet pane of 2, #1550l, 1550q 6.00 —
*w.* Booklet pane of 2, #1550m, 1550r 6.00 —
*x.* Booklet pane of 2, #1550n, 1550s 6.00 —
*y.* Booklet pane of 2, #1550o, 1550t 6.00 —
Complete booklet, #1550u, 1550v, 1550w, 1550x, 1550y 30.00

On day of issue, Nos. 1550a-1550j each sold for 78c. Complete booklet sold for €12.45.

Northern Gannet A735

Tub Gurnard A736

Brown Crab — A737

Bladder Wrack and Seaweed A738

Spotted Ray Egg Case and Shells A739

**2017, July 17 Litho. *Perf. 13¼x12¾***

**1551** Vert. strip of 5 9.50 9.50
*a.* A735 1 multi 1.90 1.90
*b.* A736 1 multi 1.90 1.90
*c.* A737 1 multi 1.90 1.90
*d.* A738 1 multi 1.90 1.90
*e.* A739 1 multi 1.90 1.90
*f.* A735 1 multi, perf. 14½ 3.00 3.00
*g.* A736 1 multi, perf. 14½ 3.00 3.00
*h.* A737 1 multi, perf. 14½ 3.00 3.00
*i.* A738 1 multi, perf. 14½ 3.00 3.00
*j.* A739 1 multi, perf. 14½ 3.00 3.00
*k.* Booklet pane of 2 #1551f 6.00 —
*l.* Booklet pane of 2 #1551g 6.00 —
*m.* Booklet pane of 2 #1551h 6.00 —
*n.* Booklet pane of 2 #1551i 6.00 —

*o.* Booklet pane of 2 #1551j 6.00 —
Complete booklet, #1551k, 1551l, 1551m, 1551n, 1551o 30.00

On day of issue, Nos. 1551a-1551j each sold for 78c. Complete booklet sold for €12.45.

Miniature Sheet

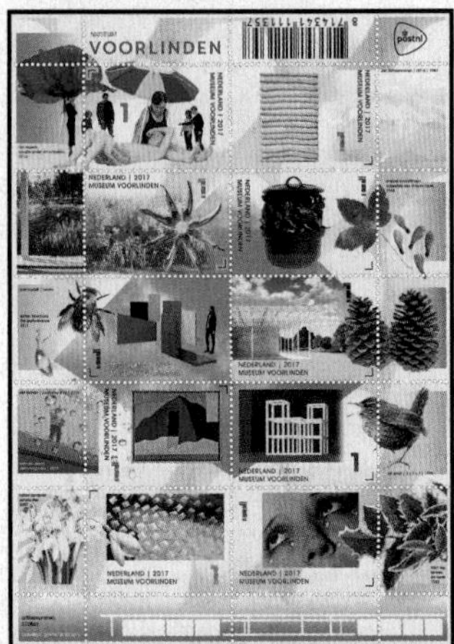

Art in Voorlinden Museum — A740

No. 1552: a, Couple Under an Umbrella, by Ron Mueck, and museum visitors. b, R81-4, by Jan Schoonhoeven. c, Flowers and Voorlinden Museum landscaping, by Piet Oudolf. d, Casserole des Moules Noire, by Marcel Broodthaers, and leaf. e, The Performance, by Esther Tielemans. f, Voorlinden Museum and pine cone. g, California #10, by Etel Adnan. h, 2x7x7 by Sol Lewitt, and bird. i, Untitled, by Robert Zandvliet, and flower. j, Larmes de Verre, by Man Ray, and leaf.

**2017, July 17 Litho. *Perf. 14½***

**1552** A740 Sheet of 10 19.00 19.00
*a.-j.* 1 Any single 1.90 1.90

On day of issue, Nos. 1552a-1552j each sold for 78c.

Souvenir Sheet

Multilateral Philatelic Exhibition, s'Hertogenbosch — A741

No. 1553: a, Zoete Lieve Gerritje Statue, St. John's Cathedral, s'Hertogenbosch. b, Duke's Palace, Remembrance Monument, Luxembourg Philharmonid, Luxembourg, Church of the Assumption, Ljubljana, Slovenia.

**2017, Aug. 25 Litho. *Perf. 14½***

**1553** A741 Sheet of 2 5.25 5.25
*a.* 1 multi 1.90 1.90
*b.* 1 Internationaal multi 3.25 3.25

On day of issue, No. 1553a sold for 78c, and No. 1553b sold for €1.33. A souvenir sheet containing No. 1553a and Luxembourg No. 1470a was given to standing order customers of Luxembourg Post, and this sheet was sold together with Netherlands No. 1553 and Luxembourg No. 1470 for €15.

Miniature Sheet

Buildings Reconstructed After World War II — A742

No. 1554: a, Velser Tunnel Ventilation Building, Velsen, 1957 (turquoise green panel at center right). b, Purfina gas station, Arnhem, 1957 (turquoise green panel at center left). c, Industriegebouw, Rotterdam, 1953, (yellow green panel at center left). d, Van Leer Drum Factory, Amstelveen, 1958 (yellow green panel at center right). e, Soesterkwartier residential district, Amersfoort, 1957 (pink panel at center right). f, Gemeenteflat (tree in front of building), Maastricht, 1950 (pink panel at center right). g, De Ploeg Weaving Mill, Bergeijk, 1958 (pale dull green panel at center right). h, Blast furnace at steel factory, IJmuiden, 1951 (pale dull green panel at center left). i, Faculty of Geodesy building, Wageningen, 1953 (orange brown panel at center left). j, Second Liberal Christian Lyceum, The Hague, 1954 (orange brown panel at center right).

***Perf. 13¼x12¾***

**2017, Sept. 11 Litho.**

**1554** A742 Sheet of 10 19.00 19.00
*a.-j.* 1 Any single 1.90 1.90

On day of issue, Nos. 1554a-1554j each sold for 78c.

Miniature Sheet

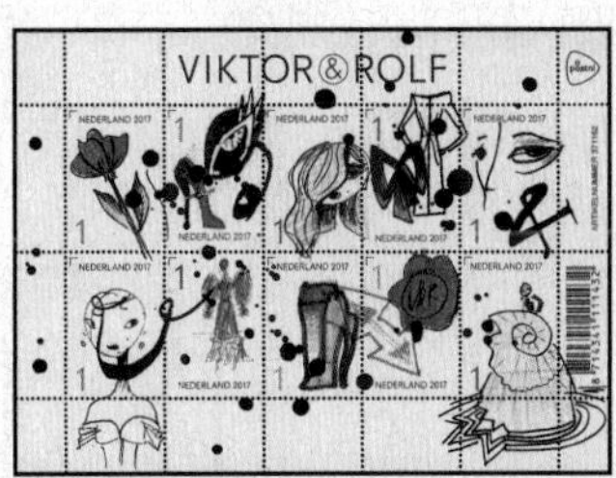

Viktor & Rolf, Fashion Designers, 25th Anniv. — A743

No. 1555 — Ink spots and drawings of: a, Flower. b, Red high-heeled shoe and eye. c, Woman's face covered by long hair. d, Dress and bow. e, Woman's face and ampersand. f, Woman's head and black curved line. g, Faceless woman wearing dress with puffed shoulders. h, Tan high-heeled shoe. i, Arrows and "V&R". j, Woman with yellow green and pink dress.

**2017, Sept. 11 Litho. *Perf. 14½***

**1555** A743 Sheet of 10 19.00 19.00
*a.-j.* 1 Any single 1.90 1.90

On day of issue, Nos. 1555a-1555j each sold for 78c.

Wood Engraving and Portrait of Princess Wilhelmina Used on 1891-96 Stamps — A744

**2017, Oct. 20 Litho. *Perf. 13¼x14***

**1556** A744 1 multi 1.90 1.90
*a.* Booklet pane of 2 6.00 6.00
Complete booklet, 5 #1556a 30.00

Stamp Day. On day of issue, No. 1556 sold for 78c. Stamps are printed tete-beche on No. 1556a. Complete booklet sold for €12.45 and contains five examples of No. 1556a, each with a different pane margin.

George Michael (1963-2016), Rock Musician — A745

String of Christmas Lights — A746

Candle Flame — A747

Woman and Stars — A748

Fork, G Clef and Musical Notes — A749

Christmas Bell and Birds — A750

Turkey A751

Stylized Christmas Tree, Hands and Accordion A752

Winter Painting and People Holding Champagne Flutes — A753

Christmas Cake — A754

***Serpentine Die Cut 11***

**2017, Nov. 20 Photo.**

**Self-Adhesive**

| | | | |
|---|---|---|---|
| **1557** | Block of 10 | 17.50 | |
| *a.* | A745 (73c) multi | 1.75 | 1.75 |
| *b.* | A746 (73c) multi | 1.75 | 1.75 |
| *c.* | A747 (73c) multi | 1.75 | 1.75 |
| *d.* | A748 (73c) multi | 1.75 | 1.75 |
| *e.* | A749 (73c) multi | 1.75 | 1.75 |
| *f.* | A750 (73c) multi | 1.75 | 1.75 |
| *g.* | A751 (73c) multi | 1.75 | 1.75 |
| *h.* | A752 (73c) multi | 1.75 | 1.75 |
| *i.* | A753 (73c) multi | 1.75 | 1.75 |
| *j.* | A754 (73c) multi | 1.75 | 1.75 |

Printed in sheets of 20 containing two each of Nos. 1557a-1557j.

## SEMI-POSTAL STAMPS

Design Symbolical of the Four Chief Means for Combating Tuberculosis: Light, Water, Air and Food — SP1

***Perf. 12½***

**1906, Dec. 21 Typo. Unwmk.**

| | | | | |
|---|---|---|---|---|
| **B1** | SP1 | 1c (+1c) rose red | 20.00 | 11.00 |
| **B2** | SP1 | 3c (+3c) pale ol grn | 30.00 | 26.00 |
| **B3** | SP1 | 5c (+5c) gray | 30.00 | 15.00 |
| | | *Nos. B1-B3 (3)* | 80.00 | *52.00* |
| | | Set, never hinged | 475.00 | |

Surtax aided the Society for the Prevention of Tuberculosis.

Nos. B1-B3 canceled-to-order "AMSTERDAM 31.07 10-12 N," sell at $3 a set.

Symbolical of Charity SP2

SP3

**1923, Dec. 15 *Perf. 11½***

| | | | | |
|---|---|---|---|---|
| **B4** | SP2 | 2c (+5c) vio bl | 17.00 | 17.00 |
| **B5** | SP3 | 10c (+5c) org red | 17.00 | 17.00 |
| | | Set, never hinged | 85.00 | |

The surtax was for the benefit of charity.

Allegory, Charity Protecting Child — SP6

**1924, Dec. 15 Photo. *Perf. 12½***

| | | | | |
|---|---|---|---|---|
| **B6** | SP6 | 2c (+2c) emer | 1.80 | 1.80 |
| **B7** | SP6 | 7½c (+3½c) dk brn | 6.75 | 8.00 |
| **B8** | SP6 | 10c (+2½c) vermilion | 4.00 | 1.80 |
| | | *Nos. B6-B8 (3)* | 12.55 | 11.60 |
| | | Set, never hinged | 26.00 | |

These stamps were sold at a premium over face value for the benefit of Child Welfare Societies.

Arms of North Brabant SP7

Arms of Gelderland SP8

Arms of South Holland — SP9

**1925, Dec. 17 *Perf. 12½***

| | | | | |
|---|---|---|---|---|
| **B9** | SP7 | 2c (+2c) grn & org | .85 | .75 |
| **B10** | SP8 | 7½c (+3½c) vio & bl | 4.25 | 4.50 |
| **B11** | SP9 | 10c (+2½c) red & org | 3.50 | .45 |
| | | *Nos. B9-B11 (3)* | 8.60 | 5.70 |
| | | Set, never hinged | 19.00 | |

Surtax went to Child Welfare Societies.

**Syncopated Perfs., Type A**

*B9a* SP7 2c (+2c) 19.00 22.00
*B10a* SP8 7½c (+3½c) 37.50 37.50
*B11a* SP9 10c (+2½c) 65.00 52.50
*Nos. B9a-B11a (3)* 121.50 112.00
Set, never hinged 300.00

Arms of Utrecht SP10

Arms of Zeeland SP11

Arms of North Holland SP12

Arms of Friesland SP13

**1926, Dec. 1 Wmk. 202 *Perf. 12½***

**B12** SP10 2c (+2c) sil & red .50 .40
**B13** SP11 5c (+3c) grn & gray bl 1.40 .75
**B14** SP12 10c (+3c) red & gold 2.10 .35
**B15** SP13 15c (+3c) ultra & yel 5.50 6.00
*Nos. B12-B15 (4)* 9.50 7.50
Set, never hinged 30.00

The surtax on these stamps was devoted to Child Welfare Societies.

**Syncopated Perfs., Type A**

*B12a* SP10 2c (+2c) 5.25 5.25
*B13a* SP11 5c (+3c) 8.25 8.25
*B14a* SP12 10c (+3c) 15.00 8.75
*B15a* SP13 15c (+3c) 16.50 16.50
*Nos. B12a-B15a (4)* 45.00 38.75
Set, never hinged 125.00

King William III — SP14

Red Cross and Doves — SP18

Designs: 3c, Queen Emma. 5c, Prince Consort Henry. 7½c, Queen Wilhelmina.

***Perf. 11½, 11½x12 B***

**1927, June Photo. Unwmk.**

**B16** SP14 2c (+2c) scar 3.25 2.75

**Engr.**

**B17** SP14 3c (+2c) dp grn 6.75 *7.50*
**B18** SP14 5c (+3c) slate bl 1.35 1.25

**Photo.**

**B19** SP14 7½c (+3½c) ultra 4.25 1.60
**B20** SP18 15c (+5c) ultra & red 9.25 8.50
*Nos. B16-B20 (5)* 24.85 21.60
Set, never hinged 65.00

60th anniversary of the Netherlands Red Cross Society. The surtaxes in parentheses were for the benefit of the Society.

Arms of Drenthe SP19

Arms of Groningen SP20

Arms of Limburg SP21

Arms of Overijssel SP22

**1927, Dec. 15 Wmk. 202 *Perf. 12½***

**B21** SP19 2c (+2c) dp rose & vio .35 .30
**B22** SP20 5c (+3c) ol grn & yel 1.50 1.25
**B23** SP21 7½c (+3½c) red & blk 3.25 .35
**B24** SP22 15c (+3c) ultra & org brn 4.75 4.25
*Nos. B21-B24 (4)* 9.85 6.15
Set, never hinged 31.00

The surtax on these stamps was for the benefit of Child Welfare Societies.

**Syncopated Perfs., Type A**

*B21a* SP19 2c (+2c) 2.25 2.25
*B22a* SP20 5c (+3c) 4.00 4.00
*B23a* SP21 7½c (+3½c) 6.00 6.00
*B24a* SP22 15c (+3c) 11.00 7.75
*Nos. B21a-B24a (4)* 23.25 20.00
Set, never hinged 75.00

Rowing — SP23

Fencing — SP24

Soccer SP25

Yachting SP26

Putting the Shot SP27

Running SP28

Riding SP29

Boxing SP30

***Perf. 11½, 12, 11½x12, 12x11½***

**1928, Mar. 27 Litho.**

**B25** SP23 1½c (+1c) dk grn 3.00 3.00
**B26** SP24 2c (+1c) red vio 3.00 3.75
**B27** SP25 3c (+1c) green 4.50 4.50
**B28** SP26 5c (+1c) lt bl 3.75 2.25
**B29** SP27 7½c (+2½c) org 3.75 2.25
**B30** SP28 10c (+2c) scarlet 6.75 5.25
**B31** SP29 15c (+2c) dk bl 9.00 5.25
**B32** SP30 30c (+3c) dk brn 19.00 19.00
*Nos. B25-B32 (8)* 52.75 45.25
Set, never hinged 170.00

The surtax on these stamps was used to help defray the expenses of the Olympic Games of 1928.

Jean Pierre Minckelers — SP31

5c, Hermann Boerhaave. 7½c, Hendrik Antoon Lorentz. 12½c, Christian Huygens.

**1928, Dec. 10 Photo. *Perf. 12x12½***

**B33** SP31 1½c (+1½c) vio .55 .40
**B34** SP31 5c (+3c) grn 1.75 .60

***Perf. 12***

**B35** SP31 7½c (+2½c) ver 3.50 .25
*a.* Perf. 12x12½ 4.75 .50
**B36** SP31 12½c (+3½c) ultra 9.75 7.50
*a.* Perf. 12x12½ 77.50 15.00
*Nos. B33-B36 (4)* 15.55 8.75
Set, never hinged 45.00

The surtax on these stamps was for the benefit of Child Welfare Societies.

Child on Dolphin — SP35

**1929, Dec. 10 Litho. *Perf. 12½***

**B37** SP35 1½c (+1½c) gray 1.75 .40
**B38** SP35 5c (+3c) blue grn 2.50 .75
**B39** SP35 6c (+4c) scarlet 2.00 .35
**B40** SP35 12½c (+3½c) dk bl 14.00 9.75
*Nos. B37-B40 (4)* 20.25 11.25
Set, never hinged 72.50

Surtax for child welfare.

**Syncopated Perfs., Type B**

*B37a* SP35 1½c (+1½c) 3.75 3.00
*B38a* SP35 5c (+3c) 4.50 4.00
*B39a* SP35 6c (+4c) 3.75 3.00
*B40a* SP35 12½c (+3½c) 18.00 14.00
*Nos. B37a-B40a (4)* 30.00 24.00
Set, never hinged 125.00

Rembrandt and His "Cloth Merchants of Amsterdam" SP36

***Perf. 11½***

**1930, Feb. 15 Engr. Unwmk.**

**B41** SP36 5c (+5c) bl grn 6.75 6.00
**B42** SP36 6c (+5c) gray blk 5.25 3.50
**B43** SP36 12½c (+5c) dp bl 9.00 8.00
*Nos. B41-B43 (3)* 21.00 17.50
Set, never hinged 62.50

Surtax for the benefit of the Rembrandt Soc.

"Spring" — SP37

5c, Summer. 6c, Autumn. 12½c, Winter.

**1930, Dec. 10 *Perf. 12½***

**B44** SP37 1½c (+1½c) lt red 1.75 .45
**B45** SP37 5c (+3c) gray grn 2.25 .60
**B46** SP37 6c (+4c) claret 1.75 .45
**B47** SP37 12½c (+3½c) lt ultra 16.00 8.50
*Nos. B44-B47 (4)* 21.75 10.00
Set, never hinged 62.50

Surtax was for Child Welfare work.

Syncopated Perfs., Type C

*B44a* SP37 1½c (+1½c) 4.00 3.75
*B45a* SP37 5c (+3c) 4.75 4.50
*B46a* SP37 6c (+4c) 4.00 3.75
*B47a* SP37 12½c (+3½c) 19.00 14.00
*Nos. B44a-B47a (4)* 31.75 26.00
Set, never hinged 85.00

Stained Glass Window and Detail of Repair Method — SP41

6c, Gouda Church and repair of window frame.

**Wmk. 202**

**1931, Oct. 1 Photo. *Perf. 12½***

**B48** SP41 1½c (+1½c) bl grn 17.00 15.00
**B49** SP41 6c (+4c) car rose 20.00 17.00
Set, never hinged 80.00

Deaf Mute Learning Lip Reading — SP43

Designs: 5c, Mentally retarded child. 6c, Blind girl learning to read Braille. 12½c, Child victim of malnutrition.

**1931, Dec. 10 *Perf. 12½***

**B50** SP43 1½c (+1½c) ver & ultra 1.90 1.25
**B51** SP43 5c (+3c) Prus bl & vio 5.25 1.25
**B52** SP43 6c (+4c) vio & grn 5.25 1.25
**B53** SP43 12½c (+3½c) ultra & dp org 29.00 21.00
*Nos. B50-B53 (4)* 41.40 24.75
Set, never hinged 125.00

The surtax was for Child Welfare work.

**Syncopated Perfs., Type C**

*B50a* SP43 1½c (+1½c) 3.75 4.00
*B51a* SP43 5c (+3c) 7.50 7.75
*B52a* SP43 6c (+4c) 7.50 7.75
*B53a* SP43 12½c (+3½c) 27.00 19.50
*Nos. B50a-B53a (4)* 45.75 39.00
Set, never hinged 150.00

Drawbridge — SP47

Designs: 2½c, Windmill and Dikes. 6c, Council House, Zierikzee. 12½c, Flower fields.

**1932, May 23 *Perf. 12½***

**B54** SP47 2½c (+1½c) turq grn & blk 7.00 5.00
**B55** SP47 6c (+4c) gray blk & blk 10.50 5.00
**B56** SP47 7½c (+3½c) brt red & blk 30.00 12.50
**B57** SP47 12½c (+2½c) ultra & blk 32.50 19.00
*Nos. B54-B57 (4)* 80.00 41.50
Set, never hinged 225.00

The surtax was for the benefit of the National Tourist Association.

Furze and Boy — SP51

Designs (Heads of children and flowers typifying the seasons): 5c, Cornflower. 6c, Sunflower. 12½c, Christmas rose.

**1932, Dec. 10 *Perf. 12½***

**B58** SP51 1½c (+1½c) brn & yel 2.10 .45
**B59** SP51 5c (+3c) red org & ultra 2.75 .75
**B60** SP51 6c (+4c) dk grn & ocher 2.10 .35
**B61** SP51 12½c (+3½c) ocher & ultra 27.50 18.00
*Nos. B58-B61 (4)* 34.45 19.55
Set, never hinged 110.00

The surtax aided Child Welfare Societies.

**Syncopated Perfs., Type C**

*B58a* SP51 1½c (+1½c) 3.50 3.50
*B59a* SP51 5c (+3c) 4.25 4.25
*B60a* SP51 6c (+4c) 4.25 4.25
*B61a* SP51 12½c (+3½c) 32.50 20.00
*Nos. B58a-B61a (4)* 44.50 32.00
Set, never hinged 135.00

Monument at Den Helder — SP55

The "Hope," A Church and Hospital Ship — SP56

Lifeboat in a Storm — SP57

Dutch Sailor and Sailors' Home — SP58

***1933, June 10*** ***Perf. 14½x13½***

| | | | | |
|---|---|---|---|---|
| **B62** | SP55 | 1½c (+1½c) dp red | 3.50 | 2.60 |
| **B63** | SP56 | 5c (+3c) bl grn & red org | 10.50 | 4.25 |
| **B64** | SP57 | 6c (+4c) dp grn | 16.00 | 3.25 |
| **B65** | SP58 | 12½c (+3½c) ultra | 24.00 | 16.00 |
| | | *Nos. B62-B65 (4)* | 54.00 | 26.10 |
| | | Set, never hinged | 135.00 | |

The surtax was for the aid of Sailors' Homes.

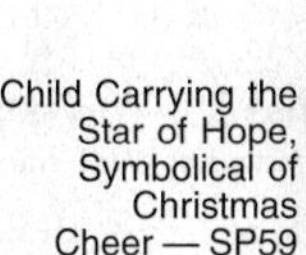

Child Carrying the Star of Hope, Symbolical of Christmas Cheer — SP59

**1933, Dec. 11** ***Perf. 12½***

| | | | | |
|---|---|---|---|---|
| **B66** | SP59 | 1½c (+1½c) sl & org brn | 1.50 | .55 |
| **B67** | SP59 | 5c (+3c) dk brn & ocher | 2.00 | .65 |
| **B68** | SP59 | 6c (+4c) bl grn & gold | 2.50 | .55 |
| **B69** | SP59 | 12½c (+3½c) dk bl & sil | 25.00 | 18.00 |
| | | *Nos. B66-B69 (4)* | 31.00 | 19.75 |
| | | Set, never hinged | 100.00 | |

The surtax aided Child Welfare Societies.

**Syncopated Perfs., Type C**

| | | | | |
|---|---|---|---|---|
| *B66a* | SP59 | 1½c (+1½c) | 1.90 | .80 |
| *B67a* | SP59 | 5c (+3c) | 2.60 | .90 |
| *B68a* | SP59 | 6c (+4c) | 3.25 | .80 |
| *B69a* | SP59 | 12½c (+3½c) | 27.50 | 24.50 |
| | | *Nos. B66a-B69a (4)* | 35.25 | 27.00 |
| | | Set, never hinged | 130.00 | |

Queen Wilhelmina SP60

Princess Juliana SP61

***Perf. 12½***

**1934, Apr. 28** **Engr.** **Unwmk.**

| | | | | |
|---|---|---|---|---|
| **B70** | SP60 | 5c (+4c) dk vio | 11.50 | 3.00 |
| **B71** | SP61 | 6c (+5c) blue | 10.50 | 3.75 |
| | | Set, never hinged | 55.00 | |

The surtax was for the benefit of the Anti-Depression Committee.

Dowager Queen Emma — SP62

**1934, Oct. 1** ***Perf. 13x14***

| | | | | |
|---|---|---|---|---|
| **B72** | SP62 | 6c (+2c) blue | 11.50 | 1.40 |
| | | Never hinged | 28.00 | |

Surtax for the Fight Tuberculosis Society.

Poor Child — SP63

***Perf. 13½x13***

**1934, Dec. 10** **Photo.** **Wmk. 202**

| | | | | |
|---|---|---|---|---|
| **B73** | SP63 | 1½c (+1½c) olive | 1.40 | .45 |
| **B74** | SP63 | 5c (+3c) rose red | 2.40 | 1.00 |
| **B75** | SP63 | 6c (+4c) bl grn | 2.40 | .25 |
| **B76** | SP63 | 12½c (+3½c) ultra | 22.50 | 16.00 |
| | | *Nos. B73-B76 (4)* | 28.70 | 17.70 |
| | | Set, never hinged | 100.00 | |

The surtax aided child welfare.

Henri D. Guyot SP64

A. J. M. Diepenbrock SP65

F. C. Donders SP66

J. P. Sweelinck SP67

***Perf. 12½ x 12, 12***

**1935, June 17** **Engr.** **Unwmk.**

| | | | | |
|---|---|---|---|---|
| **B77** | SP64 | 1½c (+1½c) dk car | 1.50 | 1.50 |
| **B78** | SP65 | 5c (+3c) blk brn | 4.00 | 4.00 |
| **B79** | SP66 | 6c (+4c) myr grn | 4.50 | .50 |
| **B80** | SP67 | 12½c (+3½c) dp bl | 24.00 | 6.00 |
| | | *Nos. B77-B80 (4)* | 34.00 | 12.00 |
| | | Set, never hinged | 100.00 | |

Surtax for social and cultural projects.

Netherlands Map, DC-3 Planes' Shadows SP68

***Perf. 14x13***

**1935, Oct. 16** **Photo.** **Wmk. 202**

| | | | | |
|---|---|---|---|---|
| **B81** | SP68 | 6c (+4c) brn | 24.00 | 7.50 |

Surtax for Natl. Aviation.

Girl Picking Apple — SP69

**1935, Dec. 4** ***Perf. 14½x13½***

| | | | | |
|---|---|---|---|---|
| **B82** | SP69 | 1½c (+1½c) crim | .50 | .55 |
| **B83** | SP69 | 5c (+3c) dk yel grn | 1.40 | 1.05 |
| **B84** | SP69 | 6c (+4c) blk brn | 1.25 | .55 |
| **B85** | SP69 | 12½c (+3½c) ultra | 20.00 | 7.50 |
| | | *Nos. B82-B85 (4)* | 23.15 | 9.65 |
| | | Set, never hinged | 110.00 | |

The surtax aided child welfare.

H. Kamerlingh Onnes — SP70

Dr. A. S. Talma — SP71

Msgr. H. J. A. M. Schaepman SP72

Desiderius Erasmus SP73

***Perf. 12½x12***

**1936, May 1** **Engr.** **Unwmk.**

| | | | | |
|---|---|---|---|---|
| **B86** | SP70 | 1½c (+1½c) brn blk | .65 | .75 |
| **B87** | SP71 | 5c (+3c) dl grn | 4.00 | *3.25* |
| **B88** | SP72 | 6c (+4c) dk red | 3.25 | .50 |
| **B89** | SP73 | 12½c (+3½c) dl bl | 11.50 | 2.50 |
| | | *Nos. B86-B89 (4)* | 19.40 | 7.00 |
| | | Set, never hinged | 67.50 | |

Surtax for social and cultural projects.

Cherub — SP74

***Perf. 14½x13½***

**1936, Dec. 1** **Photo.** **Wmk. 202**

| | | | | |
|---|---|---|---|---|
| **B90** | SP74 | 1½c (+1½c) lil gray | .50 | .30 |
| **B91** | SP74 | 5c (+3c) turq grn | 2.00 | .75 |
| **B92** | SP74 | 6c (+4c) dp red brn | 1.90 | .25 |
| **B93** | SP74 | 12½c (+3½c) ind | 14.00 | 4.75 |
| | | *Nos. B90-B93 (4)* | 18.40 | 6.05 |
| | | Set, never hinged | 52.50 | |

The surtax aided child welfare.

Jacob Maris — SP75

Franciscus de la Boe Sylvius — SP76

Joost van den Vondel SP77

Anthony van Leeuwenhoek SP78

***Perf. 12½x12***

**1937, June 1** **Engr.** **Unwmk.**

| | | | | |
|---|---|---|---|---|
| **B94** | SP75 | 1½c (+1½c) blk brn | .50 | .40 |
| **B95** | SP76 | 5c (+3c) dl grn | 4.00 | 2.75 |
| **B96** | SP77 | 6c (+4c) brn vio | 1.00 | .25 |
| **B97** | SP78 | 12½c (+3½c) dl bl | 7.00 | 1.25 |
| | | *Nos. B94-B97 (4)* | 12.50 | 4.65 |
| | | Set, never hinged | 40.00 | |

Surtax for social and cultural projects.

"The Laughing Child" after Frans Hals — SP79

***Perf. 14½x13½***

**1937, Dec. 1** **Photo.** **Wmk. 202**

| | | | | |
|---|---|---|---|---|
| **B98** | SP79 | 1½c (+1½c) blk | .25 | .25 |
| **B99** | SP79 | 3c (+2c) grn | 1.50 | 1.00 |
| **B100** | SP79 | 4c (+2c) hn brn | .60 | .45 |
| **B101** | SP79 | 5c (+3c) bl grn | .50 | .25 |
| **B102** | SP79 | 12½c (+3½c) dk bl | 7.25 | 1.40 |
| | | *Nos. B98-B102 (5)* | 10.10 | 3.35 |
| | | Set, never hinged | 35.00 | |

The surtax aided child welfare.

Marnix van Sint Aldegonde SP80

Otto Gerhard Heldring SP81

Maria Tesselschade SP82

Hermann Boerhaave SP84

Harmenszoon Rembrandt van Rijn — SP83

***Perf. 12½x12***

**1938, May 16** **Engr.** **Unwmk.**

| | | | | |
|---|---|---|---|---|
| **B103** | SP80 | 1½c (+1½c) sep | .30 | .35 |
| **B104** | SP81 | 3c (+2c) dk grn | .55 | .35 |
| **B105** | SP82 | 4c (+2c) rose lake | 1.75 | 1.75 |
| **B106** | SP83 | 5c (+3c) dk sl grn | 2.25 | .35 |
| **B107** | SP84 | 12½c (+3½c) dl bl | 7.75 | 1.00 |
| | | *Nos. B103-B107 (5)* | 12.60 | 3.80 |
| | | Set, never hinged | 34.00 | |

The surtax was for the benefit of cultural and social relief.

Child with Flowers, Bird and Fish — SP85

***Perf. 14½x13½***

**1938, Dec. 1** **Photo.** **Wmk. 202**

| | | | | |
|---|---|---|---|---|
| **B108** | SP85 | 1½c (+1½c) blk | .25 | .25 |
| **B109** | SP85 | 3c (+2c) mar | .30 | .25 |
| **B110** | SP85 | 4c (+2c) dk bl grn | .60 | .80 |

**B111** SP85 5c (+3c) hn brn .25 .25
**B112** SP85 12½c (+3½c) dp bl 9.00 1.75
*Nos. B108-B112 (5)* 10.40 3.30
Set, never hinged 35.00

The surtax aided child welfare.

Matthijs Maris — SP86

Anton Mauve — SP87

Gerard van Swieten SP88

Nikolaas Beets SP89

Peter Stuyvesant — SP90

***Perf. 12½x12***

**1939, May 1 Engr. Unwmk.**
**B113** SP86 1½c (+1½c) sepia .60 .60
**B114** SP87 2½c (+2½c) gray grn 3.00 2.75
**B115** SP88 3c (+3c) ver .80 1.00
**B116** SP89 5c (+3c) dk sl grn 2.00 .30
**B117** SP90 12½c (+3½c) indigo 5.00 .85
*Nos. B113-B117 (5)* 11.40 5.50
Set, never hinged 40.00

The surtax was for the benefit of cultural and social relief.

Child Carrying Cornucopia — SP91

***Perf. 14½x13½***

**1939, Dec. 1 Photo. Wmk. 202**
**B118** SP91 1½c (+1½c) blk .25 .25
**B119** SP91 2½c (+2½c) dk ol grn 3.75 2.00
**B120** SP91 3c (+3c) hn brn .40 .25
**B121** SP91 5c (+3c) dk grn .85 .25
**B122** SP91 12½c (+3½c) dk bl 4.00 1.00
*Nos. B118-B122 (5)* 9.25 3.75
Set, never hinged 40.00

The surtax was used for destitute children.

**Catalogue values for unused stamps in this section, from this point to the end of the section, are for Never Hinged items.**

Vincent van Gogh SP92

E. J. Potgieter SP93

Petrus Camper SP94

Jan Steen SP95

Joseph Scaliger — SP96

***Perf. 12½x12***

**1940, May 11 Engr. Wmk. 202**
**B123** SP92 1½c +1½c brn blk 4.00 .35
**B124** SP93 2½c +2½c dk grn 7.00 .65
**B125** SP94 3c +3c car 4.00 .65
**B126** SP95 5c +3c dp grn 10.00 .30
*a.* Booklet pane of 4 140.00
**B127** SP96 12½c +3½c dp bl 8.00 1.10

Surtax for social and cultural projects.

Type of 1940 Surcharged in Black

**1940, Sept. 7**
**B128** SP95 7½c +2½c on 5c +3c dk red .80 .30
*Nos. B123-B128 (6)* 33.80 3.35

Child with Flowers and Doll — SP97

***Perf. 14½x13½***

**1940, Dec. 2 Photo. Wmk. 202**
**B129** SP97 1½c +1½c dl bl gray 1.00 .25
**B130** SP97 2½c +2½c dp ol 2.75 .55
**B131** SP97 4c +3c royal bl 3.00 .60
**B132** SP97 5c +3c dk bl grn 3.00 .25
**B133** SP97 7½c +3½c hn 1.40 .25
*Nos. B129-B133 (5)* 11.15 1.90

The surtax was used for destitute children.

Dr. Antonius Mathijsen SP98

Dr. Jan Ingenhousz SP99

Aagje Deken SP100

Johannes Bosboom SP101

A. C. W. Staring — SP102

***Perf. 12½x12***

**1941, May 29 Engr. Wmk. 202**
**B134** SP98 1½c +1½c blk brn .65 .25
**B135** SP99 2½c +2½c dk sl grn .65 .25
**B136** SP100 4c +3c red .65 .25
**B137** SP101 5c +3c slate grn .65 .25
**B138** SP102 7½c +3½c rose vio .65 .25
*Nos. B134-B138 (5)* 3.25 1.25

The surtax was for cultural and social relief.

Rembrandt's Painting of Titus, His Son — SP103

***Perf. 14½x13½***

**1941, Dec. 1 Photo. Wmk. 202**
**B139** SP103 1½c +1½c vio blk .35 .25
**B140** SP103 2½c +2½c dk ol .35 .25
**B141** SP103 4c +3c royal blue .35 .25
**B142** SP103 5c +3c dp grn .35 .25
**B143** SP103 7½c +3½c dp henna brn .35 .25
*Nos. B139-B143 (5)* 1.75 1.25

The surtax aided child welfare.

Legionary
SP104 SP105

**1942, Nov. 1 *Perf. 12½x12, 12x12½***
**B144** SP104 7½c +2½c dk red .75 .50
*a.* Sheet of 10 100.00 100.00
**B145** SP105 12½c +87½c ultra 5.50 6.25
*a.* Sheet of 4 75.00 80.00

The surtax aided the Netherlands Legion.
#B144a, B145a measure 155x111mm and 94x94mm respectively.

19th Century Mail Cart — SP108

**1943, Oct. 9 Unwmk. *Perf. 12x12½***
**B148** SP108 7½c +7½c henna brn .25 .25

Issued to commemorate Stamp Day.

Child and House — SP109

#B150, Mother & Child. #B151, Mother $ Children. #B152, Child Carrying Sheaf of Wheat. #B153, Mother & Children, diff.

***Perf. 12½x12***

**1944, Mar. 6 Wmk. 202**
**B149** SP109 1½c +3½c dl blk .25 .25
**B150** SP109 4c +3½ rose lake .25 .25
**B151** SP109 5c +5c dk bl grn .25 .25
**B152** SP109 7½c +7½c dp hn brn .25 .25
**B153** SP109 10c +40c royal blue .25 .25
*Nos. B149-B153 (5)* 1.25 1.25

The surtax aided National Social Service and winter relief.

Child — SP114

**1945, Dec. 1 Photo. *Perf. 14½x13½***
**B154** SP114 1½c +2½c gray .25 .25
**B155** SP114 2½c +3½c dk bl grn .25 .25
**B156** SP114 5c +5c brn red .25 .25
**B157** SP114 7½c +4½c red .25 .25
**B158** SP114 12½c +5½c brt bl .25 .25
*Nos. B154-B158 (5)* 1.25 1.25

The surtax was for Child Welfare.

Fortuna — SP115

***Perf. 12½x12***

**1946, May 1 Engr. Unwmk.**
**B159** SP115 1½c +3½c brn blk .40 .30
**B160** SP115 2½c +5c dl grn .45 .45
**B161** SP115 5c +10c dk vio .45 .45
**B162** SP115 7½c +15c car lake .40 .30
**B163** SP115 12½c +37½c dk bl .75 .55
*Nos. B159-B163 (5)* 2.45 2.05

The surtax was for victims of World War II.

Princess Irene — SP116

Designs: Nos. B165, B167, Princess Margriet. Nos. B168-B169, Princess Beatrix.

**1946, Sept. 16**
**B164** SP116 1½c +1½c blk brn .40 .40
**B165** SP116 2½c +1½c bl grn .40 .40
**B166** SP116 4c +2c magenta .50 .40
**B167** SP116 5c +2c brown .50 .40
**B168** SP116 7½c +2½c red .40 .25
**B169** SP116 12½c +7½c dk bl .40 .50
*Nos. B164-B169 (6)* 2.60 2.35

The surtax was for child welfare and anti-tuberculosis work.

Child on Merry-go-round SP119

**1946, Dec. 2 Photo. Wmk. 202**
**B170** SP119 2c +2c lil gray .35 .30
**B171** SP119 4c +2c dk grn .35 .30
**B172** SP119 7½c +2½c brt red .35 .30
**B173** SP119 10c +5c dp plum .45 .25
**B174** SP119 20c +5c dp bl .50 .45
*Nos. B170-B174 (5)* 2.00 1.60

The surtax was for child welfare.

Dr. Hendrik van Deventer SP120

Peter Cornelisz Hooft SP121

Johan de Witt SP122

Jean F. van Royen SP123

Hugo de Groot — SP124

**1947, Aug. 1 Engr. Unwmk.**

| | | | | |
|---|---|---|---|---|
| **B175** | SP120 | 2c +2c dark red | .55 | .30 |
| **B176** | SP121 | 4c +2c dk green | .90 | .40 |
| **B177** | SP122 | 7½c +2½c dk pur brn | 1.40 | .40 |
| **B178** | SP123 | 10c +5c brown | 1.40 | .25 |
| **B179** | SP124 | 20c +5c dk blue | .85 | .40 |
| | | *Nos. B175-B179 (5)* | 5.10 | 1.75 |

The surtax was for social and cultural purposes.

Children SP125

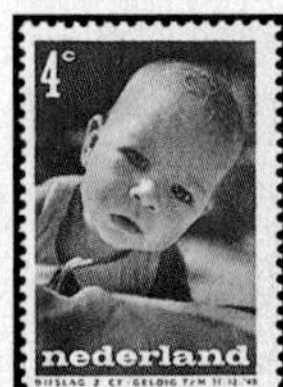
Infant SP126

**1947, Dec. 1 Photo. *Perf. 13x14***

| | | | | |
|---|---|---|---|---|
| **B180** | SP125 | 2c +2c red brn | .25 | .25 |
| **B181** | SP126 | 4c +2c bl grn | .60 | .40 |
| **B182** | SP126 | 7½c +2½c sepia | .60 | .55 |
| **B183** | SP126 | 10c +5c dk red | .80 | .25 |
| **B184** | SP125 | 20c +5c blue | .90 | .70 |
| | | *Nos. B180-B184 (5)* | 3.15 | 2.15 |

The surtax was for child welfare.

Hall of Knights, The Hague — SP127

Designs: 6c+4c, Royal Palace, Amsterdam. 10c+5c, Kneuterdyk Palace, The Hague. 20c+5c, New Church, Amsterdam.

**1948, June 17 Engr. *Perf. 13½x14***

| | | | | |
|---|---|---|---|---|
| **B185** | SP127 | 2c +2c dk brn | 1.15 | .50 |
| **B186** | SP127 | 6c +4c grn | 1.25 | .50 |
| **B187** | SP127 | 10c +5c brt red | .85 | .30 |
| **B188** | SP127 | 20c +5c deep blue | 1.25 | .70 |
| | | *Nos. B185-B188 (4)* | 4.50 | 2.00 |

The surtax was for cultural and social purposes.

Boy in Kayak — SP128

5c+3c, Swimming. 6c+4c, Sledding. 10c+5c, Swinging. 20c+8c, Figure skating.

**1948, Nov. 15 Photo. *Perf. 13x14***

| | | | | |
|---|---|---|---|---|
| **B189** | SP128 | 2c +2c yel grn | .25 | .25 |
| **B190** | SP128 | 5c +3c dk bl grn | 1.50 | .50 |
| **B191** | SP128 | 6c +4c gray | .80 | .25 |
| **B192** | SP128 | 10c +5c red | .35 | .25 |
| **B193** | SP128 | 20c +8c blue | 1.50 | .75 |
| | | *Nos. B189-B193 (5)* | 4.40 | 2.00 |

The surtax was for child welfare.

Beach Terrace SP129

Boy and Girl Hikers SP130

Campers SP131

Reaping SP132

Sailboats SP133

**1949, May 2 Wmk. 202 *Perf. 14x13***

| | | | | |
|---|---|---|---|---|
| **B194** | SP129 | 2c +2c bl & org yel | 1.10 | .25 |
| **B195** | SP130 | 5c +3c bl & yel | 1.75 | 1.00 |
| **B196** | SP131 | 6c +4c dk bl grn | 1.60 | .35 |
| **B197** | SP132 | 10c +5c bl & org yel | 1.90 | .25 |
| **B198** | SP133 | 20c +5c blue | 2.40 | 1.25 |
| | | *Nos. B194-B198 (5)* | 8.75 | 3.10 |

The surtax was for cultural and social purposes.

Hands Reaching for Sunflower — SP134

***Perf. 14½x13½***

**1949, Aug. 1 Photo. Unwmk.**

**Flower in Yellow**

| | | | | |
|---|---|---|---|---|
| **B199** | SP134 | 2c +3c gray | .95 | .25 |
| **B200** | SP134 | 6c +4c red brown | 1.50 | .30 |
| **B201** | SP134 | 10c +5c brt blue | 2.40 | .25 |
| **B202** | SP134 | 30c +10c dk brown | 5.25 | 2.40 |
| | | *Nos. B199-B202 (4)* | 10.10 | 3.20 |

The surtax was for the Red Cross and for Indonesia Relief work.

"Autumn" — SP135

5c+3c, "Summer." 6c+4c, "Spring." 10c+5c, "Winter." 20c+7c, "New Year."

**1949, Nov. 14 Engr. *Perf. 13x14***

| | | | | |
|---|---|---|---|---|
| **B203** | SP135 | 2c +3c brown | .25 | .25 |
| **B204** | SP135 | 5c +3c red | 3.50 | 1.50 |
| **B205** | SP135 | 6c +4c dull green | 2.50 | .30 |
| **B206** | SP135 | 10c +5c gray | .25 | .25 |
| **B207** | SP135 | 20c +7c blue | 3.50 | 1.50 |
| | | *Nos. B203-B207 (5)* | 10.00 | 3.80 |

The surtax was for child welfare.

Figure from PTT Monument, The Hague SP136

Grain Binder SP137

Designs: 4c+2c, Dike repairs. 5c+3c, Apartment House, Rotterdam. 10c+5c, Bridge section being towed. 20c+5c, Canal freighter.

**1950, May 2 *Perf. 12½x12, 12x12½***

| | | | | |
|---|---|---|---|---|
| **B208** | SP136 | 2c +2c dk brown | 2.10 | 1.10 |
| **B209** | SP136 | 4c +2c dk green | 6.50 | 5.75 |
| **B210** | SP136 | 5c +3c sepia | 5.50 | 4.50 |
| **B211** | SP137 | 6c +4c purple | 2.75 | .75 |
| **B212** | SP137 | 10c +5c blue gray | 3.75 | .40 |
| **B213** | SP137 | 20c +5c deep blue | 7.50 | 9.50 |
| | | *Nos. B208-B213 (6)* | 28.10 | 22.00 |

The surtax was for social and cultural works.

Church Ruins and Good Samaritan — SP138

**1950, July 17 Photo. *Perf. 12½x12***

| | | | | |
|---|---|---|---|---|
| **B214** | SP138 | 2c +2c ol brn | 4.75 | 2.40 |
| **B215** | SP138 | 5c +3c brn red | 6.25 | *7.25* |
| **B216** | SP138 | 6c +4c dp grn | 3.75 | 3.25 |
| **B217** | SP138 | 10c +5c brt lil rose | 13.50 | .80 |
| **B218** | SP138 | 20c +5c ultra | 19.00 | *24.00* |
| | | *Nos. B214-B218 (5)* | 47.25 | *37.70* |

The surtax was for the restoration of ruined churches.

Baby and Bees — SP139

Designs: 5c+3c, Boy and rooster. 6c+4c, Girl feeding birds. 10c+5c, Boy and fish. 20c+7c, Girl, butterfly and toad.

**1950, Nov. 13 *Perf. 13x12***

| | | | | |
|---|---|---|---|---|
| **B219** | SP139 | 2c +3c car | .30 | .25 |
| **B220** | SP139 | 5c +3c ol grn | 8.25 | 4.25 |
| **B221** | SP139 | 6c +4c dk bl grn | 2.40 | .65 |
| **B222** | SP139 | 10c +5c lilac | .30 | .25 |
| **B223** | SP139 | 20c +7c blue | 8.75 | 7.50 |
| | | *Nos. B219-B223 (5)* | 20.00 | 12.90 |

The surtax was to aid needy children.

Hillenraad Castle SP140

Bergh Castle SP141

Castles: 6c+4c, Hernen. 10c+5c, Rechteren. 20c+5c, Moermond.

***Perf. 12x12½, 12½x12***

**1951, May 15 Engr. Unwmk.**

| | | | | |
|---|---|---|---|---|
| **B224** | SP140 | 2c +2c purple | 1.75 | 1.00 |
| **B225** | SP141 | 5c +3c dk red | 5.50 | 6.00 |
| **B226** | SP140 | 6c +4c dk brown | 3.50 | 1.00 |
| **B227** | SP141 | 10c +5c dk green | 4.00 | .25 |
| **B228** | SP141 | 20c +5c dp blue | 5.50 | *6.00* |
| | | *Nos. B224-B228 (5)* | 20.25 | *14.25* |

The surtax was for cultural, medical and social purposes.

Girl and Windmill — SP142

Designs: 5c+3c, Boy and building construction. 6c+4c, Fisherboy and net. 10c+5c, Boy, chimneys and steelwork. 20c+7c, Girl and apartment house.

**1951, Nov. 12 Photo. *Perf. 13x14***

| | | | | |
|---|---|---|---|---|
| **B229** | SP142 | 2c +3c dp green | .60 | .25 |
| **B230** | SP142 | 5c +3c sl vio | 5.25 | 3.50 |
| **B231** | SP142 | 6c +4c dk brown | 3.50 | .70 |
| **B232** | SP142 | 10c +5c red brown | .30 | .25 |
| **B233** | SP142 | 20c +7c dp bl | 5.25 | *6.50* |
| | | *Nos. B229-B233 (5)* | 14.90 | *11.20* |

The surtax was for child welfare.

Jan van Riebeeck — SP143

**1952, Mar. *Perf. 12½x12***

| | | | | |
|---|---|---|---|---|
| **B234** | SP143 | 2c +3c dk gray | 3.25 | 2.25 |
| **B235** | SP143 | 6c +4c dk bl grn | 4.00 | 3.00 |
| **B236** | SP143 | 10c +5c brt red | 4.50 | 2.25 |
| **B237** | SP143 | 20c +5c brt blue | 3.25 | 3.00 |
| | | *Nos. B234-B237 (4)* | 15.00 | 10.50 |

Tercentenary of Van Riebeeck's landing in South Africa. Surtax was for Van Riebeeck monument fund.

Scotch Rose — SP144

Designs: 5c+3c, Marsh marigold. 6c+4c, Tulip. 10c+5c, Ox-eye daisy. 20c+5c, Cornflower.

**1952, May 1**

| | | | | |
|---|---|---|---|---|
| **B238** | SP144 | 2c +2c cer & dl grn | .60 | .50 |
| **B239** | SP144 | 5c +3c dp grn & yel | 2.40 | 3.00 |
| **B240** | SP144 | 6c +4c red & dl grn | 1.60 | 1.10 |
| **B241** | SP144 | 10c +5c org yel & dl grn | 1.20 | .35 |
| **B242** | SP144 | 20c +5c bl & dl grn | 6.25 | 5.25 |
| | | *Nos. B238-B242 (5)* | 12.05 | 10.20 |

The surtax was for social, cultural and medical purposes.

Girl and Dog — SP145

2c+3c, Boy & goat. 5c+3c, Girl on donkey. 10c+5c, Boy & kitten. 20c+7c, Boy & rabbit.

**Design in Black**

***Perf. 12x12½***

**1952, Nov. 17 Unwmk.**

| No. | Type | Value | Color | Unused | Used |
|---|---|---|---|---|---|
| **B243** | SP145 | 2c +3c | olive | .25 | .25 |
| **B244** | SP145 | 5c +3c | dp rose | 1.90 | 1.45 |
| **B245** | SP145 | 6c +4c | aqua | 1.35 | .40 |
| **B246** | SP145 | 10c +5c | org yel | .25 | .25 |
| **B247** | SP145 | 20c +7c | blue | 4.50 | 4.25 |
| | | | *Nos. B243-B247 (5)* | 8.25 | 6.60 |

The surtax was for child welfare.

No. 308 Surcharged in Black

***Perf. 13½x13***

**1953, Feb. 10 Wmk. 202**

| No. | Type | Value | Color | Unused | Used |
|---|---|---|---|---|---|
| **B248** | A76 | 10c +10c | org yel | .50 | .25 |

The surtax was for flood relief.

Hyacinth — SP146

Designs: 5c+3c, African Marigold. 6c+4c, Daffodil. 10c+5c, Anemone. 20c+5c, Iris.

**1953, May 1 Unwmk. *Perf. 12½x12***

| No. | Type | Value | Color | Unused | Used |
|---|---|---|---|---|---|
| **B249** | SP146 | 2c +2c | vio & grn | .65 | .50 |
| **B250** | SP146 | 5c +3c | dp org & grn | 2.25 | 3.25 |
| **B251** | SP146 | 6c +4c | grn & yel | 1.30 | 1.00 |
| **B252** | SP146 | 10c +5c | dk red & grn | 2.90 | .50 |
| **B253** | SP146 | 20c +5c | dp ultra & grn | 9.00 | 9.00 |
| | | | *Nos. B249-B253 (5)* | 16.10 | 14.25 |

The surtax was for social, cultural and medical purposes.

Red Cross on Shield — SP147

Designs: 6c+4c, Man holding lantern. 7c+5c, Worker and ambulance at flood. 10c+5c, Nurse giving blood transfusion. 25c+8c, Red Cross flags.

**Cross in Red**

**1953, Aug. 24 Engr.**

| No. | Type | Value | Color | Unused | Used |
|---|---|---|---|---|---|
| **B254** | SP147 | 2c +3c | dk ol | .60 | .45 |
| **B255** | SP147 | 6c +4c | dk vio brn | 3.50 | 3.25 |
| **B256** | SP147 | 7c +5c | dk gray grn | .75 | .45 |
| **B257** | SP147 | 10c +5c | red | .60 | .25 |
| **B258** | SP147 | 25c +8c | dp bl | 4.50 | 4.25 |
| | | | *Nos. B254-B258 (5)* | 9.95 | 8.65 |

The surtax was for the Red Cross.

Spade, Flag, Bucket and Girl's Head — SP148

Head of child and: 5c+3c, Apple. 7c+5c, Pigeon. 10c+5c, Sailboat. 25c+8c, Tulip.

**1953, Nov. 16 Litho. *Perf. 12x12½***

| No. | Type | Value | Color | Unused | Used |
|---|---|---|---|---|---|
| **B259** | SP148 | 2c +3c | yel & bl gray | .25 | .25 |
| **B260** | SP148 | 5c +3c | ap grn & brn car | 2.25 | 3.50 |
| **B261** | SP148 | 7c +5c | lt bl & sep | 2.25 | 1.30 |
| **B262** | SP148 | 10c +5c | ol bis & lil | .25 | .25 |
| **B263** | SP148 | 25c +8c | pink & bl grn | 6.00 | 8.00 |
| | | | *Nos. B259-B263 (5)* | 11.00 | 13.30 |

The surtax was for child welfare.

Martinus Nijhoff, Poet — SP149

5c+3c, Willem Pijper, composer. 7c+5c, H. P. Berlage, architect. 10c+5c, Johan Huizinga, historian. 25c+8c, Vincent van Gogh, painter.

**1954, May 1 Photo. *Perf. 12½x12***

| No. | Type | Value | Color | Unused | Used |
|---|---|---|---|---|---|
| **B264** | SP149 | 2c +3c | dp bl | 1.75 | 1.50 |
| **B265** | SP149 | 5c +3c | ol brn | 2.00 | 2.00 |
| **B266** | SP149 | 7c +5c | dk red | 2.60 | 1.20 |
| **B267** | SP149 | 10c +5c | dl grn | 5.25 | .60 |
| **B268** | SP149 | 25c +8c | plum | 6.75 | 7.75 |
| | | | *Nos. B264-B268 (5)* | 18.35 | 13.05 |

The surtax was for social and cultural purposes.

Boy Flying Model Plane — SP150

Portrait: 10c+4c, Albert E. Plesman.

**1954, Aug. 23 *Perf. 12½x12***

| No. | Type | Value | Color | Unused | Used |
|---|---|---|---|---|---|
| **B269** | SP150 | 2c +2c | ol grn | .75 | .65 |
| **B270** | SP150 | 10c +4c | dk gray bl | 2.10 | .65 |

The surtax was for the Netherlands Aviation Foundation.

Children Making Paper Chains — SP151

Girl Brushing Teeth — SP152

7c+5c, Boy sailing toy boat. 10c+5c, Nurse drying child. 25c+8c, Young convalescent, drawing.

***Perf. 12x12½, 12½x12***

**1954, Nov. 15**

| No. | Type | Value | Color | Unused | Used |
|---|---|---|---|---|---|
| **B271** | SP151 | 2c +3c | brn | .25 | .25 |
| **B272** | SP152 | 5c +3c | ol grn | 2.75 | 2.75 |
| **B273** | SP152 | 7c +5c | gray bl | 1.00 | .50 |
| **B274** | SP152 | 10c +5c | brn red | .25 | .25 |
| **B275** | SP151 | 25c +8c | dp bl | 5.75 | 4.75 |
| | | | *Nos. B271-B275 (5)* | 10.00 | 8.50 |

The surtax was for child welfare.

Factory, Rotterdam SP153

Amsterdam Stock Exchange SP154

5c+3c, Post office, The Hague. 10c+5c, Town hall, Hilversum. 25c+8c, Office building, The Hague.

**1955, Apr. 25 Engr.**

| No. | Type | Value | Color | Unused | Used |
|---|---|---|---|---|---|
| **B276** | SP153 | 2c +3c | brnsh bis | 1.25 | 1.00 |
| **B277** | SP153 | 5c +3c | bl grn | 2.25 | 2.75 |
| **B278** | SP154 | 7c +5c | rose brn | 1.25 | 1.00 |
| **B279** | SP153 | 10c +5c | steel bl | 1.75 | .25 |
| **B280** | SP153 | 25c +8c | choc | 6.75 | *7.00* |
| | | | *Nos. B276-B280 (5)* | 13.25 | *12.00* |

The surtax was for social and cultural purposes.

Microscope and Crab — SP155

**1955, Aug. 15 Photo. *Perf. 12½x12***

**Crab in Red**

| No. | Type | Value | Color | Unused | Used |
|---|---|---|---|---|---|
| **B281** | SP155 | 2c +3c | dk gray | .65 | .55 |
| **B282** | SP155 | 5c +3c | dk grn | 1.40 | 1.45 |
| **B283** | SP155 | 7c +5c | dk vio | 1.15 | .60 |
| **B284** | SP155 | 10c +5c | dk bl | .95 | .25 |
| **B285** | SP155 | 25c +8c | olive | 4.50 | 3.75 |
| | | | *Nos. B281-B285 (5)* | 8.65 | 6.60 |

The surtax was for cancer research.

Willem van Loon by Dirck Santvoort — SP156

Portraits: 5+3c, Boy by Jacob Adriaanszoon Backer. 7+5c, Girl by unknown artist. 10+5c, Philips Huygens by Adriaan Hanneman. 25+8c, Constantijn Huygens by Adriaan Hanneman.

**1955, Nov. 14 Unwmk.**

| No. | Type | Value | Color | Unused | Used |
|---|---|---|---|---|---|
| **B286** | SP156 | 2c +3c | dk grn | .35 | .25 |
| **B287** | SP156 | 5c +3c | dp car | 2.10 | 1.75 |
| **B288** | SP156 | 7c +5c | dl red brn | 2.10 | .65 |
| **B289** | SP156 | 10c +5c | dp bl | .35 | .25 |
| **B290** | SP156 | 25c +8c | purple | 5.50 | 5.00 |
| | | | *Nos. B286-B290 (5)* | 10.40 | 7.90 |

The surtax was for child welfare.

Farmer Wearing High Cap — SP157

Rembrandt Etchings: 5c+3c, Young Tobias with Angel. 7c+5c, Persian Wearing Fur Cap. 10c+5c, Old Blind Tobias. 25c+8c, Self-portrait of 1639.

**1956, Apr. 23 Engr. *Perf. 13½x14***

| No. | Type | Value | Color | Unused | Used |
|---|---|---|---|---|---|
| **B291** | SP157 | 2c +3c | bluish blk | 1.25 | 1.60 |
| **B292** | SP157 | 5c +3c | ol grn | 2.25 | 2.25 |
| **B293** | SP157 | 7c +5c | brown | 2.50 | 2.50 |
| **B294** | SP157 | 10c +5c | dk grn | 6.00 | .35 |
| **B295** | SP157 | 25c +8c | redsh brn | 9.25 | 9.25 |
| | | | *Nos. B291-B295 (5)* | 21.25 | 15.95 |

350th anniv. of the birth of Rembrandt van Rijn.
Surtax for social and cultural purposes.

Sailboat — SP158

Designs: 5c+3c, Woman runner. 7c+5c, Amphora depicting runners. 10c+5c, Field hockey. 25c+8c, Waterpolo player.

**1956, Aug. 27 Litho. *Perf. 12½x12***

| No. | Type | Value | Color | Unused | Used |
|---|---|---|---|---|---|
| **B296** | SP158 | 2c +3c | brt bl & blk | .70 | .80 |
| **B297** | SP158 | 5c +3c | dl yel & blk | 1.00 | 1.15 |
| **B298** | SP158 | 7c +5c | red brn & blk | 1.00 | 1.15 |
| **B299** | SP158 | 10c +5c | gray & blk | 1.25 | .40 |
| **B300** | SP158 | 25c +8c | brt grn & blk | 2.60 | *3.50* |
| | | | *Nos. B296-B300 (5)* | 6.55 | *7.00* |

16th Olympic Games at Melbourne, Nov. 22-Dec. 8, 1956.
The surtax was for the benefit of the Netherlands Olympic Committee.

Boy by Jan van Scorel — SP159

Children's Portraits: 5c+3c, Boy, 1563. 7c+5c, Girl, 1563. 10c+5c, Girl, 1590. 25c+8c, Eechie Pieters, 1592.

**1956, Nov. 12 Photo. Unwmk.**

| No. | Type | Value | Color | Unused | Used |
|---|---|---|---|---|---|
| **B301** | SP159 | 2c +3c | blk vio | .35 | .25 |
| **B302** | SP159 | 5c +3c | ol grn | 1.60 | .65 |
| **B303** | SP159 | 7c +5c | brn vio | 1.75 | 1.25 |
| **B304** | SP159 | 10c +5c | dp red | .30 | .25 |
| **B305** | SP159 | 25c +8c | dk bl | 3.25 | 2.90 |
| | | | *Nos. B301-B305 (5)* | 7.25 | 5.30 |

The surtax was for child welfare.

Motor Freighter SP160

Ships: 6c+4c, Coaster. 7c+5c, "Willem Barendsz." 10c+8c, Trawler. 30c+8c, S. S. "Nieuw Amsterdam."

**1957, May 13 Photo. *Perf. 14x13***

| No. | Type | Value | Color | Unused | Used |
|---|---|---|---|---|---|
| **B306** | SP160 | 4c +3c | brt bl | 1.00 | 1.00 |
| **B307** | SP160 | 6c +4c | brt vio | 2.00 | 2.00 |
| **B308** | SP160 | 7c +5c | dk car rose | 1.25 | 1.10 |
| **B309** | SP160 | 10c +8c | grn | 2.10 | .40 |
| **B310** | SP160 | 30c +8c | choc | 3.25 | *3.00* |
| | | | *Nos. B306-B310 (5)* | 9.60 | *7.50* |

The surtax was for social and cultural purposes.

White Pelican Feeding Young — SP161

Designs: 6c+4c, Vacation ship, "Castle of Staverden." 7c+5c, Cross and dates: 1867-1957. 10c+8c, Cross and laurel wreath. 30c+8c, Globe and Cross.

**1957, Aug. 19 Litho. *Perf. 12x12½***

**Cross in Red**

| No. | Type | Value | Color | Unused | Used |
|---|---|---|---|---|---|
| **B311** | SP161 | 4c +3c | bl & red | .65 | .60 |
| **B312** | SP161 | 6c +4c | dk grn | .85 | .85 |
| **B313** | SP161 | 7c +5c | dk grn & pink | .85 | .85 |
| **B314** | SP161 | 10c +8c | yel org | .75 | .25 |
| **B315** | SP161 | 30c +8c | vio bl | 1.90 | *1.90* |
| | | | *Nos. B311-B315 (5)* | 5.00 | *4.45* |

90th anniversary of the founding of the Netherlands Red Cross.

Girl by B. J. Blommers — SP162

Girls' Portraits by: 6c+4c, William B. Tholen. 8c+4c, Jan Sluyters. 12c+9c, Matthijs Maris. 30c+9c, Cornelis Kruseman.

**1957, Nov. 18 Photo. *Perf. 12½x12***

**B316** SP162 4c +4c dp car .30 .25
**B317** SP162 6c +4c ol grn 1.50 2.00
**B318** SP162 8c +4c gray 1.60 1.90
**B319** SP162 12c +9c dp claret .25 .25
**B320** SP162 30c +9c dk bl 4.50 4.75
*Nos. B316-B320 (5)* 8.15 9.15

The surtax was for child welfare.

Woman from Walcheren, Zeeland — SP163

Regional Costumes: 6c+4c, Marken. 8c+4c, Scheveningen. 12c+9c, Friesland. 30c+9c, Volendam.

**1958, Apr. 28 Photo. Unwmk.**

**B321** SP163 4c +4c blue .95 .60
**B322** SP163 6c +4c bister 1.60 1.60
**B323** SP163 8c +4c dk car rose 2.90 1.60
**B324** SP163 12c +9c org brn 1.60 .25
**B325** SP163 30c +9c vio 5.00 *5.25*
*Nos. B321-B325 (5)* 12.05 *9.30*

Surtax for social and cultural purposes.

Girl on Stilts and Boy on Tricycle — SP164

Children's Games: 6c+4c, Boy and girl on scooters. 8c+4c, Leapfrog. 12c+9c, Roller skating. 30c+9c, Boy in toy car and girl jumping rope.

**1958, Nov. 17 Litho.**

**B326** SP164 4c +4c lt bl .25 .25
**B327** SP164 6c +4c dp red 1.60 1.60
**B328** SP164 8c +4c brt bl grn 1.30 .75
**B329** SP164 12c +9c red org .25 .25
**B330** SP164 30c +9c dk bl 3.25 3.00
*Nos. B326-B330 (5)* 6.65 5.85

The surtax was for child welfare.

Tugs and Caisson SP165

Designs: 6c+4c, Dredger. 8c+4c, Laborers making fascine mattresses. 12c+9c, Grab cranes. 30c+9c, Sand spouter.

**1959, May 11 *Perf. 14x13***

**B331** SP165 4c +4c dk bl, *bl grn* 1.00 1.00
**B332** SP165 6c +4c red org, *gray* 1.00 1.30
**B333** SP165 8c +4c bl vio, *lt bl* 1.00 1.00
**B334** SP165 12c +9c bl grn, *brt yel* 1.75 .25
**B335** SP165 30c +9c dk brn, *brick red* 3.25 *4.50*
*Nos. B331-B335 (5)* 8.00 *8.05*

Issued to publicize the endless struggle to keep the sea out and the land dry.

The surtax was for social and cultural purposes.

Child in Playpen — SP166

Designs: 6c+4c, Playing Indian. 8c+4c, Child feeding geese. 12c+9c, Children crossing street. 30c+9c, Doing homework.

**1959, Nov. 16 *Perf. 12½x12***

**B336** SP166 4c +4c dp rose & dk bl .25 .25
**B337** SP166 6c +4c red brn & emer 1.00 1.00
**B338** SP166 8c +4c red & bl 1.75 1.10
**B339** SP166 12c +9c grnsh bl, org & gray .25 .25
**B340** SP166 30c +9c yel & bl 2.90 2.75
*Nos. B336-B340 (5)* 6.15 5.35

The surtax was for child welfare.

Refugee Woman — SP167

**1960, Apr. 7 Photo. *Perf. 13x14***

**B341** SP167 12c +8c dp claret .50 .30
**B342** SP167 30c +10c dk ol grn 2.25 2.00

Issued to publicize World Refugee Year, July 1, 1959-June 30, 1960. The surtax was for aid to refugees.

Tulip — SP168

Flowers: 6c+4c, Gorse. 8c+4c, White water-lily, horiz. 12c+8c, Red poppy. 30c+10c, Blue sea holly.

***Perf. 12½x12, 12x12½***

**1960, May 23 Unwmk.**

**B343** SP168 4c +4c gray, grn & red .95 .75
**B344** SP168 6c +4c sal, grn & yel 1.25 1.60
**B345** SP168 8c +4c multi 1.75 1.60
**B346** SP168 12c +8c dl org, red & grn 1.60 .30
**B347** SP168 30c +10c yel, grn & ultra 3.00 4.50
*Nos. B343-B347 (5)* 8.55 8.75

The surtax was for child welfare.

Girl from Marken — SP169

Regional Costumes: 6c+4c, Volendam. 8c+4c, Bunschoten. 12c+9c, Hindeloopen. 30c+9c, Huizen.

**1960, Nov. 14 *Perf. 12½x12***

**B348** SP169 4c +4c multi .35 .25
**B349** SP169 6c +4c multi 1.60 2.00
**B350** SP169 8c +4c multi 3.00 2.00
**B351** SP169 12c +9c multi .35 .25
**B352** SP169 30c +9c multi 3.75 4.50
*Nos. B348-B352 (5)* 9.05 9.00

The surtax was for child welfare.

Herring Gull — SP170

Birds: 6c+4c, Oystercatcher, horiz. 8c+4c, Curlew. 12c+8c, Avocet, horiz. 30c+10c, Lapwing.

***Perf. 12½x12, 12x12½***

**1961, Apr. 24 Litho. Unwmk.**

**B353** SP170 4c +4c yel & grnsh gray .70 .95
**B354** SP170 6c +4c fawn & blk 1.40 1.75
**B355** SP170 8c +4c ol & red brn .70 1.10
**B356** SP170 12c +8c lt bl & gray 1.90 .40
**B357** SP170 30c +10c grn & blk 1.90 2.40
*Nos. B353-B357 (5)* 6.60 6.60

The surtax was for social and cultural purposes.

St. Nicholas on his Horse — SP171

Holiday folklore: 6c+4c, Epiphany. 8c+4c, Palm Sunday. 12c+9c, Whitsun bride, Pentecost. 30c+9c, Martinmas.

**1961, Nov. 13 *Perf. 12½x12***

**B358** SP171 4c +4c brt red .25 .25
**B359** SP171 6c +4c brt bl .90 .75
**B360** SP171 8c +4c olive .80 .75
**B361** SP171 12c +9c dp grn .25 .25
**B362** SP171 30c +9c dp org 2.40 2.40
*Nos. B358-B362 (5)* 4.60 4.40

The surtax was for child welfare.

Christian Huygens' Pendulum Clock by van Ceulen — SP172

Designs: 4c+4c, Cat, Roman sculpture, horiz. 6c+4c, Fossil Ammonite. 12c+ 8c, Figurehead from admiralty ship model. 30c+10c, Guardsmen Hendrick van Berckenrode and Jacob van Lourenszz, by Frans Hals, horiz.

***Perf. 14x13, 13x14***

**1962, Apr. 27 Photo.**

**B363** SP172 4c +4c ol grn .85 .85
**B364** SP172 6c +4c gray .70 .85
**B365** SP172 8c +4c dp claret 1.00 1.25
**B366** SP172 12c +8c olive bis 1.00 .35
**B367** SP172 30c +10c bl blk 1.05 1.25
*Nos. B363-B367 (5)* 4.60 4.55

The surtax was for social and cultural purposes. Issued to publicize the International Congress of Museum Experts, July 4-11.

Children Cooking — SP173

Children's Activities: 6c+4c, Bicycling. 8c+4c, Watering flowers. 12c+9c, Feeding chickens. 30c+9c, Music making.

**1962, Nov. 12 *Perf. 12½x12***

**B368** SP173 4c +4c red .25 .25
**B369** SP173 6c +4c yel bis .75 .60
**B370** SP173 8c +4c ultra 1.05 1.15
**B371** SP173 12c +9c dp grn .25 .25
**B372** SP173 30c +9c dk car rose 1.75 1.90
*Nos. B368-B372 (5)* 4.05 4.15

The surtax was for child welfare.

Gallery Windmill — SP174

Windmills: 6c+4c, North Holland polder mill. 8c+4c, South Holland polder mill, horiz. 12c+8c, Post mill. 30c+10c, Wip mill.

***Perf. 13x14, 14x13***

**1963, Apr. 24 Litho. Unwmk.**

**B373** SP174 4c +4c dk bl .85 1.00
**B374** SP174 6c +4c dk pur .85 1.00
**B375** SP174 8c +4c dk grn 1.05 1.20
**B376** SP174 12c +8c blk 1.05 .30
**B377** SP174 30c +10c dk car 1.60 1.75
*Nos. B373-B377 (5)* 5.40 5.25

The surtax was for social and cultural purposes.

Roadside First Aid Station SP175

Designs: 6c+4c, Book collection box. 8c+4c, Crosses. 12c+9c, International aid to Africans. 30c+9c, First aid team.

**1963, Aug. 20 *Perf. 14x13***

**B378** SP175 4c +4c dk bl & red .40 .40
**B379** SP175 6c +4c dl pur & red .40 .40
**B380** SP175 8c +4c blk & red .75 .55
**B381** SP175 12c +9c red brn & red .25 .25
**B382** SP175 30c +9c yel grn & red 1.20 1.20
*Nos. B378-B382 (5)* 3.00 2.80

Centenary of the Intl. Red Cross. The surtax went to the Netherlands Red Cross.

"Aunt Lucy Sat on a Goosey" — SP176

Nursery Rhymes: 6c+4c, "In the Hague there lives a count." 8c+4c, "One day I passed a puppet's fair." 12c+9c, "Storky, storky, Billy Spoon." 30c+9c, "Ride on in a little buggy."

**1963, Nov. 12 Litho. *Perf. 13x14***

**B383** SP176 4c +4c grnsh bl & dk bl .25 .25
**B384** SP176 6c +4c org red & sl grn 1.10 .60
**B385** SP176 8c +4c dl grn & dk brn 1.60 .50
**B386** SP176 12c +9c yel & dk pur .25 .25
**B387** SP176 30c +9c rose & dk bl 1.60 1.40
*Nos. B383-B387 (5)* 4.80 3.00

The surtax was for mentally and physically handicapped children.

Seeing-Eye Dog — SP177

8c+5c, Three red deer. 12c+9c, Three kittens. 30c+9c, European bison and young.

**1964, Apr. 21 *Perf. 12x12½***

**B388** SP177 5c +5c gray ol, red & blk .35 .35
**B389** SP177 8c +5c dk red, pale brn & blk .25 .25
**B390** SP177 12c +9c dl yel, blk & gray .35 .25
**B391** SP177 30c +9c bl, gray & blk .60 .55
*Nos. B388-B391 (4)* 1.55 1.40

The surtax was for social and cultural purposes.

Child Painting — SP178

"Artistic and Creative Activities of Children": 10c+5c, Ballet dancing. 15c+10c, Girl playing the flute. 20c+10c, Little Red Riding Hood (masquerading children). 40c+15c, Boy with hammer at work bench.

***Perf. 13x14***

**1964, Nov. 17 Photo. Unwmk.**

**B392** SP178 7c +3c lt ol grn & bl .45 .35
**B393** SP178 10c +5c red, brt pink & grn .40 .35
**B394** SP178 15c +10c yel bis, blk & yel .25 .25
**B395** SP178 20c +10c brt pink, brn & red .75 .50
**B396** SP178 40c +15c bl & yel grn .95 .70
*Nos. B392-B396 (5)* 2.80 2.15

The surtax was for child welfare.

View of Veere SP179

Views: 10c+6c, Thorn. 18c+12c, Dordrecht. 20c+10c, Staveren. 40c+10c, Medemblik.

**1965, June 1 Litho. *Perf. 14x13***

**B397** SP179 8c +6c yel & blk .25 .30
**B398** SP179 10c +6c grnsh bl & blk .40 .35
**B399** SP179 18c +12c sal & blk .30 .30
**B400** SP179 20c +10c bl & blk .40 .35
**B401** SP179 40c +10c ap grn & blk .45 .45
*Nos. B397-B401 (5)* 1.80 1.75

The surtax was for social and cultural purposes.

Child SP180

Designs by Children: 10c+6c, Ship. 18c+12c, Woman, vert. 20c+10c, Child, lake and swan. 40c+10c, Tractor.

***Perf. 14x13, 13x14***

**1965, Nov. 16 Photo.**

**B402** SP180 8c +6c multi .25 .25
**B403** SP180 10c +6c multi .50 .50
**B404** SP180 18c +12c multi .25 .25
*a.* Min. sheet of 11, 5 #B402, 6 #B404 + label 16.00 *23.50*
**B405** SP180 20c +10c multi .75 .60
**B406** SP180 40c +10c multi 1.00 .85
*Nos. B402-B406 (5)* 2.75 2.45

The surtax was for child welfare.

"Help them to a safe haven" SP181

**1966, Jan. 31 Photo. *Perf. 14x13***

**B407** SP181 18c +7c blk & org yel .30 .25
**B408** SP181 40c +20c blk & red .25 .25
*a.* Min. sheet of 3, #B407, 2 #B408 1.60 1.20

The surtax was for the Intergovernmental Committee for European Migration (ICEM). The message on the stamps was given and signed by Queen Juliana.

Inkwell, Goose Quill and Book — SP182

Designs: 12c+8c, Fragment of Gysbert Japicx manuscript. 20c+10c, Knight on horseback, miniature from "Roman van Walewein" manuscript, 1350. 25c+10c, Initial "D" from "Ferguut" manuscript, 1350. 40c+20c, Print shop, 16th century woodcut.

**1966, May 3 *Perf. 13x14***

**B409** SP182 10c +5c multi .30 .35
**B410** SP182 12c +8c multi .30 .35
**B411** SP182 20c +10c multi .45 .35
**B412** SP182 25c +10c multi .60 .50
**B413** SP182 40c +20c multi .45 .50
*Nos. B409-B413 (5)* 2.10 2.05

Gysbert Japicx (1603-1666), Friesian poet, and the 200th anniversary of the founding of the Netherlands Literary Society.

The surtax was for social and cultural purposes.

Infant SP183

Designs: 12c+8c, Daughter of the painter S. C. Lixenberg. 20c+10c, Boy swimming. 25c+10c, Dominga Blazer, daughter of Carel Blazer, photographer of this set. 40c+20c, Boy and horse.

**1966, Nov. 15 Photo. *Perf. 14x13***

**B414** SP183 10c +5c dp org & bl .25 .25
**B415** SP183 12c +8c ap grn & red .25 .25
**B416** SP183 20c +10c brt bl & red .25 .25
*a.* Min. sheet of 12, 4 #B414, 5 #B415, 3 #B416 2.00 2.00
**B417** SP183 25c +10c brt rose lil & dk bl .65 .65
**B418** SP183 40c +20c dp car & dk grn .65 .65
*Nos. B414-B418 (5)* 2.05 2.05

The surtax was for child welfare.

Whelk Eggs SP184

15c+10c, Whelk. 20c+10c, Mussel with acorn shells. 25c+10c, Jellyfish. 45c+20c, Crab.

**1967, Apr. 11 Unwmk. Litho.**

**B419** SP184 12c +8c ol grn & tan .25 .25
**B420** SP184 15c +10c lt bl, ultra & blk .25 .25
**B421** SP184 20c +10c gray, blk & red .25 .25
**B422** SP184 25c +10c brn car, plum & ol brn .50 .50
**B423** SP184 45c +20c multi .70 .65
*Nos. B419-B423 (5)* 1.95 1.90

Red Cross and Dates Forming Cross SP185

15c+10c, Crosses. 20c+10c, Initials "NRK" forming cross. 25c+10c, Maltese cross and crosses. 45c+20c, "100" forming cross.

**1967, Aug. 8 *Perf. 14x13***

**B424** SP185 12c +8c dl bl & red .30 .30
**B425** SP185 15c +10c red .35 .35
**B426** SP185 20c +10c ol & red .30 .30
**B427** SP185 25c +10c ol grn & red .45 .45
**B428** SP185 45c +20c gray & red .70 .70
*Nos. B424-B428 (5)* 2.10 2.10

Centenary of the Dutch Red Cross.

"Lullaby for the Little Porcupine" — SP186

Nursery Rhymes: 15c+10c, "Little Whistling Kettle." 20c+10c, "Dikkertje Dap and the Giraffe." 25c+10c, "The Nicest Flowers." 45c+20c, "Pippeljoentje, the Little Bear."

**1967, Nov. 7 Litho. *Perf. 13x14***

**B429** SP186 12c +8c multi .25 .25
**B430** SP186 15c +10c multi .25 .25
**B431** SP186 20c +10c multi .25 .25
*a.* Min. sheet of 10, 3 #B429, 4 #B430, 3 #B431 4.00 4.00
**B432** SP186 25c +10c multi 1.10 .75
**B433** SP186 45c +20c multi 1.15 .75
*Nos. B429-B433 (5)* 3.00 2.25

The surtax was for child welfare.

St. Servatius Bridge, Maastricht SP187

Bridges: 15c+10c, Narrow Bridge, Amsterdam. 20c+10c, Railroad Bridge, Culenborg. 25c+10c, Van Brienenoord Bridge, Rotterdam. 45c+20c, Zeeland Bridge, Schelde Estuary.

**1968, Apr. 9 Photo. *Perf. 14x13***

**B434** SP187 12c +8c green .35 .35
**B435** SP187 15c +10c ol brn .50 .50
**B436** SP187 20c +10c rose red .30 .25
**B437** SP187 25c +10c gray .35 .35
**B438** SP187 45c +20c ultra .60 .60
*Nos. B434-B438 (5)* 2.10 2.05

Goblin SP188

Fairy Tale Characters: 15c+10c, Giant. 20c+10c, Witch. 25c+10c, Dragon. 45c+20c, Magician.

**1968, Nov. 12 Photo. *Perf. 14x13***

**B439** SP188 12c +8c grn, pink & blk .25 .25
**B440** SP188 15c +10c bl, pink & blk .25 .25
**B441** SP188 20c +10c bl, emer & blk .25 .25
*a.* Min. sheet of 10, 3 #B439, 4 #B440, 3 #B441 4.00 4.00
**B442** SP188 25c +10c org red, org & blk 1.25 1.25
**B443** SP188 45c +20c yel, org & blk 1.25 1.25
*Nos. B439-B443 (5)* 3.25 3.25

The surtax was for child welfare.

Villa Huis ter Heide, 1915 SP189

Contemporary Architecture: 15c+10c, House, Utrecht, 1924. 20c+10c, First open-air school, Amsterdam, 1960. 25c+10c, Burgweeshuis (orphanage), Amsterdam, 1960. 45c+20c, Netherlands Congress Building, The Hague, 1969.

**1969, Apr. 15 Photo. *Perf. 14x13***

**B444** SP189 12c +8c lt brn & sl .65 .65
**B445** SP189 15c +10c bl, gray & red .65 .65
**B446** SP189 20c +10c vio & blk .65 .65
**B447** SP189 25c +10c grn & gray .65 .65
**B448** SP189 45c +20c gray, bl & yel .65 .65
*Nos. B444-B448 (5)* 3.25 3.25

Surtax for social and cultural purposes.

Stylized Crab — SP190

**1969, Aug. 12 Photo. *Perf. 13x14***

**B449** SP190 12c +8c vio .55 .55
**B450** SP190 25c +10c org .80 .35
**B451** SP190 45c +20c bl grn 1.25 1.25
*Nos. B449-B451 (3)* 2.60 2.15

20th anniv. of the Queen Wilhelmina Fund. The surtax was for cancer research.

Child with Violin — SP191

12c+8c, Child with flute. 20c+10c, Child with drum. 25c+10c, Three children singing, horiz. 45c+20c, Two girls dancing, horiz.

**1969, Nov. 11 *Perf. 13x14, 14x13***

**B452** SP191 12c +8c ultra, blk & yel .25 .25
**B453** SP191 15c +10c blk & red .25 .25
**B454** SP191 20c +10c red, blk & yel 2.00 1.60
**B455** SP191 25c +10c yel, blk & red .25 .25
*a.* Min. sheet of 10, 4 #B452, 4 #B453, 2 #B455 5.00 5.00
**B456** SP191 45c +20c grn, blk & red 2.10 1.60
*Nos. B452-B456 (5)* 4.85 3.95

The surtax was for child welfare.

Isometric Projection from Circle to Square — SP192

Designs made by Computer: 15c+10c, Parallel planes in a cube. 20c+10c, Two overlapping scales. 25c+10c, Transition phases of concentric circles with increasing diameters. 45c+20c, Four spirals.

**Lithographed and Engraved**

**1970, Apr. 7 *Perf. 13x14***

**B457** SP192 12c +8c yel & blk .80 .80
**B458** SP192 15c +10c sil & blk .80 .80
**B459** SP192 20c +10c blk .80 .80
**B460** SP192 25c +10c brt bl & blk .80 .80
**B461** SP192 45c +20c sil & white .80 .80
*Nos. B457-B461 (5)* 4.00 4.00

Surtax for social and cultural purposes.

Bleeding Heart — SP193

**1970, July 28 Photo. *Perf. 13x14***

**B462** SP193 12c +8c org yel, red & blk .60 .60
**B463** SP193 25c +10c pink, red & blk .60 .40
**B464** SP193 45c +20c brt grn, red & blk .60 .60
*Nos. B462-B464 (3)* 1.80 1.60

The surtax was for the Netherlands Heart Foundation.

Toy Block — SP194

**1970, Nov. 10 Photo. *Perf. 13x14***

**B465** SP194 12c +8c bl, vio bl & grn .25 .25
**B466** SP194 15c +10c grn, bl & yel 1.15 1.10
**B467** SP194 20c +10c lil rose, red & vio bl 1.15 1.10
**B468** SP194 25c +10c red, yel & lil rose .25 .25
*a.* Min. sheet of 11, 9 #B465, 2 #B468 + label 6.00 6.00
**B469** SP194 45c +20c gray & blk 1.30 1.30
*Nos. B465-B469 (5)* 4.10 4.00

The surtax was for child welfare.

St. Paul — SP195

Designs: 15c+10c, "50" and people. 25c+10c, Joachim and Ann. 30c+15c, John the Baptist and the Scribes. 45c+20c, St. Anne. The sculptures are wood, 15th century, and in Dutch museums.

**1971, Apr. 20 Litho. *Perf. 13x14***

**B470** SP195 15c +10c multi .80 .80

**Lithographed and Photogravure**

**B471** SP195 20c +10c gray, grn & blk .80 .80
**B472** SP195 25c +10c buff, org & blk .80 .50
**B473** SP195 30c +15c gray, bl & blk .80 .80
**B474** SP195 45c +20c pink, ver & blk .80 .80
*Nos. B470-B474 (5)* 4.00 3.70

50th anniversary of the Federation of Netherlands Universities for Adult Education.

Detail from Borobudur — SP196

**1971, June 29 Litho. *Perf. 13x14***

**B475** SP196 45c +20c pur, yel & blk 1.60 1.60

60th birthday of Prince Bernhard. Surtax for Save Borobudur Temple Fund.

"Earth" — SP197

Designs: 20c+10c, "Air" (butterfly). 25c+10c, "Sun," horiz. 30c+15c, "Moon," horiz. 45c+20c, "Water" (child looking at reflection).

***Perf. 13x14, 14x13***

**1971, Nov. 9 Photo.**

**B476** SP197 15c +10c blk, lil & org .25 .30
**B477** SP197 20c +10c yel, blk & rose lil .25 .30
**B478** SP197 25c +10c multi .25 .30
*a.* Min. sheet of 9, 6 #B476, #B477, 2 #B478 4.50 *8.75*
**B479** SP197 30c +15c bl, blk & pur .95 .75
**B480** SP197 45c +20c grn, blk & bl 1.35 1.40
*Nos. B476-B480 (5)* 3.05 3.05

The surtax was for child welfare.

---

Luminescence

Some semipostal issues from Nos. B481-B484 onward are on phosphorescent paper.

---

Stylized Fruits — SP198

**1972, Apr. 11 Litho. *Perf. 13x14***

**B481** SP198 20c +10c shown .75 .75
**B482** SP198 25c +10c Flower .75 .75
**B483** SP198 30c +15c "Sunlit Landscape" .75 .40
**B484** SP198 45c +25c "Music" .75 .75
*Nos. B481-B484 (4)* 3.00 2.65

Summer festivals: Nos. B481-B482 publicize the Floriade, flower festival; Nos. B483-B484 the Holland Festival of Arts.

Red Cross, First Aid — SP199

Red Cross and: 25c+10c, Blood bank. 30c+15c, Disaster relief. 45c+25c, Child care.

**1972, Aug. 15 *Perf. 13x14***

**B485** SP199 20c +10c brt pink & red .40 .40
**B486** SP199 25c +10c org & red .85 .85
**B487** SP199 30c +15c blk & red .55 .40
**B488** SP199 45c +25c ultra & red .85 .85
*Nos. B485-B488 (4)* 2.65 2.50

Surtax for the Netherlands Red Cross.

Prince Willem-Alexander SP200

Photographs of Dutch Princes: 30c+10c, Johan Friso. 35c+15c, Constantijn. 50c+20c, Johan Friso, Constantijn and Willem-Alexander. All are horizontal.

***Perf. 13x14, 14x13***

**1972, Nov. 7 Photo.**

**B489** SP200 25c +15c multi .25 .25
**B490** SP200 30c +10c multi .65 .50
**B491** SP200 35c +15c multi .60 .25
*a.* Min. sheet of 7, 4 #B489, #B490, 2 #B491 + label 4.00 4.00
**B492** SP200 50c +20c multi 2.10 2.00
*Nos. B489-B492 (4)* 3.60 3.00

Surtax was for child welfare.

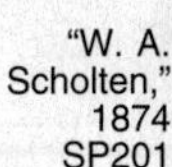

"W. A. Scholten," 1874 SP201

Ships: 25c+15c, Flagship "De Seven Provincien," 1673, vert. 35c+15c, "Veendam," 1923. 50c+20c, Zuider Zee fish well boat, 17th century, vert.

**1973, Apr. 10 Litho.**

**B493** SP201 25c +15c multi .80 .80
**B494** SP201 30c +10c multi .80 .80
**B495** SP201 35c +15c multi .80 .50
**B496** SP201 50c +20c multi .80 .80
*Nos. B493-B496 (4)* 3.20 2.90

Tercentenary of the Battle of Kijkduin and centenary of the Holland-America Line. Surtax for social and cultural purposes.

Chessboard SP202

Games: 30c+10c, Tick-tack-toe. 40c+20c, Maze. 50c+20c, Dominoes.

**1973, Nov. 13 Photo. *Perf. 13x14***

**B497** SP202 25c +15c multi .25 .25
**B498** SP202 30c +10c multi .55 .45
**B499** SP202 40c +20c multi .25 .25
*a.* Min. sheet of 6, 2 #B497, #B498, 3 #B499 4.50 4.50
**B500** SP202 50c +20c multi 1.60 1.60
*Nos. B497-B500 (4)* 2.65 2.55

Surtax was for child welfare.

Music Bands SP203

Herman Heijermans SP204

Designs: 30c+10c, Ballet dancers and traffic lights. 50c+20c, Kniertje, the fisher woman, from play by Heijermans.

**1974, Apr. 23 Litho. *Perf. 13x14***

**B501** SP203 25c +15c multi .75 .75
**B502** SP203 30c +10c multi .75 .75

**Photo.**

**B503** SP204 40c +20c multi .75 .40
**B504** SP204 50c +20c multi .75 .75
*Nos. B501-B504 (4)* 3.00 2.65

Surtax was for various social and cultural institutions.

Boy with Hoop — SP205

Designs: 35c+20c, Girl and infant. 45c+20c, Two girls. 60c+20c, Girl sitting on balustrade. Designs are from turn-of-the-century photographs.

**1974, Nov. 12 Photo. *Perf. 13x14***

**B505** SP205 30c +15c brown .25 .25
**B506** SP205 35c +20c maroon .55 .45
**B507** SP205 45c +20c black brn .55 .25
*a.* Min. sheet of 6, 4 #B505, #B506, #B507 3.00 3.00
**B508** SP205 60c +20c indigo 1.45 1.25
*Nos. B505-B508 (4)* 2.80 2.20

Surtax was for child welfare.

Beguinage, Amsterdam SP206

Cooper's Gate, Middelburg SP207

Designs: 35c+20c, St. Hubertus Hunting Lodge, horiz. 60c+20c, Orvelte Village, horiz.

***Perf. 14x13, 13x14***

**1975, Apr. 4 Litho.**

**B509** SP206 35c +20c multi .55 .50
**B510** SP206 40c +15c multi .55 .50
**B511** SP207 50c +20c multi .70 .50
**B512** SP207 60c +20c multi .90 .90
*Nos. B509-B512 (4)* 2.70 2.40

European Architectural Heritage Year 1975. Surtax was for various social and cultural institutions.

Orphans, Sculpture, 1785 SP208

40c+15c, Milkmaid, 17th cent. 50c+25c, Aymon's 4 sons on steed Bayard, 17th cent. 60c+25c, Life at orphanage, 1557. All designs are after ornamental stones from various buildings.

**1975, Nov. 11 Photo. *Perf. 14x13***

**B513** SP208 35c +15c multi .25 .25
**B514** SP208 40c +15c multi .70 .40
**B515** SP208 50c +25c multi .35 .25
*a.* Min. sheet of 5, 3 #B513, 2 #B515 + label 2.00 2.00
**B516** SP208 60c +25c multi 1.00 .70
*Nos. B513-B516 (4)* 2.30 1.60

Surtax was for child welfare.

Hedgehog SP209

Book with "ABC" and Grain; Open Field SP210

Green Frog and Spawn SP212

People and Initials of Social Security Acts SP211

***Perf. 14x13, 13x14***

**1976, Apr. 6 Litho.**

**B517** SP209 40c +20c multi .65 .50
**B518** SP210 45c +20c multi .60 .50

**Photo.**

**B519** SP211 55c +20c multi .60 .25
**B520** SP212 75c +25c multi .80 .70
*Nos. B517-B520 (4)* 2.65 1.95

Surtax for various social and cultural institutions. #B517, B520 for wildlife protection; #B518 cent. of agricultural education and 175th anniv. of elementary education legislation; #B519 75th anniv. of social legislation and the Social Insurance Bank.

Patient Surrounded by Caring Hands — SP213

**1976, Sept. 2 Litho. *Perf. 13x14***

**B521** SP213 55c +25c multi .55 .45

Dutch Anti-Rheumatism Assoc., 50th anniv.

Netherlands No. 41 — SP214

Designs: No. B523, #64. No. B524, #155. No. B525, #294. No. B526, #220.

**1976, Oct. 8 Litho. *Perf. 13x14***

**B522** SP214 55c +55c multi .75 .70
**B523** SP214 55c +55c multi .75 .70
**B524** SP214 55c +55c multi .75 .70
*a.* Strip of 3, #B522-B524 2.25 2.25

**Photo.**

**B525** SP214 75c +75c multi .75 .70
**B526** SP214 75c +75c multi .75 .70
*a.* Pair, #B525-B526 1.50 1.50
*Nos. B522-B526 (5)* 3.75 3.50

Amphilex 77 Philatelic Exhibition, Amsterdam, May 26-June 5, 1977. No. B526a printed checkerwise.

See Nos. B535-B538.

Soccer SP215

Children's Drawings: 45c+20c, Sailboat. 55c+20c, Elephant. 75c+25c, Mobile home.

**1976, Nov. 16 Photo. *Perf. 14x13***

**B527** SP215 40c +20c multi .25 .25
**B528** SP215 45c +20c multi .30 .25
**B529** SP215 55c +20c multi .35 .25
*a.* Min. sheet of 6, 2 each #B527-B529 2.40 2.40
**B530** SP215 75c +25c multi 1.10 .80
*Nos. B527-B530 (4)* 2.00 1.55

Surtax was for child welfare.

Hot Room, Thermal Bath, Heerlen SP216

45c+20c, Altar of Goddess Nehalennia, 200 A.D., Eastern Scheldt. 55c+20c, Part of oaken ship, Zwammerdam. 75c+25c, Helmet with face, Waal River at Nijmegen.

**1977, Apr. 19 Photo. *Perf. 14x13***

**B531** SP216 40c +20c multi .45 .30
**B532** SP216 45c +20c multi .50 .30
**B533** SP216 55c +20c multi .50 .30
**B534** SP216 75c +25c multi .65 .50
*Nos. B531-B534 (4)* 2.10 1.40

Archaeological finds of Roman period.

Surtax for various social and cultural institutions.

**Type of 1976**

Designs: No. B535, Netherlands #83. No. B536, Netherlands #128. No. B537, Netherlands #211. No. B538, Netherlands #302.

**1977, May 26 Litho. *Perf. 13x14***

**B535** SP214 55c +45c multi .55 .30
**B536** SP214 55c +45c multi .55 .30
*a.* Pair, #B535-B536 1.10 1.10
**B537** SP214 55c +45c multi .55 .30
**B538** SP214 55c +45c multi .55 .30
*a.* Souv. sheet of 2, #B535, B538 1.25 1.25
*b.* Pair, #B537-B538 1.10 1.10
*Nos. B535-B538 (4)* 2.20 1.20

Amphilex 77 International Philatelic Exhibition, Amsterdam May 26-June 5. No. B538a sold at Exhibition only.

Risk of Drowning — SP217

Childhood Dangers: 45c+20c, Poisoning. 55c+20c, Following ball into street. 75c+25c, Playing with matches.

**1977, Nov. 15 Photo. *Perf. 13x14***

**B539** SP217 40c +20c multi .40 .25
**B540** SP217 45c +20c multi .40 .25
**B541** SP217 55c +20c multi .40 .25
*a.* Min. sheet of 6, 2 each #B539-B541 2.50 2.40
**B542** SP217 75c +25c multi .80 .80
*Nos. B539-B542 (4)* 2.00 1.55

Surtax was for child welfare.

Anna Maria van Schuurman SP218

Delft Plate SP219

Designs: 45c+20c, Part of letter written by author Belle van Zuylen (1740-1805). 75c+25c, Makkum dish with dog.

**1978, Apr. 11 Litho. *Perf. 13x14***

**B543** SP218 40c +20c multi .40 .30
**B544** SP218 45c +20c multi .50 .30

**Photo.**

**B545** SP219 55c +20c multi .55 .30
**B546** SP219 75c +25c multi .60 .45
*Nos. B543-B546 (4)* 2.05 1.35

Dutch authors and pottery products.

Red Cross and World Map SP220

**1978, Aug. 22 Photo. *Perf. 14x13***

**B547** SP220 55c +25c multi .50 .40
*a.* Souvenir sheet of 3 1.50 1.50

Surtax was for Dutch Red Cross.

Boy Ringing Doorbell SP221

Designs: 45c+20c, Child reading book. 55c+20c, Boy writing "30x Children for Children," vert. 75c+25c, Girl at blackboard, arithmetic lesson.

***Perf. 14x13, 13x14***

**1978, Nov. 14 Photo.**

**B548** SP221 40c +20c multi .40 .25
**B549** SP221 45c +20c multi .40 .25
**B550** SP221 55c +20c multi .40 .25
*a.* Min. sheet of 6, 2 each #B548-B550 2.40 2.25
**B551** SP221 75c +25c multi .80 .65
*Nos. B548-B551 (4)* 2.00 1.40

Surtax was for child welfare.

Psalm Trilogy, by Jurriaan Andriessen SP222

Birth of Christ (detail) Stained-glass Window SP223

Designs: 45c+20c, Amsterdam Toonkunst Choir. 75c+25c, William of Orange, stained-glass window, 1603. Windows from St. John's Church, Gouda.

**1979, Apr. 3 Photo. *Perf. 13x14***

**B552** SP222 40c +20c multi .40 .30
**B553** SP222 45c +20c multi .50 .30
**B554** SP223 55c +20c multi .55 .25
**B555** SP223 75c +25c multi .60 .45
*Nos. B552-B555 (4)* 2.05 1.30

Surtax for social and cultural purposes.

Child Sleeping Under Blanket SP224

Designs: 45c+20c, Infant. 55c+20c, African boy, vert. 75c+25c, Children, vert.

**1979, Nov. 13 *Perf. 14x13, 13x14***

**B556** SP224 40c +20c blk, red & yel .40 .30
**B557** SP224 45c +20c blk & red .40 .30
**B558** SP224 55c +20c blk & yel .40 .30
*a.* Min. sheet, 2 each #B556-B558 2.75 2.75
**B559** SP224 75c +25c blk, ultra & red .75 .55
*Nos. B556-B559 (4)* 1.95 1.45

Surtax was for child welfare (in conjuction with International Year of the Child).

Roads Through Sand Dunes SP225

50c+20c, Park mansion vert. 60c+25c, Sailing. 80c+35c, Bicycling, moorlands.

***Perf. 14x13, 13x14***

**1980, Apr. 15 Litho.**

**B560** SP225 45c +20c multi .60 .30
**B561** SP225 50c +20c multi .60 .30
**B562** SP225 60c +25c multi .60 .30
**B563** SP225 80c +35c multi .80 .45
*Nos. B560-B563 (4)* 2.60 1.35

Society for the Promotion of Nature Preserves, 75th anniv. Surtax for social and cultural purposes.

Wheelchair Basketball — SP226

**1980, June 3 Litho. *Perf. 13x14***

**B564** SP226 60c +25c multi .80 .40

Olympics for the Disabled, Arnhem and Veenendaal, June 21-July 5. Surtax was for National Sports for the Handicapped Fund.

Harlequin and Girl Standing in Open Book SP227

Designs: 50c+20c, Boy on flying book, vert. 60c+30c, Boy reading King of Frogs, vert. 80c+30c, Boy "engrossed" in book.

***Perf. 14x13, 13x14***

**1980, Nov. 11 Photo.**

**B565** SP227 45c +20c multi .45 .25
**B566** SP227 50c +20c multi .55 .30
**B567** SP227 60c +30c multi .55 .25
*a.* Min. sheet of 5, 2 #B565, 3 #B567 + label 2.50 2.50
**B568** SP227 80c +30c multi .90 .60
*Nos. B565-B568 (4)* 2.45 1.40

Surtax was for child welfare.

Salt Marsh with Outlet Ditch at Low Tide — SP228

Designs: 55c+25c, Dike. 60c+25c, Land drainage. 65c+30c, Cultivated land.

**1981, Apr. 7 Photo. *Perf. 13x14***

**B569** SP228 45c +20c multi .50 .30
**B570** SP228 55c +25c multi .55 .30
**B571** SP228 60c +25c multi .65 .30
**B572** SP228 65c +30c multi .75 .30
*Nos. B569-B572 (4)* 2.45 1.20

Intl. Year of the Disabled SP229

Various people.

***Perf. 14x13, 13x14***

**1981, Nov. 10 Photo.**

**B573** SP229 45c +25c multi .45 .25
**B574** SP229 55c +20c multi, vert .50 .35
**B575** SP229 60c +25c multi, vert. .60 .35
**B576** SP229 65c +30c multi .65 .25
*a.* Min. sheet of 5, 3 #B573, 2 #B576 + label 2.50 2.40
*Nos. B573-B576 (4)* 2.20 1.20

Surtax was for child welfare.

Floriade '82, Amsterdam, Apr. — SP230

No. B578, Anemones. No. B579, Roses. No. B580, African violets.

**1982, Apr. 7 Litho. *Perf. 13½x13***

**B577** SP230 50c +20c shown .65 .35
**B578** SP230 60c +25c multi .65 .35
**B579** SP230 65c +25c multi .65 .35
**B580** SP230 70c +30c multi .65 .40
*Nos. B577-B580 (4)* 2.60 1.45

Surtax was for culture and social welfare institutions.

Birds on Child's Head — SP231

Children and Animals: 60c+20c, Boy and cat. 65c+20c, Boy and rabbit. 70c+30c, Boy and bird.

**1982, Nov. 16 Photo. *Perf. 13x14***

**B581** SP231 50c +30c multi .35 .25
**B582** SP231 60c +20c multi .50 .25
*a.* Min. sheet of 5, 4 #B581, #B582 3.00 2.75
**B583** SP231 65c +20c multi .75 .60
**B584** SP231 70c +30c multi .85 .60
*Nos. B581-B584 (4)* 2.45 1.70

Surtax was for child welfare.

Johan van Oldenbarneveldt (1547-1619), Statesman, by J. Houbraken — SP232

Paintings: 60c+25c, Willem Jansz Blaeu (1571-1638), cartographer, by Thomas de Keijser. 65c+25c, Hugo de Groot (1583-1645), statesman, by J. van Ravesteyn. 70c+30c, Portrait of Saskia van Uylenburch, by Rembrandt (1606-1669).

**1983, Apr. 19 Photo. *Perf. 14x13***

| | | | | |
|---|---|---|---|---|
| **B585** | SP232 | 50c +20c multi | .75 | .35 |
| **B586** | SP232 | 60c +25c multi | .75 | .35 |
| **B587** | SP232 | 65c +25c multi | .75 | .50 |
| **B588** | SP232 | 70c +30c multi | .75 | .50 |
| | | *Nos. B585-B588 (4)* | 3.00 | 1.70 |

Surtax was for cultural and social welfare institutions.

Red Cross Workers — SP233

Designs: 60c+20c, Principles. 65c+25c, Sociomedical work. 70c+30c, Peace.

**1983, Aug. 30 Photo. *Perf. 13x14***

| | | | | |
|---|---|---|---|---|
| **B589** | SP233 | 50c +25c multi | .75 | .45 |
| **B590** | SP233 | 60c +20c multi | .75 | .50 |
| **B591** | SP233 | 65c +25c multi | .75 | .50 |
| **B592** | SP233 | 70c +30c multi | .75 | .70 |
| *a.* | | Bklt. pane, 4 #B589, 2 #B592 | 4.75 | 4.75 |
| | | Complete booklet, #B592a | 4.75 | |
| | | *Nos. B589-B592 (4)* | 3.00 | 2.15 |

Surtax was for Red Cross.

Children's Christmas SP235

No. B596, Ox & donkey. No. B597, Snowman. No. B598, Stars. No. B599, Epiphany.

**1983, Nov. 16 Photo. *Perf. 14x13***

| | | | | |
|---|---|---|---|---|
| **B596** | SP235 | 50c +10c multi | .65 | .45 |
| **B597** | SP235 | 50c +25c multi | .40 | .25 |
| **B598** | SP235 | 60c +30c multi | .75 | .60 |
| **B599** | SP235 | 70c +30c multi | .60 | .25 |
| *a.* | | Min. sheet, 4 #B597, 2 #B599 | 3.75 | 3.25 |
| | | *Nos. B596-B599 (4)* | 2.40 | 1.55 |

Surtax was for Child Welfare.

Eurasian Lapwings SP236

Birds: 60c+25c, Ruffs. 65c+25c, Redshanks, vert. 70c+30c, Black-tailed godwits, vert.

**1984, Apr. 3 *Perf. 14x13, 13x14***

| | | | | |
|---|---|---|---|---|
| **B600** | SP236 | 50c +20c multi | .65 | .35 |
| **B601** | SP236 | 60c +25c multi | .65 | .35 |
| **B602** | SP236 | 65c +25c multi | .65 | .55 |
| **B603** | SP236 | 70c +30c multi | .65 | .55 |
| *a.* | | Bklt. pane, 2 #B600, 2 #B603 | 3.50 | 3.50 |
| | | Complete booklet, #B603a | 3.75 | |
| | | *Nos. B600-B603 (4)* | 2.60 | 1.80 |

Surtax for cultural and social welfare institutions.

FILACENTO '84 — SP237

Centenary of Organized Philately: 50c+20c, Eye, magnifying glass (36x25mm). 60c+25c, Cover, 1909 (34½x25mm). 70c+30c, Stamp club meeting, 1949 (34½x24mm).

**1984, June 13 Litho. *Perf. 14x13***

| | | | | |
|---|---|---|---|---|
| **B604** | SP237 | 50c +20c multi | .60 | .55 |
| **B605** | SP237 | 60c +25c multi | .70 | .55 |
| **B606** | SP237 | 70c +30c multi | .80 | .55 |
| *a.* | | Souv. sheet of 3, #B604-B606 | 2.50 | 2.40 |
| | | *Nos. B604-B606 (3)* | 2.10 | 1.65 |

No. B606a issued Sept. 5, 1984.

Comic Strips — SP238

No. B607, Music lesson. No. B608, Dentist. No. B609, Plumber. No. B610, King.

**1984, Nov. 14 Litho. *Perf. 13x13½***

| | | | | |
|---|---|---|---|---|
| **B607** | SP238 | 50c +25c multi | .40 | .30 |
| **B608** | SP238 | 60c +20c multi | 1.05 | .60 |
| **B609** | SP238 | 65c +20c multi | 1.15 | .80 |
| **B610** | SP238 | 70c +30c multi | .65 | .30 |
| *a.* | | Min. sheet, 4 #B607, 2 #B610 | 4.00 | 3.75 |
| | | *Nos. B607-B610 (4)* | 3.25 | 2.00 |

Surtax was for child welfare.

Winterswijk Synagogue, Holy Arc — SP239

Religious architecture: 50+20c, St. Martin's Church, Zaltbommel, vert. 65+25c, Village Congregational Church, Bolsward, vert. 70+30c, St. John's Cathedral, 'S-Hertogenbosch, detail of buttress.

***Perf. 13x14, 14x13***

**1985, Mar. 26 Photo.**

| | | | | |
|---|---|---|---|---|
| **B611** | SP239 | 50c +20c gray & brt bl | .80 | .50 |
| **B612** | SP239 | 60c +25c dk red brn, Prus bl & pck bl | .80 | .55 |
| **B613** | SP239 | 65c +25c sl bl, red brn & gray ol | .80 | .55 |
| **B614** | SP239 | 70c +30c gray, brt bl & bis | .80 | .40 |
| *a.* | | Bklt. pane, 2 #B611, 2 #B614 | 4.00 | 4.00 |
| | | Complete booklet, #B614a | 4.00 | |
| | | *Nos. B611-B614 (4)* | 3.20 | 2.00 |

Surtax for social and cultural purposes.

Traffic Safety SP240

No B615, Photograph, lock, key. No. B616, Boy, target. No. B617, Girl, hazard triangle. No. B618, Boy, traffic sign.

**1985, Nov. 13 Photo. *Perf. 13x14***

| | | | | |
|---|---|---|---|---|
| **B615** | SP240 | 50c +25c multi | .45 | .35 |
| **B616** | SP240 | 60c +20c multi | .75 | .65 |
| **B617** | SP240 | 65c +20c multi | .75 | .65 |
| **B618** | SP240 | 70c +30c multi | .85 | .35 |
| *a.* | | Souv. sheet, 4 #B615, 2 #B618 | 3.75 | 3.25 |
| | | *Nos. B615-B618 (4)* | 2.80 | 2.00 |

Surtax was for child welfare organizations.

Antique Measuring Instruments SP241

No. B619, Balance. No. B620, Clock mechanism. No. B621, Barometer. No. B622, Jacob's staff.

***Perf. 13½x13, 13x13½***

**1986, Apr. 8 Litho.**

| | | | | |
|---|---|---|---|---|
| **B619** | SP241 | 50c +20c multi | .50 | .45 |
| **B620** | SP241 | 60c +25c multi | .50 | .45 |
| **B621** | SP241 | 65c +25c multi | .50 | .45 |
| **B622** | SP241 | 70c +30c multi | .50 | .45 |
| *a.* | | Bklt. pane, 2 each #B619, B622 | 4.00 | 4.00 |
| | | Complete booklet, #B622a | 4.00 | |
| | | *Nos. B619-B622 (4)* | 2.00 | 1.80 |

Nos. B620-B621 vert.

Youth and Culture SP242

No. B623, Music. No. B624, Visual arts. No. B625, Theater.

**1986, Nov. 12 Litho. *Perf. 14x13***

| | | | | |
|---|---|---|---|---|
| **B623** | SP242 | 55c +25c multi | .75 | .45 |

***Perf. 13½x13***

| | | | | |
|---|---|---|---|---|
| **B624** | SP242 | 65c +35c multi | .90 | .45 |
| **B625** | SP242 | 75c +35c multi | 1.00 | .45 |
| *a.* | | Min. sheet of 5, #B623, 2 each #B624-B625, perf. 14x13 | 4.00 | 3.75 |
| | | *Nos. B623-B625 (3)* | 2.65 | 1.35 |

Surtax for child welfare organizations.

Traditional Industries SP243

Designs: 55c+30c, Steam pumping station, Nijkerk. 65c+35c, Water tower, Deventer. 75c+35c, Brass foundry, Joure.

**1987, Apr. 7 Photo. *Perf. 14x13***

| | | | | |
|---|---|---|---|---|
| **B626** | SP243 | 55c +30c multi | .90 | .65 |
| **B627** | SP243 | 65c +35c multi | 1.05 | .65 |
| **B628** | SP243 | 75c +35c multi | 1.20 | .85 |
| *a.* | | Bklt. pane, 2 #B626, 2 #B628 | 4.25 | 4.25 |
| | | Complete booklet, #B628a | 4.25 | |
| | | *Nos. B626-B628 (3)* | 3.15 | 2.15 |

Surtax for social and cultural welfare organizations.

Red Cross SP244

**1987, Sept. 1 Photo. *Perf. 14x13***

| | | | | |
|---|---|---|---|---|
| **B629** | SP244 | 55c +30c multi | .90 | .75 |
| **B630** | SP244 | 65c +35c multi, diff. | 1.05 | .75 |
| **B631** | SP244 | 75c +35c multi, diff. | 1.20 | .75 |
| *a.* | | Bklt. pane, 2 #B629, 2 #B631 | 4.25 | 4.25 |
| | | Complete booklet, #B631a | 4.25 | |
| | | *Nos. B629-B631 (3)* | 3.15 | 2.25 |

Surtax for nat'l. Red Cross.

Youth and Professions SP245

No. B632, Woodcutter, vert. No. B633, Sailor. No. B634, Pilot.

***Perf. 13x14, 14x13***

**1987, Nov. 11 Photo.**

| | | | | |
|---|---|---|---|---|
| **B632** | SP245 | 55c +25c multi | .90 | .60 |
| **B633** | SP245 | 65c +35c multi | 1.05 | .50 |
| **B634** | SP245 | 75c +35c multi | 1.20 | .25 |
| *a.* | | Miniature sheet of 5, #B632, 2 #B633, 2 #B634 | 4.00 | 4.00 |
| | | *Nos. B632-B634 (3)* | 3.15 | 1.35 |

Surtax for child welfare organizations.

FILACEPT '88, October 18, The Hague SP246

Designs: 55c +55c, Narcissus cyclamineus and poem "I call you flowers," by Jan Hanlo.

No. B636, Rosa gallica versicolor. No. B637, Eryngium maritimum and map of The Hague from 1270.

**1988, Feb. 23 Litho. *Perf. 13½x13***

| | | | | |
|---|---|---|---|---|
| **B635** | SP246 | 55c +55c multi | 1.00 | .90 |
| **B636** | SP246 | 75c +70c multi | 1.00 | .90 |
| **B637** | SP246 | 75c +70c multi | 1.00 | .90 |
| *a.* | | Min. sheet of 3 + 3 labels, #B635-B637 | 3.25 | 3.25 |
| | | *Nos. B635-B637 (3)* | 3.00 | 2.70 |

Surtax helped finance exhibition.

No. B637a issued Oct. 18, 1988.

Man and the Zoo — SP247

No B638, Equus quagga quagga. No. B639, Carribean sea cow. No. B640, Sam the orangutan, vert.

***Perf. 14x13, 13x14***

**1988, Mar. 22 Photo.**

| | | | | |
|---|---|---|---|---|
| **B638** | SP247 | 55c +30c multi | 1.00 | .90 |
| **B639** | SP247 | 65c +35c multi | 1.00 | 1.00 |
| **B640** | SP247 | 75c +35c multi | 1.00 | .80 |
| *a.* | | Bklt. pane, 2 #B638, 2 #B640 | 4.00 | 4.00 |
| | | Complete booklet, #B640a | 4.00 | |
| | | *Nos. B638-B640 (3)* | 3.00 | 2.70 |

Natural Artis Magistra zoological soc., 150th anniv. Surtax for social and cultural welfare organizations.

Royal Dutch Swimming Federation, Cent. SP248

Children's drawings on the theme "Children and Water." No. B641, Rain. No. B642, Getting Ready for the Race. No. B643, Swimming Test.

**1988, Nov. 16 Photo. *Perf. 14x13***

| | | | | |
|---|---|---|---|---|
| **B641** | SP248 | 55c +25c multi | .75 | .55 |
| **B642** | SP248 | 65c +35c multi | .90 | .55 |
| **B643** | SP248 | 75c +35c multi | 1.00 | .30 |
| *a.* | | Min. sheet of 5, #B641, 2 each #B642-B643 | 4.75 | 4.75 |
| | | *Nos. B641-B643 (3)* | 2.65 | 1.40 |

Surtax to benefit child welfare organizations.

Ships SP249

Designs: No. B644, Pleasure yacht (boyer), vert. No. B645, Zuiderzee fishing boat (smack). No. B646, Clipper.

***Perf. 13x14, 14x13***

**1989, Apr. 11 Photo.**

| | | | | |
|---|---|---|---|---|
| **B644** | SP249 | 55c +30c multi | 1.00 | .80 |
| **B645** | SP249 | 65c +35c multi | 1.00 | .80 |
| **B646** | SP249 | 75c +35c multi | 1.00 | .80 |
| *a.* | | Bklt. pane, #B644-B645, 2 #B646 | 4.00 | 4.00 |
| | | Complete booklet, #B646a | 4.00 | |
| | | *Nos. B644-B646 (3)* | 3.00 | 2.40 |

Surtax for social and cultural organizations.

Children's Rights SP250

**1989, Nov. 8 Litho. *Perf. 13½x13***

| | | | | |
|---|---|---|---|---|
| **B647** | SP250 | 55c +25c Housing | .75 | .55 |
| **B648** | SP250 | 65c +35c Food | .90 | .45 |
| **B649** | SP250 | 75c +35c Education | 1.00 | .35 |
| *a.* | | Min. sheet of 5, #B647, 2 each #B648-B649 | 4.00 | 4.00 |
| | | *Nos. B647-B649 (3)* | 2.65 | 1.35 |

UN Declaration of Children's Rights, 30th anniv. Surtax for child welfare.

Summer Weather SP251

No. B650, Girl, flowers. No. B651, Clouds, isobars, vert. No. B652, Weather map, vert.

***Perf. 14x13, 13x14***

**1990, Apr. 3** **Photo.**

**B650** SP251 55c +30c multi 1.00 .75
**B651** SP251 65c +35c multi 1.00 .85
**B652** SP251 75c +35c multi 1.00 .75
*a.* Bklt. pane, #B650-B651, 2 #B652 4.00 4.00
Complete booklet, #B652a 4.00
*Nos. B650-B652 (3)* 3.00 2.35

Surtax for social & cultural welfare organizations.

Children's Hobbies SP252

No. B653, Riding. No. B654, Computers. No. B655, Philately.

**1990, Nov. 7** **Litho.** ***Perf. 13½x13***

**B653** SP252 55c +25c multi .75 .75
**B654** SP252 65c +35c multi .85 .45
**B655** SP252 75c +35c multi 1.00 .25
*a.* Souv. sheet of 5, #B653, 2 each #B654-B655 4.00 4.00
*Nos. B653-B655 (3)* 2.60 1.45

Surtax for child welfare.

Dutch Farms SP253

55c+30c, Frisian farm, Wartena. 65c+35c, Guelders T-style farm, Kesteren. 75c+35c, Closed construction farm, Nuth (Limburg).

**1991, Apr. 16** **Litho.** ***Perf. 13½x13***

**B656** SP253 55c +30c multi 1.00 .90
*a.* Photo. .75 .30
**B657** SP253 65c +35c multi 1.00 .90
**B658** SP253 75c +35c multi 1.00 .90
*a.* Photo. .75 .30
*b.* Bklt. pane, 2 #B656a, 3 #B658a 4.00 4.00
Complete booklet, #B658b 4.00
*Nos. B656-B658 (3)* 3.00 2.70

Surtax for social and cultural welfare organizations.

Children Playing SP254

No. B659, Doll, robot. No. B660, Cycle race. No. B661, Hide and seek.

**1991, Nov. 6** **Litho.** ***Perf. 13½x13***

**B659** SP254 60c +30c multi .60 .30
*a.* Photo., perf. 14x13½ .60 .30
**B660** SP254 70c +35c multi .70 .70
**B661** SP254 80c +40c multi .80 .40
*a.* Photo., perf. 14x13½ .80 .40
*b.* Min. sheet, 4 #B659a, 2 #B661a 4.00 4.00
*Nos. B659-B661 (3)* 2.10 1.40

Floriade 1992, World Horticultural Exhibition SP255

Various plants and flowers.

**1992, Apr. 7** **Litho.** ***Perf. 13½x13***

**B662** SP255 60c +30c multi 1.00 1.00
*a.* Photo., perf. 14x13½ .70 .40
**B663** SP255 70c +35c multi 1.00 1.00
*a.* Photo., perf. 14x13½ .80 .70
**B664** SP255 80c +40c multi 1.00 1.00
*a.* Photo., perf. 14x13½ 3.50 3.00
*b.* Booklet pane of 6, 3 #B662a, 2 #B663a, #B664a 7.25
Complete booklet, #B664b 7.25
*Nos. B662-B664 (3)* 3.00 3.00

Surtax for social and cultural welfare organizations.

Stamps in No. 664b are tete-beche (1 pair of B662a, 1 pair of B663a, 1 pair of B662a and B664a).

Netherlands Red Cross, 125th Anniv. SP256

No. B665, Shadow of cross. No B666, Aiding victim. No. B667, Red cross on bandage.

**1992, Sept. 8** **Litho.** ***Perf. 13½x13***

**B665** SP256 60c +30c multi 1.00 1.00
*a.* Photo., perf. 14 on 3 sides .70 .40
**B666** SP256 70c +35c multi 1.00 1.00
*a.* Photo., perf. 14 on 3 sides .80 .70
**B667** SP256 80c +40c multi 1.00 1.00
*a.* Photo., perf. 14 on 3 sides 3.50 3.00
*b.* Bklt. pane, 3 #B665a, 2 #B666a, 1 #B667a 7.25
Complete booklet, #B667b 7.25
*Nos. B665-B667 (3)* 3.00 3.00

On normally centered stamps, the white border appears on the top, bottom and right sides only.

Children Making Music — SP257

No. B668, Saxophone player. No. B669, Piano player. No. B670, Bass player.

**1992, Nov. 11** **Litho.** ***Perf. 13x13½***

**B668** SP257 60c +30c multi .70 .40
*a.* Photo., perf. 13½x14 .70 .40
**B669** SP257 70c +35c multi .75 .60
*a.* Photo., perf. 13½x14 .75 .60
**B670** SP257 80c +40c multi .85 .85
*a.* Photo., perf. 13½x14 .85 .85
*b.* Min. sheet, 3 #B668a, 2 #B669a, #B670a 4.50 4.25
*Nos. B668-B670 (3)* 2.30 1.85

Senior Citizens — SP258

**1993, Apr. 20** **Litho.** ***Perf. 13x13½***

**B671** SP258 70c +35c shown 1.10 1.10
*a.* Photo., perf. 13½x14 2.75 2.75
**B672** SP258 70c +35c couple 1.10 1.10
*a.* Photo., perf. 13½x14 .80 .70
**B673** SP258 80c +40c woman 1.10 1.10
*a.* Photo., perf. 13½x14 .70 .60
*b.* Booklet pane, 1 #B671a, 2 #B672a, 3 #B673a 6.45 6.45
Complete booklet, #B673b 6.45
*Nos. B671-B673 (3)* 3.30 3.30

Children and the Media SP259

Designs: No. B674, Child wearing newspaper hat. No. B675, Elephant wearing earphones. 80c + 40c, Television, child's legs.

**1993, Nov. 17** **Litho.** ***Perf. 13½x13***

**B674** SP259 70c +35c multi .90 .90
*a.* Photo., perf. 14x13½ .90 .90
**B675** SP259 70c +35c multi .90 .90
*a.* Photo., perf. 14x13½ .90 .90
**B676** SP259 80c +40c multi .90 .90
*a.* Photo., perf. 14x13½ .90 .90
*b.* Min. sheet, 2 each #B674a-B676a 5.50 5.50
*Nos. B674-B676 (3)* 2.70 2.70

FEPAPOST '94 — SP260

Birds: 70c+60c, Branta leucopsis. 80c+70c, Luscinia svecica. 90c+80c, Anas querquedula.

**1994, Feb. 22** **Litho.** ***Perf. 14x13***

**B677** SP260 70c +60c multi 1.20 1.20
**B678** SP260 80c +70c multi 1.20 1.20
**B679** SP260 90c +80c multi 1.20 1.20
*a.* Min. sheet, #B677-B679 + 3 labels, perf. 13½x13 3.75 3.75
*Nos. B677-B679 (3)* 3.60 3.60

Issued: No. B679a, 10/17/94.

Senior Citizens — SP261

Designs: 80c+40c, Man talking on telephone seen from behind. 90c+35c, Man in suit talking on telephone.

**1994, Apr. 26** **Litho.** ***Perf. 13x13½***

**B680** SP261 70c +35c shown 1.00 .90
*a.* Photo., perf. 13½x14 .80 .70
**B681** SP261 80c +40c multi 1.00 .75
*a.* Photo., perf. 13½x14 .90 .80
**B682** SP261 90c +35c multi 1.00 1.00
*a.* Photo., perf. 13½x14 3.50 3.00
*b.* Booklet pane, 2 #B680a, 3 #B681a, #B682a 8.00
*Nos. B680-B682 (3)* 3.00 2.65

Child Welfare Stamps SP262

Designs: 70c+35c, Holding ladder for woman painting. 80c+40c, Helping to balance woman picking cherries, vert. 90c+35c, Supporting boy on top of play house, vert.

***Perf. 13½x13, 13x13½***

**1994, Nov. 9** **Litho.**

**B683** SP262 70c +35c multi .90 .50
*a.* Perf. 14x13 .90 .80
**B684** SP262 80c +40c multi .90 .50
*a.* Perf. 13x14 .90 .60
**B685** SP262 90c +35c multi 1.35 1.35
*a.* SP262 Miniature sheet, 2 #B683a, 3 #B684a, 1 #B685b 5.25 5.25
*b.* Perf. 13x14 1.35 1.35
*Nos. B683-B685 (3)* 3.15 2.35

Senior Citizens SP263

Designs: 70c+35c, Indonesia #1422 on postcard. 80c+40c, Couple seen in bus mirror. 100c+45c, Grandparents, child at zoo.

**1995, Apr. 11** **Litho.** ***Perf. 13½x13***

**B686** SP263 70c +35c multi .90 .90
**B687** SP263 80c +40c multi .90 .50
**B688** SP263 100c +45c multi .90 .90
*a.* Miniature sheet, 2 #B686, 3 #B687, 1 #B688 6.00 6.00
*Nos. B686-B688 (3)* 2.70 2.30

Child Welfare Stamps SP264

Computer drawings by children: 70c+35c, Dino, by S. Stegeman. 80c+40c, The School Teacher, by L. Ensing, vert. 100c+50c, Children and Colors, by M. Jansen.

***Perf. 13½x13, 13x13½***

**1995, Nov. 15** **Litho.**

**B689** SP264 70c +35c multi 1.10 .75
**B690** SP264 80c +40c multi 1.10 .75
**B691** SP264 100c +50c multi 1.10 1.10
*a.* Min. sheet of 6, 2 #B689, 3 #B690, 1 #B691 6.75 6.75
*Nos. B689-B691 (3)* 3.30 2.60

Senior Citizens SP265

No. B692, Swimming. No. B693, Babysitting. No. B694, Playing piano.

**1996, Apr. 23** **Litho.** ***Perf. 13¼x12¾***

**B692** SP265 70c +35c multi .95 .50
**B693** SP265 80c +40c multi .95 .50
**B694** SP265 100c +50c multi 1.75 1.10
*a.* Sheet of 6, 2 #B692, 3 #B693, 1 #B694, perf. 13x12½ 6.50 6.50
*Nos. B692-B694 (3)* 3.65 2.10

Child Welfare Stamps — SP266

Designs: 70c+35c, Baby, books. No. B696, Boy, toys. No. B697, Girl, tools.

***Perf. 12¾3x13¼***

**1996, Nov. 6** **Litho.**

**B695** SP266 70c +35 multi 1.00 .50
**B696** SP266 80c +40c multi 1.00 .50
**B697** SP266 80c +40c multi 1.00 .50
*a.* Sheet of 2 each, #B695-B697 6.00 6.00
*Nos. B695-B697 (3)* 3.00 1.50

Senior Citizens SP267

Designs: No. B698, Rose in full bloom. No. B699, Stem of rose. No. B700, Rose bud.

**1997, Apr. 15** **Litho.** ***Perf. 13¼x12¾***

**B698** SP267 80c +40c multi 1.10 .80
**B699** SP267 80c +40c multi 1.10 .80
**B700** SP267 80c +40c multi 1.10 .80
*a.* Min. sheet, 2 each #B698-B700 6.75 6.75
*Nos. B698-B700 (3)* 3.30 2.40

Netherlands Red Cross — SP268

**1997, May 27** **Litho.** ***Perf. 12¾x13¼***

**B701** SP268 80c +40c multi 1.30 1.20

Child Welfare Stamps SP269

Children's Fairy Tales: No. B702, Hunter with wolf, from "Little Red Riding Hood." No. B703, Dropping loaves of bread, from "Tom Thumb." No. B704, Man opening bottle, from "Genie in the Bottle."

*Perf. 13¼x12¾*

**1997, Nov. 12** **Litho.**

**B702** SP269 80c +40c multi 1.10 .50
**B703** SP269 80c +40c multi 1.10 .50
**B704** SP269 80c +40c multi 1.10 .50
*a.* Min. sheet of 2 each, #B702-B704 6.75 6.75
*Nos. B702-B704 (3)* 3.30 1.50

Senior Citizens SP270

#B705, Sports shoe. #B706, Note on paper. #B707, Wrapped piece of candy.

**1998, Apr. 21 Litho.** ***Perf. 13¼x12¾***

**B705** SP270 80c +40c multi 1.25 1.25
**B706** SP270 80c +40c multi 1.25 1.25
**B707** SP270 80c +40c multi 1.25 1.25
*a.* Sheet, 2 each #B705-B707 7.50 7.50
*Nos. B705-B707 (3)* 3.75 3.75

Child Welfare Stamps SP271

#B708, Elephant riding horse. #B709, Pig, rabbit decorating cake. #B710, Pig, goose, rabbit carrying flower, frog carrying flag.

*Perf. 13¼x12¾*

**1998, Nov. 11** **Litho.**

**B708** SP271 80c +40c multi 1.25 .50
**B709** SP271 80c +40c multi 1.25 .50
**B710** SP271 80c +40c multi 1.25 .50
*a.* Sheet, 2 each #B708-B710 7.50 7.50
*Nos. B708-B710 (3)* 3.75 1.50

Intl. Year of Older Persons SP272

No. B711, Woman. No. B712, Black man. No. B713, Caucasian man.

**1999, Apr. 13 Litho.** ***Perf. 13¼x12¾***

**B711** SP272 80c +40c multi 1.25 1.00
**B712** SP272 80c +40c multi 1.25 1.00
**B713** SP272 80c +40c multi 1.25 1.00
*a.* Min. sheet, 2 ea #B711-B713 7.50 7.50
*Nos. B711-B713 (3)* 3.75 3.00

Child Welfare Stamps SP273

Designs: No. B714, Boy on tow truck. No. B715, Girl and chef. No. B716, Children stamping envelope.

*Perf. 13¼x12¾*

**1999, Nov. 10** **Litho.**

**B714** SP273 80c +40c multi 1.25 .60
**B715** SP273 80c +40c multi 1.25 .60
**B716** SP273 80c +40c multi 1.25 .60
*a.* Sheet, 2 each #B714-B716 7.50 7.50
*Nos. B714-B716 (3)* 3.75 1.80

Senior Citizens SP274

No. B717, Swimmers. No. B718, Bowlers. No. B719, Fruit picker.

**2000, Apr. 4 Litho.** ***Perf. 13¼x12¾***

**B717** SP274 80c +40c multi 1.40 1.40
**B718** SP274 80c +40c multi 1.40 1.40
**B719** SP274 80c +40c multi 1.40 1.40
*a.* Souvenir sheet, 2 each #B717-B719 8.50 8.50
*Nos. B717-B719 (3)* 4.20 4.20

Souvenir Sheet

KIND EN AVONTUUR
KINDERPOSTZEGELACTIE 2000

Child Welfare — SP275

Designs: Nos. B720a, B721, Children with masks. No. B720b, Child with ghost costume. No. B720c, Child on alligator. Nos. B720d, B722, Child in boat. Nos. B720e, B723, Children cooking. No. B720f, Children in dragon costume.

**2000, Nov. 8 Litho.** ***Perf. 13¼x12¾***

**B720** SP275 Sheet of 6 5.00 5.00
*a.-f.* 80c +40c Any single .75 .75

**Self-Adhesive**

***Serpentine Die Cut 15***

**B721** SP275 80c +40c multi 2.25 1.25
**B722** SP275 80c +40c multi 2.25 1.25
**B723** SP275 80c +40c multi 2.25 1.25
*Nos. B721-B723 (3)* 6.75 3.75

Flowers SP276

Designs: No. B724a, Caryopteris. Nos. B724b, B725, Helenium. Nos. B724c, B726, Alcea rugosa. No. B724d, Euphorbia schillingii. No. B724e, B727, Centaurea dealbata. No. B724f, Inula hookeri.

**2001, Apr. 24 Litho.** ***Perf. 13¼x12¾***

**B724** Sheet of 6 6.00 6.00
*a.-f.* SP276 80c+40c Any single 1.00 1.00

***Serpentine Die Cut 14¾x15***

**Self-Adhesive**

**B725** SP276 80c +40c multi 1.40 1.40
**B726** SP276 80c +40c multi 1.40 1.40
**B727** SP276 80c +40c multi 1.40 1.40
*a.* Booklet, 10 each #B725-727 42.50
*Nos. B725-B727 (3)* 4.20 4.20

Children and Computers SP277

Black figure: No. B728a, Retrieving letter from printer. No. B728b, Crossing road with letter. No. B728c, Sliding down green vine. No. B728d, Posting letter. Nos. B728e, B729, Crossing river on log. No. B728f, Swinging on rope.

**2001, Nov. 6 Photo.** ***Perf. 14x13½***

**B728** Sheet of 6 6.75 6.75
*a.-f.* SP277 85c +40c Any single 1.00 .90

**Self-Adhesive**

***Die Cut Perf. 13¼x13***

**B729** SP277 85c +40c multi 2.50 1.50

Surtax for Dutch Children's Stamp Foundation.

SP278

SP279

SP280

SP281

SP282

Floriade 2002 — SP283

**2002, Apr. 2 Litho.** ***Perf. 14¾x14½***

**B730** SP278 39c +19c multi 1.20 .65
**B731** SP279 39c +19c multi 1.20 .65
**B732** SP280 39c +19c multi 1.20 .65
**B733** SP281 39c +19c multi 1.20 .65
**B734** SP282 39c +19c multi 1.20 .65
**B735** SP283 39c +19c multi 1.20 .65
*a.* Block of 6, #B730-B735 7.00 7.00

Nos. B730-B735 are impregnated with a floral scent.

Surtax for National Help the Aged Fund.

Blossom Walk, 10th Anniv. — SP284

**2002, Apr. 27 Litho.** ***Perf. 14¾x14½***

**B736** SP284 39c +19c multi 1.25 .90

Surtax for Red Cross.

Children — SP285

No. B737: a, Child with red head, red cat. b, Child with green head, blue father. c, Child with red head, blue ball. d, Child with yellow head, green pet dish. e, Child with brown head, legs of child. f, Child with yellow head, blue dog.

**2002, Nov. 5 Photo.** ***Perf. 14x13½***

**B737** SP285 Sheet of 6 6.75 6.75
*a.-f.* 39c +19c Any single 1.10 .85

Surtax for Dutch Children's Stamp Foundation.

Flowers — SP286

No. B738: a, Orange yellow lilies of the Incas. b, Lilac sweet peas. c, Pansies. d, Red orange and yellow trumpet creepers. e, Red campions. f, Purple, white and yellow irises.

**2003, Apr. 8 Photo.** ***Perf. 14½x14¾***

**B738** SP286 Block of 6 7.50 7.50
*a.-f.* 39c +19c Any single 1.25 1.25

Souvenir Sheet

Items in a Child's Life — SP287

No. B739: a, Note pad, radio, ballet shoes. b, Theater masks, book. c, Microphone, musical staff, paintbrush. d, Violin, soccer ball, television. e, Television, drum, light bulbs. f, Light bulbs, trombone, hat, headphones.

**2003, Nov. 4** ***Perf. 14x13½***

**B739** SP287 Sheet of 6 7.25 7.25
*a.-f.* 39c +19c Any single 1.15 .85

Flowers — SP288

No. B740 — Various flowers with background color of: a, Lilac. b, Pink. c, Brownish gray. d, Ocher. e, Blue gray. f, Olive.

**2004, Apr. 6 Photo.** ***Perf. 14¾x14½***

**B740** SP288 Block of 6 7.50 7.50
*a.-f.* 39c + 19c any single 1.25 .75

Souvenir Sheet

Fruit and Sports — SP289

No. B741: a, Watermelon, soccer. b, Lemon, rope jumping. c, Orange, cycling. d, Pear, skateboarding. e, Banana, sit-ups. f, Strawberry, weight lifting.

**2004, Nov. 9 Photo.** ***Perf. 14½***

**B741** SP289 Sheet of 6 7.50 7.50
*a.-f.* 39c +19c Any single 1.25 .85

December Stamps — SP290

No. B742 — Inscriptions: a, Novib. b, Stop AIDS Now. c, Natuurmonumenten. d, KWF Kankerbestrijding. e, UNICEF. f, Plan Nederland. g, Tros Helpt. h, Greenpeace. i, Artsen Zonder Grenzen (Doctors Without Borders). j, World Food Program.

***Serpentine Die Cut 8¾x9***

**2004, Nov. 25** **Self-Adhesive**

**B742** Block of 10 9.00 9.00
*a.-j.* SP290 29c +10c Any single .90 .80

The surtax went to the various organizations named on the stamps.

### Souvenir Sheets

SP291

Summer Stamps — SP292

No. B743 — Illustrations for children's stories and silhouette of: a, Children and barrel. b, Two children. c, Frying pan.

No. B744 — Illustrations for children's stories and silhouette of: a, Monkey. b, Cup, saucer and spoon. c, Cat playing with ball.

**2005, Apr. 5 Litho. *Perf. 13¼x13¾***

| | | | | |
|---|---|---|---|---|
| **B743** | SP291 | Sheet of 3 + 2 labels | 4.00 | 4.00 |
| *a.-c.* | | 39c +19c Any single | 1.25 | 1.25 |
| **B744** | SP292 | Sheet of 3 + 2 labels | 4.00 | 4.00 |
| *a.-c.* | | 39c +19c Any single | 1.25 | 1.25 |

### Miniature Sheet

Miffy the Bunny, by Dick Bruna — SP293

No. B745: a, Bunny and dog. b, Four bunnies. c, Bunny holding teddy bear. d, Bunny writing letter. e, White and brown bunnies. f, Six bunnies.

**2005, Nov. 8 Photo. *Perf. 14½***

| | | | | |
|---|---|---|---|---|
| **B745** | SP293 | Sheet of 6 | 8.50 | 8.50 |
| *a.-f.* | | 39c+19c Any single | 1.40 | 1.40 |

The surtax went to the Foundation for Children's Welfare Stamps. A booklet containing four panes of two stamps sold for €9.95.

SP294 SP295

SP296 SP297

SP298 SP299

SP300 SP301

Religious Art from Museum Catharijneconvent, Utrecht

SP302 SP303

***Serpentine Die Cut 8¾x9***

**2005, Nov. 24 Litho.**

| | | | |
|---|---|---|---|
| **B746** | Booklet pane of 10 | 9.50 | |
| *a.* | SP294 29c+10c multi | .95 | .95 |
| *b.* | SP295 29c+10c multi | .95 | .95 |
| *c.* | SP296 29c+10c multi | .95 | .95 |
| *d.* | SP297 29c+10c multi | .95 | .95 |
| *e.* | SP298 29c+10c multi | .95 | .95 |
| *f.* | SP299 29c+10c multi | .95 | .95 |
| *g.* | SP300 29c+10c multi | .95 | .95 |
| *h.* | SP301 29c+10c multi | .95 | .95 |
| *i.* | SP302 29c+10c multi | .95 | .95 |
| *j.* | SP303 29c+10c multi | .95 | .95 |

The surtax went to the various organizations named on the margin and backing paper of the booklet pane.

### Souvenir Sheets

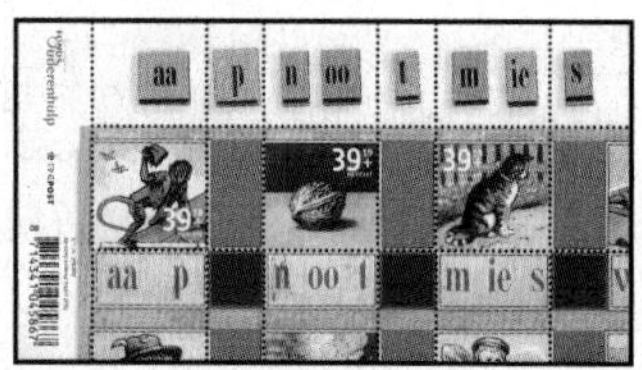

SP304

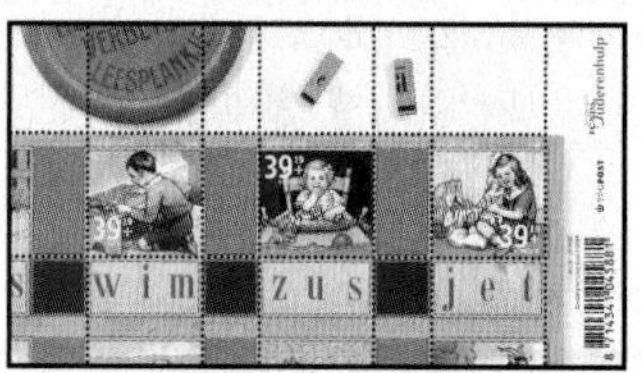

Illustrations From Reading Boards — SP305

No. B747: a, Monkey and birds. b, Walnut. c, Cat.

No. B748: a, Boy playing with game. b, Girl holding rattle. c, Girl playing with doll.

**2006, Apr. 4 Litho. *Perf. 13½x13¾***

| | | | | |
|---|---|---|---|---|
| **B747** | SP304 | Sheet of 3 + 2 labels | 4.25 | 4.25 |
| *a.-c.* | | 39c +19c Any single | 1.40 | 1.40 |
| **B748** | SP305 | Sheet of 3 + 2 labels | 4.25 | 4.25 |
| *a.-c.* | | 39c +19c Any single | 1.40 | 1.40 |

Surtax for National Fund for Care of the Elderly.

### Souvenir Sheet

Children — SP306

No. B749: a, Six children, boy in orange shirt with hands up and with foot on ball. b, Eight children, girl in red shirt with hands in air. c, Six children, girl at right standing. d, Six children, boy in orange shirt with hands down and kicking ball. e, Eight children, girl in red shirt with hands at waist. f, Six children, girl at right seated.

**2006, Nov. 7 Photo. *Perf. 14½***

| | | | | |
|---|---|---|---|---|
| **B749** | SP306 | Sheet of 6 | 9.25 | 9.25 |
| *a.-f.* | | 39c +19c Any single | 1.50 | 1.50 |

Surtax for Dutch Children's Stamp Foundation.

SP307 SP308

SP309 SP310

SP311 SP312

SP313 SP314

SP315

Children Wearing Angel Costumes — SP316

***Serpentine Die Cut 8¾x9***

**2006, Nov. 23 Litho.**

**Self-Adhesive**

| | | | |
|---|---|---|---|
| **B750** | Block of 10 | 10.50 | 10.50 |
| *a.* | SP307 29c +10c multi | 1.00 | 1.00 |
| *b.* | SP308 29c +10c multi | 1.00 | 1.00 |
| *c.* | SP309 29c +10c multi | 1.00 | 1.00 |
| *d.* | SP310 29c +10c multi | 1.00 | 1.00 |
| *e.* | SP311 29c +10c multi | 1.00 | 1.00 |
| *f.* | SP312 29c +10c multi | 1.00 | 1.00 |
| *g.* | SP313 29c +10c multi | 1.00 | 1.00 |
| *h.* | SP314 29c +10c multi | 1.00 | 1.00 |
| *i.* | SP315 29c +10c multi | 1.00 | 1.00 |
| *j.* | SP316 29c +10c multi | 1.00 | 1.00 |

The surtax went to the various organizations named in the sheet selvage.

### Souvenir Sheets

Beach Activities — SP317

No. B751: a, Woman pulling dress up in surf, boy in water. b, Woman standing in surf, children on ponies on beach. c, Children on ponies on beach, children playing on beach.

No. B752: a, Children playing on beach, family posing for photograph on beach. b, Boy waving, people in large beach chair. c, Boy on sail-powered beach cart, family digging sand at shore.

**2007, Apr. 4 Litho. *Perf. 13¼x12¾***

| | | | | |
|---|---|---|---|---|
| **B751** | SP317 | Sheet of 3 | 5.50 | 5.50 |
| *a.-c.* | | 44c +22c Any single | 1.75 | 1.75 |
| **B752** | SP317 | Sheet of 3 | 5.50 | 5.50 |
| *a.-c.* | | 44c +22c Any single | 1.75 | 1.75 |

Surtax for Natiional Fund for Senior Citizen's Help.

Netherlands Red Cross, 140th Anniv. SP318

**2007, July 19 *Perf. 13¼***

| | | | |
|---|---|---|---|
| **B753** | SP318 44c +22c multi | 1.90 | 1.90 |

Surtax for Netherlands Red Cross. Printed in sheets of 3.

### Miniature Sheet

Children and Safety — SP319

No. B754 — Child: a, Watching television. b, And building at night. c, In bed. d, And computer. e, And kitten. f, Reading book.

**2007, Nov. 6 Litho. *Perf. 14½***

| | | | | |
|---|---|---|---|---|
| **B754** | SP319 | Sheet of 6 | 12.00 | 12.00 |
| *a.-f.* | | 44c +22c any single | 2.00 | 2.00 |

Surtax for Foundation for Children's Welfare Stamps.

SP320

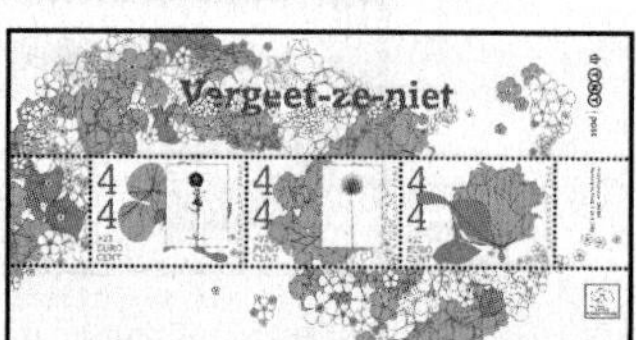


Forget-me-nots — SP321

No. B755: a, Forget-me-not, head-on view. b, Purple crane's bill geranium. c, Pink Japanese anemone.

No. B756: a, Purple larkspur. b, Globe thistle. c, Forget-me-not, side view.

**2008, Apr. 1 Litho. *Perf. 14½***

| | | | | |
|---|---|---|---|---|
| **B755** | SP320 | Sheet of 3 | 6.25 | 6.25 |
| *a.-c.* | | 44c+22c Any single | 2.00 | 2.00 |
| **B756** | SP321 | Sheet of 3 | 6.25 | 6.25 |
| *a.-c.* | | 44c+22c Any single | 2.00 | 2.00 |

Surtax for National Fund for Elderly Assistance.

### Miniature Sheet

Children's Education — SP322

No. B757 — Letters of word "Onderwijs" (education): a, "O." b, "ND." c, "ER." d, "W." e, "IJ." f, "S."

**2008, Nov. 4 Photo. *Perf. 14½***

**B757** SP322 Sheet of 6 10.00 10.00
*a.-f.* 44c +22c Any single 1.60 1.60

Surtax for Foundation for Children's Welfare Stamps.

Miniature Sheet

Elder Care — SP323

No. B758: a, Couple dancing. b, Woman with bag cart. c, Ballet dancer. d, Woman with guide dog. e, Man playing trumpet. f, Woman holding diploma.

**2009, Apr. 7 Litho. *Perf. 14½***

**B758** SP323 Sheet of 6 10.50 10.50
*a.-f.* 44c +22c Any single 1.75 1.75

Surtax for National Fund for Elderly Assistance.

Miniature Sheet

Children's Activities — SP324

No. B759 — Stylized children: a, With pencil. b, With magnifying glasses. c, Watching falling star. d, Playing. e, Reading newspaper. f, With stylized Pegasus.

**2009, Nov. 3 Photo. *Perf. 14½***

**B759** SP324 Sheet of 6 12.00 12.00
*a.-f.* 44c+22c Any single 2.00 2.00

Surtax for Foundation for Children's Welfare Stamps.

Miniature Sheet

Famous People — SP325

No. B760 — Silhouettes of: a, Ramses Shaffy (1933-2009), singer and actor. b, Fanny Blankers-Koen (1918-2004), Olympic gold medalist. c, Mies Bouwman, television personality. d, Willy Alberti (1926-85), singer. e, Dick Bruna, writer and illustrator. f, Annie M. G. Schmidt (1911-95), writer.

**2010, Apr. 27 Litho. *Perf. 14½***

**B760** SP325 Sheet of 6 10.50 10.50
*a.-f.* 44c + 22c Any single 1.75 1.75

Surtax for National Fund for Elderly Assistance.

Miniature Sheet

Children and Mathematical Symbols — SP326

No. B761: a, Boy with red shirt. b, Boy with dark gray shirt, hand near head. c, Boy with gray shirt, hand in front of chest. d, Girl with red and orange dress. e, Girl with arms clasped behind head. f, Girl with arm raised.

**2010, Nov. 9 *Perf. 14x13¾***

**B761** SP326 Sheet of 6 11.00 11.00
*a.-f.* 1 + 22c Any single 1.75 1.75

Nos. B761a-B761f each had a franking value of 44c, with the 22c surtax going to the Foundation for Children's Welfare Stamps.

Miniature Sheet

UNICEF, 65th Anniv. — SP327

No. B762: a, Child holding doll. b, Children touching globe. c, Boy holding card showing his name. d, Boy carrying branches. e, Boy looking out of broken window. f, Boy playing violin. g, Mother holding child. h, Child receiving medicine. i, Child using dog food bag as hood. j, Child blowing bubbles.

**2011, May 23 *Perf. 13¼x12¾***

| | | | | |
|---|---|---|---|---|
| **B762** | SP327 | Sheet of 10 | 19.00 | 19.00 |
| *a.-j.* | | 1 + (20c) Any single | 1.90 | 1.90 |
| *k.* | | Booklet pane of 2, #B762a-B762b | 5.75 | — |
| *l.* | | Booklet pane of 2, #B762c-B762d | 5.75 | — |
| *m.* | | Booklet pane of 2, #B762e-B762f | 5.75 | — |
| *n.* | | Booklet pane of 2, #B762g-B762h | 5.75 | — |
| *o.* | | Booklet pane of 2, #B762i-B762j | 5.75 | — |
| | | Complete booklet, #B762k-B762o | 29.00 | |

Nos. B762a-B762j each had a franking value of 46c, with the 20c surtax going to UNICEF. Complete booklet sold for €9.95.

Miniature Sheet

Children at Play — SP328

No. B763 — Child wearing: a, Orange shirt. b, Light green shirt. c, Pink shirt. d, Purple shirt. e, Blue green shirt. f, White shirt.

**2011, Oct. 29 Photo. *Perf. 14½***

**B763** SP328 Sheet of 6 11.50 11.50
*a.-f.* 1 + 23c Any single 1.90 1.90

Nos. B763a-B763f each had a franking value of 46c, with the 23c surtax going to the Foundation for Children's Welfare Stamps.

Red Cross — SP329

No. B764: a, Cross in red, text "Eerste Hulp bij ongellukken." b, Woman in cross, text "Eerste Hulp dóór iedereen." c, Hand and child's head in cross, text "Eerste Hulp vóór iedereen."

**2012, Jan. 30 Litho. *Perf. 13¼x13½***

**B764** SP329 Horiz. strip of 3 6.00 6.00
*a.-c.* 1 +25c any single 2.00 2.00

Nos. B764a-B764c each had a franking value of 50c, with the 25c surtax going to the Dutch Red Cross. No. B764 was printed in sheets containing two strips.

Miniature Sheet

Princesses — SP330

No. B765: a, Princess Catharina- Amalia. b, Princesses Alexia, Ariane and Catharina-Amalia (five buttons on blouse of Princess Ariane visible). c, Princess Ariane. d, Princesses Catharina-Amalia, Alexia and Ariane (Catharina-Amalia at left). e, Princess Alexia. f, Princesses Alexia, Ariane and Catharina-Amalia (three buttons on blouse of Princess Ariane visible).

**2012, Nov. 6 Photo. *Perf. 14½***

**B765** SP330 Sheet of 6 11.50 11.50
*a.-f.* 1 + 25c Any single 1.90 1.90

Nos. B765a-B765f each had a franking value of 50c, with the 23c surtax going to the Foundation for Children's Welfare Stamps.

Miniature Sheet

Ethiopian Children — SP331

No. B766: a, Boy, multiplication table. b, Boy holding bundle of sticks. c, Girl carrying young boy on her back. d, Girl, letters of Amharic alphabet. e, Boy, poster with pictures and English words. f, Boy carrying goat.

**2013, Nov. 4 Litho. *Perf. 14½***

**B766** SP331 Sheet of 6 14.50 14.50
*a.-f.* 1+30c Any single 2.40 2.40

Nos. B766a-B766f each had a franking value of 60c on the day of issue, with the 30c surtax going to th Foundation for Children's Welfare Stamps.

Miniature Sheet

Children in Works from the Rijksmuseum — SP332

No. B767: a, Children at the beach (36x25mm). b, Children riding donkey (36x25mm). c, Girl wearing kimono (36x25mm). d, Girl and boys near piano (36x25mm). e, Boy on skateboard (36x50mm).

**2014, Nov. 3 Litho. *Perf. 14½***
**B767** SP332 Sheet of 5 12.00 12.00
*a.-e.* 1+32c Any single 2.40 2.40

Nos. B767a-B767b had a franking value of 64c on the day of issue, with the 32c surtax going to the Foundation for Children's Welfare Stamps.

Miniature Sheet

Illustrations From Little Golden Books Series of Children's Books — SP333

No. B768: a, Sofa, toys strung together with cart containing dog and cat. b, Bird chasing cat in tree away from nest. c, Child pulling toys strung together. d, Duck, goose and house. e, Cat on mitten. f, Duck, goose, cat and pig.

**2015, Nov. 2 Litho. *Perf. 13¼***
**B768** SP333 Sheet of 6 13.50 13.50
*a.-f.* 1+34c Any single 2.25 2.25

Nos. B768a-B768f each had a franking value of 69c on the day of issue, with the 34c surcharge going to the Foundation for Children's Welfare Stamps.

Miniature Sheet

Illustrations of Bus and Passengers by Fiep Westendorp (1916-2004) — SP334

No. B769: a, Children with hats and bird cage, child cutting cake. b, Snake, turtles, birds, cat, dog, child. c, Children and chef. d, Bird and musicians. e, Eight children. f, Cats and bus driver.

**2016, Nov. 7 Litho. *Perf. 13¼x13½***
**B769** SP334 Sheet of 6 14.00 14.00
*a.-f.* 1+36c Any single 2.25 2.25

Nos. B769a-B769f each had a franking value of 73c on the day of issue, with the 36c surcharge going to the Foundation for Children's Welfare Stamps.

Miniature Sheet

Characters From *Jan, Jans, and the Children* Comic Strip, by Jan Kruis — SP335

No. B770: a, Jan and son, Gertje. b, Jans and daughter, Karlijn. c, Grandfather and cat. d, Catootje and dog. e, Jeroen holding letter. f, Cat in basket.

**2017, Oct. 9 Litho. *Perf. 14½***
**B770** SP335 Sheet of 6 16.50 16.50
*a.-f.* 1+38c Any single 2.75 2.75

Nos. B770a-B770f each had a franking value of 78c on the day of issue, with the 38c surcharge going to the Foundation for Children's Welfare Stamps.

## AIR POST STAMPS

Stylized Seagull — AP1

***Perf. 12½***

**1921, May 1 Unwmk. Typo.**
**C1** AP1 10c red 1.90 1.25
**C2** AP1 15c yellow grn 5.25 2.10
**C3** AP1 60c dp blue 23.00 .50
*Nos. C1-C3 (3)* 30.15 3.85
Set, never hinged 260.00

Nos. C1-C3 were used to pay airmail fee charged by the carrier, KLM.

Lt. G. A. Koppen — AP2

Capt. Jan van der Hoop — AP3

**Wmk. Circles (202)**

**1928, Aug. 20 Litho. *Perf. 12***
**C4** AP2 40c orange red .50 .25
**C5** AP3 75c blue green .50 .25
Set, never hinged 2.00

Mercury — AP4

***Perf. 11½***

**1929, July 16 Unwmk. Engr.**
**C6** AP4 1½g gray 2.25 1.40
**C7** AP4 4½g carmine 2.25 4.00
**C8** AP4 7½g blue green 26.00 4.00
*Nos. C6-C8 (3)* 30.50 9.40
Set, never hinged 75.00

Queen Wilhelmina — AP5

***Perf. 12½, 14x13***

**1931, Sept. 24 Photo. Wmk. 202**
**C9** AP5 36c org red & dk bl 13.00 .75
Never hinged 70.00

Fokker Pander AP6

**1933, Oct. 9 *Perf. 12½***
**C10** AP6 30c dark green .75 .75
Never hinged 1.50

Nos. C10-C12 were issued for use on special flights.

Crow in Flight AP7

**1938-53 *Perf. 13x14***
**C11** AP7 12½c dk blue & gray .35 .25
**C12** AP7 25c dk bl & gray ('53) 2.25 1.60
Set, never hinged 4.25

**Catalogue values for unused stamps in this section, from this point to the end of the section, are for Never Hinged items.**

Seagull — AP8

***Perf. 13x14***

**1951, Nov. 12 Engr. Unwmk.**
**C13** AP8 15g gray 225.00 80.00
**C14** AP8 25g blue gray 225.00 80.00
Set, hinged 250.00

Airplane AP9

**1966, Sept. 2 Litho. *Perf. 14x13***
**C15** AP9 25c gray, blk & bl .25 .35

Issued for use on special flights.

AP10

**1980, May 13 Photo. *Perf. 13x14***
**C16** AP10 1g multicolored 1.00 1.00

## REGISTRATION STAMPS

Personalized Stamp — R1

***Die Cut Perf. 12¾x12½***
**Etched on Silver Foil**

**2011, Oct. 10 Self-Adhesive**
**F1** R1 (€7) silver 19.00 19.00

The vignette portion of No. F1 could be personalized for €34.95. The image shown, depicting Piet Hein and a warship, is a generic image. Starting in 2013, stamps with different images were produced in limited quantities and sold at prices above face value were sold by Netherlands Post.

## MARINE INSURANCE STAMPS

Floating Safe Attracting Gulls — MI1

Floating Safe with Night Flare — MI2

Fantasy of Floating Safe — MI3

***Perf. 11½***

**1921, Feb. 2 Unwmk. Engr.**
**GY1** MI1 15c slate grn 11.00 *75.00*
**GY2** MI1 60c car rose 15.00 *75.00*
**GY3** MI1 75c gray brn 18.50 *75.00*
**GY4** MI2 1.50g dk blue 65.00 *425.00*
**GY5** MI2 2.25g org brn 110.00 *550.00*
**GY6** MI3 4½g black 165.00 *675.00*
**GY7** MI3 7½g red 250.00 *925.00*
*Nos. GY1-GY7 (7)* 634.50 *2,800.*
Set, never hinged 1,500.

## POSTAGE DUE STAMPS

Postage due types of Netherlands were also used for Netherlands Antilles, Netherlands Indies and Surinam in different colors.

D1

**Unwmk.**

**1870, May 15 Typo. *Perf. 13***
**J1** D1 5c brown, *org* 72.50 15.00
**J2** D1 10c violet, *bl* 150.00 20.00
*a.* Perf 12½x12 300.00 32.50

D2

Type I — 34 loops. "T" of "BETALEN" over center of loop; top branch of "E" of "TE" shorter than lower branch.
Type II — 33 loops. "T" of "BETALEN" between two loops.
Type III — 32 loops. "T" of "BETALEN" slightly to the left of loop; top branch of first "E" of "BETALEN" shorter than lower branch.
Type IV — 37 loops. Letters of "PORT" larger than in the other three types.
Imperforate varieties are proofs.

***Perf. 11½x12, 12½x12, 12½, 13½***

**1881-87 Value in Black**
**J3** D2 1c lt blue (III) 11.00 11.00
*a.* Type I 15.00 18.00
*b.* Type II 20.00 20.00
*c.* Type IV 47.50 52.50
**J4** D2 1½c lt blue (III) 15.00 15.00
*a.* Type I 18.00 18.00
*b.* Type II 24.00 24.00
*c.* Type IV 75.00 75.00
**J5** D2 2½c lt blue (III) 37.50 5.00
*a.* Type I 45.00 5.50
*b.* Type II 50.00 6.00
*c.* Type IV 210.00 125.00
**J6** D2 5c lt blue (III) ('87) 140.00 3.50
*a.* Type I 50.00 5.00
*b.* Type II 130.00 5.25
*c.* Type IV 1,250. 350.00
**J7** D2 10c lt blue (III) ('87) 92.50 4.00
*a.* Type I 115.00 4.50
*b.* Type II 125.00 5.00
*c.* Type IV 2,500. 375.00
**J8** D2 12½c lt blue (III) 95.00 25.00
*a.* Type I 165.00 40.00
*b.* Type II 130.00 45.00
*c.* Type IV 350.00 100.00
**J9** D2 15c lt blue (III) 90.00 4.00
*a.* Type I 105.00 4.50
*b.* Type II 120.00 5.00
*c.* Type IV 130.00 25.00
**J10** D2 20c lt blue (III) 35.00 4.00
*a.* Type I 47.50 4.25
*b.* Type II 50.00 5.50
*c.* Type IV 137.50 27.50
**J11** D2 25c lt blue (III) 210.00 3.50
*a.* Type I 230.00 3.00
*b.* Type II 275.00 4.50

*c.* Type IV 425.00 170.00

**Value in Red**

**J12** D2 1g lt blue (III) 85.00 30.00
*a.* Type I 85.00 37.50
*b.* Type II 100.00 40.00
*c.* Type IV 175.00 75.00
*Nos. J3-J12 (10)* 811.00 105.00

See Nos. J13-J26, J44-J60. For surcharges see Nos. J27-J28, J42-J43, J72-J75.

**1896-1910** ***Perf. 12½***

**Value in Black**

**J13** D2 ½c dk bl (I) ('01) .40 .35
**J14** D2 1c dk blue (I) 1.65 .35
*a.* Type III 2.50 3.25
**J15** D2 1½c dk blue (I) .75 .35
*a.* Type III 2.50 2.50
**J16** D2 2½c dk blue (I) 1.50 .75
*a.* Type III 3.25 .55
**J17** D2 3c dk bl (I) ('10) 1.65 1.10
**J18** D2 4c dk bl (I) ('09) 1.65 2.25
**J19** D2 5c dk blue (I) 13.00 .35
*a.* Type III 16.00 .55
**J20** D2 6½c dk bl (I) ('07) 45.00 45.00
**J21** D2 7½c dk bl (I) ('04) 1.75 .55
**J22** D2 10c dk blue (I) 35.00 .55
*a.* Type III 52.50 1.50
**J23** D2 12½c dk blue (I) 30.00 1.10
*a.* Type III 45.00 3.50
**J24** D2 15c dk blue (I) 35.00 .90
*a.* Type III 55.00 1.00
**J25** D2 20c dk blue (I) 20.00 8.00
*a.* Type III 20.00 8.75
**J26** D2 25c dk blue (I) 45.00 .75
*a.* Type III 50.00 1.00
*Nos. J13-J26 (14)* 232.35 62.35

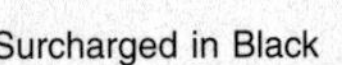

Surcharged in Black

**1906, Jan. 10** ***Perf. 12½***

**J27** D2 50c on 1g lt bl (III) 125.00 110.00
*a.* 50c on 1g light blue (I) 165.00 140.00
*b.* 50c on 1g light blue (II) 175.00 150.00

Surcharged in Red

**1906, Oct. 6**

**J28** D2 6½c on 20c dk bl (I) 5.50 5.00

Nos. 87-89 Surcharged

**1907, Nov. 1**

**J29** A13 ½c on 1c claret 1.25 1.25
**J30** A13 1c on 1c claret .50 .50
**J31** A13 1½c on 1c claret .50 .50
**J32** A13 2½c on 1c claret 1.25 1.25
**J33** A13 5c on 2½c ver 1.40 .40
**J34** A13 6½c on 2½c ver 3.50 3.50
**J35** A13 7½c on ½c blue 2.00 1.25
**J36** A13 10c on ½c blue 1.75 .75
**J37** A13 12½c on ½c blue 5.00 4.75
**J38** A13 15c on 2½c ver 6.00 4.00
**J39** A13 25c on ½c blue 9.00 8.50
**J40** A13 50c on ½c blue 42.50 40.00
**J41** A13 1g on ½c blue 60.00 55.00
*Nos. J29-J41 (13)* 134.65 121.65

Two printings of the above surcharges were made. Some values show differences in the setting of the fractions; others are practically impossible to distinguish.

No. J20 Surcharged in Red

**1909, June**

**J42** D2 4c on 6½c dark blue 5.50 5.00
Never hinged 20.00

No. J12 Surcharged in Black

**1910, July 11**

**J43** D2 3c on 1g lt bl, type III 30.00 27.50
Never hinged 100.00
*a.* Type I 37.50 40.00
Never hinged 110.00
*b.* Type II 40.00 40.00
Never hinged 125.00

**Type I**

**1912-21** ***Perf. 12½, 13½x13***

**Value in Color of Stamp**

**J44** D2 ½c pale ultra .25 .25
**J45** D2 1c pale ultra ('13) .25 .25
**J46** D2 1½c pale ultra ('15) 1.90 1.50
**J47** D2 2½c pale ultra .25 .25
**J48** D2 3c pale ultra .40 .40
**J49** D2 4c pale ultra ('13) .25 .25
**J50** D2 4½c pale ultra ('16) 5.25 5.00
**J51** D2 5c pale ultra .25 .25
**J52** D2 5½c pale ultra ('16) 5.00 5.00
**J53** D2 7c pale ultra ('21) 2.25 2.25
**J54** D2 7½c pale ultra ('13) 2.50 1.00
**J55** D2 10c pale ultra ('13) .40 .40
**J56** D2 12½c pale ultra ('13) .40 .40
**J57** D2 15c pale ultra ('13) .40 .40
**J58** D2 20c pale ultra ('20) .40 .25
**J59** D2 25c pale ultra ('17) 80.00 .60
**J60** D2 50c pale ultra ('20) .40 .25
*Nos. J44-J60 (17)* 100.55 18.70
Set, never hinged 450.00

D3

**1921-38** **Typo.** ***Perf. 12½, 13½x12½***

**J61** D3 3c pale ultra ('28) .25 .25
**J62** D3 6c pale ultra ('27) .25 .25
**J63** D3 7c pale ultra ('28) .45 .45
**J64** D3 7½c pale ultra ('26) .45 .45
**J65** D3 8c pale ultra ('38) .45 .45
**J66** D3 9c pale ultra ('30) .45 .45
**J67** D3 11c ultra ('21) 12.50 4.00
**J68** D3 12c pale ultra ('28) .45 .30
**J69** D3 25c pale ultra ('25) .45 .30
**J70** D3 30c pale ultra ('35) .45 .30
**J71** D3 1g ver ('21) .60 .30
*Nos. J61-J71 (11)* 16.75 7.50
Set, never hinged 50.00

Stamps of 1912-21 Surcharged

**1923, Dec.** ***Perf. 12½***

**J72** D2 1c on 3c ultra .75 .65
**J73** D2 2½c on 7c ultra 1.20 .65
**J74** D2 25c on 1½c ultra 8.00 .65
**J75** D2 25c on 7½c ultra 10.00 .65
*Nos. J72-J75 (4)* 19.95 2.60
Set, never hinged 57.50

Nos. 56, 58, 62, 65 Surcharged

**1924, Aug.**

**J76** A11 4c on 3c olive grn 1.10 1.10
**J77** A10 5c on 1c red .75 .40
*a.* Surcharge reading down 500.00 450.00
**J78** A10 10c on 1½c blue 1.10 .60
*a.* Tête bêche pair 8.50 10.00
**J79** A11 12½c on 5c carmine 1.50 .60
*a.* Tête bêche pair 8.50 10.00
*Nos. J76-J79 (4)* 4.45 2.70
Set, never hinged 14.50

The 11c on 22½c and 15c on 17½c exist. These were used by the postal service for accounting of parcel post fees.

**Catalogue values for unused stamps in this section, from this point to the end of the section, are for Never Hinged items.**

D5

***Perf. 13½x12½***

**1947-58** **Wmk. 202** **Photo.**

**J80** D5 1c light blue ('48) .25 .25
**J81** D5 3c light blue ('48) .40 .30
**J82** D5 4c light blue 8.50 .85
**J83** D5 5c light blue ('48) .25 .25
**J84** D5 6c light blue ('50) .35 .35
**J85** D5 7c light blue .25 .30
**J86** D5 8c light blue ('48) .25 .30
**J87** D5 10c light blue .25 .25
**J88** D5 11c light blue .35 .45
**J89** D5 12c light blue ('48) .80 .85
**J90** D5 14c light blue ('53) .80 .65
**J91** D5 15c light blue .35 .25
**J92** D5 16c light blue .70 .80
**J93** D5 20c light blue .35 .30
**J94** D5 24c light blue ('57) .95 1.10
**J95** D5 25c light blue ('48) .35 .30
**J96** D5 26c light blue ('58) 1.90 2.10
**J97** D5 30c light blue ('48) .50 .25
**J98** D5 35c light blue .65 .25
**J99** D5 40c light blue .65 .25
**J100** D5 50c light blue ('48) .80 .30
**J101** D5 60c light blue ('58) .85 .45
**J102** D5 85c light blue ('50) 13.00 .55
**J103** D5 90c light blue ('56) 2.40 .60
**J104** D5 95c light blue ('57) 2.40 .60
**J105** D5 1g carmine ('48) 1.90 .25
**J106** D5 1.75g carmine ('57) 4.50 .35
*Nos. J80-J106 (27)* 44.70 13.50

## OFFICIAL STAMPS

Regular Issues of 1898-1908 Overprinted

**1913** **Typo.** **Unwmk.** ***Perf. 12½***

**O1** A10 1c red 4.00 2.75
**O2** A10 1½c ultra 1.00 2.25
**O3** A10 2c yellow brn 7.00 7.00
**O4** A10 2½c dp green 16.00 12.00
**O5** A11 3c olive grn 4.00 1.00
**O6** A11 5c carmine rose 4.00 4.50
**O7** A11 10c gray lilac 35.00 37.50
*Nos. O1-O7 (7)* 71.00 67.00

**Same Overprint in Red on No. 58**

**1919**

**O8** A10 1½c deep blue (R) 100.00 110.00

Nos. O1 to O8 were used to defray the postage on matter relating to the Poor Laws.

Counterfeit overprints exist.

**For the International Court of Justice**

Regular Issue of 1926-33 Overprinted in Gold

**1934** **Wmk. 202** ***Perf. 12½***

**O9** A24 1½c red violet 1.50
**O10** A24 2½c deep green 1.50
**O11** A23 7½c red 2.75
**O12** A31 12½c deep ultra 22.50
**O13** A23 15c orange 2.00
**O14** A23 30c violet 2.25
*a.* Perf. 13½x12½ 2.25
*Nos. O9-O14 (6)* 32.00

**Same Overprint on No. 180 in Gold**

**1937** ***Perf. 13½x12½***

**O15** A23 12½c ultra 16.00

**"Mint" Officials**

**Nos. O9-O15, O20-O43 were sold to the public only canceled. Uncanceled, they were obtainable only by favor of an official or from UPU specimen stamps.**

Same on Regular Issue of 1940 Overprinted in Gold

**1940** ***Perf. 13½x12½***

**O16** A45 7½c bright red 27.50 7.00
**O17** A45 12½c sapphire 27.50 7.00
**O18** A45 15c lt blue 27.50 7.00
**O19** A45 30c bister 27.50 7.00
*Nos. O16-O19 (4)* 110.00 28.00

A second printing with more open letters exists. Value, $750.

Nos. 217 to 219, 221 and 223 Overprinted in Gold

**1947**

**O20** A45 7½c bright red 1.10
**O21** A45 10c brt red violet 1.10
**O22** A45 12½c sapphire 1.10
**O23** A45 20c purple 1.10
**O24** A45 25c rose brown 1.10
*Nos. O20-O24 (5)* 5.50

O1

***Perf. 14½x13½***

**1950** **Unwmk.** **Photo.**

**O25** O1 2c ultra 8.75
**O26** O1 4c olive green 8.75

Palace of Peace, The Hague — O2

Queen Juliana — O3

**1951-58** ***Perf. 12½x12***

**O27** O2 2c red brown .40
**O28** O2 3c ultra ('53) .40
**O29** O2 4c deep green .40
**O30** O2 5c olive brn ('53) .40
**O31** O2 6c olive grn ('53) .80
**O32** O2 7c red ('53) .60

**Engr.**

**O33** O3 6c brown vio 5.50
**O34** O3 10c dull green .25
**O35** O3 12c rose red .75
**O36** O3 15c rose brn ('53) .25
**O37** O3 20c dull blue .25
**O38** O3 25c violet brn .25
**O39** O3 30c rose lil ('58) .35
**O40** O3 1g slate gray .80
*Nos. O27-O40 (14)* 11.40

**1977, May** **Photo.** ***Perf. 12½x12***

**O41** O2 40c brt grnsh blue .50
**O42** O2 45c brick red .50
**O43** O2 50c brt rose lilac .50
*Nos. O41-O43 (3)* 1.50

**Catalogue values for unused stamps in this section, from this point to the end of the section, are for Never Hinged items.**

Peace Palace, The Hague — O4

Palm, Sun and Column — O4a

**1989-94** **Litho.**

| | | | | |
|---|---|---|---|---|
| O44 | O4 | 5c black & org yel | .25 | .25 |
| O45 | O4 | 10c black & blue | .25 | .25 |
| O46 | O4 | 25c black & red | .30 | .30 |
| O47 | O4 | 50c black & yel grn | .60 | .60 |
| O48 | O4 | 55c black & pink | .55 | .55 |
| O49 | O4 | 60c black & bister | .75 | .75 |
| O50 | O4 | 65c black & bl grn | .75 | .75 |
| O51 | O4 | 70c blk & gray bl | .90 | .90 |
| O52 | O4 | 75c black & yellow | .70 | .70 |
| O53 | O4 | 80c black & gray grn | 1.00 | 1.00 |
| O54 | O4 | 1g black & orange | 1.10 | 1.10 |
| O55 | O4 | 1.50g blk & blue | 1.60 | 1.60 |
| O56 | O4 | 1.60g blk & rose brn | 2.00 | 2.00 |

**Litho. & Engr.**

| | | | | |
|---|---|---|---|---|
| O57 | O4a | 5g multicolored | 5.50 | 5.50 |
| O58 | O4a | 7g multicolored | 6.50 | 6.50 |
| | | *Nos. O44-O58 (15)* | 22.75 | 22.75 |

Issued: 55c, 75c, 7g, 10/24/89; 65c, 1g, 1.50g, 5g, 10/23/90; 5c, 10c, 25c, 50c, 60c, 70c, 80c, 10/22/91; 1.60g, 11/28/94.

Intl. Court of Justice — O5

Emblem of Intl. Court of Justice — O6

**2004, Jan. 2 Litho.** ***Perf. 14¾x14½***

| | | | | |
|---|---|---|---|---|
| O59 | O5 | 39c multi | 1.00 | 1.00 |
| O60 | O6 | 61c multi | 1.60 | 1.60 |

Intl. Court of Justice — O7

Emblem of Intl. Court of Justice — O8

Doves — O9

**2011, Apr. 11** ***Perf. 13½x13¼***

| | | | | |
|---|---|---|---|---|
| O61 | O7 | 1 multi | 1.40 | 1.40 |
| O62 | O8 | 1 Europa multi | 2.40 | 2.40 |
| O63 | O9 | 1 Wereld multi | 2.75 | 2.75 |
| | | *Nos. O61-O63 (3)* | 6.55 | 6.55 |

On day of issue, Nos. O61-O63 each sold for 46c, 79c, and 95c, respectively.

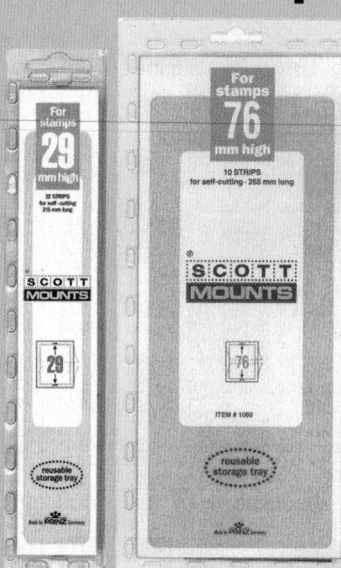

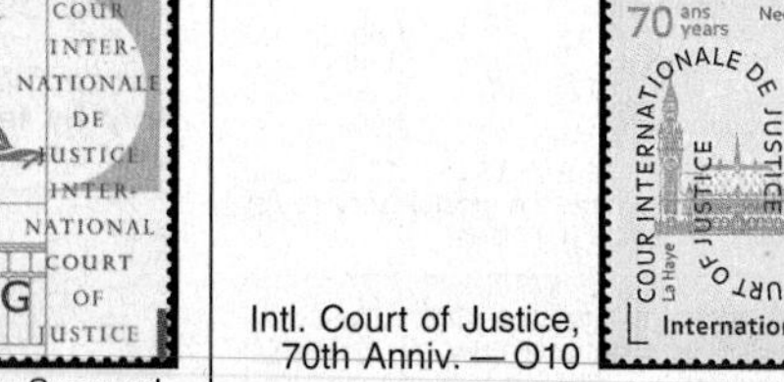

Intl. Court of Justice, 70th Anniv. — O10

**2016, Apr. 25 Litho.** ***Perf. 13½x13¼***

| | | | | |
|---|---|---|---|---|
| O64 | O10 | 1 Internationaal multi | 3.00 | 3.00 |

## NETHERLANDS ANTILLES

'ne-thər-lən̦d̦z an-'ti-lēz

### (Curaçao)

LOCATION — Two groups of islands about 500 miles apart in the West Indies, north of Venezuela
AREA — 383 sq. mi.
POP. — 207,333 (1995)
CAPITAL — Willemstad

Formerly a colony, Curaçao, Netherlands Antilles became an integral part of the Kingdom of the Netherlands under the Constitution of 1954. On Jan. 1, 1986, the island of Aruba achieved a separate status within the Kingdom and began issuing its own stamps.

100 Cents = 1 Gulden

**Catalogue values for unused stamps in this country are for Never Hinged items, beginning with Scott 164 in the regular postage section, Scott B1 in the semi-postal section, Scott C18 in the airpost section, Scott CB9 in the airpost semi-postal section, and Scott J41 in the postage due section.**

Values for unused examples of Nos. 1-44 are for stamps without gum.

**Watermark**

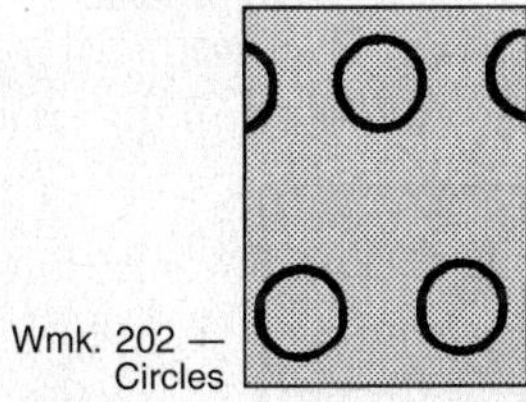

Wmk. 202 — Circles

King William III — A1

***Regular Perf. 11½, 12½, 11½x12, 12½x12, 13½x13, 14***

**1873-79 Typo. Unwmk.**

| No. | Type | Description | Unused | Used |
|---|---|---|---|---|
| 1 | A1 | 2½c green | 6.00 | 9.50 |
| 2 | A1 | 3c bister | 57.50 | *115.00* |
| 3 | A1 | 5c rose | 14.00 | 13.50 |
| 4 | A1 | 10c ultra | 80.00 | 19.00 |
| 5 | A1 | 25c brown orange | 57.50 | 9.50 |
| 6 | A1 | 50c violet | 2.00 | 1.90 |
| 7 | A1 | 2.50g bis & pur ('79) | 50.00 | 45.00 |
| | | *Nos. 1-7 (7)* | 267.00 | *213.40* |

See bluish paper note with Netherlands #7-22.

The gulden denominations, Nos. 7 and 12, are of larger size.

See 8-12. For surcharges see #18, 25-26.

***Perf. 14, Small Holes***

| No. | Type | Description | Unused | Used |
|---|---|---|---|---|
| *1b* | A1 | 2½c | 18.00 | 21.00 |
| *2b* | A1 | 3c | 70.00 | *135.00* |
| *3b* | A1 | 5c | 20.00 | 28.00 |
| *4b* | A1 | 10c | 115.00 | 97.50 |
| *5b* | A1 | 25c | 80.00 | 7.50 |
| *6b* | A1 | 50c | 40.00 | 37.50 |
| | | *Nos. 1b-6b (6)* | 343.00 | *326.50* |

"Small hole" varieties have the spaces between the holes wider than the diameter of the holes.

**1886-89 *Perf. 11½, 12½, 12½x12***

| No. | Type | Description | Unused | Used |
|---|---|---|---|---|
| 8 | A1 | 12½c yellow | 130.00 | 52.50 |
| 9 | A1 | 15c olive ('89) | 40.00 | 22.50 |
| 10 | A1 | 30c pearl gray ('89) | 45.00 | 52.50 |
| 11 | A1 | 60c olive bis ('89) | 55.00 | 19.00 |
| 12 | A1 | 1.50g lt & dk bl ('89) | 120.00 | 102.50 |
| | | *Nos. 8-12 (5)* | 390.00 | 249.00 |

Nos. 1-12 were issued without gum until 1890. Imperfs. are proofs.

Numeral — A2

**1889 *Perf. 12½***

| No. | Type | Description | Unused | Used |
|---|---|---|---|---|
| 13 | A2 | 1c gray | 1.60 | 1.60 |
| 14 | A2 | 2c violet | 1.60 | 2.25 |
| 15 | A2 | 2½c green | 5.75 | 5.25 |
| 16 | A2 | 3c bister | 6.50 | 6.00 |
| 17 | A2 | 5c rose | 25.00 | 1.90 |
| | | *Nos. 13-17 (5)* | 40.45 | 17.00 |

Black Handstamped Surcharge

**1891 *Perf. 12½x12***

**Without Gum**

| No. | Type | Description | Unused | Used |
|---|---|---|---|---|
| 18 | A1 | 25c on 30c pearl gray | 18.00 | 15.00 |

No. 18 exists with double surcharge, value $225, and with inverted surcharge, value $275.

Queen Wilhelmina — A4

**1892-96 *Perf. 12½***

| No. | Type | Description | Unused | Used |
|---|---|---|---|---|
| 19 | A4 | 10c ultra ('95) | 1.60 | 1.60 |
| 20 | A4 | 12½c green | 18.50 | 10.50 |
| 21 | A4 | 15c rose ('93) | 4.00 | 3.00 |
| 22 | A4 | 25c brown orange | 145.00 | 3.75 |
| 23 | A4 | 30c gray ('96) | 4.00 | *7.50* |
| | | *Nos. 19-23 (5)* | 173.10 | 26.35 |

No. 4 Handstamped Surcharge in Magenta

No. 10 Handstamped Surcharge in Black

**1895 *Perf. 12½, 13½x13***

| No. | Type | Description | Unused | Used |
|---|---|---|---|---|
| 25 | A1 | 2½c on 10c ultra | 16.00 | 11.50 |

***Perf. 12½x12***

| No. | Type | Description | Unused | Used |
|---|---|---|---|---|
| 26 | A1 | 2½c on 30c gray | 160.00 | 7.50 |

Nos. 25-26 exist with surcharge double or inverted.

No. 26 and No. 25, perf. 13½x13, were issued without gum.

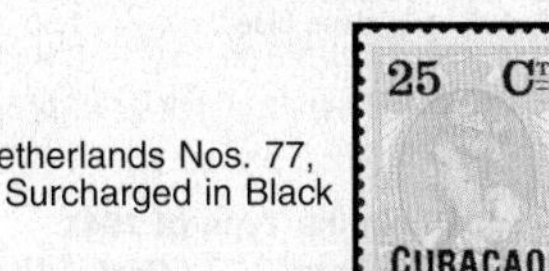


Netherlands Nos. 77, 68 Surcharged in Black

**1902, Jan. 1 *Perf. 12½***

| No. | Type | Description | Unused | Used |
|---|---|---|---|---|
| 27 | A11 | 25c on 25c car & bl | 2.00 | 1.90 |

Netherlands No. 84 Surcharged in Black

**1901, May 1 Engr. *Perf. 11½x11***

| No. | Type | Description | Unused | Used |
|---|---|---|---|---|
| 28 | A12 | 1.50g on 2.50g brn lil | 22.00 | 26.00 |

**1902, Mar. 1 Typo. *Perf. 12½***

| No. | Type | Description | Unused | Used |
|---|---|---|---|---|
| 29 | A11 | 12½c on 12½c blue | 28.00 | 9.50 |

A9

A10

**1904-08**

| No. | Type | Description | Unused | Used |
|---|---|---|---|---|
| 30 | A9 | 1c olive green | 2.00 | 1.90 |
| 31 | A9 | 2c yellow brown | 18.00 | 3.75 |
| 32 | A9 | 2½c blue green | 8.00 | .75 |
| 33 | A9 | 3c orange | 10.00 | 5.75 |
| 34 | A9 | 5c rose red | 10.00 | 1.15 |
| 35 | A9 | 7½c gray ('08) | 32.00 | 9.50 |
| 36 | A10 | 10c slate | 24.00 | 1.90 |
| 37 | A10 | 12½c deep blue | 2.00 | .75 |
| 38 | A10 | 15c brown | 20.00 | 13.50 |
| 39 | A10 | 22½c brn & ol ('08) | 20.00 | 13.50 |
| 40 | A10 | 25c violet | 24.00 | 3.75 |
| 41 | A10 | 30c brown orange | 50.00 | 17.00 |
| 42 | A10 | 50c red brown | 40.00 | 10.50 |
| | | *Nos. 30-42 (13)* | 260.00 | 83.70 |

Queen Wilhelmina — A11

**1906, Nov. 1 Engr. *Perf. 11½***

**Without Gum**

| No. | Type | Description | Unused | Used |
|---|---|---|---|---|
| 43 | A11 | 1½g red brown | 40.00 | 30.00 |
| 44 | A11 | 2½g slate blue | 40.00 | 34.00 |

A12

Queen Wilhelmina
A13 A14

***Perf. 12½, 11, 11½, 11x11½***

**1915-33 Typo.**

| No. | Type | Description | Unused | Used |
|---|---|---|---|---|
| 45 | A12 | ½c lilac ('20) | 1.60 | 1.60 |
| 46 | A12 | 1c olive green | .40 | .25 |
| 47 | A12 | 1½c blue ('20) | .40 | .25 |
| 48 | A12 | 2c yellow brn | 1.60 | 1.35 |
| 49 | A12 | 2½c green | 1.00 | .40 |
| 50 | A12 | 3c yellow | 3.00 | 1.90 |
| 51 | A12 | 3c green ('26) | 3.00 | 2.60 |
| 52 | A12 | 5c rose | 2.40 | .40 |
| 53 | A12 | 5c green ('22) | 5.00 | 2.60 |
| 54 | A12 | 5c lilac ('26) | 2.40 | .25 |
| 55 | A12 | 7½c drab | 1.45 | .25 |
| 56 | A12 | 7½c bister ('20) | 1.45 | .25 |
| 57 | A12 | 10c lilac ('22) | 5.75 | 5.75 |
| 58 | A12 | 10c rose ('26) | 5.00 | 1.90 |
| 59 | A13 | 10c car rose | 27.00 | 3.75 |
| 60 | A13 | 12½c blue | 3.00 | .75 |
| 61 | A13 | 12½c red ('22) | 2.60 | 1.90 |
| 62 | A13 | 15c olive grn | 1.00 | 1.60 |
| 63 | A13 | 15c lt blue ('26) | 5.00 | 3.00 |
| 64 | A13 | 20c blue ('22) | 8.00 | 3.00 |
| 65 | A13 | 20c olive grn ('26) | 3.25 | 2.25 |
| 66 | A13 | 22½c orange | 3.25 | 3.00 |
| 67 | A13 | 25c red violet | 4.00 | 1.60 |
| 68 | A13 | 30c slate | 4.00 | 1.60 |
| 69 | A13 | 35c sl & red ('22) | 3.25 | 6.00 |

***Perf. 11½x11, 11½, 12½, 11***

**Engr.**

| No. | Type | Description | Unused | Used |
|---|---|---|---|---|
| 70 | A14 | 50c green | 4.00 | .40 |
| 71 | A14 | 1½g violet | 18.00 | 13.50 |
| 72 | A14 | 2½g carmine | 26.00 | 24.00 |
| *a.* | | Perf. 12½ ('33) | 160.00 | *340.00* |
| | | *Nos. 45-72 (28)* | 146.80 | 86.10 |

Some stamps of 1915 were also issued without gum.

For surcharges see #74, 107-108, C1-C3.

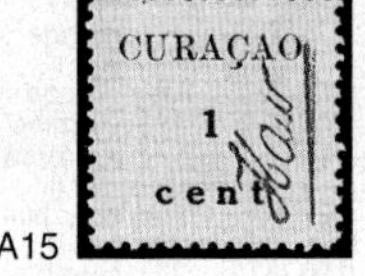


A15

**Laid Paper**
**Without Gum**

**1918, July 16 Typo. *Perf. 12***

| No. | Type | Description | Unused | Used |
|---|---|---|---|---|
| 73 | A15 | 1c black, *buff* | 6.00 | 3.75 |

"HAW" are the initials of Postmaster H. A. Willemsen.

No. 60 Surcharged in Black

**1918, Sept. 1 *Perf. 12½***

| No. | Type | Description | Unused | Used |
|---|---|---|---|---|
| 74 | A13 | 5c on 12½c blue | 4.00 | 2.60 |
| *a.* | | "5" 2½mm wide | 72.50 | 45.00 |
| *b.* | | Double surcharge | | 1,350. |
| *c.* | | As "a," double surcharge | | *1,800.* |

The "5" of No. 74 is 2.75mm wide. Illustration shows No. 74a surcharge.

Queen Wilhelmina — A16

**1923 Engr. *Perf. 11½, 11x11½***

| No. | Type | Description | Unused | Used |
|---|---|---|---|---|
| 75 | A16 | 5c green | 2.00 | 3.00 |
| 76 | A16 | 7½c olive grn | 2.00 | 3.00 |
| 77 | A16 | 10c car rose | 4.00 | 4.50 |
| 78 | A16 | 20c indigo | 4.00 | 4.50 |
| *a.* | | Perf. 11x11½ | 4.00 | 5.75 |
| 79 | A16 | 1g brown vio | 40.00 | 37.50 |
| 80 | A16 | 2½g gray black | 85.00 | *180.00* |
| 81 | A16 | 5g brown | 105.00 | *225.00* |
| *a.* | | Perf. 11x11½ | 600.00 | 475.00 |
| | | *Nos. 75-81 (7)* | 242.00 | *457.50* |

25th anniv. of the assumption of the government of the Netherlands by Queen Wilhelmina, at the age of 18.

Nos. 80-81 with clear cancel between Aug. 1, 1923 and Apr. 30, 1924, sell for considerably more.

Types of Netherlands Marine Insurance Stamps, Inscribed "CURACAO" Surcharged in Black

**1927, Oct. 3**

| No. | Type | Description | Unused | Used |
|---|---|---|---|---|
| 87 | MI1 | 3c on 15c dk green | .80 | .75 |
| 88 | MI1 | 10c on 60c car rose | .80 | .75 |
| 89 | MI1 | 12½c on 75c gray brn | .80 | .75 |
| 90 | MI2 | 15c on 1.50g dk bl | 4.00 | 3.75 |
| *a.* | | Double surcharge | *1,600.* | |
| 91 | MI2 | 25c on 2.25g org brn | 9.75 | 9.00 |
| 92 | MI3 | 30c on 4½g black | 10.50 | 9.75 |
| 93 | MI3 | 50c on 7½g red | 9.75 | 9.00 |
| | | *Nos. 87-93 (7)* | 36.40 | 33.75 |

Nos. 90, 91 and 92 have "FRANKEERZEGEL" in one line of small capitals. Nos. 90 and 91 have a heavy bar across the top of the stamp.

Queen Wilhelmina — A17

**1928-30 Engr. *Perf. 11½, 12½***
**95** A17 6c orange red ('30) 2.40 .40
*a.* Booklet pane of 6
**96** A17 7½c orange red .80 .60
**97** A17 10c carmine 1.60 .60
**98** A17 12½c red brown 1.60 1.35
*a.* Booklet pane of 6
**99** A17 15c dark blue 1.60 .60
*a.* Booklet pane of 6
**100** A17 20c blue black 6.00 .95
**101** A17 21c yellow grn ('30) 10.00 11.50
**102** A17 25c brown vio 4.00 2.10
**103** A17 27½c black ('30) 14.50 15.00
**104** A17 30c deep green 6.00 1.15
**105** A17 35c brnsh black 2.00 3.75
*Nos. 95-105 (11)* 50.50 38.00

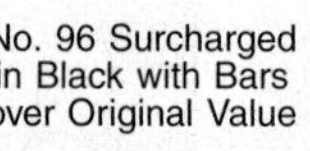

No. 96 Surcharged in Black with Bars over Original Value

**1929, Nov. 1**
**106** A17 6c on 7½c org red 1.60 1.15
*a.* Inverted surcharge 280.00 260.00

No. 51 Surcharged in Red

**1931, Mar. 1 Typo. *Perf. 12½***
**107** A12 2½c on 3c green 1.20 1.15

No. 49 Surcharged in Red

**1932, Oct. 29**
**108** A12 1½c on 2½c grn 4.00 3.75

Prince William I, Portrait by Van Key — A18

**1933 Photo. *Perf. 12½***
**109** A18 6c deep orange 2.00 1.15

400th birth anniv. of Prince William I, Count of Nassau and Prince of Orange, frequently referred to as William the Silent.

Willem Usselinx — A19

Van Walbeeck's Ship — A22

Designs: 2½c, 5c, 6c, Frederik Hendrik. 10c, 12½c, 15c, Jacob Binckes. 27½c, 30c, 50c, Cornelis Evertsen the Younger. 1.50g, 2.50g, Louis Brion.

**1934, Jan. 1 Engr. *Perf. 12½***
**110** A19 1c black 1.40 1.60
**111** A19 1½c dull violet 1.00 .40
**112** A19 2c orange 1.60 1.90
**113** A19 2½c dull green 1.20 1.60
**114** A19 5c black brn 1.20 1.60
**115** A19 6c violet bl 1.60 .40
**116** A19 10c lake 4.00 1.60
**117** A19 12½c bister brn 9.00 7.50
**118** A19 15c blue 3.00 1.90
**119** A22 20c black 4.50 3.75
**120** A22 21c brown 20.00 13.50
**121** A22 25c dull green 20.00 13.50
**122** A19 27½c brown vio 20.00 19.00
**123** A19 30c scarlet 14.00 7.50
**124** A19 50c orange 14.00 11.50
**125** A19 1.50g indigo 60.00 57.50
**126** A19 2.50g yellow grn 65.00 65.00
*Nos. 110-126 (17)* 241.50 209.75

3rd centenary of the founding of the colony.

Numeral A25

Queen Wilhelmina A26

**1936, Aug. 1 Litho. *Perf. 13½x13***
**Size: 18x22mm**
**127** A25 1c brown black .25 .25
**128** A25 1½c deep ultra .25 .25
**129** A25 2c orange .25 .25
**130** A25 2½c green .25 .25
**131** A25 5c scarlet .25 .25

**Engr.**
***Perf. 12½***
**Size: 20¼x30½mm**
**132** A26 6c brown vio .80 .25
**133** A26 10c orange red 1.20 .25
**134** A26 12½c dk bl grn 1.60 .75
**135** A26 15c dark blue 1.60 .75
**136** A26 20c orange yel 1.60 .75
**137** A26 21c dk gray 3.75 3.75
**138** A26 25c brown lake 1.60 1.15
**139** A26 27½c violet brn 3.25 3.00
**140** A26 30c olive brn .80 .70

***Perf. 13x14***
**Size: 22x33mm**
**141** A26 50c dull yel grn 4.00 .40
*a.* Perf. 14 60.00 .40
**142** A26 1.50g black brn 18.00 11.50
*a.* Perf. 14 80.00 37.50
**143** A26 2.50g rose lake 18.00 13.50
*a.* Perf. 14 20.00 19.00
*Nos. 127-143 (17)* 57.45 38.00

See Nos. 147-151. For surcharges see Nos. B1-B3.

Queen Wilhelmina — A27

***Perf. 12½x12***
**1938, Aug. 27 Photo. Wmk. 202**
**144** A27 1½c dull purple .40 .40
**145** A27 6c red orange .80 .75
**146** A27 15c royal blue 1.60 1.15
*Nos. 144-146 (3)* 2.80 2.30

Reign of Queen Wilhelmina, 40th anniv.

**Numeral Type of 1936 and**

Queen Wilhelmina — A28

**1941-42 Unwmk. Litho. *Perf. 12½***
**Thick Paper**
**Size: 17¾x22mm**
**147** A25 1c gray brn ('42) 3.00 2.60
**148** A25 1½c dull blue ('42) 9.75 .40
**149** A25 2c lt orange ('42) 9.75 8.25
**150** A25 2½c green ('42) 2.40 1.60
**151** A25 5c crimson ('42) 2.00 1.15

**Photo.**
***Perf. 12½, 13***
**Size: 18½x23mm**
**152** A28 6c rose violet 3.00 2.25
**153** A28 10c red orange 3.00 1.15
**154** A28 12½c lt green 3.25 1.15
**155** A28 15c brt ultra 8.00 2.60
**156** A28 20c orange 3.00 1.90
**157** A28 21c gray 12.00 7.50
**158** A28 25c brown lake 5.00 2.60
**159** A28 27½c deep brown 20.00 16.50
**160** A28 30c olive bis 18.00 4.50

**Size: 21x26½mm**
**161** A28 50c olive grn ('42) 24.00 .75
**162** A28 1½g gray ol ('42) 30.00 2.25
**163** A28 2½g rose lake ('42) 32.00 1.90
*Nos. 147-163 (17)* 188.15 59.05

Imperfs. are proofs.
See Nos. 174-187.

**Catalogue values for unused stamps in this section, from this point to the end of the section, are for Never Hinged items.**

Bonaire A29

St. Eustatius — A30

Designs: 2c, View of Saba. 2½c, St. Maarten. 5c, Aruba. 6c, Curaçao.

***Perf. 13x13½, 13½x13 (No. 165)***
**1943, Feb. 1 Engr. Unwmk.**
**164** A29 1c rose vio & org brn .30 .25
**165** A30 1½c dp bl & yel grn .30 .25
**166** A29 2c sl blk & org brn .60 .35
**167** A29 2½c grn & org .35 .25
**168** A29 5c red & slate blk 1.15 .25
**169** A29 6c rose lil & lt bl .85 .80
*Nos. 164-169 (6)* 3.55 2.15

Royal Family — A35

**1943, Nov. 8 *Perf. 13½x13***
**170** A35 1½c deep orange .45 .40
**171** A35 2½c red .45 .40
**172** A35 6c black 1.30 1.20
**173** A35 10c deep blue 1.30 1.20
*Nos. 170-173 (4)* 3.50 3.20

Princess Margriet Francisca of the Netherlands.

**Wilhelmina Type of 1941**
**1947 Photo. *Perf. 13½x13***
**Size: 18x22mm**
**174** A28 6c brown vio 1.60 *1.90*
**175** A28 10c orange red 1.60 *1.90*
**176** A28 12½c dk blue grn 1.60 *1.90*
**177** A28 15c dark blue 1.60 *2.25*
**178** A28 20c orange yel 1.60 *3.25*
**179** A28 21c dark gray 2.75 *3.25*
**180** A28 25c brown lake .35 .25
**181** A28 27½c chocolate 2.25 2.40
**182** A28 30c olive bister 1.90 1.30
**183** A28 50c dull yel grn 2.00 .25

***Perf. 13½x14***
**Engr.**
**Size: 25x31¼mm**
**184** A28 1½g dark brown 6.00 1.90
**185** A28 2½g rose lake 60.00 27.00
**186** A28 5g olive green 120.00 *170.00*
**187** A28 10g red orange 145.00 *275.00*
*Nos. 174-187 (14)* 348.25 492.55

Used values for Nos. 186-187 are for genuinely canceled copies clearly dated before the end of 1949.

A36

Queen Wilhelmina — A37

**1948 Unwmk. Photo. *Perf. 13½x13***
**188** A36 6c dk vio brn 1.05 .95
**189** A36 10c scarlet 1.05 *1.20*
**190** A36 12½c dk blue grn 1.05 .80
**191** A36 15c deep blue 1.05 *.95*
**192** A36 20c red orange 1.05 *1.90*
**193** A36 21c black 1.05 *1.90*
**194** A36 25c brt red vio .35 .25
**195** A36 27½c henna brn 17.50 16.00
**196** A36 30c olive brown 16.50 1.15
**197** A36 50c olive green 14.50 .25

***Perf. 12½x12***
**Engr.**
**198** A37 1.50g chocolate 28.00 6.50
*Nos. 188-198 (11)* 83.15 31.85

Queen Wilhelmina — A38

**1948, Aug. 30 *Perf. 13x14***
**199** A38 6c vermilion .70 .55
**200** A38 12½c deep blue .70 .55

Reign of Queen Wilhelmina, 50th anniv.

Queen Juliana — A39

***Perf. 14x13½***
**1948, Oct. 18 Photo. Wmk. 202**
**201** A39 6c red brown .75 .45
**202** A39 12½c dark green .75 .45

Investiture of Queen Juliana, Sept. 6, 1948. Nos. 201-202 were issued in Netherlands Sept. 6.

Ship of Ojeda — A40

Alonso de Ojeda — A41

*Perf. 14x13, 13x14*

**1949, July 26 Photo. Unwmk.**

**203** A40 6c olive green 4.00 2.25
**204** A41 12½c brown red 4.25 3.00
**205** A40 15c ultra 4.75 3.25
*Nos. 203-205 (3)* 13.00 8.50

450th anniversary of the discovery of Curaçao by Alonso de Ojeda, 1499.

Post Horns Entwined — A42

**1949, Oct. 3** ***Perf. 12x12½***

**206** A42 6c brown red 4.75 2.50
**207** A42 25c dull blue 4.75 1.30

UPU, 75th anniversary.

A43

A44

Queen Juliana — A45

**1950-79 Photo.** ***Perf. 13x13½***

**208** A43 1c red brown .25 .25
**209** A43 1½c blue .25 .25
**210** A43 2c orange .25 .25
**211** A43 2½c green 1.20 .25
**212** A43 3c purple .35 .25
**212A** A43 4c yel grn ('59) .95 .40
**213** A43 5c dark red .25 .25

***Perf. 13½x13***

**214** A44 6c deep plum 1.60 .25
**215** A44 7½c red brn ('54) 5.50 .25
**216** A44 10c red 2.25 .25
*a.* Redrawn ('79) 1.75 1.60
**217** A44 12½c dk green 2.75 .25
**218** A44 15c deep blue 2.75 .25
*a.* Redrawn ('79) .25 .25
**219** A44 20c orange 3.25 .25
*a.* Redrawn ('79) .25 .25
**220** A44 21c black 4.00 2.25
**221** A44 22½c blue grn ('54) 6.25 .25
**222** A44 25c violet 5.25 .25
*a.* Redrawn ('79) .25 .25
**223** A44 27½c henna brn 8.25 1.90
**224** A44 30c olive brown 12.50 .25
**225** A44 50c olive green 12.50 .25

***Perf. 12½x12***

**Engr.**

**226** A45 1½g slate grn 40.00 .40
**227** A45 2½g black brn 40.00 1.90
**228** A45 5g rose red 60.00 17.00
**229** A45 10g dk vio brn 190.00 65.00
*Nos. 208-229 (23)* 400.35 92.85

Nos. 216a, 218a, 219a and 222a are from booklets Nos. 427a and 428a. Background design is sharper and stamps have one or two straight edges.

See Nos. 427-429. For surcharge see No. B20.

Fort Beekenburg A46

***Perf. 13½x12½***

**1953, June 16 Photo.**

**230** A46 22½c olive brown 6.00 .90

Founding of Fort Beekenburg, 250th anniv.

Beach at Aruba A47

**1954, May 1** ***Perf. 11x11½***

**231** A47 15c dk bl, sal & dp bl 6.00 3.00

3rd congress of the Caribbean Tourist Assoc., Aruba, May 3-6.

Queen Juliana — A48

**1954, Dec. 15** ***Perf. 13½***

**232** A48 7½c olive green 1.40 1.00

Charter of the Kingdom, adopted Dec. 15, 1954. See Netherlands No. 366, Surinam No. 264.

Beach A49

Petroleum Refinery, Aruba — A50

**1955, Dec. 5 Litho.** ***Perf. 12***

**233** A49 15c chnt, bl & emer 3.25 2.60
**234** A50 25c chnt, bl & emer 4.00 3.25

Caribbean Commission, 21st meeting, Aruba.

St. Annabaai Harbor and Flags — A51

**1956, Dec. 6 Unwmk.** ***Perf. 14x13***

**235** A51 15c lt bl, blk & red .40 .40

Caribbean Commission, 10th anniversary.

Man Watching Rising Sun — A52

**1957, Mar. 14 Photo.** ***Perf. 11x11½***

**236** A52 15c black & yellow .40 .40

1st Caribbean Mental Health Conference, Aruba, Mar. 14-19.

Tourism A53

**1957, July 1 Litho.** ***Perf. 14x13***

**237** A53 7½c Saba .80 .50
**238** A53 15c St. Maarten .80 .50
**239** A53 25c St. Eustatius .80 .50
*Nos. 237-239 (3)* 2.40 1.50

Curaçao Intercontinental Hotel — A54

**1957, Oct. 12** ***Perf. 14x13***

**240** A54 15c lt ultra .40 .40

Intercontinental Hotel, Willemstad, opening.

Map of Curaçao A55

**1957, Dec. 10** ***Perf. 14x13½***

**241** A55 15c indigo & lt bl .80 .70

International Geophysical Year.

Flamingoes, Bonaire A56

Designs: 7½c, 8c, 25c, 1½g, Old buildings, Curaçao. 10c, 5g, Extinct volcano and palms, Saba. 15c, 30c, 1g, Fort Willem III, Aruba. 20c, 35c, De Ruyter obelisk, St. Eustatius. 12c, 40c, 2½g, Town Hall, St. Maarten.

**1958-59 Litho.** ***Perf. 14x13***

**Size: 33x22mm**

**242** A56 6c lt ol grn & pink 2.25 .25
**243** A56 7½c red brn & org .25 .25
**244** A56 8c dk bl & org ('59) .25 .25
**245** A56 10c gray & org yel .25 .25
**246** A56 12c bluish grn & gray ('59) .25 .25
**247** A56 15c grn & lt ultra .25 .25
*a.* 15c green & lilac .25 .25
**248** A56 20c crim & gray .25 .25
**249** A56 25c Prus bl & yel grn .30 .25
**250** A56 30c brn & bl grn .30 .25
**251** A56 35c gray & rose ('59) .40 .25
**252** A56 40c mag & grn .45 .25
**253** A56 50c grysh brn & pink .45 .25
**254** A56 1g brt red & gray 1.00 .25
**255** A56 1½g rose vio & pale brn 1.35 .25
**256** A56 2½g blue & citron 2.60 .30
**257** A56 5g lt red brn & rose lil 5.00 .60
*Nos. 242-257 (16)* 15.60 4.40

See Nos. 340-348, 400-403. For surcharge see No. B58.

Nos. 242, 244-246, and 248-257 were printed on glossy and matte paper. Nos. 243 and 247 were printed on matte paper only. No. 247a was printed on glossy paper only.

Globe A57

**1958, Oct. 16** ***Perf. 11x11½***

**258** A57 7½c blue & lake .25 .25
**259** A57 15c red & ultra .40 .40

50th anniv. of the Netherlands Antilles Radio and Telegraph Administration.

Hotel Aruba Caribbean A58

**1959, July 18** ***Perf. 14x13***

**260** A58 15c multi .40 .40

Opening of the Hotel Aruba Caribbean, Aruba.

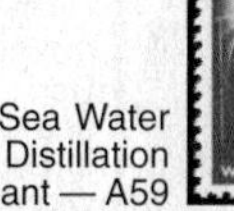

Sea Water Distillation Plant — A59

**1959, Oct. 16 Photo.** ***Perf. 14x13***

**261** A59 20c bright blue .50 .50

Opening of sea water distillation plant at Balashi, Aruba.

Netherlands Antilles Flag — A60

**1959, Dec. 14 Litho.** ***Perf. 13½***

**262** A60 10c ultra & red .50 .40
**263** A60 20c ultra, yel & red .50 .40
**264** A60 25c ultra, grn & red .50 .40
*Nos. 262-264 (3)* 1.50 1.20

5th anniv. of the new constitution (Charter of the Kingdom).

Fokker "Snip" and Map of Caribbean A61

Designs: 20c, Globe showing route flown, and plane. 25c, Map of Atlantic ocean and view of Willemstad. 35c, Map of Atlantic ocean and plane on Aruba airfield.

**1959, Dec. 22 Unwmk.** ***Perf. 14x13***

**265** A61 10c yel, lt & dk bl .80 .40
**266** A61 20c yel, lt & dk bl .80 .40
**267** A61 25c yel, lt & dk bl .80 .25
**268** A61 35c yel, lt & dk bl .80 .55
*Nos. 265-268 (4)* 3.20 1.60

25th anniv. of Netherlands-Curaçao air service.

Msgr. Martinus J. Niewindt — A62

**1960, Jan. 12 Photo.** ***Perf. 13½***

**269** A62 10c deep claret .95 .50
**270** A62 20c deep violet .95 .55
**271** A62 25c olive green .95 .55
*Nos. 269-271 (3)* 2.85 1.60

Death centenary of Monsignor Niewindt, first apostolic vicar for Curaçao.

Worker, Flag and Factories — A63

**1960, Apr. 29** ***Perf. 12½x13½***
**272** A63 20c multi .50 .50

Issued for Labor Day, May 1, 1960.

US Brig "Andrea Doria" and Gun at Fort Orange, St. Eustatius A64

**1961, Nov. 16 Litho.** ***Perf. 14x13½***
**273** A64 20c bl, red, grn & blk .80 .65

185th anniv. of 1st salute by a foreign power to the US flag flown by an American ship.

Queen Juliana and Prince Bernhard A64a

**1962, Jan. 31 Photo.** ***Perf. 14x13***
**274** A64a 10c deep orange .50 .35
**275** A64a 25c deep blue .50 .35

Silver wedding anniversary of Queen Juliana and Prince Bernhard.

Benta Player — A65

6c, Corn masher. 20c, Petji kerchief. 25c, "Jaja" (nurse) with child, sculpture.

***Perf. 12½x13½***
**1962, Mar. 14** **Photo.**
**276** A65 6c red brn & yel .40 .25
**277** A65 10c shown .40 .25
**278** A65 20c crim, ind & brt grn .40 .30
**279** A65 25c brt grn, brn & gray .40 .30
*a.* Souvenir sheet of 4, #276-279 2.00 1.25
*Nos. 276-279 (4)* 1.60 1.10

Emblem of Family Relationship A66

25c, Emblem of mental health (cross).

**1963, Apr. 17 Litho.** ***Perf. 14x13½***
**280** A66 20c dk blue & ocher .40 .40
**281** A66 25c blue & red .40 .40

Fourth Caribbean Conference for Mental Health, Curaçao, Apr. 17-23.

Dove with Olive Branch A67

**1963, July 1 Unwmk.** ***Perf. 14x13***
**282** A67 25c org yel & dk brn .40 .35

Centenary of emancipation of the slaves.

Hotel Bonaire A68

**1963, Aug. 31** ***Perf. 14x13***
**283** A68 20c dk red brown .40 .30

Opening of Hotel Bonaire on Bonaire.

Prince William of Orange Taking Oath of Allegiance — A69

**1963, Nov. 21 Photo.** ***Perf. 13½x14***
**284** A69 25c green, blk & rose .40 .35

150th anniversary of the founding of the Kingdom of the Netherlands.

Chemical Equipment A70

**1963, Dec. 10 Litho.** ***Perf. 14x13½***
**285** A70 20c bl grn, brt yel grn & red .50 .50

Opening of chemical factories on Aruba.

Airmail Letter and Wings A71

Design: 25c, Map of Caribbean, Miami-Curaçao route and planes of 1929 and 1964.

**1964, June 22 Photo.** ***Perf. 11x11½***
**286** A71 20c lt bl, red & ultra .40 .40
**287** A71 25c lt grn, bl, red & blk .40 .40

35th anniversary of the first regular Curaçao airmail service.

Map of the Caribbean A72

**1964, Nov. 30 Litho. Unwmk.**
**288** A72 20c ultra, org & dk red .40 .35

5th meeting of the Caribbean Council, Curaçao, Nov. 30-Dec. 4.

Netherlands Antilles Flags, Map of Curaçao and Crest — A73

**1964, Dec. 14 Litho.** ***Perf. 11½x11***
**289** A73 25c lt bl & multi .40 .35

10th anniversary of the Charter of the Kingdom of the Netherlands. The flags, shaped like seagulls, represent the six islands comprising the Netherlands Antilles.

Princess Beatrix — A74

**1965, Feb. 22 Photo.** ***Perf. 13½x14***
**290** A74 25c brick red .40 .40

Visit of Princess Beatrix of Netherlands.

ITU Emblem, Old and New Communication Equipment — A75

**1965, May 17 Litho.** ***Perf. 13½***
**291** A75 10c brt bl & dk bl .25 .25

ITU, centenary.

Shell Refinery, Curaçao A76

10c, Catalytic cracking installation, vert. 25c, Workers operating manifold, primary distillation plant, vert.

***Perf. 13½x14, 14x13½***
**1965, June 22** **Photo.**
**292** A76 10c blk, red & yel .40 .35
**293** A76 20c multi .40 .35
**294** A76 25c multi .40 .35
*Nos. 292-294 (3)* 1.20 1.05

50th anniv. of the oil industry in Curaçao.

Floating Market, Curaçao A77

Designs (flag and): 2c, Divi-divi tree and Haystack Mountain, Aruba. 3c, Lace, Saba. 4c, Flamingoes, Bonaire. 5c, Church ruins, St. Eustatius. 6c, Lobster, St. Maarten.

**1965, Aug. 25 Litho.** ***Perf. 14x13***
**295** A77 1c lt grn, ultra & red .25 .25
**296** A77 2c yel, ultra & red .25 .25
**297** A77 3c chlky bl, ultra & red .25 .25
**298** A77 4c org, ultra & red .25 .25
**299** A77 5c lt bl, ultra & red .25 .25
**300** A77 6c pink, ultra & red .25 .25
*Nos. 295-300 (6)* 1.50 1.50

Marine Guarding Beach — A78

**1965, Dec. 10 Photo.** ***Perf. 13x10½***
**301** A78 25c multi .25 .25

Netherlands Marine Corps, 300th anniv.

Budgerigars, Wedding Rings and Initials — A79

**1966, Mar. 10 Photo.** ***Perf. 13½x14***
**302** A79 25c gray & multi .35 .25

Issued to commemorate the marriage of Princess Beatrix and Claus van Amsberg.

M. A. de Ruyter and Map of St. Eustatius — A80

**1966, June 19 Photo.** ***Perf. 13½***
**303** A80 25c vio, ocher & lt bl .25 .25

Visit of Adm. Michiel Adriaanszoon de Ruyter (1607-1676) to St. Eustatius, 1666.

Liberal Arts and Grammar A81

10c, Rhetoric and dialectic. 20c, Arithmetic and geometry. 25c, Astronomy and music.

***Perf. 13½x12½***
**1966, Sept. 19 Litho. Unwmk.**
**304** A81 6c yel, bl & blk .25 .25
**305** A81 10c yel grn, red & blk .25 .25
**306** A81 20c bl, yel & blk .35 .25
**307** A81 25c red, yel grn & blk .35 .25
*Nos. 304-307 (4)* 1.20 1.00

25th anniversary of secondary education.

Cruiser A82

Ships: 10c, Sailing ship. 20c, Tanker. 25c, Passenger ship.

***Perf. 13½x14***
**1967, Mar. 29 Litho. Unwmk.**
**308** A82 6c lt & dk grn .35 .25
**309** A82 10c org & brn .35 .25
**310** A82 20c sep & brn .35 .25
**311** A82 25c chlky bl & dk bl .35 .25
*Nos. 308-311 (4)* 1.40 1.00

60th anniv. of *Onze Vloot* (Our Fleet), an organization which publicizes the Dutch navy and merchant marine and helps seamen.

Manuel Carlos Piar (1777-1817), Independence Hero — A83

**1967, Apr. 26 Photo.** ***Perf. 14x13***
**312** A83 20c red & blk .35 .25

Discobolus after Myron — A84

10c, Hand holding torch, & Olympic rings. 25c, Stadium, doves & Olympic rings.

**1968, Feb. 19 Litho. *Perf. 13x14***

**313** A84 10c multi .45 .30
**314** A84 20c dk brn, ol & yel .45 .30
**315** A84 25c bl, dk bl & brt yel grn .45 .30
*Nos. 313-315 (3)* 1.35 .90

19th Olympic Games, Mexico City, 10/12-27.

Friendship 500 — A84a

Designs: 20c, Beechcraft Queen Air. 25c, Friendship and DC-9.

**1968, Dec. 3 Litho. *Perf. 14x13***

**315A** A84a 10c dl yel, blk & brt bl .45 .30
**315B** A84a 20c tan, blk & brt bl .45 .30
**315C** A84a 25c sal pink, blk & brt bl .45 .30
*Nos. 315A-315C (3)* 1.35 .90

Dutch Antillean Airlines (ALM).

Map of Bonaire, Radio Mast and Waves — A85

**1969, Mar. 6 *Perf. 14x13½***

**316** A85 25c bl, emer & blk .35 .30

Opening of the relay station of the Dutch World Broadcasting System on Bonaire.

Code of Law — A86

Designs: 25c, Scales of Justice.

***Perf. 12½x13½***
**1969, May 19 Photo.**

**317** A86 20c dk grn, yel grn & gold .35 .30
**318** A86 25c vio bl, bl & gold .35 .30

Court of Justice, centenary.

ILO Emblem, Cactus and House — A87

**1969, Aug. 25 Litho. *Perf. 14x13***

**319** A87 10c bl & blk .35 .25
**320** A87 25c dk red & blk .35 .25

ILO, 50th anniversary.

Queen Juliana and Rising Sun — A87a

**1969, Dec. 12 Photo. *Perf. 14x13***

**321** A87a 25c bl & multi .45 .30

15th anniv. of the Charter of the Kingdom of the Netherlands. Phosphorescent paper.

Radio Bonaire Studio and Transmitter A88

Design: 15c, Radio waves and cross set against land, sea and air.

**1970, Feb. 5 Photo. *Perf. 12½x13½***

**322** A88 10c multi .25 .25
**323** A88 15c multi .25 .25

5th anniv. of the opening of the Trans World Missionary Radio Station, Bonaire.

Altar, St. Anna's Church, Otraband 1752 — A89

20c, Interior, Synagogue at Punda, 1732, horiz. 25c, Pulpit, Fort Church, Fort Amsterdam, 1769.

***Perf. 13½x14, 14x13½***
**1970, May 12 Photo.**

**324** A89 10c gold & multi .45 .30
**325** A89 20c gold & multi .45 .30
**326** A89 25c gold & multi .45 .30
*Nos. 324-326 (3)* 1.35 .90

St. Theresia Church, St. Nicolaas A90

**1971, Feb. 9 Litho. *Perf. 14x13½***

**327** A90 20c dl bl, gray & rose .35 .30

40th anniversary of the Parish of St. Theresia at St. Nicolaas, Aruba.

A91

**1971, Feb. 24 *Perf. 13½x14***

**328** A91 25c Lions emblem .45 .40

Lions Club in the Netherlands Antilles, 25th anniversary.

A91a

Prince Bernhard, Fokker F27, Boeing 747B.

**1971, June 29 Photo. *Perf. 13x14***

**329** A91a 45c multi .85 .60

60th birthday of Prince Bernhard.

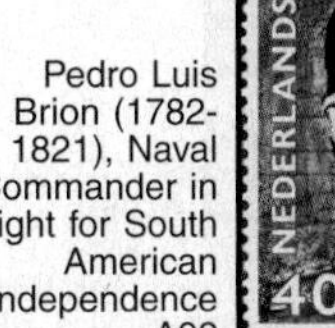

Pedro Luis Brion (1782-1821), Naval Commander in Fight for South American Independence A92

**1971, Sept. 27 Photo. *Perf. 13x12½***

**330** A92 40c multi .45 .40

Flamingoes, Bonaire A93

Designs: 1c, Queen Emma Bridge, Curaçao. 2c, The Bottom, Saba. 4c, Water tower, Aruba. 5c, Fort Amsterdam, St. Maarten. 6c, Fort Orange, St. Eustatius.

**1972, Jan. 17 Litho. *Perf. 13½x14***

**331** A93 1c yel & multi .30 .25
**332** A93 2c yel grn & multi .30 .25
**333** A93 3c dp org & multi .30 .25
**334** A93 4c brt bl & multi .30 .25
**335** A93 5c red org & multi .30 .25
**336** A93 6c lil rose & multi .30 .25
*Nos. 331-336 (6)* 1.80 1.50

Ship in Dry Dock — A94

**1972, Apr. 7 *Perf. 14x13½***

**337** A94 30c bl gray & multi .45 .40

Inauguration of large dry dock facilities in Willemstad.

Juan Enrique Irausquin — A95

**1972, June 20 Photo. *Perf. 13x14***

**338** A95 30c deep orange .45 .40

Irausquin (1904-1962), financier and patriot.

Costa Gomez — A96

**1972, Oct. 27 Litho.**

**339** A96 30c yel grn & blk .45 .40

Moises Frumencio da Costa Gomez (1907-1966), lawyer, legislator, patriot.

**Island Series Type of 1958-59**

Designs: 45c, 85c, Extinct volcano and palms, Saba. 55c, 90c, De Ruyter obelisk, St. Eustatius. 65c, 75c, 10g, Flamingoes, Bonaire. 70c, Fort Willem III, Aruba. 95c, Town Hall, St. Maarten.

**1973, Feb. 12 Litho. *Perf. 14x13***
**Size: 33x22mm**

**340** A56 45c vio bl & lt bl .50 .25
**341** A56 55c dk car rose & emer .55 .25
**342** A56 65c green & pink .80 .30
**343** A56 70c gray vio & org 1.30 .50
**344** A56 75c brt lilac & salmon .70 .50
**345** A56 85c brn ol & apple grn .80 .60
**346** A56 90c blue & ocher .95 .75
**347** A56 95c orange & yellow 1.10 .80
**348** A56 10g brt ultra & sal 8.75 4.25
*Nos. 340-348 (9)* 15.45 8.20

Mailman — A97

Designs: 15c, King William III from 1873 issue. 30c, Emblem of Netherlands Antilles postal service.

**1973, May 23 Photo. *Perf. 13x14***

**349** A97 15c lil, gold & vio .40 .35
**350** A97 20c dk grn & multi .50 .40
**351** A97 30c org & multi .50 .40
*Nos. 349-351 (3)* 1.40 1.15

Centenary of first stamps of Netherlands Antilles.

Cable Linking Aruba, Curaçao and Bonaire A98

30c, 6 stars symbolizing the islands, cable. 45c, Saba, St. Maarten and St. Eustatius linked by cable.

**1973, June 20 Litho. *Perf. 14x13***

**352** A98 15c multi .50 .45
**353** A98 30c multi .50 .45
**354** A98 45c multi .50 .45
*a.* Souvenir sheet of 3, #352-354 1.60 1.60
*Nos. 352-354 (3)* 1.50 1.35

Inauguration of the inter-island submarine cable.

Queen Juliana, Netherlands Antilles and House of Orange Colors — A99a

**Engr. & Photo.**
**1973, Sept. 4 *Perf. 12½x12***

**355** A99a 15c silver & multi .55 .55

25th anniversary of reign of Queen Juliana.

Jan Hendrik Albert Eman — A99

**1973, Oct. 17 Litho. *Perf. 13x14***

**356** A99 30c lt yel grn & blk .40 .40

Eman (1888-1957), founder of the People's Party in Aruba, member of Antillean Parliament.

Lionel Bernard Scott — A100

**1974, Jan. 28**

**357** A100 30c lt bl & multi .40 .40

Scott (1897-1966), architect and statesman.

Family at Supper — A101

Designs: 12c, Parents watching children at play. 15c, Mother and daughter sewing, father and son gardening.

**1974, Feb. 18 Litho. *Perf. 13x14***

**358** A101 6c bl & multi .30 .30
**359** A101 12c bis & multi .35 .30
**360** A101 15c grn & multi .35 .30
*Nos. 358-360 (3)* 1.00 .90

Planned parenthood and World Population Year.

Desulphurization Plant, Lago — A102

Designs: 30c, Distillation plant. 45c, Lago refinery at night.

**1974, Aug. 12 Litho. *Perf. 14x13***

**361** A102 15c lt bl, blk & yel .35 .30
**362** A102 30c lt bl, blk & yel .40 .40
**363** A102 45c dk brn & multi .55 .55
*Nos. 361-363 (3)* 1.30 1.25

Oil industry in Aruba, 50th anniversary.

UPU Emblem — A103

**1974, Oct. 9 Litho. *Perf. 13x14***

**364** A103 15c yel grn, blk & gold .50 .45
**365** A103 30c bl, blk & gold .50 .45

Centenary of Universal Postal Union.

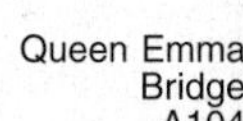

Queen Emma Bridge A104

Willemstad Bridges: 30c, Queen Juliana Bridge. 40c, Queen Wilhelmina Bridge.

**1975, Feb. 5 Litho. *Perf. 14x13***

**366** A104 20c ultra & multi .50 .45
**367** A104 30c ultra & multi .50 .45
**368** A104 40c ultra & multi .60 .55
*Nos. 366-368 (3)* 1.60 1.45

Dedication of new Queen Juliana Bridge spanning Curaçao Harbor.

Salt Crystals A105

Designs: 20c, Solar salt pond. 40c, Map of Bonaire and location of solar salt pond, vert.

***Perf. 14x13, 13x14***

**1975, Apr. 24 Litho.**

**369** A105 15c multi .55 .40
**370** A105 20c multi .55 .45
**371** A105 40c multi .65 .45
*Nos. 369-371 (3)* 1.75 1.30

Bonaire's salt industry.

Aruba Airport, 1935 and Fokker F-18 — A106

30c, Aruba Airport, 1950, & Douglas DC-9. 40c, New Princess Beatrix Airport & Boeing 727.

**1975, June 19 Litho. *Perf. 14x13***

**372** A106 15c vio & multi .45 .35
**373** A106 30c blk & multi .45 .35
**374** A106 40c yel & multi .45 .45
*Nos. 372-374 (3)* 1.35 1.15

40th anniversary of Aruba Airport.

International Women's Year Emblem A107

12c, "Women's role in social development." 20c, Embryos within female & male symbols.

**1975, Aug. 1 Photo. *Perf. 14x13***

**375** A107 6c multi .35 .25
**376** A107 12c multi .40 .30
**377** A107 20c multi .50 .40
*Nos. 375-377 (3)* 1.25 .95

International Women's Year 1975.

Beach, Aruba A108

Tourist Publicity: No. 379, Beach pavilion and boat, Bonaire. No. 380, Table Mountain and Spanish Water, Curaçao.

**1976, June 21 Litho. *Perf. 14x13***

**378** A108 40c blue & multi .55 .50
**379** A108 40c blue & multi .55 .50
**380** A108 40c blue & multi .55 .50
*Nos. 378-380 (3)* 1.65 1.50

Julio Antonio Abraham — A109

**1976, Aug. 10 Photo. *Perf. 13x14***

**381** A109 30c tan & claret .65 .45

Julio Antonio Abraham (1909-1960), founder of Democratic Party of Bonaire.

Dike and Produce — A110

**1976, Sept. 21 Litho.**

**382** A110 15c shown .50 .40
**383** A110 35c Cattle .55 .45
**384** A110 45c Fish .55 .55
*Nos. 382-384 (3)* 1.60 1.40

Agriculture, husbandry and fishing in Netherlands Antilles.

Plaque, Fort Oranje Memorial A111

Designs: 40c, Andrea Doria in St. Eustatius harbor receiving salute. 55c, Johannes de Graaff, Governor of St. Eustatius, holding Declaration of Independence.

**1976, Nov. 16 Litho. *Perf. 14x13***

**385** A111 25c multi .60 .40
**386** A111 40c multi .60 .40
**387** A111 55c multi .60 .55
*Nos. 385-387 (3)* 1.80 1.35

First gun salute to US flag, St. Eustatius, Nov. 16, 1776.

See. No. 619.

Dancer with Cactus Headdress — A112

Carnival: 35c, Woman in feather costume. 40c, Woman in pompadour costume.

**1977, Jan. 20 Litho. *Perf. 13x14***

**388** A112 25c multi .60 .45
**389** A112 35c multi .60 .45
**390** A112 40c multi .60 .45
*Nos. 388-390 (3)* 1.80 1.35

Bird Petroglyph, Aruba — A113

Indian Petroglyphs: 35c, Loops and spiral, Savonet Plantation, Curaçao. 40c, Tortoise, Onima, Bonaire.

**1977, Mar. 29**

**391** A113 25c red & multi .60 .45
**392** A113 35c brn & multi .60 .45
**393** A113 40c yel & multi .60 .45
*Nos. 391-393 (3)* 1.80 1.35

A114

Tropical Trees: 25c, Cordia Sebestena. 40c, East Indian walnut, vert. 55c, Tamarind.

**1977, July 20 *Perf. 14x13, 13x14***

**394** A114 25c blk & multi .50 .45
**395** A114 40c blk & multi .60 .45
**396** A114 55c blk & multi .65 .60
*Nos. 394-396 (3)* 1.75 1.50

A115

Designs: 20c, Chimes, Spritzer & Fuhrmann Building. 40c, Globe with Western Hemisphere and sun over Curaçao. 55c, Diamond ring and flag of Netherlands Antilles.

**1977, Sept. 27 Litho. *Perf. 13x14***

**397** A115 20c brt grn & multi .50 .45
**398** A115 40c yel & multi .60 .45
**399** A115 55c bl & multi .65 .60
*Nos. 397-399 (3)* 1.75 1.50

Spritzer & Fuhrmann, jewelers of Netherlands Antilles, 50th anniversary.

### Island Series Type of 1958-59

Designs: 20c, 35c, 55c, De Ruyter obelisk, St. Eustatius. 40c, Town Hall, St. Maarten.

***Perf. 13½ Horiz.***

**1977, Nov. 30 Photo.**

**Size: 39x22mm**

**400** A56 20c crim & gray 1.40 1.40
*a.* Bklt. pane of 6 (2 #400, 4 #402) 5.00
**401** A56 35c gray & rose 3.75 3.00
*a.* Bklt. pane of 4 (1 #401, 3 #403) 6.00
**402** A56 40c magenta & grn .50 .50
**403** A56 55c dk car rose & emer .70 .70
*Nos. 400-403 (4)* 6.35 5.60

Nos. 400-403 issued in booklets only. No. 400a has label with red inscription in size of 3 stamps; No. 401a has label with dark carmine rose inscription in size of 2 stamps.

Winding Road, Map of Saba — A116

Tourism: 35c, Ruins of Synagogue, map of St. Eustatius. 40c, Greatbay, Map of St. Maarten.

**1977, Nov. 30 Litho. *Perf. 14x13***

**404** A116 25c multi .30 .25
**405** A116 35c multi .35 .30
**406** A116 40c multi .35 .35
*Nos. 404-406 (3)* 1.00 .90

Tete-beche gutter pairs exist.

Treasure Chest A117

Designs: 20c, Logo of Netherlands Antilles Bank. 40c, Safe deposit door.

**1978, Feb. 7 Litho. *Perf. 14x13***

**407** A117 15c brt & dk bl .25 .25
**408** A117 20c org & gold .25 .25
**409** A117 40c brt & dk grn .25 .25
*Nos. 407-409 (3)* .75 .75

Bank of Netherlands Antilles, 150th anniv.

Tete-beche gutter pairs exist.

Flamboyant — A118

Flowers: 25c, Erythrina velutina. 40c, Guaiacum officinale, horiz. 55c, Gliricidia sepium, horiz.

*Perf. 13x14, 14x13*

**1978, May 31** **Litho.**

**410** A118 15c multi .25 .25
**411** A118 25c multi .25 .25
**412** A118 40c multi .40 .30
**413** A118 55c multi .50 .45
*Nos. 410-413 (4)* 1.40 1.25

Polythysana Rubrescens — A119

Butterflies: 25c, Caligo eurilochus. 35c, Prepona omphale amesis. 40c, Morpho aega.

**1978, June 20** ***Perf. 13x14***

**414** A119 15c multi .50 .30
**415** A119 25c multi .50 .30
**416** A119 35c multi .50 .35
**417** A119 40c multi .60 .45
*Nos. 414-417 (4)* 2.10 1.40

"Conserve Energy" — A120

**1978, Aug. 31** **Litho.** ***Perf. 13x14***

**418** A120 15c org & blk .30 .30
**419** A120 20c dp grn & blk .40 .30
**420** A120 40c dk red & blk .45 .40
*Nos. 418-420 (3)* 1.15 1.00

Morse Ship-to-Shore Service A121

Designs: 40c, Ship-to-shore telex service. 55c, Future radar-satellite service, vert.

*Perf. 14x13, 13x14*

**1978, Oct. 16** **Litho.**

**421** A121 20c multi .35 .35
**422** A121 40c multi .45 .45
**423** A121 55c multi .50 .50
*Nos. 421-423 (3)* 1.30 1.30

Ship-to-shore communications, 70th anniv.

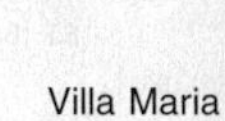

Villa Maria Waterworks A122

35c, Leonard B. Smith, vert. 40c, Opening of Queen Emma Bridge, Willemstadt, 1888.

**1978, Dec. 13**

**424** A122 25c multi .30 .25
**425** A122 35c multi .40 .30
**426** A122 40c multi .45 .40
*Nos. 424-426 (3)* 1.15 .95

L. B. Smith, engineer, 80th death anniv.

**Queen Juliana Type of 1950**

**1979, Jan. 11** **Photo.** ***Perf. 13½x13***

**427** A44 5c dp yel .25 .25
*a.* Bklt. pane of 10 (4 #427, 1 #216a, 2 #222a, 3 #429) 4.00
**428** A44 30c brown 1.05 1.05
*a.* Bklt. pane of 10 (1 #428, 4 #218a, 3 #219a, 2 #222a) 4.00
**429** A44 40c brt bl .35 .35
*Nos. 427-429 (3)* 1.65 1.65

Nos. 427-429 issued in booklets only. Nos. 427a-428a have 2 labels and selvages the size of 6 stamps. Background design of booklet stamps sharper than 1950 issue. All stamps have 1 or 2 straight edges.

Goat and Conference Emblem A123

75c, Horse & map of Curaçao. 150c, Cattle, Netherlands Antilles flag, UN & Conf. emblems.

**1979, Apr. 18** **Litho.** ***Perf. 14x13***

**437** A123 50c multi .40 .35
**438** A123 75c multi .55 .50
**439** A123 150c multi .85 .95
*a.* Souv. sheet of 3, perf. 13½x13 2.00 2.00
*Nos. 437-439 (3)* 1.80 1.80

12th Inter-American Meeting at Ministerial Level on Foot and Mouth Disease and Zoonosis Control, Curaçao, Apr. 17-20. No. 439a contains Nos. 437-439 in changed colors.

Dutch Colonial Soldier, Emblem — A124

**1979, July 4** **Litho.** ***Perf. 13x14***

**440** A124 1g multi .65 .60
*Nos. 440,B166-B167 (3)* 1.45 1.30

Netherlands Antilles Volunteer Corps, 50th anniv.

A125

Flowering Trees: 25c, Casearia Tremula. 40c, Cordia cylindro-stachya. 1.50g, Melochia tomentosa.

**1979, Sept. 3** **Litho.** ***Perf. 13x14***

**441** A125 25c multi .40 .30
**442** A125 40c multi .50 .45
**443** A125 1.50g multi 1.00 1.00
*Nos. 441-443 (3)* 1.90 1.75

A126

Designs: 65c, Dove and Netherlands flag. 1.50g, Dove and Netherlands Antilles flag.

**1979, Dec. 6** **Litho.** ***Perf. 13x14***

**444** A126 65c multi .55 .50
**445** A126 1.50g multi 1.00 1.05

Constitution, 25th anniversary.

Map of Aruba, Foundation Emblem A127

1g, Foundation headquarters, Aruba.

**1979, Dec. 18** ***Perf. 14x13***

**446** A127 95c multi .70 .70
**447** A127 1g multi .85 .85

Cultural Foundation Center, Aruba, 30th anniv.

Cupola, 1910, Fort Church — A128

**1980, Jan. 9** ***Perf. 13x14***

**448** A128 100c multi .85 .70
*Nos. 448,B172-B173 (3)* 1.65 1.50

Fort Church, Curaçao, 210th anniv. (1979).

Rotary Emblem A129

Designs: 50c, Globe and cogwheels. 85c, Cogwheel and Rotary emblem.

**1980, Feb. 22** **Litho.** ***Perf. 14x13***

**449** A129 45c multi .45 .35
**450** A129 50c multi .45 .35
**451** A129 85c multi .60 .60
*a.* Souvenir sheet of 3, #449-451, perf. 13½x13 1.75 1.60
*b.* Strip of 3, #449-451 1.60 1.60

Rotary Intl., 75th anniv. No. 451a has continuous design.

Coin Box, 1905 — A130

Post Office Savings Bank of Netherlands Antilles, 75th Anniv.: 150c, Coin box, 1980.

**1980, Apr. 2** **Litho.** ***Perf. 14x13***

**452** A130 25c multi .35 .35
**453** A130 150c multi 1.10 1.10

Netherlands Antilles No. 200, Arms — A131

60c, No. 290, royal crown.

**1980, Apr. 29** **Photo.**

**454** A131 25c shown .30 .30
**455** A131 60c multicolored .45 .45
*a.* Bklt. pane of 5 + 3 labels (#428, 2 #454, 2 #455) 3.50

Abdication of Queen Juliana of the Netherlands.
Tete-beche gutter pairs exist.

Sir Rowland Hill (1795-1879), Originator of Penny Postage A132

60c, London 1980 emblem. 1g, Airmail label.

**1980, May 6** **Litho.**

**456** A132 45c shown .40 .40
**457** A132 60c multicolored .50 .50
**458** A132 1g multicolored .80 .80
*a.* Souv. sheet of 3, perf. 13½x14 1.75 1.40
*Nos. 456-458 (3)* 1.70 1.70

London 1980 Intl. Stamp Exhibition, May 6-14. No. 458a contains Nos. 456-458 in changed colors.

Leptotila Verreauxi A133

**1980, Sept. 3** **Litho.** ***Perf. 14x13***

**459** A133 25c shown .70 .30
**460** A133 60c Mockingbird .85 .50
**461** A133 85c Coereba flaveola 1.05 .65
*Nos. 459-461 (3)* 2.60 1.45

Rudolf Theodorus Palm — A134

1g, Score, hand playing piano.

**1981, Jan. 27** **Litho.** ***Perf. 13x14***

**462** A134 60c shown .60 .60
**463** A134 1g multicolored 1.00 .85

Palm, composer, birth centenary.

Alliance Mission Emblem, Map of Aruba A135

**1981, Mar. 24** ***Perf. 14x13***

**464** A135 30c shown .35 .35
**465** A135 50c Curaçao .60 .45
**466** A135 1g Bonaire map .95 .85
*Nos. 464-466 (3)* 1.90 1.65

Evangelical Alliance Mission anniversaries: 35th in Aruba, 50th in Curaçao, 30th in Bonaire.

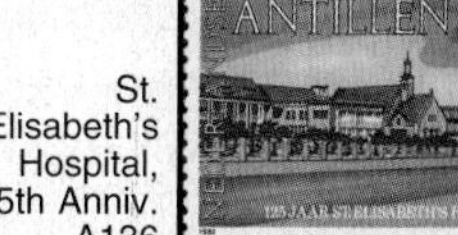


St. Elisabeth's Hospital, 125th Anniv. A136

**1981, June 24** **Litho.** ***Perf. 14x13***

**467** A136 60c Gateway .55 .55
**468** A136 1.50g shown 1.30 1.30

Oregano Blossom — A137

**1981, Nov. 24** **Litho.** ***Perf. 13x14***

**469** A137 45c shown .50 .40
**470** A137 70c Flaira .80 .65
**471** A137 100c Welisali 1.00 .80
*Nos. 469-471 (3)* 2.30 1.85

Ship Pilot Service Cent. — A138

Designs: Various ships.

**1982, Jan. 13 Litho. *Perf. 13x14***

**472** A138 70c multi 1.05 .80
**473** A138 85c multi 1.15 .85
**474** A138 1g multi 1.20 .90
*Nos. 472-474 (3)* 3.40 2.55

A139

**1982, Mar. 15 Litho. *Perf. 13x14***

**475** A139 75c Altar 1.05 .65
**476** A139 85c Building 1.15 .65
**477** A139 150c Pulpit 1.60 1.10
*Nos. 475-477 (3)* 3.80 2.40

Community Mikve Israel-Emanuel Synagogue, 250th anniv.

Flags, Peter Stuyvesant — A140

**1982, Apr. 21 Litho. *Perf. 13x14***

**478** A140 75c multicolored 1.15 .90
*a.* Souvenir sheet 1.25 1.25

US-Netherlands diplomatic relations bicentenary.
See. No. 619b.

A141

**1982, May 5**

**479** A141 35c Radar screen .65 .35
**480** A141 75c Control tower 1.05 .65
**481** A141 150c Antenna 1.60 1.10
*Nos. 479-481 (3)* 3.30 2.10

Intl. Air Traffic Controllers' Year.

A142

45c, Emblem. 85c, Mail bag. 150c, Flags of France, Netherland Antilles.

**1982, June 9 Litho. *Perf. 13x14***

**482** A142 45c multi .65 .45
**483** A142 85c multi .90 .70
**484** A142 150c multi 1.45 1.10
*a.* Souvenir sheet of 3, #482-484 3.00 2.50
*Nos. 482-484 (3)* 3.00 2.25

PHILEXFRANCE '82 Stamp Exhibition, Paris, June 11-21.

Brown Chromis A143

**1982, Sept. 15 Litho. *Perf. 14x13***

**485** A143 35c shown .85 .45
**486** A143 75c Spotted trunkfish 1.15 .80
**487** A143 85c Blue tang 1.30 .90
**488** A143 100c French angelfish 1.40 .95
*Nos. 485-488 (4)* 4.70 3.10

Natural Bridge, Aruba A144

45c, Lac-Bay, Bonaire. 100c, Willemstad, Curaçao.

**1983, Apr. 12 Litho. *Perf. 14x13***

**489** A144 35c shown .60 .45
**490** A144 45c multi .70 .55
**491** A144 100c multi 1.40 1.05
*Nos. 489-491 (3)* 2.70 2.05

World Communications Year — A145

**1983, May 17 Litho. *Perf. 13x14***

**492** A145 1g multi 1.40 1.25
*a.* Souvenir sheet 1.60 1.25

BRASILIANA '83 — A146

45c, Ship, postal building, Waaigat. 55c, Flags, emblem. 100c, Governor's Palace, Sugar Loaf Mt.

**1983, June 29 Litho. *Perf. 13x14***

**493** A146 45c multi .80 .65
**494** A146 55c multi .85 .75
**495** A146 100c multi 1.25 1.15
*a.* Souvenir sheet of 3, #493-495 3.00 2.50
*Nos. 493-495 (3)* 2.90 2.55

Fruit Tree — A147

45c, Mangifera indica. 55c, Malpighia punicifolia. 100c, Citrus aurantifolia.

**1983, Sept. 13 Litho. *Perf. 13x14***

**496** A147 45c multicolored 1.00 .65
**497** A147 55c multicolored 1.05 .70
**498** A147 100c multicolored 1.60 1.15
*Nos. 496-498 (3)* 3.65 2.50

Local Government Buildings A148

**1983, Dec. 20 Litho. *Perf. 14x13***

**499** A148 20c Saba .35 .25
**500** A148 25c St. Eustatius .35 .25
**501** A148 30c St. Maarten .40 .35
**502** A148 35c Aruba *2.40* *.40*
**503** A148 45c Bonaire .60 .45
*a.* Perf. 13½ horiz. ('86) 2.40 1.30
**504** A148 55c Curaçao .80 .55
*a.* Perf. 13½ horiz. ('86) 2.40 1.30
*b.* Bklt. pane of 4 + label (2 #503a, 504a) ('86) 10.00
*Nos. 499-504 (6)* 4.90 2.25

See Nos. 515-520, 543A-555.

Amigoe di Curaçao Newspaper Centenary A149

45c, Copy programming. 55c, Printing press. 85c, Man reading newspaper.

**1984, Jan. 5 Litho.**

**505** A149 45c multicolored .75 .60
**506** A149 55c multicolored .85 .65
**507** A149 85c multicolored 1.30 1.05
*Nos. 505-507 (3)* 2.90 2.30

40th Anniv. of Intl. Civil Aviation Org. — A150

Various emblems.

**1984, Feb. 28 Litho. *Perf. 14x13***

**508** A150 25c Winair .65 .35
**509** A150 45c ICAO .95 .60
**510** A150 55c ALM 1.05 .65
**511** A150 100c Plane 1.60 1.05
*Nos. 508-511 (4)* 4.25 2.65

Chamber of Commerce and Industry Centenary — A151

45c, Bonnet maker. 55c, Emblem. 100c, River, bridge, boat.

**1984, May 29 Litho. *Perf. 13½***

**512** A151 45c multicolored 1.20 .80
**513** A151 55c multicolored 1.25 .80
**514** A151 100c multicolored 1.75 1.10
*Nos. 512-514 (3)* 4.20 2.70

**Govt. Building Type of 1983**

**1984, June 26 Litho. *Perf. 14x13***

**515** A148 60c like 20c .65 .55
**516** A148 65c like 25c .75 .60
**517** A148 75c like 30c 1.00 .80
**518** A148 85c like 35c 3.00 .90
**519** A148 90c like 45c 1.15 .90
**520** A148 95c like 55c 1.20 .95
*Nos. 515-520 (6)* 7.75 4.70

For surcharges see Nos. B306-B307.

Local Birds — A152

45c, Tiaris bicolor. 55c, Zonotrichia capensis. 150c, Chlorostilbon mellisugus.

**1984, Sept. 18 Litho. *Perf. 14x13***

**521** A152 45c multi 1.15 .65
**522** A152 55c multi 1.30 .85
**523** A152 150c multi 2.25 1.60
*Nos. 521-523 (3)* 4.70 3.10

Eleanor Roosevelt (1884-1962) — A153

45c, At Hyde Park. 85c, Portrait. 100c, Reading to children.

**1984, Oct. 11 Litho. *Perf. 13x14***

**524** A153 45c multi .80 .55
**525** A153 85c multi 1.30 .90
**526** A153 100c multi 1.40 .95
*Nos. 524-526 (3)* 3.50 2.40

Tete-beche gutter pairs exist.

Flamingos A154

**1985, Jan. 9 Litho. *Perf. 14x13***

**527** A154 25c Adult pullets .85 .55
**528** A154 45c Juveniles 1.25 .65
**529** A154 55c Adults wading 1.25 .80
**530** A154 100c Adults flying 1.90 1.15
*Nos. 527-530 (4)* 5.25 3.15

Curaçao Masonic Lodge Bicent. — A155

45c, Compass, sun, moon and stars. 55c, Doorway, columns and 5 steps. 100c, Star, 7 steps.

**1985, Feb. 21 Litho. *Perf. 13x14***

**531** A155 45c multi 1.75 .65
**532** A155 55c multi 1.75 .85
**533** A155 100c multi 2.10 1.35
*Nos. 531-533 (3)* 5.60 2.85

UN, 40th Anniv. A156

**1985, June 5 Litho. *Perf. 14x13***

**534** A156 55c multi 1.05 .70
**535** A156 1g multi 1.60 1.15

Papiamentu, Language of the Antilles A157

45c, Pierre Lauffer (1920-1981), author and poem Patria. 55c, Waves of Papiamentu.

**1985, Sept. 4 Litho. *Perf. 14x13***

**536** A157 45c multi .70 .55
**537** A157 55c multi .85 .65

Tete-beche gutter pairs exist.

Flora — A158

5c, Calotropis procera. 10c, Capparis flexuosa. 20c, Mimosa distachya. 45c, Ipomoea nil. 55c, Heliotropium ternatum. 1.50g, Ipomoea incarnata.

**1985, Nov. 6** ***Perf. 13x14***

| | | | | |
|---|---|---|---|---|
| **538** | A158 | 5c multi | .50 | .25 |
| **539** | A158 | 10c multi | .50 | .25 |
| **540** | A158 | 20c multi | .70 | .35 |
| **541** | A158 | 45c multi | 1.05 | .55 |
| **542** | A158 | 55c multi | 1.20 | .60 |
| **543** | A158 | 1.50g multi | 1.90 | 1.30 |
| | | *Nos. 538-543 (6)* | 5.85 | 3.30 |

### Govt. Building Type of 1983

**1985-89** ***Perf. 14x13***

| | | | | |
|---|---|---|---|---|
| **543A** | A148 | 70c like 20c ('88) | 1.00 | .40 |
| **543B** | A148 | 85c like 45c ('88) | 1.15 | .45 |
| **544** | A148 | 1g like 20c | 1.40 | .90 |
| **545** | A148 | 1.50g like 25c | 1.75 | 1.15 |
| **546** | A148 | 2.50g like 30c ('86) | 2.00 | 1.60 |
| **551** | A148 | 5g like 45c ('86) | 4.00 | 3.00 |
| **554** | A148 | 10g like 55c ('87) | 8.00 | 4.75 |
| **555** | A148 | 15g like 20c ('89) | 12.00 | 7.75 |
| | | *Nos. 543A-555 (8)* | 31.30 | 20.00 |

Issued: 70c, 85c, 3/16; 1g, 1.50g, 12/4; 2.50g, 1/8; 5g, 12/3; 10g, 5/20; 15g, 2/8.

For surcharge see No. B308.

Curaçao Town Hall, 125th Anniv. A159

**1986, Jan. 8** ***Perf. 14x13, 13x14***

| | | | | |
|---|---|---|---|---|
| **561** | A159 | 5c Town Hall | .35 | .25 |
| **562** | A159 | 15c State room, vert. | .40 | .25 |
| **563** | A159 | 25c Court room | .60 | .35 |
| **564** | A159 | 55c Entrance, vert. | 1.00 | .60 |
| | | *Nos. 561-564 (4)* | 2.35 | 1.45 |

Amnesty Intl., 25th Anniv. A160

45c, Prisoner chained. 55c, Peace bird imprisoned. 100c, Prisoner behind bars.

**1986, May 28** **Litho.** ***Perf. 14x13***

| | | | | |
|---|---|---|---|---|
| **565** | A160 | 45c multi | .80 | .50 |
| **566** | A160 | 55c multi | .90 | .55 |
| **567** | A160 | 100c multi | 1.25 | .85 |
| | | *Nos. 565-567 (3)* | 2.95 | 1.90 |

Mailboxes A161

10c, PO mailbox. 25c, Steel mailbox, vert. 45c, Mailbox on brick wall, vert. 55c, Pillar box, vert.

***Perf. 14x13, 13x14***

**1986, Sept. 3** **Litho.**

| | | | | |
|---|---|---|---|---|
| **568** | A161 | 10c multi | .30 | .25 |
| **569** | A161 | 25c multi | .45 | .25 |
| **570** | A161 | 45c multi | .70 | .50 |
| **571** | A161 | 55c multi | .85 | .60 |
| | | *Nos. 568-571 (4)* | 2.30 | 1.60 |

Friars of Tilburg in the Antilles, Cent. — A162

10c, Brother Mauritius Vliegendehond, residence, 1886. 45c, Monsignor Ferdinand Kieckens, St. Thomas College, Roodeweg. 55c, Father F.S. de Beer, 1st general-superior, & college courtyard.

**1986, Nov. 13** **Litho.** ***Perf. 13x14***

| | | | | |
|---|---|---|---|---|
| **572** | A162 | 10c multi | .35 | .25 |
| **573** | A162 | 45c multi | .80 | .50 |
| **574** | A162 | 55c multi | .95 | .65 |
| | | *Nos. 572-574 (3)* | 2.10 | 1.40 |

Princess Juliana & Prince Bernhard, 50th Wedding Anniv. — A163

**1987, Jan. 7** **Litho.** ***Perf. 13x14***

| | | | | |
|---|---|---|---|---|
| **575** | A163 | 1.35g multi | 2.50 | 1.25 |
| *a.* | | Souvenir sheet | 3.00 | 2.50 |

Maduro Holding, Inc., Sesquicent. — A164

70c, Expansion map. 85c, Corporate divisions. 1.55g, S.E.L. Maduro, founder.

**1987, Jan. 26**

| | | | | |
|---|---|---|---|---|
| **576** | A164 | 70c multi | .85 | .55 |
| **577** | A164 | 85c multi | 1.05 | .65 |
| **578** | A164 | 1.55g multi | 1.75 | 1.30 |
| | | *Nos. 576-578 (3)* | 3.65 | 2.50 |

Curaçao Rotary Club, 50th Anniv. A165

15c, Map of the Antilles. 50c, Rotary headquarters. 65c, Map of Curaçao.

**1987, Apr. 2** **Litho.** ***Perf. 14x13***

| | | | | |
|---|---|---|---|---|
| **579** | A165 | 15c multicolored | .40 | .25 |
| **580** | A165 | 50c multicolored | .75 | .55 |
| **581** | A165 | 65c multicolored | 1.00 | .60 |
| | | *Nos. 579-581 (3)* | 2.15 | 1.40 |

Bolivar-Curaçao Friendship, 175th Anniv. — A166

60c, Octagon, residence of Simon Bolivar in Curaçao. 70c, Bolivarian Soc. Headquarters, 1949, Willemstad. 80c, Octagon interior (bedroom). 90c, Manual Carlos Piar, Simon Bolivar (1783-1830) & Pedro Luis Brion.

**1987, July 24** **Litho.** ***Perf. 14x13***

| | | | | |
|---|---|---|---|---|
| **582** | A166 | 60c multi | .75 | .55 |
| **583** | A166 | 70c multi | .80 | .60 |
| **584** | A166 | 80c multi | 1.05 | .80 |
| **585** | A166 | 90c multi | 1.15 | .85 |
| | | *Nos. 582-585 (4)* | 3.75 | 2.80 |

Bolivarian Society, 50th anniv. (70c, 90c).

Antilles Natl. Parks Foundation, 25th Anniv. A167

70c, Phaethon lepturus. 85c, Odocoileus virginianus curassavicus. 1.55g, Iguana iguana.

**1987, Dec. 1** **Litho.** ***Perf. 14x13***

| | | | | |
|---|---|---|---|---|
| **586** | A167 | 70c multi | .90 | .55 |
| **587** | A167 | 85c multi | 1.05 | .65 |
| **588** | A167 | 1.55g multi | 1.75 | 1.30 |
| | | *Nos. 586-588 (3)* | 3.70 | 2.50 |

The Curaçao Courant, 175th Anniv. A168

Designs: 55c, 19th Cent. printing press, lead type. 70c, Keyboard, modern press.

**1987, Dec. 11**

| | | | | |
|---|---|---|---|---|
| **589** | A168 | 55c multi | .80 | .55 |
| **590** | A168 | 70c multi | .85 | .60 |

Mijnmaatschappij Phosphate Mining Co., Curaçao, 75th Anniv. — A169

40c, William Godden, founder. 105c, Processing plant. 155c, Tafelberg.

**1988, Jan. 21**

| | | | | |
|---|---|---|---|---|
| **591** | A169 | 40c multicolored | .70 | .40 |
| **592** | A169 | 105c multicolored | 1.30 | .85 |
| **593** | A169 | 155c multicolored | 1.75 | 1.15 |
| | | *Nos. 591-593 (3)* | 3.75 | 2.40 |

States of the Netherlands Antilles, 50th Anniv. A170

Designs: 65c, John Horris Sprockel, 1st president, and natl. colors, crest. 70c, Development of state elections, women's suffrage. 155c, Natl. colors, crest, constellation representing the 5 islands and separation of Aruba.

**1988, Apr. 5** **Litho.**

| | | | | |
|---|---|---|---|---|
| **594** | A170 | 65c multi | .85 | .60 |
| **595** | A170 | 70c multi | 1.05 | .60 |
| **596** | A170 | 155c multi | 1.75 | 1.15 |
| | | *Nos. 594-596 (3)* | 3.65 | 2.35 |

Abolition of Slavery, 125th Anniv. A171

190c, Slave Wall, Curaçao.

**1988, July 1** **Litho.** ***Perf. 14x13***

| | | | | |
|---|---|---|---|---|
| **597** | A171 | 155c shown | 1.60 | 1.05 |
| **598** | A171 | 190c multicolored | 1.90 | 1.20 |

3rd Conference for Great Cities of the Americas, Curaçao, Aug. 24-27 A172

**1988, Aug. 24** **Litho.**

| | | | | |
|---|---|---|---|---|
| **599** | A172 | 80c shown | 1.05 | .60 |
| **600** | A172 | 155c Bridge, globe | 1.60 | 1.05 |

Interamerican Foundation of Cities conference on building bridges between peoples.

Charles Ernst Barend Hellmund (1896-1952) — A173

Men and women who initiated community development: 65c, Atthelo Maud Edwards Jackson (1901-1970). 90c, Nicolaas Debrot (1902-1981). 120c, William Charles De La Try Ellis (1881-1977).

**1988, Sept. 20** ***Perf. 13x14***

| | | | | |
|---|---|---|---|---|
| **601** | A173 | 55c multi | .70 | .40 |
| **602** | A173 | 65c multi | .75 | .50 |
| **603** | A173 | 90c multi | 1.20 | .75 |
| **604** | A173 | 120c multi | 1.25 | .85 |
| | | *Nos. 601-604 (4)* | 3.90 | 2.50 |

Tete-beche gutter pairs exist.

Cacti — A174

55c, Cereus hexagonus. 115c, Melocactus. 125c, Opuntia wentiana.

**1988, Dec. 13** **Litho.** ***Perf. 13x14***

| | | | | |
|---|---|---|---|---|
| **605** | A174 | 55c multicolored | .85 | .55 |
| **606** | A174 | 115c multicolored | 1.35 | .85 |
| **607** | A174 | 125c multicolored | 1.60 | 1.05 |
| | | *Nos. 605-607 (3)* | 3.80 | 2.45 |

Wildlife Protection and Curaçao Foundation for the Prevention of Cruelty to Animals A175

**1989, Mar. 9** **Litho.** ***Perf. 14x13***

| | | | | |
|---|---|---|---|---|
| **608** | A175 | 65c Crested quail | 1.30 | .75 |
| **609** | A175 | 115c Dogs, cats | 1.45 | 1.10 |

Cruise Ships at St. Maarten and Curaçao A176

**1989, May 8** **Litho.**

| | | | | |
|---|---|---|---|---|
| **610** | A176 | 70c Great Bay Harbor | 1.05 | .75 |
| **611** | A176 | 155c St. Annabay | 1.75 | 1.45 |

Tourism.

A177

Social and Political Figures: 40c, Paula Clementina Dorner (1901-1969), teacher. 55c, John Aniceto de Jongh (1885-1951), pharmacist, Parliament member. 90c, Jacobo Palm (1887-1982), composer. 120c, Abraham Mendes Chumaceiro (1841-1902), political reformer.

**1989, Sept. 20** **Litho.** ***Perf. 13x14***

| | | | | |
|---|---|---|---|---|
| **612** | A177 | 40c multi | .70 | .45 |
| **613** | A177 | 55c multi | .80 | .55 |
| **614** | A177 | 90c multi | 1.15 | .75 |
| **615** | A177 | 120c multi | 1.40 | 1.05 |
| | | *Nos. 612-615 (4)* | 4.05 | 2.80 |

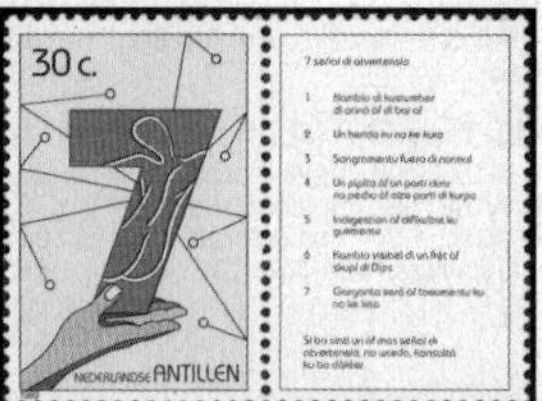


A178

30c, 7 Symptoms of cancer. 60c, Radiation treatment. 80c, Fund emblem, healthy person.

**1989, Nov. 7** **Litho.**

| | | | |
|---|---|---|---|
| **616** A178 30c multi | .60 | .45 |
| **617** A178 60c multi | .95 | .70 |
| **618** A178 80c multi | 1.15 | .70 |
| *Nos. 616-618 (3)* | 2.70 | 1.85 |

Queen Wilhelmina Fund, 40th anniv. Nos. 616-618 printed se-tenant with inscribed labels.

Souvenir Sheet

World Stamp Expo '89 and 20th UPU Congress, Washington, DC — A179

Designs: 70c, Monument, St. Eustatius, where the sovereignty of the US was 1st recognized by a foreign officer, Nov. 16, 1776. 155c, Peter Stuyvesant, flags representing bicent. of US-Antilles diplomatic relations, vert. 250c, 9-Gun salute of the *Andrea Doria.*

**1989, Nov. 17** **Litho.** ***Perf. 13***

| | | |
|---|---|---|
| **619** Sheet of 3 | 5.75 | 4.50 |
| *a.* A179 70c multicolored | 1.15 | .75 |
| *b.* A179 155c multicolored | 1.75 | 1.30 |
| *c.* A179 250c multicolored | 2.60 | 2.25 |

Fireworks A180

100c, Ornaments on tree.

**1989, Dec. 1** ***Perf. 13½x14***

| | | |
|---|---|---|
| **620** A180 30c multicolored | .60 | .40 |
| **621** A180 100c multicolored | 1.30 | .90 |

Christmas 1989 and New Year 1990. Nos. 620-621 printed se-tenant with labels inscribed "Merry X-mas and Happy New Year" in four languages.

Flowering plants — A181

30c, Tephrosia cinerea. 55c, Erithalis fruticosa. 65c, Evolvulus antillanus. 70c, Jacquinia arborea. 125c, Tournefortia gnaphalodes. 155c, Sesuvium portulacastrum.

**1990, Jan. 31** **Litho.** ***Perf. 13x14***

| | | |
|---|---|---|
| **622** A181 30c multi | .40 | .35 |
| **623** A181 55c multi | .75 | .55 |
| **624** A181 65c multi | .80 | .60 |
| **625** A181 70c multi | .90 | .70 |
| **626** A181 125c multi | 1.60 | 1.30 |
| **627** A181 155c multi | 2.00 | 1.60 |
| *Nos. 622-627 (6)* | 6.45 | 5.10 |

Dominican Nuns in the Netherlands Antilles, Cent. A182

10c, Nurse, flag, map. 55c, St. Rose Hospital and St. Martin's Home. 60c, St. Joseph School.

**1990, May 7** **Litho.** ***Perf. 14x13***

| | | |
|---|---|---|
| **628** A182 10c multicolored | .25 | .25 |
| **629** A182 55c multicolored | .75 | .50 |
| **630** A182 60c multicolored | .85 | .60 |
| *Nos. 628-630 (3)* | 1.85 | 1.35 |

A183

Poets: 40c, Carlos Alberto Nicolaas-Perez (1915-1989). 60c, Evert Stephanus Jordanus Kruythoff (1893-1967). 80c, John De Pool (1873-1947). 150c, Joseph Sickman Corsen (1853-1911).

**1990, Aug. 8** **Litho.** ***Perf. 13x14***

| | | |
|---|---|---|
| **631** A183 40c multicolored | .55 | .35 |
| **632** A183 60c multicolored | .80 | .60 |
| **633** A183 80c multicolored | 1.00 | .75 |
| **634** A183 150c multicolored | 1.75 | 1.60 |
| *Nos. 631-634 (4)* | 4.10 | 3.30 |

Netherlands Queens — A184

No. 635, Emma. No. 636, Wilhelmina. No. 637, Juliana. No. 638, Beatrix.
250c, Four Queens, horiz.

**1990, Sept. 5** ***Perf. 13x14***

| | | |
|---|---|---|
| **635** A184 100c multi | 1.45 | 1.05 |
| **636** A184 100c multi | 1.45 | 1.05 |
| **637** A184 100c multi | 1.45 | 1.05 |
| **638** A184 100c multi | 1.45 | 1.05 |
| *Nos. 635-638 (4)* | 5.80 | 4.20 |

**Souvenir Sheet**

***Perf. 14x13***

| | | |
|---|---|---|
| **639** A184 250c multi | 6.25 | 5.00 |

Oil Refining in Curaçao, 75th Anniv. A185

**1990, Oct. 1** **Litho.** ***Perf. 14x13***

| | | |
|---|---|---|
| **640** A185 100c multicolored | 1.60 | 1.25 |

Christmas A186

**1990, Dec. 5** **Litho.** ***Perf. 13½x14***

| | | |
|---|---|---|
| **641** A186 30c Gifts | .60 | .30 |
| **642** A186 100c shown | 1.60 | .95 |

25th anniv. of Bon Bisina Project (No. 641). Nos. 641-642 each printed with se-tenant label showing holiday greetings.

Express Mail Service, 5th Anniv. A187

**1991, Jan. 16** **Litho.** ***Perf. 14x13***

| | | |
|---|---|---|
| **643** A187 20g multicolored | 15.00 | 12.50 |

Fish — A188

Designs: 10c, Scuba diver, French grunt. 40c, Spotted trunkfish. 55c, Coppersweeper. 75c, Skindiver, yellow goatfish. 100c, Blackbar soldierfish.

**1991, Mar. 13** ***Perf. 13x14***

| | | |
|---|---|---|
| **644** A188 10c multicolored | .60 | .25 |
| **645** A188 40c multicolored | .70 | .50 |
| **646** A188 55c multicolored | .85 | .75 |
| **647** A188 75c multicolored | 1.05 | 1.00 |
| **648** A188 100c multicolored | 1.60 | 1.20 |
| *Nos. 644-648 (5)* | 4.80 | 3.70 |

Greetings A189

**1991, May 8** ***Perf. 14x13***

| | | |
|---|---|---|
| **649** A189 30c Good luck | .45 | .40 |
| **650** A189 30c Thank you | .45 | .40 |
| **651** A189 30c Love you | .45 | .40 |
| **652** A189 30c Happy day | .45 | .40 |
| **653** A189 30c Get well soon | .45 | .40 |
| **654** A189 30c Happy birthday | .45 | .40 |
| *Nos. 649-654 (6)* | 2.70 | 2.40 |

Lighthouses — A190

30c, Westpoint, Curaçao. 70c, Willem's Tower, Bonaire. 115c, Little Curaçao, Curaçao.

**1991, June 19** **Litho.** ***Perf. 13x14***

| | | |
|---|---|---|
| **655** A190 30c multicolored | 2.50 | 1.30 |
| **656** A190 70c multicolored | 2.50 | 1.30 |
| **657** A190 115c multicolored | 2.50 | 1.30 |
| *Nos. 655-657 (3)* | 7.50 | 3.90 |

Peter Stuyvesant College, 50th Anniv. A191

Espamer '91 — A192

**1991, July 5** ***Perf. 14x13, 13x14***

| | | |
|---|---|---|
| **658** A191 65c multicolored | .90 | .85 |
| **659** A192 125c multicolored | 1.75 | 1.75 |

Christmas A193

**1991, Dec. 2** **Litho.** ***Perf. 13½x14***

| | | |
|---|---|---|
| **660** A193 30c shown | .45 | .40 |
| **661** A193 100c Angel, shepherds | 1.40 | 1.25 |

Nos. 660-661 printed with se-tenant labels.

A194

**Litho. & Typo.**

**1991, Dec. 16** ***Perf. 13x14***

| | | |
|---|---|---|
| **662** A194 30c J. A. Correa | .80 | .45 |
| **663** A194 70c "75," coat of arms | 1.30 | .90 |
| **664** A194 155c I. H. Capriles | 1.90 | 1.60 |
| *a.* Strip of 3, #662-664 | 4.00 | 3.00 |

Maduro and Curiel's Bank NV, 75th anniv.

Odocoileus Virginianus A195

**1992, Jan. 29** **Litho.** ***Perf. 14x13***

| | | |
|---|---|---|
| **666** A195 5c Fawn | .95 | .70 |
| **667** A195 10c Two does | .95 | .70 |
| **668** A195 30c Buck | .95 | .70 |
| **669** A195 40c Buck & doe in water | .95 | .70 |
| **670** A195 200c Buck drinking | 3.00 | 2.25 |
| **671** A195 355c Buck, diff. | 5.00 | 4.00 |
| *Nos. 666-671 (6)* | 11.80 | 9.05 |

World Wildlife Fund. Nos. 670-671 are airmail and do not have the WWF emblem. Nos. 670-671 are airmail.

Souvenir Sheet

Discovery of America, 500th Anniv. — A196

Designs: a, 250c, Alhambra, Granada, Spain. b, 500c, Carthusian Monastery, Seville, Spain.

**1992, Apr. 1** **Litho.** ***Perf. 14x13***

| | | |
|---|---|---|
| **672** A196 Sheet of 2, #a.-b. | 11.50 | 9.00 |

#672a, Granada '92. #672b, Expo '92, Seville.

Discovery of America, 500th Anniv. A197

250c, Sailing ship. 500c, Map, Columbus.

**1992, May 13** **Litho.** ***Perf. 14x13***

| | | |
|---|---|---|
| **673** A197 250c multicolored | 3.25 | 2.60 |
| **674** A197 500c multicolored | 6.50 | 5.25 |

World Columbian Stamp Expo '92, Chicago.

Container Terminal, Curaçao A198

**1992, June 26**

| | | |
|---|---|---|
| **675** A198 80c multi | 1.15 | .90 |
| **676** A198 125c multi, diff. | 1.60 | 1.35 |

Famous People — A199

Designs: 30c, Angela Altagracia de Lannoy-Willems (1913-1983), politician and social activist. 40c, Lodewijk Daniel Gerharts (1901-1983), politician and promoter of tourism for Bonaire. 55c, Cyrus Wilberforce Wathey (1901-1969), businessman and philanthropist. 70c, Christiaan Winkel (1899-1962), deputy governor of Netherlands Antilles. 100c, Franciscan Nuns of Roosendaal, educational and charitable group, 150th anniversary of arrival in Curaçao.

**1992, Sept. 1 Litho. *Perf. 13x14***

| | | | | |
|---|---|---|---|---|
| **677** | A199 | 30c grn & blk, *tan* | .45 | .40 |
| **678** | A199 | 40c blue & blk, *tan* | .60 | .45 |
| **679** | A199 | 55c yel org & blk, *tan* | .75 | .60 |
| **680** | A199 | 70c lake & blk, *tan* | .85 | .70 |
| **681** | A199 | 100c blue & blk, *tan* | 1.15 | 1.15 |
| | | *Nos. 677-681 (5)* | 3.80 | 3.30 |

Queen Beatrix's 1992 Visit — A200

Designs: 70c, Queen in white hat, Prince Claus. 100c, Queen signing jubilee register. 175c, Queen in black hat, Prince Claus, native girl.

**1992, Nov. 9 Litho. *Perf. 14x13***

| | | | | |
|---|---|---|---|---|
| **682** | A200 | 70c multicolored | .95 | .80 |
| **683** | A200 | 100c multicolored | 1.30 | 1.15 |
| **684** | A200 | 175c multicolored | 2.10 | 1.90 |
| | | *Nos. 682-684 (3)* | 4.35 | 3.85 |

Queen Beatrix's accession to the throne, 12½ year anniv. (#683).

Christmas A201

30c, Nativity scene. 100c, Mary, Joseph, vert.

***Perf. 14x13½, 13½x14***

**1992, Dec. 1 Litho.**

| | | | | |
|---|---|---|---|---|
| **685** | A201 | 30c multi | .55 | .40 |
| **686** | A201 | 100c multi | 1.45 | 1.05 |

No. 686 printed with se-tenant label.

Flowers — A202

75c, Hibiscus. 90c, Helianthus annuus. 175c, Ixora. 195c, Rosea.

**1993, Feb. 3 Litho. *Perf. 13x14***

| | | | | |
|---|---|---|---|---|
| **687** | A202 | 75c multi | 1.05 | .75 |
| **688** | A202 | 90c multi | 1.25 | 1.00 |
| **689** | A202 | 175c multi | 2.10 | 1.75 |
| **690** | A202 | 195c multi | 2.40 | 2.10 |
| | | *Nos. 687-690 (4)* | 6.80 | 5.60 |

Anniversaries A203

Map of islands and: 65c, Airplane, air routes. 75c, Natl. Laboratory, scientist using microscope. 90c, Airplane at Princess Juliana Intl. Airport. 175c, Yellow and white crosses.

**1993, Mar. 9 *Perf. 14x13***

| | | | | |
|---|---|---|---|---|
| **691** | A203 | 65c multicolored | .85 | .65 |
| **692** | A203 | 75c multicolored | .95 | .70 |
| **693** | A203 | 90c multicolored | 1.15 | .95 |
| **694** | A203 | 175c multicolored | 2.00 | 1.75 |
| | | *Nos. 691-694 (4)* | 4.95 | 4.05 |

Princess Juliana Intl. Airport, 50th anniv. (#691, 693). Natl. Laboratory, 75th anniv. (#692). Princess Margaret White/Yellow Cross Foundation for District Nursing, 50th anniv. (#694).

Dogs — A204

**1993, May 26 Litho. *Perf. 13x14***

| | | | | |
|---|---|---|---|---|
| **695** | A204 | 65c Pekingese | .85 | .70 |
| **696** | A204 | 90c Poodle | 1.15 | 1.00 |
| **697** | A204 | 100c Pomeranian | 1.40 | 1.10 |
| **698** | A204 | 175c Papillon | 2.10 | 1.75 |
| | | *Nos. 695-698 (4)* | 5.50 | 4.55 |

Entry of Netherlands Antilles into UPAEP A205

Designs: 150c, Indian cave painting, Bonaire. 200c, Emblem of Brasiliana '93, flag of Netherlands Antilles. 250c, Map of Central and South America, Netherlands Antilles, Spain, and Portugal, document being signed.

**1993, July 15 Litho. *Perf. 14x13***

| | | | | |
|---|---|---|---|---|
| **699** | A205 | 150c multicolored | 2.60 | 1.60 |
| **700** | A205 | 200c multicolored | 3.00 | 2.10 |
| **701** | A205 | 250c multicolored | 3.50 | 2.60 |
| | | *Nos. 699-701 (3)* | 9.10 | 6.30 |

Brasiliana '93 (#700).

Contemporary Art — A206

**1993, July 23 Litho. *Perf. 13x14***

| | | | | |
|---|---|---|---|---|
| **702** | A206 | 90c silver & multi | 1.15 | .95 |
| **703** | A206 | 150c gold & multi | 1.75 | 1.50 |

US Consulate General in Netherlands Antilles, Bicent. A207

65c, American Consulate. 90c, Coats of Arms. 175c, Eagle in flight.

**1993, Nov. 16 Litho. *Perf. 14x13***

| | | | | |
|---|---|---|---|---|
| **704** | A207 | 65c multicolored | .80 | .70 |
| **705** | A207 | 90c multicolored | 1.20 | 1.00 |
| **706** | A207 | 175c multicolored | 2.00 | 1.75 |
| | | *Nos. 704-706 (3)* | 4.00 | 3.45 |

Christmas — A208

Designs: 30c, Mosaic of mother and child. 115c, Painting of Mary holding Christ.

**1993, Dec. 1 *Perf. 13x14***

| | | | | |
|---|---|---|---|---|
| **707** | A208 | 30c multicolored | .55 | .35 |
| **708** | A208 | 115c multicolored | 1.45 | 1.30 |

Dogs — A209

**1994, Feb. 2 Litho. *Perf. 14x13***

| | | | | |
|---|---|---|---|---|
| **709** | A209 | 65c Basset | 1.00 | .85 |
| **710** | A209 | 75c Pit bull terrier | 1.15 | .95 |
| **711** | A209 | 90c Cocker spaniel | 1.35 | 1.15 |
| **712** | A209 | 175c Chow | 2.40 | 2.00 |
| | | *Nos. 709-712 (4)* | 5.90 | 4.95 |

Birds — A210

50c, Polyborus plancus. 95c, Pavo muticus. 100c, Ara macao. 125c, Icterus icterus.

**1994, Mar. 2 Litho. *Perf. 13x14***

| | | | | |
|---|---|---|---|---|
| **713** | A210 | 50c multicolored | 1.75 | .75 |
| **714** | A210 | 95c multicolored | 1.75 | 1.35 |
| **715** | A210 | 100c multicolored | 1.75 | 1.35 |
| **716** | A210 | 125c multicolored | 2.25 | 1.60 |
| | | *Nos. 713-716 (4)* | 7.50 | 5.05 |

A211

Famous People: 65c, Joseph Husurell Lake (1925-76), politician, journalist. 75c, Efrain Jonckheer (1917-87), diplomat. 100c, Michiel Martinus Romer (1865-1937), educator. 175c, Carel Nicolaas Winkel (1882-1973), public official, social worker.

**1994, Apr. 8**

| | | | | |
|---|---|---|---|---|
| **717** | A211 | 65c olive & blk, *grn* | .80 | .80 |
| **718** | A211 | 75c brn & blk, *lt brn* | .95 | .95 |
| **719** | A211 | 100c grn & blk, *bl* | 1.25 | 1.25 |
| **720** | A211 | 175c brn & blk, *tan* | 2.25 | 2.25 |
| | | *Nos. 717-720 (4)* | 5.25 | 5.25 |

A212

1994 World Cup Soccer Championships, US: 90c, Socks, soccer shoes, horiz. 150c, Shoe, ball. 175c, Whistle, horiz.

***Perf. 14x13, 13x14***

**1994, May 4 Litho.**

| | | | | |
|---|---|---|---|---|
| **721** | A212 | 90c multicolored | 1.20 | 1.05 |
| **722** | A212 | 150c multicolored | 1.90 | 1.75 |
| **723** | A212 | 175c multicolored | 2.10 | 2.00 |
| | | *Nos. 721-723 (3)* | 5.20 | 4.80 |

A213

ILO, 75th Anniv.: 90c, Declaration, chair, gavel. 110c, "75" over heart. 200c, Wind-blown tree.

**1994, June 1 Litho. *Perf. 13x14***

| | | | | |
|---|---|---|---|---|
| **724** | A213 | 90c multicolored | 1.20 | 1.10 |
| **725** | A213 | 110c multicolored | 1.35 | 1.25 |
| **726** | A213 | 200c multicolored | 2.60 | 2.50 |
| | | *Nos. 724-726 (3)* | 5.15 | 4.85 |

Wildlife A214

Designs: 10c, Ware-wara, blenchi, parakeet, dolphin. 35c, Dolphin, pelican, troupial. 50c, Iguana, fish, lobster, sea hedgehog. 125c, Sea hedgehog, sea apple, fish, turtle, flamingos, ducks.

**1994, Aug. 4 Litho. *Perf. 14x13***

| | | | | |
|---|---|---|---|---|
| **727** | A214 | 10c multicolored | .75 | .40 |
| **728** | A214 | 35c multicolored | .75 | .55 |
| **729** | A214 | 50c multicolored | .80 | .75 |
| **730** | A214 | 125c multicolored | 1.75 | 1.75 |
| *a.* | | Souvenir sheet, #727-730 | 5.00 | 4.50 |
| | | *Nos. 727-730 (4)* | 4.05 | 3.45 |

PHILAKOREA '94 (#730a).

FEPAPOST '94 — A215

2.50g, Netherlands #277. 5g, #109.

**1994, Oct. 5 Litho. *Perf. 14x13***

| | | | | |
|---|---|---|---|---|
| **731** | A215 | 2.50g multicolored | 3.00 | 3.25 |
| **732** | A215 | 5g multicolored | 6.00 | 6.25 |
| *a.* | | Souv. sheet of 2, #731-732, perf. 13½x13 | 10.00 | 8.25 |

Christmas A216

115c, Hands holding earth.

**1994, Dec. 1 Litho. *Perf. 14x13***

| | | | | |
|---|---|---|---|---|
| **733** | A216 | 30c shown | .85 | .45 |
| **734** | A216 | 115c multicolored | 1.75 | 1.45 |

Curaçao Carnivals A217

Carnival scene and: 125c, Buildings, Willemstad. 175c, Floating market. 250c, House with thatched roof.

**1995, Jan. 19 Litho. *Perf. 14x13***

| | | | | |
|---|---|---|---|---|
| **735** | A217 | 125c multicolored | 1.60 | 1.45 |
| **736** | A217 | 175c multicolored | 2.25 | 1.90 |
| **737** | A217 | 250c multicolored | 3.00 | 2.60 |
| | | *Nos. 735-737 (3)* | 6.85 | 5.95 |

Mgr. Verriet Institute for Physically Handicapped, 50th Anniv. — A218

Design: 90c, Cedric Virginie, handicapped worker at Public Library.

**1995, Feb. 2 Litho. *Perf. 13x14***

| | | | | |
|---|---|---|---|---|
| **738** | A218 | 65c multicolored | .80 | .75 |
| **739** | A218 | 90c multicolored | 1.15 | 1.05 |

Dogs — A219

**1995, Mar. 29 Litho. *Perf. 14x13***

**740** A219 75c Doberman 1.20 1.00
**741** A219 85c Shepherd 1.45 1.20
**742** A219 100c Bouvier 1.60 1.30
**743** A219 175c St. Bernard 2.60 2.10
*Nos. 740-743 (4)* 6.85 5.60

Flags, Coats of Arms of Island Territories A220

10c, Bonaire. 35c, Curaçao. 50c, St. Maarten. 65c, Saba. 75c, St. Eustatius, natl. flag, coat of arms. 90c, Flags of territories, natl. coat of arms.

**1995, June 30 Litho. *Perf. 14x13***

**744** A220 10c multicolored .25 .30
**745** A220 35c multicolored .60 .45
**746** A220 50c multicolored .75 .60
*a.* St. Maarten flag colors reversed 60.00 —
**747** A220 65c multicolored .90 .80
**748** A220 75c multicolored 1.05 .85
**749** A220 90c multicolored 1.20 1.15
*a.* St. Maarten flag colors reversed 60.00 —
*Nos. 744-749 (6)* 4.75 4.15

Nos. 746a and 749a show the colors of the St. Maarten flag reversed: blue on top, red on bottom. Both were quickly withdrawn from sale after the error was discovered. Used examples exist.

Domestic Cats — A221

Designs: 25c, Siamese sealpoint. 60c, Maine coon. 65c, Egyptian silver mau. 90c, Angora. 150c, Persian blue smoke.

**1995, Sept. 29 Litho. *Perf. 13x14***

**750** A221 25c multicolored .70 .35
**751** A221 60c multicolored 1.05 .70
**752** A221 65c multicolored 1.15 .80
**753** A221 90c multicolored 1.40 1.15
**754** A221 150c multicolored 2.10 1.75
*Nos. 750-754 (5)* 6.40 4.75

Christmas and New Year — A222

Designs: 30c, Three Magi following star. 115c, Fireworks above houses, Handelskade.

**1995, Dec. 1 Litho. *Perf. 13½x13***

**755** A222 30c multicolored .60 .40
**756** A222 115c multicolored 1.60 1.30

Nos. 755-756 each printed with se-tenant label.

A223

Curaçao Lions Club, 50th Anniv.: 75c, List of services to community. 105c, Seal. 250c, Hands clasp.

**1996, Feb. 26 Litho. *Perf. 13x14***

**757** A223 75c multicolored 1.20 .80
**758** A223 105c multicolored 1.45 1.20
**759** A223 250c multicolored 3.25 3.00
*Nos. 757-759 (3)* 5.90 5.00

A224

**1996, Apr. 12 Litho. *Perf. 13x14***

**760** A224 85c shown .80 .65
**761** A224 175c Telegraph key 1.20 .80

Radio, cent.

A225

**1996, Apr. 12**

**762** A225 60c shown 1.15 1.05
**763** A225 75c Tornado, sun 2.10 1.90

Dr. David Ricardo Capriles Clinic, 60th anniv.

A226

**1996, May 8 Litho. *Perf. 13x14***

**764** A226 85c shown 1.15 1.15
**765** A226 225c Bible 3.00 2.60

Translation of the Bible into Papiamentu. Nos. 764-765 exist imperf. Value, set $90.

CAPEX '96 — A227

Butterflies: 5c, Agraulis vanillae. 110c, Callithea philotima. 300c, Parthenos sylvia. 750c, Euphaedra francina.

**1996, June 5 Litho. *Perf. 14x13***

**766** A227 5c multicolored .90 .25
**767** A227 110c multicolored 1.75 1.30
**768** A227 300c multicolored 4.50 3.50
*a.* Souvenir sheet of 2, #767-768 7.50 5.75
**769** A227 750c multicolored 10.50 8.50
*Nos. 766-769 (4)* 17.65 13.55

Nos. 766-769 exist imperf. Value, set $120. No. 768a exists imperf. Value, $110.

Famous Antillean Personalities A228

Designs: 40c, Mary Gertrude Johnson Hassel (1853-1939), introduced drawn thread (Spanish work) to Saba. 50c, Cornelis Marten (Papa Cornes) (1749-1852), spiritual care giver on Bonaire. 75c, Phelippi Benito Chakutoe (1891-1967), union leader. 85c, Christiaan Josef Hendrikus Engels (1907-80), physician, painter, pianist, poet.

**1996, Aug. 21 Litho. *Perf. 14x13***

**770** A228 40c orange & black .65 .50
**771** A228 50c green & black .70 .55
**772** A228 75c brown & black 1.05 .80
**773** A228 85c blue & black 1.10 1.05
*Nos. 770-773 (4)* 3.50 2.90

Horses A229

**1996, Sept. 26 Litho. *Perf. 14x13***

**774** A229 110c Shire 1.60 1.25
**775** A229 225c Shetland pony 3.25 2.50
**776** A229 275c Thoroughbred 3.50 3.25
**777** A229 350c Przewalski 4.75 4.00
*Nos. 774-777 (4)* 13.10 11.00

Christmas — A230

35c, Money bag, straw hat, candy cane, gifts, poinsettias, star. 150c, Santa Claus.

***Serpentine Die Cut 13x13½***

**1996, Dec. 2 Litho.**

**Self-Adhesive**

**778** A230 35c multicolored .80 .40
**779** A230 150c multicolored 2.00 1.60

Mushrooms A231

40c, Galerina autumnalis. 50c, Amanita virosa. 75c, Boletus edulis. 175c, Amanita muscaria.

**1997, Feb. 19 Litho. *Perf. 14x13***

**780** A231 40c multicolored 1.00 .55
**781** A231 50c multicolored 1.20 .65
**782** A231 75c multicolored 1.75 .90
**783** A231 175c multicolored 3.00 2.25
*Nos. 780-783 (4)* 6.95 4.35

Birds — A232

5c, Melopsittacus undulatus. 25c, Cacatua leadbeateri leadbeateri. 50c, Amazona barbadensis. 75c, Ardea purpurea. 85c, Chrysolampis mosquitus. 100c, Balearica pavonina. 110c, Pyrocephalus rubinus. 125c, Phoenicopteurus ruber. 200c, Pandion haliaetus. 225c, Ramphastos sulfuratus.

**1997, Mar. 26 Litho. *Perf. 13x14***

**784** A232 5c multicolored 1.10 .35
**785** A232 25c multicolored 1.35 .35
**786** A232 50c multicolored 1.60 .60
**787** A232 75c multicolored 2.00 .80
**788** A232 85c multicolored 2.10 1.00
**789** A232 100c multicolored 2.40 1.20
**790** A232 110c multicolored 2.40 1.20
**791** A232 125c multicolored 2.50 1.45
**792** A232 200c multicolored 3.50 2.25
**793** A232 225c multicolored 4.00 2.60
*Nos. 784-793 (10)* 22.95 11.80

Greetings Stamps — A233

#799A, like #794. #799B, Correspondence in 3 languages. #799C, Positivism, flower, sun. #799D, like #795. #799E, Success, rising sun. 85c, like #796. 100c, like #797. #799H, like #798. #799I, Love, silhouette of couple. 225c, like #799.

**1997, Apr. 16**

**794** A233 40c Love .55 .50
**795** A233 75c Positivism .90 .80
**796** A233 85c Mother's Day 1.05 1.05
**797** A233 100c Correspondence 1.15 1.15
**798** A233 110c Success 1.30 1.30
**799** A233 225c Congratulations 2.60 2.60
*Nos. 794-799 (6)* 7.55 7.40

**Booklet Stamps**

**Size: 21x25mm**

***Perf. 13x14 on 3 Sides***

**799A** A233 40c multicolored .75 .75
**799B** A233 40c multicolored .75 .75
**799C** A233 75c multicolored 1.15 1.15
**799D** A233 75c multicolored 1.15 1.15
**799E** A233 75c multicolored 1.15 1.15
**799F** A233 85c multicolored 1.15 1.15
**799G** A233 100c multicolored 1.60 1.60
**799H** A233 110c multicolored 1.60 1.60
**799I** A233 110c multicolored 1.60 1.60
**799J** A233 225c multicolored 3.00 3.00
*k.* Booklet pane of 10, #799A-799J + label 13.50
Complete booklet, #799k 11.75

Stamps arranged in booklet out of Scott order.

Signs of the Chinese Calendar A234

Stylized designs.

**1997, May 19 Litho. *Perf. 14x13***

**800** A234 5c Rat .25 .25
**801** A234 5c Ox .25 .25
**802** A234 5c Tiger .25 .25
**803** A234 40c Rabbit .65 .45
**804** A234 40c Dragon .65 .45
**805** A234 40c Snake .65 .45
**806** A234 75c Horse 1.05 .75
**807** A234 75c Goat 1.05 .75
**808** A234 75c Monkey 1.05 .75
**809** A234 100c Rooster 1.25 1.05
**810** A234 100c Dog 1.25 1.05
**811** A234 100c Pig 1.25 1.05
*a.* Souvenir sheet of 12, #800-811 10.25 9.75
*Nos. 800-811 (12)* 9.60 7.50

No. 811a for PACIFIC 97. Issued: 5/19/97.

Coins — A235

85c, Plaka, 2½ cent. 175c, Stuiver, 5 cent. 225c, Fuèrtè, 2½ gulden.

**1997, Aug. 6 *Perf. 13x14***

**812** A235 85c multi 1.15 1.00
**813** A235 175c multi 2.25 1.90
**814** A235 225c multi 3.00 2.50
*Nos. 812-814 (3)* 6.40 5.40

A236

Shanghai '97, Intl. Stamp Exhibition — A237

15c, Nampu Grand Bridge, Shanghai. 40c, Giant panda, horiz. 75c, Tiger, New Year 1998.
90c, Buildings in downtown Shanghai.

*Perf. 14x13, 13x14*

**1997, Nov. 19** **Litho.**

| | | | | |
|---|---|---|---|---|
| **815** | A236 15c multicolored | | .85 | .45 |
| **816** | A237 40c multicolored | | 1.30 | .90 |
| **817** | A237 75c multicolored | | 1.75 | 1.35 |
| | *Nos. 815-817 (3)* | | 3.90 | 2.70 |

**Souvenir Sheet**

| | | | |
|---|---|---|---|
| **818** | A236 90c multicolored | 3.00 | 2.75 |

No. 818 exists imperf. Value, $100.

A238

Christmas and New Year: 35c, Left panel of triptych from Roman Catholic Church, Willemstad. 150c, Champagne bottle being opened, calendar.

**1997, Dec. 1** *Perf. 13x14*

| | | | |
|---|---|---|---|
| **819** | A238 35c multicolored | .80 | .40 |
| **820** | A238 150c multicolored | 2.00 | 1.60 |

A239

Total Solar Eclipse, Curacao: 85c, Sun partially covered by moon's shadow. 110c, Outer edge of sun showing beyond moon's shadow. 225c, Total solar eclipse.
750c, Hologram of the eclipse.

**1998, Feb. 26** **Litho.** *Perf. 13x14*

| | | | |
|---|---|---|---|
| **821** | A239 85c multicolored | 1.45 | 1.20 |
| **822** | A239 110c multicolored | 2.00 | 1.40 |
| **823** | A239 225c multicolored | 3.50 | 3.00 |
| | *Nos. 821-823 (3)* | 6.95 | 5.60 |

**Souvenir Sheet**

| | | | |
|---|---|---|---|
| **824** | A239 750c multicolored | 12.50 | 11.50 |

No. 824 contains a hologram which may be damaged by soaking.

ISRAEL '98 World Stamp Exhibition — A240

Designs: 40c, Dead Sea. 75c, Zion Gate, Jerusalem. 110c, Masada.
225c, Mikvé Israel-Emanuel Synagogue, Curacao.

**1998, Apr. 29** **Litho.** *Perf. 13x14*

| | | | |
|---|---|---|---|
| **825** | A240 40c multicolored | .90 | .70 |
| **826** | A240 75c multicolored | 1.10 | .95 |
| **827** | A240 110c multicolored | 1.60 | 1.45 |
| | *Nos. 825-827 (3)* | 3.60 | 3.10 |

**Souvenir Sheet**

| | | | |
|---|---|---|---|
| **828** | A240 225c multicolored | 3.75 | 3.50 |

Elias Moreno Brandao & Sons, Car Dealership, 75th Anniv. A241

Chevrolet automobiles: 40c, 1923 Superior, Elias Moreno Brandao. 55c, 1934 Roadster. 75c, 1949 Styleline Deluxe. 110c, 1957 Bel Air Convertible. 225c, 1963 Corvette "Stingray." 500c, 1970 Chevelle SS-454.

**1998, May 4** *Perf. 14x13*

| | | | |
|---|---|---|---|
| **829** | A241 40c multicolored | 1.20 | .55 |
| **830** | A241 55c multicolored | 1.30 | .90 |
| **831** | A241 75c multicolored | 1.60 | .90 |
| **832** | A241 110c multicolored | 2.10 | 1.35 |
| **833** | A241 225c multicolored | 3.50 | 3.00 |
| **834** | A241 500c multicolored | 8.00 | 6.50 |
| | *Nos. 829-834 (6)* | 17.70 | 13.20 |

A242

Advisory Council, 50th Anniv.: 75c, Natl. flag, natl. arms. 85c, Gavel, stars, natl. arms.

**1998, June 1** **Litho.** *Perf. 13x14*

| | | | |
|---|---|---|---|
| **835** | A242 75c multicolored | 1.05 | .85 |
| **836** | A242 85c multicolored | 1.20 | 1.05 |

A243

Famous People: 40c, Christina Elizabeth Flanders (1908-96). 75c, Abraham Jesurun Dz. (1839-1918). 85c, Gerrit Simeon Newton (1884-1949). 110c, Eduardo Adriana (1925-97).

**1998, June 24** *Perf. 13*

| | | | |
|---|---|---|---|
| **837** | A243 40c multicolored | .60 | .55 |
| **838** | A243 75c multicolored | 1.05 | .90 |
| **839** | A243 85c multicolored | 1.15 | 1.05 |
| **840** | A243 110c multicolored | 1.60 | 1.35 |
| | *Nos. 837-840 (4)* | 4.40 | 3.85 |

Mailboxes — A244

**1998, July 29** **Litho.** *Perf. 13x14*

| | | | |
|---|---|---|---|
| **841** | A244 15c Ireland | .35 | .30 |
| **842** | A244 40c Nepal | .70 | .55 |
| **843** | A244 75c Uruguay | 1.15 | .90 |
| **844** | A244 85c Curacao | 1.20 | 1.20 |
| | *Nos. 841-844 (4)* | 3.40 | 2.95 |

See Nos. 932-935.

A245

Privatization of Natl. Postal Service: 75c, Globe, map of North and South America, horiz. 110c, Numbers and tree on screen. 225c, #207 and #846, horiz.

**1998, Aug. 5** *Perf. 13*

| | | | |
|---|---|---|---|
| **845** | A245 75c multicolored | 1.05 | .90 |
| **846** | A245 110c multicolored | 1.60 | 1.35 |
| **847** | A245 225c multicolored | 3.00 | 3.00 |
| | *Nos. 845-847 (3)* | 5.65 | 5.25 |

A246

Endangered Species: 5c, Black rhinoceros, horiz. 75c, White-tailed hawk. 125c, White-tailed deer, horiz. 250c, Tiger.

**1998, Aug. 26** *Perf. 13½*

| | | | |
|---|---|---|---|
| **848** | A246 5c multicolored | 1.20 | .85 |
| **849** | A246 75c multicolored | 1.60 | 1.30 |
| **850** | A246 125c multicolored | 2.40 | 1.75 |
| **851** | A246 250c multicolored | 3.75 | 3.00 |
| | *Nos. 848-851 (4)* | 8.95 | 6.90 |

Intl. Year of the Ocean A247

**1998, Sept. 30** **Litho.** *Perf. 13*

| | | | |
|---|---|---|---|
| **852** | A247 275c Mako shark | 5.25 | 3.50 |
| **853** | A247 350c Manta ray | 6.25 | 4.25 |

1998 Philatelic Exhibition, The Hague, Netherlands A248

**1998, Oct. 8** *Perf. 14x13*

| | | | |
|---|---|---|---|
| **854** | A248 225c No. 213 | 3.00 | 3.00 |
| **855** | A248 500c No. 218 | 5.75 | 5.75 |

**Souvenir Sheet**

| | | | |
|---|---|---|---|
| **856** | A248 500c Nos. 61, 218 | 6.75 | 6.50 |

Price Waterhouse Coopers in Netherlands Antilles, 60th Anniv. — A249

Emblems, company buildings in Julianaplein, minerals: 75c, Lapis lazuli. 225c, Pyrite.

**1998, Nov. 13** *Perf. 13½*

| | | | |
|---|---|---|---|
| **857** | 75c multicolored | 1.60 | 1.60 |
| **858** | 225c multicolored | 3.00 | 2.25 |
| *a.* | A249 Pair, #857-858 | 4.50 | 3.75 |

Christmas A250

Children's drawings: 35c, Christmas tree, vert. 150c, Mail box at Christmas.

*Perf. 13x14, 14x13*

**1998, Dec. 1** **Litho.**

| | | | |
|---|---|---|---|
| **859** | A250 35c multicolored | .65 | .65 |
| **860** | A250 150c multicolored | 2.10 | 1.90 |

Avila Beach Hotel, 50th Anniv. A251

Designs: 75c, Exterior view of hotel, Dr. Pieter Hendrik Maal. 110c, Beach, delonix regia. 225c, Mesquite tree, porposis juliflora.

**1999, Feb. 3** **Litho.** *Perf. 14x13*

| | | | |
|---|---|---|---|
| **861** | A251 75c multicolored | 1.10 | .90 |
| **862** | A251 110c multicolored | 1.60 | 1.35 |
| **863** | A251 225c multicolored | 3.00 | 2.75 |
| | *Nos. 861-863 (3)* | 5.70 | 5.00 |

New Year 1999 (Year of the Rabbit) and China '99, World Stamp Exhibition, Beijing A252

Designs: 75c, Rabbit, Great Wall of China. No. 865, Rabbit, Jade Pagoda, Beijing, vert. No. 866, Rabbit, landscape, vert.

*Perf. 14x13, 13x14*

**1999, Mar. 30** **Litho.**

| | | | |
|---|---|---|---|
| **864** | A252 75c multicolored | 1.60 | .90 |
| **865** | A252 225c multicolored | 3.75 | 2.60 |

**Souvenir Sheet**

*Perf. 13x13½*

| | | | |
|---|---|---|---|
| **866** | A252 225c multicolored | 4.50 | 3.50 |

Government Correctional Institute (GOG) for Youth, 50th Anniv. A253

Design, traditional musical instrument: 40c, Couple dancing, wiri. 75c, Building, bamba. 85c, Man using file and vise, triangle.

*Perf. 13x14, 14x13*

**1999, Apr. 28** **Litho.**

| | | | |
|---|---|---|---|
| **867** | A253 40c multi, vert. | .75 | .55 |
| **868** | A253 75c multi, vert. | 1.20 | .90 |
| **869** | A253 85c multi | 1.35 | 1.10 |
| | *Nos. 867-869 (3)* | 3.30 | 2.55 |

Recorded History of Curacao, 500th Anniv. A254

Curacao 500 emblem and: 75c, Ship launching. 110c, Houses on Rifwater, Otrobanda, Pasa Kontrami Bridge. 175c, #870-871. 225c, Fort Beeckenburg. 500c, #204, sailing ship.

**1999, May 19** *Perf. 14x13*

| | | | |
|---|---|---|---|
| **870** | A254 75c multicolored | 1.35 | .85 |
| **871** | A254 110c multicolored | 1.75 | 1.30 |
| **872** | A254 175c multicolored | 2.60 | 2.10 |
| **873** | A254 225c multicolored | 3.25 | 2.60 |
| **874** | A254 500c multicolored | 6.50 | 6.00 |
| | *Nos. 870-874 (5)* | 15.45 | 12.85 |

Nos. 870-874 exist imperf. Value, $120.

Wilson "Papa" Godett (1932-95), Politician — A255

**1999, May 28** *Perf. 13x14*

| | | | |
|---|---|---|---|
| **875** | A255 75c multicolored | 1.25 | 1.00 |

No. 875 exists imperf. Value, $57.50.

Millennium A256

Designs: 5c, Indians, map. 10c, Indian, ship, armored horseman. 40c, Flags of islands, Autonomy monument, Curacao, autonomy document. 75c, Telephone, #5. 85c, Airplane. 100c, Oil refinery. 110c, Satellite dish, underwater cable. 125c, Tourist ship, bridge. 225c, Island residents, music box. 350c, Birds, cacti.

**1999, Aug. 4 Litho. *Perf. 13½***
**876** A256 5c multicolored .45 .45
**877** A256 10c multicolored .45 .45
**878** A256 40c multicolored .90 .75
**879** A256 75c multicolored 1.35 1.15
**880** A256 85c multicolored 1.35 1.35
**881** A256 100c multicolored 1.35 1.35
**882** A256 110c multicolored 1.75 1.60
**883** A256 125c multicolored 2.25 2.00
**884** A256 225c multicolored 3.25 3.25
**885** A256 350c multicolored 5.00 5.00

**Size: 31x31mm**
**Self-Adhesive**
***Serpentine Die Cut 8***

**886** A256 5c multicolored .45 .45
**887** A256 10c multicolored .45 .45
**888** A256 40c multicolored .90 .75
**889** A256 75c multicolored 1.35 1.15
**890** A256 85c multicolored 1.35 1.35
**891** A256 100c multicolored 1.35 1.35
**892** A256 110c multicolored 1.75 1.60
**893** A256 125c multicolored 2.25 2.00
**894** A256 225c multicolored 3.25 3.25
**895** A256 350c multicolored 5.00 5.00
*Nos. 876-895 (20)* 36.20 34.70

A257

Designs: 150c, Church of the Conversion of St. Paul, Saba. 250c, Flamingo, Bonaire. 500c, Courthouse of Philipsburg, St. Martin.

**1999, Oct. 1 Litho. *Perf. 14x13***
**896** A257 150c multicolored 3.00 1.60
**897** A257 250c multicolored 3.75 2.75
**898** A257 500c multicolored 6.50 5.50
*Nos. 896-898 (3)* 13.25 9.85

Flowers — A258

Designs: No. 899, Allamanda. No. 900, Bougainvillea. No. 901, Gardenia jasminoides. No. 902, Saintpaulia ionantha. No. 903, Cymbidium. No. 904, Strelitzia. No. 905, Cassia fistula. No. 906, Phalaenopsis. No. 907, Doritaenopsis. No. 908, Guzmania. No. 909, Caralluma hexagona. No. 910, Catharanthus roseus.

**1999, Nov. 15 *Perf. 13½***
**899** A258 40c multicolored 1.10 1.00
**900** A258 40c multicolored 1.10 1.00
*a.* Pair, #899-900 2.25 2.25
**901** A258 40c multicolored 1.10 1.00
**902** A258 40c multicolored 1.10 1.00
*a.* Pair, #901-902 2.25 2.25
**903** A258 75c multicolored 1.25 1.10
**904** A258 75c multicolored 1.25 1.10
*a.* Pair, #903-904 2.50 2.50
**905** A258 75c multicolored 1.25 1.10
**906** A258 75c multicolored 1.25 1.10
*a.* Pair, #905-906 2.75 2.75
**907** A258 110c multicolored 2.00 1.75
**908** A258 110c multicolored 2.00 1.75
*a.* Pair, #907-908 4.00 4.00
**909** A258 225c multicolored 3.25 3.00
**910** A258 225c multicolored 3.25 3.00
*a.* Pair, #909-910 6.50 6.50
*Nos. 899-910 (12)* 19.90 17.90

Christmas A259

Year 2000 A260

**1999, Dec. 1 Litho. *Perf. 13x14***
**911** A259 35c multi .90 .40
**912** A260 150c multi 2.25 1.60

Greetings Stamps — A261

#913, 40c, #918, 150c, Hearts, roses. #914, 40c, #919, 150c, Mothers, globe. #915, 40c, Father, baby, blocks. #916, 75c, Dog in gift box. #917, 110c, Butterfly, flowers in vase. #920, 225c, Hands, rings.

**2000, Jan. 27 Litho. *Perf. 13x14***
**913-920** A261 Set of 8 12.50 11.50

New Year 2000 (Year of the Dragon) A262

**2000, Feb. 28 *Perf. 14x13***
**921** A262 110c shown 2.00 1.90

**Souvenir Sheet**

**922** A262 225c Two dragons 4.50 3.25

Fauna A263

Designs: 40c, Red eye tree toad. 75c, King penguin, vert. 85c, Killer whale, vert. 100c, African elephant, vert. 110c, Chimpanzee, vert. 225c, Indian tiger.

**2000, Mar. 29 *Perf. 14x13, 13x14***
**923-928** A263 Set of 6 14.00 11.50

Space — A264

Designs: 75c, Space Shuttle. No. 930, 225c, Astronaut, flag, space station.

**2000, June 21 Litho. *Perf. 13x14***
**929-930** A264 Set of 2 5.00 4.50

**Souvenir Sheet**
***Perf. 13x13¼***

**931** A264 225c Colonized planet 4.50 4.50

World Stamp Expo 2000, Anaheim.

**Mailbox Type of 1998**

Mailboxes from: 110c, Mexico. 175c, Dubai. 350c, England. 500c, United States.

**2000, Aug. 8 *Perf. 13x14***
**932-935** A244 Set of 4 16.50 14.00

Nos. 932-935 exist imperf. Value, set $120.

2000 Summer Olympics, Sydney — A265

75c, Cycling. No. 937, 225c, Running.

**2000, Aug. 8 Litho. *Perf. 13x14***
**936-937** A265 Set of 2 5.25 5.00

**Souvenir Sheet**

**938** A265 225c Swimming 4.50 4.50

Nos. 936-938 exist imperf. Value, set $200.

Social Insurance Bank, 40th Anniv. A266

Designs: 75c, People, islands, vert. 110c, Hands. 225c, Emblem, vert.

**2000, Sept. 1 *Perf. 13x14, 14x13***
**939-941** A266 Set of 3 6.25 5.75

Christmas A267

Songs: 40c, Jingle Bells, vert. 150c, We Wish You a Merry Christmas.

**2000, Nov. 15 *Perf. 13x14, 14x13***
**942-943** A267 Set of 2 3.25 3.25

New Year 2001 (Year of the Snake) A268

Designs: 110c, Red milk snake. 225c, Indian cobra, vert.

**2001, Jan. 17 Litho. *Perf. 14x13***
**944** A268 110c multi 2.40 1.90

**Souvenir Sheet**
***Perf. 13x14***

**945** A268 225c multi 4.50 4.50

Hong Kong 2001 Stamp Exhibition — A269

Designs: 25c, Birds in forest. 40c, Palm trees and waterfall. 110c, Spinner dolphins.

**2001, Feb. 1 *Perf. 13x14***
**946-948** A269 Set of 3 4.25 3.75

Cats and Dogs — A270

Designs: 55c, Persian shaded golden. 75c, Burmese bluepoint. 110c, Beagle and American wirehair. 175c, Golden retriever. 225c, German shepherd. 750c, British shorthair black-silver marble.

**2001, Mar. 7 Litho. *Perf. 13x14***
**949-954** A270 Set of 6 24.00 20.00

Ships — A271

Designs: 110c, Z. M. Mars. 275c, Z. M. Alphen. 350c, Z. M. Curaçao, horiz. 500c, Schooner Pioneer, horiz.

**2001, Apr. 26 *Perf. 13x14, 14x13***
**955-958** A271 Set of 4 19.00 17.50

Fedjai the Postal Worker — A272

Fedjai: 5c, On bicycle. 40c, With children. 75c, Looking at nest in mailbox. 85c, Talking with woman. 100c, Chased atop mailbox by dog. 110c, Looking at boy's stamp album.

**2001, June 5 Litho. *Perf. 13x14***
**959-964** A272 Set of 6 8.75 7.50

See No. 1012.

Cave Bats — A273

Designs: 85c, Map of bat species in Kueba Bosá. 110c, Leptonycteris nivalis curasaoe. 225c, Glosophaga elongata.

**2001, Aug. 20 Litho. *Perf. 14x13***
**965-967** A273 Set of 3 7.50 6.25

Birds — A274

No. 968: a, 10c, Trochilus polytmus. b, 85c, Pelecanus onocrotalus. c, 110c, Erythrura gouldiae. d, 175c, Passerina ciris. e, 250c, Fratercula arctica. f, 375c, Anhinga anhinga.

**2001, Sept. 28 *Perf. 12¾x13½***
**968** A274 Block of 6, #a-f 17.50 16.50

Philipsburg Methodist Church, 150th Anniv. A275

Map of St. Maarten and: 75c, Church building. 110c, Bibles.

**2001, Oct. 19 *Perf. 14x13***
**969-970** A275 Set of 2 3.50 3.25

Christmas and New Year's Day — A276

Designs: 40c, Clock, people from 8 countries. 150c, Dove, poinsettias, baby Jesus, and people from 4 countries, vert.

*Perf. 13½x12¾, 12¾x13½*

**2001, Nov. 15** **Litho.**

**971-972** A276 Set of 2 3.50 3.00

Wedding of Prince Willem-Alexander and Máxima Zorreguieta — A277

Designs: 75c, Prince. 110c, Máxima.
No. 975: a, 2.25f, Prince. b, 2.75f, Máxima.

**2002, Feb. 2 Litho.** *Perf. 12¾x14*

**973-974** A277 Set of 2 3.25 3.00

**Souvenir Sheet**

*Perf. 12¾x13½*

**975** A277 Sheet of 2, #a-b 8.75 7.50

New Year 2002 (Year of the Horse) — A278

Designs: 25c, Horse rearing. 95c, Horse's head.

**2002, Mar. 1** *Perf. 12¾x14*

**976** A278 25c multi 1.25 1.25

**Souvenir Sheet**

*Perf. 12¾x13½*

**977** A278 95c multi 3.00 2.50

Flora & Fauna A279

Designs: 50c, Chlorostilbon mellisugus and Passiflora foetida, vert. 95c, Anolis lineatus and Cordia sebestena. 120c, Odonata. 145c, Coenobita clypeatus. 285c, Polistes versicolor, vert.

*Perf. 12¾x13½, 13½x12¾*

**2002, Mar. 27** **Litho.**

**978-982** A279 Set of 5 11.00 10.00

Butterflies — A280

Designs: 25c, Dryas iulia, vert. 145c, Danaus plexippus. 400c, Mechanitis polymnia. 500c, Pyrhapygopsis socrates.

*Perf. 12¾x13½, 13½x12¾*

**2002, May 22** **Litho.**

**983-986** A280 Set of 4 17.50 16.50

**Fedjai the Postal Worker Type of 2001**

Fedjai: 10c, Jumping rope with children, horiz. 55c, Scolding dog. 95c, Delivering letter to child. 240c, Helping elderly lady across street.

*Perf. 13¾x12¾, 12¾x13¾*

**2002, July 31**

**987-990** A272 Set of 4 8.25 8.25

Amphilex 2002 Intl. Stamp Exhibition, Amsterdam — A281

Details from the 1885 version of "The Potato Eaters," by Vincent Van Gogh: 70c, 95c, 145c, 240c.
550c, Entire painting, horiz.

*Perf. 12¾x13½*

**2002, Aug. 26** **Litho.**

**991-994** A281 Set of 4 8.75 8.75

**Souvenir Sheet**

*Perf. 14x12¾*

**995** A281 550c multi 8.75 8.75

Orchids — A282

Designs: 95c, Wingfieldara casseta. 285c, Cymbidium Magna Charta. 380c, Brassolaeliocattleya. 750c, Miltonia spectabilis.

**2002, Sept. 27** *Perf. 12¾x14*

**996-999** A282 Set of 4 22.50 21.00

Christmas and New Year — A283

Designs: 95c, Christmas tree decorations. 240c, Lanterns.

**2002, Nov. 15** *Perf. 14x12¾*

**1000-1001** A283 Set of 2 5.00 4.75

Birds — A284

No. 1002: a, 5c, Buteogallus meridionalis. b, 20c, Capito niger. c, 30c, Ara macao. d, 35c, Jacamerops aurea. e, 70c, Florisuga mellivora. f, 85c, Haematoderus militaris. g, 90c, Aratinga aurea. h, 95c, Psarocolius viridis. i, 100c, Sturnella magna, horiz. j, 145c, Aratinga solstitialis, horiz. k, 240c, Trogon viridis. l, 285c, Rhamphastos tucanus.

**2002, Dec. 11 Litho.** *Perf. 13x14*

**1002** A284 Block of 12, #a-l 20.00 20.00

New Year 2003 (Year of the Ram) — A285

Chinese character and: 25c, Ram's head. 95c, Ram.

**2003, Feb. 3**

**1003** A285 25c multi 1.25 1.25

**Souvenir Sheet**

**1004** A285 95c multi 2.40 1.90

Butterflies — A286

No. 1005: a, 5c, Rhetus arcius, vert. b, 10c, Evenus teresina. c, 25c, Bhutanitis thaidina. d, 30c, Semomesia capanea. e, 45c, Papilio machaon. f, 55c, Papilio multicaudata, vert. g, 65c, Graphium weiskei, vert. h, 95c, Ancyluris formosissima venabalis, vert. i, 100c, Euphaedra neophron. j, 145c, Ornithoptera goliath samson. k, 275c, Ancyluris colubra, vert. l, 350c, Papilio lorquinianus, vert.

*Perf. 12¾x14 (vert. stamps), 14x12¾*

**2003, Apr. 23** **Litho.**

**1005** A286 Block of 12, #a-l 21.00 20.00

Printed in sheets of 2 blocks separated by a central gutter.

Miniature Sheet

Musical Instruments — A287

No. 1006: a, 20c, Trumpet. b, 75c, Percussion instruments. c, 145c, Tenor saxophone. d, 285c, Double bass.

**2003, May 28** *Perf. 12¾x14*

**1006** A287 Sheet of 4, #a-d 7.50 7.50

Johann Enschedé and Sons, Printers, 300th Anniv. — A288

No. 1007: a, 70c, 25-florin bank note, 1827. b, 95c, #4. c, 145c, Revenue stamp. d, 240c, Portion of 1967 bank note.
550c, Enschedé headquarters, Netherlands.

**2003, June 3**

**1007** A288 Sheet of 4, #a-d 8.75 8.75

**Souvenir Sheet**

**1008** A288 550c multi 7.50 7.50

Bank of the Netherlands Antilles, 175th Anniv. A289

Designs: 95c, Portion of 10-guilder banknote with serial number magnified. 145c, Road map, Bank headquarters. 285c, Early bank document, vert.

*Perf. 14x12¾, 12¾x14*

**2003, June 26**

**1009-1011** A289 Set of 3 7.00 7.00

**Fedjai, the Postal Worker Type of 2001**

Miniature Sheet

No. 1012: a, 30c, Fedjai giving gift to Angelina. b, 95c, Fedjai and Angelina at wedding. c, 145c, Fedjai taking pregnant wife on bicycle, horiz. d, 240c, Fedjai shows son to co-workers.

*Perf. 12¾x14, 14x12¾ (#1012c)*

**2003, June 31**

**1012** A272 Sheet of 4, #a-d 7.50 6.25

Ships — A290

No. 1013: a, 5c, Egyptian boat, 15th cent. B.C. b, 5c, Ship of King Tutankhamen. c, 35c, Picture from Greek vase depicting Ulysses and the Sirens. d, 35c, Egyptian river boat. e, 40c, Greek dromond. f, 40c, Illustration from 15th cent. edition of Virgil's Aeneid. g, 60c, Javanese fusta. h, 60c, Greek trade ship. i, 75c, Venetian cog, 16th cent. j, 75c, Mora from Bayeux Tapestry. k, 85c, HMS Pembroke, ship of Capt. James Cook, vert. l, 85c, Savannah, first transatlantic steamship, 1819, vert.
Illustration reduced.

*Perf. 14x12¾, 12¾x14 (vert. stamps)*

**2003, Aug. 7**

**1013** A290 Block of 12, #a-l 10.00 9.00

Miniature Sheets

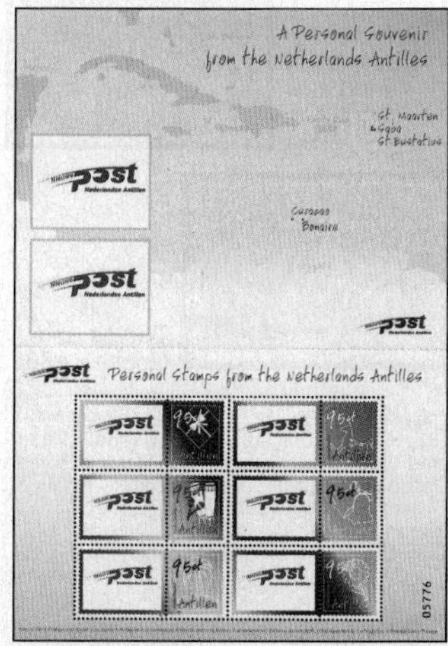


Personalized Stamps — A291

Designs: Nos. 1014a, 1015a, Gift. Nos. 1014b, 1015b, Rocking horse. Nos. 1014c, 1015c, Conga drums. Nos. 1014d, 1015d, Bells. Nos. 1014e, 1015e, Palm tree. Nos. 1014f, 1015f, Flower.

**2003, Sept. 17 Litho.** *Perf. 13¼x14*

**1014** A291 95c Sheet of 6, #a-f, + 6 labels 10.00 9.00

**1015** A291 145c Sheet of 6, #a-f, + 6 labels 15.00 14.00

Labels could be personalized. Nos. 1014-1015 each sold for $6 and $8.50 respectively in US funds.

Cats — A292

No. 1016: a, 5c, Bombay. b, 20c, Persian sealpoint. c, 25c, British shorthair blotchy. d, 50c, British blue. e, 65c, Persian chinchilla. f, 75c, Tonkinese red point. g, 85c, Balinese lilac tabbypoint. h, 95c, Persian shaded cameo. i, 100c, Burmilla. j, 145c, Chocolate tortie shaded silver eastern shorthair. k, 150c, Devon Rex silver tabby. l, 285c, Persian black tabby.

**2003, Sept. 29** ***Perf. 12¾x14***
**1016** A292 Block of 12, #a-l 18.00 17.00

Souvenir Sheet

Christmas and New Year's Day — A293

No. 1017 — Cacti with faces and Christmas lights and: a, 75c, Star. b, 240c, Clock.

**2003, Nov. 17 Litho.** ***Perf. 13x14***
**1017** A293 Sheet of 2, #a-b 3.75 3.75

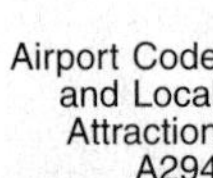

Airport Code and Local Attraction A294

Curves and Lines — A295

Designs: 50c, BON (Bonaire), slave hut. 75c, CUR (Curaçao), Handelskade, Willemstad. 95c, SAB (Saba), Holy Rosary Roman Catholic Church, Hell's Gate, Anglican Church, Valley. 120c, EUX (St. Eustatius), Simon Docker House, Fort Orange. 145c, SXM (St. Maarten), bird at sunset. 240c, CUR, Queen Emma Bridge. 285c, SXM, Simpson Bay.

**2003, Nov. 27** ***Perf. 13½x12¾***

| | | | | |
|---|---|---|---|---|
| **1018** | A294 | 50c multi | .65 | .65 |
| **1019** | A294 | 75c multi | 1.00 | 1.00 |
| **1020** | A294 | 95c multi | 1.20 | 1.20 |
| **1021** | A294 | 120c multi | 1.45 | 1.45 |
| **1022** | A294 | 145c multi | 1.60 | 1.60 |
| **1023** | A294 | 240c multi | 2.75 | 2.75 |
| **1024** | A294 | 285c multi | 3.25 | 3.25 |
| **1025** | A295 | 380c multi | 4.25 | 4.25 |
| | *Nos. 1018-1025 (8)* | | 16.15 | 16.15 |

Birth of Princess Catharina-Amalia, Dec. 7, 2003 — A296

No. 1026: a, 145c, Princess Catharina-Amalia. b, 380c, Prince Willem-Alexander and Princess Catharina-Amalia.

**2004, Jan. 16** ***Perf. 13½x13¾***
**1026** A296 Horiz. pair, #a-b 5.75 5.75
*c.* Miniature sheet, #1026a, 1026b + central label 5.75 5.75

New Year 2004 (Year of the Monkey) — A297

Designs: 95c, Golden snub-nosed monkey. 145c, Monkey holding peach, on fan.

**2004, Jan. 21** ***Perf. 13x13½***
**1027** A297 95c multi 2.00 2.00

Souvenir Sheet

**1028** A297 145c multi + 2 labels 2.50 2.50

Houses and Mansions — A298

No. 1029: a, 10c, Belvedère, L. B Smithplein 3. b, 25c, Hoogstraat 27. c, 35c, Landhuis Brievengat. d, 65c, Scharlooweg 102. e, 95c, Hoogstraat 21-25. f, 145c, Villa Maria, Van den Brandhofstraat 3 t/m 6. g, 275c, Werfstraat 6. h, 350c, Landhuis Ronde Klip.

**2004, Feb. 20** ***Perf. 13½x13***
**1029** A298 Block of 8, #a-h 11.50 11.50

See No. 1066.

Wild Animals — A299

No. 1030: a, 5c, Loxodonta africana. b, 10c, Loxodonta africana, diff. c, 25c, Loxodonta africana, diff. d, 35c, Pan troglodytes. e, 45c, Pan troglodytes, diff. f, 55c, Pan troglodytes, diff. g, 65c, Ursus maritimus. h, 95c, Ursus maritimus, diff. i, 100c, Ursus maritimus, diff. j, 145c, Panthera leo. k, 275c, Panthera leo, diff. l, 350c, Panthera leo, diff.

**2004, Mar. 31**
**1030** A299 Block of 12, #a-l 16.00 16.00

Transportation — A300

No. 1031: a, 10c, Diesel locomotive, 1977. b, 55c, Water dealer and cart, 1900. c, 75c, 1903 Ford Model A. d, 85c, Oil tanker, 2004. e, 95c, 1903 Wright Flyer. f, 145c Penny Farthing bicycles, 1871.

**2004, Apr. 27**
**1031** A300 Block of 6, #a-f 7.50 7.50

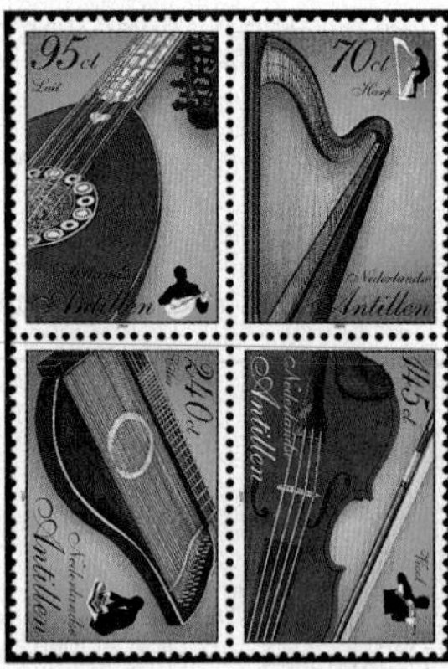

String Instruments — A301

No. 1032: a, 70c, Harp. b, 95c, Lute. c, 145c, Violin, horiz. d, 240c, Zither, horiz.

**2004, May 26** ***Perf. 13x13½, 13½x13***
**1032** A301 Block of 4, #a-d 7.50 7.50

Dogs — A302

No. 1033: a, 5c, Miniature pinscher. b, 5c, Pomeranian. c, 35c, Longhaired teckel. d, 35c, Shih tzu. e, 40c, Boxer. f, 40c, Jack Russell terrier. g, 60c, Basset hound. h, 60c, Braque de l'Ariege. i, 75c, Afghan hound. j, 75c, Old English sheepdog (bobtail). k, 85c, Entelbucher Sennen. l, 85c, Mastiff.

**2004, June 22** ***Perf. 13x13½***
**1033** A302 Block of 12, #a-l 12.50 12.50

World Stamp Championship 2004, Singapore — A303

No. 1034: a, 95c, Ship in St. Annabay Harbor, Curaçao, dragon. b, 95c, Flags of Singapore and Netherlands Antilles, lion. c, 145c, Brionplein houses, Curaçao, dragon. d, 145c, Ships at Dr. A. C. Wathey Cruise and Cargo Facility, St. Maarten, lion.
500c, Like No. 1034b.

**2004, Aug. 23** ***Perf. 13½x13***
**1034** A303 Block of 4, #a-d 5.75 5.75

**Souvenir Sheet**

**1035** A303 500c multi 5.75 5.75

Fish and Ducks A304

No. 1036: a, Pomacanthus paru. b, Epinephelus guttatus. c, Mycteroperca interstitialis. d, Holacanthus isabelita. e, Epinephelus itajara. f, Holacanthus ciliaris. g, Anas americana, Sphyreana barracuda. h, Anas discors. i, Anas bahamensis. j, Aythya affinis.

**2004, Sept. 28**

| | | | |
|---|---|---|---|
| **1036** | Block of 10 | 15.00 | 15.00 |
| *a.* | A304 30c multi | .65 | .65 |
| *b.* | A304 65c multi | .80 | .80 |
| *c.* | A304 70c multi | .90 | .90 |
| *d.* | A304 75c multi | .90 | .90 |
| *e.* | A304 85c multi | 1.00 | 1.00 |
| *f.* | A304 95c multi | 1.05 | 1.05 |
| *g.* | A304 100c multi | 1.05 | 1.05 |
| *h.* | A304 145c multi | 1.60 | 1.60 |
| *i.* | A304 250c multi | 2.60 | 2.60 |
| *j.* | A304 285c multi | 3.00 | 3.00 |

Birds — A305

Designs: 10c, Icterus icterus. 95c, Coereba flaveola. 100c, Zonotrichia capensis. 145c, Sterna hirundo. 250c, Phoenicopterus ruber. 500c, Buteo albicaudatus.

**2004, Oct. 8**
**1037-1042** A305 Set of 6 15.00 15.00

Miniature Sheets

Coats of Arms and Flags — A306

Nos. 1043 and 1044 — Arms of: a, Bonaire. b, Curacao. c, Saba. d, St. Eustatius. e, St. Maarten. f, Flags of Islands of Netherlands Antilles.

**2004, Oct. Litho.** ***Perf. 13½x13¾***
**1043** A306 95c Sheet of 6, #a-f, + 6 labels *12.50 12.50*
**1044** A306 145c Sheet of 6, #a-f, + 6 labels *20.00 20.00*

Labels on Nos. 1043-1044 could be personalized. The two sheets together sold for €12.42.

Turtles A307

Designs: 100c, Loggerhead turtle. 145c, Kemp's Ridley turtle. 240c, Green turtle. 285c, Olive Ridley turtle. 380c, Hawksbill turtle. 500c, Leatherback turtle.

**2004, Dec. 10 Litho.** ***Perf. 13½x13***
**1045-1050** A307 Set of 6 22.00 22.00

Buildings — A308

Beach Scene — A309

### Self-Adhesive

**2004** **Litho.** ***Die Cut***

| | | | | |
|---|---|---|---|---|
| **1051** | A308 145c multi | | 3.50 | 3.50 |
| **1052** | A309 145c multi | | 3.50 | 3.50 |
| *a.* | Horiz. pair, #1051-1052 | | 7.00 | |

Nos. 1051-1052 were printed in sheets of 10 containing five of each stamp at the right of the sheet. At the left of the sheet are three stamp-like vignettes lacking die cutting that were not valid for postage. The spaces at the right of the stamps where the birds are shown in the illustration was intended for personalization by customers on cruise ships that came to St. Maarten or Curacao. The three stamp-like vignettes at the left of the sheet also show the same personalized picture. Four different sheets, each depicting different birds in the space for personalization on each stamp and the three vignettes at the left of the sheet, were created as exemplars. The sheets, depicting birds or a personalized image, sold for $20 in US currency. The stamps were for postage for postcards mailed anywhere in the world.

Flowers A310

Designs: 65c, Hibiscus rosa sinensis. 76c, Plumbago auriculata. 97c, Tecoma stans. 100c, Ixora coccinea. 122c, Catharanthus roseus. 148c, Lantana camara. 240c, Tradescantia pallida. 270c, Nerium oleander. 285c, Plumeria obtusa. 350c, Bougainvillea spectabilis.

**2005, Jan. 3** **Litho.** ***Perf. 13½x13***

| | | | |
|---|---|---|---|
| **1053** | A310 65c multi | .80 | .80 |
| **1054** | A310 76c multi | .90 | .90 |
| **1055** | A310 97c multi | 1.05 | 1.05 |
| **1056** | A310 100c multi | 1.15 | 1.15 |
| **1057** | A310 122c multi | 1.30 | 1.30 |
| **1058** | A310 148c multi | 1.60 | 1.60 |
| **1059** | A310 240c multi | 2.50 | 2.50 |
| **1060** | A310 270c multi | 3.00 | 3.00 |
| **1061** | A310 285c multi | 3.00 | 3.00 |
| **1062** | A310 350c multi | 3.75 | 3.75 |
| | *Nos. 1053-1062 (10)* | 19.05 | 19.05 |

New Year 2005 (Year of the Rooster) — A311

Designs: 145c, Rooster and Chinese character. 500c, Two roosters.

**2005, Feb. 9** ***Perf. 13x13½***

**1063** A311 145c multi 1.90 1.90

### Souvenir Sheet

**1064** A311 500c multi 5.75 5.75

Souvenir Sheet

Queen Beatrix, 25th Anniv. of Reign — A312

Photos: a, Coronation, 1980. b, Giving speech, 1991. c, With Nelson Mandela, 1999. d, Visiting colonies, 1999. e, At European Parliament, 2004.

**2005, Apr. 30** ***Perf. 13¼x13¾***

| | | | |
|---|---|---|---|
| **1065** | A312 Sheet of 5 | 13.50 | 13.50 |
| *a.* | 50c multi | .75 | .75 |
| *b.* | 97c multi | 1.05 | 1.05 |
| *c.* | 145c multi | 1.50 | 1.50 |
| *d.* | 285c multi | 3.00 | 3.00 |
| *e.* | 550c multi | 5.75 | 5.75 |

### Houses & Mansions Type of 2004

No. 1066: a, 10c, Scharlooweg 76. b, 21c, Landhuis Zeelandia. c, 25c, Berg Altena. d, 35c, Landhuis Dokterstuin. e, 97c, Landhuis Santa Martha. f, 148c, Landhuis Seri Papaya. g, 270c, Landhuis Rooi Katooje. h, 300c, Plaza Horacio Hoyer 19.

**2005, May 31** ***Perf. 13½x13***

**1066** A298 Block of 8, #a-h 10.50 10.50

Paintings by Vincent van Gogh — A313

No. 1067: a, 10c, Vase with Fourteen Sunflowers, detail. b, 65c, Sunflowers, detail. c, 80c, Self-portrait. d, 120c, Sunflowers, detail, diff. e, 150c, Vase with Fourteen Sunflowers. f, 175c, Joseph Roulin.

500c, Sunflowers, detail, diff.

**2005, June 16** ***Perf. 13x13½***

**1067** A313 Block of 6, #a-f 10.00 10.00

### Souvenir Sheet

**1068** A313 500c multi 8.00 8.00

Otrobanda Section of Willemstad, 300th Anniv. (in 2007) — A314

No. 1069: a, 100c, Breedestraat. b, 150c, Wharf area. c, 285c, Rifwater. d, 500c, Brionplein bus stop.

**2005, July 28** ***Perf. 13½x13***

**1069** A314 Block of 4, #a-d 12.00 12.00

See Nos. 1108-1111, 1157-1160.

Fruit — A315

**2005, Aug. 31**

| | | | |
|---|---|---|---|
| **1070** | Block of 10 | 15.00 | 15.00 |
| *a.* | A315 25c Papaya | .50 | .50 |
| *b.* | A315 45c Pomegranates | .65 | .65 |
| *c.* | A315 70c Mango | .80 | .80 |
| *d.* | A315 75c Bananas | .90 | .90 |
| *e.* | A315 85c Cashews | 1.00 | 1.00 |
| *f.* | A315 97c Soursops | 1.05 | 1.05 |
| *g.* | A315 145c Tamarinds | 1.60 | 1.60 |
| *h.* | A315 193c Watermelons | 2.00 | 2.00 |
| *i.* | A315 270c Gennips | 3.00 | 3.00 |
| *j.* | A315 300c Sea grapes | 3.25 | 3.25 |

See Nos. 1247-1256.

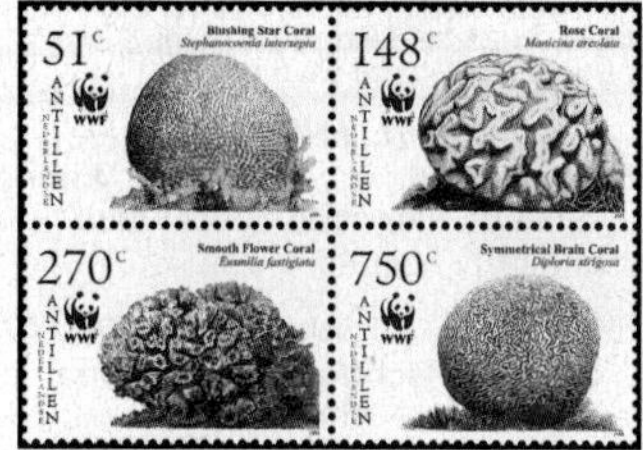

Worldwide Fund for Nature (WWF) — A316

No. 1071: a, 51c, Blushing star coral. b, 148c, Rose coral. c, 270c, Smooth flower coral. d, 750c, Symmetrical brain coral.

**2005, Sept. 29**

**1071** A316 Block of 4, #a-d 14.00 14.00

Musical Instruments A317

Designs: 55c, Bandoneon. 97c, Bagpipe, vert. 145c, Vina. 195c, Samisen, vert. 240c, Shofar. 285c, Kaha di òrgel, vert.

**2005, Nov. 8** ***Perf. 13½x13, 13x13½***

**1072-1077** A317 Set of 6 13.00 13.00

A318

Santa Claus and: 10c, Children's hands. 97c, Children, horiz. 148c, Ornament, horiz. 580c, Chair.

***Perf. 13x13½, 13½x13***

**2005, Nov. 17**

**1078-1081** A318 Set of 4 9.50 9.50

Christmas.

A319

Designs: 97c, Aerial view of St. Elizabeth Hospital, Willemstad. 145c, Stained glass window in hospital chapel. 300c, Entrance to first community hospital.

**2005, Dec. 2** ***Perf. 13x13½***

**1082-1084** A319 Set of 3 6.25 6.25

St. Elizabeth Hospital, 150th anniv.

New Year 2006 (Year of the Dog) — A320

Chinese character and: 100c, Porcelain dogs. 149c, Various dog breeds.

500c, Dog and zodiac animals.

**2006, Jan. 30** ***Perf. 13½x13***

**1085-1086** A320 Set of 2 3.25 3.25

### Souvenir Sheet

**1087** A320 500c multi 5.75 5.75

Equines A321

No. 1088: a, Turkmenian Kulan. b, Rhineland heavy draft horse. c, Donkey. d, Mule. e, Hanoverian and Arabian horses.

***Perf. 13¼x12¾***

**2006, Feb. 24** **Litho.**

| | | | |
|---|---|---|---|
| **1088** | Horiz. strip of 5 | 14.00 | 14.00 |
| *a.* | A321 50c multi | .65 | .65 |
| *b.* | A321 100c multi | 1.05 | 1.05 |
| *c.* | A321 149c multi | 1.60 | 1.60 |
| *d.* | A321 285c multi | 3.00 | 3.00 |
| *e.* | A321 550c multi | 6.00 | 6.00 |

Frogs — A322

Designs: 55c, Hyla cinerea. 100c, Dendrobates tinctorius. 149c, Dendrobates azureus. 405c, Epipedobates tricolor.

**2006, Mar. 10** ***Perf. 13¼x12¾***

**1089-1092** A322 Set of 4 9.50 9.50

Butterflies A323

Designs: 24c, Danaus chrysippus. 53c, Prepona praeneste. 100c, Caligo uranus. 149c, Ituna lamirus. 285c, Euphaedra gausape. 335c, Morpho hecuba.

**2006, Apr. 7**

**1093-1098** A323 Set of 6 11.50 11.50

Orchids A324

No. 1099: a, Brassolaeliocattleya Susan Harry M. G. R. b, Miltoniopsis Jean Sabourin. c, Promenaea xanthina Sylvan Sprite. d, Paphiopedilum Streathamense Wedgewood, vert. e, Cattleya chocoensis Linden, vert. f, Disa kewensis Rita Helen, vert.

***Perf. 13¼x12¾, 12¾x13¼ (vert. stamps)***

**2006, Apr. 26**

| | | | |
|---|---|---|---|
| **1099** | Block of 6 | 22.50 | 22.50 |
| *a.* | A324 153c multi | 1.90 | 1.90 |
| *b.* | A324 240c multi | 2.60 | 2.60 |
| *c.* | A324 285c multi | 3.25 | 3.25 |
| *d.* | A324 295c multi | 3.25 | 3.25 |
| *e.* | A324 380c multi | 4.00 | 4.00 |
| *f.* | A324 500c multi | 5.25 | 5.25 |

Automobiles A325

Designs: 51c, 1976 MGB. 100c, 1963 Studebaker Avanti. 149c, 1953 Pegaso Cabriolet. 153c, 1939 Delage Aerosport. 195c, 1924 Hispano-Suiza Boulogne. 750c, 1903 Pierce Arrow Motorette.

**2006, May 10** ***Perf. 13¼x12¾***
**1100-1105** A325 Set of 6 16.00 16.00

Washington 2006 World Philatelic Exhibition — A326

No. 1106: a, 100c, Mailboxes of United States and Netherlands Antilles. b, 100c, Queen Emma Bridge, Curaçao, George Washington Bridge, New York and New Jersey. c, 149c, UPU emblem. d, 149c, Fokker F18-Snip, Fokker F4 airplanes.
405c, U.S. Capitol, Palace of the Governor of the Netherlands Antilles.

**2006, May 26**
**1106** A326 Block of 4, #a-d 5.75 5.75

**Souvenir Sheet**

**1107** A326 405c multi 4.75 4.75

**Otrobanda Type of 2005**

Designs: 100c, Hoogstraat. 149c, Emmabrug. 335c, Pasa Kontrami. 500c, Seaman's Home.

**2006, June 16**
**1108-1111** A314 Set of 4 11.50 11.50

Greetings A327

Designs: 52c, Bless you. 55c, Love. 77c, All the best. 95c, Regards. 1.00g, Go for it. 1.49g, Tolerance. 1.53g, Positivism. 2.85g, Keep on going. 3.35g, Success. 4.05g, Be good.

**2006, July 31**
**1112-1121** A327 Set of 10 18.50 18.50

See No. 1239-1245.

Birds — A328

No. 1122: a, Taeniopygia guttata. b, Parus caeruleus, vert. c, Pitta genus. d, Pyrrhula pyrrhula, vert. e, Calospiza fastuosa. f, Cosmopsarus regius, vert. g, Coracias caudatus, vert. h, Merops apiaster, vert. i, Icterus nigrogularis. j, Dendrocopus major, vert. k, Amazona barbadensis. l, Alcedo atthis, vert.

***Perf. 13¼x12¾, 12¾x13¼ (vert. stamps)***

**2006, Aug. 18**
**1122** Block of 12 9.50 9.50
*a.-b.* A328 5c Either single .60 .60
*c.-d.* A328 35c Either single .60 .60
*e.-f.* A328 60c Either single .60 .60
*g.-h.* A328 75c Either single .65 .65
*i.-j.* A328 85c Either single .75 .75
*k.-l.* A328 100c Either single .90 .90

Miniature Sheets

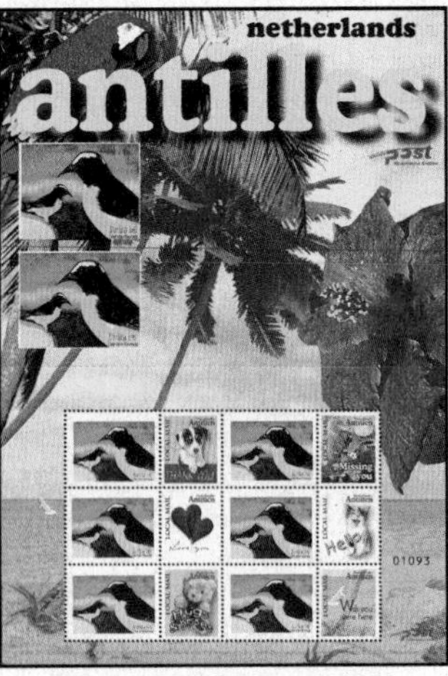


Personalized Stamps — A329

Nos. 1123 and 1124: a, Dog, "Thank you." b, Flower, "Missing you." c, Hearts, "Love you." d, Cat, "Hello." e, Teddy bear, "Hugs & kisses." f, Dolphin, "Wish you were here."

***Perf. 13¼x13¾***

**2006, Aug. 26** **Litho.**

**Stamps Inscribed "Local Mail"**

**1123** A329 (1g) Sheet of 6, #a-f, + 6 labels 11.50 11.50

**Stamps Inscribed "International Mail"**

**1124** A329 (1.49g) Sheet of 6, #a-f, + 6 labels 17.00 17.00

On day of issue, No. 1123 sold for 10g, and No. 1124 sold for 15g. Labels could be personalized. Labels shown are generic.

Rembrandt (1606-69), Painter — A330

No. 1125: a, 70c, The Nightwatch (detail of girl). b, 100c, De Staalmeesters. c, 153c, The Jewish Bride (detail). d, 285c, Self-portrait.
550c, The Nightwatch (detail of men).

***Perf. 12¾x13¼***

**2006, Sept. 28** **Litho.**
**1125** A330 Block of 4, #a-d 7.50 7.50

**Souvenir Sheet**

**1126** A330 550c multi 7.00 7.00

Souvenir Sheet

Royal Visit of Queen Beatrix — A331

No. 1127 — Various photos of Queen Beatrix with background colors of: a, 149c, Red. b, 285c, Blue. c, 335c, Yellow. d, 750c, Orange.

**2006, Nov. 13** ***Perf. 13¼x12¾***
**1127** A331 Sheet of 4, #a-d 17.00 17.00

Christmas A332

Designs: 45c, Candles. 100c, Bells. 149c, Candles. 215c, Bells. 285c, Steeple. 380c, Flower.

**2006, Nov. 15**
**1128-1133** A332 Set of 6 13.00 13.00

Fauna — A333

No. 1134: a, Cacatua leadbeateri leadbeateri. b, Aptenocytes patagonica. c, Pan troglodytes. d, Stenella longirostris. e, Anolis lineatus and Cordia sebestina, horiz. f, Passerina ciris. g, Dryas lulia. h, Bombay cat. i, Epinephelus guttatus, horiz. j, Panthera leo, horiz. k, Pomeranian dog. l, Hawksbill turtle, horiz.

***Perf. 12¾x13¼, 13¼x12¾***

**2007, Jan. 26** **Litho.**
**1134** Block of 12 15.50 15.50
*a.* A333 3c multi .40 .40
*b.* A333 25c multi .45 .45
*c.* A333 53c multi .65 .65
*d.* A333 60c multi .75 .75
*e.* A333 80c multi .90 .90
*f.* A333 81c multi .90 .90
*g.* A333 95c multi 1.10 1.10
*h.* A333 106c multi 1.20 1.20
*i.* A333 145c multi 1.60 1.60
*j.* A333 157c multi 1.60 1.60
*k.* A333 161c multi 1.60 1.60
*l.* A333 240c multi 2.50 2.50

New Year 2007 (Year of the Pig) — A334

Designs: 104c, Berkshire pig. 155c, Wart hog.
500c, Pig, vert.

**2007, Feb. 20** ***Perf. 13¼x12¾***
**1135-1136** A334 Set of 2 3.00 3.00

**Souvenir Sheet**

***Perf. 12¾x13¼***

**1137** A334 500c multi 5.75 5.75

Islands — A335

Designs: 1c, Flag of Bonaire, divers and marine life. 2c, Flag of Curaçao, royal poinciana flowers. 3c, Flag of Saba, The Bottom. 4c, Flag of Statia (St. Eustatius), cannons at Fort Orange. 5c, Flag of St. Maarten, cruise ship and pier. 104c, Map of Bonaire, flamingos, horiz. 285c, Map of Curaçao, Chobolobo Landhouse, laraha tree, horiz. 335c, Map of Saba, houses, horiz. 405c, Map of Statia, oil storage tanks, horiz. 500c, Map of St. Maarten, Guavaberry Emporium, horiz.

***Perf. 12¾x13¼, 13¼x12¾***

**2007, Mar. 1**
**1138** A335 1c multi .25 .25
**1139** A335 2c multi .25 .25
**1140** A335 3c multi .25 .25
**1141** A335 4c multi .25 .25
**1142** A335 5c multi .25 .25
**1143** A335 104c multi 1.25 1.25
**1144** A335 285c multi 3.50 3.50
**1145** A335 335c multi 4.00 4.00
**1146** A335 405c multi 4.75 4.75
**1147** A335 500c multi 6.00 6.00
*Nos. 1138-1147 (10)* 20.75 20.75

See Nos. 1221-1226.

Ananzi the Spider A336

No. 1148 — Ananzi with: a, Turtle. b, Shark. c, Parrot. d, Cow. e, Dog. f, Goat. g, Chicken. h, Donkey.

**2007, Mar. 21** ***Perf. 13¼x12¾***
**1148** Block of 8 10.00 10.00
*a.-h.* A336 104c Any single 1.25 1.25

Saba Lace Designs — A337

Various lace designs with background colors of: 59c, Red. 80c, Green. 95c, Blue. 104c, Red. 155c, Green. 159c, Blue.

**2007, Apr. 20** ***Perf. 12¾x13¼***
**1149-1154** A337 Set of 6 7.50 7.50

Marine Life — A338

No. 1155: a, School of fish and sea floor. b, Portuguese man-of-war. c, Coral reef. d, Sea turtle. e, Sea anemones. f, Fish.

**2007, May 22**
**1155** Block of 6 18.00 18.00
*a.* A338 104c multi 1.00 1.00
*b.* A338 155c multi 1.45 1.45
*c.* A338 195c multi 1.75 1.75
*d.* A338 335c multi 3.25 3.25
*e.* A338 405c multi 3.75 3.75
*f.* A338 525c multi 4.75 4.75

Fruits and Vegetables — A339

No. 1156: a, Grapes, Brussels sprouts, tomatoes, peppers and bananas. b, Pumpkins. c, Cucumber, tomatoes, corn, leeks. d, Strawberries, orange, peaches, pineapple. e, Avocados, horiz. f, Lemons, horiz. g, Peppers, corn, potato, mushrooms, horiz. h, Mangos, horiz.

***Perf. 12¾x13¼, 13¼x12¾***

**2007, June 19**
**1156** Block of 8 11.50 11.50
*a.* A339 10c multi .30 .30
*b.* A339 25c multi .30 .30
*c.* A339 35c multi .40 .40
*d.* A339 65c multi .70 .70
*e.* A339 95c multi 1.00 1.00
*f.* A339 145c multi 1.60 1.60
*g.* A339 275c multi 2.75 2.75
*h.* A339 350c multi 3.50 3.50

**Otrabanda Type of 2005**

Designs: 104c, Brionplein Square. 155c, Jopi Building and Hotel Otrabanda. 285c, Kura Hulanda. 380c, Luna Blou.

**2007, July 26** ***Perf. 13¼x12¾***
**1157-1160** A314 Set of 4 9.50 9.50

Nature — A340

No. 1161: a, 30c, Nautilus shell. b, 65c, Turtles on beach. c, 70c, Grasshopper. d, 75c, Cactus. e, 85c, Swamp. f, 95c, Bird on cactus. g, 104c, Surf spray at rocks. h, 145c, Plants near water. i, 250c, Rainbow in rainforest. j, 285c, Sun on horizon.

***Perf. 12¾x 13¼***

**2007, Aug. 22** **Litho.**
**1161** A340 Block of 10, #a-j 13.00 13.00

Paintings by Dutch Artists — A341

No. 1162: a, 104c, Portrait of a Man (probably Nicolaes Hasselaer), by Frans Hals. b, 104c, Wedding of Isaak Abrahamsz Massa and Beatrix van der Lean, by Hals. c, 155c, The Merry Drinker, by Hals. d, 155c, Serenade, by Judith Leyster.
550c, The Meagre Company, by Hals, horiz.

**2007, Sept. 20** ***Perf. 12¾x13¼***
**1162** A341 Block of 4, #a-d 7.00 7.00

**Souvenir Sheet**

***Perf. 13¼x12¾***

**1163** A341 550c multi 6.25 6.25

Dutch Royalty — A342

No. 1164: a, 50c, Queen Emma (1858-1934). b, 104c, Queen Wilhelmina (1880-1962). c, 155c, Queen Juliana (1909-2004). d, 285c, Queen Beatrix. e, 380c, Princess Máxima. f, 550c, Princess Catharina-Amalia.

**2007, Oct. 10** ***Perf. 12¾x13¼***
**1164** A342 Block of 6, #a-f 15.50 15.50

Christmas and New Year — A343

Designs: 48c, Candle. 104c, Gifts under Christmas tree. 155c, Musical notes and song lyrics, horiz. 215c, "2008" above "2007," horiz.

***Perf. 12¾x13¼, 13¼x12¾***

**2007, Nov. 15** **Litho.**
**1165-1168** A343 Set of 4 5.25 5.25

Mailboxes — A344

No. 1169 — Various mailboxes with panel color of: a, 20c, Yellow. b, 104c, Green. c, 240c, Light blue. d, 285c, Lilac. e, 380c, Orange. f, 500c, Brown.

**2007, Dec. 3** ***Perf. 12¾x13¼***
**1169** A344 Block of 6, #a-f 15.50 15.50

Lighthouses — A345

No. 1170: a, Fort Oranje, Bonaire. b, Malmok, Bonaire. c, Noordpunt, Curaçao. d, Klein Curaçao. e, Willemstoren, Bonaire. f, Bullenbaai, Curaçao.

**2008, Jan. 21**
**1170** A345 158c Block of 6, #a-f 12.00 12.00

New Year 2008 (Year of the Rat) — A346

Designs: 106c, Stylized rat. 158c, Rat. 500c, Rat on branch, horiz.

**2008, Feb. 7** ***Perf. 12¾x13¼***
**1171-1172** A346 Set of 2 3.00 3.00

**Souvenir Sheet**

***Perf. 13¼x12¾***

**1173** A346 500c multi 5.50 5.50

Dutch Royalty — A347

No. 1174: a, 75c, Princess Catharina-Amalia. b, 100c, Princess, diff. c, 125c, Crown Prince Willem-Alexander. d, 250c, Crown Prince, diff. e, 375c, Queen Beatrix. f, 500c, Queen, diff.

**2008, Feb. 28** ***Perf. 12¾x13¼***
**1174** A347 Block of 6, #a-f 15.50 15.50

Global Warming — A348

No. 1175: a, 50c, Smokestacks. b, 75c, Polar bear. c, 125c, Windmills. d, 250c, Beach and lighthouse.

**2008, Mar. 20** ***Perf. 13¼x12¾***
**1175** A348 Block of 4, #a-d 6.25 6.25

2008 Summer Olympics, Beijing — A349

No. 1176: a, 25c, Runner. b, 35c, Gymnast on rings. c, 75c, Swimmer. d, 215c, Cyclist.

**2008, Apr. 1** ***Perf. 12¾x13¼***
**1176** A349 Block of 4, #a-d 4.00 4.00

Stamp Passion Philatelic Exhibition, the Netherlands — A350

No. 1177: a, 75c, Netherlands Antilles #C14. b, 100c, Netherlands Antilles #29. c, 125c, Netherlands Antilles #CB19. d, 250c, Netherlands #O32. e, 375c, Netherlands #134. f, 500c, Netherlands Antilles #187.

**2008, Apr. 11**
**1177** A350 Block of 6, #a-f 14.00 14.00

Images of stamps shown on Nos. 1177a, 1177c and 1177e are distorted.

Catholic Diocese of Netherlands Antilles and Aruba, 50th Anniv. — A351

Designs: 59c, Chapel of Alto Vista, Aruba. 106c, Cross at Seru Largu, Bonaire. 158c, St. Ann Church, Curaçao. 240c, Sacred Heart Church, Saba. 285c, Roman Catholic Church of Oranjestad, St. Eustatius. 335c, Mary Star of the Sea Church, St. Maarten.

**2008, Apr. 28**

**1178-1183** A351 Set of 6 11.50 11.50

Dolls Depicting Women Doing Work — A352

No. 1184: a, 145c, Pounding corn (Batidó di maíshi den pilon). b, 145c, Selling fish (Bendedó di piská). c, 145c, Baking fish (Hasadó di masbangu riba bleki). d, 145c, Roasting coffee beans (Totadó di kòfi). e, 155c, Scrubbing clothes on scrub board (Labadera). f, 155c, Carrying basket of clothes (Labadó di paña na laman). g, 155c, Grinding corn on coral (Muladó di maíshi chikí riba pieda). h, 155c, Weaving hat (Trahadó di sombré).

**2008, May 15**

**1184** A352 Block of 8, #a-h 11.50 11.50

Paintings by Johannes Vermeer (1632-75) — A353

No. 1185: a, 145c, Little Street. b, 145c, Girl with Pearl Earring. c, 155c, Woman in Blue Reading Letter. d, 155c, The Love Letter. 500c, The Milkmaid.

**2008, June 23**

**1185** A353 Sheet of 4, #a-d, + 2 labels 7.50 7.50

**Souvenir Sheet**

**1186** A353 500c multi 5.75 5.75

Windows A354

Various windows.

**2008, July 8** ***Perf. 13¾***

| | | | | |
|---|---|---|---|---|
| **1187** | A354 | 5c multi | .50 | .50 |
| **1188** | A354 | 106c multi, vert. | 1.60 | 1.60 |
| **1189** | A354 | 285c multi, vert., diff. | 3.25 | 3.25 |
| *a.* | | Souvenir sheet of 5, # 1187-1189, Aruba #330, Netherlands #1311, + etiquette | 15.00 | 15.00 |

Nos. 1188-1189 were only available in No. 1189a. No. 1187 also was available in Aruba No. 332a and in Netherlands Nos. 1313a and 1313b.

Shells A355

No Country Name — A355a

Designs: 20c, Cypraea zebra. 40c, Charonia variegata. 65c, Calliostoma armillata. 106c, Strombus gigas. 158c, Pina carnea. 285c, Olivia sayana. 335c, Natica canrena. 405c, Voluta musica.

***Perf. 13¼x12¾***

**2008, Sept. 19** **Litho.**

| | | | | |
|---|---|---|---|---|
| **1190** | A355 | 20c multi | 1.00 | 1.00 |
| **1191** | A355 | 40c multi | 1.00 | 1.00 |
| **1192** | A355 | 65c multi | 1.00 | 1.00 |
| **1193** | A355a | 106c multi, without country name | 1.10 | 1.10 |
| *a.* | | With country name | 3.00 | 3.00 |
| **1194** | A355 | 158c multi | 1.60 | 1.60 |
| **1195** | A355 | 285c multi | 3.00 | 3.00 |
| **1196** | A355 | 335c multi | 3.25 | 3.25 |
| **1197** | A355 | 405c multi | 4.00 | 4.00 |
| | | *Nos. 1190-1197 (8)* | 15.95 | 15.95 |

African Animals — A356

No. 1198: a, 75c, Giraffes, vert. b, 150c, Elephants. c, 175c, Cheetahs. d, 250c, Zebras.

No. 1199, Impalas, vert.

***Perf. 13¼x12¾, 12¾x13¼ (vert. stamps)***

**2008, Oct. 2**

**1198** A356 Block of 4, #a-d 7.50 7.50

**Souvenir Sheet**

**1199** A356 250c multi 3.00 3.00

Christmas and New Year's Day — A357

Designs: 50c, Plate of basil. 106c, Flowers. 158c, Fishermen in boat. 215c, Dock.

***Perf. 13¼x12¾***

**2008, Nov. 14** **Litho.**

**1200-1203** A357 Set of 4 5.50 5.50

Traditional Costumes — A358

No. 1204: a, 100c, Antillean girl. b, 104c, Dutch boy. c, 155c, Japanese girl.

**2008, Nov. 27** ***Perf. 12¾x13¼***

**1204** A358 Horiz. strip of 3, #a-c 4.00 4.00

Birds A359

No. 1205: a, Kasuaris (cassowary). b, Struisvogel (ostrich). c, Pinguin (penguin). d, Kalkoen (wild turkey). e, Aalscholver (cormorant), horiz. f, Mandarijneend (Mandarin duck), horiz. g, Putter-distelvink (goldfinch), horiz. h, Groene reiger (green heron), horiz.

***Perf. 12¾x13¼, 13¼x12¾ (horiz. stamps)***

**2008, Dec. 12**

**1205** A359 158c Block of 8, #a-h 14.00 14.00

Flowers A360

No. 1206: a, Nelumbo nucifera. b, Chrysanthemum leucanthemum. c, Hepatica nobilis. d, Cistus incanus. e, Alamanda. f, Wise portia.

**2009, Jan. 26** **Litho.** ***Perf. 13¼x12¾***

| | | | | |
|---|---|---|---|---|
| **1206** | | Block of 6 | 16.00 | 16.00 |
| *a.* | A360 | 75c multi | .70 | .70 |
| *b.* | A360 | 150c multi | 1.10 | 1.10 |
| *c.* | A360 | 200c multi | 1.60 | 1.60 |
| *d.* | A360 | 225c multi | 2.10 | 2.10 |
| *e.* | A360 | 350c multi | 3.50 | 3.50 |
| *f.* | A360 | 500c multi | 5.00 | 5.00 |

New Year 2009 (Year of the Ox) — A361

Chinese character and: 110c, Outline of ox. 168c, Ox, horiz.

***Perf. 12¾x13¼, 13¼x12¾***

**2009, Feb. 19**

**1207-1208** A361 Set of 2 3.00 3.00

Butterflies — A362

No. 1209: a, 25c, Lycaena phlaeas. b, 35c, danaus plexippus. c, 50c, Nymphalis antiopa. d, 105c, Carterocephalus palaemon. e, 115c, Inachis io. f, 155c, Phyciodes tharos. g, 185c, Papilio glaucus. h, 240c, Dryas iulia. i, 315c, Libytheana carinenta. j, 375c, Melanis pixe. k, 400c, Asterocampa celtis. l, 1000c, Historis acheronta.

**2009, Mar. 2** ***Perf. 13¼x12¾***

**1209** A362 Block of 12, #a-l 32.00 32.00

Birds — A363

No. 1210: a, 10c, Daptrius americanus. b, 45c, Amazona amazonica. c, 80c, Querula purpurata. d, 145c, Aratinga leucophthalmus. e, 190c, Xipholena punicea. f, 235c, Celeus torquatus. g, 285c, Lamprospiza melanoleuca. h, 300c, Selenidera culik. i, 335c, Amazila viridigaster. j, 425c, Tangara gyrola. k, 450c, Nyctibius grandis. l, 500c, Galbula leucogastra.

**2009, Apr. 20** ***Perf. 12¾x13¼***

**1210** A363 Block of 12, #a-l 32.00 32.00

Telecommunications and Posts Department, Cent. — A364

Designs: 59c, Ship, telegraph operator. 110c, Person on telephone, room with radio and television. 164c, Person at computer, satellite dish, street scene.

**2009, May 18** ***Perf. 13¼x12¾***

**1211-1213** A364 Set of 3 3.50 3.50

Pianos A365

Pianos manufactured by: 175c, J. B. & Sons, 1796. 225c, J. Schantz, 1818, vert. 250c, Steinway-Welt, 1927, vert. 350c, Yamaha, 2007.

***Perf. 13¼x12¾, 12¾x13¼***

**2009, June 1**

**1214-1217** A365 Set of 4 11.50 11.50

Nos. 1214-1217 were printed in a sheet of 8 containing two of each stamp, with a central label.

Miniature Sheets

A366

A367

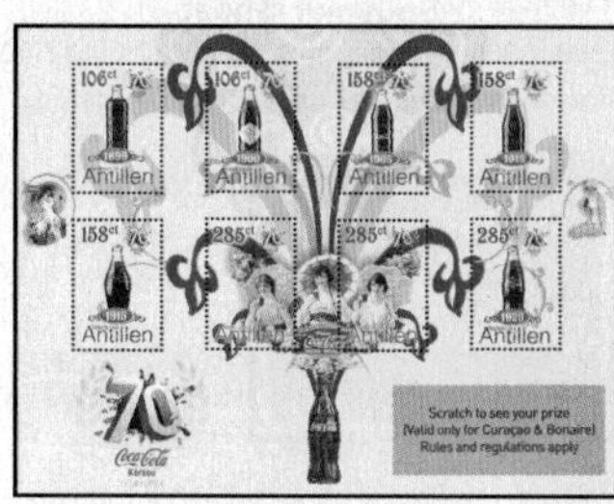

Coca-Cola Bottling on Curaçao, 70th Anniv. — A368

No. 1218 — Fria soft drinks: a, No bottle shown. b, Bottle with pink drink, parts of blue balls at UL and bottom. c, Bottle with purple drink, parts of red ball at UL and purple ball at right. d, Bottle with yellow drink, parts of green ball at UL and purple ball at LR. e, Bottle with orange drink, parts of purple ball at UL and red ball at LL. f, Bottle with red drink, parts of purple ball at UL, blue ball at LR. g, Bottle with pale pink drink, part of red ball at LR. h, Bottle with yellow-green drink, part of orange ball at LR.

No. 1219: a, Coca-Cola advertisement showing couple on beach and bottle. b, Women around counter with two Coca-Cola advertisements. c, Coca-Cola building with awning at left. d, Man at vending machine. e, Man and automobile in front of building with Coca-Cola advertisement, vert. f, Two men holding bottles of Coca-Cola. g, Men and women around a counter. h, Delivery truck.

No. 1220: a, 106c, 1899 Coca-Cola bottle. b, 106c, 1900 Coca-Cola bottle. c, 158c, 1905 Coca-Cola bottle. d, 158c, 1913 Coca-Cola bottle. e, 158c, 1915 Coca-Cola bottle. f, 285c, Woman holding glass of Coca-Cola and blue-striped umbrella. g, 285c, Woman holding glass of Coca-Cola and yellow umbrella. h, 285c, 1923 Coca-Cola bottle.

***Perf. 12¾x13¼, 13¼x12¾***

**2008, Dec. 23** **Litho.**

| | | | | |
|---|---|---|---|---|
| **1218** | A366 | 106c Sheet of 8, #a-h | 8.50 | 8.50 |
| **1219** | A367 | 158c Sheet of 8, #a-h | 13.00 | 13.00 |
| **1220** | A368 | Sheet of 8, #a-h | 15.00 | 15.00 |
| | | *Nos. 1218-1220 (3)* | 36.50 | 36.50 |

**Islands Type of 2007**

Designs: 30c, Flag of Bonaire, divers and marine life. 59c, Map of Statia, oil storage tanks, horiz. 110c, Flag of Curaçao, royal poinciana flowers. 164c, Flag of St. Maarten, cruise ship and pier. 168c, Map of bonaire, flamingos, horiz. 285c, Map of Saba, houses, horiz.

***Perf. 12¾x13¼, 13¼x12¾***

**2009, Jan.**

| | | | | |
|---|---|---|---|---|
| **1221** | A335 | 30c multi | 1.00 | 1.00 |
| **1222** | A335 | 59c multi | 1.00 | 1.00 |
| **1223** | A335 | 110c multi | 1.40 | 1.40 |
| **1224** | A335 | 164c multi | 1.60 | 1.60 |
| **1225** | A335 | 168c multi | 1.75 | 1.75 |
| **1226** | A335 | 285c multi | 3.00 | 3.00 |
| | | *Nos. 1221-1226 (6)* | 9.75 | 9.75 |

Souvenir Sheet

Birds — A369

No. 1227: a, 5g, Celeus undatus. b, 10g, Todopleura fusca.

**2009, July 20** ***Perf. 13¼x12¾***

**1227** A369 Sheet of 2, #a-b 15.00 15.00

Sailing Ships — A370

No. 1228: a, 1c, Merchantman, 200. b, 2c, Caravel, 1490. c, 3c, Naos, 1492. d, 4c, Constant, 1605. e, 5c, Merchant ship, 1620. f, 80c, Vasa, 1628. g, 220c, Hoys, 1730. h, 275c, Bark, 1750. i, 385c, Schooner, 1838. j, 475c, Sailing rig, 1884. k, 500c, Fifie, 1903. l, 750c, Junk, 1938.

**2009, Aug. 31**

**1228** A370 Block of 12, #a-l 28.00 28.00

Snakes — A371

No. 1229: a, 275c, Bothriopsis bilineata. b, 325c, Bothriechis schlegelii. c, 340c, Agkistrodeon piscivorous. d, 390c, Erythrolamprus aesculapii. e, 420c, Atropoides mexicanus. f, 450c, Bothriechis nigroviridis.

**2009, Oct. 5**

**1229** A371 Block of 6, #a-f 26.00 26.00

Aviation Pioneers A372

Designs: 59c, Freddy Johnson (1932-2001). 110c, Norman Chester Wathey (1925-2001). 164c, José Dormoy (1925-2007).

***Perf. 13¼x12¾***

**2009, Nov. 10** **Litho.**

**1230-1232** A372 Set of 3 3.50 3.50

Airplanes A373

No. 1233: a, Wright Flyer, 1903. b, DST Skysleeper, 1935. c, Cessna 170, 1948. d, Lockheed Constellation, 1943. e, De Havilland Comet, 1949. f, BAC Super VC10, 1962.

**2009, Nov. 16**

| | | | |
|---|---|---|---|
| **1233** | Block of 6 | 21.00 | 21.00 |
| *a.* | A373 55c multi | 1.00 | 1.00 |
| *b.* | A373 100c multi | 1.20 | 1.20 |
| *c.* | A373 205c multi | 2.00 | 2.00 |
| *d.* | A373 395c multi | 4.00 | 4.00 |
| *e.* | A373 645c multi | 6.00 | 6.00 |
| *f.* | A373 800c multi | 7.00 | 7.00 |

Hanukkah A374

Christmas A375

Kwanzaa A376

New Year's Day A377

**2009, Nov. 30** ***Perf. 12¾x13¼***

| | | | | |
|---|---|---|---|---|
| **1234** | A374 | 50c multi | .50 | .50 |
| **1235** | A375 | 110c multi | 1.10 | 1.10 |
| **1236** | A376 | 168c multi | 1.75 | 1.75 |
| **1237** | A377 | 215c multi | 2.25 | 2.25 |
| | | *Nos. 1234-1237 (4)* | 5.60 | 5.60 |

Fruit — A378

**2009, Dec. 28** **Litho.**

| | | | |
|---|---|---|---|
| **1238** | Block of 8 + label | 20.00 | 20.00 |
| *a.* | A378 20c Sapodilla | 1.00 | 1.00 |
| *b.* | A378 45c Pineapple | 1.00 | 1.00 |
| *c.* | A378 125c Mamey sapote | 1.30 | 1.30 |
| *d.* | A378 145c Avocado | 1.60 | 1.60 |
| *e.* | A378 160c Mangosteen | 1.60 | 1.60 |
| *f.* | A378 210c Rambutan | 2.00 | 2.00 |
| *g.* | A378 295c Pomelo | 3.00 | 3.00 |
| *h.* | A378 1000c Watermelon | 9.00 | 9.00 |

**Greetings Type of 2006**

Designs: 32c, Bless you. 60c, Love. 81c, All the best. 87c, Regards. 1.06g, Go for it. 1.57g, Tolerance. 1.61g, Positivism.

**2009** ***Perf. 13¼x12¾***

**1239-1245** A327 Set of 7 10.00 10.00

Flowers — A379

No. 1246: a, 50c, Opuntia basilaris. b, 75c, Aristolochiaceae. c, 125c, Protea cynaroides. d, 175c, Louisiana iris. e, 200c, Spontaneous frangipani. f, 250c, Red ażaleas. g, 300c, English Heritage rose. h, 350c, Aquilegia. i, 475c, Octavia Hill rose. j, 500c, Tea rose.

**2010, Jan. 25 Litho. *Perf. 13¼x12¾***

| | | | | |
|---|---|---|---|---|
| **1246** | A379 | Block of 10, #a-j | 26.00 | 26.00 |

### Fruit Type of 2005

**2010, Feb. 1 Litho. *Perf. 13¼x12¾***

| | | | | |
|---|---|---|---|---|
| **1247** | A315 | 1c Papaya | .30 | .30 |
| **1248** | A315 | 5c Pomegranates | .30 | .30 |
| **1249** | A315 | 30c Mangos | .30 | .30 |
| **1250** | A315 | 59c Bananas | .60 | .60 |
| **1251** | A315 | 79c Cashews | .80 | .80 |
| **1252** | A315 | 111c Soursops | 1.10 | 1.10 |
| **1253** | A315 | 164c Tamarinds | 1.75 | 1.75 |
| **1254** | A315 | 170c Watermelons | 1.75 | 1.75 |
| **1255** | A315 | 199c Gennips | 2.00 | 2.00 |
| **1256** | A315 | 285c Sea grapes | 3.00 | 3.00 |
| | | *Nos. 1247-1256 (10)* | 11.90 | 11.90 |

New Year 2010 (Year of the Tiger) — A380

Designs: 111c, Tiger cub. 164c, Tiger and cub. 170c, White tiger.

**2010, Feb. 1 *Perf. 12¾x13¼***

| | | | | |
|---|---|---|---|---|
| **1257-1259** | A380 | Set of 3 | 5.00 | 5.00 |

Butterflies — A381

No. 1260: a, 20c, Thersamonia thersamon. b, 50c, Acraea natalica. c, 80c, Vanessa carye. d, 100c, Apodemia mormo. e, 125c, Siproeta stelenes meridionalis. f, 175c, Anartia amathea. g, 200c, Doxocopa laure. h, 250c, Euphaedra uganda. i, 350c, Precis westermannii. j, 450c, Precis octavia. k, 500c, Euphaedra neophron. l, 700c, Vanessa cardui.

**2010, Mar. 1 *Perf. 13¼x12¾***

| | | | | |
|---|---|---|---|---|
| **1260** | A381 | Block of 12, #a-l | 34.00 | 34.00 |

Paintings by Vincent Van Gogh — A382

Designs: 200c, Self-portrait, 1888. 400c, Agostina Segatori, 1887. 500c, Arlesian Woman, 1888. 700c, Emperor Moth, 1889.

**2010, Apr. 7 *Perf. 12¾x13¼***

| | | | | |
|---|---|---|---|---|
| **1261** | A382 | 200c multi | 4.00 | 4.00 |
| **1262** | A382 | 400c multi | 4.50 | 4.50 |
| **1263** | A382 | 500c multi | 5.50 | 5.50 |
| **1264** | A382 | 700c multi | 6.75 | 6.75 |
| | | *Nos. 1261-1264 (4)* | 20.75 | 20.75 |

Nos. 1261-1264 were printed in sheets of 8 containing two of each stamp with a central label.

Birds A383

No. 1265: a, 75c, Pipra aureola. b, 150c, Neopelma chrysocephalum. c, 200c, Oxyruncus cristatus. d, 225c, Automolus rufipileatus. e, 350c, Empidonomus varius. f, 500c, Veniliornis sanguineus.

**2010, May 10**

| | | | | |
|---|---|---|---|---|
| **1265** | A383 | Block of 6, #a-f | 18.50 | 18.50 |

Ships — A384

No. 1266 — Inscriptions: a, 100c, Osberg, 800. b, 125c, Dromon, 910. c, 175c, Cocca, 1500. d, 200c, Mary, 1661. e, 250c, Houtport, 1700. f, 300c, Santissima Trinidad, 1769. g, 350c, Vrachtschip, 1800. h, 400c, Amistad, 1839. i, 450c, Oorlogsschip, 1840. j, 650c, Nederlands schip, 1850.

***Perf. 13¼x12¾***

**2010, June 14 Litho.**

| | | | | |
|---|---|---|---|---|
| **1266** | A384 | Block of 10, #a-j | 33.00 | 33.00 |

Netherlands Antilles Stamps — A385

No. 1267: a, 25c, #109. b, 50c, #140. c, 100c, #77. d, 250c, #144. e, 275c, #290. f, 300c, #75. g, 400c, #C34. h, 600c, #200.

No. 1268: a, 700c, #204. b, 800c, #141.

**2010, July 19 *Perf. 12¾x13¼***

| | | | | |
|---|---|---|---|---|
| **1267** | A385 | Block of 8, #a-h | 22.50 | 22.50 |

### Souvenir Sheet

| | | | | |
|---|---|---|---|---|
| **1268** | A385 | Sheet of 2, #a-b | 17.00 | 17.00 |

Image of stamp on No. 1267d is distorted.

TeleCuraçao, 50th Anniv. A386

Television showing: 59c, Cameraman. 111c, Transmission tower. 164c, 50th anniversary emblem.

**2010, Aug. 2 Litho. *Perf. 13¼x12¾***

| | | | | |
|---|---|---|---|---|
| **1269-1271** | A386 | Set of 3 | 3.75 | 3.75 |

Pocket Watches — A387

No. 1272 — Watches made by: a, Ulysse, 1890. b, Hampden, 1910. c, Elgin, 1924. d, Illinois, 1928. e, Vacheron, 1955.

**2010, Sept. 6 *Perf. 12¾x13¼***

| | | | | |
|---|---|---|---|---|
| **1272** | | Horiz. strip of 5 | 14.00 | 14.00 |
| *a.* | A387 | 125c multi | 2.00 | 2.00 |
| *b.* | A387 | 175c multi | 2.00 | 2.00 |
| *c.* | A387 | 250c multi | 2.50 | 2.50 |
| *d.* | A387 | 300c multi | 3.00 | 3.00 |
| *e.* | A387 | 350c multi | 3.00 | 3.00 |

On Oct. 10, 2010, the Netherlands Antilles was dissolved, being replaced by three entities: Caribbean Netherlands, Curaçao and St. Martin.

---

## SEMI-POSTAL STAMPS

**Catalogue values for unused stamps in this section are for Never Hinged items.**

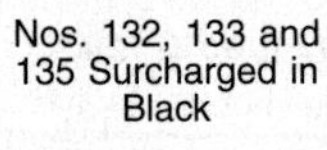

Nos. 132, 133 and 135 Surcharged in Black

**1947, Dec. 1 Unwmk. *Perf. 12½***

| | | | | |
|---|---|---|---|---|
| **B1** | A26 | 1½c + 2½c on 6c | 1.05 | 1.00 |
| **B2** | A26 | 2½c + 5c on 10c | 1.05 | 1.00 |
| **B3** | A26 | 5c + 7½c on 15c | 1.05 | 1.00 |
| | | *Nos. B1-B3 (3)* | 3.15 | 3.00 |

The surtax was for the National Inspanning Welzijnszorg in Nederlandsch Indie, relief organization for Netherlands Indies.

Curaçao Children
SP1 SP2

Design: Nos. B6, B9, Girl.

**1948, Nov. 3 Photo. *Perf. 12½x12***

| | | | | |
|---|---|---|---|---|
| **B4** | SP1 | 6c + 10c ol brn | 2.50 | 1.60 |
| **B5** | SP2 | 10c + 15c brt red | 2.50 | 1.60 |
| **B6** | SP2 | 12½c + 20c Prus grn | 2.50 | 1.75 |
| **B7** | SP1 | 15c + 25c brt bl | 2.50 | 1.75 |
| **B8** | SP2 | 20c + 30c red brn | 2.50 | 1.90 |
| **B9** | SP2 | 25c + 35c purple | 2.50 | 1.90 |
| | | *Nos. B4-B9 (6)* | 15.00 | 10.50 |

The surtax was for child welfare and the White/Yellow Cross Foundation.

Leapfrog — SP4

Designs: 5c+2½c, Flying kite. 6c+2½c, Girls swinging. 12½c+5c, "London Bridge." 25c+10c, Rolling hoops.

***Perf. 14½x13½***

**1951, Aug. 16 Unwmk.**

| | | | | |
|---|---|---|---|---|
| **B10** | SP4 | 1½c + 1c pur | 11.50 | 4.25 |
| **B11** | SP4 | 5c + 2½c brn | 11.50 | 4.25 |
| **B12** | SP4 | 6c + 2½c blue | 11.50 | 4.25 |
| **B13** | SP4 | 12½c + 5c red | 11.50 | 4.25 |
| **B14** | SP4 | 25c + 10c dl grn | 11.50 | 4.25 |
| | | *Nos. B10-B14 (5)* | 57.50 | 21.25 |

The surtax was for child welfare.

Ship and Gull — SP5

Designs: 6c+4c, Sailor and lighthouse. 12½c+7c, Prow of sailboat. 15c+10c, Ships. 25c+15c, Ship, compass and anchor.

**1952, July 16 *Perf. 13x14***

| | | | | |
|---|---|---|---|---|
| **B15** | SP5 | 1½c + 1c dk grn | 9.50 | 1.90 |
| **B16** | SP5 | 6c + 4c choc | 16.50 | 4.25 |
| **B17** | SP5 | 12½c + 7c red vio | 12.00 | 4.25 |
| **B18** | SP5 | 15c + 10c dp bl | 14.00 | 5.00 |
| **B19** | SP5 | 25c + 15c red | 13.00 | 3.75 |
| | | *Nos. B15-B19 (5)* | 65.00 | 19.15 |

The surtax was for the seamen's welfare fund.

No. 226 Surcharged in Black

**1953, Feb. 21**

| | | | | |
|---|---|---|---|---|
| **B20** | A45 | 22½c + 7½c on 1½g | 2.40 | 1.25 |

The surtax was for flood relief in the Netherlands.

Tribulus Cistoides
SP6

Flowers: 7½c+5c, Yellow hibiscus. 15c+5c, Oleander. 22½c+7½c, Cactus. 25c+10c, Red hibiscus.

**1955, May 17 Photo. *Perf. 14x13***

**Flowers in Natural Colors**

**B21** SP6 1½c + 1c bl grn & dk bl 3.00 .95

**B22** SP6 7½c + 5c dp ultra 4.00 1.90

**B23** SP6 15c + 5c ol grn 4.00 2.25

**B24** SP6 22½c + 7½c dk bl 4.00 1.90

**B25** SP6 25c + 10c ind & gray 4.00 1.90

*Nos. B21-B25 (5)* 19.00 8.90

The surtax was for child welfare.

Prince Bernhard and Queen Juliana
SP7

**1955, Oct. 19 *Perf. 11x12***

**B26** SP7 7½c + 2½c rose brn .40 .30

**B27** SP7 22½c + 7½c dp bl 1.20 .95

Royal visit to the Netherlands Antilles, Oct. 1955.

Surtax paid for a gift.

Lord Baden-Powell — SP8

**1957, Feb. 22 *Perf. 14x13½***

**B28** SP8 6c + 1½c org yel .95 .45

**B29** SP8 7½c + 2½c dp grn .95 .45

**B30** SP8 15c + 5c red .95 .45

*Nos. B28-B30 (3)* 2.85 1.35

50th anniv. of the Boy Scout movement.

Soccer Player — SP9

Map of Central America and the Caribbean
SP10

Designs: 15c+5c, Goalkeeper catching ball. 22½c+7½c, Men playing soccer.

**1957, Aug. 6 *Perf. 12x11, 11x12***

**B31** SP9 6c + 2½c org 1.90 .70

**B32** SP10 7½c + 5c dk red 1.90 1.00

**B33** SP9 15c + 5c brt bl grn 1.90 1.00

**B34** SP9 22½c + 7½c brt bl 1.90 1.00

*Nos. B31-B34 (4)* 7.60 3.70

8th Central American and Caribbean Soccer Championships, Aug. 11-25.

Surtax was for organizing costs.

American Kestrel — SP11

Birds: 7½+1½c, Yellow oriole. 15+2½c, Common ground doves. 22½+2½c, Brown-throated parakeet.

**1958, Apr. 15 Photo. *Perf. 13½x14***

**B35** SP11 2½c + 1c multi 1.75 .95

**B36** SP11 7½c + 1½c multi 1.75 .95

**B37** SP11 15c + 2½c multi 1.75 .95

**B38** SP11 22½c + 2½c multi 1.75 .95

*Nos. B35-B38 (4)* 7.00 3.80

The surtax was for child welfare.

Flag and Map — SP12

**1958, Dec. 1 Litho. *Perf. 13½***

**Cross in Red**

**B39** SP12 6c + 2c red brn .95 .45

**B40** SP12 7½c + 2½c bl grn .95 .45

**B41** SP12 15c + 5c org yel .95 .45

**B42** SP12 22½c + 7½c blue .95 .45

*Nos. B39-B42 (4)* 3.80 1.80

The surtax was for the Red Cross.

Community House, Zeeland
SP13

Historic buildings: 7½c+2½c, Molenplein. 15c+5c, Saba, vert. 22½c+7½c, Scharlooburg. 25c+7½c, Community House, Brievengat.

***Perf. 14x13½, 13½x14***

**1959, Sept. 16 Litho.**

**B43** SP13 6c + 1½c multi 1.40 .90

**B44** SP13 7½c + 2½c multi 1.40 .90

**B45** SP13 15c + 5c multi 1.40 .90

**B46** SP13 22½c + 7½c multi 1.40 .90

**B47** SP13 25c + 7½c multi 1.40 .90

*Nos. B43-B47 (5)* 7.00 4.50

The surtax went to the Foundation for the Preservation of Historical Monuments.

Fish — SP14

Designs. 10c+2c, SCUBA diver with spear gun, vert. 25c+5c, Two fish.

**1960, Aug. 24 Photo. *Perf. 13½***

**B48** SP14 10c + 2c sapphire 1.50 .85

**B49** SP14 20c + 3c multi 1.75 1.15

**B50** SP14 25c + 5c blk, brt pink & dk bl 1.75 1.15

*Nos. B48-B50 (3)* 5.00 3.15

The surtax was for the fight against cancer.

Infant — SP15

Designs: 10c+3c, Girl and doll. 20c+6c, Boy on beach. 25c+8c, Children in school.

**1961, July 24 Litho. *Perf. 13½x14***

**Designs in Black**

**B51** SP15 6c + 2c lt yel grn .55 .30

**B52** SP15 10c + 3c rose red .55 .30

**B53** SP15 20c + 6c yellow .55 .30

**B54** SP15 25c + 8c orange .55 .30

*Nos. B51-B54 (4)* 2.20 1.20

The surtax was for child welfare.

Globe and Knight
SP16

**1962, May 2 *Perf. 13½x14½***

**B55** SP16 10c + 5c green 1.10 .65

**B56** SP16 20c + 10c carmine 1.10 .65

**B57** SP16 25c + 10c dk bl 1.10 .65

*Nos. B55-B57 (3)* 3.30 1.95

Intl. Candidates Chess Tournament, Willemstad, May-June.

No. 248 Surcharged

**1963, Mar. 21**

**B58** A56 20c + 10c crimson & gray .50 .50

FAO "Freedom from Hunger" campaign.

Child and Flowers — SP17

Designs: 6c+3c, Three girls and flowers, horiz. 10c+5c, Girl with ball and trees, horiz. 20c+10c, Three boys with flags, horiz. 25c+12c, Singing boy.

***Perf. 14½x13½, 13½x14½***

**1963, Oct. 23 Photo. Unwmk.**

**B59** SP17 5c + 2c multi .40 .25

**B60** SP17 6c + 3c multi .40 .25

**B61** SP17 10c + 5c multi .40 .25

**B62** SP17 20c + 10c multi .40 .25

**B63** SP17 25c + 12c multi .40 .25

*Nos. B59-B63 (5)* 2.00 1.25

Surtax for child welfare.

Bougainvillea
SP18

Designs: 10c+5c, Wild rose. 20c+10c, Chalice flower. 25c+11c, Bellisima.

**1964, Oct. 21 *Perf. 14x13***

**Flowers in Natural Colors**

**B64** SP18 6c + 3c bl vio & blk .40 .25

**B65** SP18 10c + 5c yel brn, yel & blk .40 .25

**B66** SP18 20c + 10c dull red & blk .40 .25

**B67** SP18 25c + 11c citron & brn .40 .25

*Nos. B64-B67 (4)* 1.60 1.00

The surtax was for child welfare.

Sea Anemones and Star Coral
SP19

Corals: 6c+3c, Blue cup sponges. 10c+5c, Green cup sponges. 25c+11c, Basket sponge, knobbed brain coral and reef fish.

**1965, Nov. 10 Photo. *Perf. 14x13½***

**B68** SP19 6c + 3c multi .25 .25

**B69** SP19 10c + 5c multi .25 .25

**B70** SP19 20c + 10c multi .35 .25

**B71** SP19 25c + 11c multi .35 .25

*Nos. B68-B71 (4)* 1.20 1.00

The surtax was for child welfare.

**ICEM Type of Netherlands**

**1966, Jan. 31 Photo. *Perf. 14x13***

**B72** SP181 35c + 15c brn & dl yel .25 .25

The surtax was for the Intergovernmental Committee for European Migration (ICEM). The message on the stamps was given and signed by Queen Juliana.

Girl Cooking — SP20

Youth at Work: 10c+5c, Nurse's aide with infant. 20c+10c, Young metalworker. 25c+11c, Girl ironing.

**1966, Nov. 15 *Perf. 13½***

**B73** SP20 6c + 3c multi .25 .25

**B74** SP20 10c + 5c multi .25 .25

**B75** SP20 20c + 10c multi .25 .25

**B76** SP20 25c + 11c multi .25 .25

*Nos. B73-B76 (4)* 1.00 1.00

The surtax was for child welfare.

Helping Hands Supporting Women — SP21

**1967, July 4 Litho. *Perf. 13x14***

**B77** SP21 6c + 3c bl & blk .25 .25

**B78** SP21 10c + 5c brt pink & blk .25 .25

**B79** SP21 20c + 10c lilac .25 .25

**B80** SP21 25c + 11c dk bl .25 .25

*Nos. B77-B80 (4)* 1.00 1.00

The surtax was for various social and cultural institutions.

Nanzi the Spider and the Tiger — SP22

Nanzi Stories (Folklore): 6c+3c, Princess Longnose, vert. 10c+5c, The Turtle and the Monkey. 25c+11c, Adventure of Shon Arey, vert.

***Perf. 14x13, 13x14***

**1967, Nov. 15 Photo.**

**B81** SP22 6c + 3c dk red, pink & org .25 .25

**B82** SP22 10c + 5c vio bl & org .25 .25

**B83** SP22 20c + 10c grn & org .25 .25

**B84** SP22 25c + 11c brt bl & org .25 .25

*Nos. B81-B84 (4)* 1.00 1.00

The surtax was for child welfare.

Lintendans (Dance) and Koeoekoe House
SP23

**1968, May 29 Litho. *Perf. 14x13***

| | | | |
|---|---|---|---|
| **B85** | SP23 10c + 5c multi | .25 | .25 |
| **B86** | SP23 15c + 5c multi | .25 | .25 |
| **B87** | SP23 20c + 10c multi | .25 | .25 |
| **B88** | SP23 25c + 10c multi | .25 | .25 |
| | *Nos. B85-B88 (4)* | 1.00 | 1.00 |

The surtax was for various social and cultural institutions.

Boy and Pet Cat — SP24

Designs: 6c+3c, Boy and goat. 10c+5c, Girl and poodle. 25c+11c, Girl and duckling.

**1968, Nov. 13 Photo. *Perf. 13½***

| | | | |
|---|---|---|---|
| **B89** | SP24 6c + 3c multi | .40 | .25 |
| **B90** | SP24 10c + 5c multi | .40 | .25 |
| **B91** | SP24 20c + 10c multi | .40 | .25 |
| **B92** | SP24 25c + 11c multi | .40 | .25 |
| | *Nos. B89-B92 (4)* | 1.60 | 1.00 |

The surtax was for child welfare.

Carnival Headpiece SP25

Folklore: 15c+5c, Harvest-home festival. 20c+10c, Feast of St. John (dancers & cock). 25c+10c, "Dande" New Year's celebration.

**1969, July 23 Litho. *Perf. 13½***

| | | | |
|---|---|---|---|
| **B93** | SP25 10c + 5c multi | .30 | .25 |
| **B94** | SP25 15c + 5c multi | .30 | .25 |
| **B95** | SP25 20c + 10c multi | .35 | .30 |
| **B96** | SP25 25c + 10c multi | .35 | .30 |
| | *Nos. B93-B96 (4)* | 1.30 | 1.10 |

The surtax was for various social and cultural institutions.

Boy Playing Guitar SP26

Designs: 10c+5c, Girl with English flute. 20c+10c, Boy playing the marimula. 25c+11c, Girl playing the piano.

**1969, Nov. 3 Litho. *Perf. 14x13***

| | | | |
|---|---|---|---|
| **B97** | SP26 6c + 3c org & vio | .40 | .30 |
| **B98** | SP26 10c + 5c yel & brt grn | .40 | .35 |
| **B99** | SP26 20c + 10c bl & car | .40 | .35 |
| **B100** | SP26 25c + 11c pink & brn | .40 | .35 |
| | *Nos. B97-B100 (4)* | 1.60 | 1.35 |

The surtax was for child welfare.

Printing Press and Quill — SP27

Mass Media: 15c+5c, Filmstrip and reels. 20c+10c, Horn and radio mast. 25c+10c, Television antenna and eye focused on globe.

**1970, July 14 Litho. *Perf. 13½***

| | | | |
|---|---|---|---|
| **B101** | SP27 10c + 5c multi | .40 | .35 |
| **B102** | SP27 15c + 5c multi | .40 | .35 |
| **B103** | SP27 20c + 10c multi | .40 | .35 |
| **B104** | SP27 25c + 10c multi | .40 | .35 |
| | *Nos. B101-B104 (4)* | 1.60 | 1.40 |

The surtax was for various social and cultural institutions.

Mother and Child — SP28

Designs: 10c+5c, Girl holding piggy bank. 20c+10c, Boys wrestling (Judokas). 25c+11c, Youth carrying small boy on his shoulders.

**1970, Nov. 16 *Perf. 13½x14***

| | | | |
|---|---|---|---|
| **B105** | SP28 6c + 3c multi | .40 | .30 |
| **B106** | SP28 10c + 5c multi | .40 | .30 |
| **B107** | SP28 20c + 10c multi | .40 | .30 |
| **B108** | SP28 25c + 11c multi | .40 | .30 |
| | *Nos. B105-B108 (4)* | 1.60 | 1.20 |

The surtax was for child welfare.

Charcoal Burner SP29

Kitchen Utensils: 15c+5c, Earthenware vessel for water. 20c+10c, Baking oven. 25c+10c, Soup plate, stirrer and kneading stick.

**1971, May 12 *Perf. 14x13½***

| | | | |
|---|---|---|---|
| **B109** | SP29 10c + 5c multi | .50 | .40 |
| **B110** | SP29 15c + 5c multi | .50 | .40 |
| **B111** | SP29 20c + 10c multi | .50 | .40 |
| **B112** | SP29 25c + 10c multi | .50 | .40 |
| | *Nos. B109-B112 (4)* | 2.00 | 1.60 |

Surtax was for various social and cultural institutions.

Homemade Dolls and Comb — SP30

Homemade Toys: 20c+10c, Carts. 30c+15c, Musical top made from calabash.

**1971, Nov. 16 *Perf. 13½x14***

| | | | |
|---|---|---|---|
| **B113** | SP30 15c + 5c multi | .55 | .50 |
| **B114** | SP30 20c + 10c multi | .55 | .50 |
| **B115** | SP30 30c + 15c multi | .55 | .50 |
| | *Nos. B113-B115 (3)* | 1.65 | 1.50 |

Surtax was for child welfare.

Steel Band SP31

Designs: 20c+10c, Harvest festival (Seu). 30c+15c, Tambu dancers.

**1972, May 16**

| | | | |
|---|---|---|---|
| **B116** | SP31 15c + 5c multi | .80 | .65 |
| **B117** | SP31 20c + 10c multi | .80 | .65 |
| **B118** | SP31 30c + 15c multi | .80 | .65 |
| | *Nos. B116-B118 (3)* | 2.40 | 1.95 |

Surtax was for various social and cultural institutions.

Child at Play on Ground SP32

Designs: 20c+10c, Child playing in water. 30c+15c, Child throwing ball into air.

**1972, Nov. 14 Litho. *Perf. 14x13***

| | | | |
|---|---|---|---|
| **B119** | SP32 15c + 5c multi | .65 | .65 |
| **B120** | SP32 20c + 10c multi | .65 | .65 |
| **B121** | SP32 30c + 15c multi | .65 | .65 |
| | *Nos. B119-B121 (3)* | 1.95 | 1.95 |

Surtax was for child welfare.

Pedestrian Crossing, Traffic Sign — SP33

Designs: 15c+7c, School crossing. 40c+20c, Traffic light, road and car.

**1973, Apr. 9 Litho. *Perf. 13x14***

| | | | |
|---|---|---|---|
| **B122** | SP33 12c + 6c multi | .80 | .65 |
| **B123** | SP33 15c + 7c multi | .80 | .65 |
| **B124** | SP33 40c + 20c multi | .80 | .65 |
| | *Nos. B122-B124 (3)* | 2.40 | 1.95 |

Surtax was for various social and cultural institutions.

"1948-73" SP34

20c+10c, Children. 30c+15c, Mother & child.

**1973, Nov. 19 Litho. *Perf. 14x13***

| | | | |
|---|---|---|---|
| **B125** | SP34 15c + 5c multi | .60 | .60 |
| **B126** | SP34 20c + 10c multi | .60 | .60 |
| *a.* | Min. sheet, 2 ea #B125-B126 | 3.25 | 3.00 |
| **B127** | SP34 30c + 15c multi | .70 | .70 |
| | *Nos. B125-B127 (3)* | 1.90 | 1.90 |

Child Welfare semi-postal stamps, 25th anniv.

Girl Combing her Hair — SP35

15c+7c, Young people listening to rock music. 40c+20c, Drummer, symbolizing rock music.

**1974, Apr. 9 Litho. *Perf. 14x13***

| | | | |
|---|---|---|---|
| **B128** | SP35 12c + 6c multi | .90 | .70 |
| **B129** | SP35 15c + 7c multi | .90 | .70 |
| **B130** | SP35 40c + 20c multi | .90 | .70 |
| | *Nos. B128-B130 (3)* | 2.70 | 2.10 |

Surtax was for various social and cultural institutions.

Child, Saw and Score — SP36

Designs: 20c+10c, Footprints in circle. 30c+15c, Moon and sun. Each design includes score of a children's song.

**1974, Nov. 12 Litho. *Perf. 13x14***

| | | | |
|---|---|---|---|
| **B131** | SP36 15c + 5c multi | .90 | .60 |
| **B132** | SP36 20c + 10c multi | .90 | .60 |
| **B133** | SP36 30c + 15c multi | .90 | .60 |
| | *Nos. B131-B133 (3)* | 2.70 | 1.80 |

Surtax was for child welfare.

Carved Stone Grid, Flower Pot SP37

Jewish Tombstone, Mordecai's Procession SP38

Design: 40c+20c, Ornamental stone from facade of Jewish House, 1728.

**1975, Mar. 21 Litho. *Perf. 13x14***

| | | | |
|---|---|---|---|
| **B134** | SP37 12c + 6c multi | .60 | .60 |
| **B135** | SP38 15c + 7c multi | .60 | .60 |
| **B136** | SP37 40c + 20c multi | .60 | .60 |
| | *Nos. B134-B136 (3)* | 1.80 | 1.80 |

Surtax was for various social and cultural institutions.

Children Building Curaçao Windmill SP39

Designs: 20c+10c, Girl molding clay animal. 30c+15c, Children drawing picture.

**1975, Nov. 12 Litho. *Perf. 14x13***

| | | | |
|---|---|---|---|
| **B137** | SP39 15c + 5c multi | .60 | .60 |
| **B138** | SP39 20c + 10c multi | .60 | .60 |
| **B139** | SP39 30c + 15c multi | .60 | .60 |
| | *Nos. B137-B139 (3)* | 1.80 | 1.80 |

Surtax was for child welfare.

Carrying a Child — SP40

Designs: Different ways of carrying a child. 40c+18c is vertical.

***Perf. 14x13, 13x14***

**1976, Oct. 4 Litho.**

| | | | |
|---|---|---|---|
| **B140** | SP40 20c + 10c multi | .60 | .60 |
| **B141** | SP40 25c + 12c multi | .60 | .60 |
| **B142** | SP40 40c + 18c multi | .60 | .60 |
| | *Nos. B140-B142 (3)* | 1.80 | 1.80 |

Surtax was for child welfare.

Composite: Aces of Hearts, Clubs, Diamonds and Spades — SP41

Designs: 25c+12c, "King" and inscription. 40c+18c, Hand holding cards; map of Aruba as ace of hearts, horiz.

***Perf. 13x14, 14x13***

**1977, May 6** **Litho.**

**B143** SP41 20c + 10c red & blk .50 .35
**B144** SP41 25c + 12c multi .50 .35
*a.* Min. sheet, 2 ea #B143-B144 1.40 1.10
**B145** SP41 40c + 18c multi .65 .45
*Nos. B143-B145 (3)* 1.65 1.15

Central American and Caribbean Bridge Championships, Aruba.

**Souvenir Sheet**

**1977, May 26** ***Perf. 13½x14***

**B146** SP41 Sheet of 3 3.50 2.50

Amphilex 77 International Philatelic Exhibition, Amsterdam, May 26-June 5. No. B146 contains 3 stamps similar to Nos. B143-B145 with bright green background.

Children and Toys — SP42

Children playing with fantasy animals.

**1977, Oct. 25** **Litho.** ***Perf. 14x13***

**B147** SP42 15c + 5c multi .35 .25
**B148** SP42 20c + 10c multi .45 .35
**B149** SP42 25c + 12c multi .55 .45
**B150** SP42 40c + 18c multi .65 .45
*a.* Min. sheet, 2 ea #B148, B150 2.40 1.60
*Nos. B147-B150 (4)* 2.00 1.50

Surtax was for child welfare.

Water Skiing — SP43

Designs: 20c+10c, Sailing. 25c+12c, Soccer. 40c+18c, Baseball.

**1978, Mar. 31** **Litho.** ***Perf. 13x14***

**B151** SP43 15c + 5c multi .25 .25
**B152** SP43 20c + 10c multi .25 .25
**B153** SP43 25c + 12c multi .25 .25
**B154** SP43 40c + 18c multi .25 .25
*Nos. B151-B154 (4)* 1.00 1.00

Surtax was for sports. Tete-beche gutter pairs exist.

Red Cross SP44

**1978, Sept. 19** **Litho.** ***Perf. 14x13***

**B155** SP44 55c + 25c red & blk .40 .40
*a.* Souv. sheet of 3, perf. 13½x13 2.00 1.60

Henri Dunant (1828-1910), founder of Red Cross. Surtax for the Red Cross.

Tete-beche gutter pairs exist.

Roller Skating — SP45

Children's Activities: 20c+10c, Kite flying. 25c+12c, Playing marbles. 40c+ 18c, Bicycling.

**1978, Nov. 7** **Litho.** ***Perf. 13x14***

**B156** SP45 15c + 5c multi .45 .35
**B157** SP45 20c + 10c multi .50 .40
*a.* Min. sheet, 2 ea #B156-B157 1.75 1.50
**B158** SP45 25c + 12c multi .55 .45
**B159** SP45 40c + 18c multi .60 .50
*Nos. B156-B159 (4)* 2.10 1.70

Surtax was for child welfare.

Carnival King — SP46

25th Aruba Carnival: 75c+20c, Carnival Queen and coat of arms.

**1979, Feb. 20** **Litho.** ***Perf. 13x14***

**B160** SP46 40c + 10c multi .50 .45
**B161** SP46 75c + 20c multi .75 .70

Regatta Emblem — SP47

Designs: 35c+10c, Race. 40c+15c, Globe and yacht, horiz. 55c+25c, Yacht, birds and sun.

***Perf. 13x14, 14x13***

**1979, May 16** **Litho.**

**B162** SP47 15c + 5c multi .25 .25
**B163** SP47 35c + 10c multi .35 .30
**B164** SP47 40c + 15c multi .45 .35
**B165** SP47 55c + 25c multi .55 .40
*a.* Souv. sheet of 4, #B162-B165 1.75 1.50
*Nos. B162-B165 (4)* 1.60 1.30

12th International Sailing Regatta, Bonaire. #B164 in souvenir sheet is perf 13x14.

**Volunteer Corps Type, 1979**

15c+10c, Soldiers, 1929 and 1979. 40c+20c, Soldier guarding oil refinery, Guard emblem.

**1979, July 4** **Litho.** ***Perf. 13x14***

**B166** A124 15c + 10c multi .35 .30
**B167** A124 40c + 20c multi .45 .40

Volleyball, Olympic Rings — SP49

Girls Reading Book, IYC Emblem — SP48

IYC Emblem and Children's Drawings: 25c+12c, Infant and cat. 35c+15c, Girls walking under palm trees. 50c+20c, Children wearing adult clothing.

**1979, Oct. 24** **Litho.** ***Perf. 13x14***

**B168** SP48 20c + 10c multi .35 .35
**B169** SP48 25c + 12c multi .40 .35
**B170** SP48 35c + 15c multi .45 .40
*a.* Souv. sheet, 2 ea #B168, B170 1.50 1.60
**B171** SP48 50c + 20c multi .55 .50
*Nos. B168-B171 (4)* 1.75 1.60

International Year of the Child. Surtax for child welfare.

**Fort Church Type of 1980**

Designs: 20c+10c, Brass chandelier, 1909, horiz. 50c+25c, Pipe organ.

***Perf. 14x13, 13x14***

**1980, Jan. 9** **Litho.**

**B172** A128 20c + 10c multi .35 .35
**B173** A128 50c + 25c multi .45 .45

Designs: 25c+10c, Woman gymnast. 30c+15c, Male gymnast. 60c+25c, Basketball.

**1980, June 25** **Litho.** ***Perf. 13x14***

**B174** SP49 25c + 10c multi .35 .30
**B175** SP49 30c + 15c multi .40 .35
**B176** SP49 45c + 20c multi .55 .50
**B177** SP49 60c + 25c multi .65 .55
*a.* Souvenir sheet of 6, 3 each #B174, B177, perf. 14x13½ 2.25 1.90
*Nos. B174-B177 (4)* 1.95 1.70

22nd Summer Olympic Games, Moscow, July 19-Aug. 3.


St. Maarten Landscape SP50

Children's Drawings: 30c+15c, House in Bonaire. 40c+20c, Child at blackboard. 60c+25c, Dancers, vert.

***Perf. 14x13, 13x14***

**1980, Oct. 22** **Litho.**

**B178** SP50 25c + 10c multi .40 .25
**B179** SP50 30c + 15c multi .50 .40
**B180** SP50 40c + 20c multi .55 .45
**B181** SP50 60c + 25c multi .65 .45
*a.* Souvenir sheet of 6+ 4 labels, 3 each #B178, B181 3.00 2.25
*Nos. B178-B181 (4)* 2.10 1.55

Surtax was for child welfare.
#B178 in souvenir sheet is perf 13x14.

Girl Using Sign Language — SP51

Designs: 25c+10c, Blind woman. 30c+15c, Man in wheelchair. 45c+20c, Infant in walker.

**1981, Apr. 7** **Litho.** ***Perf. 13x14***

**B182** SP51 25c + 10c multi .45 .40
**B183** SP51 30c + 15c multi .50 .50
**B184** SP51 45c + 20c multi .65 .65
**B185** SP51 60c + 25c multi .75 .70
*Nos. B182-B185 (4)* 2.35 2.25

International Year of the Disabled. Surtax was for handicapped children.

Tennis Player — SP52

**1981, May 27** **Litho.** ***Perf. 13x14***

**B186** SP52 30c + 15c shown .60 .50
**B187** SP52 50c + 20c Diving .80 .60
**B188** SP52 70c + 25c Boxing 1.00 .80
*a.* Min. sheet of 3, #B186-B188 2.50 2.50
*Nos. B186-B188 (3)* 2.40 1.90

Surtax was for sporting events.

Den Mother and Cub Scout SP53

Scouting in Netherlands Antilles, 50th Anniv.: 70c+25c, van der Maarel, national founder. 1g+50c, Ronde Klip (headquarters).

**1981, Sept. 16** **Litho.** ***Perf. 14x13***

**B189** SP53 45c + 20c multi .95 .75
**B190** SP53 70c + 25c multi 1.20 .95
**B191** SP53 1g + 50c multi 1.60 1.35
*a.* Min. sheet of 3, #B189-B191, perf. 13½x13 4.00 3.25
*Nos. B189-B191 (3)* 3.75 3.05

Surtax was for various social and cultural institutions.

Girl and Teddy Bear — SP54

Designs: 35c+15c, Mother and child. 45c+20c, Two children. 55c+25c, Boy and cat.

**1981, Oct. 21** **Litho.** ***Perf. 13x14***

**B192** SP54 35c + 15c multi .50 .45
**B193** SP54 45c + 20c multi .60 .50
**B194** SP54 55c + 25c multi .75 .65
*a.* Min. sheet, 2 ea #B192, B194 2.50 2.00
**B195** SP54 85c + 40c multi 1.10 .95
*Nos. B192-B195 (4)* 2.95 2.55

Surtax for child welfare.

Fencing SP55

**1982, Feb. 17** **Litho.** ***Perf. 14x13***

**B196** SP55 35c + 15c shown .75 .50
**B197** SP55 45c + 20c Judo 1.00 .60
**B198** SP55 70c + 35c Soccer 1.25 .95
*a.* Miniature sheet of 2 + label 3.50 2.00
**B199** SP55 85c + 40c Bicycling 1.50 1.10
*Nos. B196-B199 (4)* 4.50 3.15

Surtax was for sporting events.

Girl Playing Accordion SP56

**1982, Oct. 20** **Litho.**

**B200** SP56 35c + 15c shown .85 .50
**B201** SP56 75c + 35c Guitar 1.40 1.00
**B202** SP56 85c + 40c Violin 1.60 1.10
*a.* Min. sheet of 3, #B200-B202 4.00 3.25
*Nos. B200-B202 (3)* 3.85 2.60

Surtax for child welfare.

Traditional House, Saba SP57

**1982, Nov. 17** **Litho.**

**B203** SP57 35c + 15c shown .95 .65
**B204** SP57 75c + 35c Aruba 1.40 .95
**B205** SP57 85c + 40c Curaçao 1.40 .95
*a.* Souv. sheet of 3, #B203-B205 4.00 3.25
*Nos. B203-B205 (3)* 3.75 2.55

Surtax was for various social and cultural institutions.

High Jump SP58

No. B207, Weight lifting. No. B208, Wind surfing.

**1983, Feb. 22** **Litho.**

**B206** SP58 35c + 15c shown .75 .60
**B207** SP58 45c + 20c multi 1.10 .75
**B208** SP58 85c + 40c multi 1.75 1.20
*Nos. B206-B208 (3)* 3.60 2.55

Surtax was for sporting events.

Child with Lizard — SP59

No. B210, Child with insects. No. B211, Child with animal.

**1983, Oct. 18** **Litho.** ***Perf. 13x14***

**B209** SP59 45c + 20c shown 1.00 .75
**B210** SP59 55c + 25c multi 1.25 .90
**B211** SP59 100c + 50c multi 2.00 1.50
*a.* Souv. sheet of 3, #B209-B211 4.50 3.25
*Nos. B209-B211 (3)* 4.25 3.15

Surtax was for Childrens' Charity.

Pre-Columbian Artifacts — SP60

**1983, Nov. 22** **Litho.** ***Perf. 13x14***

**B212** SP60 45c + 20c multi 1.00 .85
**B213** SP60 55c + 25c multi 1.25 1.00
**B214** SP60 85c + 40c multi 1.50 1.10
**B215** SP60 100c + 50c multi 1.90 1.50
*Nos. B212-B215 (4)* 5.65 4.45

Curaçao Baseball Federation, 50th Anniv. SP61

**1984, Mar. 27** **Litho.** ***Perf. 14x13***

**B216** SP61 25c + 10c Catching 1.20 .50
**B217** SP61 45c + 20c Batting 1.70 .85
**B218** SP61 55c + 25c Pitching 2.10 1.05
**B219** SP61 85c + 40c Running 2.40 1.30
*a.* Min. sheet of 3, #B217-B219 6.00 3.75
*Nos. B216-B219 (4)* 7.40 3.70

Surtax was for baseball fed., 1984 Olympics.

Microphones, Radio SP62

Designs: 55c+25c, Radio, record player. 100c+50c, Record players.

**1984, Apr. 24** **Litho.** ***Perf. 14x13***

**B220** SP62 45c + 20c multi 1.45 .90
**B221** SP62 55c + 25c multi 1.75 1.15
**B222** SP62 100c + 50c multi 2.10 1.60
*Nos. B220-B222 (3)* 5.30 3.65

Surtax was for social and cultural institutions.

Boy Reading — SP63

Designs: 55c+25c, Parents reading to children. 100c+50c, Family worship.

**1984, Nov. 7** **Litho.** ***Perf. 13x14***

**B223** SP63 45c + 20c multi 1.05 .90
**B224** SP63 55c + 25c multi 1.35 1.15
**B225** SP63 100c + 50c multi 1.75 1.45
*a.* Souv. sheet of 3, #B223-B225 4.50 3.75
*Nos. B223-B225 (3)* 4.15 3.50

Surtax was for children's charity.

Soccer Players SP64

**1985, Mar. 27** **Litho.** ***Perf. 14x13***

**B226** SP64 10c + 5c multi .60 .35
**B227** SP64 15c + 5c multi .65 .40
**B228** SP64 45c + 20c multi 1.15 .85
**B229** SP64 55c + 25c multi 1.40 1.05
**B230** SP64 85c + 40c multi 1.90 1.45
*Nos. B226-B230 (5)* 5.70 4.10

The surtax was for sporting events.

Intl. Youth Year — SP65

No. B231, Youth, computer keyboard. No. B232, Girl listening to music. No. B233, Youth breakdancing.

**1985, Apr. 29** **Litho.**

**B231** SP65 45c + 20c multi 1.20 .90
**B232** SP65 55c + 25c multi 1.60 1.15
**B233** SP65 100c + 50c multi 2.25 1.60
*Nos. B231-B233 (3)* 5.05 3.65

Surtax for youth, social and cultural organizations.

Children — SP66

No. B234, Eskimo. No. B235, African. No. B236, Asian. No. B237, Dutch. No. B238, American Indian.

**1985, Oct. 16** **Litho.** ***Perf. 13x14***

**B234** SP66 5c + 5c multi .45 .25
**B235** SP66 10c + 5c multi .55 .30
**B236** SP66 25c + 10c multi .80 .45
**B237** SP66 45c + 20c multi 1.40 .80
**B238** SP66 55c + 25c multi 1.40 .95
*a.* Souv. sheet of 3, #B236-B238 4.00 2.25
*Nos. B234-B238 (5)* 4.60 2.75

Surtax for child welfare.

Sports — SP67

No. B239, Running. No. B240, Horse racing. No. B241, Car racing. No. B242, Soccer.

**1986, Feb. 19** **Litho.** ***Perf. 13x14***

**B239** SP67 15c + 5c multi 1.05 .45
**B240** SP67 25c + 10c multi 1.25 .65
**B241** SP67 45c + 20c multi 1.60 .85
**B242** SP67 55c + 25c multi 1.75 1.05
*Nos. B239-B242 (4)* 5.65 3.00

Surtax for the natl. Sports Federation.

Handicrafts — SP68

**1986, Apr. 29**

**B243** SP68 30c + 15c Painting 1.05 .60
**B244** SP68 45c + 20c Sculpting 1.25 .65
**B245** SP68 55c + 25c Ceramics 1.50 .90
*Nos. B243-B245 (3)* 3.80 2.15

Surtax for Curaçao Social & Cultural Care.

Sports — SP69

**1986, Oct. 15** **Litho.** ***Perf. 13x14***

**B246** SP69 20c + 10c Soccer .70 .40
**B247** SP69 25c + 15c Tennis .90 .45
**B248** SP69 45c + 20c Judo 1.05 .65
**B249** SP69 55c + 25c Baseball 1.25 .85
*a.* Min. sheet of 2, #B248-B249 2.60 1.60
*Nos. B246-B249 (4)* 3.90 2.35

Surtax for the natl. Sports Foundation.

Social and Cultural Programs — SP70

No. B250, Musicians. No. B251, Handicapped. No. B252, Pavilion.

**1987, Mar. 11** **Litho.**

**B250** SP70 35c + 15c multi .80 .55
**B251** SP70 45c + 25c multi 1.25 .65
**B252** SP70 85c + 40c multi 1.60 1.05
*Nos. B250-B252 (3)* 3.65 2.25

Surtax for the Jong Wacht (Youth Guard) and the natl. Red Cross.

Boy in Various Stages of Growth SP71

**1987, Oct. 21** **Litho.** ***Perf. 14x13***

**B253** SP71 40c +15c Infant 1.00 .65
**B254** SP71 55c +25c Toddler 1.25 .85
**B255** SP71 115c +50c Boy 1.60 1.15
*a.* Souv. sheet of 3, #B253-B255 4.25 2.75
*Nos. B253-B255 (3)* 3.85 2.65

Surtax benefited Child Care programs.

Queen Emma Bridge, Cent. — SP72

55c+25c, Bridge, vert. 115c+55c, View of Willemstad Harbor and quay. 190c+60c, Flags of the Netherlands, Antilles and US, Leonard B. Smith, engineer.

**1988, May 9** ***Perf. 13x14, 14x13***

**B256** SP72 55c +25c multi 1.15 .60
**B257** SP72 115c +55c multi 1.75 1.10
**B258** SP72 190c +60c multi 3.00 2.00
*Nos. B256-B258 (3)* 5.90 3.70

Surtax for social and cultural purposes.

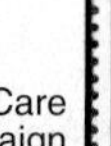

Youth Care Campaign SP73

No. B259, Girl, television. No. B260, Boy, portable stereo. No. B261, Girl, computer.

**1988, Oct. 26** **Litho.** ***Perf. 14x13***

**B259** SP73 55c +25c multi 1.05 .65
**B260** SP73 65c +30c multi 1.15 .80
**B261** SP73 115c +55c multi 1.60 1.15
*a.* Souv. sheet of 3, #B259-B261 5.25 2.75
*Nos. B259-B261 (3)* 3.80 2.60

Surtax for child welfare.

Curaçao Stamp Assoc., 50th Anniv. — SP75

Designs: 30c+10c, Type A25 and No. 461 under magnifying glass. 55c+20c, Simulated stamp (learning to use tongs). 80c+30c, Barn owl, album, magnifying glass, tongs.

**1989, Jan. 18** **Litho.** ***Perf. 13x14***

**B264** 30c +10c multi 1.25 .55
**B265** 55c +20c multi 1.25 .85
**B266** 80c +30c multi 1.25 .95
*a.* SP75 Strip of 3, #B264-B266 3.75 3.00

No. B266a has a continuous design. Surtaxed for welfare organizations.

Child and Nature SP76

No. B267, Girl, boy, tree. No. B268, Playing on beach. No. B269, Father and child.
No. B270, At the beach, diff.

**1989, Oct. 25** **Litho.** ***Perf. 14x13***

**B267** SP76 40c +15c multi 1.00 .60
**B268** SP76 65c +30c multi 1.15 .80
**B269** SP76 115c +55c multi 1.75 1.30
*Nos. B267-B269 (3)* 3.90 2.70

**Souvenir Sheet**

**B270** SP76 155c +75c multi 3.75 2.10

Surtax for child welfare.

Natl. Girl Scout Movement, 60th Anniv. — SP77

Totolika, 60th Anniv. — SP78

Natl. Boy Scout Movement, 60th Anniv. — SP79

**1990, Mar. 7** **Litho.** ***Perf. 13x14***

**B271** SP77 30c +10c multi .80 .55
**B272** SP78 40c +15c multi 1.05 .75
**B273** SP79 155c +65c multi 3.00 2.50
*Nos. B271-B273 (3)* 4.85 3.80

Parents' and Friends Association of Persons with a Mental Handicap (Totolika).
Surtax for social and cultural purposes.

SP80

**1990, June 13 Litho. *Perf. 13x14***

**B274** SP80 65c +30c multi 1.15 .75

Sport Unie Brion Trappers Soccer Club. Exists in tete-beche gutter pairs.

Anti-drug Campaign — SP81

**1990, June 13**

**B275** SP81 115c +55c multi 1.75 1.35

Exists in tete-beche gutter pairs.

Youth Care Campaign SP82

No. B276, Bees, flowers. No. B277, Dolphins. No. B278, Donkey, bicycle. No. B279, Goat, house. No. B280, Rabbit. No. B281, Lizard, moon.

**1990, Oct. 31 Litho. *Perf. 14x13***

**B276** SP82 30c +5c multi .70 .40
**B277** SP82 55c +10c multi 1.05 .60
**B278** SP82 65c +15c multi 1.15 .80
**B279** SP82 100c +20c multi 1.75 1.20
**B280** SP82 115c +25c multi 1.90 1.30
**B281** SP82 155c +55c multi 3.25 2.10
*Nos. B276-B281 (6)* 9.80 6.40

Surtax for child welfare.
See Nos. B285-B288.

Social and Cultural Care — SP83

Designs: 30c+10c, Youth philately. 65c+25c, St. Vincentius Brass Band, 50th anniv. 155c+55c, Curaçao Community Center Federation.

**1991, Apr. 3 Litho. *Perf. 14x13***

**B282** SP83 30c +10c multi .85 .60
**B283** SP83 65c +25c multi 1.35 1.00
**B284** SP83 155c +55c multi 3.00 2.25
*Nos. B282-B284 (3)* 5.20 3.85

**Youth Care Campaign Type of 1990**

Fight illiteracy: 40c+15c, Octopus holding numbers and letters. 65c+30c, Birds, blackboard. 155c+65c, Turtle telling time. No. B288a, Owl, flag. b, Books, bookworms. c, Seahorse.

**1991, Oct. 31 Litho. *Perf. 14x13***

**B285** SP82 40c +15c multi 1.15 .80
**B286** SP82 65c +30c multi 1.45 1.35
**B287** SP82 155c +65c multi 3.00 3.00
*Nos. B285-B287 (3)* 5.60 5.15

**Souvenir Sheet**

***Imperf***

**B288** Sheet of 3 6.25 5.00
*a.* SP82 55c +25c multi 2.00 1.60
*b.* SP82 100c +35c multi 2.00 1.60
*c.* SP82 115c +50c multi 2.00 1.60

Surtax for child welfare.

SP84

1992 Summer Olympics, Barcelona: a, 30c + 10c, Triangle and oval. b, 55c + 25c, Globe showing location of Netherland Antilles, flag. c, 115c + 55c, Emblem of Netherlands Antilles Olympic Committee.

**1992, Mar. 4 Litho. *Perf. 13x14***

**B289** SP84 Strip of 3, #a.-c. 4.50 3.75

Netherlands Antilles Olympic Committee, 60th Anniv.

SP85

No. B290, Spaceship. No. B291, Robot. No. B292, Extraterrestrial.
No. B293, Extraterrestrial, diff.

**1992, Oct. 28 Litho. *Perf. 13x14***

**B290** SP85 30c +10c multi .65 .50
**B291** SP85 70c +30c multi 1.15 1.15
**B292** SP85 100c +40c multi 1.75 1.60
*Nos. B290-B292 (3)* 3.55 3.25

**Souvenir Sheet**

**B293** SP85 155c +70c multi 3.50 3.25

Surtax for child welfare.

SP86

Designs: 65c+25c, Fire safety, child playing with blocks. 90c+35c, Child fastening auto safety belt, vert. 175c+75c, Child wearing flotation equipment while swimming. 35c+15c, Alert child studying.

***Perf. 14x13, 13x14***

**1993, Oct. 27 Litho.**

**B294** SP86 65c +25c multi 1.25 1.05
**B295** SP86 90c +35c multi 1.50 1.35
**B296** SP86 175c +75c multi 3.00 2.75
*Nos. B294-B296 (3)* 5.75 5.15

**Souvenir Sheet**

***Perf. 13½x13***

**B297** SP86 35c +15c Sheet of 5 + label 5.00 5.00

Surtax for child welfare.

Intl. Year of the Family — SP87

No. B298, Woman, baby. No. B299, Daughter, father. No. B300, Grandparents.
No. B301, Intl. emblem.

**1994, Oct. 26 Litho. *Perf. 13x14***

**B298** SP87 35c +15c multi .60 .55
**B299** SP87 65c +25c multi 1.10 1.05
**B300** SP87 90c +35c multi 2.00 1.75
*Nos. B298-B300 (3)* 3.70 3.35

**Souvenir Sheet**

**B301** SP87 175c +75c multi 3.75 3.75

Surtax for the benefit of the Antillean Youth Care Federation.

Slave Rebellion in Curaçao, Bicent. SP88

Designs: 30c+10c, Monument, bird with outstretched wings. 45c+15c, Bird, bell tower.

**1995, Aug. 17 Litho. *Perf. 14x13***

**B302** SP88 30c +10c multi .75 .65
**B303** SP88 45c +15c multi 1.15 1.00

Youth Philately SP89

Stamp drawings by children from: 65c+25c, Curaçao, Bonaire. 75c+35c, St. Maarten, St. Eustatius, Saba.

**1995, Aug. 17**

**B304** SP89 65c +25c multi 1.40 1.05
**B305** SP89 75c +35c multi 1.50 1.20

Nos. 516-517, 544 Surcharged in Red Brown

**1995, Sept. 22 Litho. *Perf. 14x13***

**B306** A148 65c +65c on #516 1.75 1.60
**B307** A148 75c +75c on #517 2.00 1.75
**B308** A148 1g +1g on #544 2.40 2.25
*Nos. B306-B308 (3)* 6.15 5.60

Surcharge for hurricane relief.

Child Welfare Stamps SP91

Promotion of Children's Good Deeds: 35c+15c, Helping elderly across street. 65c+25c, Reading newspaper to blind person. 90c+35c, Caring for younger sibling. 175c+75c, Giving flowers to sick person.

**1995, Oct. 25 Litho. *Perf. 14x13***

**B309** SP91 35c +15c multi .65 .60
**B310** SP91 65c +25c multi 1.15 1.05
**B311** SP91 90c +35c multi 1.45 1.35
**B312** SP91 175c +75c multi 3.00 2.75
*Nos. B309-B312 (4)* 6.25 5.75

Surtax for various youth organizations.

Child Welfare Stamps SP92

UNICEF, 50th anniv.: 40c+15c, Child wandering streets. 75c+25c, Child labor in Asia. 110c+45c, Child in wartime (former Yugoslavia), vert. 225c+100c, Caribbean poverty, vert.

***Perf. 14x13, 13x14***

**1996, Oct. 23 Litho.**

**B313** SP92 40c +15c multi .75 .65
**B314** SP92 75c +25c multi 1.30 1.20
**B315** SP92 110c +45c multi 1.90 1.75
**B316** SP92 225c +100c multi 4.00 3.75
*Nos. B313-B316 (4)* 7.95 7.35

Social and Cultural Care Stamps — SP93

Designs: 40c+15c, Curaçao Foundation for the cure and resettlement of ex-prisoners, 50th anniv. 75c+30c, ABVO (General Union of Public Servants), 60th anniv. 85+40c, 110c+50c, Red Cross Corps section, Curaçao, 65th anniv.

**1997, Jan. 16 Litho. *Perf. 13x14***

**B317** SP93 40c +15c multi .90 .65
**B318** SP93 75c +30c multi 1.30 1.20
**B319** SP93 85c +40c multi 1.60 1.60
**B320** SP93 110 +50c multi 1.90 1.75
*Nos. B317-B320 (4)* 5.70 5.20

Child Welfare Stamps SP94

Musical notes, musical instruments: 40c+15c, Drums. 75c+25c, Piano. 110c+45c, Flute. 225c+100c, Guitar.

**1997, Oct. 22 Litho. *Perf. 14x13***

**B321** SP94 40c +15c multi .80 .65
**B322** SP94 75c +25c multi 1.20 1.15
**B323** SP94 110c +45c multi 2.00 1.75
**B324** SP94 225c +100c multi 3.00 2.50
*Nos. B321-B324 (4)* 7.00 6.05

Social and Cultural Care — SP95

No. B325, Curacao Museum, 50th anniv. No. B326, Seawater Desalination, 70th anniv. 75c+25c, Water area, Lac Cai Bonaire, vert. 85c+40c, Water area, Klein-Bonaire, vert.

***Perf. 14x13, 13x14***

**1998, Mar. 9 Litho.**

**B325** SP95 40c +15c multi .85 .70
**B326** SP95 40c +15c multi .85 .70
**B327** SP95 75c +25c multi 1.45 1.30
**B328** SP95 85c +40c multi 1.90 1.75
*Nos. B325-B328 (4)* 5.05 4.45

Child Welfare Stamps — SP96

Universal Rights of the Child: 40c+15c, Child holding cutouts representing family. 75c+25c, Children eating watermelon. 110c+45c, Handicapped children drawing pictures. 225c+100c, Children holding cans with string to play telephone.

**1998, Oct. 28 Litho. *Perf. 13x14***

**B329** SP96 40c +15c multi .85 .70
**B330** SP96 75c +25c multi 1.30 1.20
**B331** SP96 110c +45c multi 2.00 1.90
**B332** SP96 225c +100c multi 4.25 4.00
*Nos. B329-B332 (4)* 8.40 7.80

Buildings — SP97

Willemstad buildings on World Heritage List: 40c+15c, Houses, Ijzerstraat neighborhood, horiz. 75c+30c, Postal Museum. 110c+50c, "Bridal Cake" building, Scharloo area, horiz.

***Perf. 14x13, 13x14***

**1999, Sept. 28** **Litho.**

| | | | |
|---|---|---|---|
| **B333** SP97 | 40c +15c multi | .80 | .70 |
| **B334** SP97 | 75c +30c multi | 1.45 | 1.30 |
| **B335** SP97 | 110c +50c multi | 2.10 | 1.90 |
| | *Nos. B333-B335 (3)* | 4.35 | 3.90 |

Sports — SP98

**1999, Oct. 27** ***Perf. 13x14***

| | | | |
|---|---|---|---|
| **B336** SP98 | 40c +15c Basketball | 1.30 | .80 |
| **B337** SP98 | 75c +25c Golf | 1.75 | 1.30 |
| **B338** SP98 | 110c +45c Fencing | 2.60 | 1.90 |
| **B339** SP98 | 225c +100c Tennis | 4.75 | 4.00 |
| | *Nos. B336-B339 (4)* | 10.40 | 8.00 |

Social and Cultural Care — SP99

Designs: 75c+30c, Children playing. 110c+50c, Chemistry lesson. 225c+100c, Arithmetic lesson, vert.

***Perf. 14x13, 13x14***

**2000, Apr. 28** **Litho.**

**B340-B342** SP99 Set of 3 8.25 7.00

Youth Care SP100

Designs: 40c+15c, Child reaching up, vert. 75c+25c, Children learning with computers. 110c+45c, Children playing with toy boat. 225c+100c, Children and map, vert.

***Perf. 13x14, 14x13***

**2000, Oct. 25** **Litho.**

**B343-B346** SP100 Set of 4 9.50 8.75

Caribbean Postal Union, 5th Anniv. — SP101

Designs: 75c+25c, Pen, emblem. 110c+45c, Emblem. 225c+100c, Globe, emblem.

**2001, May 21 Litho.** ***Perf. 13¼x13¾***

**B347-B349** SP101 Set of 3 10.00 8.25

Youth Care SP102

Designs: 40c+15c, Boy feeding baby. 75c+25c, Girls dancing, vert. 110c+45c, Boy pushing woman in wheelchair, vert.

***Perf. 13½x12¾, 12¾x13½***

**2001, Oct. 24** **Litho.**

**B350-B352** SP102 Set of 3 6.25 5.75

2002 World Cup Soccer Championships, Japan and Korea — SP103

Soccer player with: 95c+35c, Ball of flags. 145c+55c, Ball with map. 240c+110c, Ball.

**2002, June 25 Litho.** ***Perf. 12¾x14***

**B353-B355** SP103 Set of 3 11.00 10.00

Youth Care SP104

"Dialogue among civilizations:" 50c+15c, Lion and fish. 95c+35c, Kangaroo and iguana. 145c+55c, Goat and penguin. 240c+110c, Lizard and toucan.

**2002, Oct. 24** ***Perf. 14x12¾***

**B356-B359** SP104 Set of 4 11.25 11.25

Miniature Sheet

Maps of the Netherlands Antilles — SP105

No. B360: a, 25c+10c, Portion of 1688 map by Hendrick Doncker showing Curaçao and Bonaire. b, 30c+15c, Portion of Doncker map showing St. Maarten, Saba and St. Eustatius, vert. c, 55c+25c, Modern map of Curaçao and Bonaire. d, 85c+35c, Modern map of St. Maarten, Saba and St. Eustatius, vert. e, 95c+40c, Modern map of Caribbean Islands.

***Perf. 14x12¾, 12¾x14 (vert. stamps)***

**2003, Mar. 19** **Litho.**

**B360** SP105 Sheet of 5, #a-e 7.50 7.00

Miniature Sheet

Youth Care — SP106

No. B361: a, 50c+15c, Boy taking shower. b, 95c+35c, Girl with umbrella. c, 145c+55c, Boy with watering can. d, 240c+110c, Hands in water from open faucet.

**2003, Oct. 22 Litho.** ***Perf. 13x14***

**B361** SP106 Sheet of 4, #a-d 9.50 8.50

Intl. Year of Fresh Water.

Youth Care SP107

No. B362: a, Boy, girl, slave huts. b, Girl, Autonomy Monument. c, Boy, girl, broken stone walls built by slaves. d, Boy, girl, wall of plantation house. e, Boy, preamble of Netherlands Constitution.

**2004, Oct. 20** ***Perf. 13½x13***

| | | | |
|---|---|---|---|
| **B362** | Horiz. strip of 5 | 8.25 | 8.25 |
| ***a.*** | SP107 50c +15c multi | .75 | .75 |
| ***b.-c.*** | SP107 95c +35c either single | 1.50 | 1.50 |
| ***d.-e.*** | SP107 145c +55c either single | 2.25 | 2.25 |

Autonomy of the Netherlands Antilles, 50th anniv. (Nos. B362b, B362e), Intl. Year Commemorating the Struggle Against Slavery and its Abolition (Nos. B362a, B362c, B362d).

Intl. Year of Sports and Physical Education — SP108

Designs: 55c+20c, Soccer. 97c+36c, Table tennis. 148c+56c, Tennis. 240c+110c, Baseball.

**2005, Dec. 24 Litho.** ***Perf. 13x13½***

**B363-B366** SP108 Set of 4 9.50 9.50

Youth Care — SP109

Hatted globes showing: 55c+20c, North and South America. 100c+45c, Africa. 149c+61c, Europe, Africa and Asia. 285c+125c, Africa and Asia.

**2006, Oct. 23 Litho.** ***Perf. 12¾x13¼***

**B367-B370** SP109 Set of 4 8.25 8.25

Youth Care SP110

Family: 59c+26c, Praying at dinner table. 104c+46c, Respecting flag. 155c+65c, As baseball team. 285c+125c, Studying together.

**2007, Oct. 24 Litho.** ***Perf. 13¼x12¾***

**B371-B374** SP110 Set of 4 8.25 8.25

Youth Care — SP111

Potato: 59c+26c, As potato farmer. 1.06g+46c, Peeling potatoes. 1.58g+65c, Eating French fries. 2.85g+1.25g, Family.

**2008, Oct. 23 Litho.** ***Perf. 12¾x13¼***

**B375-B378** SP111 Set of 4 9.00 9.00

Intl. Year of the Potato.

Youth Care — SP112

Designs: 59c+26c, Galileo Galilei and silhouette of boy. 110c+45c, Silhouettes of stargazers and telescope. 168c+75c, Silhouettes of children watching space shuttle. 285c+125c, Men walking on Moon.

**2009, Oct. 26 Litho.** ***Perf. 12¾x13¼***

**B379-B382** SP112 Set of 4 8.50 8.50

Intl. Year of Astronomy.

## AIR POST STAMPS

Regular Issues of 1915-22 Surcharged in Black

***Perf. 12½***

**1929, July 6** **Typo.** **Unwmk.**

| | | | |
|---|---|---|---|
| **C1** A13 | 50c on 12½c red | 18.00 | 21.00 |
| **C2** A13 | 1g on 20c blue | 18.00 | 21.00 |
| **C3** A13 | 2g on 15c ol grn | 45.00 | 52.50 |
| | *Nos. C1-C3 (3)* | 81.00 | 94.50 |

Excellent forgeries exist.

Allegory, "Flight" — AP1

**1931-39** **Engr.**

| | | | |
|---|---|---|---|
| **C4** AP1 | 10c Prus grn ('34) | .25 | .25 |
| **C5** AP1 | 15c dull blue ('38) | .40 | .25 |
| **C6** AP1 | 20c red | 1.00 | .25 |
| **C7** AP1 | 25c gray ('38) | .80 | .90 |
| **C8** AP1 | 30c yellow ('39) | .40 | .40 |
| **C9** AP1 | 35c dull blue | 1.20 | 1.15 |
| **C10** AP1 | 40c green | .80 | .55 |
| **C11** AP1 | 45c orange | 2.00 | 2.00 |
| **C12** AP1 | 50c lake ('38) | 1.20 | .60 |
| **C13** AP1 | 60c brown vio | .80 | .40 |
| **C14** AP1 | 70c black | 6.50 | 2.00 |
| **C15** AP1 | 1.40g brown | 4.00 | 5.00 |
| **C16** AP1 | 2.80g bister | 5.00 | 5.25 |
| | *Nos. C4-C16 (13)* | 24.35 | 19.00 |

No. C6 Surcharged in Black

**1934, Aug. 25**

**C17** AP1 10c on 20c red 20.00 15.00

**Catalogue values for unused stamps in this section, from this point to the end of the section, are for Never Hinged items.**

Map of the Atlantic AP2

Plane over Islands AP3

Map of Curaçao, Aruba and Bonaire AP4

Planes — AP5

Plane — AP6

**1942, Oct. 20** ***Perf. 13x13½***

**C18** AP2 10c grn & bl .80 .25
**C19** AP3 15c rose car & yel grn .80 .25
**C20** AP4 20c red brn & grn .80 .25
**C21** AP5 25c dp ultra & org brn .80 .25
**C22** AP6 30c red & lt vio .80 .75
**C23** AP2 35c dk vio & ol grn 1.20 .55
**C24** AP3 40c gray ol & chnt 1.60 .55
**C25** AP4 45c dk red & blk .80 .25
**C26** AP5 50c vio & blk 2.00 .25
**C27** AP6 60c lt yel brn & dl bl 3.25 1.15
**C28** AP2 70c red brn & Prus bl 3.25 1.15
**C29** AP3 1.40g bl vio & sl grn 20.00 2.10
**C30** AP4 2.80g int bl & lt bl 28.00 5.75
**C31** AP5 5g rose lake & sl grn 45.00 19.00
**C32** AP6 10g grn & red brn 52.50 28.00
*Nos. C18-C32 (15)* 161.60 60.50

For surcharges see Nos. CB9-CB12.

Plane and Post Horn — AP7

DC-4 above Waves — AP8

**1947** **Photo.** ***Perf. 12½x12***

**C32A** AP7 6c gray blk .65 .25
**C33** AP7 10c deep red .65 .25
**C33A** AP7 12½c plum .90 .25
**C34** AP7 15c deep blue .90 .30
**C35** AP7 20c dl yel grn 1.10 .35
**C36** AP7 25c org yel 1.10 .25
**C37** AP7 30c lilac gray 1.35 .55
**C38** AP7 35c org red 1.35 .70
**C39** AP7 40c blue grn 1.35 .70
**C40** AP7 45c brt violet 1.60 1.05
**C41** AP7 50c carmine 1.60 .25
**C42** AP7 60c brt blue 2.10 .65
**C43** AP7 70c brown 3.75 1.50

**Engr.**

***Perf. 12x12½***

**C44** AP8 1.50g black 2.75 .90
**C45** AP8 2.50g dk car 15.50 4.00
**C46** AP8 5g green 32.00 8.25
**C47** AP8 7.50g dk blue 130.00 95.00
**C48** AP8 10g dk red vio 82.50 34.00
**C49** AP8 15g red org 110.00 95.00
**C50** AP8 25g chocolate 110.00 95.00
*Nos. C32A-C50 (20)* 501.15 339.20

## AIR POST SEMI-POSTAL STAMPS

Flags of the Netherlands and the House of Orange with Inscription "Netherlands Shall Rise Again" — SPAP1

**Engr. & Photo.**

**1941, Dec. 11** **Unwmk.** ***Perf. 12***

**CB1** SPAP1 10c + 10c multi 32.00 26.00
**CB2** SPAP1 15c + 25c multi 32.00 26.00
**CB3** SPAP1 20c + 25c multi 32.00 26.00
**CB4** SPAP1 25c + 25c multi 32.00 26.00
**CB5** SPAP1 30c + 50c multi 32.00 26.00
**CB6** SPAP1 35c + 50c multi 32.00 26.00
**CB7** SPAP1 40c + 50c multi 32.00 26.00
**CB8** SPAP1 50c +100c multi 32.00 26.00
*Nos. CB1-CB8 (8)* 256.00 208.00

The surtax was used by the Prince Bernhard Committee to purchase war material for the Netherlands' fighting forces in Great Britain.

**Catalogue values for unused stamps in this section, from this point to the end of the section, are for Never Hinged items.**

Nos. C29-C32 Surcharged in Black

**1943, Dec. 1** ***Perf. 13x13½***

**CB9** AP3 40c + 50c on 1.40g 9.00 8.25
**CB10** AP4 45c + 50c on 2.80g 9.00 8.25
**CB11** AP5 50c + 75c on 5g 9.00 8.25
**CB12** AP6 60c + 100c on 10g 9.00 8.25
*Nos. CB9-CB12 (4)* 36.00 33.00

The surtax was for the benefit of prisoners of war. These stamps were not sold to the public in the normal manner. All were sold in sets by advance subscription, the majority to philatelic speculators.

On No. CB9 overprint reads: "Voor / Krijgsgevangenen."

Princess Juliana — SPAP2

**Engr. & Photo.**

**1944, Aug. 16** ***Perf. 12***

**Frame in carmine & deep blue, cross in carmine**

**CB13** SPAP2 10c + 10c lt brn 2.75 2.50
**CB14** SPAP2 15c + 25c turq grn 2.75 2.50
**CB15** SPAP2 20c + 25c dk ol gray 2.75 2.50
**CB16** SPAP2 25c + 25c slate 2.75 2.50
**CB17** SPAP2 30c + 50c sepia 2.75 2.50
**CB18** SPAP2 35c + 50c chnt 2.75 2.50
**CB19** SPAP2 40c + 50c grn 2.75 2.50
**CB20** SPAP2 50c + 100c dk vio 2.75 2.50
*Nos. CB13-CB20 (8)* 22.00 20.00

The surtax was for the Red Cross.

Map of Netherlands Indies — SPAP3

Map of Netherlands — SPAP4

**Photo. & Typo.**

**1946, July 1** ***Perf. 11x11½***

**CB21** SPAP3 10c + 10c 1.75 1.60
**CB22** SPAP3 15c + 25c 1.75 1.60
**CB23** SPAP3 20c + 25c 1.75 1.60
**CB24** SPAP3 25c + 25c 1.75 1.60
**CB25** SPAP3 30c + 50c 1.75 1.60
*a.* Double impression of denomination 400.00 475.00
**CB26** SPAP3 35c + 50c 1.75 1.60
**CB27** SPAP3 40c + 75c 1.75 1.60
**CB28** SPAP3 50c + 100c 1.75 1.60
**CB29** SPAP4 10c + 10c 1.75 1.60
**CB30** SPAP4 15c + 25c 1.75 1.60
**CB31** SPAP4 20c + 25c 1.75 1.60
**CB32** SPAP4 25c + 25c 1.75 1.60
**CB33** SPAP4 30c + 50c 1.75 1.60
**CB34** SPAP4 35c + 50c 1.75 1.60
**CB35** SPAP4 40c + 75c 1.75 1.60
**CB36** SPAP4 50c + 100c 1.75 1.60
*Nos. CB21-CB36 (16)* 28.00 25.60

The surtax on Nos. CB21 to CB36 was for the National Relief Fund.

## POSTAGE DUE STAMPS

D1

Type I — 34 loops. "T" of *"BETALEN"* over center of loop, top branch of "E" of *"TE"* shorter than lower branch.

Type II — 33 loops. "T" of *"BETALEN"* over center of two loops.

Type III — 32 loops. "T" of *"BETALEN"* slightly to the left of loop, top of first "E" of *"BETALEN"* shorter than lower branch.

**Value in Black**

**1889** **Unwmk.** **Typo.** ***Perf. 12½***

**Type III**

**J1** D1 2½c green 3.00 4.50
**J2** D1 5c green 3.00 2.60
**J3** D1 10c green 35.00 34.00
**J4** D1 12½c green 400.00 210.00
**J5** D1 15c green 28.00 22.50
**J6** D1 20c green 16.00 11.50
**J7** D1 25c green 200.00 150.00
**J8** D1 30c green 14.00 11.50
**J9** D1 40c green 18.00 11.50
**J10** D1 50c green 40.00 30.00

Nos. J1-J10 were issued without gum.

**Type I**

*J1a* D1 2½c 5.00 4.50
*J2a* D1 5c 40.00 30.00
*J3a* D1 10c 45.00 35.00
*J4a* D1 12½c 450.00 225.00
*J5a* D1 15c 32.00 22.50
*J6a* D1 20c 80.00 57.50
*J7a* D1 25c 600.00 350.00
*J8a* D1 30c 80.00 67.50
*J9a* D1 40c 80.00 67.50
*J10a* D1 50c 50.00 37.50

**Type II**

*J1b* D1 2½c 8.00 5.75
*J2b* D1 5c 200.00 170.00
*J3b* D1 10c 45.00 42.50
*J4b* D1 12½c 475.00 260.00
*J5b* D1 15c 32.00 26.00
*J6b* D1 20c 450.00 425.00
*J7b* D1 25c *1,600.* *1,600.*
*J8b* D1 30c 450.00 375.00
*J9b* D1 40c 450.00 375.00
*10b* D1 50c 60.00 75.00

D2

**1892-98** **Value in Black** ***Perf. 12½***

**J11** D2 2½c green (III) .80 1.15
**J12** D2 5c green (III) 1.20 1.60
**J13** D2 10c green (III) 2.00 1.90
**J14** D2 12½c green (III) 2.00 1.90
**J15** D2 15c green (III) ('95) 3.00 1.90
**J17** D2 25c green (III) 12.00 1.15
*Nos. J11-J17 (6)* 21.00 9.60

**Type I**

*J11a* D2 2½c .80 1.15
*J12a* D2 5c 3.00 2.60
*J13a* D2 10c 3.00 2.25
*J14a* D2 12½c 2.40 1.90
**J16** D2 20c green ('95) 4.00 1.90
*J17a* D2 25c 12.00 1.90
**J18** D2 30c green ('95) 40.00 34.00
**J19** D2 40c green ('95) 50.00 34.00
**J20** D2 50c green ('95) 50.00 34.00

**Type II**

*J11b* D2 2½c 20.00 20.00
*J12b* D2 5c 1.20 1.60
*J13b* D2 10c 2.00 1.90
*J14b* D2 12½c 8.00 7.50
*J17b* D2 25c *10.00* *9.50*
*Nos. J11b-J17b (5)* 41.20 40.50

The editors would like to see documented evidence of existence the following: 15c type I; 15c, 20c, 30c, 40c, 50c type II; 20c type III.

Nos. J18-J20 are printed on porous paper.

**Type I**

**On Yellowish or White Paper**

**Value in Color of Stamp**

**1915** ***Perf. 12½, 13½x12½***

**J21** D2 2½c green .65 .75
**J22** D2 5c green .65 .75
**J23** D2 10c green .65 .75
**J24** D2 12½c green .80 1.15
**J25** D2 15c green 1.45 1.60
**J26** D2 20c green .80 1.60
**J27** D2 25c green .25 .40
**J28** D2 30c green 3.00 3.75
**J29** D2 40c green 3.00 3.75
**J30** D2 50c green 2.00 3.00
*Nos. J21-J30 (10)* 13.25 17.50

**1944** ***Perf. 11½***

*J23a* D2 10c yellow green 40.00 37.50
*J24a* D2 12½c yellow green 40.00 30.00
*J27a* D2 25c yellow green 100.00 3.75
*Nos. J23a-J27a (3)* 180.00 71.25

Nos. J23a-J27a designs are 18x22½mm; Nos. J21-J30 designs are 18x21½mm.

**Type of 1915**

**Type I**

**Value in Color of Stamp**

***Perf. 13½x13***

**1948-49** **Unwmk.** **Photo.**

**J31** D2 2½c bl grn ('48) 2.40 3.00
**J32** D2 5c bl grn ('48) 2.40 3.00
**J33** D2 10c blue green 10.00 10.50
**J34** D2 12½c blue green 10.00 5.25
**J35** D2 15c blue green 17.00 34.00
**J36** D2 20c blue green 17.00 34.00
**J37** D2 25c blue green 2.60 .75
**J38** D2 30c blue green 17.00 34.00
**J39** D2 40c blue green 17.00 34.00
**J40** D2 50c blue green 17.00 34.00
*Nos. J31-J40 (10)* 112.40 192.50

**Catalogue values for unused stamps in this section, from this point to the end of the section, are for Never Hinged items.**

D3

**1953-59** **Photo.**

| No. | Type | Value | Color | Unused | Used |
|---|---|---|---|---|---|
| J41 | D3 | 1c | dk blue grn ('59) | .25 | .40 |
| J42 | D3 | 2½c | dk blue grn | .60 | .75 |
| J43 | D3 | 5c | dk blue grn | .25 | .40 |
| J44 | D3 | 6c | dk blue grn ('59) | .75 | .90 |
| J45 | D3 | 7c | dk blue grn ('59) | .75 | .90 |
| J46 | D3 | 8c | dk blue grn ('59) | .75 | .90 |
| J47 | D3 | 9c | dk blue grn ('59) | .75 | .90 |
| J48 | D3 | 10c | dk blue grn | .30 | .40 |
| J49 | D3 | 12½c | dk blue grn | .30 | .40 |
| J50 | D3 | 15c | dk blue grn | .75 | .90 |
| J51 | D3 | 20c | dk blue grn | .75 | .90 |
| J52 | D3 | 25c | dk blue grn | .60 | .25 |
| J53 | D3 | 30c | dk blue grn | 1.60 | 1.90 |
| J54 | D3 | 35c | dk blue grn ('59) | 1.60 | 1.90 |
| J55 | D3 | 40c | dk blue grn | 1.60 | 1.90 |
| J56 | D3 | 45c | dk blue grn ('59) | 1.60 | 1.90 |
| J57 | D3 | 50c | dk blue grn | 1.60 | 1.90 |
| | | | *Nos. J41-J57 (17)* | 14.80 | 17.50 |

## NETHERLANDS INDIES

'ne-th̲ər-lən,d,z 'in-dēs

### (Dutch Indies, Indonesia)

LOCATION — East Indies
GOVT. — Dutch colony
AREA — 735,268 sq. mi.
POP. — 76,000,000 (estimated 1949)
CAPITAL — Jakarta (formerly Batavia)

Netherlands Indies consisted of the islands of Sumatra, Java, the Lesser Sundas, Madura, two thirds of Borneo, Celebes, the Moluccas, western New Guinea and many small islands.

Netherlands Indies changed its name to Indonesia in 1948. The Netherlands transferred sovereignty on Dec. 28, 1949, to the Republic of the United States of Indonesia (see "Indonesia"), except for the western part of New Guinea (see "Netherlands New Guinea"). The Republic of Indonesia was proclaimed Aug. 15, 1950.

100 Cents = 1 Gulden
100 Sen = 1 Rupiah (1949)

**Catalogue values for unused stamps in this country are for Never Hinged items, beginning with Scott 250 in the regular postage section, Scott B57 in the semi-postal section, and Scott J43 in the postage due section.**

Values for unused stamps are for examples with original gum as defined in the catalogue introduction. Very fine examples of No. 2 will have perforations touching the frameline on one or more sides due to the narrow spacing of the stamps on the plates. Stamps with perfs clear of the framelines on all four sides are scarce and will command higher prices.

**Watermarks**

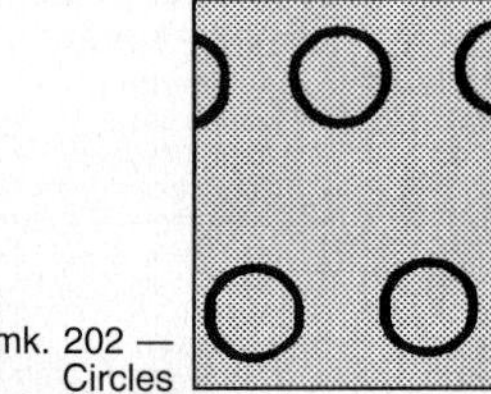

Wmk. 202 — Circles

Wmk. 228 — Small Crown and C of A Multiple

King William III — A1

**Unwmk.**

**1864, Apr. 1** **Engr.** ***Imperf.***

| No. | Type | Value | Color | Unused | Used |
|---|---|---|---|---|---|
| 1 | A1 | 10c | lake | 325.00 | 100.00 |

**1868** ***Perf. 12½x12***

| No. | Type | Value | Color | Unused | Used |
|---|---|---|---|---|---|
| 2 | A1 | 10c | lake | 1,250. | 180.00 |

Privately perforated examples of No. 1 sometimes are mistaken for No. 2.

King William III — A2

ONE CENT:
Type I — "CENT" 6mm long.
Type II — "CENT" 7½mm long.

***Perf. 11½x12, 12½, 12½x12, 13x14, 13½, 14, 13½x14***

**1870-88** **Typo.**

| No. | Type | Value | Color | Unused | Used |
|---|---|---|---|---|---|
| 3 | A2 | 1c | sl grn, type I | 20.00 | 8.00 |
| *a.* | | | Perf. 13x14, small holes | 16.00 | 6.50 |
| 4 | A2 | 1c | sl grn, type II | 9.75 | 2.40 |
| 5 | A2 | 2c | red brown | 13.00 | 5.00 |
| *a.* | | | 2c fawn | 13.00 | 5.00 |
| 6 | A2 | 2c | violet brn | 100.00 | 120.00 |
| 7 | A2 | 2½c | orange | 65.00 | 30.00 |
| 8 | A2 | 5c | pale green | 97.50 | 6.50 |
| *a.* | | | Perf. 14, small holes | 90.00 | 11.00 |
| *b.* | | | Perf. 13x14, small holes | 115.00 | 8.00 |
| 9 | A2 | 10c | orange brn | 40.00 | .40 |
| *a.* | | | Perf. 14, small holes | 35.00 | .80 |
| *b.* | | | Perf. 13x14, small holes | 57.50 | 3.25 |
| 10 | A2 | 12½c | gray | 9.75 | 3.25 |
| *a.* | | | Perf. 12½x12 | | 1,900. |
| 11 | A2 | 15c | bister | 40.00 | 3.00 |
| *a.* | | | Perf. 13x14, small holes | 57.50 | 4.00 |
| 12 | A2 | 20c | ultra | 145.00 | 3.75 |
| *a.* | | | Perf. 14, small holes | 120.00 | 4.50 |
| *b.* | | | Perf. 13x14, small holes | 160.00 | 5.75 |
| 13 | A2 | 25c | dk violet | 50.00 | 1.60 |
| *b.* | | | Perf. 13x14, small holes | 57.50 | 4.75 |
| *c.* | | | Perf. 14, large holes | 800.00 | 220.00 |
| 14 | A2 | 30c | green | 65.00 | 5.00 |
| 15 | A2 | 50c | carmine | 40.00 | 1.50 |
| *a.* | | | Perf. 14, small holes | 34.00 | 4.00 |
| *b.* | | | Perf. 13x14, small holes | 50.00 | 3.25 |
| *c.* | | | Perf. 14, large holes | 42.50 | 4.00 |
| 16 | A2 | 2.50g | green & vio | 110.00 | 26.00 |
| *b.* | | | Perf. 14, small holes | 100.00 | 28.00 |
| *c.* | | | Perf. 14, large holes | 100.00 | 28.00 |
| | | | *Nos. 3-16 (14)* | 805.00 | 216.40 |

Imperforate examples of Nos. 3-16 are proofs. The 1c red brown and 2c yellow are believed to be bogus.

"Small hole" varieties have the spaces between the holes wider than the diameter of the holes.

Numeral of Value — A3

**1883-90** ***Perf. 12½ Large Holes***

| No. | Type | Value | Color | Unused | Used |
|---|---|---|---|---|---|
| 17 | A3 | 1c | slate grn ('88) | 1.20 | .25 |
| *a.* | | | Perf. 12½x12 | 3.00 | 1.60 |
| 18 | A3 | 2c | brown ('84) | 1.20 | .25 |
| *a.* | | | Perf. 12½x12 | 3.00 | .80 |
| *b.* | | | Perf. 11½x12 | 80.00 | 50.00 |
| 19 | A3 | 2½c | yellow | 1.20 | .80 |
| *a.* | | | Perf. 12½x12 | 3.00 | 1.60 |
| *b.* | | | Perf. 11½x12 | 24.00 | 24.00 |
| 20 | A3 | 3c | lilac ('90) | 2.00 | .25 |
| 21 | A3 | 5c | green ('87) | 14.50 | .40 |
| *a.* | | | Perf. 12½, small holes | 60.00 | 26.00 |
| 22 | A3 | 5c | ultra ('90) | 14.50 | .25 |
| | | | *Nos. 17-22 (6)* | 34.60 | 2.20 |

For surcharges and overprint see Nos. 46-47, O4.

Queen Wilhelmina — A4

**1892-97** ***Perf. 12½***

| No. | Type | Value | Color | Unused | Used |
|---|---|---|---|---|---|
| 23 | A4 | 10c | orange brn ('95) | 8.00 | .40 |
| 24 | A4 | 12½c | gray ('97) | 12.00 | *32.50* |
| 25 | A4 | 15c | bister ('95) | 20.00 | 2.40 |
| 26 | A4 | 20c | ultra ('93) | 60.00 | 1.60 |
| 27 | A4 | 25c | violet | 35.00 | 2.00 |
| 28 | A4 | 30c | green ('94) | 50.00 | 3.75 |
| 29 | A4 | 50c | carmine ('93) | 40.00 | 2.00 |
| 30 | A4 | 2.50g | org brn & ultra | 140.00 | 45.00 |
| | | | *Nos. 23-30 (8)* | 365.00 | 89.65 |

For overprints see Nos. O21-O27.

Netherlands Nos. 67-69, 74, 77, 80 Surcharged in Black

**1900, July 1**

| No. | Type | Value | Color | Unused | Used |
|---|---|---|---|---|---|
| 31 | A11 | 10c | on 10c gray lil | 5.00 | .25 |
| 32 | A11 | 12½c | on 12½c blue | 5.00 | .60 |
| 33 | A11 | 15c | on 15c yel brn | 5.00 | .60 |
| 34 | A11 | 20c | on 20c yel grn | 22.00 | .60 |
| 35 | A11 | 25c | on 25c car & bl | 16.00 | .60 |
| 36 | A11 | 50c | on 50c brnz grn & red brn | 35.00 | 1.20 |

Netherlands No. 84 Surcharged in Black

**1902** ***Perf. 11½x11***

| No. | Type | Value | Color | Unused | Used |
|---|---|---|---|---|---|
| 37 | A12 | 2.50g | on 2½g brn lil | 70.00 | 20.00 |
| *a.* | | | Perf. 11 | 72.50 | 24.00 |
| | | | *Nos. 31-37 (7)* | 158.00 | 23.85 |

A6

**1902-09** ***Perf. 12½***

| No. | Type | Value | Color | Unused | Used |
|---|---|---|---|---|---|
| 38 | A6 | ½c | violet | .80 | .25 |
| 39 | A6 | 1c | olive grn | .80 | .25 |
| *a.* | | | Booklet pane of 6 | | |
| *b.* | | | Complete booklet, 4 #39a | *24.00* | |
| 40 | A6 | 2c | yellow brn | 4.00 | .25 |
| 41 | A6 | 2½c | green | 2.40 | .25 |
| *a.* | | | Booklet pane of 6 | | |
| 42 | A6 | 3c | orange | 4.00 | 1.20 |
| 43 | A6 | 4c | ultra ('09) | 14.00 | 8.50 |
| 44 | A6 | 5c | rose red | 6.00 | .25 |
| *a.* | | | Booklet pane of 6 | | |
| 45 | A6 | 7½c | gray ('08) | 4.00 | .40 |
| | | | *Nos. 38-45 (8)* | 36.00 | 11.35 |

For overprints see Nos. 63-69, 81-87, O1-O9.

**Nos. 18, 20 Surcharged**

**1902**

| No. | Type | Value | Color | Unused | Used |
|---|---|---|---|---|---|
| 46 | A3 | ½c | on 2c yel brn | .25 | .25 |
| *a.* | | | Double surcharge | 160.00 | 160.00 |
| 47 | A3 | 2½c | on 3c violet | .25 | .25 |
| *a.* | | | Double surcharge | *1,800.* | |

Queen Wilhelmina — A9

**1903-08**

| No. | Type | Value | Color | Unused | Used |
|---|---|---|---|---|---|
| 48 | A9 | 10c | slate | 5.00 | .25 |
| *a.* | | | Booklet pane of 6 | | |
| *b.* | | | Complete booklet, 4 #48a | *2,000.* | |
| 49 | A9 | 12½c | deep blue ('06) | 2.40 | .25 |
| *a.* | | | Booklet pane of 6 | | |
| *b.* | | | Complete booklet, #39a, #41a, #44a, #49a; 2 #48a | *2,000.* | |
| 50 | A9 | 15c | chocolate ('06) | 10.00 | 2.00 |
| *a.* | | | Ovptd. with 2 horiz. bars | 2.00 | .80 |
| 51 | A9 | 17½c | bister ('08) | 4.00 | .25 |
| 52 | A9 | 20c | grnsh slate | 2.40 | 1.60 |
| 53 | A9 | 20c | olive grn ('05) | 32.00 | .80 |
| 54 | A9 | 22½c | brn & ol grn ('08) | 4.00 | .30 |
| 55 | A9 | 25c | violet ('04) | 16.00 | .30 |
| 56 | A9 | 30c | orange brn | 34.00 | .40 |
| 57 | A9 | 50c | red brown ('04) | 32.00 | .40 |
| | | | *Nos. 48-57 (10)* | 141.80 | 6.55 |

For overprints and surcharges see Nos. 58, 70-78, 88-96, 139, O10-O18.

**No. 52 Surcharged in Black**

Type I

Type II

Two Types of "10":
Type I — Skinny 1 with almost straight flag.
Type II — Fat 1 with rising flag.

**1905, July 6**

| No. | Type | Value | Color | Unused | Used |
|---|---|---|---|---|---|
| 58 | A9 | 10c | on 20c grnsh slate | 3.00 | 1.20 |
| *a.* | | | Type II | 4.75 | 4.75 |

Queen Wilhelmina — A10

**1905-12** **Engr.** ***Perf. 11x11½***

| No. | Type | Value | Color | Unused | Used |
|---|---|---|---|---|---|
| 59 | A10 | 1g | dull lilac ('06) | 65.00 | .40 |
| *a.* | | | Perf. 11½x11 | 65.00 | .75 |
| *b.* | | | Perf. 11 | 80.00 | 6.00 |
| 60 | A10 | 1g | dl lil, *bl* ('12) | 60.00 | 8.00 |
| *a.* | | | Perf. 11 | 72.50 | *57.50* |
| 61 | A10 | 2½g | slate bl ('05) | 77.50 | 2.00 |
| *a.* | | | Perf. 11½ | 77.50 | 2.00 |
| *b.* | | | Perf. 11½x11 | 80.00 | 2.00 |
| *c.* | | | Perf. 11 | 900.00 | |
| 62 | A10 | 2½g | sl bl, *bl* ('12) | 120.00 | 40.00 |
| *a.* | | | Perf. 11 | 130.00 | 92.50 |
| | | | *Nos. 59-62 (4)* | 322.50 | 50.40 |

Sheets of Nos. 60 & 62 were soaked in an indigo solution.

For overprints and surcharge see Nos. 79-80, 97-98, 140, O19-O20.

Previous Issues Overprinted

**1908, July 1**

| No. | Type | Value | Color | Unused | Used |
|---|---|---|---|---|---|
| 63 | A6 | ½c | violet | .60 | .30 |
| 64 | A6 | 1c | olive grn | .60 | .30 |
| 65 | A6 | 2c | yellow brn | 2.00 | 3.00 |
| 66 | A6 | 2½c | green | 1.20 | .30 |
| 67 | A6 | 3c | orange | 1.20 | 1.20 |
| 68 | A6 | 5c | rose red | 3.25 | .40 |
| 69 | A6 | 7½c | gray | 3.00 | 3.00 |
| 70 | A9 | 10c | slate | 1.20 | .25 |
| 71 | A9 | 12½c | dp blue | 10.00 | 2.40 |
| 72 | A9 | 15c | choc (#50a) | 5.00 | 4.00 |
| 73 | A9 | 17½c | bister | 2.25 | 2.00 |
| 74 | A9 | 20c | olive grn | 10.00 | 2.40 |
| 75 | A9 | 22½c | brn & ol grn | 8.00 | 7.00 |
| 76 | A9 | 25c | violet | 8.00 | .40 |
| 77 | A9 | 30c | orange brn | 16.00 | 2.25 |
| 78 | A9 | 50c | red brown | 8.00 | .80 |
| 79 | A10 | 1g | dull lilac (#59) | 60.00 | 6.00 |
| *b.* | | | Perf. 11½x11 | 60.00 | 6.00 |
| *c.* | | | Perf. 11 | 80.00 | 8.00 |
| 80 | A10 | 2½g | slate blue (#61b) | 100.00 | 65.00 |
| | | | *Nos. 63-80 (18)* | 240.30 | 101.00 |

The above stamps were overprinted for use in the territory outside of Java and Madura, stamps overprinted "Java" being used in these latter places.

The 15c is overprinted, in addition, with two horizontal lines, 2½mm apart.

The overprint also exists on Nos. 59a-59b. Same values.

### Overprint Reading Down

| | | | | |
|---|---|---|---|---|
| *63a* | A6 | ½c | .80 | *6.00* |
| *64a* | A6 | 1c | .80 | *4.00* |
| *65a* | A6 | 2c | 4.00 | *8.00* |
| *66a* | A6 | 2½c | 1.60 | *4.00* |
| *67a* | A6 | 3c | 35.00 | *90.00* |
| *68a* | A6 | 5c | 4.00 | *3.25* |
| *70a* | A9 | 10c | 1.20 | *4.00* |
| *71a* | A9 | 12½c | 6.00 | *12.00* |
| *72a* | A9 | 15c | 32.50 | *75.00* |
| *74a* | A9 | 20c | 12.00 | 20.00 |
| *75a* | A9 | 22½c | *2,200.* | *2,800.* |
| *76a* | A9 | 25c | 8.00 | 12.00 |
| *77a* | A9 | 30c | 14.00 | 32.50 |
| *78a* | A9 | 50c | 10.00 | 24.00 |
| *79a* | A10 | 1g | 200.00 | 240.00 |
| ***d.*** | | Double overprint | *180.00* | 200.00 |
| *80a* | A10 | 2½g | *2,800.* | *4,000.* |

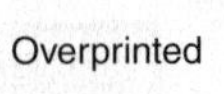
Overprinted

### 1908, July 1

| | | | | |
|---|---|---|---|---|
| **81** | A6 | ½c violet | .25 | .25 |
| ***b.*** | | Double overprint | 600.00 | |
| **82** | A6 | 1c olive grn | .60 | .40 |
| **83** | A6 | 2c yellow brn | 2.40 | 2.60 |
| **84** | A6 | 2½c green | 1.60 | .25 |
| **85** | A6 | 3c orange | 1.20 | 1.00 |
| **86** | A6 | 5c rose red | 2.40 | .25 |
| **87** | A6 | 7½c gray | 2.00 | 1.75 |
| **88** | A9 | 10c slate | 1.40 | .25 |
| **89** | A9 | 12½c deep blue | 2.00 | .80 |
| ***b.*** | | Dbl. ovpt., one inverted | 150.00 | 150.00 |
| **90** | A9 | 15c choc (on No. 50a) | 3.75 | 3.75 |
| **91** | A9 | 17½c bister | 2.00 | .80 |
| **92** | A9 | 20c olive grn | 10.00 | .80 |
| **93** | A9 | 22½c brn & ol grn | 5.25 | 3.00 |
| **94** | A9 | 25c violet | 5.25 | .40 |
| **95** | A9 | 30c orange brn | 28.00 | 3.00 |
| **96** | A9 | 50c red brown | 20.00 | .80 |
| **97** | A10 | 1g dull lilac (#59a) | 50.00 | 3.25 |
| ***b.*** | | Perf. 11 | 52.50 | 4.00 |
| **98** | A10 | 2½g slate blue (#61b) | 72.50 | 60.00 |
| | | *Nos. 81-98 (18)* | 210.60 | 83.35 |

### Inverted Overprint

| | | | | |
|---|---|---|---|---|
| *81a* | A6 | ½c | 1.25 | *4.00* |
| *82a* | A6 | 1c | .75 | *4.00* |
| *83a* | A6 | 2c | 3.00 | *12.00* |
| *84a* | A6 | 2½c | 3.25 | *8.00* |
| *85a* | A6 | 3c | 28.00 | 40.00 |
| *86a* | A6 | 5c | 3.00 | 6.00 |
| *88a* | A9 | 10c | 1.60 | *4.00* |
| *89a* | A9 | 12½c | 4.00 | 8.00 |
| *90a* | A9 | 15c | 4.00 | *16.00* |
| *92a* | A9 | 20c | 16.00 | 16.00 |
| *94a* | A9 | 25c | 6.00 | *16.00* |
| *95a* | A9 | 30c | 28.00 | 40.00 |
| *96a* | A9 | 50c | 20.00 | 28.00 |
| *97a* | A10 | 1g Perf. 11 | 160.00 | 220.00 |
| *98a* | A10 | 2½g | *2,800.* | *4,000.* |

A11

Queen Wilhelmina
A12 A13

### Typo., Litho. (#114A)

**1912-40** *Perf. 12½*

| | | | | |
|---|---|---|---|---|
| **101** | A11 | ½c lt vio | .25 | .25 |
| **102** | A11 | 1c olive grn | .25 | .25 |
| **103** | A11 | 2c yellow brn | .60 | .25 |
| **104** | A11 | 2c gray blk ('30) | .60 | .25 |
| **105** | A11 | 2½c green | 1.40 | .25 |
| **106** | A11 | 2½c lt red ('22) | .80 | .25 |
| **107** | A11 | 3c yellow | .60 | .25 |
| **108** | A11 | 3c green ('29) | 1.20 | .25 |
| **109** | A11 | 4c ultra | 1.20 | .25 |
| **110** | A11 | 4c dp grn ('28) | 1.20 | .25 |
| **111** | A11 | 4c yellow ('30) | 8.00 | 5.00 |
| **112** | A11 | 5c rose | 1.25 | .25 |
| **113** | A11 | 5c green ('22) | 1.20 | .25 |
| **114** | A11 | 5c chlky bl ('28) | .80 | .25 |
| **114A** | A11 | 5c ultra ('40) | .80 | .30 |
| **115** | A11 | 7½c bister | .80 | .25 |
| **116** | A11 | 10c lilac ('22) | 2.00 | .25 |
| **117** | A12 | 10c car rose ('14) | 1.20 | .25 |
| **118** | A12 | 12½c dull bl ('14) | 1.10 | .25 |
| **119** | A12 | 12½c red ('22) | 1.10 | .30 |
| **120** | A12 | 15c blue ('29) | 8.00 | .25 |
| **121** | A12 | 17½c red brn ('15) | 1.10 | .25 |
| **122** | A12 | 20c green ('15) | 2.00 | .25 |
| **123** | A12 | 20c blue ('22) | 2.00 | .25 |
| **124** | A12 | 20c orange ('32) | 14.00 | .30 |
| **125** | A12 | 22½c orange ('15) | 2.00 | .25 |
| **126** | A12 | 25c red vio ('15) | 2.00 | .80 |
| **127** | A12 | 30c slate ('15) | 2.00 | .25 |
| **128** | A12 | 32½c vio & red ('22) | 2.00 | .25 |
| **129** | A12 | 35c org brn ('29) | 7.25 | .60 |
| **130** | A12 | 40c green ('22) | 4.00 | .25 |

*Perf. 11½*

**Engr.**

| | | | | |
|---|---|---|---|---|
| **131** | A13 | 50c green ('13) | 6.00 | .25 |
| ***a.*** | | Perf. 11x11½ | 6.00 | .25 |
| ***b.*** | | Perf. 12½ | 6.00 | .40 |
| ***c.*** | | Vert. pair, imperf. betwn. | | *1,600.* |
| **132** | A13 | 60c dp blue ('22) | 6.00 | .25 |
| **133** | A13 | 80c orange ('22) | 6.00 | .30 |
| **134** | A13 | 1g brown ('13) | 6.00 | .25 |
| ***a.*** | | Perf. 11x11½ | 6.00 | .30 |
| **135** | A13 | 1.75g dk vio, perf, 12½ ('31) | 20.00 | 2.00 |
| **136** | A13 | 2½g car ('13) | 16.00 | .50 |
| ***a.*** | | Perf. 11x11½ | 16.00 | 4.00 |
| ***b.*** | | Perf. 12½ | 16.00 | .70 |
| | | *Nos. 101-136 (37)* | 132.70 | 17.10 |

For surcharges and overprints see Nos. 137-138, 144-150, 102a-123a, 158, 194-195, B1-B3, C1-C5.

---

Water Soluble Ink

Some values of types A11 and A12 and late printings of types A6 and A9 are in soluble ink. The design disappears when immersed in water.

---

Nos. 105, 109, 54, 59 Surcharged

**1917-18** **Typo.** *Perf. 12½*

| | | | | |
|---|---|---|---|---|
| **137** | A11 | ½c on 2½c | .30 | .30 |
| **138** | A11 | 1c on 4c ('18) | .55 | .55 |
| **139** | A9 | 17½c on 22½c ('18) | 2.00 | .75 |
| ***a.*** | | Inverted surcharge | 350.00 | 725.00 |

*Perf. 11x11½*

| | | | | |
|---|---|---|---|---|
| **140** | A10 | 30c on 1g ('18) | 6.50 | 1.75 |
| ***a.*** | | Perf. 11½x11 | 130.00 | 120.00 |
| | | *Nos. 137-140 (4)* | 9.35 | 3.35 |

### Nos. 121, 125, 131, 134 Surcharged in Red or Blue

On A12

On A13

Two types of 32½c on 50c:
I — Surcharge bars spaced as in illustration.
II — Bars more closely spaced.

**1922, Jan.** *Perf. 12½*

| | | | | |
|---|---|---|---|---|
| **144** | A12 | 12½c on 17½c (R) | .75 | .25 |
| **145** | A12 | 12½c on 22½c (R) | .75 | .25 |
| **146** | A12 | 20c on 22½c (Bl) | .75 | .25 |
| ***a.*** | | Double overprint | | *1,800.* |

*Perf. 11½, 11x11½*

| | | | | |
|---|---|---|---|---|
| **147** | A13 | 32½c on 50c (Bl) (I, perf. 11½) | 1.50 | .25 |
| ***a.*** | | Type II, perf. 11½ | 10.00 | .25 |
| ***b.*** | | Type I, perf. 11x11½ | 1,000. | 6.00 |
| ***c.*** | | Type II, perf. 11x11½ | 20.00 | 1.60 |
| **148** | A13 | 40c on 50c (R) | 4.00 | .45 |
| **149** | A13 | 60c on 1g (Bl) | 6.50 | .40 |
| **150** | A13 | 80c on 1g (R) | 8.00 | 1.20 |
| | | *Nos. 144-150 (7)* | 22.25 | 3.05 |

### Stamps of 1912-22 Overprinted in Red, Blue, Green or Black

a

b

No. 145a

**1922, Sept. 18** **Typo.** *Perf. 12½*

| | | | | |
|---|---|---|---|---|
| *102a* | A11(a) | 1c ol grn (R) | 8.00 | 8.00 |
| *103a* | A11(a) | 2c yel brn (Bl) | 8.00 | 8.00 |
| *106a* | A11(a) | 2½c lt red (G) | 57.50 | *65.00* |
| *107a* | A11(a) | 3c yellow (R) | 8.00 | 8.00 |
| *109a* | A11(a) | 4c ultra (R) | 32.50 | 40.00 |
| *113a* | A11(a) | 5c green (R) | 12.00 | 8.00 |
| *115a* | A11(a) | 7½c drab (Bl) | 8.00 | 8.00 |
| *116a* | A11(a) | 10c lilac (Bk) | 65.00 | 92.50 |
| *145a* | A12(b) | 12½c on 22½c org (Bl) | 8.00 | 8.00 |
| *121a* | A12(b) | 17½c red brn (Bk) | 8.00 | 8.00 |
| *123a* | A12(b) | 20c blue (Bk) | 8.00 | 8.00 |
| | | *Nos. 102a-123a (11)* | 223.00 | 261.50 |

Issued to publicize the 3rd Netherlands Indies Industrial Fair at Bandoeng, Java.

Nos. 102a-123a were sold at a premium for 3, 4, 5, 6, 8, 9, 10, 12½, 15, 20 and 22½ cents respectively.

Queen Wilhelmina — A15

**1923, Aug. 31** **Engr.** *Perf. 11½*

| | | | | |
|---|---|---|---|---|
| **151** | A15 | 5c myrtle green | .25 | .25 |
| ***a.*** | | Perf. 11½x11 | *1,000.* | 125.00 |
| ***b.*** | | Perf. 11x11½ | 4.00 | .75 |
| **152** | A15 | 12½c rose | .25 | .25 |
| ***a.*** | | Perf. 11x11½ | 1.25 | .25 |
| ***b.*** | | Perf. 11½x11 | 1.75 | .75 |
| ***c.*** | | Vert. pair, imperf. btwn. | *1,000.* | |
| **153** | A15 | 20c dark blue | .75 | .25 |
| ***a.*** | | Perf. 11½x11 | 4.00 | .75 |
| **154** | A15 | 50c red orange | 2.00 | .75 |
| ***a.*** | | Perf. 11x11½ | 6.00 | 1.25 |
| ***b.*** | | Perf. 11½x11 | 3.00 | .90 |
| ***c.*** | | Perf. 11 | 6.00 | 1.25 |
| **155** | A15 | 1g brown vio | 4.50 | .75 |
| ***a.*** | | Perf. 11½x11 | 8.00 | .80 |
| **156** | A15 | 2½g gray black | 40.00 | 40.00 |
| **157** | A15 | 5g orange brown | 125.00 | 140.00 |
| | | *Nos. 151-157 (7)* | 172.75 | 182.25 |

25th anniversary of the assumption of the government of the Netherlands by Queen Wilhelmina, at the age of 18.

No. 123 Surcharged

**1930, Dec. 13** **Typo.** *Perf. 12½*

| | | | | |
|---|---|---|---|---|
| **158** | A12 | 12½c on 20c bl (R) | .80 | .25 |
| ***a.*** | | Inverted surcharge | 375.00 | 725.00 |

Prince William I, Portrait by Van Key — A16

**1933, Apr. 18** **Photo.**

| | | | | |
|---|---|---|---|---|
| **163** | A16 | 12½c deep orange | 1.60 | .40 |

400th anniv. of the birth of Prince William I, Count of Nassau and Prince of Orange, frequently referred to as William the Silent.

Rice Field Scene A17

Queen Wilhelmina A18

Queen Wilhelmina A19

**1933-37** **Unwmk.** *Perf. 11½x12½*

| | | | | |
|---|---|---|---|---|
| **164** | A17 | 1c lilac gray ('34) | .25 | .25 |
| **165** | A17 | 2c plum ('34) | .25 | .25 |
| **166** | A17 | 2½c bister ('34) | .25 | .25 |
| **167** | A17 | 3c yellow grn ('34) | .25 | .25 |
| **168** | A17 | 3½c dark gray ('37) | .25 | .25 |
| **169** | A17 | 4c dk olive ('34) | 1.00 | .25 |
| **170** | A17 | 5c ultra ('34) | .25 | .25 |
| **171** | A17 | 7½c violet ('34) | 1.00 | .25 |
| **172** | A17 | 10c ver ('34) | 1.90 | .25 |
| **173** | A18 | 10c ver ('37) | .60 | .25 |
| **174** | A18 | 12½c dp org ('34) | .60 | .25 |
| ***a.*** | | 12½c light orange, perf. 12½ ('33) | 8.00 | .40 |
| **175** | A18 | 15c ultra ('34) | .60 | .25 |
| **176** | A18 | 20c plum ('34) | .80 | .25 |
| **177** | A18 | 25c blue grn ('34) | 2.25 | .25 |
| **178** | A18 | 30c lilac gray ('34) | 3.75 | .25 |
| **179** | A18 | 32½c bister ('34) | 8.00 | 8.00 |
| **180** | A18 | 35c violet ('34) | 6.00 | 2.10 |
| **181** | A18 | 40c yel grn ('34) | 3.00 | .25 |
| **182** | A18 | 42½c yellow ('34) | 3.00 | 1.25 |

**1934, Jan 16** *Perf. 12½*

| | | | | |
|---|---|---|---|---|
| **183** | A19 | 50c lilac gray | 6.00 | .25 |
| **184** | A19 | 60c ultra | 6.00 | .80 |
| **185** | A19 | 80c vermilion | 8.00 | 1.20 |
| **186** | A19 | 1g violet | 8.00 | .40 |
| **187** | A19 | 1.75g yellow grn | 20.00 | 13.50 |
| **188** | A19 | 2.50g plum | 20.00 | 2.00 |
| | | *Nos. 164-188 (25)* | 102.00 | 33.50 |

See Nos. 200-225. For overprints and surcharges see Nos. 271-275, B48, B57.

---

Water Soluble Ink

Nos. 164-188 and the first printing of No. 163 have soluble ink and the design disappears when immersed in water.

---

### Nos. C6-C7, C14, C9-C10 Surcharged in Black

a

b

**1934** **Typo.** *Perf. 12½x11½, 12½*

| | | | | |
|---|---|---|---|---|
| **189** | AP1(a) | 2c on 10c | .75 | .45 |
| **190** | AP1(a) | 2c on 20c | .75 | .25 |
| **191** | AP3(b) | 2c on 30c | .75 | 1.20 |
| **192** | AP1(a) | 42½c on 75c | 7.00 | .25 |
| **193** | AP1(a) | 42½c on 1.50g | 7.00 | .40 |
| | | *Nos. 189-193 (5)* | 16.25 | 2.55 |

### Nos. 127-128 Surcharged with New Value in Red or Black

**1937, Sept.** *Perf. 12½*

| | | | | |
|---|---|---|---|---|
| **194** | A12 | 10c on 30c (R) | 3.00 | .25 |
| ***a.*** | | Double surcharge | *675.00* | *2,400.* |
| **195** | A12 | 10c on 32½c (Bk) | 3.00 | .35 |

Wilhelmina — A20

**Perf. 12½x12**

**1938, Aug. 30 Photo. Wmk. 202**

| No. | Type | Description | Unused | Used |
|---|---|---|---|---|
| **196** | A20 | 2c dull purple | .25 | .25 |
| **197** | A20 | 10c car lake | .25 | .25 |
| **198** | A20 | 15c royal blue | 1.25 | 1.25 |
| **199** | A20 | 20c red orange | .75 | .40 |
| | | *Nos. 196-199 (4)* | 2.50 | 2.15 |

40th anniv. of the reign of Queen Wilhelmina.

**Types of 1933-37**

**1938-40 Photo. Perf. 12½x12**

| No. | Type | Description | Unused | Used |
|---|---|---|---|---|
| **200** | A17 | 1c lilac gray ('39) | .40 | *.80* |
| **201** | A17 | 2c plum ('39) | .25 | .25 |
| **202** | A17 | 2½c bister ('39) | .75 | .75 |
| **203** | A17 | 3c yellow grn ('39) | 1.50 | 1.50 |
| **205** | A17 | 4c gray ol ('39) | 1.50 | 1.50 |
| **206** | A17 | 5c ultra ('39) | .25 | .25 |
| *a.* | | Perf. 12x12½ | 1.50 | .75 |
| **207** | A17 | 7½c violet ('39) | 3.00 | 1.50 |
| **208** | A18 | 10c ver ('39) | .25 | .25 |
| **210** | A18 | 15c ultra ('39) | .25 | .25 |
| **211** | A18 | 20c plum ('39) | .25 | .25 |
| *a.* | | Perf. 12x12½ | 1.50 | .75 |
| **212** | A18 | 25c blue grn ('39) | 24.00 | 24.00 |
| **213** | A18 | 30c lilac gray ('39) | 10.00 | 5.00 |
| **215** | A18 | 35c violet ('39) | 5.75 | 1.60 |
| **216** | A18 | 40c dp yel grn ('40) | 5.75 | .25 |

**Perf. 12½**

| No. | Type | Description | Unused | Used |
|---|---|---|---|---|
| **218** | A19 | 50c lilac gray ('40) | 275.00 | |
| **219** | A19 | 60c ultra ('39) | 14.00 | 8.00 |
| **220** | A19 | 80c ver ('39) | 75.00 | 65.00 |
| **221** | A19 | 1g violet ('39) | 30.00 | 4.00 |
| **223** | A19 | 2g Prus green | 26.00 | 14.00 |
| **225** | A19 | 5g yellow brn | 24.00 | 14.00 |
| | | *Nos. 200-216,219-225 (19)* | 222.90 | 143.15 |

The note following No. 188 applies also to this issue.

The 50c was sold only at the philatelic window in Amsterdam.

War Dance of Nias Island — A23

Legong Dancer of Bali — A24

Wayang Wong Dancer of Java A25

Padjogé Dancer, Southern Celebes A26

Dyak Dancer of Borneo — A27

**1941 Unwmk. Perf. 12½**

| No. | Type | Description | Unused | Used |
|---|---|---|---|---|
| **228** | A23 | 2½c rose violet | .60 | .80 |
| **229** | A24 | 3c green | .60 | .80 |
| **230** | A25 | 4c olive green | .50 | .80 |
| **231** | A26 | 5c blue | .25 | .25 |
| **232** | A27 | 7½c dark violet | .60 | .35 |
| | | *Nos. 228-232 (5)* | 2.55 | 3.00 |

See Nos. 279-280, 293, N38.

Imperfs. are printers waste.

A28

Queen Wilhelmina A28a

**1941 Perf. 12½**

**Size: 18x22¾mm**

| No. | Type | Description | Unused | Used |
|---|---|---|---|---|
| **234** | A28 | 10c red orange | .80 | .40 |
| *a.* | | Perf. 13½ | .40 | .40 |
| **235** | A28 | 15c ultra | 4.00 | 4.00 |
| **236** | A28 | 17½c orange | 2.00 | 2.00 |
| **237** | A28 | 20c plum | 40.00 | 120.00 |
| **238** | A28 | 25c Prus green | 50.00 | 1.75 |
| **239** | A28 | 30c olive bis | 7.00 | 3.25 |
| **240** | A28 | 35c purple | 160.00 | *400.00* |
| **241** | A28 | 40c yellow grn | 18.50 | 8.00 |

**Perf. 13½**

**Size: 20½x26mm**

| No. | Type | Description | Unused | Used |
|---|---|---|---|---|
| **242** | A28 | 50c car lake | 7.25 | 1.60 |
| **243** | A28 | 60c ultra | 6.50 | 1.60 |
| **244** | A28 | 80c red orange | 6.50 | 1.60 |
| **245** | A28 | 1g purple | 6.50 | .80 |
| **246** | A28 | 2g Prus green | 20.00 | 2.40 |
| **247** | A28 | 5g bis, perf. 12½ | 350.00 | *3,000.* |
| **248** | A28 | 10g green | 42.50 | 24.00 |

**Size: 26x32mm**

| No. | Type | Description | Unused | Used |
|---|---|---|---|---|
| **249** | A28a | 25g orange | 260.00 | 160.00 |
| | | *Nos. 234-249 (16)* | 981.55 | *3,731.* |

Nos. 242-246 come with pin-perf 13½. Small hole, large hole, comb and line perforation varieties exist.

Nos. 242-246 exist on thick paper in darker colors. These are proofs.

The 10c comes in two types: 1¼mm between "10" and "CENT," and 1¾mm.

For overprints and surcharge see Nos. 276-278, J43-J46.

**Catalogue values for unused stamps in this section, from this point to the end of the section, are for Never Hinged items.**

Rice Fields — A29

Barge on Java Lake — A30

University of Medicine, Batavia A31

Palms on Shore — A32

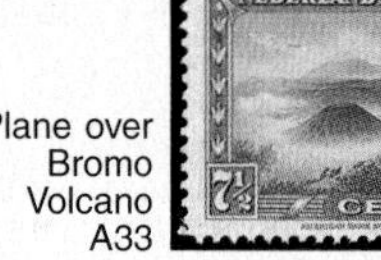

Plane over Bromo Volcano A33

Queen Wilhelmina
A34 A35

**1945-46, Oct. 1 Engr. Perf. 12**

| No. | Type | Description | Unused | Used |
|---|---|---|---|---|
| **250** | A29 | 1c green | .60 | .25 |
| **251** | A30 | 2c rose lilac | .60 | .35 |
| **252** | A31 | 2½c dull lilac | .60 | .25 |
| **253** | A32 | 5c blue | .40 | .25 |
| **254** | A33 | 7½c olive gray | .80 | .25 |
| **255** | A34 | 10c red brown | .40 | .25 |
| **256** | A34 | 15c dark blue | .40 | .25 |
| **257** | A34 | 17½c rose lake | .40 | .25 |
| **258** | A34 | 20c sepia | .40 | .25 |
| **259** | A34 | 30c slate gray | .40 | .25 |
| **260** | A35 | 60c gray black | .80 | .25 |
| **261** | A35 | 1g blue green | 1.20 | .25 |
| **262** | A35 | 2½g red orange | 3.75 | .75 |
| | | *Nos. 250-262 (13)* | 10.75 | 3.85 |

For surcharge see No. 304.

Issued: 15c, 1946, others 10/1/45.

Railway Viaduct Near Soekaboemi A36

Dam and Power Station A37

Palm Tree and Menangkabau House — A38

Huts on Piles A39

Buddhist Stupas A40

**Perf. 14½x14**

**1946 Typo. Wmk. 228**

| No. | Type | Description | Unused | Used |
|---|---|---|---|---|
| **263** | A36 | 1c dark green | .35 | .25 |
| **264** | A37 | 2c black brown | .35 | .25 |
| **265** | A38 | 2½c scarlet | .35 | .25 |
| **266** | A39 | 5c indigo | .35 | .25 |
| **267** | A40 | 7½c ultra | .35 | .25 |
| | | *Nos. 263-267 (5)* | 1.75 | 1.25 |

**Nos. 265, 267, 263 Surcharged**

**1947, Sept. 25**

| No. | Type | Description | Unused | Used |
|---|---|---|---|---|
| **268** | A38 | 3c on 2½c scar | .35 | .25 |
| **269** | A40 | 3c on 7½c ultra | .35 | .25 |
| *a.* | | Double surcharge | 200.00 | 200.00 |
| **270** | A36 | 4c on 1c dk green | .35 | .25 |
| | | *Nos. 268-270 (3)* | 1.05 | .75 |

**No. 219 Surcharged with New Value and Bars in Red**

**1947, Sept. 25 Wmk. 202 Perf. 12½**

| No. | Type | Description | Unused | Used |
|---|---|---|---|---|
| **271** | A19 | 45c on 60c ultra | 1.45 | 1.00 |

**Nos. 212, 218 and 220 Overprinted "1947" in Red or Black**

**1947, Sept. 25 Perf. 12½x12, 12½**

| No. | Type | Description | Unused | Used |
|---|---|---|---|---|
| **272** | A18 | 25c blue green (R) | .40 | .25 |
| *a.* | | Unwmkd. | | 260.00 |
| **273** | A19 | 50c lilac gray (R) | .80 | .35 |
| **274** | A19 | 80c vermilion | 1.20 | 1.20 |
| *a.* | | Unwmkd. | 500.00 | 240.00 |
| | | *Nos. 272-274 (3)* | 2.40 | 1.80 |

Bar above "1947" on No. 274.

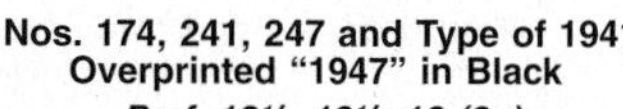
**Nos. 174, 241, 247 and Type of 1941 Overprinted "1947" in Black**

**Perf. 12½, 12½x12 (2g)**

**1947, Sept. 25 Unwmk.**

| No. | Type | Description | Unused | Used |
|---|---|---|---|---|
| **275** | A18 | 12½c deep orange | .40 | .25 |
| **276** | A28 | 40c yellow green | .80 | .25 |
| **277** | A28 | 2g Prus green | 4.00 | 1.40 |
| **278** | A28 | 5g bister | 11.00 | 9.75 |
| | | *Nos. 275-278 (4)* | 16.20 | 11.65 |

The overprint is vertical on Nos. 276-278.

**Dancer Types of 1941, 1945**

**1948, May 13 Litho. Perf. 12½**

| No. | Type | Description | Unused | Used |
|---|---|---|---|---|
| **279** | OS21 | 3c rose red | .25 | .25 |
| **280** | A24 | 4c dull olive grn | .25 | .25 |

Queen Wilhelmina — A41

**1948 Photo. Perf. 12½**

**Size: 18x22mm**

| No. | Type | Description | Unused | Used |
|---|---|---|---|---|
| **281** | A41 | 15c red orange | .80 | 2.00 |
| **282** | A41 | 20c brt blue | .30 | .30 |
| **283** | A41 | 25c dk green | .30 | .30 |
| **284** | A41 | 40c dp yellow grn | .30 | .30 |
| **285** | A41 | 45c plum | .60 | .80 |
| **286** | A41 | 50c red brown | .50 | .30 |
| **287** | A41 | 80c brt red | .60 | .60 |

**Perf. 13**

**Size: 20½x26mm**

| No. | Type | Description | Unused | Used |
|---|---|---|---|---|
| **288** | A41 | 1g deep violet | .30 | .30 |
| *a.* | | Perf. 12½ x 12 | 1.20 | .60 |
| **289** | A41 | 10g green | 32.50 | 15.00 |
| **290** | A41 | 25g orange | 60.00 | 60.00 |
| | | *Nos. 281-290 (10)* | 96.20 | 79.90 |

See Nos. 291-292. For overprints see Nos. 294-303.

**Wilhelmina Type of 1948 Inscribed "1898-1948"**

**1948, Aug. 31 Perf. 12½x12**

**Size: 21x26½mm**

| No. | Type | Description | Unused | Used |
|---|---|---|---|---|
| **291** | A41 | 15c orange | .40 | .40 |
| **292** | A41 | 20c ultra | .40 | .30 |

Reign of Queen Wilhelmina, 50th anniv.

**Dancer Type of 1941**

**1948, Sept. Photo. Perf. 12½**

| No. | Type | Description | Unused | Used |
|---|---|---|---|---|
| **293** | A27 | 7½c olive bister | .80 | .75 |

**Juliana Type of Netherlands 1948**

**Perf. 14½x13½**

**1948, Sept. 25 Wmk. 202**

| No. | Type | Description | Unused | Used |
|---|---|---|---|---|
| **293A** | A75 | 15c red orange | .50 | .35 |
| **293B** | A75 | 20c deep ultra | .50 | .35 |

Investiture of Queen Juliana, Sept. 6, 1948.

**Indonesia**

Nos. 281 to 287 Overprinted in Black

Two types of overprint:
I — Shiny ink, bar 1.8mm wide. By G. C. T. van Dorp & Co.
II — Dull ink, bar 2.2mm. By G. Kolff & Co.

**1948 Perf. 12½**

| No. | Type | Description | Unused | Used |
|---|---|---|---|---|
| **294** | A41 | 15c red orange (I) | 1.75 | .25 |
| *a.* | | Type II | .95 | .25 |
| **295** | A41 | 20c bright blue (I) | .25 | .25 |
| *a.* | | Type II | .50 | .25 |
| **296** | A41 | 25c dark green (I) | .25 | .25 |
| *a.* | | Type II | .25 | .25 |
| **297** | A41 | 40c dp yel grn (I) | .25 | .25 |
| **298** | A41 | 45c plum ('49) (II) | 1.10 | .90 |
| **299** | A41 | 50c red brn ('49) (II) | .25 | .25 |
| **300** | A41 | 80c bright red (I) | 1.00 | .25 |
| *a.* | | Type II | 1.10 | .25 |

Nos. 288-290 Overprinted in Black

**Two Bars**
*Perf. 12½x12*

**301** A41 1g deep violet 1.25 .25
*a.* As #301, with three bars 8.00 .35
*b.* Perf. 13 2.75 .30

*Perf. 13*

**302** A41 10g green 92.50 30.00
**303** A41 25g orange 125.00 57.50
*Nos. 294-303 (10)* 223.60 90.15

**Same Overprint in Black on No. 262**

**1949 Engr. *Perf. 12***
**Bars 28½mm long**

**304** A35 2½g red orange 52.50 9.75

A42

Tjandi Puntadewa Temple Entrance, East Java — A43

Detail, Temple of the Dead, Bedjuning, Bali A44

Menangkabau House, Sumatra A45

Toradja House, Celebes — A46

Designs: 5r, 10r, 25r, Temple entrance.

*Perf. 12½, 11½*

**1949 Unwmk. Photo.**

**307** A42 1s gray .30 .25
*a.* Perf. 11½ .60 .80
**308** A42 2s claret .60 .25
*a.* Perf. 11½ 30.00 *30.00*
**309** A42 2½s olive brown .30 .25
*a.* Perf. 11½ .30 .25
**310** A42 3s rose pink .60 .25
*a.* Perf. 11½ 1.50 1.40
**311** A42 4s green .60 .60
**312** A42 5s blue .30 .25
*a.* Perf. 11½ 1.10 .25
**313** A42 7½s dark green .60 .25
*a.* Perf. 11½ 1.10 .60
**314** A42 10s violet .30 .25
*a.* Perf. 11½ *475.00*
**315** A42 12½s brt red 1.90 .25
*a.* Perf. 11½ 2.25 1.75
**316** A43 15s rose red .30 .25
*a.* Perf. 12½ 1.75 .60
**317** A43 20s gray black .30 .25
*a.* Perf. 12½ .95 .25
**318** A43 25s ultra .30 .25
*a.* Perf. 12½ .95 .25
**319** A44 30s brt red 1.10 .25
*a.* Perf. 12½ 1.10 .25
**320** A44 40s gray green .60 .25
*a.* Perf. 12½ .30 .25
**321** A44 45s claret .60 3.75
*a.* Perf. 12½ 2.75 .50
**322** A45 50s orange brn .60 .25
*a.* Perf. 12½ 1.50 .25
**323** A45 60s brown .80 1.90
*a.* Perf. 12½ 1.50 .25
**324** A45 80s scarlet 1.15 .25
*a.* Perf. 12½ 4.00 .25

The 4s is perf. 12½. The 25s, 30s, 40s, 50s, 60s come both 12½ and 11½, same values.

*Perf. 12½, 12¼*

**325** A46 1r purple .80 .25
*a.* Perf. 12¼ .80 .25
**326** A46 2r gray green 4.75 .25
*a.* Perf. 12¼ 4.75 .25
**327** A46 3r red violet 95.00 .25
**328** A46 5r dk brown 67.50 .40
**329** A46 10r gray 82.50 1.90
**330** A46 25r orange brn .80 1.90
*Nos. 307-330 (24)* 262.60 14.95

Nos. 307-330 remained on sale in Indonesia Republic post offices until May 23, 1958, and were valid for postage until June 30, 1958.

For surcharge, see Indonesia Nos. 335-358.

Nos. 325-330 exist with both large and small holes.

Globe and Arms of Bern — A48

**1949, Oct. 1 *Perf. 12½***

**331** A48 15s bright red 1.15 .40
**332** A48 25s ultra 1.15 .40

Nos. 307-330 remained on sale in Indonesia Republic post offices until May 23, 1958, and were valid for postage until June 30, 1958.

75th anniv. of UPU.

See Indonesia (republic) for subsequent listings.

---

## SEMI-POSTAL STAMPS

Regular Issue of 1912-14 Surcharged in Carmine

**1915, June 10 Unwmk. *Perf. 12½***

**B1** A11 1c + 5c ol grn 4.50 4.50
**B2** A11 5c + 5c rose 4.50 4.50
**B3** A12 10c + 5c rose 7.25 7.25
*Nos. B1-B3 (3)* 16.25 16.25

Surtax for the Red Cross.

Bali Temple SP1

Watchtower SP2

Menangkabau Compound — SP3

Borobudur Temple, Java SP4

*Perf. 11½x11, 11x11½*

**1930, Dec. 1 Photo.**

**B4** SP1 2c (+ 1c) vio & brn 1.00 .80
**B5** SP2 5c (+ 2½c) dk grn & brn 4.75 2.50
**B6** SP3 12½c (+ 2½c) dp red & brn 3.25 .50
**B7** SP4 15c (+ 5c) ultra & brn 5.75 5.75
*Nos. B4-B7 (4)* 14.75 9.55

Surtax for youth care.

Farmer and Carabao SP5

5c, Fishermen. 12½c, Dancers. 15c, Musicians.

**1931, Dec. 1 Engr. *Perf. 12½***

**B8** SP5 2c (+ 1c) olive bis 3.00 2.00
**B9** SP5 5c (+ 2½c) bl grn 4.25 3.75
**B10** SP5 12½c (+ 2½c) dp red 3.25 .55
**B11** SP5 15c (+ 5c) dl bl 8.25 7.00
*Nos. B8-B11 (4)* 18.75 13.30

The surtax was for the aid of the Leper Colony at Salatiga.

Weaving SP9

5c, Plaiting rattan. 12½c, Woman batik dyer. 15c, Coppersmith.

**1932, Dec. 1 Photo. *Perf. 12½***

**B12** SP9 2c (+ 1c) dp vio & bis .40 .40
**B13** SP9 5c (+ 2½c) dp grn & bis 2.50 2.00
**B14** SP9 12½c (+ 2½c) brt rose & bis .85 .30
**B15** SP9 15c (+ 5c) bl & bis 3.25 3.00
*Nos. B12-B15 (4)* 7.00 5.70

The surtax was donated to the Salvation Army.

Woman and Lotus — SP13

Designs: 5c, "The Light that Shows the Way." 12½c, YMCA emblem. 15c, Jobless man.

**1933, Dec. 1 *Perf. 12½***

**B16** SP13 2c (+ 1c) red vio & ol bis .65 .30
**B17** SP13 5c (+ 2½c) grn & ol bis 2.25 1.90
**B18** SP13 12½c (+ 2½c) ver & ol bis 2.50 .30
**B19** SP13 15c (+ 5c) bl & ol bis 2.75 2.00
*Nos. B16-B19 (4)* 8.15 4.50

The surtax was for the Amsterdam Young Men's Society for Relief of the Poor in Netherlands Indies.

Dowager Queen Emma — SP17

**1934, Sept. 15 *Perf. 13x14***

**B20** SP17 12½c (+ 2½c) blk brn 1.25 .45

Issued in memory of the late Dowager Queen Emma of Netherlands. The surtax was for the Anti-Tuberculosis Society.

A Pioneer at Work — SP18

Designs: 5c, Cavalryman rescuing wounded native. 12½c, Artilleryman under fire. 15c, Bugler.

**1935 *Perf. 12½***

**B21** SP18 2c (+ 1c) dp mag & bis 1.25 1.00
**B22** SP18 5c (+ 2½c) grn & bis 3.25 2.25
**B23** SP18 12½c (+ 2½c) red org & bis 3.25 .25
**B24** SP18 15c (+ 5c) brt bl & bis 4.50 4.50
*Nos. B21-B24 (4)* 12.25 8.00

The surtax was for the Indies Committee of the Christian Military Association for the East and West Indies.

Child Welfare Work — SP22

**1936, Dec. 1 Size: 23x20mm**

**B25** SP22 2c (+ 1c) plum 1.00 .60

**Size: 30x26½mm**

**B26** SP22 5c (+ 2½c) gray vio 1.25 1.10
**B27** SP22 7½c (+ 2½c) dk vio 1.25 1.25
**B28** SP22 12½c (+ 2½c) red org 1.25 .30
**B29** SP22 15c (+5c) brt bl 2.00 1.75
*Nos. B25-B29 (5)* 6.75 5.00

Surtax for Salvation Army.

Boy Scouts — SP23

**1937, May 1**

**B30** SP23 7½c + 2½c dk ol brn 1.25 1.00
**B31** SP23 12½c + 2½c rose car 1.25 .50

Fifth Boy Scout World Jamboree, Vogelenzang, Netherlands, July 31-Aug. 13, 1937. Surtax for Netherlands Indies Scout Association.

Sifting Rice — SP24

Designs: 3½c, Mother and children. 7½c, Plowing with carabao team. 10c, Carabao team and cart. 20c, Native couple.

**1937, Dec. 1**

**B32** SP24 2c (+ 1c) dk brn & org 1.10 .80
**B33** SP24 3½c (+ 1½c) gray 1.10 .80
**B34** SP24 7½c (+ 2½c) Prus grn & org 1.25 .95
**B35** SP24 10c (+ 2½c) car & org 1.25 .25
**B36** SP24 20c (+ 5c) brt bl 1.25 1.10
*Nos. B32-B36 (5)* 5.95 3.90

Surtax for the Public Relief Fund for indigenous poor.

Modern Plane — SP28

Design: 20c, Plane nose facing left.

**Wmk. 202**

**1938, Oct. 15 Photo. *Perf. 12½***

**B36A** SP28 17½c (+5c) olive brn .85 .85
**B36B** SP28 20c (+5c) slate .85 .55

10th anniversary of the Dutch East Indies Royal Air Lines (K. N. I. L. M.).

Surtax for the Aviation Fund in the Netherlands Indies.

Nun and Child
SP29 SP30

Designs: 7½c, Nurse examining child's arm. 10c, Nurse bathing baby. 20c, Nun bandaging child's head.

**1938, Dec. 1 Wmk. 202 *Perf. 12½***

| | | | | |
|---|---|---|---|---|
| **B37** | SP29 | 2c (+ 1c) vio | .60 | .45 |

***Perf. 11½x12***

| | | | | |
|---|---|---|---|---|
| **B38** | SP30 | 3½c (+ 1½c) brt grn | 1.00 | .90 |

***Perf. 12x11½***

| | | | | |
|---|---|---|---|---|
| **B39** | SP30 | 7½c (+ 2½c) cop red | .80 | .85 |
| **B40** | SP30 | 10c (+ 2½c) ver | .90 | .25 |
| **B41** | SP30 | 20c (+ 5c) brt ultra | 1.00 | .95 |
| | | *Nos. B37-B41 (5)* | 4.30 | 3.40 |

The surtax was for the Central Mission Bureau in Batavia.

Social Workers
SP34

Indonesian Nurse Tending Patient
SP35

European Nurse Tending Patient — SP36

***Perf. 13x11½, 11½x13***

**1939, Dec. 1 Photo.**

| | | | | |
|---|---|---|---|---|
| **B42** | SP34 | 2c (+ 1c) purple | .25 | .25 |
| **B43** | SP35 | 3½c (+ 1½c) bl grn & pale bl grn | .30 | .25 |
| **B44** | SP34 | 7½c (+ 2½c) cop brn | .25 | .25 |
| **B45** | SP35 | 10c (+ 2½c) scar & pink | 1.40 | .80 |
| **B46** | SP36 | 10c (+ 2½c) scar | 1.40 | .80 |
| **B47** | SP36 | 20c (+ 5c) dk bl | .40 | .35 |
| | | *Nos. B42-B47 (6)* | 4.00 | 2.70 |

No. B44 shows native social workers.

Nos. B45 and B46 were issued se-tenant vertically and horizontally. The surtax was used for the Bureau of Social Service.

No. 174 Surcharged in Brown

**1940, Dec. 2 Unwmk. *Perf. 12x12½***

| | | | | |
|---|---|---|---|---|
| **B48** | A18 | 10c + 5c on 12½c dp org | 1.10 | .40 |

SP37

Netherlands coat of arms and inscription "Netherlands Shall Rise Again"

**1941, May 10 Litho. *Perf. 12½***

| | | | | |
|---|---|---|---|---|
| **B49** | SP37 | 5c + 5c multi | .25 | .25 |
| **B50** | SP37 | 10c + 10c multi | .25 | .25 |
| **B51** | SP37 | 1g + 1g multi | 9.00 | 6.75 |
| | | *Nos. B49-B51 (3)* | 9.50 | 7.25 |

The surtax was used to purchase fighter planes for Dutch pilots fighting with the Royal Air Force in Great Britain.

SP38

Designs: 2c, Doctor and child, 3½c, Rice eater. 7½c, Nurse and patient. 10c, Nurse and children. 15c, Basket weaver.

**1941, Sept. 22 Photo.**

| | | | | |
|---|---|---|---|---|
| **B52** | SP38 | 2c (+ 1c) yel grn | .60 | .55 |
| **B53** | SP38 | 3½c (+ 1½c) vio brn | 4.00 | 3.50 |
| **B54** | SP38 | 7½c (+ 2½c) vio | 3.25 | 2.75 |
| **B55** | SP38 | 10c (+ 2½c) dk red | .90 | .25 |
| **B56** | SP38 | 15c (+ 5c) saph | 9.50 | 6.00 |
| | | *Nos. B52-B56 (5)* | 18.25 | 13.05 |

The surtax was used for various charities.

**Catalogue values for unused stamps in this section, from this point to the end of the section, are for Never Hinged items.**

**Indonesia**

No. 208 Surcharged in Black

***Perf. 12½x12***

**1948, Feb. 2 Wmk. 202**

| | | | | |
|---|---|---|---|---|
| **B57** | A18 | 15c + 10c on 10c | .25 | .25 |
| *a.* | | Inverted surcharge | 210.00 | 210.00 |

The surtax was for war victims and other charitable purposes.

## AIR POST STAMPS

**Regular Issues of 1913-1923 Surcharged in Black or Blue**

Nos. 119 & 126 Surcharged

No. 133 Surcharged

No. 134 Surcharged

No. 136 Surcharged

***Perf. 12½, 11½***

**1928, Sept. 20 Unwmk.**

| | | | | |
|---|---|---|---|---|
| **C1** | A12 | 10c on 12½c red | 1.25 | 1.25 |
| **C2** | A12 | 20c on 25c red vio | 3.00 | 3.00 |
| **C3** | A13 | 40c on 80c org | 3.00 | 3.00 |
| **C4** | A13 | 75c on 1g brn (Bl) | 1.25 | 1.25 |
| **C5** | A13 | 1½g on 2½g car | 8.00 | 8.00 |
| | | *Nos. C1-C5 (5)* | 16.50 | 16.50 |

On Nos. C4 and C5 there are stars over the original values and the airplane is of different shape. On No. C3 there are no bars under "OST."

Planes over Temple
AP1

**1928, Dec. 1 Litho. *Perf. 12½x11½***

| | | | | |
|---|---|---|---|---|
| **C6** | AP1 | 10c red violet | .40 | .25 |
| **C7** | AP1 | 20c brown | 1.00 | .75 |
| **C8** | AP1 | 40c rose | 1.20 | .75 |
| **C9** | AP1 | 75c green | 3.25 | .25 |
| **C10** | AP1 | 1.50g orange | 6.25 | .75 |
| | | *Nos. C6-C10 (5)* | 12.10 | 2.75 |

For surcharges see Nos. 189-190, 192-193, C11-C12, C17.

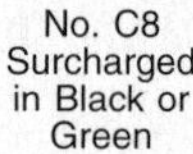

No. C8 Surcharged in Black or Green

**1930-32**

| | | | | |
|---|---|---|---|---|
| **C11** | AP1 | 30c on 40c rose | 2.00 | .25 |
| **C12** | AP1 | 30c on 40c rose (G) ('32) | 2.40 | .25 |

Pilot at Controls of Plane
AP2

**1931, Apr. 1 Photo. *Perf. 12½***

| | | | | |
|---|---|---|---|---|
| **C13** | AP2 | 1g blue & brown | 16.00 | *18.00* |

Issued for the first air mail flight from Java to Australia.

Landscape and Garudas
AP3

**1931, May**

| | | | | |
|---|---|---|---|---|
| **C14** | AP3 | 30c red violet | 3.25 | .25 |
| **C15** | AP3 | 4½g bright blue | 9.00 | 3.25 |
| **C16** | AP3 | 7½g yellow green | 12.00 | 4.50 |
| | | *Nos. C14-C16 (3)* | 24.25 | 8.00 |

For surcharge see No. 191.

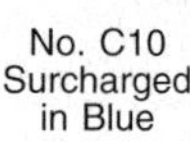

No. C10 Surcharged in Blue

**1932, July 21 *Perf. 12½x11½***

| | | | | |
|---|---|---|---|---|
| **C17** | AP1 | 50c on 1.50g org | 3.25 | .60 |
| *a.* | | Inverted surcharge | *2,200.* | *2,800.* |

Airplane
AP4

**1933, Oct. 18 Photo. *Perf. 12½***

| | | | | |
|---|---|---|---|---|
| **C18** | AP4 | 30c deep blue | 1.50 | 1.50 |

## MARINE INSURANCE STAMPS

Floating Safe Attracting Gulls — MI1

Floating Safe with Night Flare — MI2

Artistic Fantasy of Floating Safe — MI3

***Perf. 11½***

**1921, Nov. 1 Unwmk. Engr.**

| | | | | |
|---|---|---|---|---|
| **GY1** | MI1 | 15c slate green | 12.50 | *60.00* |
| **GY2** | MI1 | 60c rose | 12.50 | *90.00* |
| **GY3** | MI1 | 75c gray brn | 12.50 | *120.00* |
| **GY4** | MI2 | 1.50g dark blue | 37.50 | *325.00* |
| **GY5** | MI2 | 2.25g org brn | 45.00 | *475.00* |
| **GY6** | MI3 | 4½g black | 80.00 | *800.00* |
| **GY7** | MI3 | 7½g red | 100.00 | *925.00* |
| | | *Nos. GY1-GY7 (7)* | 300.00 | *2,795.* |

## POSTAGE DUE STAMPS

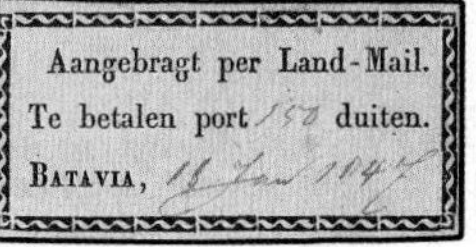


D1

D2

**1845-46 Unwmk. Typeset *Imperf.***

**Bluish Paper**

| | | | |
|---|---|---|---|
| **J1** | D1 | black ('46) | *1,650.* |
| **J2** | D2 | black | *2,000.* |
| *a.* | | "Maill" instead of "Mail" | *3,200.* |

D3

**1874 Typo. *Perf. 12½x12, 13x14***

| | | | | |
|---|---|---|---|---|
| **J3** | D3 | 5c ocher | 300.00 | 275.00 |
| **J4** | D3 | 10c green, *yel* | 240.00 | 155.00 |
| **J5** | D3 | 15c ocher, *org* | 40.00 | 24.00 |
| *a.* | | Perf. 11½x12 | 65.00 | 65.00 |
| **J6** | D3 | 20c green, *blue* | 60.00 | 24.00 |
| *a.* | | Perf. 11½x12 | 110.00 | 45.00 |
| | | *Nos. J3-J6 (4)* | 640.00 | 478.00 |

D4

Type I — 34 loops. "T" of "Betalen" over center of loop, top branch of "E" of "Te" shorter than lower branch.

Type II — 33 loops. "T" of "Betalen" over center of two loops.

Type III — 32 loops. "T" of "Betalen" slightly to the left of loop, top branch of first "E" of "Betalen" shorter than lower branch.

Type IV — 37 loops and letters of "PORT" larger than in the other three types.

**Value in Black**

***Perf. 11½x12, 12½, 12½x12, 13½***

**1882-88 Type III**

| | | | | |
|---|---|---|---|---|
| **J7** | D4 | 2½c carmine | .75 | 1.25 |
| **J8** | D4 | 5c carmine | .75 | .75 |
| **J9** | D4 | 10c carmine | 4.00 | 4.00 |
| **J10** | D4 | 15c carmine | 4.00 | 3.25 |
| **J11** | D4 | 20c carmine | 100.00 | .75 |
| **J12** | D4 | 30c carmine | 3.75 | 4.50 |
| **J13** | D4 | 40c carmine | 2.40 | 3.25 |
| **J14** | D4 | 50c deep salmon | 1.25 | 1.60 |
| **J15** | D4 | 75c carmine | 1.25 | 1.60 |
| | | *Nos. J7-J15 (9)* | 118.15 | 20.95 |

**Type I**

| | | | | |
|---|---|---|---|---|
| *J7a* | D4 | 2½c carmine | .75 | 1.60 |
| *J8a* | D4 | 5c carmine | .75 | 1.25 |
| *J9a* | D4 | 10c carmine | 5.00 | 6.00 |
| *J10a* | D4 | 15c carmine | 5.00 | 5.75 |
| *J11a* | D4 | 20c carmine | 120.00 | 1.25 |
| *J12a* | D4 | 30c carmine | 6.00 | 8.00 |
| *J13a* | D4 | 40c carmine | 2.40 | 3.25 |

*J14a* D4 50c deep salmon 2.00 2.40
*J15a* D4 75c carmine 1.25 2.00
*Nos. J7a-J15a (9)* 143.15 31.50

**Type II**

*J7b* D4 2½c carmine .75 2.00
*J8b* D4 5c carmine .75 1.25
*J9b* D4 10c carmine 6.00 6.00
*J10b* D4 15c carmine 6.00 6.00
*J11b* D4 20c carmine 120.00 3.25
*J12b* D4 30c carmine 10.00 10.00
*J13b* D4 40c carmine 3.25 4.00
*J14b* D4 50c deep salmon 2.00 2.50
*J15b* D4 75c carmine 1.60 2.50
*Nos. J7b-J15b (9)* 150.35 37.50

**Type IV**

*J7c* D4 2½c carmine 4.00 6.00
*J8c* D4 5c carmine 2.00 6.00
*J9c* D4 10c carmine 27.50 40.00
*J10c* D4 15c carmine 24.00 27.50
*J11c* D4 20c carmine 250.00 12.50
*J13c* D4 40c carmine 4.00 6.00
*J14c* D4 50c deep salmon 16.00 *24.00*
*J15c* D4 75c carmine 2.50 6.00
*Nos. J7c-J15c (8)* 330.00 128.00

D5

**1892-95 Type I *Perf. 12½***

**J16** D5 10c carmine 2.50 .40
**J17** D5 15c carmine ('95) 22.00 3.00
**J18** D5 20c carmine 5.50 .25
*Nos. J16-J18 (3)* 30.00 3.65

**Type III**

*J16a* D5 10c dull red 5.00 3.00
*J18a* D5 20c dull red 6.00 2.00

**Type II**

*J16b* D5 10c dull red 16.00 16.00
*J18b* D5 20c dull red 10.00 10.00

**1906-09 Type I**

**J19** D5 2½c carmine ('08) 1.60 .30
**J20** D5 5c carmine ('09) 5.00 .25
**J21** D5 30c carmine 30.00 10.00
**J22** D5 40c carmine ('09) 26.00 3.25
**J23** D5 50c carmine ('09) 18.00 1.60
**J24** D5 75c carmine ('09) 34.00 5.25
*Nos. J19-J24 (6)* 114.60 20.65

**Value in Color of Stamp**

**1913-39 *Perf. 12½***

**J25** D5 1c salmon ('39) .25 *25.00*
**J26** D5 2½c salmon .25 .25
**J27** D5 3½c salmon ('39) .25 *25.00*
**J28** D5 5c salmon .25 .25
**J29** D5 7½c salmon ('22) .25 .25
**J30** D5 10c salmon .25 .25
**J31** D5 12½c salmon ('22) 3.25 .40
**J32** D5 15c salmon 3.25 .40
**J33** D5 20c salmon .25 .25
**J34** D5 25c salmon ('22) .25 .25
**J35** D5 30c salmon .25 .25
**J36** D5 37½c salmon ('30) 18.00 20.00
**J37** D5 40c salmon .25 .25
**J38** D5 50c salmon 2.40 .25
**J39** D5 75c salmon 3.25 2.40
*Nos. J25-J39 (15)* 32.65 75.45

**Thick White Paper**
**Invisible Gum**
**Numerals Slightly Larger**

**1941 Litho. *Perf. 12½***

*J25a* D5 1c light red .75 *12.00*
*J28a* D5 5c light red .75 12.00
*J30a* D5 10c light red 8.00 24.00
*J32a* D5 15c light red 1.00 12.00
*J33a* D5 20c light red .80 12.00
*J35a* D5 30c light red 1.25 12.00
*J37a* D5 40c light red 1.00 12.00
*Nos. J25a-J37a (7)* 13.55 96.00

**No. J36 Surcharged with New Value**

**1937, Oct. 1 Unwmk. *Perf. 12½***

**J40** D5 20c on 37½c salmon .80 .40

D6

**1939-40**

**J41** D6 1g salmon 6.00 8.00
**J42** D6 1g blue ('40) .40 *4.00*
*a.* 1g lt bl, thick paper, invisible gum .80 *12.00*

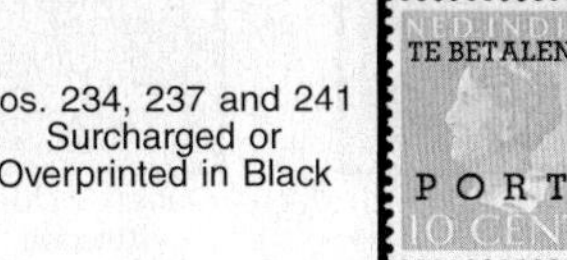
**Catalogue values for unused stamps in this section, from this point to the end of the section, are for Never Hinged items.**

Nos. 234, 237 and 241 Surcharged or Overprinted in Black

**1946, Mar. 11 Photo.**

**J43** A28 2½c on 10c red org 1.25 1.25
**J44** A28 10c red orange 2.00 2.00
**J45** A28 20c plum 6.00 6.00
**J46** A28 40c yellow green 45.00 45.00
*Nos. J43-J46 (4)* 54.25 54.25

D7

***Perf. 14½x14***

**1946, Aug. 14 Wmk. 228 Typo.**

**J47** D7 1c purple .75 1.25
**J48** D7 2½c brn org 2.00 2.00
**J49** D7 3½c ultra .75 1.25
**J50** D7 5c red orange .75 1.25
**J51** D7 7½c Prus green .75 1.25
**J52** D7 10c deep magenta .75 1.25
**J53** D7 20c light ultra .75 1.25
**J54** D7 25c olive .75 1.25
**J55** D7 30c red brown 1.25 1.50
**J56** D7 40c yellow grn 1.25 1.50
**J57** D7 50c yellow 1.60 1.50
**J58** D7 75c aqua 1.60 1.50
**J59** D7 100c apple green 1.60 1.50
*Nos. J47-J59 (13)* 14.55 18.25

**1948 Litho. Unwmk. *Perf. 12½***

**J59A** D7 2½c brown orange 1.25 *2.00*

## OFFICIAL STAMPS

Regular Issues of 1883-1909 Overprinted

DIENST.

***Perf. 12½***

**1911, Oct. 1 Typo. Unwmk.**

**O1** A6 ½c violet 1.00 8.00
**O2** A6 1c olive grn .25 .80
**O3** A6 2c yellow brn .25 .25
**O4** A3 2½c yellow .75 .75
**O5** A6 2½c blue grn 2.00 2.00
**O6** A6 3c orange .65 .65
**O7** A6 4c ultra .25 .25
**O8** A6 5c rose red 1.20 1.00
*b.* Double overprint *1,600.* *400.00*
**O9** A6 7½c gray 3.00 3.00
**O10** A9 10c slate .25 .25
**O11** A9 12½c deep blue 3.00 3.00
**O12** A9 15c chocolate 1.00 1.00
*a.* Overprinted with two bars 40.00 *120.00*
*b.* As "a," "Dienst" inverted 50.00
**O13** A9 17½c bister 4.00 3.00
**O14** A9 20c olive grn 1.00 .65
**O15** A9 22½c brn & ol grn 4.00 4.00
**O16** A9 25c violet 2.40 2.00
**O17** A9 30c orange brn 1.25 .75
**O18** A9 50c red brown 16.00 10.00
**O19** A10 1g dull lilac 4.00 2.00
**O20** A10 2½g slate blue 34.00 35.00
*Nos. O1-O20 (20)* 80.25 78.35

The overprint reads diagonally downward on Nos. O1-O3 and O5-O9.

**Overprint Inverted**

*O1a* A6 ½c 60.00 *120.00*
*O2a* A6 1c 4.00 *20.00*
*O3a* A6 2c 4.00 *20.00*
*O5a* A6 2½c 12.00 *28.00*
*O6a* A6 3c 120.00 *40.00*
*O8a* A6 5c 4.00 *20.00*
*O10a* A9 10c 4.00 *8.00*
*O11a* A9 12½c 40.00 *60.00*
*O14a* A9 20c 200.00 60.00
*O16a* A9 25c *1,400.* *1,400.*
*O17a* A9 30c 200.00 120.00
*O18a* A9 50c 40.00 32.50
*O19a* A10 1g *575.00* *1,000.*
*O20a* A10 2½g 240.00 *650.00*

Regular Issue of 1892-1894 Overprinted

**1911, Oct. 1**

**O21** A4 10c orange brn 2.40 1.60
**O22** A4 12½c gray 4.00 *12.00*
**O23** A4 15c bister 4.00 4.00
**O24** A4 20c blue 4.00 2.40
**O25** A4 25c lilac 16.00 10.00
**O26** A4 50c carmine 4.00 2.00
**O27** A4 2.50g org brn & bl 67.50 65.00
*Nos. O21-O27 (7)* 101.90 97.00

**Inverted Overprints**

*O21a* A4 10c *15.00* *50.00*
*O22a* A4 12½c *425.00* *400.00*
*O23a* A4 15c *425.00* *325.00*
*O24a* A4 20c *165.00* *175.00*
*O25a* A4 25c *800.00* *900.00*
*O26a* A4 50c *15.00* *75.00*
*O27a* A4 2.50g *1,150.* *1,450.*

Handstamped overprints exist on Nos. O21, O26, O27. Handstamps differ from machine overprints in that the ink is flatter, the quality is poorer, and the "D" is usually slightly angled. The machined printed overprints are always parallel.

A handstamped "D" exists on regular-issue No. 28; however, this was created in limited quantities and was never issued. Value, $2,200.

## OCCUPATION STAMPS

### Issued under Japanese Occupation

During the Japanese occupation of the Netherlands Indies, 1942-45, the occupation forces applied a great variety of overprints to supplies of Netherlands Indies stamps of 1933-42. A few typical examples are shown above.

Most of these overprinted stamps were for use in limited areas, such as Java, Sumatra, Bangka and Billiton, etc. The anchor overprints were applied by the Japanese naval authorities for areas under their control.

For a time, stamps of Straits Settlements and some of the Malayan states, with Japanese overprints, were used in Sumatra and the Riouw archipelago. Stamps of Japan without overprint were also used in the Netherlands Indies during the occupation.

### For Use in Java and Sumatra

100 Sen (Cents) = 1 Rupee (Gulden)

Globe Showing Japanese Empire — OS1

Farmer Plowing Rice Field — OS2

Mt. Semeru, Java's Highest Active Volcano — OS3

Bantam Bay, Northwest Java — OS4

**Values in Sen**

***Perf. 12½***

**1943, Mar. 9 Unwmk. Litho.**

**N1** OS1 2s red brown 2.50 4.25
**N2** OS2 3½s carmine 1.75 1.25
**N3** OS3 5s green 5.00 1.25
**N4** OS4 10s light blue 15.00 2.50
*Nos. N1-N4 (4)* 24.25 9.25

Issued to mark the anniversary of Japan's "Victory" in Java.

### For Use in Java (also Sumatra, Borneo and Malaya)

Javanese Dancer OS5

Javanese Puppet OS6

Buddha Statue, Borobudur OS7

Map of Java OS8

Sacred Dancer of Djokja Palace, and Borobudur OS9

Bird of Vishnu, Map of Java and Mt. Semeru OS10

Plowing with Carabao OS11

Terraced Rice Fields OS12

**Values in Cents, Sen or Rupees**

**1943-44 Unwmk. *Perf. 12½***

**N5** OS5 3½c rose red 2.00 1.00
**N6** OS6 5s yellow grn 3.50 .80
**N7** OS7 10c dk blue 4.00 .60
**N8** OS8 20c gray olive 1.40 .80
**N9** OS9 40c rose lilac 3.50 1.20
**N10** OS10 60c red orange 2.50 1.20
**N11** OS11 80s fawn ('44) 4.50 3.75
**N12** OS12 1r violet ('44) 22.50 3.00
*Nos. N5-N12 (8)* 43.90 12.35

Indies Soldier — OS13

**1943, Apr.**

| | | | | |
|---|---|---|---|---|
| **N13** | OS13 | 3½c rose | 11.00 | 10.00 |
| **N14** | OS13 | 10c blue | 35.00 | 4.25 |

Issued to commemorate reaching the postal savings goal of 5,000,000 gulden.

### For Use in Sumatra

Batta Tribal House OS14

Menangkabau House OS15

Plowing with Carabao OS16

Nias Island Scene OS17

Carabao Canyon — OS18

**1943 Unwmk. *Perf. 12½***

| | | | | |
|---|---|---|---|---|
| **N15** | OS14 | 1c olive green | .55 | 1.00 |
| **N16** | OS14 | 2c brt yel brn | .55 | 1.00 |
| **N17** | OS14 | 3c bluish green | .55 | 1.00 |
| **N18** | OS15 | 3½c rose red | 2.10 | 1.00 |
| **N19** | OS15 | 4c ultra | 1.25 | 1.00 |
| **N20** | OS15 | 5c red orange | 1.50 | 1.00 |
| **N21** | OS16 | 10c blue gray | 4.75 | .50 |
| **N22** | OS16 | 20c orange brn | 1.00 | .50 |
| **N23** | OS17 | 30c red violet | 2.25 | 1.00 |
| **N24** | OS17 | 40c dull brown | 2.50 | 1.00 |
| **N25** | OS18 | 50c bister brn | 2.50 | 2.50 |
| **N26** | OS18 | 1r lt blue vio | 35.00 | 5.00 |
| | | *Nos. N15-N26 (12)* | 54.50 | 16.50 |

### For Use in the Lesser Sunda Islands, Molucca Archipelago and Districts of Celebes and South Borneo Controlled by the Japanese Navy

Japanese Flag, Island Scene OS19

Mt. Fuji, Kite, Flag, Map of East Indies OS20

Values in Cents and Gulden

**1943 Wmk. 257 Typo. *Perf. 13***

| | | | | |
|---|---|---|---|---|
| **N27** | OS19 | 2c brown | 1.25 | *11.50* |
| **N28** | OS19 | 3c yellow grn | 1.25 | *10.50* |
| **N29** | OS19 | 3½c brown org | 4.00 | *10.50* |
| **N30** | OS19 | 5c blue | .80 | *3.75* |
| **N31** | OS19 | 10c carmine | 1.00 | *3.75* |
| **N32** | OS19 | 15c ultra | 1.20 | *10.00* |
| **N33** | OS19 | 20c dull violet | 1.75 | *3.75* |
| | | **Engr.** | | |
| **N34** | OS20 | 25c orange | 6.00 | *11.50* |
| **N35** | OS20 | 30c blue | 6.00 | *6.25* |
| **N36** | OS20 | 50c slate green | 8.50 | *9.00* |
| **N37** | OS20 | 1g brown lilac | 37.50 | *20.00* |
| | | *Nos. N27-N37 (11)* | 69.25 | *100.50* |

### Issued under Nationalist Occupation

Menari Dancer of Amboina — OS21

***Perf. 12½***

**1945, Aug. Photo. Unwmk.**

| | | | | |
|---|---|---|---|---|
| **N38** | OS21 | 2c carmine | .25 | .35 |

This stamp was prepared in 1941 or 1942 by Netherlands Indies authorities as an addition to the 1941 "dancers" set, but was issued in 1945 by the Nationalists (Indonesian Republic). It was not recognized by the Dutch. Exists imperforate.

## NETHERLANDS NEW GUINEA

'ne-t͟hər-lənd͜z 'nü 'gi-nē

(Dutch New Guinea)

LOCATION — Western half of New Guinea, southwest Pacific Ocean
GOVT. — Former Overseas Territory of the Netherlands
AREA — 151,789 sq. mi.
POP. — 730,000 (est. 1958)
CAPITAL — Hollandia

Netherlands New Guinea came under temporary United Nations administration Oct. 1, 1962, when stamps of this territory overprinted "UNTEA" were introduced to replace issues of Netherlands New Guinea. See West New Guinea (West Irian) in Vol. 6.

100 Cents = 1 Gulden

**Catalogue values for all unused stamps in this country are for Never Hinged items.**

A1

A2

Queen Juliana — A3

***Perf. 12½x13½***

**1950-52 Unwmk. Photo.**

| | | | | |
|---|---|---|---|---|
| **1** | A1 | 1c slate blue | .35 | .25 |
| **2** | A1 | 2c deep org | .35 | .25 |
| **3** | A1 | 2½c olive brn | .50 | .25 |
| **4** | A1 | 3c deep plum | 1.75 | 1.60 |
| **5** | A1 | 4c blue grn | 1.75 | 1.25 |
| **6** | A1 | 5c ultra | 3.50 | .25 |
| **7** | A1 | 7½c org brown | .55 | .25 |
| **8** | A1 | 10c purple | 1.75 | .25 |
| **9** | A1 | 12½c crimson | 1.75 | 1.60 |
| | | ***Perf. 13½x12½*** | | |
| **10** | A2 | 15c brown org | 2.50 | .75 |
| **11** | A2 | 20c blue | 1.15 | .25 |
| **12** | A2 | 25c orange red | 1.15 | .25 |
| **13** | A2 | 30c dp blue ('52) | 10.00 | .40 |
| **14** | A2 | 40c blue grn | 1.75 | .25 |
| **15** | A2 | 45c brown ('52) | 5.50 | .80 |
| **16** | A2 | 50c deep orange | 1.50 | .25 |
| **17** | A2 | 55c brown blk ('52) | 10.00 | .60 |
| **18** | A2 | 80c purple | 12.00 | 3.00 |
| | | **Engr. *Perf. 12½x12*** | | |
| **19** | A3 | 1g red | 15.00 | .40 |
| **20** | A3 | 2g yellow brn ('52) | 12.00 | 1.40 |
| **21** | A3 | 5g dk olive grn | 17.50 | 1.40 |
| | | *Nos. 1-21 (21)* | 102.30 | 15.70 |

For surcharges see Nos. B1-B3.

Bird of Paradise — A4

Queen Victoria Crowned Pigeon — A5

Queen Juliana — A6

10c, 15c, 20c, Bird of Paradise with raised wings.

**Photo.; Litho. (Nos. 24, 26, 28)**

**1954-60 *Perf. 12½x12***

| | | | | |
|---|---|---|---|---|
| **22** | A4 | 1c ver & yel ('58) | .40 | .25 |
| **23** | A4 | 5c choc & yel | .40 | .25 |
| **24** | A5 | 7c org red, bl & brn vio ('59) | .55 | .35 |
| **25** | A4 | 10c aqua & red brn | .40 | .25 |
| **26** | A5 | 12c grn, bl & brn vio ('59) | .55 | .35 |
| **27** | A4 | 15c dp yel & red brn | .40 | .25 |
| **28** | A5 | 17c brn vio & bl ('59) | .55 | .25 |
| **29** | A4 | 20c lt bl grn & red brn ('56) | 1.20 | .60 |
| **30** | A6 | 25c red | .40 | .25 |
| **31** | A6 | 30c deep blue | .55 | .25 |
| **32** | A6 | 40c dp orange ('60) | 2.50 | 2.00 |
| **33** | A6 | 45c dk olive ('58) | 1.20 | 1.25 |
| **34** | A6 | 55c dk blue grn | .75 | .25 |
| **35** | A6 | 80c dl gray vio | 1.60 | .40 |
| **36** | A6 | 85c dk vio brn ('56) | 2.00 | .55 |
| **37** | A6 | 1g plum ('59) | 5.25 | 2.25 |
| | | *Nos. 22-37 (16)* | 18.70 | 9.75 |

Stamps overprinted "UNTEA" are listed under West Irian in Vol. 6.
For surcharges see Nos. B4-B6.

Papuan Watching Helicopter — A7

**1959, Apr. 10 Photo. *Perf. 11½x11***

| | | | | |
|---|---|---|---|---|
| **38** | A7 | 55c red brown & blue | 1.75 | 1.00 |

1959 expedition to the Star Mountains of New Guinea.

Mourning Woman — A8

**1960, Apr. 7 Unwmk. *Perf. 13x14***

| | | | | |
|---|---|---|---|---|
| **39** | A8 | 25c blue | .75 | .60 |
| **40** | A8 | 30c yellow bister | .75 | .60 |

World Refugee Year, 7/1/59-6/30/60.

Council Building A9

**1961, Apr. 5 Litho. *Perf. 11x11½***

| | | | | |
|---|---|---|---|---|
| **41** | A9 | 25c bluish green | .30 | *.40* |
| **42** | A9 | 30c rose | .30 | *.40* |

Inauguration of the New Council.

School Children Crossing Street — A10

Design: 30c, Men looking at traffic sign.

**1962, Mar. 16 Photo. *Perf. 14x13***

| | | | | |
|---|---|---|---|---|
| **43** | A10 | 25c dp blue & red | .40 | .40 |
| **44** | A10 | 30c brt green & red | .40 | .40 |

Need for road safety.

Queen Juliana and Prince Bernhard A11

**1962, Apr. 28 Unwmk. *Perf. 14x13***

| | | | | |
|---|---|---|---|---|
| **45** | A11 | 55c olive brown | .40 | *.50* |

Silver wedding anniv.

Tropical Beach A12

Design: 30c, Palm trees on beach.

**1962, July 18 *Perf. 14x13***

| | | | | |
|---|---|---|---|---|
| **46** | A12 | 25c multicolored | .30 | *.40* |
| **47** | A12 | 30c multicolored | .30 | *.40* |

5th So. Pacific Conf., Pago Pago, July 1962.

### SEMI-POSTAL STAMPS

Regular Issue of 1950-52 Surcharged in Black

***Perf. 12½x13½***

**1953, Feb. 9 Unwmk. Photo.**

| | | | | |
|---|---|---|---|---|
| **B1** | A1 | 5c + 5c ultra | 12.00 | 9.50 |
| | | ***Perf. 13½x12½*** | | |
| **B2** | A2 | 15c + 10c brn org | 12.00 | 9.50 |
| **B3** | A2 | 25c + 10c org red | 12.00 | 9.50 |
| | | *Nos. B1-B3 (3)* | 36.00 | 28.50 |

The tax was for flood relief work in the Netherlands.

Nos. 23, 25, 27 Surcharged in Red

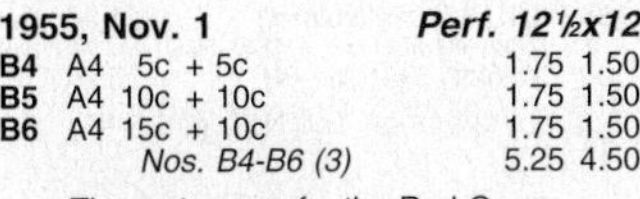

**1955, Nov. 1** *Perf. 12½x12*
**B4** A4 5c + 5c 1.75 1.50
**B5** A4 10c + 10c 1.75 1.50
**B6** A4 15c + 10c 1.75 1.50
*Nos. B4-B6 (3)* 5.25 4.50

The surtax was for the Red Cross.

Leprosarium SP1

10c+5c, 30c+10c, Young Papuan and huts.

*Perf. 12x12½*

**1956, Dec. 15** **Unwmk.** **Photo.**
**B7** SP1 5c + 5c dk slate grn 1.25 .95
**B8** SP1 10c + 5c brn violet 1.25 .95
**B9** SP1 25c + 10c brt blue 1.25 .95
**B10** SP1 30c + 10c ocher 1.25 .95
*Nos. B7-B10 (4)* 5.00 3.80

The surtax was for the fight against leprosy.

Papuan Girl and Beach Scene — SP2

10c+5c, 30c+10c, Papuan boy and pile dwelling.

**1957, Oct. 1** *Perf. 12½x12*
**B11** SP2 5c + 5c maroon 1.25 .95
**B12** SP2 10c + 5c slate grn 1.25 .95
**B13** SP2 25c + 10c brown 1.25 .95
**B14** SP2 30c + 10c dark blue 1.25 .95
*Nos. B11-B14 (4)* 5.00 3.80

The surtax was to fight infant mortality.

Ancestral Image, North Coast New Guinea — SP3

Design: 10c+5c, 30c+10c, Bowl in form of human figure, Asmat-Papua.

**1958, Oct. 1** **Litho.** *Perf. 12½x12*
**B15** SP3 5c + 5c bl, blk & red 1.25 .95
**B16** SP3 10c + 5c rose lake, blk, red & yel 1.25 .95
**B17** SP3 25c + 10c bl grn, blk & red 1.25 .95
**B18** SP3 30c + 10c ol gray, blk, red & yel 1.25 .95
*Nos. B15-B18 (4)* 5.00 3.80

The surtax was for the Red Cross.

Bignonia — SP4

Flowers: 10c+5c, Orchid. 25c+10c, Rhododendron. 30c+10c, Gesneriacea.

**1959, Nov. 16** **Photo.** *Perf. 12½x13*
**B19** SP4 5c + 5c car rose & grn .80 .70
**B20** SP4 10c + 5c ol, yel & lil .80 .70
**B21** SP4 25c + 10c red, org & grn .80 .70
**B22** SP4 30c + 10c vio & grn .80 .70
*Nos. B19-B22 (4)* 3.20 2.80

Birdwing SP5

Various Butterflies.

*Perf. 13x12½*

**1960, Sept. 1** **Unwmk.** **Litho.**
**B23** SP5 5c + 5c lt bl, blk, emer & yel 1.40 1.25
**B24** SP5 10c + 5c sal, blk & bl 1.40 1.25
**B25** SP5 25c + 10c yel, blk & org red 1.40 1.25
**B26** SP5 30c + 10c lt grn, brn & yel 1.40 1.25
*Nos. B23-B26 (4)* 5.60 5.00

Surtax for social care.

Rhinoceros Beetle and Coconut Palm Leaf — SP6

Beetles & leaves of host plants: 10c+5c, Ectocemus 10-maculatus Montri, a primitive weevil. 25c+10c, Stag beetle. 30c+10c, Tortoise beetle.

**1961, Sept. 15** *Perf. 13x12½*
**Beetles in Natural Colors**
**B27** SP6 5c + 5c deep org .70 .50
**B28** SP6 10c + 5c lt ultra .70 .50
**B29** SP6 25c + 10c citron .70 .50
**B30** SP6 30c + 10c green .70 .50
*Nos. B27-B30 (4)* 2.80 2.00

Surtax for social care.

Crab — SP7

Designs: 10c+5c, Lobster, vert. 25c+10c, Spiny lobster, vert. 30c+10c, Shrimp.

*Perf. 14x13, 13x14*

**1962, Sept. 17** **Unwmk.**
**B31** SP7 5c + 5c red, grn, brn & yel .30 .25
**B32** SP7 10c + 5c Prus bl & yel .30 .25
**B33** SP7 25c + 10c multicolored .30 .25
**B34** SP7 30c + 10c bl, org red & yel .35 .30
*Nos. B31-B34 (4)* 1.25 1.05

The surtax on Nos. B19-B34 went to various social works organizations.

## POSTAGE DUE STAMPS

D1

*Perf. 13½x12½*

**1957** **Photo.** **Unwmk.**
**J1** D1 1c vermilion .50 .45
**J2** D1 5c vermilion 1.25 *1.10*
**J3** D1 10c vermilion 2.75 *2.50*
**J4** D1 25c vermilion 3.25 2.90
**J5** D1 40c vermilion 3.25 2.90
**J6** D1 1g blue 5.25 *5.25*
*Nos. J1-J6 (6)* 16.25 15.10

# NEVIS

'nē-vəs

LOCATION — West Indies, southeast of Puerto Rico
GOVT. — A former presidency of the Leeward Islands Colony (British)
AREA — 36 sq. mi.
POP. — 8,794 (1991)

Nevis stamps were discontinued in 1890 and replaced by those of the Leeward Islands. From 1903 to 1956 stamps of St. Kitts-Nevis and Leeward Islands were used concurrently. From 1956 to 1980 stamps of St. Kitts-Nevis were used. While still a part of St. Kitts-Nevis, Nevis started issuing stamps in 1980.

See Leeward Islands and St. Kitts-Nevis.

12 Pence = 1 Shilling
100 Cents = 1 Dollar

**Catalogue values for unused stamps in this country are for Never Hinged items, beginning with Scott 100 in the regular postage section and Scott O1 in the officials section.**

Unused examples of Nos. 1-8 almost always have no original gum, and they are valued without gum. These stamps with original gum are worth more. Other issues are valued with original gum as defined in the catalogue introduction. Very fine examples of Nos. 1-8, will have perforations touching the design on at least one side due to the narrow spacing of the stamps on the plates. Stamps with perfs clear of the design on all four sides are scarce and will command higher prices.

Medicinal Spring
A1 A2

A3

A4

**1861** **Unwmk.** **Engr.** *Perf. 13*
**Bluish Wove Paper**
**1** A1 1p lake rose 325.00 140.00
**2** A2 4p dull rose 950.00 200.00
**3** A3 6p gray 775.00 260.00
**4** A4 1sh green 1,100. 250.00
**Grayish Wove Paper**
**5** A1 1p lake rose 115.00 60.00
**6** A2 4p dull rose 170.00 80.00
**7** A3 6p lilac gray 175.00 65.00
**8** A4 1sh green 400.00 95.00

**1867** **White Wove Paper** *Perf. 15*
**9** A1 1p red 67.50 55.00
**10** A2 4p orange 155.00 25.00
**11** A4 1sh yellow green 925.00 125.00
**12** A4 1sh blue green 325.00 45.00
**Laid Paper**
**13** A4 1sh yel green *25,000.* 6,750.
Manuscript cancel 3,000.

No. 13 values are for stamps with design cut into on one or two sides.

**1876** **Wove Paper** **Litho.**
**14** A1 1p rose 35.00 25.00
**14A** A1 1p red 45.00 30.00
*b.* 1p vermilion 45.00 45.00
*c.* Imperf., pair *1,900.*
*d.* Half used as ½p on cover *4,500.*

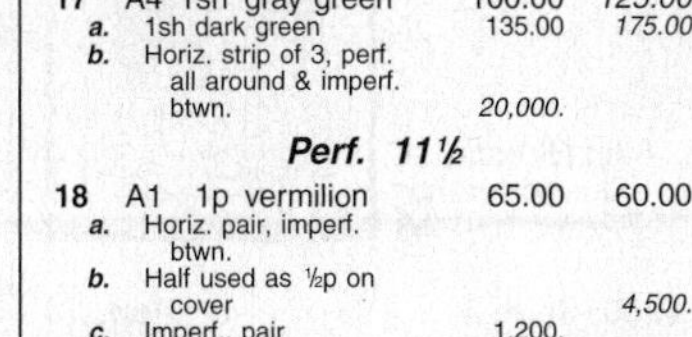

**15** A2 4p orange 190.00 45.00
*a.* Imperf.
*b.* Vert. pair, imperf. between *12,750.*
**16** A3 6p olive gray 250.00 250.00
**17** A4 1sh gray green 100.00 *125.00*
*a.* 1sh dark green 135.00 *175.00*
*b.* Horiz. strip of 3, perf. all around & imperf. btwn. *20,000.*

*Perf. 11½*

**18** A1 1p vermilion 65.00 60.00
*a.* Horiz. pair, imperf. btwn.
*b.* Half used as ½p on cover *4,500.*
*c.* Imperf., pair 1,200.
*Nos. 14-18 (6)* 685.00 535.00

Queen Victoria — A5

**1879-80** **Typo.** **Wmk. 1** *Perf. 14*
**19** A5 1p violet ('80) 90.00 55.00
*a.* Diagonal half used as ½p on cover *1,500.*
**20** A5 2½p red brown 175.00 100.00

**1882-90** **Wmk. Crown and CA (2)**
**21** A5 ½p green ('83) 14.00 *27.50*
**22** A5 1p violet 125.00 50.00
*a.* Half used as ½p on cover 900.00
**23a** A5 1p carmine ('84) 20.00 20.00
**24** A5 2½p red brown 140.00 55.00
**25** A5 2½p ultra ('84) 24.00 27.50
**26** A5 4p blue 400.00 55.00
**27** A5 4p gray ('84) 25.00 10.00
**28** A5 6p green ('83) 500.00 400.00
**29** A5 6p brown org ('86) 27.50 *77.50*
**30** A5 1sh violet ('90) 125.00 *225.00*
*Nos. 21-30 (10)* 1,401. *947.50*

Half of No. 22 Surcharged in Black or Violet

**1883**
**31** A5 ½p on half of 1p 1,100. 60.00
*a.* Double surcharge 450.00
*b.* Unsevered pair *7,500.*
*c.* Surcharged on half of 1p revenue stamp 600.00
**32** A5 ½p on half of 1p (V) 1,250. 55.00
*a.* Double surcharge 450.00
*b.* Unsevered pair *7,500.* 850.00
*c.* Surcharged on half of 1p revenue stamp 600.00

Surcharge reads up or down.

**Catalogue values for unused stamps in this section, from this point to the end of the section, are for Never Hinged items.**

**St. Kitts-Nevis Nos. 357-369 Ovptd.**

*Perf. 14½x14*

**1980, June 23** **Litho.** **Wmk. 373**
**100** A61 5c multicolored .25 .25
**101** A61 10c multicolored .25 .25
**102** A61 12c multicolored .25 .30
**103** A61 15c multicolored .25 .25
**104** A61 25c multicolored .25 .25
*a.* Unwatermarked .80 *1.50*
**105** A61 30c multicolored .25 .25
**106** A61 40c multicolored .30 .30
**107** A61 45c multicolored .75 .50
**108** A61 50c multicolored .30 .30
**109** A61 55c multicolored .40 .25
**110** A61 $1 multicolored .30 .30
*a.* Unwatermarked 2.50 *5.00*
**111** A61 $5 multicolored 1.50 1.00
**112** A61 $10 multicolored 2.50 1.50
*Nos. 100-112 (13)* 7.55 5.70

The bars cover "St. Christopher" and "Anguilla."

80th Birthday of Queen Mother Elizabeth — A6

**1980, Sept. 4** ***Perf. 14***
113 A6 $2 multicolored .40 .50

Ships and Boats — A6a

5c, Nevis lighter. 30c, Local fishing boat. 55c, *Caona*. $3, Windjammer's S.V. *Polynesia*.

**1980, Oct. 8**
114 A6a 5c multicolored .25 .25
115 A6a 30c multicolored .25 .25
116 A6a 55c multicolored .25 .25

**Size: 38x52mm**

117 A6a $3 multicolored .65 .65
a. Perf. 12½x12 .65 .65
b. Booklet pane of 3 #117a 2.00
*Nos. 114-117 (4)* 1.40 1.40

No. 117b separated into three parts by roulettes running vert. through the margin surrounding the stamps. For overprint see No. 538.

Christmas — A7

**1980, Nov. 20** ***Perf. 14***
118 A7 5c Mother and child .30 .30
119 A7 30c Heralding angel .30 .30
120 A7 $2.50 Three kings .60 .60
*Nos. 118-120 (3)* 1.20 1.20

Landmarks — A8

A9

5c, Charlestown Pier. 10c, Court House & Library. 15c, New River Mill. 20c, Nelson Museum. 25c, St. James' Parish Church. 30c, Nevis Lane. 40c, Zetland Plantation. 45c, Nisbet Plantation. 50c, Pinney's Beach. 55c, Eva Wilkin's Studio. $1, Nevis at dawn. $2.50, Ft. Charles ruins. $5, Old Bath House. $10, Nisbet's Beach.

**1981, Feb. 5**

**No Date Imprint Below Design**

121 A8 5c multicolored .25 .25
122 A8 10c multicolored .25 .25
123 A9 15c multicolored .25 .25
124 A9 20c multicolored .25 .25
125 A9 25c multicolored .25 .25
126 A9 30c multicolored .25 .25
127 A9 40c multicolored .25 .25
128 A9 45c multicolored .25 .25
129 A9 50c multicolored .25 .25
130 A9 55c multicolored .30 .30
131 A9 $1 multicolored .55 .55
132 A9 $2.50 multicolored .75 .75
133 A9 $5 multicolored 1.50 1.50
134 A9 $10 multicolored 3.00 3.00
*Nos. 121-134 (14)* 8.35 8.35

For surcharges see Nos. 169-181.

**1982, June 9**

**Inscribed "1982" Below Design**

121a A8 5c multicolored .30 .30
122a A8 10c multicolored .30 .30
123a A9 15c multicolored .25 .25
124a A9 20c multicolored .25 .25
125a A9 25c multicolored .25 .25
126a A9 30c multicolored .25 .25
127a A9 40c multicolored .25 .25
128a A9 45c multicolored .25 .25
129a A9 50c multicolored .25 .25
130a A9 55c multicolored .30 .30
131a A9 $1 multicolored .55 .55
132a A9 $2.50 multicolored .75 .75
133a A9 $5 multicolored 1.50 1.50
134a A9 $10 multicolored 3.00 3.00
*Nos. 121a-134a (14)* 8.45 8.45

**1983**

**Inscribed "1983" Below Design**

124b A9 20c multicolored .50 .25
125b A9 25c multicolored .50 .25
126b A9 30c multicolored .50 .25
127b A9 40c multicolored .50 .25
128b A9 45c multicolored .50 .25
129b A9 50c multicolored .50 .25
130b A9 55c multicolored .50 .25
132b A9 $2.50 multicolored 1.50 1.25
*Nos. 124b-132b (8)* 5.00 3.00

Prince Charles, Lady Diana, Royal Yacht Charlotte A9a

Prince Charles and Lady Diana — A9b

No. 135, Couple, *Royal Caroline*. No. 136, Couple. No. 137, Couple, *Royal Sovereign*. No. 139, Couple, HMY *Britannia*.

**1981, June 23 Wmk. 373** ***Perf. 14***
135 A9a 55c multicolored .25 .25
a. Bklt. pane of 4, perf. 12, unwmkd. 1.10 1.10
136 A9b 55c multicolored .25 .25
137 A9a $2 multicolored .65 .65
138 A9b $2 like No. 136 .65 .65
a. Bklt. pane of 2, perf. 12, unwmkd. 1.75 1.75
139 A9a $5 multicolored 1.25 1.25
140 A9b $5 like No. 136 1.25 1.25
*Nos. 135-140 (6)* 4.30 4.30

**Souvenir Sheet**

**1981, Dec. 14** ***Perf. 12***
141 A9b $4.50 like No. 136 2.00 2.00

Stamps of the same denomination issued in sheets of 7 (6 type A9a and 1 type A9b).
For surcharges see Nos. 453-454.

Butterflies A10

5c, Zebra. 30c, Malachite. 55c, Southern dagger tail. $2, Large orange sulphur.

**1982, Feb. 16** ***Perf. 14***
142 A10 5c multicolored .25 .25
143 A10 30c multicolored .25 .25
144 A10 55c multicolored .25 .25
145 A10 $2 multicolored 1.25 1.25
*Nos. 142-145 (4)* 2.00 2.00

For overprint see No. 452.

**1983, June 8**

30c, Tropical chequered skipper. 55c, Caribbean buckeye, vert. $1.10, Common long-tailed skipper, vert. $2, Mimic.

146 A10 30c multicolored .45 .45
147 A10 55c multicolored .45 .45
148 A10 $1.10 multicolored .65 .65
149 A10 $2 multicolored .90 .90
*Nos. 146-149 (4)* 2.45 2.45

21st Birthday of Princess Diana, July 1 — A11

30c, Caroline of Brunswick. 55c, Brunswick arms. $5, Diana.

**1982, June 22** ***Perf. 13½x14***
150 A11 30c multi .25 .25
151 A11 55c multi .30 .30
152 A11 $5 multi 1.20 1.20
*Nos. 150-152 (3)* 1.75 1.75

For surcharge see No. 449.

**Nos. 150-152 Overprinted "ROYAL BABY"**

**1982, July 12**
153 A11 30c multicolored .25 .25
154 A11 55c multicolored .35 .35
155 A11 $5 multicolored 1.40 1.40
*Nos. 153-155 (3)* 2.00 2.00

Birth of Prince William of Wales, June 21.

Scouting, 75th Anniv. — A12

**1982, Aug. 18**
156 A12 5c Cycling .35 .35
157 A12 30c Running .45 .45
158 A12 $2.50 Building campfire .90 .90
*Nos. 156-158 (3)* 1.70 1.70

For overprints see Nos. 447, 455.

Christmas — A13

Illustrations by youths — 15c, Eugene Seabrookes. 30c, Kharenzabeth Glasgow. $1.50, David Grant. $2.50, Leonard Huggins.
Nos. 159-160 vert.

**1982, Oct. 20** ***Perf. 13½x14, 14x13½***
159 A13 15c multicolored .30 .30
160 A13 30c multicolored .30 .30
161 A13 $1.50 multicolored .40 .40
162 A13 $2.50 multicolored .75 .75
*Nos. 159-162 (4)* 1.75 1.75

Coral — A14

15c, Tube sponge. 30c, Stinging coral. 55c, Flower coral. $3, Sea rod, red fire sponge.

**1983, Jan. 12** ***Perf. 14***
163 A14 15c multicolored .25 .25
164 A14 30c multicolored .40 .40
165 A14 55c multicolored .40 .40
166 A14 $3 multicolored 1.20 1.20
a. Souvenir sheet of 4, #163-166 2.40 2.40
*Nos. 163-166 (4)* 2.25 2.25

For overprints see Nos. 446, 448.

Commonwealth Day — A15

55c, HMS *Boreas* off Nevis. $2, Lord Nelson, *Boreas*.

**1983, Mar. 14**
167 A15 55c multicolored .25 .25
168 A15 $2 multicolored .65 .65

**Nos. 121a and 123a-134a Ovptd.**

No. 169

No. 170-181



**1983, Sept. 19**
169 A8 5c multicolored .25 .25
c. Overprint larger with serifed letters 1.25 *2.25*
170 A9 15c multicolored .25 .25
171 A9 20c multicolored .25 .25
172 A9 25c multicolored .25 .25
173 A9 30c multicolored .25 .25
174 A9 40c multicolored .25 .30
175 A9 45c multicolored .30 .40
176 A9 50c multicolored .30 .40
177 A9 55c multicolored .35 .45
178 A9 $1 multicolored .45 .45
179 A9 $2.50 multicolored .45 .70
180 A9 $5 multicolored .55 .85
181 A9 $10 multicolored .75 1.10
*Nos. 169-181 (13)* 4.65 5.90

The overprints on Nos. 169a and 169c were applied locally.

**Nos. 121, 123-127, 130-134 Ovptd.**

**1983**
169a A8 5c multicolored, larger ovpt. 15.00 12.00
170a A9 15c multicolored 42.50 42.50
171a A9 20c multicolored 6.00 6.00
172a A9 25c multicolored 6.00 6.00
173a A9 30c multicolored 1.10 1.10
174a A9 40c multicolored 1.00 1.00
177a A9 55c multicolored 1.00 1.00
178a A9 $1 multicolored 1.00 1.00
179a A9 $2.50 multicolored 1.40 1.40
180a A9 $5 multicolored 2.50 2.50
181a A9 $10 multicolored 4.50 4.50
*Nos. 169a-181a (11)* 82.00 79.00

**Nos. 124b-132b and Additional values inscribed "1983" Ovptd.**

**1983**
170b A9 15c multicolored 1.75 1.00
171b A9 20c multicolored 1.75 1.00
172b A9 25c multicolored 1.75 1.00
173b A9 30c multicolored 1.75 1.00
174b A9 40c multicolored 1.75 1.00
175b A9 45c multicolored 1.75 1.00
176b A9 50c multicolored 1.75 1.00
177b A9 55c multicolored 1.75 1.00
178b A9 $1 multicolored 2.25 1.25
179b A9 $2.50 multicolored 1.75 1.00
180b A9 $5 multicolored 3.00 3.00
181b A9 $10 multicolored 6.00 6.00
*Nos. 170b-181b (12)* 27.00 19.25

1st Manned Flight, Bicent. A16

10c, Montgolfier Balloon, 1783, vert. 45c, Lindbergh's Sikorsky S-38 carrying mail, 1929. 50c, Beechcraft Twin Bonanza. $2.50, Sea Harrier, 1st operational V/STOL fighter.

**1983, Sept. 28 Wmk. 380**

**182** A16 10c multicolored .25 .25
**183** A16 45c multicolored .25 .25
**184** A16 50c multicolored .25 .25
**185** A16 $2.50 multicolored .50 .50
*a.* Souvenir sheet of 4, #182-185 1.75 1.75
*Nos. 182-185 (4)* 1.25 1.25

Christmas A17

**1983, Nov. 7**

**186** A17 5c Nativity .25 .25
**187** A17 30c Shepherds, flock .25 .25
**188** A17 55c Angels .25 .25
**189** A17 $3 Youths .90 .90
*a.* Souvenir sheet of 4, #186-189 1.50 1.50
*Nos. 186-189 (4)* 1.65 1.65

**Leaders of the World**

**Large quantities of some Leaders of the World issues were sold at a fraction of face value when the printer was liquidated.**

A18

Leaders of the World: Locomotives — No. 190, 1882 Class Wee Bogie, UK. No. 191, 1968 JNR Class EF81, Japan. No. 192, 1878 Snowdon Ranger, UK. No. 193, 1927 P.O. Class 5500, France. No. 194, 1859 Connor Single Class. No. 195, 1904 Large Belpaire Passenger, UK. No. 196, 1829 Stourbridge Lion, US. No. 197, 1934 Cock O' The North. No. 198, 1945 County of Oxford, GB. No. 199, 1940 SNCF Class 240P, France. No. 200, 1851 Comet, UK. No. 201, 1904 County Class, UK. No. 202, 1926 JNR Class 7000, Japan. No. 203, 1877 Nord L'Outrance, France. No. 204, 1919 CM St.P&P Bipolar, US. No. 205, 1897 Palatinate Railway Class P3, Germany. No. 206, 1908 Class 8H, UK. No. 207, 1927 King George V. No. 208, 1951 Britannia. No. 209, 1924 Pendennis Castle. No. 210, 1960 Evening Star. No. 211, 1934 Stanier Class 5, GB. No. 212, 1946 Winston Churchill Battle of Britain. No. 213, 1935 Mallard A4. No. 214, 1899 Q.R. Class PB-15, Australia. No. 215, 1836 C&St.L Dorchester, Canada. No. 216, 1953 U.P. Gas Turbine, US. No. 217, 1969 U.P. Centennial Class, US. No. 218, 1866 No. 23 Class A, UK. No. 219, 1955 NY, NH & HR FL9, US. No. 220, 1837 B&O Lafayette, US. No. 221, 1964 JNR Shin-Kansen, Japan. No. 222, 1928 DRG Class 64, Germany. No. 223, 1882 D&RGR Class C-16, US.

**1983-86 Litho. Unwmk. *Perf. 12½***

**Se-tenant Pairs, #a.-b.**

**a. — Side and front views.**

**b. — Action scene.**

**190** A18 1c multicolored .25 .25
**191** A18 5c multicolored .25 .25
**192** A18 5c multicolored .25 .25
**193** A18 10c multicolored .25 .25
**194** A18 15c multicolored .25 .25
**195** A18 30c multicolored .25 .25
**196** A18 30c multicolored .25 .25
**197** A18 45c multicolored .25 .25
**198** A18 55c multicolored .25 .25
**199** A18 60c multicolored .25 .25
**200** A18 60c multicolored .25 .25
**201** A18 60c multicolored .25 .25
**202** A18 60c multicolored .25 .25
**203** A18 75c multicolored .30 .30
**204** A18 75c multicolored .30 .30
**205** A18 75c multicolored .30 .30
**206** A18 90c multicolored .30 .30
**207** A18 $1 multicolored .35 .35
**208** A18 $1 multicolored .35 .35
**209** A18 $1 multicolored .35 .35
**210** A18 $1 multicolored .35 .35
**211** A18 $1 multicolored .35 .35
**212** A18 $1 multicolored .35 .35
**213** A18 $1 multicolored .35 .35
**214** A18 $1 multicolored .35 .35
**215** A18 $1 multicolored .35 .35
**216** A18 $1.50 multicolored .50 .50
**217** A18 $1.50 multicolored .50 .50
**218** A18 $2 multicolored .70 .70
**219** A18 $2 multicolored .70 .70
**220** A18 $2 multicolored .70 .70
**221** A18 $2.50 multicolored 1.00 1.00
**222** A18 $2.50 multicolored 1.00 1.00
**223** A18 $3 multicolored 1.00 1.00
*Nos. 190-223 (34)* 13.70 13.70

Issued: #190, 200, 218, 4/26/85; #191, 193, 199, 221, 10/29/84; #192, 195, 201, 203, 214, 222, 7/26/85; #194, 197, 202, 204, 215, 217, 220, 223, 10/1/86; #196, 205, 216, 219, 1/30/86; #198, 206-213, 11/10/83.

British Monarchs, Scenes from History — A20

#258a, Boer War. #258b, Queen Victoria. #259a, Signing of the Magna Carta. #259b, King John. #260a, Victoria, diff. #260b, Osborne House. #261a, John, diff. #261b, Newark Castle, Nottinghamshire. #262a, Battle of Dettingen. #262b, King George II. #263a, George II, diff. #263b, Bank of England, 1732. #264a, George II's coat of arms. #264b, George II, diff. #265a, John's coat of arms. #265b, John, diff. #266a, Victoria's coat of arms. #266b, Victoria, diff.

**1984**

**258** A20 5c Pair, #a.-b. .25 .25
**259** A20 5c Pair, #a.-b. .25 .25
**260** A20 50c Pair, #a.-b. .25 .25
**261** A20 55c Pair, #a.-b. .25 .25
**262** A20 60c Pair, #a.-b. .25 .25
**263** A20 75c Pair, #a.-b. .25 .25
**264** A20 $1 Pair, #a.-b. .25 .25
**265** A20 $2 Pair, #a.-b. .60 .60
**266** A20 $3 Pair, #a.-b. .50 .50
*Nos. 258-266 (9)* 2.85 2.85

Issued: #258, 260, 262-264, 266, 4/11; others, 11/20.

Tourism A22

No. 276, Golden Rock Inn. No. 277, Rest Haven Inn. No. 278, Cliffdwellers Hotel. No. 279, Pinney's Beach Hotel.

**1984, May 16 Wmk. 380 *Perf. 14***

**276** A22 55c multicolored .40 .40
**277** A22 55c multicolored .40 .40
**278** A22 55c multicolored .40 .40
**279** A22 55c multicolored .40 .40
*Nos. 276-279 (4)* 1.60 1.60

Seal of the Colony — A22a

**1984, June 8 Wmk. 380 *Perf. 14***

**279A** A22a $15 dull red 1.60 5.25

**Tourism Type of 1984**

No. 280, Croney's Old Manor Hotel. No. 281, Montpelier Plantation Inn. No. 282, Nisbet's Plantation Inn. No. 283, Zetland Plantation Inn.

**1985, Feb. 12**

**280** A22 $1.20 multicolored .60 .60
**281** A22 $1.20 multicolored .60 .60
**282** A22 $1.20 multicolored .60 .60
**283** A22 $1.20 multicolored .60 .60
*Nos. 280-283 (4)* 2.40 2.40

A23

Leaders of the World: Classic cars — No. 285, 1932 Cadillac V16 Fleetwood Convertible, US. No. 286, 1935 Delahaye Type 35 Cabriolet, France. No. 287, 1916 Packard Twin Six Touring Car, US. No. 288, 1929 Lagonda Speed Model Touring Car, GB. No. 289, 1958 Ferrari Testarossa, Italy. No. 290, 1934 Voisin Aerodyne, France. No. 291, 1912 Sunbeam Coupe De L'Auto, GB. No. 292, 1936 Adler Trumpf, Germany. No. 293, 1886 Daimler 2-Cylinder, Germany. No. 294, 1930 Riley Brooklands Nine, UK. No. 295, 1967 Jaguar E-Type 4.2 Liter, GB. No. 296, 1970 Porsche 911 S Targa, Germany. No. 297, 1948 Cisitalia Pinnifarina Coupe, Italy. No. 298, 1885 Benz Three-wheeler, Germany. No. 299, 1966 Alfa Romeo GTA, Italy. No. 300, 1947 Volkswagen Beetle, Germany. No. 301, 1963 Buick Riviera. No. 302, 1947 MG TC, GB. No. 303, 1960 Cooper Climax, UK. No. 304, 1957 Maserati Tipo 250F, Italy. No. 305, 1913 Pierce Arrow Type 66, US. No. 306, 1904 Ford 999, US. No. 307, 1980 Porsche 928S, Germany. No. 308, 1910 Oldsmobile Limited, US. No. 309, 1951 Jaguar C-Type, UK. No. 310, 1928 Willys-Knight 66A, US. No. 311, 1933 MG K3 Magnette, GB. No. 312, 1937 Lincoln Zephyr, US. No. 313, 1937 ERA 1.5 I B Type, UK. No. 314, 1953 Studebaker Starliner, US. No. 315, 1926 Pontiac 2-door, US. No. 316, 1966 Cobra Roadster 289, US. No. 317, 1930 MG M-Type Midget, UK. No. 318, 1966 Aston Martin DB6 Hardtop, GB. No. 319, 1932 Pierce Arrow V12, US. No. 320, 1971 Rolls Royce Corniche, UK. No. 321, 1953 Chevrolet Corvette, US. No. 322, 1919 Cunningham V-8, US.

**1984-86 Unwmk. *Perf. 12½***

**Se-tenant Pairs, #a.-b.**

**a. — Side and front views.**

**b. — Action scene.**

**285** A23 1c multicolored .25 .25
**286** A23 1c multicolored .25 .25
**287** A23 5c multicolored .25 .25
**288** A23 5c multicolored .25 .25
**289** A23 5c multicolored .25 .25
**290** A23 10c multicolored .25 .25
**291** A23 10c multicolored .25 .25
**292** A23 10c multicolored .25 .25
**293** A23 15c multicolored .25 .25
**294** A23 15c multicolored .25 .25
**295** A23 30c multicolored .25 .25
**296** A23 35c multicolored .25 .25
**297** A23 35c multicolored .25 .25
**298** A23 45c multicolored .25 .25
**299** A23 45c multicolored .25 .25
**300** A23 50c multicolored .25 .25
**301** A23 50c multicolored .25 .25
**302** A23 55c multicolored .25 .25
**303** A23 60c multicolored .25 .25
**304** A23 60c multicolored .25 .25
**305** A23 60c multicolored .25 .25
**306** A23 75c multicolored .25 .25
**307** A23 75c multicolored .25 .25
**308** A23 75c multicolored .25 .25
**309** A23 $1 multicolored .30 .30
**310** A23 $1 multicolored .30 .30
**311** A23 $1.15 multicolored .35 .35
**312** A23 $1.50 multicolored .40 .40
**313** A23 $1.50 multicolored .40 .40
**314** A23 $1.75 multicolored .45 .45
**315** A23 $2 multicolored .55 .55
**316** A23 $2.50 multicolored .70 .70
**317** A23 $2.50 multicolored .70 .70
**318** A23 $3 multicolored .75 .75
**319** A23 $3 multicolored .75 .75
**320** A23 $3 multicolored .75 .75
**321** A23 $3 multicolored .75 .75
**322** A23 $3 multicolored .75 .75
*Nos. 285-322 (38)* 13.90 13.90

Issued: #285, 287, 293, 296, 298, 302, 316, 318, 7/25/84; #286, 289-290, 301, 303, 306, 317, 320, 2/20/85; #288, 295, 300, 319, 10/23/84; #291, 297, 307, 311-312, 315, 10/4/85; #292, 303, 308-309, 313, 321, 1/30/86; #294, 299, 305, 310, 314, 322, 8/15/86.

Culturama Carnival, 10th Anniv. A24a

30c, Carpentry. 55c, Weaving mats and baskets. $1, Ceramics. $3, Carnival queen, folk dancers.

**Wmk. 380**

**1984, Aug. 1 Litho. *Perf. 14***

**361** A24a 30c multicolored .25 .25
**362** A24a 55c multicolored .25 .25
**363** A24a $1 multicolored .25 .25
**364** A24a $3 multicolored .65 .65
*Nos. 361-364 (4)* 1.40 1.40

Flowers — A24b

5c, Yellow bell. 10c, Plumbago. 15c, Flamboyant. 20c, Eyelash orchid. 30c, Bougainvillea. 40c, Hibiscus. 50c, Night-blooming cereus. 55c, Yellow mahoe. 60c, Spider lily. 75c, Scarlet cordia. $1, Shell ginger. $3, Blue petrea. $5, Coral hibiscus. $10, Passion flower.

**1984, Aug. 8**

**No Date Imprint Below Design**

**365** A24b 5c multi .25 .25
**366** A24b 10c multi .25 .25
**367** A24b 15c multi .25 .25
**368** A24b 20c multi .25 .25
*a.* Inscribed "1986" .55 .35
**369** A24b 30c multi .25 .25
**370** A24b 40c multi .25 .25
*a.* Inscribed "1986" .40 .35
**371** A24b 50c multi .25 .25
**372** A24b 55c multi .25 .25
**373** A24b 60c multi .30 .30
**374** A24b 75c multi .35 .35
**375** A24b $1 multi .30 .40
**376** A24b $3 multi .60 1.10
**377** A24b $5 multi 1.10 2.00
**378** A24b $10 multi 2.25 3.50
*Nos. 365-378 (14)* 6.90 9.65

Nos. 368a and 370a issued 7/23/86.

Independence of St. Kitts and Nevis, 1st Anniv. — A26

15c, Picking cotton. 55c, Hamilton House. $1.10, Self-sufficiency in food production. $3, Pinney's Beach.

**1984, Sept. 18**

**379** A26 15c multi .25 .25
**380** A26 55c multi .25 .25
**381** A26 $1.10 multi .35 .35
**382** A26 $3 multi .60 1.00
*Nos. 379-382 (4)* 1.45 1.85

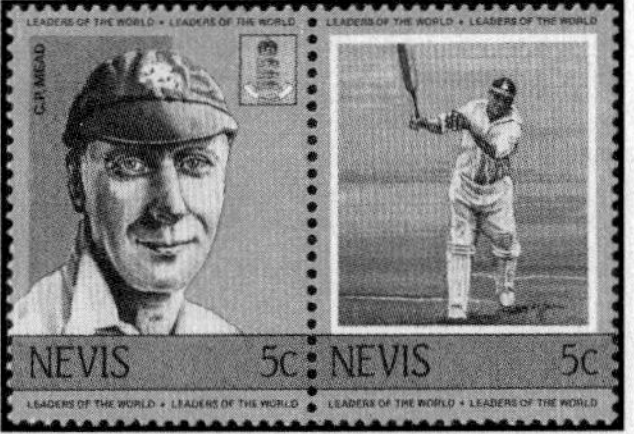

Leaders of the World — A27

Cricket players and team emblems and match scenes: No. 383, C.P. Mead, England. No. 384, J.D. Love, Yorkshire. No. 385, S.J. Dennis, Yorkshire. No. 386, J.B. Statham, England. No. 387, Sir Learie Constantine,

West Indies. No. 388, B.W. Luckhurst, Kent. No. 389, Sir Leonard Hutton, England. No. 390, B.L. D'Oliveira, England.

**Pairs, #a.-b.**

**1984 Unwmk. *Perf. 12½***

| | | | | |
|---|---|---|---|---|
| **383** | A27 | 5c multicolored | .25 | .25 |
| **384** | A27 | 5c multicolored | .25 | .25 |
| **385** | A27 | 15c multicolored | .25 | .25 |
| **386** | A27 | 25c multicolored | .25 | .25 |
| **387** | A27 | 55c multicolored | .25 | .25 |
| **388** | A27 | 55c multicolored | .25 | .25 |
| **389** | A27 | $2.50 multicolored | .50 | 1.25 |
| **390** | A27 | $2.50 multicolored | .50 | 1.25 |
| | | *Nos. 383-390 (8)* | 2.50 | 4.00 |

Issued: #383, 386, 389, 10/23; others, 11/20.

Christmas A29

Musicians from local bands: 15c, Flutist and drummer of the Honeybees Band. 40c, Guitar and barhow players of the Canary Birds Band. 60c, Shell All Stars steel band. $3, Choir, organist, St. John's Church, Fig Tree.

**1984, Nov. 2 Wmk. 380 *Perf. 14***

| | | | | |
|---|---|---|---|---|
| **399-402** | A29 | Set of 4 | 2.25 | 2.25 |

Birds A30

**1985, Mar. 19**

| | | | | |
|---|---|---|---|---|
| **403** | A30 | 20c Broad-winged hawk | 1.10 | .25 |
| **404** | A30 | 40c Red-tailed hawk | 1.25 | .35 |
| **405** | A30 | 60c Little blue heron | 1.25 | .45 |
| **406** | A30 | $3 Great white heron | 2.75 | 2.25 |
| | | *Nos. 403-406 (4)* | 6.35 | 3.30 |

Leaders of the World — A31

Birds: #407a, Painted bunting. #407b, Golden-crowned kinglet. #408a, Eastern bluebird. #408b, Northern cardinal. #409a, Common flicker. #409b, Western tanager. #410a, Belted kingfisher. #410b, Mangrove cuckoo. #411a, Yellow warbler. #411b, Cerulean warbler. #412a, Sage thrasher. #412b, Evening grosbeak. #413a, Burrowing owl. #413b, Long-eared owl. #414a, Blackburnian warbler. #414b, Northern oriole.

**1985 Unwmk. *Perf. 12½***

| | | | | |
|---|---|---|---|---|
| **407** | A31 | 1c Pair, #a.-b. | .25 | .25 |
| **408** | A31 | 5c Pair, #a.-b. | .25 | .25 |
| **409** | A31 | 40c Pair, #a.-b. | .35 | .35 |
| **410** | A31 | 55c Pair, #a.-b. | .40 | .40 |
| **411** | A31 | 60c Pair, #a.-b. | .45 | .45 |
| **412** | A31 | 60c Pair, #a.-b. | .45 | .45 |
| **413** | A31 | $2 Pair, #a.-b. | 1.25 | 1.25 |
| **414** | A31 | $2.50 Pair, #a.-b. | 1.50 | 1.50 |
| | | *Nos. 407-414 (8)* | 4.90 | 4.90 |

John J. Audubon, ornithologist, birth bicent.
Issued: 1c, 40c, #412, $2.50, 6/3; others, 3/25.

Girl Guides, 75th Anniv. — A32

15c, Troop, horiz. 60c, Uniforms, 1910, 1985. $1, Lord and Lady Baden-Powell. $3, Princess Margaret.

**1985, June 17 Wmk. 380 *Perf. 14***

| | | | | |
|---|---|---|---|---|
| **423** | A32 | 15c multicolored | .25 | .25 |
| **424** | A32 | 60c multicolored | .25 | .25 |
| **425** | A32 | $1 multicolored | .30 | .30 |
| **426** | A32 | $3 multicolored | .80 | 1.25 |
| | | *Nos. 423-426 (4)* | 1.60 | 2.05 |

Queen Mother Elizabeth — A33

#427a, 432a, Black hat, white plume. #427b, 432b, Blue hat, pink feathers. #428a, Blue hat. #428b, Tiara. #429a, Violet & blue hat. #429b, Blue hat. #430a, 433a, Light blue hat. #430b, 433b, Black hat. #431a, As a child, c. 1910. #431b, Queen consort, c. 1945.

**1985, July 31 Unwmk. *Perf. 12½***

| | | | | |
|---|---|---|---|---|
| **427** | A33 | 45c Pair, #a.-b. | .25 | .25 |
| **428** | A33 | 75c Pair, #a.-b. | .30 | .30 |
| **429** | A33 | $1.20 Pair, #a.-b. | .55 | .55 |
| **430** | A33 | $1.50 Pair, #a.-b. | .70 | .70 |
| | | *Nos. 427-430 (4)* | 1.80 | 1.80 |

**Souvenir Sheets**

| | | | | |
|---|---|---|---|---|
| **431** | A33 | $2 Sheet of 2, #a.-b. | 2.00 | 2.00 |
| **432** | A33 | $3.50 Sheet of 2, #a.-b. | 2.00 | 2.00 |
| **433** | A33 | $6 Sheet of 2, #a.-b. | 4.00 | 4.00 |

Issued: #432-433, 12/27; others, 7/31.
For overprints see No. 450.

Great Western Railway, 150th Anniv. — A34

Railway engineers and their achievements: #438a, Isambard Brunel. #438b, Royal Albert Bridge, 1859. #439a, William Dean. #439b, *Lord of the Isles*, 1895. #440a, *Lode Star*, 1907. #440b, G.J. Churchward. #441a, Pendennis Castle Class, 1924. #441b, C.B. Collett.

**1985, Aug. 31**

| | | | | |
|---|---|---|---|---|
| **438** | A34 | 25c Pair, #a.-b. | .25 | .25 |
| **439** | A34 | 50c Pair, #a.-b. | .30 | .30 |
| **440** | A34 | $1 Pair, #a.-b. | .50 | .50 |
| **441** | A34 | $2.50 Pair, #a.-b. | 1.30 | 1.30 |
| | | *Nos. 438-441 (4)* | 2.35 | 2.35 |

**Nos. 163, 157, 164, 151, 427, 144, 139-140 and 158 Ovptd. or Srchd. "CARIBBEAN ROYAL VISIT 1985" in 2 or 3 Lines**

***Perf. 14, 12½ (45c)***

**1985, Oct. 23 Wmk. as Before**

| | | | | |
|---|---|---|---|---|
| **446** | A14 | 15c No. 163 | 1.00 | 1.00 |
| **447** | A12 | 30c No. 157 | 2.00 | 2.00 |
| **448** | A14 | 30c No. 164 | 1.00 | 1.00 |
| **449** | A11 | 40c on 55c No. 151 | 2.25 | 2.25 |
| **450** | A33 | 45c Pair, #a.-b. | 3.00 | 3.00 |
| **452** | A10 | 55c No. 144 | 2.25 | 2.25 |
| **453** | A9a | $1.50 on $5 No. 139 | 3.75 | 3.75 |
| **454** | A9b | $1.50 on $5 No. 140 | 13.00 | *15.00* |
| **455** | A12 | $2.50 No. 158 | 4.00 | 4.00 |
| | | *Nos. 446-455 (9)* | 32.25 | 34.25 |

Christmas A36

Anglican, Roman Catholic and Methodist churches — 10c, St. Paul's, Charlestown. 40c, St. Theresa, Charlestown. 60c, Methodist Church, Gingerland. $3, St. Thomas, Lowland.

**1985, Nov. 5 Wmk. 380 *Perf. 15***

| | | | | |
|---|---|---|---|---|
| **456** | A36 | 10c multicolored | .25 | .25 |
| **457** | A36 | 40c multicolored | .30 | .30 |
| **458** | A36 | 60c multicolored | .40 | .40 |
| **459** | A36 | $3 multicolored | 1.25 | 1.25 |
| | | *Nos. 456-459 (4)* | 2.20 | 2.20 |

Spitfire Fighter Plane, 50th Anniv. — A37

$1, Prototype K.5054, 1936. $2.50, Mk.1A, 1940. $3, Mk.XII, 1944. $4, Mk.XXIV, 1948. $6, Seafire Mk.III.

**1986, Mar. 24 Unwmk. *Perf. 12½***

| | | | | |
|---|---|---|---|---|
| **460** | A37 | $1 multi | .30 | .30 |
| **461** | A37 | $2.50 multi | .70 | .70 |
| **462** | A37 | $3 multi | .80 | .80 |
| **463** | A37 | $4 multi | 1.20 | 1.20 |
| | | *Nos. 460-463 (4)* | 3.00 | 3.00 |

**Souvenir Sheet**

| | | | | |
|---|---|---|---|---|
| **464** | A37 | $6 multi | 3.00 | 3.00 |

No. 464 exists imperf. Value, $12.50 unused.

Discovery of America, 500th Anniv. (in 1992) — A38

#465a, American Indian. #465b, Columbus trading with Indians. #466a, Columbus's coat of arms. #466b, Breadfruit. #467a, Galleons. #467b, Columbus.

**1986, Apr. 11**

| | | | | |
|---|---|---|---|---|
| **465** | A38 | 75c Pair, #a.-b. | .90 | .90 |
| **466** | A38 | $1.75 Pair, #a.-b. | 2.25 | 2.25 |
| **467** | A38 | $2.50 Pair, #a.-b. | 3.25 | 3.25 |
| | | *Nos. 465-467 (3)* | 6.40 | 6.40 |

**Souvenir Sheet**

| | | | | |
|---|---|---|---|---|
| **468** | A38 | $6 Columbus, diff. | 6.50 | 6.50 |

Printed in continuous designs picturing various maps of Columbus's voyages.

Queen Elizabeth II, 60th Birthday — A39

Various portraits.

**1986, Apr. 21**

| | | | | |
|---|---|---|---|---|
| **472** | A39 | 5c multicolored | .25 | .25 |
| **473** | A39 | 75c multicolored | .25 | .25 |
| **474** | A39 | $2 multicolored | .50 | .50 |
| **475** | A39 | $8 multi, vert. | 2.00 | 2.00 |
| | | *Nos. 472-475 (4)* | 3.00 | 3.00 |

**Souvenir Sheet**

| | | | | |
|---|---|---|---|---|
| **476** | A39 | $10 multicolored | 6.00 | 6.00 |

1986 World Cup Soccer Championships, Mexico — A40

1c, Character trademark. 2c, Brazilian player. 5c, Danish player. 10c, Brazilian, diff. 20c, Denmark vs. Spain. 30c, Paraguay vs. Chile. 60c, Italy vs. W. Germany. 75c, Danish team. $1, Paraguayan team. $1.75, Brazilian team. $3, Italy vs. England. $6, Italian team.

**Size of 75c, $1, $1.75, $6: 56x35½mm**

***Perf. 15, 12½ (75c, $1, $1.75, $6)***

**1986, May 16**

| | | | | |
|---|---|---|---|---|
| **477** | A40 | 1c multicolored | .25 | .25 |
| **478** | A40 | 2c multicolored | .25 | .25 |
| **479** | A40 | 5c multicolored | .25 | .25 |
| **480** | A40 | 10c multicolored | .25 | .25 |
| **481** | A40 | 20c multicolored | .25 | .25 |
| **482** | A40 | 30c multicolored | .25 | .25 |
| **483** | A40 | 60c multicolored | .35 | .35 |
| **484** | A40 | 75c multicolored | .50 | .50 |
| **485** | A40 | $1 multicolored | .70 | .70 |
| **486** | A40 | $1.75 multicolored | .80 | .80 |
| **487** | A40 | $3 multicolored | 1.30 | 1.30 |
| **488** | A40 | $6 multicolored | 2.50 | 2.50 |
| | | *Nos. 477-488 (12)* | 7.65 | 7.65 |

**Souvenir Sheets**

***Perf. 12½***

| | | | | |
|---|---|---|---|---|
| **489** | A40 | $1.50 like $1.75 | 1.90 | 1.90 |
| **490** | A40 | $2 like $6 | 2.10 | 2.10 |

***Perf. 15***

| | | | | |
|---|---|---|---|---|
| **491** | A40 | $2 like 20c | 2.10 | 2.10 |
| **492** | A40 | $2.50 like 60c | 2.50 | 2.50 |
| **493** | A40 | $4 like 30c | 3.50 | 3.50 |

Nos. 478-483 and 487 vert.

Local Industry A41

**1986, July 18 Wmk. 380 *Perf. 14***

| | | | | |
|---|---|---|---|---|
| **494** | A41 | 15c Textile | .35 | .35 |
| **495** | A41 | 40c Carpentry | .50 | .50 |
| **496** | A41 | $1.20 Agriculture | 1.40 | 1.40 |
| **497** | A41 | $3 Fishing | 3.25 | 3.25 |
| | | *Nos. 494-497 (4)* | 5.50 | 5.50 |

A42

Wedding of Prince Andrew and Sarah Ferguson — A43

#498a, Andrew. #498b, Sarah. #499a, Andrew at the races, horiz. #499b, Andrew in Africa, horiz.

**1986, July 23 Unwmk. *Perf. 12½***

| | | | | |
|---|---|---|---|---|
| **498** | A42 | 60c Pair, #a.-b. | .40 | .40 |

**499** A42 $2 Pair, #a.-b. 1.25 1.25

### Souvenir Sheet

**500** A43 $10 Couple on Balcony 4.25 4.25

Printed in vert. and horiz. pairs.
For overprints see Nos. 521-522.

Coral — A44

**1986, Sept. 8 Wmk. 380 *Perf. 15***

**503** A44 15c Gorgonia .25 .25
**504** A44 60c Fire coral .30 .30
**505** A44 $2 Elkhorn coral 1.00 1.00
**506** A44 $3 Feather star 1.30 1.30
*Nos. 503-506 (4)* 2.85 2.85

A45

Statue of Liberty, Cent. — A46

15c, Statue, World Trade Center. 25c, Statue, tall ship. 40c, Under renovation (front). 60c, Renovation (side). 75c, Statue, Operation Sail. $1, Tall ship. $1.50, Renovation (arm, head). $2, Ship flying Liberty flag. $2.50, Statue, Manhattan. $3, Workers on scaffold.

$3.50, Statue at dusk. $4, Head. $4.50, Torch struck by lightning. $5, Torch, blazing sun.

All stamps are vertical except the $1 & $2.

**1986, Oct. 28 Unwmk. *Perf. 14***

**507** A45 15c multicolored .25 .25
**508** A45 25c multicolored .25 .25
**509** A45 40c multicolored .25 .25
**510** A45 60c multicolored .40 .40
**511** A45 75c multicolored .50 .50
**512** A45 $1 multicolored .65 .65
**513** A45 $1.50 multicolored .85 .85
**514** A45 $2 multicolored 1.10 1.10
**515** A45 $2.50 multicolored 1.25 1.25
**516** A45 $3 multicolored 1.60 1.60
*Nos. 507-516 (10)* 7.10 7.10

### Souvenir Sheets

**517** A46 $3.50 multicolored 2.10 2.10
**518** A46 $4 multicolored 2.25 2.25
**519** A46 $4.50 multicolored 2.50 2.50
**520** A46 $5 multicolored 2.75 2.75

### Nos. 498-499 Ovptd. "Congratulations to T.R.H. The Duke & Duchess of York"

**1986, Nov. 17 *Perf. 12½***

**521** A42 60c Pair, #a.-b. .45 .45
**522** A42 $2 Pair, #a.-b. 1.50 1.50

Sports A47

**1986, Nov. 21 *Perf. 14***

**525** A47 10c Sailing .30 .30
**526** A47 25c Netball .30 .30
**527** A47 $2 Cricket 2.10 2.10
**528** A47 $3 Basketball 3.25 3.25
*Nos. 525-528 (4)* 5.95 5.95

Christmas — A48

Churches: 10c, St. George's Anglican Church, Gingerland. 40c, Methodist Church, Fountain. $1, Charlestown Methodist Church. $5, Wesleyan Holiness Church, Brown Hill.

**1986, Dec. 8**

**529** A48 10c multicolored .25 .25
**530** A48 40c multicolored .30 .30
**531** A48 $1 multicolored .75 .75
**532** A48 $5 multicolored 3.25 3.25
*Nos. 529-532 (4)* 4.55 4.55

US Constitution — A49

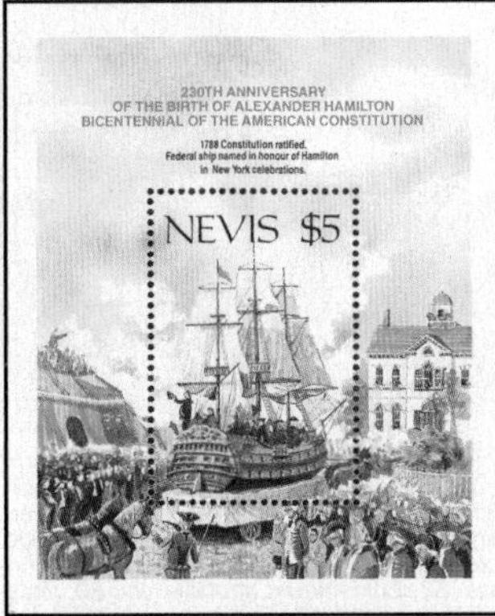


Christening of the Hamilton, 1788 — A50

US Constitution, bicent. and 230th anniv. of the birth of Alexander Hamilton: 40c, Alexander Hamilton, Hamilton House. 60c, Hamilton. $2, George Washington and members of the 1st presidential cabinet.

**1987, Jan. 11**

**533** A49 15c shown .25 .25
**534** A49 40c multicolored .30 .30
**535** A49 60c multicolored .45 .45
**536** A49 $2 multicolored 1.10 1.10
*Nos. 533-536 (4)* 2.10 2.10

### Souvenir Sheet

**537** A50 $5 shown 8.50 8.50

### No. 117 Overprinted

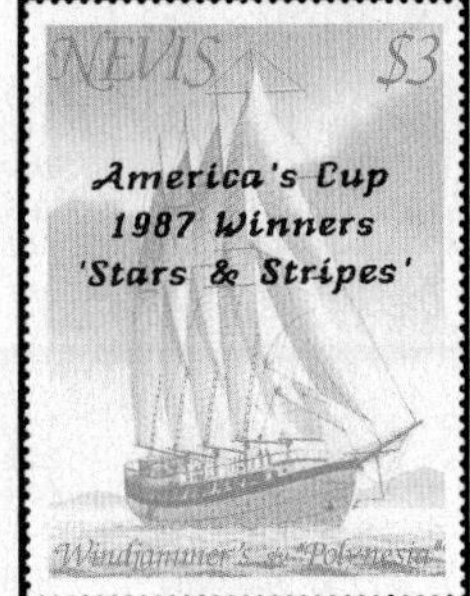


**1987, Feb. 20 Wmk. 373**

**538** A6a $3 multicolored 1.60 1.60

Wedding of Capt. Horatio Nelson and Frances Nisbet, Bicent. A51

**1987, Mar. 11 Wmk. 380**

**539** A51 15c Fig Tree Church .35 .35
**540** A51 60c Frances Nisbet .85 .85
**541** A51 $1 HMS *Boreas* 1.40 1.40
**542** A51 $3 Capt. Nelson 3.25 3.25
*Nos. 539-542 (4)* 5.85 5.85

### Souvenir Sheet

**543** Sheet of 2, #542, 543a 6.00 6.00
*a.* A51 $3 like No. 540 3.50 3.50

A52

#544a, Queen angelfish. #544b, Blue angelfish. #545a, Blue thum. #545b, Red thum. #546a, Red hind. #546b, Rock hind. #547a, Coney Butterfish. #547b, Coney butterfish, diff.

**1987, July 22 Unwmk. *Perf. 15***

**544** A52 60c Pair, #a.-b. .70 .70
**545** A52 $1 Pair, #a.-b. 1.25 1.25
**546** A52 $1.50 Pair, #a.-b. 1.75 1.75
**547** A52 $2.50 Pair, #a.-b. 3.00 3.00
*Nos. 544-547 (4)* 6.70 6.70

Mushrooms — A53

15c, Panaeolus antillarum. 50c, Pycnoporus sanguineus. $2, Gymnopilus chrysopellus. $3, Cantharellus cinnabarinus.

**1987, Oct. 16 Wmk. 384 *Perf. 14***

**552** A53 15c multicolored .40 .40
**553** A53 50c multicolored 1.00 1.00
**554** A53 $2 multicolored 3.00 3.00
**555** A53 $3 multicolored 3.50 3.50
*Nos. 552-555 (4)* 7.90 7.90

Christmas — A54

**1987, Dec. 4 *Perf. 14½***

**556** A54 10c Rag doll .25 .25
**557** A54 40c Coconut boat .25 .25
**558** A54 $1.20 Sandbox cart .70 .70
**559** A54 $5 Two-wheeled cart 2.25 2.25
*Nos. 556-559 (4)* 3.45 3.45

Sea Shells — A55

**1988, Feb. 15 *Perf. 14x14½***

**560** A55 15c Hawk-wing conch .30 .30
**561** A55 40c Roostertail conch .45 .45
**562** A55 60c Emperor helmet .60 .60
**563** A55 $2 Queen conch 1.60 1.60
**564** A55 $3 King helmet 2.10 2.10
*Nos. 560-564 (5)* 5.05 5.05

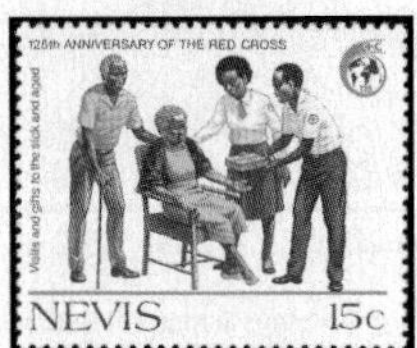


Intl. Red Cross and Red Crescent Organizations, 125th Annivs. — A56

Activities: 15c, Visiting the sick and the elderly. 40c, First aid training. 60c, Wheelchairs for the disabled. $5, Disaster relief.

**1988, June 20 *Perf. 14½x14***

**565** A56 15c multicolored .25 .25
**566** A56 40c multicolored .30 .30
**567** A56 60c multicolored .45 .45
**568** A56 $5 multicolored 3.00 3.00
*Nos. 565-568 (4)* 4.00 4.00

1988 Summer Olympics, Seoul — A57

**1988, Aug. 26 *Perf. 14***

**569** Strip of 4 3.75 3.75
*a.* A57 10c Runner at starting block .25 .25
*b.* A57 $1.20 Leaving block .70 .70
*c.* A57 $2 Full stride 1.20 1.20
*d.* A57 $3 Crossing finish line 1.75 1.75
*e.* Souvenir sheet of 4, #569a-569d 3.75 3.75

Printed se-tenant in a continuous design. Stamps in No. 569e are 23½x36½.

Independence, 5th Anniv. — A58

**1988, Sept. 19 Wmk. 373 *Perf. 14½***

**570** A58 $5 multicolored 3.25 3.25

Common Design Types pictured following the introduction.

### Lloyds of London
Common Design Type

Designs: 15c, Act of Parliament incorporating Lloyds, 1871. 60c, *Cunard Countess* in Nevis Harbor, horiz. $2.50, Space shuttle, deployment of satellite in space, horiz. $3, *Viking Princess* on fire in the Caribbean, 1966.

**1988, Oct. 31 Wmk. 384 *Perf. 14***

**571** CD341 15c multicolored .45 .45
**572** CD341 60c multicolored .90 .90
**573** CD341 $2.50 multicolored 2.50 2.50
**574** CD341 $3 multicolored 4.50 4.50
*Nos. 571-574 (4)* 8.35 8.35

Christmas Flowers — A59

**1988, Nov. 7 *Perf. 14½***

**575** A59 15c Poinsettia .25 .25
**576** A59 40c Tiger claws .25 .25
**577** A59 60c Sorrel flower .35 .35
**578** A59 $1 Christmas candle .60 .60
**579** A59 $5 Snow bush 2.40 2.40
*Nos. 575-579 (5)* 3.85 3.85

Battle of Frigate Bay, 1782 — A60

Exhibition emblem & maps. #580a-580c in a continuous design.

**1989, Apr. 17 *Perf. 14***

**580** A60 Strip of 3 3.75 3.75
*a.* 50c multicolored .30 .30
*b.* $1.20 multicolored .80 .80
*c.* $2 multicolored 1.40 1.40

**Size: 34x47mm**

***Perf. 14x13½***

**581** A60 $3 Map of Nevis, 1764 3.25 3.25

French revolution bicent., PHILEXFRANCE '89.

Nocturnal Insects and Frogs — A61

**1989, May 15**

**582** A61 10c Cicada .30 .30
**583** A61 40c Grasshopper .50 .50
**584** A61 60c Cricket .85 .85
**585** A61 $5 Tree frog 4.50 4.50
*a.* Souvenir sheet of 4, #582-585 7.50 7.50
*Nos. 582-585 (4)* 6.15 6.15

### Moon Landing, 20th Anniv.
Common Design Type

*Apollo 12:* 15c, Vehicle Assembly Building, Kennedy Space Center. 40c, Crew members Charles Conrad Jr., Richard Gordon and Alan Bean. $2, Mission emblem. $3, Moon operation in the Sun's glare. $6, Buzz Aldrin deploying passive seismic experiment package on the lunar surface, Apollo 11 mission.

**1989, July 20 *Perf. 14x13½***

**Size of Nos. 587-588: 29x29mm**

**586** CD342 15c multicolored .25 .25
**587** CD342 40c multicolored .25 .25
**588** CD342 $2 multicolored 1.25 1.25
**589** CD342 $3 multicolored 1.75 1.75
*Nos. 586-589 (4)* 3.50 3.50

**Souvenir Sheet**

**590** CD342 $6 multicolored 4.00 4.00

Queen Conchs *(Strombus gigas)* A62

**1990, Jan. 31**

**591** A62 10c shown .35 .35
**592** A62 40c Conch, diff .65 .65
**593** A62 60c Conch, diff 1.50 1.50
**594** A62 $1 Conch, diff 2.25 2.25
*Nos. 591-594 (4)* 4.75 4.75

**Souvenir Sheet**

**595** A62 $5 Fish and coral 5.75 5.75

World Wildlife Fund.

Wyon Portrait of Victoria — A63

40c, Engine-turned background. 60c, Heath's engraving. $4, Inscriptions added. $5, Completed design.

***Perf. 14x15***

**1990, May 3 Litho. Unwmk.**

**596** A63 15c brn, blk, tan .25 .25
**597** A63 40c grn, blk, lt grn .30 .30
**598** A63 60c blk, gray .50 .50
**599** A63 $4 blue, blk, lt blue 3.00 3.00
*Nos. 596-599 (4)* 4.05 4.05

**Souvenir Sheet**

**600** A63 $5 multicolored 5.25 5.25

Penny Black, 150th anniv. No. 600 for Stamp World London '90.

A64

**1990, May 3 *Perf. 13½***

**601** A64 15c brown .25 .25
**602** A64 40c deep green .30 .30
**603** A64 60c violet .50 .50
**604** A64 $4 bright ultra 3.50 3.50
*Nos. 601-604 (4)* 4.55 4.55

**Souvenir Sheet**

**605** A64 $5 gray, lake & buff 5.50 5.50

Penny Black 150th anniversary and commemoration of the Thurn & Taxis postal service.

Crabs A65

Designs include UPAE and discovery of America anniversary emblems.

**1990, June 25 Litho. *Perf. 14***

**606** A65 5c Sand fiddler .25 .25
**607** A65 15c Great land crab .25 .25
**608** A65 20c Blue crab .30 .30
**609** A65 40c Stone crab .40 .40
**610** A65 60c Mountain crab .60 .60
**611** A65 $2 Sargassum crab 1.40 1.40
**612** A65 $3 Yellow box crab 2.00 2.00
**613** A65 $4 Spiny spider crab 2.75 2.75
*Nos. 606-613 (8)* 7.95 7.95

**Souvenir Sheets**

**614** A65 $5 Wharf crab 4.00 4.00
**615** A65 $5 Sally lightfoot 4.00 4.00

Queen Mother 90th Birthday
A66 A67

**1990, July 5**

**616** A66 $2 shown 1.50 1.50
**617** A67 $2 shown 1.50 1.50
**618** A66 $2 Queen Consort, diff. 1.50 1.50
*a.* Strip of 3, #616-618 4.50 4.50

**Souvenir Sheet**

**619** A67 $6 Coronation Portrait, diff. 5.00 5.00

Nos. 616-618 printed in sheet of 9.

A68

Players from participating countries.

**1990, Oct. 1 Litho. *Perf. 14***

**620** A68 10c Cameroun .25 .25
**621** A68 25c Czechoslovakia .25 .25
**622** A68 $2.50 England 2.25 2.25
**623** A68 $5 West Germany 4.75 4.75
*Nos. 620-623 (4)* 7.50 7.50

**Souvenir Sheets**

**624** A68 $5 Spain 4.00 4.00
**625** A68 $5 Argentina 4.00 4.00

World Cup Soccer Championships, Italy.

A69

Christmas (Orchids): 10c, Cattleya deckeri. 15c, Epidendrum ciliare. 20c, Epidendrum fragrans. 40c, Epidendrum ibaguense. 60c, Epidendrum latifolium. $1.20, Maxillaria conferta. $2, Epidendrum strobiliferum. $3, Brassavola cucullata. $5, Rodriguezia lanceolata.

**Unwmk.**

**1990, Nov. 19 Litho. *Perf. 14***

**626** A69 10c multicolored .30 .30
**627** A69 15c multicolored .30 .30
**628** A69 20c multicolored .30 .30
**629** A69 40c multicolored .45 .45
**630** A69 60c multicolored .70 .70
**631** A69 $1.20 multicolored 1.30 1.30
**632** A69 $2 multicolored 2.25 2.25
**633** A69 $3 multicolored 3.50 3.50
*Nos. 626-633 (8)* 9.10 9.10

**Souvenir Sheet**

**634** A69 $5 multicolored 8.00 8.00

Peter Paul Rubens (1577-1640), Painter A70

Details from The Feast of Achelous: 10c, Pitchers. 40c, Woman at table. 60c, Two women. $4, Achelous feasting. $5, Complete painting, horiz.

**1991, Jan. 14 Litho. *Perf. 13½***

**635** A70 10c multicolored .30 .30
**636** A70 40c multicolored .50 .50
**637** A70 60c multicolored .80 .80
**638** A70 $4 multicolored 4.25 4.25
*Nos. 635-638 (4)* 5.85 5.85

**Souvenir Sheet**

**639** A70 $5 multicolored 6.25 6.25

Butterflies A71

5c, Gulf fritillary. 10c, Orion. 15c, Dagger wing. 20c, Red anartia. 25c, Caribbean buckeye. 40c, Zebra. 50c, Southern dagger tail. 60c, Silver spot. 75c, Doris. $1, Mimic. $3, Monarch. $5, Small blue grecian. $10, Tiger. $20, Flambeau.

**1991, Mar. *Perf. 14***

**No Date Imprint Below Design**

**640** A71 5c multicolored .25 .25
**641** A71 10c multicolored .25 .25
**642** A71 15c multicolored .25 .25
**643** A71 20c multicolored .25 .25
**644** A71 25c multicolored .25 .25
**645** A71 40c multicolored .35 .35
**646** A71 50c multicolored .50 .50
**647** A71 60c multicolored .55 .55
**648** A71 75c multicolored .65 .65
**649** A71 $1 multicolored .90 .90
**650** A71 $3 multicolored 2.75 2.75
**651** A71 $5 multicolored 4.50 4.50
**652** A71 $10 multicolored 9.00 9.00
**653** A71 $20 multicolored 18.00 18.00
*Nos. 640-653 (14)* 38.45 38.45

For overprints see Nos. O41-O54.

**1992, Mar. 1 "1992" Below Design**

*640a* A71 5c multicolored .25 .25
*641a* A71 10c multicolored .25 .25
*642a* A71 15c multicolored .25 .25
*643a* A71 20c multicolored .25 .25
*644a* A71 25c multicolored .30 .25
*645a* A71 40c multicolored .40 .25
*646a* A71 50c multicolored .50 .50
*648b* A71 75c multicolored .65 .65
**648A** A71 80c multicolored 1.50 1.50
*649a* A71 $1 multicolored .90 .90
*650a* A71 $3 multicolored 2.75 2.75
*651a* A71 $5 multicolored 4.50 4.50
*652a* A71 $10 multicolored 9.00 9.00
*653a* A71 $20 multicolored 18.00 18.00
*Nos. 640a-653a (14)* 39.50 39.30

**1994 "1994" Below Design**

*640b* A71 5c multicolored .40 .40
*641b* A71 10c multicolored .40 .40
*644b* A71 25c multicolored .40 .40
*646b* A71 50c multicolored .40 .40
*648Ab* A71 80c multicolored 1.75 1.75
*Nos. 640b-648Ab (5)* 3.35 3.35

Space Exploration-Discovery Voyages — A72

15c, Viking Mars lander. 40c, Apollo 11 liftoff. 60c, Skylab. 75c, Salyut 6. $1, Voyager 1. $2, Venera 7. $4, Gemini 4. $5, Luna 3.

No. 662, Sailing ship, vert. No. 663, Columbus' landfall.

**1991, Apr. 22 Litho. *Perf. 14***

**654** A72 15c multi .25 .25
**655** A72 40c multi .30 .30
**656** A72 60c multi .45 .45
**657** A72 75c multi .55 .55
**658** A72 $1 multi .75 .75
**659** A72 $2 multi 1.25 1.25
**660** A72 $4 multi 2.50 2.50
**661** A72 $5 multi 3.25 3.25
*Nos. 654-661 (8)* 9.30 9.30

**Souvenir Sheet**

**662** A72 $6 multi 5.50 5.50
**663** A72 $6 multi 5.50 5.50

Discovery of America, 500th anniv. (in 1992) (No. 663).

Miniature Sheet

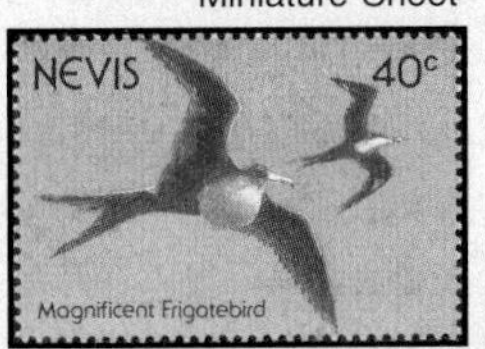


Birds
A73

Designs: a, Magnificent frigatebird. b, Roseate tern. c, Red-tailed hawk. d, Zenaida dove. e, Bananaquit. f, American kestrel. g, Grey kingbird. h, Prothonotary warbler. i, Blue-hooded euphonia. j, Antillean crested hummingbird. k, White-tailed tropicbird. l, Yellow-bellied sapsucker. m, Green-throated carib. n, Purple-throated carib. o, Black-bellied tree duck. p, Ringed kingfisher. q, Burrowing owl. r, Ruddy turnstone. s, Great white heron. t, Yellow-crowned night heron.

**1991, May 28**

| | | | | |
|---|---|---|---|---|
| **664** | A73 | 40c Sheet of 20, #a.-t. | 16.00 | 16.00 |

**Souvenir Sheet**

| | | | | |
|---|---|---|---|---|
| **665** | A73 | $6 Great egret | 11.00 | 11.00 |

**Royal Family Birthday, Anniversary**

Common Design Type

No. 674, Elizabeth, Philip. No. 675, Charles, Diana & family.

**1991, July 5 Litho. *Perf. 14***

| | | | | |
|---|---|---|---|---|
| **666** | CD347 | 10c multicolored | .30 | .30 |
| **667** | CD347 | 15c multicolored | .30 | .30 |
| **668** | CD347 | 40c multicolored | .45 | .45 |
| **669** | CD347 | 50c multicolored | .60 | .60 |
| **670** | CD347 | $1 multicolored | 1.00 | 1.00 |
| **671** | CD347 | $2 multicolored | 2.00 | 2.00 |
| **672** | CD347 | $4 multicolored | 4.00 | 4.00 |
| **673** | CD347 | $5 multicolored | 5.00 | 5.00 |
| | | *Nos. 666-673 (8)* | 13.65 | 13.65 |

**Souvenir Sheets**

| | | | | |
|---|---|---|---|---|
| **674** | CD347 | $5 multicolored | 6.00 | 6.00 |
| **675** | CD347 | $5 multicolored | 6.00 | 6.00 |

10c, 50c, $1, Nos. 673, 675, Charles and Diana, 10th Wedding Anniv. Others, Queen Elizabeth II 65th birthday.

Japanese Trains
A74

Locomotives: 10c, C62 Steam, vert. 15c, C56 Steam. 40c, Streamlined C55, steam. 60c, Class 1400 Steam. $1, Class 485 bonnet type rail diesel car, vert. $2, C61 Steam, vert. $3, Class 485 express train. $4, Class 7000 electric train. No. 684, D51 Steam. No. 685, Hikari bullet train.

**1991, Aug. 12**

| | | | | |
|---|---|---|---|---|
| **676-683** | A74 | Set of 8 | 14.00 | 14.00 |

**Souvenir Sheets**

| | | | | |
|---|---|---|---|---|
| **684-685** | A74 | $5 Set of 2 | 11.00 | 11.00 |

Phila Nippon '91.

Christmas
A75

Paintings by Albrecht Durer: 10c, Mary Being Crowned by an Angel. 40c, Mary with the Pear. 60c, Mary in a Halo. $3, Mary with the Crown of Stars and Scepter. No. 690, The Holy Family. No. 691, Mary at the Yard Gate.

**1991, Dec. 20 Litho. *Perf. 13½***

| | | | | |
|---|---|---|---|---|
| **686** | A75 | 10c yel green & blk | .25 | .25 |
| **687** | A75 | 40c org brown & blk | .30 | .30 |
| **688** | A75 | 60c blue & black | .45 | .45 |
| **689** | A75 | $3 brt magenta & blk | 1.90 | 1.90 |
| | | *Nos. 686-689 (4)* | 2.90 | 2.90 |

**Souvenir Sheets**

| | | | | |
|---|---|---|---|---|
| **690** | A75 | $6 black | 8.00 | 8.00 |
| **691** | A75 | $6 black | 8.00 | 8.00 |

A76

Mushrooms: 15c, Marasmius haematocephalus. 40c, Psilocybe cubensis. 60c, Hygrocybe acutoconica. 75c, Hygrocybe occidentalis. $1, Boletellus cubensis. $2, Gymnopilus chrysopellus. $4, Cantharellus cinnabarinus. $5, Chlorophyllum molybdites. No. 700, Our Lady of the Snows (8 mushrooms). No. 701, Our Lady of the Snows (4 mushrooms), diff.

**1991, Dec. 20 Litho. *Perf. 14***

| | | | | |
|---|---|---|---|---|
| **692-699** | A76 | Set of 8 | 10.00 | 10.00 |

**Souvenir Sheet**

| | | | | |
|---|---|---|---|---|
| **700-701** | A76 | $6 Set of 2 | 10.00 | 10.00 |

**Queen Elizabeth II's Accession to the Throne, 40th Anniv.**

Common Design Type

**1992, Feb. 26 Litho. *Perf. 14***

| | | | | |
|---|---|---|---|---|
| **702** | CD348 | 10c multicolored | .25 | .25 |
| **703** | CD348 | 40c multicolored | .30 | .30 |
| **704** | CD348 | $1 multicolored | .75 | .75 |
| **705** | CD348 | $5 multicolored | 3.50 | 3.50 |
| | | *Nos. 702-705 (4)* | 4.80 | 4.80 |

**Souvenir Sheets**

| | | | | |
|---|---|---|---|---|
| **706** | CD348 | $6 Queen, people on beach | 4.50 | 4.50 |
| **707** | CD348 | $6 Queen, seashell | 4.50 | 4.50 |

A77

Gold medalists: 20c, Monique Knol, France, cycling. 25c, Roger Kingdom, US, 110-meter hurdles. 50c, Yugoslavia, water polo. 80c, Anja Fichtel, West Germany, foil. $1, Said Aouita, Morocco, 5000-meters. $1.50, Yuri Sedykh, USSR, hammer throw. $3, Yelena Shushunova, USSR, gymnastics. $5, Vladimir Artemov, USSR, gymnastics. No. 716, Florence Griffith-Joyner, US, 100-meter dash. No. 717, Naim Suleymanoglu, Turkey, weight lifting.

**1992, May 7 Litho. *Perf. 14***

| | | | | |
|---|---|---|---|---|
| **708-715** | A77 | Set of 8 | 11.50 | 11.50 |

**Souvenir Sheets**

| | | | | |
|---|---|---|---|---|
| **716-717** | A77 | $6 Set of 2 | 8.25 | 8.25 |

1992 Summer Olympics, Barcelona. All athletes except those on $1 and $1.50 won gold medals in 1988. No. 715 incorrectly spelled "Valimir."

Spanish Art — A78

Designs: 20c, Landscape, by Mariano Fortuny, vert. 25c, Dona Juana la Loca, by Francisco Pradilla Ortiz. 50c, Idyll, by Fortuny, vert. 80c, Old Man in the Sun, by Fortuny, vert. $1, $2, The Painter's Children in the Japanese Salon (different details), vert., by Fortuny. $3, Still Life (Sea Bream and Oranges), by Luis Eugenio Melendez. $5, Still Life (Box of Sweets, Pastry, and Other Objects), by Melendez, vert. No. 726, Moroccans by Fortuny. No. 727, Bullfight, by Fortuny.

***Perf. 13x13½, 13½x13***

**1992, June 1 Litho.**

| | | | | |
|---|---|---|---|---|
| **718-725** | A78 | Set of 8 | 12.50 | 12.50 |

**Size: 120x95mm**

***Imperf***

| | | | | |
|---|---|---|---|---|
| **726-727** | A78 | $6 Set of 2 | 8.25 | 8.25 |

Granada '92.

A79

**1992, July 6 *Perf. 14***

| | | | | |
|---|---|---|---|---|
| **728** | A79 | 20c Early compass | .30 | .60 |
| **729** | A79 | 50c Manatee | .60 | .60 |
| **730** | A79 | 80c Green turtle | .90 | .90 |
| **731** | A79 | $1.50 Santa Maria | 1.60 | 1.60 |
| **732** | A79 | $3 Queen Isabella | 3.00 | 3.00 |
| **733** | A79 | $5 Pineapple | 5.50 | 5.50 |
| | | *Nos. 728-733 (6)* | 11.90 | 12.20 |

**Souvenir Sheets**

| | | | | |
|---|---|---|---|---|
| **734** | A79 | $6 Storm petrel, horiz. | 5.50 | 5.50 |
| **735** | A79 | $6 Pepper, horiz. | 5.50 | 5.50 |

Discovery of America, 500th anniv. World Columbian Stamp Expo '92, Chicago.

A80

**1992, Aug. 24 *Perf. 14½***

| | | | | |
|---|---|---|---|---|
| **736** | A80 | $1 Coming ashore | .80 | .80 |
| **737** | A80 | $2 Natives, ships | 1.50 | 1.50 |

Discovery of America, 500th anniv. Organization of East Caribbean States.

Wolfgang Amadeus Mozart, Bicent. of Death (in 1991) — A81

**1992, Oct. Litho. *Perf. 14***

| | | | | |
|---|---|---|---|---|
| **738** | A81 | $3 multicolored | 3.00 | 3.00 |

**Souvenir Sheet**

| | | | | |
|---|---|---|---|---|
| **739** | A81 | $6 Don Giovanni | 5.25 | 5.25 |

Mickey's Portrait Gallery
A82

10c, Minnie Mouse, 1930. 15c, Mickey Mouse. 40c, Donald Duck. 80c, Mickey Mouse, 1930. $1, Daisy Duck. $2, Pluto. $4, Goofy. $5, Goofy, 1932.

No. 748, Plane Crazy. No. 749, Mickey, Home Sweet Home, horiz.

**1992, Nov. 9 Litho. *Perf. 13½x14***

| | | | | |
|---|---|---|---|---|
| **740** | A82 | 10c multicolored | .25 | .25 |
| **741** | A82 | 15c multicolored | .35 | .35 |
| **742** | A82 | 40c multicolored | .45 | .45 |
| **743** | A82 | 80c multicolored | .75 | .75 |
| **744** | A82 | $1 multicolored | 1.00 | 1.00 |
| **745** | A82 | $2 multicolored | 1.75 | 1.75 |
| **746** | A82 | $4 multicolored | 3.50 | 3.50 |
| **747** | A82 | $5 multicolored | 4.00 | 4.00 |
| | | *Nos. 740-747 (8)* | 12.05 | 12.05 |

**Souvenir Sheet**

***Perf. 14x13½***

| | | | | |
|---|---|---|---|---|
| **748** | A82 | $6 multicolored | 6.00 | 6.00 |
| **749** | A82 | $6 multicolored | 6.00 | 6.00 |

Christmas
A83

Details or entire paintings: 20c, The Virgin and Child Between Two Saints, by Giovanni Bellini. 40c, The Virgin and Child Surrounded by Four Angels, by Master of the Castello Nativity. 50c, Virgin and Child Surrounded by Angels with St. Frediano and St. Augustine, by Fra Filippo Lippi. 80c, The Virgin and Child Between St. Peter and St. Sebastian, by Giovanni Bellini. $1, The Virgin and Child with St. Julian and St. Nicholas of Myra, by Lorenzo Di Credi. $2, Saint Bernardino and a Female Saint Presenting a Donor to Virgin and Child, by Francesco Bissolo. $4, Madonna and Child with Four Cherubs, Ascribed to Barthel Bruyn. $5, The Virgin and Child, by Quentin Metsys. No. 758, The Virgin and Child Surrounded by Two Angels, by Perugino. No. 759, Madonna and Child with the Infant St. John and Archangel Gabriel, by Sandro Botticelli.

**1992, Nov. 16 Litho. *Perf. 13½x14***

| | | | | |
|---|---|---|---|---|
| **750-757** | A83 | Set of 8 | 11.00 | 11.00 |

**Souvenir Sheet**

| | | | | |
|---|---|---|---|---|
| **758-759** | A83 | $6 Set of 2 | 10.00 | 10.00 |

Empire State Building, New York City — A84

**1992, Oct. 28 Litho. *Perf. 14***

| | | | | |
|---|---|---|---|---|
| **760** | A84 | $6 multicolored | 5.50 | 5.50 |

Postage Stamp Mega Event '92, New York City.

A85

A89

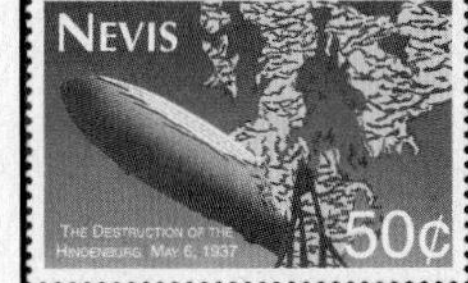


A86

A87

A88

A90

A92

A91

Anniversaries and Events — A93

Designs: 15c, Japanese launch vehicle H-2. 50c, Hindenburg on fire, 1937. 75c, Charles de Gaulle, Konrad Adenauer. No. 764, Horatio Nelson Museum, Nevis. No. 765, Red Cross emblem, Nevis. No. 766, America's Cup yacht *Resolute*, 1920, vert. No. 767, St. Thomas Anglican Church. No. 768, Care Bear, butterfly and flower. No. 770, Blue whale. No. 771, WHO, ICN, FAO emblems, graph showing population growth. vert. No. 772, Lion, Lion's Intl. emblem. No. 773, John F. Kennedy, Adenauer. No. 774, Lebaudy, first flying machine with mechanical engine. No. 775, Soviet Energia launch vehicle SL-17.

Elvis Presley: No. 776a, Portrait. b, With guitar. c, With microphone.

Details or entire paintings, by Georges de La Tour: No. 777a, The Cheater (left). b, The Cheater (center). c, The Cheater (right). d, St. Joseph, the Carpenter. e, Saint Thomas. f, Adoration of the Shepherds (left). g, Adoration of the Shepherds (right). h, La Madeleine a La Veilleuse.

No. 778, Care Bear, palm tree, vert. No. 779, Manned maneuvering unit in space. No. 780, Count Zeppelin taking off from Goppingen for Friedrichshafen. No. 781, Adenauer. No. 782, America's Cup yacht. No. 783, The Angel Departing from the Family of Tobias, by Rembrandt.

**1993 Litho. *Perf. 14***

**761** A85 15c multicolored .25 .25
**762** A86 50c multicolored .40 .40
**763** A87 75c multicolored .80 .80
**764** A88 80c multicolored .90 .90
**765** A88 80c multicolored .90 .90
**766** A89 80c multicolored .60 .60
**767** A88 80c multicolored .60 .60
**768** A90 80c multicolored .60 .60
**770** A88 $1 multicolored .75 .75
**771** A91 $3 multicolored 3.50 3.50
**772** A85 $3 multicolored 3.00 3.00
**773** A87 $5 multicolored 3.00 3.00
**774** A86 $5 multicolored 3.50 3.50
**775** A85 $5 multicolored 3.50 3.50

***Perf. 14***

**776** A92 $1 Strip of 3, #a.-c. 2.00 2.00
*Nos. 761-776 (15)* 24.30 24.30

**Miniature Sheet**

***Perf. 12***

**777** A93 $1 Sheet of 8, #a.-h. + label 8.00 8.00

**Souvenir Sheets**

***Perf. 14***

**778** A90 $2 multicolored 1.25 1.25
**779** A85 $6 multicolored 5.25 5.25
**780** A86 $6 multicolored 5.25 5.25
**781** A87 $6 multicolored 5.50 5.50
**782** A89 $6 multicolored 4.00 4.00

***Perf. 14½***

**783** A92 $6 multicolored 6.00 6.00

Intl. Space Year (#761, 775, 779). Count Zeppelin, 75th anniv. of death (#762, 774, 780). Konrad Adenauer, 25th anniv. of death (#763, 773, 781). Anglican Church in Nevis, 150th anniv. Opening of Horatio Nelson Museum (#764). Nevis and St. Kitts Red Cross, 50th anniv. (#765). America's Cup yacht race (#766, 782). (#767). Lions Intl., 75th anniv. (#772). Earth Summit, Rio de Janeiro (#768, 770, 778). Intl. Conference on Nutrition, Rome (#771). Elvis Presley, 15th death anniv. (in 1992) (#776). Louvre Art Museum, bicent. (#777, 783).

Nos. 779-781 have continuous designs.
No. 783 contains one 55x89mm stamp.
Issued: No. 767, Mar.; others, Jan. 14.

Tropical Flowers — A94

**1993, Mar. 26 Litho. *Perf. 14***

**784** A94 10c Frangipani .25 .25
**785** A94 25c Bougainvillea .25 .25
**786** A94 50c Allamanda .50 .50
**787** A94 80c Anthurium .80 .80
**788** A94 $1 Ixora 1.00 1.00
**789** A94 $2 Hibiscus 2.00 2.00
**790** A94 $4 Shrimp plant 4.00 4.00
**791** A94 $5 Coral vine 5.00 5.00
*Nos. 784-791 (8)* 13.80 13.80

**Souvenir Sheets**

**792** A94 $6 Lantana 5.00 5.00
**793** A94 $6 Petrea 5.00 5.00

Butterflies A95

10c, Antillean blue. 25c, Cuban crescentspot. 50c, Ruddy daggerwing. 80c, Little yellow. $1, Atala. $1.50, Orange-barred giant sulphur. $4, Tropic queen. $5, Malachite.

No. 802, Polydamas swallowtail. No. 803, West Indian Buckeye.

**1993, May 17 Litho. *Perf. 14***

**794** A95 10c multicolored .30 .30
**795** A95 25c multicolored .30 .30
**796** A95 50c multicolored .60 .60
**797** A95 80c multicolored .90 .90
**798** A95 $1 multicolored 1.00 1.00
**799** A95 $1.50 multicolored 1.40 1.40
**800** A95 $4 multicolored 4.00 4.00
**801** A95 $5 multicolored 5.00 5.00
*Nos. 794-801 (8)* 13.50 13.50

**Souvenir Sheets**

**802** A95 $6 multicolored 5.75 5.75
*a.* Ovptd. in sheet margin 5.00 5.00
**803** A95 $6 multicolored 5.75 5.75
*a.* Ovptd. in sheet margin 5.00 5.00

Location of Hong Kong '94 emblem on Nos. 802a-803a varies.

Nos. 802a, 803a issued Feb. 18, 1994.

Miniature Sheet

Coronation of Queen Elizabeth II, 40th Anniv. A96

Designs: a, 10c, Official coronation photograph. b, 80c, Queen, wearing Imperial Crown of State. c, $2, Queen, sitting on throne during ceremony. d, $4, Prince Charles kissing mother's hand.

$6, Portrait, "Riding on Worcran in the Great Park at Windsor," by Susan Crawford, 1977.

**1993, June 2 Litho. *Perf. 13½x14***

**804** A96 Sheet, 2 ea #a.-d. 10.00 10.00

**Souvenir Sheet**

***Perf. 14***

**805** A96 $6 multicolored 4.00 4.00

No. 805 contains one 28x42mm stamp.

Independence of St. Kitts and Nevis, 10th Anniv. — A97

Designs: 25c, Natl. flag, anthem. 80c, Brown pelican, map of St. Kitts and Nevis.

**1993, Sept. 19 Litho. *Perf. 13½***

**807** A97 25c multicolored .50 .50
**808** A97 80c multicolored 1.50 1.50

1994 World Cup Soccer Championships, US — A98

Soccer players: 10c, Garaba, Hungary; Platini, France. 25c, Maradona, Argentina; Bergomi, Italy. 50c, Fernandez, France; Rats, Russia. 80c, Munoz, Spain. $1, Elkjaer, Denmark; Goicoechea, Spain. $2, Coelho, Brazil; Tigana, France. $3, Troglio, Argentina; Alejnikov, Russia. No. 816, $5, Karas, Poland; Costa, Brazil.

Each $5: No. 817, Belloumi, Algeria. No. 818, Steven, England, vert.

**1993, Nov. 9 Litho. *Perf. 14***

**809-816** A98 Set of 8 14.00 14.00

**Souvenir Sheets**

**817-818** A98 Set of 2 22.50 22.50

Christmas A99

Works by Albrecht Durer: 20c, Annunciation of Mary. 40c, The Nativity. 50c, Holy Family on a Grassy Bank. 80c, The Presentation of Christ in the Temple. $1, Virgin in Glory on the Crescent. $1.60, The Nativity, diff. $3, Madonna and Child. $5, The Presentation of Christ in the Temple (detail).

Each $6: No. 827, Mary with Child and the Long-Tailed Monkey, by Durer. No. 828, The Rest on the Flight into Egypt, by Fragonard, horiz.

**1993, Nov. 30 *Perf. 13***

**819-826** A99 Set of 8 12.50 12.50

**Souvenir Sheets**

**827-828** A99 Set of 2 20.00 20.00

Tuff Mickey — A100

Disney's Mickey Mouse playing: 10c, Basketball. 50c, Volleyball. $1, Soccer. $5, Boxing.

No. 837, $6, Tug-of-war. No. 838, Ringing carnival bell with hammer, vert.

Disney's Minnie Mouse: 25c, Welcome to my island, vert. 80c, Sunny and snappy, vert. $1.50, Happy hoopin', vert. $4, Jumping for joy, vert.

***Perf. 14x13½, 13½x14***

**1994, Mar. 15 Litho.**

**829** A100 10c multicolored .25 .25
**830** A100 25c multicolored .25 .25
**831** A100 50c multicolored .55 .55
**832** A100 80c multicolored .80 .80
**833** A100 $1 multicolored .90 .90
**834** A100 $1.50 multicolored 1.30 1.30
**835** A100 $4 multicolored 3.50 3.50
**836** A100 $5 multicolored 4.50 4.50
*Nos. 829-836 (8)* 12.05 12.05

**Souvenir Sheets**

**837** A100 $6 multicolored 12.00 12.00
**838** A100 $6 multicolored 12.00 12.00

Hummel Figurines — A101

Designs: 5c, Umbrella Girl. 25c, For Father. 50c, Apple Tree Girl. 80c, March Winds. $1, Have the Sun in Your Heart. $1.60, Blue Belle. $2, Winter Fun. $5, Apple Tree Boy.

**1994, Apr. 6 Litho. *Perf. 14***

**839-846** A101 Set of 8 11.50 11.50
*845a* Souv. sheet, #839, 843-845 4.00 4.00
*846a* Souv. sheet, #840-842, 846 6.50 6.50

Beekeeping — A102

Designs: 50c, Beekeeper cutting wild nest of bees. 80c, Group of beekeepers, 1987. $1.60, Decapping frames of honey. $3, Queen bee rearing.

$6, Queen bee, worker bees, woman extracting honey.

**1994, June 13 Litho. *Perf. 14***

**847-850** A102 Set of 4 7.75 7.75

**Souvenir Sheet**

**851** A102 $6 multicolored 7.50 7.50
*a.* Ovptd. in sheet margin 5.50 5.50

No. 851a Overprinted "2nd Caribbean Beekeeping Congress / August 14-18, 2000" in sheet margin. Issued 8/14/00.

Issued: No. 851a, 8/17/00.

Miniature Sheet

Cats — A103

Designs: a, Blue point Himalayan. b, Black & white Persian. c, Cream Persian. d, Red Persian. e, Persian. f, Persian black smoke. g, Chocolate smoke Persian. h, Black Persian.
Each $6: No. 853, Brown tabby Persian. No. 854, Silver tabby Persian.

**1994, July 20**
**852** A103 80c Sheet of 8, #a.-h. 7.00 7.00

**Souvenir Sheets**
**853-854** A103 Set of 2 21.00 21.00

Marine Life A104

Marine Life A104a

Designs: 10c, Striped burrfish. 25c, Black coral, white & yellow, vert. 40c, Black coral, white & red, vert. 50c, Black coral, yellow & green, vert. 80c, Black coral, spiral-shaped, vert. $1, Blue-striped grunt. $1.60, Blue angelfish. $3, Cocoa damselfish.
No. 864a, Flameback angelfish. b, Reef bass. c, Honey gregory. d, Saddle squirrelfish. e, Cobalt chromis. f, Cleaner goby. g, Slendertail cardinalfish. h, Royal gramma.
Each $6: No. 865, Sailfish, vert. No. 866, Blue marlin.

**1994, July 25 Litho. *Perf. 14***
**856-863** A104 Set of 8 8.00 8.00
*860a* Strip of 4, #857-860 4.00 4.00
*860b* Min. sheet, 3 each #857-860 13.00 13.00

**Miniature Sheet of 8**
**864** A104a 50c #a.-h. 9.50 9.50
*i.* Ovptd. in sheet margin 4.00 4.00

**Souvenir Sheets**
**865-866** A104a Set of 2 24.00 24.00

Nos. 857-860, World Wildlife Fund. No. 864i overprinted in sheet margin with PHILAKOREA '94 emblem.
Issued: #864i, 8/16; #860b, 7/25.

Local Architecture — A105

Designs: 25c, Residence, Barnes Ghaut Village. 50c, House above grocery store, Newcastle. $1, Treasury Building, Charlestown. $5, House above supermarket, Charlestown. $6, Apartment houses.

**1994, Aug. 22**
**867-870** A105 Set of 4 8.00 8.00

**Souvenir Sheet**
**871** A105 $6 multicolored 5.25 5.25

Order of the Caribbean Community — A106

First award recipients: 25c, William Demas, economist, Trinidad and Tobago. 50c, Sir Shridath Ramphal, statesman, Guyana. $1, Derek Walcott, writer, Nobel Laureate, St. Lucia.

**1994, Sept. 1**
**872-874** A106 Set of 3 3.25 3.25

Miniature Sheet of 8

PHILAKOREA '94 — A107

Folding screen, longevity symbols embroidered on silk, Late Choson Dynasty: a, #1. b, #2. c, #3. d, #4. e, #5. f, #6. g, #7. h, #8.

**1994 Litho. *Perf. 14***
**875** A107 50c #a.-h. 5.00 5.00

Christmas — A108

Different details from paintings: 20c, 40c, 50c, $5, The Virgin Mary as Queen of Heaven, by Jan Provost. 80c, $1, $1.60, $3, Adoration of the Magi, by Workshop of Hugo van der Goes.
No. 884, The Virgin Mary as Queen of Heaven (complete). $6, Adoration of the Magi (complete).

**1994, Dec. 1 Litho. *Perf. 14***
**876-883** A108 Set of 8 10.00 10.00

**Souvenir Sheets**
**884** A108 $5 multicolored 5.25 5.25
**885** A108 $6 multicolored 6.25 6.25

Disney Valentines — A109

Designs: 10c, Mickey, Minnie. 25c, Donald, Daisy. 50c, Pluto, Fifi. 80c, Clarabelle, Horace Horsecollar. $1, Pluto, Figaro. $1.50, Polly, Peter Penguin. $4, Prunella Pullet, Hick Rooster. $5, Jenny Wren, Cock Robin.
Each $6: No. 894, Minnie, vert. No. 895, Daisy, vert.

**1995, Feb. 14 Litho. *Perf. 14x13½***
**886-893** A109 Set of 8 11.50 11.50

**Souvenir Sheets**
***Perf. 13½x14***
**894-895** A109 Set of 2 11.50 11.50

Birds — A110

Designs: 50c, Hooded merganser. 80c, Green-backed heron. $2, Double crested cormorant. $3, Ruddy duck.
Hummingbirds: No. 900a, Rufous-breasted hermit. b, Purple-throated carib. c, Green mango. d, Bahama woodstar. e, Hispaniolan emerald. f, Antillean crested. g, Green-throated carib. h, Antillean mango. i, Vervian. j, Jamaican mango. k, Cuban emerald. l, Blue-headed.
Each $6: No. 901, Black skimmer. No. 902, Snowy plover.

**1995, Mar. 30 Litho. *Perf. 14***
**896-899** A110 Set of 4 3.75 3.75

**Miniature Sheet of 12**
**900** A110 50c #a.-l. 10.00 10.00

**Souvenir Sheets**
**901-902** A110 Set of 2 10.00 10.00

Dogs A111

Designs: 25c, Pointer. 50c, Old Danish pointer. $1, German short-haired pointer. $2, English setter.
No. 907a, Irish setter. b, Weimaraner. c, Gordon setter. d, Britanny spaniel. e, American cocker spaniel. f, English cocker spaniel. g, Labrador retriever. h, Golden retriever. i, Flat-coated retriever.
Each $6: #908, Bloodhound. #909, German shepherd.

**1995, May 23 Litho. *Perf. 14***
**903-906** A111 Set of 4 2.75 2.75

**Miniature Sheet of 9**
**907** A111 80c #a.-i. 11.00 11.00

**Souvenir Sheets**
**908-909** A111 Set of 2 11.00 11.00

Cacti — A112

Designs: 40c, Schulumbergera truncata. 50c, Echinocereus pectinatus. 80c, Mammillaria zelmanniana alba. $1.60, Lobivia hertriehiana. $2, Hamatocactus setispinus. $3, Astrophytum myriostigma.
Each $6: No. 916, Opuntia robusta. No. 917, Rhipsalidopsis gaertneri.

**1995, June 20 Litho. *Perf. 14***
**910-915** A112 Set of 6 6.50 6.50

**Souvenir Sheets**
**916-917** A112 Set of 2 10.00 10.00

Miniature Sheets of 6 or 8

End of World War II, 50th Anniv. — A113

Famous World War II Personalities: No. 918: a, Clark Gable. b, Audie Murphy. c, Glenn Miller. d, Joe Louis. e, Jimmy Doolittle. f, John Hersey. g, John F. Kennedy. h, Jimmy Stewart.
Planes: No. 919: a, F4F Wildcat. b, F4U-1A Corsair. c, Vought SB2U Vindicator. d, F6-F Hellcat. e, SDB Dauntless. f, TBF-1 Avenger.
Each $6: No. 920, Jimmy Doolittle, vert. No. 921, Fighter plane landing on aircraft carrier.

**1995, July 20**
**918** A113 $1.25 #a.-h. + label 10.00 10.00
**919** A113 $2 #a.-f. + label 11.00 11.00

**Souvenir Sheets**
**920-921** A113 Set of 2 15.00 15.00

UN, 50th Anniv. — A114

People of various races: No. 922a, $1.25, Two men, child. b, $1.60, Man wearing turban, man with beard, woman. c, $3, Two men in business suits, woman.
$6, Nelson Mandela.

**1995, July 20 Litho. *Perf. 14***
**922** A114 Strip of 3, #a.-c. 4.25 4.25

**Souvenir Sheet**
**923** A114 $6 multicolored 4.50 4.50

No. 922 is a continuous design.

1995 Boy Scout Jamboree, Holland — A115

Scouts in various activities: No. 924a, $1, Two wearing backpacks. b, $2, One holding rope, one wearing backpack. c, $4, One crossing rope bridge, one looking at map, natl. flag.
$6, Scout in kayak.

**1995, July 20**
**924** A115 Strip of 3, #a.-c. 5.50 5.50

**Souvenir Sheet**
**925** A115 $6 multicolored 6.00 6.00

No. 924 is a continuous design.

Rotary Intl., 90th Anniv. A116

Designs: $5, Rotary emblem, natl. flag.
$6, Rotary emblem, beach.

**1995, July 20**
**926** A116 $5 multicolored 4.00 4.00

**Souvenir Sheet**
**927** A116 $6 multicolored 4.75 4.75

Queen Mother, 95th Birthday — A117

No. 928: a, Drawing. b, Pink hat. c, Formal portrait. d, Green blue hat.
$6, Wearing crown jewels.

**1995, July 20 *Perf. 13½x14***
**928** A117 $1.50 Block or strip of 4, #a.-d. 4.50 4.50

**Souvenir Sheet**
**928E** A117 $6 multicolored 4.75 4.75

No. 928 was issued in sheets of 2.
Sheets of Nos. 928 and 928E exist with margins overprinted with black border and text "In Memoriam 1900-2002."

FAO, 50th anniv. — A118

No. 929a, 40c, Woman with tan sari over head. b, $2, FAO emblem, two infants. c, $3, Woman with blue sari over head.
$6, Man with hands around hoe handle.

**1995, July 20** *Perf. 14*
**929** A118 Strip of 3, #a.-c. 4.25 4.25

**Souvenir Sheet**

**930** A118 $6 multicolored 4.75 4.75

No. 929 is a continuous design.

Miniature Sheet of 9

Nobel Prize Recipients — A119

No. 931: a, Emil A. von Behring, medicine, 1901. b, Wilhelm Roentgen, physics, 1901. c, Paul J.L. Heyse, literature, 1910. d, Le Duc Tho, peace, 1973. e, Yasunari Kawabata, 1968. f, Tsung-Dao Lee, physics, 1957. g, Werner Heisenberg, physics, 1932. h, Johannes Stark, physics, 1919. i, Wilhelm Wien, physics, 1911.
$6, Kenzaburo Oe, literature, 1994.

**1995, July 20**
**931** A119 $1.25 #a.-i. 9.50 9.50

**Souvenir Sheet**

**932** A119 $6 multicolored 4.75 4.75

Souvenir Sheet

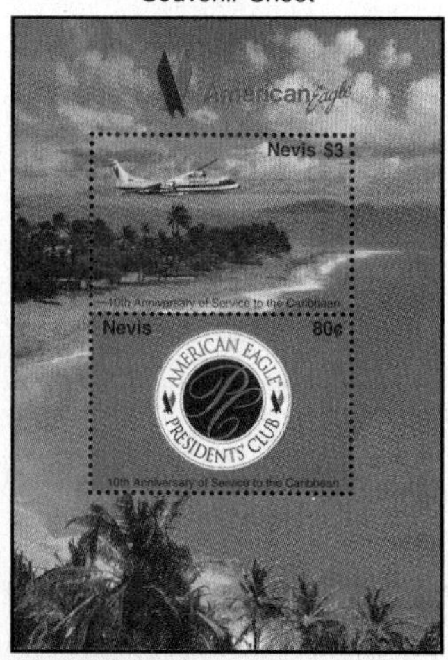

American Eagle Service, 10th Anniv. — A120

a, 80c, President's Club Emblem. b, $3, Airplane over beach.

**1995, Aug. 28** **Litho.** *Perf. 14*
**933** A120 Sheet of 2, #a.-b. 3.75 3.75

Miniature Sheet of 16

Marine Life — A121

No. 934: a, Great egrets. b, 17th cent. ship. c, Marlin. d, Herring gulls. e, Nassau groupers. f, Manta ray. g, Leopard shark, hammerhead shark. h, Hourglass dolphins. i, Spanish hogfish. j, Jellyfish, sea horses. k, Angel fish. l, Hawsbill turtle. m, Octopus vulgaris (i, j, m). n, Moray eel (o). o, Queen angelfish, butterflyfish. p, Ghost crab, sea star.
Each $6: No. 935, Nassau grouper. No. 936, Queen angelfish, vert.

**1995, Sept. 1**
**934** A121 50c #a.-p. 8.00 8.00

**Souvenir Sheets**

**935-936** A121 Set of 2 11.00 11.00

Singapore '95 (#935-936).

Natl. Telephone Co., SKANTEL Ltd., 10th Anniv. — A122

Designs: $1, Repairman working on telephone. $1.50, Company sign on building.
$5, Front of SKANTEL's Nevis office, horiz.

**1995, Oct. 23** **Litho.** *Perf. 14*
**937** A122 $1 multicolored .90 .90
**938** A122 $1.50 multicolored 1.25 1.25

**Souvenir Sheet**

**939** A122 $5 multicolored 4.50 4.50

Christmas Paintings, by Duccio di Buoninsegna (1250-1318) — A123

Details or entire paintings: 20c, Rucellai Madonna and Child. 50c, Border angel from Rucellai Madonna facing left. 80c, Madonna and Child. $1, The Annuniciation. $1.60, Madonna and Child. $3, Border angel from Rucellai Madonna facing right.
No. 946, Nativity with Prophets Isiah and Ezekiel. No. 947, Crevole Madonna.

**1995, Dec. 1** **Litho.** *Perf. 13½x14*
**940-945** A123 Set of 6 7.50 7.50

**Souvenir Sheets**

**946** A123 $5 multicolored 4.75 4.75
**947** A123 $6 multicolored 5.50 5.50

Four Seasons Resort, 5th Anniv. A124

Designs: 25c, Beach, resort buildings. 50c, Sailboats on beach. 80c, Golf course. $2, Premier Simeon Daniel laying cornerstone.
$6, Lounge chair on beach, sunset.

**1996, Feb. 14** **Litho.** *Perf. 14*
**948-951** A124 Set of 4 2.75 2.75

**Souvenir Sheet**

**952** A124 $6 multicolored 4.75 4.75

New Year 1996 (Year of the Rat) — A125

Rat, various plant life, with olive margin: Nos. 953: a, Looking up at butterfly. b, Crawling left. c, Looking up at horsefly. d, Looking up at dragonfly.
Nos. 954a-954d: like Nos. 953a-953d, with yellow brown margin.
$3, Berries above rat.

**1996, Feb, 28**
**953** A125 $1 Block of 4, #a.-d. 3.00 3.00

**Miniature Sheet**

**954** A125 $1 Sheet of 4, #a.-d. 3.00 3.00

**Souvenir Sheet**

**955** A125 $3 multicolored 3.00 3.00

No. 953 was issued in sheets of 16 stamps.

Pagodas of China A126

#956: a, Qian Qing Gong, 1420, Beijing. b, Qi Nian Dian, Temple of Heaven, Beijing. c, Zhongnanhai, Beijing. d, Da Zing Hall, Shenyang Palace. e, Temple of the Sleeping Buddha, Beijing. f, Huang Qiong Yu, Alter of Heaven, Beijing. g, Grand Bell Temple, Beijing. h, Imperial Palace, Beijing. i, Pu Tuo Temple.
$6, Summer Palace of emperor Wan Yanliang, 1153, Beijing, vert.

**1996, May 15** **Litho.** *Perf. 14*
**956** A126 $1 Sheet of 9, #a.-i. 6.75 6.75

**Souvenir Sheet**

**957** A126 $6 multicolored 4.50 4.50

CHINA '96, 9th Asian Intl. Philatelic Exhibition (#956).

Queen Elizabeth II, 70th Birthday — A127

Queen wearing: a, Blue dress, pearls. b, Formal white dress. c, Purple dress, hat.
$6, In uniform at trooping of the color.

**1996, May 15** **Litho.** *Perf. 13½x14*
**958** A127 $2 Strip of 3, #a.-c. 3.75 3.75

**Souvenir Sheet**

**959** A127 $6 multicolored 3.75 3.75

No. 958 was issued in sheets of 9 stamps with each strip in a different order.

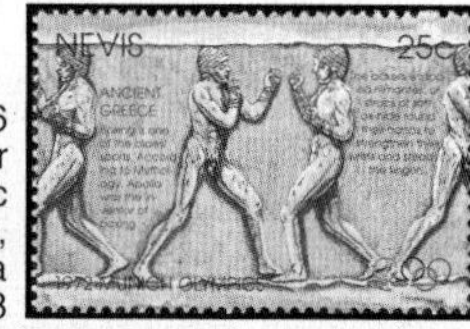

1996 Summer Olympic Games, Atlanta A128

Designs: 25c, Ancient Greek athletes boxing. 50c, Mark Spitz, gold medalist, swimming, 1972. 80c, Siegbert Horn, kayak singles gold medalist, 1972. $3, Siegestor Triumphal Arch, Munich, vert.
Pictures inside gold medals: No. 964, vert.: a, Jim Thorpe. b, Glenn Morris. c, Bob Mathias. d, Rafer Johnson. e, Bill Toomey. f, Nikolay Avilov. g, Bruce Jenner. h, Daley Thompson. i, Christian Schenk.
Each $5: No. 965, Willi Holdorf, vert. No. 966, Hans-Joachim Walde, silver medal, vert.

**1996, May 28** *Perf. 14*
**960-963** A128 Set of 4 3.75 3.75
**964** A128 $1 Sheet of 9, #a.-i. 7.25 7.25

**Souvenir Sheets**

**965-966** A128 Set of 2 15.00 15.00

Olymphilex '96 (#965).

UNESCO, 50th Anniv. — A129

25c, Cave paintings, Tassili N'Ajjer, Algeria. $2, Tikal Natl. Park, Guatemala, vert. $3, Temple of Hera at Samos, Greece.
$6, Pueblo, Taos, US.

**1996, July 1** **Litho.** *Perf. 14*
**967-969** A129 Set of 3 4.75 4.75

**Souvenir Sheet**

**970** A129 $6 multicolored 4.50 4.50

UNICEF, 50th Anniv. A130

25c, Children reading book. 50c, Girl receiving innoculation. $4, Faces of young people.
$6, Girl, vert.

**1996, July 1**
**971-973** A130 Set of 3 4.50 4.50

**Souvenir Sheet**

**974** A130 $6 multicolored 4.50 4.50

Disney's Sweethearts — A131

Designs: a, Pocahontas, John Smith, Flit. b, Mowgli, The Girl, Kaa. c, Belle, Beast, Mrs. Potts, Chip. d, Cinderella, Prince Charming, Jaq. e, Pinocchio, Dutch Girl Marionette, Jiminy Cricket. f, Grace Martin, Henry Coy. g, Snow White, Prince. h, Aladdin, Jasmine, Abu. i, Pecos Bill, Slue Foot Sue.
Each $6: No. 977, Sleeping Beauty, Prince Phillip, vert. No. 978, Ariel, Eric.

*Perf. 14x13½, 13½x14*

**1996, June 17** **Litho.**
**975** A131 $2 Sheet of 9, #a.-i. 21.00 21.00

**Souvenir Sheets**

**977-978** A131 Set of 2 13.00 13.00

A number has been reserved for an additional sheet with this set.

American Academy of Ophthalmology, Cent. — A132

**1996, July 1 Litho. *Perf. 14***
**979** A132 $5 multicolored 4.00 4.00

Flowers — A133

Designs: 25c, Rothmannia longiflora. 50c, Gloriosa simplex. $2, Catharanthus roseus. $3, Plumbago auriculata.

No. 984: a, Monodora myristica. b, Giraffa camelopardalis. c, Adansonia digitata. d, Ansellia gigantea. e, Geissorhiza rochensis. f, Arctotis venusta. g, Gladiohis cardinalis. h, Eucomis bicolor. i, Protea obtusifolia.

$5, Stelitzia reginae.

**1996, Sept. 24 Litho. *Perf. 14***
**980-983** A133 Set of 4 4.25 4.25
**984** A133 $1 Sheet of 9, #a.-i. 6.75 6.75

**Souvenir Sheet**

**985** A133 $5 multicolored 3.75 3.75

Christmas A134

Designs: 25c, Western meadowlark, vert. 50c, American goldfinch. 80c, Santa in sleigh, reindeer. $1, Western meadowlark, diff., vert. $1.60, Mockingbird, vert. $5, Yellow-rumped caleque.

Each $6: No. 992, Macaw. No. 993, Vermilion flycatcher.

**1996, Dec. 2 Litho. *Perf. 14***
**986-991** A134 Set of 6 7.25 7.25

**Souvenir Sheets**

**992-993** A134 Set of 2 9.00 9.00

New Year 1997 (Year of the Ox) — A135

Painting, "Five Oxen," by Han Huang: a, 50c. b, 80c. c, $1.60. d, $2.

**1997, Jan. 16 Litho. *Perf. 14x15***
**994** A135 Sheet of 4, #a.-d. + label 4.25 4.25

A136

Pandas: a, Eating leaves on branch. b, Face, eating. c, Paws holding object. d, Hanging upside down. e, Lying between tree branch. f, Climbing tree.

$5, Mother, cub.

**1997, Feb. 12 Litho. *Perf. 14***
**995** A136 $1.60 Sheet of 6, #a.-f. 9.50 9.50

**Souvenir Sheet**

**996** A136 $5 multicolored 3.75 3.75

Hong Kong '97.

A137

Cricket Players: 25c, Elquemedo Willet. 80c, Stuart Williams. $2, Keith Arthurton.

Each $5: No. 1000, Willet, Arthurton, Williams, 1990 Nevis team. No. 1001, Williams, Arthurton, 1994 West Indies team, vert.

**1997, May 1 Litho. *Perf. 14***
**997-999** A137 Set of 3 2.25 2.25

**Souvenir Sheets**

**1000-1001** A137 Set of 2 7.50 7.50

Queen Elizabeth II, Prince Philip, 50th Wedding Anniv. A138

No. 1002: a, Queen Elizabeth II. b, Royal arms. c, Prince, Queen in red hat. d, Queen in blue coat, Prince. e, Caernarfon Castle. f, Prince Philip.

$5, Queen wearing crown.

**1997, May 29 Litho. *Perf. 14***
**1002** A138 $1 Sheet of 6, #a.-f. 5.00 5.00

**Souvenir Sheet**

**1003** A138 $5 multicolored 4.00 4.00

Paintings by Hiroshige (1797-1858) A139

No. 1004: a, Scattered Pines, Tone River. b, Nakagawa River Mouth. c, Niijuku Ferry. d, Horie and Nekozane. e, View of Konodai and the Tone River. f, Maple Trees at Mama, Tekona Shrine & Bridge.

Each $6: No. 1005, Mitsumata Wakarenofuchi. No. 1006, Moto-Hachinan Shrine, Sunamura.

**1997, May 29 *Perf. 13½x14***
**1004** A139 $1.60 Sheet of 6, #a.-f. 8.00 8.00

**Souvenir Sheets**

**1005-1006** A139 Set of 2 9.00 9.00

Paul Harris (1868-1947), Founder of Rotary Intl. — A140

$2, Literacy promotion, portrait of Harris.

$5, Rotary Village Corps coaching soccer for youths in Chile.

**1997, May 29 *Perf. 14***
**1007** A140 $2 multicolored 1.75 1.75

**Souvenir Sheet**

**1008** A140 $5 multicolored 3.75 3.75

Heinrich von Stephan (1831-97) A141

No. 1009: a, Russian Reindeer Post, 1859. b, Von Stephan, UPU emblem. c, Steamboat, City of Cairo, 1800's.

$5, Portrait of Von Stephan, Bavarian postal messenger, 1640.

**1997, May 29**
**1009** A141 $1.60 Sheet of 3, #a.-c. 3.50 3.50

**Souvenir Sheet**

**1010** A141 $5 multicolored 3.75 3.75

PACIFIC 97.

Butterflies and Moths A142

10c, Crimson speckled. 25c, Purple emperor. 50c, Regent skipper. 80c, Provence burnet moth. $1, Common wall butterfly. $4, Cruiser butterfly.

No. 1017: a, Red-lined geometrid. b, Boisduval's autumnal moth. c, Blue pansy. d, Common clubtail. e, Tufted jungle queen. f, Lesser marbled fritillary. g, Peacock royal. h, Emperor gum moth. i, Orange swallow-tailed moth.

Each $5: No. 1018, Jersey tiger. No. 1019, Japanese emperor.

**1997, May 12 Litho. *Perf. 14***
**1011-1016** A142 Set of 6 5.50 5.50
**1017** A142 $1 Sheet of 9, #a.-i. 7.25 7.25

**Souvenir Sheets**

**1018-1019** A142 Set of 2 7.50 7.50

Souvenir Sheet

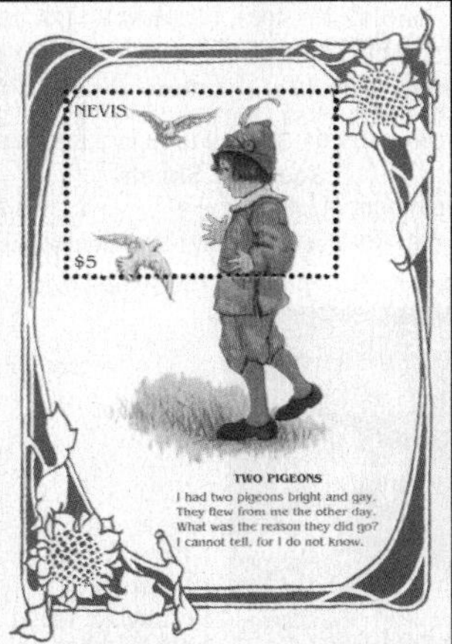


Mother Goose — A143

**1997, May 29**
**1020** A143 $5 Boy, two pigeons 3.75 3.75

Golf Courses of the World A144

Designs: a, Augusta National, U.S. b, Cabo Del Sol, Mexico. c, Cypress Point, U.S. d, Lost City, South Africa. e, Moscow Country Club, Russia. f, New South Wales, Australia. g, Royal Montreal, Canada. h, St. Andrews, Scotland. i, Four Seasons Resort, Nevis.

**1997, July 15**
**1021** A144 $1 Sheet of 9, #a.-i. 7.50 7.50

Mushrooms A145

Designs: 25c, Cantharellus cibarius. 50c, Stropharia aeruginosa. $3, Lactarius turpis. $4, Entoloma Jypeatum.

No. 1026: a, Suillus luteus. b, Amanita musearia. c, Lactarius rufus. d, Amanita rubescens. e, Armillaria mellea. f, Russula sardonia.

No. 1027: a, Boletus edulis. b, Pholiota lenta. c, Cortinarius bolaris. d, Coprinus picaceus. e, Amanita phalloides. f, Cystolepiota aspera.

Each $5: No. 1028, Gymnopilus junonius. No. 1029, Galerina mutabilis, philiota auriuella.

**1997, Aug. 12 Litho. *Perf. 13***
**1022-1025** A145 Set of 4 6.00 6.00

**Sheets of 6**

**1026** A145 80c #a.-f. 3.75 3.75
**1027** A145 $1 #a.-f. 4.50 4.50

**Souvenir Sheets**

**1028-1029** A145 Set of 2 8.00 8.00

Diana, Princess of Wales (1961-97) — A146

Various portraits.

**1997, Sept. 19 Litho. *Perf. 14***
**1030** A146 $1 Sheet of 9, #a.-i. 7.50 7.50

Trains A147

Designs: 10c, New Pacific type, Victorian Government Railways, Australia. 50c, Express locomotive, Imperial Government Railways, Japan. 80c, Turbine driven locomotive, London, Midland & Scottish Railway. $1, Electric passenger & freight locomotive, Swiss Federal Railways. $2, 3 cylinder compound express locomotive, London, Midland, Scottish Railway. $3, Express locomotive Kestrel, Great Northern Railway, Ireland.

No. 1037: a, 2-8-2 Mikado, Sudan Government Railways. b, Mohammed Ali El Kebir locomotive, Egyptian State Railways. c, "Schools" class locomotive, Southern Railway. d, Drum Battery Train, Great Southern Railways, Ireland. e, "Pacific" express locomotive, German State Railways. f, Mixed traffic locomotive, Canton-Hankow Railway, China.

Each $5: No. 1038, "King" class express, Great Western Railway. No. 1039, High pressure locomotive, London, Midland and Scottish Railway.

**1997, Sept. 29 Litho. *Perf. 14***
**1031-1036** A147 Set of 6 6.25 6.25
**1037** A147 $1.50 Sheet of 6, #a.-f. 7.25 7.25

**Souvenir Sheets**

**1038-1039** A147 Set of 2 8.00 8.00

Christmas — A148

Entire paintings or details: 20c, 25c, Diff. details from Selection of Angels, by Durer. 50c, Andromeda and Perseus, by Rubens. 80c, $1.60, Diff. details from Astronomy, by Raphael. $5, Holy Trinity, by Raphael.
Each $5: No. 1046, Ezekiel's Vision, by Raphael, horiz. No. 1047, Justice, by Rapahel, horiz.

**1997, Nov. 26 Litho. *Perf. 14***
**1040-1045** A148 Set of 6 7.00 7.00

**Souvenir Sheets**
**1046-1047** A148 Set of 2 7.50 7.50

New Year 1998 (Year of the Tiger) — A149

Tigers: No. 1048: a, Jumping right. b, Looking back over shoulder. c, Jumping left. d, Looking forward.
No. 1049, Tiger, vert.

**1998, Jan. 19 Litho. *Perf. 14***
**1048** A149 80c Sheet of 4, #a.-d. 4.00 4.00

**Souvenir Sheet**
**1049** A149 $2 multicolored 2.25 2.25

Social Security of St. Kitts and Nevis, 20th Anniv. A150

Designs: 30c, Logo, vert. $1.20, Front of Social Security building.
$6, Social Security staff, Charlestown, Nevis.

**1998, Feb. 2 Litho. *Perf. 13***
**1050** A150 30c multicolored .30 .30
**1051** A150 $1.20 multicolored .90 .90

**Souvenir Sheet**
***Perf. 13½x13***
**1052** A150 $6 multicolored 4.50 4.50

No. 1052 contains one 56x36mm stamp.

Fruit — A151

**1998, Mar. 9 *Perf. 14***
**No Year Imprint Below Design**

**1053** A151 5c Soursop .25 .25
**1054** A151 10c Carambola .25 .25
**1055** A151 25c Guava .25 .25
**1056** A151 30c Papaya .25 .25
**1057** A151 50c Mango .40 .40
**1058** A151 60c Golden apple .45 .45
**1059** A151 80c Pineapple .60 .60
**1060** A151 90c Watermelon .70 .70
**1061** A151 $1 Bananas .75 .75
**1062** A151 $1.80 Orange 1.40 1.40
**1063** A151 $3 Honeydew 2.25 2.25
**1064** A151 $5 Cantaloupe 3.75 3.75
**1065** A151 $10 Pomegranate 7.50 7.50
**1066** A151 $20 Cashew 15.00 15.00
*Nos. 1053-1066 (14)* 33.80 33.80

For overprints see #O55-O66.

**2000, Mar. 22**
**Inscribed "2000" Below Design**

*1054a* A151 10c multicolored .25 .25
*1056a* A151 30c multicolored .40 .25
*1059a* A151 80c multicolored .90 .60
*1062a* A151 $1.80 multicolored 1.75 1.40
*1064a* A151 $5 multicolored 4.00 4.00
*1065a* A151 $10 multicolored 7.50 7.50
*Nos. 1054a-1065a (6)* 14.80 14.00

Endangered Species — A152

Designs: 30c, Fish eagle. 80c, Summer tangers. 90c, Orangutan. $1.20, Tiger. $2, Cape pangolin. $3, Moatzin.
No. 1073: a, Chimpanzee. b, Keel-billed toucan. c, Chaco peccary. d, Spadefoot toad. e, Howler monkey. f, Alaskan brown bear. g, Koala. h, Brown pelican. i, Iguana.
Each $5: No. 1074, Mandrill. No. 1075, Polar bear.

**1998, Mar. 31 Litho. *Perf. 14***
**1067-1072** A152 Set of 6 6.50 6.50
**1073** A152 $1 Sheet of 9, #a.-i. 7.00 7.00

**Souvenir Sheets**
**1074-1075** A152 Set of 2 8.50 8.50

Aircraft A153

Designs: 10c, Boeing 747 200B. 90c, Cessna 185 Skywagon. $1.80, McDonnell Douglas DC-9 SO. $5, Airbus A300 B4.
No. 1080: a, Northrop B-2A. b, Lockheed SR-71A. c, Beechcraft T-44A. d, Sukhoi Su-27UB. e, Hawker Siddeley (BAe) Harrier GR.MK1. f, Boeing E-3A Sentry. g, Convair B-36H. h, IAI Kfir C2.
Each $5: No. 1081, Lockheed F-117A. No. 1082, Concorde G-BOAA.

**1998, May 19 Litho. *Perf. 14***
**1076-1079** A153 Set of 4 6.25 6.25
**1080** A153 $1 Sheet of 8, #a.-h. 6.50 6.50

**Souvenir Sheets**
**1081-1082** A153 Set of 2 8.25 8.25

#1081-1082 each contain 1 57x42mm stamp.

Chaim Topol Portraying Tevye from "Fiddler on the Roof" — A154

**1998, May 17 Litho. *Perf. 13½***
**1083** A154 $1.60 multicolored 1.75 1.75

Israel '98. Issued in sheets of 6.

Voice of Nevis (VON) Radio, 10th Anniv. A155

20c, Logo of Nevis Broadcasting Co., vert. 30c, Evered "Webbo" Herbert, station manager at controls. $1.20, Exterior of offices and studios.
$5, Merritt Herbert, managing director, opening ceremony, 1988.

**1998, June 18 *Perf. 14***
**1084-1086** A155 Set of 3 1.60 1.60

**Souvenir Sheet**
**1087** A155 $5 multicolored 4.00 4.00

Intl. Year of the Ocean A156

30c, Butterflyfish. 80c, Bicolor cherub. $1.20, Silver badgerfish. $2, Asfur angelfish.
No. 1092, vert: a, Copperbanded butterflyfish. b, Forcepsfish. c, Double-saddled butterflyfish. d, Blue surgeonfish. e, Orbiculate batfish. f, Undulated triggerfish. g, Rock beauty. h, Flamefish. i, Queen angelfish.
No. 1093: a, Pygama cardinal fish. b, Wimplefish. c, Long-nosed filefish. d, Oriental sweetlips. e, Blue spotted boxfish. f, Blue stripe angelfish. g, Goldrim tang. h, Royal gramma. i, Common clownfish.
Each $5: No. 1094, Longhorned cowfish, vert. No. 1095, Red-faced batfish, vert.

**1998, Aug. 18 Litho. *Perf. 14***
**1088-1091** A156 Set of 4 5.75 5.75
**1092** A156 90c Sheet of 9, #a.-i. 6.00 6.00
**1093** A156 $1 Sheet of 9, #a.-i. 6.75 6.75

**Souvenir Sheets**
**1094-1095** A156 Set of 2 8.50 8.50

Diana, Princess of Wales (1961-97) A157

**1998, Oct. 15 Litho. *Perf. 14***
**1096** A157 $1 multicolored .80 .80

No. 1096 was issued in sheets of 6.

Mahatma Gandhi (1869-1948) A158

Portraits: No. 1097, In South Africa, 1914. No. 1098, At Downing Street, London.

**1998, Oct. 15**
**1097** A158 $1 multicolored .90 .90
**1098** A158 $1 multicolored .90 .90

Nos. 1097-1098 were each issued in sheets of 6.

Royal Air Force, 80th Anniv. A159

Aircraft — #1100: a, Panavia Tornado F3 ADV. b, Panavia Tornado F3 IDV. c, Tristar K Mk1 Tanker refueling Panavia Tornado. d, Panavia Tornado GRl.
Each $5: No. 1101, Wessex helicopter, fighter plane. No. 1102, Early aircraft, birds.

**1998, Oct. 15 Litho. *Perf. 14***
**1100** A159 $2 Sheet of 4, #a.-d. 7.00 7.00

**Souvenir Sheets**
**1101-1102** A159 Set of 2 9.25 9.25

1998 World Scouting Jamboree, Chile — A160

Designs: a, Four Boy Scouts from around the world. b, Boy Scout accompanying Gettysburg veterans, 1913. c, First black troop, Virginia, 1928.

**1998, Oct. 15**
**1103** A160 $3 Sheet of 3, #a.-c. 7.50 7.50

Independence, 15th Anniv. — A161

Design: Prime Minister Kennedy Simmonds receiving constitutional instruments from Princess Margaret, Countess of Snowden.

**1998, Oct. 15 Litho. *Perf. 14***
**1104** A161 $1 multicolored .95 .95

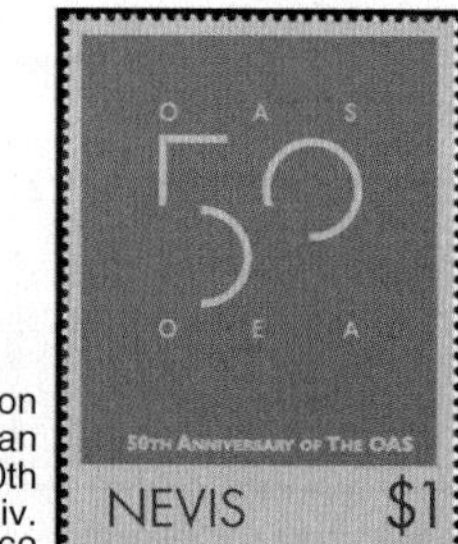

Organization of American States, 50th Anniv. A162

**1998, Oct. 15 *Perf. 14***
**1105** A162 $1 multicolored .75 .75

Enzo Ferrari (1898-1988), Automobile Manufacturer — A163

No. 1106: a, 365 California. b, Pininfarina's P6. c, 250 LM.
$5, 212 Export Spyder.

**1998, Oct. 15**
**1106** A163 $2 Sheet of 3, #a.-c. 5.50 5.50

**Souvenir Sheet**
**1107** A163 $5 multicolored 4.75 4.75

No. 1107 contains one 91x35mm stamp.

Christmas — A164

Designs: 25c, Kitten, Santa. 60c, Kitten, ornament. 80c, Kitten in sock, vert. 90c, Puppy, presents. $1, Cherub sleeping, birds. $3, Child making snowball, vert.
Each $5: No. 1114, Family, vert. No. 1115, Two dogs.

**1998, Nov. 24 Litho. *Perf. 14***
**1108-1113** A164 Set of 6 5.25 5.25

**Souvenir Sheets**

**1114-1115** A164 Set of 2 7.75 7.75

New Year 1999 (Year of the Rabbit) — A165

Color of pairs of rabbits — #1116: a, brown & gray. b, brown & white. c, brown. d, white & black spotted.
$5, Adult white rabbit, 3 bunnies.

**1999, Jan. 4 Litho. *Perf. 14***
**1116** A165 $1.60 Sheet of 4, #a.-d. 5.25 5.25

**Souvenir Sheet**

**1117** A165 $5 multicolored 4.50 4.50

No. 1117 contains one 58x47mm stamp.

Disney Characters Playing Basketball A166

Basketball in background — #1118, each $1: a, Mickey in green. b, Donald. c, Minnie. d, Goofy. e, One of Donald's nephews. f, Goofy, Mickey. g, Mickey in purple. h, Huey, Dewey, Louie.
Green & white background — #1119, each $1: a, Mickey in purple. b, Goofy. c, Minnie in puple. d, Mickey in yellow & gray. e, Minnie in yellow. f, Donald. g, Donald & Mickey. h, One of Donald's nephews.
No. 1120, $5, Minnie, green bow, horiz. No. 1121, $5, Minnie, purple bow, horiz. No. 1122, $6, Mickey in purple, horiz. No. 1123, $6, Mickey in yellow, horiz.

***Perf. 13½x14, 14x13½***
**1998, Dec. 24 Litho.**

**Sheets of 8, #a-h**

**1118-1119** A166 Set of 2 17.00 17.00

**Souvenir Sheets**

**1120-1121** A166 Set of 2 8.75 8.75
**1122-1123** A166 Set of 2 11.00 11.00

Mickey Mouse, 70th anniv.

1998 World Cup Soccer Players — A167

No. 1124: a, Laurent Blanc, France. b, Dennis Bergkamp, Holland. c, David Sukor, Croatia. d, Ronaldo, Brazil. e, Didier Deschamps, France. f, Patrick Kluivert, Holland. g, Rivaldo, Brazil. h, Zinedine Zidane, France.
$5, Zinedine Zidane, close-up.

**1999, Jan. 18 *Perf. 13½***
**1124** A167 $1 Sheet of 8, #a.-h. 6.25 6.25

**Souvenir Sheet**

**1125** A167 $5 multicolored 4.00 4.00

Australia '99, World Stamp Expo A168

Dinosaurs: 30c, Kritosaurus. 60c, Oviraptor. 80c, Eustreptospondylus. $1.20, Tenontosaurus. $2, Ouranosaurus. $3, Muttaburrasaurus.
No. 1132, $1.20: a, Edmontosaurus. b, Avimimus. c, Minmi. d, Segnosaurus. e, Kentrosaurus. f, Deinonychus.
No. 1133, #1.20: a, Saltasaurus. b, Compsoganthus c, Hadrosaurus. d, Tuojiangosaurus. e, Euoplocephalus. f, Anchisaurus.
Each $5: #1134, Triceratops. #1135, Stegosaurus.

**1999, Feb. 22 Litho. *Perf. 14***
**1126-1131** A168 Set of 6 6.50 6.50

**Sheets of 6, #a-f**

**1132-1133** A168 Set of 2 11.50 11.50

**Souvenir Sheets**

**1134-1135** A168 Set of 2 8.00 8.00

World Leaders of the 20th Century — A169

No. 1136: a, Emperor Haile Selassie (1892-1975), Ethiopia. b, Selassie, Ethiopian warriors, flag. c, David Ben-Gurion (1886-1973), Prime Minister of Israel. d, Ben-Gurion, Israeli flag. e, Pres. Franklin Roosevelt (1882-1945), Eleanor Roosevelt (1884-1962), UN emblem. f, Roosevelts campaigning, US GI in combat. g, Mao Tse-tung (1893-1976), Chinese leader, 1934 Long March. h, Poster of Mao, soldier.
Each $5: No. 1137, Gandhi. No. 1138, Nelson Mandela.

**1999, Mar. 8**
**1136** A169 90c Sheet of 8, #a.-h. 6.75 6.75

**Souvenir Sheets**

**1137-1138** A169 Set of 2 8.00 8.00

#1136b-1136c, 1136f-1136g are each 53x38mm.

Birds A170

No. 1139, each $1.60: a, Yellow warbler. b, Common yellowthroat. c, Painted bunting. d, Belted kingfisher. e, American kestrel. f, Northern oriole.
No. 1140, each $1.60: a, Malachite kingfisher. b, Lilac-breasted roller. c, Swallow-tailed bee-eater. d, Eurasian jay. e, Black-collared apalis. f, Gray-backed camaroptera.
Each $5: No. 1141, Banaquit. No. 1142, Ground scraper thrush, vert.

**1999, May 10 Litho. *Perf. 14***

**Sheets of 6, #a-f**

**1139-1140** A170 Set of 2 15.00 15.00

**Souvenir Sheets**

**1141-1142** A170 Set of 2 8.00 8.00

Orchids A171

Designs: 20c, Phaius hybrid, vert. 25c, Cuitlauzina pendula, vert. 50c, Bletilla striata, vert. 80c, Cymbidium "Showgirl," vert. $1.60, Zygopetalum crinitium. $3, Dendrobium nobile.
No. 1149, vert, each $1: a, Cattleya pumpernickel. b, Odontocidium Arthur Elle. c, Neostylis Lou Sneary. d, Phalaenopsis Aprodite. e, Arkundina graminieolia. f, Cymbidium Hunter's Point. g, Rynchoatylis coelestis. h, Cymbidium Elf's castle.
No. 1150, vert, each $1: a, Cattleya intermedia. b, Cattleya Sophia Martin. c, Phalaenopsis Little Hal. d, Laeliocattleya alisal "Rodeo." e, Laelia lucasiana fournieri. f, Cymbidium Red beauty. g, Sobralia sp. h, Promenaea xanthina.
Each $5: No. 1151, Philippine wind orchid. No. 1152, Dragon's mouth.

**1999, June 15 Litho. *Perf. 14***
**1143-1148** A171 Set of 6 5.50 5.50

**Sheets of 8, #a-h**

**1149-1150** A171 14.50 14.50

**Souvenir Sheets**

**1151-1152** A171 Set of 2 8.00 8.00

Wedding of Prince Edward and Sophie Rhys-Jones A172

No. 1153, each $2: a, Sophie in checked suit. b, Couple walking across grass. c, Sophie in black hat, suit, d, Prince Edward in white shirt.
No. 1154, each $2: a, Couple standing in front of building. b, Sophie wearing large hat. c, Sophie in black dress. d, Edward in striped shirt.
Each $5: No. 1155, Couple posing for engagement photo, horiz. No. 1156, Edward kissing Sophie, horiz.

**1999, June 19 Litho. *Perf. 14¼***

**Sheets of 4, #a-d**

**1153-1154** A172 Set of 2 12.50 12.50

**Souvenir Sheets**

**1155-1156** A172 Set of 2 8.00 8.00

IBRA '99, World Stamp Exhibition, Nuremberg — A173

Beuth 2-2-2 locomotive and: 30c, Baden #1. 80c, Brunswick #1.
Sailing ship Kruzenshstern and: 90c, Bergedorf #2 & #1a. $1, Bremen #1.
$5, Regensburg air post label on cover.

**1999, July 1 *Perf. 14x14½***
**1157-1160** A173 Set of 4 2.75 2.75

**Souvenir Sheet**

**1161** A173 $5 multicolored 3.50 3.50

**Souvenir Sheets**

PhilexFrance '99, World Philatelic Exhibition — A174

Trains: No. 1162, $5: First Class Carriage, 1837. No. 1163, $5: 141.R Mixed Traffic 2-8-2, 1949.

**1999, July 1 *Perf. 14x13½***
**1162-1163** A174 Set of 2 8.25 8.25

Paintings by Hokusai (1760-1849) A175

Details or entire paintings — #1164: a, (Five) Women Returning Home at Sunset. b, The Blind. c, (Four) Women Returning Home at Sunset. d, A Young Man on a White Horse. e, The Blind (man with beard). f, A Peasant Crossing a Bridge.
No. 1165: a, Poppies (one in bloom). b, The Blind (man with goatee). c, Poppies. d, Abe No Nakamaro Gazing at the Moon from a Terrace. e, The Blind. f, Cranes on a Snowy Pine.
Each $5: No. 1166, Carp in a Waterfall. No. 1167, A Rider in the Snow.

**1999, July 1 *Perf. 13½x14***

**Sheets of 6**

**1164** A175 $1 #a.-f. 4.50 4.50
**1165** A175 $1.60 #a.-f. 7.25 7.25

**Souvenir Sheets**

**1166-1167** A175 Set of 2 8.25 8.25

Culturama Festival, 25th Anniv. — A176

Designs: 30c, Steel drummers. 80c, Clowns. $1.80, Masqueraders with "Big Drum." No. 1171, $5, String band.
No. 1172, Masquerade dancers.

**1999, July 1 Litho. *Perf. 14***
**1168-1171** A176 Set of 4 6.25 6.25

**Souvenir Sheet**

**1172** A176 $5 multicolored 4.00 4.00

No. 1172 contains one 51x38mm stamp.

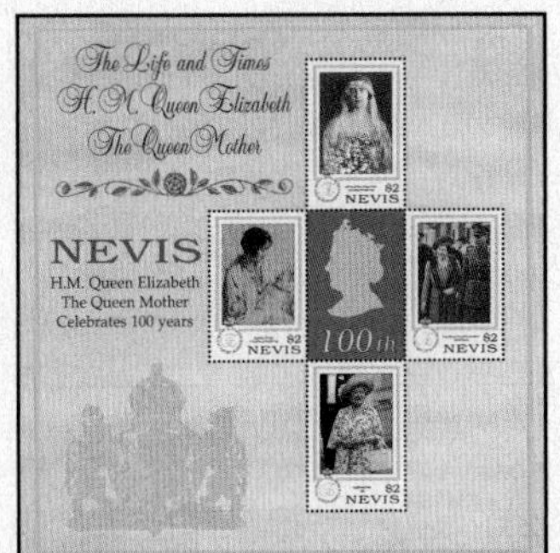

Queen Mother — A177

Queen Mother (b. 1900): No. 1173: a, In bridal gown, 1923. b, With Princess Elizabeth, 1926. c, With King George VI in World War II. d, Wearing hat, 1983.
$6, Wearing tiara, 1957.

**Gold Frames**

**1999, Aug. 4 Sheet of 4 *Perf. 14***
**1173** A177 $2 #a.-d., + label 6.25 6.25

**Souvenir Sheet**
***Perf. 13¾***

**1174** A177 $6 multicolored 4.75 4.75

No. 1174 contains one 38x51mm stamp.
See Nos. 1287-1288.

Christmas — A178

30c, Adoration of the Magi, by Albrecht Durer. 90c, Canigiani Holy Family, by Raphael. $1.20, The Nativity, by Durer. $1.80, Madonna Surrounded by Angels, by Peter Paul Rubens. $3, Madonna Surrounded by Saints, by Rubens.
$5, Madonna and Child by a Window, by Durer, horiz.

**1999, Nov. 12 Litho. *Perf. 14***
**1175-1179** A178 Set of 5 5.75 5.75

**Souvenir Sheet**

**1180** A178 $5 multicolored 4.00 4.00

Millennium A179

Scenes of Four Seasons Resort: a, Aerial view. b, Palm tree, beach. c, Golf course. d, Couple on beach.

**1999 Litho. *Perf. 14¼x13¾***
**1181** A179 30c Sheet of 4, #a.-d. .90 .90

Flowers A180

Various flowers making up a photomosaic of Princess Diana.

**1999, Dec. 31 Litho. *Perf. 13¾***
**1182** A180 $1 Sheet of 8, #a.-h. 6.50 6.50

New Year 2000 (Year of the Dragon) — A181

No. 1183: a, Dragon showing 9 claws. b, Dragon showing 10 claws. c, Dragon showing 5 claws. d, Dragon showing 8 claws.
$5, Dragon, vert.

**2000, Feb. 5 *Perf. 14***
**1183** A181 $1.60 Sheet of 4, #a.-d. 4.75 4.75

**Souvenir Sheet**
***Perf. 13¾***

**1184** A181 $5 multi 4.25 4.25

No. 1184 contains one 38x50mm stamp.

Millennium A182

No. 1185 — Highlights of 1700-1750: a, Jonathan Swift writes "Gulliver's Travels." b, Manchu Dynasty flourishes in China. c, Bartolomeo Cristofori invents piano. d, Capt. William Kidd hanged for piracy. e, Astronomer William Herschel born. f, George I succeeds Queen Anne as British ruler. g, Russian treaty with China. h, Bubonic plague hits Austria and Germany. i, Kaigetsudo paints "Standing Woman." j, Queen Anne ascends to English throne. k, Anders Celsius invents centigrade scale for thermometer. l, Vitus Bering discovers Alaska and Aleutian Islands. m, Edmond Halley predicts return of comet. n, John and Charles Wesley found Methodism movement. o, Isaac Newton publishes "Opticks." p, England and Scotland form Great Britain (60x40mm). q, Johann Sebastian Bach composes "The Well-Tempered Clavier."
No. 1186 — Highlights of the 1990s: a, Boris Yeltsin becomes prime minister of Russian Federation. b, Gulf War begins. c, Civil War in Bosnia. d, Signing of the Oslo Accords. e, John Major, Albert Reynolds search for peace in Northern Ireland. f, F.W. De Klerk, Nelson Mandela end apartheid in South Africa. g, Cal Ripken, Jr. breaks record for most consecutive baseball games played. h, Kobe, Japan earthquake. i, Inca girl, believed to be 500 years old, found in ice. j, Sojourner beams back images from Mars. k, Dr. Ian Wilmot clones sheep "Dolly." l, Princess Diana dies in car crash. m, Hong Kong returned to China. n, Septuplets born and survive. o, Guggenheim Museum in Bilbao, Spain completed. p, Countdown to year 2000 (60x40mm). q, Pres. William J. Clinton impeached.

**2000, Jan. 4 Litho. *Perf. 12¾x12½***

**Sheets of 17**

**1185** A182 30c #a.-q., + label 5.00 5.00
**1186** A182 50c #a.-q., + label 7.25 7.25

Misspellings and historical inaccuracies abound on Nos. 1185-1186.

Tropical Fish A183

Designs: 30c, Spotted scat. 80c, Platy variatus. 90c, Emerald betta. $4, Cowfish.
No. 1191, each $1: a, Oriental sweetlips. b, Royal gramma. c, Threadfin butterflyfish. d, Yellow tang. e, Bicolor angelfish. f, Catalina goby. g, False cleanerfish. h, Powder blue surgeon.
No. 1192, each $1: a, Sailfin tang. b, Black-capped gramma. c, Majestic snapper. d, Purple firefish. e, Clown trigger. f, Yellow long-nose. g, Clown wrasse. h, Yellow-headed jawfish.
Each $5: No. 1193, Clown coris. No. 1194, Clown killifish.

**2000, Mar. 27 *Perf. 14***
**1187-1190** A183 Set of 4 5.00 5.00

**Sheets of 8, #a.-h.**

**1191-1192** A183 Set of 2 13.00 13.00

**Souvenir Sheets**

**1193-1194** A183 Set of 2 8.00 8.00

Dogs — A184

Designs: 10c, Miniature pinscher. 20c, Pyrenean mountain dog. 30c, Welsh Springer spaniel. 80c, Alaskan malamute. $2, Bearded collie. $3, Amercian cocker spaniel.
No. 1201, horiz.: a, Beagle. b, Basset hound. c, St. Bernard. d, Rough collie. e, Shih tzu. f, American bulldog.
No. 1202, horiz.: a, Irish red and white setter. b, Dalmatian. c, Pomeranian. d, Chihuahua. e, English sheepdog. f, Samoyed.
Each $5: No. 1203, Leonberger. No. 1204, Longhaired miniature dachshund, horiz.

**2000, May 1 Litho. *Perf. 14***
**1195-1200** A184 Set of 6 5.25 5.25
**1201** A184 90c Sheet of 6, #a-f 4.50 4.50
**1202** A184 $1 Sheet of 6, #a-f 5.00 5.00

**Souvenir Sheets**

**1203-1204** A184 Set of 2 8.50 8.50

100th Test Match at Lord's Ground — A185

Designs: $2, Elquemede Willett. $3, Keith Arthurton.
$5, Lord's Ground, horiz.

**2000, June 10**
**1205-1206** A185 Set of 2 4.00 4.00

**Souvenir Sheet**

**1207** A185 $5 multi 4.00 4.00

First Zeppelin Flight, Cent. — A186

No. 1208: a, LZ-129. b, LZ-1. c, LZ-11.
$5, LZ-127.

**2000, June 10 *Perf. 14***
**1208** A186 $3 Sheet of 3, #a-c 7.00 7.00

**Souvenir Sheet**
***Perf. 14¼***

**1209** A186 $5 multi 4.25 4.25

No. 1208 contains three 38x25mm stamps.

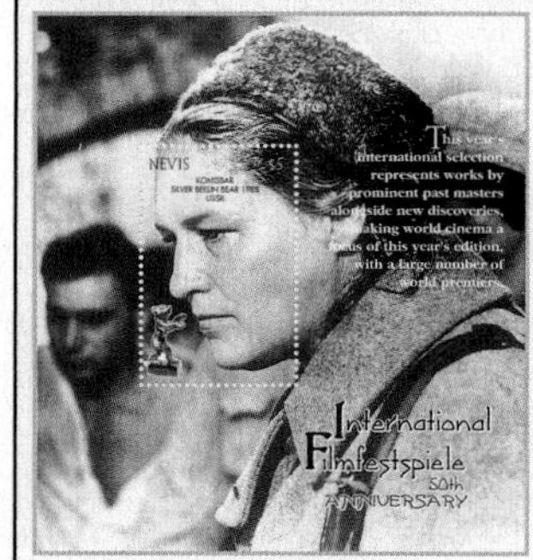

Berlin Film Festival, 50th Anniv. — A187

No. 1210: a, Rani Radovi. b, Salvatore Giuliano. c, Schoenzeit für Füchse. d, Shirley MacLaine. e, Simone Signoret. f, Sohrab Shahid Saless.
$5, Komissar.

**2000, June 10 *Perf. 14***
**1210** A187 $1.60 Sheet of 6, #a-f 7.50 7.50

**Souvenir Sheet**

**1211** A187 $5 multi 4.25 4.25

Spacecraft — A188

No. 1212, each $1.60: a, Mars IV probe. b, Mars Water. c, Mars 1. d, Viking. e, Mariner 7. f, Mars Surveyor.
No. 1213, each $1.60: a, Mariner 9. b, Mars 3. c, Mariner 4. d, Planet B. e, Mars Express Lander. f, Mars Express.
Each $5: No. 1214, Mars Observer. No. 1215, Mars Climate Observer, vert.

**2000, June 10 Sheets of 6, #a-f**
**1212-1213** A188 Set of 2 15.00 15.00

**Souvenir Sheets**

**1214-1215** A188 Set of 2 8.00 8.00

Souvenir Sheets

2000 Summer Olympics, Sydney — A189

No. 1216: a, Gisela Mauermeyer. b, Uneven bars. c, Wembley Stadium, London, and British flag. d, Ancient Greek horse racing.

**2000, June 10**
**1216** A189 $2 Sheet of 4, #a-d 5.00 5.00

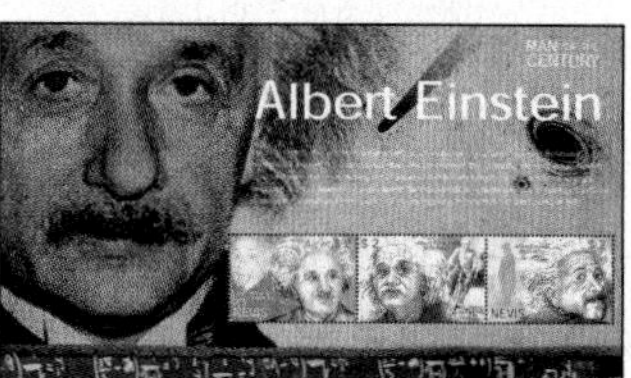

Albert Einstein (1879-1955) — A190

No. 1217: a, Sticking out tongue. b, Riding bicycle. c, Wearing hat.

**2000, June 10**
**1217** A190 $2 Sheet of 3, #a-c 5.00 5.00

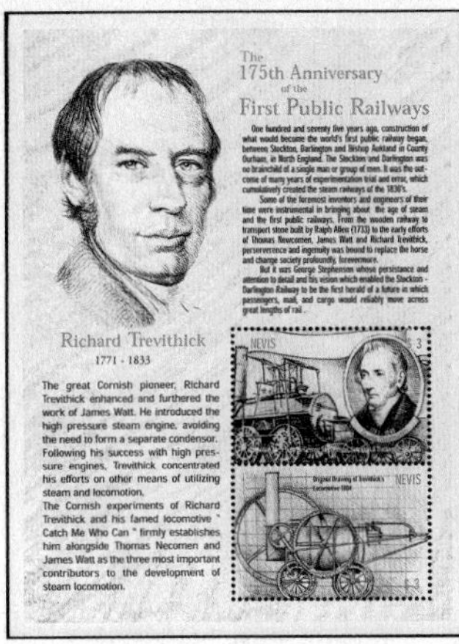


Public Railways, 175th Anniv. — A191

No. 1218: a, Locomotion No. 1, George Stephenson. b, Trevithick's 1804 drawing of locomotive.

**2000, June 10**
**1218** A191 $3 Sheet of 2, #a-b 4.50 4.50

Johann Sebastian Bach (1685-1750) — A192

**2000, June 10**
**1219** A192 $5 multi 4.25 4.25

Prince William, 18th Birthday — A193

No. 1220: a, Reaching to shake hand. b, In ski gear. c, With jacket open. d, In sweater. $5, In suit and tie.

**2000, June 21** ***Perf. 14***
**1220** A193 $1.60 Sheet of 4, #a-d 4.75 4.75

**Souvenir Sheet**

***Perf. 13¾***

**1221** A193 $5 multi 4.00 4.00

No. 1220 contains four 28x42mm stamps.

Souvenir Sheets

Bob Hope, Entertainer — A194

No. 1222: a, Wearing Air Force Ranger uniform. b, With Sammy Davis, Jr. c, With wife, Dolores. d, On golf course. e, In suit behind microphone. f, Walking.

**2000, July 10** ***Perf. 14***
**1222** A194 $1 Sheet of 6, #a-f 5.25 5.25

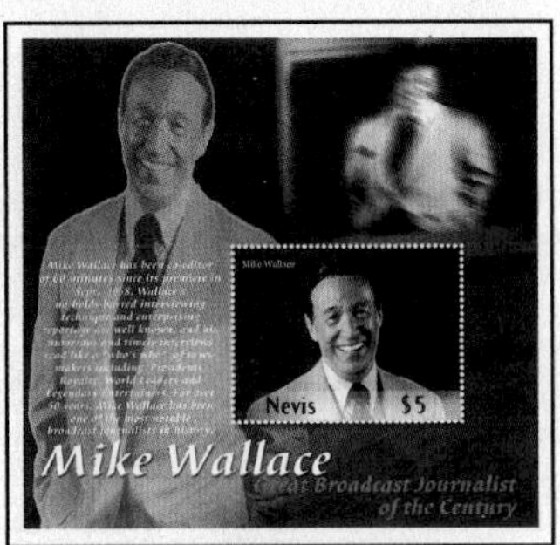


Mike Wallace, Broadcast Journalist — A195

**2000, July 10** ***Perf. 13¾***
**1223** A195 $5 multi 4.25 4.25

Carifesta VII — A196

Designs: 30c, Emblem. 90c, Festival participants. $1.20, Dancer.

**2000, Aug. 17** ***Perf. 14***
**1224-1226** A196 Set of 3 2.25 2.25

Monarchs — A197

No. 1227: a, King Edward III of England, 1327-77. b, Holy Roman Emperor Charles V (Charles I of Spain), 1520-56. c, Holy Roman Emperor Joseph II of Austria-Hungary, 1780-90. d, King Henry II of Germany, 1002-24. e, King Louis IV of France, 936-54. f, King Louis II of Bavaria, 1864-86.
$5, King Louis IX of France, 1226-70.

**2000, Aug. 1** **Litho.** ***Perf. 13¾***
**1227** A197 $1.60 Sheet of 6, #a-f 8.00 8.00

**Souvenir Sheet**

**1228** A197 $5 multi 4.25 4.25

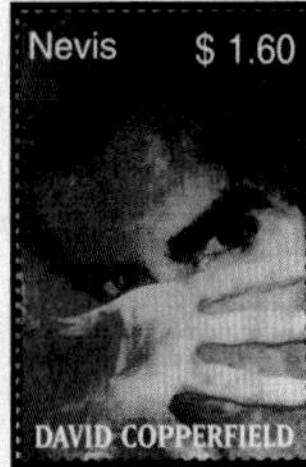


David Copperfield, Magician — A198

**2000, Aug. 10** ***Perf. 14***
**1229** A198 $1.60 multi 2.00 2.00

Printed in sheets of 4.

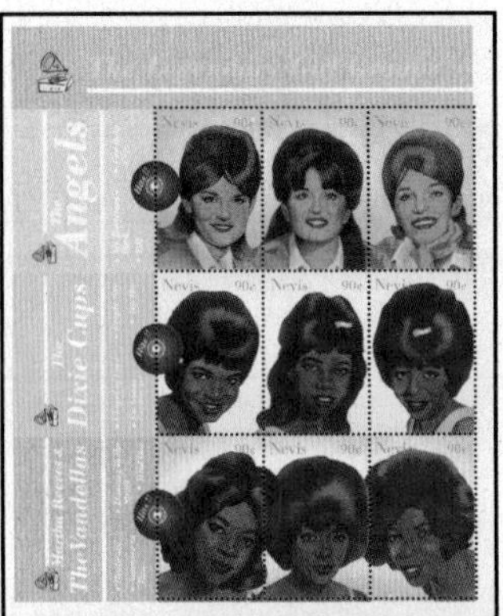


Female Singing Groups — A199

Singers from the Angels (a-c, blue background), Dixie Cups (d-f, yellow background) and Martha Reeves and the Vandellas (g-i, pink background): a, Record half. b, Woman with long hair. c, Woman with hand on chin. d, Record half. e, Woman with mole on cheek. f, Woman, no mole. g, Record half. h, Woman, not showing teeth. i, Woman showing teeth.

**2000, Aug. 10**
**1230** A199 90c Sheet of 9, #a-i 6.75 6.75

Butterflies A200

Designs: 30c, Zebra. 80c, Julia. $1.60, Small flambeau. $5, Purple mort bleu.
No. 1235, $1: a, Ruddy dagger. b, Common morpho. c, Banded king shoemaker. d, Figure of eight. e, Grecian shoemaker. f, Mosaic.
No. 1236, $1: a, White peacock. b, Hewitson's blue hairstreak. c, Tiger pierid. d, Gold drop helicopsis. e, Cramer's mesene. f, Red-banded pereute.
No. 1237, $5, Common mechanitis. No. 1238, $5, Hewitson's pierella.

**2001, Mar. 22**
**1231-1234** A200 Set of 4 6.00 6.00

**Sheets of 6, #a-f**

**1235-1236** A200 Set of 2 9.50 9.50

**Souvenir Sheets**

**1237-1238** A200 Set of 2 7.75 7.75

Flowers A201

Designs: 30c, Golden elegance oriental lily. 80c, Frangipani. $1.60, Garden zinnia. $5, Rose elegance lily.
No. 1243, 90c: a, Star of the march. b, Tiger lily. c, Mont Blanc lily. d, Torch ginger. e, Cattleya orchid. f, Saint John's wort.
No. 1244, $1: a, Culebra. b, Rubellum lily. c, Silver elegance oriental lily. d, Chinese hibiscus. e, Tiger lily. f, Royal poinciana.
No. 1245, $1.60: a, Epiphyte. b, Enchantment lily. c, Glory lily. d, Purple granadilla. e, Jacaranda. f, Shrimp plant.
No. 1246, $5, Dahlia. No. 1247, $5, Bird of Paradise.

**2000, Oct. 30**
**1239-1242** A201 Set of 4 6.00 6.00

**Sheets of 6, #a-f**

**1243-1245** A201 Set of 3 17.00 17.00

**Souvenir Sheets**

**1246-1247** A201 Set of 2 7.75 7.75

The Stamp Show 2000, London (Nos. 1243-1247).

Christmas — A203

Designs: 30c, The Coronation of the Virgin, by Diego Velazquez, vert. 80c, The Immaculate Conception, by Velazquez, vert. 90c, Madonna and Child, by Titian. $1.20, Madonna and Child With St. John the Baptist and St. Catherine, by Titian.
$6, Madonna and Child With St. Catherine, by Titian.

**2000, Dec. 4** **Litho.** ***Perf. 13½***
**1249-1252** A203 Set of 4 2.40 2.40

**Souvenir Sheet**

**1253** A203 $6 multi 4.50 4.50

New Year 2001 (Year of the Snake) — A204

No. 1254: a, Snake coiled on branch, facing right. b, Snake coiled on branch, facing left. c, Snake on ground, facing right. d, Snake on ground, facing left.
$5, Snake raising head.

**2001, Jan. 4** ***Perf. 14***
**1254** A204 $1.60 Sheet of 4, #a-d 4.75 4.75

**Souvenir Sheet**

**1255** A204 $5 multi 3.75 3.75

195th Annual Leeward Islands Methodist Church District Conference — A205

Churches: a, Charlestown. b, Jessups. c, Clifton. d, Trinity. e, Combermere. f, Gingerland. g, New River.

**2001, Jan. 23**

**1256** A205 50c Sheet of 7, #a-g 2.60 2.60

Garden of Eden — A206

No. 1257, $1.60: a, Red-crested woodpecker, unicorn. b, African elephant. c, Siberian tiger. d, Greater flamingo, Adam and Eve. e, Hippopotamus. f, Harlequin frog.

No. 1258, $1.60: a, Giraffe. b, Rainbow boa constrictor. c, Mountain cottontail rabbit. d, Bluebuck antelope. e, Red fox. f, Box turtle.

No. 1259, $5, Bald eagle. No. 1260, $5, Blue and gold macaw, vert. No. 1261, $5, Toucan, vert. No. 1262, $5, Koala, vert.

**2001, Jan. 31** ***Perf. 14***

**Sheets of 6, #a-f**

**1257-1258** A206 Set of 2 14.50 14.50

**Souvenir Sheets**

**1259-1262** A206 Set of 4 15.00 15.00

Mushrooms A207

Designs: 20c, Clavulinopsis corniculata. 25c, Cantharellus cibarius. 50c, Chlorociboria aeruginascens. 80c, Auricularia auricula judae. $2, Peziza vesiculosa. $3, Mycena acicula.

No. 1269, $1: a, Entoloma incanum. b, Entoloma nitidum. c, Stropharia cyanea. d, Otidea onotica. e, Aleuria aurantia. f, Mitrula paludosa. g, Gyromitra esculenta. h, Helvella crispa. i, Morchella semilibera.

No. 1270, $5, Omphalotus olearius. No. 1271, $5, Russula sardonia.

**2001, May 15** **Litho.** ***Perf. 14***

**1263-1268** A207 Set of 6 5.25 5.25

**1269** A207 $1 Sheet of 9, #a-i 7.00 7.00

**Souvenir Sheets**

**1270-1271** A207 Set of 2 7.75 7.75

Tale of Prince Shotoku — A208

No. 1272, $2: a, Conception of Prince Shotoku. b, At six. c, At ten. d, At eleven.

No. 1273, $2: a, At sixteen (soldiers at gate). b, At sixteen (soldiers on horseback). c, At thirty-seven. d, At forty-four.

**2001, May 31** ***Perf. 13¾***

**Sheets of 4, #a-d**

**1272-1273** A208 Set of 2 12.00 12.00

Phila Nippon '01, Japan.

Queen Victoria (1819-1901) — A209

No. 1274: a, Prince Albert. b, Queen Victoria (flower in hair). c, Alexandrina Victoria. d, Duchess of Kent. e, Queen Victoria (as old woman). f, Prince of Wales.

$5, Queen Victoria (with tiara).

**2001, July 9** **Litho.** ***Perf. 14***

**1274** A209 $1.20 Sheet of 6, #a-f 5.50 5.50

**Souvenir Sheet**

**1275** A209 $5 multi 3.75 3.75

Queen Elizabeth II, 75th Birthday — A210

No. 1276: a, Blue hat. b, Tiara. c, Yellow hat. d, Tan hat. e, Red hat. f, No hat.

$5, Blue hat, diff.

**2001, July 9**

**1276** A210 90c Sheet of 6, #a-f 4.00 4.00

**Souvenir Sheet**

**1277** A210 $5 multi 3.75 3.75

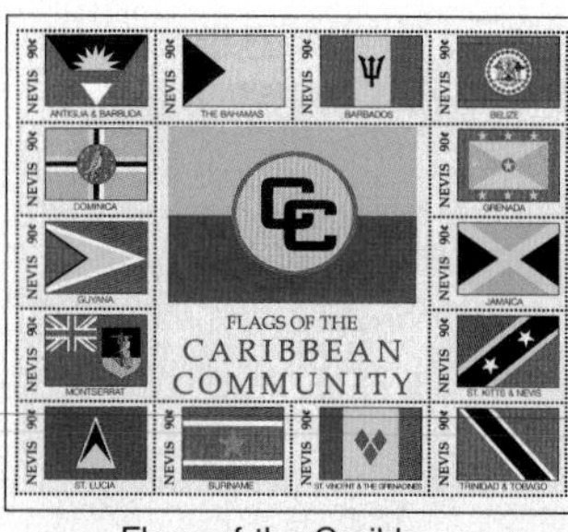


Flags of the Caribbean Community — A211

No. 1278: a, Antigua & Barbuda. b, Bahamas. c, Barbados. d, Belize. e, Dominica. f, Grenada. g, Guyana. h, Jamaica. i, Montserrat. j, St. Kitts & Nevis. k, St. Lucia. l, Surinam. m, St. Vincent & the Grenadines. n, Trinidad & Tobago.

**2001, Dec. 3** **Litho.** ***Perf. 14***

**1278** A211 90c Sheet of 14, #a-n 9.50 9.50

Christmas A212

Flowers: 30c, Christmas candle, vert. 90c, Poinsettia. $1.20, Snowbush. $3, Tiger claw, vert.

**2001, Dec. 3**

**1279-1282** A212 Set of 4 4.00 4.00

2002 World Cup Soccer Championships, Japan and Korea — A213

No. 1283, $1.60: a, Moracana Stadium, Brazil, 1950. b, Ferenc Puskas, 1954. c, Luis Bellini, 1958. d, Mauro, 1962. e, Cap, 1966. f, Banner, 1970.

No. 1284, $1.60: a, Passarella, 1978. b, Dino Zoff, 1982. c, Azteca Stadium, Mexico, 1986. d, San Siro Stadium, Italy, 1990. e, Dennis Bergkamp, Netherlands, 1994. f, Stade de France, 1998.

No. 1285, $5, Head from Jules Rimet Cup, 1930. No. 1286, $5, Head and globe from World Cup trophy, 2002.

**2001, Dec. 10** ***Perf. 13¾x14¼***

**Sheets of 6, #a-f**

**1283-1284** A213 Set of 2 14.50 14.50

**Souvenir Sheets**

***Perf. 14½x14¼***

**1285-1286** A213 Set of 2 7.50 7.50

**Queen Mother Type of 1999 Redrawn**

No. 1287: a, In bridal gown, 1923. b, With Princess Elizabeth, 1926. c, With King George VI in World War II. d, Wearing hat, 1983.

$6, Wearing tiara, 1957.

**2001, Dec. 13** ***Perf. 14***

**Yellow Orange Frames**

**1287** A177 $2 Sheet of 4, #a-d, + label 6.00 6.00

**Souvenir Sheet**

***Perf. 13¾***

**1288** A177 $6 multi 4.50 4.50

Queen Mother's 101st birthday. No. 1288 contains one 38x51mm stamp with a bluer background than that found on No. 1174. Sheet margins of Nos. 1287-1288 lack embossing and gold arms and frames found on Nos. 1173-1174.

Reign of Queen Elizabeth II, 50th Anniv. — A214

No. 1289: a, Queen with Prince Philip. b, Prince Philip. c, Queen with yellow dress. d, Queen touching horse.

$5, Queen with Prince Philip, diff.

**2002, Feb. 6** ***Perf. 14¼***

**1289** A214 $2 Sheet of 4, #a-d 6.00 6.00

**Souvenir Sheet**

**1290** A214 $5 multi 3.75 3.75

New Year 2002 (Year of the Horse) — A215

Horse paintings by Ren Renfa: a, Brown and white horse. b, Horse with ribs showing. c, Horse with tassel under neck. d, Gray horse.

**2002, Mar. 4** ***Perf. 13¼***

**1291** A215 $1.60 Sheet of 4, #a-d 4.75 4.75

Insects, Birds and Whales — A216

No. 1292, $1.20: a, Beechey's bee. b, Banded king shoemaker butterfly. c, Streaked sphinx caterpillar. d, Hercules beetle. e, South American palm beetle. f, Giant katydid.

No. 1293, $1.60: a, Roseate spoonbill. b, White-tailed tropicbird. c, Ruby-throated tropicbird. d, Black skimmer. e, Black-necked stilt. f, Mourning dove.

No. 1294, $1.60: a, Sperm whale. b, Sperm and killer whales. c, Minke whales. d, Fin whale. e, Blainville's beaked whale. f, Pygmy sperm whale.

No. 1295, $5, Click beetle. No. 1296, $5, Royal tern. No. 1297, $5, Humpback whale, vert.

**2002, Aug. 15** **Litho.** ***Perf. 14***

**Sheets of 6, #a-f**

**1292-1294** A216 Set of 3 21.00 21.00

**Souvenir Sheets**

**1295-1297** A216 Set of 3 12.00 12.00

APS Stampshow (#1293).

United We Stand — A217

**2002, Aug. 26**

**1298** A217 $2 multi 1.50 1.50

Printed in sheets of 4.

2002 Winter Olympics, Salt Lake City — A218

Designs: No. 1299, $2, Figure skating. No. 1300, $2, Freestyle skiing.

**2002, Aug. 26**

**1299-1300** A218 Set of 2 3.00 3.00
*a.* Souvenir sheet, #1299-1300 3.00 3.00

Intl. Year of Mountains — A219

No. 1301: a, Mt. Assiniboine, Canada. b, Mt. Atitlán, Guatemala. c, Mt. Adams, US. d, Matterhorn, Switzerland and Italy. e, Mt. Dhaulagiri, Nepal. f, Mt. Chamlang, Nepal.
$5, Mt. Kvaenangen, Norway.

**2002, Aug. 26**

**1301** A219 $2 Sheet of 6, #a-f 9.00 9.00

**Souvenir Sheet**

**1302** A219 $5 multi 3.75 3.75

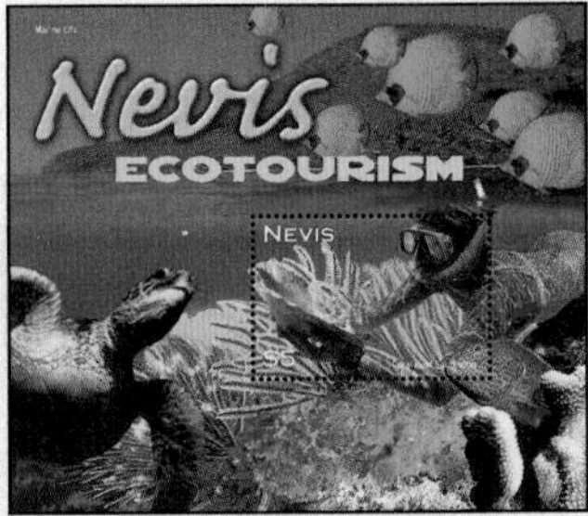

Ecotourism — A220

No. 1303: a, Horseback riding on beach. b, Windsurfing. c, Pinney's Beach. d, Cross-country hike. e, Robert T. Jones Golf Course. f, Scuba safaris.
$5, Coral reef snorkeling.

**2002, Aug. 26**

**1303** A220 $1.60 Sheet of 6, #a-f 7.25 7.25

**Souvenir Sheet**

**1304** A220 $5 multi 3.75 3.75

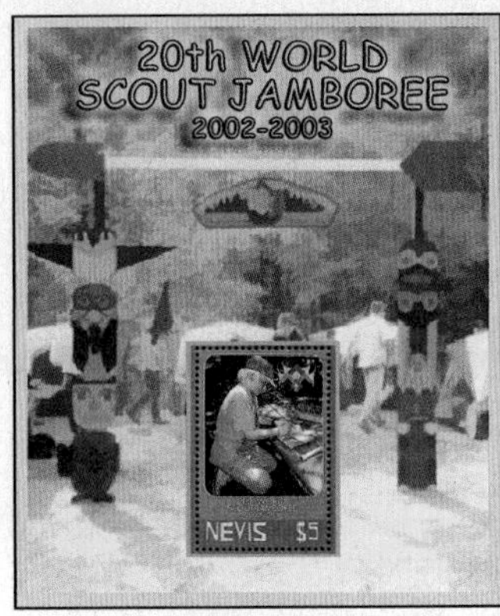

20th World Scout Jamboree, Thailand — A221

No. 1305: a, Scouts in two canoes. b, Scouts in one canoe. c, Scout on rope bridge. d, Scouts in inflatable rafts.
$5, Scout working on leatherwork project.

**2002, Aug. 26**

**1305** A221 $2 Sheet of 4, #a-d 6.00 6.00

**Souvenir Sheet**

**1306** A221 $5 multi 3.75 3.75

Souvenir Sheet

Artwork of Eva Wilkin (1898-1989) — A222

No. 1307: a, Unnamed painting of windmill. b, Nevis Peak (sepia toned). c, Fig Tree Church. d, Nevis Peak (full color).

**2002, Sept. 23**

**1307** A222 $1.20 Sheet of 4, #a-d 3.75 3.75

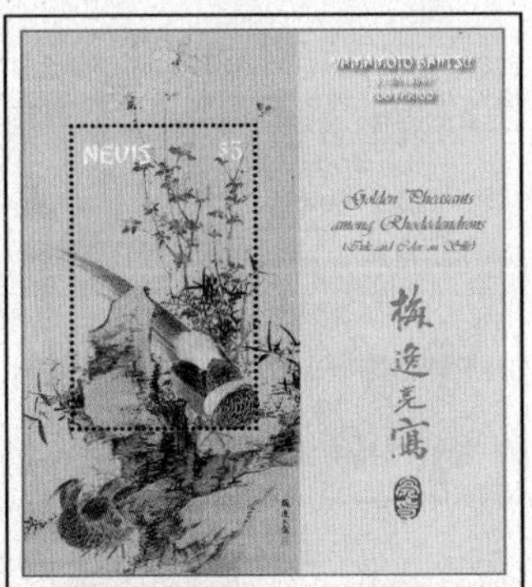
Japanese Art — A223

No. 1308: a, Golden Pheasants and Loquat, by Shoei Kano. b, Flowers and Birds of the Four Seasons (snow-covered branches), by Koson Ikeda. c, Pheasants and Azaleas, by Kano. d, Flowers and Birds of the Four Seasons (tree and hill), by Ikeda.
No. 1309, $3: a, Flying bird from Birds and Flowers of Summer and Autumn, by Terutada Shikibu. b, Red flower, from Birds and Flowers of Summer and Autumn, by Shikibu
No. 1310, $3: a, White flower from Birds and Flowers of Summer and Autumn, by Shikibu. b, Perched bird from Birds and Flowers of Summer and Autumn, by Shikibu.
No. 1311, $3, horiz.: a, Bird facing right, from Two Birds on Willow and Peach Trees, by Buson Yosa. b, Bird facing left, from Two Birds on Willow and Peach Trees, by Yosa.
No. 1312, $5, Golden Pheasants Among Rhododendrons, by Baiitsu Yamamoto. No. 1313, $5, Muskrat and Camellias, by Neko Jako, horiz.

**2002** ***Perf. 14x14¾***

**1308** A223 $2 Sheet of 4, #a-d 6.00 6.00

**Sheets of 2, #a-b**

***Perf. 13¾***

**1309-1311** A223 Set of 3 13.50 13.50

**Souvenir Sheets**

**1312-1313** A223 Set of 2 7.50 7.50

No. 1308 contains four 29x80mm stamps.

2002 World Cup Soccer Championship Quarterfinal Matches — A224

No. 1314, $1.20: a, Claudio Reyna and Torsten Frings. b, Michael Ballack and Eddie Pope. c, Sebastian Kehl and Brian McBride. d, Puyol and Eul Yong Lee. e, Jin Cheul Choi and Gaizka Mendieta. f, Juan Valeron and Jin Cheul Choi.
No. 1315, $1.60: a, Emile Heskey and Edmilson. b, Rivaldo and Sol Campbell. c, Ronaldinho and Nicky Butt. d, Ilhan Mansiz and Omar Daf. e, Hasan Sas and Papa Bouba Diop. f, Lamine Diatta and Hakan Sukur.
No. 1316, $3: a, Sebastian Kehl. b, Frankie Hejduk.
No. 1317, $3: a, Hong Myung Bo. b, Gaizka Mendieta.
No. 1318, $3: a, David Beckham and Roque Junior. b, Paul Scholes and Rivaldo.
No. 1319, $3: a, Alpay Ozalan. b, Khalilou Fadiga.

**2002, Nov. 4** **Litho.** ***Perf. 13¼***

**Sheets of 6, #a-f**

**1314-1315** A224 Set of 2 12.50 12.50

**Souvenir Sheets of 2, #a-b**

**1316-1319** A224 Set of 4 18.00 18.00

Christmas — A225

Religious art: 30c, Madonna and Child Enthroned with Saints, by Perugino. 80c, Adoration of the Magi, by Domenico Ghirlandaio. 90c, San Zaccaria Altarpiece, by Giovanni Bellini. $1.20, Presentation at the Temple, by Bellini. $5, Madonna and Child, by Simone Martini.
$6, Maestà, by Martini.

**2002, Nov. 4** ***Perf. 14¼***

**1320-1324** A225 Set of 5 6.25 6.25

**Souvenir Sheet**

***Perf. 14x14¼***

**1325** A225 $6 multi 4.50 4.50

New Year 2003 (Year of the Ram) — A226

**2003, Feb. 10** ***Perf. 14x13¾***

**1326** A226 $2 multi 2.00 2.00

Printed in sheets of 4.

Pres. John F. Kennedy (1917-63) — A227

No. 1327, $2: a, Robert and Edward Kennedy. b, John F. Kennedy. c, Joseph P., Jr., and John F. Kennedy as children. d, Robert and John F. Kennedy.
No. 1328, $2: a, Taking oath of office, 1961. b, At cabinet oath ceremony, 1961. c, With Russian foreign minister Andrei Gromyko, 1963. d, Cuban Missile Crisis, 1962.

**2003, Mar. 10** **Litho.** ***Perf. 14***

**Sheets of 4, #a-d**

**1327-1328** A227 Set of 2 12.00 12.00

Elvis Presley (1935-77) — A228

**2003, Mar. 10** **Litho.** ***Perf. 14***

**1329** A228 $1.60 multi 1.25 1.25

Printed in sheets of 6.

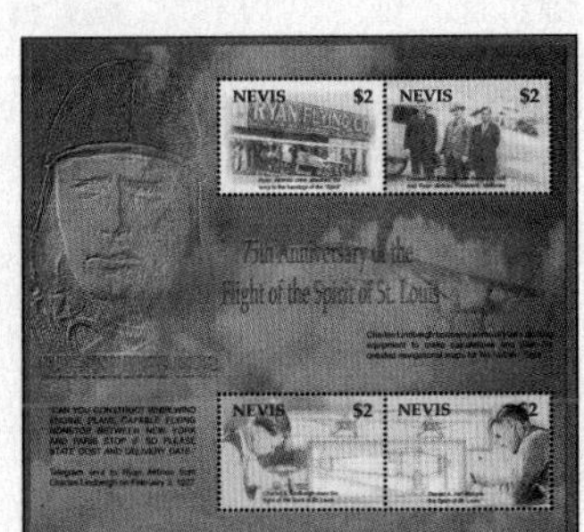
First Non-Stop Solo Transatlantic Flight, 75th Anniv. — A229

No. 1330, $2: a, Ryan Airlines crew attaches wing to fuselage of the Spirit of St. Louis. b, Charles Lindbergh, Donald Hall and President of Ryan Flying Co. c, Lindbergh planning flight. d, Hall designing Spirit of St. Louis.
No. 1331, $2: a, Hall. b, Lindbergh. c, Automobile towing Spirit of St. Louis from Ryan factory. d, Spirit of St. Louis being towed at Curtiss Field.

**2003, Mar. 10** **Sheets of 4, #a-d**

**1330-1331** A229 Set of 2 12.00 12.00

Princess Diana (1961-97) — A230

No. 1332: a, Wearing blue dress. b, Wearing blue dress, pearl necklace. c, Wearing black gown. d, Wearing hat.
$5, Wearing black dress and necklace.

**2003, Mar. 10** ***Perf. 12¼***
**1332** A230 $2 Sheet of 4, #a-d 6.00 6.00

**Souvenir Sheet**

**1333** A230 $5 multi 3.75 3.75

Marlene Dietrich (1901-92) — A231

No. 1334: a, With cigarette, country name at right. b, With cigarette, country name at left. c, Close-up. d, Wearing hat and white jacket.
$5, Wearing dress.

**2003, Mar. 10** ***Perf. 14***
**1334** A231 $1.60 Sheet, #a-b, 2 each #c-d 7.25 7.25

**Souvenir Sheet**

**1335** A231 $5 multi 3.75 3.75

Coronation of Queen Elizabeth II, 50th Anniv. — A232

No. 1336: a, Queen as young woman. b, Queen as older woman. c, Queen wearing glasses.
$5, Queen wearing tiara.

**2003, May 13**
**1336** A232 $3 Sheet of 3, #a-c 6.75 6.75

**Souvenir Sheet**

**1337** A232 $5 multi 3.75 3.75

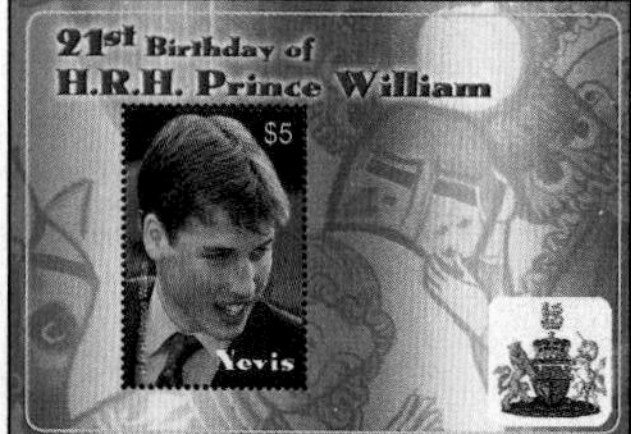

Prince William, 21st Birthday — A233

No. 1338: a, Wearing suit, showing teeth. b, Wearing suit. c, Wearing sweater.
$5, Wearing suit, diff.

**2003, May 13**
**1338** A233 $3 Sheet of 3, #a-c 6.75 6.75

**Souvenir Sheet**

**1339** A233 $5 multi 3.75 3.75

Powered Flight, Cent. — A234

No. 1340: a, A. V. Roe triplane. b, A. V. Roe Type D biplane. c, Avro Type F. d, Avro 504.
$5, Avro 561.

**2003, May 13**
**1340** A234 $1.80 Sheet of 4, #a-d 5.75 5.75

**Souvenir Sheet**

**1341** A234 $5 multi 4.00 4.00

Teddy Bears, Cent. (in 2002) — A235

No. 1342: a, Abraham Lincoln bear. b, Napoleon bear. c, King Henry VIII bear. d, Charlie Chaplin bear.
$5, Baseball bear.

**2003, May 13** ***Perf. 13¼***
**1342** A235 $2 Sheet of 4, #a-d 6.25 6.25

**Souvenir Sheet**

**1343** A235 $5 multi 4.00 4.00

Tour de France Bicycle Race, Cent. — A236

No. 1344: a, Gustave Garrigou, 1911. b, Odile Defraye, 1912. c, Philippe Thys, 1913. d, Thys, 1914.
$5, François Faber.

**2003, May 13**
**1344** A236 $2 Sheet of 4, #a-d 6.00 6.00

**Souvenir Sheet**

**1345** A236 $5 multi 3.75 3.75

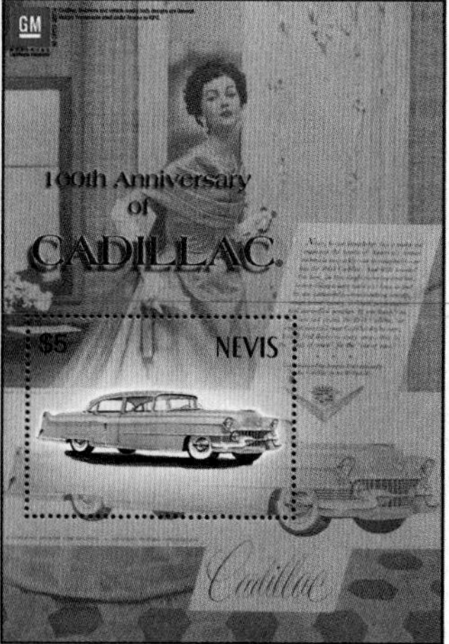

General Motors Automobiles — A237

No. 1346, $2 — Cadillacs: a, 1933 355-C V8 sedan. b, 1953 Eldorado. c, 1977 Coupe de Ville. d, 1980 Seville Elegante.
No. 1347, $2 — Corvettes: a, 1970. b, 1974. c, 1971. d, 1973.
No. 1348, $5, 1954 Cadillac. No. 1349, $5, 1997 C5 Corvette.

**2003, May 13**

**Sheets of 4, #a-d**

**1346-1347** A237 Set of 2 12.00 12.00

**Souvenir Sheets**

**1348-1349** A237 Set of 2 7.50 7.50

Orchids A238

Designs: 20c, Phalaenopsis joline, vert. $1.20, Vanda thonglor, vert. No. 1352, $2, Potinara. $3, Lycaste aquila.
No. 1354, $2: a, Brassolaelia cattleya. b, Cymbidium claricon. c, Calanthe vestita. d, Odontoglossum crispum.
$5, Odontioda brocade.

**2003, Oct. 24** ***Perf. 14***
**1350-1353** A238 Set of 4 5.00 5.00
**1354** A238 $2 Sheet of 4, #a-d 6.25 6.25

**Souvenir Sheet**

**1355** A238 $5 multi 4.00 4.00

Butterflies A239

Designs: 30c, Perisama bonplandii. 90c, Danaus formosa. $1, Amauris vashti. $3, Lycorea ceres.
No. 1360: a, Kallima rumia. b, Nessaea ancaeus. c, Callicore cajetani. d, Hamadryas guatemalena.
$5, Euphaedra medon.

**2003, Oct. 24**
**1356-1359** A239 Set of 4 4.25 4.25
**1360** A239 $2 Sheet of 4, #a-d 6.25 6.25

**Souvenir Sheet**

**1361** A239 $5 multi 4.00 4.00

Marine Life A240

Designs: 30c, Epinephelus striatus, vert. 80c, Acropora, vert. 90c, Myripristis hexagona. No. 1365, $5, Trichechus manatus.
No. 1366: a, Lioices latus. b, Chelmon rostratus. c, Epinephelus merra. d, Acanthurus coeruleus.
No. 1367, $5, Haemulon sciurus.

**2003, Oct. 24**
**1362-1365** A240 Set of 4 5.50 5.50
**1366** A240 $2 Sheet of 4, #a-d 6.25 6.25

**Souvenir Sheet**

**1367** A240 $5 multi 4.00 4.00

Christmas A241

Designs: 30c, Madonna of the Magnificat, by Botticelli. 90c, Madonna with the Long Neck, by Il Parmigianino. $1.20, Virgin and Child With St. Anne, by Leonardo da Vinci. $5, Madonna and Child and Scenes from the Life of St. Anne, by Filippo Lippi.
$6, Conestabile Madonna, by Raphael.

**2003, Nov. 5** ***Perf. 14¼***
**1368-1371** A241 Set of 4 5.50 5.50

**Souvenir Sheet**

**1372** A241 $6 multi 4.50 4.50

World AIDS Day A242

National flag, AIDS ribbon and: 90c, Stylized men. $1.20, Map.

**2003, Dec. 1** ***Perf. 14***
**1373-1374** A242 Set of 2 1.60 1.60

New Year 2004 (Year of the Monkey) A243

Designs: $1.60, Monkey King and Chinese text. $3, Monkey King.

**2004, Feb. 16 Litho.** ***Perf. 13¼***
**1375** A243 $1.60 red & black 1.50 1.50

**Souvenir Sheet**

***Perf. 13¼x13***

**1376** A243 $3 multi 2.50 2.50

No. 1375 printed in sheets of 4. No. 1376 contains one 30x40mm stamp.

Girl Guides in Nevis, 50th Anniv. — A244

Designs: 30c, Badges. 90c, Guide and guide leader, horiz. $1.20, Lady Olave Baden-Powell. $5, Guides wearing t-shirts.

**2004, Feb. 22** ***Perf. 14***
**1377-1380** A244 Set of 4 5.50 5.50

Paintings in the Hermitage, St. Petersburg, Russia — A245

Designs: 30c, Still Life with a Drapery, by Paul Cézanne. 90c, The Smoker, by Cézanne, vert. $2, Girl with a Fan, by Pierre Auguste Renoir, vert. No. 1384, $5, Grove, by André Derain, vert.

No. 1385, Lady in the Garden (Sainte Adresse), by Claude Monet.

**2004, Mar. 4** ***Perf. 13¼***

**1381-1384** A245 Set of 4 6.25 6.25

***Imperf***

**Size: 94x74mm**

**1385** A245 $5 multi 3.75 3.75

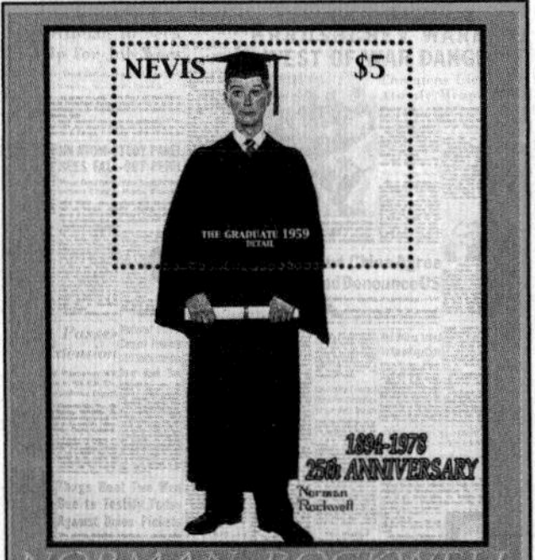

Paintings by Norman Rockwell (1894-1978) — A246

No. 1386, vert.: a, The Morning After. b, Solitaire. c, Easter Morning. d, Walking to Church.

$5, The Graduate.

**2004, Mar. 4** ***Perf. 13¼***

**1386** A246 $2 Sheet of 4, #a-d 6.00 6.00

**Souvenir Sheet**

**1387** A246 $5 multi 3.75 3.75

Paintings by Pablo Picasso (1881-1973) — A247

No. 1388, $2: a, Woman with a Hat. b, Seated Woman. c, Portrait of Nusch Eluard. d, Woman in a Straw Hat.

No. 1389, $2: a, L'Arlésienne. b, The Mirror. c, Repose. d, Portrait of Paul Eluard.

No. 1390, Portrait of Nusch Eluard, diff. No. 1391, Reclining Woman with a Book, horiz.

**2004, Mar. 4** ***Perf. 13¼***

**Sheets of 4, #a-d**

**1388-1389** A247 Set of 2 12.00 12.00

***Imperf***

**1390** A247 $5 shown 3.75 3.75

**Size: 100x75mm**

**1391** A247 $5 multi 3.75 3.75

ASDA Mega-Event, New York (#1389).

A248

Marilyn Monroe — A249

No. 1393 — Placement of stamp on sheet: a, UL. b, UR. c, LL. d, LR.

**2004, June 17** ***Perf. 13½x13¼***

**1392** A248 60c multi .45 .45

***Perf. 13¼***

**1393** A249 $2 Sheet of 4, #a-d 6.00 6.00

John Denver (1943-97), Musician — A250

Placement of stamp on sheet: a, Top left. b, Top right. c, Bottom left. d, Bottom right.

**2004, June 17** ***Perf. 13¾x13½***

**1394** A250 $1.20 Sheet of 4, #a-d 3.75 3.75

2004 Summer Olympics, Athens A251

Designs: 30c, Commemorative medal, 1968 Mexico City Olympics. 90c, Pentathlon. $1.80, Avery Brundage, Intl. Olympic Committee President. $3, Women's tennis, 1920 Antwerp Olympics, horiz.

**2004, Sept. 7** **Litho.** ***Perf. 14¼***

**1395-1398** A251 Set of 4 4.50 4.50

Intl. Year of Peace — A252

No. 1399: a, Country name at right, dove's feet not visible. b, Country name at left. c, Country name at right, dove's feet visible.

**2004, Sept. 7**

**1399** A252 $3 Sheet of 3, #a-c 6.75 6.75

**Souvenir Sheet**

Deng Xiaoping (1904-97), Chinese Leader — A253

**2004, Sept. 7** ***Perf. 14***

**1400** A253 $5 multi 3.75 3.75

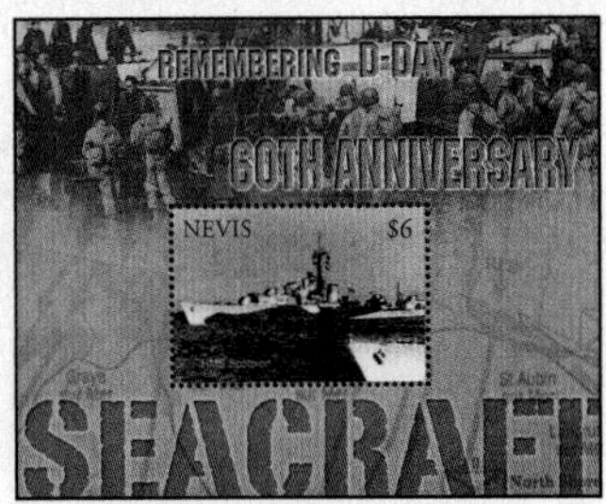

D-Day, 60th Anniv. — A254

No. 1401: a, HMCS Penetang. b, Landing Craft Infantry (Large). c, LCT (6). d, Landing Craft Tank (Rocket). e, Landing Barge Kitchen. f, Battleship Texas.

$6, HMS Scorpion.

**2004, Sept. 7**

**1401** A254 $1.20 Sheet of 6, #a-f 5.50 5.50

**Souvenir Sheet**

**1402** A254 $6 multi 4.50 4.50

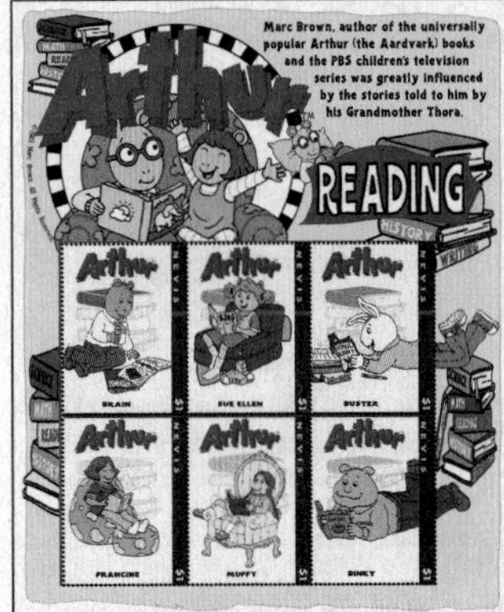

Arthur and Friends — A255

No. 1403 — Characters reading: a, Brain. b, Sue Ellen. c, Buster. d, Francine. e, Muffy. f, Binky.

No. 1404, $2 — Characters, with purple background: a, Arthur. b, D. W. c, Francine, looking right. d, Buster, diff.

No. 1405, $2 — Characters, with lilac background: a, Binky, diff. b, Sue Ellen, diff. c, Brain, diff. d, Francine, looking left.

**2004, June 17** **Litho.** ***Perf. 14¼***

**1403** A255 $1 Sheet of 6, #a-f 4.50 4.50

**Sheets of 4, #a-d**

**1404-1405** A255 Set of 2 12.00 12.00

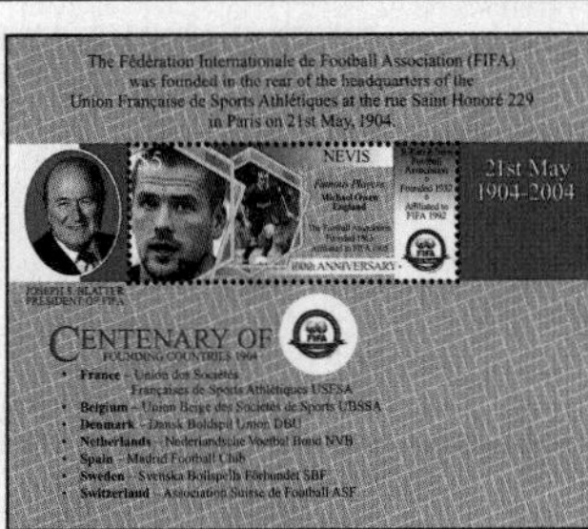

FIFA (Fédération Internationale de Football Association), Cent. — A256

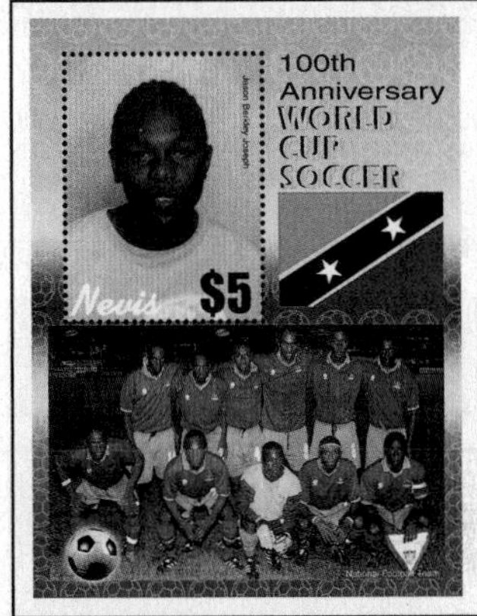

Jason Berkley Joseph, Soccer Player — A257

No. 1406: a, Nery Pumpido. b, Gary Lineker. c, Thomas Hassler. d, Sol Campbell.

No. 1407, Michael Owen.

**2004, Nov. 29** ***Perf. 12¾x12½***

**1406** A256 $2 Sheet of 4, #a-d 6.00 6.00

**Souvenir Sheets**

**1407** A256 $5 multi 3.75 3.75

**1408** A257 $5 multi 3.75 3.75

Marginal inscription on No. 1408, "100th Anniversary World Cup Soccer" is incorrect as the first World Cup was held in 1930.

Elvis Presley (1935-77) A258

No. 1409 — Wearing checked shirt: a, Blue background. b, Bright red violet background.

No. 1410 — Color of sweater: a, Red. b, Orange yellow. c, Blue. d, Blue green. e, Red violet. f, Bright green.

**2004, Nov. 29** ***Perf. 13½x13¼***

**1409** A258 $1.20 Pair, #a-b 1.90 1.90

**1410** A258 $1.20 Sheet of 6, #a-f 5.50 5.50

No. 1409 printed in sheets of 3 pairs.

Christmas A259

Paintings by Norman Rockwell: 25c, Santa's Good Boys. 30c, Ride 'em Cowboy. 90c, Christmas Sing Merrilie. No. 1414, $5, The Christmas Newsstand.
No. 1415, $5, Is He Coming.

**2004, Dec. 1** ***Perf. 12***
**1411-1414** A259 Set of 4 5.00 5.00

***Imperf***

**Size: 63x73mm**

**1415** A259 $5 multi 3.75 3.75

Locomotives, 200th Anniv. — A260

No. 1416: a, Steam Idyll, Indonesia. b, 2-8-2, Syria. c, Narrow gauge Mallet 0-4-4-0T, Portugal. d, Western Pacific Bo-Bo Road Switcher, US.
$5, LMS 5305, Great Britain.

**2004, Dec. 13** ***Perf. 13¼x13½***
**1416** A260 $3 Sheet of 4, #a-d 9.00 9.00

**Souvenir Sheet**

**1417** A260 $5 multi 3.75 3.75

Reptiles and Amphibians — A261

No. 1418: a, Gekko gecko. b, Eyelash viper. c, Green iguana. d, Whistling frog.
$5, Hawksbill turtle.

**2005, Jan. 10** ***Perf. 14***
**1418** A261 $1.20 Sheet of 4, #a-d 4.00 4.00

**Souvenir Sheet**

**1419** A261 $5 multi 4.00 4.00

Mushrooms — A262

No. 1420: a, Xeromphalina campanella. b, Calvatia sculpta. c, Mitrula elegans. d, Aleuria aurantia.
$5, Scarlet cup.

**2005, Jan. 10**
**1420** A262 $2 Sheet of 4, #a-d 6.25 6.25

**Souvenir Sheet**

**1421** A262 $5 multi 4.00 4.00

Hummingbirds — A263

No. 1422: a, Rufous hummingbird. b, Green-crowned brilliant. c, Ruby-throated hummingbird. d, Purple-throated Carib.
$5, Magnificent hummingbird.

**2005, Jan. 10** **Litho.** ***Perf. 14***
**1422** A263 $2 Sheet of 4, #a-d 6.25 6.25

**Souvenir Sheet**

**1423** A263 $5 multi 4.00 4.00

Sharks — A264

No. 1424: a, Zebra shark. b, Caribbean reef shark. c, Blue shark. d, Bronze whaler.
$5, Blacktip reef shark.

**2005, Jan. 10**
**1424** A264 $2 Sheet of 4, #a-d 6.25 6.25

**Souvenir Sheet**

**1425** A264 $5 multi 4.00 4.00

Artist's Depictions of Hawksbill Turtles — A265

Artist: 30c, Leon Silcott. 90c, Kris Liburd. $1.20, Alice Webber. $5, Jeuaunito Huggins.

**2005, Jan. 10**
**1426-1429** A265 Set of 4 6.00 6.00

Souvenir Sheet

New Year 2005 (Year of the Rooster) — A266

No. 1430: a, Rooster, blue green background. b, Rooster silhouette, light green background. c, Rooster silhouette, blue background. d, Rooster, red violet background.

**2005, Jan. 17** ***Perf. 12***
**1430** A266 75c Sheet of 4, #a-d 2.50 2.50

Friedrich von Schiller (1759-1805), Writer — A267

No. 1431: a, Schiller, country name in pink. b, Schiller, country name in blue. c, Schiller's birthplace, Marbach, Germany.
$5, Statue of Schiller, Chicago.

**2005, May 16** ***Perf. 12¾***
**1431** A267 $3 Sheet of 3, #a-c 6.75 6.75

**Souvenir Sheet**

**1432** A267 $5 multi 3.75 3.75

Rotary International, Cent. — A268

No. 1433, vert.: a, Barefoot child. b, Vaccination of child. c, Child with crutches and braces.
$5, Woman and children.

**2005, May 16**
**1433** A268 $3 Sheet of 3, #a-c 6.75 6.75

**Souvenir Sheet**

**1434** A268 $5 multi 3.75 3.75

Hans Christian Andersen (1805-75), Author — A269

No. 1435: a, The Little Mermaid. b, Thumbelina. c, The Snow Queen. d, The Emperor's New Clothes.
$6, Andersen.

**2005, May 16**
**1435** A269 $2 Sheet of 4, #a-d 6.00 6.00

**Souvenir Sheet**

**1436** A269 $6 multi 4.50 4.50

World Cup Soccer Championships, 75th Anniv. — A270

No. 1437: a, Brazil, 1958 champions. b, Scene from 1958 Brazil-Sweden final. c, Rasunda Stadium, Stockholm. d, Pele.
$5, 1958 Brazil team celebrating victory.

**2005, May 16** **Litho.**
**1437** A270 $2 Sheet of 4, #a-d 6.00 6.00

**Souvenir Sheet**

**1438** A270 $5 multi 3.75 3.75

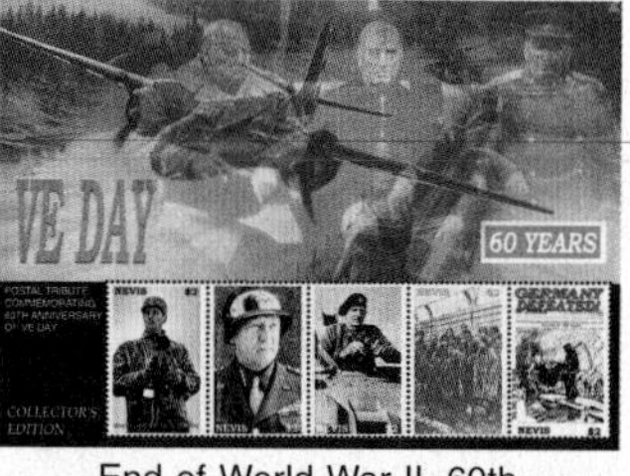

End of World War II, 60th Anniv. — A271

No. 1439, $2: a, Gen. Charles de Gaulle. b, Gen. George S. Patton. c, Field Marshal Bernard Montgomery. d, Liberation of concentration camps. e, Political cartoon about end of war.
No. 1440, $2, horiz.: a, Flight crew of the Enola Gay. b, Atomic bomb mushroom cloud. c, Souvenir of Japanese surrender ceremony. d, Japanese delegation on USS Missouri. e, Gen. Douglas MacArthur speaking at surrender ceremony.

**2005, May 16** ***Perf. 12¾***

**Sheets of 5, #a-e**

**1439-1440** A271 Set of 2 15.00 15.00

Battle of Trafalgar, Bicent. — A272

Various ships and: 30c, Admiral William Cornwallis. 90c, Capt. Maurice Suckling. $1.20, Fleet Admiral Earl Howe. $3, Sir John Jervis.
$5, Earl Howe on the quarterdeck of the Queen Charlotte.

**2005, May 16** ***Perf. 12¾***
**1441-1444** A272 Set of 4 4.25 4.25

**Souvenir Sheet**

***Perf. 12***

**1445** A272 $5 multi 3.75 3.75

A273

Prehistoric Animals — A274

Designs: 30c, Tyrannosaurus rex. No. 1447, $5, Hadrosaur.
No. 1448, $1.20: a, Apatosaurus. b, Camarasaurus. c, Iguanodon. d, Edmontosaurus. e, Centrosaurus. f, Euoplocephalus.
No. 1449, $1.20: a, Ouranosaurus. b, Parasaurolophus. c, Psittacosaurus. d, Stegosaurus. e, Scelidosaurus. f, Hypsilophodon.
No. 1450, $1.20, vert.: a, Deinotherium. b, Platybelodon. c, Palaeoloxodon. d, Arsinotherium. e, Procoptodon. f, Macrauchenia.
No. 1451, $5, Brontotherium. No. 1452, $5, Daspletosaurus. No. 1453, $5, Pliosaur.

**2005, June 7** *Perf. 12¾*
**1446-1447** A273 Set of 2 4.00 4.00

**Sheets of 6, #a-f**

**1448-1450** A274 Set of 3 16.50 16.50

**Souvenir Sheets**

**1451-1453** A274 Set of 3 11.50 11.50

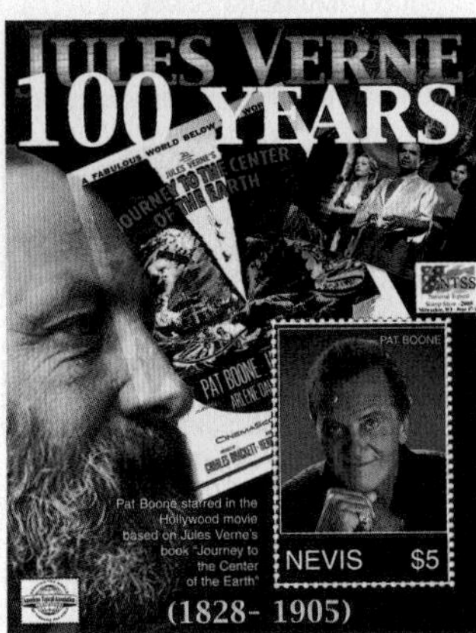

Jules Verne (1828-1905), Writer — A275

No. 1454 — Story characters: a, Captain Nemo, *20,000 Leagues Under the Sea.* b, Michael Strogoff, *Michael Strogoff.* c, Phileas Fogg, *Around the World in 80 Days.* d, Captain Cyrus Smith, *Mysterious Island.*
$5, Pat Boone, actor in movie, *Journey to the Center of the Earth.*

**2005, June 17**
**1454** A275 $2 Sheet of 4, #a-d 6.00 6.00

**Souvenir Sheet**

**1455** A275 $5 multi 3.75 3.75

2005 National Topical Stamp Show, Milwaukee (#1455).

Vatican City No. 66 — A276

Pope John Paul II (1920-2005) A277

**2005, July 12** *Perf. 13x13¼*
**1456** A276 90c multi .70 .70

*Perf. 13½x13¼*

**1457** A277 $4 multi 3.00 3.00

National Basketball Association Players — A278

Designs: No. 1458, $1, Shareef-Abdur Rahim (shown), Portland Trail Blazers. No. 1459, $1, Shaun Livingston, Los Angeles Clippers. No. 1460, $1, Vince Carter, New Jersey Nets. No. 1461, $1, Rasheed Wallace, Detroit Pistons.
No. 1462: a, Theo Ratliff, Portland Trail Blazers. b, Portland Trail Blazers emblem.

**2005, July 26** *Perf. 14*
**1458-1461** A278 Set of 4 3.00 3.00
**1462** A278 $1 Sheet, 10 #1462a, 2 #1462b 9.00 9.00

Souvenir Sheet

Sun Yat-sen (1866-1925), Chinese Leader — A279

No. 1463: a, Wearing blue suit, harbor in background. b, Wearing suit and tie. c, Wearing blue suit, statue in background. d, Wearing brown red suit.

**2005, Aug. 19** **Litho.** *Perf. 14*
**1463** A279 $2 Sheet of 4, #a-d 6.00 6.00

Taipei 2005 Intl. Stamp Exhibition.

Christmas — A280

Designs: 25c, Madonna and the Angels, by Fra Angelico. 30c, Madonna and the Child, by Fra Filippo Lippi. 90c, Madonna and Child, by Giotto. $4, Madonna of the Chair, by Raphael.
$5, Adoration of the Magi, by Giovanni Batista Tiepolo, horiz.

**2005, Dec. 1** *Perf. 13½*
**1464-1467** A280 Set of 4 4.25 4.25

**Souvenir Sheet**

**1468** A280 $5 multi 3.75 3.75

U.S. Forest Service, Cent. (in 2005) — A281

No. 1469, vert.: a, Eldorado National Forest, California. b, Pisgah National Forest, North Carolina. c, Chattahoochee-Oconee National Forests, Georgia. d, Nantahala National Forest, North Carolina. e, Bridger-Teton National Forest, Wyoming. f, Mount Hood National Forest, Oregon.
No. 1470, $6, Klamath National Forest, California. No. 1471, $6, The Source Rain Forest Walk, Nevis, vert.

**2006, Jan. 3**
**1469** A281 $1.60 Sheet of 6, #a-f 7.25 7.25

**Souvenir Sheets**

**1470-1471** A281 Set of 2 9.00 9.00

A Dog, by Ren Xun — A282

**2006, Jan. 3**
**1472** A282 75c multi .70 .70

New Year 2006 (Year of the Dog). Printed in sheets of 4.

Queen Elizabeth II, 80th Anniv. — A283

No. 1473 — Queen wearing: a, Black hat with feather. b, No hat. c, Tiara. d, White hat.
$5, As young woman.

**2006, Mar. 20** **Litho.** *Perf. 13¼*
**1473** A283 $2 Sheet of 4, #a-d 6.00 6.00

**Souvenir Sheet**

**1474** A283 $5 multi 3.75 3.75

2006 Winter Olympics, Turin — A284

Designs: 25c, U.S. #1796. 30c, Italy #705. 90c, Italy #707. $1.20, Emblem of 1980 Lake Placid Winter Olympics, vert. $4, Italy #708. $5, Emblem of 1956 Cortina d'Ampezzo Winter Olympics.

*Perf. 14¼ (25c, $1.20), 13¼*

**2006, Apr. 24**
**1475-1480** A284 Set of 6 8.75 8.75

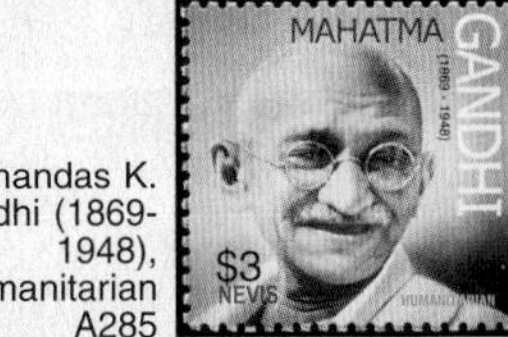

Mohandas K. Gandhi (1869-1948), Humanitarian A285

**2006, May 27** *Perf. 12x11½*
**1481** A285 $3 multi 2.25 2.25

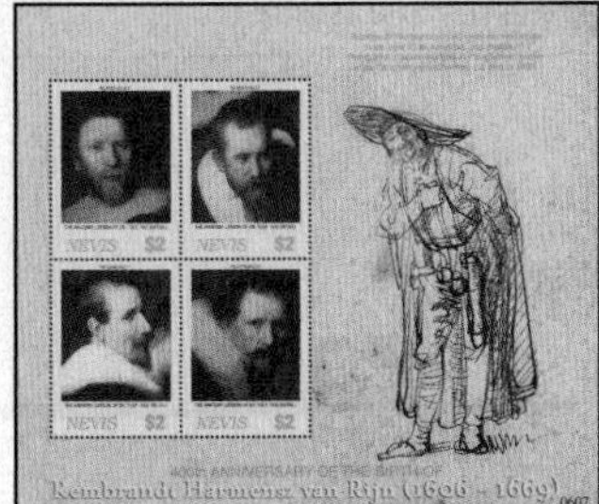

Rembrandt (1606-69), Painter — A286

No. 1482 — Various men from The Anatomy Lesson of Dr. Tulp.
$6, Bald-headed Old Man.

**2006, June 23** *Perf. 13¼*
**1482** A286 $2 Sheet of 4, a-d 6.00 6.00

***Imperf***

**Size: 70x100mm**

**1483** A286 $6 multi 4.50 4.50

Miniature Sheets

Space Achievements — A287

No. 1484 — Apollo-Soyuz: a, Liftoff of Saturn IB rocket . b, Astronaut Donald K. Slayton, Cosmonaut Aleksei A. Leonov. c, Liftoff of Soyuz 19. d, Soyuz in space. e, American and Soviet crews, model of docked spacecraft. f, Apollo in space.
No. 1485 — Viking I: a, Liftoff of Titan Centaur rocket. b, Viking I in flight. c, Model of Viking I on Mars. d, Mars.

**2006, Sept. 11** *Perf. 13¼*
**1484** A287 $2 Sheet of 6, #a-f 9.00 9.00
**1485** A287 $3 Sheet of 4, #a-d 9.00 9.00

Christmas A288

Designs: 25c, Charlestown Christmas tree. 30c, Snowman decoration. 90c, Reindeer decorations. $4, Christmas tree and gifts, vert.
$6, Santa Claus and children.

**2006, Dec. 8**
**1486-1489** A288 Set of 4 4.25 4.25

**Souvenir Sheet**

**1490** A288 $6 multi 4.50 4.50

Scouting, Cent. A289

Designs: $3, Flags, Map of Great Britain and Ireland. $5, Flags, bird, map, horiz.

**2007, Jan. 29** **Litho.** *Perf. 13¼*
**1491** A289 $3 multi 2.25 2.25

**Souvenir Sheet**

**1492** A289 $5 multi 3.75 3.75

No. 1491 printed in sheets of 4.

Miniature Sheet

Marilyn Monroe (1926-62), Actress — A290

No. 1493 — Monroe: a, With head tilted. b, Wearing necklace. c, With lips closed. d, Wearing sash.

**2007, Jan. 29**
**1493** A290 $2 Sheet of 4, #a-d 6.00 6.00

Cricket World Cup — A291

Designs: 90c, Cricket World Cup emblem, flag of St. Kitts and Nevis, map of Nevis. $2, Emblem and Runako Morton.
$6, Emblem.

**2007, May 1** ***Perf. 14***
**1494-1495** A291 Set of 2 2.25 2.25

**Souvenir Sheet**

**1496** A291 $6 multi 4.50 4.50

Shells — A292

Designs: 10c, Flame helmet. 25c, Rooster tail conch. 30c, Beaded periwinkle. 60c, Emperor helmet. 80c, Scotch bonnet. 90c Milk conch. $1, Beaded periwinkle, diff. $1.20, Alphabet cone. $1.80, Measled cowrie. $3, King helmet. $5, Atlantic hairy triton. $10, White-lined mitre. $20, Reticulated cowrie.

**2007, July 5** ***Perf. 12½x13¼***

| | | | | |
|---|---|---|---|---|
| **1497** | A292 | 10c multi | .25 | .25 |
| **1498** | A292 | 25c multi | .25 | .25 |
| **1499** | A292 | 30c multi | .30 | .30 |
| **1500** | A292 | 60c multi | .50 | .50 |
| **1501** | A292 | 80c multi | .65 | .65 |
| **1502** | A292 | 90c multi | .75 | .75 |
| **1503** | A292 | $1 multi | .80 | .80 |
| **1504** | A292 | $1.20 multi | 1.00 | 1.00 |
| **1505** | A292 | $1.80 multi | 1.50 | 1.50 |
| **1506** | A292 | $3 multi | 2.40 | 2.40 |
| **1507** | A292 | $5 multi | 4.00 | 4.00 |
| **1508** | A292 | $10 multi | 7.75 | 7.75 |
| **1509** | A292 | $20 multi | 16.00 | 16.00 |
| | *Nos. 1497-1509 (13)* | | 36.15 | 36.15 |

Worldwide Fund for Nature (WWF) — A293

No. 1510 — Rainbow parrotfish: a, Facing left, white coral above fish. b, Two parrotfish. c, Facing left, ocean floor below fish. d, Facing right.

**2007, July 23** ***Perf. 13½***
**1510** Strip of 4 4.00 4.00
***a.-d.*** A293 $1.20 Any single .95 .95
***e.*** Miniature sheet, 2 each #1510a-1510d 7.75 7.75

Flowers — A294

No. 1511: a, Wild cilliment. b, Jumbie beads. c, Wild sage. d, Blood flower.
$6, Pink trumpet.

**2007, July 23** ***Perf. 13¼***
**1511** A294 $2 Sheet of 4, #a-d 6.25 6.25

**Souvenir Sheet**

**1512** A294 $6 multi 4.75 4.75

Butterflies — A295

No. 1513: a, Zetides swallowtail. b, Hahnel's Amazon swallowtail. c, Haitian mimic. d, Marbled white.
$6, Three-tailed tiger swallowtail.

**2007, July 23**
**1513** A295 $2 Sheet of 4, #a-d 6.25 6.25

**Souvenir Sheet**

**1514** A295 $6 multi 4.75 4.75

Miniature Sheet

Elvis Presley (1935-77) — A296

No. 1515 — Various photographs of Presley with: a, Denomination in white, country name in violet, laces showing on shirt. b, Denomination in blue. c, Denomination in bister. d, Denomination and country name in pink. e, Denomination in white, country name in pink. f, Denomination in white, country name in violet, laces not showing on shirt.

**2007, Aug. 13**
**1515** A296 $1.20 Sheet of 6, #a-f 5.50 5.50

Princess Diana (1961-97) — A297

No. 1516: a, With head on hands. b, Wearing black dress. c, Wearing pink jacket. d, Wearing white dress.
$6, Wearing hat.

**2007, Aug. 13**
**1516** A297 $2 Sheet of 4, #a-d 6.00 6.00

**Souvenir Sheet**

**1517** A297 $6 multi 4.50 4.50

Miniature Sheets

Concorde — A298

No. 1518, $1.20 — Concorde with portions of globe in background: a, Western United States. b, Central United States. c, Atlantic Ocean and Eastern Canada. d, Central Pacific Ocean. e, Central America. f, Northeastern South America.

No. 1519, $1.20 — Concorde with: a, Green frame, white denomination. b, Red frame, blue denomination. c, Green frame, yellow denomination. d, Red frame, yellow denomination. e, Green frame, blue denomination. f, Red frame, white denomination.

**2007, Aug. 13 Litho.** ***Perf. 13¼***

**Sheets of 6, #a-f**

**1518-1519** A298 Set of 2 11.00 11.00

Pope Benedict XVI — A299

**2007, Oct. 24**
**1520** A299 $1 multi .75 .75

Printed in sheets of 8.

Miniature Sheet

Wedding of Queen Elizabeth II and Prince Philip, 60th Anniv. — A300

No. 1521 — Couple: a, Queen wearing tiara. b, Waving. c, Wearing feathered hats. d, In gilded coach, Queen in blue, waving. e, In coach, Queen with red hat, waving. f, On balcony, Queen waving.

**2007, Oct. 24**
**1521** A300 $1.20 Sheet of 6, #a-f 5.50 5.50

Miniature Sheet

Inauguration of Pres. John F. Kennedy, 46th Anniv. — A301

No. 1522: a, Jacqueline Kennedy. b, John F. Kennedy, hands at side. c, John F. Kennedy, clapping. d, Vice president Lyndon B. Johnson.

**2007, Nov. 28**
**1522** A301 $3 Sheet of 4, #a-d 9.00 9.00

First Helicopter Flight, Cent. — A302

No. 1523, horiz.: a, Westland Sea King. b, Schweizer N330TT. c, Sikorsky R-4/R-5. d, PZL Swidnik.
$6, MIL V-12.

**2007, Nov. 28**
**1523** A302 $3 Sheet of 4, #a-d 9.00 9.00

**Souvenir Sheet**

**1524** A302 $6 multi 4.50 4.50

Paintings by Qi Baishi (1864-1957) — A303

No. 1525: a, Begonias and Rock. b, Mother and Child. c, Fish and Bait. d, Solitary Hero.
$6, Chrysanthemums and Insects.

**2007, Nov. 28** ***Perf. 12½***
**1525** A303 $3 Sheet of 4, #a-d 9.00 9.00

**Souvenir Sheet**

***Perf. 13¼***

**1526** A303 $6 multi 4.50 4.50

No. 1525 contains four 32x80mm stamps.

Christmas A304

Paintings: 25c, The Rest on the Flight Into Egypt, by Federico Barocci. 30c, The Annunciation, by Barocci. 90c, The Annunciation, by Cavalier d'Arpino. $4, The Rest on the Flight Into Egypt, by Francesco Mancini.

$5, The Virgin and Child Between Saints Peter and Paul and the Twelve Magistrates of the Rota, by Antoniazzo Romano.

**2007, Dec. 3** ***Perf. 11¼x11½***

**1527-1530** A304 Set of 4 4.25 4.25

**Souvenir Sheet**

***Perf. 13½***

**1531** A304 $5 multi 3.75 3.75

Miniature Sheet

Ferrari Automobiles, 60th Anniv. — A305

No. 1532: a, 1997 F 355 F1 GTS. b, 1985 412. c, 1964 158 F1. d, 1953 375 MM. e, 1967 330 P4. f, 1978 512 BB LM. g, 1974 312 B3-74. h, 1982 308 GTB Quattrovalvole.

**2007, Dec. 10** ***Perf. 13¼***

**1532** A305 $1 Sheet of 8, #a-h 6.00 6.00

Miniature Sheet

2008 Summer Olympics, Beijing — A306

No. 1533: a, Cycling. b, Kayaking. c, Sailing. d, Equestrian.

**2008, Mar. 8** **Litho.** ***Perf. 12¾***

**1533** A306 $2 Sheet of 4, #a-d 6.00 6.00

Israel 2008 Intl. Philatelic Exhibition — A307

No. 1534 — Sites in Israel: a, Mt. Masada. b, Red Sea and mountains. c, Dead Sea. d, Sea of Galilee.

$5, Mt. Hermon.

**2008, May 21** **Litho.** ***Perf. 11½x11¼***

**1534** A307 $1.50 Sheet of 4, #a-d 4.50 4.50

**Souvenir Sheet**

**1535** A307 $5 multi 3.75 3.75

32nd America's Cup Yacht Races — A308

No. 1536 — Various yachts: a, $1.20. b, $1.80. c, $3. d, $5.

**2007, Dec. 31** **Litho.** ***Perf. 13½***

**1536** A308 Block of 4, #a-d 8.25 8.25

No. 1536 was not made available until late 2008.

Miniature Sheets

A309

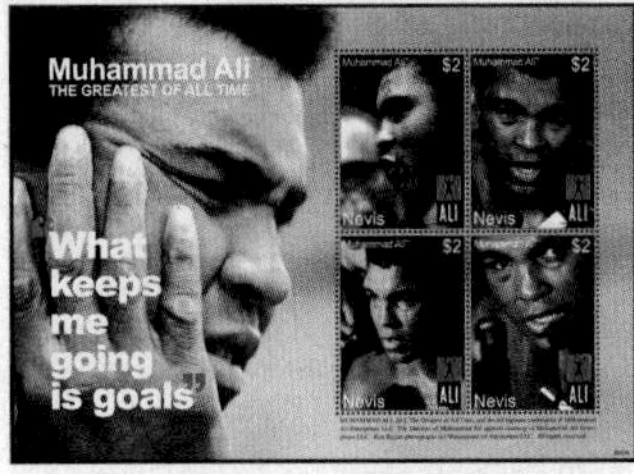

Muhammad Ali, Boxer — A310

No. 1537 — Ali: a, In ring with fists at side. b, In ring, opponent at right. c, In ring, opponent punching. d, With arm on ropes. e, With arms raised. f, Receiving trophy.

No. 1538 — Ali: a, Facing left, face in background. b, With microphones, at bottom. c, Facing left, with microphone at left. d, With large microphone at LL.

**2008, Sept. 3** **Litho.** ***Perf. 11½x12***

**1537** A309 $1.80 Sheet of 6, #a-f 8.25 8.25

***Perf. 13¼***

**1538** A310 $2 Sheet of 4, #a-d 6.25 6.25

Miniature Sheet

Elvis Presley (1935-77) — A311

No. 1539 — Presley with guitar: a, Microphone at right, both hands on guitar. b, Microphone at left, hand on neck of guitar. c, With audience at LL. d, Microphone at left, no hands shown. e, Wearing blue shirt. f, Microphone at right, with hands off guitar.

**2008, Sept. 3** ***Perf. 13¼***

**1539** A311 $1.80 Sheet of 6, #a-f 8.25 8.25

Miniature Sheet

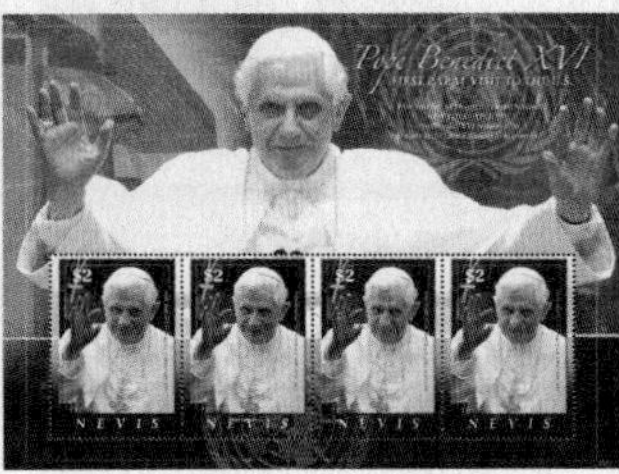

Visit to New York of Pope Benedict XVI — A312

No. 1540 — Pope Benedict XVI and background with: a, Gray spot to left of "N" in "Nevis." b, Left half of United Nations emblem. c, Right half of United Nations Emblem. d, Gray spot between "E" and "V" in "Nevis."

**2008, Sept. 17**

**1540** A312 $2 Sheet of 4, #a-d 6.25 6.25

Geothermal Well — A313

**2008, Sept. 19** ***Perf. 11½***

**1541** A313 $5 multi 4.00 4.00

Independence, 25th anniv.

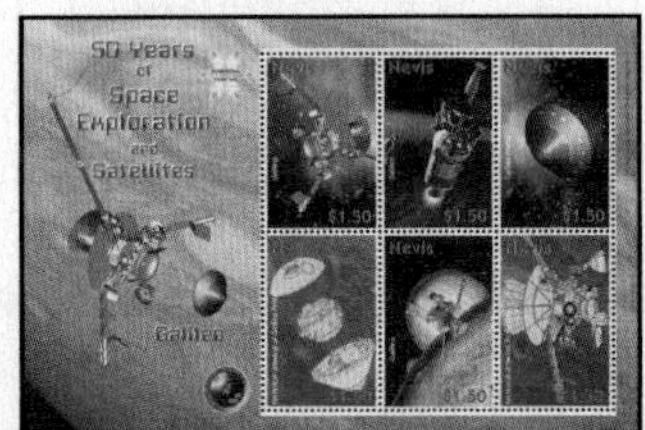

A314

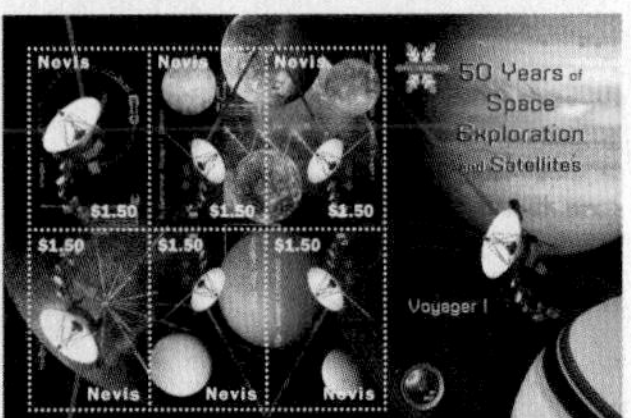

Space Exploration, 50th Anniv. — A315

No. 1542: a, Galileo spacecraft with arms extended, stars in background. b, Galileo on booster rocket. c, Galileo probe. d, Technical drawing of Galileo probe. e, Galileo, planet and moon. f, Technical drawing of Galileo.

No. 1543: a, Voyager 1 and ring diagram. b, Io, Ganymede, Voyager 1 and Callisto. c, Ganymede, Europa, Callisto and Voyager 1. d, Voyager 1 and radiating line diagram. e, Voyager 1, Titan and Dione. f, Titan, Voyager 1 and Enceladus.

No. 1544: a, Technical drawing of Apollo 11 command module. b, Saturn V rocket on launch pad. c, Edwin E. Aldrin on Moon. d, Technical drawing of Apollo 11 lunar module.

No. 1545: a, Van Allen radiation belt. b, Technical drawing of Explorer 1. c, James Van Allen. d, Explorer 1 above Earth.

**2008, Dec. 3** ***Perf. 13¼***

**1542** A314 $1.50 Sheet of 6, #a-f 7.00 7.00

**1543** A315 $1.50 Sheet of 6, #a-f 7.00 7.00

**1544** A314 $2 Sheet of 4, #a-d 6.25 6.25

**1545** A315 $2 Sheet of 4, #a-d 6.25 6.25

Christmas A316

Traditional holiday foods: 25c, Roast pig. 30c, Fruit cake. 80c, Pumpkin pie. 90c, Sorrel drink. $2, Fruit cake, diff.

$6, Baked ham and turkey, vert.

**2008, Dec. 5** ***Perf. 11½***

**1546-1550** A316 Set of 5 3.25 3.25

**Souvenir Sheet**

**1551** A316 $6 multi 4.75 4.75

Miniature Sheet

Inauguration of U.S. President Barack Obama — A317

No. 1552 — Pres. Obama and, in background: a, Window. b, Flag and chair. c, White House and flowers. d, Chair.

**2009, Jan. 20** **Litho.** ***Perf. 11½x12***

**1552** A317 $3 Sheet of 4, #a-d 9.25 9.25

Agricultural Open Day, 15th Anniv. A318

Designs: 25c, Fruits and packaged foods. 30c, Fruits. 90c, Goats. $5, Workers propagating plants.

$6, Entertainment at fair.

**2009, Mar. 26** ***Perf. 11½***

**1553-1556** A318 Set of 4 5.00 5.00

**Souvenir Sheet**

***Perf. 13½***

**1557** A318 $6 multi 4.75 4.75

No. 1557 contains one 51x37mm stamp.

Miniature Sheets

A319

China 2009 World Stamp Exhibition, Luoyang — A320

No. 1558 — Olympic Sports: a, Shooting. b, Field hockey. c, Taekwondo. d, Softball.

No. 1559 — Emperor Hsuan-yeh (Kangxi) (1654-1722): a, Wearing blue robe. b, Wearing Robe with blue sleeves. c, Wearing robe with yellow sleeves. d, At desk.

**2009, Apr. 10** ***Perf. 14x14¾***

**1558** A319 $1.40 Sheet of 4, #a-d 4.25 4.25

***Perf. 12¾x12½***

**1559** A320 $1.40 Sheet of 4, #a-d 4.25 4.25

Charles Darwin (1809-82), Naturalist — A321

No. 1560, horiz.: a, Marine iguana. b, Statue of Darwin, Shrewsbury, England. c, Platypus. d, Vampire bat. e, Painting of Darwin by George Richmond. f, Large ground finch.
$6, 1881 colorized photograph of Darwin

**2009, June 15** ***Perf. 11½***

**1560** A321 $2 Sheet of 6, #a-f 9.00 9.00

**Souvenir Sheet**

***Perf. 13¼***

**1561** A321 $6 multi 4.50 4.50

No. 1560 contains six 40x30mm stamps.

Dolphins and Whales — A322

No. 1562: a, Amazon River dolphin. b, Indus river dolphin. c, Atlantic white-sided dolphin. d, La Plata dolphin. e, Peale's dolphin. f, White-beaked dolphin.

No. 1563: a, Long-finned pilot whale. b, Short-finned pilot whale.

No. 1564: a, Killer whale. b, Pygmy killer whale.

**2009, June 15** ***Perf. 13¼***

**1562** A322 $2 Sheet of 6, #a-f 9.00 9.00

**Souvenir Sheets**

**1563** A322 $3 Sheet of 2, #a-b 4.50 4.50

**1564** A322 $3 Sheet of 2, #a-b 4.50 4.50

Souvenir Sheets

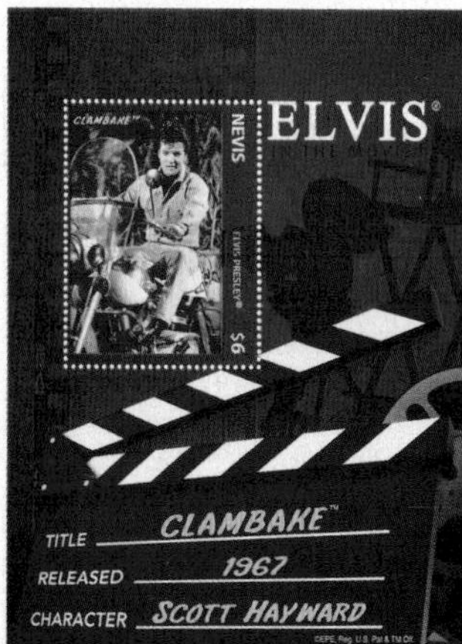


A323

A324

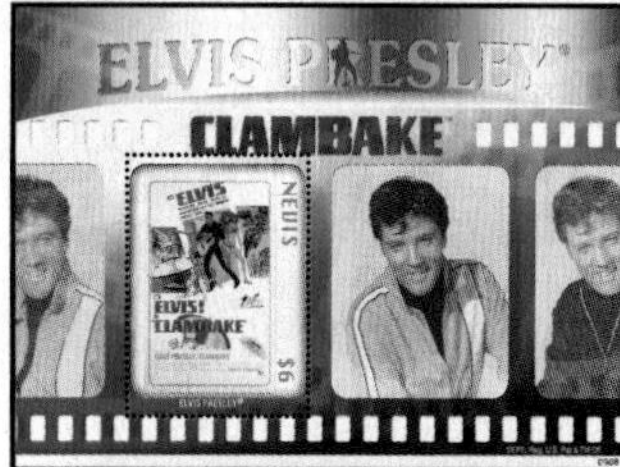


A325

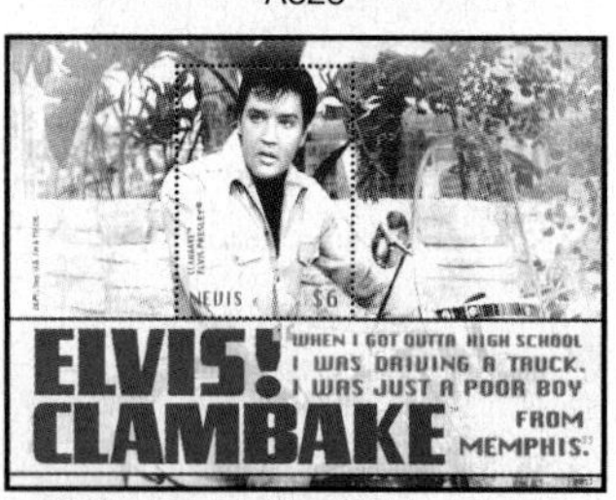


Elvis Presley (1935-77) — A326

**2009, June 15** ***Perf. 13¼***

**1565** A323 $6 multi 4.50 4.50

**1566** A324 $6 multi 4.50 4.50

**1567** A325 $6 multi 4.50 4.50

**1568** A326 $6 multi 4.50 4.50

*Nos. 1565-1568 (4)* 18.00 18.00

Miniature Sheet

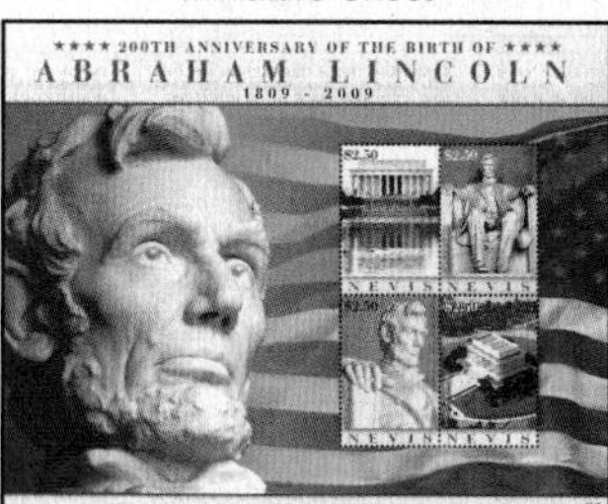


Pres. Abraham Lincoln (1809-65) — A327

No. 1569: a, Lincoln Memorial and Reflecting Pool. b, Front view of Lincoln sculpture in Lincoln Memorial. c, Head and hand of Lincoln sculpture. d, Aerial view of Lincoln Memorial.

**2009, Aug. 20**

**1569** A327 $2.50 Sheet of 4, #a-d 7.50 7.50

Miniature Sheet

The Three Stooges — A328

No. 1570: a, Moe Howard, Curly Howard and Larry Fine. b, Curly Howard. c, Moe Howard. d, Larry Fine.

**2009, Aug. 20** ***Perf. 11½***

**1570** A328 $2.50 Sheet of 4, #a-d 7.50 7.50

Miniature Sheet

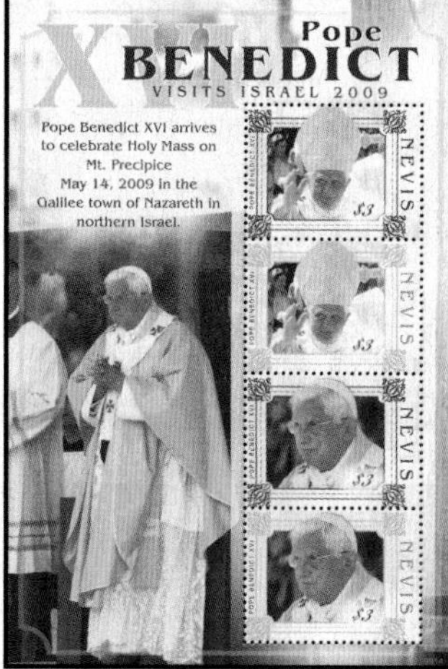


Pope Benedict XVI — A329

No. 1571 — Pope Benedict XVI: a, Wearing miter, brown frame. b, Wearing miter, bister frame. c, Wearing zucchetto and eyeglasses, brown frame. d, Wearing zucchetto and eyeglasses, bister frame.

**2009, Aug. 20**

**1571** A329 $3 Sheet of 4, #a-d 9.00 9.00

Miniature Sheets

A330

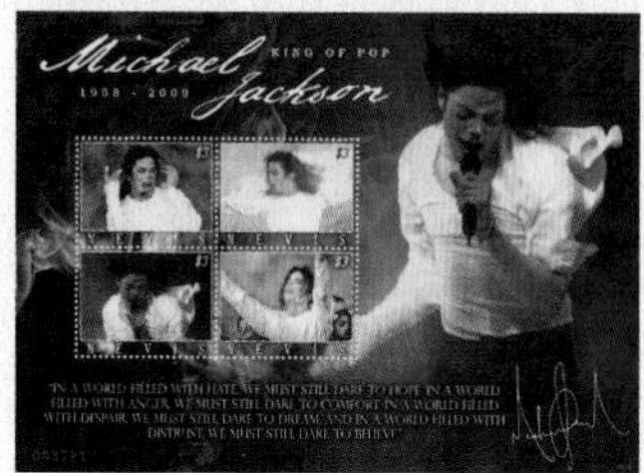


Michael Jackson (1958-2009) — A331

No. 1572 — Jackson with country name in: a, Blue. b, Yellow. c, Lilac. d, Red.

No. 1573 — Jackson: a, With microphone near mouth, hands raised. b, With arms extended to side. c, Holding microphone. d, With people in background.

***Perf. 11¼x11½***

**2009, Sept. 25** **Litho.**

**1572** A330 $2 Sheet of 4, #a-d 6.00 6.00

***Perf. 11½x12***

**1573** A331 $3 Sheet of 4, #a-d 9.00 9.00

Worldwide Fund for Nature (WWF) A332

No. 1574 — Caribbean reef squid with denomination in: a, Pink and blue. b, Pink. c, Orange and red. d, Green and blue.

**2009, Dec. 1** ***Perf. 13¼***

**1574** Strip or block of 4 6.00 6.00

*a.-d.* A332 $2 Any single 1.50 1.50

*e.* Sheet of 8, 2 each #1574a-1574d 12.00 12.00

Flowers A333

Designs: 25c, Genipa americana. 50c, Clusia rosea. 80c, Browallia americana. 90c, Bidens alba. $1, Begonia odorata. $5, Jatropha gossypiifolia.

No. 1581: a, Crantzia cristata. b, Selaginella flabellata. c, Hibiscus tiliaceus. d, Heliconia psittacorum.

**2009, Dec. 1** **Litho.** ***Perf. 13x13¼***

**1575-1580** A333 Set of 6 6.25 6.25

**1581** A333 $2.50 Sheet of 4, #a-d 7.50 7.50

Christmas A334

Designs: 25c, Magi on camels. 30c, Holy Family. 90c, Magus and camel in stars. $5, Holy Family and angels.

**2009, Dec. 7** **Litho.** ***Perf. 14¾x14¼***

**1582-1585** A334 Set of 4 5.00 5.00

First Man on the Moon, 40th Anniv. — A335

No. 1586: a, Astronaut Neil Armstrong, Saturn V rocket. b, Astronauts Edwin "Buzz" Aldrin and Michael Collins. c, Apollo 11 command module, Moon. d, Apollo 11 lunar module leaving Moon.
$6, Armstrong and lunar module.

**2009, Dec. 30** **Litho.** ***Perf. 11½x12***

**1586** A335 $2.50 Sheet of 4, #a-d 7.75 7.75

**Souvenir Sheet**

***Perf. 11½x11¼***

**1587** A335 $6 multi 4.75 4.75

Intl. Year of Astronomy.

Miniature Sheet

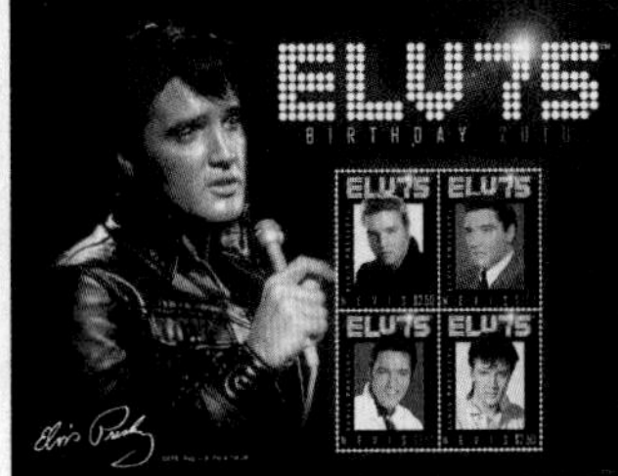


Elvis Presley (1935-77) — A336

No. 1588 — Presley wearing: a, Black jacket. b, Brown suit and blue shirt. c, White shirt with red neckerchief. d, Blue shirt.

**2010, Mar. 2 Litho.** ***Perf. 12x11½***
**1588** A336 $2.50 Sheet of 4, #a-d 7.75 7.75

Ferrari Race Cars and Parts A337

No. 1589, $1.25: a, Engine diagram of 1947 125 S. b, 1947 125 S.
No. 1590, $1.25: a, Engine of 1951 500 F2. b, 1951 500 F2.
No. 1591, $1.25: a, Exhaust pipe of 1953 553 F2. b, 1953 553 F2.
No. 1592, $1.25: a, Engine of 1957 Dino 156 F2. b, 1957 Dino 156 F2.

**2010, Mar. 2** ***Perf. 12***
**Vert. Pairs, #a-b**
**1589-1592** A337 Set of 4 7.75 7.75

Mushrooms A338

Designs: 25c, Psilocybe guilartensis. 80c, Alboleptonia flavifolia. $1, Agaricus sp. $5, Psilocybe caerulescens.
No. 1597: a, Psilocybe portoricensis. b, Boletus ruborculus. c, Psilocybe plutonia (one). d, Alboleptonia largentii. e, Psilocybe plutonia (three). f, Collybia aurea.

**2010, Mar. 24 Litho.** ***Perf. 11½***
**1593-1596** A338 Set of 4 5.25 5.25
**1597** A338 $1.50 Sheet of 6, #a-f 6.75 6.75

A339

A340

Birds — A341

Designs: 30c, Great blue heron. 90c, Magnificent frigatebird. $1, Masked booby. $5, Great egret.
No. 1602: a, White-tailed tropicbird. b, Audubon's shearwater. c, Red-billed tropicbird. d, Leach's storm petrel.
No. 1603: a, Brown pelican. b, Brown booby.

**2010, May 21** ***Perf. 11½***
**1598-1601** A339 Set of 4 5.50 5.50
**1602** A340 $2 Sheet of 4, #a-d 6.00 6.00

**Souvenir Sheet**
***Perf. 11½x12***
**1603** A341 $3 Sheet of 2, #a-b 4.50 4.50

Miniature Sheets

A342

Election of Pres. John F. Kennedy, 50th Anniv. — A343

No. 1604 — Denomination in red: a, Kennedy. b, USSR Premier Nikita Khrushchev. c, Khrushchev on sofa. d, Kennedy on sofa.
No. 1605 — Denomination in white: a, Pres. Richard M. Nixon, color photograph. b, Kennedy, color photograph. c, Kennedy, black-and-white photograph. d, Nixon, black-and-white photograph.

**2010, May 21 Litho.** ***Perf. 13¼***
**1604** A342 $3 Sheet of 4, #a-d 9.00 9.00
**1605** A343 $3 Sheet of 4, #a-d 9.00 9.00

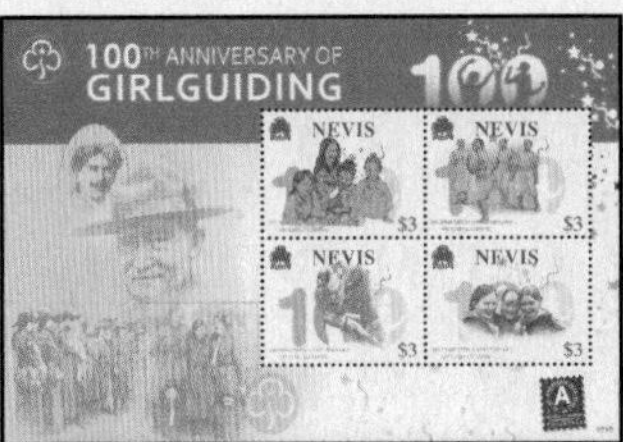


Girl Guides, Cent. — A344

No. 1606: a, Four Girl Guides and adult leader. b, Four Girl Guides. c, Girl Guide climbing rock. d, Three Girl Guides.
$6, Four Girl Guides, vert.

**2010, May 21** ***Perf. 11½x12***
**1606** A344 $3 Sheet of 4, #a-d 9.00 9.00

**Souvenir Sheet**
***Perf. 11¼x11½***
**1607** A344 $6 multi 4.50 4.50

A345

Whales — A346

Designs: $1.20, Minke whale. $1.80, Northern right whale. $3, Fin whale. $5, Sei whale.
$6, Blue whale.

**2010, July 14** ***Perf. 13x13¼***
**1608-1611** A345 Set of 4 8.25 8.25

**Souvenir Sheet**
**1612** A346 $6 multi 4.50 4.50

Souvenir Sheet

Sea Mammals — A347

No. 1613: a, Caribbean monk seal. b, West Indian manatee.

**2010, July 14**
**1613** A347 $3 Sheet of 2, #a-b 4.50 4.50

Miniature Sheet

John F. Kennedy's 1960 US Presidential Campaign Buttons — A348

No. 1614: a, "Vote Kennedy for President." b, "For President John F. Kennedy." c, "Kennedy Johnson." d, "America Needs Kennedy Johnson."

**2010, Sept. 8** ***Perf.***
**1614** A348 $2 Sheet of 4, #a-d 6.00 6.00

Orchids — A349

No. 1615, horiz.: a, Heart-lipped brassavola. b, Waunakee Sunset. c, Moss-loving cranichis. d, Longclaw orchid. e, Golden yellow cattleya. f, Fat Cat.
$6, Von Martin's brassavola.

**2010, Sept. 8** ***Perf. 11½x12***
**1615** A349 $2 Sheet of 6, #a-f 9.00 9.00

**Souvenir Sheet**
***Perf. 11½***
**1616** A349 $6 multi 4.50 4.50

Henri Dunant (1828-1910), Founder of Red Cross — A350

No. 1617 — Dunant and: a, Bertha von Suttner. b, Victor Hugo. c, Charles Dickens. d, Harriet Beecher Stowe.
$6, Dunant and scene of abolition of slavery in Washington, DC.

**2010, Sept. 8** ***Perf. 13x13¼***
**1617** A350 $2.50 Sheet of 4, #a-d 7.50 7.50

**Souvenir Sheet**
**1618** A350 $6 multi 4.50 4.50

A351

Princess Diana (1961-97) — A352

No. 1619 — Princess Diana wearing: a, Black hat, black jacket. b, Black and white hat, white dress. c, Tiara.
$3, White dress, no hat.

**2010, Dec. 6** ***Perf. 12***
**1619** A351 $2 Vert. strip of 3, #a-c 4.50 4.50
**1620** A352 $3 multi 2.25 2.25

No. 1619 was printed in sheets containing 2 of each stamp. No. 1620 was printed in sheets of 4.

Christmas A353

Paintings: 30c, Annunciation, by Paolo Uccello. 90c, The Altarpiece of the Rose Garlands, by Albrecht Dürer. $1.80, Like 30c. $2, Sistine Madonna, by Raphael. $2.30, Like $2. $3, The Adoration of the Magi, by Giotto di Bondone.

**2010, Dec. 6** ***Perf. 12***
**1621-1626** A353 Set of 6 7.75 7.75

A354

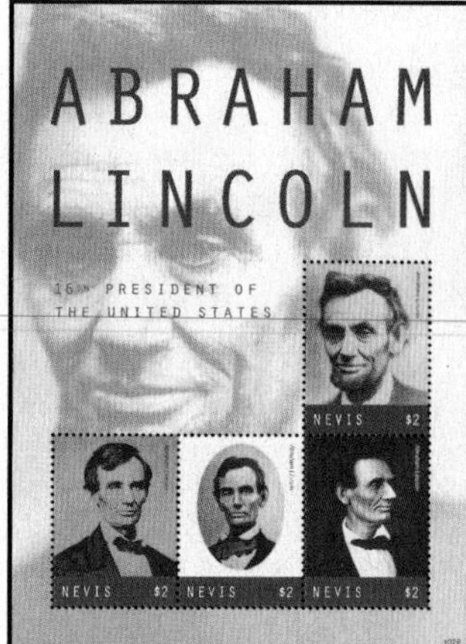


Pres. Abraham Lincoln (1809-65) — A355

No. 1628 — Lincoln: a, With buff background. b, With gray background. c, Oval photograph. d, With black background.

**2010, Dec. 10** ***Perf. 11½***
**1627** A354 $2 black 1.50 1.50
**1628** A355 $2 Sheet of 4, #a-d 6.00 6.00

Bank of Nevis — A356

Designs: 30c, Old building. $5, New building.

**2010, Dec. 9 Litho.** ***Perf. 11¼x11½***
**1629-1630** A356 Set of 2 4.00 4.00

Pope John Paul II (1920-2005) A357

Pope John Paul II wearing: $3, Miter. $4, Red hat.

**2010, Dec. 10** ***Perf. 14x14¾***
**1631-1632** A357 Set of 2 5.25 5.25

No. 1631 was printed in sheets of 4; No. 1632, in sheets of 3.

Elvis Presley (1935-77) A358

Presley wearing: No. 1633, $3, Black jacket, white shirt. No. 1634, $3, Red shirt.

**2010, Dec. 10**
**1633-1634** A358 Set of 2 4.50 4.50

Nos. 1633-1634 each were printed in sheets of 4.

2010 World Cup Soccer Championships, South Africa — A359

No. 1635, $1.50: a, Marek Hamsik. b, Giovanni Van Bronckhorst. c, Robert Vittek. d, Eljero Elia. e, Miroslav Stoch. f, Dirk Kuyt.
No. 1636, $1.50: a, Lucio. b, Alexis Sanchez. c, Dani Alves. d, Arturo Vidal. e, Gilberto Silva. f, Rodrigo Tello.
No. 1637, $1.50: a, Liedson. b, Xavi Hernandez. c, Simao. d, Jasper Juinen. e, Cristiano Ronaldo. f, David Villa.
No. 1638, $1.50: a, Paulo Da Silva. b, Yoshito Okubo. c, Edgar Barreto. d, Yuichi Komano. e, Cristian Riveros. f, Yasuhito Endo.
No. 1639, $1.50: a, Netherlands coach Bert van Marwijk. b, Joris Mathijsen.
No. 1640, $1.50: a, Brazil coach Dunga. b, Kaka.
No. 1641, $1.50: a, Spain coach Vicente del Bosque. b, Sergio Ramos.
No. 1642, $1.50: a, Paraguay coach Gerardo Martino. b, Roque Santa Cruz.

**2010, Dec. 10** ***Perf. 12***
**Sheets of 6, #a-f**
**1635-1638** A359 Set of 4 27.00 27.00
**Souvenir Sheets of 2, #a-b**
**1639-1642** A359 Set of 4 9.00 9.00

Trip to India of U.S. President Barack Obama — A360

No. 1643: a, Barack and Michelle Obama leaving Air Force One. b, Pres. Obama addressing Indian students in Mumbai. c, Pres. Obama signing Mumbai terrorist attacks condolence book. d, Pres. Obama and Indian Prime Minister Manmohan Singh. $6, Pres. Obama addressing Indian students in Mumbai, horiz.

**2010, Dec. 10** ***Perf. 14¼x14¾***
**1643** A360 $3 Sheet of 4, #a-d 9.00 9.00
**Souvenir Sheet**
***Perf. 14¾x14¼***
**1644** A360 $6 multi 4.50 4.50

Indipex 2011, New Delhi.

Engagement of Prince William and Catherine Middleton — A361

No. 1645: a, Arms of Prince William (38mm diameter). b, Buckingham Palace (86x40mm arc-shaped). c, Catherine Middleton, black-and-white photo (86x40mm arc-shaped). d, Prince William, black-and-white photo (86x40mm arc-shaped).
No. 1646: a, Couple (86x40mm arc-shaped). b, Catherine Middleton, color photo (86x40mm arc-shaped). c, Prince William, color photo (86x40mm arc-shaped). $6, Couple, diff.

**2010, Dec. 30** ***Perf. 13***
**1645** A361 $3 Sheet of 4, #a-d 9.00 9.00
**1646** A361 $3 Sheet of 4, #1645a, 1646a-1646c 9.00 9.00
**Souvenir Sheet**
***Perf. 11½x11¼***
**1647** A361 $6 multi 4.50 4.50

No. 1647 contains one 40x30mm stamp.

Miniature Sheets

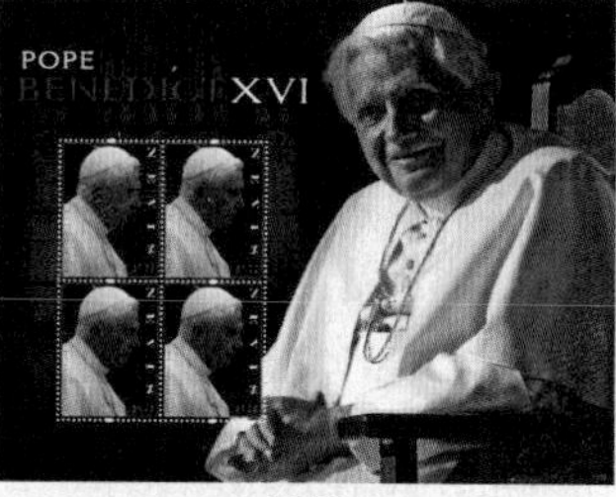

A362

Pope Benedict XVI — A363

No. 1648 — Pope Benedict XVI with: a, Part of white stole outside frame line at LR. b, Black areas outside of frame line.
No. 1649 — Pope Benedict with: a, Windows under "N," "V" and "S" in country name. b, Protruding corner of ceiling to left of "N" in country name. c, White area under "N" in country name. d, Cross and head of statue under "V" of country name.

**2011, Mar. 30** ***Perf. 13 Syncopated***
**1648** A362 $3 Sheet of 4, #1648a, 3 #1648b 9.00 9.00
**1649** A363 $3 Sheet of 4, #a-d 9.00 9.00

Mohandas K. Gandhi (1869-1948), Indian Nationalist A364

Gandhi and: No. 1650, $3, Orange panel at bottom. No. 1651, $3, Red brown panel at left.

**2011, Mar. 30** ***Perf. 12***
**1650-1651** A364 Set of 2 4.50 4.50

Nos. 1650-1651 each were printed in sheets of 4.

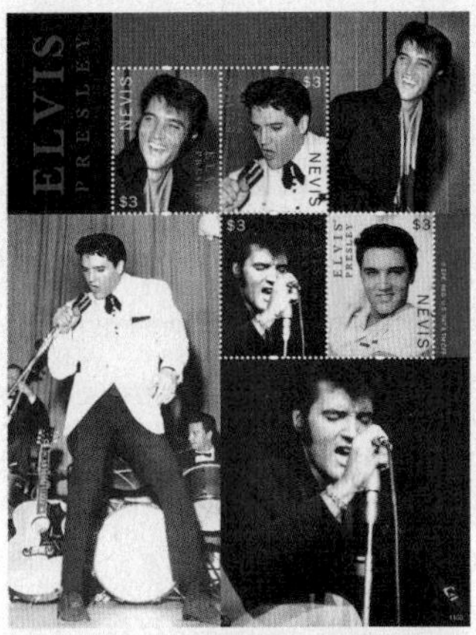

A365

A366

A367

A368

A369

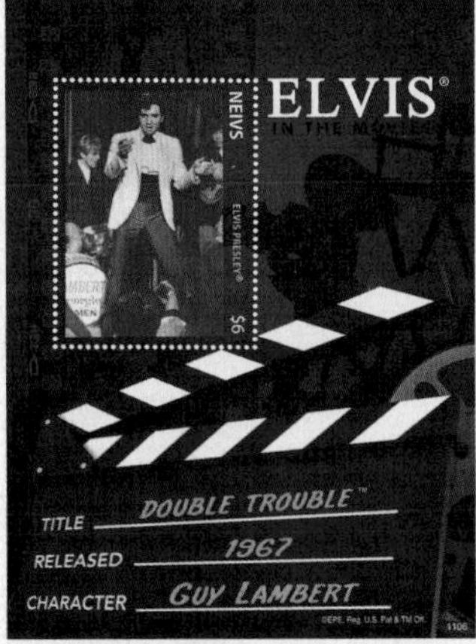

Elvis Presley (1935-77) — A370

No. 1652 — Presley and: a, Country name in white at UL. b, Country name in black at LR, Presley holding microphone. c, No country name. d, Country name in black at LL, no microphone shown.

No. 1653 — Presley: a, Head and neck only. b, Wearing hat. c, Wearing jacket. d, Touching his chin.

**2011, Mar. 30** ***Perf. 13 Syncopated***

**1652** A365 $3 Sheet of 4, #a-d 9.00 9.00
**1653** A366 $3 Sheet of 4, #a-d 9.00 9.00

**Souvenir Sheets**

***Perf. 12½***

**1654** A367 $6 multi 4.50 4.50
**1655** A368 $6 multi 4.50 4.50
**1656** A369 $6 multi 4.50 4.50
**1657** A370 $6 multi 4.50 4.50
*Nos. 1654-1657 (4)* 18.00 18.00

Miniature Sheets

Cats — A371

No. 1658, $2.50: a, Maine Coon cat. b, Norwegian Forest cat. c, Ragdoll cat. d, Turkish Angora cat.

No. 1659: $2.50: a, Russian Blue cat. b, Siamese cat. c, Abyssinan cat. d, Bombay cat.

**2011, Apr. 4** ***Perf. 12***

**Sheets of 4, #a-d**

**1658-1659** A371 Set of 2 15.00 15.00

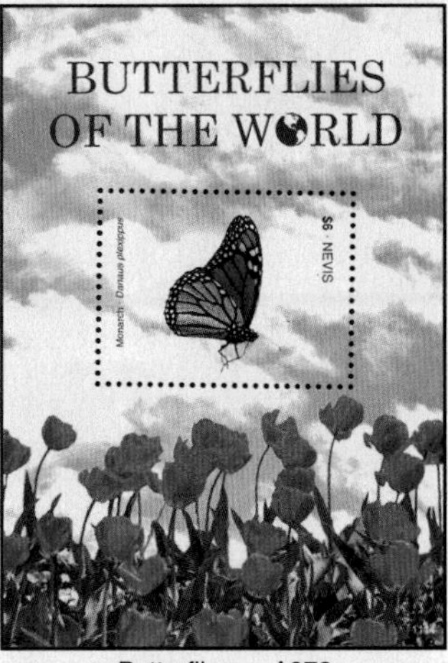

Butterflies — A372

No. 1660: a, Meadow argus. b, Gulf fritillary. c, Eastern tiger swallowtail. d, Gabb's checkerspot. e, Indian leafwing. f, Blue diadem. $6, Monarch butterfly.

**2011, Apr. 4** ***Perf. 13 Syncopated***

**1660** A372 $2 Sheet of 6, #a-f 9.00 9.00

**Souvenir Sheet**

***Perf. 12***

**1661** A372 $6 multi 4.50 4.50

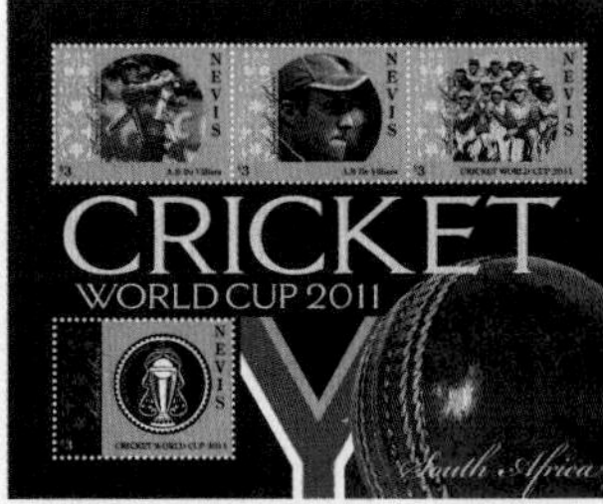

British Royalty — A373

Designs: No. 1662, Prince Philip.

No. 1663 — Queen Elizabeth II wearing: a, White dress. b, Lilac dress.

No. 1664, King George V. No. 1665, King George VI.

**2011, Apr. 4** ***Perf. 13 Syncopated***

**1662** A373 $2 multi 1.50 1.50
**1663** A373 $2 Pair, #a-b 3.00 3.00
**1664** A373 $3 multi 2.25 2.25
**1665** A373 $3 multi 2.25 2.25
*Nos. 1662-1665 (4)* 9.00 9.00

Nos. 1662, 1664-1665 each were printed in sheets of 4. No. 1663 was printed in sheet containing two pairs.

Miniature Sheets

2011 Cricket World Cup, India, Bangladesh and Sri Lanka — A374

No. 1666 — Inscribed "South Africa," with dull orange background: a, A. B. De Villiers batting. b, Close-up of De Villiers. c, Posed photograph of South Africa team. d, Cricket World Cup.

No. 1667 — Inscribed "South Africa," with orange background: a, Like #1666a. b, Like #1666b. c, South Africa team celebrating. d, Like #1666d.

No. 1668 — Inscribed "Pakistan," with olive green background: a, Shoaib Akhtar running. b, Close-up of Akhtar. c, Pakistan team. d Like #1666d.

No. 1669 — Inscribed "Sri Lanka," with red brown background: a, Kumar Sangakkara on cricket pitch. b, Close-up of Sangakkara. c, Sri Lanka team. d, Like #1666d.

No. 1670 — Inscribed "West Indies," with dark red background: a, Chris Gayle holding on cricket bat. b, Close-up of Gayle. c, West Indies team. d, Like #1666d.

**2011, Apr. 4** ***Perf. 12***

**1666** A374 $3 Sheet of 4, #a-d 9.00 9.00
**1667** A374 $3 Sheet of 4, #a-d 9.00 9.00
**1668** A374 $3 Sheet of 4, #a-d 9.00 9.00
**1669** A374 $3 Sheet of 4, #a-d 9.00 9.00
**1670** A374 $3 Sheet of 4, #a-d 9.00 9.00
*Nos. 1666-1670 (5)* 45.00 45.00

Wedding of Prince William and Catherine Middleton — A375

No. 1671: a, Groom facing right. b, Bride waving.

No. 1672: a, Bride. b, Groom facing forward. c, Couple in coach, facing left, groom waving.

No. 1673: a, Couple standing. b, Couple in coach, facing right, groom waving.

**2011, Apr. 29** **Litho.** ***Perf. 12***

**1671** A375 $3 Pair, #a-b 4.50 4.50
**1672** A375 $3 Sheet of 4, #1672a-1672b, 2 #1672c 9.00 9.00

**Souvenir Sheet**

**1673** A375 $6 Sheet of 2, #a-b 9.00 9.00

No. 1671 was printed in sheets containing two pairs.

Miniature Sheets

Pres. Abraham Lincoln (1809-65) — A376

No. 1674, $2: a, Union soldier. b, Civil War era illustration with shield, books, wounded snake. c, Union soldiers in trenches. d, Lincoln.

No. 1675, $2 — Lincoln and quotes: a, "Government of the people, by the people, for the people shall not perish from the Earth." b, "The best way to destroy an enemy is to make him a friend." c, "A house divided against itself cannot stand." d, "Avoid popularity if you would have peace."

**2011, June 20** ***Perf. 13 Syncopated***

**Sheets of 4, #a-d**

**1674-1675** A376 Set of 2 12.00 12.00

U.S. Civil War, 150th anniv.

Miniature Sheets

Princess Diana (1961-97) — A377

No. 1676, $2 — Red panel, Princess Diana: a, Facing forward, wearing dress with dark collar. b, Wearing sailor's cap. c, Facing left, wearing striped blouse. d, Wearing maroon hat.

No. 1677, $2 — Yellow panel, Princess Diana wearing: a, Purple jacket. b, Black and white hat. c, Black jacket. d, Red dress.

**2011, June 20** ***Perf. 12***

**Sheets of 4, #a-d**

**1676-1677** A377 Set of 2 12.00 12.00

A378

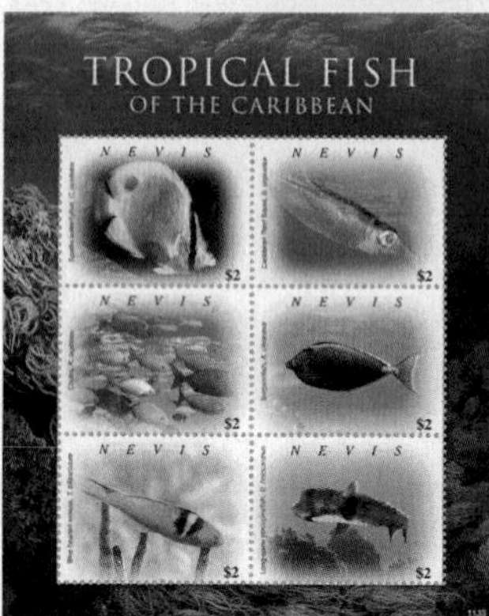

A379

Marine Life — A380

Designs: 10c, Blue stripe grunt. 30c, Red hind. 40c, Red snapper. $5, Old wife.

No. 1682: a, Spotfin butterflyfish. b, Caribbean reef squid. c, Chubs. d, Surgeonfish. e, Blue-headed wrasse. f, Long-spine porcupinefish.

$6, Anemonefish.

**2011, July 6** ***Perf. 12***

**1678-1681** A378 Set of 4 4.25 4.25
**1682** A379 $2 Sheet of 6, #a-f 9.00 9.00

**Souvenir Sheet**

**1683** A380 $6 multi 4.50 4.50

Shells — A381

Designs: 20c, Scaphella junonia. 30c, Strombus gigas. $1.80, Busycon contrarium. $5, Arca zebra.

No. 1688: a, Charonia variegata. b, Cypraea aurantium. c, Cyphoma gibbosa. d, Chicoreus articulatus.

No. 1689, $6, Thais deltoidea. No. 1690, $6, Cittarium pica.

**2011, July 25** ***Perf. 12***

**1684-1687** A381 Set of 4 5.50 5.50

***Perf. 13 Syncopated***

**1688** A381 $2.50 Sheet of 4, #a-d 7.50 7.50

**Souvenir Sheets**

**1689-1690** A381 Set of 2 9.00 9.00

Pres. John F. Kennedy (1917-63) — A382

No. 1691 — Kennedy: a, In front of window next to other man. b, With lectern visible. c, With other man in front of microphones. d, Greeting youths.

$6, Kennedy on path shoveled in snow.

**2011, Aug. 29** ***Perf. 12***

**1691** A382 $3 Sheet of 4, #a-d 9.00 9.00

**Souvenir Sheet**

**1692** A382 $6 multi 4.50 4.50

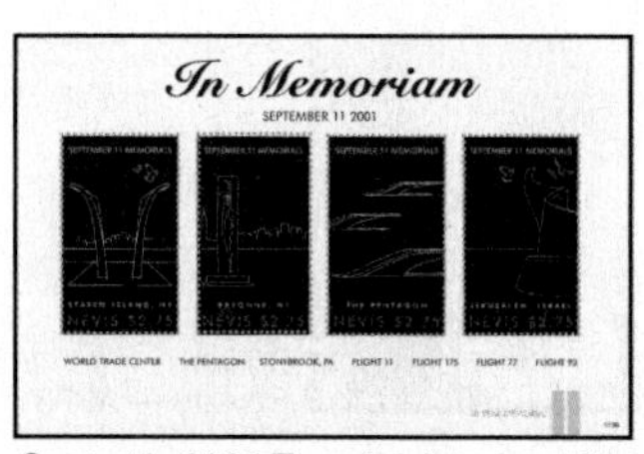

Sept. 11, 2001 Terrorist Attacks, 10th Anniv. — A383

No. 1693 — Memorials at: a, Staten Island, New York. b, Bayonne, New Jersey. c, Pentagon. d, Jerusalem, Israel.

$6, Ground Zero Reflecting Pools.

**2011, Sept. 9** **Litho.**

**1693** A383 $2.75 Sheet of 4, #a-d 8.25 8.25

**Souvenir Sheet**

**1694** A383 $2.75 multi 4.50 4.50

Miniature Sheet

Inter Milan Soccer Team — A384

No. 1695: a, Team photo, 1910. b, Giorgio Muggiani, team founder. c, Angelo Moratti, past president of team. d, Heleno Herrera, coach. e, Team celebrating 2011 TIM Cup championship. f, Giacinto Facchetti, player and team president. g, Sandro Mazzola, player. h, Mario Corso, player. i, Luis Suarez, player.

**2011, Sept. 13** ***Perf. 12¾***

**1695** A384 $1.50 Sheet of 9, #a-i 10.00 10.00

A385

Dogs — A386

No. 1696: a, Alaskan malamute. b, Yorkshire terrier. c, Black Labrador retriever. d, Dachshund.

$6, Beagle.

**2011, Oct. 14** ***Perf. 13 Syncopated***

**1696** A385 $2.75 Sheet of 4, #a-d 8.25 8.25

**Souvenir Sheet**

**1697** A386 $6 multi 4.50 4.50

Christmas A387

Paintings by Melchior Broederlam: 25c, Annunciation. 30c, Visitation. 90c, Presentation in the Temple. $5, Flight into Egypt.

**2011, Nov. 7** ***Perf. 12***

**1698-1701** A387 Set of 4 4.75 4.75

Reptiles — A388

No. 1702: a, Anegada ground iguana. b, Antilles racer. c, Brown anole. d, Lesser Antillean iguana.

$6, Anegada ground iguana, horiz.

**2011, Nov. 14** **Litho.** ***Perf. 12***

**1702** A388 $3 Sheet of 4, #a-d 9.00 9.00

**Souvenir Sheet**

***Perf. 12½***

**1703** A388 $6 multi 4.50 4.50

No. 1703 contains one 51x38mm stamp.

Miniature Sheets

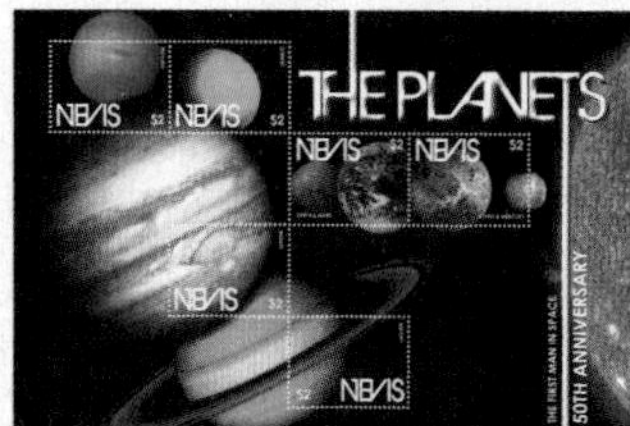

First Man in Space, 50th Anniv. — A389

No. 1704 — Planets: a, Neptune. b, Uranus. c, Earth and Mars. d, Venus and Mercury. e, Jupiter. f, Saturn.

No. 1705 — Phases of the Moon: a, Full (country name in black). b, Waxing gibbous ("N" of country name in white). c, First quarter ("NE" and part of "V" of country name in white). d, Waxing crescent (country name in white).

**2011, Dec. 16** ***Perf. 12½x12***

**1704** A389 $2 Sheet of 6, #a-f 9.00 9.00

***Perf. 13***

**1705** A389 $3 Sheet of 4, #a-d 9.00 9.00

No. 1705 contains four 35mm diameter stamps.

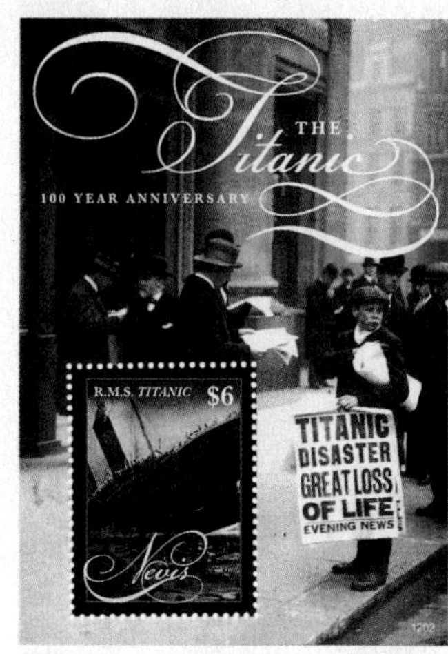

Sinking of the Titanic, Cent. — A390

No. 1706: a, Stowaway on rope. b, Grand Staircase of the Olympic. c, Titanic at Southampton dock. d, Reading and writing room.

$6, Titanic sinking.

**2012, Feb. 8** ***Perf. 13 Syncopated***

**1706** A390 $3 Sheet of 4, #a-d 9.00 9.00

**Souvenir Sheet**

***Perf. 12***

**1707** A390 $6 multi 4.50 4.50

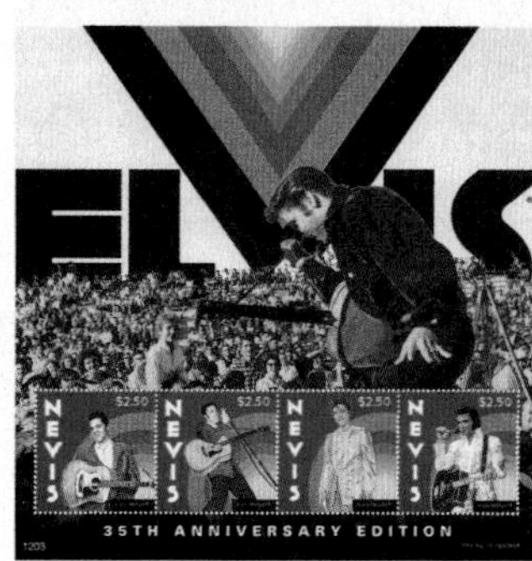

Elvis Presley (1935-77) — A391

No. 1708 — Presley: a, With guitar and gray suit, no microphone. b, With guitar, gray suit, microphone on stand. c, With beige suit. d, With guitar, white suit, holding microphone.

$9, Presley in gray suit playing guitar.

**2012, Mar. 26** ***Perf. 12***

**1708** A391 $2.50 Sheet of 4, #a-d 7.50 7.50

**Souvenir Sheet**

***Perf. 13¼***

**1709** A391 $9 multi 6.75 6.75

Medicinal Spring — A392

Nevis Coat of Arms — A393

**2012, June 14** *Perf. 11¼*

**1710** A392 $100 multi 75.00 75.00
**1711** A393 $150 multi 110.00 110.00

Reign of Queen Elizabeth II, 60th Anniv. — A394

No. 1712 — Various photographs of Queen Elizabeth II with denomination at: a, LR. b, LL. c, UR. d, UL.
$10, Queen Elizabeth II wearing tiara.

**2012, July 25** *Perf. 13¾*

**1712** A394 $3 Sheet of 4, #a-d 9.00 9.00

**Souvenir Sheet**

**1713** A394 $10 multi 7.50 7.50

Charles Dickens (1812-70), Writer — A395

Designs: $3.50, Dickens.
No. 1715: a, Books by Dickens. b, Dickens, diff.

**2012, Aug. 7** **Litho.**

**1714** A395 $3.50 multi 2.60 2.60

**Souvenir Sheet**

**1715** A395 $4.50 Sheet of 2, #a-b 6.75 6.75

No. 1714 was printed in sheets of 4.

Miniature Sheet

Stingrays — A396

No. 1716: a, Caribbean whiptail. b, Lesseer electric ray. c, Giant manta ray. d, Southern stingray. e, Spotted eagle ray.

**2012, Aug. 7** *Perf. 12*

**1716** A396 $3 Sheet of 5, #a-e 11.00 11.00

Illustrations From *Peter Pan,* by James M. Barrie (1860-1937) — A397

No. 1717 — Various illustrations with upper panel in: a, Green. b, Yellow green. c, Dull brown. d, Blue.
$6, Yellow green panel at right.

**2012, Aug. 9** ***Perf. 13 Syncopated***

**1717** A397 $3 Sheet of 4, #a-d 9.00 9.00

**Souvenir Sheet**

**1718** A397 $6 multi 4.50 4.50

Miniature Sheet

Butterflies — A398

No. 1719: a, Hamadryas amphinome. b, Lycorea halia atergatis. c, Marpesia eleuchea bahamensis. d, Pyrisitia proterpia, with antennae. e, Pyrisitia proterpia, without antennae. f, Pyrrhocalles antiqua.

**2012, Nov. 28** *Perf. 12*

**1719** A398 $2.50 Sheet of 6, #a-f 11.00 11.00

Beetles — A399

No. 1720: a, Lema biornata. b, Lema splendida. c, Lema minuta. d, Lema dorsalis.
No. 1721: a, Stilodes heydeni. b, Stilodes leoparda.

**2012, Nov. 28** *Perf. 13¾*

**1720** A399 $2.50 Sheet of 4, #a-d 7.50 7.50

**Souvenir Sheet**

**1721** A399 $4 Sheet of 2, #a-b 6.00 6.00

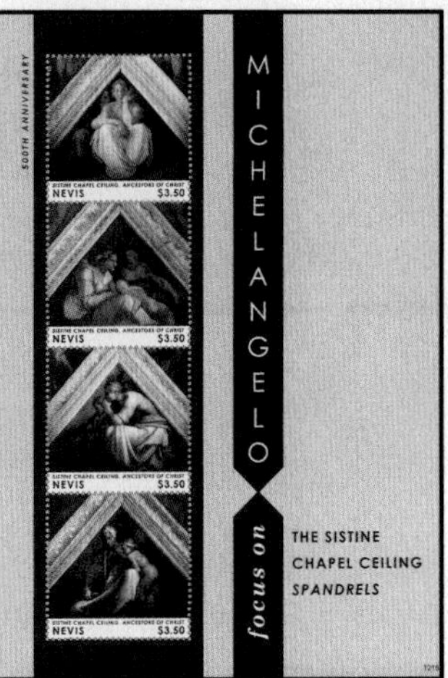

Painting of the Sistine Chapel Ceiling by Michelangelo, 500th Anniv. — A400

No. 1722 — Details from Ancestors of Christ: a, Man with hand at face. b, Woman, man and infant. c, Woman kissing child. d, Woman and naked child at right.
$9, The Creation of Adam, horiz.

**2012, Nov. 28** *Perf. 13¾*

**1722** A400 $3.50 Sheet of 4, #a-d 10.50 10.50

**Souvenir Sheet**

***Perf. 12***

**1723** A400 $9 multi 6.75 6.75

No. 1723 contains one 80x30mm stamp.

Souvenir Sheets

Elvis Presley (1935-77) — A401

Presley: No. 1724, $9, Playing guitar, purple frame, country name in red. No. 1725, $9, With two women, black frame and country name. No. 1726, $9, With band, playing guitar, red frame and country name. No. 1727, $9, Holding microphone, red frame and country name. No. 1728, $9, Holding microphone, gray frame and country name.

**2012, Nov. 28** *Perf. 12¾*

**1724-1728** A401 Set of 5 34.00 34.00

Christmas A402

Paintings by Caravaggio: 25c, Adoration of the Shepherds. 30c, Annunciation. 90c, Holy Family with St. John the Baptist. $1, Nativity with St. Francis and St. Lawrence. $3, Rest on the Flight into Egypt. $5, Madonna of the Rosary.

**2012, Nov. 28** **Litho.**

**1729-1734** A402 Set of 6 7.75 7.75

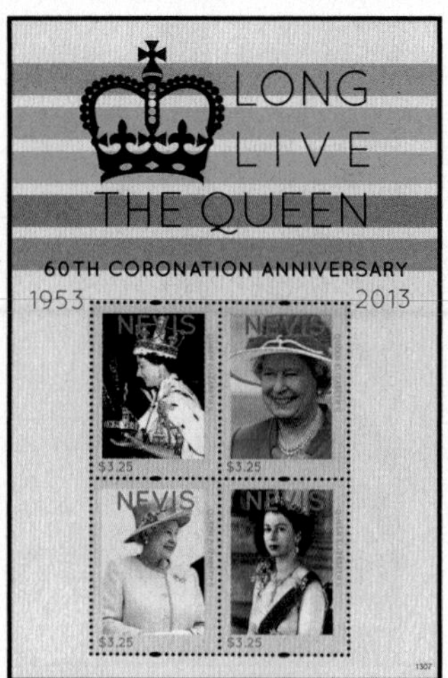


Coronation of Queen Elizabeth II, 60th Anniv. — A403

No. 1735 — Queen Elizabeth II: a, Holding orb. b, Wearing blue hat. c, Wearing pink hat. d, Wearing sash.
$9, Queen Elizabeth II wearing crown, waving.

**2013, Apr. 13** ***Perf. 13 Syncopated***
**1735** A403 $3.25 Sheet of 4, #a-d 9.75 9.75

**Souvenir Sheet**

**1736** A403 $9 multi 6.75 6,75

Miniature Sheets

Crossword Puzzles, Cent. — A404

No. 1737, $2 — Stamps with green panels and numbered squares: a, 1-5, 14, 17, 20, 23-25. b, 6-9, 15, 18, 21, 26-27. c, 10-13, 16, 19, 22. d, 28-29, 32-33, 37, 42, 45-48. e, 30, 34-36, 38, 43, 49-50. f, 31, 39-41, 44, 51. g, 52, 57, 60, 66, 69. h, 53-54, 58, 61-63, 67, 70. i, 55-56, 59, 64-65, 68, 71.
No. 1738, $2 — Stamps with red panels and numbered squares: a, 1-5, 14, 17, 20, 22, 23. b, 6-9, 15, 18, 21, 24. c, 10-13, 16, 19. d, 25, 29, 32-33, 37, 40-43. e, 26-27, 30, 34, 44. f, 28, 31, 35-36, 38-39, 45. g, 46-47, 49, 52, 56, 59. h, 48, 50-51, 53, 57, 60. i, 54-55, 58, 61.

**2013, Apr. 3** ***Perf. 13¾***

**Sheets of 9, #a-i**

**1737-1738** A404 Set of 2 27.00 27.00

On Nos. 1737-1738, crossword puzzle clues are in sheet margins and puzzle answers are printed on the backs of the stamps.

Personalizable Stamp — A405

**2013, Apr. 22** ***Perf. 14x14¾***
**1739** A405 $3 multi 2.25 2.25

No. 1739 was printed in sheets of 9 and presumably could be personalized for an extra fee.

World Radio Day — A406

No. 1740 — Radio antennae and concentric circles with United Nations emblem at: a, UL. b, UR. c, LL. d, LR.
$8, Radio antenna, concentric circles, United Nations emblem at LL.

**2013, Apr. 25** ***Perf. 12***
**1740** A406 $3 Sheet of 4, #a-d 9.00 9.00

**Souvenir Sheet**

**1741** A406 $8 multi 6.00 6.00

Hummingbirds — A407

No. 1742: a, Antillean mango. b, Ruby-throated hummingbird. c, Purple-throated carib. d, Long-billed starthroat.
No. 1743: a, Green-throated carib. b, Tufted coquette.

**2013, Apr. 25** ***Perf. 13¾***
**1742** A407 $3.25 Sheet of 4, #a-d 9.75 9.75

**Souvenir Sheet**

**1743** A407 $4.50 Sheet of 2, #a-b 6.75 6.75

Nos. 1742 and 1743 exist imperf. Value, set $25.

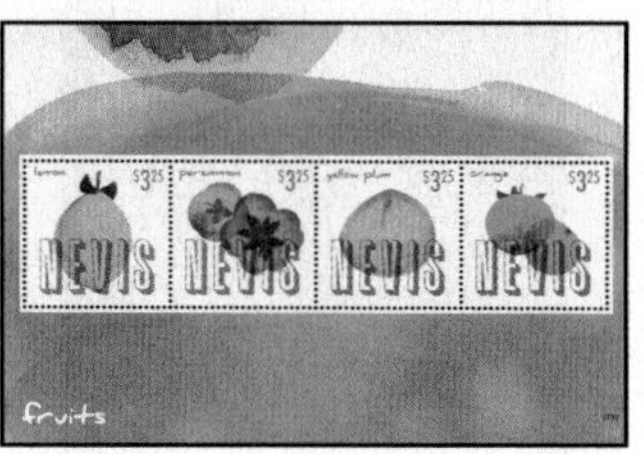


Bees — A408

No. 1744: a, Bicyrtes quadrifasciatus. b, Bembix americana. c, Ammophila apicalis. d, Ectemnius continuus.
$8, Bicyrtes quadrifasciatus, diff.

**2013, Apr. 25** ***Perf. 12***
**1744** A408 $4 Sheet of 4, #a-d 12.00 12.00

**Souvenir Sheet**

**1745** A408 $8 multi 6.00 6.00

Fruit — A409

No. 1746: a, Lemon. b, Persimmons. c, Yellow plum. d, Oranges.
$9, Peach, vert.

**2013, June 3** ***Perf. 13¾***
**1746** A409 $3.25 Sheet of 4, #a-d 9.75 9.75

**Souvenir Sheet**

***Perf. 12½***

**1747** A409 $9 multi 6.75 6.75

No. 1747 contains one 38x51mm stamp.

Turtles — A410

No. 1748: a, Desert tortoise. b, African helmeted turtle. c, Redbelly turtle. d, Red-eared slider.
$9, Gulf Coast box turtle.

**2013, June 3** ***Perf. 13 Syncopated***
**1748** A410 $3.25 Sheet of 4, #a-d 9.75 9.75

**Souvenir Sheet**

**1749** A410 $9 multi 6.75 6.75

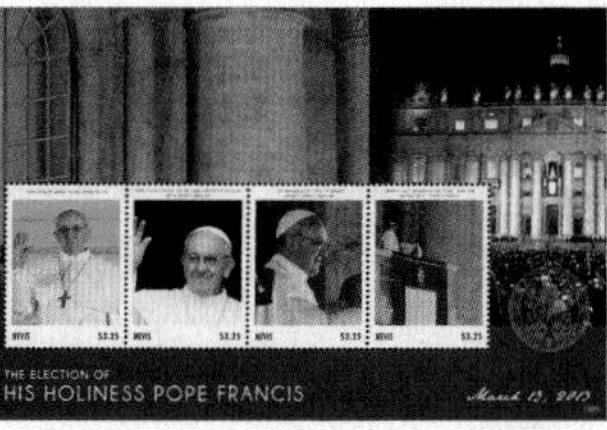

Parrots — A411

No. 1750: a, Imperial amazon. b, Cuban amazon. c, Hispanolian parrot. d, St. Vincent amazon.
$9, St. Lucia amazon, vert.

**2013, June 3** ***Perf. 13¾***
**1750** A411 $3.25 Sheet of 4, #a-d 9.75 9.75

**Souvenir Sheet**

***Perf. 12½***

**1751** A411 $9 multi 6.75 6.75

No. 1751 contains one 38x51mm stamp.

Election of Pope Francis — A412

No. 1752 — Pope Francis: a, Waving, orange background. b, Waving, black background. c, Facing right. d, On balcony with assistant.
$9, Pope Francis, assistant with microphone.

**2013, June 3** ***Perf. 14***
**1752** A412 $3.25 Sheet of 4, #a-d 9.75 9.75

**Souvenir Sheet**

***Perf. 12½***

**1753** A412 $9 multi 6.75 6.75

No. 1753 contains one 38x51mm stamp.

Souvenir Sheet

Elvis Presley (1935-77) — A413

**Litho., Margin Embossed**

**2013, July 8** ***Imperf.***

**Without Gum**

**1754** A413 $20 black 15.00 15.00



Birth of Prince George of Cambridge — A414

No. 1755: a, Duke and Duchess of Cambridge, Prince George. b, Prince George. c, Duchess of Cambridge, Prince George. d, Duke of Cambridge, Prince George.
No. 1756: a, Duke and Duchess of Cambridge, Prince George, diff. b, Prince George, diff.

**2013, Sept. 10** **Litho.** ***Perf. 12x12½***
**1755** A414 $3.25 Sheet of 4, #a-d 9.75 9.75

**Souvenir Sheet**

**1756** A414 $4.75 Sheet of 2, #a-b 7.00 7.00

Flora of Thailand — A415

No. 1757: a, Pineapple. b, Papayas. c, Red pineapple. d, Plumeria. e, Magnolia. f, Camellia.
$9, Bromeliad, vert.

**2013, Aug. 26 Litho. *Perf. 13¾***

**1757** A415 $2.50 Sheet of 6, #a-f 11.50 11.50

**Souvenir Sheet**

***Perf. 12½***

**1758** A415 $9 multi 6.75 6.75

Thailand 2013 World Stamp Exhibition, Bangkok. No. 1758 contains one 38x51mm stamp.

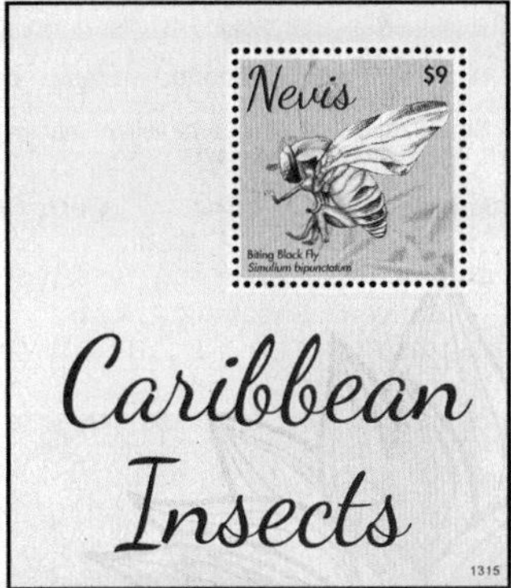


Insects — A416

No. 1759: a, Citrus root weevil. b, West Indian firetail. c, Catarina. d, Field cricket.
$9, Biting black fly.

**2013, Sept. 17 Litho. *Perf. 12½***

**1759** A416 $3.50 Sheet of 4, #a-d 10.50 10.50

**Souvenir Sheet**

**1760** A416 $9 multi 6.75 6.75

Independence, 30th Anniv. — A417

Designs: 30c, Soldiers handling flag. $5, National anthem, vert. (30x50mm). $10, Soldiers on parade.
$9, Map of St. Kitts and Nevis, vert.

***Perf. 12½x13¼, 12 ($5)***

**2013, Sept. 19 Litho.**

**1761-1763** A417 Set of 3 11.50 11.50

**Souvenir Sheet**

***Perf. 13¼x12½***

**1764** A417 $9 multi 6.75 6.75

Christmas A418

Paintings by Carlo Crivelli: 30c, Adoration of the Shepherds. 90c, Christ Blessing. $2, Immaculate Conception. $5, Madonna d'Ancona.

**2013, Dec. 2 Litho. *Perf. 12½***

**1765-1768** A418 Set of 4 6.25 6.25

Fish — A419

Designs: 10c, Barred hogfish. 15c, Bluefaced angelfish (Pomacanthus xanthometopon). 20c, Comb grouper. 30c, Spotfin hogfish. 90c, Yellow jack. $1, Broadbarred firefish. $1.20, Queen angelfish. $2, Stoplight parrotfish. $3, Tiger grouper. $5, Titan triggerfish. $10, Blue-striped grunt. $20, Flameback angelfish.

**2013, Dec. 4 Litho. *Perf. 13¾***

| | | | | | |
|---|---|---|---|---|---|
| **1769** | A419 | 10c | multi | .25 | .25 |
| **1770** | A419 | 15c | multi | .25 | .25 |
| **1771** | A419 | 20c | multi | .25 | .25 |
| **1772** | A419 | 30c | multi | .25 | .25 |
| **1773** | A419 | 90c | multi | .65 | .65 |
| **1774** | A419 | $1 | multi | .75 | .75 |
| **1775** | A419 | $1.20 | multi | .90 | .90 |
| **1776** | A419 | $2 | multi | 1.50 | 1.50 |
| **1777** | A419 | $3 | multi | 2.25 | 2.25 |
| **1778** | A419 | $5 | multi | 3.75 | 3.75 |
| **1779** | A419 | $10 | multi | 7.50 | 7.50 |
| **1780** | A419 | $20 | multi | 15.00 | 15.00 |
| | *Nos. 1769-1780 (12)* | | | 33.30 | 33.30 |

A420

A421

A422

Nelson Mandela (1918-2013), President of South Africa — A423

No. 1782 — Mandela: a, Wearing blue and white shirt with AIDS ribbon below top button. b, Wearing black and white shirt, person in background. c, Waving. d, Wearing black and white shirt.

**2013, Dec. 15 Litho. *Perf. 13¾***

**1781** A420 $4 multi 3.00 3.00
**1782** A421 $4 Sheet of 4, #a-d 12.00 12.00

**Souvenir Sheets**

**1783** A422 $14 multi 10.50 10.50
**1784** A423 $14 multi 10.50 10.50

No. 1781 was printed in sheets of 4.

Coffee — A424

No. 1785: a, Cup of coffee. b, Leaves and roasted beans. c, Coffee berries.
$9, Roasted bean.

**2013, Nov. 18 Litho. *Perf. 12½***

**1785** A424 $3.75 Sheet of 3, #a-c 8.50 8.50

**Souvenir Sheet**

**1786** A424 $9 multi 6.75 6.75

2013 Brasiliana Intl. Philatelic Exhibition, Rio de Janeiro.

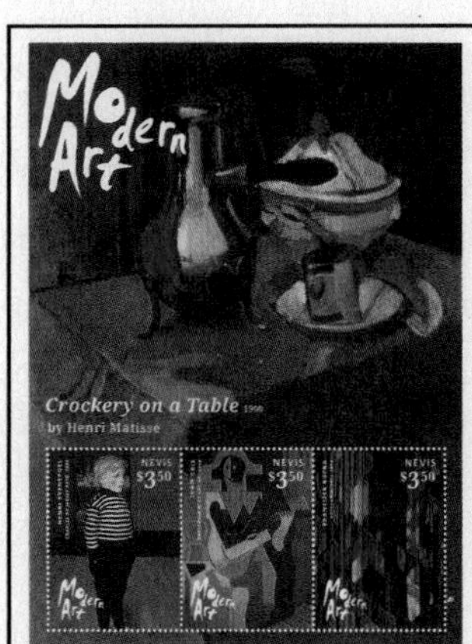


Modern Art — A425

No. 1787, $3.50: a, Charles au Jersey Rayé, by Henri Evenepoel. b, Harlequin with Guitar, by Juan Gris. c, Katedrala, by Frantisek Kupka.

No. 1788, $3.50: a, Madras Rouge, by Henri Matisse. b, Nude with a Parrot, by George Bellows. c, The Old Guitarist, by Pablo Picasso.

No. 1789, $9, Senecio, by Paul Klee. No. 1790, $9, Udnie, by Francis Picabia.

**2014, Jan. 3 Litho. *Perf. 12¾***

**Sheets of 3, #a-c**

**1787-1788** A425 Set of 2 15.50 15.50

**Souvenir Sheets**

**1789-1790** A425 Set of 2 13.50 13.50

Alexander Hamilton (1755-1804), First U.S. Treasury Secretary — A426

Designs: 30c, Portrait of Hamilton. 90c, Statue of Hamilton, U.S. Treasury Building. $10, Parchment scrolls.
$9, Nevis Heritage Center, horiz.

**2014, Jan. 11 Litho. *Perf. 14***

**1791-1793** A426 Set of 3 8.50 8.50

**Souvenir Sheet**

***Perf. 12***

**1794** A426 $9 multi 6.75 6.75

No. 1794 contains one 50x30mm stamp.

Miniature Sheets

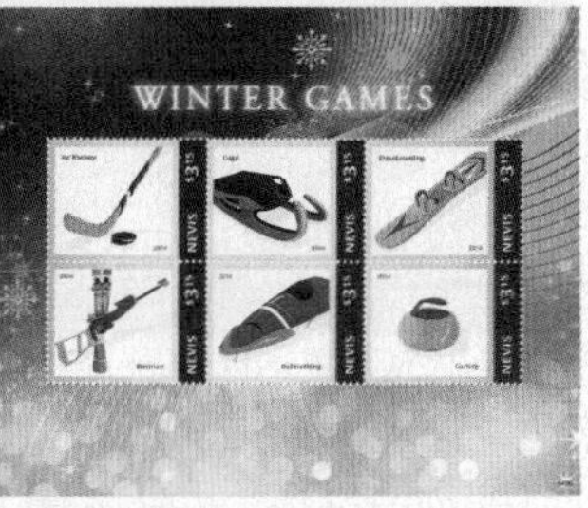


2014 Winter Olympics, Sochi, Russia — A427

No. 1795: a, Ice hockey stick and puck. b, Luge. c, Snowboard. d, Biathlon skis and rifle. e, Bobsled. f, Curling stone.

No. 1796, vert.: a, Ski jumping. b, Speed skating. c, Alpine skiing. d, Figure skating.

**2014, Mar. 5 Litho. *Perf. 12***

**1795** A427 $3.15 Sheet of 6, #a-f 14.00 14.00
**1796** A427 $4.75 Sheet of 4, #a-d 14.00 14.00

No. 1796 contains four 30x50mm stamps.

World War I, Cent. — A428

No. 1797, $3.15: a, Recruitment station, Trafalgar Square, London, 1914. b, Man wearing body armor, 1915. c, French machine gunners take position, 1917. d, Fort Brady, 1915. e, World War I photographer, 1917. f, Medical officer in a gas mask, 1915.

No. 1798, $3.15 — War posters from: a, France, 1915. b, Great Britain, 1914. c, United States, 1914. d, Germany, 1914. e, Australia, 1914. f, Italy, 1914.

No. 1799, $5: a, French soldiers in a trench at Berry-au-Bac, 1914. b, French soldier standing in the entrance to a trench, 1914.

No. 1800, $5 — War recruitment posters from: a, Great Britain, 1914. b, United States, 1917.

**2014, Mar. 5 Litho. *Perf. 12¾***

**Sheets of 6, #a-f**

**1797-1798** A428 Set of 2 28.00 28.00

**Souvenir Sheets of 2, #a-b**

**1799-1800** A428 Set of 2 15.00 15.00

Characters from *Downton Abbey* Television Series — A429

No. 1801: a, Anna. b, Ivy. c, Daisy. d, Alfred Nugent.
$9, Tom Branson and Lady Sybil Crawley, horiz.

**2014, Mar. 5 Litho. *Perf. 14***

**1801** A429 $3.25 Sheet of 4, #a-d 9.75 9.75

**Souvenir Sheet**

**1802** A429 $9 multi 6.75 6.75

Worldwide Fund for Nature (WWF) — A430

Nos. 1803 and 1804 — Caribbean reef shark: a, One shark, nose pointing to UR. b, Two sharks and fish. c, One shark with nose pointing to UL and fish. d, One shark with nose pointing left and fish.

**2014, Apr. 2 Litho. *Perf. 14***

**1803** A430 $2.50 Block or vert. strip of 4, #a-d 7.50 7.50
**1804** A430 $2.75 Block or vert. strip of 4, #a-d 8.25 8.25

Berlin Wall Graffiti Art — A431

No. 1805: a, Dove, ball and chain. b, Pink stylized face. c, Reproduction of inner left cover of Pink Floyd's *The Wall* album (Marching hammers and broken wall). d, Soldier and barbed wire. e, Hand with upraised, chained thumb. f, Hands at prison window, chain.
No. 1806: a, Two stylized heads. b, Reproduction of inner right cover of Pink Floyd's *The Wall* album (mother, teacher and creature).

**2014, June 23 Litho. *Perf. 12¾***

**1805** A431 $3 Sheet of 6, #a-f 13.50 13.50

**Souvenir Sheet**

**1806** A431 $5 Sheet of 2, #a-b 7.50 7.50

Fall of Berlin Wall, 25th anniv.

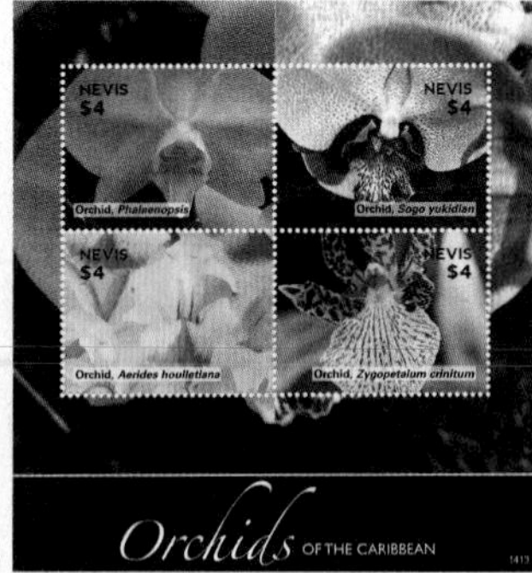


Orchids — A432

No. 1807: a, Phalaenopsis. b, Phalaenopsis Sogo Yukidian. c, Aerides houllettiana. d, Zygopetalum crinitum.
No. 1808: a, Laelia gouldiana. b, Miltonia regnellii. c, Epidendrum fulgens. d, Cattleya alaorii.
No. 1809, vert.: a, Pink phalaenopsis, diff. b, Miltonia. No. 1810, vert.: a, Yellow phalaenopsis. b, Miltoniopsis.

**2014, July 7 Litho. *Perf. 14***

**1807** A432 $4 Sheet of 4, #a-d 12.00 12.00
**1808** A432 $4 Sheet of 4, #a-d 12.00 12.00

**Souvenir Sheet**

**1809** A432 $9 Sheet of 2, #a-b 13.50 13.50
**1810** A432 $9 Sheet of 2, #a-b 13.50 13.50

Nevis Financial Services Department, 30th Anniv. A433

Background color: 30c, Purple. $2, Greenish blue. $5, Blue.

**2014, June 20 Litho. *Perf. 13¼***

**1811-1813** A433 Set of 3 5.50 5.50

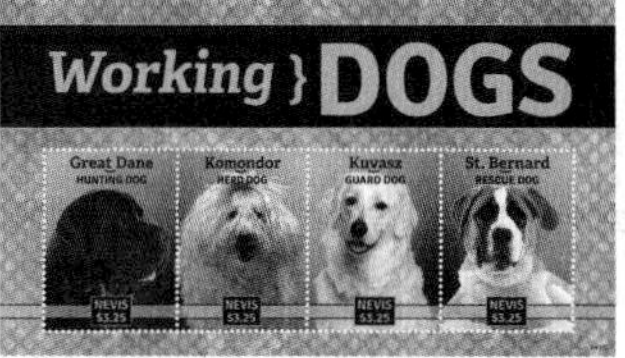


Dogs — A434

No. 1814, $3.25: a, Great Dane. b, Komondor. c, Kuvasz. d, St. Bernard.
No. 1815, $3.25: a, Italian greyhound. b, Pomeranian. c, Chihuahua. d, Japanese chin.
No. 1816, $5: a, Newfoundland. b, Alaskan malamute.
No. 1817, $5: a, Mini pinshcer. b, Chinese crested.

**2014, Aug. 14 Litho. *Perf. 14***

**Sheets of 4, #a-d**

**1814-1815** A434 Set of 2 19.50 19.50

**Souvenir Sheets of 2, #a-b**

**1816-1817** A434 Set of 2 15.00 15.00

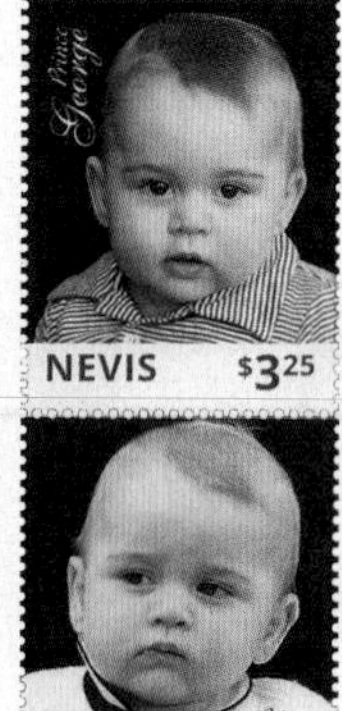


A435

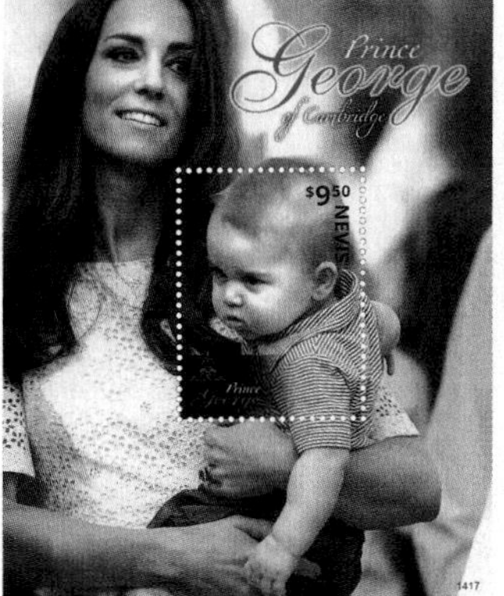


Prince George of Cambridge — A436

No. 1818 — Prince George wearing: a, Blue and white striped shirt. b, White shirt.
No. 1819, $9.50, Prince George (shown). No. 1820, $9.50, Prince George (close-up).

**2014, Aug. 14 Litho. *Perf. 14***

**1818** A435 $3.25 Vert. pair, #a-b 5.00 5.00

**Souvenir Sheets**

***Perf. 12***

**1819-1820** A436 Set of 2 14.00 14.00

No. 1818 was printed in sheets containing three pairs. One example of No. 1818b has a different background, showing the shirt and tie of Prince William.

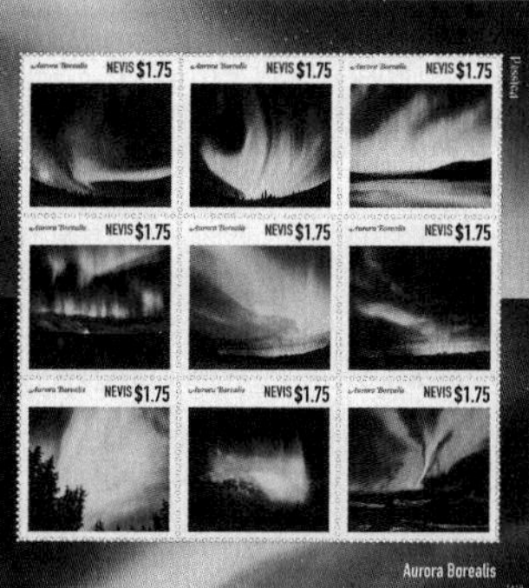


Aurora Borealis — A437

No. 1821, Various depictions of the Aurora Borealis, as shown.
$10, Aurora Borealis, diff.

**2014, Sept. 3 Litho. *Perf. 13¾***

**1821** A437 $1.75 Sheet of 9, #a-i 12.00 12.00

**Souvenir Sheet**

**1822** A437 $10 multi 7.50 7.50

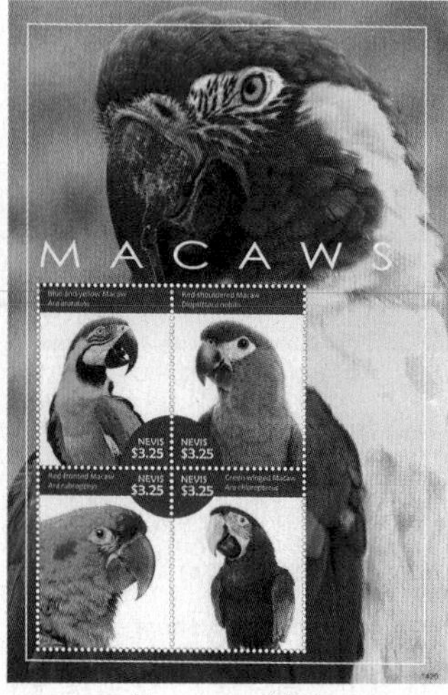


Macaws — A438

No. 1823, $3.25: a, Blue and yellow macaw. b, Red-shouldered macaw. c, Red-fronted macaw. d, Green-winged macaw.
No. 1824, $3.25: a, Indigo macaw. b, Hyacinth macaw. c, Blue-headed macaw. d, Great green macaw.
No. 1825, $5: a, Scarlet macaaw. b, Golden-collared macaw.
No. 1826, $5: a, Blue and yellow macaw, diff. b, Blue-throated macaw.

**2014, Sept. 3 Litho. *Perf. 14***

**Sheets of 4, #a-d**

**1823-1824** A438 Set of 2 19.50 19.50

**Souvenir Sheets of 2, #a-b**

**1825-1826** A438 Set of 2 15.00 15.00

Ducks — A439

No. 1827, $3.25: a, Marbled duck. b, Tufted duck. c, Barrow's goldeneye. d, King eider.
No. 1828, $3.25: a, Wood duck. b, Rosy-billed pochard. c, Puna teal. d, Maned duck.
No. 1829, $10, Indian whistling ducks, vert. No. 1830, $10, Yellow-billed ducks, vert.

**2014, Sept. 4 Litho. *Perf. 13¾***

**Sheets of 4, #a-d**

**1827-1828** A439 Set of 2 19.50 19.50

**Souvenir Sheets**

***Perf. 12***

**1829-1830** A439 Set of 2 15.00 15.00

Nos. 1829-1830 each contain one 30x40mm stamp.

A440

Coral Reefs — A441

Various corals and fish, as shown.

**2014, Sept. 4 Litho. *Perf. 12***

**1831** A440 $3.25 Sheet of 8, #a-h 19.50 19.50

**Souvenir Sheet**

**1832** A441 $5 Sheet of 2, #a-b 7.50 7.50

Visit of Pope Francis to Israel A442

Designs: $1.25, Pope Francis seated with Israeli President Shimon Peres.

No. 1834 — Pope Francis: a, Standing at Church of the Holy Sepulchre. b, Kneeling at Church of the Holy Sepulchre. c, At Yad Vashem Holocaust Museum. d, At Dome of the Rock.

No. 1835, $9.50, Pope Francis facing left. and praying at Yad Vashem Holocaust Museum. No. 1836, $9.50, Pope Francis facing right and praying at the Wailing Wall.

**2014, Oct. 14 Litho. *Perf. 14***

**1833** A442 $1.25 multi .95 .95

***Perf. 12***

**1834** A442 $3.25 Sheet of 4, #a-d 9.75 9.75

**Souvenir Sheets**

**1835-1836** A442 Set of 2 14.00 14.00

Cicely Tyson, Actress — A443

**2014, Jan. 1 Litho. *Perf. 14***

**1837** A443 $3.25 multi 2.40 2.40

No. 1837 was printed in sheets of 4.

40th Culturama Festival — A444

Designs: $5, Crowd watching perfomers. No. 1839, $10, Dancers and crowd.

No. 1840, $10, King Meeko and King Dis and Dat, musicians.

**2014, Aug. 1 Litho. *Perf. 13¼x12½***

**1838-1839** A444 Set of 2 11.00 11.00

**Souvenir Sheet**

***Perf. 12x12½***

**1840** A444 $10 multi 7.50 7.50

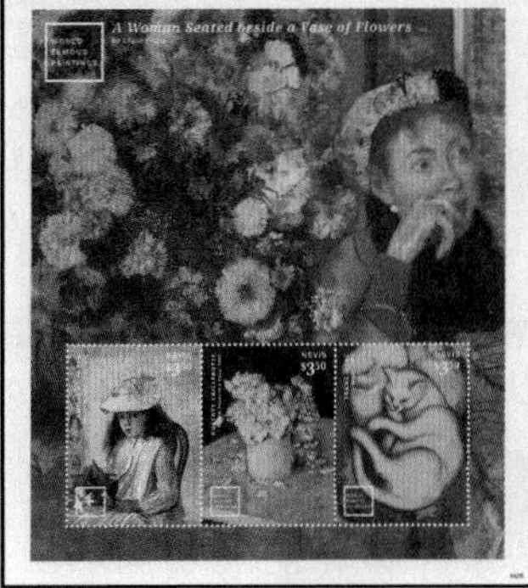

Paintings — A445

No. 1841, $3.50: a, The Artist's Daughter, by Camille Pissarro. b, Yellow Roses in a Vase, by Gustave Caillebotte. c, Kitten, by Franz Marc.

No. 1842, $3.50: a, Clump of Chrysanthemums, by Caillebotte. b, Woman Combing Her Hair, by Edgar Degas. c, Still Life with a Curtain, by Paul Gauguin.

No. 1843, $10, Road in Maine, by Edward Hopper. No. 1844, $10, Baby Reaching for an Apple, by Mary Cassatt.

**2014, Oct. 14 Litho. *Perf. 12¾x12½***

**Sheets of 3, #a-c**

**1841-1842** A445 Set of 2 15.50 15.50

**Size:100x100mm**

***Imperf***

**1843-1844** A445 Set of 2 15.00 15.00

Christmas A446

Paintings by Raphael: 30c, Madonna of Foligno. 90c, The Transfiguration. $2, Madonna of Loreto. $5, Madonna del Baldacchino.

**2014, Oct. 24 Litho. *Perf. 12½***

**1845-1848** A446 Set of 4 6.00 6.00

Steam Locomotives of 1857 — A447

No. 1849, $3.25: a, Queen Class of Engines. b, Fourth and Fifth Lots Coupled. c, Eight Feet Passenger Engine. d, Third Lot Coupled.

No. 1850, $3.25: a, Five Feet Tank Engine. b, Sixth and Seventh Lots Coupled. c, Bogie Engine. d, Six Feet Tank Engine.

No. 1851, $10, Seven Feet Coupled Engine. No. 1852, $10, 6 Feet 6 Inches Coupled.

**2014, Nov. 3 Litho. *Perf. 12***

**Sheets of 4, #a-d**

**1849-1850** A447 Set of 2 19.50 19.50

**Souvenir Sheets**

**1851-1852** A447 Set of 2 15.00 15.00

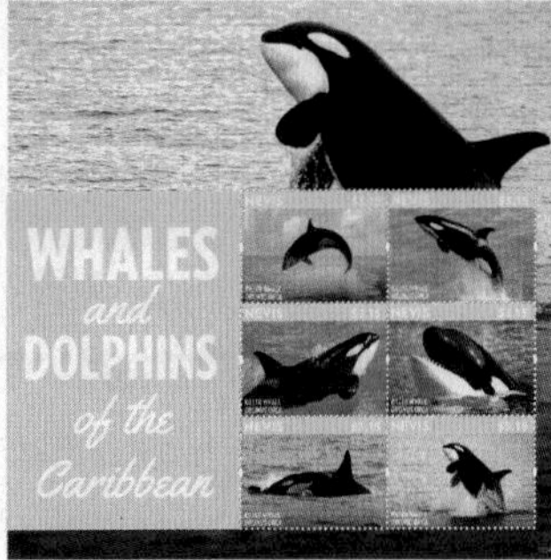

A448

Whales and Dolphins — A449

No. 1853, Various photographs of killer whale, as shown.

No. 1854, Various photographs of humpback whale, as shown.

No. 1855, $10, Pygmy killer whale. No. 1856, $10, Sperm whale.

***Perf. 13 Syncopated***

**2014, Dec. 16 Litho.**

**1853** A448 $3.15 Sheet of 6, #a-f 14.00 14.00

**1854** A449 $3.25 Sheet of 4, #a-d 9.75 9.75

**Souvenir Sheets**

**1855-1856** A449 Set of 2 15.00 15.00

Rosetta Mission — A450

No. 1857: a, Philae landing on Comet 67P. b, Philae passing Earth. c, Philae passing Mars. d, Philae break away.

$10, Philae's descent to Comet 67P.

**2015, Jan. 1 Litho. *Perf. 13¾***

**1857** A450 $3.25 Sheet of 4, #a-d 9.75 9.75

**Souvenir Sheet**

**1858** A450 $10 multi 7.50 7.50

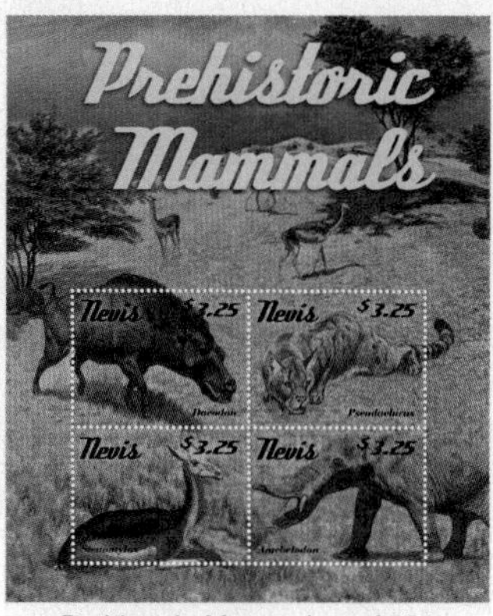

Prehistoric Mammals — A451

No. 1859, $3.25: a, Daeodon. b, Pseudaelurus. c, Stenomylus. d, Amebelodon.

No. 1860, $3.25: a, Megacerops. b, Synthetoceras. c, Merychyrus. d, Prosthennops.

No. 1861, $10, Saber-toothed cat. No. 1862, $10, Woolly mammoth.

**2015, Jan. 21 Litho. *Perf. 14***

**Sheets of 4, #a-d**

**1859-1860** A451 Set of 2 19.50 19.50

**Souvenir Sheets**

***Perf. 12***

**1861-1862** A451 Set of 2 15.00 15.00

Volcanoes — A452

No. 1863: a, Klyuchevskoy Volcano, Russia (80x30mm). b, Popocatépetl Volcano, Mexico (40x30mm). c, Kamchatka Volcano, Russia (40x60mm). d, Kilauea Volcano, U.S. (40x30mm). e, Nevis Peak, Nevis (40x30mm). f, Yasur Volcano, Vanuatu (40x30mm).

$10, Mt. Fuji, Japan.

**2015, Mar. 2 Litho. *Perf. 14***

**1863** A452 $3.15 Sheet of 6, #a-f 14.00 14.00

**Souvenir Sheet**

***Perf. 12***

**1864** A452 $10 multi 7.50 7.50

No. 1864 contains one 65x32mm triangular stamp.

Birds — A453

No. 1865: a, Scarlet ibis on tree branch. b, Greater flamingo. c, Scarlet ibis on rock with wings extended. d, Roseate spoonbill. e, Scarlet ibis on rock looking left. f, Caribbean flamingo.

$10, Caribbean flamingo, diff.

**2015, Mar. 2 Litho. *Perf. 14***

**1865** A453 $4 Sheet of 6, #a-f 18.00 18.00

**Souvenir Sheet**

**1866** A453 $10 multi 7.50 7.50

No. 1866 contains one 30x80mm stamp.

Loggerhead Sea Turtles — A454

No. 1867, Various photographs.
$10, Loggerhead sea turtle, diff.

**2015, Mar. 24 Litho. *Perf. 14***

**1867** A454 $3.15 Sheet of 6, #a-f 14.00 14.00

**Souvenir Sheet**

***Perf. 12***

**1868** A454 $10 multi 7.50 7.50

Pope Benedict XVI — A455

No. 1869: a, Pope Benedict XVI on balcony with arms extended. b, Pope Benedict XVI wearing red zucchetto. c, Smoke announcing election of Pope Benedict XVI. d, Crowd at inauguration of Pope Benedict XVI. e, Pope Benedict XVI wearing miter. f, Pope Benedict XVI wearing white zucchetto.
$10, Pope Benedict XVI seated.

**2015, Mar. 24 Litho. *Perf. 14***

**1869** A455 $3.15 Sheet of 6, #a-f 14.00 14.00

**Souvenir Sheet**

***Perf. 12***

**1870** A455 $10 multi 7.50 7.50

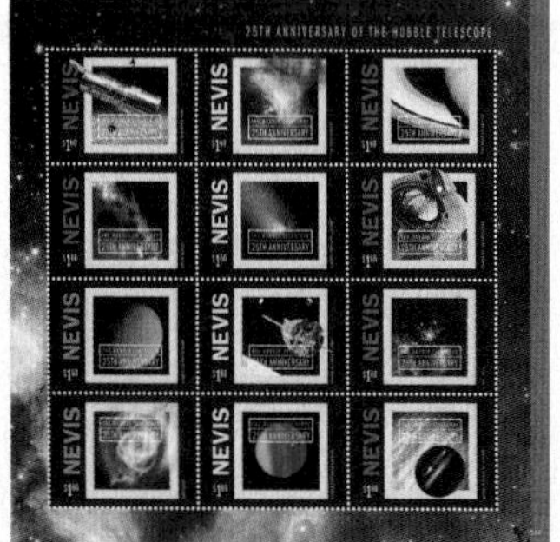

Hubble Space Telescope, 25th Anniv. — A456

No. 1871: a, Hubble Space Telescope above Earth. b, Crab Nebula. c, Rings of Saturn. d, Orion Nebula. e, Comet. f, Astronaut repairing telescope. g, Mars. h, Hubble Space Telescope, Earth at LL corner. i, NGC 3603. j, NGC 6543. k, Neptune. l, A moon in front of Jupiter.
$10, Hubble Space Telescope, diff.

**2015, Mar. 24 Litho. *Perf. 14***

**1871** A456 $1.60 Sheet of 12, #a-l 14.50 14.50

**Souvenir Sheet**

***Perf. 12½***

**1872** A456 $10 multi 7.50 7.50

No. 1872 contains one 51x38mm stamp.

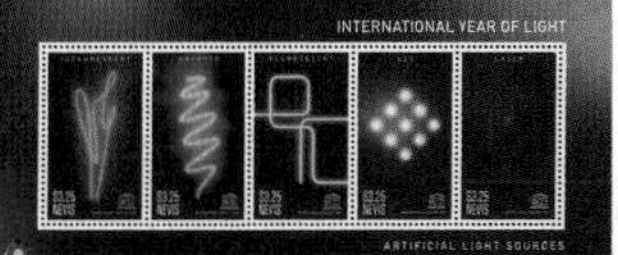

International Year of Light — A457

No. 1873 — UNESCO emblem, light and inscription: a, Incandescent. b, Halogen. c, Fluorescent. d, LED. e, Laser.
$10, UNESCO emblem and "2015 / International / Year of / Light."

**2015, Apr. 15 Litho. *Perf. 12***

**1873** A457 $3.25 Sheet of 5, #a-e 12.00 12.00

**Souvenir Sheet**

***Perf. 12¾***

**1874** A457 $10 multi 7.50 7.50

No. 1874 contains one 38x51mm stamp.

English Lighthouses — A458

No. 1875: a, Roker Pier Lighthouse. b, Beachy Head Lighthouse. c, New Lighthouse at Dungeness. d, Smeaton's Tower. e, St. Catherine's Lighthouse. f, Flamborough Head Lighthouse.
$10, Needles Lighthouse.

**2015, Apr. 15 Litho. *Perf. 14***

**1875** A458 $3.15 Sheet of 6, #a-f 14.00 14.00

**Souvenir Sheet**

**1876** A458 $10 multi 7.50 7.50

Europhilex Stamp Exhibition, London.

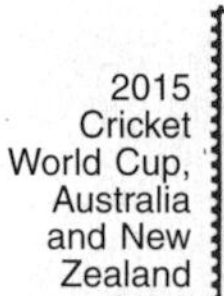

2015 Cricket World Cup, Australia and New Zealand A459

Designs: $4, Hagley Oval, Christchurch, New Zealand.
$10, Cricket World Cup, vert.

**2015, May 4 Litho. *Perf. 14***

**1877** A459 $4 multi 3.00 3.00

**Souvenir Sheet**

***Perf. 12***

**1878** A459 $10 multi 7.50 7.50

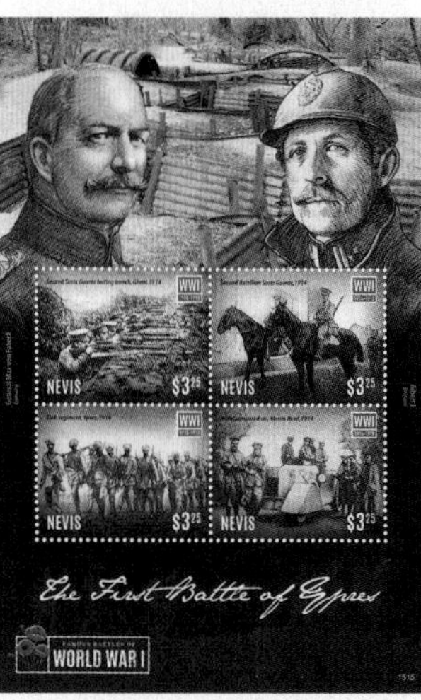

First Battle of Ypres, Cent. (in 2014) — A460

No. 1879: a, Second Scots Guards testing trench, Ghent. b, Second Battalion Scots Guards. c, Sikh Regiment, Ypres. d, Naval armored car, Menin Road.
$10, British medics aid wounded comrade.

**2015, Nov. 1 Litho. *Perf. 12***

**1879** A460 $3.25 Sheet of 4, #a-d 9.75 9.75

**Souvenir Sheet**

***Perf. 12½***

**1880** A460 $10 multi 7.50 7.50

No. 1880 contains one 51x38mm stamp.

Christmas — A461

Paintings by Bartolomé Esteban Murillo: 30c, The Annunciation. 90c, Nativity. $2, Madonna and Child. $5, Adoration of the Shepherds.

**2015, Nov. 2 Litho. *Perf. 14***

**1881-1884** A461 Set of 4 6.00 6.00

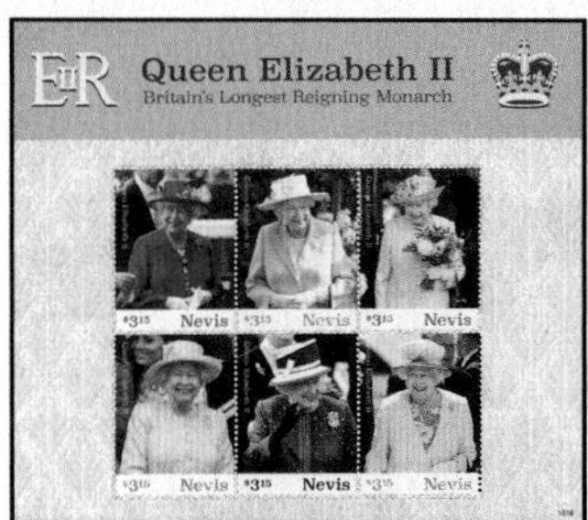

Queen Elizabeth II, Longest-Reigning British Monarch — A462

No. 1885 — Various photographs of Queen Elizabeth II with denomination in: a, Magenta. b, Turquoise green. c, Violet gray. d, Ochre, e, Black. f, Gray.
$10, Queen Elizabeth II wearing pink and white dress.

**2015, Nov. 25 Litho. *Perf. 14***

**1885** A462 $3.15 Sheet of 6, #a-f 14.00 14.00

**Souvenir Sheet**

***Perf. 12¾***

**1886** A462 $10 multi 7.50 7.50

No. 1886 contains one 38x51mm stamp.

Flowers — A463

No. 1887: a, Royal poinciana. b, Hibiscus. c, Bromeliad. d, Paper flower. e, Moth orchid. f, Flamingo flower.
$10, Red palulu, vert.

**2015, Dec. 7 Litho. *Perf. 14***

**1887** A463 $3.15 Sheet of 6, #a-f 14.00 14.00

**Souvenir Sheet**

***Perf. 12***

**1888** A463 $10 multi 7.50 7.50

No. 1888 contains one 30x50mm stamp.

Bank of Nevis Limited, 30th Anniv. A464

Designs: 30c, Bank building. 90c, Bank building, diff. $5, Sir Simeon Daniel (1934-2012), premier of Nevis, bank founder, vert.

**2015, Dec. 9 Litho. *Perf. 14***

**1889-1891** A464 Set of 3 4.75 4.75

Kingfishers — A465

No. 1892: a, Belted kingfisher. b, Ringed kingfisher. c, Green and rufous kingfisher. d, Green kingfisher, showing breast. e, Amazon kingfisher. f, Green kingfisher, showing back.
$10, Belted kingfisher in flight.

**2015, Dec. 17 Litho. *Perf. 13¾***

**1892** A465 $3.15 Sheet of 6, #a-f 14.00 14.00

**Souvenir Sheet**

**1893** A465 $10 multi 7.50 7.50

Visit of Pope Francis to New York City — A466

No. 1894, Various photographs of Pope Francis, as shown.
$10, Pope Francis looking forward with left arm raised.

**2015, Dec. 17 Litho. *Perf. 14***

**1894** A466 $3.15 Sheet of 6, #a-f 14.00 14.00

**Souvenir Sheet**

***Perf. 12***

**1895** A466 $10 multi 7.50 7.50

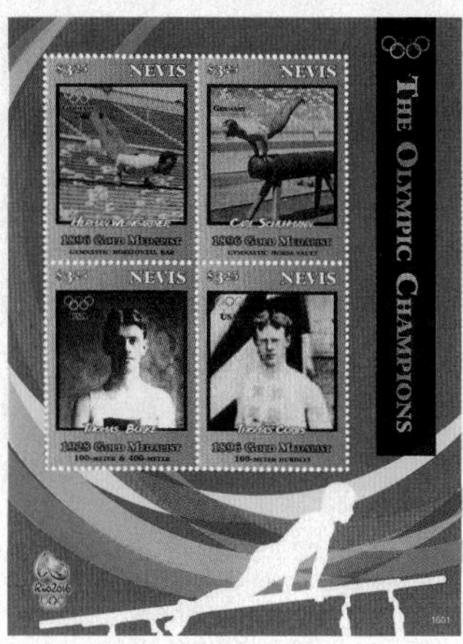

1896 Olympic Champions — A467

No. 1896: a, Herman Weingärtner, horizontal bar. b, Carl Schuhmann, horse vault. c, Thomas Burke, 100-meter and 400-meter race. d, Thomas Curtis, 100-meter hurdles.
$10, Alfred Flatow, parallel bars.

**2015, Dec. 21 Litho. *Perf. 14***

**1896** A467 $3.25 Sheet of 4, #a-d 9.75 9.75

**Souvenir Sheet**

***Perf. 12½***

**1897** A467 $10 multi 7.50 7.50

No. 1897 contains one 38x51mm stamp.

Dolphins — A468

No. 1898: a, Rough-toothed dolphin. b, Atlantic spotted dolphin. c, Striped dolphin. d, Common bottlenose dolphin. e, Risso's dolphin. f, Fraser's dolphin.
$10, Short-beaked common dolphin.

**2016, Jan. 28 Litho. *Perf. 14***

**1898** A468 $4 Sheet of 6, #a-f 18.00 18.00

**Souvenir Sheet**

***Perf. 12***

**1899** A468 $10 multi 7.50 7.50

No. 1899 contains one 80x30mm stamp.

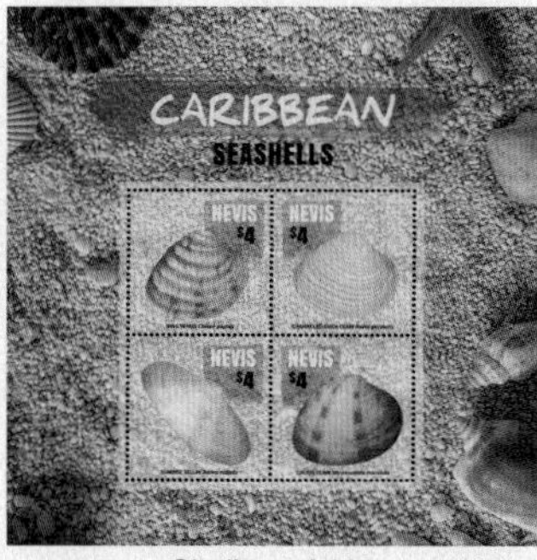

Shells — A469

No. 1900: a, King venus. b, Channeled duck clam. c, Sunrise tellin. d, Calico clam.
$10, Royal comb venus, horiz.

**2016, Jan. 28 Litho. *Perf. 13¾***

**1900** A469 $4 Sheet of 4, #a-d 12.00 12.00

**Souvenir Sheet**

***Perf. 12½***

**1901** A469 $10 multi 7.50 7.50

No. 1901 contains one 51x38mm stamp.

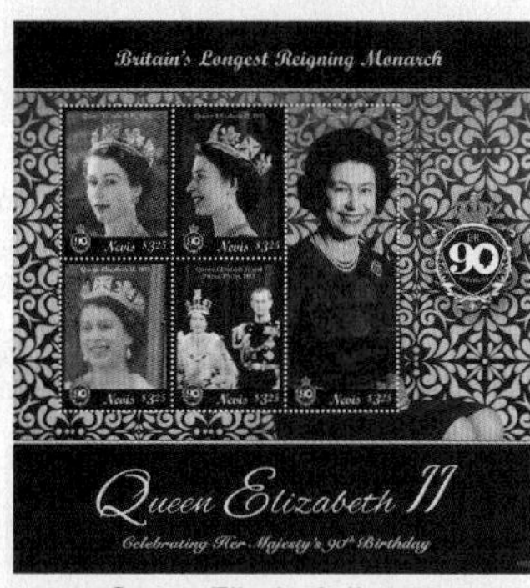

Queen Elizabeth II, 90th Birthday — A470

No. 1902: a, Queen Elizabeth II wearing pearl necklace (30x40mm). b, Queen Elizabeth II wearing long earring, looking left (30x40mm). c, Queen Elizabeth II wearing teardrop earrings (30x40mm). d, Queen Elizabeth II and Prince Philip (30x40mm). e, Queen Elizabeth II in 1970 (30x80mm).
$13, Queen Elizabeth II in 1987.

**2016, Apr. 1 Litho. *Perf. 14***

**1902** A470 $3.25 Sheet of 5, #a-e 12.00 12.00

**Souvenir Sheet**

***Perf. 12***

**1903** A470 $13 multi 9.75 9.75

No. 1903 contains one 30x50mm stamp.

2016 World Stamp Show, New York — A471

No. 1904 — New York City landmarks: a, Central Park. b, Statue of Liberty. c, Grand Central Terminal. d, Brooklyn Bridge.
$8, New York skyline.

**2016, Apr. 29 Litho. *Perf. 12***

**1904** A471 $4 Sheet of 4, #a-d 12.00 12.00

**Souvenir Sheet**

***Perf. 14***

**1905** A471 $8 multi 6.00 6.00

No. 1905 contains one 60x80mm stamp.

September 11, 2001 Terrorist Attacks, 15th Anniv. — A472

No. 1906: a, Flag on World Trade Center rubble. b, World Trade Center. c, New York firefighters at World Trade Center. d, Pentagon 9/11 Memorial. e, Flight 93 National Memorial. f, 9/11 Memorial, Staten Island, New York.
No. 1907: a, Flag hanging from Pentagon. b, Pentagon. c, World Trade Center, diff. d, Tribute in Light.
$14, Tribute in Light, diff.

**2016, May 26 Litho. *Perf. 13¾***

**1906** A472 $3.25 Sheet of 6, #a-f 14.50 14.50

**1907** A472 $3.50 Sheet of 4, #a-d 10.50 10.50

**Souvenir Sheet**

**1908** A472 $14 multi 10.50 10.50

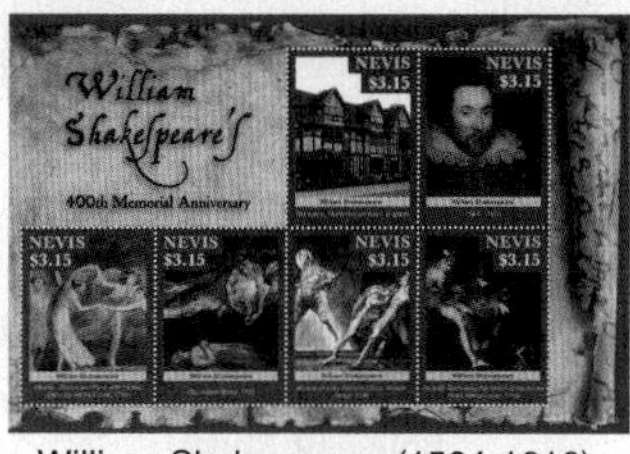

William Shakespeare (1564-1616), Writer — A473

No. 1909: a, Shakespeare's birthplace, Stratford-on-Avon, England. b, Shakespeare. c, Oberon, Titania and Puck with Fairies Dancing, painting by Henry Fuseli. d, Pity, painting by William Blake. e, Hamlet and His Father's Ghost, painting by Blake. f, Macbeth Consulting the Vision of the Armed Head, painting by Fuseli.
$12, Shakespeare, diff.

**2016, June 1 Litho. *Perf. 12½***

**1909** A473 $3.15 Sheet of 6, #a-f 14.00 14.00

**Souvenir Sheet**

***Perf.***

**1910** A473 $12 multi 9.00 9.00

No. 1910 contains one 33x43mm oval stamp.

Pres. Barack Obama's Visit to Saudi Arabia — A474

No. 1911: a, Pres. Obama, U.S. flag (40x60mm). b, Pres. Obama behind microphone (80x30mm). c, King Salman of Saudi Arabia (40x60mm). d, Pres. Obama and King Salman standing in front of emblem (40x30mm). e, Pres. Obama and King Salman walking (40x30mm).
No. 1912: a, Pres. Obama, U.S. flag. b, King Salman, Saudi Arabia flag.

**2016, Oct. 18 Litho. *Perf. 14***

**1911** A474 $4 Sheet of 5, #a-e 15.00 15.00

**Souvenir Sheet**

***Perf. 12½***

**1912** A474 $7 Sheet of 2, #a-b 10.50 10.50

No. 1912 contains two 38x51mm stamps.

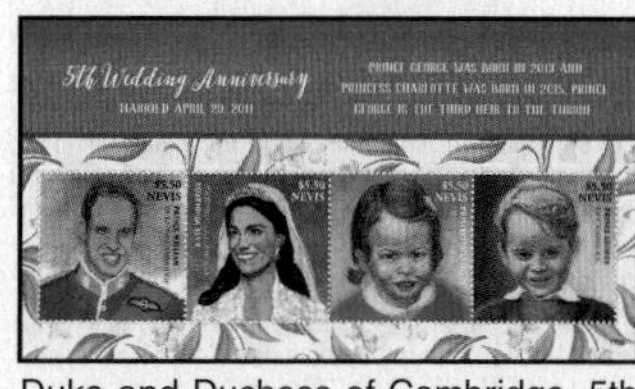

Duke and Duchess of Cambridge, 5th Wedding Anniversary — A475

No. 1913: a, Duke of Cambridge. b, Duchess of Cambridge. c, Princess Charlotte. d, Prince George.
$10, Duke and Duchess of Cambridge kissing at wedding, vert.

**2017, Mar. 14 Litho. *Perf. 13¾***

**1913** A475 $5.50 Sheet of 4, #a-d 16.50 16.50

**Souvenir Sheet**

***Perf. 12½***

**1914** A475 $10 multi 7.50 7.50

No. 1914 contains one 38x51mm stamp.

Princess Diana (1961-97) — A476

No. 1915 — Princess Diana: a, With Princes William and Harry, horse. b, Carrying Prince Harry. c, With Princes William and Harry on fence. d, Leaning over Prince William's shoulder. e, With Princes William and Harry, wearing suits. f, With hands together talking to Prince William.
No. 1916 — Princess Diana, Princes Charles, William and Harry with: a, Building in background. b, Trees in background.

**2017, Apr. 14 Litho. *Perf. 14***

**1915** A476 $3.50 Sheet of 6, #a-f 15.50 15.50

**Souvenir Sheet**

**1916** A476 $7.50 Sheet of 2, #a-b 11.00 11.00

*Star Trek* Television Shows, 50th Anniv. (in 2016) — A477

No. 1917 — Scenes from *Star Trek: The Next Generation* episodes: a, The Pegasus. b, Unification II. c, Q Who. d, Deja Q. e, Rascals. f, All Good Things. . .
$12, Scene from Darmok episode.

**2017, Apr. 24 Litho. *Perf. 12***

**1917** A477 $4 Sheet of 6, #a-f 18.00 18.00

**Souvenir Sheet**

***Perf. 12½***

**1918** A477 $12 multi 9.00 9.00

No. 1918 contains one 51x38mm stamp.

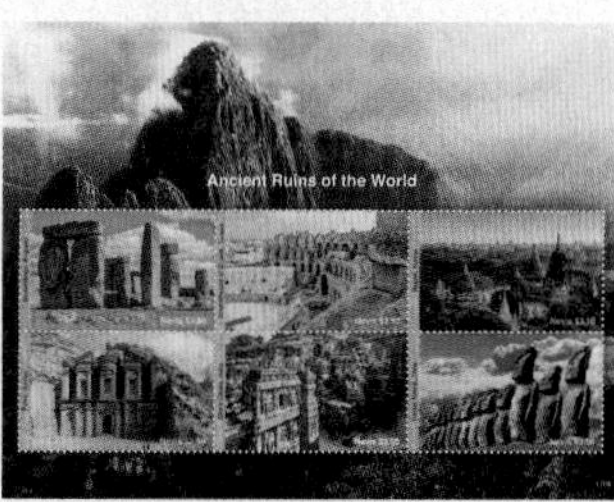

Ancient Ruins — A478

No. 1919: a, Stonehenge, England. b, Amphitheater of El Djem, Tunisia. c, Bagan, Burma. d, Petra, Jordan. e, Ellora Caves, India. f, Moai, Easter Island, Chile.
$10, Machu Picchu, Peru.

**2017, June 7 Litho. *Perf. 12***

**1919** A478 $3.50 Sheet of 6, #a-f 15.50 15.50

**Souvenir Sheet**

**1920** A478 $10 multi 7.50 7.50

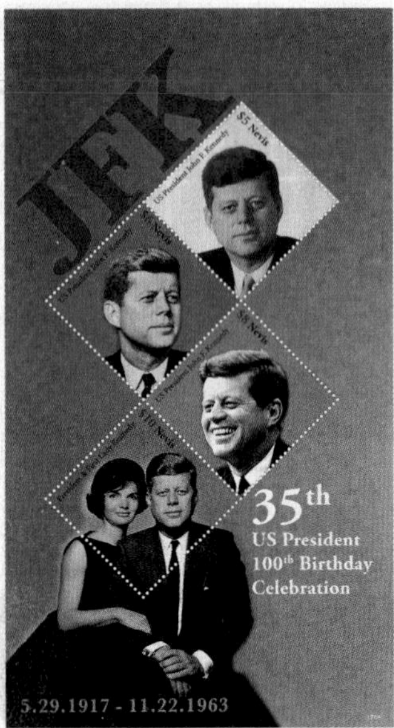


A479

A480

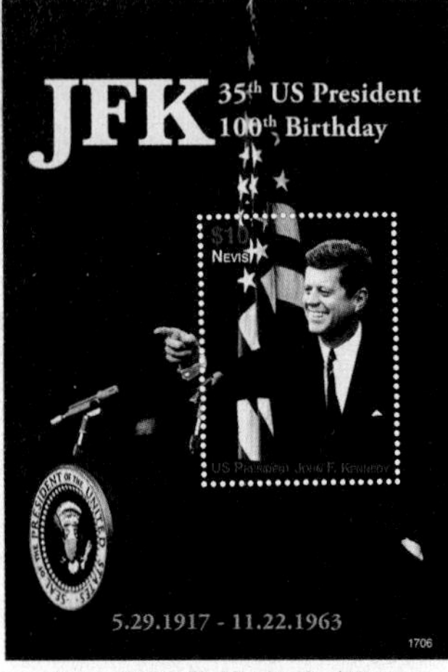


Pres. John F. Kennedy (1917-63) — A481

No. 1921: a, $5, Pres. Kennedy facing forward. b, $6, Pres. Kennedy facing right. c, $8, Pres. Kennedy facing left. d, $10, Pres. Kennedy and wife, Jacqueline.

No. 1922, vert. — Pres. Kennedy: a, Seated at desk. b, Pointing. c, Wearing Navy cap. d, Facing left.

No. 1923, Pres. Kennedy and U.S. flag, vert.

**2017, June 7 Litho. *Perf. 13¾***

**1921** A479 Sheet of 4, #a-d 21.50 21.50

***Perf. 14***

**1922** A480 $5.50 Sheet of 4, #a-d 16.50 16.50

**Souvenir Sheet**

**1923** A481 $10 multi 7.50 7.50

Piping Plovers — A482

No. 1924: a, Chick (entire bird). b, Adult (head).

$10, Two birds, vert.

**2017, June 22 Litho. *Perf.***

**1924** A482 $7.50 Sheet of 2, #a-b 11.00 11.00

**Souvenir Sheet**

***Perf. 12½***

**1925** A482 $10 multi 7.50 7.50

No. 1925 contains one 38x51mm stamp.

Animals — A483

No. 1926: a, Naked mole rat. b, Cydno longwing butterfly. c, Saint Croix sheep. d, Asian garden dormouse.

$15, Cave cricket, vert.

**2017, Apr. 14 Litho. *Perf. 12¾***

**1926** A483 $4 Sheet of 4, #a-d 12.00 12.00

**Souvenir Sheet**

**1927** A483 $15 multi 11.00 11.00

Miniature Sheets

Tree Flowers — A484

No. 1928, $5.50: a, Tulip tree. b, Royal poinciana. c, Shaving brush tree. d, Geiger tree.

No. 1929, $5.50: a, Golden shower tree. b, Jacaranda. c, Japanese cherry. d, Southern magnolia.

**2017, June 22 Litho. *Perf. 14***

**Sheets of 4, #a-d**

**1928-1929** A484 Set of 2 32.50 32.50

Miniature Sheet

Brown Pelicans — A485

No. 1930: a, One pelican in flight. b, Two pelicans in flight. c, Pelican on rock, denomination in black. d, Pelican, denomination in yellow. e, Juvenile pelican facing left. f, Pelican hatchling and egg.

**2017, Sept. 28 Litho. *Perf. 13¾***

**1930** A485 $4 Sheet of 6, #a-f 18.00 18.00

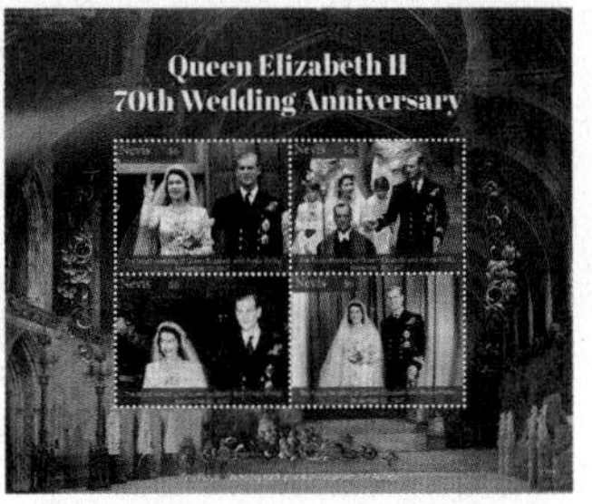


70th Wedding Anniversary of Queen Elizabeth II and Prince Philip — A486

No. 1931: a, Couple, bride waving. b, Couple with attendants. c, Couple passing line of people. d, Formal photograph of couple.

$12, Couple with family and attendants.

**2017, Sept. 28 Litho. *Perf. 14***

**1931** A486 $6 Sheet of 4, #a-d 18.00 18.00

**Souvenir Sheet**

**1932** A486 $12 multi 9.00 9.00

No. 1932 contains one 80x30mm stamp.

Inhabitants of Coral Reefs — A487

No. 1933: a, Diamond blenny. b, Caribbean reef shark. c, Green sea turtle. d, Flamingo tongue snail. e, Fairy basslet. f, Green moray eel.

No. 1934, $12, Longsnout seahorse, vert.

No. 1935, $12, Green sea turtle, vert.

**2017, Dec. 4 Litho. *Perf. 14***

**1933** A487 $4 Sheet of 6, #a-f 18.00 18.00

**Souvenir Sheets**

**1934-1935** A487 Set of 2 18.00 18.00

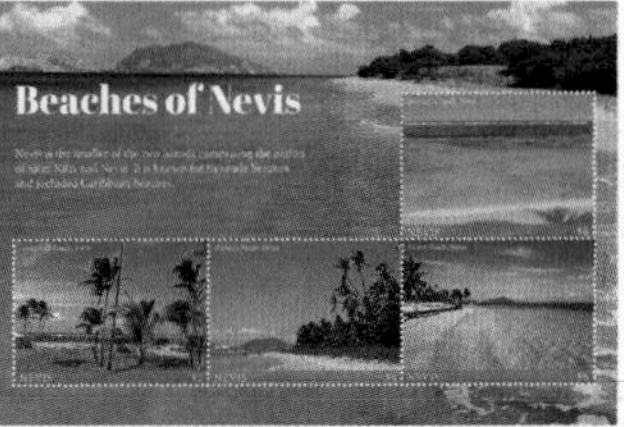


Nevis Beaches — A488

No. 1936: a, $2, Long Haul Beach. b, $4, Pinney's Beach. c, $6, Nisbet Beach. d, $8, Newcastle Beach.

No. 1937: a, $7, Pinney's Beach, diff. b, $8, Oualie Beach.

**2017, Dec. 22 Litho. *Perf. 13¼***

**1936** A488 Sheet of 4, #a-d 15.00 15.00

**Souvenir Sheet**

***Perf. 12½x13¼***

**1937** A488 Sheet of 2, #a-b 11.00 11.00

No. 1937 contains two 40x30mm stamps.

Miniature Sheet

British Royalty — A489

No. 1938: a, Queen Elizabeth II. b, Duke and Duchess of Cambridge. c, Prince George and Princess Charlotte of Cambridge. d, Prince Harry and fiancée Meghan Markle.

**2018, Jan. 24 Litho. *Perf. 12½x13¼***

**1938** A489 $7 Sheet of 4, #a-d 21.00 21.00

---

## OFFICIAL STAMPS

**Catalogue values for unused stamps in this section are for Never Hinged items.**

**Nos. 103-112 Ovptd. "OFFICIAL"**

***Perf. 14½x14***

**1980, July 30 Litho. Wmk. 373**

| | | | | |
|---|---|---|---|---|
| **O1** | A61 | 15c multicolored | .25 | .25 |
| **O2** | A61 | 25c multicolored | .25 | .25 |
| **O3** | A61 | 30c multicolored | .25 | .25 |
| **O4** | A61 | 40c multicolored | .25 | .25 |
| **O5** | A61 | 45c multicolored | .25 | .25 |
| **O6** | A61 | 50c multicolored | .25 | .25 |
| **O7** | A61 | 55c multicolored | .25 | .25 |
| **O8** | A61 | $1 multicolored | .30 | .30 |
| **O9** | A61 | $5 multicolored | 1.60 | 1.60 |
| **O10** | A61 | $10 multicolored | 2.75 | 2.75 |
| | | *Nos. O1-O10 (10)* | 6.40 | 6.40 |

Inverted or double overprints exist on some denominations.

**Nos. 123-134 Ovptd. "OFFICIAL"**

**1981, Mar. *Perf. 14***

| | | | | |
|---|---|---|---|---|
| **O11** | A9 | 15c multicolored | .25 | .25 |
| **O12** | A9 | 20c multicolored | .25 | .25 |
| **O13** | A9 | 25c multicolored | .25 | .25 |
| **O14** | A9 | 30c multicolored | .25 | .25 |
| **O15** | A9 | 40c multicolored | .25 | .25 |
| **O16** | A9 | 45c multicolored | .25 | .25 |
| **O17** | A9 | 50c multicolored | .25 | .25 |
| **O18** | A9 | 55c multicolored | .25 | .25 |
| **O19** | A9 | $1 multicolored | .35 | .35 |
| **O20** | A9 | $2.50 multicolored | .80 | .80 |
| **O21** | A9 | $5 multicolored | 1.60 | 1.60 |
| **O22** | A9 | $10 multicolored | 2.75 | 2.75 |
| | | *Nos. O11-O22 (12)* | 7.50 | 7.50 |

**Nos. 135-140 Ovptd. or Surcharged "OFFICIAL" in Blue or Black**

**1983, Feb. 2**

| | | | | |
|---|---|---|---|---|
| **O23** | A9a | 45c on $2 #137 | .30 | .30 |
| **O24** | A9b | 45c on $2 #138 | .30 | .30 |
| **O25** | A9a | 55c #135 | .40 | .40 |
| **O26** | A9b | 55c #136 | .40 | .40 |

O27 A9a $1.10 on $5 #139 (Bk) .80 .80
O28 A9b $1.10 on $5 #140 (Bk) .80 .80
*Nos. O23-O28 (6)* 3.00 3.00

Inverted or double overprints exist on some denominations.

### Nos. 367-378 Ovptd. "OFFICIAL"

**1985, Jan. 2 Wmk. 380**
O29 A24b 15c multicolored .30 .30
O30 A24b 20c multicolored .30 .30
O31 A24b 30c multicolored .30 .30
O32 A24b 40c multicolored .30 .30
O33 A24b 50c multicolored .35 .35
O34 A24b 55c multicolored .35 .35
O35 A24b 60c multicolored .35 .35
O36 A24b 75c multicolored .45 .45
O37 A24b $1 multicolored .65 .65
O38 A24b $3 multicolored 1.90 1.90
O39 A24b $5 multicolored 3.25 3.25
O40 A24b $10 multicolored 6.50 6.50
*Nos. O29-O40 (12)* 15.00 15.00

### Nos. 640-646, 648-653 Ovptd. "OFFICIAL"

**1993 Litho. *Perf. 14***
O41 A71 5c multicolored .30 .30
O42 A71 10c multicolored .30 .30
O43 A71 15c multicolored .30 .30
O44 A71 20c multicolored .30 .30
O45 A71 25c multicolored .30 .30
O46 A71 40c multicolored .35 .35
O47 A71 50c multicolored .50 .50
O48 A71 75c multicolored .70 .70
O49 A71 80c multicolored .75 .75
O50 A71 $1 multicolored .95 .95
O51 A71 $3 multicolored 2.75 2.75
O52 A71 $5 multicolored 4.75 4.75
O53 A71 $10 multicolored 9.25 9.25
O54 A71 $20 multicolored 18.00 18.00
*Nos. O41-O54 (14)* 39.50 39.50

Dated "1992."

### Nos. 1055-1066 Ovptd. "OFFICIAL"

**1999, Mar. 22 Litho. *Perf. 14***
O55 A151 25c multicolored .25 .25
O56 A151 30c multicolored .25 .25
O57 A151 50c multicolored .40 .40
O58 A151 60c multicolored .45 .45
O59 A151 80c multicolored .60 .60
O60 A151 90c multicolored .70 .70
O61 A151 $1 multicolored .75 .75
O62 A151 $1.80 multicolored 1.40 1.40
O63 A151 $3 multicolored 2.25 2.25
O64 A151 $5 multicolored 3.75 3.75
O65 A151 $10 multicolored 7.50 7.50
O66 A151 $20 multicolored 15.00 15.00
*Nos. O55-O66 (12)* 33.30 33.30

## NEW BRITAIN

'nü 'bri-tən

LOCATION — South Pacific Ocean, northeast of New Guinea
GOVT. — Australian military government
AREA — 13,000 sq. mi. (approx.)
POP. — 50,600 (approx.)
CAPITAL — Rabaul

The island Neu-Pommern, a part of former German New Guinea, was captured during World War I by Australian troops and named New Britain. Following the war it was mandated to Australia and designated a part of the Mandated Territory of New Guinea. See German New Guinea, North West Pacific Islands and New Guinea.

12 Pence = 1 Shilling

### Stamps of German New Guinea, 1900, Surcharged

Kaiser's Yacht "The Hohenzollern"
A3 A4

### First Setting
### Surcharge lines spaced 6mm on 1p-8p, 4mm on 1sh-5sh

***Perf. 14, 14½***

**1914, Oct. 17 Unwmk.**
1 A3 1p on 3pf brown 750.00 875.00
2 A3 1p on 5pf green 95.00 200.00
3 A3 2p on 10pf car 100.00 260.00
4 A3 2p on 20pf ultra 100.00 200.00
a. "2d." dbl., "G.R.I." omitted 6,000.
b. Inverted surcharge 16,500.
5 A3 2½p on 10pf car 105.00 220.00
6 A3 2½p on 20pf ultra 120.00 250.00
a. Inverted surcharge
7 A3 3p on 25pf org & blk, *yel* 375.00 475.00
8 A3 3p on 30pf org & blk, *sal* 475.00 525.00
a. Double surcharge 15,000. 15,000.
b. Triple surcharge
9 A3 4p on 40pf lake & black 475.00 625.00
a. Double surcharge 4,100. 5,000.
b. Inverted surcharge 16,250.
c. "4d." omitted
10 A3 5p on 50pf pur & blk, *sal* 850.00 1,100.
a. Double surcharge 16,250.
11 A3 8p on 80pf lake & blk, *rose* 1,050. 1,650.
a. No period after "8d" 4,600.
b. Surcharged "G.R.I. 4d" (error) 15,250.
12 A4 1sh on 1m car 5,500. 4,750.
13 A4 2sh on 2m blue 3,750. 4,500.
a. Surcharged "G.R.I. 5s" (error) 45,000.
b. Surcharged "G.R.I. 2d" corrected by hand-stamped "s" 55,000.
14 A4 3sh on 3m blk vio 6,000. 7,750.
a. No period after "I" 14,000. 14,000.
15 A4 5sh on 5m slate & car 14,000. 16,500.
a. No period after "I" 18,500. 23,000.
b. Surcharged "G.R.I. 1s" (error) 87,500.

"G.R.I." stands for Georgius Rex Imperator.

### Second Setting
### Surcharge lines spaced 5mm on 1p-8p, 5½mm on 1sh-5sh

**1914, Dec. 16**
16 A3 1p on 3pf brown 110.00 120.00
a. Double surcharge 1,500. 1,850.
b. "I" for "1" 825.00
c. "1" with straight top serif 160.00 190.00
d. Inverted surcharge 6,000. —
e. "4" for "1" 17,500.
f. Small "1" 350.00
g. Double surcharge, one inverted 8,000.
17 A3 1p on 5pf green 37.50 55.00
a. Double surcharge 5,250.
b. "G. I. R." 13,000. 14,000.
c. "d" inverted 3,750.
d. No periods after "G R I" 11,000.
e. Small "1" 140.00 210.00
f. "1d" double —
g. No period after "1d"
h. Triple surcharge
18 A3 2p on 10pf car 50.00 65.00
a. Double surcharge 16,250. 16,250.
b. Dbl. surch., one inverted 13,000.
c. Surcharged "G. I. R., 3d" (error) 13,000.
d. Surcharged "1d" (error) 12,500. 12,500.
e. Period before "G" 11,000.
f. No period after "2d" 200.00 275.00
g. Inverted surcharge
h. "2d" double, one inverted
j. Pair, #18, 20 30,000.
19 A3 2p on 20pf ultra 50.00 75.00
a. Double surcharge 3,500. 5,250.
b. Double surch., one inverted 5,000. 6,500.
c. "R" inverted 9,250.
d. Surcharged "1d" (error) 13,000. 14,000.
f. Inverted surcharge 11,500. 13,500.
h. Pair, one without surcharge 25,000.
i. Vertical pair, #19, 21 20,000. 23,000.
20 A3 2½p on 10pf car 250.00 375.00
21 A3 2½p on 20pf ultra 2,100. 2,500.
a. Double surcharge, one invtd.
b. "2½" triple
c. Surcharged "3d" in pair with normal 42,500.
22 A3 3p on 25pf org & blk, *yel* 190.00 275.00
a. Double surcharge 11,000. 13,000.
b. Inverted surcharge 11,000. 13,000.
c. "G. R. I." only
d. "G. I. R."
e. Pair, one without surcharge 15,000.
f. Surcharged "G. I. R., 5d" (error)
g. Surcharged "1d" (error) 22,000.
23 A3 3p on 30pf org & blk, *sal* 175.00 240.00
a. Double surcharge 4,000. 4,600.
b. Double surcharge, one invtd. 4,500. 5,500.
c. "d" inverted
d. Surcharged "1d" (error) 12,000. 16,000.
e. Triple surcharge
g. Double inverted surcharge 13,000. 14,000.
h. Pair, one without surcharge 14,000.
24 A3 4p on 40pf lake & blk 185.00 300.00
a. Double surcharge 3,500. —
b. Double surcharge, both invtd. 13,000.
c. Double surcharge, one invtd. 5,250.
d. Inverted surcharge 9,250.
e. Surcharged "1d" (error) 9,000.
f. "1" on "4"
g. As "e," inverted 20,000.
h. Surcharge "G.R.I. 3d," double (error) 27,500.
i. No period after "I" 3,500.
25 A3 5p on 50pf pur & blk, *sal* 350.00 400.00
a. Double surcharge 4,500. 5,500.
b. Double surcharge, one invtd. 10,500. 10,500.
c. "5" omitted
d. Inverted surcharge 10,000. 10,000.
e. Double inverted surcharge 13,000. 14,000.
f. "G. I. R."
g. Surcharge "G.R.I. 3d" (error) 23,000.
26 A3 8p on 80pf lake & blk, *rose* 475.00 650.00
a. Double surcharge 7,000. 8,250.
b. Double surcharge, one invtd. 7,000. 8,250.
c. Triple surcharge 9,500. 10,000.
d. No period after "8d"
e. Inverted surcharge 14,000. 14,000.
f. Surcharged "3d" (error) 18,500. 18,500.
27 A4 1sh on 1m car 5,250. 8,250.
a. No period after "I" 12,000.
28 A4 2sh on 2m bl 5,500. 8,750.
a. Surcharged "5s" (error)
b. Double surcharge
c. No period after "I" 13,000.
29 A4 3sh on 3m blk vio 10,000. 16,250.
a. No periods after "R I"
b. "G.R.I." double 45,000.
29C A4 5sh on 5m sl & car 42,500. 45,000.
d. No periods after "R I"
e. Surcharged "1s"

### Nos. 18-19 Surcharged with Large "1"

**1915, Jan.**
29F A3 1(p) on 2p on 10pf carmine 32,500. 30,000.
29G A3 1(p) on 2p on 20pf ultramarine 30,000. 17,500.

### Same Surcharge on Stamps of Marshall Islands

**1914**
30 A3 1p on 3pf brn 110.00 170.00
a. Inverted surcharge 9,250.
31 A3 1p on 5pf green 90.00 130.00
a. Double surcharge 3,800. 5,000.
b. No period after "d"
c. Inverted surcharge 5,250.
32 A3 2p on 10pf car 27.50 50.00
a. Double surcharge 3,800.
b. Double surcharge, one invtd. 5,500.
c. Surcharge sideways 10,500.
d. No period after "2d"
e. No period after "G" 875.00
f. Inverted surcharge 7,000.
33 A3 2p on 20 pf ultra 30.00 50.00
a. No period after "d" 80.00 150.00
b. Double surcharge 4,000. 5,250.
c. Double surcharge, one invtd. 9,750. 10,500.
d. Inverted surcharge 11,000. 11,000.
e. "I" omitted
34 A3 3p on 25pf org & blk, *yel* 475.00 600.00
a. Double surcharge 4,250. 5,000.
b. Double surcharge, one invtd. 4,700.
c. No period after "d" 925.00 1,250.
d. Inverted surcharge 13,000.
35 A3 3p on 30pf org & blk, *sal* 475.00 600.00
a. No period after "d" 925.00 1,200.
b. Inverted surcharge 9,000. 9,500.
c. Double surcharge 7,000.
d. Double surcharge, one invtd.
36 A3 4p on 40pf lake & blk 175.00 250.00
a. No period after "d" 475.00 700.00
b. Double surcharge 7,000. 8,000.
c. "4d" omitted
d. "1d" on "4d"
e. No period after "R"
f. Inverted surcharge 11,000.
g. Surcharged "1d" (error) 17,500.
h. Surcharged "G.R.I. 3d" (error)
37 A3 5p on 50pf pur & blk, *sal* 300.00 375.00
a. "d" omitted 2,250.
b. Double surcharge 10,500.
c. "5d" double
d. Inverted surcharge 16,500.
38 A3 8p on 80pf lake & blk, *rose* 525.00 775.00
a. Inverted surcharge 11,500.
b. Double surcharge 10,000.
c. Double surcharge, one invtd.
d. Triple surcharge 16,500.
e. Double surcharge, both inverted 13,250. 14,000.
39 A4 1sh on 1m car 4,100. 5,500.
a. Double surcharge 45,000.
b. Dbl. surch., one with "s1" for "1s"
c. No period after "I" 6,500. 9,250.
d. Additional surcharge "1d" 50,000.
40 A4 2sh on 2m blue 2,000. 4,500.
a. Double surcharge, one invtd. 45,000. 45,000.
b. Double surcharge 45,000.
c. Large "S"
d. No period after "I" 3,750. 6,500.
41 A4 3sh on 3m blk vio 6,500. 9,750.
a. Double surcharge 42,500. 45,000.
b. No period after "I" 8,750.
c. No period after "R I"
d. Inverted surcharge
42 A4 5sh on 5m sl & car 14,000. 15,000.
a. Double surcharge, one invtd. 75,000.

See Nos. 44-45.

A5

### Surcharged in Black on Registration Label
### Town Name in Sans-Serif Letters

**1914 *Perf. 12***
43 A5 3p black & red (Rabaul) 300.00 350.00
a. Double surcharge (Rabaul) 5,500. 7,000.
44 A5 3p black & red (Friedrich Wilhelmshaven) 275.00 875.00
45 A5 3p black & red (Herbertshohe) 325.00 875.00
46 A5 3p black & red (Kawieng) 350.00 700.00
a. Double surcharge
47 A5 3p black & red (Kieta) 500.00 875.00
a. Pair, one without surcharge 16,500.
48 A5 3p black & red (Manus) 325.00 925.00
a. Double surcharge 9,250.
49 A5 3p black & red (Deulon) 27,500. 30,000.
50 A5 3p black & red (Stephansort) 4,500.

Nos. 44, 46 and 48 exist with town name in letters with serifs. The varieties Deutsch-Neuguinea, Deutsch Neu-Guinea, etc., are known. For detailed listings see the *Scott Classic Specialized Catalogue of Stamps and Covers.*

Nos. 32-33 Surcharged with Large "1"

**1915**
51 A3 1p on 2p on 10pf 275. 300.
a. "1" double 16,500.
b. "1" inverted 20,000. 20,000.
52 A3 1p on 2p on 20pf 4,000. 2,750.
a. "1" inverted 20,000. 20,000.

The stamps of Marshall Islands surcharged "G. R. I." and new values in British currency were all used in New Britain and are therefore listed here.

### Stamps of Marshall Islands Surcharged
### Surcharge lines spaced 6mm apart

53 A3 1p on 3pf brown 3,750.
a. Inverted surcharge 16,000.
54 A3 1p on 5pf green 3,750.
a. Inverted surcharge 16,500.
55 A3 2p on 10pf car 4,750.
56 A3 2p on 20pf ultra 4,250.
a. Inverted surcharge 17,000.
57 A3 2½p on 10pf car 30,000.
58 A3 2½p on 20pf ultra 45,000.
59 A3 3p on 25pf org & blk, *yel* 7,000.
60 A3 3p on 30pf org & blk, *sal* 7,000.
61 A3 4p on 40pf lake & blk 7,000.
a. Inverted surcharge 18,000.
62 A3 5p on 50pf pur & blk, *sal* 6,500.
63 A3 8p on 80pf lake & blk, *rose* 7,500.
a. Inverted surcharge 20,000.

### Surcharge lines spaced 5½mm apart

64 A4 1sh on 1m car 17,500.
a. Large "S" 22,500.
65 A4 2sh on 2m bl 14,500.
a. Large "S" 20,000.
66 A4 3sh on 3m blk vi-ol 30,000.
a. Large "S" 40,000.
67 A4 5sh on 5m sl & car 45,000.
a. Large "S" 52,500.

### OFFICIAL STAMPS

O1

**German New Guinea Nos. 7-8 Surcharged**

**1915 Unwmk. *Perf. 14***
**O1** O1 1p on 3pf brown 36.00 *80.00*
a. Double surcharge 5,500.
**O2** O1 1p on 5pf green 110.00 *150.00*

## NEW CALEDONIA

'nü ˌka-lə-'dō-nyə

LOCATION — Island in the South Pacific Ocean, east of Queensland, Australia
GOVT. — French Overseas Territory
AREA — 7,172 sq. mi.
POP. — 197,361 (1999 est.)
CAPITAL — Noumea

Dependencies of New Caledonia are the Loyalty Islands, Isle of Pines, Huon Islands and Chesterfield Islands.

100 Centimes = 1 Franc

**Catalogue values for unused stamps in this country are for Never Hinged items, beginning with Scott 252 in the regular postage section, Scott B10 in the semi-postal section, Scott C14 in the airpost section, Scott J32 in the postage due section, and Scott O1 in the official section.**

**Watermark**

TOR C
CARTO
TOR C
CARTO

Wmk. 385

Napoleon III — A1

**1859 Unwmk. Litho. *Imperf.***
**Without Gum**
**1** A1 10c black 250.00 250.00

Fifty varieties. Counterfeits abound. See No. 315.

**Type of French Colonies, 1877 Surcharged in Black**

Nos. 2-5

Nos. 6-7

**1881-83**
**2** A8 5c on 40c red, *straw* ('82) 425.00 425.00
a. Inverted surcharge 1,600. 1,600.
b. Double surcharge 1,350.
c. Double surcharge, both inverted 1,900. 1,900.
**3** A8 05c on 40c red, *straw* ('83) 40.00 40.00
**4** A8 25c on 35c dp vio, *yel* 300.00 300.00
a. Inverted surcharge 950.00 950.00
**5** A8 25c on 75c rose car, *rose* ('82) 400.00 400.00
a. Inverted surcharge 1,250. 1,250.

**1883-84**
**6** A8 5c on 40c red, *straw* ('84) 26.50 26.50
a. Inverted surcharge 26.50 26.50
**7** A8 5c on 75c rose car, *rose* ('83) 52.50 52.50
a. Inverted surcharge 75.00 75.00

In type "a" surcharge, the narrower-spaced letters measure 14½mm, and an early printing of No. 4 measures 13½mm. Type "b" letters measure 18mm.

**French Colonies No. 59 Surcharged in Black**

No. 8

Nos. 9-10

**1886 *Perf. 14x13½***
**8** A9 5c on 1fr 32.50 26.50
a. Inverted surcharge 45.00 45.00
b. Double surcharge 200.00 200.00
c. Double surcharge, one inverted 225.00 225.00
**9** A9 5c on 1fr 32.50 30.00
a. Inverted surcharge 60.00 60.00
b. Double surcharge 200.00 200.00
c. Double surcharge, one inverted 225.00 225.00

**French Colonies No. 29 Surcharged**
***Imperf***
**10** A8 5c on 1fr *10,000. 11,500.*

**Types of French Colonies, 1877-86, Surcharged in Black**

Nos. 11, 13

No. 12

**1891-92 *Imperf.***
**11** A8 10c on 40c red, *straw* ('92) 45.00 40.00
a. Inverted surcharge 42.50 37.50
b. Double surcharge 100.00 100.00
c. Double surcharge, one inverted 190.00 190.00
d. No period after "10c" 125.00 125.00

***Perf. 14x13½***
**12** A9 10c on 30c brn, *bis* 25.00 22.50
a. Inverted surcharge 25.00 22.50
b. Double surcharge 67.50 67.50
c. Double surcharge, inverted 60.00 60.00
d. Double surcharge, one inverted 100.00 100.00
**13** A9 10c on 40c red, *straw* ('92) 26.00 26.00
a. Inverted surcharge 26.00 26.00
b. No period after "10c" 60.00 60.00
c. Double surcharge 67.50 67.50
d. Double surcharge, one inverted 110.00 100.00
*Nos. 11-13 (3)* 96.00 88.50

Variety "double surcharge, one inverted" exists on Nos. 11-13. Value slightly higher than for "double surcharge."

Types of French Colonies, 1877-86, Handstamped in Black — g

**1892 *Imperf.***
**16** A8 20c red, *grn* 350.00 *400.00*
a. Inverted surcharge 850.00 900.00
**17** A8 35c violet, *org* 75.00 75.00
a. Pair, one stamp without surcharge 950.00
**18** A8 40c red, *straw* *1,500.*
**19** A8 1fr bronz grn, *straw* 300.00 300.00

The 1c, 2c, 4c and 75c of type A8 are believed not to have been officially made or actually used.

**1892 *Perf. 14x13½***
**23** A9 5c green, *grnsh* 19.00 15.00
a. Pair, one stamp without overprint 600.00
**24** A9 10c blk, *lavender* 140.00 82.50
**25** A9 15c blue 110.00 60.00
a. Pair, one stamp without overprint 825.00
**26** A9 20c red, *grn* 110.00 60.00
**27** A9 25c yellow, *straw* 30.00 22.50
**28** A9 25c black, *rose* 110.00 37.50
**29** A9 30c brown, *bis* 90.00 75.00
**30** A9 35c violet, *org* 240.00 190.00
a. Inverted overprint 650.00
b. Pair, one stamp without overprint 1,350.
**32** A9 75c carmine, *rose* 225.00 190.00
a. Pair, one stamp without overprint 1,350.
**33** A9 1fr bronz grn, *straw* 190.00 175.00
*Nos. 23-33 (10)* 1,264. 907.50

The note following No. 19 also applies to the 1c, 2c, 4c and 40c of type A9.

Surcharged in Blue or Black — h

**1892-93 *Imperf.***
**34** A8 10c on 1fr brnz grn, *straw* (Bl) *5,250. 4,500.*

***Perf. 14x13½***
**35** A9 5c on 20c red, *grn* (Bk) 27.50 22.50
a. Inverted surcharge 125.00 125.00
b. Double surcharge 82.50 100,00
**36** A9 5c on 75c car, *rose* (Bk) 22.50 16.50
a. Inverted surcharge 125.00 125.00
b. Double surcharge 82.50 82.50
**37** A9 5c on 75c car, *rose* (Bl) 18.50 15.00
a. Inverted surcharge 125.00 125.00
b. Double surcharge 82.50 82.50
**38** A9 10c on 1fr brnz grn, *straw* (Bk) 21.00 15.00
a. Inverted surcharge 600.00 600.00
**39** A9 10c on 1fr brnz grn, *straw* (Bl) 22.50 21.00
a. Inverted surcharge 125.00 125.00
b. Double surcharge 85.00 85.00
*Nos. 35-39 (5)* 112.00 90.00

Navigation and Commerce — A12

**1892-1904 Typo. *Perf. 14x13½***
**Name of Colony in Blue or Carmine**
**40** A12 1c black, *blue* 1.10 1.10
**41** A12 2c brown, *buff* 1.90 1.90
**42** A12 4c claret, *lav* 2.50 2.25
**43** A12 5c green, *grnsh* 4.00 1.90
**44** A12 5c yellow green ('00) 2.25 1.50
**45** A12 10c blk, *lavender* 9.00 5.25
**46** A12 10c rose red ('00) 11.00 1.50
**47** A12 15c bl, quadrille paper 30.00 3.50
**48** A12 15c gray ('00) 20.00 1.50
**49** A12 20c red, *grn* 20.00 10.50
**50** A12 25c black, *rose* 25.00 6.75
**51** A12 25c blue ('00) 22.00 10.50
**52** A12 30c brown, *bis* 25.00 13.50
**53** A12 40c red, *straw* 26.00 13.50
**54** A12 50c carmine, *rose* 67.50 37.50
**55** A12 50c brn, *az* (name in car) ('00) 125.00 85.00
**56** A12 50c brn, *az* (name in bl) ('04) 65.00 42.50
**57** A12 75c violet, *org* 37.50 26.50
**58** A12 1fr bronz grn, *straw* 45.00 26.50
*Nos. 40-58 (19)* 539.75 293.15

Perf. 13½x14 stamps are counterfeits.
For overprints and surcharges see Nos. 59-87, 117-121.

**Nos. 41-42, 52, 57-58 Surcharged in Black**

j

**1900-01**
**59** A12 (h) 5c on 2c ('01) 22.50 19.00
a. Double surcharge 140.00 140.00
b. Inverted surcharge 125.00 125.00
Never hinged 210.00
**60** A12 (h) 5c on 4c 4.50 4.50
a. Inverted surcharge 82.50 82.50
b. Double surcharge 87.50 87.50
**61** A12 (j) 15c on 30c 5.25 4.50
a. Inverted surcharge 75.00 75.00
b. Double surcharge 67.50 67.50
**62** A12 (j) 15c on 75c ('01) 20.00 17.50
a. Pair, one without surcharge —
b. Inverted surcharge 130.00 130.00
c. Double surcharge 140.00 140.00
**63** A12 (j) 15c on 1fr ('01) 26.50 26.50
a. Double surcharge 175.00 175.00
b. Inverted surcharge 175.00 175.00
*Nos. 59-63 (5)* 78.75 72.00

**Nos. 52-53 Surcharged in Black**

k

**1902**
**64** A12 (k) 5c on 30c 10.50 9.00
a. Inverted surcharge 52.50 52.50
**65** A12 (k) 15c on 40c 10.50 8.25
a. Inverted surcharge 52.50 52.50

**Jubilee Issue**

Stamps of 1892-1900 Overprinted in Blue, Red, Black or Gold

**1903**
**66** A12 1c blk, *lil bl* (Bl) 3.00 3.00
a. Inverted overprint *290.00 290.00*
**67** A12 2c brown, *buff* (Bl) 5.25 4.50
**68** A12 4c claret, *lav* (Bl) 7.50 6.00
a. Double overprint *375.00 375.00*
**69** A12 5c dk grn, *grnsh* (R) 7.50 4.50
**70** A12 5c yellow green (R) 10.00 9.00
**71** A12 10c blk, *lav* (R) 19.00 16.00
**72** A12 10c blk, *lav* (double G & Bk) 11.50 9.00
**73** A12 15c gray (R) 15.00 11.50
**74** A12 20c red, *grn* (Bl) 22.00 19.00
**75** A12 25c blk, *rose* (Bl) 19.50 19.00
a. Double overprint 325.00
**76** A12 30c brown, *bis* (R) 26.50 22.50
**77** A12 40c red, *straw* (Bl) 34.00 30.00
**78** A12 50c car, *rose* (Bl) 60.00 52.50
a. Pair, one without overprint *300.00*
**79** A12 75c vio, *org* (Bk) 77.50 72.50
a. Dbl. ovpt. in blk and red *500.00*
**80** A12 1fr brnz grn, *straw* (Bl) 120.00 115.00
a. Dbl. ovpt., one in red *525.00 525.00*
*Nos. 66-80 (15)* 438.25 394.00

**With Additional Surcharge of New Value in Blue**

(a)

(b)

(c)

**81** A12 (a) 1c on 2c #67 1.90 1.90
a. Numeral double *115.00 115.00*
b. Numeral only 400.00
**82** A12 (b) 2c on 4c #68 3.50 3.50
**83** A12 (a) 4c on 5c #69 2.25 2.25
a. Small "4" *650.00 650.00*
**84** A12 (c) 4c on 5c #70 3.00 3.00
a. Pair, one without numeral

| No. | Type | Description | Unused | Used |
|---|---|---|---|---|
| 85 | A12 (b) | 10c on 15c #73 | 3.00 | 3.00 |
| 86 | A12 (b) | 15c on 20c #74 | 3.75 | 3.75 |
| 87 | A12 (b) | 20c on 25c #75 | 9.00 | 9.00 |
| | | *Nos. 81-87 (7)* | 26.40 | 26.40 |

50 years of French occupation.

Surcharge on Nos. 81-83, 85-86 is horizontal, reading down.

There are three types of numeral on No. 83. The numeral on No. 84 is identical with that of No. 83a except that its position is upright.

Nos. 66-87 are known with "I" of "TENAIRE" missing.

Kagu A16 Landscape A17

Ship — A18

**1905-28 Typo. *Perf. 14x13½***

| No. | Type | Description | Unused | Used |
|---|---|---|---|---|
| 88 | A16 | 1c blk, *green* | .30 | .30 |
| 89 | A16 | 2c red brown | .30 | .30 |
| 90 | A16 | 4c bl, *org* | .45 | .45 |
| 91 | A16 | 5c pale green | .55 | .55 |
| 92 | A16 | 5c dl bl ('21) | .40 | .40 |
| 93 | A16 | 10c carmine | 1.90 | 1.25 |
| 94 | A16 | 10c green ('21) | .75 | .75 |
| 95 | A16 | 10c red, *pink* ('25) | .85 | .85 |
| 96 | A16 | 15c violet | .90 | .85 |
| 97 | A17 | 20c brown | .55 | .55 |
| 98 | A17 | 25c blue, *grn* | 1.05 | .60 |
| 99 | A17 | 25c red, *yel* ('21) | .75 | .75 |
| 100 | A17 | 30c brn, *org* | 1.40 | .85 |
| 101 | A17 | 30c dp rose ('21) | 2.50 | 2.50 |
| 102 | A17 | 30c org ('25) | .60 | .60 |
| 103 | A17 | 35c blk, *yellow* | .75 | .75 |
| 104 | A17 | 40c car, *grn* | 1.25 | 1.05 |
| 105 | A17 | 45c vio brn, *lav* | .75 | .75 |
| 106 | A17 | 50c car, *org* | 3.25 | 3.00 |
| 107 | A17 | 50c dk bl ('21) | 1.75 | 1.75 |
| 108 | A17 | 50c gray ('25) | 1.05 | 1.05 |
| 109 | A17 | 65c dp bl ('28) | .90 | .90 |
| 110 | A17 | 75c ol grn, *straw* | .85 | .70 |
| 111 | A17 | 75c bl, *bluish* ('25) | .90 | .90 |
| 112 | A17 | 75c violet ('27) | 1.15 | 1.15 |
| 113 | A18 | 1fr bl, *yel grn* | 1.30 | 1.05 |
| 114 | A18 | 1fr dp bl ('25) | 1.90 | 1.90 |
| 115 | A18 | 2fr car, *bl* | 3.50 | 2.25 |
| 116 | A18 | 5fr blk, *straw* | 6.75 | 6.75 |
| | | *Nos. 88-116 (29)* | 39.30 | 35.50 |

See Nos. 311, 317a. For surcharges see Nos. 122-135, B1-B3, Q1-Q3.

Nos. 96, 98, 103, 106, 113 and 115, pasted on cardboard and handstamped "TRESORIER PAYEUR DE LA NOUVELLE CALEDONIE" were used as emergency currency in 1914.

**Stamps of 1892-1904 Surcharged in Carmine or Black**

**1912**

| No. | Type | Description | Unused | Used |
|---|---|---|---|---|
| 117 | A12 | 5c on 15c gray (C) | 1.50 | *1.90* |
| *a.* | | Inverted surcharge | 210.00 | 210.00 |
| 118 | A12 | 5c on 20c red, *grn* | 1.50 | *1.90* |
| 119 | A12 | 5c on 30c brn, *bis* (C) | 2.25 | *3.00* |
| 120 | A12 | 10c on 40c red, *straw* | 3.25 | *3.25* |
| 121 | A12 | 10c on 50c brn, *az* (C) | 3.25 | *4.25* |
| | | *Nos. 117-121 (5)* | 11.75 | 14.30 |

Two spacings between the surcharged numerals are found on Nos. 117 to 121. For detailed listings, see the *Scott Classic Specialized Catalogue of Stamps and Covers.*

No. 96 Surcharged in Brown

**1918**

| No. | Type | Description | Unused | Used |
|---|---|---|---|---|
| 122 | A16 | 5c on 15c violet | 1.90 | 1.90 |
| *a.* | | Double surcharge | 75.00 | 75.00 |
| *b.* | | Inverted surcharge | 45.00 | 45.00 |

The color of the surcharge on No. 122 varies from red to dark brown.

No. 96 Surcharged

**1922**

| No. | Type | Description | Unused | Used |
|---|---|---|---|---|
| 123 | A16 | 5c on 15c vio (R) | .60 | .60 |
| *a.* | | Double surcharge | 75.00 | 75.00 |

**Stamps and Types of 1905-28 Surcharged in Red or Black**

No. 124

No. 127

**1924-27**

| No. | Type | Description | Unused | Used |
|---|---|---|---|---|
| 124 | A16 | 25c on 15c vio | .75 | .75 |
| *a.* | | Double surcharge | 75.00 | |
| *b.* | | Double surcharge, one inverted | 110.00 | |
| 125 | A18 | 25c on 2fr car, *bl* | .85 | .85 |
| 126 | A18 | 25c on 5fr blk, *straw* | .90 | .90 |
| *a.* | | Double surcharge | 125.00 | 125.00 |
| *b.* | | Triple surcharge | 225.00 | 210.00 |
| 127 | A17 | 60c on 75c bl grn (R) | .75 | .75 |
| 128 | A17 | 65c on 45c red brn | 2.00 | 2.00 |
| 129 | A17 | 85c on 45c red brn | 2.00 | 2.00 |
| 130 | A17 | 90c on 75c dp rose | 1.05 | 1.05 |
| 131 | A18 | 1.25fr on 1fr dp bl (R) | .90 | .90 |
| 132 | A18 | 1.50fr on 1fr dp bl, *bl* | 1.60 | 1.60 |
| 133 | A18 | 3fr on 5fr red vio | 2.10 | 2.10 |
| 134 | A18 | 10fr on 5fr ol, *lav* (R) | 7.50 | 7.50 |
| 135 | A18 | 20fr on 5fr vio rose, *org* | 14.50 | 14.50 |
| | | *Nos. 124-135 (12)* | 34.90 | 34.90 |

Issue years: Nos. 125-127, 1924. Nos. 124, 128-129, 1925. Nos. 131, 134, 1926. Nos. 130, 132-133, 135, 1927.

Bay of Palétuviers Point A19

Landscape with Chief's House A20

Admiral de Bougainville and Count de La Pérouse — A21

**1928-40 Typo.**

| No. | Type | Description | Unused | Used |
|---|---|---|---|---|
| 136 | A19 | 1c brn vio & ind | .25 | .25 |
| 137 | A19 | 2c dk brn & yel grn | .25 | .25 |
| 137B | A19 | 3c brn vio & ind | .30 | .30 |
| 138 | A19 | 4c org & Prus grn | .25 | .25 |
| 139 | A19 | 5c Prus bl & dp ol | .45 | .45 |
| 140 | A19 | 10c gray lil & dk brn | .30 | .30 |
| 141 | A19 | 15c yel brn & dp bl | .55 | .55 |
| 142 | A19 | 20c brn red & dk brn | .55 | .55 |
| 143 | A19 | 25c dk grn & dk brn | .70 | .55 |
| 144 | A20 | 30c gray grn & bl grn | .60 | .60 |
| 145 | A20 | 35c blk & brt vio | .90 | .90 |
| 146 | A20 | 40c brt red & olvn | .55 | .55 |
| 147 | A20 | 45c dp bl & red org | 1.60 | 1.30 |
| 147A | A20 | 45c bl grn & dl grn | 1.05 | 1.05 |
| 148 | A20 | 50c vio & brn | .85 | .85 |
| 149 | A20 | 55c vio bl & car | 3.50 | 2.25 |
| 150 | A20 | 60c vio bl & car | .75 | .75 |
| 151 | A20 | 65c org brn & bl | 1.30 | 1.15 |
| 152 | A20 | 70c dp rose & brn | .60 | .60 |
| 153 | A20 | 75c Prus bl & ol gray | 1.40 | 1.15 |
| 154 | A20 | 80c red brn & grn | 1.15 | 1.00 |
| 155 | A20 | 85c grn & brn | 2.00 | 1.30 |
| 156 | A20 | 90c dp red & brt red | 1.30 | .90 |
| 157 | A20 | 90c ol grn & rose red | 1.05 | 1.05 |
| 158 | A21 | 1fr dp ol & sal red | 7.25 | 4.25 |
| 159 | A21 | 1fr rose red & dk car | 2.25 | 1.75 |
| 160 | A21 | 1fr brn red & grn | 1.05 | 1.05 |
| 161 | A21 | 1.10fr grn & brn | 12.00 | 12.00 |
| 162 | A21 | 1.25fr brn red & grn | 1.20 | 1.20 |
| 163 | A21 | 1.25fr rose red & dk car | 1.15 | 1.15 |
| 164 | A21 | 1.40fr dk bl & red org | 1.20 | 1.20 |
| 165 | A21 | 1.50fr dp bl & bl | .90 | .90 |
| 166 | A21 | 1.60fr dp grn & brn | 1.35 | 1.35 |
| 167 | A21 | 1.75fr dk bl & red org | 1.05 | 1.05 |
| 168 | A21 | 1.75fr violet bl | 1.50 | 1.05 |
| 169 | A21 | 2fr red org & brn | .90 | .75 |
| 170 | A21 | 2.25fr vio bl | 1.20 | 1.20 |
| 171 | A21 | 2.50fr brn & lt brn | 1.75 | 1.75 |
| 172 | A21 | 3fr mag & brn | .75 | .75 |
| 173 | A21 | 5fr dk bl & brn | 1.15 | 1.15 |
| 174 | A21 | 10fr vio & brn, *pnksh* | 1.30 | 1.30 |
| 175 | A21 | 20fr red & brn, *yel* | 2.75 | 2.75 |
| | | *Nos. 136-175 (42)* | 62.90 | 55.45 |

The 35c in Prussian green and dark green without overprint is listed as Wallis and Futuna No. 53a.

Issue years: 35c, 70c, 85c, #162, 167, 1933; 55c, 80c, #159, 168, 1938; #157, 163, 2.25fr, 1939; 3c, 60c, 1.40fr, 1.60fr, 2.50fr, 147A, 160, 1940; others, 1928.

For overprints see #180-207, 217-251, Q4-Q6.

Common Design Types pictured following the introduction.

**Colonial Exposition Issue**

Common Design Types

**1931 Engr. *Perf. 12½***

**Country Name Typo. in Black**

| No. | Type | Description | Unused | Used |
|---|---|---|---|---|
| 176 | CD70 | 40c dp green | 6.00 | 6.00 |
| 177 | CD71 | 50c violet | 6.00 | 6.00 |
| 178 | CD72 | 90c red orange | 6.00 | 6.00 |
| 179 | CD73 | 1.50fr dull blue | 6.00 | 6.00 |
| | | *Nos. 176-179 (4)* | 24.00 | 24.00 |

**Paris-Nouméa Flight Issue**

Regular Issue of 1928 Overprinted

**1932 *Perf. 14x13½***

| No. | Type | Description | Unused | Used |
|---|---|---|---|---|
| 180 | A20 | 40c brt red & olvn | 475.00 | *500.00* |
| 181 | A20 | 50c vio & brn | 475.00 | *500.00* |

Arrival on Apr. 5, 1932 at Nouméa, of the French aviators, Verneilh, Dévé and Munch.

Excellent forgeries exist of #180-181.

**Types of 1928-33 Overprinted in Black or Red**

**1933**

| No. | Type | Description | Unused | Used |
|---|---|---|---|---|
| 182 | A19 | 1c red vio & dl bl | 6.50 | *7.00* |
| 183 | A19 | 2c dk brn & yel grn | 6.50 | *7.00* |
| 184 | A19 | 4c dl org & Prus bl | 6.50 | *7.00* |
| 185 | A19 | 5c Prus grn & ol (R) | 6.50 | *7.00* |
| 186 | A19 | 10c gray lil & dk brn (R) | 6.50 | *7.00* |
| 187 | A19 | 15c yel brn & dp bl (R) | 6.50 | *7.00* |
| 188 | A19 | 20c brn red & dk brn | 6.50 | *7.00* |
| 189 | A19 | 25c dk grn & dk brn (R) | 6.50 | *7.00* |
| 190 | A20 | 30c gray grn & bl grn (R) | 6.75 | *7.50* |
| 191 | A20 | 35c blk & lt vio | 6.75 | *7.50* |
| 192 | A20 | 40c brt red & olvn | 6.75 | *7.00* |
| 193 | A20 | 45c dp bl & red org | 6.75 | *7.50* |
| 194 | A20 | 50c vio & brn | 6.75 | *7.00* |
| 195 | A20 | 70c dp rose & brn | 7.50 | *8.00* |
| 196 | A20 | 75c Prus bl & ol gray (R) | 7.50 | *8.00* |
| 197 | A20 | 85c grn & brn | 7.50 | *8.00* |
| 198 | A20 | 90c dp red & brt red | 9.50 | *10.00* |
| 199 | A21 | 1fr dp ol & sal red | 9.50 | *10.00* |
| 200 | A21 | 1.25fr brn red & grn | 9.50 | *10.00* |
| 201 | A21 | 1.50fr dp bl & bl (R) | 9.50 | *10.00* |
| 202 | A21 | 1.75fr dk bl & red org | 9.50 | *10.00* |
| 203 | A21 | 2fr red org & brn | 9.50 | *10.00* |
| 204 | A21 | 3fr mag & brn | 9.50 | *10.00* |
| 205 | A21 | 5fr dk bl & brn (R) | 9.50 | *10.00* |
| 206 | A21 | 10fr vio & brn, *pnksh* | 10.00 | *11.00* |
| 207 | A21 | 20fr red & brn, *yel* | 10.00 | *11.00* |
| | | *Nos. 182-207 (26)* | 204.25 | 218.50 |

1st anniv., Paris-Noumea flight. Plane centered on Nos. 190-207.

**Paris International Exposition Issue**

Common Design Types

**1937 Engr. *Perf. 13***

| No. | Type | Description | Unused | Used |
|---|---|---|---|---|
| 208 | CD74 | 20c dp vio | 2.75 | 2.75 |
| 209 | CD75 | 30c dk grn | 2.75 | 2.75 |
| 210 | CD76 | 40c car rose | 2.75 | 2.75 |
| 211 | CD77 | 50c dk brn & bl | 2.75 | 2.75 |
| 212 | CD78 | 90c red | 2.75 | 2.75 |
| 213 | CD79 | 1.50fr ultra | 2.75 | 2.75 |
| | | *Nos. 208-213 (6)* | 16.50 | 16.50 |

**Colonial Arts Exhibition Issue**

**Souvenir Sheet**

Common Design Type

**1937 *Imperf.***

| No. | Type | Description | Unused | Used |
|---|---|---|---|---|
| 214 | CD78 | 3fr sepia | 22.50 | *34.00* |

**New York World's Fair Issue**

Common Design Type

**1939 *Perf. 12½x12***

| No. | Type | Description | Unused | Used |
|---|---|---|---|---|
| 215 | CD82 | 1.25fr car lake | 1.60 | 1.60 |
| 216 | CD82 | 2.25fr ultra | 1.75 | 1.75 |

Nouméa Roadstead and Marshal Pétain

**1941 Engr. *Perf. 12½x12***

| No. | Type | Description | Unused | Used |
|---|---|---|---|---|
| 216A | A21a | 1fr bluish green | .75 | |
| 216B | A21a | 2.50fr dark blue | .75 | |

Nos. 216A-216B were issued by the Vichy government in France, but were not placed on sale in the colony.

For surcharges, see Nos. B12A-B12B.

**Types of 1928-40 Overprinted in Black**

**1941** *Perf. 14x13½*

| No. | Type | Description | Unused | Used |
|---|---|---|---|---|
| **217** | A19 | 1c red vio & dl bl | 13.50 | 13.50 |
| **218** | A19 | 2c dk brn & yel grn | 13.50 | 13.50 |
| **219** | A19 | 3c brn vio & ind | 13.50 | 13.50 |
| **220** | A19 | 4c dl org & Prus bl | 13.50 | 13.50 |
| **221** | A19 | 5c Prus bl & dp ol | 13.50 | 13.50 |
| **222** | A19 | 10c gray lil & dk brn | 13.50 | 13.50 |
| **223** | A19 | 15c yel brn & dp bl | 18.00 | 18.00 |
| **224** | A19 | 20c brn red & dk brn | 18.00 | 18.00 |
| **225** | A19 | 25c dk grn & dk brn | 18.00 | 18.00 |
| **226** | A20 | 30c gray grn & bl grn | 18.00 | 18.00 |
| **227** | A20 | 35c blk & brt vio | 18.00 | 18.00 |
| **228** | A20 | 40c brt red & olvn | 18.00 | 18.00 |
| **229** | A20 | 45c bl grn & dl grn | 18.00 | 18.00 |
| **230** | A20 | 50c vio & brn | 18.00 | 18.00 |
| **231** | A20 | 55c vio bl & car | 18.00 | 18.00 |
| **232** | A20 | 60c vio bl & car | 18.00 | 18.00 |
| **233** | A20 | 65c org brn & bl | 18.00 | 18.00 |
| **234** | A20 | 70c dp rose & brn | 18.00 | 18.00 |
| **235** | A20 | 75c Prus bl & ol gray | 18.00 | 18.00 |
| **236** | A20 | 80c red brn & grn | 18.00 | 18.00 |
| **237** | A20 | 85c grn & brn | 18.00 | 18.00 |
| **238** | A20 | 90c dp red & brt red | 18.00 | 18.00 |
| **239** | A21 | 1fr rose red & dk car | 18.00 | 18.00 |
| **240** | A21 | 1.25fr brn red & grn | 18.00 | 18.00 |
| **241** | A21 | 1.40fr dk bl & red org | 18.00 | 18.00 |
| **242** | A21 | 1.50fr dp bl & bl | 18.00 | 18.00 |
| **243** | A21 | 1.60fr dp grn & brn | 18.00 | 18.00 |
| **244** | A21 | 1.75fr dk bl & red org | 18.00 | 18.00 |
| **245** | A21 | 2fr red org & brn | 18.00 | 18.00 |
| **246** | A21 | 2.25fr vio bl | 18.00 | 18.00 |
| **247** | A21 | 2.50fr brn & lt brn | 22.00 | 19.50 |
| **248** | A21 | 3fr mag & brn | 22.00 | 19.50 |
| **249** | A21 | 5fr dk bl & brn | 22.00 | 19.50 |
| **250** | A21 | 10fr vio & brn, *pnksh* | 22.00 | 22.00 |
| **251** | A21 | 20fr red & brn, *yel* | 23.50 | 23.50 |
| | | *Nos. 217-251 (35)* | 624.50 | 617.00 |
| | | Set, never hinged | 875.00 | |

Issued to note this colony's affiliation with the "Free France" movement.

**Catalogue values for unused stamps in this section, from this point to the end of the section, are for Never Hinged items.**

Kagu
A22

**1942** **Photo.** *Perf. 14½x14*

| No. | Type | Description | Unused | Used |
|---|---|---|---|---|
| **252** | A22 | 5c brown | .40 | .25 |
| **253** | A22 | 10c dk gray bl | .45 | .30 |
| **254** | A22 | 25c emerald | .70 | .30 |
| **255** | A22 | 30c red org | .70 | .45 |
| **256** | A22 | 40c dk slate grn | .70 | .45 |
| **257** | A22 | 80c dl red brn | .70 | .45 |
| **258** | A22 | 1fr rose vio | .90 | .70 |
| **259** | A22 | 1.50fr red | .90 | .70 |
| **260** | A22 | 2fr gray blk | 1.30 | 1.10 |
| **261** | A22 | 2.50fr brt ultra | 1.30 | 1.10 |
| **262** | A22 | 4fr dl vio | 1.30 | 1.10 |
| **263** | A22 | 5fr bister | 1.30 | 1.10 |
| **264** | A22 | 10fr dp brn | 1.60 | 1.50 |
| **265** | A22 | 20fr dp grn | 2.50 | 2.25 |
| | | *Nos. 252-265 (14)* | 14.75 | 11.75 |

**Types of 1928 Without "RF"**

**1944** **Typo.** *Perf. 14x13½*

| No. | Type | Description | Unused | Used |
|---|---|---|---|---|
| **265A** | A19 | 10c gray lil & dk brn | .75 | |
| **265B** | A20 | 60c vio bl & car | 1.50 | |

Nos. 265A-265B were issued by the Vichy government in France, but were not placed on sale in the colony.

**Stamps of 1942 Surcharged in Carmine or Black**

**1945-46** **Unwmk.** *Perf. 14½x14*

| No. | Type | Description | Unused | Used |
|---|---|---|---|---|
| **266** | A22 | 50c on 5c (C) ('46) | 1.60 | 1.50 |
| **267** | A22 | 60c on 5c (C) | 1.60 | 1.50 |
| **268** | A22 | 70c on 5c (C) | 1.60 | 1.50 |
| **269** | A22 | 1.20fr on 5c (C) | .85 | .75 |
| **270** | A22 | 2.40fr on 25c | .85 | .75 |
| **271** | A22 | 3fr on 25c ('46) | 1.00 | .75 |
| **272** | A22 | 4.50fr on 25c | 1.90 | 1.10 |
| **273** | A22 | 15fr on 2.50fr (C) | 2.60 | 2.00 |
| | | *Nos. 266-273 (8)* | 12.00 | 9.85 |

**Eboue Issue**

Common Design Type

**1945** **Engr.** *Perf. 13*

| No. | Type | Description | Unused | Used |
|---|---|---|---|---|
| **274** | CD91 | 2fr black | .90 | .90 |
| **275** | CD91 | 25fr Prus grn | 2.50 | 2.10 |

Kagus
A23

Ducos
Sanatorium
A24

Porcupine
Isle — A25

Nickel
Foundry
A26

"Towers of
Notre
Dame"
A27

Chieftain's
House — A28

**1948** **Unwmk.** **Photo.** *Perf. 13½x13*

| No. | Type | Description | Unused | Used |
|---|---|---|---|---|
| **276** | A23 | 10c yel & gray brn | .30 | .30 |
| **277** | A23 | 30c bl grn & gray brn | .30 | .30 |
| **278** | A23 | 40c org & gray brn | .30 | .30 |
| **279** | A24 | 50c pink & gray blk | .60 | .45 |
| **280** | A24 | 60c yel & brn | .60 | .60 |
| **281** | A24 | 80c pale bl grn & bl grn | .60 | .60 |
| **282** | A25 | 1fr brn, vio & org | .75 | .60 |
| **283** | A25 | 1.20fr brn & bl | .75 | .60 |
| **284** | A25 | 1.50fr dk bl & yel | .90 | .70 |
| **285** | A26 | 2fr turq grn & brnsh blk | .75 | .60 |
| **286** | A26 | 2.40fr car & peach | 1.20 | .85 |
| **287** | A26 | 3fr pale org & vio | 7.50 | 2.00 |
| **288** | A26 | 4fr lt bl & dk bl | 2.10 | 1.00 |
| **289** | A27 | 5fr sal & dk vio | 2.75 | 1.10 |
| **290** | A27 | 6fr yel & brn | 2.75 | 1.60 |
| **291** | A27 | 10fr pale org & dk bl | 2.75 | 1.60 |
| **292** | A28 | 15fr red brn & bl gray | 3.50 | 1.75 |
| **293** | A28 | 20fr vio & yel | 3.50 | 2.25 |
| **294** | A28 | 25fr dk bl & pale org | 4.50 | 3.50 |
| | | *Nos. 276-294 (19)* | 36.40 | 20.70 |

**Military Medal Issue**

Common Design Type

**1952** **Engr. & Typo.** *Perf. 13*

| No. | Type | Description | Unused | Used |
|---|---|---|---|---|
| **295** | CD101 | 2fr multi | 6.50 | 6.00 |

Admiral Bruni d'Entrecasteaux and his Two Frigates — A29

Designs: 2fr, Msgr. Douarre and Cathedral of Nouméa. 6fr, Admiral Dumont d'Urville and map. 13fr, Admiral Auguste Febvrier-Despointes and Nouméa roadstead.

**1953, Sept. 24** **Engr.**

| No. | Type | Description | Unused | Used |
|---|---|---|---|---|
| **296** | A29 | 1.50fr org brn & dp claret | 7.25 | 5.50 |
| **297** | A29 | 2fr ind & aqua | 6.00 | 3.50 |
| **298** | A29 | 6fr dk brn, bl & car | 11.00 | 6.00 |
| **299** | A29 | 13fr bl grn & dk grnsh bl | 12.50 | 7.00 |
| | | *Nos. 296-299 (4)* | 36.75 | 22.00 |

Centenary of the presence of the French in New Caledonia.

"Towers of Notre Dame" — A30

Coffee
A31

**1955, Nov. 21** **Unwmk.** *Perf. 13*

| No. | Type | Description | Unused | Used |
|---|---|---|---|---|
| **300** | A30 | 2.50fr dk brn, ultra & grn | 1.90 | 1.05 |
| **301** | A30 | 3fr grn, ultra & red brn | 8.25 | 4.00 |
| **302** | A31 | 9fr vio bl & indigo | 3.00 | 1.05 |
| | | *Nos. 300-302 (3)* | 13.15 | 6.10 |

**FIDES Issue**

Common Design Type

Design: Dumbea Dam.

**1956, Oct. 22** **Engr.** *Perf. 13x12½*

| No. | Type | Description | Unused | Used |
|---|---|---|---|---|
| **303** | CD103 | 3fr grn & bl | 1.90 | 1.10 |

**Flower Issue**

Common Design Type

Designs: 4fr, Xanthostemon. 15fr, Hibiscus.

**1958, July 7** **Photo.** *Perf. 12x12½*

| No. | Type | Description | Unused | Used |
|---|---|---|---|---|
| **304** | CD104 | 4fr multi | 2.75 | 1.25 |
| **305** | CD104 | 15fr grn, red & yel | 5.25 | 1.75 |

Imperforates

Most stamps of New Caledonia from 1958 onward exist imperforate, in trial colors, or in small presentation sheets in which the stamps are printed in changed colors.

**Human Rights Issue**

Common Design Type

**1958, Dec. 10** **Engr.** *Perf. 13*

| No. | Type | Description | Unused | Used |
|---|---|---|---|---|
| **306** | CD105 | 7fr car & dk bl | 2.00 | 1.50 |

Brachyrus
Zebra — A32

Lienardella
Fasciata
A33

Designs: 10fr, Glaucus and Spirographe. 26fr, Fluorescent corals.

**1959, Mar. 21** **Engr.** *Perf. 13*

| No. | Type | Description | Unused | Used |
|---|---|---|---|---|
| **307** | A32 | 1fr lil gray & red brn | .75 | .55 |
| **308** | A33 | 3fr bl, grn & red | 1.75 | .60 |
| **309** | A32 | 10fr dk brn, Prus bl & org brn | 2.50 | 1.00 |
| **310** | A33 | 26fr multi | 4.50 | 4.50 |
| | | *Nos. 307-310 (4)* | 9.50 | 6.65 |

**Types of 1859, 1905 and**

Girl
Operating
Check
Writer
A34

Telephone
Receiver
and
Exchange
A35

Port-de-France (Nouméa) in 1859 — A36

Designs: 9fr, Wayside mailbox and mail bus, vert. 33fr, like 19fr without stamps.

*Perf. 13½x13, 13*

**1960, May 20** **Unwmk.**

| No. | Type | Description | Unused | Used |
|---|---|---|---|---|
| **311** | A16 | 4fr red | 1.00 | .55 |
| **312** | A34 | 5fr claret & org brn | 1.20 | .75 |
| **313** | A36 | 9fr dk grn & brn | 1.20 | .75 |
| **314** | A35 | 12fr bl & blk | 1.50 | .90 |
| **315** | A1 | 13fr slate blue | 3.75 | 2.00 |
| **316** | A36 | 19fr bl grn, dl grn & red | 3.75 | 1.25 |
| **317** | A36 | 33fr Prus bl & dl red | 4.00 | 2.75 |
| *a.* | | Souv. sheet of 3, #315, 311, 317 + label | 12.50 | 12.50 |
| | | *Nos. 311-317 (7)* | 16.40 | 8.95 |

Cent. of postal service and stamps in New Caledonia.

No. 317a has label between 4fr and 33fr stamps.

Melanesian
Sailing
Canoes
A37

Designs: 4fr, Spear fisherman, vert. 5fr, Sail Rock and sailboats, Noumea.

**1962, July 2** **Engr.** *Perf. 13*

| No. | Type | Description | Unused | Used |
|---|---|---|---|---|
| **318** | A37 | 2fr slate grn, ultra & brn | 1.10 | .55 |
| **319** | A37 | 4fr brn, car & grn | 1.40 | .55 |
| **320** | A37 | 5fr sepia, grn & bl | 1.75 | .75 |
| | | *Nos. 318-320 (3)* | 4.25 | 1.85 |

See Nos. C29-C32.

Map of Australia and South Pacific — A37a

**1962, July 18 Photo. *Perf. 13x12***

**321** A37a 15fr multi 3.00 1.90

Fifth South Pacific Conf., Pago Pago, 1962.

Air Currents over Map of New Caledonia and South Pacific, Barograph and Compass Rose — A38

**1962, Nov. 5 *Perf. 12x12½***

**322** A38 50fr multi 7.50 6.00

3rd regional assembly of the World Meteorological Association, Noumea, November 1962.

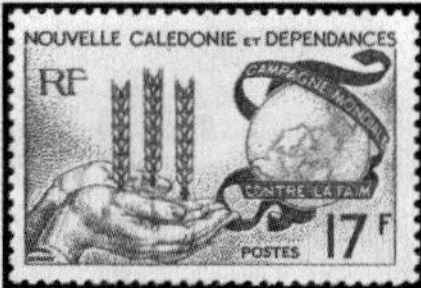


Wheat Emblem and Globe A38a

**1963, Mar. 21 Engr. *Perf. 13***

**323** A38a 17fr choc & dk bl 3.50 1.75

FAO "Freedom from Hunger" campaign.

Relay Race — A39

***Perf. 12½***

**1963, Aug. 29 Unwmk. Photo.**

**324** A39 1fr shown 1.20 .60
**325** A39 7fr Tennis 1.75 .90
**326** A39 10fr Soccer 2.40 1.50
**327** A39 27fr Javelin 4.25 2.75
*Nos. 324-327 (4)* 9.60 5.75

South Pacific Games, Suva, Aug. 29-Sept. 7.

### Red Cross Centenary Issue
Common Design Type

**1963 Sept. 2 Engr. *Perf. 13***

**328** CD113 37fr bl, gray & car 8.00 6.75

### Human Rights Issue
Common Design Type

**1963, Dec. 10 Unwmk. *Perf. 13***

**329** CD117 50fr sl grn & dp claret 7.00 6.00

Bikkia Fritillarioides — A40

Flowers: 1fr, Freycinettia Sp. 3fr, Xanthostemon Francii. 4fr, Psidiomyrtus locellatus. 5fr, Callistemon suberosum. 7fr, Montrouziera sphaeroidea, horiz. 10fr, Ixora collina, horiz. 17fr, Deplanchea speciosa.

**Photogravure; Lithographed (2fr, 3fr)**

**1964-65 *Perf. 13x12½***

**330** A40 1fr multi 1.00 .55
**331** A40 2fr multi 1.00 .60
**332** A40 3fr multi 1.60 .75
**333** A40 4fr multi ('65) 3.00 .90
**334** A40 5fr multi ('65) 3.75 1.25
**335** A40 7fr multi 4.75 1.60
**336** A40 10fr multi 5.50 1.75
**337** A40 17fr multi 8.50 4.25
*Nos. 330-337 (8)* 29.10 11.65

Sea Squirts — A41

Design: 10fr, Alcyonium catalai. 17fr, Shrimp (hymenocera elegans).

**1964-65 Engr. *Perf. 13***

**338** A41 7fr dk bl, org & brn 1.75 1.00
**339** A41 10fr dk red & dk vio bl ('65) 2.75 1.10
**340** A41 17fr dk bl, mag & grn 4.75 2.50
*Nos. 338-340 (3)* 9.25 4.60

Nouméa Aquarium. See Nos. C41-C43.

### Philatec Issue
Common Design Type

**1964, Apr. 9 Unwmk. *Perf. 13***

**341** CD118 40fr dk vio, grn & choc 6.50 6.50

De Gaulle's 1940 Poster "A Tous les Francais" A42

**1965, Sept. 20 Engr. *Perf. 13***

**342** A42 20fr red, bl & blk 12.50 8.25

25th anniv. of the rallying of the Free French.

Amedee Lighthouse — A43

**1965, Nov. 25**

**343** A43 8fr dk vio bl, bis & grn 2.60 1.00

Centenary of the Amedee lighthouse.

Games' Emblem — A44

**1966, Mar. 1 Engr. *Perf. 13***

**344** A44 8fr dk red, brt bl & blk 1.50 .90

2nd So. Pacific Games, Nouméa, Dec. 1966.

Red-throated Parrot Finch — A45

Design: 3fr, Giant imperial pigeon.

**1966, Oct. 10 Litho. *Perf. 13x12½***
**Size: 22x37mm**

**345** A45 1fr green & multi 3.00 1.50
**346** A45 3fr citron & multi 5.00 1.90

See #361-366, 380-381, C48-C49A, C70-C71.

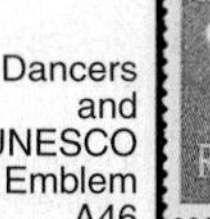

Dancers and UNESCO Emblem A46

**1966, Nov. 4 Engr. *Perf. 13***

**347** A46 16fr pur, ocher & grn 2.40 1.40

20th anniv. of UNESCO.

High Jump and Games' Emblem A47

**1966, Dec. 8 Engr. *Perf. 13***

**348** A47 17fr shown 3.00 1.25
**349** A47 20fr Hurdling 4.25 2.10
**350** A47 40fr Running 5.50 2.40
**351** A47 100fr Swimming 9.50 6.25
*a.* Souv. sheet of 4, #348-351 + label 35.00 35.00
*Nos. 348-351 (4)* 22.25 12.00

2nd So. Pacific Games, Nouméa, Dec. 8-18.

Lekine Cliffs A48

**1967, Jan. 14 Engr. *Perf. 13***

**352** A48 17fr brt grn, ultra & sl grn 2.40 2.00

Magenta Stadium, Nouméa A49

Design: 20fr, Ouen Toro Municipal Swimming Pool, Nouméa.

**1967, June 5 Photo. *Perf. 12x13***

**353** A49 10fr multi 1.50 .85
**354** A49 20fr multi 3.50 1.60

ITY Emblem, Beach at Nouméa A50

**1967, June 19 Engr. *Perf. 13***

**355** A50 30fr multi 4.75 2.60

Issued for International Tourist Year, 1967.

19th Century Mailman A51

**1967, July 12**

**356** A51 7fr dk car, bl grn & brn 3.00 1.40

Issued for Stamp Day.

Papilio Montrouzieri — A52

Butterflies: 9fr, Polyura clitarchus. 13fr, 15fr, Hypolimnas bolina, male and female respectively.

**1967-68 Engr. *Perf. 13***
**Size: 36x22mm**

**357** A52 7fr lt grn, blk & ultra 4.75 1.25
**358** A52 9fr brn, lil & ind ('68) 5.75 1.50
**359** A52 13fr vio bl, brn org & dk brn 7.00 2.50
**360** A52 15fr dk brn, bl & yel 10.00 4.50
*Nos. 357-360,C51-C53 (7)* 58.50 24.25

Issued: 9fr, 3/26/68; others, 8/10/67.

### Bird Type of 1966

Birds: 1fr, New Caledonian grass warbler. 2fr, New Caledonia whistler. 3fr, New Caledonia white-throated pigeon. 4fr, Kagus. 5fr, Crested parakeet. 10fr, Crow honey-eater.

**1967-68 Photo. *Perf. 13x12½***
**Size: 22x37mm**

**361** A45 1fr multi 1.50 1.00
**362** A45 2fr multi 2.00 1.25
**363** A45 3fr multi 2.50 1.40
**364** A45 4fr grn & multi 4.00 2.50
**365** A45 5fr lt yel & multi 7.00 3.25
**366** A45 10fr pink & multi 12.00 4.25
*Nos. 361-366 (6)* 29.00 13.65

Issued: #364-366, 12/16/67; others 5/14/68.

### WHO Anniversary Issue
Common Design Type

**1968, May 4 Engr. *Perf. 13***

**367** CD126 20fr mar, vio & dk bl grn 4.00 2.25

Ferrying Mail Truck Across Tontouta River, 1900 A53

**1968, Sept. 2 Engr. *Perf. 13***

**368** A53 9fr dk red brn, grn & ultra 3.75 1.60

Issued for Stamp Day, 1968.

### Human Rights Year Issue
Common Design Type

**1968, Aug. 10 Engr. *Perf. 13***

**369** CD127 12fr sl grn, dp car & org yel 2.75 1.50

Conus Geographus — A54

**1968, Nov. 9 Engr. *Perf. 13***
**Size: 36x22mm**

**370** A54 10fr dk brn, brt bl & gray 4.25 2.25
*Nos. 370,C58-C60 (4)* 37.75 13.50

Car on Road A55

**1968, Dec. 26 Engr. *Perf. 13***

**371** A55 25fr dp bl, sl grn & hn brn 7.50 3.75

2nd Automobile Safari of New Caledonia.

Cattle Dip — A56

**1969, May 10 Engr. *Perf. 13***
**Size: 36x22mm**

**372** A56 9fr shown 2.50 1.00
**373** A56 25fr Cattle branding 3.50 1.75
*Nos. 372-373,C64 (3)* 13.00 6.00

Cattle breeding in New Caledonia.

Murex Haustellum A57

Sea Shells: 5fr, Venus comb. 15fr, Murex ramosus.

**1969, June 21 Engr. *Perf. 13***
**Size: 35½x22mm**

**374** A57 2fr ver, bl & brn 1.75 .90
**375** A57 5fr dl red, pur & beige 3.75 1.20
**376** A57 15fr ver, dl grn & gray 6.00 2.40
*Nos. 374-376,C65 (4)* 35.50 16.00

Judo A58

**1969, Aug. 7 Engr. *Perf. 13***
**Size: 36x22mm**

**377** A58 19fr shown 3.75 1.90
**378** A58 20fr Boxers 3.75 1.90
*Nos. 377-378,C66-C67 (4)* 19.50 8.80

3rd South Pacific Games. Port Moresby, Papua and New Guinea, Aug. 13-23.

**ILO Issue**
Common Design Type

**1969, Nov. 24 Engr. *Perf. 13***

**379** CD131 12fr org, brn vio & brn 2.25 1.10

**Bird Type of 1966**

15fr, Friarbird. 30fr, Sacred kingfisher.

**1970, Feb. 19 Photo. *Perf. 13***
**Size: 22x37mm**

**380** A45 15fr yel grn & multi 8.25 3.25
**381** A45 30fr pale salmon & multi 12.00 5.50
*Nos. 380-381,C70-C71 (4)* 59.75 22.75

**UPU Headquarters Issue**
Common Design Type

**1970, May 20 Engr. *Perf. 13***

**382** CD133 12fr brn, gray & dk car 3.00 1.50

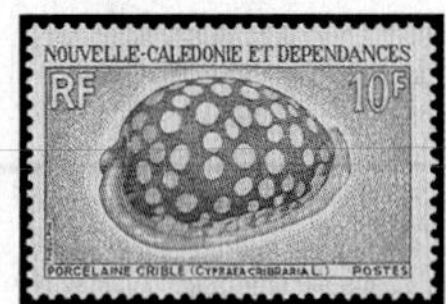


Porcelain Sieve Shell A59

Designs: 1fr, Strombus epidromis linne, vert. No. 385, Strombus variabilis swainson, vert. 21fr, Mole porcelain shell.

**1970 Size: 22x36mm, 36x22mm**

**383** A59 1fr brt grn & multi 2.25 .75
**384** A59 10fr rose & multi 5.25 1.50
**385** A59 10fr blk & multi 6.75 2.40
**386** A59 21fr bl grn, brn & dk brn 10.00 4.00
*Nos. 383-386,C73-C76 (8)* 64.50 25.65

See Nos. 395-396, C89-C90.

Packet Ship "Natal," 1883 A60

**1970, July 23 Engr. *Perf. 13***

**387** A60 9fr Prus bl, blk & brt grn 4.00 1.40

Issued for Stamp Day.

Dumbea Railroad Post Office A61

**1971, Mar. 13 Engr. *Perf. 13***

**388** A61 10fr red, slate grn & blk 5.00 2.00

Stamp Day, 1971.

Racing Yachts — A62

**1971, Apr. 17 Engr. *Perf. 13***

**389** A62 16fr bl, Prus bl & sl grn *5.00* 3.00

Third sailing cruise from Whangarei, New Zealand, to Nouméa.

Morse Recorder, Communications Satellite — A63

**1971, May 17 Engr. *Perf. 13***

**390** A63 19fr red, lake & org 4.00 1.25

3rd World Telecommunications Day.

Weight Lifting — A64

**1971, June 24 Engr. *Perf. 13***

**391** A64 11fr shown 2.50 1.00
**392** A64 23fr Basketball 3.75 1.50
*Nos. 391-392,C82-C83 (4)* 18.00 8.75

4th South Pacific Games, Papeete, French Polynesia, Sept. 8-19.

**De Gaulle Issue**
Common Design Type

Designs: 34fr, Pres. de Gaulle, 1970. 100fr, Gen. de Gaulle, 1940.

**1971, Nov. 9**

**393** CD134 34fr dk pur & blk 8.00 3.75
**394** CD134 100fr dk pur & blk 15.00 8.00

**Sea Shell Type of 1970**

Designs: 1fr, Scorpion conch, vert. 3fr, Common spider conch., vert.

**1972, Mar. 4 Engr. *Perf. 13***
**Size: 22x36mm**

**395** A59 1fr vio & dk brn 2.00 .70
**396** A59 3fr grn & ocher 3.00 .80
*Nos. 395-396,C89-C90 (4)* 19.50 8.50

Carved Wooden Pillow — A66

1fr, Doorpost, Goa. 5fr, Monstrance. 12fr, Tchamba mask.

**1972-73 Photo. *Perf. 12½x13***

**397** A66 1fr multi ('73) 1.75 .40
**398** A66 2fr shown 1.75 .65
**399** A66 5fr multi 2.00 .80
**400** A66 12fr multi 5.00 1.25
*Nos. 397-400,C102-C103 (6)* 18.00 6.10

Objects from Nouméa Museum. Issued: 2fr-15fr, 8/5.

Chamber of Commerce Emblem — A67

**1972, Dec. 16**

**401** A67 12fr blk, yel & brt bl 1.75 .90

Junior Chamber of Commerce, 10th anniv.

Tchamba Mask — A68

**1973, Mar. 15 Engr. *Perf. 13***

**402** A68 12fr lilac 8.25 2.00
*a.* Booklet pane of 5 200.00

No. 402 issued in booklets only.
See No. C99.

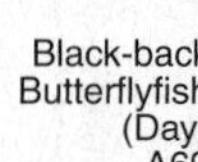

Black-back Butterflyfish (Day) A69

**1973, June 23 Photo. *Perf. 13x12½***

**403** A69 8fr shown 2.50 1.00
**404** A69 14fr same fish (night) 3.75 1.50
*Nos. 403-404,C105 (3)* 11.25 4.50

Nouméa Aquarium.

Emblem A70

**1973, July 21 *Perf. 13***

**405** A70 20fr grn, yel & vio bl 2.25 .80

School Coordinating Office, 10th anniv.

"Nature Protection" — A72

**1974, June 22 Photo. *Perf. 13x12½***

**406** A72 7fr multi 1.50 .55

Scorched Landscape A73

**1975, Feb. 7 Photo. *Perf. 13***

**407** A73 20fr multi 2.25 1.10

"Prevent brush fires."

Calanthe Veratrifolia — A74

Design: 11fr, Liperanthus gigas.

**1975, May 30 Photo. *Perf. 13***

**408** A74 8fr pur & multi 3.00 1.00
**409** A74 11fr dk bl & multi 3.50 1.00
*Nos. 408-409,C125 (3)* 12.50 4.25

Orchids. See Nos. 425-426.

Festival Emblem — A75

**1975, Sept. 6 Photo. *Perf. 12½x13***
**410** A75 12fr ultra, org & yel 2.00 .70

Melanesia 2000 Festival.

Birds in Flight — A76

**1975, Oct. 18 Photo. *Perf. 13½x13***
**411** A76 5fr ocher, yel & blk 1.75 .55

Nouméa Ornithological Society, 10th anniversary.

Georges Pompidou — A77

**1975, Dec. 6 Engr. *Perf. 13***
**412** A77 26fr dk grn, blk & sl 3.25 1.25

Pompidou (1911-74), president of France.

Sea Birds A78

***Perf. 13x12½, 12½x13***
**1976, Feb. 26 Photo.**
**413** A78 1fr Brown booby 1.25 .45
**414** A78 2fr Blue-faced booby 1.75 .70
**415** A78 8fr Red-footed booby, vert. 3.00 1.10
*Nos. 413-415 (3)* 6.00 2.25

Festival Emblem A79

**1976, Mar. 13 Litho. *Perf. 12½***
**416** A79 27fr bl, org & blk 2.50 .90

Rotorua 1976, South Pacific Arts Festival, New Zealand.

Lion and Lions Emblem — A80

**1976, Mar. 13 Photo. *Perf. 12½x13***
**417** A80 49fr multi 5.00 2.00

Lions Club of Nouméa, 15th anniversary.

Music Pavilion — A81

Design: 30fr, Fountain, vert.

**1976, July 3 Litho. *Perf. 12½***
**418** A81 25fr multi 1.75 .70
**419** A81 30fr blue & multi 2.25 1.00

Old Nouméa.

Polluted Shore — A82

**1976, Aug. 21 Photo. *Perf. 13***
**420** A82 20fr dp bl & multi 2.50 .90

Nature protection.

South Pacific People A83

**1976, Oct. 23 Photo. *Perf. 13***
**421** A83 20fr bl & multi 2.25 .90

16th South Pacific Commission Conference, Nouméa, Oct. 1976.

Giant Grasshopper — A84

**1977, Feb. 21 Engr. *Perf. 13***
**422** A84 26fr shown 2.00 1.25
**423** A84 31fr Beetle and larvae 3.00 1.40

Ground Satellite Station, Nouméa — A85

**1977, Apr. 16 Litho. *Perf. 13***
**424** A85 29fr multi 2.75 1.10

**Orchid Type of 1975**

Designs: 22fr, Phajus daenikeri. 44fr, Dendrobium finetianum.

**1977, May 23 Photo. *Perf. 13***
**425** A74 22fr brn & multi 3.75 1.25
**426** A74 44fr bl & multi 4.25 1.90

Mask, Palms, "Stamps" — A86

**1977, June 25 Photo. *Perf. 13***
**427** A86 35fr multi 2.00 1.00

Philately in school, Philatelic Exhibition, La Perouse Lyceum, Nouméa.

Trees A87

**1977, July 23 Photo. *Perf. 13***
**428** A87 20fr multi 1.50 .75

Nature protection.

Congress Emblem — A88

**1977, Aug. 6 Photo. *Perf. 13***
**429** A88 200fr multi 9.25 5.50

French Junior Economic Chambers Congress, Nouméa.

Young Frigate Bird — A89

Black-naped Tern — A89a

Sooty Terns — A89b

**1977-78 Photo. *Perf. 13***
**430** A89 16fr multi 5.75 1.00
**431** A89a 22fr multi 2.25 1.10
**432** A89b 40fr multi 3.75 1.50
*Nos. 430-432,C138 (4)* 17.75 5.20

Issued: 16fr, 9/17/77; 22fr, 40fr, 2/11/78.

Mare and Foal — A90

**1977, Nov. 19 Engr. *Perf. 13***
**433** A90 5fr multi 2.00 .55

10th anniversary of the Society for Promotion of Caledonian Horses.

Araucaria Montana — A91

**1978, Mar. 17 Photo. *Perf. 12½x13***
**434** A91 16fr multi 1.25 .55

See No. C149.

Halityle Regularis — A92

**1978, May 20 Photo. *Perf. 13***
**436** A92 10fr vio bl & multi 1.60 .45

Nouméa Aquarium.

Stylized Turtle and Globe A93

**1978, May 20**
**437** A93 30fr multi 3.00 1.10

Protection of the turtle.

Flying Fox — A94

**1978, June 10**
**438** A94 20fr multi 4.50 1.50

Nature protection.

Maurice Leenhardt — A95

**1978, Aug. 12 Engr. *Perf. 13***
439 A95 37fr multi 2.00 1.25

Pastor Maurice Leenhardt (1878-1954).

Soccer Player, League Emblem — A96

**1978, Nov. 4 Photo. *Perf. 13***
440 A96 26fr multi 4.50 2.50

New Caledonia Soccer League, 50th anniversary.

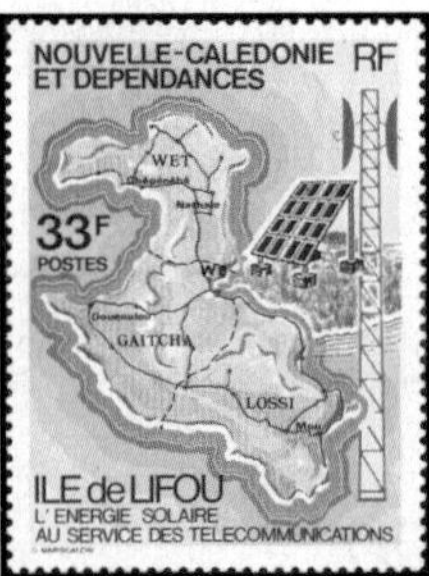
Lifu Island A97

**1978, Dec. 9 Litho. *Perf. 13***
441 A97 33fr multi 2.25 1.75

Petroglyph, Mère — A98

**1979, Jan. 27 Engr. *Perf. 13***
442 A98 10fr brick red 1.40 .55

Map of Ouvea — A99

Design: 31fr, Map of Mare Island, horiz.

***Perf. 12½x13, 13x12½***

**1979, Feb. 17 Photo.**
443 A99 11fr multi 1.25 .55
444 A99 31fr multi 1.75 .75

House at Artillery Point — A100

**1979, Apr. 28 Photo. *Perf. 13***
445 A100 20fr multi 2.00 1.50

Auguste Escoffier — A101

**1979, July 21 Engr. *Perf. 12½x13***
446 A101 24fr multi 1.50 1.50

Auguste Escoffier Hotel School.

Regatta and Games Emblem A102

**1979, Aug. 11 Photo. *Perf. 13***
447 A102 16fr multi 2.00 .70

6th South Pacific Games, Suva, Fiji, Aug. 27-Sept. 8.

Agathis Ovata A103

**1979, Oct. 20 Photo. *Perf. 13x12½***
448 A103 5fr shown 1.50 .35
449 A103 34fr Cyathea intermedia 2.00 .75

Pouembout Rodeo A104

**1979, Oct. 27 Engr. *Perf. 13x12½***
450 A104 12fr multi 1.75 .55

Bantamia Merleti A105

**1979, Dec. 1 Photo. *Perf. 13x11½***
451 A105 23fr multi 1.75 .70

Fluorescent corals from Nouméa Aquarium.

Map of Pine Tree Island, Fishermen with Nets A106

**1980, Jan. 12 Photo. *Perf. 13x12½***
452 A106 23fr multi 1.60 .45

Hibbertia Virotii A107

**1980, Apr. 19 Photo. *Perf. 13x12½***
453 A107 11fr shown 1.40 .65
454 A107 12fr Grevillea meisneri 1.40 .65

Philately at School — A108

**1980, May 10 Litho. *Perf. 12½***
455 A108 30fr multi 1.75 .55

Prevention of Traffic Accidents A109

**1980, July 5 Photo. *Perf. 13x12½***
456 A109 15fr multi 1.20 .35

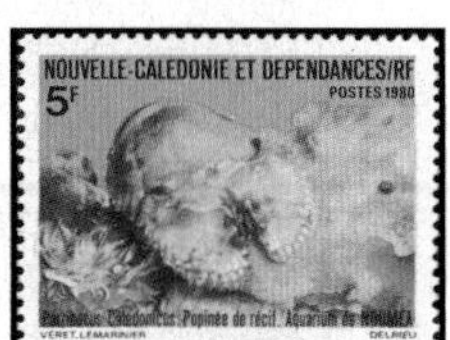
Parribacus Caledonicus — A110

Noumea Aquarium Crustacea: 8fr, Panulirus versicolor.

**1980, Aug. 23 Litho. *Perf. 13x13½***
457 A110 5fr multi .75 .35
458 A110 8fr multi 1.00 .55

Solar Energy A111

**1980, Oct. 11 Photo. *Perf. 13x12½***
459 A111 23fr multi 1.50 .70

Manta Birostris A112

25fr, Carcharhinus amblyrhnchos.

**1981, Feb. 18 Photo. *Perf. 13x12½***
460 A112 23fr shown 2.50 .90
461 A112 25fr multicolored 2.50 .90

Belep Islands A113

**1981, Mar. 4**
462 A113 26fr multi 1.25 .55

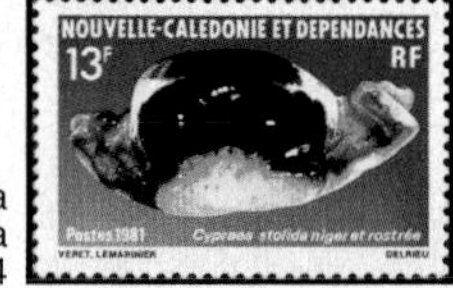
Cypraea Stolida A114

1fr, Cymbiola rossiniana, vert. 2fr, Connus floccatus, vert.

**1981, June 17 Photo. *Perf. 13***
463 A114 1fr multicolored .95 .50
464 A114 2fr multicolored 1.00 .65
465 A114 13fr shown 1.90 .75
*Nos. 463-465 (3)* 3.85 1.90

See Nos. 470-471.

Corvette Constantine, 1854 — A115

25fr, Aviso le Phoque, 1853.

**1981, July 22 Engr. *Perf. 13***
466 A115 10fr shown 1.40 .55
467 A115 25fr multicolored 2.10 1.10

See Nos. 476-477.

Intl. Year of the Disabled A116

**1981, Sept. 2 Litho. *Perf. 12½***
468 A116 45fr multicolored 1.90 .85

Nature Preservation A117

**1981, Nov. 7 Photo. *Perf. 13***
469 A117 28fr multicolored 2.25 .90

**Marine Life Type of 1981**

**1982, Jan. 20 Photo. *Perf. 13x13½***
470 A114 13fr Calappa calappa 1.50 .80
471 A114 25fr Etisus splendidus 2.25 1.10

Chalcantite A118

**1982, Mar. 17 Photo. *Perf. 13x13½***

**472** A118 15fr shown 2.25 1.10
**473** A118 30fr Anorthosite 3.00 1.10

Melaleuca Quinquenervia — A119

20fr, Savannah trees, vert.

**1982, June 23 Photo. *Perf. 13***

**474** A119 20fr multicolored 1.25 .70
**475** A119 29fr shown 1.50 .70

**Ship Type of 1981**

44fr, Barque Le Cher. 59fr, Naval dispatch vessel Kersaint.

**1982, July 7 Engr.**

**476** A115 44fr multicolored 2.10 1.00
**477** A115 59fr multicolored 2.75 1.00

Ateou Tribe Traditional House — A120

**1982, Oct. 13 Photo. *Perf. 13½x13***

**478** A120 52fr multicolored 1.75 .90

Grey's Ptilope — A121

**1982, Nov. 6**

**479** A121 32fr shown 1.75 .70
**480** A121 35fr Caledonian lori-quet 2.00 .90

Central Education Coordination Office — A122

**1982, Nov. 27 Litho. *Perf. 13½x13***

**481** A122 48fr Boat 1.75 .75

Bernheim Library, Noumea — A123

**1982, Dec. 15 Engr. *Perf. 13***

**482** A123 36fr multicolored 1.10 .55

Caledonian Orchids A123a

10fr, Dendrobium oppositifolium. 15fr, Dendrobium munificum. 29fr, Dendrobium fractiflexum.

**1983, Feb. 16 Photo. *Perf. 13x13½***

**482A** A123a 10fr multicolored .75 .35
**482B** A123a 15fr multicolored 1.10 .45
**482C** A123a 29fr multicolored 1.75 .90
*Nos. 482A-482C (3)* 3.60 1.70

Xanthostemon Aurantiacum — A124

1fr, Crinum asiaticum. 2fr, Xanthostemon aurantiacum. 4fr, Metrosideros demonstrans, vert.

**1983, Mar. 23 Litho. *Perf. 13***

**483** A124 1fr multicolored .45 .35
**484** A124 2fr multicolored .45 .65
**485** A124 4fr multicolored .45 .35
*Nos. 483-485 (3)* 1.35 1.35

25th Anniv. of Posts and Telecommunications Dept. — A125

Telephones and post offices.

**1983, Apr. 30 Litho. *Perf. 13***

**486** A125 30fr multicolored 1.10 .45
**487** A125 40fr multicolored 1.20 .75
**488** A125 50fr multicolored 1.75 .80
*a.* Souvenir sheet of 3 11.00 10.00
*b.* Strip of 3, #486-488 5.50 5.50

No. 488a contains Nos. 486-488 with changed background colors.

Local Snakes A126

**1983, June 22 Photo. *Perf. 13***

**489** A126 31fr Laticauda laticauda 1.75 .75
**490** A126 33fr Laticauda colubrina 2.00 .85

A127

**1983, Aug. 10 Engr.**

**491** A127 16fr Volleyball 1.25 .65

7th South Pacific Games, Sept.

Nature Protection A128

**1983, Oct. 12 Photo. *Perf. 12½***

**492** A128 56fr multi 2.00 1.00

Birds of Prey A129

34fr, Tyto Alba Lifuensis, vert. 37fr, Pandion Haliaetus.

**1983, Nov. 16 Litho. *Perf. 13***

**493** A129 34fr multicolored 2.00 .95
**494** A129 37fr multicolored 2.50 1.25

Local Shells — A130

5fr, Conus chenui. 15fr, Conus moluccensis. 20fr, Conus optimus.

**1984, Jan. 11 Litho. & Engr.**

**495** A130 5fr multicolored 1.00 .60
**496** A130 15fr multicolored 1.10 .60
**497** A130 20fr multicolored 1.40 .80
*Nos. 495-497 (3)* 3.50 2.00

See Nos. 521-522.

Steamers A131

**1984, Feb. 8 Engr.**

**498** A131 18fr St. Joseph 1.00 .65
**499** A131 31fr St. Antoine 1.50 .85

Arms of Noumea — A132

**1984, Apr. 11 Litho. *Perf. 12½x13***

**500** A132 35fr multi 1.25 .65

See No. 546, 607, C214.

Environmental Preservation — A133

**1984, May 23 *Perf. 13***

**501** A133 65fr Island scene 2.25 .90

Orchids — A134

16fr, Diplocaulobium ou-hinnae. 38fr, Acianthus atepalus.

**1984, July 18 Litho. *Perf. 12***

**502** A134 16fr multicolored 1.50 .75
**503** A134 38fr multicolored 2.00 1.10

Cent. of Public Schooling A135

**1984, Oct. 11 Litho. *Perf. 13½x13***

**504** A135 59fr Schoolhouse 2.00 .90

Kagu — A137

**1985-86 Engr. *Perf. 13***

**511** A137 1fr brt bl .60 .60
**512** A137 2fr green .60 .60
**513** A137 3fr brt org .60 .60
**514** A137 4fr brt grn .60 .60
**515** A137 5fr dp rose lil .60 .60
**516** A137 35fr crimson 1.25 .90
**517** A137 38fr vermilion 1.25 1.00
**518** A137 40fr brt rose ('86) 1.40 .70
*Nos. 511-518 (8)* 6.90 5.60

Issued: 1, 2, 5, 38fr, 5/22; 3, 4, 35fr, 2/13; 40fr, 7/30.

See types A179, A179a.

**Sea Shell Type of 1984**

**Lithographed and Engraved**

**1985, Feb. 27 *Perf. 13***

**521** A130 55fr Conus bullatus 1.50 .90
**522** A130 72fr Conus lamberti 2.00 1.40

25th World Meteorological Day — A138

17fr, Radio communication, storm.

**1985, Mar. 20 Litho.**

**523** A138 17fr multicolored .85 .85

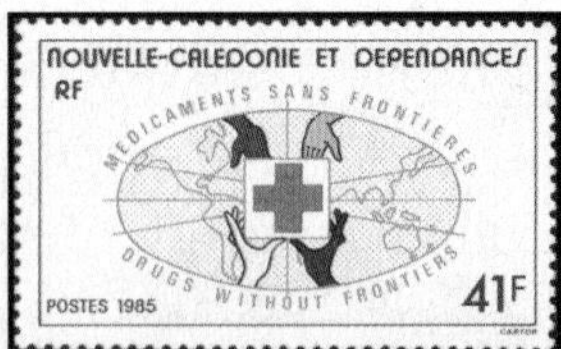

Red Cross, Medicine Without Frontiers — A139

**1985, Apr. 10** ***Perf. 12½***
**524** A139 41fr multi 1.50 .80

Telephone Switching Center Inauguration — A140

**1985, Apr. 24**
**525** A140 70fr E 10 B installation 1.75 1.00

Marguerite La Foa Suspension Bridge A141

**1985, May 10** **Engr.** ***Perf. 13***
**526** A141 44fr brt bl & red brn 1.75 .90

Historical Preservation Association.

Le Cagou Philatelic Society — A142

**1985, June 15** **Litho.**
**527** A142 220fr multi 5.75 4.00
*a.* Souvenir sheet, perf. 12½ 8.50 8.50

No. 527a sold for 230fr.

4th Pacific Arts Festival — A143

**1985, July 3** ***Perf. 13½***
**Black Overprint**
**528** A143 55fr multi 1.50 1.00
**529** A143 75fr multi 2.25 1.40

Not issued without overprint. Festival was transferred to French Polynesia.

Intl. Youth Year — A144

**1985, July 24** **Litho.** ***Perf. 13***
**530** A144 59fr multi 2.00 .80

Amedee Lighthouse Electrification — A145

**1985, Aug. 13**
**531** A145 89fr multi 2.25 1.10

Environmental Conservation A146

**1985, Sept. 18**
**532** A146 100fr Planting trees 2.50 1.10

Birds A147

**1985, Dec. 18** ***Perf. 12½***
**533** A147 50fr Poule sultane 1.75 1.00
**534** A147 60fr Merle caledonien 2.75 1.10

Noumea Aquarium A148

10fr, Pomacanthus imperator. 17fr, Rhinopias aphanes.

**1986, Feb. 19** **Litho.** ***Perf. 12½x13***
**535** A148 10fr multicolored .55 .35
**536** A148 17fr multicolored .75 .60

Kanumera Bay, Isle of Pines — A149

**1986, Mar. 26** **Litho.** ***Perf. 12½***
**537** A149 50fr shown 1.25 .70
**538** A149 55fr Inland village 1.40 .80

See Nos. 547-548, 617-618.

Geckos A150

20fr, Bavayia sauvagii. 45fr, Rhacodactylus leachianus.

**1986, Apr. 16** ***Perf. 12½x13***
**539** A150 20fr multicolored 1.10 .75
**540** A150 45fr multicolored 1.50 .85

1986 World Cup Soccer Championships, Mexico — A151

**1986, May 28** ***Perf. 13***
**541** A151 60fr multi 1.50 1.00

1st Pharmacy in New Caledonia, 120th Anniv. — A152

**1986, June 25** **Litho.** ***Perf. 13***
**542** A152 80fr multi 2.25 1.25

Orchids A153

44fr, Coelogynae licastioides. 58fr, Calanthe langei.

**1986, July 16** ***Perf. 12½x13***
**543** A153 44fr multicolored 1.50 .80
**544** A153 58fr multicolored 1.75 .90

STAMPEX '86, Adelaide — A154

**1986, Aug. 4** ***Perf. 12½***
**545** A154 110fr Bird 3.00 1.40

**Arms Type of 1984**

**1986, Oct. 11** **Litho.** ***Perf. 13½***
**546** A132 94fr Mont Dore 3.00 1.10

**Landscape Type of 1986**

40fr, West landscape, vert. 76fr, South Landscape.

**1986, Oct. 29** **Litho.** ***Perf. 12½***
**547** A149 40fr multicolored 1.10 .70
**548** A149 76fr multicolored 1.75 .80

Flowers A156

Niponthes vieillardi, Syzygium ngayense, Archidendropsis Paivana, Scavola balansae.

**1986, Nov. 12** ***Perf. 12½***
**549** A156 73fr multi 1.90 .90

Nature Protection Assoc.

A157

**1986, Nov. 26** ***Perf. 13x12½***
**550** A157 350fr Emblem 8.00 4.25

Noumea Lions Club, 25th anniv.

A158

Paintings: 74fr, Moret Point, by A. Sisley. 140fr, Butterfly Chase, by B. Morisot.

**1986, Dec. 23** **Litho.** ***Perf. 13***
**551** A158 74fr multi 2.25 1.40
**552** A158 140fr multi 4.00 1.60

America's Cup — A159

**1987, Jan. 28** ***Perf. 13½***
**553** A159 30fr Challenge France 1.50 .90
**554** A159 70fr French Kiss 1.90 1.10

Plants, Butterflies A160

46fr, Anona squamosa, Graphium gelon. 54fr, Albizzia granulosa, Polyura gamma.

**1987, Feb. 25** **Litho.** ***Perf. 13x12½***
**555** A160 46fr multi 2.50 .90
**556** A160 54fr multi 3.00 1.50

Pirogues A161

**1987, May 13** **Engr.** ***Perf. 13x12½***
**557** A161 72fr from Isle of Pines 1.75 1.00
**558** A161 90fr from Ouvea 2.25 1.25

New Town Hall, Mont Dore A162

**1987, May 23** **Litho.** ***Perf. 12½x13***
**559** A162 92fr multi 2.10 1.00

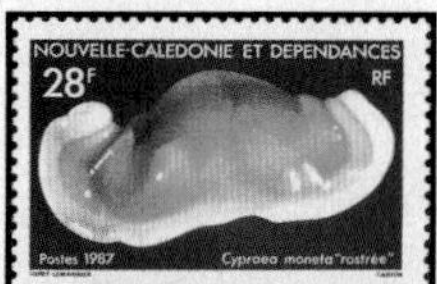

Seashells A163

**1987, June 24** *Perf. 13*
**560** A163 28fr Cypraea moneta 1.00 .65
**561** A163 36fr Cypraea martini 1.50 .70

8th South Pacific Games — A164

**1987, July 8** *Perf. 12½x13*
**562** A164 40fr multi 1.25 .55

A165

**1987, July 22** *Perf. 13½*
**563** A165 270fr multi 5.75 2.75

Soroptimist Int'l. 13th Convention, Melbourne, July 26-31.

Birds A166

18fr, Zosterops xanthochroa. 21fr, Falco peregrinus nesiotes, vert.

**1987, Aug. 26** *Perf. 13*
**564** A166 18fr multicolored .90 .35
**565** A166 21fr multicolored 1.10 .35

South Pacific Commission, 40th Anniv. — A167

**1987, Oct. 14** **Litho.** *Perf. 13*
**566** A167 200fr multi 5.00 2.50

Philately at School A168

**1987, Oct. 21** *Perf. 12½*
**567** A168 15fr multi .90 .50

8th South Pacific Games, Noumea — A169

**1987, Dec. 8** **Litho.** *Perf. 12½*
**568** A169 20fr Golf 1.25 .50
**569** A169 30fr Rugby 1.75 1.20
**570** A169 100fr Long jump 3.00 1.25
*Nos. 568-570 (3)* 6.00 2.95

Map, Ships, La Perouse — A170

**1988, Feb. 10** **Engr.** *Perf. 13*
**571** A170 36fr dark rose lil 1.50 .70

Disappearance of La Perouse expedition, 200th anniv., and Jean-Francois de Galaup (1741-1788), Comte de La Perouse.

French University of the South Pacific at Noumea and Papeete A171

**1988, Feb. 24** **Litho.** *Perf. 13x12½*
**572** A171 400fr multi 9.25 4.25

Tropical Fish A172

30fr, Pomacanthus semicirculatus. 46fr, Glyphidodontops cyaneus.

**1988, Mar. 23** **Litho.** *Perf. 13*
**573** A172 30fr multicolored 1.10 .55
**574** A172 46fr multicolored 1.50 .80

Intl. Red Cross and Red Crescent Organizations, 125th Annivs. — A173

**1988, Apr. 27**
**575** A173 300fr multi 7.50 3.75

Regional Housing A174

Designs: 19fr, Mwaringou, Canala Region, vert. 21fr, Nathalo, Lifou.

**1988, Apr. 13** **Engr.** *Perf. 13*
**576** A174 19fr emer grn, brt blue & red brn .85 .50
**577** A174 21fr brt blue, emer grn & red brn .85 .50

Medicinal Plants A175

**1988, May 18** **Litho.** *Perf. 13x12½*
**578** A175 28fr Ochrosia elliptica 1.10 .55
**579** A175 64fr Rauvolfia levenetii 2.10 1.10

No. 579 is airmail.

Living Fossils — A176

51fr, Gymnocrinus richeri.

**1988, June 11** *Perf. 13*
**580** A176 51fr multicolored 2.25 .90

Bourail Museum and Historical Soc. — A177

**1988, June 25** **Litho.** *Perf. 13*
**581** A177 120fr multi 3.00 1.60

SYDPEX '88 — A178

Designs: No. 582, La Perouse aboard *La Boussole*, gazing through spyglass at the First Fleet in Botany Bay, Jan. 24, 1788. No. 583, Capt. Phillip and crew ashore on Botany Bay watching the approach of La Perouse's ships *La Boussole* and *L'Astrolabe*.

**1988, July 30** **Litho.** *Perf. 13x12½*
**582** A178 42fr multi 1.50 .90
**583** A178 42fr multi 1.50 .90
*a.* Souvenir sheet of 2, #582-583, perf. 13x13½ 4.75 4.25
*b.* Strip of 2, #582-583 + label 3.50 3.00

No. 583a sold for 120fr.

Kagu — A179

**1988-90** **Engr.** *Perf. 13*
**584** A179 1fr bright blue .50 .25
**585** A179 2fr green .50 .25
**586** A179 3fr bright orange .75 .25
**587** A179 4fr bright green .75 .25
**588** A179 5fr deep rose lilac 1.00 .25
**589** A179 28fr orange 1.00 .25
**590** A179 40fr bright rose 1.10 .25
*Nos. 584-590 (7)* 5.60 1.75

Issued: 40fr, 8/10/88; 1fr, 4fr, 1/25/89; 2fr, 3fr, 5fr, 4/19/89; 28fr, 1/15/90.
See Type A137.

Kagu — A179a

**1990-93** **Engr.** *Perf. 13*
**591** A179a 1fr dark blue .25 .25
**592** A179a 2fr bright green .25 .25
**593** A179a 3fr brt yel org .30 .25
**594** A179a 4fr dark green .30 .25
**595** A179a 5fr bright violet .30 .25
**596** A179a 9fr blue black .35 .25
**597** A179a 12fr orange .40 .25
**598** A179a 40fr lilac rose 1.00 .25
**599** A179a 50fr red 1.40 .30
*Nos. 591-599 (9)* 4.55 2.30

Issued: 50fr, 9/5/90; 1fr-5fr, 1/9/91; 40fr, 1/15/92; 9fr, 12fr, 1/25/93.
See Type A137 and Nos. 675, 683. For surcharge see No. 685.

1988 Summer Olympics, Seoul — A180

**1988, Sept. 14** *Perf. 12½x12*
**600** A180 150fr multi 4.00 2.00

Pasteur Institute, Noumea, Cent. A181

**1988, Sept. 28** **Engr.** *Perf. 13*
**601** A181 100fr blk, brt ultra & dark red 2.50 1.25

Writers — A182

72fr, Georges Baudoux (1870-1949). 73fr, Jean Mariotti (1901-1975).

**1988, Oct. 15** **Engr.** *Perf. 13*
**602** A182 72fr multicolored 2.00 1.00
**603** A182 73fr multicolored 2.00 1.00

No. 603 is airmail.

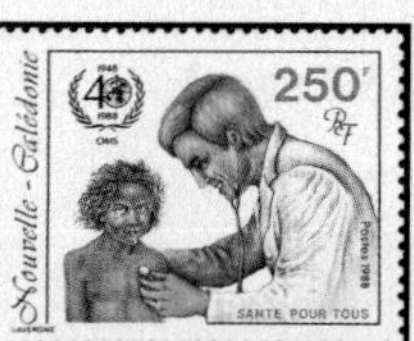

WHO, 40th Anniv. A183

**1988, Nov. 16** **Litho.** *Perf. 13x12½*
**604** A183 250fr multi 6.00 2.75

### Art Type of 1984 Without "ET DEPENDANCES"

Paintings by artists of the Pacific: 54fr, *Land of Men*, by L. Bunckley. 92fr, *The Latin Quarter*, by Marik.

**1988, Dec. 7**
**605** AP113 54fr multi 2.25 1.00
**606** AP113 92fr multi 3.00 1.40

**Arms Type of 1984 Without "ET DEPENDANCES"**

**1989, Feb. 22 Litho.** ***Perf. 13½***
**607** A132 200fr Koumac 4.50 2.00

Indigenous Flora A184

80fr, Parasitaxus ustus, vert. 90fr, Tristaniopsis guillainii.

**1989, Mar. 22 Litho.** ***Perf. 13½***
**608** A184 80fr multicolored 2.00 1.10
**609** A184 90fr multicolored 2.50 1.40

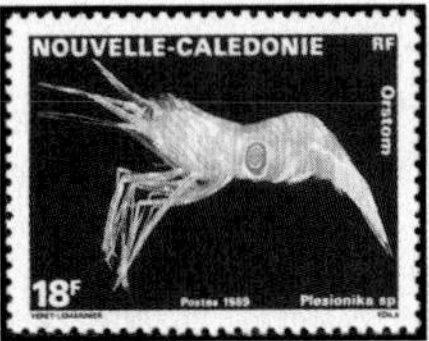

Marine Life A185

**1989, May 17 Litho.** ***Perf. 12½x13***
**610** A185 18fr Plesionika 1.10 .60
**611** A185 66fr Ocosia apia 1.90 1.00
**612** A185 110fr Latiaxis 2.75 1.60
*Nos. 610-612 (3)* 5.75 3.20

See Nos. 652-653.

French Revolution, Bicent. — A186

40fr, Liberty. 58fr, Equality. 76fr, Fraternity. 180fr, Liberty, Equality, Fraternity.

**1989, July 7 Litho.** ***Perf. 13½***
**613** A186 40fr multi 1.75 .60
**614** A186 58fr multi 1.75 .75
**615** A186 76fr multi 1.75 1.00
*Nos. 613-615 (3)* 5.25 2.35

**Souvenir Sheet**

**616** A186 180fr multi 5.50 5.50

Nos. 614-616 are airmail.

**Landscape Type of 1986 Without "ET DEPENDANCES"**

64fr, La Poule rookery, Hienghene. 180fr, Ouaieme ferry.

**1989, Aug. 23 Litho.** ***Perf. 13***
**617** A149 64fr multicolored 1.50 .75
**618** A149 180fr multicolored 4.00 1.60

No. 617 is airmail.

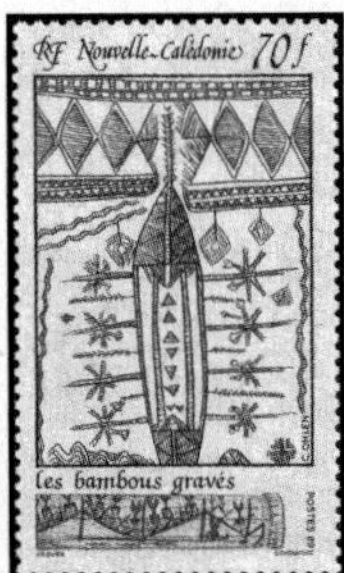

Carved Bamboo — A187

**Litho. & Engr.**

**1989, Sept. 27** ***Perf. 12½x13***
**619** A187 70fr multicolored 1.75 .70

See No. C216.

A188

**1989, Oct. 25 Litho.** ***Perf. 13***
**620** A188 350fr multicolored 8.50 3.50

Hobie-Cat 14 10th World Championships, Nov. 3, Noumea.

Natl. Historical Soc., 20th Anniv. — A189

Cover of *Moeurs: Superstitions of New Caledonians,* cover of book on Melanesian oral literature and historians G. Pisier, R.P. Neyret and A. Surleau.

**1989, Nov. 3 Engr.**
**621** A189 74fr brown & black 2.00 .80

Ft. Teremba — A190

**1989, Nov. 18 Engr.**
**622** A190 100fr bl grn & dk org 2.50 1.40

Marguerite Historical Preservation Soc.

Impressionist Paintings — A191

Designs: 130fr, The Escape of Rochefort, by Manet. 270fr, Self-portrait, by Courbet.

**1989, Dec. 6 Litho.** ***Perf. 13½***
**623** A191 130fr multicolored 3.25 1.90
**624** A191 270fr multicolored 7.50 4.00

Fr. Patrick O'Reilly (1900-1988), Writer — A192

**1990, Jan. 24 Engr.** ***Perf. 13x13½***
**625** A192 170fr blk & plum 4.25 1.90

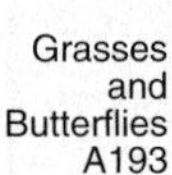

Grasses and Butterflies A193

Various Cyperacea costularia and Paratisiphone lyrnessa: 18fr, Female. 50fr, Female, diff. 94fr, Male.

**1990, Feb. 21 Litho.** ***Perf. 13½***
**626** A193 18fr shown 1.90 .60
**627** A193 50fr multicolored .90 .50
**628** A193 94fr multicolored 3.25 1.25
*Nos. 626-628 (3)* 6.05 2.35

Nos. 626 and 628 are airmail.

A194

**1990, Mar. 16 Engr.** ***Perf. 12½x13***
**629** A194 85fr Kanakan money 1.90 .80
**630** A194 140fr money, diff. 3.50 1.40

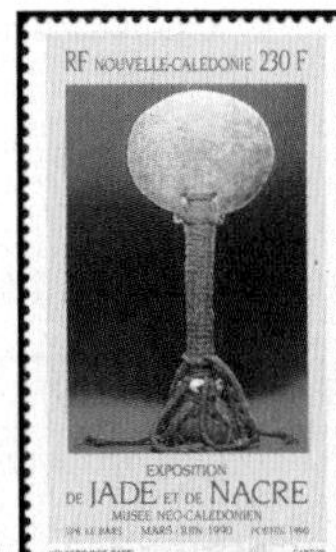

A195

**1990, Mar. 16 Litho.** ***Perf. 13x13½***
**631** A195 230fr multicolored 5.25 2.50

Jade and mother of pearl exhibition, New Caledonian Museum.

Noumea Aquarium A196

10fr, Phyllidia ocellata. 42fr, Chromodoris kuniei, vert.

**1990, Apr. 25** ***Perf. 13x12½, 12½x13***
**632** A196 10fr multicolored .45 .45
**633** A196 42fr multicolored 1.50 .70

Petroglyphs A197

**1990, July 11 Engr.** ***Perf. 13***
**634** A197 40fr Neounda 1.25 .55
**635** A197 58fr Kassducou 1.75 .90

No. 635 is airmail.

Meeting Center of the Pacific — A198

**1990, July 25 Litho.** ***Perf. 13***
**636** A198 320fr multicolored 7.00 3.00

World Cup Soccer Championships, Italy — A199

**1990, May 30 Litho.** ***Perf. 13***
**637** A199 240fr multicolored 6.00 3.00

Flowers A200

105fr, Gardenia aubryi. 130fr, Hibbertia baudouinii.

**1990, Nov. 7** ***Perf. 13x12½***
**638** A200 105fr multicolored 2.50 1.25
**639** A200 130fr multicolored 3.00 2.00

La Maison Celieres by M. Petron A201

365fr, Le Mont-Dore de Jade by C. Degroiselle.

**1990, Dec. 5** ***Perf. 12½***
**640** A201 110fr multicolored 2.50 1.25
**641** A201 365fr multicolored 9.00 2.75

No. 640 is airmail.

Writers — A202

Designs: #642, Louise Michel (1830-1905). #643, Charles B. Nething (1867-1947).

**1991, Mar. 20 Engr.** ***Perf. 13***
**642** 125fr rose lil & bl 3.00 1.50
**643** 125fr brn & bl 3.00 1.50
*a.* A202 Pair, #642-643 + label 6.50 6.00

Native Huts — A203

**1991, May 15 Litho.** ***Perf. 12***
**644** A203 12fr Houailou .75 .40
**645** A203 35fr Hienghene 1.00 .60

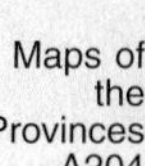

Maps of the Provinces A204

**1991, June 17 Litho. *Perf. 13½***

| | | | |
|---|---|---|---|
| **646** | A204 45fr Northern | 1.00 | .45 |
| **647** | A204 45fr Island | 1.00 | .45 |
| **648** | A204 45fr Southern | 1.00 | .45 |
| *a.* | Strip of 3, #646-648 | 3.50 | 3.25 |

Orchids — A205

55fr, Dendrobium biflorum. 70fr, Dendrobium closterium.

**1991, July 24 Litho. *Perf. 13***

| | | | |
|---|---|---|---|
| **649** | A205 55fr multicolored | 1.60 | .80 |
| **650** | A205 70fr multicolored | 2.25 | 1.00 |

French Institute of Scientific Research — A206

**1991, Aug. 26**

| | | | |
|---|---|---|---|
| **651** | A206 170fr multicolored | 3.75 | 1.75 |

**Marine Life Type of 1989**

60fr, Monocentris japonicus. 100fr, Tristigenys niphonia.

**1991, Aug. 26 Litho. *Perf. 12***

| | | | |
|---|---|---|---|
| **652** | A185 60fr multicolored | 1.50 | .80 |
| **653** | A185 100fr multicolored | 2.50 | 1.10 |

9th South Pacific Games, Papua New Guinea A207

**1991, Sept. 6 *Perf. 12½***

| | | | |
|---|---|---|---|
| **654** | A207 170fr multicolored | 3.50 | 1.50 |

Vietnamese in New Caledonia, Cent. — A208

**1991, Sept. 8 Engr. *Perf. 13x12½***

| | | | |
|---|---|---|---|
| **655** | A208 300fr multicolored | 6.50 | 2.50 |

Lions Club of New Caledonia, 30th Anniv. — A209

**1991, Oct. 5 Litho. *Perf. 12½***

| | | | |
|---|---|---|---|
| **656** | A209 192fr multicolored | 5.50 | 2.75 |

First Commercial Harvesting of Sandalwood, 150th Anniv. — A210

**1991, Oct. 23 Engr. *Perf. 13***

| | | | |
|---|---|---|---|
| **657** | A210 200fr multicolored | 5.25 | 2.75 |

Phila Nippon '91 — A211

Plants and butterflies: 8fr, Phillantus, Eurema hecabe. 15fr, Pipturus incanus, Hypolimnas octocula. 20fr, Stachytarpheta urticaefolia, Precis villida. 26fr, Malaisia scandens, Cyrestis telamon.

Butterflies: No. 662a, Cyrestis telamon, vert. b, Hypolimnas octocula, vert. c, Eurema hecabe, vert. d, Precis villida, vert.

**1991, Nov. 16 Litho. *Perf. 12½***

| | | | |
|---|---|---|---|
| **658** | A211 8fr multicolored | .25 | .25 |
| **659** | A211 15fr multicolored | .35 | .35 |
| **660** | A211 20fr multicolored | .45 | .35 |
| **661** | A211 26fr multicolored | .70 | .45 |
| *a.* | Strip of 4, #658-661 + label | 2.75 | 2.50 |

**Souvenir Sheet**

| | | | |
|---|---|---|---|
| **662** | A211 75fr Sheet of 4, #a.-d. | 12.00 | 12.00 |

Central Bank for Economic Cooperation, 50th Anniv. — A212

Designs: No. 663, Nickel processing plant, dam. No. 664, Private home, tourist hotels.

**1991, Dec. 2 Litho. *Perf. 13***

| | | | |
|---|---|---|---|
| **663** | 76fr multicolored | 1.90 | 1.00 |
| **664** | 76fr multicolored | 1.90 | 1.00 |
| *a.* | A212 Pair, #663-664 + label | 4.00 | 4.00 |

Preservation of Nature — A213

15fr, Madeleine waterfalls.

**1992, Mar. 25 Litho. *Perf. 13***

| | | | |
|---|---|---|---|
| **665** | A213 15fr multicolored | .60 | .45 |
| *a.* | Souv. sheet, perf. 12½ | 4.00 | 4.00 |

No. 665a sold for 150fr.

Immigration of First Japanese to New Caledonia, Cent. — A214

**1992, June 11 Litho. *Perf. 13x12½***

| | | | |
|---|---|---|---|
| **666** | 95fr yellow & multi | 2.25 | 1.25 |
| **667** | 95fr gray & multi | 2.25 | 1.25 |
| *a.* | A214 Pair, #666-667 + label | 4.50 | 4.50 |

Arrival of American Armed Forces, 50th Anniv. — A215

**1992, Aug. 13**

| | | | |
|---|---|---|---|
| **668** | A215 50fr multicolored | 1.50 | .60 |

Lagoon Protection — A216

**1993, Feb. 23 Litho. *Perf. 13***

| | | | |
|---|---|---|---|
| **669** | A216 120fr multicolored | 2.75 | 1.25 |

**Kagu Type of 1990**

**1993-94 Engr. *Perf. 13***

| | | | |
|---|---|---|---|
| **675** | A179a 55fr red | 2.00 | 1.25 |
| **676** | A179a (60fr) claret | 1.50 | .60 |

**Self-Adhesive**

**Litho.**

***Die Cut Perf. 10***

| | | | |
|---|---|---|---|
| **681** | A179a 5fr bright lilac | 1.40 | 1.40 |
| *a.* | Bklt. pane, 8+8, gutter btwn. | 22.50 | |
| **683** | A179a 55fr red | 3.50 | 3.50 |
| *a.* | Bklt. pane, 8+8, gutter btwn. | 57.50 | |

Issued: Nos. 675, 683, 4/7/93; No. 676, 1/27/94; No. 681, 2/94.

No. 676 sold for 60fr on day of issue.

By their nature, Nos. 681a, 683a are complete booklets. The peelable paper backing serves as a booklet cover.

This is an expanding set. Numbers may change.

No. 599 Surcharged

**1993 Engr. *Perf. 13***

| | | | |
|---|---|---|---|
| **685** | A179a 55fr on 50fr red | 1.40 | .70 |

Philately in School — A217

**1993, Apr. 7 Litho. *Perf. 13½***

| | | | |
|---|---|---|---|
| **686** | A217 25fr multicolored | .60 | .30 |

For overprint see No. 690.

Miniature Sheet of 13

Town Coats of Arms A218

Designs: a, Bourail. b, Noumea. c, Canala. d, Kone. e, Paita. f, Dumbea. g, Koumac. h, Ponerhouen. i, Kaamoo Hyehen. j, Mont Dore. k, Thio. l, Kaala-Gomen. m, Touho.

**1993, Dec. 10 Litho. *Perf. 13½***

| | | | |
|---|---|---|---|
| **687** | A218 70fr #a.-m., + 2 labels | 40.00 | 40.00 |

Souvenir Sheet

Hong Kong '94 — A219

Wildlife: a, Panda. b, Kagu.

**1994, Feb. 18 Litho. *Perf. 13***

| | | | |
|---|---|---|---|
| **688** | A219 105fr Sheet of 2, #a.-b. | 8.25 | 8.25 |

First Postal Delivery Route, 50th Anniv. — A220

**1994, Apr. 28 Engr. *Perf. 13***

| | | | |
|---|---|---|---|
| **689** | A220 15fr multicolored | .50 | .25 |

No. 686 Ovptd. in Blue

**1994, Apr. 22 Litho. *Perf. 13½***

| | | | |
|---|---|---|---|
| **690** | A217 25fr multicolored | .70 | .35 |

Headquarters of New Caledonian Post Office — A222

**1994, June 25 Litho. *Perf. 13½x13***

| | | | |
|---|---|---|---|
| **691** | Strip of 4, #a.-d. | 8.00 | 8.00 |
| *a.* | A222 30fr 1859 | .75 | .45 |
| *b.* | A222 60fr 1936 | 1.50 | .80 |
| *c.* | A222 90fr 1967 | 2.10 | 1.40 |
| *d.* | A222 120fr 1993 | 3.00 | 1.75 |

Pacific Sculpture — A223

**1994, June 25 Litho. *Perf. 13x13½***

| | | | |
|---|---|---|---|
| **693** | A223 60fr multicolored | 1.50 | .70 |

Chambeyronia Macrocarpa A224

**1994, July 7 Litho. *Perf. 13x13½***
**694** A224 90fr multicolored 2.25 1.10

### No. J46 Overprinted With Bar Over "Timbre Taxe"

**1994, Aug. 8 Litho. *Perf. 13***
**696** D5 5fr multicolored 17.50 —

Stag A227

**1994, Aug. 14 Litho. *Perf. 13½***
**697** A227 150fr multicolored 3.50 1.60

Jacques Nervat, Writer — A228

**1994, Sept. 15 *Perf. 13x13½***
**698** A228 175fr multicolored 4.00 1.90

Frigate Nivose A229

No. 699, 30fr, Ship at sea. No. 700, 30fr, Ship along shore. No. 701, 30fr, Ship docked. No. 702, 60fr, Painting of frigate, map of island, ship's crest. No. 703, 60fr, Ship's bell. No. 704, 60fr, Sailor looking at ship.

**1994, Oct. 7 Litho. *Perf. 13½***

**Booklet Stamps**

| | | | | |
|---|---|---|---|---|
| **699** | A229 30fr multicolored | 1.10 | .45 |
| **700** | A229 30fr multicolored | 1.10 | .45 |
| **701** | A229 30fr multicolored | 1.10 | .35 |
| **702** | A229 60fr multicolored | 1.75 | .80 |
| **703** | A229 60fr multicolored | 1.75 | .80 |
| **704** | A229 60fr multicolored | 1.75 | .80 |
| *a.* | Booklet pane, #699-704 | 9.00 | |
| | Booklet, 4 #704a | 40.00 | |

Philately at School A230

**1994, Nov. 4 Litho. *Perf. 13½***
**705** A230 30fr multicolored .90 .35

For overprint see No. 749

Christmas A231

Top of bell starts below: a, Second "o." b, Third "e." c, "a." d, "C." e, Second "e."

**1994, Dec. 17**
**706** Strip of 5 4.75 4.25
*a.-e.* A231 30fr Any single .85 .55

Nos. 706a-706e differ in location of the red ball, yellow bell and statue. No.706 is designed for stereoscopic viewing.

Le Monde Newspaper, 50th Anniv. — A232

**1994, Dec. 17**
**707** A232 90fr multicolored 2.75 1.60

Louis Pasteur (1822-95) — A233

**1995, Feb. 13 Litho. *Perf. 13***
**708** A233 120fr No. 601 2.75 1.40

Charles de Gaulle (1890-1970) — A234

**Litho. & Embossed**

**1995, Mar. 28 *Perf. 13***
**709** A234 1000fr blue & gold 18.00 15.00

Teacher's Training College for the French Territories in the Pacific — A235

**1995, Apr. 24 Litho. *Perf. 13***
**710** A235 100fr multicolored 2.25 1.25

See French Polynesia No. 656 and Wallis & Futuna No. C182.

Sylviornis Neo-Caledonia, Fossil Bird — A236

**1995, May 16 Litho. *Perf. 13x13½***
**711** A236 60fr multicolored 1.75 .70

10th Sunshine Triathlon — A237

**1995, May 26 Engr. *Perf. 13x12½***
**712** A237 60fr multicolored 1.50 .90

Creation of the CFP Franc, 1945 A238

Top of tree at left points to: a, Second "e." b, Second "l." c, First "l." d, First "e."

**1995, June 8 Litho. *Perf. 13x13½***
**713** A238 10fr Strip of 4, #a.-d. 1.50 1.50

Nos. 713a-713d show coin rotating clockwise with trees, hut at different locations. No. 713 is designed for stereoscopic viewing.

1st New Caledonian Deputy in French Natl. Assembly, 50th Anniv. A239

**1995, June 8 *Perf. 13½***
**714** A239 60fr multicolored 1.50 .70

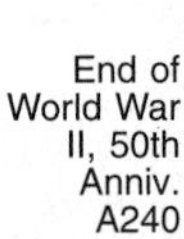

End of World War II, 50th Anniv. A240

**1995, June 8 *Perf. 13x13½***
**715** A240 90fr multicolored 1.50 .60

UN, 50th Anniv. A241

**1995, June 8**
**716** A241 90fr multicolored 2.25 .90

Sebertia Acuminata A242

**1995, July 28 Litho. *Perf. 13x13½***
**717** A242 60fr multicolored 1.50 .60

Singapore '95 — A243

Sea birds: 5fr, Anous stolidus. 10fr, Larus novaehollandiae. 20fr, Sterna dougallii. 35fr, Pandion haliaetus. 65fr, Sula sula. 125fr, Fregata minor.

**1995, Aug. 24 Litho. *Perf. 13x13½***

| | | | |
|---|---|---|---|
| **718** | A243 5fr multicolored | .25 | .25 |
| **719** | A243 10fr multicolored | .35 | .25 |
| **720** | A243 20fr multicolored | .40 | .25 |
| **721** | A243 35fr multicolored | .80 | .55 |
| **722** | A243 65fr multicolored | 1.40 | 1.10 |
| **723** | A243 125fr multicolored | 3.00 | 1.60 |
| *a.* | Souvenir sheet, #718-723 + label | 7.50 | 7.50 |
| | *Nos. 718-723 (6)* | 6.20 | 4.00 |

10th South Pacific Games A244

**1995, Aug. 24**
**724** A244 90fr multicolored 2.10 1.10

Sculpture, The Lizard Man, by Dick Bone — A248

**1995, Oct. 25 Litho. *Perf. 13***
**730** A248 65fr multicolored 1.25 .75

Gargariscus Prionocephalus — A249

**1995, Dec. 15 Litho. *Perf. 13***
**731** A249 100fr multicolored 2.25 1.00

Francis Carco (1886-1958), Poet & Novelist — A250

**1995, Nov. 15 Litho. *Perf. 13x13½***
**732** A250 95fr multicolored 2.25 1.25

Ancient Pottery — A251

**1996, Apr. 12 Litho. *Perf. 13***
**733** A251 65fr multicolored 1.60 .90

Endemic Rubiaceous Plants — A252

Designs: 65fr, Captaincookia margaretae. 95fr, Ixora cauliflora.

**1996, Apr. 17**
**734** A252 65fr multicolored 1.50 .60
**735** A252 95fr multicolored 2.10 .90

7th Va'a (Outrigger Canoe) World Championship, Noumea, New Caledonia — A253

Designs: a, 30fr, Islander standing on shore with early version of canoe. b, 65fr, Early single-hull canoe with islanders. c, 95fr, Early catamaran, people rowing. d, 125fr, Modern racing canoe.

**1996, May 10 Litho. *Perf. 13***
**736** A253 Strip of 4, #a.-d. 6.50 6.50

No. 736 is a continuous design.

CHINA '96 — A254

Marine life: 25fr, Halieutaea stellata. 40fr, Perotrochus deforgesi. 65fr, Mursia musorstomia. 125fr, Metacrinus levii.

**1996, May 18**
**737** A254 25fr multicolored .55 .35
**738** A254 40fr multicolored .85 .65
**739** A254 65fr multicolored 1.50 .90
**740** A254 125fr multicolored 2.75 1.60
*Nos. 737-740 (4)* 5.65 3.50

Nos. 737-740 were each issued in sheets of 10 + 5 labels.

On Nos. 737-740 portions of the design were applied by a thermographic process producing a shiny, raised effect.

*737a* Booklet pane of 6 5.00
*738a* Booklet pane of 6 6.50
*739a* Booklet pane of 6 12.50
*740a* Booklet pane of 6 25.00
Complete booklet, #737a-740a 49.00

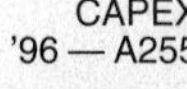

CAPEX '96 — A255

Orchids: 5fr, Sarcochilus koghiensis. 10fr, Phaius robertsii. 25fr, Megastylis montana. 65fr, Dendrobium macrophyllum. 95fr, Dendrobium virotii. 125fr, Ephemerantha comata.

**1996, June 25 Litho. *Perf. 13***
**741** A255 5fr multicolored .25 .25
**742** A255 10fr multicolored .40 .25
**743** A255 25fr multicolored .65 .35
**744** A255 65fr multicolored 1.40 .65
**745** A255 95fr multicolored 2.25 1.00
**746** A255 125fr multicolored 2.50 1.25
***a.*** Booklet pane of 6, #741-746 7.75
Souvenir booklet, 4 #746a 38.00
*Nos. 741-746 (6)* 7.45 3.75

Nos. 741-746 were each issued in sheets of 10 + 5 labels.

**No. 705 Ovptd. with UNICEF Emblem in Blue**

**1996, Sept. 12 Litho. *Perf. 13½***
**749** A230 30fr multicolored .75 .45

UNICEF, 50th anniv.

Ordination of the First Melanesian Priests A258

**1996, Oct. 9 Litho. *Perf. 13***
**750** A258 160fr multicolored 3.50 1.90

Portions of the design on No. 750 were applied by a thermographic process producing a shiny, raised effect.

7th Festival of South Pacific Arts A259

Designs: 100fr, Dancer, face carving. 105fr, Wood carvings of women. 200fr, Painting by Paula Boi. 500fr, Gaica Dance, Lifou.

**1996, Oct. 9**
**751** A259 100fr multicolored 2.25 1.25
**752** A259 105fr multicolored 2.25 1.25
**753** A259 200fr multicolored 4.00 2.25
**754** A259 500fr multicolored 9.00 5.75
*Nos. 751-754 (4)* 17.50 10.50

No. 751 is airmail.

French Pres. Francois Mitterrand (1916-96) — A260

**1997, Mar. 14 Litho. *Perf. 13***
**755** A260 1000fr multicolored 18.00 11.00

Alphonse Daudet (1840-97), Writer — A261

Designs: No. 756, "Letters from a Windmill." No. 757, "Le Petit Chose." No. 758, "Tartarin of Tarascon." No. 759, Daudet writing.

**1997, May 14 *Perf. 13***
**756** A261 65fr multicolored 1.50 1.50
**757** A261 65fr multicolored 1.50 1.50
**758** A261 65fr multicolored 1.50 1.50
**759** A261 65fr multicolored 1.50 1.50
***a.*** Souvenir sheet, #756-759 6.50 6.50

Henri La Fleur, First Senator of New Caledonia — A262

**1997, June 12 Litho. *Perf. 13***
**760** A262 105fr multicolored 2.40 1.25

Insects A263

Designs: a, Tectocoris diophthalmus. b, Kanakia gigas. c, Aenetus cohici.

**1997, June 25 Litho. *Perf. 13x12½***
**761** A263 65fr Strip of 3, #a.-c. 4.50 4.00

Jacques Iekawe (1946-92), First Melanesian Prefect — A264

**1997, July 23 Litho. *Perf. 13***
**762** A264 250fr multicolored 5.00 2.50

Kagu — A265

**1997, Aug. 13 Engr. *Perf. 13***
**763** A265 95fr blue 2.10 1.25

See Nos. 772-773C, 878-879, 897.

Horse Racing A266

No. 764, Harness racing. No. 765, Thoroughbred racing.

**1997, Sept. 20 Litho. *Perf. 13***
**764** A266 65fr multicolored 1.75 .80
**765** A266 65fr multicolored 1.75 .80

Early Engraving of "View of Port de France" (Noumea) — A267

**Photo. & Engr.**

**1997, Sept. 22 *Perf. 13x12½***
**766** A267 95fr multicolored 2.00 1.25

See No. 802.

A268

**1997, Sept. 22 Litho. *Perf. 13***
**767** A268 150fr multicolored 3.00 1.75

First Melanesian election, 50th anniv.

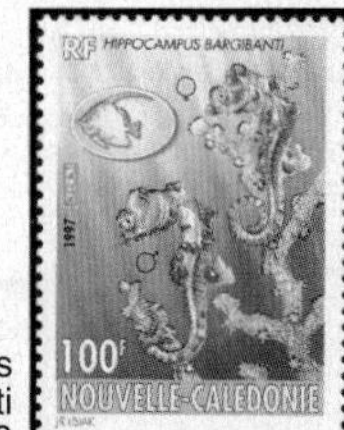


Hippocampus Bargibanti A269

**1997, Nov. 3 Litho. *Perf. 13½x13***
**768** A269 100fr multicolored 2.25 1.50

5th World Conf. on Fish of the Indo-Pacific. Issued in sheets of 10+5 labels.

South Pacific Arts A270

Designs: a, Doka wood carvings. b, Beizam dance mask. c, Abstract painting of primative life by Yvette Bouquet.

**1997, Nov. 3 *Perf. 13***
**769** A270 100fr Strip of 3, #a.-c. 6.00 6.00

Christmas A271

Designs: 95fr, Santa on surfboard pulled by dolphins. 100fr, Dolphin with banner in mouth.

**1997, Nov. 17**
**770** A271 95fr multicolored 2.00 1.00
**771** A271 100fr multicolored 2.00 1.00

Nos. 770-771 issued in sheets of 10+5 labels.

**Kagu Type of 1997**

**1997-98 Engr. *Perf. 13***

**772** A265 30fr orange 1.00 .35
**773** A265 (70fr) red 1.60 .75

**Booklet Stamps Self-Adhesive**

**Litho.**

***Serpentine Die Cut 11***

**773A** A265 (70fr) red 2.00 .45
*b.* Booklet pane of 10 22.50

**Engr.**

***Serpentine Die Cut 6¾ Vert.***

**773C** A265 (70fr) red — —
*d.* Booklet pane of 10 —

The peelable paper backing of No. 773A serves as a booklet cover.

Issued: 30fr, 1997; No. 773A, 1/2/98; No. 773C, 2004.

A272

Mushrooms: #774, Lentinus tuber-regium. #775, Volvaria bombycina. #776, Morchella anteridiformis.

**1998, Jan. 22 Litho. *Perf. 13***

**774** A272 70fr multicolored 1.40 .80
**775** A272 70fr multicolored 1.40 .80
**776** A272 70fr multicolored 1.40 .80
*Nos. 774-776 (3)* 4.20 2.40

A273

Artifacts from Territorial Museum: 105fr, Mask, Northern Region. 110fr, "Dulon" door frame pillar, Central Region.

**1998, Mar. 17 Litho. *Perf. 13***

**777** A273 105fr multicolored 2.00 1.10
**778** A273 110fr multicolored 2.10 1.10

Paul Gauguin (1848-1903) — A274

**1998, May 15 Litho. *Perf. 13***

**779** A274 405fr multicolored 8.00 5.00

1998 World Cup Soccer Championships, France — A280

**1998, June 5 Photo. *Perf. 12½***

**787** A280 100fr multicolored 2.00 1.25

A281

Jean-Marie Tjibaou Cultural Center — A282

Designs: 30fr, "Mitimitia," artwork by Fatu Feu'u. No. 789, Jean-Marie Tjibaou (1936-89), Melanesian political leader. No. 790, Exterior view of building, vert. 105fr, "Man Bird," painting by Mathias Kauage.

**1998, June 21 Litho. *Perf. 13x13½***

**788** A281 30fr multicolored .75 .35
*a.* Booklet pane of 6 4.50
**789** A281 70fr multicolored 1.50 .85
*a.* Booklet pane of 6 9.00
**790** A281 70fr multicolored 1.50 .85
*a.* Booklet pane of 6 9.00
**791** A282 105fr multicolored 2.25 1.25
*a.* Booklet pane of 6 15.00
Complete booklet, #788a, 789a, 790a, 791a 40.00
*Nos. 788-791 (4)* 6.00 3.30

Abolition of Slavery, 150th Anniv. — A283

**1998, July 21 Engr. *Perf. 13***

**792** A283 130fr multicolored 2.50 1.50

Postman, Dogs A284

**1998, Aug. 20 Litho. *Perf. 13***

**793** A284 70fr multicolored 1.75 .85

Arab Presence in New Caledonia, Cent. A285

**1998, Sept. 4**

**794** A285 80fr multicolored 1.75 1.00

A286

Vasco da Gama's Voyage to India, 500th Anniv. A287

No. 795: a, Port in India. b, Da Gama at Cape of Good Hope, ships at sea. c, Da Gama meeting with Indians. d, Da Gama's picture in crest.

No. 796: a, Map of route. b, Vasco da Gama. c, Ship at anchor.

**1998, Sept. 4**

**795** A286 100fr Strip of 4, #a.-d. 8.00 8.00

**Souvenir Sheet**

**796** A287 70fr Sheet of 3, #a.-c. 5.00 5.00

Portugal '98 Intl. Philatelic Exhibition.

A288

**Litho. & Engr.**

**1998, Sept. 25 *Perf. 12½x13***

**797** A288 110fr multicolored 2.25 2.25

Vincent Bouquet (1893-1971), High Chief.

A289

World Wildlife Fund — Kagu: 5fr, Male. 10fr, Female. 15fr, Two in grass. 70fr, Two in dirt, one ruffling feathers.

**1998, Oct. 20 Litho. *Perf. 13***

**798** A289 5fr multicolored .30 .25
**799** A289 10fr multicolored .40 .25
**800** A289 15fr multicolored .60 .25
**801** A289 70fr multicolored 1.75 1.25
*Nos. 798-801 (4)* 3.05 2.00

**Early Engraving Type of 1997**

**1998, Nov. 4 Engr. *Perf. 13x12½***

**802** A267 155fr Nou Island 3.00 2.00

Universal Declaration of Human Rights, 50th Anniv. — A290

**1998, Nov. 4 Engr. *Perf. 13***

**803** A290 70fr blk, bl & bl grn 1.75 1.40

Columnar Pine A291

**1998, Nov. 5 Litho. *Perf. 13x13½***

**804** A291 100fr shown 2.25 2.00
**805** A291 100fr Coast, forest 2.25 2.00

A292

Post and Telecommunications, 40th Anniv.: #806, Switchboard, bicycle, early post office. #807, Cell phone, microwave relay, motorcycle.

**1998, Nov. 27 Litho. *Perf. 13½x13***

**806** A292 70fr multicolored 1.60 1.60
**807** A292 70fr multicolored 1.60 1.60
*a.* Pair, #806-807 + label 3.50 3.50

A293

Underwater scenes (Greetings Stamps): No. 808, Fish, coral forming flower, Happy Anniversary. No. 809, Fish up close, Happy New Year. No. 810, Open treasure chest, Best Wishes. No. 811, Fish, starfish forming Christmas tree, Merry Christmas.

**1998, Dec. 1**

**808** A293 100fr multicolored 2.00 1.50
**809** A293 100fr multicolored 2.00 1.50
**810** A293 100fr multicolored 2.00 1.50
**811** A293 100fr multicolored 2.00 1.50
*Nos. 808-811 (4)* 8.00 6.00

Monument to the Disappearance of the Ship Monique, 20th Anniv. — A294

**1998, Dec. 1 *Perf. 13***

**812** A294 130fr multicolored 2.75 2.00

Arachnids
A295

Designs: No. 813, Argiope aetherea. No. 814, Barycheloides alluvviophilus. No. 815, Latrodectus hasselti. No. 816, Crytophora moluccensis.

**1999, Mar. 19 Litho.** ***Perf. 13x13½***
**813** A295 70fr multicolored 1.60 1.40
**814** A295 70fr multicolored 1.60 1.40
**815** A295 70fr multicolored 1.60 1.40
**816** A295 70fr multicolored 1.60 1.40
*Nos. 813-816 (4)* 6.40 5.60

Carcharodon Megalodon — A296

Designs: 100fr, Fossil tooth of megalodon.
No. 818: a, Shark swimming with mouth open, vert. b, Comparison of shark to man and carcharodon carcharias. c, Fossil tooth on bottom of ocean.

**1999, Mar. 19** ***Perf. 12½***
**817** A296 100fr multicolored 2.25 1.50

**Souvenir Sheet**
***Perf. 13***
**818** A296 70fr Sheet of 3, #a.-c. 4.50 4.50

Nos. 818a is 30x40mm and 818b is 40x30mm.
Australia '99, World Stamp Expo (#818).

Paul Bloc (1883-1970), Writer — A297

**1999, Apr. 23 Engr.** ***Perf. 13x12½***
**819** A297 105fr grn, bl grn & brn 2.25 1.50

Traditional Musical Instruments
A298

**1999, May 20 Litho.** ***Perf. 13½x13***
**820** A298 30fr Bwanjep .75 .60
**821** A298 70fr Sonnailles 1.50 1.40
**822** A298 100fr Flutes 2.25 2.00
*Nos. 820-822 (3)* 4.50 4.00

11th South Pacific Games, Guam
A299

**1999, May 20** ***Perf. 13x13¼***
**823** A299 5fr Track & field .25 .25
**824** A299 10fr Tennis .25 .25
**825** A299 30fr Karate .75 .60
**826** A299 70fr Baseball 1.60 1.40
*Nos. 823-826 (4)* 2.85 2.50

Overseas Transport Squadron 52, Humanitarian Missions — A300

**1999, June 18** ***Perf. 13***
**827** A300 135fr multicolored 2.75 1.75

Escoffier Hotel Catering and Business School, Noumea, 20th Anniv. — A301

**1999, June 17 Litho.** ***Perf. 13***
**828** A301 70fr Building, computer 1.40 1.00
*a.* Pair + central label 3.00 2.50
**829** A301 70fr Building, chef's hat 1.40 1.00
*a.* Pair + central label 3.00 2.50

New Caledonia's First Postage Stamp, 140th Anniv. — A302

Designs: No. 830, #1.
No. 831: a, Two #1. b, #1, diff. c, #1 up close. d, like #830. e, Design A265, image of Napolean III from #1, "1999."

**1999, July 2 Photo.** ***Perf. 13¼***
**830** A302 70fr multicolored 1.75 1.40

**Souvenir Sheet**
***Perf. 12***
**831** Sheet of 5 27.50 27.50
*a.* A302 100fr Engraved 2.50 2.50
*b.* A302 100fr Litho., thermograph 2.50 2.50
*c.* A302 100fr Litho. 2.50 2.50
*d.* A302 100fr Litho. & embossed 2.50 2.50
*e.* A302 700fr Litho., hologram 15.00 15.00

Nos. 831a-831d are each 36x28mm. No. 831e is 44x35mm. Portions of the design on No. 831b were applied by a thermographic process producing a shiny, raised effect. No. 831e contains a holographic image. Soaking in water may affect the hologram.
PhilexFrance '99 (#831).

Tourism
A303

**1999, Sept. 28 Litho.** ***Perf. 13¼***
**832** A303 5fr Fish, vegetables .25 .25
**833** A303 30fr Lobster dish .75 .55
**834** A303 70fr Tourist huts 1.50 1.25
**835** A303 100fr Hotel pool 2.25 1.90
*Nos. 832-835 (4)* 4.75 3.95

Ratification of Noumea Accord, 1998 — A304

**1999, Nov. 10 Litho.** ***Perf. 13x13½***
**836** A304 70fr multi 1.75 1.25

Aji Aboro Dance
A305

**1999, Nov. 10**
**837** A305 70fr multi 1.50 1.25

Château Hagen — A306

**1999, Nov. 18** ***Perf. 13***
**838** A306 155fr multi 3.50 2.75

Nature Protection — A307

**1999, Dec. 7**
**839** A307 30fr multi .75 .50

Greetings — A308

Designs: No. 840, "Joyeux Noel." No. 841, "Félicitations." No. 842, "Bon Anniversaire." No. 843, "Meilleurs Voeux 2000."

**1999, Dec. 20**
**840** A308 100fr multi 2.00 1.50
**841** A308 100fr multi 2.00 1.50
**842** A308 100fr multi 2.00 1.50
**843** A308 100fr multi 2.00 1.50
*Nos. 840-843 (4)* 8.00 6.00

Amédée Lighthouse
A309

**2000, Mar. 7 Litho.** ***Perf. 13½x12***
**844** A309 100fr multi 2.25 1.60

Ship Emile Renouf — A310

**2000, Apr. 19 Engr.** ***Perf. 13x13¼***
**845** A310 135fr multi 3.50 2.25

Painting by Giles Subileau — A311

**2000, June 15 Litho.** ***Perf. 13***
**846** A311 155fr multi 3.00 2.25

**Souvenir Sheet**

New Year 2000 (Year of the Dragon) — A312

Denomination: a, at R. b, at L.

**2000, June 15**
**847** A312 105fr Sheet of 2, #a-b 5.00 4.50

Antoine de Saint-Exupéry (1900-44), Aviator, Writer — A313

**2000, July 7**
**848** A313 130fr multi 3.00 2.75

World Stamp Expo 2000, Anaheim.

Noumea Aquarium
A314

Designs: No. 849, Hymenocera elegans. No. 850, Fluorescent corals. No. 851, Chelinus undulatus.

**2000, July 7** ***Perf. 13x13¼***
**849-851** A314 70fr Set of 3 5.50 3.50

Mangrove Heart A315

**2000, Aug. 10 Photo. *Perf. 13***
**852** A315 100fr multi 2.50 1.40

Value is for copy with surrounding selvage.

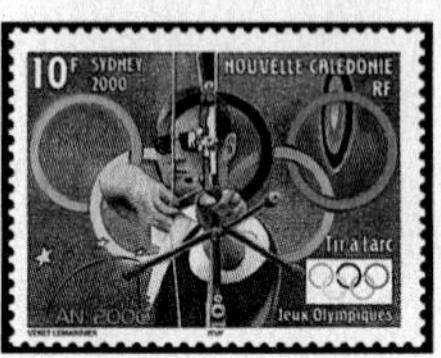

2000 Summer Olympics, Sydney A316

Designs: 10fr, Archery. 30fr, Boxing. 80fr, Cycling. 100fr, Fencing.

**2000, Sept. 15 Litho. *Perf. 13x13¼***
**853-856** A316 Set of 4 4.50 4.50

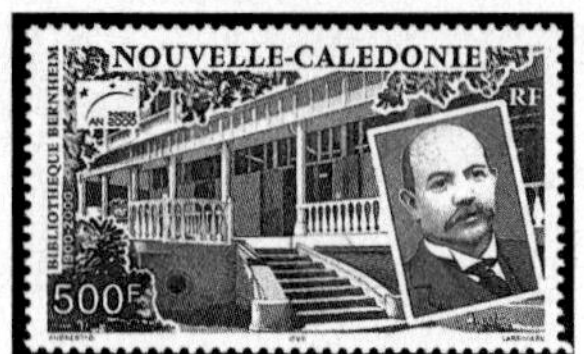

Lucien Bernheim (1856-1917), Library Founder, and Bernheim Library, Cent. — A317

**2000, Oct. 24 Engr. *Perf. 13***
**857** A317 500fr multi 11.00 7.25

A318

8th Pacific Arts Festival — A319

Kanak money and background colors of: 90fr, Orange. 105fr, Dark blue.

Festival emblem and works of art — No. 860: a, White denomination at UL, "RF" at UR. b, White denomination and "RF" at UL. c, Yellow denomination. d, White denomination at UR.

**2000, Oct. 24 *Perf. 13x13¼***
**858-859** A318 Set of 2 4.50 3.00

**Souvenir Sheet**

**860** A319 70fr Sheet of 4, #a-d 6.25 6.25

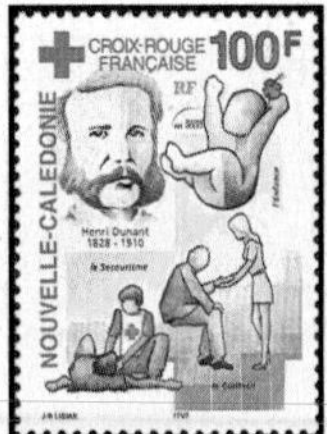

Red Cross — A320

**2000, Nov. 9 Litho. *Perf. 13¼x13***
**861** A320 100fr multi 2.25 2.00

Queen Hortense (1848-1900) A321

**2000, Nov. 9 Engr. *Perf. 12½x13***
**862** A321 110fr multi 2.50 2.25

Northern Province Landscapes — A322

a, Fisherman in canoe. b, Motorboat near beach and cliffs. c, Fisherman on raft.

**2000, Nov. 9 Litho. *Perf. 13x13¼***
**863** A322 Horiz. strip of 3 6.50 6.50
*a.-c.* 100fr Any single 2.00 1.50

Philately in School — A323

Children's art by: a, Kévyn Pamoiloun. b, Lise-Marie Samanich. c, Alexandre Mandin.

**2000, Nov. 14 *Perf. 13¼x13***
**864** A323 Horiz. strip of 3 4.50 3.50
*a.-c.* 70fr Any single 1.40 1.10

Christmas, Holy Year 2000 A324

**2000, Dec. 19 *Perf. 13***
**865** A324 100fr multi 2.00 1.60

Portions of the design were applied by a thermographic process producing a shiny, raised effect.

Greetings — A325

Kagu and: No. 866, "Meilleurs voeux de bonheur." No. 867, "Vive les vacances." No. 868, Félicitations.

**2000, Dec. 19 *Perf. 13¼x13***
**866-868** A325 100fr Set of 3 6.75 6.00

No. 868 printed se-tenant with two labels.

New Year 2001 (Year of the Snake) — A326

Designs: 100fr, Snake on beach, snake wearing robe.

No. 870: a, Snake in flowers. b, Snake in city.

**2001, Feb. 15 Litho. *Perf. 13***
**869** A326 100fr multi 2.50 2.00

**Souvenir Sheet**

***Perf. 13½x13***

**870** A326 70fr Sheet of 2, #a-b 4.25 4.25

Size of Nos. 870a-870b: 30x40mm.

Sailing Ship France II — A327

**2001, Apr. 18 Engr. *Perf. 13x13¼***
**871** A327 110fr multi 2.50 2.25

Noumea Aquarium — A328

Nautilus macromphalus: a, Conjoined pair. b, Anatomical cross-section. c, Pair separated.

**2001, May 22 Litho.**
**872** A328 Horiz. strip of 3 7.00 7.00
*a.-c.* 100fr Any single 2.25 1.50

Corvus Moneduliodes and Tools — A329

**2001, June 14 *Perf. 13***
**873** A329 70fr multi 1.60 1.50

Operation Cetacean — A330

No. 874: a, Pair of Megaptera novaeangliae underwater. b, Whales breaching surface.

**2001, July 18 *Perf. 13x13¼***
**874** A330 Horiz. pair with central label 5.00 5.00
*a.-b.* 100fr Any single 2.25 1.50

See Vanuatu Nos. 785-787.

The Keeper of Gaia, the Eden, by Ito Waia — A331

Vision From Oceania, by Jipé Le-Bars — A332

**2001, Aug. 22 *Perf. 13***
**875** A331 70fr multi 1.60 1.25
**876** A332 110fr multi 2.25 2.00

Year of Dialogue Among Civilizations A333

**2001, Sept. 19 Litho. *Perf. 13x13¼***
**877** A333 265fr multi 6.50 5.50

**Kagu Type of 1997**

**2001 Engr. *Perf. 13***
**878** A265 100fr bright blue 2.50 2.50

**Self-Adhesive**

**Litho.**

***Serpentine Die Cut 11***

**879** A265 100fr bright blue 2.75 2.50
*a.* Booklet pane of 10 32.50

Issued: No. 878, 9/23; No. 879, 9/20.

For surcharge see No. 972.

The Lonely Boatman, by Marik — A334

**2001, Oct. 11 Litho. *Perf. 13***
**880** A334 110fr multi 2.25 2.25

Underwater Observatory — A335

**2001, Oct. 11**
**881** A335 135fr multi 2.75 1.25

Qanono Church, Lifou — A336

**2001, Oct. 11**
**882** A336 500fr multi 10.00 8.00

Fernande Le Riche (1884-1967), Novelist — A337

**2001, Nov. 8**
**883** A337 155fr brown & blue 3.00 3.00

First Olympic Gold Medal Won by a New Caledonian A338

**2001, Nov. 8** ***Perf. 13x13¼***
**884** A338 265fr multi 5.50 5.00

Kitesurfing A339

**2001, Nov. 16** ***Perf. 13***
**885** A339 100fr multi 2.50 2.00

"The Book, My Friend" Literacy Campaign A340

**2001, Nov. 27** ***Perf. 13x13¼***
**886** A340 70fr multi 1.75 1.40

Lifou Scenes — A341

No. 887: a, Easo. b, Jokin.

**2001, Nov. 27** ***Perf. 13¼x13***
**887** A341 100fr Vert. pair, #a-b 4.75 4.50

Greetings A342

Flying fox and: No. 888, 100fr, Joyeux Noel (Merry Christmas). No. 889, 100fr, Meilleurs voeux (Best wishes). No. 890, 100fr, Vive la fete (Long live the holiday).

**2001, Dec. 7** ***Perf. 13x13¼***
**888-890** A342 Set of 3 6.50 6.00

New Year 2002 (Year of the Horse) — A343

Designs: 100fr, Horse, other zodiac animals.
No. 892, vert.: a, Horse. b, Seahorse.

**2002, Feb. 7** ***Perf. 13***
**891** A343 100fr multi 2.50 2.25

**Souvenir Sheet**

**892** A343 70fr Sheet of 2, #a-b 3.50 3.25

Love A344

**2002, Feb. 13**
**893** A344 100fr multi 2.50 2.00

Value is for stamp with surrounding selvage.

Cricket — A345

**2002, Mar. 20** **Litho.** ***Perf. 13***
**894** A345 100fr multi 2.50 2.00

Ancient Hatchet — A346

**2002, Mar. 20** **Litho.**
**895** A346 505fr multi 11.00 10.00

Portions of the design were applied by a thermographic process producing a shiny, raised effect.

Hobie Cat 16 World Championships — A347

**2002, Apr. 1** **Litho.** ***Perf. 13***
**896** A347 70fr multi 1.75 1.40

**Kagu Type of 1997**

**2002, Apr. 15** **Engr.** ***Perf. 13***
**897** A265 5fr purple .30 .25

2002 World Cup Soccer Championships, Japan and Korea — A348

**2002, May 15** **Photo.**
**898** A348 100fr multi 2.75 2.00

Values are for stamp with surrounding selvage.

Souvenir Sheet

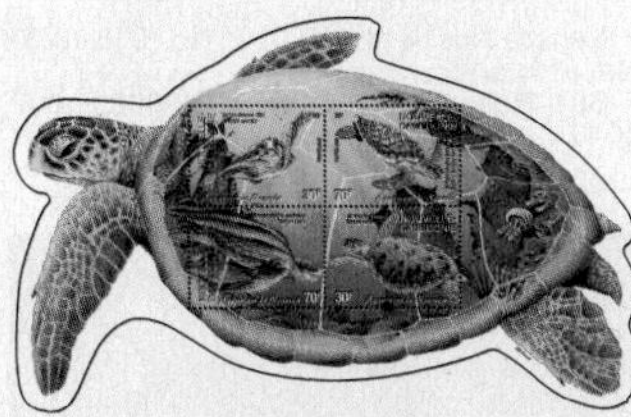
Turtles at Noumea Aquarium — A349

No. 899: a, 30fr, Caretta caretta. b, 70fr, Eretmochelys imbricat. c, 70fr, Dermochelys coriacea. d, 30fr, Chelonia mydas.

**2002, May 15** **Litho.** ***Perf. 13x13¼***
**899** A349 Sheet of 4, #a-d 4.75 4.75
*e.* As #899, with inscription added in margin 4.75 4.75

Issued: No. 899e, 10/24/03. Inscription in margin of No. 899e reads "Coupe du monde 2003 / Champion du monde."

Corvette Alcmene and Map — A350

**2002, June 13** **Engr.** ***Perf. 13x13¼***
**900** A350 210fr multi 4.75 4.00

Coffee — A351

No. 901: a, Coffee plant and beans. b, Bean roasters. c, Coffee makers, woman, cup of coffee.

**2002, June 13** **Litho.**
**901** A351 Horiz. strip of 3 5.00 5.00
*a.-c.* 70fr Any single 1.50 1.40

No. 901 was impregnated with coffee scent.

Edmond Caillard (1912-91), Astronomer — A352

**2002, June 26** **Engr.**
**902** A352 70fr multi 1.75 1.50

Statue of Emma Piffault (1861-77), by Michel Rocton — A353

**2002, July 17** **Litho.** ***Perf. 13¼x13***
**903** A353 10fr multi .40 .25

Noumea Circus School — A354

**2002, Aug. 30** ***Perf. 13***
**904** A354 70fr multi 1.75 1.40

Illustrations From Books by Jean Mariotti — A355

**2002, Sept. 18**
**905** A355 70fr multi 1.60 1.40

Operation Cetacean — A356

No. 906: a, Adult and young of Physeter macrocephalus. b, Physeter macrocephalus and squid.

**2002, Sept. 18** ***Perf. 13x13¼***
**906** A356 Horiz. pair with central label 4.75 4.75
*a.-b.* 100fr Either single 2.25 2.00

See Norfolk Island No. 783.

Intl. Year of Mountains — A357

**2002, Nov. 7 Litho.** ***Perf. 13***
**907** A357 100fr multi 2.50 2.00

Christmas and New Year's Day — A358

**2002, Nov. 7**
**908** A358 100fr multi 2.25 2.00

Bourail Fort Powder Magazine — A359

**2002, Nov. 7 Engr.** ***Perf. 13x12½***
**909** A359 1000fr multi 20.00 18.00

Mel Me Mec, by Adrien Trohmae — A360

**2002, Nov. 28 Litho.** ***Perf. 13***
**910** A360 100fr multi 2.50 2.00

New Year 2003 (Year of the Ram) A361

**2003, Jan. 29**
**911** A361 100fr multi 2.50 2.00

Printed in sheets of 10 + 2 labels.

Valentine's Day — A362

**2003, Jan. 29 Photo.** ***Perf. 13***
**912** A362 100fr multi 2.50 2.00

Values are for stamps with surrounding selvage.

Jubilee Issue, Cent. — A363

**2003 Litho.** ***Perf. 13¼x13***
**913** A363 70fr No. 77 1.75 1.40

**Booklet Stamp**
**Size: 19x25mm**

**913A** A363 70fr No. 77 1.75 1.40
*b.* Booklet pane of 10 17.50 —

Issued: No. 913, 2/7. No. 913A, 8/20.

Kagu — A364

**2003 Engr.** ***Perf. 13***

| | | | | |
|---|---|---|---|---|
| **914** A364 | 10fr green | .25 | .25 |
| **915** A364 | 15fr brown | .35 | .25 |
| **916** A364 | 30fr orange | .80 | .60 |
| **917** A364 | (70fr) red | 1.60 | 1.40 |
| | *Nos. 914-917 (4)* | 3.00 | 2.50 |

**Booklet Stamps**
**Litho. & Embossed**
***Perf. 13¼x13¾***

**918** A364 70fr gray & silver 1.75 1.40
*a.* Booklet pane of 10 17.50 —
Complete booklet, #913Ab, 918a 35.00

**Engr.**
***Serpentine Die Cut 6¾ Vert.***
**Self-Adhesive**

**919** A364 (70fr) red 1.90 1.40
*a.* Booklet pane of 10 20.00

Issued: Nos. 914-917, 2/7; No. 918, 8/20; No. 919, 5/15.

See Nos. 938, 965-966, 985-986, 1007, 1070.

Fish at Nouméa Aquarium — A365

No. 920: a, Epinephelus maculatus. b, Plectropomus leopardus. c, Cromileptes altivelis.

**2003, Apr. 9 Photo.** ***Perf. 12¾***
**920** A365 70fr Horiz. strip of 3, #a-c 5.00 4.00

Greater Nouméa High School — A366

**2003, May 14 Litho.** ***Perf. 13***
**921** A366 70fr multi 1.50 1.40

Operation Cetacean — A367

No. 922: a, Dugong swimming (79x29mm). b, Dugong feeding (40x29mm).

**2003, June 11** ***Perf. 13x13¼***
**922** A367 100fr Horiz. pair, #a-b 5.00 4.00

12th South Pacific Games, Suva, Fiji — A368

Designs: 5fr, Trapshooting. 30fr, Rugby. 70fr, Squash.

**2003, June 11**
**923-925** A368 Set of 3 2.50 2.10

Man Picking Fruit From a Tree, by Paul Gauguin (1848-1903) A369

**2003, June 25 Photo.** ***Perf. 13***
**926** A369 100fr multi 2.50 1.90

Aircalin, 20th Anniv. — A370

**2003, July 9 Litho.**
**927** A370 100fr multi 2.50 1.90

Governor Paul Feillet (1857-1903) A371

**2003, July 9 Engr.** ***Perf. 12½x13***
**928** A371 100fr bl grn & ol grn 2.00 1.50

Souvenir Sheet

Paintings by Paul Gauguin — A372

No. 929: a, Study of Heads of Tahitian Women. b, Still Life with Maori Statuette.

**2003, Aug. 20 Litho.** ***Perf. 13***
**929** A372 100fr Sheet of 2, #a-b 5.00 4.50

German Shepherd — A373

**2003, Oct. 8**
**930** A373 105fr multi 2.50 2.10

Le Phoque, Le Prony and Le Catinat in Balade Roadstead, 1853 — A374

**2003, Oct. 8 Engr.** ***Perf. 13x12½***
**931** A374 110fr multi 2.75 2.10

Robert Tatin d'Avesnières (1925-82), Painter — A375

**2003, Oct. 8 Litho.** ***Perf. 13***
**932** A375 135fr multi 3.25 2.60

Souvenir Sheet

Geckos — A376

No. 933: a, 30fr, Bavayia cyclura. b, 30fr, Rhacodactylus chahoua. c, 70fr, Rhacodactylus ciliatus. d, 70fr, Eurydactylodes vieillardi.

**2003, Oct. 8** ***Perf. 13x13¼***
**933** A376 Sheet of 4, #a-d 5.50 5.50

Ouen Island — A377

**2003, Nov. 6** *Perf. 13*
**934** A377 100fr multi 2.50 1.90

Merry Christmas and Happy New Year
A378

**2003, Nov. 6**
**935** A378 100fr multi 2.50 1.90

New Year 2004 (Year of the Monkey) — A379

Designs: 70fr, Monkeys, Hong Kong skyline. No. 937: a, Tiger and woman. b, Monkey on horse.

**2004, Jan. 30** **Litho.** *Perf. 13*
**936** A379 70fr multi 1.75 1.50

**Souvenir Sheet**
***Perf. 13¼x13***
**Litho. With Foil Application**

**937** A379 100fr Sheet of 2, #a-b 5.00 5.00

2004 Hong Kong Stamp Expo. No. 937 contains two 30x40mm stamps.

**Kagu Type of 2003**

**2004, Feb. 11** **Engr.** *Perf. 13*
**938** A364 100fr blue 2.50 2.10

For surcharge see No. 973.

Love
A380

**2004, Feb. 11** **Photo.**
**939** A380 100fr multi 2.50 2.10

Values are for stamps with surrounding selvage.

Stamp Day — A381

**2004, May 15** **Litho.**
**940** A381 105fr multi 2.50 2.10

Railroads in New Caledonia — A382

**2004, May 15** **Engr.** *Perf. 13x12½*
**941** A382 155fr multi 3.50 3.00

Rays — A383

No. 942: a, Dasyatis kuhlii. b, Aetobatus narinari. c, Taeniura meyeni.

**2004, May 15** **Litho.** *Perf. 13x13¼*
**942** A383 Horiz. strip of 3 7.25 7.25
*a.-c.* 100fr Any single 2.25 2.00

**Souvenir Sheet**

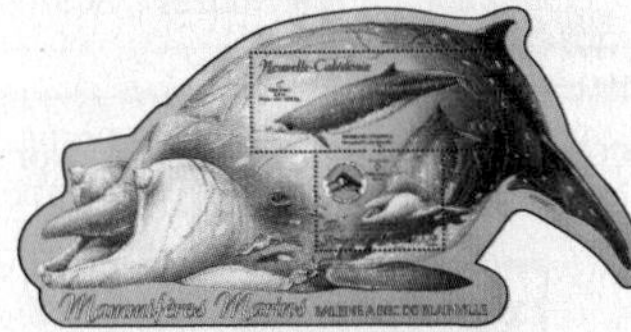
Mesoplodon Densirostris — A384

No. 943: a, Male (79x29mm). b, Female (40x29mm).

**2004, May 15**
**943** A384 100fr Sheet of 2, #a-b 5.00 5.00

Operation Cetacean.

Flowers — A385

No. 944: a, Oxera sulfurea. b, Turbina inopinata. c, Gardenia urvillei.

**2004, June 26**
**944** A385 Horiz. strip of 3 7.25 7.25
*a.-c.* 100fr Any single 2.25 2.00

Sandalwood — A386

Designs: 200fr, Sandalwood sculpture, house.
No. 946: a, Fruit and flowers. b, Sandalwood oil extraction machinery. c, Flowerpot.

**2004, June 26** *Perf. 13*
**945** A386 200fr multi 4.75 4.25

**Souvenir Sheet**
***Perf. 13x13¼***

**946** A386 100fr Sheet of 3, #a-c 7.25 7.25

No. 946 contains three 40x29mm stamps.

Noumea, 150th Anniv. — A387

**2004, July 8** **Litho.** *Perf. 13*
**947** A387 70fr multi 1.60 1.50

**Miniature Sheet**

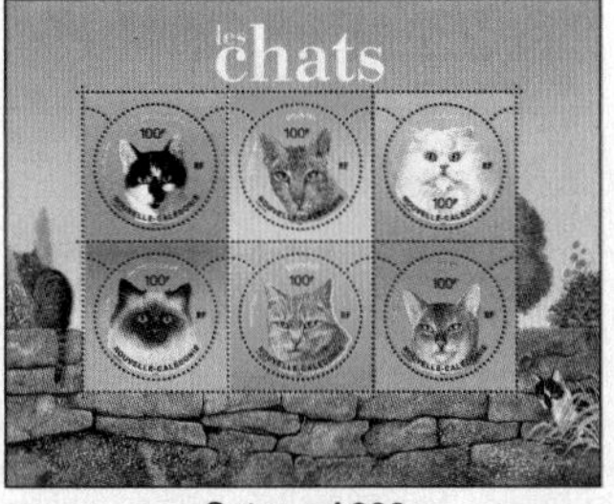
Cats — A388

No. 948: a, Mixed breed. b, Oriental. c, Persian. d, Birman. e, European. f, Abyssinian.

**2004, July 25**
**948** A388 100fr Sheet of 6, #a-f 14.50 12.50

2004 Summer Olympics, Athens
A389

Designs: No. 949, 70fr, Women's rhythmic gymnastics. No. 950, 70fr, Women's 4x400m relay. No. 951, 70fr, Beach volleyball.

**2004, Aug. 5** *Perf. 13x13¼*
**949-951** A389 Set of 3 5.00 4.50

Symposium on French Research in the Pacific — A390

No. 952: a, Butterfly, hut. b, Dolphin, woman.

**2004, Aug. 10** *Perf. 13*
**952** A390 Pair 4.75 4.75
*a.-b.* 100fr Either single 2.25 2.00

Belep Island and Walla Bay — A391

**2004, Nov. 10**
**953** A391 100fr multi 2.50 2.25

Tradimodernition, by Nathalie Deschamps — A392

**2004, Nov. 10**
**954** A392 505fr multi 12.00 11.00

Christmas — A393

**2004, Dec. 8**
**955** A393 100fr multi 2.50 2.25

A394

New Year 2005 (Year of the Rooster) — A395

No. 957: a, Rooster. b, Monkey.

**2005, Feb. 9** **Litho.** *Perf. 13*
**956** A394 100fr multi 2.50 2.25

**Souvenir Sheet**
***Perf. 13¼x13***

**957** A395 100fr Sheet of 2, #a-b 4.75 4.50

Rotary International, Cent.
A396

**2005, Feb. 23** **Photo.** *Perf. 12½*
**958** A396 110fr multi 2.75 2.50

Values are for stamps with surrounding selvage.

Francophone Week — A397

**2005, Mar. 17 Litho. *Perf. 13x13¼***
**959** A397 135fr multi 3.25 3.00

Printed in sheets of 10 + 5 labels. See Wallis & Futuna Islands No. 600.

20th International Triathlon, Noumea — A398

**2005, Apr. 22 Litho. *Perf. 13***
**960** A398 80fr multi 2.00 1.75

Coastal Tour Ship — A399

**2005, May 21**
**961** A399 75fr multi 1.90 1.60

New Caledonian Railways — A400

**2005, May 21**
**962** A400 745fr multi 18.00 15.00

Dolphins — A401

No. 963: a, Stenella attenuata. b, Turciop truncatus. c, Stenella longirostris.

**2005, May 21 *Perf. 13x13¼***
**963** A401 Horiz. strip of 3 7.75 7.75
***a.-c.*** 100fr Any single 2.25 2.00

For surcharge, see No. 971.

**Souvenir Sheet**

Sharks — A402

No. 964: a, Carcharinus melanopterus. b, Nebrius ferrugineus.

**2005, July 20 *Perf. 13***
**964** A402 110fr Sheet of 2, #a-b 5.25 4.50

**Kagu Type of 2003**

**2005, Aug. 10 Engr. *Perf. 13***
**965** A364 1fr sky blue .25 .25
**966** A364 3fr brt yel green .60 .25

Luengoni Beach, Lifou — A403

**2005, Aug. 24 Litho.**
**967** A403 85fr multi 2.00 1.75

Parakeets A404

Designs: No. 968, 75fr, Eunymphicus uvaeensis. No. 969, 75fr, Eunymphicus cornutus. No. 970, 75fr, Cyanoramphus saisseti.

**2005, Aug. 24 *Perf. 13x13¼***
**968-970** A404 Set of 3 5.50 4.75

**No. 963 Surcharged in Silver**

and Nos. 878 and 938 Surcharged

**Methods and Perfs as Before**

**2005**
**971** Horiz. strip of 3 (#963) 7.00 7.00
***a.-c.*** A401 100fr +10fr Any single 2.25 2.25
**972** A265 100fr +10fr bright blue (#878) 2.25 2.25
**973** A364 100fr +10fr blue (#938) 2.25 2.25
*Nos. 971-973 (3)* 11.50 11.50

Issued: No. 971, July. Nos. 972-973, Oct.

World Health Organization West Pacific Region Conference, Noumea — A405

**2005, Sept. 14 Litho. *Perf. 13x13¼***
**974** A405 150fr multi 3.75 3.00

World Peace Day — A406

**2005, Sept. 21 *Perf. 13¼x13***
**975** A406 85fr multi 2.00 1.75

Governor Eugène du Bouzet (1805-67) A407

**2005, Nov. 10 Engr.**
**976** A407 500fr multi 12.50 10.00

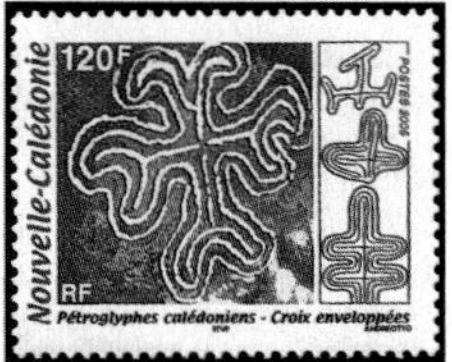
Petroglyphs — A408

Designs: No. 977, 120fr, Enclosed crosses. No. 978, 120fr, Petroglyph, Balade. No. 979, 120fr, Ouaré Petroglyph, Hienghène.

**2005, Nov. 10 *Perf. 13x12¾***
**977-979** A408 Set of 3 8.75 7.25

Common Destiny, Artwork by Ito Waia and Adjé A409

**2005, Dec. 7 Litho. *Perf. 13***
**980** A409 190fr multi 4.75 4.00

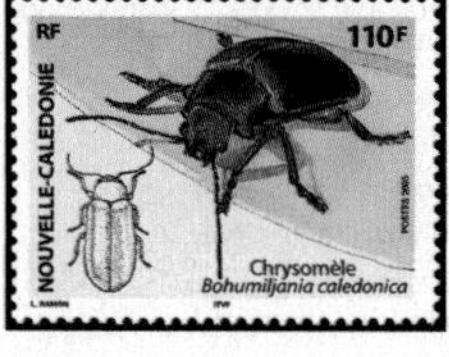
Insects A410

Designs: No. 981, 110fr, Bohumiljania caledonica. No. 982, 110fr, Bohumiljania humboldti. No. 983, 110fr, Cazeresia montana.

**2005, Dec. 7 *Perf. 13x13¼***
**981-983** A410 Set of 3 8.00 6.75

Christmas A411

**2005, Dec. 8 *Perf. 13¼x13***
**984** A411 110fr multi 2.75 2.25

**Kagu Type of 2003**

**2006 Engr. *Perf. 13***
**985** A364 110fr dk blue gray 2.75 2.25

**Booklet Stamp**
**Self-Adhesive**
***Serpentine Die Cut 6¾ Vert.***

**986** A364 110fr dk blue gray 2.75 2.25
***a.*** Booklet pane of 10 30.00

Issued: No. 985, 1/18. No. 986, June.

Nokanhoui Islet — A412

**2006, Mar. 9 Litho. *Perf. 13***
**987** A412 110fr multi 2.75 2.25

Automobiles — A413

No. 988: a, 1903 Georges Richard. b, 1925 Renault NN. c, 1925 Citroen Tréfle.

**2006, Mar. 23 *Perf. 13x13¼***
**988** A413 Horiz. strip of 3 8.00 8.00
***a.-c.*** 110fr Any single 2.50 2.25

New Caledonian Red Cross, 60th Anniv. — A414

**2006, Apr. 12 Litho. *Perf. 13¼x13***
**989** A414 75fr red & black 1.90 1.60

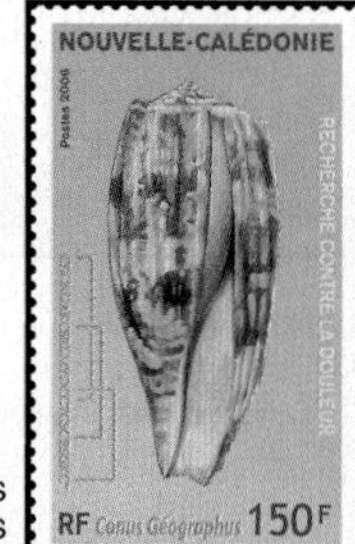
Conus Geographus A415

**2006, Apr. 12 Litho. *Perf. 13***
**990** A415 150fr multi 3.75 3.25

11th World Congress on Pain, New Caledonia, 2005. Portions of the design were applied by a thermographic process producing a shiny, raised effect.

Arrival of French Colonists, 80th Anniv. — A416

**2006, May 23 Engr. *Perf. 13x12¾***
**991** A416 180fr multi 4.50 3.75

2006 World Cup Soccer Championships, Germany — A417

**2006, June 8 Litho. *Perf. 13***
**992** A417 110fr multi 2.75 2.25

BirdLife International A418

Designs: No. 993, 75fr, Charmosyna diadema. No. 994, 75fr, Aegotheles savesi. No. 995, 75fr, Gallirallus lafresnayanis.

**2006, June 17 *Perf. 13¼x13***
**993-995** A418 Set of 3 5.50 4.75

Souvenir Sheet

Endangered Birds — A419

No. 996: a, Charmosyna diadema. b, Aegotheles savesi, vert. c, Gallirallus lafresnayanis.

**2006, June 17**
**996** A419 110fr Sheet of 3, #a-c 8.00 7.00

Creeper Flowers — A420

No. 997: a, Artia balansae. b, Oxera brevicalyx. c, Canavalia favieri.

**2006, June 17 *Perf. 13x13¼***
**997** A420 Horiz. strip of 3 8.00 8.00
***a.-c.*** 110fr Any single 2.50 2.25

Mobile Post Office — A421

**2006, Aug. 5 Engr. *Perf. 13x12¾***
**998** A421 75fr multi 1.75 1.60

Stamp Day.

New Caledonian Evacuee Voluntary Aid Association, 25th Anniv. — A422

**2006, Aug. 5 Litho. *Perf. 13¼x13***
**999** A422 85fr multi 2.00 1.90

17th South Pacific Regional Environment Program Conference, Noumea — A423

**2006, Sept. 11 Litho. *Perf. 13***
**1000** A423 190fr multi 4.00 4.00

Nakale 7547 Locomotive of New Caledonia Railroad — A424

**2006, Sept. 19 Engr. *Perf. 13x13¼***
**1001** A424 320fr multi 6.75 6.75

Kaneka Music, 20th Anniv. A425

**2006, Nov. 8 Litho. *Perf. 13x13½***
**1002** A425 75fr multi 1.90 1.75

Mobilis Mobile Phone Service, 10th Anniv. — A426

**2006, Nov. 8 *Perf. 13***
**1003** A426 75fr multi 1.90 1.75

Wooden Players Puppet Theater, 30th Anniv. — A427

**2006, Nov. 8**
**1004** A427 280fr multi 7.00 6.25

Christmas A428

**Litho. & Engr.**

**2006, Nov. 9 *Perf. 13***
**1005** A428 110fr multi 2.75 2.50

Lizard Man, Sculpture by Joseph Poukiou A429

**2006, Dec. 13 Litho.**
**1006** A429 110fr multi 2.75 2.40

**Kagu Type of 2003**

**2007, Jan. 25 Engr. *Perf. 13***
**1007** A364 5fr purple .35 .25

New Year 2007 (Year of the Pig) A430

**2007, Feb. 6 Litho. *Perf. 13***
**1008** A430 110fr multi 2.50 2.50

Printed in sheets of 10 + central label.

General Secretariat of the South Pacific Community, 60th Anniv. — A431

**2007, Feb. 6**
**1009** A431 120fr multi 2.75 2.75

Audit Office, Bicent. A432

**2007, Mar. 17 Engr. *Perf. 13¼***
**1010** A432 110fr multi 2.50 2.50

Treaty of Rome, 50th Anniv. A433

**2007, May 10 Litho. *Perf. 13x13¼***
**1011** A433 110fr multi 2.50 2.50

13th South Pacific Games, Samoa — A434

**2007, June 13 Litho. *Perf. 13***
**1012** A434 75fr multi 1.75 1.75

Submarine Cable Between Noumea and Sydney — A435

**2007, June 13 Litho. & Engr.**
**1013** A435 280fr multi 6.50 6.50

Fish A436

Designs: 35fr, Siganus lineatus. 75fr, Lutianus adetii. 110fr, Naso unicornis.

**2007, June 13 Litho. *Perf. 13x13½***
**1014-1016** A436 Set of 3 5.00 5.00

Natl. Sea Rescue Society, 40th Anniv. — A437

**2007, Aug. 3 *Perf. 13***
**1017** A437 75fr multi 1.75 1.75

BirdLife International — A438

Endangered birds: 35fr, Gymnomyza aubryana. 75fr, Coracina analis. 110fr, Rhynochetos jubatus.

**2007, Aug. 3** ***Perf. 13x13¼***
**1018-1020** A438 Set of 3 5.00 5.00

A439

A440

A441

A442

A443

A444

A445

A446

A447

Mailboxes
A448

**2007, Aug. 3** ***Perf. 13¼x13, 13x13¼***

| | | | |
|---|---|---|---|
| **1021** | Booklet pane of 10 | 17.50 | 17.50 |
| *a.* | A439 75fr multi | 1.75 | 1.75 |
| *b.* | A440 75fr multi | 1.75 | 1.75 |
| *c.* | A441 75fr multi | 1.75 | 1.75 |
| *d.* | A442 75fr multi | 1.75 | 1.75 |
| *e.* | A443 75fr multi | 1.75 | 1.75 |
| *f.* | A444 75fr multi | 1.75 | 1.75 |
| *g.* | A445 75fr multi | 1.75 | 1.75 |
| *h.* | A446 75fr multi | 1.75 | 1.75 |
| *i.* | A447 75fr multi | 1.75 | 1.75 |
| *j.* | A448 75fr multi | 1.75 | 1.75 |
| | Complete booklet, #1021 | 17.50 | |

Stamp Day.

Souvenir Sheet

Kagu Philatelic Club, 60th Anniv. — A449

No. 1022: a, Magnifying glass over New Caledonia #262 on cover. b, Kagu.

**Litho. & Silk Screened**
**2007, Aug. 3** ***Perf. 13x13¼***
**1022** A449 110fr Sheet of 2, #a-b 5.00 5.00

Season of New Hebrides Culture in New Zealand — A450

**2007, Aug. 16** **Litho.** ***Perf. 13***
**1023** A450 190fr multi 4.50 4.50

New Aquarium of New Caledonia — A451

No. 1024 — Entrance of new aquarium and: a, Gymnothorax polyranodon (40x30mm). b, Entrance of old aquarium. (80x30mm). c, Monodactylus argenteus (40x30mm). d, Negaprion brevirostris (40x30mm). e, Pseudanthias bicolor (40x30mm).

**2007, Aug. 31** ***Perf. 13x13¼***
**1024** A451 110fr Booklet pane of 5, #a-e 13.00 13.00
Complete booklet, 2 #1024 26.00

2007 Rugby World Cup, France
A452

**2007, Sept. 5** **Photo.** ***Perf.***
**1025** A452 110fr multi 2.60 2.60

Jules Repiquet (1874-1960), Governor of New Caledonia, 1914-23 — A453

**2007, Oct. 10** **Engr.** ***Perf. 13x13¼***
**1026** A453 320fr multi 7.75 7.75

Tropical Fruits
A454

Designs: 35fr, Bananas and passion fruits. 75fr, Vanilla beans, vert. 110fr, Pineapples and lychees.

***Perf. 13x13¼, 13¼x13***
**2007, Nov. 8** **Litho.**
**1027-1029** A454 Set of 3 5.50 5.50

The banana, vanilla bean and pineapple portions of these stamps are covered with scratch-and-sniff coatings having those fragrances.

La Montagnarde Locomotive, New Caledonian Railways — A455

**2007, Nov. 8** **Engr.** ***Perf. 13x13¼***
**1030** A455 400fr multi 10.00 10.00

Tao Waterfall
A456

**2007, Nov. 8** **Litho.** ***Perf. 13***
**1031** A456 110fr multi 2.75 2.75

The Damned, Performance by Najib Guerfi Dance Company — A457

**2007, Nov. 8**
**1032** A457 110fr multi 2.75 2.75

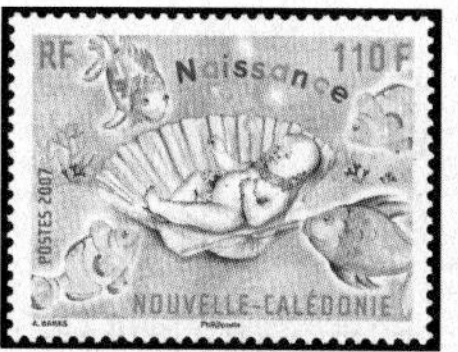
Birth Announcement — A458

**2007, Nov. 8** ***Perf. 13x13¼***
**1033** A458 110fr multi 2.75 2.75

New Year's Greetings
A459

**2007, Nov. 8**
**1034** A459 110fr multi 2.75 2.75

Rooftop Totem — A460

**2007, Dec. 5** **Litho.** ***Perf. 13***
**1035** A460 110fr multi 2.75 2.75

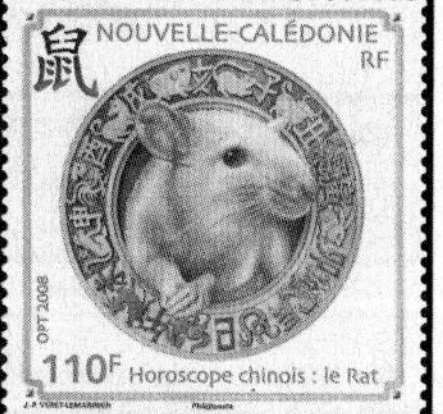
New Year 2008 (Year of the Rat)
A461

**2008, Feb. 6** **Litho.** ***Perf. 13***
**1036** A461 110fr multi 3.00 3.00

Academic Palms, Bicent. — A462

**Litho. & Embossed**

**2008, Mar. 17** *Perf. 13x13¼*
**1037** A462 110fr multi 3.00 3.00

Tjibaou Cultural Center, 10th Anniv. — A463

**2008, June 14** **Litho.** *Perf. 13*
**1038** A463 120fr multi 3.25 3.25

Matignon Accords, 20th Anniv. — A464

**2008, June 14**
**1039** A464 430fr multi 11.50 11.50

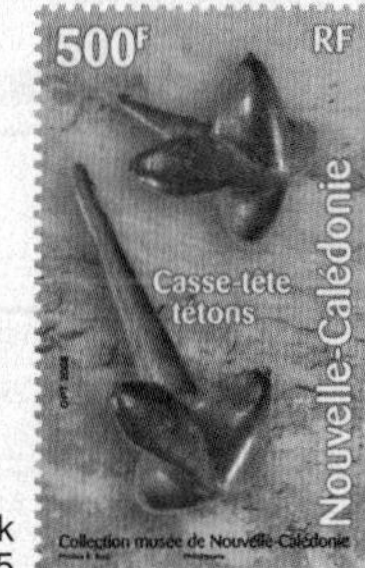

Kanak Ax — A465

**2008, June 14**
**1040** A465 500fr multi 13.50 13.50

BirdLife International — A466

Endangered birds: No. 1041, 110fr, Pterodroma leucoptera. No. 1042, 110fr, Pseudobulweria rostrata. No. 1043, 110fr, Nesofregatta fuliginosa.

**2008, June 14** *Perf. 13x13¼*
**1041-1043** A466 Set of 3 8.75 8.75

Fruit A467

Designs: No. 1044, 110fr, Citrus nobilis. No. 1045, 110fr, Mangifera indica. No. 1046, 110fr, Carica papaya.

**2008, June 14**
**1044-1046** A467 Set of 3 8.75 8.75

2008 Summer Olympics, Beijing A468

Designs: No. 1047, 75fr, Weight lifting. No. 1048, 75fr, Table tennis. No. 1049, 75fr, Taekwondo.

**2008, July 31**
**1047-1049** A468 Set of 3 5.75 5.75

Office of Posts and Telecommunications, 50th Anniv. — A469

Designs: No. 1050, 75fr, New Caledonia #314, dish antennas, cable, map of South Pacific. No. 1051, 75fr, New Caledonia #311, savings card, person at computer. No. 1052, 75fr, New Caledonia #C106, mailbox, mail sorter.

**2008, July 31**
**1050-1052** A469 Set of 3 5.75 5.75

Miniature Sheet

Telecommunications History — A470

No. 1053: a, Telegraph. b, Radio telephone. c, Satellite and antenna. d, Fiber-optic cables and flowers.

**2008, July 31** *Perf. 13¼x13*
**1053** A470 75fr Sheet of 4, #a-d 7.50 7.50

Kagu — A471

*Serpentine Die Cut 6¾x7¾*

**2008** **Self-Adhesive** **Litho.**
**1054** A471 (75fr) red & multi 4.50 4.50
**1055** A471 110fr blue & multi 5.25 5.25

Nos. 1054 and 1055 each were issued in sheets of 20 and 25. Sheets of 20 of each stamp sold for 3800fr and 4500fr, respectively, and sheets of 25 sold for 4125fr and 5000fr, respectively. The left part of the stamp, which cannot be separated from the stamp, could be personalized if desired. The left part of the stamp shown has a generic image that was utilized if a customer did not provide an image for personalization.

Koné Fort — A472

**2008, Oct. 3** **Engr.** *Perf. 13x12¾*
**1056** A472 220fr multi 5.00 5.00

Fifth French Republic, 50th Anniv. — A473

**2008, Oct. 14** *Perf. 13x13¼*
**1057** A473 290fr blue & red 6.25 6.25

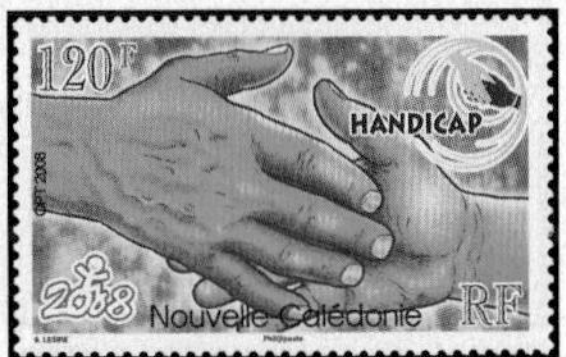

Handicap Awareness — A474

**2008, Nov. 6** **Litho.** *Perf. 13*
**1058** A474 120fr multi 2.60 2.60

Diahot River — A475

No. 1059 — View of river with denomination color of: a, Green. b, Blue violet.

**2008, Nov. 6**
**1059** A475 Horiz. pair + central label 5.00 5.00
*a.-b.* 110fr Either single 2.50 2.50

Christmas A476

**2008, Nov. 6** *Perf. 13¼x13*
**1060** A476 110fr multi 2.50 2.50

14th Pacific Games, New Caledonia A477

**2008, Dec. 12** *Perf. 13*
**1061** A477 110fr multi 2.50 2.50

Miniature Sheet

New Caledonia Lagoons UNESCO World Heritage Site — A478

No. 1062: a, Birds from Entrecasteaux Reefs Zone. b, Snake from Northeastern Coastal Zone, horiz. c, Sea turtles from Beautemps-Beaupré Zone, horiz. d, Fish from Great Northern Lagoon Zone. e, Dugong from Western Coastal Zone. f, Whale from Great Southern Lagoon Zone, horiz.

*Perf. 13¼x13, 13x13¼ (horiz. stamps)*

**2008, Dec. 12**
**1062** A478 75fr Sheet of 6, #a-f 10.50 10.50

Fish — A479

No. 1063 — Fish sold at local fish markets: a, Lethrinus atkinsoni. b, Chlorurus microrhinos. c Lethrinus nebulosus.

**2009, Mar. 25** **Litho.** *Perf. 13x13¼*
**1063** A479 Horiz. strip of 3 5.00 5.00
*a.-c.* 75fr Any single 1.60 1.60

New Year 2009 (Year of the Ox) A480

**2009, Apr. 8** *Perf. 13*
**1064** A480 75fr multi 1.75 1.75

Souvenir Sheet

New Year 2009 (Year of the Ox) — A481

No. 1065 — Ox: a, Standing. b, Charging.

**2009, Apr. 8** **Litho.** *Perf. 13*
**1065** A481 110fr Sheet of 2, #a-b 5.00 5.00

The Turtle Bearer, Sculpture by Tein Thavouvace — A482

**2009, May 14** **Litho.** ***Perf. 13***
**1066** A482 180fr multi 4.25 4.25

BirdLife International — A483

No. 1067 — Terns: a, Sterna nereis. b, Sterna sumatrana. c, Sterna dougalli.

**2009, June 10** ***Perf. 13x13¼***
**1067** A483 Horiz. strip of 3 5.25 5.25
*a.-c.* 75fr Any single 1.75 1.75

Jean-Pierre Jeunet Cinema, La Foa, 10th Anniv. — A484

**2009, June 26** ***Perf. 13***
**1068** A484 75fr multi 1.75 1.75

Third France-Oceania Summit, Noumea — A485

No. 1069 — Earth in: a, Hands. b, Flower.

**2009, July 16**
**1069** A485 110fr Pair, #a-b 5.25 5.25

**Kagu Type of 2003**
***Serpentine Die Cut 7½ Vert.***
**2009, July** **Litho.**
**Booklet Stamp**
**Self-Adhesive**

**1070** A364 (75fr) red 1.75 1.75
*a.* Booklet pane of 10 17.50

A486 Kagu — A487

**2009, Aug. 6** **Engr.** ***Perf. 13***
**1071** A486 5fr purple .25 .25
**1072** A486 10fr green .25 .25
*a.* Dated "2014" .25 .25
**1073** A486 (75fr) red 1.75 1.75
**1074** A486 110fr dark blue 2.60 2.60

**Litho. With Three-Dimensional Plastic Affixed**
***Perf. 16***
**Self-Adhesive**
**1075** A487 500fr multi 12.00 12.00

**Litho.**
***Serpentine Die Cut 7½ Vert.***
**Booklet Stamp**
**1076** A486 (75fr) red 1.75 1.75
*a.* Booklet pane of 10 17.50
*b.* As #1076, serpentine die cut 6¾ vert., with "Phil@poste" printer's inscription at bottom 1.60 1.60
*c.* Booklet pane of 10 #1076b 16.00
*d.* As "b," dated "2014" 1.75 1.75
*e.* Booklet pane of 10 #1076d 17.50
*f.* As "b," dated "2016" 1.40 1.40
*g.* Booklet pane of 10 #1076f 14.00
*Nos. 1071-1076 (6)* 18.60 18.60

No. 1075 printed in sheets of 4.
Issued: Nos. 1076b, 1076c, June 2010; Nos. 1076d, 1076e, July 2014.
See No. 1131.

Intl. Year of Astronomy — A488

**2009, Aug. 6** **Litho.** ***Perf. 13***
**1077** A488 110fr multi 2.60 2.60

Miniature Sheet

New Caledonia Postal Service, 150th Anniv. — A489

No. 1078 — Modes of mail delivery: a, Coach. b, Horse, vert. c, Automobile. d, Mail deliverer on foot, vert.

**2009, Aug. 6** ***Perf. 13¼***
**1078** A489 110fr Sheet of 4, #a-d 10.50 10.50

Personalized Stamps — A490a

***Serpentine Die Cut 6¾x8***
**2009, Sept.** **Litho.**
**Self-Adhesive**
**1079A** A490a (75fr) red & multi — —
**1079B** A490a 110fr blue & multi — —

Nos. 1079A and 1079B were issued in sheets of 20 and 25. The personalized part of the stamp is at left. The illustration is that of a generic image used for both No. 1079A and 1079B. Sheets with other personalized images sold for more than the face value.

14th Pacific Games, New Caledonia A491

**2009, Nov. 5** **Litho.** ***Perf. 13***
**1080** A491 75fr multi 1.90 1.90

Western Coastal Zone of Lagoons of New Caledonia UNESCO World Heritage Site — A492

**2009, Nov. 5**
**1081** A492 75fr multi 1.90 1.90

Christmas A493

**2009, Nov. 5** ***Perf. 13x13¼***
**1082** A493 110fr multi 2.75 2.75

Canala Barracks — A494

**2009, Nov. 5** **Engr.**
**1083** A494 120fr multi 3.00 3.00

Maritime History Museum, Noumea, 10th Anniv. — A495

No. 1084: a, Ships and museum. b, Ship and map.

**2009, Nov. 5** **Litho.**
**1084** A495 75fr Horiz. pair, #a-b 3.75 3.75

A496

Tontouta River — A497

**2009, Nov. 5** ***Perf. 13***
**1085** Horiz. pair + central label 5.50 5.50
*a.* A496 110fr multi 2.75 2.75
*b.* A497 110fr multi 2.75 2.75

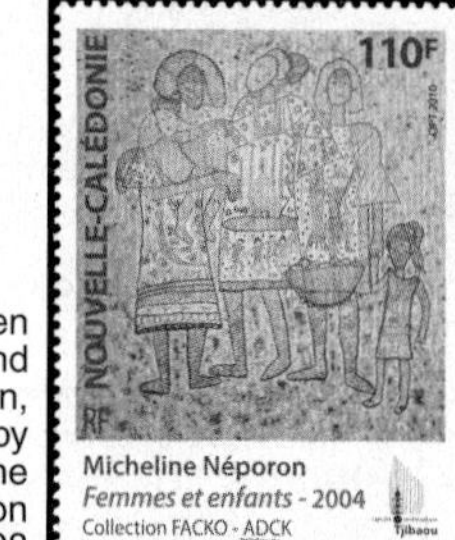


Women and Children, by Micheline Néporon A498

**2010, Mar. 8** **Litho.** ***Perf. 13***
**1086** A498 110fr multi 2.50 2.50

Intl. Women's Day.

Champlain Alliance, 25th Anniv. A499

**2010, Mar. 18** ***Perf. 13x13¼***
**1087** A499 110fr multi 2.50 2.50

Fish — A500

No. 1089 — Fish sold at local fish markets: a, Acanthocybium solandri. b, Thunnus albacares. c, Coryphaena hippurus.

**2010, Mar. 18**
**1088** A500 Horiz. strip of 3 5.25 5.25
*a.-c.* 75fr multi 1.75 1.75

New Year 2010 (Year of the Tiger) A501

**2010, Mar. 18** ***Perf. 13***
**1089** A501 110fr multi 2.50 2.50

Dumbea River — A502

No. 1090: a, River bends. b, Canoers on river, bridge.

**2010, Mar. 18**
**1090** A502 Horiz. pair + central label 5.00 5.00
*a.-b.* 110fr Either single 2.50 2.50

14th Va'a (Outrigger Canoe) World Championships, Anse Vata Bay — A503

**2010, May 3 Litho.** *Perf. 13x13¼*
**1091** A503 75fr multi 1.75 1.75

French Pavilion, Expo 2010, Shanghai — A504

**2010, June 14** *Perf. 13*
**1092** A504 110fr multi 2.40 2.40

Mueo Fort — A505

**2010, Aug. 5 Engr.** *Perf. 13x13¼*
**1093** A505 75fr multi 1.75 1.75

2010 Youth Olympics, Singapore — A506

**2010, Aug. 5 Litho.** *Perf. 13*
**1094** A506 75fr multi 1.75 1.75

St. Joseph's Cathedral, Noumea A507

**2010, Aug. 5 Litho. & Engr.**
**1095** A507 1000fr multi 22.50 22.50

Nickel Mining — A508

No. 1096: a, Open-pit mine. b, Smelter. c, Ship transport.

**Litho. With Foil Application**

**2010, Aug. 5** *Perf. 13x12¾*
**1096** A508 75fr Horiz. strip of 3, #a-c 5.00 5.00

Miniature Sheet

Flora and Fauna of Grandes Fougères Park — A509

No. 1097: a, Pteropus ornatus. b, Ducula goliath. c, Cyathea sp. d, Calanthe langel.

**2010, Aug. 5 Litho.** *Perf. 13¼x13*
**1097** A509 110fr Sheet of 4, #a-d 9.75 9.75

14th Pacific Games, New Caledonia — A510

**2010, Aug. 27** *Perf. 13*
**1098** A510 75fr multi 1.60 1.60

Fourth Melanesian Arts Festival — A511

**2010, Sept. 8**
**1099** A511 180fr multi 4.00 4.00

Governor Henri Sautot (1885-1963) — A512

**2010, Sept. 16 Engr.** *Perf. 13x13¼*
**1100** A512 250fr multi 6.00 6.00

New Caledonia's alliance with Free France, 70th anniv.

Road Safety A513

Designs: No. 1101, 75fr, Car with drunk driver. No. 1102, 75fr, Woman with baby stroller in crosswalk escaping speeding motorcyclist.

**2010, Oct. 13 Litho.** *Perf. 13x13¼*
**1101-1102** A513 Set of 2 3.50 3.50

Great Northern Lagoon UNESCO World Heritage Site — A514

**2010, Nov. 3** *Perf. 13*
**1103** A514 75fr multi 1.75 1.75

New Caledonia House, Paris — A515

**2010, Nov. 3**
**1104** A515 110fr multi 2.50 2.50

Intl. Year of Biodiversity A516

**2010, Nov. 3** *Perf. 13¼*
**1105** A516 110fr multi 2.50 2.50

Christmas A517

**2010, Nov. 3** *Perf. 13x13¼*
**1106** A517 110fr multi 2.50 2.50

New Year 2011 (Year of the Rabbit) A518

**2011, Feb. 2** *Perf. 13*
**1107** A518 110fr multi 2.50 2.50

Printed in sheets of 10 + central label.

Inauguration of Digital High Definition Television Transmission — A519

**2011, Feb. 2** *Perf. 13x13¼*
**1108** A519 75fr multi 1.75 1.75

14th Pacific Games, New Caledonia A520

**2011, Mar. 17** *Perf. 13*
**1109** A520 110fr multi 2.75 2.75

Rivers — A521

No. 1110: a, Pourina River. b, Ouinné River.

**2011, Mar. 17 Litho.**
**1110** A521 Horiz. pair + central label 5.50 5.50
*a.-b.* 110fr Either single 2.75 2.75

Transcaledonian Adventure Race, 20th Anniv. — A522

**2011, June 23** *Perf. 13x13¼*
**1111** A522 75fr multi 1.75 1.75

Podoserpula Miranda — A523

**2011, June 23** *Perf. 13¼x13*
**1112** A523 110fr multi 2.60 2.60

Ouégoa Fort — A524

**2011, Aug. 5 Engr.** *Perf. 13x13¼*
**1113** A524 75fr multi 1.90 1.90

Ouvea and Beautemps-Beaupré Lagoon Area UNESCO World Heritage Site — A525

**2011, Aug. 5 Litho.** *Perf. 13*
**1114** A525 75fr multi 1.90 1.90

Intl. Year of Forests — A526

**2011, Aug. 5**
**1115** A526 120fr multi 3.00 3.00

Miniature Sheet

Rivière Bleue Provincial Park — A527

No. 1116: a, Syzygium acre. b, Montrouziera gabriellae. c, Waterfall. d, Rhynochetos jubatus.

**2011, Aug. 5 Photo.** ***Perf. 13¼x13***
**1116** A527 110fr Sheet of 4, #a-d 11.00 11.00

Kanak Traditional Games A528

**2011, Aug. 27 Litho.** ***Perf. 13x13¼***
**1117** A528 75fr multi 1.75 1.75

Souvenir Sheet

14th Pacific Games, Noumea — A529

No. 1118 — Emblem and: a, Medal. b, Torch. c, Flame basin.

**Photo. Photo & Embossed (#1118a)**
**2011, Aug. 27** ***Perf. 13¼x13***
**1118** A529 110fr Sheet of 3, #a-c 7.75 7.75

Ruins and Chimney of Nimba Sugar Factory, Dumbea — A530

**2011, Nov. 3 Engr.** ***Perf. 13x13¼***
**1119** A530 450fr multi 10.50 10.50

Animals and Scenery A531

Designs: No. 1120, 110fr, Cerf rusa (rusa deer). No. 1121, 110fr, Tricot rayé (striped jersey snake). No. 1122, 110fr, Lindéralique Cliffs. No. 1123, 110fr, Ilôt Canard, vert.

***Perf. 13x13¼, 13¼x13***
**2011, Nov. 3 Litho.**
**1120-1123** A531 Set of 4 10.50 10.50

Christmas A532

**2011, Nov. 3** ***Perf. 13¼x13***
**1124** A532 110fr multi 2.60 2.60

Jacques Lafleur (1932-2010), Politician — A533

**2011, Dec. 1 Engr.** ***Perf. 12¼x13***
**1125** A533 1000fr multi 22.50 22.50

New Year 2012 (Year of the Dragon) A534

**2012, Jan. 23 Litho.** ***Perf. 13***
**1126** A534 75fr multi 1.75 1.75

Printed in sheets of 10 + central label.

St. Valentine's Day — A535

**2012, Jan. 23**
**1127** A535 110fr multi 2.50 2.50

Values are for stamps with surrounding selvage.

Voh, 120th Anniv. — A536

No. 1128: a, Coffee plantation. b, Mine.

**2012, Jan. 23** ***Perf. 13x13¼***
**1128** A536 110fr Horiz. pair, #a-b 5.00 5.00

Southern Backpacking Trail — A537

**2012, Mar. 5** ***Perf. 13¼x13***
**1129** A537 110fr multi 2.50 2.50

Ouaménie Sugar Works Chimney A538

**2012, May 4 Engr.** ***Perf. 12¼x13***
**1130** A538 750fr multi 16.00 16.00

**Kagu Type of 2009**

**2012, June 5 Engr.** ***Perf. 13***
**1131** A486 30fr orange .65 .65
*a.* Dated "2014" .60 .60

Nudibranchs — A539

Designs: 75fr, Glossodoris cruenta. 85fr, Halgerda sp., vert. 120fr, Noumea catalai.

***Perf. 13x13¼, 13¼x13***
**2012, July 6 Litho.**
**1132-1134** A539 Set of 3 5.75 5.75

Souvenir Sheet

Japanese Presence on New Caledonia, 120th Anniv. — A540

No. 1135: a, Memorial. b, Nickel miner with pick, horiz. c, Mine worker with ore cart, horiz.

***Perf. 13¼x13, 13x13¼***
**2012, July 6 Photo.**
**1135** A540 110fr Sheet of 3, #a-c 6.75 6.75

Amborella Trichopoda A541

**2012, Aug. 6 Litho.** ***Perf. 13¼x13***
**1136** A541 180fr multi 4.00 4.00

2012 Paralympics, London — A542

Designs: No. 1137, 75fr, Wheelchair race. No. 1138, 75fr, Shot put.

**2012, Aug. 6** ***Perf. 13x13¼***
**1137-1138** A542 Set of 2 3.25 3.25

Local Scenes — A543

Designs: No. 1139, 110fr, Bonhomme de Bourail rock formation. No. 1140, 110fr, Hut made of coconut palm fronds, Maré. No. 1141, 110fr, Mouth of Koumac River. No. 1142, 110fr, Cowboys and cattle.

**2012, Aug. 6** ***Perf. 13***
**1139-1142** A543 Set of 4 9.50 9.50

Souvenir Sheet

Michel Corbasson Zoo and Forest, Noumea, 50th Anniv. — A544

No. 1143: a, Rhacodactylus leachianus. b, Corvus moneduloides. c, Pittosporum tanianum.

**2012, Sept. 25** ***Perf. 13¼x13***
**1143** A544 110fr Sheet of 3, #a-c 7.25 7.25

National Tree Planting Campaign A545

**2012, Sept. 26** ***Perf. 13***
**1144** A545 75fr multi 1.60 1.60

3G Technology A546

**2012, Sept. 26** *Perf. 13x13¼*
**1145** A546 280fr multi 6.00 6.00

Whales in Great Southern Lagoon Zone — A547

**2012, Nov. 9** *Perf. 13*
**1146** A547 75fr multi 1.60 1.60

Mangrove Forest A548

**2012, Nov. 9** **Litho.**
**1147** A548 75fr multi 1.60 1.60

Christmas A549

**2012, Nov. 9** *Perf. 13x13¼*
**1148** A549 110fr multi 2.40 2.40

New Year 2013 (Year of the Snake) A550

**2013, Feb. 7** **Litho.** *Perf. 13*
**1149** A550 110fr multi 2.40 2.40

Encastreaux Reefs Area — A551

**2013, Mar. 7**
**1150** A551 110fr multi 2.40 2.40

Opening of La Tontouta Intl. Airport, Noumea — A552

**2013, Mar. 19**
**1151** A552 110fr multi 2.40 2.40

Bacouya Sugar Factory Chimney — A553

**2013, May 13** **Engr.** *Perf. 13x12¼*
**1152** A553 120fr multi 2.75 2.75

Red Cross South Pacific Regional Intervention Platform — A554

**2013, June 7** **Litho.** *Perf. 13*
**1153** A554 75fr multi 1.75 1.75

Opening of Calédoscope, New Philatelic Office — A555

**2013, June 7** **Litho.** *Perf. 14½*
**1154** A555 75fr multi 1.75 1.75

Naso Unicornis — A556

**2013, June 7** **Engr.** *Perf. 13*
**1155** A556 110fr blue 2.50 2.50

Marine Life in Lagoons A557

No. 1156: a, Plectorpomus leopardus, Epinephelus polyphekadion. b, Carcharhinus amblyrhynchos. c, Scomberomorus commerson. d, Chelonia mydas. e, Caranx melampygus. f, Tridacna maxima, Forcipiger flavissimus. g, Chromis viridis. h, Panulirus penicillatus. i, Myripristis berndti. j, Lutjanus kasmira.

***Serpentine Die Cut 11***
**2013, June 8** **Litho.**
**Self-Adhesive**

**1156** Booklet pane of 10 25.00
*a.-j.* A557 110fr Any single 2.50 2.50

Re-opening of Maritime History Museum — A558

**2013, June 28** **Litho.** *Perf. 13*
**1157** A558 110fr multi 2.40 2.40

Opening of Nouville Penitentiary Museum — A559

**2013, Aug. 7** **Litho.** *Perf. 13*
**1158** A559 280fr multi 6.25 6.25

Birth of a Girl — A560

Birth of a Boy — A561

**2013, Aug. 8** **Litho.** *Perf. 13¼x13*
**1159** A560 110fr multi 2.50 2.50
**1160** A561 110fr multi 2.50 2.50

World Swimming Championships for the Intellectually Disabled, Dumbea — A562

**2013, Aug. 19** **Litho.** *Perf. 13*
**1161** A562 120fr multi 2.75 2.75

Captaincookia Tree — A563

**2013, Sept. 9** **Litho.** *Perf. 13¼x13*
**1162** A563 85fr multi 1.90 1.90

Pouembout Dovecote — A564

**2013, Sept. 9** **Litho.** *Perf. 13¼x13*
**1163** A564 180fr multi 4.00 4.00

Wildlife and Landscapes — A565

Designs: 85fr, Fruit bat and bougainvillea flowers. 110fr, 500-Franc Note Beach, Hienghène. 190fr, Warrior's Leap, Maré Island, vert. 250fr, Thio and Bota Méré, vert.

***Perf. 13x13¼, 13¼x13***
**2013, Nov. 6** **Litho.**
**1164-1167** A565 Set of 4 14.50 14.50

Beekeeping — A566

No. 1168: a, Jars of honey, honeydipper, flower, beekeeper checking hives. b, Bees and hives.

**2013, Nov. 6** **Litho.** *Perf. 13*
**1168** A566 110fr Horiz. pair, #a-b 5.00 5.00

Miniature Sheet

Orchids — A567

No. 1169: a, Eria karicouyensis. b, Earina deplanchei, vert. c, Eriaxis rigida, vert. d, Dendrobium poissonianum.

***Perf. 13x13¼, 13¼x13***
**2013, Sept. 10** **Litho.**
**1169** A567 110fr Sheet of 4, #a-d 10.00 10.00

Christmas A568

**2013, Nov. 6** **Litho.** *Perf. 13x13¼*
**1170** A568 110fr multi 2.50 2.50

Miniature Sheet

New Banknotes — A569

No. 1171: a, 75fr, 500-franc banknote. b, 75fr, 1000-franc banknote. c, 110fr, 5000-franc banknote. d, 110fr, 10,000-franc banknote.

**Litho. & Silk-screened**

**2014, Jan. 20** ***Perf. 13x12¾***
**1171** A569 Sheet of 4, #a-d 8.50 8.50

New Year 2014 (Year of the Horse) A570

**2014, Feb. 3 Litho.** ***Perf. 13***
**1172** A570 110fr multi 2.50 2.50

No. 1172 was printed in sheets of 10 + central label.

Exhibition at Tjibaou Cultural Center of Kanak Art — A571

**2014, Mar. 15 Litho.** ***Perf. 12¾x13***
**1173** A571 110fr multi 2.60 2.60

North and East Coastal Zone UNESCO World Heritage Site — A572

**2014, Apr. 22 Litho.** ***Perf. 13¼x13***
**1174** A572 110fr multi 2.60 2.60

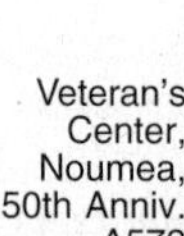

Veteran's Center, Noumea, 50th Anniv. A573

**2014, May 16 Litho.** ***Perf. 13x13¼***
**1175** A573 150fr multi 3.50 3.50

Cajoulle House, Koné — A574

**2014, May 16 Engr.** ***Perf. 13x13¼***
**1176** A574 750fr multi 17.00 17.00

World Blood Donor Day — A575

**2014, June 6 Litho.** ***Perf. 13***
**1177** A575 110fr multi 2.50 2.50

Landscapes and Wildlife — A576

Designs: 75fr, Koné Coral Reef. 110fr, Golden damselfish (poisson-demoiselle), horiz. 120fr, Horned parakeet (perruche), horiz. 190fr, Drowned Forest (La Fôret Noyée).

***Perf. 13¼x13, 13x13¼***

**2014, June 6 Litho.**
**1178-1181** A576 Set of 4 11.50 11.50

Marine Rescue Service, 10th Anniv. — A577

**Litho. & Engr.**

**2014, Sept. 8** ***Perf. 13***
**1182** A577 110fr multi 2.40 2.40

Souvenir Sheet

Flora and Fauna of the Mining Scrubland — A578

No. 1183: a, Red-throated parrotfinch (Diamant psittaculaire). b, Grevillea gillivrayi, vert. c, Deplanchea sessilifolia.

***Perf. 13x13¼, 13¼x13***

**2014, Sept. 8 Photo.**
**1183** A578 110fr Sheet of 3, #a-c 7.00 7.00

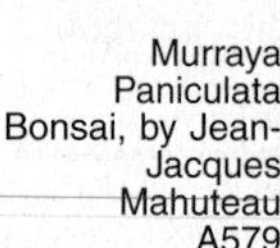

Murraya Paniculata Bonsai, by Jean-Jacques Mahuteau A579

**2014, Oct. 6 Litho.** ***Perf. 13¼x13***
**1184** A579 150fr multi 3.25 3.25

Isle of Pines Penitentiary — A580

**2014, Oct. 6 Engr.** ***Perf. 13x12½***
**1185** A580 280fr multi 6.00 6.00

Papilio Montrouzieri A581

**Litho. & Embossed With Foil Application**

**2014, Nov. 6** ***Perf. 13½***
**1186** A581 180fr multi 3.75 3.75

Niaouli Flowers and Oil Distillation — A582

**2014, Nov. 6 Litho.** ***Perf. 13***
**1187** A582 190fr multi 4.00 4.00

No. 1187 is impregnated with a niaouli scent.

Kanak Weaving A583

**Litho. & Embossed**

**2014, Nov. 6** ***Perf. 13***
**1188** A583 250fr multi 5.25 5.25

Christmas A584

**2014, Nov. 6 Litho.** ***Perf. 13x13¼***
**1189** A584 110fr multi 2.40 2.40

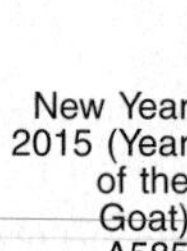

New Year 2015 (Year of the Goat) A585

**2015, Feb. 19 Litho.** ***Perf. 13***
**1190** A585 110fr multi 2.10 2.10

No. 1190 was printed in sheets of 10 + central label.

Dick Ukeiwe (1928-2013), Senator — A586

**2015, Feb. 19 Engr.** ***Perf. 13¼***
**1191** A586 500fr dark blue & brown 9.25 9.25

Pittosporum Tanianum A587

**2015, Mar. 19 Litho.** ***Perf. 13x13¼***
**1192** A587 120fr multi 2.25 2.25

Kô Salt Marshes, Poingam — A588

**2015, Apr. 22 Litho.** ***Perf. 13***
**1193** A588 450fr multi 8.50 8.50

Children's Art — A589

Designs: No. 1194, Wildlife, by Eliot-Louis Hatterer.

No. 1195, horiz.: a, Building, tree and Sun, by Emmanuelle Hnawang. b, Flower and snake, by Thomas Bodeouarou.

**2015, June 5 Litho.** ***Perf. 13¼x13***
**1194** A589 75fr multi 1.40 1.40

***Perf. 13x13¼***

**1195** Horiz. pair + central label 2.80 2.80
*a.-b.* A589 75fr Either single 1.40 1.40

World War I, Cent. A590

No. 1196 — Military medals and: a, Soldiers boarding the Sontay. b, Battle of the Serre. c, Soldiers returning home on the El Kantara.

**2015, June 5 Litho. *Perf. 13x13¼***
**1196** Horiz. strip of 3 2.00 2.00
***a.-c.*** A590 35fr Any single .65 .65

Souvenir Sheet

Birds — A591

No. 1197: a, Nycticorax caledonicus. b, Egretta sacra albolineata, horiz. c, Egretta novaehollandiae nana.

***Perf. 13¼x13, 13x13¼***
**2015, June 5 Litho.**
**1197** A591 110fr Sheet of 3, #a-c 6.25 6.25

Maxat, First Yam Farming Cycle — A592

**2015, July 20 Litho. *Perf. 13***
**1198** A592 110fr multi 2.10 2.10

New Caledonia Ornithological Society, 50th Anniv. — A593

**2015, Aug. 5 Litho. *Perf. 13***
**1199** A593 180fr multi 3.50 3.50

Château Escande, Poya — A594

**2015, Sept. 15 Engr. *Perf. 13x12½***
**1200** A594 750fr multi 14.00 14.00

First Lighting of Amédée Lighthouse, 150th Anniv. — A595

**2015, Nov. 5 Litho. *Perf. 13***
**1201** A595 110fr multi 2.00 2.00

Flowers A596

No. 1202: a, Arthroclianthus deplanchei. b, Thiollierea campanulata. c, Xanthostemon aurantiacus. d, Deplanchea speciosa. e, Xanthostemon sulfureus. f, Deplanchea sessifolia. g, Boronella pancheri. h, Artia balansae. i, Virotia angustifolia. j, Arthroclianthus microbotrys.

***Serpentine Die Cut 11***
**2015, Nov. 5 Litho.**
**Self-Adhesive**
**1202** Booklet pane of 10 20.00
***a.-j.*** A596 110fr Any single 2.00 2.00

Miniature Sheet

Turtles — A597

No. 1203 — Inscriptions: a, Tortue bonne écaille. b, Tortue grosse tête. c, Tortue verte, horiz. d, Tortue luth, horiz.

**2015, Nov. 5 Photo. *Perf. 13½x13***
**1203** A597 110fr Sheet of 4, #a-d 8.00 8.00

Christmas — A598

**Litho. & Thermographed**
**2015, Nov. 5 *Perf. 13 on 3 Sides***
**1204** A598 110fr multi 2.00 2.00

New Year 2016 (Year of the Monkey) A599

**2016, Feb. 8 Litho. *Perf. 13***
**1205** A599 110fr multi 2.00 2.00

No. 1205 was printed in sheets of 10 + central label.

Conifers and Palm Trees — A600

**2016, Mar. 14 Litho. *Perf. 13***
**1206** A600 120fr multi 2.40 2.40

Tiga Island — A601

**2016, Apr. 14 Litho. *Perf. 13***
**1207** A601 110fr multi 2.10 2.10

Marriage A602

**2016, May 12 Litho. *Perf. 13x13¼***
**1208** A602 75fr multi 1.40 1.40

Statue of Kanak Soldier of World War I — A603

**2016, June 3 Litho. *Perf. 13***
**1209** A603 110fr multi 2.10 2.10

Shell Engraved by Convict A604

**Litho. & Silk-Screened**
**2016, June 10 *Perf. 13x13¼***
**1210** A604 75fr multi 1.40 1.40

Fiber Optic Communications — A605

**2016, June 10 Litho. *Perf. 13x13¼***
**1211** A605 75fr multi 1.40 1.40

Natural Park of the Coral Sea — A606

**2016, June 10 Litho. *Perf. 13***
**1212** A606 110fr multi 2.10 2.10

Astronomy in New Caledonia A607

**2016, Aug. 5 Litho. *Perf. 14¼x14***
**1213** A607 450fr multi 8.50 8.50

Janisel House, Pouébo A608

**2016, Sept. 12 Litho. *Perf. 13x13¼***
**1214** A608 110fr multi 2.10 2.10

Dr. René Catala (1901-88), Biologist — A609

**2016, Sept. 12 Litho. *Perf. 13***
**1215** A609 120fr multi + label 2.25 2.25

Horat, Second Yam Farming Cycle — A610

**2016, Oct. 10 Litho. *Perf. 13***
**1216** A610 120fr multi 2.25 2.25

Ocean Liner Le Calédonien — A611

**2016, Nov. 3 Litho. *Perf. 13***
**1217** A611 110fr multi 2.00 2.00

Miniature Sheet

Items With Spirals — A612

No. 1218: a, Hippocampus kuda (seahorse). b, Spirobranchus giganteus (Christmas tree worms), horiz. c, Cyathea intermedia (tree fern). d, Nautilus macromphalus (nautilus), horiz.

**2016, Nov. 3 Litho. *Perf. 13¼***
**1218** A612 110fr Sheet of 4, #a-d 8.00 8.00

Kagu — A613

**2016, Nov. 3 Litho. *Perf. 13***
**Background Color**
**1219** A613 5fr reddish lilac .25 .25
**1220** A613 10fr light green .25 .25
**1221** A613 30fr cerise .55 .55
*Nos. 1219-1221 (3)* 1.05 1.05

**Booklet Stamps**
**Self-Adhesive**
***Serpentine Die Cut 6¾ Vert.***
**1222** A613 (75fr) dark red 1.40 1.40
*a.* Booklet pane of 10 14.00
**1223** A613 (120fr) yel orange 2.25 2.25
*a.* Booklet pane of 10 22.50

Christmas and New Year's Day A614

**2016, Nov. 3 Litho. *Perf. 13x13¼***
**1224** A614 110fr multi 2.00 2.00

New Year 2017 (Year of the Rooster) A615

**2017, Feb. 1 Litho. *Perf. 13¼***
**1225** A615 75fr multi 1.40 1.40

No. 1225 was printed in sheets of 10 + central label.

Roger Gervolino (1909-91), Politician — A616

**2017, Mar. 14 Engr. *Perf. 13***
**1226** A616 1000fr dk blue & dk brn 18.00 18.00

Mixed Battalion of the Pacific, Cent. — A619

**2017, May 15 Litho. *Perf. 13***
**1229** A619 120fr multi 2.25 2.25

Lions Clubs International, Cent. — A620

**2017, July 6 Litho. *Perf. 13¼x13***
**1230** A620 75fr multi 1.50 1.50

Buildings — A622

No. 1232: a, Beaumont House, Moindou. b, Round houses, Isle of Pines.

**2017, July 7 Litho. *Perf. 13x13¼***
**1232** A622 75fr Horiz. pair, #a-b, + central label 3.00 3.00

Kagu Philatelic Club, 70th Anniv. A625

**2017, Nov. 8 Litho. *Perf. 13x13¼***
**1235** A625 75fr multi 1.50 1.50

Wênit, Third Yam Farming Cycle — A626

**2017, Nov. 9 Litho. *Perf. 13***
**1236** A626 75fr multi 1.50 1.50

Caves and Water Holes A627

No. 1237 — Inscriptions: a, Grotte de Koumac. b, Pléiades du Nord. c, Trou Feuillet. d, Trou bleu. e, Trou d'eau à la Rivière Bleue. f, Trou d'eau d'Anawa. g, Grotte de la Reine Hortense. h, Aquarium naturel. i, Trou de Bone. j, Grotte du Diable.

***Serpentine Die Cut 11***
**2017, Nov. 9 Litho.**
**Self-Adhesive**
**1237** Booklet pane of 10 22.50
*a.-j.* A627 110fr Any single 2.25 2.25

Christmas — A628

**2017, Nov. 9 Litho. *Perf. 13¼x13***
**1238** A628 110fr multi 2.25 2.25

## SEMI-POSTAL STAMPS

No. 93 Surcharged

**1915 Unwmk. *Perf. 14x13½***
**B1** A16 10c + 5c carmine 1.50 1.50
*a.* Inverted surcharge 75.00 75.00
*b.* Cross omitted 100.00 —
*c.* Double surcharge 160.00 160.00

Regular Issue of 1905 Surcharged

**1917**
**B2** A16 10c + 5c rose 1.50 1.30
*a.* Double surcharge 130.00 —
**B3** A16 15c + 5c violet 1.50 1.40

**Curie Issue**
Common Design Type
**1938, Oct. 24 *Perf. 13***
**B4** CD80 1.75fr + 50c brt ultra 16.50 17.50

**French Revolution Issue**
Common Design Type
**1939, July 5 Photo.**
**Name and Value Typo. in Black**
**B5** CD83 45c + 25c green 13.50 13.50
**B6** CD83 70c + 30c brown 13.50 13.50
**B7** CD83 90c + 35c red org 13.50 13.50
**B8** CD83 1.25fr + 1fr rose pink 13.50 13.50
**B9** CD83 2.25fr + 2fr blue 13.50 13.50
*Nos. B5-B9 (5)* 67.50 67.50

**Catalogue values for unused stamps in this section, from this point to the end of the section, are for Never Hinged items.**

**Common Design Type and**

Dumont d'Urville's ship, "Zélée" — SP2

New Caledonian Militiaman SP3

**1941 Photo. *Perf. 13½***
**B10** SP2 1fr + 1fr red 2.25
**B11** CD86 1.50fr + 3fr maroon 2.25
**B12** SP3 2.50fr + 1fr dk blue 2.25
*Nos. B10-B12 (3)* 6.75

Nos. B10-B12 were issued by the Vichy government in France, but were not placed on sale in New Caledonia.

Nos. 216A-216B Srchd. in Black or Red

**1944 Engr. *Perf. 12½x12***
**B12A** 50c + 1.50fr on 2.50fr deep blue (R) 1.00
**B12B** + 2.50fr on 1fr green 1.25

Colonial Development Fund.

Nos. B12A-B12B were issued by the Vichy government in France, but were not placed on sale in New Caledonia.

**Red Cross Issue**
Common Design Type
**1944 *Perf. 14½x14***
**B13** CD90 5fr + 20fr brt scar 1.50 1.50

The surtax was for the French Red Cross and national relief.

**Tropical Medicine Issue**
Common Design Type
**1950, May 15 Engr. *Perf. 13***
**B14** CD100 10fr + 2fr red brn & sepia 6.75 5.25

The surtax was for charitable work.

## AIR POST STAMPS

Seaplane Over Pacific Ocean AP1

**1938-40 Unwmk. Engr. *Perf. 13***
**C1** AP1 65c deep violet 1.00 1.00
*a.* "65c" omitted 225.00
**C2** AP1 4.50fr red 1.60 1.60
**C3** AP1 7fr dk bl grn ('40) 1.15 .85
**C4** AP1 9fr ultra 3.00 2.60
**C5** AP1 20fr dk org ('40) 2.25 2.25
**C6** AP1 50fr black ('40) 3.75 3.25
*Nos. C1-C6 (6)* 12.75 11.55

**Type of 1938-40 Without "RF"**
**1942-43**
**C6A** AP1 65c deep violet .30
**C6B** AP1 4.50fr red .30
**C6C** AP1 5fr yellow brown .55
**C6D** AP1 9fr ultramarine .45
**C6E** AP1 10fr brown lilac 1.00
**C6F** AP1 20fr dark orange 1.60
**C6G** AP1 50fr black 1.75
*Nos. C6A-C6G (7)* 5.95

Nos. C6A-C6G were issued by the Vichy government in France, but were not placed on sale in New Caledonia.

Common Design Type
**1942 Unwmk. *Perf. 14½x14***
**C7** CD87 1fr dk orange .70 .70
**C8** CD87 1.50fr brt red .70 .70
**C9** CD87 5fr brown red .70 .70
**C10** CD87 10fr black 1.10 .70
**C11** CD87 25fr ultra 1.40 1.25
**C12** CD87 50fr dk green 2.00 1.25
**C13** CD87 100fr plum 2.25 2.00
*Nos. C7-C13 (7)* 8.85 7.30

Eagle — AP1a

**1944 *Perf. 13***
**C13A** AP1a 100fr gray green & blue green 1.50

No. C13A was issued by the Vichy government in France, but was not placed on sale in New Caledonia.

**Catalogue values for unused stamps in this section, from this point to the end of the section, are for Never Hinged items.**

**Victory Issue**
Common Design Type
**1946, May 8 Engr. *Perf. 12½***
**C14** CD92 8fr brt ultra 1.50 1.25

**Chad to Rhine Issue**
Common Design Types
**1946, June 6**
**C15** CD93 5fr black 1.75 1.60
**C16** CD94 10fr carmine 1.75 1.60
**C17** CD95 15fr dk blue 1.75 1.60

**C18** CD96 20fr orange brn 1.75 1.60
**C19** CD97 25fr olive grn 2.40 2.00
**C20** CD98 50fr dk rose vio 4.00 3.50
*Nos. C15-C20 (6)* 13.40 11.90

St. Vincent Bay — AP2

Planes over Islands — AP3

View of Nouméa — AP4

*Perf. 13x12½, 12½x13*

**1948, Mar. 1 Photo. Unwmk.**
**C21** AP2 50fr org & rose vio 6.00 4.00
**C22** AP3 100fr bl grn & sl bl 10.50 4.50
**C23** AP4 200fr brown & yel 16.50 8.50
*Nos. C21-C23 (3)* 33.00 17.00

### UPU Issue
Common Design Type

**1949, Nov. 21 Engr. *Perf. 13***
**C24** CD99 10fr multicolored 7.50 5.00

### Liberation Issue
Common Design Type

**1954, June 6**
**C25** CD102 3fr indigo & ultra 7.50 5.00

Conveyor for Nickel Ore — AP5

**1955, Nov. 21 Unwmk. *Perf. 13***
**C26** AP5 14fr indigo & sepia 4.00 1.50

Rock Formations, Bourail — AP6

**1959, Mar. 21**
**C27** AP6 200fr lt bl, brn & grn 34.00 15.00

Yaté Dam — AP7

**1959, Sept. 21 Engr.**
**C28** AP7 50fr grn, brt bl & sepia 7.50 4.50

Dedication of Yaté Dam.

Fisherman with Throw-net — AP8

Skin Diver Shooting Bumphead Surgeonfish — AP9

20fr, Nautilus shell. 100fr, Yaté rock.

**1962 Unwmk. *Perf. 13***
**C29** AP8 15fr red, Prus grn & sep 4.75 2.25
**C30** AP9 20fr dk sl grn & org ver 9.50 3.75
**C31** AP9 25fr red brn, gray & bl 9.50 4.50
**C32** AP9 100fr dk brn, dk bl & sl grn 16.00 11.50
*Nos. C29-C32 (4)* 39.75 22.00

### Telstar Issue
Common Design Type

**1962, Dec. 4 Unwmk. *Perf. 13***
**C33** CD111 200fr dk bl, choc & grnsh bl 25.00 18.50

Nickel Mining, Houailou — AP10

**1964, May 14 Photo.**
**C34** AP10 30fr multi 4.00 2.50

Isle of Pines — AP11

**1964, Dec. 7 Engr. *Perf. 13***
**C35** AP11 50fr dk bl, sl grn & choc 5.75 2.60

Phyllobranchus — AP12

Design: 27fr, Paracanthurus teuthis (fish).

**1964, Dec. 21 Photo.**
**C36** AP12 27fr red brn, yel, dp bl & blk 7.50 3.50
**C37** AP12 37fr bl, brn & yel 9.00 5.00

Issued to publicize the Nouméa Aquarium.

Greco-Roman Wrestling — AP13

**1964, Dec. 28 Engr.**
**C38** AP13 10fr brt grn, pink & blk 18.00 15.00

18th Olympic Games, Tokyo, Oct. 10-25.

Nimbus Weather Satellite over New Caledonia AP14

**1965, Mar. 23 Photo. *Perf. 13x12½***
**C39** AP14 9fr multi 3.75 3.00

Fifth World Meteorological Day.

### ITU Issue
Common Design Type

**1965, May 17 Engr. *Perf. 13***
**C40** CD120 40fr lt bl, lil rose & lt brn 10.00 8.00

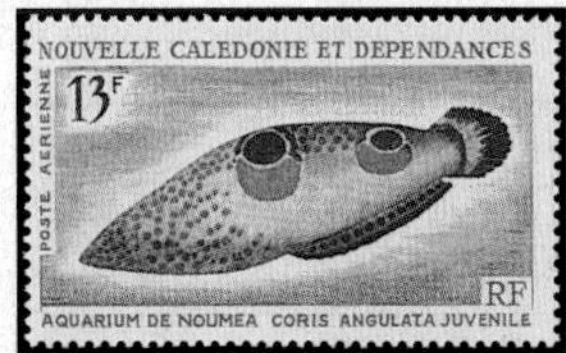


Coris Angulata (Young Fish) — AP15

15fr, Adolescent fish. 25fr, Adult fish.

**1965, Dec. 6 Engr. *Perf. 13***
**C41** AP15 13fr red org, ol bis & blk 4.00 1.50
**C42** AP15 15fr ind, sl grn & bis 6.00 2.00
**C43** AP15 25fr ind & yel grn 8.00 4.00
*Nos. C41-C43 (3)* 18.00 7.50

Issued to publicize the Nouméa Aquarium.

### French Satellite A-1 Issue
Common Design Type

Designs: 8fr, Diamant rocket and launching installations. 12fr, A-1 satellite.

**1966, Jan. 10 Engr. *Perf. 13***
**C44** CD121 8fr rose brn, ultra & Prus bl 2.00 1.60
**C45** CD121 12fr ultra, Prus bl & rose brn 3.00 3.00
*a.* Strip of 2, #C44-C45 + label 7.00 7.00

### French Satellite D-1 Issue
Common Design Type

**1966, May 16 Engr. *Perf. 13***
**C46** CD122 10fr dl bl, ocher & sep 2.25 2.00

Port-de-France, 1866 — AP16

**1966, June 2**
**C47** AP16 30fr dk red, bl & ind 4.25 3.00

Port-de-France changing name to Nouméa, cent.

### Bird Type of Regular Issue

Designs: 27fr, Uvea crested parakeet. 37fr, Scarlet honey eater. 50fr, Two cloven-feathered doves.

**1966-68 Photo. *Perf. 13***
**Size: 26x46mm**
**C48** A45 27fr pink & multi 7.50 4.00
**C49** A45 37fr grn & multi 10.00 5.00
**Size: 27x48mm**
**C49A** A45 50fr multi ('68) 13.00 7.50
*Nos. C48-C49A (3)* 30.50 16.50

Issued: 27fr, 37fr, Oct. 10; 50fr, May 14.

Sailboats and Map of New Caledonia-New Zealand Route — AP17

**1967, Apr. 15 Engr. *Perf. 13***
**C50** AP17 25fr brt grn, dp ultra & red 6.75 3.75

2nd sailboat race from Whangarei, New Zealand, to Nouméa, New Caledonia.

### Butterfly Type of Regular Issue

Butterflies: 19fr, Danaus plexippus. 29fr, Hippotion celerio. 85fr, Delias elipsis.

**1967-68 Engr. *Perf. 13***
**Size: 48x27mm**
**C51** A52 19fr multi ('68) 6.50 3.00
**C52** A52 29fr multi ('68) 9.50 4.00
**C53** A52 85fr red, dk brn & yel 15.00 7.50
*Nos. C51-C53 (3)* 31.00 14.50

Issued: 85fr, Aug. 10; others, Mar. 26.

Jules Garnier, Garnierite and Mine — AP18

**1967, Oct. 9 Engr. *Perf. 13***
**C54** AP18 70fr bl gray, brn & yel grn 9.00 5.25

Discovery of garnierite (nickel ore), cent.

Lifu Island — AP19

**1967, Oct. 28 Photo. *Perf. 13***
**C55** AP19 200fr multi 14.00 7.50

Skier, Snowflake and Olympic Emblem — AP20

**1967, Nov. 16 Engr. *Perf. 13***
**C56** AP20 100fr brn red, sl grn & brt bl 14.00 7.50

10th Winter Olympic Games, Grenoble, France, Feb. 6-18, 1968.

**Sea Shell Type of Regular Issue**

Designs: 39fr, Conus lienardi. 40fr, Conus cabriti. 70fr, Conus coccineus.

**1968, Nov. 9 Engr. *Perf. 13***
**C58** A54 39fr bl grn, brn & gray 8.25 2.75
**C59** A54 40fr blk, brn red & ol 8.25 3.00
**C60** A54 70fr brn, pur & gray 17.00 5.50
*Nos. C58-C60 (3)* 33.50 11.25

Maré Dancers — AP21

**1968, Nov. 30 Engr. *Perf. 13***
**C61** AP21 60fr grn, ultra & hn brn 7.50 5.00

World Map and Caudron C 600 "Aiglon" — AP22

**1969, Mar. 24 Engr. *Perf. 13***
**C62** AP22 29fr lil, dk bl & dk car 5.00 2.25

Stamp Day and honoring the 1st flight from Nouméa to Paris of Henri Martinet & Paul Klein, Mar. 24, 1939.

**Concorde Issue**
Common Design Type

**1969, Apr. 17 Engr. *Perf. 13***
**C63** CD129 100fr sl grn & brt grn 27.50 20.00

**Cattle Type of Regular Issue**

Design: 50fr, Cowboy and herd.

**1969, May 10 Engr. *Perf. 13***
**Size: 48x27mm**
**C64** A56 50fr sl grn, dk brn & red brn 7.00 3.25

**Sea Shell Type of Regular Issue, 1969**

Design: 100fr, Black murex.

**1969, June 21 Engr. *Perf. 13***
**Size: 48x27mm**
**C65** A57 100fr lake, bl & blk 24.00 11.50

**Sports Type of 1969**

30fr, Woman diver. 39fr, Shot put, vert.

**1969, Aug. 7 Engr. *Perf. 13***
**Size: 48x27mm, 27x48mm**
**C66** A58 30fr dk brn, bl & blk 5.25 2.00
**C67** A58 39fr dk ol, brt grn & ol 6.75 3.00

Napoleon in Coronation Robes, by François P. Gerard AP23

**1969, Oct. 2 Photo. *Perf. 12½x12***
**C68** AP23 40fr lil & multi 14.00 10.00

200th birth anniv. of Napoleon Bonaparte (1769-1821).

Air France Plane over Outrigger Canoe — AP24

**1969, Oct. 2 Engr. *Perf. 13***
**C69** AP24 50fr slate grn, sky bl & choc 5.50 3.25

20th anniversary of the inauguration of the Nouméa to Paris airline.

**Bird Type of Regular Issue**

39fr, Emerald doves. 100fr, Whistling kite.

**1970, Feb. 19 Photo. *Perf. 13***
**Size: 27x48mm**
**C70** A45 39fr multi 13.50 4.00
**C71** A45 100fr lt bl & multi 26.00 10.00

Planes Circling Globe and Paris-Nouméa Route — AP25

**1970, May 6 Engr. *Perf. 13***
**C72** AP25 200fr vio, org brn & grnsh bl 17.50 9.75

10th anniversary of the Paris to Nouméa flight: "French Wings Around the World."

**Shell Type of Regular Issue, 1970**

22fr, Strombus sinautus humphrey, vert. 33fr, Argus porcelain shell. 34fr, Strombus vomer, vert. 60fr, Card porcelain shell.

**1970 Engr. *Perf. 13***
**Size: 27x48mm, 48x27mm**
**C73** A59 22fr bl & multi 7.25 3.00
**C74** A59 33fr brn & gray bl 9.00 4.50
**C75** A59 34fr pur & multi 9.00 3.50
**C76** A59 60fr lt grn & brn 15.00 6.00
*Nos. C73-C76 (4)* 40.25 17.00

See Nos. C89-C90.

Bicyclists on Map of New Caledonia — AP26

**1970, Aug. 20 Engr. *Perf. 13***
**C77** AP26 40fr bl, ultra & choc 6.75 3.25

The 4th Bicycling Race of New Caledonia.

Mt. Fuji and Monorail Train — AP27

45fr, Map of Japan and Buddha statue.

**1970, Sept. 3 Photo. *Perf. 13x12½***
**C78** AP27 20fr blk, bl & yel grn 4.50 1.90
**C79** AP27 45fr mar, lt bl & ol 6.00 3.25

EXPO '70 International Exposition, Osaka, Japan, Mar. 15-Sept. 13.

Racing Yachts AP28

**1971, Feb. 23 Engr. *Perf. 13***
**C80** AP28 20fr grn, blk & ver 3.75 1.25

First challenge in New Zealand waters for the One Ton Cup ocean race.

Lt. Col. Broche and Map of Mediterranean — AP29

**1971, May 5 Photo. *Perf. 12½***
**C81** AP29 60fr multi 7.50 4.00

30th anniversary of Battalion of the Pacific.

Pole Vault — AP30

**1971, June 24 Engr. *Perf. 13***
**C82** AP30 25fr shown 3.75 2.00
**C83** AP30 100fr Archery 8.00 4.25

4th South Pacific Games, Papeete, French Polynesia, Sept. 8-19.

Port de Plaisance, Nouméa — AP31

**1971, Sept. 27 Photo. *Perf. 13***
**C84** AP31 200fr multi 16.00 7.00

Golden Eagle and Pilot's Leaflet — AP32

**1971, Nov. 20 Engr. *Perf. 13***
**C85** AP32 90fr dk brn, org & indigo 8.25 3.75

1st flight New Caledonia — Australia with Victor Roffey piloting the Golden Eagle, 40th anniv.

Skiing and Sapporo '72 Emblem — AP33

**1972, Jan. 22 Engr. *Perf. 13***
**C86** AP33 50fr brt bl, car & sl grn 6.00 2.75

11th Winter Olympic Games, Sapporo, Japan, Feb. 3-13.

South Pacific Commission Headquarters, Nouméa — AP34

**1972, Feb. 5 Photo.**
**C87** AP34 18fr bl & multi 2.25 .85

South Pacific Commission, 25th anniv.

St. Mark's Basilica, Venice — AP35

**1972, Feb. 5 Engr.**
**C88** AP35 20fr lt grn, bl & grn 4.25 1.25

UNESCO campaign to save Venice.

**Shell Type of Regular Issue, 1970**

Designs: 25fr, Orange spider conch, vert. 50fr, Chiragra spider conch, vert.

**1972, Mar. 4 Engr. *Perf. 13***
**Size: 27x48mm**

**C89** A59 25fr dp car & dk brn 6.50 3.00
**C90** A59 50fr grn, brn & rose car 8.00 4.00

Breguet F-ALMV and Globe — AP36

**1972, Apr. 5 Engr. *Perf. 13***
**C91** AP36 110fr brt rose lil, bl & grn 8.00 6.00

40th anniversary of the first Paris-Nouméa flight, Mar. 9-Apr. 5, 1932.

Round House and Festival Emblem — AP37

**1972, May 13**
**C92** AP37 24fr org, bl & brn 3.00 1.50

So. Pacific Festival of Arts, Fiji, May 6-20.

Hurdles and Olympic Rings — AP38

**1972, Sept. 2 Engr. *Perf. 13***
**C93** AP38 72fr vio, bl & red lil 7.50 3.75

20th Olympic Games, Munich, Aug. 26-Sept. 11.

New Post Office, Noumea — AP39

**1972, Nov. 25 Engr. *Perf. 13***
**C94** AP39 23fr brn, brt bl & grn 2.25 1.00

Molière and Scenes from Plays — AP40

**1973, Feb. 24 Engr. *Perf. 13***
**C95** AP40 50fr multi 7.50 2.75

300th anniversary of the death of Molière (Jean Baptiste Poquelin, 1622-1673), French actor and playwright.

Woodlands — AP41

Designs: 18fr, Palm trees on coast, vert. 21fr, Waterfall, vert.

**1973, Feb. 24 Photo.**
**C96** AP41 11fr gold & multi 2.00 1.00
**C97** AP41 18fr gold & multi 3.00 1.50
**C98** AP41 21fr gold & multi 4.00 1.50
*Nos. C96-C98 (3)* 9.00 4.00

Concorde — AP42

**1973, Mar. 15 Engr. *Perf. 13***
**C99** AP42 23fr blue 12.50 5.00
*a.* Booklet pane of 5 250.00

No. C99 issued in booklets only.

El Kantara in Panama Canal — AP43

**1973, Mar. 24 Engr. *Perf. 13***
**C100** AP43 60fr brn, yel grn & blk 7.50 3.25

50th anniversary of steamship connection Marseilles to Nouméa through Panama Canal.

Sun, Earth, Wind God and Satellite — AP44

**1973, Mar. 24**
**C101** AP44 80fr multi 7.00 2.75

Centenary of intl. meteorological cooperation and 13th World Meteorological Day.

**Museum Type of Regular Issue**

Designs: 16fr, Carved arrows and arrowhead. 40fr, Carved entrance to chief's house.

**1973, Apr. 30 Photo. *Perf. 12½x13***
**C102** A66 16fr multi 3.00 1.00
**C103** A66 40fr multi 4.50 2.00

DC-10 over Map of Route Paris to Nouméa — AP45

**1973, May 26 Engr. *Perf. 13***
**C104** AP45 100fr brn, ultra & sl grn 7.50 3.50

First direct flight by DC-10, Nouméa to Paris.

**Fish Type of Regular Issue**

32fr, Old and young olive surgeonfish.

**1973, June 23 Photo. *Perf. 13x12½***
**C105** A69 32fr multi 5.00 2.00

Coach, 1880 — AP46

**1973, Sept. 22 Engr. *Perf. 13***
**C106** AP46 15fr choc, bl & sl grn 2.50 1.25

Stamp Day 1973.

Landscape — AP47

West Coast Landscapes: 8fr, Rocky path, vert. 26fr, Trees on shore.

**1974, Feb. 23 Photo. *Perf. 13***
**C107** AP47 8fr gold & multi 1.60 .90
**C108** AP47 22fr gold & multi 2.25 1.40
**C109** AP47 26fr gold & multi 3.75 1.50
*Nos. C107-C109 (3)* 7.60 3.80

Anse-Vata, Scientific Center, Nouméa — AP48

**1974, Mar. 23 Photo. *Perf. 13x12½***
**C110** AP48 50fr multi 3.25 2.00

Ovula Ovum AP49

**1974, Mar. 23**
**C111** AP49 3fr shown 1.50 .55
**C112** AP49 32fr Hydatina 4.00 1.10
**C113** AP49 37fr Dolium perdix 4.50 2.10
*Nos. C111-C113 (3)* 10.00 3.75

Nouméa Aquarium.

Capt. Cook, Map of Grande Terre and "Endeavour" — AP50

Designs: 25fr, Jean F. de la Perouse, his ship and map of Grande Terre. 28fr, French sailor, 18th century, on board ship, vert. 30fr, Antoine R. J. d'Entrecasteaux, ship and map. 36fr, Dumont d'Urville, ship and map of Loyalty Islands.

**1974, Sept. 4 Engr. *Perf. 13***
**C114** AP50 20fr multi 2.00 1.00
**C115** AP50 25fr multi 3.00 1.60
**C116** AP50 28fr multi 4.00 1.60
**C117** AP50 30fr multi 5.00 2.00
**C118** AP50 36fr multi 9.00 2.50
*Nos. C114-C118 (5)* 23.00 8.70

Discovery and exploration of New Caledonia and Loyalty Islands.

UPU Emblem and Symbolic Design — AP51

**1974, Oct. 9 Engr. *Perf. 13***
**C119** AP51 95fr multi 6.00 2.75

Centenary of Universal Postal Union.

Abstract Design — AP52

**1974, Oct. 26 Photo. *Perf. 13***
**C120** AP52 80fr bl, blk & org 5.00 2.00

ARPHILA 75, Philatelic Exhibition, Paris, June 6-16, 1975.

Hôtel Chateau-Royal, Nouméa — AP53

**1975, Jan. 20 Photo. *Perf. 13***
**C121** AP53 22fr multi 2.25 1.25

Cricket — AP54

Designs: 25fr, Bougna ceremony (food offering). 31fr, Pilou dance.

**1975, Apr. 5 Photo. *Perf. 13***
**C122** AP54 3fr bl & multi 1.25 .45
**C123** AP54 25fr olive grn & multi 2.50 .70
**C124** AP54 31fr yel grn & multi 3.00 1.10
*Nos. C122-C124 (3)* 6.75 2.25

Tourist publicity.

**Orchid Type of 1975**

Design: 42fr, Eriaxis rigida.

**1975, May 30**
**C125** A74 42fr grn & multi 6.00 2.25

Globe as "Flower" with "Stamps" and leaves — AP55

**1975, June 7 Engr. *Perf. 13***

**C126** AP55 105fr multi 7.00 2.75

ARPHILA 75 International Philatelic Exhibition, Paris, June 6-16.

Discus and Games' Emblem — AP56

50fr, Volleyball and Games' emblem.

**1975, Aug. 23 Photo. *Perf. 13x12½***

**C127** AP56 24fr emer, pur & dk bl 2.00 1.00

**C128** AP56 50fr multi 3.50 2.00

5th South Pacific Games, Guam, Aug. 1-10.

Concorde — AP57

**1976, Jan. 21 Engr. *Perf. 13***

**C129** AP57 147fr car & ultra 12.00 7.00

First commercial flight of supersonic jet Concorde, Paris-Rio de Janeiro, Jan. 21.

For surcharge see No. C141.

Telephones 1876 and 1976, Satellite — AP58

**1976, Apr. 12 Photo. *Perf. 13***

**C130** AP58 36fr multi 3.50 1.25

Centenary of first telephone call by Alexander Graham Bell, Mar. 10, 1876.

Battle Scene — AP59

**1976, June 14 Engr. *Perf. 13***

**C131** AP59 24fr red brn & ver 2.75 1.25

American Bicentennial.

Runners and Maple Leaf — AP60

**1976, July 24 Engr. *Perf. 13***

**C132** AP60 33fr car, vio & brn 2.25 1.25

21st Olympic Games, Montreal, Canada, July 17-Aug. 1.

Whimsical Bird as Student and Collector AP61

**1976, Aug. 21 Photo.**

**C133** AP61 42fr multi 3.50 1.50

Philately in School, Philatelic Exhibition in La Perouse Lyceum, Nouméa.

Old City Hall, Nouméa — AP62

Design: 125fr, New City Hall, Nouméa.

**1976, Oct. 22 Photo. *Perf. 13***

**C134** AP62 75fr multi 5.00 2.75

**C135** AP62 125fr multi 7.25 3.25

Lagoon, Women and Festival Symbols AP63

**1977, Jan. 15 Photo. *Perf. 13x12½***

**C136** AP63 11fr multi 2.00 1.00

Summer Festival 1977, Nouméa.

Training Children in Toy Cars — AP64

**1977, Mar. 12 Litho. *Perf. 13***

**C137** AP64 50fr multi 3.00 1.60

Road safety training.

**Bird Type of 1977**

Design: 42fr, Male frigate bird, horiz.

**1977, Sept. 17 Photo. *Perf. 13***

**C138** A89 42fr multi 6.00 1.60

Magenta Airport and Routes — AP65

Design: 57fr, La Tontouta airport.

**1977, Oct. 22 Litho. *Perf. 13***

**C139** AP65 24fr multi 1.75 1.00

**C140** AP65 57fr multi 3.50 2.00

**No. C129 Surcharged in Violet Blue**

**1977, Nov. 22 Engr. *Perf. 13***

**C141** AP57 147fr car & ultra 14.00 9.00

Concorde, 1st commercial flight Paris-NY.

Old Nouméa, by H. Didonna — AP66

Valley of the Settlers, by Jean Kreber — AP67

**1977, Nov. 26 Photo. *Perf. 13***

**C142** AP66 41fr gold & multi 3.00 1.50

**Engr.**

**C143** AP67 42fr red brn & dk brn 3.00 1.50

"Underwater Carnival," Aubusson Tapestry — AP68

**1978, June 17 Photo. *Perf. 13***

**C144** AP68 105fr multi 5.50 2.25

"The Hare and the Tortoise" — AP69

**1978, Aug. 19 Photo. *Perf. 13x13½***

**C145** AP69 35fr multi 4.50 1.50

School philately.

Bourail School Children, Map and Conus Shell — AP70

**1978, Sept. 30 Engr. *Perf. 13***

**C146** AP70 41fr multi 3.00 1.25

Promotion of topical philately in Bourail public schools.

Old and New Candles — AP71

**1978, Oct. 28 Photo. *Perf. 13***

**C147** AP71 36fr multi 2.00 .75

Third Caledonian Senior Citizens' Day.

Faubourg Blanchot, by Lacouture — AP72

**1978, Nov. 25 Photo. *Perf. 13***

**C148** AP72 24fr multi 1.75 1.00

**Type of 1978**

Design: 42fr, Amyema scandens, horiz.

**1978, Mar. 17 *Perf. 13x12½***

**C149** A91 42fr multi 3.50 1.60

Orbiting Weather Satellites, WMO Emblem AP73

**1979, Mar. 24 Photo. *Perf. 13***

**C150** AP73 53fr multi 2.50 1.25

First world-wide satellite system in the atmosphere.

Ships and Emblem — AP74

**1979, Mar. 31 Engr.**

**C151** AP74 49fr multi 2.10 1.10

Chamber of Commerce and Industry, centenary.

Child's Drawing, IYC Emblem AP75

**1979, Apr. 21** **Photo.** ***Perf. 13***
**C152** AP75 35fr multi 2.10 1.10

International Year of the Child.

Surf Casting AP76

Design: 30fr, Swordfish fishing.

**1979, May 26** **Litho.** ***Perf. 12½***
**C153** AP76 29fr multi 2.00 1.00
**C154** AP76 30fr multi 2.00 1.00

Port-de-France, 1854, and de Montravel — AP77

**1979, June 16** **Engr.** ***Perf. 13***
**C155** AP77 75fr multi 4.25 2.25

125th anniversary of Noumea, formerly Port-de-France, founded by L. Tardy de Montravel.

The Eel Queen, Kanaka Legend — AP78

**1979, July 7** **Photo.** ***Perf. 13***
**C156** AP78 42fr multi 3.00 1.75

Nature protection.

Map of New Caledonia, Postmark, Five Races — AP79

**1979, Aug. 18** **Photo.** ***Perf. 13***
**C157** AP79 27fr multi 1.75 .90

New Caledonian youth and philately.

Orstom Center, Noumea, Orstom Emblem — AP80

**1979, Sept. 17** **Photo.** ***Perf. 13***
**C158** AP80 25fr multi 1.75 1.00

Old Post Office, Noumea, New Caledonia No. 1, Hill — AP81

**1979, Nov. 17** **Engr.**
**C159** AP81 150fr multi 5.25 2.00

Sir Rowland Hill (1795-1879), originator of penny postage.

Pirogue AP82

**1980, Jan. 26** **Engr.** ***Perf. 13***
**C160** AP82 45fr multi 1.75 .90

Rotary Intl., 75th Anniv. — AP83

**1980, Feb. 23** **Photo.** ***Perf. 13***
**C161** AP83 100fr multi 4.50 1.60

Man Holding Dolphinfish AP84

39fr, Fishermen, sail fish, vert.

**1980, Mar. 29** **Photo.** ***Perf. 13x12½***
**C162** AP84 34fr shown 1.75 1.00
**C163** AP84 39fr multicolored 2.50 1.25

Coral Seas Air Rally — AP85

**1980, June 7** **Engr.** ***Perf. 13***
**C164** AP85 31fr multi 1.75 .90

Carved Alligator, Boat — AP86

**1980, June 21** **Photo.**
**C165** AP86 27fr multi 1.50 .55

South Pacific Arts Festival, Port Moresby, Papua New Guinea.

New Caledonian Kiwanis, 10th Anniversary — AP87

**1980, Sept. 10** **Photo.** ***Perf. 13***
**C166** AP87 50fr multi 1.90 .90

View of Old Noumea — AP88

**1980, Oct. 25** **Photo.** ***Perf. 13½***
**C167** AP88 33fr multi 1.60 .90

Charles de Gaulle, 10th Anniversary of Death — AP89

**1980, Nov. 15** **Engr.** ***Perf. 13***
**C168** AP89 120fr multi 6.00 3.50

Fluorescent Coral, Noumea Aquarium AP90

**1980, Dec. 13** **Photo.** ***Perf. 13x13½***
**C169** AP90 60fr multi 3.00 1.10

Xeronema Moorei AP91

51fr, Geissois pruinosa.

**1981, Mar. 18** **Photo.** ***Perf. 13x12½***
**C170** AP91 38fr shown 1.50 1.25
**C171** AP91 51fr multicolored 2.00 1.40

Yuri Gagarin and Vostok I — AP92

20th Anniversary of First Space Flights: 155fr, Alan B. Shepard, Freedom 7.

**1981, Apr. 8** **Engr.** ***Perf. 13***
**C172** AP92 64fr multi 2.75 1.10
**C173** AP92 155fr multi 4.50 2.10
*a.* Souv. sheet of 2, #C172-C173 15.00 15.00

No. C173a sold for 225fr.

40th Anniv. of Departure of Pacific Batallion — AP93

**1981, May 5** **Photo.** ***Perf. 13***
**C174** AP93 29fr multi 3.00 1.10

Ecinometra Mathaei AP94

51fr, Prionocidaris verticillata.

**1981, Aug. 5** **Photo.** ***Perf. 13x13½***
**C175** AP94 38fr shown 1.50 .80
**C176** AP94 51fr multicolored 2.25 .95

No. 4, Post Office Building AP95

**1981, Sept. 16** **Photo.** ***Perf. 13x13½***
**C177** AP95 41fr multi 1.75 .90

Stamp Day.

Old Noumea Latin Quarter — AP96

**1981, Oct. 14** **Photo.** ***Perf. 13½***
**C178** AP96 43fr multi 1.75 .75

New Caledonia to Australia Airmail Flight by Victor Roffey, 50th Anniv. AP97

**1981, Nov. 21 Engr. *Perf. 13***
**C179** AP97 37fr multi 1.50 .75

Rousette AP98

**1982, Feb. 24 Engr. *Perf. 13***
**C180** AP98 38fr shown 1.50 .75
**C181** AP98 51fr Kagu 2.00 .85

See Nos. C188B-C188C.

50th Anniv. of Paris-Noumea Flight — AP99

250fr, Pilots, map, plane.

**1982, Apr. 5 Engr. *Perf. 13***
**C182** AP99 250fr multi 7.00 3.50

Scouting Year — AP100

**1982, Apr. 21 Photo. *Perf. 13½x13***
**C183** AP100 40fr multi 1.50 .80

PHILEXFRANCE '82 Intl. Stamp Show, Paris, June 11-21 — AP101

**1982, May 12 Engr. *Perf. 13***
**C184** AP101 150fr multi 3.25 2.00

1982 World Cup AP102

**1982, June 9 Photo. *Perf. 13x13½***
**C185** AP102 74fr multi 2.10 1.00

French Overseas Possessions Week, Sept. 18-25 — AP103

100fr, Map, kagu, citizens.

**1982, Sept. 17 *Perf. 13x12½***
**C186** AP103 100fr multicolored 2.75 1.00

Gypsum, Poya Mines AP104

59fr, Silica gel, Kone mine.

**1983, Jan. 15 Photo. *Perf. 13x13½***
**C187** AP104 44fr shown 2.50 1.10
**C188** AP104 59fr multicolored 3.50 1.40

World Communications Year — AP104a

Design: WCY emblem, map, globe.

**1983, Mar. 9 Litho. *Perf. 13***
**C188A** AP104a 170fr multi 4.00 1.50

**Aircraft Type of 1982**

46fr, Pou-du-Ciel. 61fr, L'Aiglon Caudron.

**1983, July 6 Engr. *Perf. 13***
**C188B** AP98 46fr multi 1.50 .75
**C188C** AP98 61fr multi 2.50 1.25

Temple and Dancers — AP105

**1983, July 20 Litho. *Perf. 12½x12***
**C189** AP105 47fr multi 1.50 .80

BANGKOK '83 Intl. Stamp Show, Aug. 4-13.

Oueholle Tribe, Straw Hut — AP106

**1983, Sept. 7 Litho. *Perf. 13***
**C190** AP106 76fr multi 2.25 1.10

Loyalty Islander by the Shore, by R. Mascart AP107

Paintings: 350fr, The Guitarist from Mare Island, by P. Neilly.

**1983, Dec. 7 Photo. *Perf. 13***
**C191** AP107 100fr multi 3.75 1.75
**C192** AP107 350fr multi 9.00 5.25

Noumea Aquarium Fish AP108

46fr, Amphiprion clarkii. 61fr, Centropyge bicolor.

**1984, Mar. 7 Photo. *Perf. 13***
**C193** AP108 46fr multi 2.25 .90
**C194** AP108 61fr multi 2.75 1.25

Local Plants — AP109

51fr, Araucaria columnaris. 67fr, Pritchardiopsis jeanneneyi.

**1984, Apr. 25 Litho. *Perf. 12½x13***
**C195** AP109 51fr multi 2.00 .90
**C196** AP109 67fr multi 2.75 1.25

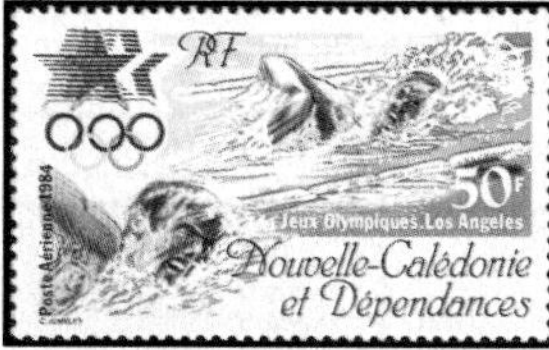
1984 Summer Olympics — AP110

**1984, June 20 Photo. *Perf. 13½x13***
**C197** AP110 50fr Swimming 1.75 1.10
**C198** AP110 83fr Wind surfing 3.50 1.60
**C199** AP110 200fr Running 6.00 2.75
*Nos. C197-C199 (3)* 11.25 5.45

Ausipex '84 — AP111

**1984, Sept. 21 Engr. *Perf. 13***
**C200** AP111 150fr Exhibition Hall 4.50 2.25
*a.* Souvenir sheet 6.00 6.00

Se-tenant with label showing exhibition emblem. No. C200a contains No. C200 in changed colors.

Army Day — AP112

**1984, Oct. 27 Litho. *Perf. 13½x13***
**C201** AP112 51fr multi 1.60 1.00

Woman Fishing for Crabs, by Mme. Bonnet de Larbogne — AP113

Painting: 300fr, Cook Discovering New Caledonia, by Pilioko.

**1984, Nov. 8 Litho. *Perf. 13x12½***
**C202** AP113 120fr multi 3.50 1.75
**C203** AP113 300fr multi 8.00 4.50

See Nos. 605-606.

Transpac Dragon Rapide, Map AP114

**1985, Oct. 2 Litho. *Perf. 13½***
**C204** AP114 80fr multi 2.50 1.25

Internal air services, 30th anniv.

UN, 40th Anniv. AP115

***Perf. 12½x13***
**1985, Oct. 25 Wmk. 385**
**C205** AP115 250fr multi 5.50 2.00

Jules Garnier High School AP116

**1985, Nov. 13 Unwmk. *Perf. 13***
**C206** AP116 400fr multi 10.00 4.25

Paris-Noumea Scheduled Flights, 30th Anniv. — AP117

**1986, Jan. 6**
**C207** AP117 72fr multi 2.25 1.25

Nou Island Livestock Warehouse — AP118

**1986, June 14 Engr. *Perf. 13***
**C208** AP118 230fr Prus bl, sep & brn 5.25 2.75

ATR-42 Inaugural Service AP119

**1986, Aug. 13 Litho. *Perf. 12½x13***
**C209** AP119 18fr multi .90 .75

STOCKHOLMIA '86 — AP120

**1986, Aug. 29 Engr. *Perf. 13***
**C210** AP120 108fr No. 1 3.00 1.50

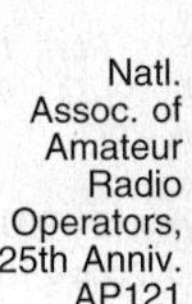

Natl. Assoc. of Amateur Radio Operators, 25th Anniv. AP121

**1987, Jan. 7 Litho. *Perf. 12½***
**C211** AP121 64fr multi 1.75 .85

Nature Conservation, Fight Noise Pollution — AP122

**1987, Mar. 25 Litho. *Perf. 13x12½***
**C212** AP122 150fr multi 4.00 1.75

French Cricket Federation AP123

**1987, Nov. 25 Litho. *Perf. 12½***
**C213** AP123 94fr multi 2.50 1.75

**Arms Type of 1984**

**1988, Jan. 13 *Perf. 12½x13***
**C214** A132 76fr Dumbea 2.50 1.00

Rotary Intl. Anti-Polio Campaign — AP124

**1988, Oct. 26 Litho. *Perf. 13½***
**C215** AP124 220fr multi 5.25 2.75

**Bamboo Type of 1989**
**Litho. & Engr.**

**1989, Sept. 27 *Perf. 12½x13***
**C216** A187 44fr multi 1.25 .65

De Gaulle's Call For French Resistance, 50th Anniv. AP125

**1990, June 20 Litho. *Perf. 12½***
**C217** AP125 160fr multicolored 4.00 1.75

Military Cemetery, New Zealand — AP126

Auckland 1990: #C219, Brigadier William Walter Dove.

**1990, Aug. 24 *Perf. 13***
**C218** AP126 80fr multi 2.00 1.00
**C219** AP126 80fr multi 2.00 1.00
*a.* Pair, #C218-C219 + label 4.50 4.50

Souvenir Sheet

New Zealand 1990 — AP126a

**1990, Aug. 25 Litho. *Perf. 13x12½***
**C219B** AP126a 150fr multi 6.00 5.00

Crustaceans AP127

30fr, Munidopsis sp. Orstom. 60fr, Lyreidius tridentatus.

**1990, Oct. 17 Litho. *Perf. 12½x13***
**C220** AP127 30fr multi 1.00 .55
**C221** AP127 60fr multi 2.00 1.10

30th South Pacific Conference — AP128

**1990, Oct. 29 Litho. *Perf. 13***
**C222** AP128 85fr multicolored 2.10 1.10

Gen. Charles de Gaulle (1890-1970) AP129

**1990, Nov. 21 Engr. *Perf. 13***
**C223** AP129 410fr dk blue 9.00 3.50

Scenic Views — AP130

**1991, Feb. 13 Litho. *Perf. 13***
**C224** AP130 36fr Fayawa-Ouvea Bay .90 .50
**C225** AP130 90fr shown 2.40 1.25

See No. C246.

New Caledonian Cricket Players by Marcel Moutouh — AP131

Design: 435fr, Saint Louis by Janine Goetz.

**1991, Dec. 18 *Perf. 13x12½***
**C226** AP131 130fr multicolored 3.00 2.00
**C227** AP131 435fr multicolored 10.00 5.00

See Nos. C236, C242, C260.

Blue River Nature Park — AP132

**1992, Feb. 6 Litho. *Perf. 12½***
**C228** AP132 400fr multicolored 9.25 4.75
*a.* Souvenir sheet of 1 10.50 10.50

No. C228a sold for 450fr and was issued 2/5/92.

Native Pottery AP133

**Photo. & Engr.**

**1992, Apr. 9 *Perf. 12½x13***
**C229** AP133 25fr black & orange .75 .30

Expo '92, Seville AP134

**1992, Apr. 25 Litho. *Perf. 13***
**C230** AP134 10fr multicolored .35 .25

Discovery of America, 500th Anniv. AP135

#C234: a, Erik the Red, Viking longship. b, Columbus, coat of arms. c, Amerigo Vespucci.

**1992, May 22 Litho. *Perf. 13½***
**C231** AP135 80fr Pinta 2.00 1.00
**C232** AP135 80fr Santa Maria 2.00 1.00
**C233** AP135 80fr Nina 2.00 1.00
*a.* Strip of 3, #C231-C233 6.00 6.00
*b.* Bklt. pane of 3, #C231-C233 10.00 10.00

**Souvenir Sheet**
***Perf. 12½***

**C234** AP135 110fr Sheet of 3, #a.-c. 10.00 10.00

World Columbian Stamp Expo '92, Chicago. No. C234 sold for 360fr.

1992 Summer Olympics, Barcelona — AP136

260fr, Synchronized swimming.

**1992, July 25 *Perf. 13***
**C235** AP136 260fr multi 6.75 3.25

**Painters of the Pacific Type of 1991**

Design: 205fr, Wahpa, by Paul Mascart

**1992, Sept. 28 Litho. *Perf. 12½x13***
**C236** AP131 205fr multicolored 5.00 2.50

Australian Bouvier — AP138

**1992, Oct. 4** ***Perf. 12***
**C237** AP138 175fr multicolored 5.25 2.40

Exploration of New Caledonian Coast by Chevalier d'Entrecasteaux, Bicent. — AP139

**1992, Nov. 18 Engr.** ***Perf. 13***
**C238** AP139 110fr bl grn, ocher & olive grn 3.00 1.25

Shells — AP140

30fr, Amalda fuscolingua. 50fr, Cassis abbotti.

**1992, Nov. 26 Litho.** ***Perf. 13½x13***
**C239** AP140 30fr multi 1.00 .35
**C240** AP140 50fr multi 1.50 .75

The vignettes on Nos. C239-C240 were applied by a thermographic process, producing a shiny, raised effect.

AP141

Comic Strip Characters from "La Brousse en Folie," by Bernard Berger: a, Dede. b. Torton Marcel in Mimine II. c, Tathan. d, Joinville.

**1992, Dec. 9 Litho.** ***Perf. 13½***
**C241** AP141 80fr Strip of 4, #a.-d. 8.50 8.50

**Painters of the Pacific Type of 1991**

Design: 150fr, Noumea, 1890, by Gaston Roullet (1847-1925).

**1993, Mar. 25 Litho.** ***Perf. 13x12½***
**C242** AP131 150fr multicolored 3.50 1.75

Extraction of Attar from Niaouli Flowers (Melaleuca Quinquenervia), Cent. — AP142

**1993, Apr. 28** ***Perf. 13***
**C243** AP142 85fr multicolored 2.00 1.00

Nicolaus Copernicus (1473-1543) — AP143

**1993, May 5 Engr.** ***Perf. 13***
**C244** AP143 110fr multicolored 3.00 1.25

Polska '93.

Noumea Temple, Cent. AP144

**1993, June 16 Litho.** ***Perf. 12½x13***
**C245** AP144 400fr multicolored 8.00 4.50

**Scenic Views Type of 1991**

**1993, July 8 Litho.** ***Perf. 13***
**C246** AP130 85fr Malabou 2.00 1.00

Little Train of Thio — AP145

**1993, July 24 Engr.** ***Perf. 13***
**C247** AP145 115fr multicolored 3.00 1.40

AP146

**1993, Aug. 18 Litho.**
**C248** AP146 100fr multicolored 2.50 1.10

Henri Rochefort (1831-1913), writer.

Bangkok '93 — AP147

No. C249, Vanda coerulea. No. C250, Megastylis paradoxa. 140fr, Royal Palace, Bangkok, horiz.

**1993, Oct. 1** ***Perf. 13½***
**C249** AP147 30fr multicolored 1.00 .35
**C250** AP147 30fr multicolored 1.00 .35

**Souvenir Sheet**

***Perf. 13***

**C251** AP147 140fr multicolored 3.50 3.50

No. C251 contains one 52x40mm stamp.

Air Caledonia, 10th Anniv. — AP148

**1993, Oct. 9** ***Perf. 13***
**C252** AP148 85fr multicolored 2.25 1.10

New Caledonia-Australia Telephone Cable, Cent. — AP149

**1993, Oct. 15 Engr.** ***Perf. 13x12½***
**C253** AP149 200fr blue & black 4.75 2.25

Oxpleurodon Orbiculatus — AP150

**1993, Oct. 15 Litho.** ***Perf. 13½***
**C254** AP150 250fr multicolored 6.00 2.75

Portions of the design on No. C254 were applied by a thermographic process producing a shiny, raised effect.

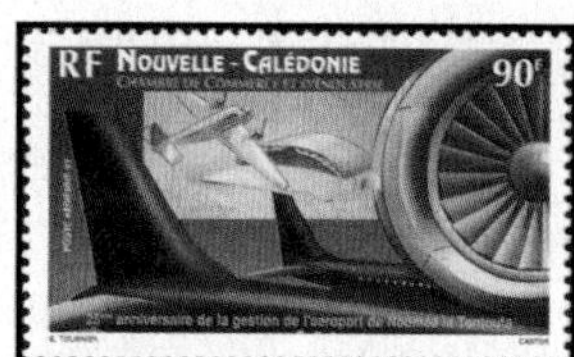

Tontouta Airport, Noumea, 25th Anniv. — AP151

**1993, Nov. 29 Litho.** ***Perf. 13***
**C255** AP151 90fr multicolored 2.25 1.00

Christmas — AP152

**1993, Dec. 9 Litho.**
**C256** AP152 120fr multicolored 3.00 1.25

Portions of the design on No. C256 were applied by a thermographic process producing a shiny, raised effect.

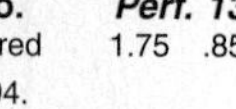

New Year 1994 (Year of the Dog) AP153

**1994, Feb. 18 Litho.** ***Perf. 13***
**C257** AP153 60fr multicolored 1.75 .85

Hong Kong '94.

First Airbus A340 Flight, Paris-Noumea — AP154

**1994, Mar. 31 Litho.** ***Die Cut 8***

**Self-Adhesive**

**C258** AP154 90fr multicolored 2.75 1.25

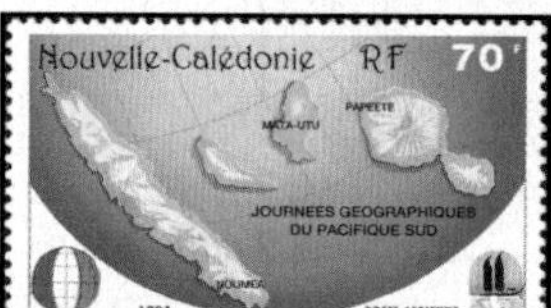

South Pacific Geography Day — AP155

**1994, May 10 Litho.** ***Perf. 13***
**C259** AP155 70fr multicolored 1.75 .85

See Wallis and Futuna No. C177.

**Painters of the Pacific Type of 1991**

Design: 120fr, Legende du Poulpe, by Micheline Neporon.

**1994, June 24 Litho.** ***Perf. 13***
**C260** AP131 120fr multicolored 2.75 1.40

Pottery, Museum of Noumea AP156

**1994, July 6 Litho.** ***Perf. 12½x13***
**C261** AP156 95fr multicolored 2.25 1.10

1994 World Cup Soccer Championships, U.S. — AP156a

**1994, July 12 Litho.** ***Perf. 13***
**C261A** AP156a 105fr multicolored 2.50 1.50

Intl. Year of the Family AP157

PHILAKOREA '94 — AP158

Korean cuisine: No. C263a, Rice, celery, carrots, peppers. b, Lettuce, cabbage, garlic. c, Onions. d, Shrimp, oysters.

**1994, Aug. 17** *Perf. 13½x13*
**C262** AP157 60fr multicolored 2.25 1.00

**Souvenir Sheet**
*Perf. 12½*

**C263** Sheet of 4 4.75 4.75
*a.-d.* AP158 35fr any single 1.10 1.00

Research Ship Atalante — AP159

**1994, Aug. 26** *Perf. 13*
**C264** AP159 120fr multicolored 2.75 1.50

Masons in New Caledonia, 125th Anniv. — AP160

**1994, Sept. 16** *Perf. 13*
**C265** AP160 350fr multicolored 8.00 3.75

Participation in First European Stamp Show — AP161

**1994, Oct. 15 Litho.** *Perf. 13*
**C266** AP161 90fr Island 2.00 1.00
**C267** AP161 90fr Herding cattle 2.00 1.00
*a.* Pair, #C266-C267 + label 4.50 4.50

ORSTOM, 50th Anniv. — AP162

**1994, Nov. 14 Photo.** *Perf. 13*
**C268** AP162 95fr multicolored 2.50 1.25

Tiebaghi Mine — AP163

**1994, Nov. 24 Litho.**
**C269** AP163 90fr multicolored 2.75 1.00

South Pacific Tourism Year AP164

**1995, Mar. 15 Litho.** *Perf. 13½*
**C270** AP164 90fr multicolored 3.00 1.00

35th South Pacific Conference, Noumea — AP165

**1995, Oct. 25 Litho.** *Perf. 13*
**C271** AP165 500fr multicolored 9.00 5.00

Kanak Dances AP166

**1995, Dec. 8 Litho.** *Perf. 13x13½*
**C272** AP166 95fr Ouaré 2.25 1.00
**C273** AP166 100fr Pothé 2.50 1.00

Mekosuchus Inexpactatus — AP167

**1996, Feb. 23 Litho.** *Perf. 13x13½*
**C274** AP167 125fr multicolored 2.75 1.50

Indonesian Centenary AP168

**1996, July 20**
**C275** AP168 130fr multicolored 3.00 3.00

Louis Brauquier (1900-76), Writer — AP169

**1996, Aug. 7 Litho.** *Perf. 12½*
**C276** AP169 95fr multicolored 2.25 1.10

Ile Nou Ground Station, 20th Anniv. AP170

125fr, Guglielmo Marconi, telegraph wires.

**1996, Sept. 26 Litho.** *Perf. 13*
**C277** AP170 95f multicolored 2.25 1.10
**C278** AP170 125fr multicolored 2.75 1.50
*a.* Pair, #C277-C278 + label 5.00 5.00

Radio, cent. (#C278).

Regional Views — AP171

**1996, Nov. 7 Litho.** *Perf. 13*
**C279** AP171 95fr Great reef 2.25 1.10
**C280** AP171 95fr Mount Koghi 2.25 1.10
*a.* Pair, #C279-C280 + label 4.75 4.75

50th Autumn Philatelic Salon.

Christmas AP172

**1996, Nov. 25** *Perf. 13½x13*
**C281** AP172 95fr multicolored 2.25 1.10

Horned Turtle Meiolania AP173

**1997, Jan. 8 Litho.** *Perf. 13*
**C282** AP173 95fr multicolored 2.25 1.25

Portions of the design were applied by a thermographic process producing a shiny, raised effect.

South Pacific Commission, 50th Anniv. — AP174

**1997, Feb. 7 Litho.** *Perf. 13X13½*
**C283** AP174 100fr multicolored 2.25 1.10

Hong Kong '97 AP175

New Year 1997 (Year of the Ox) — #C285: a, Water buffalo pulling plow. b, Cattle in pasture.

**1997, Feb. 12** *Perf. 13*
**C284** AP175 95fr multicolored 2.50 1.10

**Sheet of 2**
*Perf. 13x13½*

**C285** AP175 75fr #a.-b. 3.50 3.25

No. C285 contains two 40x30mm stamps.

Melanesian Pottery — AP176

Lapita pottery c. 1200-1000 B.C.: No. C286, With stylized faces. No. C287, With labyrinth pattern.

**1997, May 14 Litho.** *Perf. 13*
**C286** AP176 95fr multicolored 2.25 2.25
**C287** AP176 95fr multicolored 2.25 2.25

TRAPAS, French Airlines in the South Pacific, 1947-50 — AP177

Airplane, emblem, map showing: No. C288, Australia, New Herbrides, Suva, Tahiti, New Zealand. No. C289, Koumac, Poindimie, Noumea, Isle of Pines.

**Photo. & Engr.**

**1997, Aug. 12** *Perf. 13*
**C288** AP177 95fr multicolored 2.10 2.10
**C289** AP177 95fr multicolored 2.10 2.10
*a.* Pair, #C288-C289 4.25 4.25

Regular Paris-Noumea Air Service, 50th Anniv. — AP178

**1999, Sept. 29 Photo. *Perf. 13x12½***

| | | | | |
|---|---|---|---|---|
| **C290** | AP178 | 100fr multicolored | 2.50 | 2.00 |

Inauguration of Noumea-Osaka Air Service — AP179

**2001, Oct. 11 Litho. *Perf. 13***

| | | | | |
|---|---|---|---|---|
| **C291** | AP179 | 110fr multi | 2.25 | 2.25 |

## AIR POST SEMI-POSTAL STAMPS

**French Revolution Issue**

Common Design Type

**Unwmk.**

**1939, July 5 Photo. *Perf. 13***

**Name and Value Typo. in Orange**

| | | | | |
|---|---|---|---|---|
| **CB1** | CD83 | 4.50fr + 4fr brn blk | 34.00 | 34.00 |

Father & Child — SPAP1

**1942, June 22 Engr. *Perf. 13***

| | | | |
|---|---|---|---|
| **CB2** | SPAP1 | 1.50fr + 3.50fr green | 2.25 |
| **CB3** | SPAP1 | 2fr + 6fr yel brn | 2.25 |

Native children's welfare fund.

Nos. CB2-CB3 were issued by the Vichy government in France, but were not placed on sale in New Caledonia.

**Colonial Education Fund**

Common Design Type

**1942, June 22**

| | | | |
|---|---|---|---|
| **CB4** | CD86a | 1.20fr + 1.80fr blue & red | 2.25 |

No. CB4 was issued by the Vichy government in France, but was not placed on sale in New Caledonia.

## POSTAGE DUE STAMPS

For a short time in 1894, 5, 10, 15, 20, 25 and 30c postage stamps (Nos. 43, 45, 47, 49, 50 and 52) were overprinted with a "T" in an inverted triangle and used as Postage Due stamps.

French Colonies Postage Due Stamps Overprinted in Carmine, Blue or Silver

**1903 Unwmk. *Imperf.***

| | | | | |
|---|---|---|---|---|
| **J1** | D1 | 5c blue (C) | 3.75 | 3.75 |
| **J2** | D1 | 10c brown (C) | 11.50 | 11.50 |
| **J3** | D1 | 15c yel grn (C) | 22.50 | 11.50 |
| **J4** | D1 | 30c carmine (Bl) | 19.00 | 15.00 |
| **J5** | D1 | 50c violet (Bl) | 65.00 | 22.50 |
| **J6** | D1 | 60c brn, *buff* (Bl) | 260.00 | 95.00 |
| **J7** | D1 | 1fr rose, *buff* (S) | 42.50 | 26.00 |
| *b.* | | Double overprint | 225.00 | 225.00 |
| **J8** | D1 | 2fr red brn (Bl) | 1,300. | 1,300. |
| | | *Nos. J1-J8 (8)* | 1,724. | 1,485. |

Nos. J1 to J8 are known with the "I" in "TENAIRE" missing.

Fifty years of French occupation.

Men Poling Boat — D2

**1906 Typo. *Perf. 13½x14***

| | | | | |
|---|---|---|---|---|
| **J9** | D2 | 5c ultra, *azure* | .70 | *.75* |
| **J10** | D2 | 10c vio brn, *buff* | .70 | *.75* |
| **J11** | D2 | 15c grn, *greenish* | 1.00 | *1.10* |
| **J12** | D2 | 20c blk, *yellow* | 1.00 | *1.10* |
| **J13** | D2 | 30c carmine | 1.35 | *1.50* |
| **J14** | D2 | 50c ultra, *buff* | 2.25 | 2.25 |
| **J15** | D2 | 60c brn, *azure* | 1.50 | *1.90* |
| **J16** | D2 | 1fr dk grn, *straw* | 2.25 | *2.75* |
| | | *Nos. J9-J16 (8)* | 10.75 | *12.10* |

Type of 1906 Issue Surcharged

**1926-27**

| | | | | |
|---|---|---|---|---|
| **J17** | D2 | 2fr on 1fr vio | 5.75 | *6.25* |
| **J18** | D2 | 3fr on 1fr org brn | 5.75 | *6.25* |

Malayan Sambar — D3

**1928 Typo.**

| | | | | |
|---|---|---|---|---|
| **J19** | D3 | 2c sl bl & dp brn | .25 | *.40* |
| **J20** | D3 | 4c brn red & bl grn | .45 | *.60* |
| **J21** | D3 | 5c red org & bl blk | .60 | *.75* |
| **J22** | D3 | 10c mag & Prus bl | .60 | *.75* |
| **J23** | D3 | 15c dl grn & scar | .60 | *.75* |
| **J24** | D3 | 20c mar & ol grn | 1.05 | *1.10* |
| **J25** | D3 | 25c bis brn & sl bl | .75 | *.90* |
| **J26** | D3 | 30c bl grn & ol grn | 1.05 | *1.10* |
| **J27** | D3 | 50c lt brn & dk red | 1.35 | *1.50* |
| **J28** | D3 | 60c mag & brt rose | 1.35 | *1.50* |
| **J29** | D3 | 1fr dl bl & Prus grn | 1.75 | *1.90* |
| **J30** | D3 | 2fr dk red & ol grn | 1.90 | *2.25* |
| **J31** | D3 | 3fr violet & brn | 2.75 | *3.00* |
| | | *Nos. J19-J31 (13)* | 14.45 | *16.50* |

**Catalogue values for unused stamps in this section, from this point to the end of the section, are for Never Hinged items.**

D4

**1948 Unwmk. Photo. *Perf. 13***

| | | | | |
|---|---|---|---|---|
| **J32** | D4 | 10c violet | .30 | .30 |
| **J33** | D4 | 30c brown | .40 | .40 |
| **J34** | D4 | 50c blue green | .60 | .60 |
| **J35** | D4 | 1fr orange | .60 | .60 |
| **J36** | D4 | 2fr red violet | .75 | .75 |
| **J37** | D4 | 3fr red brown | .75 | .75 |
| **J38** | D4 | 4fr dull blue | 1.10 | 1.10 |
| **J39** | D4 | 5fr henna brown | 1.10 | 1.10 |
| **J40** | D4 | 10fr slate green | 1.75 | 1.75 |
| **J41** | D4 | 20fr violet blue | 2.40 | 2.40 |
| | | *Nos. J32-J41 (10)* | 9.75 | 9.75 |

Bat — D5

**1983 Litho. *Perf. 13***

| | | | | |
|---|---|---|---|---|
| **J42** | D5 | 1fr multi | .25 | .25 |
| **J43** | D5 | 2fr multi | .30 | .30 |
| **J44** | D5 | 3fr multi | .30 | .30 |
| **J45** | D5 | 4fr multi | .45 | .45 |
| **J46** | D5 | 5fr multi | .55 | .55 |
| **J47** | D5 | 10fr multi | .75 | .75 |
| **J48** | D5 | 20fr multi | .90 | .90 |
| **J49** | D5 | 40fr multi | 1.40 | 1.40 |
| **J50** | D5 | 50fr multi | 1.75 | 1.75 |
| | | *Nos. J42-J50 (9)* | 6.65 | 6.65 |

For overprint see No. 696.

## MILITARY STAMPS

Stamps of the above types, although issued by officials, were unauthorized and practically a private speculation.

## OFFICIAL STAMPS

**Catalogue values for unused stamps in this section are for Never Hinged items.**

Ancestor Pole — O1

Various carved ancestor poles.

**1959 Unwmk. Typo. *Perf. 14x13***

| | | | | |
|---|---|---|---|---|
| **O1** | O1 | 1fr org yel | .45 | .45 |
| **O2** | O1 | 3fr lt bl grn | .45 | .45 |
| **O3** | O1 | 4fr purple | .60 | .60 |
| **O4** | O1 | 5fr ultra | .75 | .75 |
| **O5** | O1 | 9fr black | 1.00 | 1.00 |
| **O6** | O1 | 10fr brt vio | 1.40 | 1.40 |
| **O7** | O1 | 13fr yel grn | 1.50 | 1.50 |
| **O8** | O1 | 15fr lt bl | 2.00 | 2.00 |
| **O9** | O1 | 24fr red lilac | 2.40 | 2.40 |
| **O10** | O1 | 26fr deep org | 2.75 | 2.75 |
| **O11** | O1 | 50fr green | 5.75 | 5.75 |
| **O12** | O1 | 100fr chocolate | 11.00 | 11.00 |
| **O13** | O1 | 200fr red | 20.00 | 20.00 |
| | | *Nos. O1-O13 (13)* | 50.05 | 50.05 |

Carved Wooden Pillow — O2

**Vignette: Green, Red Brown (2, 29, 31, 35, 38, 65, 76fr), Brown (40fr), Blue (58fr)**

**1973-87 Photo. *Perf. 13***

| | | | | |
|---|---|---|---|---|
| **O14** | O2 | 1fr yellow | .30 | .30 |
| **O14A** | O2 | 2fr green ('87) | .25 | .25 |
| **O15** | O2 | 3fr tan | .45 | .45 |
| **O16** | O2 | 4fr pale violet | .60 | .60 |
| **O17** | O2 | 5fr lilac rose | .60 | .60 |
| **O18** | O2 | 9fr light blue | 1.00 | 1.00 |
| **O19** | O2 | 10fr orange | 1.10 | 1.10 |
| **O20** | O2 | 11fr bright lilac ('76) | .60 | .60 |
| **O21** | O2 | 12fr bl grn ('73) | 1.25 | 1.25 |
| **O22** | O2 | 15fr green ('76) | .70 | .70 |
| **O23** | O2 | 20fr rose ('76) | .75 | .75 |
| **O24** | O2 | 23fr red ('80) | 1.00 | 1.00 |
| **O25** | O2 | 24fr Prus bl ('76) | 1.00 | 1.00 |
| **O25A** | O2 | 25fr gray ('81) | 1.30 | 1.30 |
| **O26** | O2 | 26fr yellow ('76) | 1.05 | 1.05 |
| **O26A** | O2 | 29fr dl grn ('83) | 1.30 | 1.30 |
| **O26B** | O2 | 31fr yellow ('82) | 1.40 | 1.40 |
| **O26C** | O2 | 35fr yellow ('84) | 1.50 | 1.50 |
| **O27** | O2 | 36fr dp lil rose ('76) | 1.30 | 1.30 |
| **O27A** | O2 | 38fr tan | 1.50 | 1.50 |
| **O27B** | O2 | 40fr blue ('87) | 1.30 | 1.30 |
| **O28** | O2 | 42fr bister ('76) | 1.50 | 1.50 |
| **O29** | O2 | 50fr blue ('76) | 1.50 | 1.50 |
| **O29A** | O2 | 58fr blue grn ('87) | 1.75 | 1.75 |
| **O29B** | O2 | 65fr lilac ('84) | 1.90 | 1.90 |
| **O29C** | O2 | 76fr brt yel ('87) | 2.25 | 2.25 |
| **O30** | O2 | 100fr red ('76) | 2.75 | 2.75 |
| **O31** | O2 | 200fr orange ('76) | 5.00 | 5.00 |
| | | *Nos. O14-O31 (28)* | 36.90 | 36.90 |

## PARCEL POST STAMPS

Type of Regular Issue of 1905-28 Srchd. or Ovptd.

**1926 Unwmk. *Perf. 14x13½***

| | | | | |
|---|---|---|---|---|
| **Q1** | A18 | 50c on 5fr olive, *lav* | 1.30 | *1.90* |
| **Q2** | A18 | 1fr deep blue | 1.75 | *2.75* |
| **Q3** | A18 | 2fr car, *bluish* | 2.10 | *3.00* |
| | | *Nos. Q1-Q3 (3)* | 5.15 | *7.65* |

Regular Issue of 1928 Overprinted

Colis Postaux

**1930**

| | | | | |
|---|---|---|---|---|
| **Q4** | A20 | 50c violet & brown | 1.30 | *1.90* |
| **Q5** | A21 | 1fr dp ol & sal red | 1.75 | *2.75* |
| **Q6** | A21 | 2fr red org & brn | 2.10 | *3.00* |
| | | *Nos. Q4-Q6 (3)* | 5.15 | 7.65 |

# NEW GUINEA

'nü 'gi-nē

LOCATION — On an island of the same name in the South Pacific Ocean, north of Australia.
GOVT. — Mandate administered by Australia
AREA — 93,000 sq. mi.
POP. — 675,369 (1940)
CAPITAL — Rabaul

The territory occupies the northeastern part of the island and includes New Britain and other nearby islands. It was formerly a German possession and should not be confused with British New Guinea (Papua) which is in the southeastern part of the same island, nor Netherlands New Guinea. For previous issues see German New Guinea, New Britain, North West Pacific Islands. Issues for 1952 and later are listed under Papua.

12 Pence = 1 Shilling
20 Shillings = 1 Pound

Native Huts — A1

**1925-28 Engr. *Perf. 11***

| No. | Type | Denomination / Color | Unused | Used |
|---|---|---|---|---|
| 1 | A1 | ½p orange | 2.75 | *8.00* |
| 2 | A1 | 1p yellow green | 2.75 | *6.25* |
| 3 | A1 | 1½p vermilion ('26) | 3.75 | *3.00* |
| 4 | A1 | 2p claret | 7.25 | *5.00* |
| 5 | A1 | 3p deep blue | 8.00 | 4.50 |
| 6 | A1 | 4p olive green | 15.00 | *26.00* |
| 7 | A1 | 6p yel bister ('28) | 6.50 | *55.00* |
| *a.* | | 6p light brown | 22.50 | *55.00* |
| *b.* | | 6p olive bister ('27) | 15.00 | *52.50* |
| 8 | A1 | 9p deep violet | 15.00 | *50.00* |
| 9 | A1 | 1sh gray green | 17.50 | *30.00* |
| 10 | A1 | 2sh red brown | 35.00 | *55.00* |
| 11 | A1 | 5sh olive bister | 55.00 | 75.00 |
| 12 | A1 | 10sh dull rose | 120.00 | *200.00* |
| 13 | A1 | £1 grnsh gray | 210.00 | *325.00* |
| | | *Nos. 1-13 (13)* | 498.50 | 842.75 |

For overprints see Nos. C1-C13, O1-O9.

Bird of Paradise — A2

**1931, Aug. 2**

| No. | Type | Denomination / Color | Unused | Used |
|---|---|---|---|---|
| 18 | A2 | 1p light green | 4.50 | *7.50* |
| 19 | A2 | 1½p red | 5.75 | *11.50* |
| 20 | A2 | 2p violet brown | 5.75 | 2.50 |
| 21 | A2 | 3p deep blue | 5.75 | 5.50 |
| 22 | A2 | 4p olive green | 7.50 | *32.50* |
| 23 | A2 | 5p slate green | 9.00 | *24.00* |
| 24 | A2 | 6p bister | 8.00 | *25.00* |
| 25 | A2 | 9p dull violet | 9.50 | *21.00* |
| 26 | A2 | 1sh bluish gray | 7.00 | *17.00* |
| 27 | A2 | 2sh red brown | 11.50 | *50.00* |
| 28 | A2 | 5sh olive brown | 47.50 | *62.50* |
| 29 | A2 | 10sh rose red | 120.00 | *150.00* |
| 30 | A2 | £1 gray | 250.00 | *300.00* |
| | | *Nos. 18-30 (13)* | 491.75 | *709.00* |

10th anniversary of Australian Mandate.
For overprints see #C14-C27, O12-O22.

### Type of 1931 without date scrolls

**1932-34 *Perf. 11***

| No. | Type | Denomination / Color | Unused | Used |
|---|---|---|---|---|
| 31 | A2 | 1p light green | 8.00 | .25 |
| 32 | A2 | 1½p violet brown | 8.00 | *20.00* |
| 33 | A2 | 2p red | 5.50 | .25 |
| 34 | A2 | 2½p dp grn ('34) | 7.50 | *27.50* |
| 35 | A2 | 3p gray blue | 8.00 | 1.25 |
| 36 | A2 | 3½p magenta ('34) | 15.00 | *22.50* |
| 37 | A2 | 4p olive green | 7.00 | *7.00* |
| 38 | A2 | 5p slate green | 7.25 | .80 |
| 39 | A2 | 6p bister | 7.50 | *5.50* |
| 40 | A2 | 9p dull violet | 11.00 | *27.50* |
| 41 | A2 | 1sh bluish gray | 7.00 | *11.50* |
| 42 | A2 | 2sh red brown | 5.00 | *19.00* |
| 43 | A2 | 5sh olive brown | 32.50 | *50.00* |
| 44 | A2 | 10sh rose red | 60.00 | *80.00* |
| 45 | A2 | £1 gray | 120.00 | *110.00* |
| | | *Nos. 31-45 (15)* | 309.25 | *383.05* |

For overprints see #46-47, C28-C43, O23-O35. See footnote following C43.

### Silver Jubilee Issue

Stamps of 1932-34 Overprinted

**1935, June 27 Glazed Paper**

| No. | Type | Denomination / Color | Unused | Used |
|---|---|---|---|---|
| 46 | A2 | 1p light green | 1.10 | .85 |
| 47 | A2 | 2p red | 3.25 | .85 |
| | | Set, never hinged | 6.50 | |

King George VI — A3

**1937, May 18 Engr.**

| No. | Type | Denomination / Color | Unused | Used |
|---|---|---|---|---|
| 48 | A3 | 2p salmon rose | .30 | *1.60* |
| 49 | A3 | 3p blue | .30 | *1.90* |
| 50 | A3 | 5p green | .35 | *1.90* |
| 51 | A3 | 1sh brown violet | .45 | *2.50* |
| | | *Nos. 48-51 (4)* | 1.40 | *7.90* |
| | | Set, never hinged | 2.50 | |

Coronation of George VI and Queen Elizabeth.

## AIR POST STAMPS

Regular Issues of 1925-28 Overprinted

**1931, June *Perf. 11***

| No. | Type | Denomination / Color | Unused | Used |
|---|---|---|---|---|
| C1 | A1 | ½p orange | 1.75 | *9.50* |
| C2 | A1 | 1p yellow green | 1.75 | *5.75* |
| C3 | A1 | 1½p vermilion | 1.40 | *8.50* |
| C4 | A1 | 2p claret | 1.40 | *8.00* |
| C5 | A1 | 3p deep blue | 2.00 | *15.00* |
| C6 | A1 | 4p olive green | 1.40 | *10.00* |
| C7 | A1 | 6p light brown | 2.00 | *16.00* |
| C8 | A1 | 9p deep violet | 3.50 | *19.00* |
| C9 | A1 | 1sh gray green | 3.50 | *19.00* |
| C10 | A1 | 2sh red brown | 8.00 | *50.00* |
| C11 | A1 | 5sh ol bister | 22.50 | *75.00* |
| C12 | A1 | 10sh light red | 92.50 | *120.00* |
| C13 | A1 | £1 grnsh gray | 170.00 | *290.00* |
| | | *Nos. C1-C13 (13)* | 311.70 | *645.75* |

Type of Regular Issue of 1931 and Nos. 18-30 Overprinted

**1931, Aug.**

| No. | Type | Denomination / Color | Unused | Used |
|---|---|---|---|---|
| C14 | A2 | ½p orange | 3.75 | 3.75 |
| C15 | A2 | 1p light green | 4.50 | *7.50* |
| C16 | A2 | 1½p red | 4.25 | *11.50* |
| C17 | A2 | 2p violet brown | 4.25 | 3.50 |
| C18 | A2 | 3p deep blue | 7.00 | *7.00* |
| C19 | A2 | 4p olive green | 7.00 | 7.00 |
| C20 | A2 | 5p slate green | 7.00 | 12.50 |
| C21 | A2 | 6p bister | 8.00 | *30.00* |
| C22 | A2 | 9p dull violet | 9.00 | *17.00* |
| C23 | A2 | 1sh bluish gray | 8.50 | *17.00* |
| C24 | A2 | 2sh red brown | 18.00 | *55.00* |
| C25 | A2 | 5sh olive brown | 47.50 | *80.00* |
| C26 | A2 | 10sh rose red | 87.50 | *140.00* |
| C27 | A2 | £1 gray | 150.00 | *290.00* |
| | | *Nos. C14-C27 (14)* | 366.25 | *681.75* |

10th anniversary of Australian Mandate.

### Same Overprint on Type of Regular Issue of 1932-34 and Nos. 31-45

**1932-34 *Perf. 11***

| No. | Type | Denomination / Color | Unused | Used |
|---|---|---|---|---|
| C28 | A2 | ½p orange | .65 | *1.75* |
| C29 | A2 | 1p light green | 1.40 | *2.50* |
| C30 | A2 | 1½p violet brown | 2.00 | *11.50* |
| C31 | A2 | 2p red | 2.00 | *.35* |
| C32 | A2 | 2½p dp grn ('34) | 8.75 | 2.75 |
| C33 | A2 | 3p gray blue | 3.75 | 3.50 |
| C34 | A2 | 3½p mag ('34) | 5.25 | *3.75* |
| C35 | A2 | 4p olive green | 5.00 | *11.50* |
| C36 | A2 | 5p slate green | 8.00 | *8.50* |
| C37 | A2 | 6p bister | 5.00 | *17.00* |
| C38 | A2 | 9p dull violet | 7.00 | *10.00* |
| C39 | A2 | 1sh bluish gray | 7.00 | *12.50* |
| C40 | A2 | 2sh red brown | 14.00 | *55.00* |
| C41 | A2 | 5sh olive brown | 55.00 | *65.00* |
| C42 | A2 | 10sh rose red | 100.00 | 92.50 |
| C43 | A2 | £1 gray | 87.50 | 62.50 |
| | | *Nos. C28-C43 (16)* | 312.30 | *360.60* |

No. C28 exists without overprint, but is believed not to have been issued in this condition. Value $200.

Plane over Bulolo Goldfield AP1

**1935, May 1 Engr. Unwmk.**

| No. | Type | Denomination / Color | Unused | Used |
|---|---|---|---|---|
| C44 | AP1 | £2 violet | 350.00 | 160.00 |
| C45 | AP1 | £5 green | 750.00 | 550.00 |

AP2

**1939, Mar. 1**

| No. | Type | Denomination / Color | Unused | Used |
|---|---|---|---|---|
| C46 | AP2 | ½p orange | 2.50 | *9.25* |
| C47 | AP2 | 1p green | 2.00 | *5.00* |
| C48 | AP2 | 1½p vio brown | 2.50 | *19.00* |
| C49 | AP2 | 2p red orange | 5.00 | 4.00 |
| C50 | AP2 | 3p dark blue | 11.00 | *21.00* |
| C51 | AP2 | 4p ol bister | 9.00 | 9.75 |
| C52 | AP2 | 5p slate grn | 8.50 | 4.50 |
| C53 | AP2 | 6p bister brn | 25.00 | *30.00* |
| C54 | AP2 | 9p dl violet | 27.50 | *45.00* |
| C55 | AP2 | 1sh sage grn | 27.50 | 32.50 |
| C56 | AP2 | 2sh car lake | 50.00 | *75.00* |
| C57 | AP2 | 5sh ol brown | 110.00 | *160.00* |
| C58 | AP2 | 10sh rose red | 350.00 | *425.00* |
| C59 | AP2 | £1 grnsh gray | 90.00 | *150.00* |
| | | *Nos. C46-C59 (14)* | 720.50 | *990.00* |
| | | Set, never hinged | 1,200. | |

## OFFICIAL STAMPS

Regular Issue of 1925 Overprinted

**1925-29 Unwmk. *Perf. 11***

| No. | Type | Denomination / Color | Unused | Used |
|---|---|---|---|---|
| O1 | A1 | 1p yellow green | 5.00 | *5.00* |
| O2 | A1 | 1½p vermilion ('29) | 6.25 | *19.00* |
| O3 | A1 | 2p claret | 3.25 | *4.25* |
| O4 | A1 | 3p deep blue | 6.00 | *10.00* |
| O5 | A1 | 4p olive green | 5.00 | *9.75* |
| O6 | A1 | 6p yel bister ('29) | 8.00 | *40.00* |
| *a.* | | 6p olive bister | 29.00 | *40.00* |
| O7 | A1 | 9p deep violet | 4.50 | *40.00* |
| O8 | A1 | 1sh gray green | 6.25 | *40.00* |
| O9 | A1 | 2sh red brown | 42.50 | *70.00* |
| | | *Nos. O1-O9 (9)* | 86.75 | *238.00* |

Nos. 18-28 Overprinted

**1931, Aug. 2**

| No. | Type | Denomination / Color | Unused | Used |
|---|---|---|---|---|
| O12 | A2 | 1p light green | 12.00 | *14.00* |
| O13 | A2 | 1½p red | 12.00 | *13.50* |
| O14 | A2 | 2p violet brown | 12.00 | *8.00* |
| O15 | A2 | 3p deep blue | 7.50 | *7.00* |
| O16 | A2 | 4p olive green | 7.00 | *9.75* |
| O17 | A2 | 5p slate green | 11.50 | *13.50* |
| O18 | A2 | 6p bister | 16.00 | *19.00* |
| O19 | A2 | 9p dull violet | 18.00 | *32.50* |
| O20 | A2 | 1sh bluish gray | 18.00 | *32.50* |
| O21 | A2 | 2sh red brown | 45.00 | *80.00* |
| O22 | A2 | 5sh olive brown | 110.00 | *200.00* |
| | | *Nos. O12-O22 (11)* | 269.00 | *429.75* |

10th anniversary of Australian Mandate.

### Same Overprint on Nos. 31-43

**1932-34**

| No. | Type | Denomination / Color | Unused | Used |
|---|---|---|---|---|
| O23 | A2 | 1p light green | 19.00 | *20.00* |
| O24 | A2 | 1½p violet brown | 19.00 | *20.00* |
| O25 | A2 | 2p red | 19.50 | *3.75* |
| O26 | A2 | 2½p dp green ('34) | 10.00 | *12.50* |
| O27 | A2 | 3p gray blue | 11.50 | *42.50* |
| O28 | A2 | 3½p magenta ('34) | 8.00 | *10.00* |
| O29 | A2 | 4p olive green | 21.00 | *32.50* |
| O30 | A2 | 5p slate green | 10.00 | *30.00* |
| O31 | A2 | 6p bister | 25.00 | *55.00* |
| O32 | A2 | 9p dull violet | 16.00 | *50.00* |
| O33 | A2 | 1sh bluish gray | 17.50 | *32.50* |
| O34 | A2 | 2sh red brown | 40.00 | *85.00* |
| O35 | A2 | 5sh olive brown | 140.00 | *190.00* |
| | | *Nos. O23-O35 (13)* | 356.50 | *583.75* |

# NEW HEBRIDES, BRITISH

'nü 'he-brə-ˌdēz

LOCATION — A group of islands in the South Pacific Ocean northeast of New Caledonia
GOVT. — Condominium under the joint administration of Great Britain and France
AREA — 5,790 sq. mi.
POP. — 100,000 (est. 1976)
CAPITAL — Vila (Port-Vila)

Stamps were issued by both Great Britain and France. In 1911 a joint issue bore the coats of arms of both countries. The British stamps bore the arms of Great Britain and the value in British currency on the right and the French arms and value at the left. On the French stamps the positions were reversed. After World War II when the franc dropped in value, both series were sold for their value in francs.

New Hebrides became the independent state of Vanuatu in 1980.

12 Pence = 1 Shilling
100 Centimes = 1 Franc
100 Centimes = 1 Hebrides Franc (FNH) (1977)

**French issues (inscribed "Nouvelles Hebrides") follow after No. J20.**

**Catalogue values for unused stamps in this country are for Never Hinged items, beginning with Scott 62 in the regular postage section, Scott J11 in the postage due section.**

### British Issues

Stamps of Fiji, 1903-06, Overprinted

**1908-09 Wmk. 2 *Perf. 14***

**Colored Bar Covers "FIJI" on #2-6, 9**

1 A22 ½p grn & pale grn ('09) 60.00 *87.50*
2 A22 2p vio & orange 1.50 *1.75*
3 A22 2½p vio & ultra, *bl* 1.50 *1.75*
4 A22 5p vio & green 1.60 *3.25*
5 A22 6p vio & car rose 3.75 *3.50*
6 A22 1sh grn & car rose 145.00 *300.00*
*Nos. 1-6 (6)* 213.35 *397.75*

**Wmk. Multiple Crown and CA (3)**

7 A22 ½p gray green 1.00 *5.00*
8 A22 1p carmine .80 *1.00*
*a.* Pair, one without overprint *10,000.*
9 A22 1sh grn & car rose ('09) 25.00 *4.25*
*Nos. 7-9 (3)* 26.80 *10.25*

Nos. 2-6, 9 are on chalk-surfaced paper.

Stamps of Fiji, 1904-11, Overprinted in Black or Red

**1910, Dec. 15**

10 A22 ½p green 3.50 *25.00*
11 A22 1p carmine 11.00 *8.50*
12 A22 2p gray 1.00 *3.00*
13 A22 2½p ultra 1.10 *6.00*
14 A22 5p violet & ol grn 2.25 *5.50*
15 A22 6p violet 2.50 *7.50*
16 A22 1sh black, *grn* (R) 3.00 *7.50*
*Nos. 10-16 (7)* 24.35 *63.00*

Nos. 14-16 are on chalk-surfaced paper.

Native Idols — A1

**1911, July 25 Engr. Wmk. 3**

17 A1 ½p pale green 1.00 *1.75*
18 A1 1p red 4.00 2.00
19 A1 2p gray 7.00 3.00
20 A1 2½p ultramarine 4.75 *5.75*
21 A1 5p olive green 4.50 *6.00*
22 A1 6p claret 3.00 *5.00*
23 A1 1sh black, *green* 2.75 *12.00*
24 A1 2sh violet, *blue* 22.50 *20.00*
25 A1 5sh green, *yel* 32.50 *50.00*
*Nos. 17-25 (9)* 82.00 *105.50*

See Nos. 33-37. For surcharges see Nos. 26-29, 38-39, French Issues No. 36.

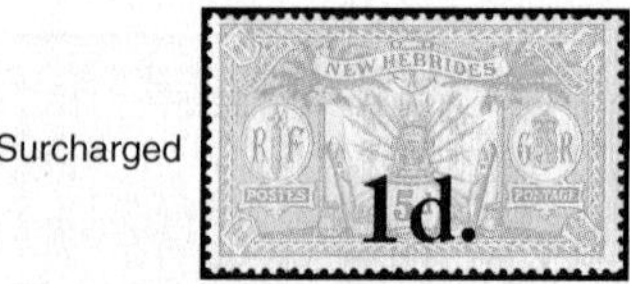


Surcharged

**1920-21**

26 A1 1p on 5p ol grn ('21) 10.00 *60.00*
*a.* Inverted surcharge 4,500.
27 A1 1p on 1sh blk, *grn* 4.00 *13.00*
28 A1 1p on 2sh vio, *blue* 1.50 *10.00*
29 A1 1p on 5sh grn, *yel* 1.25 *10.00*

**On French Issue No. 16**

30 A2 2p on 40c red, *yel* ('21) 2.00 *22.00*
*Nos. 26-30 (5)* 18.75 *115.00*

French Issue No. 27

**Wmk. R F in Sheet**

31 A2 2p on 40c red, *yel* ('21) 125.00 *700.00*

The letters "R.F." are the initials of "Republique Francaise." They are large double-lined Roman capitals, about 120mm high. About one-fourth of the stamps in each sheet show portions of the watermark, the other stamps are without watermark.

No. 26a is considered by some to be printers' waste.

**Type of 1911 Issue**

**1921, Oct. Wmk. 4**

33 A1 1p rose red 2.50 *14.50*
34 A1 2p gray 4.00 *45.00*
37 A1 6p claret 14.00 *80.00*
*Nos. 33-37 (3)* 20.50 *139.50*

For surcharge see No. 40.

**Stamps of 1911-21 Surcharged with New Values as in 1920-21**

**1924, May 1 Wmk. 3**

38 A1 1p on ½p pale green 4.00 *22.50*
39 A1 5p on 2½p ultra 7.50 *27.50*
*a.* Inverted surcharge 3,500.

**Wmk. 4**

40 A1 3p on 1p rose red 4.50 *10.00*
*Nos. 38-40 (3)* 16.00 *60.00*

No. 39a is considered by some to be printers' waste.

A3

The values at the lower right denote the currency and amount for which the stamps were to be sold. The English stamps could be bought at the French post office in French money.

**1925 Engr.**

41 A3 ½p (5c) black 1.25 *20.00*
42 A3 1p (10c) green 1.00 *17.50*
43 A3 2p (20c) grnsh gray 1.75 *2.75*
44 A3 2½p (25c) brown 1.00 *14.00*
45 A3 5p (50c) ultra 3.25 *2.75*
46 A3 6p (60c) claret 4.00 *15.00*
47 A3 1sh (1.25fr) blk, *grn* 3.50 *18.00*
48 A3 2sh (2.50fr) vio, *bl* 6.25 *20.00*
49 A3 5sh (6.25fr) grn, *yel* 6.25 *27.50*
*Nos. 41-49 (9)* 28.25 *137.50*

Beach Scene A5

**1938, June 1 Wmk. 4 *Perf. 12***

50 A5 5c green 1.75 *4.00*
51 A5 10c dark orange 2.00 *2.00*
52 A5 15c violet 2.50 *3.00*
53 A5 20c rose red 2.75 *3.25*
54 A5 25c brown 1.50 *2.75*
55 A5 30c dark blue 3.00 2.50
56 A5 40c olive green 3.25 *5.50*
57 A5 50c brown vio 1.25 *1.50*
58 A5 1fr car, *emerald* 6.50 *9.00*
59 A5 2fr dk blue, *emer* 22.50 22.50
60 A5 5fr red, *yellow* 40.00 50.00
61 A5 10fr violet, *blue* 125.00 80.00
*Nos. 50-61 (12)* 212.00 186.00
Set, never hinged 300.00

**Catalogue values for unused stamps in this section, from this point to the end of the section, are for Never Hinged items.**

Common Design Types pictured following the introduction.

**UPU Issue**

Common Design Type

**1949, Oct. 10 Engr. *Perf. 13½***

62 CD309 10c red orange .35 *.90*
63 CD309 15c violet .35 *1.00*
64 CD309 30c violet blue .40 *1.10*
65 CD309 50c rose violet .50 *1.25*
*Nos. 62-65 (4)* 1.60 *4.25*

Outrigger Canoes with Sails — A6

Designs: 25c, 30c, 40c and 50c, Native Carving. 1fr, 2fr and 5fr, Island couple.

**1953, Apr. 30 *Perf. 12½***

66 A6 5c green 1.00 *1.25*
67 A6 10c red 1.10 .35
68 A6 15c yellow 1.10 .25
69 A6 20c ultramarine 1.10 .25
70 A6 25c olive .90 .25
71 A6 30c light brown .90 .25
72 A6 40c black brown 1.10 .40
73 A6 50c violet 1.40 .50
74 A6 1fr deep orange 5.75 1.75
75 A6 2fr red violet 6.00 *9.00*
76 A6 5fr scarlet 9.00 *22.50*
*Nos. 66-76 (11)* 29.35 *36.75*

**Coronation Issue**

Common Design Type

**1953, June 2 *Perf. 13½x13***

77 CD312 10c car & black .75 .60

Discovery of New Hebrides, 1606 — A7

20c, 50c, Britannia, Marianne, Flags & Mask.

***Perf. 14½x14***

**1956, Oct. 20 Photo. Wmk. 4**

78 A7 5c emerald .25 .25
79 A7 10c crimson .25 .25
80 A7 20c ultramarine .25 .25
81 A7 50c purple .25 .25
*Nos. 78-81 (4)* 1.00 1.00

50th anniv. of the establishment of the Anglo-French Condominium.

Port Vila and Iririki Islet — A8

Designs: 25c, 30c, 40c, 50c, Tropical river and spear fisherman. 1fr, 2fr, 5fr, Woman drinking from coconut (inscribed: "Franco-British Alliance 4th March 1947").

**1957, Sept. 3 Engr. *Perf. 13½x13***

82 A8 5c green .45 *1.00*
83 A8 10c red .40 .25
84 A8 15c orange yellow .55 *1.00*
85 A8 20c ultramarine .45 .25
86 A8 25c olive .50 .25
87 A8 30c light brown .50 .25
88 A8 40c sepia .50 .25
89 A8 50c violet .75 .25
90 A8 1fr orange 1.10 1.10
91 A8 2fr rose lilac 4.50 2.75
92 A8 5fr black 10.00 5.50
*Nos. 82-92 (11)* 19.70 12.85

**Freedom from Hunger Issue**

Common Design Type

***Perf. 14x14½***

**1963, Sept. 2 Photo. Wmk. 314**

93 CD314 60c green .60 .25

**Red Cross Centenary Issue**

Common Design Type with Royal Cipher and "RF" Replacing Queen's Portrait

**1963, Sept. 2 Litho. *Perf. 13***

94 CD315 15c black & red .40 .25
95 CD315 45c ultra & red .60 .25

Copra Industry A9

Designs: 5c, Manganese loading, Forari Wharf. 10c, Cacao. 20c, Map of New Hebrides, tuna, marlin, ships. 25c, Striped triggerfish. 30c, Pearly nautilus (mollusk). 40c, 60c, Turkeyfish. 50c, Lined tang (fish). 1fr, Cardinal honey-eater and hibiscus. 2fr, Buff-bellied flycatcher. 3fr, Thicket warbler. 5fr, White-collared kingfisher.

**Wmk. 314 (10c, 20c, 40c, 60c, 3fr); Unwmkd. (others)**

***Perf. 12½ (10c, 20c, 40c, 60c); 14 (3fr); 13 (others)***

**Photo. (10c, 20c, 40c, 60c, 3fr); Engraved (others)**

**1963-67**

96 A9 5c Prus bl, pur brn & cl ('66) 1.75 .50
*a.* 5c prus blue & claret ('72) 45.00 37.50
97 A9 10c brt grn, org brn & dk brn ('65) .25 .25
98 A9 15c dk pur, yel & brn .25 .25
99 A9 20c brt blue, gray & cit ('65) .55 .25
100 A9 25c vio, rose lil & org brn ('66) .75 .50
101 A9 30c lilac, brn & cit 1.00 .75
102 A9 40c dk bl & ver ('65) 1.25 1.50
103 A9 50c Prus bl, yel & green 1.10 .80
103A A9 60c dk bl & ver ('67) 1.00 .50
104 A9 1fr blue grn, blk & red ('66) 3.00 3.50
105 A9 2fr ol, blk & brn 4.00 2.00
106 A9 3fr org grn, brt grn & blk ('65) 10.00 7.00
107 A9 5fr indigo, dp bl & gray ('67) 15.00 *20.00*
*Nos. 96-107 (13)* 39.90 37.80

For surcharge see No. 141.

ITU Emblem CD317

***Perf. 11x11½***

**1965, May 17 Litho. Wmk. 314**

108 CD317 15c ver & ol bister .25 .25
109 CD317 60c ultra & ver .40 .25

**Intl. Cooperation Year Issue**

Common Design Type with Royal Cipher and "RF" Replacing Queen's Portrait

**1965, Sept. 24** *Perf. 14½*

**110** CD318 5c blue grn & claret .25 .25
**111** CD318 55c lt violet & green .25 .25

**Churchill Memorial Issue**

Common Design Type with Royal Cipher and "RF" Replacing Queen's Portrait

**1966, Jan. 24 Photo.** *Perf. 14*

**112** CD319 5c multicolored .30 .25
**113** CD319 15c multicolored .50 .25
**114** CD319 25c multicolored .75 .25
**115** CD319 30c multicolored .75 .25
*Nos. 112-115 (4)* 2.30 1.00

**World Cup Soccer Issue**

Common Design Type with Royal Cipher and "RF" Replacing Queen's Portrait

**1966, July 1 Litho.** *Perf. 14*

**116** CD321 20c multicolored .30 .30
**117** CD321 40c multicolored .70 .70

**WHO Headquarters Issue**

Common Design Type with Royal Cipher and "RF" Replacing Queen's Portrait

**1966, Sept. 20 Litho.** *Perf. 14*

**118** CD322 25c multicolored .25 .25
**119** CD322 60c multicolored .50 .25

**UNESCO Anniversary Issue**

Common Design Type with Royal Cipher and "RF" Replacing Queen's Portrait

**1966, Dec. 1 Litho.** *Perf. 14*

**120** CD323 15c "Education" .35 .35
**121** CD323 30c "Science" .60 .60
**122** CD323 45c "Culture" .95 .95
*Nos. 120-122 (3)* 1.90 1.90

Coast Watchers — A11

25c, Map of South Pacific war zone, US Marine and Australian soldier. 60c, Australian cruiser Canberra. 1fr, Flying fortress taking off from Bauer Field, & view of Vila.

*Perf. 14x13*

**1967, Sept. 26 Photo. Wmk. 314**

**123** A11 15c lt blue & multi .25 .25
**124** A11 25c yellow & multi .30 .30
**125** A11 60c multicolored .75 .75
**126** A11 1fr pale salmon & multi 1.00 1.00
*Nos. 123-126 (4)* 2.30 2.30

25th anniv. of the Allied Forces' campaign in the South Pacific War Zone.

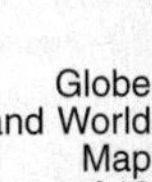

Globe and World Map A12

Designs: 25c, Ships La Boudeuse and L'Etoile and map of Bougainville Strait. 60c, Louis Antoine de Bougainville, ship's figure-head and bougainvillaea.

**1968, May 23 Engr.** *Perf. 13*

**127** A12 15c ver, emer & dull vio .25 .25
**128** A12 25c ultra, olive & brn .25 .25
**129** A12 60c magenta, grn & brn .30 .25
*Nos. 127-129 (3)* .80 .75

200th anniv. of Louis Antoine de Bougainville's (1729-1811) voyage around the world.

Concorde Airliner A13

Design: 60c, Concorde, sideview.

**1968, Oct. 9 Litho.** *Perf. 14x13½*

**130** A13 25c vio bl, red & lt bl .30 .25
**131** A13 60c red, ultra & black .60 .50

Development of the Concorde supersonic airliner, a joint Anglo-French project to produce a high speed plane.

Kauri Pine — A14

*Perf. 14x14½*

**1969, June 30 Wmk. 314**

**132** A14 20c brown & multi .30 .30

New Hebrides timber industry. Issued in sheets of 9 (3x3) on simulated wood grain background.

Relay Race, French and British Flags — A15

Design: 1fr, Runner at right.

*Perf. 12½x13*

**1969, Aug. 13 Photo. Unwmk.**

**133** A15 25c ultra, car, brn & gold .25 .25
**134** A15 1fr brn, car, ultra & gold .25 .25

3rd South Pacific Games, Port Moresby, Papua and New Guinea, Aug. 13-23.

Land Diver, Pentecost Island — A16

Designs: 15c, Diver in starting position on tower. 1fr, Diver nearing ground.

**Wmk. 314**

**1969, Oct. 15 Litho.** *Perf. 12½*

**135** A16 15c yellow & multi .25 .25
**136** A16 25c pink & multi .25 .25
**137** A16 1fr gray & multi .25 .25
*Nos. 135-137 (3)* .75 .75

UPU Headquarters and Monument, Bern — A17

**Unwmk.**

**1970, May 20 Engr.** *Perf. 13*

**138** A17 1.05fr org, lilac & slate .30 .30

Opening of the new UPU Headquarters, Bern.

Charles de Gaulle — A18

**1970, July 20 Photo.** *Perf. 13*

**139** A18 65c brown & multi .25 .25
**140** A18 1.10fr dp blue & multi .75 .75

30th anniv. of the rallying to the Free French.
For overprints see Nos. 144-145.

No. 99 Surcharged

**1970, Oct. 15 Wmk. 314** *Perf. 12½*

**141** A9 35c on 20c multi .30 .30

Virgin and Child, by Giovanni Bellini — A19

Christmas: 50c, Virgin and Child, by Giovanni Cima.

*Perf. 14½x14*

**1970, Nov. 30 Litho. Wmk. 314**

**142** A19 15c tan & multi .25 .25
**143** A19 50c lt green & multi .25 .25

Nos. 139-140 Overprinted in Black and Gold

**Unwmk.**

**1971, Jan. 19 Photo.** *Perf. 13*

**144** A18 65c brown & multi .25 .25
**145** A18 1.10fr dp blue & multi .35 .35

In memory of Gen. Charles de Gaulle (1890-1970), President of France.

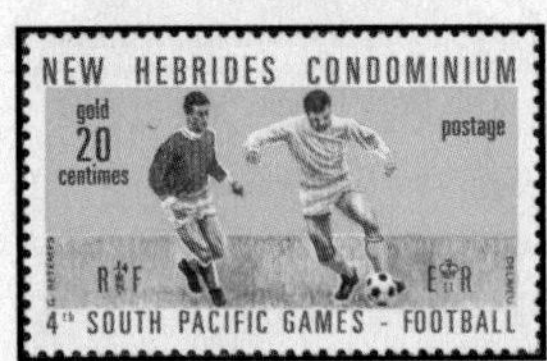


Soccer — A20

Design: 65c, Basketball, vert.

**1971, July 13 Photo.** *Perf. 12½*

**146** A20 20c multicolored .25 .25
**147** A20 65c multicolored .25 .25

4th South Pacific Games, Papeete, French Polynesia, Sept. 8-19.

Kauri Pine, Cone and Arms of Royal Society — A21

*Perf. 14½x14*

**1971, Sept. 7 Litho. Wmk. 314**

**148** A21 65c multicolored .30 .30

Royal Society of London for the Advancement of Science expedition to study vegetation and fauna, July 1-October.

Adoration of the Shepherds, by Louis Le Nain — A22

Design: 50c, Adoration of the Shepherds, by Jacopo Tintoretto.

**1971, Nov. 23** *Perf. 14x13½*

**149** A22 25c lt green & multi .25 .25
**150** A22 50c lt blue & multi .25 .25

Christmas. See Nos. 167-168.

Drover Mk III — A23

Airplanes: 25c, Sandringham seaplane. 30c, Dragon Rapide. 65c, Caravelle.

*Perf. 13½x13*

**1972, Feb. 29 Photo. Unwmk.**

**151** A23 20c lt green & multi .25 .25
**152** A23 25c ultra & multi .25 .25
**153** A23 30c orange & multi .45 .45
**154** A23 65c dk blue & multi .90 .90
*Nos. 151-154 (4)* 1.85 1.85

Headdress, South Malekula — A24

Baker's Pigeon — A25

Artifacts: 15c, Slit gong and carved figure, North Ambrym. 1fr, Carved figures, North Ambrym. 3fr, Ceremonial headdress, South Malekula.

Birds: 20c, Red-headed parrot-finch. 35c, Chestnut-bellied kingfisher. 2fr, Green palm lorikeet.

Sea shells: 25c, Cribraria fischeri. 30c, Oliva rubrolabiata. 65c, Strombus plicatus. 5fr, Turbo marmoratus.

**1972, July 24 Photo.** ***Perf. 12½x13***

| No. | Type | Description | Unused | Used |
|---|---|---|---|---|
| **155** | A24 | 5c plum & multi | .25 | .25 |
| **156** | A25 | 10c blue & multi | .25 | .25 |
| **157** | A24 | 15c red & multi | .30 | .40 |
| **158** | A25 | 20c org brown & multi | .35 | .50 |
| **159** | A24 | 25c dp blue & multi | .50 | .80 |
| **160** | A24 | 30c dk green & multi | .65 | .85 |
| **161** | A25 | 35c gray bl & multi | .70 | 1.10 |
| **162** | A24 | 65c dk green & multi | 1.25 | 3.75 |
| **163** | A24 | 1fr orange & multi | 2.00 | 3.00 |
| **164** | A25 | 2fr multicolored | 4.50 | 4.50 |
| **165** | A24 | 3fr yellow & multi | 5.75 | 6.75 |
| **166** | A24 | 5fr pink & multi | 9.00 | 13.50 |
| | | *Nos. 155-166 (12)* | 25.50 | 35.65 |

For overprints and surcharges see #181-182, 217-228.

**Christmas Type of 1971**

Designs: 25c, Adoration of the Magi (detail), by Bartholomaeus Spranger. 70c, Virgin and Child, by Jan Provoost.

***Perf. 14x13½***

**1972, Sept. 25 Litho. Wmk. 314**

| No. | Type | Description | Unused | Used |
|---|---|---|---|---|
| **167** | A22 | 25c lt green & multi | .25 | .25 |
| **168** | A22 | 70c lt blue & multi | .25 | .25 |

**Silver Wedding Issue, 1972**

Common Design Type

Design: Elizabeth II and Prince Philip.

**1972, Nov. 20 Photo.** ***Perf. 14x14½***

| No. | Type | Description | Unused | Used |
|---|---|---|---|---|
| **169** | CD324 | 35c vio black & multi | .25 | .25 |
| **170** | CD324 | 65c olive & multi | .25 | .25 |

Dendrobium Teretifolium — A26

Orchids: 30c, Ephemerantha comata. 35c, Spathoglottis petri. 65c, Dendrobium mohlianum.

**1973, Feb. 26 Litho.** ***Perf. 14***

| No. | Type | Description | Unused | Used |
|---|---|---|---|---|
| **171** | A26 | 25c blue vio & multi | .40 | .25 |
| **172** | A26 | 30c multicolored | .60 | .35 |
| **173** | A26 | 35c violet & multi | .75 | .45 |
| **174** | A26 | 65c dk green & multi | 1.25 | .60 |
| | | *Nos. 171-174 (4)* | 3.00 | 1.65 |

New Wharf, Vila — A27

Design: 70c, New wharf, horiz.

**1973, May 14 Wmk. 314**

| No. | Type | Description | Unused | Used |
|---|---|---|---|---|
| **175** | A27 | 25c multicolored | .25 | .25 |
| **176** | A27 | 70c multicolored | .30 | .30 |

New wharf at Vila, finished Nov. 1972.

Wild Horses, Tanna Island A28

70c, Yasur Volcano, Tanna.

***Perf. 13x12½***

**1973, Aug. 13 Photo. Unwmk.**

| No. | Type | Description | Unused | Used |
|---|---|---|---|---|
| **177** | A28 | 35c shown | .45 | .45 |
| **178** | A28 | 70c multicolored | 1.25 | .90 |

Mother and Child, by Marcel Moutouh — A29

Christmas: 70c, Star over Lagoon, by Tatin d'Avesnieres.

***Perf. 14x13½***

**1973, Nov. 19 Litho. Wmk. 314**

| No. | Type | Description | Unused | Used |
|---|---|---|---|---|
| **179** | A29 | 35c tan & multi | .25 | .25 |
| **180** | A29 | 70c lilac rose & multi | .25 | .25 |

Nos. 161 and 164 Overprinted in Red or Black

***Perf. 12½x13***

**1974, Feb. 11 Photo. Unwmk.**

| No. | Type | Description | Unused | Used |
|---|---|---|---|---|
| **181** | A25 | 35c multicolored (R) | .35 | .25 |
| **182** | A25 | 2fr multicolored (B) | .75 | .60 |

Visit of British Royal Family, Feb. 11-12.

Pacific Dove A30

Designs: 35c, Night swallowtail. 70c, Green sea turtle. 1.15fr, Flying fox.

**1974, Feb. 11** ***Perf. 13x12½***

| No. | Type | Description | Unused | Used |
|---|---|---|---|---|
| **183** | A30 | 25c gray & multi | .75 | .25 |
| **184** | A30 | 35c gray & multi | 1.10 | .30 |
| **185** | A30 | 70c gray & multi | 1.90 | 1.00 |
| **186** | A30 | 1.15fr gray & multi | 3.25 | 1.75 |
| | | *Nos. 183-186 (4)* | 7.00 | 3.30 |

Nature conservation.

Old Post Office, Vila — A31

Design: 70c, New Post Office.

**1974, May 6 Unwmk.** ***Perf. 12***

| No. | Type | Description | Unused | Used |
|---|---|---|---|---|
| **187** | A31 | 35c blue & multi | .25 | .25 |
| **188** | A31 | 70c red & multi | .25 | .25 |
| *a.* | | Pair, #187-188 | .50 | .50 |

Opening of New Post Office, May, 1974.

Capt. Cook and Tanna Island A32

#190, William Wales, & boat landing on island. #191, William Hodges painting islanders & landscape. 1.15fr, Capt. Cook, "Resolution" & map of New Hebrides.

**Wmk. 314**

**1974, Aug. 1 Litho.** ***Perf. 13***

**Size: 40x25mm**

| No. | Type | Description | Unused | Used |
|---|---|---|---|---|
| **189** | A32 | 35c multicolored | 1.50 | 1.00 |
| **190** | A32 | 35c multicolored | 1.50 | 1.00 |
| **191** | A32 | 35c multicolored | 1.50 | 1.00 |
| *a.* | | Strip of 3, #189-191 | 4.75 | *5.50* |

***Perf. 11***

**Size: 58x34mm**

| No. | Type | Description | Unused | Used |
|---|---|---|---|---|
| **192** | A32 | 1.15fr lilac & multi | 3.00 | 3.00 |
| | | *Nos. 189-192 (4)* | 7.50 | 6.00 |

Bicentenary of the discovery of the New Hebrides by Capt. Cook. No. 191a has continuous design.

Exchange of Letters, UPU Emblem A33

***Perf. 13x12½***

**1974, Oct. 9 Photo. Unwmk.**

| No. | Type | Description | Unused | Used |
|---|---|---|---|---|
| **193** | A33 | 70c multicolored | .30 | .30 |

Centenary of Universal Postal Union.

Nativity, by Gerard van Honthorst — A34

Christmas: 35c, Adoration of the Kings, by Velazquez, vert.

**Wmk. 314**

**1974, Nov. 14 Litho.** ***Perf. 13½***

| No. | Type | Description | Unused | Used |
|---|---|---|---|---|
| **194** | A34 | 35c multicolored | .25 | .25 |
| **195** | A34 | 70c multicolored | .25 | .25 |

Charolais Bull — A35

**1975, Apr. 29 Engr.** ***Perf. 13***

| No. | Type | Description | Unused | Used |
|---|---|---|---|---|
| **196** | A35 | 10fr multicolored | 10.00 | *20.00* |

For surcharge see No. 229.

A36

**1975, Aug. 5 Litho.** ***Perf. 14x13½***

| No. | Type | Description | Unused | Used |
|---|---|---|---|---|
| **197** | A36 | 25c Kayak race | .25 | .25 |
| **198** | A36 | 35c Camp cooks | .25 | .25 |
| **199** | A36 | 1fr Map makers | .65 | .65 |
| **200** | A36 | 5fr Fishermen | 4.50 | 4.50 |
| | | *Nos. 197-200 (4)* | 5.65 | 5.65 |

Nordjamb 75, 14th Boy Scout Jamboree, Lillehammer, Norway, July 29-Aug. 7.

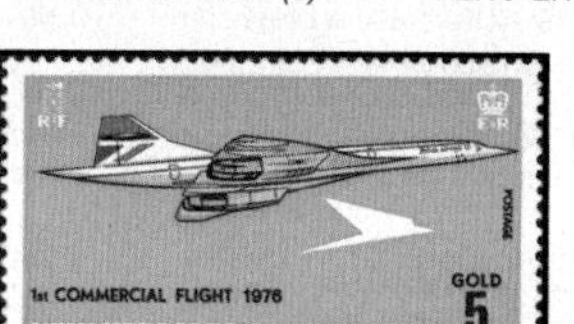

A37

Christmas (After Michelangelo): 35c, Pitti Madonna. 70c, Bruges Madonna. 2.50fr, Taddei Madonna.

***Perf. 14½x14***

**1975, Nov. 11 Litho. Wmk. 373**

| No. | Type | Description | Unused | Used |
|---|---|---|---|---|
| **201** | A37 | 35c ol green & multi | .25 | .25 |
| **202** | A37 | 70c brown & multi | .45 | .45 |
| **203** | A37 | 2.50fr blue & multi | 1.40 | 1.40 |
| | | *Nos. 201-203 (3)* | 2.10 | 2.10 |


Concorde, British Airways Colors and Emblem — A38

**Unwmk.**

**1976, Jan. 30 Typo.** ***Perf. 13***

| No. | Type | Description | Unused | Used |
|---|---|---|---|---|
| **204** | A38 | 5fr blue & multi | 7.50 | 7.50 |

First commercial flight of supersonic jet Concorde from London to Bahrain, Jan. 21.

Telephones, 1876 and 1976 — A39

Designs: 70c, Alexander Graham Bell. 1.15fr, Nouméa earth station and satellite.

**1976, Mar. 31 Photo.** ***Perf. 13***

| No. | Type | Description | Unused | Used |
|---|---|---|---|---|
| **205** | A39 | 25c black, car & blue | .30 | .30 |
| **206** | A39 | 70c black & multi | .40 | .40 |
| **207** | A39 | 1.15fr black, org & vio bl | 1.00 | 1.00 |
| | | *Nos. 205-207 (3)* | 1.70 | 1.70 |

Centenary of first telephone call by Alexander Graham Bell, Mar. 10, 1876.

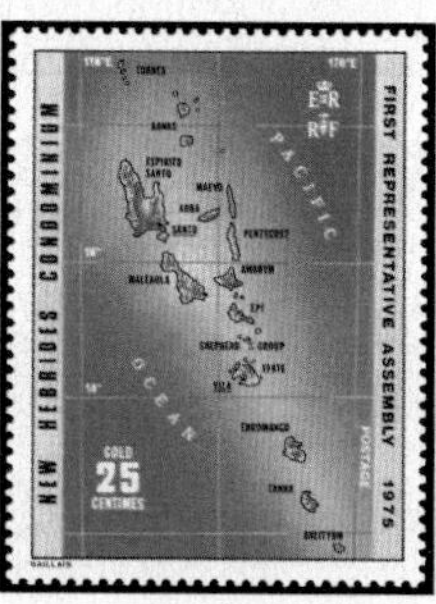

Map of New Hebrides A40

View of Santo A41

Design: 2fr, View of Vila.

**1976, June 29 Photo. *Perf. 13***

| | | | | |
|---|---|---|---|---|
| **208** | A40 | 25c blue & multi | .30 | .30 |
| **209** | A41 | 1fr multicolored | .70 | .70 |
| **210** | A41 | 2fr multicolored | 1.50 | 1.50 |
| | | *Nos. 208-210 (3)* | 2.50 | 2.50 |

Opening of First Representative Assembly, June 29 (25c); first Santo Municipal Council (1fr); first Vila Municipal Council (2fr).

See Nos. 263-264 for types of design A40 surcharged.

Flight into Egypt, by Francisco Vieira Lusitano — A42

Christmas (Portuguese 16th Cent. Paintings): 70c, Adoration of the Shepherds. 2.50fr, Adoration of the Kings.

**Wmk. 373**

**1976, Nov. 8 Litho. *Perf. 14***

| | | | | |
|---|---|---|---|---|
| **211** | A42 | 35c purple & multi | .25 | .25 |
| **212** | A42 | 70c blue & multi | .25 | .25 |
| **213** | A42 | 2.50fr lt green & multi | .60 | .60 |
| | | *Nos. 211-213 (3)* | 1.10 | 1.10 |

Queen's Visit, 1974 — A43

70c, Imperial state crown. 2fr, The blessing.

**1977, Feb. 7 *Perf. 14x13½***

| | | | | |
|---|---|---|---|---|
| **214** | A43 | 35c lt green & multi | .25 | .25 |
| **215** | A43 | 70c blue & multi | .25 | .25 |
| **216** | A43 | 2fr pink & multi | .25 | .25 |
| | | *Nos. 214-216 (3)* | .75 | .75 |

25th anniv. of the reign of Elizabeth II.

**Nos. 155-166, 196 Surcharged**

**Paris Overprints**

***Perf. 12½x13***

**1977, July 1 Photo. Unwmk.**

| | | | | |
|---|---|---|---|---|
| **217** | A24 | 5fr on 5c multi | .50 | *.60* |
| **218** | A25 | 10fr on 10c multi | .80 | .40 |
| **219** | A24 | 15fr on 15c multi | .65 | *1.75* |
| **220** | A25 | 20fr on 20c multi | 1.30 | .60 |
| **221** | A24 | 25fr on 25c multi | 1.75 | 2.00 |
| **222** | A24 | 30fr on 30c multi | 1.75 | 1.25 |
| **223** | A25 | 35fr on 35c multi | 1.75 | 1.50 |
| **224** | A24 | 40fr on 65c multi | 1.50 | 1.50 |
| **225** | A24 | 50fr on 1fr multi | 1.10 | 2.00 |
| **226** | A25 | 70fr on 2fr multi | 6.75 | 1.00 |
| **227** | A24 | 100fr on 3fr multi | 1.20 | *4.00* |
| **228** | A24 | 200fr on 5fr multi | 5.50 | *14.00* |

**Wmk. 314**

**Engr. *Perf. 13***

| | | | | |
|---|---|---|---|---|
| **229** | A35 | 500fr on 10fr multi | 15.00 | 17.50 |
| | | *Nos. 217-229 (13)* | 39.55 | 48.10 |

**Nos. 155//166, 196 Surcharged with New Value, "FNH" and Bars**

FNH a  FNH b  FNH c  25 FNH d

**Port Vila Overprints**

Two settings of 35fr and 200fr surcharges: type 1, 1.4mm between new value and "FNH"; type 2, 2.1mm between value and "FNH."

***Perf. 12½x13***

**1977-78 Photo. Unwmk.**

| | | | | |
|---|---|---|---|---|
| *217a* | A24 | 5fr on 5c (a) | .60 | .25 |
| *218a* | A25 | 10fr on 10c (b) | .85 | .25 |
| *219a* | A24 | 15fr on 15c (c) | 2.00 | 1.00 |
| *221a* | A24 | 25fr on 25c (d) | 60.00 | 24.00 |
| *222a* | A24 | 30fr on 30c (d) | 275.00 | 75.00 |
| *223a* | A25 | 35fr on 35c (d), type 1 | 3.50 | .90 |
| ***b.*** | | Type 2 | 6.00 | 1.20 |
| *224a* | A24 | 40fr on 65c (d) | 1.75 | .65 |
| *225a* | A24 | 50fr on 1fr (d) | 50.00 | 30.00 |
| *227a* | A24 | 100fr on (d) | 50.00 | *30.00* |
| *228a* | A24 | 200fr on 5fr (d), type 1 | 20.00 | 15.00 |
| ***b.*** | | Type 2 | — | — |
| *229a* | A35 | 500fr on 10fr (d) | 22.50 | 16.00 |
| | | *Nos. 217a-229a (11)* | 486.20 | 193.05 |

The 50fr and 100fr values were sold only through the philatelic bureau.

Issued: 10fr, 7/10; 15fr, 7/18; 5fr, 8/10; #228a, 8/22; 25fr, 30fr, #223a, 9/10; 40fr, 9/12; 500fr, 9/14; #223b, 1/6/78; #228b, 1/13/78.

Erromango and Kaori Tree — A44

Designs: 10fr, Archipelago and man making copra. 15fr, Espiritu Santo Island and cattle. 20fr, Efate Island and Post Office, Vila. 25fr, Malakula Island and headdresses. 30fr, Aoba and Maewo Islands and pig tusks. 35fr, Pentecost Island and land diving. 40fr, Tanna Island and Prophet John Frum's Red Cross. 50fr, Shepherd Island and canoe with sail. 70fr, Banks Island and dancers. 100fr, Ambrym Island and carvings. 200fr, Aneityum Island and decorated baskets. 500fr, Torres Islands and fishing with bow and arrow.

**1977-78 Wmk. 373 Litho. *Perf. 14***

| | | | | |
|---|---|---|---|---|
| **238** | A44 | 5fr multicolored | .25 | .25 |
| **239** | A44 | 10fr multicolored | .25 | .25 |
| **240** | A44 | 15fr multicolored | .25 | .25 |
| **241** | A44 | 20fr multicolored | .30 | .30 |
| **242** | A44 | 25fr multicolored | .40 | .40 |
| **243** | A44 | 30fr multicolored | .50 | .50 |
| **244** | A44 | 35fr multicolored | .55 | .55 |
| **245** | A44 | 40fr multicolored | .60 | .60 |
| **246** | A44 | 50fr multicolored | 1.25 | .75 |
| **247** | A44 | 70fr multicolored | 1.50 | *2.00* |
| **248** | A44 | 100fr multicolored | 1.75 | 1.25 |
| **249** | A44 | 200fr multicolored | 2.50 | 2.50 |
| **250** | A44 | 500fr multicolored | 5.50 | 7.50 |
| | | *Nos. 238-250 (13)* | 15.60 | 17.10 |

Issue dates: 5fr, 20fr, 50fr, 100fr, 200fr, Sept. 7; 15fr, 25fr, 30fr, 40fr, Nov. 23, 1977; 10fr, 35fr, 70fr, 500fr, May 9, 1978.

Tempi Madonna, by Raphael — A45

Christmas: 15fr, Virgin and Child, by Gerard David. 30fr, Virgin and Child, by Pompeo Batoni.

**1977, Dec. 8 Litho. *Perf. 12***

| | | | | |
|---|---|---|---|---|
| **251** | A45 | 10fr multicolored | .25 | .25 |
| **252** | A45 | 15fr multicolored | .25 | .25 |
| **253** | A45 | 30fr multicolored | .30 | .30 |
| | | *Nos. 251-253 (3)* | .80 | .80 |

British Airways Concorde over New York City — A46

20fr, British Airways Concorde over London. 30fr, Air France Concorde over Washington. 40fr, Air France Concorde over Paris.

**1978, May 9 Wmk. 373 *Perf. 14***

| | | | | |
|---|---|---|---|---|
| **254** | A46 | 10fr multicolored | .85 | .50 |
| **255** | A46 | 20fr multicolored | 1.10 | 1.10 |
| **256** | A46 | 30fr multicolored | 1.50 | 1.50 |
| **257** | A46 | 40fr multicolored | 1.75 | 1.75 |
| | | *Nos. 254-257 (4)* | 5.20 | 4.85 |

Concorde, 1st commercial flight, Paris to NYC.

**Elizabeth II Coronation Anniversary Issue**

Common Design Types

Souvenir Sheet

**1978, June 2 Unwmk. *Perf. 15***

| | | | |
|---|---|---|---|
| **258** | Sheet of 6 | 1.75 | 1.75 |
| ***a.*** | CD326 40fr White horse of Hanover | .25 | .25 |
| ***b.*** | CD327 40fr Elizabeth II | .25 | .25 |
| ***c.*** | CD328 40fr Gallic cock | .25 | .25 |

No. 258 contains 2 se-tenant strips of Nos. 258a-258c, separated by horizontal gutter with commemorative and descriptive inscriptions and showing central part of coronation procession with coach.

Virgin and Child, by Dürer — A47

Dürer Paintings: 15fr, Virgin and Child with St. Anne. 30fr, Virgin and Child with Goldfinch. 40fr, Virgin and Child with Pear.

***Perf. 14x13½***

**1978, Dec. 1 Litho. Wmk. 373**

| | | | | |
|---|---|---|---|---|
| **259** | A47 | 10fr multicolored | .25 | .25 |
| **260** | A47 | 15fr multicolored | .25 | .25 |
| **261** | A47 | 30fr multicolored | .25 | .25 |
| **262** | A47 | 40fr multicolored | .25 | .25 |
| | | *Nos. 259-262 (4)* | 1.00 | 1.00 |

Christmas and 450th death anniv. of Albrecht Dürer (1471-1528), German painter.

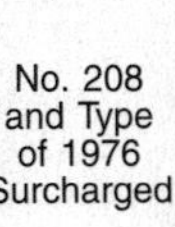
No. 208 and Type of 1976 Surcharged

**Longitude changed to "166E."**

**1979, Jan. 11 Photo. *Perf. 13***

| | | | | |
|---|---|---|---|---|
| **263** | A40 | 10fr on 25c bl & multi | .25 | .25 |
| **264** | A40 | 40fr on 25c lt grn & multi | .25 | .25 |

1st anniv. of Internal Self-Government.

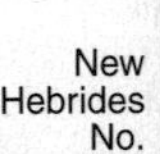
New Hebrides No. 50 — A48

Rowland Hill and New Hebrides Stamps: 20fr, No. 136. 40fr, No. 43.

**1979, Sept. 10 Litho. *Perf. 14***

| | | | | |
|---|---|---|---|---|
| **265** | A48 | 10fr multicolored | .25 | .25 |
| **266** | A48 | 20fr multicolored | .25 | .25 |
| ***a.*** | | Souvenir sheet of 2 | .90 | .90 |
| **267** | A48 | 40fr multicolored | .40 | .40 |
| | | *Nos. 265-267 (3)* | .90 | .90 |

Sir Rowland Hill (1795-1879), originator of penny postage. No. 266a contains New Hebrides, British, No. 266, and French, No. 286; margin shows Mulready envelope.

Arts Festival — A49

Designs: 10fr, Clubs and spears. 20fr, Ritual puppet. 40fr, Headdress.

**1979, Nov. 16 Wmk. 373 *Perf. 14***

| | | | | |
|---|---|---|---|---|
| **268** | A49 | 5fr multicolored | .25 | .25 |
| **269** | A49 | 10fr multicolored | .25 | .25 |
| **270** | A49 | 20fr multicolored | .25 | .25 |
| **271** | A49 | 40fr multicolored | .40 | .40 |
| | | *Nos. 268-271 (4)* | 1.15 | 1.15 |

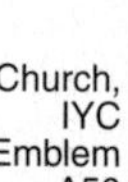
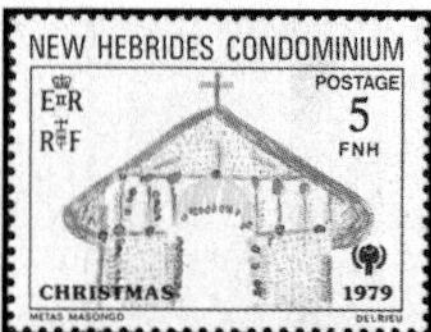


Church, IYC Emblem A50

IYC Emblem, Children's Drawings: 10fr, Father Christmas. 20fr, Cross and Bible, vert. 40fr, Stars, candle and Santa Claus, vert.

**1979, Dec. 4** *Perf. 13x13½*

| | | | | |
|---|---|---|---|---|
| **272** | A50 | 5fr multicolored | .25 | .25 |
| **273** | A50 | 10fr multicolored | .25 | .25 |
| **274** | A50 | 20fr multicolored | .25 | .25 |
| **275** | A50 | 40fr multicolored | .35 | .35 |
| | | *Nos. 272-275 (4)* | 1.10 | 1.10 |

Christmas; Intl. Year of the Child.

White-bellied Honeyeater — A51

**1980, Feb. 27** **Litho.** *Perf. 14*

| | | | | |
|---|---|---|---|---|
| **276** | A51 | 10fr shown | .85 | .25 |
| **277** | A51 | 20fr Scarlet robins | 1.10 | .45 |
| **278** | A51 | 30fr Yellow white-eyes | 1.50 | .65 |
| **279** | A51 | 40fr Fan-tailed brush cuckoo | 1.75 | .85 |
| | | *Nos. 276-279 (4)* | 5.20 | 2.20 |

New Hebrides stamps were replaced in 1980 by those of Vanuatu.

### POSTAGE DUE STAMPS

**British Issues**

Type of 1925 Overprinted

**1925, June** **Engr.** **Wmk. 4** *Perf. 14*

| | | | | |
|---|---|---|---|---|
| **J1** | A3 | 1p (10c) green | 37.50 | 1.25 |
| **J2** | A3 | 2p (20c) gray | 40.00 | 1.25 |
| **J3** | A3 | 3p (30c) carmine | 40.00 | 3.25 |
| **J4** | A3 | 5p (50c) ultra | 45.00 | 5.50 |
| **J5** | A3 | 10p (1fr) car, *blue* | 52.50 | 6.50 |
| | | *Nos. J1-J5 (5)* | 215.00 | 17.75 |

Values for Nos. J1-J5 are for toned stamps.

**Regular Stamps of 1938 Overprinted in Black**

**1938, June 1** *Perf. 12*

| | | | | |
|---|---|---|---|---|
| **J6** | A5 | 5c green | 20.00 | *32.50* |
| **J7** | A5 | 10c dark orange | 20.00 | *32.50* |
| **J8** | A5 | 20c rose red | 22.50 | *50.00* |
| **J9** | A5 | 40c olive green | 27.50 | *57.50* |
| **J10** | A5 | 1fr car, *emerald* | 35.00 | *67.50* |
| | | *Nos. J6-J10 (5)* | 125.00 | *240.00* |

**Catalogue values for unused stamps in this section, from this point to the end of the section, are for Never Hinged items.**

**Regular Stamps of 1953 Overprinted in Black**

**1953, Apr. 30** *Perf. 12½*

| | | | | |
|---|---|---|---|---|
| **J11** | A6 | 5c green | 4.75 | *13.50* |
| **J12** | A6 | 10c red | 2.25 | *11.00* |
| **J13** | A6 | 20c ultramarine | 6.00 | *20.00* |
| **J14** | A6 | 40c black brown | 8.50 | *37.50* |
| **J15** | A6 | 1fr deep orange | 5.50 | *45.00* |
| | | *Nos. J11-J15 (5)* | 27.00 | *127.00* |

**Same on Nos. 82-83, 85, 88 and 90**

**1957, Sept. 3** *Perf. 13½x13*

| | | | | |
|---|---|---|---|---|
| **J16** | A8 | 5c green | .25 | *1.00* |
| **J17** | A8 | 10c red | .35 | *1.25* |
| **J18** | A8 | 20c ultramarine | .75 | *1.50* |
| **J19** | A8 | 40c sepia | 1.00 | *2.50* |
| **J20** | A8 | 1fr orange | 2.00 | *3.50* |
| | | *Nos. J16-J20 (5)* | 4.35 | *9.75* |

## NEW HEBRIDES, FRENCH

'nü 'he-brə-ˌdēz

LOCATION — A group of islands in the South Pacific Ocean lying north of New Caledonia

GOVT. — Condominium under the joint administration of Great Britain and France

AREA — 5,790 sq. mi.

POP. — 100,000 (est. 1976)

CAPITAL — Port-Vila (Vila)

Postage stamps are issued by both Great Britain and France. In 1911 a joint issue was made bearing the coats of arms of both countries. The British stamps bore the coat of arms of Great Britain and the value in British currency on the right and the French coat of arms and values at the left. On the French stamps the positions were reversed. This resulted in some confusion when the value of the French franc decreased following World War I but the situation was corrected by arranging that both series of stamps be sold for their value as expressed in French currency.

12 Pence = 1 Shilling
100 Centimes = 1 Franc
New Hebrides Franc (FNH) — 1977

**Catalogue values for unused stamps in this country are for Never Hinged items, beginning with Scott 79 in the regular postage section, Scott J16 in the postage due section.**

**French Issues**

**Stamps of New Caledonia, 1905, Overprinted in Black or Red**

Nos. 1-4

No. 5

**1908** **Unwmk.** *Perf. 14x13½*

| | | | | |
|---|---|---|---|---|
| **1** | A16 | 5c green | 13.50 | *5.00* |
| **2** | A16 | 10c rose | 13.50 | *4.75* |
| **3** | A17 | 25c blue, *grnsh* (R) | 9.50 | *4.00* |
| **4** | A17 | 50c carmine, *org* | 8.50 | *6.50* |
| **5** | A18 | 1fr bl, *yel grn* (R) | 29.00 | *22.50* |
| | | *Nos. 1-5 (5)* | 74.00 | *42.75* |

For overprints and surcharges see #6-10, 33-35.

Stamps of 1908 with Additional Overprint

**1910**

| | | | | |
|---|---|---|---|---|
| **6** | A16 | 5c green | 8.00 | *3.00* |
| **7** | A16 | 10c rose | 8.00 | *1.75* |
| **8** | A17 | 25c blue, *grnsh* (R) | 3.50 | *4.50* |
| **9** | A17 | 50c red, *orange* | 12.00 | *27.50* |
| **10** | A18 | 1fr bl, *yel grn* (R) | 30.00 | *22.50* |
| | | *Nos. 6-10 (5)* | 61.50 | *59.25* |

A2

*Perf. 14*

**1911, July 12** **Engr.** **Wmk. 3**

| | | | | |
|---|---|---|---|---|
| **11** | A2 | 5c pale green | 1.00 | *3.00* |
| **12** | A2 | 10c red | .55 | *1.10* |
| **13** | A2 | 20c gray | 2.00 | *3.00* |
| **14** | A2 | 25c ultramarine | 2.75 | *7.00* |
| **15** | A2 | 30c vio, *yellow* | 6.50 | *6.50* |
| **16** | A2 | 40c red, *yellow* | 4.00 | *7.50* |
| **17** | A2 | 50c olive green | 4.00 | *7.50* |
| **18** | A2 | 75c brn orange | 7.00 | *30.00* |
| **19** | A2 | 1fr brn red, *bl* | 6.00 | *7.00* |
| **20** | A2 | 2fr violet | 12.00 | *22.50* |
| **21** | A2 | 5fr brn red, *grn* | 14.00 | *47.50* |
| | | *Nos. 11-21 (11)* | 59.80 | *142.60* |

For surcharges see Nos. 36-37, 43 and British issue No. 30.

**1912** **Wmk. R F in Sheet**

| | | | | |
|---|---|---|---|---|
| **22** | A2 | 5c pale green | 1.75 | *5.50* |
| **23** | A2 | 10c red | 1.75 | *6.00* |
| **24** | A2 | 20c gray | 2.10 | *2.40* |
| **25** | A2 | 25c ultramarine | 2.50 | *5.00* |
| **26** | A2 | 30c vio, *yellow* | 2.50 | *17.00* |
| **27** | A2 | 40c red, *yellow* | 24.00 | *80.00* |
| **28** | A2 | 50c olive green | 18.00 | *35.00* |
| **29** | A2 | 75c brn orange | 9.00 | *42.50* |
| **30** | A2 | 1fr brn red, *bl* | 9.00 | *10.00* |
| **31** | A2 | 2fr violet | 9.25 | *50.00* |
| **32** | A2 | 5fr brn red, *grn* | 32.50 | *57.50* |
| | | *Nos. 22-32 (11)* | 112.35 | 310.90 |

In the watermark, "R F" (République Française initials) are large double-lined Roman capitals, about 120mm high. About one-fourth of the stamps in each sheet show parts of the watermark. The other stamps are without watermark.

For surcharges see Nos. 38-42 and British issue No. 31.

Nos. 9 and 8 Surcharged

**1920** **Unwmk.** *Perf. 14x13½*

| | | | | |
|---|---|---|---|---|
| **33** | A17 | 5c on 50c red, *org* | 2.50 | *22.00* |
| **34** | A17 | 10c on 25c bl, *grnsh* | .75 | *1.50* |

**Same Surcharge on No. 4**

| | | | | |
|---|---|---|---|---|
| **35** | A17 | 5c on 50c red, *org* | 800.00 | *1,000.* |

British Issue No. 21 and French Issue No. 15 Surcharged

**1921** **Wmk. 3** *Perf. 14*

| | | | | |
|---|---|---|---|---|
| **36** | A1 | 10c on 5p ol grn | 16.00 | *50.00* |
| **37** | A2 | 20c on 30c vio, *yel* | 15.00 | *65.00* |

**Nos. 27 and 26 Surcharged**

**1921** **Wmk. R F in Sheet**

| | | | | |
|---|---|---|---|---|
| **38** | A2 | 5c on 40c red, *yel* | 27.50 | *100.00* |
| **39** | A2 | 20c on 30c vio, *yel* | 11.50 | *80.00* |

**Stamps of 1910-12 Surcharged with New Values as in 1920-21**

**1924**

| | | | | |
|---|---|---|---|---|
| **40** | A2 | 10c on 5c pale grn | 2.75 | 11.00 |
| **41** | A2 | 30c on 10c red | 2.75 | 3.00 |
| **42** | A2 | 50c on 25c ultra | 4.50 | 20.00 |

**Wmk. 3**

| | | | | |
|---|---|---|---|---|
| **43** | A2 | 50c on 25c ultra | 45.00 | *110.00* |
| | | *Nos. 40-43 (4)* | 55.00 | 144.00 |

A4

The values at the lower right denote the currency and amount for which the stamps were to be sold. The stamps could be purchased at the French post office and used to pay postage at the English rates.

**1925** **Engr.** **Wmk. R F in Sheet**

| | | | | |
|---|---|---|---|---|
| **44** | A4 | 5c (½p) black | .90 | *13.00* |
| **45** | A4 | 10c (1p) green | 1.00 | *9.00* |
| **46** | A4 | 20c (2p) grnsh gray | 4.25 | *3.75* |
| **47** | A4 | 25c (2½p) brown | 1.50 | *9.00* |
| **48** | A4 | 30c (3p) carmine | 1.75 | *18.00* |
| **49** | A4 | 40c (4p) car, *org* | 3.25 | *16.00* |
| **50** | A4 | 50c (5p) ultra | 2.00 | *11.00* |
| **51** | A4 | 75c (7½p) bis brn | 1.75 | *22.00* |
| **52** | A4 | 1fr (10p) car, *blue* | 3.00 | *14.50* |
| **53** | A4 | 2fr (1sh 8p) gray vio | 2.75 | 37.50 |
| **54** | A4 | 5fr (4sh) car, *grnsh* | 5.00 | *37.50* |
| | | *Nos. 44-54 (11)* | 27.15 | *191.25* |

For overprints see Nos. J1-J5.

Beach Scene A6

**1938** *Perf. 12*

| | | | | |
|---|---|---|---|---|
| **55** | A6 | 5c green | 3.00 | *9.75* |
| **56** | A6 | 10c dark orange | 3.25 | *3.25* |
| **57** | A6 | 15c violet | 3.25 | *8.00* |
| **58** | A6 | 20c rose red | 3.25 | *5.50* |
| **59** | A6 | 25c brown | 6.50 | *7.75* |
| **60** | A6 | 30c dark blue | 6.50 | *8.00* |
| **61** | A6 | 40c olive grn | 3.50 | *14.50* |
| **62** | A6 | 50c brown violet | 3.50 | *5.50* |
| **63** | A6 | 1fr dk car, *grn* | 4.00 | *8.50* |
| **64** | A6 | 2fr blue, *grn* | 27.50 | *42.50* |
| **65** | A6 | 5fr red, *yellow* | 40.00 | *67.50* |
| **66** | A6 | 10fr vio, *blue* | 87.50 | *145.00* |
| | | *Nos. 55-66 (12)* | 191.75 | *325.75* |
| | | Set, never hinged | 375.00 | |

For overprints see Nos. 67-78, J6-J15.

Stamps of 1938 Ovptd. in Black

**1941**

| | | | | |
|---|---|---|---|---|
| **67** | A6 | 5c green | 1.25 | *25.00* |
| **68** | A6 | 10c dark orange | 3.50 | *24.00* |
| **69** | A6 | 15c violet | 5.50 | *40.00* |
| **70** | A6 | 20c rose red | 15.50 | *30.00* |
| **71** | A6 | 25c brown | 16.50 | *40.00* |
| **72** | A6 | 30c dark blue | 17.00 | *35.00* |
| **73** | A6 | 40c olive green | 17.00 | *40.00* |
| **74** | A6 | 50c brn violet | 14.50 | *35.00* |
| **75** | A6 | 1fr dk car, *grn* | 14.50 | *37.50* |
| **76** | A6 | 2fr blue, *grn* | 13.50 | *37.50* |

**77** A6 5fr red, *yellow* 11.00 *37.50*
**78** A6 10fr vio, *blue* 10.00 *40.00*
*Nos. 67-78 (12)* 139.75 421.50
Set, never hinged 245.00

**Catalogue values for unused stamps in this section, from this point to the end of the section, are for Never Hinged items.**

### UPU Issue
Common Design Type
**Wmk. RF in Sheet**

**1949 Engr. *Perf. 13½x14***
**79** CD309 10c red orange 3.50 3.50
**80** CD309 15c violet 4.75 4.75
**81** CD309 30c violet blue 7.50 7.50
**82** CD309 50c rose violet 8.50 8.50
*Nos. 79-82 (4)* 24.25 24.25

Some stamps in each sheet show part of the watermark; others show none.

Common Design Types pictured following the introduction.

A8

5c, 10c, 15c, 20c, Canoes with sails. 25c, 30c, 40c, 50c, Native carving. 1fr, 2fr, 5fr, Natives.

**1953 *Perf. 12½***
**83** A8 5c green 2.75 *6.75*
**84** A8 10c red 5.50 *6.75*
**85** A8 15c yellow 5.50 *7.00*
**86** A8 20c ultramarine 5.75 *5.50*
**87** A8 25c olive 3.00 *5.50*
**88** A8 30c light brown 1.50 *5.50*
**89** A8 40c black brown 1.75 *5.75*
**90** A8 50c violet 1.75 *4.75*
**91** A8 1fr deep orange 12.50 *11.00*
**92** A8 2fr red violet 16.50 *42.00*
**93** A8 5fr scarlet 17.00 *70.00*
*Nos. 83-93 (11)* 73.50 *170.50*

For overprints see Nos. J16-J20.

Discovery of New Hebrides, 1606 — A9

20c, 50c, Britannia, Marianne, Flags and Mask.

***Perf. 14½x14***
**1956, Oct. 20 Unwmk. Photo.**
**94** A9 5c emerald 1.25 1.25
**95** A9 10c crimson 1.40 1.40
**96** A9 20c ultramarine 1.25 1.25
**97** A9 50c purple 1.25 1.25
*Nos. 94-97 (4)* 5.15 5.15

50th anniv. of the establishment of the Anglo-French Condominium.

Port Vila and Iririki Islet — A10

Designs: 25c, 30c, 40c, 50c, Tropical river and spear fisherman. 1fr, 2fr, 5fr, Woman drinking from coconut (inscribed: "Alliance Franco-Britannique 4 Mars 1947").

**Wmk. RF in Sheet**

**1957 Engr. *Perf. 13½x13***
**98** A10 5c green .60 *1.25*
**99** A10 10c red .90 *.85*
**100** A10 15c orange yel 1.00 *1.50*
**101** A10 20c ultramarine 1.25 *1.50*
**102** A10 25c olive 1.25 *1.25*
**103** A10 30c light brown 1.75 *1.75*
**104** A10 40c sepia 2.00 *2.25*
**105** A10 50c violet 2.50 *3.50*
**106** A10 1fr orange 6.75 *9.00*
**107** A10 2fr rose lilac 14.50 *20.00*
**108** A10 5fr black 28.00 *40.00*
*Nos. 98-108 (11)* 60.50 *82.85*

For overprints see Nos. J21-J25.

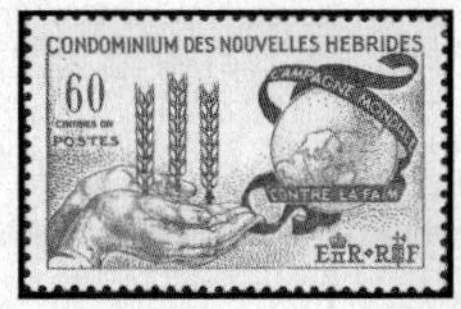

Wheat Emblem and Globe A10a

**1963, Sept. 2 Unwmk. *Perf. 13***
**109** A10a 60c org brn & slate grn 19.00 19.00

FAO "Freedom from Hunger" campaign.

Centenary Emblem — A11

**1963, Sept. 2 Unwmk.**
**110** A11 15c org, gray & car 12.50 12.50
**111** A11 45c bis, gray & car 18.50 18.50

Centenary of International Red Cross.

Copra Industry A12

Designs: 5c, Manganese loading, Forari Wharf. 10c, Cacao. 20c, Map of New Hebrides, tuna, marlin and ships. 25c, Striped triggerfish. 30c, Nautilus. 40c, 60c, Turkeyfish (pterois volitans). 50c, Lined tang (fish). 1fr, Cardinal honeyeater and hibiscus. 2fr, Buff-bellied flycatcher. 3fr, Thicket warbler. 5fr, White-collared kingfisher.

***Perf. 12½ (10c, 20c, 40c, 60c); 14 (3fr); 13 (others)***
**Photo. (10c, 20c, 40c, 60c, 3fr); Engr. (others)**

**1963-67 Unwmk.**
**112** A12 5c Prus bl, pur brn & cl ('66) .65 .65
*a.* 5c prus blue & claret ('72) 57.50 *60.00*
**113** A12 10c brt grn, org brn & dk brn ("RF" at left) ('65) 2.10 1.60
**114** A12 15c dk pur, yel & brn .80 .80
**115** A12 20c brt bl, gray & cit ("RF" at left) ('65) 3.00 2.75
**116** A12 25c vio, rose lil & org brn ('66) .80 .80
**117** A12 30c lil, brn & citron 6.00 1.60
**118** A12 40c dk bl & ver ('65) 5.50 5.50
**119** A12 50c Prus bl, yel & grn 5.00 2.40
**119A** A12 60c dk bl & ver ('67) 1.90 1.50
**120** A12 1fr bl grn, blk & red ('66) 3.75 3.75
**121** A12 2fr ol, blk & brn 17.50 9.00
**122** A12 3fr org brn, brt grn & blk ("RF" at left) ('65) 16.00 *22.50*
**123** A12 5fr ind, dp bl & gray ('67) 30.00 30.00
*Nos. 112-123 (13)* 93.00 82.85

See #146-148. For surcharge see #160.

Telegraph, Syncom Satellite and ITU Emblem — A13

**1965, May 17 Unwmk. *Perf. 13***
**124** A13 15c dk red brn, brt bl & emer 11.50 9.00
**125** A13 60c Prus grn, mag & sl 29.00 25.00

ITU, centenary.

### Intl. Cooperation Year Issue
Common Design Type with Royal Cipher and "RF" Replacing Queen's Portrait

**1965, Oct. 24 Litho. *Perf. 14½***
**126** CD318 5c blue grn & claret 4.00 4.00
**127** CD318 55c lt violet & grn 8.00 8.00

International Cooperation Year.

### Churchill Memorial Issue
Common Design Type with Royal Cipher and "RF" Replacing Queen's Portrait

**1966, Jan. 24 Photo. *Perf. 14***
**Design in Black, Gold and Carmine Rose**
**128** CD319 5c brt blue 1.00 1.00
**129** CD319 15c green 1.50 1.50
**130** CD319 25c brown 3.25 3.25
**131** CD319 30c violet 4.50 4.50
*Nos. 128-131 (4)* 10.25 10.25

### World Cup Soccer Issue
Common Design Type with Royal Cipher and "RF" Replacing Queen's Portrait

**1966, July 1 Litho. *Perf. 14***
**132** CD321 20c multicolored 2.75 2.75
**133** CD321 40c multicolored 4.25 4.25

### WHO Headquarters Issue
Common Design Type with Royal Cipher and "RF" Replacing Queen's Portrait

**1966, Sept. 20 Litho. *Perf. 14***
**134** CD322 25c multicolored 3.75 3.75
**135** CD322 60c multicolored 5.00 5.00

### UNESCO Anniversary Issue
Common Design Type with Royal Cipher and "RF" Replacing Queen's Portrait

**1966, Dec. 1 Litho. *Perf. 14***
**136** CD323 15c "Education" 1.50 1.50
**137** CD323 30c "Science" 3.00 3.00
**138** CD323 45c "Culture" 3.25 3.25
*Nos. 136-138 (3)* 7.75 7.75

US Marine, Australian Soldier and Map of South Pacific War Zone — A19

Designs: 15c, The coast watchers. 60c, Australian cruiser Canberra. 1fr, Flying fortress taking off from Bauer Field, and view of Vila.

***Perf. 14x13***
**1967, Sept. 26 Photo. Unwmk.**
**139** A19 15c lt blue & multi 1.10 1.10
**140** A19 25c yellow & multi 1.25 1.25
**141** A19 60c multicolored 2.00 2.00
**142** A19 1fr pale salmon & multi 2.50 2.50
*Nos. 139-142 (4)* 6.85 6.85

25th anniv. of the Allied Forces' campaign in the South Pacific War Zone.

L. A. de Bougainville, Ship's Figurehead and Bougainvillea — A20

15c, Globe & world map. 25c, Ships La Boudeuse & L'Etoile & map of Bougainville Strait.

**1968, May 23 Engr. *Perf. 13***
**143** A20 15c ver, emer & dl vio .45 .45
**144** A20 25c ultra, ol & brn .65 .65
**145** A20 60c mag, grn & brn 1.15 1.15
*Nos. 143-145 (3)* 2.25 2.25

200th anniv. of Louis Antoine de Bougainville's (1729-1811) voyage around the world.

### Type of 1963-67 Redrawn, "E II R" at left, "RF" at Right
Designs as before.

**1968, Aug. 5 Photo. *Perf. 12½***
**146** A12 10c brt grn, org brn & dk brn 1.00 1.00
**147** A12 20c brt bl, gray & citron 1.40 1.40

***Perf. 14***
**148** A12 3fr org brn, brt grn & blk 9.50 9.50
*Nos. 146-148 (3)* 11.90 11.90

On Nos. 113, 115 and 122 "RF" is at left and "E II R" is at right.
For surcharge see No. 160.

Concorde Supersonic Airliner — A21

Design: 25c, Concorde seen from above.

**1968, Oct. 9 Litho. *Perf. 14x13½***
**149** A21 25c vio bl, red & lt bl 3.00 2.50
**150** A21 60c red, ultra & blk 6.50 5.00

Development of the Concorde supersonic airliner, a joint Anglo-French project.

Kauri Pine — A22

**1969, June 30 *Perf. 14½x14***
**151** A22 20c brown & multi .60 .60

New Hebrides timber industry. Issued in sheets of 9 (3x3) on simulated wood grain background.

Relay Race, British and French Flags — A23

**1969, Aug. 13 Photo. *Perf. 12½x13***
**152** A23 25c shown .85 .85
**153** A23 1fr Runner at right 1.60 1.60

3rd South Pacific Games, Port Moresby, Papua and New Guinea, Aug. 13-23.

Land Diver at Start, Pentecost Island — A24

**1969, Oct. 15 Litho. *Perf. 12½***

154 A24 15c shown .50 .50
155 A24 25c Diver in mid-air .60 .60
156 A24 1fr Diver near ground 2.00 2.00
*Nos. 154-156 (3)* 3.10 3.10

Land divers of Pentecost Island.

UPU Headquarters and Monument, Bern — A25

**1970, May 20 Engr. *Perf. 13***

157 A25 1.05fr org, lilac & slate 1.00 1.00

New UPU Headquarters, Bern.

Charles de Gaulle — A26

**1970, July 20 Photo. *Perf. 13***

158 A26 65c brown & multi 2.00 2.00
159 A26 1.10fr dp blue & multi 2.75 2.75

Rallying of the Free French, 30th anniv. For overprints see Nos. 163-164.

No. 147 Surcharged

**1970, Oct. 15 Photo. *Perf. 12½***

160 A12 35c on 20c multi .50 *.60*

Virgin and Child, by Giovanni Bellini — A27

50c, Virgin and Child, by Giovanni Cima.

**1970, Nov. 30 Litho. *Perf. 14½x14***

161 A27 15c tan & multi .25 .25
162 A27 50c lt grn & multi .50 .35

Christmas. See Nos. 186-187.

Nos. 158-159 Overprinted in Gold and Black

**1971, Jan. 19 Photo. *Perf. 13***

163 A26 65c brown & multi .85 .85
164 A26 1.10fr dp blue & multi 2.00 2.00

In memory of Gen. Charles de Gaulle (1890-1970), President of France.

Soccer — A28

Design: 65c, Basketball, vert.

**1971, July 13 Photo. *Perf. 12½***

165 A28 20c multicolored .75 .75
166 A28 65c multicolored 1.25 1.25

4th South Pacific Games, Papeete, French Polynesia, Sept. 8-19.

Breadfruit Tree and Fruit, Society Arms — A29

***Perf. 14½x14***

**1971, Sept. 7 Litho. Unwmk.**

167 A29 65c multicolored 1.75 1.75

Expedition of the Royal Society of London for the Advancement of Science to study vegetation and fauna, July 1-October.

Adoration of the Shepherds, by Louis Le Nain — A30

Christmas: 50c, Adoration of the Shepherds, by Jacopo Tintoretto.

**1971, Nov. 23 *Perf. 14x13½***

168 A30 25c lt green & multi .60 .60
169 A30 50c lt blue & multi .90 .90

Drover Mk III — A31

Airplanes: 25c, Sandringham seaplane. 30c, Dragon Rapide. 65c, Caravelle.

**1972, Feb. 29 Photo. *Perf. 13½x13***

170 A31 20c lt green & multi .90 .90
171 A31 25c ultra & multi 1.00 1.00
172 A31 30c orange & multi 1.10 1.10
173 A31 65c dk blue & multi 3.00 3.00
*Nos. 170-173 (4)* 6.00 6.00

Headdress, South Malekula — A32

Baker's Pigeon — A33

Artifacts: 15c, Slit gong and carved figure, North Ambrym. 1fr, Carved figures, North Ambrym. 3fr, Ceremonial headdress, South Malekula.

Birds: 20c, Red-headed parrot-finch. 35c, Chestnut-bellied kingfisher. 2fr, Green palm lorikeet.

Sea Shells: 25c, Cribraria fischeri. 30c, Oliva rubrolabiata. 65c, Strombus plicatus. 5fr, Turbo marmoratus.

**1972, July 24 Photo. *Perf. 12½x13***

174 A32 5c plum & multi .30 *1.00*
175 A33 10c blue & multi 2.25 *1.75*
176 A32 15c red & multi .35 1.00
177 A33 20c org brn & multi 2.50 1.50
178 A32 25c dp blue & multi 1.75 1.60
179 A32 30c dk green & multi 1.75 *1.75*
180 A33 35c gray bl & multi 3.00 2.50
181 A32 65c dk green & multi 3.75 3.00
182 A32 1fr orange & multi 2.75 *4.25*
183 A33 2fr multicolored 25.00 15.00
184 A32 3fr yellow & multi 9.75 *17.50*
185 A32 5fr pink & multi 21.00 *30.00*
*Nos. 174-185 (12)* 74.15 *80.85*

For overprints see Nos. 200-201. For surcharges see Nos. 236-247.

**Christmas Type of 1970**

Christmas: 25c, Adoration of the Magi (detail), by Bartholomaeus Spranger. 70c, Virgin and Child, by Jan Provoost.

**1972, Sept. 25 Litho. *Perf. 14x13½***

186 A27 25c lt green & multi .50 .50
187 A27 70c lt blue & multi .75 .75

**Silver Wedding Issue**

Common Design Type With Royal Cipher and "RF" (at Right)

Design: Elizabeth II and Prince Philip.

***Perf. 14x14½***

**1972, Nov. 20 Photo. Wmk. 314**

188 CD324 35c violet blk & multi .45 .45
189 CD324 65c olive & multi .60 .60

Dendrobium Teretifolium — A35

Orchids: 30c, Ephemerantha comata. 35c, Spathoglottis petri. 65c, Dendrobium mohlianum.

**Unwmk.**

**1973, Feb. 26 Litho. *Perf. 14***

190 A35 25c blue vio & multi 2.00 2.00
191 A35 30c multicolored 2.00 2.00
192 A35 35c violet & multi 3.00 3.00
193 A35 65c dk green & multi 5.75 5.75
*Nos. 190-193 (4)* 12.75 12.75

New Wharf, Vila — A36

**1973, May 14 Litho. *Perf. 14***

194 A36 25c shown .85 .85
195 A36 70c New Wharf, horiz. 1.50 1.50

New wharf at Vila, completed Nov. 1972.

Wild Horses, Tanna A37

Design: 70c, Yasur Volcano, Tanna.

**1973, Aug. 13 Photo. *Perf. 13x13½***

196 A37 35c multicolored 2.75 2.75
197 A37 70c multicolored 3.50 3.50

Christmas A38

35c, Mother and Child, by Marcel Moutouh. 70c, Star over Lagoon, by Tatin D'Avesnieres.

**1973, Nov. 19 Litho. *Perf. 14x13½***

198 A38 35c tan & multi .60 .60
199 A38 70c lil rose & multi .90 .90

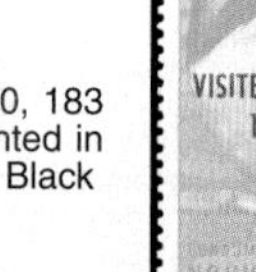


Nos. 180, 183 Overprinted in Red or Black

**1974, Feb. 11 Photo. *Perf. 12½x13***

200 A33 35c multi (R) 3.00 1.10
201 A33 2fr multi (B) 8.50 7.50

Visit of British Royal Family, Feb. 15-16.

Pacific Dove A39

Designs: 35c, Night swallowtail. 70c, Green sea turtle. 1.15fr, Flying fox.

**1974, Feb. 11** ***Perf. 13x12½***

| | | | | |
|---|---|---|---|---|
| **202** | A39 | 25c gray & multi | 4.50 | 3.00 |
| **203** | A39 | 35c gray & multi | 5.50 | 2.50 |
| **204** | A39 | 70c gray & multi | 6.75 | 4.75 |
| **205** | A39 | 1.15fr gray & multi | 7.75 | 9.50 |
| | | *Nos. 202-205 (4)* | 24.50 | 19.75 |

Nature conservation.

Old Post Office, Vila — A40

Design: 70c, New Post Office.

**Unwmk.**

**1974, May 6** **Photo.** ***Perf. 12***

| | | | | |
|---|---|---|---|---|
| **206** | A40 | 35c blue & multi | .60 | .50 |
| **207** | A40 | 70c red & multi | 1.10 | .90 |
| *a.* | | Pair, #206-207 | 2.25 | 2.25 |

Opening of New Post Office, May, 1974.

Capt. Cook and Tanna Island A41

Designs: No. 209, William Wales and boat landing on island. No. 210, William Hodges painting islanders and landscape. 1.15fr, Capt. Cook, "Resolution" and map of New Hebrides.

**1974, Aug. 1** **Litho.** ***Perf. 13***

**Size: 40x25mm**

| | | | | |
|---|---|---|---|---|
| **208** | A41 | 35c multicolored | 4.50 | 2.75 |
| **209** | A41 | 35c multicolored | 4.50 | 2.75 |
| **210** | A41 | 35c multicolored | 4.50 | 2.75 |
| *a.* | | Strip of 3, #208-210 | 18.00 | 18.00 |

**Size: 58x34mm**

***Perf. 11***

| | | | | |
|---|---|---|---|---|
| **211** | A41 | 1.15fr lilac & multi | 7.50 | 7.50 |

Bicentenary of the discovery of the New Hebrides by Capt. James Cook.

No. 210a has a continuous design.

Exchange of Letters, UPU Emblem A42

**1974, Oct. 9** **Photo.** ***Perf. 13x12½***

| | | | | |
|---|---|---|---|---|
| **212** | A42 | 70c multicolored | 1.50 | 1.50 |

Centenary of Universal Postal Union.

Nativity, by Gerard Van Honthorst — A43

Christmas: 35c, Adoration of the Kings, by Velazquez, vert.

**1974, Nov. 14** **Litho.** ***Perf. 13½***

| | | | | |
|---|---|---|---|---|
| **213** | A43 | 35c multicolored | .25 | .25 |
| **214** | A43 | 70c multicolored | .50 | .50 |

Charolais Bull — A44

**1975, Apr. 29** **Engr.** ***Perf. 13***

| | | | | |
|---|---|---|---|---|
| **215** | A44 | 10fr multicolored | 27.50 | *30.00* |

For surcharge see No. 248.

Nordjamb Emblem, Kayaks — A45

**1975, Aug. 5** **Litho.** ***Perf. 14x13½***

| | | | | |
|---|---|---|---|---|
| **216** | A45 | 25c shown | .60 | .50 |
| **217** | A45 | 35c Camp cooks | .80 | .70 |
| **218** | A45 | 1fr Map makers | 1.75 | 1.75 |
| **219** | A45 | 5fr Fishermen | 8.50 | 8.50 |
| | | *Nos. 216-219 (4)* | 11.65 | 11.45 |

Nordjamb 75, 14th Boy Scout Jamboree, Lillehammer, Norway, July 29-Aug. 7.

Pitti Madonna, by Michelangelo A46

Christmas (After Michelangelo): 70c, Bruges Madonna. 2.50fr, Taddei Madonna.

**1975, Nov. 11** **Litho.** ***Perf. 14½x14***

| | | | | |
|---|---|---|---|---|
| **220** | A46 | 35c multicolored | .55 | .55 |
| **221** | A46 | 70c brown & multi | .70 | .70 |
| **222** | A46 | 2.50fr blue & multi | 2.75 | 2.75 |
| | | *Nos. 220-222 (3)* | 4.00 | 4.00 |

Concorde, Air France Colors and Emblem — A47

**1976, Jan. 30** **Typo.** ***Perf. 13***

| | | | | |
|---|---|---|---|---|
| **223** | A47 | 5fr blue & multi | 13.50 | 13.50 |

1st commercial flight of supersonic jet Concorde from Paris to Rio, Jan. 21.

Telephones, 1876 and 1976 — A48

Designs: 70c, Alexander Graham Bell. 1.15fr, Nouméa Earth Station and satellite.

**1976, Mar. 31** **Photo.** ***Perf. 13***

| | | | | |
|---|---|---|---|---|
| **224** | A48 | 25c black, car & bl | .50 | .50 |
| **225** | A48 | 70c black & multi | 1.50 | 1.50 |
| **226** | A48 | 1.15fr blk, org & vio bl | 2.00 | 2.00 |
| | | *Nos. 224-226 (3)* | 4.00 | 4.00 |

Centenary of first telephone call by Alexander Graham Bell, Mar. 10, 1876.

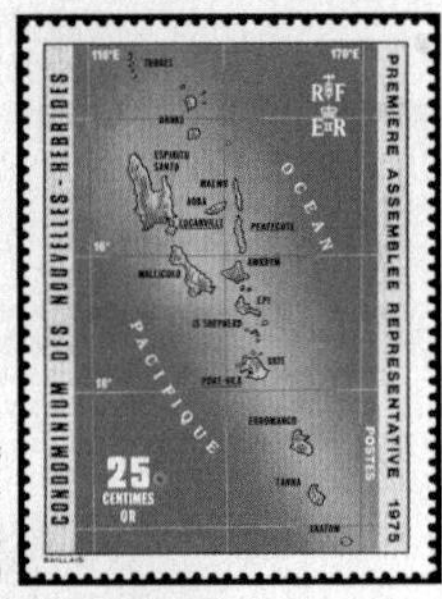


Map of New Hebrides A49

View of Luganville (Santo) A50

Design: 2fr, View of Vila.

**1976, June 29** **Unwmk.** ***Perf. 13***

| | | | | |
|---|---|---|---|---|
| **227** | A49 | 25c blue & multi | .55 | .45 |
| **228** | A50 | 1fr multicolored | 1.25 | 1.00 |
| **229** | A50 | 2fr multicolored | 3.00 | 3.00 |
| | | *Nos. 227-229 (3)* | 4.80 | 4.45 |

Opening of first Representative Assembly, June 29, 1976 (25c); first Luganville (Santo) Municipal Council (1fr); first Vila Municipal Council (2fr).

Nos. 228-229 exist with lower inscription reading "Premiere Assemblée Representative 1975" instead of "Premiere Municipalite de Luganville" on 1fr and "Premiere Municipalite de Port-Vila" on 2fr.

For surcharges, see No. 283-284.

Flight into Egypt, by Francisco Vieira Lusitano — A51

Portuguese 16th Cent. Paintings: 70c, Adoration of the Shepherds. 2.50fr, Adoration of the Kings.

**1976, Nov. 8** **Litho.** ***Perf. 14***

| | | | | |
|---|---|---|---|---|
| **230** | A51 | 35c purple & multi | .45 | .35 |
| **231** | A51 | 70c blue & multi | .65 | .55 |
| **232** | A51 | 2.50fr multicolored | 2.00 | 2.00 |
| | | *Nos. 230-232 (3)* | 3.10 | 2.90 |

Christmas 1976.

Queen's Visit, 1974 — A52

70c, Imperial State crown. 2fr, The blessing.

**1977, Feb. 7** **Litho.** ***Perf. 14x13½***

| | | | | |
|---|---|---|---|---|
| **233** | A52 | 35c lt green & multi | .35 | .25 |
| **234** | A52 | 70c blue & multi | .55 | .50 |
| **235** | A52 | 2fr pink & multi | 1.00 | 1.00 |
| | | *Nos. 233-235 (3)* | 1.90 | 1.75 |

Reign of Queen Elizabeth II, 25th anniv.

**Nos. 174-185, 215 Surcharged**

**Paris Overprints**

**1977, July 1** **Photo.** ***Perf. 12½x13***

| | | | | |
|---|---|---|---|---|
| **236** | A32 | 5fr on 5c multi | 1.75 | 1.75 |
| **237** | A33 | 10fr on 10c multi | 2.75 | 1.50 |
| **238** | A32 | 15fr on 15c multi | 1.50 | 1.50 |
| **239** | A33 | 20fr on 20c multi | 3.00 | 1.75 |
| **240** | A32 | 25fr on 25c multi | 2.75 | 2.00 |
| **241** | A32 | 30fr on 30c multi | 2.75 | 2.50 |
| **242** | A33 | 35fr on 35c multi | 4.50 | 4.00 |
| **243** | A32 | 40fr on 65c multi | 3.50 | 3.00 |
| **244** | A32 | 50fr on 1fr multi | 2.25 | *3.00* |
| **245** | A33 | 70fr on 2fr multi | 7.50 | 4.00 |
| **246** | A32 | 100fr on 3fr multi | 3.00 | *6.00* |
| **247** | A32 | 200fr on 5fr multi | 10.00 | *25.00* |

**Engr.**

***Perf. 13***

| | | | | |
|---|---|---|---|---|
| **248** | A44 | 500fr on 10fr multi | 20.00 | *42.50* |
| | | *Nos. 236-248 (13)* | 65.25 | *98.50* |

**Nos. 174/185, 215 Surcharged with New Value, "FNH" and Bars**

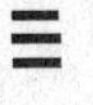

FNH a FNH b FNH c 25 FNH d

**Port Vila Overprints**

Two settings of 35fr and 200fr surcharges: type 1, 1.4mm between new value and "FNH"; type 2, 2.1mm between value and "FNH."

***Perf. 12½x13***

**1977-78** **Photo.** **Unwmk.**

| | | | | |
|---|---|---|---|---|
| *236a* | A32 | 5fr on 5c (a) | 3.00 | 3.00 |
| *237a* | A33 | 10fr on 10c (b) | 3.50 | 2.50 |
| *238a* | A32 | 15fr on 15c (c) | 5.00 | 3.25 |
| *240a* | A32 | 25fr on 25c (d) | 120.00 | 80.00 |
| *241a* | A32 | 30fr on 30c (d) | 250.00 | 80.00 |

*242a* A33 35fr on 35c (d), type 1 8.00 6.50
**b.** Type 2 37.50 22.50
*243a* A32 40fr on 65c (d) 7.00 7.00
*244a* A32 50fr on 1fr multi 80.00
*245a* A33 70fr on 2fr multi 80.00
*246a* A32 100fr on 3fr multi 80.00
*247a* A32 200fr on 5fr (d), type 1 55.00 *65.00*
**b.** Type 2 65.00 65.00
*248a* A44 500fr on 10fr (d) 65.00 *75.00*
*Nos. 236a-248a (12)* 756.50 322.25

The 50fr, 70fr and 100fr values were sold only through the philatelic bureau.

Issued: 15fr, 7/18; 10fr, 7/20; 5fr, 8/10#247a, 8/22; 25fr, 30fr, #242a, 9/10; 40fr, 9/12; 500fr, 9/14; #242b, 1/6/78; #247b, 1/13/78.

Espiritu Santo and Cattle — A53

Designs: 5fr, Erromango Island and Kaori tree. 10fr, Archipelago and man making copra. 20fr, Efate Island and Post Office, Vila. 25fr, Malakula Island and headdresses. 30fr, Aoba and Maewo Islands and pig tusks. 35fr, Pentecost Island and land diving. 40fr, Tanna Island and Prophet John Frum's Red Cross. 50fr, Shepherd Island and canoe with sail. 70fr, Banks Island and dancers. 100fr, Ambrym Island and carvings. 200fr, Aneityum Island and decorated baskets. 500fr, Torres Islands and fishing with bow and arrow.

**1977-78 Litho. *Perf. 14***

**258** A53 5fr multicolored .25 .25
**259** A53 10fr multicolored .40 .70
**260** A53 15fr multicolored .50 .70
**261** A53 20fr multicolored .60 .90
**262** A53 25fr multicolored .75 1.00
**263** A53 30fr multicolored 1.00 1.10
**264** A53 35fr multicolored 1.10 1.10
**265** A53 40fr multicolored 1.25 1.25
**266** A53 50fr multicolored 1.50 2.00
**267** A53 70fr multicolored 2.50 3.25
**268** A53 100fr multicolored 3.50 5.00
**269** A53 200fr multicolored 6.75 10.00
**270** A53 500fr multicolored 14.00 24.00
*Nos. 258-270 (13)* 34.10 51.25

Issued: 5fr, 20fr, 50fr, 100fr, 200fr, 9/7/77; 15fr, 25fr, 30fr, 40fr, 11/23/77; 10fr, 35fr, 70fr, 500fr, 5/9/78.

Tempi Madonna, by Raphael — A54

Christmas: 15fr, Virgin and Child, by Gerard David. 30fr, Virgin and Child, by Pompeo Batoni.

**1977, Dec. 8 Litho. *Perf. 12***

**271** A54 10fr multicolored .35 .35
**272** A54 15fr multicolored .50 .35
**273** A54 30fr multicolored .90 .90
*Nos. 271-273 (3)* 1.75 1.60

British Airways Concorde over New York — A55

Designs: 20fr, British Airways Concorde over London. 30fr, Air France Concorde over Washington. 40fr, Air France Concorde over Paris.

**1978, May 9 Litho. *Perf. 14***

**274** A55 10fr multicolored 2.00 1.50
**275** A55 20fr multicolored 2.75 1.75
**276** A55 30fr multicolored 3.25 2.25
**277** A55 40fr multicolored 4.50 3.50
*Nos. 274-277 (4)* 12.50 9.00

**Elizabeth II Coronation Anniversary Issue**

Common Design Types
Souvenir Sheet

**1978, June 2 Litho. *Perf. 15***

**278** Sheet of 6 3.50 3.50
**a.** CD326 40fr White Horse of Hanover .25 .25
**b.** CD327 40fr Elizabeth II .25 .25
**c.** CD328 40fr Gallic cock .25 .25

No. 278 contains 2 se-tenant strips of Nos. 278a-278c, separated by horizontal gutter with commemorative and descriptive inscriptions and showing central part of coronation procession with coach.

Virgin and Child, by Dürer — A58

Christmas, Paintings by Albrecht Durer (1471-1528): 15fr, Virgin and Child with St. Anne. 30fr, Virgin and Child with Goldfinch. 40fr, Virgin and Child with Pear.

**1978, Dec. 1 Litho. *Perf. 14x13½***

**279** A58 10fr multicolored .25 .25
**280** A58 15fr multicolored .25 .25
**281** A58 30fr multicolored .25 .25
**282** A58 40fr multicolored .35 .35
*Nos. 279-282 (4)* 1.10 1.10

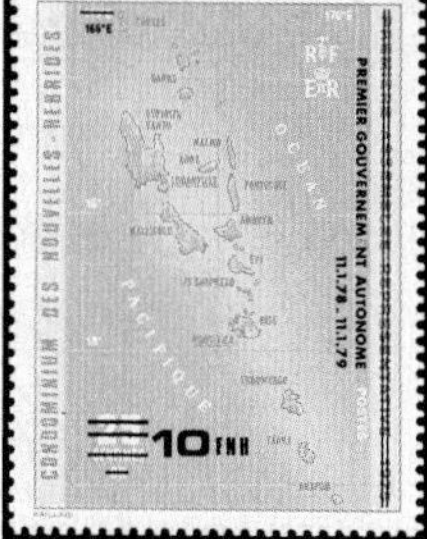


No. 227 and Type of 1976 Surcharged

**1979, Jan. 11 Photo. *Perf. 13***

**283** A49 10fr on 25c bl & multi 1.00 1.00
**284** A49 40fr on 25c lt grn & multi 2.00 2.00

First anniv. of Internal Self-Government.

New Hebrides No. 155 and Hill Statue A59

Rowland Hill and New Hebrides Stamps: 10fr, No. 55. 40fr, No. 46.

**1979, Sept. 10 Litho. *Perf. 14***

**285** A59 10fr multicolored .25 .25
**286** A59 20fr multicolored .25 .25
**287** A59 40fr multicolored .40 .40
*Nos. 285-287 (3)* .90 .90

Sir Rowland Hill (1795-1879), originator of penny postage. A souvenir sheet containing No. 286 and British issue No. 266 is listed as No. 266a under New Hebrides, British issues.

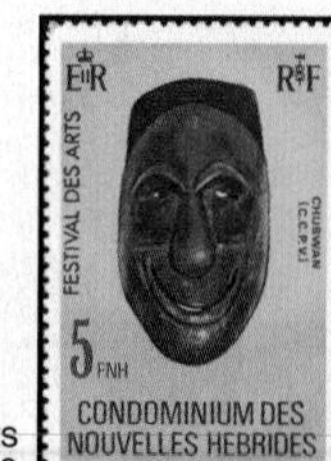


Arts Festival — A60

Designs: 10fr, Clubs and spears. 20fr, Ritual puppet. 40fr, Headdress.

**1979, Nov. 16 Litho. *Perf. 14***

**288** A60 5fr multicolored .25 .25
**289** A60 10fr multicolored .25 .25
**290** A60 20fr multicolored .40 .40
**291** A60 40fr multicolored .65 .65
*Nos. 288-291 (4)* 1.55 1.55

Church, IYC Emblem A61

IYC Emblem, Children's Drawings: 10fr, Father Christmas. 20fr, Cross and Bible, vert. 40fr, Stars, candle and Santa Claus, vert.

**1979, Dec. 4 *Perf. 13x13½***

**292** A61 5fr multicolored .70 .60
**293** A61 10fr multicolored 1.00 .60
**294** A61 20fr multicolored 1.40 .90
**295** A61 40fr multicolored 1.75 1.75
*Nos. 292-295 (4)* 4.85 3.85

Christmas; Intl. Year of the Child.

White-bellied Honeyeater — A62

20fr, Scarlet robins. 30fr, Yellow white-eyes. 40fr, Fan-tailed brush cuckoo.

**1980, Feb. 27 Litho. *Perf. 14***

**296** A62 10fr shown .85 .85
**297** A62 20fr multi 1.40 1.60
**298** A62 30fr multi 2.75 2.75
**299** A62 40fr multi 3.25 3.25
*Nos. 296-299 (4)* 8.25 8.45

Stamps of Vanuatu replaced those of New Hebrides in 1980.

---

## POSTAGE DUE STAMPS

### French Issues

Nos. 45-46, 48, 50, 52 Overprinted

**1925 Wmk. R F in Sheet *Perf. 14***

**J1** A4 10c green 50.00 4.75
**J2** A4 20c greenish gray 50.00 4.75
**J3** A4 30c carmine 50.00 4.75
**J4** A4 50c ultramarine 50.00 4.75
**J5** A4 1fr carmine, *blue* 50.00 4.75
*Nos. J1-J5 (5)* 250.00 23.75

**Nos. 55-56, 58, 61, 63 Overprinted**

**1938 *Perf. 12***

**J6** A6 5c green 11.00 *65.00*
**J7** A6 10c dark orange 12.50 *65.00*
**J8** A6 20c rose red 14.50 *70.00*
**J9** A6 40c olive green 30.00 *140.00*
**J10** A6 1fr dark car, *green* 35.00 *160.00*
*Nos. J6-J10 (5)* 103.00 *500.00*

**Nos. J6-J10 Overprinted like Nos. 67-78**

**1941**

**J11** A6 5c green 11.00 *42.50*
**J12** A6 10c dark orange 11.00 *42.50*
**J13** A6 20c rose red 11.00 *42.50*
**J14** A6 40c olive green 13.00 *42.50*
**J15** A6 1fr dk car, *green* 12.00 *42.50*
*Nos. J11-J15 (5)* 58.00 *212.50*

**Catalogue values for unused stamps in this section, from this point to the end of the section, are for Never Hinged items.**

Nos. 83-84, 86, 89, 91 Overprinted

**1953 Unwmk. *Perf. 12½***

**J16** A8 5c green 6.00 *13.50*
**J17** A8 10c red 8.00 *18.00*
**J18** A8 20c ultramarine 14.00 *30.00*
**J19** A8 40c black brown 19.00 *55.00*
**J20** A8 1fr deep orange 27.50 *60.00*
*Nos. J16-J20 (5)* 74.50 *176.50*

**Nos. 98-99, 101, 104, 106 Overprinted "TIMBRE-TAXE"**

**Wmk. R F in Sheet**

**1957 Engr. *Perf. 13½x13***

**J21** A10 5c green 1.25 *3.50*
**J22** A10 10c red 1.50 *4.25*
**J23** A10 20c ultramarine 1.75 *5.25*
**J24** A10 40c sepia 6.75 *19.00*
**J25** A10 1fr orange 16.00 *45.00*
*Nos. J21-J25 (5)* 27.25 *77.00*

## NEW REPUBLIC

'nü ri-'pə-blik

LOCATION — In South Africa, located in the northern part of the present province of Natal
GOVT. — A former Republic
CAPITAL — Vryheid

New Republic was created in 1884 by Boer adventurers from Transvaal who proclaimed Dinizulu king of Zululand and claimed as their reward a large tract of country as their own, which they called New Republic. This area was excepted when Great Britain annexed Zululand in 1887, but New Republic became a part of Transvaal in 1888 and was included in the Union of South Africa.

12 Pence = 1 Shilling
20 Shillings = 1 Pound

New Republic stamps were individually handstamped on gummed and perforated sheets of paper. Naturally many of the impressions are misaligned and touch or intersect the perforations. Values are for stamps with good color and, for Nos. 37-64, sharp embossing. The alignment does not materially alter the value of the stamp.

A1

### Handstamped

**1886 Unwmk. *Perf. 11½***

**1** A1 1p violet, *yel* 20.00 22.50
 *a.* "d" omitted, in pair with normal 2,750.
**1A** A1 1p black, *yel* *3,250.*
**2** A1 2p violet, *yel* 22.50 *27.50*
 *a.* "d" omitterd 4,750.
 *b.* As "a", without date
 *c.* tete-beche pair —
**3** A1 3p violet, *yel* 50.00 *60.00*
 *a.* Double impression
 *b.* "d" omitted (Oct. 13 '86) *4,750.*
 *c.* Tete-beche pair —
**4** A1 4p violet, *yel* 85.00
 *a.* Without date
 *b.* "4d" omitted, in pair with normal *3,000.*
**5** A1 6p violet, *yel* 65.00 *70.00*
 *a.* Double impression
 *b.* "6d" omitted in pair with normal —
**6** A1 9p violet, *yel* 125.00
**7** A1 1sh violet, *yel* 125.00
 *a.* "1/S" 800.00
 *b.* "1s" omitted in pair with normal —
**8** A1 1/6 violet, *yel* 120.00
 *a.* Without date
 *b.* "1s6d" 600.00
 *c.* as "b", tete-beche pair —
 *d.* as "b", "d" omitted 150.00
**9** A1 2sh violet, *yel* 75.00
 *a.* tete-beche pair 875.00
**10** A1 2sh6p violet, *yel* 190.00
 *a.* Without date
 *b.* "2/6" 190.00
**11** A1 4sh violet, *yel*
 *a.* "4/s" 825.00
**12** A1 5sh violet, *yel* 55.00 *65.00*
 *a.* Without date
 *b.* "s" omitted, in pair with normal 3,500.
**13** A1 5/6 violet, *yel* 300.00
 *a.* "5s6d" 550.00
**14** A1 7sh6p violet, *yel* 175.00
 *a.* "7/6" 250.00
**15** A1 10sh violet, *yel* 225.00 *275.00*
 *a.* Tete-beche pair —
**16** A1 10sh6p violet, *yel* 250.00
 *b.* "d" omitted 225.00
**16A** A1 13sh violet, *yel* 600.00
**17** A1 £1 violet, *yel* 150.00
 *a.* Tete-beche pair 650.00
**18** A1 30sh violet, *yel* 150.00
 *a.* tete-beche pair 750.00

### Granite Paper

**19** A1 1p violet, *gray* 30.00 *35.00*
 *a.* "d" omitted 750.00
 *b.* "1" omitted in pair with normal —
**20** A1 2p violet, *gray* 22.50 *25.00*
 *a.* "ZUID AFRIKA" omitted
 *b.* "d" omitted *1,350.*
 *c.* "2d." omitted in pair with normal —
**21** A1 3p violet, *gray* 40.00 37.50
 *a.* tete-beche pair 375.00
**22** A1 4p violet, *gray* 55.00 *60.00*
**23** A1 6p violet, *gray* 95.00 *95.00*
 *a.* "6" omitted in pair with normal *2,750.*
**24** A1 9p violet, *gray* 150.00
**25** A1 1sh violet, *gray* 45.00 50.00
 *a.* tete-beche pair 425.00
 *b.* "1s." omitted in pair with normal 2,750.
**26** A1 1sh6p violet, *gray* 125.00
 *a.* tete-beche pair 750.00
 *b.* "1/6" 190.00
 *c.* "d" omitted —
**27** A1 2sh violet, *gray* 150.00
 *a.* "2s." omitted in pair with normal *3,250.*
**28** A1 2sh6p violet, *gray* 3,500.
 *a.* "2/6" 250.00
**29** A1 4sh violet, *gray* 525.00
**30** A1 5sh6p violet, *gray* 425.00
 *a.* "5/6" 325.00
 *b.* As "a," "/" omitted —
 *c.* As "a," "6" omitted *4,500.*
**31** A1 7/6 violet, *gray* 325.00
 *a.* 7s. 6d violet gray 450.00
**32** A1 10sh violet, *gray* 225.00 225.00
 *a.* tete-beche pair 525.00
 *f.* "s" omitted —
**32B** A1 10sh 6p vio, *gray* 275.00
 *c.* Without date —
 *d.* tete-beche pair
 *e.* "d" omitted 600.00
**33** A1 12sh violet, *gray* 450.00
**34** A1 13sh violet, *gray* 550.00
**35** A1 £1 violet, *gray* 375.00
**36** A1 30sh violet, *gray* 325.00

### Same with Embossed Arms

**37** A1 1p violet, *yel* 22.50 *25.00*
 *a.* Arms inverted 30.00 35.00
 *b.* Arms tete-beche, pair 125.00 *135.00*
 *c.* tete-beche pair *950.00*
**38** A1 2p violet, *yel* 27.50 *30.00*
 *a.* Arms inverted 30.00 35.00
**39** A1 4p violet, *yel* 80.00 85.00
 *a.* Arms inverted 125.00 87.50
 *b.* Arms tete-beche, pair 350.00
**40** A1 6p violet, *yel* 375.00

### Granite Paper

**41** A1 1p violet, *gray* 30.00 30.00
 *a.* Imperf. vert., pair
 *b.* Arms inverted 40.00 45.00
 *c.* Arms tete-beche, pair 550.00
**42** A1 2p violet, *gray* 30.00 30.00
 *a.* Imperf. horiz., pair
 *b.* Arms inverted 55.00 *65.00*
 *c.* Arms tete-beche, pair 550.00

There were several printings of the above stamps and the date upon them varies from "JAN 86" and "7 JAN 86" to "20 JAN 87."

Nos. 7, 8, 10, 13, 14, 26, 28 and 30 have the denomination expressed in two ways. Example: "1s 6d" or "1/6."

A2

**1887 Arms Embossed**

**43** A2 3p violet, *yel* 27.50 *27.50*
 *a.* Arms inverted 30.00 32.50
 *b.* tete-beche pair 375.00 450.00
 *c.* Imperf. vert., pair
 *d.* Arms omitted
 *e.* Arms tete-beche, pair 225.00
 *f.* Arms sideways 375.00
**44** A2 4p violet, *yel* 20.00 20.00
 *a.* Arms inverted 25.00 25.00
**45** A2 6p violet, *yel* 17.50 *17.50*
 *a.* Arms inverted 50.00 50.00
 *b.* Arms omitted 95.00
 *c.* Arms tete-beche, pair 375.00
**46** A2 9p violet, *yel* 17.50 *20.00*
 *a.* Arms inverted 250.00
 *b.* Arms tete-beche, pair 425.00
**47** A2 1sh violet, *yel* 20.00 *20.00*
 *a.* Arms inverted 75.00
 *b.* Arms omitted
**48** A2 1sh6p violet, *yel* 55.00 45.00
**49** A2 2sh violet, *yel* 42.50 *45.00*
 *a.* Arms inverted 65.00 60.00
 *b.* Arms omitted 150.00
**50** A2 2sh6p violet, *yel* 40.00 *40.00*
 *a.* Arms inverted 45.00 *45.00*
**50B** A2 3sh violet, *yel* 65.00 65.00
 *c.* Arms inverted 80.00 *80.00*
 *d.* Arms tete-beche, pair 600.00
**51** A2 4sh violet, *yel* 650.00
 *a.* Arms omitted —
 *b.* "4/s" 65.00 65.00
 *c.* As "b," arms omitted 275.00
**51B** A2 4/s violet, *yel*
 *a.* Arms omitted
**52** A2 5sh violet, *yel* 60.00 60.00
 *a.* Imperf. vert., pair
 *b.* Arms inverted — 175.00
**53** A2 5sh6p violet, *yel* 30.00 *35.00*
**54** A2 7sh6p violet, *yel* 35.00 *37.50*
 *a.* Arms inverted 125.00
 *b.* Arms tete-beche, pair
**55** A2 10sh violet, *yel* 32.50 *35.00*
 *a.* Arms inverted 40.00
 *b.* Arms omitted 135.00 90.00
 *c.* Imperf. vert., pair
 *d.* Arms tete-beche, pair 150.00
**56** A2 10sh6p violet, *yel* 30.00 *32.50*
 *a.* Imperf. vert., pair
 *b.* Arms inverted 55.00
 *c.* Arms omitted
**57** A2 £1 violet, *yel* 75.00 85.00
 *a.* Arms inverted 80.00
 *b.* tete-beche pair 650.00 750.00
**58** A2 30sh violet, *yel* 225.00

### Granite Paper

**59** A2 1p violet, *gray* 32.50 20.00
 *a.* Arms omitted 150.00 150.00
 *b.* Arms inverted 30.00 30.00
 *c.* Imperf. vert., pair
 *d.* tete-beche pair 650.00
 *e.* Arms tete-beche, pair —
 *f.* Arms sideways —
**60** A2 2p violet, *gray* 20.00 20.00
 *a.* Arms omitted 135.00 125.00
 *b.* Arms inverted 55.00 55.00
 *c.* tete-beche pair 425.00
 *d.* Arms tete-beche, pair —
**61** A2 3p violet, *gray* 35.00 35.00
 *a.* Arms inverted 65.00 65.00
 *b.* tete-beche pair 450.00
 *c.* Arms tete-beche, pair —
**62** A2 4p violet, *gray* 30.00 27.50
 *a.* Arms inverted 110.00
 *b.* Tete-beche, pair 375.00
 *c.* Arms tete-beche, pair 300.00
**63** A2 6p violet, *gray* 35.00 35.00
 *a.* Arms inverted 110.00
**64** A2 1sh6p violet, *gray* 50.00 42.50
 *a.* Arms inverted 175.00
 *b.* Arms tete-beche, pair 475.00
**65** A2 2/6 violet, *gray* — *1,150.*
 *Nos. 59-64 (6)* 202.50 180.00

These stamps were valid only in New Republic.

All these stamps may have been valid for postage but bona-fide canceled examples of any but the 1p and 2p stamps are quite rare.

## NEW ZEALAND

'nü 'zē-lənd

LOCATION — Group of islands in the south Pacific Ocean, southeast of Australia
GOVT. — Self-governing dominion of the British Commonwealth
AREA — 107,241 sq. mi.
POP. — 3,662,265 (1999 est.)
CAPITAL — Wellington

12 Pence = 1 Shilling
20 Shillings = 1 Pound
100 Cents = 1 Dollar (1967)

**Catalogue values for unused stamps in this country are for Never Hinged items, beginning with Scott 246 in the regular postage section, Scott AR99 in the postal-fiscal section, Scott B9 in the semi-postal section, Scott J21 in the postage due section, Scott O92 in the officials section, Scott OY29 in the Life Insurance Department section, and Scott L1 in Ross Dependency.**

### Watermarks

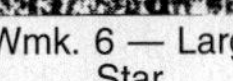
Wmk. 6 — Large Star

Wmk. 59 — N Z

Wmk. 60 — Lozenges

This watermark includes the vertical word "INVICTA" once in each quarter of the sheet.

Wmk. 61 — N Z and Star Close Together

Wmk. 62 — N Z and Star Wide Apart

On watermark 61 the margins of the sheets are watermarked "NEW ZEALAND POSTAGE" and parts of the double-lined letters of these words are frequently found on the stamps. It occasionally happens that a stamp shows no watermark whatever.

Wmk. 63 — Double-lined N Z and Star

Wmk. 64 — Small Star Only

Wmk. 253 — Multiple N Z and Star

Wmk. 387

Values for unused stamps are for examples with original gum as defined in the catalogue introduction.

Very fine examples of the perforated issues between Nos. 7a-69, AR1-AR30, J1-J11, OY1-OY9 and P1-P4 will have perforations touching the framelines or design on one or more sides due to the narrow spacing of the stamps on the plates and imperfect perforating methods.

The rouletted and serrate rouletted stamps of the same period rarely have complete roulettes and are valued as sound and showing partial roulettes. Stamps with complete roulettes range from very scarce to very rare, are seldom traded, and command great premiums.

Victoria — A1

**London Print**

**Wmk. 6**

**1855, July 20 Engr. *Imperf.***

**White Paper**

1 A1 1p dull carmine *85,000.* *20,000.*
2 A1 2p deep blue *40,000.* 775.
3 A1 1sh yellow green *55,000.* *6,000.*
*a.* Half used as 6p on cover *42,500.*

The blueing of Nos. 2 and 3 was caused by chemical action in the printing process.

**Auckland Print**

**1855-58 Blue Paper Unwmk.**

4 A1 1p orange red 14,000. 2,200.
5 Al 2p blue ('56) 4,000. 325.
6 Al 1sh green ('58) *50,000.* 4,250.
*a.* Half used as 6p on cover *27,500.*

Nos. 4-6 may be found with parts of the papermaker's name in double-lined letters.

**1857-61 Unwmk.**

**Thin Hard or Thick Soft White Paper**

7 A1 1p orange ('58) 4,000. 825.
*e.* 1p org vermilion, Wmk. 6 ('56) *36,000.*
8 A1 2p blue ('58) 1,450. 200.
9 A1 6p brown ('59) 3,000. 325.
*e.* 6p bister brown ('59) 4,250. 600.
*f.* 6p chestnut ('59) 5,000. 650.
*h.* 6p pale brown 2,850. 350.
10 A1 1sh blue grn ('61) 18,500. 2,250.
*e.* 1sh emerald ('58) 22,000. 1,850.

No. 7e is identical to a shade of No. 7. The only currently known example is a pair on a cover front. To qualify as No. 7e, a stamp must be on piece or on cover with a cancellation dated prior to 1862.

**1859 *Pin Rouletted 9-10***

*7a* A1 1p dull orange 6,000.
*8a* A1 2p blue 3,800.
*9a* A1 6p brown 4,600.
*10a* A1 1sh greenish blue 8,250.

**1859 *Serrate Rouletted 16, 18***

*7b* A1 1p dull orange 5,500.
*8b* A1 2p blue 4,100.
*9b* A1 6p brown 3,800.
*g.* 6p chestnut 7,750.
*10b* A1 1sh greenish blue 7,000.

Value for No. 10b is for a damaged stamp.

**1859 *Rouletted 7***

*7c* A1 1p dull orange *9,750.* 5,500.
*f.* Pair, imperf between —
*8c* A1 2p blue *8,250.* 3,500.
*9c* A1 6p brown *7,750.* 4,750.
*l.* Pair, imperf. between 27,500. 13,000.
*10c* A1 1sh greenish blue — 5,750.
*10d* A1 1sh emerald green — 5,250.

Roulettes are seldom complete or intact. Values for Nos. 7c to 10d are for stamps with partial roulettes.

**1862 *Perf. 13***

*7d* A1 1p orange vermilion 8,000.
*8d* A1 2p blue 8,250. 3,800.
*9d* A1 6p brown *7,000.*

See No. 26.

**1862-63 Wmk. 6 *Imperf.***

11 A1 1p orange ver 1,050. 275.00
*d.* 1p carmine vermilion ('63) 475.00 300.00
*e.* 1p vermilion 800.00 275.00
12 A1 2p deep blue 950.00 100.00
*d.* 2p slate blue 2,000. 200.00
*e.* Double impression 4,250.
*g.* 2p blue, worn plate 950.00 95.00
13 A1 3p brown lilac ('63) 750.00 95.00
14 A1 6p red brn ('63) 1,700. 115.00
*d.* 6p black brown 2,000. 130.00
*e.* 6p brown ('63) 2,100. 125.00
15 A1 1sh yellow green 2,500. 375.00
*d.* 1sh deep green 2,750. 650.00

See No. 7e.

**1862 *Pin Rouletted 9-10***

*12a* A1 2p deep blue — 3,100.
*14a* A1 6p black brown — 4,250.

**1862 *Serrate Rouletted 16, 18***

*11b* A1 1p orange vermilion 11,500. 2,400.
*12b* A1 2p blue — 1,500.
*13b* A1 3p brown lilac 6,000. 1,850.
*14b* A1 6p black brown — 2,250.
*15b* A1 1sh yellow green 4,500.

**1862 *Rouletted 7***

*11c* A1 1p vermilion 4,750. 850.
*12c* A1 2p blue 3,750. 500.
*13c* A1 3p brown lilac 3,800. 900.
*14c* A1 6p red brown 3,500. 525.
*15c* A1 1sh green 4,500. 950.

The 1p, 2p, 6p and 1sh come in two or more shades.

**1863 *Perf. 13***

16 A1 1p carmine ver 2,500. 425.00
17 A1 2p blue, no plate wear 2,500. 450.00
18 A1 3p brown lilac 3,250. 525.00
19 A1 6p red brown 1,500. 120.00
*c.* As "b," horiz. pair, imperf. btwn. —
20 A1 1sh green 2,850. 375.00

The 1p, 2p, 6p and 1sh come in two or more shades. See the *Scott Classic Specialized Catalogue.*

**1862 Unwmk. *Imperf.***

**Pelure Paper**

21 A1 1p vermilion 15,000. 2,750.
*b.* Rouletted 7 6,500.
*c.* Serrate perf.13 11,000.
22 A1 2p pale dull ultra 5,250. 1,000.
*c.* 2p gray blue 7,000. 1,000.
23 A1 3p brown lilac *50,000.*
24 A1 6p black brown 3,300. 400.
*b.* Rouletted 7 4,250. *525.*
*c.* Serrate rouletted 15 — *6,000.*
*d.* Serrate rouletted 13 *6,250.*
25 A1 1sh deep yel green 14,500. 1,100.
*b.* 1sh deep green 14,500. *1,250.*
*c.* Rouletted 7 15,000. *2,500.*
*d.* Serrate rouletted 15 *5,000.*
*e.* "Y" rouletted 18 *5,000.*

No. 23 was never placed in use.

**1863 *Perf. 13***

*21a* A1 1p vermilion 15,000. 3,500.
*22a* A1 2p gray blue 9,000. 1,100.
*b.* 2p pale dull ultramarine 8,000. 1,100.
*24a* A1 6p black brown 8,000. 400.
*25a* A1 1sh deep green 14,000. 2,100.

**1863 Unwmk. *Perf. 13***

**Thick White Paper**

26 A1 2p dull dark blue 3,750. 900.
*a.* Imperf. 2,000. 1,150.
*b.* Pin Roulette 9-10 *2,500.*

Nos. 26 and 26a differ from 8 and 8d by a white patch of wear at right of head.

**1864 Wmk. 59 *Imperf.***

27 A1 1p carmine ver 950. 325.
28 A1 2p blue 1,750. 275.
29 A1 6p red brown 5,250. 750.
30 A1 1sh green 3,250. 350.

**1864 *Rouletted 7***

*27a* A1 1p carmine vermilion 6,250. 4,000.
*28a* A1 2p blue 2,500. 775.
*29a* A1 6p deep red brown 7,250. 3,100.
*30a* A1 1sh green 4,250. 1,150.

**1864 *Perf. 12½***

27B A1 1p carmine ver 12,000. 5,000.
28B A1 2p blue 450. 80.
29B A1 6p red brown 625. 70.
30B A1 1sh dp yel green 7,750. 3,100.

**1864 *Perf. 13***

27C A1 1p carmine ver 11,500. 5,250.
*d.* "Y" roulette 18 *7,000.*
28C A1 2p blue 1,250. 210.
30C A1 1sh yellow green 2,600. 800.
*d.* Horiz. pair, imperf. btwn. *45,000.*
*e.* Perf. 6½x13 4,750.

**1864-71 Wmk. 6 *Perf. 12½***

31 A1 1p vermilion 225.00 42.50
*a.* 1p orange ('71) 600.00 95.00
*b.* 1p pale org & ver 275.00 42.50
*c.* 1p Imperf. pair 4,500. 2,750.
*d.* 1p Vert. pair, imperf. btwn.
32 A1 2p blue 225.00 22.00
*a.* 2p blue, worn plate 325.00 30.00
*b.* Horiz. pair, imperf. btwn. (#32) *5,250.*
*c.* Perf. 10x12½ 19,000.
*d.* Imperf., pair (#32) *3,250.* *2,250.*
*e.* indigo ('65), plate II 325.00 *75.00*
*f.* As "e", horiz. pair, imperf. btwn.
33 A1 3p lilac 165.00 35.00
*a.* 3p mauve 850.00 90.00
*b.* Imperf. pair (#33) *4,500.* *2,000.*
*c.* As "a", imperf. pair *5,000.* *2,000.*
*d.* 3p brown lilac 2,600. 800.00
34 A1 4p deep rose ('65) 3,250. 275.00
35 A1 4p yellow ('65) 250.00 130.00
*a.* 4p orange yellow *2,350.* 1,000.
36 A1 6p red brown 325.00 27.50
*a.* 6p brown 375.00 42.50
*b.* Horiz. pair, imperf. btwn. 3,000. 3,000.
*c.* Imperf. pair 2,250. 3,250.
37 A1 1sh yellow green 325.00 125.00
*c.* Imperf., pair 5,500. 4,250.

The 1p, 2p and 6p come in two or more shades.

*Imperforate examples of the 1p pale orange, worn plate; 2p dull blue and 6p dull chocolate brown are official reprints. Value, each $100.*

**1871 Wmk. 6 *Perf. 10***

38 A1 1p deep brown 950.00 130.00

**1871 *Perf. 12½***

39 A1 1p brown 250.00 55.00
*a.* Imperf., pair 3,500. 2,250.
*b.* Vert. pair, imperf. horiz. 3,500. 5,750.
40 A1 2p orange 190.00 31.00
*a.* 2p vermilion 225.00 35.00
*b.* Imperf., pair 3,000. *4,750.*
41 A1 6p blue 500.00 75.00
*Nos. 39-41 (3)* 940.00 161.00

**1871 *Perf. 10x12½***

42 A1 1p brown 425.00 55.00
43 A1 2p orange 300.00 42.50
44 A1 6p blue 2,400. 575.00
*c.* Vert. pair, imperf. btwn. *6,000.* —
*d.* Horiz. pair, imperf. vert. —
*Nos. 42-44 (3)* 3,125. 672.50

**1873 Wmk. 59 *Perf. 12½***

45 A1 1p brown 11,000.
46 A1 2p vermilion 1,600. 400.00
*a.* Imperf., pair *4,750.*

**1873 Unwmk. *Perf. 12½***

47 A1 1p brown 1,150. 260.00
48 A1 2p vermilion 160.00 60.00
49 A1 4p yellow orange 225.00 *2,100.*

The watermark "T.H. SAUNDERS" in double-line capitals falls on 32 of the 240 stamps in a sheet. The 1p and 2p also are known with script "WT & CO" watermark.

**1873 Wmk. 60**

50 A1 2p vermilion *3,500.* 925.

A2

A3

A4

A5

A6

A7

**1874 Typo. Wmk. 62 *Perf. 12½***

51 A2 1p violet 120.00 15.50
*a.* Bluish paper 240.00 45.00
*b.* Imperf. pair 1,750.
*c.* Perf. 12x12½ 1,650. 400.00
52 A3 2p rose 120.00 9.00
*a.* Bluish paper 240.00 42.50
*b.* Perf. 12 1,300. 210.00
*c.* Perf. 12x12½ 1,300. 350.00
53 A4 3p brown 210.00 85.00
*a.* Bluish paper 400.00 110.00
54 A5 4p claret 315.00 75.00
*a.* Bluish paper 625.00 125.00
55 A6 6p blue 275.00 13.50
*a.* Bluish paper 475.00 60.00
56 A7 1sh green 625.00 40.00
*a.* Bluish paper 1,150. 200.00
*Nos. 51-56 (6)* 1,665. 238.00

**1874 *Perf. 12½, 10***

*51f* A2 1p violet 175.00 45.00
*g.* Bluish paper 275.00 65.00
*52f* A3 2p rose 250.00 95.00
*g.* Bluish paper 600.00 110.00
*53f* A4 3p brown 225.00 90.00
*g.* Bluish paper 425.00 125.00
*54f* A5 4p claret 850.00 165.00
*g.* Bluish paper 425.00 125.00
*55f* A6 6p blue 325.00 55.00
*g.* Bluish paper 475.00 110.00
*56f* A7 1sh green 700.00 150.00
*g.* Bluish paper 1,200. 275.00
*h.* Vert. pair, imperf. between *6,750.*

**1878 *Perf. 12x11½***

*51i* A2 1p violet 65.00 9.00
*52i* A3 2p rose 70.00 8.00
*54i* A5 4p claret 210.00 60.00
*55i* A6 6p blue 140.00 12.50
*56i* A7 1sh green 225.00 50.00

**1875 Wmk. 6 *Perf. 12½***

57 A2 1p violet 2,000. 310.00
58 A3 2p rose 775.00 45.00

A8

**1878 Wmk. 62** ***Perf. 12x11½***

**59** A8 2sh deep rose 750.00 450.00
**60** A8 5sh gray 800.00 500.00

No. 60 has numeral "5" in each of the four spandrels.
Beware of cleaned fiscally used examples of Nos. 59-60.

A9

A10

A11

A12

A13

A14 A15

***Perf. 10, 11, 11½, 12, 12½ and Compound***

**1882-98**

**61** A9 1p rose 9.00 .25
*a.* Vert. pair, imperf. horiz. *1,100.*
*b.* Perf. 12x11½ 55.00 7.50
*c.* Perf. 12½ 500.00 305.00
*d.* Imperf., pair *1,100.*
**62** A10 2p violet 16.00 1.00
*a.* Vert. pair, imperf. btwn. *950.00*
*b.* Perf. 12½ 500.00 500.00
*c.* Imperf., pair *1,000.*
**63** A11 3p orange 60.00 9.50
*a.* 3p yellow ('99) 62.50 15.00
**64** A12 4p blue green ('97) 62.50 5.00
*a.* Perf. 10x11 ('96) 110.00 13.50
**65** A13 6p brown 82.50 8.50
*b.* 6p brown, thin coarse paper ('98) 140.00 14.50
**66** A14 8p blue ('98) 85.00 65.00
**67** A15 1sh red brown ('97) 120.00 14.00
*d.* Vert. pair, imperf. btwn. *1,800.*
*Nos. 61-67 (7)* 435.00 103.25

See #87. For overprints see #O1-O2, O5, O7-O8.

A15a

A16

A17

**1891-95**

**67A** A15a ½p black ('95) 9.00 .25
*b.* Perf. 12x11½ 45.00 *90.00*

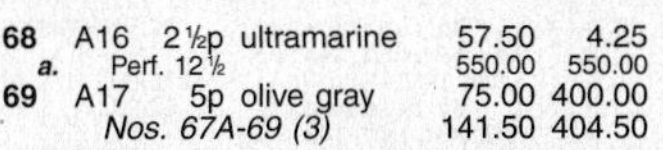

**68** A16 2½p ultramarine 57.50 4.25
*a.* Perf. 12½ 550.00 550.00
**69** A17 5p olive gray 75.00 400.00
*Nos. 67A-69 (3)* 141.50 404.50

In 1893 advertisements were printed on the backs of Nos. 61-67, 68-69.
See #86C. For overprints see #O3-O4, O9.

Mt. Cook — A18

Lake Taupo — A19

Pembroke Peak — A20

Mt. Earnslaw, Lake Wakitipu — A21

Mt. Earnslaw, Lake Wakitipu — A22

Huia, Sacred Birds — A23

White Terrace, Rotomahana A24

Otira Gorge and Mt. Ruapehu A25

Kiwi A26

Maori Canoe A27

Pink Terrace, Rotomahana A28

Kea & Kaka (Hawk-billed Parrots) A29

Milford Sound — A30

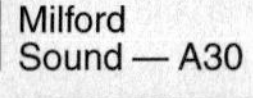

Mt. Cook — A31

***Perf. 12 to 16***

**1898, Apr. 5 Engr. Unwmk.**

**70** A18 ½p lilac gray 9.00 1.65
*a.* Horiz. or vert. pair, imperf. btwn. 1,750. 1,450.
**71** A19 1p yel brn & bl 6.00 .75
*a.* Horiz. or vert. pair, imperf. btwn. 1,350. 1,350.
*b.* Imperf. pair 950.00 850.00
**72** A20 2p rose brown 57.50 .30
*a.* Horiz. pair, imperf. vert. 650.00
*b.* Vert. pair, imperf. btwn. 1,300.
**73** A21 2½p bl *(Wakitipu)* 16.00 *47.50*
**74** A22 2½p bl *(Wakatipu)* 50.00 9.00
**75** A23 3p orange brn 35.00 9.00
**76** A24 4p rose 17.00 *21.00*
**77** A25 5p red brown 95.00 200.00
*a.* 5p violet brown 65.00 *25.00*
**78** A26 6p green 85.00 50.00
**79** A27 8p dull blue 75.00 50.00
**80** A28 9p lilac 70.00 42.50
**81** A29 1sh dull red 100.00 30.00
*a.* Pair, imperf. between 5,250.
**82** A30 2sh blue green 275.00 160.00
*a.* Vert. pair, imperf. btwn. 5,500. 5,250.
**83** A31 5sh vermilion 375.00 *525.00*
*Nos. 70-83 (14)* 1,266. *1,147.*

The 5sh stamps are often found with revenue cancellations that are embossed or show a crown on the top of a circle. These are worth much less.
See Nos. 84, 88-89, 91-98, 99B, 102, 104, 106-107, 111-112, 114-121, 126-128, 1508-1521. For overprint see No. O10.

A32 A33

**1900 Wmk. 63** ***Perf. 11***

**Thick Soft Wove Paper**

**84** A18 ½p green 9.00 2.00
**85** A32 1p carmine rose 14.00 .25
*a.* 1p lake 50.00 6.50
*b.* 1p crimson 14.00 .25
*c.* As "b," pair, imperf. btwn. 1,650. 1,750.
*d.* As "c," horiz. pair, imperf. vert. 650.00
**86** A33 2p red violet 15.00 .75
*a.* Pair, imperf. btwn. 1,450.
*Nos. 84-86 (3)* 38.00 3.00

Nos. 84 and 86 are re-engravings of Nos. 70 and 72 and are slightly smaller.
See No. 110. For Handstamp see No. O18.

A34

**1899-1900 Wmk. 63**

**86C** A15a ½p black ('00) 9.00 *18.00*
**87** A10 2p violet ('00) 30.00 20.00

**Unwmk.**

**88** A22 2½p blue 21.00 4.00
*a.* Horiz. pair, imperf. vert. 1,500.
*b.* Vert. pair, imperf. btwn. 650.00 —
**89** A23 3p org brown 27.50 2.50
*a.* Horiz. pair, imperf. vert. 700.00
*b.* Horiz. pair, imperf. btwn. 1,525.
**90** A34 4p yel brn & bl ('00) 6.50 4.00
**91** A25 5p red brown 50.00 9.00
*a.* 5p violet brown 60.00 9.00
*b.* Pair, imperf. between *3,250.*
**92** A26 6p green 70.00 *75.00*
**93** A26 6p rose ('00) 50.00 8.50
*a.* 6p carmine 50.00 8.00
*d.* As #93, horiz. pair, imperf. vert. 600.00
*g.* As #93, horiz. pair, imperf. btwn. 1,400.
**94** A27 8p dark blue 50.00 20.00
**95** A28 9p red lilac 60.00 37.50
**96** A29 1sh red 70.00 11.00
**97** A30 2sh blue green 215.00 60.00
**98** A31 5sh vermilion 300.00 400.00
Revenue cancel 27.50
*Nos. 86C-98 (13)* 959.00 669.50

See #113. For overprints see #O11-O15.
The 5sh stamps are often found with revenue cancellations that are embossed or show a crown on the top of a circle. These are worth much less.

"Commerce" — A35

**1901, Jan. 1 Unwmk.** ***Perf. 12 to 16***

**99** A35 1p carmine 7.00 4.50

Universal Penny Postage.
See Nos. 100, 103, 105, 108, 129. For overprint see Nos. 121a, O16, O18, O24, O32. Compare design A35 with A42.

Boer War Contingent A36

**1901 Wmk. 63** ***Perf. 11***

**Thick Soft Paper**

**99B** A18 ½p green 14.00 7.50
*c.* Pair, imperf. btwn. 650.00
**100** A35 1p carmine 10.00 .40
*a.* Horiz. pair, imperf. vert. 425.00 350.00
**101** A36 1½p brown org 10.00 4.00
*a.* Vert. pair, imperf. horiz. 1,200.
*b.* As "d," imperf. pair 1,250.
*c.* Horiz. pair, imperf. vert. 1,300.
*Nos. 99B-101 (3)* 34.00 11.90

***Perf. 14***

*99Bd* A18 ½p green 24.00 7.00
*100c* A35 1p carmine 70.00 23.00
*d.* Horiz. pair, imperf. vert. 350.00

***Perf. 14x11***

*99Be* A18 ½p green 12.00 16.50
*100e* A35 1p carmine 300.00 125.00

***Perf. 11x14***

*99Bf* A18 ½p green 14.00 27.50
*100f* A35 1p carmine 2,400. 925.00

***Perf. 11, 14 mixed***

*99Bg* A18 ½p green 60.00 90.00
*100g* A35 1p carmine 300.00 125.00

No. 101 was issued to honor the New Zealand forces in the South African War.
See No. 109.

**Thin Hard Paper**

***Perf. 14***

**102** A18 ½p green 42.50 42.50
*a.* Horiz. pair, imperf. vert. 400.00
**103** A35 1p carmine 18.00 8.00
*a.* Horiz. pair, imperf. vert. 300.00
*b.* Vert. pair, imperf. horiz. 300.00

***Perf. 11***

*102c* A18 ½p green 95.00 125.00
*103c* A35 1p carmine 165.00 145.00

***Perf. 14x11***

*102d* A18 ½p green 50.00 70.00
*103d* A35 1p carmine 35.00 20.00

***Perf. 11x14***

*102e* A18 ½p green 26.00 55.00
*103e* A35 1p carmine 10.00 4.00

***Perf. 11, 14 mixed***

*102f* A18 ½p green 70.00 105.00
*103f* A35 1p carmine 82.50 87.50

**1902 Unwmk.** ***Perf. 14***

**104** A18 ½p green 35.00 8.50
**105** A35 1p carmine 12.50 4.25

***Perf. 11***

*104a* A18 ½p green 200.00 210.00

***Perf. 14x11***

*104b* A18 ½p green 145.00 210.00
*105b* A35 1p carmine 125.00 145.00

***Perf. 11x14***

*104c* A18 ½p green 200.00 350.00
*105c* A35 1p carmine 145.00 200.00

***Perf. 11, 14 mixed***

*104d* A18 ½p green 175.00 250.00
*105d* A35 1p carmine 130.00 175.00

**1902** ***Perf. 11***

**Thin White Wove Paper**

**106** A26 6p rose red 65.00 80.00
*a.* Watermarked letters 120.00 130.00

The sheets of No. 106 are watermarked with the words "LISBON SUPERFINE" in two lines, covering 10 stamps. Value, block of 10 *$4,000.*

**1902-07 Wmk. 61** ***Perf. 14***

**107** A18 ½p green 9.00 2.75
*a.* Horiz. pair, imperf. vert. 300.00
**108** A35 1p carmine 4.25 .25
*d.* Horiz. pair, imperf. vert. 200.00
*e.* Vert. pair, imperf. horiz. 200.00
*f.* Booklet pane of 6 275.00
**109** A36 1½p brown org ('07) 25.00 *55.00*
**110** A33 2p dull vio ('03) 12.00 2.75

**111** A22 2½p blue 30.00 5.00
**112** A23 3p org brown 32.50 8.00
*a.* Horiz. pair, imperf. vert. 1,000.
**113** A34 4p yel brn & bl 10.00 4.50
*a.* Horiz. pair, imperf. vert. 650.00
*b.* Vert. pair, imperf. horiz. 650.00
**114** A25 5p red brown 40.00 16.00
**115** A26 6p rose red 60.00 9.00
**116** A27 8p steel blue 45.00 11.50
**117** A28 9p red violet 45.00 8.00
**118** A29 1sh pale red 175.00 60.00
**119** A30 2sh green 150.00 32.50
**120** A31 5sh deep red 240.00 *300.00*
*Nos. 107-120 (14)* 877.75 515.25

The unique example of No. 113 with inverted center is used and is in the New Zealand National Philatelic Collection.

**1902-03** ***Perf. 11***
*107e* A18 ½p green 70.00 *120.00*
*108k* A35 1p carmine *800.00* *800.00*
*111e* A22 2½p blue 35.00 11.00
*112e* A23 3p yellow brown 37.50 3.50
*113e* A34 4p yel brn & bl 6.00 *75.00*
*f.* Horiz. pair, imperf. vert. *650.00*
*114e* A25 5p deep brown 55.00 7.50
*115e* A26 6p rose 40.00 8.00
*h* Horiz. pair, imperf. vert. 850.00
*116e* A27 8p deep blue 55.00 11.50
*g.* Horiz. pair, imperf. vert. 2,000.
*h.* Vert. pair, imperf. horiz. 2,000.
*117e* A28 9p red violet 70.00 11.00
*118e* A29 1sh orange red 75.00 7.50
*119e* A30 2sh blue green 190.00 42.50
*120e* A31 5sh vermilion 275.00 *3.75*
*Nos. (12)* 1,709. 1,101.

**1902-07** ***Perf. compound 11 and 14***
*107i* A18 ½p green, perf. 14x11 ('02) 30.00 *125.00*
*j.* Perf 11x14 30.00 *90.00*
*108i* A35 1p carmine, perf 14x11 ('02) 100.00 *125.00*
*m.* Perf. 11x14 150.00 *150.00*
*109i* A36 1½p chestnut ('07) *1,600.*
*110i* A33 2p dull violet ('03) *500.00* *400.00*
*112i* A23 3p orange brown *1,000.* *750.00*
*113i* A34 4p yel brn & blue ('03) *450.00* *450.00*
*114i* A25 5p red brown ('06) *1,800.* *1,500.*
*115i* A26 6p rose carmine ('07) *450.00* *450.00*
*116i* A27 8p steel blue ('07) *1,500.* *1,500.*
*117i* A28 9p red violet ('06) *1,750.* *1,600.*
*120i* A31 5sh deep red ('06) *3,500.* *3,250.*

**1903-07** ***Perf. mixed 11 and 14***
*107k* A18 ½p green 40.00 *77.50*
*108o* A35 1p carmine 35.00 *55.00*
*109k* A36 1½p chestnut ('07) *1,600.*
*110k* A33 2p dull violet ('03) *450.00* 325.00
*112k* A23 3p orange brown ('06) *1,000.* *750.00*
*113k* A34 4p yel brn & blue ('03) *425.00* *450.00*
*114k* A25 5p red brown ('06) *1,400.* *200.00*
*115k* A26 6p rose carmine ('07) *450.00* *450.00*
*116k* A27 8p steel blue ('07) *1,500.* *1,500.*
*117k* A28 9p red violet ('06) *1,650.* *1,600.*
*119k* A30 2sh blue green ('06) *1,750.* *1,800.*
*120k* A31 5sh deep red ('06) *3,500.* *3,250.*

Wmk. 61 is normally sideways on 3p, 5p, 6p, 8p and 1sh. The 6p exists with wmk. upright. The 1sh exists with wmk. upright and inverted.

See No. 129. For overprints see Nos. O17-O22.

The 5sh stamps are often found with revenue cancellations that are embossed or show a crown on the top of a circle. These are worth much less.

**1903** **Unwmk.** ***Perf. 11***
**Laid Paper**
**121** A30 2sh blue green 225.00 *250.00*

### No. 108a Overprinted in Green: "King Edward VII Land" in Two Lines Reading Up

**1908, Jan. 15** ***Perf. 14***
*121a* A35 1p rose carmine 475.00 42.50
*b.* Double overprint *1,600.*

In 1908 a quantity of the 1p carmine (A35) was overprinted "King Edward VII Land" and taken on a Shackleton expedition to the Antarctic. Because of the weather Shackleton landed at Victoria Land instead. The stamp was never sold to the public at face value. See No. 121a.

Similar conditions prevailed for the 1909-12 ½p green and 1p carmine overprinted "VICTORIA LAND." See Nos. 130d-131d.

### Christchurch Exhibition Issue

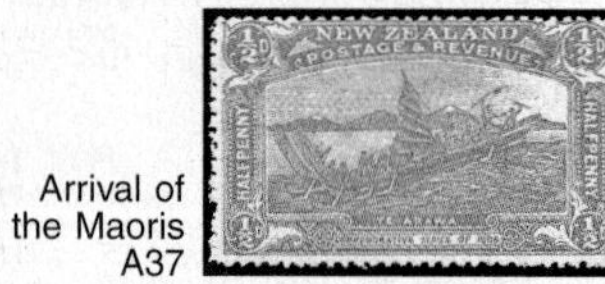
Arrival of the Maoris A37

Maori Art — A38

Landing of Capt. Cook A39

Annexation of New Zealand A40

**Wmk. 61**
**1906, Nov.** **Typo.** ***Perf. 14***
**122** A37 ½p emerald 37.50 *37.50*
**123** A38 1p vermilion 18.00 27.50
**124** A39 3p blue & brown 60.00 *115.00*
**125** A40 6p gray grn & rose 220.00 *425.00*
*Nos. 122-125 (4)* 335.50 *605.00*

Value for No. 123a is for a fine example.

### Designs of 1902-07 Issue, but smaller

**1907-08** **Engr.** ***Perf. 14x15***
**126** A23 3p orange brown *55.00* 17.50
**127** A26 6p carmine rose *55.00* 11.50
**128** A29 1sh orange red *125.00* 26.00
*Nos. 126-128 (3)* *235.00* 55.00

***Perf. 14x13, 13½ Compound***
*126a* A23 3p orange brown 60.00 55.00
*127a* A26 6p carmine red 475.00 190.00
*128a* A29 1sh orange red 155.00 70.00

***Perf. 14***
*126b* A23 3p orange brown 100.00 30.00
*127b* A26 6p carmine red 50.00 11.00

The small stamps are about 21mm high, those of 1898-1902 about 23mm.

### Type of 1902 Redrawn

**1908** **Typo.** ***Perf. 14x14½***
**129** A35 1p carmine 40.00 3.00

REDRAWN, 1p: The lines of shading in the globe are diagonal and the other lines of the design are generally thicker than on No. 108.

Edward VII A41

"Commerce" A42

**1909-12** ***Perf. 14x14½***
**130** A41 ½p yellow green 7.25 .55
*a.* Booklet pane of 6 *225.00*
*b.* Booklet pane 5 + label *775.00*
*c.* Imperf., pair 250.00
**131** A42 1p carmine 2.00 .25
*a.* Imperf., pair 410.00
*b.* Booklet pane of 6 225.00

***Perf. 14x14½***
**Engr.**
**Various Frames**
**132** A41 2p mauve 25.00 7.25
**133** A41 3p orange brown 27.50 1.40
**134** A41 4p red orange 32.50 *27.50*
**135** A41 4p yellow ('12) 22.50 *13.50*
**136** A41 5p red brown 22.00 5.00
**137** A41 6p carmine rose 50.00 1.75
**138** A41 8p deep blue 20.00 3.25
**139** A41 1sh vermilion 75.00 6.75
*Nos. 130-139 (10)* 283.75 67.20

***Perf. 14***
*133a* A41 3p orange brown 55.00 22.00
*134a* A41 4p red orange 22.00 16.50
*136a* A41 5p red brown 29.00 5.00
*137a* A41 6p carmine rose 45.00 11.00
*138a* A41 8p deep blue 50.00 100.00
*d.* No wmk. 110.00 200.00
*139a* A41 1sh vermilion 65.00 15.00

***Perf. 14x13½***
*133b* A41 3p orange brown 82.50 145.00
*c.* Vert. pair, perf. 14x13½ and 14x14½ 275.00 475.00
*136b* A41 5p red brown 21.00 3.25
*c.* Vert. pair, perf. 14x13½ and 14x14½ 275.00 475.00
*137b* A41 6p carmine rose 82.50 145.00
*c.* Vert. pair, perf. 14x13½ and 14x14½ 275.00 475.00
*138b* A41 8p deep blue 50.00 3.25
*c.* Vert. pair, perf. 14x13½ and 14x14½ 275.00 475.00

See No. 177. For overprints see Nos. 130d-131d, 130e-137e, O33-O37, O49, O54; Cook Islands No. 49.

### Nos. 130-131 Overprinted in Black: "VICTORIA LAND" in Two Lines

**1911-13**
*130d* A41 ½p yellow green *1,100.* *950.00*
*131d* A42 1p carmine 70.00 *150.00*

See note after No. 120.
Issue dates: 1p, Feb. 9; ½p, Jan. 18, 1913.

Stamps of 1909 Overprinted in Black

**1913**
*130e* A41 ½p yellow green 25.00 *55.00*
*131e* A42 1p carmine 35.00 *45.00*
*133e* A41 3p orange brown 250.00 *400.00*
*137e* A41 6p carmine rose 300.00 *500.00*
*Nos. 130e-137e (4)* 610.00 *1,000.*

This issue was valid only within New Zealand and to Australia from Dec. 1, 1913, to Feb. 28, 1914. The Auckland Stamp Collectors Club inspired this issue.

King George V — A43

**1915** **Typo.** ***Perf. 14x15***
**144** A43 ½p yellow green 2.00 .25
*b.* Booklet pane of 6 *150.00*

See Nos. 163-164, 176, 178. For overprints see Nos. O41, O45-O46, MR1; Cook Islands No. 48.

A44

A45

**1915-22** **Engr.** ***Perf. 14x13½***
**145** A44 1½p gray 4.25 2.00
*a.* Perf. 14x14½ 5.50 2.00
*b.* Vert. pair, both perfs 39.00 *110.00*
**146** A45 2p purple 14.50 *45.00*
*a.* Perf. 14x14½ 7.75 *55.00*
*b.* Vert. pair, both perfs 30.00 *175.00*
**147** A45 2p org yel ('16) 9.50 *35.00*
*a.* Perf. 14x14½ 9.50 *35.00*
*b.* Vert. pair, both perfs 23.00 *275.00*
**148** A44 2½p dull blue 3.50 *7.50*
*a.* Perf. 14x14½ 10.00 *35.00*
*b.* Vert. pair, both perfs 45.00 *200.00*
**149** A45 3p violet brown 16.50 1.40
*a.* Vert. pair, both perfs 55.00 *150.00*
*b.* Perf. 14x14½ 13.00 2.25
**150** A45 4p orange yellow 4.75 *60.00*
*a.* Vert. pair, both perfs 30.00 *275.00*
*b.* Perf. 14x14½ 4.75 *60.00*
**151** A45 4p purple ('16) 22.50 .55
*a.* Perf. 14x14½ 7.50 .55
*b.* Vert. pair, both perfs 65.00 *165.00*
**152** A44 4½p dark green 25.00 *26.00*
*a.* Perf. 14x14½ 15.00 *60.00*
*b.* Vert. pair, both perfs 60.00 *190.00*
**153** A45 5p light blue ('21) 19.00 1.10
*a.* Imperf., pair 250.00 200.00
*b.* Perf. 14x14½ 13.00 *42.50*
*c.* Vert. pair, both perfs 90.00 *275.00*
**154** A45 6p carmine rose 13.00 .55
*a.* Horiz. pair, imperf. vert.
*b.* Perf. 14x14½ 11.00 .65
*c.* Vert. pair, both perfs 70.00 *155.00*
**155** A44 7½p red brown 22.50 *26.00*
*a.* Perf. 14x14½ 12.00 *90.00*
*b.* Vert. pair, both perfs 55.00 *250.00*
**156** A45 8p blue ('21) 25.00 *50.00*
*a.* Perf. 14x14½ 9.50 *60.00*
*b.* Vert. pair, both perfs 42.50 *200.00*
**157** A45 8p red brown ('22) 35.00 4.00
**158** A45 9p olive green 30.00 5.00
*a.* Imperf., pair *1,500.*
*b.* Perf. 14x14½ 16.50 *32.50*
*c.* Vert. pair, both perfs 82.50 *250.00*
**159** A45 1sh vermilion 30.00 .60
*a.* Imperf., pair 450.00
*b.* Perf. 14x14½ 15.00 .55
*c.* Vert. pair, both perfs 82.50 *300.00*
*Nos. 145-159 (15)* 275.00 264.70

Nos. 145-156, 158-159 exist in vert. pairs with perf 14x13½ on top and perf 14x14½ on the bottom. These sell for a premium. The 5p and No. 151c exist with the perf varieties reversed. These are rare. No. 157 only comes perf 14x13½.

The former Nos. 151a and 151b probably were listed from sheets with No. 151d. They probably do not exist.

For overprints see Nos. O47-O48, O50-O53; Cook Islands Nos. 53-60.

A46

A47

No. 160

No. 161

The engr. stamps have a background of geometric lathe-work; the typo. stamps have a background of crossed dotted lines.

Type A43 has three diamonds at each side of the crown, type A46 has two, and type A47 has one.

**1916-19** **Typo.** ***Perf. 14x15***
**160** A46 1½p gray black 9.00 1.40
**161** A47 1½p gray black 11.00 .60
**162** A47 1½p brown org ('18) 42.50 *1.00*
*a.* Perf. 14 9.50 *45.00*
**163** A43 2p yellow 2.60 .25
*a.* Perf. 14 3.00 .25
**164** A43 3p chocolate ('19) 12.00 1.50
*a.* Perf. 14 9.50 4.00
*Nos. 160-164 (5)* 77.10 4.75

In 1916 the 1½, 2, 3 and 6p of the 1915-16 issue and the 8p of the 1909 issue were printed on paper intended for the long rectangular stamps of the 1902-07 issue. In this paper the watermarks are set wide apart, so that the smaller stamps often show only a small part of the watermark or miss it altogether.

For overprints see Nos. O42-O44; Cook Islands Nos. 50-52.

### Victory Issue

"Peace" and British Lion — A48

Peace and Lion — A49

Maori Chief — A50

British Lion — A51

"Victory" — A52

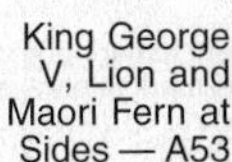

King George V, Lion and Maori Fern at Sides — A53

**1920, Jan. 27** *Perf. 14*

| No. | Type | Description | Unused | Used |
|---|---|---|---|---|
| 165 | A48 | ½p yellow green | 3.25 | 2.75 |
| 166 | A49 | 1p carmine | 4.50 | .65 |
| 167 | A50 | 1½p brown orange | 3.50 | .55 |
| 168 | A51 | 3p black brown | 15.00 | *16.00* |
| 169 | A52 | 6p purple | 17.00 | *19.00* |
| 170 | A53 | 1sh vermilion | 25.00 | *55.00* |
| | | *Nos. 165-170 (6)* | 68.25 | *93.95* |

No. 165 Surcharged in Red

**1922, Mar.**

| No. | Type | Description | Unused | Used |
|---|---|---|---|---|
| 174 | A48 | 2p on ½p yellow green | 6.00 | 1.50 |

Map of New Zealand — A54

**1923** **Typo.** *Perf. 14x15*

| No. | Type | Description | Unused | Used |
|---|---|---|---|---|
| 175 | A54 | 1p carmine rose | 4.75 | .70 |

Restoration of Penny Postage. The paper varies from thin to thick.

### Types of 1909-15
### N Z and Star 'watermark' printed on back, usually in blue

**1925** **Unwmk.** *Perf. 14x14½*

| No. | Type | Description | Unused | Used |
|---|---|---|---|---|
| 176 | A43 | ½p yellow green | 3.50 | *3.50* |
| 177 | A42 | 1p carmine | 3.50 | .90 |
| 178 | A43 | 2p yellow | 20.00 | *62.50* |
| | | *Nos. 176-178 (3)* | 27.00 | *66.90* |

Exhibition Buildings A55

**1925, Nov. 17** **Wmk. 61**

**Surface Tinted Paper**

| No. | Type | Description | Unused | Used |
|---|---|---|---|---|
| 179 | A55 | ½p yel green, *grnsh* | 3.50 | *16.50* |
| 180 | A55 | 1p car rose, *pink* | 4.25 | *7.50* |
| 181 | A55 | 4p red violet, *lilac* | 37.50 | *80.00* |
| | | *Nos. 179-181 (3)* | 45.25 | *104.00* |

Dunedin Exhibition.

George V in Admiral's Uniform A56

In Field Marshal's Uniform A57

**1926** *Perf. 14*

| No. | Type | Description | Unused | Used |
|---|---|---|---|---|
| 182 | A56 | 2sh blue | 70.00 | 35.00 |
| a. | | 2sh dark blue | 65.00 | *67.50* |
| 183 | A56 | 3sh violet | 130.00 | *175.00* |
| a. | | 3sh deep violet | 110.00 | *190.00* |
| 184 | A57 | 1p rose red | 1.25 | .25 |
| a. | | Booklet pane of 6 | 150.00 | |
| b. | | Imperf., pair | 250.00 | |
| c. | | Perf. 14x14½ | .70 | .55 |
| | | *Nos. 182-184 (3)* | 201.25 | 210.25 |

For overprints see Nos. O55-O56 and Cook Islands Nos. 74-75.

Pied Fantail and Clematis A58

Kiwi and Cabbage Palm A59

Maori Woman Cooking in Boiling Spring A60

Maori Council House (Whare) A61

Mt. Cook and Mountain Lilies A62

Maori Girl Wearing Tiki — A63

Mitre Peak — A64

Striped Marlin A65

Harvesting — A66

Tuatara Lizard — A67

Maori Panel from Door — A68

Tui or Parson Bird — A69

Capt. Cook Landing at Poverty Bay — A70

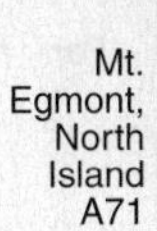

Mt. Egmont, North Island A71

***Perf. 13½-14x13½, 13-14x13½ (189, 192, 197, 198), 13½x14 (193), 14x14½ (195), 14 (191)***

**1935, May 1** **Engr.** **Wmk. 61**

| No. | Type | Description | Unused | Used |
|---|---|---|---|---|
| 185 | A58 | ½p bright green | 3.00 | 1.50 |
| 186 | A59 | 1p copper red | 2.50 | 1.00 |
| c. | | Perf. 13½x14 | 82.50 | 65.00 |
| 186A | A59 | 1p copper red, re-engraved | 9.00 | 4.00 |
| b. | | Booklet pane of 6 + ad labels | *80.00* | |
| 187 | A60 | 1½p red brown | 16.00 | *22.00* |
| a. | | Perf. 13½x14 | 6.50 | 13.00 |
| 188 | A61 | 2p red orange | 4.00 | 2.50 |
| 189 | A62 | 2½p dull blue & dk brown | 15.00 | *45.00* |
| a. | | Perf. 13½x14 | 10.00 | 30.00 |
| 190 | A63 | 3p chocolate | 13.50 | 4.00 |
| 191 | A64 | 4p blk brn & blk | 5.00 | 3.25 |
| 192 | A65 | 5p violet blue | 26.00 | *35.00* |
| a. | | Perf. 13½x14 | 28.00 | 55.00 |
| 193 | A66 | 6p red | 9.00 | *12.00* |
| 194 | A67 | 8p dark brown | 14.00 | *21.00* |

**Litho.**

**Size: 18x21½mm**

| No. | Type | Description | Unused | Used |
|---|---|---|---|---|
| 195 | A68 | 9p blk & scar | 16.00 | 7.00 |

**Engr.**

| No. | Type | Description | Unused | Used |
|---|---|---|---|---|
| 196 | A69 | 1sh dk sl green | 25.00 | 20.00 |
| 197 | A70 | 2sh olive green | 50.00 | 50.00 |
| a. | | Perf. 13½x14 | 70.00 | 65.00 |
| 198 | A71 | 3sh yel brn & brn black | 25.00 | *55.00* |
| a. | | Perf. 13½x14 | 25.00 | 65.00 |
| | | *Nos. 185-198 (15)* | 233.00 | 283.25 |
| | | Set, never hinged | 500.00 | |

On No. 186A, the horizontal lines in the sky are much darker.

The 2½p, 5p, 2sh and 3sh are perf. 13½ vertically; perf. 13-14 horizontally on each stamp.

See Nos. 203-216, 244-245. For overprints see Nos. O58-O71, O90.

### Silver Jubilee Issue

Queen Mary and King George V A72

**1935, May 7** *Perf. 11x11½*

| No. | Type | Description | Unused | Used |
|---|---|---|---|---|
| 199 | A72 | ½p blue green | .75 | 1.00 |
| 200 | A72 | 1p dark car rose | 1.00 | .75 |
| 201 | A72 | 6p vermilion | 20.00 | *30.00* |
| | | *Nos. 199-201 (3)* | 21.75 | *31.75* |
| | | Set, never hinged | 29.00 | |

25th anniv. of the reign of King George V.

### Types of 1935
***Perf. 13½-14x13½***

**1936-42** **Wmk. 253**

| No. | Type | Description | Unused | Used |
|---|---|---|---|---|
| 203 | A58 | ½p bright green | 2.00 | .25 |
| 204 | A59 | 1p copper red | 2.00 | .25 |
| 205 | A60 | 1½p red brown | 9.50 | 6.00 |
| 206 | A61 | 2p red orange | .25 | .25 |
| a. | | Perf. 14 | 16.50 | .90 |
| b. | | Perf. 14x14½-15 | 21.00 | *25.00* |
| c. | | Perf. 12½ | 4.00 | .25 |
| 207 | A62 | 2½p dull blue & dk brn | 1.50 | *6.00* |
| a. | | Perf. 14 | 10.00 | 1.65 |
| b. | | Perf. 13-14x13½ | 12.00 | 28.00 |
| 208 | A63 | 3p chocolate | 20.00 | 1.50 |
| 209 | A64 | 4p blk brn & blk | 10.00 | 1.25 |
| a. | | Perf. 12½ | 50.00 | 20.00 |
| b. | | Perf. 14 | 70.00 | 145.00 |
| c. | | Perf. 14x14¼ | 1.25 | .25 |
| 210 | A65 | 5p violet blue | 2.50 | 1.25 |
| a. | | Perf. 12½ | 16.00 | 14.00 |
| b. | | Perf. 13-14x13½ | 30.00 | 3.75 |
| 211 | A66 | 6p red, perf. 13½x14 | 27.50 | 2.00 |
| a. | | Perf. 12½ | 1.75 | 5.00 |
| b. | | Perf. 14½x14 | 1.50 | .25 |
| 212 | A67 | 8p dark brown | 17.50 | 7.75 |
| a. | | Perf. 12½ | 2.25 | 1.60 |
| b. | | Perf. 14½x14 | 4.50 | 1.75 |

**Litho.**

**Size: 18x21½mm**

| No. | Type | Description | Unused | Used |
|---|---|---|---|---|
| 213 | A68 | 9p gray & scarlet, perf.14x15 | 30.00 | 4.00 |
| a. | | 9p black & scarlet, perf. 14x14½ | 32.50 | 4.25 |

**Engr.**

| No. | Type | Description | Unused | Used |
|---|---|---|---|---|
| 214 | A69 | 1sh dk sl grn | 3.50 | 1.25 |
| a. | | Perf. 12½ | 35.00 | 25.00 |
| 215 | A70 | 2sh olive green | 6.50 | 1.50 |
| a. | | Perf. 13½x14 | 175.00 | 4.00 |
| b. | | Perf. 12½ | 12.50 | 9.50 |
| c. | | Perf. 13-14x13½ | 55.00 | 12.00 |
| 216 | A71 | 3sh yel brn & blk brn | 5.50 | 3.25 |
| a. | | Perf. 12½ ('41) | 45.00 | 50.00 |
| b. | | Perf. 13-14x13½ | 55.00 | 14.00 |
| | | *Nos. 203-216 (14)* | 138.25 | 36.50 |
| | | Set, never hinged | 180.00 | |

Perf. 13-14x13½ is perforated 13 on half of each horizontal side and 14 on the other half.

Wool Industry A73

Butter Industry A74

Sheep Farming A75

Apple Industry A76

Shipping A77

**1936, Oct. 1** **Wmk. 61** *Perf. 11*

| No. | Type | Description | Unused | Used |
|---|---|---|---|---|
| 218 | A73 | ½p deep green | .25 | .30 |
| 219 | A74 | 1p red | .25 | .25 |
| 220 | A75 | 2½p deep blue | 1.25 | *4.00* |
| 221 | A76 | 4p dark purple | 1.00 | *3.00* |
| 222 | A77 | 6p red brown | 2.00 | *3.50* |
| | | *Nos. 218-222 (5)* | 4.75 | *11.05* |
| | | Set, never hinged | 6.50 | |

Congress of the Chambers of Commerce of the British Empire held in New Zealand.

Queen Elizabeth and King George VI A78

***Perf. 13½x13***

**1937, May 13** **Wmk. 253**

| No. | Type | Description | Unused | Used |
|---|---|---|---|---|
| 223 | A78 | 1p rose carmine | .25 | .25 |
| 224 | A78 | 2½p dark blue | .50 | *1.25* |
| 225 | A78 | 6p vermilion | .65 | *1.25* |
| | | *Nos. 223-225 (3)* | 1.40 | *2.75* |
| | | Set, never hinged | 2.25 | |

Coronation of George VI and Elizabeth.

A79

A80

**1938-44** **Engr.** *Perf. 13½*

| No. | Type | Description | Unused | Used |
|---|---|---|---|---|
| 226 | A79 | ½p emerald | 4.75 | .25 |
| 226B | A79 | ½p brown org ('41) | .25 | .30 |
| 227 | A79 | 1p rose red | 3.75 | .25 |
| 227A | A79 | 1p lt blue grn ('41) | .25 | .25 |
| 228 | A80 | 1½p violet brown | 19.00 | 3.25 |
| 228B | A80 | 1½p red ('44) | .25 | .35 |
| 228C | A80 | 3p blue ('41) | .25 | .25 |
| | | *Nos. 226-228C (7)* | 28.50 | 4.90 |
| | | Set, never hinged | 40.00 | |

See Nos. 258-264. For surcharges and overprints see Nos. 242-243, 279, 285, O72-O74, O88-O89, O92-O97.

Landing of the Maoris in 1350 A81

Captain Cook, His Map of New Zealand, 1769, H.M.S. Endeavour
A82

Victoria, Edward VII, George V, Edward VIII and George VI — A83

Abel Tasman, Ship, and Chart of West Coast of New Zealand
A84

Treaty of Waitangi, 1840 — A85

Pioneer Settlers Landing on Petone Beach, 1840
A86

The Progress of Transport
A87

H.M.S. "Britomart" at Akaroa — A88

Route of Ship Carrying First Shipment of Frozen Mutton to England — A89

Maori Council
A90

Gold Mining in 1861 and Modern Gold Dredge
A91

Giant Kauri — A92

***Perf. 13½x14 (236), 13x13½, 14x13½ (233)***

**1940, Jan. 2 Engr. Wmk. 253**

**229** A81 ½p dk blue green .30 .25
**230** A82 1p scarlet & sepia 2.25 .25
**231** A83 1½p brt vio & ultra .25 .60
**232** A84 2p blk brn & Prus grn 1.10 .25
**233** A85 2½p dk bl & myr grn 1.50 1.00
**234** A86 3p dp plum & dk vio 2.75 1.00
**235** A87 4p dk red vio & vio brn 10.00 1.60
**236** A88 5p brown & lt bl 6.00 4.00
**237** A89 6p vio & brt grn 8.00 1.50
**238** A90 7p org red & black 1.25 *4.50*
**239** A90 8p org red & black 8.00 5.00
**240** A91 9p dp org & olive 5.50 2.25
**241** A92 1sh dk sl grn & ol 10.00 4.00
*Nos. 229-241 (13)* 56.90 26.20
Set, never hinged 95.00

Centenary of British sovereignty established by the treaty of Waitangi.

Imperfs of #229-241 exist. These probably are plate proofs.

For surcharge and overprints see Nos. 246, O76-O86.

**Stamps of 1938 Surcharged with New Values in Black**

**1941 Wmk. 253 *Perf. 13½***

**242** A79 1p on ½p emerald 1.00 .25
**243** A80 2p on 1½p violet brn 1.00 .25
Set, never hinged 3.50

**Type of 1935 Redrawn**

**1941 Typo. Wmk. 61 *Perf. 14x15***

**Size: 17½x20½mm**

**244** A68 9p int black & scarlet 70.00 30.00

**Wmk. 253**

**245** A68 9p int black & scarlet 4.00 3.50
Set, never hinged 160.00

**Catalogue values for unused stamps in this section, from this point to the end of the section, are for Never Hinged items.**

No 231 Srchd. in Black

**1944 *Perf. 13½x13***

**246** A83 10p on 1½p brt vio & ultra .45 .45

**Peace Issue**

Lake Matheson
A93

Parliament House, Wellington — A94

St. Paul's Cathedral, London — A95

The Royal Family — A96

Badge of Royal New Zealand Air Force
A97

New Zealand Army Overseas Badge
A98

Badge of Royal Navy
A99

New Zealand Coat of Arms
A100

Knight, Window of Wellington Boys' College
A101

Natl. Memorial Campanile, Wellington
A103

Southern Alps and Chapel Altar
A102

**Engr.; Photo. (1½p, 1sh)**

***Perf. 13x13½, 13½x13***

**1946, Apr. 1 Wmk. 253**

**247** A93 ½p choc & dk bl grn .25 *.60*
**248** A94 1p emerald .25 .25
**249** A95 1½p scarlet .25 .25
**250** A96 2p rose violet .25 .25
**251** A97 3p dk grn & ultra .25 .25
**252** A98 4p brn org & ol grn .25 .25
**253** A99 5p ultra & blue grn .75 .75
**254** A100 6p org red & red brn .25 .25
**255** A101 8p brown lake & blk .30 .30
**256** A102 9p black & brt bl .30 .30
**257** A103 1sh gray black .75 .35
*Nos. 247-257 (11)* 3.85 3.80

Return to peace at the close of WWII.
Imperfs exist from the printer's archives.

**George VI Type of 1938 and**

King George VI — A104

**1947 Engr. *Perf. 13½***

**258** A80 2p orange .30 .25
**260** A80 4p rose lilac .65 .65
**261** A80 5p gray .85 .75
**262** A80 6p rose carmine .85 .25
**263** A80 8p deep violet .90 .90
**264** A80 9p chocolate 1.60 .45

***Perf. 14***

**265** A104 1sh dk car rose & chnt .55 .55
**266** A104 1sh3p ultra & chnt 2.00 1.00
**267** A104 2sh dk grn & brn org 5.00 1.50
**268** A104 3sh gray blk & chnt 3.75 3.00
*Nos. 258-268 (10)* 16.45 9.30

Nos. 265-267 have watermark either upright or sideways. On No. 268 watermark is always sideways.

For overprints see Nos. O98-O99.

"John Wickliffe" and "Philip Laing"
A105

Cromwell, Otago
A106

First Church, Dunedin — A107

University of Otago
A108

**1948, Feb. 23 *Perf. 13½***

**269** A105 1p green & blue .25 .25
**270** A106 2p brown & green .25 .25
**271** A107 3p violet .30 .30
**272** A108 6p lilac rose & gray blk .30 .30
*Nos. 269-272 (4)* 1.10 1.10

Otago Province settlement, cent.

**A Royal Visit set of four was prepared but not issued. Examples of the 3p have appeared in the stamp market.**

A109

**Black Surcharge**

**Wmk. 253**

**1950, July 28 Typo. *Perf. 14***

**273** A109 1½p rose red .40 .40

See Nos. 367, 404A-404D, AR46-69.

Cathedral at Christchurch — A110

"They Passed this Way"
A111

3p, John Robert Godley. 6p, Canterbury University College. 1sh, View of Timaru.

**1950, Nov. 20 Engr. *Perf. 13x13½***
**274** A110 1p blue grn & blue .40 .40
**275** A111 2p car & red org .40 .40
**276** A110 3p indigo & blue .40 .40
**277** A111 6p brown & blue .55 .55
**278** A111 1sh claret & blue .70 .70
*Nos. 274-278 (5)* 2.45 2.45

Centenary of the founding of Canterbury Provincial District.
Imperfs of #274-278 exist.

### No. 227A Surcharged in Black

**1952, Dec. *Perf. 13½***
**279** A79 3p on 1p lt blue green .30 .25

### Coronation Issue

Buckingham Palace and Elizabeth II — A112

Queen Elizabeth II — A113

Westminster Abbey — A114

Designs: 4p, Queen Elizabeth and state coach. 1sh6p, Crown and royal scepter.

***Perf. 13x12½, 14x14½ (3p, 8p)***
**Engr., Photo. (3p, 8p)**
**1953, May 25**
**280** A112 2p ultramarine .40 .35
**281** A113 3p brown .35 .25
**282** A112 4p carmine 1.50 1.50
**283** A114 8p slate black 1.00 1.00
**284** A112 1sh6p vio blue & pur 2.50 2.50
*Nos. 280-284 (5)* 5.75 5.60

See Nos. 1869-1873.

### No. 226B Surcharged in Black

**1953, Sept. *Perf. 13½***
**285** A79 1p on ½p brown orange .40 .25

Queen Elizabeth II — A115

Queen Elizabeth II and Duke of Edinburgh A116

***Perf. 12½x13½, 13½x13***
**1953, Dec. 9 Engr.**
**286** A115 3p lilac .25 .25
**287** A116 4p deep blue .25 .25

Visit of Queen Elizabeth II and the Duke of Edinburgh.

A117

A118

A119

**1953-57 *Perf. 13½***
**288** A117 ½p gray .25 .30
**289** A117 1p orange .25 .25
**290** A117 1½p rose brown .25 .25
**291** A117 2p blue green .25 .25
**292** A117 3p red .25 .25
**293** A117 4p blue .35 .30
**294** A117 6p rose violet .65 .90
**295** A117 8p rose car .50 .50
**296** A118 9p emer & org brn .50 .30
**297** A118 1sh car & blk .75 .25
**298** A118 1sh6p blue & blk 1.75 .40
**298A** A118 1sh9p org & blk 7.00 1.00
**298B** A119 2sh6p redsh brn 22.50 5.50
**299** A119 3sh blue green 11.00 .45
**300** A119 5sh rose car 26.00 3.75
**301** A119 10sh vio blue 52.50 14.50
*Nos. 288-301 (16)* 124.75 29.15

The 1½p was issued in 1953; 1sh9p and 2sh6p in 1957; all others in 1954.

No. 298A exists on both ordinary and chalky paper.

Two dies of the 1sh differ in shading on the sleeve.

Imperfs of Nos. 298B-301 and tete-beche pairs of No. 301 and 312 exist from the printer's archives.

See Nos. 306-312. For surcharge see No. 320.

Maori Mailman A120

Queen Elizabeth II A121

Douglas DC-3 A122

***Perf. 13½ (2p), 14 (3p), 13 (4p)***
**1955, July 18 Wmk. 253**
**302** A120 2p deep grn & brn .25 .25
**303** A121 3p claret .25 .25
**304** A122 4p ultra & black .45 .45
*Nos. 302-304 (3)* .95 .95

Cent. of New Zealand's 1st postage stamps.

### Type of 1953-54 Redrawn

**1955-59 Wmk. 253 *Perf. 13½***
**306** A117 1p orange ('56) .45 .25
**307** A117 1½p rose brown .50 .35
**308** A117 2p bl grn ('56) .40 .25
**309** A117 3p vermilion ('56) .30 .25
**310** A117 4p blue ('58) 1.25 .70
**311** A117 6p violet 7.00 .25
**312** A117 8p brown red ('59) 3.25 4.25
*Nos. 306-312 (7)* 13.15 6.30

The numeral has been enlarged and the ornament in the lower right corner omitted.

Nos. 306, 308-310 exist on both ordinary and chalky paper.

Imperfs exist.

For surcharges see Nos. 319, 354.

Whalers of Foveaux Strait A123

"Agriculture" with Cow and Sheep — A124

Notornis (Takahe) — A125

**1956, Jan. *Perf. 13x12½, 13 (8p)***
**313** A123 2p deep green .30 .25
**314** A124 3p sepia .25 .25
**315** A125 8p car & blue vio 1.10 .90
*Nos. 313-315 (3)* 1.65 1.40

Southland centennial.

Lamb and Map of New Zealand — A126

Lamb, S. S. "Dunedin" and Refrigeration Ship — A127

***Perf. 14x14½, 14½x14***
**1957, Feb. 15 Photo.**
**316** A126 4p bright blue .50 .75
**317** A127 8p brick red .75 1.00

New Zealand Meat Export Trade, 75th anniv.

Sir Truby King — A128

**1957, May 14 Engr. *Perf. 13***
**318** A128 3p rose red .25 .25

Plunket Society, 50th anniversary.

Imperfs exist. These probably are plate proofs.

Nos. 307, 290 Surcharged

**1958, Jan. 15 *Perf. 13½***
**319** A117 2p on 1½p (#307) .45 .25
*a.* Small surcharge .25 .25
**320** A117 2p on 1½p (#290) 160.00 175.00
*a.* Small surcharge —

Surcharge measures 9½mm vert. on Nos. 319-320; 9mm on No. 319a-320a. Diameter of dot 4½mm on Nos. 319-320; 3¾mm on No. 319a-320a.

Counterfeits exist.

Sir Charles Kingsford-Smith and "Southern Cross" — A129

***Perf. 14x14½***
**1958, Aug. 27 Engr. Wmk. 253**
**321** A129 6p brt violet blue .45 .55

1st air crossing of the Tasman Sea, 30th anniv. See footnote under No. 2322.

See Australia No. 310.

Nelson Diocese Seal — A129a

**1958, Sept. 29 *Perf. 13***
**322** A129a 3p carmine rose .25 .25

Centenary of Nelson City.

Imperfs exist. These probably are plate proofs.

Statue of "Pania," Napier — A130

Gannet Sanctuary, Cape Kidnappers A131

Design: 8p, Maori shearing sheep.

***Perf. 13½x14½, 14½x14***
**1958, Nov. 3 Photo. Wmk. 253**
**323** A130 2p yellow green .25 .25
**324** A131 3p ultramarine .25 .25
**325** A130 8p red brown .85 1.25
*Nos. 323-325 (3)* 1.35 1.75

Centenary of Hawkes Bay province.

Jamboree Kiwi Badge — A132

**1959, Jan. 5 Engr. *Perf. 13***
**326** A132 3p car rose & brown .30 .25

Pan-Pacific Scout Jamboree, Auckland, Jan. 3-10.

"Endeavour" at Ship Cove — A133

Designs: 3p, Shipping wool at Wairau bar, 1857. 8p, Salt Industry, Grassmere.

**1959, Mar. 2 Photo. *Perf. 14½x14***
**327** A133 2p green .30 .25
**328** A133 3p dark blue .30 .25
**329** A133 8p brown 1.10 1.25
*Nos. 327-329 (3)* 1.70 1.75

Centenary of Marlborough Province.

The Explorer — A134

Westland Centennial: 3p, The Gold Digger. 8p, The Pioneer Woman.

**1960, May 16** ***Perf. 14x14½***

**330** A134 2p green .25 .25
**331** A134 3p orange .30 .25
**332** A134 8p gray 1.00 1.75
*Nos. 330-332 (3)* 1.55 2.25

Kaka Beak Flower A135

Timber Industry A136

Tiki A137

Maori Rock Drawing A138

Butter Making A139

Designs: ½p, Manuka flower. 1p, Karaka flower. 2½p, Titoki flower. 3p, Kowhai flower. 4p, Hibiscus. 5p, Mountain daisy. 6p, Clematis. 7p, Koromiko flower. 8p, Rata flower. 9p, Flag. 1sh3p, Rainbow trout. 1sh9p, Plane spraying farmland. 3sh, Ngauruhoe Volcano, Tongariro National Park. 5sh, Sutherland Falls. 10sh, Tasman Glacier, Mount Cook. £1, Pohutu Geyser.

***Perf. 14½x14, 14x14½***

**1960-66 Photo. Wmk. 253**

**333** A135 ½p dp car, grn & pale bl .25 .25
*b.* Green omitted 475.00
*c.* Pale blue omitted 350.00 275.00
**334** A135 1p brn, org & grn .25 .25
*b.* Orange omitted 675.00 400.00
*c.* Perf. 14½x13, wmkd. sideways 1.50 *2.75*
**335** A135 2p grn, rose car, blk & yel .25 .25
*b.* Black omitted 550.00
*c.* Yellow omitted 600.00
**336** A135 2½p blk, grn, red & brn .90 .25
*a.* Brown omitted 300.00
*b.* Green & red omitted 950.00
*c.* Green omitted 400.00
*d.* Red omitted 850.00 850.00
**337** A135 3p Prus bl, yel, brn & grn .30 .25
*b.* Yellow omitted 200.00
*c.* Brown omitted 250.00
*d.* Green omitted 350.00
*e.* Perf. 14½x13, wmkd. sideways 1.50 *2.75*
**338** A135 4p bl, grn, yel & lil .40 .25
*a.* Yellow omitted 900.00
*b.* Lilac omitted 650.00 500.00
**339** A135 5p pur, blk, yel & grn .90 .25
*a.* Yellow omitted 425.00 350.00
**340** A135 6p dp grn, lt grn & lil .50 .25
*a.* Light green omitted 450.00 350.00
*b.* Lilac omitted 450.00
**340C** A135 7p pink, red, grn & yel 1.00 *1.25*
**341** A135 8p gray, grn, pink & yel .45 .25
**342** A136 9p ultra & car .45 .25
*a.* Carmine omitted 575.00
**343** A136 1sh grn & brn .50 .25
**344** A137 1sh3p bl, brn & carmine 2.75 .25
*a.* Carmine omitted 875.00
**345** A137 1sh6p org brn & ol grn 1.00 .25
**346** A136 1sh9p pale brn 12.00 .50
**347** A138 2sh buff & blk 1.00 .25
**348** A139 2sh6p red brn & yel 1.50 1.00
*a.* Yellow omitted 1,450. 825.00
**349** A139 3sh gray brn 21.00 1.00
**350** A138 5sh dk grn 1.75 .80
**351** A139 10sh blue 3.00 .60
**352** A138 £1 magenta 10.00 7.25
*Nos. 333-352 (21)* 60.15 15.90

Nos. 334c and 337e were issued in coils.

Only on chalky paper: 2½p, 5p, 7p. On ordinary and chalky paper: 1p, 3p, 4p, 6p, 1sh9p, 2sh, 3sh, 5sh, 10sh. Others on ordinary paper only.

Issued: 2p, 4p, 1sh, 1sh3p, 1sh6p, 1sh9p, 2sh, 2sh6p, 3sh, 5sh, 10sh, £1, 7/11/60; ½p, 1p, 3p, 6p, 8p, 9p, 9/1/60; 2½p, 11/1/61; 5p, 5/14/62; 7p, 3/16/66; #334c, 11/63; #337e, 10/3/63.

See Nos. 360-361, 382-404.

Adoration of the Shepherds, by Rembrandt A140

***Perf. 11½x12***

**1960, Nov. 1 Wmk. 253**

**353** A140 2p dp brn & red, *cream* .30 .25
*a.* Red omitted *450.00 450.00*

Christmas. See No. 355.

**No. 309 Surcharged with New Value and Bars**

Two types of surcharge:
Type I — "2½d" is 5½mm wide.
Type II — "2½d" is 5mm wide.

**1961, Sept. 1 Engr.** ***Perf. 13½***

**354** A117 2½p on 3p vermilion, I .40 .25
*a.* Type II .40 .25

**Christmas Type of 1960**

2½p, Adoration of the Magi, by Dürer.

**1961, Oct. 16 Photo.** ***Perf. 14½x14***
**Size: 30x34mm**

**355** A140 2½p multicolored .25 .25

Morse Key and Port Hills, Lyttelton, 1862 A141

Design: 8p, Teleprinter and tape, 1962.

**1962, June 1 Wmk. 253**

**356** A141 3p dk brn & grn .25 .25
*a.* Green omitted 3,000.
**357** A141 8p dk red & gray .70 .70
*a.* Imperf., pair 2,600.
*b.* Gray omitted 2,300.

Centenary of the New Zealand telegraph.

Madonna in Prayer by Sassoferrato A142

**1962, Oct. 15** ***Perf. 14½x14***

**358** A142 2½p multicolored .25 .25

Christmas.

Holy Family by Titian A143

**1963, Oct. 14 Photo.** ***Perf. 12½***

**359** A143 2½p multicolored .25 .25
*a.* Imperf., pair *300.00*
*b.* Yellow omitted *500.00*

Christmas.

**Types of 1960-62**

1sh9p, Plane spraying farmland. 3sh, Ngauruhoe volcano, Tongariro National Park.

**1963-64** ***Perf. 14½x14***

**360** A136 1sh9p brt blue, grn & yel 2.50 1.00
**361** A139 3sh bl, grn & bis 2.00 1.75

Issued: 1sh9p, 11/4/63; 3sh, 4/1/64.

Old and New Engines A144

1sh9p, Express train and Mt. Ruapehu.

**1963, Nov. 25** ***Perf. 14***

**362** A144 3p multicolored .40 .25
*a.* Blue (sky) omitted *550.00*
**363** A144 1sh9p bl, blk, yel & carmine 2.25 1.50
*a.* Carmine (value) omitted *2,500.*

Centenary of New Zealand Railways.

Cable Around World and Under Sea A144a

**1963, Dec. 3 Unwmk.** ***Perf. 13½***

**364** A144a 8p yel, car, blk & bl .90 *1.25*

Opening of the Commonwealth Pacific (telephone) cable service (COMPAC).

See Australia No. 381.

Map of New Zealand and Steering Wheel A145

***Perf. 14½x14***

**1964, May 1 Wmk. 253**

**365** A145 3p multicolored .30 .25

National Road Safety Campaign.

Rev. Samuel Marsden Conducting First Christian Service, Rangihoua Bay, Christmas 1814 — A146

**1964, Oct. 12** ***Perf. 14x13½***

**366** A146 2½p multicolored .25 .25

Christmas.

**Postal-Fiscal Type of 1950**

**1964, Dec. 14 Typo.** ***Perf. 14***
**Black Surcharge**

**367** A109 7p rose red .50 *1.10*

**ANZAC Issue**

Anzac Cove, Gallipoli A147

Design: 5p, Anzac Cove and poppy.

***Perf. 12½***

**1965, Apr. 14 Unwmk. Photo.**

**368** A147 4p light brown .25 .25
**369** A147 5p green & red .25 *.40*

50th anniv. of the landing of the Australian and New Zealand Army Corps, ANZAC, at Gallipoli, Turkey, Apr. 25, 1915.

ITU Emblem, Old and New Communication Equipment — A148

***Perf. 14½x14***

**1965, May 17 Photo. Wmk. 253**

**370** A148 9p lt brown & dk blue .55 .35

Centenary of the ITU.

Sir Winston Spencer Churchill (1874-1965) A148a

**1965, May 24 Unwmk.** ***Perf. 13½***

**371** A148a 7p lt blue, gray & blk .30 *.40*

See Australia No. 389.

Provincial Council Building, Wellington A149

***Perf. 14½x14***

**1965, July 26 Photo. Wmk. 253**

**372** A149 4p multicolored .25 .25

Centenary of the establishment of Wellington as seat of government. The design is from a water color by L. B. Temple, 1867.

ICY Emblem A150

**1965, Sept. 28 Litho.** ***Perf. 14***

**373** A150 4p ol bister & dk red .25 .25

International Cooperation Year.

"The Two Trinities" by Murillo — A151

**1965, Oct. 11 Photo. *Perf. 13½x14***

**374** A151 3p multicolored .25 .25
*a.* Gold omitted 1,500.

Christmas.

Parliament House, Wellington and Commonwealth Parliamentary Association Emblem — A152

Designs: 4p, Arms of New Zealand and Queen Elizabeth II. 2sh, Wellington from Mt. Victoria.

**1965, Nov. 30 Unwmk. *Perf. 14***

**375** A152 4p multicolored .30 .25
*a.* Blue omitted *1,000.*
**376** A152 9p multicolored .60 .60
**377** A152 2sh multicolored 4.75 4.75
*a.* Red omitted *950.00*
*Nos. 375-377 (3)* 5.65 5.60

11th Commonwealth Parliamentary Assoc. Conf.

Scout Emblem, Maori Pattern — A153

***Perf. 14x14½***

**1966, Jan. 5 Photo. Wmk. 253**

**378** A153 4p green & gold .25 .25
*a.* Gold omitted *1,100.*

4th National Scout Jamboree, Trentham.

Virgin with Child, by Carlo Maratta — A154

**1966, Oct. 3 Wmk. 253 *Perf. 14***

**379** A154 3p multicolored .25 .25
*a.* Red omitted *350.00*

Christmas.

Queens Victoria and Elizabeth II — A155

New Zealand PO Savings Bank cent.: 9p, Reverse of half sovereign, 1867, and 1967 dollar.

***Perf. 14x14½***

**1967, Feb. 3 Photo. Wmk. 253**

**380** A155 4p plum, gold & black .25 .25
**381** A155 9p dk grn, bl, blk, sil & gold .25 .25

**Decimal Currency**

Types of 1960-62

Designs: ½c, Manuka flower. 1c, Karaka flower. 2c, Kaka beak flower. 2½c, Kowhai flower. 3c, Hibiscus. 4c, Mountain daisy. 5c, Clematis. 6c, Koromiko flower. 7c, Rata flower. 7½c, Brown trout. 8c, Flag. 10c, Timber industry. 15c, Tiki. 20c, Maori rock drawing. 25c, Butter making. 28c, Fox Glacier, Westland National Park. 30c, Ngauruhoe Volcano, Tongarino National Park. 50c, Sutherland Falls. $1, Tasman Glacier, Mount Cook. $2, Pohutu Geyser.

**Wmk. 253, Unwmkd. (#400)**

**1967-70 Photo. *Various Perfs.***

**382** A135 ½c multicolored .25 .25
*a.* Pale blue omitted *325.00*
**383** A135 1c multicolored .25 .25
*a.* Booklet pane of 5 + label 2.25
**384** A135 2c multicolored .25 .25
**385** A135 2½c multicolored .25 .25
*a.* Dark blue omitted *3,750.*
**386** A135 3c multicolored .25 .25
**387** A135 4c multicolored .30 .25
**388** A135 5c multicolored .50 .50
**389** A135 6c multicolored .50 *1.00*
**390** A135 7c multicolored .60 *1.00*
**391** A137 7½c multicolored .50 .50
**392** A136 8c ultra & car .60 .60
*a.* Red omitted *1,200.*
**393** A136 10c grn & brn .60 .60
**394** A137 15c org brn & slate grn 2.25 2.25
**395** A137 15c grn, sl grn & red ('68) 1.00 1.00
**396** A138 20c buff & black 1.00 .25
**397** A139 25c brown & yel 1.25 *2.00*
**398** A138 28c multi ('68) .75 .25
**399** A139 30c multicolored 1.75 .40
**400** A139 30c multi ('70) 5.00 3.00
**401** A138 50c dark green 2.00 .75
**402** A139 $1 blue 11.00 1.50
**403** A138 $2 magenta 7.50 5.00
**404** A138 $2 multi ('68) 30.00 15.00
*Nos. 382-404 (23)* 68.35 37.10

Perf. 13½x14: ½c to 3c, 5c, 7c. Perf. 14½x14: 4c, 6c, 8c, 10c, 25c, 30c, $1.

Perf. 13½: 7½c. Perf. 14x14½: 15c, 20c, 28c, 50c, $2.

Issued: 7½c, 8/29/67; No. 395, 3/19/68; 28c, 7/30/68; No. 404, 12/10/68; No. 400, 1970; others, 7/10/67.

The 7½c was issued to commemorate the centenary of the brown trout's introduction to New Zealand, and retained as part of the regular series.

No. 395 has been redrawn. The "c" on No. 395 lacks serif; No. 394 has serif.

No. 391 exists with watermarks either sideways or upright.

Coat of Arms — A155a

**Decimal Currency**

**1967, July 10 Wmk. 253 *Perf. 14***

**404A** A155a $4 purple 4.00 2.00
**404B** A155a $6 green 6.00 4.00
*a.* Unwmk. ('87) 9.00 4.50
**404C** A155a $8 light blue 8.00 4.75
*a.* Unwmk. ('87) 9.50 *12.00*
**404D** A155a $10 dark blue 10.00 *4.00*
*a.* Unwmk. ('87) 11.00 9.00
*Nos. 404A-404D (4)* 28.00 14.75

See Nos. AR46-AR69.

Adoration of the Shepherds, by Poussin — A156

***Perf. 13½x14***

**1967, Oct. 3 Photo. Wmk. 253**

**405** A156 2½c multicolored .25 .25

Christmas.

Sir James Hector — A157

Design: 4c, Mt. Aspiring, aurora australis and Southern Cross.

**1967, Oct. 10 Litho. *Perf. 14***

**406** A157 4c multicolored .25 .25
**407** A157 8c multicolored .35 *.55*

Centenary of the Royal Society of New Zealand to Promote Science.

Maori Bible — A158

**1968, Apr. 23 Litho. *Perf. 13½***

**408** A158 3c multicolored .25 .25
*a.* Gold omitted *160.00*

Publication of the Bible in Maori, cent.

Soldiers of Two Eras and Tank A159

10c, Airmen of two eras, insigne & plane. 28c, Sailors of two eras, insigne & battleships.

**1968, May 7 *Perf. 14x13½***

**409** A159 4c multicolored .25 .25
**410** A159 10c multicolored .50 .50
**411** A159 28c multicolored 1.50 1.50
*Nos. 409-411 (3)* 2.25 2.25

Issued to honor the Armed Services.

"Universal Suffrage" A160

Human Rights Flame A161

***Perf. 13½***

**1968, Sept. 19 Photo. Unwmk.**

**412** A160 3c ol grn, lt bl & grn .25 .25
**413** A161 10c dp grn, yel & red .30 .30

75th anniv. of universal suffrage in New Zealand; Intl. Human Rights Year.

Adoration of the Holy Child, by Gerard van Honthorst A162

***Perf. 14x14½***

**1968, Oct. 1 Wmk. 253**

**414** A162 2½c multicolored .25 .25

Christmas.

Romney Marsh Sheep and Woolmark on Carpet A163

Designs: 7c, Trawler and catch. 8c, Apples and orchard. 10c, Radiata pines and stacked lumber. 20c, Cargo hoist and grazing cattle. 25c, Dairy farm in Taranaki, Mt. Egmont and crated dairy products.

**Wmk. 253 (10c, 18c, 25c); others Unwmkd.**

***Perf. 13½; 14½x14 (10c, 25c)***

**1968-69 Litho.; Photo. (10c, 25c)**

**415** A163 7c multi ('69) .90 .90
**416** A163 8c multi ('69) .75 .75
**417** A163 10c multi .50 .25
*a.* Green omitted *950.00*
**418** A163 18c multi ('69) 1.25 .55
**419** A163 20c multi ('69) 1.00 .25
**420** A163 25c multi 2.25 1.75
*Nos. 415-420 (6)* 6.65 4.45

ILO Emblem A164

***Perf. 14½x14***

**1969, Feb. 11 Photo. Wmk. 253**

**421** A164 7c scarlet & black .35 .35

50th anniv. of the ILO.

Law Society Coat of Arms — A165

Designs: 3c, Supreme Court Building, Auckland, horiz. 18c, "Justice" from memorial window of the University of Canterbury Hall, Christchurch.

**1969, Apr. 8 Litho. *Perf. 13½***

**422** A165 3c multicolored .25 .25
**423** A165 10c multicolored .40 .40
**424** A165 18c multicolored .65 .65
*Nos. 422-424 (3)* 1.30 1.30

Centenary of New Zealand Law Society.

Otago University — A166

Design: 10c, Conferring degree and arms of the University, horiz.

**1969, June 3**

**425** A166 3c multicolored .25 .25
**426** A166 10c multicolored .35 .35

Centenary of the University of Otago.

Oldest House in New Zealand, Kerikeri A167

Design: 6c, Bay of Islands.

**1969, Aug. 18 Litho. Wmk. 253**

**427** A167 4c multicolored .30 .30
**428** A167 6c multicolored .75 .75

Early European settlements in New Zealand on the 150th anniv. of the founding of Kerikeri, the oldest existing European settlement.

Nativity, by Federico Fiori — A168

*Perf. 13½x14*

**1969, Oct. 1 Photo. Wmk. 253**

**429** A168 2½c multicolored .25 .25

**Unwmk.**

**430** A168 2½c multicolored .25 .25

Christmas.

Capt. Cook, Transit of Venus and Octant A169

Designs: 6c, Joseph Banks and bark Endeavour. 18c, Dr. Daniel Solander and matata branch (rhabdothamnus solandri). 28c, Queen Elizabeth II and map showing Cook's chart of 1769.

**1969, Oct. 9** ***Perf. 14½x14***

**431** A169 4c dk bl, blk & brt rose .50 .50
- *a.* Imperf., pair 425.00

**432** A169 6c sl grn & choc 1.25 *1.25*

**433** A169 18c choc, sl grn & black 2.00 2.00

**434** A169 28c dk ultra, blk & brt rose 3.50 *3.50*
- *a.* Souv. sheet of 4, #431-434 18.50 18.50

*Nos. 431-434 (4)* 7.25 7.25

Cook's landing in New Zealand, bicent.

Child Drinking Milk, and Cattle A170

7c, Wheat and child with empty bowl.

**1969, Nov. 18 Photo.** ***Perf. 13***

**435** A170 7c multicolored 1.25 1.25

**436** A170 8c multicolored 1.25 1.25

25th anniv. of CORSO (Council of Organizations for Relief Services Overseas).

Cardigan Bay A171

**1970, Jan. 28 Unwmk.** ***Perf. 11½***

**Granite Paper**

**437** A171 10c multicolored .40 .40

Return to New Zealand from the US of Cardigan Bay, 1st standard bred light-harness race horse to win a million dollars in stake money.

Glade Copper Butterfly A172

Scarlet Parrotfish A173

New Zealand Coat of Arms and Queen Elizabeth II — A174

Egmont National Park A176

Hauraki Gulf Maritime Park — A177

Maori Fishhook A175

Designs: 1c, Red admiral butterfly. 2c, Tussock butterfly. 2½c, Magpie moth. 3c, Lichen moth. 4c, Puriri moth. 6c, Sea horses. 7c, Leatherjackets (fish). 7½c, Garfish. 8c, John dory (fish). 18c, Maori club. 20c, Maori tattoo pattern. 30c, Mt. Cook National Park (chamois). 50c, Abel Tasman National Park. $1, Geothermal power plant. $2, Helicopter over field, molecule (agricultural technology).

**1970-71 Wmk. 253** ***Perf. 13½x13***

**438** A172 ½c ultra & multi .25 .25

**439** A172 1c dp bis & multi .25 .25
- *a.* Bklt. pane of 3 + 3 labels ('71) 2.50
- *b.* Red omitted 275.00

**440** A172 2c ol grn & multi .25 .25
- *a.* Black omitted 400.00

**441** A172 2½c yel & multi .30 .25

**442** A172 3c brown & multi .25 .25

**443** A172 4c dk brown & multi .25 .25
- *a.* Bright green omitted 250.00 110.00

**444** A173 5c dk green & multi .35 *.80*

**445** A173 6c dp car & multi .45 .80

**446** A173 7c brn red & multi .50 1.50

**447** A173 7½c dk vio & multi .75 .75

**448** A173 8c blue grn & multi .50 .25

***Perf. 14½x14***

**449** A174 10c dk bl, sil, red & ultra .45 .25

***Perf. 14x13, 13x14***

**450** A175 15c brick red, sal & blk .75 .50
- *a.* Brick red omitted 700.00

**451** A177 18c yel grn, blk & red brn .75 .50

**452** A175 20c yel brn & blk .75 .25

Nos. 439, 442 and 443 exist with watermark either sideways or upright.

***Perf. 13½x12½***

**Unwmk.**

**453** A176 23c bl, grn & blk .60 .30

**Litho.**

***Perf. 13½***

**454** A177 25c gray & multi 1.25 .50
- *a.* Perf. 14 ('76) .60 .50

**455** A177 30c tan & multi .60 .25
- *a.* Perf. 14 ('76) 1.25 1.75

**Photo.**

***Perf. 13½x12½***

**456** A176 50c sl grn & multi .75 .25
- *a.* Apple grn omitted 27.50
- *b.* Buff omitted 55.00
- *c.* Slate grn omitted 350.00

***Perf. 11½***

**Granite Paper**

**457** A175 $1 lt ultra & multi 1.50 1.00

**458** A175 $2 ol & multi 3.25 1.50

*Nos. 438-458 (21)* 14.75 10.90

The 10c for the visit of Queen Elizabeth II, Prince Philip and Princess Anne.

Issued: 10c, 3/12/70; ½c-4c, 9/2/70; 5c-8c, 11/4/70; 15c-20c, 1/20/71; 25c-50c, 9/1/71; $1-$2, 4/14/71; 23c, 12/1/71.

See Nos. 533-546. For surcharge see No. 480.

EXPO '70 Emblem, Geyser Restaurant — A178

Designs: 8c, EXPO '70 emblem and New Zealand Pavilion. 18c, EXPO '70 emblem and bush walk (part of N.Z. exhibit).

***Perf. 13x13½***

**1970, Apr. 8 Photo. Unwmk.**

**459** A178 7c multicolored .75 .75

**460** A178 8c multicolored .75 .75

**461** A178 18c multicolored 1.50 1.50

*Nos. 459-461 (3)* 3.00 3.00

EXPO '70 Intl. Expo., Osaka, Japan.

UN Headquarters, New York — A179

UN, 25th anniv.: 10c, Plowing toward the sun and "25" with laurel.

**1970, June 24 Litho.** ***Perf. 13½***

**462** A179 3c multicolored .25 .25

**463** A179 10c yellow & red .35 .35

Adoration, by Correggio — A180

Tower, Catholic Church, Sockburn A181

Christmas: 3c, Holy Family, stained glass window, First Presbyterian Church, Invercargill.

**1970, Oct. 1 Unwmk.** ***Perf. 12½***

**464** A180 2½c multicolored .25 .25

**465** A180 3c multicolored .25 .25
- *a.* Green omitted 275.00

**466** A181 10c silver, org & blk .45 .45

*Nos. 464-466 (3)* .95 .95

Chatham Islands Mollymawk — A182

**1970, Dec. 2 Photo.** ***Perf. 13x13½***

**467** A182 1c Chatham Islands lily .25 .25

**468** A182 2c shown .25 .25

G Clef, Emblem and Spinning Wheel A183

Rotary Emblem and Map of New Zealand A184

**1971, Feb. 10 Photo.** ***Perf. 13x13½***

**469** A183 4c multicolored .25 .25

**470** A184 10c lemon, dk blue & gold .35 .35

50th anniv. of Country Women's Inst. (4c) and Rotary Intl. in New Zealand (10c).

Ocean Racer A185

8c, One Ton Cup and blueprint of racing yacht.

**1971, Mar. 3 Litho.** ***Perf. 13½x13***

**471** A185 5c blue, blk & red .25 .25

**472** A185 8c ultra & black .65 .65

First challenge in New Zealand waters for the One Ton Cup ocean race.

Coats of Arms A186

**1971, May 12 Photo.** ***Perf. 13x13½***

**473** A186 3c Palmerston North .25 .25

**474** A186 4c Auckland .25 .25

**475** A186 5c Invercargill .30 .30

*Nos. 473-475 (3)* .80 .80

Centenary of New Zealand cities.

Map of Antarctica — A187

**1971, June 9 Photo.** ***Perf. 13x13½***

**476** A187 6c dk blue, pur & grn 1.40 *1.40*

10th anniv. of the Antarctic Treaty pledging peaceful uses of and scientific cooperation in Antarctica.

Child on Swing — A188

**1971, June 9** ***Perf. 13½x13***

**477** A1887c yellow & multi 1.00 1.00

25th anniv. of UNICEF.

Opening of New Zealand's 1st Satellite Earth Station near Warkworth A189

**1971, July 14** ***Perf. 11½***

**478** A189 8c Radar Station .75 .75

**479** A189 10c Satellite .75 .75

No. 441 Surcharged

**1971 Wmk. 253** ***Perf. 13½x13***

**480** A172 4c on 2½c multi .45 .25
- *a.* Narrow bars .25 .25

Surcharge typographed on No. 480, photogravure or typographed on No. 480a.

Holy Night, by Carlo Maratta — A190

The Three Kings — A191

Christmas: 4c, Annunciation, stained glass window, St. Luke's Anglican Church, Havelock North.

*Perf. 13x13½*

**1971, Oct. 6 Photo. Unwmk.**

**481** A190 3c orange & multi .25 .25
**482** A191 4c multicolored .25 .25
**483** A191 10c dk blue & multi .50 .50
*Nos. 481-483 (3)* 1.00 1.00

World Rose Convention — A192

**1971, Nov. 3** ***Perf. 11½***

**484** A192 2c Tiffany rose .25 .25
**485** A192 5c Peace rose .35 .35
**486** A192 8c Chrysler Imperial rose .85 .85
*Nos. 484-486 (3)* 1.45 1.45

Rutherford and Alpha Particles Passing Atomic Nucleus A193

7c, Lord Rutherford, by Sir Oswald Birley, and formula of disintegration of nitrogen atom.

**1971, Dec. 1 Litho.** ***Perf. 13½x13***

**487** A193 1c gray & multi .25 .25
**488** A193 7c multicolored .75 .75

Centenary of the birth of Ernest Lord Rutherford (1871-1937), physicist.

Benz, 1895 — A194

Vintage Cars: 4c, Oldsmobile, 1904. 5c, Model T Ford, 1914. 6c, Cadillac service car, 1915. 8c, Chrysler, 1924. 10c, Austin 7, 1923.

**1972, Feb. 2** ***Perf. 14x14½***

**489** A194 3c brn, car & multi .25 .25
**490** A194 4c brt lilac & multi .25 .25
**491** A194 5c lilac rose & multi .30 .30
**492** A194 6c gray grn & multi .40 .40
**493** A194 8c vio blue & multi .60 .60
**494** A194 10c sepia & multi .75 .75
*Nos. 489-494 (6)* 2.55 2.55

13th International Vintage Car Rally, New Zealand, Feb. 1972.

Asian-Oceanic Postal Union — A195

Designs: 3c, Wanganui City arms and Drurie Hill tower, vert. 5c, De Havilland DH89 and Boeing 737 planes, vert. 8c, French frigate and Maori palisade at Moturoa, vert. 10c, Stone cairn at Kaeo (site of first Methodist mission).

**1972, Apr. 5** ***Perf. 13x14, 14x13***

**495** A195 3c violet & multi .30 .30
**496** A195 4c brn org, blk & brn .30 .30
**497** A195 5c blue & multi .45 .45
**498** A195 8c green & multi 1.25 1.25
**499** A195 10c olive, yel & blk 1.50 1.50
*Nos. 495-499 (5)* 3.80 3.80

Cent. of Council government at Wanganui (3c); 10th anniv. of Asian-Oceanic Postal Union (4c); 25th anniv. of Nat. Airways Corp. (5c); bicent. of the landing by Marion du Fresne at the Bay of Islands (8c); 150th anniv. of the Methodist Church in New Zealand (10c).

Black Scree Cotula — A196

Alpine Plants: 6c, North Is. edelweiss. 8c, Haast's buttercup. 10c, Brown mountain daisy.

**1972, June 7 Litho.** ***Perf. 13x14***

**500** A196 4c orange & multi .55 .55
**501** A196 6c dp blue & multi .70 .70
**502** A196 8c rose lilac & multi 1.10 1.10
**503** A196 10c yel green & multi 1.50 1.50
*Nos. 500-503 (4)* 3.85 3.85

Madonna and Child, by Murillo — A197

Christmas: 5c, Resurrection, stained-glass window, St. John's Methodist Church, Levin. 10c, Pohutukawa (New Zealand's Christmas flower).

**1972, Oct. 4 Photo.** ***Perf. 11½***

**504** A197 3c gray & multi .25 .25
**505** A197 5c gray & multi .25 .25
**506** A197 10c gray & multi .65 .65
*Nos. 504-506 (3)* 1.15 1.15

New Zealand Lakes — A198

**1972, Dec. 6 Photo. Unwmk.**

**507** A198 6c Waikaremoana 1.25 1.25
**508** A198 8c Hayes 1.50 1.50
**509** A198 18c Wakatipu 2.25 *2.25*
**510** A198 23c Rotomahana 3.00 *3.00*
*Nos. 507-510 (4)* 8.00 8.00

Old Pollen Street A199

Coal Mining and Landscape A200

Cloister, University of Canterbury A201

Forest, Birds and Lake A202

Rowing and Olympic Emblems A203

Progress Chart A204

**1973, Feb. 7 Litho.** ***Perf. 13½x13***

**511** A199 3c ocher & multi .25 .25
**512** A200 4c blue & multi .25 .25
**513** A201 5c multicolored .25 .25
**514** A202 6c blue & multi .50 .50
**515** A203 8c multicolored .60 .60
**516** A204 10c blue & multi .60 .60
*Nos. 511-516 (6)* 2.45 2.45

Centenaries of Thames and Westport Boroughs (3c, 4c); centenary of the Univ. of Canterbury, Christchurch (5c); 50th anniv. of Royal Forest and Bird Protection Soc. (6c); success of New Zealand rowing team at 20th Olympic Games (8c); 25th anniv. of the Economic Commission for Asia and the Far East (ECAFE, 10c).

Class W Locomotive, 1889 — A205

New Zealand Steam Locomotives: 4c, Class X, 1908. 5c, "Passchendaele" Ab Class. 10c, Ja Class, last steam locomotive.

**1973, Apr. 4 Litho.** ***Perf. 14½***

**517** A205 3c lt green & multi .35 .25
**518** A205 4c lil rose & multi .35 .25
**519** A205 5c lt blue & multi .45 .45
**520** A205 10c cream & multi 1.75 1.75
*Nos. 517-520 (4)* 2.90 2.70

Maori Woman and Child, by Hodgkins — A206

Paintings by Frances Hodgkins: 8c, The Hill Top. 10c, Barn in Picardy. 18c, Self-portrait, Still Life.

**1973, June 6 Photo.** ***Perf. 12x11½***

**521** A206 5c multicolored .50 .50
**522** A206 8c multicolored .90 .90
**523** A206 10c multicolored .90 .90
**524** A206 18c multicolored 1.50 1.50
*Nos. 521-524 (4)* 3.80 3.80

Christmas in New Zealand — A207

Christmas: 3c, Tempi Madonna, by Raphael. 5c, Three Kings, stained-glass window, St. Theresa's R.C. Church, Auckland.

**1973, Oct. 3 Photo.** ***Perf. 12½x13½***

**525** A207 3c gold & multi .25 .25
**526** A207 5c gold & multi .25 .25
**527** A207 10c gold & multi .50 .50
*Nos. 525-527 (3)* 1.00 1.00

Mt. Ngauruhoe A208

6c, Mitre Peak. 18c, Mt. Sefton, horiz. 23c, Burnett Range, horiz.

***Perf. 13x13½, 13½x13***

**1973, Dec. 5 Photo.**

**528** A208 6c multi .65 .65
**529** A208 8c shown .85 .85
**530** A208 18c multi 1.60 1.60
**531** A208 23c multi 1.90 1.90
*Nos. 528-531 (4)* 5.00 5.00

### Types of 1970-71

Designs as before.

***Perf. 13½x13***

**1973-76 Photo. Unwmk.**

**533** A172 1c multicolored .60 *1.00*
*a.* Bklt. pane of 3 + 3 labels ('74) 2.50
**534** A172 2c multicolored .30 .25
**536** A172 3c multicolored .50 .50
**537** A172 4c multicolored .45 .25
**538** A173 5c multicolored .60 .60
**539** A173 6c multicolored 1.50 1.50
**540** A173 7c multicolored 4.00 2.75
**542** A173 8c multicolored 4.75 3.50

***Perf. 14x13½***

**543** A174 10c multicolored 1.25 .25

***Perf. 13x14, 14x13***

**544** A175 15c multicolored .50 .50
**545** A177 18c multicolored 2.00 .60
**546** A175 20c yel brn & blk .80 .80
*Nos. 533-546 (12)* 17.25 12.50

Issued: 2c, 10c, 6/73; 1c, 4c, 6c, 9/7/73; 5c, 1973; 3c, 7c, 8c, 18c, 20c, 1974; 15c, 8/2/76.

For surcharges see Nos. 630-631.

Hurdles and Games' Emblem — A209

Designs: 5c, Paraplegic ballplayer. 10c, Bicycling. 18c, Rifle shooting. 23c, Lawn bowling. 4c, 10c, 18c and 23c stamps also show Commonwealth Games' emblem.

**1974, Jan. 9 Litho.** ***Perf. 13x13½***

**547** A209 4c yellow & multi .30 .30
**548** A209 5c violet & black .30 .30
**549** A209 10c brt red & multi .70 .70
**550** A209 18c brown & multi .45 .45
**551** A209 23c yel green & multi .55 .55
*Nos. 547-551 (5)* 2.30 2.30

10th British Commonwealth Games, Christchurch, 1/24-2/2. #548 for the 4th Paraplegic Games, Dunedin, 1/10-20.

Souvenir Sheet

New Zealand Day — A210

**1974, Feb. 6 Litho. *Perf. 13***

| | | | | |
|---|---|---|---|---|
| **552** | A210 | Sheet of 5 | 1.60 | 1.60 |
| *a.* | | 4c Treaty House, Waitangi | .25 | .25 |
| *b.* | | 4c Parliament extension buildings | .25 | .25 |
| *c.* | | 4c Signing Treaty of Waitangi | .25 | .25 |
| *d.* | | 4c Queen Elizabeth II | .25 | .25 |
| *e.* | | 4c Integrated school | .25 | .25 |

New Zealand Day (Waitangi Day). No. 552 has marginal inscription and imprint.

"Spirit of Napier" Fountain — A211

Clock Tower, Bern — A212

Design: 8c, UPU emblem.

**1974, Apr. 3 Photo. *Perf. 11½***

| | | | | |
|---|---|---|---|---|
| **553** | A211 | 4c blue green & multi | .25 | .25 |
| **554** | A212 | 5c brown & multi | .25 | .25 |
| **555** | A212 | 8c lemon & multi | .60 | .60 |
| | | *Nos. 553-555 (3)* | 1.10 | 1.10 |

Centenaries of Napier (4c); UPU (5c, 8c).

Boeing Seaplane, 1919 A213

Designs: 4c, Lockheed Electra, 1937. 5c, Bristol freighter, 1958. 23c, Empire S30 flying boat, 1940.

**1974, June 5 Litho. *Perf. 14x13***

| | | | | |
|---|---|---|---|---|
| **556** | A213 | 3c multicolored | .35 | .35 |
| **557** | A213 | 4c multicolored | .40 | .40 |
| **558** | A213 | 5c multicolored | .40 | .40 |
| **559** | A213 | 23c multicolored | 1.60 | 1.60 |
| | | *Nos. 556-559 (4)* | 2.75 | 2.75 |

Development of New Zealand's air transport.

Adoration of the Kings, by Conrad Witz — A214

Christmas: 5c, Angels, stained glass window, St. Paul's Church, Wellington. 10c, Christmas lily (lilium candidum).

**1974, Oct. 2 Photo. *Perf. 11½***
**Granite Paper**

| | | | | |
|---|---|---|---|---|
| **560** | A214 | 3c olive & multi | .25 | .25 |
| **561** | A214 | 5c lilac & multi | .25 | .25 |
| **562** | A214 | 10c orange & multi | .50 | .50 |
| | | *Nos. 560-562 (3)* | 1.00 | 1.00 |

Offshore Islands A215

**1974, Dec. 4 Photo. *Perf. 13½x13***

| | | | | |
|---|---|---|---|---|
| **563** | A215 | 6c Great Barrier | .40 | .40 |
| **564** | A215 | 8c Stewart | .60 | .60 |
| **565** | A215 | 18c White | .85 | .85 |
| **566** | A215 | 23c The Brothers | 1.00 | 1.00 |
| | | *Nos. 563-566 (4)* | 2.85 | 2.85 |

Child Using Walker A216

Farm Woman and Children A217

IWY Symbol A218

Otago Medical School A219

**1975, Feb. 5 Litho. *Perf. 13½x13***

| | | | | |
|---|---|---|---|---|
| **567** | A216 | 3c orange & multi | .25 | .25 |
| **568** | A217 | 5c green & multi | .25 | .25 |
| **569** | A218 | 10c blue & multi | .25 | .25 |
| **570** | A219 | 18c multicolored | .50 | .50 |
| | | *Nos. 567-570 (4)* | 1.25 | 1.25 |

New Zealand Crippled Children's Soc., 40th anniv. (3c); Women's Division Federated Farmers of N. Z., 50th anniv. (5c); IWY (10c); Otago Medical School cent. (18c).

Scow "Lake Erie," 1873 A220

Historic Sailing Ships: 5c, Schooner "Herald," 1826. 8c, Brigantine "New Zealander," 1828. 10c, Topsail schooner "Jessie Kelly," 1866. 18c, Barque "Tory," 1834. 23c, Clipper "Rangitiki," 1863.

**1975, Apr. 2 Litho. *Perf. 13½x13***

| | | | | |
|---|---|---|---|---|
| **571** | A220 | 4c vermilion & blk | .30 | .30 |
| **572** | A220 | 5c grnsh blue & blk | .30 | .30 |
| **573** | A220 | 8c yellow & black | .45 | .45 |
| **574** | A220 | 10c yellow grn & blk | .55 | .55 |
| **575** | A220 | 18c brown & black | .80 | .80 |
| **576** | A220 | 23c dull lilac & blk | .85 | .85 |
| | | *Nos. 571-576 (6)* | 3.25 | 3.25 |

State Forest Parks A221

**1975, June 4 Photo. *Perf. 13½x13***

| | | | | |
|---|---|---|---|---|
| **577** | A221 | 6c Lake Sumner | .50 | .50 |
| **578** | A221 | 8c North West Nelson | .80 | .80 |
| **579** | A221 | 18c Kaweka | 1.00 | 1.00 |
| **580** | A221 | 23c Coromandel | 1.25 | 1.25 |
| | | *Nos. 577-580 (4)* | 3.55 | 3.55 |

Virgin and Child, by Zanobi Machiavelli (1418-1479) — A222

Stained Glass Window, Greendale Methodist/Presbyterian Church — A223

Christmas: 10c, Medieval ships and doves.

***Perf. 13½x14, 14x13½***
**1975, Oct. 1 Photo.**

| | | | | |
|---|---|---|---|---|
| **581** | A222 | 3c multicolored | .25 | .25 |
| **582** | A223 | 5c multicolored | .25 | .25 |
| **583** | A223 | 10c multicolored | .45 | .45 |
| | | *Nos. 581-583 (3)* | .95 | .95 |

Sterling Silver — A224

Roses: 2c, Lilli Marlene. 3c, Queen Elizabeth. 4c, Super star. 5c, Diamond jubilee. 6c, Cresset. 7c, Michele Meilland. 8c, Josephine Bruce. 9c, Iceberg.

**1975, Nov. 26 Photo. *Perf. 14½x14***

| | | | | |
|---|---|---|---|---|
| **584** | A224 | 1c multicolored | .25 | .25 |
| **585** | A224 | 2c orange & multi | .25 | .25 |
| **586** | A224 | 3c ultra & multi | .25 | .25 |
| *a.* | | Perf. 14½ ('79) | .25 | .25 |
| **587** | A224 | 4c purple & multi | .25 | .25 |
| **588** | A224 | 5c brown & multi | .25 | .25 |
| **589** | A224 | 6c multicolored ('76) | .25 | .25 |
| *a.* | | Perf. 14½ | .50 | .50 |
| **590** | A224 | 7c multicolored ('76) | .25 | .25 |
| *a.* | | Perf. 14½ | .70 | .60 |
| **591** | A224 | 8c yellow & multi ('76) | .25 | .25 |
| *a.* | | Perf. 14½ | .70 | .60 |
| **592** | A224 | 9c blue & multi | .25 | .25 |
| | | *Nos. 584-592 (9)* | 2.25 | 2.25 |

For surcharges see Nos. 693, 695, 718.

Family and Mothers' League Emblem A225

Designs: 7c, "Weight, measure, temperature and capacity." 8c, 1st emigrant ship "William Bryan" and Mt. Egmont. 10c, Maori and Caucasian women and YWCA emblem. 25c, Telecommunications network on Goode's equal area projection.

**1976, Feb. 4 Litho. *Perf. 14***

| | | | | |
|---|---|---|---|---|
| **593** | A225 | 6c olive & multi | .25 | .25 |
| **594** | A225 | 7c lilac & multi | .25 | .25 |
| **595** | A225 | 8c red & multi | .25 | .25 |
| **596** | A225 | 10c yellow & multi | .25 | .25 |
| **597** | A225 | 25c tan & multi | .35 | .35 |
| | | *Nos. 593-597 (5)* | 1.35 | 1.35 |

League of Mothers of New Zealand, 50th anniv. (6c); Metric conversion, 1976 (7c); cent. of New Plymouth (8c); YWCA in New Zealand, 50th anniv. (10c); cent. of link into intl. telecommunications network (25c).

Gig A226

Farm Vehicles: 7c, Thornycroft truck. 8c, Scandi wagon. 9c, Traction engine. 10c, Wool wagon. 25c, One-horse cart.

**1976, Apr. 7 Litho. *Perf. 14x13½***

| | | | | |
|---|---|---|---|---|
| **598** | A226 | 6c dk olive & multi | .25 | .25 |
| **599** | A226 | 7c gray & multi | .25 | .25 |
| **600** | A226 | 8c dk blue & multi | .40 | .40 |
| **601** | A226 | 9c maroon & multi | .30 | .30 |
| **602** | A226 | 10c brown & multi | .30 | .30 |
| **603** | A226 | 25c multicolored | .90 | .90 |
| | | *Nos. 598-603 (6)* | 2.40 | 2.40 |

Purakaunui Falls — A227

Waterfalls: 14c, Marakopa Falls. 15c, Bridal Veil Falls. 16c, Papakorito Falls.

**1976, June 2 Photo. *Perf. 11½***

| | | | | |
|---|---|---|---|---|
| **604** | A227 | 10c blue & multi | .35 | .35 |
| **605** | A227 | 14c lilac & multi | .50 | .50 |
| **606** | A227 | 15c ocher & multi | .60 | .60 |
| **607** | A227 | 16c multicolored | .75 | .75 |
| | | *Nos. 604-607 (4)* | 2.20 | 2.20 |

Nativity, Carved Ivory, Spain, 16th Century — A228

Christmas: 11c, Risen Christ, St. Joseph's Church, Grey Lynn, Auckland, horiz. 18c, "Hark the Herald Angels Sing," horiz.

***Perf. 14x14½, 14½x14***
**1976, Oct. 6 Photo.**

| | | | | |
|---|---|---|---|---|
| **608** | A228 | 7c ocher & multi | .25 | .25 |
| **609** | A228 | 11c ocher & multi | .35 | .35 |
| **610** | A228 | 18c ocher & multi | .45 | .45 |
| | | *Nos. 608-610 (3)* | 1.05 | 1.05 |

Maripi (Carved Wooden Knife) — A229

Maori Artifacts: 12c, Putorino, carved flute. 13c, Wahaika, hardwood club. 14c, Kotiate, violin-shaped weapon.

**1976, Nov. 24 Photo. *Perf. 11½***
**Granite Paper**

| | | | | |
|---|---|---|---|---|
| **611** | A229 | 11c multicolored | .25 | .25 |
| **612** | A229 | 12c multicolored | .25 | .25 |
| **613** | A229 | 13c multicolored | .25 | .25 |
| **614** | A229 | 14c multicolored | .25 | .25 |
| | | *Nos. 611-614 (4)* | 1.00 | 1.00 |

Arms of Hamilton A230

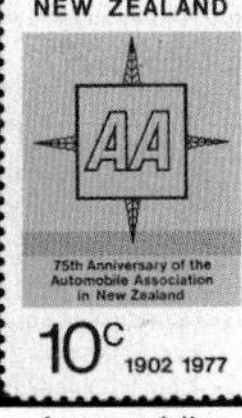


Automobile Assoc. Emblem A231

Designs: No. 616, Arms of Gisborne. No. 617, Arms of Masterton. No. 619, Emblem of Royal Australasian College of Surgeons.

**1977, Jan. 19 Litho. *Perf. 13x13½***

| | | | | |
|---|---|---|---|---|
| **615** | A230 | 8c multicolored | .25 | .25 |
| **616** | A230 | 8c multicolored | .25 | .25 |
| **617** | A230 | 8c multicolored | .25 | .25 |
| *a.* | | Strip of 3, #615-617 | .75 | .75 |

**618** A231 10c multicolored .30 .35
**619** A230 10c multicolored .30 .35
*a.* Pair, #618-619 .60 *.75*
*Nos. 615-619 (5)* 1.35 1.45

Centenaries of Hamilton, Gisborne and Masterton (cities); 75th anniv. of the New Zealand Automobile Assoc. and 50th anniv. of the Royal Australasian College of Surgeons.

Souvenir Sheet

Queen Elizabeth II, 1976 — A232

Designs: Various portraits.

**1977, Feb. Photo. *Perf. 14x14½***
**620** A232 Sheet of 5 1.25 *1.25*
*a.-e.* 8c single stamp .25 .25
*f.* Sheet imperf. *1,350.*

25th anniv. of the reign of Elizabeth II.

Physical Education, Maori Culture A233

Education Dept., Geography, Science A234

#623, Special school for the deaf; kindergarten. #624, Language class. #625, Home economics, correspondence school, teacher training.

**1977, Apr. 6 Litho. *Perf. 13x13½***
**621** A233 8c shown .40 .40
**622** A234 8c shown .40 .40
**623** A233 8c multicolored .40 .40
**624** A234 8c multicolored .40 .40
**625** A233 8c multicolored .40 .40
*a.* Strip of 5, #621-625 2.50 2.50
*Nos. 621-625 (5)* 2.00 2.00

Cent. of Education Act, establishing Dept. of Education.

Karitane Beach — A235

Seascapes and beach scenes: 16c, Ocean Beach, Mount Maunganui. 18c, Piha Beach. 30c, Kaikoura Coast.

**1977, June 1 Photo. *Perf. 14½***
**626** A235 10c multicolored .25 .25
**627** A235 16c multicolored .30 .30
**628** A235 18c multicolored .30 .30
**629** A235 30c multicolored .35 .35
*Nos. 626-629 (4)* 1.20 1.20

**Nos. 536-537 Surcharged with New Value and Heavy Bar**

**1977 Unwmk. *Perf. 13½x13***
**630** A172 7c on 3c multicolored .35 .35
**631** A172 8c on 4c multicolored .35 .35

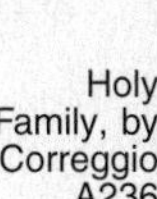

Holy Family, by Correggio A236

Window, St. Michael's and All Angels Church — A237

Partridge in a Pear Tree — A238

**1977, Oct. 5 Photo. *Perf. 11½***
**632** A236 7c multicolored .25 .25
**633** A237 16c multicolored .30 .30
**634** A238 23c multicolored .50 .50
*Nos. 632-634 (3)* 1.05 1.05

Christmas.

Merryweather Manual Pump, 1860 — A239

Fire Fighting Equipment: 11c, 2-wheel hose reel and ladder, 1880. 12c, Shand Mason Steam Fire Engine, 1873. 23c, Chemical fire engine, 1888.

**1977, Dec. 7 Litho. *Perf. 14x13½***
**635** A239 10c multicolored .25 .25
**636** A239 11c multicolored .25 .25
**637** A239 12c multicolored .25 .25
**638** A239 23c multicolored .30 .30
*Nos. 635-638 (4)* 1.05 1.05

A240

A240a

Parliament Building, Wellington — A241

**1977-82 Photo. *Perf. 14½***
**648** A240 10c ultra & multi .25 .25
*a.* Perf. 14½x14 .80 .50

***Perf. 14½x14***
**649** A240a 24c blue & lt green .30 .25
*a.* Perf. 13x12½ .45 .25

***Perf. 13***
**650** A241 $5 multicolored 4.00 2.00
*Nos. 648-650 (3)* 4.55 2.50

Issued: No. 648, 2/79; No. 648a, 12/7/77; $5, 12/2/81; No. 649, 4/1/82; No. 649a, 12/13/82.

For surcharge see No. 694.

A242

**Coil Stamps**

**1978 Photo. *Perf. 13½x13***
**651** A242 1c red lilac .25 .25
**652** A242 2c orange .25 .25
**653** A242 5c brown .25 .25

***Perf. 14½x14***
**654** A242 10c ultramarine .25 .25
*Nos. 651-654 (4)* 1.00 1.00

Issue dates: 10c, May 3; others, June 9.

Ashburton A244

Stratford A245

Old Telephone — A246

Bay of Islands A247

**1978, Feb. 1 Litho. *Perf. 14***
**656** A244 10c multicolored .25 .25
**657** A245 10c multicolored .25 .25
*a.* Pair, #656-657 .50 .50
**658** A246 12c multicolored .25 .25
**659** A247 20c multicolored .30 .30
*Nos. 656-659 (4)* 1.05 1.05

Cent. of the cities of Ashburton, Stratford, the NZ Telephone Co. and Bay of Islands County.

Lincoln Univ. College of Agriculture, Cent. — A248

Designs: 10c, Students and Ivey Hall. 12c, Grazing sheep. 15c, Mechanical fertilization. 16c, Furrow, plow and tractor. 20c, Combine harvester. 30c, Grazing cattle.

**1978, Apr. 26 *Perf. 14½***
**660** A248 10c multicolored .25 .25
**661** A248 12c multicolored .25 .25
**662** A248 15c multicolored .25 .25
**663** A248 16c multicolored .25 .25
**664** A248 20c multicolored .25 .25
**665** A248 30c multicolored .30 .30
*Nos. 660-665 (6)* 1.55 1.55

Maui Gas Drilling Platform — A249

The sea and its resources: 15c, Fishing boat. 20c, Map of New Zealand and 200-mile limit. 23c, Whale and bottle-nosed dolphins. 35c, Kingfish, snapper, grouper and squid.

**1978, June 7 Litho. *Perf. 13½x14***
**666** A249 12c multicolored .25 .25
**667** A249 15c multicolored .25 .25
**668** A249 20c multicolored .25 .25
**669** A249 23c multicolored .30 .30
**670** A249 35c multicolored .45 .45
*Nos. 666-670 (5)* 1.50 1.50

All Saints Church, Howick A250

Christmas: 7c, Holy Family, by El Greco, vert. 23c, Beach scene.

**1978, Oct. 4 Photo. *Perf. 11½***
**671** A250 7c gold & multi .25 .25
**672** A250 16c gold & multi .30 .30
**673** A250 23c gold & multi .35 .35
*Nos. 671-673 (3)* .90 .90

Sea Shells — A251

20c, Paua (Haliotis Iris). 30c, Toheroa (paphies ventricosa). 40c, Coarse dosinia (dosinia anus). 50c, Spiny murex (poirieria zelandica).

**1978, Nov. 29 Photo. *Perf. 13x12½***
**674** A251 20c multicolored .25 .25
**675** A251 30c multicolored .30 .25
**676** A251 40c multicolored .45 .30
**677** A251 50c multicolored .55 .40
*Nos. 674-677 (4)* 1.55 1.20

See Nos. 696-697.

Julius Vogel — A252

19th cent. NZ statesmen: No. 679, George Grey. No. 680, Richard John Seddon.

**1979, Feb. 7 Litho. *Perf. 13x13½***
**678** A252 10c light & dark brown .25 .25
**679** A252 10c light & dark brown .25 .25
**680** A252 10c light & dark brown .25 .25
*a.* Strip of 3, #678-680 1.10 1.10

Riverlands Cottage, Blenheim — A253

Early NZ Architecture: 12c, Mission House, Waimate North, 1831-32. 15c, The Elms, Anglican Church Mission, Tauranga, 1847. 20c, Provincial Council Buildings, Christchurch, 1859.

**1979, Apr. 4 *Perf. 13½x13***
**681** A253 10c multicolored .25 .25
**682** A253 12c multicolored .25 .25
**683** A253 15c black & gray .25 .25
**684** A253 20c multicolored .25 .25
*Nos. 681-684 (4)* 1.00 1.00

Whangaroa Harbor — A254

Small Harbors: 20c, Kawau Island. 23c, Akaroa Harbor, vert. 35c, Picton Harbor, vert.

***Perf. 13x13½, 13½x13***
**1979, June 6 Photo.**
**685** A254 15c multicolored .25 .25
**686** A254 20c multicolored .25 .25
**687** A254 23c multicolored .30 .30
**688** A254 35c multicolored .40 .40
*Nos. 685-688 (4)* 1.20 1.20

IYC
A255

**1979, June 6 Litho. *Perf. 14***
**689** A255 10c Children playing .25 .25

Virgin and Child, by Lorenzo Ghiberti — A256

Christmas: 25c, Christ Church, Russell, 1835. 35c, Pohutukawa ("Christmas") tree.

**1979, Oct. 3 Photo. *Perf. 11½***
**690** A256 10c multicolored .25 .25
**691** A256 25c multicolored .35 .35
**692** A256 35c multicolored .45 .45
*Nos. 690-692 (3)* 1.05 1.05

**Nos. 591a, 648 and 589a Surcharged**

**1979, Sept. *Perf. 14½, 14½x14 (14c)***
**693** A224 4c on 8c multi .25 .25
**694** A240 14c on 10c multi .25 .25
**695** A224 17c on 6c multi .25 .25
*Nos. 693-695 (3)* .75 .75

**Shell Type of 1978**

$1, Scallop (pecten novaezelandiae). $2, Circular saw (astraea heliotropium).

**1979, Nov. 26 Photo. *Perf. 13x12½***
**696** A251 $1 multicolored 1.25 .75
**697** A251 $2 multicolored 2.50 1.00

Debating Chamber, House of Parliament
A257

**1979, Nov. 26 Litho. *Perf. 14x13½***
**698** A257 14c shown .25 .25
**699** A257 20c Mace, black rod .25 .25
**700** A257 30c Wall hanging .40 .40
*Nos. 698-700 (3)* .90 .90

25th Commonwealth Parliamentary Conference, Wellington, Nov. 26-Dec. 2.

NZ No. 1
A258

**1980, Feb. 7 Litho. *Perf. 14x13½***
**701** A258 14c shown .25 .25
**702** A258 14c No. 2 .25 .25
**703** A258 14c No. 3 .25 .25
*a.* Souvenir sheet of 3, #701-703 2.00 2.00
*b.* Strip of 3, #701-703 .75 .75

NZ postage stamps, 125th anniv. No. 703a publicizes Zeapex '80 Intl. Stamp Exhib., Auckland, Aug. 23-31; it sold for 52c, of which 10c went to exhib. fund.

Maori Wood Carving, Tudor Towers
A259

Earina Autumnalis and Thelymitra Venosa — A260

Tractor Plowing, Golden Plow Trophy
A261

**1980, Feb. 7 *Perf. 14½***
**704** A259 17c multicolored .25 .25
**705** A260 25c multicolored .35 .35
**706** A261 30c multicolored .45 .45
*Nos. 704-706 (3)* 1.05 1.05

Rotorua cent.; Intl. Orchid Conf., Auckland, Oct.; World Plowing Championship, Christchurch, May.

Ewelme Cottage, Parnell, 1864
A262

Early NZ Architecture: 17c, Broadgreen, Nelson, 1855. 25c, Courthouse, Oamaru, 1822, 30c, Government Buildings, Wellington, 1877.

**1980, Apr. 2 Litho. *Perf. 13½x13***
**707** A262 14c multicolored .25 .25
**708** A262 17c multicolored .25 .25
**709** A262 25c green & black .30 .30
**710** A262 30c multicolored .35 .35
*Nos. 707-710 (4)* 1.15 1.15

Harbors
A263

**1980, June 4 Photo. *Perf. 13x13½***
**711** A263 25c Auckland .30 .20
**712** A263 30c Wellington .35 .35
**713** A263 35c Lyttelton .40 .40
**714** A263 50c Port Chalmers .65 .65
*Nos. 711-714 (4)* 1.70 1.60

Madonna and Child with Cherubim, by Andrea della Robbia — A264

25c, St. Mary's Church, New Plymouth. 35c, Picnic.

**1980, Oct. 1 Photo. *Perf. 12***
**715** A264 10c shown .25 .25
**716** A264 25c multi .30 .30
**717** A264 35c multi .40 .40
*Nos. 715-717 (3)* .95 .95

Christmas.

**No. 590 Surcharged**

**1980, Sept. 29 Photo. *Perf. 14½x14***
**718** A224 20c on 7c multicolored .25 .25

Te Heu Heu Tukino IV, Ngati Tuwharetoa Tribal Chief — A265

Maori Leaders: 25c, Te Hau-Takiri Wharepapa. 35c, Princess Te Puea Herangi. 45, Apirana Ngata. 60c, Hakopa Te Ata-o-tu.

**1980, Nov. 26 *Perf. 13***
**719** A265 15c multicolored .25 .25
**720** A265 25c multicolored .25 .25
**721** A265 35c multicolored .35 .35
**722** A265 45c multicolored .55 .55
**723** A265 60c multicolored .60 .60
*Nos. 719-723 (5)* 2.00 2.00

Henry A. Feilding, Borough Emblem
A266

**1981, Feb. 4 Litho. *Perf. 14½***
**724** A266 20c multicolored .30 .25

Borough of Feilding centenary.

IYD
A267

**1981, Feb. 4**
**725** A267 25c orange & black .35 .35

Family and Dog — A268

25c, Grandparents. 30c, Parents reading to children. 35c, Family outing.

**1981, Apr. 1 Litho. *Perf. 13***
**726** A268 20c shown .25 .25
**727** A268 25c multi .30 .30
**728** A268 30c multi .35 .35
**729** A268 35c multi .40 .40
*Nos. 726-729 (4)* 1.30 1.30

Shotover River — A269

30c, Kaiauai River, vert. 35c, Mangahao River, vert. 60c, Cleddau River.

**1981, June 3 Photo. *Perf. 13½***
**730** A269 30c multi .35 .35
**731** A269 35c multi .40 .40
**732** A269 40c shown .50 .50
**733** A269 60c multi .65 .65
*Nos. 730-733 (4)* 1.90 1.90

Prince Charles and Lady Diana
A270

No. 735, St. Paul's Cathedral.

**1981, July 29 Litho. *Perf. 14½***
**734** A270 20c shown .30 .25
**735** A270 20c multi .30 .25
*a.* Pair, #734-735 .60 .60

Royal Wedding.

Golden Tainui — A271

Christmas: 14c, Madonna and Child, by Marco d'Oggiono, 15th cent. 30c, St. John's Church, Wakefield.

**1981, Oct. Photo. *Perf. 11½***
**Granite Paper**
**736** A271 14c multicolored .25 .25
**737** A271 30c multicolored .30 .30
**738** A271 40c multicolored .45 .45
*Nos. 736-738 (3)* 1.00 1.00

SPCA Centenary
A272

Intl. Science Year
A273

Centenaries: No. 739, Tauranga. No. 740, Hawera. 30c, Frozen meat exports.

**1982, Feb. 3 Litho. *Perf. 14½***
**739** A272 20c multicolored .25 .25
**740** A272 20c multicolored .25 .25
*a.* Pair, #739-740 .60 .60
**741** A272 25c multicolored .30 .30
**742** A272 30c multicolored .40 .40
**743** A273 35c multicolored .45 .45
*Nos. 739-743 (5)* 1.65 1.65

Alberton Farmhouse, Auckland, 1867 — A274

25c, Caccia Birch, Palmerston North, 1893. 30c, Dunedin Railway Station, 1904. 35c, PO, Ophir, 1886.

**1982, Apr. 7 Litho.**
**744** A274 20c shown .25 .25
**745** A274 25c multicolored .30 .30
**746** A274 30c multicolored .45 .45
**747** A274 35c multicolored .45 .45
*Nos. 744-747 (4)* 1.45 1.45

Summer, Kaiteriteri
A275

40c, Autumn, Queenstown. 45c, Winter, Mt. Ngauruhoe. 70c, Spring, Wairarapa.

**1982, June 2 Photo. *Perf. 13½***
**748** A275 35c shown .40 .40
**749** A275 40c multicolored .45 .45
**750** A275 45c multicolored .50 .50
**751** A275 70c multicolored .85 .85
*Nos. 748-751 (4)* 2.20 2.20

Madonna with Child and Two Angels, by Piero di Cosimo — A276

Christmas: 35c, Rangiatea Maori Church, Otaki. 45c, Surf life-saving patrol.

**1982, Oct. 6 Photo.** ***Perf. 14***

| | | | | |
|---|---|---|---|---|
| **752** | A276 | 18c multicolored | .25 | .25 |
| **753** | A276 | 35c multicolored | .35 | .35 |
| **754** | A276 | 45c multicolored | .60 | .60 |
| | | *Nos. 752-754 (3)* | 1.20 | 1.20 |

Nephrite A277

Fruit Export A278

**1982-83 Litho.**

| | | | | |
|---|---|---|---|---|
| **755** | A277 | 1c shown | .25 | .25 |
| *a.* | | Perf 13x12½ | .40 | .40 |
| **756** | A277 | 2c Agate | .25 | .25 |
| *a.* | | Perf 13x12½ | 1.10 | 1.10 |
| **757** | A277 | 3c Iron pyrites | .25 | .25 |
| **758** | A277 | 4c Amethyst | .25 | .25 |
| **759** | A277 | 5c Carnelian | .25 | .25 |
| **760** | A277 | 9c Native sulphur | .25 | .25 |
| **761** | A278 | 10c Grapes | .25 | .25 |
| **762** | A278 | 20c Citrus fruit | .30 | .25 |
| **763** | A278 | 30c Nectarines | .35 | .25 |
| **764** | A278 | 40c Apples | .40 | .25 |
| **765** | A278 | 50c Kiwifruit | .45 | .25 |
| | | *Nos. 755-765 (11)* | 3.25 | 2.75 |

Issued: A277, Dec. 1; A278, Dec. 7, 1983.

Native Birds — A279

**1985-89** ***Perf. 14½***

| | | | | |
|---|---|---|---|---|
| **766** | A279 | 30c Kakapo | .75 | .25 |
| **767** | A279 | 45c Falcon | 1.25 | .50 |
| **768** | A279 | $1 Kokako | 1.25 | .45 |
| **769** | A279 | $2 Black Robin | 2.50 | .70 |
| *a.* | | Souvenir sheet of one | 11.00 | 11.00 |
| **770** | A279 | $3 Stitchbird | 4.00 | 2.75 |
| **770A** | A279 | $4 Saddleback | 4.75 | 3.25 |
| | | *Nos. 766-770A (6)* | 14.50 | 7.90 |

No. 769a for PHILEXFRANCE '89 and has margin picturing progressive proofs of No. 769. No. 769a sold for $3.50.

Issued: $1, $2, 4/24; $3, $4, 4/23/86; 30c, 45c, 5/1/86; No. 769a, 7/7/89.

See Nos. 830-835, 919-933.

Salvation Army in NZ Cent. — A280

Univ. of Auckland Cent. — A281

NZ-Australia Closer Economic Relationship Agreement — A282

Introduction of Rainbow Trout Cent. — A283

WCY — A284

***Perf. 14, 14x13½ (35c)***

**1983, Feb. 2 Litho.**

| | | | | |
|---|---|---|---|---|
| **771** | A280 | 24c multicolored | .25 | .25 |
| **772** | A281 | 30c multicolored | .30 | .30 |
| **773** | A282 | 35c multicolored | .35 | .35 |
| **774** | A283 | 40c multicolored | .60 | .60 |
| **775** | A284 | 45c multicolored | .70 | .70 |
| | | *Nos. 771-775 (5)* | 2.20 | 2.20 |

A285

24c, Queen Elizabeth II. 35c, Maori rock painting. 40c, Wool industry logos. 45c, Arms.

**1983, Mar. 14 Litho.** ***Perf. 14***

| | | | | |
|---|---|---|---|---|
| **776** | A285 | 24c multicolored | .30 | .30 |
| **777** | A285 | 35c multicolored | .35 | .35 |
| **778** | A285 | 40c multicolored | .45 | .45 |
| **779** | A285 | 45c multicolored | .65 | .65 |
| | | *Nos. 776-779 (4)* | 1.75 | 1.75 |

Commonwealth Day.

Island Bay, by Rita Angus (1908-1970) A286

Landscapes.

**1983, Apr. 6 Litho.** ***Perf. 14½***

| | | | | |
|---|---|---|---|---|
| **780** | A286 | 24c shown | .35 | .35 |
| **781** | A286 | 30c Central Otago | .45 | .45 |
| **782** | A286 | 35c Wanaka | .50 | .50 |
| **783** | A286 | 45c Tree, Greymouth | .60 | .60 |
| | | *Nos. 780-783 (4)* | 1.90 | 1.90 |

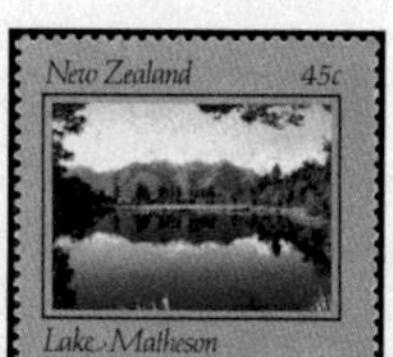


Lake Matheson A287

***Perf. 13½x13, 13x13½***

**1983, June 1 Photo.**

| | | | | |
|---|---|---|---|---|
| **784** | A287 | 35c Mt. Egmont, vert. | .40 | .40 |
| **785** | A287 | 40c Cooks Bay, vert. | .50 | .50 |
| **786** | A287 | 45c shown | .60 | .60 |
| **787** | A287 | 70c Lake Alexandrina | .95 | .95 |
| | | *Nos. 784-787 (4)* | 2.45 | 2.45 |

Christmas 1983 — A288

18c, Holy Family of the Oak Tree, by Raphael. 35c, St. Patrick's Church, Greymouth. 45c, Star, poinsettias.

**1983, Oct. 5 Photo.** ***Perf. 12***

| | | | | |
|---|---|---|---|---|
| **788** | A288 | 18c multicolored | .25 | .25 |
| **789** | A288 | 35c multicolored | .45 | .45 |
| **790** | A288 | 45c multicolored | .70 | .70 |
| | | *Nos. 788-790 (3)* | 1.40 | 1.40 |

Antarctic Research A289

**1984, Feb. 1 Litho.** ***Perf. 13½x13***

| | | | | |
|---|---|---|---|---|
| **791** | A289 | 24c Geology | .35 | .35 |
| **792** | A289 | 40c Biology | .55 | .55 |
| **793** | A289 | 58c Glaciology | .90 | .90 |
| **794** | A289 | 70c Meteorology | .95 | .95 |
| *a.* | | Souvenir sheet of 4, #791-794 | 3.00 | 3.00 |
| | | *Nos. 791-794 (4)* | 2.75 | 2.75 |

Ferry Mountaineer, Lake Wakatipu, 1879 — A290

40c, Waikana, Otago Harbor, 1909. 58c, Britannia, Waitemata Harbor, 1885. 70c, Wakatere, Firth of Thames, 1896.

**1984, Apr. 4 Litho.** ***Perf. 13½***

| | | | | |
|---|---|---|---|---|
| **795** | A290 | 24c shown | .40 | .40 |
| **796** | A290 | 40c multicolored | .50 | .50 |
| **797** | A290 | 58c multicolored | .65 | .65 |
| **798** | A290 | 70c multicolored | .90 | .90 |
| | | *Nos. 795-798 (4)* | 2.45 | 2.45 |

Skier, Mount Hutt — A291

**1984, June 6 Litho.** ***Perf. 13½x13***

| | | | | |
|---|---|---|---|---|
| **799** | A291 | 35c shown | .40 | .40 |
| **800** | A291 | 40c Coronet Peak | .50 | .50 |
| **801** | A291 | 45c Turoa | .60 | .60 |
| **802** | A291 | 70c Whakapapa | .85 | .85 |
| | | *Nos. 799-802 (4)* | 2.35 | 2.35 |

Hamilton's Frog A292

**1984, July 11** ***Perf. 13½***

| | | | | |
|---|---|---|---|---|
| **803** | A292 | 24c shown | .25 | .25 |
| **804** | A292 | 24c Great barrier skink | .25 | .25 |
| *a.* | | Pair, #803-804 | .80 | .80 |
| **805** | A292 | 30c Harlequin gecko | .30 | .30 |
| **806** | A292 | 58c Otago skink | .60 | .60 |
| **807** | A292 | 70c Gold-striped gecko | .80 | .80 |
| | | *Nos. 803-807 (5)* | 2.20 | 2.20 |

No. 804a has continuous design.

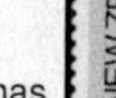

Christmas A293

Designs: 18c, Adoration of the Shepherds, by Lorenzo Di Credi. 35c, Old St. Paul's Church, Wellington, vert. 45c, Bell, vert.

***Perf. 13½x14, 14x13½***

**1984, Sept. 26 Photo.**

| | | | | |
|---|---|---|---|---|
| **808** | A293 | 18c multicolored | .25 | .25 |
| **809** | A293 | 35c multicolored | .35 | .35 |
| **810** | A293 | 45c multicolored | .50 | .50 |
| | | *Nos. 808-810 (3)* | 1.10 | 1.10 |

Military History A294

24c, South Africa, 1901. 40c, France, 1917. 58c, North Africa, 1942. 70c, Korea & South-east Asia, 1950-72.

**1984, Nov. 7 Litho.** ***Perf. 15x14***

| | | | | |
|---|---|---|---|---|
| **811** | A294 | 24c multi | .40 | .40 |
| **812** | A294 | 40c multi | .60 | .60 |
| **813** | A294 | 58c multi | .80 | .80 |
| **814** | A294 | 70c multi | .90 | .90 |
| *a.* | | Souvenir sheet of 4, #811-814 | 2.75 | *2.75* |
| | | *Nos. 811-814 (4)* | 2.70 | 2.70 |

St. John Ambulance Assoc. Cent. in NZ A295

**1985, Jan. 16 Litho.** ***Perf. 14***

| | | | | |
|---|---|---|---|---|
| **815** | A295 | 24c multicolored | .25 | .25 |
| **816** | A295 | 30c multicolored | .30 | .30 |
| **817** | A295 | 40c multicolored | .45 | .45 |
| | | *Nos. 815-817 (3)* | 1.00 | 1.00 |

Early Transportation — A296

24c, Nelson Horse Tram, 1862. 30c, Graham's Town-Steam, 1871. 35c, Dunedin Cable Car, 1881. 40c, Auckland Electric, 1902. 45c, Wellington Electric, 1904. 58c, Christchurch Electric, 1905.

**1985, Mar. 6 Litho.** ***Perf. 13½***

| | | | | |
|---|---|---|---|---|
| **818** | A296 | 24c multicolored | .40 | .25 |
| **819** | A296 | 30c multicolored | .40 | .40 |
| **820** | A296 | 35c multicolored | .45 | .45 |
| **821** | A296 | 40c multicolored | .50 | .50 |
| **822** | A296 | 45c multicolored | .55 | .55 |
| **823** | A296 | 58c multicolored | .60 | .60 |
| | | *Nos. 818-823 (6)* | 2.90 | 2.75 |

Bridges A297

35c, Shotover. 40c, Alexandra. 45c, South Rangitikei, vert. 70c, Twin Bridges, vert.

**1985, June 12 Photo.** ***Perf. 11½***

| | | | | |
|---|---|---|---|---|
| **824** | A297 | 35c multicolored | .45 | .45 |
| **825** | A297 | 40c multicolored | .50 | .50 |
| **826** | A297 | 45c multicolored | .65 | .65 |
| **827** | A297 | 70c multicolored | .90 | .90 |
| | | *Nos. 824-827 (4)* | 2.50 | 2.50 |

**Bird Type of 1985 and**

Elizabeth II — A298

**1985-89 Litho. *Perf. 14½x14***
**828** A298 25c multicolored .40 .40
**829** A298 35c multicolored .60 .60

***Perf. 14½***
**830** A279 40c Blue duck .65 .25
**831** A279 60c Brown teal 1.00 .65
**832** A279 70c Paradise shelduck 1.05 .75
*a.* Souvenir sheet of 1 *10.00 10.00*
**835** A279 $5 Takahe 7.00 6.00
*Nos. 828-835 (6)* 10.70 8.65

Size of 70c, 22x27mm.
No. 832a for World Stamp Expo '89. Sold for $1.50.
Issued: 25c, 35c, 7/1/85; 40c, 60c, 2/2/87; 70c, 6/7/88; $5, 4/20/88; #832a, 11/17/89.

Christmas A301

Carol "Silent Night, Holy Night," by Joseph Mohr (1792-1848), Austrian clergyman.

***Perf. 13½x12½***
**1985, Sept. 18 Litho.**
**836** A301 18c Stable .25 .25
**837** A301 40c Shepherds .55 .55
**838** A301 50c Angels .60 .60
*Nos. 836-838 (3)* 1.40 1.40

Navy Ships A302

25c, Philomel, 1914-1947. 45c, Achilles, 1936-1946. 60c, Rotoiti, 1949-1965. 75c, Canterbury, 1971-.

**1985, Nov. 6 Litho. *Perf. 13½***
**839** A302 25c multicolored .40 .25
**840** A302 45c multicolored .75 .75
**841** A302 60c multicolored 1.00 1.00
**842** A302 75c multicolored 1.25 1.25
*a.* Souvenir sheet of 4, #839-842 4.00 *4.00*
*Nos. 839-842 (4)* 3.40 3.25

Police Force Act, Cent. — A303

Designs: a, Radio operators, 1940-1985. b, Mounted policeman, 1890, forensic specialist in mobile lab, 1985. c, Police station, 1895, policewoman and badge, 1985. d, 1920 motorcycle, 1940s car, modern patrol cars and graphologist. e, Original Mt. Cook Training Center and modern Police College, Poriria.

**1986, Jan. 15 *Perf. 14½x14***
**843** Strip of 5 2.00 2.00
*a.-e.* A303 25c any single .35 .25

Intl. Peace Year — A304

**1986, Mar. 5 *Perf. 13½x13***
**844** 25c Tree .35 .25
**845** 25c Dove .35 .25
*a.* A304 Pair, #844-845 .80 .70

Motorcycles — A305

35c, 1920 Indian Power Plus. 45c, 1927 Norton CS1. 60c, 1930 BSA Sloper. 75c, 1915 Triumph Model H.

**1986, Mar. 5**
**846** A305 35c multicolored .50 .50
**847** A305 45c multi .60 .60
**848** A305 60c multi .75 .75
**849** A305 75c multi .95 .95
*Nos. 846-849 (4)* 2.80 2.80

Knight's Point — A306

**1986, June 11 Litho. *Perf. 14***
**850** A306 55c shown .65 .65
**851** A306 60c Beck's Bay .70 .70
**852** A306 65c Doubtless Bay .75 .75
**853** A306 80c Wainui Bay .80 .80
*a.* Miniature sheet of one 1.90 1.90
*Nos. 850-853 (4)* 2.90 2.90

No. 853a sold for $1.20. Surtax benefited the "NZ 1990" executive committee.
No. 853a exists with Stockholmia '86 emblem. This sheet was sold only at the exhibition.

The Twelve Days of Christmas — A307

**1986, Sept. 17 Photo. *Perf. 14½***
**854** A307 25c First day .35 .25
**855** A307 55c Second .55 .55
**856** A307 65c Third .90 .90
*Nos. 854-856 (3)* 1.80 1.70

Music — A308

**1986, Nov. 5 Litho. *Perf. 14½x14***
**857** A308 30c Conductor .45 .30
**858** A308 60c Brass band .60 .60
**859** A308 80c Highland pipe band .95 .95
**860** A308 $1 Country music 1.10 1.10
*Nos. 857-860 (4)* 3.10 2.95

Tourism — A309

60c, Boating. 70c, Aviation. 80c, Camping. 85c, Windsurfing. $1.05, Mountain climbing. $1.30, White water rafting.

**1987, Jan. 14 *Perf. 14½x14***
**861** A309 60c multi .75 .75
**862** A309 70c multi .90 .90
**863** A309 80c multi 1.00 1.00
**864** A309 85c multi 1.10 1.10
**865** A309 $1.05 multi 1.25 1.25
**866** A309 $1.30 multi 1.50 1.50
*Nos. 861-866 (6)* 6.50 6.50

Blue Water Classics A310

40c, Southern Cross Cup. 80c, Admiral's Cup. $1.05, Kenwood Cup. $1.30, America's Cup.

**1987, Feb. 2 *Perf. 14x14½***
**867** A310 40c multi .60 .35
**868** A310 80c multi 1.00 1.00
**869** A310 $1.05 multi 1.25 1.25
**870** A310 $1.30 multi 1.50 1.50
*Nos. 867-870 (4)* 4.35 4.10

Vesting Day — A311

a, Motor vehicles, plane. b, Train, bicycle.

**1987, Apr. 1 Litho. *Perf. 13½***
**871** A311 Pair 1.75 1.75
*a.-b.* 40c any single .60 .40

Establishment of NZ Post Ltd., Apr. 1, replacing the NZ PO.

Royal NZ Air Force, 50th Anniv. A312

Designs: 40c, Avro 626, Wigram Airfield, c. 1937. 70c, P-40 Kittyhawks. 80c, Sunderland seaplane. 85c, A4 Skyhawks.

**1987, Apr. 15 *Perf. 14x14½***
**872** A312 40c multicolored .60 .60
**873** A312 70c multicolored 1.00 1.00
**874** A312 80c multicolored 1.10 1.10
**875** A312 85c multicolored 1.25 1.25
*a.* Souvenir sheet of 4, #872-875 5.50 5.50
*b.* As "a," ovptd. with CAPEX '87 emblem in margin 10.00 10.00
*Nos. 872-875 (4)* 3.95 3.95

Natl. Parks System, Cent. — A313

**1987, June 17 Litho. *Perf. 14½***
**876** A313 70c Urewera .85 1.00
**877** A313 80c Mt. Cook .90 1.10
**878** A313 85c Fiordland 1.00 1.10
**879** A313 $1.30 Tongariro 1.75 2.10
*a.* Souvenir sheet of one 3.50 3.50
*b.* As "a," ovptd. with CAPEX '87 emblem in margin 11.00 11.00
*Nos. 876-879 (4)* 4.50 5.30

No. 879a sold for $1.70 to benefit the NZ 1990 World Phil. Exhib., Auckland.

Christmas Carols — A314

35c, Hark! The Herald Angels Sing. 70c, Away in a Manger. 85c, We Three Kings of Orient Are.

**1987, Sept. 16 Litho. *Perf. 14x14½***
**880** A314 35c multi .50 .40
**881** A314 70c multi .90 .90
**882** A314 85c multi 1.25 1.25
*Nos. 880-882 (3)* 2.65 2.55

Maori Fiber Art — A315

**1987, Nov. 4 Litho. *Perf. 12***
**883** A315 40c Knot .55 .45
**884** A315 60c Binding .75 .75
**885** A315 80c Plait .95 .95
**886** A315 85c Flax fiber 1.00 1.00
*Nos. 883-886 (4)* 3.25 3.15

Royal Phil. Soc. of NZ, Cent. A316

Portrait of Queen Victoria by Chalon — A317

Queen Elizabeth II and: No. 887, No. 61 (blue background). No. 888, No. 62 (red background).

**1988, Jan. 13 *Perf. 14x14½***
**887** A316 40c multicolored .55 .45
**888** A316 40c multicolored .55 .45
*a.* Pair, #887-888 1.25 1.25

**Souvenir Sheet**
**889** A317 $1 multicolored 2.75 2.75
*a.* Overprinted with SYDPEX '88 emblem in margin 30.00 30.00

NZ Electrification, Cent. — A318

**1988, Jan. 13 *Perf. 14x14½***
**890** A318 40c Geothermal .45 .45
**891** A318 60c Thermal .55 .55
**892** A318 70c Gas .75 .75
**893** A318 80c Hydroelectric 1.00 1.00
*Nos. 890-893 (4)* 2.75 2.75

Maori Rafter Paintings — A319

**1988, Mar. 2 Litho. *Perf. 14½***

| No. | Type | Description | Unused | Used |
|---|---|---|---|---|
| **894** | A319 | 40c Mangopare | .65 | .65 |
| **895** | A319 | 40c Koru | .65 | .65 |
| **896** | A319 | 40c Raupunga | .65 | .65 |
| **897** | A319 | 60c Koiri | .95 | .95 |
| | | *Nos. 894-897 (4)* | 2.90 | 2.90 |

Greetings Messages A320

**1988, May 18 Litho. *Perf. 13½x13***

**Booklet Stamps**

| No. | Type | Description | Unused | Used |
|---|---|---|---|---|
| **898** | A320 | 40c Good luck | .75 | .75 |
| **899** | A320 | 40c Keeping in touch | .75 | .75 |
| **900** | A320 | 40c Happy birthday | .75 | .75 |

**Size: 41x27mm**

| No. | Type | Description | Unused | Used |
|---|---|---|---|---|
| **901** | A320 | 40c Congratulations | .75 | .75 |
| **902** | A320 | 40c Get well soon | .75 | .75 |
| *a.* | | Bklt. pane of 5, #898-902 | 4.25 | |

Landscapes A321

**1988, June 8 *Perf. 14½***

| No. | Type | Description | Unused | Used |
|---|---|---|---|---|
| **903** | A321 | 70c Milford Track | .80 | .80 |
| **904** | A321 | 80c Heaphy Track | .85 | .85 |
| **905** | A321 | 85c Copland Track | .95 | .95 |
| **906** | A321 | $1.30 Routeburn Track | *1.50* | 1.50 |
| *a.* | | Miniature sheet of one | 2.75 | 2.75 |
| | | *Nos. 903-906 (4)* | 4.10 | 4.10 |

No. 906a sold for $1.70 to benefit the exhibition.

**NEW ZEALAND 1990**
**Souvenir Sheets**

**Four souvenir sheets were sold by the New Zealand post to benefit NEW ZEALAND 1990 World Stamp Exhibition. They each contain three $1 and one $2 "stamps" picturing antarctic scenes. They are not valid for postage.**

Australia Bicentennial A322

Caricature: Kiwi and koala around campfire.

**1988, June 21**

| No. | Type | Description | Unused | Used |
|---|---|---|---|---|
| **907** | A322 | 40c multicolored | .55 | .55 |

See Australia No. 1086.

Christmas Carols — A323

Illuminated manuscripts: 35c, O, Come All Ye Faithful, by John Francis Wade, 1742. 70c, Hark! the Herald Angels Sing. 80c, Ding Dong! Merrily on High. 85c, The First Noel, first published in Davies & Gilbert's Some Ancient Christmas Carols, 1832.

**1988, Sept. 14 Litho. *Perf. 14½***

| No. | Type | Description | Unused | Used |
|---|---|---|---|---|
| **908** | A323 | 35c multicolored | .55 | .40 |
| **909** | A323 | 70c multicolored | .95 | .95 |
| **910** | A323 | 80c multicolored | 1.00 | 1.00 |
| **911** | A323 | 85c multicolored | 1.10 | 1.10 |
| | | *Nos. 908-911 (4)* | 3.60 | 3.45 |

New Zealand Heritage A324

The Land. Paintings by 19th cent. artists: 40c, Lake Pukaki, 1862, by John Gully. 60c, On the Grass Plain Below Lake Arthur, 1846, by William Fox. 70c, View of Auckland, 1873, by John Hoyte. 80c, Mt. Egmont from the Southward, 1840, by Charles Heaphy. $1.05, Anakiwa, Queen Charlotte Sound, 1871, by John Kinder. $1.30, White Terraces, Lake Rotomahana, 1880, by Charles Barraud.

**1988, Oct. 5 Litho. *Perf. 14x14½***

| No. | Type | Description | Unused | Used |
|---|---|---|---|---|
| **912** | A324 | 40c multicolored | .50 | .25 |
| **913** | A324 | 60c multicolored | .70 | .70 |
| **914** | A324 | 70c multicolored | .90 | .90 |
| **915** | A324 | 80c multicolored | 1.00 | 1.00 |
| **916** | A324 | $1.05 multicolored | 1.20 | 1.20 |
| **917** | A324 | $1.30 multicolored | 1.40 | 1.40 |
| | | *Nos. 912-917 (6)* | 5.70 | 5.45 |

Kiwi A325

**1988, Oct. 19 Engr. *Perf. 14½***

| No. | Type | Description | Unused | Used |
|---|---|---|---|---|
| **918** | A325 | $1 green | 2.50 | 2.50 |
| *a.* | | Booklet pane of 6 | 12.50 | |
| *b.* | | Litho. | 2.50 | 2.50 |

Value is for stamp with surrounding selvage. No. 918 issued in booklets only.
No. 918b is from No. 1161a.
See Nos. 1027, 1161, 1445, 1635, 1787, 2368-2370.

**Bird Type of 1985**

5c, Spotless crake. 10c, Banded dotterel. 20c, Yellowhead. 30c, Silvereye. 40c, Brown kiwi. 45c, Rock wren. 50c, Kingfisher. 60c, Spotted shag. No. 927, Fiordland crested penguin. No. 928, New Zealand falcon. 90c, South Island robin. $10, Little spotted kiwi.

**1988-95 Litho. *Perf. 14½x14***

**Sizes: $10, 26x31½mm, Others, 22x27mm**

| No. | Type | Description | Unused | Used |
|---|---|---|---|---|
| **919** | A279 | 5c multi | .25 | .25 |
| **920** | A279 | 10c multi | .25 | .25 |
| **921** | A279 | 20c multi | .30 | .25 |
| *a.* | | Perf. 13½ | .75 | .75 |
| **922** | A279 | 30c multi | .45 | .25 |
| **923** | A279 | 40c multi | .65 | .30 |
| *c.* | | Perf. 13½x13 | 3.00 | 3.00 |
| **924** | A279 | 45c multi | .70 | .25 |
| *b.* | | Booklet pane of 10 | 6.50 | |
| **925** | A279 | 50c multi | .80 | .35 |
| **926** | A279 | 60c multi | .95 | .80 |
| *a.* | | Sheet of 8, #919-926 | 5.00 | 5.00 |
| *b.* | | Perf. 13½ | 7.00 | 7.00 |
| **927** | A279 | 80c multi | 1.25 | 1.00 |
| **928** | A279 | 80c multi | 1.25 | 1.00 |
| | | Complete booklet, 10 #928 | 12.50 | |
| *c.* | | Perf. 12 on 3 sides | 4.00 | 4.00 |
| *d.* | | As "c," booklet pane of 10 | 40.00 | |
| | | Complete booklet, #928d | 40.00 | |
| **929** | A279 | 90c multi | 1.40 | 1.25 |
| **930** | A279 | $10 multi | 9.50 | 6.75 |
| *d.* | | Souv. sheet of 1 | 20.00 | 20.00 |

**Self-Adhesive**

***Die Cut Perf 11½***

| No. | Type | Description | Unused | Used |
|---|---|---|---|---|
| **931** | A279 | 40c like #923 | .65 | .50 |
| **932** | A279 | 45c like #924 | .70 | .55 |

***Die Cut Perf 10½x11***

| No. | Type | Description | Unused | Used |
|---|---|---|---|---|
| **933** | A279 | 45c like #924 | .70 | .55 |
| | | *Nos. 919-933 (15)* | 19.80 | 14.30 |

No. 933 has a darker blue background than No. 932 and has perf "teeth" at the corners while No. 932 does not. Perf "teeth" on the top and left side are staggered to line up with perf "holes" on the bottom and right on No. 933. "Teeth" line up with "teeth" on No. 932.

PHILAKOREA '94 (#926a). POST'X '95 Postal Exhibition (#930d).

Issued: $10, 4/19/89; #931, 4/17/91; 5c, #924, 932, 7/1/91; #933, 1991; #928, 3/31/93; #926a, 8/16/94; #930d, 2/3/95; #921a, 926b, 9/22/95; #923c, 11/8/89; others, 11/2/88.

Whales of the Southern Oceans A326

60c, Humpback. 70c, Killer. 80c, Southern right. 85c, Blue. $1.05, Southern bottlenose. $1.30, Sperm.

**1988, Nov. 2 Litho. *Perf. 13½***

| No. | Type | Description | Unused | Used |
|---|---|---|---|---|
| **936** | A326 | 60c multi | .95 | .95 |
| **937** | A326 | 70c multi | 1.00 | 1.00 |
| **938** | A326 | 80c multi | 1.10 | 1.10 |
| **939** | A326 | 85c multi | 1.25 | 1.25 |
| **940** | A326 | $1.05 multi | 1.50 | 1.50 |
| **941** | A326 | $1.30 multi | 1.75 | 1.75 |
| | | *Nos. 936-941 (6)* | 7.55 | 7.55 |

Wildflowers A327

**1989, Jan. 18 Litho. *Perf. 14½***

| No. | Type | Description | Unused | Used |
|---|---|---|---|---|
| **942** | A327 | 40c Clover | .55 | .55 |
| **943** | A327 | 60c Lotus | .75 | .75 |
| **944** | A327 | 70c Montbretia | .80 | .80 |
| **945** | A327 | 80c Wild ginger | .95 | .95 |
| | | *Nos. 942-945 (4)* | 3.05 | 3.05 |

Authors — A328

Portraits: 40c, Katherine Mansfield (1888-1923). 60c, James K. Baxter (1926-1972). 70c, Bruce Mason (1921-1982). 80c, Ngaio Marsh (1899-1982).

**1989, Mar. 1 Litho. *Perf. 12½***

| No. | Type | Description | Unused | Used |
|---|---|---|---|---|
| **946** | A328 | 40c multicolored | .45 | .45 |
| **947** | A328 | 60c multicolored | .65 | .65 |
| **948** | A328 | 70c multicolored | .70 | .70 |
| **949** | A328 | 80c multicolored | .80 | .80 |
| | | *Nos. 946-949 (4)* | 2.60 | 2.60 |

New Zealand Heritage A329

The people.

**1989, May 17 *Perf. 14x14½***

| No. | Type | Description | Unused | Used |
|---|---|---|---|---|
| **950** | A329 | 40c Moriori | .60 | .35 |
| **951** | A329 | 60c Prospectors | .85 | .85 |
| **952** | A329 | 70c Land settlers | .70 | .70 |
| **953** | A329 | 80c Whalers | .85 | .85 |
| **954** | A329 | $1.05 Missionaries | .95 | .95 |
| **955** | A329 | $1.30 Maori | 1.25 | 1.25 |
| | | *Nos. 950-955 (6)* | 5.20 | 4.95 |

Trees — A330

**1989, June 7**

| No. | Type | Description | Unused | Used |
|---|---|---|---|---|
| **956** | A330 | 80c Kahikatea | .90 | .90 |
| **957** | A330 | 85c Rimu | .95 | .95 |
| **958** | A330 | $1.05 Totara | 1.25 | 1.25 |
| **959** | A330 | $1.30 Kauri | 1.40 | 1.40 |
| *a.* | | Miniature sheet of one | 3.00 | 3.00 |
| | | *Nos. 956-959 (4)* | 4.50 | 4.50 |

No. 959a sold for $1.80. Surtax benefited the "NZ 1990" executive committee.

Christmas — A331

Star of Bethlehem illuminating settings: 35c, View of One Tree Hill from a bedroom window. 65c, A shepherd overlooking snow-capped mountains. 80c, Boats in harbor. $1, Earth.

**1989, Sept. 13 Litho. *Perf. 14½***

| No. | Type | Description | Unused | Used |
|---|---|---|---|---|
| **960** | A331 | 35c multicolored | .40 | .25 |
| *a.* | | Booklet pane of 10 | 5.50 | |
| **961** | A331 | 65c multicolored | .75 | .75 |
| **962** | A331 | 80c multicolored | .95 | .95 |
| **963** | A331 | $1 multicolored | 1.10 | 1.10 |
| | | *Nos. 960-963 (4)* | 3.20 | 3.05 |

New Zealand Heritage A332

The sea.

**1989, Oct. 11 Litho. *Perf. 14x14½***

| No. | Type | Description | Unused | Used |
|---|---|---|---|---|
| **964** | A332 | 40c Windsurfing | .50 | .25 |
| **965** | A332 | 60c Fishing | .65 | .65 |
| **966** | A332 | 65c Swordfish | .90 | .90 |
| **967** | A332 | 80c Harbor | 1.00 | 1.00 |
| **968** | A332 | $1 Gulls over coast | 1.25 | 1.25 |
| **969** | A332 | $1.50 Container ship | 1.90 | 1.90 |
| | | *Nos. 964-969 (6)* | 6.20 | 5.95 |

14th Commonwealth Games, Auckland, Jan. 24-Feb. 3, 1990 — A333

No. 970, Emblem. No. 971, Goldie character trademark. No. 972, Gymnastics. No. 973, Weight lifting. No. 974, Swimming. No. 975, Cycling. No. 976, Lawn bowling. No. 977, Hurdles.

**1989, Nov. 8 *Perf. 14½***

| No. | Type | Description | Unused | Used |
|---|---|---|---|---|
| **970** | A333 | 40c multi | .45 | .45 |
| **971** | A333 | 40c multi | .45 | .45 |
| *a.* | | Souvenir sheet of 2, #970-971, sailboats ('90) | 2.75 | 2.75 |
| *b.* | | As "a," stadium ('90) | 2.75 | 2.75 |
| **972** | A333 | 40c multi | .45 | .45 |
| **973** | A333 | 50c multi | .55 | .55 |
| **974** | A333 | 65c multi | .75 | .75 |
| **975** | A333 | 80c multi | .95 | .95 |
| **976** | A333 | $1 multi | 1.00 | 1.00 |
| **977** | A333 | $1.80 multi | 1.50 | 1.50 |
| | | *Nos. 970-977 (8)* | 6.10 | 6.10 |

Air New Zealand, 50th Anniv. A334

**1990, Jan. 17** *Perf. 13½x14½*

**978** A334 80c multicolored 1.50 1.25

Souvenir Sheet

Treaty of Waitangi, 150th Anniv. — A335

Painting by Leonard Mitchell: a, Maori chief signing the treaty. b, Chief Hone Heke shaking hand of Lt.-Gov. William Hobson.

**1990, Jan. 17** *Perf. 13½*

**979** A335 Sheet of 2 3.50 3.50
*a.-b.* 40c any single 1.40 1.40

New Zealand Heritage A336

The Ships: No. 980, Polynesian double-hulled canoe, c. 1000. No. 981, Endeavour. No. 982, Tory. No. 983, Crusader. No. 984, Edwin Fox. No. 985, Arawa.

**1990, Mar. 7** **Litho.** *Perf. 14x14½*

**980** A336 40c multi .60 .25
**981** A336 50c multi .75 .75
*a.* Souvenir sheet of 1 20.00 20.00
**982** A336 60c multi .90 .90
**983** A336 80c multi 1.40 1.40
**984** A336 $1 multi 1.50 1.50
**985** A336 $1.50 multi 2.00 2.00
*Nos. 980-985 (6)* 7.15 6.80

No. 981a for Stamp World London '90. Sold for $1.30. Issued May 3.

Miniature Sheet

Orchids — A337

Designs: a, Sun. b, Spider. c, Winika. d, Greenhood. e, Odd-leaved orchid.

**1990, Apr. 18** **Litho.** *Perf. 14½*

**986** Sheet of 5 7.00 7.00
*a.-d.* A337 40c any single 1.00 1.00
*e.* A337 80c multicolored 2.00 2.00

No. 986 sold for $4.90. Surcharge for the intl. stamp exhibition, Auckland, Aug. 24-Sept 2. Imperf. sheets were available only in season tickets which were sold for $25. Value, $35

New Zealand Heritage A338

The Achievers: 40c, Grace Neill (1846-1926), nurse, journalist. 50c, Jean Batten (1909-1982), aviator. 60c, Katherine Sheppard (1848-1934), social worker. 80c, Richard Pearse (1877-1953), inventor. $1, Gov.-Gen. Bernard Freyberg (1889-1963). $1.50, Peter Buck (1877-1951), cabinet minister.

**1990, May 16** **Litho.** *Perf. 14x14½*

**987** A338 40c multicolored .65 .30
**988** A338 50c multicolored .80 .80
**989** A338 60c multicolored .95 .95
**990** A338 80c multicolored 1.25 1.25
**991** A338 $1 multicolored 1.50 1.50
**992** A338 $1.50 multicolored 1.75 1.75
*Nos. 987-992 (6)* 6.90 6.55

Akaroa Harbor — A339

Early Settlements: $1, Durie Hill, Wanganui River. $1.50, Mt. Victoria, Wellington. $1.80, Rangitoto Island, Takapuna Beach, Auckland.

**1990, June 13** **Litho.** *Perf. 14½*

**993** A339 80c multicolored 1.00 1.00
**994** A339 $1 multicolored 1.40 1.40
**995** A339 $1.50 multicolored 2.25 2.25
**996** A339 $1.80 multicolored 2.50 2.50
*a.* Souvenir sheet of 1 4.25 4.25
*Nos. 993-996 (4)* 7.15 7.15

No. 996a sold for $2.30. Surtax for world philatelic expo, New Zealand '90.

New Zealand Heritage A340

The Maori: 40c, Legend of Rangi and Papa. 50c, Maori feather cloak. 60c, Song. 80c, Maori tattoo. $1, War canoe prow. $1.50, Maori war dance.

**1990, Aug. 24** **Litho.** *Perf. 14*

**997** A340 40c multicolored .55 .30
**998** A340 50c multicolored .65 .65
**999** A340 60c multicolored .75 .75
**1000** A340 80c multicolored .85 .85
**1001** A340 $1 multicolored 1.25 1.25
**1002** A340 $1.50 multicolored 1.75 1.75
*Nos. 997-1002 (6)* 5.80 5.55

Souvenir Sheet

First Postage Stamps, 150th Anniv. — A341

Designs: a, Victoria. b, Edward VII. c, George V. d, Edward VIII. e, George VI. f, Elizabeth II.

**1990, Aug. 29** **Engr.** *Perf. 14½x14*

**1003** A341 40c Sheet of 6 5.25 5.25
*a.-f.* any single .75 .75

Christmas — A342

Various angels.

**1990, Sept. 12** **Litho.** *Perf. 14*

**1004** A342 40c multicolored .55 .40
**1005** A342 $1 multicolored 1.25 .25
**1006** A342 $1.50 multicolored 2.00 1.25
**1007** A342 $1.80 multicolored 2.25 2.00
*Nos. 1004-1007 (4)* 6.05 3.90

Antarctic Petrel — A343

50c, Wilson's storm petrel. 60c, Snow petrel. 80c, Antarctic fulmar. $1, Chinstrap penguin. $1.50, Emperor penguin.

**1990, Nov. 7** *Perf. 13½x13*

**1008** A343 40c shown .65 .35
**1009** A343 50c multicolored .80 .70
**1010** A343 60c multicolored .95 .85
**1011** A343 80c multicolored 1.25 1.10
**1012** A343 $1 multicolored 1.60 1.60
**1013** A343 $1.50 multicolored 2.40 2.25
*Nos. 1008-1013 (6)* 7.65 6.85

Sheep — A344

**1991, Jan. 23** **Litho.** *Perf. 14½*

**1014** A344 40c Coopworth .55 .25
**1015** A344 60c Perendale .80 .80
**1016** A344 80c Corriedale 1.00 1.00
**1017** A344 $1 Drysdale 1.25 1.25
**1018** A344 $1.50 South Suffolk 1.75 1.75
**1019** A344 $1.80 Romney 2.00 2.00
*Nos. 1014-1019 (6)* 7.35 7.05

Map, Royal Albatross, Designs from Moriori House, Moriori Man, Nikau Palm, Tree Carving — A345

Design: 80c, Map, sailing ship, carving, petroglyph, Moriori house, Tommy Solomon, last full-blooded Moriori.

**1991, Mar. 6** **Litho.** *Perf. 13½*

**1020** A345 40c shown .65 .55
**1021** A345 80c multicolored 1.25 1.10

Discovery of the Chatham Islands, Bicent.

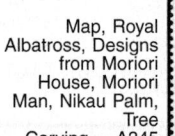

New Zealand Football (Soccer) Assoc., Cent. A346

Designs: a, Goal. b, 5 players, referee.

**1991, Mar. 6**

**1022** Pair 2.50 2.50
*a.-b.* A346 80c any single 1.25 1.25

Tuatara A347

Designs: No. 1023, Juvenile. No. 1024, In burrow. No. 1025, Female. No. 1026, Male.

**1991, Apr. 17** **Litho.** *Perf. 14½*

**Denomination Color**

**1023** A347 40c gray blue 1.00 1.00
**1024** A347 40c dark brown 1.00 1.00
**1025** A347 40c olive green 1.00 1.00
**1026** A347 40c orange brown 1.00 1.00
*Nos. 1023-1026 (4)* 4.00 4.00

**Kiwi Type of 1988**

**1991, Apr. 17** **Engr.** *Perf. 14½*

**1027** A325 $1 red 1.60 1.25
*a.* Litho. 1.75 1.50

Value is for stamp with surrounding selvage. No. 1027a is from Nos.1161a, 1635a.

Happy Birthday — A348

Thinking of You — A349

No. 1028, Clown face. No. 1029, Balloons. No. 1030, Birthday hat. No. 1031, Present. No. 1032, Cake & candles. No. 1033 Cat, front paws on window sill. No. 1034, Cat, slippers. No. 1035, Cat, alarm clock. No. 1036, Cat sitting on window sill. No. 1037, Cat walking by door.

**1991, May 15** **Litho.** *Perf. 14x13½*

**Size of Nos. 1031-1032, 1036-1037: 41x27mm**

**1028** A348 40c multi .90 .90
**1029** A348 40c multi .90 .90
**1030** A348 40c multi .90 .90
**1031** A348 40c multi .90 .90
**1032** A348 40c multi .90 .90
*a.* Bklt. pane of 5, #1028-1032 6.00
**1033** A349 40c shown .90 .90
**1034** A349 40c multi .90 .90
**1035** A349 40c multi .90 .90
**1036** A349 40c multi .90 .90
**1037** A349 40c multi .90 .90
*a.* Bklt. pane of 5, #1033-1037 6.00
*Nos. 1028-1037 (10)* 9.00 9.00

See Nos. 1044-1053.

Rock Formations A350

40c, Punakaiki Rocks. 50c, Moeraki Boulders. 80c, Organ Pipes. $1, Castle Hill. $1.50, Te Kaukau Point. $1.80, Ahuriri River Clay Cliffs.

**1991, June 12** **Litho.** *Perf. 14½*

**1038** A350 40c multicolored .60 .35
**1039** A350 50c multicolored .75 .75
**1040** A350 80c multicolored 1.10 1.10
**1041** A350 $1 multicolored 1.25 1.25
**1042** A350 $1.50 multicolored 2.00 2.00
**1043** A350 $1.80 multicolored 2.25 2.25
*Nos. 1038-1043 (6)* 7.95 7.70

**Greetings Types**

**1991, July 1** **Litho.** *Perf. 14x13½*

**Size of Nos. 1047-1048, 1052-1053: 41x27mm**

**1044** A348 45c like #1028 .90 .90
**1045** A348 45c like #1029 .90 .90
**1046** A348 45c like #1030 .90 .90
**1047** A348 45c like #1031 .90 .90
**1048** A348 45c like #1032 .90 .90
*a.* Bklt. pane of 5, #1044-1048 5.50
**1049** A349 45c like #1033 .90 .90
**1050** A349 45c like #1034 .90 .90
**1051** A349 45c like #1035 .90 .90
**1052** A349 45c like #1036 .90 .90
**1053** A349 45c like #1037 .90 .90
*a.* Bklt. pane of 5, #1049-1053 5.50
*Nos. 1044-1053 (10)* 9.00 9.00

1991 Rugby World Cup — A351

**1991, Aug. 21 Litho. *Perf. 14½x14***

**1054** A351 80c Children's 1.00 1.00
**1055** A351 $1 Women's 1.10 1.10
**1056** A351 $1.50 Senior 2.00 2.00
**1057** A351 $1.80 All Blacks 2.25 2.25
*a.* Souvenir sheet of 1 4.00 4.00
*b.* As "a," with Phila Nippon '91 emblem in margin *12.50 12.50*
*Nos. 1054-1057 (4)* 6.35 6.35

No. 1057a sold for $2.40 to benefit philatelic trust for hobby support.

Christmas A352

No. 1058, Shepherds. No. 1059, Wise men, camels. No. 1060, Mary, Baby Jesus. No. 1061, Wise man, gift. No. 1062, Star. No. 1063, Crown. No. 1064, Angel.

**1991, Sept. 18 Litho. *Perf. 13½x14***

**1058** A352 45c multi .55 .55
**1059** A352 45c multi .55 .55
**1060** A352 45c multi .55 .55
**1061** A352 45c multi .55 .55
*a.* Block of 4, #1058-1061 3.00 3.00
**1062** A352 65c multi .90 .90
**1063** A352 $1 multi 1.50 1.50
**1064** A352 $1.50 multi 2.00 2.00
*Nos. 1058-1064 (7)* 6.60 6.60

Butterflies A354

$1, Forest ringlet. $2, Southern blue. $3, Yellow admiral. $4, Common copper. $5, Red admiral.

**1991-2008 Litho. *Perf. 14¼***

**1075** A354 $1 multi 1.40 1.10
*a.* Perf. 14x14½ on 3 sides 5.00 5.00
*b.* Booklet pane of 5 + 5 labels Perf. 14x14½ on 3 sides 25.00
Complete booklet, #1075b 25.00
*c.* Perf. 13¾x14¼ 2.00 2.00
**1076** A354 $2 multi 3.00 2.25
*a.* Perf. 13¾x14¼ 15.00 15.00
**1077** A354 $3 multi 4.00 3.50
*a.* Souvenir sheet of 1 10.00 10.00
*b.* Perf. 13¾x14¼ 15.00 15.00
**1078** A354 $4 multi 5.00 3.00
*a.* Perf. 13¾x14¼ 7.00 5.25
*b.* Perf. 14 ('08) 6.25 4.50
**1079** A354 $5 multi 6.50 5.00
*a.* Perf. 13¾x14¼ 8.50 6.00
*Nos. 1075-1079 (5)* 19.90 14.85

No. 1077a issued later for Phila Nippon '91.
Issued: #1075, 1075a, 1076, 1077, 11/6/91; $4-$5, 1/25/95; #1075b, 9/1/95; #1078a, 10/97; #1079a, 10/9/96; #1075c, 1076a, 11/6/96; #1077b, Aug. 1996..

Mount Cook — A356

**Die Stamped & Engr.**
***Perf. 14½x15***

**1994, Feb. 18 Wmk. 387**

**1084** A356 $20 gold & blue 22.50 15.00

1992 America's Cup Competition A357

45c, KZ7 Kiwi Magic, 1987. 80c, KZ1 New Zealand, 1988. $1, America, 1851. $1.50, New Zealand, 1992.

**1992, Jan. 22 Litho. *Perf. 14x14½***

**1085** A357 45c multicolored .60 .25
**1086** A357 80c multicolored .95 .95
**1087** A357 $1 multicolored 1.25 1.25
**1088** A357 $1.50 multicolored 1.50 1.50
*Nos. 1085-1088 (4)* 4.30 3.95

Sighting of New Zealand by Abel Tasman, 350th Anniv. A358

**1992, Mar. 12 *Perf. 13½x14½***

**1089** A358 45c Heemskerck .60 .30
**1090** A358 80c Zeehaen 1.00 1.00
**1091** A358 $1 Santa Maria 1.40 1.40
**1092** A358 $1.50 Pinta and Nina 1.75 1.75
*a.* Souvenir sheet of 2, #1091-1092, Perf. 14x14½ 7.50 7.50
*Nos. 1089-1092 (4)* 4.75 4.45

Discovery of America, 500th anniv. (#1091-1092).
Issue date: No. 1092a, May 22. World Columbian Stamp Expo (#1092a).

1992 Summer Olympics, Barcelona A359

**1992, Apr. 3 Litho. *Perf. 13½***

**1093** A359 45c Runners .70 .60

Antarctic Seals — A360

45c, Weddell seal. 50c, Crabeater seal. 65c, Leopard seal. 80c, Ross seal. $1, Southern elephant seal. $1.80, Hooker's sea lion.

**1992, Apr. 8 *Perf. 14x13½***

**1094** A360 45c multi .70 .60
**1095** A360 50c multi .80 .70
**1096** A360 65c multi 1.00 .85
**1097** A360 80c multi 1.25 1.00
**1098** A360 $1 multi 1.60 1.40
**1099** A360 $1.80 multi 2.75 2.50
*Nos. 1094-1099 (6)* 8.10 7.05

1992 Summer Olympics, Barcelona A361

**1992, May 13 Litho. *Perf. 13½***

**1100** A361 45c Cycling .65 .40
**1101** A361 80c Archery 1.00 1.00
**1102** A361 $1 Equestrian 1.25 1.25
**1103** A361 $1.50 Board sailing 1.75 1.75
*a.* Souvenir sheet of 4, #1100-1103, perf 14x14½ 5.75 5.75
*b.* No. 1103a overprinted 11.00 11.00
*Nos. 1100-1103 (4)* 4.65 4.40

No. 1103b overprint consists of World Columbian Stamp Expo emblem in sheet margin. Issue date: No. 1103b, May 22.

Glaciers A362

45c, Glacier ice. 50c, Tasman glacier. 80c, Snowball glacier. $1, Brewster glacier. $1.50, Fox glacier. $1.80, Franz Josef glacier.

**1992, June 12**

**1104** A362 45c multicolored .60 .30
**1105** A362 50c multicolored .70 .70
**1106** A362 80c multicolored .85 .85
**1107** A362 $1 multicolored 1.25 1.25
**1108** A362 $1.50 multicolored 1.60 1.60
**1109** A362 $1.80 multicolored 1.75 1.75
*Nos. 1104-1109 (6)* 6.75 6.45

Camellias — A363

45c, Grand finale. 50c, Showa-no-sakae. 80c, Sugar dream. $1, Night rider. $1.50, E.G. Waterhouse. $1.80, Dr. Clifford Parks.

**1992, July 8 *Perf. 14½***

**1110** A363 45c multicolored .60 .30
**1111** A363 50c multicolored .70 .70
**1112** A363 80c multicolored .90 .90
**1113** A363 $1 multicolored 1.10 1.10
**1114** A363 $1.50 multicolored 1.50 1.50
**1115** A363 $1.80 multicolored 1.75 1.75
*Nos. 1110-1115 (6)* 6.55 6.25

Scenic Views of New Zealand — A364

No. 1116, Tree, hills. No. 1117, Hills, stream. No. 1118, Hills, mountain tops. No. 1119, Glacier. No. 1120, Trees, green hills. No. 1121, Tree branch, rapids. No. 1122, Rocky shoreline. No. 1123, Fjord. No. 1124, Glacial runoff. No. 1125, Vegetation, stream.

**1992, Sept. 1 Litho. *Perf. 14x14½***
**Booklet Stamps**

**1116** A364 45c multicolored .65 .65
**1117** A364 45c multicolored .65 .65
**1118** A364 45c multicolored .65 .65
**1119** A364 45c multicolored .65 .65
**1120** A364 45c multicolored .65 .65
**1121** A364 45c multicolored .65 .65
**1122** A364 45c multicolored .65 .65
**1123** A364 45c multicolored .65 .65
**1124** A364 45c multicolored .65 .65
**1125** A364 45c multicolored .65 .65
*a.* Bklt. pane of 10, #1116-1125 8.75
*Nos. 1116-1125 (10)* 6.50 6.50

No. 1125a has continous design.

Christmas — A365

No. 1126, Two reindeer over village. No. 1127, Two reindeer pulling Santa's sleigh. No. 1128, Christmas tree in window. No. 1129, Two children looking out window. 65c, Fireplace, stockings. $1, Church. $1.50, People beneath pohutukawa tree at beach.

**1992, Sept. 16 *Perf. 14½***

**1126** A365 45c multicolored .50 .50
**1127** A365 45c multicolored .50 .50
**1128** A365 45c multicolored .50 .50
**1129** A365 45c multicolored .50 .50
*a.* Block of 4, #1126-1129 2.50 2.50
**1130** A365 65c multicolored .75 .75
**1131** A365 $1 multicolored 1.00 1.00
**1132** A365 $1.50 multicolored 1.75 1.75
*Nos. 1126-1132 (7)* 5.50 5.50

No. 1129a has continous design.

A366

The Emerging Years: The 1920s: 45c, Flaming youth. 50c, Birth of broadcasting. 80c, All Blacks rugby player. $1, The swaggie. $1.50, Motorcar brings freedom. $1.80, Arrival of the air age.

**1992, Nov. 4 Litho. *Perf. 13½***

**1133** A366 45c multicolored .50 .25
**1134** A366 50c multicolored .55 .35
**1135** A366 80c multicolored .85 .85
**1136** A366 $1 multicolored .95 .95
**1137** A366 $1.50 multicolored 1.75 1.75
**1138** A366 $1.80 multicolored 2.00 2.00
*Nos. 1133-1138 (6)* 6.60 6.15

Royal Doulton Ceramics A367

45c, Character jug, "Old Charley." 50c, Plate from "Bunnykins" series. 80c, Maori art tea ware. $1, Hand painted "Ophelia" plate. $1.50, Burslem figurine of St. George. $1.80, Salt glazed vase.

**1993, Jan. 20 Litho. *Perf. 13***

**1139** A367 45c multicolored .50 .25
**1140** A367 50c multicolored .55 .55
**1141** A367 80c multicolored .85 .85
**1142** A367 $1 multicolored 1.00 1.00
**1143** A367 $1.50 multicolored 1.50 1.50
**1144** A367 $1.80 multicolored 1.75 1.75
*a.* Souvenir sheet of 1 2.50 2.50
*Nos. 1139-1144 (6)* 6.15 5.90

A368

The Emerging Years: The 1930's: 45c, Buttons and bows, the new femininity. 50c, The Great Depression. 80c, Race horse, Phar Lap. $1, State housing. $1.50, Free milk for schools. $1.80, The talkies.

**1993, Feb. 17 Litho. *Perf. 14½x14***

**1145** A368 45c multicolored .55 .25
**1146** A368 50c multicolored .60 .60
**1147** A368 80c multicolored .95 .95
**1148** A368 $1 multicolored 1.00 1.00
**1149** A368 $1.50 multicolored 1.50 1.50
**1150** A368 $1.80 multicolored 1.75 1.75
*Nos. 1145-1150 (6)* 6.35 6.05

Woman Suffrage, Cent. — A369

45c, First vote. 80c, War work. $1, Child care. $1.50, Contemporary women.

**1993, Mar. 31 Litho. *Perf. 13½***
**1151** A369 45c multicolored .55 .25
**1152** A369 80c multicolored .85 .85
**1153** A369 $1 multicolored .95 .95
**1154** A369 $1.50 multicolored 2.40 2.40
*Nos. 1151-1154 (4)* 4.75 4.45

Thermal Wonders A370

45c, Champagne Pool. 50c, Boiling mud, Rotorua. 80c, Emerald Pool. $1, Hakereteke Falls. $1.50, Warbrick Terrace. $1.80, Pohutu Geyser.

**1993, May 5 Litho. *Perf. 12***
**1155** A370 45c multicolored .55 .25
**1156** A370 50c multicolored .65 .65
**1157** A370 80c multicolored 1.00 1.00
**1158** A370 $1 multicolored 1.10 1.10
**1159** A370 $1.50 multicolored 1.50 1.50
**1160** A370 $1.80 multicolored 2.00 2.00
*a.* Souvenir sheet of 1 3.50 3.50
*Nos. 1155-1160 (6)* 6.80 6.50

No. 1160a inscribed with Bangkok '93 emblem in sheet margin. Issue date: No. 1160a, Oct. 1.

**Kiwi Type of 1988**

**1993, June 9 Engr. *Perf. 14½***
**1161** A325 $1 blue 1.50 1.50
*a.* Souv. sheet of 3, #918b, 1027a, 1161 8.50 8.50
*b.* Litho. 2.25 1.75
*c.* Souv. sheet of 3, #918b, 1027a, 1161b 6.00 6.00

Taipei '93, Asian Intl. Stamp Exhibition (#1161a), Hong Kong '94 (#1161c).
Value is for stamp with surrounding selvage.
Issued: #1161a, 8/14/93; #1161c, 2/18/94.
See No. 1635a.

Species Unique to New Zealand A371

Designs: No. 1162, Yellow-eyed penguin, Hector's dolphin, New Zealand fur seal. 1162A, Taiko, Mt. Cook lily, blue duck. 1162B, Giant snail, rock wren, Hamilton's frog. 1162C, Kaka, Chatham Island pigeon, giant weta.
No. 1163, Tusked weta.

**1993, June 9 Litho. *Perf. 14x14½***
**1162** A371 45c multicolored .85 .85
**1162A** A371 45c multicolored .85 .85
**1162B** A371 45c multicolored .85 .85
**1162C** A371 45c multicolored .85 .85
*d.* As #1162-1162C, block of 4 4.25 4.25
**1163** A371 45c multicolored 1.00 1.00
*a.* Booklet pane of 10 10.00 —
Complete booklet 10.50
*Nos. 1162-1163 (5)* 4.40 4.40

World Wildlife Fund.
Nos. 1162-1162C were issued both in sheets containing individual designs and in sheets containing the four values setenant (#1162d).

Christmas — A372

Christmas designs: No. 1164, Flowers from pohutukawa tree, denomination at UL. No. 1165, Like #1164, denomination at UR. No. 1166, Present with yellow ribbon, denomination at LL. No. 1167, Present with red ribbon, denomination at LR. $1.00, Ornaments, cracker, sailboats. $1.50, Wreath, sailboats, present.

**1993, Sept. 1 Litho. *Perf. 14½x14***
**1164** A372 45c multicolored .60 .60
**1165** A372 45c multicolored .60 .60
**1166** A372 45c multicolored .60 .60
**1167** A372 45c multicolored .60 .60
*a.* Block of 4, #1164-1167 2.75 2.75
**1168** A372 $1 multicolored 1.25 1.10
**1169** A372 $1.50 multicolored 2.00 1.75
*Nos. 1164-1169 (6)* 5.65 5.25

**Booklet Stamps**
***Perf. 12***

*1164a* A372 45c multicolored 1.00 1.00
*1165a* A372 45c multicolored 1.00 1.00
*1166a* A372 45c multicolored 1.00 1.00
*1167b* A372 45c multicolored 1.00 1.00
*c.* Bklt. pane, 2 ea #1166a, 1167b, 3 ea #1164a-1165a 17.50

At least one edge of No. 1167c is guillotined.

Fish — A373

Designs: No. 1170, Paua (#1175). No. 1171, Greenshell mussels. No. 1172, Terakihi (#1171). No. 1173, Salmon (#1172). No. 1174, Southern bluefin tuna, albacore tuna, kahawai (#1173). No. 1175, Rock lobster (#1171). No. 1176, Snapper (#1177). No. 1177, Grouper ("Groper," #1178). No. 1178, Orange roughy (#1179). No. 1179, Squid, hoki, oreo dory (#1173, #1174, #1178).

**1993, Sept. 1 *Perf. 13½***
**Booklet Stamps**
**1170** A373 45c multicolored .80 .80
**1171** A373 45c multicolored .80 .80
**1172** A373 45c multicolored .80 .80
**1173** A373 45c multicolored .80 .80
**1174** A373 45c multicolored .80 .80
**1175** A373 45c multicolored .80 .80
**1176** A373 45c multicolored .80 .80
**1177** A373 45c multicolored .80 .80
**1178** A373 45c multicolored .80 .80
**1179** A373 45c multicolored .80 .80
*a.* Booklet pane of 10, #1170-1179 + 2 labels 10.00
*Nos. 1170-1179 (10)* 8.00 8.00

Nos. 1179a has continuous design.

Dinosaurs — A374

**1993, Oct. 1**
**1180** A374 45c Sauropod .60 .50
**1181** A374 80c Pterosaur 1.10 1.10
**1182** A374 $1 Ankylosaur 1.25 1.25
**1183** A374 $1.20 Mauisaurus 1.50 1.50
**1184** A374 $1.50 Carnosaur 1.60 1.60
*a.* Souvenir sheet of 1, perf. 14½x14 2.25 2.00
*b.* As "a," inscribed with Bangkok '93 emblem 3.00 2.75
*Nos. 1180-1184 (5)* 6.05 5.95

**Booklet Stamp**
**Size: 25½x23½mm**
***Perf. 12***

**1185** A374 45c Carnosaur, sauropod .70 .55
*a.* Booklet pane of 10 + 2 labels 7.00 7.00

The 1940s — A375

Designs: 45c, New Zealand at war. 50c, Crop dusting. 80c, State produces hydroelectricity. $1, New Zealand Marching Assoc. $1.50, The American invasion. $1.80, Victory.

**1993, Nov. 3 Litho. *Perf. 14***
**1186** A375 45c multicolored .65 .30
**1187** A375 50c multicolored .75 .75
**1188** A375 80c multicolored 1.10 1.10
**1189** A375 $1 multicolored 1.40 1.40
**1190** A375 $1.50 multicolored 2.00 2.00
**1191** A375 $1.80 multicolored 2.25 2.25
*Nos. 1186-1191 (6)* 8.15 7.80

Outdoor Adventure Sports — A376

45c, Bungy jumping. 80c, Trout fishing. $1, Jet boating, horiz. $1.50, Tramping. $1.80, Heli-skiing.

**1994, Jan. 19 Litho. *Perf. 12***
**1192** A376 45c multicolored .60 .30
**1193** A376 80c multicolored .95 .95
**1194** A376 $1 multicolored 1.25 1.25
**1195** A376 $1.50 multicolored 1.75 1.75
**1196** A376 $1.80 multicolored 2.00 2.00
*a.* Souvenir sheet of 1 3.75 3.75
*Nos. 1192-1196 (5)* 6.55 6.25

No. 1196a inscribed in sheet margin with Hong Kong '94 emblem and text in English and Chinese. Issue date: No. 1196a, Feb. 18.

White Water Rafting — A377

**1994, Jan. 19 Litho. *Perf. 12***
**Booklet Stamp**
**1197** A377 45c multicolored .55 .55
*a.* Booklet pane of 10 + 4 labels 6.00

Whitbread Trans-Global Yacht Race — A378

**1994, Jan. 19 *Perf. 15***
**1198** A378 $1 Endeavour 1.40 1.40

Used value is for stamp with complete selvage.

The 1950's — A379

Designs: 45c, Rock and roll. 80c, Conquest of Mt. Everest. $1, Aunt Daisy, "Good Morning Everybody." $1.20, Royal visit, 1953. $1.50, Opo, the Friendly Dolphin. $1.80, The Coat Hanger (Auckland Harbor Bridge.)

**1994, Mar. 24 Litho. *Perf. 14***
**1199** A379 45c multicolored .60 .30
**1200** A379 80c multicolored .95 .95
**1201** A379 $1 multicolored 1.25 1.25
**1202** A379 $1.20 multicolored 1.50 1.50
**1203** A379 $1.50 multicolored 1.75 1.75
**1204** A379 $1.80 multicolored 2.25 2.25
*Nos. 1199-1204 (6)* 8.30 8.00

Scenic Views of the Four Seasons A380

Designs: 45c, Winter, Mt. Cook, Mt. Cook lily. 70c, Spring, Lake Hawea, kowhai flower. $1.50, Summer, Opononi, pohutukawa flower. $1.80, Autumn, Mt. Cook, Lake Pukaki, puriri flower.

**1994, Apr. 27 *Perf. 12***
**1205** A380 45c multicolored .50 .30
**1206** A380 70c multicolored .85 .85
**1207** A380 $1.50 multicolored 1.25 1.25
**1208** A380 $1.80 multicolored 1.75 1.75
*a.* Strip of 4, #1205-1208 5.00 5.00
*Nos. 1205-1208 (4)* 4.35 4.15

Paua Shell — A381

Pavlova Dessert A382

Jandals — A383

Bush Shirt — A384

Buzzy Bee Toy — A385

Kiwi Fruit — A386

Kiwiana: #1211, Hokey pokey ice cream. #1212, Fish and chips. #1216, Black singlet, gumboots. #1217, Rugby shoes, ball.

**1994, Apr. 27 Litho. *Perf. 12***
**Booklet Stamps**
**1209** A381 45c shown .55 .55
**1210** A382 45c shown .55 .55
**1211** A381 45c multicolored .55 .55
**1212** A382 45c multicolored .55 .55
**1213** A383 45c shown .55 .55

**1214** A384 45c shown .55 .55
**1215** A385 45c shown .55 .55
**1216** A384 45c multicolored .55 .55
**1217** A385 45c multicolored .55 .55
**1218** A386 45c shown .55 .55
*a.* Booklet pane of 10, #1209-1218 7.50
*Nos. 1209-1218 (10)* 5.50 5.50

Maori Myths — A387

Designs: 45c, Maui pulls up Te Ika (the fish). 80c, Rona is snatched up by Marama (moon). $1, Maui attacks Tuna (eel). $1.20, Tane separates Rangi (sky) and Papa (earth). $1.50, Matakauri slays Giant of Wakatipu. $1.80, Panenehu shows Koura (crayfish) to Tangaroa.

**1994, June 8** *Perf. 13*
**1219** A387 45c multicolored .65 .35
**1220** A387 80c multicolored .95 .95
**1221** A387 $1 multicolored 1.25 1.25
**1222** A387 $1.20 multicolored 1.50 1.50
**1223** A387 $1.50 multicolored 1.90 1.90
**1224** A387 $1.80 multicolored 2.25 2.25
*Nos. 1219-1224 (6)* 8.50 8.20

First Manned Moon Landing, 25th Anniv. — A388

**1994, July 20** **Litho.** *Perf. 12*
**1225** A388 $1.50 multicolored 2.25 2.25

No. 1225 has a holographic image. Soaking in water may affect the hologram.

People Reaching People — A389

***Serpentine Die Cut 11***
**1994, July 20** **Photo.**
**Self-Adhesive**
**1226** A389 45c multicolored .60 .50
*a.* Arrow partially covering hole in "B," serpentine die cut 11¼ *2.00* .75

No. 1226a issued Aug. 1995.
See No. 1311.

Wild Animals A390

No. 1227, Hippopotamus. No. 1228, Spider monkey. No. 1229, Giant panda. No. 1230, Polar bear. No. 1231, African elephant. No. 1232, White rhinoceros. No. 1233, African lion. No. 1234, Plains zebra. No. 1235, Giraffe. No. 1236, Siberian tiger.

**1994, Aug. 16** **Litho.** *Perf. 14*
**1227** A390 45c multicolored .75 .75
**1228** A390 45c multicolored .75 .75
**1229** A390 45c multicolored .75 .75
**1230** A390 45c multicolored .75 .75
**1231** A390 45c multicolored .75 .75
**1232** A390 45c multicolored .75 .75
**1233** A390 45c multicolored .75 .75
**1234** A390 45c multicolored .75 .75
**1235** A390 45c multicolored .75 .75
**1236** A390 45c multicolored .75 .75
*a.* Block of 10, #1227-1236 9.00 9.00
*b.* Souvenir sheet of 6, #1229-1231, 1233, 1235-1236 4.50 4.50
*Nos. 1227-1236 (10)* 7.50 7.50

PHILAKOREA '94 (#1236b). Nos. 1227-1236 printed in sheets of 100. Because of the design of these sheets, blocks or strips of Nos. 1227-1236 exist in 10 different arrangements. Value assigned to No. 1236a applies to all arrangements.

Christmas A391

Designs: No. 1237, Children, Nativity scene. 70c, Magi, father, child. 80c, Carolers, stained glass window. $1, Carolers, Christmas tree. $1.50, Children, candles. $1.80, Father, mother, infant.

No. 1243, Children, Christmas tree, Santa.

**1994, Sept. 21** **Litho.** *Perf. 14*
**1237** A391 45c multicolored .60 .50
**1238** A391 70c multicolored .90 .90
**1239** A391 80c multicolored 1.10 1.10
**1240** A391 $1 multicolored 1.25 1.25
*a.* Souv. sheet, 1 ea #1237-1240 4.00 4.00
**1241** A391 $1.50 multicolored 1.50 1.50
**1242** A391 $1.80 multicolored 1.75 1.75
*Nos. 1237-1242 (6)* 7.10 7.00

**Booklet Stamp**
**Size: 30x25mm**
**1243** A391 45c multicolored .55 .55
*a.* Booklet pane of 10 7.00

Cricket in New Zealand, Cent. — A392

Beach Cricket — A393

No. 1248: a, Woman with striped bathing suit in ocean. b, Person on bodyboard in ocean. c, Child holding float toy at water's edge. d, Boy with beach ball. e, Man holding ice cream cone. f, Beach umbrella at LL. g, Man in blue and red shorts holding cricket bat. h, Woman with cap holding cricket bat. i, Child with pail and shovel. j, Sunbather reading newspaper.

**1994, Nov. 2** *Perf. 13½*
**1244** A392 45c Batting .60 .40
**1245** A392 80c Bowling 1.10 .80
**1246** A392 $1 Wicketkeeping 1.25 1.25
**1247** A392 $1.80 Fielding 2.00 2.00
*Nos. 1244-1247 (4)* 4.95 4.45

*Perf. 12*
**1248** 45c Bklt. pane of 10 8.00 8.00
*a.-j.* A393 Any single .70 .55

New Zealand at Night A394

**1995, Feb. 22** **Litho.** *Perf. 12*
**1249** A394 45c Auckland .65 .30
**1250** A394 80c Wellington 1.00 .60
**1251** A394 $1 Christchurch 1.40 1.00
**1252** A394 $1.20 Dunedin 1.60 1.60
**1253** A394 $1.50 Rotorua 1.75 1.75
**1254** A394 $1.80 Queenstown 2.00 2.00
*a.* Souv. sheet of 6, #1249-1254 25.00 25.00
*Nos. 1249-1254 (6)* 8.40 7.25

Singapore '95, Jakarta '95 (#1254a). Issued: No. 1254a, 9/1/95.

Golf Courses — A395

**1995, Mar. 22** **Litho.** *Perf. 14*
**1255** A395 45c Waitangi .65 .35
**1256** A395 80c New Plymouth 1.00 1.00
**1257** A395 $1.20 Rotorua 1.50 1.50
**1258** A395 $1.80 Queenstown 2.50 2.50
*Nos. 1255-1258 (4)* 5.65 5.35

Environmental Protection A396

No. 1259, Native fauna, flora. No. 1260, Plant native trees, shrubs. No. 1261, Protect marine mammals. No. 1262, Conserve power, water. No. 1263, Enjoy natural environment. No. 1264, Control animal pests. No. 1265, Eliminate noxious plants. No. 1266, Return undersized catches. No. 1267, Control air, water quality. No. 1268, Dispose of trash properly.

**1995, Mar. 22**
**1259** A396 45c multicolored .65 .65
**1260** A396 45c multicolored .65 .65
**1261** A396 45c multicolored .65 .65
**1262** A396 45c multicolored .65 .65
**1263** A396 45c multicolored .65 .65
**1264** A396 45c multicolored .65 .65
**1265** A396 45c multicolored .65 .65
**1266** A396 45c multicolored .65 .65
**1267** A396 45c multicolored .65 .65
**1268** A396 45c multicolored .65 .65
*a.* Booklet pane, #1259-1268 7.50
Complete booklet, #1268a 8.00
*Nos. 1259-1268 (10)* 6.50 6.50

Maori Language — A397

Designs: 45c, Treasured Language Nest. 70c, Sing to awaken the spirit. 80c, Acquire knowledge through stories. $1, The welcoming call. $1.50, Recite the genealogies that link people. $1.80, Tell the lore of the people.

**1995, May 3** **Litho.** *Perf. 13½*
**1269** A397 45c multicolored .60 .25
**1270** A397 70c multicolored .90 .90
**1271** A397 80c multicolored 1.10 1.10
**1272** A397 $1 multicolored 1.25 1.25
**1273** A397 $1.50 multicolored 2.00 2.00
**1274** A397 $1.80 multicolored 2.25 2.25
*Nos. 1269-1274 (6)* 8.10 7.75

Asian Development Bank, 28th Meeting of the Board of Governors, Auckland — A398

Design: $1.50, Pacific Basin Economic Council, 28th Intl. Meeting, Auckland.

**1995, May 3**
**1275** A398 $1 Map shown 1.25 1.25
**1276** A398 $1.50 Map of Pacific 2.00 2.00

Team New Zealand, 1995 America's Cup Winner — A399

**1995, May 16** *Perf. 12*
**1277** A399 45c Black Magic yacht .70 .60

Rugby League, Cent. A400

Designs: No. 1278, Club Rugby League, Lion Red Cup. No. 1282, Trans Tasman. $1, Mini League. $1.50, George Smith, Albert Baskerville, Early Rugby League. $1.80, Intl. Rugby League, Courtney Intl. Goodwill Trophy.

**1995, July 26** **Litho.** *Perf. 14*
**1278** A400 45c multicolored .65 .25
**1279** A400 $1 multicolored 1.40 1.40
**1280** A400 $1.50 multicolored 2.10 2.10
**1281** A400 $1.80 multicolored 2.50 2.50
*a.* Souvenir sheet of 1 3.00 3.00
*Nos. 1278-1281 (4)* 6.65 6.25

**Booklet Stamp**
***Perf. 12 on 3 Sides***
**1282** A400 45c multicolored .60 .60
*a.* Booklet pane of 10 7.00
Complete booklet, #1282a 7.00

#1281a exists imperf from a "Limited Edition" album.

From 1995 onward, New Zealand Post has released a series of "Limited Edition" albums in editions of 2,000. Some contain souvenir sheets unique to these albums.

Farm Animals — A401

**1995** **Litho.** *Perf. 14x14½*
**Booklet Stamps**
**1283** A401 40c Sheep .50 .50
**1284** A401 40c Deer .50 .50
**1285** A401 40c Horses .50 .50
**1286** A401 40c Cattle .50 .50
**1287** A401 40c Goats .50 .50
**1288** A401 40c Turkey .50 .50
**1289** A401 40c Ducks .50 .50
**1290** A401 40c Chickens .50 .50
**1291** A401 40c Pigs .50 .50
**1292** A401 40c Border collie .50 .50
*a.* Bklt. pane of 10, #1283-1292 6.25
Complete booklet 6.75
**1293** A401 45c Sheep .75 .75
**1294** A401 45c Deer .75 .75
**1295** A401 45c Horses .75 .75
**1296** A401 45c Cattle .75 .75
**1297** A401 45c Goats .75 .75
**1298** A401 45c Turkey .75 .75
**1299** A401 45c Ducks .75 .75
**1300** A401 45c Chickens .75 .75
**1301** A401 45c Pigs .75 .75
**1302** A401 45c Border collie .75 .75
*a.* Bklt. pane of 10, #1293-1302 8.25
Complete booklet, #1302a 8.75
*b.* Souvenir sheet of 5, #1298-1302, perf. 12 4.25 4.25
*Nos. 1283-1302 (20)* 12.50 12.50

Singapore '95 (#1302b).
#1302b exists imperf.
Issued: #1302a, 9/1/95; #1292a, 10/2/95.

Christmas A402

Stained glass windows: 40c, 45c, Archangel Gabriel. No. 1309A, Angel with trumpet. 70c, Mary. 80c, Shepherds. $1, Madonna and Child. $1.50, Two wise men. $1.80, One wise man.

**1995** *Perf. 12*

| | | | | |
|---|---|---|---|---|
| **1303** | A402 | 40c multi | .60 | .25 |
| **1304** | A402 | 45c multi | .65 | .35 |
| **1305** | A402 | 70c multi | .95 | .95 |
| **1306** | A402 | 80c multi | 1.00 | 1.00 |
| **1307** | A402 | $1 multi | 1.25 | 1.25 |
| **1308** | A402 | $1.50 multi | 2.25 | 2.25 |
| **1309** | A402 | $1.80 multi | 2.50 | 2.50 |
| | | *Nos. 1303-1309 (7)* | 9.20 | 8.55 |

**Booklet Stamp**
**Size: 25x30mm**
***Perf. 14½x14***

**1309A** A402 40c multi .55 .55
*b.* Booklet pane of 10 6.50
Complete booklet, #1309b 6.50

Issued: 45c-$1.80, 9/1; #1303, 10/2; #1309A, 11/9.

Nos. 1303-1309 exist in a souvenir sheet from a "Limited Edition" pack.

Nuclear Disarmament A403

**1995, Sept. 1 Litho.** *Perf. 13½*
**1310** A403 $1 multicolored 1.40 1.40

**People Reaching People Type of 1994**
***Serpentine Die Cut 11***
**1995, Oct. 2 Photo.**
**Self-Adhesive**

**1311** A389 40c multicolored 1.50 .50
*a.* Arrow partially covering hole in "B," serpentine die cut 11¼ 1.00 1.00

No. 1311a, Nov. 1995.

**Scenic Views**

Mitre Peak — A404

**1995, Oct. 2 Litho.** *Perf. 13½*
**1312** A404 40c multicolored .65 .55
*a.* Perf 12 .65 .60
*b.* As "a," miniature sheet of 10 6.50

Southpex '96 Stamp Show (No. 1312a).

See Nos. 1345-1360, 1405, 1412, 1636-1640, 1679-1680, 1909, 1929.

UN, 50th Anniv. — A405

**1995, Oct. 4** *Perf. 14½*
**1313** A405 $1.80 multicolored 2.50 2.50

Famous Living New Zealanders — A406

Person, career field: 40c, Dame Kiri Te Kanawa, performing arts. 80c, Charles Upham, service, business, development. $1, Barry Crump, fine arts, literature. $1.20, Sir Brian Barratt-Boyes, science, medicine, education. $1.50, Dame Whina Cooper, community leader, social campaigner. $1.80, Sir Richard Hadlee, sports.

**1995, Oct. 4** *Perf. 12*

| | | | | |
|---|---|---|---|---|
| **1314** | A406 | 40c multicolored | .90 | .45 |
| **1315** | A406 | 80c multicolored | 1.10 | .85 |
| **1316** | A406 | $1 multicolored | 1.25 | 1.25 |
| **1317** | A406 | $1.20 multicolored | 1.50 | 1.50 |
| **1318** | A406 | $1.50 multicolored | 2.00 | 2.00 |
| **1319** | A406 | $1.80 multicolored | 2.50 | 2.50 |
| | | *Nos. 1314-1319 (6)* | 9.25 | 8.55 |

Nos. 1314-1319 issued with se-tenant tab inscribed "STAMP / MONTH / OCTOBER / 1995."

Commonwealth Heads of Government Meeting, Auckland — A407

Designs: 40c, Fern, sky, globe, $1.80, Fern, sea, national flag.

**1995, Nov. 9 Litho.** *Perf. 14*
**1320** A407 40c multicolored .65 .50
**1321** A407 $1.80 multicolored 2.75 2.50

Racehorses A408

40c, Kiwi. 80c, Rough Habit. $1, Blossom Lady. $1.20, Il Vicolo. $1.50, Horlicks. $1.80, Bonecrusher.

**1996, Jan. 24 Litho.** *Perf. 13½x14*

| | | | | |
|---|---|---|---|---|
| **1322** | A408 | 40c multi | .75 | .25 |
| **1323** | A408 | 80c multi | 1.00 | 1.00 |
| **1324** | A408 | $1 multi | 1.25 | 1.25 |
| **1325** | A408 | $1.20 multi | 1.75 | 1.75 |
| **1326** | A408 | $1.50 multi | 2.00 | 2.00 |
| **1327** | A408 | $1.80 multi | 2.50 | 2.50 |
| | | *Nos. 1322-1327 (6)* | 9.25 | 8.75 |

**Booklet**

**1328** A408 Souvenir bklt. *19.00*

No. 1328 contains one booklet pane of Nos. 1322-1327, perf. 14, and individual panes of 1 each Nos. 1322-1327.

Maori Crafts — A409

**1996, Feb. 21 Litho.** *Perf. 14x13½*

| | | | | |
|---|---|---|---|---|
| **1329** | A409 | 40c Basket | .45 | .25 |
| **1330** | A409 | 80c Weapon | .85 | .85 |
| **1331** | A409 | $1 Embroidery | 1.10 | 1.10 |
| **1332** | A409 | $1.20 Greenstone | 1.50 | 1.50 |
| **1333** | A409 | $1.50 Gourd | 1.75 | 1.75 |
| *a.* | | Souvenir sheet of 3, #1329, 1330, 1333, perf. 13 | 5.50 | 5.50 |
| **1334** | A409 | $1.80 Cloak | 2.00 | 2.00 |
| | | *Nos. 1329-1334 (6)* | 7.65 | 7.45 |

No. 1333a for Hong Kong '97. Issued 2/12/97.

Seashore — A410

Designs: No. 1335, Black-backed gull. No. 1336, Sea cucumber, spiny starfish. No. 1337, Common shrimp. No. 1338, Gaudy nudibranch. No. 1339, Large rock crab, clingfish. No. 1340, Snake skin chiton, red rock crab. No. 1341, Estuarine triplefin, cat's eye shell. No. 1342, Cushion star, sea horse. No. 1343, Blue-eyed triplefin, yaldwyn's triplefin. No. 1344, Common octopus.

**1996, Feb. 21** *Perf. 14x14½*
**Booklet Stamps**

| | | | | |
|---|---|---|---|---|
| **1335** | A410 | 40c multicolored | .55 | .55 |
| **1336** | A410 | 40c multicolored | .55 | .55 |
| **1337** | A410 | 40c multicolored | .55 | .55 |
| **1338** | A410 | 40c multicolored | .55 | .55 |
| **1339** | A410 | 40c multicolored | .55 | .55 |
| **1340** | A410 | 40c multicolored | .55 | .55 |
| **1341** | A410 | 40c multicolored | .55 | .55 |
| **1342** | A410 | 40c multicolored | .55 | .55 |
| **1343** | A410 | 40c multicolored | .55 | .55 |
| **1344** | A410 | 40c multicolored | .55 | .55 |
| *a.* | | Booklet pane, Nos. 1335-1344 | 6.50 | |
| | | Complete booklet, No. 1344a | 6.75 | |
| | | *Nos. 1335-1344 (10)* | 5.50 | 5.50 |

No. 1344a has a continuous design.

***Serpentine Die Cut 11½***
**1996, Aug. 7 Litho.**
**Booklet Stamps**
**Self-Adhesive**

| | | | | |
|---|---|---|---|---|
| **1344B** | A410 | 40c like #1335 | 1.25 | 1.25 |
| **1344C** | A410 | 40c like #1336 | 1.25 | 1.25 |
| **1344D** | A410 | 40c like #1337 | 1.25 | 1.25 |
| **1344E** | A410 | 40c like #1338 | 1.25 | 1.25 |
| **1344F** | A410 | 40c like #1339 | 1.25 | 1.25 |
| **1344G** | A410 | 40c like #1340 | 1.25 | 1.25 |
| **1344H** | A410 | 40c like #1341 | 1.25 | 1.25 |
| **1344I** | A410 | 40c like #1342 | 1.25 | 1.25 |
| **1344J** | A410 | 40c like #1343 | 1.25 | 1.25 |
| **1344K** | A410 | 40c like #1344 | 1.25 | 1.25 |
| *l.* | | Bklt pane, #1344B-1344K | 14.00 | |
| | | *Nos. 1344B-1344K (10)* | 12.50 | 12.50 |

No. 1344Kl is a complete booklet. The peelable paper backing serves as a booklet cover.

**Scenic Views Type of 1995**

5c, Mt. Cook, horiz. 10c, Champagne Pool, horiz. 20c, Cape Reinga, horiz. 30c, Mackenzie Country, horiz. 50c, Mt. Ngauruhoe, horiz. 60c, Lake Wanaka. 70c, Giant Kauri-Tane Mahuta. 80c, Doubtful Sound. 90c, Waitomo Limestone Cave.

No. 1354, Tory Channel, Marlborough Sounds. No. 1355, Lake Wakatipu. No. 1356, Lake Matheson. No. 1357, Fox Glacier. No. 1358, Mt. Egmont, Taranaki. No. 1359, Piercy Island, Bay of Islands. No. 1354-1359 horiz.

**1996, Mar. 27 Litho.** *Perf. 13½*

| | | | | |
|---|---|---|---|---|
| **1345** | A404 | 5c multicolored | .25 | .25 |
| **1346** | A404 | 10c multicolored | .25 | .25 |
| **1347** | A404 | 20c multicolored | .25 | .25 |
| **1348** | A404 | 30c multicolored | .35 | .35 |
| **1349** | A404 | 50c multicolored | .50 | .50 |
| *a.* | | Souv. sheet of 4, #1346-1349 | 3.00 | 3.00 |
| **1350** | A404 | 60c multicolored | .70 | .70 |
| **1351** | A404 | 70c multicolored | .80 | .80 |
| **1352** | A404 | 80c multicolored | 1.00 | 1.00 |
| **1353** | A404 | 90c multicolored | 1.25 | 1.25 |
| *a.* | | Souv. sheet of 4, #1350-1353 | 6.50 | 6.50 |
| | | *Nos. 1345-1353 (9)* | 5.35 | 5.35 |

CHINA '96 (#1349a). CAPEX '96 (#1353a.)

See No. 1405.

***Serpentine Die Cut 11¼***
**1996, May 1 Photo.**
**Size: 26x21mm**
**Self-Adhesive**

| | | | | |
|---|---|---|---|---|
| **1354** | A404 | 40c multicolored | .55 | .55 |
| **1355** | A404 | 40c multicolored | .55 | .55 |
| **1356** | A404 | 40c multicolored | .55 | .55 |
| **1357** | A404 | 40c multicolored | .55 | .55 |
| **1358** | A404 | 40c multicolored | .55 | .55 |
| **1359** | A404 | 40c multicolored | .55 | .55 |
| *a.* | | Strip of 6, Nos. 1354-1359 | 3.50 | 3.50 |
| *k.* | | Sheet of 10, #1356, 1359, 2 each #1354-1355, 1357-1358 | *35.00* | |
| *l.* | | Sheet of 10, #1355, 1358, 2 each #1354, 1356-1357, 1359 | *35.00* | |
| *m.* | | Sheet of 10, #1354, 1357, 2 each #1355-1356, 1358-1359 | *35.00* | |
| | | *Nos. 1354-1359 (6)* | 3.30 | 3.30 |

***Serpentine Die Cut 10x9¾***
**1998, Jan. 14 Litho.**
**Booklet Stamps**
**Size: 26x21mm**
**Self-Adhesive**

| | | | | |
|---|---|---|---|---|
| **1359B** | A404 | 40c like #1358 | .55 | .55 |
| **1359C** | A404 | 40c like #1357 | .55 | .55 |
| **1359D** | A404 | 40c like #1359 | .55 | .55 |
| **1359E** | A404 | 40c like #1356 | .55 | .55 |
| **1359F** | A404 | 40c like #1354 | .55 | .55 |
| *h.* | | "Marlborough Sounds" omitted | *17.50* | |
| **1359G** | A404 | 40c like #1355 | .55 | .55 |
| *i.* | | Booklet pane, #1359D, 1359F, 1359Fh, 1359G, 2 #1359B-1359C, 1359E | *19.00* | |
| *j.* | | Booklet pane #1359D, 1359G, 2 each #1359B, 1359C, 1359E, 1359F | 5.50 | |
| *n.* | | Coil strip of 6, #1359B-1359G | 3.60 | |
| | | *Nos. 1359B-1359G (6)* | 3.30 | 3.30 |

No. 1359Gi is a complete booklet.

***Serpentine Die Cut 11½***
**1996, Aug. 7 Litho.**
**Size: 33x22mm**
**Self-Adhesive**

Design: $1, Pohutukawa tree, horiz.

**1360** A404 $1 multicolored 1.40 1.40
*a.* Booklet pane of 5 7.00

By its nature No. 1360a is a complete booklet. The peelable paper backing serves as a booklet cover. The outside of the cover contains 5 peelable international airpost labels.

Rescue Services — A411

40c, Fire service, ambulance. 80c, Civil defense. $1, Air sea rescue. $1.50, Air ambulance, rescue helicopter. $1.80, Mountain rescue, Red Cross.

**1996, Mar. 27** *Perf. 14½x15*

| | | | | |
|---|---|---|---|---|
| **1361** | A411 | 40c multicolored | .60 | .45 |
| **1362** | A411 | 80c multicolored | 1.00 | 1.00 |
| **1363** | A411 | $1 multicolored | 1.25 | 1.25 |
| **1364** | A411 | $1.50 multicolored | 2.00 | 2.00 |
| **1365** | A411 | $1.80 multicolored | 2.50 | 2.50 |
| | | *Nos. 1361-1365 (5)* | 7.35 | 7.20 |

Wildlife A412

Designs: 40c, Yellow-eyed penguin, vert. 80c, Royal albatross. $1, White heron. $1.20, Sperm whale. $1.50, Fur seal, vert. $1.80, Bottlenose dolphin, vert.

**1996, May 1 Litho. *Perf. 14***

**1366** A412 40c multicolored .70 .50
**1367** A412 80c multicolored 1.25 .90
**1368** A412 $1 multicolored 1.40 1.40
**1369** A412 $1.20 multicolored 1.50 1.50
**1370** A412 $1.50 multicolored 1.75 1.75
*a.* Sheet of 2, #1368, 1370 6.50 6.50
**1371** A412 $1.80 multicolored 2.00 2.00
*a.* Sheet of 2, #1367, 1371 5.00 5.00
*b.* Block, #1366-1371, + 2 labels 9.50 9.50
*Nos. 1366-1371 (6)* 8.60 8.05

No. 1370a for CHINA '96. Issued May 18. No. 1371a for Taipei '96. Issued Oct. 2.

New Zealand Symphony Orchestra, 50th Anniv. — A413

**1996, July 10 Litho. *Perf. 15x14½***

**1372** A413 40c Violin .60 .50
**1373** A413 80c French horn 1.10 1.10

1996 Summer Olympics, Atlanta A414

**1996, July 10 *Perf. 14½***

**1374** A414 40c Swimming .75 .30
**1375** A414 80c Cycling 1.40 1.40
**1376** A414 $1 Athletics 1.50 1.50
**1377** A414 $1.50 Rowing 1.75 1.75
**1378** A414 $1.80 Yachting 2.00 2.00
*a.* Sheet of 5, #1374-1378 8.00 8.00
*Nos. 1374-1378 (5)* 7.40 6.95

Used value is for stamp with complete selvage.

A miniature sheet containing #1374-1378, both perf and imperf within the sheet, exists. This comes from a "Limited Edition" collectors' pack.

See No. 1383.

A415

Motion pictures, cent.: 40c, Hinemoa. 80c, Broken Barrier. $1.50, Goodbye Pork Pie. $1.80, Once Were Warriors.

**1996, Aug. 7 Litho. *Perf. 14½x15***

**1379** A415 40c multicolored .60 .35
**1380** A415 80c multicolored 1.10 1.10
**1381** A415 $1.50 multicolored 1.75 1.75
**1382** A415 $1.80 multicolored 2.00 2.00
*Nos. 1379-1382 (4)* 5.45 5.20

Nos. 1379-1382 are printed se-tenant with scratch and win labels for a contest available to New Zealand residents. Values 25% more with unscratched labels attached.

**1996 Summer Olympics Type**

Design: Danyon Loader, swimmer, Blyth Tait, horseman, 1996 gold medalists from New Zealand.

**1996, Aug. 28 Litho. *Perf. 14½***

**1383** A414 40c multicolored .65 .65

Used value is for stamp with complete selvage.

Leaves in selvage printed in six different patterns.

Beehive Ballot Box — A416

**1996, Sept. 4 *Perf. 12***

**1384** A416 40c multicolored .65 .50

Mixed member proportional election, 1966. No. 1384 was issued in sheets of 10.

Christmas A417

Scenes from the Christmas story: No. 1385, Following the star. 70c, Shepherd finding baby in manger. 80c, Angel's announcement to shepherd. $1, The Nativity. $1.50, Journey to Bethlehem. $1.80, The annunciation.

No. 1391, Adoration of the Magi. No. 1392, Heavenly host praising God.

**1996, Sept. 4 *Perf. 14***

**1385** A417 40c multicolored .60 .30
**1386** A417 70c multicolored 1.00 1.00
**1387** A417 80c multicolored 1.10 1.10
**1388** A417 $1 multicolored 1.25 1.25
**1389** A417 $1.50 multicolored 1.75 1.75
**1390** A417 $1.80 multicolored 2.00 2.00
*Nos. 1385-1390 (6)* 7.70 7.40

**Size: 29x24mm**

**Self-Adhesive**

***Serpentine Die Cut 11½***

**1391** A417 40c multicolored .65 .55
*a.* Booklet pane 10 6.50
**1392** A417 40c multicolored .65 .55

By its nature No. 1391a is a complete booklet. The peelable paper backing serves as a booklet cover.

Extinct Birds A418

No. 1393, 40c, Adzebill. 80c, Laughing owl. $1, Piopio. $1.20, Huia. $1.50, Giant eagle. $1.80, Giant moa. No. 1399, 40c, Stout-legged wren.

**1996, Oct. 2 Litho. *Perf. 13½***

**1393** A418 40c multi .60 .45
**1394** A418 80c multi 1.10 1.10
**1395** A418 $1 multi 1.50 1.50
**1396** A418 $1.20 multi 1.60 1.60
**1397** A418 $1.50 multi 2.00 2.00
**1398** A418 $1.80 multi 2.25 2.25
*a.* Souvenir sheet 3.00 3.00
*b.* As "a," with added inscription 4.50 4.50
*Nos. 1393-1398 (6)* 9.05 8.90

**Size: 29x24mm**

**Self-Adhesive**

***Serpentine Die Cut 11½***

**1399** A418 40c multi .65 .55
*a.* Booklet pane of 10 6.50

Inscriptions on backs of Nos. 1393-1398 describe each species. By its nature No. 1399a is a complete booklet. The peelable backing serves as a booklet cover.

No. 1398b contains Taipei '96 exhibition emblem in sheet margin.

Scenic Gardens — A419

Designs: 40c, Seymour Square Gardens, Blenheim. 80c, Pukekura Park Gardens, New Plymouth. $1, Wintergarden, Auckland. $1.50, Botanic Gardens, Christchurch. $1.80, Marine Parade Gardens, Napier.

**1996, Nov. 13 Litho. *Perf. 13½***

**1400** A419 40c multicolored .55 .45
**1401** A419 80c multicolored 1.00 1.00
**1402** A419 $1 multicolored 1.25 1.25
**1403** A419 $1.50 multicolored 1.75 1.75
**1404** A419 $1.80 multicolored 2.25 2.25
*Nos. 1400-1404 (5)* 6.80 6.70

New Zealand Post produced and distributed three souvenir sheets as rewards for purchases made from the post office during 1996. The sheets were not available through normal philatelic channels. The sheets are inscribed "NEW ZEALAND POST / Best of 1996" and the Stamp Points emblem. Each sheet contains 3 stamps; #1327, 1365, 1334; #1378, 1382, 1371; #1390, 1404, 1398.

**Scenic Views Type of 1995**

***Serpentine Die Cut 11½***

**1996, Nov. 1 Litho.**

**Size: 21x26mm**

**Self-Adhesive**

**1405** A404 80c like No. 1352 1.10 1.10
*a.* Booklet pane of 10 12.50

By its nature No. 1405a is a complete booklet. The peelable paper backing serves as a booklet cover. The outside of the cover contains 10 peelable international airpost labels.

Cattle — A420

40c, Holstein-Friesian. 80c, Jersey. $1, Simmental. $1.20, Ayrshire. $1.50, Angus. $1.80, Hereford.

**1997, Jan. 15 *Perf. 14x14½***

**1406** A420 40c multi .65 .30
**1407** A420 80c multi 1.25 1.10
**1408** A420 $1 multi 1.60 1.40
**1409** A420 $1.20 multi 1.75 1.75
**1410** A420 $1.50 multi 2.00 2.00
*a.* Souvenir sheet of 3, #1407, 1408, 1410 9.00 9.00
**1411** A420 $1.80 multi 2.25 2.25
*Nos. 1406-1411 (6)* 9.50 8.80

No. 1410a for Hong Kong '97. Issued 2/12/97.

Souvenir Sheets

The 1997 sheets contain: Nos. 1411, 1418, 1434; Nos. 1440, 1444, 1451; Nos. 1445, 1457, 1475.

See note following No. 1404.

**Scenic Views Type of 1995**

**1997, Feb. 12 Litho. *Perf. 13½***

**Size: 37x32mm**

**1412** A404 $10 Mt. Ruapehu 15.00 11.50

Discoverers — A421

40c, James Cook. 80c, Kupe. $1, Maui, vert. $1.20, Jean de Surville, vert. $1.50, Dumont d'Urville. $1.80, Abel Tasman.

**1997, Feb. 12 *Perf. 14***

**1413** A421 40c multicolored .75 .50
**1414** A421 80c multicolored 1.10 1.10
**1415** A421 $1 multicolored 1.40 1.40
**1416** A421 $1.20 multicolored 1.75 1.75
**1417** A421 $1.50 multicolored 2.25 2.25
**1418** A421 $1.80 multicolored 2.50 2.50
*Nos. 1413-1418 (6)* 9.75 9.50

#1413-1418 exist in sheet of 6 created for a hard-bound millennium book that sold for $129.

"Wackiest Letterboxes" — A422

***Serpentine Die Cut 11¼***

**1997, Mar. 19 Litho.**

**Self-Adhesive**

**Booklet Stamps**

**1419** A422 40c Log house .55 .55
**1420** A422 40c Owl .55 .55
**1421** A422 40c Whale .55 .55
**1422** A422 40c "Kilroy is Back" .55 .55
**1423** A422 40c House of twigs .55 .55
**1424** A422 40c Scottish piper .55 .55
**1425** A422 40c Diving helmet .55 .55
**1426** A422 40c Airplane .55 .55
**1427** A422 40c Water faucet .55 .55
**1428** A422 40c Painted buildings .55 .55
*a.* Bklt. pane of 10, #1419-1428 7.00
*b.* Sheet of 10, #1419-1428 18.00
*Nos. 1419-1428 (10)* 5.50 5.50

By its nature No. 1428a is a complete booklet. The peelable paper backing serves as a booklet cover.

Vineyards — A423

40c, Central Otago. 80c, Hawke's Bay. $1, Marlborough. $1.20, Canterbury, Waipara. $1.50, Gisborne. $1.80, Auckland, Waiheke.

**1997, Mar. 19 *Perf. 14***

**1429** A423 40c multicolored .50 .30
*a.* Booklet pane of 1 .65
**1430** A423 80c multicolored 1.10 1.10
*a.* Booklet pane of 1 1.10
**1431** A423 $1 multicolored 1.50 1.50
*a.* Booklet pane of 1 1.50
**1432** A423 $1.20 multicolored 1.75 1.75
*a.* Booklet pane of 1 1.75
**1433** A423 $1.50 multicolored 2.50 2.50
*a.* Booklet pane of 1 2.50
*b.* Souvenir sheet of 3, #1429, 1431, 1433 8.50 8.50
**1434** A423 $1.80 multicolored 2.50 2.50
*a.* Booklet pane of 1 2.50
*b.* Bklt. pane of 6, #1429-1434 10.00
Complete booklet, #1429a, 1430a, 1431a, 1432a, 1433a, 1434a, 1434b 21.00
*Nos. 1429-1434 (6)* 9.85 9.65

No. 1433b for PACIFIC 97. Issued: 5/29.

Pigeon Mail Service, Cent. A424

Design: 1899 local stamp.

**1997, May 7 Litho. *Perf. 14***

**1435** A424 40c red .65 .65
**1436** A424 80c blue 1.25 1.25
*a.* Souv. sheet, 2 ea #1435-1436 9.50 9.50
*b.* As "a," diff. inscription 6.00 6.00

No. 1436a for PACIFIC 97. Issued: 5/29.

No. 1436b was inscribed in sheet margin for AUPEX '97 National Stamp Exhibition, Auckland. Issued 11/13.

Paintings by Colin McCahon (1919-87) — A425

Designs: 40c, The Promised Land, 1948. $1, Six Days in Nelson and Canterbury, 1950. $1.50, Northland Panels, 1958. $1.80, Moby Dick is sighted off Muriwai Beach, 1972.

**1997, May 7**

**1437** A425 40c multicolored .65 .30
**1438** A425 $1 multicolored 1.25 1.25
**1439** A425 $1.50 multicolored 2.00 2.00
**1440** A425 $1.80 multicolored 2.25 2.25
*Nos. 1437-1440 (4)* 6.15 5.80

See Nos. 1597-1600.

Fly Fishing — A426

Designs: 40c, Red setter fly, rainbow trout. $1, Grey ghost fly, sea-run brown trout. $1.50, Twilight beauty fly, brook trout. $1.80, Hare & copper fly, brown trout.

**1997, June 18 Litho. *Perf. 13***

**1441** A426 40c multicolored .60 .40
**1442** A426 $1 multicolored 1.50 1.50
**1443** A426 $1.50 multicolored 2.00 2.00
**1444** A426 $1.80 multicolored 2.25 2.25
*a.* Souv. sheet of 2, #1441, 1444 6.00 6.00
*Nos. 1441-1444 (4)* 6.35 6.15

No.1444a issued 5/13/98 for Israel '98 World Stamp Exhibition, Tel Aviv.

### Kiwi Type of 1988

**1997, Aug. 6 Litho. *Perf. 14½***

**1445** A325 $1 violet 1.25 1.25

Value is for stamp with surrounding selvage. Selvage comes with and without gold sunbursts.

See No. 1635a.

Scenic Trains A426a

Name of train, area scene, map of train route: 40c, Overlander, Paremata, Wellington, Wellington-Auckland. 80c, Trans-Alpine, Southern Alps, Christchurch-Greymouth. $1, Southerner, Canterbury, Invercargill-Christchurch. $1.20, Coastal Pacific, Kaikoura Coast, Christchurch-Picton. $1.50, Bay Express, Central Hawke's Bay, Wellington-Napier. $1.80, Kaimai Express, Tauranga Harbor, Tauranga-Auckland.

**1997, Aug. 6 *Perf. 14x14½***

**1446** A426a 40c multicolored .60 .40
**1447** A426a 80c multicolored 1.10 1.00
**1448** A426a $1 multicolored 1.25 1.25
**1449** A426a $1.20 multicolored 1.50 1.50
**1450** A426a $1.50 multicolored 2.00 2.00
*a.* Sheet of 3, #1447-1448, 1450 7.50 7.50
**1451** A426a $1.80 multicolored 2.25 2.25
*Nos. 1446-1451 (6)* 8.70 8.40

No. 1450a issued 5/13/98 for Israel '98 World Stamp Exhibition, Tel Aviv.

Nos. 1446-1451 exist in a sheet of 6 from a "Limited Edition" album.

Christmas A427

Scenes from first Christian service, Rangihoua Bay, and words from Christmas carol, "Te Harinui:" No. 1452, Samuel Marsden's ship, Active. 70c, Marsden preaching from pulpit. 80c, Marsden extending hand to local chiefs. $1, Mother, children from Rangihoua. $1.50, Maori and Pakeha hands, Marsden's memorial cross. $1.80, Pohutukawa flowers, Rangihoua Bay. No. 1458, Cross marking spot of service, flowers, bay.

**1997, Sept. 3 Litho. *Perf. 14***

**1452** A427 40c multicolored .60 .25
**1453** A427 70c multicolored .90 .90
**1454** A427 80c multicolored 1.00 1.00
**1455** A427 $1 multicolored 1.25 1.25
**1456** A427 $1.50 multicolored 1.75 1.75
**1457** A427 $1.80 multicolored 2.00 2.00
*a.* Block of 6, #1452-1457 10.00 10.00
*Nos. 1452-1457 (6)* 7.50 7.15

### Self-Adhesive

### Size: 30x24mm

### *Serpentine Die Cut 10*

**1458** A427 40c multicolored .50 .50
*a.* Booklet pane of 10 6.50

By its nature No. 1458a is a complete booklet. The peelable paper backing serves as a booklet cover.

"Creepy Crawlies" — A428

### *Serpentine Die Cut 11¼*

**1997, Oct. 1 Litho.**

### Booklet Stamps

**1459** A428 40c Huhu beetle .55 .55
**1460** A428 40c Giant land snail .55 .55
**1461** A428 40c Giant weta .55 .55
**1462** A428 40c Giant dragonfly .55 .55
**1463** A428 40c Peripatus .55 .55
**1464** A428 40c Cicada .55 .55
**1465** A428 40c Puriri moth .55 .55
**1466** A428 40c Veined slug .55 .55
**1467** A428 40c Katipo .55 .55
**1468** A428 40c Flaxweevil .55 .55
*a.* Booklet pane, #1459-1468 6.25
*b.* Sheet of 10, #1459-1468 10.00
*Nos. 1459-1468 (10)* 5.50 5.50

By its nature No. 1468a is a complete booklet. The peelable paper backing serves as a booklet cover.

China-New Zealand Stamp Expo — A429

**1997, Oct. 9 *Perf. 14***

**1469** 40c Rosa rugosa .65 .50
**1470** 40c Aotearoa-New Zealand .65 .50
*a.* A429 Pair, #1469-1470 1.40 1.10
*b.* Souvenir sheet, #1470a 2.00 2.00
*c.* As "b," diff. inscription 2.00 2.00

No. 1470c inscribed in gold and black in sheet margin for Shanghai 1997 Intl. Stamp & Coin Expo. Issued: 11/19/97.

See People's Republic of China Nos. 2797-2798.

Queen Elizabeth II and Prince Philip, 50th Wedding Anniv. — A430

**1997, Nov. 12 Litho. *Perf. 12***

**1471** A430 40c multicolored .65 .45

Issued in sheets of 10.

Cartoonists A431

"Kiwis Taking on the World:" 40c, Kiwi flying on bee, by Garrick Tremain. $1, Kiwi using world as egg and having it for breakfast, by Jim Hubbard. $1.50, Kiwi in yacht race against the world, by Eric Heath. $1.80, Man with chain saw, trees on mountainside cut as peace symbol, by Burton Silver.

**1997, Nov. 12 *Perf. 14***

**1472** A431 40c multicolored .65 .30
**1473** A431 $1 multicolored 1.25 1.25
**1474** A431 $1.50 multicolored 1.75 1.75
**1475** A431 $1.80 multicolored 2.50 2.50
*Nos. 1472-1475 (4)* 6.15 5.80

Performing Arts — A432

**1998, Jan. 14 Litho. *Perf. 13½***

**1476** A432 40c Modern dance .60 .35
*a.* Booklet pane of 1 .60
**1477** A432 80c Music 1.00 .95
*a.* Booklet pane of 1 1.00
*b.* Perf 14 2.50 2.50
**1478** A432 $1 Opera 1.25 1.25
*a.* Booklet pane of 1 1.25
**1479** A432 $1.20 Theater 1.50 1.50
*a.* Booklet pane of 1 1.50
**1480** A432 $1.50 Song 2.00 2.00
*a.* Booklet pane of 1 2.00
**1481** A432 $1.80 Ballet 2.25 2.25
*a.* Booklet pane of 1 2.25
*b.* Bklt. pane of 6, #1476-1481 11.00
Complete booklet, 1 each #1476a-1481a, 1481b 22.50
*c.* Perf 14 5.50 5.50
*Nos. 1476-1481 (6)* 8.60 8.30

Museum of New Zealand Te Papa Tongarewa — A433

40c, People at entrance. $1.80, Waterfront location.

**1998, Feb. 11 Litho. *Perf. 14***

**1482** A433 40c multicolored .50 .45
**1483** A433 $1.80 multicolored 2.00 2.00

### Souvenir Sheets

The 1998 sheets contain: Nos. 1489, 1483, 1481; Nos. 1491, 1521, 1525; Nos. 1531, 1537, 1562.

See note following No. 1404.

Domestic Cat — A434

**1998, Feb. 11 *Perf. 13½***

**1484** A434 40c Moggy .55 .30
**1485** A434 80c Burmese 1.00 1.00
**1486** A434 $1 Birman 1.10 1.10
**1487** A434 $1.20 British blue 1.25 1.25
**1488** A434 $1.50 Persian 1.75 1.75
**1489** A434 $1.80 Siamese 2.25 2.25
*a.* Souvenir sheet of 3, #1484, #1486, #1489 6.00 6.00
*Nos. 1484-1489 (6)* 7.90 7.65

Memorial Statues — A435

40c, "With Great Respect to the Mehmetcik, Gallipoli" (Turkish soldier carrying wounded ANZAC). $1.80, "Mother with Children," Natl. War Memorial, Wellington.

**1998, Mar. 18 Litho. *Perf. 13½***

**1490** A435 40c multicolored .50 .40
**1491** A435 $1.80 multicolored 2.00 2.00

See Turkey Nos. 2695-2696.

New Zealand's Multi-cultural Society — A436

Designs: 40c, The Maori. 80c, British/European settlers, 1840-1914. $1, Fortune seekers, 1800-1920. $1.20, Post-war British/European migrants, 1945-70. $1.50, Pacific Islanders, from 1960. $1.80, Asian arrivals, 1980s-90s.

**1998, Mar. 18 *Perf. 14***

**1492** A436 40c multicolored .55 .25
**1493** A436 80c multicolored 1.10 .90
**1494** A436 $1 multicolored 1.40 1.10
**1495** A436 $1.20 multicolored 1.50 1.50
**1496** A436 $1.50 multicolored 1.75 1.75
**1497** A436 $1.80 multicolored 2.00 2.00
*Nos. 1492-1497 (6)* 8.30 7.50

Nos. 1492-1497 exist in sheet of 6 created for a hard-bound millennium book that sold for $129.

"Stay in Touch" Greetings Stamps A437

Designs: No. 1498, Young and older person hugging, vert. No. 1499, Middle-aged couple wading in water at beach, vert. No. 1500, Characters giving "high five," vert. No. 1501, Stylized boy pointing way to old woman, vert. No. 1502, Cartoon of woman with tears embracing man. No. 1503, Couple kissing. No. 1504, Older couple with faces together. No. 1505, Two boys arm in arm in swimming pool. No. 1506, Stylized couple, clouds. No. 1507, Stylized couple seated on sofa.

*Die Cut Perf. 10x10¼, 10¼x10*

**1998, Apr. 15 Litho.**

**Booklet Stamps**

**Self-Adhesive**

**1498** A437 40c multicolored .50 .50
**1499** A437 40c multicolored .50 .50
**1500** A437 40c multicolored .50 .50
**1501** A437 40c multicolored .50 .50
*a.* Sheet of 4, #1498-1501 5.00
**1502** A437 40c multicolored .50 .50
**1503** A437 40c multicolored .50 .50
**1504** A437 40c multicolored .50 .50
**1505** A437 40c multicolored .50 .50
**1506** A437 40c multicolored .50 .50
**1507** A437 40c multicolored .50 .50
*a.* Booklet pane, #1498-1507 6.50
*b.* Sheet of 6, #1502-1507 10.00
*Nos. 1498-1507 (10)* 5.00 5.00

The peelable paper backing of No. 1507a serves as a booklet cover.

**Types of 1898**

**1998, May 20 Litho. *Perf. 14x14½***

**1508** A18 40c Mt. Cook .55 .55
**1509** A19 40c Lake Taupo .55 .55
**1510** A20 40c Pembroke Peak .55 .55
**1511** A23 40c Huia .55 .55
**1512** A24 40c White Terrace .55 .55
**1513** A26 40c Kiwi .55 .55
**1514** A27 40c Maori canoe .55 .55
**1515** A29 40c Hawk-billed parrots .55 .55

***Perf. 14½***

**1516** A21 80c Wakitipu 1.00 1.00
**1517** A22 80c Wakatipu 1.00 1.00
*a.* Souvenir sheet of 2, 1516-1517 4.75 4.75
**1518** A25 $1 Otira Gorge 1.25 1.25
**1519** A28 $1.20 Pink Terrace 1.50 1.50
**1520** A30 $1.50 Milford Sound 1.75 1.75
*a.* Sheet of 2, #1517, 1520 4.00 4.00
**1521** A31 $1.80 Mt. Cook 2.00 2.00
*Nos. 1508-1521 (14)* 12.90 12.90

No. 1517a issued 8/7/98 for Tarapex '98, Natl. Stamp Exhibition.
No. 1520a issued 10/23/98 for Italia '98.

Paintings by Peter McIntyre A438

Designs: 40c, Wounded at Cassino, 1944. $1, The Cliffs of Rangitikei, c. 1958. $1.50, Maori Children, King Country, 1963. $1.80, The Anglican Church, Kakahi, 1972.

**1998, June 24 Litho. *Perf. 13½***

**1522** A438 40c multicolored .45 .30
**1523** A438 $1 multicolored 1.10 1.10
**1524** A438 $1.50 multicolored 1.50 1.50
**1525** A438 $1.80 multicolored 1.75 1.75
*a.* Souvenir sheet, #1524-1525, perf 14 6.00 6.00
*Nos. 1522-1525 (4)* 4.80 4.65

No. 1525a issued 10/23/98 for Italia '98.
Nos. 1524-1525 exist in an imperf souvenir sheet from a "Limited Edition" album.

Scenic Skies — A439

40c, Cambridge. 80c, Lake Wanaka. $1, Mt. Maunganui. $1.20, Kaikoura. $1.50, Whakatane. $1.80, Lindis Pass.

**1998, July 29 Litho. *Perf. 14½***

**1526** A439 40c multi .60 .25
**1527** A439 80c multi 1.10 .90
**1528** A439 $1 multi 1.25 1.10
**1529** A439 $1.20 multi 1.40 1.40
**1530** A439 $1.50 multi 2.00 2.00
**1531** A439 $1.80 multi 2.25 2.25
*a.* Souv. sheet of 2, #1526, 1531 3.75 3.75
*Nos. 1526-1531 (6)* 8.60 7.90

No. 1531a issued 3/19/99 for Australia '99 World Stamp Expo.

Christmas A440

Designs: 40c, Madonna and Child. 70c, Shepherds approaching nativity scene. 80c, Joseph, Mary, Christ Child. $1, Magus. $1.50, Magi with gifts. $1.80, Angel telling shepherds about Messiah.

**1998, Sept. 2 Litho. *Perf. 13x14***

**1532** A440 40c multicolored .55 .25
**1533** A440 70c multicolored .90 .80
**1534** A440 80c multicolored 1.10 .90
**1535** A440 $1 multicolored 1.25 1.25
**1536** A440 $1.50 multicolored 1.75 1.75
**1537** A440 $1.80 multicolored 2.00 2.00
*Nos. 1532-1537 (6)* 7.55 6.95

**Self-adhesive**

**Size: 24x30mm**

***Serpentine Die Cut 11½***

**1538** A440 40c multicolored .50 .40
*a.* Booklet pane of 10 6.50

No. 1538a is a complete booklet. The peelable paper backing serves as a booklet cover.

Marine Life — A441

**1998, Oct. 7 Litho. *Perf. 14***

**1539** A441 40c Moonfish .45 .45
**1540** A441 40c Mako shark .45 .45
**1541** A441 40c Yellowfin tuna .45 .45
**1542** A441 40c Giant squid .45 .45
*a.* Block of 4, #1539-1542 2.50 2.50
**1543** A441 80c Striped marlin .90 .90
**1544** A441 80c Porcupine fish .90 .90
*a.* Souvenir sheet of 4, #1539-1540, #1543-1544 5.25 5.25
**1545** A441 80c Eagle ray .90 .90
**1546** A441 80c Sandager's wrasse .90 .90
*a.* Block of 4, #1543-1546 4.75 4.75
*b.* Souvenir sheet of 4, #1541-1542, 1545-1546 8.00 8.00
*Nos. 1539-1546 (8)* 5.40 5.40

No. 1544a issued 3/19/99 for Australia '99, World Stamp Expo. No. 1546b was issued 7/2/99 for PhilexFrance '99, World Philatelic Exhibition.
#1539-1546 exist in sheets of 8 from a "Limited Edition" album.

Famous Town Icons
A442 A443

Designs: No. 1547, L&P bottle, Paeroa. No. 1548, Carrot, Ohakune. No. 1549, Brown trout, Gore. No. 1550, Crayfish, Kaikoura. No. 1551, Sheep shearer, Te Kuiti. No. 1552, Pania of the Reef, Napier. No. 1553, Paua shell, Riverton. No. 1554, Kiwifruit, Te Puke. No. 1555, Border collie, Tekapo. No. 1556, Cow, Hawera.

***Serpentine Die Cut 11½***

**1998, Oct. 7 Litho.**

**Self-Adhesive**

**1547** A442 40c multicolored .45 .45
**1548** A442 40c multicolored .45 .45
**1549** A443 40c multicolored .45 .45
**1550** A443 40c multicolored .45 .45
**1551** A443 40c multicolored .45 .45
**1552** A443 40c multicolored .45 .45

**Size: 25x30mm**

**1553** A443 40c multicolored .45 .45
**1554** A443 40c multicolored .45 .45
**1555** A443 40c multicolored .45 .45
**1556** A443 40c multicolored .45 .45
*a.* Sheet of 10, #1547-1556 10.00
*b.* Booklet pane, #1547-1556 5.75
*Nos. 1547-1556 (10)* 4.50 4.50

No. 1556b is a complete booklet. The peelable paper backing serves as a booklet cover.

Urban Transformation — A444

**1998, Nov. 11 Litho. *Perf. 14x14½***

**1557** A444 40c Wellington .60 .35
**1558** A444 80c Auckland 1.00 .65
**1559** A444 $1 Christchurch 1.10 1.10
**1560** A444 $1.20 Westport 1.40 1.40
**1561** A444 $1.50 Tauranga 1.75 1.75
**1562** A444 $1.80 Dunedin 2.25 2.25
*Nos. 1557-1562 (6)* 8.10 7.50

#1557-1562 exist in sheet of 6 created for a hard-bound Millennium book that sold for $129.

Native Tree Flowers — A445

40c, Kotukutuku. 80c, Poroporo. $1, Kowhai. $1.20, Weeping broom. $1.50, Teteaweka. $1.80, Southern rata.

**1999, Jan. 13 Litho. *Perf. 14½x14***

**1563** A445 40c multi .50 .25
**1564** A445 80c multi .85 .85
*a.* Souv. sheet of 2, #1563-1564 3.50 3.50
**1565** A445 $1 multi .95 .95
**1566** A445 $1.20 multi 1.10 1.10
**1567** A445 $1.50 multi 1.50 1.50
**1568** A445 $1.80 multi 2.00 2.00
*Nos. 1563-1568 (6)* 6.90 6.65

No. 1564a was issued 8/21/99 for China 1999 World Philatelic Exhibition.
Nos. 1567-1568 exist in a souvenir sheet from a "Limited Edition" album.

**Souvenir Sheets**

The 1999 sheets contain: Nos. 1568, 1572, 1578; Nos. 1584, 1600, 1607; Nos. 1613, 1620, 1627.
See note following No. 1404.

Art Deco Buildings — A446

40c, Civic Theatre, Auckland. $1, Masonic Hotel, Napier. $1.50, Medical and Dental Offices, Hastings. $1.80, Buller County Offices, Westport.

**1999, Feb. 10 Litho. *Perf. 14***

**1569** A446 40c multicolored .70 .25
**1570** A446 $1 multicolored 1.75 1.00
**1571** A446 $1.50 multicolored 1.75 1.75
**1572** A446 $1.80 multicolored 2.00 2.00
*Nos. 1569-1572 (4)* 6.20 5.00

Popular Pets — A447

Designs: 40c, Labrador puppy. 80c, Netherland dwarf rabbit. $1, Rabbit, tabby kitten. $1.20, Lamb. $1.50, Welsh pony. $1.80, Budgies.

**1999, Feb. 10**

**1573** A447 40c multicolored .50 .35
**1574** A447 80c multicolored 1.00 .60
**1575** A447 $1 multicolored 1.25 1.25
*a.* Souvenir sheet, #1573-1575 4.25 4.25
*b.* Souvenir sheet, #1573, 1575 5.50 5.50
**1576** A447 $1.20 multicolored 1.50 1.50
**1577** A447 $1.50 multicolored 1.75 1.75
**1578** A447 $1.80 multicolored 2.25 2.25
*Nos. 1573-1578 (6)* 8.25 7.70

New Year 1999, Year of the Rabbit (#1575a).
No. 1575b was issued 8/21/99 for China 1999 World Philatelic Exhibition.

Nostalgia A448

**1999, Mar. 10 Litho. *Perf. 14***

**1579** A448 40c Toys .70 .25
**1580** A448 80c Food 1.00 1.00
**1581** A448 $1 Transport 1.25 1.25
**1582** A448 $1.20 Household 1.50 1.50
**1583** A448 $1.50 Collectibles 1.75 1.75
**1584** A448 $1.80 Garden 2.00 2.00
*Nos. 1579-1584 (6)* 8.20 7.75

#1579-1584 exist in sheet of 6 created for a hard-bound Millennium book that sold for $129.

Victoria University of Wellington, Cent. A449

**1999, Apr. 7 Litho. *Perf. 14***

**1585** A449 40c multicolored .55 .45

1999 New Zealand U-Bix Rugby Super 12 — A450

Auckland Blues: a, Kicking ball. b, Running with ball.
Chiefs: c, Being tackled. d, Catching ball.
Wellington Hurricanes: e, Being tackled. f, Passing.
Canterbury Crusaders: g, Catching ball. h, Kicking ball.
Otago Highlanders: i, Falling down with ball. j, Running with ball.

**1999, Apr. 7** ***Perf. 14½***

**1586** A450 40c Sheet of 10, #a.-j. 12.50 12.50

**Booklet Stamps**

**Self-Adhesive**

***Die Cut Perf. 12***

**1587** A450 40c like #1586a .60 .45
**1588** A450 40c like #1586b .60 .45
*a.* Bklt. pane, 5 ea #1587-1588 6.50
**1589** A450 40c like #1586c .60 .45
**1590** A450 40c like #1586d .60 .45
*a.* Bklt. pane, 5 ea #1589-1590 6.50
**1591** A450 40c like #1586e .60 .45
**1592** A450 40c like #1586f .60 .45
*a.* Bklt. pane, 5 ea #1591-1592 6.50
**1593** A450 40c like #1586g .60 .45
**1594** A450 40c like #1586h .60 .45
*a.* Bklt. pane, 5 ea #1593-1594 6.50
**1595** A450 40c like #1586i .60 .45
**1596** A450 40c like #1586j .60 .45
*a.* Bklt. pane, 5 ea #1595-1596 6.50

Nos. 1587-1588, 1589-1590, 1591-1592, 1593-1594, 1595-1596 were also issued as pairs without surrounding selvage.
Nos. 1588a, 1590a, 1592a, 1594a and 1596a are all complete booklets.

**Paintings Type of 1997**

Paintings by Doris Lusk: 40c, The Lake, Tuai, 1948. $1, The Pumping Station, 1958. $1.50, Arcade Awning, St. Mark's Square, Venice (2), 1976. $1.80, Tuan St. II, 1982.

**1999, June 16 Litho.** ***Perf. 14***

**1597** A425 40c multicolored .60 .25
**1598** A425 $1 multicolored 1.25 1.25
**1599** A425 $1.50 multicolored 1.50 1.50
**1600** A425 $1.80 multicolored 2.25 2.25
*a.* Souv. sheet of 2, #1597, 1600 5.00 5.00
*Nos. 1597-1600 (4)* 5.60 5.25

No. 1600a was issued 7/2/99 for Philex-France '99, World Philatelic Exhibition.

Asia-Pacific Economic Cooperation (APEC) — A451

**1999, July 21 Litho.** ***Perf. 14***

**1601** A451 40c multicolored .50 .45

Scenic Walks A452

Designs: 40c, West Ruggedy Beach, Stewart Island. 80c, Ice Lake, Butler Valley, Westland. $1, Tonga Bay, Abel Tasman Natl. Park. $1.20, East Matakitaki Valley, Nelson Lakes Natl. Park. $1.50, Great Barrier Island. $1.80, Mt. Taranaki/Egmont.

**1999, July 28**

**1602** A452 40c multicolored .50 .25
*a.* Booklet pane of 1 .55
**1603** A452 80c multicolored .85 .85
*a.* Booklet pane of 1 .95
**1604** A452 $1 multicolored 1.00 1.00
*a.* Booklet pane of 1 1.10
**1605** A452 $1.20 multicolored 1.40 1.40
*a.* Booklet pane of 1 1.50
**1606** A452 $1.50 multicolored 2.00 2.00
*a.* Booklet pane of 1 2.25
**1607** A452 $1.80 multicolored 2.25 2.25
*a.* Booklet pane of 1 2.50
*b.* Bklt. pane of 6, #1602-1607 11.00
Complete booklet, 1 each #1602a-1607a, 1607b 22.50
*c.* Souvenir sheet of 1 3.50 3.50
*Nos. 1602-1607 (6)* 8.00 7.75

Issued: No. 1607c, 10/1.

Christmas A453

40c, Baby in manger. 80c, Virgin Mary. $1.10, Joseph and Mary. $1.20, Angel with harp. $1.50, Shepherds. $1.80, Three Magi.
No. 1614, Baby in manger.

**1999, Sept. 8 Litho.** ***Perf. 13***

**1608** A453 40c multicolored .50 .25
**1609** A453 80c multicolored 1.00 1.00
**1610** A453 $1.10 multicolored 1.40 1.40
**1611** A453 $1.20 multicolored 1.50 1.50
**1612** A453 $1.50 multicolored 1.75 1.75
**1613** A453 $1.80 multicolored 2.00 2.00
*Nos. 1608-1613 (6)* 8.15 7.90

**Self-Adhesive**

**Size: 23x27mm**

***Die Cut Perf. 9½x10***

**1614** A453 40c multicolored .50 .25
*a.* Booklet pane of 10 6.00

No. 1614a is a complete booklet.

Yachting — A454

**1999, Oct. 20 Litho.** ***Perf. 14***

**1615** A454 40c P Class .60 .25
**1616** A454 80c Laser 1.00 .85
**1617** A454 $1.10 18-foot skiff 1.25 1.25
**1618** A454 $1.20 Hobie Cat 1.40 1.40
**1619** A454 $1.50 Racing yacht 1.50 1.50
**1620** A454 $1.80 Cruising yacht 1.75 1.75
*a.* Souvenir sheet of 6, #1615-1620 8.50 8.50
*Nos. 1615-1620 (6)* 7.50 7.00

Nos. 1615-1620 exist in an imperf souvenir sheet from a "Limited Edition" album.

**Self-Adhesive**

**Size: 25x30mm**

***Die Cut Perf. 9½x10***

**1621** A454 40c Optimist .45 .40
*a.* Booklet pane of 10 6.00

No. 1621a is a complete booklet.

Millennium — A455

New Zealanders Leading the Way: 40c, Women, ballot box. 80c, Airplane of Richard Pearse, pioneer aviator. $1.10, Lord Ernest Rutherford, physicist. $1.20, Jet boat. $1.50, Sir Edmund Hillary, Mt. Everest. $1.80, Anti-nuclear protesters.

**1999, Nov. 17 Litho.** ***Perf. 14x14¼***

**1622** A455 40c multicolored .60 .25
**1623** A455 80c multicolored 1.10 .60
**1624** A455 $1.10 multicolored 1.50 1.50
**1625** A455 $1.20 multicolored 1.60 1.60
**1626** A455 $1.50 multicolored 1.75 1.75
**1627** A455 $1.80 multicolored 2.00 2.00
*Nos. 1622-1627 (6)* 8.55 7.70

Nos. 1622-1627 exist in sheet of 6 created for a hard-bound millennium book that sold for $129.

Year 2000 A456

**2000, Jan. 1 Litho.** ***Perf. 14¼***

**1628** A456 40c multi .65 .45
*a.* Miniature sheet of 10 6.50 4.50

No. 1628 exists in a sheet of 6 created for a hard-bound Millennium book that sold for $129.
The third stamp in the left column on No. 1628a is missing the map and sun emblem between the time and country name.

New Year 2000 (Year of the Dragon) — A457

Spirits and guardians: 40c, Araiteuru. 80c, Kurangaituku. $1.10, Te Hoata and Te Pupu. $1.20, Patupaiarehe. $1.50, Te Ngarara-huarau. $1.80, Tuhirangi.

**2000, Feb. 9 Litho.** ***Perf. 14***

**1629** A457 40c multi .60 .25
**1630** A457 80c multi .90 .45
**1631** A457 $1.10 multi 1.25 1.25
**1632** A457 $1.20 multi 1.50 1.50
**1633** A457 $1.50 multi 1.75 1.75
**1634** A457 $1.80 multi 2.25 2.25
*a.* Souv. sheet of 2, #1633-1634 5.25 5.25
*Nos. 1629-1634 (6)* 8.25 7.45

Nos. 1631-1632 exist in a souvenir sheet from a "Limited Edition" album.

**Kiwi Type of 1988**

**2000, Mar. 6 Litho.** ***Perf. 14½***

**1635** A325 $1.10 gold 1.50 1.50
*a.* Souv. sheet, #918b, 1027a, 1161b, 1445, 1635 8.25 8.25

Used value is for stamp with complete selvage.
#1635a issued 7/7 for World Stamp Expo 2000, Anaheim.

The 2000 sheets contain: #1694, 1635, 1671; #1662, 1634, 1638; #1677, 1665, 1656. See note following #1404.

**Scenic Views Type of 1995**

$1, Taiaroa Head. $1.10, Kaikoura Coast. $2, Great Barrier Is. $3, Cape Kidnappers.

**2000 Litho.** ***Perf. 13¼x13½***

**Size: 27x22mm**

**1636** A404 $1 multi 1.50 1.00
**1637** A404 $1.10 multi 1.60 1.10
**1638** A404 $2 multi 2.25 1.75
**1639** A404 $3 multi 2.75 2.50
*a.* Souv. sheet, #1636, 1638-1639 9.00 9.00
*Nos. 1636-1639 (4)* 8.10 6.35

**Self-Adhesive**

**Booklet Stamp**

***Die Cut Perf 10x9¾***

**1640** A404 $1.10 Like #1637 1.50 1.10
*a.* Booklet, 5 #1640 + 5 etiquettes 8.75

The Stamp Show 2000, London (No. 1639a).
Issued: #1639a, 5/22; #1640, 4/3; others, 3/6.

New Zealand Popular Culture — A458

Kiwi with: #1641, Insulated cooler. #1642, Pipis. #1643, Inflatable beach cushion. #1644, Chocolate fish. #1645, Beach house and surf board. #1646, Barbecue. #1647, Ug boots. #1648, Anzac biscuit. #1649, Hot dog. #1650, Meat pie.

***Die Cut Perf. 9¾x10***

**2000, Apr. 3 Litho.**

**Booklet Stamps**

**Self-Adhesive**

**1641** A458 40c multi .55 .45
**1642** A458 40c multi .55 .45
**1643** A458 40c multi .55 .45
**1644** A458 40c multi .55 .45
**1645** A458 40c multi .55 .45
**1646** A458 40c multi .55 .45
**1647** A458 40c multi .55 .45
**1648** A458 40c multi .55 .45
**1649** A458 40c multi .55 .45
**1650** A458 40c multi .55 .45
*a.* Booklet, #1641-1650 6.00
*b.* Sheet, #1641-1650 6.00
*Nos. 1641-1650 (10)* 5.50 4.50

No. 1650b has plain backing paper.

Automobiles A459

40c, Volkswagen Beetle. 80c, Ford Zephyr MK I. $1.10, Morris Mini MK II. $1.20, Holden HQ Kingswood. $1.50, Honda Civic EB2. $1.80, Toyota Corolla.

**2000, June 1** ***Perf. 14***

**1651** A459 40c claret .55 .35
*a.* Booklet pane of 1 .55
**1652** A459 80c blue .90 .65
*a.* Booklet pane of 1 .90
**1653** A459 $1.10 brown 1.25 1.25
*a.* Booklet pane of 1 1.25
**1654** A459 $1.20 green 1.50 1.50
*a.* Booklet pane of 1 1.50
**1655** A459 $1.50 olive grn 2.00 2.00
*a.* Booklet pane of 1 2.00
**1656** A459 $1.80 violet 2.25 2.25
*a.* Booklet pane of 1 2.25
*b.* Booklet pane, #1651-1656 9.00
Booklet, #1651a-1656a, 1656b 18.00
*Nos. 1651-1656 (6)* 8.45 8.00

A miniature sheet containing #1651-1656, both perf and imperf within the sheet, exists. This comes from a "Limited Edition" album.

Scenic Reflections A460

Designs: 40c, Lake Lyndon. 80c, Lake Wakatipu. $1.10, Mt. Ruapehu. $1.20, Rainbow Mountain Scenic Reserve. $1.50, Tairua Harbor. $1.80, Lake Alexandrina.

**2000, July 7 Litho. *Perf. 14***

| | | | | |
|---|---|---|---|---|
| **1657** | A460 | 40c multi | .60 | .35 |
| **1658** | A460 | 80c multi | 1.10 | .55 |
| **1659** | A460 | $1.10 multi | 1.25 | 1.00 |
| **1660** | A460 | $1.20 multi | 1.50 | 1.50 |
| **1661** | A460 | $1.50 multi | 1.75 | 1.75 |
| **1662** | A460 | $1.80 multi | 2.00 | 2.00 |
| *a.* | | Souvenir Sheet, #1657, 1662 | 4.00 | 4.00 |
| | | *Nos. 1657-1662 (6)* | 8.20 | 7.15 |

No. 1662a issued 10/5/00 for Canpex 2000 Stamp Exhibition, Christchurch.

Queen Mother's 100th Birthday A461

Queen Mother in: 40c, 1907. $1.10, 1966. $1.80, 1997.

**2000, Aug. 4**

| | | | | |
|---|---|---|---|---|
| **1663** | A461 | 40c multi | .60 | .35 |
| **1664** | A461 | $1.10 multi | 1.25 | 1.00 |
| **1665** | A461 | $1.80 multi | 2.50 | 2.00 |
| *a.* | | Souvenir sheet, #1663-1665 | 4.25 | 4.25 |
| | | *Nos. 1663-1665 (3)* | 4.35 | 3.35 |

Sports A462

**2000, Aug. 4 *Perf. 14x14¼***

| | | | | |
|---|---|---|---|---|
| **1666** | A462 | 40c Rowing | .60 | .35 |
| **1667** | A462 | 80c Equestrian | 1.00 | .55 |
| **1668** | A462 | $1.10 Cycling | 1.50 | 1.00 |
| **1669** | A462 | $1.20 Triathlon | 1.50 | 1.50 |
| **1670** | A462 | $1.50 Lawn bowling | 1.75 | 1.75 |
| **1671** | A462 | $1.80 Netball | 2.00 | 2.25 |
| | | *Nos. 1666-1671 (6)* | 8.35 | 7.40 |

2000 Summer Olympics, Sydney (Nos. 1666-1669).

Christmas A463

Designs: 40c, Madonna and child. 80c, Mary, Joseph and donkey. $1.10, Baby Jesus, cow, lamb. $1.20, Archangel. $1.50, Shepherd and lamb. $1.80, Magi.

**2000, Sept. 6 *Perf. 14***

| | | | | |
|---|---|---|---|---|
| **1672** | A463 | 40c multi | .60 | .25 |
| **1673** | A463 | 80c multi | 1.00 | .60 |
| **1674** | A463 | $1.10 multi | 1.40 | 1.40 |
| **1675** | A463 | $1.20 multi | 1.60 | 1.60 |
| **1676** | A463 | $1.50 multi | 1.75 | 1.75 |
| **1677** | A463 | $1.80 multi | 2.00 | 2.00 |
| | | *Nos. 1672-1677 (6)* | 8.35 | 7.60 |

**Self-Adhesive**

**Size: 30x25mm**

***Serpentine Die Cut 11¼x11***

| | | | | |
|---|---|---|---|---|
| **1678** | A463 | 40c multi | .60 | .25 |
| *a.* | | Booklet of 10 | 6.50 | |

Issued: No. 1678a, 11/1/00.

**Scenic Views Type of 1995**

Designs: 90c, Rangitoto Island. $1.30, Lake Camp, South Canterbury.

**2000 Litho. *Perf. 13¼x13½***

**Size: 27x22mm**

| | | | | |
|---|---|---|---|---|
| **1679** | A404 | 90c multi | 1.25 | .75 |
| **1680** | A404 | $1.30 multi | 1.75 | 1.10 |
| *a.* | | Souvenir sheet, #1636-1637, 1679-1680 | 6.00 | 6.00 |

Issued: Nos. 1679-1680, 10/2/00; No. 1680a, 3/16/01. 2001: A Stamp Odyssey Philatelic Exhibition, Invercargill (#1680a).

Teddy Bears and Dolls — A464

Designs: 40c+5c, Teddy bear "Geronimo," by Rose Hill. 80c+5c, Antique French and wooden Schoenhut dolls. $1.10, Chad Valley bear. $1.20, Doll "Poppy," by Debbie Pointon. $1.50, Teddy bears "Swanni," by Robin Rive, and "Dear John," by Rose Hill. $1.80, Doll "Lia," by Gloria Young, and teddy bear.

**2000, Oct. 5 *Perf. 14½x14¾***

| | | | | |
|---|---|---|---|---|
| **1681** | A464 | 40c +5c multi | .65 | .40 |
| **1682** | A464 | 80c +5c multi | 1.25 | .70 |
| *a.* | | Souvenir sheet, #1681-1682 | 2.75 | 2.75 |
| **1683** | A464 | $1.10 multi | 1.40 | 1.40 |
| **1684** | A464 | $1.20 multi | 1.60 | 1.60 |
| **1685** | A464 | $1.50 multi | 1.75 | 1.75 |
| **1686** | A464 | $1.80 multi | 2.00 | 2.00 |
| *a.* | | Block of 6, #1681-1686 | 9.50 | 9.50 |

**Coil Stamp**

**Size: 30x25mm**

**Self-Adhesive**

***Serpentine Die Cut 11¼***

| | | | | |
|---|---|---|---|---|
| **1687** | A464 | 40c +5c multi | .55 | .40 |

Endangered Birds — A465

Designs: No. 1688, Lesser kestrel. No. 1689, Orange fronted parakeet. 80c, Black stilt. $1.10, Stewart Island fernbird. $1.20, Kakapo. $1.50, North Island weka. $1.80, Okarito brown kiwi.

**2000, Nov. 4 *Perf. 14***

| | | | | |
|---|---|---|---|---|
| **1688** | A465 | 40c multi | .60 | .35 |
| **1689** | A465 | 40c multi | .60 | .35 |
| *a.* | | Pair, #1688-1689 | 1.75 | 1.75 |
| **1690** | A465 | 80c multi | 1.25 | .90 |
| **1691** | A465 | $1.10 multi | 1.40 | 1.40 |
| **1692** | A465 | $1.20 multi | 1.50 | 1.50 |
| **1693** | A465 | $1.50 multi | 1.75 | 1.75 |
| **1694** | A465 | $1.80 multi | 2.00 | 2.00 |
| *a.* | | Souvenir sheet, #1693-1694 | 5.75 | 5.75 |
| | | *Nos. 1688-1694 (7)* | 9.10 | 8.25 |

Nos. 1689-1690 exist in a souvenir sheet from a "Limited Edition" album.

Issued: No. 1694a, 2/1/01. Hong Kong 2001 Stamp Exhibition (#1694a). See France Nos. 2790-2791.

Penny Universal Postage, Cent. — A466

Methods of mail delivery: a, Steamship. b, Horse-drawn coach. c, Early mail truck. d, Paddle steamer. e, Railway traveling post office. f, Airplane with front cargo hatch. g, Bicycle. h, Tractor trailer. i, Airplane with side cargo hatch. j, Computer mouse.

**2001, Jan. 1**

| | | | | |
|---|---|---|---|---|
| **1695** | | Sheet of 10 | 5.75 | 5.75 |
| *a.-j.* | | A466 40c Any single | .55 | .55 |
| *k.* | | As No. 1695, with Belgica 2001 sheet margin | 6.00 | 6.00 |

No. 1695k has no perforations running through sheet margin.

Marine Reptiles — A467

Designs: 40c, Green turtle. 80c, Leathery turtle. 90c, Loggerhead turtle. $1.30, Hawksbill turtle. $1.50, Banded sea snake. $2, Yellow-bellied sea snake.

**2001, Feb. 1**

| | | | | |
|---|---|---|---|---|
| **1696** | A467 | 40c multi | .75 | .25 |
| **1697** | A467 | 80c multi | 1.10 | .65 |
| **1698** | A467 | 90c multi | 1.25 | 1.25 |
| **1699** | A467 | $1.30 multi | 1.75 | 1.75 |
| **1700** | A467 | $1.50 multi | 2.00 | 2.00 |
| **1701** | A467 | $2 multi | 2.25 | 2.25 |
| *a.* | | Souvenir sheet, #1700-1701 | 5.00 | 5.00 |
| | | *Nos. 1696-1701 (6)* | 9.10 | 8.15 |

New Year 2001 (Year of the snake) (#1701a).

Flowers A468

**2001, Mar. 7**

| | | | | |
|---|---|---|---|---|
| **1702** | A468 | 40c Camellia | .55 | .35 |
| **1703** | A468 | 80c Siberian iris | .90 | .55 |
| **1704** | A468 | 90c Daffodil | 1.10 | 1.10 |
| **1705** | A468 | $1.30 Chrysanthemum | 1.50 | 1.50 |
| **1706** | A468 | $1.50 Sweet pea | 1.75 | 1.75 |
| **1707** | A468 | $2 Petunia | 2.50 | 2.50 |
| *a.* | | Souvenir sheet, #1702-1707 | 8.25 | 8.25 |
| | | *Nos. 1702-1707 (6)* | 8.30 | 7.75 |

No. 1707a exists imperf from a "Limited Edition" album.

Art From Nature A469

**2001, Apr. 4 Litho. *Perf. 14¼***

| | | | | |
|---|---|---|---|---|
| **1708** | A469 | 40c Greenstone | .55 | .35 |
| **1709** | A469 | 80c Oamaru stone | .90 | .55 |
| **1710** | A469 | 90c Paua | 1.10 | 1.10 |
| **1711** | A469 | $1.30 Kauri gum | 1.50 | 1.50 |
| **1712** | A469 | $1.50 Flax | 1.75 | 1.75 |
| **1713** | A469 | $2 Fern | 2.50 | 2.50 |
| | | *Nos. 1708-1713 (6)* | 8.30 | 7.75 |

Within sheets of 25 printed for each stamp are four blocks of four showing a circular design, made by rotating each stamp design 90 degrees.

Aircraft A470

Designs: 40c, Douglas DC-3. 80c, Fletcher FU24 Topdresser. 90c, De Havilland DH82A Tiger Moth. $1.30, Fokker FVIIb/3m. $1.50, De Havilland DH100 Vampire. $2, Boeing & Westervelt Seaplane.

**2001, May 2 *Perf. 14x14¼***

| | | | | |
|---|---|---|---|---|
| **1714** | A470 | 40c multi | .60 | .35 |
| *a.* | | Booklet pane of 1 | .60 | |
| **1715** | A470 | 80c multi | .90 | .65 |
| *a.* | | Booklet pane of 1 | .90 | |
| **1716** | A470 | 90c multi | 1.25 | 1.25 |
| *a.* | | Booklet pane of 1 | 1.25 | |
| **1717** | A470 | $1.30 multi | 1.50 | 1.50 |
| *a.* | | Booklet pane of 1 | 1.50 | |
| **1718** | A470 | $1.50 multi | 1.75 | 1.75 |
| *a.* | | Booklet pane of 1 | 1.75 | |

| | | | | |
|---|---|---|---|---|
| **1719** | A470 | $2 multi | 2.50 | 2.50 |
| *a.* | | Booklet pane of 1 | 2.50 | |
| *b.* | | Booklet pane, #1714-1719 | 10.00 | |
| | | Booklet, #1714a-1719a, 1719b | 20.00 | |
| | | *Nos. 1714-1719 (6)* | 8.50 | 8.00 |

Greetings — A471

No. 1720: a, Heart. b, Balloons. c, Flower. d, Gift. e, Trumpet.

No. 1721: a, Candles. b, Stars. c, Roses and candle. d, Picture frame. e, Letter and fountain pen.

**2001, June 6 *Perf. 14½x14***

| | | | | |
|---|---|---|---|---|
| **1720** | | Vert. strip of 5 + 5 labels | 2.75 | 2.75 |
| *a.-e.* | | A471 40c Any single + label | .50 | .50 |
| **1721** | | Vert. strip of 5 + 5 labels | 5.75 | 5.75 |
| *a.-e.* | | A471 90c Any single + label | .90 | .90 |

Labels could be personalized on sheets that sold for $15.95 and $27.95 respectively.

Government Tourist Office, Cent. — A472

Designs: 40c, Bungee jumper, Queenstown. 80c, Canoeing on Lake Rotoiti. 90c, Sightseers on Mt. Alfred. $1.30, Fishing in Glenorchy River. $1.50, Kayakers in Abel Tasman Natl. Park. $2, Hiker in Fiordland Natl. Park.

**2001 Litho. *Perf. 14¼***

| | | | | |
|---|---|---|---|---|
| **1722** | A472 | 40c multi | .50 | .25 |
| **1723** | A472 | 80c multi | .90 | .90 |
| **1724** | A472 | 90c multi | 1.10 | 1.10 |
| **1725** | A472 | $1.30 multi | 1.50 | 1.50 |
| **1726** | A472 | $1.50 multi | 1.75 | 1.75 |
| **1727** | A472 | $2 multi | 2.25 | 2.25 |
| *a.* | | Souvenir sheet, #1726-1727 | 4.75 | 4.75 |

**Size: 26x21mm**

***Serpentine Die Cut 11¼x11***

**Self-Adhesive**

| | | | | |
|---|---|---|---|---|
| **1728** | A472 | 40c multi | .60 | .50 |
| *a.* | | Booklet of 10 + 10 etiquettes | 6.50 | |
| **1729** | A472 | 90c multi | 1.25 | 1.25 |
| *a.* | | Booklet of 10 + 10 etiquettes | 14.00 | |
| **1730** | A472 | $1.50 multi | 2.25 | 2.25 |
| *a.* | | Horiz. strip, #1728-1730 | 4.50 | |
| *b.* | | Booklet of 5 + 5 etiquettes | 12.00 | |

**Coil Stamp**

**Size: 26x21mm**

**Self-Adhesive**

***Serpentine Die Cut 10x9¾***

| | | | | |
|---|---|---|---|---|
| **1730C** | A472 | 40c Like #1722 | .55 | .35 |
| | | *Nos. 1722-1730C (10)* | 12.65 | 12.10 |

Phila Nippon '01, Japan (No. 1727a).
Issued: No. 1727a, 8/1; others, 7/4.

A sheet containing 3 each of Nos. 1722-1727 was included in a book that sold for $69.95.

Christmas — A473

Designs: 40c, In Excelsis Gloria. 80c, Away in the Manger. 90c, Joy to the World. $1.30, Angels We Have Heard on High. $1.50, O Holy Night. $2, While Shepherds Watched Their Flocks.

**2001, Sept. 5** *Perf. 13¼x13¾*

**1731** A473 40c multi .60 .25
**1732** A473 80c multi 1.10 .50
**1733** A473 90c multi 1.25 1.25
**1734** A473 $1.30 multi 1.50 1.50
**1735** A473 $1.50 multi 1.75 1.75
**1736** A473 $2 multi 2.00 2.00

**Size: 21x26mm**

***Serpentine Die Cut 9¾x10***

**Self-Adhesive**

**1737** A473 40c multi .65 .25
a. Booklet of 10 6.50
*Nos. 1731-1737 (7)* 8.85 7.50

Issued: No. 1737a, 11/7/01.

Visit of Queen Elizabeth II, Oct. 2001 — A474

Queen in past visits: 40c, Arriving for opening of Parliament, 1953. 80c, With crowd, 1970. 90c, With crowd, 1977. $1.30, With crowd, 1986. $1.50, At Commonwealth Games, 1990. $2, 2001 portrait.

**2001, Oct. 3** **Litho.** *Perf. 14*

**1738** A474 40c multi .65 .35
**1739** A474 80c multi 1.10 .60
**1740** A474 90c multi 1.25 1.25
**1741** A474 $1.30 multi 1.50 1.50
**1742** A474 $1.50 multi 1.75 1.75
**1743** A474 $2 multi 2.25 2.25
a. Horiz. strip, #1738-1743 8.50 8.50
*Nos. 1738-1743 (6)* 8.50 7.70

Nos. 1738-1743 exist in a souvenir sheet from a "Limited Edition" album. Nos. 1738-1743 also exist imperf.

Penguins A475

Designs: 40c, Rockhopper. 80c, Little blue. 90c, Snares crested. $1.30, Erect-crested. $1.50, Fiordland crested. $2, Yellow-eyed.

**2001, Nov. 7** *Perf. 14¼*

**1744** A475 40c multi .75 .40
**1745** A475 80c multi 1.10 .60
**1746** A475 90c multi 1.25 1.25
**1747** A475 $1.30 multi 1.75 1.75
**1748** A475 $1.50 multi 2.00 2.00
**1749** A475 $2 multi 2.25 2.25
*Nos. 1744-1749 (6)* 9.10 8.25

Filming in New Zealand of The Lord of the Rings Trilogy — A476

Scenes from "The Lord of the Rings: The Fellowship of the Ring:" 40c, Gandalf the Gray and Saruman the White, vert. 80c, Lady Galadriel, vert. 90c, Sam Gamgee and Frodo Baggins. $1.30, Guardian of Rivendell, vert. $1.50, Strider, vert. $2, Boromir, son of Denethor.

***Perf. 14½x14, 14x14½***

**2001, Dec. 4** **Litho.**

**1750** A476 40c multi .75 .50
a. Souvenir sheet of 1 2.25 1.75
b. Sheet of 10 #1750 7.50 —
**1751** A476 80c multi 1.75 1.75
a. Souvenir sheet of 1 4.00 3.50
**1752** A476 90c multi 2.00 2.00
a. Souvenir sheet of 1 4.75 4.00
**1753** A476 $1.30 multi 2.75 2.75
a. Souvenir sheet of 1 6.50 5.75
**1754** A476 $1.50 multi 3.00 3.00
a. Souvenir sheet of 1 7.50 6.50
**1755** A476 $2 multi 4.00 4.00
a. Souvenir sheet of 1 11.00 8.75
b. Souvenir sheet, #1754-1755 8.00 8.00
c. Souvenir sheet, #1750, 1753, 1755 9.50 9.50

**Self-Adhesive**

***Serpentine Die Cut 10x10¼, 10¼x10***

**Size: 22x33mm, 33x22mm**

**1756** A476 40c multi .85 .85
**1757** A476 80c multi 2.00 2.00
**1758** A476 90c multi 2.25 2.25
**1759** A476 $1.30 multi 3.00 3.00
**1760** A476 $1.50 multi 3.25 3.25
**1761** A476 $2 multi 4.25 4.25
a. Pane, #1756-1761 *16.00*
b. Booklet pane, #1757, 1759-1761, 4 #1756, 2 #1758 *35.00*
*Nos. 1750-1761 (12)* 29.85 29.60

Issued: No. 1755b, 8/30/02; No. 1755c, 4/5/02. Other values, 12/4/01.

No. 1755b issued for Amphilex 2002 World Stamp Exhibition, Amsterdam; No. 1755c issued for Northpex 2002.

See Nos. 1835-1846, 1897-1908.

New Year 2002 (Year of the Horse) A477

Champion race horses: 40c, Christian Cullen. 80c, Lyell Creek. 90c, Yulestar. $1.30, Sunline. $1.50, Ethereal. $2, Zabeel.

**2002, Feb. 7** *Perf. 14*

**1762** A477 40c multi .55 .35
**1763** A477 80c multi .90 .90
**1764** A477 90c multi 1.10 1.10
**1765** A477 $1.30 multi 1.50 1.50
**1766** A477 $1.50 multi 1.75 1.75
a. Souvenir sheet, #1765-1766 4.50 4.50
**1767** A477 $2 multi 2.50 2.50
*Nos. 1762-1767 (6)* 8.30 8.10

Fungi — A478

Designs: 40c, Hygrocybe rubrocarnosa. 80c, Entoloma hochstetteri. 90c, Aseroe rubra. $1.30, Hericium coralloides. $1.50, Thaxterogaster porphyreus. $2, Ramaria aureorhiza.

**2002, Mar. 6** **Litho.** *Perf. 14*

**1768** A478 40c multi .60 .40
**1769** A478 80c multi 1.10 .60
**1770** A478 90c multi 1.25 1.25
**1771** A478 $1.30 multi 1.75 1.75
**1772** A478 $1.50 multi 2.00 2.00
**1773** A478 $2 multi 2.25 2.25
a. Souvenir sheet, #1768-1773 9.00 9.00
*Nos. 1768-1773 (6)* 8.95 8.25

No. 1773a exists as an imperforate souvenir sheet from a "Limited Edition" album.

A479

A480

Architectural Heritage — A481

Designs: 40c, War Memorial Museum, Auckland. 80c, Stone Store, Kerikeri. 90c, Arts Center, Christchurch. $1.30, Government buildings, Wellington. $1.50, Railway Station, Dunedin. $2, Sky Tower, Auckland.

**2002, Apr. 3** **Litho.** *Perf. 14½x14*

**1774** A479 40c multi .65 .30
a. Booklet pane of 1 .65 —
**1775** A480 80c multi 1.10 .75
a. Booklet pane of 1 1.10 —
**1776** A481 90c multi 1.25 1.00
a. Booklet pane of 1 1.25 —
**1777** A481 $1.30 multi 1.50 1.50
a. Booklet pane of 1 1.50 —
**1778** A480 $1.50 multi 1.75 1.75
a. Booklet pane of 1 1.75 —
**1779** A479 $2 multi 2.00 2.00
a. Booklet pane of 1 2.00 —
b. Block of 6, #1774-1779 10.00 10.00
c. Booklet pane, #1779b 11.00 —
Booklet, #1774a-1779a, 1779c 20.00
*Nos. 1774-1779 (6)* 8.25 7.30

Booklet containing Nos. 1774a-1779a, 1779c sold for $16.95.

Art from Sweden and New Zealand A482

Designs: No. 1780, Maori basket, by Willa Rogers, New Zealand. No. 1781, Starfish Vessel, by Graeme Priddle, New Zealand. 80c, Catch II, by Raewyn Atkinson, New Zealand. 90c, Silver brooch, by Gavin Hithings, New Zealand. $1.30, Glass towers, by Emma Camden, New Zealand. $1.50, Pacific Rim, by Merilyn Wiseman. $2, Rain Forest, glass vase by Ola Höglund, Sweden.

**Litho. & Engr. (#1780, 1786), Litho.**

***Perf. 12½x12¾ (#1780, 1786), 14***

**2002, May 2**

**1780** A482 40c multi .60 .35
**1781** A482 40c multi .60 .35
**1782** A482 80c multi 1.10 .65
**1783** A482 90c multi 1.25 1.25
**1784** A482 $1.30 multi 1.50 1.50
**1785** A482 $1.50 multi 1.75 1.75
**1786** A482 $2 multi 2.00 2.00
*Nos. 1780-1786 (7)* 8.80 7.85

See Sweden No. 2440.

Nos. 1780-1786 exist in a souvenir sheet from a "Limited Edition" album.

**Kiwi Type of 1988**

**2002, June 5** **Litho.** *Perf. 14½*

**1787** A325 $1.50 brown 2.00 1.50
a. Souvenir sheet of 3 7.00 7.00

Used value is for stamp with complete selvage.

Issued: No. 1787a, 11/12/10. Palmpex 2010 Stamp Show, Palmerston North (No. 1787a).

Queen Mother Elizabeth (1900-2002) A483

**2002, June 5** *Perf. 14¼*

**1788** A483 $2 multi 2.25 2.00

Children's Book Festival Stamp Design Contest Winners A484

Art by: No. 1789, Anna Poland, Cardinal McKeefry School, Wellington. No. 1790, Hee Su Kim, Glendowie Primary School, Auckland. No. 1791, Jayne Bruce, Rangiora Borough School, Rangiora. No. 1792, Teigan Stafford-Bush (bird), Ararimu School, Auckland. No. 1793, Hazel Gilbert, Gonville School, Wanganui. No. 1794, Gerard Mackle, Temuka High School, Temuka. No. 1795, Maria Rodgers, Salford School, Invercargill. No. 1796, Paul Read (hand and ball), Ararimu School, Auckland. No. 1797, Four students, Glendene Primary School, Auckland. No. 1798, Olivia Duncan, Takapuna Normal Intermediate School, Auckland.

**2002, June 5** *Perf. 14*

**1789** A484 40c multi .75 .75
**1790** A484 40c multi .75 .75
**1791** A484 40c multi .75 .75
**1792** A484 40c multi .75 .75
**1793** A484 40c multi .75 .75
**1794** A484 40c multi .75 .75
**1795** A484 40c multi .75 .75
**1796** A484 40c multi .75 .75
**1797** A484 40c multi .75 .75
**1798** A484 40c multi .75 .75
a. Block of 10, #1789-1798 7.75 7.75
b. Sheet of 10, #1789-1798 8.00 8.00
*Nos. 1789-1798 (10)* 7.50 7.50

Scenic Coastlines A485

Designs: 40c, Tongaporutu Cliffs, Taranaki. 80c, Lottin Point, East Cape. 90c, Curio Bay, Catlins. $1.30, Kaikoura Coast. $1.50, Meybille Bay, West Coast. $2, Papanui Point, Raglan.

**2002, July 3** *Perf. 14*

**1799** A485 40c multi .50 .30
**1800** A485 80c multi 1.00 .60
**1801** A485 90c multi 1.25 1.25
**1802** A485 $1.30 multi 1.50 1.50
**1803** A485 $1.50 multi 1.75 1.75
**1804** A485 $2 multi 2.00 2.00

**Size: 28x22mm**

**Self-Adhesive**

***Serpentine Die Cut 10x9¾***

**1805** A485 40c multi .55 .55
a. Booklet pane of 10 6.50
b. Serpentine die cut 11 .70 .70
c. Booklet pane of 10 #1805b 7.50
**1806** A485 90c multi 1.25 1.25
a. Booklet pane of 10 14.00
**1807** A485 $1.50 multi 2.40 1.50
a. Booklet pane of 5 12.00
b. Coil strip of 3, #1805-1807 4.50

**Coil Stamp**

**Size: 28x22mm**

**Self-Adhesive**

***Die Cut Perf. 12¾***

**1808** A485 40c multi .55 .40
*Nos. 1799-1808 (10)* 12.75 11.10

Christmas A487

Church interiors: 40c, Saint Werenfried Catholic Church, Waihi Village, Tokaannu. 80c, St. David's Anglican Church, Christchurch. 90c, Orthodox Church of the Transfiguration of Our Lord, Masterton. $1.30, Cathedral of the Holy Spirit, Palmerston North. $1.50, Cathedral of St. Paul, Wellington. $2, Cathedral of the Blessed Sacrament, Christchurch.

**2002, Sept. 4** *Perf. 14¼*

**1812** A487 40c multi .50 .25
**1813** A487 80c multi 1.00 .45
**1814** A487 90c multi 1.25 1.00
**1815** A487 $1.30 multi 1.75 1.75
**1816** A487 $1.50 multi 2.00 2.00
**1817** A487 $2 multi 2.25 2.25

**Coil Stamp**

**Size: 21x26mm**

**Self-Adhesive**

***Die Cut Perf. 13x12¾***

**1818** A487 40c multi .55 .25

**Booklet Stamp**

**Size: 21x26mm**

**Self-Adhesive**

***Die Cut Perf 9¾x10***

**1818A** A487 40c Like No. 1818 .55 .25
b. Booklet pane of 10 6.50
*Nos. 1812-1818A (8)* 9.85 8.20

Issued: No. 1818A, 11/6/02.

Scene Locations from *The Lord of the Rings* Movie Trilogy
A512

Designs: Nos. 1956, 1965, Skippers Canyon. Nos. 1957, 1964, Skippers Canyon (Ford of Bruinden) with actors. Nos. 1958, 1967, Mount Olympus. No. 1959, 1966, Mount Olympus (South of Rivendell) with actors. No. 1960, Erewhon. No. 1961, Erewhon (Edoras) with actors. No. 1962, Tongariro National Park. No. 1963, Tongariro National Park (Emyn Muil) with actors.

**2004, July 7** *Perf. 14*

**1956** A512 45c multi .65 .65
**1957** A512 45c multi .65 .65
*a.* Vert. pair, #1956-1957 1.40 1.40
**1958** A512 90c multi 1.25 1.25
**1959** A512 90c multi 1.25 1.25
*a.* Vert. pair, #1958-1959 2.75 2.75
**1960** A512 $1.50 multi 2.25 2.25
**1961** A512 $1.50 multi 2.25 2.25
*a.* Vert. pair, #1960-1961 4.75 4.75
*b.* Souvenir sheet, #1958-1961 7.25 7.25
**1962** A512 $2 multi 3.00 3.00
**1963** A512 $2 multi 3.00 3.00
*a.* Vert. pair, #1962-1963 6.50 6.50
*b.* Horiz. block of 8, #1956-1963 15.50 15.50
*c.* Souvenir sheet, #1956-1963 15.50 15.50

No. 1963c exists imperf from a "Limited Edition" album.

**Self-Adhesive**

***Serpentine Die Cut 11¼***

**Size: 30x25mm**

**1964** A512 45c multi .60 .60
**1965** A512 45c multi .60 .60
**1966** A512 90c multi 1.25 1.25
**1967** A512 90c multi 1.25 1.25
*a.* Block of 4, #1964-1967 4.00
*b.* Booklet pane, 3 each #1964-1965, 2 each #1966-1967 9.25
*Nos. 1956-1967 (12)* 18.00 18.00

No. 1961b issued 8/28. World Stamp Championship (No. 1961b).

2004 Summer Olympics, Athens — A513

Gold medalists: 45c, John Walker, 1500 meters, Montreal, 1976. 90c, Yvette Williams, long jump, Helsinki, 1952. $1.50, Ian Ferguson and Paul MacDonald, 500 meters kayak doubles, Seoul, 1988. $2, Peter Snell, 800 meters, Rome, 1960.

**Litho. with 3-Dimensional Plastic Affixed**

***Serpentine Die Cut 10¾***

**2004, Aug. 2** **Self-Adhesive**

**1968** A513 45c multi .65 .50
**1969** A513 90c multi 1.00 .80
**1970** A513 $1.50 multi 1.75 1.75
**1971** A513 $2 multi 2.25 2.25
*a.* Horiz. strip of 4, #1968-1971 7.00
*Nos. 1968-1971 (4)* 5.65 5.30

**Tourist Attractions Type of 2003**

Designs: No. 1972, Lake Wakatipu, Queenstown. No. 1973, Kaikoura. No. 1974, Bath House, Rotorua. No. 1975, Pohutu Geyser, Rotorua. No. 1976, Mitre Peak, Milford Sound. No. 1977, Hawke's Bay.

**2004-05** **Litho.** *Perf. 13¼x13½*

**1972** A496 $1.50 multi 1.90 1.90
*a.* Perf. 14x14¼ 1.90 1.90
**1973** A496 $1.50 multi 1.90 1.90
**1974** A496 $1.50 multi 1.90 1.90
**1975** A496 $1.50 multi 1.90 1.90
*a.* Souvenir sheet, #1973, 1975 5.00 5.00
**1976** A496 $1.50 multi 1.90 1.90
*a.* Perf. 14x14¼ 1.90 1.90
*b.* Souvenir sheet, #1972a, 1976a 4.50 4.50
**1977** A496 $1.50 multi 1.90 1.90
*a.* Souvenir sheet, #1639, 1977 7.25 7.25
*Nos. 1972-1977 (6)* 11.40 11.40

Issued: Nos. 1972-1977, 8/28; No. 1977a, 10/29 for Baypex 2004; No. 1975a, 8/18/05 for Taipei 2005 Stamp Exhibition; Nos. 1972a, 1976a, 1976b, 8/3/07. Bangkok 2007 Asian International Stamp Exhibition (#1976b).

A514

Christmas — A515

Designs: 45c, Candle, wine bottle, turkey, ham. 90c, Hangi. $1, Christmas cards, fruit cake. $1.35, Barbecued shrimp. $1.50, Wine bottle, pie and salad. $2, Candelabra, pavlova and plum pudding.

**2004, Oct. 4** *Perf. 14¼*

**1978** A514 45c multi .60 .25
**1979** A514 90c multi 1.25 .50
**1980** A514 $1.35 multi 1.50 1.50
**1981** A514 $1.50 multi 1.75 1.75
**1982** A514 $2 multi 2.50 2.50
*Nos. 1978-1982 (5)* 7.60 6.50

**Self-Adhesive**

***Serpentine Die Cut 9½x10***

**1983** A515 45c multi .60 .40
*a.* Booklet pane of 10 7.00
**1984** A515 90c multi 1.10 1.00
**1985** A515 $1 multi 1.40 1.40
*a.* Booklet pane of 8 + 8 etiquettes 13.00
*b.* Horiz. strip, #1983-1985 3.75 3.75
*Nos. 1983-1985 (3)* 3.10 2.80

Extreme Sports
A516

Designs: 45c, Whitewater rafting. 90c, Snow sports. $1.35, Skydiving. $1.50, Jet boating. $2, Bungy jumping.

**2004, Dec. 1** *Perf. 14*

**1986** A516 45c multi .55 .25
*a.* Booklet pane of 1 .75 —
**1987** A516 90c multi 1.00 .65
*a.* Booklet pane of 1 1.50 —
**1988** A516 $1.35 multi 1.50 1.50
*a.* Booklet pane of 1 2.00 —
**1989** A516 $1.50 multi 1.75 1.75
*a.* Booklet pane of 1 2.50 —
**1990** A516 $2 multi 2.75 2.75
*a.* Booklet pane of 1 3.25 —
*b.* Booklet pane, #1986-1990 12.00 —
Complete booklet, #1986a, 1987a, 1988a, 1989a, 1990a, 1990b 24.00
*Nos. 1986-1990 (5)* 7.55 6.90

Complete booklet sold for $14.95.

---

The 2004 sheets contain: #1914, 1920, 1925, 1934, 1940, 1954, 1962, 1982, 1990. See note following #1404.

---

Farm Animals — A517

Designs: 45c, Ewe (with horns) and lambs. 90c, Scottish border collies. $1.35, Pigs. $1.50, Rooster and chicken. $2, Rooster and chicken, diff.

**2005, Jan. 12** *Perf. 14*

**1991** A517 45c multi .60 .45
**1992** A517 90c multi 1.25 .75
**1993** A517 $1.35 multi 1.50 1.50
**1994** A517 $1.50 multi 1.75 1.75
**1995** A517 $2 multi 2.75 2.75
*a.* Horiz. strip, #1991-1995 10.00 10.00
*b.* Souvenir sheet, #1994-1995 5.25 5.25
*Nos. 1991-1995 (5)* 7.85 7.20

Nos. 1991-1995 exist in a souvenir sheet from a "Limited Edition" album.

**Self-Adhesive**

**Size: 22x27mm**

***Serpentine Die Cut 11x11¼***

**1996** A517 45c multi .50 .60
*a.* Booklet pane of 10 6.50

New Year 2005 (Year of the Cock) (No. 1995b).

Community Groups
A518

Designs: No. 1997, Canoeists, YMCA emblem. No. 1998, Three people holding cement, Rotary International emblem. No. 1999, People building track bed, Lions International emblem. No. 2000, Four people jumping, YMCA emblem. No. 2001, People building wall, Rotary International emblem. No. 2002, Miniature train, Lions International emblem.

**2005, Feb. 2** **Litho.** *Perf. 14*

**1997** A518 45c multi .50 .40
**1998** A518 45c multi .50 .40
**1999** A518 45c multi .50 .40
**2000** A518 $1.50 multi 2.00 2.00
*a.* Horiz. pair, #1997, 2000, + central label 3.00 3.00
*b.* Miniature sheet, 3 #2000a 8.00 8.00
**2001** A518 $1.50 multi 2.00 2.00
*a.* Horiz. pair, #1998, 2001, + central label 3.00 3.00
*b.* Miniature sheet, 3 #2001a 8.00 8.00
**2002** A518 $1.50 multi 2.00 2.00
*a.* Horiz. pair, #1999, 2002, + central label 3.00 3.00
*b.* Miniature sheet, #2000a, 2001a, 2002a 8.00 8.00
*c.* Miniature sheet, 3 #2002a 8.25 8.25
*Nos. 1997-2002 (6)* 7.50 7.20

New Zealand Postage Stamps, 150th Anniv. — A519

**2005, Mar. 2** **Litho.** *Perf. 14*

**2003** A519 45c No. 1 .60 .35
**2004** A519 90c No. P1 1.10 .75
**2005** A519 $1.35 No. OY5 1.50 1.50
**2006** A519 $1.50 No. 83 1.75 1.75
**2007** A519 $2 No. 99 2.75 2.75
*a.* Souvenir sheet, #2003-2007 8.75 8.75
*Nos. 2003-2007 (5)* 7.70 7.10

**2005, Apr. 6** **Litho.** *Perf. 14*

**2008** A519 45c No. 123a .60 .60
**2009** A519 90c No. B3 1.10 .75
**2010** A519 $1.35 No. C7 1.50 1.50
**2011** A519 $1.50 No. 256 1.75 1.75
**2012** A519 $2 No. 301 2.75 2.75
*a.* Souvenir sheet, #2008-2012 8.75 8.75
*b.* Souvenir sheet, #2007, 2012 6.50 6.50
*Nos. 2008-2012 (5)* 7.70 7.35

No. 2012b issued 4/21 for Pacific Explorer 2005 World Stamp Expo, Sydney.

**Size: 25x30mm**

**Self-Adhesive**

**Coil Stamps**

***Serpentine Die Cut 12¾***

**2013** A519 45c No. 123a .55 .55
**2014** A519 90c No. B3 1.00 1.00
*a.* Horiz. pair, #2013-2014 2.25

**Booklet Stamps**

***Serpentine Die Cut 11x11¼***

**2015** A519 45c No. 123a .60 .50
*a.* Booklet pane of 10 7.00
**2016** A519 90c No. B3 1.10 1.10
*a.* Booklet pane of 10 12.00
*Nos. 2013-2016 (4)* 3.25 3.15

**2005, June 1** **Litho.** *Perf. 14*

**2017** A519 45c No. 369 .60 .25
**2018** A519 90c No. 918 1.10 .75
**2019** A519 $1.35 No. 989 1.50 1.50
**2020** A519 $1.50 No. 1219 1.75 1.75
*a.* Souvenir sheet, #2006, 2011, 2020 7.25 7.25
**2021** A519 $2 No. 1878 2.75 2.75
*a.* Souvenir sheet, #2017-2021 10.00 10.00
*Nos. 2017-2021 (5)* 7.70 7.00

No. 2020a issued 11/17 for New Zealand 2005 National Stamp Show, Auckland.

A miniature sheet containing Nos. 2003-2012 and 2017-2021 was sold only with a commemorative book.

Cafés — A520

**2005, May 4** **Litho.** *Die Cut*

**Self-Adhesive**

**2022** A520 45c 1910s .60 .35
**2023** A520 90c 1940s 1.25 .75
**2024** A520 $1.35 1970s 1.50 1.50
**2025** A520 $1.50 1990s 2.00 2.00
**2026** A520 $2 2005 2.75 2.75
*a.* Horiz. strip, #2022-2026 10.00
*Nos. 2022-2026 (5)* 8.10 7.35

Rugby Team Shirts
A521

Shirts of: Nos. 2027, 2029, All Blacks. Nos. 2028, 2030, British & Irish Lions.

**2005, June 1** *Die Cut*

**Self-Adhesive**

**2027** A521 45c multi .55 .55
**2028** A521 45c multi .55 .55
*a.* Horiz. pair, #2027-2028 1.30
**2029** A521 $1.50 multi 2.00 2.00
**2030** A521 $1.50 multi 2.00 2.00
*a.* Horiz. pair, #2029-2030 4.50
*Nos. 2027-2030 (4)* 5.10 5.10

Miniature Sheet

Greetings Stamps — A522

No. 2031: a, Kiwi. b, Pohutukawa flower. c, Champagne flutes. d, Balloons. e, Wedding rings. f, Gift. g, Baby's hand. h, New Zealand on globe. i, Kiwi. j, Fern.

**2005, July 6** *Perf. 14*

**2031** A522 Sheet of 10 12.50 12.50
*a.-g.* 45c Any single .60 .50
*h.* $1.50 multi 2.10 1.75
*i.-j.* $2 Either single 3.00 3.00
*k.* Sheet of 20 #2031a + 20 labels 25.00 —
*l.* Sheet of 20 #2031b + 20 labels 25.00 —
*m.* Sheet of 20 #2031c + 20 labels 25.00 —
*n.* Sheet of 20 #2031d + 20 labels 25.00 —
*o.* Sheet of 20 #2031e + 20 labels 25.00 —
*p.* Sheet of 20 #2031f + 20 labels 25.00 —
*q.* Sheet of 20 #2031g + 20 labels 25.00 —
*r.* Sheet of 20 #2031h + 20 labels 50.00 —

| | | | |
|---|---|---|---|
| *s.* | Sheet of 20 #2031i + 20 labels | 70.00 | — |
| *t.* | Sheet of 20 #2031j + 20 labels | 70.00 | — |

Nos. 2031k-2031q each sold for $19.95; No. 2031r sold for $44.95; Nos. 2031s-2031t each sold for $54.95.

Examples of Nos. 2031a and 2031h without the "2005" year date were produced in sheets of 20 stamps + 20 labels for the Washington 2006 World Philatelic Exhibition and sold only at that show.

See Nos. 2070, 2120.

Worldwide Fund for Nature (WWF)
A523

Kakapo and text: No. 2032, "Nocturnal bird living on the forest floor." No. 2033, "Endangered — only 86 known surviving." No. 2034, "Relies heavily on camouflage for defence." No. 2035, "Night Parrot unique to New Zealand."

**2005, Aug. 3**

| | | | | |
|---|---|---|---|---|
| **2032** | A523 45c multi | | .70 | .70 |
| **2033** | A523 45c multi | | .70 | .70 |
| **2034** | A523 45c multi | | .70 | .70 |
| **2035** | A523 45c multi | | .70 | .70 |
| *a.* | Strip of 4, #2032-2035 | | 2.75 | 2.75 |
| | *Nos. 2032-2035 (4)* | | 2.80 | 2.80 |

A524

Christmas — A525

Designs: 45c, Baby Jesus. 90c, Mary and Joseph. $1.35, Shepherd and sheep. $1.50, Magi. $2, Star of Bethlehem.

**2005 Litho. *Perf. 14¼***

| | | | |
|---|---|---|---|
| **2036** | A524 45c multi | .60 | .30 |
| **2037** | A524 90c multi | 1.10 | .70 |
| **2038** | A524 $1.35 multi | 1.50 | 1.50 |
| **2039** | A524 $1.50 multi | 1.75 | 1.75 |
| **2040** | A524 $2 multi | 2.75 | 2.75 |
| *a.* | Horiz. strip, #2036-2040 | 9.50 | 9.50 |
| | *Nos. 2036-2040 (5)* | 7.70 | 7.00 |

**Booklet Stamps**

**Size: 22x27mm**

**Self-Adhesive**

***Serpentine Die Cut 11x11¼***

| | | | |
|---|---|---|---|
| **2041** | A524 45c multi | .65 | .55 |
| *a.* | Booklet pane of 10 | 7.00 | |
| **2042** | A525 $1 multi | 1.40 | 1.40 |
| *a.* | Booklet pane of 10 | 14.00 | |

Issued: $1, 10/5; Nos. 2036-2041, 11/2.

Premiere of Movie, *King Kong* — A526

Characters: 45c, King Kong. 90c, Carl Denham. $1.35, Ann Darrow. $1.50, Jack Driscoll. $2, Darrow and Driscoll.

**2005, Oct. 19 *Perf. 14¾***

| | | | |
|---|---|---|---|
| **2043** | A526 45c multi | .70 | .70 |
| **2044** | A526 90c multi | 1.40 | 1.40 |
| **2045** | A526 $1.35 multi | 2.10 | 2.10 |
| **2046** | A526 $1.50 multi | 2.40 | 2.40 |
| **2047** | A526 $2 multi | 3.25 | 3.25 |
| *a.* | Horiz. strip, #2043-2047 | 10.00 | 10.00 |
| *b.* | Souvenir sheet, #2047a | 10.00 | 10.00 |
| | *Nos. 2043-2047 (5)* | 9.85 | 9.85 |

Premiere of Film *Narnia: The Lion, The Witch and the Wardrobe*
A527

Designs: 45c, Lucy and the Wardrobe. 90c, Lucy, Edmund, Peter and Susan, horiz. $1.35, White Witch and Edmund, horiz. $1.50, Frozen Army. $2, Aslan and Lucy, horiz.

***Perf. 14x14¼, 14¼x14***

**2005, Dec. 1 Litho.**

| | | | |
|---|---|---|---|
| **2048** | A527 45c multi | .70 | .70 |
| *a.* | Souvenir sheet of 1 | 1.00 | 1.00 |
| **2049** | A527 90c multi | 1.40 | 1.40 |
| *a.* | Souvenir sheet of 1 | 1.90 | 1.90 |
| **2050** | A527 $1.35 multi | 2.10 | 2.10 |
| *a.* | Souvenir sheet of 1 | 3.00 | 3.00 |
| **2051** | A527 $1.50 multi | 2.40 | 2.40 |
| *a.* | Souvenir sheet of 1 | 3.25 | 3.25 |
| **2052** | A527 $2 multi | 3.25 | 3.25 |
| *a.* | Souvenir sheet of 1 | 4.25 | 4.25 |
| | *Nos. 2048-2052 (5)* | 9.85 | 9.85 |
| | Set of 5 souvenir sheets of 1 each, #2048a//2052a | 13.40 | 13.40 |

**Self-Adhesive**

***Serpentine Die Cut 12½x12, 12x12½***

| | | | |
|---|---|---|---|
| **2053** | Sheet of 5 | 10.00 | |
| *a.* | A527 45c multi, 26x37mm | .70 | .70 |
| *b.* | A527 90c multi, 37x26mm | 1.40 | 1.40 |
| *c.* | A527 $1.35 multi, 37x26mm | 2.10 | 2.10 |
| *d.* | A527 $1.50 multi, 26x37mm | 2.40 | 2.40 |
| *e.* | A527 $2 multi, 37x26mm | 3.25 | 3.25 |

Nos. 2048a-2052a sold as a set for $8.70.

The 2005 sheets contain: #2003, 2006, 2007, 2008, 2011, 2012, 2017, 2020, 2021. See note following #1404.

New Year 2006 (Year of the Dog) — A528

Designs: 45c, Labrador retriever. 90c, German shepherd. $1.35, Jack Russell terrier. $1.50, Golden retriever. $2, Huntaway.

**Litho. & Embossed**

**2006, Jan. 4 *Perf. 14***

| | | | |
|---|---|---|---|
| **2054** | A528 45c multi | .60 | .30 |

**Litho.**

| | | | |
|---|---|---|---|
| **2055** | A528 90c multi | 1.10 | 1.10 |
| **2056** | A528 $1.35 multi | 1.50 | 1.50 |
| **2057** | A528 $1.50 multi | 2.00 | 2.00 |
| **2058** | A528 $2 multi | 2.75 | 2.75 |
| *a.* | Souvenir sheet, #2057-2058 | 5.75 | 5.75 |
| | *Nos. 2054-2058 (5)* | 7.95 | 7.65 |

No. 2058a exists imperf in a limited edition album.

**Self-Adhesive**

**Size: 25x30mm Coil Stamp**

**Coil Stamp**

***Die Cut Perf. 12¾***

| | | | |
|---|---|---|---|
| **2059** | A528 45c multi | .65 | .55 |

**Booklet Stamp**

***Serpentine Die Cut 11x11¼***

| | | | |
|---|---|---|---|
| **2060** | A528 45c multi | .65 | .55 |
| *a.* | Booklet pane of 10 | 7.00 | |

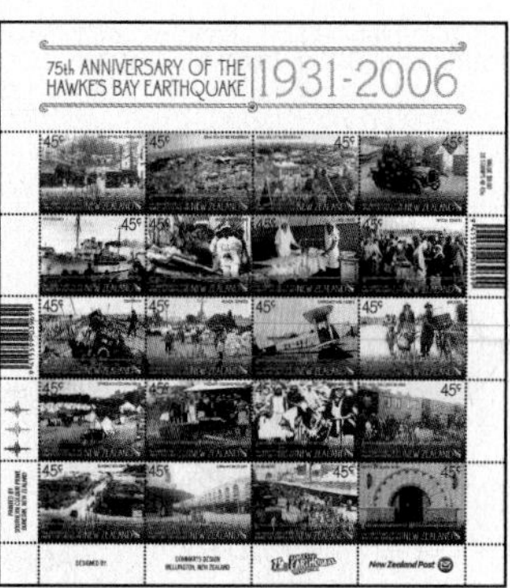


Hawke's Bay Earthquake, 75th Anniv. — A529

No. 2061: a, Napier before the earthquake. b, Aerial view of the devastation (denomination at left). c, Aerial view of the devastation (denomination at right). d, Fire service. e, HMS Veronica. f, HMS Veronica sailors. g, Red Cross. h, Rescue services. i, Devastation. j, Medical services. k, Emergency mail flights. l, Refugees. m, Emergency accommodation. n, Makeshift cooking facilities. o, Community spirit. p, Refugees evacuated by train. q, Building industry. r, A new Art Deco city. s, Celebrations. t, Hawke's Bay region today.

**2006, Feb. 3 Litho. *Perf. 14***

| | | | |
|---|---|---|---|
| **2061** | A529 Sheet of 20 | 14.00 | 14.00 |
| *a.-t.* | 45c Any single | .70 | .70 |
| *u.* | Booklet pane, 2 each #2061a-2061c | 4.75 | — |
| *v.* | Booklet pane, 2 each #2061r-2061t | 4.75 | — |
| *w.* | Booklet pane, 2 each #2061d-2061f | 4.75 | — |
| *x.* | Booklet pane, 2 each #2061g-2061h + 2 labels | 3.25 | — |
| *y.* | Booklet pane, 2 each #2061i, 2061k, 2061p | 4.75 | — |
| *z.* | Booklet pane, 2 each #2061j, 2061l, 2061m | 4.75 | — |
| *aa.* | Booklet pane, 2 each #2061n, 2061o, 2061q | 4.75 | — |
| | Complete booklet, #2061u-2061aa | 32.50 | |

Complete booklet sold for $19.95.

**Tourist Attractions Type of 2003**

Designs: No. 2062, Franz Josef Glacier, West Coast. No. 2063, Halfmoon Bay, Stewart Island. No. 2064, Cathedral Cove, Coromandel. No. 2065, Mount Taranaki. No. 2066, Huka Falls, Taupo. No. 2067, Lake Wanaka.

**2006, Mar. 1 *Perf. 13¼x13½***

| | | | |
|---|---|---|---|
| **2062** | A496 $1.50 multi | 2.00 | 2.00 |
| **2063** | A496 $1.50 multi | 2.00 | 2.00 |
| **2064** | A496 $1.50 multi | 2.00 | 2.00 |
| **2065** | A496 $1.50 multi | 2.00 | 2.00 |
| **2066** | A496 $1.50 multi | 2.00 | 2.00 |
| **2067** | A496 $1.50 multi | 2.00 | 2.00 |
| | *Nos. 2062-2067 (6)* | 12.00 | 12.00 |

Queen Elizabeth II, 80th Birthday
A530

**Litho. & Embossed with Foil Application**

**2006, Apr. 21 *Perf. 13½***

| | | | |
|---|---|---|---|
| **2068** | A530 $5 dk bl & multi | 8.00 | 8.00 |
| *a.* | $5 Prussian blue & multi | 8.00 | 8.00 |
| *b.* | Souvenir sheet, #2068a, Jersey #1215a | 27.50 | 27.50 |

Printed in sheets of 4.

No. 2068b sold for $17.50. See Jersey No. 1215.

Miniature Sheet

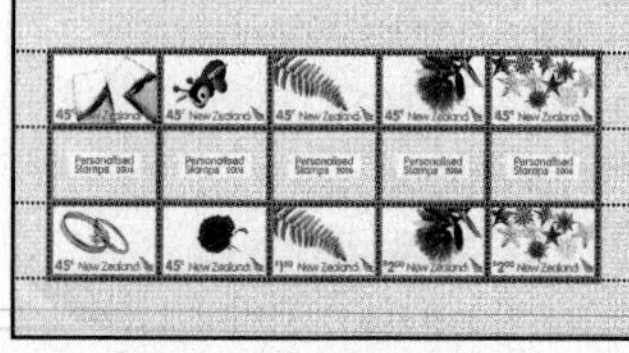

Greetings Stamps — A531

No. 2069: a, Champagne flutes. b, Child's toy. c, Fern. d, Pohutukawa flower. e, Stars. f, Wedding and engagement rings. g, Rose. h, Fern. i, Pohutukawa flower. j, Stars.

**2006, May 3 Litho. *Perf. 14***

| | | | |
|---|---|---|---|
| **2069** | A531 Sheet of 10 + 5 labels | 14.00 | 14.00 |
| *a.-g.* | 45c Any single | .70 | .70 |
| *h.* | $1.50 multi | 2.40 | 2.40 |
| *i.-j.* | $2 Either single | 3.25 | 3.25 |
| *k.* | Souvenir sheet, #2069i, 2 #2069h | 8.00 | 8.00 |
| *l.* | Sheet of 20 #2069h + 20 labels | 67.50 | — |
| *m.* | Sheet of 20 #2069i + 20 labels | 82.50 | — |
| *n.* | Sheet of 20 #2069j + 20 labels | 82.50 | — |

No. 2069k issued 11/16. Belgica'06 World Philatelic Exhibition, Brussels (#2069k).

Nos. 2069l-2069n issued 2007. No. 2069l sold for $44.90; Nos. 2069m and 2069n, each sold for $54.90. Labels could be personalized.

A sheet of 20 #2069c + 20 labels depicting New Zealand's America's Cup Emirates Team yacht sold for $19.90. Labels on this sheet could not be personalized.

See Nos. 2138, 2292, 2326-2327, 2412.

**Greetings Type of 2005 Redrawn**

Souvenir Sheet

No. 2070: a, Like #2031i, without "2005" year date. b, Like #2031j, without "2005" year date.

**2006, May 27 Litho. *Perf. 14***

| | | | |
|---|---|---|---|
| **2070** | Sheet of 2 + central label | 6.50 | 6.50 |
| *a.-b.* | A522 $2 Either single | 3.25 | 3.25 |
| *c.* | Souvenir sheet, #2070a-2070b | 6.75 | 6.75 |

Washington 2006 World Philatelic Exhibition.

No. 2070c issued 11/2. Kiwipex 2006 National Stamp Exhibition, Christchurch (#2070c). No. 2070c lacks label, and sold for $5, with the extra $1 going to the NZ Philatelic Foundation.

A set of five gummed stamps, a self-adhesive coil stamp and a self-adhesive booklet stamp depicting Traditional Maori Performing Arts was prepared for release on June 7, 2006 but was withdrawn on June 2. Some mail orders for these stamps were fulfilled and shipped out inadvertantly prior to June 7, but apparently no examples were sold over post office counters. The editors request any evidence of sale of any of these stamps over post office counters.

Renewable Energy
A532

Designs: 45c, Wind farm, Tararua. 90c, Roxburgh Hydroelectric Dam. $1.35, Biogas facility, Waikato. $1.50, Geothermal Power Station, Wairakei. $2, Solar panels on Cape Reinga Lighthouse, vert.

**2006, July 5**

| | | | |
|---|---|---|---|
| **2071** | A532 45c multi | .70 | .70 |
| **2072** | A532 90c multi | 1.40 | 1.40 |
| **2073** | A532 $1.35 multi | 2.10 | 2.10 |
| **2074** | A532 $1.50 multi | 2.40 | 2.40 |
| **2075** | A532 $2 multi | 3.25 | 3.25 |
| | *Nos. 2071-2075 (5)* | 9.85 | 9.85 |

Fruits and Vegetables A533

Slogan "5 + a day," and: 45c+5c, Tomatoes and "5." 90c+10c, Oranges and "+." $1.35, Onions and "a" (30x30mm). $1.50, Kiwi fruit and "Day," horiz. $2, Radicchio and hand.

**2006, Aug. 2 Litho. *Perf. 14***

|  |  | | |
|---|---|---|---|
| **2076** | A533 45c +5c multi | .70 | .70 |
| **2077** | A533 90c +10c multi | 1.40 | 1.40 |
| **2078** | A533 $1.35 multi | 2.10 | 2.10 |
| **2079** | A533 $1.50 multi | 2.40 | 2.40 |
| **2080** | A533 $2 multi | 3.25 | 3.25 |
| *a.* | Souvenir sheet, #2076-2080 | 10.00 | 10.00 |
| | *Nos. 2076-2080 (5)* | 9.85 | 9.85 |

**Self-Adhesive**

**Size: 24x29mm**

***Serpentine Die Cut 9¾x10***

|  |  | | |
|---|---|---|---|
| **2081** | A533 45c +5c multi | .70 | .70 |

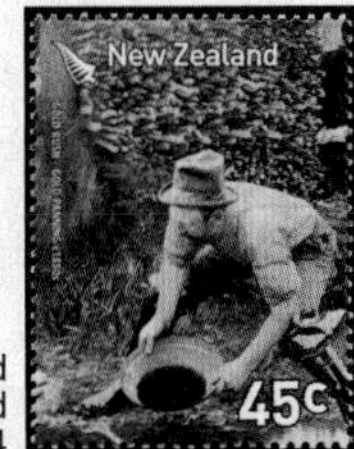


New Zealand Gold Rush — A534

Designs: 45c, Gold panner, c. 1880. 90c, Miners, Kuranui Creek, c. 1868, horiz. $1.35, Chinese miners, Tuapeka, c. 1900, horiz. $1.50, Gold escort coach, Roxburgh, 1901, horiz. $2, Dunedin harbor, c. 1900, horiz.

**2006, Sept. 9 *Perf. 14***

|  |  | | |
|---|---|---|---|
| **2082** | A534 45c multi | .70 | .70 |
| **2083** | A534 90c multi | 1.40 | 1.40 |
| **2084** | A534 $1.35 multi | 2.10 | 2.10 |
| **2085** | A534 $1.50 multi | 2.40 | 2.40 |
| **2086** | A534 $2 multi | 3.25 | 3.25 |
| | *Nos. 2082-2086 (5)* | 9.85 | 9.85 |

**Souvenir Sheet**

**Litho. With Foil Application**

|  |  | | |
|---|---|---|---|
| **2087** | Sheet of 5 | 10.00 | 10.00 |
| *a.* | A534 45c gold & multi | .70 | .70 |
| *b.* | A534 90c gold & multi | 1.40 | 1.40 |
| *c.* | A534 $1.35 gold & multi | 2.10 | 2.10 |
| *d.* | A534 $1.50 gold & multi | 2.40 | 2.40 |
| *e.* | A534 $2 gold & multi | 3.25 | 3.25 |

Portions of the design of Nos. 2082 and 2087a are printed with a thermochromic ink that changes color when warmed that is applied by a thermographic process producing a shiny, raised effect.

No. 2087 exists imperf in a limited edition album.

Christmas A535

Children's art by: Nos. 2088, 2098, Hanna McLachlan. No. 2089, Isla Hewitt. No. 2090, Caitlin Davidson. No. 2091, Maria Petersen. No. 2092, Deborah Yoon. No. 2093, Hannah Webster. 90c, Pierce Higginson. $1.35, Rosa Tucker. $1.50, Sylvie Webby. $2, Gemma Baldock.

**2006, Oct. 4 Litho. *Perf. 14¼***

|  |  | | |
|---|---|---|---|
| **2088** | A535 45c multi | .70 | .70 |
| **2089** | A535 45c multi | .70 | .70 |
| **2090** | A535 45c multi | .70 | .70 |
| **2091** | A535 45c multi | .70 | .70 |
| **2092** | A535 45c multi | .70 | .70 |
| **2093** | A535 45c multi | .70 | .70 |
| *a.* | Miniature sheet, #2088-2093 | 4.25 | 4.25 |
| *b.* | Horiz. strip of 5, #2089-2093 | 3.50 | 3.50 |
| **2094** | A535 90c multi | 1.40 | 1.40 |
| **2095** | A535 $1.35 multi | 2.10 | 2.10 |
| **2096** | A535 $1.50 multi | 2.40 | 2.40 |
| **2097** | A535 $2 multi | 3.25 | 3.25 |
| | *Nos. 2088-2097 (10)* | 13.35 | 13.35 |

**Self-Adhesive**

**Size: 21x26mm**

***Serpentine Die Cut 9¾x10***

|  |  | | |
|---|---|---|---|
| **2098** | A535 45c multi | .70 | .70 |
| *a.* | Booklet pane of 10 | 7.00 | |
| **2099** | A535 $1.50 multi | 2.40 | 2.40 |
| *a.* | Horiz. pair, #2098-2099 | 3.00 | |
| *b.* | Booklet pane of 10 | 24.00 | |

No. 2099b sold for $13.50.

Summer Festivals A536

Designs: 45c, Dragon boat racing. 90c, Race day. $1.35, Teddy Bears' Picnic. $1.50, Outdoor concerts. $2, Jazz festivals.

**2006, Nov. 1 *Perf. 14¼***

|  |  | | |
|---|---|---|---|
| **2100** | A536 45c multi | .70 | .70 |
| **2101** | A536 90c multi | 1.40 | 1.40 |
| **2102** | A536 $1.35 multi | 2.10 | 2.10 |
| **2103** | A536 $1.50 multi | 2.40 | 2.40 |
| **2104** | A536 $2 multi | 3.25 | 3.25 |
| *a.* | Horiz. strip of 5, #2100-2104 | 10.00 | 10.00 |
| *b.* | Miniature sheet, #2104a | 10.00 | 10.00 |
| | *Nos. 2100-2104 (5)* | 9.85 | 9.85 |

The 2006 sheets contain: #2058, 2061e, 2066, 2069i, 2075, 2080, 2086, 2097, 2104. See note following #1404.

Scott Base, Antarctica, 50th Anniv. — A537

Designs: 45c, Opening ceremony, 1957. 90c, Scott Base, 1990. $1.35, Aerial view, 2000. $1.50, Sign, 2003-04. $2, Aerial view, 2005.

**2007, Jan. 20 *Perf. 14¼x14***

|  |  | | |
|---|---|---|---|
| **2105** | A537 45c multi | .70 | .70 |
| *a.* | Souvenir sheet of 1 | 1.00 | 1.00 |
| **2106** | A537 90c multi | 1.40 | 1.40 |
| *a.* | Souvenir sheet of 1 | 1.90 | 1.90 |
| **2107** | A537 $1.35 multi | 2.10 | 2.10 |
| *a.* | Souvenir sheet of 1 | 2.75 | 2.75 |
| **2108** | A537 $1.50 multi | 2.40 | 2.40 |
| *a.* | Souvenir sheet of 1 | 3.50 | 3.50 |
| **2109** | A537 $2 multi | 3.25 | 3.25 |
| *a.* | Souvenir sheet of 1 | 4.50 | 4.50 |
| | *Nos. 2105-2109 (5)* | 9.85 | 9.85 |

Nos. 2105a-2109a sold as a set for $8.70. The souvenir sheets exist overprinted in a limited edition album.

New Year 2007 (Year of the Pig) A538

Pig breeds: 45c, Kunekune. 90c, Kunekune, diff. $1.35, Arapawa. $1.50, Auckland Island. $2, Kunekune, diff.

**2007, Feb. 7 *Perf. 14½x14***

|  |  | | |
|---|---|---|---|
| **2110** | A538 45c multi | .70 | .70 |
| **2111** | A538 90c multi | 1.40 | 1.40 |
| **2112** | A538 $1.35 multi | 2.10 | 2.10 |
| **2113** | A538 $1.50 multi | 2.40 | 2.40 |
| **2114** | A538 $2 multi | 3.25 | 3.25 |
| *a.* | Souvenir sheet, #2113-2114 | 5.75 | 5.75 |

Nos. 2111-2112 exist in a souvenir sheet in a limited edition album.

Indigenous Animals — A539

Designs: 45c, Tuatara. 90c, Kiwi. $1.35, Hamilton's frog. $1.50, Yellow-eyed penguin. $2, Hector's dolphin.

***Serpentine Die Cut***

**2007, Mar. 7 Litho.**

**Self-Adhesive**

|  |  | | |
|---|---|---|---|
| **2115** | A539 45c multi | .65 | .65 |
| **2116** | A539 90c multi | 1.25 | 1.25 |
| **2117** | A539 $1.35 multi | 1.90 | 1.90 |
| **2118** | A539 $1.50 multi | 2.10 | 2.10 |
| **2119** | A539 $2 multi | 2.75 | 2.75 |
| *a.* | Horiz. strip of 5, #2115-2119 | 8.65 | |

**Greetings Type of 2005 Redrawn**

**Souvenir Sheet**

**2007, Mar. 30 Litho. *Perf. 14***

|  |  | | |
|---|---|---|---|
| **2120** | Sheet , #2075, 2120a | 6.00 | 6.00 |
| *a.* | A531 $2 Like #2069i, without "2006" year date | 3.00 | 3.00 |

Northland 2007 National Stamp Exhibition, Whangarei.

Centenaries — A540

Designs: No. 2121, Scouts and Lieutenant Colonel David Cossgrove, founder of scouting movement in New Zealand. No. 2122, Infant, nurse, Dr. Frederic Truby King, founder of Plunket Society. No. 2123, Rugby players, Hercules "Bumper" Wright, first team captain. No. 2124, Sister of Compassion teaching children, Suzanne Aubert, founder of Sisters of Compassion. $1, Plunket Society emblem, family. $1.50, Sisters of Compassion emblem, women reading book. No. 2127, New Zealand Rugby League emblem, rugby players. No. 2128, Scouting emblem, scouts.

**2007, Apr. 24 *Perf. 14***

|  |  | | |
|---|---|---|---|
| **2121** | A540 50c multi | .75 | .75 |
| **2122** | A540 50c multi | .75 | .75 |
| **2123** | A540 50c multi | .75 | .75 |
| **2124** | A540 50c multi | .75 | .75 |
| *a.* | Horiz. strip of 4, #2121-2124 | 4.00 | 4.00 |
| **2125** | A540 $1 multi | 1.50 | 1.50 |
| **2126** | A540 $1.50 multi | 2.25 | 2.25 |
| **2127** | A540 $2 multi | 3.00 | 3.00 |
| **2128** | A540 $2 multi | 3.00 | 3.00 |
| *a.* | Block of 8, #2121-2128 | 12.75 | 12.75 |
| *b.* | Horiz. pair, #2127-2128 | 9.00 | 9.00 |

**Tourist Attractions Type of 2003**

Designs: 5c, Whakarewarewa geothermal area. 10c, Central Otago. 20c, Rainbow Falls, Northland. 50c, Lake Coleridge. $1, Rangitoto Island. $2.50, Abel Tasman National Park. $3, Tongaporutu, Taranaki.

**2007, May 9 *Perf. 13¼x13½***

|  |  | | |
|---|---|---|---|
| **2129** | A496 5c multi | .25 | .25 |
| **2130** | A496 10c multi | .25 | .25 |
| **2131** | A496 20c multi | .30 | .30 |
| **2132** | A496 50c multi | .75 | .75 |
| **2133** | A496 $1 multi | 1.50 | 1.50 |
| **2134** | A496 $2.50 multi | 3.75 | 3.75 |
| **2135** | A496 $3 multi | 4.50 | 4.50 |
| | *Nos. 2129-2135 (7)* | 11.30 | 11.30 |

**Self-Adhesive**

***Serpentine Die Cut 10x9½***

|  |  | | |
|---|---|---|---|
| **2136** | A496 50c multi | .75 | .75 |
| *a.* | Booklet pane of 10 | 7.50 | |
| **2137** | A496 $1 multi | 1.50 | 1.50 |
| *a.* | Horiz. pair, #2136-2137 | 2.25 | 2.25 |
| *b.* | Booklet pane of 10 | 15.00 | |

**Greetings Type of 2006 Redrawn**

No. 2138: a, Child's toy. b, Pohutukawa flower. c, Wedding and engagement rings. d, Fern. e, Champagne flutes. f, Rose. g, Stars.

**2007, May 9 *Perf. 14***

|  |  | | |
|---|---|---|---|
| **2138** | A531 Sheet of 7 + 8 labels | 5.25 | 5.25 |
| *a.-g.* | 50c Any single | .75 | .75 |
| *h.* | Sheet of 20 #2138a + 20 labels | 32.50 | — |
| *i.* | Sheet of 20 #2138b + 20 labels | 32.50 | — |
| *j.* | Sheet of 20 #2138c + 20 labels | 32.50 | — |
| *k.* | Sheet of 20 #2138d + 20 labels | 32.50 | — |
| *l.* | Sheet of 20 #2138e + 20 labels | 32.50 | — |
| *m.* | Sheet of 20 #2138f + 20 labels | 32.50 | — |
| *n.* | Sheet of 20 #2138g + 20 labels | 32.50 | — |

Nos. 2138h-2138n each sold for $20.90.

Southern Skies and Observatories — A541

Designs: 50c, Southern Cross, Stardome Observatory. $1, Pleiades, McLellan Mt. John Observatory. $1.50, Trifid Nebula, Ward Observatory. $2, Southern Pinwheel, MOA telescope, Mt. John Observatory. $2.50, Large Magellanic Cloud, Southern African Large Telescope.

**2007, June 6 *Perf. 13x13¼***

|  |  | | |
|---|---|---|---|
| **2139** | A541 50c multi | .80 | .80 |
| *a.* | Perf. 14 | 1.00 | 1.00 |
| *b.* | Booklet pane of 1 #2139a | 1.00 | — |
| **2140** | A541 $1 multi | 1.60 | 1.60 |
| *a.* | Perf. 14 | 2.00 | 2.00 |
| *b.* | Booklet pane of 1 #2140a | 2.00 | — |
| **2141** | A541 $1.50 multi | 2.40 | 2.40 |
| *a.* | Perf. 14 | 3.00 | 3.00 |
| *b.* | Booklet pane of 1 #2141a | 3.00 | — |
| **2142** | A541 $2 multi | 3.00 | 3.00 |
| *a.* | Perf. 14 | 4.25 | 4.25 |
| *b.* | Booklet pane of 1 #2142a | 4.25 | — |
| **2143** | A541 $2.50 multi | 3.75 | 3.75 |
| *a.* | Perf. 14 | 5.25 | 5.25 |
| *b.* | Booklet pane of 1 #2143a | 5.25 | — |
| *c.* | Booklet pane of 5, #2139a-2143a | 15.50 | — |
| | Complete booklet, #2139b, 2140b, 2141b, 2142b, 2143b, 2143c | 31.00 | |
| *d.* | Souvenir sheet, #2142a, 2143a | 6.75 | 6.75 |
| | *Nos. 2139-2143 (5)* | 11.55 | 11.55 |

No. 2143d issued 8/31. Huttpex 2007 Stampshow (#2143d).

Miniature Sheet

New Zealand Slang — A542

No. 2144 — Designs: a, "Good as gold," gold nugget. b, "Sweet as," kiwi fruit. c, "She'll be right," hand with thumb up. d, "Hissy fit," insect. e, "Sparrow fart," sun in sky. f, "Cuz," kiwi bird. g, "Away laughing," sandals. h, "Tiki tour," road sign. i, "Away with the fairies," cookies. j, "Wop-wops," house. k, "Hard yakka," shirt. l, "Cods wollop," fish. m, "Boots and all," rugby ball and athletic shoes. n, "Shark and taties," fish and chips. o, "Knackered," boots. p, "Laughing gear," mug. q, "Everyman and his dog," dog. r, "Bit of a dag," sheep. s, "Dreaded lurgy," box of tissues. t, "Rark up," hand pointing.

**2007, July 4 *Perf. 14***

|  |  | | |
|---|---|---|---|
| **2144** | A542 Sheet of 20 | 16.00 | 16.00 |
| *a.-t.* | 50c Any single | .80 | .80 |

Portions of the design were covered with a thermographic ink that allowed printing below (definitinons of the slang phrases) to appear when the ink was warmed.

Technical Innovations by New Zealanders
A543

Designs: 50c, Gallagher electric fence. $1, Spreadable butter. $1.50, Mountain buggy. $2, Hamilton jet boat. $2.50, Tranquilizer gun.

**2007, Aug. 1**

| No. | Type | Denomination | Unused | Used |
|---|---|---|---|---|
| 2145 | A543 | 50c multi | .75 | .75 |
| 2146 | A543 | $1 multi | 1.50 | 1.50 |
| 2147 | A543 | $1.50 multi | 2.25 | 2.25 |
| 2148 | A543 | $2 multi | 3.00 | 3.00 |
| 2149 | A543 | $2.50 multi | 3.75 | 3.75 |
| | | *Nos. 2145-2149 (5)* | 11.25 | 11.25 |

Nos. 2145-2149 exist in a souvenir sheet in a limited edition album.

Wedding of Queen Elizabeth II and Prince Philip, 60th Anniv. — A544

Queen and Prince: 50c, In 2007. $2, On wedding day, 1947.

**2007, Sept. 5 Litho. *Perf. 14***

| No. | Type | Denomination | Unused | Used |
|---|---|---|---|---|
| 2150 | A544 | 50c multi | .70 | .70 |
| 2151 | A544 | $2 multi | 2.75 | 2.75 |
| *a.* | | Souvenir sheet, #2150-2151 | 3.50 | 3.50 |

Christmas
A545

Children's art by: 50c, Sione Vao. $1, Reece Cateley. $1.50, Emily Wang. $2, Alexandra Eathorne. $2.50, Jake Hooper.

**2007, Oct. 3 *Perf. 14¼***

| No. | Type | Denomination | Unused | Used |
|---|---|---|---|---|
| 2152 | A545 | 50c multi | .80 | .80 |
| 2153 | A545 | $1 multi | 1.50 | 1.50 |
| 2154 | A545 | $1.50 multi | 2.40 | 2.40 |
| 2155 | A545 | $2 multi | 3.00 | 3.00 |
| 2156 | A545 | $2.50 multi | 4.00 | 4.00 |
| | | *Nos. 2152-2156 (5)* | 11.70 | 11.70 |

**Size: 25x30mm**

**Self-Adhesive**

**Coil Stamps**

***Die Cut Perf. 13x12¾***

| No. | Type | Denomination | Unused | Used |
|---|---|---|---|---|
| 2157 | A545 | 50c multi | .80 | .80 |
| 2158 | A545 | $1.50 multi | 2.40 | 2.40 |
| *a.* | | Horiz. pair, #2157-2158 | 3.25 | |

**Booklet Stamps**

***Serpentine Die Cut 11x11¼***

| No. | Type | Denomination | Unused | Used |
|---|---|---|---|---|
| 2159 | A545 | 50c multi | .80 | .80 |
| *a.* | | Booket pane of 10 | 8.00 | |
| 2160 | A545 | $1.50 multi | 2.10 | 2.10 |
| *a.* | | Booklet pane of 10 | 21.00 | |

No. 2160a sold for $13.50.

Miniature Sheet

Greetings Stamps — A546

No. 2161: a, "Go You Good Thing." b, "Look Who It Is." c, "Love Always." d, "Thanks a Million." e, "We've Got News." f, "Wish You Were Here." g, "Time to Celebrate." h, "Kia Ora." i, "You Gotta Love Christmas." j, Chinese characters.

**2007, Nov. 7 *Perf. 14***

| No. | Type | Description | Unused | Used |
|---|---|---|---|---|
| 2161 | A546 | Sheet of 10 + 5 labels | 13.00 | 13.00 |
| *a.-f.* | | 50c Any single | .75 | .75 |
| *g.-h.* | | $1 Either single | 1.50 | 1.50 |
| *i.* | | $1.50 multi | 2.40 | 2.40 |
| *j.* | | $2 multi | 3.00 | 3.00 |
| *k.* | | Sheet of 20 #2161c + 20 labels | 32.50 | — |
| *l.* | | Sheet of 20 #2161d + 20 labels | 32.50 | — |
| *m.* | | Sheet of 20 #2161e + 20 labels | 32.50 | — |
| *n.* | | Sheet of 20 #2161f + 20 labels | 32.50 | — |
| *o.* | | Sheet of 20 #2161g + 20 labels | 47.50 | — |
| *p.* | | Sheet of 20 #2161h + 20 labels | 47.50 | — |
| *q.* | | Sheet of 20 #2161i + 20 labels | 70.00 | — |
| *r.* | | Sheet of 20 #2161j + 20 labels | 85.00 | — |
| *s.* | | As #2161h, perf 13¼x13½ (2224b) | 1.25 | 1.25 |
| *t.* | | As #2161j, perf 13¼x13½ (2224b) | 2.40 | 2.40 |

Nos. 2161k-2161n each sold for $20.90; Nos. 2161o-2161p, for $30.90; No. 2161q, for $44.90; No. 2161r, for $54.90. Labels were personalizable on Nos. 2161k-2161r. Issued: Nos. 2161s, 2161t, 4/1/09.

The 2007 sheets contain: #2114, 2109, 2142; #2127, 2128, 2148; #2155, 2151, 2161j. See note following #1404.

Reefs
A547

Marine life from: 50c, Dusky Sound, Fiordland. $1, Mayor Island, Bay of Plenty. $1.50, Fiordland. $2, Volkner Rocks, White Island, Bay of Plenty.

**2008, Jan. 9 Litho. *Perf. 13x13¼***

| No. | Type | Denomination | Unused | Used |
|---|---|---|---|---|
| 2162 | A547 | 50c multi | .80 | .80 |
| 2163 | A547 | $1 multi | 1.60 | 1.60 |
| 2164 | A547 | $1.50 multi | 2.40 | 2.40 |
| 2165 | A547 | $2 multi | 3.25 | 3.25 |
| *a.* | | Souvenir sheet, #2162-2165 | 8.25 | 8.25 |
| | | *Nos. 2162-2165 (4)* | 8.05 | 8.05 |

**Self-Adhesive**

**Size: 26x21mm**

***Serpentine Die Cut 11¼***

| No. | Type | Denomination | Unused | Used |
|---|---|---|---|---|
| 2166 | A547 | 50c multi | .80 | .80 |
| *a.* | | Booklet pane of 10 | 8.00 | |
| 2167 | A547 | $1 multi | 1.60 | 1.60 |
| *a.* | | Horiz. pair, #2166-2167 | 2.40 | |
| *b.* | | Booklet pane of 10 #2167 | 16.00 | |

Pocket Pets
A548

**2008, Feb. 7 *Perf. 14***

| No. | Type | Denomination | Unused | Used |
|---|---|---|---|---|
| 2168 | A548 | 50c Rabbits | .80 | .80 |
| 2169 | A548 | $1 Guinea pigs | 1.60 | 1.60 |
| 2170 | A548 | $1.50 Rats | 2.40 | 2.40 |
| 2171 | A548 | $2 Mice | 3.25 | 3.25 |
| *a.* | | Souvenir sheet, #2170-2171 | 5.75 | 5.75 |
| *b.* | | As #2171, perf. 13½x13¼ | 3.25 | 3.25 |
| *c.* | | Souvenir sheet, #2161j, 2171b | 6.50 | 6.50 |

New Year 2008 (Year of the Rat), No. 2171a.

Nos. 2171b, 2171c issued 3/7. Taipei 2008 International Stamp Exhibition (#2171c).

Weather Extremes
A549

Designs: No. 2172, Drought, Gisborne, 1998. No. 2173, Wind, Auckland, 2007. $1, Storm, Wellington, 2001. $1.50, Flooding, Hikurangi, 2007. $2, Snow storm, Southland, 2001. $2.50, Heat, Matarangi, 2005.

**2008, Mar. 5 Litho. *Perf. 14***

| No. | Type | Denomination | Unused | Used |
|---|---|---|---|---|
| 2172 | A549 | 50c multi | .80 | .80 |
| 2173 | A549 | 50c multi | .80 | .80 |
| 2174 | A549 | $1 multi | 1.60 | 1.60 |
| 2175 | A549 | $1.50 multi | 2.40 | 2.40 |
| 2176 | A549 | $2 multi | 3.25 | 3.25 |
| 2177 | A549 | $2.50 multi | 4.00 | 4.00 |
| | | *Nos. 2172-2177 (6)* | 12.85 | 12.85 |

Nos. 2172-2177 exist in a souvenir sheet in a limited edition album.

Australian and New Zealand Army Corps (ANZAC)
A550

Designs: No. 2178, Dawn Parade. No. 2179, Soldiers at Gallipoli, 1915. $1, Soldiers at Western Front, 1916-18. $1.50, Chalk kiwi made by soldiers, England, 1919. $2, Soldier's Haka dance, Egypt, 1941. $2.50, Soldiers in Viet Nam, 1965-71.

**2008, Apr. 2**

| No. | Type | Description | Unused | Used |
|---|---|---|---|---|
| 2178 | A550 | 50c multi | .80 | .80 |
| *a.* | | Booklet pane of 1 | 1.00 | — |
| 2179 | A550 | 50c multi | .80 | .80 |
| *a.* | | Booklet pane of 1 | 1.00 | — |
| 2180 | A550 | $1 multi | 1.60 | 1.60 |
| *a.* | | Booklet pane of 1 | 2.00 | — |
| 2181 | A550 | $1.50 multi | 2.40 | 2.40 |
| *a.* | | Booklet pane of 1 | 3.00 | — |
| *b.* | | Souvenir sheet, #2179-2181 | 3.50 | 3.50 |
| 2182 | A550 | $2 multi | 3.25 | 3.25 |
| *a.* | | Booklet pane of 1 | 4.00 | — |
| 2183 | A550 | $2.50 multi | 4.00 | 4.00 |
| *a.* | | Booklet pane of 1 | 5.00 | — |
| *b.* | | Booklet pane of 6, #2178-2183 | 16.00 | — |
| | | Complete booklet, #2178a, 2179a, 2180a, 2181a, 2182a, 2183a, 2183b | 32.00 | |
| | | *Nos. 2178-2183 (6)* | 12.85 | 12.85 |

No. 2181b issued 10/20. End of World War I, 90th anniv. (#2181b).

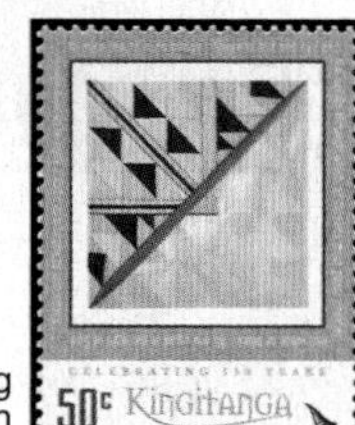


Maori King Movement, 150th Anniv. — A551

Various unnamed artworks by Fred Graham and English text: 50c, "There is but one eye of the needle. . ." $1.50, "Taupiri is the mountain. . ." $2.50, "After I am gone. . .," horiz.

**2008, May 2 Litho. *Perf. 14***

| No. | Type | Denomination | Unused | Used |
|---|---|---|---|---|
| 2184 | A551 | 50c multi | .80 | .80 |
| 2185 | A551 | $1.50 multi | 2.40 | 2.40 |
| 2186 | A551 | $2.50 multi | 4.00 | 4.00 |
| | | *Nos. 2184-2186 (3)* | 7.20 | 7.20 |

Premiere of Film, *The Chronicles of Narnia: Prince Caspian* — A552

Designs: 50c, The Pevensie children. $1, Queen Susan. $1.50, High King Peter. $2, Prince Caspian.

**2008, May 7 *Perf. 14½x14***

| No. | Type | Description | Unused | Used |
|---|---|---|---|---|
| 2187 | A552 | 50c multi | .80 | .80 |
| *a.* | | Souvenir sheet of 1 | 1.10 | 1.10 |
| 2188 | A552 | $1 multi | 1.60 | 1.60 |
| *a.* | | Souvenir sheet of 1 | 2.25 | 2.25 |
| 2189 | A552 | $1.50 multi | 2.40 | 2.40 |
| *a.* | | Souvenir sheet of 1 | 3.25 | 3.25 |
| 2190 | A552 | $2 multi | 3.25 | 3.25 |
| *a.* | | Souvenir sheet of 1 | 4.50 | 4.50 |
| | | *Nos. 2187-2190 (4)* | 8.05 | 8.05 |

Nos. 2187a-2190a were sold as a set for $7.

Matariki (Maori New Year)
A553

Inscriptions: No. 2191, Ranginui. No. 2192, Te Moana nui a Kiwa. $1, Papatuanuku. $1.50, Whakapapa. $2, Takoha. $2.50, Te Tau Hou.

**2008, June 5 Litho. *Perf. 14***

| No. | Type | Description | Unused | Used |
|---|---|---|---|---|
| 2191 | A553 | 50c multi | .80 | .80 |
| 2192 | A553 | 50c multi | .80 | .80 |
| 2193 | A553 | $1 multi | 1.60 | 1.60 |
| 2194 | A553 | $1.50 multi | 2.40 | 2.40 |
| 2195 | A553 | $2 multi | 3.25 | 3.25 |
| *a.* | | Souvenir sheet, #2192, 2194, 2195 | 6.50 | 6.50 |
| 2196 | A553 | $2.50 multi | 4.00 | 4.00 |
| *a.* | | Miniature sheet, #2191-2196, perf. 13½x13¼ | 13.00 | 13.00 |
| | | *Nos. 2191-2196 (6)* | 12.85 | 12.85 |

No. 2195a issued 9/18. Vienna Intl. Postage Stamp Exhibition (#2195a).

No. 2196a exists as an imperf miniature sheet from a limited edition album.

2008 Summer Olympics, Beijing — A554

**2008, July 2 *Perf. 14¼***

| No. | Type | Denomination | Unused | Used |
|---|---|---|---|---|
| 2197 | A554 | 50c Rowing | .80 | .80 |
| 2198 | A554 | 50c Cycling | .80 | .80 |
| 2199 | A554 | $1 Kayaking | 1.60 | 1.60 |
| 2200 | A554 | $2 Running | 3.00 | 3.00 |
| | | *Nos. 2197-2200 (4)* | 6.20 | 6.20 |

Compare with Type SP82.

Miniature Sheet

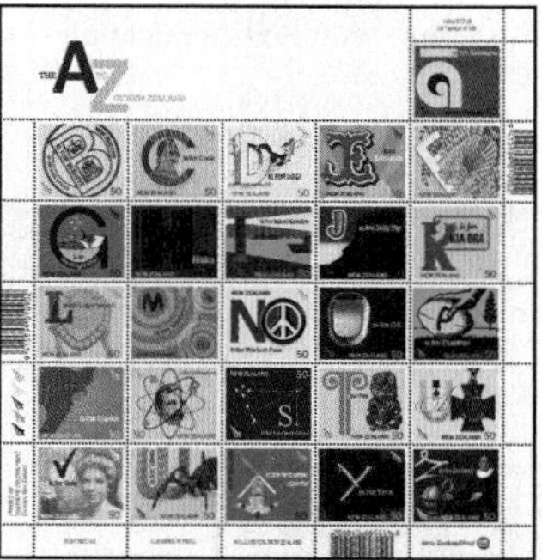

Alphabet — A555

No. 2201 — Inscriptions: a, A is for Aotearoa (Maori name for New Zealand). b, B is for Beehive (Parliament Building). c, C is for Cook (Capt. James Cook). d, D is for Dog (comic strip character). e, E is for Edmonds (Thomas J. Edmonds, cookbook producer). f, F is for Fantail (bird). g, G is for Goodnight Kiwi (cartoon). h, H is for Haka (Maori dance). i, I is for Interislander (ferry). j, J is for Jelly tip (ice cream bar). k, K is for Kia ora. l, L is for Log O'Wood (rugby trophy). m, M is for Mudpools. n, N is for Nuclear free. o, O is for O.E. (overseas experience). p, P is for Pinetree (Colin "Pinetree" Meads, rugby player). q, Q is for Quake. r, R is for Rutherford (Sir Ernest Rutherford, chemist and physicist). s, S is for Southern Cross (constellation). t, T is for Tiki (rock carving). u, U is for Upham (Capt. Charles Upham, war hero). v, V is for Vote. w, W is for Weta (insect). x, X is for X-treme sports. y, Y is for Yarn. z, Z is for Zeeland (Dutch province for which New Zealand was named).

**2008, Aug. 6 *Perf. 14¼***

| No. | Type | Description | Unused | Used |
|---|---|---|---|---|
| 2201 | A555 | Sheet of 26 | 18.50 | 18.50 |
| *a.-z.* | | 50c Any single | .70 | .70 |

North Island Main Trunk Line, Cent.
A556

Designs: 50c, Last spike ceremony, Manganui-o-te-Ao, 1908. $1, Locomotive at Taumarunui Station, 1958. $1.50, Train on Makatote Viaduct, 1963. $2, Train on Raurimi Spiral, 1964. $2.50, Train on Hapuawhenua Viaduct, 2003.

**2008, Sept. 3 Litho. *Perf. 14***

**2202** A556 50c multi .70 .70
**2203** A556 $1 multi 1.40 1.40
**2204** A556 $1.50 multi 2.00 2.00
**2205** A556 $2 multi 2.75 2.75
**2206** A556 $2.50 multi 3.50 3.50
*Nos. 2202-2206 (5)* 10.35 10.35

Christmas
A557

Winning art in children's stamp design competition: 50c, Sheep With Stocking Cap, by Kirsten Fisher-Marsters. $2, Pohutukawa and Koru, by Tamara Jenkin. $2.50, Kiwi and Pohutukawa, by Molly Bruhns.

**2008, Oct. 1 *Perf. 14¼***

**2207** A557 50c multi .70 .70
**2208** A557 $2 multi 2.75 2.75
**2209** A557 $2.50 multi 3.25 3.25
*Nos. 2207-2209 (3)* 6.70 6.70

Christmas
A558

Designs: 50c, Nativity. $1, Holy Family. $1.50, Madonna and Child.

**2008, Oct. 1 *Perf. 14¼***

**2210** A558 50c multi .70 .70
**2211** A558 $1 multi 1.40 1.40
**2212** A558 $1.50 multi 2.00 2.00
*Nos. 2210-2212 (3)* 4.10 4.10

**Size: 21x26mm**

**Self-Adhesive**

**Coil Stamps**

***Die Cut Perf. 12¾***

**2213** A558 50c multi .70 .70
**2214** A558 $1.50 multi 2.00 2.00
*a.* Horiz. pair, #2213-2214 2.75

**Booklet Stamps**

***Serpentine Die Cut 11¼***

**2215** A558 50c multi .70 .70
*a.* Booklet pane of 10 7.00
**2216** A558 $1.50 multi 2.00 2.00
*a.* Booklet pane of 10 20.00
*Nos. 2213-2216 (4)* 5.40 5.40

Sir Edmund Hillary (1919-2008), Mountaineer
A559

New Zealand flag and: 50c, Hillary. $1, Hillary and Tenzing Norgay on Mt. Everest, 1953. $1.50, Hillary on Trans-Antarctic Expedition, 1958. $2, Hillary with Nepalese people, 1964. $2.50, Hillary at Order of the Garter ceremony, 1995.

**2008, Nov. 5 Litho. *Perf. 14¾***

**2217** A559 50c multi .60 .60
*a.* Perf. 14 .75 .75
**2218** A559 $1 multi 1.25 1.25
*a.* Perf. 14 1.50 1.50
**2219** A559 $1.50 multi 1.75 1.75
**2220** A559 $2 multi 2.40 2.40
**2221** A559 $2.50 multi 3.00 3.00
*a.* Perf. 14 3.75 3.75
*b.* Souvenir sheet, #2217a, 2218a, 2221a, + specimen of #1084 6.00 6.00
*Nos. 2217-2221 (5)* 9.00 9.00

Timpex 2009 National Stamp Exhibition, Timaru (Nos. 2217a, 2218a, 2221a-b); Issued 10/16/09.

**Tourist Attractions Type of 2003**

**Souvenir Sheet**

No. 2222: a, Like #2065, without year date. b, Like #2135, without year date.

**2008, Nov. 7 *Perf. 13¼x13½***

**2222** Sheet of 2 5.50 5.50
*a.* A496 $1.50 multi 1.75 1.75
*b.* A496 $3 multi 3.75 3.75

Tarapex 2008 Philatelic Exhibition, New Plymouth.

The 2008 sheets contain: #2165, 2171, 2177; #2183, 2186, 2196; #2206, 2212, 2221. See note following #1404.

New Year 2009 (Year of the Ox) — A560

Designs: 50c, Chinese character for "ox." $1, Ox. $2, Chinese lanterns and Auckland Harbor Bridge.

**2009, Jan. 7 *Perf. 13¼x13***

**2223** A560 50c multi .60 .60
**2224** A560 $1 multi 1.25 1.25
*a.* Perf. 13¼x13½ 1.25 1.25
*b.* Souvenir sheet, #2161s, 2161t, 2224a 5.00 5.00
**2225** A560 $2 multi 2.40 2.40
*a.* Souvenir sheet, #2223-2225 4.25 4.25
*Nos. 2223-2225 (3)* 4.25 4.25

China 2009 World Stamp Exhibition, Luoyand (#2224b). Issued: Nos. 2224a, 2224b, 4/1.

Lighthouses — A561

Designs: 50c, Pencarrow Lighthouse. $1, Dog Island Lighthouse. $1.50, Cape Brett Lighthouse. $2, Cape Egmont Lighthouse. $2.50, Cape Reinga Lighthouse.

**2009, Jan. 7 *Perf. 13x13¼***

**2226** A561 50c multi .60 .60
**2227** A561 $1 multi 1.25 1.25
**2228** A561 $1.50 multi 1.75 1.75
**2229** A561 $2 multi 2.40 2.40
**2230** A561 $2.50 multi 3.00 3.00
*Nos. 2226-2230 (5)* 9.00 9.00

Motor Sports Champions
A562

Designs: 50c, Scott Dixon. $1, Bruce McLaren. $1.50, Ivan Mauger. $2, Denny Hulme. $2.50, Hugh Anderson.

**2009, Feb. 4 Litho. *Perf. 14***

**2231** A562 50c multi .50 .50
**2232** A562 $1 multi 1.00 1.00
**2233** A562 $1.50 multi 1.50 1.50
**2234** A562 $2 multi 2.10 2.10
**2235** A562 $2.50 multi 2.60 2.60
*a.* Sheet, #2231-2235 7.75 7.75
*Nos. 2231-2235 (5)* 7.70 7.70

**Self-Adhesive**

**Size: 26x21mm**

***Serpentine Die Cut 10x9¾***

**2236** A562 50c multi .50 .50
*a.* Booklet pane of 10 5.00
**2237** A562 $1 multi 1.00 1.00
*a.* Booklet pane of 10 10.00
*b.* Horiz. pair, #2236-2237 1.50

**Tourist Attractions Type of 2003**

**2009, Mar. 4 Litho. *Perf. 13¼x13½***

**2238** Sheet of 2 #2238a 3.00 3.00
*a.* A496 $1.50 Like #2062, without year date 1.50 1.50

Intl. Polar Year.

Giants of New Zealand — A563

Designs: 50c, Giant moa. $1, Colossal squid. $1.50 Southern right whale. $2, Giant eagle. $2.50, Giant weta.

**2009, Mar. 4 *Perf. 14½***

**2239** A563 50c multi .75 .75
**2240** A563 $1 multi 1.50 1.50
**2241** A563 $1.50 multi 2.00 2.00
**2242** A563 $2 multi 2.50 2.50
**2243** A563 $2.50 multi 3.00 3.00
*a.* Miniature sheet, #2239-2243 8.00 8.00
*Nos. 2239-2243 (5)* 9.75 9.75

Australian and New Zealand Army Corps (ANZAC)
A564

Poppy and: No. 2244, Funeral procession of the Unknown Warrior. No. 2245, New Zealand Maori Pioneer Battalion, World War I. $1, New Zealand No. 75 Squadron of the Royal Air Force, World War II. $1.50, HMS Achilles, World War II. $2, Kayforce soldiers, Korean War. $2.50, ANZAC Battalion, Vietnam War.

**2009, Apr. 1 Litho. *Perf. 13½x13¼***

**2244** A564 50c multi .60 .60
*a.* Perf. 14 .70 .70
*b.* Booklet pane of 1 #2244a .70 —
**2245** A564 50c multi .60 .60
*a.* Perf. 14 .70 .70
*b.* Booklet pane of 1 #2245a .70 —
**2246** A564 $1 multi 1.25 1.25
*a.* Perf. 14 1.50 1.50
*b.* Booklet pane of 1 #2246a 1.50 —
**2247** A564 $1.50 multi 1.75 1.75
*a.* Perf. 14 2.25 2.25
*b.* Booklet pane of 1 #2247a 2.25 —
**2248** A564 $2 multi 2.40 2.40
*a.* Perf. 14 3.00 3.00
*b.* Booklet pane of 1 #2248a 3.00 —
**2249** A564 $2.50 multi 3.00 3.00
*a.* Perf. 14 3.75 3.75
*b.* Booklet pane of 1 #2249a 3.75 —
*c.* Booklet pane of 6, #2244a, 2245a, 2246a, 2247a, 2248a, 2249a 12.00 —
Complete booklet, #2244b, 2245b, 2246b, 2247b, 2248b, 2249b, 2249c 24.00
*Nos. 2244-2249 (6)* 9.60 9.60

Complete booklet sold for $19.90.

Auckland Harbour Bridge, 50th Anniv.
A565

Various views of bridge with inscription: 50c, Opening Day 1959. $1, Our Bridge 2009. $1.50, Our Icon 1961. $2, Our Link 2009.

**2009, May 1 *Perf. 13½x13¼***

**2250** A565 50c multi .60 .60
**2251** A565 $1 multi 1.25 1.25
**2252** A565 $1.50 multi 1.75 1.75
**2253** A565 $2 multi 2.25 2.25
*Nos. 2250-2253 (4)* 5.85 5.85

**Self-Adhesive**

***Serpentine Die Cut 9½x10***

**2254** A565 50c multi .60 .60

Miniature Sheets

Matariki (Maori New Year) — A566

Nos. 2255 and 2256 — Various heitikis: a, Heitiki in Te Maori Exhibition. b, Heitiki carved by Raponi. c, Corian heitiki carved by Rangi Kipa. d, Female greenstone heitiki. e, Heitiki in Museum of New Zealand. f, Whalebone heitiki carved by Rangi Hetet.

***Perf. 13¼x13½***

**2009, June 24 Litho.**

**2255** A566 Sheet of 6 11.50 11.50
*a.* 50c multi .60 .60
*b.* $1 multi 1.25 1.25
*c.* $1.50 multi 1.90 1.90
*d.* $1.80 multi 2.25 2.25
*e.* $2 multi 2.50 2.50
*f.* $2.30 multi 3.00 3.00

**Self-Adhesive**

***Serpentine Die Cut 10x9½***

**2256** A566 Sheet of 6 11.50 11.50
*a.* 50c multi .60 .60
*b.* $1 multi 1.25 1.25
*c.* $1.50 multi 1.90 1.90
*d.* $1.80 multi 2.25 2.25
*e.* $2 multi 2.50 2.50
*f.* $2.30 multi 3.00 3.00

**Tourist Attractions Type of 2003**

Designs: 30c, Tolaga Bay. $1.80, Russell. $2.30, Lake Wanaka. $2.80, Auckland. $3.30, Rakaia River. $4, Wellington.

**2009, July 1 *Perf. 13¼x13½***

**2257** A496 30c multi .40 .40
**2258** A496 $1.80 multi 2.25 2.25
**2259** A496 $2.30 multi 3.00 3.00
**2260** A496 $2.80 multi 3.50 3.50
**2261** A496 $3.30 multi 4.25 4.25
**2262** A496 $4 multi 5.00 5.00
*Nos. 2257-2262 (6)* 18.40 18.40

**Self-Adhesive**

***Serpentine Die Cut 10x9½***

**2263** A496 $1.80 multi 2.25 2.25
*a.* Booklet pane of 5 11.50

Miniature Sheet

Tiki Tour of New Zealand — A567

No. 2264 — Parts of map of New Zealand and: a, Signpost and lighthouse, Cape Reinga, fisherman and red snapper, Tane Mahuta, quill pen, Stone Store, Kerikeri. b, Bird, boat on Hole in the Rock tour, dolphin. c, White heron, Maori snaring the Sun. d, Bird, airplane, yachts. e, Rangitoto Island volcano, Sky tower, Auckland, L&P Bottle, Paeroa, bird, surf boat, hibiscus, car and trailer. f, Fishing boat and marlin. g, Balloons, Maori canoe, bull playing rugby. h, Balloon, rower, statue of sheep shearer, Te Kuiti, trout, kiwifruit, Maori carving, Rotorua Mud Pools. i, Pohutukawa tree blossom, meeting house, surfer, horse and rider. j, Maui gas rig, Mt. Taranaki, hang glider, Wind Wand sculpture. k, Rubber boot, apple, pear, windmills, Waimarie River cruise boat, highway sign, Viking helmet, giant kiwi. l, Tractor and wagon, gannet, Pania of the Reef, Napier. m, Westport Municipal Building, statue, Greymouth, Pancake Rocks, Punakaiki. n, Mussel, fisherman, grapes, glass blowers and bottle. o, Birds, statue of Richard Seddon, daffodil, windsurfer, Cook Strait ferry, Golden Shears, Masterton, Westpac Stadium, Wellington. p, Mount Cook lily, bulldozer lifting coal, statue of Mackenzie sheep dog, Lake Tekapo. q, Red deer, punt on Avon River, trailer for selling crayfish, French flags, Chalice, sculpture by Neil Dawson, Christchurch. r, Birds, boat, whale, fish. s, Crayfish, black robin, fishing boat. t, Kayakers, skier, mountains, jetboat on Shotover River. u, Kea, biplane, clams, Museum, Oamaru, clock, Alexandra. v, Kakapo, Museum, Invercargill, Burt Munro motorcycle, musician at Country and Western Festival, Gore. w, Moeraki Boulders, Larnach Castle, Dunedin, curler, seal. x, Stewart Island shag, blue cod, Chain sculpture, Oban.

**2009, Aug. 5** ***Perf. 14¼***

**2264** A567 Sheet of 24 + label 16.00 16.00
*a.-x.* 50c Any single .65 .65

Kiwistamps — A568

Designs: No. 2265, Cricket ball, bails and wickets. No. 2266, Kiwi fruit. No. 2267, Highway route sign. No. 2268, Wind turbine and man with broken umbrella. No. 2269, Rotary lawn mower. No. 2270, Trailer. No. 2271, Wall decorations (three birds). No. 2272, Fish and chips. No. 2273, Jacket on barbed-wire fence. No. 2274, Hot dog and barbecue.

***Serpentine Die Cut 9¾x10***

**2009, Sept. 7** **Litho.**

**Self-Adhesive**

**2265** A568 (50c) multi .75 .75
*a.* Serpentine die cut 11x11¼ .75 .75
*b.* As "a," with silver text .75 .75
*c.* Serpentine die cut 10x9¾ .75 .75
*d.* As "c," with silver text .75 .75
**2266** A568 (50c) multi .75 .75
*a.* Serpentine die cut 11x11¼ .75 .75
*b.* As "a," with silver text .75 .75
*c.* Serpentine die cut 10x9¾ .75 .75
*d.* As "c," with silver text .75 .75
**2267** A568 (50c) multi .75 .75
*a.* Serpentine die cut 11x11¼ .75 .75
*b.* As "a," with silver text .75 .75
*c.* Serpentine die cut 10x9¾ .75 .75
*d.* As "c," with silver text .75 .75
**2268** A568 (50c) multi .75 .75
*a.* Serpentine die cut 11x11¼ .75 .75
*b.* As "a," with silver text .75 .75
*c.* Serpentine die cut 10x9¾ .75 .75
*d.* As "c," with silver text .75 .75
**2269** A568 (50c) multi .75 .75
*a.* Serpentine die cut 11x11¼ .75 .75
*b.* As "a," with silver text .75 .75
*c.* Serpentine die cut 10x9¾ .75 .75
*d.* As "c," with silver text .75 .75
**2270** A568 (50c) multi .75 .75
*a.* Serpentine die cut 11x11¼ .75 .75
*b.* As "a," with silver text .75 .75
*c.* Serpentine die cut 10x9¾ .75 .75
*d.* As "c," with silver text .75 .75
**2271** A568 (50c) multi .75 .75
*a.* Serpentine die cut 11x11¼ .75 .75
*b.* As "a," with silver text .75 .75
*c.* Serpentine die cut 10x9¾ .75 .75
*d.* As "c," with silver text .75 .75
**2272** A568 (50c) multi .75 .75
*a.* Serpentine die cut 11x11¼ .75 .75
*b.* As "a," with silver text .75 .75
*c.* Serpentine die cut 10x9¾ .75 .75
*d.* As "c," with silver text .75 .75
**2273** A568 (50c) multi .75 .75
*a.* Serpentine die cut 11x11¼ .75 .75
*b.* As "a," with silver text .75 .75
*c.* Serpentine die cut 10x9¾ .75 .75
*d.* As "c," with silver text .75 .75
**2274** A568 (50c) multi .75 .75
*a.* Serpentine die cut 11x11¼ .75 .75
*b.* As "a," with silver text .75 .75
*c.* Serpentine die cut 10x9¾ .75 .75
*d.* As "c," with silver text .75 .75
*e.* Block of 10, #2265-2274 7.50
*f.* Booklet pane of 10, #2265a-2274a 7.50
*g.* Booklet pane of 10, #2265b-2274b 7.50
*h.* Vert. coil strip of 10, #2265-2274 7.50
*Nos. 2265-2274 (10)* 7.50 7.50

A569

A570

Christmas A571

Designs: Nos. 2275, 2281, Adoration of the Shepherds. No. 2276, Chair and Pohutukawa Tree, by Felix Wang. $1, Holy Family. $1.80, Adoration of the Magi. $2.30, New Zealand Pigeon, by Dannielle Aldworth. $2.80, Child, Gifts and Christmas Tree, by Apurv Bakshi.

**2009, Oct. 7** **Litho.** ***Perf. 14¼***

**2275** A569 50c multi .75 .75
**2276** A570 50c multi .75 .75
**2277** A569 $1 multi 1.50 1.50
**2278** A569 $1.80 multi 2.60 2.60
**2279** A570 $2.30 multi 3.50 3.50
**2280** A570 $2.80 multi 4.00 4.00
*Nos. 2275-2280 (6)* 13.10 13.10

**Self-Adhesive**

***Serpentine Die Cut 10x9½***

**2281** A571 50c multi .75 .75
*a.* Booklet pane of 10 7.50
**2282** A571 $1.80 multi 2.60 2.60
*a.* Booklet pane of 10 26.00
*b.* Horiz. pair, #2281-2282 3.50

No. 2282a sold for $15.

Sir Peter Blake (1948-2001), Yachtsman A572

Photograph of Blake and New Zealand flag with inscription at lower right: 50c, Inspirational leader. $1, Yachtsman. $1.80, Record breaker. $2.30, Passionate Kiwi. $2.80, Environmentalist.

**2009, Nov. 25** ***Perf. 13¼x13½***

**2283** A572 50c multi .75 .75
**2284** A572 $1 multi 1.50 1.50
**2285** A572 $1.80 multi 2.60 2.60
**2286** A572 $2.30 multi 3.25 3.25
**2287** A572 $2.80 multi 4.00 4.00
*a.* Souvenir sheet, #2283-2287 12.50 12.50
*Nos. 2283-2287 (5)* 12.10 12.10

The 2009 sheets contain: #2230, 2225, 2235; #2249, 2243, 2253; #2256f, 2278, 2287. See note following #1404.

New Year 2010 (Year of the Tiger) — A573

Designs: 50c, Chinese character for "tiger." $1, Tiger. $1.80 Tiger's head. $2.30, Bird and Wellington Beehive.

**2010, Jan. 6** ***Perf. 14***

**2288** A573 50c multi .70 .70
*a.* Perf. 13½ .70 .70
**2289** A573 $1 multi 1.40 1.40
*a.* Perf. 13½ 1.40 1.40
**2290** A573 $1.80 multi 2.60 2.60
*a.* Perf. 13½ 2.60 2.60
**2291** A573 $2.30 multi 3.25 3.25
*a.* Perf. 13½ 3.25 3.25
*b.* Souvenir sheet, #2288a-2291a 8.00 8.00
*Nos. 2288-2291 (4)* 7.95 7.95

**Greetings Type of 2006 Redrawn Without Silver Frames**

No. 2292: a, Heitiki. b, Champagne flutes. c, Wedding and engagement rings. d, Pohutukawa flower.

**2010, Feb. 10** **Litho.** ***Perf. 15x14½***

**2292** Sheet of 4 + 2 labels 12.50 12.50
*a.* A531 $1.80 multi 2.60 2.60
*b.-d.* A531 $2.30 Any single 3.25 3.25
*e.* Sheet of 20 #2292a + 20 labels 72.50 72.50
*f.* Sheet of 20 #2292b + 20 labels 85.00 85.00
*g.* Sheet of 20 #2292c + 20 labels 85.00 85.00
*h.* Sheet of 20 #2292d + 20 labels 85.00 85.00

Labels are not personalizable on No. 2292.
No. 2292e sold for $50.90. Nos. 2292f-2292h each sold for $60.90. Labels could ber personalized on Nos. 2292e-2292h.

Prehistoric Animals — A574

Designs: 50c, Allosaurus. $1, Anhanguera. $1.80, Titanosaurus. $2.30, Moanasaurus. $2.80, Mauisaurus.

**2010, Mar. 3** **Litho.** ***Perf. 14¾***

**2293** A574 50c multi .70 .70
**2294** A574 $1 multi 1.40 1.40
**2295** A574 $1.80 multi 2.50 2.50
**2296** A574 $2.30 multi 3.25 3.25
**2297** A574 $2.80 multi 4.00 4.00
*Nos. 2293-2297 (5)* 11.85 11.85

**Self-Adhesive**

***Serpentine Die Cut 10x9¾***

**2298** Sheet of 5 12.00
*a.* A574 50c multi .70 .70
*b.* A574 $1 multi 1.40 1.40
*c.* A574 $1.80 multi 2.50 2.50
*d.* A574 $2.30 multi 3.25 3.25
*e.* A574 $2.80 multi 4.00 4.00

ANZAC Remembrance — A575

Designs: No. 2299, Silhouette of soldier. No. 2300, Gallipoli veterans marching on ANZAC Day, 1958. $1, Posthumous Victoria Cross ceremony for Te Moana-nui-a-Kiwa, 1943. $1.80, Nurses placing wreath in Cairo cemetery on ANZAC Day, 1940. $2.30, Unveiling of ANZAC War Memorial, Port Said, Egypt, 1932. $2.80, Veteran visiting Sangro War Cemetery, Italy, 2004.

**2010, Apr. 7** **Litho.** ***Perf. 13½x13¼***

**2299** A575 50c multi .75 .75
*a.* Perf. 14 .80 .80
*b.* Booklet pane of 1, perf. 14 .80 —
**2300** A575 50c multi .75 .75
*a.* Perf. 14 .80 .80
*b.* Booklet pane of 1, perf. 14 .80 —
**2301** A575 $1 multi 1.50 1.50
*a.* Perf. 14 1.60 1.60
*b.* Booklet pane of 1, perf. 14 1.60 —
**2302** A575 $1.80 multi 2.60 2.60
*a.* Perf. 14 3.00 3.00
*b.* Booklet pane of 1, perf. 14 3.00 —
**2303** A575 $2.30 multi 3.25 3.25
*a.* Perf. 14 3.75 3.75
*b.* Booklet pane of 1, perf. 14 3.75 —
**2304** A575 $2.80 multi 4.00 4.00
*a.* Perf. 14 4.50 4.50
*b.* Booklet pane of 1, perf. 14 4.50 —
*c.* Booklet pane of 6, #2299a-2304a 14.50 —
Complete booklet, #2299b-2304b, 2304c 29.00
*d.* Souvenir sheet of 3, #2299a, 2303a, 2304a 9.25 9.25
*Nos. 2299-2304 (6)* 12.85 12.85

Complete booklet sold for $19.90.
Issued: No. 2304d, 4/30. London 2010 Festival of Stamps (No. 2304d).

Expo 2010, Shanghai — A576

Designs: 50c, Pohutukawas and peonies. $1, Kaitiaki and Fu Dog. $1.80, Tane and Pan Gu. $2.30, Auckland and Shanghai. $2.80, Heitiki and Cong.

**2010, Apr. 30** **Litho.** ***Perf. 14***

**2305** A576 50c multi .75 .75
**2306** A576 $1 multi 1.50 1.50
**2307** A576 $1.80 multi 2.60 2.60
**2308** A576 $2.30 multi 3.50 3.50
**2309** A576 $2.80 multi 4.25 4.25
*a.* Horiz. strip of 5, #2305-2309 13.00 13.00
*b.* Sheet of 5, #2305-2309, without back printing 13.00 13.00
*Nos. 2305-2309 (5)* 12.60 12.60

Maori Rugby, Cent. — A577

Designs: 50c, Centenary jersey. $1.80, Centenary emblem.

**2010, June 9**

**2310** A577 50c multi .70 .70
**2311** A577 $1.80 multi 2.50 2.50
*a.* Souvenir sheet of 2, #2310-2311 3.25 3.25

Traditional Maori Kites A578

Designs: 50c, Manu Aute. $1, Manu Patiki, vert. $1.80, Manu Taratahi, vert. $2.30, Upoko Tangata.

**2010, June 9**

**2312** A578 50c multi .70 .70
**2313** A578 $1 multi 1.40 1.40
**2314** A578 $1.80 multi 2.50 2.50
**2315** A578 $2.30 multi 3.25 3.25
*a.* Souvenir sheet of 4, #2312-2315 8.00 8.00
*Nos. 2312-2315 (4)* 7.85 7.85

**Tourist Attractions Type of 2003**

Designs: $1.20, Mitre Peak, Milford Sound. $1.90, Queenstown. $2.40, Lake Rotorua. $2.90, Kaikoura. $3.40, Christchurch.

**2010, Aug. 4** ***Perf. 13¼x13½***

**2316** A496 $1.20 multi 1.75 1.75
**2317** A496 $1.90 multi 2.75 2.75
**2318** A496 $2.40 multi 3.50 3.50
*a.* Souvenir sheet of 3, #2316-2318 8.50 8.50

**2319** A496 $2.90 multi 4.25 4.25
**2320** A496 $3.40 multi 5.00 5.00
*a.* Souvenir sheet of 2, #2319-2320 9.00 9.00
*Nos. 2316-2320 (5)* 17.25 17.25

### Self-Adhesive

***Serpentine Die Cut 10x9½***

**2321** A496 $1.20 multi 1.75 1.75
*a.* Booklet pane of 10 17.50
**2322** A496 $1.90 multi 2.75 2.75
*a.* Booklet pane of 5 14.00

Issued: No. 2318a, 2/12/11. Indipex 2011 (#2318a). Christchurch 2016 Stamp & Postcard Exhibition (No. 2320a). Issued: No. 2320a, 11/18/16. No. 2320a contains a lithographed perf. 14½ reproduction of No. 321 that is not valid for postage.

Emblem of All Blacks Rugby Team A579

**2010, Aug. 4** ***Perf. 13½x13¼***

**2323** A579 60c black .90 .90
**2324** A579 $1.90 black 2.75 2.75
*a.* Miniature sheet of 6 60.00 60.00

### Souvenir Sheet

**2325** Sheet of 4, #2323, 2324, 2325a, 2325b 7.50 7.50
*a.* A579 60c black, 32x17mm, perf. 15x14½ .90 .90
*b.* A579 $1.90 black, 32x17mm, perf. 15x14½ .90 .90
*c.* Sheet of 20 #2325a + 20 labels 34.00 34.00
*d.* Sheet of 20 #2325b + 20 labels 77.50 77.50

2011 Rugby World Cup victory of New Zealand rugby team (No. 2324a). Issued: No. 2324a, 10/28/11. No. 2324a sold for $19.90.

No. 2325c sold for $22.90. No. 2325d sold for $52.90. Labels could be personalized on Nos. 2325c-2325d. In 2011, No. 2325c was made available for the same price with labels that could not be personalized.

See Nos. 2410-2411, 2519-2521.

### Greetings Stamps Type of 2006 Without Silver Frames

No. 2326: a, Champagne flutes. b, Child's toy. c, Fern. d, Pohutukawa flower. e, Wedding and engagement rings. f, Rose. g, Heitiki. h, Teddy bear.

No. 2327: a, Heitiki. b, Champagne flutes. c, Wedding and engagement rings. d, Pohutukawa flower.

**2010, Sept. 9** ***Perf. 15x14½***

**2326** A531 Sheet of 8 + 4 labels 7.25 7.25
*a.-h.* 60c Any single .90 .90
*i.* Sheet of 20 #2326a + 20 labels 34.00 34.00
*j.* Sheet of 20 #2326b + 20 labels 34.00 34.00
*k.* Sheet of 20 #2326c + 20 labels 34.00 34.00
*l.* Sheet of 20 #2326d + 20 labels 34.00 34.00
*m.* Sheet of 20 #2326e + 20 labels 34.00 34.00
*n.* Sheet of 20 #2326f + 20 labels 34.00 34.00
*o.* Sheet of 20 #2326g + 20 labels 34.00 34.00
*p.* Sheet of 20 #2326h + 20 labels 34.00 34.00
**2327** A531 Sheet of 4 + 2 labels 13.50 13.50
*a.* $1.90 multi 2.75 2.75
*b.-d.* $2.40 Any single 3.50 3.50
*e.* Sheet of 20 #2327a + 20 labels 77.50 77.50
*f.* Sheet of 20 #2327b + 20 labels 92.50 92.50
*g.* Sheet of 20 #2327c + 20 labels 92.50 92.50
*h.* Sheet of 20 #2327d + 20 labels 92.50 92.50

Nos. 2326i-2326p each sold for $22.90. No. 2327e sold for $52.90. Nos. 2327f-2327h each sold for $62.90. Labels could be personalized on Nos. 2326i-2326p, 2327e-2327h.

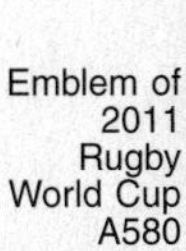

60c
IRB
RUGBY
WORLD CUP
2011
NEW ZEALAND


Emblem of 2011 Rugby World Cup A580

**2010, Sept. 9** ***Perf. 13½x13¼***

**2328** A580 60c multi .90 .90
**2329** A580 $1.90 multi 2.75 2.75

### Souvenir Sheet

**2330** Sheet of 4, #2328, 2329, 2330a, 2330b 7.50 7.50
*a.* A580 60c multi, 32x17mm, perf. 15x14½ .90 .90
*b.* A580 $1.90 multi, 32x17mm, perf. 15x14½ .90 .90
*c.* Sheet of 20 #2330a + 20 labels 34.00 34.00
*d.* Sheet of 20 #2330b + 20 labels 77.50 77.50

No. 2330c sold for $22.90. No. 2330d sold for $52.90. Labels could be personalized on Nos. 2330c-2330d. In 2011, No. 2330c was made available for the same price with labels that could not be personalized.

Miniature Sheet

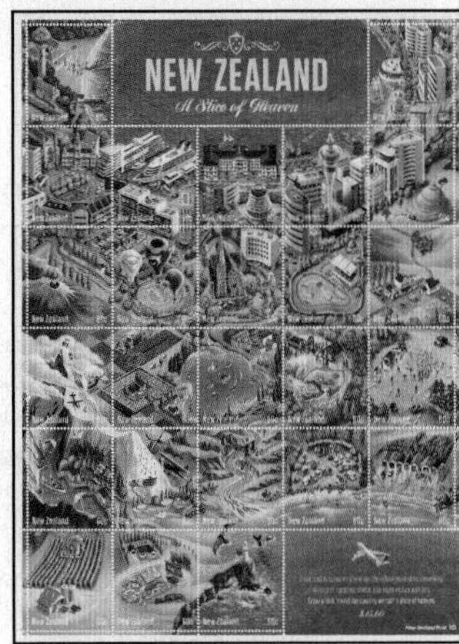


"A Slice of Heaven" — A581

No. 2331: a, Tane Mahuta kauri tree, Stone Store, Kerikeri, Waitangi Treaty Grounds, boat at dock. b, Carter Fountain, Oriental Bay, buildings. c, The Octagon, St. Paul's Cathedral, Dunedin. d, Cruise ship, Princes Wharf, Auckland. e, The Beehive, Wellington. f, Sky Tower, Auckland Ferry Terminal. g, Obelisk on grave of Sir John Logan Campbell on One Tree Hill, cable car, buildings. h, Mount Ruapehu (volcano), punts on Avon River, Christchurch. i, Fairfield Bridge, hot-air balloons over Basin Reserve Cricket Grounds, Wellington. j, Christchurch Cathedral, Bridge of Remembrance. k, Horse racing track. l, Road, small town, war memorial, sheep in field. m, Mountain climbers with flag on Mt. Cook, ski plane, helicopter. n, Farm house, storage shed, plowed field, cows in pasture, shore of Lake Taupo. o, Lake Taupo, Huka Falls. p, Champagne Pool, geyser, mud pool. q, Rugby field. r, TSS Earnslaw on Lake Wakatipu, parasailers, Queenstown. s, Biplane and glider over ski and golf resort. t, Suspension bridge over river, river mouth. u, Trailer park near beach, Moeraki Boulders. v, Line of boatsheds, Tihati Bay. w, Farmhouse, barn, tractor, silos. x, House, sheep pens, truck. y, Nugget Point Lighthouse, whale.

**2010, Oct. 6** ***Perf. 14¼***

**2331** A581 Sheet of 25 22.50 22.50
*a.-y.* 60c Any single .90 .90

Christmas A582

New Zealand Christmas stamps of the past: 60c, #353. $1.20, #465. $1.90, #692. $2.40, #790. $2.90, #1672.

**2010, Oct. 20** ***Perf. 13¼x13½***

### Stamps Without White Frames

**2332** A582 60c multi .95 .95
**2333** A582 $1.20 multi 1.90 1.90
**2334** A582 $1.90 multi 3.00 3.00
**2335** A582 $2.40 multi 4.00 4.00
**2336** A582 $2.90 multi 4.75 4.75
*Nos. 2332-2336 (5)* 14.60 14.60

### Stamps With White Frames

### Coil Stamps

### Self-Adhesive

### Size: 21x26mm

***Die Cut Perf. 12¾***

**2337** A582 60c multi .95 .95
**2338** A582 $1.90 multi 3.00 3.00
*a.* Horiz. pair, #2337-2338 4.00

### Booklet Stamps

***Serpentine Die Cut 11¼***

**2339** A582 60c multi .95 .95
*a.* Booklet pane of 10 9.50
**2340** A582 $1.90 multi 3.00 3.00
*a.* Booklet pane of 10 30.00
*Nos. 2337-2340 (4)* 7.90 7.90

New Zealand Christmas stamps, 50th anniv. No. 2339a sold for $5.40 and No. 2340a sold for $16.

Volunteer Lifeguard Clubs, Cent. A583

Designs: 60c, Surf lifeguard and beach flag. $1.20, Lifeguards on inflatable rescue boat. $1.90, Lifeguards on ski paddlers. $2.40, Lifeguards on surf boat. $2.90, Lifeguards marching on beach.

**2010, Nov. 3** ***Perf. 13x13¼***

**2341** A583 60c multi .95 .95
**2342** A583 $1.20 multi 1.90 1.90
**2343** A583 $1.90 multi 3.00 3.00
**2344** A583 $2.40 multi 4.00 4.00
**2345** A583 $2.90 multi 4.75 4.75
*Nos. 2341-2345 (5)* 14.60 14.60

The 2010 sheets contain: #2291, 2297, 2304; #2309, 2315, B198; #2319, 2336, 2345. See note following #1404.

New Year 2011 (Year of the Rabbit) — A584

Designs: 60c, Chinese character for "rabbit." $1.20, Paper-cut rabbit. $1.90, Rabbit. $2.40, Kite, Christchurch Cathedral.

**2011, Jan. 12 Litho.** ***Perf. 13½x13***

**2346** A584 60c multi .95 .95
**2347** A584 $1.20 multi 1.90 1.90
**2348** A584 $1.90 multi 3.00 3.00
**2349** A584 $2.40 multi 3.75 3.75
*a.* Souvenir sheet, #2346-2349 9.75 9.75
*Nos. 2346-2349 (4)* 9.60 9.60

Miniature Sheets

Kapa Haka — A585

Nos. 2350 and 2351: a, Whakaeke. b, Poi. c, Waiata-a-ringa. d, Haka. e, Whakawatea. f, Moteatea.

**2011, Feb. 17** ***Perf. 13¼x13½***

**2350** A585 Sheet of 6 15.00 15.00
*a.-b.* 60c Either single .90 .90
*c.* $1.20 multi 1.90 1.90
*d.* $1.90 multi 3.00 3.00
*e.* $2.40 multi 3.75 3.75
*f.* $2.90 multi 4.50 4.50

### Self-Adhesive

***Serpentine Die Cut 10x9½***

**2351** A585 Sheet of 6 15.00 15.00
*a.-b.* 60c Either single .90 .90
*c.* $1.20 multi 1.90 1.90
*d.* $1.90 multi 3.00 3.00
*e.* $2.40 multi 3.75 3.75
*f.* $2.90 multi 4.50 4.50

Kiwistamps A586

Designs: Nos. 2352, 2357, Hokey pokey ice cream cone. Nos. 2353, 2358, Kiwi crossing road sign. Nos. 2354, 2359, People on beach. Nos. 2355, 2360, Trout fisherman. Nos. 2356, 2361, Mountain biking.

***Serpentine Die Cut 10x9¾***

**2011, Mar. 23** **Litho.**

### Self-Adhesive

### Coil Stamps

**2352** A586 (60c) multi .95 .95
**2353** A586 (60c) multi .95 .95
**2354** A586 (60c) multi .95 .95
**2355** A586 (60c) multi .95 .95
**2356** A586 (60c) multi .95 .95
*a.* Horiz. strip of 5, #2352-2356 4.75
*Nos. 2352-2356 (5)* 4.75 4.75

### Booklet Stamps

***Serpentine Die Cut 11***

**2357** A586 (60c) multi .95 .95
**2358** A586 (60c) multi .95 .95
**2359** A586 (60c) multi .95 .95
**2360** A586 (60c) multi .95 .95
**2361** A586 (60c) multi .95 .95
*a.* Booklet pane of 10, 2 each #2357-2361 9.50
*Nos. 2357-2361 (5)* 4.75 4.75



Wedding of Prince William and Catherine Middleton A587

Prince William and Catherine Middleton with Prince William wearing: No. 2362, Suit and tie. No. 2363, Sweater.

**2011, Mar. 23** ***Perf. 14½x14¾***

**2362** A587 $2.40 multi 3.75 3.75
**2363** A587 $2.40 multi 3.75 3.75
*a.* Horiz. pair, #2362-2363 7.50 7.50
*b.* Souvenir sheet of 2, #2362-2363 7.50 7.50

New Zealand's Victoria Cross Recipients A588

No. 2364: a, Charles Heaphy. b, William James Hardham. c, Cyril Royston Guyton Bassett. d, Donald Forrester Brown. e, Samuel Frickleton. f, Leslie Wilton Andrew. g, Henry James Nicholas. h, Richard Charles Travis. i, Samuel Forsyth. j, Reginald Stanley Judson. k, Harry John Laurent. l, James Crichton. m, John Gildroy Grant. n, James Edward Allen Ward. o, Charles Hazlitt Upham. p, Alfred Clive Hulme. q, John Daniel Hinton. r, Keith Elliott.s, Moana-nui-a-Kiwa Ngarimu. t, Lloyd Allen Trigg. u, Leonard Henry Trent. v, Bill Henry Apiata (medal only).

**2011, Apr. 14** ***Perf. 13¼x13½***

**2364** Miniature sheet of 22 22.00 22.00
*a.-v.* A588 60c Any single 1.00 1.00

Miniature Sheet

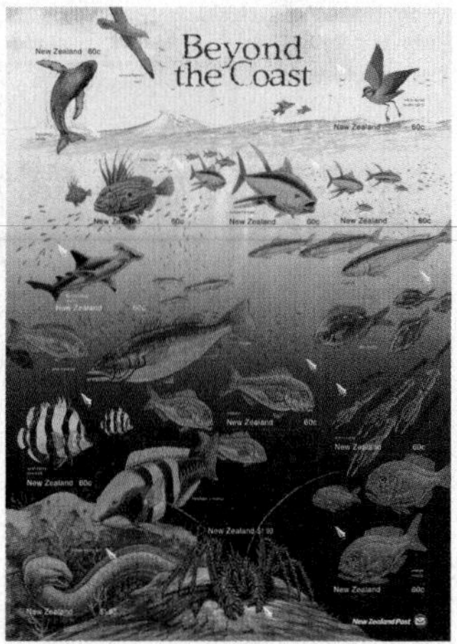


Life Beyond the Coast — A589

No. 2365: a, Humpback whale. b, White-faced storm petrel, horiz. c, John Dory, horiz. d, Yellowfin tuna, horiz. e, Kingfish, horiz. f, Hammerhead shark, horiz. g, Snapper, horiz. h, Arrow squid, horiz. i, Lord Howe coralfish. j, Orange roughy, horiz. k, Yellow moray eel, horiz. l, King crab.

***Serpentine Die Cut 10x9½, 9½x10***

**2011, May 4 Self-Adhesive**

**2365** A589 Sheet of 12 15.50
*a.-j.* 60c Any single .95 .95
*k.-l.* $1.90 Either single 3.00 3.00

Miniature Sheet

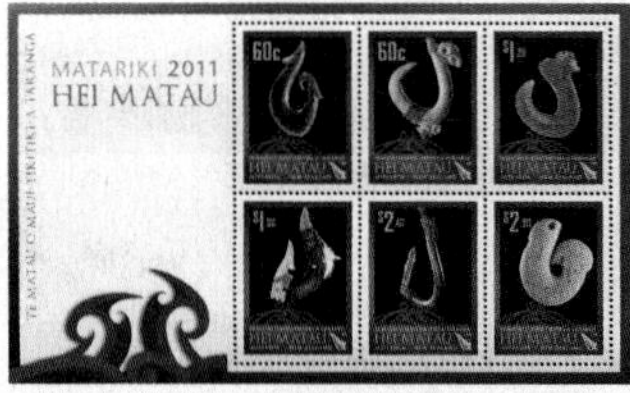


Matariki (Maori New Year) — A590

Nos. 2366 and 2367 — Various hei mataus (decorative fish hooks): a, Green pounamu fish hook by Lewis Gardiner. b, White whalebone fish hook, c. 1500-1800, in Museum of New Zealand. c, Inanga fish hook, c. 1800, in Museum of New Zealand. d, Pounamu, whalebone, feathers and flax fiber fish hook by Gardiner. e, Wooden fish hook, c. 1800, in Auckland War Memorial Museum. f, Whalebone fish hook, c. 1750-1850, in Museum of New Zealand.

**2011, June 1 Litho. *Perf. 13¼x13½***

**2366** A590 Sheet of 6 16.00 16.00
*a.-b.* 60c Either single 1.00 1.00
*c.* $1.20 multi 2.00 2.00
*d.* $1.90 multi 3.25 3.25
*e.* $2.40 multi 4.00 4.00
*f.* $2.90 multi 4.75 4.75

**Self-Adhesive**

***Serpentine Die Cut 10x9½***

**2367** A590 Sheet of 6 16.00 16.00
*a.-b.* 60c Either single 1.00 1.00
*c.* $1.20 multi 2.00 2.00
*d.* $1.90 multi 3.25 3.25
*e.* $2.40 multi 4.00 4.00
*f.* $2.90 multi 4.75 4.75

**Kiwi Type of 1988**

**2011 Litho. *Perf. 14½***

**2368** A325 $1.20 black 2.00 2.00
**2369** A325 $1.90 silver 3.25 3.25
*a.* Souvenir sheet, #2369, 2 #2324 9.75 9.75
**2370** A325 $2.40 blue 4.00 4.00
*a.* Horiz. strip of 3, #2368-2370 9.25 9.25
*b.* Souvenir sheet of 3, #2368-2370 8.75 8.75
*Nos. 2368-2370 (3)* 9.25 9.25

Issued: Nos. 2368-2370, 7/6; No. 2369a, 7/28. No. 2370b, 11/11. Philanippon 2011 World Stamp Exhibition, Yokohama (#2369a). China 2011 Intl. Stamp Exhibition, Wuxi, China (#2370b).

Values for Nos. 2368-2370 are for stamps with surrounding selvage.

Miniature Sheet

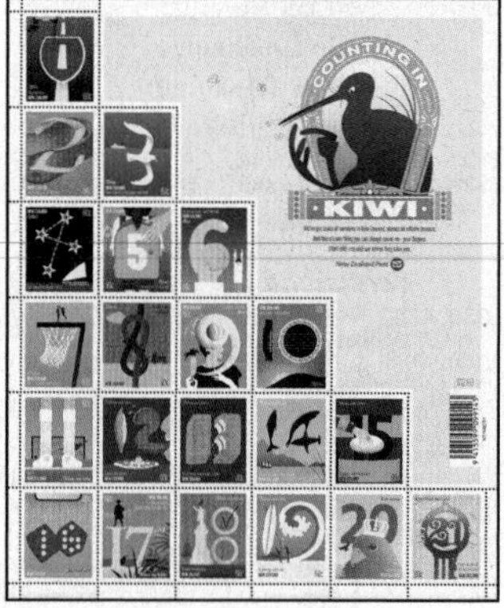


Numbers — A591

No. 2371 — Maori words for numbers and stylized numbers: a, 1 (State Highway 1 sign). b, 2 (2 beach sandals). c, 3 (sea gull, Cook Strait ferry). d, 4 (stars in Southern Cross, sailboat) e, 5 (child with backpack). f, 6 (hand, cricket umpire). g, 7 (netball goal and players). h, 8 (barbed wire, tractor). i, 9 (woman in fancy clothes, race horse). j, 10 (guitar). k, 11 (legs of soccer player). l, 12 (oyster shell, tongue, plate of oysters). m, 13 (Lamington cakes). n, 14 (dolphins, outrigger canoes in national parks). o, 15 (hand on rugby ball). p, 16 (dice hanging from rear-view mirror). q, 17 (Capt. James Cook and year of his arrival in New Zealand). r, 18 (bird on statue, ballot circles, Parliament building). s, 19 (surf board and wave). t, 20 (parrot with crown). u, 21 (key and streamers).

**2011, Aug. 10 *Perf. 14***

**2371** A591 Sheet of 21 21.00 21.00
*a.-u.* 60c Any single 1.00 1.00

Webb Ellis Cup, Trophy of Rugby World Cup A592

**Litho. With 3-Dimensional Plastic Affixed**

***Serpentine Die Cut 10¼***

**2011, Sept. 7 Self-Adhesive**

**2372** A592 $15 multi 25.00 25.00

The New Zealand Experience A593

Designs: No. 2373, Backpacker, paraglider, camp, hikers, mountains. No. 2374, Sailboaters, motor boat, sailboarder. $1.20, Fisherman and fish. $1.90, Maoris. $2.40, Skier, helicopter. $2.90, Bungee jumper, whitewater raft, hot air balloon.

**2011, Sept. 7 Litho. *Perf. 14***

**2373** A593 60c multi .95 .95
**2374** A593 60c multi .95 .95
**2375** A593 $1.20 multi 1.90 1.90
**2376** A593 $1.90 multi 3.00 3.00
**2377** A593 $2.40 multi 3.75 3.75
**2378** A593 $2.90 multi 4.50 4.50
*a.* Souvenir sheet of 6, #2373-2378 15.50 15.50
*Nos. 2373-2378 (6)* 15.05 15.05

A594

Christmas — A595

Star of Bethlehem and: 60c, Baby Jesus and livestock. $1.20, Angel appearing to shepherds. $1.90, Holy Family. $2.40, Adoration of the Shepherds. $2.90, Adoration of the Magi.

**2011, Nov. 2 Litho. *Perf. 14¼***

**2379** A594 60c multi .95 .95
**2380** A594 $1.20 multi 1.90 1.90
**2381** A594 $1.90 multi 3.00 3.00
**2382** A594 $2.40 multi 4.00 4.00
**2383** A594 $2.90 multi 4.75 4.75
*Nos. 2379-2383 (5)* 14.60 14.60

**Self-Adhesive**

***Serpentine Die Cut 9¾x10***

**2384** A595 60c multi .95 .95
**2385** A595 $1.90 multi 3.00 3.00
*a.* Booklet pane of 10 30.00
**2386** A595 $2.40 multi 4.00 4.00
*a.* Horiz. sheet of 3, #2384-2386 8.00
*b.* Booklet pane of 10 40.00

**Booklet Stamp**

***Serpentine Die Cut 11¼***

**2387** A595 60c multi .95 .95
*a.* Booklet pane of 10 9.50
*Nos. 2384-2387 (4)* 8.90 8.90

Nos. 2385a and 2386b sold for $17.10 and $21.60, respectively. A se-tenant strip of Nos. 2379-2383 was not put on sale but was a reward for standing order customers.

The 2011 sheets contain: #2349, 2362, 2350f; #2364v, B202, 2366f; #2378, 2370, 2383. See note following #1404.

New Year 2012 (Year of the Dragon) — A596

Designs: 60c, Chinese character for "dragon." $1.20, Dragon. $1.90, Dragon lantern. $2.40, Dunedin Railroad Station, swallows.

**2012, Jan. 5 Litho. *Perf. 13¼x13½***

**2388** A596 60c multi 1.00 1.00
**2389** A596 $1.20 multi 2.00 2.00
**2390** A596 $1.90 multi 3.25 3.25
**2391** A596 $2.40 multi 4.00 4.00
*a.* Souvenir sheet of 4, #2388-2391 10.50 10.50
*b.* Souvenir sheet of 3, #2388, 2390, 2391 8.25 8.25
*Nos. 2388-2391 (4)* 10.25 10.25

Issued: No. 2391b, 11/2. 2012 Beijing Intl. Stamp and Coin Expo (#2391b).

**Tourist Attractions Type of 2003**

***Serpentine Die Cut 10x9½***

**2012, Feb. 1 Litho.**

**Self-Adhesive**

**2392** A496 $2.40 Lake Rotorua 4.00 4.00
*a.* Booklet pane of 5 + 2 etiquettes 20.00
*2392b* Dated "2010" 3.25 3.25
*2392c* Booklet pane of 5 #2392b + 2 etiquettes 16.50

Issued: Nos. 2392b, 2392c, 2015.

Native Trees — A597

Designs: 60c, Pohutukawa. $1.20, Cabbage tree. $1.90, Kowhai. $2.40, Nikau. $2.90, Manuka.

**2012, Feb. 1 *Perf. 13¼x13½***

**2393** A597 60c multi 1.00 1.00
**2394** A597 $1.20 multi 2.00 2.00
**2395** A597 $1.90 multi 3.25 3.25
**2396** A597 $2.40 multi 4.00 4.00
*a.* Souvenir sheet of 3, #2393, 2395, 2396 8.25 8.25
**2397** A597 $2.90 multi 5.00 5.00
*a.* Souvenir sheet of 5, #2393-2397 15.50 15.50
*Nos. 2393-2397 (5)* 15.25 15.25

Issued: No. 2396a, 6/18. Indonesia 2012 World Stamp Championship and Exhibition, Jakarta (#2396a).

Miniature Sheet

Royal New Zealand Air Force, 75th Anniv. — A598

No. 2398 — Inscriptions: a, The Beginning. b, Air Training corps. c, WWII Europe. d, Women's Auxiliary Air Force. e, WWII Pacific. f, Aerial Topdressing. g, Territorial Air Force. h, Sout East Asia. i, ANZAC. j, Naval Support. k, Transport. l, Peacekeeping. m, Search and Rescue. n, Remembrance. o, The Future.

**2012, Mar. 15 *Perf. 14½***

**2398** A598 Sheet of 15 15.00 15.00
*a.-o.* 60c Any single 1.00 1.00
*p.* Booklet pane of 4, 2 each #2398a-2398b 4.50 —
*q.* Booklet pane of 4, 2 each #2398c-2398d 4.50 —
*r.* Booklet pane of 4, 2 each #2398e-2398f 4.50 —
*s.* Booklet pane of 4, 2 each #2398g-2398h 4.50 —
*t.* Booklet pane of 4, 2 each #2398i-2398j 4.50 —
*u.* Booklet pane of 4, 2 each #2398k-2398l 4.50 —
*v.* Booklet pane of 4, 2 each #2398m, 2398o 4.50 —
*w.* Booklet pane of 2 #2398n 2.25 —
Complete booklet, #2398p-2398w 34.00

Complete booklet sold for $19.90.

Reign of Queen Elizabeth II, 60th Anniv. — A599

Photographs of: No. 2399, Queen, 2012. No. 2400, Queen and Prince Philip, 2012. $1.40, Queen and Prince Philip, 1986. $1.90, Queen and Prince Philip, 1981. $2.40, Queen and Prince Philip, 1977. $2.90, Queen, 1953.

**Litho. With Foil Application**

**2012, May 9** *Perf. 13¼x13½*

**2399** A599 70c multi 1.10 1.10
**2400** A599 70c multi 1.10 1.10
**2401** A599 $1.40 multi 2.25 2.25
**2402** A599 $1.90 multi 3.00 3.00
**2403** A599 $2.40 multi 3.75 3.75
**2404** A599 $2.90 multi 4.50 4.50
*a.* Souvenir sheet of 6, #2399-2404 16.00 16.00
*b.* Souvenir sheet of 3, #2399, 2402, 2404 9.25 9.25
*Nos. 2399-2404 (6)* 15.70 15.70

Issued: No. 2404b, 10/12. 2012 New Zealand National Stamp Exhibition, Blenheim (#2404b).

**Tourist Attractions Type of 2003**

Designs: $1.40, Cape Reinga Lighthouse. $2.10, Stewart Island. $3.50, Lake Matheson.

**2012, May 23 Litho.** *Perf. 13¼x13½*

**2405** A496 $1.40 multi 2.25 2.25
**2406** A496 $2.10 multi 3.25 3.25
**2407** A496 $3.50 multi 5.50 5.50
*Nos. 2405-2407 (3)* 11.00 11.00

**Self-Adhesive**

***Serpentine Die Cut 10x9½***

**2408** A496 $1.40 multi 2.25 2.25
*a.* Booklet pane of 10 22.50
**2409** A496 $2.10 multi 3.25 3.25
*a.* Booklet pane of 5 16.50
*b.* Horiz. pair, #2408-2409 5.50

**All Blacks Type of 2010**

**2012, May 23** *Perf. 13½x13¼*

**2410** A579 70c black 1.10 1.10

**Souvenir Sheet**

**2411** Sheet of 2, #2410, 2411a 2.25 2.25
*a.* A579 70c black, 32x17mm, perf. 15x14½ 1.10 1.10

**Greetings Stamps Type of 2006 Without Silver Frames**

No. 2412: a, Champagne flutes. b, Child's toy. c, Fern. d, Pohutukawa flower. e, Wedding and engagement rings. f, Rose. g, Heitiki. h, Tedddy bear.

**2012, June 6** *Perf. 15x14½*

**2412** A531 Sheet of 8 + 4 labels 9.00 9.00
*a.-h.* 70c Any single 1.10 1.10

Miniature Sheets

Maori Rock Art — A600

Nos. 2413 and 2414: a, Pouakai, Pareora. b, Tiki, Maerewhenua. c, Mohiki, Opihi. d, Te Puawaitanga, Waitaki. e, Tiki, Te Ana a Wai. f, Taniwha, Opihi.

**2012, June 6** *Perf. 13½x13¼*

**2413** A600 Sheet of 6 16.00 16.00
*a.-b.* 70c Either single 1.10 1.10
*c.* $1.40 multi 2.25 2.25
*d.* $1.90 multi 3.00 3.00
*e.* $2.40 multi 3.75 3.75
*f.* $2.90 multi 4.50 4.50

**Self-Adhesive**

***Serpentine Die Cut 9½x10***

**2414** A600 Sheet of 6 16.00 16.00
*a.-b.* 70c Either single 1.10 1.10
*c.* $1.40 multi 2.25 2.25
*d.* $1.90 multi 3.00 3.00
*e.* $2.40 multi 3.75 3.75
*f.* $2.90 multi 4.50 4.50

Miniature Sheet

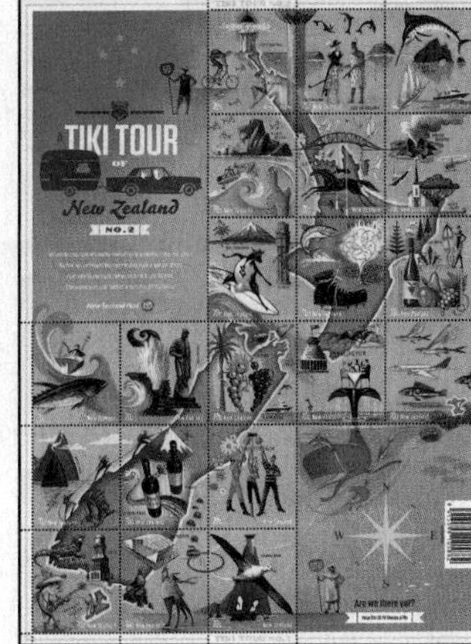


Tiki Tour of New Zealand — A601

No. 2415 — Places named on map of New Zealand: a, Cape Reinga, Ninety Mile Beach, Kaitaia. b, Whangarei, Bay of Islands. c, Cape Brett. d, Lion Rock. e, Auckland, Hamilton, Tauranga. f, White Island, East Cape. g, Mt. Taranaki, New Plymouth, Hawera. h, Rotorua, Taupo, Palmerston North. i, Gisborne, Napier. j, No place names (fish, boat, waves). k, Westport, Greymouth. l, Golden Bay, Nelson, Cook Strait, Kaikoura. m, Wellington, Castlepoint. n, Chatham Islands. o, Mitre Peak, Milford Sound. p, Queenstown, Aoraki (Mount Cook), Timaru. q, Christchurch, Ashburton. r, Gore, Invercargill, Foveaux Strait, Stewart Island. s, Dunedin. t, Taiaroa Head.

**2012, July 4** *Perf. 14¼*

**2415** A601 Sheet of 20 22.00 22.00
*a.-t.* 70c Any single 1.10 1.10

Samoan Head Combs — A602

Designs: 70c, Fu'a. $1.40, Niu. $1.90, Maota. $2.40, Tatau. $2.90, Malumalu.

**2012, Aug. 1** *Perf. 14*

**2416** A602 70c multi 1.25 1.25
**2417** A602 $1.40 multi 2.40 2.40
**2418** A602 $1.90 multi 3.25 3.25
**2419** A602 $2.40 multi 4.00 4.00
**2420** A602 $2.90 multi 4.75 4.75
*a.* Souvenir sheet of 5, #2416-2420 16.00 16.00
*Nos. 2416-2420 (5)* 15.65 15.65

Ships A603

Designs: 70c, Aramoana. $1.40, Waka. $1.90, Earnslaw. $2.40, Dunedin. $2.90, Rotomahana.

**2012, Sept. 5**

**2421** A603 70c multi 1.25 1.25
**2422** A603 $1.40 multi 2.25 2.25
**2423** A603 $1.90 multi 3.25 3.25
**2424** A603 $2.40 multi 4.00 4.00
**2425** A603 $2.90 multi 4.75 4.75
*a.* Souvenir sheet of 5, #2421-2425 15.50 15.50
*Nos. 2421-2425 (5)* 15.50 15.50

A604

Christmas — A605

Designs: 70c, Holy Family. $1.40, Adoration of the Shepherds. $1.90, Angel. $2.40 Adoration of the Magi. $2.90, Magi and camels.

**2012, Oct. 3** *Perf. 14*

**2426** A604 70c multi 1.25 1.25
**2427** A604 $1.40 multi 2.25 2.25
**2428** A604 $1.90 multi 3.25 3.25
**2429** A604 $2.40 multi 4.00 4.00
**2430** A604 $2.90 multi 4.75 4.75
*Nos. 2426-2430 (5)* 15.50 15.50

**Self-Adhesive**

***Serpentine Die Cut 11x11¼***

**2431** A605 70c multi 1.25 1.25
*a.* Booklet pane of 10 12.50
**2432** A605 $1.90 multi 3.25 3.25
*a.* Booklet pane of 10 + 10 etiquettes 32.50
**2433** A605 $2.40 multi 4.00 4.00
*a.* Booklet pane of 10 + 10 etiquettes 40.00
*b.* Horiz. sheet of 3, #2431-2433 8.50
*Nos. 2431-2433 (3)* 8.50 8.50

Nos. 2432 and 2433 are air mail. No. 2432a sold for $17.10. No. 2433a sold for $21.60.

Premiere of Movie *The Hobbit: An Unexpected Journey*

A606 A607

Characters: 70c, Bilbo Baggins. $1.40, Gollum. $1.90, Gandalf, horiz. $2.10, Thorin Oakenshield, horiz. $2.40, Radagast. $2.90, Elrond.

**2012, Nov. 1** *Perf. 14½x14, 14x14½*

**2434** A606 70c multi 1.25 1.25
*a.* Souvenir sheet of 1 1.50 1.50
**2435** A606 $1.40 multi 2.40 2.40
*a.* Souvenir sheet of 1 3.00 3.00
**2436** A606 $1.90 multi 3.25 3.25
*a.* Souvenir sheet of 1 4.00 4.00
**2437** A606 $2.10 multi 3.50 3.50
*a.* Souvenir sheet of 1 4.50 4.50
**2438** A606 $2.40 multi 4.00 4.00
*a.* Souvenir sheet of 1 5.00 5.00
**2439** A606 $2.90 multi 4.75 4.75
*a.* Souvenir sheet of 1 6.25 6.25
*Nos. 2434-2439 (6)* 19.15 19.15

**Self-Adhesive**

***Serpentine Die Cut 11¼***

**2440** Sheet of 6 19.50
*a.* A607 70c multi 1.25 1.25
*b.* A607 $1.40 multi 2.40 2.40
*c.* A607 $1.90 multi 3.25 3.25
*d.* A607 $2.10 multi 3.50 3.50
*e.* A607 $2.40 multi 4.00 4.00
*f.* A607 $2.90 multi 4.75 4.75
*g.* Booklet pane of 10, #2440c-2440f, 4 #2440a, 2 #2440b 25.50

Nos. 2434a-2439a sold as a set of 6 sheets for $14.40.

New Year 2013 (Year of the Snake) — A608

Designs: 70c, Chinese character for "snake." $1.40, Snake. $1.90, Snake on lantern. $2.40, Lanterns and Skyline Gondola, Queenstown.

**2013, Jan. 9** *Perf. 13¼x13*

**2441** A608 70c multi 1.25 1.25
**2442** A608 $1.40 multi 2.40 2.40
**2443** A608 $1.90 multi 3.25 3.25
**2444** A608 $2.40 multi 4.00 4.00
*a.* Souvenir sheet of 4, #2441-2444 11.00 11.00
*Nos. 2441-2444 (4)* 10.90 10.90

Ferns A609

Designs: 70c, Hen and chickens fern. $1.40, Kidney fern. $1.90, Colenso's hard fern. $2.40, Umbrella fern. $2.90, Silver fern.

**2013, Feb. 7** *Perf. 13x13¼*

**2445** A609 70c multi 1.25 1.25
**2446** A609 $1.40 multi 2.40 2.40
**2447** A609 $1.90 multi 3.25 3.25
**2448** A609 $2.40 multi 4.00 4.00
**2449** A609 $2.90 multi 5.00 5.00
*a.* Souvenir sheet of 5, #2445-2449 16.00 16.00
*b.* Souvenir sheet of 2, #2448-2449, perf. 13½ 13.00 13.00
*Nos. 2445-2449 (5)* 15.90 15.90

Issued: No. 2449b, 9/13. Upper Hutt 2013 National Stamp Show (#2449b). No. 2449b sold for $7.80, with $2.50 of that amount going to the Philatelic Trust.

Children's Books by Margaret Mahy (1936-2012) — A610

Designs: 70c, A Lion in the Meadow. $1.40, A Summery Saturday Morning. $1.90, The Word Witch. $2.40, The Great White Man-Eating Shark. $2.90, The Changeover.

**2013, Mar. 13** *Perf. 14*

**2450** A610 70c multi 1.25 1.25
**2451** A610 $1.40 multi 2.40 2.40
**2452** A610 $1.90 multi 3.25 3.25
**2453** A610 $2.40 multi 4.00 4.00
**2454** A610 $2.90 multi 4.75 4.75
*a.* Souvenir sheet of 5, #2450-2454 16.00 16.00
*Nos. 2450-2454 (5)* 15.65 15.65

New Zealand Defense Force Missions Abroad A611

Mission in: No. 2455, Afghanistan. No. 2456, Timor. 140c, Solomon Islands. 190c, Bosnia and Herzegovina. 240c, Antarctica. 290c, Korea.

**2013, Apr. 10**

**2455** A611 70c multi 1.25 1.25
*a.* Booklet pane of 1 1.25 1.25
**2456** A611 70c multi 1.25 1.25
*a.* Booklet pane of 1 1.25 1.25
**2457** A611 140c multi 2.40 2.40
*a.* Booklet pane of 1 2.40 2.40
**2458** A611 190c multi 3.25 3.25
*a.* Booklet pane of 1 3.25 3.25

| | | | | |
|---|---|---|---|---|
| **2459** | A611 | 240c multi | 4.00 | 4.00 |
| *a.* | | Booklet pane of 1 | 4.00 | 4.00 |
| **2460** | A611 | 290c multi | 5.00 | 5.00 |
| *a.* | | Booklet pane of 1 | 5.00 | 5.00 |
| *b.* | | Booklet pane of 6, #2455-2460 | 17.50 | — |
| | | Complete booklet, #2455a, 2456a, 2457a, 2458a, 2459a, 2460a, 2460b | 35.00 | |
| | | *Nos. 2455-2460 (6)* | 17.15 | 17.15 |

Complete booklet sold for $19.90.

Coronation of Queen Elizabeth II, 60th Anniv. — A612

Depictions of Queen Elizabeth II used on New Zealand currency by: No. 2461, Mary Gillick, 1953. No. 2462, Gillick, re-engraved in 1956. $1.40, Arnold Machin, 1967. $1.90, James Berry, 1979. $2.40, Raphael Maklouf, 1986. $2.90, Ian Rank-Broadley, 1999.

**Litho. & Embossed With Foil Application**

**2013**

| | | | | |
|---|---|---|---|---|
| **2461** | A612 | 70c multi | 1.25 | 1.25 |
| **2462** | A612 | 70c multi | 1.25 | 1.25 |
| **2463** | A612 | $1.40 multi | 2.25 | 2.25 |
| **2464** | A612 | $1.90 multi | 3.00 | 3.00 |
| **2465** | A612 | $2.40 multi | 4.00 | 4.00 |
| **2466** | A612 | $2.90 multi | 4.75 | 4.75 |
| *a.* | | Souvenir sheet of 6, #2461-2466 | 16.50 | 16.50 |
| *b.* | | Souvenir sheet of 3, #2461, 2463, 2466 | 8.25 | 8.25 |
| | | *Nos. 2461-2466 (6)* | 16.50 | 16.50 |

Australia 2013 World Stamp Exhibition, Melbourne (#24266b). Issued: Nos. 2461-2466, 2466a, 5/8; No. 2466b, 5/10.

Miniature Sheets

Matariki (Maori New Year) — A613

Nos. 2467 and 2468 — Koru patterns: a, Piko. b, Manu Tukutuku. c, Nguru. d, Pataka. e, Kotiate. f, Patiki.

**2013, June 5 Litho. *Perf. 13¾x13½***

| | | | | |
|---|---|---|---|---|
| **2467** | A613 | Sheet of 6 | 16.50 | 16.50 |
| *a.-b.* | | 70c Either single | 1.25 | 1.25 |
| *c.* | | $1.40 multi | 2.25 | 2.25 |
| *d.* | | $1.90 multi | 3.00 | 3.00 |
| *e.* | | $2.40 multi | 4.00 | 4.00 |
| *f.* | | $2.90 multi | 4.75 | 4.75 |

**Self-Adhesive**

***Serpentine Die Cut 9½x10***

| | | | | |
|---|---|---|---|---|
| **2468** | A613 | Sheet of 6 | 16.50 | 16.50 |
| *a.-b.* | | 70c Either single | 1.25 | 1.25 |
| *c.* | | $1.40 multi | 2.25 | 2.25 |
| *d.* | | $1.90 multi | 3.00 | 3.00 |
| *e.* | | $2.40 multi | 4.00 | 4.00 |
| *f.* | | $2.90 multi | 4.75 | 4.75 |

Honey Bees A614

Designs: 70c, Bee collecting nectar. 140c, Bees at hive entrance. 190c, Bees on honeycomb. 240c, Apiarist collecting honey. 290c, Harvested honeycomb.

**2013, July 3 *Perf. 14***

| | | | | |
|---|---|---|---|---|
| **2469** | A614 | 70c multi | 1.25 | 1.25 |
| **2470** | A614 | 140c multi | 2.25 | 2.25 |
| **2471** | A614 | 190c multi | 3.00 | 3.00 |
| **2472** | A614 | 240c multi | 4.00 | 4.00 |
| **2473** | A614 | 290c multi | 4.75 | 4.75 |
| *a.* | | Souvenir sheet of 5, #2469-2473 | 15.50 | 15.50 |
| | | *Nos. 2469-2473 (5)* | 15.25 | 15.25 |

Classic Travel Posters — A615

No. 2474 — Travel poster depicting: a, Woman in bathing suit, Napier Carnival. b, Fishing boat and fish. c, Tree fern. d, Rata blossom, Franz Josef Glacier. e, Fisherman in river. f, Wellington. g, Contrail of TEAL Airlines emblem going through mouth of Maori carving, mountains. h, Queenstown. i, Timaru by the Sea. j, Lake and mountains. k, Man reaching for hand, Tauranga. l, Kea. m, Bus touring the Southern Alps. n, Marlborough Sounds. o, Sheep drover on horse, sheep herd, dog. p, Basket weaver. q, Skier at Mt. Cook. r, Mt. Egmont. s, Maori statues, mountains, geyser. t, Swimmers at Blue Baths, Rotorua.

**2013, Aug. 7 *Perf. 14x14½***

| | | | | |
|---|---|---|---|---|
| **2474** | A615 | Sheet of 20 | 22.00 | 22.00 |
| *a.-t.* | | 70c Any single | 1.10 | 1.10 |

Coastlines and Lighthouses — A616

Designs: 70c, Castlepoint. $1.40, Nugget Point. $1.90, East Cape. $2.40, Pencarrow Head. $2.90, Cape Campbell.

**2013, Sept. 4 *Perf. 13¼x13½***

| | | | | |
|---|---|---|---|---|
| **2475** | A616 | 70c multi | 1.10 | 1.10 |
| **2476** | A616 | $1.40 multi | 2.25 | 2.25 |
| **2477** | A616 | $1.90 multi | 3.00 | 3.00 |
| **2478** | A616 | $2.40 multi | 4.00 | 4.00 |
| **2479** | A616 | $2.90 multi | 4.75 | 4.75 |
| *a.* | | Souvenir sheet of 5, #2475-2479 | 15.50 | 15.50 |
| | | *Nos. 2475-2479 (5)* | 15.10 | 15.10 |

Birth of Prince George of Cambridge A617

Designs: 70c, Duke, Duchess of Cambridge, Prince George. $1.90, Duke of Cambridge holding Prince George. $2.40, Duke, Duchess of Cambridge, Prince George, diff. $2.90, Duchess of Cambridge holding Prince George.

**2013, Sept. 11 *Perf. 14¾***

| | | | | |
|---|---|---|---|---|
| **2480** | A617 | 70c multi | 1.25 | 1.25 |
| **2481** | A617 | $1.90 multi | 3.25 | 3.25 |
| **2482** | A617 | $2.40 multi | 4.00 | 4.00 |
| **2483** | A617 | $2.90 multi | 4.75 | 4.75 |
| *a.* | | Horiz. strip of 4, #2480-2483 | 13.50 | 13.50 |
| | | *Nos. 2480-2483 (4)* | 13.25 | 13.25 |

A618

Christmas — A619

Designs: 70c, Child receiving gift. $1.40, Christmas lunch. $1.90, Children decorating Christmas tree. $2.40, Children playing cricket on beach. $2.90, People singing Christmas carols.

**2013, Oct. 2 *Perf. 14¼***

| | | | | |
|---|---|---|---|---|
| **2484** | A618 | 70c multi | 1.25 | 1.25 |
| **2485** | A618 | $1.40 multi | 2.40 | 2.40 |
| **2486** | A618 | $1.90 multi | 3.25 | 3.25 |
| **2487** | A618 | $2.40 multi | 4.00 | 4.00 |
| **2488** | A618 | $2.90 multi | 5.00 | 5.00 |
| | | *Nos. 2484-2488 (5)* | 15.90 | 15.90 |

**Self-Adhesive**

***Serpentine Die Cut 9½x10¼***

| | | | |
|---|---|---|---|
| **2489** | Sheet of 3 | 8.50 | |
| *a.* | A619 70c multi | 1.25 | 1.25 |
| *b.* | A619 $1.90 multi | 3.25 | 3.25 |
| *c.* | A619 $2.40 multi | 4.00 | 4.00 |
| *d.* | Booklet pane of 10 #2489a | 12.50 | |
| *e.* | Booklet pane of 10 #2489b | 32.50 | |
| *f.* | Booklet pane of 10 #2489c | 40.00 | |

No. 2489a doesn not have a blue airmail panel at the bottom of the stamp. No. 2489e sold for $17.10. No. 2489f sold for $21.60.

Premiere of Movie *The Hobbit: The Desolation of Smaug*

A620 A621

Designs: 70c, Thorin Oakenshield. $1.40, Gandalf. $1.90, Tauriel, horiz. $2.10, Bilbo Baggins, horiz. $2.40, Legolas Greenleaf. $2.90, Bard the Bowman.

**2013, Nov. 1 *Perf. 14½x14, 14x14½***

| | | | | |
|---|---|---|---|---|
| **2490** | A620 | 70c multi | 1.25 | 1.25 |
| *a.* | | Souvenir sheet of 1 | 1.50 | 1.50 |
| **2491** | A620 | $1.40 multi | 2.40 | 2.40 |
| *a.* | | Souvenir sheet of 1 | 3.00 | 3.00 |
| **2492** | A620 | $1.90 multi | 3.25 | 3.25 |
| *a.* | | Souvenir sheet of 1 | 4.00 | 4.00 |
| **2493** | A620 | $2.10 multi | 3.50 | 3.50 |
| *a.* | | Souvenir sheet of 1 | 4.50 | 4.50 |
| **2494** | A620 | $2.40 multi | 4.00 | 4.00 |
| *a.* | | Souvenir sheet of 1 | 5.00 | 5.00 |
| **2495** | A620 | $2.90 multi | 5.00 | 5.00 |
| *a.* | | Souvenir sheet of 1 | 6.25 | 6.25 |
| | | *Nos. 2490-2495 (6)* | 19.40 | 19.40 |

**Self-Adhesive**

***Serpentine Die Cut 10¼x10, 10x10¼***

| | | | |
|---|---|---|---|
| **2496** | Sheet of 6 | 19.50 | |
| *a.* | A621 70c multi | 1.25 | 1.25 |
| *b.* | A621 $1.40 multi | 2.40 | 2.40 |
| *c.* | A621 $1.90 multi | 3.25 | 3.25 |
| *d.* | A621 $2.10 multi | 3.50 | 3.50 |
| *e.* | A621 $2.40 multi | 4.00 | 4.00 |
| *f.* | A621 $2.90 multi | 5.00 | 5.00 |
| *g.* | Booklet pane of 10, #2496c-2496f, 4 #2496a, 2 #2496b | 26.00 | |

Nos. 2490a-2495a were sold as a set for $14.40.

New Year 2014 (Year of the Horse) — A622

Designs: 70c, Chinese character for "horse." $1.40, Horse. $1.90, Horse jumping over hurdle. $2.40, Rotorua Museum, Chinese lantern.

**2014, Jan. 8 Litho. *Perf. 13½x13***

| | | | | |
|---|---|---|---|---|
| **2497** | A622 | 70c multi | 1.25 | 1.25 |
| **2498** | A622 | $1.40 multi | 2.40 | 2.40 |
| **2499** | A622 | $1.90 multi | 3.25 | 3.25 |
| **2500** | A000 | $2.40 multi | 4.00 | 4.00 |
| *a.* | | Souvenir sheet of 4, #2497-2500 | 11.00 | 11.00 |
| | | *Nos. 2497-2500 (4)* | 10.90 | 10.90 |

Seaweeds A623

Map of New Zealand and: 70c, Hormosira banksii. $1.40, Landsburgia quercifolia. $1.90, Caulerpa brownii. $2.40, Marginariella boryana. $2.90, Pterocladia lucida.

**2014, Feb. 5 Litho. *Perf. 14***

| | | | | |
|---|---|---|---|---|
| **2501** | A623 | 70c multi | 1.25 | 1.25 |
| *a.* | | Perf. 13¼x13½ | 1.25 | 1.25 |
| **2502** | A623 | $1.40 multi | 2.40 | 2.40 |
| *a.* | | Perf. 13¼x13½ | 2.40 | 2.40 |
| **2503** | A623 | $1.90 multi | 3.25 | 3.25 |
| *a.* | | Perf. 13¼x13½ | 3.25 | 3.25 |
| **2504** | A623 | $2.40 multi | 4.00 | 4.00 |
| *a.* | | Perf. 13¼x13½ | 4.00 | 4.00 |
| **2505** | A623 | $2.90 multi | 5.00 | 5.00 |
| *a.* | | Perf. 13¼x13½ | 5.00 | 5.00 |
| *b.* | | Souvenir sheet of 5, #2501a-2505a | 16.00 | 16.00 |
| | | *Nos. 2501-2505 (5)* | 15.90 | 15.90 |

Houses A624

Designs: 70c, Colonial cottage. $1.40, Villa. $1.90, Californian bungalow. $2.40, Art Deco. $2.90, State house.

**2014, Mar. 5 Litho. *Perf. 14***

| | | | | |
|---|---|---|---|---|
| **2506** | A624 | 70c multi | 1.25 | 1.25 |
| **2507** | A624 | $1.40 multi | 2.40 | 2.40 |
| **2508** | A624 | $1.90 multi | 3.25 | 3.25 |
| **2509** | A624 | $2.40 multi | 4.00 | 4.00 |
| **2510** | A624 | $2.90 multi | 5.00 | 5.00 |
| *a.* | | Souvenir sheet of 5, #2506-2510 | 5.00 | 5.00 |
| | | *Nos. 2506-2510 (5)* | 15.90 | 15.90 |

World War II Poster Art — A625

Posters inscribed: No. 2511, Duty Calls the Youth of New Zealand. No. 2512, Help Farm for Victory. $1.40, The Air Force Needs Men! $1.90, Navy Week. $2.40, Army Week. $2.90, Taringa Whakarongo!

**2014, Apr. 2 Litho. *Perf. 14¾***

| | | | | |
|---|---|---|---|---|
| **2511** | A625 | 70c multi | 1.25 | 1.25 |
| *a.* | | Perf. 13 | 1.25 | 1.25 |
| *b.* | | Booklet pane of 1, #2511a | 1.25 | — |

**2512** A625 70c multi 1.25 1.25
a. Perf. 13 1.25 1.25
b. Booklet pane of 1, #2512a 1.25 —
**2513** A625 $1.40 multi 2.40 2.40
a. Perf. 13 2.40 2.40
b. Booklet pane of 1, #2513a 2.40 —
**2514** A625 $1.90 multi 3.25 3.25
a. Perf. 13 3.25 3.25
b. Booklet pane of 1, #2514a 3.25 —
**2515** A625 $2.40 multi 4.00 4.00
a. Perf. 13 4.00 4.00
b. Booklet pane of 1, #2515a 4.00 —
**2516** A625 $2.90 multi 5.00 5.00
a. Perf. 13 5.00 5.00
b. Booklet pane of 1, #2516a 5.00 —
c. Booklet pane of 6, #2511a-2516a 17.50 —
Complete booklet, #2511b, 2512b, 2513b, 2514b, 2515b, 2516b, 2516c 35.00
*Nos. 2511-2516 (6)* 17.15 17.15

Complete booklet sold for $19.90.

Visit to New Zealand of Duke and Duchess of Cambridge and Prince George A626

Various photos of Duke, Duchess and Prince.

**2014, Apr. 7 Litho. *Perf. 14½***
**2517** A626 70c multi 1.25 1.25
**2518** A626 $2.40 multi 4.25 4.25

### All Blacks Type of 2010

**2014, May 7 Litho. *Perf. 13½x13¼***
**2519** A579 80c black 1.40 1.40
**2520** A579 $2.50 black 4.25 4.25

### Souvenir Sheet

**2521** Sheet of 4, #2519, 2520, 2521a, 2521b 11.50 11.50
a. A579 80c black, 32x17mm, perf. 15x14½ 1.40 1.40
b. A579 $2.50 black, 32x17mm, perf. 15x14½ 4.25 4.25

Tourist Attractions A627

Designs: 60c, Franz Josef Glacier. $1.60, Moeraki Boulders. $2, Mount Taranaki. $2.50, Pancake Rocks. $3.60, Waikato River.

**2014, May 7 Litho. *Perf. 13¼***
**2522** A627 60c multi 1.00 1.00
**2523** A627 $1.60 multi 2.75 2.75
**2524** A627 $2.50 multi 4.25 4.25
**2525** A627 $3.60 multi 6.25 6.25
*Nos. 2522-2525 (4)* 14.25 14.25

### Self-Adhesive

***Serpentine Die Cut 10x9½***
**2526** A627 $2 multi 3.50 3.50
a. Booklet pane of 5 17.50
**2527** A627 $2.50 multi 4.25 4.25
a. Pair, #2526-2527 7.75
b. Booklet pane of 5 21.50

See Nos. 2644-2651.

### Miniature Sheets

Personalized Stamps — A628

No. 2528: a, Wedding rings. b, Fern fiddlehead. c, "Love." d, Champagne flutes. e, Teddy bear. f, Pohutukawa flowers. g, Cupcake with birthday candles. h, Bunch of balloons.

No. 2529: a, Wedding rings. b, Fern fiddlehead. c, Champagne flutes. d, Pohutukawa flowers.

**2014, May 7 Litho. *Perf. 15x14½***
**2528** A628 Sheet of 8 + 4 labels 11.50 11.50
a.-h. 80c Any single 1.40 1.40
**2529** A628 Sheet of 4 + 2 labels 15.50 15.50
a.-b. $2 Either single 3.50 3.50
c.-d. $2.50 Either single 4.25 4.25

### Miniature Sheets

Matariki — A629

Nos. 2530 and 2531 — Maori art depicting the story of Papatuanuku and Ranginui: a, Te Wehenga o Rangi Raua ko Papa, by Cliff Whiting, b, Rangi and Papa, by Phil Mokaraka Berry. c, Te Whakamamae o te Wehenga, by Kura Te Waru Rewiri. d, The Separtation of Rangi and Papa, by Fred Graham, horiz. e, The Children of Rangi and Papa, by Pauline Kahurangi Yearbury, horiz. f, The Ranginui Doorway, by Robert Jahnke, horiz.

**2014, June 4 Litho. *Perf. 13½***
**2530** A629 Sheet of 6 18.50 18.50
a.-b. 80c Either single 1.40 1.40
c. $1.40 multi 2.40 2.40
d. $2 multi 3.50 3.50
e. $2.50 multi 4.25 4.25
f. $3 multi 5.25 5.25

### Self-Adhesive

***Serpentine Die Cut 10x9½ (vert. stamps), 9½x10 (horiz. stamps)***
**2531** A629 Sheet of 6 18.50
a.-b. 80c Either single 1.40 1.40
c. $1.40 multi 2.40 2.40
d. $2 multi 3.50 3.50
e. $2.50 multi 4.25 4.25
f. $3 multi 5.25 5.25

### Miniature Sheet

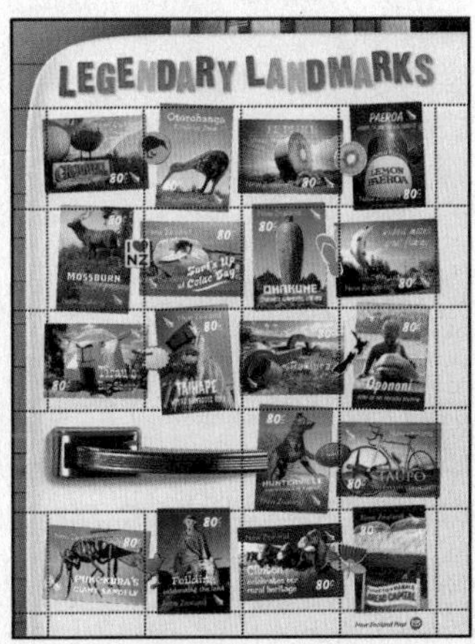


Landmarks — A630

No. 2532: a, Sculptures of peaches, Cromwell. b, Kiwi statue, Otorohanga. c, Kiwi fruit slice statue, Te Puke. d, Lemon and Paeroa bottle statue, Paeroa. e, Deer statue, Mossburn. f, Surfer statue, Colac Bay. g, Carrot statue, Ohakune. h, Fish statue, Rakaia. i, Sheep building, Tirau. j, Gumboot sculpture, Taihape. k, Chain sculpture, Raikura. l, Statue of boy and bottlenose dolphin, Opononi. m, Dog statue, Hunterville. n, Bicycle sculpture, Taupo. o, Sandfly sculpture, Pukekura. p, Sculpture of man and dog, Feilding. q, Clydesdale horses sculptures, Clinton. r, Sculpture of bread loaves, Manaia.

**2014, July 2 Litho. *Perf. 14½***
**2532** A630 Sheet of 18 + label 25.50 25.50
a.-r. 80c Any single 1.40 1.40

World War I, Cent. — A631

Designs: No. 2533, Lord Kitchener. No. 2534, Poster for military training. No. 2535, Announcement of war. No. 2536, Melville Mirfin in military uniform. No. 2537, Photograph of Mirfin family. No. 2538, Departure of troop ships. No. 2539, Training camp. No. 2540, Street scene, Karaka Bay. No. 2541, Letter from Mirfin from Samoa. No. 2542, New Zealand soldiers in Egypt.

**2014, July 29 Litho. *Perf. 14½***
**2533** A631 80c multi 1.40 1.40
a. Booklet pane of 1 2.00 —
**2534** A631 80c multi 1.40 1.40
a. Booklet pane of 1 2.00 —
**2535** A631 80c multi 1.40 1.40
a. Booklet pane of 1 2.00 —
**2536** A631 80c multi 1.40 1.40
a. Booklet pane of 1 2.00 —
**2537** A631 80c multi 1.40 1.40
a. Booklet pane of 1 2.00 —
**2538** A631 80c multi 1.40 1.40
a. Booklet pane of 1 2.00 —
b. Booklet pane of 6, #2533-2538 12.00 —
c. Block of 6, #2533-2538 8.50 8.50
d. Souvenir sheet, #2533-2538 8.50 8.50
**2539** A631 $2 multi 3.50 3.50
a. Booklet pane of 1 5.00 —
**2540** A631 $2 multi 3.50 3.50
a. Booklet pane of 1 5.00 —
b. Horiz. pair, #2539-2540 7.00 7.00
**2541** A631 $2.50 multi 4.25 4.25
a. Booklet pane of 1 6.25 —
**2542** A631 $2.50 multi 4.25 4.25
a. Booklet pane of 1 6.25 —
b. Booklet pane of 4, #2539-2542 22.50 —
Complete booklet, #2533a, 2534a, 2535a, 2536a, 2537a, 2538a, 2538b, 2539a, 2540a, 2541a, 2542a, 2542b 69.00
c. Horiz. pair, #2541-2542 8.50 8.50
d. Souvenir sheet of 4, #2539-2542 15.50 15.50
e. Souvenir sheet of 10, #2533-2542 24.00 24.00
f. Souvenir sheet of 3, #2538, 2539, 2542 12.50 12.50
*Nos. 2533-2542 (10)* 23.90 23.90

Issued: No. 2542f, 11/14. Baypex 2014 National Stamp Exhibition, Hawke's Bay (No. 2542f). No. 2542f sold for $7.80 with surtax going to the Philatelic Trust. Complete booklet sold for $39.90. See Nos. 2574-2683, 2633-2642, 2715-2724, 2782-2791.

Endangered Seabirds — A632

Designs: 80c, Antipodean albatross. $1.40, New Zealand fairy tern. $2, Chatham Island shag. $2.50, Black-billed gull. $3, Chatham Island taiko.

**2014, Sept. 3 Litho. *Perf. 14***
**2543** A632 80c multi 1.25 1.25
a. Perf. 13½x13¼ 1.25 1.25
**2544** A632 $1.40 multi 2.25 2.25
a. Perf. 13½x13¼ 2.25 2.25
**2545** A632 $2 multi 3.25 3.25
a. Perf. 13½x13¼ 3.25 3.25
**2546** A632 $2.50 multi 4.00 4.00
a. Perf. 13½x13¼ 4.00 4.00
**2547** A632 $3 multi 4.75 4.75
a. Perf. 13½x13¼ 4.75 4.75
b. Souvenir sheet of 5, #2543a, 2544a, 2545a, 2546a, 2547a 15.50 15.50
*Nos. 2543-2547 (5)* 15.50 15.50

The silhouettes of birds were printed with thermochromic ink, which disappeared when warmed.

A633 Christmas — A634

Children in Nativity play depicting: 80c, Mary and Jesus. $1.40, Joseph. $2, Wise Man. $2.50, Angel. $3, Shepherd.

**2014, Oct. 1 Litho. *Perf. 14***
**2548** A633 80c multi 1.25 1.25
**2549** A633 $1.40 multi 2.25 2.25
**2550** A633 $2 multi 3.25 3.25
**2551** A633 $2.50 multi 4.00 4.00
**2552** A633 $3 multi 4.75 4.75
*Nos. 2548-2552 (5)* 15.50 15.50

### Self-Adhesive

***Serpentine Die Cut 10x9½***
**2553** Sheet of 3 8.50
a. A634 80c multi 1.25 1.25
b. A634 $2 multi 3.25 3.25
c. A634 $2.50 multi 4.00 4.00
d. Booklet pane of 10 #2553a 12.50
e. Booklet pane of 10 #2553b 32.50
f. Booklet pane of 10 #2553c 40.00

Nos. 2553b and 2553c are airmail. No. 2553e sold for $18. No. 2553f sold for $22.50.

### Souvenir Sheet

Premiere of Movie *The Hobbit: The Battle of the Five Armies* — A635

Design: Characters from movie in costume.

**2014, Oct. 15 Litho. *Perf. 14¾x14½***
**2554** A635 Sheet of 2 5.25 5.25
a. 80c multi 1.25 1.25
b. $2.50 multi 4.00 4.00

Nos. 2554a and 2554b were each available in sheets of 20 + 20 personalizable labels.

Premiere of Movie *The Hobbit: The Battle of the Five Armies*
A636 A637

Designs: 80c, Smaug. $1.40, Bilbo Baggins. $2, Gandalf, horiz. $2.10, Thranduil, horiz. Nos. 2559, 2562e, Bard the Bowman. $3, Tauriel. No. 2561, Door to Bag End.

***Perf. 14½x14, 14x14½***
**2014, Nov. 12 Litho.**
**2555** A636 80c multi 1.25 1.25
a. Souvenir sheet of 1 1.60 1.60
**2556** A636 $1.40 multi 2.25 2.25
a. Souvenir sheet of 1 2.75 2.75
**2557** A636 $2 multi 3.00 3.00
a. Souvenir sheet of 1 4.00 4.00
**2558** A636 $2.10 multi 3.25 3.25
a. Souvenir sheet of 1 4.25 4.25
**2559** A636 $2.50 multi 4.00 4.00
a. Souvenir sheet of 1 5.00 5.00
**2560** A636 $3 multi 4.75 4.75
a. Souvenir sheet of 1 5.75 5.75

### Litho. & Thermography

**2561** A636 $2.50 multi 4.00 4.00
a. Souvenir sheet of 1 5.00 5.00
*Nos. 2555-2561 (7)* 22.50 22.50

### Self-Adhesive

### Litho.

***Serpentine Die Cut 10¼x10, 10x10¼***
**2562** Sheet of 6 18.50
a. A637 80c multi 1.25 1.25
b. A637 $1.40 multi 2.25 2.25
c. A637 $2 multi 3.00 3.00
d. A637 $2.10 multi 3.25 3.25
e. A637 $2.50 multi 4.00 4.00
f. A637 $3 multi 4.75 4.75
g. Booklet pane of 10, #2562c-2562f, 4 #2562a, 2 #2562b 24.50

Particles of wood from the movie set are embedded in the thermographic ink on No. 2561. Nos. 2555a-2561a sold as a set for $17.80.

New Year 2015 (Year of the Sheep) — A638

Designs: 80c, Chinese character for "sheep." $1.40, Sheep in paper-cut design. $2, Sheep and fence, New Zealand. $2.50, Church of the Good Shepherd, Tekapo, and Chinese kite.

**2015, Jan. 14 Litho. *Perf. 14***

2563 A638 80c multi 1.25 1.25
a. Perf. 13¼x13½ 1.25 1.25
2564 A638 $1.40 multi 2.10 2.10
a. Perf. 13¼x13½ 2.10 2.10
2565 A638 $2 multi 3.00 3.00
a. Perf. 13¼x13½ 3.00 3.00
2566 A638 $2.50 multi 3.75 3.75
a. Perf. 13¼x13½ 3.75 3.75
b. Souvenir sheet of 4, #2563a-2566a 10.50 10.50
*Nos. 2563-2566 (4)* 10.10 10.10

Air New Zealand, 75th Anniv. — A639

Designs: 80c, Short S-30 Flying Boat on first Auckland-Sydney flight, 1940. $1.40, Airplanes, Stewardess Margaret Gould, child, pilot, 1948. $2, Tasman Empire Airways Ltd. 1951-60 Coral Route baggage label. $2.50, Children and flight attendant, 1977. $3, Air New Zealand Boeing 787-9 taking off.

**2015, Jan. 14 Litho. *Perf. 14¾***

2567 A639 80c multi 1.25 1.25
2568 A639 $1.40 multi 2.10 2.10
2569 A639 $2 multi 3.00 3.00
2570 A639 $2.50 multi 3.75 3.75
2571 A639 $3 multi 4.50 4.50
a. Souvenir sheet of 5, #2567-2571 15.00 15.00
*Nos. 2567-2571 (5)* 14.60 14.60

Souvenir Sheet

Treaty of Waitangi, 175th Anniv. — A640

***Perf. 14x14½***

**2015, Feb. 4 Litho. Wmk. 387**

2572 A640 $2.50 multi 3.75 3.75

Miniature Sheet

2015 ICC Cricket World Cup Tournament, Australia and New Zealand — A641

No. 2573 — Tournament emblem on cricket ball with flag of competing team: a, India (dark blue ball, red stitching). b, England (white ball, red stitching). c, South Africa (green ball, orange stitching). d, Pakistan (yellow green ball, yellow stitching). e, United Arab Emirates (gray ball, red stitching). f, Sri Lanka (dark blue ball, yellow stitching). g, West Indies (red violet ball, orange stitching). h, Afghanistan (blue ball, red stitching). i, Ireland (green ball, blue stitching). j, Bangladesh (red ball, green stitching). k, Australia (yellow ball, black stitching). l, New Zealand (gray ball, black stitching). m, Zimbabwe (red ball, white stitching). n, Scotland (deep blue ball, blue stitching).

**Unwmk.**

**2015, Feb. 4 Litho. *Die Cut***

**Self-Adhesive**

2573 A641 Sheet of 14 17.50
a.-n. 80c Any single 1.25 1.25

**World War I, Cent. Type of 2014**

Designs: No. 2574, Evelyn Brooke, nurse. No. 2575, Postcard from Egypt. No. 2576, Landing at Anzac Cove. No. 2577, Chunuk Bair. No. 2578, Casualties return. No. 2579, Marquette Memorial. No. 2580, The Sapper and His Donkey, painting by Horace Moore-Jones. No. 2581, War census poster. No. 2582, Hospital ship Maheno. No. 2583, An Enduting Bond, poster by Otho Hewett.

**2015, Mar. 23 Litho. *Perf. 14½***

2574 A631 80c multi 1.25 1.25
a. Booklet pane of 1 1.75 —
2575 A631 80c multi 1.25 1.25
a. Booklet pane of 1 1.75 —
2576 A631 80c multi 1.25 1.25
a. Booklet pane of 1 1.75 —
2577 A631 80c multi 1.25 1.25
a. Booklet pane of 1 1.75 —
2578 A631 80c multi 1.25 1.25
a. Booklet pane of 1 1.75 —
2579 A631 80c multi 1.25 1.25
a. Booklet pane of 1 1.75 —
b. Booklet pane of 6, #2574-2579 10.50 —
c. Block of 6, #2574-2579 7.50 7.50
d. Souvenir sheet of 6, #2574-2579 7.50 7.50
2580 A631 $2 multi 3.00 3.00
a. Booklet pane of 1 4.50 —
2581 A631 $2 multi 3.00 3.00
a. Booklet pane of 1 4.50 —
b. Horiz. pair, #2580-2581 6.00 6.00
2582 A631 $2.50 multi 3.75 3.75
a. Booklet pane of 1 5.50 —
b. Souvenir sheet of 3, #2576, 2580, 2582 7.25 7.25
2583 A631 $2.50 multi 3.75 3.75
a. Booklet pane of 1 5.50 —
b. Booklet pane of 4, #2580-2583 20.00 —
Complete booklet, #2574a, 2575a, 2576a, 2577a, 2578a, 2579a, 2579b, 2580a, 2581a, 2582a, 2583a, 2583b 61.00
c. Horiz. pair, #2582-2583 7.50 7.50
d. Souvenir sheet of 4, #2580-2583 13.50 13.50
e. Souvenir sheet of 10, #2574-2583 21.00 21.00
*Nos. 2574-2583 (10)* 21.00 21.00

Complete booklet sold for $39.90.
Issued: No. 2582b, 10/23/15. 2015, Capital Stamp Show, Wellington, (No. 2582b).

Australian and New Zealand Army Corps, Cent. — A642

Soldier and bugler with bugler facing: 80c, Right. $2, Left.

**2015, Apr. 7 Litho. *Perf. 14½x14***

2584 A642 80c multi 1.25 1.25
2585 A642 $2 multi 3.00 3.00
a. Souvenir sheet of 2, #2584-2585 4.25 4.25

See Australia Nos. 4271-4274.

Shells — A643

Designs: 80c, Silver paua. $1.40, Scott's murex. $2, Golden volute. $2.50, Fan shell. $3, Opal top shell.

**2015, May 6 Litho. *Perf. 14***

2586 A643 80c multi 1.25 1.25
a. Perf. 13¼x13½ 1.25 1.25
2587 A643 $1.40 multi 2.10 2.10
a. Perf. 13¼x13½ 2.10 2.10
2588 A643 $2 multi 3.00 3.00
a. Perf. 13¼x13½ 3.00 3.00
2589 A643 $2.50 multi 3.75 3.75
a. Perf. 13¼x13½ 3.75 3.75
2590 A643 $3 multi 4.50 4.50
a. Perf. 13¼x13½ 4.50 4.50
b. Souvenir sheet of 5, #2586a-2590a 15.00 15.00
*Nos. 2586-2590 (5)* 14.60 14.60

Miniature Sheets

Matariki (Maori New Year) — A644

Nos. 2591 and 2592 — Kowhaiwhai: a, Digiwhaiwhai, by Johnson Witehira. b, Tenei Au Tenei Au, by Kura Te Waru Rewiri. c, Haki, by Kylie Tiuka. d, Banner Moon, by Buck Nin, horiz. e, Part of Te Hatete o Te Reo Series, by Ngatai Taepa, horiz. f, Taona Marama, by Sandy Adsett, horiz.

**2015, June 3 Litho. *Perf. 14***

2591 A644 Sheet of 6 14.50 14.50
a.-b. 80c Either single 1.10 1.10
c. $1.40 multi 1.90 1.90
d. $2 multi 2.75 2.75
e. $2.50 multi 3.50 3.50
f. $3 multi 4.00 4.00

**Self-Adhesive**

***Serpentine Die Cut 10x9½ (vert. stamps), 9½x10 (horiz. stamps)***

2592 A644 Sheet of 6 14.50 14.50
a.-b. 80c Either single 1.10 1.10
c. $1.40 multi 1.90 1.90
d. $2 multi 2.75 2.75
e. $2.50 multi 3.50 3.50
f. $3 multi 4.00 4.00

Miniature Sheet

Popular New Zealand Foods — A645

No. 2593: a, Aspargaus rolls. b, Kiwi onion dip. c, Puha and pork. d, Bluff oyster. e, Meat loaf. f, Hokey pokey ice cream. g, Shrimp cocktail. h, Cheese rolls. i, Pikelets. j, Lamington cake. k, Mince on toast. l, Whitebait fritters. m, Curried egg. n, Saveloy sausage and sauce. o, Bacon and egg pie. p, Pavlova. q, Fairy bread. r, Mouse trap.

**2015, July 1 Litho. *Perf. 14¼x14¾***

2593 A645 Sheet of 18 20.00 20.00
a.-r. 80c Any single 1.10 1.10

UNESCO World Heritage Sites — A646

Designs: 80c, Emerald Lakes, Tongariro National Park. $1.40, Franz Josef Glacier, Te Wahipounamu-South West New Zealand. $2, Enderby Island, New Zealand Sub-Antarctic Islands. $2.20, Mount Ngauruhoe, Tongariro National Park. $2.50, Lake Mackenzie, Te Wahipounamu-South West New Zealand. $3, Campbell Island, New Zealand Sub-Antarctic Islands.

**2015, Aug. 5 Litho. *Perf. 14***

2594 A646 80c multi 1.00 1.00
2595 A646 $1.40 multi 1.75 1.75
2596 A646 $2 multi 2.50 2.50
2597 A646 $2.20 multi 2.75 2.75
2598 A646 $2.50 multi 3.25 3.25
2599 A646 $3 multi 3.75 3.75
a. Souvenir sheet of 6, #2594-2599 15.00 15.00
*Nos. 2594-2599 (6)* 15.00 15.00

Parliament House, Wellington A647

**2015, Aug. 14 Litho. *Perf. 14¼***

2600 A647 $2.50 multi 3.25 3.25
a. Souvenir sheet of 3, #2600, Australia #4331, Singapore #1743 5.75 5.75

See Australia Nos. 4331-4333, Singapore Nos. 1743-1745.
No. 2600a sold for $4.50 and was released for Singapore 2015 International Stamp Exhibition.

All Blacks Rugby Team Uniform Shirt — A648

**Litho. With Fabric Affixed**

**2015, Sept. 2 *Perf. 13¼x13½***

2601 A648 $15 multi 19.00 19.00

No. 2601 was sold individually in a folder.

Queen Elizabeth II, Longest-Reigning British Monarch — A649

Photograph of Queen Elizabeth II from: No. 2602, 1950s. No. 2603, 1960s. $1.40, 1970s. $2, 1980s. $2.20, 1990s. $2.50, 2000s. $3, 2010s.

**2015, Oct. 7 Litho. *Perf. 14¾x14¼***

2602 A649 80c multi 1.10 1.10
2603 A649 80c multi 1.10 1.10
2604 A649 $1.40 multi 1.90 1.90
2605 A649 $2 multi 2.75 2.75
2606 A649 $2.20 multi 3.00 3.00
2607 A649 $2.50 multi 3.50 3.50
2608 A649 $3 multi 4.00 4.00
a. Souvenir sheet of 7, #2602-2608 17.50 17.50
*Nos. 2602-2608 (7)* 17.35 17.35

Christmas

A650 A651

Stained-glass windows: 80c, Angel, St. Mark's Church, Carterton. $1.40, Dove, St. Aidan's Anglican Church, Remuera. $2, Madonna and Child, St. Mary's-in-Holy Trinity Cathedral, Parnell. $2.50, Pohutukawa flower, Christchurch Hospital Nurses Memorial Chapel. $3, Wise Men, St. Benedict's Church, Auckland.

**2015, Nov. 4 Litho. *Perf. 14***

**2609** A650 80c multi 1.10 1.10
**2610** A650 $1.40 multi 1.90 1.90
**2611** A650 $2 multi 2.75 2.75
**2612** A650 $2.50 multi 3.50 3.50
**2613** A650 $3 multi 4.00 4.00
*Nos. 2609-2613 (5)* 13.25 13.25

**Miniature Sheet**
**Translucent Paper**

**2614** Sheet of 5 13.50 13.50
*a.* A650 80c multi 1.10 1.10
*b.* A650 $1.40 multi 1.90 1.90
*c.* A650 $2 multi 2.75 2.75
*d.* A650 $2.50 multi 3.50 3.50
*e.* A650 $3 multi 4.00 4.00

**Self-Adhesive**
***Serpentine Die Cut 9½x10***

**2615** A651 80c multi 1.10 1.10
*a.* Booklet pane of 10 9.00
**2616** A651 $2 multi 2.75 2.75
*a.* Booklet pane of 10 + 10 etiquettes 27.50
**2617** A651 $2.50 multi 3.50 3.50
*a.* Booklet pane of 10 + 10 etiquettes 35.00
*b.* Horiz. strip of 3, #2615-2617 7.50
*Nos. 2615-2617 (3)* 7.35 7.35

No. 2616a sold for $18. No. 2617a sold for $22.50.

New Year 2016 (Year of the Monkey) — A652

Designs: 80c, Chinese character for "monkey." $1.40, Monkey in paper-cut design. $2, Monkey hanging from branch. $2.50, Bar-tailed godwit and Monkey Island.

**2016, Jan. 13 Litho. *Perf. 14***

**2618** A652 80c multi 1.10 1.10
*a.* Perf. 13¼x13½ 1.10 1.10
**2619** A652 $1.40 multi 1.90 1.90
*a.* Perf. 13¼x13½ 1.90 1.90
**2620** A652 $2 multi 2.60 2.60
*a.* Perf. 13¼x13½ 2.60 2.60
**2621** A652 $2.50 multi 3.25 3.25
*a.* Perf. 13¼x13½ 3.25 3.25
*b.* Souvenir sheet of 4, #2618a-2621a 9.00 9.00
*Nos. 2618-2621 (4)* 8.85 8.85

Returned and Services' Association, Cent. A653

Inscription: 80c, The returned. $1.40, The poppy. $2, Supporting those who served. $2.20, At the RSA. $2.50, The badge. $3, We will remember them.

**2016, Feb. 3 Litho. *Perf. 14¼x14¾***

**2622** A653 80c multi 1.10 1.10
**2623** A653 $1.40 multi 1.90 1.90
**2624** A653 $2 multi 2.75 2.75
**2625** A653 $2.20 multi 3.00 3.00
**2626** A653 $2.50 multi 3.50 3.50
**2627** A653 $3 multi 4.00 4.00
*a.* Souvenir sheet of 6, #2622-2627 16.50 16.50
*Nos. 2622-2627 (6)* 16.25 16.25

Glowworms
A654 A655

Glowworms from: 80c, Mangawhitikau Cave. $1.40, Nikau Cave. $2, Ruakuri Cave. $2.50, Waipu Cave.

**2016, Mar. 2 Litho. *Perf. 14½x14***

**2628** A654 80c multi 1.10 1.10
**2629** A654 $1.40 multi 1.90 1.90
**2630** A654 $2 multi 2.75 2.75
**2631** A654 $2.50 multi 3.50 3.50
*a.* Souvenir sheet of 4, #2628-2631 9.25 9.25
*Nos. 2628-2631 (4)* 9.25 9.25

**Self-Adhesive**
***Serpentine Die Cut 10x9½***

**2632** A655 $2 multi 2.75 2.75
*a.* Booklet pane of 10 27.50

No. 2632 was issued with backing paper with and without printing on the reverse.

**World War I, Cent. Type of 2014**

Designs: No. 2633, Solomon Isaacs, member of New Zealand Expeditionary Force. No. 2634, Pioneer Battalion. No. 2635, Inscriptions in Arras Tunnels. No. 2636, Newspaper story announcing introduction of conscription. No. 2637, New Zealand troops in the Middle East. No. 2638, Troops in trenches during the Somme Offensive. No. 2639, First ANZAC Day. No. 2640, Soldiers away from the front at Bloomsbury Square headquarters of New Zealand Expeditionary Force. No. 2641, Battle of Jutland. No. 2642, The home front (Kaikoura, New Zealand Post Office).

**2016, Apr. 6 Litho. *Perf. 14½***

**2633** A631 80c multi 1.10 1.10
*a.* Booklet pane of 1 1.60 —
**2634** A631 80c multi 1.10 1.10
*a.* Booklet pane of 1 1.60 —
**2635** A631 80c multi 1.10 1.10
*a.* Booklet pane of 1 1.60 —
**2636** A631 80c multi 1.10 1.10
*a.* Booklet pane of 1 1.60 —
**2637** A631 80c multi 1.10 1.10
*a.* Booklet pane of 1 1.60 —
**2638** A631 80c multi 1.10 1.10
*a.* Booklet pane of 1 1.60 —
*b.* Booklet pane of 6, #2633-2638 9.50 —
*c.* Block of 6, #2633-2638 6.60 6.60
*d.* Souvenir sheet, #2633-2638 6.60 6.60
**2639** A631 $2 multi 2.75 2.75
*a.* Booklet pane of 1 4.00 —
**2640** A631 $2 multi 2.75 2.75
*a.* Booklet pane of 1 4.00 —
*b.* Horiz. pair, #2639-2640 5.50 5.50
**2641** A631 $2.50 multi 3.50 3.50
*a.* Booklet pane of 1 5.00 —
**2642** A631 $2.50 multi 3.50 3.50
*a.* Booklet pane of 1 5.00 —
*b.* Booklet pane of 4, #2639-2642 17.50 —
Complete booklet, #2633a, 2634a, 2635a, 2636a, 2637a, 2638a, 2638b, 2639a, 2640a, 2641a, 2642a, 2642b 55.00
*c.* Horiz. pair, #2641-2642 7.00 7.00
*d.* Souvenir sheet of 4, #2639-2642 12.50 12.50
*e.* Souvenir sheet of 10, #2633-2642 19.50 19.50
*Nos. 2633-2642 (10)* 19.10 19.10

Complete booklet sold for $39.90.

**Souvenir Sheet**

Queen Elizabeth II, 90th Birthday — A656

No. 2643: a, Infant Princess Elizabeth with King George VI and Queen Mother Elizabeth, 1926, Princess Elizabeth with infant Prince Charles, 1949, Queen Elizabeth II on visit to New Zealand, 1995. b, Princess Elizabeth as young girl, 1936, Queen Elizabeth II opening New Zealand's Parliament, 1963, Queen Elizabeth II on visit to New Zealand, 2002. d, Princess Elizabeth in wedding dress, 1947, Queen Elizabeth II on visit to New Zealand, 1977, Queen Elizabeth II attending ANZAC centenary commemorations, 2015.

**Litho. With 3-Dimensional Plastic Affixed**

**2016, May 4 *Die Cut***

**Self-Adhesive**

**2643** A656 Sheet of 3 21.00 21.00
*a.-c.* $5 Any single 7.00 7.00

**Tourist Attractions Type of 2014**

Designs: 40c, Church of the Good Shepherd, Lake Tekapo. 80c, Chatham Islands. $2.20, Awaroa Bay, Abel Tasman Scenic Reserve. $2.70, Vineyard, Marlborough. $3.30, Dunedin Railway Station. $3.80, Te Mata Peak, Hawke's Bay.

**2016, May 18 Litho. *Perf. 13¼x13½***

**2644** A627 40c multi .55 .55
**2645** A627 80c multi 1.10 1.10
**2646** A627 $2.20 multi 3.00 3.00
**2647** A627 $2.70 multi 3.75 3.75
**2648** A627 $3.30 multi 4.50 4.50
**2649** A627 $3.80 multi 5.25 5.25
*Nos. 2644-2649 (6)* 18.15 18.15

**Self-Adhesive**
***Serpentine Die Cut 10x9½***

**2650** A627 $2.20 multi 3.00 3.00
*a.* Booklet pane of 5 15.00
**2651** A627 $2.70 multi 3.75 3.75
*a.* Horiz. pair, #2650-2651 6.75
*b.* Booklet pane of 5 19.00

**Miniature Sheets**

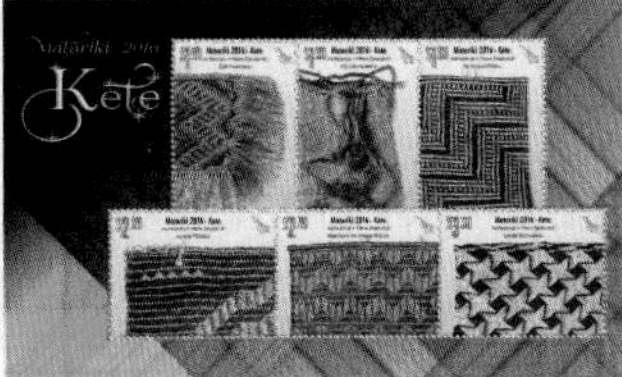


Matariki (Maori New Year) — A657

Nos. 2652 and 2653 — Kete woven by: a, Cori Marsters. b, Pip Devonshire. c, Te Atiwei Ririnui. d, Audra Potaka, horiz. e, Matthew McIntyre Wilson, horiz. f, Sonia Snowden, horiz.

**2016, June 1 Litho. *Perf. 13½***

**2652** A657 Sheet of 6 17.00 17.00
*a.-b.* $1 Either single 1.40 1.40
*c.* $1.80 multi 2.50 2.50
*d.* $2.20 multi 3.00 3.00
*e.* $2.70 multi 3.75 3.75
*f.* $3.30 multi 4.50 4.50

**Self-Adhesive**
***Serpentine Die Cut 10x9½ (vert. stamps), 9½x10 (horiz. stamps)***

**2653** A657 Sheet of 6 17.00 17.00
*a.-b.* $1 Either single 1.40 1.40
*c.* $1.80 multi 2.50 2.50
*d.* $2.20 multi 3.00 3.00
*e.* $2.70 multi 3.75 3.75
*f.* $3.30 multi 4.50 4.50

**Miniature Sheet**

Personalized Stamps — A658

No. 2654: a and i, Wedding rings. b and h, Fern fiddlehead. c, "Love." d, Champagne flutes. e, Teddy bear. f and j, Pohutukawa flowers. g, Buch of balloons.

**2016, June 22 Litho. *Perf. 15x14½***

**2654** A658 Sheet of 10 + 5 labels 21.00 21.00
*a.-g.* $1 Any single 1.50 1.50
*h.-i.* $2.20 Either single 3.25 3.25
*j.* $2.70 multi 4.00 4.00

Track A659

Boxing — A660

Canoeing — A661

Swimming — A662

Equestrian — A663

Field Hockey — A664

Triathlon — A665

Cycling — A666

Rowing — A667

Sailing — A668

**2016, July 6 Litho. *Perf. 14¼***

**2655** A659 $1 multi 1.50 1.50
**2656** A660 $1 multi 1.50 1.50
**2657** A661 $1 multi 1.50 1.50
**2658** A662 $1 multi 1.50 1.50
**2659** A663 $1 multi 1.50 1.50
**2660** A664 $1 multi 1.50 1.50
**2661** A665 $1 multi 1.50 1.50
**2662** A666 $1 multi 1.50 1.50
**2663** A667 $1 multi 1.50 1.50
**2664** A668 $1 multi 1.50 1.50
*a.* Block of 10, #2655-2664 15.00 15.00
*b.* Souvenir sheet of 10, #2655-2664 15.00 15.00

New Zealand Medalists at the 2016 Summer Olympics, Rio de Janeiro — A669

Designs: No. 2665, Natalie Rooney, women's trap shooting silver medalist. No. 2666, Women's rugby sevens team, silver medalist. No. 2667, Eric Murray and Hamish Bond, men's rowing pair gold medalists. No. 2668, Luuka Jones, women's kayaking single slalom silver medalist. No. 2669, Ethan Mitchell, Sam Webster and Eddie Dawkins, men's team sprint track cycling silver medalists. No. 2670, Genevieve Behrent and Rebecca Scown, women's rowing pair silver medalists. No. 2671, Valerie Adams, women's shot put silver medalist. No. 2672, Mahe Drysdale, men's single scull rowing gold medalist. No. 2673, Lisa Carrington, women's 200-meter single kayaking sprint gold medalist. No. 2674, Sam Meech, men's Laser class sailing bronze medalist. No. 2675, Lisa Carrington, women's 500-meter single kayaking sprint bronze medalist. No. 2676, Jo Aleh and Polly Powrie, women's 470 class sailing silver medalists. No. 2677, Peter Burling and Blair Tuke, men's 49er class sailing gold medalists. No. 2678, Molly Meech and Alex Maloney, women's 49erFX class sailing silver medalists. No. 2679, Tomas Walsh, men's shot put bronze medalist. No. 2680, Eliza McCartney, women's pole vault bronze medalist. No. 2681, Lydia Ko, women's golf silver medalist. No. 2682, Nick Willis, men's 1500-meter race bronze medalist.

**2016 Litho. *Perf. 14¼***

| | | | | |
|---|---|---|---|---|
| **2665** | A669 $1 multi | | 1.50 | 1.50 |
| **2666** | A669 $1 multi | | 1.50 | 1.50 |
| **2667** | A669 $1 multi | | 1.50 | 1.50 |
| **2668** | A669 $1 multi | | 1.50 | 1.50 |
| **2669** | A669 $1 multi | | 1.50 | 1.50 |
| **2670** | A669 $1 multi | | 1.50 | 1.50 |
| **2671** | A669 $1 multi | | 1.50 | 1.50 |
| **2672** | A669 $1 multi | | 1.50 | 1.50 |
| **2673** | A669 $1 multi | | 1.50 | 1.50 |
| **2674** | A669 $1 multi | | 1.50 | 1.50 |
| **2675** | A669 $1 multi | | 1.50 | 1.50 |
| **2676** | A669 $1 multi | | 1.50 | 1.50 |
| **2677** | A669 $1 multi | | 1.50 | 1.50 |
| **2678** | A669 $1 multi | | 1.50 | 1.50 |
| **2679** | A669 $1 multi | | 1.50 | 1.50 |
| **2680** | A669 $1 multi | | 1.50 | 1.50 |
| **2681** | A669 $1 multi | | 1.50 | 1.50 |
| **2682** | A669 $1 multi | | 1.50 | 1.50 |
| *a.* | Souvenir sheet of 18, #2665-2682 | | 27.00 | 27.00 |
| | *Nos. 2665-2682 (18)* | | 27.00 | 27.00 |

Issued: No. 2665, 8/8; Nos. 2666-2669, 8/12; Nos. 2670-2672, 8/15; Nos. 2673-2674, 8/18; Nos. 2675-2679, 8/19; Nos. 2680-2682, 2682a, 8/22.

Miniature Sheet

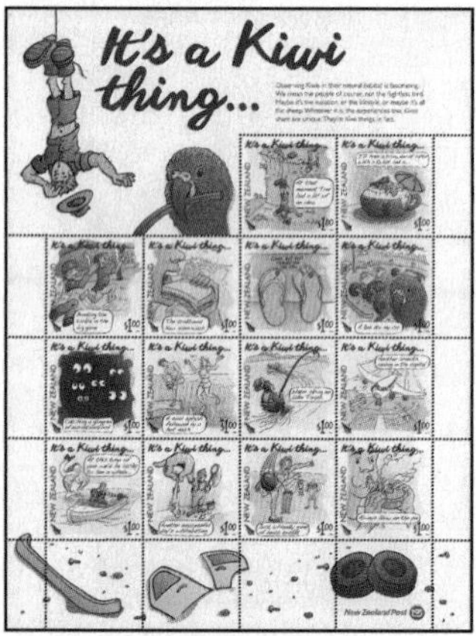


"It's a Kiwi Thing" — A670

No. 2683 — Inscriptions: a, At that moment Trev had a bit of an idea. b, I'll have a trim decaf latte with a twist and a . . . c, Breaking the tackle in the big game. d, The traditional Kiwi sand-wich. e, Gone but not forgotten 2011-2014. f, A kea ate my car. g, Catching a glimpse of our national bird. h, A cool splash followed by a hot dash. i, Water skiing on Lake Taupo. j, Another smooth landing in the capital. k, At this time of year we'd be lucky to see a whale . . . l, Another successful day's whitebaiting. m, Just a friendly game of beach cricket. n, Always blow on the pie.

**2016, Sept. 7 Litho. *Perf. 14¼x14½***

| | | | |
|---|---|---|---|
| **2683** | A670 Sheet of 14 | 21.00 | 21.00 |
| *a.-n.* | $1 Any single | 1.50 | 1.50 |

Royal New Zealand Navy, 75th Anniv. — A671

Designs: No. 2684, Sailors from HMS Neptune. No. 2685, Ship in Korean conflict. $1.80, Woman sailor using sextant. $2.20, Ship and helicopter supporting United Nations peacekeepers. $2.70, Sailor in Christchurch disaster relief efforts. $3.30, Sailor with his children.

**2016, Oct. 5 Litho. *Perf. 14½x14¼***

| | | | |
|---|---|---|---|
| **2684** | A671 $1 multi | 1.50 | 1.50 |
| **2685** | A671 $1 multi | 1.50 | 1.50 |
| **2686** | A671 $1.80 multi | 2.75 | 2.75 |
| **2687** | A671 $2.20 multi | 3.25 | 3.25 |
| **2688** | A671 $2.70 multi | 4.00 | 4.00 |
| **2689** | A671 $3.30 multi | 5.00 | 5.00 |
| *a.* | Souvenir sheet of 6, #2684-2689 | 18.00 | 18.00 |
| | *Nos. 2684-2689 (6)* | 18.00 | 18.00 |

Souvenir Sheet

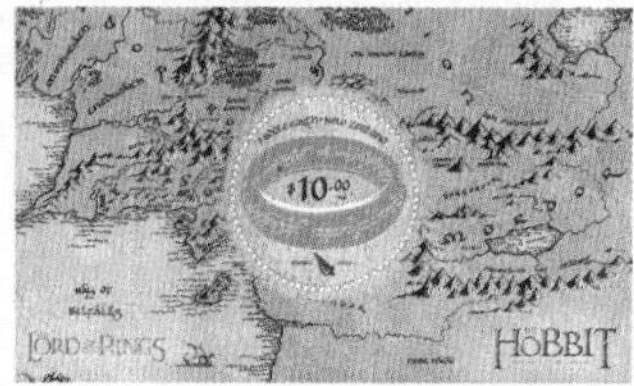


The One Ring From *The Lord of the Rings* — A672

**Litho. & Embossed With Foil Application**

**2016, Oct. 19 *Perf.***

| | | | |
|---|---|---|---|
| **2690** | A672 $10 multi | 15.50 | 15.50 |

No. 2690 sold for $10.50.

A673

Christmas — A674

Designs: $1, Infant Jesus. $1.80, Joseph. $2.20, Shepherd. $2.70, Virgin Mary. $3.30, Magus.

**2016, Nov. 2 Litho. *Perf. 14x14¼***

| | | | |
|---|---|---|---|
| **2691** | A673 $1 multi | 1.50 | 1.50 |
| **2692** | A673 $1.80 multi | 2.75 | 2.75 |
| **2693** | A673 $2.20 multi | 3.25 | 3.25 |
| **2694** | A673 $2.70 multi | 4.00 | 4.00 |
| **2695** | A673 $3.30 multi | 5.00 | 5.00 |
| *a.* | Souvenir sheet of 5, #2691-2695 | 16.50 | 16.50 |
| | *Nos. 2691-2695 (5)* | 16.50 | 16.50 |

**Self-Adhesive**

***Serpentine Die Cut 9½x10***

| | | | |
|---|---|---|---|
| **2696** | A674 $1 multi | 1.50 | 1.50 |
| *a.* | Booklet pane of 10 | 15.00 | |
| **2697** | A674 $2.20 multi | 3.25 | 3.25 |
| *a.* | Booklet pane of 10 + 10 labels | 32.50 | |
| **2698** | A674 $2.70 multi | 4.00 | 4.00 |
| *a.* | Booklet pane of 10 + 10 labels | 40.00 | |
| *b.* | Horiz. strip of 3, #2696-2698 | 11.50 | |
| | *Nos. 2696-2698 (3)* | 8.75 | 8.75 |

No. 2697a sold for $19.80, No. 2698a, for $24.30.

New Year 2017 (Year of the Rooster) — A675

Designs: $1, Chinese character for "rooster." $1.80, Paper-cut rooster. $2.20, Rooster. $2.70, Auckland War Memorial Museum, Chinese lantern.

**2017, Jan. 11 Litho. *Perf. 13¼x13***

| | | | |
|---|---|---|---|
| **2699** | A675 $1 multi | 1.50 | 1.50 |
| **2700** | A675 $1.80 multi | 2.60 | 2.60 |
| **2701** | A675 $2.20 multi | 3.25 | 3.25 |
| **2702** | A675 $2.70 multi | 4.00 | 4.00 |
| | *Nos. 2699-2702 (4)* | 11.35 | 11.35 |
| *a.* | Souvenir sheet of 4, #2699-2702 | 11.50 | 11.50 |

Southern Lights — A676

Various depictions of Southern Lights (Aurora Australis) from Mackenzie Basin.

**2017, Feb. 8 Litho. *Perf. 14½x14***

| | | | |
|---|---|---|---|
| **2703** | A676 $1 multi | 1.40 | 1.40 |
| **2704** | A676 $1.80 multi | 2.60 | 2.60 |
| **2705** | A676 $2 multi | 3.00 | 3.00 |
| **2706** | A676 $2.20 multi | 3.25 | 3.25 |
| **2707** | A676 $2.70 multi | 4.00 | 4.00 |
| **2708** | A676 $3.30 multi | 4.75 | 4.75 |
| | *Nos. 2703-2708 (6)* | 19.00 | 19.00 |

**Miniature Sheet**

**Litho. With Foil Application**

| | | | |
|---|---|---|---|
| **2709** | Sheet of 6 | 19.00 | 19.00 |
| *a.* | A676 $1 Like #2703 | 1.40 | 1.40 |
| *b.* | A676 $1.80 Like #2704 | 2.60 | 2.60 |
| *c.* | A676 $2 Like #2705 | 3.00 | 3.00 |
| *d.* | A676 $2.20 Like #2706 | 3.25 | 3.25 |
| *e.* | A676 $2.70 Like #2707 | 4.00 | 4.00 |
| *f.* | A676 $3.30 Like #2708 | 4.75 | 4.75 |

Freshwater Fish — A677

Designs: $1, Lowland longjaw galaxias. $1.80, Redfin bully. $2.20, Longfin eel. $2.70, Lamprey. $3.30, Torrentfish.

**2017, Mar. 1 Litho. *Perf. 14x14½***

| | | | |
|---|---|---|---|
| **2710** | A677 $1 multi | 1.40 | 1.40 |
| **2711** | A677 $1.80 multi | 2.60 | 2.60 |
| **2712** | A677 $2.20 multi | 3.25 | 3.25 |
| **2713** | A677 $2.70 multi | 4.00 | 4.00 |
| **2714** | A677 $3.30 multi | 4.75 | 4.75 |
| *a.* | Souvenir sheet of 5, #2710-2714 | 16.00 | 16.00 |
| | *Nos. 2710-2714 (5)* | 16.00 | 16.00 |

**World War I, Cent. Type of 2014**

Designs: No. 2715, Ellen Knight, mother who lost three sons in World War I. No. 2716, New Zealand officers near Beersheba mosque. No. 2717, Postmarks of Sling Camp, England. No. 2718, Tank at Battle of Messines. No. 2719, Hospital staffers in plastic surgery operating room. No. 2720, People looking at graves at Passchendaele battlefield. No. 2721, Soldiers marching at Battle of Messines. No. 2722, Notice of closing of New Zealand bars at 6 o'clock. No. 2723, SS Port Kembla, sunk off New Zealand coast. No. 2724, Women working at Census and Statistics Office Military Service Section.

**2017, Apr. 5 Litho. *Perf. 14½***

| | | | |
|---|---|---|---|
| **2715** | A631 $1 multi | 1.40 | 1.40 |
| *a.* | Booklet pane of 1 | 1.75 | — |
| **2716** | A631 $1 multi | 1.40 | 1.40 |
| *a.* | Booklet pane of 1 | 1.75 | — |
| **2717** | A631 $1 multi | 1.40 | 1.40 |
| *a.* | Booklet pane of 1 | 1.75 | — |
| **2718** | A631 $1 multi | 1.40 | 1.40 |
| *a.* | Booklet pane of 1 | 1.75 | — |
| **2719** | A631 $1 multi | 1.40 | 1.40 |
| *a.* | Booklet pane of 1 | 1.75 | — |
| **2720** | A631 $1 multi | 1.40 | 1.40 |
| *a.* | Booklet pane of 1 | 1.75 | — |
| *b.* | Booklet pane of 6, #2715-2720 | 11.00 | — |
| *c.* | Block of 6, #2715-2720 | 8.50 | 8.50 |
| *d.* | Souvenir sheet, #2715-2720 | 8.50 | 8.50 |
| **2721** | A631 $2.20 multi | 3.25 | 3.25 |
| *a.* | Booklet pane of 1 | 4.00 | — |
| **2722** | A631 $2.20 multi | 3.25 | 3.25 |
| *a.* | Booklet pane of 1 | 4.00 | — |
| *b.* | Horiz. pair, #2721-2722 | 6.50 | 6.50 |
| **2723** | A631 $2.70 multi | 3.75 | 3.75 |
| *a.* | Booklet pane of 1 | 4.75 | — |
| **2724** | A631 $2.70 multi | 3.75 | 3.75 |
| *a.* | Booklet pane of 1 | 4.75 | — |
| *b.* | Booklet pane of 4, #2721-2724 | 17.50 | — |
| | Complete booklet, #2715a, 2716a, 2717a, 2718a, 2719a, 2720a, 2720b, 2721a, 2722a, 2723a, 2724a, 2724b | 57.00 | |
| *c.* | Horiz. pair, #2723-2724 | 7.50 | 7.50 |
| *d.* | Souvenir sheet of 4, #2721-2724 | 14.00 | 14.00 |
| *e.* | Souvenir sheet of 10, #2715-2724 | 22.50 | 22.50 |
| | *Nos. 2715-2724 (10)* | 22.40 | 22.40 |

Complete booklet sold for $39.90.

Miniature Sheet

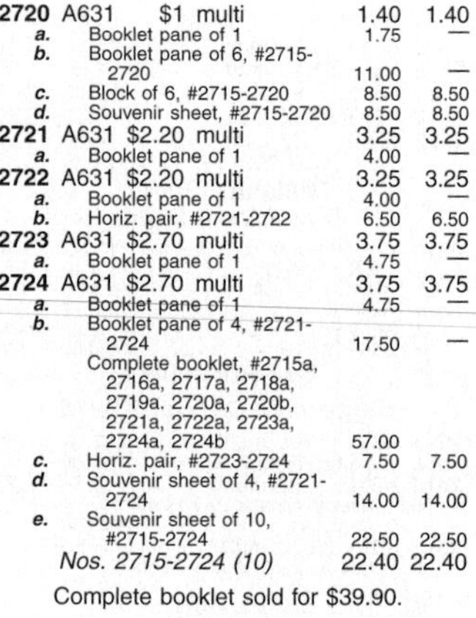


British and Irish Lions Rugby Team's 2017 Tour of New Zealand — A678

No. 2725 — Lion from team emblem and parts of map of New Zealand showing: a, Whangarei area. b, Auckland area. c, Hamilton area. d, Rotorua area. e, Wellington area. f, Christchurch area. g, Dunedin area.

**2017, May 3 Litho. *Perf. 14x14¼***

| | | | |
|---|---|---|---|
| **2725** | A678 Sheet of 7 | 28.00 | 28.00 |
| *a.-g.* | $2.70 Any single | 4.00 | 4.00 |

Opening of He Tohu Exhibition at National Library, Wellington — A679

Historic and modern people and text: $1, Declaration of Independence of the United Tribes of New Zealand, 1835. $2, Treaty of Waitangi, 1840. $2.20, Women's Suffrage Petition, 1893.

**2017, May 17 Litho. *Perf. 14x14¼***

| | | | |
|---|---|---|---|
| **2726** | A679 $1 multi | 1.40 | 1.40 |
| **2727** | A679 $2 multi | 3.00 | 3.00 |
| **2728** | A679 $2.20 multi | 3.25 | 3.25 |
| | *Nos. 2726-2728 (3)* | 7.65 | 7.65 |

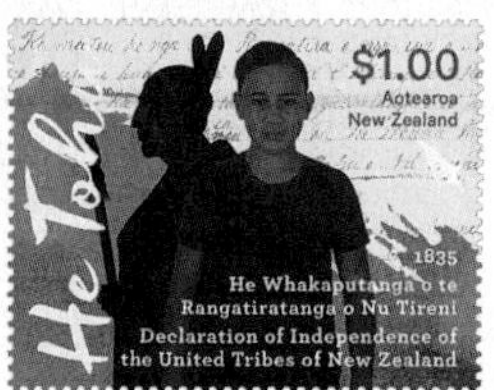


Scenery — A680

Designs: $2.30, Mangamaunu, Kaikoura. $4.30, Manu Bay, Raglan.

**2017, June 7 Litho. *Perf. 13¼x13½***

| | | | |
|---|---|---|---|
| **2729** | A680 $2.30 multi | 3.50 | 3.50 |
| **2730** | A680 $4.30 multi | 6.25 | 6.25 |

Surfing Areas — A681

Designs: $1, Piha Bar, Piha. $2.20, Manu Bay, Raglan. $2.30, Surf Highway 45, Taranaki. $2.70, Mangamaunu, Kaikoura. $3.30, Aramoana Spit, Dunedin.

**2017, June 7 Litho. *Perf. 14x14½***

**2731** A681 $1 multi 1.50 1.50
**2732** A681 $2.20 multi 3.25 3.25
**2733** A681 $2.30 multi 3.50 3.50
**2734** A681 $2.70 multi 4.00 4.00
**2735** A681 $3.30 multi 5.00 5.00
*a.* Souvenir sheet of 5, #2731-2735 17.50 17.50
*Nos. 2731-2735 (5)* 17.25 17.25

A682

A683

A684

A685

A686

A687

Victory of Emirates Team New Zealand in 2017 America's Cup Yacht Race
A687

**2017, July 3 Litho. *Perf. 13½x13¼***

**2736** Sheet of 6 29.00 29.00
*a.* A682 $2.70 multi 4.75 4.75
*b.* A683 $2.70 multi 4.75 4.75
*c.* A684 $2.70 multi 4.75 4.75
*d.* A685 $2.70 multi 4.75 4.75
*e.* A686 $2.70 multi 4.75 4.75
*f.* A687 $2.70 multi 4.75 4.75

No. 2736 sold for $19.90.

Miniature Sheet

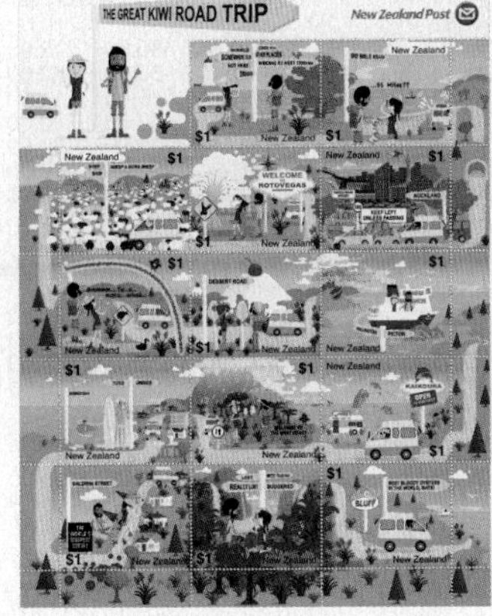


Great Kiwi Road Trip — A688

No. 2737 — Tourists and: a, Lighthouse and seven directional signs. b, Directional sign for 90 Mile Beach. c, Three directional signs for Sheep. d, "Welcome to Rotovegas" sign. e, Directional sign for Auckland. f, Directional sign for Taumatawhakatangihangakoauauotamateaturipukakapikimaungahoronukupokaiwhenuakitanatahu. g, Directional sign for Dessert Road. h, Directional signs for Wellington and Picton. i, Three directional signs for Sumner Beach, Togs and Undies. j, "Welcome to the West Coast" sign. k, Kaikoura sign. l, Directional sign for Baldwin Street. m, Waterfalls and four directional signs. n, Directional sign for best oysters.

**2017, July 12 Litho. *Perf. 14½x14***

**2737** A688 Sheet of 14 21.00 21.00
*a.-n.* $1 Any single 1.50 1.50

Native Birds
A689

Designs: $1, Campbell Island teal. $2.20, Black stilt. $2.30, North Island kaka. $2.70, South Island saddleback. $3.30, Northern New Zealand dotterel.

**2017, Aug. 2 Litho. *Perf. 14½x14***

**2738** A689 $1 multi 1.50 1.50
*a.* Perf. 14¼x14 1.50 1.50
**2739** A689 $2.20 multi 3.25 3.25
*a.* Perf. 14¼x14 3.25 3.25
**2740** A689 $2.30 multi 3.50 3.50
*a.* Perf. 14¼x14 3.50 3.50
*b.* Souvenir sheet of 3, #2738-2740 7.75 7.75
**2741** A689 $2.70 multi 4.00 4.00
*a.* Perf. 14¼x14 4.00 4.00
**2742** A689 $3.30 multi 4.75 4.75
*a.* Perf. 14¼x14 4.75 4.75
*b.* Souvenir sheet of 5, #2738a-2742a 17.00 17.00
*Nos. 2738-2742 (5)* 17.00 17.00

Royalpex 2017 National Stamp Exhibition, Hamilton (No. 2740b). Issued: No. 2740b, 11/24.

Miniature Sheet

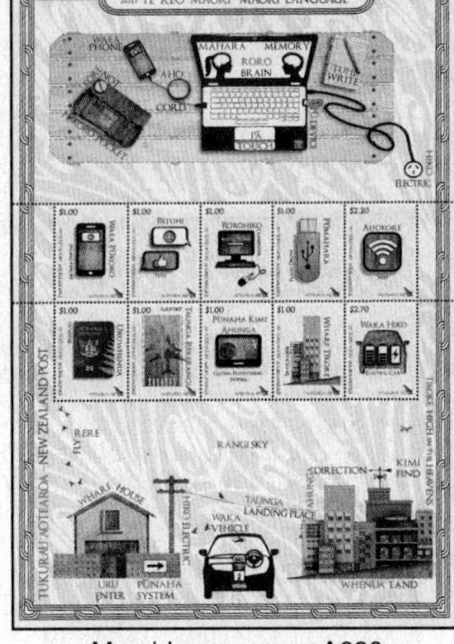


Maori Language — A690

No. 2743 — English and Maori words for modern objects: a, Mobile phone. b, Text. c, Computer. d, Flash drive. e, Passport. f, Airport. g, Global positioning system. h, Skyscraper. i, Wifi. j, Electric car.

**2017, Sept. 6 Litho. *Perf. 13¼***

**2743** A690 Sheet of 10 18.50 18.50
*a.-h.* $1 Any single 1.40 1.40
*i.* $2.20 multi 3.25 3.25
*j.* $2.70 multi 4.00 4.00

Herbs and Vegetables — A691

Designs: Nos. 2744, 2750a, Basil. Nos. 2745, 2750b, Carrots. $2.20, Parsley. $2.30, Chives. $2.70, Broccoli. $3.30, Lettuce.

***Perf. 14x14¼ on 3 sides, Rouletted 9½ on diagonal sides***

**2017, Oct. 4 Litho.**

**2744** A691 $1 multi 1.40 1.40
**2745** A691 $1 multi 1.40 1.40
**2746** A691 $2.20 multi 3.25 3.25
**2747** A691 $2.30 multi 3.50 3.50
**2748** A691 $2.70 multi 4.00 4.00
**2749** A691 $3.30 multi 4.75 4.75
*Nos. 2744-2749 (6)* 18.30 18.30

**Miniature Sheet**
**Stamps With Circle and "Plant Me" at Bottom**

**2750** Sheet of 6 18.50 18.50
*a.-b.* A691 $1 Either single 1.40 1.40
*c.* A691 $2.20 multi 3.25 3.25
*d.* A691 $2.30 multi 3.50 3.50
*e.* A691 $2.70 multi 4.00 4.00
*f.* A691 $3.30 multi 4.75 4.75

Examples of No. 2750 sold in New Zealand had seeds affixed to the bottom of each stamp. The stamps could be planted so the seeds could sprout. Inthernational purchasers of No. 2750 were only sent examples without seeds affixed.

70th Wedding Anniversary of Queen Elizabeth II and Prince Philip — A692

Designs: $1, Engagement photograph. $2, Wedding photograph. $2.20, Queen Elizabeth II, Prince Philip and their children. $2.30, Queen Elizabeth II and Prince Philip. $2.70, Queen Elizabeth II, Princes, Philip, Charles, William, Harry, Duchess of Cambridge and Princess Charlotte. $3.30, Queen Elizabeth II and Prince Philip, diff.

**Litho. With Foil Application**

**2017, Nov. 20 *Perf. 14¼***

**2751** A692 $1 sil & multi 1.40 1.40
**2752** A692 $2 sil & multi 2.75 2.75
**2753** A692 $2.20 sil & multi 3.00 3.00
**2754** A692 $2.30 sil & multi 3.25 3.25
**2755** A692 $2.70 sil & multi 3.75 3.75
**2756** A692 $3.30 sil & multi 4.50 4.50
*a.* Souvenir sheet of 6, #2751-2756 19.00 19.00
*Nos. 2751-2756 (6)* 18.65 18.65

A693

Christmas — A694

Quilled: $1, Angel. $2.20, Christmas ornament. $2.30, Star. $2.70, Bell. $3.30, Wreath.

**2017, Dec. 6 Litho. *Perf. 14¼***

**2757** A693 $1 multi 1.50 1.50
**2758** A693 $2.20 multi 3.25 3.25
**2759** A693 $2.30 multi 3.25 3.25
**2760** A693 $2.70 multi 4.00 4.00
**2761** A693 $3.30 multi 4.75 4.75
*a.* Souvenir sheet of 5, #2757-2761 17.00 17.00
*Nos. 2757-2761 (5)* 16.75 16.75

**Self-Adhesive**
***Serpentine Die Cut 9½x10***

**2762** A694 $1 multi 1.50 1.50
*a.* Booklet pane of 10 15.00
**2763** A694 $2.20 multi 3.25 3.25
*a.* Booklet pane of 10 32.50
**2764** A694 $2.70 multi 4.00 4.00
*a.* Booklet pane of 10 40.00
*b.* Horiz. strip of 3, #2762-2764 8.75
*Nos. 2762-2764 (3)* 8.75 8.75

Nos. 2763 and 2764 are airmail. No. 2763a sold for $19.80. No. 2764a sold for $24.30.

New Year 2018 (Year of the Dog) — A695

Designs: $1, Chinese character for "dog." $2.20, Paper-cut dog. $2.20, Dog and sheep. $2.70, Sheepdog Memorial, Lake Tekapo and birds.

**2018, Jan. 10 Litho. *Perf. 13¼x13***

**2765** A695 $1 multi 1.50 1.50
**2766** A695 $2.20 multi 3.25 3.25
**2767** A695 $2.70 multi 4.00 4.00
**2768** A695 $3.30 multi 5.00 5.00
*a.* Souvenir sheet of 4, #2765-2768 14.00 14.00
*Nos. 2765-2768 (4)* 13.75 13.75

New Zealand in Space
A696

No. 2769: a, Electron rocket being delivered to launch pad. b, Rocket on launch pad. c,

Humanity Star satellite. d, Aerial view of launch facility. e, Rocket launch. f, Satellite in space.

**2018, Jan. 25 Litho. *Perf. 13½x13¼***

| No. | Description | Unused | Used |
|---|---|---|---|
| **2769** | Sheet of 6 | 29.50 | 29.50 |
| *a.* | A696 $1 multi | 2.00 | 2.00 |
| *b.* | A696 $2 multi | 4.25 | 4.25 |
| *c.* | A696 $2.20 multi | 4.50 | 4.50 |
| *d.* | A696 $2.70 multi | 5.75 | 5.75 |
| *e.* | A696 $3 multi | 6.25 | 6.25 |
| *f.* | A696 $3.30 multi | 6.75 | 6.75 |

No. 2769 sold for $19.90.

Bicycle Trails — A697

Designs: No. 2770, $1, Alps 2 Ocean Trail. No. 2771, $1, Mountains to Sea Trail. $2, Otago Central Rail Trail. $2.20, Old Ghost Road. $2.70, Queen Charlotte Track. $3.30, Timber Trail.

**2018, Feb. 7 Litho. *Perf. 14x14½***

| No. | Type | Description | Unused | Used |
|---|---|---|---|---|
| **2770** | A697 | $1 multi | 1.50 | 1.50 |
| **2771** | A697 | $1 multi | 1.50 | 1.50 |
| **2772** | A697 | $2 multi | 3.00 | 3.00 |
| **2773** | A697 | $2.20 multi | 3.25 | 3.25 |
| **2774** | A697 | $2.70 multi | 4.00 | 4.00 |
| **2775** | A697 | $3.30 multi | 4.75 | 4.75 |
| *a.* | | Souvenir sheet of 6, #2770-2775 | 18.00 | 18.00 |
| | | *Nos. 2770-2775 (6)* | 18.00 | 18.00 |

Wahine Ferry Disaster, 50th Anniv. — A698

Inscription: No. 2776, $1, World's Finest Drive-on Vessel. No. 2777, $1, Wahine in Trouble. $2, Waiting to Abandon Ship. $2.20, Lifeboats Make Land. $2.70, Hundreds Rescued From Wellington Harbor. $3.30, Aranui Passes Wahine Wreck.

**2018, Mar. 7 Litho. *Perf. 14½x14***

| No. | Type | Description | Unused | Used |
|---|---|---|---|---|
| **2776** | A698 | $1 multi | 1.50 | 1.50 |
| **2777** | A698 | $1 multi | 1.50 | 1.50 |
| **2778** | A698 | $2 multi | 3.00 | 3.00 |
| **2779** | A698 | $2.20 multi | 3.25 | 3.25 |
| **2780** | A698 | $2.70 multi | 4.00 | 4.00 |
| **2781** | A698 | $3.30 multi | 4.75 | 4.75 |
| *a.* | | Souvenir sheet of 6, #2776-2781 | 18.00 | 18.00 |
| | | *Nos. 2776-2781 (6)* | 18.00 | 18.00 |

### World War I, Cent. Type of 2014

Designs: No. 2782, Private Arthur Gordon (1895-1978), advocate for disabled veterans. No. 2783, Hundred Days Offensive. No. 2784, Medicine Depot for treating victims of influenza pandemic. No. 2785, Demobilized soldier in New Zealand with family. No. 2786, Resettlement of veterans. No. 2787, Sopwith Camel biplane in air battle. No. 2788, Auckland Town Hall with lights celebrating armistice. No. 2789, Return of Maori Battalion. No. 2790, New Zealand soldiersat Le Quesnoy on stained-glass window of St. Andrew's Anglican Church, Cambridge, England. No. 2791, Emblem of War Amputees' Association.

**2018, Apr. 4 Litho. *Perf. 14½***

| No. | Type | Description | Unused | Used |
|---|---|---|---|---|
| **2782** | A631 | $1 multi | 1.50 | 1.50 |
| *a.* | | Booklet pane of 1 | 1.90 | — |
| **2783** | A631 | $1 multi | 1.50 | 1.50 |
| *a.* | | Booklet pane of 1 | 1.90 | — |
| **2784** | A631 | $1 multi | 1.50 | 1.50 |
| *a.* | | Booklet pane of 1 | 1.90 | — |
| **2785** | A631 | $1 multi | 1.50 | 1.50 |
| *a.* | | Booklet pane of 1 | 1.90 | — |
| **2786** | A631 | $1 multi | 1.50 | 1.50 |
| *a.* | | Booklet pane of 1 | 1.90 | — |
| **2787** | A631 | $1 multi | 1.50 | 1.50 |
| *a.* | | Booklet pane of 1 | 1.90 | — |
| *b.* | | Block of 6, #2782-2787 | 9.00 | 9.00 |
| *c.* | | Souvenir sheet of 6, #2782-2787 | 9.00 | 9.00 |
| **2788** | A631 | $2.20 multi | 3.25 | 3.25 |
| *a.* | | Booklet pane of 1 | 4.00 | — |
| *b.* | | Booklet pane of 6, #2782-2786, 2788 | 13.00 | — |
| **2789** | A631 | $2.20 multi | 3.25 | 3.25 |
| *a.* | | Booklet pane of 1 | 4.00 | — |
| *b.* | | Horiz. pair, #2788-2789 | 6.50 | 6.50 |
| **2790** | A631 | $2.70 multi | 4.00 | 4.00 |
| *a.* | | Booklet pane of 1 | 5.00 | — |
| **2791** | A631 | $2.70 multi | 4.00 | 4.00 |
| *a.* | | Booklet pane of 1 | 5.00 | — |
| *b.* | | Booklet pane of 4, #2787, 2789-2791 | 16.00 | — |
| | | Complete booklet, #2782a, 2783a, 2784a, 2785a, 2786a. 2787a, 2788a, 2788b, 2789a, 2790a, 2791a, 2791b | 58.50 | |
| *c.* | | Horiz. pair, #2790-2791 | 8.00 | 8.00 |
| *d.* | | Souvenir sheet of 4, #2788-2791 | 14.50 | 14.50 |
| *e.* | | Souvenir sheet of 10, #2782-2791 | 23.50 | 23.50 |
| | | *Nos. 2782-2791 (10)* | 23.50 | 23.50 |

Complete booklet sold for $39.90.

## POSTAL-FISCAL STAMPS

In 1881 fiscal stamps of New Zealand of denominations over one shilling were made acceptable for postal duty. Values for canceled stamps are for postal cancellations. Denominations above £5 appear to have been used primarily for fiscal purposes.

Queen Victoria
PF1 PF2

***Perf. 11, 12, 12½***

**1882 Typo. Wmk. 62**

| No. | Type | Description | Unused | Used |
|---|---|---|---|---|
| **AR1** | PF1 | 2sh blue | 125.00 | 20.00 |
| **AR2** | PF1 | 2sh6p dk brown | 125.00 | 20.00 |
| **AR3** | PF1 | 3sh violet | 225.00 | 25.00 |
| **AR4** | PF1 | 4sh brown vio | 325.00 | 40.00 |
| **AR5** | PF1 | 4sh red brn | 275.00 | 40.00 |
| **AR6** | PF1 | 5sh green | 325.00 | 40.00 |
| **AR7** | PF1 | 6sh rose | 500.00 | 65.00 |
| **AR8** | PF1 | 7sh ultra | 550.00 | 150.00 |
| **AR9** | PF1 | 7sh6p ol gray | 1,500. | 500.00 |
| **AR10** | PF1 | 8sh dull blue | 525.00 | 125.00 |
| **AR11** | PF1 | 9sh org red | 900.00 | 300.00 |
| **AR12** | PF1 | 10sh red brn | 350.00 | 75.00 |

**1882-90**

| No. | Type | Description | Unused | Used |
|---|---|---|---|---|
| **AR13** | PF2 | 15sh dk grn | 1,500. | 400.00 |
| **AR15** | PF2 | £1 rose | 700.00 | 150.00 |
| **AR16** | PF2 | 25sh blue | | — |
| **AR17** | PF2 | 30sh brown | | — |
| **AR18** | PF2 | £1 15sh yellow | | — |
| **AR19** | PF2 | £2 purple | | — |

PF3 PF4

| No. | Type | Description | Unused | Used |
|---|---|---|---|---|
| **AR20** | PF3 | £2 10sh red brn | | — |
| **AR21** | PF3 | £3 yel green | | — |
| **AR22** | PF3 | £3 10sh rose | | — |
| **AR23** | PF3 | £4 ultra | | — |
| **AR24** | PF3 | £4 10sh ol brn | | — |
| **AR25** | PF3 | £5 dark blue | | — |
| **AR26** | PF4 | £6 org red | | — |
| **AR27** | PF4 | £7 brn red | | — |
| **AR28** | PF4 | £8 green | | — |
| **AR29** | PF4 | £9 rose | | — |
| **AR30** | PF4 | £10 blue | | — |
| **AR30A** | PF4 | £20 yellow | — | — |

No. AR31

### With "COUNTERPART" at Bottom

**1901**

| No. | Type | Description | Unused | Used |
|---|---|---|---|---|
| **AR31** | PF1 | 2sh6p brown | 300.00 | *400.00* |

***Perf. 11, 14, 14½x14***

**1903-15 Wmk. 61**

| No. | Type | Description | Unused | Used |
|---|---|---|---|---|
| **AR32** | PF1 | 2sh blue ('07) | 80.00 | 12.00 |
| **AR33** | PF1 | 2sh6p brown | 80.00 | 12.00 |
| **AR34** | PF1 | 3sh violet | 175.00 | 14.00 |
| **AR35** | PF1 | 4sh brn red | 200.00 | 30.00 |
| **AR36** | PF1 | 5sh grn ('06) | 225.00 | 30.00 |
| **AR37** | PF1 | 6sh rose | 375.00 | 50.00 |
| **AR38** | PF1 | 7sh dull blue | 400.00 | 80.00 |
| **AR39** | PF1 | 7sh6p ol gray ('06) | 1,500. | 400.00 |
| **AR40** | PF1 | 8sh dk blue | 450.00 | 75.00 |
| **AR41** | PF1 | 9sh dl org ('06) | 600.00 | 200.00 |
| **AR42** | PF1 | 10sh dp clar | 250.00 | 50.00 |
| **AR43** | PF2 | 15sh blue grn | 1,350. | 350.00 |
| **AR44** | PF2 | £1 rose | 500.00 | 150.00 |

***Perf. 14½***

| No. | Type | Description | Unused | Used |
|---|---|---|---|---|
| **AR45** | PF2 | £2 dp vio ('25) | 600.00 | 150.00 |
| *a.* | | Perf. 14 | 700.00 | 150.00 |
| | | *Nos. AR32-AR45 (14)* | 6,785. | 1,603. |

For overprints see Cook Islands Nos. 67-71.

Coat of Arms — PF5

**1931-39 Wmk. 61 *Perf. 14***

**Type PF5 (Various Frames)**

| No. | Description | Unused | Used |
|---|---|---|---|
| **AR46** | 1sh3p lemon | 30.00 | 40.00 |
| **AR47** | 1sh3p org ('32) | 8.00 | 9.00 |
| **AR48** | 2sh6p brown | 16.00 | 5.25 |
| **AR49** | 4sh dull red ('32) | 17.00 | 7.50 |
| **AR50** | 5sh green | 21.00 | 12.50 |
| **AR51** | 6sh brt rose ('32) | 37.50 | 15.00 |
| **AR52** | 7sh gray blue | 32.50 | 25.00 |
| **AR53** | 7sh6p olive gray ('32) | 75.00 | 92.50 |
| **AR54** | 8sh dark blue | 50.00 | 37.50 |
| **AR55** | 9sh brn org | 52.50 | 32.50 |
| **AR56** | 10sh dark car | 27.50 | 10.50 |
| **AR57** | 12sh6p brn vio ('35) | 250.00 | 250.00 |
| **AR58** | 15sh ol grn ('32) | 70.00 | 42.50 |
| **AR59** | £1 pink ('32) | 75.00 | 22.50 |
| **AR60** | 25sh turq bl ('38) | 550.00 | 600.00 |
| **AR61** | 30sh dk brn ('36) | 300.00 | 200.00 |
| **AR62** | 35sh yel ('37) | 6,000. | *7,500.* |
| **AR63** | £2 vio ('33) | 400.00 | 70.00 |
| **AR64** | £2 10sh dk red ('36) | 400.00 | *550.00* |
| **AR65** | £3 lt grn ('32) | 400.00 | 210.00 |
| **AR66** | £3 10sh rose ('39) | 2,250. | 2,250. |
| **AR67** | £4 light blue | 400.00 | 175.00 |
| **AR68** | £4 10sh dk ol gray ('39) | 2,500. | 2,500. |
| **AR69** | £5 dk blue ('32) | 400.00 | 100.00 |

For overprints see Cook Islands Nos. 80-83.

No. AR62 Surcharged in Black

**1939 *Perf. 14***

| No. | Description | Unused | Used |
|---|---|---|---|
| **AR70** | PF5 35sh on 35sh yel | 500.00 | 350.00 |

### Type PF5 Surcharged in Black

**1940**

| No. | Description | Unused | Used |
|---|---|---|---|
| **AR71** | 3sh6p on 3sh6p dl green | 28.50 | 21.00 |
| **AR72** | 5sh6p on 5sh6p rose lilac | 60.00 | 57.50 |
| **AR73** | 11sh on 11sh pale yellow | 125.00 | 150.00 |
| **AR74** | 22sh on 22sh scar | 275.00 | 350.00 |
| | *Nos. AR71-AR74 (4)* | 488.50 | 578.50 |

### Type of 1931

**1940-58 Wmk. 253 *Perf. 14***

**Type PF5 (Various Frames)**

| No. | Description | Unused | Used |
|---|---|---|---|
| **AR75** | 1sh3p orange | 5.75 | .60 |
| **AR76** | 2sh6p brown | 5.75 | .60 |
| **AR77** | 4sh dull red | 6.75 | .60 |
| **AR78** | 5sh green | 11.50 | .90 |
| **AR79** | 6sh brt rose | 20.00 | 4.00 |
| **AR80** | 7sh gray bl | 20.00 | 6.75 |
| **AR81** | 7sh6p ol gray ('50) | 70.00 | *70.00* |
| **AR82** | 8sh dk blue | 45.00 | 25.00 |
| **AR83** | 9sh orange ('46) | 50.00 | 30.00 |
| **AR84** | 10sh dk carmine | 25.00 | 3.25 |
| **AR85** | 15sh olive ('45) | 55.00 | 20.00 |
| **AR86** | £1 pink('45) | 29.00 | 8.50 |
| *a.* | Perf. 14x13½ ('58) | 32.50 | 15.00 |
| **AR87** | 25sh blue ('46) | 500.00 | *550.00* |
| **AR88** | 30sh choc ('46) | 250.00 | 200.00 |
| **AR89** | £2 violet ('46) | 100.00 | 60.00 |
| **AR90** | £2 10sh dk red ('51) | 400.00 | *525.00* |
| **AR91** | £3 lt grn ('46) | 150.00 | 125.00 |
| **AR92** | £3 10sh rose ('48) | 2,300. | *2,500.* |
| **AR93** | £4 lt blue ('52) | 150.00 | 160.00 |
| **AR94** | £5 dk blue ('40) | 175.00 | 150.00 |

### Type PF5 Surcharged in Black

**1942-45 Wmk. 253**

| No. | Description | Unused | Used |
|---|---|---|---|
| **AR95** | 3sh6p on 3sh6p grn | 12.50 | 8.00 |
| **AR96** | 5sh6p on 5sh6p rose lil ('44) | 26.00 | 8.50 |
| **AR97** | 11sh on 11sh yel | 67.50 | 52.50 |
| **AR98** | 22sh on 22sh car ('45) | 325.00 | *275.00* |
| | *Nos. AR95-AR98 (4)* | 431.00 | 344.00 |

**Catalogue values for unused stamps in this section, from this point to the end of the section, are for Never Hinged items.**

### Type of 1931 Redrawn Surcharged in Black

**1953 Typo.**

| No. | Description | Unused | Used |
|---|---|---|---|
| **AR99** | PF5 3sh6p on 3sh6p green | 32.50 | 35.00 |

Denomination of basic stamp is in small, sans-serif capitals without period after "sixpence."

### Type of 1931

**1955 Wmk. 253 *Perf. 14***

**Denomination in Black**

| No. | Description | Unused | Used |
|---|---|---|---|
| **AR100** | PF5 1sh3p orange | 2.75 | .90 |

**1956 Denomination in Blue**

| No. | Description | Unused | Used |
|---|---|---|---|
| **AR101** | PF5 1sh3p orange yel | 17.50 | 14.50 |

For decimal-currency postage stamps of design No. PF5, see Nos. 404A-404D, 404Ba, 404Ca, 404Da.

## SEMI-POSTAL STAMPS

Nurse — SP1

### Inscribed: "Help Stamp out Tuberculosis, 1929"

**Wmk. 61**

**1929, Dec. 11 Typo. *Perf. 14***

| No. | Description | Unused | Used |
|---|---|---|---|
| **B1** | SP1 1p + 1p scarlet | 12.50 | *20.00* |

Nurse — SP2

### Inscribed: "Help Promote Health, 1930"

**1930, Oct. 29**

| No. | Description | Unused | Used |
|---|---|---|---|
| **B2** | SP2 1p + 1p scarlet | 30.00 | *45.00* |

Boy — SP3

**1931, Oct. 31** *Perf. 14½x14*

| | | | |
|---|---|---|---|
| **B3** | SP3 1p + 1p scarlet | 100.00 | 90.00 |
| **B4** | SP3 2p + 1p dark blue | 100.00 | 75.00 |

Hygeia, Goddess of Health — SP4

**1932, Nov. 18** **Engr.** *Perf. 14*

| | | | |
|---|---|---|---|
| **B5** | SP4 1p + 1p carmine | 22.50 | *30.00* |
| | Never hinged | 55.00 | |

Road to Health — SP5

**1933, Nov. 8**

| | | | |
|---|---|---|---|
| **B6** | SP5 1p + 1p carmine | 15.00 | *20.00* |
| | Never hinged | 35.00 | |

Crusader — SP6

**1934, Oct. 25** *Perf. 14x13½*

| | | | |
|---|---|---|---|
| **B7** | SP6 1p + 1p dark carmine | 12.50 | *20.00* |
| | Never hinged | 25.00 | |

Child at Bathing Beach — SP7

**1935, Sept. 30** *Perf. 11*

| | | | |
|---|---|---|---|
| **B8** | SP7 1p + 1p scarlet | 3.00 | 3.25 |
| | Never hinged | 5.00 | |

**Catalogue values for unused stamps in this section, from this point to the end of the section, are for Never Hinged items.**

Anzac — SP8

**1936, Apr. 27**

| | | | |
|---|---|---|---|
| **B9** | SP8 ½p + ½p green | .70 | *2.00* |
| **B10** | SP8 1p + 1p red | .70 | *1.60* |

21st anniv. of Anzac landing at Gallipoli.

"Health" SP9

**1936, Nov. 2**

| | | | |
|---|---|---|---|
| **B11** | SP9 1p + 1p red | 2.00 | *4.25* |

Boy Hiker — SP10

**1937, Oct. 1**

| | | | |
|---|---|---|---|
| **B12** | SP10 1p + 1p red | 3.00 | *4.00* |

Children at Play — SP11

*Perf. 14x13½*

**1938, Oct. 1** **Wmk. 253**

| | | | |
|---|---|---|---|
| **B13** | SP11 1p + 1p red | 6.25 | 3.25 |

Children at Play — SP12

**Black Surcharge**

**1939, Oct. 16** **Wmk. 61** *Perf. 11½*

| | | | |
|---|---|---|---|
| **B14** | SP12 1p on ½p + ½p grn | 5.00 | 5.00 |
| **B15** | SP12 2p on 1p + 1p scar | 5.00 | 5.00 |

Children at Play — SP12a

**1940, Oct. 1**

| | | | |
|---|---|---|---|
| **B16** | SP12a 1p + ½p green | 16.00 | 17.50 |
| **B17** | SP12a 2p + 1p org brown | 16.00 | 17.50 |

The surtax was used to help maintain children's health camps.

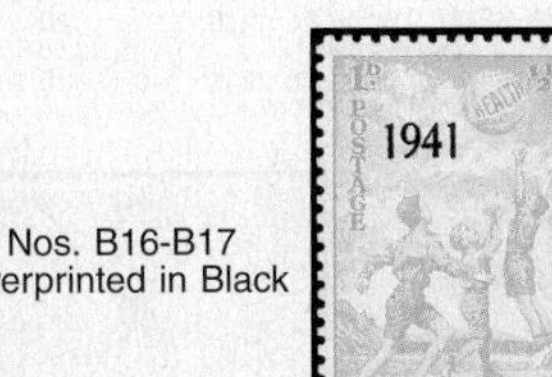

Nos. B16-B17 Overprinted in Black

**1941, Oct. 4** *Perf. 11½*

| | | | |
|---|---|---|---|
| **B18** | SP12a 1p + ½p green | 3.00 | *3.50* |
| **B19** | SP12a 2p + 1p org brown | 3.00 | *3.50* |

Children in Swing — SP13

**1942, Oct. 1** **Engr.**

| | | | |
|---|---|---|---|
| **B20** | SP13 1p + ½p green | .35 | *1.10* |
| **B21** | SP13 2p + 1p dp org brown | .35 | *1.10* |

**Imperf plate proofs on card exist for #B22-B27, B32-B33, B38-B39, B46-B48, B59-B60. Imperfs exist for B44-B45, B49-B51. These are from the printer's archives.**

Princess Elizabeth — SP14

Design: 1p+1/2p, Princess Margaret Rose.

**1943, Oct. 1** **Wmk. 253** *Perf. 12*

| | | | |
|---|---|---|---|
| **B22** | SP14 1p + ½p dark green | .25 | .40 |
| *a.* | Vert. pair, imperf. between | 12,500. | |
| **B23** | SP14 2p + 1p red brown | .25 | .40 |
| *a.* | Vert. pair, imperf. between | 12,500. | |

Princesses Margaret Rose and Elizabeth SP16

**1944, Oct. 9** *Perf. 13½*

| | | | |
|---|---|---|---|
| **B24** | SP16 1p + ½p blue green | .35 | .45 |
| **B25** | SP16 2p + 1p chalky blue | .35 | .35 |

Peter Pan Statue, London — SP17

**1945, Oct. 1**

| | | | |
|---|---|---|---|
| **B26** | SP17 1p + ½p gray grn & bis brn | .25 | .35 |
| **B27** | SP17 2p + 1p car & ol bis | .25 | .35 |

Soldier Helping Child over Stile SP18

**1946, Oct. 24** *Perf. 13½x13*

| | | | |
|---|---|---|---|
| **B28** | SP18 1p + ½p dk grn & org brn | .25 | .35 |
| **B29** | SP18 2p + 1p dk brn & org brn | .25 | .35 |

Statue of Eros, London — SP19

**1947, Oct. 1** **Engr.** *Perf. 13x13½*

| | | | |
|---|---|---|---|
| **B30** | SP19 1p + ½p deep green | .25 | .35 |
| **B31** | SP19 2p + 1p deep carmine | .25 | .35 |

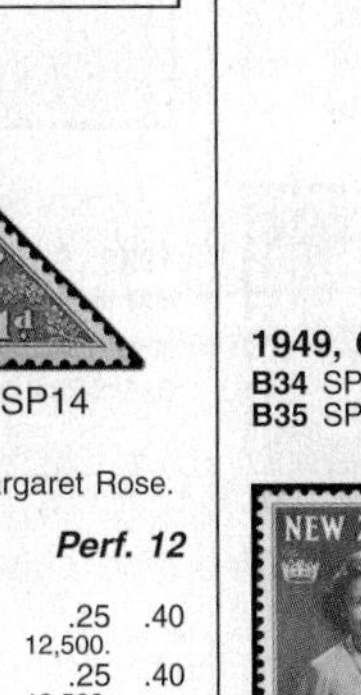

Children's Health Camp SP20

**1948, Oct. 1** *Perf. 13½x13*

| | | | |
|---|---|---|---|
| **B32** | SP20 1p + ½p blue grn & ultra | .25 | .35 |
| **B33** | SP20 2p + 1p red & dk brn | .25 | .35 |

Nurse and Child — SP21

**1949, Oct. 3** **Photo.** *Perf. 14x14½*

| | | | |
|---|---|---|---|
| **B34** | SP21 1p + ½p deep green | .30 | .35 |
| **B35** | SP21 2p + 1p ultramarine | .30 | .35 |

Princess Elizabeth and Prince Charles — SP22

**1950, Oct. 2**

| | | | |
|---|---|---|---|
| **B36** | SP22 1p + ½p green | .25 | .35 |
| **B37** | SP22 2p + 1p violet brown | .25 | .35 |

Racing Yachts SP23

*Perf. 13½x13*

**1951, Nov. 1** **Engr.** **Wmk. 253**

| | | | |
|---|---|---|---|
| **B38** | SP23 1½p + ½p red & yel | .25 | *.35* |
| **B39** | SP23 2p + 1p dp grn & yel | .25 | .35 |

Princess Anne SP24

Prince Charles SP25

*Perf. 14x14½*

**1952, Oct. 1** **Wmk. 253** **Photo.**

| | | | |
|---|---|---|---|
| **B40** | SP24 1½p + ½p crimson | .25 | .35 |
| **B41** | SP25 2p + 1p brown | .25 | .35 |

Girl Guides Marching SP26

Boy Scouts at Camp SP27

**1953, Oct. 7**

B42 SP26 1½p + ½p bright blue .25 .35
B43 SP27 2p + 1p deep green .25 .35

The border of No. B43 consists of Morse code reading "Health" at top and bottom and "New Zealand" on each side. On No. B42 the top border line is replaced by "Health" in Morse code.

Young Mountain Climber Studying Map — SP28

**1954, Oct. 4 Engr. *Perf. 13½***

B44 SP28 1½p + ½p pur & brn .25 .35
B45 SP28 2p + 1p vio gray & brn .25 .35

Child's Head — SP29

**1955, Oct. 3 Wmk. 253 *Perf. 13***

B46 SP29 1½p + ½p brn org & sep .25 .35
B47 SP29 2p + 1p grn & org brn .25 .35
B48 SP29 3p + 1p car & sepia .25 .35
*Nos. B46-B48 (3)* .75 1.05

Children Picking Apples — SP30

**1956, Sept. 24**

B49 SP30 1½p + ½p chocolate .25 .35
B50 SP30 2p + 1p blue green .25 .35
B51 SP30 3p + 1p dk car .25 .35
*Nos. B49-B51 (3)* .75 1.05

Life-Saving Team SP31

3p+1p, Children playing and boy in canoe.

**1957, Sept. 25 *Perf. 13½***

B52 SP31 2p + 1p emer & blk .25 .35
a. Miniature sheet of 6 7.25 25.00
B53 SP31 3p + 1p car & ultra .25 .35
a. Miniature sheet of 6 7.25 25.00

The watermark is sideways on Nos. B52a and B53a. In a second printing, the watermark is upright; values double.

Girls' Life Brigade Cadet — SP32

Design: 3p+1p, Bugler, Boys' Brigade.

**1958, Aug. 20 Photo. *Perf. 14x14½***

B54 SP32 2p + 1p green .25 .45
a. Miniature sheet of 6 5.00 25.00
B55 SP32 3p + 1p ultramarine .25 .45
a. Miniature sheet of 6 5.00 25.00

75th anniv. of the founding of the Boys' Brigade.

The surtax on this and other preceding semi-postals was for the maintenance of children's health camps.

Globes and Red Cross Flag SP33

**1959, June 3 *Perf. 14½x14***

B56 SP33 3p + 1p ultra & car .25 .25
a. Red Cross omitted 2,000.

The surtax was for the Red Cross.

Gray Teal (Tete) — SP34

Design: 3p+1p, Pied stilt (Poaka).

**1959, Sept. 16 *Perf. 14x14½***

B57 SP34 2p + 1p pink, blk, yel & gray .60 .75
a. Miniature sheet of 6 6.00 20.00
B58 SP34 3p + 1p blue, black & pink .60 .75
a. Miniature sheet of 6 6.00 20.00
b. Pink omitted 160.00

Sacred Kingfisher (Kotare) — SP35

Design: 3p+1p, NZ pigeon (Kereru).

**1960, Aug. 10 Engr. *Perf. 13x13½***

B59 SP35 2p + 1p grnsh blue & sepia .60 .85
a. Min. sheet of 6, perf. 11½x11 13.00 22.50
B60 SP35 3p + 1p org & sepia .60 .85
a. Min. sheet of 6, perf. 11½x11 13.00 22.50

**Type of 1959**

Birds: 2p+1p, Great white egret (Kotuku). 3p+1p, New Zealand falcon (Karearea).

**1961, Aug. 2 Wmk. 253**

B61 SP34 2p + 1p pale lil & blk .60 .80
a. Miniature sheet of 6 13.00 22.50
B62 SP34 3p + 1p yel grn & blk brn .60 .80
a. Miniature sheet of 6 13.00 22.50

**Type of 1959**

Birds: 2½p+1p, Red-fronted parakeet (Kakariki). 3p+1p, Saddleback (Tieke).

**1962, Oct. 3 Photo. *Perf. 15x14***

B63 SP34 2½p + 1p lt bl, blk, grn & org .60 .80
a. Miniature sheet of 6 20.00 27.50
B64 SP34 3p + 1p salmon, blk, grn & org .60 .80
a. Miniature sheet of 6 20.00 27.50
b. Orange omitted 2,750.

Prince Andrew — SP36

Design: 3p+1p, Prince without book.

**1963, Aug. 7 Engr. *Perf. 14***

B65 SP36 2½p + 1p ultra .35 .80
a. Miniature sheet of 6 13.00 22.50
B66 SP36 3p + 1p rose car .35 .25
a. Miniature sheet of 6 13.00 22.50

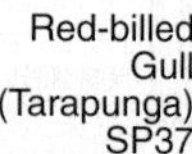

Red-billed Gull (Tarapunga) SP37

Design: 3p+1p, Blue penguin (Korora).

**1964, Aug. 5 Photo. *Perf. 14***

B67 SP37 2½p + 1p lt bl, pale yel, red & blk .45 .75
a. Miniature sheet of 8 22.50 35.00
b. Red omitted 325.00 225.00
c. Yellow omitted
B68 SP37 3p + 1p blue, yel & blk .45 .75
a. Miniature sheet of 8 22.50 35.00

Kaka — SP38

Design: 4p+1p, Fantail (Piwakawaka).

**1965, Aug. 4 *Perf. 14x14½***

B69 SP38 3p + 1p gray, red, brn & yellow .60 .85
a. Miniature sheet of 6 11.00 27.50
B70 SP38 4p + 1p yel, blk, emer & brn .60 .85
a. Miniature sheet of 6 11.00 27.50
b. As No. B70, green omitted 2,000. 2,000.

Bellbird & Bough of Kowhai Tree — SP39

4p+1p, Flightless rail (Weka) and fern.

**1966, Aug. 3 Photo. Wmk. 253**

B71 SP39 3p + 1p lt bl & multi .60 .85
a. Miniature sheet of 6 9.00 25.00
B72 SP39 4p + 1p lt grn & multi .60 .85
a. Miniature sheet of 6 9.00 25.00
b. Brown omitted 2,250.

National Team Rugby Player and Boy — SP40

Design: 3c+1c, Man and boy placing ball for place kick, horiz.

**1967, Aug. 2 *Perf. 14½x14, 14x14½***

B73 SP40 2½c + 1c multi .25 .25
a. Miniature sheet of 6 10.00 20.00
B74 SP40 3c + 1c multi .25 .25
a. Miniature sheet of 6 10.00 20.00

Boy Running and Olympic Rings — SP41

3c+1c, Girl swimming and Olympic rings.

**1968, Aug. 7 *Perf. 14½x14***

B75 SP41 2½c + 1c multi .25 .25
a. Miniature sheet of 6 9.50 22.50
b. As No. B75, blue omitted 400.00

B76 SP41 3c + 1c multi .25 .25
a. Miniature sheet of 6 9.50 22.50
b. Red omitted, from No. B76a 3,350. 2,000.
c. Dark blue omitted, from No. B76a 2,250.

Boys Playing Cricket SP42

Dr. Elizabeth Gunn — SP43

Design: 3c+1c, playing cricket.

***Perf. 13½x13, 13x13½***

**1969, Aug. 6 Litho. Unwmk.**

B77 SP42 2½c + 1c multi .45 .75
a. Miniature sheet of 6 10.00 25.00
B78 SP42 3c + 1c multi .45 .75
a. Miniature sheet of 6 10.00 25.00
B79 SP43 4c + 1c multi .45 2.50
*Nos. B77-B79 (3)* 1.35 4.00

50th anniv. of Children's Health Camps, founded by Dr. Elizabeth Gunn.

Boys Playing Soccer SP44

2½c+1c, Girls playing basketball, vert.

**1970, Aug. 5 Unwmk. *Perf. 13½***

B80 SP44 2½c + 1c multi .30 .80
a. Miniature sheet of 6 10.00 26.00
B81 SP44 3c + 1c multi .30 .80
a. Miniature sheet of 6 10.00 26.00

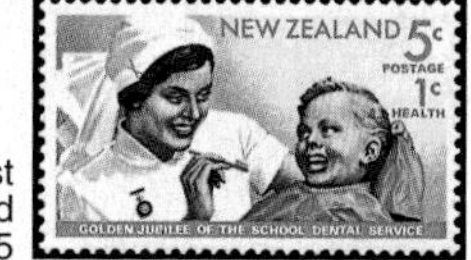

Hygienist and Child SP45

Designs: 3c+1c, Girls playing hockey. 4c+1c, Boys playing hockey.

**1971, Aug. 4 Litho. *Perf. 13½***

B82 SP45 3c + 1c multicolored .50 .75
a. Miniature sheet of 6 10.00 22.50
B83 SP45 4c + 1c multicolored .50 .75
a. Miniature sheet of 6 10.00 22.50
B84 SP45 5c + 1c multicolored 1.00 2.25
*Nos. B82-B84 (3)* 2.00 3.75

50th anniv. of School Dental Service (No. B84).

Boy Playing Tennis — SP46

Design: 4c+1c, Girl playing tennis.

**1972, Aug. 2 Litho. *Perf. 13x13½***

B85 SP46 3c + 1c gray & lt brn .35 .60
a. Miniature sheet of 6 9.50 20.00
B86 SP46 4c + 1c brown, yel & gray .35 .60
a. Miniature sheet of 6 9.50 20.00

Prince Edward — SP47

**1973, Aug. 1** **Photo.**
**B87** SP47 3c + 1c grn & brn .35 .60
a. Miniature sheet of 6 9.00 *20.00*
**B88** SP47 4c + 1c dk red & blk .35 .60
a. Miniature sheet of 6 9.00 *20.00*

Children with Cat and Dog — SP48

Designs: 4c+1c, Girl with dogs and cat. 5c+1c, Children and dogs.

**1974, Aug. 7** **Litho.** ***Perf. 13½x14***
**B89** SP48 3c + 1c multicolored .25 .60
**B90** SP48 4c + 1c multicolored .30 .60
a. Miniature sheet of 10 20.00 *40.00*
**B91** SP48 5c + 1c multicolored 1.10 1.75
*Nos. B89-B91 (3)* 1.65 2.95

Girl Feeding Lamb SP49

Designs: 4c+1c, Boy with hen and chicks. 5c+1c, Boy with duck and duckling.

**1975, Aug. 6** **Litho.** ***Perf. 14x13½***
**B92** SP49 3c + 1c multicolored .25 .35
**B93** SP49 4c + 1c multicolored .25 .35
a. Miniature sheet of 10 15.00 *40.00*
**B94** SP49 5c + 1c multicolored .75 *1.75*
*Nos. B92-B94 (3)* 1.25 2.45

Boy and Piebald Pony — SP50

Designs: 8c+1c, Farm girl and calf. 10c+1c, 2 girls watching nest-bound thrush.

**1976, Aug. 4** **Litho.** ***Perf. 13½x14***
**B95** SP50 7c + 1c multicolored .25 .35
**B96** SP50 8c + 1c multicolored .25 .35
**B97** SP50 10c + 1c multicolored .45 *.90*
a. Min. sheet, 2 each #B95-B97 4.25 *6.00*
*Nos. B95-B97 (3)* .95 1.60

Girl and Bluebird — SP51

8c+2c, Boy & frog. 10c+2c, Girl & butterfly.

**1977, Aug. 3** **Litho.** ***Perf. 13½x14***
**B98** SP51 7c + 2c multi .25 .60
**B99** SP51 8c + 2c multi .25 .65
**B100** SP51 10c + 2c multi .50 *1.10*
a. Miniature sheet of 6 2.50 *6.50*
*Nos. B98-B100 (3)* 1.00 2.35

No. B100a contains 2 each of Nos. B98-B100 in 2 strips of continuous design.

NZ No. B1 SP52

Heart Surgery SP53

**1978, Aug. 2** **Litho.** ***Perf. 13½x14***
**B101** SP52 10c + 2c multi .35 .40
**B102** SP53 12c + 2c multi .35 .45
a. Min. sheet, 3 ea #B101-B102 1.40 *4.00*

50th Health Stamp issue (No. B101) and National Heart Foundation (No. B102).

No. B102a exists in two printings: with "HARRISON & SONS LTD., LONDON" imprint at bottom left margin (valued) and with imprint more centered across three bottom stamps (apparently very scarce). Both varieties are known on first day covers.

Demoiselle Fish SP54

Designs: No. B104, Sea urchin. 12c+2c, Underwater photographer and red mullet, vert.

**1979, July 25** ***Perf. 13½x13, 13x13½***
**B103** SP54 10c + 2c multi .35 .70
**B104** SP54 10c + 2c multi .35 .70
a. Pair, #B103-B104 .70 1.25
**B105** SP54 12c + 2c multi .35 .70
a. Min. sheet, 2 ea #B103-B105 1.50 *2.75*
*Nos. B103-B105 (3)* 1.05 2.10

Children Surf Casting SP55

No. B107, Wharf Fishing. B108, Underwater fishing.

**1980, Aug. 6** **Litho.** ***Perf. 13½x13***
**B106** SP55 14c + 2c shown .35 .95
**B107** SP55 14c + 2c multi .35 .95
a. Pair, #B106-B107 .70 1.75
**B108** SP55 17c + 2c multi .35 .65
a. Min. sheet, 2 ea #B106-B108 1.90 *3.25*
*Nos. B106-B108 (3)* 1.05 2.55

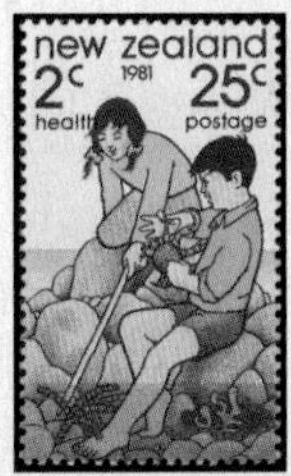

Boy and Girl at Rock Pool — SP56

**1981, Aug. 5** **Litho.** ***Perf. 14½***
**B109** SP56 20c + 2c Girl, starfish .30 .75
**B110** SP56 20c + 2c Boy fishing .30 .75
a. Pair, #B109-B110 .60 1.50
**B111** SP56 25c + 2c shown .30 .40
a. Min. sheet, 2 ea #B109-B111 1.50 3.50
*Nos. B109-B111 (3)* .90 1.90

Cocker Spaniel — SP57

**1982, Aug. 4** **Litho.** ***Perf. 13x13½***
**B112** SP57 24c + 2c Labrador .90 1.10
**B113** SP57 24c + 2c Border collie .90 1.10
a. Pair, #B112-B113 1.90 2.25
**B114** SP57 30c + 2c shown .90 1.10
a. Min. sheet, 2 each #B112-B114, perf. 14x13½ 5.00 7.50
*Nos. B112-B114 (3)* 2.70 3.30

Persian Cat — SP58

**1983, Aug. 3** **Litho.** ***Perf. 14½***
**B115** SP58 24 + 2c Tabby .70 .85
**B116** SP58 24 + 2c Siamese .70 .85
a. Pair, #B115-B116 1.40 1.75
**B117** SP58 30 + 2c shown .95 1.10
a. Min. sheet, 2 ea #B115-B117 3.00 3.50
*Nos. B115-B117 (3)* 2.35 2.80

Thoroughbreds — SP59

**1984, Aug. 1** **Litho.** ***Perf. 13½x13***
**B118** SP59 24c + 2c Clydesdales .60 .85
**B119** SP59 24c + 2c Shetlands .60 .85
a. Pair, #B118-B119 1.25 1.75
**B120** SP59 30c + 2c shown .60 .85
a. Min. sheet, 2 ea #B118-B120 2.50 3.75
*Nos. B118-B120 (3)* 1.80 2.55

Health — SP60

Princess Diana and: No. B121, Prince William. No. B122, Prince Henry. No. B123, Princes Charles, William and Henry.

**1985, July 31** **Litho.** ***Perf. 13½***
**B121** SP60 25c + 2c multi 1.00 1.50
**B122** SP60 25c + 2c multi 1.00 1.50
a. Pair, #B121-B122 2.10 3.00
**B123** SP60 35c + 2c multi 1.00 1.50
a. Min. sheet, 2 ea #B121-B123 4.75 7.00
*Nos. B121-B123 (3)* 3.00 4.50

Surtax for children's health camps.

Children's Drawings — SP61

No. B125, Children playing. No. B126, Skipping rope, horiz.

**1986, July 30** **Litho.** ***Perf. 14½x14***
**B124** SP61 30c + 3c shown .50 .75
**B125** SP61 30c + 3c multi .50 .75
a. Pair, #B124-B125 1.00 1.50
**B126** SP61 45c + 3c multi .75 .90
a. Min. sheet, 2 ea #B124-B126 3.50 4.00
*Nos. B124-B126 (3)* 1.75 2.40

Surtax for children's health camps.

No. B126a exists with Stockholmia '86 emblem. This sheet was sold only at the exhibition.

Children's Drawings SP62

**1987, July 29** **Litho.** ***Perf. 14½***
**B127** SP62 40c + 3c shown .90 1.75
**B128** SP62 40c + 3c Swimming .90 1.75
a. Pair, #B127-B128 1.90 3.50
**B129** SP62 60c + 3c Riding horse, vert. 1.50 7.75
a. Min. sheet, 2 ea #B127-B129 6.50 11.00
*Nos. B127-B129 (3)* 3.30 11.25

Surtax benefited children's health camps.

1988 Summer Olympics, Seoul — SP63

**1988, July 27** **Litho.** ***Perf. 14½***
**B130** SP63 40c + 3c Swimming .70 .80
**B131** SP63 60c + 3c Running .95 1.25
**B132** SP63 70c + 3c Rowing 1.10 1.25
**B133** SP63 80c + 3c Equestrian 1.25 1.60
a. Souv. sheet of 4, #B130-B133 4.00 5.00
*Nos. B130-B133 (4)* 4.00 4.90

Children's Health — SP64

Designs: No. B134, Duke and Duchess of York, Princess Beatrice. No. B135, Duchess, princess. No. B136, Princess.

**1989, July 23**
**B134** SP64 40c + 3c multi .90 1.75
**B135** SP64 40c + 3c multi .90 1.75
a. Pair, #B134-B135 1.90 3.50
**B136** SP64 80c + 3c multi 1.60 2.00
a. Min. sheet, 2 ea #B134-B136 6.75 8.75
b. As "a," overprinted with World Stamp Expo '89 emblem in margin 17.50 17.50
*Nos. B134-B136 (3)* 3.40 5.50

Athletes SP65

40c+5c, Jack Lovelock (1910-1949), runner. 80c+5c, George Nepia (1905-1986), rugby player.

**1990, July 25** **Litho.** ***Perf. 14½x14***
**B137** SP65 40c +5c multi .60 .95
**B138** SP65 80c +5c multi 1.25 1.60
a. Min. sheet, 2 ea #B137-B138 3.75 4.25

Hector's Dolphin SP66

**1991, July 24 Litho. *Perf. 14½***

**B139** SP66 45c +5c 3 Swimming 1.00 1.40
**B140** SP66 80c +5c 2 Jumping 1.40 2.25
*a.* Souv. sheet, 2 ea #B139-B140 5.75 7.50

Surtax benefited children's health camps.

Anthony F. Wilding (1883-1915), Tennis Player — SP67

Design: No. B142, C.S. "Stewie" Dempster (1903-1974), cricket player.

**1992, Aug. 12 Litho. *Perf. 14x13½***

**B141** SP67 45c +5c multi 1.10 1.40
**B142** SP67 80c +5c multi 1.40 1.75
*a.* Souv. sheet, 2 each #B141-B142, perf. 14½ 4.50 6.25

Surtax for children's health camps.

SP68

**1993, July 21 Litho. *Perf. 13½x14***

**B143** SP68 45c +5c Boy, puppy .80 1.00
**B144** SP68 80c +5c Girl, kitten 1.40 1.75
*a.* Souvenir sheet, 2 each #B143-B144, perf. 14½ 4.50 5.00
*b.* As "a," inscribed in sheet margin 7.00 7.00

Surtax for children's health camps.

No. B144b inscribed with "TAIPEI '93" emblem.

Issue date: No. B144b, Aug. 14.

SP69

Children's Health Camps, 75th Anniv.: No. B145, #B15, Children playing with ball. No. B146, #B34, Nurse holding child. No. B147, #B79, Children reading. 80c+5c, #B4, Boy.

**1994, July 20 Litho. *Perf. 14***

**B145** SP69 45c +5c multi .80 .90
**B146** SP69 45c +5c multi .80 .90
**B147** SP69 45c +5c multi .80 .90
**B148** SP69 80c +5c multi 1.40 1.40
*a.* Souv. sheet of 4, #B145-B148 4.50 5.00
*Nos. B145-B148 (4)* 3.80 4.10

Surtax for children's health camps.

Children's Health Camps — SP70

Designs: 45c+5c, Boy on skateboard. 80c+5c, Child on bicycle.

**1995, June 21 Litho. *Perf. 14½***

**B149** SP70 45c +5c multi .85 1.25
**B150** SP70 80c +5c multi 2.10 2.10
*a.* Souv. sheet, 2 ea #B149-B150 4.75 5.75
*b.* As "a," with added inscription 8.00 8.00

No. B150b inscribed with Stampex '95 emblem in sheet margin.

Surtax for children's health camps.

SP71

Children's Health: Nos. B151, B153, Infant buckled into child safety seat. 80c, Child holding adult's hand on pedestrian crossing.

**1996, June 5 Litho. *Perf. 14x13½***

**B151** SP71 40c +5c multi .80 .95
**B152** SP71 80c +5c multi 1.40 1.50
*a.* Souvenir sheet, 2 each Nos. B151-B152, perf. 14x14½ 4.00 4.00
*b.* As "a" with added inscription 5.50 5.50

**Self-Adhesive**

***Serpentine Die Cut 11½***

**B153** SP71 40c +5c multi .60 .85

No. B152b inscribed with CAPEX '96 emblem in sheet margin.

SP72

**Original Design**

**1996, June 5 Litho. *Perf. 14x13½***

**B154** SP72 40c +5c multi *1,000.* 1,200.

**Self-Adhesive**

***Serpentine Die Cut 11½***

**B155** SP72 40c +5c multi 1,750. 1,750.

Nos. B154 and B155 were withdrawn before issue by New Zealand Post. Slightly over 1,000 examples of No. B154 and 500 examples of No. B155 were sold in error by two post offices within three days of June 5. A total of 402 examples of the souvenir sheet containing No. B154 were made available by the printer, but none were sold at post offices.

The stamps were withdrawn because the inclusion of the stuffed animal indicated that the infant was improperly belted into the vehicle.

Children's Health SP73

Children's designs of "Healthy Living:" No. B156, Child on beach. 80c+5c, Child riding horse on waterfront. No. B158, Mosaic of person collecting fruit from tree, vert.

**1997, June 18 Litho. *Perf. 14***

**B156** SP73 40c +5c multi .80 .85
**B157** SP73 80c +5c multi 1.40 1.40

**Souvenir Sheet**

**B157A** Sheet of 3, #B156-B157, B157Ab 3.50 3.50
*b.* SP73 40c +5c like #B158 2.00 2.00

**Size: 25x36mm**

**Self-Adhesive**

***Serpentine Die Cut 10½***

**B158** SP73 40c +5c multi .75 .70

Children's Water Safety — SP74

Designs: 40c+5c, Child in life jacket. 80c+5c Child learning to swim.

**1998, June 24 Litho. *Perf. 13½***

**B159** SP74 40c +5c multicolored .75 .60
**B160** SP74 80c +5c multicolored 1.40 1.40
*a.* Sheet, 2 each #B159-B160 4.25 4.25

**Size: 25x38mm**

**Self-Adhesive**

***Serpentine Die Cut 11½***

**B161** SP74 40c +5c multicolored .75 .45

Children's Health SP75

Scenes from children's books: #B162, Hairy Maclary's Bone, by Lynley Dodd. #B163, Lion in the Meadow, by Margaret Mahy. 80c+5c, Greedy Cat, by Joy Cowley.

***Serpentine Die Cut 10¼***

**1999, June 16 Litho.**

**Self-Adhesive (#B162)**

**B162** SP75 40c +5c multi .75 .60

***Perf. 14¼***

**B163** SP75 40c +5c multi .75 .60
**B164** SP75 80c +5c multi 1.40 1.40

**Souvenir Sheet**

**B165** Sheet of 3, #B163-B164, B165a 3.50 3.50
*a.* SP75 40c +5c like #B162 2.00 2.00

Nos. B162, B165a are 37x26mm.

For 2000 semi-postals, see Nos. 1681, 1682, 1682a and 1687.

Children's Health SP76

Designs: No. B166, Four cyclists. 90c+5c, Cyclist in air. No. B168, Cyclist riding through puddle.

**2001, Aug. 1 Litho. *Perf. 14***

**B166** SP76 40c +5c multi .75 .60
*a.* Sheet of 10 7.50 7.50
**B167** SP76 90c +5c multi 1.50 1.40
*a.* Souvenir sheet, #B166-B167 2.10 2.10

**Size: 30x25mm**

***Serpentine Die Cut 10x9¾***

**Self-Adhesive**

**B168** SP76 40c +5c multi .60 .60
*Nos. B166-B168 (3)* 2.85 2.60

Healthy Living SP77

Designs: B169, 40c+5c, Fruits. 90c+5c, Vegetables.

No. B171a, Fruits, diff. B172, Fruits diff. (like B171a).

**2002, Aug. 7 *Perf. 14¼x14***

**B169** SP77 40c +5c multi .75 .60
**B170** SP77 90c +5c multi 1.50 1.50

**Souvenir Sheet**

**B171** Sheet, #B169-B170, B171a 3.50 3.50
*a.* SP77 40c +5c multi (21x26mm) 2.00 2.00

**Coil Stamp**

**Size: 21x26mm**

**Self-Adhesive**

***Serpentine Die Cut 9¾x10***

**B172** SP77 40c +5c multi .75 .50

Children's Health SP78

Designs: No. B173, 40c+5c, Children on swings. 90c+5c, Child with ball, girl playing hopscotch.

Nos. B175a, B176, 40c+ 5c, Girl on monkey bars.

**2003, Aug. 6 Litho. *Perf. 14***

**B173** SP78 40c +5c multi .75 .55
**B174** SP78 90c +5c multi 1.50 1.50

**Souvenir Sheet**

**B175** Sheet, #B173-B174, B175a 3.50 3.50
*a.* SP78 40c +5c multi (21x26mm), perf. 14½x14 2.00 2.00

**Coil Stamp**

**Size: 21x26mm**

**Self-Adhesive**

***Serpentine Die Cut 9¾x10***

**B176** SP78 40c +5c multi .75 .55

Children's Health — SP79

Designs: No. B177, Children playing with beach ball in water. No. B178, People in boat. Nos. B179a, B180, People fishing.

**2004, Sept. 1 Litho. *Perf. 14***

**B177** SP79 45c +5c multi .75 .65
**B178** SP79 90c +5c multi 1.50 1.50

**Souvenir Sheet**

**B179** Sheet, #B177-B178, B179a 3.50 3.50
*a.* SP79 45c +5c multi (22x27mm), perf. 14¼x14 2.00 2.00

**Self-Adhesive**

**Size: 22x27mm**

***Serpentine Die Cut 9½x10***

**B180** SP79 45c +5c multi .75 .65

Children's Health — SP80

Designs: No. B181, Girl and horse. 90c+5c, Boy and rabbit. Nos. B183a, B184, Children and dog.

**2005, Aug. 3 Litho. *Perf. 14***

**B181** SP80 45c +5c multi .75 .65
**B182** SP80 90c +5c multi 1.50 1.50
**B183** Souvenir sheet, #B181-B182, B183a 3.50 3.50
*a.* SP80 45c +5c multi, 20x25mm, perf. 14½x14 2.00 2.00

**Self-Adhesive**

**Size: 20x25mm**

***Serpentine Die Cut 9½x10***

**B184** SP80 45c +5c multi .75 .65



Children's Health — SP81

Designs: No. B185, Girl releasing dove. $1+10c, Boy with origami bird. Nos. B187a, B188, Two children, peace lily (25x30mm).

**2007, Sept. 5 Litho. *Perf. 14***

**B185** SP81 50c +10c multi .85 .85
 a. Perf. 13½ .85 .85
**B186** SP81 $1 +10c multi 1.50 1.50
 a. Perf. 13½ 1.50 1.50

**Souvenir Sheet**

**B187** Sheet, #B185-B186, B187a 3.75 3.75
 a. SP81 50c +10c multi, perf. 14½x14 2.50 2.50
 b. As "a," perf. 14½x13½x14½x14 2.00 2.00
 c. Souvenir sheet, #B185a, B186a, B187b 3.25 3.25

**Self-Adhesive**

***Serpentine Die Cut 9½x10***

**B188** SP81 50c +10c multi .85 .85

Surtax for Children's Health Camps.

Children's Health — SP82

Child: No. B189, Cycling. $1+10c, Kayaking. Nos. B191a, B192, Running.

**2008, July 2 Litho. *Perf. 14¼***

**B189** SP82 50c +10c multi .75 .75
**B190** SP82 $1 +10c multi 1.50 1.50

**Souvenir Sheet**

**B191** Sheet, #B189-B190, B191a 4.00 4.00
 a. SP82 50c +10c multi (36x36mm), perf. 14x14½ 1.75 1.75

**Self-Adhesive**

***Serpentine Die Cut 9¾***

**Size: 34x34mm**

**B192** SP82 50c +10c multi .95 .95

Surtax for Children's Health Camps.

Children's Health Stamps, 80th Anniv. — SP83

Stamps in color: No. B193, #B151. $1+10c, #B5. Nos. B195a, B196, #B23.

**2009, Sept. 7 Litho. *Perf. 13¼x13½***

**B193** SP83 50c +10c multi .90 .90
 a. Perf. 14 1.00 1.00
**B194** SP83 $1 +10c multi 1.60 1.60
 a. Perf. 14 1.75 1.75

**Souvenir Sheet**

**B195** Sheet, #B193a, B194a, B195a 3.75 3.50
 a. SP83 50c+10c multi, perf. 14½x14, 22x27mm 2.00 2.00

**Self-Adhesive**

***Serpentine Die Cut 9½x10***

**Size: 21x26mm**

**B196** SP83 50c +10c multi .90 .90

Surtax for Children's Health Camps.

Butterflies SP84

Designs: No. B197, Monarch butterfly. $1+10c, Tussock butterfly. Nos. B199a, B200, Boulder copper butterfly, vert. (25x30mm).

**2010, July 7 Litho. *Perf. 14***

**B197** SP84 50c + 10c multi .75 .75
**B198** SP84 $1 +10c multi 1.50 1.50

**Souvenir Sheet**

**B199** Sheet of 3, #B197-B198, B199a 3.75 3.75
 a. SP84 50c +10c multi 1.50 1.50

**Self-Adhesive**

***Serpentine Die Cut 9½x10***

**B200** SP84 50c +10c multi 1.00 1.00

Surtax for Children's Health Camps.

Flightless Birds SP85

Designs: No. B201, Kiwi. $1.20+10c, Kakapo. Nos. B203a, B204, Takahe, vert. (25x30mm).

**2011, July 6 Litho. *Perf. 14***

**B201** SP85 60c + 10c multi 1.10 1.10
**B202** SP85 $1.20 +10c multi 2.25 2.25

**Souvenir Sheet**

**B203** Sheet of 3, #B201-B202, B203a 5.00 5.00
 a. SP85 60c +10c multi 1.60 1.60

**Self-Adhesive**

***Serpentine Die Cut 9½x10***

**B204** SP85 60c +10c multi 1.25 1.25

Surtax for Children's Health Camps.

New Zealand Sea Lions SP86

Designs: No. B205, Sea lion pup. $1.40+10c, Adolescent male sea lion. Nos. B207a, B208, Head of sea lion pup, vert. (23x27mm).

**2012, Aug. 1 *Perf. 14***

**B205** SP86 70c + 10c multi 1.25 1.25
**B206** SP86 $1.40 +10c multi 2.50 2.50

**Souvenir Sheet**

**B207** Sheet of 3, #B205-B206, B207a 5.75 5.75
 a. SP86 70c +10c multi 2.00 2.00

**Self-Adhesive**

***Serpentine Die Cut 9½x10***

**B208** SP86 70c +10c multi 1.40 1.40

Surtax for New Zealand Foundation for Child and Family Health and Development.

Children and Farm Pets — SP87

Designs: No. B209, Boy and lamb. $1.40 + 10c, Girl and piglets. Nos. B211a, B212, Boy and goat (22x27mm).

**2013, Sept. 4 *Perf. 14***

**B209** SP87 70c +10c multi 1.25 1.25
 a. Perf. 13½ 1.25 1.25
**B210** SP87 $1.40 +10c multi 2.40 2.40
 a. Perf. 13½ 2.40 2.40

**Souvenir Sheet**

***Perf. 13½***

**B211** Sheet of 3, #B209a, B210a, B211a 5.00 5.00
 a. SP87 70c +10c multi 1.25 1.25

**Self-Adhesive**

***Serpentine Die Cut 9½x10***

**B212** SP87 70c +10c multi 1.25 1.25

Surtax for Stand Children's Services.

Children and Vegetables SP88

Designs: No. B213, Girl and carrots. $1.40 + 10c, Boy and apples. Nos. B215a, B216, Boy and pumpkin.

**2014, Sept. 3 Litho. *Perf. 14***

**B213** SP88 80c +10c multi 1.40 1.40
 a. Perf. 13½ 1.40 1.40
**B214** SP88 $1.40 +10c multi 2.40 2.40
 a. Perf. 13½ 2.40 2.40

**Souvenir Sheet**

**B215** Sheet of 3, #B213a, B214a, B215a 5.25 5.25
 a. SP88 80c +10c multi (22x27mm) 1.40 1.40

**Self-Adhesive**

**Size: 21x26mm**

**B216** SP88 80c +10c multi 1.40 1.40

Surtax for Stand Children's Services Tu Maia Whanau.

Children and Sun Protection SP89

Designs: No. B217, Girl under beach umbrella. $1.40+10c, Girl wearing hat with ear flaps putting sun screen on hands. $2+10c, Girl with large hat over head. Nos. B220a, B221, Boy, large pair of sunglasses.

**2015, Sept. 2 Litho. *Perf. 14***

**B217** SP89 80c +10c multi 1.25 1.25
 a. Perf. 13¼x13½ 1.25 1.25
**B218** SP89 $1.40 +10c multi 1.90 1.90
 a. Perf. 13¼x13½ 1.90 1.90
**B219** SP89 $2 +10c multi 2.75 2.75
 a. Perf. 13¼x13½ 2.75 2.75
 *Nos. B217-B219 (3)* 5.90 5.90

**Miniature Sheet**

**B220** Sheet of 4, #B217a, B218a, B219a, B220a 7.25 7.25
 a. SP89 80c+10c multi, perf. 13¼x13½, 25x30mm 1.25 1.25

**Self-Adhesive**

**Size: 25x30mm**

***Serpentine Die Cut 9½x10***

**B221** SP89 80c +10c multi 1.25 1.25

Surtax for Stand Children's Services Tu Maia Whanau.

Children's Health — SP90

Designs: $1+10c, Child with rugby ball, child holding end of rope. $1.80+10c, Children playing tug-of-war. $2.20+10c, Child holding end of rope, children stretching.

**2016, Sept. 7 Litho. *Perf. 14¼***

**B222** SP90 $1 +10c multi 1.60 1.60
**B223** SP90 $1.80 +10c multi 2.75 2.75
**B224** SP90 $2.20 +10c multi 3.50 3.50
 a. Horiz. strip of 3, #B222-B224 8.00 8.00
 b. Souvenir sheet of 3, #B222-B224 8.00 8.00
 *Nos. B222-B224 (3)* 7.85 7.85

Surtax for Stand Children's Services Tu Maia Whanau.

## AIR POST STAMPS

Plane over Lake Manapouri AP1

***Perf. 14x14½***

**1931, Nov. 10 Typo. Wmk. 61**

**C1** AP1 3p chocolate 27.50 22.50
 a. Perf. 14x15 150.00 *500.00*
**C2** AP1 4p dark violet 27.50 27.50
**C3** AP1 7p orange 30.00 27.50
 *Nos. C1-C3 (3)* 85.00 77.50

Most examples of No. C1a are poorly centered.

Type of 1931 Surcharged in Red

**1931, Dec. 18 *Perf. 14x14½***

**C4** AP1 5p on 3p yel green 20.00 25.00

Type of 1931 Overprinted in Dark Blue

**1934, Jan. 17**

**C5** AP1 7p bright blue 50.00 55.00

1st official air mail flight between NZ and Australia.

Airplane over Landing Field AP2

**1935, May 4 Engr. *Perf. 14***

**C6** AP2 1p rose carmine 1.10 .80
**C7** AP2 3p dark violet 5.75 3.75
**C8** AP2 6p gray blue 11.50 5.75
 *Nos. C6-C8 (3)* 18.35 10.30
 Set, never hinged 40.00

## SPECIAL DELIVERY STAMPS

SD1

***Perf. 14x14½,14x15***

**1903-26 Typo. Wmk. 61**

**E1** SD1 6p purple & red ('26) 60.00 40.00
 a. 6p violet & red, perf. 11 70.00 50.00

Mail Car — SD2

**1939, Aug. 16 Engr. *Perf. 14***

**E2** SD2 6p violet 1.75 6.00

## POSTAGE DUE STAMPS

D1

**Wmk. 62**

**1899, Dec. 1 Typo. *Perf. 11***

**J1** D1 ½p green & red 8.00 *19.00*
*a.* No period after "D" 75.00 60.00
**J2** D1 1p green & red 12.50 2.10
**J3** D1 2p green & red 40.00 6.25
**J4** D1 3p green & red 20.00 6.00
**J5** D1 4p green & red 42.50 25.00
**J6** D1 5p green & red 45.00 *60.00*
**J7** D1 6p green & red 45.00 *60.00*
**J8** D1 8p green & red 110.00 *150.00*
**J9** D1 10p green & red 175.00 *225.00*
**J10** D1 1sh green & red 140.00 100.00
**J11** D1 2sh green & red 225.00 *300.00*
*Nos. J1-J11 (11)* 863.00 953.35

Nos. J1-J11 may be found with N. Z. and D. varying in size.

D2

**1902, Feb. 28 Unwmk.**

**J12** D2 ½p gray grn & red 3.00 7.50

**Wmk. 61**

**J13** D2 ½p gray grn & red 3.00 2.10
**J14** D2 1p gray grn & red 12.00 4.00
**J15** D2 2p gray grn & red 150.00 150.00

**1904-28 *Perf. 14, 14x14½***

**J16** D2 ½p green & car 3.75 4.25
**J17** D2 1p green & car 7.00 1.00
**J18** D2 2p green & car 9.00 3.50
**J19** D2 3p grn & rose ('28) 50.00 25.00
*Nos. J16-J19 (4)* 69.75 33.75

### N Z and Star printed on the back in Blue

**1925 Unwmk. *Perf. 14x14½, 14x15***

**J20** D2 ½p green & rose 4.00 *26.00*
**J21** D2 2p green & rose 9.00 *35.00*

**Catalogue values for unused stamps in this section, from this point to the end of the section, are for Never Hinged items.**

D3

**1939 Wmk. 61 Typo. *Perf. 15x14***

**J22** D3 ½p turquoise green 13.00 *9.00*
**J23** D3 1p rose pink 5.00 .60
**J24** D3 2p ultramarine 9.00 1.75
**J25** D3 3p brown orange 26.00 29.00
*Nos. J22-J25 (4)* 53.00 40.35

**1945-49 Wmk. 253**

**J27** D3 1p rose pink ('49) 5.00 25.00
**J28** D3 2p ultramarine ('47) 7.00 9.00
**J29** D3 3p brown orange 15.00 5.75
*Nos. J27-J29 (3)* 27.00 39.75

The use of postage due stamps was discontinued in Sept., 1951.

## WAR TAX STAMP

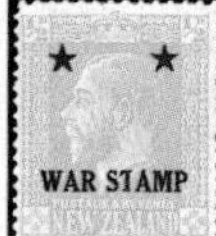
No. 144 Overprinted in Black

***Perf. 14x14½***

**1915, Sept. 24 Wmk. 61**

**MR1** A43 ½p green 2.10 .60

## OFFICIAL STAMPS

Regular Issues of 1882-92 Overprinted & Handstamped

**1892 Wmk. 62 *Perf as Before***

### Rose or Magenta Handstamp

**O1** A9 1p rose *600.*
**O2** A10 2p violet *800.*
**O3** A16 2½p ultramarine *700.*
**O4** A17 5p olive gray *1,000.*
**O5** A13 6p brown *1,200.*

### Violet Handstamp

**O6** N1 ½p rose *1,000.*
**O7** A9 1p rose *600.*
**O8** A10 2p violet

### Handstamped on No. 67A in Rose

**1899 *Perf. 10, 10x11***

**O9** A15a ½p black *600.*

### Handstamped on No. 79 in Violet

**Unwmk. *Perf. 14, 15***

**O10** A27 8p dull blue *1,200.*

Hstmpd. on Stamps of 1899-1900 in Violet

**1902 *Perf. 11***

**O11** A22 2½p blue *650.*
**O12** A23 3p org brown *1,000.*
**O13** A25 5p red brown *900.*
**O14** A27 8p dark blue *1,000.*

### Green Handstamp

**O15** A25 5p red brown *900.*

### Handstamped on Stamp of 1901 in Violet

**Wmk. 63 *Perf. 11***

**O16** A35 1p carmine *600.*

### Handstamped on Stamps of 1902-07 in Violet or Magenta

**1905-07 Wmk. 61 *Perf. 11, 14***

**O17** A18 ½p green *600.*
**O18** A35 1p carmine *600.*
**O19** A22 2½p blue *700.*
**O20** A25 5p red brown
**O21** A27 8p deep blue
**O22** A30 2sh blue green *5,000.*

The "O. P. S. O." handstamp is usually struck diagonally, reading up, but on No. O19 it also occurs horizontally. The letters stand for "On Public Service Only."

Overprinted in Black

### On Stamps of 1902-07

**1907 *Perf. 14, 14x13, 14x14½***

**O23** A18 ½p green 12.00 2.00
**O24** A35 1p carmine 12.00 1.00
*a.* Booklet pane of 6 110.00
**O25** A33 2p violet 20.00 2.00
**O26** A23 3p orange brn 60.00 6.00
**O27** A26 6p carmine rose 250.00 40.00
*a.* Horiz. pair, imperf. vert. *925.00*
**O28** A29 1sh brown red 125.00 25.00
**O29** A30 2sh blue green 175.00 150.00
*a.* Horiz. pair, imperf. vert. *1,400.*
**O30** A31 5sh vermilion 350.00 350.00
*Nos. O23-O30 (8)* 1,004. 576.00

### On No. 127

***Perf. 14x13, 14x14½***

**O31** A26 6p carmine rose 325.00 65.00

### On No. 129

**1909 *Perf. 14x14½***

**O32** A35 1p car (redrawn) 90.00 3.00

### On Nos. 130-131, 133, 137, 139

**1910 *Perf. 14, 14x13½, 14x14½***

**O33** A41 ½p yel grn 10.00 1.00
*a.* Inverted overprint 1,600.
**O34** A42 1p carmine 3.75 .25
**O35** A41 3p org brn 20.00 2.00
**O36** A41 6p car rose 30.00 10.00
**O37** A41 1sh vermilion 70.00 40.00
*Nos. O33-O37 (5)* 133.75 53.25

For 3p see note on perf varieties following No. 139.

On Postal-Fiscal Stamps Nos. AR32, AR36, AR44

**1911-14**

**O38** PF1 2sh blue ('14) 75.00 52.50
**O39** PF1 5sh green ('13) 125.00 *200.00*
**O40** PF2 £1 rose 1,000. 625.00
*Nos. O38-O40 (3)* 1,200. 877.50

### On Stamps of 1909-19

***Perf. 14x13½, 14x14½, 14x15]***

**1915-19 Typo.**

**O41** A43 ½p green 1.60 .25
**O42** A46 1½p gray black ('16) 8.00 3.00
**O43** A47 1½p gray black ('16) 5.75 1.00
**O44** A47 1½p brown org ('19) 5.75 .60
**O45** A43 2p yellow ('17) 5.75 .50
**O46** A43 3p chocolate ('19) 16.00 1.50

**Engr.**

**O47** A45 3p vio brn ('16) 8.00 1.50
**O48** A45 6p car rose ('16) 12.00 1.00
**O49** A41 8p dp bl (R) ('16) 20.00 *30.00*
**O50** A45 1sh vermilion ('16) 7.50 2.25
*a.* 1sh orange 15.00 *20.00*
*Nos. O41-O50 (10)* 90.35 *41.60*

For 8p see note on perf varieties following No. 139.

**1922 On No. 157**

**O51** A45 8p red brown 125.00 *200.00*

**1925 On Nos. 151, 158**

**O52** A45 4p purple 20.00 4.25
**O53** A45 9p olive green 45.00 42.50

### On No. 177

**1925 *Perf. 14x14½***

**O54** A42 1p carmine 5.00 5.00

### On Nos. 184, 182

**1927-28 Wmk. 61 *Perf. 14, 14½x14***

**O55** A57 1p rose red 2.50 .25
**O56** A56 2sh blue 125.00 140.00

### On No. AR50

**1933 *Perf. 14***

**O57** PF5 5sh green 450.00 450.00

Nos. 186, 187, 196 Overprinted in Black

**1936 *Perf. 14x13½, 13½x14, 14***

**O58** A59 1p copper red 2.00 1.40
**O59** A60 1½p red brown 14.00 *30.00*
**O60** A69 1sh dark slate grn 30.00 *52.50*
*Nos. O58-O60 (3)* 46.00 83.90
Set, never hinged 120.00

### Same Overprint Horizontally in Black or Green on Stamps of 1936

***Perf. 12½, 13½, 13x13½, 14x13½, 13½x14, 14***

**1936-42 Wmk. 253**

**O61** A58 ½p brt grn ('37) 1.50 5.25
**O62** A59 1p copper red 3.00 .60
**O63** A60 1½p red brown 4.00 5.25
**O64** A61 2p red org ('38) 1.00 .25
*a.* Perf. 12½ ('42) 110.00 62.50
**O65** A62 2½p dk gray & dk brown 8.00 24.00
**O66** A63 3p choc ('38) 27.50 4.00
**O67** A64 4p blk brn & blk 5.00 1.10
**O68** A66 6p red ('37) 5.75 .35
**O68B** A67 8p dp brn ('42) 8.50 20.00
**O69** A68 9p blk & scar (G) ('38) 80.00 45.00
**O70** A69 1sh dk slate grn 14.00 1.60
*a.* Perf. 12½ ('42) 27.50 1.75

Overprint Vertical

**O71** A70 2sh ol grn ('37) 24.00 8.50
*a.* Perf. 12½ ('42) 90.00 25.00
*Nos. O61-O71 (12)* 182.25 115.90
Set, never hinged 550.00

### Same Overprint Horizontally in Black on Nos. 226, 227, 228

**1938**

**O72** A79 ½p emerald 5.75 1.75
**O73** A79 1p rose red 7.25 .30
**O74** A80 1½p violet brn 37.50 10.50
*Nos. O72-O74 (3)* 50.50 12.55
Set, never hinged 95.00

### Same Overprint on No. AR50

**1938 Wmk. 61 *Perf. 14***

**O75** PF5 5sh green 75.00 47.50

Nos. 229-235, 237, 239-241 Overprinted in Red or Black

***Perf. 13½x13, 13x13½, 14x13½***

**1940 Wmk. 253**

**O76** A81 ½p dk bl grn (R) .60 .75
*a.* "ff" joined 29.00 70.00
**O77** A82 1p scar & sepia 2.25 .30
*a.* "ff" joined 29.00 70.00
**O78** A83 1½p brt vio & ultra 1.10 *4.25*
**O79** A84 2p blk brn & Prus grn 2.25 .30
*a.* "ff" joined 35.00 70.00
**O80** A85 2½p dk bl & myr grn 1.40 4.50
*a.* "ff" joined 29.00 77.50
**O81** A86 3p dp plum & dk vio (R) 5.75 .95
*a.* "ff" joined 24.00 55.00
**O82** A87 4p dk red vio & vio brn 14.50 1.60
*a.* "ff" joined 70.00 92.50
**O83** A89 6p vio & brt grn 14.50 1.60
*a.* "ff" joined 40.00 80.00
**O84** A90 8p org red & blk 14.50 13.00
*a.* "ff" joined 40.00 110.00
**O85** A91 9p dp org & olive 5.75 5.75
**O86** A92 1sh dk sl grn & ol 35.00 5.25
*Nos. O76-O86 (11)* 97.60 38.25
Set, never hinged 190.00

Nos. 227A, 228C Overprinted in Black

**1941 Wmk. 253 *Perf. 13½***

**O88** A79 1p light blue green .30 .30
**O89** A80 3p blue .75 .30
Set, never hinged 2.25

### Same Overprint on No. 245

**1944 *Perf. 14x15***

**Size: 17¼x20¼mm**

**O90** A68 9p int black & scar 20.00 17.00
Never Hinged 60.00

### Same Overprint on No. AR78

***Perf. 14***

**O91** PF5 5sh green 12.00 7.00
Never Hinged 20.00

**Catalogue values for unused stamps in this section, from this point to the end of the section, are for Never Hinged items.**

### Same Ovpt. on Stamps of 1941-47

**1946-51 *Perf. 13½, 14***

**O92** A79 ½p brn org ('46) 1.75 1.25
**O92B** A80 1½p red 5.75 1.25
**O93** A80 2p orange .90 .30
**O94** A80 4p rose lilac 4.00 1.25

**O95** A80 6p rose carmine 5.75 1.25
**O96** A80 8p deep violet 10.00 4.50
**O97** A80 9p chocolate 11.50 5.75
**O98** A104 1sh dk car rose & chestnut 11.50 1.75
**O99** A104 2sh dk grn & brn org 26.00 8.50
*Nos. O92-O99 (9)* 77.15 25.80

Queen Elizabeth II — O1

***Perf. 13½x13***

**1954, Mar. 1 Engr. Wmk. 253**

**O100** O1 1p orange 1.10 .50
**O101** O1 1½p rose brown 4.25 5.75
**O102** O1 2p green .45 .25
**O103** O1 3p red .45 .25
**O104** O1 4p blue 1.10 .60
**O105** O1 9p rose carmine 10.50 2.50
**O106** O1 1sh rose violet 1.10 .25
*Nos. O100-O106 (7)* 18.95 10.10

Exist imperf.

**Nos. O102, O101 Surcharged with New Value and Dots**

**1959-61**

**O107** O1 2½p on 2p green ('61) 1.10 1.75
**O108** O1 6p on 1½p rose brn .60 1.25

Exist imperf.

**1963, Mar. 1**

**O109** O1 2½p dark olive 4.00 1.75
**O111** O1 3sh slate 47.50 57.50

Exist imperf.

## LIFE INSURANCE

Lighthouses — LI1

***Perf. 10, 11, 10x11, 12x11½***

**1891, Jan. 2 Typo. Wmk. 62**

**OY1** LI1 ½p purple 110.00 7.00
**OY2** LI1 1p blue 80.00 2.00
**OY3** LI1 2p red brown 150.00 4.25
**OY4** LI1 3p chocolate 425.00 22.50
**OY5** LI1 6p green 550.00 70.00
**OY6** LI1 1sh rose pink 800.00 140.00
*Nos. OY1-OY6 (6)* 2,115. 245.75

Stamps from outside rows of the sheets sometimes lack watermark.

**1903-04 Wmk. 61 *Perf. 11, 14x11***

**OY7** LI1 ½p purple 120.00 7.00
**OY8** LI1 1p blue 75.00 1.10
**OY9** LI1 2p red brown 200.00 10.00
*Nos. OY7-OY9 (3)* 395.00 18.10

Lighthouses — LI2

**1905-32 *Perf. 11, 14, 14x14½***

**OY10** LI2 ½p yel grn ('13) 1.40 .90
**OY11** LI2 ½p green ('32) 5.75 2.75
**OY12** LI2 1p blue ('06) 375.00 29.00
**OY13** LI2 1p dp rose ('13) 9.75 1.10
**OY14** LI2 1p scarlet ('31) 4.25 2.00
**OY15** LI2 1½p gray ('17) 14.00 4.25
**OY16** LI2 1½p brn org ('19) 1.75 1.40
**OY17** LI2 2p red brown 2,750. 200.00
**OY18** LI2 2p violet ('13) 20.00 17.00
**OY19** LI2 2p yellow ('21) 6.00 6.00
**OY20** LI2 3p ocher ('13) 29.00 20.00
**OY21** LI2 3p choc ('31) 11.00 26.00
**OY22** LI2 6p car rose ('13) 20.00 26.00
**OY23** LI2 6p pink ('31) 20.00 45.00
*Nos. OY10-OY23 (14)* 3,268. 381.40

#OY15, OY16 have "POSTAGE" at each side.

Stamps from outside rows of the sheets sometimes lack watermark.

**1946-47 Wmk. 253 *Perf. 14x15***

**OY24** LI2 ½p yel grn ('47) 1.90 1.90
**OY25** LI2 1p scarlet 1.40 1.25
**OY26** LI2 2p yellow 2.25 *15.00*
**OY27** LI2 3p chocolate 10.50 *30.00*
**OY28** LI2 6p pink ('47) 8.50 *25.00*
*Nos. OY24-OY28 (5)* 24.55 73.15
Set, never hinged 42.50

**Catalogue values for unused stamps in this section, from this point to the end of the section, are for Never Hinged items.**

**New Zealand Lighthouses**

Castlepoint LI3

Taiaroa — LI4

Cape Palliser LI5

Cape Campbell LI6

Eddystone (England) LI7

Stephens Island LI8

The Brothers LI9

Cape Brett — LI10

***Perf. 13½x13, 13x13½***

**1947-65 Engr. Wmk. 253**

**OY29** LI3 ½p dk grn & red orange 1.75 1.70
**OY30** LI4 1p dk ol grn & blue 1.75 1.10
**OY31** LI5 2p int bl & gray .90 .90
**OY32** LI6 2½p ultra & blk ('63) 11.00 15.00
**OY33** LI7 3p red vio & bl 3.50 .75
**OY34** LI8 4p dk brn & org 4.50 1.75
*a.* Wmkd. sideways ('65) 4.50 16.00
**OY35** LI9 6p dk brn & bl 4.25 2.50
**OY36** LI10 1sh red brn & bl 4.25 3.50
*Nos. OY29-OY36 (8)* 31.90 27.20

Set first issued Aug. 1, 1947.
Exist imperf.

**Nos. OY30, OY32-OY33, OY34a, OY35-OY36 and Types Surcharged**

No. OY37

No. OY38

***Perf. 13½x13, 13x13½***

**1967-68 Engr. Wmk. 253**

**OY37** LI4 1c on 1p 2.50 4.75
*a.* Wmkd. upright ('68) 1.10 4.75
**OY38** LI6 2c on 2½p 11.00 16.00
**OY39** LI7 2½c on 3p, wmkd. upright 1.75 5.50
*a.* Watermarked sideways ('68) 2.75 5.50
**OY40** LI8 3c on 4p 5.25 6.25
**OY41** LI9 5c on 6p .85 7.00
**OY42** LI10 10c on 1sh, wmkd. sideways .85 4.75
*a.* Watermarked upright 2.40 11.50
*Nos. OY37-OY42 (6)* 22.20 44.25

The surcharge is different on each stamp and is adjusted to obliterate old denomination. One dot only on 2½c.

Set first issued July 10, 1967.

Moeraki Point Lighthouse — LI11

Lighthouses: 2½c, Puysegur Point, horiz. 3c, Baring Head. 4c, Cape Egmont, horiz. 8c, East Cape. 10c, Farewell Spit. 15c, Dog Island.

***Perf. 13x13½, 13½x13, 14 (8c, 10c)***

**1969-76 Litho. Unwmk.**

**OY43** LI11 ½c pur, bl & yel .75 2.00
**OY44** LI11 2½c yel, ultra & grn .60 1.40
**OY45** LI11 3c yellow & brown .60 .85
**OY46** LI11 4c lt ultra & ocher .60 1.10
**OY47** LI11 8c multicolored .60 3.25
**OY48** LI11 10c multicolored .40 3.25
**OY49** LI11 15c multicolored .40 2.40
*a.* Perf. 14 ('78) 1.00 2.50
*Nos. OY43-OY49 (7)* 3.95 14.25

Cent. of Government Life Insurance Office.

Issued: #OY47-OY48, 11/17/76; others 3/27/69.

**No. OY44 Surcharged with New Value and 4 Diagonal Bars**

***Perf. 13½x13***

**1978, Mar. 8 Litho. Wmk. 253**

**OY50** LI11 25c on 2½c multi .85 2.00

Lighthouse — LI12

**1981, June 3 Litho. *Perf. 14½***

**OY51** LI12 5c multicolored .25 .25
**OY52** LI12 10c multicolored .25 .25
**OY53** LI12 20c multicolored .25 .25
**OY54** LI12 30c multicolored .30 .30
**OY55** LI12 40c multicolored .35 .35
**OY56** LI12 50c multicolored .35 .50
*Nos. OY51-OY56 (6)* 1.75 1.90

Government Life Insurance Stamps have been discontinued.

## NEWSPAPER STAMPS

Queen Victoria — N1

**Wmk. 59**

**1873, Jan. 1 Typo. *Perf. 10***

**P1** N1 ½p rose 140.00 47.50
*a.* Perf. 12½x10 160.00 75.00
*b.* Perf. 12½ 210.00 75.00

The "N Z" watermark is widely spaced and intended for larger stamps. About a third of the stamps in each sheet are unwatermarked. They are worth a slight premium.

For overprint, see No. O6.

**1875, Jan. Wmk. 64 *Perf. 12½***

**P3** N1 ½p rose 25.00 5.00
*a.* Pair, imperf. between 800.00 500.00
*b.* Perf. 12 70.00 12.50

**1892 Wmk. 62 *Perf. 12½***

**P4** N1 ½p bright rose 11.00 1.50
*a.* Unwatermarked 20.00 10.00

## ROSS DEPENDENCY

**Catalogue values for unused stamps in this section are for Never Hinged items.**

H.M.S. Erebus and Mount Erebus A1

Ernest H. Shackleton and Robert F. Scott — A2

Map Showing Location of Ross Dependency A3

Queen Elizabeth II A4

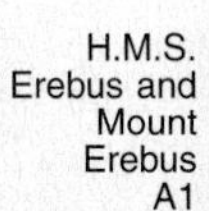

***Perf. 14, 13 (A4)***

**1957, Jan. 11 Engr. Wmk. 253**

**L1** A1 3p dark blue 3.00 1.25
**L2** A2 4p dark carmine 3.00 1.25
**L3** A3 8p ultra & car rose 3.00 1.25
**L4** A4 1sh6p dull violet 3.00 1.25
*Nos. L1-L4 (4)* 12.00 5.00

**1967, July 10**

**L5** A1 2c dark blue 21.00 15.00
**L6** A2 3c dark carmine 12.00 10.00
**L7** A3 7c ultra & car rose 12.00 10.00
**L8** A4 15c dull violet 12.00 10.00
*Nos. L5-L8 (4)* 57.00 45.00

Skua — A5

Scott Base — A6

Designs: 4c, Hercules plane unloading at Williams Field. 5c, Shackleton's hut, Cape Royds. 8c, Naval supply ship Endeavour unloading. 18c, Tabular ice floe.

*Perf. 13x13½*

**1972, Jan. 18 Litho. Unwmk.**

| No. | Description | Unused | Used |
|---|---|---|---|
| L9 | A5 3c lt bl, blk & gray | 1.00 | 1.75 |
| L10 | A5 4c black & violet | .25 | 1.75 |
| L11 | A5 5c rose lil, blk & gray | .25 | 1.75 |
| L12 | A5 8c blk, dk gray & brn | .25 | 1.75 |

*Perf. 14½x14*

| No. | Description | Unused | Used |
|---|---|---|---|
| L13 | A6 10c slate grn, brt grn & blk | .25 | 1.90 |
| a. | Perf. 14½x13½ ('79) | .70 | 1.75 |
| L14 | A6 18c pur & black | .25 | 1.90 |
| a. | Perf. 14½x13½ ('79) | 1.60 | 3.00 |
| | *Nos. L9-L14 (6)* | 2.25 | 10.80 |

25th Anniv. of Scott Base — A7

5c, Adelie penguins. 10c, Tracked vehicles. 30c, Field party, Upper Taylor Valley. 40c, Vanda Station. 50c, Scott's hut, Cape Evans, 1911.

**1982, Jan. 20 Litho. *Perf. 15½***

| No. | Description | Unused | Used |
|---|---|---|---|
| L15 | A7 5c multicolored | 1.40 | 1.60 |
| L16 | A7 10c multicolored | .25 | .75 |
| L17 | A7 20c shown | .25 | .75 |
| L18 | A7 30c multicolored | .25 | .45 |
| L19 | A7 40c multicolored | .25 | .45 |
| L20 | A7 50c multicolored | .25 | .45 |
| | *Nos. L15-L20 (6)* | 2.65 | 4.45 |

Wildlife — A8

5c, South polar skua. 10c, Snow petrel chick. 20c, Black-browed albatross. 45c, Emperor penguins. 50c, Chinstrap penguins. 70c, Adelie penguins. 80c, Elephant seals. $1, Leopard seal. $2, Weddell seal. $3, Crabeater seal pup.

**1994-95 Litho. *Perf. 13½***

| No. | Description | Unused | Used |
|---|---|---|---|
| L21 | A8 5c multicolored | .25 | .25 |
| L22 | A8 10c multicolored | .25 | .25 |
| L23 | A8 20c multicolored | .30 | .30 |
| L23A | A8 40c like No. 24 | .65 | .65 |
| L24 | A8 45c multicolored | .70 | .70 |
| L25 | A8 50c multicolored | .80 | .80 |
| L26 | A8 70c multicolored | 1.10 | 1.10 |
| L27 | A8 80c multicolored | 1.25 | 1.25 |
| L28 | A8 $1 multicolored | 1.60 | 1.60 |
| L29 | A8 $2 multicolored | 3.25 | 3.25 |
| L30 | A8 $3 multicolored | 4.75 | 4.75 |
| | *Nos. L21-L30 (11)* | 14.90 | 14.90 |

Issued: 40c, 10/2/95; others, 11/2/94.

Antarctic Explorers A9

Explorer, ships: 40c, James Cook, Resolution & Adventure. 80c, James Clark Ross, Erebus & Terror. $1, Roald Amundsen, Fram. $1.20, Robert Falcon Scott, Terra Nova. $1.50, Ernest Henry Shackleton, Endurance. $1.80, Richard Evelyn Byrd, Floyd Bennett (airplane).

**1995, Nov. 9 Litho. *Perf. 14½***

| No. | Description | Unused | Used |
|---|---|---|---|
| L31 | A9 40c multicolored | .65 | .65 |
| L32 | A9 80c multicolored | 1.25 | 1.25 |
| L33 | A9 $1 multicolored | 1.60 | 1.60 |
| L34 | A9 $1.20 multicolored | 1.90 | 1.90 |
| L35 | A9 $1.50 multicolored | 2.40 | 2.40 |
| L36 | A9 $1.80 multicolored | 2.75 | 2.75 |
| | *Nos. L31-L36 (6)* | 10.55 | 10.55 |

Antarctic Landscapes — A10

Designs: 40c, Inside ice cave, vert. 80c, Base of glacier, vert. $1, Glacier ice fall, vert. $1.20, Climbers on crater rim. $1.50, Pressure ridges. $1.80, Fumarole ice tower.

**1996, Nov. 13 Litho. *Perf. 14***

| No. | Description | Unused | Used |
|---|---|---|---|
| L37 | A10 40c multicolored | .65 | .65 |
| L38 | A10 80c multicolored | 1.25 | 1.25 |
| L39 | A10 $1 multicolored | 1.60 | 1.60 |
| L40 | A10 $1.20 multicolored | 1.90 | 1.90 |
| L41 | A10 $1.50 multicolored | 2.40 | 2.40 |
| L42 | A10 $1.80 multicolored | 2.75 | 2.75 |
| | *Nos. L37-L42 (6)* | 10.55 | 10.55 |

Antarctic Sea Birds — A11

40c, Snow petrel. 80c, Cape petrel. $1, Antarctic prion. $1.20, Antarctic fulmar. $1.50, Antarctic petrel. $1.80, Antarctic tern.

**1997, Nov. 12 Litho. *Perf. 14***

| No. | Description | Unused | Used |
|---|---|---|---|
| L43 | A11 40c multi | .65 | .65 |
| L44 | A11 80c multi | 1.25 | 1.25 |
| L45 | A11 $1 multi | 1.75 | 1.50 |
| L46 | A11 $1.20 multi | 2.25 | 2.00 |
| L47 | A11 $1.50 multi | 2.50 | 2.25 |
| L48 | A11 $1.80 multi | 3.00 | 15.00 |
| | *Nos. L43-L48 (6)* | 11.40 | 22.65 |
| L48A | Block of 6, #L45, L48, L48b-L48e | 20.00 | 20.00 |
| b. | A11 40c As #L43, without WWF emblem | .90 | .90 |
| c. | A11 80c As #L44, without WWF emblem | 1.75 | 1.75 |
| d. | A11 $1.20 As #L46, without WWF emblem | 2.75 | 2.75 |
| e. | A11 $1.50 As #L47, without WWF emblem | 3.50 | 3.50 |

World Wildlife Fund. Nos. L43-L44, L46-L47 have WWF emblem. Nos. L45 and L48 do not have emblem.

Ice Formations A12

Designs: 40c, Sculptured sea ice. 80c, Glacial tongue. $1, Stranded tabular iceberg. $1.20, Autumn at Cape Evans. $1.50, Sea ice in summer thaw. $1.80, Sunset on tabular icebergs.

**1998, Nov. 11 Litho. *Perf. 14***

| No. | Description | Unused | Used |
|---|---|---|---|
| L49 | A12 40c multicolored | .65 | .65 |
| L50 | A12 80c multicolored | 1.25 | 1.25 |
| L51 | A12 $1 multicolored | 1.60 | 1.60 |
| L52 | A12 $1.20 multicolored | 1.90 | 1.90 |
| L53 | A12 $1.50 multicolored | 2.40 | 2.40 |
| L54 | A12 $1.80 multicolored | 2.75 | 2.75 |
| a. | Block of 6, #L49-L54 | 15.00 | 15.00 |
| | *Nos. L49-L54 (6)* | 10.55 | 10.55 |

Night Skies A13

Designs: 40c, Sea smoke, McMurdo Sound. 80c, Alpenglow, Mt. Erebus. $1.10, Sunset, Black Island. $1.20, Pressure ridges, Ross Sea. $1.50, Evening light, Ross Island. $1.80, Mother of pearl clouds, Ross Island.

**1999, Nov. 17 Litho. *Perf. 14***

| No. | Description | Unused | Used |
|---|---|---|---|
| L55 | A13 40c multicolored | .65 | .65 |
| L56 | A13 80c multicolored | 1.25 | 1.25 |
| L57 | A13 $1.10 multicolored | 1.75 | 1.75 |
| L58 | A13 $1.20 multicolored | 1.90 | 1.90 |
| L59 | A13 $1.50 multicolored | 2.40 | 2.40 |
| L60 | A13 $1.80 multicolored | 2.75 | 2.75 |
| | *Nos. L55-L60 (6)* | 10.70 | 10.70 |

Antarctic Transportation — A14

Designs: 40c, RNZAF C130 Hercules. 80c, Hagglunds BV206 All-terrain carrier. $1.10, Tracked 4x4 motorbike. $1.20, ASV Track truck. $1.50, Squirrel helicopter. $1.80, Elan Skidoo.

**2000, Nov. 4 Litho. *Perf. 14***

| No. | Description | Unused | Used |
|---|---|---|---|
| L61 | A14 40c multi | .65 | .65 |
| L62 | A14 80c multi | 1.25 | 1.25 |
| L63 | A14 $1.10 multi | 1.75 | 1.75 |
| L64 | A14 $1.20 multi | 1.90 | 1.90 |
| L65 | A14 $1.50 multi | 2.40 | 2.40 |
| L66 | A14 $1.80 multi | 2.75 | 2.75 |
| | *Nos. L61-L66 (6)* | 10.70 | 10.70 |

### Penguins Type of 2001 of New Zealand

Designs: 40c, Emperor. 80c, Adelie. 90c, Emperor, diff. $1.30, Adelie, diff. $1.50, Emperor, diff. $2, Adelie, diff.

**2001, Nov. 7 *Perf. 14¼***

| No. | Description | Unused | Used |
|---|---|---|---|
| L67 | A475 40c multi | .65 | .65 |
| L68 | A475 80c multi | 1.25 | 1.25 |
| L69 | A475 90c multi | 1.40 | 1.40 |
| L70 | A475 $1.30 multi | 2.10 | 2.10 |
| L71 | A475 $1.50 multi | 2.40 | 2.40 |
| L72 | A475 $2 multi | 3.25 | 3.25 |
| | *Nos. L67-L72 (6)* | 11.05 | 11.05 |

Discovery Expedition of Capt. Robert Falcon Scott, 1901-04 A15

Designs: 40c, Three men with sleds. 80c, HMS Discovery. 90c, HMS Discovery trapped in ice. $1.30, Edward Wilson, Ernest Shackleton and sleds. $1.50, Explorers with flags and dog. $2, Base hut.

**2002, Nov. 6 Litho. *Perf. 14***

| No. | Description | Unused | Used |
|---|---|---|---|
| L73 | A15 40c multi | .65 | .65 |
| L74 | A15 80c multi | 1.25 | 1.25 |
| L75 | A15 90c multi | 1.40 | 1.40 |
| L76 | A15 $1.30 multi | 2.10 | 2.10 |
| L77 | A15 $1.50 multi | 2.40 | 2.40 |
| L78 | A15 $2 multi | 3.25 | 3.25 |
| | *Nos. L73-L78 (6)* | 11.05 | 11.05 |

Marine Life — A16

Designs: 40c, Odontaster validus. 90c, Beroe cucumis. $1.30, Macroptychaster accrescens. $1.50, Sterechinus neumayeri. $2, Perkinsiana littoralis.

**2003, Oct. 1 Litho. *Perf. 13x13¼***

| No. | Description | Unused | Used |
|---|---|---|---|
| L79 | A16 40c multi | .65 | .65 |
| L80 | A16 90c multi | 1.40 | 1.40 |
| L81 | A16 $1.30 multi | 2.10 | 2.10 |
| L82 | A16 $1.50 multi | 2.40 | 2.40 |
| L83 | A16 $2 multi | 3.25 | 3.25 |
| | *Nos. L79-L83 (5)* | 9.80 | 9.80 |

Emperor Penguins and Map of Antarctica — A17

Various pictures of penguins.

**2004, Nov. 3 Litho. *Perf. 13¼x14***

**Color of Denomination**

| No. | Description | Unused | Used |
|---|---|---|---|
| L84 | A17 45c yellow orange | .70 | .70 |
| L85 | A17 90c dark brown | 1.40 | 1.40 |
| L86 | A17 $1.35 lilac | 2.10 | 2.10 |
| L87 | A17 $1.50 red brown | 2.40 | 2.40 |
| L88 | A17 $2 gray blue | 3.25 | 3.25 |
| | *Nos. L84-L88 (5)* | 9.85 | 9.85 |

Photographs — A18

Designs: 45c, Dry Valleys, by Craig Potton. 90c, Emperor Penguins, by Andris Apse. $1.35, Fur Seal, by Mark Mitchell. $1.50, Captain Scott's Hut, by Colin Monteath. $2. Minke Whale, by Kim Westerskov.

**2005, Nov. 2 Litho. *Perf. 13¼***

| No. | Description | Unused | Used |
|---|---|---|---|
| L89 | A18 45c multi | .70 | .70 |
| L90 | A18 90c multi | 1.40 | 1.40 |
| L91 | A18 $1.35 multi | 2.10 | 2.10 |
| L92 | A18 $1.50 multi | 2.40 | 2.40 |
| L93 | A18 $2 multi | 3.25 | 3.25 |
| | *Nos. L89-L93 (5)* | 9.85 | 9.85 |

A sheet containing Nos. L89-L93 was in a limited edition album.

New Zealand Antarctic Program, 50th Anniv. A19

Designs: 45c, Biologist. 90c, Hydrologist. $1.35, Geologist. $1.50, Meteorologist. $2, Marine biologist.

**2006, Nov. 1 Litho. *Perf. 14***

| No. | Description | Unused | Used |
|---|---|---|---|
| L94 | A19 45c multi | .70 | .70 |
| L95 | A19 90c multi | 1.40 | 1.40 |
| L96 | A19 $1.35 multi | 2.10 | 2.10 |
| L97 | A19 $1.50 multi | 2.40 | 2.40 |
| L98 | A19 $2 multi | 3.25 | 3.25 |
| | *Nos. L94-L98 (5)* | 9.85 | 9.85 |

Commonwealth Trans-Antarctic Expedition, 50th Anniv. — A20

Designs: 50c, Man and Beaver airplane. $1, Man and sled. $1.50, Sled dogs. $2, TE20 Ferguson tractor. $2.50, HMNZS Endeavour.

**2007, Nov. 7 Litho. *Perf. 14***

| No. | Description | Unused | Used |
|---|---|---|---|
| L99 | A20 50c multi | .80 | .80 |
| L100 | A20 $1 multi | 1.50 | 1.50 |
| L101 | A20 $1.50 multi | 2.40 | 2.40 |
| L102 | A20 $2 multi | 3.25 | 3.25 |
| L103 | A20 $2.50 multi | 4.00 | 4.00 |
| a. | Souvenir sheet, #L102-L103 | 7.25 | 7.25 |
| | *Nos. L99-L103 (5)* | 11.95 | 11.95 |

1907-09 British Antarctic Expedition A21

Designs: 50c, Departure of Nimrod from Lyttleton. $1, Expedition Hut, Cape Royds. $1.50, First vehicle on Antarctica. $2, First men to reach South Magnetic Pole. $2.50, First ascent of Mt. Erebus.

**2008, Nov. 5 Litho. *Perf. 13½x13¼***

| | | | | |
|---|---|---|---|---|
| **L104** | A21 | 50c multi | .80 | .80 |
| **L105** | A21 | $1 multi | 1.50 | 1.50 |
| **L106** | A21 | $1.50 multi | 2.40 | 2.40 |
| **L107** | A21 | $2 multi | 3.25 | 3.25 |
| **L108** | A21 | $2.50 multi | 4.00 | 4.00 |
| | | *Nos. L104-L108 (5)* | 11.95 | 11.95 |

Signing of Antarctic Treaty, 50th Anniv. — A22

Mountains and: 50c, Map of Antarctica. $1, Penguins. $1.80, Scientist and equipment. $2.30, Flags. $2.80, Seal.

***Perf. 13¼x13½***

**2009, Nov. 25 Litho.**

| | | | | |
|---|---|---|---|---|
| **L109** | A22 | 50c multi | .75 | .75 |
| **L110** | A22 | $1 multi | 1.50 | 1.50 |
| **L111** | A22 | $1.80 multi | 2.60 | 2.60 |
| **L112** | A22 | $2.30 multi | 3.25 | 3.25 |
| **L113** | A22 | $2.80 multi | 4.00 | 4.00 |
| | | *Nos. L109-L113 (5)* | 12.10 | 12.10 |

Whales — A23

Designs: 60c, Sperm whale. $1.20, Minke whale. $1.90, Sei whale. $2.40, Killer whale. $2.90, Humpback whale.

**2010, Nov. 17 Litho. *Perf. 15x14¾***

| | | | | |
|---|---|---|---|---|
| **L114** | A23 | 60c multi | .95 | .95 |
| **L115** | A23 | $1.20 multi | 1.90 | 1.90 |
| **L116** | A23 | $1.90 multi | 3.00 | 3.00 |
| **L117** | A23 | $2.40 multi | 3.75 | 3.75 |
| **L118** | A23 | $2.90 multi | 4.50 | 4.50 |
| *a.* | | Souvenir sheet of 5, #L114-L118 | 14.50 | 14.50 |
| | | *Nos. L114-L118 (5)* | 14.10 | 14.10 |

Race to the South Pole A24

Map of Antarctica and: 60c, Roald Amundsen and ship, Fram. $1.20, Men of Amundsen's expedition. $1.90, Robert Falcon Scott and ship Terra Nova. $2.40, Men of Scott expedition, cross on cairn. $2.90, Flags of United Kingdom and Norway.

**2011, Nov. 2 *Perf. 13½x13¼***

| | | | | |
|---|---|---|---|---|
| **L119** | A24 | 60c multi | .95 | .95 |
| **L120** | A24 | $1.20 multi | 1.90 | 1.90 |
| **L121** | A24 | $1.90 multi | 3.00 | 3.00 |
| **L122** | A24 | $2.40 multi | 4.00 | 4.00 |
| *a.* | | Souvenir sheet of 2, #L121-L122 | 10.00 | 10.00 |
| **L123** | A24 | $2.90 multi | 4.75 | 4.75 |
| *a.* | | Souvenir sheet of 5, #L119-L123 | 15.00 | 15.00 |
| | | *Nos. L119-L123 (5)* | 14.60 | 14.60 |

Issued: No. L122a, 1/14/12. Christchurch Philatelic Society Centennial Stamp and Postcard Exhibition (#L122a).

Antarctic Landscapes — A25

Designs: 70c, Mount Erebus. $1.40, Beardmore Glacier. $1.90, Lake Vanda. $2.40, Cape Adare. $2.90, Ross Ice Shelf.

**2012, Nov. 21**

| | | | | |
|---|---|---|---|---|
| **L124** | A25 | 70c multi | 1.25 | 1.25 |
| **L125** | A25 | $1.40 multi | 2.40 | 2.40 |
| **L126** | A25 | $1.90 multi | 3.25 | 3.25 |
| **L127** | A25 | $2.40 multi | 4.00 | 4.00 |
| **L128** | A25 | $2.90 multi | 4.75 | 4.75 |
| *a.* | | Souvenir sheet of 5, #L124-L128 | 16.00 | 16.00 |
| | | *Nos. L124-L128 (5)* | 15.65 | 15.65 |

Antarctic Food Web — A26

Designs: 70c, Antarctic krill. $1.40, Lesser snow petrel. $1.90, Adélie penguin. $2.40, Crabeater seal. $2.90, Blue whale.

**2013, Nov. 20 Litho. *Perf. 14***

| | | | | |
|---|---|---|---|---|
| **L129** | A26 | 70c multi | 1.25 | 1.25 |
| **L130** | A26 | $1.40 multi | 2.40 | 2.40 |
| **L131** | A26 | $1.90 multi | 3.25 | 3.25 |
| **L132** | A26 | $2.40 multi | 4.00 | 4.00 |
| **L133** | A26 | $2.90 multi | 4.75 | 4.75 |
| *a.* | | Souvenir sheet of 5, #L129-L133 | 16.00 | 16.00 |
| | | *Nos. L129-L133 (5)* | 15.65 | 15.65 |

Penguins A27

Designs: 80c, Emperor penguins. $1.40, Adélie penguin. $2, Macaroni penguins. $2.50, Gentoo penguin and eggs. $3, Chinstrap penguin.

**2014, Nov. 19 Litho. *Perf. 14½***

| | | | | |
|---|---|---|---|---|
| **L134** | A27 | 80c multi | 1.25 | 1.25 |
| **L135** | A27 | $1.40 multi | 2.25 | 2.25 |
| **L136** | A27 | $2 multi | 3.25 | 3.25 |
| **L137** | A27 | $2.50 multi | 4.00 | 4.00 |
| **L138** | A27 | $3 multi | 4.75 | 4.75 |
| *a.* | | Souvenir sheet of 1 + label | 4.75 | 4.75 |
| *b.* | | Souvenir sheet of 5, #L134-L138 | 15.50 | 15.50 |
| | | *Nos. L134-L138 (5)* | 15.50 | 15.50 |

Values for Nos. L134-L138 are for stamps with surrounding selvage. See Greenland No. 679a.

Imperial Trans-Antarctic Expedition, Cent. — A28

Designs: No. L139, S.Y. Endurance. No. L140, Ocean Camp. $1.40, Expedition members in boat going from Elephant Island to South Georgia. $2, S.Y. Aurora. $2.50, Expedition members laying depots. $3, Rescue of the Ross Sea Party.

**2015, Nov. 4 Litho. *Perf. 14x14½***

| | | | | |
|---|---|---|---|---|
| **L139** | A28 | 80c multi | 1.10 | 1.10 |
| **L140** | A28 | 80c multi | 1.10 | 1.10 |
| **L141** | A28 | $1.40 multi | 1.90 | 1.90 |
| *a.* | | Souvenir sheet of 3, #L139-L141 | 4.25 | 4.25 |
| **L142** | A28 | $2 multi | 2.75 | 2.75 |
| **L143** | A28 | $2.50 multi | 3.50 | 3.50 |
| **L144** | A28 | $3 multi | 4.00 | 4.00 |
| *a.* | | Souvenir sheet of 3, #L142-L144 | 10.50 | 10.50 |
| | | *Nos. L139-L144 (6)* | 14.35 | 14.35 |

Creatures of the Antarctic Sea Floor — A29

Designs: $1, Stalked crinoid. $1.80, Sea star. $2.20, Sponge. $2.70, Hydroid. $3.30, Sea spider.

**2016, Nov. 16 Litho. *Perf. 14½x14***

| | | | | |
|---|---|---|---|---|
| **L145** | A29 | $1 multi | 1.40 | 1.40 |
| **L146** | A29 | $1.80 multi | 2.60 | 2.60 |
| **L147** | A29 | $2.20 multi | 3.25 | 3.25 |
| **L148** | A29 | $2.70 multi | 4.00 | 4.00 |
| **L149** | A29 | $3.30 multi | 4.75 | 4.75 |
| *a.* | | Souvenir sheet of 5, #L145-L149 | 16.00 | 16.00 |
| | | *Nos. L145-L149 (5)* | 16.00 | 16.00 |

Historic Huts and Items Found In Them — A30

Designs: $1, Captain Robert Falcon Scott's Discovery Hut. $2, Box, bottle, kettle and crate in Discovery Hut. $2.20, Sir Ernest Shackleton's Nimrod Hut. $2.30, Stove, kettles and canister in Nimrod Hut. $2.70, Scott's Terra Nova Hut. $3.30, Letter, bottles and pencils in Terra Nova Hut.

**2017, Sept. 20 Litho. *Perf. 14½***

| | | | | |
|---|---|---|---|---|
| **L150** | A30 | $1 multi | 1.40 | 1.40 |
| **L151** | A30 | $2 multi | 3.00 | 3.00 |
| **L152** | A30 | $2.20 multi | 3.25 | 3.25 |
| **L153** | A30 | $2.30 multi | 3.50 | 3.50 |
| **L154** | A30 | $2.70 multi | 4.00 | 4.00 |
| **L155** | A30 | $3.30 multi | 4.75 | 4.75 |
| *a.* | | Souvenir sheet of 6, #L150-L155 | 20.00 | 20.00 |
| | | *Nos. L150-L155 (6)* | 19.90 | 19.90 |

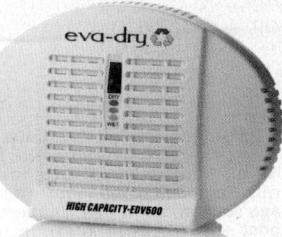

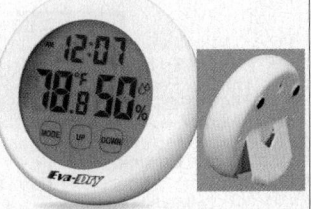

# NICARAGUA

ˌni-kə-ˈrä-gwə

LOCATION — Central America, between Honduras and Costa Rica
GOVT. — Republic
AREA — 50,439 sq. mi.
POP. — 4,384,400 (1997 est.)
CAPITAL — Managua

100 Centavos = 1 Peso
100 Centavos = 1 Córdoba (1913)

**Catalogue values for unused stamps in this country are for Never Hinged items, beginning with Scott 689 in the regular postage section, Scott C261 in the airpost section, Scott CO37 in the airpost official section, and Scott RA60 in the postal tax section.**

## ISSUES OF THE REPUBLIC

### Watermarks

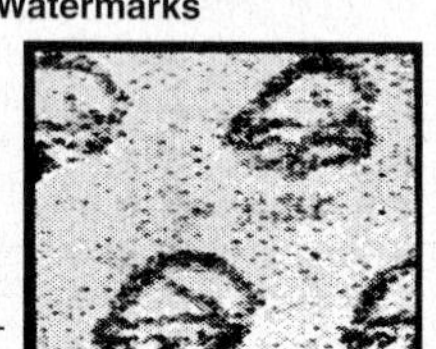

Wmk. 117 — Liberty Cap

Wmk. 209 — Multiple Ovals

Liberty Cap on Mountain Peak; From Seal of Country — A1

**Unwmk.**

**1862, Dec. 2 Engr. *Perf. 12***

**Yellowish Paper**

| No. | Design | Value | Unused | Used |
|---|---|---|---|---|
| **1** | A1 | 2c dark blue | 75.00 | 20.00 |
| **2** | A1 | 5c black | 150.00 | 60.00 |

Designs of Nos. 1-2 measure 22½x18½mm. Perforations are invariably rough.

Values are for stamps without gum. Examples with gum sell for more. Nos. 1-2 were canceled only by pen.

There is one reported cover of No. 1, two of No. 2.

See No. C509.

A2 A3

**1869-71 White Paper**

| No. | Design | Value | Unused | Used |
|---|---|---|---|---|
| **3** | A1 | 1c bister ('71) | 3.00 | 1.25 |
| **4** | A1 | 2c blue | 3.00 | 1.25 |
| **5** | A1 | 5c black | 100.00 | 1.00 |
| **6** | A2 | 10c vermilion | 4.00 | 1.75 |
| **7** | A3 | 25c green | 7.50 | 4.00 |
| | | *Nos. 3-7 (5)* | 117.50 | 9.25 |

Designs of Nos. 3-7 measure 22½x19mm. Perforations are clean cut.

There are two reported covers of No. 5, five of No. 7.

**1878-80 *Rouletted 8½***

| No. | Design | Value | Unused | Used |
|---|---|---|---|---|
| **8** | A1 | 1c brown | 2.00 | 1.25 |
| **9** | A1 | 2c blue | 2.00 | 1.25 |
| **10** | A1 | 5c black | 50.00 | 1.00 |
| **11** | A2 | 10c ver ('80) | 2.50 | 1.50 |
| **12** | A3 | 25c green ('79) | 2.50 | 4.00 |
| | | *Nos. 8-12 (5)* | 59.00 | 9.00 |

Most values exist on thicker soft paper.

Stamps with letter/numeral cancellations other than "3 G," "6 M," "9 C" sell for more.

*Nos. 3-12 were reprinted in 1892. The corresponding values of the two series are printed in the same shades which is not usually true of the originals. They are, however, similar to some of the original shades and the only certain test is comparison. Originals have thin white gum; reprints have rather thick yellowish gum. Value 50c each. Unused examples of Nos. 3-12 without gum should be presumed to be reprints. Nos. 5 and 10 unused are extremely scarce and should be purchased with original gum and should be expertized.*

Seal of Nicaragua — A4

**1882 Engr. *Perf. 12***

| No. | Design | Value | Unused | Used |
|---|---|---|---|---|
| **13** | A4 | 1c green | .25 | .25 |
| **14** | A4 | 2c carmine | .25 | .25 |
| **15** | A4 | 5c blue | .30 | .25 |
| **16** | A4 | 10c dull violet | .40 | *.75* |
| **17** | A4 | 15c yellow | .80 | *25.00* |
| **18** | A4 | 20c slate gray | 1.60 | *5.00* |
| **19** | A4 | 50c dull violet | 2.25 | *25.00* |
| | | *Nos. 13-19 (7)* | 5.85 | *56.50* |

Used Values

of Nos. 13-120 are for stamps with genuine cancellations applied while the stamps were valid. Various counterfeit cancellations exist.

Locomotive and Telegraph Key — A5

**1890 Engr.**

| No. | Design | Value | Unused | Used |
|---|---|---|---|---|
| **20** | A5 | 1c yellow brown | .25 | .30 |
| **21** | A5 | 2c vermilion | .25 | .30 |
| **22** | A5 | 5c deep blue | .25 | .30 |
| **23** | A5 | 10c lilac gray | .25 | .30 |
| **24** | A5 | 20c red | .25 | *.30* |
| **25** | A5 | 50c purple | .25 | *.30* |
| **26** | A5 | 1p brown | .25 | *.40* |
| **27** | A5 | 2p dark green | .25 | *.40* |
| **28** | A5 | 5p lake | .25 | *.50* |
| **29** | A5 | 10p orange | .25 | *.50* |
| | | *Nos. 20-29 (10)* | 2.50 | |

The issues of 1890-1899 were printed by the Hamilton Bank Note Co., New York, to the order of N. F. Seebeck who held a contract for stamps with the government of Nicaragua. Reprints were made, for sale to collectors, of the 1896, 1897 and 1898, postage, postage due and official stamps. See notes following those issues.

For overprints see Nos. O1-O10.

Perforation Varieties

Imperfs and part perfs of all the Seebeck issues, Nos. 20-120, exist for all except originals of the 1898 issue, Nos. 99-109M.

Goddess of Plenty — A6

**1891 Engr.**

| No. | Design | Value | Unused | Used |
|---|---|---|---|---|
| **30** | A6 | 1c yellow brn | .25 | .35 |
| **31** | A6 | 2c red | .25 | .35 |
| **32** | A6 | 5c dk blue | .25 | .25 |
| **33** | A6 | 10c slate | .25 | .50 |
| **34** | A6 | 20c plum | .25 | *2.00* |
| **35** | A6 | 50c purple | .25 | *5.00* |
| **36** | A6 | 1p black brn | .25 | *5.00* |
| **37** | A6 | 2p green | .25 | *8.50* |
| **38** | A6 | 5p brown red | .25 | |
| **39** | A6 | 10p orange | .25 | |
| | | *Nos. 30-39 (10)* | 2.50 | |

For overprints see Nos. O11-O20.

Columbus Sighting Land — A7

**1892 Engr.**

| No. | Design | Value | Unused | Used |
|---|---|---|---|---|
| **40** | A7 | 1c yellow brn | .25 | .25 |
| **41** | A7 | 2c vermilion | .25 | .25 |
| **42** | A7 | 5c dk blue | .25 | .25 |
| **43** | A7 | 10c slate | .25 | .25 |
| **44** | A7 | 20c plum | .25 | *2.00* |
| **45** | A7 | 50c purple | .25 | *7.00* |
| **46** | A7 | 1p brown | .25 | *7.00* |
| **47** | A7 | 2p blue grn | .25 | *8.50* |
| **48** | A7 | 5p rose lake | .25 | |
| **49** | A7 | 10p orange | .25 | |
| | | *Nos. 40-49 (10)* | 2.50 | |

Commemorative of the 400th anniversary of the discovery of America by Columbus.

Stamps of the 1892 design were printed in other colors than those listed and overprinted "Telegrafos". The 1c blue, 10c orange, 20c slate, 50c plum and 2p vermilion are telegraph stamps which did not receive the overprint.

For overprints see Nos. O21-O30.

Arms — A8

**1893 Engr.**

| No. | Design | Value | Unused | Used |
|---|---|---|---|---|
| **51** | A8 | 1c yellow brn | .25 | .25 |
| **52** | A8 | 2c vermilion | .25 | .25 |
| **53** | A8 | 5c dk blue | .25 | .25 |
| **54** | A8 | 10c slate | .25 | .25 |
| **55** | A8 | 20c dull red | .25 | *1.50* |
| **56** | A8 | 50c violet | .25 | *4.00* |
| **57** | A8 | 1p dk brown | .25 | *7.00* |
| **58** | A8 | 2p blue green | .25 | *8.50* |
| **59** | A8 | 5p rose lake | .25 | |
| **60** | A8 | 10p orange | .25 | |
| | | *Nos. 51-60 (10)* | 2.50 | |

The 1c blue and 2c dark brown are telegraph stamps which did not receive the "Telegrafos" overprint.

For overprints see Nos. O31-O41.

"Victory" — A9

**1894 Engr.**

| No. | Design | Value | Unused | Used |
|---|---|---|---|---|
| **61** | A9 | 1c yellow brn | .30 | *.30* |
| **62** | A9 | 2c vermilion | .30 | *.30* |
| **63** | A9 | 5c dp blue | .30 | *.30* |
| **64** | A9 | 10c slate | .30 | *.30* |
| **65** | A9 | 20c lake | .30 | *2.00* |
| **66** | A9 | 50c purple | .30 | *5.00* |
| **67** | A9 | 1p brown | .40 | *9.50* |
| **68** | A9 | 2p green | .40 | *17.50* |
| **69** | A9 | 5p brown red | .50 | *45.00* |
| **70** | A9 | 10p orange | .50 | *45.00* |
| | | *Nos. 61-70 (10)* | 3.60 | 125.20 |

There were three printings of this issue. Only the first is known postally used. Unused values are for the third printing.

Used values are for stamps with "DIRECCION" cancels in black that were removed from post office new year cards.

Specialists believe the 25c yellow green, type A9, is a telegraph denomination never issued for postal purposes. Stamps in other colors are telegraph stamps without the usual "Telegrafos" overprint.

For overprints see Nos. O42-O51.

Coat of Arms — A10

**1895 Engr.**

| No. | Design | Value | Unused | Used |
|---|---|---|---|---|
| **71** | A10 | 1c yellow brn | .25 | .30 |
| **72** | A10 | 2c vermilion | .25 | .30 |
| **73** | A10 | 5c deep blue | .25 | .25 |
| **74** | A10 | 10c slate | .25 | .25 |
| **75** | A10 | 20c claret | .25 | *.75* |
| **76** | A10 | 50c light violet | 50.00 | *5.00* |
| **77** | A10 | 1p dark brown | .25 | *5.00* |
| **78** | A10 | 2p deep green | .25 | *8.00* |
| **79** | A10 | 5p brown red | .25 | *11.00* |
| **80** | A10 | 10p orange | .25 | |
| | | *Nos. 71-80 (10)* | 52.25 | |

Frames of Nos. 71-80 differ for each denomination.

A 50c violet blue exists. Its status is questioned. Value 25c.

There was little proper use of No. 80. Canceled examples are almost always c-t-o or have faked cancels.

For overprints see Nos. O52-O71.

Map of Nicaragua — A11

**1896 Engr.**

| No. | Design | Value | Unused | Used |
|---|---|---|---|---|
| **81** | A11 | 1c violet | .30 | *1.00* |
| **82** | A11 | 2c blue grn | .30 | *.50* |
| **83** | A11 | 5c brt rose | .30 | *.30* |
| **84** | A11 | 10c blue | .50 | *.50* |
| **85** | A11 | 20c bister brn | 3.00 | *4.00* |
| **86** | A11 | 50c blue gray | .60 | *8.00* |
| **87** | A11 | 1p black | .75 | *11.00* |
| **88** | A11 | 2p claret | .75 | *15.00* |
| **89** | A11 | 5p deep blue | .75 | *15.00* |
| | | *Nos. 81-89 (9)* | 7.25 | *55.30* |

There were two printings of this issue. Only the first is known postally used. Unused values are for the second printing.

See italic note after No. 109M.

For overprints see Nos. O82-O117.

**Wmk. 117**

| No. | Design | Value | Unused | Used |
|---|---|---|---|---|
| **89A** | A11 | 1c violet | 3.75 | .90 |
| **89B** | A11 | 2c bl grn | 3.75 | 1.25 |
| **89C** | A11 | 5c brt rose | 15.00 | .30 |
| **89D** | A11 | 10c blue | 25.00 | .90 |
| **89E** | A11 | 20c bis brn | 22.50 | 4.25 |
| **89F** | A11 | 50c bl gray | 42.50 | *9.00* |
| **89G** | A11 | 1p black | 37.50 | *12.50* |
| **89H** | A11 | 2p claret | | *18.00* |
| **89I** | A11 | 5p dp bl | | *40.00* |

**Same, dated 1897**

**1897 Engr. Unwmk.**

| No. | Design | Value | Unused | Used |
|---|---|---|---|---|
| **90** | A11 | 1c violet | .50 | .50 |
| **91** | A11 | 2c bl grn | .50 | .60 |
| **92** | A11 | 5c brt rose | .50 | .30 |
| **93** | A11 | 10c blue | 6.25 | .75 |
| **94** | A11 | 20c bis brn | 2.50 | *3.75* |
| **95** | A11 | 50c bl gray | 9.00 | *9.50* |
| **96** | A11 | 1p black | 9.00 | *15.00* |
| **97** | A11 | 2p claret | 20.00 | *19.00* |
| **98** | A11 | 5p dp bl | 20.00 | *42.50* |
| | | *Nos. 90-98 (9)* | 68.25 | *91.90* |

See italic note after No. 109M.

**Wmk. 117**

| No. | Design | Value | Unused | Used |
|---|---|---|---|---|
| **98A** | A11 | 1c violet | 14.00 | .50 |
| **98B** | A11 | 2c bl grn | 14.00 | .50 |
| **98C** | A11 | 5c brt rose | 20.00 | .40 |
| **98D** | A11 | 10c blue | 22.50 | .90 |
| **98E** | A11 | 20c bis brn | 22.50 | 4.25 |
| **98F** | A11 | 50c bl gray | 22.50 | *8.00* |
| **98G** | A11 | 1p black | 25.00 | *16.00* |
| **98H** | A11 | 2p claret | 25.00 | *25.00* |
| **98I** | A11 | 5p dp bl | 125.00 | *50.00* |
| | | *Nos. 98A-98I (9)* | 290.50 | *105.55* |

Coat of Arms of "Republic of Central America" — A12

**1898 Engr. Wmk. 117**

| No. | Design | Value | Unused | Used |
|---|---|---|---|---|
| **99** | A12 | 1c brown | .25 | .40 |
| **100** | A12 | 2c slate | .25 | .40 |
| **101** | A12 | 4c red brown | .25 | .50 |
| **102** | A12 | 5c olive green | 40.00 | 22.50 |
| **103** | A12 | 10c violet | 15.00 | .60 |
| **104** | A12 | 15c ultra | .40 | 1.50 |
| **105** | A12 | 20c blue | 10.00 | 2.00 |
| **106** | A12 | 50c yellow | 10.00 | *9.50* |
| **107** | A12 | 1p violet blue | .40 | *16.00* |
| **108** | A12 | 2p brown | 19.00 | *22.50* |
| **109** | A12 | 5p orange | 25.00 | *32.50* |
| | | *Nos. 99-109 (11)* | 120.55 | *108.40* |

**Unwmk.**

| No. | Design | Value | Unused | Used |
|---|---|---|---|---|
| **109A** | A12 | 1c brown | 1.25 | .30 |
| **109B** | A12 | 2c slate | 1.25 | |
| **109D** | A12 | 4c red brown | 2.25 | .60 |
| **109E** | A12 | 5c olive green | 25.00 | .25 |
| **109G** | A12 | 10c violet | 25.00 | .60 |
| **109H** | A12 | 15c ultra | 25.00 | |

**109I** A12 20c blue 25.00
**109J** A12 50c yellow 25.00
**109K** A12 1p deep ultra 25.00
**109L** A12 2p olive brown 25.00
**109M** A12 5p orange 25.00
*Nos. 109A-109M (11)* 204.75

The paper of Nos. 109A to 109M is slightly thicker and more opaque than that of Nos. 81 to 89 and 90 to 98. The 5c and 10c also exist on very thin, semi-transparent paper.

*Many reprints of Nos. 81-98, 98F-98H, 99-109M are on thick, porous paper, with and without watermark. The watermark is sideways. Paper of the originals is thinner for Nos. 81-109 but thicker for Nos. 109A-109M. Value 25c each.*

*In addition, reprints of Nos. 81-89 and 90-98 exist on thin paper, but with shades differing slightly from those of originals.*

For overprints see Nos. O118-O128.

"Justice" — A13

**1899** **Litho.**

**110** A13 1c gray grn .25 *.35*
**111** A13 2c brown .25 *.25*
**112** A13 4c dp rose .35 *.40*
**113** A13 5c dp bl .25 *.25*
**114** A13 10c buff .25 *.30*
**115** A13 15c chocolate .25 *.65*
**116** A13 20c dk grn .35 *.75*
**117** A13 50c brt rose .25 *3.00*
**118** A13 1p red .25 *8.50*
**119** A13 2p violet .25 *20.00*
**120** A13 5p lt bl .25 *25.00*
*Nos. 110-120 (11)* 2.95 *59.45*

Nos. 110-120 exist imperf. and in horizontal pairs imperf. between.

Nos. 110-111, 113 exist perf 6x12 due to defective perforating equipment.

For overprints see Nos. O129-O139.

Mt. Momotombo A14

**Imprint: "American Bank Note Co. NY"**

**1900, Jan. 1** **Engr.**

**121** A14 1c plum .65 .25
**122** A14 2c vermilion .65 .25
**123** A14 3c green .90 .25
**124** A14 4c ol grn 1.25 .25
**125** A14 5c dk bl 4.00 .25
**126** A14 6c car rose 14.00 5.00
**127** A14 10c violet 7.00 .25
**128** A14 15c ultra 8.00 .65
**129** A14 20c brown 8.00 .65
**130** A14 50c lake 7.00 1.10
**131** A14 1p yellow 12.00 4.00
**132** A14 2p salmon 10.00 2.25
**133** A14 5p black 10.00 3.00
*Nos. 121-133 (13)* 83.45 18.15

Used values for #123, 126, 130-133 are for canceled to order examples.

See Nos. 159-161. For overprints and surcharges see Nos. 134-136, 144-151, 162-163, 175-178, O150-O154, 1L1-1L13, 1L16-1L19, 1L20, 2L1-2L10, 2L16-2L24, 2L36-2L39.

Mt. Momotombo — A14a

**1902** **White Wove Paper** ***Imperf.***
**Size: 55x52mm**

**133A** A14a 5c blue
**133B** A14a 10c red violet
**133C** A14a 20c brown
**133D** A14a 30c black green
**133E** A14a 50c red

**51x51mm**

**133F** A14a 2c dk red, *buff*
**133G** A14a 4c red brown, *buff*

Nos. 133A-133G are documented on covers postmarked from 1902-04. Specimen pairs and blocks are from sheets of 35 (Nos. 133A-133E) or 28 (Nos. 133F-133G) sold in the 1990 American Bank Note Company archives sale. Nos. 133A-133G are not cutouts from similar postal envelopes issued in 1900.

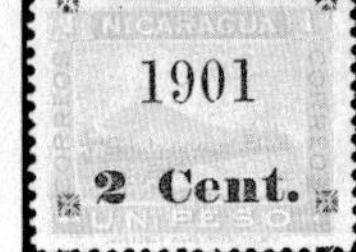


Nos. 131-133 Surcharged in Black or Red

**1901, Mar. 5**

**134** A14 2c on 1p yel 5.00 4.50
*a.* Bar below date 16.00 *9.00*
*b.* Inverted surcharge *35.00*
*c.* Double surcharge *50.00*
**135** A14 10c on 5p blk (R) 12.00 4.50
*a.* Bar below date 17.50 8.00
**136** A14 20c on 2p salmon 7.50 7.50
*a.* Bar below date 14.00 10.00
*Nos. 134-136 (3)* 24.50 16.50

A 2c surcharge on No. 121, the 1c plum, was not put on sale, though some are known used from a few sheets distributed by the post office to "government friends." Value, *$250.00.*

*The 2c on 1p yellow without ornaments is a reprint.*

Postage Due Stamps of 1900 Overprinted in Black or Gold

**1901, Mar.**

**137** D3 1c plum 4.50 3.50
**138** D3 2c vermilion 4.50 3.50
**139** D3 5c dk bl 6.00 3.50
**140** D3 10c pur (G) 8.50 8.50
*a.* Double overprint 14.00 14.00
**141** D3 20c org brn 10.00 10.00
**142** D3 30c dk grn 10.00 6.50
**143** D3 50c lake 8.50 4.00
*a.* "1091" for "1901" 35.00 35.00
*b.* "Correo" 37.50
*Nos. 137-143 (7)* 52.00 39.50

In 1904 an imitation of this overprint was made to fill a dealer's order. The date is at top and "Correos" at bottom. The overprint is printed in black, sideways on the 1c and 2c and upright on the 5c and 10c. Some examples of the 2c were further surcharged "1 Centavo." None of these stamps was ever regularly used.

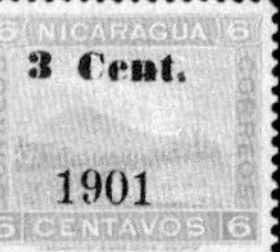


Nos. 126, 131-133 Surcharged

**1901, Oct. 20** **Black Surcharge**

**144** A14 3c on 6c rose 12.00 5.00
*a.* Bar below value 13.00 5.50
*b.* Inverted surcharge 14.00 8.00
*c.* Double surcharge 14.00 8.00
*d.* Double surch., one inverted 25.00 25.00
**145** A14 4c on 6c rose 8.00 4.00
*a.* Bar below value 9.00 4.50
*b.* "1 cent" instead of "4 cent" 11.00 8.00
*c.* Double surcharge 20.00 20.00
**146** A14 5c on 1p yellow 6.00 4.00
*a.* Three bars below value 7.00 4.50
*b.* Ornaments at each side of "1901" 30.00 4.50
*c.* Double surcharge, one in red 17.50 15.00
**147** A14 10c on 2p salmon 6.50 4.00
*a.* Inverted surcharge 30.00 27.50
*b.* Double surcharge

**Blue Surcharge**

**148** A14 3c on 6c rose 9.00 4.50
*a.* Bar below value 10.00 5.50
*b.* Double surcharge 11.00 8.00
**149** A14 4c on 6c rose 12.00 5.00
*a.* Bar below value 13.00 7.50
*b.* "1 cent" instead of "4 cent" 20.00 10.00
*c.* Inverted surcharge 25.00 20.00

**Red Surcharge**

**150** A14 5c on 1p yellow 8.00 6.50
*a.* Three bars below value 10.00 7.00
*b.* Ornaments at each side of "1901" 10.00 7.00
*c.* Inverted surcharge 20.00 12.00
*d.* Double surcharge, inverted 22.50 17.50
**151** A14 20c on 5p black 5.50 3.50
*a.* Inverted surcharge 20.00 16.00
*b.* Double surcharge 22.50 22.50
*c.* Triple surcharge
*Nos. 144-151 (8)* 67.00 36.50

In 1904 a series was surcharged as above, but with "Centavos" spelled out. About the same time No. 122 was surcharged "1 cent." and "1901," "1902" or "1904." All of these surcharges were made to fill a dealer's order and none of the stamps was regularly issued or used.

Postage Due Stamps of 1900 Overprinted in Black

**1901, Oct.**

**152** D3 1c red violet 1.00 .40
*a.* Ornaments at each side of the stamp 10.00 .65
*b.* Ornaments at each side of "1901" 1.10 .65
*c.* "Correos" in italics 1.50 1.50
*d.* Double overprint 14.00 14.00
**153** D3 2c vermilion .75 .40
*a.* Double overprint 8.50 5.50
**154** D3 5c dark blue 1.00 .60
*a.* Double overprint, one inverted
*b.* Double overprint 7.00 7.00
**155** D3 10c purple 1.00 .60
*b.* Double overprint 10.00 10.00
*c.* Double overprint, one inverted 12.00 12.00
**156** D3 20c org brn 1.50 1.25
*b.* Double overprint 7.00 7.00
**157** D3 30c dk grn 1.00 1.10
*a.* Double overprint 9.00 9.00
*b.* Inverted overprint 19.00 19.00
**158** D3 50c lake 1.00 1.10
*a.* Triple overprint 25.00 25.00
*b.* Double overprint 16.00 16.00
*Nos. 152-158 (7)* 7.25 5.45

One stamp in each group of 25 has the 2nd "o" of "Correos" italic. Value twice normal.

**Momotombo Type of 1900**
Without Imprint

**1902** **Litho.** ***Perf. 14***

**159** A14 5c blue .50 .25
*a.* Imperf., pair 3.75
**160** A14 5c carmine .50 .25
*a.* Imperf., pair 3.75
**161** A14 10c violet 1.50 .25
*a.* Imperf., pair 3.75
*Nos. 159-161 (3)* 2.50 .75

No. 161 was privately surcharged 6c, 1p and 5p in black in 1903. Not fully authorized but known postally used. Value of c-t-o peso denominations, $5 each.

Nos. 121 and 122 Surcharged in Black

**1902, Oct.** ***Perf. 12***

**162** A14 15c on 2c ver 4.00 .75
*a.* Double surcharge 32.50
*b.* Blue surcharge 90.00
**163** A14 30c on 1c plum 3.00 2.25
*a.* Double surcharge 12.00
*b.* Inverted surcharge 27.50

Counterfeits of No. 163 exist in slightly smaller type.

President José Santos Zelaya — A15

**1903, Jan.** **Engr.**

**167** A15 1c emer & blk .45 .50
**168** A15 2c rose & blk 1.00 .50
**169** A15 5c ultra & blk .50 .50
**170** A15 10c yel & blk .50 *.85*
**171** A15 15c lake & blk 1.75 *2.00*
**172** A15 20c vio & blk 1.75 *2.00*
**173** A15 50c ol & blk 1.75 *5.00*
**174** A15 1p red brn & blk 2.00 *6.00*
*Nos. 167-174 (8)* 9.70 *17.35*

10th anniv. of 1st election of Pres. Zelaya.

The so-called color errors-1c orange yellow and black, 2c ultramarine and black, 5c lake and black and 10c emerald and black-were also delivered to postal authorities. They were intended for official use though not issued as such. Value, $4 each.

**No. 161 Surcharged in Blue**

Nos. 175-176

No. 177

**1904-05**

**175** A14 5c on 10c vio ('05) 1.75 .25
*a.* Inverted surcharge 5.50 3.00
*b.* Without ornaments 2.00 .70
*c.* Character for "cents" inverted 1.75 .40
*d.* As "b," inverted
*e.* As "c," inverted 2.75 2.75
*f.* Double surcharge 25.00 8.00
*g.* "5" omitted 2.75 2.75
**176** A14 15c on 10c vio ('05) .90 .30
*a.* Inverted surcharge 4.00 1.40
*b.* Without ornaments 2.00 1.40
*c.* Character for "cents" inverted 2.50 1.10
*d.* As "b," inverted
*e.* As "c," inverted 5.00 1.75
*f.* Imperf. 7.00
*h.* As "a," imperf. 10.00 9.00
*i.* Double surcharge 16.00 14.00
**177** A14 15c on 10c vio 4.50 2.75
*a.* Inverted surcharge 7.00 6.00
*b.* "Centcvos" 7.00 4.50
*c.* "5" of "15" omitted 12.50
*d.* As "b," inverted 8.50 8.50
*e.* Double surcharge 11.00 11.00
*f.* Double surcharge, inverted 13.00 13.00
*g.* Imperf., pair 9.00 9.00
*Nos. 175-177 (3)* 7.15 3.30

There are two settings of the surcharge on No. 175. In the 1st the character for "cents" and the figure "5" are 2mm apart and in the 2nd 4mm.

The 2c vermilion, No. 122, with surcharge "1 cent. / 1904" was not issued.

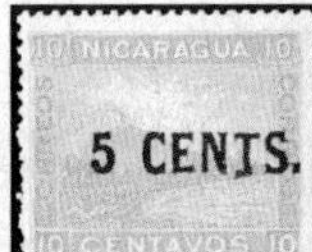


No. 161 Surcharged in Black

**1905, June**

**178** A14 5c on 10c violet .60 .35
*a.* Inverted surcharge 13.50 10.00
*b.* Double surcharge 4.50 4.50
*c.* Surcharge in blue *75.00*

Coat of Arms — A18

**Imprint: "American Bank Note Co. NY"**

**1905, July 25** **Engr.** ***Perf. 12***

**179** A18 1c green .30 .25
**180** A18 2c car rose .30 .25
**181** A18 3c violet .45 .25
**182** A18 4c org red .45 .25
**183** A18 5c blue .45 .25
**184** A18 6c slate .60 .40
**185** A18 10c yel brn .85 .25
**186** A18 15c brn olive .75 .35
**187** A18 20c lake .60 .40
**188** A18 50c orange 3.00 1.50
**189** A18 1p black 1.50 1.50
**190** A18 2p dk grn 1.50 2.00
**191** A18 5p violet 1.75 2.50
*Nos. 179-191 (13)* 12.50 10.15

See Nos. 202-208, 237-248. For overprints and surcharges see Nos. 193-201, 212-216, 235-236, 249-265, O187-O198, O210-O222, 1L21-1L62, 1L73-1L95, 1LO1-1LO3, 2L26-2L35, 2L42-2L46, 2L48-2L72, 2LO1-2LO4.

Nos. 179-184 and 191 Surcharged in Black or Red Reading Up or Down

**1906-08**

**193** A18 10c on 2c car rose (up) 7.00 4.50
*a.* Surcharge reading down 13.00 13.00
**194** A18 10c on 3c vio (up) .80 .25
*a.* "¢" normal 2.75 1.35
*b.* Double surcharge 4.50 4.50
*c.* Double surch., up and down 7.00 5.00
*d.* Pair, one without surcharge 9.50
*e.* Surcharge reading down .30 .25
**195** A18 10c on 4c org red (up) ('08) *35.00 15.00*
*a.* Surcharge reading down *32.50 26.00*
**196** A18 15c on 1c grn (up) .60 .30
*a.* Double surcharge 7.50 7.50
*b.* Dbl. surch., one reading down 11.00 11.00
*c.* Surcharge reading down .70 .35
**197** A18 20c on 2c car rose (down) ('07) .50 .30
*a.* Double surcharge 13.00 13.00
*b.* Surcharge reading up 37.50 32.50
*c.* "V" omitted 10.00 10.00
**198** A18 20c on 5c bl (down) .90 .50
*a.* Surcharge reading up 35.00
**199** A18 50c on 6c sl (R) (down) .80 .50
*a.* Double surcharge
*b.* Surcharge reading up 30.00 30.00
*c.* Yellow brown surcharge .80 .40
**200** A18 1p on 5p vio (down) ('07) 42.50 18.00
*Nos. 193-200 (8)* *88.10 39.35*

There are several settings of these surcharges and many varieties in the shapes of the figures, the spacing, etc.

Surcharged in Red Vertically Reading Up

**1908, May**

**201** A18 35c on 6c slate 3.50 2.25
*a.* Double surcharge (R) 25.00
*b.* Double surcharge (R + Bk) 65.00
*c.* Carmine surcharge 3.50 2.25

### Arms Type of 1905

Imprint: "Waterlow & Sons, Ltd."

**1907, Feb.** ***Perf. 14 to 15***

**202** A18 1c green .70 .40
**203** A18 2c rose .80 .25
**204** A18 4c brn org 2.00 .30
**205** A18 10c yel brn 3.00 .25
**206** A18 15c brn olive 4.50 .90
**207** A18 20c lake 8.00 1.25
**208** A18 50c orange 20.00 4.25
*Nos. 202-208 (7)* 39.00 7.60

Nos. 202-204, 207-208 Surcharged in Black or Blue (Bl) Reading Down

**1907-08**

**212** A18 10c on 2c rose 1.50 .50
*a.* Double surcharge 10.00
*b.* "Vale" only 22.50
*c.* Surcharge reading up 14.00 6.50
**213** A18 10c on 4c brn org (up) ('08) 2.25 .85
*a.* Double surcharge 10.00
*b.* Surcharge reading down 10.00
**214** A18 10c on 20c lake ('08) 3.25 1.40
*b.* Surcharge reading up 80.00
**215** A18 10c on 50c org (Bl) ('08) 2.00 .60
**216** A18 15c on 1c grn ('08) 32.50 4.00
*Nos. 212-216 (5)* 41.50 7.35

Several settings of this surcharge provide varieties of numeral font, spacing, etc.

Revenue Stamps Overprinted "CORREO-1908" — A19

**1908, June**

**217** A19 5c yel & blk .60 .40
*a.* "CORROE" 2.75 2.75
*b.* Overprint reading down 7.00
*c.* Double overprint 13.00
**218** A19 10c lt bl & blk .50 .25
*a.* Double overprint 4.50 4.50
*b.* Overprint reading down .50 .25
*c.* Double overprint, up and down 13.00 13.00
**219** A19 1p yel brn & blk .50 *2.00*
*a.* "CORROE" 10.00 *12.00*
**220** A19 2p pearl gray & blk .50 *2.50*
*a.* "CORROE" 10.00 10.00
*Nos. 217-220 (4)* 2.10 *5.15*

The overprint exists on a 5p in green (value $200) and on a 50p in black (value $300).

Revenue Stamps Surcharged Vertically Reading Up in Red (1c, 15c), Blue(2c), Green (4c) or Orange (35c)

**221** A19 1c on 5c yel & blk .40 .25
*a.* "1008" 2.00 *3.00*
*b.* "8908" 2.00 *3.00*
*c.* Surcharge reading down 4.00 4.00
*d.* Double surcharge 4.00 4.00
**222** A19 2c on 5c yel & blk .50 .30
*b.* "ORREO" 1.75 1.75
*c.* "1008" 1.75 1.75
*d.* "8908" 2.50 *5.50*
*f.* Double surcharge 7.00 7.00
*g.* Double surcharge, one inverted 7.00 7.00
*h.* Surcharge reading down 9.00 9.00
**223** A19 4c on 5c yel & blk .65 .35
*a.* "ORREO" 3.50 *7.50*
*b.* "1008" 2.00 2.00
*c.* "8908" 2.00 2.00
**224** A19 15c on 50c ol & blk .60 .40
*a.* "1008" 7.50 *11.50*
*b.* "8908" 4.00 4.00
*c.* Surcharge reading down 10.00 10.00
**225** A19 35c on 50c ol & blk 4.00 1.00
*a.* Double surcharge, one inverted 12.00 12.00
*b.* Surcharge reading down 12.00 12.00
*c.* Double surcharge, one in black
*Nos. 221-225 (5)* 6.15 2.30

For surcharges and overprints see Nos. 225D-225H, 230-234, 266-278, 1L63-1L72A, 1L96-1L106, 2L47.

Revenue Stamps Surcharged Vertically Reading Up in Blue, Black or Orange

**1908, Nov.**

**225D** A19 2c on 5c yel org & blk (Bl) 20.00 12.50
*e.* "9c" instead of "2c" 75.00 75.00
**225F** A19 10c on 50c ol & blk (Bk) *850.00 325.00*
*g.* Double surcharge *425.00*
**225H** A19 35c on 50c ol & blk (O) 17.50 10.00

In this setting there are three types of the character for "cents."

### Revenue Stamps Overprinted or Surcharged in Various Colors

No. 226

No. 227

**1908, Dec.**

**226** 2c org (Bk) 3.50 2.00
*a.* Double overprint 6.00 6.00
*b.* Overprint reading up 5.00 5.00
**227** 4c on 2c org (Bk) 1.75 .90
*a.* Surcharge reading up 5.00 5.00
*b.* Blue surcharge 80.00 80.00
**228** 5c on 2c org (Bl) 1.50 .60
*a.* Surcharge reading up 6.00 6.00
**229** 10c on 2c org (G) 1.50 .30
*a.* "1988" for "1908" 4.00 3.00
*b.* Surcharge reading up 5.00 5.00
*c.* "¢" inverted 4.00 4.00
*d.* Double surcharge 7.50
*Nos. 226-229 (4)* 8.25 3.80

Two printings of No. 229 exist. In the first, the initial of "VALE" is a small capital, and in the second a large capital.

The overprint "Correos-1908." 35mm long, handstamped on 1c blue revenue stamp of type A20, is private and fraudulent.

Revenue Stamps Surcharged in Various Colors

**1909, Feb.** **Color: Olive & Black**

**230** A19 1c on 50c (V) 4.00 1.60
**231** A19 2c on 50c (Br) 7.00 3.00
**232** A19 4c on 50c (G) 7.00 3.00
**233** A19 5c on 50c (C) 4.00 1.75
*a.* Double surcharge 12.50 12.50
**234** A19 10c on 50c (Bk) 1.10 .75
*Nos. 230-234 (5)* 23.10 10.10

Nos. 230 to 234 are found with three types of the character for "cents."

Nos. 190 and 191 Surcharged in Black

**1909, Mar.** ***Perf. 12***

**235** A18 10c on 2p dk grn 20.00 12.00
**236** A18 10c on 5p vio *100.00 70.00*

There are three types of the character for "cents."

### Arms Type of 1905

Imprint: "American Bank Note Co. NY"

**1909, Mar.**

**237** A18 1c yel grn .35 .25
**238** A18 2c vermilion .35 .25
**239** A18 3c red org .35 .25
**240** A18 4c violet .35 .25
**241** A18 5c dp bl .35 .25
**242** A18 6c gray brn 3.00 1.50
**243** A18 10c lake .85 .25
**244** A18 15c black .85 .25
**245** A18 20c brn olive .85 .25
**246** A18 50c dp grn 1.25 .40
**247** A18 1p yellow 1.25 .40
**248** A18 2p car rose 1.00 .40
*Nos. 237-248 (12)* 10.80 4.70

Nos. 239 and 244, Surcharged in Black or Red

**1910, July**

**249** A18 2c on 3c red org 2.75 1.10
**250** A18 10c on 15c blk (R) 1.25 .30
*a.* "VLEA" 3.50 2.00
*b.* Double surcharge 17.50 17.50

There are two types of the character for "cents."

Nos. 239, 244, 245 Surcharged in Black or Red

**1910**

**252** A18 2c on 3c (Bk) 1.50 1.25
*a.* Double surcharge 6.00 6.00
*b.* Pair, one without surcharge
*c.* "Vale" omitted 10.00 10.00
**254** A18 5c on 20c (R) .40 .30
*a.* Double surcharge (R) 6.00 5.00
*b.* Inverted surcharge (R) 10.00 *32.50*
*c.* Black surcharge 100.00
*d.* Double surcharge (Bk) 140.00
*e.* Inverted surcharge (Bk) 110.00
**255** A18 10c on 15c (Bk) .90 .30
*a.* "c" omitted 2.00 1.10
*b.* "10c" omitted 2.50 1.50
*c.* Inverted surcharge 4.00 4.00
*d.* Double surcharge 6.00 6.00
*e.* Double surch., one inverted 14.00 *18.50*
*Nos. 252-255 (3)* 2.80 1.85

There are several minor varieties in this setting, such as italic "L" and "E" and fancy "V" in "VALE," small italic "C," and italic "I" for "1" in "10."

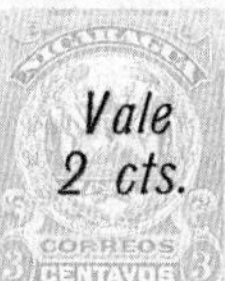

Nos. 239, 244, 246 and 247, Surcharged in Black

**1910, Dec. 10**

**256** A18 2c on 3c red org .85 .45
*a.* Without period 1.00 .75
*b.* Inverted surcharge 6.00 6.00
*c.* Double surcharge 6.00 6.00
**257** A18 10c on 15c blk 2.00 .75
*a.* Without period 3.50 1.25
*b.* Double surcharge 6.00 3.00
*c.* Inverted surcharge 10.00 *18.00*
**258** A18 10c on 50c dp grn 1.25 .40
*a.* Without period 1.50 .75
*b.* Double surcharge 10.00 *26.00*
*c.* Inverted surcharge 3.00 3.00
**259** A18 10c on 1p yel .90 .40
*a.* Without period 1.25 .75
*b.* Double surcharge 3.00 3.00
*Nos. 256-259 (4)* 5.00 2.00

The 15c on 50c deep green is a telegraph stamp from which the "Telegrafos" overprint was omitted. It appears to have been pressed into postal service, as all examples are used with postal cancels. Value $450.

Nos. 240, 244-248 Surcharged in Black

Surcharge as on Nos. 256-259 but lines wider apart.

**1911, Mar.**

**260** A18 2c on 4c vio .30 .25
*a.* Without period .35 .30
*b.* Double surcharge 3.50 3.00
*c.* Double surcharge, inverted 4.00 4.00
*d.* Double surcharge, one invtd. 9.00 *17.50*
*e.* Inverted surcharge 10.00 *18.50*
**261** A18 5c on 20c brn ol .30 .25
*a.* Without period .60 .50
*b.* Double surcharge 2.50 2.50
*c.* Inverted surcharge 2.50 2.00
*d.* Double surcharge, one invtd. 6.00 6.00
**262** A18 10c on 15c blk .40 .25
*a.* Without period 1.00 .50
*b.* "Yale" 12.00 12.00
*c.* Double surcharge 3.00 3.00
*d.* Inverted surcharge 3.00 3.00
*e.* Double surch., one inverted 5.00 4.00
*f.* Double surch., both inverted 12.00 12.00
**263** A18 10c on 50c dp grn .25 .25
*a.* Without period 1.00 .50
*b.* Double surcharge 3.00 2.50
*c.* Double surcharge, one invtd. 5.00 4.00
*d.* Inverted surcharge 5.00 5.00
**264** A18 10c on 1p yel 1.50 .40
*a.* Without period 2.00 1.50
*b.* Double surcharge 4.00 4.00
*c.* Double surcharge, one invtd. 7.50

**265** A18 10c on 2p car rose .60 .50
- *a.* Without period 2.00 1.50
- *b.* Double surcharge 2.50 2.50
- *c.* Double surcharge, one invtd. 6.00 6.00
- *d.* Inverted surcharge 6.00 6.00

*Nos. 260-265 (6)* 3.35 1.90

Revenue Stamps Surcharged in Black

**1911, Apr. 10** *Perf. 14 to 15*

**266** A19 2c on 5p dl bl 1.00 *1.25*
- *a.* Without period 1.25 *1.50*
- *b.* Double surcharge 2.50 2.00

**267** A19 2c on 5p ultra .35 *.40*
- *a.* Without period .75 *1.25*
- *b.* Double surcharge *3.50*

**268** A19 5c on 10p pink .75 .40
- *a.* Without period 1.50 1.00
- *b.* "cte" for "cts" 1.50 1.00
- *c.* Double surcharge 4.00 4.00
- *d.* Inverted surcharge 2.50 2.50

**269** A19 10c on 25c lilac .40 .25
- *a.* Without period 1.00 .75
- *b.* "cte" for "cts" 1.25 1.00
- *c.* Inverted surcharge 4.00 4.00
- *d.* Double surcharge 2.50 2.50
- *e.* Double surcharge, one inverted 4.00 4.00

**270** A19 10c on 2p gray .40 .25
- *a.* Without period 1.00 .75
- *b.* "cte" for "cts" 1.25 1.00
- *c.* Double surcharge 5.00 5.00
- *d.* Double surcharge, one inverted 4.00 3.00

**271** A19 35c on 1p brown .40 .30
- *a.* Without period 1.00 .75
- *b.* "cte" for "cts" 1.25 1.00
- *c.* "Corre" 1.50 1.50
- *d.* Double surcharge 2.50 2.50
- *e.* Double surcharge, one inverted 2.50 2.50
- *f.* Double surcharge inverted 3.00 3.00
- *g.* Inverted surcharge *5.00*

*Nos. 266-271 (6)* 3.30 2.85

These surcharges are in settings of twenty-five. One stamp in each setting has a large square period after "cts" and two have no period. One of the 2c has no space between "02" and "cts" and one 5c has a small thin "s" in "Correos."

Surcharged in Black

**1911, June**

**272** A19 5c on 2p gray 1.50 1.00
- *a.* Inverted surcharge 6.00 5.00

In this setting one stamp has a large square period and another has a thick up-right "c" in "cts."

Surcharged in Black

**1911, June 12**

**273** A19 5c on 25c lilac 1.50 1.25
**274** A19 5c on 50c ol grn 5.00 5.00
**275** A19 5c on 5p blue 7.00 7.00
**276** A19 5c on 5p ultra 7.50 6.00
- *a.* Inverted surcharge 45.00

**277** A19 5c on 50p ver 6.25 5.00
**278** A19 10c on 50c ol grn 1.50 .50

*Nos. 273-278 (6)* 28.75 24.75

This setting has the large square period and the thick "c" in "cts." Many of the stamps have no period after "cts." Owing to broken type and defective impressions letters sometimes appear to be omitted.

A21

Revenue Stamps Surcharged on the Back in Black

a b

Railroad coupon tax stamps (1st class red and 2nd class blue) are the basic stamps of Nos. 279-294. They were first surcharged for revenue use in 1903 in two types: I — "Timbre Fiscal" and "ctvs." II — "TIMBRE FISCAL" and "cents" (originally intended for use in Bluefields).

**1911, July**

**279** A21 (a) 2c on 5c on 2 bl .25 .30
- *a.* New value in yellow on face 6.00 6.00
- *b.* New value in black on face 10.00 5.00
- *c.* New value in red on face *100.00*
- *d.* Inverted surcharge .75
- *e.* Double surch., one inverted 7.50 7.50
- *f.* "TIMBRE FISCAL" in black .75 .75

**280** A21 (b) 2c on 5c on 2 bl .25 .30
- *a.* New value in yellow on face 3.00 3.00
- *b.* New value in black on face 9.00 4.00
- *c.* New value in red on face *100.00*
- *d.* Inverted surcharge .90 1.00
- *e.* Double surch., one inverted 7.50 7.50
- *f.* "TIMBRE FISCAL" in black 1.00 1.00

**281** A21 (a) 5c on 5c on 2 bl .25 .25
- *a.* Inverted surcharge .50 .35
- *b.* "TIMBRE FISCAL" in black 1.00 1.00
- *c.* New value in yellow on face

**282** A21 (b) 5c on 5c on 2 bl .25 .25
- *a.* Inverted surcharge .40 .35
- *b.* "TIMBRE FISCAL" in black 1.00 1.00
- *c.* New value in yellow on face

**283** A21 (a) 10c on 5c on 2 bl .25 .25
- *a.* Inverted surcharge .75 .50
- *b.* "TIMBRE FISCAL" in black 1.00 1.00
- *c.* New value in yellow on face *100.00*
- *d.* Double surcharge 6.00 6.00

**284** A21 (b) 10c on 5c on 2 bl .25 .25
- *a.* Inverted surcharge .75 .50
- *b.* "TIMBRE FISCAL" in black 1.00 1.00
- *c.* Double surcharge 6.00 6.00
- *d.* New value in yellow on face *110.00*

**285** A21 (a) 15c on 10c on 1 red .25 .25
- *a.* Inverted surcharge 1.00 1.25
- *b.* "Timbre Fiscal" double 5.00

**286** A21 (b) 15c on 10c on 1 red .40 .35
- *a.* Inverted surcharge 1.00 1.00
- *b.* "Timbre Fiscal" double 5.00

*Nos. 279-286 (8)* 2.15 2.20

These surcharges are in settings of 20. For listing, they are separated into small and large figures, but there are many other varieties due to type and arrangement.

The colored surcharges on the face of the stamps were trial printings. These were then surcharged in black on the reverse. The olive yellow surcharge on the face of the 2c was later applied to prevent use as a 5c revenue stamps. Other colors known on the face are orange and green. Forgeries exist.

For overprints and surcharges see Nos. 287-294, O223-O244, 1L107-1L108.

Surcharged on the Face in Black

**1911, Oct.**

**287** A21 2c on 10c on 1 red 6.50 6.50
- *a.* Inverted surcharge 1.40 1.40
- *b.* Double surcharge 10.00 10.00

**288** A21 20c on 10c on 1 red 4.50 4.50
- *a.* Inverted surcharge 5.25 5.00

**289** A21 50c on 10c on 1 red 5.25 4.50
- *a.* Inverted surcharge 10.00 10.00

*Nos. 287-289 (3)* 16.25 15.50

There are two varieties of the figures "2" and "5" in this setting.

Surcharged on the Back in Black

**1911, Nov.**

**289B** A21 5c on 10c on 1 red 37.50
- *c.* Inverted surcharge 20.00

**289D** A21 10c on 10c on 1 red 12.50
- *e.* Inverted surcharge 24.00

Surcharged on the Face

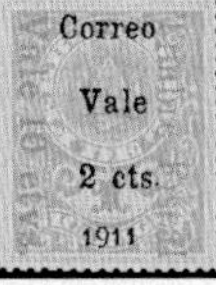


**1911, Dec.**

**Dark Blue Postal Surcharge**

**290** A21 2c on 10c on 1 red .25 .25
- *a.* Inverted surcharge 2.50 2.50
- *b.* Double surcharge 5.00 5.00

**291** A21 5c on 10c on 1 red .30 .25
- *a.* Double surcharge 2.50 2.50
- *b.* Inverted surcharge 2.50 2.50

**292** A21 10c on 10c on 1 red .35 .25
- *a.* Inverted surcharge 2.50 2.50
- *b.* Double surcharge 2.50 2.50
- *c.* "TIMBRE FISCAL" on back 3.50 3.50

**Black Postal Surcharge**

**293** A21 10c on 10c on 1 red 1.50 1.00
- *a.* Inverted surcharge 7.00 7.00
- *b.* New value surch. on back 12.00 12.00

**Red Postal Surcharge**

**293C** A21 5c on 5c on 2 blue 1.40 1.25
- *d.* "TIMBRE FISCAL" in black 2.50 1.75
- *e.* "5" omitted 3.75 3.75
- *f.* Inverted surcharge 4.75 4.75

*Nos. 290-293C (5)* 3.80 3.00

Bar Overprinted on No. O234 in Dark Blue

**294** A21 10c on 10c on 1 red 1.25 1.00
- *a.* Inverted surcharge 2.50 2.50
- *b.* Bar at foot of stamp 5.00 5.00

Nos. 290-294 each have three varieties of the numerals in the surcharge.

"Liberty" — A22

Coat of Arms — A23

**1912, Jan.** **Engr.** *Perf. 14, 15*

**295** A22 1c yel grn .30 .25
**296** A22 2c carmine .40 .25
**297** A22 3c yel brn .30 .25
**298** A22 4c brn vio .30 .25
**299** A22 5c blue & blk .25 .25
**300** A22 6c olive bister .30 .80
**301** A22 10c red brn .25 .25
**302** A22 15c vio .25 .25
**303** A22 20c red .25 .25
**304** A22 25c blue grn & blk .30 .25
**305** A23 35c grn & chnt 2.00 1.50
**306** A22 50c lt blue 1.00 .40
**307** A22 1p org 1.40 2.00
**308** A22 2p dark blue grn 1.50 2.25
**309** A22 5p blk 3.50 3.50

*Nos. 295-309 (15)* 12.30 12.70

For overprints and surcharges see Nos. 310-324, 337A-348, 395-396, O245-O259.

No. 305 Surcharged in Violet

**1913, Mar.**

**310** A23 15c on 35c .40 .25
- *a.* "ats" for "cts" 7.50 6.00

Stamps of 1912 Surcharged in Red or Black

**1913-14**

**311** A22 ½c on 3c yel brn (R) .40 .35
- *a.* "Corooba" 2.50 2.50
- *b.* "do" for "de" 2.50 2.50
- *c.* Inverted surcharge 22.50

**312** A22 ½c on 15c vio (R) .25 .25
- *a.* "Corooba" 1.00 1.00
- *b.* "do" for "de" 1.25 1.25

**313** A22 ½c on 1p org .75 .25
- *a.* "VALB" 3.00 *5.00*
- *b.* "ALE" 4.00 3.50
- *c.* "LE" 6.00 5.00
- *d.* "VALE" omitted 3.50 3.50

**314** A22 1c on 3c yel brn .95 .60
**315** A22 1c on 4c brn vio .75 .25
**316** A22 1c on 50c lt blue .25 .25
**317** A22 1c on 5p blk .25 .25
**318** A22 2c on 4c brn vio .35 .25
- *a.* "do" for "de" 3.00 *12.00*

**319** A22 2c on 20c red 3.50 *4.50*
- *a.* "do" for "de" 17.50 12.50

**320** A22 2c on 25c blue grn & blk .35 .25
- *a.* "do" for "de" 3.50 2.50

**321** A23 2c on 35c grn & chnt .25 .40
- *a.* "9131" 4.00 *7.50*
- *b.* "do" for "de" 2.50 2.00

**322** A22 2c on 50c lt blue .25 .25
- *a.* "do" for "de" 2.00 *4.00*

**323** A22 2c on 2p dark blue grn .25 .25
- *a.* "VALB" 1.25 1.25
- *b.* "ALE" 2.50 1.25
- *c.* "VALE" omitted 6.00
- *d.* "VALE" and "dos" omitted 6.00

**324** A22 3c on 6c olive bis .25 .25
- *a.* "VALB" *35.00*

*Nos. 311-324 (14)* 8.80 8.35

Nos. 311, 312 surcharged in black were not regularly issued.

**Surcharged on Zelaya Issue of 1912**

**325** Z2 ½c on 2c ver .60 *1.25*
- *a.* "Corooba" 1.25 1.25
- *b.* "do" for "de" 1.25 1.25

**326** Z2 1c on 3c org brn .50 .25
**327** Z2 1c on 4c car .50 .25
**328** Z2 1c on 6c red brn .40 .25
**329** Z2 1c on 20c dark vio .50 .25
**330** Z2 1c on 25c grn & blk .50 .25
**331** Z2 2c on 1c yel grn ('14) 6.75 1.25
- *a.* "Centavos" 7.50 1.50

**332** Z2 2c on 25c grn & blk 2.25 *3.00*
**333** Z2 5c on 35c brn & blk .40 .25
**334** Z2 5c on 50c ol grn .40 .25
- *a.* Double surcharge 22.50

**335** Z2 6c on 1p org .50 .25
**336** Z2 10c on 2p org brn .90 .25
**337** Z2 1p on 5p dk bl grn 1.00 .40

*Nos. 325-337 (13)* 15.20 8.15

On No. 331 the surcharge has a space of 2½mm between "Vale" and "dos."

**Space between "Vale" and "dos" 2½mm instead of 1mm, "de Cordoba" in different type.**

**1914, Feb.**

**337A** A22 2c on 4c brn vio 27.50 4.00
- *b.* "Ccntavos" 12.00

**337C** A22 2c on 20c red 13.00 3.75
- *d.* "Ccntavos" 4.00

**337E** A22 2c on 25c bl grn & blk 6.00
- *f.* "Ccntavos" 12.00

**337G** A23 2c on 35c grn & chnt 8.50
- *h.* "Ccntavos" 15.00

**337I** A22 2c on 50c lt bl 22.50 4.00
- *j.* "Ccntavos" 10.00

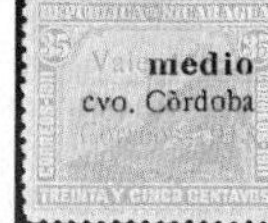


No. 310 with Additional Surcharge

**1913, Dec.**

**337K** A23 ½c on 15c on 35c *300.00*

The word "Medio" is usually in heavy-faced, shaded letters. It is also in thinner, unshaded letters and in letters from both fonts mixed.

No. 310 Surcharged in Black and Violet

**338** A23 ½c on 15c on 35c .50 .25
- *a.* Double surcharge 3.50
- *b.* Inverted surcharge 3.50
- *c.* Surcharged on No. 305 12.00

**339** A23 1c on 15c on 35c .25 .25
- *a.* Double surcharge 4.00

Official Stamps of 1912 Surcharged

**1914, Feb.**

**340** A22 1c on 25c lt bl .40 .25
- *a.* Double surcharge 9.00

**341** A23 1c on 35c lt bl .40 .25
- *a.* "0.10" for "0.01" 10.00 10.00

**341B** A22 1c on 50c lt bl *200.00*

**342** A22 1c on 1p lt bl .25 .25

**342A** A22 2c on 20c lt bl *200.00 150.00*
- *b.* "0.12" for "0.02"

**343** A22 2c on 50c lt bl .40 .25
- *a.* "0.12" for "0.02" 150.00

**344** A22 2c on 2p lt bl .40 .25

**345** A22 2c on 5p lt bl *250.00*

**346** A22 5c on 5p lt bl .25 .25

**Red Surcharge**

**347** A22 5c on 1p lt bl *140.00*

**348** A22 5c on 5p lt bl *500.00*

National Palace, Managua — A24

León Cathedral — A25

**Various Frames**

**1914, May 13 Engr. *Perf. 12***

**349** A24 ½c lt blue .85 .25

**350** A24 1c dk green .85 .25

**351** A25 2c red orange .85 .25

**352** A24 3c red brown 1.25 .30

**353** A25 4c scarlet 1.25 .40

**354** A24 5c gray black .45 .25

**355** A25 6c black brn 9.00 5.50

**356** A25 10c orange yel .85 .25

**357** A24 15c dp violet 5.75 2.00

**358** A25 20c slate 11.00 5.50

**359** A24 25c orange 1.50 .45

**360** A25 50c pale blue 1.40 .40

*Nos. 349-360 (12)* 35.00 15.80

In 1924 the 5c, 10c, 25c, 50c were issued in slightly larger size, 27x22¾mm. The original set was 26x22½mm.

No. 356 with overprint "Union Panamericana 1890-1940" in green is of private origin.

See Nos. 408-415, 483-495, 513-523, 652-664. For overprints and surcharges see Nos. 361-394, 397-400, 416-419, 427-479, 500, 540-548, 580-586, 600-648, 671-673, 684-685, C1-C3, C9-C13, C49-C66, C92-C105, C121-C134, C147-C149, C155-C163, C174-C185, CO1-CO24, O260-O294, O296-O319, O332-O376, RA1-RA5, RA10-RA11, RA26-RA35, RA39-RA40, RA44, RA47, RA52.

No. 355 Surcharged in Black

**1915, Sept.**

**361** A25 5c on 6c blk brn 1.50 .40
- *a.* Double surcharge 7.00 7.00

Stamps of 1914 Surcharged in Black or Red

**1918-19 New Value in Figures**

**362** A24 1c on 3c red brn 6.50 2.25
- *a.* Double surch., one invtd. 12.50

**363** A25 2c on 4c scarlet 32.50 22.50

**364** A24 5c on 15c dp vio (R) 7.50 1.50
- *a.* Double surcharge 12.00

**364C** A24 5c on 15c dp vio 350.00

Surcharged in Black

**365** A25 2c on 20c slate 110.00 60.00
- *a.* "ppr" for "por" *500.00 300.00*
- *b.* Double surcharge *300.00*
- *c.* "Cordobo" *500.00 300.00*

**365D** A25 5c on 20c slate — *200.00*
- *e.* Double surcharge (Bk + R) *300.00*
- *f.* "Cordobo" *300.00*

The surcharge on No. 365 is in blue black, and that on No. 365D usually has an admixture of red.

Used only at Bluefields and Rama.

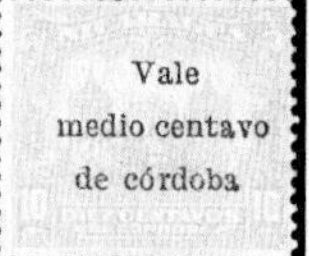


Surcharged in Black, Red or Violet

**New Value in Words**

**366** A25 ½c on 6c blk brn 4.00 1.50
- *a.* "Meio" 15.00
- *b.* Double surcharge 12.00

**367** A25 ½c on 10c yellow 2.50 .30
- *a.* "Val" for "Vale" 3.00
- *b.* "Codoba" 3.00
- *c.* Inverted surcharge 5.00
- *d.* Double surch., one inverted 10.00

**368** A24 ½c on 15c dp vio 2.50 .60
- *a.* Double surcharge 7.50
- *b.* "Codoba" 4.00
- *c.* "Meio" 6.00

**369** A24 ½c on 25c orange 5.00 2.00
- *a.* Double surcharge 8.00
- *b.* Double surch., one inverted 6.00

**370** A25 ½c on 50c pale bl 2.50 .30
- *a.* "Meio" 6.00
- *b.* Double surcharge 5.00
- *c.* Double surch., one inverted 7.00

**371** A25 ½c on 50c pale bl (R) 4.50 1.50
- *a.* Double surcharge 10.00

**372** A24 1c on 3c red brn 3.00 .30
- *a.* Double surcharge 3.50

**373** A25 1c on 6c blk brn 12.50 3.50
- *a.* Double surcharge 9.00

**374** A25 1c on 10c yellow 24.00 8.00
- *a.* "nu" for "un" 22.50

**375** A24 1c on 15c dp vio 4.50 .75
- *a.* Double surcharge 10.00
- *b.* "Codoba" 6.00

**376** A25 1c on 20c slate *200.00 100.00*
- *a.* Black surch. normal and red surch. invtd. *150.00*
- *b.* Double surch., red & black *150.00*
- *c.* Blue surcharge *200.00*

**377** A25 1c on 20c sl (V) 110.00 70.00
- *a.* Double surcharge (V + Bk) *150.00*

**378** A25 1c on 20c sl (R) 2.50 .30
- *a.* Double surch., one inverted
- *b.* "Val" for "Vale" 3.50 3.00

**379** A24 1c on 25c orange 4.50 1.00
- *a.* Double surcharge 11.00

**380** A25 1c on 50c pale bl 14.00 4.50
- *a.* Double surcharge 17.50

**381** A25 2c on 4c scarlet 3.50 .30
- *a.* Double surcharge 10.00
- *b.* "centavo" 5.00
- *c.* "Val" for "Vale"

**382** A25 2c on 6c blk brn 24.00 8.00
- *a.* "Centavoss"
- *b.* "Cordobas"

**383** A25 2c on 10c yellow 24.00 4.50
- *a.* "centavo"

**384** A25 2c on 20c sl (R) 13.00 3.25
- *a.* "pe" for "de" 15.00
- *b.* Double surch., red & blk 27.50
- *c.* "centavo" 12.00
- *d.* Double surcharge (R) 17.50

**385** A24 2c on 25c orange 5.50 .40
- *a.* "Vle" for "Vale" 7.50
- *b.* "Codoba" 7.50
- *c.* Inverted surcharge 10.00

**386** A25 5c on 6c blk brn 10.00 4.25
- *a.* Double surcharge 13.50

**387** A24 5c on 15c dp vio 3.50 .60
- *a.* "cincoun" for "cinco" 15.00
- *b.* "Vle" for "Vale" 12.50
- *c.* "Codoba" 12.50

*Nos. 366-387 (22)* 479.50 215.85

No. 378 is surcharged in light red and brown red: the latter color is frequently offered as the violet surcharge (No. 377).

Official Stamps of 1915 Surcharged in Black or Blue

**1919-21**

**388** A24 1c on 25c lt blue 1.50 .25
- *a.* Double surcharge 10.00
- *b.* Inverted surcharge 12.00

**389** A25 2c on 50c lt blue 1.50 .25
- *a.* "centavo" 4.00 4.00
- *b.* Double surcharge 12.00

**390** A25 10c on 20c lt blue 1.40 .40
- *a.* "centovos" 5.00 5.00
- *b.* Double surcharge 8.00

**390F** A25 10c on 20c lt bl (Bl) 65.00

*Nos. 388-390 (3)* 4.40 .90

There are numerous varieties of omitted, inverted and italic letters in the foregoing surcharges.

No. 358 Surcharged in Black

Types of the numerals

I II III IV

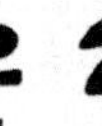
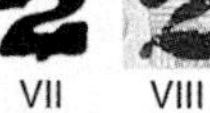

V VI VII VIII

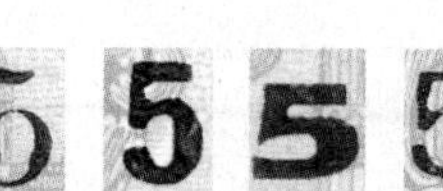

I II III IV

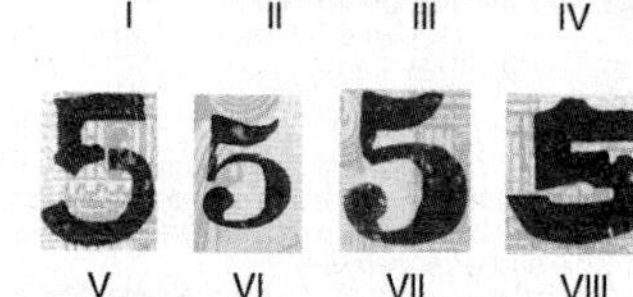

V VI VII VIII

**1919, May**

**391** A25 2c on 20c (I) *200.00 150.00*
- *a.* Type II
- *b.* Type III
- *c.* Type IV
- *d.* Type VI
- *e.* Type VIII

**392** A25 5c on 20c (I) 110.00 50.00
- *a.* Type II 110.00 45.00
- *b.* Type III 125.00 55.00
- *c.* Type IV 125.00 50.00
- *d.* Type V 140.00 60.00
- *e.* Type VI 140.00 60.00
- *f.* Type VII 400.00 250.00
- *h.* Double surch., one inverted

No. 358 Surcharged in Black

**393** A25 2 Cents on 20c (I) *200.00 150.00*
- *a.* Type II
- *b.* Type III
- *c.* Type IV
- *d.* Type V
- *e.* Type VI
- *f.* Type VII

**393G** A25 5 Cents on 20c sl, (VIII) 140.00 55.00

Nos. 391-393G used only at Bluefields and Rama.

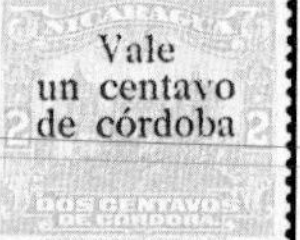


No. 351 Surcharged in Black

**1920, Jan.**

**394** A25 1c on 2c red org 1.50 .25
- *a.* Inverted surcharge
- *b.* Double surcharge

No. 394 stamps with uppercase "VALE" in surcharge are believed to be unauthorized surcharges.

Official Stamps of 1912 Overprinted in Carmine

**1921, Mar.**

**395** A22 1c lt blue 1.50 .60
- *a.* "Parricular" 5.00 5.00
- *b.* Inverted overprint 10.00

**396** A22 5c lt blue 1.50 .40
- *a.* "Parricular" 5.00 5.00

Official Stamps of 1915 Surcharged in Carmine

**1921, May**

**397** A25 ½c on 2c light blue .50 .25
- *a.* "Mddio" 2.50 2.50

**398** A25 ½c on 4c light blue 1.25 .25
- *a.* "Mddio" 2.50 2.50

**399** A24 1c on 3c light blue 1.25 .30

*Nos. 397-399 (3)* 3.00 .80

No. 354 Surcharged in Red

**1921, Aug.**

**400** A24 ½c on 5c gray blk .75 .75

Trial printings of this stamp were surcharged in yellow, black and red, and yellow and red. Some of these were used for postage.

Gen. Manuel José Arce — A26

José Cecilio del Valle — A27

Miguel Larreinaga A28

Gen. Fernando Chamorro A29

Gen. Máximo Jérez — A30

Gen. Pedro Joaquín Chamorro — A31

Rubén Darío — A32

**1921, Sept.** **Engr.**

**401** A26 ½c lt bl & blk 1.60 1.60
**402** A27 1c grn & blk 1.60 1.60
**403** A28 2c rose red & blk 1.60 1.60
**404** A29 5c ultra & blk 1.60 1.60
**405** A30 10c org & blk 1.60 1.60
**406** A31 25c yel & blk 1.60 1.60
**407** A32 50c vio & blk 1.60 1.60
*Nos. 401-407 (7)* 11.20 11.20

Centenary of independence.

For overprints and surcharges see Nos. 420-421, RA12-RA16, RA19-RA23.

### Types of 1914 Issue

**1922** **Various Frames**

**408** A24 ½c green .25 .25
**409** A24 1c violet .25 .25
**410** A25 2c car rose .25 .25
**411** A24 3c ol gray .30 .25
**411A** A25 4c vermilion .35 .25
**412** A25 6c red brn .25 .25
**413** A24 15c brown .35 .25
**414** A25 20c bis brn .50 .25
**415** A25 1cor blk brn .90 .50
*Nos. 408-415 (9)* 3.40 2.50

In 1924 Nos. 408-415 were issued in slightly larger size, 27x22¾mm. The original set was 26x22½mm.

Nos. 408, 410 exist with signature controls. See note before No. 600. Same values.

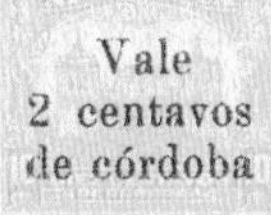


No. 356 Surcharged in Black

**1922, Nov.**

**416** A25 1c on 10c org yel 1.00 .35
**417** A25 2c on 10c org yel 1.00 .25

Nos. 354 and 356 Surcharged in Red

Vale
2 centavos
de córdoba

**1923, Jan.**

**418** A24 1c on 5c gray blk 1.25 .25
**419** A25 2c on 10c org yel 1.25 .25
*a.* Inverted surcharge

Nos. 401 and 402 Overprinted in Red

**1923**

**420** A26 ½c lt blue & blk 7.50 7.50
**421** A27 1c green & blk 2.50 .85
*a.* Double overprint 7.50

Francisco Hernández de Córdoba — A33

**1924** **Engr.**

**422** A33 1c deep green 2.50 .30
**423** A33 2c carmine rose 2.50 .30
**424** A33 5c deep blue 2.00 .30
**425** A33 10c bister brn 2.00 .60
*Nos. 422-425 (4)* 9.00 1.50

Founding of León & Granada, 400th anniv.

For overprint & surcharges see #499, 536, O295.

Stamps of 1914-22 Overprinted

### Black, Red or Blue Overprint

**1927, May 3**

**427** A24 ½c green (Bk) .25 .25
**428** A24 1c violet (R) .25 .25
*a.* Double overprint 3.00
**428B** A24 1c violet (Bk) 85.00 55.00
**429** A25 2c car rose (Bk) .25 .25
*a.* Inverted overprint 5.00
*b.* Double overprint 5.00
**430** A24 3c ol gray (Bk) 1.25 1.25
*a.* Inverted overprint 5.00
*b.* Double overprint 6.00
*c.* Double ovpt., one inverted 9.00 7.00
**430D** A24 3c ol gray (Bl) 8.00 3.25
**431** A25 4c ver (Bk) 16.00 13.00
*a.* Inverted overprint 30.00
**432** A24 5c gray blk (R) 1.25 .25
*a.* Inverted overprint 7.50
**432B** A24 5c gray blk (Bk) .75 .25
*c.* Double ovpt., one inverted 8.00
*d.* Double overprint 8.00
**433** A25 6c red brn (Bk) 13.00 11.00
*a.* Inverted overprint 17.50
*b.* Double overprint
*c.* "1297" for "1927" 250.00
**434** A25 10c yellow (Bl) .65 .40
*a.* Double overprint 12.50
*b.* Double ovpt., one inverted 10.00
**435** A24 15c brown (Bk) 6.00 2.50
**436** A25 20c bis brn (Bk) 6.00 2.50
*a.* Double overprint 17.50
**437** A24 25c orange (Bk) 27.50 5.00
**438** A25 50c pale bl (Bk) 7.50 3.00
**439** A25 1cor blk brn (Bk) 15.00 9.00
*Nos. 427-439 (16)* 188.65 107.15

Most stamps of this group exist with tall "1" in "1927." Counterfeits exist of normal stamps and errors of Nos. 427-478.

**1927, May 19** **Violet Overprint**

**440** A24 ½c green .25 .25
*a.* Inverted overprint 2.00 2.00
*b.* Double overprint 2.00 2.00
**441** A24 1c violet .25 .25
*a.* Double overprint 2.00 2.00
**442** A25 2c car rose .25 .25
*a.* Double overprint 2.00 2.00
*b.* "1927" double 5.00
*d.* Double ovpt., one inverted 2.00 2.00
**443** A24 3c ol gray .25 .25
*a.* Inverted overprint 6.00
*b.* Overprinted "1927" only 12.00
*c.* Double ovpt., one inverted 6.00
**444** A25 4c vermilion 37.50 27.50
*a.* Inverted overprint 75.00
**445** A24 5c gray blk 1.00 .25
*a.* Double overprint, one inverted 6.00
**446** A25 6c red brn 37.50 27.50
*a.* Inverted overprint 75.00
**447** A25 10c yellow .35 .25
*a.* Double overprint 2.00 2.00
**448** A24 15c brown .75 .30
*a.* Double overprint 5.00
*b.* Double overprint, one inverted 8.00
**449** A25 20c bis brn .35 .25
*a.* Double overprint
**450** A24 25c orange .40 .25
**451** A25 50c pale bl .40 .25
*a.* Double ovpt., one inverted 4.00 4.00
**452** A25 1cor blk brn .75 .25
*a.* Double overprint 3.00
*b.* "1927" double 5.00
*c.* Double ovpt., one inverted 6.00
*Nos. 440-452 (13)* 80.00 57.80

Stamps of 1914-22 Overprinted in Violet

**1928, Jan. 3**

**453** A24 ½c green .25 .25
*a.* Double overprint 3.00
*b.* Double overprint, one inverted 4.00
**454** A24 1c violet .25 .25
*a.* Inverted overprint 2.00
*b.* Double overprint 2.00
*c.* Double overprint, one inverted 2.00
*d.* "928" for "1928" 2.50
**455** A25 2c car rose .25 .25
*a.* Inverted overprint 2.00
*b.* Double overprint 2.00
*c.* "1928" omitted 5.00
*d.* "928" for "1928" 2.50
*e.* As "d," inverted
*f.* "19" for "1928"
**456** A24 3c ol gray .40 .25
**457** A25 4c vermilion .25 .25
**458** A24 5c gray blk .25 .25
*a.* Double overprint 5.00
*b.* Double overprint, one inverted 5.00
**459** A25 6c red brn .25 .25
**460** A25 10c yellow .25 .25
*a.* Double overprint 2.50
*c.* Inverted overprint
**461** A24 15c brown .35 .25
**462** A25 20c bis brn .50 .25
*a.* Double overprint
**463** A24 25c orange .75 .25
*a.* Double overprint, one inverted 4.00
**464** A25 50c pale bl 1.25 .25
**465** A25 1cor blk brn 1.25 .35
*Nos. 453-465 (13)* 6.25 3.35

Stamps of 1914-22 Overprinted in Violet

**1928, June 11**

**466** A24 ½c green .25 .25
**467** A24 1c violet .25 .25
*a.* "928" omitted
**469** A24 3c ol gray .75 .25
*a.* Double overprint 6.00
**470** A25 4c vermilion .35 .25
**471** A24 5c gray blk .25 .25
*a.* Double overprint 4.00
**472** A25 6c red brn .40 .25
*a.* Double overprint 5.00
**473** A25 10c yellow .50 .25
**474** A24 15c brown 1.75 .25
*a.* Double overprint
**475** A25 20c bis brn 2.00 .25
**476** A24 25c orange 2.00 .25
*a.* Double overprint, one inverted 6.00
**477** A25 50c pale bl 2.00 .25
**478** A25 1cor blk brn 5.00 2.50
*a.* Double overprint 10.00
*Nos. 466-478 (12)* 15.50 5.25

No. 410 with above overprint in black was not regularly issued.

No. 470 with Additional Surcharge in Violet

**1928**

**479** A25 2c on 4c ver 1.25 .35
*a.* Double surcharge 9.00

A34

### Inscribed: "Timbre Telegrafico"

**1928** **Red Surcharge**

**480** A34 1c on 5c bl & blk .30 .25
*a.* Double surcharge 5.00
*b.* Double surcharge, one inverted
**481** A34 2c on 5c bl & blk .30 .25
*a.* Double surcharge 5.00
**482** A34 3c on 5c bl & blk .30 .25
*Nos. 480-482 (3)* .90 .75

Stamps similar to Nos. 481-482, but with surcharge in black and with basic stamp inscribed "Timbre Fiscal," are of private origin.

See designs A36, A37, A44, PT1, PT4, PT6, PT7.

### Types of 1914 Issue

**1928** **Various Frames**

**483** A24 ½c org red .40 .25
**484** A24 1c orange .40 .25
**485** A25 2c green .40 .25
**486** A24 3c dp vio .40 .25
**487** A25 4c brown .40 .25
**488** A24 5c yellow .40 .25
**489** A25 6c lt bl .40 .25
**490** A25 10c dk bl .90 .25
**491** A24 15c car rose 1.40 .50
**492** A25 20c dk grn 1.40 .50
**493** A24 25c blk brn 27.50 6.00
**494** A25 50c bis brn 3.25 1.00
**495** A25 1cor dl vio 6.25 3.00
*Nos. 483-495 (13)* 43.50 13.00

No. 425 Overprinted in Violet

**1929**

**499** A33 10c bis brn .75 .60

No. 408 Overprinted in Red

**1929**

**500** A24 ½c green (R) .25 .25
*a.* Inverted overprint 5.50
*b.* Double overprint 5.00
*c.* Double overprint, one inverted 5.00

A36

### Ovptd. Horiz. in Black "R. de T." Surcharged Vert. in Red

**1929**

**504** A36 1c on 5c bl & blk (R) .25 .25
*a.* Inverted surcharge 3.00
*b.* Surcharged "0.10" for "0.01" 3.00
*c.* "0.0" instead of "0.01" 5.00
**509** A36 2c on 5c bl & blk (R) .25 .25
*a.* Double surcharge 2.50
*b.* Double surcharge, one inverted 3.50
*c.* Inverted surcharge 5.00

### Overprinted Horizontally in Black "R. de C." Surcharged Vertically in Red

**510** A36 2c on 5c bl & blk (R) 22.50 1.25
*a.* Dbl. surcharge, one inverted 25.00

A37

### Surcharged in Red

**511** A37 1c on 10c dk grn & blk (R) .25 .25
*a.* Double surcharge
**512** A37 2c on 5c bl & blk (R) .25 .25
*Nos. 504-512 (5)* 23.50 2.25

The varieties tall "1" in "0.01" and "O$" for "C$" are found in this surcharge.

Nos. 500, 504, 509-512 and RA38 were surcharged in red and sold in large quantities to the public. Surcharges in various other colors were distributed only to a favored few and not regularly sold at the post offices.

### Types of 1914 Issue

**1929-31** **Various Frames**

**513** A24 1c ol grn .25 .25
**514** A24 3c lt bl .30 .25
**515** A25 4c dk bl ('31) .30 .25
**516** A24 5c ol brn .40 .25
**517** A25 6c bis brn ('31) .50 .30
**518** A25 10c lt brn ('31) .60 .25
**519** A24 15c org red ('31) .90 .25
**520** A25 20c org ('31) 1.25 .35
**521** A24 25c dk vio .25 .25

**522** A25 50c grn ('31) .50 .25
**523** A25 1cor yel ('31) 4.50 1.25
*Nos. 513-523 (11)* 9.75 3.90

Nos. 513-523 exist with signature controls. See note before No. 600. Same values.

New Post Office at Managua — A38

**1930, Sept. 15** **Engr.**

**525** A38 ½c olive gray 1.25 1.25
**526** A38 1c carmine 1.25 1.25
**527** A38 2c red org .90 .90
**528** A38 3c orange 1.75 1.75
**529** A38 4c yellow 1.75 1.75
**530** A38 5c ol grn 2.25 2.25
**531** A38 6c bl grn 2.25 2.25
**532** A38 10c black 2.75 2.75
**533** A38 25c dp bl 5.50 5.50
**534** A38 50c ultra 9.00 9.00
**535** A38 1cor dp vio 25.00 25.00
*Nos. 525-535 (11)* 53.65 53.65

Opening of the new general post office at Managua. The stamps were on sale on day of issuance and for an emergency in April, 1931.

No. 499 Surcharged in Black and Red

**1931, May 29**

**536** A33 2c on 10c bis brn .50 1.60
*a.* Red surcharge omitted 2.50
*b.* Red surcharge double 5.00
*c.* Red surcharge inverted 6.00
*d.* Red surcharge double, one invtd.

Surcharge exists in brown.

Types of 1914-31 Issue Overprinted

**1931, June 11**

**540** A24 ½c green .35 .25
*a.* Double overprint .80
*b.* Double ovpt., one inverted 1.40
*c.* Inverted overprint .80
**541** A24 1c ol grn .35 .25
*a.* Double overprint .80
*b.* Double ovpt., one inverted 1.40
*c.* Inverted overprint
**542** A25 2c car rose .35 .25
*a.* Double overprint .80
*b.* Double ovpt., both inverted 2.50
*c.* Inverted overprint 1.40
**543** A24 3c lt bl .35 .25
*a.* Double overprint .80
*b.* Double ovpt., one inverted 1.40
*c.* Inverted overprint 1.40
**544** A24 5c yellow 4.00 2.25
**545** A24 5c ol brn 1.25 .25
*a.* Double overprint 4.50
*b.* Inverted overprint 4.50
**546** A24 15c org red 1.50 .40
*a.* Double overprint 3.50
**547** A24 25c blk brn 12.00 6.50
*a.* Double overprint 13.00 7.00
*b.* Inverted overprint 13.00 7.00
**548** A24 25c dk vio 4.50 2.50
*a.* Double overprint 10.00
*Nos. 540-548 (9)* 24.65 12.90

Counterfeits exist of the scarcer values. The 4c brown and 6c light blue with this overprint are bogus.

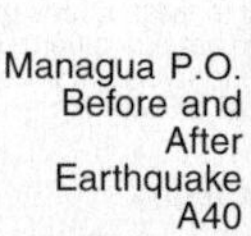

Managua P.O. Before and After Earthquake A40

**1932, Jan. 1** **Litho.** ***Perf. 11½***
**Soft porous paper, Without gum**

**556** A40 ½c emerald 1.50
**557** A40 1c yel brn 1.90
**558** A40 2c dp car 1.50
**559** A40 3c ultra 1.50
**560** A40 4c dp ultra 1.50
**561** A40 5c yel brn 1.60
**562** A40 6c gray brn 1.60
**563** A40 10c yel brn 2.50
**564** A40 15c dl rose 3.75
**565** A40 20c orange 3.50
**566** A40 25c dk vio 2.50
**567** A40 50c emerald 2.50
**568** A40 1cor yellow 6.25
*Nos. 556-568 (13)* 32.10

Issued in commemoration of the earthquake at Managua, Mar. 31, 1931. The stamps were on sale on Jan. 1, 1932, only. The money received from this sale was for the reconstruction of the Post Office building and for the improvement of the postal service. Many shades exist.

Sheets of 10.

*Reprints are on thin hard paper and do not have the faint horiz. ribbing that is on the front or back of the originals. Fake cancels abound. Value 75 cents each.*

See Nos. C20-C24. For overprints and surcharges see Nos. C32-C43, C47-C48.

**Rivas Railroad Issue**

"Fill" at El Nacascolo — A41

1c, Wharf at San Jorge. 5c, Rivas Station. 10c, San Juan del Sur. 15c, Train at Rivas Station.

**1932, Dec. 17** **Litho.** ***Perf. 12***
**Soft porous paper**

**570** A41 1c yellow 16.00
*a.* 1c ocher 18.00
**571** A41 2c carmine 16.00
**572** A41 5c blk brn 16.00
**573** A41 10c chocolate 16.00
**574** A41 15c yellow 16.00
*a.* 15c deep orange 18.00
*Nos. 570-574 (5)* 80.00

Inauguration of the railroad from San Jorge to San Juan del Sur. On sale only on Dec. 17, 1932.

Sheets of 4, without gum. See #C67-C71.

*Reprints exist on five different papers ranging from thick soft light cream to thin very hard paper and do not have the faint horiz. ribbing that is normally on the front or back of the originals. Originals are on very white paper. Value of reprints, $5 each.*

**Leon-Sauce Railroad Issue**

Bridge No. 2 at Santa Lucia — A42

Designs: 1c, Environs of El Sauce. 5c, Santa Lucia. 10c, Works at Km. 64. 15c, Rock cut at Santa Lucia.

**1932, Dec. 30** ***Perf. 12***
**Soft porous paper**

**575** A42 1c orange 16.00
**576** A42 2c carmine 16.00
**577** A42 5c blk brn 16.00
**578** A42 10c brown 16.00
**579** A42 15c orange 16.00
*Nos. 575-579 (5)* 80.00

Inauguration of the railroad from Leon to El Sauce. On sale only on Dec. 30, 1932.

Sheets of 4, without gum. See #C72-C76.

*Reprints exist on thin hard paper and do not have the faint horiz. ribbing that is on the front or back of the originals. Value $5 each.*

Nos. 514-515, 543 Surcharged in Red

**1932, Dec. 10**

**580** A24 1c on 3c lt bl (514) .35 .25
*a.* Double surcharge 3.50
**581** A24 1c on 3c lt bl (543) 4.00 3.50
**582** A25 2c on 4c dk bl (515) .25 .25
*a.* Double surcharge 2.50
*Nos. 580-582 (3)* 4.60 4.00

Nos. 514, 516, 545 and 518 Surcharged in Black or Red

**1933**

**583** A24 1c on 3c lt bl (Bk) (514) .25 .25
*a.* "Censavo" 4.00 2.25
*b.* Double surcharge, one inverted 4.00
**584** A24 1c on 5c ol brn (R) (516) .25 .25
*a.* Inverted surcharge
*b.* Double surcharge
**585** A24 1c on 5c ol brn (R) (545) 6.50 5.00
*a.* Red surcharge double 12.00
**586** A25 2c on 10c lt brn (Bk) (518) .25 .25
*a.* Double surcharge 7.00 2.50
*b.* Inverted surcharge 6.00 3.50
*c.* Double surcharge, one inverted 7.00 2.50
*Nos. 583-586 (4)* 7.25 5.75

On No. 586 "Vale Dos" measures 13mm and 14mm.

No. 583 with green surcharge and No. 586 with red surcharge are bogus.

**Flag of the Race Issue**

Flag with Three Crosses for Three Ships of Columbus A43

**1933, Aug. 3** **Litho.** ***Rouletted 9***
**Without gum**

**587** A43 ½c emerald 1.75 1.75
**588** A43 1c green 1.50 1.50
**589** A43 2c red 1.50 1.50
**590** A43 3c dp rose 1.50 1.50
**591** A43 4c orange 1.50 1.50
**592** A43 5c yellow 1.75 1.75
**593** A43 10c dp brn 1.75 1.75
**594** A43 15c dk brn 1.75 1.75
**595** A43 20c vio bl 1.75 1.75
**596** A43 25c dl bl 1.75 1.75
**597** A43 30c violet 4.50 4.50
**598** A43 50c red vio 4.50 4.50
**599** A43 1cor ol brn 4.50 4.50
*Nos. 587-599 (13)* 30.00 30.00

Commemorating the raising of the symbolical "Flag of the Race"; also the 441st anniversary of the sailing of Columbus for the New World, Aug. 3, 1492. Printed in sheets of 10.

See Nos. C77-C87, O320-O331.

---

In October, 1933, various postage, airmail and official stamps of current issues were overprinted with facsimile signatures of the Minister of Public Works and the Postmaster-General. These overprints are control marks.

---

Nos. 410 and 513 Overprinted in Black

**1935** ***Perf. 12***

**600** A24 1c ol grn .25 .25
*a.* Inverted overprint 1.40 1.60
*b.* Double overprint 1.40 1.60
*c.* Double overprint, one inverted 1.60 1.60
**601** A25 2c car rose .25 .25
*a.* Inverted overprint 1.60
*b.* Double overprint 1.60
*c.* Double overprint, one inverted 1.60
*d.* Double overprint, both inverted 2.50 2.25

**No. 517 Surcharged in Red as in 1932**

**1936, June**

**602** A25 ½c on 6c bis brn .35 .25
*a.* "Ccentavo" .80 .80
*b.* Double surcharge 3.50 3.50

Regular Issues of 1929-35 Overprinted in Blue

**1935, Dec.**

**603** A25 ½c on 6c bis brn .65 .25
**604** A24 1c ol grn (#600) .80 .25
**605** A25 2c car rose (#601) .80 .25
*a.* Black overprint inverted 6.00
**606** A24 3c lt bl .80 .25
**607** A24 5c ol brn 1.00 .25
**608** A25 10c lt brn 1.60 .80
*Nos. 603-608 (6)* 5.65 2.05

Nos. 606-608 have signature control overprint. See note before No. 600.

**Same Overprint in Red**

**1936, Jan.**

**609** A24 ½c dk grn .25 .25
**610** A25 ½c on 6c bis brn (602) .25 .25
*a.* Double surch., one inverted 6.00 6.00
**611** A24 1c ol grn (513) .25 .25
**612** A24 1c ol grn (600) .25 .25
**613** A25 2c car rose (410) .50 .25
**614** A25 2c car rose (601) .25 .25
*a.* Black overprint inverted 12.00 2.50
*b.* Black ovpt. double, one invtd. 12.00 3.50
**615** A24 3c lt bl .25 .25
**616** A25 4c dk bl .25 .25
**617** A24 5c ol brn .25 .25
**618** A25 6c bis brn .25 .25
**619** A25 10c lt brn .50 .25
**620** A24 15c org red .25 .25
**621** A25 20c orange .80 .25
**622** A24 25c dk vio .25 .25
**623** A25 50c green .35 .25
**624** A25 1cor yellow .40 .25
*Nos. 609-624 (16)* 5.30 4.00

Red or blue "Resello 1935" overprint may be found inverted or double. Red and blue overprints on same stamp are bogus.

Nos. 615-624 have signature control overprint. See note before No. 600.

Regular Issues of 1922-29 Overprinted in Carmine

**1936, May**

**625** A24 ½c green .25 .25
**626** A24 1c olive green .25 .25
**627** A25 2c carmine rose .50 .25
**628** A24 3c light blue .25 .25
*Nos. 625-628 (4)* 1.25 1.00

No. 628 has signature control overprint. See note before No. 600.

Nos. 514, 516 Surcharged in Black

**1936, June**

**629** A24 1c on 3c lt bl .25 .25
*a.* "1396" for "1936" 1.00 1.00
*b.* "Un" omitted 4.50 1.40
*c.* Inverted surcharge 1.60 1.60
*d.* Double surcharge 1.60 1.60
**630** A24 2c on 5c ol brn .25 .25
*a.* "1396" for "1936" 1.40 1.40
*b.* Double surcharge 3.50 3.50

Regular Issues of 1929-31 Surcharged in Black or Red

**1936**

**631** A24 ½c on 15c org red (R) .25 .25
*a.* Double surcharge 5.00
**632** A25 1c on 4c dk bl (Bk) .25 .25
**633** A24 1c on 5c ol brn (Bk) .25 .25
**634** A25 1c on 6c bis brn (Bk) .40 .25
*a.* "1939" instead of "1936" 2.50 1.60
**635** A24 1c on 15c org red (Bk) .25 .25
*a.* "1939" instead of "1936" 2.50 1.60
**636** A25 1c on 20c org (Bk) .25 .25
*a.* "1939" intead of "1936" 2.50 1.60
*b.* Double surcharge 4.00

**637** A25 1c on 20c org (R) .25 .25
**638** A25 2c on 10c lt brn (Bk) .25 .25
**639** A24 2c on 15c org red (Bk) 1.00 .80
**640** A25 2c on 20c org (Bk) .50 .25
**641** A24 2c on 25c dk vio (R) .35 .25
**642** A24 2c on 25c dk vio (Bk) .35 .25
*a.* "1939" instead of "1936" 2.50 1.60
**643** A25 2c on 50c grn (Bk) .35 .25
*a.* "1939" instead of "1936" 2.50 1.60
**644** A25 2c on 1 cor yel (Bk) .35 .25
*a.* "1939" instead of "1936" 2.50 1.60
**645** A25 3c on 4c dk bl (Bk) .65 .50
*a.* "1939" instead of "1936" 2.50 1.60
*b.* "s" of "Centavos" omitted and "r" of "Tres" inverted 2.50
*Nos. 631-645 (15)* 5.70 4.55

Nos. 634, 639, 643-644 exist with and without signature controls. Same values, except for No. 639, which is rare without the signature control. Nos. 635-636, 642, 645 do not have signature controls. Others have signature controls only. See note before No. 600.

Regular Issues of 1929-31 Overprinted in Black

**1936, Aug.**

**646** A24 3c lt bl .35 .25
**647** A24 5c ol brn .25 .25
**648** A25 10c lt brn .50 .35
*Nos. 646-648 (3)* 1.10 .85

No. 648 bears script control mark.

A44

**1936, Oct. 19** **Red Surcharge**

**649** A44 1c on 5c grn & blk .25 .25
**650** A44 2c on 5c grn & blk .25 .25

**Types of 1914**

**1937, Jan. 1** **Engr.**

**652** A24 ½c black .25 .25
**653** A24 1c car rose .25 .25
**654** A25 2c dp bl .25 .25
**655** A24 3c chocolate .25 .25
**656** A25 4c yellow .25 .25
**657** A24 5c org red .25 .25
**658** A25 6c dl vio .25 .25
**659** A25 10c ol grn .25 .25
**660** A24 15c green .25 .25
**661** A25 20c red brn .25 .25
**663** A25 50c brown .35 .25
**664** A25 1cor ultra .60 .25
*Nos. 652-664 (12)* 3.45 3.00

See note after No. 360.

Mail Carrier — A45

Designs: 1c, Mule carrying mail. 2c, Mail coach. 3c, Sailboat. 5c, Steamship. 7½c, Train.

**1937, Dec.** **Litho.** ***Perf. 11***

**665** A45 ½c green .25 .25
**666** A45 1c magenta .25 .25
**667** A45 2c brown .25 .25
**668** A45 3c purple .25 .25
**669** A45 5c blue .25 .25
**670** A45 7½c red org .55 .35
*Nos. 665-670 (6)* 1.80 1.60

75th anniv. of the postal service in Nicaragua.

Nos. 665-670 exists printed on several different kinds of paper: medium thick porous white paper, a thinner whitish toned paper, and a thin hard brownish tone paper.

Nos. 665-670 were also issued in sheets of 4. Value, set of sheets $20.

The miniature sheets are ungummed, and also exist imperf. and part-perf.

Nos. 359, 663 and 664 Surcharged in Red

**1938** ***Perf. 12***

**671** A24 3c on 25c org .25 .25
**672** A25 5c on 50c brn .25 .25
*a.* "e" of "Vale" omitted 1.60 1.00
**673** A25 6c on 1cor ultra .25 .25
*Nos. 671-673 (3)* .75 .75

No. 672 has a script signature control and the surcharge is in three lines.

Dario Park A46

**1939, Jan.** **Engr.** ***Perf. 12½***

**674** A46 1½c yel grn .25 .25
**675** A46 2c dp rose .25 .25
**676** A46 3c brt bl .25 .25
**677** A46 6c brn org .25 .25
**678** A46 7½c dp grn .25 .25
**679** A46 10c blk brn .25 .25
**680** A46 15c orange .25 .25
**681** A46 25c lt vio .25 .25
**682** A46 50c brt yel grn .25 .25
**683** A46 1cor yellow .65 .40
*Nos. 674-683 (10)* 2.90 2.65

Nos. 660 and 661 Surcharged in Red

**1939** ***Perf. 12***

**684** A24 1c on 15c grn .25 .25
*a.* Inverted surcharge 2.00 2.00
**685** A25 1c on 20c red brn .25 .25

**No. C236 Surcharged in Carmine**

**1941** **Unwmk.** ***Perf. 12***

**686** AP14 10c on 1c brt grn 1.00 .25
*a.* Double surcharge 10.00 2.50
*b.* Inverted surcharge 10.00 2.50

Rubén Darío A47

**1941, Dec.** **Engr.** ***Perf. 12½***

**687** A47 10c red .40 .25
*Nos. 687,C257-C260 (5)* 2.00 1.30

25th anniversary of the death of Rubén Darío, poet and writer.

**No. C236 Surcharged in Carmine**

**1943** ***Perf. 12***

**688** AP14 10c on 1c brt grn 4.00 .25
*a.* Inverted surcharge 10.00
*b.* Double surcharge 10.00

**Catalogue values for unused stamps in this section, from this point to the end of the section, are for Never Hinged items.**

"Victory" — A48

**1943, Dec. 8** **Engr.**

**689** A48 10c vio & cerise .25 .25
**690** A48 30c org brn & cerise .25 .25

2nd anniv. of Nicaragua's declaration of war against the Axis. See Nos. C261-C262.

Columbus and Lighthouse — A49

**1945, Sept. 1** **Unwmk.** ***Perf. 12½***

**691** A49 4c dk grn & blk .25 .25
**692** A49 6c org & blk .25 .25
**693** A49 8c dp rose & blk .35 .35
**694** A49 10c bl & blk .40 .40
*Nos. 691-694,C266-C271 (10)* 6.30 5.50

Issued in honor of the discovery of America by Columbus and the Columbus Lighthouse near Ciudad Trujillo, Dominican Republic.

Franklin D. Roosevelt, Philatelist A50

Roosevelt Signing Declaration of War Against Japan — A51

8c, F. D. Roosevelt, Winston Churchill. 16c, Gen. Henri Giraud, Roosevelt, de Gaulle & Churchill. 32c, Stalin, Roosevelt, Churchill. 50c, Sculptured head of Roosevelt.

**Engraved, Center Photogravure**

**1946, June 15** **Unwmk.** ***Perf. 12½***

**Frame in Black**

**695** A50 4c sl grn .25 .25
**696** A50 8c violet .30 .30
**697** A51 10c ultra .30 .30
**698** A50 16c rose red .40 .40
**699** A50 32c org brn .30 .30
**700** A51 50c gray .30 .30
*Nos. 695-700,C272-C276 (11)* 11.50 11.50

Issued to honor US Pres. Franklin D. Roosevelt (1882-1945). See Nos. C272-C276.

Projected Provincial Seminary — A56

Designs: 4c, Metropolitan Cathedral, Managua. 5c, Sanitation Building. 6c, Municipal Building. 75c, Communications Building.

**1947, Jan. 10** **Frame in Black**

**701** A56 4c carmine .25 .25
**702** A56 5c blue .25 .25
**703** A56 6c green .25 .25
**704** A56 10c olive .25 .25
**705** A56 75c golden brn .30 .30
*Nos. 701-705,C277-C282 (11)* 4.80 4.30

Centenary of the founding of the city of Managua. See Nos. C277-C282.

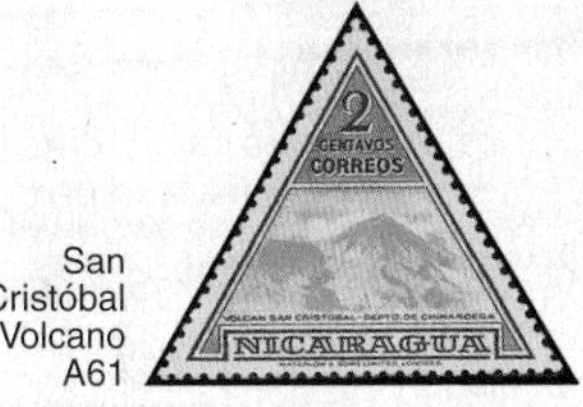


San Cristóbal Volcano A61

Designs: 3c, Tomb of Rubén Dario. 4c, Grandstand. 5c, Soldiers' monument. 6c, Sugar cane. 8c, Tropical fruit. 10c, Cotton industry. 20c, Horse race. 30c, Nicaraguan coffee. 50c, Steer. 1cor, Agriculture.

**Engraved, Center Photogravure**

**1947, Aug. 29** **Frame in Black**

**706** A61 2c orange .25 .25
**707** A61 3c violet .25 .25
**708** A61 4c gray .25 .25
**709** A61 5c rose car .55 .25
**710** A61 6c green .30 .25
**711** A61 8c org brn .40 .25
**712** A61 10c red .55 .25
**713** A61 20c brt ultra 1.90 .50
**714** A61 30c rose lilac 1.50 .50
**715** A61 50c dp claret 3.25 .95
**716** A61 1cor brn org 1.10 .50
*Nos. 706-716,C283-C295 (24)* 35.30 29.20

The frames differ for each denomination. For surcharge see No. 769.

Softball A62

Boy Scout, Badge and Flag — A63

Designs: 3c, Pole vault. 4c, Diving. 5c, Bicycling. 10c, Proposed stadium. 15c, Baseball. 25c, Boxing. 35c, Basketball. 40c, Regatta. 60c, Table tennis. 1 cor, Soccer. 2 cor, Tennis.

**1949, July 15** **Photo.** ***Perf. 12***

**717** A62 1c henna brn .45 .25
**718** A63 2c ultra .80 .25
**719** A63 3c bl grn .45 .25
**720** A62 4c dp claret .30 .25
**721** A63 5c orange .65 .25
**722** A62 10c emerald .65 .25
**723** A62 15c cerise .90 .25
**724** A63 25c brt bl .90 .25
**725** A63 35c olive grn 1.75 .25
**726** A62 40c violet 2.50 .30
**727** A62 60c olive gray 3.00 .40

**728** A62 1cor scarlet 4.00 1.25
**729** A62 2cor red vio 7.00 2.50
*Nos. 717-729 (13)* 23.35 6.70
*Nos. 717-729,C296-C308 (26)* 57.45 17.25

10th World Series of Amateur Baseball, 1948.

Each denomination was also issued in a souvenir sheet containing four stamps and marginal inscriptions. Value, set of 13 sheets, $375.

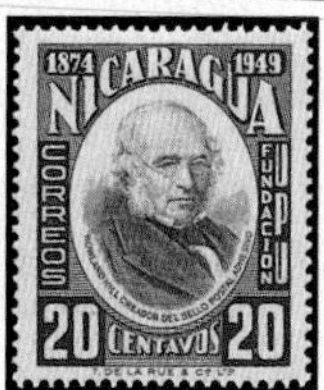
Rowland Hill — A64

Designs: 25c, Heinrich von Stephan. 75c, UPU Monument. 80c, Congress medal, obverse. 4cor, as 80c, reverse.

**1950, Nov. 23 Engr. *Perf. 13***

**Frame in Black**

**730** A64 20c car lake .25 .25
**731** A64 25c yel grn .25 .25
**732** A64 75c ultra .50 .25
**733** A64 80c green .25 .25
**734** A64 4cor blue 1.00 .80
*Nos. 730-734 (5)* 2.25 1.80
*Nos. 730-734,C309-C315,CO45-CO50 (18)* 11.45 9.45

75th anniv. (in 1949) of the UPU.

Each denomination was also issued in a souvenir sheet containing 4 stamps. Size: 115x123mm. Value, set of 5 sheets, $30.

For surcharge see #771.

Queen Isabella I — A65

Ships of Columbus A66

Designs: 98c, Santa Maria. 1.20cor, Map. 1.76cor, Portrait facing left.

**1952, June 25 *Perf. 11½***

**735** A65 10c lilac rose .25 .25
**736** A66 96c deep ultra .75 .75
**737** A65 98c carmine .75 .75
**738** A65 1.20cor brown .90 .90
**739** A65 1.76cor red violet 1.25 1.25
*a.* Souvenir sheet of 5, #735-739 10.00 3.75
*Nos. 735-739 (5)* 3.90 3.90
*Nos. 735-739,C316-C320 (10)* 16.40 13.90

Queen Isabella I of Spain, 500th birth anniv.

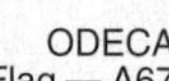

ODECA Flag — A67

Designs: 5c, Map of Central America. 6c, Arms of ODECA. 15c, Presidents of Five Central American Republics. 50c, ODECA Charter and Flags.

**1953, Apr. 15 *Perf. 13½x14***

**740** A67 4c dk bl .25 .25
**741** A67 5c emerald .25 .25
**742** A67 6c lt brn .25 .25
**743** A67 15c lt ol grn .25 .25
**744** A67 50c blk brn .25 .25
*Nos. 740-744,C321-C325 (10)* 3.00 2.90

Founding of the Organization of the Central American States (ODECA).

For surcharge see #767.

Pres. Carlos Solorzano — A68

Presidents: 6c, Diego Manuel Chamorro. 8c, Adolfo Diaz. 15c, Gen. Anastasio Somoza. 50c, Gen. Emiliano Chamorro.

**Heads in Gray Black**

**Engr. (frames); Photo. (heads)**

**1953, June 25 *Perf. 12½***

**745** A68 4c dk car rose .25 .25
**746** A68 6c dp ultra .25 .25
**747** A68 8c brown .25 .25
**748** A68 15c car rose .25 .25
**749** A68 50c bl grn .25 .25
*Nos. 745-749,C326-C338 (18)* 5.15 5.00

For surcharges see Nos. 768, 853.

Sculptor and UN Emblem — A69

4c, Arms of Nicaragua. 5c, Globe. 15c, Candle & Charter. 1cor, Flags of Nicaragua & UN.

***Perf. 13½***

**1954, Apr. 30 Engr. Unwmk.**

**750** A69 3c olive .25 .25
**751** A69 4c olive green .25 .25
**752** A69 5c emerald .25 .25
**753** A69 15c deep green .90 .25
**754** A69 1cor blue green .75 .30
*Nos. 750-754,C339-C345 (12)* 11.05 7.30

UN Organization.

Capt. Dean L. Ray, USAF — A70

Designs: 2c, Sabre jet plane. 3c, Plane, type A-20. 4c, B-24 bomber. 5c, Plane, type AT-6. 15c, Gen. Anastasio Somoza. 1cor, Air Force emblem.

**Frame in Black**

**Engraved; Center Photogravure**

**1954, Nov. 5 *Perf. 13***

**755** A70 1c gray .25 .25
**756** A70 2c gray .25 .25
**757** A70 3c dk gray grn .25 .25
**758** A70 4c orange .25 .25
**759** A70 5c emerald .25 .25
**760** A70 15c aqua .25 .25
**761** A70 1cor purple .25 .25
*Nos. 755-761,C346-C352 (14)* 3.80 3.70

National Air Force.

Rotary Slogans and Wreath — A71

Map of the World and Rotary Emblem A72

20c, Handclasp, Rotary emblem & globe. 35c, Flags of Nicaragua & Rotary. 90c, Paul P. Harris.

**1955, Aug. 30 Photo. *Perf. 11½***

**Granite Paper.**

**762** A71 15c dp orange .25 .25
**763** A71 20c dk olive grn .25 .25
**764** A71 35c red violet .25 .25
**765** A72 40c carmine .25 .25
**766** A71 90c black & gray .35 .35
*a.* Souvenir sheet of 5, #762-766 5.75 4.25
*Nos. 762-766,C353-C362 (15)* 4.05 4.00

50th anniversary of Rotary International.

For surcharges see Nos. 770, 772, 876.

Issues of 1947-55 Surcharged in Various Colors

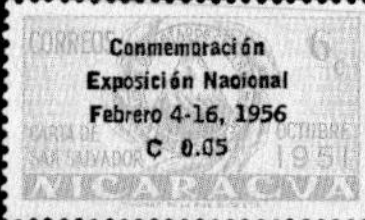


***Perf. 13½x14, 12½, 11½, 13***

**Engraved, Photogravure**

**1956, Feb. 4 Unwmk.**

**767** A67 5c on 6c lt brn .25 .25
**768** A68 5c on 6c ultra & gray blk (Ult) .25 .25
**769** A61 5c on 8c blk & org brn .25 .25
**770** A71 15c on 35c red vio (G) .25 .25
**771** A64 15c on 80c blk & grn .25 .25
**772** A71 15c on 90c blk & gray (Bl) .25 .25
*Nos. 767-772,C363-C366 (10)* 3.05 3.00

Spacing of surcharge varies to fit shape of stamps.

National Exhibition, Feb. 4-16, 1956.

Gen. Máximo Jerez — A73

Battle of San Jacinto A74

10c, Gen. Fernando Chamorro. 25c, Burning of Granada. 50c, Gen. José Dolores Estrada.

***Perf. 12½x12, 12, 12½***

**1956, Sept. 14 Engr.**

**773** A73 5c brown .25 .25
**774** A73 10c dk car rose .25 .25
**775** A74 15c blue gray .25 .25
**776** A74 25c brt red .25 .25
**777** A73 50c brt red vio .40 .25
*Nos. 773-777,C367-C371 (10)* 4.80 4.40

National War, cent.

Boy Scout — A75

Designs: 15c, Cub Scout. 20c, Boy Scout. 25c, Lord Baden-Powell. 50c, Joseph A. Harrison.

***Perf. 13½x14***

**1957, Apr. 9 Photo. Unwmk.**

**778** A75 10c violet & ol .25 .25
**779** A75 15c dp plum & gray blk .25 .25
**780** A75 20c ultra & brn .25 .25
**781** A75 25c dl red brn & dp bluish grn .25 .25
**782** A75 50c red & olive .25 .25
*a.* Souvenir sheet of 5, #778-782, imperf. 3.25 2.50
*Nos. 778-782,C377-C386 (15)* 3.80 3.80

Centenary of the birth of Lord Baden-Powell, founder of the Boy Scouts.

For surcharge see #C754.

Pres. Luis A. Somoza — A76

**Portrait in Dark Brown**

**1957, July 2 *Perf. 14x13½***

**783** A76 10c brt red .25 .25
**784** A76 15c deep blue .25 .25
**785** A76 35c rose violet .25 .25
**786** A76 50c brown .30 .25
**787** A76 75c gray green .65 .55
*Nos. 783-787,C387-C391 (10)* 3.95 3.80

President Luis A. Somoza.

Leon Cathedral A77

Bishop Pereira y Castellon — A78

Designs: 5c, Managua Cathedral. 15c, Archbishop Lezcano y Ortega. 50c, De la Merced Church, Granada. 1cor, Father Mariano Dubon.

**Centers in Olive Gray**

**1957, July 12 *Perf. 13½x14, 14x13½***

**788** A77 5c dull green .25 .25
**789** A78 10c dk purple .25 .25
**790** A78 15c dk blue .25 .25
**791** A77 20c dk brown .30 .25
**792** A77 50c dk slate grn .35 .25
**793** A78 1cor dk violet .65 .30
*Nos. 788-793,C392-C397 (12)* 6.65 3.60

Honoring the Catholic Church in Nicaragua.

M. S. Honduras A79

5c, Gen. Anastasio Somoza & freighter. 6c, M. S. Guatemala. 10c, M. S. Salvador. 15c, Ship between globes. 50c, Globes & ship.

**1957, Oct. 15 Litho. *Perf. 14***

**794** A79 4c green, bl & blk .25 .25
**795** A79 5c multi .25 .25
**796** A79 6c red, bl & blk .25 .25
**797** A79 10c brn, bl grn & blk .25 .25
**798** A79 15c dk car, ultra & ol brn .25 .25
**799** A79 50c violet, bl & mar .40 .25
*Nos. 794-799,C398-C403 (12)* 4.75 4.60

Issued to honor Nicaragua's Merchant Marine. For surcharge see No. C691.

Melvin Jones and Lions Emblem A80

Designs: 5c, Arms of Central American Republics. 20c, Dr. Teodoro A. Arias. 50c, Edward G. Barry. 75c, Motto and emblem. 1.50 cor, Map of Central America.

**Emblem in Yellow, Red and Blue**

**1958, May 8 Unwmk. *Perf. 14***

| | | | | |
|---|---|---|---|---|
| **800** | A80 | 5c blue & multi | .25 | .25 |
| **801** | A80 | 10c blue & org | .25 | .25 |
| **802** | A80 | 20c blue & olive | .25 | .25 |
| **803** | A80 | 50c blue & lilac | .25 | .25 |
| **804** | A80 | 75c blue & pink | .35 | .25 |
| **805** | A80 | 1.50cor blue, gray ol & sal | .60 | .45 |
| *a.* | | Souvenir sheet of 6, #800-805 | 3.25 | 2.50 |
| | | *Nos. 800-805,C410-C415 (12)* | 5.30 | 4.70 |

17th convention of Lions Intl. of Central America, May, 1958.
For surcharge see #C686.

St. Jean Baptiste De La Salle — A81

Christian Brothers: 5c, Arms of La Salle. 10c, School, Managua, horiz. 20c, Bro. Carlos. 50c, Bro. Antonio. 75c, Bro. Julio. 1cor, Bro. Argeo.

**1958, July 13 Photo. *Perf. 14***

| | | | | |
|---|---|---|---|---|
| **806** | A81 | 5c car, bl & yel | .25 | .25 |
| **807** | A81 | 10c emer, blk & ultra | .25 | .25 |
| **808** | A81 | 15c red brn, bis & blk | .25 | .25 |
| **809** | A81 | 20c car, bis & blk | .25 | .25 |
| **810** | A81 | 50c org, bis & brn blk | .25 | .25 |
| **811** | A81 | 75c bl, lt grn & dk brn | .25 | .25 |
| **812** | A81 | 1cor vio, bis & grnsh blk | .30 | .30 |
| | | *Nos. 806-812,C416-C423 (15)* | 6.85 | 5.65 |

For surcharges see Nos. C539A, C755-C756.

UN Emblem and Globe — A82

15c, UNESCO building. 25c, 45c, "UNESCO." 40c, UNESCO building and Eiffel tower.

**1958, Dec. 15 Litho. *Perf. 11½***

| | | | | |
|---|---|---|---|---|
| **813** | A82 | 10c brt pink & bl | .25 | .25 |
| **814** | A82 | 15c blue & brt pink | .25 | .25 |
| **815** | A82 | 25c green & brn | .25 | .25 |
| **816** | A82 | 40c red org & blk | .25 | .25 |
| **817** | A82 | 45c dk bl & rose lil | .25 | .25 |
| **818** | A82 | 50c brown & grn | .25 | .25 |
| *a.* | | Miniature sheet of 6, #813-818 | 1.25 | .75 |
| | | *Nos. 813-818,C424-C429 (12)* | 5.30 | 4.10 |

UNESCO Headquarters in Paris opening, Nov. 3.

Pope John XXIII and Cardinal Spellman — A83

Designs: 10c, Spellman coat of arms. 15c, Cardinal Spellman. 20c, Human rosary and Cardinal, horiz. 25c, Cardinal with Ruben Dario order.

**1959, Nov. 26 Unwmk. *Perf. 12½***

| | | | | |
|---|---|---|---|---|
| **819** | A83 | 5c grnsh bl & brn | .25 | .25 |
| **820** | A83 | 10c yel, bl & car | .25 | .25 |
| **821** | A83 | 15c dk grn, blk & dk car | .25 | .25 |
| **822** | A83 | 20c yel, dk bl & grn | .25 | .25 |
| **823** | A83 | 25c ultra, vio & mag | .25 | .25 |
| *a.* | | Min. sheet of 5, #819-823, perf. or imperf. | 1.50 | 1.00 |
| | | *Nos. 819-823,C430-C436 (12)* | 4.90 | 3.90 |

Cardinal Spellman's visit to Managua, Feb. 1958.
For surcharges see #C638, C747, C752.

Abraham Lincoln — A84

**Center in Black**

**1960, Jan. Engr. *Perf. 13x13½***

| | | | | |
|---|---|---|---|---|
| **824** | A84 | 5c dp carmine | .25 | .25 |
| **825** | A84 | 10c green | .25 | .25 |
| **826** | A84 | 15c dp orange | .25 | .25 |
| **827** | A84 | 1cor plum | .25 | .25 |
| **828** | A84 | 2cor ultra | .35 | .30 |
| *a.* | | Souv. sheet of 5, #824-828, imperf. | .90 | .90 |
| | | *Nos. 824-828,C437-C442 (11)* | 4.00 | 3.50 |

150th anniv. of the birth of Abraham Lincoln.
For surcharges see #C500, C539, C637, C680, C753.

Nos. 824-828 Overprinted in Red

**1960, Sept. 19 Center in Black**

| | | | | |
|---|---|---|---|---|
| **829** | A84 | 5c deep carmine | .25 | .25 |
| **830** | A84 | 10c green | .25 | .25 |
| **831** | A84 | 15c deep orange | .25 | .25 |
| **832** | A84 | 1cor plum | .25 | .25 |
| **833** | A84 | 2cor ultra | .50 | .40 |
| | | *Nos. 829-833,C446-C451 (11)* | 4.45 | 3.85 |

Issued for the Red Cross to aid earthquake victims in Chile.

Gen. Tomas Martinez and Pres. Luis A. Somoza — A85

5c, Official decrees. 10c, Two envelopes.

***Perf. 13½***

**1961, Aug. 29 Unwmk. Litho.**

| | | | | |
|---|---|---|---|---|
| **834** | A85 | 5c grnsh bl & lt brn | .25 | .25 |
| **835** | A85 | 10c green & lt brn | .25 | .25 |
| **836** | A85 | 15c pink & brn | .25 | .25 |
| | | *Nos. 834-836 (3)* | .75 | .75 |

Cent. (in 1960) of the postal rates regulation.

Arms of Nueva Segovia — A86

Coats of Arms: 3c, León. 4c, Managua. 5c, Granada. 6c, Rivas.

**Arms in Original Colors; Black Inscriptions**

**1962, Nov. 22 *Perf. 12½x13***

| | | | | |
|---|---|---|---|---|
| **837** | A86 | 2c pink | .25 | .25 |
| **838** | A86 | 3c lt blue | .25 | .25 |
| **839** | A86 | 4c pale lilac | .25 | .25 |
| **840** | A86 | 5c yellow | .25 | .25 |
| **841** | A86 | 6c buff | .25 | .25 |
| | | *Nos. 837-841,C510-C514 (10)* | 3.15 | 3.05 |

For surcharge see #854.

**No. RA73 Overprinted in Red: "CORREOS"**

**1964 Photo. *Perf. 11½***

| | | | | |
|---|---|---|---|---|
| **842** | PT13 | 5c gray, red & org | .25 | .25 |
| *a.* | | Inverted overprint | | |

Nos. RA66-RA75 Overprinted

**1965 Photo. *Perf. 11½***

**Orchids in Natural Colors**

| | | | | |
|---|---|---|---|---|
| **843** | PT13 | 5c pale lilac & grn | .60 | .30 |
| **844** | PT13 | 5c yellow & grn | .60 | .30 |
| **845** | PT13 | 5c pink & grn | .60 | .30 |
| **846** | PT13 | 5c pale vio & grn | .60 | .30 |
| **847** | PT13 | 5c lt grnsh bl & red | .60 | .30 |
| **848** | PT13 | 5c buff & lil | .60 | .30 |
| **849** | PT13 | 5c yel grn & brn | .60 | .30 |
| **850** | PT13 | 5c gray & red | .60 | .30 |
| **851** | PT13 | 5c lt blue & dk bl | .60 | .30 |
| **852** | PT13 | 5c lt green & brn | .60 | .30 |
| | | *Nos. 843-852 (10)* | 6.00 | 3.00 |

Seventh Central American Scout Camporee at El Coyotete. This overprint was also applied to each stamp on souvenir sheet No. C386a. Value, $15.
Use of Nos. 843-852 for postage was authorized by official decree.

**Nos. 746 and 841 Surcharged with New Value and "RESELLO"**

**1968, May Engr. *Perf. 12½***

| | | | | |
|---|---|---|---|---|
| **853** | A68 | 5c on 6c dp ultra & gray blk | .50 | .50 |

**Litho. *Perf. 12½x13***

| | | | | |
|---|---|---|---|---|
| **854** | A86 | 5c on 6c multi | .50 | .50 |

Nos. RA66-RA67, RA69 and RA71 Overprinted

**1969 Photo. *Perf. 11½***

**Orchids in Natural Colors**

| | | | | |
|---|---|---|---|---|
| **855** | PT13 | 5c pale lil & grn | .60 | .60 |
| **856** | PT13 | 5c yellow & grn | .60 | .60 |
| **857** | PT13 | 5c pale vio & grn | .60 | .60 |
| **858** | PT13 | 5c buff & lilac | .60 | .60 |
| | | *Nos. 855-858 (4)* | 2.40 | 2.40 |

Nos. RA66-RA75 Overprinted

**1969 Photo. *Perf. 11½***

**Orchids in Natural Colors**

| | | | | |
|---|---|---|---|---|
| **859** | PT13 | 5c pale lil & grn | .50 | .30 |
| **860** | PT13 | 5c yellow & grn | .50 | .30 |
| **861** | PT13 | 5c pink & grn | .50 | .30 |
| **862** | PT13 | 5c pale vio & grn | .50 | .30 |
| **863** | PT13 | 5c lt grnsh bl & red | .50 | .30 |
| **864** | PT13 | 5c buff & lil | .50 | .30 |
| **865** | PT13 | 5c yel grn & brn | .50 | .30 |
| **866** | PT13 | 5c gray & red | .50 | .30 |
| **867** | PT13 | 5c lt & dk blue | .50 | .30 |
| **868** | PT13 | 5c lt grn & brn | .50 | .30 |
| | | *Nos. 859-868 (10)* | 5.00 | 3.00 |

International Labor Organization, 50th anniv.

Pelé, Brazil — A87

Soccer Players: 10c, Ferenc Puskás, Hungary. 15c, Sir Stanley Matthews, England. 40c, Alfredo di Stefano, Argentina. 2cor, Giacinto Facchetti, Italy. 3cor, Lev Yashin, USSR. 5cor, Franz Beckenbauer, West Germany.

**1970, May 11 Litho. *Perf. 13½***

| | | | | |
|---|---|---|---|---|
| **869** | A87 | 5c multicolored | .25 | .25 |
| **870** | A87 | 10c multicolored | .25 | .25 |
| **871** | A87 | 15c multicolored | .25 | .25 |
| **872** | A87 | 40c multicolored | .30 | .25 |
| **873** | A87 | 2cor multicolored | 1.00 | .75 |
| **874** | A87 | 3cor multicolored | 1.30 | .90 |
| **875** | A87 | 5cor multicolored | 1.50 | 1.25 |
| | | *Nos. 869-875,C712-C716 (12)* | 8.70 | 6.80 |

Issued to honor the winners of the 1970 poll for the International Soccer Hall of Fame. Names of players and their achievements printed in black on back of stamps.
For surcharges and overprint see Nos. 899-900, C786-C788.

No. 766 Surcharged & Overprinted in Black

**1971, Mar. Photo. *Perf. 11***

| | | | | |
|---|---|---|---|---|
| **876** | A71 | 30c on 90c blk & gray | *200.00* | *100.00* |

Egyptian Using Fingers to Count — A88

Symbolic Designs of Scientific Formulas: 15c, Newton's law (gravity). 20c, Einstein's theory (relativity). 1cor, Tsiolkovski's law (speed of rockets). 2cor, Maxwell's law (electromagnetism).

**1971, May 15 Litho. *Perf. 13½***

| | | | | |
|---|---|---|---|---|
| **877** | A88 | 10c lt bl & multi | .25 | .25 |
| **878** | A88 | 15c lt bl & multi | .25 | .25 |
| **879** | A88 | 20c lt bl & multi | .30 | .25 |
| **880** | A88 | 1cor lt bl & multi | 1.00 | .60 |
| **881** | A88 | 2cor lt bl & multi | 2.10 | 1.25 |
| | | *Nos. 877-881,C761-C765 (10)* | 7.90 | 4.45 |

Mathematical equations which changed the world. On the back of each stamp is a descriptive paragraph.
See Nos. C761-C765.

Symbols of Civilization, Peace Emblem with Globe — A89

**1971, Sept. 6 Litho. *Perf. 14***

| | | | | |
|---|---|---|---|---|
| **882** | A89 | 10c blk & bl | .25 | .25 |
| **883** | A89 | 15c vio bl, bl & blk | .25 | .25 |
| **884** | A89 | 20c brn bl & blk | .25 | .25 |
| **885** | A89 | 40c emer, bl & blk | .30 | .30 |
| **886** | A89 | 50c mag, bl & blk | .40 | .40 |
| **887** | A89 | 80c org, bl & blk | .60 | .60 |
| **888** | A89 | 1cor ol, bl & blk | .75 | .75 |
| **889** | A89 | 2cor vio, bl & blk | 1.50 | 1.50 |
| | | *Nos. 882-889 (8)* | 4.30 | 4.30 |

"Is there a formula for peace?" issue.

Moses with Tablets of the Law, by Rembrandt A90

The Ten Commandments (Paintings): 15c, Moses and the Burning Bush, by Botticelli (I). 20c, Jephthah's Daughter, by Degas, (II), horiz. 30c, St. Vincent Ferrer Preaching in Verona, by Domenico Morone (III). 35c, The Nakedness of Noah, by Michelangelo (IV), horiz. 40c, Cain and Abel, by Francesco Trevisani (V), horiz. 50c, Potiphar's wife, by Rembrandt (VI). 60c, Isaac Blessing Jacob, by Gerbrand van den Eeckhout (VII), horiz. 75c, Susanna and the Elders, by Rubens (VIII), horiz.

**1971, Nov. 1** ***Perf. 11***

**890** A90 10c ocher & multi .25 .25
**891** A90 15c ocher & multi .25 .25
**892** A90 20c ocher & multi .25 .25
**893** A90 30c ocher & multi .25 .25
**894** A90 35c ocher & multi .25 .25
**895** A90 40c ocher & multi .25 .25
**896** A90 50c ocher & multi .35 .35
**897** A90 60c ocher & multi .55 .50
**898** A90 75c ocher & multi .80 .75
*Nos. 890-898,C776-C777 (11)* 5.80 4.35

Descriptive inscriptions printed in gray on back of stamps.

Nos. 873-874 Surcharged

**1972, Mar. 20** **Litho.** ***Perf. 13½***

**899** A87 40c on 2cor multi .25 .25
**900** A87 50c on 3cor multi .30 .25
*Nos. 899-900,C786-C788 (5)* 2.40 2.00

20th Olympic Games, Munich, 8/26-9/10.

Nos. RA66-RA69, RA71-RA74 Overprinted in Blue

**1972, July 29** **Photo.** ***Perf. 11½***
**Granite Paper**

**901** PT13 5c (#RA66) .30 .25
**902** PT13 5c (#RA67) .30 .25
**903** PT13 5c (#RA68) .30 .25
**904** PT13 5c (#RA69) .30 .25
**905** PT13 5c (#RA71) .30 .25
**906** PT13 5c (#RA72) .30 .25
**907** PT13 5c (#RA73) .30 .25
**908** PT13 5c (#RA74) .30 .25
*Nos. 901-908 (8)* 2.40 2.00

Gown by Givenchy, Paris — A91

**1973, July 26** **Litho.** ***Perf. 13½***

**909** A91 1cor shown .30 .25
**910** A91 2cor Hartnell, London .55 .50
**911** A91 5cor Balmain, Paris 1.40 1.20
*Nos. 909-911,C839-C844 (9)* 3.75 3.45

Gowns by famous designers, modeled by Nicaraguan women. Inscriptions on back printed on top of gum give description of gown in Spanish and English.

Nos. 909-911 in perf. 11, see No. C844a.

Christmas A92

2c, 5c, Virginia O'Hanlon writing letter, father. 3c, 15c, letter. 4c, 20c, Virginia, father reading letter.

**1973, Nov. 15** **Litho.** ***Perf. 15***

**912** A92 2c multicolored .25 .25
**913** A92 3c multicolored .25 .25
**914** A92 4c multicolored .25 .25
**915** A92 5c multicolored .25 .25
**916** A92 15c multicolored .25 .25
**917** A92 20c multicolored .25 .25
*Nos. 912-917,C846-C848 (9)* 3.50 3.50

Sir Winston Churchill (1874-1965) A93

Designs: 2c, Churchill speaking. 3c, Military planning. 4c, Cigar, lamp. 5c, Churchill with Roosevelt and Stalin. 10c, Churchill walking ashore from landing craft.

**1974, Apr. 30** ***Perf. 14½***

**918** A93 2c multicolored .25 .25
**919** A93 3c multicolored .25 .25
**920** A93 4c multicolored .25 .25
**921** A93 5c multicolored .25 .25
**922** A93 10c multicolored .25 .25
*Nos. 918-922,C849-C850 (7)* 4.40 4.40

World Cup Soccer Championships, Munich — A94

Scenes from previous World Cup Championships with flags and scores of finalists.

**1974, May 8** ***Perf. 14½***

**923** A94 1c 1930 .25 .25
**924** A94 2c 1934 .25 .25
**925** A94 3c 1938 .25 .25
**926** A94 4c 1950 .25 .25
**927** A94 5c 1954 .25 .25
**928** A94 10c 1958 .25 .25
**929** A94 15c 1962 .25 .25
**930** A94 20c 1966 .25 .25
**931** A94 25c 1970 .25 .25
*Nos. 923-931,C853 (10)* 5.00 5.00

For overprint see No. C856.

A95

Wild Flowers and Cacti: 2c, Hollyhocks. 3c, Paguira insignis. 4c, Morning glory. 5c, Pereschia autumnalis. 10c, Cultivated morning glory. 15c, Hibiscus. 20c, Pagoda tree blossoms.

**1974, June 11** **Litho.** ***Perf. 14***

**932** A95 2c grn & multi .25 .25
**933** A95 3c grn & multi .25 .25
**934** A95 4c grn & multi .25 .25
**935** A95 5c grn & multi .25 .25
**936** A95 10c grn & multi .25 .25
**937** A95 15c grn & multi .25 .25
**938** A95 20c grn & multi .25 .25
*Nos. 932-938,C854-C855 (9)* 2.80 2.55

Nicaraguan Stamps — A96

**1974, July 10** ***Perf. 14½***

**939** A96 2c No. 670 .25 .25
**940** A96 3c No. 669 .25 .25
**941** A96 4c No. C110, horiz. .25 .25
**942** A96 5c No. 667 .25 .25
**943** A96 10c No. 666 .25 .25
**944** A96 20c No. 665 .25 .25
*Nos. 939-944,C855A-C855C (9)* 4.05 4.05

UPU, Cent.

Four-toed Anteater A97

Designs: 2c, Puma. 3c, Raccoon. 4c, Ocelot. 5c, Kinkajou. 10c, Coypu. 15c, Peccary. 20c, Tapir.

**1974, Sept. 10** **Litho.** ***Perf. 14½***

**946** A97 1c multi .25 .25
**947** A97 2c multi .25 .25
**948** A97 3c multi .25 .25
**949** A97 4c multi .25 .25
**950** A97 5c multi .25 .25
**951** A97 10c multi .25 .25
**952** A97 15c multi .25 .25
**953** A97 20c multi .25 .25
*Nos. 946-953,C857-C858 (10)* 3.65 3.45

Wild animals from San Diego and London Zoos.

Prophet Zacharias, by Michelangelo A98

Works of Michelangelo: 2c, The Last Judgment. 3c, The Creation of Adam, horiz. 4c, Sistine Chapel. 5c, Moses. 10c, Mouscron Madonna. 15c, David. 20c, Doni Madonna.

**1974, Dec. 15**

**954** A98 1c dp rose & multi .25 .25
**955** A98 2c yellow & multi .25 .25
**956** A98 3c sal & multi .25 .25
**957** A98 4c blue & multi .25 .25
**958** A98 5c tan & multi .25 .25
**959** A98 10c multicolored .25 .25
**960** A98 15c multicolored .25 .25
**961** A98 20c blue & multi .25 .25
*Nos. 954-961,C859-C862 (12)* 3.50 3.40

Christmas 1974 and 500th birth anniversary of Michelangelo Buonarroti (1475-1564), Italian painter, sculptor and architect.

Giovanni Martinelli, Othello A99

Opera Singers and Scores: 2c, Tito Gobbi, Simone Boccanegra. 3c, Lotte Lehmann, Der Rosenkavalier. 4c, Lauritz Melchior, Parsifal. 5c, Nellie Melba, La Traviata. 15c, Jussi Bjoerling, La Bohème. 20c, Birgit Nilsson, Turandot.

**1975, Jan. 22** ***Perf. 14x13½***

**962** A99 1c rose lil & multi .25 .25
**963** A99 2c brt bl & multi .25 .25
**964** A99 3c yel & multi .25 .25
**965** A99 4c dl bl & multi .25 .25
**966** A99 5c org & multi .25 .25
**967** A99 15c lake & multi .25 .25
**968** A99 20c gray & multi .25 .25
*Nos. 962-968,C863-C870 (15)* 6.45 4.15

Famous opera singers.

Jesus Condemned A100

Stations of the Cross: 2c, Jesus Carries the Cross. 3c, Jesus falls the first time. 4c, Jesus meets his mother. 5c, Simon of Cyrene carries the Cross. 15c, St. Veronica wipes Jesus' face. 20c, Jesus falls the second time. 25c, Jesus meets the women of Jerusalem. 35c, Jesus falls the third time. Designs from Leon Cathedral.

**1975, Mar. 20** ***Perf. 14½***

**969** A100 1c ultra & multi .25 .25
**970** A100 2c ultra & multi .25 .25
**971** A100 3c ultra & multi .25 .25
**972** A100 4c ultra & multi .25 .25
**973** A100 5c ultra & multi .25 .25
**974** A100 15c ultra & multi .25 .25
**975** A100 20c ultra & multi .25 .25
**976** A100 25c ultra & multi .25 .25
**977** A100 35c ultra & multi .25 .25
*Nos. 969-977,C871-C875 (14)* 4.15 4.05

Easter 1975.

The Spirit of 76, by Archibald M. Willard — A101

Designs: 2c, Pitt Addressing Parliament, by K. A. Hickel. 3c, The Midnight Ride of Paul Revere, horiz. 4c, Statue of George III Demolished, by W. Walcutt, horiz. 5c, Boston Massacre. 10c, Colonial coin and seal, horiz. 15c, Boston Tea Party, horiz. 20c, Thomas Jefferson, by Rembrandt Peale. 25c, Benjamin Franklin, by Charles Willson Peale. 30c, Signing Declaration of Independence, by John Trumbull, horiz. 35c, Surrender of Cornwallis, by Trumbull, horiz.

**1975, Apr. 16** ***Perf. 14***

**978** A101 1c tan & multi .25 .25
**979** A101 2c tan & multi .25 .25
**980** A101 3c tan & multi .25 .25
**981** A101 4c tan & multi .25 .25
**982** A101 5c tan & multi .25 .25
**983** A101 10c tan & multi .25 .25

**984** A101 15c tan & multi .25 .25
**985** A101 20c tan & multi .25 .25
**986** A101 25c tan & multi .25 .25
**987** A101 30c tan & multi .25 .25
**988** A101 35c tan & multi .25 .25
*Nos. 978-988,C876-C879 (15)* 6.20 5.85

American Bicentennial.

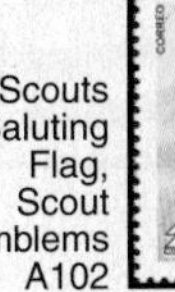

Scouts Saluting Flag, Scout Emblems — A102

2c, Two-men canoe. 3c, Scouts of various races shaking hands. 4c, Scout cooking. 5c, Entrance to Camp Nicaragua. 20c, Group discussion.

**1975, Aug. 15** ***Perf. 14½***
**989** A102 1c multi .25 .25
**990** A102 2c multi .25 .25
**991** A102 3c multi .25 .25
**992** A102 4c multi .25 .25
**993** A102 5c multi .25 .25
**994** A102 20c multi .25 .25
*Nos. 989-994,C880-C883 (10)* 4.05 3.50

Nordjamb 75, 14th World Boy Scout Jamboree, Lillehammer, Norway, July 29-Aug. 7.

Pres. Somoza, Map and Arms of Nicaragua — A103

**1975, Sept. 10** ***Perf. 14***
**995** A103 20c multi .25 .25
**996** A103 40c org & multi .25 .25
*Nos. 995-996,C884-C886 (5)* 6.75 5.50

Reelection of Pres. Anastasio Somoza D.

King's College Choir, Cambridge — A104

Famous Choirs: 2c, Einsiedeln Abbey. 3c, Regensburg. 4c, Vienna Choir Boys. 5c, Sistine Chapel. 15c, Westminster Cathedral. 20c, Mormon Tabernacle.

**1975, Nov. 15** ***Perf. 14½***
**997** A104 1c silver & multi .25 .25
**998** A104 2c silver & multi .25 .25
**999** A104 3c silver & multi .25 .25
**1000** A104 4c silver & multi .25 .25
**1001** A104 5c silver & multi .25 .25
**1002** A104 15c silver & multi .25 .25
**1003** A104 20c silver & multi .25 .25
*Nos. 997-1003,C887-C890 (11)* 4.00 3.40

Christmas 1975.

The Chess Players, by Ludovico Carracci — A105

History of Chess: 2c, Arabs Playing Chess, by Delacroix. 3c, Cardinals Playing Chess, by Victor Marais-Milton. 4c, Albrecht V of Bavaria and Anne of Austria Playing Chess, by Hans Muelich, vert. 5c, Chess Players, Persian manuscript, 14th century. 10c, Origin of Chess, Indian miniature, 17th century. 15c, Napoleon Playing Chess at Schönbrunn, by Antoni Uniechowski, vert. 20c, The Chess Game, by J. E. Hummel.

**1976, Jan. 8** ***Perf. 14½***
**1004** A105 1c brn & multi .25 .25
**1005** A105 2c lt vio & multi .25 .25
**1006** A105 3c ocher & multi .25 .25
**1007** A105 4c multi .25 .25
**1008** A105 5c multi .25 .25
**1009** A105 10c multi .25 .25
**1010** A105 15c blue & multi .25 .25
**1011** A105 20c ocher & multi .25 .25
*Nos. 1004-1011,C891-C893 (11)* 4.50 4.05

Olympic Rings, Danish Crew — A107

Winners, Rowing and Sculling Events: 2c, East Germany, 1972. 3c, Italy, 1968. 4c, Great Britain, 1936. 5c, France, 1952. 35c, US, 1920, vert.

**1976, Sept. 7** **Litho.** ***Perf. 14***
**1022** A107 1c blue & multi .25 .25
**1023** A107 2c blue & multi .25 .25
**1024** A107 3c blue & multi .25 .25
**1025** A107 4c blue & multi .25 .25
**1026** A107 5c blue & multi .25 .25
**1027** A107 35c blue & multi .25 .25
*Nos. 1022-1027,C902-C905 (10)* 6.75 6.00

Candlelight — A108

#1028, The Smoke Signal, by Frederic Remington. #1029, Space Signal Monitoring Center. #1031, Edison's laboratory & light bulb. #1032, Agriculture, 1776. #1033, Agriculture, 1976. #1034, Harvard College, 1726. #1035, Harvard University, 1976. #1036, Horse-drawn carriage. #1037, Boeing 747.

**1976, May 25** **Litho.** ***Perf. 13½***
**1028** A108 1c gray & multi .25 .25
**1029** A108 1c gray & multi .25 .25
*a.* Pair, #1028-1029 .25 .25
**1030** A108 2c gray & multi .25 .25
**1031** A108 2c gray & multi .25 .25
*a.* Pair, #1030-1031 .25 .25
**1032** A108 3c gray & multi .25 .25
**1033** A108 3c gray & multi .25 .25
*a.* Pair, #1032-1033 .25 .25
**1034** A108 4c gray & multi .25 .25
**1035** A108 4c gray & multi .25 .25
*a.* Pair, #1034-1035 .25 .25
**1036** A108 5c gray & multi .25 .25
**1037** A108 5c gray & multi .25 .25
*a.* Pair, #1036-1037 .25 .25
*Nos. 1028-1037,C907-C912 (16)* 5.60 4.80

American Bicentennial, 200 years of progress.

Mauritius No. 2 — A109

Rare Stamps: 2c, Western Australia #3a. 3c, Mauritius #1. 4c, Jamaica #83a. 5c, US #C3a. 10c, Basel #3L1. 25c, Canada #387a.

**1976, Dec.** ***Perf. 14***
**1038** A109 1c multi .25 .25
**1039** A109 2c multi .25 .25
**1040** A109 3c multi .25 .25
**1041** A109 4c multi .25 .25
**1042** A109 5c multi .25 .25
**1043** A109 10c multi .25 .25
**1044** A109 25c multi .25 .25
*Nos. 1038-1044,C913-C917 (12)* 4.65 4.40

Back inscriptions printed on top of gum describe illustrated stamp.

Zeppelin in Flight — A110

1c, Zeppelin in hangar. 3c, Giffard's dirigible airship, 1852. 4c, Zeppelin on raising stilts coming out of hangar. 5c, Zeppelin ready for take-off.

**1977, Oct. 31** **Litho.** ***Perf. 14½***
**1045** A110 1c multi .25 .25
**1046** A110 2c multi .25 .25
**1047** A110 3c multi .25 .25
**1048** A110 4c multi .25 .25
**1049** A110 5c multi .25 .25
*Nos. 1045-1049,C921-C924 (9)* 4.90 4.00

75th anniversary of Zeppelin.

Lindbergh, Map of Nicaragua — A111

2c, Spirit of St. Louis, map of Nicaragua. 3c, Lindbergh, vert. 4c, Spirit of St. Louis & NYC-Paris route. 5c, Lindbergh & Spirit of St. Louis. 20c, Lindbergh, NYC-Paris route & plane.

**1977, Nov. 30**
**1050** A111 1c multi .25 .25
**1051** A111 2c multi .25 .25
**1052** A111 3c multi .25 .25
**1053** A111 4c multi .25 .25
**1054** A111 5c multi .25 .25
**1055** A111 20c multi .25 .25
*Nos. 1050-1055,C926-C929 (10)* 4.40 3.90

Charles A. Lindbergh's solo transatlantic flight from NYC to Paris, 50th anniv.

Nutcracker Suite — A112

1c, Christmas party. 2c, Dancing dolls. 3c, Clara and Snowflakes. 4c, Snowflake and prince. 5c, Snowflake dance. 15c, Sugarplum fairy and prince. 40c, Waltz of the flowers. 90c, Chinese tea dance. 1cor, Bonbonnière. 10cor, Arabian coffee dance.

**1977, Dec. 12**
**1056** A112 1c multi .25 .25
**1057** A112 2c multi .25 .25
**1058** A112 3c multi .25 .25
**1059** A112 4c multi .25 .25
**1060** A112 5c multi .25 .25
**1061** A112 15c multi .25 .25
**1062** A112 40c multi .25 .25
**1063** A112 90c multi .25 .25
**1064** A112 1cor multi .30 .25
**1065** A112 10cor multi 2.25 2.00
*Nos. 1056-1065 (10)* 4.55 4.25

Christmas 1977. See No. C931.

Mr. and Mrs. Andrews, by Gainsborough — A113

Paintings: 2c, Giovanna Bacelli, by Gainsborough. 3c, Blue Boy by Gainsborough. 4c, Francis I, by Titian. 5c, Charles V in Battle of Muhlberg, by Titian. 25c, Sacred Love, by Titian.

**1978, Jan. 11** **Litho.** ***Perf. 14½***
**1066** A113 1c multi .25 .25
**1067** A113 2c multi .25 .25
**1068** A113 3c multi .25 .25
**1069** A113 4c multi .25 .25
**1070** A113 5c multi .25 .25
**1071** A113 25c multi .25 .25
*Nos. 1066-1071,C932-C933 (8)* 4.70 3.95

Thomas Gainsborough (1727-1788), 250th birth anniv.; Titian (1477-1576), 500th birth anniv.

Gothic Portal, Lower Church, Assisi — A114

Designs: 2c, St. Francis preaching to the birds. 3c, St. Francis, painting. 4c, St. Francis and Franciscan saints, 15th century tapestry. 5c, Portiuncola, cell of St. Francis, now in church of St. Mary of the Angels, Assisi. 15c, Blessing of St. Francis for Brother Leo (parchment). 25c, Stained-glass window, Upper Church of St. Francis, Assisi.

**1978, Feb. 23** **Litho.** ***Perf. 14½***
**1072** A114 1c red & multi .25 .25
**1073** A114 2c brt grn & multi .25 .25
**1074** A114 3c bl grn & multi .25 .25
**1075** A114 4c ultra & multi .25 .25
**1076** A114 5c rose & multi .25 .25
**1077** A114 15c yel & multi .25 .25
**1078** A114 25c ocher & multi .25 .25
*Nos. 1072-1078,C935-C936 (9)* 3.90 3.75

St. Francis of Assisi (1182-1266), 750th anniversary of his canonization, and in honor of Our Lady of the Immaculate Conception, patron saint of Nicaragua.

Passenger and Freight Locomotives — A115

Locomotives: 2c, Lightweight freight. 3c, American. 4c, Heavy freight Baldwin. 5c, Light freight and passenger Baldwin. 15c, Presidential coach.

**1978, Apr. 7** **Litho.** ***Perf. 14½***
**1079** A115 1c lil & multi .25 .25
**1080** A115 2c rose lil & multi .25 .25
**1081** A115 3c bl & multi .25 .25
**1082** A115 4c ol & multi .30 .25
**1083** A115 5c yel & multi .30 .25
**1084** A115 15c dp org & multi .45 .25
*Nos. 1079-1084,C938-C940 (9)* 6.55 4.15

Centenary of Nicaraguan railroads.

Michael Strogoff, by Jules Verne — A116

Jules Verne Books: 2c, The Mysterious Island. 3c, Journey to the Center of the Earth (battle of the sea monsters). 4c, Five Weeks in a Balloon.

**1978, Aug.** **Litho.** ***Perf. 14½***
**1085** A116 1c multi .25 .25
**1086** A116 2c multi .25 .25
**1087** A116 3c multi .25 .25
**1088** A116 4c multi .25 .25
*Nos. 1085-1088,C942-C943 (6)* 3.00 2.75

Jules Verne (1828-1905), science fiction writer.

Montgolfier Balloon — A117

1c, Icarus. 3c, Wright Brothers' Flyer A. 4c, Orville Wright at control of Flyer, 1908.

***Perf. 14½, horiz.***

**1978, Sept. 29** **Litho.**

**1089** A117 1c multi, horiz. .25 .25
**1090** A117 2c multi .25 .25
**1091** A117 3c multi, horiz. .25 .25
**1092** A117 4c multi .25 .25
*Nos. 1089-1092,C945-C946 (6)* 2.65 2.25

History of aviation & 75th anniv. of 1st powered flight.

Ernst Ocwirk and Alfredo Di Stefano — A118

Soccer Players: 25c, Ralf Edstroem and Oswaldo Piazza.

**1978, Oct. 25** **Litho.** ***Perf. 13½x14***

**1093** A118 20c multicolored .25 .25
**1094** A118 25c multicolored .25 .25
*Nos. 1093-1094,C948-C949 (4)* 1.75 1.60

11th World Soccer Cup Championship, Argentina, June 1-25. See No. C950.

St. Peter, by Goya — A119

Paintings: 15c, St. Gregory, by Goya.

**1978, Dec. 12** **Litho.** ***Perf. 13½x14***

**1095** A119 10c multi .25 .25
**1096** A119 15c multi .25 .25
*Nos. 1095-1096,C951-C952 (4)* 2.30 1.85

Christmas 1978. See No. C953.

San Cristobal Volcano and Map — A120

Designs: No. 1098, Lake Cosiguina. No. 1099, Telica Volcano. No. 1100, Lake Jiloa.

**1978, Dec. 29** ***Perf. 14x13½***

**1097** A120 5c multi .25 .25
**1098** A120 5c multi .25 .25
*a.* Pair, #1097-1098 .25 .25
**1099** A120 20c multi .25 .25
**1100** A120 20c multi .25 .25
*a.* Pair, #1099-1100 .25 .25
*Nos. 1097-1100,C954-C961 (12)* 6.30 5.30

Volcanos, lakes and their locations.

Overprinted in Silver or Red — A120a

Overprint reads: 1979 / ANO DE LA LIBERACION / OLYMPIC RINGS / PARTICIPACION NICARAGUA / OLIMPIADAS 1980 / Litografia Nacional, Portugal symbol

International Year of the Child: 20c, Carousel. 90c, Playing soccer. 2cor, Collecting stamps. 2.20cor, Playing with model train, plane. 10cor, Playing baseball.

**1980, Apr. 7** **Litho.** ***Perf. 13¾x14¼***

**Overprinted in Silver**

**1101** A120a 20c multi
*e.* Red ovpt.
**1101A** A120a 90c multi
*f.* Red ovpt.
**1101B** A120a 2cor multi
*g.* Red ovpt.
**1101C** A120a 2.20cor multi
*h.* Red ovpt.
**1101D** A120a 10cor multi
*i.* Red ovpt.
*Nos. 1101-1101D (5)* 5.00 5.00

Overprinted for Year of Liberation and 1980 Olympic Games.

Nos. 1101-1101D, 1101e-1101i were not issued without overprint.

Nos. 1101A-1101D are airmail.

Overprinted in Red or Silver — A120b

Overprint reads like Nos. 1101-1101D

Designs: 20c, North American Indian messenger. 35c, Post rider on horse. 1cor, Prestamp cover to London, horiz. 1.80cor, Sir Rowland Hill (1795-1897), postal reformer. 2.20cor, Block of six of Great Britain #1, horiz. 5cor, Nicaragua Zeppelin cover to Germany, horiz.

**1980, Apr. 7** **Litho.** ***Perf. 14½***

**Overprinted in Red**

**1102** A120b 20c multi — —
*f.* Silver overprint
**1102A** A120b 35c multi — —
*g.* Silver overprint
**1102B** A120b 1cor multi — —
*h.* Silver overprint
**1102C** A120b 1.80cor multi — —
*i.* Silver overprint
**1102D** A120b 2.20cor multi — —
*j.* Silver overprint
**1102E** A120b 5cor multi — —
*k.* Silver overprint

Overprinted for Year of Liberation and 1980 Olympic Games. Nos. 1102-1102E, 1102f-1102k were not issued without overprint. Nos. 1102C-1102E are airmail.

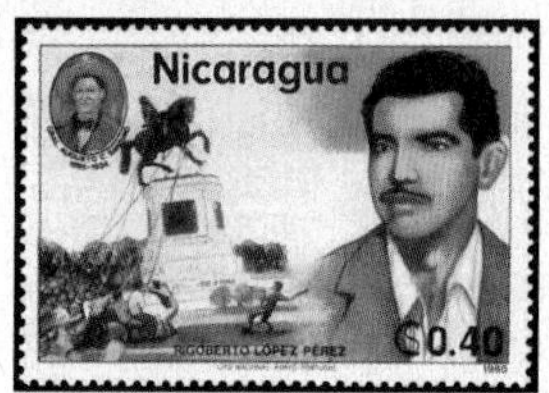


Overprinted in Silver — A120c

Overprint reads: 1979 / ANO DE LA LIBERACION / OLYMPIC RINGS / PARTICIPACION NICARAGUA / OLIMPIADAS 1980 / Litografia Nacional, Portugal symbol

Albert Einstein and: 5c, Albert Schweitzer. 10c, Theory of Relativity; 15c, Trylon & Perisphere, NY World's Fair, 1939. 20c, J. Robert Oppenheimer. 25c, Wailing Wall, Jerusalem. 1cor, Nobel Prize Medal. 2.75cor, Spaceship, radio telescope antenna.

**Overprinted in Silver**

**1980, Apr. 7** **Litho.** ***Perf. 14¾***

**1103** A120c 5c multi
**1103A** A120c 10c multi
**1103B** A120c 15c multi
**1103C** A120c 20c multi
**1103D** A120c 25c multi
**1103E** A120c 1cor multi
**1103F** A120c 2.75cor multi
*Nos. 1103-1103F (7)* 5.50 5.50

Overprinted for Intl. Year of the Child, Year of Liberation and 1980 Olympic Games.

Nos. 1103-1103F were not issued without overprint. Nos. 1103E-1103F are airmail.

The editors would like to examine the set overprinted in red.

1st Anniv. of the Revolution — A120d

Sandino portrait and: 40c, Rigoberto Lopez Perez. 75c, Street fighters. 1cor, Literacy Logo, Intl. Solidarity with Nicaragua, vert. 1.25cor, German Pomares Ordonez, jungle fighters. 1.85cor, Crowd celebrating, vert. 2.50cor, Carlos Fonseca, campfire, FSLN. 5cor, Map of Central America, Flag of Nicarauga, vert. 10cor, Literacy statement, rural scene.

**1980, July 19** **Litho.** ***Perf. 14***

**1104** A120d 40c multi
**1104A** A120d 75c multi
**1104B** A120d 1cor multi
**1104C** A120d 1.25cor multi
**1104D** A120d 1.85cor multi
**1104E** A120d 2.50cor multi
**1104F** A120d 5cor multi

**Souvenir Sheet**

***Perf. 14½x14¼***

**1104G** A120d 10cor multi

---

Numbers have been reserved for two sheets of 6 and a souvenir sheet overprinted for the 1980 Literacy Year, the Intl. Year of the Child, 1980 Olympic Games, and other subjects. The editors would like to examine all three items.

---

Intl. Year of the Child Type of 1980 Overprinted in Black — A120f

Overprint reads: 1980 ANO DE LA ALFABETIZACION and Litografia Nacional, Portugal symbol

***Perf. 13¾x14¼***

**1980, Dec. 20** **Litho.**

**1106** A120f 20c like #1101
**1106A** A120f 90c like #1101A
**1106B** A120f 2cor like #1101B
**1106C** A120f 2.20cor like #1101C
**1106D** A120f 10cor like #1101D

Nos. 1106-1106D were not issued without overprint. Nos. 1106A-1106D are airmail.

A number has been reserved for a souvenir sheet issued with this set. The editors would like to examine the sheet.

**Einstein Type of 1980**

Overprinted in Gold and Black: 1980 ANO DE LA ALFABETIZACION, Litografia Nacional, Portugal symbol and

A120g

Additional overprints read: No. 1107, YURI GAGARIN / 12/IV/1961 / LER HOMBRE EN EL ESPACIO. No. 1107A, Space Shuttle and LUNABA 1981. No. 1107B, Space Shuttle. Nos. 1107C, 1107E, 1107F, 1980 ANO DE LA ALFABETIZACION and Litografia Nacional, Portugal symbol. No. 1107D, Apollo XI / 16/VII/1969 / LER HONBRE A LA LUNA. No. 1107G, Einstin and Gandhi, with LUNOJOD 1 Overprint. No. 1107H, Einstin holding clipboard, with Space Shuttle, LUNABA 1981, PLANETA SATURNO 1980 and VOYAGER overprints.

**1981, May 15** **Litho.** ***Perf. 14½***

**1107** A120g 5c like #1103
**1107A** A120g 10c like #1103A
**1107B** A120g 15c like #1103B
**1107C** A120g 20c like #1103C
**1107D** A120g 25c like #1103D
**1107E** A120g 1cor like #1103E
**1107F** A120g 2.75cor like #1103F
**1107G** A120g 10cor multi

**Souvenir Sheet**

***Perf. 14¾***

**1107H** A120g 10cor on 20cor multi

Nos. 1107-1107H were not issued without overprint. Nos. 1107E-1107H are airmail.

Souvenir Sheet

Quetzal — A121

**1981, May 18** **Litho.** ***Perf. 13***

**1108** A121 10cor multi 2.50 1.25

WIPA 1981 Phil. Exhib., Vienna, May 22-31.

1982 World Cup A122

Various soccer players and stadiums.

**1981, June 25** ***Perf. 12x12½***

**1109** A122 5c multi .25 .25
**1109A** A122 20c multi .25 .25
**1109B** A122 25c multi .25 .25
**1109C** A122 30c multi .25 .25
**1109D** A122 50c multi .25 .25
**1109E** A122 4cor multi .45 .25
**1109F** A122 5cor multi .55 .30
**1109G** A122 10cor multi 1.10 .65
*Nos. 1109-1109G (8)* 3.35 2.45

**Souvenir Sheet**

***Perf. 13***

**1109H** A122 10cor multi 2.00 1.00

2nd Anniv. of Revolution — A123

**1981, July 19** *Perf. 12½x12*

**1110** A123 50c Adult education .25 .25
*Nos. 1110,C975E-C975G (4)* 8.50 1.20

20th Anniv. of the FSLN A124

**1981, July 23**

**1111** A124 50c Armed citizen .25 .25

See No. C976.

Postal Union of Spain and the Americas, 12th Congress, Managua — A125

**1981, Aug. 10**

**1112** A125 50c Mailman .25 .25
*Nos. 1112,C977-C979 (4)* 1.40 1.10

Natl. Literacy Campaign, 1st Anniv. — A125a

Designs: 5c, "S"ahino, man counting on fingers. 20c, "A"rmadillo, children marching. 30c, "N"utria, teacher with 2 women. 40c, "D"anto, teacher with 5 people.60c, "I"guana, teacher with 3 adults, hut. 6cor, "N"icaragua, map of Nicaragua with graph. 9cor, "O"so hormiguera, UNESCO Krupskaya medal.

**1981, August** **Litho.** *Perf. 14*

**1113** A125a 5c multi
**1113A** A125a 10c multi
**1113B** A125a 30c multi
**1113C** A125a 40c multi
**1113D** A125a 60c multi
**1113E** A125a 6cor multi
**1113F** A125a 9cor multi
*Nos. 1113-1103F (7)* 4.00 4.00

Aquatic Flowers (Nymphaea...) A126

**1981, Sept. 15** *Perf. 12½*

**1114** A126 50c Capensis .25 .25
**1115** A126 1cor Daubenyana .25 .25
**1116** A126 1.20cor Marliacea .25 .25
**1117** A126 1.80cor GT Moore .35 .25
**1118** A126 2cor Lotus .40 .25
**1119** A126 2.50cor BG Berry .55 .30
*Nos. 1114-1119,C981 (7)* 3.45 2.45

Tropical Fish A127

50c, Cheirodon axelrodi. 1cor, Poecilia reticulata. 1.85cor, Anostomus anostomus. 2.10cor, Corydoras arcuatus. 2.50cor, Cynolebias nigripinnis.

**1981, Oct. 19**

**1120** A127 50c multicolored .25 .25
**1121** A127 1cor multicolored .25 .25
**1122** A127 1.85cor multicolored .35 .25
**1123** A127 2.10cor multicolored .45 .25
**1124** A127 2.50cor multicolored .55 .30
*Nos. 1120-1124,C983-C984 (7)* 3.35 1.90

Dryocopus Lineatus — A128

1.20cor, Ramphastos sulfuratus, horiz. 1.80cor, Aratinga finschi, horiz. 2cor, Ara macao.

**1981, Nov. 30** *Perf. 12½*

**1125** A128 50c multi .30 .25
**1126** A128 1.20cor multi .45 .25
**1127** A128 1.80cor multi .55 .25
**1128** A128 2cor multi .65 .25
*Nos. 1125-1128,C986-C988 (7)* 5.75 2.45

Space Communications — A129

Various communications satellites.

**1981, Dec. 15** *Perf. 13x12½*

**1129** A129 50c multi .25 .25
**1130** A129 1cor multi .25 .25
**1131** A129 1.50cor multi .25 .25
**1132** A129 2cor multi .30 .25
*Nos. 1129-1132,C989-C991 (7)* 4.05 1.90

Vaporcito 93 A130

1cor, Vulcan Iron Works, 1946. 1.20cor, 1911. 1.80cor, Hoist & Derriel, 1909. 2cor, U-10B, 1956. 2.50cor, Ferrobus, 1945.

**1981, Dec. 30** *Perf. 12½*

**1133** A130 50c multi .25 .25
**1134** A130 1cor multi .30 .25
**1135** A130 1.20cor multi .35 .25
**1136** A130 1.80cor multi .50 .25
**1137** A130 2cor multi .55 .25
**1138** A130 2.50cor multi .75 .30
*Nos. 1133-1138,C992 (7)* 4.95 2.30

1982 World Cup — A131

Designs: Various soccer players. 3.50cor horiz.

**1982, Jan. 25**

**1139** A131 5c multi .25 .25
**1140** A131 20c multi .25 .25
**1141** A131 25c multi .25 .25
**1142** A131 2.50cor multi .40 .35
**1143** A131 3.50cor multi .55 .35
*Nos. 1139-1143,C993-C994 (7)* 3.70 2.55

Cocker Spaniels A132

20c, German shepherds. 25c, English setters. 2.50cor, Brittany spaniels.

**1982, Feb. 18**

**1144** A132 5c multi .25 .25
**1145** A132 20c multi .25 .25
**1146** A132 25c multi .25 .25
**1147** A132 2.50cor multi .45 .30
*Nos. 1144-1147,C996-C998 (7)* 3.45 2.15

Dynamine Myrrhina A133

1.20cor, Eunica alcmena. 1.50cor, Callizona acesta. 2cor, Adelpha leuceria.

**1982, Mar. 26**

**1148** A133 50c multi .30 .25
**1149** A133 1.20cor multi .40 .25
**1150** A133 1.50cor multi .45 .25
**1151** A133 2cor multi .50 .25
*Nos. 1148-1151,C1000-C1002 (7)* 4.45 2.00

Satellite A134

Designs: Various satellites. 5c, 50c, 1.50cor, 2.50cor horiz.

**1982, Apr. 12**

**1152** A134 5c multi .25 .25
**1153** A134 15c multi .25 .25
**1154** A134 50c multi .25 .25
**1155** A134 1.50cor multi .25 .25
**1156** A134 2.50cor multi .45 .25
*Nos. 1152-1156,C1003-C1004 (7)* 3.20 2.15

UPU Membership Centenary — A135

**1982, May 1** **Litho.** *Perf. 13*

**1157** A135 50c Mail coach .25 .25
**1158** A135 1.20cor Ship .25 .25
*Nos. 1157-1158,C1005-C1006 (4)* 2.00 1.45

14th Central American and Caribbean Games (Cuba '82) — A136

**1982, May 13**

**1159** A136 10c Bicycling .25 .25
**1160** A136 15c Swimming, horiz. .25 .25
**1161** A136 25c Basketball .25 .25
**1162** A136 50c Weight lifting .25 .25
*Nos. 1159-1162,C1007-C1009 (7)* 4.00 2.35

3rd Anniv. of Revolution — A137

**1982, July 19**

**1163** A137 50c multi .25 .25
*Nos. 1163,C1012-C1014 (4)* 2.50 1.50

George Washington (1732-1799) A138

19th Century Paintings. 50c, Mount Vernon. 1cor, Signing the Constitution, horiz. 2cor, Riding through Trenton.
Size of 50c: 45x35mm.

*Perf. 13x12½, 12½x13*

**1982, June 20** **Litho.**

**1164** A138 50c multicolored .25 .25
**1165** A138 1cor multicolored .25 .25
**1166** A138 2cor multicolored .40 .25
*Nos. 1164-1166,C1015-C1018 (7)* 3.90 2.35

Flower Arrangement, by R. Penalba A139

Paintings: 50c, Masked Dancers, by M. Garcia, horiz. 1cor, The Couple, by R. Perez. 1.20cor, Canales Valley, by A. Mejias, horiz. 1.85cor, Portrait of Mrs. Castellon, by T. Jerez. 2cor, Street Vendors, by L. Cerrato. 10cor, Cock Fight, by Gallos P. Ortiz.

**1982, Aug. 17** *Perf. 13*

**1167** A139 25c multi .25 .25
**1168** A139 50c multi .25 .25
**1169** A139 1cor multi .25 .25
**1170** A139 1.20cor multi .25 .25
**1171** A139 1.85cor multi .30 .25
**1172** A139 2cor multi .30 .25
*Nos. 1167-1172,C1019 (7)* 3.60 2.30

**Souvenir Sheet**

**1173** A139 10cor multi 2.00 1.00

No. 1173 contains one 36x28mm stamp.

George Dimitrov, First Pres. of Bulgaria — A140

50c, Lenin, Dimitrov, 1921.

**1982, Sept. 9**

**1174** A140 50c multicolored .25 .25
*Nos. 1174,C1020-C1021 (3)* 1.50 .90

26th Anniv. of End of Dictatorship — A141

50c, Ausberto Narvaez. 2.50cor, Cornelio Silva.

**1982, Sept. 21** *Perf. 13x12½*

**1175** A141 50c multi .25 .25
**1176** A141 2.50cor multi .50 .30
*Nos. 1175-1176,C1022-C1023 (4)* 2.35 1.55

Ruins, Leon Viejo A142

1cor, Ruben Dario Theater and Park. 1.20cor, Independence Plaza, Granada. 1.80cor, Corn Island. 2cor, Santiago Volcano crater, Masaya.

**1982, Sept. 25** *Perf. 13*

**1177** A142 50c multi .25 .25
**1178** A142 1cor multi .25 .25
**1179** A142 1.20cor multi .25 .25
**1180** A142 1.80cor multi .30 .25
**1181** A142 2cor multi .30 .25
*Nos. 1177-1181,C1024-C1025 (7)* 2.20 1.75

Karl Marx (1818-1883) — A143

**1982, Oct. 4** *Perf. 12½*

**1182** A143 1cor Marx, birthplace .25 .25

Se-tenant with label showing Communist Manifesto titlepage. See No. C1026.

World Food Day (Oct. 16) A144

50c, Picking fruit. 1cor, Farm workers, vert. 2cor, Cutting sugar cane. 10cor, Emblems.

**1982, Oct. 10** *Perf. 13*

**1183** A144 50c multicolored .25 .25
**1184** A144 1cor multicolored .25 .25
**1185** A144 2cor multicolored .30 .25
**1186** A144 10cor multicolored 1.50 1.25
*Nos. 1183-1186 (4)* 2.30 2.00

Discovery of America, 490th Anniv. — A145

50c, Santa Maria. 1cor, Nina. 1.50cor, Pinta. 2cor, Columbus, fleet.

**1982, Oct. 12** *Perf. 12½x13*

**1187** A145 50c multi .25 .25
**1188** A145 1cor multi .25 .25
**1189** A145 1.50cor multi .30 .25
**1190** A145 2cor multi .40 .30
*Nos. 1187-1190,C1027-C1029 (7)* 3.70 2.40

A146

50c, Lobelia laxiflora. 1.20cor, Bombacopsis quinata. 1.80cor, Mimosa albida. 2cor, Epidendrum alatum.

**1982, Nov. 13** *Perf. 12½*

**1191** A146 50c multi .25 .25
**1192** A146 1.20cor multi .25 .25
**1193** A146 1.80cor multi .40 .25
**1194** A146 2cor multi .40 .25
*Nos. 1191-1194,C1031-C1033 (7)* 3.40 2.00

A147

10c, Coral snake. 50c, Iguana, horiz. 2cor, Lachesis muta, horiz.

**1982, Dec. 10** *Perf. 13*

**1195** A147 10c multi .25 .25
**1196** A147 50c multi .25 .25
**1197** A147 2cor multi .40 .25
*Nos. 1195-1197,C1034-C1037 (7)* 7.30 2.05

Telecommunications Day — A148

50c, Radio transmission station. 1cor, Telcor building, Managua.

**1982, Dec. 12** **Litho.** *Perf. 12½*

**1198** A148 50c multicolored .25 .25
**1199** A148 1cor multicolored .25 .25

50c airmail.

Jose Marti, Cuban Independence Hero, 130th Birth Anniv. — A149

**1983, Jan. 28** *Perf. 13*

**1200** A149 1cor multi .25 .25

Boxing — A150

1cor, Gymnast. 1.50cor, Running. 2cor, Weightlifting. 4cor, Women's discus. 5cor, Basketball. 6cor, Bicycling. 15cor, Sailing.

**1983, Jan. 31** *Perf. 12½*

**1201** A150 50c shown .25 .25
**1202** A150 1cor multi .25 .25
**1203** A150 1.50cor multi .25 .25
**1204** A150 2cor multi .40 .25
**1205** A150 4cor multi .75 .30
**1206** A150 5cor multi .95 .40
**1207** A150 6cor multi 1.15 .50
*Nos. 1201-1207 (7)* 4.00 2.20

**Souvenir Sheet**

*Perf. 13*

**1208** A150 15cor multi 2.25 1.25

23rd Olympic Games, Los Angeles, July 28-Aug. 12, 1984. Nos. 1205-1208 airmail. No. 1208 contains one 31x39mm stamp.

Local Flowers — A151

No. 1209, Bixa orellana. No. 1210, Brassavola nodosa. No. 1211, Cattleya lueddemanniana. No. 1212, Cochlospermum spec. No. 1213, Hibiscus rosa-sinensis. No. 1214, Laella spec. No. 1215, Malvaviscus arboreus. No. 1216, Neomarica coerulea. No. 1217, Plumeria rubra. No. 1218, Senecio spec. No. 1219, Sobralla macrantha. No. 1220, Stachytarpheta indica. No. 1221, Tabebula ochraceae. No. 1222, Tagetes erecta. No. 1223, Tecoma stans. No. 1224, Thumbergia alata.

**1983, Feb. 5** *Perf. 12½*

**1209** A151 1cor black .25 .25
**1210** A151 1cor olive green .25 .25
**1211** A151 1cor olive grey .25 .25
**1212** A151 1cor apple green .25 .25
**1213** A151 1cor brown rose .25 .25
**1214** A151 1cor deep magenta .25 .25
**1215** A151 1cor blue green .25 .25
**1216** A151 1cor ultramarine .25 .25
**1217** A151 1cor dull vermilion .25 .25
**1218** A151 1cor brown ochre .25 .25
**1219** A151 1cor deep purple .25 .25
**1220** A151 1cor light blue .25 .25
**1221** A151 1cor bluish violet .25 .25
**1222** A151 1cor orange yellow .25 .25
**1223** A151 1cor bright magenta .25 .25
**1224** A151 1cor dp turq grn .25 .25
*Nos. 1209-1224 (16)* 4.00 4.00

See #1515-1530, 1592-1607, 1828-1843.

Visit of Pope John Paul II A152

50c, Peace banner. 1cor, Map, girl picking coffee beans. 4cor, Pres. Rafael Rivas, Pope. 7cor, Pope, Managua Cathedral.
15cor, Pope, vert.

**1983, Mar. 4** *Perf. 13*

**1225** A152 50c multicolored .25 .25
**1226** A152 1cor multicolored .25 .25
**1227** A152 4cor multicolored 1.10 .60
**1228** A152 7cor multicolored 1.90 1.00
*Nos. 1225-1228 (4)* 3.50 2.10

**Souvenir Sheet**

**1229** A152 15cor multicolored 3.25 1.75

Nos. 1227-1229 airmail. No. 1229 contains one 31x39mm stamp.

Nocturnal Moths — A153

15c, Xilophanes chiron. 50c, Protoparce ochus. 65c, Pholus lasbruscae. 1cor, Amphypterus gannascus. 1.50cor, Pholus licaon. 2cor, Agrius cingulata. 10cor, Rothschildia jurulla, vert.

**1983, Mar. 10**

**1230** A153 15c multi .25 .25
**1231** A153 50c multi .25 .25
**1232** A153 65c multi .30 .25
**1233** A153 1cor multi .35 .25
**1234** A153 1.50cor multi .40 .25
**1235** A153 2cor multi .45 .25
**1236** A153 10cor multi 1.90 .80
*Nos. 1230-1236 (7)* 3.90 2.30

No. 1236 airmail.

26th Anniv. of the Anti-Somoza Movement — A154

Various monuments and churches — 50c, Church of Subtiava, Leon. 1cor, La Immaculata Castle, Rio San Juan. 2cor, La Recolección Church, Leon, vert. 4cor, Ruben Dario monument, Managua, vert.

**1983, Mar. 25** *Perf. 12½*

**1237** A154 50c multi .25 .25
**1238** A154 1cor multi .25 .25
**1239** A154 2cor multi .35 .25
**1240** A154 4cor multi .65 .40
*Nos. 1237-1240 (4)* 1.50 1.15

Nos. 1237-1239 has "correos" above date. No. 1240 has "aereo" above date.

Railroad Cars A155

15c, Passenger. 65c, Freight. 1cor, Tank. 1.50cor, Ore. 4cor, Rail bus. 5cor, Dump truck. 7cor, Rail bus, diff.

**1983, Apr. 15**

**1241** A155 15c multi .25 .25
**1242** A155 65c multi .25 .25
**1243** A155 1cor multi .25 .25
**1244** A155 1.50cor multi .25 .25
**1245** A155 4cor multi .55 .30
**1246** A155 5cor multi .70 .40
**1247** A155 7cor multi .95 .50
*Nos. 1241-1247 (7)* 3.20 2.20

Nos. 1245-1247 airmail.

Red Cross Flood Rescue A156

1cor, Putting patient in ambulance. 4cor, 1972 earthquake & fire rescue. 5cor, Nurse examining soldier, 1979 Liberation War.

**1983, May 8** ***Perf. 13***

**1248** A156 50c multi .25 .25
**1249** A156 1cor multi .25 .25
**1250** A156 4cor multi .65 .40
**1251** A156 5cor multi .70 .40
*Nos. 1248-1251 (4)* 1.85 1.30

4cor, 5cor airmail. 4cor vert.

World Communications Year — A157

**1983, May 17**

**1252** A157 1cor multi .40 .25

9th Pan-American Games, Aug. — A158

15c, Baseball. 50c, Water polo. 65c, Running. 1cor, Women's basketball, vert. 2cor, Weightlifting, vert. 7cor, Fencing. 8cor, Gymnastics.
15cor, Boxing.

**1983, May 30** **Litho.** ***Perf. 13***

**1253** A158 15c multi .25 .25
**1254** A158 50c multi .25 .25
**1255** A158 65c multi .25 .25
**1256** A158 1cor multi .25 .25
**1257** A158 2cor multi .35 .25
**1258** A158 7cor multi 1.10 .55
**1259** A158 8cor multi 1.25 .65
*Nos. 1253-1259 (7)* 3.70 2.45

**Souvenir Sheet**

**1260** A158 15cor multi 2.50 1.25

Nos. 1258-1260 airmail. No. 1260 contains one 39x31mm stamp.

4th Anniv. of Revolution — A159

1cor, Port of Corinto. 2cor, Telecommunications Bldg., Leon.

**1983, July 19** **Litho.** ***Perf. 12½***

**1261** A159 1cor multicolored .25 .25
**1262** A159 2cor multicolored .40 .25

Founders of FSLN (Sandinista Party) — A160

**1983, July 23** **Litho.** ***Perf. 13***

**1263** A160 50c multi .25 .25
**1264** A160 1cor multi .25 .25
**1265** A160 4cor multi, vert. .60 .35
*Nos. 1263-1265 (3)* 1.10 .85

No. 1265, airmail, 33x44mm.

Simon Bolivar, 200th Birth Anniv. A161

50c, Bolivar and Sandino. 1cor, Bolivar on horseback, vert.

**1983, July 24** **Litho.** ***Perf. 12½***

**1266** A161 50c multicolored .25 .25
**1267** A161 1cor multicolored .25 .25

14th Winter Olympic Games, Sarajevo, Yugoslavia, Feb. 8-19, 1984 — A162

50c, Speed skating. 1cor, Slalom. 1.50cor, Luge. 2cor, Ski jumping. 4cor, Ice dancing. 5cor, Skiing. 6cor, Biathlon.

**1983, Aug. 5** **Litho.** ***Perf. 13***

**1268** A162 50c multi .25 .25
**1269** A162 1cor multi .25 .25
**1270** A162 1.50cor multi .25 .25
**1271** A162 2cor multi .40 .25
**1272** A162 4cor multi .65 .35
**1273** A162 5cor multi .75 .40
**1274** A162 6cor multi 1.00 .50
*Nos. 1268-1274 (7)* 3.55 2.25

**Souvenir Sheet**

**1983, Aug. 25** **Litho.** ***Perf. 13***

**1275** A162 15cor Hockey 2.50 1.40

No. 1275 contains one 39x32mm stamp. Nos. 1272-1275 airmail.

Chess Moves — A163

**1983, Aug. 20** **Litho.** ***Perf. 13***

**1276** A163 15c Pawn .25 .25
**1277** A163 65c Knight .25 .25
**1278** A163 1cor Bishop .25 .25
**1279** A163 2cor Castle .35 .25
**1280** A163 4cor Queen .60 .35
**1281** A163 5cor King .70 .40
**1282** A163 7cor Player 1.00 .55
*Nos. 1276-1282 (7)* 3.40 2.30

Nos. 1280-1282 airmail.

Archaeological Finds — A164

**1983, Aug. 20** ***Perf. 13x12½***

**1283** A164 50c Stone figurine .25 .25
**1284** A164 1cor Covered dish .25 .25
**1285** A164 2cor Vase .40 .25
**1286** A164 4cor Platter .70 .35
*Nos. 1283-1286 (4)* 1.60 1.10

No. 1286 airmail.

Madonna of the Chair, by Raphael (1483-1517) A165

Paintings: 1cor, The Eszterhazy Madonna. 1.50cor, Sistine Madonna. 2cor, Madonna of the Linnet. 4cor, Madonna of the Meadow. 5cor, La Belle Jardiniere. 6cor, Adoration of the Kings. 15cor, Madonna de Foligno. 4, 5, 6, 15cor airmail.

**1983, Sept. 15**

**1287** A165 50c multi .25 .25
**1288** A165 1cor multi .25 .25
**1289** A165 1.50cor multi .25 .25
**1290** A165 2cor multi .35 .25
**1291** A165 4cor multi .60 .35
**1292** A165 5cor multi .70 .40
**1293** A165 6cor multi .90 .45
*Nos. 1287-1293 (7)* 3.30 2.20

**Souvenir Sheet**

**1984, Sept. 15** **Litho.** ***Perf. 13***

**1293A** A165 15cor multi 2.75 1.25

Mining Industry Nationalization — A166

1cor, Pouring molten metal. 4cor, Mine headstock, workers.

**1983, Oct. 2** ***Perf. 13***

**1294** A166 1cor multicolored .25 .25
**1295** A166 4cor multicolored .60 .40

4cor airmail.

Ship-to-Shore Communications — A167

**1983, Oct. 7** ***Perf. 12½***

**1296** A167 1cor shown .25 .25
**1297** A167 4cor Radio tower, view .60 .40

FRACAP '83, Federation of Central American and Panamanian Radio Amateurs Cong., Oct. 7-9.

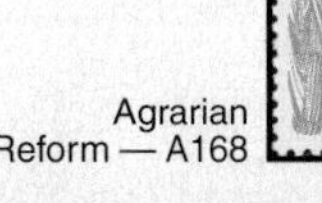


Agrarian Reform — A168

**1983, Oct. 16**

**1298** A168 1cor Tobacco .25 .25
**1299** A168 2cor Cotton .35 .25
**1300** A168 4cor Corn .60 .25
**1301** A168 5cor Sugar cane .70 .35
**1302** A168 6cor Cattle .90 .40
**1303** A168 7cor Rice paddy 1.00 .45
**1304** A168 8cor Coffee beans 1.20 .55
**1305** A168 10cor Bananas 1.50 .65
*Nos. 1298-1305 (8)* 6.50 3.15

See Nos. 1531-1538, 1608-1615.

Fire Engine A169

Various Fire Engines.

**1983, Oct. 17** ***Perf. 13***

**1306** A169 50c multi .25 .25
**1307** A169 1cor multi .25 .25
**1308** A169 1.50cor multi .25 .25
**1309** A169 2cor multi .35 .25
**1310** A169 4cor multi .60 .35
**1311** A169 5cor multi .70 .40
**1312** A169 6cor multi .90 .45
*Nos. 1306-1312 (7)* 3.30 2.20

Nos. 1308-1311 airmail.

Nicaraguan-Cuban Solidarity — A170

1cor, José Marti, Gen. Sandino. 4cor, Education, health, industry.

**1983, Oct. 24**

**1313** A170 1cor multicolored .25 .25
**1314** A170 4cor multicolored .60 .40

4cor airmail.

A171

Christmas (Adoration of the Kings Paintings by): 50c, Hugo van der Goes. 1 cor, Ghirlandaio. 2cor, El Greco. 7cor, Konrad von Soest. 7cor airmail.

**1983, Dec. 1**

**1315** A171 50c multi .25 .25
**1316** A171 1cor multi .25 .25
**1317** A171 2cor multi .30 .25
**1318** A171 7cor multi 1.20 .40
*Nos. 1315-1318 (4)* 2.00 1.15

A172

**1984, Jan. 10**

**1319** A172 50c Biathlon .25 .25
**1320** A172 50c Bobsledding .25 .25
**1321** A172 1cor Speed skating .25 .25
**1322** A172 1cor Slalom .25 .25
**1323** A172 4cor Downhill skiing .65 .35
**1324** A172 5cor Ice dancing .80 .40
**1325** A172 10cor Ski jumping 1.40 .75
*Nos. 1319-1325 (7)* 3.85 2.50

**Souvenir Sheet**

**1326** A172 15cor Hockey 3.50 1.75

1984 Winter Olympics. No. 1326 contains one 31x39mm stamp. Nos. 1323-1326 airmail.

Domestic Cats — A173

No. 1327, Chinchilla. No. 1328, Long-haired Angel. No. 1329, Red tabby. No. 1330, Tortoiseshell. No. 1331, Siamese. No. 1332, Blue Burmese. No. 1333, Silver long-haired.

**1984, Feb. 15** *Perf. 12½*

**1327** A173 50c multicolored .25 .25
**1328** A173 50c multicolored .25 .25
**1329** A173 1cor multicolored .40 .25
**1330** A173 2cor multicolored .60 .25
**1331** A173 3cor multicolored .50 .30
**1332** A173 4cor multicolored 1.00 .40
**1333** A173 7cor multicolored 2.00 .60
*Nos. 1327-1333 (7)* 5.00 2.30

Nos. 1331, 1333 airmail.

Augusto Cesar Sandino (d. 1934) — A174

**1984, Feb. 21**

**1334** A174 1cor Arms .25 .25
**1335** A174 4cor Portrait .60 .40

4cor airmail.

Intl. Women's Day — A175

**1984, Mar. 8**

**1336** A175 1cor Blanca Arauz .40 .25

Bee-pollinated Flowers A176

No. 1337, Poinsettia. No. 1338, Sunflower. No. 1339, Antigonan leptopus. No. 1340, Cassia alata. No. 1341, Bidens pilosa. No. 1342, Althea rosea. No. 1343, Rivea corymbosa.

**1984, Mar. 20**

**1337** A176 50c multicolored .25 .25
**1338** A176 50c multicolored .25 .25
**1339** A176 1cor multicolored .25 .25
**1340** A176 1cor multicolored .25 .25
**1341** A176 3cor multicolored .40 .25
**1342** A176 4cor multicolored .60 .35
**1343** A176 5cor multicolored .70 .40
*Nos. 1337-1343 (7)* 2.70 2.00

Nos. 1341-1343 airmail.

Space Annivs. — A177

No. 1344, Soyuz 6,7,8, 1969. No. 1345, Soyuz 6,7,8, diff. No. 1346, Apollo 11, 1969. No. 1347, Luna 1, 1959. No. 1348, Luna 2, 1959. No. 1349, Luna 3, 1959. No. 1350, Painting by Koroliov, 1934.

**1984, Apr. 20**

**1344** A177 50c multicolored .25 .25
**1345** A177 50c multicolored .25 .25
**1346** A177 1cor multicolored .25 .25
**1347** A177 2cor multicolored .35 .25
**1348** A177 3cor multicolored .50 .25
**1349** A177 4cor multicolored .65 .35
**1350** A177 9cor multicolored 1.40 .50
*Nos. 1344-1350 (7)* 3.65 2.10

Nos. 1348-1350 airmail.

Noli Me Tangere, by Correggio A178

No. 1352, Madonna of San Girolamo. No. 1353, Allegory of the Virtues. No. 1354, Allegory of Placer. No. 1355, Ganimedes. No. 1356, Danae. No. 1357, Leda.

No. 1358, St. John the Evangelist.

**1984, May 17** **Litho.** *Perf. 12½*

**1351** A178 50c shown .25 .25
**1352** A178 50c multicolored .25 .25
**1353** A178 1cor multicolored .25 .25
**1354** A178 2cor multicolored .35 .25
**1355** A178 3cor multicolored .50 .25
**1356** A178 5cor multicolored .80 .40
**1357** A178 8cor multicolored 1.25 .65
*Nos. 1351-1357 (7)* 3.65 2.30

**Souvenir Sheet**

**1358** A178 15cor multicolored 3.25 1.25

No. 1358 contains one 31x39mm stamp. Nos. 1355-1358 airmail.

Vintage Cars A179

No. 1359, Abadal, 1914. No. 1360, Daimler, 1886, vert. No. 1361, Ford, 1903, vert. No. 1362, Renault, 1899, vert. No. 1363, Rolls Royce, 1910. No. 1364, Metallurgique, 1907. No. 1365, Bugatti Mode 40.

**1984, May 18**

**1359** A179 1cor multicolored .25 .25
**1360** A179 1cor multicolored .25 .25
**1361** A179 2cor multicolored .35 .25
**1362** A179 2cor multicolored .35 .25
**1363** A179 3cor multicolored .50 .25
**1364** A179 4cor multicolored .65 .35
**1365** A179 7cor multicolored 1.10 .60
*Nos. 1359-1365 (7)* 3.45 2.20

Birth sesquicentennial of Gottlieb Daimler. Nos. 1363-1365 airmail.

1984 Summer Olympics A180

**1984, July 6**

**1366** A180 50c Volleyball .25 .25
**1367** A180 50c Basketball .25 .25
**1368** A180 1cor Field hockey .25 .25
**1369** A180 2cor Tennis .35 .25
**1370** A180 3cor Soccer .50 .25
**1371** A180 4cor Water polo .65 .35
**1372** A180 9cor Net ball 1.40 .70
*Nos. 1366-1372 (7)* 3.65 2.30

**Souvenir Sheet**

*Perf. 13*

**1373** A180 15cor Baseball 2.25 1.25

No. 1373 contains one 40x31mm stamp. Nos. 1370-1373 airmail and horiz.

5th Anniv. of Revolution — A181

**1984, July 19**

**1374** A181 50c Construction .25 .25
**1375** A181 1cor Transportation .25 .25
**1376** A181 4cor Agriculture .65 .35
**1377** A181 7cor Govt. building 1.25 .55
*Nos. 1374-1377 (4)* 2.40 1.40

Nos. 1376-1377 airmail.

UNESCO Nature Conservation Campaign — A182

50c, Children dependent on nature. 1cor, Forest. 2cor, River. 10cor, Seedlings, field, vert.

**1984, Aug. 3** *Perf. 12½x13, 13x12½*

**1378** A182 50c multicolored .25 .25
**1379** A182 1cor multicolored .25 .25
**1380** A182 2cor multicolored .35 .25
**1381** A182 10cor multicolored 1.50 .80
*Nos. 1378-1381 (4)* 2.35 1.55

No. 1381 airmail.

Nicaraguan Red Cross, 50th Anniv. — A183

**1984, Sept. 16** *Perf. 12½x12*

**1382** A183 1cor Air ambulance .25 .25
**1383** A183 7cor Battle field 1.00 .55

No. 1383 airmail.

History of Baseball — A184

Portraits and national colors: #1384, Ventura Escalante, Dominican Republic. #1385, Daniel Herrera, Mexico. #1386, Adalberto Herrera, Venezuela. #1387, Roberto Clemente, Puerto Rico. #1388, Carlos Colas, Cuba. #1389, Stanley Cayasso, Nicaragua. #1390, Babe Ruth, US.

**1984, Oct. 25** **Litho.** *Perf. 12½*

**1384** A184 50c multi .25 .25
**1385** A184 50c multi .25 .25
**1386** A184 1cor multi .35 .25
**1387** A184 1cor multi .35 .25
**1388** A184 3cor multi .90 .25
**1389** A184 4cor multi 1.25 .25
**1390** A184 5cor multi 1.50 .35
*Nos. 1384-1390 (7)* 4.85 1.85

Nos. 1388-1390 are airmail.

Tapirus Bairdii A185

**1984, Dec. 28** *Perf. 13*

**1391** A185 25c In water .30 .25
**1392** A185 25c In field .30 .25
**1393** A185 3cor Baring teeth .70 .25
**1394** A185 4cor Female and young .90 .25
*Nos. 1391-1394 (4)* 2.20 1.00

Wildlife conservation. Nos. 1393-1394 are airmail. Compare with type A202.

1986 World Cup Soccer Championships, Mexico — A186

Evolution of soccer.

**1985, Jan. 20**

**1395** A186 50c 1314 .25 .25
**1396** A186 50c 1500 .25 .25
**1397** A186 1cor 1846 .25 .25
**1398** A186 1cor 1872 .25 .25
**1399** A186 2cor 1883 .25 .25
**1400** A186 4cor 1890 .40 .25
**1401** A186 6cor 1953 .60 .30
*Nos. 1395-1401 (7)* 2.25 1.80

**Souvenir Sheet**

*Perf. 12½*

**1402** A186 10cor 1985 2.00 1.00

Nos. 1399-1402 are airmail. No. 1402 contains one 40x32mm stamp.

Mushrooms A187

No. 1403, Boletus calopus. No. 1404, Strobilomyces retisporus. No. 1405, Boletus luridus. No. 1406, Xerocomus illudens. No. 1407, Gyrodon merulioides. No. 1408, Tylopilus plumbeoviolaceus. No. 1409, Gyroporus castaneus.

**1985, Feb. 20**

**1403** A187 50c multicolored .25 .25
**1404** A187 50c multicolored .25 .25
**1405** A187 1cor multicolored .25 .25
**1406** A187 1cor multicolored .25 .25
**1407** A187 4cor multicolored .50 .25
**1408** A187 5cor multicolored .60 .25
**1409** A187 8cor multicolored 1.00 .40
*Nos. 1403-1409 (7)* 3.10 1.90

Nos. 1406-1409 are airmail.

Postal Union of the Americas and Spain, 13th Congress
A188

UPAE emblem and: 1cor, Chasqui, mail runner and map of Realejo-Nicaragua route. 7cor, Monoplane and Nicaraguan air network.

**1985, Mar. 11** ***Perf. 12½x13***

**1410** A188 1cor multi .55 .25
**1411** A188 7cor multi 2.10 .40

No. 1411 is airmail.

Locomotives — A189

**1985, Apr. 5** ***Perf. 12½***

**1412** A189 1cor Electric .25 .25
**1413** A189 1cor Steam .25 .25
**1414** A189 9cor Steam, diff. .80 .25
**1415** A189 9cor Tram .80 .25
**1416** A189 15cor Steam, diff. 1.40 .40
**1417** A189 21cor Steam, diff. 2.00 .35
*Nos. 1412-1417 (6)* 5.50 1.75

**Souvenir Sheet**

***Perf. 13***

**1418** A189 42cor steam, diff. 5.75 5.75

German Railroads, 150th Anniv. #1418 also for 100th anniv. of Nicaraguan railroads. #1418 contains one 40x32mm stamp. #1414-1418 are airmail.

Motorcycle Cent. — A190

**1985, Apr. 30** **Litho.** ***Perf. 12½***

**1419** A190 50c F.N., 1928 .25 .25
**1420** A190 50c Douglas, 1928 .25 .25
**1421** A190 1cor Puch, 1938 .40 .25
**1422** A190 2cor Wanderer, 1939 .50 .25
**1423** A190 4cor Honda, 1949 1.00 .25
**1424** A190 5cor BMW, 1984 1.40 .25
**1425** A190 7cor Honda, 1984 1.75 .40
*Nos. 1419-1425 (7)* 5.55 1.90

Nos. 1419-1425 se-tenant with labels picturing manufacturers' trademarks. Nos. 1422-1425 are airmail.

Flowers — A194

No. 1454, Metelea quirosii. No. 1455, Ipomea nil. No. 1456, Lysichitum americanum. No. 1457, Clusia sp. No. 1458, Vanilla planifolia. No. 1459, Stemmadenia obovata.

**1985, May 20** **Litho.** ***Perf. 13***

**1454** A194 50c multicolored .25 .25
**1455** A194 50c multicolored .25 .25
**1456** A194 1cor multicolored .40 .25
**1457** A194 2cor multicolored .70 .25
**1458** A194 4cor multicolored 1.40 .35
**1459** A194 7cor multicolored 2.50 .60
*a.* Miniature sheet of 6, #1454-1459 5.75
*Nos. 1454-1459 (6)* 5.50 1.95

Nos. 1457-1459 are airmail.
Stamps in No. 1459a do not have white border.

End of World War II, 40th Anniv. — A195

9.50cor, German army surrenders. 28cor, Nuremberg trials, horiz.

**1985, May** ***Perf. 12x12½, 12½x12***

**1460** A195 9.50cor multi .80 .35
**1461** A195 28cor multi 2.25 1.00

No. 1461 is airmail.

Lenin, 115th Birth Anniv. A196

Design: 21cor, Lenin speaking to workers.

**1985, June** **Litho.** ***Perf. 12x12½***

**1462** A196 4cor multicolored .50 .25
**1463** A196 21cor multicolored 2.50 1.10

**Souvenir Sheet**

Argentina '85 — A197

**1985, June 5** **Litho.** ***Perf. 13***

**1464** A197 75cor multicolored 4.25 2.00

World Stamp Exposition.

Birds — A198

No. 1465, Ring-neck pheasant. No. 1466, Chicken. No. 1467, Guinea hen. No. 1468, Goose. No. 1469, Turkey. No. 1470, Duck.

**1985, Aug. 25**

**1465** A198 50c multi .25 .25
**1466** A198 50c multi .25 .25
**1467** A198 1cor multi .30 .25
**1468** A198 2cor multi .60 .25
**1469** A198 6cor multi 1.90 .60
**1470** A198 8cor multi 2.40 .80
*Nos. 1465-1470 (6)* 5.70 2.40

Intl. Music Year A199

No. 1471, Luis A. Delgadillo, vert. No. 1473, Parade. No. 1474, Managua Cathedral. No. 1475, Masked dancer. No. 1476, Parade, diff.

**1985, Sept. 1**

**1471** A199 1cor multicolored .25 .25
**1472** A199 1cor shown .25 .25
**1473** A199 9cor multicolored .90 .35
**1474** A199 9cor multicolored .90 .35
**1475** A199 15cor multicolored 1.40 .55
**1476** A199 21cor multicolored 1.90 .75
*Nos. 1471-1476 (6)* 5.60 2.50

Nos. 1473-1476 are airmail.

Natl. Fire Brigade, 6th Anniv. A200

No. 1477, Fire station. No. 1478, Fire truck. No. 1480, Ambulance. No. 1481, Airport fire truck. No. 1482, Waterfront fire. No. 1483, Hose team, fire.

**1985, Oct. 18**

**1477** A200 1cor multi .25 .25
**1478** A200 1cor multi .25 .25
**1479** A200 1cor shown .25 .25
**1480** A200 3cor multi .30 .25
**1481** A200 9cor multi .90 .30
**1482** A200 15cor multi 1.50 .50
**1483** A200 21cor multi 2.10 .75
*a.* Min. sheet of 7, #1474-1483 + 2 labels 5.50
*Nos. 1477-1483 (7)* 5.55 2.55

Stamps from No. 1483a have orange borders. Nos. 1480-1483 are airmail.

Halley's Comet — A201

No. 1484, Edmond Halley. No. 1485, Map of comet's track, 1910. No. 1486, Tycho Brahe's observatory. No. 1487, Astrolabe, map. No. 1488, Telescopes. No. 1489, Telescope designs.

**1985, Nov. 26**

**1484** A201 1cor multicolored .25 .25
**1485** A201 3cor multicolored .35 .25
**1486** A201 3cor multicolored .35 .25
**1487** A201 9cor multicolored .90 .25
**1488** A201 15cor multicolored 1.50 .40
**1489** A201 21cor multicolored 2.25 .60
*Nos. 1484-1489 (6)* 5.60 2.00

Nos. 1487-1489 are airmail.

Tapirus Bairdii A202

**1985, Dec. 30**

**1490** A202 1cor Eating .40 .25
**1491** A202 3cor Drinking .60 .25
**1492** A202 5cor Grazing in field 1.00 .25
**1493** A202 9cor With young 1.90 .45
*Nos. 1490-1493 (4)* 3.90 1.20

Nos. 1491-1493 are airmail.

Roses — A203

**1986, Jan. 15** ***Perf. 12½***

**1494** A203 1cor Spinosissima .25 .25
**1495** A203 1cor Canina .25 .25
**1496** A203 3cor Eglanteria .40 .25
**1497** A203 5cor Rubrifolia .40 .25
**1498** A203 9cor Foetida .40 .25
**1499** A203 100cor Rugosa 4.00 1.10
*Nos. 1494-1499 (6)* 5.70 2.35

Nos. 1497-1499 are airmail.

Birds — A204

No. 1500, Colibri topacio. No. 1501, Paraulata picodorado. No. 1502, Troupial. No. 1503, Vereron pintado. No. 1504, Tordo ruisenor. No. 1505, Buho real. No. 1506, Gran kiskadee.

**1986, Feb. 10** ***Perf. 13x12½***

**1500** A204 1cor multi .25 .25
**1501** A204 3cor multi .30 .25
**1502** A204 3cor multi .30 .25
**1503** A204 5cor multi .30 .25
**1504** A204 10cor multi .45 .25
**1505** A204 21cor multi .90 .25
**1506** A204 75cor multi 3.00 1.10
*Nos. 1500-1506 (7)* 5.50 2.60

Nos. 1504-1506 are airmail.

A205

World Cup Soccer Championships, Mexico: Soccer players and pre-Columbian artifacts. No. 1514, Player's foot, ball.

**1986, Mar. 20** *Perf. 12½*

**Shirt Colors**

| | | | | |
|---|---|---|---|---|
| **1507** | A205 | 1cor blue & yel | .25 | .25 |
| **1508** | A205 | 1cor yel & green | .25 | .25 |
| **1509** | A205 | 3cor blue & white | .25 | .25 |
| **1510** | A205 | 3cor red & white | .25 | .25 |
| **1511** | A205 | 5cor red | .25 | .25 |
| **1512** | A205 | 9cor blk & yel | .25 | .25 |
| **1513** | A205 | 100cor red & grn | 2.25 | 1.10 |
| | | *Nos. 1507-1513 (7)* | 3.75 | 2.60 |

**Souvenir Sheet**

*Perf. 13*

| | | | | |
|---|---|---|---|---|
| **1514** | A205 | 100cor multicolored | 2.50 | 1.25 |

Nos. 1509-1514 are airmail.

**Flower Type of 1983**

**1986, Mar.** **Litho.** *Perf. 12½*

| | | | | |
|---|---|---|---|---|
| **1515** | A151 | 5cor like #1209 | .35 | .25 |
| **1516** | A151 | 5cor like #1210 | .35 | .25 |
| **1517** | A151 | 5cor like #1211 | .35 | .25 |
| **1518** | A151 | 5cor like #1212 | .35 | .25 |
| **1519** | A151 | 5cor like #1213 | .35 | .25 |
| **1520** | A151 | 5cor like #1214 | .35 | .25 |
| **1521** | A151 | 5cor like #1215 | .35 | .25 |
| **1522** | A151 | 5cor like #1216 | .35 | .25 |
| **1523** | A151 | 5cor like #1217 | .35 | .25 |
| **1524** | A151 | 5cor like #1218 | .35 | .25 |
| **1525** | A151 | 5cor like #1219 | .35 | .25 |
| **1526** | A151 | 5cor like #1220 | .35 | .25 |
| **1527** | A151 | 5cor like #1221 | .35 | .25 |
| **1528** | A151 | 5cor like #1222 | .35 | .25 |
| **1529** | A151 | 5cor like #1223 | .35 | .25 |
| **1530** | A151 | 5cor like #1224 | .35 | .25 |
| | | *Nos. 1515-1530 (16)* | 5.60 | 4.00 |

**Agrarian Reform Type of 1983**

**1986, Apr. 15** *Perf. 12½*

| | | | | |
|---|---|---|---|---|
| **1531** | A168 | 1cor dk brown | .25 | .25 |
| **1532** | A168 | 9cor purple | .25 | .25 |
| **1533** | A168 | 15cor rose violet | .30 | .25 |
| **1534** | A168 | 21cor dk car rose | .45 | .25 |
| **1535** | A168 | 33cor orange | .75 | .35 |
| **1536** | A168 | 42cor green | .95 | .45 |
| **1537** | A168 | 50cor brown | 1.10 | .55 |
| **1538** | A168 | 100cor blue | 2.25 | 1.10 |
| | | *Nos. 1531-1538 (8)* | 6.30 | 3.45 |

Writers A207

No. 1539, Alfonso Cortes. No. 1540, Salomon de la Selva. No. 1541, Azarias H. Pallais. No. 1542, Ruben Dario. No. 1543, Pablo Neruda. No. 1544, Alfonso Reyes. No. 1545, Pedro Henriquez Urena.

**1986, Apr. 23** *Perf. 12½x13*

| | | | | |
|---|---|---|---|---|
| **1539** | A207 | 1cor multicolored | .25 | .25 |
| **1540** | A207 | 3cor multicolored | .25 | .25 |
| **1541** | A207 | 3cor multicolored | .25 | .25 |
| **1542** | A207 | 5cor multicolored | .25 | .25 |
| **1543** | A207 | 9cor multicolored | .30 | .25 |
| **1544** | A207 | 15cor multicolored | .45 | .25 |
| **1545** | A207 | 100cor multicolored | 3.50 | 1.10 |
| | | *Nos. 1539-1545 (7)* | 5.25 | 2.60 |

Nos. 1544-1545 are airmail.

Nuts & Fruits — A208

No. 1546, Maranon (cashew). No. 1547, Zapote. No. 1548, Pitahaya. No. 1549, Granadilla. No. 1550, Anona. No. 1551, Melocoton (starfruit). No. 1552, Mamey.

**1986, June 20** *Perf. 12x12½*

| | | | | |
|---|---|---|---|---|
| **1546** | A208 | 1cor multicolored | .25 | .25 |
| **1547** | A208 | 1cor multicolored | .25 | .25 |
| **1548** | A208 | 3cor multicolored | .30 | .25 |
| **1549** | A208 | 3cor multicolored | .30 | .25 |
| **1550** | A208 | 5cor multicolored | .30 | .25 |
| **1551** | A208 | 21cor multicolored | .75 | .25 |
| **1552** | A208 | 100cor multicolored | 3.25 | 1.10 |
| | | *Nos. 1546-1552 (7)* | 5.40 | 2.60 |

FAO, 40th Anniv. Nos. 1550-1552 are airmail.

Lockheed L-1011 Tristar — A209

Airplanes: No. 1554, YAK 40. No. 1555, BAC 1-11. No. 1556, Boeing 747. 9cor, A-300. 15cor, TU-154. No. 1559, Concorde, vert. No. 1560, Fairchild 340.

**1986, Aug. 22** *Perf. 12½*

| | | | | |
|---|---|---|---|---|
| **1553** | A209 | 1cor multicolored | .25 | .25 |
| **1554** | A209 | 1cor multicolored | .25 | .25 |
| **1555** | A209 | 3cor multicolored | .25 | .25 |
| **1556** | A209 | 3cor multicolored | .30 | .25 |
| **1557** | A209 | 9cor multicolored | .40 | .25 |
| **1558** | A209 | 15cor multicolored | .50 | .25 |
| **1559** | A209 | 100cor multicolored | 3.50 | 1.10 |
| | | *Nos. 1553-1559 (7)* | 5.45 | 2.60 |

**Souvenir Sheet**

*Perf. 13*

| | | | | |
|---|---|---|---|---|
| **1560** | A209 | 100cor multicolored | 3.75 | 3.75 |

Stockholmia '86. No. 1560 contains one 40x32mm stamp.

Nos. 1557-1560 airmail.

A210

A210a

Discovery of America, 500th Anniv. (in 1992) — A210b

No. 1561, 1 of Columbus' ships. No. 1562, 2 of Columbus' ships. No. 1563, Juan de la Cosa. No. 1564, Columbus. No. 1565, Ferdinand, Isabella. No. 1566, Columbus before throne.

**1986, Oct. 12** *Perf. 12½x12*

| | | | | |
|---|---|---|---|---|
| **1561** | A210 | 1cor multi | .25 | .25 |
| **1562** | A210 | 1cor multi | .25 | .25 |
| *a.* | | Pair, #1561-1562 | .25 | .25 |
| *b.* | | Souv. sheet of 2, #1561-1562 | .30 | .25 |

*Perf. 12x12½*

| | | | | |
|---|---|---|---|---|
| **1563** | A210a | 9cor multi | .30 | .25 |
| **1564** | A210a | 9cor multi | .30 | .25 |
| *a.* | | Pair, #1563-1564 | .65 | .25 |
| **1565** | A210b | 21cor multi | .80 | .25 |
| **1566** | A210b | 100cor multi | 3.50 | 1.10 |
| *a.* | | Pair, #1565-1566 | 4.50 | 1.40 |
| *b.* | | Souv. sheet of 4, #1563-1566 | 5.00 | 1.50 |
| | | *Nos. 1561-1566 (6)* | 5.40 | 2.35 |

Nos. 1563-1566 are airmail. Nos. 1564a, 1566a have continuous design.

Butterflies A211

No. 1567, Theritas coronata. No. 1568, Charayes nitebis. No. 1569, Salamis cacta. No. 1570, Papilio maacki. No. 1571, Euphaedro cyparissa. No. 1572, Palaeochrysophonus hippothoe. No. 1573, Ritra aurea.

**1986, Dec. 12** *Perf. 12½*

| | | | | |
|---|---|---|---|---|
| **1567** | A211 | 10cor multi | .45 | .25 |
| **1568** | A211 | 15cor multi | .70 | .25 |
| **1569** | A211 | 15cor multi | .70 | .25 |
| **1570** | A211 | 15cor multi | .70 | .25 |
| **1571** | A211 | 25cor multi | 1.10 | .30 |
| **1572** | A211 | 25cor multi | 1.10 | .30 |
| **1573** | A211 | 30cor multi | 1.50 | .35 |
| | | *Nos. 1567-1573 (7)* | 6.25 | 1.95 |

Nos. 1568-1573 are airmail.

Ruben Dario Order of Cultural Independence A212

Dario Order Winning Writers: No. 1574, Ernesto Mejia Sanchez. No. 1575, Fernando Gordillo C. No. 1576, Francisco Perez Estrada. 30cor, Julio Cortazar. 60cor, Enrique Fernandez Morales.

**1987, Jan. 18** **Litho.** *Perf. 13*

| | | | | |
|---|---|---|---|---|
| **1574** | A212 | 10cor multicolored | .25 | .25 |
| **1575** | A212 | 10cor multicolored | .25 | .25 |
| **1576** | A212 | 10cor multicolored | .25 | .25 |
| **1577** | A212 | 15cor multicolored | .30 | .25 |
| **1578** | A212 | 30cor multicolored | .65 | .30 |
| **1579** | A212 | 60cor multicolored | 1.25 | .65 |
| *a.* | | Strip of 6, #1574-1579 | 2.90 | 1.50 |
| *b.* | | Min. sheet of 6, #1574-1579 | 2.90 | 2.90 |

1988 Winter Olympics, Calgary — A213

#1580, Speed skating. #1581, Ice hockey. #1582, Women's figure skating. #1583, Ski jumping. 20cor, Biathalon. 30cor, Slalom skiing. 40cor, Downhill skiing. 110cor, Ice hockey, diff., horiz.

**1987, Feb. 3** *Perf. 13*

| | | | | |
|---|---|---|---|---|
| **1580** | A213 | 10cor multi | .45 | .25 |
| **1581** | A213 | 10cor multi | .45 | .25 |
| **1582** | A213 | 15cor multi | .60 | .25 |
| **1583** | A213 | 15cor multi | .60 | .25 |
| **1584** | A213 | 20cor multi | .75 | .25 |
| **1585** | A213 | 30cor multi | 1.10 | .30 |
| **1586** | A213 | 40cor multi | 1.75 | .40 |
| | | *Nos. 1580-1586 (7)* | 5.70 | 1.95 |

**Souvenir Sheet**

*Perf. 12½*

| | | | | |
|---|---|---|---|---|
| **1587** | A213 | 110cor multi | 3.75 | 3.75 |

Nos. 1582-1587 are airmail. No. 1587 contains one 40x32mm stamp.

Children's Welfare Campaign A214

No. 1588, Growth & development. No. 1589, Vaccination. No. 1590, Rehydration. No. 1591, Breastfeeding.

**1987, Mar. 18** *Perf. 13*

| | | | | |
|---|---|---|---|---|
| **1588** | A214 | 10cor multi | .25 | .25 |
| **1589** | A214 | 25cor multi | .90 | .30 |
| **1590** | A214 | 30cor multi | 1.50 | .35 |
| **1591** | A214 | 50cor multi | 5.00 | .60 |
| | | *Nos. 1588-1591 (4)* | 7.65 | 1.50 |

Nos. 1589-1591 are airmail. For surcharges, see Nos. 1674A-1674D.

**Flower Type of 1983**

No. 1592, Bixa orellana. No. 1593, Brassavola nodosa. No. 1594, Cattleya lueddemanniana. No. 1595, Cochlospermum spec. No. 1596, Hibiscus rosa-sinensis. No. 1597, Laelia spec. No. 1598, Malvaviscus arboreus. No. 1599, Neomarica coerulea. No. 1600, Plumeria rubra. No. 1601, Senecio spec. No. 1602, Sobralia macrantha. No. 1603, Stachytarpheta indica. No. 1604, Tabebula ochraceae. No. 1605, Tagetes erecta. No. 1606, Tecoma stans. No. 1607, Thumbergia alata.

**1987, Mar. 25** *Perf. 12½*

| | | | | |
|---|---|---|---|---|
| **1592** | A151 | 10cor black | .35 | .25 |
| **1593** | A151 | 10cor olive green | .35 | .25 |
| **1594** | A151 | 10cor olive grey | .35 | .25 |
| **1595** | A151 | 10cor apple green | .35 | .25 |
| **1596** | A151 | 10cor brown rose | .35 | .25 |
| **1597** | A151 | 10cor deep magenta | .35 | .25 |
| **1598** | A151 | 10cor blue green | .35 | .25 |
| **1599** | A151 | 10cor ultramarine | .35 | .25 |
| **1600** | A151 | 10cor dull vermilion | .35 | .25 |
| **1601** | A151 | 10cor brown ochre | .35 | .25 |
| **1602** | A151 | 10cor deep purple | .35 | .25 |
| **1603** | A151 | 10cor light blue | .35 | .25 |
| **1604** | A151 | 10cor bluish violet | .35 | .25 |
| **1605** | A151 | 10cor orange yellow | .35 | .25 |
| **1606** | A151 | 10cor bright magenta | .35 | .25 |
| **1607** | A151 | 10cor dp turq grn | .35 | .25 |
| | | *Nos. 1592-1607 (16)* | 5.60 | 4.00 |

**Agrarian Reform Type of 1983 Inscribed "1987"**

Designs: No. 1608, Tobacco. No. 1609, Cotton. 15cor, Corn. 25cor, Sugar. 30cor, Cattle. 50cor, Coffee Beans. 60cor, Rice. 100cor, Bananas.

**1987, Mar. 25** *Perf. 12½*

| | | | | |
|---|---|---|---|---|
| **1608** | A168 | 10cor dk brown | .30 | .25 |
| **1609** | A168 | 10cor purple | .30 | .25 |
| **1610** | A168 | 15cor rose violet | .45 | .25 |
| **1611** | A168 | 25cor dk car rose | .70 | .35 |
| **1612** | A168 | 30cor orange | .85 | .45 |
| **1613** | A168 | 50cor brown | 1.40 | .65 |
| **1614** | A168 | 60cor green | 1.75 | .90 |
| **1615** | A168 | 100cor blue | 2.75 | 1.40 |
| | | *Nos. 1608-1615 (8)* | 8.50 | 4.50 |

77th Interparliamentary Conf., Managua — A215

**1987, Apr. 27**

| | | | | |
|---|---|---|---|---|
| **1616** | A215 | 10cor multicolored | .25 | .25 |

Prehistoric Creatures — A216

**1987, May 25** *Perf. 13*
**1617** A216 10cor Mammoth .35 .25
**1618** A216 10cor Dimetrodon .35 .25
**1619** A216 10cor Triceratops .35 .25
**1620** A216 15cor Dinichthys .60 .25
**1621** A216 15cor Uintaterium .60 .25
**1622** A216 30cor Pteranodon 1.25 .25
**1623** A216 40cor Tilosaurus 1.75 .30
*Nos. 1617-1623 (7)* 5.25 1.80

Nos. 1620-1623 are airmail.

CAPEX '87 — A217

Various tennis players in action: No. 1624, Male player. No. 1625, Female player serving. No. 1626, Male player at net. No. 1627, Female player at line, racquet at left side. No. 1628, Female player, racquet behind her ready to hit ball. No. 1629, Female player, both hands on racquet above head. No. 1630, Male player, one hand hold racquet above head.
No. 1631, Doubles partners, vert.

**1987, June 2** *Perf. 13*
**1624** A217 10cor multi .30 .25
**1625** A217 10cor multi .30 .25
**1626** A217 15cor multi .60 .25
**1627** A217 15cor multi .60 .25
**1628** A217 20cor multi .70 .25
**1629** A217 30cor multi 1.25 .30
**1630** A217 40cor multi 1.90 .40
*Nos. 1624-1630 (7)* 5.65 1.95

**Souvenir Sheet**
*Perf. 12½*
**1631** A217 110cor multi 3.75 3.75

Nos. 1626-1631 are airmail. No. 1631 contains one 32x40mm stamp.

Dogs — A218

No. 1632, Doberman pinscher. No. 1633, Bull Mastiff. No. 1634, Japanese Spaniel. No. 1635, Keeshond. No. 1636, Chihuahua. No. 1637, St. Bernard. No. 1638, West Gotha spitz.

**1987, June 25** *Perf. 13*
**1632** A218 10cor multicolored .25 .25
**1633** A218 10cor multicolored .25 .25
**1634** A218 15cor multicolored .60 .25
**1635** A218 15cor multicolored .60 .25
**1636** A218 20cor multicolored .80 .25
**1637** A218 30cor multicolored 1.25 .30
**1638** A218 40cor multicolored 1.75 .40
*Nos. 1632-1638 (7)* 5.50 1.95

Nos. 1634-1638 are airmail.

Cacti A219

No. 1639, Lophocereus schottii. No. 1640, Opuntia acanthocarpa. No. 1641, Echinocereus engelmanii. No. 1642, Lemaireocereus thurberi. No. 1643, Saguaros. No. 1644, Opuntia fulgida. No. 1645, Opuntia ficus.

**1987, July 25** *Perf. 12½*
**1639** A219 10cor multicolored .30 .25
**1640** A219 10cor multicolored .30 .25
**1641** A219 10cor multicolored .30 .25
**1642** A219 20cor multicolored .80 .25
**1643** A219 20cor multicolored .80 .25
**1644** A219 30cor multicolored 1.25 .30
**1645** A219 50cor multicolored 2.00 .50
*Nos. 1639-1645 (7)* 5.75 2.05

Nos. 1642-1645 are airmail.

10th Pan American Games, Indianapolis — A220

No. 1646, High jump. No. 1647, Volleyball. No. 1648, Sprinter. No. 1649, Gymnastics. No. 1650, Baseball. No. 1651, Synchronized swimming. No. 1652, Weightlifting.
110cor, Rhythmic gymnastics.

**1987, Aug. 7** *Perf. 13*
**1646** A220 10cor multi .30 .25
**1647** A220 10cor multi .30 .25
**1648** A220 15cor multi .55 .25
**1649** A220 15cor multi .55 .25
**1650** A220 20cor multi .70 .30
**1651** A220 30cor multi 1.10 .45
**1652** A220 40cor multi 1.50 .60
*Nos. 1646-1652 (7)* 5.00 2.35

**Souvenir Sheet**
**1653** A220 110cor multi 3.50 3.50

Nos. 1648-1653 are airmail. No. 1653 contains one 32x40mm stamp. Nos. 1651-1653 are vert.

Satellites A221

**1987, Oct. 4**
**1654** A221 10cor Sputnik .30 .25
**1655** A221 10cor Cosmos .30 .25
**1656** A221 15cor Proton .50 .25
**1657** A221 25cor Meteor .90 .25
**1658** A221 25cor Luna .90 .25
**1659** A221 30cor Electron 1.00 .30
**1660** A221 50cor Mars 1 1.60 .50
*Nos. 1654-1660 (7)* 5.50 2.05

Cosmonauts' Day. Nos. 1656-1660 are airmail.

Fish A222

Designs: No. 1661, Tarpon atlanticus. No. 1662, Cichlasoma managuense. No. 1663, Atractoteus tropicus. No. 1664, Astyana fasciatus. No. 1665, Cichlasoma citrimellum. 20cor, Cichlosoma dowi. 50cor, Caracharhinus nicaraguensis.

**1987, Oct. 18** *Perf. 12½*
**1661** A222 10cor multicolored .35 .25
**1662** A222 10cor multicolored .35 .25
**1663** A222 10cor multicolored .35 .25
**1664** A222 15cor multicolored .60 .25
**1665** A222 15cor multicolored .60 .25
**1666** A222 20cor multicolored .80 .25
**1667** A222 50cor multicolored 2.00 .50
*Nos. 1661-1667 (7)* 5.05 2.00

Nos. 1663-1667 are airmail.

October Revolution, 70th Anniv. — A223

Designs: 30cor, Cruiser Aurora, horiz. 50cor, USSR natl. arms.

**1987, Nov. 7** *Perf. 13*
**1668** A223 10cor multicolored .25 .25
**1669** A223 30cor multicolored .60 .35
**1670** A223 50cor multicolored 1.00 .60
*Nos. 1668-1670 (3)* 1.85 1.20

Nos. 1669-1670 are airmail.

Christmas Paintings by L. Saenz — A224

10cor, Nativity. 20cor, Adoration of the Magi. 25cor, Adoration of the Magi, diff. 50cor, Nativity, diff.

**1987, Nov. 15** *Perf. 13*
**1671** A224 10cor multicolored .25 .25
**1672** A224 20cor multicolored .35 .25
**1673** A224 25cor multicolored .40 .25
**1674** A224 50cor multicolored .80 .40
*Nos. 1671-1674 (4)* 1.80 1.15

Nos. 1588-1591 Surcharged

**Methods and Perfs As Before**
**1987, Dec. 26**
**1674A** A214 400cor on 10cor #1588 — 5.00
**1674B** A214 600cor on 50cor #1591 — —
**1674C** A214 1000cor on 25cor #1589 — —
**1674D** A214 5000cor on 30cor #1590 — —
Nos. 1674A-1674D (4) *30.00*

1988 Winter Olymmpics, Calgary — A225

No. 1675, Biathlon. No. 1676, Cross-country skiing, vert. No. 1677, Hockey, vert. No. 1678, Women's figure skating, vert. No. 1679, Slalom skiing, vert. No. 1680, Ski jumping. No. 1681, Men's downhill skiing, vert.
No. 1682, Pairs figure skating.

**1988, Jan. 30** **Litho.** *Perf. 12½*
**1675** A225 10cor multicolored .25 .25
**1676** A225 10cor multicolored .25 .25
**1677** A225 15cor multicolored .50 .25
**1678** A225 20cor multicolored .75 .25
**1679** A225 25cor multicolored 1.00 .30
**1680** A225 30cor multicolored 1.10 .40
**1681** A225 40cor multicolored 1.50 .50
*Nos. 1675-1681 (7)* 5.35 2.20

**Souvenir Sheet**
*Perf. 13*
**1682** A225 100cor multicolored 3.75 3.75

Nos. 1675-1681 printed with se-tenant label showing Canadian flag and wildlife.
No. 1682 contains one 40x32mm stamp.

Nicaraguan Journalists Assoc., 10th Anniv. — A226

Design: 5cor, Churches of St. Francis Xavier and Fatima, and speaker addressing journalists, horiz.

**1988, Feb. 10**
**1683** A226 1cor shown .25 .25
**1684** A226 5cor multicolored .75 .40

No. 1684 is airmail.

1988 Summer Olympics, Seoul — A227

**1988, Feb. 28**
**1685** A227 10cor Gymnastics .25 .25
**1686** A227 10cor Basketball .25 .25
**1687** A227 15cor Volleyball .50 .25
**1688** A227 20cor Long jump .75 .25
**1689** A227 25cor Soccer 1.00 .25
**1690** A227 30cor Water polo 1.10 .40
**1691** A227 40cor Boxing 1.75 .55
*Nos. 1685-1691 (7)* 5.60 2.20

**Souvenir Sheet**
**1692** A227 100cor Baseball 3.75 3.75

No. 1692 contains one 40x32mm stamp.

European Soccer Championships, Essen — A228

Designs: Various soccer players in action.

**1988, Apr. 14** *Perf. 13x12½, 12½x13*
**1693** A228 50c multicolored .35 .25
**1694** A228 1cor multicolored .35 .25
**1695** A228 2cor multi, vert. .40 .25
**1696** A228 3cor multi, vert. .70 .25
**1697** A228 4cor multi, vert. .95 .25
**1698** A228 5cor multi, vert. 1.25 .35
**1699** A228 6cor multicolored 1.50 .40
*Nos. 1693-1699 (7)* 5.50 2.00

**Souvenir Sheet**
*Perf. 13*
**1700** A228 15cor multi, vert. 3.75 3.75

Nos. 1695-1700 are airmail. No. 1700 contains one 32x40mm stamp.

Sandinista Revolution, 9th Anniv. — A229

**1988, July 19** *Perf. 13*

**1701** A229 1cor shown .25 .25
**1702** A229 5cor Volcanoes, dove .60 .30

No. 1702 is airmail.

Animals — A230

10c, Bear, cub. 15c, Lion, cubs. 25c, Spaniel, pups. 50c, Wild boars. 4cor, Cheetah, cubs. 7cor, Hyenas. 8cor, Fox, kit.
15cor, House cat, kittens, vert.

**1988, Mar. 3** *Perf. 13x12½*

**1703** A230 10c multi .25 .25
**1704** A230 15c multi .25 .25
**1705** A230 25c multi .25 .25
**1706** A230 50c multi .25 .25
**1707** A230 4cor multi 1.10 .35
**1708** A230 7cor multi 1.60 .70
**1709** A230 8cor multi 2.00 .80
*Nos. 1703-1709 (7)* 5.70 2.85

**Souvenir Sheet**

*Perf. 12½*

**1710** A230 15cor multi 3.75 3.75

Nos. 1707-1710 are airmail. No. 1710 contains one 32x40mm stamp.

Helicopters — A231

**1988, June 1** *Perf. 12½x12*

**1711** A231 4cor B-206B-JRIII .25 .25
**1712** A231 12cor BK-117A-3 .25 .25
**1713** A231 16cor B-360 .50 .25
**1714** A231 20cor 109-MRII .60 .25
**1715** A231 24cor S-61 .80 .25
**1716** A231 28cor SA-365N-D2 .90 .25
**1717** A231 56cor S-76 1.75 .50
*Nos. 1711-1717 (7)* 5.05 2.00

**Souvenir Sheet**

*Perf. 13*

**1718** A231 120cor NH-90 3.75 3.75

Nos. 1712-1718 are airmail. No. 1718 contains one 40x32mm stamp.

Shells — A232

4cor, Strombus pugilis. 12cor, Polymita picta. 16cor, Architectonica maximum. 20cor, Pectens laqueatus. 24cor, Guildfordia triumphans. 28cor, Ranella pustulosa. 50cor, Trochus maculatus.

**1988, Sept. 20** *Perf. 13*

**1719** A232 4cor multicolored .25 .25
**1720** A232 12cor multicolored .30 .25
**1721** A232 16cor multicolored .50 .25
**1722** A232 20cor multicolored .70 .25
**1723** A232 24cor multicolored .90 .25
**1724** A232 28cor multicolored .95 .30
**1725** A232 50cor multicolored 1.75 .50
*Nos. 1719-1725 (7)* 5.35 2.05

Nos. 1720-1725 are airmail.

Insects — A233

4cor, Chrysina macropus. 12cor, Plusiotis victoriana. 16cor, Ceratotrupes bolivari. 20cor, Gymnetosoma stellata. 24cor, Euphoria lineoligera. 28cor, Euphoria candezei. 50cor, Sulcophanaeus chryseicollis.

**1988, Nov. 10**

**1726** A233 4cor multicolored .25 .25
**1727** A233 12cor multicolored .40 .25
**1728** A233 16cor multicolored .55 .25
**1729** A233 20cor multicolored .80 .25
**1730** A233 24cor multicolored .95 .25
**1731** A233 28cor multicolored 1.05 .30
**1732** A233 50cor multicolored 1.75 .50
*Nos. 1726-1732 (7)* 5.75 2.05

Nos. 1727-1732 are airmail.

Heroes of the Revolution — A234

Designs: 4cor, Casimiro Sotelo Montenegro. 12cor, Ricardo Morales Aviles. 16cor, Silvio Mayorga Delgado. 20cor, Pedro Arauz Palacios. 24cor, Oscar A. Turcios Chavarrias. 28cor, Julio C. Buitrago Urroz. 50cor, Jose B. Escobar Perez. 100cor, Eduardo E. Contreras Escobar.

**1988, Aug. 27** *Perf. 12½x12*

**1733** A234 4cor sky blue .25 .25
**1734** A234 12cor red lilac .25 .25
**1735** A234 16cor yel grn .30 .25
**1736** A234 20cor org brown .40 .25
**1737** A234 24cor brown .45 .25
**1738** A234 28cor purple .55 .30
**1739** A234 50cor henna brn .95 .50
**1740** A234 100cor plum 1.90 .95
*Nos. 1733-1740 (8)* 5.05 3.00

Nos. 1734-1740 are airmail.

Flowers — A235

Designs: 4cor, Acacia baileyana. 12cor, Anigozanthos manglesii. 16cor, Telopia speciosissima. 20cor, Eucalyptus ficifolia. 24cor, Boronia heterophylla. 28cor, Callistemon speciosus. 30cor, Nymphaea caerulea, horiz. 50cor, Clianthus formosus.

**1988, Aug. 30** *Perf. 13*

**1741** A235 4cor multicolored .25 .25
**1742** A235 12cor multicolored .35 .25
**1743** A235 16cor multicolored .45 .25
**1744** A235 20cor multicolored .60 .25
**1745** A235 24cor multicolored .70 .25
**1746** A235 28cor multicolored .80 .50
**1747** A235 30cor multicolored .90 .30
**1748** A235 50cor multicolored 1.50 .45
*Nos. 1741-1748 (8)* 5.55 2.50

Nos. 1742-1748 are airmail.

Pre-Columbian Art — A236

Designs: 4cor, Zapotec funeral urn. 12cor, Mochica ceramic kneeling man. 16cor, Mochica ceramic head. 20cor, Taina ceramic vase. 28cor, Nazca cup, horiz. 100cor, Inca pipe, horiz. 120cor, Aztec ceramic vessel, horiz.

**1988, Oct. 12** *Perf. 12x12½, 12½x12*

**1749** A236 4cor multi + label .25 .25
**1750** A236 12cor multi + label .35 .25
**1751** A236 16cor multi + label .45 .25
**1752** A236 20cor multi + label .60 .25
**1753** A236 28cor multi + label .80 .30
**1754** A236 100cor multi + label 2.75 1.00
*Nos. 1749-1754 (6)* 5.20 2.30

**Souvenir Sheet**

*Perf. 13x13½*

**1755** A236 120cor multicolored 3.75 3.75

Discovery of America, 500th anniv. (in 1992). Nos. 1750-1755 are airmail. No. 1755 contains one 40x32mm stamp.

Publication of Blue, by Ruben Dario, Cent. — A237

**1988, Oct. 12** *Perf. 12x12½*

**1756** A237 25cor multi + label .45 .25

No. 1756 is airmail.

Tourism — A238

4cor, Pochomil. 12cor, Granada. 20cor, Olof Palme Convention Center. 24cor, Masaya Volcano Natl. Park. 28cor, La Boquita. 30cor, Xiloa. 50cor, Hotels of Managua.
160cor, Montelimar.

**1989, Feb. 5** *Perf. 12½x12*

**1757** A238 4cor multicolored .25 .25
**1758** A238 12cor multicolored .35 .25
**1759** A238 20cor multicolored .65 .25
**1760** A238 24cor multicolored .70 .25
**1761** A238 28cor multicolored .90 .25
**1762** A238 30cor multicolored .95 .25
**1763** A238 50cor multicolored 1.75 .45
*Nos. 1757-1763 (7)* 5.55 1.95

**Souvenir Sheet**

*Perf. 13*

**1764** A238 160cor multicolored 3.75 3.75

Nos. 1758-1764 are airmail. No. 1764 contains one 40x32mm stamp.

French Revolution, Bicentennial — A240

Designs: 50cor, Procession of the Estates General, Versailles. 300cor, Oath of the Tennis Court. 600cor, 14th of July, vert. 1000cor, Dancing Around the Liberty Tree. 2000cor, Liberty Guiding the People, vert. 3000cor, Storming the Bastille. 5000cor, Lafayette Swearing Allegiance to the Constitution, vert. 9000cor, La Marsiellaise, vert.

***Perf. 12½x13 (50cor), 13x12½ (600, 2000cor), 12½***

**1989, July 14**

**Sizes: 50cor, 40x25mm**

**600cor, 2000cor, 33x44mm**

**1773** A240 50cor multicolored .25 .25
**1774** A240 300cor shown .25 .25
**1775** A240 600cor multicolored .30 .25
**1776** A240 1000cor multicolored .45 .25
**1777** A240 2000cor multicolored .80 .30
**1778** A240 3000cor multicolored 1.40 .40
**1779** A240 5000cor multicolored 2.10 .65
*Nos. 1773-1779 (7)* 5.55 2.35

**Souvenir Sheet**

*Perf. 12½*

**1780** A240 9000cor multicolored 4.50 4.50

Philexfrance '89. #1774-1780 are airmail. #1780 contains one 32x40mm stamp.

Currency Reform

Currency reform took place Mar. 4, 1990. Until stamps in the new currency were issued, mail was to be handstamped "Franqueo Pagado," (Postage Paid). Stamps were not used again until Apr. 25, 1991. The following four sets and one airmail set were sold by the post office but were not valid for postage.

Ships

Stamp World London '90: 500cor, Director. 1000cor, Independence. 3000cor, Orizaba. 5000cor, SS Lewis. 10,000cor, Golden Rule. 30,000cor, Santiago de Cuba. 75,000cor, Bahia de Corinto. 100,000cor, North Star.

**1990, Apr. 3** *Perf. 12½x12*

Set of 7 5.50

**Souvenir Sheet**

*Perf. 12½*

75,000cor 4.25

World Cup Soccer Championships, Italy

Designs: Various soccer players in action.

**1990, Apr. 30** *Perf. 13*

Set of 7 5.50

**Souvenir Sheet**

*Perf. 12½*

75,000cor 4.00

1992 Winter Olympics, Albertville

Designs: 500cor, Ski jumping. 1000cor, Downhill skiing. 3000cor, Figure skating, vert. 5000cor, Speed skating, vert. 10,000cor, Biathlon, vert. 30,000cor, Cross country skiing, vert. 75,000cor, Two-man bobsled, vert. 100,000cor, Ice hockey, vert.

**1990, July 25** *Perf. 13*
Set of 7 5.50

### Souvenir Sheet
*Perf. 12½*

75,000cor 4.00

1992 Summer Olympics, Barcelona

Designs: 500cor, Javelin. 1000cor, Steeplechase. 3000cor, Handball. 5000cor, Basketball. 10,000cor, Gymnastics. 30,000cor, Cycling. 75,000cor, Soccer. 100,000cor, Boxing, horiz.

**1990, Aug. 10** *Perf. 13*
Set of 7 5.50

### Souvenir Sheet

75,000cor 4.00

Birds A245

Designs: No. 1813, Apteryx owenii. No. 1814, Notornis mantelli. 10c, Cyanoramphus novaezelandiae. 20c, Gallirallus australis. 30c, Rhynochetos jubatus, vert. 60c, Nestor notabilis. 70c, Strigops habroptilus. 1.50cor, Cygnus atratus.

**1990, Aug. 14** **Litho.** *Perf. 12½*
**1813** A245 5c multicolored .25 .25
**1814** A245 5c multicolored .25 .25
**1815** A245 10c multicolored .25 .25
**1816** A245 20c multicolored .50 .25
**1817** A245 30c multicolored .85 .30
**1818** A245 60c multicolored 1.75 .65
**1819** A245 70c multicolored 2.00 .75
*Nos. 1813-1819 (7)* 5.85 2.70

### Souvenir Sheet

**1820** A245 1.50cor multicolored 4.00 3.75

New Zealand '90, Intl. Philatelic Exhibition.

Fauna A246

No. 1821, Panthera onca. No. 1822, Felis pardalis, vert. No. 1823, Atelles geoffrogi, vert. No. 1824, Tapirus bairdi. No. 1825, Dasypus novencintus. No. 1826, Canis latrans. No. 1827, Choloepus hoffmanni.

**1990, Oct. 10**
**1821** A246 5c multicolored .25 .25
**1822** A246 5c multicolored .25 .25
**1823** A246 10c multicolored .25 .25
**1824** A246 20c multicolored .50 .25
**1825** A246 30c multicolored .85 .30
**1826** A246 60c multicolored 1.60 .65
**1827** A246 70c multicolored 2.00 .75
*Nos. 1821-1827 (7)* 5.70 2.70

FAO, 45th anniv.

### Flower Type of 1983 Redrawn Without Date

**1991, Apr. 24** **Litho.** *Perf. 14x13½*
**Size: 19x22mm**
**1828** A151 1cor like #1220 .40 .25
**1829** A151 2cor like #1212 .80 .25
**1830** A151 3cor like #1218 1.25 .25
**1831** A151 4cor like #1219 1.60 .25
**1832** A151 5cor like #1217 2.00 .25
**1833** A151 6cor like #1210 2.40 .25
**1834** A151 7cor like #1216 2.75 .25
**1835** A151 8cor like #1215 3.25 .25
**1836** A151 9cor like #1211 3.50 .25
**1837** A151 10cor like #1221 4.00 .25
**1838** A151 11cor like #1214 4.50 .25
**1839** A151 12cor like #1222 4.75 .25
**1840** A151 13cor like #1213 5.25 .25
**1841** A151 14cor like #1224 5.50 .25
**1842** A151 15cor like #1223 6.00 .25
**1843** A151 16cor like #1209 6.50 .25
*Nos. 1828-1843 (16)* 54.45 4.00

Dr. Pedro Joaquin Chamorro — A247

**1991, Apr. 25** *Perf. 14½x14*
**1844** A247 2.25cor multicolored .95 .45

1990 World Cup Soccer Championships, Italy — A248

Designs: No. 1845, Two players. No. 1846, Four players, vert. 50c, Two players, referee. 1cor, Germany, five players, vert. 1.50cor, One player, vert. 3cor, Argentina, five players, vert. 3.50cor, Italian players. 7.50cor, German team with trophy.

**1991, July 16** *Perf. 14x14½, 14½x14*
**1845** A248 25c multicolored .25 .25
**1846** A248 25c multicolored .25 .25
**1847** A248 50c multicolored .25 .25
**1848** A248 1cor multicolored .40 .25
**1849** A248 1.50cor multicolored .60 .30
**1850** A248 3cor multicolored 1.25 .60
**1851** A248 3.50cor multicolored 1.40 .70
*Nos. 1845-1851 (7)* 4.40 2.60

### Souvenir Sheet

**1852** A248 7.50cor multicolored 3.00 1.50
*a.* Overprinted in sheet margin ('93) 3.25 1.60

No. 1852a overprint reads "COPA DE FOOTBALL / U.S.A. '94."

Butterflies — A249

Designs: No. 1853, Prepona praeneste. No. 1854, Anartia fatima. 50c, Eryphanis aesacus. 1cor, Heliconius melpomene. 1.50cor, Chlosyne janais. 3cor, Marpesia iole. 3.50cor, Metamorpha epaphus. 7.50cor, Morpho peleides.

**1991, July 16** *Perf. 14½x14*
**1853** A249 25c multicolored .25 .25
**1854** A249 25c multicolored .25 .25
**1855** A249 50c multicolored .25 .25
**1856** A249 1cor multicolored .40 .25
**1857** A249 1.50cor multicolored .60 .30
**1858** A249 3cor multicolored 1.25 .60
**1859** A249 3.50cor multicolored 1.40 .70
*Nos. 1853-1859 (7)* 4.40 2.60

### Souvenir Sheet

**1860** A249 7.50cor multicolored 3.00 1.50

Fauna of Rainforest — A250

No. 1861 a, Yellow-headed amazon. b, Toucan. c, Scarlet macaw (lapa roja). d, Quetzal. e, Spider monkey (mono arana). f, Capuchin monkey. g, Sloth (cucala). h, Oropendola. i, Violet sabrewing (colibri violeta). j, Tamandua. k, Jaguarundi. l, Boa constrictor. m, Iguana. n, Jaguar. o, White-necked jacobin. p, Doxocopa clothilda. q, Dismorphia deione. r, Golden arrow-poison frog (rana venenosa). s, Callithomia hezia. t, Chameleon.

**1991, Aug. 7** **Litho.** *Perf. 14x14½*
**1861** A250 2.25cor Sheet of 20, #a.-t. 24.00 12.00

America Issue — A251

2.25cor, Concepcion volcano.

**1990, Oct. 12** *Perf. 14½x14*
**1862** A251 2.25cor multi 2.00 .55

Orchids A252

Designs: No. 1863, Isochilus major. No. 1864, Cycnoches ventricosum. 50c, Vanilla odorata. 1cor, Helleriella nicaraguensis. 1.50cor, Barkeria spectabilis. 3cor, Maxillaria hedwigae. 3.50cor, Cattleya aurantiaca. 7.50cor, Psygmorchis pusilla, vert.

**1991** **Litho.** *Perf. 14x14½*
**1863** A252 25c multicolored .25 .25
**1864** A252 25c multicolored .25 .25
**1865** A252 50c multicolored .25 .25
**1866** A252 1cor multicolored .35 .25
**1867** A252 1.50cor multicolored .60 .25
**1868** A252 3cor multicolored 1.10 .50
**1869** A252 3.50cor multicolored 1.40 .55
*Nos. 1863-1869 (7)* 4.20 2.30

### Souvenir Sheet
*Perf. 14½x14*

**1870** A252 7.50cor multicolored 3.00 1.50

Locomotives of South America — A253

Various steam locomotives.

**1991, Apr. 21** *Perf. 14½x14*
**1871** A253 25c Bolivia .25 .25
**1872** A253 25c Peru .25 .25
**1873** A253 50c Argentina .25 .25
**1874** A253 1.50cor Chile .60 .25
**1875** A253 2cor Colombia .80 .30
**1876** A253 3cor Brazil 1.10 .50
**1877** A253 3.50cor Paraguay 1.30 .55
*Nos. 1871-1877 (7)* 4.55 2.35

### Souvenir Sheets

**1878** A253 7.50cor Nicaragua 3.50 3.00
**1879** A253 7.50cor Guatemala 3.50 3.00

Birds — A254

Designs: 50c, Eumomota supercilliosa. 75c, Trogon collaris. 1cor, Electron platyrhynchum. 1.50cor, Teleonema filicauda. 1.75cor, Tangara chilensis, horiz. No. 1885, Pharomachrus mocino. No. 1886, Phlegopsis nigromaculata. No. 1887, Hylophylax naevioides, horiz. No. 1888, Aulacorhynchus haematopygius, horiz.

**1991** *Perf. 14½x14, 14x14½*
**1880** A254 50c multicolored .25 .25
**1881** A254 75c multicolored .30 .25
**1882** A254 1cor multicolored .40 .25
**1883** A254 1.50cor multicolored .65 .25
**1884** A254 1.75cor multicolored .70 .30
**1885** A254 2.25cor multicolored 1.00 .35
**1886** A254 2.25cor multicolored 1.00 .35
*Nos. 1880-1886 (7)* 4.30 2.00

### Souvenir Sheets

**1887** A254 7.50cor multicolored 3.00 3.00
**1888** A254 7.50cor multicolored 3.00 3.00

Paintings by Vincent Van Gogh A255

Designs: No. 1889, Head of a Peasant Woman Wearing a Bonnet. No. 1890, One-Eyed Man. 50c, Self-Portrait. 1cor, Vase with Carnations and Other Flowers. 1.50cor, Vase with Zinnias and Geraniums. 3cor, Portrait of Pere Tanguy. 3.50cor, Portrait of a Man, horiz. 7.50cor, Path Lined with Poplars, horiz.

**1991** *Perf. 14x13½, 13½x14*
**1889** A255 25c multicolored .25 .25
**1890** A255 25c multicolored .25 .25
**1891** A255 50c multicolored .30 .25
**1892** A255 1cor multicolored .40 .25
**1893** A255 1.50cor multicolored .65 .25
**1894** A255 3cor multicolored 1.20 .50
**1895** A255 3.50cor multicolored 1.60 .55
*Nos. 1889-1895 (7)* 4.65 2.30

**Size: 128x102mm**
*Imperf*

**1896** A255 7.50cor multicolored 2.50 1.25

Phila Nippon '91 A256

Designs: 25c, Golden Hall. 50c, Phoenix Hall. 1cor, Bunraku puppet head. 1.50cor, Japanese cranes. 2.50cor, Himeji Castle. 3cor, Statue of the Guardian. 3.50cor, Kabuki warrior. 7.50cor, Vase.

**1991** *Perf. 14x14½*
**1897** A256 25c multicolored .25 .25
**1898** A256 50c multicolored .25 .25
**1899** A256 1cor multicolored .45 .25
**1900** A256 1.50cor multicolored .65 .25
**1901** A256 2.50cor multicolored 1.00 .40

**1902** A256 3cor multicolored 1.25 .50
**1903** A256 3.50cor multicolored 1.40 .55
*Nos. 1897-1903 (7)* 5.25 2.45

**Souvenir Sheet**

**1904** A256 7.50cor multicolored 3.00 3.00

Inscriptions are switched on 50c and 2.50cor.

Child's Drawing A257

**1991**

**1905** A257 2.25cor multicolored 1.10 .45

Central American Bank of Economic Integration, 30th Anniv. — A258

**1991, Aug. 1 Litho. *Perf. 14***

**1906** A258 1.50cor multicolored 1.05 .50

No. 1906 printed with se-tenant label.

Discovery of America, 500th Anniv. (in 1992) — A259

**1991, Oct. 12 *Perf. 14½x14***

**1907** A259 2.25cor Columbus' fleet 1.05 .75

Swiss Confederation, 700th Anniv. (in 1991) — A260

**1992, Aug. 1 Litho. *Perf. 14x14½***

**1908** A260 2.25cor black & red 1.80 .75

Contemporary Art — A261

Designs: No. 1909, Pitcher, by Jose Ortiz. No. 1910, Black jar, by Lorenza Pineda Cooperative, vert. 50c, Vase, by Elio Gutierrez, vert. 1cor, Christ on Cross, by Jose de Los Santos, vert. 1.50cor, Sculpture of family, by Erasmo Moya, vert. 3cor, Bird and fish, by Silvio Chavarria Cooperative. 3.50cor, Filigree jar, by Maria de Los Angeles Bermudez, vert. 7.50cor, Masks by Jose Flores.

***Perf. 14x14½, 14½x14***

**1992, Sept. 17 Litho.**

**1909** A261 25c multicolored .25 .25
**1910** A261 25c multicolored .25 .25
**1911** A261 50c multicolored .25 .25
**1912** A261 1cor multicolored .45 .25
**1913** A261 1.50cor multicolored .65 .30
**1914** A261 3cor multicolored 1.25 .65
**1915** A261 3.50cor multicolored 1.50 .75
*Nos. 1909-1915 (7)* 4.60 2.70

***Imperf***

**Size: 100x70mm**

**1916** A261 7.50cor multicolored 3.25 1.60

**Miniature Sheet**

Fauna and Flora of Rainforest — A262

No. 1917: a, Colibri magnifico (b). b, Aguila arpia (f). c, Orchids. d, Toucan, Mariposa morpho. e, Quetzal (i). f, Guardabarranco (g, k). g, Mono aullador (howler monkey). h, Perezoso (sloth). i, Mono ardilla (squirrel monkey). j, Guacamaya (macaw) (n). k, Boa esmeralda, Tanagra escarlata (emerald boa, scarlet tanager). l, Rana flecha venenosa (arrow frog). m, Jaguar. n, Oso hormiguero (anteater) (o). o, Ocelot. p, Coati.

**1992, Nov. 12 *Perf. 14½x14***

**1917** A262 1.50cor Sheet of 16, #a.-p. 12.00 6.00

1992 Winter Olympics, Albertville A263

No. 1918, Ice hockey. No. 1919, 4-man bobsled. No. 1920, Combined slalom, vert. No. 1921, Speed skating. No. 1922, Cross-country skiing. No. 1923, Double luge. No. 1924, Ski jumping, vert. No. 1925, Slalom.

***Perf. 14x14½, 14½x14***

**1992, Sept. 17**

**1918** A263 25c multi .25 .25
**1919** A263 25c multi .25 .25
**1920** A263 50c multi .25 .25
**1921** A263 1cor multi .45 .25
**1922** A263 1.50cor multi .65 .30
**1923** A263 3cor multi 1.40 .65
**1924** A263 3.50cor multi 1.50 .75
*Nos. 1918-1924 (7)* 4.75 2.70

***Imperf***

**Size: 100x70mm**

**1925** A263 7.50cor multi 3.25 1.60
*a.* Overprinted ('93) 3.25 1.60

No. 1925a overprint reads "JUEGOS PRE OLIMPICOS DE INVIERNO / LILLEHAMMER, NORUEGA."

1992 Summer Olympics, Barcelona A264

No. 1926, Javelin. No. 1927, Fencing. No. 1928, Basketball. No. 1929, 1500-meter race. No. 1930, Long jump. No. 1931, Women's 10,000-meter race. No. 1932, Equestrian. No. 1933, Canoeing

***Perf. 14x14½, 14½x14***

**1992, Sept. 17 Litho.**

**1926** A264 25c multi .25 .25
**1927** A264 25c multi .25 .25
**1928** A264 50c multi .25 .25
**1929** A264 1.50cor multi .65 .30
**1930** A264 2cor multi .85 .40
**1931** A264 3cor multi 1.25 .65
**1932** A264 3.50cor multi 1.50 .75
*Nos. 1926-1932 (7)* 5.00 2.85

***Imperf***

**Size: 100x70mm**

**1933** A264 7.50cor multi 3.25 1.60
*a.* Overprinted ('93) 3.25 1.60

Nos. 1927-1932 are vert. Dated 1991.

No. 1933a overprint reads "JUEGOS PRE OLIMPICOS DE VERANO / ATLANTA, GA. / ESTADOS UNIDOS DE AMERICA."

Father R. M. Fabretto and Children A265

**1992, Nov. 12 Litho. *Perf. 14x14½***

**1934** A265 2.25cor multicolored .95 .50

Nicaraguan Natives, by Claudia Gordillo — A266

**1992, Nov. 12**

**1935** A266 2.25cor black & brn .95 .50

Nicaraguan Caciques, by Milton Jose Cruz — A267

**1992, Nov. 12**

**1936** A267 2.25cor multicolored .95 .50

Contemporary Paintings — A268

Paintings by: No. 1937, Alberto Ycaza, vert. No. 1938, Alejandro Arostegui, vert. 50c, Bernard Dreyfus. 1.50cor, Orlando Sobalvarro. 2cor, Hugo Palma. 3cor, Omar D'Leon. 3.50cor, Carlos Montenegro, vert. 7.50cor, Federico Nordalm.

***Perf. 14½x14, 14x14½***

**1992, Nov. 12**

**1937** A268 25c multicolored .25 .25
**1938** A268 25c multicolored .25 .25
**1939** A268 50c multicolored .25 .25
**1940** A268 1.50cor multicolored .65 .30
**1941** A268 2cor multicolored .85 .40
**1942** A268 3cor multicolored 1.25 .65
**1943** A268 3.50cor multicolored 1.50 .75
*Nos. 1937-1943 (7)* 5.00 2.85

***Imperf***

**Size: 100x70mm**

**1944** A268 7.50cor multicolored 3.25 1.60

Monument to Columbus, Rivas — A269

**1993, Mar. 22 *Perf. 14½x14***

**1945** A269 2.25cor multicolored 1.50 .50

UPAEP issue. Dated 1992.

Catholic Religion in Nicaragua, 460th Anniv. — A270

Designs: 25c, Eucharistic gonfalon. 50c, Statue of Virgin Mary. 1cor, Document, 1792-93. 1.50cor, Baptismal font. 2cor, Statue of Madonna and Child. 2.25cor, Monsignor Diego Alvarez Osario. 3cor, Christ on cross.

**1993, Mar. 22**

**1946** A270 25c multicolored .25 .25
**1947** A270 50c multicolored .25 .25
**1948** A270 1cor multicolored .40 .25
**1949** A270 1.50cor multicolored .65 .30
**1950** A270 2cor multicolored .85 .40
**1951** A270 2.25cor multicolored .95 .50
**1952** A270 3cor multicolored 1.25 .65
*Nos. 1946-1952 (7)* 4.60 2.60

Dated 1992.

A271

Archdiocese of Managua: a, 3cor, Cathedral of the Immaculate Conception. b, 4cor, Cross, map.

**1993, Apr. 30**

**1953** A271 Pair, #a.-b. 3.00 1.75

Dated 1992.

A272

Player, country: 50c, Brolin, Sweden. No. 1955, Karas, Poland; Costa, Brazil. No. 1956, Bossis, Platini, France. 1.50cor, Schumacher, Germany. 2cor, Zubizarreta, Spain. 2.50cor, Matthaeus, Germany; Maradona, Argentina. 3.50cor, Robson, England; Santos, Portugal. 10cor, Biyik, Cameroun; Valderrama, Colombia.

**1994, Jan. 28 Litho. *Perf. 14***

**1954** A272 50c multicolored .25 .25
**1955** A272 1cor multicolored .40 .25
**1956** A272 1cor multicolored .40 .25
**1957** A272 1.50cor multicolored .65 .30
**1958** A272 2cor multicolored .85 .40
**1959** A272 2.50cor multicolored 1.10 .55
**1960** A272 3.50cor multicolored 1.50 .75
*Nos. 1954-1960 (7)* 5.15 2.75

**Souvenir Sheet**

**1961** A272 10cor multicolored 4.25 2.00

1994 World Cup Soccer Championships, US.

Sonatina, by Alma Iris Prez — A272a

**1993, Oct. 29 Litho. *Perf. 13½x14***

**1961A** A272a 3cor multicolored 1.00 1.00

Butterflyfish A273

No. 1962: a, Chaetodon lunula. b, Chaetodon rainfordi. c, Chaetodon reticulatus. d, Chaetodon auriga. e, Heniochus acuminatus. f, Coradion fulvocinctus. g, Chaetodon speculum. h, Chaetodon lineolatus. i, Chaetodon bennetti. j, Chaetodon melanotus. k, Chaetodon aureus. l. Chaetodon ephippium. m, Hemitaurichthys polylepis. n, Chaetodon semeion. o, Chaetodon kleinii. p, Chelmon rostratus.

**1993, Nov. 18 Litho. *Perf. 14***

**1962** Sheet of 16 10.00 7.50
*a.-p.* A273 1.50cor Any single .40 .30
*q.* Inscribed with Bangkok '93 emblem in sheet margin 10.00 7.50
*r.* Inscribed with Indopex '93 emblem in sheet margin 10.00 7.50
*s.* Inscribed with Taipei '93 emblem in sheet margin 10.00 7.50

Issue date: No. 1962, Nov. 1, 1993.
No. 1962 is without any show emblem in sheet margin.

1994 Winter Olympics, Lillehammer, 1996 Summer Olympics, Atlanta — A274

No. 1963, Downhill skiing. No. 1964, Fourman bobsled. No. 1965, Swimming. No. 1966, Diving. No. 1967, Speed skating. No. 1968, Race walking. No. 1969, Hurdles. No. 1970, Ski jumping. No. 1971, Women's gymnastics. No. 1972, Women's figure skating. No. 1973, Pairs figure skating. No. 1974, Javelin. No. 1975, Biathlon. No. 1976, Running.
No. 1977, Torch, hands. No. 1978, Flags.

**1993, Nov. 18**

**1963** A274 25c multicolored .25 .25
**1964** A274 25c multicolored .25 .25
**1965** A274 25c multicolored .25 .25
**1966** A274 25c multicolored .25 .25
**1967** A274 50c multicolored .25 .25
**1968** A274 50c multicolored .25 .25
**1969** A274 1cor multicolored .40 .25
**1970** A274 1.50cor multicolored .65 .30
**1971** A274 1.50cor multicolored .65 .30
**1972** A274 2cor multicolored .85 .40
**1973** A274 3cor multicolored 1.25 .65
**1974** A274 3cor multicolored 1.25 .65
**1975** A274 3.50cor multicolored 1.50 .75
**1976** A274 3.50cor multicolored 1.50 .75
*Nos. 1963-1976 (14)* 9.55 5.55

**Souvenir Sheets**

**1977** A274 7.50cor multicolored 3.25 1.50
**1978** A274 7.50cor multicolored 4.25 1.50

1994 Winter Olympics (#1963-1964, 1967, 1970, 1972-1973, 1975, 1978). Others, 1996 Summer Olympics.

Pan-American Health Organization, 90th Anniv. — A275

**1993, June 16 *Perf. 14½***

**1979** A275 3cor multicolored 1.25 .65

Organization of American States, 23rd General Assembly — A276

**1993, June 7 *Perf. 13½x14***

**1980** A276 3cor multicolored 1.25 .65

Christmas — A276a

Paintings: 1cor, Holy Family, by unknown painter. 4cor, Birth of Christ, by Lezamon.

**1994, Feb. 23 Litho. *Perf. 13½x14***

**1980A** A276a 1cor multicolored .35 .25
**1980B** A276a 4cor multicolored 1.40 .70

Fauna and Flora of Rainforest — A277

No. 1981: a, Bromeliacae. b, Tilmatura dupontii. c, Anolis biporcatus (b). d, Fulgara laternaria. e, Bradypus. f, Spizaetus ornatus. g, Cotinga amabilis. h, Bothrops schlegelii. i, Odontoglossum. j, Agalychnis callidryas. k, Heliconius spaho. l, Passiflora vitifolia.
No. 1982, Dasyprocta punctata. No. 1983, Melinaea lilis.

**1994, Jan. 20 *Perf. 14***

**1981** A277 2cor Sheet of 12, #a.-l. 14.00 7.50

**Souvenir Sheets**

**1982** A277 10cor multicolored 3.50 1.75
**1983** A277 10cor multicolored 3.50 1.75

Graf Zeppelin A281

Astronomers — A279

**1994, Feb. 18 Litho. *Perf. 14***

**1984** A278 1.50cor Sheet of 16, #a.-p. 10.00 6.00

No. 1984 — Butterflies: a, Callicore patelina. b, Chlosyne narva. c, Anteos maerula. d, Marpesia petreus. e, Pierella helvetia. f, Eurytides epidaus. g, Heliconius doris. h, Smyrna blomfildia. i, Eueides lybia. j, Adelpha heraclea. k, Heliconius hecale. l, Parides montezuma. m, Morpho polyphemus. n, Eresia alsina. o, Prepona omphale. p, Morpho granadensis.

No. 1985 — Copernicus and: a, Satellite. b, Tycho Brahe (1546-1601), making observations. c, Galileo probe, Galileo. d, Isaac Newton, Newton telescope. e, Giotto probe to Halley's comet, Edmund Halley. f, James Bradley (1693-1762), Grenwich Observatory. g, 1793 telescope, William Herschel (1738-1822). h, John Goodricke (1764-86), stellar eclipse. i, Gottingen observatory, Karl Fredrich Gauss (1777-1855). j, Friedrich Bessell (1784-1846), astronomical instrument. k, Harvard College Observatory, William Granch (1783-1859). l, George B. Airy (1801-92), stellar disc. m, Lowell Observatory, Flagstaff, Arizona, Percival Lowell (1855-1916). n, George A. Halle (1868-1938), solar spectrograph. o, Space telescope, Edwin Hubble (1889-1953). p, Gerard Kuiper (1905-73), Uranus' moon Miranda.
10cor, Nicolas Copernicus, interstellar probe.

**1994, Apr. 4**

**1985** A279 1.50cor Sheet of 16, #a.-p. 9.00 4.50

**Souvenir Sheet**

**1986** A279 10cor multicolored 3.50 2.00

Automotive Anniversaries — A280

No. 1987: a, 1886 Benz three-wheel car. b, 1909 Benz Blitzen. c, 1923 Mercedes Benz 24/100/140. d, 1928 Mercedes Benz SSK. e, 1934 Mercedes Benz Cabriolet 500k. f, 1949 Mercedes Benz 170S. g, 1954 Mercedes Benz W196. h, 1954 Mercedes Benz 300SL. i, 1896 Ford four-wheel car. j, 1920 Ford taxi. k, 1928 Ford Roadster. l, 1932 Ford V-8. m, 1937 Ford 78 (V-8). n, 1939 Ford 91 Deluxe Tudor Sedan. o, 1946 Ford V-8 Sedan Coupe. p, 1958 Ford Custom 300.
10cor, Henry Ford (1863-1947), 1903 Ford Model A; Karl Benz (1844-1929), 1897 Benz 5CH.

**1994, Apr. 5**

**1987** A280 1.50cor Sheet of 16, #a.-p. 9.00 4.50

**Souvenir Sheet**

**1988** A280 10cor multicolored 3.50 2.00

First Benz four-wheeled vehicle, cent. (Nos. 1987a-1987h). First Ford gasoline engine, cent. (Nos. 1987i-1987p).

No. 1989 — Graf Zeppelin and: a, Dr. Hugo Eckener, Count Zeppelin (inside cabin). b, New York City, 1928. c, Tokyo, 1929. d, San Simeon, California, 1929. e, Col. Charles Lindbergh, Dr. Hugo Eckener, 1929. f, Moscow, 1930. g, Paris, 1930. h, Cairo, 1931. i, Arctic waters. j, Rio de Janeiro, 1932. k, London, 1935. l, St. Peter's Basilica, Vatican City. m, Swiss Alps. n, Brandenburg Gate. o, Eckener in control room. p, Ernest A. Lehman, DO-X.
No. 1990, Graf Zeppelin, Count Zeppelin. No. 1991, Zeppelin, Eckener.

**1994, Apr. 6**

**1989** A281 1.50cor Sheet of 16. #a.-p. 9.00 4.50

**Souvenir Sheets**

**1990** A281 10cor multicolored 3.50 1.75
**1991** A281 10cor multicolored 3.50 1.75

Dr. Hugo Eckener (1868-1954) (#1991).

Contemporary Crafts — A282

Designs: No. 1992, 50c, Basket weaving, by Rosalia Sevilla, horiz. No. 1993, 50c, Wood carving, by Julio Lopez. No. 1994, 1cor, Woman carrying sack, by Indiana Robleto. No. 1995, 1cor, Church, by Auxiliadora Bush. 2.50cor, Carving, by Jose de Los Santos. 3cor, Costumed doll with horse's head, by Ines Gutierrez de Chong. 4cor, Ceramic container, by Elio Gutierrez.
10cor, Metate, by Saul Carballo.

***Perf. 13½x14, 14x13½***

**1994, Feb. 15 Litho.**

**1992-1998** A282 Set of 7 4.25 2.00

***Imperf***

**Size: 96x66mm**

**1999** A282 10cor multicolored 3.25 1.60

Dated 1993.

Stone Carvings, Chontal Culture — A283

Color of inscription tablet: No. 2000, 50c, Yellow. No. 2001, 50c, Yellow brown. No. 2002, 1cor, Green. No. 2003, 1cor, Yellow green. 2.50cor, Greenish blue. 3cor, Blue. 4cor, Grey green.
10cor, Two stone totems seen against landscape painting.

**1994, Feb. 23 *Perf. 14***

**2000-2006** A283 Set of 7 4.25 2.00

***Imperf***

**Size: 96x66mm**

**2007** A283 10cor multicolored 3.25 1.60

Dated 1993.

Contemporary Art — A284

Designs: No. 2008, 50c, Lady Embroidering, by Guillermo Rivas Navas. No. 2009, 50c, Virgin of Nicaragua, by Cella Lacayo. No. 2010, 1cor, The Dance, by June Beer. No. 2011, 1cor, Song of Peace, by Alejandro Canales. 2.50cor, Fruits, by Genaro Lugo, horiz. 3cor, Figures and Fragments, by Leonel Vanegas. 4cor, Eruption of Volcano of Water, by Asilia Guillen, horiz.
10cor, Still life, by Alejandro Alonso Rochi.

**1994, Mar. 15** ***Perf. 14x13½, 13½x14***
**2008-2014** A284 Set of 7 4.25 2.00

***Imperf***

**Size: 96x66mm**

**2015** A284 10cor multicolored 3.25 1.60

Dated 1993.

Prominent Nicaraguan Philatelists — A285

Designs: 1cor, Gabriel Horvilleur (1907-91). 3cor, Jose S. Cuadra A. (1932-92). 4cor, Alfredo Pertz (1864-1948).

**1994, Apr. 18** **Litho.** ***Perf. 14***
**2016-2018** A285 Set of 3 2.75 1.40

Dated 1993.

First Tree Conference of Nicaragua A286

**1994, June 5** ***Perf. 14x13½***
**2019** A286 4cor multicolored 1.40 .70

Souvenir Sheets

Reported Alien Sightings — A287

Date and location of sighting: No. 2020, 60cor, July 21, 1991, Missouri. No. 2021, 60cor, July 28, 1965, Argentina. No. 2022, 60cor, Aug. 21, 1955, Kentucky. No. 2023, 60cor, Oct. 25, 1973, Pennsylvania. No. 2024, 60cor, Sept. 19, 1961, New Hampshire. No. 2025, 60cor, Nov. 7, 1989, Kansas. No. 2026, 60cor, Sept. 26, 1976, Grand Canary Island. No. 2027, 60cor, May 8, 1973, Texas.

**1994, May 25** **Litho.** ***Perf. 14***
**2020-2027** A287 Set of 8 *150.00 60.00*

Sacred Art — A288

Designs: No. 2028, 50c, Pulpit, Cathedral of Leon. No. 2029, 50c, Statue of Saint Ann, Chinandega Parish. No. 2030, 1cor, Statue of St. Joseph, San Pedro Parish, Rivas. No. 2031, 1cor, Statue of St. James, Jinotepe Parish. 2.50cor, Chalice, Subtiava Temple, Leon. 3cor, Processional cross, Nequinohoma Parish, Masaya. 4cor, Crucifix, Temple of Miracles, Managua. 10cor, Silver frontal, San Pedro Parish, Rivas.

**1994, July 11** **Litho.** ***Perf. 14***
**2028-2034** A288 Set of 7 4.25 2.25

**Size: 96x66mm**

***Imperf***

**2036** A288 10cor multicolored 3.50 1.75

No. 2035 is unassigned.

A289

**1994, July 4** **Litho.** ***Perf. 14***
**2037** A289 3cor multicolored 1.00 1.00

Intl. Conference of New or Restored Democracies.

A290

**1994, Aug. 2**
**2038** A290 4cor multicolored 1.50 1.50

32nd World Amateur Baseball Championships.

PHILAKOREA '94 — A291

No. 2039: a, Soraksan. b, Statue of Kim Yu-Shin. c, Solitary Rock. d, Waterfall, Hallasan Valley. e, Mirukpong and Pisondae. f, Chonbuldong Valley. g, Bridge of the Seven Nymphs. h, Piryong Falls.

No. 2040, Boy on first birthday, gifts of fruit.

**1994, Aug. 16**
**2039** A291 1.50cor Sheet of 8, #a.-h. 4.00 4.00

**Souvenir Sheet**

**2040** A291 10cor multicolored 3.00 3.00

Dinosaurs A292

No. 2041: a, Tyrannosaurus rex. b, Plateosaurus (f-g). c, Pteranodon (b). d, Camarasaurus (c). e, Euplocephalus. f, Sacuanjoche. g, Deinonychus (h). h, Chasmosaurus (d). i, Dimorphodon. j, Ametriorhynchids (i). k, Ichthyosaurus (j). l, Pterapsis, Compsognathus. m, Cephalopod. n, Archelon (o). o, Griphognatus, Gyroptychius. p, Plesiosaur (o), Navtiloid.

**1994, Sept. 1**
**2041** A292 1.50cor Sheet of 16, #a.-p. 9.50 8.50

1994 World Cup Soccer Championships, US — A293

Players: a, Rai. b, Freddy Rincon. c, Luis Garcia. d, Thomas Dooley. e, Franco Baresi. f, Tony Meola. g, Enzo Francescoli. h, Roy Wegerle.

No. 2043, 10cor, Faustino Asprilla. No. 2044, 10cor, Adolfo Valencia, horiz.

**1994, Sept. 19**
**2042** A293 3cor Sheet of 8, #a.-h. 8.50 7.50

**Souvenir Sheets**

**2043-2044** A293 Set of 2 6.00 6.00

D-Day, 50th Anniv. A294

No. 2045: a, British fighter plane. b, C-47 transports dropping paratroopers. c, HMS Mauritius bombards Houlgate. d, Mulberry artificial harbor. e, Churchill tank. f, Landing craft approaching beach.

**1994, Sept. 26**
**2045** A294 3cor Sheet of 6, #a.-f. 7.25 6.00

Ruben Dario National Theater, 25th Anniv. — A295

**1994, Sept. 30**
**2046** A295 3cor multicolored 1.10 1.00

A296

Intl. Olympic Committee, Cent. — A297

Gold Medalists: No. 2047, Cassius Clay (Muhammad Ali), boxing, 1960. No. 2048, Renate Stecher, track, 1972, 1976. 10cor, Claudia Pechstein, speed skating, 1994.

**1994, Oct. 3**
**2047** A296 3.50cor multicolored 1.25 1.25
**2048** A296 3.50cor multicolored 1.25 1.25

**Souvenir Sheet**

**2049** A297 10cor multicolored 3.25 3.25

La Carreta Nagua, by Erick Joanello Montoya A298

**1994, Oct. 19**
**2050** A298 4cor multicolored 1.25 1.25

Motion Pictures, Cent. — A299

No. 2051 — Film and director: a, The Kid, Charlie Chaplin. b, Citizen Kane, Orson Welles. c, Lawrence of Arabia, David Lean. d, Ivan the Terrible, Sergei Eisenstein. e, Metropolis, Fritz Lang. f, The Ten Commandments, Cecil B. DeMille. g, Gandhi, Richard Attenborough. h, Casablanca, Michael Curtis. i, Platoon, Oliver Stone. j, The Godfather, Francis Ford Coppola. k, 2001: A Space Odyssey, Stanley Kubrick. l, The Ocean Depths, Jean Renoir.

No. 2052, Gone With the Wind, Victor Fleming.

**1994, Nov. 14**
**2051** A299 2cor Sheet of 12, #a.-l. 8.00 8.00

**Souvenir Sheet**

**2052** A299 15cor multicolored 5.00 5.00

Wildlife A300

No. 2053: a, Nyticorax nyticorax. b, Ara macao. c, Bulbulcus ibis. d, Coragyps atratus. e, Epicrates cenchria. f, Cyanerpes cyaneus. g, Ortalis vetula. h, Bradypus griseus. i, Felis onca. j, Anhinga anhinga. k, Tapirus bairdi. l, Myrmecophaga jubata. m, Iguana iguana. n, Chelydra serpentina. o, Dendrocygna autumnalis. p, Felis paradalis.

**1994, Oct. 31**
**2053** A300 2cor Sheet of 16, #a.-p. 10.00 10.00

First Manned Moon Landing, 25th Anniv. — A301

No. 2054: a, Docking command, lunar modules. b, Lift-off. c, Entering lunar orbit. d, Footprint on moon. e, Separation of first stage. f, Trans-lunar insertion. g, Lander descending toward moon. h, Astronaut on moon.

No. 2055, 10cor, Astronaut saluting, flag. No. 2056, 10cor, Astronauts in quarantine, horiz.

**1994, Oct. 17**
**2054** A301 3cor Sheet of 8, #a.-h. 9.50 8.00

**Souvenir Sheets**

**2055-2056** A301 Set of 2 6.50 6.50

Nos. 2055-2056 each contain one 29x47mm stamp.

Contemporary Paintings by Rodrigo Penalba — A302

Designs: 50c, Discovery of America. 1cor, Portrait of Maurice. 1.50cor, Portrait of Franco. 2cor, Portrait of Mimi Hammer. 2.50cor, Seated Woman. 3cor, Still Life, horiz. 4cor, Portrait of Maria Augusta. 15cor, Entrance to Anticoli.

**1994, Nov. 15**

**2057-2063** A302 Set of 7 4.75 4.75

**Size: 66x96mm**

***Imperf***

**2064** A302 15cor multicolored 4.75 4.75

Domestic Cats — A303

No. 2065: a, Chocolate point Himalayan. b, Red Somalian. c, American long hair. d, Russian blue. e, Scottish folded ear. f, Persian chinchilla. g, Egyptian mau. h, Manx blue cream. i, Burmese blue Malaysian. j, Balinesian seal point. k, Oriental long-haired blue. l, Persian chinchilla cameo. m, Angora. n, Siamese. o, Burmese seal point. p, Mixed red.

15cor, Golden shoulder Persian.

**1994, Dec. 20 Litho. *Perf. 14***

**2065** A303 1.50cor Sheet of 16, #a.-p. 9.00 8.00

**Souvenir Sheet**

**2066** A303 15cor multicolored 5.00 5.00

No. 2066 contains one 38x51mm stamp.

Wild Fowl A304

No. 2067 — Penelopina nigra: a, 50c, Male, female on tree branch. b, 1cor, Head of male, male on tree branch. c, 2.50cor, Head of female, female on tree branch. d, 3cor, Male spreading wings, female.

No. 2068, Heads of male and female Penelopina nigra. No. 2069, Anhinga anhinga.

**1994, Dec. 20 Litho. *Perf. 14***

**2067** A304 Vert. strip of 4, #a.-d. 2.75 2.25

**Souvenir Sheets**

**2068** A304 15cor multi 7.00 7.00
**2069** A304 15cor multi 5.50 5.50

World Wildlife Fund (#2067).

No. 2067 was issued in minature sheets of 3 strips.

Sculpture — A305

Designs: 50c, Truth, by Aparicio Arthola. 1cor, Owl, by Orlando Sobalvarro. 1.50cor, Small Music Player, by Noel Flores Castro. 2cor, Exodus II, by Miguel Angel Abarca. 2.50cor, Raza, by Fernando Saravia. 3cor, Dolor Incognito, by Edith Gron. 4cor, Heron, by Ernesto Cardenal.

No. 2077, 15cor, Atlante, by Jorge Navas Cordonero. No. 2078, 15cor, Motherhood, by Rodrigo Penalba.

**1995, Feb. 23 Litho. *Perf. 14½***

**2070-2076** A305 Set of 7 4.50 4.50

**Size: 66x96mm**

***Imperf***

**2077-2078** A305 Set of 2 9.00 9.00

Historic Landmarks — A306

Designs: 50c, Animas Chapel, Granada, vert. 1cor, San Francisco Convent, Granada. 1.50cor, Santiago Tower, Leon, vert. 2cor, Santa Ana Church, Nindiri. 2.50cor, Santa Ana Church, Nandaime, vert. 3cor, Lion Gate, Granada. 4cor, Castle of the Immaculate Conception, Rio San Juan.

15cor, Hacienda San Jacinto, Managua.

**1995 Litho. *Perf. 14***

**2079-2085** A306 Set of 7 4.50 4.50

**Size: 96x66mm**

**2086** A306 15cor multicolored 4.50 4.50

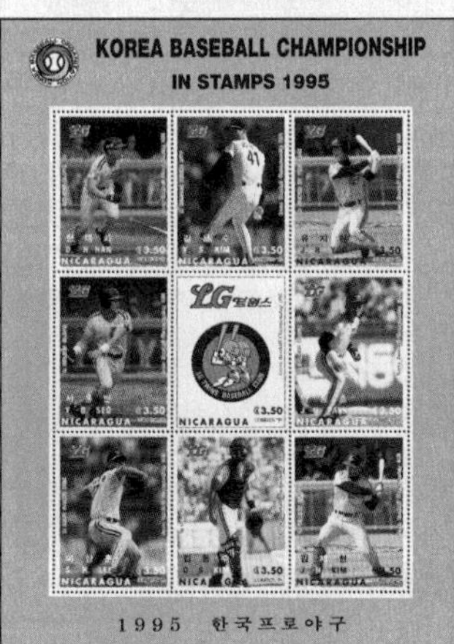


Korean Baseball Championships — A307

No. 2087, 3.50cor — LG Twins: No. 2087a, D.H. Han. b, Y.S. Kim. c, J.H. Yoo. d, Y.B. Seo. e, Team logo. f, J.H. Park. g, S.H. Lee. h, D.S. Kim. i, J.H. Kim.

No. 2088, 3.50cor — Samsung Lions: a, J.L. Ryu. b, S.Y. Kim. c, S.R. Kim. d, B.C. Dong. e, Team logo. f, K.W. Kang. g, C.S. Park. h, J.H. Yang. i, T.H. Kim.

No. 2089, 3.50cor — SBW Raiders: a, H.J. Park. b, K.J. Cho. c, K.T. Kim. d, W.H. Kim. e, Team logo. f, I.H. Baik. g, S.K. Park. h, K.L. Kim. i, J.S. Park.

No. 2090, 3.50cor — Doosan OB Bears: a, M.S. Lee. b, C.S. Park. c, H.S. Lim. d, K.W. Kim. e, Team logo. f, J.S. Kim. g, T.H. Kim. h, H.S. Kim. i, S.J. Kim.

No. 2091, 3.50cor — Pacific Dolphins: a, M.W. Jung. b, K.K. Kim. c, H.J. Kim. d, M.T. Chung. e, Team logo. f, B.W. An. g, D.G. Yoon. h, S.D. Choi. i, D.K. Kim.

No. 2092, 3.50cor — Hanwha Eagles: a, J.H. Jang. b, Y.D. Han. c, K.D. Lee. d, J.S. Park. e, Team logo. f, M.C. Jeong. g, J.W. Song. h, J.G. Kang. i, D.S. Koo.

No. 2093, 3.50cor — Lotte Giants: a, H.K. Yoon. b, D.H. Park. c, H.K. Joo. d, E.G. Kim. e, Team logo. f, J.T. Park. g, P.S. Kong. h, J.S. Yeom. i, M.H. Kim.

No. 2094, 3.50cor — Haitai Tigers: a, D.Y. Sun. b, J.B. Lee. c, J.S. Kim. d, S.H. Kim. e, Team logo. f, G.C. Lee. g, G.H. Cho. h, S.H. Kim. i, S.C. Lee.

**1995, Mar. 25 Litho. *Perf. 14***

**Sheets of 9, #a-i**

**2087-2094** A307 Set of 8 77.50 77.50

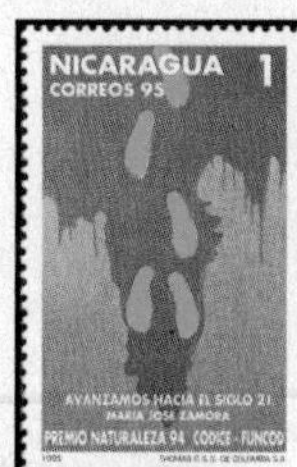


Nature Paintings — A308

Designs: 1cor, Advancing Forward, by Maria Jose Zamora. 2cor, Natural Death, by Rafael Castellon. 4cor, Captives of Water, by Alvaro Gutierrez.

**1995, Apr. 4 Litho. *Perf. 14***

**2095-2097** A308 Set of 3 2.25 2.25

British-Nicaragua Expedition, San Juan River — A309

**1995, May 5**

**2098** A309 4cor multicolored 1.25 1.25

Boaco Festival — A310

**1995, May 10**

**2099** A310 4cor multicolored 1.25 1.25

Printed with se-tenant label.

Contemporary Paintings, by Armando Morales — A311

Designs: 50c, Ferry Boat. 1cor, Oliverio Castañeda, vert. 1.50cor, Sitting Nude, vert. 2cor, Señoritas at the Port of Cabeza. 2.50cor, The Automobile and Company, vert. 3cor, Bullfight, vert. 4cor, Still life.

15cor, Woman Sleeping.

**1995, Oct. 31 Litho. *Perf. 14***

**2100-2106** A311 Set of 7 4.50 4.50

**Size: 96x66mm**

**2107** A311 15cor multicolored 4.50 4.50

Louis Pasteur (1822-95) — A312

**1995, Sept. 28 Litho. *Perf. 14***

**2108** A312 4cor multicolored 1.25 1.25

First Place in Childrens' Painting Contest A313

Nature scene, by Brenda Jarquin Gutierrez.

**1995, Oct. 9**

**2109** A313 3cor multicolored .90 .90

Animals A314

No. 2110: a, Crocodile. b, Opossum. c, Zahina. d, Guardatinale. e, Frog. f, Iguana. g, Macaw. h, Capybara. i, Vampire bat.

No. 2111, 15cor, Jaguar, vert. No. 2112, 15cor, Eagle, vert.

**1995, Oct. 9**

**2110** A314 2.50cor Sheet of 9, #a.-i. 6.75 6.75

**Souvenir Sheets**

**2111-2112** A314 Set of 2 10.00 9.00

Issued: #2112, 4/15; #2110-2111, 10/9.

FAO, 50th Anniv. — A315

**1995, Oct. 16**

**2113** A315 4cor multicolored 1.25 1.25

UN, 50th Anniv. — A316

No. 2114: a, 3cor, UN flag, doves, rainbow. b, 4cor, Rainbow, lion, lamb. c, 5cor, Rainbow, dove on soldier's helmet.

No. 2115, Children holding hands under sun, dove.

**1995, Oct. 31**

**2114** A316 Strip of 3, #a.-c. 3.75 3.75

**Souvenir Sheet**

**2115** A316 10cor multicolored 3.00 3.00

No. 2114 is a continuous design.

Rotary Intl., 90th Anniv. — A317

**1995, Nov. 17**

**2116** A317 15cor Paul Harris, logo 4.50 4.50

**Souvenir Sheet**

**2117** A317 25cor Old, new logos 7.50 7.50

Butterflies, Moths — A318

No. 2118: a, Cyrestis camillus. b, Salamis cacta. c, Charaxes castor. d, Danaus formosa. e, Graphium ridleyanus. f, Hewitsonia boisduvali. g, Charaxes zoolina. h, Kallima cymodoce i, Precis westermanni. j, Papilo antimachus. k, Cymothoe sangaris. l, Papillo zalmoxis.

No. 2119, Danaus formosa, vert.

**1995, Nov. 17**

**2118** A318 2.50cor Sheet of 12, #a.-l. 9.00 9.00

**Souvenir Sheet**

**2119** A318 15cor multicolored 4.50 4.50

1996 Summer Olympics, Atlanta — A319

No. 2120: a, Michael Jordan. b, Heike Henkel. c, Linford Christie. d, Vitaly Chtcherbo. e, Heike Drechsler. f, Mark Tewksbury.

Pierre de Coubertin and: No. 2121, 20cor, Javelin thrower, horiz. No. 2122, 20cor, Runner.

**1995, Dec. 1 Litho. *Perf. 14***

**2120** A319 5cor Sheet of 6, #a.-f. 9.00 9.00

**Souvenir Sheets**

**2121-2122** A319 Set of 2 12.00 12.00

John Lennon (1940-80) — A320

**1995, Dec. 8**

**2123** A320 2cor multicolored 1.00 .60

Issued in sheets of 16.

Trains A321

Designs: No. 2124, 2cor, Mombasa mail train, Uganda. No. 2125, 2cor, Steam locomotive, East Africa. No. 2126, 2cor, Electric locomotive, South Africa. No. 2127, 2cor, Beyer-Garrat steam locomotive, South Africa. No. 2128, 2cor, Beyer-Garrat steam locomotive, Rhodesia. No. 2129, 2cor, Class 30 steam locomotive, East Africa.

No. 2130: a, New York Central & Hudson River RR 4-4-0, #999, US. b, Australian Class 638, 4-6-2, Pacific. c, Baldwin 2-10-2, Bolivia. d, Vulcan 4-8-4, China. e, Paris-Orleans 4-6-2 Pacific, France. f, Class 062, 4-6-4, Japan.

No. 2131, 15cor, Siberian cargo train. No. 2132, 15cor, Midland 4-4-0 train, Great Britain. No. 2133, 15cor, Soviet steam locomotive.

**1995, Dec. 11**

**2124-2129** A321 Set of 6 4.00 3.75

**Miniature Sheet**

**2130** A321 4cor Sheet of 6, #a.-f. 7.25 7.25

**Souvenir Sheets**

**2131-2133** A321 Set of 3 13.50 13.50

#2131-2133 each contain one 85x28mm stamp.

Establishment of Nobel Prize Fund, Cent. — A322

No. 2134: a, Otto Meyerhof, medicine, 1922. b, Léon Bourgeois, peace, 1920. c, James Franck, physics, 1925. d, Leo Esaki, physics, 1973. e, Miguel Angel Asturias, literature, 1967. f, Henri Bergson, literature, 1927. g, Friedrich Bergius, chemistry, 1931. h, Klaus von Klitzing, physics, 1985. i, Eisaku Sato, Japan, peace, 1974.

No. 2135: a, Wilhelm C. Roentgen, physics, 1901. b, Theodor Mommsen, literature, 1902. c, Philipp E.A. von Lenard, physics, 1905. d, Walther H. Nernst, chemistry, 1920. e, Hans Spemann, medicine, 1935. f, Jean Paul Sartre, literature, 1964. g, T.S. Eliot, literature, 1948. h, Albert Camus, literature, 1957. i, Ludwig Quidde, peace, 1927. j, Werner Heisenberg, physics, 1932. k, Joseph Brodsky, literature, 1987. l, Carl von Ossietzky, peace, 1935.

No. 2136, 15cor, Sin-itiro Tomonaga, physics, 1965. No. 2137, 15cor, Johannes Stark, physics, 1919. No. 2138, 15cor, Oscar Arias Sánchez, peace, 1987.

**1995, Dec. 11**

**2134** A322 2.50cor Sheet of 9, #a.-i. 6.75 6.75

**2135** A322 2.50cor Sheet of 12, #a.-l. 9.00 9.00

**Souvenir Sheets**

**2136-2138** A322 Set of 3 13.50 13.50

Orchids A323

No. 2139: a, Cattleya dowinana. b, Odontoglossum maculatum. c, Barkeria lindleyana. d, Rossioglossum grnde. e, Brassavpia digbyana. f, Miltonia schroederiana. g, Ondidium ornithorhynchum. h, Odontoglossum cervantesii. i, Chysis tricostata.

No. 2140: a, Lycaste auburn. b, Lemboglossum cordatum. c, Cyrtochilum macranthum. d, Miltassia Aztec "Nalo." e, Masdevaltia ignea. f, Oncidium sniffen "Jennifer Dauro." g, Brassolaeliocattleya Alma Kee. h, Ascocenda blue boy. i, Phalaenopsis.

15cor, Odontogiossum uro-skinneri.

**1995, Dec. 15**

**2139** A323 2.50cor Sheet of 9, #a.-i. 6.75 6.75

**2140** A323 3cor Sheet of 9, #a.-i. 8.25 8.25

**Souvenir Sheet**

**2141** A323 15cor multicolored 4.50 4.50

World War II, 50th Anniv. A324

No. 2142: a, Patton's troops crossing the Rhine. b, Churchill, Roosevelt, and Stalin at Yalta. c, US flag being raised at Iwo Jima. d, Marine infantry taking possession of Okinawa. e, US troops greeting Russian troops at Torgau. f, Liberation of concentration camps. g, Signing UN Charter, June 1945. h, Ships arriving at Tokyo after war's end.

10cor, German Bf-109 fighter plane.

**1996, Jan. 24 Litho. *Perf. 14***

**2142** A324 3cor Sheet of 8, #a.-h. + label 7.25 7.25

**Souvenir Sheet**

**2143** A324 10cor multicolored 3.00 3.00

Miniature Sheet

Exotic Birds — A325

No. 2144: a, Paradisiaea apoda. b, Dryocopus galeatus. c, Psarisomus dalhousiae (g). d, Psarocolius montezuma. e, Halcyon pileata. f, Calocitta formosa. g, Ara chloroptera. h, Platycercus eximius. i, Polyplectron emphanum. j, Cariama cristata. k, Opisthocomus hoatzin. l, Coracias cyanogaster.

10cor, Dryocopus galeatus.

**1996, Feb. 1**

**2144** A325 2cor Sheet of 12, #a.-l. 7.25 7.25

**Souvenir Sheet**

**2145** A325 10cor multicolored 3.00 3.00

Town of Rivas, 275th Anniv. — A326

**1995, Sept. 23 Litho. *Perf. 14***

**2146** A326 3cor multi +label .90 .90

Christmas A327

**1995, Dec. 8**

**2147** A327 4cor multicolored 1.25 1.25

20th Century Writers — A328

No. 2148 — Writer, country flag: a, C. Drummond de Andrade (1902-87), Brazil. b, Cesar Vallejo (1892-1938), Peru. c, J. Luis Borges (1899-1986), Argentina. d, James Joyce (1882-1941), Italy. e, Marcel Proust (1871-1922), France. f, William Faulkner (1897-1962), US. g, Vladmir Maiakovski (1893-1930), Russia. h, Ezra Pound (1885-1972), US. i, Franz Kafka (1883-1924), Czechoslovakia. j, T.S. Eliot (188-1965), United Kingdom. k, Rainer Rilke (1875-1926), Austria. l, Federico G. Lorca (1898-1936), Spain.

**1995, Oct. 15 *Perf. 14½x14***

**2148** A328 3cor Sheet of 12, #a.-l. 12.50 12.50

Classic Sailing Ships A329

No. 2149, 2.50cor: a, Mayflower, England. b, Young America, US. c, Preussen, Germany. d, Lateen-rigged pirate ship, Caribbean Sea. e, Cutty Sark, England. f, Square-rigged pirate ship, Caribbean Sea. g, Galeón, Spain. h, The Sun King, France. i, Santa Maria, Spain.

No. 2150, 2.50cor: a, HMS Bounty, England. b, The President, US. c, Prince William, Holland. d, Flying Cloud, US. e, Markab, Nile River, Egypt. f, Europa, Holland. g, Vasa, Sweden. h, Foochow junk, China. i, San Gabriel, Portugal.

No. 2151, 15cor, Passat, Germany. No. 2152, 15cor, Japanese junk, vert.

**1996, Jan. 10 Litho. *Perf. 14***

**Sheets of 9, #a-i**

**2149-2150** A329 Set of 2 13.50 13.50

**Souvenir Sheets**

**2151-2152** A329 Set of 2 9.00 9.00

Visit of Pope John Paul II — A330

**1996, Feb. 7**

**2153** A330 5cor multicolored 1.50 1.50

Puppies — A331

Various breeds: No. 2154, 1cor, Holding red leash in mouth. No. 2155, 1cor, With red bandanna around neck. No. 2156, 2cor, Spaniel playing with ball. No. 2157, 2cor, With dog biscuit in mouth. No. 2158, 3cor, Akita. No. 2159, 3cor, Bull dog. No. 2160, 4cor, With newspaper in mouth. No. 2161, 4cor, Dalmatian with cat.

No. 2162, 16cor, Bending down on front paws. No. 2163, 16cor, Poodle.

**1996, Mar. 6**

**2154-2161** A331 Set of 8 7.25 7.25

**Souvenir Sheets**

**2162-2163** A331 Set of 2 9.50 9.50

Famous Women — A332

No. 2164: a, Indira Gandhi. b, Mme. Chiang Kai-shek. c, Mother Teresa. d, Marie Curie. e, Margaret Thatcher. f, Eleanor Roosevelt. g, Eva Perón. h, Golda Meir. i, Violeta Barrios de Chamorro.

No. 2165, 15cor, Jacqueline Kennedy Onassis, vert. No. 2166, 15cor, Aung San Suu Kyi, vert. No. 2167, 15cor, Valentina Tereshkova, vert.

**1996, Mar. 8 *Perf. 14x13½***

**2164** A332 2.50cor Sheet of 9, #a.-i. 7.25 7.25

**Souvenir Sheets**

***Perf. 13½x14***

**2165-2167** A332 Set of 3 13.50 13.50

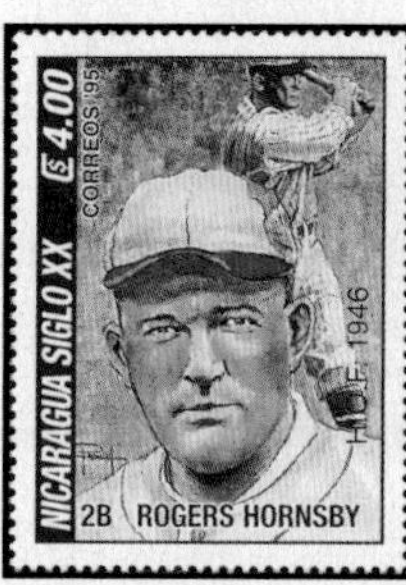
Members of Baseball's Hall of Fame A333

No. 2168 — Player, year inducted: a, Lou Gehrig, 1944. b, Rogers Hornsby, 1946. c, Mike Schmidt, 1995. d, Honus Wagner, 1936. e, Ty Cobb, 1936. f, Roberto Clemente, 1973. g, Babe Ruth, 1936. h, Johnny Bench, 1987. i, Tom Seaver, 1993.
10cor, Reggie Jackson, 1993.

**1996, Mar. 15 Litho. *Perf. 13½x14***
**2168** A333 4cor Sheet of 9, #a.-i. 11.00 11.00

**Souvenir Sheet**
**2169** A333 10cor multicolored 9.25 9.25

1996 Summer Olympics, Atlanta A334

Designs: 1cor, Takehide Nakatani, Japan. 2cor, Olympic Stadium, Tokyo, 1964. 3cor, Al Oerter, US, vert. 10cor, Discus thrower from ancient games.
No. 2174, 2.50cor, vert. — Gold medal winners in boxing: a, Andrew Maynard, U.S. b, Rudi Fink, Germany. c, Peter Lessov, Bulgaria. d, Angel Herrera, Cuba. e, Patrizio Oliva, Italy. f, Armando Martinez, Cuba. g, Slobodan Kacar, Yugoslavia. h, Teofilo Stevenson, Cuba. i, George Foreman, U.S.
No. 2175, 2.50cor — Events: a, Basketball. b, Baseball. c, Boxing. d, Long jump. e, Judo. f, Team handball. g, Volleyball. h, Water polo. i, Tennis.
25cor, Cassius Clay (Muhammad Ali), US.

**1996, Mar. 28 *Perf. 14***
**2170-2173** A334 Set of 4 4.75 4.75

**Sheets of 9, #a-i**
**2174-2175** A334 Set of 2 13.50 13.50

**Souvenir Sheet**
**2176** A334 25cor multicolored 7.50 7.50

Race Horses A335

Carousel Horses — A336

Race horses: 1cor, "Wave." 2cor, "Charming Traveler." 2.50cor, "Noble Vagabond." No. 2180, 3cor, "Golden Dancer," vert. No. 2181, 3cor, "Wave Runner." No. 2182, 4cor, "Ebony Champion." No. 2183, 4cor, "Wave Tamer."
Antique carousel horses: No. 2184a, Persian light infantry horse, 18th cent. b, Italian parade horse, 15th cent. c, German armored horse, 15th cent. d, Turkish light infantry horse, 17th cent.
16cor, "Proud Heart." 25cor, German armored horse, 16th cent.

**1996, Apr. 15**
**2177-2183** A335 Set of 7 6.00 6.00
**2184** A336 2cor Sheet of 4, #a.-d. 2.50 2.50

**Souvenir Sheets**
**2185** A335 16cor multi 6.50 6.50
**2186** A336 25cor multi 7.50 7.50

Marine Life A337

No. 2187, 2.50cor: a, Butterflyfish (d). b, Barracuda (a). c, Manatee. d, Jellyfish. e, Octopus (b, d, f, g, h). f, Small yellow-striped fish. g, Lemon shark. h, Striped fish. i, Red fish.
No. 2188, 2.50cor: a, Reef shark. b, Diver, hammerhead shark (c, e). c, Moray eel (f). d, Macrela ojos de caballo (a, b, e). e, Hammerhead shark. f, Butterflyfish. g, Mediterranean grouper. h, Octopus, diff. i, Manta ray.
No. 2189, 20cor, Angelfish. No. 2190, 20cor, Saddleback butterflyfish.

**1996, Apr. 29 Litho. *Perf. 14***

**Sheets of 9, #a-i**
**2187-2188** A337 Set of 2 14.50 14.50

**Souvenir Sheets**
**2189-2190** A337 Set of 2 13.00 13.00

Chinese Lunar Calendar A338

Year signs: a, Rat. b, Ox. c, Tiger. d, Hare. e, Dragon. f, Snake. g, Horse. h, Sheep. i, Monkey. j, Rooster. k, Dog. l, Boar.

**1996, May 6**
**2191** A338 2cor Sheet of 12, #a.-l. 6.50 6.50
China'96.

Central American Integration System (SICA) A339

**1996, May 8 *Perf. 14½***
**2192** A339 5cor multicolored 1.60 1.60

20th Century Events A340

No. 2193: a, Russian revolution, 1917. b, Chinese revolution, 1945. c, Creation of the UN, 1945. d, Tearing down the Berlin Wall, 1989. e, World War I, vert. f, Creation of the State of Israel, 1948, vert. g, World War II, vert. h, 2nd Vatican Council, 1962-65, vert. i, Atom bombing of Hiroshima, 1945. j, Viet Nam War, 1962-73. k, Persian Gulf War, 1991. l, End of Apartheid, 1991.

**1996 *Perf. 14***
**2193** A340 3cor Sheet of 12, #a.-l. + label 11.50 11.50

Souvenir Sheet

New Year 1997 (Year of the Ox) — A341

**1996 Litho. *Perf. 15x14***
**2194** A341 10cor multicolored 3.00 3.00

Wuhan Huanghelou — A342

**1996, May 20 Litho. *Perf. 14***
**2195** A342 4cor multicolored 1.50 1.50

China '96. No. 2195 was not available until March 1997. No. 2195 comes in a souvenir sheet of 1.

Red Parrot, by Ernesto Cardenal — A343

**1996, June 5 Litho. *Perf. 14½x14***
**2196** A343 4cor multicolored 1.25 1.25

Friendship Between Nicaragua and Republic of China A344

Designs: 10cor, Painting, "Landscape with Bags," by Fredrico Nordalm, vert. 20cor, Dr. Lee Teng-Hui, Pres. of Republic of China and Violeta Barrios de Chamorro, President of Nicaragua.

***Perf. 14½x14, 14x14½***
**1996, June 26 Litho.**
**2197** A344 10cor multicolored 1.75 1.75
**2198** A344 20cor multicolored 3.50 3.50

Violeta Barrios de Chamorro, President, 1990-96 A345

***Serpentine Die Cut***
**1997, Jan. 27 Litho.**

**Self-Adhesive**
**2199** A345 3cor multicolored .90 .90
*a.* Booklet pane of 9 + 2 labels 8.25

The peelable paper backing serves as a booklet cover.

"Plan International," Intl. Children's Organization, 60th Anniv. — A346

**1997, Feb. 24 *Serpentine Die Cut***

**Self-Adhesive**
**2200** A346 7.50cor multicolored 2.25 2.25
*a.* Booklet pane of 12 27.00

The peelable paper backing serves as a booklet cover.

"Iberoamerica," Spanish-America Art Exhibition — A347

Painting, "Night with Two Figures," by Alejandro Aróstegui.

**1998, May 8 *Perf. 13½***
**2201** A347 7.50cor multicolored 2.00 2.00

Butterflies — A348

No. 2202: a, Metamorpha stelenes. b, Erateina staudingeri. c, Premolis semirufa. d, Heliconius eisini. e, Phoebis phlea. f, Dione juno. g, Helicopis cupido. h, Catonephele numili. i, Anteos clorinde.
No. 2203, 25cor, Thecla coronata. No. 2204, 25cor, Ufefheisa bela.

**1999, Mar. 15 Litho. *Perf. 14***
**2202** A348 2.50cor Sheet of 9, #a.-i. 5.00 5.00

**Souvenir Sheets**
**2203-2204** A348 Set of 2 15.50 15.50
Dated 1996.

Fauna of Central America — A349

No. 2205, 2cor: a, Red banded parrot. b, Sloth. c, Porcupine. d, Toucan. e, Howler monkey. f, Anteater. g, Kinkajou. h, Owl monkey. i, Red-footed land turtle. j, Red deer. k, Armadillo. l, Paca.
No. 2206, 2cor: a, Vulture. b, Tarantula. c, Palm viper. d, Ocelot. e, Fighting spider. f, Large fruit bat. g, Jaguar. h, Venomous tree frog. i, Viper. j, Grison. k, Rattlesnake. l, Puma.
No. 2207, 25cor, Tapir. No. 2208, 25cor, Caiman.

**1999, Mar. 15 Sheets of 12, #a-l**

**2205-2206** A349 Set of 2 9.00 9.00

**Souvenir Sheets**

**2207-2208** A349 Set of 2 9.00 9.00

Dated 1996.

Endangered Species — A350

No. 2209, 2.50cor: a, Owls, gorilla. b, Cheetahs. c, Giraffes. d, Gazelle, elephants. e, Elephants. f, Lion, okapi. g, Rhinoceros. h, Hippopotamus. i, Lion.

No. 2210, 2.50cor, vert: a, Lemurs. b, Blue gliding parrot. c, Toucan. d, Boa. e, Jaguar. f, Margay. g, Loris. h, White egret. i, Armadillo.

No. 2211, 2.50cor, vert: a, Prezwalski horse. b, Red deer. c, Zebra. d, Golden lion monkey. e, African elephant. f, Black bear. g, Tiger. h, Orangutan. i, Snow leopard.

25cor, Chimpanzee. 25.50cor, Panda, vert.

**1999, Mar. 15 Sheets of 9, #a-i**

**2209-2211** A350 Set of 3 14.00 14.00

**Souvenir Sheets**

**2212** A350 25cor multi 4.50 4.50
**2213** A350 25.50cor multi 4.75 4.75

Dated 1996.

India's Independence, 50th Anniv. — A351

**1998, Aug. 13 Litho. *Perf. 14½***

**2214** A351 3cor blue & multi .50 .50
**2215** A351 9cor brn yel & multi 1.50 1.50

Dated 1997.

Nature Reserves and Natl. Parks A352

Designs: 1.50cor, Mombacho Volcano Nature Reserve. 2.50cor, La Flor Wildlife Refuge. 3cor, Zapatera Archipelago Natl. Park. 3.50cor, Miraflor Nature Reserve. 5cor, Cosigüina Volcano Natl. Park. 6.50cor, Masaya Volcano Natl. Park. 7.50cor, Juan Venado Island Nature Reserve. 8cor, Escalante Chacocente River Wildlife Refuge. 10cor, Protected Areas, Natl. Park System.

12cor, Trees, first Biosphere Reserve.

**1998, Aug. 20 *Perf. 10½***

**2216** A352 1.50cor multicolored .25 .25
**2217** A352 2.50cor multicolored .45 .45
**2218** A352 3cor multicolored .50 .50
**2219** A352 3.50cor multicolored .60 .60
**2220** A352 5cor multicolored .85 .85
**2221** A352 6.50cor multicolored 1.10 1.10
**2222** A352 7.50cor multicolored 1.25 1.25
**2223** A352 8cor multicolored 1.40 1.40
**2224** A352 10cor multicolored 1.75 1.75
*Nos. 2216-2224 (9)* 8.15 8.15

**Size: 65x95mm**

***Imperf***

**2225** A352 12cor multicolored 2.60 2.00

National Museum, Cent A353

**1998, Aug. 25**

**2226** A353 3.50cor Footprints .80 .60

Paintings by Rodrigo Peñalba (1908-1979) A354

Designs: 2.50cor, "Descendimiento." 3.50cor, "Victoria y Piere With Child." 5cor, "Motherhood."

10cor, "El Güegüense."

**1998, Aug. 26 *Perf. 10½***

**2227** A354 2.50cor multicolored .45 .45
**2228** A354 3.50cor multicolored .60 .60
**2229** A354 5cor multicolored .85 .85
*Nos. 2227-2229 (3)* 1.90 1.90

**Size: 95x65mm**

***Imperf***

**2230** A354 10cor multicolored 1.90 1.75

Child's Painting, "Children Love Peace" — A355

**1998, Aug. 28 *Perf. 14½***

**2231** A355 50c multicolored .30 .25

Dated 1997.

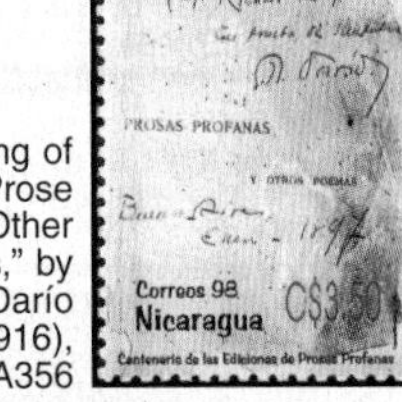


Publishing of "Profane Prose and Other Poems," by Rubén Darío (1867-1916), Cent. — A356

**1998, Sept. 11 *Perf. 10½***

**2232** A356 3.50cor shown .60 .60
**2233** A356 5cor Portrait .85 .85

Naturaleza '98 — A357

Painting by Bayron Gómez Chavarría.

**1998, Sept. 25**

**2234** A357 3.50cor multicolored .80 .60

World Stamp Day — A358

**1998, Oct. 9**

**2235** A358 6.50cor multicolored 1.10 1.10

Dialogue of Nicaragua A359

**1998, Oct. 12**

**2236** A359 5cor multicolored .85 .85

Famous Nicaraguan Women — A360

America issue: 3.50cor, Lolita Soriano de Guerrero (b. 1922), writer. 7.50cor, Violeta Barrios de Chamorro (b. 1929), former president.

**1998, Oct. 16**

**2237** A360 3.50cor multicolored .60 .60
**2238** A360 7.50cor multicolored 1.40 1.25

Universal Declaration of Human Rights, 50th Anniv. A361

**1998, Dec. 10 *Perf. 13½***

**2239** A361 12cor multicolored 2.10 2.10

Christmas — A362

Nativity scenes: 50c, Molded miniature, vert. 1cor, Drawing on pottery, vert. 2cor, Adoration of the Magi. 3cor, Painting.

7.50cor, Painting of angel over modern village.

**1998, Dec. 14 *Perf. 14***

**2240** A362 50c multicolored .25 .25
**2241** A362 1cor multicolored .25 .25
**2242** A362 2cor multicolored .35 .35
**2243** A362 3cor multicolored .50 .50
*Nos. 2240-2243 (4)* 1.35 1.35

**Size: 95x64mm**

***Imperf***

**2244** A362 7.50cor multicolored 1.25 1.25

Dated 1997.

Managua Earthquake, 25th Anniv. (in 1997) — A363

Designs: 3cor, Managua in 1997, vert. 7.50cor, Devastation after earthquake in 1972. 10.50cor, Buildings toppling, clock, vert.

**1998, Dec. 23**

**2245** A363 3cor multicolored .50 .50
**2246** A363 7.50cor multicolored 1.25 1.25

**Souvenir Sheet**

**2247** A363 10.50cor multicolored 1.75 1.75

Dated 1997.

Diana, Princess of Wales (1961-97) — A364

Designs: 5cor, Wearing hat. 7.50cor, Wearing tiara. 10cor, Wearing white dress.

**1999, Apr. 29 Litho. *Perf. 13½***

**2248-2250** A364 Set of 3 3.75 3.75

Nos. 2248-2250 were each issued in sheets of 6.

Butterflies A365

Designs: 3.50cor, Papilionidae ornithoptera. 8cor, Nymphalidae cepheuptychia. 12.50cor, Pieridae phoebis.

No. 2254: a, Nymphalidae eryphanis. b, Nymphalidae callicore. c, Nymphalidae hypolimmas. d, Nymphalidae precis. e, Papilionidae troides. f, Nymphalidae cithaerias. g, Papilionidae parides. h, Nymphalidae heliconius. i, Nymphalidae morpho.

15cor, Papilionidae papilio.

**1999, Apr. 30 *Perf. 14***

**2251-2253** A365 Set of 3 4.25 4.25
**2254** A365 9cor Sheet of 9, #a.-i. 14.00 14.00

**Souvenir Sheet**

**2255** A365 15cor multicolored 3.25 3.25

Sailing Ships — A366

Paintings: 2cor, Eagle, 1851, US. 4cor, Contest, 1800, US. 5cor, Architect, 1847, US. 10cor, Edward O'Brien, 1863, UK.

No. 2260, vert: a, HMS Rodney, 1830, UK. b, Boyne, 1700's, Great Britain. c, Castor, 1800's, UK. d, Mutin, 1800's, UK. e, Britainnia, 1820, UK. f, Gouden Leeuw, 1600, Holland. g, Hercules, 1600, Holland. h, Resolution, 1667, Great Britain. i, Royal George, 1756, Great Britain. j, Vanguard, 1700's, Great Britain. k, Prince Royal, 1600, Great Britain. l, Zeven Provincien, 1600, Holland.

No. 2261, 15cor, Pamir, 1905, US. No. 2262, 15cor, Great Expedition, 1700's, Great Britain.

**1999, May 31 Litho. *Perf. 14x13½***
2256-2259 A366 Set of 4 3.75 3.75
***Perf. 14½x14¼***
2260 A366 3cor Sheet of 12, #a.-l. 6.50 6.50

**Souvenir Sheets**
***Perf. 13½x14***
2261-2262 A366 Set of 2 5.50 5.50

No. 2260 contains twelve 28x36mm stamps.

Flora and Fauna A367

Designs: 5cor, Anteos clorinde. 6cor, Coereba flaveola. No. 2265, 7.50cor, Rynchops niger. No. 2266, 7.50cor, Chaetodon striatus.

No. 2267, vert: a, Palm tree. b, Phaethon lepturus. c, Cinclocerthia ruficauda. d, Myadestes genibarbis. e, Rosa sinesis. f, Cyanophala bicolor. g, Delphinus delphis. h, Anolis carolinensis (l). i, Dynastes tityus. j, Heliconia psittacorum. k, Iguana iguana (j). l, Propona meander.

No. 2268, 10cor, Ceryle torquata, vert. No. 2269, 10cor, Anisotremus virginicus.

**1999, June 14 *Perf. 14x14¼***
2263-2266 A367 Set of 4 4.75 4.75
***Perf. 14¼x14***
2267 A367 5cor Sheet of 12, #a.-l. 11.00 11.00

**Souvenir Sheet**
2268-2269 A367 Set of 2 4.50 4.50

No. 2267 l is inscribed 3cor, but the editors believe the sheet was sold as sheet of 5cor stamps.

Birds — A368

Designs: 5cor, Eudyptes chrysocome. 5.50cor, Spheniscus magellanious. 6cor, Pygoscelis antarctica. 7.50cor, Magadyptes antipodes.

No. 2274, horiz.: a, Phalacrocorax punctatus featherstoni. b, Phalacrocorax bougainvillii. c, Anhinga anhinga. d, Phalacrocorax punctatus punctatus. e, Phalacrocorax sulcirostris. f, Pelecanus occidentalis.

No. 2275, 12cor, Aptenodytes forsteri, horiz. No. 2276, 12cor, Pygoscelis papua.

**1999, May 25 Litho. *Perf. 14***
2270-2273 A368 Set of 4 4.00 4.00
2274 A368 6cor Sheet of 6, #a.-f. 6.00 6.00

**Souvenir Sheets**
2275-2276 A368 Set of 2 4.00 4.00

Dated 1998.

Dinosaurs A369

No. 2277: a, Sordes. b, Dimorphodon. c, Anurognathus. d, Rhamphorhynchus. e, Pterodaustro. f, Pteranodon.

No. 2278: a, Macroplata. b, Coelurus. c, "Stegosaurus." d, "Corythosaurus." e, Thadeosaurus. f, "Brachisaurus."

No. 2279, 12cor, Platecarpus. No. 2280, 12cor, Pterodactylus.

**1999, June 1 Litho. *Perf. 14***
2277 A369 5cor Sheet of 6, #a.-f. 5.00 5.00
2278 A369 6cor Sheet of 6, #a.-f. 6.00 6.00

**Souvenir Sheets**
2279-2280 A369 Set of 2 4.00 4.00

Dated 1998. Stamp inscriptions on Nos. 2278c, 2278d and 2278f, and perhaps others, are incorrect or misspelled.

Trains A370

Designs: 1cor, U25B, Rock Island Line. 5cor, C-630 Santa Fe Railroad. 6.50cor, Class D. D. 40 AX, Union Pacific Railroad. 7.50cor, F Series B. B. EMD, Maryland Department of Transportation.

No. 2285: a, CR Alco RS11. b, Metra EMD F40. c, British Columbia Railways GF6C. d, Amtrak AEM7. e, C-40-9, Norfolk Southern. f, C-630, Reading Railroad.

No. 2286: a, British Columbia Railways GF6C, diff. b, Indian Railways WDM C-C. c, Class 421, Australia. d, Class M821, Australia. e, LRC B.B., Via Canada. f, GM Class X, Victorian Railways, Australia.

No. 2287, 15cor, Queen Victoria. No. 2288, 15cor, Donald Smith driving last spike of Trans-Canada Railway, vert.

**1999, June 28 Litho. *Perf. 14***
2281-2284 A370 Set of 4 3.25 3.25
2285 A370 5cor Sheet of 6, #a.-f. 5.00 5.00
2286 A370 6cor Sheet of 6, #a.-f. 6.00 6.00

**Souvenir Sheets**
2287-2288 A370 Set of 2 5.00 5.00

Dated 1998. Stamp inscription on No. 2284, and perhaps others, is misspelled.

Mushrooms and Insects — A371

No. 2289: a, Tricholoma ustaloides, leaf beetle. b, Tricholoma pardinum, grasshopper. c, Amanita echinocephala, crickets. d, Tricholoma saponaceum, red-tipped clearwing moth. e, Amanita inaurata, hanging scorpionfly. f, Amanita rubescens, assassin bug.

No. 2290: a, Amanita citrina, banded agrion. b, Cryoptotrama asprata, clouded yellow butterfly. c, Amanita gemmata, mayfly. d, Catathelasma imperiale, variable reed beetle. e, Collybia fusipes, black swallowtail caterpillar. f, Collybia butyracea, South African savannah grasshopper.

No. 2291, 12.50cor, Tricholomopsis rutilans, lesser cloverleaf weevil. No. 2292, 12.50cor, Tricholoma virgatum, rose weevil.

**1999, Oct. 27 Litho. *Perf. 13¼x13½***
2289 A371 5.50cor Sheet of 6, #a.-f. 5.50 5.50
2290 A371 7.50cor Sheet of 6, #a.-f. 7.25 7.25

**Souvenir Sheets**
2291-2292 A371 Set of 2 4.00 4.00

Dated 1998.

Ballooning — A372

No. 2293, 12cor: a, Solo Spirit 3. b, Emblem of Breitling Orbiter 3, first balloon to make non-stop circumnavigation, 1999. c, ICO Global.

No. 2294, 12cor: a, Breitling Orbiter 3 over mountains. b, Leonardo da Vinci. c, Brian Jones and Bertrand Piccard, pilots of Breitling Orbiter 3.

No. 2295, 12cor: a, Tiberius Cavallo. b, Breitling Orbiter 3 on ground. c, Piccard and Jones, diff.

No. 2296, 12cor: a, Jones. b, Breitling Orbiter 3 in flight. c, Piccard.

No. 2297, 25cor, Jean-Francois Pilatre de Rozier. No. 2298, 25cor, Jean-Pierre Blanchard. No. 2299, 25cor, Madame Thible. No. 2300, 25cor, J. A. C. Charles.

**1999, Nov. 12 *Perf. 13½x13¼***
**Sheets of 3, #a-c**
2293-2296 A372 Set of 4 24.00 24.00

**Souvenir Sheets**
2297-2300 A372 Set of 4 16.00 16.00

Dated 1998.

Orchids — A373

Designs: 2cor, Cattleya, skinneri. 4cor, Lycaste aromatica. 5cor, Odontoglossum cervantesii. 10cor, Brassia verrucosa.

No. 2305, 3cor: a, Odontoglossum rossii. b, Cattleya aurantiaca. c, Encyclia cordigera. d, Phragmipedium bessae. e, Brassavola nodosa. f, Cattleya forbesii.

No. 2306, 3cor: a, Barkeria spectabilis. b, Dracula erythrochaete. c, Cochleanthes discolor. d, Encyclia cochleata. e, Lycaste aromatica. f, Brassia maculata.

No. 2307, 25cor, Odontoglossum rossii, diff. No. 2308, 25cor, Phragmipedium longifolium.

**1999, Nov. 10**
2301-2304 A373 Set of 4 4.00 3.50

**Sheets of 6, #a.-f.**
2305-2306 A373 Set of 2 7.25 6.00

**Souvenir Sheets**
2307-2308 A373 Set of 2 8.00 8.00

Rubén Darío Natl. Theater, 30th Anniv. A374

**1999, Dec. 6 *Perf. 13¼x13½***
2309 A374 7.50cor multi 1.25 1.25

Inter-American Development Bank, 40th Anniv. — A375

**1999, Nov. 18 *Perf. 13¼***
2310 A375 7.50cor multi 1.25 1.25

America Issue, A New Millennium Without Arms — A376

**1999, Nov. 25 *Perf. 13½***
2311 A376 7.50cor multi 1.25 1.25

Japanese-Nicaraguan Friendship — A377

Designs: a, 3.50cor, Fishing boats, Puertos Cabezas. b, 9cor, Hospital. c, 5cor, Combine in field. d, 6cor, Japanese school. e, 7.50cor, Bridge on Pan-American Highway. f, 8cor, Aqueduct.

**1999, Nov. 12 *Perf. 13x13¼***
2312 A377 Sheet of 6, #a.-f. 7.50 7.50

UPU, 125th Anniv. — A378

**1999, Dec. 20 Litho. *Perf. 13½***
2313 A378 7.50cor multi 1.40 1.40

Cities of Granada and León, 475th Anniv. A379

No. 2314 — Granada: a, City Hall. b, Guadalupe Church. c, Buildings on central square. d, Houses with porches. e, House of the Leones. f, El Consulado Street.

No. 2315 — León: a, Cathedral. b, Municipal theater. c, La Recolección Church. d, Rubén Dario Museum. e, Post and Telegraph office. f, Cural de Subtiava house.

**1999, Dec. 13 *Perf. 13x13½***
2314 A379 3.50cor Sheet of 6, #a.-f. 3.50 3.50
2315 A379 7.50cor Sheet of 6, #a.-f. 7.25 7.25

Dogs and Cats — A380

Designs: 1cor, Azawakh. 2cor, Chihuahua. 2.50cor, Chocolate colorpoint Birman, horiz. 3cor, Norwegian Forest cat, horiz.

No. 2320: a, Clumber spaniel. b, Australian shepherd. c, German wire-haired pointer. d, Unnnamed. e, Ibizan hound. f, Norwegian elkhound.

No. 2321, horiz.: a, Blue European Shorthair. b, Turkish Angora. c, Red Tiffany. d, Persian. e, Calico Shorthair. f, Russian Blue.

No. 2322, 12cor, Braque du Bourbonnais. No. 2323, 12cor, Burmese, horiz.

*Perf. 13¾x13½, 13½x13¾*

**2000, July 20** **Litho.**

**2316-2319** A380 Set of 4 1.50 1.50
**2320** A380 6cor Sheet of 6, #a-f 6.25 6.25
**2321** A380 6.50cor Sheet of 6, #a-f 6.75 6.75

**Souvenir Sheets**

**2322-2323** A380 Set of 2 4.25 4.25

No. 2322 contains one 42x56mm stamp; No. 2323 contains one 56x42mm stamp.

Trains A381

Designs: 3cor, Class 470 APT-P, Great Britain. 4cor, X-2000, Sweden. 5cor, XPT, Australia. 10cor, High speed train, Great Britain.

No. 2328: a, Metro North B-25-7. b, Long Island Railroad EMD DE30. c, EMD F40 PHM-2C. d, Pennsylvania Railroad GG1. e, New Jersey Transit MK GP40 FH-2. f, Amtrak EMD F59 PHI.

No. 2329: a, DM-3, Sweden. b, EW 165, New Zealand. c, Class 87, Great Britain. d, Class 40, Great Britain. e, GE 6/6, Switzerland. f, Class 277, Spain.

No. 2330, Metra EMD P69PN-AC. No. 2331, Class 44, Great Britain.

**2000, Aug. 21** **Litho.** ***Perf. 14***

**2324-2327** A381 Set of 4 3.75 3.75

**Sheets of 6, #a-f**

**2328-2329** A381 3cor Set of 2 6.25 6.25

**Souvenir Sheets**

**2330-2331** A381 25cor Set of 2 8.50 8.50

Marine Life A382

Designs: 3.50cor, Great white shark. 5cor, Humpback whale. 6cor, Sea turtle. 9cor, Sperm whale.

No. 2336, 7.50cor: a, Puffer fish. b, Manta ray. c, Black grouper. d, Tiger grouper. e, Golden-tailed eel. f, Atlantic squid.

No. 2337, 7.50cor: a, Hawksbill turtle. b, Moon jellyfish. c, Caribbean reef shark. d, Turtle. e, Spotted dolphin. f, Southern sting ray.

No. 2338, Tiger shark. No. 2339, Spotted dolphins.

**2000, Aug. 22** ***Perf. 14***

**2332-2335** A382 Set of 4 4.00 4.00

**Sheets of 6, #a-f**

**2336-2337** A382 Set of 2 17.50 17.50

**Souvenir Sheets**

**2338-2339** A382 25cor Set of 2 9.50 9.50

Queen Mother, 100th Birthday — A383

No. 2340: a, As young woman. b, In 1970. c, With King George VI. d, As old woman.

**Litho. (Margin Embossed)**

**2000, July 25** ***Perf. 14***

**2340** A383 10cor Sheet of 4, #a-d + label 7.00 7.00

**Souvenir Sheet**

***Perf. 13¾***

**2341** A383 25cor In 1948 4.25 4.25

No. 2341 contains one 38x51mm stamp.

History of Aviation — A384

No. 2342, 7.50cor: a, Montgolfier balloon (blue background), vert. b, Hawker Hart. c, Lysander. d, Bleriot and Fox Moth, vert. e, Harrier. f, VC10.

No. 2343, 7.50cor: a, Montgolfier balloon (tan background), vert. b, Bristol F2B. c, Jet Provost. d, Avro 504K and Redwing II trainer, vert. e, Hunter. f, Wessex.

No. 2344, 25cor, Spartan Arrow (top) and Tiger Moth. No. 2345, 25cor, Tiger Moth (top) and Spartan Arrow.

**2000, July 27** **Litho.** ***Perf. 14½x14***

**Sheets of 6, #a-d**

**2342-2343** A384 Set of 2 15.00 15.00

**Souvenir Sheets**

**2344-2345** A384 Set of 2 8.50 8.50

Size of Nos. 2342a, 2342d, 2343a, 2343d: 41x60mm.

Birds — A385

Designs: 5cor, Cotinga amabilis. 7.50cor, Galbula ruficauda. 10cor, Guiraca caerulea. 12.50cor, Momotus momota.

No. 2350: a, Ara macao. b, Amazona ochrocephala. c, Chloroceryle americana. d, Archilocus colubris. e, Pharamachrus mocinno. f, Ramphastos sulfuratus. g, Coereba flaveola. h, Piculus rubiginosus. i, Passerina ciris. j, Busarellus nigricollis.

No. 2351, 25cor, Aulacorhynchus prasinus. No. 2352, 25cor, Ceryle alcyon.

**2000, Aug. 23** ***Perf. 14***

**2346-2349** A385 Set of 4 7.00 7.00
**2350** A385 3cor Sheet of 10, #a-j 6.00 6.00

**Souvenir Sheets**

**2351-2352** A385 Set of 2 8.50 8.50

Space Exploration — A386

No. 2353, 5cor: a, Donald K. Slayton. b, M. Scott Carpenter. c, Walter M. Schirra. d, John H. Glenn, Jr. e, L. Gordon Cooper. f, Virgil I. Grissom. g, Mercury Redsone 3 rocket. h, Alan B. Shepard.

No. 2354, 5cor, horiz.: a, Recovery of Mercury 8. b, View of Earth from space. c, Carpenter in life raft. d, Shepard in water. e, USS Intrepid. f, Friendship 7. g, Mercury 9 splashdown. h, Recovery of Mercury 6.

No. 2355, 25cor, Glenn, diff. No. 2356, 25cor, Shepard, horiz.

**2000, Aug. 25** **Litho.**

**Sheets of 8, #a-h**

**2353-2354** A386 Set of 2 14.00 14.00

**Souvenir Sheets**

**2355-2356** A386 Set of 2 8.50 8.50

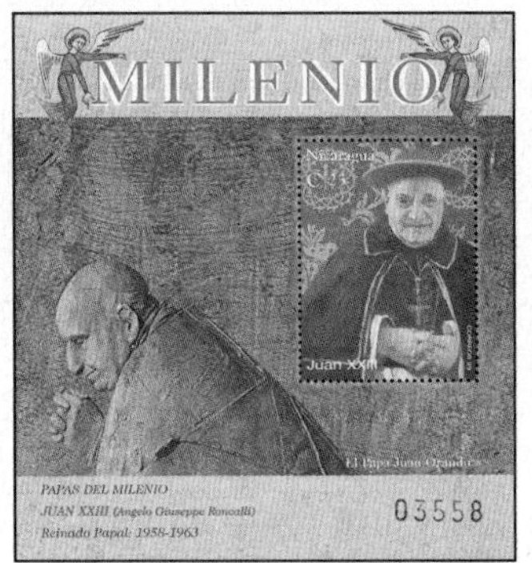

Millennium — A387

No. 2357: a, Pope Leo XIII. b, Rerum Novarum. c, Pope Pius X. d, Revision of ecclesiastic music. e, Pope Benedict XV. f, Canonization of Joan of Arc. g, Pope Pius XI. h, Establishment of Radio Vatican. i, Pope John XXIII. j, Peace symbol. k, Pope Paul VI. l, Arms of Paul VI. m, Pope John Paul I. n, Lamb and cross. o, Pope John Paul II. p, Globe, hands holding dove.

No. 2358, 25cor, John XXIII. No. 2359, 25cor, John Paul II.

**2000, Sept. 7** ***Perf. 13¼***

**2357** A387 3cor Sheet of 16, #a-p + label 9.50 9.50

**Souvenir Sheets**

**2358-2359** A387 Set of 2 10.00 10.00

No. 2357 contains sixteen 30x40mm stamps.

Butterflies — A388

No. 2360, 8cor: a, Catonephele numilla esite. b, Marpesia marcella. c, Heliconius hecalesia. d, Actinote thalia anteas. e, Doxocopa larentia cherubina. f, Napeogenes tolosa mombachoensis.

No. 2361, 9cor: a, Heliconius cydno galanthus. b, Nessaea agiaura. c, Godyris zavaleta sosunga. d, Caligo atreus dionysos. e, Morpho amatonte. f, Eryphanis polyxena lycomedon.

No. 2362, 25cor, Papilio garamas. No. 2363, 25cor, Cithaerias menander.

**2000, Sept. 27** ***Perf. 14***

**Sheets of 6, #a-f**

**2360-2361** A388 Set of 2 22.50 22.50

**Souvenir Sheets**

**2362-2363** A388 Set of 2 10.00 10.00

20th Century National Leaders — A389

No. 2364, 5cor: a, Kemal Ataturk, dam. b, Ataturk, Turkish flag, horiz. c, John F. Kennedy, wife Jacqueline, Soviet missiles, horiz. d, John F. Kennedy, rocket. e, Winston Churchill, bomb explosion. f, Churchill, airplane, horiz. g, Jomo Kenyatta, tribesman, animals, horiz. h, Kenyatta, Mt. Kenya.

No. 2365, 5cor: a, Indira Gandhi. b, Indira Gandhi, soldier, elephant, horiz. c, Ronald Reagan, airplanes, horiz. d, Reagan, American flags. e, Lenin. f, Lenin, hammer and sickle, horiz. g, Charles de Gaulle, Eiffel Tower, horiz. h, De Gaulle, monument.

No. 2366, 25cor, Chiang Kai-shek. No. 2367, 25cor, Theodore Roosevelt.

**2000, Oct. 5** ***Perf. 14***

**Sheets of 8, #a-h**

**2364-2365** A389 Set of 2 14.00 14.00

**Souvenir Sheets**

**2366-2367** A389 Set of 2 8.50 8.50

Horizontal stamps are 56x42mm.

Lions Intl. — A390

No. 2368, horiz.: a, Melvin Jones and other founding members, Chicago, 1917. b, Old headquarters building, Chicago. c, Helen Keller and dog. d, UN Secretary General Kofi Annan greeting Lions Intl. Pres. Kajit Habananda. e, Jones and globe. f, André de Villiers, winner of 1998-99 Peace Poster contest.

**2000, Oct. 26** **Litho.**

**2368** A390 5cor Sheet of 6, #a-f 6.00 6.00

**Souvenir Sheet**

**2369** A390 25cor Melvin Jones 5.50 5.50

Rotary Intl. — A391

No. 2370: a, Clowns and child in Great Britain. b, Polio vaccination in Egypt. c, Burkina Faso natives at well. d, School for girls in Nepal. e, Assisting the disabled in Australia. f, Discussing problem of urban violence.

**2000, Oct. 26** *Perf. 14*
**2370** A391 7cor Sheet of 6, #a-f 7.25 7.25

**Souvenir Sheet**

**2371** A391 25cor Rotary emblem 4.25 4.25

Campaign Against AIDS A392

**2000, Dec. 1** **Litho.** *Perf. 13¼*
**2372** A392 7.50cor multi 1.60 1.60

Third Conference of States Signing Ottawa Convention — A393

Designs: 7.50cor, People, world map. 10cor, People opposing land mines on globe.

**2001, Sept. 18** *Perf. 13x13½*
**2373-2374** A393 Set of 2 3.25 3.25

Miniature Sheet

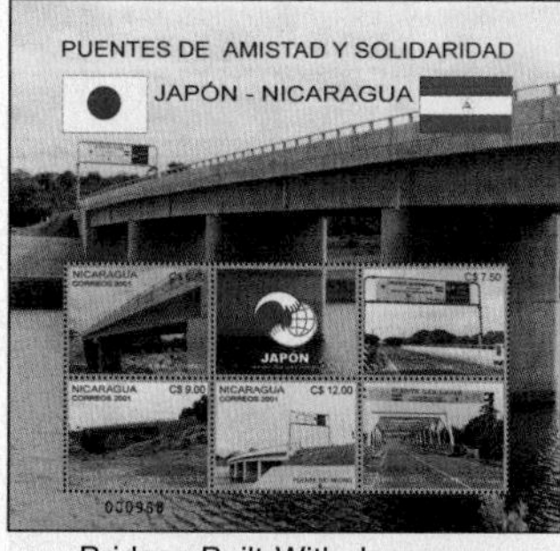


Bridges Built With Japanese Assistance — A394

No. 2375: a, 6.50cor, Tamarindo Bridge. b, 7.50cor, Ochomogo Bridge. c, 9cor, Gil González Bridge. d, 10cor, Las Lajas Bridge. e, 12cor, Río Negro Bridge.

**2001, Oct. 23** *Perf. 13x13¼*
**2375** A394 Sheet of 5, #a-e, + label 8.00 8.00

World Post Day — A395

**2001, Nov. 21** *Perf. 13½*
**2376** A395 6.50cor multi 1.40 1.40

Dated 2000.

America Issue — Old Léon Ruins, UNESCO World Heritage Site A396

**2001, Nov. 23** *Perf. 13½*
**2377** A396 10cor multi 1.90 1.90

Order of Piarists in Nicaragua, 50th Anniv. — A397

*Perf. 13¼x13½*

**2001, Nov. 27** **Litho.**
**2378** A397 7cor multi 1.25 1.25

Dated 2000.

Miniature Sheet

Endangered Wildlife — A398

No. 2379: a, 5cor, Rhamphastos swaisonii. b, 6.50cor, Amazona auropalliata. c, 8cor, Buteo magnirostris. d, 9cor, Atteles geoffroyi. 10cor, Leopardus wiedii. 12cor, Puma concolor.

**2001, Nov. 27** *Perf. 13¼x13*
**2379** A398 Sheet of 6, #a-f 7.50 7.50

Dated 2000.

SOS Children's Villages, 50th Anniv. — A399

**2001, Dec. 6** *Perf. 13¼x13½*
**2380** A399 5.50cor multi 1.00 1.00

Dated 2000.

Miguel Cardinal Obando Bravo A400

**2002, Jan. 3** **Litho.** *Perf. 13½*
**2381** A400 6.50cor multi 1.25 1.25

Souvenir Sheet

Friendship Between Nicaragua and People's Republic of China — A401

No. 2382: a, 3cor, President's House, Managua. b, 7.50cor, Ministry of Foreign Affairs Building, Managua.

**2002, Jan. 4** **Litho.** *Perf. 13x13¼*
**2382** A401 Sheet of 2, #a-b — —

Visit of UN Secretary General Kofi Annan to Nicaragua A402

**2002, Mar. 15** **Litho.** *Perf. 13¼*
**2383** A402 14cor multi 2.25 2.25

Sister Maria Romero A403

**2002, Apr. 9** *Perf. 13x13¼*
**2384** A403 7.50cor multi 1.50 1.50

Discovery of Nicaragua, 500th Anniv. A404

Design: 12cor, Natives watching ships on horizon, vert.

**2002, Sept. 12** **Litho.** *Perf. 13x13¼*
**2385** A404 7.50cor shown 1.50 1.50

**Souvenir Sheet**

*Perf. 13¼x13*

**2386** A404 12cor multi 2.75 2.00

America Issue - Youth, Education and Literacy — A405

**2002, Nov. 29** **Litho.** *Perf. 13¼x13*
**2387** A405 7.50cor multi 1.50 1.50

Canonization of St. Josemaría Escrivá de Balaguer — A406

**2002, Nov. 28** *Perf. 13x13¼*
**2388** A406 2.50cor multi .50 .50

Port of Corinto A407

**2002, Dec. 10**
**2389** A407 5cor multi 1.00 1.00

Managua Earthquake, 30th Anniv. — A408

Pictures of earthquake damage: 3.50cor, Avenida del Mercado Central. 7.50cor, Managua Cathedral, vert.

*Perf. 13¼x13½, 13½x13¼*

**2002, Dec. 13**
**2390-2391** A408 Set of 2 2.25 2.25

Visit of Grand Duke Henri and Princess Maria Teresa of Luxembourg A409

**2003, Feb. 5** *Perf. 13¼x13*
**2392** A409 12cor multi 2.50 2.50

Paintings — A410

Designs: 3cor, En Diriamba de Nicaragua, Capturaronme Amigo, by Roger Pérez de la Rocha. 5cor, San Gabriel Arcangel, by Orlando Sobalvarro. 6.50cor, Ava Fénix, by Alejandro Aróstegui. 7.50cor, Abstracción de Frutas, by Leonel Vanegas. 8cor, Suite en Turquesa y Azules, by Bernard Dreyfus, horiz. 9cor, Ana III, by Armando Morales, horiz. 10cor, Coloso IV, by Arnoldo Guillén, horiz.

*Perf. 14x13½, 13½x14*

**2003, Oct. 23** **Litho.**
**2393-2399** A410 Set of 7 8.50 8.50

Souvenir Sheet

Pontificate of Pope John Paul II, 25th Anniv. — A411

No. 2400: a, 3cor, Pope wearing zucchetto. b, 10cor, Pope wearing miter.

**2003, Oct. 28 Litho.** ***Perf. 13¼x13***
**2400** A411 Sheet of 2, #a-b 2.50 2.50

Christian Brothers (La Salle Order) in Nicaragua, Cent. — A412

Designs: 3cor, San Juan de Dios Hospice, horiz. 5cor, Brother Octavio de Jesús. 6.50cor, Brother Bodrán Marie. 7.50cor, Brother Agustin Hervé. 9cor, Brother Vauthier de Jesús. 10cor, Father Mariano Dubón.
12cor, St. Jean-Baptiste de la Salle.

***Perf. 13½x14, 14x13½***
**2003, Nov. 14** **Litho.**
**2401-2406** A412 Set of 6 7.00 7.00

**Souvenir Sheet**

**2407** A412 12cor multi 2.50 2.50

Insects — A413

No. 2408, 6.50cor: a, Fulgora laternaria. b, Acraephia perspicillata. c, Copidocephala guttata. d, Pterodictya reticularis. e, Phrictus quinquepartitus. f, Odontoptera carrenoi.
No. 2409, 8cor: a, Golofa pizarro. b, Phaneus pyrois. c, Plusiotis aurigans. d, Polyphylla concurrens. e, Dynastes hercules septentrionalis. f, Phaneus demon excelsus.

**2003, Nov. 19** ***Perf. 13x13½***
**Sheets of 6, #a-f**
**2408-2409** A413 Set of 2 14.00 14.00

Contemporary Crafts — A414

Designs: 3cor, Marble sculpture, vert. 5cor, Dolls. 6.50cor, Balsa wood fish and birds. 7.50cor, Cord and jipijapa hats. 8cor, Ceramics. 9cor, Saddle. 10cor, Clay rendition of Léon Cathedral.

***Perf. 14x13½, 13½x14***
**2003, Nov. 20**
**2410-2416** A414 Set of 7 8.00 8.00

Lake and River Mail Steamships A415

Designs: 3cor, Victoria. 5cor, Irma. 6.50cor, Hollenbeck. 7.50cor, Managua.

**2003, Nov. 28** ***Perf. 13½x14***
**2417-2420** A415 Set of 4 3.50 3.50

America Issue - Flora and Fauna A416

Designs: 10cor, Corytophanes cristatus. 12.50cor, Guaiacum sanctum.

**2003, Dec. 4** ***Perf. 13x13¼***
**2421-2422** A416 Set of 2 3.75 3.75

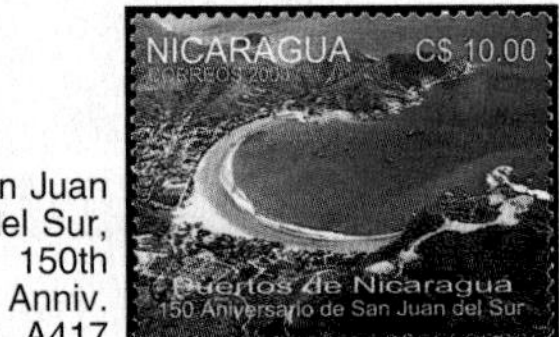

San Juan del Sur, 150th Anniv. A417

**2003, Dec. 9** **Litho.**
**2423** A417 10cor multi 1.75 1.75

Miniature Sheet

Toyota Motor Vehicles — A418

No. 2424: a, 1936 Model AA. b, 1936 Model AB Phaeton. c, 1947 Model SA. d, 1951 Model BJ. e, 1955 Model Crown RSD. f, 1958 Model FJ28VA.

**2003, Dec. 11**
**2424** A418 7.50cor Sheet of 6, #a-f 6.00 6.00

Publication of Tierras Solares, by Rubén Darío, Cent. A419

**2004, June 22** ***Perf. 13x13¼***
**2425** A419 10cor multi 1.75 1.75

Flora A420

Designs: 3cor, Tabebuia rosea. 5cor, Cassia fistula. 6.50cor, Delonix regia.

**2004, June 24**
**2426-2428** A420 Set of 3 2.60 2.60

America Issue - Environmental Protection — A421

Designs: No. 2429, 7.50cor, Bosawas Río Bocay Biosphere Reserve. No. 2430, 7.50cor, Cerro Kilambé Nature Reserve.

**2004, June 30**
**2429-2430** A421 Set of 2 2.75 2.75

2004 Summer Olympics, Athens — A422

Designs: 7.50cor, Track athletes. 10cor, Swimmers. 12cor, Rifleman.

**2004, Aug. 13** ***Perf. 13¼x13***
**2431-2433** A422 Set of 3 4.75 4.75

Central American Student's Games, Managua A423

Designs: 3cor, Judo. 5cor, Soccer, baseball. 6.50cor, High jump, swimming.

**2004, Sept. 17**
**2434-2436** A423 Set of 3 2.75 2.75

Birds — A424

Designs: 5cor, Selenidera spectabilis. 6.50cor, Nycticorax nycticorax. 7.50cor, Caracara plancus. 10cor, Myiozetetes similis.

**2004, Sept. 28** **Litho.**
**2437-2440** A424 Set of 4 5.00 5.00

Granada Railroad Station A425

**2004, Oct. 8** ***Perf. 13x13¼***
**2441** A425 3cor multi .50 .40

Tourist Attractions A426

Designs: No. 2442, 7.50cor, Río Tapou, Río San Juan Forest Refuge. No. 2443, 7.50cor, Mombacho Volcano Natural Reserve.

**2004, Oct. 12**
**2442-2443** A426 Set of 2 2.50 2.50

Contemporary Paintings — A427

Designs: 3cor, Frutas Ocultas, by Federico Nordalm. 7.50cor, Nicaraguapa, by Efrén Medina, vert. 10cor, Bambues, by Genaro Lugo.

**2004, Nov. 4** ***Perf. 13x13¼, 13¼x13***
**2444-2446** A427 Set of 3 3.50 3.50

Dogma of the Immaculate Conception, 150th Anniv. — A428

**2004, Dec. 6** ***Perf. 13¼x13***
**2447** A428 3cor multi .50 .40

Pablo Neruda (1904-73), Poet — A429

**2004, Dec. 16**
**2448** A429 7.50cor multi 1.25 1.25

Publication of *Songs of Life and Hope*, by Rubén Darío, Cent. — A430

**2005, Feb. 7 Litho.** ***Perf. 13¼x13½***
**2449** A430 7.50col multi + label 1.40 1.40

Souvenir Sheet

Nicaragua — Japan Diplomatic Relations, 70th Anniv. — A431

No. 2450: a, 3col, Adult volunteer teaching student. b, 7.50col, Momotombo Volcano. c, 10col, Vado Bridge, Bocana de Paiwas. d, 12col, Flowers.

**2005, Feb. 21** ***Perf. 13x13¼***
**2450** A431 Sheet of 4, #a-d 5.00 5.00

Orchids — A432

Designs: 3.50cor, Eleanthus hymeniformis. 5cor, Laelia superbens. 6.50cor, Cattleya aurentiaca. 7.50cor, Bletia roezlii. 10cor, Dimerandra emarginata. 12cor, Epidendrum werckleii.
25cor, Cyhysis tricostata.

**2005** **Litho.** ***Perf. 13¼x13***
**2451-2456** A432 Set of 6 6.25 6.25

**Souvenir Sheet**

**2457** A432 25cor multi 3.75 3.75

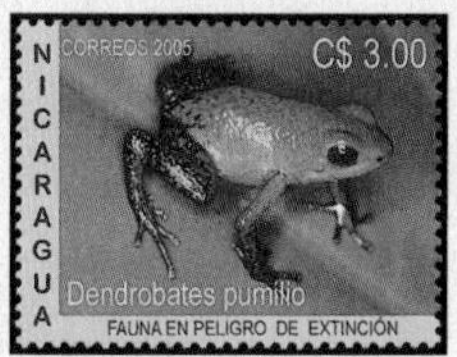

Endangered Reptiles and Amphibians — A433

Designs: 3cor, Dendrobates pumilio. 6.50cor, Drymodius melanotropis. 7.50cor, Cochranella granulosa. 10cor, Bolitoglossa mombachoensis. 12cor, Caiman crocodilus. 15cor, Polychrus gutturosus.
25cor, Lepidochelys olivacea.

**2005** **Litho.** ***Perf. 13x13¼***
**2458-2463** A433 Set of 6 7.75 7.75

**Souvenir Sheet**

**2464** A433 25cor multi 3.75 3.75

Intl. Year of Microcredit A434

**2005** **Litho.** ***Perf. 13¼x13***
**2465** A434 3.50cor multi .60 .45

Europa Stamps, 50th Anniv. A435

Designs: Nos. 2466, 2470a, 14cor, Morpho peleides. Nos. 2467, 2470b, 14cor, Amazona autumnalis. Nos. 2468, 2470c, 15cor, Rubén Dario Monument. Nos. 2469, 2470d, 25cor, Antigua Cathedral, Managua.

**2005, Dec. 12** ***Perf. 13¾x13½***
**2466-2469** A435 Set of 4 10.00 10.00

**Souvenir Sheet**

***Imperf***

**2470** A435 Sheet of 4, #a-d 15.00 15.00

No. 2470 contains four 40x30mm stamps.

Souvenir Sheet

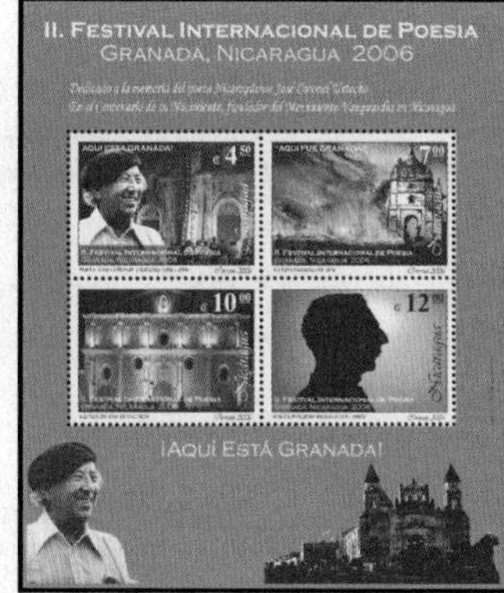

Second Intl. Poetry Festival, Granada — A436

No. 2471: a, 4.50cor, Jose Coronel Urtecho (1906-94), poet. b, 7cor, Guadalupe Church, 1856. c, 10cor, Church of St. Francis. d, 12cor, Joaquin Pasos (1914-47), poet.

**2006** **Litho.** ***Perf. 14***
**2471** A436 Sheet of 4, #a-d 4.75 4.75

Environmental Protection — A437

Designs: 4.50cor, Casmerodius albus. 11.50cor, Amazilia tzacatl. 13.50cor, Jacana spinosa. 14.50cor, Mico River.

**2007** **Litho.** ***Perf. 13x13¼***
**2472-2475** A437 Set of 4 6.50 6.50

Gen. Augusto C. Sandino (1893-1934) A438

Various photographs of Sandino: 8.50cor, 10.50cor, 12.50cor.

**2007** ***Perf. 13¼x13***
**2476-2478** A438 Set of 3 5.00 5.00

Land Mine Clearance Program, 15th Anniv. A439

**2007** **Litho.** ***Perf. 13x13¼***
**2479** A439 19cor multi 3.25 3.25

Literacy Campaign, 27th Anniv. — A440

Various literacy campaign workers and students: 1cor, 2cor, 2.50cor, 4.50cor.

**2007** ***Perf. 13¼x13***
**2480-2483** A440 Set of 4 1.75 1.75

Second Edition of "Cantos de Vida y Esperanza," by Rubén Darío — A441

Designs: 4cor, Baptismal font, León Cathedral. 10cor, Photograph of Darío at age 5. 13.50cor, Birthplace of Darío, monument. 16cor, Portrait of Darío as diplomat in Spain.

**2007, May 4** **Litho.** ***Perf. 13¼x13***
**2484-2487** A441 Set of 4 6.50 6.50

Port Facilities A442

Designs: 1cor, Port of Corinto. 2cor, Port of Rama. 5cor, Port of Granada. 10cor, Port of San Juan del Sur. 15cor, Port of Sandino. 25cor, Salvador Allende Port.

**2009, Apr. 28** **Litho.** ***Perf. 10½***
**2488-2493** A442 Set of 6 7.50 7.50

Gen. Augusto C. Sandino (1895-1934) A443

Designs: No. 2494, 10cor, Sandino and wife, Blanca Aráuz. No. 2495, 10cor, Statue of Sandino.

**2009, May 18** **Litho.** ***Perf. 10½***
**2494-2495** A443 Set of 2 3.00 3.00

Víctor Raúl Haya de la Torre (1895-1979), President of Peruvian Constitutional Assembly — A444

**2009, May 27** **Litho.** ***Perf. 10½***
**2496** A444 12cor multi 1.90 1.90

Nicaraguan Social Security Institute, 50th Anniv. A445

50th anniversary emblem and: 4cor, Nurse examining child. 14cor, Hands, map of Nicaragua. 16cor, Elderly women. 25cor, Workman wearing air filter.

**2009, July 30** **Litho.** ***Perf. 10½***
**2497-2500** A445 Set of 4 8.00 8.00

A446

Sandinista Revolution, 30th Anniv. A447

Designs: 4cor, General Augusto C. Sandino. 5cor, Victory celebration, July 19, 1979. 60cor, Soldier.

**2009, July 30**
**2501** A446 4cor multi .60 .60
**2502** A446 5cor multi .80 .80
**2503** A447 60cor multi 8.00 8.00
*Nos. 2501-2503 (3)* 9.40 9.40

Caribbean Coast Autonomy Law, 22nd Anniv. A448

Designs: 6.50cor, Creole children. 10cor, Map and Mayagna people. 14cor, Garifuna people, vert. 60cor, Dancers wrapping ribbons around pole.

**2009, Oct. 9** **Litho.** ***Perf. 10½***
**2504-2507** A448 Set of 4 8.75 8.75

Central American Court of Justice, 17th Anniv. — A449

**2009**
**2508** A449 25cor multi 2.40 2.40

Central Bank of Nicaragua, 50th Anniv. A450

Designs: No. 2509, 15cor, 50th anniversary emblem. No. 2510, 15cor, Nicaraguan banknotes.

**2010, Jan. 6**
**2509-2510** A450 Set of 2 3.00 3.00

National Assembly, 25th Anniv. A451

**2010, Jan. 9**
**2511** A451 60cor multi 5.75 5.75

Venezuelan Independence, Bicent. — A452

**2010**
**2512** A452 60cor multi 5.50 5.50

Mexican Revolution, Cent. — A453

Mexican Independence, Bicent. — A454

**2010** ***Imperf.***
**2513** A453 10cor multi .95 .95
**2514** A454 13.50cor multi 1.40 1.40

Miniature Sheet

Ecuadoran Independence, Bicent. — A455

No. 2515: a, 50c, Manuel Rodríguez de Quiroga. b, 4cor, Eugenio de Santa Cruz y Espejo. c, 5cor, Juan Salinas. d, 6.50cor, José Joaquín Olmedo. e, 10cor, Juan Pio Montufar.

**2010** ***Perf. 10½***
**2515** A455 Sheet of 5, #a-e, + label 2.40 2.40

Postal Union of the Americas, Spain and Portugal (UPAEP), Cent. — A456

**2011, Sept. 1**
**2516** A456 12cor multi 1.10 1.10

Bernardo O'Higgins (1778-1842), Chilean General — A457

**2011**
**2517** A457 15cor multi 1.40 1.40

José de San Martín (1778-1850), Argentine General — A458

**2011**
**2518** A458 25cor multi 2.25 2.25

Argentine independence, bicent.

Souvenir Sheet

Preservation of Polar Regions and Glaciers — A459

**2011** **Litho.**
**2519** A459 50.50cor multi 6.00 6.00

Miniature Sheet

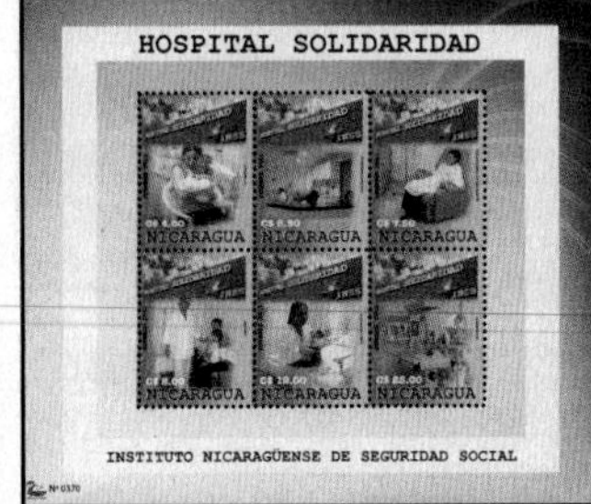

Solidarity Hospital, Managua — A460

No. 2520: a, 4cor, Woman in chair holding infant in neo-natal unit. b, 6.50cor, Nurse's station. c, 7.50cor, Woman in chair receiving chemotherapy. d, 8cor, Pediatrician, mother and child. e, 12cor, Woman sitting on hospital bed holding infant. f, 25cor, Pediatrics unit equipment.

**2011** ***Perf. 10½***
**2520** A460 Sheet of 6, #a-f 10.00 10.00

Central American Parliament, 20th Anniv. — A461

**2011, Aug. 9** **Litho.** ***Perf. 10½***
**2521** A461 16cor multi — —

Colombian Independence, Bicent. (in 2010) — A462

**2012, Feb. 29** **Litho.** ***Perf. 10½***
**2522** A462 50.50cor multi 4.50 4.50

Dated 2011.

Paintings — A463

Designs: No. 2523, 50c, La Embarcacíon, by Leonel Vanegas. No. 2524, 50c, La Princesa Está Triste, by Vanegas. No. 2525, 1cor, La Montaña Mágica, by Leoncio Sáenz. No. 2426, 1cor, La Gigantona I, by Sáenz. No. 2527, 2cor, No Olvides Monimbó, by Roger Pérez de la Rocha. No. 2528, 2cor, Campesinas, by Pérez de la Rocha. 10cor, Amanecer, by Arnoldo Guillén. 13.50cor, Esta Tierra ni se Vende, ni se Rinde, Guillén. 15cor, Metamorfosis de las Mujeres del Cua, by Orlando Sobalvarro. 16cor, Verano, by Sobalvarro.

**2012, Sept. 6**
**2523-2532** A463 Set of 10 5.25 5.25

Miniature Sheet

San Juan River — A464

No. 2533: a, 1cor, El Castillo. b, 4cor, River and its shores. c, 5cor, Crocodylus acutus. d, 10cor, Ctenosaura similis. e, 14cor, Mellisuga helenae. f, 50cor, Egretta alba.

**2012, Sept. 6**
**2533** A464 Sheet of 6, #a-f 10.00 10.00

Miniature Sheet

Diplomatic Relations Between Nicaragua and South Korea, 50th Anniv. — A465

No. 2534: a, 4cor, Solar panels. b, 5cor, Water pump, Juigalpa. c, 13.50cor, Machinery in factory. d, 25cor, Building in free trade zone.

**2012, Sept. 30**
**2534** A465 Sheet of 4, #a-d 4.00 4.00

Souvenir Sheet

Cádiz Constitution (First Spanish Constitution), Bicent. — A466

**2012, Oct. 16**
**2535** A466 100cor multi 8.50 8.50

Souvenir Sheet

Spanish Agency for Intl. Development Cooperation, 25th Anniv. — A467

**2013, Nov. 21** **Litho.** ***Perf. 10½***
**2536** A467 25cor multi 2.00 2.00

America Issue — A468

Flags and Hugo Chávez (1954-2013), President of Venezuela: 5cor, Waving. 10cor, Holding map of South America.

**2014, Mar. 5 Litho. *Perf. 10½***
**2537-2538** A468 Set of 2 2.25 2.25

Miniature Sheet

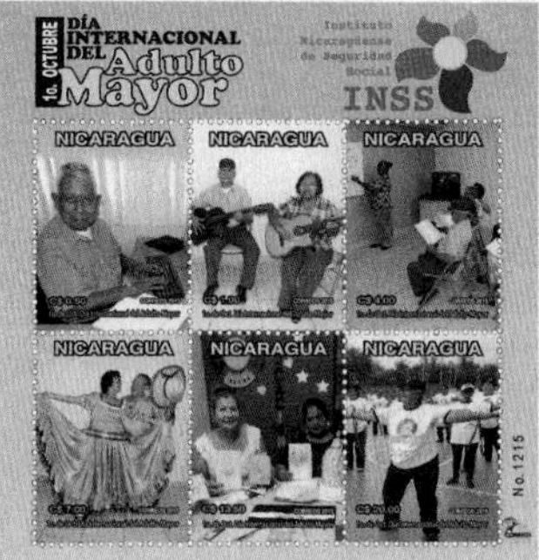


International Day of Older Persons — A469

No. 2539: a, 50c, Man using computer. b, 1cor, Man and woman with guitars. c, 4cor, Teacher and students in classroom. d, 7cor, Dancers. e, 13.50cor, Women holding greeting cards. f, 20cor, People exercising.

**2015, Oct. 1 Litho. *Perf. 10½***
**2539** A469 Sheet of 6, #a-f 3.50 3.50

Rubén Darío (1867-1916), Poet — A470

**2015, Oct. 15 Litho. *Perf. 13½***
**2540** A470 60cor multi 4.50 4.50

## AIR POST STAMPS

Counterfeits exist of almost all scarce surcharges among Nos. C1-C66.

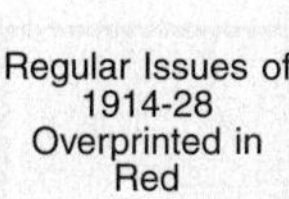

Regular Issues of 1914-28 Overprinted in Red

**1929, May 15 Unwmk. *Perf. 12***
**C1** A24 25c orange 1.75 1.75
*a.* Double overprint, one inverted 50.00
*b.* Inverted overprint 50.00
*c.* Double overprint 50.00
**C2** A24 25c blk brn 2.25 2.25
*a.* Double overprint, one inverted 50.00
*b.* Double overprint 50.00
*c.* Inverted overprint 30.00

There are numerous varieties in the setting of the overprint. The most important are: Large "1" in "1929" and large "A" in "Aereo" and "P. A. A."

### Similar Overprint on Regular Issue of 1929 in Red

**1929, June**
**C3** A24 25c dk vio 1.25 .75
*a.* Double overprint 50.00
*b.* Inverted overprint 50.00
*c.* Double overprint, one inverted 50.00
*Nos. C1-C3 (3)* 5.25 4.75

The stamps in the bottom row of the sheet have the letters "P. A. A." larger than usual.

Similar overprints, some including an airplane, have been applied to postage issues of 1914-20, officials of 1926 and Nos. 401-407. These are, at best, essays.

Airplanes over Mt. Momotombo — AP1

**1929, Dec. 15 Engr.**
**C4** AP1 25c olive blk .50 .40
**C5** AP1 50c blk brn .75 .75
**C6** AP1 1cor org red 1.00 1.00
*Nos. C4-C6 (3)* 2.25 2.15

See Nos. C18-C19, C164-C168. For surcharges and overprints see Nos. C7-C8, C14-C17, C25-C31, C106-C120, C135-C146, C150-C154, C169-C173, CO25-CO29.

No. C4 Surcharged in Red or Black

**1930, May 15**
**C7** AP1 15c on 25c ol blk (R) .50 .40
*a.* "$" inverted 3.50
*b.* Double surcharge (R + Bk) 7.00
*c.* As "b," red normal, blk invtd. 7.00
*d.* Double red surch., one inverted 7.00
**C8** AP1 20c on 25c ol blk (Bk) .75 .60
*a.* "$" inverted 7.00
*b.* Inverted surcharge 15.00

Nos. C1, C2 and C3 Surcharged in Green

**1931, June 7**
**C9** A24 15c on 25c org 70.00 50.00
**C10** A24 15c on 25c blk brn 100.00 100.00
**C11** A24 15c on 25c dk vio 15.00 15.00
*c.* Inverted surcharge 47.50
**C12** A24 20c on 25c dk vio 10.00 10.00
*c.* Inverted surcharge 100.00
*d.* Double surcharge 100.00
**C13** A24 20c on 25c blk brn *375.00*

No. C13 was not regularly issued.

**"1391"**

*C9a* A24 15c on 25c
*C10a* A24 15c on 25c
*C11a* A24 15c on 25c 60.00
*d.* As "a," inverted 400.00
*C12a* A24 20c on 25c *75.00*
*e.* As "a," inverted 400.00
*g.* As "a," double 400.00
*C13a* A24 20c on 25c

**"1921"**

*C9b* A24 15c on 25c
*C10b* A24 15c on 25c 400.00
*C11b* A24 15c on 25c 60.00
*e.* As "b," inverted 400.00
*C12b* A24 20c on 25c *100.00*
*f.* As "b," inverted 400.00
*h.* As "b," double 400.00
*C13b* A24 20c on 25c

Nos. C8, C4-C6 Surcharged in Blue

**1931, June**
**C14** AP1 15c on 20c on 25c 26.00 9.00
*b.* Blue surcharge inverted 37.50
*c.* "$" in blk, surch. invtd. 50.00
*d.* Blue surch. dbl., one invtd. 30.00
**C15** AP1 15c on 25c 5.50 5.50
*b.* Blue surcharge inverted 100.00
*c.* Double surch., one invtd. 25.00
**C16** AP1 15c on 50c 40.00 40.00
**C17** AP1 15c on 1cor 100.00 100.00
*Nos. C14-C17 (4)* 171.50 154.50

**"1391"**

*C14a* AP1 15c on 20c on 25c 50.00
*C15a* AP1 15c on 25c 30.00
*C16a* AP1 15c on 50c 80.00
*C17a* AP1 15c on 1cor 225.00
*Nos. C14a-C17a (4)* 385.00

### Momotombo Type of 1929

**1931, July 8**
**C18** AP1 15c deep violet .25 .25
**C19** AP1 20c deep green .40 .40

Managua Post Office Before and After Earthquake AP2

### Without gum, Soft porous paper

**1932, Jan. 1 Litho. *Perf. 11***
**C20** AP2 15c lilac 1.50 *1.25*
*a.* 15c violet 22.50
*b.* Vert. pair, imperf. btwn. 35.00
**C21** AP2 20c emerald 2.00
*b.* Horizontal pair, imperf. between 35.00
**C22** AP2 25c yel brn 6.50
*b.* Vertical pair, imperf. between 60.00
**C23** AP2 50c yel brn 8.00
**C24** AP2 1cor dp car 12.00
*a.* Vert. or horiz. pair, imperf. btwn. 80.00
*Nos. C20-C24 (5)* 30.00

Sheets of 10. See note after No. 568.

For overprint and surcharges see #C44-C46.

*Reprints: see note following No. 568. Value $1 each.*

Nos. C5 and C6 Surcharged in Red or Black

**1932, July 12 *Perf. 12***
**C25** AP1 30c on 50c (Bk) 1.50 1.50
*a.* "Valc" 25.00
*b.* Double surcharge 15.00
*c.* Double surch., one inverted 15.00
*d.* Period omitted after "O" 25.00
*e.* As "a," double 300.00
**C26** AP1 35c on 50c (R) 1.50 1.50
*a.* "Valc" 30.00
*b.* Double surcharge 12.00
*c.* Double surch., one inverted 12.00
*d.* As "a," double 300.00
**C27** AP1 35c on 50c (Bk) 35.00 35.00
*a.* "Valc" 250.00
**C28** AP1 40c on 1cor (Bk) 1.75 1.75
*a.* "Valc" 25.00
*b.* Double surcharge 15.00
*c.* Double surch., one inverted 15.00
*d.* Inverted surcharge 15.00
*e.* As "a," inverted 300.00
*f.* As "a," double 300.00
**C29** AP1 55c on 1cor (R) 1.75 1.75
*a.* "Valc" 25.00
*b.* Double surcharge 12.00
*c.* Double surch., one inverted 12.00
*d.* Inverted surcharge 12.00
*e.* As "a," inverted 300.00
*f.* As "a," double 300.00
*Nos. C25-C29 (5)* 41.50 41.50

No. C18 Overprinted in Red

**1932, Sept. 11**
**C30** AP1 15c dp vio 70.00 70.00
*a.* "Aerreo" 150.00 150.00
*b.* Invtd. "m" in "Septiembre" 150.00

International Air Mail Week.

No. C6 Surcharged

**1932, Oct. 12**
**C31** AP1 8c on 1 cor org red 20.00 20.00
*a.* "1232" 30.00 30.00
*b.* 2nd "u" of "Inauguracion" is an "n" 30.00 30.00

Inauguration of airmail service to the interior.

Regular Issue of 1932 Overprinted in Red

**1932, Oct. 24 *Perf. 11½***

### Without Gum

**C32** A40 1c yel brn 20.00 20.00
*a.* Inverted overprint 125.00 125.00
**C33** A40 2c carmine 20.00 20.00
*a.* Inverted overprint 125.00 125.00
*b.* Double overprint 100.00 100.00
**C34** A40 3c ultra 9.50 9.50
*a.* Inverted overprint 150.00 150.00
*b.* As "a," vert. pair, imperf. btwn. 500.00
**C35** A40 4c dp ultra 9.50 9.50
*a.* Inverted overprint 125.00 125.00
*b.* Double overprint 100.00 100.00
*c.* Vert. or horiz. pair, imperf. btwn. 300.00
**C36** A40 5c yel brn 9.50 9.50
*a.* Inverted overprint 125.00 125.00
*b.* Vert. pair, imperf. btwn. 75.00
**C37** A40 6c gray brn 9.50 9.50
*a.* Inverted overprint 100.00 100.00
**C38** A40 50c green 9.00 9.00
*a.* Inverted overprint 125.00 125.00
**C39** A40 1cor yellow 9.50 9.50
*a.* Inverted overprint 125.00 125.00
*b.* Horiz. pair, imperf. btwn. 200.00
*Nos. C32-C39 (8)* 96.50 96.50

Nos. 564, C20-C21 exist overprinted as C32-C39. The editors believe they were not regularly issued.

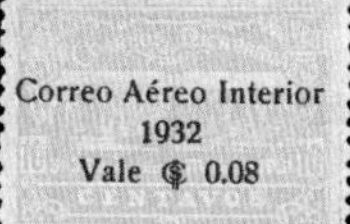


Surcharged in Red

**1932, Oct. 24**
**C40** A40 8c on 10c yel brn 9.00 9.00
*a.* Inverted surcharge 125.00 125.00
**C41** A40 16c on 20c org 9.00 9.00
*a.* Inverted surcharge 125.00 125.00
**C42** A40 24c on 25c dp vio 9.00 9.00
*a.* Inverted surcharge 125.00 125.00
*b.* Horiz. pair, imperf. vert. 300.00

### Surcharged in Red as No. C40 but without the word "Vale"

**C43** A40 8c on 10c yel brn 45.00 45.00
*a.* Inverted surcharge 125.00 125.00
*b.* Horiz. pair, imperf. vert. 300.00

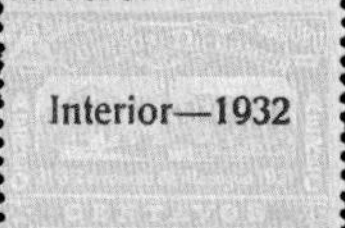


No. C22 Overprinted in Red

**1932, Oct. 24**
**C44** AP2 25c yel brn 8.00 8.00
*a.* Inverted overprint 125.00 125.00

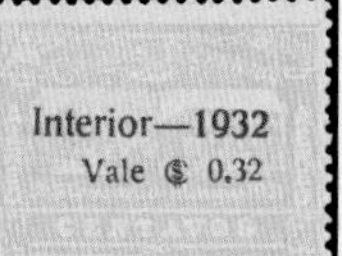


Nos. C23 and C24 Surcharged in Red

**1932, Oct. 24**
**C45** AP2 32c on 50c yel brn 9.50 9.50
*a.* Inverted surcharge 125.00 125.00
*b.* "Interior-1932" inverted 150.00 150.00
*c.* "Vale $0.32" inverted 150.00 150.00
*d.* Horiz. pair, imperf. btwn. 200.00

**C46** AP2 40c on 1cor car 7.00 7.00
*a.* Inverted surcharge 125.00 125.00
*b.* "Vale $0.40" inverted 200.00 200.00

### Nos. 557-558 Overprinted in Black like Nos. C32 to C39

**1932, Nov. 16**

**C47** A40 1c yel brn 25.00 22.50
*a.* "1232" 45.00 45.00
*b.* Inverted overprint 125.00 125.00
*c.* Double ovpt., one invtd. 125.00 125.00
*d.* As "a," inverted 500.00
**C48** A40 2c dp car 20.00 17.50
*a.* "1232" 45.00 45.00
*b.* Inverted overprint 125.00 125.00
*c.* As "a," inverted 500.00

Excellent counterfeits exist of Nos. C27, C30-C48. Forged overprints and surcharges as on Nos. C32-C48 exist on reprints of Nos. C20-C24.

Regular Issue of 1914-32 Surcharged in Black

**1932** *Perf. 12*

**C49** A25 1c on 2c brt rose .65 .30
**C50** A24 2c on 3c lt bl .65 .30
**C51** A25 3c on 4c dk bl .65 .30
**C52** A24 4c on 5c gray brn .65 .30
**C53** A25 5c on 6c ol brn .65 .30
**C54** A25 6c on 10c lt brn .65 .30
*a.* Double surcharge 25.00
**C55** A24 8c on 15c org red .65 .30
**C56** A25 16c on 20c org .65 .35
**C57** A24 24c on 25c dk vio 2.50 1.00
**C58** A24 25c on 25c dk vio 2.50 1.00
*a.* Double surcharge 25.00
**C59** A25 32c on 50c grn 2.50 1.25
**C60** A25 40c on 50c grn 3.00 1.40
**C61** A25 50c on 1cor yel 4.25 2.25
**C62** A25 1cor on 1cor yel 6.50 3.00
*Nos. C49-C62 (14)* 26.45 12.35

Nos. C49-C62 exist with inverted surcharge.

In addition to C49 to C62, four other stamps, Type A25, exist with this surcharge:
40c on 50c bister brown, black surcharge.
1cor on 2c bright rose, black surcharge.
1cor on 1cor yellow, red surcharge.
1cor on 1cor dull violet, black surcharge.

The editors believe they were not regularly issued.

### Surcharged on Nos. 548, 547

**1932**

**C65** A24 24c on 25c dk vio 45.00 45.00
**C66** A24 25c on 25c blk brn 50.00 50.00

Counterfeits of Nos. C65 and C66 are plentiful.

### Rivas Railroad Issue

La Chocolata Cut — AP3

El Nacascola — AP4

Designs: 25c, Cuesta cut. 50c, Mole of San Juan del Sur. 1cor, View of El Estero.

**1932, Dec.** **Litho.**

**Soft porous paper**

**C67** AP3 15c dk vio 20.00
**C68** AP4 20c bl grn 20.00
**C69** AP4 25c dk brn 20.00
**C70** AP4 50c blk brn 20.00
**C71** AP4 1cor rose red 20.00
*Nos. C67-C71 (5)* 100.00

Inauguration of the railroad from San Jorge to San Juan del Sur, Dec. 18, 1932. Printed in sheets of 4, without gum.

*Reprints: see note following No. 574. Value, $6 each.*

### Leon-Sauce Railroad Issue

"Fill" at Santa Lucia River — AP5

Designs: 15c, Bridge at Santa Lucia. 25c, Malpaicillo Station. 50c, Panoramic view. 1cor, San Andres.

**1932, Dec. 30** **Soft porous paper**

**C72** AP5 15c purple 20.00
**C73** AP5 20c bl grn 20.00
**C74** AP5 25c dk brn 20.00
**C75** AP5 50c blk brn 20.00
**C76** AP5 1cor rose red 20.00
*Nos. C72-C76 (5)* 100.00

Inauguration of the railroad from Leon to El Sauce, 12/30/32. Sheets of 4, without gum.

*Reprints: see note following No. 579. Value, $6 each.*

### Flag of the Race Issue

**1933, Aug. 3** **Litho.** ***Rouletted 9***

**Without gum**

**C77** A43 1c dk brn 1.50 1.50
**C78** A43 2c red vio 1.50 1.50
**C79** A43 4c violet 2.50 2.25
**C80** A43 5c dl bl 2.25 2.25
**C81** A43 6c vio bl 2.25 2.25
**C82** A43 8c dp brn .70 .70
**C83** A43 15c ol brn .70 .70
**C84** A43 20c yellow 2.25 2.25
*a.* Horiz. pair, imperf. btwn. 15.00
*b.* Horiz. pair, imperf. vert. 15.00
**C85** A43 25c orange 2.25 2.25
**C86** A43 50c rose 2.25 2.25
**C87** A43 1cor green 11.00 11.00
*Nos. C77-C87 (11)* 29.15 28.90

See note after No. 599. Printed in sheets of 10.

*Reprints exist, shades differ from postage and official stamps.*

**Imperf., Pairs**

*C78a* A43 2c 14.00
*C79a* A43 4c 10.00
*C81a* A43 6c 10.00
*C82a* A43 8c 10.00
*C83a* A43 15c 10.00
*C87a* A43 1cor 30.00

AP7

**1933, Nov.** ***Perf. 12***

**C88** AP7 10c bis brn 1.60 1.60
*a.* Vert. pair, imperf. between 35.00
**C89** AP7 15c violet 1.25 1.25
*a.* Vert. pair, imperf. between 37.50
**C90** AP7 25c red 1.50 1.50
*a.* Horiz. pair, imperf. between 22.50
**C91** AP7 50c dp bl 1.60 1.60
*Nos. C88-C91 (4)* 5.95 5.95

Intl. Air Post Week, Nov. 6-11, 1933. Printed in sheets of 4. Counterfeits exist.

Stamps and Types of 1928-31 Surcharged in Black

**1933, Nov. 3**

**C92** A25 1c on 2c grn .25 .25
**C93** A24 2c on 3c ol gray .25 .25
**C94** A25 3c on 4c car rose .25 .25
**C95** A24 4c on 5c lt bl .25 .25
**C96** A25 5c on 6c dk bl .25 .25
**C97** A25 6c on 10c ol brn .25 .25
**C98** A24 8c on 15c bis brn .25 .25
**C99** A25 16c on 20c brn .25 .25
**C100** A24 24c on 25c ver .25 .25
**C101** A24 25c on 25c org .25 .25
**C102** A25 32c on 50c vio .25 .25
**C103** A25 40c on 50c grn .25 .25
**C104** A25 50c on 1cor yel .25 .25
**C105** A25 1cor on 1cor org red .35 .25
*Nos. C92-C105 (14)* 3.60 3.50

Nos. C100, C102-C105 exist without script control overprint. Value, each $1.50.

Type of Air Post Stamps of 1929 Surcharged in Black

**1933, Oct. 28**

**C106** AP1 30c on 50c org red *2.00* .25
**C107** AP1 35c on 50c lt bl *2.00* .25
**C108** AP1 40c on 1cor yel *5.00* .25
**C109** AP1 55c on 1cor grn *4.00* .25
*Nos. C106-C109 (4)* *13.00* 1.00

No. C19 Surcharged in Red

**1934, Mar. 31**

**C110** AP1 10c on 20c grn .30 .25
*a.* Inverted surcharge 15.00
*b.* Double surcharge, one inverted 15.00
*c.* "Ceutroamericano" 10.00

No. C110 with black surcharge is believed to be of private origin.

No. C4 Surcharged in Red

**1935, Aug.**

**C111** AP1 10c on 25c ol blk .25 .25
*a.* Small "v" in "vale" (R) 5.00
*b.* "centrvos" (R) 5.00
*c.* Double surcharge (R) 25.00
*d.* Inverted surcharge (R) 25.00
*g.* As "a," inverted 400.00
*h.* As "a," double 400.00

No. C111 with blue surcharge is believed to be private origin.

The editors do not recognize the Nicaraguan air post stamps overprinted in red "VALIDO 1935" in two lines and with or without script control marks as having been issued primarily for postal purposes.

Nos C4-C6, C18-C19 Overprinted Vertically in Blue, Reading Up:

**1935-36**

**C112** AP1 15c dp vio 1.00 1.00
**C113** AP1 20c dp grn 1.75 1.75
**C114** AP1 25c ol blk 2.25 2.25
**C115** AP1 50c blk brn 5.00 5.00
**C116** AP1 1cor org red 40.00 40.00
*Nos. C112-C116 (5)* 50.00 50.00

### Same Overprint on Nos. C106-C109 Reading Up or Down

**C117** AP1 30c on 50c org red 1.50 1.40
**C118** AP1 35c on 50c lt bl 6.50 6.50
**C119** AP1 40c on 1cor yel 6.50 6.50
**C120** AP1 55c on 1cor grn 6.50 6.50
*Nos. C117-C120 (4)* 21.00 20.90
*Nos. C112-C120 (9)* 71.00 70.90

### Same Overprint in Red on Nos. C92-C105

**1936**

**C121** A25 1c on 2c grn .25 .25
**C122** A24 2c on 3c ol gray .25 .25
**C123** A25 3c on 4c car rose .25 .25
**C124** A24 4c on 5c lt bl .25 .25
**C125** A25 5c on 6c dk bl .25 .25
**C126** A25 6c on 10c ol brn .25 .25
**C127** A24 8c on 15c bis brn .25 .25
**C128** A25 16c on 20c brn .30 .25
**C129** A24 24c on 25c ver .50 .30
**C130** A24 25c on 25c org .35 .25
**C131** A25 32c on 50c vio .35 .25
**C132** A25 40c on 50c grn 1.00 .50
**C133** A25 50c on 1cor yel .85 .25
**C134** A25 1cor on 1cor org red 3.50 .65
*Nos. C121-C134 (14)* 8.60 4.20

Nos. C121 to C134 are handstamped with script control mark.

### Overprint Reading Down on No. C110

**C135** AP1 10c on 20c grn *350.00*

This stamp has been extensively counterfeited.

### Overprinted in Red on Nos. C4 to C6, C18 and C19

**C136** AP1 15c dp vio 1.00 .25
**C137** AP1 20c dp grn 1.25 .60
**C138** AP1 25c ol blk 1.25 .55
**C139** AP1 50c blk brn 1.00 .55
**C140** AP1 1cor org red 3.25 .55

### On Nos. C106 to C109

**C141** AP1 30c on 50c org red 2.25 .60
**C142** AP1 35c on 50c lt bl 2.25 .40
**C143** AP1 40c on 1cor yel 2.25 .55
**C144** AP1 55c on 1cor grn 2.25 .50

### Same Overprint in Red or Blue on No. C111 Reading Up or Down

**C145** AP1 10c on 25c, down 3.00 .45
*a.* "Centrvos" 25.00
**C146** AP1 10c on 25c (Bl), up 6.00 1.00
*a.* "Centrvos" 25.00
*Nos. C136-C146 (11)* 25.75 6.00

Overprint on No. C145 is at right, on No. C146 in center.

Nos. C92, C93 and C98 Overprinted in Black

**1936**

**C147** A25 1c on 2c grn 2.00 .25
**C148** A24 2c on 3c ol gray 2.00 .25
*a.* "Resello 1936" dbl., one invtd. 7.50
**C149** A24 8c on 15c bis brn 2.00 .25
*Nos. C147-C149 (3)* 6.00 .75

With script control handstamp.

Nos. C5 and C6 Surcharged in Red

**1936, Nov. 26**

**C150** AP1 15c on 50c blk brn .40 .25
**C151** AP1 15c on 1cor org red .40 .25

Nos. C18 and C19 Overprinted in Carmine

**1936, July 2**

C152 AP1 15c dp vio .60 .25
C153 AP1 20c dp grn .60 .25

Overprint reading up or down.

No. C4 Surcharged and Overprinted in Red

C154 AP1 10c on 25c olive blk .50 .30
*a.* Surch. and ovpt. inverted 3.50

**Same Overprint in Carmine on Nos. C92 to C99**

C155 A25 1c on 2c green .75 .25
C156 A24 2c on 3c olive gray 4.00 2.00
C157 A25 3c on 4c car rose .75 .25
C158 A24 4c on 5c light blue .75 .25
C159 A25 5c on 6c dark blue .75 .25
C160 A25 6c on 10c olive brn .75 .25
C161 A24 8c on 15c bister brn .75 .25
C162 A25 16c on 20c brown .75 .25
*Nos. C154-C162 (9)* 9.75 4.05

No. 518 Overprinted in Black

C163 A25 10c lt brn .75 .25
*a.* Overprint inverted 3.50
*b.* Double overprint 3.50

Two fonts are found in the sheet of #C163.

**Momotombo Type of 1929**

**1937**

C164 AP1 15c yel org 1.00 .25
C165 AP1 20c org red 1.00 .25
C166 AP1 25c black 1.00 .25
C167 AP1 50c violet 1.00 .25
C168 AP1 1cor orange 4.50 .25
*Nos. C164-C168 (5)* 8.50 1.25

Surcharged in Black

**1937**

C169 AP1 30c on 50c car rose 1.25 .25
C170 AP1 35c on 50c olive grn 1.25 .25
C171 AP1 40c on 1cor green 1.25 .25
C172 AP1 55c on 1cor blue 1.25 .25
*Nos. C169-C172 (4)* 5.00 1.00

No. C168 Surcharged in Violet

**1937 Unwmk. *Perf. 12***

C173 AP1 10c on 1cor org .45 .25
*a.* "Centauos" 10.00

**No. C98 with Additional Overprint "1937"**

C174 A24 8c on 15c bis brn .65 .25
*a.* "1937" double 6.50

**Nos. C92-C102 with Additional Overprint in Blue reading "HABILITADO 1937"**

C175 A25 1c on 2c grn .90 .25
*a.* Blue overprint double *3.50*
C176 A24 2c on 3c ol gray .90 .25
*a.* Double surch., one inverted *3.50*
C177 A25 3c on 4c car rose .90 .25
C178 A24 4c on 5c lt bl .90 .25
C179 A25 5c on 6c dk bl .90 .25
C180 A25 6c on 10c ol brn .90 .25
C181 A24 8c on 15c bis brn .90 .25
*a.* "Habilitado 1937" double 4.50
C182 A25 16c on 20c brn .90 .25
*a.* Double surcharge 3.50
C183 A24 24c on 25c ver .90 .25
C184 A24 25c on 25c org .90 .25
C185 A25 32c on 50c vio .90 .25
*Nos. C175-C185 (11)* 9.90 2.75

Map of Nicaragua AP8

**For Foreign Postage**

**1937, July 30 Engr.**

C186 AP8 10c green .40 .25
C187 AP8 15c dp bl .40 .25
C188 AP8 20c yellow .40 .25
C189 AP8 25c bl vio .40 .25
C190 AP8 30c rose car .40 .25
C191 AP8 50c org yel .50 .25
C192 AP8 1cor ol grn 1.00 .55
*Nos. C186-C192 (7)* 3.50 2.05

Presidential Palace AP9

**For Domestic Postage**

C193 AP9 1c rose car .40 .25
C194 AP9 2c dp bl .40 .25
C195 AP9 3c ol grn .40 .25
C196 AP9 4c black .40 .25
C197 AP9 5c dk vio .40 .25
C198 AP9 6c chocolate .40 .25
C199 AP9 8c bl vio .40 .25
C200 AP9 16c org yel .40 .25
C201 AP9 24c yellow .40 .25
C202 AP9 25c yel grn .40 .25
*Nos. C193-C202 (10)* 4.00 2.50

No. C201 with green overprint "Union Panamericana 1890-1940" is of private origin.

Managua AP10

Designs: 15c, Presidential Palace. 20c, Map of South America. 25c, Map of Central America. 30c, Map of North America. 35c, Lagoon of Tiscapa, Managua. 40c, Road Scene. 45c, Park. 50c, Another park. 55c, Scene in San Juan del Sur. 75c, Tipitapa River. 1cor, Landscape.

**Wmk. 209**

**1937, Sept. 17 Typo. *Perf. 11***

**Center in Dark Blue**

C203 AP10 10c yel grn 2.25 1.20
C204 AP10 15c orange 2.25 1.40
C205 AP10 20c red 1.75 1.00
C206 AP10 25c vio brn 1.75 1.00
*a.* Center, double impression —
C207 AP10 30c bl grn 1.75 1.00
*a.* Great Lakes omitted 40.00 40.00
C208 AP10 35c lemon .75 .45
C209 AP10 40c green .75 .40
C210 AP10 45c brt vio .75 .35
C211 AP10 50c rose lil .75 .35
*a.* Vert. pair, imperf. btwn. 140.00
C212 AP10 55c lt bl .75 .35
C213 AP10 75c gray grn .75 .35

**Center in Brown Red**

C214 AP10 1cor dk bl 1.75 .50
*Nos. C203-C214 (12)* 16.00 8.35

150th anniv. of the Constitution of the US.

Diriangen — AP11

Designs: 4c, 10c, Nicarao. 5c, 15c, Bartolomé de Las Casas. 8c, 20c, Columbus.

**For Domestic Postage**

Without gum

**1937, Oct. 12 Unwmk. *Perf. 11***

C215 AP11 1c green .25 .25
C216 AP11 4c brn car .25 .25
C217 AP11 5c dk vio .25 .25
*a.* Without imprint .40
C218 AP11 8c dp bl .25 .25
*a.* Without imprint .50

**For Foreign Postage**

**Wmk. 209**

**With Gum**

C219 AP11 10c lt brn .25 .25
C220 AP11 15c pale bl .25 .25
*a.* Without imprint 1.00
C221 AP11 20c pale rose .25 .25
*Nos. C215-C221 (7)* 1.75 1.75

Nos. C215-C221 printed in sheets of 4.

**Imperf., Pairs**

*C215a* AP11 1c .25 .25
*C216a* AP11 4c .25 .25
*C217b* AP11 5c .25 .25
*C217c* AP11 5c Without imprint
*C218b* AP11 8c .25
*C218c* AP11 8c Without imprint
*C219a* AP11 10c .25 .25
*C220b* AP11 15c .25 .25
*C220c* AP11 15c Without imprint
*C221a* AP11 20c .35 .35

Gen. Tomas Martinez — AP11a

Design: 10c-50c, Gen. Anastasio Somoza.

**For Domestic Postage**

Without Gum

***Perf. 11½, Imperf.***

**1938, Jan. 18 Typo. Unwmk.**

**Center in Black**

C221B AP11a 1c orange .25 .25
C221C AP11a 5c red vio .25 .25
C221D AP11a 8c dk bl .25 .25
C221E AP11a 16c brown .25 .25
*f.* Sheet of 4, 1c, 5c, 8c, 16c 1.75 1.75

**For Foreign Postage**

C221G AP11a 10c green .25 .25
C221H AP11a 15c dk bl .25 .25
C221J AP11a 25c violet .40 .40
C221K AP11a 50c carmine .50 .45
*m.* Sheet of 4, 10c, 15c, 25c, 50c 1.75 1.75
*Nos. C221B-C221K (8)* 2.40 2.35

75th anniv. of postal service in Nicaragua. Printed in sheets of four.

Stamps of type AP11a exist in changed colors and with inverted centers, double centers and frames printed on the back. These varieties were private fabrications.

Lake Managua AP12

President Anastasio Somoza — AP13

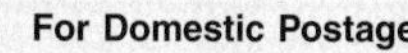

**For Domestic Postage**

**1939 Unwmk. Engr. *Perf. 12½***

C222 AP12 2c dp bl .25 .25
C223 AP12 3c green .25 .25
C224 AP12 8c pale lil .25 .25
C225 AP12 16c orange .25 .25
C226 AP12 24c yellow .25 .25
C227 AP12 32c dk grn .25 .25
C228 AP12 50c dp rose .25 .25

**For Foreign Postage**

C229 AP13 10c dk brn .25 .25
C230 AP13 15c dk bl .25 .25
C231 AP13 20c org yel .25 .25
C232 AP13 25c dk pur .25 .25
C233 AP13 30c lake .25 .25
C234 AP13 50c dp org .25 .25
C235 AP13 1cor dk ol grn .35 .40
*Nos. C222-C235 (14)* 3.60 3.65

**For Domestic Postage**

Will Rogers and View of Managua AP14

Designs: 2c, Rogers standing beside plane. 3c, Leaving airport office. 4c, Rogers and US Marines. 5c, Managua after earthquake.

**1939, Mar. 31 Engr. *Perf. 12***

C236 AP14 1c brt grn .25 .25
C237 AP14 2c org red .25 .25
C238 AP14 3c lt ultra .25 .25
C239 AP14 4c dk bl .25 .25
C240 AP14 5c rose car .25 .25
*Nos. C236-C240 (5)* 1.25 1.25

Will Rogers' flight to Managua after the earthquake, Mar. 31, 1931.

For surcharges see Nos. 686, 688.

Pres. Anastasio Somoza in US House of Representatives — AP19

President Somoza and US Capitol AP20

President Somoza, Tower of the Sun and Trylon and Perisphere AP21

**For Domestic Postage**

**1940, Feb. 1**

C241 AP19 4c red brn .25 .25
C242 AP20 8c blk brn .25 .25
C243 AP19 16c grnsh bl .25 .25
C244 AP20 20c brt plum .50 .30
C245 AP21 32c scarlet .25 .25

**For Foreign Postage**

C246 AP19 25c dp bl .25 .25
C247 AP19 30c black .25 .25
C248 AP20 50c rose pink .45 .40
C249 AP21 60c green .50 .30
C250 AP19 65c dk vio brn .50 .25
C251 AP19 90c ol grn .65 .30
C252 AP21 1cor violet 1.00 .55
*Nos. C241-C252 (12)* 5.10 3.60

Visit of Pres. Somoza to US in 1939.

For surcharge see No. C636.

L. S. Rowe, Statue of Liberty, Nicaraguan Coastline, Flags of 21 American Republics, US Shield and Arms of Nicaragua — AP22

**1940, Aug. 2 Engr. *Perf. 12½***

| | | | | |
|---|---|---|---|---|
| C253 | AP22 | 1.25cor multi | 2.00 | 1.00 |

50th anniversary of Pan American Union.
For overprint see No. C493.

First Nicaraguan Postage Stamp and Sir Rowland Hill — AP23

**1941, Apr. 4**

| | | | | |
|---|---|---|---|---|
| C254 | AP23 | 2cor brown | 2.50 | .80 |
| C255 | AP23 | 3cor dk bl | 8.25 | 1.40 |
| C256 | AP23 | 5cor carmine | 22.50 | 3.50 |
| | | *Nos. C254-C256 (3)* | 33.25 | 5.70 |

Centenary of the first postage stamp.
Nos. C254-C256 imperf. are proofs.

Rubén Darío AP24

**1941, Dec. 23**

| | | | | |
|---|---|---|---|---|
| C257 | AP24 | 20c pale lil | .25 | .25 |
| C258 | AP24 | 35c yel grn | .30 | .25 |
| C259 | AP24 | 40c org yel | .40 | .25 |
| C260 | AP24 | 60c lt bl | .65 | .30 |
| | | *Nos. C257-C260 (4)* | 1.60 | 1.05 |

25th anniversary of the death of Rubén Dario, poet and writer.

**Catalogue values for unused stamps in this section, from this point to the end of the section, are for Never Hinged items.**

### Victory Type

**1943, Dec. 8 *Perf. 12***

| | | | | |
|---|---|---|---|---|
| C261 | A48 | 40c dk bl grn & cer | .25 | .25 |
| C262 | A48 | 60c lt bl & cer | .30 | .25 |

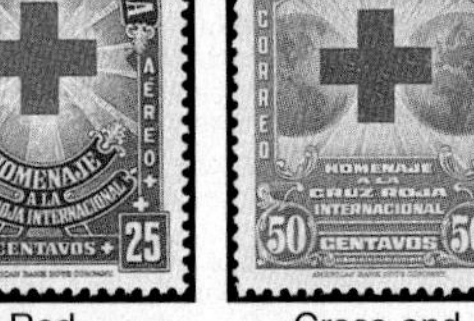

Red Cross — AP26 Cross and Globes — AP27

Red Cross Workers AP28

**1944, Oct. 12 Engr.**

| | | | | |
|---|---|---|---|---|
| C263 | AP26 | 25c red lil & car | .65 | .30 |
| C264 | AP27 | 50c ol brn & car | 1.00 | .55 |
| C265 | AP28 | 1cor dk bl grn & car | 2.00 | 2.00 |
| | | *Nos. C263-C265 (3)* | 3.65 | 2.85 |

International Red Cross Society, 80th anniv.

Caravels of Columbus and Columbus Lighthouse AP29

Landing of Columbus AP30

**1945, Sept. 1 *Perf. 12½***

| | | | | |
|---|---|---|---|---|
| C266 | AP29 | 20c dp grn & gray | .25 | .25 |
| C267 | AP29 | 35c dk car & blk | .35 | .30 |
| C268 | AP29 | 75c ol grn & rose pink | .50 | .40 |
| C269 | AP29 | 90c brick red & aqua | .80 | .75 |
| C270 | AP29 | 1cor blk & pale bl | .90 | .30 |
| C271 | AP30 | 2.50cor dk bl & car rose | 2.25 | 2.25 |
| | | *Nos. C266-C271 (6)* | 5.05 | 4.25 |

Issued in honor of the discovery of America by Columbus and the Columbus Lighthouse near Ciudad Trujillo, Dominican Republic.

### Roosevelt Types

Designs: 25c, Franklin D. Roosevelt and Winston Churchill. 75c, Roosevelt signing declaration of war against Japan. 1cor, Gen. Henri Giraud, Roosevelt, Gen. Charles de Gaulle and Churchill. 3cor, Stalin, Roosevelt and Churchill. 5cor, Sculptured head of Roosevelt.

### Engraved, Center Photogravure

**1946, June 15 *Perf. 12½***

**Frame in Black**

| | | | | |
|---|---|---|---|---|
| C272 | A50 | 25c orange | .25 | .25 |
| *a.* | | Horiz. pair, imperf. btwn. | 225.00 | |
| *b.* | | Imperf., pair | 175.00 | |
| C273 | A51 | 75c carmine | .25 | .25 |
| *a.* | | Imperf., pair | 175.00 | |
| C274 | A50 | 1cor dark green | .40 | .40 |
| C275 | A50 | 3cor violet | 3.75 | 3.75 |
| C276 | A51 | 5cor greenish blue | 5.00 | 5.00 |
| | | *Nos. C272-C276 (5)* | 9.65 | 9.65 |

Issued to honor Franklin D. Roosevelt.

Projected Provincial Seminary — AP36

Designs: 20c, Communications Building. 35c, Sanitation Building. 90c, National Bank. 1cor, Municipal Building. 2.50cor, National Palace.

**1947, Jan. 10 Frame in Black**

| | | | | |
|---|---|---|---|---|
| C277 | AP36 | 5c violet | .25 | .25 |
| *a.* | | Imperf., pair | 125.00 | |
| C278 | AP36 | 20c gray grn | .25 | .25 |
| C279 | AP36 | 35c orange | .25 | .25 |
| C280 | AP36 | 90c red lil | .40 | .30 |
| C281 | AP36 | 1cor brown | .60 | .45 |
| C282 | AP36 | 2.50cor rose lil | 1.75 | 1.50 |
| | | *Nos. C277-C282 (6)* | 3.50 | 3.00 |

City of Managua centenary.

Rubén Darío Monument — AP42

Designs: 6c, Tapir. 8c, Stone Highway. 10c, Genizaro Dam. 20c, Detail of Dario Monument. 25c, Sulphurous Lake of Nejapa. 35c, Mercedes Airport. 50c, Prinzapolka River delta. 1cor, Tipitapa Spa. 1.50cor, Tipitapa River. 5cor, United States Embassy. 10cor, Indian fruit vendor. 25cor, Franklin D. Roosevelt Monument.

### Engraved, Center Photogravure

**1947, Aug. 29 Unwmk. *Perf. 12½***

| | | | | |
|---|---|---|---|---|
| C283 | AP42 | 5c dk bl grn & rose car | .25 | .25 |
| C284 | AP42 | 6c blk & yel | .25 | .25 |
| C285 | AP42 | 8c car & ol | .25 | .25 |
| C286 | AP42 | 10c brn & bl | .25 | .25 |
| C287 | AP42 | 20c bl vio & org | .30 | .30 |
| C288 | AP42 | 25c brn red & emer | .35 | .35 |
| C289 | AP42 | 35c gray & bis | .30 | .30 |
| C290 | AP42 | 50c pur & sep | .25 | .25 |
| C291 | AP42 | 1cor blk & lil rose | .75 | .75 |
| C292 | AP42 | 1.50cor red brn & aqua | .80 | .80 |
| C293 | AP42 | 5cor choc & car rose | 6.25 | 6.25 |
| C294 | AP42 | 10cor vio & dk brn | 5.00 | 5.00 |
| C295 | AP42 | 25cor dk bl grn & yel | 10.00 | 10.00 |
| | | *Nos. C283-C295 (13)* | 25.00 | 25.00 |

The frames differ for each denomination.
For surcharge see No. C750.

Tennis — AP43

Designs: 2c, Soccer. 3c, Table tennis. 4c, Proposed stadium. 5c, Regatta. 15c, Basketball. 25c, Boxing. 30c, Baseball. 40c, Bicycling. 75c, Diving. 1cor, Pole vault. 2cor, Boy Scouts. 5cor, Softball.

**1949, July Photo. *Perf. 12***

| | | | | |
|---|---|---|---|---|
| C296 | AP43 | 1c cerise | .35 | .25 |
| C297 | AP43 | 2c ol gray | .35 | .25 |
| C298 | AP43 | 3c scarlet | .35 | .25 |
| C299 | AP43 | 4c dk bl gray | .35 | .25 |
| C300 | AP43 | 5c aqua | .35 | .25 |
| C301 | AP43 | 15c bl grn | .35 | .25 |
| C302 | AP43 | 25c red vio | 3.00 | .30 |
| C303 | AP43 | 30c red brn | 2.75 | .30 |
| C304 | AP43 | 40c violet | .75 | .30 |
| C305 | AP43 | 75c magenta | 7.50 | 2.75 |
| C306 | AP43 | 1cor lt bl | 9.00 | 1.40 |
| C307 | AP43 | 2cor brn ol | 4.00 | 1.75 |
| C308 | AP43 | 5cor lt grn | 5.00 | 2.25 |
| *a.* | | Set of 13 souv. sheets of 4 | *450.00* | *450.00* |
| | | *Nos. C296-C308 (13)* | 34.10 | 10.55 |

10th World Series of Amateur Baseball, 1948.

Rowland Hill — AP44

Designs: 20c, Heinrich von Stephan. 25c, First UPU Bldg. 30c, UPU Bldg., Bern. 85c, UPU Monument. 1.10cor, Congress medal, obverse. 2.14cor, as 1.10cor, reverse.

**1950, Nov. 23 Engr. *Perf. 13***

**Frames in Black**

| | | | | |
|---|---|---|---|---|
| C309 | AP44 | 16c cerise | .25 | .25 |
| C310 | AP44 | 20c orange | .25 | .25 |
| C311 | AP44 | 25c gray | .25 | .25 |
| C312 | AP44 | 30c cerise | .40 | .25 |
| C313 | AP44 | 85c dk bl grn | .75 | .65 |
| C314 | AP44 | 1.10cor chnt brn | 1.50 | .45 |
| C315 | AP44 | 2.14cor ol grn | 2.25 | 2.25 |
| | | *Nos. C309-C315 (7)* | 5.65 | 4.35 |

75th anniv. (in 1949) of the UPU.
Each denomination was also issued in a souvenir sheet containing four stamps and marginal inscriptions. Size: 126x114mm. Value, set of 7 sheets, $35.
For surcharges see Nos. C501, C758.

### Queen Isabela I Type

Designs: 2.30cor, Portrait facing left. 2.80cor, Map. 3cor, Santa Maria. 3.30cor, Columbus' ships. 3.60cor, Portrait facing right.

**1952, June 25 Unwmk. *Perf. 11½***

| | | | | |
|---|---|---|---|---|
| C316 | A65 | 2.30cor rose car | 2.50 | 2.00 |
| C317 | A65 | 2.80cor red org | 2.25 | 1.75 |
| C318 | A65 | 3cor green | 2.50 | 2.00 |
| C319 | A66 | 3.30cor lt bl | 2.50 | 2.00 |
| C320 | A65 | 3.60cor yel grn | 2.75 | 2.25 |
| *a.* | | Souv. sheet of 5, #C316-C320 | 12.50 | 12.50 |
| | | *Nos. C316-C320 (5)* | 12.50 | 10.00 |

For overprint see No. C445.

Arms of ODECA AP47

Designs: 25c, ODECA Flag. 30c, Presidents of five Central American countries. 60c, ODECA Charter and Flags. 1cor, Map of Central America.

**1953, Apr. 15 *Perf. 13½x14***

| | | | | |
|---|---|---|---|---|
| C321 | AP47 | 20c red lil | .25 | .25 |
| C322 | AP47 | 25c lt bl | .25 | .25 |
| C323 | AP47 | 30c sepia | .25 | .25 |
| C324 | AP47 | 60c dk bl grn | .30 | .25 |
| C325 | AP47 | 1cor dk vio | .70 | .65 |
| | | *Nos. C321-C325 (5)* | 1.75 | 1.65 |

Founding of the Organization of Central American States (ODECA).

Leonardo Arguello — AP48

Presidents: 5c, Gen. Jose Maria Moncada. 20c, Juan Bautista Sacasa. 25c, Gen. Jose Santos Zelaya. 30c, Gen. Anastasio Somoza. 35c, Gen. Tomas Martinez. 40c, Fernando Guzman. 45c, Vicente Cuadra. 50c, Pedro Joaquin Chamorro. 60c, Gen. Joaquin Zavala. 85c, Adan Cardenas. 1.10cor, Evaristo Carazo. 1.20cor, Roberto Sacasa.

### Engraved (frames); Photogravure (heads)

**1953, June 25 *Perf. 12½***

**Heads in Gray Black**

| | | | | |
|---|---|---|---|---|
| C326 | AP48 | 4c dp car | .25 | .25 |
| C327 | AP48 | 5c dp org | .25 | .25 |
| C328 | AP48 | 20c dk Prus bl | .25 | .25 |
| C329 | AP48 | 25c blue | .25 | .25 |
| C330 | AP48 | 30c red brn | .25 | .25 |
| C331 | AP48 | 35c dp grn | .25 | .25 |
| C332 | AP48 | 40c dk vio brn | .25 | .25 |
| C333 | AP48 | 45c olive | .25 | .25 |
| C334 | AP48 | 50c carmine | .30 | .25 |
| C335 | AP48 | 60c ultra | .30 | .25 |
| C336 | AP48 | 85c brown | .40 | .35 |
| C337 | AP48 | 1.10cor purple | .45 | .45 |
| C338 | AP48 | 1.20cor ol bis | .45 | .45 |
| | | *Nos. C326-C338 (13)* | 3.90 | 3.75 |

For surcharges see Nos. C363-C364, C757.

Torch and UN Emblem — AP49

Designs: 4c, Raised hands. 5c, Candle and charter. 30c, Flags of Nicaragua and UN. 2cor, Globe. 3cor, Arms of Nicaragua. 5cor, Type A69 inscribed "Aereo."

**1954, Apr. 30 Engr. *Perf. 13½***

| | | | | |
|---|---|---|---|---|
| C339 | AP49 | 3c rose pink | .25 | .25 |
| C340 | AP49 | 4c dp org | .25 | .25 |
| C341 | AP49 | 5c red | .25 | .25 |
| C342 | AP49 | 30c cerise | 1.00 | .25 |
| C343 | AP49 | 2cor magenta | 1.40 | 1.00 |
| C344 | AP49 | 3cor org brn | 2.50 | 1.75 |
| C345 | AP49 | 5cor brn vio | 3.00 | 2.25 |
| | | *Nos. C339-C345 (7)* | 8.65 | 6.00 |

Honoring the United Nations.
For overprint & surcharge see #C366, C443.

Capt. Dean L. Ray, USAF — AP50

Designs: 15c, Sabre jet plane. 20c, Air Force emblem. 25c, National Air Force hangars. 30c, Gen. A. Somoza. 50c, AT-6's in formation. 1cor, Plane, type P-38.

**Frame in Black**
**Engraved; Center Photogravure**

**1954, Nov. 5** *Perf. 13*
**C346** AP50 10c gray .25 .25
**C347** AP50 15c gray .25 .25
**C348** AP50 20c claret .25 .25
**C349** AP50 25c red .25 .25
**C350** AP50 30c ultra .25 .25
**C351** AP50 50c blue .45 .45
**C352** AP50 1cor green .35 .25
*Nos. C346-C352 (7)* 2.05 1.95

Issued to honor the National Air Force.

**Rotary Intl. Type**

Designs: 1c, 1cor, Paul P. Harris. 2c, 50c, Handclasp, Rotary emblem and globe. 3c, 45c, Map of world and Rotary emblem. 4c, 30c, Rotary slogans and wreath. 5c, 25c, Flags of Nicaragua and Rotary.

*Perf. 11½*
**1955, Aug. 30 Unwmk. Photo.**
**Granite Paper**
**C353** A71 1c vermilion .25 .25
**C354** A71 2c ultra .25 .25
**C355** A72 3c pck grn .25 .25
**C356** A71 4c violet .25 .25
**C357** A71 5c org brn .25 .25
**C358** A71 25c brt grnsh bl .25 .25
**C359** A71 30c dl pur .25 .25
**C360** A72 45c lil rose .35 .30
**C361** A71 50c lt bl grn .25 .25
**C362** A71 1cor ultra .35 .35
*a.* Souv. sheet of 5, #C358-C362 9.50 9.50
*Nos. C353-C362 (10)* 2.70 2.65

For surcharge see No. C365.

Nos. C331, C333, C360, C345 Surcharged in Green or Black

**Engraved, Photogravure**
**1956, Feb. 4** *Perf. 13½x13, 11½*
**C363** AP48 30c on 35c (G) .25 .25
**C364** AP48 30c on 45c (G) .25 .25
**C365** A72 30c on 45c .25 .25
**C366** AP49 2cor on 5cor .80 .75
*Nos. C363-C366 (4)* 1.55 1.50

National Exhibition, Feb. 4-16, 1956.
See note after No. 772.

Gen. Jose D. Estrada — AP53

The Stoning of Andres Castro AP54

1.50 cor, Emanuel Mongalo. 2.50 cor, Battle of Rivas. 10 cor, Com. Hiram Paulding.

**1956, Sept. 14 Engr.** *Perf. 12½*
**C367** AP53 30c dk car rose .25 .25
**C368** AP54 60c chocolate .25 .25
**C369** AP53 1.50cor green .25 .25
**C370** AP54 2.50cor dk ultra .40 .40
**C371** AP53 10cor red org 2.25 2.00
*Nos. C367-C371 (5)* 3.40 3.15

Centenary of the National War.
For overprint and surcharge see #C444, C751.

President Somoza — AP55

**1957, Feb. 1 Photo.** *Perf. 14x13½*
**Various Frames: Centers in Black**
**C372** AP55 15c gray blk .25 .25
**C373** AP55 30c indigo .25 .25
**C374** AP55 2cor purple 1.00 1.00
**C375** AP55 3cor dk grn 2.00 2.00
**C376** AP55 5cor dk brn 3.25 3.25
*Nos. C372-C376 (5)* 6.75 6.75

President Anastasio Somoza, 1896-1956.

**Type of Regular Issue and**

Handshake and Globe — AP56

Designs: 4c, Scout emblem, globe and Lord Baden-Powell. 5c, Cub Scout. 6c, Crossed flags and Scout emblem. 8c, Scout symbols. 30c, Joseph A. Harrison. 40c, Pres. Somoza receiving decoration at first Central American Camporee. 75c, Explorer Scout. 85c, Boy Scout. 1cor, Lord Baden-Powell.

**1957, Apr. 9 Unwmk.** *Perf. 13½x14*
**C377** AP56 3c red org & ol .25 .25
**C378** A75 4c dk brn & dk Prus grn .25 .25
**C379** A75 5c grn & brn .25 .25
**C380** A75 6c pur & ol .25 .25
**C381** A75 8c grnsh blk & red .25 .25
**C382** A75 30c Prus grn & gray .25 .25
**C383** AP56 40c dk bl & grysh blk .25 .25
**C384** A75 75c mar & brn .25 .25
**C385** A75 85c red & gray .25 .25
**C386** A75 1cor dl red brn & sl grn .30 .30
*a.* Souv. sheet of 5, #C382-C386, imperf. 2.50 2.50
*Nos. C377-C386 (10)* 2.55 2.55

Centenary of the birth of Lord Baden-Powell, founder of the Boy Scouts.
No. C386a with each stamp overprinted "CAMPOREE SCOUT 1965" was issued in 1965 along with Nos. 843-852. Value, sheet $10.
For surcharge see No. C754.

Pres. Luis A. Somoza — AP57

**1957, July 2** *Perf. 14x13½*
**Portrait in Dark Brown**
**C387** AP57 20c dp bl .25 .25
**C388** AP57 25c lil rose .25 .25
**C389** AP57 30c blk brn .25 .25
**C390** AP57 40c grnsh bl .25 .25
**C391** AP57 2cor brt vio 1.25 1.25
*Nos. C387-C391 (5)* 2.25 2.25

Issued to honor President Luis A. Somoza.

**Church Types of Regular Issue**

Designs: 30c, Archbishop Lezcano y Ortega. 60c, Managua Cathedral. 75c, Bishop Pereira y Castellon. 90c, Leon Cathedral. 1.50cor, De la Merced Church, Granada. 2cor, Father Mariano Dubon.

**1957, July 16 Unwmk.**
**Centers in Olive Gray**
**C392** A78 30c dk grn .35 .25
**C393** A77 60c chocolate .35 .25
**C394** A78 75c dk bl .35 .25
**C395** A77 90c brt red .55 .30
**C396** A77 1.50cor Prus grn 1.25 .40
**C397** A78 2cor brt pur 1.75 .60
*Nos. C392-C397 (6)* 4.60 2.05

**Merchant Marine Type of 1957**

Designs: 25c, M. S. Managua. 30c, Ship's wheel and map. 50c, Pennants. 60c, M. S. Costa Rica. 1 cor, M. S. Nicarao. 2.50 cor, Flag, globe & ship.

**1957, Oct. 24 Litho.** *Perf. 14*
**C398** A79 25c ultra grysh bl & gray .25 .25
**C399** A79 30c red brn, gray & yel .25 .25
**C400** A79 50c vio, ol gray & bl .30 .30
**C401** A79 60c lake, grnsh bl & blk .35 .35
**C402** A79 1cor crim, brt bl & blk .45 .45
**C403** A79 2.50cor blk, bl & red brn 1.50 1.50
*Nos. C398-C403 (6)* 3.10 3.10

For surcharge see No. C691.

Fair Emblem — AP58

Designs: 30c, 2cor, Arms of Nicaragua. 45c, 10cor, Pavilion of Nicaragua, Brussels.

**1958, Apr. 17 Unwmk.** *Perf. 14*
**C404** AP58 25c bluish grn, blk & yel .25 .25
**C405** AP58 30c multi .25 .25
**C406** AP58 45c bis, bl & blk .25 .25
**C407** AP58 1cor pale brn, lt bl & blk .25 .25
**C408** AP58 2cor multi .40 .30
**C409** AP58 10cor pale bl, lil & brn 2.10 1.60
*a.* Souv. sheet of 6, #C404-C409 12.00 12.00
*Nos. C404-C409 (6)* 3.50 2.90

World's Fair, Brussels, Apr. 17-Oct. 19.

**Lions Type of Regular Issue**

Designs: 30c, Dr. Teodoro A. Arias. 60c, Arms of Central American Republics. 90c, Edward G. Barry. 1.25cor, Melvin Jones. 2cor, Motto and emblem. 3cor, Map of Central America.

**1958, May 8 Litho.**
**Emblem in Yellow, Red and Blue**
**C410** A80 30c bl & org .25 .25
**C411** A80 60c multi .25 .25
**C412** A80 90c blue .35 .30
**C413** A80 1.25cor bl & ol .45 .40
**C414** A80 2cor bl & grn .80 .70
**C415** A80 3cor bl, lil & pink 1.25 1.10
*a.* Souv. sheet of 6, #C410-C415 4.25 4.25
*Nos. C410-C415 (6)* 3.35 3.00

For surcharge see No. C686.

**Christian Brothers Type of 1958**

Designs: 30c, Arms of La Salle. 60c, School, Managua, horiz 85c, St. Jean Baptiste De La Salle. 90c, Bro. Carlos. 1.25cor, Bro. Julio. 1.50cor, Bro. Antonio. 1.75cor, Bro. Argeo. 2cor, Bro. Eugenio.

**1958, July 13 Photo.** *Perf. 14*
**C416** A81 30c bl, car & yel .25 .25
**C417** A81 60c gray, brn & lil .35 .25
**C418** A81 85c red, bl & grnsh blk .35 .30
**C419** A81 90c ol grn, ocher & blk .50 .35
**C420** A81 1.25cor car, ocher & blk .70 .50
**C421** A81 1.50cor lt grn, gray & vio blk .80 .55
**C422** A81 1.75cor brn, bl & grnsh blk .85 .65
**C423** A81 2cor ol grn, gray & vio blk 1.25 1.00
*Nos. C416-C423 (8)* 5.05 3.85

For surcharges see Nos. C539A, C755-C756.

UNESCO Building, Paris — AP59

75c, 5cor, "UNESCO." 90c, 3cor, UNESCO building, Eiffel tower. 1cor, Emblem, globe.

*Perf. 11½*
**1958, Dec. 15 Unwmk. Litho.**
**C424** AP59 60c brt pink & bl .30 .25
**C425** AP59 75c grn & red brn .30 .25
**C426** AP59 90c lt brn & grn .30 .25
**C427** AP59 1cor ultra & brt pink .30 .25
**C428** AP59 3cor gray & org 1.00 .65
**C429** AP59 5cor rose lil & dk bl 1.60 .95
*a.* Min. sheet of 6, #C424-C429 4.00 4.00
*Nos. C424-C429 (6)* 3.80 2.60

UNESCO Headquarters Opening in Paris, Nov. 3.
For overprints see Nos. C494-C499.

**Type of Regular Issue, 1959 and**

Nicaraguan, Papal and US Flags — AP60

Designs: 35c, Pope John XXIII and Cardinal Spellman. 1cor, Spellman coat of arms. 1.05cor, Cardinal Spellman. 1.50cor, Human rosary and Cardinal, horiz. 2cor, Cardinal with Ruben Dario order.

**1959, Nov. 26** *Perf. 12½*
**C430** AP60 30c vio bl, yel & red .25 .25
**C431** A83 35c dp org & grnsh blk .25 .25
**C432** A83 1cor yel, bl & car .25 .25
**C433** A83 1.05cor red, blk & dk car .40 .30
**C434** A83 1.50cor dk bl & yel .40 .30
**C435** A83 2cor multi .50 .40
**C436** AP60 5cor multi 1.60 .90
*a.* Min. sheet of 7, #C430-C436, perf. or imperf. 4.00 4.00
*Nos. C430-C436 (7)* 3.65 2.65

Visit of Cardinal Spellman to Managua, Feb. 1958.
For surcharges see #C538, C638, C747, C752.

**Type of Lincoln Regular Issue and**

AP61

*Perf. 13x13½, 13½x13*
**1960, Jan. 21 Engr. Unwmk.**
**Portrait in Black**
**C437** A84 30c indigo .25 .25
**C438** A84 35c brt car .25 .25
**C439** A84 70c plum .25 .25
**C440** A84 1.05cor emerald .25 .25
**C441** A84 1.50cor violet .40 .30
**C442** AP61 5cor int blk & bis 1.25 .90
*a.* Souv. sheet of 6, #C437-C442, imperf. 4.00 4.00
*Nos. C437-C442 (6)* 2.65 2.20

150th anniv. of the birth of Abraham Lincoln.
For overprints and surcharges see Nos. C446-C451, C500, C539, C637, C680, C753.

Nos. C343, C370 and C318 Overprinted

**1960, July 4 Engr.**
**C443** AP49 2cor magenta .90 .70
**C444** AP54 2.50cor dk ultra .90 .75
**C445** A65 3cor green 1.25 1.10
*Nos. C443-C445 (3)* 3.05 2.55

10th anniversary of the Philatelic Club of San Jose, Costa Rica.

Nos. C437-C442 Overprinted in Red

*Perf. 13x13½, 13½x13*

**1960, Sept. 19 Unwmk.**

**Center in Black**

| | | | | |
|---|---|---|---|---|
| **C446** | A84 | 30c indigo | .25 | .25 |
| **C447** | A84 | 35c brt car | .25 | .25 |
| **C448** | A84 | 70c plum | .25 | .25 |
| **C449** | A84 | 1.05cor emerald | .30 | .25 |
| **C450** | A84 | 1.50cor violet | .50 | .35 |
| **C451** | AP61 | 5cor int blk & bis | 1.40 | 1.10 |
| | | *Nos. C446-C451 (6)* | 2.95 | 2.45 |

Issued for the Red Cross to aid earthquake victims in Chile. The overprint on No. C451 is horizontal and always inverted.

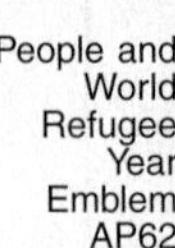

People and World Refugee Year Emblem AP62

5cor, Crosses, globe and WRY emblem.

**1961, Dec. 30 Litho.** ***Perf. 11x11½***

| | | | | |
|---|---|---|---|---|
| **C452** | AP62 | 2cor multi | .50 | .30 |
| **C453** | AP62 | 5cor multi | 1.00 | .65 |
| *a.* | | Souv. sheet of 2, #C452-C453 | 2.50 | 2.50 |

World Refugee Year, July 1, 1959-June 30, 1960.

Consular Service Stamps Surcharged in Red, Black or Blue — AP63

**Unwmk.**

**1961, Feb. 21 Engr.** ***Perf. 12***

**Red Marginal Number**

| | | | | |
|---|---|---|---|---|
| **C454** | AP63 | 20c on 50c dp bl (R) | .25 | .25 |
| **C455** | AP63 | 20c on 1cor grnsh blk (R) | .25 | .25 |
| **C456** | AP63 | 20c on 2cor grn (R) | .25 | .25 |
| **C457** | AP63 | 20c on 3cor dk car | .25 | .25 |
| **C458** | AP63 | 20c on 5cor org (Bl) | .25 | .25 |
| **C459** | AP63 | 20c on 10cor vio (R) | .25 | .25 |
| **C460** | AP63 | 20c on 20cor red brn (R) | .25 | .25 |
| **C461** | AP63 | 20c on 50cor brn (R) | .25 | .25 |
| **C462** | AP63 | 20c on 100cor mag | .25 | .25 |
| | | *Nos. C454-C462 (9)* | 2.25 | 2.25 |

See Nos. CO51-CO59, RA63-RA64.

Charles L. Mullins, Anastasio Somoza and Franklin D. Roosevelt AP64

Standard Bearers with Flags of Nicaragua and Academy — AP65

Designs: 25c, 70c, Flags of Nicaragua and Academy. 30c, 1.05cor, Directors of Academy: Fred T. Cruse, LeRoy Bartlett, Jr., John F. Greco, Anastasio Somoza Debayle, Francisco Boza, Elias Monge. 40c, 2cor, Academy Emblem. 45c, 5cor, Anastasio Somoza Debayle and Luis Somoza Debayle.

*Perf. 11x11½, 11½x11*

**1961, Feb. 24 Litho. Unwmk.**

| | | | | |
|---|---|---|---|---|
| **C463** | AP64 | 20c rose, gray & buff | .25 | .25 |
| **C464** | AP65 | 25c bl, red & blk | .25 | .25 |
| **C465** | AP64 | 30c bl, gray & yel | .25 | .25 |
| **C466** | AP65 | 35c multi | .25 | .25 |
| **C467** | AP65 | 40c multi | .25 | .25 |
| **C468** | AP64 | 45c pink, gray & buff | .25 | .25 |
| *a.* | | Min. sheet of 6, #C463-C468, imperf. | .90 | .70 |
| **C469** | AP64 | 60c brn, gray & buff | .25 | .25 |
| **C470** | AP65 | 70c multi | .25 | .25 |
| **C471** | AP64 | 1.05cor clar, gray & yel | .25 | .25 |
| **C472** | AP65 | 1.50cor multi | .25 | .25 |
| **C473** | AP65 | 2cor multi | .30 | .25 |
| **C474** | AP64 | 5cor gray & buff | .70 | .55 |
| *a.* | | Min. sheet of 6, #C469-C474, imperf. | 3.50 | 3.50 |
| | | *Nos. C463-C474 (12)* | 3.50 | 3.30 |

20th anniversary (in 1959) of the founding of the Military Academy of Nicaragua.

In 1977, Nos. C468a and C474a were overprinted in black: "1927-1977 50 ANIVERSARIO / Guardia Nacional de Nicaragua." Value, $8.75 for both.

For surcharges see Nos. C692, C748, C759.

Emblem of Junior Chamber of Commerce — AP66

Designs: 2c, 15c, Globe showing map of Americas, horiz. 4c, 35c, Globe and initials, horiz. 5c, 70c, Chamber credo. 6c, 1.05cor, Handclasp. 10c, 5cor, Regional map.

*Perf. 11x11½, 11½x11*

**1961, May 16 Unwmk.**

| | | | | |
|---|---|---|---|---|
| **C475** | AP66 | 2c multi | .25 | .25 |
| **C476** | AP66 | 3c yel & blk | .25 | .25 |
| **C477** | AP66 | 4c multi | .25 | .25 |
| **C478** | AP66 | 5c crim & blk | .25 | .25 |
| **C479** | AP66 | 6c brn, yel & blk | .25 | .25 |
| **C480** | AP66 | 10c org, blk & lt bl | .25 | .25 |
| **C481** | AP66 | 15c bl, blk & grn | .25 | .25 |
| **C482** | AP66 | 30c bl & blk | .25 | .25 |
| **C483** | AP66 | 35c multi | .25 | .25 |
| **C484** | AP66 | 70c yel, blk & crim | .25 | .25 |
| **C485** | AP66 | 1.05cor multi | .25 | .25 |
| **C486** | AP66 | 5cor multi | .55 | .55 |
| | | *Nos. C475-C486 (12)* | 3.30 | 3.30 |

13th Regional Congress of the Junior Chamber of Commerce of Nicaragua and the Intl. Junior Chamber of Commerce.

The imperforates of Nos. C475-C486 were not authorized.

For overprints and surcharges see Nos. C504-C508, C537, C634, C687, C749.

Rigoberto Cabezas — AP67

Map of Costa Rica and View of Cartago AP68

Designs: 45c, Newspaper. 70c, Building. 2cor, Cabezas quotation. 10cor, Map of lower Nicaragua with Masaya area.

**1961, Aug. 29 Litho.** ***Perf. 13½***

| | | | | |
|---|---|---|---|---|
| **C487** | AP67 | 20c org & dk bl | .25 | .25 |
| **C488** | AP68 | 40c lt bl & claret | .25 | .25 |
| **C489** | AP68 | 45c citron & brn | .25 | .25 |
| **C490** | AP68 | 70c beige & grn | .25 | .25 |
| **C491** | AP68 | 2cor pink & dk bl | .30 | .25 |
| **C492** | AP68 | 10cor grnsh bl & cl | 1.40 | 1.10 |
| | | *Nos. C487-C492 (6)* | 2.70 | 2.35 |

Centenary of the birth of Rigoberto Cabezas, who acquired the Mosquito Territory (Atlantic Littoral) for Nicaragua.

**No. C253 Overprinted in Red: "Convención Filatélica-Centro-América-Panama-San Salvador-27 Julio 1961"**

**1961, Aug. 23 Engr.** ***Perf. 12½***

| | | | | |
|---|---|---|---|---|
| **C493** | AP22 | 1.25cor multi | .90 | .90 |
| *a.* | | Inverted overprint | 75.00 | |

Central American Philatelic Convention, San Salvador, July 27.

**Nos. C424-C429 Overprinted in Red: "Homenaje a Hammarskjold Sept. 18-1961"**

**1961 Litho.** ***Perf. 11½***

| | | | | |
|---|---|---|---|---|
| **C494** | AP59 | 60c brt pink & bl | .25 | .25 |
| **C495** | AP59 | 75c grn & red brn | .30 | .30 |
| **C496** | AP59 | 90c lt brn & grn | .30 | .30 |
| **C497** | AP59 | 1cor ultra & brt pink | .30 | .30 |
| **C498** | AP59 | 3cor gray & org | .65 | .65 |
| **C499** | AP59 | 5cor rose lil & dk bl | 1.75 | 1.75 |
| | | *Nos. C494-C499 (6)* | 3.55 | 3.55 |

Issued in memory of Dag Hammarskjold, Secretary General of the United Nations, 1953-61.

Nos. C314 and C440 Surcharged in Red

*Perf. 13x13½, 13*

**1962, Jan. 20 Engr.**

| | | | | |
|---|---|---|---|---|
| **C500** | A84 | 1cor on 1.05cor | .25 | .25 |
| **C501** | AP44 | 1cor on 1.10cor | .25 | .25 |

UNESCO Emblem and Crowd — AP69

Design: 5cor, UNESCO and UN Emblems.

**Unwmk.**

**1962, Feb. 26 Photo.** ***Perf. 12***

| | | | | |
|---|---|---|---|---|
| **C502** | AP69 | 2cor multi | .40 | .25 |
| **C503** | AP69 | 5cor multi | .85 | .70 |
| *a.* | | Souv. sheet of 2, #C502-C503, imperf. | 1.25 | 1.25 |

15th anniv. (in 1961) of UNESCO.

Nos. C480 and C483-C486 Overprinted

*Perf. 11x11½, 11½x11*

**1962, July Litho.**

| | | | | |
|---|---|---|---|---|
| **C504** | AP66 | 10c multi | .30 | .25 |
| **C505** | AP66 | 35c multi | .40 | .25 |
| **C506** | AP66 | 70c multi | .50 | .30 |
| **C507** | AP66 | 1.05cor multi | .65 | .45 |
| **C508** | AP66 | 5cor multi | 1.10 | 1.40 |
| | | *Nos. C504-C508 (5)* | 2.95 | 2.65 |

WHO drive to eradicate malaria.

Souvenir Sheet

Stamps and Postmarks of 1862 — AP69a

**1962, Sept. 9 Litho.** ***Imperf.***

| | | | | |
|---|---|---|---|---|
| **C509** | AP69a | 7cor multi | 3.50 | 2.75 |

Cent. of Nicaraguan postage stamps.

**Arms Type of Regular Issue, 1962**

30c, Nueva Segovia. 50c, León. 1cor, Managua. 2cor, Granada. 5cor, Rivas.

**1962, Nov. 22** ***Perf. 12½x13***

**Arms in Original Colors; Black Inscriptions**

| | | | | |
|---|---|---|---|---|
| **C510** | A86 | 30c rose | .25 | .25 |
| **C511** | A86 | 50c salmon | .25 | .25 |
| **C512** | A86 | 1cor lt grn | .25 | .25 |
| **C513** | A86 | 2cor gray | .30 | .30 |
| **C514** | A86 | 5cor lt bl | .85 | .75 |
| | | *Nos. C510-C514 (5)* | 1.90 | 1.80 |

Liberty Bell AP70

**1963, May 15 Litho.** ***Perf. 13x12***

| | | | | |
|---|---|---|---|---|
| **C515** | AP70 | 30c lt bl, blk & ol bis | .25 | .25 |

Sesquicentennial of the 1st Nicaraguan declaration of Independence (in 1961).

Paulist Brother Comforting Boy — AP71

60c, Nun comforting girl. 2cor, St. Vincent de Paul and St. Louisa de Marillac, horiz.

**1963, May 15 Photo.** ***Perf. 13½***

| | | | | |
|---|---|---|---|---|
| **C516** | AP71 | 60c gray & ocher | .25 | .25 |
| **C517** | AP71 | 1cor salmon & blk | .30 | .25 |
| **C518** | AP71 | 2cor crimson & blk | .50 | .50 |
| | | *Nos. C516-C518 (3)* | 1.05 | 1.00 |

300th anniv. of the deaths of St. Vincent de Paul and St. Louisa de Marillac (in 1960).

Map of Central America — AP72

**Lithographed and Engraved**

**1963, Aug. 2 Unwmk.** ***Perf. 12***

| | | | | |
|---|---|---|---|---|
| **C519** | AP72 | 1cor bl & yel | .25 | .25 |

Issued to honor the Federation of Central American Philatelic Societies.

Cross over World — AP73

**1963, Aug. 6**
**C520** AP73 20c yel & red .25 .25

Vatican II, the 21st Ecumenical Council of the Roman Catholic Church.

Wheat and Map of Nicaragua AP74

Design: 25c, Dead tree on parched earth.

**1963, Aug. 6**
**C521** AP74 10c lt grn & grn .25 .25
**C522** AP74 25c yel & dk brn .25 .25

FAO "Freedom from Hunger" campaign.

Boxing — AP75

**Lithographed and Engraved**
**1963, Dec. 12 Unwmk. *Perf. 12***
**C523** AP75 2c shown .25 .25
**C524** AP75 3c Running .25 .25
**C525** AP75 4c Underwater .25 .25
**C526** AP75 5c Soccer .25 .25
**C527** AP75 6c Baseball .25 .25
**C528** AP75 10c Tennis .25 .25
**C529** AP75 15c Bicycling .25 .25
**C530** AP75 20c Motorcycling .25 .25
**C531** AP75 35c Chess .25 .25
**C532** AP75 60c Deep-sea fishing .30 .30
**C533** AP75 1cor Table tennis .40 .40
**C534** AP75 2cor Basketball .80 .80
**C535** AP75 5cor Golf 2.00 2.00
*Nos. C523-C535 (13)* 5.75 5.75

Publicizing the 1964 Olympic Games.
For overprints and surcharge see Nos. C553-C558, C635.

**Central American Independence Issue**

Flags of Central American States — AP75a

**1964, Sept. 15 Litho. *Perf. 13x13½***
**Size: 27x43mm**
**C536** AP75a 40c multi .25 .25

**Nos. C479, C430, C437 and C416 Surcharged in Black or Red**

a

b

**1964 Litho. *Perf. 11½x11***
**C537** AP66 (a) 5c on 6c .25 .25
***Perf. 12½***
**C538** AP60 (a) 10c on 30c .50 .25
**Engr.**
***Perf. 13x13½***
**C539** A84 (a) 15c on 30c (R) .65 .25
**Photo.**
***Perf. 14***
**C539A** A81 (b) 20c on 30c .25 .25
*Nos. C537-C539A (4)* 1.65 1.00

Floating Red Cross Station AP76

Designs: 5c, Alliance for Progress emblem, vert. 15c, Highway. 20c, Plowing with tractors, and sun. 25c, Housing development. 30c, Presidents Somoza and Kennedy and World Bank Chairman Eugene Black. 35c, Adult education. 40c, Smokestacks.

**1964, Oct. 15 Litho. *Perf. 12***
**C540** AP76 5c yel, brt bl, grn & gray .25 .25
**C541** AP76 10c multi .25 .25
**C542** AP76 15c multi .25 .25
**C543** AP76 20c org brn, yel & blk .25 .25
**C544** AP76 25c multi .25 .25
**C545** AP76 30c dk bl, blk & brn .25 .25
**C546** AP76 35c lil rose, dk red & blk .25 .25
**C547** AP76 40c dp car, blk & yel 3.00 .25
*Nos. C540-C547 (8)* 4.75 2.00

Alliance for Progress.
For surcharges see Nos. C677, C693.

Map of Central America and Central American States AP77

Designs (Map of Central America and): 25c, Grain. 40c, Cogwheels. 50c, Heads of cattle.

**1964, Nov. 30 Litho. *Perf. 12***
**C548** AP77 15c ultra & multi .25 .25
**C549** AP77 25c multi .25 .25
**C550** AP77 40c multi .25 .25
**C551** AP77 50c multi .25 .25
*Nos. C548-C551 (4)* 1.00 1.00

Central American Common Market.
For surcharge see No. C678.

**Nos. C523-C525, C527 and C533-C534 Overprinted: "OLIMPIADAS / TOKYO-1964"**

**Lithographed and Engraved**
**1964, Dec. 19 Unwmk. *Perf. 12***
**C553** AP75 2c multi .25 .25
**C554** AP75 3c multi .25 .25
**C555** AP75 4c multi .25 .25
**C556** AP75 6c multi .25 .25
**C557** AP75 1cor multi 2.25 2.00
**C558** AP75 2cor multi 2.75 2.50
*Nos. C553-C558 (6)* 6.00 5.50

18th Olympic Games, Tokyo, Oct. 10-25.

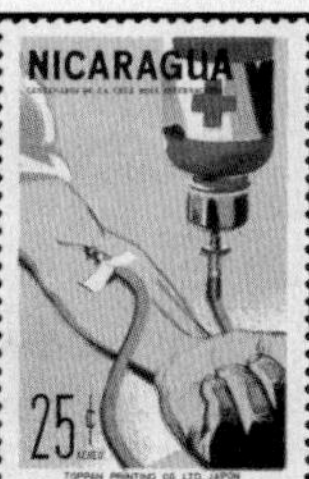

Blood Transfusion AP78

Designs: 20c, Volunteers and priest rescuing wounded man. 40c, Landscape during storm. 10cor, Red Cross over map of Nicaragua.

**1965, Jan. 28 Litho. *Perf. 12***
**C559** AP78 20c yel, blk & red .25 .25
**C560** AP78 25c red, blk & ol bis .25 .25
**C561** AP78 40c grn, blk & red .25 .25
**C562** AP78 10cor multi 1.75 1.10
*Nos. C559-C562 (4)* 2.50 1.85

Centenary (in 1963) of the Intl. Red Cross.

Stele — AP79

Antique Indian artifacts: 5c, Three jadeite statuettes, horiz. 15c, Dog, horiz. 20c, Talamanca pendant. 25c, Decorated pottery bowl and vase, horiz. 30c, Stone pestle and mortar on animal base. 35c, Three statuettes, horiz. 40c, Idol on animal pedestal. 50c, Decorated pottery bowl and vase. 60c, Vase and metate (tripod bowl), horiz. 1cor, Metate.

***Perf. 13½x13, 13x13½***
**1965, Mar. 24 Litho. Unwmk.**
**Black Margin and Inscription**
**C563** AP79 5c yel & multi .30 .25
**C564** AP79 10c multi .30 .25
**C565** AP79 15c multi .30 .25
**C566** AP79 20c sal & dk brn .30 .25
**C567** AP79 25c lil & multi .30 .25
**C568** AP79 30c lt grn & multi .30 .25
**C569** AP79 35c multi .30 .25
**C570** AP79 40c cit & multi .30 .25
**C571** AP79 50c ocher & multi .30 .25
**C572** AP79 60c multi .30 .25
**C573** AP79 1cor car & multi .40 .25
*Nos. C563-C573 (11)* 3.40 2.75

For surcharges see Nos. C596-597, C679, C688-C690.

Pres. John F. Kennedy (1917-63) — AP80

**Photogravure & Lithographed**
**1965, Apr. 28 *Perf. 12½x13½***
**C574** AP80 35c blk & brt grn .25 .25
**C575** AP80 75c blk & brt pink .35 .25
**C576** AP80 1.10cor blk & dk bl .50 .40
**C577** AP80 2cor blk & yel brn 1.25 1.00
*Nos. C574-C577 (4)* 2.35 1.90
Set of 4 souvenir sheets 5.50 5.50

Nos. C574-C577 each exist in souvenir sheets containing one imperf. block of 4.
For surcharge see No. C760.

Andrés Bello AP81

**1965, Oct. 15 Litho. *Perf. 14***
**C578** AP81 10c dk brn & red brn .25 .25
**C579** AP81 15c ind & lt bl .25 .25
**C580** AP81 45c blk & dl lil .25 .25
**C581** AP81 80c blk & yel grn .25 .25
**C582** AP81 1cor dk brn & yel .25 .25
**C583** AP81 2cor blk & gray .30 .30
*Nos. C578-C583 (6)* 1.55 1.55

Centenary of the death of Andrés Bello (1780?-1864), Venezuelan writer and educator.

Winston Churchill — AP82

Winston Churchill: 35c, 1cor, Broadcasting, horiz. 60c, 3cor, On military inspection. 75c, As young officer.

**1966, Feb. 7 Unwmk. *Perf. 14***
**C584** AP82 20c cer & blk .25 .25
**C585** AP82 35c dk ol grn & blk .25 .25
**C586** AP82 60c brn & blk .25 .25
**C587** AP82 75c rose red .30 .25
**C588** AP82 1cor vio blk .45 .25
**C589** AP82 2cor lil & blk .80 .50
*a.* Souv. sheet of 4 3.25 3.25
**C590** AP82 3cor ind & blk 1.25 .70
*Nos. C584-C590 (7)* 3.55 2.45

Sir Winston Spencer Churchill (1874-1965), statesman and World War II leader.
No. C589a contains four imperf. stamps similar to Nos. C586-C589 with simulated perforations.

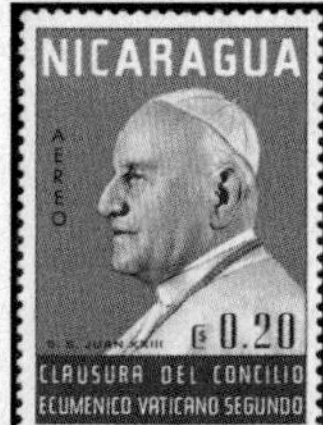

Pope John XXIII — AP83

35c, Pope Paul VI. 1cor, Archbishop Gonzalez y Robleto. 2cor, St. Peter's, Rome. 3cor, Arms of Pope John XXIII & St. Peter's.

**1966, Dec. 15 Litho. *Perf. 13***
**C591** AP83 20c multi .25 .25
**C592** AP83 35c multi .25 .25
**C593** AP83 1cor multi .25 .25
**C594** AP83 2cor multi .40 .35
**C595** AP83 3cor multi .65 .50
*Nos. C591-C595 (5)* 1.80 1.60

Closing of the Ecumenical Council, Vatican II.

Nos. C571-C572 Surcharged in Red

**1967 *Perf. 13x13½, 13½x13***
**C596** AP79 10c on 50c multi .25 .25
**C597** AP79 15c on 60c multi .25 .25

Rubén Dario and Birthplace — AP84

Portrait and: 10c, Monument, Managua. 20c, Leon Cathedral, site of Dario's tomb. 40c, Centaurs. 75c, Swans. 1cor, Roman triumphal march. 2cor, St. Francis and the Wolf. 5cor, "Faith" defeating "Death."

**1967, Jan. 18 Litho. *Perf. 13***

| | | | | |
|---|---|---|---|---|
| **C598** | AP84 | 5c lt brn, tan & blk | .25 | .25 |
| **C599** | AP84 | 10c org, pale org & blk | .25 | .25 |
| **C600** | AP84 | 20c vio, lt bl & blk | .25 | .25 |
| **C601** | AP84 | 40c grn, dk grn & blk | .25 | .25 |
| *a.* | | Souv. sheet of 4, #C598-C601 | 1.00 | 1.00 |
| **C602** | AP84 | 75c ultra, pale bl & blk | .25 | .25 |
| **C603** | AP84 | 1cor red, pale red & blk | .25 | .25 |
| **C604** | AP84 | 2cor rose pink, car & blk | .30 | .30 |
| **C605** | AP84 | 5cor dp ultra, vio bl, & blk | .75 | .65 |
| *a.* | | Souv. sheet of 4, #C602-C605 | 3.50 | 3.50 |
| | | *Nos. C598-C605 (8)* | 2.55 | 2.45 |

Rubén Dario (pen name of Felix Rubén Garcia Sarmiento, 1867-1916), poet, newspaper correspondent and diplomat.

Sheets were issued perf. and imperf.

Megalura Peleus AP85

Designs: Various butterflies. 5c, 10c, 30c, 35c, 50c and 1cor are vertical.

**1967, Apr. 20 Litho. *Perf. 14***

| | | | | |
|---|---|---|---|---|
| **C606** | AP85 | 5c multi | .30 | .25 |
| **C607** | AP85 | 10c multi | .35 | .25 |
| **C608** | AP85 | 15c multi | .45 | .25 |
| **C609** | AP85 | 20c multi | .75 | .25 |
| **C610** | AP85 | 25c multi | 1.00 | .25 |
| **C611** | AP85 | 30c multi | 1.10 | .25 |
| **C612** | AP85 | 35c multi | 1.25 | .25 |
| **C613** | AP85 | 40c multi | 1.40 | .25 |
| **C614** | AP85 | 50c multi | 1.50 | .25 |
| **C615** | AP85 | 60c multi | 2.00 | .30 |
| **C616** | AP85 | 1cor multi | 3.00 | .30 |
| **C617** | AP85 | 2cor multi | 6.50 | 1.00 |
| | | *Nos. C606-C617 (12)* | 19.60 | 3.85 |

Com. James McDivitt and Maj. Edward H. White AP86

Gemini 4 Space Flight: 10c, 40c, Rocket launching and astronauts. 15c, 75c, Edward H. White walking in space. 20c, 1cor, Recovery of capsule.

**1967, Sept. 20 Litho. *Perf. 13***

| | | | | |
|---|---|---|---|---|
| **C618** | AP86 | 5c red & multi | .25 | .25 |
| **C619** | AP86 | 10c org & multi | .25 | .25 |
| **C620** | AP86 | 15c multi | .25 | .25 |
| **C621** | AP86 | 20c multi | .25 | .25 |
| **C622** | AP86 | 35c ol & multi | .25 | .25 |
| **C623** | AP86 | 40c ultra & multi | .25 | .25 |
| **C624** | AP86 | 75c brn & multi | .30 | .30 |
| **C625** | AP86 | 1cor multi | .40 | .40 |
| | | *Nos. C618-C625 (8)* | 2.20 | 2.20 |

Saquanjoche, National Flower of Nicaragua — AP87

National Flowers: No. C626, White nun orchid, Guatemala. No. C627, Rose, Honduras. No. C629, Maquilishuat, Salvador. No. C630, Purple guaria orchid, Costa Rica.

**1967, Nov. 22 Litho. *Perf. 13½***

| | | | | |
|---|---|---|---|---|
| **C626** | AP87 | 40c multi | .45 | .25 |
| **C627** | AP87 | 40c multi | .45 | .25 |
| **C628** | AP87 | 40c multi | .45 | .25 |
| **C629** | AP87 | 40c multi | .45 | .25 |
| **C630** | AP87 | 40c multi | .45 | .25 |
| *a.* | | Strip of 5, #C626-C630 | 5.00 | 3.75 |

5th anniversary of the General Treaty for Central American Economic Integration.

Presidents of Nicaragua and Mexico — AP88

Designs: 40c Pres. Gustavo Diáz Ordaz of Mexico and Pres. René Schick of Nicaragua signing statement, horiz. 1cor, President Diáz.

**1968, Feb. 28 Litho. *Perf. 12½***

| | | | | |
|---|---|---|---|---|
| **C631** | AP88 | 20c black | .25 | .25 |
| **C632** | AP88 | 40c slate grn | .25 | .25 |
| **C633** | AP88 | 1cor dp brn | .25 | .25 |
| | | *Nos. C631-C633 (3)* | .75 | .75 |

Issued to commemorate the visit of the President of Mexico, Gustavo Diáz Ordaz.

### Nos. C479, C527, C242, C440 and C434 Surcharged "Resello" and New Value in Black, Red (#C637) or Yellow (#C638)

**1968, May Litho.; Engr.**

| | | | | |
|---|---|---|---|---|
| **C634** | AP66 | 5c on 6c multi | .25 | .25 |
| **C635** | AP75 | 5c on 6c multi | .25 | .25 |
| **C636** | AP20 | 5c on 8c blk brn | .25 | .25 |
| **C637** | A84 | 1cor on 1.05cor emer & blk | .25 | .25 |
| **C638** | A83 | 1cor on 1.50cor dk bl & yel | .25 | .25 |
| | | *Nos. C634-C638 (5)* | 1.25 | 1.25 |

Mangos — AP89

**1968, May 15 Litho. *Perf. 14***

| | | | | |
|---|---|---|---|---|
| **C639** | AP89 | 5c shown | .25 | .25 |
| **C640** | AP89 | 10c Pineapples | .25 | .25 |
| **C641** | AP89 | 15c Orange | .25 | .25 |
| **C642** | AP89 | 20c Papaya | .30 | .25 |
| **C643** | AP89 | 30c Bananas | .40 | .25 |
| **C644** | AP89 | 35c Avocado | .55 | .25 |
| **C645** | AP89 | 50c Watermelon | .55 | .25 |
| **C646** | AP89 | 75c Cashews | .55 | .30 |
| **C647** | AP89 | 1cor Sapodilla | .65 | .30 |
| **C648** | AP89 | 2cor Cacao | 1.10 | .45 |
| | | *Nos. C639-C648 (10)* | 4.85 | 2.80 |

The Last Judgment, by Michelangelo — AP90

Paintings: 10c, The Crucifixion, by Fra Angelo, horiz. 35c, Madonna with Child and St. John, by Raphael. 2cor, The Disrobing of Christ, by El Greco. 3cor, The Immaculate Conception, by Murillo. 5cor, Christ of St. John of the Cross, by Salvador Dali.

**1968, July 22 Litho. *Perf. 12½***

| | | | | |
|---|---|---|---|---|
| **C649** | AP90 | 10c gold & multi | .25 | .25 |
| **C650** | AP90 | 15c gold & multi | .25 | .25 |
| **C651** | AP90 | 35c gold & multi | .25 | .25 |
| **C652** | AP90 | 2cor gold & multi | .45 | .40 |
| **C653** | AP90 | 3cor gold & multi | .65 | .55 |
| | | *Nos. C649-C653 (5)* | 1.85 | 1.70 |

**Miniature Sheet**

| | | | | |
|---|---|---|---|---|
| **C654** | AP90 | 5cor gold & multi | 2.75 | 2.75 |

### Nos. C649-C652 Overprinted: "Visita de S.S. Paulo VI C.E. de Bogota 1968"

**1968, Oct. 25 Litho. *Perf. 12½***

| | | | | |
|---|---|---|---|---|
| **C655** | AP90 | 10c gold & multi | .25 | .25 |
| **C656** | AP90 | 15c gold & multi | .25 | .25 |
| **C657** | AP90 | 35c gold & multi | .25 | .25 |
| **C658** | AP90 | 2cor gold & multi | .50 | .40 |
| | | *Nos. C655-C658 (4)* | 1.25 | 1.15 |

Visit of Pope Paul VI to Bogota, Colombia, Aug. 22-24. The overprint has 3 lines on the 10c stamp and 5 lines on others.

Basketball AP91

Sports: 15c, Fencing, horiz. 20c, Diving. 35c, Running. 50c, Hurdling, horiz. 75c, Weight lifting. 1cor, Boxing, horiz. 2cor, Soccer.

**1968, Nov. 28 Litho. *Perf. 14***

| | | | | |
|---|---|---|---|---|
| **C659** | AP91 | 10c multi | .25 | .25 |
| **C660** | AP91 | 15c org red, blk & gray | .25 | .25 |
| **C661** | AP91 | 20c multi | .25 | .25 |
| **C662** | AP91 | 35c multi | .25 | .25 |
| **C663** | AP91 | 50c multi | .25 | .25 |
| **C664** | AP91 | 75c multi | .25 | .25 |
| **C665** | AP91 | 1cor yel & multi | .30 | .30 |
| **C666** | AP91 | 2cor gray & multi | .80 | .80 |
| *a.* | | Souv. sheet of 4, #C663-C666 | 1.75 | 1.75 |
| | | *Nos. C659-C666 (8)* | 2.60 | 2.60 |

19th Olympic Games, Mexico City, 10/12-27.

Cichlasoma Citrinellum — AP92

Fish: 15c, Cichlasoma nicaraguensis. 20c, Carp. 30c, Gar (lepisosteus tropicus). 35c, Swordfish. 50c, Phylipnus dormitor, vert. 75c, Tarpon atlanticus, vert. 1cor, Eulamia nicaraguensis, vert. 2cor, Sailfish, vert. 3cor, Sawfish, vert.

***Perf. 13½x13, 13x13½***

**1969, Mar. 12 Litho.**

| | | | | |
|---|---|---|---|---|
| **C667** | AP92 | 10c vio bl & multi | .35 | .25 |
| **C668** | AP92 | 15c org & multi | .35 | .25 |
| **C669** | AP92 | 20c grn & multi | .35 | .25 |
| **C670** | AP92 | 30c pur & multi | .35 | .25 |
| **C671** | AP92 | 35c yel & multi | .35 | .25 |
| **C672** | AP92 | 50c brn & multi | .35 | .25 |
| **C673** | AP92 | 75c ultra & multi | .35 | .25 |
| **C674** | AP92 | 1cor org & multi | .35 | .25 |
| **C675** | AP92 | 2cor dk bl & multi | .60 | .25 |
| **C676** | AP92 | 3cor multi | .90 | .40 |
| *a.* | | Min. sheet of 4, #C673-C676 | 4.25 | 4.25 |
| | | *Nos. C667-C676 (10)* | 4.30 | 2.65 |

Nos. C544, C549, C567 and C439 Srchd. in Black or Red

**1969, Mar. Litho. *Perf. 12, 13½x13***

| | | | | |
|---|---|---|---|---|
| **C677** | AP76 | 10c on 25c multi | .25 | .25 |
| **C678** | AP77 | 10c on 25c multi | .25 | .25 |
| **C679** | AP79 | 15c on 25c multi | .25 | .25 |

**Engr.**

| | | | | |
|---|---|---|---|---|
| **C680** | A84 | 50c on 70c (R) | .25 | .25 |
| | | *Nos. C677-C680 (4)* | 1.00 | 1.00 |

Size of 50c surcharge: 11½x9mm.

View, Exhibition Tower and Emblem — AP93

**1969, May 30 Litho. *Perf. 13½x13***

| | | | | |
|---|---|---|---|---|
| **C681** | AP93 | 30c dk vio bl & red | .25 | .25 |
| **C682** | AP93 | 35c blk & red | .25 | .25 |
| **C683** | AP93 | 75c car rose & vio bl | .25 | .25 |
| **C684** | AP93 | 1cor dp plum & blk | .25 | .25 |
| **C685** | AP93 | 2cor dk brn & blk | .45 | .35 |
| *a.* | | Souv. sheet of 4, #C681-C682, C684-C685 | 1.25 | 1.25 |
| | | *Nos. C681-C685 (5)* | 1.45 | 1.35 |

HEMISFAIR 1968 Exhibition.

Nos. C410, C482, C567-C569, C399, C465, C546 Srchd. in Black or Red

**1969 Litho. *Perfs. as before***

| | | | | |
|---|---|---|---|---|
| **C686** | A80 | 10c on 30c multi | .55 | .25 |
| **C687** | AP66 | 10c on 30c bl & blk (R) | .55 | .25 |
| **C688** | AP79 | 10c on 25c multi | .55 | .25 |
| **C689** | AP79 | 10c on 30c multi | .55 | .25 |
| **C690** | AP79 | 15c on 35c multi (R) | .55 | .25 |
| **C691** | A79 | 20c on 30c multi | .55 | .25 |
| **C692** | AP64 | 20c on 30c multi | .55 | .25 |
| **C693** | AP76 | 20c on 35c multi | .55 | .25 |
| | | *Nos. C686-C693 (8)* | 4.40 | 2.00 |

Products of Nicaragua AP94

5c, Minerals (miner). 10c, Fishing. 15c, Bananas. 20c, Timber (truck). 35c, Coffee. 40c, Sugar cane. 60c, Cotton. 75c, Rice and corn. 1cor, Tobacco. 2cor, Meat.

**1969, Sept. 22 Litho. *Perf. 13x13½***

| | | | | |
|---|---|---|---|---|
| **C694** | AP94 | 5c gold & multi | .25 | .25 |
| **C695** | AP94 | 10c gold & multi | .25 | .25 |
| **C696** | AP94 | 15c gold & multi | .25 | .25 |
| **C697** | AP94 | 20c gold & multi | .25 | .25 |
| **C698** | AP94 | 35c gold & multi | .25 | .25 |
| **C699** | AP94 | 40c gold & multi | .25 | .25 |
| **C700** | AP94 | 60c gold & multi | .25 | .25 |
| **C701** | AP94 | 75c gold & multi | .25 | .25 |
| **C702** | AP94 | 1cor gold & multi | .25 | .25 |
| **C703** | AP94 | 2cor gold & multi | .40 | .25 |
| | | *Nos. C694-C703 (10)* | 2.65 | 2.50 |

Woman Carrying Jar, Conference Emblem — AP95

**1970, Feb. 26 Litho. *Perf. 13½x14***

| | | | | |
|---|---|---|---|---|
| **C704** | AP95 | 10c multi | .25 | .25 |
| **C705** | AP95 | 15c grn & multi | .25 | .25 |
| **C706** | AP95 | 20c ultra & multi | .25 | .25 |
| **C707** | AP95 | 35c multi | .25 | .25 |
| **C708** | AP95 | 50c multi | .25 | .25 |
| **C709** | AP95 | 75c multi | .25 | .25 |
| **C710** | AP95 | 1cor lil & multi | .45 | .30 |
| **C711** | AP95 | 2cor multi | .85 | .50 |
| | | *Nos. C704-C711 (8)* | 2.80 | 2.30 |

8th Inter-American Conf. on Savings & Loans.

**Soccer Type of Regular Issue and**

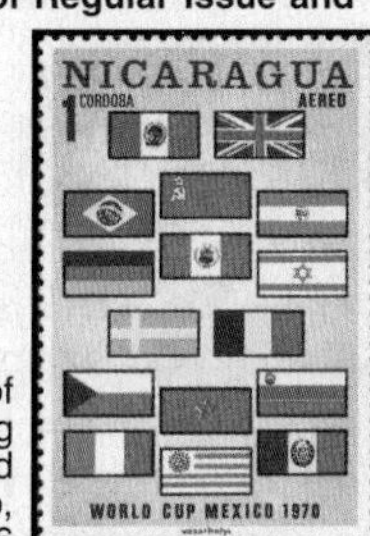


Flags of Participating Nations, World Cup, 1970 — AP96

Soccer Players: 20c, Djalma Santos, Brazil. 80c, Billy Wright, England. 4cor, Jozef Bozsik, Hungary. 5cor, Bobby Charlton, England.

**1970, May 11 Litho. *Perf. 13½***

**C712** A87 20c multi .25 .25
**C713** A87 80c multi .30 .25
**C714** AP96 1cor multi .40 .25
**C715** A87 4cor multi 1.40 .90
**C716** A87 5cor multi 1.50 1.25
*Nos. C712-C716 (5)* 3.85 2.90

Issued to honor the winners of the 1970 poll for the International Soccer Hall of Fame. No. C714 also publicizes the 9th World Soccer Championships for the Jules Rimet Cup, Mexico City, May 30-June 21, 1970.

Names of players and their achievements printed in black on back of stamps.

For overprint and surcharges see Nos. C786-788.

EXPO Emblem, Mt. Fuji and Torii — AP97

**1970, July 5 Litho. *Perf. 13½x14***

**C717** AP97 25c multi .25 .25
**C718** AP97 30c multi .25 .25
**C719** AP97 35c multi .25 .25
**C720** AP97 75c multi .25 .25
**C721** AP97 1.50cor multi .40 .30
**C722** AP97 3cor multi .75 .75
*a.* Souv. sheet of 3, #C720-C722, imperf. 1.00 1.00
*Nos. C717-C722 (6)* 2.15 2.05

EXPO '70 International Exhibition, Osaka, Japan, Mar. 15-Sept. 13, 1970.

Moon Landing, Apollo 11 Emblem and Nicaragua Flag AP98

Apollo 11 Emblem, Nicaragua Flag and: 40c, 75c, Moon surface and landing capsule. 60c, 1cor, Astronaut planting US flag.

**1970, Aug. 12 Litho. *Perf. 14***

**C723** AP98 35c multi .25 .25
**C724** AP98 40c multi .25 .25
**C725** AP98 60c pink & multi .25 .25
**C726** AP98 75c yel & multi .25 .25
**C727** AP98 1cor vio & multi .40 .25
**C728** AP98 2cor org & multi .65 .40
*Nos. C723-C728 (6)* 2.05 1.65

Man's 1st landing on the moon, July 20, 1969. See note after US No. C76.

Franklin D. Roosevelt — AP99

Roosevelt Portraits: 15c, 1cor, as stamp collector. 20c, 50c, 2cor, Full face.

**1970, Oct. 12**

**C729** AP99 10c blk & bluish blk .25 .25
**C730** AP99 15c blk & brn vio .25 .25
**C731** AP99 20c blk & ol grn .25 .25
**C732** AP99 35c blk & brn vio .25 .25
**C733** AP99 50c brown .25 .25
**C734** AP99 75c blue .25 .25
**C735** AP99 1cor rose red .25 .25
**C736** AP99 2cor black .40 .25
*Nos. C729-C736 (8)* 2.15 2.00

Franklin Delano Roosevelt (1882-1945).

Christmas 1970 — AP100

Paintings: Nos. C737, C742, Annunciation, by Matthias Grunewald. Nos. C738, C743, Nativity, by El Greco. Nos. C739, C744, Adoration of the Magi, by Albrecht Dürer. Nos. C740, C745, Virgin and Child, by J. van Hemessen. Nos. C741, C746, Holy Shepherd, Portuguese School, 16th century.

**1970, Dec. 1 Litho. *Perf. 14***

**C737** AP100 10c multi .25 .25
**C738** AP100 10c multi .25 .25
**C739** AP100 10c multi .25 .25
**C740** AP100 10c multi .25 .25
**C741** AP100 10c multi .25 .25
**C742** AP100 15c multi .25 .25
**C743** AP100 20c multi .25 .25
**C744** AP100 35c multi .25 .25
**C745** AP100 75c multi .25 .25
**C746** AP100 1cor multi .25 .25
*Nos. C737-C746 (10)* 2.50 2.50

Nos. C737-C741 printed se-tenant.

Issues of 1947-67 Surcharged

**1971, Mar.**

**C747** A83 10c on 1.05cor, #C433 .30 .30
**C748** AP64 10c on 1.05cor, #C471 .30 .30
**C749** AP66 10c on 1.05cor, #C485 .30 .30
**C750** AP42 15c on 1.50cor, #C292 .40 .40
**C751** AP53 15c on 1.50cor, #C369 .40 .40
**C752** A83 15c on 1.50cor, #C434 .40 .40
**C753** A84 15c on 1.50cor, #C441 .40 .40
**C754** A75 20c on 85c, #C385 .50 .50
**C755** A81 20c on 85c, #C418 .50 .50
**C756** A81 25c on 90c, #C419 .70 .70
**C757** AP48 30c on 1.10cor, #C337 .85 .85
**C758** AP44 40c on 1.10cor, #C314 1.10 1.10
**C759** AP65 40c on 1.50cor, #C472 1.10 1.10
**C760** AP80 1cor on 1.10cor, #C576 2.75 2.75
*Nos. C747-C760 (14)* 10.00 10.00

The arrangement of the surcharge differs on each stamp.

**Mathematics Type of Regular Issue**

Symbolic Designs of Scientific Formulae: 25c, Napier's law (logarithms). 30c, Pythagorean theorem (length of sides of right-angled triangle). 40c, Boltzman's equation (movement of gases). 1cor, Broglie's law (motion of particles of matter). 2cor, Archimedes' principle (displacement of mass).

**1971, May 15 Litho. *Perf. 13½***

**C761** A88 25c lt bl & multi .25 .25
**C762** A88 30c lt bl & multi .30 .25
**C763** A88 40c lt bl & multi .45 .25
**C764** A88 1cor lt bl & multi 1.10 .35
**C765** A88 2cor lt bl & multi 1.90 .75
*Nos. C761-C765 (5)* 4.00 1.85

On the back of each stamp is a descriptive paragraph.

Montezuma Oropendola AP101

Birds: 15c, Turquoise-browed motmot. 20c, Magpie-jay. 25c, Scissor-tailed flycatchers. 30c, Spot-breasted oriole, horiz. 35c, Rufous-naped wren. 40c, Great kiskadee. 75c, Red-legged honeycreeper, horiz. 1cor, Great-tailed grackle, horiz. 2cor, Belted kingfisher.

**1971, Oct. 15 Litho. *Perf. 14***

**C766** AP101 10c multi .40 .25
**C767** AP101 15c multi .40 .25
**C768** AP101 20c gray & multi .40 .25
**C769** AP101 25c multi .40 .25
**C770** AP101 30c multi .40 .25
**C771** AP101 35c multi .45 .25
**C772** AP101 40c multi .45 .25
**C773** AP101 75c yel & multi .55 .25
**C774** AP101 1cor org & multi .70 .25
**C775** AP101 2cor org & multi 1.20 .30
*Nos. C766-C775 (10)* 5.35 2.55

**Ten Commandments Type of Regular Issue**

Designs: 1cor, Bathsheba at her Bath, by Rembrandt (IX). 2cor, Naboth's Vineyard, by James Smetham (X).

**1971, Nov. 1 *Perf. 11***

**C776** A90 1cor ocher & multi 1.00 .45
**C777** A90 2cor ocher & multi 1.60 .80

Descriptive inscriptions printed in gray on back of stamps.

U Thant, Anastasio Somoza, UN Emblem AP102

**1972, Feb. 15 *Perf. 14x13½***

**C778** AP102 10c pink & mar .25 .25
**C779** AP102 15c green .25 .25
**C780** AP102 20c blue .25 .25
**C781** AP102 25c rose claret .25 .25
**C782** AP102 30c org & brn .25 .25
**C783** AP102 40c gray & sl grn .25 .25
**C784** AP102 1cor ol grn .25 .25
**C785** AP102 2cor brown .45 .25
*Nos. C778-C785 (8)* 2.20 2.00

25th anniv. of the United Nations (in 1970).

**Nos. C713, C715, C716 Surcharged or Overprinted Like Nos. 899-900**

**1972, Mar. 20 Litho. *Perf. 13½***

**C786** A87 20c on 80c multi .30 .25
**C787** A87 60c on 4cor multi .30 .25
**C788** A87 5cor multi 1.25 1.00
*Nos. C786-C788 (3)* 1.85 1.50

20th Olympic Games, Munich, 8/26-9/11.

Ceramic Figure, Map of Nicaragua — AP103

Pre-Columbian ceramics (700-1200 A.D.) found at sites indicated on map of Nicaragua.

**1972, Sept. 16 Litho. *Perf. 14x13½***

**C789** AP103 10c blue & multi .25 .25
**C790** AP103 15c blue & multi .25 .25
**C791** AP103 20c blue & multi .25 .25
**C792** AP103 25c blue & multi .25 .25
**C793** AP103 30c blue & multi .25 .25
**C794** AP103 35c blue & multi .25 .25
**C795** AP103 40c blue & multi .25 .25
**C796** AP103 50c blue & multi .25 .25
**C797** AP103 60c blue & multi .25 .25
**C798** AP103 80c blue & multi .25 .25
**C799** AP103 1cor blue & multi .25 .25
**C800** AP103 2cor blue & multi .40 .25
*Nos. C789-C800 (12)* 3.15 3.00

Lord Peter Wimsey, by Dorothy L. Sayers AP104

Designs (Book and): 10c, Philip Marlowe, by Raymond Chandler. 15c, Sam Spade, by Dashiell Hammett. 20c, Perry Mason, by Erle S. Gardner. 25c, Nero Wolfe, by Rex Stout. 35c, Auguste Dupin, by Edgar Allan Poe. 40c, Ellery Queen, by Frederick Dannay and Manfred B. Lee. 50c, Father Brown, by G. K. Chesterton. 60c, Charlie Chan, by Earl Derr Biggers. 80c, Inspector Maigret, by Georges Simenon. 1cor, Hercule Poirot, by Agatha Christie. 2cor, Sherlock Holmes, by A. Conan Doyle.

**1972, Nov. 13 Litho. *Perf. 14x13½***

**C801** AP104 5c blue & multi .30 .25
**C802** AP104 10c blue & multi .30 .25
**C803** AP104 15c blue & multi .30 .25
**C804** AP104 20c blue & multi .30 .25
**C805** AP104 25c blue & multi .30 .25
**C806** AP104 35c blue & multi .40 .25
**C807** AP104 40c blue & multi .40 .25
**C808** AP104 50c blue & multi .50 .30
**C809** AP104 60c blue & multi .70 .40
**C810** AP104 80c blue & multi .85 .50
**C811** AP104 1cor blue & multi 1.10 .65
**C812** AP104 2cor blue & multi 2.25 1.25
*Nos. C801-C812 (12)* 7.70 4.85

50th anniv. of INTERPOL, intl. police organization. Designs show famous fictional detectives. Inscriptions on back, printed on top of gum, give thumbnail sketch of character and author.

Shepherds Following Star AP105

Legend of the Christmas Rose: 15c, Adoration of the kings and shepherds. 20c, Shepherd girl alone crying. 35c, Angel appears to girl. 40c, Christmas rose (Helleborus niger). 60c, Girl thanks angel. 80c, Girl and Holy Family. 1cor, Girl presents rose to Christ Child. 2cor, Adoration.

**1972, Dec. 20**

**C813** AP105 10c multi .25 .25
**C814** AP105 15c multi .25 .25
**C815** AP105 20c multi .25 .25
**C816** AP105 35c multi .25 .25
**C817** AP105 40c multi .25 .25
**C818** AP105 60c multi .25 .25
**C819** AP105 80c multi .25 .25
**C820** AP105 1cor multi .25 .25
**C821** AP105 2cor multi .40 .30
*a.* Souv. sheet of 9, #C813-C821 1.25 1.25
*Nos. C813-C821 (9)* 2.40 2.30

Christmas 1972.

No. C821a exists with red marginal overprint, "TERREMOTO DESASTRE," for the Managua earthquake of Dec. 22-23, 1972. It was sold abroad, starting in Jan. 1973.

Sir Walter Raleigh, Patent to Settle New World — AP106

Events and Quotations from Contemporary Illustrations: 15c, Mayflower Compact, 1620. 20c, Acquittal of Peter Zenger, 1735, vert. 25c, William Pitt, 1766, vert. 30c, British revenue stamp for use in America No. RM31, vert. 35c, "Join or Die" serpent, 1768. 40c, Boston Massacre and State House, 1770, vert. 50c, Boston Tea Party and 3p coin, 1774. 60c, Patrick Henry, 1775, vert. 75c, Battle scene ("Our cause is just, our union is perfect," 1775). 80c, Declaration of Independence, 1776. 1cor, Liberty Bell, Philadelphia. 2cor, Seal of US, 1782, vert.

**1973, Feb. 22 Photo. *Perf. 13½***

**C822** AP106 10c olive & multi .25 .25
**C823** AP106 15c olive & multi .25 .25
**C824** AP106 20c olive & multi .25 .25

**C825** AP106 25c olive & multi .25 .25
**C826** AP106 30c olive & multi .25 .25
**C827** AP106 35c ol, gold & blk .35 .25
**C828** AP106 40c olive & multi .35 .25
**C829** AP106 50c olive & multi .35 .35
**C830** AP106 60c olive & multi .40 .35
**C831** AP106 75c olive & multi .50 .40
**C832** AP106 80c olive & multi .50 .40
**C833** AP106 1cor olive & multi .80 .50
**C834** AP106 2cor olive & multi 1.50 1.00
*Nos. C822-C834 (13)* 6.00 4.75

Inscriptions on back, printed on top of gum, give brief description of subject and event.

Baseball, Player and Map of Nicaragua AP107

**1973, May 25 Litho.** ***Perf. 13½x14***
**C835** AP107 15c lil & multi .25 .25
**C836** AP107 20c multi .25 .25
**C837** AP107 40c multi .25 .25
**C838** AP107 10cor multi 1.75 1.50
*a.* Souvenir sheet of 4 10.00 10.00
*Nos. C835-C838 (4)* 2.50 2.25

20th International Baseball Championships, Managua, Nov. 15-Dec. 5, 1972. No. C838a contains 4 stamps similar to Nos. C835-C838 with changed background colors (15c, olive; 20c, gray; 40c, lt. green; 10cor, lilac), and 5 labels.

### Fashion Type of 1973

10c, Lourdes Nicaragua. 15c, Halston, New York. 20c, Pino Lancetti, Rome. 35c, Madame Ges, Paris. 40c, Irene Galitzine, Rome. 80c, Pedro Rodriguez, Barcelona.

**1973, July 26 Litho.** ***Perf. 13½***
**C839** A91 10c multicolored .25 .25
**C840** A91 15c multicolored .25 .25
**C841** A91 20c multicolored .25 .25
**C842** A91 35c multicolored .25 .25
**C843** A91 40c multicolored .25 .25
**C844** A91 80c multicolored .25 .25
*a.* Souv. sheet of 9, #909-911, C839-C844, perf. 11 + 3 labels *12.00 12.00*
*Nos. C839-C844 (6)* 1.50 1.50

Inscriptions on back printed on top of gum give description of gown in Spanish and English.

### Type of Air Post Semi-Postal Issue

Design: 2cor, Pediatric surgery.

**1973, Sept. 25**
**C845** SPAP1 2cor multi .40 .35
*Nos. C845,CB1-CB11 (12)* 5.45 3.55

Planned Children's Hospital. Inscription on back, printed on top of gum gives brief description of subject shown.
See Nos. CB1-CB11.

### Christmas Type

1cor, Virginia O'Hanlon writing letter, father. 2cor, Letter. 4cor, Virginia, father reading letter.

**1973, Nov. 15 Litho.** ***Perf. 15***
**C846** A92 1cor multicolored .30 .30
**C847** A92 2cor multicolored .60 .60
**C848** A92 4cor multicolored 1.10 1.10
*a.* Souvenir sheet of 3, #C846-C848, perf. 14½ 4.00 4.00
*Nos. C846-C848 (3)* 2.00 2.00

### Churchill Type

#C851, Silhouette, Parliament. #C852, Silhouette, #10 Downing St. 5cor, Showing "V" sign. 6cor, "Bulldog" Churchill protecting England.

**1974, Apr. 30** ***Perf. 14½***
**C849** A93 5cor multicolored 1.40 1.40
**C850** A93 6cor multicolored 1.75 1.75

**Souvenir Sheets**

***Perf. 15***
**C851** A93 4cor blk, org & bl 1.40 1.40
**C852** A93 4cor blk, org, & grn 1.40 1.40

Nos. C851-C852 contain one 28x42mm stamp.

### World Cup Type

Scenes from previous World Cup Championships with flags and scores of finalists.

**1974, May 8** ***Perf. 14½***
**C853** A94 10cor Flags of participants 2.75 2.75

**Souvenir Sheets**
**C853A** A94 4cor like No. 928 1.10 1.10
**C853B** A94 5cor like No. 930 1.40 1.40

For overprint see No. C856.

### Flower Type of 1974

Wild Flowers and Cacti: 1 cor, Centrosema. 3 cor, Night-blooming cereus.

**1974, June 11 Litho.** ***Perf. 14***
**C854** A95 1cor green & multi .30 .25
**C855** A95 3cor green & multi .75 .55

### Nicaraguan Stamps Type

**1974, July 10** ***Perf. 14½***
**C855A** A96 40c #835 .25 .25
**C855B** A96 3cor #C313, horiz. .90 .90
**C855C** A96 5cor #734 1.40 1.40
*Nos. C855A-C855C (3)* 2.55 2.55

**Souvenir Sheet**

***Imperf***
**C855D** Sheet of 3 2.25
*e.* A96 1cor #665 .30
*f.* A96 2cor #C110, horiz. .55
*g.* A96 4cor Globe, stars 1.40

UPU, Cent.

No. C853 Ovptd.

**1974, July 12**
**C856** A94 10cor Flags 2.75 2.25

### Animal Type of 1974

3cor, Colorado deer. 5cor, Jaguar.

**1974, Sept. 10 Litho.** ***Perf. 14½***
**C857** A97 3cor multi .65 .55
**C858** A97 5cor multi 1.00 .90

### Christmas Type of 1974

Works of Michelangelo: 40c, Madonna of the Stairs. 80c, Pitti Madonna. 2cor, Pietà. 5cor, Self-portrait.

**1974, Dec. 15**
**C859** A98 40c multi .25 .25
**C860** A98 80c multi .25 .25
**C861** A98 2cor multi .30 .25
**C862** A98 5cor multi .70 .65
*Nos. C859-C862 (4)* 1.50 1.40

An imperf. souvenir sheet exists containing 2cor and 5cor stamps. Value, $3.50.

### Opera Type of 1975

Opera Singers and Scores: 25c, Rosa Ponselle, Norma. 35c, Giuseppe de Luca, Rigoletto. 40c, Joan Sutherland, La Figlia del Reggimento. 50c, Ezio Pinza, Don Giovanni. 60c, Kirsten Flagstad, Tristan and Isolde. 80c, Maria Callas, Tosca. 2cor, Fyodor Chaliapin, Boris Godunov. 5cor, Enrico Caruso, La Juive.

**1975, Jan. 22** ***Perf. 14x13½***
**C863** A99 25c grn & multi .30 .25
**C864** A99 35c multi .30 .25
**C865** A99 40c multi .30 .25
**C866** A99 50c org & multi .30 .25
**C867** A99 60c rose & multi .30 .25
**C868** A99 80c lake & multi .40 .25
**C869** A99 2cor sep & multi .80 .25
**C870** A99 5cor multi 2.00 .65
*a.* Souvenir sheet of 3 4.00 4.00
*Nos. C863-C870 (8)* 4.70 2.40

No. C870a contains one each of Nos. C869-C870 and a 1cor with design and colors of No. C868. Exists imperf.

### Easter Type of 1975

Stations of the Cross: 40c, Jesus stripped of his clothes. 50c, Jesus nailed to the Cross. 80c, Jesus dies on the Cross. 1cor, Descent from the Cross. 5cor, Jesus laid in the tomb.

**1975, Mar. 20** ***Perf. 14½***
**C871** A100 40c ultra & multi .25 .25
**C872** A100 50c ultra & multi .25 .25
**C873** A100 80c ultra & multi .25 .25
**C874** A100 1cor ultra & multi .25 .25
**C875** A100 5cor ultra & multi .90 .80
*Nos. C871-C875 (5)* 1.90 1.80

### American Bicentennal Type of 1975

Designs: 40c, Washington's Farewell, 1783. 50c, Washington Addressing Continental Congress by J. B. Stearns. 2cor, Washington Arriving for Inauguration. 5cor, Statue of Liberty and flags of 1776 and 1976. 40c, 50c, 2cor, horiz.

**1975, Apr. 16** ***Perf. 14***
**C876** A101 40c tan & multi .25 .25
**C877** A101 50c tan & multi .30 .25
**C878** A101 2cor tan & multi .90 .70
**C879** A101 5cor tan & multi 2.00 1.90
*Nos. C876-C879 (4)* 3.45 3.10

Perf. and imperf. 7cor souv. sheets exist. Value, $3.50.

### Nordjamb 75 Type of 1975

Designs (Scout and Nordjamb Emblems and): 35c, Camp. 40c, Scout musicians. 1cor, Campfire. 10cor, Lord Baden-Powell.

**1975, Aug. 15** ***Perf. 14½***
**C880** A102 35c multi .25 .25
**C881** A102 40c multi .25 .25
**C882** A102 1cor multi .30 .25
**C883** A102 10cor multi 1.75 1.25
*Nos. C880-C883 (4)* 2.55 2.00

Two airmail souvenir sheets of 2 exist. One, perf., contains 2cor and 3cor with designs of Nos. 992 and 990. The other, imperf., contains 2cor and 3cor with designs of Nos. 993 and C882. Size: 125x101mm. Value, pair $18.

### Pres. Somoza Type of 1975

**1975, Sept. 10** ***Perf. 14***
**C884** A103 1cor vio & multi .25 .25
**C885** A103 10cor bl & multi 2.00 1.75
**C886** A103 20cor multi 4.00 3.00
*Nos. C884-C886 (3)* 6.25 5.00

### Choir Type of 1975

Famous Choirs: 50c, Montserrat Abbey. 1cor, St. Florian Choir Boys. 2cor, Choir Boys of the Wooden Cross, vert. 5cor, Boys and Pope Paul VI (Pueri Cantores International Federation).

**1975, Nov. 15** ***Perf. 14½***
**C887** A104 50c sil & multi .25 .25
**C888** A104 1cor sil & multi .25 .25
**C889** A104 2cor sil & multi .35 .30
**C890** A104 5cor sil & multi 1.40 .85
*Nos. C887-C890 (4)* 2.25 1.65

A 10cor imperf. souvenir sheet exists (Oberndorf Memorial Chapel Choir and score of "Holy Night-Silent Night"). Value, $12.50.

### Chess Type of 1976

Designs: 40c, The Chess Players, by Thomas Eakins. 2cor, Bobby Fischer and Boris Spasski in Reykjavik, 1972. 5cor, Shakespeare and Ben Johnson Playing Chess, by Karel van Mander.

**1976, Jan. 8** ***Perf. 14½***
**C891** A105 40c multi .25 .25
**C892** A105 2cor vio & multi .75 .55
**C893** A105 5cor multi 1.50 1.25
*Nos. C891-C893 (3)* 2.50 2.05

A souvenir sheet contains one each of Nos. C892-C893, perf. and imperf. Size: 143x67mm. Value, pair $10.

### Olympic Winner Type 1976

Winners, Rowing and Sculling Events: 55c, USSR, 1956, 1960, 1964, vert. 70c, New Zealand, 1972, vert. 90c, New Zealand, 1968. 10cor, Women's rowing crew, US, 1976, vert. 20cor, US, 1956.

**1976, Sept. 7 Litho.** ***Perf. 14***
**C902** A107 55c bl & multi .25 .25
**C903** A107 70c bl & multi .25 .25
**C904** A107 90c bl & multi .25 .25
**C905** A107 20cor bl & multi 4.50 3.75
*Nos. C902-C905 (4)* 5.25 4.50

**Souvenir Sheet**
**C906** A107 10cor multi 3.00 2.00

No. C906 for the 1st participation of women in Olympic rowing events, size of stamp: 37x50mm.

The overprint "Republica Democratica Alemana Vencedor en 1976" was applied in 1976 to No. C905 in black in 3 lines and to the margin of No. C906 in gold in 2 lines.

### Bicentennial Type of 1976

American Bicentennial Emblem and: #C907, Philadelphia, 1776. #C908, Washington, 1976. #C909, John Paul Jones' ships. #C910, Atomic submarine. #C911, Wagon train. #C912, Diesel train.

**1976, May 25 Litho.** ***Perf. 13½***
**C907** A108 80c multi .25 .25
**C908** A108 80c multi .25 .25
*a.* Pair, #C907-C908 .35 .30
**C909** A108 2.75cor multi .50 .40
**C910** A108 2.75cor multi .50 .40
*a.* Pair, #C909-C910 1.00 .80
**C911** A108 4cor multi .80 .50
**C912** A108 4cor multi .80 .50
*a.* Pair, #C911-C912 1.75 1.00
*Nos. C907-C912 (6)* 3.10 2.30

A souvenir sheet contains two 10cor stamps showing George Washington and Gerald R. Ford with their families. Size: 140x111mm. Value, $5.

### Rare Stamps Type of 1976

Rare Stamps: 40c, Hawaii #1. 1cor, Great Britain #1. 2cor, British Guiana #13. 5cor, Honduras #C12. 10cor, Newfoundland #C1.

**1976, Dec.** ***Perf. 14***
**C913** A109 40c multi .25 .25
**C914** A109 1cor multi .25 .25
**C915** A109 2cor multi .30 .25
**C916** A109 5cor multi .70 .65
**C917** A109 10cor multi 1.40 1.25
*Nos. C913-C917 (5)* 2.90 2.65

Inscriptions on back printed on top of gum give description of illustrated stamp. A 4cor imperf. souvenir sheet shows 1881 Great Britain-Nicaragua combination cover. Size: 140x101mm. Value, $2.

Olga Nuñez de Saballos — AP108

Designs: 1cor, Josefa Toledo de Aguerri. 10cor, Hope Portocarrero de Somoza.

**1977, Feb. Litho.** ***Perf. 13½***
**C918** AP108 35c multi .25 .25
**C919** AP108 1cor red & multi .25 .25
**C920** AP108 10cor multi 2.00 1.75
*Nos. C918-C920 (3)* 2.50 2.25

Famous Nicaraguan women and for International Women's Year (in 1975).

### Zeppelin Type of 1977

Designs: 35c, Ville de Paris airship. 70c, Zeppelin "Schwaben." 3cor, Zeppelin in flight. 10cor, Vickers "Mayfly" before take-off. 20cor, Zeppelin with leadlines extended.

**1977, Oct. 31 Litho.** ***Perf. 14½***
**C921** A110 35c multi .25 .25
**C922** A110 70c multi .25 .25
**C923** A110 3cor multi .65 .50
**C924** A110 10cor multi 2.50 1.75
*Nos. C921-C924 (4)* 3.65 2.75

**Souvenir Sheet**
**C925** A110 20cor multi 5.00 2.75

### Lindbergh Type of 1977

Designs: 55c, Lindbergh's plane approaching Nicaraguan airfield, 1928. 80c, Spirit of St. Louis and map of New York-Paris route. 2cor, Plane flying off Nicaragua's Pacific Coast. 10cor, Lindbergh flying past Momotombo Volcano on way to Managua. 20cor, Spirit of St. Louis.

**1977, Nov. 30**
**C926** A111 55c multi .25 .25
**C927** A111 80c multi .25 .25
**C928** A111 2cor multi .40 .30
**C929** A111 10cor multi 2.00 1.60
*Nos. C926-C929 (4)* 2.90 2.40

**Souvenir Sheet**
**C930** A111 20cor multi 5.00 3.50

### Christmas Type of 1977

Souvenir Sheet

Design: 20cor, Finale of Nutcracker Suite.

**1977, Dec. 12**
**C931** A112 20cor multi 4.50 4.50

### Painting Type of 1978

Rubens Paintings: 5cor, Hippopotamus and Crocodile Hunt. 100cor, Duke de Lerma on Horseback. 20cor, Self-portrait.

**1978, Jan. 11 Litho.** ***Perf. 14½***
**C932** A113 5cor multi 1.10 .85

**C933** A113 10cor multi 2.10 1.60

**Souvenir Sheet**

**C934** A113 20cor multi 5.75 4.00

Peter Paul Rubens (1577-1640), 400th birth anniversary.

### St. Francis Type of 1978

Designs: 80c, St. Francis and the wolf. 10cor, St. Francis, painting. 20cor, Our Lady of Conception, statue in Church of El Viejo.

**1978, Feb. 23 Litho. *Perf. 14½***

**C935** A114 80c lt brn & multi .25 .25
**C936** A114 10cor bl & multi 1.90 1.75

**Souvenir Sheet**

**C937** A114 20cor multi 3.50 2.50

### Railroad Type of 1978

Locomotives: 35c, Light-weight American. 4cor, Heavy Baldwin. 10cor, Juniata, 13-ton. 20cor, Map of route system.

**1978, Apr. 7 Litho. *Perf. 14½***

**C938** A115 35c lt grn & multi .50 .25
**C939** A115 4cor dp org & multi 1.50 .90
**C940** A115 10cor cit & multi 2.75 1.50
*Nos. C938-C940 (3)* 4.75 2.65

**Souvenir Sheet**

**C941** A115 20cor multi 11.50 4.00

### Jules Verne Type of 1978

Designs: 90c, 20,000 Leagues under the Sea. 10cor, Around the World in 80 Days. 20cor, From the Earth to the Moon.

**1978, Aug. Litho. *Perf. 14½***

**C942** A116 90c multi .25 .25
**C943** A116 10cor multi 1.75 1.50

**Souvenir Sheet**

**C944** A116 20cor multi 7.50 5.00

### Aviation History Type of 1978

Designs: 55c, Igor Sikorsky in his helicopter, 1913, horiz. 10cor, Space shuttle, horiz. 20cor, Flyer III, horiz.

**1978, Sept. 29 Litho. *Perf. 14½***

**C945** A117 55c multi .25 .25
**C946** A117 10cor multi 1.40 1.00

**Souvenir Sheet**

**C947** A117 20cor multi 5.00 4.00

### Soccer Type of 1978

Soccer Players: 50c, Denis Law and Franz Beckenbauer. 5cor, Dino Zoff and Pelé. 20cor, Dominique Rocheteau and Johan Neeskens.

**1978, Oct. 25 Litho. *Perf. 13½x14***

**C948** A118 50c multi .25 .25
**C949** A118 5cor multi 1.00 .85

**Souvenir Sheet**

**C950** A118 20cor multi 5.00 4.00

### Christmas Type of 1978

Paintings: 3cor, Apostles John and Peter, by Dürer. 10cor, Apostles Paul and Mark, by Dürer. 20cor, Virgin and Child with Garlands, by Dürer.

**1978, Dec. 12 Litho. *Perf. 13½x14***

**C951** A119 3cor multi .40 .35
**C952** A119 10cor multi 1.40 1.00

**Souvenir Sheet**

**C953** A119 20cor multi 5.00 2.50

### Volcano Type of 1978

Designs: No. C954, Cerro Negro Volcano. No. C955, Lake Masaya. No. C956, Momotombo Volcano. No. C957, Lake Asososca. No. C958, Mombacho Volcano. No. C959, Lake Apoyo. No. C960, Concepcion Volcano. No. C961, Lake Tiscapa.

**1978, Dec. 29 *Perf. 14x13½***

**C954** A120 35c multi .25 .25
**C955** A120 35c multi .25 .25
*a.* Pair, #C549-C955 .30 .30
**C956** A120 90c multi .25 .25
**C957** A120 90c multi .25 .25
*a.* Pair, #C956-C957 .35 .30
**C958** A120 1cor multi .25 .25
**C959** A120 1cor multi .25 .25
*a.* Pair, #C958-C959 .40 .30
**C960** A120 10cor multi 1.90 1.40
**C961** A120 10cor multi 1.90 1.40
*a.* Pair, #C960-C961 4.00 3.00
*Nos. C954-C961 (8)* 5.30 4.30

Bernardo O'Higgins AP109

**1979, Mar. 7 Litho. *Perf. 14***

**C962** AP109 20cor multi 4.25 3.25

Bernardo O'Higgins (1778-1842), Chilean soldier and statesman.

Red Ginger and Rubythroated Hummingbird — AP110

Designs: 55c, Orchid. 70c, Poinsettia. 80c, Flower and bees. 2cor, Lignum vitae and blue morpho butterfly. 4cor, Cattleya.

**1979, Apr. 6 Litho. *Perf. 14x13½***

**C963** AP110 50c multi .25 .25
**C964** AP110 55c multi .25 .25
**C965** AP110 70c multi .25 .25
**C966** AP110 80c multi .25 .25
**C967** AP110 2cor multi .60 .30
**C968** AP110 4cor multi 1.25 .50
*Nos. C963-C968 (6)* 2.85 1.80

Endangered Turtles Overprinted in Red — AP110a

Overprint reads: 1979 / ANO DE LA LIBERACION / OLYMPIC RINGS / PARTICIPACION NICARAGUA / OLIMPIADAS 1980 / Litografia Nacional, Portugal symbol

Turtles: 90c, Loggerhead. 2cor, Correoso. 2.20cor, Ridley. 10cor, Pico Halcón.

**1980, Apr. 7 Litho. *Perf. 14¼x13¾***

**C969** AP110a 90c multi
**C969A** AP110a 2cor multi
**C969B** AP110a 2.20cor multi
**C969C** AP110a 10cor multi
*Nos. C969-C969C (4)* 7.00 7.00

Overprinted for Year of Liberation and 1980 Olympic Games.

Nos. C969-C969C were not issued without overprints.

**Souvenir Sheet**

Intl. Year of the Child — AP110b

Designs: a, 5cor, like #1101C. b, 15cor, Dr. Hermann Gmeiner.

**1980, May 3 Litho. *Perf. 14½***

**C970** AP110b Sheet of 2, #a-b. 21.00

No. C970 exists imperf.

---

Numbers have been reserved for 4 souvenir sheets celebrating the Year of Liberation and featuring Rowland Hill, Albert Einstein and Endangered Turtles. The editors would like to examine these sheets.

Numbers have been reserved for miniature sheets celebrating Natl. Literacy Campaign overprinted on Nos. C436a, C503a, C937, C415a, C509, C722a and C925. The editors would like to examine these sheets.

---

### No. C930 Overprinted in Gold, Purple and Green

**1980, Sept. 30 *Perf. 14½***

**C973** A111 20cor multi

**Souvenir Sheet**

Overprinted & Surcharged in Black & Silver — AP110h

Overprint reads: 1980 ANO DE LA ALFABETIZACION / 1980 MOSCU and Litografia Nacional, Portugal symbol

**1980, Dec. 20 Litho. *Perf. 14½***

**C974F** AP110h 10cor on 20cor multi

Overprinted & surcharged for Literacy Year.

No. 974F was not issued without surcharge.

Numbers have been reserved for 6 additional stamps in this set. The editors would like to examine these stamps.

Endangered Turtles Type of 1980 Overprinted in Red — AP110j

Overprint reads: 1980 ANO DE LA ALFABETIZACION and Litografia Nacional, Portugal symbol

No. C975D, Green (Verde) turtle.

**1981, May 15 Litho. *Perf. 14¼x13¾***

**C975** AP110j 90c like #C969
**C975A** AP110j 2cor like #C969A
**C975B** AP110j 2.20cor like #C969B
**C975C** AP110j 10cor like #C969C

**Souvenir Sheet**

**C975D** AP110j 5cor on 20cor multi *15.00*

Overprinted for Literacy Year.

Nos. C975-C975D were not issues without overprints and surcharge.

### Revolution Type of 1981

**1981, July 19 Litho. *Perf. 12½x12***

**C975E** A123 2.10cor March 1.25 .25
**C975F** A123 3cor Construction 2.00 .25
**C975G** A123 6cor Health programs 5.00 .45
*Nos. C975E-C975G (3)* 8.25 .95

### FSLN Type of 1981

**1981, July 23**

**C976** A124 4cor Founder .55 .35

### Postal Union Type of 1981

**1981, Aug. 10**

**C977** A125 2.10cor Pony express .25 .25
**C978** A125 3cor Headquarters .30 .25
**C979** A125 6cor Members' flags .60 .35
*Nos. C977-C979 (3)* 1.15 .85

1300th Anniv. of Bulgaria — AP112

**1981, Sept. 2 *Imperf.***

**C980** AP112 10cor multi 2.50 1.00

Size: 96x70mm.

### Aquatic Flower Type of 1981

10cor, Nymphaea gladstoniana.

**1981, Sept. 15 *Perf. 12½***

**C981** A126 10cor multi 1.40 .90

**Souvenir Sheet**

Panda Bear — AP113

**1981, Oct. 9 *Perf. 13***

**C982** AP113 10cor multi 1.75 1.00

Philatokyo Stamp Exhibition, Tokyo.

### Tropical Fish Type of 1981

3.50cor, Pterolebias longipinnis. 4cor, Xiphophorus helleri.

**1981, Oct. 19 *Perf. 12½***

**C983** A127 3.50cor multi .70 .30
**C984** A127 4cor multi .80 .30

**Souvenir Sheet**

Frigate — AP114

**1981, Nov. 2 *Perf. 13***

**C985** AP114 10cor multi 1.75 1.00

Espamer '81 Stamp Exhibition, Buenos Aires, Nov. 13-22.

### Bird Type of 1981

3cor, Trogon massena. 4cor, Campylopterus hemileucurus, horiz. 6cor, Momotus momota.

**1981, Nov. 30** ***Perf. 12½***

**C986** A128 3cor multicolored .80 .30
**C987** A128 4cor multicolored 1.00 .40
**C988** A128 6cor multicolored 2.00 .75
*Nos. C986-C988 (3)* 3.80 1.45

### Satellite Type of 1981

**1981, Dec. 15** ***Perf. 13x12½***

**C989** A129 3cor multi .75 .25
**C990** A129 4cor multi 1.00 .30
**C991** A129 5cor multi 1.25 .35
*Nos. C989-C991 (3)* 3.00 .90

### Railroad Type of 1981

**1981, Dec. 30** ***Perf. 12½***

**C992** A130 6cor Ferrobus, 1967 2.25 .75

### World Cup Type of 1982

**1982, Jan. 25**

**C993** A131 4cor multi .60 .30
**C994** A131 10cor multi, horiz. 1.40 .80

**Souvenir Sheet**

***Perf. 13***

**C995** A131 10cor multi 2.75 1.10

No. C995 contains one 39x31mm stamp.

### Dog Type of 1982

**1982, Feb. 18**

**C996** A132 3cor Boxers .60 .30
**C997** A132 3.50cor Pointers .65 .30
**C998** A132 6cor Collies 1.00 .50
*Nos. C996-C998 (3)* 2.25 1.10

Intl. ITU Congress — AP115

**1982, Mar. 12**

**C999** AP115 25cor multi 3.50 2.25

### Butterfly Type of 1982

3cor, Parides iphidamas. 3.50cor, Consul hippona. 4cor, Morpho peleides.

**1982, Mar. 26**

**C1000** A133 3cor multi .80 .30
**C1001** A133 3.50cor multi .90 .30
**C1002** A133 4cor multi 1.10 .40
*Nos. C1000-C1002 (3)* 2.80 1.00

### Satellite Type of 1982

**1982, Apr. 12**

**C1003** A134 5cor multi, horiz. .75 .40
**C1004** A134 6cor multi 1.00 .50

### UPU Type of 1982

**1982, May 1** **Litho.** ***Perf. 13***

**C1005** A135 3.50cor Train .40 .25
**C1006** A135 10cor Jet 1.10 .70

### Sports Type of 1982

2.50cor, Women's volleyball, vert. 3cor, Boxing. 9cor, Soccer.
10cor, Baseball, vert.

**1982, May 13**

**C1007** A136 2.50cor multi .50 .25
**C1008** A136 3cor multi .60 .30
**C1009** A136 9cor multi 1.90 .80
*Nos. C1007-C1009 (3)* 3.00 1.35

**Souvenir Sheet**

**C1010** A136 10cor multi 2.00 .80

No. C1010 contains one 29x36mm stamp.

Souvenir Sheet

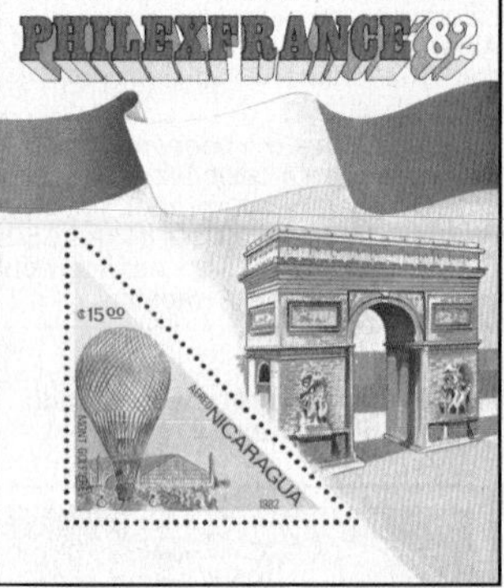


PHILEXFRANCE '82 Intl. Stamp Exhibition, Paris, June 11-21 — AP116

**1982, June 9** ***Perf. 13x12½***

**C1011** AP116 15cor multi 2.75 1.25

### Revolution Type of 1982

Symbolic doves. 2.50cor, 4cor vert.

**1982, July 19** ***Perf. 13***

**C1012** A137 2.50cor multi .45 .25
**C1013** A137 4cor multi .70 .40
**C1014** A137 6cor multi 1.10 .60
*Nos. C1012-C1014 (3)* 2.25 1.25

### Washington Type of 1982

2.50cor, Crossing the Delaware. 3.50cor, At Valley Forge. 4cor, Battle of Trenton. 6cor, Washington in Princeton.

***Perf. 12½x13, 13x12½***

**1982, June 20** **Litho.**

**C1015** A138 2.50cor multi, horiz. .50 .25
**C1016** A138 3.50cor multi, horiz. .65 .35
**C1017** A138 4cor multi .75 .40
**C1018** A138 6cor multi 1.10 .60
*Nos. C1015-C1018 (4)* 3.00 1.60

### Painting Type of 1982

9cor, Seated Woman, by A. Morales.

**1982, Aug. 17** ***Perf. 13***

**C1019** A139 9cor multi 2.00 .80

### Dimitrov Type of 1982

2.50cor, Dimitrov, Yikov, Sofia, 1946. 4cor, Portrait, flag.

**1982, Sept. 9**

**C1020** A140 2.50cor multi .45 .25
**C1021** A140 4cor multi .80 .40

### Dictatorship Type of 1982

4cor, Rigoberto Lopez Perez. 6cor, Edwin Castro.

**1982, Sept. 21** ***Perf. 13x12½***

**C1022** A141 4cor multi .60 .40
**C1023** A141 6cor multi 1.00 .60

### Tourism Type of 1982

2.50cor, Coyotepe Fortress, Masaya. 3.50cor, Velazquez Park, Managua.

**1982, Sept. 25** ***Perf. 13***

**C1024** A142 2.50cor multi .40 .25
**C1025** A142 3.50cor multi .45 .25

### Marx Type of 1982

4cor, Marx, Highgate Monument.

**1982, Oct. 4** ***Perf. 12½***

**C1026** A143 4cor multi .55 .35

### Discovery of America Type of 1982

2.50cor, Trans-atlantic voyage. 4cor, Landing of Columbus. 7cor, Death of Columbus.
10cor, Columbus' fleet.

**1982, Oct. 12** ***Perf. 12½x13***

**C1027** A145 2.50cor multi .50 .25
**C1028** A145 4cor multi .75 .40
**C1029** A145 7cor multi 1.25 .70
*a.* Sheet, 2 each #1187-1190, C1027-C1029, + 2 labels — —
*Nos. C1027-C1029 (3)* 2.50 1.35

**Souvenir Sheet**

***Perf. 13***

**C1030** A145 10cor multi 2.25 1.10

No. C1030 contains one 31x39mm stamp.

### Flower Type of 1982

2.50cor, Pasiflora foetida. 3.50cor, Clitoria sp. 5cor, Russelia sarmentosa.

**1982, Nov. 13** ***Perf. 12½***

**C1031** A146 2.50cor multi .60 .25
**C1032** A146 3.50cor multi .70 .30
**C1033** A146 5cor multi .80 .45
*Nos. C1031-C1033 (3)* 2.10 1.00

### Reptile Type of 1982

2.50cor, Turtle, horiz. 3cor, Boa constrictor. 3.50cor, Crocodile, horiz. 5cor, Sistrurus catenatus, horiz.

**1982, Dec. 10** ***Perf. 13***

**C1034** A147 2.50cor multi 1.25 .25
**C1035** A147 3cor multi 1.40 .30
**C1036** A147 3.50cor multi 1.50 .30
**C1037** A147 5cor multi 2.25 .45
*Nos. C1034-C1037 (4)* 6.40 1.30

Non-aligned States Conference, Jan. 12-14 — AP117

**1983, Jan. 10** **Litho.** ***Perf. 12½x13***

**C1038** AP117 4cor multi .90 .40

Geothermal Electricity Generating Plant, Momotombo Volcano — AP118

**1983, Feb. 25** ***Perf. 13***

**C1039** AP118 2.50cor multi .40 .25

Souvenir Sheet

TEMBAL '83 Philatelic Exhibition, Basel, Switzerland — AP119

**1983, May 21** **Litho.** ***Perf. 13***

**C1040** AP119 15cor Chamoix 2.40 1.40

Souvenir Sheet

1st Nicaraguan Philatelic Exhibition — AP120

10cor, Nicaragua Airlines jet.

**1983, July 17** **Litho.** ***Perf. 13***

**C1041** AP120 10cor multi 2.40 1.40

Armed Forces AP121

4cor, Frontier guards, watch dog.

**1983, Sept. 2** **Litho.** ***Perf. 13***

**C1042** AP121 4cor multi .40 .25

Souvenir Sheet

BRASILIANA '83 Intl. Stamp Show, Rio de Janeiro, July 29-Aug. 7 — AP122

**1983**

**C1043** AP122 15cor Jaguar 5.00 1.75

Cuban Revolution, 25th Anniv. AP122a

6cor, Castro, Guevara, flag.

**1984, Jan. 1** **Litho.** ***Perf. 13***

**C1043A** AP122a 4cor shown .80 .40
**C1043B** AP122a 6cor multi 1.20 .60

Souvenir Sheet

Cardinal Infante Don Fernando, by Diego Velazquez — AP123

**1984, May 2** **Litho.** ***Perf. 13***

**C1044** AP123 15cor multi 3.75 1.25

ESPANA '84.

Souvenir Sheet

Hamburg '84 — AP124

**1984, June 19 Litho.** ***Perf. 13***
**C1045** AP124 15cor Dirigible 3.75 1.25

1984 UPU Congress — AP125

15cor, Mail transport.

**1984, June 24** ***Perf. 12½***
**C1046** AP125 15cor multi 2.00 1.00

Souvenir Sheet

Expofilnic '84 (2nd Natl. Stamp Exhibition) — AP126

15cor, Communications Museum.

**1984, July 15**
**C1047** AP126 15cor multi 2.00 1.00

Souvenir Sheet

Ausipex '84 — AP127

**1984, Sept. 21**
**C1048** AP127 15cor Explorer ship 2.00 1.00

Souvenir Sheet

OLYMPHILEX '85 — AP128

**1985, Mar. 18 Litho.** ***Perf. 12½***
**C1049** AP128 15cor Bicycle race 1.50 .75

Souvenir Sheet

ESPAMER '85, Havana, Mar. 19-24 — AP129

10cor, Crocodylus rhombifer.

**1985, Mar. 19**
**C1050** AP129 10cor multi 1.50 .75

Victory of Sandanista Revolution, 6th Anniv. AP134

**1985, July 19 Litho.** ***Perf. 12½***
**C1125** AP134 9cor Soldier, flag .90 .60
**C1126** AP134 9cor Sugar mill .90 .60

Benjamin Zeledon, Birth Cent. — AP135

**1985, Oct. 4 Litho.** ***Perf. 12½***
**C1127** AP135 15cor multicolored .90 .40

Henri Dunant (1828-1910), Founder of Red Cross — AP136

15cor, Dunant, air ambulance.

**1985, Oct. 10** ***Perf. 12½x12***
**C1128** AP136 3cor shown .30 .25
**C1129** AP136 15cor multi 1.10 .45
*a.* Pair, #C1128-C1129 + label 2.25 1.50

Nicaraguan Stamps, 125th Anniv. AP137

**1986, May 22** ***Perf. 12½x13***
**C1130** AP137 30cor No. C1 .80 .30
**C1131** AP137 40cor No. 174 1.00 .40
**C1132** AP137 50cor No. 48 1.25 .50
**C1133** AP137 100cor No. 1 2.40 1.10
*Nos. C1130-C1133 (4)* 5.45 2.30

Intl. Peace Year — AP138

**1986, July 19** ***Perf. 12½***
**C1134** AP138 5cor shown .25 .25
**C1135** AP138 10cor Globe, dove .25 .25

Carlos Fonseca, 10th Death Anniv. — AP139

**1986, Aug. 11 Litho.** ***Perf. 12½***
**C1136** AP139 15cor multicolored .30 .25

Formation of the Sandinista Front, 25th anniv.

AP140

**1986, Nov. 20** ***Perf. 13***
**C1137** AP140 15cor Rhinoceros .40 .25
**C1138** AP140 15cor Zebra .40 .25
**C1139** AP140 25cor Elephant .55 .30
**C1140** AP140 25cor Giraffe .55 .30
**C1141** AP140 50cor Mandrill 1.20 .55
**C1142** AP140 50cor Tiger 1.20 .55
*Nos. C1137-C1142 (6)* 4.30 2.20

AP141

World Cup Soccer Championships, Mexico: Various soccer players and natl. flags.

**1986, Dec. 20** ***Perf. 13***

**Shirt Colors**

**C1143** AP141 10cor blue .30 .25
**C1144** AP141 10cor blk & white .30 .25
**C1145** AP141 10cor blue & white .30 .25
**C1146** AP141 15cor pink & white .45 .25
**C1147** AP141 15cor grn & blk .45 .25
**C1148** AP141 25cor blk & white, red .70 .30
**C1149** AP141 50cor grn & yel, red, horiz. 1.40 .55
*Nos. C1143-C1149 (7)* 3.90 2.10

**Souvenir Sheet**

***Perf. 12½***

**C1150** AP141 100cor blk & white, bl & white 2.75 1.10

Vassil Levski, 150th Birth Anniv. — AP142

**1987, Apr. 18** ***Perf. 13***
**C1151** AP142 30cor multicolored .70 .30

Intl. Year of Shelter for the Homeless — AP143

**1987, Aug. 2**
**C1152** AP143 20cor multicolored .55 .25
**C1153** AP143 30cor Housing, diff. .85 .35

For surcharges, see Nos. C1160B-C1160C.

Souvenir Sheet

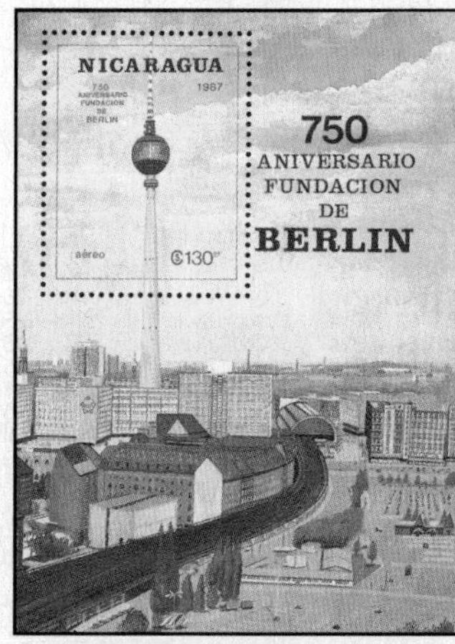


Berlin, 750th Anniv. — AP144

**1987, Sept. 25 Litho.** ***Perf. 13***
**C1154** AP144 130cor multi 3.50 1.00

Discovery of America, 500th Anniv. (in 1992) — AP145

No. C1155, Indian village. No. C1156, Sailing ships. No. C1157, Battle in village. No.

C1158, Battle, prisoners. No. C1159, Spanish town. No. C1160, Cathedral.

**1987, Oct. 12** ***Perf. 13***

| | | | |
|---|---|---|---|
| **C1155** AP145 15cor multicolored | .50 | .25 |
| **C1156** AP145 15cor multicolored | .50 | .25 |
| **C1157** AP145 20cor multicolored | .65 | .25 |
| **C1158** AP145 30cor multicolored | 1.00 | .30 |
| **C1159** AP145 40cor multicolored | 1.40 | .40 |
| **C1160** AP145 50cor multicolored | 1.60 | .50 |
| *a.* Min. sheet of 6, #C1155-C1160 | 5.75 | 5.75 |
| *Nos. C1155-C1160 (6)* | 5.65 | 1.95 |

**Nos. C1152-C1153 Surcharged**

**Methods and Perfs As Before**

**1987, Dec. 26**

| | | |
|---|---|---|
| **C1160B** AP143 200cor on 20cor #C1152 | — | — |
| **C1160C** AP143 3000cor on 30cor #C1153 | — | — |
| Nos. C1160B-C1160C (2) | 35.00 | — |

Cuban Revolution, 30th Anniv. — AP146

**1989, Jan. 1** ***Perf. 13***

| | | |
|---|---|---|
| **C1161** AP146 20cor multicolored | .75 | .25 |

AP147

Designs: Various soccer players in action.

**1989, Feb. 20** ***Perf. 13x12½***

| | | |
|---|---|---|
| **C1162** AP147 100cor multi | .30 | .25 |
| **C1163** AP147 200cor multi | .30 | .25 |
| **C1164** AP147 600cor multi | .30 | .25 |
| **C1165** AP147 1000cor multi | .45 | .25 |
| **C1166** AP147 2000cor multi | .90 | .45 |
| **C1167** AP147 3000cor multi | 1.40 | .40 |
| **C1168** AP147 5000cor multi | 2.10 | .65 |
| *Nos. C1162-C1168 (7)* | 5.75 | 2.50 |

**Souvenir Sheet**

***Perf. 13***

| | | |
|---|---|---|
| **C1169** AP147 9000cor multi | 4.00 | 2.25 |

World Cup Soccer Championships, Italy. No. C1169 contains one 32x40mm stamp.

AP148

Design: 9000cor, Concepcion Volcano.

**1989, July 19** ***Perf. 13***

| | | |
|---|---|---|
| **C1170** AP148 300cor multi | .25 | .25 |

**Souvenir Sheet**

| | | |
|---|---|---|
| **C1171** AP148 9000cor multi | 3.00 | 2.25 |

Sandinista Revolution, 10th Anniv. No. C1171 contains one 40x32mm stamp.

AP149

Birds: 100cor, Anhinga anhinga. 200cor, Elanoides forficatus. 600cor, Eumomota superciliosa. 1000cor, Setophaga picta. 2000cor, Taraba major, horiz. 3000cor, Onychorhynchus mexicanus. 5000cor, Myrmotherula axillaris, horiz. 9000cor, Amazona ochrocephala.

**1989, July 18** ***Perf. 13x12½, 12½x13***

| | | |
|---|---|---|
| **C1172** AP149 100cor multi | .25 | .25 |
| **C1173** AP149 200cor multi | .25 | .25 |
| **C1174** AP149 600cor multi | .25 | .25 |
| **C1175** AP149 1000cor multi | .40 | .25 |
| **C1176** AP149 2000cor multi | .90 | .30 |
| **C1177** AP149 3000cor multi | 1.40 | .45 |
| **C1178** AP149 5000cor multi | 2.40 | .75 |
| *Nos. C1172-C1178 (7)* | 5.85 | 2.50 |

**Souvenir Sheet**

***Perf. 13***

| | | |
|---|---|---|
| **C1179** AP149 9000cor multi | 4.00 | 2.00 |

Brasiliana '89. No. C1179 contains one 32x40mm stamp.

AP150

Designs: 50cor, Downhill skiing. 300cor, Ice hockey. 600cor, Ski jumping. 1000cor, Pairs figure skating. 2000cor, Biathalon. 3000cor, Slalom skiing. 5000cor, Cross country skiing. 9000cor, Two-man luge.

**1989, Mar. 25** ***Perf. 13***

| | | |
|---|---|---|
| **C1180** AP150 50cor multi | .60 | .25 |
| **C1181** AP150 300cor multi | .60 | .25 |
| **C1182** AP150 600cor multi | .60 | .25 |
| **C1183** AP150 1000cor multi | .60 | .25 |
| **C1184** AP150 2000cor multi | 1.00 | .25 |
| **C1185** AP150 3000cor multi | 1.10 | .25 |
| **C1186** AP150 5000cor multi | 1.25 | .25 |
| *Nos. C1180-C1186 (7)* | 5.75 | 1.75 |

**Souvenir Sheet**

| | | |
|---|---|---|
| **C1187** AP150 9000cor multi | 4.00 | 2.00 |

1992 Winter Olympics, Albertville. No. C1187 contains one 32x40mm stamp.

AP151

Designs: 100cor, Water polo. 200cor, Running. 600cor, Diving. 1000cor, Gymnastics. 2000cor, Weight lifting. 3000cor, Volleyball. 5000cor, Wrestling. 9000cor, Field hockey.

**1989, Apr. 23**

| | | |
|---|---|---|
| **C1188** AP151 100cor multi | .60 | .25 |
| **C1189** AP151 200cor multi | .60 | .25 |
| **C1190** AP151 600cor multi | .60 | .25 |
| **C1191** AP151 1000cor multi | .60 | .25 |
| **C1192** AP151 2000cor multi | 1.00 | .25 |
| **C1193** AP151 3000cor multi | 1.10 | .25 |
| **C1194** AP151 5000cor multi | 1.25 | .25 |
| *Nos. C1188-C1194 (7)* | 5.75 | 1.75 |

**Souvenir Sheet**

| | | |
|---|---|---|
| **C1195** AP151 9000cor multi | 3.75 | .45 |

1992 Summer Olympics, Barcelona. No. C1195 contains one 32x40mm stamp.

AP152

**1989, Oct. 12**

| | | |
|---|---|---|
| **C1196** AP152 2000cor Vase | .70 | .30 |

Discovery of America, 500th Anniv. (in 1992).

---

Currency Reform

Currency reform took place Mar. 4, 1990. Until stamps in the new currency were issued, mail was to be hand-stamped "Franqueo Pagado," (Postage Paid). Stamps were not used again until Apr. 25, 1991. The following set was sold by the post office but was not valid for postage. Value $5.65

---

Mushrooms

Designs: 500cor, Morchella esculenta. 1000cor, Boletus edulis. 5000cor, Lactarius deliciosus. 10,000cor, Panellus stipticus. 20,000cor, Craterellus cornucopioides. 40,000cor, Cantharellus cibarius. 50,000cor, Armillariella mellea.

**1990, July 15** ***Perf. 13***

500cor-50,000cor

---

## AIR POST SEMI-POSTAL STAMPS

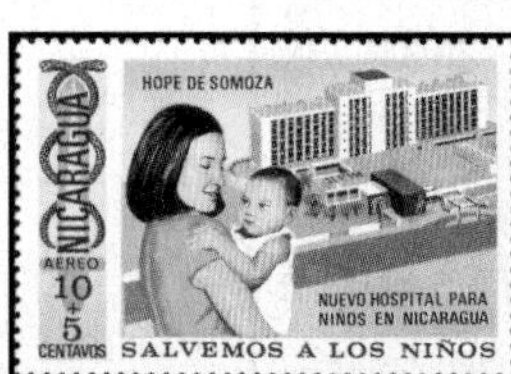


Mrs. Somoza and Children's Hospital — SPAP1

Designs: 5c+5c, Children and weight chart. 15c+5c, Incubator and Da Vinci's "Child in Womb." 20c+5c, Smallpox vaccination. 30c+5c, Water purification. 35c+5c, 1cor+50c, like 10c+5c. 50c+10c, Antibiotics. 60c+15c, Malaria control. 70c+10c, Laboratory. 80c+20c, Gastroenteritis (sick and well babies).

**1973, Sept. 25 Litho.** ***Perf. 13½x14***

| | | |
|---|---|---|
| **CB1** SPAP1 5c + 5c multi | .25 | .25 |
| **CB2** SPAP1 10c + 5c multi | .25 | .25 |
| **CB3** SPAP1 15c + 5c multi | .30 | .25 |
| **CB4** SPAP1 20c + 5c multi | .30 | .25 |
| **CB5** SPAP1 30c + 5c multi | .30 | .25 |
| **CB6** SPAP1 35c + 5c multi | .30 | .25 |
| **CB7** SPAP1 50c + 10c multi | .30 | .25 |
| **CB8** SPAP1 60c + 15c multi | .50 | .30 |
| **CB9** SPAP1 70c + 10c multi | .75 | .30 |
| **CB10** SPAP1 80c + 20c multi | .85 | .40 |
| **CB11** SPAP1 1cor + 50c multi | .95 | .45 |
| *Nos. CB1-CB11 (11)* | 5.05 | 3.20 |

The surtax was for hospital building fund.

See No. C845. Inscriptions on back, printed on top of gum give brief description of subjects shown.

---

## AIR POST OFFICIAL STAMPS

OA1

**"Typewritten" Overprint on #O293**

**1929, Aug.** **Unwmk.** ***Perf. 12***

| | | |
|---|---|---|
| **CO1** OA1 25c orange | 50.00 | 45.00 |

Excellent counterfeits of No. CO1 are plentiful.

Official Stamps of 1926 Ovptd. in Dark Blue

**1929, Sept. 15**

| | | |
|---|---|---|
| **CO2** A24 25c orange | .50 | .50 |
| *a.* Inverted overprint | 25.00 | |
| *b.* Double overprint | 25.00 | |
| **CO3** A25 50c pale bl | .75 | .75 |
| *a.* Inverted overprint | 25.00 | |
| *b.* Double overprint | 25.00 | |
| *c.* Double overprint, one inverted | 25.00 | |

Nos. O308-O312 Overprinted in Black

**1932, Feb.**

| | | |
|---|---|---|
| **CO4** A24 15c org red | .40 | .40 |
| *a.* Inverted overprint | 25.00 | |
| *b.* Double overprint | 25.00 | |
| *c.* Double overprint, one invtd. | 25.00 | |
| **CO5** A25 20c orange | .45 | .45 |
| *a.* Double overprint | 25.00 | |
| **CO6** A24 25c dk vio | .45 | .45 |
| **CO7** A25 50c green | .55 | .55 |
| **CO8** A25 1cor yellow | 1.00 | 1.00 |
| *Nos. CO4-CO8 (5)* | 2.85 | 2.85 |

Nos. CO4-CO5, CO7-CO8 exist with signature control overprint. Value, each, $2.50.

**Overprinted on Stamp No. 547**

| | | |
|---|---|---|
| **CO9** A24 25c blk brn | 42.50 | 42.50 |

The varieties "OFICAL", "OFIAIAL" and "CORROE" occur in the setting and are found on each stamp of the series.

Counterfeits of No. CO9 are plentiful.

Stamp No. CO4 with overprint "1931" in addition is believed to be of private origin.

**Type of Regular Issue of 1914 Overprinted Like Nos. CO4-CO8**

**1933**

| | | |
|---|---|---|
| **CO10** A24 25c olive | .25 | .25 |
| **CO11** A25 50c ol grn | .25 | .25 |
| **CO12** A25 1cor org red | .40 | .40 |

**On Stamps of 1914-28**

| | | |
|---|---|---|
| **CO13** A24 15c dp vio | .25 | .25 |
| **CO14** A25 20c dp grn | .25 | .25 |
| *Nos. CO10-CO14 (5)* | 1.40 | 1.40 |

Nos. CO10-CO14 exist without signature control mark. Value, each $2.50.

Air Post Official Stamps of 1932-33 Ovptd. in Blue

**1935**

| | | |
|---|---|---|
| **CO15** A24 15c dp vio | 1.00 | .80 |
| **CO16** A25 20c dp grn | 2.00 | 1.60 |
| **CO17** A24 25c olive | 3.00 | 2.50 |
| **CO18** A25 50c ol grn | 35.00 | 30.00 |
| **CO19** A25 1cor org red | 40.00 | 37.50 |
| *Nos. CO15-CO19 (5)* | 81.00 | 72.40 |

**Overprinted in Red**

| | | | | |
|---|---|---|---|---|
| **CO20** | A24 | 15c dp vio | .25 | .25 |
| **CO21** | A25 | 20c dp grn | .25 | .25 |
| **CO22** | A24 | 25c olive | .25 | .25 |
| **CO23** | A25 | 50c ol grn | .80 | .80 |
| **CO24** | A25 | 1cor org red | .80 | .80 |
| | | *Nos. CO20-CO24 (5)* | 2.35 | 2.35 |

Nos. CO15 to CO24 are handstamped with script control mark. Counterfeits of blue overprint are plentiful.

The editors do not recognize the Nicaraguan air post Official stamps overprinted in red "VALIDO 1935" in two lines and with or without script control marks as having been issued primarily for postal purposes.

Nos. C164-C168 Overprinted in Black

**1937**

| | | | | |
|---|---|---|---|---|
| **CO25** | AP1 | 15c yel org | .80 | .55 |
| **CO26** | AP1 | 20c org red | .80 | .60 |
| **CO27** | AP1 | 25c black | .80 | .70 |
| **CO28** | AP1 | 50c violet | .80 | .70 |
| **CO29** | AP1 | 1cor orange | .80 | .70 |
| | | *Nos. CO25-CO29 (5)* | 4.00 | 3.25 |

Pres. Anastasio Somoza — OA2

**1939, Feb. 7 Engr. *Perf. 12½***

| | | | | |
|---|---|---|---|---|
| **CO30** | OA2 | 10c brown | .25 | .25 |
| **CO31** | OA2 | 15c dk bl | .25 | .25 |
| **CO32** | OA2 | 20c yellow | .25 | .25 |
| **CO33** | OA2 | 25c dk pur | .25 | .25 |
| **CO34** | OA2 | 30c lake | .25 | .25 |
| **CO35** | OA2 | 50c dp org | .65 | .65 |
| **CO36** | OA2 | 1cor dk ol grn | 1.25 | 1.25 |
| | | *Nos. CO30-CO36 (7)* | 3.15 | 3.15 |

**Catalogue values for unused stamps in this section, from this point to the end of the section, are for Never Hinged items.**

Mercedes Airport — OA3

Designs: 10c, Sulphurous Lake of Nejapa. 15c, Ruben Dario Monument. 20c, Tapir. 25c, Genizaro Dam. 50c, Tipitapa Spa. 1cor, Stone Highway. 2.50cor, Franklin D. Roosevelt Monument.

**Engraved, Center Photogravure**
**1947, Aug. 29**
**Various Frames in Black**

| | | | | |
|---|---|---|---|---|
| **CO37** | OA3 | 5c org brn | .50 | .25 |
| **CO38** | OA3 | 10c blue | .50 | .25 |
| **CO39** | OA3 | 15c violet | .50 | .25 |
| **CO40** | OA3 | 20c red org | .50 | .25 |
| **CO41** | OA3 | 25c blue | .50 | .25 |
| **CO42** | OA3 | 50c car rose | .50 | .25 |
| **CO43** | OA3 | 1cor slate | .70 | .45 |
| **CO44** | OA3 | 2.50cor red brn | 2.00 | 1.25 |
| | | *Nos. CO37-CO44 (8)* | 5.70 | 3.20 |

Rowland Hill — OA4

Designs: 10c, Heinrich von Stephan. 25c, 1st UPU Bldg. 50c, UPU Bldg., Bern. 1cor, UPU Monument. 2.60cor, Congress medal, reverse.

**1950, Nov. 23 Engr. *Perf. 13***
**Frames in Black**

| | | | | |
|---|---|---|---|---|
| **CO45** | OA4 | 5c rose vio | .25 | .25 |
| **CO46** | OA4 | 10c dp grn | .25 | .25 |
| **CO47** | OA4 | 25c rose vio | .25 | .25 |
| **CO48** | OA4 | 50c dp org | .25 | .25 |
| **CO49** | OA4 | 1cor ultra | .30 | .30 |
| **CO50** | OA4 | 2.60cor gray blk | 2.25 | 2.00 |
| | | *Nos. CO45-CO50 (6)* | 3.55 | 3.30 |

75th anniv. (in 1949) of the UPU.

Each denomination was also issued in a souvenir sheet containing four stamps and marginal inscriptions. Size: 121x96mm. Value, set of 6 sheets, $35.

**Consular Service Stamps Surcharged "Oficial Aéreo" and New Denomination in Red, Black or Blue**

**1961, Nov. Unwmk. Engr. *Perf. 12***
**Red Marginal Number**

| | | | | |
|---|---|---|---|---|
| **CO51** | AP63 | 10c on 1cor grnsh blk (R) | .25 | .25 |
| **CO52** | AP63 | 15c on 20cor red brn (R) | .25 | .25 |
| **CO53** | AP63 | 20c on 100cor mag | .25 | .25 |
| **CO54** | AP63 | 25c on 50c dp bl (R) | .25 | .25 |
| **CO55** | AP63 | 35c on 50cor brn (R) | .25 | .25 |
| **CO56** | AP63 | 50c on 3cor dk car | .25 | .25 |
| **CO57** | AP63 | 1cor on 2cor grn (R) | .25 | .25 |
| **CO58** | AP63 | 2cor on 5cor org (Bl) | .40 | .40 |
| **CO59** | AP63 | 5cor on 10cor vio (R) | 1.00 | 1.00 |
| | | *Nos. CO51-CO59 (9)* | 3.15 | 3.15 |

## POSTAGE DUE STAMPS

D1

**1896 Unwmk. Engr. *Perf. 12***

| | | | | |
|---|---|---|---|---|
| **J1** | D1 | 1c orange | .50 | *1.25* |
| **J2** | D1 | 2c orange | .50 | *1.25* |
| **J3** | D1 | 5c orange | .50 | *1.25* |
| **J4** | D1 | 10c orange | .50 | *1.25* |
| **J5** | D1 | 20c orange | .50 | *1.25* |
| **J6** | D1 | 30c orange | .50 | *1.25* |
| **J7** | D1 | 50c orange | .50 | *1.50* |
| | | *Nos. J1-J7 (7)* | 3.50 | *9.00* |

**Wmk. 117**

| | | | | |
|---|---|---|---|---|
| **J8** | D1 | 1c orange | 1.00 | *1.50* |
| **J9** | D1 | 2c orange | 1.00 | *1.50* |
| **J10** | D1 | 5c orange | 1.00 | *1.50* |
| **J11** | D1 | 10c orange | 1.00 | *1.50* |
| **J12** | D1 | 20c orange | 1.25 | *1.50* |
| **J13** | D1 | 30c orange | 1.00 | *1.50* |
| **J14** | D1 | 50c orange | 1.00 | *1.50* |
| | | *Nos. J8-J14 (7)* | 7.25 | *10.50* |

**1897 Unwmk.**

| | | | | |
|---|---|---|---|---|
| **J15** | D1 | 1c violet | .50 | *1.50* |
| **J16** | D1 | 2c violet | .50 | *1.50* |
| **J17** | D1 | 5c violet | .50 | *1.50* |
| **J18** | D1 | 10c violet | .50 | *1.50* |
| **J19** | D1 | 20c violet | 1.25 | *2.00* |
| **J20** | D1 | 30c violet | .50 | *1.50* |
| **J21** | D1 | 50c violet | .50 | *1.50* |
| | | *Nos. J15-J21 (7)* | 4.25 | *11.00* |

**Wmk. 117**

| | | | | |
|---|---|---|---|---|
| **J22** | D1 | 1c violet | .50 | *1.50* |
| **J23** | D1 | 2c violet | .50 | *1.50* |
| **J24** | D1 | 5c violet | .50 | *1.50* |
| **J25** | D1 | 10c violet | .50 | *1.50* |
| **J26** | D1 | 20c violet | 1.00 | *2.00* |
| **J27** | D1 | 30c violet | .50 | *1.50* |
| **J28** | D1 | 50c violet | .50 | *1.50* |
| | | *Nos. J22-J28 (7)* | 4.00 | *11.00* |

*Reprints of Nos. J8-J28 are on thick, porous paper. Color of 1896 reprints, reddish orange; or 1897 reprints, reddish violet. On watermarked reprints, liberty cap is sideways. Value 25c each.*

D2

**1898 Litho. Unwmk.**

| | | | | |
|---|---|---|---|---|
| **J29** | D2 | 1c blue green | .25 | *2.00* |
| **J30** | D2 | 2c blue green | .25 | *2.00* |
| **J31** | D2 | 5c blue green | .25 | *2.00* |
| **J32** | D2 | 10c blue green | .25 | *2.00* |
| **J33** | D2 | 20c blue green | .25 | *2.00* |
| **J34** | D2 | 30c blue green | .25 | *2.00* |
| **J35** | D2 | 50c blue green | .25 | *2.00* |
| | | *Nos. J29-J35 (7)* | 1.75 | *14.00* |

**1899**

| | | | | |
|---|---|---|---|---|
| **J36** | D2 | 1c carmine | .25 | *2.00* |
| **J37** | D2 | 2c carmine | .25 | *2.00* |
| **J38** | D2 | 5c carmine | .25 | *2.00* |
| **J39** | D2 | 10c carmine | .25 | *2.00* |
| **J40** | D2 | 20c carmine | .25 | *2.00* |
| **J41** | D2 | 50c carmine | .25 | *2.00* |
| | | *Nos. J36-J41 (6)* | 1.50 | *12.00* |

Some denominations are found in se-tenant pairs.

Various counterfeit cancellations exist on #J1-J41.

D3

**1900 Engr.**

| | | | |
|---|---|---|---|
| **J42** | D3 | 1c plum | .75 |
| **J43** | D3 | 2c vermilion | .75 |
| **J44** | D3 | 5c dk bl | .75 |
| **J45** | D3 | 10c purple | .75 |
| **J46** | D3 | 20c org brn | .75 |
| **J47** | D3 | 30c dk grn | 1.50 |
| **J48** | D3 | 50c lake | 1.50 |
| | | *Nos. J42-J48 (7)* | 6.75 |

Nos. J42-J48 were not placed in use as postage due stamps. They were only issued with "Postage" overprints. See Nos. 137-143, 152-158, O72-O81, 2L11-2L15, 2L25, 2L40-2L41.

## OFFICIAL STAMPS

Types of Postage Stamps Overprinted in Red Diagonally Reading up

**1890 Unwmk. Engr. *Perf. 12***

| | | | | |
|---|---|---|---|---|
| **O1** | A5 | 1c ultra | .25 | *.30* |
| **O2** | A5 | 2c ultra | .25 | *.30* |
| **O3** | A5 | 5c ultra | .25 | *.30* |
| **O4** | A5 | 10c ultra | .25 | *.40* |
| **O5** | A5 | 20c ultra | .25 | *.45* |
| **O6** | A5 | 50c ultra | .25 | *.75* |
| **O7** | A5 | 1p ultra | .25 | *1.25* |
| **O8** | A5 | 2p ultra | .25 | *1.60* |
| **O9** | A5 | 5p ultra | .25 | *2.40* |
| **O10** | A5 | 10p ultra | .25 | *4.00* |
| | | *Nos. O1-O10 (10)* | 2.50 | *11.75* |

All values of the 1890 issue are known without overprint and most of them with inverted or double overprint, or without overprint and imperforate. There is no evidence that they were issued in these forms.

Official stamps of 1890-1899 are scarce with genuine cancellations. Forged cancellations are plentiful.

Overprinted Vertically Reading Up

**1891 Litho.**

| | | | | |
|---|---|---|---|---|
| **O11** | A6 | 1c green | .25 | *.30* |
| **O12** | A6 | 2c green | .25 | *.30* |
| **O13** | A6 | 5c green | .25 | *.30* |
| **O14** | A6 | 10c green | .25 | *.30* |
| **O15** | A6 | 20c green | .25 | *.50* |
| **O16** | A6 | 50c green | .25 | *1.10* |
| **O17** | A6 | 1p green | .25 | *1.25* |
| **O18** | A6 | 2p green | .25 | *1.30* |
| **O19** | A6 | 5p green | .35 | *2.40* |
| **O20** | A6 | 10p green | .50 | *4.00* |
| | | *Nos. O11-O20 (10)* | 2.85 | *11.75* |

All values of this issue except the 2c and 5p exist without overprint and several with double overprint. They are not known to have been issued in this form.

Many of the denominations may be found in se-tenant pairs.

Overprinted in Dark Blue

**1892 Engr.**

| | | | | |
|---|---|---|---|---|
| **O21** | A7 | 1c yellow brown | .25 | *.30* |
| **O22** | A7 | 2c yellow brown | .25 | *.30* |
| **O23** | A7 | 5c yellow brown | .25 | *.30* |
| **O24** | A7 | 10c yellow brown | .25 | *.30* |
| **O25** | A7 | 20c yellow brown | .25 | *.50* |
| **O26** | A7 | 50c yellow brown | .25 | *1.00* |
| **O27** | A7 | 1p yellow brown | .25 | *1.25* |
| **O28** | A7 | 2p yellow brown | .25 | *1.60* |
| **O29** | A7 | 5p yellow brown | .25 | *2.40* |
| **O30** | A7 | 10p yellow brown | .25 | *4.00* |
| | | *Nos. O21-O30 (10)* | 2.50 | *11.95* |

The 2c and 1p are known without overprint and several values exist with double or inverted overprint. These probably were not regularly issued.

Commemorative of the 400th anniversary of the discovery of America by Christopher Columbus.

Overprinted in Red

**1893 Engr.**

| | | | | |
|---|---|---|---|---|
| **O31** | A8 | 1c slate | .25 | *.30* |
| **O32** | A8 | 2c slate | .25 | *.30* |
| **O33** | A8 | 5c slate | .25 | *.30* |
| **O34** | A8 | 10c slate | .25 | *.30* |
| **O35** | A8 | 20c slate | .25 | *.50* |
| **O36** | A8 | 25c slate | .25 | *.75* |
| **O37** | A8 | 50c slate | .25 | *.85* |
| **O38** | A8 | 1p slate | .25 | *1.00* |
| **O39** | A8 | 2p slate | .25 | *2.00* |
| **O40** | A8 | 5p slate | .25 | *2.50* |
| **O41** | A8 | 10p slate | .25 | *5.50* |
| | | *Nos. O31-O41 (11)* | 2.75 | *14.30* |

The 2, 5, 10, 20, 25, 50c and 5p are known without overprint but probably were not regularly issued. Some values exist with double or inverted overprints.

Overprinted in Black

**1894**

| | | | | |
|---|---|---|---|---|
| **O42** | A9 | 1c orange | .30 | *.35* |
| **O43** | A9 | 2c orange | .30 | *.35* |
| **O44** | A9 | 5c orange | .30 | *.35* |
| **O45** | A9 | 10c orange | .30 | *.35* |
| **O46** | A9 | 20c orange | .30 | *.50* |
| **O47** | A9 | 50c orange | .30 | *.75* |
| **O48** | A9 | 1p orange | .30 | *1.50* |
| **O49** | A9 | 2p orange | .30 | *2.00* |
| **O50** | A9 | 5p orange | 2.00 | *3.00* |
| **O51** | A9 | 10p orange | 2.00 | *4.00* |
| | | *Nos. O42-O51 (10)* | 6.40 | *13.15* |

*Reprints are yellow.*

Overprinted in Dark Blue

**1895**

| | | | | |
|---|---|---|---|---|
| **O52** | A10 | 1c green | .25 | *.35* |
| **O53** | A10 | 2c green | .25 | *.35* |
| **O54** | A10 | 5c green | .25 | *.35* |

**O55** A10 10c green .25 *.35*
**O56** A10 20c green .25 *.50*
**O57** A10 50c green .25 *1.00*
**O58** A10 1p green .25 *1.50*
**O59** A10 2p green .25 *2.00*
**O60** A10 5p green .25 *3.00*
**O61** A10 10p green .25 *4.00*
*Nos. O52-O61 (10)* 2.50 *13.40*

**Wmk. 117**

**O62** A10 1c green
**O63** A10 2c green
**O64** A10 5c green
**O65** A10 10c green
**O66** A10 20c green
**O67** A10 50c green
**O68** A10 1p green
**O69** A10 2p green
**O70** A10 5p green
**O71** A10 10p green

Nos. O62-O71 probably exist only as reprints. Value, each 15 cents.

Postage Due Stamps of Same Date Handstamped in Violet

**1896** **Unwmk.**

**O72** D1 1c orange 7.00
**O73** D1 2c orange 7.00
**O74** D1 5c orange 5.00
**O75** D1 10c orange 5.00
**O76** D1 20c orange 10.00
*Nos. O72-O76 (5)* 34.00

**Wmk. 117**

**O77** D1 1c orange 7.00
**O78** D1 2c orange 7.00
**O79** D1 5c orange 4.00
**O80** D1 10c orange 4.00
**O81** D1 20c orange 4.00
*Nos. O77-O81 (5)* 26.00

Nos. O72-O81 were handstamped in rows of five. Several handstamps were used, one of which had the variety "Oftcial." Most varieties are known inverted and double.
Forgeries exist.

Types of Postage Stamps Overprinted in Red

**1896** **Unwmk.**

**O82** A11 1c red 2.50 3.00
**O83** A11 2c red 2.50 3.00
**O84** A11 5c red 2.50 3.00
**O85** A11 10c red 2.50 3.00
**O86** A11 20c red 3.00 3.00
**O87** A11 50c red 5.00 *5.00*
**O88** A11 1p red 12.00 *12.00*
**O89** A11 2p red 12.00 *12.00*
**O90** A11 5p red 16.00 *16.00*
*Nos. O82-O90 (9)* 58.00 *60.00*

**Wmk. 117**

**O91** A11 1c red 3.00 3.50
**O92** A11 2c red 3.00 3.50
**O93** A11 5c red 3.00 3.50
**O94** A11 10c red 3.00 3.50
**O95** A11 20c red 5.00 5.00
**O96** A11 50c red 3.00 *5.00*
**O97** A11 1p red 14.00 *14.00*
**O98** A11 2p red 16.00 *16.00*
**O99** A11 5p red 25.00 *25.00*
*Nos. O91-O99 (9)* 75.00 *79.00*

Used values for Nos. O88-O90, O97-O99 are for CTO examples. Postally used examples are not known.

**Same, Dated 1897**

**1897** **Unwmk.**

**O100** A11 1c red 3.00 3.00
**O101** A11 2c red 3.00 3.00
**O102** A11 5c red 3.00 2.50
**O103** A11 10c red 3.00 3.00
**O104** A11 20c red 3.00 4.00
**O105** A11 50c red 5.00 *5.00*
**O106** A11 1p red 12.00 *12.00*
**O107** A11 2p red 12.00 *12.00*
**O108** A11 5p red 16.00 *16.00*
*Nos. O100-O108 (9)* 60.00 *60.50*

**Wmk. 117**

**O109** A11 1c red 5.00 5.00
**O110** A11 2c red 5.00 5.00
**O111** A11 5c red 5.00 5.00
**O112** A11 10c red 10.00 10.00
**O113** A11 20c red 10.00 10.00
**O114** A11 50c red 12.00 *12.00*
**O115** A11 1p red 20.00 *20.00*

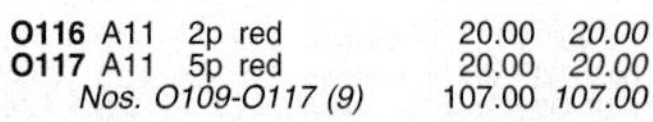
**O116** A11 2p red 20.00 *20.00*
**O117** A11 5p red 20.00 *20.00*
*Nos. O109-O117 (9)* 107.00 *107.00*

*Reprints of Nos. O82-O117 are described in notes after No. 109M. Value 15c each.*

Used values for Nos. O106-O108, O115-O117 are for CTO examples. Postally used examples are not known.

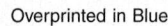

Overprinted in Blue

**1898** **Unwmk.**

**O118** A12 1c carmine 3.25 3.25
**O119** A12 2c carmine 3.25 3.25
**O120** A12 4c carmine 3.25 3.25
**O121** A12 5c carmine 2.50 2.50
**O122** A12 10c carmine 4.00 4.00
**O123** A12 15c carmine 6.00 6.00
**O124** A12 20c carmine 6.00 6.00
**O125** A12 50c carmine 8.50 *8.50*
**O126** A12 1p carmine 11.00 *11.00*
**O127** A12 2p carmine 11.00 *11.00*
**O128** A12 5p carmine 11.00 *11.00*
*Nos. O118-O128 (11)* 69.75 *69.75*

*Stamps of this set with sideways watermark 117 or with black overprint are reprints. Value 25c each.*

Used values for Nos. O126-O128 are for CTO examples. Postally used examples are not known.

Overprinted in Dark Blue

**1899**

**O129** A13 1c gray grn .35 *1.00*
**O130** A13 2c bis brn .35 *1.00*
**O131** A13 4c lake .35 *1.00*
**O132** A13 5c dk bl .35 *.50*
**O133** A13 10c buff .35 *1.00*
**O134** A13 15c chocolate .35 *2.00*
**O135** A13 20c dk grn .35 *3.00*
**O136** A13 50c car rose .35 *3.00*
**O137** A13 1p red .35 *10.00*
**O138** A13 2p violet .35 *10.00*
**O139** A13 5p lt bl .35 *15.00*
*Nos. O129-O139 (11)* 3.85 *47.50*

Counterfeit cancellations on Nos. O129-O139 are plentiful.

"Justice" — O5

**1900** **Engr.**

**O140** O5 1c plum .60 .60
**O141** O5 2c vermilion .50 .50
**O142** O5 4c ol grn .60 .60
**O143** O5 5c dk bl 1.25 .45
**O144** O5 10c purple 1.25 .35
**O145** O5 20c brown .90 .35
**O146** O5 50c lake 1.25 .50
**O147** O5 1p ultra 3.50 2.50
**O148** O5 2p brn org 4.00 4.00
**O149** O5 5p grnsh blk 5.00 5.00
*Nos. O140-O149 (10)* 18.85 14.85

For surcharges see Nos. O155-O157.

Nos. 123, 161 Surcharged in Black

**1903** ***Perf. 12, 14***

**O150** A14 1c on 10c violet .25 .30
*a.* "Centovo" 1.00
*b.* "Contavo" 1.00
*c.* With ornaments .30
*d.* Inverted surcharge 1.00
*e.* "1" omitted at upper left 2.00
**O151** A14 2c on 3c green .30 .40
*a.* "Centovos" 1.00
*b.* "Contavos" 1.00
*c.* With ornaments .35
*d.* Inverted surcharge 1.00
**O152** A14 4c on 3c green 1.25 1.25
*a.* "Centovos" 2.50
*b.* "Contavos" 2.50
*c.* With ornaments 2.50
*d.* Inverted surcharge
**O153** A14 4c on 10c violet 1.25 1.25
*a.* "Centovos" 2.50
*b.* "Contavos" 2.50
*c.* With ornaments 2.00
*d.* Inverted surcharge
**O154** A14 5c on 3c green .25 .25
*a.* "Centovos" 1.00
*b.* "Contavos" 1.00
*c.* With ornaments .30
*d.* Double surcharge 2.00
*e.* Inverted surcharge
*Nos. O150-O154 (5)* 3.30 3.45

These surcharges are set up to cover 25 stamps. Some of the settings have bars or pieces of fancy border type below "OFICIAL." There are 5 varieties on #O150, 3 on #O151, 1 each on #O152, O153, O154.

In 1904 #O151 was reprinted to fill a dealer's order. This printing lacks the small figure at the upper right. It includes the variety "OFICILA." At the same time the same setting was printed in carmine on official stamps of 1900, 1c on 10c violet and 2c on 1p ultramarine. Also the 1, 2 and 5p official stamps of 1900 were surcharged with new values and the dates 1901 or 1902 in various colors, inverted, etc. It is doubtful if any of these varieties were ever in Nicaragua and certain that none of them ever did legitimate postal duty.

No. O145 Surcharged in Black

**1904** ***Perf. 12***

**O155** O5 10c on 20c brn .25 .25
*a.* No period after "Ctvs" 1.00 .75
**O156** O5 30c on 20c brn .25 .25
**O157** O5 50c on 20c brn .50 .35
*a.* Lower "50" omitted 2.50 2.50
*b.* Upper figures omitted 2.50 2.50
*c.* Top left and lower figures omitted 3.50 3.50
*Nos. O155-O157 (3)* 1.00 .85

Coat of Arms — O6

**1905, July 25** **Engr.**

**O158** O6 1c green .25 .25
**O159** O6 2c rose .25 .25
**O160** O6 5c blue .25 .25
**O161** O6 10c yel brn .25 .25
**O162** O6 20c orange .25 .25
**O163** O6 50c brn ol .25 .25
**O164** O6 1p lake .25 .25
**O165** O6 2p violet .25 .25
**O166** O6 5p gray blk .25 .25
*Nos. O158-O166 (9)* 2.25 2.25

Surcharged Vertically Up or Down

**1907**

**O167** O6 10c on 1c grn .75 .75
**O168** O6 10c on 2c rose 25.00 22.50
**O169** O6 20c on 2c rose 22.50 *26.00*
**O170** O6 50c on 1c grn 1.50 1.50
**O171** O6 50c on 2c rose 22.50 *23.00*

Surcharged

**O172** O6 1p on 2c rose 1.50 1.50
**O173** O6 2p on 2c rose 1.50 1.50
**O174** O6 3p on 2c rose 1.50 1.50
**O175** O6 4p on 2c rose
**O176** O6 4p on 5c blue 2.25 2.25

The setting for this surcharge includes various letters from wrong fonts, the figure "1" for "l" in "Vale" and an "l" for "1" in "$1.00."

Surcharged

**O177** O6 20c on 1c green 1.00 1.00
*a.* Double surcharge 5.00 5.00
*Nos. O167-O174,O176-O177 (10)* 80.00 81.50

The preceding surcharges are vertical, reading both up and down.

**Revenue Stamps Surcharged**

O7

**1907** ***Perf. 14 to 15***

**O178** O7 10c on 2c org (Bk) .25 .25
**O179** O7 35c on 1c bl (R) .25 .25
*a.* Inverted surcharge 3.00 3.00
**O180** O7 70c on 1c bl (V) .25 .25
*a.* Inverted surcharge 3.00 3.00
**O181** O7 70c on 1c bl (O) .25 .25
*a.* Inverted surcharge 3.00 3.00
**O182** O7 1p on 2c org (G) .25 .25
*a.* Inverted surcharge 14.00 14.00
**O183** O7 2p on 2c org (Br) .25 .25
**O184** O7 3p on 5c brn (Bl) .25 .25
**O185** O7 4p on 5c brn (G) .25 .25
*a.* Double surcharge 3.00 3.00
**O186** O7 5p on 5c brn (G) .25 .25
*a.* Inverted surcharge 3.50 3.50
*Nos. O178-O186 (9)* 2.25 2.25

Letters and figures from several fonts were mixed in these surcharges.
See Nos. O199-O209.

No. 202 Surcharged

**1907, Nov.**

**Black or Blue Black Surcharge**

**O187** A18 10c on 1c grn 15.00 15.00
**O188** A18 15c on 1c grn 15.00 20.00
**O189** A18 20c on 1c grn 15.00 15.00
**O190** A18 50c on 1c grn 15.00 20.00

**Red Surcharge**

**O191** A18 1(un)p on 1c grn 14.00 15.00
**O192** A18 2(dos)p on 1c grn 14.00 15.00
*Nos. O187-O192 (6)* 88.00 100.00

No. 181 Surcharged

**1908 Yellow Surcharge** *Perf. 12*

| | | | | |
|---|---|---|---|---|
| O193 | A18 | 10c on 3c vio | 15.00 | 15.00 |
| O194 | A18 | 15c on 3c vio | 15.00 | 15.00 |
| O195 | A18 | 20c on 3c vio | 15.00 | 15.00 |
| O196 | A18 | 35c on 3c vio | 15.00 | 15.00 |
| O197 | A18 | 50c on 3c vio | 15.00 | 15.00 |
| | | *Nos. O193-O197 (5)* | 75.00 | 75.00 |

**Black Surcharge**

| | | | | |
|---|---|---|---|---|
| O198 | A18 | 35c on 3c vio | *100.00* | *100.00* |

### Revenue Stamps Surcharged like 1907 Issue Dated "1908"

**1908** *Perf. 14 to 15*

| | | | | |
|---|---|---|---|---|
| O199 | O7 | 10c on 1c bl (V) | .75 | .50 |
| *a.* | | Inverted surcharge | 3.50 | 3.50 |
| O200 | O7 | 35c on 1c bl (Bk) | .75 | .50 |
| *a.* | | Inverted surcharge | 3.50 | 3.50 |
| *b.* | | Double surcharge | 4.00 | 4.00 |
| O201 | O7 | 50c on 1c bl (R) | .75 | .50 |
| O202 | O7 | 1p on 1c bl (Br) | 37.50 | 37.50 |
| *a.* | | Inverted surcharge | 65.00 | 65.00 |
| O203 | O7 | 2p on 1c bl (G) | .90 | .75 |
| O204 | O7 | 10c on 2c org (Bk) | 1.10 | .65 |
| O205 | O7 | 35c on 2c org (R) | 1.10 | .65 |
| *a.* | | Double surcharge | 3.50 | |
| O206 | O7 | 50c on 2c org (Bk) | 1.10 | .65 |
| O207 | O7 | 70c on 2c org (Bl) | 1.10 | .65 |
| O208 | O7 | 1p on 2c org (G) | 1.10 | .65 |
| O209 | O7 | 2p on 2c org (Br) | 1.10 | .65 |
| | | *Nos. O199-O209 (11)* | 47.25 | 43.65 |

There are several minor varieties in the figures, etc., in these surcharges.

Nos. 243-248 Overprinted in Black

**1909** *Perf. 12*

| | | | | |
|---|---|---|---|---|
| O210 | A18 | 10c lake | .25 | .25 |
| *a.* | | Double overprint | 2.50 | 2.50 |
| O211 | A18 | 15c black | .60 | .50 |
| O212 | A18 | 20c brn ol | 1.00 | .75 |
| O213 | A18 | 50c dp grn | 1.50 | 1.00 |
| O214 | A18 | 1p yellow | 1.75 | 1.25 |
| O215 | A18 | 2p car rose | 6.50 | 2.00 |
| | | *Nos. O210-O215 (6)* | 11.60 | 5.75 |

Overprinted in Black

**1910**

| | | | | |
|---|---|---|---|---|
| O216 | A18 | 15c black | 1.50 | 1.25 |
| *a.* | | Double overprint | 4.00 | 4.00 |
| O217 | A18 | 20c brn ol | 2.50 | 2.00 |
| O218 | A18 | 50c dp grn | 2.50 | 2.00 |
| O219 | A18 | 1p yellow | 2.75 | 2.50 |
| *a.* | | Inverted overprint | 16.00 | 7.50 |
| O220 | A18 | 2p car rose | 4.00 | 3.00 |
| | | *Nos. O216-O220 (5)* | 13.25 | 10.75 |

### Nos. 239-240 Surcharged in Black

No. O221

No. O222

**1911**

| | | | | |
|---|---|---|---|---|
| O221 | A18 | 5c on 3c red org | 10.00 | 6.00 |
| O222 | A18 | 10c on 4c vio | 12.00 | 5.00 |
| *a.* | | Double surcharge | 24.00 | 24.00 |
| *b.* | | Pair, one without new value | 35.00 | |

Revenue Stamps Surcharged in Black

**1911, Nov.** *Perf. 14 to 15*

| | | | | |
|---|---|---|---|---|
| O223 | A21 | 10c on 10c on 1 red | 3.00 | 3.00 |
| *a.* | | Inverted surcharge | 4.50 | |
| *b.* | | Double surcharge | 4.50 | |
| O224 | A21 | 15c on 10c on 1 red | 3.00 | 3.00 |
| *a.* | | Inverted surcharge | 5.00 | |
| *b.* | | Double surcharge | 4.50 | |
| O225 | A21 | 20c on 10c on 1 red | 3.00 | 3.00 |
| *a.* | | Inverted surcharge | 5.00 | |
| O226 | A21 | 50c on 10c on 1 red | 3.75 | 3.75 |
| *a.* | | Inverted surcharge | 4.50 | |
| O227 | A21 | 1p on 10c on 1 red | 5.00 | *7.00* |
| *a.* | | Inverted surcharge | 6.00 | |
| O228 | A21 | 2p on 10c on 1 red | 5.50 | *10.00* |
| *a.* | | Inverted surcharge | 7.50 | |
| *b.* | | Double surcharge | 7.50 | |
| | | *Nos. O223-O228 (6)* | 23.25 | 29.75 |

Surcharged in Black

**1911, Nov.**

| | | | | |
|---|---|---|---|---|
| O229 | A21 | 10c on 10c on 1 red | 22.50 | |
| O230 | A21 | 15c on 10c on 1 red | 22.50 | |
| O231 | A21 | 20c on 10c on 1 red | 22.50 | |
| O232 | A21 | 50c on 10c on 1 red | 16.00 | |
| | | *Nos. O229-O232 (4)* | 83.50 | |

Surcharged in Black

**1911, Dec.**

| | | | | |
|---|---|---|---|---|
| O233 | A21 | 5c on 10c on 1 red | 4.50 | *6.00* |
| *a.* | | Double surcharge | 7.50 | |
| *b.* | | Inverted surcharge | 7.50 | |
| *c.* | | "5" omitted | 6.00 | |
| O234 | A21 | 10c on 10c on 1 red | 5.50 | *7.00* |
| O235 | A21 | 15c on 10c on 1 red | 6.00 | *7.50* |
| O236 | A21 | 20c on 10c on 1 red | 6.50 | *8.50* |
| O237 | A21 | 50c on 10c on 1 red | 7.50 | *10.00* |
| | | *Nos. O233-O237 (5)* | 30.00 | 39.00 |

Nos. O233 to O237 have a surcharge on the back like Nos. 285 and 286 with "15 cts" obliterated by a heavy horizontal bar.

Surcharged Vertically in Black

**1912**

| | | | | |
|---|---|---|---|---|
| O238 | A21 | 5c on 10c on 1 red | 8.00 | 8.00 |
| O239 | A21 | 10c on 10c on 1 red | 8.00 | 8.00 |
| O240 | A21 | 15c on 10c on 1 red | 8.00 | 8.00 |
| O241 | A21 | 20c on 10c on 1 red | 8.00 | 8.00 |
| O242 | A21 | 35c on 10c on 1 red | 8.00 | 8.00 |
| O243 | A21 | 50c on 10c on 1 red | 8.00 | 8.00 |
| O244 | A21 | 1p on 10c on 1 red | 8.00 | 8.00 |
| | | *Nos. O238-O244 (7)* | 56.00 | 56.00 |

Nos. O238 to O244 are printed on Nos. 285 and 286 but the surcharge on the back is obliterated by a vertical bar.

Types of Regular Issue of 1912 Overprinted in Black

**1912** *Perf. 12*

| | | | | |
|---|---|---|---|---|
| O245 | A22 | 1c light blue | .25 | .25 |
| O246 | A22 | 2c light blue | .25 | .25 |
| O247 | A22 | 3c light blue | .25 | .25 |
| O248 | A22 | 4c light blue | .25 | .25 |
| O249 | A22 | 5c light blue | .25 | .25 |
| O250 | A22 | 6c light blue | .35 | .25 |
| O251 | A22 | 10c light blue | .35 | .25 |
| O252 | A22 | 15c light blue | .35 | .25 |
| O253 | A22 | 20c light blue | .35 | .25 |
| O254 | A22 | 25c light blue | .35 | .25 |
| O255 | A23 | 35c light blue | .40 | .25 |
| O256 | A22 | 50c light blue | 3.75 | 2.00 |
| O257 | A22 | 1p light blue | .65 | .45 |
| O258 | A22 | 2p light blue | .75 | .55 |
| O259 | A22 | 5p light blue | 1.00 | .75 |
| | | *Nos. O245-O259 (15)* | 9.55 | 6.50 |

On the 35c the overprint is 15½mm wide, on the other values it is 13mm.

Types of Regular Issue of 1914 Overprinted in Black

**1915, May**

| | | | | |
|---|---|---|---|---|
| O260 | A24 | 1c light blue | .25 | .25 |
| O261 | A25 | 2c light blue | .25 | .25 |
| O262 | A24 | 3c light blue | .25 | .25 |
| O263 | A25 | 4c light blue | .25 | .25 |
| O264 | A24 | 5c light blue | .25 | .25 |
| O265 | A25 | 6c light blue | .25 | .25 |
| O266 | A25 | 10c light blue | .25 | .25 |
| O267 | A24 | 15c light blue | .25 | .25 |
| O268 | A25 | 20c light blue | .25 | .25 |
| O269 | A24 | 25c light blue | .30 | .30 |
| O270 | A25 | 50c light blue | .60 | .60 |
| | | *Nos. O260-O270 (11)* | 3.15 | 3.15 |

Regular Issues of 1914-22 Overprinted in Red

**1925**

| | | | | |
|---|---|---|---|---|
| O271 | A24 | ½c dp grn | .25 | .25 |
| *a.* | | Double overprint | 2.50 | 2.50 |
| O272 | A24 | 1c violet | .25 | .25 |
| O273 | A25 | 2c car rose | .25 | .25 |
| O274 | A24 | 3c ol grn | .25 | .25 |
| O275 | A25 | 4c vermilion | .25 | .25 |
| *a.* | | Double overprint | *4.00* | *4.00* |
| O276 | A24 | 5c black | .25 | .25 |
| *a.* | | Double overprint | *4.00* | *4.00* |
| O277 | A25 | 6c red brn | .25 | .25 |
| O278 | A25 | 10c yellow | .30 | .30 |
| *a.* | | Double overprint | *4.25* | *4.25* |
| O279 | A24 | 15c red brn | .40 | .40 |
| O280 | A25 | 20c bis brn | .50 | .50 |
| O281 | A24 | 25c orange | .60 | .60 |
| *a.* | | Inverted overprint | *60.00* | *40.00* |
| O282 | A25 | 50c pale bl | .75 | .75 |
| *a.* | | Double overprint | *20.00* | *20.00* |
| | | *Nos. O271-O282 (12)* | 4.30 | 4.30 |

Type II overprint has "f" and "i" separated. Comes on Nos. O272-O274 and O276.

Regular Issues of 1914-22 Overprinted in Black

**1926**

| | | | | |
|---|---|---|---|---|
| O283 | A24 | ½c dk grn | .25 | .25 |
| O284 | A24 | 1c dp vio | .25 | .25 |
| O285 | A25 | 2c car rose | .25 | .25 |
| O286 | A24 | 3c ol gray | .25 | .25 |
| O287 | A25 | 4c vermilion | .25 | .25 |
| O288 | A24 | 5c gray blk | .25 | .25 |
| O289 | A25 | 6c red brn | .25 | .25 |
| O290 | A25 | 10c yellow | .25 | .25 |
| O291 | A24 | 15c dp brn | .25 | .25 |
| O292 | A25 | 20c bis brn | .25 | .25 |
| O293 | A24 | 25c orange | .25 | .25 |
| O294 | A25 | 50c pale bl | .25 | .25 |
| | | *Nos. O283-O294 (12)* | 3.00 | 3.00 |

No. 499 Surcharged in Black

**1931**

| | | | | |
|---|---|---|---|---|
| O295 | A33 | 5c on 10c bis brn | .25 | .25 |

Nos. 517-518 Overprinted in Red

**1931**

| | | | | |
|---|---|---|---|---|
| O296 | A25 | 6c bis brn | .25 | .25 |
| O297 | A25 | 10c lt brn | .25 | .25 |

Nos. 541, 543, 545 With Additional Overprint in Red

| | | | | |
|---|---|---|---|---|
| O298 | A24 | 1c ol grn | .25 | .25 |
| O299 | A24 | 3c lt bl | .25 | .25 |
| *a.* | | "OFICIAL" inverted | .80 | .80 |
| O300 | A24 | 5c gray brn | .25 | .25 |
| *a.* | | "1931" double | .80 | .80 |
| | | *Nos. O298-O300 (3)* | .75 | .75 |

Regular Issues of 1914-31 Overprinted in Black

**1932, Feb. 6**

| | | | | |
|---|---|---|---|---|
| O301 | A24 | 1c ol grn | .25 | .25 |
| *a.* | | Double overprint | 1.40 | 1.40 |
| O302 | A25 | 2c brt rose | .25 | .25 |
| *a.* | | Double overprint | 1.40 | 1.40 |
| O303 | A24 | 3c lt bl | .25 | .25 |
| *a.* | | Double overprint | .50 | .50 |
| O304 | A25 | 4c dk bl | .25 | .25 |
| O305 | A24 | 5c ol brn | .25 | .25 |
| O306 | A25 | 6c bis brn | .25 | .25 |
| *a.* | | Double overprint | 2.00 | 2.00 |
| O307 | A25 | 10c lt brn | .30 | .25 |
| O308 | A24 | 15c org red | .40 | .25 |
| *a.* | | Double overprint | 2.25 | 2.25 |
| O309 | A25 | 20c orange | .70 | .35 |
| O310 | A24 | 25c dk vio | 2.00 | .50 |
| O311 | A25 | 50c green | .25 | .25 |
| O312 | A25 | 1cor yellow | .25 | .25 |
| | | *Nos. O301-O312 (12)* | 5.40 | 3.35 |

With Additional Overprint in Black

**1932, Feb. 6**

| | | | | |
|---|---|---|---|---|
| O313 | A24 | 1c ol grn | 5.50 | 5.50 |
| O314 | A25 | 2c brt rose | 6.50 | 6.50 |
| *a.* | | Double overprint | 8.25 | 8.25 |
| O315 | A24 | 3c lt bl | 5.00 | 5.00 |
| O316 | A24 | 5c ol brn | 5.00 | 5.00 |
| O317 | A24 | 15c org red | .65 | .65 |
| O318 | A24 | 25c blk brn | .65 | .65 |
| O319 | A24 | 25c dk vio | 1.50 | 1.50 |
| | | *Nos. O313-O319 (7)* | 24.80 | 24.80 |

The variety "OFIAIAL" occurs once in each sheet of Nos. O301 to O319 inclusive.

Despite the 1932 release date, the "1931" overprint on Nos. O313-O319 is correct.

### Flag of the Race Issue

**1933, Aug. 9 Litho.** *Rouletted 9*

**Without gum**

| | | | | |
|---|---|---|---|---|
| O320 | A43 | 1c orange | 1.25 | 1.25 |
| O321 | A43 | 2c yellow | 1.25 | 1.25 |
| O322 | A43 | 3c dk brn | 1.25 | 1.25 |
| O323 | A43 | 4c dp brn | 1.25 | 1.25 |
| O324 | A43 | 5c gray brn | 1.25 | 1.25 |
| O325 | A43 | 6c dp ultra | 1.50 | 1.50 |
| O326 | A43 | 10c dp vio | 1.50 | 1.50 |
| O327 | A43 | 15c red vio | 1.50 | 1.50 |
| O328 | A43 | 20c dp grn | 1.50 | 1.50 |
| O329 | A43 | 25c green | 2.50 | 2.50 |
| O330 | A43 | 50c carmine | 3.00 | 3.00 |
| O331 | A43 | 1cor red | 5.00 | 5.00 |
| | | *Nos. O320-O331 (12)* | 22.75 | 22.75 |

See note after No. 599.

*Reprints of Nos. O320-O331 exist.*

A 25c dull blue exists. Its status is questioned.

Regular Issue of 1914-31 Overprinted in Red

**1933, Nov.** *Perf. 12*

| | | | | |
|---|---|---|---|---|
| O332 | A24 | 1c ol grn | .25 | .25 |
| O333 | A25 | 2c brt rose | .25 | .25 |
| O334 | A24 | 3c lt bl | .25 | .25 |
| O335 | A25 | 4c dk bl | .25 | .25 |
| O336 | A24 | 5c ol brn | .25 | .25 |
| O337 | A25 | 6c bis brn | .25 | .25 |
| O338 | A25 | 10c lt brn | .25 | .25 |
| O339 | A24 | 15c red org | .25 | .25 |
| O340 | A25 | 20c orange | .25 | .25 |

**O341** A24 25c dk vio .25 .25
**O342** A25 50c green .25 .25
**O343** A25 1cor yellow .35 .25
*Nos. O332-O343 (12)* 3.10 3.00

Nos. O332-O343 exist with or without signature control overprint. Values are the same.

### Official Stamps of 1933 Overprinted as Nos. CO15-CO19 in Blue

**1935, Dec.**
**O344** A24 1c ol grn .65 .40
**O345** A25 2c brt rose .65 .50
**O346** A24 3c lt bl 1.60 .50
**O347** A25 4c dk bl 1.60 1.60
**O348** A24 5c ol brn 1.60 1.60
**O349** A25 6c bis brn 2.00 2.00
**O350** A25 10c lt brn 2.00 2.00
**O351** A24 15c org red 27.50 27.50
**O352** A25 20c orange 27.50 27.50
**O353** A24 25c dk vio 27.50 27.50
**O354** A25 50c green 27.50 27.50
**O355** A25 1cor yellow 27.50 27.50
*Nos. O344-O355 (12)* 147.60 146.10

Nos. O344-O355 have signature control overprints. Counterfeits of overprint abound.

### Same Overprinted in Red

**1936, Jan.**
**O356** A24 1c ol grn .25 .25
**O357** A25 2c brt rose .25 .25
**O358** A24 3c lt bl .25 .25
*a.* Double overprint
**O359** A25 4c dk bl .25 .25
**O360** A24 5c ol brn .25 .25
**O361** A25 6c bis brn .25 .25
**O362** A25 10c lt brn .25 .25
**O363** A24 15c org red .25 .25
**O364** A25 20c orange .25 .25
**O365** A24 25c dk vio .25 .25
**O366** A25 50c green .25 .25
**O367** A25 1cor yellow .35 .35
*Nos. O356-O367 (12)* 3.10 3.10

Nos. O356-O367 have signature control overprints.

Nos. 653 to 655, 657, 659 660, 662 to 664 Overprinted in Black

**1937**
**O368** A24 1c car rose .25 .25
**O369** A25 2c dp bl .25 .25
**O370** A24 3c chocolate .25 .25
**O371** A24 5c org red .35 .25
**O372** A25 10c ol grn .65 .40
**O373** A24 15c green .80 .50
**O374** A24 25c orange 1.00 .65
**O375** A25 50c brown 1.40 .80
**O376** A25 1cor ultra 2.50 1.25
*Nos. O368-O376 (9)* 7.45 4.60

Islands of the Great Lake
O9

**1939, Jan. Engr. *Perf. 12½***
**O377** O9 2c rose red 1.00 .25
**O378** O9 3c lt bl 1.00 .25
**O379** O9 6c brn org 1.00 .25
**O380** O9 7½c dp grn 1.00 .25
**O381** O9 10c blk brn 1.00 .25
**O382** O9 15c orange 1.00 .25
**O383** O9 25c dk vio 1.50 .25
**O384** O9 50c brt yel grn 4.00 .75
*Nos. O377-O384 (8)* 11.50 2.50

---

## POSTAL TAX STAMPS

Official Stamps of 1915 Surcharged in Black

**1921, July Unwmk. *Perf. 12***
**RA1** A24 1c on 5c lt bl 1.50 .60
**RA2** A25 1c on 6c lt bl .65 .25
*a.* Double surcharge, one inverted
**RA3** A25 1c on 10c lt bl 1.00 .25
*a.* Double surcharge 3.50 3.50
**RA4** A24 1c on 15c lt bl 1.50 .25
*a.* Double surcharge, one inverted 5.00 5.00
*Nos. RA1-RA4 (4)* 4.65 1.35

"R de C" signifies "Reconstruccion de Comunicaciones." The stamps were intended to provide a fund for rebuilding the General Post Office which was burned in April, 1921. One stamp was required on each letter or parcel, in addition to the regular postage. In the setting of one hundred there are five stamps with antique "C" and twenty-one with "R" and "C" smaller than in the illustration. One or more stamps in the setting have a dotted bar, as illustrated over No. 388, instead of the double bar.

The use of the "R de C" stamps for the payment of regular postage was not permitted.

Official Stamp of 1915 Overprinted in Black

**1921, July**
**RA5** A24 1c light blue 6.00 1.75

This stamp is known with the dotted bar as illustrated over No. 388, instead of the double bar.

Coat of Arms — PT1

**1921, Sept. Red Surcharge**
**RA6** PT1 1c on 1c ver & blk .25 .25
**RA7** PT1 1c on 2c grn & blk .25 .25
*a.* Double surcharge 3.00 3.00
*b.* Double surcharge, one inverted 4.00 4.00
**RA8** PT1 1c on 4c org & blk .25 .25
*a.* Double surcharge 4.00 4.00
**RA9** PT1 1c on 15c dk bl & blk .25 .25
*a.* Double surcharge 3.00 3.00
*Nos. RA6-RA9 (4)* 1.00 1.00

PT2

**1922, Feb. Black Surcharge**
**RA10** PT2 1c on 10c yellow .25 .25
*a.* Period after "de" .50 .40
*b.* Double surcharge 2.00 2.00
*c.* Double inverted surcharge 3.75 3.75
*d.* Inverted surcharge 3.00 3.00
*e.* Without period after "C" 1.00 1.00

No. 409 Overprinted in Black

**1922**
**RA11** A24 1c violet .25 .25
*a.* Double overprint 2.00 2.00

This stamp with the overprint in red is a trial printing.

Nos. 402, 404-407 Surcharged in Black

**1922, June**
**RA12** A27 1c on 1c grn & blk .75 .75
**RA13** A29 1c on 5c ultra & blk .75 .75
**RA14** A30 1c on 10c org & blk .75 .40
**RA15** A31 1c on 25c yel & blk .75 .30
*a.* Inverted surcharge 5.00 5.00
**RA16** A32 1c on 50c vio & blk .30 .25
*a.* Double surcharge 4.00 4.00
*Nos. RA12-RA16 (5)* 3.30 2.45

PT3

### Surcharge in Red or Dark Blue

**1922, Oct. *Perf. 11½***
**RA17** PT3 1c yellow (R) .25 .25
*a.* No period after "C" 1.00 1.00
**RA18** PT3 1c violet (DBl) .25 .25
*a.* No period after "C" 1.00 1.00

Surcharge is inverted on 22 out of 50 of No. RA17, 23 out of 50 of No. RA18.
See No. RA24.

Nos. 403-407 Surcharged in Black

**1923 *Perf. 12***
**RA19** A28 1c on 2c rose red & black .50 .45
**RA20** A29 1c on 5c ultra & blk .55 .25
**RA21** A30 1c on 10c org & blk .25 .25
**RA22** A31 1c on 25c yel & blk .35 .30
**RA23** A32 1c on 50c vio & blk .25 .25
*Nos. RA19-RA23 (5)* 1.90 1.50

The variety no period after "R" occurs twice on each sheet.

### Red Surcharge
### Wmk. Coat of Arms in Sheet
***Perf. 11½***

**RA24** PT3 1c pale blue .25 .25

### Type of 1921 Issue

Without Surcharge of New Value

### Unwmk.

**RA25** PT1 1c ver & blk .25 .25
*a.* Double overprint, one inverted 3.00 3.00

No. 409 Overprinted in Blue

**1924**
**RA26** A24 1c violet .25 .25
*a.* Double overprint 8.00 8.00

There are two settings of the overprint on No. RA26, with "1924" 5½mm or 6½mm wide.

No. 409 Overprinted in Blue

**1925**
**RA27** A24 1c violet .25 .25

No. 409 Overprinted in Blue

**1926**
**RA28** A24 1c violet .25 .25

No. RA28 Overprinted in Various Colors

**1927**
**RA29** A24 1c vio (R) .25 .25
*a.* Double overprint (R) 2.00 2.00
*b.* Inverted overprint (R) 3.00 3.00
**RA30** A24 1c vio (V) .25 .25
*a.* Double overprint 2.50 2.50
*b.* Inverted overprint 2.50 2.50
**RA31** A24 1c vio (Bl) .25 .25
*a.* Double overprint 5.00 5.00
**RA32** A24 1c vio (Bk) .25 .25
*a.* Double ovpt., one invtd. 4.25 4.25
*b.* Double overprint 4.25 4.25

### Same Overprint on No. RA27

**RA33** A24 1c vio (Bk) 15.00 10.00
*Nos. RA29-RA33 (5)* 16.00 11.00

No. RA28 Overprinted in Violet

**1928**
**RA34** A24 1c violet .25 .25
*a.* Double overprint 2.00 2.00
*b.* "928" 1.00 1.00

### Similar to No. RA34 but 8mm space between "Resello" and "1928"
### Black Overprint

**RA35** A24 1c violet .40 .25
*a.* "1828" 2.00 2.00

PT4

### Inscribed "Timbre Telegrafico"
Horiz. Srch. in Black, Vert. Srch. in Red

**RA36** PT4 1c on 5c bl & blk .60 .25
*a.* Comma after "R" 1.25 1.25
*b.* No period after "R" 1.25 1.25
*c.* No periods after "R" and "C" 1.25 1.25

("CORREOS" at right) — PT5

**1928 Engr. *Perf. 12***
**RA37** PT5 1c plum .25 .25

See Nos. RA41-RA43. For overprints see Nos. RA45-RA46, RA48-RA51.

PT6

**1929 Red Surcharge**

**RA38** PT6 1c on 5c bl & blk .25 .25
- *a.* Inverted surcharge 3.00 3.00
- *b.* Double surcharge 2.00 2.00
- *c.* Double surcharge, one inverted 2.00 2.00
- *d.* Period after "de" 1.25 1.25
- *e.* Comma after "R" 1.25 1.25

See note after No. 512.

Regular Issue of 1928 Overprinted in Blue

**RA39** A24 1c red orange .25 .25

No. RA39 exists both with and without signature control overprint.

An additional overprint, "1929" in black or blue on No. RA39, is fraudulent.

No. 513 Overprinted in Red

**1929**

**RA40** A24 1c ol grn .25 .25
- *a.* Double overprint .75 .75

No. RA40 is known with overprint in black, and with overprint inverted. These varieties were not regularly issued, but copies have been canceled by favor.

**Type of 1928 Issue Inscribed at right "COMUNICACIONES"**

**1930-37**

**RA41** PT5 1c carmine .25 .25
**RA42** PT5 1c orange ('33) .25 .25
**RA43** PT5 1c green ('37) .25 .25
*Nos. RA41-RA43 (3)* .75 .75

No. RA42 has signature control. See note before No. 600.

No. RA39 Overprinted in Black

**1931**

**RA44** A24 1c red orange .25 .25
- *a.* "1931" double overprint .35 .35
- *b.* "1931" double ovpt., one invtd. .40 .40

No. RA44 exists with signature control overprint. See note before No. 600. Value is the same.

No. RA42 Overprinted Vertically, up or down, in Black

**1935**

**RA45** PT5 1c orange .25 .25
- *a.* Double overprint 1.00 1.00
- *b.* Double ovpt., one inverted

No. RA45 and RA45a Overprinted Vertically, Reading Down, in Blue

**RA46** PT5 1c orange .50 .25
- *a.* Black overprint double 2.00 2.00

**Same Overprint in Red on Nos. RA39, RA42 and RA45**

**RA47** A24 1c red org (#RA39) *50.00 50.00*
**RA48** PT5 1c org (#RA42) .25 .25
**RA49** PT5 1c org (#RA45) .25 .25
- *a.* Black overprint double .80 .80

Overprint is horizontal on No. RA47 and vertical, reading down, on Nos. RA48-RA49.

No. RA48 exists with signature control overprint. See note before No. 600. Same values.

No. RA42 Overprinted Vertically, Reading Down, in Carmine

**1935 Unwmk. *Perf. 12***

**RA50** PT5 1c orange .25 .25

**No. RA45 with Additional Overprint "1936", Vertically, Reading Down, in Red**

**1936**

**RA51** PT5 1c orange .50 .25

**No. RA39 with Additional Overprint "1936" in Red**

**RA52** A24 1c red orange .50 .25

No. RA52 exists only with script control mark.

PT7

**1936 Vertical Surcharge in Red**

**RA53** PT7 1c on 5c grn & blk .25 .25
- *a.* "Cenavo" 1.40 1.40
- *b.* "Centavos" 1.40 1.40

**Horizontal Surcharge in Red**

**RA54** PT7 1c on 5c grn & blk .25 .25
- *a.* Double surcharge 1.40 1.40

Baseball Player PT8

**1937 Typo. *Perf. 11***

**RA55** PT8 1c carmine .60 .25
**RA56** PT8 1c yellow .60 .25
**RA57** PT8 1c blue .60 .25
**RA58** PT8 1c green .60 .25
- *b.* Sheet of 4, #RA55-RA58 8.00 3.00

*Nos. RA55-RA58 (4)* 2.40 1.00

Issued for the benefit of the Central American Caribbean Games of 1937.

Control mark in red is variously placed. See dark oval below "OLIMPICO" in illustration.

**Tête bêche Pairs**

*RA55a* PT8 1c 1.25 1.25
*RA56a* PT8 1c 1.25 1.25
*RA57a* PT8 1c 1.25 1.25
*RA58a* PT8 1c 1.25 1.25
*Nos. RA55a-RA58a (4)* 5.00 5.00

**Catalogue values for unused stamps in this section, from this point to the end of the section, are for Never Hinged items.**

Proposed Natl. Stadium, Managua — PT9

**1949 Photo. *Perf. 12***

**RA60** PT9 5c greenish blue .25 .25
- *a.* Souvenir sheet of 4 12.00 12.00

10th World Series of Amateur Baseball, 1948. The tax was used toward the erection of a national stadium at Managua.

**Type Similar to 1949, with "Correos" omitted**

**1952**

**RA61** PT9 5c magenta .25 .25

The tax was used toward the erection of a national stadium at Managua.

PT10

**1956 Engr. *Perf. 12½x12***

**RA62** PT10 5c deep ultra .25 .25

The tax was used for social welfare.

PT11

PT11a

**Surcharged in Red or Black**

**1959 Unwmk. *Perf. 12***

**Red Marginal Number**

**RA63** PT11 5c on 50c vio bl (R) .25 .25
**RA64** PT11a 5c on 50c vio bl (B) .25 .25

Nos. RA63-RA64 are surcharged on consular revenue stamps. Surcharge reads "Sobre Tasa Postal CO.O5." Vertical surcharge on No. RA63, horizontal on No. RA64.

Jesus and Children — PT12

**1959 Photo. *Perf. 16***

**RA65** PT12 5c ultra .25 .25

Hexisia Bidentata — PT13

Orchids: No. RA67, Schomburgkia tibicinus. No. RA68, Stanhopea ecornuta. No. RA69, Lycaste macrophylla. No. RA70, Maxillaria tenuifolia. No. RA71, Cattleya skinneri. No. RA72, Cycnoches egertonianum. No. RA73, Bletia roezlii. No. RA74, Sobralia pleiantha. No. RA75, Oncidium cebolleta and ascendens.

**1962, Feb. Photo. *Perf. 11½***

**Granite Paper**

**Orchids in Natural Colors**

**RA66** PT13 5c pale lil & grn .25 .25
**RA67** PT13 5c yel & grn .25 .25
**RA68** PT13 5c pink & grn .25 .25
**RA69** PT13 5c pale vio & grn .25 .25
**RA70** PT13 5c lt grnsh bl & red .25 .25
**RA71** PT13 5c buff & lil .25 .25
**RA72** PT13 5c yel grn & brn .25 .25
**RA73** PT13 5c gray & red .25 .25
**RA74** PT13 5c lt bl & dk bl .25 .25
**RA75** PT13 5c lt grn & brn .25 .25
*Nos. RA66-RA75 (10)* 2.50 2.50

For overprints see #842-852, 855-868, 901-908.

Exist imperf. Value, each pair $100.

## PROVINCE OF ZELAYA

### (Bluefields)

A province of Nicaragua lying along the eastern coast. Special postage stamps for this section were made necessary because for a period two currencies, which differed materially in value, were in use in Nicaragua. Silver money was used in Zelaya and Cabo Gracias a Dios while the rest of Nicaragua used paper money. Later the money of the entire country was placed on a gold basis.

Dangerous counterfeits exist of most of the Bluefields overprints.

Regular Issues of 1900-05 Handstamped in Black (4 or more types)

**1904-05 Unwmk. *Perf. 12, 14***

**On Engraved Stamps of 1900**

**1L1** A14 1c plum 1.50 .75
**1L2** A14 2c vermilion 1.50 .75
**1L3** A14 3c green 1.90 1.50
**1L4** A14 4c ol grn 11.00 9.00
**1L5** A14 15c ultra 3.00 1.90
**1L6** A14 20c brown 3.00 1.90
**1L7** A14 50c lake 10.50 9.00
**1L8** A14 1p yellow 21.00
**1L9** A14 2p salmon 30.00
**1L10** A14 5p black 37.50
*Nos. 1L1-1L10 (10)* 120.90
*Nos. 1L1-1L7 (7)* 24.80

**On Lithographed Stamps of 1902**

**1L11** A14 5c blue 3.00 .75
**1L12** A14 5c carmine 1.90 .90
**1L13** A14 10c violet 1.50 .75
*Nos. 1L11-1L13 (3)* 6.40 2.40

**On Postage Due Stamps Overprinted "1901 Correos"**

**1L14** D3 20c brn (No. 156) 4.50 1.90
**1L15** D3 50c lake (No. 158) — —

**On Surcharged Stamps of 1904-05**

**1L16** A14 5c on 10c (#175) 1.50 1.10
**1L17** A14 5c on 10c (#178) 3.00 1.50
**1L18** A14 15c on 10c vio (#176) 1.50 1.50
**1L19** A14 15c on 10c vio (#177) 14.00 4.50
*Nos. 1L16-1L19 (4)* 20.00 8.60

**On Surcharged Stamp of 1901**

**1L20** A14 20c on 5p blk 18.00 3.00

**On Regular Issue of 1905**

**1906-07 *Perf. 12***

**1L21** A18 1c green .30 .30
**1L22** A18 2c car rose .30 .30
**1L23** A18 3c violet .30 .30
**1L24** A18 4c org red .45 .45
**1L25** A18 5c blue .25 .25
**1L26** A18 10c yel brn 3.00 1.50
**1L27** A18 15c brn ol 4.50 1.75
**1L28** A18 20c lake 9.00 7.50
**1L29** A18 50c orange 35.00 30.00
**1L30** A18 1p black 30.00 27.50
**1L31** A18 2p dk grn 37.50
**1L32** A18 5p violet 45.00
*Nos. 1L21-1L32 (12)* 165.60
*Nos. 1L21-1L30 (10)* 69.85

**On Surcharged Stamps of 1906-08**

**1L33** A18 10c on 3c vio .40 .40
**1L34** A18 15c on 1c grn .50 .50
**1L35** A18 20c on 2c rose 3.50 3.50
**1L36** A18 20c on 5c bl 1.50 1.50
**1L37** A18 50c on 6c sl (R) 1.50 3.00
*Nos. 1L33-1L37 (5)* 7.40 8.90

Handstamped

Stamps with the above overprints were made to fill dealers' orders but were never regularly issued or used. Stamps with similar overprints handstamped are bogus.

Surcharged Stamps of 1906 Overprinted in Red, Black or Blue

1L38 A18 15c on 1c grn (R) 2.75 2.75
 a. Red overprint inverted
1L39 A18 20c on 2c rose (Bk) 1.90 1.90
1L40 A18 20c on 5c bl (R) 3.00 3.00
1L41 A18 50c on 6c sl (Bl) 14.00 14.00
 *Nos. 1L38-1L41 (4)* 21.65 21.65

Stamps of the 1905 issue overprinted as above No. 1L38 or similarly overprinted but with only 2¼mm space between "B" and "Dpto. Zelaya" were made to fill dealers' orders but not placed in use.

No. 205 Handstamped in Black

***Perf. 14 to 15***

1L42 A18 10c yel brn 24.00 24.00

Stamps of 1907 Overprinted in Red or Black

1L43 A18 15c brn ol (R) 3.00 3.00
1L44 A18 20c lake .90 .90
 a. Inverted overprint 11.00 11.00

With Additional Surcharge

1L45 A18 5c brn org .50 .45
 a. Inverted surcharge 7.50 7.50

With Additional Surcharge

1L46 A18 5c on 4c brn org 12.00 12.00

### On Provisional Postage Stamps of 1907-08 in Black or Blue

1L47 A18 10c on 2c rose (Bl) 4.50 4.50
1L48 A18 10c on 2c rose *300.00*
1L48A A18 10c on 4c brn org *300.00*
1L49 A18 10c on 20c lake 3.00 3.00
1L50 A18 10c on 50c org (Bl) 3.00 2.25

Arms Type of 1907 Overprinted in Black or Violet

**1907**

1L51 A18 1c green .30 .25
1L52 A18 2c rose .30 .25
1L53 A18 3c violet .40 .40
1L54 A18 4c brn org .45 .45
1L55 A18 5c blue 4.50 2.25
1L56 A18 10c yel brn .40 .30
1L57 A18 15c brn ol .75 .40
1L58 A18 20c lake .75 .45
1L59 A18 50c orange 2.25 1.50
1L60 A18 1p blk (V) 2.25 1.50
1L61 A18 2p dk grn 2.25 1.90
1L62 A18 5p violet 3.75 2.25
 *Nos. 1L51-1L62 (12)* 18.35 11.90

Nos. 217-225 Overprinted in Green

**1908**

1L63 A19 1c on 5c yel & blk (R) .45 .40
1L64 A19 2c on 5c yel & blk (Bl) .45 .40
1L65 A19 4c on 5c yel & blk (G) .45 .40
 a. Overprint reading down 11.00 11.00
 b. Double overprint, reading up and down 18.00 18.00
1L66 A19 5c yel & blk .45 .45
 a. "CORROE" 4.50
 b. Double overprint 11.00 11.00
 c. Double overprint, reading up and down 19.00 19.00
 d. "CORREO 1908" double 15.00 15.00
1L67 A19 10c lt bl & blk .45 .45
 a. Ovpt. reading down .50 .50
 b. "CORREO 1908" triple 37.50
1L68 A19 15c on 50c ol & blk (R) .90 .90
 a. "1008" 4.50
 b. "8908" 4.50
1L69 A19 35c on 50c ol & blk 1.40 1.40
1L70 A19 1p yel brn & blk 1.90 1.90
 a. "CORROE" 12.00 12.00
1L71 A19 2p pearl gray & blk 2.25 2.25
 a. "CORROE" 15.00 15.00
 *Nos. 1L63-1L71 (9)* 8.70 8.55

### Overprinted Horizontally in Black or Green

1L72 A19 5c yel & blk 9.00 7.50
1L72A A19 2p pearl gray & blk (G) *300.00*

On Nos. 1L72-1L72A, space between "B" and "Dpto. Zelaya" is 13mm.

Nos. 237-248 Overprinted in Black

### Imprint: "American Bank Note Co. NY"

**1909** ***Perf. 12***

1L73 A18 1c yel grn .25 .25
1L74 A18 2c vermilion .25 .25
 a. Inverted overprint
1L75 A18 3c red org .25 .25
1L76 A18 4c violet .25 .25
1L77 A18 5c dp bl .30 .25
 a. Inverted overprint 9.00 9.00
 b. "B" inverted 7.50 7.50
 c. Double overprint 12.00 12.00
1L78 A18 6c gray brn 4.50 3.00
1L79 A18 10c lake .30 .30
 a. "B" inverted 9.00 9.00
1L80 A18 15c black .45 .40
 a. "B" inverted 11.00 11.00
 b. Inverted overprint 12.00 12.00
 c. Double overprint 14.00 14.00
1L81 A18 20c brn ol .50 .50
 a. "B" inverted 19.00 19.00
1L82 A18 50c dp grn 1.50 1.50
1L83 A18 1p yellow 5.00 2.25
1L84 A18 2p car rose 6.00 3.00
 a. Double overprint 27.50 27.50
 *Nos. 1L73-1L84 (12)* 19.55 12.20

One stamp in each sheet has the "o" of "Dpto." sideways.

Overprinted in Black

**1910**

1L85 A18 3c red org .40 .40
1L86 A18 4c violet .40 .40
 a. Inverted overprint 14.00 14.00
1L87 A18 15c black 4.50 2.25
1L88 A18 20c brn ol .25 .30
1L89 A18 50c dp grn .30 .40
1L90 A18 1p yellow .30 .45
 a. Inverted overprint 7.50
1L91 A18 2p car rose .40 .75
 *Nos. 1L85-1L91 (7)* 6.55 4.95

No. 243 Overprinted and Surcharged in Black, Green & Carmine

**1910**

1L92 A18 5c on 10c lake 3.75 3.00

There are three types of the letter "B." It is stated that this stamp was used exclusively for postal purposes and not for telegrams.

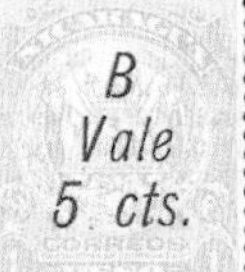


No. 247 Surcharged in Black

**1911**

1L93 A18 5c on 1p yellow .75 .75
 a. Double surcharge 14.00
1L94 A18 10c on 1p yellow 1.50 1.50
1L95 A18 15c on 1p yellow .75 .75
 a. Inverted surcharge 9.00
 b. Double surcharge 9.00
 c. Double surcharge, one invtd. 9.00
 *Nos. 1L93-1L95 (3)* 3.00 3.00

Revenue Stamps Surcharged in Black

***Perf. 14 to 15***

1L96 A19 5c on 25c lilac .75 1.10
 a. Without period 1.50 1.50
 b. Inverted surcharge 9.00 9.00
1L97 A19 10c on 1p yel brn 1.10 .75
 a. Without period 1.90 1.90
 b. "01" for "10" 9.00 7.50
 c. Inverted surcharge 13.00 13.00

Surcharged in Black

1L98 A19 5c on 1p yel brn 1.50 1.50
 a. Without period 2.25
 b. "50" for "05" 14.00 14.00
 c. Inverted surcharge 15.00 15.00
1L99 A19 5c on 10p pink 1.50 1.50
 a. Without period 2.25 2.25
 b. "50" for "05" 11.00 11.00
1L100 A19 10c on 1p yel brn 82.50 82.50
 a. Without period 95.00 95.00
1L101 A19 10c on 25p grn .75 .75
 a. Without period 2.25 2.25
 b. "1" for "10" 7.50
1L102 A19 10c on 50p ver 11.00 11.00
 a. Without period 16.00
 b. "1" for "10" 22.50
 *Nos. 1L98-1L102 (5)* 97.25 97.25

### With Additional Overprint "1904"

1L103 A19 5c on 10p pink 14.00 14.00
 a. Without period 24.00 24.00
 b. "50" for "05" 110.00 110.00
1L104 A19 10c on 2p gray .75 .75
 a. Without period 1.90
 b. "1" for "10" 7.50
1L105 A19 10c on 25p grn 92.50
 a. Without period 100.00
1L106 A19 10c on 50p ver 7.50 7.50
 a. Without period 14.00
 b. "1" for "10" 18.00
 c. Inverted surcharge

The surcharges on Nos. 1L96 to 1L106 are in settings of twenty-five. One stamp in each setting has a large square period after "cts" and another has a thick upright "c" in that word. There are two types of "1904".

No. 293C Overprinted

**1911**

1L107 A21 5c on 5c on 2 bl (R) 32.50
 a. "5" omitted 37.50
 b. Red overprint inverted 40.00
 c. As "a" and "b" 47.50

### Same Overprint On Nos. 290, 291, 292 and 289D with Lines of Surcharge spaced 2½mm apart Reading Down

1L107D A21 2c on 10c on 1 red *250.00*
 e. Overprint reading up *250.00*
1L107F A21 5c on 10c on 1 red *150.00*
1L107G A21 10c on 10c on 1 red (#292) *200.00*
1L108 A21 10c on 10c on 1 red (#289D) *200.00*

Locomotive — Z2

**1912** **Engr.** ***Perf. 14***

1L109 Z2 1c yel grn 1.50 .50
1L110 Z2 2c vermilion 1.25 .25
1L111 Z2 3c org brn 1.50 .45
1L112 Z2 4c carmine 1.50 .30
1L113 Z2 5c dp bl 1.50 .45
1L114 Z2 6c red brn 9.00 3.50
1L115 Z2 10c slate 1.50 .30
1L116 Z2 15c dl lil 1.50 .60
1L117 Z2 20c bl vio 1.50 .60
1L118 Z2 25c grn & blk 2.25 .80
1L119 Z2 35c brn & blk 3.00 1.25
1L120 Z2 50c ol grn 3.00 1.25
1L121 Z2 1p orange 4.00 1.75

**1L122** Z2 2p org brn 7.50 3.25
**1L123** Z2 5p dk bl grn 18.00 7.50
*Nos. 1L109-1L123 (15)* 58.50 22.75

The stamps of this issue were for use in all places on the Atlantic Coast of Nicaragua where the currency was on a silver basis.

For surcharges see Nos. 325-337.

## OFFICIAL STAMPS

Regular Issue of 1909 Overprinted in Black

**1909** **Unwmk.** ***Perf. 12***
**1LO1** A18 20c brn ol 15.00 12.00
*a.* Double overprint 30.00

No. O216 Overprinted in Black

**1LO2** A18 15c black 15.00 10.00

**Same Overprint on Official Stamp of 1911**

**1911**
**1LO3** A18 5c on 3c red org 22.50 17.50

## CABO GRACIAS A DIOS

A cape and seaport town in the extreme northeast of Nicaragua. The name was coined by Spanish explorers who had great difficulty finding a landing place along the Nicaraguan coast and when eventually locating this harbor expressed their relief by designating the point "Cape Thanks to God." Special postage stamps came into use for the same reasons as the Zelaya issues. See Zelaya.

Dangerous counterfeits exist of most of the Cabo Gracias a Dios overprints. Special caution should be taken with double and inverted handstamps of Nos. 2L1-2L25, as most are counterfeits. Expert opinion is required.

Regular Issues of 1900-04 Handstamped in Violet

**On Engraved Stamps of 1900**

**1904-05** **Unwmk.** ***Perf. 12, 14***
**2L1** A14 1c plum 2.25 1.10
**2L2** A14 2c vermilion 4.50 1.25
**2L3** A14 3c green 6.00 4.50
**2L4** A14 4c ol grn 9.75 9.75
**2L5** A14 15c ultra 35.00 22.50
**2L6** A14 20c brown 3.00 2.25
*Nos. 2L1-2L6 (6)* 60.50 41.35

**On Lithographed Stamps of 1902**

**2L7** A14 5c blue 24.00 24.00
**2L8** A14 10c violet 24.00 24.00

**On Surcharged Stamps of 1904**

**2L9** A16 5c on 10c vio 22.50 22.50
**2L10** A16 15c on 10c vio

**On Postage Due Stamps**
**Violet Handstamp**

**2L11** D3 20c org brn (#141) 5.00 1.25
**2L12** D3 20c org brn (#156) 3.50 1.25
**2L13** D3 30c dk grn (#157) 14.00 14.00
**2L14** D3 50c lake (#158) 3.75 .75
*Nos. 2L11-2L14 (4)* 26.25 17.25

**Black Handstamp**

**2L15** D3 30c dk grn (#157) 24.00 24.00

Stamps of 1900-05 Handstamped in Violet

**On Engraved Stamps of 1900**

**2L16** A14 1c plum 2.75 2.25
**2L17** A14 2c vermilion 27.50 24.00
**2L18** A14 3c green 37.50 27.50
**2L19** A14 4c ol grn 40.00 37.50
**2L20** A14 15c ultra 45.00 45.00
*Nos. 2L16-2L20 (5)* 152.75 136.25

**On Lithographed Stamps of 1902**

**2L22** A14 5c dk bl 95.00 50.00
**2L23** A14 10c violet 27.50 24.00

**On Surcharged Stamp of 1904**

**2L24** A14 5c on 10c vio

**On Postage Due Stamp**

**2L25** D3 20c org brn (#141)

The editors have no evidence that stamps with this handstamp were issued. Examples were sent to the UPU and covers are known.

Stamps of 1900-08 Handstamped in Violet

**1905** **On Stamps of 1905**
**2L26** A18 1c green 1.10 1.10
**2L27** A18 2c car rose 1.50 1.50
**2L28** A18 3c violet 1.50 1.50
**2L29** A18 4c org red 3.75 3.75
**2L30** A18 5c blue 1.50 1.10
**2L31** A18 6c slate 3.75 3.75
**2L32** A18 10c yel brn 3.00 1.90
**2L33** A18 15c brn ol 4.50 4.50
**2L34** A18 1p black 20.00 20.00
**2L35** A18 2p dk grn 35.00 35.00
*Nos. 2L26-2L35 (10)* 75.60 74.10

**Magenta Handstamp**

*2L26a* A18 1c 3.75 3.00
*2L27a* A18 2c 3.00 2.75
*2L28a* A18 3c 3.75 3.00
*2L30a* A18 5c 7.50 6.00
*2L33a* A18 15c 13.50 11.00
*Nos. 2L26a-2L33a (5)* 31.50 25.75

**On Stamps of 1900-04**

**2L36** A14 5c on 10c vio 14.00 14.00
**2L37** A14 10c violet
**2L38** A14 20c brown 12.00 12.00
**2L39** A14 20c on 5p blk 95.00

**On Postage Due Stamps Overprinted "Correos"**

**2L40** D3 20c org brn (#141) 9.00 9.00
**2L41** D3 20c org brn (#156) 5.00 4.50

**On Surcharged Stamps of 1906-08**

**2L42** A18 10c on 3c vio *250.00*
**2L43** A18 20c on 5c blue 9.00 9.00
**2L44** A18 50c on 6c slate 24.00 24.00

**On Stamps of 1907**
***Perf. 14 to 15***

**2L44A** A18 2c rose *250.00*
**2L45** A18 10c yel brn *100.00 75.00*
**2L46** A18 15c brn ol *90.00 75.00*

**On Provisional Stamp of 1908 in Magenta**

**2L47** A19 5c yel & blk 7.50 7.50

Stamps with the above large handstamp in black instead of violet, are bogus. There are also excellent counterfeits in violet.

The foregoing overprints being handstamped are found in various positions, especially the last type.

Stamps of 1907 Type A18, Overprinted in Black or Violet

**1907**
**2L48** A18 1c green .35 .30
*a.* Vert. pair, imperf. btwn. —
**2L49** A18 2c rose .35 .30
**2L50** A18 3c violet .35 .30
*a.* Vert. pair, imperf. btwn. *350.00*
**2L51** A18 4c brn org .50 .40
**2L52** A18 5c blue .60 .50
**2L53** A18 10c yel brn .50 .40
**2L54** A18 15c brn ol .85 .75
**2L55** A18 20c lake .85 .75
**2L56** A18 50c orange 2.25 1.50
**2L57** A18 1p blk (V) 2.50 1.90
**2L58** A18 2p dk grn 3.50 2.25
**2L59** A18 5p violet 5.00 3.75
*Nos. 2L48-2L59 (12)* 17.60 13.10

Nos. 237-248 Overprinted in Black

**Imprint: American Bank Note Co.**

**1909** ***Perf. 12***
**2L60** A18 1c yel grn .35 .40
**2L61** A18 2c vermilion .35 .40
**2L62** A18 3c red org .35 .40
**2L63** A18 4c violet .35 .40
**2L64** A18 5c dp bl .35 .60
**2L65** A18 6c gray brn 6.00 6.00
**2L66** A18 10c lake .60 .75
**2L67** A18 15c black .90 .90
**2L68** A18 20c brn ol 1.00 *4.00*
**2L69** A18 50c dp grn 2.50 2.50
**2L70** A18 1p yellow 4.00 4.00
**2L71** A18 2p car rose 5.75 5.75
*Nos. 2L60-2L71 (12)* 22.50 26.10

No. 199 Overprinted Vertically

**2L72** A18 50c on 6c slate (R) 7.50 7.50

## CABO GRACIAS A DIOS OFFICIAL STAMPS

Official Stamps of 1907 Overprinted in Red or Violet

**1907**
**2LO1** A18 10c on 1c green *60.00*
**2LO2** A18 15c on 1c green *75.00*
**2LO3** A18 20c on 1c green *100.00*
**2LO4** A18 50c on 1c green *125.00*

# NIGER

ˈnī-jər

LOCATION — Northern Africa, directly north of Nigeria
GOVT. — Republic
AREA — 458,075 sq. mi.
POP. — 9,962,242 (1999 est.)
CAPITAL — Niamey

The colony, formed in 1922, was originally a military territory. The Republic of the Niger was proclaimed December 18, 1958. In the period between issues of the colony and the republic, stamps of French West Africa were used. Full independence from France was proclaimed August 3, 1960.

100 Centimes = 1 Franc

**Catalogue values for unused stamps in this country are for Never Hinged items, beginning with Scott 91 in the regular postage section, Scott B14 in the semi-postal section, Scott C14 in the airpost section, Scott J22 in the postage due section, and Scott O1 in the official section.**

**Watermark**

Wmk. 385

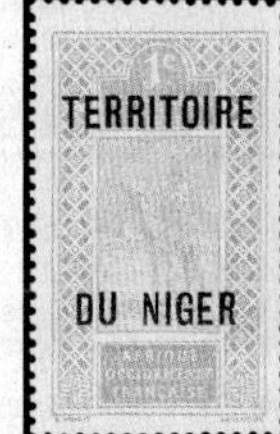


Stamps of Upper Senegal and Niger Type of 1914, Overprinted

In the overprint, normal spacing between the words "DU" and "NIGER" is 2½mm. In one position (72) of all sheets in the first printing, the space between the two words is 3mm.

**1921-26** **Unwmk.** ***Perf. 13½x14***
**1** A4 1c brn vio & vio .25 *.40*
**2** A4 2c dk gray & dl vio .25 *.40*
**3** A4 4c black & blue .35 *.50*
**4** A4 5c ol brn & dk brn .30 *.50*
**5** A4 10c yel grn & bl grn 1.60 *2.00*
**6** A4 10c mag, *bluish* ('26) .95 *1.20*
**7** A4 15c red brn & org .40 *.55*
**8** A4 20c brn vio & blk .35 *.50*
**9** A4 25c blk & bl grn .80 *.80*
**10** A4 30c red org & rose 2.75 *3.50*
**11** A4 30c bl grn & red org ('26) .80 *.80*
**12** A4 35c rose & violet .95 *1.20*
**13** A4 40c gray & rose .95 *1.20*
**14** A4 45c blue & ol brn 1.40 *1.40*
**15** A4 50c ultra & bl .80 *1.20*
**16** A4 50c dk gray & bl vio ('25) 1.60 *1.60*
**17** A4 60c org red ('26) 1.40 *2.00*
**18** A4 75c yel & ol brn 1.40 *1.60*
**19** A4 1fr dk brn & dl vio 1.60 *2.00*
**20** A4 2fr green & blue 1.60 *2.00*
**21** A4 5fr violet & blk 2.75 *4.00*
*Nos. 1-21 (21)* 23.25 *29.35*

Types of 1921 Surcharged in Black or Red

**1922-26**

| No. | Type | Description | Unused | Used |
|---|---|---|---|---|
| 22 | A4 | 25c on 15c red brn & org ('25) | .95 | .80 |
| a. | | Multiple surcharge | 260.00 | |
| b. | | "25c" inverted | 140.00 | |
| 23 | A4 | 25c on 2fr grn & bl (R) ('24) | .90 | .80 |
| 24 | A4 | 25c on 5fr vio & blk (R) ('24) | .95 | .80 |
| a. | | Double surcharge | 225.00 | |
| 25 | A4 | 60c on 75c vio, *pnksh* | .90 | *1.20* |
| 26 | A4 | 65c on 45c bl & ol brn ('25) | 2.75 | *3.50* |
| 27 | A4 | 85c on 75c yel & ol brn ('25) | 2.75 | *3.50* |
| 28 | A4 | 1.25fr on 1fr dp bl & lt bl (R) ('26) | 1.10 | *1.20* |
| a. | | Surcharge omitted | 260.00 | |
| b. | | As "a," in pair with unsurcharged stamp | 1,700. | |
| | | *Nos. 22-28 (7)* | 10.30 | 11.80 |

Nos. 22-24 are surcharged "25c," No. 28, "1f25." Nos. 25-27 are surcharged like illustration.

Drawing Water from Well — A2

Zinder Fortress — A4

Boat on Niger River — A3

***Perf. 13x14, 13½x14, 14x13, 14x13½***

**1926-40** **Typo.**

| No. | Type | Description | Unused | Used |
|---|---|---|---|---|
| 29 | A2 | 1c lil rose & ol | .25 | *.40* |
| 30 | A2 | 2c dk gray & dl red | .25 | *.40* |
| 31 | A2 | 3c red vio & ol gray ('40) | .25 | *.40* |
| 32 | A2 | 4c amber & gray | .25 | *.40* |
| 33 | A2 | 5c ver & yel grn | .25 | *.40* |
| 34 | A2 | 10c dp bl & Prus bl | .25 | *.40* |
| 35 | A2 | 15c gray grn & yel grn | .55 | *.80* |
| 36 | A2 | 15c gray lil & lt red ('28) | .40 | .40 |
| 37 | A3 | 20c Prus grn & ol brn | .40 | *.55* |
| 38 | A3 | 25c black & dl red | .40 | .50 |
| 39 | A3 | 30c bl grn & yel grn | .80 | *1.20* |
| 40 | A3 | 30c yel & red vio ('40) | .30 | *.50* |
| 41 | A3 | 35c brn org & turq bl, *bluish* | .80 | *1.20* |
| 42 | A3 | 35c bl grn & dl grn ('38) | 1.20 | *1.60* |
| 43 | A3 | 40c red brn & slate | .40 | *.50* |
| 44 | A3 | 45c yel & red vio | 1.60 | *1.90* |
| 45 | A3 | 45c bl grn & dl grn ('40) | .30 | *.50* |
| 46 | A3 | 50c scar & grn, *grnsh* | .40 | .40 |
| 47 | A3 | 55c dk car & brn ('38) | 2.00 | 2.00 |
| 48 | A3 | 60c dk car & brn ('40) | .55 | *.70* |
| 49 | A3 | 65c ol grn & rose | .40 | *.55* |
| 50 | A3 | 70c ol grn & rose ('40) | 2.00 | *2.50* |
| 51 | A3 | 75c grn & vio, *pink* | 2.00 | *2.25* |
| a. | | Center and value double | 225.00 | |
| 52 | A3 | 80c cl & ol grn ('38) | 1.60 | *2.00* |
| 53 | A3 | 90c brn red & ver | 1.60 | *1.90* |
| 54 | A3 | 90c brt rose & yel grn ('39) | 2.00 | *2.40* |
| 55 | A4 | 1fr rose & yel grn | 8.00 | 8.75 |
| 56 | A4 | 1fr dk red & red org ('38) | 2.00 | *2.40* |
| 57 | A4 | 1fr grn & red ('40) | .80 | .80 |
| 58 | A4 | 1.10fr ol brn & grn | 4.00 | *6.50* |
| 59 | A4 | 1.25fr grn & red ('33) | 2.40 | 2.40 |
| 60 | A4 | 1.25fr dk red & red org ('39) | .80 | *1.20* |
| 61 | A4 | 1.40fr red vio & dk brn ('40) | .80 | *1.50* |
| 62 | A4 | 1.50fr dp bl & pale bl | .55 | *.70* |
| 63 | A4 | 1.60fr ol brn & grn ('40) | 1.75 | *2.00* |
| 64 | A4 | 1.75fr red vio & dk brn ('33) | 1.60 | 2.40 |
| 65 | A4 | 1.75fr dk bl & vio bl ('38) | 1.25 | *1.60* |
| 66 | A4 | 2fr red org & ol brn | .30 | *.50* |
| 67 | A4 | 2.25fr dk bl & vio bl ('39) | 1.20 | *1.60* |
| 68 | A4 | 2.50fr blk brn ('40) | 1.20 | *1.60* |
| 69 | A4 | 3fr dl vio & blk ('27) | .55 | *.80* |
| 70 | A4 | 5fr vio brn & blk, *pink* | .80 | *1.20* |
| 71 | A4 | 10fr chlky bl & mag | 1.60 | *2.00* |
| 72 | A4 | 20fr yel grn & red org | 1.60 | *2.00* |
| | | *Nos. 29-72 (44)* | 52.40 | *66.70* |

For surcharges see Nos. B7-B10.

Common Design Types pictured following the introduction.

### Colonial Exposition Issue

Common Design Types

**1931** **Typo.** ***Perf. 12½***

**Name of Country in Black**

| No. | Type | Description | Unused | Used |
|---|---|---|---|---|
| 73 | CD70 | 40c deep green | 5.00 | 5.00 |
| 74 | CD71 | 50c violet | 5.00 | 5.00 |
| 75 | CD72 | 90c red orange | 5.75 | 5.75 |
| 76 | CD73 | 1.50fr dull blue | 5.75 | 5.75 |
| | | *Nos. 73-76 (4)* | 21.50 | 21.50 |

### Paris International Exposition Issue

Common Design Types

**1937** ***Perf. 13***

| No. | Type | Description | Unused | Used |
|---|---|---|---|---|
| 77 | CD74 | 20c deep violet | 2.00 | 2.00 |
| 78 | CD75 | 30c dark green | 2.00 | 2.00 |
| 79 | CD76 | 40c carmine rose | 2.00 | 2.00 |
| 80 | CD77 | 50c dark brown | 1.60 | 1.60 |
| 81 | CD78 | 90c red | 1.60 | 1.60 |
| 82 | CD79 | 1.50fr ultra | 2.00 | 2.00 |
| | | *Nos. 77-82 (6)* | 11.20 | 11.20 |

### Colonial Arts Exhibition Issue

Souvenir Sheet

Common Design Type

**1937** ***Imperf.***

| No. | Type | Description | Unused | Used |
|---|---|---|---|---|
| 83 | CD74 | 3fr magenta | 10.00 | *14.00* |

### Caillie Issue

Common Design Type

**1939** ***Perf. 12½x12***

| No. | Type | Description | Unused | Used |
|---|---|---|---|---|
| 84 | CD81 | 90c org brn & org | .35 | .35 |
| 85 | CD81 | 2fr brt violet | .35 | 1.00 |
| 86 | CD81 | 2.25fr ultra & dk bl | .35 | 1.00 |
| | | *Nos. 84-86 (3)* | 1.05 | 2.35 |

### New York World's Fair Issue

Common Design Type

**1939, May 10**

| No. | Type | Description | Unused | Used |
|---|---|---|---|---|
| 87 | CD82 | 1.25fr car lake | .70 | 1.40 |
| 88 | CD82 | 2.25fr ultra | .70 | 1.40 |

Zinder Fortress and Marshal Pétain — A5

**1941 Unwmk. Engr.** ***Perf. 12x12½***

| No. | Type | Description | Unused | Used |
|---|---|---|---|---|
| 89 | A5 | 1fr green | .35 | |
| 90 | A5 | 2.50fr dark blue | .35 | |
| | | Set, never hinged | 1.40 | |

Nos. 89-90 were issued by the Vichy government in France, but were not placed on sale in Niger.

For surcharges, see Nos. B13A-B13B.

**See French West Africa No. 68 for additional stamp inscribed "Niger" and "Afrique Occidentale Francaise."**

**Catalogue values for unused stamps in this section, from this point to the end of the section, are for Never Hinged items.**

### Republic of the Niger

Giraffes — A6

1fr, 2fr, Crested cranes. 5fr, 7fr, Saddle-billed storks. 15fr, 20fr, Barbary sheep. 25fr, 30fr, Giraffes. 50fr, 60fr, Ostriches. 85fr, 100fr, Lion.

**1959-60 Unwmk. Engr.** ***Perf. 13***

| No. | Type | Description | Unused | Used |
|---|---|---|---|---|
| 91 | A6 | 1fr multi | .35 | .25 |
| 92 | A6 | 2fr multi | .35 | .25 |
| 93 | A6 | 5fr blk, car & ol | .50 | .25 |
| 94 | A6 | 7fr grn, blk & red | .60 | .25 |
| 95 | A6 | 15fr grnsh bl & dk brn | .25 | .25 |
| 96 | A6 | 20fr vio, blk & ind | .25 | .25 |
| 97 | A6 | 25fr multi | .35 | .25 |
| 98 | A6 | 30fr multi | .45 | .30 |
| 99 | A6 | 50fr ind & org brn | 4.75 | .70 |
| 100 | A6 | 60fr dk brn & emer | 6.50 | 1.00 |
| 101 | A6 | 85fr org brn & bis | 2.25 | .80 |
| 102 | A6 | 100fr bis & yel grn | 3.00 | 1.25 |
| | | *Nos. 91-102 (12)* | 19.60 | 5.80 |

Issue years: #97, 1959; others, 1960.

For surcharge see No. 103.

Imperforates

Most stamps of the republic exist imperforate in issued and trial colors, and also in small presentation sheets in issued color.

No. 102 Surcharged

**1960**

| No. | Type | Description | Unused | Used |
|---|---|---|---|---|
| 103 | A6 | 200fr on 100fr | 14.00 | 14.00 |

Niger's independence.

### C.C.T.A. Issue

Common Design Type

**1960 Engr.** ***Perf. 13***

| No. | Type | Description | Unused | Used |
|---|---|---|---|---|
| 104 | CD106 | 25fr buff & red brn | .85 | .45 |

Emblem of the Entente — A6a

**1960, May 29 Photo.** ***Perf. 13x13½***

| No. | Type | Description | Unused | Used |
|---|---|---|---|---|
| 105 | A6a | 25fr multi | .85 | .45 |

1st anniversary of the Entente (Dahomey, Ivory Coast, Niger and Upper Volta).

Pres. Diori Hamani — A7

**1960, Dec. 18 Engr.** ***Perf. 13***

| No. | Type | Description | Unused | Used |
|---|---|---|---|---|
| 106 | A7 | 25fr ol bis & blk | .60 | .30 |

2nd anniversary of the proclamation of the Republic of the Niger.

Manatee A8

**1962, Jan. 29 Unwmk.** ***Perf. 13***

| No. | Type | Description | Unused | Used |
|---|---|---|---|---|
| 107 | A8 | 50c grn & dk sl grn | .40 | .25 |
| 108 | A8 | 10fr red brn & dk grn | .65 | .25 |

### Abidjan Games Issue

Common Design Type

25fr, Basketball & Soccer. 85fr, Track, horiz.

**1962, May 26 Photo.** ***Perf. 12x12½***

| No. | Type | Description | Unused | Used |
|---|---|---|---|---|
| 109 | CD109 | 15fr multi | .40 | .25 |
| 110 | CD109 | 25fr multi | .60 | .25 |
| 111 | CD109 | 85fr multi | 1.60 | .60 |
| | | *Nos. 109-111 (3)* | 2.60 | 1.10 |

### African-Malgache Union Issue

Common Design Type

**1962, Sept. 8** ***Perf. 12½x12***

| No. | Type | Description | Unused | Used |
|---|---|---|---|---|
| 112 | CD110 | 30fr multi | .80 | .40 |

Pres. Diori Hamani and Map of Niger in Africa A10

**1962, Dec. 18 Photo.** ***Perf. 12½x12***

| No. | Type | Description | Unused | Used |
|---|---|---|---|---|
| 113 | A10 | 25fr multi | .60 | .25 |

Woman Runner — A11

15fr, Swimming, horiz. 45fr, Volleyball.

**Unwmk.**

**1963, Apr. 11 Engr.** ***Perf. 13***

| No. | Type | Description | Unused | Used |
|---|---|---|---|---|
| 114 | A11 | 15fr brt bl & dk brn | .25 | .25 |
| 115 | A11 | 25fr dk brn & red | .60 | .25 |
| 116 | A11 | 45fr grn & blk | 1.10 | .40 |
| | | *Nos. 114-116 (3)* | 1.95 | .90 |

Friendship Games, Dakar, Apr. 11-21.

Woodworker — A12

10fr, Tanners, horiz. 25fr, Goldsmith. 30fr, Mat makers, horiz. 85fr, Decoy maker.

*Perf. 12x12½, 12½x12*

**1963, Aug. 30 Photo.**

**117** A12 5fr brn & multi .25 .25
**118** A12 10fr dk grn & multi .35 .25
**119** A12 25fr blk & multi .60 .25
**120** A12 30fr vio & multi .90 .30
**121** A12 85fr dk bl & multi 2.00 .80
*Nos. 117-121,C26 (6)* 6.85 3.35

Berberi (Nuba) Woman's Costume — A13

Costume Museum, Niamey — A14

Costumes: 20fr, Hausa woman. 25fr, Tuareg woman. 30fr, Tuareg man. 60fr, Djerma woman.

*Perf. 12x12½, 12½x12*

**1963, Oct. 15 Photo.**

**122** A13 15fr multi .35 .25
**123** A13 20fr blk & bl .50 .25
**124** A13 25fr multi .70 .25
**125** A13 30fr multi .75 .25
**126** A13 60fr multi 1.75 .60
**127** A14 85fr multi 2.00 .70
*Nos. 122-127 (6)* 6.05 2.30

Man, Globe and Scales — A15

**Unwmk.**

**1963, Dec. 10 Engr. *Perf. 13***

**128** A15 25fr lt ol grn, ultra & brn org .65 .30

15th anniversary of the Universal Declaration of Human Rights.

Parkinsonia Aculeata — A16

Plumeria Rubra — A16a

Flowers: 10fr, Russelia equisetiformis. 15fr, Red sage (lantana). 20fr, Argyreia nervosa. 25fr, Luffa cylindrica. 30fr, Hibiscus rosa sinensis. 50fr, Catharanthus roseus. 60fr, Caesalpinia pulcherrima.

**1964-65 Photo. *Perf. 13½x13***

**129** A16 5fr dk red, grn & yel .75 .30
**130** A16 10fr multi .60 .30
**131** A16 15fr multi 1.00 .40
**132** A16 20fr multi 1.00 .40
**133** A16 25fr multi 1.00 .40
**134** A16 30fr multi 1.25 .55
**135** A16a 45fr multi ('65) 2.25 .85
**136** A16a 50fr dk red, brt pink & grn ('65) 2.25 .85
**137** A16a 60fr multi ('65) 4.00 1.10
*Nos. 129-137 (9)* 14.10 5.15

On No. 135 "PLUMERIA" is spelled incorrectly.

Solar Flares and IQSY Emblem — A17

**1964, May 12 Engr. *Perf. 13***

**138** A17 30fr dp org, vio & blk .60 .45

International Quiet Sun Year, 1964-65.

Mobile Medical Unit — A18

30fr, Mobile children's clinic. 50fr, Mobile women's clinic. 60fr, Outdoor medical laboratory.

**1964, May 26**

**139** A18 25fr bl, org & ol .40 .25
**140** A18 30fr multi .50 .25
**141** A18 50fr vio, org & bl .80 .30
**142** A18 60fr grnsh bl, org & dk brn .90 .40
*Nos. 139-142 (4)* 2.60 1.20

Nigerian mobile health education organization, OMNES (Organisation Médicale Mobile Nigérienne d'Education Sanitaire).

**Cooperation Issue**

Common Design Type

**1964, Nov. 7 Unwmk. *Perf. 13***

**143** CD119 50fr vio, dk brn & org .80 .40

Tuareg Tent of Azawak A19

Designs: 20fr, Songhai house. 25fr, Wogo and Kourtey tents. 30fr, Djerma house. 60fr, Huts of Sorkawa fishermen. 85fr, Hausa town house.

**1964-65 Engr.**

**144** A19 15fr ultra, dl grn & red brn .25 .25
**145** A19 20fr multi .30 .25
**146** A19 25fr Prus bl, dk brn & org brn .40 .25
**147** A19 30fr multi ('65) .50 .30
**148** A19 60fr red, grn & bis ('65) 1.00 .30
**149** A19 85fr multi ('65) 1.40 .50
*Nos. 144-149 (6)* 3.85 1.85

Leprosy Examination — A20

**1964, Dec. 15 Photo. *Perf. 13x12½***

**150** A20 50fr multi .70 .45

Issued to publicize the fight against leprosy.

Abraham Lincoln — A21

**1965, Apr. 3 *Perf. 13x12½***

**151** A21 50fr vio bl, blk, & ocher .70 .45

Centenary of death of Abraham Lincoln.

Teaching with Radio and Pictures — A22

Designs: 25fr, Woman studying arithmetic: "A better life through knowledge." 30fr, Adult education class. 50fr, Map of Niger and 5 tribesmen, "Literacy for adults."

**1965, Apr. 16 Engr. *Perf. 13***

**152** A22 20fr dk bl, dk brn & ocher .40 .25
**153** A22 25fr sl grn, brn & ol brn .50 .25
**154** A22 30fr red, sl grn & vio brn .60 .25
**155** A22 50fr dp bl, brn & vio brn .85 .35
*Nos. 152-155 (4)* 2.35 1.10

Issued to promote adult education and "a better life through knowledge."

Ader Portable Telephone — A23

Designs: 30fr, Wheatstone telegraph interrupter. 50fr, Early telewriter.

**1965, May 17 Unwmk. *Perf. 13***

**156** A23 25fr red brn, dk grn & ind .60 .25
**157** A23 30fr lil, slate grn & red .70 .30
**158** A23 50fr red, slate grn & pur 1.00 .40
*Nos. 156-158 (3)* 2.30 .95

International Telecommunication Union, cent.

Runner — A24

Designs: 10fr, Hurdler, horiz. 20fr, Pole vaulter, horiz. 30fr, Long jumper.

**1965, July 1 Engr. *Perf. 13***

**159** A24 10fr brn, ocher & blk .25 .25
**160** A24 15fr gray, brn & red .45 .25
**161** A24 20fr dk grn, brn & vio bl .60 .25
**162** A24 30fr maroon, brn & grn .70 .25
*Nos. 159-162 (4)* 2.00 1.00

African Games, Brazzaville, July 18-25.

Radio Interview and Club Emblem A25

45fr, Recording folk music, vert. 50fr, Group listening to broadcast, vert. 60fr, Public debate.

**1965, Oct. 1 Engr. *Perf. 13***

**163** A25 30fr brt vio, emer & red brn .40 .25
**164** A25 45fr blk, car & buff .55 .25
**165** A25 50fr dk car, bl & lt brn .60 .30
**166** A25 60fr bis, ultra & brn .75 .35
*Nos. 163-166 (4)* 2.30 1.15

Issued to promote radio clubs.

Water Cycle — A26

**1966, Feb. 28 Engr. *Perf. 13***

**167** A26 50fr vio, ocher & bl .80 .35

Hydrological Decade, 1965-74.

Carvings, Mask and Headdresses — A27

50fr, Carvings and wall decorations. 60fr, Carvings and arch. 100fr, Architecture and handicraft.

**1966, Apr. 12**

**168** A27 30fr red brn, blk & brt grn .55 .35
**169** A27 50fr brt bl, ocher & pur .80 .35
**170** A27 60fr car lake, dl pur & yel brn .90 .50
**171** A27 100fr brt red, bl & blk 1.75 .90
*Nos. 168-171 (4)* 4.00 2.10

Intl. Negro Arts Festival, Dakar, Senegal, Apr. 1-24.

Soccer Player — A28

50fr, Goalkeeper, horiz. 60fr, Player kicking ball.

**1966, June 17 Engr. *Perf. 13***

**172** A28 30fr dk brn, brt bl & rose red .60 .30
**173** A28 50fr bl, choc & emer .75 .35
**174** A28 60fr bl, lil & brn .90 .45
*Nos. 172-174 (3)* 2.25 1.10

8th World Soccer Cup Championship, Wembley, England, July 11-30.

Color Guard — A29

20fr, Parachutist, horiz. 45fr, Tanks, horiz.

*Perf. 12½x13, 13x12½*

**1966, Aug. 23 Photo.**

**175** A29 20fr multi .40 .25
**176** A29 30fr multi .50 .25
**177** A29 45fr multi .65 .30
*Nos. 175-177 (3)* 1.55 .80

5th anniv. of the National Armed Forces.

Cow Receiving Injection A30

**1966, Sept. 26 Litho. *Perf. 12½x13***
178 A30 45fr org brn, bl & blk 1.25 .50

Campaign against cattle plague.

UNESCO Emblem — A31

**1966, Nov. 4 Litho. *Perf. 13x12½***
179 A31 50fr multi .70 .40

20th anniversary of UNESCO.

Cement Works Malbaza A32

Designs: 10fr, Furnace, vert. 20fr, Electric center. 50fr, Handling of raw material.

**1966, Dec. 17 Engr. *Perf. 13***
180 A32 10fr ind, brn & org .30 .25
181 A32 20fr dk ol grn & dl bl .45 .25
182 A32 30fr bl, gray & red brn .45 .25
183 A32 50fr ind, bl & brn .70 .30
*Nos. 180-183 (4)* 1.90 1.05

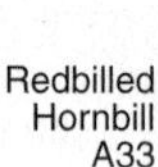

Redbilled Hornbill A33

Birds: 2fr, Pied kingfisher. 30fr, Barbary shrike. 45fr, 65fr, Little weaver and nest. 70fr, Chestnut-bellied sand grouse.

**1967-81 Engr. *Perf. 13***
184 A33 1fr red, sl grn & dk brn .70 .35
185 A33 2fr brn, brt grn & blk .70 .35
186 A33 30fr multi 3.50 .65
187 A33 45fr multi 1.75 .40
188 A33 65fr multi ('81) 3.25 .75
189 A33 70fr multi 3.25 .65
*Nos. 184-189 (6)* 13.15 3.15

Issued: 1fr, 2fr, 30fr, 2/8; 45fr, 70fr, 11/18; 65fr, 9/81. See #237.

Villard-de-Lans and Olympic Emblem — A34

Olympic Emblem and Mountains: 45fr, Autrans and ski jump. 60fr, Saint Nizier du Moucherotte and ski jump. 90fr, Chamrousse and course for downhill and slalom races.

**1967, Feb. 24**
190 A34 30fr grn, ultra & brn .50 .25
191 A34 45fr grn, ultra & brn .70 .40
192 A34 60fr grn, ultra & brn .95 .50
193 A34 90fr grn, ultra & brn 1.40 .75
*Nos. 190-193 (4)* 3.55 1.90

10th Winter Olympic Games, Grenoble, 1968.

Lions Emblem and Family — A35

**1967, Mar. 4**
194 A35 50fr dk grn, brn red & ultra 1.00 .40

Lions International, 50th anniversary.

ITY Emblem, Views, Globe and Plane A36

**1967, Apr. 28 Engr. *Perf. 13***
195 A36 45fr vio, brt grn & red lil .70 .35

International Tourist Year, 1967.

1967 Jamboree Emblem and Scouts — A37

Designs (Jamboree Emblem and): 45fr, Scouts gathering from all directions, horiz. 80fr, Campfire.

**1967, May 25 Engr. *Perf. 13***
196 A37 30fr mar, Prus bl & ol .50 .25
197 A37 45fr org, vio bl & brn ol .70 .30
198 A37 80fr multi 1.40 .75
*Nos. 196-198 (3)* 2.60 1.30

12th Boy Scout World Jamboree, Farragut State Park, Idaho, Aug. 1-9.

Red Cross Aides Carrying Sick Man — A38

Designs: 50fr, Nurse, mother and infant. 60fr, Physician examining woman.

**1967, July 13 Engr. *Perf. 13***
199 A38 45fr blk, grn & car .65 .30
200 A38 50fr grn, blk & car .90 .50
201 A38 60fr blk, grn & car 1.25 .55
*Nos. 199-201 (3)* 2.80 1.35

Issued for the Red Cross.

### Europafrica Issue

Map of Europe and Africa — A39

**1967, July 20 Photo. *Perf. 12½x12***
202 A39 50fr multi .75 .30

Women and UN Emblem — A40

**1967, Oct. 21 Engr. *Perf. 13***
203 A40 50fr brn, brt bl & yel .70 .40

UN Commission on Status of Women.

### Monetary Union Issue
Common Design Type

**1967, Nov. 4 Engr. *Perf. 13***
204 CD125 30fr grn & dk gray .45 .25

Human Rights Flame, Globe, People and Statue of Liberty A41

**1968, Feb. 19 Engr. *Perf. 13***
205 A41 50fr brn, indigo & brt bl .70 .40

International Human Rights Year.

Woman Dancing and WHO Emblem — A42

**1968, Apr. 8 Engr. *Perf. 13***
206 A42 50fr brt bl, blk & red brn .75 .40

20th anniv. of WHO.

Gray Hornbill A43

Birds: 10fr, Woodland kingfisher. 15fr, Senegalese coucal. 20fr, Rose-ringed parakeets. 25fr, Abyssinian roller. 50fr, Cattle egret.

### Dated "1968"

**1968, Nov. 15 Photo. *Perf. 12½x13***
207 A43 5fr dk grn & multi .60 .40
208 A43 10fr grn & multi .70 .40
209 A43 15fr bl vio & multi 1.25 .40
210 A43 20fr pink & multi 1.25 .50
211 A43 25fr ol & multi 2.00 .60
212 A43 50fr pur & multi 2.75 1.50
*Nos. 207-212 (6)* 8.55 3.80

See Nos. 233-236, 316.

ILO Emblem and "Labor Supporting the World" A44

**1969, Apr. 22 Engr. *Perf. 13***
213 A44 30fr yel grn & dk car .50 .25
214 A44 50fr dk car & yel grn .65 .40

50th anniv. of the World Labor Organization.

Red Crosses, Mother and Child — A45

Designs: 50fr, People, globe, red crosses, horiz. 70fr, Man with gift parcel and red crosses.

**1969, May 5 Engr. *Perf. 13***
215 A45 45fr bl, red & brn ol .80 .25
216 A45 50fr dk grn, red & gray .80 .35
217 A45 70fr ocher, red & dk brn 1.25 .60
*Nos. 215-217 (3)* 2.85 1.20

50th anniv. of the League of Red Cross Societies.

Mouth and Ear — A46

**1969, May 20 Photo. *Perf. 12½x12***
218 A46 100fr multi 1.25 .55

First (cultural) Conference of French-speaking Community at Niamey.

National Administration College — A47

**1969, July 8 Photo. *Perf. 12½x12***
219 A47 30fr emer & dp org .60 .30

### Development Bank Issue
Common Design Type

**1969, Sept. 10 Engr. *Perf. 13***
220 CD130 30fr pur, grn & ocher .60 .30

### ASECNA Issue
Common Design Type

**1969, Dec. 12 Engr. *Perf. 12***
221 CD132 100fr car rose 1.25 .70

Classical Pavilion, National Museum A48

Pavilions, National Museum: 45fr, Temporary exhibitions. 50fr, Audio-visual. 70fr, Nigerian musical instruments. 100fr, Craftsmanship.

**1970, Feb. 23 Engr. *Perf. 13***
222 A48 30fr brt bl, sl grn & brn .40 .25
223 A48 45fr emer, Prus bl & brn .55 .25
224 A48 50fr sl grn, vio bl & brn .60 .25
225 A48 70fr brn, sl grn & lt bl .90 .45
226 A48 100fr sl grn, vio bl & brn 1.40 .60
*Nos. 222-226 (5)* 3.85 1.80

Map of Africa and Vaccination Gun — A49

**1970, Mar. 31 Engr. *Perf. 13***
227 A49 50fr ultra, dp yel grn & mag .75 .40

Issued to commemorate the 100 millionth smallpox vaccination in West Africa.

Mexican Figurine and Soccer Player A50

Designs: 70fr, Figurine, globe and soccer ball. 90fr, Figurine and 2 soccer players.

**1970, Apr. 25**

**228** A50 40fr dk brn, red lil & emer .75 .35
**229** A50 70fr red brn, bl & plum 1.05 .50
**230** A50 90fr blk & red 1.40 .70
*Nos. 228-230 (3)* 3.20 1.55

9th World Soccer Championship for the Jules Rimet Cup, Mexico City, 5/29-6/21.

**UPU Headquarters Issue**
Common Design Type

**1970, May 20 Engr. *Perf. 13***

**231** CD133 30fr brn, dk gray & dk red .40 .25
**232** CD133 60fr vio bl, dk car & vio .80 .35

**Bird Types of 1967-68**

Birds: 5fr, Gray hornbill. 10fr, Woodland kingfisher. 15fr, Senegalese coucal. 20fr, Rose-ringed parakeets. 40fr, Red bishop.

**Dated "1970"**

**1970-71 Photo. *Perf. 13***

**233** A43 5fr multi ('71) .40 .25
**234** A43 10fr multi ('71) .40 .25
**235** A43 15fr multi ('71) .65 .25
**236** A43 20fr multi ('71) .90 .30

**Engr.**

**237** A33 40fr multi 3.00 1.00
*Nos. 233-237 (5)* 5.35 2.05

Issue dates: 40fr, Dec. 9; others Jan. 4.

World Map with Niamey in Center A51

**1971, Mar. 3 Photo. *Perf. 12½x12***

**238** A51 40fr brn & multi .75 .40

First anniversary of founding of the cooperative agency of French-speaking countries.
For overprint see No. 289.

Scout Emblem, Merit Badges, Mt. Fuji, Japanese Flag — A52

Designs: 40fr, Boy Scouts and flags, vert. 45fr, Map of Japan, Boy Scouts and compass rose, vert. 50fr, Tent and "Jamboree."

**1971, July 5 Engr. *Perf. 13***

**239** A52 35fr rose lil, dp car & org .50 .25
**240** A52 40fr dk pur, grn & mar .55 .25
**241** A52 45fr ultra, cop red & grn .70 .30
**242** A52 50fr multi .80 .30
*Nos. 239-242 (4)* 2.55 1.10

13th Boy Scout World Jamboree, Asagiri Plain, Japan, Aug. 2-10.

Maps of Europe and Africa — A53

**1971, July 29 Photo. *Perf. 13x12***

**243** A53 50fr lt bl & multi .80 .35

Renewal of the agreement on economic association between Europe and Africa, 2nd anniv.

Broad-tailed Whydah A54

**1971, Aug. 17 *Perf. 12½x12***

**244** A54 35fr yel grn & multi 3.25 1.25

See No. 443.

Garaya, Haoussa — A55

Stringed Instruments of Niger: 25fr, Gouroumi, Haoussa. 30fr, Molo, Djerma. 40fr, Godjie, Djerma-Sonrai. 45fr, Inzad, Tuareg. 50fr, Kountigui, Sonrai.

**1971-72 Engr. *Perf. 13***

**245** A55 25fr red, emer & brn .45 .25
**246** A55 30fr emer, pur & brn .50 .25
**247** A55 35fr brn red, emer & ind .55 .40
**248** A55 40fr emer, org & dk brn .65 .45
**249** A55 45fr Prus bl, grn & bis .85 .50
**250** A55 50fr blk, red & brn 1.10 .60
*Nos. 245-250 (6)* 4.10 2.45

Issued: 35, 40, 45fr, 10/13/71; others, 6/16/72.

UNICEF Emblem, Children of 4 Races — A56

**1971, Dec. 11 Photo. *Perf. 11***

**251** A56 50fr multi .65 .40

25th anniversary of UNICEF.

Star with Globe, Book, UNESCO Emblem A57

Design: 40fr, Boy reading, UNESCO emblem, sailing ship, plane, mosque.

**1972, Mar. 27 Engr. *Perf. 13***

**252** A57 35fr mag & emer .30 .25
**253** A57 40fr dk car & Prus bl .65 .25

International Book Year 1972.

Cattle Egret A58

**1972, July 31 Photo. *Perf. 12½x12***

**254** A58 50fr tan & multi 5.25 2.75

See No. 425.

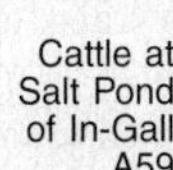

Cattle at Salt Pond of In-Gall A59

40fr, Cattle wading in pond.

**1972, Aug. 25 *Perf. 13***

**255** A59 35fr shown .85 .40
**256** A59 40fr multicolored 1.25 .45

Salt cure for cattle.
For surcharge see No. 282.

Lottery Drum — A60

**1972, Sept. 18**

**257** A60 35fr multi .65 .40

6th anniversary of the national lottery.

**West African Monetary Union Issue**
Common Design Type

Design: 40fr, African couple, city, village and commemorative coin.

**1972, Nov. 2 Engr. *Perf. 13***

**258** CD136 40fr brn, lil & gray .55 .30

Dromedary Race — A61

Design: 40fr, Horse race.

**1972, Dec. 15 Engr. *Perf. 13***

**259** A61 35fr brt bl, dk red & brn .90 .45
**260** A61 40fr sl grn, mar & brn 1.25 .65

Pole Vault, Map of Africa — A62

Map of Africa and: 40fr, Basketball. 45fr, Boxing. 75fr, Soccer.

**1973, Jan. 15 Engr. *Perf. 13***

**261** A62 35fr claret & multi .35 .25
**262** A62 40fr grn & multi .45 .25
**263** A62 45fr red & multi .55 .30
**264** A62 75fr dk bl & multi .75 .40
*Nos. 261-264 (4)* 2.10 1.20

2nd African Games, Lagos, Nigeria, 1/7-18.

Knight, Pawn, Chessboard A63

**1973, Feb. 16 Engr. *Perf. 13***

**265** A63 100fr dl red, sl grn & bl 3.00 1.25

World Chess Championship, Reykjavik, Iceland, July-Sept. 1972.

Abutilon Pannosum — A64

Rare African Flowers: 45fr, Crotalaria barkae. 60fr, Dichrostachys cinerea. 80fr, Caralluma decaisneana.

**1973, Feb. 26 Photo. *Perf. 12x12½***

**266** A64 30fr dk vio & multi .75 .40
**267** A64 45fr red & multi .90 .40
**268** A64 60fr ultra & multi 1.25 .50
**269** A64 80fr ocher & multi 1.75 .60
*Nos. 266-269 (4)* 4.65 1.90

Interpol Emblem — A65

**1973, Mar. 13 Typo. *Perf. 13x12½***

**270** A65 50fr brt grn & multi .60 .40

50th anniversary of International Criminal Police Organization (INTERPOL).

Dr. Hansen, Microscope and Petri Dish — A66

**1973, Mar. 29 Engr. *Perf. 13***

**271** A66 50fr vio bl, sl grn & dk brn 1.25 .50

Centenary of the discovery by Dr. Armauer G. Hansen of the Hansen bacillus, the cause of leprosy.

Nurse Treating Infant, UN and Red Cross Emblems — A67

**1973, Apr. 3 Engr. *Perf. 13***

**272** A67 50fr red, bl & brn .60 .25

25th anniversary of WHO.

Crocodile A68

Animals from W National Park: 35fr, Elephant. 40fr, Hippopotamus. 80fr, Wart hog.

**1973, June 5 Typo. *Perf. 12½x13***

**273** A68 25fr gray & blk .90 .25
**274** A68 35fr blk, gold & gray 1.25 .30
**275** A68 40fr red, lt bl & blk 1.25 .35
**276** A68 80fr multi 2.50 .50
*Nos. 273-276 (4)* 5.90 1.40

Eclipse over Mountains A69

**1973, June 21 Engr.** ***Perf. 13***

| | | | | |
|---|---|---|---|---|
| **277** | A69 | 40fr dk vio bl | .60 | .40 |

Solar eclipse, June 30, 1973.

Palominos — A70

Horses: 75fr, French trotters. 80fr, English thoroughbreds. 100fr, Arabian thoroughbreds.

**1973, Aug. 1 Photo.** ***Perf. 13x12½***

| | | | | |
|---|---|---|---|---|
| **278** | A70 | 50fr ultra & multi | 1.00 | .45 |
| **279** | A70 | 75fr gray & multi | 1.40 | .50 |
| **280** | A70 | 80fr emer & multi | 1.75 | .65 |
| **281** | A70 | 100fr ocher & multi | 2.25 | .85 |
| | | *Nos. 278-281 (4)* | 6.40 | 2.45 |

### No. 255 Srchd. and Ovptd. in Ultramarine

**1973, Aug. 16** ***Perf. 13***

| | | | | |
|---|---|---|---|---|
| **282** | A59 | 100fr on 35fr multi | 1.60 | 1.00 |

African solidarity in drought emergency.

Diesel Engine and Rudolf Diesel A71

Designs: Various Diesel locomotives.

**1973, Sept. 7** ***Perf. 13x12½***

| | | | | |
|---|---|---|---|---|
| **283** | A71 | 25fr gray, choc & Prus bl | .70 | .25 |
| **284** | A71 | 50fr sl bl, gray & dk grn | 1.25 | .40 |
| **285** | A71 | 75fr red lil, sl bl & gray | 1.60 | .65 |
| **286** | A71 | 125fr brt grn, vio bl & car | 2.75 | 1.10 |
| | | *Nos. 283-286 (4)* | 6.30 | 2.40 |

Rudolf Diesel (1858-1913), inventor of an internal combustion engine, later called Diesel engine.

### African Postal Union Issue
Common Design Type

**1973, Sept. 12 Engr.** ***Perf. 13***

| | | | | |
|---|---|---|---|---|
| **287** | CD137 | 100fr ol, dk car & sl grn | .90 | .60 |

TV Set, Map of Niger, Children A72

**1973, Oct. 1 Engr.** ***Perf. 13***

| | | | | |
|---|---|---|---|---|
| **288** | A72 | 50fr car, ultra & brn | .75 | .35 |

Educational television.

Type of 1971 Overprinted

**1973, Oct. 12 Photo.** ***Perf. 13***

| | | | | |
|---|---|---|---|---|
| **289** | A51 | 40fr red & multi | .75 | .30 |

3rd Conference of French-speaking countries, Liège, Sept. 15-Oct. 14.

Apollo of Belvedère — A73

Classic Sculpture: No. 291, Venus of Milo. No. 292, Hercules. No. 293, Atlas.

**1973, Oct. 15** **Engr.**

| | | | | |
|---|---|---|---|---|
| **290** | A73 | 50fr brn & sl grn | 1.00 | .45 |
| **291** | A73 | 50fr rose car & pur | 1.00 | .45 |
| **292** | A73 | 50fr red brn & dk brn | 1.00 | .45 |
| **293** | A73 | 50fr red brn & blk | 1.00 | .45 |
| | | *Nos. 290-293 (4)* | 4.00 | 1.80 |

Beehive, Bees and Globes A74

**1973, Oct. 31 Engr.** ***Perf. 13***

| | | | | |
|---|---|---|---|---|
| **294** | A74 | 40fr dl red, ocher & dl bl | .75 | .30 |

World Savings Day.

Tcherka Songhai Blanket — A75

Design: 35fr, Kounta Songhai blanket, vert.

***Perf. 12½x13, 13x12½***

**1973, Dec. 17** **Photo.**

| | | | | |
|---|---|---|---|---|
| **295** | A75 | 35fr brn & multi | .75 | .40 |
| **296** | A75 | 40fr brn & multi | .75 | .45 |

Textiles of Niger.

WPY Emblem, Infant and Globe A76

**1974, Mar. 4 Engr.** ***Perf. 13***

| | | | | |
|---|---|---|---|---|
| **297** | A76 | 50fr multi | .70 | .35 |

World Population Year 1974.

Locomotives, 1938 and 1948 — A77

75fr, Locomotive, 1893. 100fr, Locomotives, 1866 and 1939. 150fr, Locomotives, 1829.

**1974, May 24 Engr.** ***Perf. 13***

| | | | | |
|---|---|---|---|---|
| **298** | A77 | 50fr shown | .95 | .40 |
| **299** | A77 | 75fr multicolored | 1.50 | .55 |
| **300** | A77 | 100fr multicolored | 2.10 | .85 |
| **301** | A77 | 150fr multicolored | 3.25 | 1.40 |
| | | *Nos. 298-301 (4)* | 7.80 | 3.20 |

Map and Flags of Members A78

**1974, May 29 Photo.** ***Perf. 13x12½***

| | | | | |
|---|---|---|---|---|
| **302** | A78 | 40fr bl & multi | .70 | .35 |

15th anniversary of the Council of Accord.

Marconi Sending Radio Signals to Australia — A79

**1974, July 1 Engr.** ***Perf. 13***

| | | | | |
|---|---|---|---|---|
| **303** | A79 | 50fr pur, bl & dk brn | .75 | .35 |

Centenary of the birth of Guglielmo Marconi (1874-1937), Italian inventor and physicist.

Hand Holding Sapling — A80

**1974, Aug. 2 Engr.** ***Perf. 13***

| | | | | |
|---|---|---|---|---|
| **304** | A80 | 35fr multi | .75 | .35 |

National Tree Week.

Camel Saddle — A81

Design: 50fr, 3 sculptured horses, horiz.

**1974, Aug. 20 Engr.** ***Perf. 13***

| | | | | |
|---|---|---|---|---|
| **305** | A81 | 40fr ol brn, bl & red | .60 | .30 |
| **306** | A81 | 50fr ol brn, bl & red | .75 | .35 |

Chopin and Polish Eagle A82

Design: No. 308, Ludwig van Beethoven and allegory of Ninth Symphony.

**1974**

| | | | | |
|---|---|---|---|---|
| **307** | A82 | 100fr multi | 2.00 | .80 |
| **308** | A82 | 100fr multi | 2.00 | .80 |

125th anniversary of the death of Frederic Chopin (1810-1849), composer and 150th anniversary of Beethoven's Ninth Symphony, composed 1823.

Issue dates: #307, Sept. 4; #308, Sept. 19.

Don-Don Drum — A83

**1974, Nov. 12 Engr.** ***Perf. 13***

| | | | | |
|---|---|---|---|---|
| **309** | A83 | 60fr multi | 1.10 | .55 |

Tenere Tree, Compass Rose and Caravan — A84

**1974, Nov. 24 Engr.** ***Perf. 13***

| | | | | |
|---|---|---|---|---|
| **310** | A84 | 50fr multi | 2.50 | 1.10 |

Tenere tree, a landmark in Sahara Desert, first death anniversary.

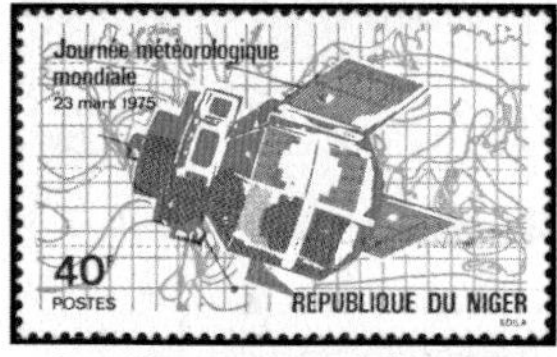

Satellite over World Weather Map — A85

**1975, Mar. 23 Litho.** ***Perf. 13***

| | | | | |
|---|---|---|---|---|
| **311** | A85 | 40fr bl, blk & red | .60 | .30 |

World Meteorological Day, Mar. 23, 1975.

"City of Truro," English, 1903 — A86

Locomotives and Flags: 75fr, "5.003," Germany, 1937. 100fr, "The General," United States, 1863. 125fr, "Electric BB 15.000," France, 1971.

**1975, Apr. 24 Typo.** ***Perf. 13***

| | | | | |
|---|---|---|---|---|
| **312** | A86 | 50fr org & multi | 1.50 | .35 |
| **313** | A86 | 75fr yel grn & multi | 2.00 | .65 |
| **314** | A86 | 100fr lt bl & multi | 2.40 | .80 |
| **315** | A86 | 125fr multi | 3.00 | 1.00 |
| | | *Nos. 312-315 (4)* | 8.90 | 2.80 |

### Bird Type of 1968 Dated "1975"

**1975, Apr. Photo.** ***Perf. 13***

| | | | | |
|---|---|---|---|---|
| **316** | A43 | 25fr ol & multi | 2.00 | .60 |

Zabira Leather Bag — A87

Handicrafts: 40fr, Damier tapestry. 45fr, Vase. 60fr, Gourd flask.

**1975, May 28 Litho. *Perf. 12½***

**317** A87 35fr dp bl & multi .35 .25
**318** A87 40fr dp grn & multi .50 .30
**319** A87 45fr brn & multi .70 .40
**320** A87 60fr dp org & multi 1.10 .40
*Nos. 317-320 (4)* 2.65 1.35

Mother and Child, IWY Emblem — A88

**1975, June 9 Engr. *Perf. 13***

**321** A88 50fr claret, brn & bl .80 .35

International Women's Year 1975.

Dr. Schweitzer and Lambarene Hospital — A89

**1975, June 23 Engr. *Perf. 13***

**322** A89 100fr brn, grn & blk 1.40 .75

Dr. Albert Schweitzer (1875-1965), medical missionary.

Peugeot, 1892 — A90

Early Autos: 75fr, Daimler, 1895. 100fr, Fiat, 1899. 125fr, Cadillac, 1903.

**1975, July 16 Engr. *Perf. 13***

**323** A90 50fr rose & vio bl 1.05 .40
**324** A90 75fr bl & vio brn 1.60 .45
**325** A90 100fr brt grn & mag 2.50 .70
**326** A90 125fr brick red & brt grn 2.75 .80
*Nos. 323-326 (4)* 7.90 2.35

Sun, Tree and Earth — A91

**1975, Aug. 2 Engr. *Perf. 13***

**327** A91 40fr multi .80 .35

National Tree Week.

Boxing — A92

Designs: 35fr, Boxing, horiz. 45fr, Wrestling, horiz. 50fr, Wrestling.

**1975, Aug. 25 Engr. *Perf. 13***

**328** A92 35fr blk, org & brn .45 .25
**329** A92 40fr bl grn, brn & blk .50 .30
**330** A92 45fr blk, brt bl & brn .80 .35
**331** A92 50fr red, brn & blk .85 .40
*Nos. 328-331 (4)* 2.60 1.30

Lion's Head Tetradrachm, Leontini, 460 B.C. — A93

Greek Coins: 75fr, Owl tetradrachm, Athens, 500 B.C. 100fr, Crab didrachm, Himera, 480 B.C. 125fr, Minotaur tetradrachm, Gela, 460 B.C.

**1975, Sept. 12 Engr. *Perf. 13***

**332** A93 50fr red, dl bl & blk .90 .30
**333** A93 75fr lil, brt bl & blk 1.25 .35
**334** A93 100fr bl, org & blk 1.60 .60
**335** A93 125fr grn, pur & blk 2.25 .70
*Nos. 332-335 (4)* 6.00 1.95

Starving Family A94

45fr, Animal skeletons. 60fr, Truck bringing food.

**1975, Oct. 21 Engr. *Perf. 13x12½***

**336** A94 40fr multi .80 .40
**337** A94 45fr ultra & brn 1.50 .60
**338** A94 60fr grn, org & dk bl 1.35 .50
*Nos. 336-338 (3)* 3.65 1.50

Fight against drought.

Niger River Crossing — A95

Designs: 45fr, Entrance to Boubon camp. 50fr, Camp building.

**1975, Nov. 10 Litho. *Perf. 12½***

**339** A95 40fr multi .70 .30
**340** A95 45fr multi .75 .30
**341** A95 50fr multi .80 .40
*Nos. 339-341 (3)* 2.25 1.00

Tourist publicity.

Teacher and Pupils A96

Each stamp has different inscription in center.

**1976, Jan. 12 Photo. *Perf. 13***

**342** A96 25fr ol & multi .25 .25
**343** A96 30fr vio bl & multi .25 .25
**344** A96 40fr multi .25 .25
**345** A96 50fr multi .40 .25
**346** A96 60fr multi .50 .25
*Nos. 342-346 (5)* 1.65 1.25

Literacy campaign 1976.
For overprints see Nos. 371-375.

12th Winter Olympic Games, Innsbruck — A97

**1976, Feb. 20 Litho. *Perf. 14x13½***

**347** A97 40fr Ice hockey .35 .25
**348** A97 50fr Luge .55 .30
**349** A97 150fr Ski jump 1.10 .60
*Nos. 347-349,C266-C267 (5)* 5.75 3.15

Satellite, Telephone, ITU Emblem — A98

**1976, Mar. 10 Litho. *Perf. 13***

**350** A98 100fr org, bl & vio bl 1.25 .60

Centenary of first telephone call by Alexander Graham Bell, Mar. 10, 1876.

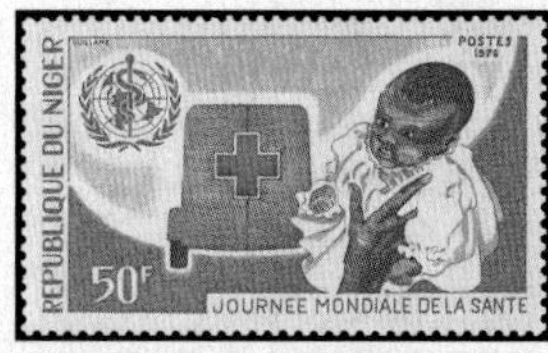


WHO Emblem, Red Cross Truck, Infant — A99

**1976, Apr. 7 Engr. *Perf. 13***

**351** A99 50fr multi .75 .25

World Health Day 1976.

Statue of Liberty and Washington Crossing the Delaware — A100

50fr, Statue of Liberty and call to arms.

**1976, Apr. 8 Litho. *Perf. 14x13½***

**352** A100 40fr multi .30 .25
**353** A100 50fr multi .40 .25
*Nos. 352-353,C269-C271 (5)* 6.05 2.45

American Bicentennial.

The Army Helping in Development — A101

Design: 50fr, Food distribution, vert.

***Perf. 12½x13, 13x12½***

**1976, Apr. 15 Litho.**

**354** A101 50fr multi .45 .25
**355** A101 100fr multi .90 .40

National Armed Forces, 2nd anniv. of takeover.

### Europafrica Issue

Maps, Concorde, Ship and Grain — A102

**1976, June 9 Litho. *Perf. 13***

**356** A102 100fr multi 1.25 .50

Road Building A103

Design: 30fr, Rice cultivation.

**1976, June 26 *Perf. 12½***

**357** A103 25fr multi .25 .25
**358** A103 30fr multi .40 .25

Community labor.

Motobecane 125, France — A104

Motorcycles: 75fr, Norton Challenge, England. 100fr, BMW 90 S, Germany. 125fr, Kawasaki 1000, Japan.

**1976, July 16 Engr. *Perf. 13***

| | | | | |
|---|---|---|---|---|
| **359** | A104 | 50fr vio bl & multi | .70 | .30 |
| **360** | A104 | 75fr dp grn & multi | 1.00 | .35 |
| **361** | A104 | 100fr dk brn & multi | 1.50 | .70 |
| **362** | A104 | 125fr slate & multi | 1.75 | .80 |
| | | *Nos. 359-362 (4)* | 4.95 | 2.15 |

Boxing
A105

Designs: 50fr, Basketball. 60fr, Soccer. 80fr, Cycling, horiz. 100fr, Judo, horiz.

**1976, July 17 Litho. *Perf. 14***

| | | | | |
|---|---|---|---|---|
| **363** | A105 | 40fr multi | .50 | .30 |
| **364** | A105 | 50fr multi | .60 | .30 |
| **365** | A105 | 60fr multi | .70 | .30 |
| **366** | A105 | 80fr multi | .80 | .30 |
| **367** | A105 | 100fr multi | 1.10 | .35 |
| | | *Nos. 363-367 (5)* | 3.70 | 1.55 |

21st Summer Olympic games, Montreal. See No. C279.

Map of Niger, Planting Seedlings
A106

Designs: 50fr, Woman watering seedling, vert. 60fr, Women planting seedlings, vert.

**1976, Aug. 1 Litho. *Perf. 12½x13***

| | | | | |
|---|---|---|---|---|
| **368** | A106 | 40fr org & multi | .45 | .25 |
| **369** | A106 | 50fr yel & multi | .55 | .30 |
| **370** | A106 | 60fr grn & multi | .70 | .35 |
| | | *Nos. 368-370 (3)* | 1.70 | .90 |

Reclamation of Sahel Region.

### Nos. 342-346 Overprinted: "JOURNEE / INTERNATIONALE / DE L'ALPHABETISATION"

**1976, Sept. 8 Photo. *Perf. 13***

| | | | | |
|---|---|---|---|---|
| **371** | A96 | 25fr ol & multi | .25 | .25 |
| **372** | A96 | 30fr vio bl & multi | .25 | .25 |
| **373** | A96 | 40fr multi | .30 | .25 |
| **374** | A96 | 50fr multi | .40 | .25 |
| **375** | A96 | 60fr multi | .45 | .30 |
| | | *Nos. 371-375 (5)* | 1.65 | 1.30 |

Literacy campaign.

Hairdresser — A107

Designs: 40fr, Woman weaving straw, vert. 50fr, Women potters, vert.

**1976, Oct. 6 *Perf. 13***

| | | | | |
|---|---|---|---|---|
| **376** | A107 | 40fr buff & multi | .45 | .25 |
| **377** | A107 | 45fr bl & multi | .50 | .25 |
| **378** | A107 | 50fr red & multi | .70 | .30 |
| | | *Nos. 376-378 (3)* | 1.65 | .80 |

Niger Women's Association.

Rock Carvings
A108

Archaeology: 50fr, Neolithic sculptures. 60fr, Dinosaur skeleton.

**1976, Nov. 15 Photo. *Perf. 13x12½***

| | | | | |
|---|---|---|---|---|
| **379** | A108 | 40fr blk, sl & yel | 2.25 | .55 |
| **380** | A108 | 50fr blk, red & bis | 2.50 | .55 |
| **381** | A108 | 60fr bis, blk & brn | 5.00 | .75 |
| | | *Nos. 379-381 (3)* | 9.75 | 1.85 |

Benin Head — A109

Weaver, Dancers and Musicians — A110

**1977, Jan. 15 Engr. *Perf. 13***

| | | | | |
|---|---|---|---|---|
| **382** | A109 | 40fr dk brn | .45 | .25 |
| **383** | A110 | 50fr gray bl | 1.00 | .30 |

2nd World Black and African Festival, Lagos, Nigeria, Jan. 15-Feb. 12.

First Aid, Student, Blackboard and Plow — A111

Designs: Inscriptions on blackboard differ on each denomination.

**1977, Jan. 23 Photo. *Perf. 12½x13***

| | | | | |
|---|---|---|---|---|
| **384** | A111 | 40fr multi | .40 | .25 |
| **385** | A111 | 50fr multi | .50 | .30 |
| **386** | A111 | 60fr multi | .70 | .40 |
| | | *Nos. 384-386 (3)* | 1.60 | .95 |

Literacy campaign.

Midwife — A112

Design: 50fr, Midwife examining newborn.

**1977, Feb. 23 Litho. *Perf. 13***

| | | | | |
|---|---|---|---|---|
| **387** | A112 | 40fr multi | .45 | .25 |
| **388** | A112 | 50fr multi | .75 | .30 |

Village health service.

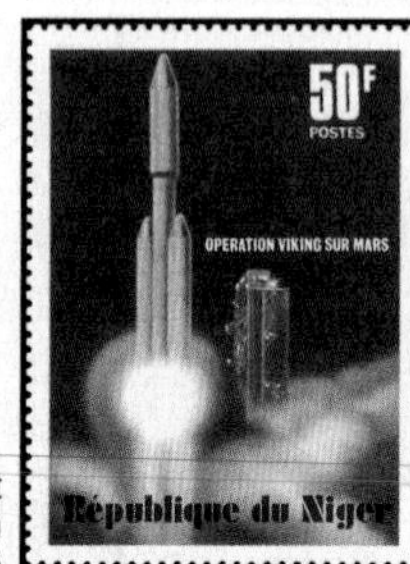


Titan Rocket Launch
A113

80fr, Viking orbiter near Mars, horiz.

**1977, Mar. 15 Litho. *Perf. 14***

| | | | | |
|---|---|---|---|---|
| **389** | A113 | 50fr multi | .45 | .25 |
| **390** | A113 | 80fr multi | .75 | .25 |
| | | *Nos. 389-390,C283-C285 (5)* | 4.70 | 1.80 |

Viking Mars project.

For overprints see #497-498, C295-C297.

Marabous
A114

Design: 90fr, Harnessed antelopes.

**1977, Mar. 18 Engr. *Perf. 13***

| | | | | |
|---|---|---|---|---|
| **391** | A114 | 80fr multi | 2.00 | 1.00 |
| **392** | A114 | 90fr multi | 2.25 | 1.00 |

Nature protection.

Weather Map, Satellite, WMO Emblem
A115

**1977, Mar. 23**

| | | | | |
|---|---|---|---|---|
| **393** | A115 | 100fr multi | 1.25 | .60 |

World Meteorological Day.

Group Gymnastics — A116

50fr, High jump. 80fr, Folk singers.

**1977, Apr. 7 Litho. *Perf. 13x12½***

| | | | | |
|---|---|---|---|---|
| **394** | A116 | 40fr dl yel & multi | .45 | .25 |
| **395** | A116 | 50fr bl & multi | .60 | .30 |
| **396** | A116 | 80fr org & multi | .75 | .35 |
| | | *Nos. 394-396 (3)* | 1.80 | .90 |

2nd Tahoua Youth Festival, Apr. 7-14.

Red Cross, WHO Emblems and Children — A117

**1977, Apr. 25 Engr. *Perf. 13***

| | | | | |
|---|---|---|---|---|
| **397** | A117 | 80fr lil, org & red | .85 | .40 |

World Health Day: "Immunization means protection of your children."

Eye with WHO Emblem, and Sword Killing Fly — A118

**1977, May 7**

| | | | | |
|---|---|---|---|---|
| **398** | A118 | 100fr multi | 1.25 | .60 |

Fight against onchocerciasis, a roundworm infection, transmitted by flies, causing blindness.

Guirka Tahoua Dance
A119

50fr, Mailfilafili Gaya. 80fr, Naguihinayan Loga.

**1977, June 7 Photo. *Perf. 13x12½***

| | | | | |
|---|---|---|---|---|
| **399** | A119 | 40fr multi | .55 | .30 |
| **400** | A119 | 50fr multi | .75 | .40 |
| **401** | A119 | 80fr multi | 1.10 | .55 |
| | | *Nos. 399-401 (3)* | 2.40 | 1.25 |

Popular arts and traditions.

Cavalry — A120

Traditional chief's cavalry, different groups.

**1977, July 7 Litho. *Perf. 13x12½***

| | | | | |
|---|---|---|---|---|
| **402** | A120 | 40fr multi | .70 | .40 |
| **403** | A120 | 50fr multi | .80 | .45 |
| **404** | A120 | 60fr multi | 1.20 | .60 |
| | | *Nos. 402-404 (3)* | 2.70 | 1.45 |

Planting and Cultivating — A121

**1977, Aug. 10**

| | | | | |
|---|---|---|---|---|
| **405** | A121 | 40fr multi | .60 | .30 |

Reclamation of Sahel Region.

Albert John Luthuli Peace — A122

Designs: 80fr, Maurice Maeterlinck, literature. 100fr, Allan L. Hodgkin, medicine. 150fr, Albert Camus, literature. 200fr, Paul Ehrlich, medicine.

**1977, Aug. 20 Litho. *Perf. 14***

| | | | | |
|---|---|---|---|---|
| **406** | A122 | 50fr multi | .35 | .25 |
| **407** | A122 | 80fr multi | .45 | .25 |
| **408** | A122 | 100fr multi | .70 | .25 |
| **409** | A122 | 150fr multi | 1.10 | .40 |
| **410** | A122 | 200fr multi | 1.50 | .50 |
| | | *Nos. 406-410 (5)* | 4.10 | 1.65 |

Nobel prize winners. See No. C287.

Mao Tse-tung — A123

**1977, Sept. 9 Engr. *Perf. 13***

| | | | | |
|---|---|---|---|---|
| **411** | A123 | 100fr blk & red | 3.75 | 1.50 |

Argentina '78 Emblem, Soccer Players and Coach, Vittorio Pozzo, Italy — A124

Designs (Argentina '78 emblem, soccer players and coach): 50fr, Vincente Feola, Spain. 80fr, Aymore Moreira, Portugal. 100fr, Sir Alf Ramsey, England. 200fr, Helmut Schoen, Germany. 500fr, Sepp Herberger, Germany.

**1977, Oct. 12 Litho. *Perf. 13½***

| | | | | |
|---|---|---|---|---|
| **412** | A124 | 40fr multi | .40 | .25 |
| **413** | A124 | 50fr multi | .50 | .25 |
| **414** | A124 | 80fr multi | .65 | .25 |
| **415** | A124 | 100fr multi | 1.10 | .35 |
| **416** | A124 | 200fr multi | 1.75 | .65 |
| | | *Nos. 412-416 (5)* | 4.40 | 1.75 |

**Souvenir Sheet**

| | | | | |
|---|---|---|---|---|
| **417** | A124 | 500fr multi | 4.25 | 1.75 |

World Cup Soccer championship, Argentina '78.

For overprints see Nos. 453-458.

Horse's Head, Parthenon and UNESCO Emblem — A125

**1977, Nov. 12 Engr. *Perf. 13***

| | | | | |
|---|---|---|---|---|
| **418** | A125 | 100fr multi | 1.75 | .75 |

Woman Carrying Water Pots — A126

Design: 50fr, Women pounding corn.

**1977, Nov. 23 Photo. *Perf. 12½x13***

| | | | | |
|---|---|---|---|---|
| **419** | A126 | 40fr multi | .45 | .25 |
| **420** | A126 | 50fr red & multi | .55 | .30 |

Niger Women's Association.

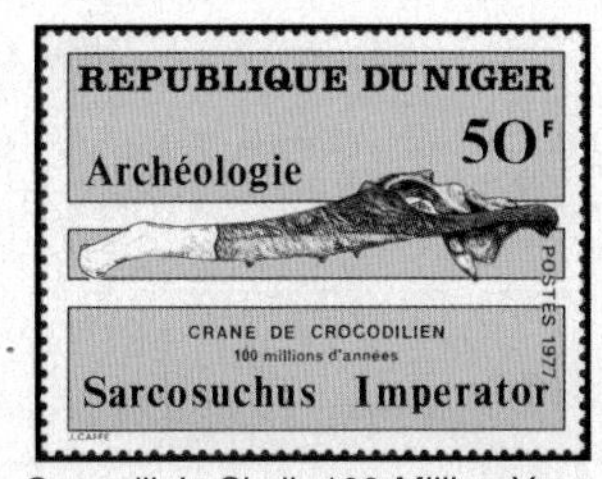


Crocodile's Skull, 100 Million Years Old — A127

Design: 80fr, Neolithic flint tools.

**1977, Dec. 14 *Perf. 13***

| | | | | |
|---|---|---|---|---|
| **421** | A127 | 50fr multi | 1.10 | .55 |
| **422** | A127 | 80fr multi | 1.50 | .80 |

Raoul Follereau and Lepers A128

40fr, Raoul Follereau and woman leper, vert.

**1978, Jan. 28 Engr. *Perf. 13***

| | | | | |
|---|---|---|---|---|
| **423** | A128 | 40fr multi | .45 | .25 |
| **424** | A128 | 50fr multi | .50 | .30 |

25th anniversary of Leprosy Day. Follereau (1903-1977) was "Apostle to the Lepers" and educator of the blind.

**Bird Type of 1972 Redrawn**

**1978, Feb. Photo. *Perf. 13***

| | | | | |
|---|---|---|---|---|
| **425** | A58 | 50fr tan & multi | 2.50 | 1.00 |

No. 425 is dated "1978" and has only designer's name in imprint. No. 254 has printer's name also.

Assumption, by Rubens A129

Rubens Paintings: 70fr, Rubens and Friends, horiz. 100fr, History of Marie de Medici. 150fr, Alathea Talbot and Family. 200fr, Marquise de Spinola. 500fr, Virgin and St. Ildefonso.

**1978, Feb. 25 Litho. *Perf. 14***

| | | | | |
|---|---|---|---|---|
| **426** | A129 | 50fr multi | .40 | .25 |
| **427** | A129 | 70fr multi | .45 | .25 |
| **428** | A129 | 100fr multi | .85 | .30 |
| **429** | A129 | 150fr multi | 1.25 | .40 |
| **430** | A129 | 200fr multi | 1.80 | .50 |
| | | *Nos. 426-430 (5)* | 4.75 | 1.70 |

**Souvenir Sheet**

***Perf. 13½***

| | | | | |
|---|---|---|---|---|
| **431** | A129 | 500fr gold & multi | 5.00 | 1.50 |

Peter Paul Rubens (1577-1640), 400th birth anniversary.

Shot Put A130

**1978, Mar. 22 Photo. *Perf. 13***

| | | | | |
|---|---|---|---|---|
| **432** | A130 | 40fr shown | .30 | .25 |
| **433** | A130 | 50fr Volleyball | .40 | .25 |
| **434** | A130 | 60fr Long jump | .45 | .25 |
| **435** | A130 | 100fr Javelin | .80 | .35 |
| | | *Nos. 432-435 (4)* | 1.95 | 1.10 |

Natl. University Games' Championships.

First Aid and Red Crosses A131

**1978, May 13 Litho.**

| | | | | |
|---|---|---|---|---|
| **436** | A131 | 40fr red & multi | .35 | .25 |

Niger Red Cross.

Goudel Earth Station A132

**1978, May 23**

| | | | | |
|---|---|---|---|---|
| **437** | A132 | 100fr multi | .75 | .40 |

Soccer Ball, Flags of Participants A133

Argentina '78 Emblem and: 50fr, Ball in net. 100fr, Globe with South America, Soccer field. 200fr, Two players, horiz. 300fr, Player and globe.

**1978, June 18 Litho. *Perf. 13½***

| | | | | |
|---|---|---|---|---|
| **438** | A133 | 40fr multi | .30 | .25 |
| **439** | A133 | 50fr multi | .50 | .25 |
| **440** | A133 | 100fr multi | .75 | .35 |
| **441** | A133 | 200fr multi | 1.50 | .60 |
| | | *Nos. 438-441 (4)* | 3.05 | 1.45 |

**Souvenir Sheet**

| | | | | |
|---|---|---|---|---|
| **442** | A133 | 300fr multi | 2.50 | 1.25 |

11th World Cup Soccer Championship, Argentina, June 1-25.

**Bird Type of 1971 Redrawn**

**1978, June Photo. *Perf. 13***

| | | | | |
|---|---|---|---|---|
| **443** | A54 | 35fr bl & multi | 3.25 | .80 |

No. 443 has no year date, nor Delrieu imprint.

Post Office, Niamey — A134

Design: 60fr, Post Office, different view.

**1978, Aug. 12 Litho.**

| | | | | |
|---|---|---|---|---|
| **444** | A134 | 40fr multi | .30 | .25 |
| **445** | A134 | 60fr multi | .45 | .25 |

Goudel Water Works A135

**1978, Sept. 25 Photo. *Perf. 13***

| | | | | |
|---|---|---|---|---|
| **446** | A135 | 100fr multi | .85 | .55 |

Giraffe — A136

Animals and Wildlife Fund Emblem: 50fr, Ostrich. 70fr, Cheetah. 150fr, Oryx, horiz. 200fr, Addax, horiz. 300fr, Hartebeest, horiz.

**1978, Nov. 20 Litho. *Perf. 15***

| | | | | |
|---|---|---|---|---|
| **447** | A136 | 40fr multi | *1.00* | .50 |
| **448** | A136 | 50fr multi | *1.75* | .60 |
| **449** | A136 | 70fr multi | *2.40* | .80 |
| **450** | A136 | 150fr multi | *5.00* | 1.40 |
| **451** | A136 | 200fr multi | *8.00* | 2.00 |
| **452** | A136 | 300fr multi | *10.00* | 2.75 |
| | | *Nos. 447-452 (6)* | *28.15* | 8.05 |

Endangered species.

**Nos. 412-417 Overprinted in Silver**

a

b

c

d 

e 

**1978, Dec. 1** ***Perf. 13½***

| | | | | |
|---|---|---|---|---|
| **453** | A124(a) | 40fr multi | .35 | .25 |
| **454** | A124(b) | 50fr multi | .45 | .25 |
| **455** | A124(c) | 80fr multi | .70 | .30 |
| **456** | A124(d) | 100fr multi | 1.00 | .40 |
| **457** | A124(e) | 200fr multi | 1.75 | .75 |
| | | *Nos. 453-457 (5)* | 4.25 | 1.95 |

**Souvenir Sheet**

| | | | | |
|---|---|---|---|---|
| **458** | A124(e) | 500fr multi | 4.25 | 1.75 |

Winners, World Soccer Cup Championship, Argentina, June 1-25.

Tinguizi — A137

Musicians: No. 460, Dan Gourmou. No. 461, Chetima Ganga, horiz.

**1978, Dec. 11** **Litho.** ***Perf. 13***

| | | | | |
|---|---|---|---|---|
| **459** | A137 | 100fr multi | 1.00 | .50 |
| **460** | A137 | 100fr multi | 1.00 | .50 |
| **461** | A137 | 100fr multi | 1.00 | .50 |
| | | *Nos. 459-461 (3)* | 3.00 | 1.50 |

Virgin Mary, by Dürer A138

50fr, The Homecoming, by Honoré Daumier (1808-79). 150fr, 200fr, 500fr, Virgin and Child, by Albrecht Dürer (1471-1528), diff.

**1979, Jan. 31** **Litho.** ***Perf. 13½***

| | | | | |
|---|---|---|---|---|
| **462** | A138 | 50fr multi | .70 | .25 |
| **463** | A138 | 100fr multi | .75 | .30 |
| **464** | A138 | 150fr multi | 1.25 | .40 |
| **465** | A138 | 200fr multi | 1.75 | .60 |
| | | *Nos. 462-465 (4)* | 4.45 | 1.55 |

**Souvenir Sheet**

| | | | | |
|---|---|---|---|---|
| **466** | A138 | 500fr multi | 4.50 | 1.50 |

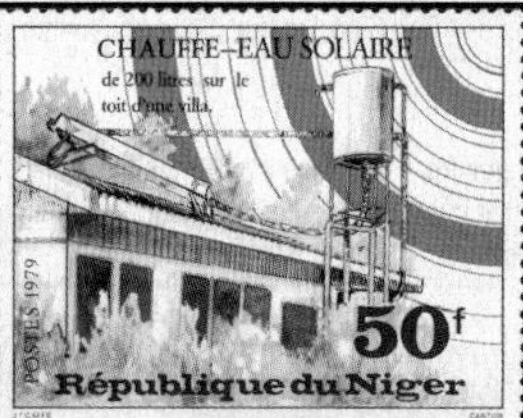

Solar Panels and Tank — A139

Design: 40fr, Tank and panels on roof, vert.

**1979, Feb. 28** ***Perf. 12½x12, 12x12½***

| | | | | |
|---|---|---|---|---|
| **467** | A139 | 40fr multi | .35 | .25 |
| **468** | A139 | 50fr multi | .45 | .25 |

Hot water from solar heat.

Children with Building Blocks — A140

Children and IYC Emblem: 100fr, Reading books. 150fr, With model plane.

**1979, Apr. 10** **Litho.** ***Perf. 13½***

| | | | | |
|---|---|---|---|---|
| **469** | A140 | 40fr multi | .40 | .25 |
| **470** | A140 | 100fr multi | .80 | .30 |
| **471** | A140 | 150fr multi | 1.60 | .40 |
| | | *Nos. 469-471 (3)* | 2.80 | .95 |

International Year of the Child.

The Langa, Traditional Sport A141

Design: 50fr, The langa, diff.

**1979, Apr. 10** **Litho.** ***Perf. 12½x12***

| | | | | |
|---|---|---|---|---|
| **472** | A141 | 40fr multi | .35 | .25 |
| **473** | A141 | 50fr multi | .45 | .25 |

Rowland Hill, Mail Truck and France No. 8 — A142

Designs (Hill and): 100fr, Canoes and Austria #P4. 150fr, Air Niger plane and US #122. 200fr, Streamlined mail train and Canada type A6. 400fr, Electric train and Niger #51.

**1979, June 6** **Litho.** ***Perf. 14***

| | | | | |
|---|---|---|---|---|
| **474** | A142 | 40fr multi | .50 | .25 |
| **475** | A142 | 100fr multi | 1.00 | .30 |
| **476** | A142 | 150fr multi | 1.50 | .40 |
| **477** | A142 | 200fr multi | 1.80 | .55 |
| | | *Nos. 474-477 (4)* | 4.80 | 1.50 |

**Souvenir Sheet**

| | | | | |
|---|---|---|---|---|
| **478** | A142 | 400fr multi | 4.00 | 1.50 |

Sir Rowland Hill (1795-1879), originator of penny postage.

Zabira Handbag and Niger No. 135 — A143

Design: 150fr, Heads with communications waves, world map, UPU emblem and satellite.

**1979, June 8** **Litho.** ***Perf. 12x12½***

| | | | | |
|---|---|---|---|---|
| **479** | A143 | 50fr multi | 1.25 | .60 |

**Engr.** ***Perf. 13***

| | | | | |
|---|---|---|---|---|
| **480** | A143 | 150fr brt red & ultra | 3.25 | 1.60 |

Philexafrique II, Libreville, Gabon, June 8-17. Nos. 479, 480 each printed in sheets of 10 and 5 labels showing exhibition emblem.

Djermakoye Palace — A144

**1979, Sept. 26** **Litho.** ***Perf. 13x12½***

| | | | | |
|---|---|---|---|---|
| **481** | A144 | 100fr multi | .75 | .40 |

Bororo Festive Headdress — A145

60fr, Bororo women's traditional costumes.

***Perf. 13x12½, 12½x13***

**1979, Sept. 26**

| | | | | |
|---|---|---|---|---|
| **482** | A145 | 45fr multi | .35 | .25 |
| **483** | A145 | 60fr multi, vert. | .50 | .30 |

Annual Bororo Festival.

Olympic Emblem, Flame and Boxers — A146

Designs: 100fr, 150fr, 250fr, 500fr, Olympic emblem, flame and boxers, diff.

**1979, Oct. 6** ***Perf. 13½***

| | | | | |
|---|---|---|---|---|
| **484** | A146 | 45fr multi | .40 | .25 |
| **485** | A146 | 100fr multi | .85 | .30 |
| **486** | A146 | 150fr multi | 1.30 | .40 |
| **487** | A146 | 250fr multi | 2.25 | .65 |
| | | *Nos. 484-487 (4)* | 4.80 | 1.60 |

**Souvenir Sheet**

| | | | | |
|---|---|---|---|---|
| **488** | A146 | 500fr multi | 4.00 | 1.75 |

Pre-Olympic Year.

John Alcock, Arthur Whitten Brown, Vickers-Vimy Biplane — A147

**1979, Sept. 3** ***Perf. 13½***

| | | | | |
|---|---|---|---|---|
| **489** | A147 | 100fr multi | 1.25 | .50 |

First Transatlantic flight, 60th anniversary.

Road and Traffic Safety — A148

**1979, Nov. 20** **Litho.** ***Perf. 12½***

| | | | | |
|---|---|---|---|---|
| **490** | A148 | 45fr multi | .45 | .30 |

Four-Man Bobsledding, Lake Placid '80 Emblem — A149

Lake Placid '80 Emblem and: 60fr, Downhill skiing. 100fr, Speed skating. 150fr, Two-man bobsledding. 200fr, Figure skating. 300fr, Cross-country skiing.

**1979, Dec. 10** ***Perf. 14½***

| | | | | |
|---|---|---|---|---|
| **491** | A149 | 40fr multi | .30 | .25 |
| **492** | A149 | 60fr multi | .45 | .25 |
| **493** | A149 | 100fr multi | .75 | .30 |
| **494** | A149 | 150fr multi | 1.10 | .40 |
| **495** | A149 | 200fr multi | 1.50 | .75 |
| | | *Nos. 491-495 (5)* | 4.10 | 1.95 |

**Souvenir Sheet**

| | | | | |
|---|---|---|---|---|
| **496** | A149 | 300fr multi | 2.50 | 1.00 |

13th Winter Olympic Games, Lake Placid, NY, Feb. 12-24, 1980.

For overprints see Nos. 501-506.

Nos. 389, 390 Overprinted in Silver or Black

**1979, Dec. 20** **Litho.** ***Perf. 14***

| | | | | |
|---|---|---|---|---|
| **497** | A113 | 50fr multi (S) | .35 | .25 |
| **498** | A113 | 80fr multi | .60 | .30 |
| | | *Nos. 497-498,C295-C296 (4)* | 3.80 | 2.10 |

Apollo 11 moon landing, 10th anniv. See #C297.

Court of Sultan of Zinder — A150

**1980, Mar. 25 Litho. *Perf. 13x12½***

**499** A150 45fr shown .35 .25
**500** A150 60fr Sultan's court, diff. .45 .25

### Nos. 491-496 Overprinted

(a)

(b)

(c)

(d)

(e)

(f)

**1980, Mar. 31 Litho. *Perf. 14½***

**501** A149 (a) 40fr multi .30 .25
**502** A149 (b) 60fr multi .45 .25
**503** A149 (c) 100fr multi .75 .40
**504** A149 (d) 150fr multi 1.10 .50
**505** A149 (e) 200fr multi 1.50 .70
*Nos. 501-505 (5)* 4.10 2.10

### Souvenir Sheet

**506** A149 (f) 300fr multi 2.40 1.50

Javelin, Olympic Rings — A151

90fr, Walking. 100fr, High jump, horiz. 300fr, Marathon runners, horiz.
500fr, High jump, horiz.

**1980, Apr. 17**

**507** A151 60fr shown .45 .25
**508** A151 90fr multi .75 .25
**509** A151 100fr multi .90 .30
**510** A151 300fr multi 2.00 .80
*Nos. 507-510 (4)* 4.10 1.60

### Souvenir Sheet

**511** A151 500fr multi 3.50 1.50

22nd Summer Olympic Games, Moscow, July 19-Aug. 3.
For overprints see Nos. 527-531.

Man Smoking Cigarette, Runner — A152

**1980, Apr. 7 *Perf. 13***

**512** A152 100fr multi .70 .40

World Health Day; fight against cigarette smoking.

Health Year A153

**1980, May 15 Photo. *Perf. 13x12½***

**513** A153 150fr multi 1.10 .65

Shimbashi-Yokohama Locomotive — A154

60fr, American type. 90fr, German Reichsbahn series 61. 100fr, Prussian Staatsbahn P2. 130fr, L'Aigle.
425fr, Stephenson's Rocket.

**1980, June Litho. *Perf. 12½***

**514** A154 45fr shown .55 .30
**515** A154 60fr multicolored .80 .35
**516** A154 90fr multicolored 1.05 .50
**517** A154 100fr multicolored 1.40 .65
**518** A154 130fr multicolored 1.75 .85
*Nos. 514-518 (5)* 5.55 2.65

### Souvenir Sheet

**519** A154 425fr multicolored 7.50 2.25

For overprint see No. 674.

Steve Biko, 4th Anniversary of Death — A155

**1980, Sept. 12 Litho. *Perf. 13***

**520** A155 150fr org & blk 1.00 .60

Soccer Players — A156

Designs: Various soccer scenes.

**1980, Oct. 15 *Perf. 12½***

**521** A156 45fr multi .30 .25
**522** A156 60fr multi .40 .25
**523** A156 90fr multi .70 .25
**524** A156 100fr multi .80 .30
**525** A156 130fr multi .90 .35
*Nos. 521-525 (5)* 3.10 1.40

### Souvenir Sheet

**526** A156 425fr multi 4.00 1.25

World Soccer Cup 1982.

### Nos. 507-511 Overprinted in Gold with Winner's Name and Country

**1980, Sept. 27 Litho. *Perf. 14½***

**527** A151 60fr multi .45 .25
**528** A151 90fr multi .70 .30
**529** A151 100fr multi .80 .35
**530** A151 300fr multi 2.40 1.00
*Nos. 527-530 (4)* 4.35 1.90

### Souvenir Sheet

**531** A151 500fr multi, horiz. 4.00 2.50

African Postal Union, 5th Anniversary A157

**1980, Dec. 24 Photo. *Perf. 13½***

**532** A157 100fr multi .75 .40

Terra Cotta Kareygorou Head — A158

Designs: Terra Cotta Kareygorou Statues, 5th-12th cent. 45fr, 150fr, horiz.

**1981, Jan. 23 Litho. *Perf. 13***

**533** A158 45fr multi .30 .25
**534** A158 60fr multi .45 .25
**535** A158 90fr multi .60 .30
**536** A158 150fr multi 1.10 .50
*Nos. 533-536 (4)* 2.45 1.30

Ostrich — A159

**1981, Mar. 17 Litho. *Perf. 12½***

**537** A159 10fr shown 1.10 .30
**538** A159 20fr Oryx .40 .30
**539** A159 25fr Gazelle .40 .30
**540** A159 30fr Great bustard 1.80 .60
**541** A159 60fr Giraffe .75 .40
**542** A159 150fr Addax 1.80 .80
*Nos. 537-542 (6)* 6.25 2.70

7th Anniv. of the F.A.N. A160

**1981, Apr. 14 Litho. *Perf. 13***

**543** A160 100fr multi .75 .40

One-armed Archer — A161

**1981, Apr. 24 Engr.**

**544** A161 50fr shown .70 .30
**545** A161 100fr Draftsman 1.10 .60

Intl. Year of the Disabled.

Scene from Mahalba Ballet, 1980 Youth Festival, Dosso A162

**1981, May 17 Litho.**

**546** A162 100fr shown .75 .40
**547** A162 100fr Ballet, diff. .75 .40

Prince Charles and Lady Diana, Coach — A163

Designs: Couple and coaches.

**1981, July 15 Litho. *Perf. 14½***

**548** A163 150fr multi 1.10 .45
**549** A163 200fr multi 1.40 .65
**550** A163 300fr multi 2.00 .90
*Nos. 548-550 (3)* 4.50 2.00

### Souvenir Sheet

**551** A163 400fr multi 3.00 1.50

Royal wedding.
For overprints see Nos. 595-598.

Hegira 1500th Anniv. — A164

**1981, July 15 *Perf. 13½x13***

**552** A164 100fr multi .80 .40

Alexander Fleming (1881-1955) A165

**1981, Aug. 6 Engr. *Perf. 13***
**553** A165 150fr multi 2.00 .95

25th Intl. Letter Writing Week, Oct. 6-12 — A167

**1981, Oct. 9 Surcharged in Black**
**554** A167 65fr on 40fr multi .55 .30
**555** A167 85fr on 60fr multi .75 .50

Nos. 554-555 not issued without surcharge.

World Food Day — A168

**1981, Oct. 16 Litho.**
**556** A168 100fr multi .75 .40

Espana '82 World Cup Soccer — A169

Designs: Various soccer players.

**1981, Nov. 18 Litho. *Perf. 14x13½***
**557** A169 40fr multi .30 .25
**558** A169 65fr multi .50 .25
**559** A169 85fr multi .60 .25
**560** A169 150fr multi 1.10 .45
**561** A169 300fr multi 2.00 .90
*Nos. 557-561 (5)* 4.50 2.10

**Souvenir Sheet**

**562** A169 500fr multi 4.00 1.75

For overprints see Nos. 603-608.

75th Anniv. of Grand Prix — A170

Designs: Winners and their cars — 20fr, Peugeot, 1912. 40fr, Bugatti, 1924. 65fr, Lotus-Climax, 1962. 85fr, Georges Boillot, 1912. 150fr, Phil Hill, 1960.
450fr, Race.

**1981, Nov. 30 *Perf. 14***
**563** A170 20fr multicolored .40 .25
**564** A170 40fr multicolored .55 .25
**565** A170 65fr multicolored .80 .25
**566** A170 85fr multicolored 1.00 .50
**567** A170 150fr multicolored 1.50 .80
*Nos. 563-567 (5)* 4.25 2.05

**Souvenir Sheet**

**568** A170 450fr multicolored 5.00 1.75

For overprint see No. 675.

Christmas 1981 — A171

Designs: Virgin and Child paintings.

**1981, Dec. 24**
**569** A171 100fr Botticelli .80 .35
**570** A171 200fr Botticini 1.40 .75
**571** A171 300fr Botticelli, diff. 2.40 1.00
*Nos. 569-571 (3)* 4.60 2.10

School Gardens A172

**1982, Feb. 19 Litho. *Perf. 13x13½***
**572** A172 65fr shown .55 .30
**573** A172 85fr Garden, diff. .70 .45

L'Estaque, by Georges Braque (1882-1963) — A173

Anniversaries: 120fr, Arturo Toscanini (1867-1957), vert. 140fr, Fruit on a Table, by Edouard Manet (1832-1883). 300fr, George Washington (1732-99), vert. 400fr, Goethe (1749-1832), vert. Nos. 579-580, 21st birthday of Diana, Princess of Wales (portraits), vert.

**1982, Mar. 8 Litho. *Perf. 13***
**574** A173 120fr multi 1.15 .45
**575** A173 140fr multi 1.60 .50
**576** A173 200fr multi 2.75 .75
**577** A173 300fr multi 3.25 1.15
**578** A173 400fr multi 4.00 1.50
**579** A173 500fr multi 5.00 2.00
*Nos. 574-579 (6)* 17.75 6.35

**Souvenir Sheet**

**580** A173 500fr multi 4.00 1.75

Palace of Congress — A174

**1982, Mar. 17**
**581** A174 150fr multi 1.25 .70

7th Youth Festival, Agadez — A175

65fr, Martial arts, horiz. 100fr, Wrestling.

**1982, Apr. 7 *Perf. 12½***
**582** A175 65fr multicolored .50 .30
**583** A175 100fr multicolored .90 .50

Reafforestation Campaign — A176

**1982, Apr. 16 *Perf. 13***
**584** A176 150fr Tree planting 1.20 .50
**585** A176 200fr Trees, Desert 1.40 .75

For overprints see Nos. 668-669.

Scouting Year A177

65fr, Canoeing, two boys sitting. 85fr, Scouts in rubber boat. 130fr, Canoeing, two boys standing. 200fr, Rafting.
400fr, Beach scene.

**1982, May 13**
**586** A177 65fr multi .60 .25
**587** A177 85fr multi .85 .30
**588** A177 130fr multi 1.25 .45
**589** A177 200fr multi 1.75 .75
*Nos. 586-589 (4)* 4.45 1.75

**Souvenir Sheet**

**590** A177 400fr multi 3.25 1.75

For overprint see No. 673.

A178

**1982, June 6**
**591** A178 100fr multi .90 .40

13th Meeting of Islamic Countries Foreign Affairs Ministers, Niamey, Aug. 20-27.

West African Economic Community — A179

**1982, June 28**
**592** A179 200fr Map 1.25 .85

Fishermen in Canoe A180

**1982, July 18 *Perf. 13x12½***
**593** A180 65fr shown .60 .35
**594** A180 85fr Bringing in nets .75 .40

**Nos. 548-551 Overprinted in Blue: "NAISSANCE ROYALE 1982"**

**1982, Aug. 4 *Perf. 14½***
**595** A163 150fr multi 1.10 .50
**596** A163 200fr multi 1.40 .70
**597** A163 300fr multi 2.40 1.00
*Nos. 595-597 (3)* 4.90 2.20

**Souvenir Sheet**

**598** A163 400fr multi 2.75 1.50

Flautist, by Norman Rockwell A181

85fr, Clerk. 110fr, Teacher and Pupil. 150fr, Girl Shopper.

**1982, Sept. 10 Litho. *Perf. 14***
**599** A181 65fr shown .50 .25
**600** A181 85fr multi .70 .30
**601** A181 110fr multi .90 .35
**602** A181 150fr multi 1.25 .50
*Nos. 599-602 (4)* 3.35 1.40

**Nos. 557-562 Overprinted with Past and Present Winners in Black on Silver**

**1982, Sept. 28 *Perf. 14x13½***
**603** A169 40fr multi .30 .25
**604** A169 65fr multi .45 .25
**605** A169 85fr multi .55 .30
**606** A169 150fr multi 1.20 .45
**607** A169 300fr multi 2.25 1.10
*Nos. 603-607 (5)* 4.75 2.35

**Souvenir Sheet**

**608** A169 500fr multi 4.00 2.75

Italy's victory in 1982 World Cup.

ITU Plenipotentiaries Conference, Nairobi, Sept. — A182

**1982, Sept. 28 *Perf. 13***
**609** A182 130fr black & blue .90 .50

Laboratory Workers A183

Various laboratory workers.

**1982, Nov. 9 Litho. *Perf. 13***
**610** A183 65fr multi .60 .35
**611** A183 115fr multi .90 .55

Self-sufficiency in Food Production — A184

**1983, Feb. 16 Litho. *Perf. 13½x13***

| | | | | |
|---|---|---|---|---|
| **612** | A184 | 65fr Rice harvest | .60 | .30 |
| **613** | A184 | 85fr Planting rice, vert. | .90 | .40 |

Grand Ducal Madonna, by Raphael A185

Raphael Paintings: 65fr, Miraculous Catch of Fishes. 100fr, Deliverance of St. Peter. 150fr, Sistine Madonna. 200fr, Christ on the Way to Calvary. 300fr, Deposition. 400fr, Transfiguration. 500fr, St. Michael Slaying the Dragon.

**1983, Mar. 30 Litho. *Perf. 14***

| | | | | |
|---|---|---|---|---|
| **614** | A185 | 65fr multi, vert. | .50 | .25 |
| **615** | A185 | 85fr multi | .60 | .25 |
| **616** | A185 | 100fr multi, vert. | .80 | .25 |
| **617** | A185 | 150fr multi | 1.10 | .40 |
| **618** | A185 | 200fr multi | 1.40 | .55 |
| **619** | A185 | 300fr multi, vert. | 2.00 | .80 |
| **620** | A185 | 400fr multi | 3.00 | 1.10 |
| **621** | A185 | 500fr multi | 4.00 | 1.25 |
| | | *Nos. 614-621 (8)* | 13.40 | 4.85 |

African Economic Commission, 25th Anniv. — A186

**1983, Mar. 18 *Perf. 12½x13***

| | | | | |
|---|---|---|---|---|
| **622** | A186 | 120fr multi | .90 | .45 |
| **623** | A186 | 200fr multi | 1.40 | .85 |

Army Surveyors A187

**1983, Apr. 14 *Perf. 13x12½***

| | | | | |
|---|---|---|---|---|
| **624** | A187 | 85fr shown | .60 | .40 |
| **625** | A187 | 150fr Road building | 1.10 | .75 |

Agadez Court A188

**1983, Apr. 26 Litho. *Perf. 13x12½***

| | | | | |
|---|---|---|---|---|
| **626** | A188 | 65fr multi | .45 | .25 |

Mail Van — A189

**1983, June 25 Litho.**

| | | | | |
|---|---|---|---|---|
| **627** | A189 | 65fr Van | .45 | .40 |
| **628** | A189 | 100fr Van, map | .75 | .45 |

Palestine Solidarity — A190

**1983, Aug. 21 Litho. *Perf. 12½***

| | | | | |
|---|---|---|---|---|
| **629** | A190 | 65fr multi | .60 | .25 |

Intl. Literacy Year — A191

Various adult education classes. 65fr, 150fr vert.

***Perf. 13½x14½, 14½x13½***

**1983, Sept. 8 Litho.**

| | | | | |
|---|---|---|---|---|
| **630** | A191 | 40fr multi | .35 | .25 |
| **631** | A191 | 65fr multi | .45 | .25 |
| **632** | A191 | 85fr multi | .60 | .30 |
| **633** | A191 | 100fr multi | .75 | .40 |
| **634** | A191 | 150fr multi | 1.25 | .90 |
| | | *Nos. 630-634 (5)* | 3.40 | 2.10 |

7th Ballet Festival of Dosso Dept. A192

Various dancers.

**1983, Oct. 7 *Perf. 14½x13½***

| | | | | |
|---|---|---|---|---|
| **635** | A192 | 65fr multi | .50 | .35 |
| **636** | A192 | 85fr multi | .70 | .45 |
| **637** | A192 | 120fr multi | 1.10 | .60 |
| | | *Nos. 635-637 (3)* | 2.30 | 1.40 |

World Communications Year — A193

80fr, Post Office, mail van. 120fr, Sorting mail. 150fr, Emblem, vert.

**1983, Oct. 18 *Perf. 13x12½, 12½x13***

| | | | | |
|---|---|---|---|---|
| **638** | A193 | 80fr multi | .60 | .45 |
| **639** | A193 | 120fr multi | .85 | .50 |
| **640** | A193 | 150fr multi | 1.25 | .60 |
| | | *Nos. 638-640 (3)* | 2.70 | 1.55 |

Solar Energy For Television — A194

**1983, Nov. 26 *Perf. 13***

| | | | | |
|---|---|---|---|---|
| **641** | A194 | 85fr Antenna | .60 | .40 |
| **642** | A194 | 130fr Car | 1.00 | .40 |

Local Butterflies — A195

75fr, Hypolimnas misippus. 120fr, Papilio demodocus. 250fr, Vanessa antiopa. 350fr, Charesex jasius. 500fr, Danaus chrisippus.

**1983, Dec. 9 *Perf. 12½***

| | | | | |
|---|---|---|---|---|
| **643** | A195 | 75fr multicolored | .90 | .40 |
| **644** | A195 | 120fr multicolored | 1.25 | .50 |
| **645** | A195 | 250fr multicolored | 2.25 | .90 |
| **646** | A195 | 350fr multicolored | 3.50 | 1.25 |
| **647** | A195 | 500fr multicolored | 5.50 | 1.60 |
| | | *Nos. 643-647 (5)* | 13.40 | 4.65 |

SAMARIYA Natl. Development Movement — A196

**1984, Jan. 18 Litho. *Perf. 13x13½***

| | | | | |
|---|---|---|---|---|
| **648** | A196 | 80fr multi | .60 | .40 |

Alestes Bouboni A197

**1984, Mar. 28 Litho. *Perf. 13***

| | | | | |
|---|---|---|---|---|
| **649** | A197 | 120fr multi | 3.00 | .80 |

Military Pentathlon A198

**1984, Apr. 10**

| | | | | |
|---|---|---|---|---|
| **650** | A198 | 120fr Hurdles | .85 | .40 |
| **651** | A198 | 140fr Shooting | 1.00 | .60 |

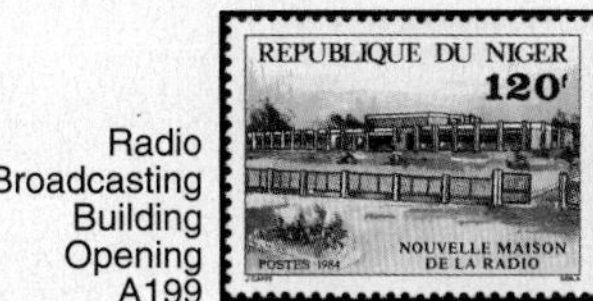

Radio Broadcasting Building Opening A199

**1984, May 14 Litho. *Perf. 13***

| | | | | |
|---|---|---|---|---|
| **652** | A199 | 120fr multi | .90 | .40 |

25th Anniv. of Council of Unity — A200

**1984, May 29 *Perf. 12½***

| | | | | |
|---|---|---|---|---|
| **653** | A200 | 65fr multi | .45 | .35 |
| **654** | A200 | 85fr multi | .75 | .45 |

Renault, 1902 — A201

80fr, Paris. 100fr, Gottlieb Daimler. 120fr, Three-master Jacques Coeur. 150fr, Barque Bosphorus. 250fr, Delage D8. 300fr, Three-master Comet. 400fr, Maybach Zeppelin.
Vintage cars (#656, 658, 660, 662) & ships.

**1984, June 12 *Perf. 12½***

| | | | | |
|---|---|---|---|---|
| **655** | A201 | 80fr multicolored | .60 | .30 |
| **656** | A201 | 100fr multicolored | .75 | .40 |
| **657** | A201 | 120fr multicolored | .75 | .40 |
| **658** | A201 | 140fr shown | 1.00 | .50 |
| **659** | A201 | 150fr multicolored | 1.10 | .60 |
| **660** | A201 | 250fr multicolored | 1.90 | .75 |
| **661** | A201 | 300fr multicolored | 2.00 | .75 |
| **662** | A201 | 400fr multicolored | 3.00 | 1.00 |
| | | *Nos. 655-662 (8)* | 11.10 | 4.70 |

1984 UPU Congress A202

**1984, June 20 Engr. *Perf. 13x12½***

| | | | | |
|---|---|---|---|---|
| **663** | A202 | 300fr Ship, emblems | 3.00 | 1.75 |

Ayerou Market Place A203

**1984, July 18 Litho. *Perf. 12½***

| | | | | |
|---|---|---|---|---|
| **664** | A203 | 80fr shown | .75 | .50 |
| **665** | A203 | 120fr River scene | 1.10 | .60 |

Vipere Echis Leucogaster — A204

**1984, Aug. 16 *Perf. 13x12½***

| | | | | |
|---|---|---|---|---|
| **666** | A204 | 80fr multi | 1.05 | .55 |

West African Union, CEAO, 10th Anniv. A205

**1984, Oct. 26 Litho. *Perf. 13½***
**667** A205 80fr multi .60 .40

UN Disarmament Campaign, 20th Anniv. — A205a

**1984, Oct. 31 *Perf. 13***
**667A** A205a 400fr brt grn & blk 2.75 1.50
**667B** A205a 500fr brt bl & blk 3.25 2.00

**Nos. 584-585 Overprinted "Aide au Sahel 84"**

**1984 Litho. *Perf. 13***
**668** A176 150fr multi 1.40 .75
**669** A176 200fr multi 1.60 1.10

World Tourism Organization, 10th Anniv. — A206

**1984, Jan. 2 Litho. *Perf. 12½***
**670** A206 110fr WTO emblem .90 .45

Infant Survival Campaign A207

85fr, Breastfeeding. 110fr, Weighing child, giving liquids.

**1985, Jan. 28 Litho. *Perf. 12½***
**671** A207 85fr multi .65 .35
**672** A207 110fr multi .90 .50

**Nos. 590, 519 and 568 Overprinted with Exhibitions in Red**

Souvenir Sheets

***Perf. 13, 12½, 14***

**1985, Mar. 11 Litho.**
**673** A177 400fr MOPHILA '85 / HAMBOURG 4.50 4.50
**674** A154 425fr TSUKUBA EXPO '85 4.50 4.50
**675** A170 450fr ROME, ITALIA '85 emblem 4.50 4.50

See Nos. C356-C357.

Technical & Cultural Cooperation Agency, 15th Anniv. — A208

**1985, Mar. 20 *Perf. 13***
**676** A208 110fr vio, brn & car rose .75 .40

8th Niamey Festival A209

Gaya Ballet Troupe. No. 678 vert.

**1985, Apr. 8 *Perf. 12½x13, 13x12½***
**677** A209 85fr multi .60 .40
**678** A209 110fr multi .75 .55
**679** A209 150fr multi 1.10 .70
*Nos. 677-679 (3)* 2.45 1.65

Intl. Youth Year — A210

Authors and scenes from novels: 85fr, Jack London (1876-1916). 105fr, Joseph Kessel (1898-1979). 250fr, Herman Melville. 450fr, Rudyard Kipling.

**1985, Apr. 29 *Perf. 13***
**680** A210 85fr multi .75 .35
**681** A210 105fr multi .80 .40
**682** A210 250fr multi 2.00 .90
**683** A210 450fr multi 3.50 1.75
*Nos. 680-683 (4)* 7.05 3.40

PHILEXAFRICA '85, Lome, Togo — A211

**1985, May 6 *Perf. 13x12½***
**684** A211 200fr Tree planting 1.50 1.10
**685** A211 200fr Industry 1.50 1.10
*a.* Pair, Nos. 684-685 + label 4.50 4.50

Victor Hugo and His Son Francois, by A. de Chatillon — A212

**1985, May 22 *Perf. 12½***
**686** A212 500fr multi 4.00 1.80

Europafrica A213

**1985, June 3 *Perf. 13***
**687** A213 110fr multi .95 .50

World Wildlife Fund — A214

50fr, 60fr, Addax. 85fr, 110fr, Oryx.

**1985, June 15**
**688** A214 50fr Head, vert. *2.75 .65*
**689** A214 60fr Grazing *3.50 .85*
**690** A214 85fr Two adults *4.25 1.05*
**691** A214 110fr Head, vert. *5.50 1.25*
*Nos. 688-691 (4)* *16.00 3.80*

Environ-destroying Species — A215

85fr, Oedaleus sp. 110fr, Dysdercus volkeri. 150fr, Tolyposporium ehrenbergii, Sclerospora graminicola, horiz. 210fr, Passer luteus. 390fr, Quelea quelea.

**1985, July 1 *Perf. 13x12½, 12½x13***
**692** A215 85fr multi .90 .35
**693** A215 110fr multi 1.00 .40
**694** A215 150fr multi 1.60 .60
**695** A215 210fr multi 2.25 .90
**696** A215 390fr multi 4.25 1.75
*Nos. 692-696 (5)* 10.00 4.00

**Official Type of 1988 and**

Cross of Agadez — A216

**1985-94 Engr. *Perf. 13***
**697** A216 85fr green .75 .40
**698** O2 110fr brown 1.00 .50
**699** A216 125fr blue green —
**700** A216 175fr emerald —
**701** A216 210fr orange — —

Issued: 85fr, 110fr, 7/85; 125fr, 175fr, 210fr, 5/15/94.

Natl. Independence, 25th Anniv. — A217

**1985, Aug. 3 Litho. *Perf. 13x12½***
**707** A217 110fr multi .90 .40

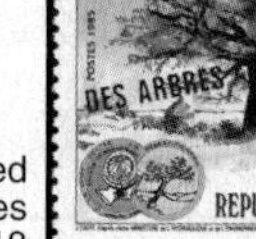


Protected Trees A218

Designs: 30fr, No. 711, Adansonia digitata and pod, vert. 85fr, 210fr, Acacia albida. No. 710, 390fr, Adansonia digitata, diff. Nos. 708-710 inscribed "DES ARBRES POUR LE NIGER."

**1985 *Perf. 13x12½, 12½x13***
**708** A218 30fr grn & multi .55 .40
**709** A218 85fr brn & multi .85 .50
**710** A218 110fr mag & multi 1.20 .60
**711** A218 110fr blk & multi 1.05 .55
**712** A218 210fr blk & multi 1.75 1.10
**713** A218 390fr blk & multi 3.50 1.60
*Nos. 708-713 (6)* 8.90 4.75

Issued: #708-710, 10/1; #711-713, 8/19.

Niamey-Bamako Motorboat Race — A219

110fr, Boats on Niger River. 150fr, Helicopter, competitor. 250fr, Motorboat, map.

**1985, Sept. 16 *Perf. 13½***
**714** A219 110fr multicolored .75 .40
**715** A219 150fr multicolored 1.00 .60
**716** A219 250fr multicolored 1.90 1.00
*Nos. 714-716 (3)* 3.65 2.00

Mushrooms — A220

85fr, Boletus. 110fr, Hypholoma fasciculare. 200fr, Coprinus comatus. 300fr, Agaricus arvensis. 400fr, Geastrum fimbriatum.

**1985, Oct. 3**
**717** A220 85fr multicolored .80 .35
**718** A220 110fr multicolored 1.10 .40
**719** A220 200fr multicolored 1.90 .75
**720** A220 300fr multicolored 3.25 1.10
**721** A220 400fr multicolored 4.25 1.60
*Nos. 717-721 (5)* 11.30 4.20

Nos. 717-719 vert.

PHILEXAFRICA '85, Lome, Togo — A221

No. 722, Village water pump. No. 723, Children playing dili.

**1985, Oct. 21 *Perf. 13x12½***
**722** A221 250fr multicolored 2.00 1.25
**723** A221 250fr multicolored 2.00 1.25
*a.* Pair, Nos. 722-723 4.50 4.50

61st World Savings Day
A222

**1985, Oct. 31** *Perf. 12½x13*
**724** A222 210fr multi 1.60 .90

European Music Year
A223

Traditional instruments.

**1985, Nov. 4** *Perf. 13½*
**725** A223 150fr Gouroumi, vert. 1.25 .80
**726** A223 210fr Gassou 1.75 1.25
**727** A223 390fr Algaita, vert. 3.00 1.75
*Nos. 725-727 (3)* 6.00 3.80

**Souvenir Sheet**

***Perf. 12½***

**728** A223 500fr Biti 4.00 4.00

Civil Statutes Reform — A224

**1986, Jan. 2** **Litho.** *Perf. 13x12½*
**729** A224 85fr Natl. identity card .60 .40
**730** A224 110fr Family services .85 .50

Traffic Safety — A225

**1986, Mar. 26** **Litho.** *Perf. 12½x13*
**731** A225 85fr Obey signs .60 .35
**732** A225 110fr Speed restriction .85 .50

Artists — A226

60fr, Oumarou Ganda, filmmaker. 85fr, Ida Na Dadaou, entertainer. 100fr, Dan Gourmou, entertainer. 130fr, Koungoui, comedian.

**1986, Apr. 11** *Perf. 12½*
**733** A226 60fr multi .45 .30
**734** A226 85fr multi .60 .40
**735** A226 100fr multi .75 .50
**736** A226 130fr multi 1.00 .55
*Nos. 733-736 (4)* 2.80 1.75

Hunger Relief Campaign, Trucks of Hope — A227

85fr, Relief supply truck. 110fr, Mother, child, vert.

**1986, Aug. 27** **Litho.** *Perf. 12½*
**737** A227 85fr multicolored .75 .40
**738** A227 110fr multicolored 1.00 .50

Intl. Solidarity Day — A228

200fr, Nelson Mandela and Walter Sisulu, Robben Island prison camp. 300fr, Mandela.

**1986, Oct. 8** *Perf. 13½*
**739** A228 200fr multi 1.80 .90
**740** A228 300fr multi 2.75 1.40

FAO, 40th Anniv.
A229

50fr, Cooperative peanut farm. 60fr, Fight desert encroachment. 85fr, Irrigation management. 100fr, Breeding livestock. 110fr, Afforestation.

**1986, Oct. 16** *Perf. 13*
**741** A229 50fr multicolored .40 .30
**742** A229 60fr multicolored .45 .30
**743** A229 85fr multicolored .60 .40
**744** A229 100fr multicolored .75 .40
**745** A229 110fr multicolored 1.00 .40
*Nos. 741-745 (5)* 3.20 1.80

Improved Housing for a Healthier Niger — A230

**1987, Feb. 26** **Litho.** *Perf. 13½*
**746** A230 85fr Albarka .75 .30
**747** A230 110fr Mai Sauki .95 .50

Insects Protecting Growing Crops — A231

**1987, Mar. 26** *Perf. 13x12½*
**748** A231 85fr Sphodromantis 1.00 .50
**749** A231 110fr Delta 1.50 .60
**750** A231 120fr Cicindela 1.75 .85
*Nos. 748-750 (3)* 4.25 1.95

Liptako-Gourma Telecommunications Link Inauguration — A232

**1987, Apr. 10** *Perf. 13½*
**751** A232 110fr multi .75 .50

Samuel Morse — A233

120fr, Telegraph key, operator, horiz. 350fr, Receiver, horiz.

**1987, May 21** **Litho.** *Perf. 12x12½*
**752** A233 120fr multicolored .75 .40
**753** A233 200fr shown 1.50 .75
**754** A233 350fr multicolored 3.00 1.50
*Nos. 752-754 (3)* 5.25 2.65

Invention of the telegraph, 150th anniv.

1988 Seoul Summer Olympics — A234

**1987, July 15**
**755** A234 85fr Tennis .55 .40
**756** A234 110fr Pole vault .85 .40
**757** A234 250fr Soccer 2.00 .85
*Nos. 755-757 (3)* 3.40 1.65

**Souvenir Sheet**

**758** A234 500fr Running 4.00 2.75

1988 Winter Olympics, Calgary — A235

85fr, Ice hockey. 110fr, Speed skating. 250fr, Pairs figure skating.
500fr, Downhill skiing.

**1987, July 28** **Litho.** *Perf. 12½*
**759** A235 85fr multi .60 .35
**760** A235 110fr multi .85 .40
**761** A235 250fr multi 2.00 .85
*Nos. 759-761 (3)* 3.45 1.60

**Souvenir Sheet**

**762** A235 500fr multi 4.00 2.75

For overprints see Nos. 783-785.

African Games, Nairobi — A236

**1987, Aug. 5** *Perf. 13*
**763** A236 85fr Runners .60 .35
**764** A236 110fr High jump .75 .40
**765** A236 200fr Hurdles 1.50 .75
**766** A236 400fr Javelin 3.00 1.50
*Nos. 763-766 (4)* 5.85 3.00

Natl. Tourism Office, 10th Anniv.
A237

85fr, Chief's stool, scepter, vert. 110fr, Nomad, caravan, scepter. 120fr, Moslem village. 200fr, Bridge over Niger River.

**1987, Sept. 10** *Perf. 13½*
**767** A237 85fr multicolored .50 .35
**768** A237 110fr multicolored 1.00 .40
**769** A237 120fr multicolored 1.00 .40
**770** A237 200fr multicolored 1.75 .75
*Nos. 767-770 (4)* 4.25 1.90

Aga Khan Architecture Prize, 1986 — A238

85fr, Yaama Mosque, dawn. 110fr, At night. 250fr, In daylight.

**1987, Oct. 7** *Perf. 13*
**771** A238 85fr multi .60 .30
**772** A238 110fr multi .80 .40
**773** A238 250fr multi 1.75 .90
*Nos. 771-773 (3)* 3.15 1.60

Niamey Court of Appeal
A239

**1987, Nov. 17** *Perf. 13x12½*
**774** A239 85fr multi .60 .30
**775** A239 110fr multi .75 .40
**776** A239 140fr multi 1.00 .50
*Nos. 774-776 (3)* 2.35 1.20

Christmas 1987 — A240

Paintings: 110fr, The Holy Family with Lamb, by Raphael. 500fr, The Adoration of the Magi, by Hans Memling (c. 1430-1494).

**Wmk. 385**

**1987, Dec. 24** **Litho.** *Perf. 12½*
**777** A240 110fr multi 1.00 .50

**Souvenir Sheet**

**778** A240 500fr multi 4.00 2.50

No. 778 is airmail.

Modern Services for a Healthy Community — A241

**1988, Jan. 21** ***Perf. 13***
**779** A241 85fr Water drainage .95 .55
**780** A241 110fr Sewage 1.10 .70
**781** A241 165fr Garbage removal 1.90 .95
*Nos. 779-781 (3)* 3.95 2.20

Dan-Gourmou Prize — A242

**1988, Feb. 16 Litho.** ***Perf. 13½***
**782** A242 85fr multi 1.10 .70

Natl. modern music competition.

**Nos. 759-761 Ovptd. "Medaille d'or" and Name of Winner in Gold**

**1988, Mar. 29** ***Perf. 12½***
**783** A235 85fr USSR .60 .40
**784** A235 110fr Gusafson, Sweden .80 .50
**785** A235 250fr Gordeeva and Grinkov, USSR 2.00 1.20
*Nos. 783-785 (3)* 3.40 2.10

New Market Building, Niamey A243

**1988, Apr. 9 Litho.** ***Perf. 13x12½***
**786** A243 85fr multi .75 .40

WHO 40th Anniv., Universal Immunization Campaign — A244

**1988, May 26 Litho.** ***Perf. 12½x13***
**787** A244 85fr Mother and child .65 .40
**788** A244 110fr Visiting doctor .90 .45

Organization for African Unity (OAU), 25th Anniv. — A245

**1988, June 28** ***Perf. 12½***
**789** A245 85fr multi .65 .35

Construction of a Sand Break to Arrest Desert Encroachment — A246

**1988, Sept. 27 Litho.** ***Perf. 12½x13***
**790** A246 85fr multi 1.10 .50

Intl. Red Cross and Red Crescent Organizations, 125th Annivs. — A247

**1988, Oct. 26** ***Perf. 13x12½***
**791** A247 85fr multi .60 .35
**792** A247 110fr multi .80 .40

Niger Press Agency A248

**1989, Jan. 31 Litho.** ***Perf. 12½***
**793** A248 85fr blk, org & grn .65 .35

Fight Against AIDS — A249

**1989, Feb. 28** ***Perf. 13½***
**794** A249 85fr multi .65 .35
**795** A249 110fr multi .80 .40

Intl. Maritime Organization, 30th Anniv. — A250

**1989, Mar. 29 Litho.** ***Perf. 12½x13***
**796** A250 100fr multi .90 .40
**797** A250 120fr multi 1.20 .50

FAN Seizure of Government, 15th Anniv. — A251

85fr, Gen. Ali Saibou. 110fr, Raising of the flag.

**1989, Apr. 14**
**798** A251 85fr multi .60 .30
**799** A251 110fr multi .80 .35

PHILEXFRANCE '89 — A252

100fr, Eiffel Tower. 200fr, Simulated stamps.

**1989, July 1 Litho.** ***Perf. 13***
**800** A252 100fr multi .75 .40
**801** A252 200fr multi 1.50 .70

French Revolution, Bicent. — A253

250fr, Planting a tree for liberty.

**1989, July 1**
**802** A253 250fr multicolored 2.25 1.10

Zinder Regional Museum — A253a

***Perf. 14¾x14¼***
**1989, Aug. 23** **Litho.**
**802A** A253a 85fr multicolored *20.00*

African Development Bank, 25th Anniv. — A254

**1989, Aug. 30 Litho.** ***Perf. 13½***
**803** A254 100fr multicolored .75 .35

Communication and Postal Organization of West Africa (CAPTEAO), 30th Anniv. — A255

**1989, July 3 Litho.** ***Perf. 13½***
**804** A255 85fr multicolored .65 .35

Verdant Field, Field After Locust Plague — A256

**1989, Oct. 1 Litho.** ***Perf. 13***
**805** A256 85fr multicolored 1.25 .35

Lumiere Brothers, Film Pioneers A256a

Designs: 150fr, Auguste Lumiere (1862-1954). 250fr, Louis Lumiere (1864-1948).

**1989, Nov. 21 Litho.** ***Perf. 13½***
**805A** A256a 150fr multicolored 1.50 .75
**805B** A256a 250fr multicolored 2.25 1.00
**805C** A256a 400fr multicolored 3.50 1.75
*Nos. 805A-805C (3)* 7.25 3.50

Rural Development Council, 30th Anniv. — A256b

**1989 Litho.** ***Perf. 15x14***
**805D** A256b 75fr multicolored *20.00*

Flora — A257

10fr, Russelia equisetiformis. 20fr, Argyreia nervosa. 30fr, Hibiscus rosa-sinensis. 50fr, Catharanthus roseus. 100fr, Cymothoe sangaris, horiz.

**1989, Dec. 12 Litho.** ***Perf. 13***
**806** A257 10fr multicolored .25 .25
**807** A257 20fr multicolored .25 .25
**808** A257 30fr multicolored .25 .25
**809** A257 50fr multicolored .45 .25
**810** A257 100fr multicolored 1.00 .40
*Nos. 806-810 (5)* 2.20 1.40

Dunes of Temet A257a

**1989 Litho.** ***Perf. 15x14***
**810A** A257a 145fr Caravan *55.00 45.00*
**810B** A257a 165fr shown *55.00 45.00*

Pan-African Postal Union, 10th Anniv. — A258

**1990, Jan. 18** ***Perf. 12½***
**811** A258 120fr multicolored 1.00 .50

Intl. Literacy Year — A259

**1990, Feb. 27** ***Perf. 13½x13***

| | | | | |
|---|---|---|---|---|
| **812** | A259 | 85fr shown | .65 | .30 |
| **813** | A259 | 110fr Class, diff. | .95 | .40 |

Islamic Conference Organization, 20th anniv. — A260

**1990, Mar. 15** ***Perf. 13x12½***

| | | | | |
|---|---|---|---|---|
| **814** | A260 | 85fr OCI emblem | .70 | .35 |

U.S. Congressman Mickey Leland — A261

**1990, Mar. 29** **Litho.** ***Perf. 13½***

| | | | | |
|---|---|---|---|---|
| **815** | A261 | 300fr multicolored | 2.40 | 1.25 |
| **816** | A261 | 500fr multicolored | 4.00 | 2.00 |

Leland died Aug. 7, 1989 in a plane crash on a humanitarian mission.

Natl. Development Society, 1st Anniv. — A262

**1990, May 15** **Litho.** ***Perf. 13½***

| | | | | |
|---|---|---|---|---|
| **817** | A262 | 85fr multicolored | .70 | .35 |

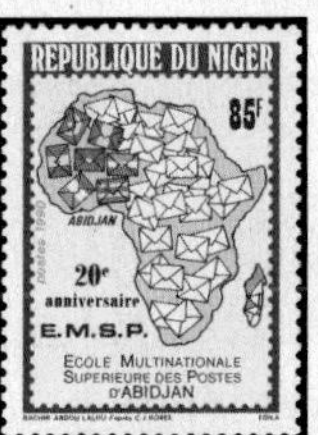


Multinational Postal School, 20th Anniv. — A263

**1990, May 31** ***Perf. 13x12½***

| | | | | |
|---|---|---|---|---|
| **818** | A263 | 85fr multicolored | .75 | .35 |

1992 Summer Olympics, Barcelona — A263a

**1990, June 4** **Litho.** ***Perf. 13½***

| | | | | |
|---|---|---|---|---|
| **818A** | A263a | 85fr Gymnastics | .65 | .30 |
| **818B** | A263a | 110fr Hurdles | .85 | .40 |
| **818C** | A263a | 250fr Running | 2.00 | 1.00 |
| **818D** | A263a | 400fr Equestrian | 3.00 | 1.50 |
| **818E** | A263a | 500fr Long jump | 4.00 | 2.00 |
| | | *Nos. 818A-818E (5)* | 10.50 | 5.20 |

**Souvenir Sheet**

| | | | | |
|---|---|---|---|---|
| **818F** | A263a | 600fr Cycling | 4.75 | 2.75 |

Nos. 818D-818F are airmail.

Independence, 30th Anniv. — A264

**1990, Aug. 3** ***Perf. 12½***

| | | | | |
|---|---|---|---|---|
| **819** | A264 | 85fr gray grn & multi | .60 | .35 |
| **820** | A264 | 110fr buff & multi | .90 | .45 |

UN Development Program, 40th Anniv. — A265

**1990, Oct. 24** **Litho.** ***Perf. 13½***

| | | | | |
|---|---|---|---|---|
| **821** | A265 | 100fr multicolored | .80 | .40 |

A266

Butterflies and Mushrooms — A266a

Designs: 85fr, Amanita rubescens. 110fr, Graphum pylades. 200fr, Pseudacraea hostilia. 250fr, Russula virescens. 400fr, Boletus impolitus. 500fr, Precis octavia. 600fr, Cantharellus cibarius & pseudacraea boisduvali.

**1991, Jan. 15** **Litho.** ***Perf. 13½***

| | | | | |
|---|---|---|---|---|
| **822** | A266 | 85fr multicolored | .65 | .30 |
| **823** | A266 | 110fr multicolored | .75 | .40 |
| **824** | A266 | 200fr multicolored | 1.20 | .80 |
| **825** | A266 | 250fr multicolored | 2.25 | 1.00 |
| **826** | A266 | 400fr multicolored | 3.25 | 1.50 |
| **827** | A266 | 500fr multicolored | 3.50 | 1.60 |
| | | *Nos. 822-827 (6)* | 11.60 | 5.60 |

**Souvenir Sheet**

| | | | | |
|---|---|---|---|---|
| **828** | A266a | 600fr multicolored | 5.00 | 5.00 |

Nos. 826-828 are airmail. No. 828 contains one 30x38mm stamp.

Palestinian Uprising — A267

**1991, Mar. 30** **Litho.** ***Perf. 12½***

| | | | | |
|---|---|---|---|---|
| **829** | A267 | 110fr multicolored | 1.00 | .45 |

Christopher Columbus (1451-1506) A268

Hypothetical portraits and: 85fr, Santa Maria. 110fr, Frigata, Portuguese caravel, 15th cent. 200fr, Four-masted caravel, 16th cent. 250fr, Estremadura, Spanish caravel, 1511. 400fr, Vija, Portuguese caravel, 1600. 500fr, Pinta. 600fr, Nina.

**1991, Mar. 19** **Litho.** ***Perf. 13½***

| | | | | |
|---|---|---|---|---|
| **830** | A268 | 85fr multicolored | .75 | .35 |
| **831** | A268 | 110fr multicolored | .90 | .40 |
| **832** | A268 | 200fr multicolored | 1.60 | .80 |
| **833** | A268 | 250fr multicolored | 2.00 | 1.00 |
| **834** | A268 | 400fr multicolored | 3.25 | 1.40 |
| **835** | A268 | 500fr multicolored | 3.75 | 1.90 |
| | | *Nos. 830-835 (6)* | 12.25 | 5.85 |

**Souvenir Sheet**

| | | | | |
|---|---|---|---|---|
| **835A** | A268 | 600fr multicolored | 5.00 | 4.00 |

Nos. 834-835A are airmail.

Timia Falls — A269

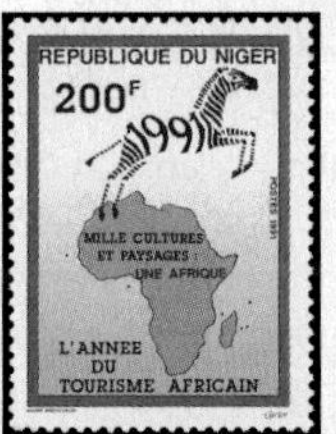


African Tourism Year — A270

Designs: 85fr, Boubon Market, horiz. 130fr, Ruins of Assode, horiz.

**1991, July 10**

| | | | | |
|---|---|---|---|---|
| **836** | A269 | 85fr multicolored | .70 | .30 |
| **837** | A269 | 110fr multicolored | .95 | .45 |
| **838** | A269 | 130fr multicolored | 1.10 | .50 |
| **839** | A270 | 200fr multicolored | 1.75 | .85 |
| | | *Nos. 836-839 (4)* | 4.50 | 2.10 |

Anniversaries and Events — A270a

85fr, Chess players Anatoly Karpov and Garry Kasparov. 110fr, Race car drivers Ayrton Senna and Alain Prost. 200fr, An official swears allegiance to the constitution, Honoré-Gabriel Riqueti (Comte de Mirabeau). 250fr, Gen. Dwight D. Eisenhower, Winston Churchill, Field Marshal Bernard Montgomery and Republic P-4D Thunderbolt. 400fr, Charles de Gaulle and Konrad Adenauer. 500fr, German Chancellor Helmut Kohl, Brandenburg Gate. 600fr, Pope John Paul II's visit to Africa.

**1991, July 15** **Litho.** ***Perf. 13½***

| | | | | |
|---|---|---|---|---|
| **839A** | A270a | 85fr multicolored | .45 | .25 |
| **839B** | A270a | 110fr multicolored | .60 | .25 |
| **839C** | A270a | 200fr multicolored | 1.10 | .35 |
| **839D** | A270a | 250fr multicolored | 6.00 | 1.25 |
| **839E** | A270a | 400fr multicolored | 2.25 | .75 |
| **839F** | A270a | 500fr multicolored | 2.75 | .85 |
| **839G** | A270a | 600fr multicolored | 5.00 | 5.00 |
| | | *Nos. 839A-839G (7)* | 18.15 | 8.70 |

French Revolution, bicent. (#839C). Franco-German Cooperation Agreement, 28th anniv. (#839E). #839E is airmail & exists in a souvenir sheet of 1. German reunification (#839F). Nos. 839F and 839G are airmail and exist in souvenir sheets of 1.

For surcharge see No. 865.

Women's Hairstyles A271

**1991**

| | | | | |
|---|---|---|---|---|
| **840** | A271 | 85fr multicolored | .95 | .30 |
| **841** | A271 | 110fr multicolored | 1.25 | .40 |
| **842** | A271 | 165fr multicolored | 1.90 | .65 |
| **843** | A271 | 200fr multicolored | 2.10 | .75 |
| | | *Nos. 840-843 (4)* | 6.20 | 2.10 |

Transportation — A271a

Design: 85fr, Earth Resources Satellite, ERS-1, Japan; 110fr, EXOS-D satellite for observation of the Aurora Borealis, Japan; 200fr, Louis Favre (1826-1879), Congo-Ocean locomotive BB 415; 250fr, Congo-Ocean locomotive BB.BB.301; 400fr, Locomotive BB BB 302; 500fr, Anglo-French Concorde, F117 stealth fighter, US. 600fr, George Nagelmacker (1845-1905), Orient Express.

**1991, Oct. 15** **Litho.** ***Perf. 13½x13¼***

| | | | | |
|---|---|---|---|---|
| **843A** | A271a | 85fr multi | .45 | .25 |
| **843B** | A271a | 110fr multi | .60 | .25 |
| **843C** | A271a | 200fr multi | 2.10 | .35 |
| **843D** | A271a | 250fr multi | 2.50 | .40 |
| **843E** | A271a | 400fr multi | 3.75 | .55 |
| **843F** | A271a | 500fr multi | 2.75 | .50 |
| | | *Nos. 843A-843F (6)* | 12.15 | 2.30 |

**Souvenir Sheet**

| | | | | |
|---|---|---|---|---|
| **843G** | A271a | 600fr multi | 2.75 | .50 |

Nos. 843E-843G are airmail. Nos. 843A-843F exist in souvenir sheets of one. A souvenir sheet of 3 containing Nos. 843A-843B, 843F exists.

Natl. Conference of Niger — A272

**1991, Dec. 17** **Litho.** ***Perf. 12½***

| | | | | |
|---|---|---|---|---|
| **844** | A272 | 85fr multicolored | .70 | .35 |

House Built Without Wood A273

**1992, May 25** **Litho.** ***Perf. 12½***

| | | | | |
|---|---|---|---|---|
| **845** | A273 | 85fr multicolored | .75 | .40 |

World Population Day — A274

Designs: 85fr, Assembling world puzzle. 110fr, Globe on a kite string.

**1992, July 11 Litho. *Perf. 12½***
**846** A274 85fr multicolored .75 .40
**847** A274 110fr multicolored .95 .50

Discovery of America, 500th Anniv. — A275

**1992, Sept. 16 *Perf. 13***
**848** A275 250fr multicolored 2.25 1.10

Hadjia Haoua Issa (1927-1990), Singer — A276

**1992, Sept. 23 *Perf. 12½x13***
**849** A276 150fr multicolored 1.25 .65

Intl. Conference on Nutrition, Rome — A277

**1992 Litho. *Perf. 12½***
**850** A277 145fr tan & multi 1.40 .60
**851** A277 350fr blue & multi 3.00 1.50

African School of Meteorology and Civil Aviation, 30th Anniv. — A278

**1993, Feb. 7 *Perf. 13½***
**852** A278 110fr bl, grn & blk .90 .45

Environmental Protection A279

**1993, June 26 Litho. *Perf. 12½***
**853** A279 85fr salmon & multi .75 .40
**854** A279 165fr green & multi 1.50 .75

World Population Day A280

110fr, Buildings, person with globe as head, tree.

**1993, July 11 Litho. *Perf. 13½***
**855** A280 85fr multicolored .65 .30
**856** A280 110fr multicolored .85 .40

Holy City of Jerusalem — A281

**1993, Nov. 8 Litho. *Perf. 13x12½***
**857** A281 110fr multicolored .95 .45

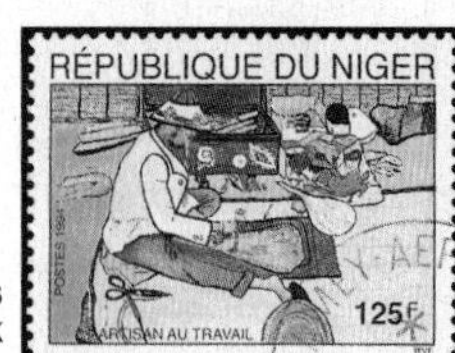

Artisans at Work — A282b

**1994 Litho. *Perf. 13x13¼***
**857D** A282b 125fr Tailor —
**857E** A282b 175fr Weaver, vert. — —

Nelson Mandela, F.W. De Klerk, Winners of 1993 Nobel Peace Prize — A282

**1994, Feb. 11 Litho. *Perf. 13***
**858** A282 270fr multicolored 1.10 .55

Landscapes — A282a

**1994 Litho. *Perf. 12½x13***
**858B** A282a 110fr Hills —
**858C** A282a 165fr Mountain —

An 85fr stamp was released with this set. The editors would like to examine that stamp.

Cultural Cooperation & Technique Agency, 25th Anniv. — A283

**1995 Litho. *Perf. 13½x13***
**859** A283 100fr multicolored .50 .25

Animals Used for Transportation — A284

500fr, Donkey cart. 1000fr, Man, saddled horse.

**1995 *Perf. 13x13½***
**860** A284 500fr multi 1.75 1.10
**861** A284 1000fr multi 4.00 2.25

Economic Community of West African States (ECOWAS), 20th Anniv. — A285

**1995 Litho. *Perf. 13½***
**862** A285 125fr multicolored .70 .35

Cattle Ranching A286

Design: 300fr, Irrigating fields.

**1995 *Perf. 13½x13***
**863** A286 125fr shown .60 .35
**864** A286 300fr multicolored 1.20 .75

**Souvenir Sheet of No. 839E Ovptd.**

**1995, Nov. 8 Litho. *Perf. 13½***
**865** A270a 400fr multicolored *6.50 4.00*

African Development Bank, 30th Anniv. — A287

**1995 Litho. *Perf. 14***
**866** A287 300fr green & red 1.25 .80

Boy Scouts A288

350fr, Robert Baden-Powell. 500fr, Scout saluting.

**1996 *Perf. 13½***
**867** A288 350fr multicolored 1.25 .75
**868** A288 500fr multicolored 2.00 1.20

Nos. 867-868 exist imperf. and in souvenir sheets of 1 both perf. and imperf.

UN, UNICEF, 50th Anniv. — A289

Designs: 150fr, Child with head bandaged, UNICEF emblem. 225fr, Boy carrying bowl of food on head, dove, globes. 475fr, Woman, boy playing on artillery piece, space station Mir. 550fr, Boy, race car driver Michael Schumacher, UNICEF emblem.

**1996**
**869** A289 150fr multicolored .70 .35
**870** A289 225fr multicolored 1.00 .50
**871** A289 475fr multicolored 2.25 1.10
*a.* Sheet of 2, #870-871 + label *11.00 5.50*
**872** A289 550fr multicolored 2.50 1.25
*a.* Sheet of 2, #869, 872 + label *11.00 5.50*
*Nos. 869-872 (4)* 6.45 3.20

Entertainers — A290

No. 873, Bob Marley. No. 874, Janis Joplin. No. 874A, Madonna. No. 875, Jerry Garcia. No. 876, Elvis Presley. No. 877, Marilyn Monroe. No. 878, John Lennon. No. 879, Monroe, diff. No. 880, Presley, diff.
No. 881, Presley, diff. No. 882, Monroe, diff.

**1996**
**873** A290 175fr multicolored .70 .45
**874** A290 300fr multicolored 1.10 .90
**874A** A290 400fr multicolored 1.60 1.20
**875** A290 600fr multicolored 2.50 1.75
**876** A290 700fr multicolored 2.75 2.10
**877** A290 700fr multicolored 2.75 2.10
**878** A290 750fr multicolored 3.25 2.25
**879** A290 800fr multicolored 3.25 2.40
**880** A290 800fr multicolored 3.25 2.40
*Nos. 873-880 (9)* 21.15 15.55

**Souvenir Sheets**

**881** A290 2000fr multicolored 7.00 6.00
**882** A290 2000fr multicolored 7.00 6.00

Nos. 873-882 exist imperf. and in souvenir sheets of 1 both perf. and imperf.
No. 874A exists in a souvenir sheet of 1.

Butterflies A291

Boy Scout Jamboree emblem and: 150fr, Chrysiridia riphearia. 200fr, Palla ussheri. 750fr, Mylothris chloris. 800fr, Papilo dardanus.

**1996 Litho. *Perf. 13½***

| | | | | |
|---|---|---|---|---|
| **883** | A291 150fr multicolored | .60 | .35 |
| **884** | A291 200fr multicolored | .80 | .50 |
| **885** | A291 750fr multicolored | 2.75 | 2.25 |
| **886** | A291 800fr multicolored | 2.90 | 2.40 |
| | *Nos. 883-886 (4)* | 7.05 | 5.50 |

Nos. 883-886 exist imperf. and in souvenir sheets of 1 both perf. and imperf.

Wild Animals — A292

Boy Scout Jamboree emblem, Rotary emblem and: 150fr, Erythrocebus patas. 200fr, Panthera pardus. 900fr, Balearica regulorum. 1000fr, Alcelaphus buselaphus.
2000fr, Panthera leo.

**1996**

| | | | |
|---|---|---|---|
| **887** | A292 150fr multicolored | .55 | .35 |
| **888** | A292 200fr multicolored | .70 | .55 |
| **889** | A292 900fr multicolored | 3.00 | 2.50 |
| **890** | A292 1000fr multicolored | 3.50 | 2.75 |
| | *Nos. 887-890 (4)* | 7.75 | 6.15 |

**Souvenir Sheet**

**891** A292 2000fr multicolored 7.00 6.00

Nos. 887-890 exist in souvenir sheets of 1.

Rotary International A292a

Designs: 200fr, Boy holding fruits and vegetables. 700fr, Girl holding sheaves of grain.

**1996 Litho. *Perf. 13½***

| | | | |
|---|---|---|---|
| **891A** | A292a 200fr multicolored | .90 | .55 |
| **891B** | A292a 700fr multicolored | 3.00 | 1.90 |

Intl. Red Cross and Lions Intl. — A293

Designs: 250fr, Jean-Henri Dunant as young man. 300fr, Lions Intl. emblems, boy with books. 400fr, Dunant as old man. 600fr, Older boy carrying younger boy, Lions Intl. emblems.

**1996 Litho. *Perf. 13½***

| | | | |
|---|---|---|---|
| **892** | A293 250fr multicolored | .90 | .60 |
| **893** | A293 300fr multicolored | 1.05 | .55 |
| **894** | A293 400fr multicolored | 1.50 | 1.25 |
| **895** | A293 600fr multicolored | 2.25 | 1.75 |
| | *Nos. 892-895 (4)* | 5.70 | 4.15 |

Traditional Musical Instruments A294

**1996 Litho. *Perf. 13½***

| | | | |
|---|---|---|---|
| **896** | A294 125fr violet & multi | .55 | .30 |
| **897** | A294 175fr pink & multi | .80 | .40 |

Sports A295

**1996**

| | | | |
|---|---|---|---|
| **898** | A295 300fr Golf | 1.05 | .70 |
| **899** | A295 500fr Tennis | 1.75 | 1.40 |
| **900** | A295 700fr Table tennis | 2.60 | 1.80 |
| | *Nos. 898-900 (3)* | 5.40 | 3.90 |

Nos. 898-900 exist in souvenir sheets of one.

1996 Summer Olympic Games, Atlanta A296

Designs: 250fr, Track & field. 350fr, Women's gymnastics, table tennis. 400fr, Tennis, swimming. 600fr, Hurdles, pole vault.
1500fr, Men's track and field.

**1996 Litho. *Perf. 13½***

| | | | |
|---|---|---|---|
| **901** | A296 250fr multicolored | .90 | .60 |
| **902** | A296 350fr multicolored | 1.25 | 1.05 |
| **903** | A296 400fr multicolored | 1.50 | 1.25 |
| **904** | A296 600fr multicolored | 2.10 | 1.80 |
| | *Nos. 901-904 (4)* | 5.75 | 4.70 |

**Souvenir Sheet**

**904A** A296 1500fr multicolored 6.00 6.00

Souvenir Sheet

CHINA '96 — A297

Statues from Yunguang Grottoes, Datong, China: a, Head of Buddha. b, Side view.

**1996**

**905** A297 140fr Sheet of 2, #a.-b. 2.00 1.00

1998 Winter Olympic Games, Nagano A298

**1996**

| | | | |
|---|---|---|---|
| **906** | A298 85fr Hockey | .40 | .25 |
| **907** | A298 200fr Downhill skiing | .90 | .45 |
| **908** | A298 400fr Slalom skiing | 1.75 | .90 |
| **909** | A298 500fr Pairs figure skating | 2.25 | 1.10 |
| | *Nos. 906-909 (4)* | 5.30 | 2.70 |

Nos. 906-909 were not issued without metallic blue overprint on stamps dated 1991. Nos. 908-909 are airmail.

Nos. 906-909 exist with red metallic overprint. A 600fr souvenir sheet with red metallic overprint exists in limited quantities.

Formula I Race Car Drivers A299

Designs: 450fr, Jacques Villeneuve. 2000fr, Ayrton Senna (1960-94).

**1996**

**910** A299 450fr multicolored 1.60 .80

**Souvenir Sheet**

**911** A299 2000fr multicolored 7.00 6.00

No. 910 exists in souvenir sheet of 1. No. 911 contains one 39x57mm stamp.

Tockus Nasutus A300

Coracias Abyssinica — A301

Designs: 15fr, Psittacula krameri. 25fr, Coracias abyssinica. 35fr, Bulbucus ibis.

**1996 Litho. *Perf. 13½x13***

| | | |
|---|---|---|
| **912** | A300 5fr multi | — |
| **912A** | A300 15fr multi | |
| **912B** | A300 25fr multi | — |
| **912C** | A300 35fr multi | |

***Perf. 13***

| | | |
|---|---|---|
| **913** | A301 25fr multi | |
| **914** | A301 35fr multi | |

Compare type A300 to types A301 and A309. The editors would like to examine two stamps of type A301 with 5fr and 15fr denominations.

1998 Winter Olympic Games, Nagano, Japan A302

**1996 Litho. *Perf. 13x13½***

| | | | |
|---|---|---|---|
| **915** | A302 125fr Ice hockey | .55 | .30 |
| **916** | A302 175fr Slalom skiing | .75 | .35 |
| **917** | A302 700fr Pairs figure skating | 3.00 | 1.50 |
| **918** | A302 800fr Speed skating | 3.50 | 1.75 |
| | *Nos. 915-918 (4)* | 7.80 | 3.90 |

**Souvenir Sheet**

**919** A302 1500fr Downhill skiing 6.50 3.25

No. 919 contains one 57x51mm stamp.
Nos. 915-918 exist in souvenir sheets of 1.

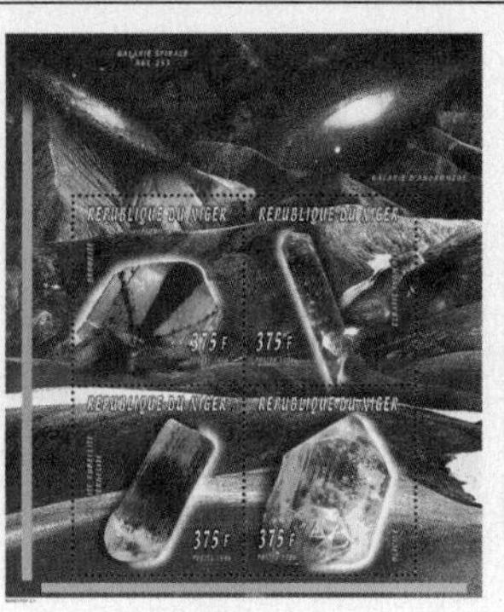

Minerals — A303

No. 920: a, Brookite. b, Elbaite indicolite. c. Elbaite rubellite verdelite. d, Olivine.

No. 921: a, Topaz. b, Autunite. c, Leucite. d, Struvite.

**1996 Litho. *Perf. 13½***

| | | | |
|---|---|---|---|
| **920** | A303 375fr Sheet of 4, #a.-d. | 5.50 | 3.25 |
| **921** | A303 500fr Sheet of 4, #a.-d. | 7.00 | 4.50 |

**Souvenir Sheet**

**922** A303 2000fr Pyrargyrite 6.50 3.25

No. 922 contains one 42x39mm stamp.

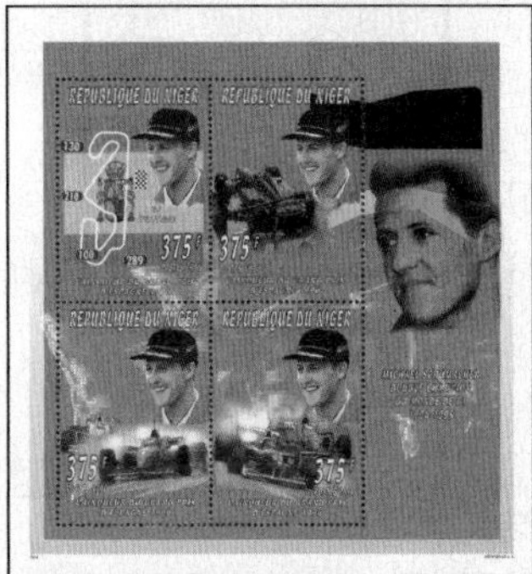

World Driving Champion Michael Schumacher — A304

Schumacher: a, Grand Prix of Spain. b, In race car in pit. c, Ahead of another car. d, Behind another car.

**1996 Litho. *Perf. 13½***

**923** A304 375fr Sheet of 4, #a.-d. 5.50 4.00

German Soccer Team, Euro '96 Champions — A305

No. 924: a, Oliver Bierhoff, player jumping up. b, Bierhoff, player holding up arms. c, ChancellorHelmut Kohl, Queen Elizabeth II, Klinsmann. d, Stadium, Mathias Sammer. logos.

**1996 Litho. *Perf. 13½***

**924** A305 400fr Sheet of 4, #a.-d. 6.00 4.50

Dinosaurs — A306

No. 925: a, Ouranosaurus. b, Spinosaurus. c, Polacanthus. d, Deinonychus.
No. 926: a, Camptosaurus. b, Allosaurus. c, Nodosaurus. d, Kritosaurus.
2000fr, Protoceratops, oviraptor, horiz.

**1996**

**925** A306 300fr Sheet of 4, #a.-d. 7.00 7.00
**926** A306 450fr Sheet of 4, #a.-d. 11.00 11.00

**Souvenir Sheet**

**927** A306 2000fr multicolored 6.75 6.00

France '98, World Soccer Cup Championships — A307

World Cup Trophy and: 125fr, American player. 175fr, Brazilian player. 750fr, Italian player. 1000fr, German player.
1500fr, Player in action scene.

**1996**

**928** A307 125fr multicolored .55 .30
**929** A307 175fr multicolored .75 .45
**930** A307 750fr multicolored 3.25 1.90
**931** A307 1000fr multicolored 4.25 2.40
*Nos. 928-931 (4)* 8.80 5.05

**Souvenir Sheet**

**932** A307 1500fr multicolored 6.00 4.00

No. 932 contains one 57x51mm stamp.

New Year 1997 (Year of the Ox) — A308

**1997 Litho. *Perf. 13½***

**933** A308 500fr shown 2.00 1.00
**934** A308 500fr Riding three oxen 2.00 1.00

Nos. 933-934 exist in souvenir sheets of 1, design extending to perfs on No. 933.

Birds A309

5fr, Tockus nasutus. 15fr, Psittacula kramer. 25fr, Coracias abyssinica. 35fr, Bulbucus ibis.

**1997 Litho. *Perf. 13½***

**935** A309 5fr multicolored .30 .25
**936** A309 15fr multicolored .30 .25
**937** A309 25fr multicolored .30 .25
**938** A309 35fr multicolored .30 .25
*Nos. 935-938 (4)* 1.20 1.00

See No. 1050.

19th Dakar-Agades-Dakar Rally — A310

Designs: 125fr, Truck, child in traditional dress. 175fr, Ostrich, three-wheel vehicle. 300fr, Camel, heavy-duty support truck. 500fr, Motorcycles.

**1997**

**939** A310 125fr multicolored .50 .30
**940** A310 175fr multicolored .70 .40
**941** A310 300fr multicolored 1.20 .75
**942** A310 500fr multicolored 1.90 1.25
*a.* Souvenir sheet, #939-942 4.50 4.50
*b.* Strip of 4, #939-942 4.50 4.50

Deng Xiaoping (1904-97), Chinese Leader — A311

Designs: a, Deng, flag, eating at table, Deng as young man. b, Farming with oxen, Deng holding girl, flag. c, Flag, Deng with soldiers, camp. d, Deng bathing, ships in port, combining grain, launching space vehicle. e, Huts, heavy equipment vehicle, men working. f, Airplane, man holding up flask, operating room, Deng.

**1997**

**943** A311 150fr Sheet of 6, #a.-f. 3.50 2.00

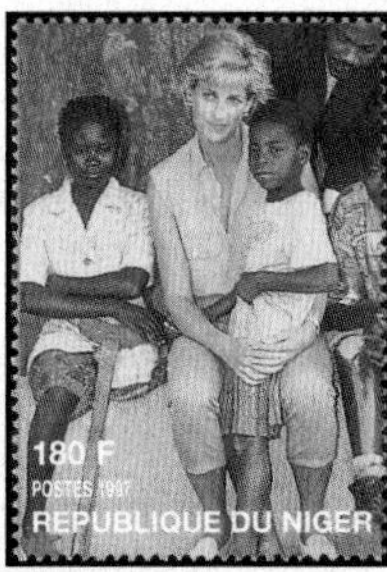


Diana, Princess of Wales (1961-97) A312

No. 944: Various portraits performing humanitarin deeds, on world tours, with various figures.
No. 945: Various portraits in designer dresses.
No. 946: With Mother Teresa (in margin).

**1997, Sept. 30 Litho. *Perf. 13½***

**944** A312 180fr Sheet of 9, #a.-i. 6.50 4.00
**945** A312 180fr Sheet of 9, #a.-i. 6.50 4.00

**Souvenir Sheets**

**946** A312 2000fr multicolored 7.25 5.00
**947** A312 4000fr multicolored 14.00 14.00

No. 947 contains one 40x46mm stamp depicting Princess Diana in red coat, holding bouquet.
A number of other stamps and souvenir sheets having similar type fonts depicting Princess Diana exist. These were declared to be not authorized by Niger postal authorites.

Famous Americans — A313

No. 948 — Various portraits: a-b, John F. Kennedy. c-d, Pres. Bill Clinton.
No. 949 — Various pprtraits: a, Kennedy. b, Dr. Martin Luther King (1929-68). c-d, Clinton.
2000fr, John F. Kennedy.

**1997 Litho. *Perf. 13½***

**948** A313 350fr Sheet of 4, #a.-d. 4.75 3.00
**949** A313 400fr Sheet of 4, #a.-d. 5.75 5.75

**Souvenir Sheet**

**950** A313 2000fr multicolored 6.75 4.00

No. 950 contains one 42x60mm stamp.

Stars of American Cinema — A314

No. 951: a, Eddie Murphy. b, Elizabeth Taylor. c, Bruce Willis. d, James Dean. e, Clint Eastwood. f, Elvis Presley. g, Michelle Pfeiffer. h, Marilyn Monroe. i, Robert Redford.

**1997 Litho. *Perf. 13½***

**951** A314 300fr Sheet of 9, #a.-i. 10.50 6.00

Communications — A315

No. 952: a, 80fr, Satellite transmission, radios. b, 100fr, Computers. c, 60fr, Cellular phone transmission around world. d, 120fr, Hand holding car phone. e, 180fr, Satellite, earth. f, 50fr, Transmission tower, cellular phone.

**1997**

**952** A315 Sheet of 6, #a.-f. 2.25 1.10

Prof. Abdou Moumouni Dioffo — A316

**1997 Litho. *Perf. 13½x13***

**953** A316 125fr multicolored *125.00*

Methods of Transportation — A317

Bicycles, motorcycles: No. 954: a, Jan Ullrich, 1997 Tour de France winner, Eiffel Tower. b, Diana 250, Harley Davidson. c, MK VIII motorcycle, bicycles of 1819, 1875. d, Brands Match Motorcycle Race, Great Britain.
Modern locomotives, country flags: No. 955: a, Pendolino ETR 470, Italy. b, Rame TGV 112, France. c, Eurostar, France, Belgium, UK. d, Intercity Express ICE train, Germany.
Early locomotives, country flags: No. 956: a, Trevithick, UK. b, Pacific North Chapelon, France. c, Buddicom, UK, France. d, PLM "C", France.
Trains of Switzerland: No. 957: a, Crocodile, St. Gothard. b, RE 460. c, Red Streak, RAE 2/4 1001. d, Limmat.
Classic cars, modern sports cars: No. 958: a, Mercedes 300 SL Gullwing, Mercedes E320 Cabriolet. b, Aston Martin V8, Aston Martin DBR2. c. Ferrari F50, Ferrari 250 GT Berlinette. d, Ford Thunderbird, Ford GT40.
Air flight: No. 959: a, Clement Ader's Avion 111, dirigible R101. b, Concorde jet, X36 NASA/MCDD prototype. c, Aile volante FW900, Airbus A340. d, Gaudron GIII, Montgolfier's balloon.
Space travel: No. 960: a, HII rocket, Japan, Copernicus. b, Galileo, Ariane rocket. c, Space shuttle, Neil Armstrong. d, Yuri Gagarin, orbital space station, Soyuz.
1500fr, Swiss train, RE 4/4 II 11349, vert. No. 962, Hubble Space Telescope, Concorde jet. No. 963, TGV mail train, 1958 Chevrolet Corvette.

**1997 Litho. *Perf. 13½***

**954** A317 300fr Sheet of 4, #a.-d. 4.00 4.00
**955** A317 350fr Sheet of 4, #a.-d. 5.00 5.00
**956** A317 375fr Sheet of 4, #a.-d. 5.00 5.00
**957** A317 400fr Sheet of 4, #a.-d. 6.00 6.00
**958** A317 450fr Sheet of 4, #a.-d. 6.00 6.00
**959** A317 500fr Sheet of 4, #a.-d. 6.75 6.75
**960** A317 600fr Sheet of 4, #a.-d. 7.50 7.50

**Souvenir Sheets**

**961** A317 1500fr multicolored 5.75 5.75
**962** A317 2000fr multicolored 6.75 6.75
**963** A317 2000fr multicolored 6.75 6.75

Swiss Railroad, 150th anniv. (#957, #961). Nos. 961-963 each contain one 50x60mm stamp.

Diana, Princess of Wales (1961-97) — A318

Various portraits.
1500fr, Wearing red dress. No. 966, Wearing blue dress.

**1997 Litho. *Perf. 13½***

| | | | | |
|---|---|---|---|---|
| **964** | A318 | 250fr Sheet of 9, #a.-i. | 8.75 | 4.50 |
| **964J** | A318 | 300fr Sheet of 9, #k.-s. | 10.50 | 5.25 |

**Souvenir Sheets**

| | | | | |
|---|---|---|---|---|
| **965** | A318 | 1500fr multicolored | 5.25 | 3.50 |
| **966** | A318 | 2000fr multicolored | 7.00 | 4.50 |

Nos. 965-966 contain one 42x60mm stamp.

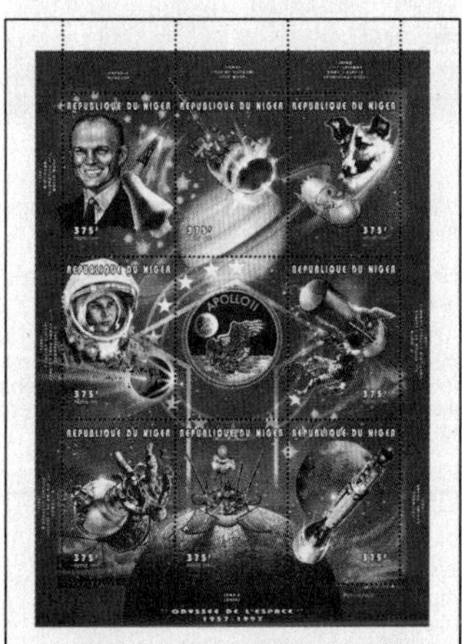

Man in Space — A319

No. 967: a, John Glenn, Mercury capsule. b, Cassini/Huygens satellite. c, Laika, first dog in space, Sputnik 2. d, Valentina Tereshkova, first woman in space, Vostok 6. e. Edward White, first American to walk in space, Gemini 4. f, Alexi Leonov, first Soviet to walk in space. g, Luna 9. h, Gemini capsule docked to Agena.

No. 968: a, Skylab space station. b, Pioneer 13, Venus 2. c, Giotto probe, Halley's Comet. d, Apollo-Soyuz mission. e, Mariner 10. f, Viking 1. g, Venera 11. h, Surveyor 1.

No. 969, 2000fr, Yuri Gagarin, first man in space, Sergei Korolev, RD107 rocket. No. 970, 2000fr, John F. Kennedy, Apollo 11, Neil Armstrong, first man to set foot on the moon.

**1997 Litho. *Perf. 13½***

| | | | | |
|---|---|---|---|---|
| **967** | A319 | 375fr Sheet of 8 + label | 10.00 | 8.00 |
| **968** | A319 | 450fr Sheet of 8 + label | 13.00 | 9.00 |

**Souvenir Sheets**

| | | | | |
|---|---|---|---|---|
| **969-970** | A319 | Set of 2 | 14.00 | 10.00 |

Nos. 969-970 each contain one 42x60mm stamp.

Pres. Ibrahim Mainassara-Bare — A320

**1997 Litho. & Embossed *Perf. 13½***

| | | | | |
|---|---|---|---|---|
| **971** | A320 | 500fr gold & multi | 1.75 | 1.10 |

Scouting, Intl., 90th Anniv. (in 1997) — A321

No. 972 — Scout and: a, Lion. b, Rhinoceros. c, Giraffe. d, Elephant.

No. 972E — Girl Scout: f, Building bird house. g, Examining flower with magnifying glass. h, Identifying flower from book. i, Playing with bird.

No. 973: a, Butterfly. b, Bird with berries in mouth. c, Bird. d, Brown & white butterfly.

No. 974: a, Holding up rock to light. b, Using magnifying glass. c, Looking at rock. d, On hands and knees.

No. 975 — Scout, mushroom, with background color of: a, Yellow. b, White. c, Pink. d, Green.

2000fr, Robert Baden-Powell, Scouts chasing butterflies, mushroom.

**1998 Litho.**

| | | | | |
|---|---|---|---|---|
| **972** | A321 | 350fr Sheet of 4, #a.-d. | 5.00 | 2.75 |
| **972E** | A321 | 400fr Sheet of 4, #f.-i. | 5.75 | 3.50 |
| **973** | A321 | 450fr Sheet of 4, #a.-d. | 6.50 | 3.75 |
| **974** | A321 | 500fr Sheet of 4, #a.-d. | 7.00 | 4.00 |
| **975** | A321 | 600fr Sheet of 4, #a.-d. | 8.50 | 4.75 |

**Souvenir Sheet**

| | | | | |
|---|---|---|---|---|
| **975E** | A321 | 2000fr multicolored | 7.00 | 4.00 |

Greenpeace — A322

No. 976 — Turtles: a, Being caught in net. b, One swimming right. c, Mating. d, One swimming left.

**1998**

| | | | | |
|---|---|---|---|---|
| **976** | A322 | 400fr Block of 4, #a-d | 9.00 | 4.50 |
| *e.* | | Souvenir sheet, #976 | 16.00 | 16.00 |

Sheets overprinted "CHINA 99 World Philatelic Exhibition" are not authorized.

A323

No. 977 — Turtles: a, Pelomedusa subruta. b, Megacephalum shiui. c, Eretmochelus imbricata. d, Platycephala platycephala. e, Spinifera spinifera. f, Malayemys subtrijuga.

No. 978 — Raptors: a, Aquila uerreauxii. b, Asia otus. c, Bubo bubo. d, Surnia ulula. e, Asio flammeus. f, Falco biarnicus.

No. 979 — Orchids: a, Oeceoclades saundersiana. b, Paphiopedilum venustum. c, Maxillaria picta. d, Masdevallia triangularis. e, Zugopetalum. f, Encyllia nemoralis.

No. 980 — Butterflies: a, Danaus plexippus. b, Leto venus. c, Callioratis millari. d, Hippotion celerio. e, Euchloron megaera. f, Teracotona euprepia.

No. 981 — Mushrooms: a, Phaeolepotia aurea. b, Disciotis venosa. c, Gomphidius glutinosus. d, Amanita vaginata. e, Tremellodon gelatinosum. f, Voluariella voluacea.

**1998, Sept. 29 Litho. *Perf. 13½***

| | | | | |
|---|---|---|---|---|
| **977** | A323 | 250fr Sheet of 6, #a.-f. | 5.50 | 2.50 |
| **978** | A323 | 300fr Sheet of 6, #a.-f. | 6.50 | 3.75 |
| **979** | A323 | 350fr Sheet of 6, #a.-f. | 7.50 | 4.00 |
| **980** | A323 | 400fr Sheet of 6, #a.-f. | 8.50 | 4.75 |
| **981** | A323 | 450fr Sheet of 6, #a.-f. | 9.75 | 5.25 |

Marine Life — A324

No. 982: a, Tursiops truncatus. b, Phocoenoides dalli. c, Sousa teuszii. d, Stegostoma fasciatum. e, Delphinus delphis, balaenoptera musculus. f, Carcharodon carcharias. g, Argonauta argo, heterodontus portusjacksoni. h, Mitsukurina owstoni. i, Sphyrna mokarran. j, Homarus gammarus, prostheceraeus vittatus. k, Glossodoris valenciennesi, cephalopodes decapodes. l, Nemertien anople, elysia viridis.

**1998, Sept. 29 Litho. *Perf. 13½***

| | | | | |
|---|---|---|---|---|
| **982** | A324 | 175fr Sheet of 12, #a-l | 8.00 | 4.00 |

World Wildlife Fund A325

Gazella dorcas: No. 983, Doe, fawn. No. 984, Adult lying down. No. 985, Two adults standing still. No. 986 Adult walking.

**1998**

| | | | | |
|---|---|---|---|---|
| **983** | A325 | 250fr multicolored | 1.40 | .85 |
| **984** | A325 | 250fr multicolored | 1.40 | .85 |
| **985** | A325 | 250fr multicolored | 1.40 | .85 |
| **986** | A325 | 250fr multicolored | 1.40 | .85 |
| *a.* | | Se-tenant block of 4 | 8.00 | 6.00 |
| *b.* | | Souvenir sheet, #983-986 | 40.00 | 35.00 |
| | | *Nos. 983-986 (4)* | 5.60 | 3.40 |

Similar items without WWF emblem are not authorized.

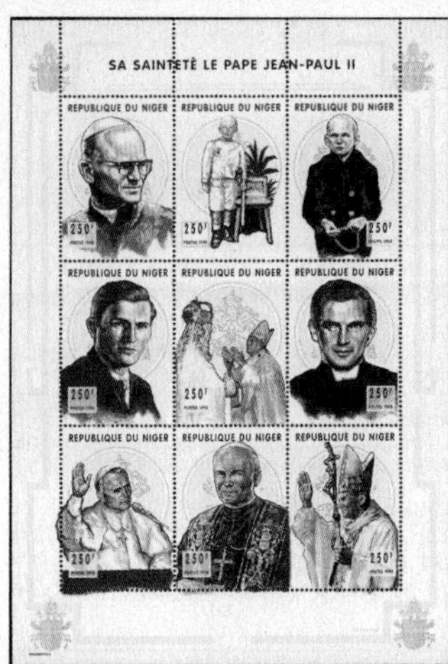


Pope John Paul II — A326

Various portraits of pontiff thoughout his life.

**1998, Sept. 29 Litho. *Perf. 13½***

| | | | | |
|---|---|---|---|---|
| **987** | A326 | 250fr Sheet of 9, #a.-i. | 8.75 | 4.50 |

**Souvenir Sheet**

| | | | | |
|---|---|---|---|---|
| **988** | A326 | 2000fr multicolored | 7.75 | 4.00 |

No. 988 contains one 57x51mm stamp.

Frank Sinatra (1915-98) — A327

Various portraits.

**1998**

| | | | | |
|---|---|---|---|---|
| **989** | A327 | 300fr Sheet of 9, #a.-i. | 10.50 | 6.00 |

Explorers — A328

No. 990: a, Juan Sebastian del Cano (1476-1526), commander of vessel that completed circumnavigation of globe. b, Globe, sailing ships. c, Ferdinand Magellan (1480-1521).

No. 991 — Vasco da Gama (1469-1524): a. Portrait. b, Angels, explorers, soldiers, flag. c, Sailing ship, da Gama's tomb, Lisbon.

No. 992 — Aviator Roland Garros (1888-1918): a, Arriving at Utrecht. b, Flying across Mediterranean, 1913. c, Portrait.

**1998, Sept. 29**

| | | | | |
|---|---|---|---|---|
| **990** | A328 | 350fr Sheet of 3, #a.-c. | 4.00 | 2.00 |
| **991** | A328 | 400fr Sheet of 3, #a.-c. | 4.75 | 2.25 |
| **992** | A328 | 450fr Sheet of 3, #a.-c. | 5.25 | 2.50 |

Nos. 990b, 991b, 992b are 60x51mm.

Jacques-Yves Cousteau (1910-97), Environmentalist — A329

No. 993: a, Whales. b, Fish, diver, whales, sled dog team. c, Portrait of Cousteau surrounded by ship, explorers in polar region, whale, fish.

No. 994: a, Cousteau, children, bird. b, Ship, marine life. c, Cousteau in diving gear, fish.

**1998, Sept. 29**

**993** A329 500fr Sheet of 3, #a.-c. 5.75 3.00
**994** A329 600fr Sheet of 3, #a.-c. 7.00 3.50

Nos. 993b and 994b are 60x51mm.

1998 World Cup Soccer Championships, France — A330

No. 995: a, Emmanuel Petit. b, Zinedine Zidane. c, Fabien Barthez. d, Lilian Thuram. e, Didier Deschamps. f, Youri Djorkaeff. g, Marcel Desailly, Christian Karembeu. h, Bixente Lizarazu. i, Frank Leboeuf, Stephane Guivarc'h.

**1998**

**995** A330 250fr Sheet of 9, #a.-i. 8.75 4.50

A331

FIMA Niger '98 African Fashion Festival — A332

**1998 Litho. *Perf. 13½x13***

**996** A331 175fr multi 1.20 .75
**997** A332 225fr multi 1.50 .75

Flowers — A333

Designs: 10fr, Roses and anemone. 20fr, Asystasia vogeliana, horiz. 30fr, Agrumes, horiz. 40fr, Angraecum sesquipedale. 45fr, Dissotis rotundifolia. 50fr, Hibiscus rosa-sinensis. 100fr, Datura.

**1998 Litho. *Perf. 13¼x13½***

**997A** A333 10fr multi — —
**997B** A333 20fr multi — —
**997C** A333 30fr multi — —
**997D** A333 40fr multi — —
**997E** A333 45fr multi — —
**998** A333 50fr multi — —
**999** A333 100fr multi — —

A number of items inscribed "Republique du Niger" were not authorized by Niger postal authorities. These include:

Dated 1996: Overprinted 500fr souvenir sheet for 20th anniv. first commercial flight of the Concorde.

Dated 1998: Martin Luther King, Jr., 2000fr souvenir sheet;

Ferrari automobile, 2000fr stamp and souvenir sheet;

Trains, 650fr sheet of 4, 2500fr souvenir sheet, two 3000fr souvenir sheets;

Titanic, 650fr sheet of 4, four 650fr souvenir sheets, 2500fr souvenir sheet;

Paintings by Toulouse-Lautrec, Gauguin, Renoir, Matisse, Delacroix, Van Gogh, sheets of nine 250fr, 300fr, 375fr 400fr, 425fr, 500fr stamps, sheet of three 725fr Matisse stamps, 200fr, Delacroix souvenir sheet;

French and Italian performers, sheet of nine 675fr stamps;

Sailing vessels, sheets of four 525fr, 875fr stamps;

Events of the 20th Century, 3 sheets of nine 225fr stamps, 2 sheets of nine 375fr stamps, 3 sheets of nine 500fr stamps, fourteen 225fr souvenir sheets, three 2000fr souvenir sheets;

Space events of the 20th Century, two 2000fr souvenir sheets;

Papal visits, sheet of nine 500fr stamps, sheet of two 1500fr stamps;

Cats, sheetlet of 5 stamps, various denominations, 500fr souvenir sheet;

African Music, sheet of nine 225fr stamps;

Pinocchio, sheet of nine 200fr stamps;

Dated 1999: History of the Cinema (Marilyn Monroe), sheet of nine 275fr stamps, 2000fr souvenir sheet;

History of American Cinema (various actors), sheet of nine 400fr stamps;

John F. Kennedy, Jr., sheet of nine 500fr stamps;

Sheets of nine stamps of various denominations depicting Cats, Panda, Dinosaurs, Kennedy Space Center, Mushrooms, Butterflies, Eagles, Tiger Woods, Chess Pieces (2 different sheets);

Sheets of six stamps of various denominations depicting Butterflies, Cartoon Network Cartoon Characters.

Additional issues may be added to this list.

Wildlife — A334

Designs: No. 1000, 180fr, Tiger, Rotary emblem, vert. No. 1001, 250fr, Tigers, Lions emblem. No. 1002, 375fr, Tiger, Scouting, scouting jamboree emblems. 500fr, Owl, vert.

No. 1003, vert. — Rotary emblem and: a, Lions. b, Leopard. c, Red-headed cranes. d, Owl. e, Buzzards. f, Gazelles (long horns). g, Elands (twisted horns). h, Antelope (short horns).

No. 1004 — Lions emblem and: a, Lion, looking left. b, Lion, lioness. c, Lion reclining. d, Leopards. e, Leopard on rock. f, Lion, looking right. g, Lion in grass. h, Lion cub.

No. 1005 — Scouting and scouting jamboree emblems and: a, Leopard, mouth open. b, Leopard overlooking plains. c, Leopard looking right. d, Cat. e, Pair of leopards. f, Leopard and trees. g, Leopard reclining. h, Leopard standing on rock.

1000fr, Tiger in water, horiz. 2500fr, Leopards.

**1998 Litho. *Perf. 13½***

**1000-1002** A334 Set of 3
**1003** A334 180fr Sheet of 9, #a-h, 1000
**1004** A334 250fr Sheet of 9, #a-h, 1001
**1005** A334 375fr Sheet of 9, #a-h, 1002

**Souvenir Sheets**

**1005I** A334 500fr multi — —
**1006** A334 1000fr mutli
**1007** A334 2500fr multi

New Year 1998, Year of the Tiger, Nos. 1000-1002, 1006. Nos. 1006-1007 each contain one 46x40mm stamp.

No. 1005I contains one 40x46mm stamp. Italia '98 Intl. Philatelic Exhibition (No. 1005I).

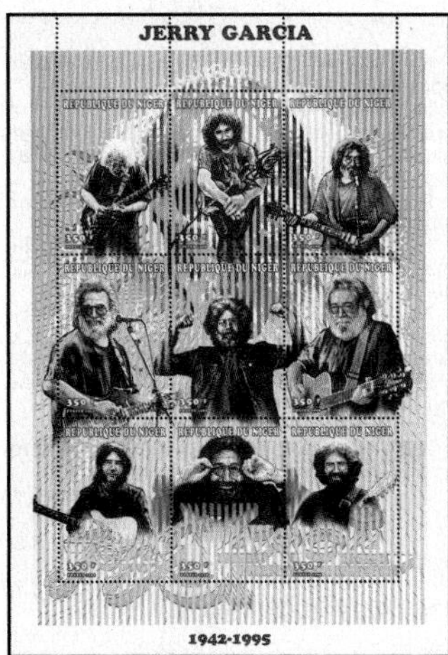


Jerry Garcia — A335

No. 1008: a, In brown shirt. b, In blue shirt, with flower. c, In yellow shirt. d, in green shirt. e, With fists clenched. f, In blue shirt. g, In black jacket. h, Holding glasses. i, In black shirt, with black guitar strap.

**1998**

**1008** A335 350fr Sheet of 9, #a-i 10.00 10.00

Dogs and Birds — A336

No. 1009, 100fr — Scouting emblem and: a, Beagle, butterfly. b, Airedale terrier, Italia 98 emblem. c, Doberman pinscher, butterfly. d, Small white dog, Italia emblem. e, Husky pup, Concorde. f, White Eskimo dog, Italia emblem. g, Dalmatian, butterfly. h, Retriever, butterfly. i, Pit bull, butterfly.

No. 1010, 300fr — a-i, Scouting jamboree emblem and various penguins.

No. 1011, 500fr — a-i, Various parrots.

**1999 Sheets of 9, #a-i**

**1009-1011** A336 Set of 3 *15.00 15.00*

Intl. Year of the Ocean (No. 1010). Dated 1998.

Sailing — A337

No. 1012: a, Sailboat, lighthouse. b, Man, woman in sailboat. c, Sailor, large waves. d, Yachts racing.

**1999**

**1012** A337 750fr Sheet of 4, #a-d

Dated 1998. Sheets of four 525fr and 875fr stamps were not authorized by Niger Post.

Trains — A338

Various trains. Sheets of 4, each stamp denominated: 225fr, 325fr, 375fr, 500fr.

**1999 Sheets of 4, #a-d**

**1013-1017** A338 Set of 5

Dated 1998. PhilexFrance 99 (#1017). A sheet of four similar stamps with 650fr denominations, 750fr souvenir sheet, 2500fr souvenir sheet, and two 3000fr souvenir sheets were not authorized by Niger Post.

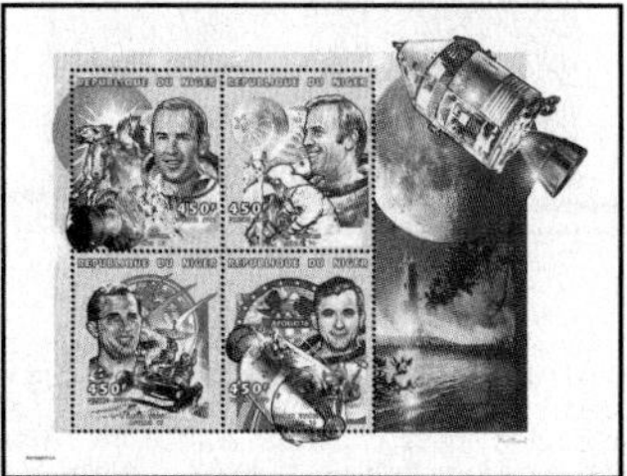

Astronauts — A339

No. 1018, 450fr: a, James Lovell. b, Alan Shepard. c, David Scott. d, John Young.

No. 1019, 500fr: a, Neil Armstrong. b, Michael Collins. c, Edwin Aldrin. d, Alan Bean.

No. 1020, 600fr: a, Walter Schirra. b, Robert Crippen. c, Thomas Stafford. d, Owen Garriott.

No. 1021, 750fr: a, John Glenn. b, Gordon Cooper. c, Scott Carpenter. d, Virgil Grissom.

2000fr, Collins, Armstrong and Aldrin.

**1999 Sheets of 4, #a-d**

**1018-1021** A339 Set of 4 *40.00 40.00*

**Souvenir Sheet**

**1022** A339 2000fr multi *9.00 9.00*

No. 1022 contains one 56x51mm stamp.

Chess — A340

No. 1023, 350fr: a, Tigran Petrosian. b, Robert Fischer. c, Boris Spassky. d, Viktor Korchnoi. e, Garry Kasparov. f, Anatoly Karpov.
No. 1024, 400fr: a, Richard Reti. b, Alexander Alekhine. c, Max Euwe. d, Paul Keres. e, Mikhail Botvinnik. f, Mikhail Tal.
No. 1025, 500fr: a, Philidor. b, Adolf Anderssen. c, Joseph Henry Blackburne. d, Emanuel Lasker. e, Frank Marshall. f, José Raul Capablanca.
2000fr, head of Kasparov, Leo Tolstoy playing chess.

**1999 Sheets of 6, #a-f**
**1023-1025** A340 Set of 3 *35.00 35.00*

**Souvenir Sheet**

**1026** A340 2000fr multi *10.00 10.00*

Nos. 1023-1025 each contain six 51x36mm stamps. Dated 1998.

Baseball Players — A341

No. 1027, 200fr, Various views of Lou Gehrig.
No. 1028, 250fr, Various views of Ty Cobb.
Nos. 1029, 1031, Gehrig, diff. Nos. 1030, 1032, Cobb, diff.

**1999 Sheets of 9, #a-i**
**1027-1028** A341 Set of 2 *19.00 19.00*

**Souvenir Sheets**

**1029-1030** A341 1500fr Set of 2 *15.00 15.00*
**1031-1032** A341 2000fr Set of 2 *15.00 15.00*

Animals and Mushrooms — A342

No. 1033, 300fr: a, Snake. b, Tortoise. c, Scorpion. d, Lizard.
No. 1034, 400fr: a, Vulture. b, Gray cuckoo. c, Jackdaw. d, Turtle dove.
No. 1035, 600fr: a, Ham the chimpanzee. b, Laika the dog. c, Cat. d, Spider.
No. 1036, 750fr: a, Nymphalidae palla. b, Nymphalidae perle. c, Nymphalidae diademe-bleu. d, Nymphalidae pirate.
No. 1037, 1000fr: a, Cliotcybe rouge brique. b, Lactaire a odeur de camphre. c, Strophaire vert-de-gris. d, Lepiote a ecailles aigues.
Illustration reduced.

**1999, Nov. 23 Sheets of 4, #a-d**
**1033-1037** A342 Set of 5 *50.00 50.00*

Council of the Entente, 40th Anniv. A343

**1999, May 29 Litho. *Perf. 13x13¼***
**1039** A343 175fr multi 2.00 2.00

An additional stamp was issued in this set. The editors would like to examine any examples.

First French Stamps, 150th Anniv. A344

**Litho. With Hologram Applied**
**1999, Oct. 7 *Perf. 13***
**1040** A344 200fr France Type A1 1.50 1.50

Fire Fighting Equipment — A345

No. 1041 — Automobiles: a, Bugatti Type 37. b, Chevrolet Corvette. c, Lotus Elise. d, Ferrari 550 Maranello.
No. 1042: a, Canadair airplane. b, Hook and ladder truck. c, Water pumper of middle ages. d, 1914 pumper.
No. 1043 — Trains: a, Union Pacific, 1869. b, Prussian State Railway P8, 1905. c, Pennsylvania Railroad T1, 1942. d, German Railways Series 015, 1962.
No. 1044 — Airplanes: a, De Havilland Comet. b, Airbus A340. c, Boeing 747. d, Concorde.
No. 1045 — Trains: a, Diesel-electric locomotive. b, Bullet train, Japan. c, Thalys. d, X2000, China.
No. 1046 — Spacecraft: a, Atlas rocket, Mercury capsule. b, RD-107 Soyuz. c, Saturn V rocket, Apollo capsule. d, Space shuttle.

**1999, Nov. 23 Litho. *Perf. 13½***
**1041** A345 450fr Sheet of 4, #a-d *10.00 10.00*
**1042** A345 500fr Sheet of 4, #a-d *11.50 11.50*
**1043** A345 600fr Sheet of 4, #a-d *13.00 13.00*
**1044** A345 650fr Sheet of 4, #a-d *14.50 14.50*
**1045** A345 750fr Sheet of 4, #a-d *16.00 16.00*
**1046** A345 800fr Sheet of 4, #a-d *12.50 12.50*

Intl. Anti-Desertification Day — A346

Designs: 150fr, Trenches. 200fr, Men in field. 225fr, Trees in desert.

**2000, June 17 Litho. *Perf. 13½***
**1047-1049** A346 Set of 3 1.75 1.75

**Bird Type of 1997**

**2000, June 20 *Perf. 13¼***
**1050** A309 150fr Psittacula krameri 1.00 1.00

2000 Summer Olympics, Sydney — A347

No. 1051: a, 50fr, Men's singles, badminton. b, 50fr, Men's doubles, badminton. c, 50fr, Softball. d, 50fr, Men's floor exercises. e, 50fr, Women's singles, badminton. f, 50fr, Women's doubles, badminton. g, 50fr, Baseball. h, 50fr, Men's long horse vault. i, 50fr, Women's cycling. j, 50fr, Women's pursuit cycling. k, 50fr, Women's road race cycling. l, 50fr, Women's shot put. m, 900fr, Men's singles, table tennis. n, 900fr, Men's doubles, table tennis. o, 900fr, Women's singles, table tennis. p, 900fr, Women's doubles, table tennis.
No. 1052: a, 100fr, Women's freestyle swimming. b, 100fr, Women's butterfly. c, 100fr, Men's prone rifle. d, 100fr, Women's sport pistol. e, 100fr, Women's 3-meter diving. f, 100fr, Women's 10-meter diving. g, 100fr, Women's three-position rifle. h, 100fr, Women's double trap. i, 100fr, Women's beach volleyball. j, 100fr, Women's volleyball. k, 100fr, Women's handball. l, 100fr, Men's sailboarding. m, 700fr, Women's kayak singles. n, 700fr, Women's kayak pairs. o, 700fr, Women's kayak fours. p, 700fr, Women's eight-oared shell with coxswain.

**2000, July 27 Litho.**
**Sheets of 16, #a-p**
**1051-1052** A347 Set of 2 *70.00 70.00*

Modern and Prehistoric Fauna — A348

No. 1053, 200fr — Butterflies: a, Epiphora bauhiniae. b, Cymothoe sangaris. c, Cyrestris camillus. d, Precis clelia. e, Precis octavia amestris. f, Nudaurelia zambesina.
No. 1054, 200fr — Insects: a, Stenocara eburnea. b, Chalcocoris anchorago. c, Scarabaeus aeratus. d, Pseudocreobotra wahlbergi. e, Schistocera gregaria. f, Anopheles gambiae.
No. 1055, 225fr — Prehistoric winged animals: a, Sordes pilosus. b, Quetzalcoatlus. c, Dimorphodon. d, Podopteryx. e, Archaeopteryx. f, Pteranodon.
No. 1056, 225fr — Birds: a, Bec-en-sabot. b, Euplecte ingnicolore. c, Spreo royal. d, Calao trompette. e, Pseudocanari parasite. f, Gonolek rouge et noir.
No. 1057, 400fr — Cats: a, Egyptian mau. b, Domestic. c, African wildcat. d, Chat dore. e, Chat a pieds noirs. f, Chat des sables.
No. 1058, 400fr — Dogs: a, Chien du pharaon. b, Saluki. c, Rhodesian ridgeback. d, Beagle. e, Spitz. f, Basenji.
No. 1059, 450fr — Modern and prehistoric African animals: a, Proconsul africanus. b, Chimpanzee. c, Metamynodon planifrons. d, Black rhinoceros. e, Hyrachius eximus. f, White rhinoceros.
No. 1060, 450fr — Modern and prehistoric African animals: a, Canis familiaris. b, Black and white basenji. c, Hipparion mediterraneum. d, Burchell zebra. e, Moeritherium. f, African elephant.
No. 1061, 475fr — Modern and prehistoric reptiles: a, Palaeobatrachus. b, African frog. c, Metoposaurus. d, Salamander. e, Tylosaurus. f, Varan du Nil.
No. 1062, 475fr — Modern and prehistoric African animals: a, Basilosaurus. b, Solalie du Cameroun. c, Mesosaurus. d, Cordylus giganteus. e, Sarcosuchus. f, Nile crocodile

**2000, Oct. 27 *Perf. 13¼***
**Sheets of 6, #a-f**
**1053-1062** A348 Set of 10 *120.00 120.00*

2002 World Cup Soccer Championships, Japan and Korea — A349

No. 1063, 400fr: a, Castro. b, Orsi. c, Piola. d, Ghiggia.
No. 1064, 400fr: a, Morlock. b, Pele. c, Amarildo. d, Hurst.
No. 1065, 400fr: a, Jairzinho. b, Müller. c, Kempes. d, Rossi.
No. 1066, 400fr: a, Burruchaga. b, Brehme. c, Dunga. d, Petit.

**2001, Jan. 16 Sheets of 4, #a-d**
**1063-1066** A349 Set of 4 22.50 22.50

Dated 2000.

Universal Postal Union, 125th Anniv. (in 1999) — A350

No. 1067, 150fr — Ships: a, Transat, Citta di Catania. b, Great Eastern, Julius Caesar. c, Caledonia, Mercury. d, Braganza, Westland.
No. 1068, 225fr — Vehicles: a, Horse-drawn omnibus, postal bus. b, 1899 automobile, rural omnibus. c, 1904 van, postal automobile and bicycle. d, 1906 automobile, Swiss postal bus.
No. 1069, 450fr — Trains: a, 25NC Modder Kimberley locomotive, CDJR diesel. b, Pacific Karoo, Budd diesel. c, 141 Maghreb locomotive, EAR Diesel-electric locomotive. d, 230 Series 6 C.G.A., Postal TGV train.
No. 1070, 500fr — Airplanes: a, Late-28, Super Constellation. b, Douglas DC-4, Nord Atlas. c, Boeing 707, Concorde. d, Boeing 747, Airbus A3XX.
No. 1071, 550fr — Spacecraft: a, 1934 postal rocket, Asian telecommunications satellite. b, Space capsules. c, Apollo 15, Astra 1 H telecommunications satellite. d, Voyager, Space Station and shuttle.
No. 1072, 700fr — Trains: a, 230 locomotive, Senegal, 141 locomotive, Tanganyika. b, 141 locomotive, Niger. 242 locomotive, South Africa. c, 130+031 locomotive, Ivory Coast, Garrat 242+242. d, 040 locomotive, Cameroun, 14R locomotive.

**2001, Jan. 16 *Perf. 13¼***
**Sheets of 4, #a-d**
**1067-1072** A350 Set of 6 50.00 50.00

Dated 2000.

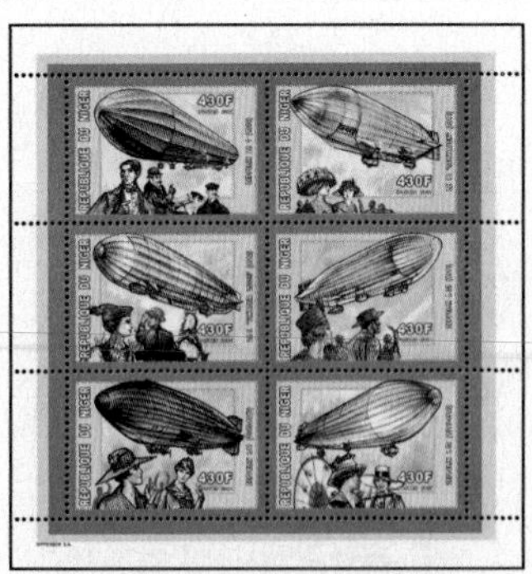

Zeppelins and Satellites — A351

No. 1073, 430fr — Zeppelins: a, LZ-1. b, LZ-10 Schwaben. c, LZ II Viktoria Luise. d, L-30. e, L-11. f, L-59.

No. 1074, 460fr — Zeppelins: a, LZ-120 Bodensee. b, L-72 Dixmude. c, LZ-127 Graf Zeppelin. d, LZ-129 Hindenburg. e, LZ-130. f, D-LZFN.

No. 1075, 750fr, vert. — Satellites: a, Meteosat. b, GOMS. c, GMS. d, Insat 1A. e, GOES. f, FY-2.

**2001, June 20** **Litho.**

**Sheets of 6, #a-f**

**1073-1075** A351 Set of 3 40.00 40.00

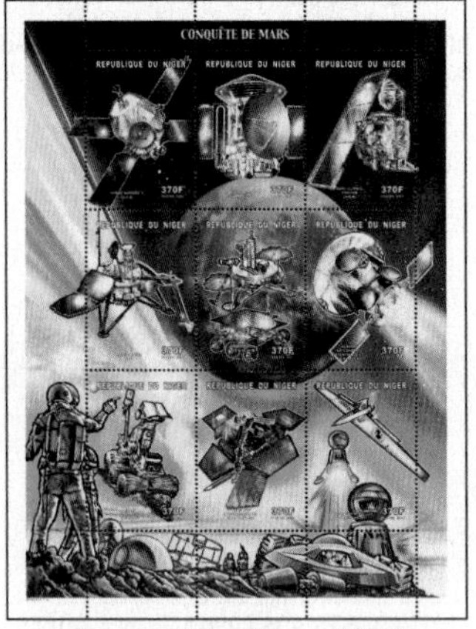


Space Exploration — A352

No. 1076, 370fr — Conquest of Mars: a, Mariner 9. b, Mars 3. c, Mars Climate Orbiter. d, Mars Lander. e, Mars Rover. f, Netlander. g, Robot on Mars. h, Beagle 2. i, Ames Research plane for Mars.

No. 1077, 390fr — Orbital and Lunar Exploration: a, Yuri Gagarin, Vostok capsule. b, John Glenn, Mercury capsule. c, Space shuttle. d, Alan Shepard, Apollo 14. e, Neil Armstrong, Apollo 11. f, Charles Conrad, Apollo 12. g, Edward White, Gemini 4. h, James Irwin, Apollo 15. i, Lunar base and shuttle.

No. 1078, 490fr — Planetary and Interstellar Exploration: a, Pioneer 10. b, Mariner 10. c, Venera 13. d, Pioneer 13, Venus 2. e, Probe for detecting "Big Bang." f, Interstellar spacecraft. g, Inhabited space station. h, Giotto probe, Astronaut on comet. i, Galileo probe.

**2001, June 20** **Litho.**

**Sheets of 9, #a-i**

**1076-1078** A352 Set of 3 50.00 50.00

African History — A353

No. 1079, 390fr: a, Gahna Empire, 10th cent. b, Kankou Moussa, Emperor of Mali, 1324. c, Sankore, University of Tombouctou, 15th cent. d, Sonni Ali Ber, Songhai Emperor. e, Bantu migrations, 15th and 16th cents. f, Slave trade, 1513.

No. 1080, 490fr: a, Ramses II, 1301-1235 B.C., Battle of Qadesh. b, Mummification. c, Religion. d, Instruction. e, Justice. f, Artisans.

No. 1081, 530fr: a, Djoser, Third Dynasty, 2650 B.C. b, Rahotep and wife, Fourth Dynasty, 2570 B.C. c, Cheops and Pyramid, Fourth Dynasty, 2600 B.C. d, Chephren, Fourth Dynasty, 2500 B.C. e, Akhenaton and Nefertiti, 18th Dynasty, 1372-1354 B.C. f, Tutankhamen, 18th Dynasty, 1354-1346 B.C.

**2001, July 24** **Litho.**

**Sheets of 6, #a-f**

**1079-1081** A353 Set of 3 35.00 35.00

Air Chiriet — A354

**2001** ***Perf. 13x13¼***

**1082** A354 150fr multi 1.00 1.00

Intl. Volunteers Year — A355

**2001**

**1083** A355 150fr multi 1.00 1.00

Birds, Butterflies, Meteorites, and Mushrooms — A356

No. 1084, 530fr — Birds: a, Falco peregrinus. b, Falco biarmicus. c, Vultur gryphus.

No. 1085, 575fr — Butterflies: a, Junonia orithya. b, Salamis parhassus. c, Amauris echeria.

No. 1086, 750fr — Meteorites: a, P. Pallas, 1772. b, Iron meteorite. c, Bouvante rock.

No. 1087, 825fr — Mushrooms: a, Otidea onotica. b, Lentinus sajor-caju. c, Pleurotus luteoalbus.

**2002, Apr. 24** ***Perf. 13¼***

**Sheets of 3, #a-c**

**1084-1087** A356 Set of 4 27.50 27.50

Souvenir sheets of 1 of each of the individual stamps exist.

Cow's Head A357

**2002, Sept. 17** **Litho.** ***Perf. 13¼***

**1088** A357 50fr multi .50 .50

Toubou Spears — A358

**2002, Sept. 17** **Litho.** ***Perf. 13x12½***

**1089** A358 100fr multi .90 .90

Birds — A359

**2002, Sept. 17** **Litho.** ***Perf. 13***

**1090** A359 225fr multi 1.10 1.10

Hippopotamus in Captivity — A360

Boudouma Cow A361

Boudouma Calf — A362

**2003, Dec. 3** **Litho.** ***Perf. 13x13¼***

**1091** A360 100fr multi *.60 .60*

***Perf. 13***

**1092** A361 150fr multi *.80 .80*

***Perf. 13¼***

**1093** A362 225fr multi *1.10 1.10*

*Nos. 1091-1093 (3) 2.50 2.50*

Values for No. 1092 are for stamps with surrounding selvage.

Pottery — A363

Camel and Rider A364

**2004** ***Perf. 13x13¼***

**1094** A363 150fr multi 1.00 1.00

***Perf. 13***

**1095** A364 1000fr multi *5.00 5.00*

Values for No. 1095 are for stamps with surrounding selvage.

In Universal Postal Union Circular 388, issued Nov. 28, 2005, Niger postal officials declared illegal additional items bearing the inscription "Republique du Niger." As this circular contains a somewhat unintelligible list of items which lacks specifics as to denominations found on the illegal items or the sizes of sheets, some of the items may be duplicative of items mentioned in the note on illegal stamps following No. 999. Also, because of the lack of clarity of the list, some catalogued items may now be items cited as "illegal" in Circular 388. The text of this circular can be seen on the UPU's WNS website, www.wnsstamps.ch.

Emblem of 2005 Francophone Games — A365

**2005, May 12** **Litho.** ***Perf. 13x13¼***

**1096** A365 150fr multi .65 .65

World Summit on the Information Society, Tunis — A366

**2005, May 26** ***Perf. 13¼***

**1097** A366 225fr multi 1.25 1.25

Mascot of 2005 Francophone Games — A367

**2005, Aug. 22** ***Perf. 13***

**1098** A367 225fr multi 1.00 1.00

Léopold Sédar Senghor (1906-2001), First President of Senegal — A368

**2006, Apr. 6** **Litho.** ***Perf. 12¾***

**1099** A368 175fr multi .85 .85

Pres. Tandja Mamadou — A369

**2006, July 14**

**1100** A369 750fr multi 3.50 3.50

Boubou Hama (1906-82), Writer — A370

Background colors: 150fr, Green. 175fr, Orange brown. 325fr, Light blue.

**2006, Sept. 23** **Litho.** ***Perf. 13x12¾***

**1101-1103** A370 Set of 3 3.50 3.50

Messenger From Madaoua — A371

**2006, Nov. 6** **Litho.** ***Perf. 13x12¾***

**1104** A371 25fr multi —

Dated 2004.

24th UPU Congress, Geneva, Switzerland — A373

**2007, Nov. 9** **Litho.** ***Perf. 13***

**1106** A373 500fr multi 2.25 2.25

Values are for stamps with surrounding selvage. UPU Congress was moved to Geneva after political violence in Nairobi, Kenya.

Wildlife A374

Designs: 200fr, Giraffes. 400fr, Addax. 600fr, Ostriches.

**2007, Nov. 9** ***Perf. 12¾***

**1107-1109** A374 Set of 3 5.50 5.50

Grain Grinding A375

Bororo Dance A376

Chief's Guard A377

**2008, Aug. 8** ***Perf. 12¾***

**1110** A375 100fr multi .45 .45
**1111** A376 350fr multi 1.60 1.60
**1112** A377 1000fr multi 4.75 4.75
*Nos. 1110-1112 (3)* 6.80 6.80

Women At Well — A378

Hunters — A379

**2009, Nov. 20** ***Perf. 13***

**1113** A378 300fr multi 1.40 1.40
**1114** A379 450fr multi 2.10 2.10

Téra-téra Blanket A381

Women's Hairstyles A382

**2010, June 4** ***Perf. 12¾***

**1115** A380 500fr multi 1.90 1.90

***Perf. 13***

**1116** A381 700fr multi 2.60 2.60

***Perf. 13¼***

**1117** A382 1500fr multi 5.50 5.50
*Nos. 1115-1117 (3)* 10.00 10.00

Values for No. 1116 are for stamps with surrounding selvage.

Independence, 50th Anniv. — A383

**2010, June 30** ***Perf. 13***

**1118** A383 1000fr multi 4.00 4.00

Hut of Sultan Usman Dan Fodio (1754-1817) — A384

Lété Island A385

**2011, May 30** ***Perf. 12¾***

**1119** A384 175fr multi .80 .80
**1120** A385 320fr multi 1.40 1.40

Violet de Galmi Onions A386

Djado Ruins A387

Gen. Salou Djibo, Head of State of Niger — A388

**2011, Oct. 19**

**1121** A386 500fr multi 2.10 2.10
**1122** A387 735fr multi 3.25 3.25
**1123** A388 1000fr multi 4.25 4.25
*Nos. 1121-1123 (3)* 9.60 9.60

Worldwide Fund for Nature (WWF) — A389

Wildlife — A390

No. 1124 — Giraffa camelopardalis peralta with: a, WWF emblem at LR, animal name at UR. b, WWF emblem at UL, animal name at bottom. c, WWF emblem at LR, animal name at UL. d, WWF emblem at UR, animal name at bottom.

No. 1125, 750fr — Hippopotamus amphibius: a, Denomination at UR, head down, facing right. b, Denomination at UL. c, Denomination at UR, head up at right. d, Denomination at UR, head up at left.

No. 1126, 750fr — Syncerus caffer: a, Denomination at UR, animal name at UL. b, Denomination at UL, animal name at top, animal facing right. c, Denomination at UL, animal name at top, animal facing left. d, Denomination at UR, animal name at LL.

No. 1127, 750fr — Foxes: a, Vulpes rueppellii, animal name at UL. b, Vulpes zerda, animal name at UL, end of name even with top of denomination. c, Vulpes zerda, animal name at left, end of name lower than denomination. d, Vulpes rueppellii, animal name at LR.

No. 1128, 750fr — Hyenas: a, Crocuta crocuta, animal name at LL. b, Hyaena hyaena, animal name at UR. c, Hyaena hyaena, animal name at UL. d, Crocuta crocuta, animal name at top.

No. 1129, 750fr — Antelopes: a, Oryx dammah. b, Ammotragus lervia. c, Nanger dama. d, Tragelaphus eurycerus.

No. 1130, 750fr — Primates: a, Galago senegalensis. b, Chlorocebus tantalus. c, Erythrocebus patas. d, Papio anubis.

No. 1131, 750fr — Bats: a, Eidolon helvum. b, Micropteropus pusillus. c, Lavia frons. d, Nycteris thebaica.

No. 1132, 750fr — Lions and leopards: a, Male Panthera leo. b, One Panthera pardus. c, Two Panthera pardus. d, Two female Panthera leo.

No. 1133, 750fr — Wildcats: a, Felis silvestris lybica. b, Felis margarita. c, Leptailurus serval. d, Felis margarita airensis.

No. 1134, 750fr — Lycaon pictus: a, Denomination at UR, animal name at UL. b, Denomination at UL, animal name at UR. c, Denomination at UL, animal name at top center. d, Denomination at UR, animal name at top center.

No. 1135, 750fr — Loxodonta africana: a, Denomination at right center, animal name at UL. b, Denomination at UR, animal name at UL. c, Denomination at UL, animal name at left. d, Denomination at UR, animal name at right center.

No. 1136, 750fr — Trichechus senegalensis: a, Animal name at UL, left flipper above "b" in "République." b, Animal name at UL, right flipper above "d" in "du." c, Animal name at UL, right fin above space between "République" and "du." d, Animal name at LL.

No. 1137, 750fr — Owls: a, Scotopelia peli. b, Glaucidium perlatum. c, Otus senegalensis. d, Ptilopsis leucotis.

No. 1138, 750fr — Doves: a, Colombar waalia. b, Oena capensis. c, Columba guinea. d, Columba arquatrix.

No. 1139, 750fr — Parrots: a, Poicephalus robustus. b, Psittacula krameri, animal name below denomination. c, Psittacula krameri, animal name to left of denomination. d, Psittacus erithacus, Psittacula krameri.

No. 1140, 750fr — Birds: a, Chalcomitra senegalensis. b, Hedydipna platurus. c, Cinnyris pulchella. d, Cinnyris cupreus.

No. 1141, 750fr — Water birds: a, Ardea cinerea in flight. b, Ardeola rufiventris. c, Ardea cinerea with fish. d, Ardea goliath.

No. 1142, 750fr — Birds of prey: a, Circaetus cinereus. b, Hieraaetus pennatus. c, Aquila rapax. d, Aquila pomarina.

No. 1143, 750fr — Butterflies: a, Pinacopteryx eriphia. b, Colotis antevippe with orange wing tips. c, Colotis antevippe with yellow and black coloratiion. d, Zizeeria knysna.

No. 1144, 750fr — Butterflies: a, Catopsilia florella. b, Coeliades forestan. c, Acraea neobule. d, Hypolimnas misippus.

No. 1145, 750fr — Fish: a, Hemichromis fasciatus. b, Fundulosoma thierryi. c, Aphyosemion bitaeniatum. d, Arnoldichthys spilopterus.

No. 1146, 750fr — Turtles: a, Psammobates geometricus. b, Pelomedusa subrufa. c, Pelusios niger. d, Astrochelys yniphora.

No. 1147, 750fr — Crocodiles: a, Crocodylus niloticus, animal name at UL. b, Crocodylus cataphractus, denomination at UL. c, Crocodylus cataphractus, denomination at UR. d, Crocodylus niloticus, animal name at LL.

No. 1148, 750fr — Snakes: a, Dasypeltis sahelensis. b, Dromophis praeornatus. c, Dromophis lineatus. d, Dasypeltis gansi.

No. 1149, 2500fr, Giraffa camelopardalis peralta, diff. No. 1150, 2500fr, Hippopotamus amphibius, diff. No. 1151, 2500fr, Syncerus caffer, diff. No. 1152, 2500fr, Vulpes rueppellii, diff. No. 1153, 2500fr, Crocuta crocuta, diff. No. 1154, 2500fr, Ammotragus lervia, diff. No. 1155, 2500fr, Papio anubis, diff. No. 1156, 2500fr, Micropteropus pusillus, diff. No. 1157, 2500fr, Panthera pardus, diff. No. 1158, 2500fr, Caracal caracal. No. 1159, 2500fr, Lycaon pictus, diff. No. 1160, 2500fr, Loxodonta africana, diff. No. 1161, 2500fr, Trichechus senegalensis, diff. No. 1162, 2500fr, Bubo ascalaphus. No. 1163, 2500fr, Colombar waalia, diff. No. 1164, 2500fr, Psittacus erithacus, diff. No. 1165, 2500fr, Cinnyris coccinigastrus. No. 1166, 2500fr, Ardea cinerea, diff. No. 1167, 2500fr, Falco naumanii. No. 1168, 2500fr, Spialia spio. No. 1169, 2500fr, Danaus chysippus. No. 1170, 2500fr, Oreochromis aureus. No. 1171, 2500fr, Pelusios sinuatus. No. 1172, 2500fr, Crocodylus niloticus, diff. No. 1173, 2500fr, Atracaspis microlepidota.

**2013, Mar. 1** ***Perf. 13¼x13***

**1124** Strip of 4 12.00 12.00
***a.-d.*** A389 750fr Any single 3.00 3.00
***e.*** Souvenir sheet of 8, 2 each #1124a-1124d, + 2 labels 24.00 24.00

**Sheets of 4, #a-d**

***Perf. 13¼***

**1125-1148** A390 Set of 24 285.00 285.00

**Souvenir Sheets**

**1149-1173** A390 Set of 25 250.00 250.00

Pres. Issoufou Mahamadou A391

**2013, Mar. 8** ***Perf. 13¼x13***

**1174** A391 500fr multi 2.00 2.00

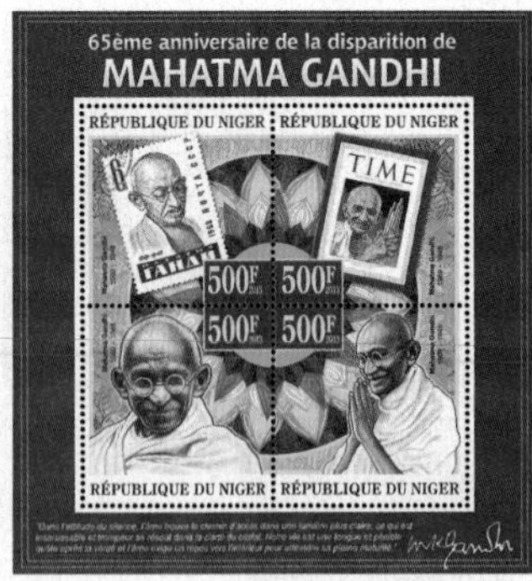


A392

No. 1175, 500fr — Mahatma Gandhi (1869-1948), Indian independence leader: a, On Russia #3639, denomination at LR. b, On cover of *Time* magazine, denomination at LL. c, Denomination at UR. d, With hands together, denomination at UL.

No. 1176, 500fr — Yang Liwei, Chinese astronaut, and Shenzhou 5 with: a, Denomination at LR. b, Denomination at LL. c, Denomination at UR. d, Denomination at UL.

No. 1177, 675fr — Pope Benedict XVI with: a, Denomination at LR. b, Denomination at LL. c, Denomination at UR. d, Denomination at UL.

No. 1178, 675fr — Garry Kasparov, chess champion, and chess pieces with: a, Denomination at LR. b, Denomination at LL. c, Denomination at UR. d, Denomination at UL.

No. 1179, 675fr — Cat breeds: a, Cymric. b, Maine coon cat. c, Persian. d, Oriental.

No. 1180, 675fr — Small dog breeds: a, Chihuahua. b, Spitz. c, Russian toy terrier. d, Yorkshire terrier.

No. 1181, 750fr — Paintings by Albrecht Dürer (1471-1528): a, Portrait of Barbara Dürer, denomination at LR. b, Nativity, denomination at LL. c, Young Hare, denomination at UR. d, Feast of the Rosary, denomination at UL.

No. 1182, 750fr — Paintings by Paul Signac (1863-1935): a, Calvados, denomination at LR. b, Road to Gennevilliers, denomination at LL. c, The Gas Tanks at Clichy, denomination at UR. d, The Railroad at Bois Colombes, denomination at UL.

No. 1183, 750fr — Paintings by Joan Miró (1893-1983): a, Carneval d'Arlequin, denomination at LR. b, Catalan Landscape (The Hunter), denomination at LL. c, Circus, denomination at UR. d, The Poetess, denomination at UL.

No. 1184, 750fr — Bobby Fischer (1943-2008), chess champion: a, On Iceland #1203, denomination at LR. b, On cover of *Life* magazine, denomination at LL. c, With chess pieces, denomination at UR. d, With chess pieces, denomination at UL.

No. 1185, 750fr — Audrey Hepburn (1929-93), actress: a, Wearing red dress. b, With Peter O'Toole. c, With Cary Grant. d, With Gregory Peck.

No. 1186, 750fr — Ancient Egyptian monuments: a, Sculpted head of Amenhotep III. Temple of Horus. b, Bust of Nefertiti. c, Sphinx and Pyramids. d, Pyramids.

No. 1187, 750fr — Lighthouses: a, Biloxi Lighthouse, U.S. b, Rotesand Lighthouse, Germany. c, Execution Rocks Lighthouse, U.S. d, Coney Island Lighthouse, U.S.

No. 1188, 750fr — Cessation of Concorde flights, 10th anniv.: a, Concorde, Buckingham Palace, Queen Elizabeth II, Prince Philip. b, Concorde, Heathrow Airport, Brian Trubshaw, pilot. c, Concorde, Tower Bridge, British flag. d, Concorde, Arc de Triomphe, French flag.

No. 1189, 750fr — Space Shuttle Columbia disaster, 10th anniv.: a, Explosion. b, Columbia, map of U.S.. c, Memorial to Columbia astronauts. d, Columbia on launch pad.

No. 1190, 750fr — Tour de France bicycle race, cent.: a, Lucien Petit-Breton. b, Philippe Thys. c, Greg LeMond. d, Cadel Evans.

No. 1191, 750fr — 2013 African Cup of Nations soccer tournament: a, Two players, denomination at LR. b, One player, denomination at LL. c, One player, denomination at UR. d, Two players, denomination at UL.

No. 1192, 750fr — 2014 Winter Olympics, Sochi: a, Luge. b, Figure skating. c, Ice hockey. d, Speed skating.

No. 1193, 750fr — Dinosaurs: a, Jobaria tiguidensis. b, Afrovenator abakensis. c, Spinophorosaurus nigerensis. d, Suchomimus tenerensis.

No. 1194, 825fr — Paintings by Vincent van Gogh (1853-90): a, Portrait of Postman Joseph Roulin, denomination at LR. b, Self-portrait, Agostina Segatori Sitting in the Cafe du Tambourin, denomination at LL. c, Self-portrait, Olive Trees, denomination at UR. d, The Drinkers, denomination at UL.

No. 1195, 825fr — Hamadou Djibo Issaka, Nigerien rower at 2012 Summer Olympics: a, Denomination at LR. b, Denomination at LL. c, Denomination at UR. d, Denomination at UL.

No. 1196, 825fr — Scouting: a, Scouts building bridge, denomination at LR. b, Scout at campfire, denomination at LL. c, Map, Scout with pocket watch. d, Scouts erecting tents, denomination at UL.

No. 1197, 825fr — Rotary International Flood Aid to Niger: a, Denomination at LR. b, Denomination at LL. c, Denomination at UR. d, Denomination at UL.

No. 1198, 825fr — Scenes from the Djado Plateau: a, Denomination at LR. b, Denomination at LL. c, Denomination at UR. d, Denomination at UL.

No. 1199, 825fr — Minerals of Niger: a, Diamond, denomination at LR. b, Gold, denomination at LL. c, Tin, denomination at UR. d, Silver, denomination at UL.

No. 1200, 2000fr, Gandhi, diff. No. 1201, 2000fr, Yang Liwei and Shenzhou 5, diff. No. 1202, 2000fr, Pope Benedict XVI, diff. No. 1203, 2000fr, Kasparov, diff. No. 1204, 2000fr, Cymric cat, diff. No. 1205, 2000fr, Papillon. No. 1206, 2500fr, Adoration of the Magi, by Dürer. No. 1207, 2500fr, Evening Calm, Concarneau, by Signac. No. 1208, 2500fr, Women and Birds at Sunrise, by Miró. No. 1209, 2500fr, Fischer, diff. No. 1210, 2500fr, Hepburn and husband, Mel Ferrer. No. 1211, 2500fr, Bust of Nefertiti, diff. No. 1212, 2500fr, Mohegan Lighthouse, U.S. No. 1213, 2500fr, Concorde and London. No. 1214, 2500fr, Crew of Space Shuttle Columbia flight STS-107. No. 1215, 2500fr, Bradley Wiggins, cyclist. No. 1216, 2500fr, Two soccer players, diff. No. 1217, 2500fr, Freestyle skiing. No. 1218, 2500fr, Kryptops palaios. No. 1219, 3000fr, Pietà, by van Gogh. No. 1220, 3000fr, Issaka, diff. No. 1221, 3000fr, Scouts and tent. No. 1222, 3000fr, Map of Niger, Rotary International emblem, child and Gaston Kaba, Niamey Rotary president. No. 1223, 3000fr, Djado Plateau rock painting. No. 1224, 3000fr, Salt, map of Niger.

**2013, Apr. 15** ***Perf. 13¼***

**Sheets of 4, #a-d**

**1175-1199** A392 Set of 25 290.00 290.00

**Souvenir Sheets**

**1200-1224** A392 Set of 25 250.00 250.00

A393

No. 1225, 750fr — Yuri Gagarin (1934-68), first man in space: a, Blue panel, Gagarin without cap at left. b, Red panel, Gagarin wearing space helmet at left. c, Red panel, Gagarin wearing military cap at left. d, Blue panel, Gagarin wearing military cap.

No. 1226, 750fr — Space tourism: a, International Space Station, XCOR Lynx Mark II. b, WhiteKnightTwo, SpaceShipOne. c, SpaceShipTwo. d, International Space Station, Astrium Suborbital Space Plane.

No. 1227, 750fr — Steam trains: a, South African Class 26. b, LNER Peppercorn Class A1 60163 Tornado. c, LB&SCR Class B4. d, Reading Blue Mountain & Northern Railway 425.

No. 1228, 750fr — High-speed trains: a, Acela Express, New York City skyline. b, Chinese CRH380A UEM, Yongdinghe Bridge, Beijing. c, Maglev train, Shanghai. d, Alfa train, Lisbon, Portugal skyline.

No. 1229, 750fr — Ships and lighthouses: a, Barque Europa, 2007. b, Mahatao Lighthouse, Philippines. c, Amerigo Vespucci, 1976. d, Isle of May Lighthouse, Scotland.

No. 1230, 750fr — French airplanes: a, Concorde. b, Dassault Rafale. c, Breguet 14. d, Dassault Mirage F1.

No. 1231, 750fr — Fire trucks: a, SACFS Isuzu 800. b, Atego Mercedes-Benz LF 10/6 Ziegler. c, Valdosta, Georgia Airport E-7 fire truck. d, Kronenburg MAC 11.

No. 1232, 750fr — Motorcycles and actors: a, 1953 Triumph Thunderbird, Marlon Brando. b, 1955 Triumph TR5, James Dean, Marilyn Monroe. c, 1934 Harley-Davidson RL, Clark Gable. d, 1940 Indian Four Cylinder, Steve McQueen.

No. 1233, 750fr — Elvis Presley (1935-77), with panel color of: a, Blue. b, Purple. c, Olive green. d, Red.

No. 1234, 750fr — Marilyn Monroe (1926-62), with panel color of: a, Prussian blue. b, Red. c, Violet. d, Brown orange.

No. 1235, 750fr — 60th anniv. of coronation of Queen Elizabeth II, with panel color of: a, Blue. b, Red. c, Green. d, Brown orange.

No. 1236, 750fr — Pope Francis, with panel color of: a, Blue. b, Brown orange. c, Green. d, Red.

No. 1237, 750fr — Dr. Albert Schweitzer (1875-1965), 1952 Nobel Peace laureate, with panel color of: a, Dark brown. b, Prussian blue. c, Dark blue. d, Brown orange.

No. 1238, 750fr — Louis Pasteur (1822-95), microbiologist, with panel colors of: a, Brown. b, Prussian blue. c, Dark blue. d, Brown orange.

No. 1239, 750fr — Mao Zedong (1893-1976), Chinese Communist leader: a, Holding book at right, gray panel. b, Clapping at right, brown orange panel. c, Holding book at right, brown orange panel. d, With raised arm at right, gray panel.

No. 1240, 750fr — Table tennis players: a, Zhang Jike. b, Ding Ning. c, Ma Long. d, Xu Xin.

No. 1241, 750fr — Paul Cézanne (1839-1906), painter, and: a, Compotier, Pitcher and Fruit, 1894. b, Mont Saint-Victoire and Chateau Noir, 1904-06. c, Lac d'Annecy, 1896. d, Apples and Oranges, 1899.

No. 1242, 750fr — Pierre-Auguste Renoir (1841-1919), painter, and: a, Luncheon of the Boating Party, 1881. b, La Grenouillère, 1869. c, Chestnut Tree in Bloom, 1881. d, Madame Georges Charpentier and Her Children, 1878.

No. 1243, 750fr — Volcanoes and minerals: a, Chaíten Volcano, Chile, Vanadinite. b, Popocatépetl, Mexico, Calcite. c, Tungurahua, Ecuador, Hemimorphite. d, Redoubt Volcano, Alaska, Calcite and hematite.

No. 1244, 750fr — Dolphins and shells: a, Lagenorhynchus obscurus. b, Turbinella pyrum. c, Cymbiola vespertilio. d, Tursiops truncatus.

No. 1245, 750fr — Owls and mushrooms: a, Tyto alba, unnamed mushrooms. b, Gomphidus glutinosus, unnamed owl. c, Bubo virginianus, unnamed mushrooms. d, Sarcodon imbricatus, unnamed owl.

No. 1246, 750fr — Orchids and butterflies: a, Encyclia vitellina, unnamed butterflies. b, Papilio maackii, unnamed orchid. c, Vanda sanderiana, unnamed butterflies. d, Bhutanitis lidderdalii, unnamed orchid.

No. 1247, 750fr — Year of the Horse: a, Horse, brown orange panel. b, Two horses, blue panel. c, Two horses, purple panel. d, Horse, black panel.

No. 1248, 2500fr, Gagarin, diff. No. 1249, 2500fr, Richard Branson, SpaceShip Two. No. 1250, 2500fr, Southern Railway Class Ps-4. No. 1251, 2500fr, Shinkansen Series 800, Japan. No. 1252, 2500fr, Fastnet Lighthouse, Ireland, and ship. No. 1253, 2500fr, Blériot XI. No. 1254, 2500fr, Oshkosh Striker T-3000. No. 1255, 2500fr, 1964 Triumph Tiger 100, Bob Dylan. No. 1256, 2500fr, Presley, diff. No. 1257, 2500fr, Monroe, diff. No. 1258, 2500fr, Queen Elizabeth II, diff. No. 1259, 2500fr, Pope Francis, diff. No. 1260, 2500fr, Schweitzer, diff. No. 1261, 2500fr, Pasteur, diff. No. 1262, 2500fr, Mao Zedong, diff. No. 1263, 2500fr, Timo Boll, table tennis player. No. 1264, 2500fr, Cézanne, Mont Sainte-Victoire, 1885-87. No. 1265, 2500fr, Renoir, Ball at the Moulin de la Galette, 1876. No. 1266, 2500fr, Mount Etna, Italy, Pyrite. No. 1267, 2500fr, Stenella coeruleoalba. No. 1268, 2500fr, Strix aluco, unnamed mushrooms. No. 1269, 2500fr, Atrophaneura hector, unnamed orchid. No. 1270, 2500fr, Horse, diff.

**2013, July 1** **Litho.** ***Perf. 13¼***

**Sheets of 4, #a-d**

**1225-1247** A393 Set of 23 275.00 275.00

**Souvenir Sheets**

**1248-1270** A393 Set of 23 230.00 230.00

2013 China International Collection Expo (Nos. 1239, 1262).

Photography by Sergey Tkachenko and Russian Philatelic Items — A394

No. 1271 — Photograph and: a, Post card depicting Graf Zeppelin. b, Russia #C24. c, Russia #C21. d, Russia #C20.

2500fr, Photograph and Russia #6016.

**2013, July 1** **Litho.** ***Perf. 12¾x13¼***

**1271** A394 750fr Sheet of 4, #a-d 12.00 12.00

**Souvenir Sheet**

**1272** A394 2500fr multi 10.00 10.00

Souvenir Sheet

Mao Zedong (1893-1976), Chinese Communist Leader — A395

**2013, July 1 Litho. *Perf. 12¾x13¼***
**On Wood Veneer**
**Self-Adhesive**

**1273** A395 6500fr multi 26.00 26.00

Souvenir Sheet

Peng Liyuan, Singer and Wife of Xi Jinping, President of People's Republic of China — A396

**2013, July 1 Litho. *Perf. 12¾x13¼***
**On Wood Veneer**
**Self-Adhesive**

**1274** A396 6500fr multi 26.00 26.00

Cooperation Between Niger and Algeria — A397

***Perf. 12¾x13¼***

**2013, Sept. 10 Litho.**

**1275** A397 1060fr multi 4.50 4.50

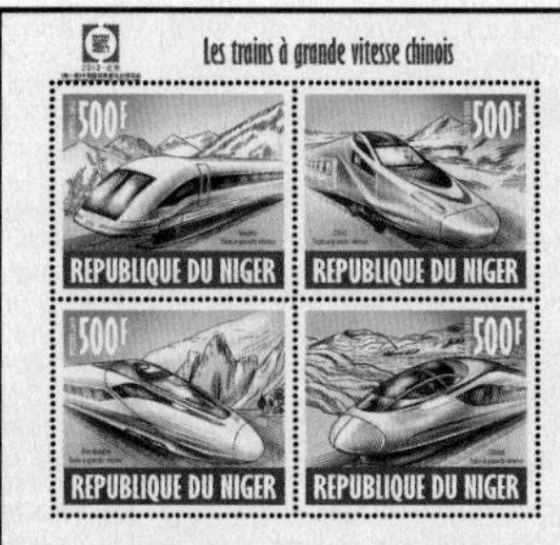


A398

No. 1276, 500fr — Chinese high-speed trains: a, Maglev. b, CRH5. c, Bombardier. d, CRH6A.

No. 1277, 500fr — Shenzhou 10: a, Astronaut Wang Yaping, Shenzhou 10. b, Astronaut Nie Haisheng, Shenzhou 10. c, Astronaut Zhang Xiaoguang, rocket on launch pad. d, Shenzhou 10 and emblem.

No. 1278, 675fr — Nanger Dama: a, Head of gazelle facing left, gazelle in background. b, Gazelle leaping. c, Gazelle resting. d, Adult and juvenile gazelles.

No. 1279, 675fr — African mammals: a, Equus burchelli. b, Phacochoerus africanus. c, Hippopotamus amphibius. d, Alcelaphus buselaphus caama.

No. 1280, 675fr — Wildcats: a, Caracal caracal. b, Leptailurus serval. c, Acinonyx jubatus. d, Panthera pardus.

No. 1281, 750fr — Whales: a, Megaptera novaeangliae. b, Balaenoptera borealis. c, Balaenoptera musculus. d, Eschrichtius robustus.

No. 1282, 750fr — Apis mellifera and flowers: a, Chaenomeles japonica. b, Tanacetum parthenium. c, Paeonia cambessedesii. d, Odontoglossum rossii.

No. 1283, 750fr — Birds: a, Halcyon malimbica. b, Caprimulgus eximius. c, Scopus umbretta. d, Musophaga violacea.

No. 1284, 750fr — Reptiles: a, Python regius. b, Crocodylus niloticus. c, Varanus griseus. d, Trionyx triunguis.

No. 1285, 750fr — Campaign against malaria: a, Red Cross worker feeling head of sick child. b, Children under mosquito netting, mosquito at right. c, Children under mosquito netting, mosquito at left. d, Red Cross worker wearing gloves treating sick child.

No. 1286, 750fr — Prehistoric man: a, Homo georgicus. b, Homo neanderthalensis. c, Homo tyrolensis. d, Homo erectus.

No. 1287, 750fr — Military aircraft: a, Argentine Air Force Douglas A-4 Skyhawk. b, Iranian Air Force F14 Tomcat. c, U.S. Air Force Northrop Grumman RQ-4 Global Hawk. d, U.S. Air Force Lockheed Martin F35B Stealth fighter.

No. 1288, 750fr — Special transportation: a, BMW R1200RT police motorcycle. b, Agusta A-109 K2 helicopter ambulance. c, Pierce Arrow 105-foot X-ladder fire truck. d, Chevrolet C4500 ambulance.

No. 1289, 750fr — Famous cricket players: a, Inzamam-ul-Haq. b, Malcolm Marshall. c, Sanath Jayasuriya. d, Sachin Tendulkar.

No. 1290, 750fr — Pierre de Coubertin (1863-1937), founder of International Olympic Committee, and: a, Runner. b, High jumper. c, Wrestlers. d, Gymnast.

No. 1291, 750fr — Giuseppe Verdi (1813-1901), composer, and performers from opera: a, Rigoletto. b, Hermani. c, Macbeth. d, La Pucelle d'Orléans (Giovanna d'Arco).

No. 1292, 750fr — Richard Wagner (1813-83), composer, and performers from opera: a, Lohengrin. b, Tristan and Isolde. c, The Mastersingers of Nuremberg (Les Maîtres Chanteurs de Nuremberg). d, The Flying Dutchman (Le Vaisseau Fantôme).

No. 1293, 750fr — Nelson Mandela (1918-2013), President of South Africa, and: a, Princess Diana. b, Dove. c, Michael Jackson. d, Bill Gates.

No. 1294, 750fr — Pope John Paul II (1920-2005): a, Waving. b, Seated. c, Seated holding crucifix. d, Standing and praying.

No. 1295, 750fr — Grace Kelly (1929-82), actress and Princess of Monaco: a, Wearing red dress in background. b, In scene from *To Catch a Thief,* 1955. c, In scene from *Dial M for Murder,* 1954. d, Wearing blue dress in background.

No. 1296, 750fr — Paintings by Francisco Goya (1746-1828): a, Witches' Sabbath, 1798. b, The Grape Harvest, 1787. c, The Parasol, 1777. d, Gaspar Melchor de Jovellanos, 1798.

No. 1297, 750fr — Paintings by American Impressionists: a, The Hammock, by Joseph DeCamp. b, Five O'Clock, by Guy Rose. c, Madonna of the Apples, by Joseph Kleitsch. d, Marjorie and Little Edmund, by Edmund C. Tarbell.

No. 1298, 750fr — Paintings by Pablo Picasso (1881-1973): a, Woman at Fountain, 1901. b, Still Life with a Bull's Skull, 1939. c, Science and Charity, 1897. d, The Red Armchair, 1931 (incorrect inscription).

No. 1299, 750fr — Birth of Prince George of Cambridge: a, Prince Charles, Princess Diana and Prince William. b, Duke and Duchess of Cambridge with Prince George outside hospital. c, Duke and Duchess of Cambridge with Prince George in nursery. d, Princess Diana, Princes William and Harry.

No. 1300, 875fr — Rotary International emblem and: a, Paul P. Harris (1868-1947), founder of Rotary International, Acraea neobule. b, Polio virus. c, Rotarians giving baby polio vaccine, Hypolimnas misippus. d, Hands touching, Colotis danae.

No. 1301, 2000fr, CRH3 train. No. 1302, 2000fr, Nanger dama, diff. No. 1303, 2000fr, Ceratotherium simum. No. 1304, 2000fr, Panthera leo. No. 1305, 2500fr, Wang Yaping, Shenzhou 10, diff. No. 1306, 2500fr, Orcinus orca. No. 1307, 2500fr, Apis mellifera, Raphanus sativus. No. 1308, 2500fr, Halcyon chelicuti. No. 1309, 2500fr, Geochelone sulcata. No. 1310, 2500fr, Red Cross emblem, medical worker giving child an injection. No. 1311, 2500fr, Homo neanderthalensis, cave drawing. No. 1312, 2500fr, Russian Air Force Sukhoi PAK FA. No. 1313, 2500fr, Ford F150 fire truck. No. 1314, 2500fr, Cricket player Andrew Flintoff. No. 1315, 2500fr, Coubertin, meeting of International Olympic Committee. No. 1316, 2500fr, Verdi. No. 1317, 2500fr, Wagner. No. 1318, 2500fr, Mandela and Queen Elizabeth II. No. 1319, 2500fr, Popes John Paul II and Benedict XVI. No. 1320, 2500fr, Kelly. No. 1321, 2500fr, Two Boys with a Giant Mastiff, by Goya. No. 1322, 2500fr, Spring on the Riviera, by Rose. No. 1323, 2500fr, Bullfight, by Picasso. No. 1324, 2500fr, Duke and Duchess of Cambridge, Prince George, vert. No. 1325, 3000fr, Harris, Rotary International emblem, Charaxes jasius.

**2013, Sept. 30 Litho. *Perf. 13¼***
**Sheets of 4, #a-d**

**1276-1300** A398 Set of 25 300.00 300.00

**Souvenir Sheets**

**1301-1325** A398 Set of 25 255.00 255.00

A399

A400

A401

Chinese Chang'e 3 Mission to the Moon — A402

***Perf. 12¾x13¼***

**2013, Dec. 20 Litho.**

| | | | |
|---|---|---|---|
| **1326** | Horiz. strip of 4 | 13.00 | 13.00 |
| *a.* | A399 750fr multi | 3.25 | 3.25 |
| *b.* | A400 750fr multi | 3.25 | 3.25 |
| *c.* | A401 750fr multi | 3.25 | 3.25 |
| *d.* | A402 750fr multi | 3.25 | 3.25 |

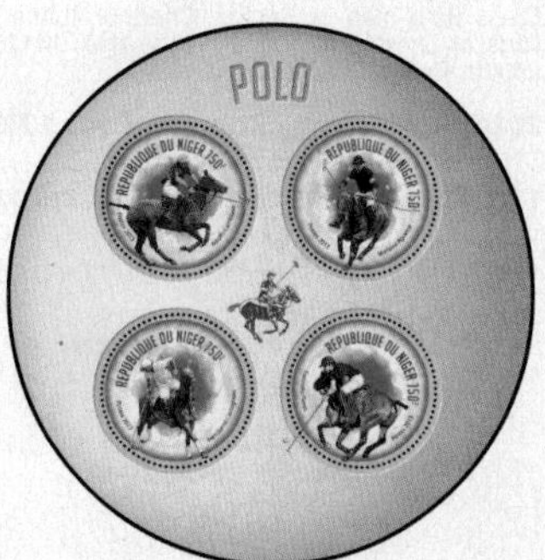


Polo — A403

No. 1327 — Polo players on horses: a, Adolfo Cambiaso. b, Mariano Aguerre. c, Bartolomé Castagnola. d, Facundo Pieres.

2500fr, Polo player on horse.

**2013, Dec. 20 Litho. *Perf.***

**1327** A403 750fr Sheet of 4, #a-d 13.00 13.00

**Souvenir Sheet**

**1328** A403 2500fr multi 10.50 10.50

A404

No. 1329, 750fr — Pan troglodytes: a, Sitting on rock. b, Sitting next to tree, looking forward. c, Adult and juvenile. d, Sitting on branch looking left.

No. 1330, 750fr — Dugong dugon with Latin name: a, At LL, animal facing left. b, At UR, animal facing forward. c, At UR, with animal's head touching sea floor. d, At LL, with animal looking forward.

No. 1331, 750fr — Dolphins: a, Tursiops truncatus, Latin name at LR. b, Two Tursiops truncatus, Latin name at LL. c, Two Tursiops truncatus, Latin name at UR. d, Two Delphinus delphi.

No. 1332, 750fr — Tropical fish: a, Chelmon rostratus. b, Pygoplites diacanthus. c, Chaetodon auriga. d, Amphiprion ocellaris.

No. 1333, 750fr — Turtles: a, Geochelone sulcata. b, Chelonoidis denticulata. c, Geochelone nigra. d, Trachemys scripta elegans.

No. 1334, 750fr — Dinosaurs: a, Diceratops. b, Dicraeosaurus. c, Diplodocus. d, Tyrannosaurus.

No. 1335, 750fr — Endangered animals: a, Eretmochelys imbricata. b, Ailuropoda melanoleuca. c, Loxodonta cyclotis. d, Panthera pardus orientalis.

No. 1336, 750fr — Climate change: a, Arctocephalus gazella on shore. b, Ursus maritimus in water. c, Giraffa camelopardalis in water. d, Odobenus rosmarus on ice.

No. 1337, 750fr — Orchids: a, Paphiopedilum callosum. b, Cattleya auera. c, Cattleya labiata. d, Miltonia spectabilis.

No. 1338, 750fr — Mushrooms: a, Macrolepiota procera. b, Sarcodon imbricatus. c, Cantharellus cibarius. d, Leccinum aurantiacum.

No. 1339, 750fr — Minerals: a, Jasper. b, Amethyst. c, Malachite. d, Smoky quartz.

No. 1340, 750fr — Lighthouses: a, Rubjerg Knude Lighthouse, Denmark. b, Green Cape Lighthouse, Australia (incorrect inscription on stamp). c, Fingal Head Lighthouse, Australia (incorrect inscription on stamp). d, Hov Fyr Lighthouse, Denmark.

No. 1341, 750fr — Windmills in: a, Campo de Criptana, Spain. b, Kuzelov, Czech Republic. c, Kinderdijk, Netherlands. d, Volendam, Netherlands.

No. 1342, 750fr — Japanese high-speed trains: a, E3 Series Shinkansen. b, 700 Series Shinkansen. c, E2 Series Shinkansen. d, E3 R1 Akita Shinkansen.

No. 1343, 750fr — Fire trucks: a, Ural. b, 1938 Quad. c, Magirus-Deutz LF 16-TS. d, Steam-driven wagon.

No. 1344, 750fr — Ferrari automobiles: a, F40. b, 458. c, FF. d, "Enzo Ferrari".

No. 1345, 750fr — Chess: a, White piece tilting wooden king on white square. b, White and black queens. c, Timer. d, Player holding white piece tilting wooden king on black square.

No. 1346, 750fr — Campaign against AIDS: a, Women wearing head covering, child. b, Mother and infant meeting with doctor. c, Woman. d, Doctor examining infant held in woman's arms.

No. 1347, 750fr — Niger culture: a, Aerial view of desert village. b, Buildings in Agadez. c, Mural. d, Mountains in desert.

No. 1348, 750fr — Composers: a, Joseph Haydn (1732-1809). b, Johann Sebastian Bach (1685-1750). c, Robert Schumann (1810-56). d, Wolfgang Amadeus Mozart (1756-91).

No. 1349, 750fr — Paintings by Eugène Delacroix (1798-1863): a, Combat of Horsemen in the Countryside, 1824. b, The Dying Turk, 1825-30. c, Horse Frightened by a Storm, 1824. d, A Mortally Wounded Brigand Quenches His Thirst, 1825.

No. 1350, 750fr — Pope Benedix XVI with top inscription: a, In white on one line. b, In black on two lines. c, In white on two lines. d, In black on three lines.

No. 1351, 750fr — Nelson Mandela (1918-2013), President of South Africa: a, With hand clenched at LL. b, Waving. c, Saluting. d, With flag of South Africa.

No. 1352, 2500fr, Adult and juvenile Pan troglodytes, diff. No. 1353, 2500fr, Dugong dugon, diff. No. 1354, 2500fr, Tursiops truncatus, diff. No. 1355, 2500fr, Heniochus acuminatus. No. 1356, 2500fr, Chelonia mydas. No. 1357, 2500fr, Spinosaurus. No. 1358, 2500fr, Diceros bicornis. No. 1359, 2500fr, Pygoscelis papua. No. 1360, 2500fr, Oncidium altissimum. No. 1361, 2500fr, Boletus edulis. No. 1362, 2500fr, Chalcedony. No. 1363, 2500fr, Michigan City East Lighthouse, Michigan City, Indiana. No. 1364, 2500fr, Windmill at Lithuanian Ethnographic Museum. No. 1365, 2500fr, E3-2000 Series Shinkansen. No. 1366, 2500fr, Mercedes-Benz Zetros fire truck. No. 1367, 2500fr, Enzo Ferrari (1898-1988), automobile manufacturer. No. 1368, 2500fr, Chess board and timer. No. 1369, 2500fr, Two women, infant, red cross. No. 1370, 2500fr, Sahara Desert rock paintings. No. 1371, 2500fr, Ludwig van Beethoven (1770-1827), composer. No. 1372, 2500fr, The Combat of the Giaour and Hassan, by Delacroix. No. 1373, 2500fr, Pope Benedict XVI, diff. No. 1374, 2500fr, Mandela with fist raised. No. 1375, 2500fr, Mandela and flag of South Africa, diff.

**2013, Dec. 20 Litho. *Perf. 13¼***
**Sheets of 4, #a-d**

**1329-1351** A404 Set of 23 290.00 290.00

**Souvenir Sheets**

**1352-1375** A404 Set of 24 250.00 250.00

Millet — A405

**2014, Apr. 25 Litho. *Perf. 13¼x13***

**1376** A405 35fr multi .25 .25

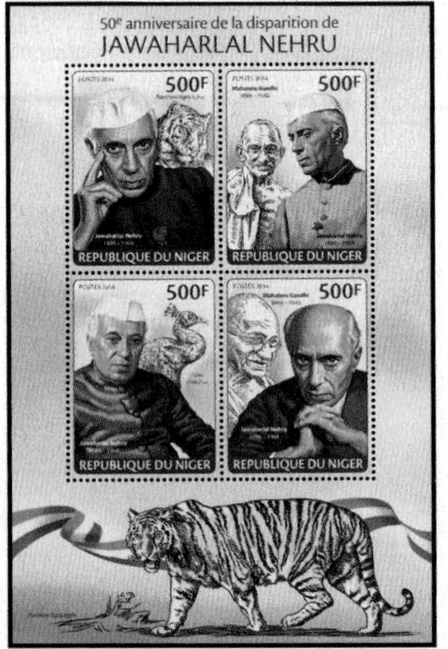


A406

No. 1377, 500fr — Jawaharlal Nehru (1889-1964), First Prime Minister of India, and: a, Panthera tigris tigris. b, Mahatma Gandhi (1869-1948), Indian nationalist leader (Nehru wearing hat). c, Pavo cristatus. d, Gandhi (Nehru without hat).

No. 1378, 500fr — Diplomatic relations between Niger and People's Republic of China, 40th anniv.: a, Flags of Niger and People's Republic of China, Great Wall of China, ruins of Djado, Niger. b, Flags, Niger Prime Minister Senyi Oumarou and Chinese President Hu Jintao shaking hands. c, Flags, Cheiffou Amadou and Wang Gang shaking hands. d, Flags, 2012 meeting of Presidents of Niger and People's Republic of China.

No. 1379, 675fr — Charles Lindbergh (1902-74), aviator, and airplane: a, Lindbergh wearing cap. b, Lindbergh wearing headgear and goggles, standing. c, Lindbergh without hat. d, Lindbergh wearing headgear and goggles, in cockpit.

No. 1380, 675fr — Louis Renault (1877-1944), automobile manufacturer: a, At right of car. b, Driving car. c, With head above car roof. d, At left of car.

No. 1381, 675fr — Giacomo Puccini (1858-1924), opera composer: a, Theater in background. b, Poster for *Tosca* in background. c, With Giuseppe Verdi (1813-1901). d, With character from *Turandot* in background.

No. 1382, 750fr — Jean-Philippe Rameau (1683-1764), composer, and: a, Cathedral of St. Benignus, Dijon, France. b, Dulcimer. c, Baroque lute. d, Harpsichord.

No. 1383, 750fr — Joséphine de Beauharnais (1763-1814), first wife of Napoleon Bonaparte: a, With head on chair, Napoleon standing. b, In her Malmaison bedroom. c, Standing, with Napoleon. d, Seated, her portrait in background.

No. 1384, 750fr — Charlie Chaplin (1889-1977), actor: a, Holding hat. b, With legs above head, holding cane. c, Reading. d, Touching bottom of shoe.

No. 1385, 750fr — Yuri Gagarin (1934-68), first man in space: a, Receiving flowers from girl. b, Wearing space helmet. c, Wearing military uniform, Vostok 1 in flight. d, Wearing space suit, no helmet.

No. 1386, 750fr — Pope Francis: a, Wearing miter, dove flying in background. b, With cardinals in background. c, Standing on platform, cardinals in background. d, Wearing zucchetto, dove flying in background.

No. 1387, 750fr — Joe DiMaggio (1914-99), baseball player, and his wife, Marilyn Monroe (1926-62), actress: a, DiMaggio wearing brown suit. b, DiMaggio wearing baseball uniform. c, Monroe alone. d, DiMaggio wearing green suit.

No. 1388, 750fr — Ayrton Senna (1960-94), race car driver: a, Driving blue race car. b, Holding trophy. c, Flag of Brazil in background. d, Driving yellow car.

No. 1389, 750fr — 2014 Winter Olympics, Sochi, Russia: a, Ski jumper. b, Figure skater. c, Ice hockey player. d, Snowboarder.

No. 1390, 750fr — 2014 World Cup Soccer Championships, Brazil: a, Player in blue shirt and player in green shirt. b, Player in yellow orange shirt. c, Player in light yellow shirt. d, Player in light blue shirt and player in light yellow shirt.

No. 1391, 750fr — Start of World War I, cent.: a, Carrier pigeon. b, Fokker Dr.I airplane of Manfred von Richtofen c, Renault Ft tank. d, German soldiers wearing gas masks.

No. 1392, 750fr — USS Nautilus, 60th anniv.: a, Entire ship at surface. b, Submarine submerging. c, Fore of submarine at surface. d, Submarine and wake.

No. 1393, 750fr — English Channel Tunnel, 20th anniv.: a, British Rail Class 92, flags of Great Britain and France. b, Eurotunnel Class 9, Eiffel Tower, flag of France. c, ICE3, Tower Bridge, flag of Great Britain. d, Eurostar Class 373, flags of Great Britain and France.

No. 1394, 750fr — Red List of Endangered Animals, 50th anniv.: a, Procolobus kirkii. b, Onychogalea fraenata. c, Gyps rueppellii. d, Balearica regulorum.

No. 1395, 2000fr, Nehru, Gandhi, flag of India. No. 1396, 2000fr, Prime Minister Oumarou shaking hands with Chinese Premier Wen Jiabao, flags of Niger and People's Republic of China. No. 1397, 2000fr, Lindbergh, map of transatlantic flight. No. 1398, 2000fr, Renault and tank. No. 1399, 2000fr, Puccini and poster for *La Bohàme.* No. 1400, 2500fr, Rameau and Baroque guitar. No. 1401, 2500fr, Napoleon Bonaparte and Josàphine de Beauharnais, diff. No. 1402, 2500fr, Chaplin in and out of stage makeup. No. 1403, 2500fr, Gagarin and Vostok 1, diff. No. 1404, 2500fr, Pope Francis and two cardinals. No. 1405, 2500fr, DiMaggio in baseball uniform. No. 1406, 2500fr, Senna and race car, diff. No. 1407, 2500fr, Biathlon. No. 1408, 2500fr, Two soccer players, diff. No. 1409, 2500fr, Assassination of Archduke Franz Ferdinand. No. 1410, 2500fr, Launch of USS Nautilus. No. 1411, 2500fr, Eurostar Class 320, map of English Channel Tunnel, flags of Great Britain and France. No. 1412, 2500fr, Panthera tigris sumatrae.

**2014, Apr. 25 Litho. *Perf. 13¼***
**Sheets of 4, #a-d**

**1377-1394** A406 Set of 18 215.00 215.00

**Souvenir Sheets**

**1395-1412** A406 Set of 18 180.00 180.00

Works of Famous Artists — A407

No. 1413, 750fr — Alphonse Mucha (1860-1939): a, Poster for F. Champenois, 1897. b, The Precious Stones Series, 1900. c, The Celebration of Svantovit on Rügen, 1912. d, Fate, 1920.

No. 1414, 750fr — Edvard Munch (1863-1944): a, Self-portrait with a Bottle of Wine, 1906. b, The Girls on the Bridge, 1901. c, Two Human Beings: The Lonely Ones, 1933-35. d, Separation, 1896.

No. 1415, 750fr — Frida Kahlo (1907-54): a, The Wounded Deer, 1946. b, Self-portrait Along the Border of Mexico and the United States, 1932. c, The Bride Frightened at Seeing Life Opened, 1944. d, The Two Fridas, 1939.

No. 1416, 750fr — Henri de Toulouse-Lautrec (1864-1901): a, Self-portrait in Front of a Mirror, 1883. b, Count Alphonse de Toulouse-Lautrec Driving a Four Horse Hitch, 1881. c, Portrait of Suzanne Valadon, 1888. d, In Bed, 1893.

No. 1417, 750fr — Salvador Dalí (1904-89): a, Apparition of a Face and Fruit Dish on a Beach, 1938. b, Atavism at Twilight, 1934. c, Metamorphosis of Narcissus, 1937. d, Paranoiac-Critical Solitude, 1935.

No. 1418, 750fr — Wassily Kandinsky (1866-1944): a, Autumn Landscape, 1911. b, Transverse Line, 1923. c, Green Emptyness, 1930. d, In Blue, 1925.

No. 1419, 750fr — William Hogarth (1697-1764): a, The Distrest Poet, 1729. b, The Life of a Libertine, 1732-35. c, The Graham Children, 1742. d, Marriage à la Mode: The Toilette, 1743-45.

No. 1420, 2500fr, Spring, by Mucha, 1896. No. 1421, 2500fr, Cendres, by Munch, 1924. No. 1422, 2500fr, Without Hope, by Kahlo, 1945. No. 1423, 2500fr, At the Moulin Rouge, by Toulouse-Lautrec, 1892-95. No. 1424, 2500fr, The Persistence of Memory, by Dalí, 1931. No. 1425, 2500fr, Murnau, A Village Street, by Kandinsky, 1908. No. 1426, 2500fr, Columbus Breaking the Egg, 1752.

**2014, Apr. 25 Litho. *Perf. 13¼***
**Sheets of 4, #a-d**

**1413-1419** A407 Set of 7 90.00 90.00

**Souvenir Sheets**

**1420-1426** A407 Set of 7 75.00 75.00

A408

No. 1427, 750fr — St. John Paul II (1920-2005), and: a, St. Peter's Basilica, holding crucifix. b, Castel Sant'Angelo. c, St. Peter's Basilica, waving. d, Pope Francis.

No. 1428, 750fr — Deng Xiaoping (1904-97), paramount leader of People's Republic of China, and: a, Mao Zedong (1893-1976) and other Chinese leaders. b, City Skyline, flag of People's Republic of China. c, Chinese temple, flag of People's Republic of China. d, Mao Zedong.

No. 1429, 750fr — Postage stamps of various countries: a, Russia #6178, Tokelau #389. b, Australia #3563, Falkland Islands #1031. c, Australia #3562, Russia #7302. d, Australia #3561, Jamaica #1057.

No. 1430, 2500fr, St. John Paul II and his papal coat of arms. No. 1431, 2500fr, Deng Xiaoping, Mao Zedong, flowers, map of People's Republic of China. No. 1432, 2500fr, Australia #3564, Christmas Island #487a.

**Litho. With Foil Application (#1427, 1430), Litho.**

**2014, June 25 *Perf. 13¼***
**Sheets of 4, #a-d**

**1427-1429** A408 Set of 3 37.50 37.50

**Souvenir Sheets**

**1430-1432** A408 Set of 3 32.00 32.00

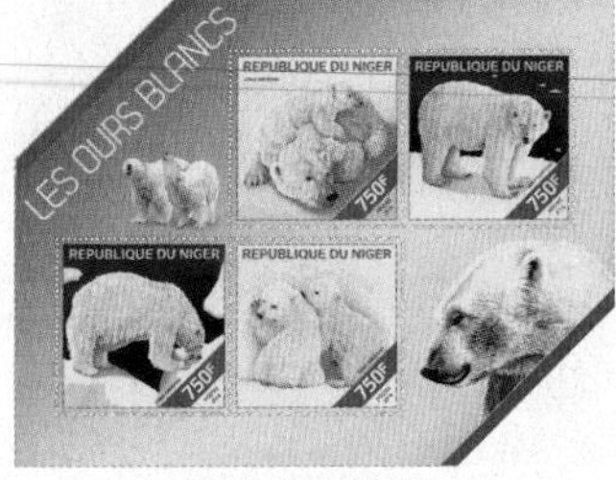


Animals — A409

No. 1433, 750fr — Ursus maritimus: a, Cub on adult polar bear. b, Adult polar bear on ice. c, Adult polar bear crossing gap in ice. d,Two polar bear cubs.

No. 1434, 750fr — Ailuropoda melanoleuca: a, Head and paws of giant panda. b, Giant panda sitting and eating. c, Giant panda reclining and eating. d, Giant panda climbing rock.

No. 1435, 750fr — Gorillas: a, Gorilla gorilla diehli. b, Gorilla gorilla gorilla. c, Gorilla beringei graueri. d, Gorilla gorilla.

No. 1436, 750fr — Rhinoceroses: a, Diceros bicornis. b, Rhinoceros unicornis. c, Dicerorhinus sumatrensis. d, Rhinoceros sondaicus.

No. 1437, 750fr — Bovids: a, Bubalus bubalis. b, Bos primigenius indicus. c, Ovis aries. d, Gazella dorcas.

No. 1438, 750fr — Sea lions: a, Otaria flavescens. b, Phocarctos hookeri. c, Adult and juvenile Zalophus californianus. d, One Zalophus californianus.

No. 1439, 750fr — Wild cats: a, Panthera leo. b, Panthera tigris tigris. c, Panthera onca. d, Acinonyx jubatus.

No. 1440, 750fr — Domesticated cats: a, Japanese bobtail. b, Himalayan. c, Munchkin. d, Singapura.

No. 1441, 750fr — Dogs: a, West Highland white terriers. b, Field spaniel. c, Parson Russell terriers. d, Basset hounds.

No. 1442, 750fr — Elephants: a, Three juvenile Loxodonta africana. b, Two adult Loxodonta africana. c, One Loxodonta africana. d, Elephas maximus.

No. 1443, 750fr — Horses: a, Bavarian Warmblood. b, East Bulgarian. c, Icelandic. d, Gypsy Cob.

No. 1444, 750fr — Dolphins: a, Delphinus delphis. b, Sotalia guianensis. c, Tursiops aduncus. d, Sousa chinensis.

No. 1445, 750fr — Orcinas orca: a, Dorsal fin at UR. b, Dorsal fin at UL. c, Backflipping. d, With open mouth.

No. 1446, 750fr — Fish: a, Parambassis ranga. b, Pterapogon kauderni. c, Centropyge loricula. d, Pterophyllum scalare.

No. 1447, 750fr — Owls: a, Megascops asio. b, Strix occidentalis. c, Bubo virginianus. d, Strix nebulosa.

No. 1448, 750fr — Birds of prey: a, Pithecophaga jefferyi. b, Accipiter soloensis. c, Elanus leucurus. d, Gypaetus barbatus.

No. 1449, 750fr — Water birds: a, Fratercula arctica. b, Ardea herodias. c, Aethia cristatella. d, Podiceps nigricollis nigricollis.

No. 1450, 750fr — Butterflies: a, Danaus plexippus. b, Siproeta epaphus. c, Talicada nyseus. d, Diaethria neglecta.

No. 1451, 750fr — Turtles: a, Chelydra serpentina. b, Terrapene carolina. c, Stigmochelys pardalis. d, Clemmys guttata.

No. 1452, 750fr — Varanus komodensis: a, Komodo dragon facing left. b, Komodo dragon, head and tail facing right, tongue extended. c, Komodo dragon, head facing right, tongue extended. d, Komodo dragon facing left, mouth open.

No. 1453, 750fr — Extinct animals: a, Megaladapis. b, Macrotis leucura. c, Pinguinus impennis. d, Diceros bicornis longipes.

No. 1454, 2500fr, Ursus maritimus, diff. No. 1455, 2500fr, Adult and juvenile Ailuropoda melanoleuca. No. 1456, 2500fr, Three Gorilla gorilla. No. 1457, 2500fr, Ceratotherium simum simum. No. 1458, 2500fr, Antilope cervicapra. No. 1459, 2500fr, Phocarctos hookeri and bird. No. 1460, 2500fr, Neofelis nebulosa. No. 1461, 2500fr, Abyssinian cat. No. 1462, 2500fr, Russian toy dogs. No. 1463, 2500fr, Loxodonta africana, diff. No. 1464, 2500fr, Marwari horse. No. 1465, 2500fr, Delphinus delphis, diff. No. 1466, 2500fr, Orcinus orca, diff. No. 1467, 2500fr, Pomacanthus annularis. No. 1468, 2500fr, Tyto alba. No. 1469, 2500fr, Harpia harpyja. No. 1470, 2500fr, Aix galericulata. No. 1471, 2500fr, Danaus plexippus, diff. No. 1472, 2500fr, Chelonia mydas. No. 1473, 2500fr, Varanus komodoensis, diff. No. 1474, 2500fr, Palaeopropithecus.

**2014, June 25 Litho. *Perf. 13¼***
**Sheets of 4, #a-d**

**1433-1453** A409 Set of 21 260.00 260.00

**Souvenir Sheets**

**1454-1474** A409 Set of 21 220.00 220.00

Souvenir Sheet

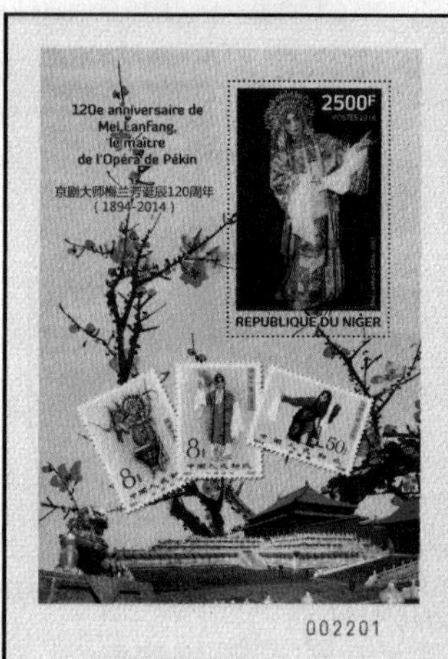


Mei Lanfang (1894-1961), Chinese Opera Actor — A410

***Perf. 12¾x13¼***
**2014, June 25 Litho.**
**Self-Adhesive**
**On Silk**

**1475** A410 2500fr multi 10.50 10.50

2014 World Cup Soccer Championships, Brazil — A411

No. 1476: a, Emblem of 2014 World Cup, flag of Brazil with soccer ball in place of constellation in sky (150x80mm). b, World Cup (150x240mm). c, Flag of Brazil with soccer ball in place of constellation in sky, mascot of 2014 World Cup (150x80mm).

**2014, June 25 Litho. *Perf. 13¼x13***

**1476** Sheet of 3 + 40 labels 6.50 6.50
***a.-c.*** A411 500fr Any single 2.10 2.10

## SEMI-POSTAL STAMPS

**Curie Issue**
Common Design Type

**1938 Unwmk. Engr. *Perf. 13***

**B1** CD80 1.75fr + 50c brt ultra 15.00 15.00

**French Revolution Issue**
Common Design Type

**1939 Photo. *Perf. 13***
**Name and Value Typo. in Black**

**B2** CD83 45c + 25c grn 12.00 12.00
**B3** CD83 70c + 30c brn 12.00 12.00
**B4** CD83 90c + 35c red org 12.00 12.00
**B5** CD83 1.25fr + 1fr rose pink 12.00 12.00
**B6** CD83 2.25fr + 2fr blue 12.00 12.00
*Nos. B2-B6 (5)* 60.00 60.00

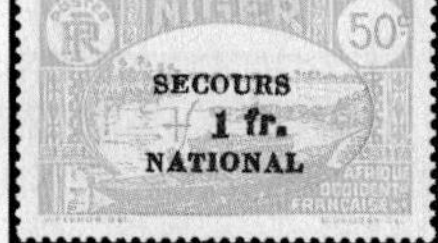


Stamps of 1926-38, Surcharged in Black

**1941 *Perf. 14x13½, 13½x14***

**B7** A3 50c + 1fr scar & grn, *grnsh* 3.25 3.25
**B8** A3 80c + 2fr cl & ol grn 7.25 7.25
**B9** A4 1.50fr + 2fr dp bl & pale bl 7.25 7.25
**B10** A4 2fr + 3fr red org & ol brn 7.25 7.25
*Nos. B7-B10 (4)* 25.00 25.00

**Common Design Type and**

Colonial Cavalry — SP1

Soldiers and Tank SP2

**1941 Unwmk. Photo. *Perf. 13½***

**B11** SP2 1fr + 1fr red 1.10
**B12** CD86 1.50fr + 3fr claret 1.10
**B13** SP1 2.50fr + 1fr blue 1.10
*Nos. B11-B13 (3)* 3.30
Set, never hinged 5.25

Nos. B11-B13 were issued by the Vichy government in France, but were not placed on sale in Niger.

Nos. 89-90 Surcharged in Black or Red

**1944 Engr. *Perf. 12x12½***

**B13A** 50c + 1.50fr on 2.50fr deep blue (R) .35
**B13B** + 2.50fr on 1fr green .35
Set, never hinged 1.40

Colonial Development Fund.
Nos. B13A-B13B were issued by the Vichy government in France, but were not placed on sale in Niger.

**Catalogue values for unused stamps in this section, from this point to the end of the section, are for Never Hinged items.**

**Republic of the Niger**
**Anti-Malaria Issue**
Common Design Type

***Perf. 12½x12***
**1962, Apr. 7 Engr. Unwmk.**

**B14** CD108 25fr + 5fr brn .60 .60

**Freedom from Hunger Issue**
Common Design Type

**1963, Mar. 21 *Perf. 13***

**B15** CD112 25fr + 5fr gray ol, red lil & brn .60 .60

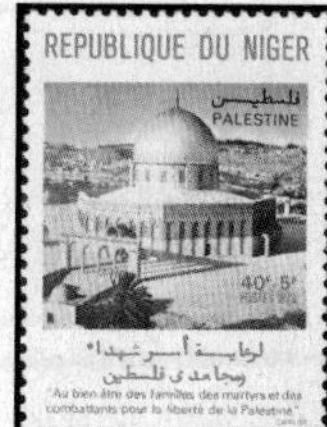


Dome of the Rock — SP3

**1978, Dec. 11 Litho. *Perf. 12½***

**B16** SP3 40fr + 5fr multi .45 .30

Surtax was for Palestinian fighters and their families.

## AIR POST STAMPS

Common Design Type

**1940 Unwmk. Engr. *Perf. 12½x12***

**C1** CD85 1.90fr ultra .35 .35
**C2** CD85 2.90fr dk red .35 .35
**C3** CD85 4.50fr dk gray grn .70 .70
**C4** CD85 4.90fr yel bis .70 .70
**C5** CD85 6.90fr dp org 1.40 1.40
*Nos. C1-C5 (5)* 3.50 3.50

Common Design Types

**1942**

**C6** CD88 50c car & bl .30
**C7** CD88 1fr brn & blk .35
**C8** CD88 2fr multi .70
**C9** CD88 3fr multi .70
**C10** CD88 5fr vio & brn red .70

**Frame Engraved, Center Typographed**

**C11** CD89 10fr multi 1.00
**C12** CD89 20fr multi 1.40
**C13** CD89 50fr multi 1.75
*Nos. C6-C13 (8)* 6.90
Set, never hinged 10.00

There is doubt whether Nos. C6-C13 were officially placed in use. They were issued by the Vichy government.

**Catalogue values for unused stamps in this section, from this point to the end of the section, are for Never Hinged items.**

**Republic of the Niger**

Wild Animals, W National Park — AP1

**1960, Apr. 11 Engr. *Perf. 13***

**C14** AP1 500fr multi 17.50 8.00

For overprint see No. C112.

Nubian Carmine Bee-eater — AP2

**1961, Dec. 18 Unwmk. *Perf. 13***

**C15** AP2 200fr multi 8.00 3.00

UN Headquarters and Emblem, Niger Flag and Map — AP3

**1961, Dec. 16**

**C20** AP3 25fr multi .60 .35
**C21** AP3 100fr multi 2.00 1.25

Niger's admission to the United Nations.
For overprints see Nos. C28-C29.

**Air Afrique Issue**
Common Design Type

**1962, Feb. 17 Unwmk. *Perf. 13***

**C22** CD107 100fr multi 1.75 .90

Mosque at Agadez and UPU Emblem — AP4

Designs: 85fr, Gaya Bridge. 100fr, Presidential Palace, Niamey.

**1963, June 12 Photo. *Perf. 12½***

**C23** AP4 50fr multi .90 .50
**C24** AP4 85fr multi 1.60 .70
**C25** AP4 100fr multi 1.60 .80
*Nos. C23-C25 (3)* 4.10 2.00

2nd anniv. of Niger's admission to the UPU.

**Type of Regular Issue, 1963**

Design: 100fr, Building boats (kadei), horiz.

**1963, Aug. 30 *Perf. 12½x12***
**Size: 47x27mm**

**C26** A12 100fr multi 2.75 1.50

**African Postal Union Issue**
Common Design Type

**1963, Sept. 8 *Perf. 12½***

**C27** CD114 85fr multi 1.25 .60

**Nos. C20-C21 Overprinted in Red**

**1963, Sept. 30 Engr. *Perf. 13***

**C28** AP3 25fr multi .75 .50
**C29** AP3 100fr multi 1.75 .90

Centenary of International Red Cross.

White and Black before Rising Sun — AP5

**1963, Oct. 25 Photo. *Perf. 12x13***

**C30** AP5 50fr multi 3.00 2.25

See note after Mauritania No. C28.

Peanut Cultivation — AP6

Designs: 45fr, Camels transporting peanuts to market. 85fr, Men closing bags. 100fr, Loading bags on truck.

**1963, Nov. 5 Engr. *Perf. 13***

| | | | | |
|---|---|---|---|---|
| **C31** | AP6 | 20fr grn, bl & red brn | .60 | .25 |
| **C32** | AP6 | 45fr red brn, bl & grn | 1.00 | .40 |
| **C33** | AP6 | 85fr multi | 2.00 | .70 |
| **C34** | AP6 | 100fr red brn, ol bis & bl | 2.25 | 1.00 |
| *a.* | | Souv. sheet of 4, #C31-C34 | 6.00 | 6.00 |
| | | *Nos. C31-C34 (4)* | 5.85 | 2.35 |

To publicize Niger's peanut industry.

**1963 Air Afrique Issue**
Common Design Type

**1963, Nov. 19 Photo. *Perf. 13x12***

**C35** CD115 50fr multi .90 .50

Telstar and Capricornus and Sagittarius Constellations — AP7

100fr, Relay satellite, Leo & Virgo constellations.

**1964, Feb. 11 Engr. *Perf. 13***

| | | | | |
|---|---|---|---|---|
| **C36** | AP7 | 25fr olive gray & vio | .50 | .30 |
| **C37** | AP7 | 100fr grn & rose claret | 1.40 | .85 |

Ramses II Holding Crook and Flail, Abu Simbel — AP8

**1964, Mar. 9**

| | | | | |
|---|---|---|---|---|
| **C38** | AP8 | 25fr bis brn & dl bl grn | .80 | .50 |
| **C39** | AP8 | 30fr dk bl & org brn | 1.25 | .65 |
| **C40** | AP8 | 50fr dp claret & dk bl | 2.25 | 1.25 |
| | | *Nos. C38-C40 (3)* | 4.30 | 2.40 |

Issued to publicize the UNESCO world campaign to save historic monuments in Nubia.

Tiros I Weather Satellite over Globe and WMO Emblem — AP9

**1964, Mar. 23 Unwmk. *Perf. 13***

**C41** AP9 50fr emer, dk bl & choc 1.25 .65

4th World Meteorological Day, Mar. 23.

Rocket, Stars and "Stamp" — AP10

**1964, June 5 Engr.**

**C42** AP10 50fr dk bl & magenta 1.10 .65

"PHILATEC," International Philatelic and Postal Techniques Exhibition, Paris, June 5-21, 1964.

**Europafrica Issue, 1963**
Common Design Type

50fr, European & African shaking hands, emblems of industry & agriculture.

**1964, July 20 Photo. *Perf. 12x13***

**C43** CD116 50fr multi .85 .50

John F. Kennedy — AP11

***Perf. 12½***

**1964, Sept. 25 Unwmk. Photo.**

| | | | | |
|---|---|---|---|---|
| **C44** | AP11 | 100fr multi | 1.90 | 1.25 |
| *a.* | | Souvenir sheet of 4 | 8.50 | 8.50 |

President John F. Kennedy (1917-1963).

Discobolus and Discus Thrower — AP12

60fr, Water polo, horiz. 85fr, Relay race, horiz. 250fr, Torch bearer & Pierre de Coubertin.

**1964, Oct. 10 Engr. *Perf. 13***

| | | | | |
|---|---|---|---|---|
| **C45** | AP12 | 60fr red brn & sl grn | 1.00 | .50 |
| **C46** | AP12 | 85fr ultra & red brn | 1.50 | .60 |
| **C47** | AP12 | 100fr brt grn, dk red & sl | 1.50 | .70 |
| **C48** | AP12 | 250fr yel brn, brt grn & sl | 3.50 | 1.75 |
| *a.* | | Min. sheet of 4, #C45-C48 | 11.00 | 11.00 |
| | | *Nos. C45-C48 (4)* | 7.50 | 3.55 |

18th Olympic Games, Tokyo, Oct. 10-25.

Pope John XXIII (1881-1963) AP13

**1965, June 3 Photo. *Perf. 12½x13***

**C49** AP13 100fr multi 1.50 .75

Hand Crushing Crab — AP14

**1965, July 15 Engr. *Perf. 13***

**C50** AP14 100fr yel grn, blk & brn 1.40 .85

Issued to publicize the fight against cancer.

Sir Winston Churchill — AP15

***Perf. 12½x13***

**1965, Sept. 3 Photo. Unwmk.**

**C51** AP15 100fr multi 1.40 .85

Symbols of Agriculture, Industry, Education AP16

**1965, Oct. 24 Engr. *Perf. 13***

**C52** AP16 50fr henna brn, blk & ol .90 .50

International Cooperation Year, 1965.

Flags and Niamey Fair — AP17

**1965, Dec. 10 Photo. *Perf. 13x12½***

**C53** AP17 100fr multi 1.40 .80

International Fair at Niamey.

Dr. Schweitzer, Crippled Hands and Symbols of Medicine, Religion and Music — AP18

**1966, Jan. 4 Photo. *Perf. 12½x13***

**C54** AP18 50fr multi 1.00 .50

Weather Survey Frigate and WMO Emblem — AP19

**1966, Mar. 23 Engr. *Perf. 13***

**C55** AP19 50fr brt rose lil, dl grn & dk vio bl 1.50 .60

6th World Meteorological Day, Mar. 23.

Edward H. White Floating in Space and Gemini IV — AP20

#C57, Alexei A. Leonov & Voskhod II.

**1966, Mar. 30**

| | | | | |
|---|---|---|---|---|
| **C56** | AP20 | 50fr dk red brn, blk & brt grn | 1.00 | .50 |
| **C57** | AP20 | 50fr pur, slate & org | 1.00 | .50 |

Issued to honor astronauts Edward H. White and Alexei A. Leonov.

A-1 Satellite and Earth — AP21

45fr, Diamant rocket and launching pad. 90fr, FR-1 satellite. 100fr, D-1 satellite.

**1966, May 12 Photo. *Perf. 13***

| | | | | |
|---|---|---|---|---|
| **C58** | AP21 | 45fr multi, vert. | .75 | .45 |
| **C59** | AP21 | 60fr multi | .90 | .50 |
| **C60** | AP21 | 90fr multi | 1.10 | .70 |
| **C61** | AP21 | 100fr multi | 1.75 | .90 |
| | | *Nos. C58-C61 (4)* | 4.50 | 2.55 |

French achievements in space.

Maps of Europe and Africa and Symbols of Industry — AP22

**1966, July 20 Photo. *Perf. 12x13***

**C62** AP22 50fr multi .80 .40

Third anniversary of economic agreement between the European Economic Community and the African and Malgache Union.

**Air Afrique Issue, 1966**
Common Design Type

**1966, Aug. 31 Photo. *Perf. 13***

**C63** CD123 30fr gray, yel grn & blk .65 .35

Gemini 6 and 7 — AP23

**1966, Oct. 14 Engr. *Perf. 13***

**C64** AP23 50fr Voskhod 1, vert. .80 .40
**C65** AP23 100fr shown 1.60 .75

Russian & American achievements in space.

Torii and Atom Destroying Crab — AP24

**1966, Dec. 2 Photo. *Perf. 13***

**C66** AP24 100fr dp claret, brn, vio & bl grn 1.50 .70

9th Intl. Anticancer Cong., Tokyo, Oct. 23-29.

New Mosque, Niamey — AP25

**1967, Jan. 11 Engr. *Perf. 13***

**C67** AP25 100fr grn & brt bl 1.75 .80

Albrecht Dürer, Self-portrait AP26

Self-portraits: 100fr, Jacques Louis David. 250fr, Ferdinand Delacroix.

**1967, Jan. 27 Photo. *Perf. 12½***

**C68** AP26 50fr multi 1.10 .70
**C69** AP26 100fr multi 2.00 1.00
**C70** AP26 250fr multi 4.50 2.25
*Nos. C68-C70 (3)* 7.60 3.95

See No. C98.

Maritime Weather Station — AP27

**1967, Mar. 23 Engr. *Perf. 13***

**C71** AP27 50fr brt bl, dk car rose & blk 1.50 .70

7th World Meteorological Day.

View of EXPO '67, Montreal — AP28

**1967, Apr. 28 Engr. *Perf. 13***

**C72** AP28 100fr lil, brt bl & blk 1.25 .70

Issued for EXPO '67, International Exhibition, Montreal, Apr. 28-Oct. 27, 1967.

Audio-visual Center, Stylized Eye and People — AP29

**1967, June 22 Engr. *Perf. 13***

**C73** AP29 100fr brt bl, pur & grn 1.25 .60

National Audio-Visual Center.

Konrad Adenauer (1876-1967), Chancellor of West Germany (1949-63) — AP30

**1967, Aug. 11 Photo. *Perf. 12½***

**C74** AP30 100fr dk bl, gray & sep 1.75 .70
*a.* Souv. sheet of 4 7.50 7.50

### African Postal Union Issue, 1967

Common Design Type

**1967, Sept. 9 Engr. *Perf. 13***

**C75** CD124 100fr emer, red & brt lil 1.40 .60

Jesus Teaching in the Temple, by Ingres — AP31

Design: 150fr, Jesus Giving the Keys to St. Peter, by Ingres, vert.

**1967, Oct. 2 Photo. *Perf. 12½***

**C76** AP31 100fr multi 2.25 1.10
**C77** AP31 150fr multi 3.25 1.60

Jean Dominique Ingres (1780-1867), French painter.

Children and UNICEF Emblem — AP32

**1967, Dec. 11 Engr. *Perf. 13***

**C78** AP32 100fr bl, brn & grn 1.50 .85

21st anniv. of UNICEF.

O.C.A.M. Emblem — AP33

**1968, Jan. 12 Engr. *Perf. 13***

**C79** AP33 100fr brt bl, grn & org 1.25 .55

Conf. of the Organization Communitée Afrique et Malgache (OCAM), Niamey, Jan. 1968.

Vincent van Gogh, Self-portrait AP34

Self-portraits: 50fr, Jean Baptiste Camille Corot. 150fr, Francisco de Goya.

**1968, Jan. 29 Photo. *Perf. 12½***

**C80** AP34 50fr multi 1.00 .45
**C81** AP34 150fr multi 2.75 1.10
**C82** AP34 200fr multi 4.25 1.75
*Nos. C80-C82 (3)* 8.00 3.30

See No. C98.

Breguet 27 — AP35

Planes: 80fr, Potez 25 on the ground. 100fr, Potez 25 in the air.

**1968, Mar. 14 Engr. *Perf. 13***

**C83** AP35 45fr ind, car & dk grn 1.00 .40
**C84** AP35 80fr indigo, bl & brn 1.50 .75
**C85** AP35 100fr sky bl, brn blk & dk grn 2.50 .90
*Nos. C83-C85 (3)* 5.00 2.05

25th anniversary of air mail service between France and Niger.

Splendid Glossy Starling — AP36

Design: 100fr, Amethyst starling, vert.

**1968-69 Photo. *Perf. 13***

**C86** AP36 100fr gold & multi ('69) 5.00 1.10

**Engr.**

**C87** AP36 250fr mag, sl grn & brt bl 3.25 1.40

See No. C255.

Dandy Horse, 1818, and Racer, 1968 — AP37

**1968, May 17 Engr. *Perf. 13***

**C88** AP37 100fr bl grn & red 2.25 .75

150th anniversary of the invention of the bicycle.

Sheet Bend Knot — AP37a

**1968, July 20 Photo. *Perf. 13***

**C89** AP37a 50fr gray, blk, red & grn .80 .45

Fifth anniversary of economic agreement between the European Economic Community and the African and Malgache Union.

Fencing — AP38

Designs: 100fr, Jackknife dive, vert. 150fr, Weight lifting, vert. 200fr, Equestrian.

**1968, Sept. 10 Engr. *Perf. 13***

**C90** AP38 50fr pur & blk .60 .40
**C91** AP38 100fr choc, ultra & blk 1.10 .60
**C92** AP38 150fr choc & org 1.60 .75
**C93** AP38 200fr brn, emer & ind 2.25 1.50
*a.* Min. sheet of 4, #C90-C93 7.50 7.50
*Nos. C90-C93 (4)* 5.55 3.25

19th Olympic Games, Mexico City, 10/12-27.

No. C93a is folded down the vertical gutter separating Nos. C90-C91 se-tenant at left and Nos. C92-C93 se-tenant at right.

Robert F. Kennedy — AP39

#C95, John F. Kennedy. #C96, Rev. Dr. Martin Luther King, Jr. #C97, Mahatma Gandhi.

**1968, Oct. 4 Photo. *Perf. 12½***

**C94** AP39 100fr blk & pale org 1.25 .70
**C95** AP39 100fr blk & aqua 1.40 .70
**C96** AP39 100fr blk & bluish gray 1.25 .70
**C97** AP39 100fr blk & yel 1.25 .70
*a.* Souv. sheet of 4, #C94-C97 6.50 6.50
*Nos. C94-C97 (4)* 5.15 2.80

Issued to honor proponents of non-violence.

**PHILEXAFRIQUE Issue**
Painting Type of 1968

Design: 100fr, Interior Minister Paré, by J. L. La Neuville (1748-1826).

**1968, Oct. 25 Photo. *Perf. 12½***
**C98** AP34 100fr multi 3.00 2.50

Issued to publicize PHILEXAFRIQUE, Philatelic Exhibition in Abidjan, Feb. 14-23, 1969. Printed with alternating light blue label.

Arms and Flags of Niger — AP40

**1968, Dec. 17 Litho. *Perf. 13***
**C99** AP40 100fr multi 1.50 .65

10th anniv. of the proclamation of the Republic.

Bonaparte as First Consul, by Ingres AP41

Paintings: 100fr, Napoleon Visiting the Plague House in Jaffa, by Antoine Jean Gros. 150fr, Napoleon on the Imperial Throne, by Jean Auguste Dominique Ingres. 200fr, Napoleon's March Through France, by Jean Louis Ernest Meissonier, horiz.

***Perf. 12½x12, 12x12½***

**1969, Jan. 20 Photo.**
**C100** AP41 50fr multi 1.90 .95
**C101** AP41 100fr grn & multi 3.00 1.50
**C102** AP41 150fr pur & multi 4.00 1.75
**C103** AP41 200fr brn & multi 6.00 3.00
*Nos. C100-C103 (4)* 14.90 7.20

Napoleon Bonaparte (1769-1821).

**2nd PHILEXAFRIQUE Issue**
Common Design Type

Designs: 50fr, Niger No. 41 and giraffes.

**1969, Feb. 14 Engr. *Perf. 13***
**C104** CD128 50fr slate, brn & org 2.75 1.90

Weather Observation Plane in Storm and Anemometer — AP42

**1969, Mar. 23 Engr. *Perf. 13***
**C105** AP42 50fr blk, brt bl & grn .75 .45

9th World Meteorological Day.

Panhard Levassor, 1900 — AP43

Early Automobiles: 45fr, De Dion Bouton 8, 1904. 50fr, Opel, 1909. 70fr, Daimler, 1910. 100fr, Vermorel 12/16, 1912.

**1969, Apr. 15 Engr. *Perf. 13***
**C106** AP43 25fr gray, lt grn & bl grn .55 .30
**C107** AP43 45fr gray, bl & vio .70 .30
**C108** AP43 50fr gray, yel bis & brn 1.60 .40
**C109** AP43 70fr gray, brt pink & brt lil 2.00 .65
**C110** AP43 100fr gray, lem & sl grn 2.25 .90
*Nos. C106-C110 (5)* 7.10 2.55

Apollo 8 Trip around Moon AP44

**Embossed on Gold Foil**

**1969, Mar. 31 *Die-cut Perf. 10½***
**C111** AP44 1000fr gold 20.00 20.00

US Apollo 8 mission, which put the 1st men into orbit around the moon, Dec. 21-27, 1968.

No. C14 Overprinted in Red

**1969, July 25 Engr. *Perf. 13***
**C112** AP1 500fr multi 8.00 8.00

See note after Mali No. C80.

Toys — AP45

**1969, Oct. 13 Engr. *Perf. 13***
**C113** AP45 100fr bl, red brn & grn 1.40 .55

International Nuremberg Toy Fair.

**Europafrica Issue**

Links — AP46

**1969, Oct. 30 Photo.**
**C114** AP46 50fr vio, yel & blk .75 .50

Camels and Motor Caravan Crossing Desert — AP47

100fr, Motor caravan crossing mountainous region. 150fr, Motor caravan in African village. 200fr, Map of Africa showing tour, Citroen B-2 tractor, African & European men shaking hands.

**1969, Nov. 22 Engr. *Perf. 13***
**C115** AP47 50fr lil, pink & brn .95 .40
**C116** AP47 100fr dk car rose, lt bl & vio bl 2.00 .75
**C117** AP47 150fr multi 2.50 1.25
**C118** AP47 200fr sl grn, bl & blk 4.00 1.75
*Nos. C115-C118 (4)* 9.45 4.15

Black Tour across Africa from Colomb-Bechar, Algeria, to Mombassa, Dar es Salaam, Mozambique, Tananarive and the Cape of Good Hope.

EXPO '70 at Osaka — AP48

**1970, Mar. 25 Photo. *Perf. 12½***
**C119** AP48 100fr multi 1.25 .60

Issued to publicize EXPO '70 International Exhibition, Osaka, Japan, Mar. 15-Sept. 13.

Education Year Emblem and Education Symbols — AP49

**1970, Apr. 6 Engr. *Perf. 13***
**C120** AP49 100fr plum, red & gray 1.25 .60

Issued for International Education Year.

Rotary Emblem, Globe and Niamey Club Emblem — AP50

**1970, Apr. 30 Photo. *Perf. 12½***
**C121** AP50 100fr gold & multi 1.60 .80

65th anniversary of Rotary International.

Modern Plane, Clement Ader and his Flying Machine — AP51

Designs: 100fr, Joseph and Jacques Montgolfier, rocket and balloon. 150fr, Isaac Newton, planetary system and trajectories. 200fr, Galileo Galilei, spaceship and trajectories. 250fr, Leonardo da Vinci, his flying machine, and plane.

**1970, May 11 Engr. *Perf. 13***
**C122** AP51 50fr bl, cop red & sl .90 .40
**C123** AP51 100fr cop red, bl & sl 1.60 .80
**C124** AP51 150fr brn, grn & ocher 1.75 1.00
**C125** AP51 200fr dk car rose, dp vio & bis 2.40 1.40
**C126** AP51 250fr cop red, gray & pur 3.75 1.75
*Nos. C122-C126 (5)* 10.40 5.35

Pioneers of space research.

For overprints and surcharges see Nos. C129-C130, C141-C142.

Bay of Naples, Buildings, Mt. Vesuvius and Niger No. 97 — AP52

**1970, May 5 Photo. *Perf. 12½***
**C127** AP52 100fr multi 1.25 .55

Issued to publicize the 10th Europa Philatelic Exhibition, Naples, Italy, May 2-10.

TV Tube, Books, Microscope, Globe and ITU Emblem — AP53

**1970, May 16 Engr. *Perf. 13***
**C128** AP53 100fr grn, brn & red 1.40 .70

Issued for World Telecommunications Day.

**Nos. C123 and C125 Overprinted: "Solidarité Spatiale / Apollo XIII / 11-17 Avril 1970"**

**1970, June 6 Engr. *Perf. 13***
**C129** AP51 100fr multi 1.25 .60
**C130** AP51 200fr multi 2.25 .80

Abortive flight of Apollo 13, 4/11-17/70.

UN Emblem, Man, Woman and Doves — AP54

**1970, June 26 Photo. *Perf. 12½***
**C131** AP54 100fr brt bl, dk bl & org 1.25 .60
**C132** AP54 150fr multi 1.75 .80

25th anniversary of the United Nations.

European and African Men, Globe and Fleur-de-lis — AP55

**Lithographed; Embossed on Gold Foil**

**1970, July 22 *Perf. 12½***
**C133** AP55 250fr gold & ultra 4.00 4.00

French Language Cong., Niamey, Mar. 1970.

### Europafrica Issue

European and African Women — AP56

**1970, July 29 Engr. *Perf. 13***
**C134** AP56 50fr slate grn & dl red .75 .40

EXPO Emblem, Geisha and Torii — AP57

Design: 150fr, EXPO emblem, exhibition at night and character from Noh play.

**1970, Sept. 16 Engr. *Perf. 13***
**C135** AP57 100fr multi 1.10 .50
**C136** AP57 150fr bl, dk brn & grn 1.60 .65

EXPO '70 International Exhibition, Osaka, Japan, Mar. 15-Sept. 13.

Gymnast on Parallel Bars — AP58

Sports: 100fr, Vaulting, horiz. 150fr, Flying jump, horiz. 200fr, Rings.

**1970, Oct. 26 Engr. *Perf. 13***
**C137** AP58 50fr brt bl .65 .40
**C138** AP58 100fr brt grn 1.40 .70
**C139** AP58 150fr brt rose lil 2.25 .95
**C140** AP58 200fr red org 2.75 1.25
*Nos. C137-C140 (4)* 7.05 3.30

17th World Gymnastics Championships, Ljubljana, Oct. 22-27.

### Nos. C124 and C126 Surcharged and Overprinted: "LUNA 16 - Sept. 1970 / PREMIERS PRELEVEMENTS / AUTOMATIQUES SUR LA LUNE"

**1970, Nov. 5**
**C141** AP51 100fr on 150fr multi 1.60 .65
**C142** AP51 200fr on 250fr multi 3.25 1.30

Unmanned moon probe of the Russian space ship Luna 16, Sept. 12-24.

Beethoven and Piano — AP59

Design: 150fr, Beethoven and dancers with dove, symbolic of Ode to Joy.

**1970, Nov. 18 Photo. *Perf. 12½***
**C143** AP59 100fr multi 1.60 .60
**C144** AP59 150fr multi 2.40 .90

Ludwig van Beethoven (1770-1827), composer.

John F. Kennedy Bridge, Niamey — AP60

**1970, Dec. 18 Photo. *Perf. 12½***
**C145** AP60 100fr multicolored 1.40 .60

Proclamation of the Republic, 12th anniv.

Gamal Abdel Nasser (1918-70), President of Egypt — AP61

Design: 200fr, Nasser with raised arm.

**1971, Jan. 5 Photo. *Perf. 12½***
**C146** AP61 100fr blk, org brn & grn 1.00 .50
**C147** AP61 200fr grn, org & blk brn 1.75 .85

Charles de Gaulle AP62

### Embossed on Gold Foil

**1971, Jan. 22 *Die-cut Perf. 10***
**C148** AP62 1000fr gold *65.00 65.00*

In memory of Gen. Charles de Gaulle (1890-1970), President of France.

Olympic Rings and "Munich" — AP63

**1971, Jan. 29 Engr. *Perf. 13***
**C149** AP63 150fr dk bl, rose lil & grn 1.90 .80

1972 Summer Olympic Games, Munich.

Landing Module over Moon — AP64

**1971, Feb. 5 Engr. *Perf. 13***
**C150** AP64 250fr ultra, sl grn & org 3.00 1.75

Apollo 14 mission, Jan. 31-Feb. 9.

Masks of Hate — AP65

200fr, People & 4-leaf clover (symbol of unity).

**1971, Mar. 20 Engr. *Perf. 13***
**C151** AP65 100fr red, sl & brt bl 1.10 .45
**C152** AP65 200fr slate, red & grn 2.25 .85

Intl. Year against Racial Discrimination.

Map of Africa and Telecommunications System — AP66

**1971, Apr. 6 Photo. *Perf. 12½***
**C153** AP66 100fr grn & multi .80 .45

Pan-African telecommunications system.

African Mask and Japan No. 580 — AP67

Design: 100fr, Japanese actors, stamps of Niger, No. 95 on cover and No. 170.

**1971, Apr. 23 Engr. *Perf. 13***
**C154** AP67 50fr dk brn, emer & blk .80 .45
**C155** AP67 100fr brn & multi 1.40 .60

Philatokyo 71, Tokyo Philatelic Exposition, Apr. 19-29.

Longwood, St. Helena, by Carle Vernet — AP68

Napoleon Bonaparte: 200fr, Napoleon's body on camp bed, by Marryat.

**1971, May 5 Photo. *Perf. 13***
**C156** AP68 150fr gold & multi 2.25 .75
**C157** AP68 200fr gold & multi 3.25 1.25

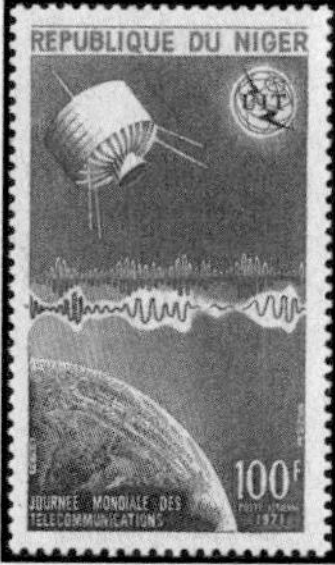


Satellite, Waves and Earth — AP69

**1971, May 17 Engr. *Perf. 13***
**C158** AP69 100fr org, ultra & dk brn 1.40 .60

3rd World Telecommunications Day.

Olympic Rings, Athletes and Torch — AP70

Designs: 50fr, Pierre de Coubertin, discus throwers, horiz. 150fr, Runners, horiz.

**1971, June 10**
**C159** AP70 50fr red & slate .80 .30
**C160** AP70 100fr sl, brn & grn 1.25 .50
**C161** AP70 150fr plum, bl & rose lil 2.10 1.10
*Nos. C159-C161 (3)* 4.15 1.90

75th anniv. of modern Olympic Games.

Astronauts and Landing Module on Moon — AP71

**1971, July 26 Engr. *Perf. 13***
**C162** AP71 150fr red brn, pur & sl 1.90 .85

US Apollo 15 moon mission, 7/26-8/7/71.

Charles de Gaulle — AP72

**1971, Nov. 9 Photo. *Perf. 12½x12***
**C163** AP72 250r multi 8.00 5.00

First anniversary of the death of Charles de Gaulle (1890-1970), president of France.

### African Postal Union Issue, 1971
Common Design Type

Design: 100fr, Water carrier, cattle and UAMPT headquarters, Brazzaville, Congo.

**1971, Nov. 13 Photo. *Perf. 13x13½***
**C164** CD135 100fr blue & multi 1.25 .60

Al Hariri Holding Audience, Baghdad, 1237 — AP73

Designs from Mohammedan Miniatures: 150fr, Archangel Israfil, late 14th century, vert. 200fr, Horsemen, 1210.

**1971, Nov. 25** ***Perf. 13***

**C165** AP73 100fr multi 1.25 .60
**C166** AP73 150fr multi 2.00 .95
**C167** AP73 200fr multi 3.00 1.75
*Nos. C165-C167 (3)* 6.25 3.30

Louis Armstrong AP74

Design: 150fr, Armstrong with trumpet.

**1971, Dec. 6**

**C168** AP74 100fr multi 2.00 .75
**C169** AP74 150fr multi 3.00 1.00

Armstrong (1900-71), American jazz musician.

Adoration of the Kings, by Di Bartolo — AP75

Christmas (Paintings): 150fr, Nativity, by Domenico Ghirlandaio, vert. 200fr, Adoration of the Shepherds, by Il Perugino.

**1971, Dec. 24** **Photo.** ***Perf. 13***

**C170** AP75 100fr blk & multi 1.25 .55
**C171** AP75 150fr blk & multi 2.00 .80
**C172** AP75 200fr blk & multi 2.50 1.20
*Nos. C170-C172 (3)* 5.75 2.55

See Nos. C210-C212, C232-C234.

Presidents Pompidou and Diori Hamani, Flags of Niger and France — AP76

**1972, Jan. 22**

**C173** AP76 250fr multi 7.00 4.00

Visit of President Georges Pompidou of France, Jan. 1972.

Snowflakes, Olympic Torch and Emblem — AP77

Design: 100fr, Torii made of ski poles and skis, and dwarf tree, vert.

**1972, Jan. 27** **Engr.**

**C174** AP77 100fr dk vio, grn & car 1.25 .55
**C175** AP77 150fr dk vio, lil & red 1.90 .75
*a.* Souv. sheet of 2, #C174-C175 3.25 3.25

11th Winter Olympic Games, Sapporo, Japan, Feb. 3-13.

The Masked Ball, by Guardi — AP78

50fr, 100fr, 150fr, Details from "The Masked Ball," by Francesco Guardi (1712-93); all vert.

**1972, Feb. 7** **Photo.**

**C176** AP78 50fr gold & multi 1.10 .50
**C177** AP78 100fr gold & multi 1.75 .85
**C178** AP78 150fr gold & multi 2.75 1.10
**C179** AP78 200fr gold & multi 3.25 1.40
*Nos. C176-C179 (4)* 8.85 3.85

UNESCO campaign to save Venice.
See Nos. C215-C216.

Johannes Brahms and "Lullaby" — AP79

**1972, Mar. 17** **Engr.** ***Perf. 13***

**C180** AP79 100fr multicolored 1.90 .75

75th anniversary of death of Johannes Brahms (1833-1897), German composer.

Scout Sign and Tents — AP80

**1972, Mar. 22**

**C181** AP80 150fr pur, org & slate bl 1.75 .75

World Boy Scout Seminar, Cotonou, Dahomey, March 1972.

Surgical Team, Heart-shaped Globe and Emblem — AP81

**1972** **Engr.** ***Perf. 13***

**C182** AP81 100fr dp brn & car 1.40 .60

"Your heart is your health," World Health Day.

Famous Aircraft — AP82

50fr, Bleriot XI Crossing English Channel. 75fr, Spirit of St. Louis crossing Atlantic. 100fr, 1st flight of Concorde supersonic jet.

**1972, Apr. 24**

**C183** AP82 50fr shown .90 .40
**C184** AP82 75fr multicolored 1.40 .55
**C185** AP82 100fr multicolored 2.50 1.40
*Nos. C183-C185 (3)* 4.80 2.35

ITU Emblem, Satellite, Stars and Earth — AP83

**1972, May 17** **Engr.** ***Perf. 13***

**C186** AP83 100fr pur, car & blk 1.40 .60

4th World Telecommunications Day.

20th Olympic Games, Munich — AP84

50fr, Boxing and Opera House. 100fr, Broad jump & City Hall. 150fr, Soccer & Church of the Theatines, vert. 200fr, Running and Propylaeum.

**1972, May 26**

**C187** AP84 50fr blue & grn .70 .30
**C188** AP84 100fr yel grn & dk brn 1.00 .50
**C189** AP84 150fr org red & dk brn 1.60 .70
**C190** AP84 200fr violet & dk brn 2.10 .90
*a.* Min. sheet of 4, #C187-C190 6.50 6.50
*Nos. C187-C190 (4)* 5.40 2.40

For overprints see Nos. C196-C199.

"Alexander Graham Bell," Telephone — AP85

**1972, July 7**

**C191** AP85 100fr car, dk pur & slate 1.25 .60

Alexander Graham Bell (1847-1922), inventor of the telephone. Stamp pictures Samuel F. B. Morse.

### Europafrica Issue

Stylized Maps of Africa and Europe — AP86

**1972, July 29** **Engr.** ***Perf. 13***

**C192** AP86 50fr red brn, bl & grn .60 .25

Mail Runner, UPU Emblem — AP87

Designs: 100fr, Mail truck, UPU emblem. 150fr, Mail plane, UPU emblem.

**1972, Oct. 9** **Engr.** ***Perf. 13***

**C193** AP87 50fr multicolored .80 .40
**C194** AP87 100fr multicolored 1.25 .65
**C195** AP87 150fr multicolored 2.00 .95
*Nos. C193-C195 (3)* 4.05 2.00

Universal Postal Union Day.

### Nos. C187-C190 Overprinted in Red or Violet Blue

(a)

(b)

(c)

(d)

**1972, Nov. 10**

**C196** AP84(a) 50fr multi (R) .65 .35
**C197** AP84(b) 100fr multi (R) 1.00 .50
**C198** AP84(c) 150fr multi (VBl) 1.75 .80
**C199** AP84(d) 200fr multi (R) 2.25 .95
*Nos. C196-C199 (4)* 5.65 2.60

Gold medal winners in 20th Olympic Games: Emilio Correa, Cuba, welterweight boxing; Victor Saneev, USSR, triple jump; Poland, soccer; Frank Shorter, US, marathon.

Fables — AP88

25fr, The Crow and The Fox. 50fr, The Lion and the Mouse. 75fr, The Monkey and the Leopard.

**1972, Nov. 23**

**C200** AP88 25fr emer, blk & brn 1.10 .40
**C201** AP88 50fr brt pink, bl grn & brn 1.50 .50
**C202** AP88 75fr lt brn, grn & dk brn 2.40 .80
*Nos. C200-C202 (3)* 5.00 1.70

Jean de La Fontaine (1621-1695), French fabulist.

Astronauts on Moon — AP89

**1972, Dec. 12 Photo. *Perf. 13***

**C203** AP89 250fr multi 3.25 1.50

Apollo 17 US moon mission, Dec. 7-19.

Young Athlete AP90

Design: 100fr, Head of Hermes.

**1973, Feb. 7 Engr. *Perf. 13***

**C204** AP90 50fr dk car .60 .35
**C205** AP90 100fr purple 1.25 .50

Treasures of antiquity.

Boy Scouts and Radio Transmission — AP91

Niger Boy Scouts: 50fr, Red Cross, first aid. 100fr, Scout and gazelle. 150fr, Scouts with gazelle and bird.

**1973, Mar. 21 Engr. *Perf. 13***

**C206** AP91 25fr multicolored .40 .30
**C207** AP91 50fr multicolored .75 .35
**C208** AP91 100fr multicolored 1.25 .60
**C209** AP91 150fr multicolored 1.60 .75
*Nos. C206-C209 (4)* 4.00 2.00

For overprints see Nos. C217-C218.

### Christmas Type of 1971

Paintings: 50fr, Crucifixion, by Hugo van der Goes, vert. 100fr, Burial of Christ, by Cima da Conegliano. 150fr, Pietà, by Giovanni Bellini.

**1973, Apr. 20 Photo. *Perf. 13***

**C210** AP75 50fr gold & multi .70 .30
**C211** AP75 100fr gold & multi 1.40 .55
**C212** AP75 150fr gold & multi 2.00 .70
*Nos. C210-C212 (3)* 4.10 1.55

Easter 1973.

Air Afrique Plane and Mail Truck — AP92

**1973, Apr. 30 Engr. *Perf. 13***

**C213** AP92 100fr brt grn, choc & car 1.60 .65

Stamp Day 1973.

WMO Emblem, Pyramids with Weather Symbols, Satellite — AP93

**1973, May 7**

**C214** AP93 100fr multicolored 1.25 .50

Cent. of intl. meteorological cooperation.

### Painting Type of 1972

Paintings by Delacroix: 150fr, Prowling lioness. 200fr, Tigress and cub.

**1973, May 22 Photo. *Perf. 13x12½***

**C215** AP78 150fr blk & multi 2.75 1.40
**C216** AP78 200fr blk & multi 4.50 2.25

175th anniversary of the birth of Ferdinand Delacroix (1798-1863), French painter.

### Nos. C208-C209 Overprinted

**1973, July 19 Engr. *Perf. 13***

**C217** AP91 100fr multi 1.25 .55
**C218** AP91 150fr multi 1.75 .80

Boy Scout 24th World Jamboree, Nairobi, Kenya, July 16-21.

Head and City Hall, Brussels AP93a

**1973, Sept. 17 Engr. *Perf. 13***

**C219** AP93a 100fr multicolored 1.25 .80

Africa Weeks, Brussels, Sept. 15-30, 1973.

Men Emptying Cornucopia, FAO Emblem, People — AP94

**1973, Nov. 2 Engr. *Perf. 13***

**C220** AP94 50fr ultra, pur & ver .80 .35

10th anniversary of the World Food Program.

AP95

Copernicus, Sputnik 1, Heliocentric System.

**1973, Nov. 12**

**C221** AP95 150fr mag, vio bl & brn 1.75 .90

AP96

**1973, Nov. 22 Photo. *Perf. 12½***

**C222** AP96 100fr reddsh brn & multi 1.25 .60

### Souvenir Sheet

***Perf. 13***

**C223** AP96 200fr dp ultra & multi 2.40 2.40

10th anniv. of the death of Pres. John F. Kennedy.

Barge on Niger River — AP97

Design: 75fr, Tug Baban Maza.

**1974, Jan. 18 Engr. *Perf. 13***

**C224** AP97 50fr mar, vio bl & grn 1.00 .50
**C225** AP97 75fr yel grn, bl & lil rose 1.40 .50

1st anniv. of the upstream voyage of the Flotilla of Hope.

Lenin — AP98

**1974, Jan. 21**

**C226** AP98 50fr dk red brn 2.10 .60

Skiers AP99

**1974, Feb. 8 Engr. *Perf. 11½x11***

**C227** AP99 200fr bl, sepia & car 3.00 1.20

50th anniversary of the first Winter Olympic Games, Chamonix, France.

Soccer and Emblem — AP100

Designs: Various views of soccer game.

**1974, Apr. 8 Engr. *Perf. 13***

**C228** AP100 75fr vio & blk .85 .40
**C229** AP100 150fr brn, lt & sl grn 1.75 .75
**C230** AP100 200fr Prus bl, grn & brn 2.40 1.25
*Nos. C228-C230 (3)* 5.00 2.40

### Souvenir Sheet

**C231** AP100 250fr yel grn, brn & ol brn 3.25 3.25

World Soccer Championship, Munich, June 13-July 7.
For overprint see No. C239.

### Christmas Type of 1971

Paintings: 50fr, Crucifixion, by Matthias Grunewald. 75fr, Avignon Pietà, attributed to Enguerrand Quarton. 125fr, Burial of Christ, by G. Isenmann.

**1974, Apr. 12 Litho. *Perf. 13x12½***

**C232** AP75 50fr blk & multi .70 .30
**C233** AP75 75fr blk & multi .95 .40
**C234** AP75 125fr blk & multi 1.60 .70
*Nos. C232-C234 (3)* 3.25 1.40

Easter 1974.

21st Chess Olympiad, Nice, June 6-30 — AP101

**1974, June 3 Engr. *Perf. 13***
**C235** AP101 50fr Knights 2.10 .75
**C236** AP101 75fr Kings 2.60 1.25

Astronaut and Apollo 11 Badge AP102

**1974, July 20 Engr. *Perf. 13***
**C237** AP102 150fr multi 1.60 .75

5th anniversary of the first manned moon landing.

### Europafrica Issue

The Rhinoceros, by Pietro Longhi — AP103

**1974, Aug. 10 Photo. *Perf. 12½x13***
**C238** AP103 250fr multi 7.50 4.00

### No. C231 Overprinted in Red

### Souvenir Sheet

**1974, Sept. 27 Engr. *Perf. 13***
**C239** AP100 250fr multi 3.25 3.25

World Cup Soccer Championship, Munich, 1974, victory of German Federal Republic.

Caucasian Woman, Envelope, UPU Emblem and Jets — AP104

Designs (UPU emblem, Envelope and): 100fr, Oriental woman and trains. 150fr, Indian woman and ships. 200fr, Black woman and buses.

**1974, Oct. 9 Engr. *Perf. 13***
**C240** AP104 50fr multi .75 .35
**C241** AP104 100fr multi 1.40 .45
**C242** AP104 150fr bl & multi 2.00 .75
**C243** AP104 200fr multi 2.75 1.20
*Nos. C240-C243 (4)* 6.90 2.75

Centenary of Universal Postal Union.

Skylab over Africa — AP105

**1974, Nov. 4 Engr. *Perf. 13***
**C244** AP105 100fr multi 1.25 .50

Virgin and Child, by Correggio AP106

150fr, Virgin and Child with St. Hilary, by Filippo Lippi. 200fr, Virgin and Child, by Murillo.

**1974, Dec. 24 Litho. *Perf. 12½x13***
**C245** AP106 100fr multi 1.25 .45
**C246** AP106 150fr multi 2.00 .65
**C247** AP106 200fr multi 2.50 1.00
*Nos. C245-C247 (3)* 5.75 2.10

Christmas 1974. See Nos. C252-C254, C260-C262, C280-C282.

Apollo and Emblem AP107

Designs (Emblem of Soyuz-Apollo Space Docking): 100fr, Docking in space over earth. 150fr, Soyuz in space.

**1975, Jan. 31 Engr. *Perf. 13***
**C248** AP107 50fr bl & multi .55 .35
**C249** AP107 100fr multi 1.00 .50
**C250** AP107 150fr multi 1.60 .70
*Nos. C248-C250 (3)* 3.15 1.55

Russo-American space cooperation. For overprints see Nos. C263-C265.

### Europafrica Issue

European and African Women, Globe — AP108

**1975, Feb. 28 Engr. *Perf. 13***
**C251** AP108 250fr brn, lil & red 3.00 1.50

### Painting Type of 1974

Easter: 75fr, Jesus in Garden of Olives, by Delacroix, horiz. 125fr, Crucifixion, by El Greco. 150fr, Resurrection, by Leonard Limosin.

***Perf. 13x12½, 12½x13***
**1975, Mar. 27 Litho.**
**C252** AP106 75fr multi .75 .35
**C253** AP106 125fr multi 1.40 .50
**C254** AP106 150fr multi 1.75 .75
*Nos. C252-C254 (3)* 3.90 1.60

### Bird Type of 1968-69 Dated "1975"

100fr, Cinnyricinclus leucogaster, vert.

**1975, Apr. Photo. *Perf. 13***
**C255** AP36 100fr gold & multi 3.00 1.30

Lt. Col. Seyni Kountche AP109

**1975, Apr. 15 Litho. *Perf. 12½x13***
**C256** AP109 100fr multi 1.40 .60

Military Government, first anniversary.

Shot Put, Maple Leaf, Montreal Olympic Emblem AP110

Design: 200fr, Gymnast on rings, Canadian flag, Montreal Olympic emblem.

**1975, Oct. 6 Engr. *Perf. 13***
**C257** AP110 150fr blk & red 1.40 .70
**C258** AP110 200fr red & blk 2.00 1.00

Pre-Olympic Year 1975.

UN Emblem and Dove — AP111

**1975, Nov. 26 Engr. *Perf. 13***
**C259** AP111 100fr grn & bl 1.00 .50

United Nations, 30th anniversary.

### Painting Type of 1974

50fr, Virgin of Seville, by Murillo. 75fr, Adoration of the Shepherds, by Tintoretto, horiz. 125fr, Virgin with Angels, Florentine, 15th cent.

**1975, Dec. 24 Litho. *Perf. 12½x13***
**C260** AP106 50fr multi .55 .35
**C261** AP106 75fr multi .85 .45
**C262** AP106 125fr multi 1.40 .80
*Nos. C260-C262 (3)* 2.80 1.60

Christmas 1975.

Nos. C248-C250 Ovptd.

**1975, Dec. 30 Engr. *Perf. 13***
**C263** AP107 50fr bl & multi .70 .25
**C264** AP107 100fr multi .90 .55
**C265** AP107 150fr multi 1.60 .90
*Nos. C263-C265 (3)* 3.20 1.70

Apollo-Soyuz link-up in space, July 17, 1975.

### 12th Winter Olympic Games Type, 1976

Designs: 200fr, Women's figure skating. 300fr, Biathlon. 500fr, Speed skating.

**1976, Feb. 20 Litho. *Perf. 14x13½***
**C266** A97 200fr multi 1.50 .80
**C267** A97 300fr multi 2.25 1.20

### Souvenir Sheet

**C268** A97 500fr multi 4.25 2.00

### American Bicentennial Type, 1976

Design (Statue of Liberty and): 150fr, Joseph Warren, martyr at Bunker Hill. 200fr, John Paul Jones on the bridge of the "Bonhomme Richard." 300fr, Molly Pitcher, Monmouth battle heroine. 500fr, Start of the fighting.

**1976, Apr. 8**
**C269** A100 150fr multi 1.20 .40
**C270** A100 200fr multi 1.75 .70
**C271** A100 300fr multi 2.40 .85
*Nos. C269-C271 (3)* 4.95 1.85

### Souvenir Sheet

**C272** A100 500fr multi 4.25 1.60

LZ-129 over Lake Constance — AP112

Designs: 50fr, LZ-3 over Würzburg. 150fr, LZ-9 over Friedrichshafen. 200fr, LZ-2 over Rothenburg, vert. 300fr, LZ-130 over Essen. 500fr, LZ-127 over the Swiss Alps.

**1976, May 18 Litho. *Perf. 11***
**C273** AP112 40fr multi .50 .25
**C274** AP112 50fr multi .60 .25
**C275** AP112 150fr multi 1.75 .50
**C276** AP112 200fr multi 2.00 .55
**C277** AP112 300fr multi 3.00 .70
*Nos. C273-C277 (5)* 7.85 2.25

### Souvenir Sheet

**C278** AP112 500fr multi 5.00 2.00

75th anniversary of the Zeppelin.

### Olympic Games Issue
Souvenir Sheet

**1976, July 17 Litho. *Perf. 14***
**C279** A105 150fr Sprint 1.60 .80

### Christmas Type of 1974

Paintings: 50fr, Nativity, by Rubens. 100fr, Virgin and Child, by Correggio. 150fr, Adoration of the Kings, by Gerard David, horiz.

**1976, Dec. 24 Litho. *Perf. 12½***
**C280** AP106 50fr multi .60 .25
**C281** AP106 100fr multi 1.25 .50
**C282** AP106 150fr multi 2.00 .85
*Nos. C280-C282 (3)* 3.85 1.60

Christmas 1976.

### Viking Mars Project Issue

100fr, Viking lander & nprobe, horiz. 150fr, Descent phases of Viking lander. 200fr, Titan rocket start for Mars. 400fr, Viking orbiter in flight.

**1977, Mar. 15 Litho. *Perf. 14***
**C283** A113 100fr multi .80 .25
**C284** A113 150fr multi 1.10 .45
**C285** A113 200fr multi 1.60 .60
*Nos. C283-C285 (3)* 3.50 1.10

### Souvenir Sheet

**C286** A113 400fr multi 3.25 1.25

For overprints see Nos. C295-C297.

### Nobel Prize Issue
Souvenir Sheet

Design: 500fr, Theodore Roosevelt, peace.

**1977, Aug. 20 Litho. *Perf. 14***
**C287** A122 500fr multi 4.50 1.25

Games' Emblem, Wheels and Colors AP113

150fr, Rings, colors and Games' emblem.

**1978, July 13 Litho. *Perf. 12½x13***

| | | | |
|---|---|---|---|
| **C288** AP113 40fr multi | .40 | .30 |
| **C289** AP113 150fr multi | 1.40 | .60 |

Third African Games, Algiers, July 13-28.

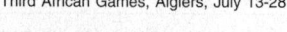

Emblem AP114

**1978, Oct. 6 Litho. *Perf. 13***

**C290** AP114 150fr multi 1.25 .60

Niger Broadcasting Company, 20th anniversary.

**Philexafrique II — Essen Issue**

Common Design Types

Designs: No. C291, Giraffes and Niger No. 92. No. C292, Eagle and Oldenburg No. 7.

**1978, Nov. 1 Litho. *Perf. 13x12½***

| | | |
|---|---|---|
| **C291** CD138 100fr multi | 2.25 | 1.40 |
| **C292** CD139 100fr multi | 2.25 | 1.40 |
| *a.* Pair, #C291-C292 + label | 6.00 | 5.00 |

View of Campus and Laying Cornerstone — AP115

**1978, Dec. 11 Litho. *Perf. 12½***

**C293** AP115 100fr multi .80 .40

Islamic University of Niger.

Control Tower, Emblem, Plane, Map of Niger AP116

**1979, Dec. 12 Litho. *Perf. 12½***

**C294** AP116 150fr multi 1.25 .65

ASECNA (Air Safety Board), 20th anniversary.

Nos. C284-C286 Overprinted in Silver or Black

**1979, Dec. 20 Litho. *Perf. 14***

**C295** A113 150fr multi 1.25 .70

**C296** A113 200fr multi (S) 1.60 .85

**Souvenir Sheet**

**C297** A113 400fr multi 3.25 2.00

Apollo 11 moon landing, 10th anniversary.

Gaweye Hotel AP117

**1980, Jan. 10 Litho. *Perf. 13***

**C298** AP117 100fr multi .80 .40

Self-portrait, by Rembrandt AP118

Rembrandt Portraits: 90fr, Hendrickje at the Window. 100fr, Old Man. 130fr, Maria Trip. 200fr, Self-portrait, diff. 400fr, Saskia.

**1981, Feb. 12 Litho. *Perf. 12½***

| | | |
|---|---|---|
| **C299** AP118 60fr multi | .45 | .25 |
| **C300** AP118 90fr multi | .70 | .25 |
| **C301** AP118 100fr multi | .80 | .30 |
| **C302** AP118 130fr multi | 1.10 | .40 |
| **C303** AP118 200fr multi | 1.60 | .40 |
| **C304** AP118 400fr multi | 3.25 | 1.00 |
| *Nos. C299-C304 (6)* | 7.90 | 2.60 |

Apollo 11, 1969 — AP119

Space Conquest: Views of Columbia space shuttle, 1981.

**1981, Mar. 30 Litho. *Perf. 12½***

| | | |
|---|---|---|
| **C305** AP119 100fr multi | .80 | .30 |
| **C306** AP119 150fr multi | 1.25 | .35 |
| **C307** AP119 200fr multi | 1.40 | .45 |
| **C308** AP119 300fr multi | 2.25 | .75 |
| *Nos. C305-C308 (4)* | 5.70 | 1.85 |

**Souvenir Sheet**

**C309** AP119 500fr multi 4.00 1.25

For overprint see No. C356.

Girl in a Room, by Picasso — AP120

Picasso Birth Centenary: 60fr, Olga in an Armchair. 90fr, Family of Acrobats. 120fr, Three Musicians. 200fr, Paul on a Donkey. All vert.

**1981, June 25 Litho. *Perf. 12½***

| | | |
|---|---|---|
| **C310** AP120 60fr multi | .50 | .25 |
| **C311** AP120 90fr multi | .80 | .30 |
| **C312** AP120 120fr multi | 1.00 | .40 |
| **C313** AP120 200fr multi | 1.75 | .60 |
| **C314** AP120 400fr multi | 3.50 | 1.10 |
| *Nos. C310-C314 (5)* | 7.55 | 2.65 |

Christmas 1982 AP121

Rubens Paintings — 200fr, Adoration of the Kings. 300fr, Mystical Marriage of St. Catherine. 400fr, Virgin and Child.

**1982, Dec. 24 Litho. *Perf. 14***

| | | |
|---|---|---|
| **C315** AP121 200fr multi | 1.40 | .30 |
| **C316** AP121 300fr multi | 2.10 | .65 |
| **C317** AP121 400fr multi | 2.75 | .80 |
| *Nos. C315-C317 (3)* | 6.25 | 1.75 |

Manned Flight Bicentenary AP122

65fr, Montgolfiere balloon, 1783, vert. 85fr, Hydrogen balloon, 1783, vert. 200fr, Zeppelin. 250fr, Farman plane. 300fr, Concorde. 500fr, Apollo 11, vert.

**1983, Jan. 24**

| | | |
|---|---|---|
| **C318** AP122 65fr multi | .50 | .25 |
| **C319** AP122 85fr multi | .75 | .25 |
| **C320** AP122 200fr multi | 1.50 | .40 |
| **C321** AP122 250fr multi | 2.00 | .55 |
| **C322** AP122 300fr multi | 2.25 | .65 |
| **C323** AP122 500fr multi | 4.00 | 1.00 |
| *Nos. C318-C323 (6)* | 11.00 | 3.10 |

Pre-Olympic Year — AP123

**1983, May 25 Litho. *Perf. 13***

| | | |
|---|---|---|
| **C324** AP123 85fr Javelin | .60 | .25 |
| **C325** AP123 200fr Shot put | 1.60 | .55 |
| **C326** AP123 250fr Hammer, vert. | 1.90 | .70 |
| **C327** AP123 300fr Discus | 2.40 | .80 |
| *Nos. C324-C327 (4)* | 6.50 | 2.30 |

**Souvenir Sheet**

**C328** AP123 500fr Shot put, diff. 4.00 1.25

For overprint see No. C357.

Christmas 1983 — AP124

Botticelli Paintings — 120fr, Virgin and Child with Angels, vert. 350fr, Adoration of the Kings. 500fr, Virgin of the Pomegranate, vert.

**Wmk. 385 Cartor**

**1983 Litho. *Perf. 13***

| | | |
|---|---|---|
| **C329** AP124 120fr multi | .90 | .35 |
| **C330** AP124 350fr multi | 2.75 | .75 |
| **C331** AP124 500fr multi | 3.75 | 1.10 |
| *Nos. C329-C331 (3)* | 7.40 | 2.20 |

1984 Summer Olympics — AP125

80fr, Sprint. 120fr, Pole vault. 140fr, High jump. 200fr, Triple jump, vert. 350fr, Long jump, vert.

500fr, 110-meter hurdles.

**Unwmk.**

**1984, Feb. 22 Litho. *Perf. 13***

| | | |
|---|---|---|
| **C332** AP125 80fr multi | .55 | .25 |
| **C333** AP125 120fr multi | .80 | .25 |
| **C334** AP125 140fr multi | 1.25 | .40 |
| **C335** AP125 200fr multi | 1.75 | .40 |
| **C336** AP125 350fr multi | 2.75 | .90 |
| *Nos. C332-C336 (5)* | 7.10 | 2.20 |

**Souvenir Sheet**

**C337** AP125 500fr multi 3.50 1.25

**1984, Oct. 8 Litho.**

Designs: Winners of various track events: 80fr, Carl Lewis, vert. 120fr, J. Cruz, vert. 140fr, A. Cova, vert. 300fr, Al Joyner, vert.

500fr, D. Mogenburg, high jump.

| | | |
|---|---|---|
| **C338** AP125 80fr multi | .55 | .35 |
| **C339** AP125 120fr multi | .90 | .45 |
| **C340** AP125 140fr multi | 1.00 | .50 |
| **C341** AP125 300fr multi | 2.10 | 1.10 |
| *Nos. C338-C341 (4)* | 4.55 | 2.40 |

**Souvenir Sheet**

**C342** AP125 500fr multi 3.50 2.00

World Soccer Cup — AP126

**1984, Nov. 19 Litho. *Perf. 13***

| | | |
|---|---|---|
| **C345** AP126 150fr multi | 1.00 | .60 |
| **C346** AP126 250fr multi | 1.75 | 1.05 |
| **C347** AP126 450fr multi | 3.25 | 1.60 |
| **C348** AP126 500fr multi | 3.50 | 1.90 |
| *Nos. C345-C348 (4)* | 9.50 | 5.15 |

Christmas 1984 AP127

Paintings: 100fr, The Visitation, by Ghirlandajo. 200fr, Virgin and Child, by the Master of Santa Verdiana. 400fr, Virgin and Child, by J. Koning.

**1984, Dec. 24 Litho. *Perf. 13***

| | | |
|---|---|---|
| **C349** AP127 100fr multi | .80 | .45 |
| **C350** AP127 200fr multi | 1.60 | .95 |
| **C351** AP127 400fr multi | 3.25 | 1.40 |
| *Nos. C349-C351 (3)* | 5.65 | 2.80 |

Audubon Birth Bicentennial — AP128

110fr, Himantopus mexicanus. 140fr, Phoenicopterus ruber, vert. 200fr, Fratercula arctica. 350fr, Sterna paradisaea, vert.

**1985, Feb. 6 Litho. *Perf. 13***

| | | | | |
|---|---|---|---|---|
| **C352** | AP128 | 110fr multi | .90 | .50 |
| **C353** | AP128 | 140fr multi | 1.40 | .55 |
| **C354** | AP128 | 200fr multi | 1.75 | .85 |
| **C355** | AP128 | 350fr multi | 3.25 | 1.40 |
| | | *Nos. C352-C355 (4)* | 7.30 | 3.30 |

**Nos. C309, C328 Ovptd. in Silver with Exhibition Emblems**

**1985, Mar. 11 Litho. *Perf. 12½, 13***

| | | | | |
|---|---|---|---|---|
| **C356** | AP119 | 500fr ARGENTINA '85 BUENOS AIRES | 4.75 | 3.00 |
| **C357** | AP123 | 500fr OLYMPHILEX '85 LAUSANNE | 4.75 | 3.00 |

Religious Paintings by Bartolome Murillo (1617-1682) AP129

110fr, Virgin of the Rosary. 250fr, The Immaculate Conception. 390fr, Virgin of Seville.

**1985, Dec. 19 Litho. *Perf. 13***

| | | | | |
|---|---|---|---|---|
| **C358** | AP129 | 110fr multi | .80 | .45 |
| **C359** | AP129 | 250fr multi | 1.90 | .85 |
| **C360** | AP129 | 390fr multi | 3.25 | 1.40 |
| | | *Nos. C358-C360 (3)* | 5.95 | 2.70 |

Christmas 1985.

Halley's Comet — AP130

110fr, Over Paris, 1910. 130fr, Over New York. 200fr, Giotto space probe. 300fr, Vega probe. 390fr, Planet A probe.

**1985, Dec. 26**

| | | | | |
|---|---|---|---|---|
| **C361** | AP130 | 110fr multi | .80 | .40 |
| **C362** | AP130 | 130fr multi | 1.00 | .55 |
| **C363** | AP130 | 200fr multi | 1.75 | .80 |
| **C364** | AP130 | 300fr multi | 2.50 | 1.20 |
| **C365** | AP130 | 390fr multi | 3.25 | 1.60 |
| | | *Nos. C361-C365 (5)* | 9.30 | 4.55 |

Martin Luther King, Jr. (1929-1968), Civil Rights Activist — AP131

**1986, Apr. 28 Litho. *Perf. 13½***

| | | | | |
|---|---|---|---|---|
| **C366** | AP131 | 500fr multi | 4.00 | 2.00 |

1986 World Cup Soccer Championships, Mexico — AP132

Various soccer plays, stamps and labels.

**1986, May 21 *Perf. 13***

| | | | | |
|---|---|---|---|---|
| **C367** | AP132 | 130fr No. 228 | .90 | .40 |
| **C368** | AP132 | 210fr No. 229 | 1.40 | .70 |
| **C369** | AP132 | 390fr No. 230 | 2.75 | 1.25 |
| **C370** | AP132 | 400fr Aztec drawing | 2.75 | 1.25 |
| | | *Nos. C367-C370 (4)* | 7.80 | 3.60 |

**Souvenir Sheet**

| | | | | |
|---|---|---|---|---|
| **C371** | AP132 | 500fr World Cup | 3.50 | 2.25 |

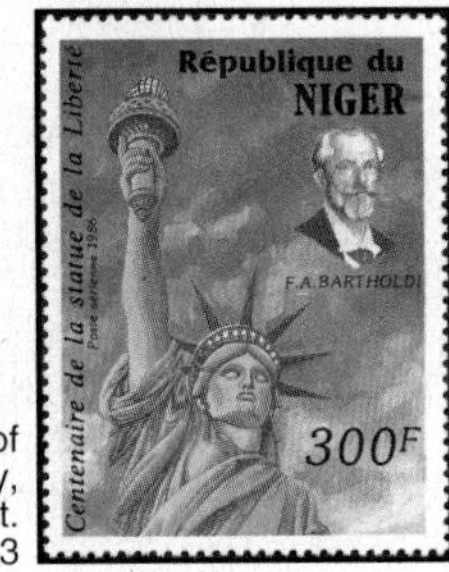


Statue of Liberty, Cent. AP133

300fr, Bartholdi, statue.

**1986, June 19**

| | | | | |
|---|---|---|---|---|
| **C372** | AP133 | 300fr multi | 2.40 | 1.25 |

1988 Summer Olympics, Seoul AP134

Olympic Rings, Pierre de Coubertin and: 85fr, One-man kayak, vert. 165fr, Crew racing. 200fr, Two-man kayak. 600fr, One-man kayak, diff., vert. 750fr, One-man kayak, diff., vert.

**1988, June 22 Litho. *Perf. 13***

| | | | | |
|---|---|---|---|---|
| **C373** | AP134 | 85fr multi | .65 | .30 |
| **C374** | AP134 | 165fr multi | 1.25 | .60 |
| **C375** | AP134 | 200fr multi | 1.60 | .80 |
| **C376** | AP134 | 600fr multi | 4.50 | 2.25 |
| | | *Nos. C373-C376 (4)* | 8.00 | 3.95 |

**Souvenir Sheet**

| | | | | |
|---|---|---|---|---|
| **C377** | AP134 | 750fr multi | 6.00 | 4.50 |

First Moon Landing, 20th Anniv. AP135

200fr, Launch. 300fr, Crew. 350fr, Lunar experiments. 400fr, Raising flag.

**1989, July 27 Litho. *Perf. 13***

| | | | | |
|---|---|---|---|---|
| **C378** | AP135 | 200fr multi | 1.60 | .75 |
| **C379** | AP135 | 300fr multi | 2.40 | 1.25 |
| **C380** | AP135 | 350fr multi | 2.75 | 1.40 |
| **C381** | AP135 | 400fr multi | 3.25 | 1.50 |
| | | *Nos. C378-C381 (4)* | 10.00 | 4.90 |

1990 World Cup Soccer Championships, Italy — AP136

Athletes & views or symbols of Italian cities.

**1990, Mar. 6 Litho. *Perf. 13***

| | | | | |
|---|---|---|---|---|
| **C382** | AP136 | 130fr Florence | .90 | .40 |
| **C383** | AP136 | 210fr Verona | 1.50 | .75 |
| **C384** | AP136 | 500fr Bari | 3.50 | 1.75 |
| **C385** | AP136 | 600fr Rome | 4.25 | 2.10 |
| | | *Nos. C382-C385 (4)* | 10.15 | 5.00 |

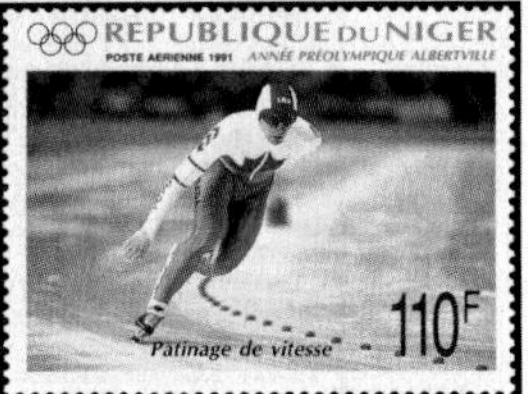


1992 Winter Olympics, Albertville — AP138

110fr, Speed skating. 300fr, Ice hockey. 500fr, Downhill skiing. 600fr, Luge.

**1991, Mar. 28 Litho. *Perf. 13***

| | | | | |
|---|---|---|---|---|
| **C392** | AP138 | 110fr multicolored | .80 | .35 |
| **C393** | AP138 | 300fr multicolored | 2.40 | 1.25 |
| **C394** | AP138 | 500fr multicolored | 4.00 | 2.00 |
| **C395** | AP138 | 600fr multicolored | 4.75 | 2.40 |
| | | *Nos. C392-C395 (4)* | 11.95 | 6.00 |

## AIR POST SEMI-POSTAL STAMPS

**Dahomey types SPAP1-SPAP3 inscribed Niger**

***Perf. 13½x12½, 13 (#CB3)***

**Photo, Engr. (#CB3)**

**1942, June 22**

| | | | | |
|---|---|---|---|---|
| **CB1** | SPAP1 | 1.50fr + 3.50fr green | .35 | *5.00* |
| **CB2** | SPAP2 | 2fr + 6fr brown | .35 | *5.00* |
| **CB3** | SPAP3 | 3fr + 9fr car red | .35 | *5.00* |
| | | *Nos. CB1-CB3 (3)* | 1.05 | 15.00 |
| | | Set, never hinged | 2.00 | |

Native children's welfare fund.

**Colonial Education Fund**

Common Design Type

***Perf. 12½x13½***

**1942, June 22 Engr.**

| | | | | |
|---|---|---|---|---|
| **CB4** | CD86a | 1.20fr + 1.80fr blue & red | .35 | *5.00* |
| | | Never hinged | .70 | |

## POSTAGE DUE STAMPS

1914 Upper Senegal and Niger Postage Due Stamps Ovptd.

**1921 Unwmk. *Perf. 14x13½***

| | | | | |
|---|---|---|---|---|
| **J1** | D1 | 5c green | .70 | *.95* |
| **J2** | D1 | 10c rose | .70 | *.95* |
| **J3** | D1 | 15c gray | .70 | *1.05* |
| **J4** | D1 | 20c brown | .70 | *1.05* |
| **J5** | D1 | 30c blue | .70 | *1.20* |
| **J6** | D1 | 50c black | .70 | *1.20* |
| **J7** | D1 | 60c orange | 1.40 | *2.00* |
| **J8** | D1 | 1fr violet | 1.40 | *2.00* |
| | | *Nos. J1-J8 (8)* | 7.00 | *10.40* |

Caravansary Near Timbuktu D2

**1927 Typo.**

| | | | | |
|---|---|---|---|---|
| **J9** | D2 | 2c dk bl & red | .35 | *.35* |
| **J10** | D2 | 4c ver & blk | .35 | *.35* |
| **J11** | D2 | 5c org & vio | .35 | *.35* |
| **J12** | D2 | 10c red brn & blk vio | .35 | *.35* |
| **J13** | D2 | 15c grn & org | .35 | .35 |
| **J14** | D2 | 20c cer & ol brn | .35 | .70 |
| **J15** | D2 | 25c blk & ol brn | .35 | *.70* |
| **J16** | D2 | 30c dl vio & blk | 1.40 | *1.40* |
| **J17** | D2 | 50c dp red, *grnsh* | .70 | *1.10* |
| **J18** | D2 | 60c gray vio & org, *bluish* | .70 | .70 |
| **J19** | D2 | 1fr ind & ultra, *bluish* | 1.00 | *1.20* |
| **J20** | D2 | 2fr rose red & vio | 1.10 | *1.40* |
| **J21** | D2 | 3fr org brn & ultra | 1.75 | 2.00 |
| | | *Nos. J9-J21 (13)* | 9.10 | *10.95* |

**Catalogue values for unused stamps in this section, from this point to the end of the section, are for Never Hinged items.**

**Republic of the Niger**

Cross of Agadez D3

Native Metalcraft: 3fr, 5fr, 10fr, Cross of Iferouane. 15fr, 20fr, 50fr, Cross of Tahoua.

***Perf. 12½***

**1962, July 1 Unwmk. Photo.**

| | | | | |
|---|---|---|---|---|
| **J22** | D3 | 50c emerald | .25 | .25 |
| **J23** | D3 | 1fr violet | .25 | .25 |
| **J24** | D3 | 2fr slate green | .25 | .25 |
| **J25** | D3 | 3fr lilac rose | .25 | .25 |
| **J26** | D3 | 5fr green | .25 | .25 |
| **J27** | D3 | 10fr orange | .25 | .25 |
| **J28** | D3 | 15fr deep blue | .25 | .25 |
| **J29** | D3 | 20fr carmine | .25 | .25 |
| **J30** | D3 | 50fr chocolate | .35 | .35 |
| | | *Nos. J22-J30 (9)* | 2.35 | 2.35 |

**1993 Litho. *Perf. 12½***

**Designs as Before**

**Size: 50x50mm**

| | | | | |
|---|---|---|---|---|
| **J31** | D3 | 5fr green | .25 | .25 |
| **J32** | D3 | 10fr orange | .25 | .25 |
| **J33** | D3 | 15fr blue | .25 | .25 |
| **J34** | D3 | 20fr red | .25 | .25 |
| **J35** | D3 | 50fr chocolate | .40 | .40 |
| | | *Nos. J31-J35 (5)* | 1.40 | 1.40 |

Imprint on Nos. J31-J35 is in black.

## OFFICIAL STAMPS

**Catalogue values for unused stamps in this section are for Never Hinged items.**

Djerma Girl Carrying Jug — O1

**Denomination in Black**

***Perf. 14x13½***

**1962-71 Typo. Unwmk.**

| | | | | |
|---|---|---|---|---|
| **O1** | O1 | 1fr dark purple | .25 | .25 |
| **O2** | O1 | 2fr yel grn | .25 | .25 |
| **O3** | O1 | 5fr brt blue | .25 | .25 |
| **O4** | O1 | 10fr deep red | .25 | .25 |
| **O5** | O1 | 20fr vio blue | .25 | .25 |
| **O6** | O1 | 25fr orange | .25 | .25 |
| **O7** | O1 | 30fr light blue ('65) | .30 | .25 |
| **O8** | O1 | 35fr pale grn ('71) | .40 | .30 |
| **O9** | O1 | 40fr brown ('71) | .40 | .30 |
| **O10** | O1 | 50fr black | .40 | .30 |

| | | | | |
|---|---|---|---|---|
| **O11** | O1 | 60fr rose red | .60 | .35 |
| **O12** | O1 | 85fr blue green | .90 | .35 |
| **O13** | O1 | 100fr red lilac | .95 | .35 |
| **O14** | O1 | 200fr dark blue | 2.00 | .75 |
| | | *Nos. O1-O14 (14)* | 7.45 | 4.45 |

Djerma Girl Carrying Jug — O2

**Denomination Same Color As Design**

**1988, Nov. Typo. *Perf. 13***

| | | | | |
|---|---|---|---|---|
| **O15** | O2 | 5fr brt blue | .25 | .25 |
| **O16** | O2 | 10fr henna brn | .25 | .25 |
| **O17** | O2 | 20fr vio blue | .25 | .25 |
| **O18** | O2 | 50fr greenish blk | .50 | .25 |

**1989-96(?)**

| | | | | |
|---|---|---|---|---|
| **O19** | O2 | 15fr bright yellow | .25 | .25 |
| **O20** | O2 | 45fr orange | .30 | .25 |
| **O21** | O2 | 85fr blue green | | |
| **O22** | O2 | 100fr red lilac | | |

Issued: 15, 45fr, 3/89; 85, 100fr, 1996(?).

See No. 698.

## NIGER COAST PROTECTORATE

'nī-jər 'kōst prə-'tek-t(ə-)rət

### (Oil Rivers Protectorate)

LOCATION — West coast of Africa on Gulf of Guinea

GOVT. — British Protectorate

This territory was originally known as the Oil Rivers Protectorate, and its affairs were conducted by the British Royal Niger Company. The Company surrendered its charter to the Crown in 1899. In 1900 all of the territories formerly controlled by the Royal Niger Company were incorporated into the two protectorates of Northern and Southern Nigeria, the latter absorbing the area formerly known as Niger Coast Protectorate. In 1914 Northern and Southern Nigeria joined to form the Crown Colony of Nigeria. (See Nigeria, Northern Nigeria, Southern Nigeria and Lagos.)

12 Pence = 1 Shilling

Stamps of Great Britain, 1881-87, Overprinted in Black

**1892 Wmk. 30 *Perf. 14***

| | | | | |
|---|---|---|---|---|
| **1** | A54 | ½p vermilion | 22.50 | 13.00 |
| **2** | A40 | 1p lilac | 13.00 | 11.00 |
| *a.* | | "OIL RIVERS" at top | *10,000.* | |
| *b.* | | Half used as ½p on cover | | *2,750.* |
| **3** | A56 | 2p green & car | 40.00 | 9.50 |
| *a.* | | Half used as 1p on cover | | *2,500.* |
| **4** | A57 | 2½p violet, *bl* | 10.00 | 2.75 |
| **5** | A61 | 5p lilac & blue | 20.00 | 7.25 |
| **6** | A65 | 1sh green | 77.50 | *100.00* |
| | | *Nos. 1-6 (6)* | 183.00 | 143.50 |

For surcharges see Nos. 7-36, 50.

**Dangerous forgeries exist of all surcharges.**

No. 2 Surcharged in Red or Violet

**1893**

| | | | | |
|---|---|---|---|---|
| **7** | A40 | ½p on half of 1p (R) | 175. | 160. |
| *c.* | | Unsevered pair | 550. | 500. |
| *d.* | | As "c," surcharge inverted and dividing line reversed | | *27,500.* |
| *e.* | | "½" omitted | | |
| *f.* | | Straight top to "1" in "½" | 390. | *400.* |
| *g.* | | Double surcharge in pair with normal | | *2,100.* |
| **7A** | A40 | ½p on half of 1p (V) | *7,750.* | *5,500.* |
| *b.* | | Surcharge double | *27,500.* | |
| *c.* | | Unsevered pair | *20,000.* | *17,500.* |

Nos. 3-6 Handstamp Srchd. in Violet, Red, Carmine, Bluish Black, Deep Blue, Green or Black

**1893 Wmk. 30 *Perf. 14***

| | | | | |
|---|---|---|---|---|
| **8** | A56 | ½p on 2p (V) | *525.* | 325. |
| *a.* | | Surcharge inverted | *19,000.* | |
| *b.* | | Surcharge diagonal, inverted | *18,500.* | |
| **9** | A57 | ½p on 2½p (V) | 14,000. | |
| **10** | A57 | ½p on 2½p (R) | 425. | 275. |
| *a.* | | Surcharge inverted | *12,500.* | |
| *b.* | | Surcharge diagonal, inverted | *14,500.* | |
| **11** | A57 | ½p on 2½p (C) | *25,000.* | *24,500.* |
| **12** | A57 | ½p on 2½p (B) | *40,000.* | — |
| **13** | A57 | ½p on 2½p (G) | 550. | |

| | | | | |
|---|---|---|---|---|
| **14** | A56 | ½p on 2p (V) | 500. | 375. |
| **15** | A56 | ½p on 2p (Bl) | 2,200. | 825. |
| **16** | A57 | ½p on 2½p (V) | *7,750.* | |
| **17** | A57 | ½p on 2½p (R) | 650. | *775.* |
| **18** | A57 | ½p on 2½p (Bl) | 475. | 450. |
| **19** | A57 | ½p on 2½p (G) | 500. | *550.* |

| | | | | |
|---|---|---|---|---|
| **20** | A56 | ½p on 2p (V) | 550. | 775. |
| *a.* | | Surcharge inverted | *17,500.* | |
| **21** | A57 | ½p on 2½p (R) | 600. | 475. |
| *a.* | | Surcharge inverted | *20,000.* | |
| *b.* | | Surcharge diagonal, inverted | *8,250.* | |
| **22** | A57 | ½p on 2½p (C) | 475. | 500. |
| **23** | A57 | ½p on 2½p (Bl Bk) | *5,500.* | |
| **24** | A57 | ½p on 2½p (Bl) | 475. | *525.* |
| **25** | A57 | ½p on 2½p (G) | 325. | 275. |
| *a.* | | Surcharge diagonal, inverted | | |
| **26** | A57 | ½p on 2½p (Bk) | *4,750.* | |
| *a.* | | Surcharge inverted | *15,500.* | |
| *b.* | | Surcharge diagonal, inverted | *13,500.* | |

| | | | | |
|---|---|---|---|---|
| **27** | A57 | ½p on 2½p (R) | *10,000.* | |
| **28** | A57 | ½p on 2½p (G) | 550. | 500. |

| | | | | |
|---|---|---|---|---|
| **29** | A56 | 1sh on 2p (V) | 500. | 425. |
| *a.* | | Surcharge inverted | *13,500.* | |
| *b.* | | Surcharge diagonal, inverted | *12,500.* | |
| **30** | A56 | 1sh on 2p (R) | 825. | *4,500.* |
| *a.* | | Surcharge inverted | *18,000.* | |
| **31** | A56 | 1sh on 2p (Bk) | *6,500.* | |
| *a.* | | Surcharge inverted | *21,000.* | |

| | | | | |
|---|---|---|---|---|
| **32** | A56 | 5sh on 2d (V) | *10,000.* | *11,500.* |
| *a.* | | Surcharge inverted | *55,000.* | |
| **33** | A61 | 10sh on 5p (R) | *7,250.* | *11,000.* |
| *a.* | | Surcharge inverted | *55,000.* | |
| **34** | A65 | 20sh on 1sh (V) | *165,000.* | |
| *a.* | | Surcharge inverted | *190,000.* | |
| **35** | A65 | 20sh on 1sh (R) | *145,000.* | |
| **36** | A65 | 20sh on 1sh (Bk) | *145,000.* | |

The handstamped 1893 surcharges are known inverted, vertical, etc.

Queen Victoria

A8 A9

A10

A11

A12

A13

**1893 Unwmk. *Perf. 12 to 15***

| | | | | |
|---|---|---|---|---|
| **37** | A8 | ½p vermilion | 9.00 | *11.00* |
| **38** | A9 | 1p light blue | 5.75 | 5.25 |
| *a.* | | Half used as ½p on cover | | *825.00* |
| **39** | A10 | 2p green | 22.00 | 20.00 |
| *a.* | | Half used as 1p on cover | | *1,000.* |
| *b.* | | Horiz. pair, imperf. between | | *17,500.* |
| **40** | A11 | 2½p car lake | 20.00 | 4.50 |
| **41** | A12 | 5p gray lilac | 24.00 | 15.00 |
| *a.* | | 5p lilac | 16.50 | 24.00 |
| **42** | A13 | 1sh black | 15.50 | 16.00 |
| | | *Nos. 37-42 (6)* | 96.25 | 71.75 |

For surcharge see No. 49.

A15

A16

A17

A18

A19

A20

**1894 Engr.**

| | | | | |
|---|---|---|---|---|
| **43** | A15 | ½p yel green | 5.50 | 5.50 |
| **44** | A16 | 1p vermilion | 15.00 | 9.50 |
| *a.* | | 1p orange vermilion | 25.00 | 17.50 |
| *b.* | | Diagonal half, used as ½p on cover | | 875.00 |
| **45** | A17 | 2p car lake | 35.00 | 7.25 |
| *a.* | | Half used as 1p on cover | | — |
| **46** | A18 | 2½p blue | 10.00 | 4.50 |
| **47** | A19 | 5p dp violet | 14.00 | 6.00 |
| **48** | A20 | 1sh black | 70.00 | 8.50 |
| | | *Nos. 43-48 (6)* | 149.50 | 41.25 |

See #55-59, 61. For surcharges see #51-54.

**Halves of Nos. 38, 3 & 44 Srchd. in Red, Blue, Violet or Black**

No. 49

No. 50

Nos. 51-53

**1894**

| | | | | |
|---|---|---|---|---|
| **49** | A9 | ½p on half of 1p (R) | 1,300. | 425. |
| *a.* | | Inverted surcharge | *15,500.* | |

***Perf. 14***

**Wmk. 30**

| | | | | |
|---|---|---|---|---|
| **50** | A56 | 1p on half of 2p (R) | 1,950. | 425. |
| *a.* | | Double surcharge | 7,250. | 1,350. |
| *b.* | | Inverted surcharge | | 2,250. |

***Perf. 12 to 15***

**Unwmk.**

| | | | | |
|---|---|---|---|---|
| **51** | A16 | ½p on half of 1p (Bl) | 3,850. | 550. |
| *a.* | | Double surcharge | | |
| **52** | A16 | ½p on half of 1p (V) | 4,400. | 775. |
| **53** | A16 | ½p on half of 1p (Bk) | *6,000.* | *1,100.* |

This surcharge is found on both vertical and diagonal halves of the 1p.

No. 46 Surcharged in Black

**1894**

| | | | | |
|---|---|---|---|---|
| **54** | A18 | ½p on 2½p blue | 475. | 275. |
| *a.* | | Double surcharge | 8,750. | 2,500. |

The surcharge is found in eight types. The "OIE" variety is broken type.

A27

A28

A29

**1897-98** **Wmk. 2**

55 A15 ½p yel green 3.50 3.00
56 A16 1p vermilion 9.00 1.60
a. 1p orange-vermilion 3.00 1.50
57 A17 2p car lake 4.75 2.50
58 A18 2½p blue 17.50 3.25
a. 2½p slate blue 7.50 3.00
59 A19 5p dp violet 22.50 *90.00*
a. 5p purple 13.00 *95.00*
60 A27 6p yel brn ('98) 8.00 *10.00*
61 A20 1sh black 17.50 *32.50*
62 A28 2sh6p olive bister 24.00 *90.00*
63 A29 10sh dp pur ('98) 140.00 *250.00*
a. 10sh bright purple 135.00 *225.00*
*Nos. 55-63 (9)* 246.75 *482.85*

The stamps of Niger Coast Protectorate were superseded in Jan. 1900, by those of Northern and Southern Nigeria.

## NIGERIA

nī-ˈjir-ē-ə

LOCATION — West coast of Africa, bordering on the Gulf of Guinea
GOVT. — Republic
AREA — 356,669 sq. mi.
POP. — 113,828,587 (1999 est.)
CAPITAL — Abuja

The colony and protectorate were formed in 1914 by the union of Northern and Southern Nigeria. The mandated territory of Cameroons (British) was also attached for administrative purposes. The Federation of Nigeria was formed in 1960. It became a republic in 1963. See Niger Coast Protectorate, Lagos, Northern Nigeria and Southern Nigeria.

12 Pence = 1 Shilling
20 Shillings = 1 Pound
100 Kobo = 1 Naira (1973)

**Catalogue values for unused stamps in this country are for Never Hinged items, beginning with Scott 71 in the regular postage section, Scott B1 in the semi-postal section and Scott J1 in the postage due section.**

**Watermarks**

Wmk. 335 — FN Multiple

Wmk. 379 — NIGERIA in Continuous Wavy Lines

King George V — A1

Numerals of 3p, 4p, 6p, 5sh and £1 of type A1 are in color on plain tablet.

Dies I and II are described at front of this volume.

**Die I**
**Ordinary Paper**
**Wmk. Multiple Crown and CA (3)**

**1914-27** **Typo.** ***Perf. 14***

1 A1 ½p green 5.50 .70
a. Booklet pane of 6
2 A1 1p carmine 5.25 .25
a. Booklet pane of 6
b. 1p scarlet ('16) 16.00 .25
3 A1 2p gray 9.00 2.00
a. 2p slate gray ('18) 10.00 .85
4 A1 2½p ultramarine 10.00 8.00
a. 2½p dull blue ('15) 27.50 11.00

**Chalky Paper**

5 A1 3p violet, *yel* 1.60 3.00
6 A1 4p blk & red, *yel* 1.10 *5.25*
7 A1 6p dull vio & red vio 10.00 11.00
8 A1 1sh black, *green* 1.60 *10.00*
a. 1sh black, *emerald* 1.40 *15.00*
b. 1sh black, *bl grn*, ol back 60.00 *60.00*
c. As "a," olive back ('20) 9.00 *52.50*
9 A1 2sh6p blk & red, *bl* 17.50 7.25
10 A1 5sh grn & red, *yel*, white back 22.00 *62.50*
11 A1 10sh grn & red, *grn* 72.50 *100.00*
a. 10sh grn & red, *emer* 40.00 *125.00*
b. 10sh green & red, *blue grn*, olive back 1,200. *1,850.*
c. As "a," olive back 160.00 250.00
12 A1 £1 vio & blk, *red* 190.00 *260.00*
a. Die II ('27) 275.00 *350.00*
*Nos. 1-12 (12)* 346.05 *469.95*

**Surface-colored Paper**

13 A1 3p violet, *yel* 3.50 *12.00*
14 A1 4p black & red, *yel* 1.60 *11.50*
15 A1 1sh black, *green* 1.60 *25.00*
a. 1sh black, *emerald* *225.00*
16 A1 5sh grn & red, *yel* 21.00 *55.00*
17 A1 10sh grn & red, *grn* 50.00 *180.00*
*Nos. 13-17 (5)* 77.70 *283.50*

**Die II**

**1921-33** **Ordinary Paper** **Wmk. 4**

18 A1 ½p green 6.50 .90
a. Die I 1.25 .60
19 A1 1p carmine 1.75 .55
a. Booklet pane of 6 27.50
b. Die I 3.25 .35
c. Booklet pane of 6, Die I 37.50
20 A1 1½p orange ('31) 9.25 .35
21 A1 2p gray 10.00 .50
a. Die I 1.60 *8.00*
b. Booklet pane of 6, Die I 55.00
22 A1 2p red brown ('27) 5.00 1.00
a. Booklet pane of 6 60.00
23 A1 2p dk brown ('28) 4.50 .25
a. Booklet pane of 6 50.00
b. Die I ('32) 6.00 .75
24 A1 2½p ultra (die I) 1.25 *13.50*
25 A1 3p dp violet 11.00 1.10
a. Die I ('24) 6.00 5.00
26 A1 3p ultra ('31) 10.00 1.10

**Chalky Paper**

27 A1 4p blk & red, *yel* .70 .60
a. Die I ('32) 6.25 7.75
28 A1 6p dull vio & red vio 8.00 *9.00*
a. Die I 14.00 *42.50*
29 A1 1sh black, *emerald* 7.25 2.25
30 A1 2sh6p blk & red, *bl* 7.25 *52.50*
a. Die I ('32) 50.00 *85.00*
31 A1 5sh green & red, *yel* ('26) 16.00 *80.00*
a. Die I ('32) 75.00 *250.00*
32 A1 10sh green & red, *emer* 67.50 *225.00*
a. Die I ('32) 130.00 *500.00*
*Nos. 18-32 (15)* 165.95 388.60

**Silver Jubilee Issue**
Common Design Type

**1935, May 6** **Engr.** ***Perf. 11x12***

34 CD301 1½p black & ultra 1.00 *1.50*
35 CD301 2p indigo & green 2.00 2.00
36 CD301 3p ultra & brown 3.50 *19.00*
37 CD301 1sh brown vio & ind 11.00 *47.50*
*Nos. 34-37 (4)* 17.50 *70.00*
Set, never hinged 24.00

Wharf at Apapa — A2

Picking Cacao Pods — A3

Dredging for Tin — A4

Timber — A5

Fishing Village — A6

Ginning Cotton — A7

Minaret at Habe — A8

Fulani Cattle — A9

Victoria-Buea Road — A10

Oil Palms A11

View of Niger at Jebba A12

Nigerian Canoe A13

**1936, Feb. 1** ***Perf. 11½x13***

38 A2 ½p green 1.50 1.40
39 A3 1p rose car .50 .40
40 A4 1½p brown 2.00 .40
a. Perf. 12½x13½ 85.00 4.50
41 A5 2p black .50 *.80*
42 A6 3p dark blue 2.00 1.50
a. Perf. 12½x13½ 150.00 25.00
43 A7 4p red brown 2.50 2.00
44 A8 6p dull violet .70 .60
45 A9 1sh olive green 2.25 *5.00*

***Perf. 14***

46 A10 2sh6p ultra & blk 8.00 *40.00*
47 A11 5sh ol grn & blk 22.00 *60.00*
48 A12 10sh slate & blk 90.00 *140.00*
49 A13 £1 orange & blk 130.00 *200.00*
*Nos. 38-49 (12)* 261.95 *452.10*
Set, never hinged 400.00

Common Design Types pictured following the introduction.

**Coronation Issue**
Common Design Type

**1937, May 12** ***Perf. 11x11½***

50 CD302 1p dark carmine .50 *2.00*
51 CD302 1½p dark brown 1.25 *2.50*
52 CD302 3p deep ultra 1.50 *4.00*
*Nos. 50-52 (3)* 3.25 8.50
Set, never hinged 6.50

George VI — A14

Victoria-Buea Road — A15

Niger at Jebba A16

**1938-51** **Wmk. 4** ***Perf. 12***

53 A14 ½p deep green .25 .25
a. Perf. 11½ ('50) 1.40 *1.75*
54 A14 1p dk carmine .40 .30
55 A14 1½p red brown .25 .25
a. Perf. 11½ ('50) .25 .25
56 A14 2p black .25 *3.00*
57 A14 2½p orange ('41) .25 *3.00*
58 A14 3p deep blue .25 .25
59 A14 4p orange 32.50 4.00
60 A14 6p brown violet .30 .25
a. Perf. 11½ ('51) 1.40 .60
61 A14 1sh olive green .40 .25
a. Perf. 11½ ('50) .90 .25
62 A14 1sh3p turq blue ('40) .60 .70
a. Perf. 11½ ('50) 2.10 .70
63 A15 2sh6p ultra & blk ('51) 1.50 4.50
a. Perf. 13½ ('42) 2.25 *7.00*
b. Perf. 14 ('42) 2.00 *3.50*
c. Perf. 13x11½ 37.50 24.00
64 A16 5sh org & blk, perf. 13½ ('42) 4.50 *4.50*
a. Perf. 12 ('49) 5.50 4.00
b. Perf. 14 ('48) 6.75 3.00
c. Perf. 13x11½ 67.50 21.00

**1944, Dec. 1** ***Perf. 12***

65 A14 1p red violet .25 .30
a. Perf. 11½ ('50) .60 .60
66 A14 2p deep red .25 *3.00*
a. Perf. 11½ ('50) .35 *.70*
67 A14 3p black .25 *3.50*
68 A14 4p dark blue .25 *4.00*
*Nos. 53-68 (16)* 42.45 *32.05*
Set, never hinged 75.00

Issue date: Nos. 65a, 66a, Feb. 15.

**Catalogue values for unused stamps in this section, from this point to the end of the section, are for Never Hinged items.**

**Peace Issue**
Common Design Type

**1946, Oct. 21** **Engr.** ***Perf. 13½x14***

71 CD303 1½p brown .35 .25
72 CD303 4p deep blue .35 *2.50*

**Silver Wedding Issue**
Common Design Types

**1948, Dec. 20** **Photo.** ***Perf. 14x14½***

73 CD304 1p brt red violet .35 .30

***Perf. 11½x11***

**Engraved; Name Typographed**

74 CD305 5sh brown orange 17.50 *22.50*

**UPU Issue**
Common Design Types

**Engr.; Name Typo. on 3p, 6p**
***Perf. 13½, 11x11½***

**1949, Oct. 10** **Wmk. 4**

75 CD306 1p red violet .25 .25
76 CD307 3p indigo .35 *3.50*
77 CD308 6p rose violet .80 *3.50*
78 CD309 1sh olive 1.40 *2.00*
*Nos. 75-78 (4)* 2.80 *9.25*

### Coronation Issue
Common Design Type

**1953, June 2 Engr. *Perf. 13½x13***

| | | | | |
|---|---|---|---|---|
| 79 | CD312 1½p brt grn & blk | | .45 | .25 |

Manilla (Bracelet) Currency A17

Olokun Head, Ife — A18

Designs: 1p, Bornu horsemen. 1½p, Peanuts, Kano City. 2p, Mining tin. 3p, Jebba Bridge over Niger River. 4p, Cocoa industry. 1sh, Logging. 2sh6p, Victoria harbor. 5sh, Loading palm oil. 10sh, Goats and Fulani cattle. £1, Lagos waterfront, 19th and 20th centuries.

**1953, Sept. 1 *Perf. 14***

**Size: 35½x22½mm**

| | | | | |
|---|---|---|---|---|
| 80 | A17 | ½p red org & blk | .25 | .25 |
| 81 | A17 | 1p ol gray & blk | .25 | .25 |
| 82 | A17 | 1½p blue green | .50 | .25 |
| 83 | A17 | 2p bister & blk | 4.00 | .30 |
| 84 | A17 | 3p purple & blk | .50 | .30 |
| 85 | A17 | 4p ultra & black | 2.50 | .25 |
| 86 | A18 | 6p blk & org brn | .30 | .25 |
| 87 | A17 | 1sh brn vio & blk | .50 | .25 |

**Size: 40½x24½mm**

| | | | | |
|---|---|---|---|---|
| 88 | A17 | 2sh6p green & black | 16.00 | 1.25 |
| 89 | A17 | 5sh ver & black | 5.50 | 1.40 |
| 90 | A17 | 10sh red brn & blk | 24.00 | 3.25 |

**Size: 42x31½mm**

| | | | | |
|---|---|---|---|---|
| 91 | A17 | £1 violet & black | 32.50 | 16.00 |
| | | *Nos. 80-91 (12)* | 86.80 | 24.00 |

Booklet panes of 4 of Nos. 80, 81, 84, 87 were issued in 1957. They are identical to margin blocks of 4 from sheets.

See No. 93.

No. 83 Overprinted in Black

**1956, Jan. 28 Wmk. 4 *Perf. 13½***

| | | | | |
|---|---|---|---|---|
| 92 | A17 2p bister & black | | .40 | .30 |

Visit of Queen Elizabeth II to Nigeria, Jan.-Feb., 1956.

### Mining Tin Type of 1953

Two types:
I — Broken row of dots between "G" and miner's head.
II — Complete row of dots.

**1956-57**

| | | | |
|---|---|---|---|
| 93 | A17 2p bluish gray (shades) (I) | 3.00 | 2.00 |
| *b.* | 2p gray (shades) (II) | 4.75 | .40 |

Booklet pane of 4 of No. 93 was issued in 1957. See note after No. 91.

Ambas Bay, Victoria Harbor A19

**Wmk. 314**

**1958, Dec. 1 Engr. *Perf. 13½***

| | | | |
|---|---|---|---|
| 94 | A19 3p purple & black | .40 | .30 |

Cent. of the founding of Victoria, Southern Cameroons.

**1959, Mar. 14**

3p, Lugard Hall, Kaduna. 1sh, Kano Mosque.

| | | | | |
|---|---|---|---|---|
| 95 | A19 | 3p purple & black | .30 | .25 |
| 96 | A19 | 1sh green & black | .75 | .50 |

Attainment of self-government by the Northern Region, Mar. 15, 1959.

### Federation of Nigeria

Federal Legislature A20

3p, Man Paddling Canoe. 6p, Federal Supreme Court. 1sh3p, Map of Africa, dove and torch.

**Wmk. 335**

**1960, Oct. 1 Photo. *Perf. 13½***

**Size: 35x22mm**

| | | | | |
|---|---|---|---|---|
| 97 | A20 | 1p carmine & black | .25 | .25 |
| 98 | A20 | 3p blue & black | .25 | .25 |
| 99 | A20 | 6p dk red brn & emer | .25 | .25 |

**Size: 39½x23½mm**

| | | | | |
|---|---|---|---|---|
| 100 | A20 | 1sh3p ultra & yellow | .25 | .25 |
| | | *Nos. 97-100 (4)* | 1.00 | 1.00 |

Nigeria's independence, Oct. 1, 1960.

Peanuts — A21

Central Bank, Lagos A22

Designs: 1p, Coal miner. 1½p, Adult education. 2p, Potter. 3p, Oyo carver. 4p, Weaver. 6p, Benin mask. 1sh, Yellow-casqued hornbill. 1sh3p, Camel train and map. 5sh, Nigeria museum and sculpture. 10sh, Kano airport. £1, Lagos terminal.

***Perf. 14½x14***

**1961, Jan. 1 Wmk. 335**

| | | | | |
|---|---|---|---|---|
| 101 | A21 | ½p emerald | .30 | *.60* |
| 102 | A21 | 1p purple | .80 | .30 |
| *a.* | | Booklet pane of 6 | 5.00 | |
| 103 | A21 | 1½p rose red | .80 | *2.25* |
| 104 | A21 | 2p ultra | .30 | .30 |
| 105 | A21 | 3p dk grn | .40 | .30 |
| *a.* | | Booklet pane of 6 | 2.50 | |
| 106 | A21 | 4p blue | .30 | *2.00* |
| 107 | A21 | 6p blk & yel | .80 | .30 |
| *a.* | | Booklet pane of 6 | 5.00 | |
| *b.* | | Yellow omitted | *2,750.* | *1,300.* |
| 108 | A21 | 1sh yel grn | 4.00 | .30 |
| 109 | A21 | 1sh3p orange | 1.50 | .30 |
| *a.* | | Booklet pane of 6 | 9.00 | |
| 110 | A22 | 2sh6p yellow & blk | 2.75 | .30 |
| 111 | A22 | 5sh emer & blk | 1.25 | 1.25 |
| 112 | A22 | 10sh dp ultra & blk | 3.75 | 3.75 |
| 113 | A22 | £1 dp car & blk | 13.00 | *14.00* |
| | | *Nos. 101-113 (13)* | 29.95 | 25.95 |

For overprint see No. 198.

Globe and Train A23

**1961, July 25 Wmk. 335**

| | | | | |
|---|---|---|---|---|
| 114 | A23 | 1p shown | .25 | .25 |
| 115 | A23 | 3p Truck | .25 | .25 |
| 116 | A23 | 1sh3p Plane | .35 | .35 |
| 117 | A23 | 2sh6p Ship | .80 | .80 |
| | | *Nos. 114-117 (4)* | 1.65 | 1.65 |

Nigeria's admission to the UPU.

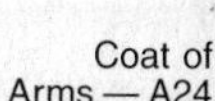

Coat of Arms — A24

Map and Natural Resources — A25

Designs: 6p, Eagle carrying banner. 1sh3p, Flying eagles forming flag. 2sh6p, Young couple looking at flag and government building.

***Perf. 14½x14, 14x14½***

**1961, Oct. 1 Photo. Wmk. 335**

| | | | | |
|---|---|---|---|---|
| 118 | A24 | 3p multicolored | .25 | .25 |
| 119 | A25 | 4p org, yel grn & dk red | .25 | .25 |
| 120 | A25 | 6p emerald | .25 | .25 |
| 121 | A25 | 1sh3p ultra, emer & gray | .25 | .25 |
| 122 | A25 | 2sh6p blue, emer & sep | .50 | .50 |
| | | *Nos. 118-122 (5)* | 1.50 | 1.50 |

First anniversary of independence.

Map of Africa and Staff of Aesculapius — A26

Map of Africa and: 3p, Lyre, book and scroll. 6p, Cogwheel. 1sh, Radio beacon. 1sh3p, Hands holding globe.

**1962, Jan. 25 *Perf. 14x14½***

| | | | | |
|---|---|---|---|---|
| 123 | A26 | 1p bister | .25 | .25 |
| 124 | A26 | 3p deep magenta | .25 | .25 |
| 125 | A26 | 6p blue green | .25 | .25 |
| 126 | A26 | 1sh chestnut | .25 | .25 |
| 127 | A26 | 1sh3p bright blue | .25 | .25 |
| | | *Nos. 123-127 (5)* | 1.25 | 1.25 |

Issued to honor the conference of heads of state of African and Malagasy Governments.

Malaria Eradication Emblem and Larvae — A27

Emblem and: 6p, Man with spray gun. 1sh3p, Plane spraying insecticide. 2sh6p, Microscope, retort and patient.

**1962, Apr. 7 *Perf. 14½***

| | | | | |
|---|---|---|---|---|
| 128 | A27 | 3p emer, brn & ver | .25 | .25 |
| 129 | A27 | 6p lil rose & dk blue | .25 | .25 |
| 130 | A27 | 1sh3p dk blue & lil rose | .25 | .25 |
| 131 | A27 | 2sh6p yel brown & blue | .30 | .80 |
| | | *Nos. 128-131 (4)* | 1.05 | 1.55 |

WHO drive to eradicate malaria.

National Monument, Lagos A28

Ife Bronze Head and Flag — A29

***Perf. 14½x14, 14x14½***

**1962, Oct. 1 Wmk. 335 Photo.**

| | | | | |
|---|---|---|---|---|
| 132 | A28 | 3p lt ultra & emer | .25 | .25 |
| *a.* | | Emerald omitted | 800.00 | 475.00 |
| 133 | A29 | 5sh vio, emer & org red | 1.25 | 1.25 |

Second anniversary of independence.

Fair Emblem — A30

Designs (horizontal): 6p, "Wheels of Industry." 1sh, Cornucopia, goods and trucks. 2sh6p, Oil derricks and tanker.

**1962, Oct. 27 Wmk. 335**

| | | | | |
|---|---|---|---|---|
| 134 | A30 | 1p brown olive & org | .25 | .25 |
| 135 | A30 | 6p crimson & blk | .25 | .25 |
| 136 | A30 | 1sh dp orange & blk | .25 | .25 |
| 137 | A30 | 2sh6p dk ultra, yel & blk | .30 | .25 |
| | | *Nos. 134-137 (4)* | 1.05 | 1.00 |

Lagos Intl. Trade Fair, Oct. 27-Nov. 8.

Globe and Arrows — A31

4p, Natl. Hall & Commonwealth emblem, horiz. 1sh3p, Palm tree, emblem & doves.

**1962, Nov. 5**

| | | | | |
|---|---|---|---|---|
| 138 | A31 | 2½p sky blue | .25 | *1.00* |
| 139 | A31 | 4p dp rose & slate bl | .25 | .25 |
| 140 | A31 | 1sh3p gray & yellow | .25 | .25 |
| | | *Nos. 138-140 (3)* | .75 | 1.50 |

8th Commonwealth Parliamentary Conf., Lagos.

Herdsman with Cattle — A32

Design: 6p, Tractor and corn, horiz.

**1963, Mar. 21 Photo. *Perf. 14½***

| | | | | |
|---|---|---|---|---|
| 141 | A32 | 3p olive green | 1.10 | .25 |
| 142 | A32 | 6p brt lilac rose | 1.40 | .25 |

FAO "Freedom from Hunger" campaign.

US Mercury Capsule over Kano Tracking Station — A33

Design: 1sh3p, Syncom II satellite and US tracking ship "Kingsport," Lagos harbor.

**1963, June 21** *Perf. 14½*

**143** A33 6p dk blue & yel grn .25 .25
**144** A33 1sh3p black & dp green .30 .30

Peaceful uses of outer space.
Printed in sheets of 12 (4x3) with ornamental borders and inscriptions.

Nigerian and Greek Scouts Shaking Hands and Jamboree Emblem — A34

1sh, Scouts dancing around campfire.

**1963, Aug. 1** **Photo.** *Perf. 14*

**145** A34 3p gray olive & red .30 .25
**146** A34 1sh red & black .60 .60
*a.* Souvenir sheet of 2, #145-146 1.60 1.60

11th Boy Scout Jamboree, Marathon, Greece, Aug. 1963.

**Republic**

First Aid — A35

Designs: 6p, Blood donors and ambulances. 1sh3p, Helping the needy.

**1963, Sept. 1** **Wmk. 335** *Perf. 14½*

**147** A35 3p dk blue & red .35 .25
**148** A35 6p dk green & red .55 .30
**149** A35 1sh3p black & red 1.50 1.00
*a.* Souvenir sheet of 4, #149 12.00 12.00
*Nos. 147-149 (3)* 2.40 1.55

Cent. of the Intl. Red Cross.

Pres. Nnamdi Azikiwe and State House — A36

Designs: 1sh3p, President and Federal Supreme Court. 2sh6p, President and Parliament Building.

**1963, Oct. 1** **Unwmk.** *Perf. 14x13*

**150** A36 3p dull grn & yel grn .25 .25
**151** A36 1sh3p brown & bister .25 .25
*a.* Bister (head) omitted
**152** A36 2sh6p vio bl & brt grnsh bl .25 .25
*Nos. 150-152 (3)* .75 .75

Independence Day, Oct. 1, 1963.

"Freedom of Worship" — A37

3p, Charter & broken whip, horiz. 1sh3p, "Freedom from Want." 2sh6p, "Freedom of Speech."

**1963, Dec. 10** **Wmk. 335** *Perf. 13*

**153** A37 3p vermilion .25 .25
**154** A37 6p green .25 .25
**155** A37 1sh3p deep ultra .25 .25
**156** A37 2sh6p red lilac .30 .30
*Nos. 153-156 (4)* 1.05 1.05

15th anniv. of the Universal Declaration of Human Rights.

Queen Nefertari — A38

**1964, Mar. 8** **Photo.** *Perf. 14*

**157** A38 6p shown 1.00 .35
**158** A38 2sh6p Ramses II 2.00 2.25

UNESCO world campaign to save historic monuments in Nubia.

John F. Kennedy, US and Nigerian Flags A39

1sh3p, Kennedy bust & laurel. 5sh, Kennedy coin (US), flags of US & Nigeria at half-mast.

**1964, Aug. 20** **Unwmk.** *Perf. 13x14*

**159** A39 1sh3p black & lt vio .25 .25
**160** A39 2sh6p multicolored .65 .75
**161** A39 5sh multicolored 1.40 1.75
*a.* Souvenir sheet of 4 7.50 7.50
*Nos. 159-161 (3)* 2.30 2.75

Pres. John F. Kennedy (1917-63). No. 161a contains 4 imperf. stamps similar to No. 161 with simulated perforations.

Pres. Nnamdi Azikiwe — A40

Herbert Macaulay — A41

Design: 2sh6p, King Jaja of Opobo.

*Perf. 14x13, 14*

**1964, Oct. 1** **Photo.** **Unwmk.**

**162** A40 3p red brown .25 .25
**163** A41 1sh3p green .25 .25
**164** A41 2sh6p slate green .60 .60
*Nos. 162-164 (3)* 1.10 1.10

First anniversary of the Republic.

Boxing Gloves and Torch A42

Hurdling — A43

6p, High jump. 1sh3p, Woman runner, vert.

**1964, Oct.** *Perf. 14½*

**165** A42 3p olive grn & sepia .25 .25
**166** A42 6p dk blue & emer .35 .35
**167** A42 1sh3p olive & brown .55 .55

*Perf. 14*

**168** A43 2sh6p orange red & brn 1.50 1.50
*a.* Souvenir sheet of 4 4.25 4.25
*Nos. 165-168 (4)* 2.65 2.65

18th Olympic Games, Tokyo, Oct. 10-25.
No. 168a contains 4 imperf. stamps similar to No. 168 with simulated perforations.

Mountain Climbing Scouts — A44

3p, Golden Jubilee emblem. 6p, Nigeria's Scout emblem & merit badges. 1sh3p, Lord Baden-Powell & Nigerian Boy Scout.

**1965, Jan.** **Photo.** *Perf. 14½*

**169** A44 1p brown .25 .25
**170** A44 3p emer, blk & red .25 .25
**171** A44 6p yel grn, red & blk .25 .25
**172** A44 1sh3p sep, yel & dk grn .35 .75
*a.* Souvenir sheet of 4 7.25 7.25
*Nos. 169-172 (4)* 1.10 1.50

Founding of the Nigerian Boy Scouts, 50th anniv.
No. 172a contains four imperf. stamps similar to No. 172 with simulated perforation.

IQSY Emblem and Telstar, Map of Africa — A45

1sh3p, Explorer XII over map of Africa.

**1965, Apr. 1** **Unwmk.** *Perf. 14x13*

**173** A45 6p grnsh bl & vio .25 .25
**174** A45 1sh3p lilac & green .30 .30

Intl. Quiet Sun Year, 1964-65. Printed in sheets of 12 (4x3) with ornamental borders and inscriptions.

ITU Emblem, Drummer, Man at Desk and Telephone A46

Cent. of the ITU: 1sh3p, ITU emblem and telecommunication tower, vert. 5sh, ITU emblem, Syncom satellite and map of Africa showing Nigeria.

*Perf. 11x11½, 11½x11*

**1965, Aug. 2** **Photo.** **Unwmk.**

**175** A46 3p ocher, red & blk .30 .25
**176** A46 1sh3p ultra, grn & blk 1.50 1.50
**177** A46 5sh multicolored 6.00 6.00
*Nos. 175-177 (3)* 7.80 7.75

ICY Emblem, Diesel Locomotive and Camel Caravan A47

ICY Emblem and: 1sh, Students and hospital, Lagos. 2sh6p, Kainji Dam, Niger River.

*Perf. 14x15*

**1965, Sept. 1** **Wmk. 335**

**178** A47 3p orange, grn & car 3.50 .35
**179** A47 1sh ultra, blk & yel 3.00 .50
**180** A47 2sh6p ultra, yel & grn 10.00 7.50
*Nos. 178-180 (3)* 16.50 8.35

Intl. Cooperation Year and 20th anniv. of the UN.

Stone Images, Ikom — A48

Designs: 3p, Carved frieze, horiz. 5sh, Seated man, Taba bronze.

*Perf. 14x15, 15x14*

**1965, Oct. 1** **Photo.** **Unwmk.**

**181** A48 3p ocher, blk & red .25 .25
**182** A48 1sh3p lt ultra, grn & reddish brn .25 .25
**183** A48 5sh emer, dk brn & reddish brn .60 1.25
*Nos. 181-183 (3)* 1.10 1.75

Second anniversary of the Republic.

Elephants A49

Designs: ½p, Lioness and cubs, vert. 1½p, Splendid sunbird. 2p, Weaverbirds. 3p, Cheetah. 4p, Leopard and cubs. 6p, Saddle-billed storks, vert. 9p, Gray parrots. 1sh, Kingfishers. 1sh3p, Crowned cranes. 2sh6p, Buffon's kobs (antelopes). 5sh, Giraffes. 10sh, Hippopotami, vert. £1, Buffalos.

**"MAURICE FIEVET" below Design**

*Perf. 12x12½, 12½x12, 14x13½ (1p, 2p, 3p, 4p, 9p)*

**1965-66** **Photo.**

**Size: 23x38mm, 38x23mm**

**184** A49 ½p multicolored 1.00 *2.50*
**185** A49 1p red & multi .50 .25
**186** A49 1½p lt blue & multi 8.00 *9.50*
**187** A49 2p brt red & multi 3.75 .25
*a.* White "2d" ('70) 4.50 2.50
**188** A49 3p brt grn, yel & dl brn 1.25 .30
**189** A49 4p lilac & multi .30 .25
*a.* Perf 12½x12 .60 *3.00*
*b.* "4" 5mm wide ('71) 60.00 8.00
**190** A49 6p violet & multi 2.10 .40
**191** A49 9p blue & orange 3.00 .60

*Perf. 12½*

**Size: 45x26mm, 26x45mm**

**192** A49 1sh gray & multi 5.00 .60
*a.* Red omitted
**193** A49 1sh3p brt bl & multi 9.00 2.00
**194** A49 2sh6p dk brn, yel & ocher 1.00 *2.00*
**195** A49 5sh brn, yel & red brown 2.25 3.50
**196** A49 10sh grnsh bl & multi 7.00 3.25
**197** A49 £1 brt grn & multi 18.50 9.00
*Nos. 184-197 (14)* 62.65 34.40

The designer's name, Maurice Fievet, appears at right or left, in small or large capitals. Nos. 187a and 189b have "MAURICE FIEVET" at right, 5mm wide. No. 187a has "2d" in white instead of yellow. No. 189b has "REPUBLIC" and "4d" larger, bolder.
Issued: ½p, 1p, 11/1/65; 2p, 4/1/66; 1½p, #189a, 6p, 1sh, 1sh3p, 2sh6p, 5sh, 10sh, 1£, 5/2/66; 3p, 9p, 10/17/66; 4p, 1966.
Nine values were overprinted "F. G. N./ F. G. N." (Federal Government of Nigeria) in 1968. They were not issued, but some were sold by accident in 1968. Later the Nigerian Philatelic Service sold examples, stating they were not postally valid. However, some were used by government agencies in 1969.
See Nos. 258-267.

**No. 110 Overprinted in Red: "COMMONWEALTH / P.M. MEETING / 11. Jan. 1966"**

*Perf. 14½x14*

**1966, Jan. 11** **Photo.** **Wmk. 335**

**198** A22 2sh6p yellow & black .35 .35

Conf. of British Commonwealth Prime Ministers, Lagos.

YWCA Building, Lagos
A50

**Unwmk.**

**1966, Sept. 1 Litho. *Perf. 14***

**199** A50 4p yel, green & multi .25 .25
**200** A50 9p brt green & multi .25 .50

60th anniv. of the Nigerian YWCA.

Lineman and Telephone
A51

Designs: 4p, Flag and letter carrying pigeon, vert. 2sh6p, Niger Bridge.

***Perf. 14½x14, 14x14½***

**1966, Oct. 1 Photo. Wmk. 335**

**201** A51 4p green .25 .25
**202** A51 1sh6p lilac, blk & sep .30 .50
**203** A51 2sh6p multicolored .70 1.75
*Nos. 201-203 (3)* 1.25 2.50

Third anniversary of the Republic.

Book, Chemical Apparatus, Carved Head and UNESCO Emblem
A52

**1966, Nov. 4 *Perf. 14½x14***

**204** A52 4p dl org, mar & blk .50 .25
**205** A52 1sh6p bl grn, plum & blk 1.75 2.50
**206** A52 2sh6p pink, plum & blk 3.50 6.00
*Nos. 204-206 (3)* 5.75 8.75

20th anniv. of UNESCO.

Surveyors and Hydrological Decade Emblem — A53

Design: 2sh6p, Water depth gauge on dam and Hydrological Decade emblem, vert.

***Perf. 14½x14, 14x14½***

**1967, Feb. 1 Photo. Wmk. 335**

**207** A53 4p multicolored .25 .25
**208** A53 2sh6p multicolored .50 1.25

Hydrological Decade (UNESCO), 1965-74.

Weather Satellite Orbiting Earth
A54

1sh6p, Storm over land & sea & World Meteorological Organization emblem.

**1967, Mar. 23 Photo. *Perf. 14½x14***

**209** A54 4p dp ultra & brt rose .25 .25
**210** A54 1sh6p ultra & yellow .65 .90

World Meteorological Day, March 23.

Eyo Masqueraders — A55

1sh6p, Acrobat. 2sh6p, Stilt dancer, vert.

***Perf. 11x11½, 11½x11***

**1967, Oct. 1 Photo. Unwmk.**

**211** A55 4p multicolored .25 .25
**212** A55 1sh6p turq bl & multi .50 1.25
**213** A55 2sh6p pale grn & multi .75 2.50
*Nos. 211-213 (3)* 1.50 4.00

4th anniversary of the Federal Republic.

Vaccination of Cattle
A56

**1967, Dec. 1 *Perf. 14½x14***

**214** A56 4p maroon & multi .25 .25
**215** A56 1sh6p ultra & multi .70 *1.25*

Campaign to eradicate cattle plague.

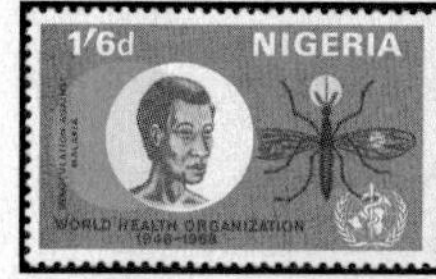


Anopheles Mosquito and Sick Man — A57

20th anniv. of the WHO: 4p, WHO emblem and vaccination.

**1968, Apr. 7 Litho. *Perf. 14***

**216** A57 4p dp lil rose & blk .25 .25
**217** A57 1sh6p org yel & blk .55 .80

Shackled Hands, Map of Nigeria and Human Rights Flame
A58

Design: 1sh6p, Flag of Nigeria and human rights flame, vert.

**1968, July 1 Photo. *Perf. 14***

**218** A58 4p dp blue, yel & blk .25 .25
**219** A58 1sh6p green, blk & red .45 .80

International Human Rights Year.

Hand and Doves — A59

**1968, Oct. 1 Unwmk. *Perf. 14***

**220** A59 4p brt blue & multi .25 .25
**221** A59 1sh6p black & multi .25 .25

5th anniversary of the Federal Republic.

Olympic Rings, Nigerian Flag and Athletes
A60

4p, Map of Nigeria and Olympic rings.

**1968, Oct. 14 Photo. *Perf. 14***

**222** A60 4p red, blk & emer .25 .25
**223** A60 1sh6p multicolored .50 .35

19th Olympic Games, Mexico City, 10/12-27.

G.P.O., Lagos
A61

**1969, Apr. 11 Unwmk. *Perf. 14***

**224** A61 4p emerald & black .25 .25
**225** A61 1sh6p dk blue & black .25 .40

Opening of the Nigerian Philatelic Service of the GPO, Lagos.

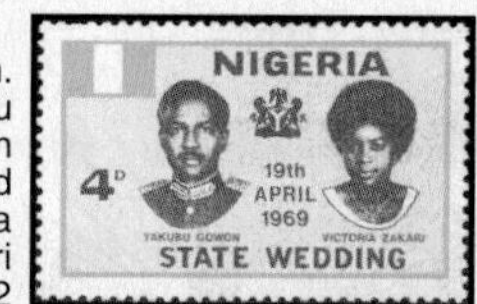


Gen. Yakubu Gowon and Victoria Zakari
A62

***Perf. 13x13½***

**1969, Sept. 20 Litho. Unwmk.**

**226** A62 4p emerald & choc .30 .25
**227** A62 1sh6p emerald & black .70 .45

Wedding of Yakubu Gowon, head of state of Nigeria, and Miss Victoria Zakari, Apr. 19, 1969.

Development Bank Emblem and "5" — A63

Design: 1sh6p, Emblem and rays.

**1969, Oct. 18 Litho. *Perf. 14***

**228** A63 4p dk bl, blk & org .25 .25
**229** A63 1sh6p dk pur, yel & blk .35 *1.00*

African Development Bank, 5th anniv.

ILO Emblem
A64

50th anniv. of the ILO: 1sh6p, ILO emblem and world map.

**1969, Nov. 15 Photo.**

**230** A64 4p purple & black .25 .25
**231** A64 1sh6p green & black .65 *1.25*

Tourist Year Emblem and Musicians — A65

Designs: 4p, Olumo Rock and Tourist Year emblem, horiz. 1sh6p, Assob Falls.

**1969, Dec. 30 Photo. *Perf. 14***

**232** A65 4p blue & multi .25 .25
**233** A65 1sh emerald & black .30 .30
**234** A65 1sh6p multicolored 1.25 .85
*Nos. 232-234 (3)* 1.80 1.40

International Year of African Tourism.

12-Spoke Wheel and Arms of Nigeria — A66

Designs: 4p, Map of Nigeria and tree with 12 fruits representing 12 tribes. 1sh6p, People bound by common destiny and map of Nigeria. 2sh, Torch with 12 flames and map of Africa, horiz.

***Perf. 11½x11, 11x11½***

**1970, May 28 Photo. Unwmk.**

**235** A66 4p gold, blue & blk .25 .25
**236** A66 1sh gold & multi .25 .25
**237** A66 1sh6p green & black .25 .25
**238** A66 2sh bl, org, gold & black .25 .25
*Nos. 235-238 (4)* 1.00 1.00

Establishment of a 12-state administrative structure in Nigeria.

Opening of New UPU Headquarters, Bern — A67

**1970, June 29 Unwmk. *Perf. 14***

**239** A67 4p purple & yellow .30 .25
**240** A67 1sh6p blue & vio blue .45 .35

UN Emblem and Charter — A68

25th anniv. of the UN: 1sh6p, UN emblem and headquarters, New York.

**1970, Sept. 1 Photo. *Perf. 14***

**241** A68 4p brn org, buff & blk .25 .25
**242** A68 1sh6p dk bl, gold & bis brn .25 .25

Student — A69

Designs: 2p, Oil drilling platform. 6p, Durbar horsemen. 9p, Soldier and sailors raising flag. 1sh, Soccer player. 1sh6p, Parliament Building. 2sh, Kainji Dam. 2sh6p, Export products: Timber, rubber, peanuts, cocoa and palm produce.

**1970, Sept. 30 Litho. *Perf. 14x13½***

**243** A69 2p blue & multi .25 .25
**244** A69 4p blue & multi .25 .25
**245** A69 6p blue & multi .30 .25
**246** A69 9p blue & multi .45 .25
**247** A69 1sh blue & multi .45 .25
**248** A69 1sh6p blue & multi .45 .40
**249** A69 2sh blue & multi .80 .90
**250** A69 2sh6p blue & multi .80 1.00
*Nos. 243-250 (8)* 3.75 3.55

Ten years of independence.

Black and White Men Uprooting Racism — A70

Designs: 4p, Black and white school children and globe, horiz. 1sh6p, World map with black and white stripes. 2sh, Black and white men, shoulder to shoulder, horiz.

***Perf. 13½x14, 14x13½***

**1971, Mar. 22 Photo. Unwmk.**

**251** A70 4p multicolored .25 .25
**252** A70 1sh yellow & multi .25 .25
**253** A70 1sh6p blue, yel & blk .25 .65
**254** A70 2sh multicolored .25 1.25
*Nos. 251-254 (4)* 1.00 2.40

Intl. year against racial discrimination.

Ibibio Mask, c. 1900 — A71

Nigerian Antiquities: 1sh3p, Bronze mask of a King of Benin, c. 1700. 1sh9p, Bronze figure of a King of Ife.

**1971, Sept. 30 *Perf. 13½x14***

**255** A71 4p lt blue & black .25 .25
**256** A71 1sh3p yellow bis & blk .25 .35
**257** A71 1sh9p apple grn, dp grn & blk .25 1.00
*Nos. 255-257 (3)* .75 1.60

**Type of 1965-66 Redrawn**

Imprint: "N.S.P. & M. Co. Ltd."
Added to "MAURICE FIEVET"

***Perf. 13x13½; 14x13½ (6p)***

**1969-72 Photo.**

**Size: 38x23mm**

**258** A49 1p red & multi 3.00 2.25
**259** A49 2p brt red & multi 4.00 1.50
**260** A49 3p multi ('71) .75 *2.00*
**261** A49 4p lilac & multi 8.50 .25
**262** A49 6p brt vio & multi ('71) 2.25 .25
**263** A49 9p dl bl & dp org ('70) 7.00 .50

**Size: 45x26mm**

**264** A49 1sh multi ('71) 3.00 .25
**265** A49 1sh3p multi ('71) 11.00 3.50
**266** A49 2sh6p multi ('72) 15.00 7.00
**267** A49 5sh multi ('72) 3.50 *17.50*
*Nos. 258-267 (10)* 58.00 35.00

"Maurice Fievet" imprint on No. 259 exists in two lengths, 5mm and 5½mm.

"Maurice Fievet" imprint on No. 260 exists in two lengths, 5½mm and 8½mm.

UNICEF Emblem and Children — A72

UNICEF 25th anniv.: 1sh3p, Mother and child. 1sh9p, African mother carrying child on back.

**1971, Dec. 11 *Perf. 14***

**270** A72 4p purple & yellow .25 .25
**271** A72 1sh3p org, pur & plum .25 *.45*
**272** A72 1sh9p blue & dk blue .25 *.90*
*Nos. 270-272 (3)* .75 1.60

Satellite Earth Station — A73

Various views of satellite communications earth station, Lanlate, Nigeria. All horiz.

**1971, Dec. 30 Photo. *Perf. 14***

**273** A73 4p multicolored .25 .25
**274** A73 1sh3p blue, blk & grn .25 .65
**275** A73 1sh9p orange & blk .30 .95
**276** A73 3sh brt pink & blk .55 1.75
*Nos. 273-276 (4)* 1.35 3.60

Satellite communications earth station, Lanlate, Nigeria.

Fair Emblem — A74

Fair Emblem and: 1sh3p, Map of Africa, horiz. 1sh9p, Globe with map of Africa.

***Perf. 13½x13, 13x13½***

**1972, Feb. 23 Litho.**

**277** A74 4p multicolored .25 .25
**278** A74 1sh3p dull pur, yel & gold .25 *.40*
**279** A74 1sh9p orange, yel & blk .25 *1.25*
*Nos. 277-279 (3)* .75 1.90

First All-Africa Trade Fair, Nairobi, Kenya, Feb. 23-Mar. 5.

Traffic A75

Designs: 1sh3p, Traffic flow at circle. 1sh9p, Car and truck on road. 3sh, Intersection with lights and pedestrians.

**1972, June 23 Photo. *Perf. 13x13½***

**280** A75 4p orange & blk .50 .25
**281** A75 1sh3p lt blue & multi 1.50 1.00
**282** A75 1sh9p emerald & multi 1.75 1.25
**283** A75 3sh yellow & multi 3.00 *3.50*
*Nos. 280-283 (4)* 6.75 6.00

Introduction of right-hand driving in Nigeria, Apr. 2, 1972.

Nok Style Terra-cotta Head, Katsina Ala — A76

1sh3p, Roped bronze vessel, Igbo Ukwu. 1sh9p, Bone harpoon, Daima, horiz.

***Perf. 13½x13, 13x13½***

**1972, Sept. 1 Litho.**

**284** A76 4p dk blue & multi .25 .25
**285** A76 1sh3p gold & multi .45 *.60*
**286** A76 1sh9p dp blue & multi .55 *1.60*
*Nos. 284-286 (3)* 1.25 2.45

All-Nigeria Festival of the Arts, Kaduna, Dec. 9.

Games Emblem and Soccer A77

Designs: 5k, Running. 18k, Table tennis. 25k, Stadium, vert.

**1973, Jan. 8 Litho. *Perf. 13x13½***

**287** A77 5k lilac, blue & blk .25 .25
**288** A77 12k multicolored .35 .55
**289** A77 18k yellow & multi .60 *1.10*
**290** A77 25k brown & multi 1.00 *1.50*
*Nos. 287-290 (4)* 2.20 3.40

2nd All-Africa Games, Lagos, Jan. 7-18.

Hides and Skins A78

Designs: 2k, Natural gas tanks. 3k, Cement works. 5k, Cattle ranching. 7k, Lumbermill. 8k, Oil refinery. 10k, Leopards, Yankari Game Reserve. 12k, New civic building. 15k, Sugar cane harvesting. 18k, Palm oil production, vert. 20k, Vaccine production. 25k, Modern docks. 30k, Argungu Fishing Festival, vert. 35k, Textile industry. 50k, Pottery, vert. 1n, Eko Bridge. 2n, Teaching Hospital, Lagos.

**Imprint at left: "N S P & M Co Ltd"**

6mm on Litho. Stamps, 5¼ mm on Photo. Stamps

**Litho.; Photo. (50k)**

**1973-74 Unwmk. *Perf. 14***

**291** A78 1k multi, buff imprint *.25* *.25*
**292** A78 2k multi ('74) *3.00* *.90*
**293** A78 3k multi ('74) *.25* *.25*
**294** A78 5k grn & multi ('74) *3.75* *.90*
**295** A78 7k multicolored *.35* *1.25*
**296** A78 8k multicolored *.40* *.25*
**297** A78 10k multicolored *5.00* *.25*
**298** A78 12k multicolored *.50* *2.00*
**299** A78 15k multicolored *.35* *.60*
**300** A78 18k multicolored *.55* *.30*
**301** A78 20k multicolored *.65* *.30*
**302** A78 25k multicolored *.85* *.45*
**303** A78 30k multicolored *.50* *1.50*
**304** A78 35k multicolored *6.00* *4.00*
**305** A78 50k black background *2.00* *2.50*
**306** A78 1n multicolored *1.00* *.90*
**307** A78 2n multicolored *1.00* *2.25*
*Nos. 291-307 (17)* *26.40* *18.85*

Imprint on 35k has periods.

**Imprint at left: "N S P & M Co Ltd"**

**1973 Photo., Imprint 5¼mm**

*291a* A78 1k multi, dk grn foliage *1.00* *.75*
*291b* A78 1k multi, brt grn foliage *.25* *.25*
*292a* A78 2k multicolored *.35* *.25*
*294a* A78 5k multi, emer fields *.60* *.75*
*294b* A78 5k multi, yel grn fields *.50* *.25*
*297a* A78 10k multicolored *.75* *.80*
*298a* A78 12k multicolored *12.00* *10.00*
*300a* A78 18k multicolored *12.00* *2.00*
*301a* A78 20k multicolored *13.00* *3.00*
*303a* A78 30k multicolored *12.00* *7.50*
*305a* A78 50k dk brn background *.75* *.90*
*306a* A78 1n multicolored *2.00* *4.00*
*Nos. 291a-306a (12)* *55.20* *30.45*

Nos. 300a, 305a and 306a have periods in the imprint. The liquid in the flasks is gray on No. 301, black on No. 301a, and blue on No. 301b.

**1975-80 Wmk. 379**

*291c* A78 1k multi, dk grn foliage *1.50* *2.00*
*292b* A78 2k multi ('75) *1.75* *.25*
*293a* A78 3k multi ('75) *.25* *.25*
*294c* A78 5k emerald fields ('76) *2.25* *.25*
*295a* A78 7k multi ('80) *3.50* *3.50*
*296a* A78 8k multi ('76) *1.75* *2.00*
*297b* A78 10k multi ('76) *2.00* *.25*
*299a* A78 15k multicolored *3.00*
*300b* A78 18k multi ('78) *4.25* *4.00*
*301b* A78 20k multi, pale pink table, door, windows ('79) *3.25* *3.50*
*302a* A78 25k multi, pur barges *3.25* *.25*
*302b* A78 25k multi, brn barges *3.25* *.25*
*305b* A78 50k dk brn background, grn imprint *3.50* *3.75*
*307a* A78 2n multicolored *5.50* *6.50*

OAU Headquarters — A79

Designs: 18k, OAU flag, vert. 30k, Stairs leading to OAU emblem, vert.

**1973, May 25 Litho. *Perf. 14***

**308** A79 5k blue & multi .25 .25
**309** A79 18k olive grn & multi .35 *.50*
**310** A79 30k lilac & multi .55 *.80*
*Nos. 308-310 (3)* 1.15 1.55

Org. for African Unity, 10th anniv.

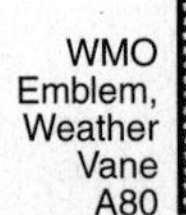
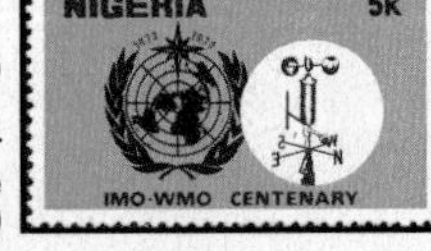


WMO Emblem, Weather Vane A80

**1973, Sept. 4 Litho. *Perf. 13***

**311** A80 5k multicolored .30 .25
**312** A80 30k multicolored 1.50 *2.25*

Cent. of intl. meteorological cooperation.

View of Ibadan University A81

Designs: 12k, Campus, crest and graph showing growth, vert. 18k, Campus, students and crest. 30k, Teaching hospital.

**1973, Nov. 17 *Perf. 14***

**313** A81 5k lt blue & multi .25 .25
**314** A81 12k lilac & multi .25 .30
**315** A81 18k orange & multi .45 .40
**316** A81 30k blue, org & blk .65 *.80*
*Nos. 313-316 (4)* 1.60 1.75

University of Ibadan, 25th anniversary.

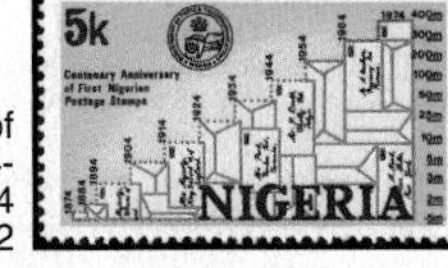


Growth of Mail, 1874-1974 A82

12k, Nigerian Post emblem & Northern Nigeria #18A. 18k, Postal emblem & Lagos #1. 30k, Map of Nigeria &means of transportation.

**1974, June 10 Litho. *Perf. 14***

**317** A82 5k green, black & org .25 .25
**318** A82 12k green & multi .60 .60
**319** A82 18k green, lilac & blk 1.00 1.00
**320** A82 30k black & multi 1.75 1.75
*Nos. 317-320 (4)* 3.60 3.60

Centenary of first Nigerian postage stamps.

Globe and UPU Emblem A83

UPU cent.: 18k, World map and means of transportation. 30k, Letters.

**1974, Oct. 9**

**321** A83 5k blue & multi .25 .25
**322** A83 18k orange & multi 2.50 .60
**323** A83 30k brown & multi 2.00 1.75
*Nos. 321-323 (3)* 4.75 2.60

Hungry and Well-fed Children — A84

Designs: 12k, Chicken farm, horiz. 30k, Irrigation project.

**1974, Nov. 25 Litho. *Perf. 14***

**324** A84 5k orange, blk & grn .25 .25
**325** A84 12k multicolored .35 .50
**326** A84 30k multicolored .80 *1.50*
*Nos. 324-326 (3)* 1.40 2.25

Freedom from Hunger.

A85

Map of Nigeria with Telex Network, Teleprinter — A86

**1975, July 3 Litho. *Perf. 14***

| | | | | |
|---|---|---|---|---|
| **327** | A85 | 5k multicolored | .25 | .25 |
| **328** | A85 | 12k multicolored | .25 | .25 |
| **329** | A86 | 18k multicolored | .30 | .30 |
| **330** | A86 | 30k multicolored | .55 | .55 |
| | | *Nos. 327-330 (4)* | 1.35 | 1.35 |

Inauguration of Nigeria Telex Network.

Queen Amina of Zaria (1536-1566) — A87

**1975, Aug. 18 Litho. *Perf. 14***

| | | | | |
|---|---|---|---|---|
| **331** | A87 | 5k multicolored | .25 | .25 |
| **332** | A87 | 18k multicolored | 1.10 | .90 |
| **333** | A87 | 30k multicolored | 1.40 | *1.75* |
| | | *Nos. 331-333 (3)* | 2.75 | 2.90 |

International Women's Year.

Alexander Graham Bell — A88

Designs: 18k, Hands beating gong, modern telephone operator, horiz. 25k, Telephones, 1876, 1976.

**1976, Mar. 10 Wmk. 379**

| | | | | |
|---|---|---|---|---|
| **334** | A88 | 5k pink, black & ocher | .25 | .25 |
| **335** | A88 | 18k deep lilac & multi | .45 | .55 |
| **336** | A88 | 25k lt bl, vio bl & blk | .90 | 1.10 |
| | | *Nos. 334-336 (3)* | 1.60 | 1.90 |

Centenary of first telephone call by Alexander Graham Bell, Mar. 10, 1876.

Children Going to School — A89

Designs: 5k, Child learning to write, horiz. 25k, Classroom.

**1976, Sept. 20 Litho. *Perf. 14***

| | | | | |
|---|---|---|---|---|
| **337** | A89 | 5k multicolored | .25 | .25 |
| **338** | A89 | 18k multicolored | .55 | .75 |
| **339** | A89 | 25k multicolored | .70 | 1.00 |
| | | *Nos. 337-339 (3)* | 1.50 | 2.00 |

Launching of universal primary education in 1976.

Traditional Musical Instruments A90

5k, Carved mask (festival emblem). 10k, Natl. Arts Theater, Lagos. 12k, Nigerian & African women's hair styles. 30k, Nigerian carvings.

**1976-77 Wmk. 379**

| | | | | |
|---|---|---|---|---|
| **340** | A90 | 5k black, gold & grn | .25 | .25 |
| **341** | A90 | 10k multicolored | .40 | .40 |
| **342** | A90 | 12k multicolored | .75 | .75 |
| **343** | A90 | 18k brown, ocher & blk | .90 | .90 |
| **344** | A90 | 30k multicolored | 1.10 | 1.25 |
| | | *Nos. 340-344 (5)* | 3.40 | 3.55 |

2nd World Black and African Festival of Arts and Culture, Lagos, Jan. 15-Feb. 12, 1977. Issued: 5k, 18k, 11/1; others 1/15/77.

Gen. Muhammed Broadcasting and Map of Nigeria — A91

Designs: 18k, Gen. Muhammed as Commander in Chief, vert. 30k, in battle dress, vert.

**1977, Feb. 13 Litho. *Perf. 14***

| | | | | |
|---|---|---|---|---|
| **345** | A91 | 5k multicolored | .25 | .25 |
| **346** | A91 | 18k multicolored | .45 | .45 |
| **347** | A91 | 30k multicolored | .80 | .80 |
| | | *Nos. 345-347 (3)* | 1.50 | 1.50 |

Gen. Murtala Ramat Muhammed, Head of State and Commander in Chief, 1st death anniversary.

Scouts Clearing Street A92

5k, Senior and Junior Boy Scouts saluting, vert. 25k, Scouts working on farm. 30k, African Scout Jamboree emblem, map of Africa.

**1977, Apr. 1 Wmk. 379**

| | | | | |
|---|---|---|---|---|
| **348** | A92 | 5k multicolored | .30 | .30 |
| **349** | A92 | 18k multicolored | .70 | .70 |
| **350** | A92 | 25k multicolored | .90 | 1.10 |
| **351** | A92 | 30k multicolored | 1.25 | 1.75 |
| | | *Nos. 348-351 (4)* | 3.15 | 3.85 |

First All-Africa Boy Scout Jamboree, Sherehills, Jos, Nigeria, Apr. 2-8, 1977.

Trade Fair Emblem A93

Emblem and: 5k, View of Fair grounds. 30k, Weaver and potter.

**1977, Nov. 27 Litho. *Perf. 13***

| | | | | |
|---|---|---|---|---|
| **352** | A93 | 5k multicolored | .25 | .25 |
| **353** | A93 | 18k multicolored | .35 | .35 |
| **354** | A93 | 30k multicolored | .65 | .65 |
| | | *Nos. 352-354 (3)* | 1.25 | 1.25 |

1st Lagos Intl. Trade Fair, Nov. 27-Dec. 11.

Nigeria's 13 Universities A94

12k, Map of West African highways and telecommunications network. 18k, Training of technicians, and cogwheel. 30k, World map and map of Argentina with Buenos Aires.

**1978, Apr. 28 Wmk. 379**

| | | | | |
|---|---|---|---|---|
| **355** | A94 | 5k multicolored | .25 | .25 |
| **356** | A94 | 12k multicolored | .25 | .25 |
| **357** | A94 | 18k multicolored | .30 | .30 |
| **358** | A94 | 30k multicolored | .65 | .65 |
| | | *Nos. 355-358 (4)* | 1.45 | 1.45 |

Global Conf. on Technical Cooperation among Developing Countries, Buenos Aires.

Antenna and ITU Emblem A95

**1978, May 17 Litho. *Perf. 14***

| | | | | |
|---|---|---|---|---|
| **359** | A95 | 30k multicolored | .75 | .75 |

10th World Telecommunications Day.

Students on Cassava Plantation A96

"Operation Feed the Nation": 18k, Woman working in backyard vegetable garden. 30k, Plantain harvest, vert.

**1978, July 7 Litho. *Perf. 14***

| | | | | |
|---|---|---|---|---|
| **360** | A96 | 5k multicolored | .25 | .25 |
| **361** | A96 | 18k multicolored | .30 | .30 |
| **362** | A96 | 30k multicolored | .50 | .50 |
| | | *Nos. 360-362 (3)* | 1.05 | 1.05 |

Mother Holding Sick Child A97

Designs: 12k, Sick boy at health station. 18k, Vaccination of children. 30k, Syringe and WHO emblem, vert.

**1978, Aug. 31 Wmk. 379**

| | | | | |
|---|---|---|---|---|
| **363** | A97 | 5k multicolored | .25 | .25 |
| **364** | A97 | 12k multicolored | .30 | .30 |
| **365** | A97 | 18k multicolored | .45 | .45 |
| **366** | A97 | 30k multicolored | .75 | .75 |
| | | *Nos. 363-366 (4)* | 1.75 | 1.75 |

Global eradication of smallpox.

Bronze Horseman from Benin — A98

Nigerian antiquities: 5k, Nok terracotta figure from Bwari. 12k, Bronze snail and animal from Igbo-Ukwu. 18k, Bronze statue of a king of Ife.

**1978, Oct. 27 Litho. *Perf. 14***

| | | | | |
|---|---|---|---|---|
| **367** | A98 | 5k multicolored | .25 | .25 |
| **368** | A98 | 12k multicolored, horiz. | .25 | .25 |
| **369** | A98 | 18k multicolored | .30 | .30 |
| **370** | A98 | 30k multicolored | .50 | .50 |
| | | *Nos. 367-370 (4)* | 1.30 | 1.30 |

Anti-Apartheid Emblem — A99

**1978, Dec. 10 *Perf. 14***

| | | | | |
|---|---|---|---|---|
| **371** | A99 | 18k red, yellow & black | .35 | .35 |

Anti-Apartheid Year.

Wright Brothers, Flyer A A100

18k, Nigerian Air Force fighters in formation.

**1978, Dec. 28**

| | | | | |
|---|---|---|---|---|
| **372** | A100 | 5k multicolored | .30 | .30 |
| **373** | A100 | 18k multicolored | .60 | .60 |

75th anniversary of powered flight.

Murtala Muhammed Airport A101

**1979, Mar. 15 Litho. *Perf. 14***

| | | | | |
|---|---|---|---|---|
| **374** | A101 | 5k bright blue & black | .50 | .30 |

Inauguration of Murtala Muhammed Airport.

Young Stamp Collector A102

**1979, Apr. 11**

| | | | | |
|---|---|---|---|---|
| **375** | A102 | 5k multicolored | .35 | .25 |

Philatelic Week; Natl. Philatelic Service, 10th anniv.

Mother Nursing Child, IYC Emblem A103

18k, Children at study. 25k, Children at play, vert.

**1979, June 28 Wmk. 379 *Perf. 14***

| | | | | |
|---|---|---|---|---|
| **376** | A103 | 5k multicolored | .25 | .25 |
| **377** | A103 | 18k multicolored | .30 | .30 |
| **378** | A103 | 25k multicolored | .35 | .35 |
| | | *Nos. 376-378 (3)* | .90 | .90 |

International Year of the Child.

A104

Design: 10k, Preparation of audio-visual material. 30k, Adult education class.

**1979, July 25 Photo. & Engr.**

| | | | | |
|---|---|---|---|---|
| **379** | A104 | 10k multicolored | .25 | .25 |
| **380** | A104 | 30k multicolored | .40 | .40 |

Intl. Bureau of Education, Geneva, 50th anniv.

Necom House, Lagos — A105

**1979, Sept. 20 Litho. *Perf. 13½x14***

| | | | | |
|---|---|---|---|---|
| **381** | A105 | 10k multicolored | .30 | .30 |

Intl. Radio Consultative Committee (CCIR) of the ITU, 50th anniv.

Trainees and Survey Equipment A106

**1979, Dec. 12 Photo. *Perf. 14***

**382** A106 10k multicolored .30 .30

Economic Commission for Africa, 21st anniv.

Soccer Cup and Ball on Map of Nigeria A107

**1980, Mar. 8**

**383** A107 10k shown .25 .25
**384** A107 30k Player, vert. .60 .60

12th African Cup of Nations Soccer Championship, Lagos and Ibadan, Mar.

Swimming, Moscow '80 Emblem A108

10k, Wrestling, vert. 20k, Long jump, vert. 45k, Women's basketball, vert.

**Litho. & Engr.**

**1980, July 19 *Perf. 14***

**385** A108 10k multi .25 .25
**386** A108 20k multi .25 .25
**387** A108 30k shown .30 .30
**388** A108 45k multi .35 .35
*Nos. 385-388 (4)* 1.15 1.15

22nd Summer Olympic Games, Moscow, July 19-Aug. 3.

Men Holding OPEC Emblem A109

45k, Anniversary emblem, vert.

**1980, Sept. 15 Litho. & Engr.**

**389** A109 10k shown .25 .25
**390** A109 45k multi .75 .75

OPEC, 20th anniversary.

First Steam Locomotive in Nigeria A110

20k, Unloading freight car. 30k, Freight train.

**1980, Oct. 2 Wmk. 379 *Perf. 14***

**391** A110 10k shown .50 .50
**392** A110 20k multi 1.40 1.40
**393** A110 30k multi 2.10 2.10
*Nos. 391-393 (3)* 4.00 4.00

Nigerian Railway Corp., 75th anniv.

Technician Performing Quality Control Test A111

**1980, Oct. 14**

**394** A111 10k Scale, ruler, vert. .25 .25
**395** A111 30k shown .45 .45

World Standards Day.

Map of West Africa showing ECOWAS Members, Modes of Communication — A112

25k, Transportation. 30k, Map, cow, cocoa. 45k, Map, industrial symbols.

**1980, Nov. 5 Litho. & Engr.**

**396** A112 10k shown .25 .25
**396A** A112 25k multi .30 .30
**397** A112 30k multi .40 .40
**398** A112 45k multi .55 .55
*Nos. 396-398 (4)* 1.50 1.50

Woman with Cane Sweeping — A113

30k, Amputee photographer.

**Wmk. 379**

**1981, June 25 Litho. *Perf. 14***

**399** A113 10k shown .25 .25
**400** A113 30k multi .50 .50

Intl. Year of the Disabled.

World Food Day A114

10k, Pres. Shenu Shagari. 25k, Produce, vert. 30k, Tomato crop, vert. 45k, Pig farm.

**1981, Oct. 16 Litho. & Engr.**

**401** A114 10k multi .25 .25
**402** A114 25k multi .30 .30
**403** A114 30k multi .40 .40
**404** A114 45k multi .55 .55
*Nos. 401-404 (4)* 1.50 1.50

Anti-apartheid Year — A115

30k, Soweto riot. 45k, Police hitting man, vert.

**1981, Dec. 10 Litho.**

**405** A115 30k multi .40 .55
**406** A115 45k multi .60 1.00

Scouting Year A116

30k, Animal first aid. 45k, Baden-Powell, scouts.

**1982, Feb. 22 Litho. *Perf. 14***

**407** A116 30k multi .60 .65
**408** A116 45k multi 1.10 1.25

TB Bacillus Centenary A117

10k, Inoculation. 30k, Research. 45k, Patient being x-rayed, vert.

**1982, Mar. 24 Litho. *Perf. 14***

**409** A117 10k multi .30 .30
**410** A117 30k multi .50 .60
**411** A117 45k multi .80 1.40
*Nos. 409-411 (3)* 1.60 2.30

10th Anniv. of UN Conference on Human Environment — A118

10k, Keep your environment clean. 20k, Check air pollution. 30k, Preserve natural environment. 45k, Reafforestation concerns all.

**1982, June 10 Litho.**

**412** A118 10k multicolored .25 .25
**413** A118 20k multicolored .25 .35
**414** A118 30k multicolored .35 .50
**415** A118 45k multicolored .60 .80
*Nos. 412-415 (4)* 1.45 1.90

Salamis Parnassus A119

20k, Papilio zalmoxis. 30k, Pachylophus beckeri. 45k, Papilio hesperus.

**1982, Sept. 15 Litho.**

**416** A119 10k shown .35 .25
**417** A119 20k multi .65 .55
**418** A119 30k multi 1.00 1.00
**419** A119 45k multi 1.50 1.40
*Nos. 416-419 (4)* 3.50 3.20

25th Anniv. of Natl. Museum A120

10k, Statuettes, vert. 20k, Bronze leopard. 30k, Soapstone seated figure, vert. 45k, Wooden helmet mask.

**1982, Nov. 18 Wmk. 379**

**420** A120 10k multi .25 .25
**421** A120 20k multi .35 .35
**422** A120 30k multi .40 .40
**423** A120 45k multi .60 .60
*Nos. 420-423 (4)* 1.60 1.60

Family Day — A121

10k, Extended family, house, horiz. 30k, Family.

**1983, Mar. 8 Litho. *Perf. 14***

**424** A121 10k multicolored .25 .25
**425** A121 30k multicolored .50 .50

Commonwealth Day — A122

10k, Satellite view, horiz. 25k, Natl. Assembly buildings, horiz. 30k, Oil exploration. 45k, Runners.

**1983, Mar. 14**

**426** A122 10k multicolored .25 .25
**427** A122 25k multicolored .35 .35
**428** A122 30k multicolored .45 .45
**429** A122 45k multicolored .55 .55
*Nos. 426-429 (4)* 1.60 1.60

10th Anniv. of Natl. Youth Service Corps A123

**1983, May 25 Litho. *Perf. 14***

**430** A123 10k Construction .25 .25
**431** A123 25k Climbing wall, vert. .45 .45
**432** A123 30k Marching, vert. .65 .65
*Nos. 430-432 (3)* 1.35 1.35

World Communications Year — A124

10k, Mailman, vert. 25k, Newspaper stand. 30k, Traditional horn messenger. 45k, TV news broadcast.

**Wmk. 379**

**1983, July 22 Litho. *Perf. 14***

**433** A124 10k multicolored .25 .25
**434** A124 25k multicolored .35 .35
**435** A124 30k multicolored .55 .55
**436** A124 45k multicolored .45 .45
*Nos. 433-436 (4)* 1.60 1.60

World Fishery A125

**1983, Sept. 22 Litho. Wmk. 379**

**437** A125 10k Pink shrimp .30 .30
**438** A125 25k Long neck croaker .45 .45
**439** A125 30k Barracuda .55 .55
**440** A125 45k Fishing technique .65 .65
*Nos. 437-440 (4)* 1.95 1.95

Boys' Brigade, 75th Anniv. A126

10k, Boys, emblem, vert. 30k, Food production. 45k, Skill training.

**1983, Oct. 14 *Perf. 14***

**441** A126 10k multicolored .30 .30
**442** A126 30k multicolored 1.50 1.50
**443** A126 45k multicolored 2.25 2.25
*Nos. 441-443 (3)* 4.05 4.05

Fight Against Polio Campaign A127

**1984, Feb. 29 Litho. *Perf. 14***

**444** A127 10k Crippled boy, vert. .25 .25
**445** A127 25k Vaccination .60 .60
**446** A127 30k Healthy child, vert. .80 .80
*Nos. 444-446 (3)* 1.65 1.65

Hartebeests — A128

10k, Waterbuck, vert. 30k, Buffalo. 45k, African golden monkey, vert.

Federal Environmental Protection Agency, 10th Anniv. — A209

5n, Water resources. 10n, Natural resources. 20n, Endangered species. 30n, One earth, one family.

**1999, June 8** **Litho.** ***Perf. 13***

| | | | | |
|---|---|---|---|---|
| **697** | A209 | 5n multicolored | .50 | .50 |
| **698** | A209 | 10n multicolored | .75 | .75 |
| **699** | A209 | 20n multicolored | 1.75 | 1.75 |
| **700** | A209 | 30n multicolored | 2.50 | 2.50 |
| | | *Nos. 697-700 (4)* | 5.50 | 5.50 |

NICON Insurance Corp., 30th Anniv. A210

Emblem and: 5n, Airplane, ship, oil refinery, vert. 30n, Building.

***Perf. 12¾x13, 13x12¾***

**1999, Aug. 31** **Litho.**

| | | | | |
|---|---|---|---|---|
| **701** | A210 | 5n multi | .40 | .40 |
| **702** | A210 | 30n multi | 2.00 | 2.00 |

Millennium A211

Designs: 10n, Map of Northern and Southern Protectorates, 1900-14. 20n, Map of Nigeria, 1914. 30n, Coat of arms. 40n, Map of 36 states, 1996.

**2000** **Litho.** ***Perf. 13***

**703-706** A211 Set of 4 2.10 2.10

World Meteorological Organization, 50th Anniv. — A212

Designs: 10n, Sunshine hour recorder, vert. 30n, Meteorological station.

**2000** ***Perf. 12¾x13, 13x12¾***

**707-708** A212 Set of 2 1.00 1.00

Return to Democracy A213

Designs: 10n, Flag, "Freedom of the press," vert. 20n, Scales of justice. 30n, Legislative mace, vert. 40n, Pres. Olusegun Obasanjo, flag, vert.

**2000** ***Perf. 14¾***

| | | | | |
|---|---|---|---|---|
| **709-712** | A213 | Set of 4 | 3.25 | 3.25 |
| *712a* | | Souvenir sheet, #709-712 | 5.00 | 5.00 |

2000 Summer Olympics, Sydney A214

Designs: 10n, Boxing. 20n, Weight lifting. 30n, Soccer. 40n, Soccer, diff.

**2000, Sept. 7** **Litho.** ***Perf. 13x12¾***

| | | | | |
|---|---|---|---|---|
| **713-716** | A214 | Set of 4 | 3.25 | 3.25 |
| *716a* | | Souvenir sheet, #713-716 + 4 labels | 5.00 | 5.00 |

A215

Independence, 40th anniv.: 10n, Obafemi Awolowo (1909-87), promoter of federal constitution. 20n, Prime Minister Abubakar Tafawa Balewa (1912-66). 30n, Pres. Nnamdi Azikiwe (1904-96). 40n, Liquified gas refinery, horiz. 50n, Ship carrying exports, horiz.

***Perf. 12¾x13, 13x12¾***

**2000, Sept. 27** **Litho.**

**717-721** A215 Set of 5 3.75 3.75

A216

Fruit: 20n, Hug plum. 30n, White star apple. 40n, African breadfruit. 50n, Akee apple.

**2001, Jan. 16** ***Perf. 14***

**722-725** A216 Set of 4 3.00 3.00

Nigeria Daily Times Newspaper, 75th Anniv. A217

Designs: 20n, Corporate headquarters, Lagos. 30n, First issue. 40n, Daily Times complex, Lagos. 50n, Masthead.

**2001, June 1** **Litho.** ***Perf. 13x12¾***

**726-729** A217 Set of 4 3.25 3.25

Fauna A218

Designs: 10n, Broad-tailed paradise whydahs, vert. 15n, Fire-bellied woodpeckers, vert. 20n, Grant's zebras. 25n, Aardvark. 30n, Preuss's guenon, vert. 40n, Giant ground pangolin. 50n, Bonobo. 100n, Red-eared guenon, vert.

**2001, June 15** ***Perf. 14***

| | | | | |
|---|---|---|---|---|
| **730** | A218 | 10n multi | .40 | .25 |
| **731** | A218 | 15n multi | .50 | .25 |
| **732** | A218 | 20n multi | .60 | .35 |
| *a.* | | Thinner inscriptions, perf. 13x13¼ ('05) | .30 | .30 |
| **733** | A218 | 25n multi | .70 | .45 |
| **734** | A218 | 30n multi | .80 | .60 |
| **735** | A218 | 40n multi | .90 | .80 |
| **736** | A218 | 50n multi | 1.00 | .90 |
| *a.* | | Thinner inscriptions, perf. 13x13¼ ('05) | .80 | .80 |
| **737** | A218 | 100n multi | 2.50 | 2.00 |
| *a.* | | Perf. 13¼x13 | — | — |
| | | *Nos. 730-737 (8)* | 7.40 | 5.60 |

Inscriptions vary widely in size and style. Issued: Nos. 732a, 736a, 737a, 2005.

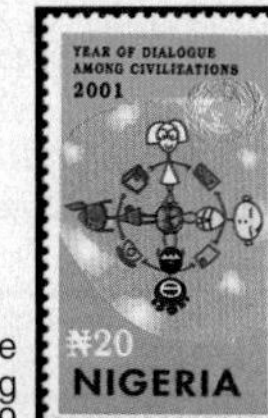

Year of Dialogue Among Civilizations — A219

**2001, Oct. 9** **Litho.** ***Perf. 13***

**738** A219 20n multi .90 .90

New Millennium A220

Designs: 20n, Peace. 30n, Age of globalization. 40n, Reconciliation. 50n, Love.

**2002, Feb. 13** **Litho.** ***Perf. 13x12¾***

**739-742** A220 Set of 4 3.00 3.00

Crops A221

Designs: 20n, Kola nuts. 30n, Oil palm. 40n, Cassava. 50n, Corn, vert.

**2002, May 10** ***Perf. 13x12¾, 12¾x13***

**743-746** A221 Set of 4 2.60 2.60

2002 World Cup Soccer Championships, Japan and Korea — A222

Emblem and: 20n, Nigerian player and opponent, vert. 30n, Globe and soccer balls, vert. 40n, Player's legs and ball. 50n, World Cup trophy, vert.

***Perf. 12¾x13, 13x12¾***

**2002, June 14**

**747-750** A222 Set of 4 2.75 2.75

World AIDS Day — A223

Designs: 20n, Nurse, patient, flowers. 50n, AIDS counseling.

**2003, May 3** **Litho.** ***Perf. 13x12¾***

| | | | | |
|---|---|---|---|---|
| **751-752** | A223 | Set of 2 | 1.70 | 1.70 |
| *752a* | | Souvenir sheet, #751-752 | 3.50 | 3.50 |

A224

Universal basic education: 20n, Students. 50n, Student writing, horiz.

***Perf. 12¾x13, 13x12¾***

**2003, Sept. 22** **Litho.**

**753-754** A224 Set of 2 2.00 2.00

A225

Eighth All Africa Games: 20n, Runner. 30n, High jump, horiz. 40n, Taekwondo, horiz. 50n, Long jump

**2003, Oct. 4**

| | | | | |
|---|---|---|---|---|
| **755-758** | A225 | Set of 4 | 2.50 | 2.50 |
| *758a* | | Souvenir sheet, #755-758 + 4 labels | 3.00 | 3.00 |

Worldwide Fund for Nature (WWF) A226

Side-striped jackal: 20n, Adult and pups. 40n, Adult in grass. 80n, Two adults. 100n, Adult in grass, diff.

**2003, Dec. 12** ***Perf. 13x12¾***

| | | | | |
|---|---|---|---|---|
| **759-762** | A226 | Set of 4 | 4.25 | 3.75 |
| *762a* | | Block of 4, #759-762 | 4.75 | 4.75 |

Commonwealth Heads of Government Meeting, Abuja — A227

Emblem and: 20n, Map of Nigeria. 50n, Flag of Nigeria, vert.

***Perf. 13x12¾, 12¾x13***

**2003, Dec. 7** **Litho.**

**763-764** A227 Set of 2 2.00 2.00

2004 Summer Olympics, Athens — A228

Designs: 50n, Runners. 120n, Basketball.

**2004, Aug. 18** **Litho.** ***Perf. 12¾x13***

| | | | | |
|---|---|---|---|---|
| **765-766** | A228 | Set of 2 | 3.00 | 3.00 |
| *766a* | | Souvenir sheet of 2, #765-766, + 4 labels | — | — |

No. 766a sold for 150n.

A229

A232

A230

Winning Children's Stamp Art Contest Designs — A231

*Perf. 12¾x13, 13x12¾*

**2004, Oct. 29** **Litho.**

| | | | |
|---|---|---|---|
| **767** A229 50n multi | .75 | .75 |
| **768** A230 90n multi | 1.40 | 1.40 |
| **769** A231 120n multi | 1.90 | 1.90 |
| **770** A232 150n multi | 2.25 | 2.25 |
| *a.* Souvenir sheet, #767-770, + 12 labels | 6.50 | 6.50 |
| *Nos. 767-770 (4)* | 6.30 | 6.30 |

Rotary International, Cent. — A233

Designs: 50n, "100" with Rotary emblems for zeroes. 120n, Rotary emblem and world map.

**2005, Aug. 9** **Litho.** ***Perf. 13x12¾***

| | | |
|---|---|---|
| **771-772** Set of 2 | 3.50 | 3.50 |
| *772a* A233 Horiz. pair, #771-772 | 3.50 | 3.50 |

Nigerian Postage Stamps, 131st Anniv. A234

Designs: 50n, Text in simulated stamp. 90n, Map of Nigeria, simulated stamp. 120n, Map of Nigeria, years "1874" and "2005." 150n, Nigeria #118, 746, vert.

**2005, Oct. 9** ***Perf. 13x12¾, 12¾x13***

| | | |
|---|---|---|
| **773-776** A234 Set of 4 | 6.50 | 6.50 |

World Summit on the Information Society, Tunis A235

Summit emblems, globe and: 20n, Nigeria Post emblem. 50n, Postman on motorcycle, vert. 120n, Like 20n.

*Perf. 13x12¾, 12¾x13*

**2005, Nov. 4** **Litho.**

| | | |
|---|---|---|
| **777-779** A235 Set of 3 | 3.50 | 3.50 |

Writers A236

Designs: 20n, Prof. Chinua Achebe. 40n, Dr. Abubakar Imam (1911-81). 50n, Prof. Wole Soyinka.

**2006, Jan. 18** ***Perf. 13x12¾***

| | | |
|---|---|---|
| **780-782** A236 Set of 3 | 1.75 | 1.75 |

Scholars — A237

Designs: No. 783, 50n, No. 786, 100n, Prof. Ayodele Awojobi (1937-84), engineer. No. 784, 50n, No. 787, 120n, Prof. Gabriel Oyibo, mathematician. No. 785, 50n, No. 788, 150n, Philip Emeagwali, computer scientist.

**2006, Jan. 18** ***Perf. 12¾x13***

| | | |
|---|---|---|
| **783-788** A237 Set of 6 | 8.25 | 8.25 |

Dated 2005.

52nd Commonwealth Parliamentary Conference, Abuja — A238

Designs: No. 789, International Conference Center. No. 790, National Assembly Building. No. 791: a, 20n, Like No. 789 with smaller-sized denomination in green and white. b, 50n, Like No. 790 with denomination in green.

**2006, Sept. 4** **Litho.** ***Perf. 13x12¾***

| | | |
|---|---|---|
| **789** A238 20n multi | — | — |
| **790** A238 50n multi | — | — |

**Souvenir Sheet**

***Imperf***

| | | |
|---|---|---|
| **791** A238 Sheet of 2, #a-b | — | — |

Queen Elizabeth II, 80th Birthday A239

Designs: 20n, Queen at public ceremony, in pink hat. 50n, Queen in pink hat, vert.

**2006, Oct. 9** **Litho.** ***Perf. 13***

| | | |
|---|---|---|
| **792-793** A239 Set of 2 | 1.40 | 1.40 |

Agbani Darego, 2001 Miss World — A240

Darego and: 20n, Map of Nigeria. 50n, Map of world, horiz.

**2006, Nov. 9**

| | | |
|---|---|---|
| **794-795** A240 Set of 2 | 1.10 | 1.10 |

Abuja, 30th Anniv. A241

Designs: 20n, Gate, fireworks, palm trees, map of Nigeria. 50n, Emblem, hands beating drum, vert.

**2006, Dec. 13**

| | | |
|---|---|---|
| **796-797** A241 Set of 2 | 1.10 | 1.10 |

143rd Extraordinary Conference of OPEC, Abuja — A242

**2006, Dec. 14**

| | | |
|---|---|---|
| **798** A242 50n multi | .80 | .80 |

The editors have been shown numerous examples of this stamp on cover, but Nigerian postal authorities state that it was issued "strictly for the validation of documents, and not for postage," and that use of the stamp on mail was probably done out of ignorance.

Mungo Park (1771-1806), Explorer — A243

Park and: 20n, Monument. 50n, River, horiz.

**2007, Mar. 29** **Litho.** ***Perf. 13***

| | | |
|---|---|---|
| **799-800** A243 Set of 2 | 1.10 | 1.10 |

Second World Black and African Festival of Arts and Culture, 30th Anniv. A244

**2007, Mar. 29** **Litho.** ***Perf. 13***

| | | |
|---|---|---|
| **801** A244 50n multi | .80 | .80 |
| *h.* Sheet of 2 #801, imperf. | — | — |

24th UPU Congress — A244a

Ceremonial costumes: No. 801A, Fulani man. No. 801B, Igbo man and woman. No. 801C, South Zone man and woman. No. 801D, Tiv man and woman, horiz. No. 801E, 50n, Yoruba man and woman. No. 801F, North East Zone women.

*Perf. 13x12¾, 12¾x13*

**2007, Oct. 9** **Litho.**

| | | |
|---|---|---|
| **801A** A244a 20n multi | — | — |
| **801B** A244a 20n multi | — | — |
| **801C** A244a 30n multi | | — |
| **801D** A244a 30n multi | | — |
| **801E** A244a 50n multi | | — |
| **801F** A244a 50n multi | | — |
| *g.* Souvenir sheet of 6, #801A-801F, imperf. | — | — |

The 24th UPU Congress, scheduled to be held in Nairobi, was moved to Geneva, Switzerland, because of political unrest in Kenya.

A245

Cross river gorilla: 20n, Adult. 50n, Two adults, horiz. 100n, Adult and juvenile, horiz. 150n, Head.

**2008, Mar. 26** **Litho.** ***Perf. 13***

| | | |
|---|---|---|
| **802-805** A245 Set of 4 | 5.00 | 5.00 |

Worldwide Fund for Nature (WWF).

A246

Designs: 20n, Hands, money. 50n, Campaign to end violation of 419 law. 100n, Clasped hands.

**2008, Apr. 10**

| | | |
|---|---|---|
| **806-808** A246 Set of 3 | 3.00 | 3.00 |
| *808a* Souvenir sheet of 3, #806-808, imperf. | — | — |

Economic & Financial Crimes Commission anti-corruption campaign.

Nos. 806-809 exist without printer's imprint. Their issue status is uncertain. Value, set $110.

2008 Summer Olympics, Beijing A247

Designs: 20n, Runners at finish line. 50n, Soccer. 100n, Wrestling, vert.

**2008, Aug. 8**

| | | |
|---|---|---|
| **809-811** A247 Set of 3 | 3.00 | 3.00 |

Federal Road Safety Commission, 20th Anniv. — A247a — 811A

**2008, Nov. 13** **Litho.** ***Perf. 13***

| | | |
|---|---|---|
| **811A** A247a 50n multi | 1.25 | 1.00 |

Nigerian Institute of Advanced Legal Studies A248

**2009, Sept. 4** **Litho.** ***Perf. 13***

| | | |
|---|---|---|
| **812** A248 50n multi | .65 | .65 |

Pan-African Postal Union, 30th Anniv. — A248a

**2010, Jan. 8** **Litho.** ***Perf. 13x12¾***

| | | |
|---|---|---|
| **812A** A248a 50n multi | 1.00 | 1.00 |

Dated 2009.

Return to Democracy, 10th Anniv. A249

Designs: No. 813, 50n, Nigerian flag, Pres. Umaru Musa Yar'Adua. No. 814, 50n, Mace, scales of justice, barrister's wig, vert.

***Perf. 13x12¾, 12¾x13***

**2010, Apr. 6** **Litho.**

**813-814** A249 Set of 2 1.75 1.75

Dated 2009.

GT Bank, 20th Anniv. A250

Woman, globe, 20th anniversary emblem, bank emblem and background color of: 20n, Red. 50n, Gray. 100n, Pale yellow. 120n, Gray green.

**2010, July 14** **Litho.** ***Perf. 13x12¾***

**815-818** A250 Set of 4 5.50 5.50

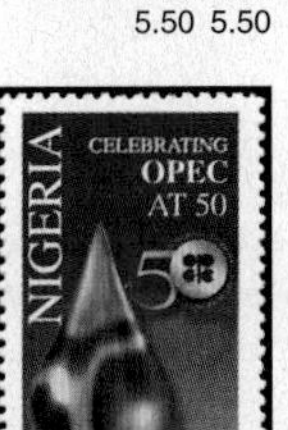


Organization of Petroleum Exporting Countries, 50th Anniv. — A251

Designs: 50n, Oil droplet, 50th anniversary emblem. 120n, 50th anniversary emblem.

**2010, Aug. 12** **Litho.** ***Perf. 12¾x13***

**819-820** A251 Set of 2 3.00 3.00

2010 World Cup Soccer Championships, South Africa — A252

Design: 20n, Two soccer players and ball. 30n, Soccer ball, globe, World Cup, vert. 50n, Soccer players and stadium.

**2010** ***Perf. 13x12¾, 12¾x13***

**821** A252 20n multi *.50* —
**821A** A252 30n multi *1.00* —
**821B** A252 50n multi *1.75* —

Terracotta Head — A253

Terracotta Head — A253a

Bronze Bowl — A254

Igbo-Ukwu Bronze Bowl — A254a

Slave Chain A255

Lander Brothers Anchorage A256

Lander Brothers Anchorage — A256a

Nok Terracotta Head — A257

Monkey Colony, Lagwa-Mbaise A258

Elephants, Yankari Game Reserve — A258a

Argungu Fishing Festival, Kebbi State A259

Seated Human Figurine — A260

Lander Brothers Anchorage — A260a

***Perf. 12¼x12½, 13 (Nos. 822A, 823A, 825A, 826, 827, 828), 12½x12¼ (No. 827A)***

**Litho. With Hologram Applied**

**2010-11**

**822** A253 20n multi *.75* —
**822A** A253a 20n multi — —
**823** A254 30n multi — —
**823A** A254a 30n multi — —
**824** A255 50n multi — —
**825** A256 50n multi — —
**825A** A256a 50n multi — —
**826** A257 50n multi — —
**827** A258 50n multi — —
**827A** A260a 50n multi (round hologram) — —
**827B** A258a 90n multi — —
**828** A259 100n multi — *4.00*
**829** A260 120n multi *3.50* —

**Litho.**

***Perf. 12¾x13***

**829A** A260a 50n multi *20.00 20.00*

Issued: No. 822A, 823A, 825A, 2011; No. 829A, 2010; others, 10/9/2010. No. 822A is dated 2010. No. 829A is dated 2009.

Independence, 50th Anniv. — A261

Nigerian arms and: 20n, Nigerian flag on pole, man holding pole with British flag, 50th anniv. emblem. 30n, Map and symbols of Nigeria. No. 832, 50n, Four men and Nigerian flag, 50th anniv. emblem, horiz. (77x22mm). No. 833, 50n, Photographs of Nigerian crops and industries, 50th anniv. emblem, horiz. (53x37mm).

***Perf. 13, 13¼ (#832), 13¼x13 (#833)***

**2010** **Litho.**

**830-833** A261 Set of 4 3.50 3.50

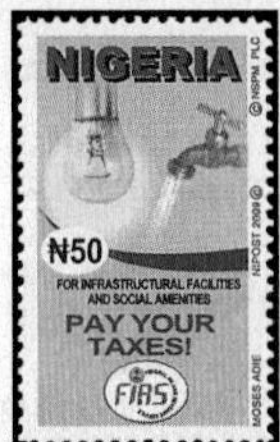


Federal Inland Revenue Service — A262

Emblem of Federal Inland Revenue Service and: 20n, Heart, map of Nigeria. 50n, Light bulb, water faucet. 100n, Taxcard.

**2011** **Litho.** ***Perf. 13***

**834** A262 20n multi *.75* —
**835** A262 50n multi *1.25* —
**836** A262 100n multi *2.50* —

Dated 2009.

Benue State A263

Map of Benue State and: 20n, Gugur Waterfall. 30n, Food basket. 50n, Senator Joseph Sawuan Tarka (1932-80). 100n, Benue Bridge.

**2011** **Litho.** ***Perf. 13***

**837-840** A263 Set of 4 4.50 4.50
*840a* Souvenir sheet of 4, #837-840, imperf. *14.00 14.00*

Nigerian Institute of Management, 50th Anniv. — A264

**2011, Sept. 27**

**841** A264 50n multi 1.00 1.00
*a.* Souvenir sheet of 1, imperf. — —

Phila Africa 2012 Stamp Exhibition — A265

**2012, Jan. 31**

**842** A265 50n multi 1.00 1.00

An imperforate souvenir sheet of 1 sold for 400n.

Enugu, Cent. (in 2009) — A266

**2012, Sept. 27** **Litho.** ***Perf. 12¾x13***

**843** A266 50n multi — —

Ahmadu Bello University, Zaria, 50th Anniv. — A267

50th Anniv. emblem and: Nos. 844, 848, Sir Ahmadu Bello (1910-66), Premier of Northern Nigeria. Nos. 845, 849, Ahmadu Bello University Senate Building, horiz. 90n, University crest. 120n, Shika brown chickens, horiz.

**Litho. With Hologram Applied**

**2012, Nov. 24** ***Perf. 13***

**844** A267 50n multi — —
**845** A267 50n multi — —
**846** A267 90n multi — —
**847** A267 120n multi — —

**Litho.**

***Perf. 13¼x14***

**Booklet Stamps**

**848** A267 50n multi — —
**849** A267 50n multi — —
**850** A267 90n multi — —
**851** A267 120n multi — —
*a.* Booklet pane of 4, #848-851 —
Complete booklet, 3 #851a —

Diplomatic Relations Between Nigeria and Philippines, 50th Anniv. A268

Flags of Philippines and Nigeria and: 50n, Coat of arms of Nigeria, daisy. 120n, Coat of arms of Philippines, sampaguita.

**Litho. With Hologram Applied**

**2013, Dec. 24** ***Perf. 12¾x13¼***

**853** A268 50n multi — —
**854** A268 120n multi — —

See Philippines No. 3511.

Civilian Leaders of Nigerians — A269

Designs: Nos. 855, 862a, 50n, Nnamdi Azikwe (1904-96), President and Governor-General. Nos. 856, 862b, 50n, Sir Abubakar Tafawa Balewa (1912-96), Prime Minister. Nos. 857, 862c, 50n, Alhajlaliyu Shehu Shagari, President. Nos. 858, 862d, 50n, Goodluck Ebele Jonathan, President. Nos. 859, 862e, 50n, Ernest Shonekan, President. Nos. 860, 862f, 50n, Olusegun Obasanjo, President. Nos. 861, 862g, 50n, Umaru Musa Yar'Adua (1951-2010), President.

**Litho. With Hologram**

**2014, Nov. 27** *Perf. 13½*

**855-861** A269 Set of 7 — —

**Souvenir Sheet**

**Litho.**

***Imperf***

**862** A269 Sheet of 7, #a-g — —

Nigeria, Cent. A270

Designs: Nos. 863, 867a, 50n, Fist, map of Nigeria. Nos. 864, 867b, 50n, People lifting map of Nigeria. Nos. 865, 867c, 100n, Chief Obafemi Awolowo (1909-87), Sir Ahmadu Bello (1910-66), Dr. Nnamdi Azikwe (1904-96). Nos, 866, 867d, 120n, Sir Frederick Lord Lugard (1858-1945), colonial administrator.

**Litho. With Hologram**

**2014** *Perf. 14*

**863-866** A270 Set of 4 — —

**Souvenir Sheet**

**Litho.**

***Imperf***

**867** A270 Sheet of 4, #a-d — —

Famous Nigerian Buildings A271

Designs: Nos. 868, 874a, 50n, Amalgamation House, Calabar. Nos. 869, 874b, 50n, Lord Lugard Court, Lokoja. Nos. 870, 874c, 50n, Seat of Administriation of Lord Lugar (now Kogi State Government House), Lokoja. Nos. 871, 874d, 50n, National Assembly, Abuja, Nigeria #97. Nos. 872, 874e, 50n, Supreme Court, Abuja, Nigeria #98. Nos. 873, 874f, 50n, State House, Marina, Lagos, Presidential Villa, Abuja.

**Litho. With Hologram**

**2014** *Perf. 13½x13¾*

**868-873** A271 Set of 6 — —

**Souvenir Sheet**

**Litho.**

***Imperf***

**874** A271 Sheet of 6, #a-f — —

Nigeria, cent.

Economic Community of West African States (ECOWAS), 40th Anniv. A272

**2015, May 28 Litho.** *Perf. 13x13¼*

**875** A272 50n multi — —

No. 875 comes in sheets of 25.

University of Nigeria, 55th Anniv. A273

Designs: No. 876, 50n, University crest, emblem of West African University Games. No. 877, 50n, Prof. Benjamin C. Ozumba, University Vice-Chancellor, university crest and games emblem. 100n, Dr. George M. Johnson, first Vice-Chancellor, university crest and games emblem. 120n, Dr. Nnamdi Azikwe, founder, university crest and games emblem.

**2015, Oct. 23 Litho.** *Perf. 14x13½*

**876-879** A273 Set of 4 — —

*879a* Souvenir sheet of 4, #876-879, imperf. — —

University of Nigeria, host of 2015 West African University Games.

**University of Nigeria Type of 2015**

Designs: No. 879B, 50n, Like #876. No. 879C, 50n, Like #877. No. 879D, 100n, Like #878. No. 879E, 120n, Like #879.

**Litho. With Hologram Affixed**

**2015, Oct. 23** *Perf. 14x13½*

**879B-879E** A273 Set of 4 — —

Anti-Corruption Campaign — A274

Inscriptions: No. 880, 50n, Say no to theft. No. 881, 50n, Say no to bunkering. No. 882, 50n, Say no to fraud. No. 883, 50n, Say no to bribery.

**Litho. With Hologram**

**2016, Nov. 7** *Perf. 12½x13¼*

**880-883** A274 Set of 4 — —

*883a* Souvenir sheet of 4, #880-883 — —

## SEMI-POSTAL STAMPS

**Catalogue values for unused stamps in this section are for Never Hinged items.**

Children Drinking Milk at Orphanage SP1

Designs: 1sh6p+3p, Civilian first aid, vert. 2sh6p+3p, Military first aid.

**1966, Dec. 1 Photo.** *Perf. 14½x14*

| | | | | |
|---|---|---|---|---|
| **B1** | SP1 | 4p + 1p pur, blk & red | .35 | .35 |
| **B2** | SP1 | 1sh6p + 3p multi | .80 | .80 |
| **B3** | SP1 | 2sh6p + 3p multi | 1.25 | 1.25 |
| | | *Nos. B1-B3 (3)* | 2.40 | 2.40 |

The surtax was for the Nigerian Red Cross.

Dr. Armauer G. Hansen — SP2

**1973, July 30 Litho.** *Perf. 14*

**B4** SP2 5k + 2k blk, brn & buff .50 *1.00*

Centenary of the discovery of the Hansen bacillus, the cause of leprosy. The surtax was for the Nigerian Anti-Leprosy Association.

Nigeria '99, FIFA World Youth Championships — SP3

5n+5n, Soccer ball, FIFA emblem. 10n+5n, Throwing ball. 20n+5n, Kicking ball into goal. 30n+5n, Map of Nigeria. 40n+5n, FIFA emblem, eagle, soccer ball. 50n+5n, Tackling.

**1999, Mar. 31 Litho.** *Perf. 13x14*

| | | | | |
|---|---|---|---|---|
| **B5** | SP3 | 5n +5n multi | .25 | .25 |
| **B6** | SP3 | 10n +5n multi | .30 | .30 |
| **B7** | SP3 | 20n +5n multi | .55 | .55 |
| **B8** | SP3 | 30n +5n multi | .65 | .65 |
| **B9** | SP3 | 40n +5n multi | .90 | .90 |
| **B10** | SP3 | 50n +5n multi | 1.20 | 1.20 |
| *a.* | | Souvenir sheet of 6, #B5-B10 | 3.75 | 3.75 |
| | | *Nos. B5-B10 (6)* | 3.85 | 3.85 |

## POSTAGE DUE STAMPS

**Catalogue values for unused stamps in this section are for Never Hinged items.**

D1

*Perf. 14½x14*

**1959, Jan. 4 Wmk. 4 Litho.**

| | | | | |
|---|---|---|---|---|
| **J1** | D1 | 1p orange | .25 | *1.00* |
| **J2** | D1 | 2p orange | .25 | *1.25* |
| **J3** | D1 | 3p orange | .25 | *1.75* |
| **J4** | D1 | 6p orange | .80 | *6.25* |
| **J5** | D1 | 1sh black | 1.25 | *11.00* |
| | | *Nos. J1-J5 (5)* | 2.80 | *21.25* |

**1961, Aug. 1 Wmk. 335**

| | | | | |
|---|---|---|---|---|
| **J6** | D1 | 1p red | .25 | *.40* |
| **J7** | D1 | 2p blue | .25 | *.50* |
| **J8** | D1 | 3p emerald | .25 | *.75* |
| **J9** | D1 | 6p yellow | .25 | *2.00* |
| **J10** | D1 | 1sh dark blue | .40 | *4.00* |
| | | *Nos. J6-J10 (5)* | 1.40 | *7.65* |

D2

*Perf. 12½x13½*

**1973, May 3 Litho. Unwmk.**

| | | | | |
|---|---|---|---|---|
| **J11** | D2 | 2k red | .25 | .25 |
| **J12** | D2 | 3k blue | .25 | .25 |
| **J13** | D2 | 5k orange | .25 | .25 |
| **J14** | D2 | 10k yellow green | .25 | .25 |
| | | *Nos. J11-J14 (4)* | 1.00 | 1.00 |

**1987-94** ***Rouletted 9***

| | | | | |
|---|---|---|---|---|
| **J15** | D2 | 2k red | 1.75 | *2.50* |
| **J16** | D2 | 5k yellow | 4.50 | *5.00* |
| **J17** | D2 | 10k green | 9.00 | *10.00* |
| | | *Nos. J15-J17 (3)* | 15.25 | *17.50* |

D3

**2004 Litho.** *Perf. 12¾*

| | | | | |
|---|---|---|---|---|
| **J18** | D3 | 20n yel green | *.75* | — |
| **J19** | D3 | 40n red | *.95* | — |

# NIUE

nē-'ü-ˌā

LOCATION — Island in the south Pacific Ocean, northeast of New Zealand
GOVT. — Self-government, in free association with New Zealand
AREA — 100 sq. mi.
POP. — 1,708 (1997 est.)
CAPITAL — Alofi

Niue, also known as Savage Island, was annexed to New Zealand in 1901 with the Cook Islands. Niue achieved internal self-government in 1974.

12 Pence = 1 Shilling
20 Shillings = 1 Pound
100 Cents = 1 Dollar (1967)

**Catalogue values for unused stamps in this country are for Never Hinged items, beginning with Scott 90 in the regular postage section, Scott B1 in the semi-postal section, Scott C1 in the air post section, and Scott O1 in the officials section.**

### Watermarks

Wmk. 61 — Single-lined NZ and Star Close Together

Wmk. 253 — NZ and Star

New Zealand No. 100 Handstamped in Green

**1902 Wmk. 63 *Perf. 11***
**Thick Soft Paper**

1 A35 1p carmine 375.00 375.00

### Stamps of New Zealand Surcharged in Carmine, Vermilion or Blue

1/2p

1p

2 1/2p

***Perf. 14***
***Thin Hard Paper***

3 A18 ½p green (C) 5.50 *7.00*
a. Inverted surcharge 325.00 *600.00*
b. Double surcharge 1,200.
4 A35 1p carmine (Bl), perf. 11x14 2.00 *4.25*
a. No period after "PENI" 50.00 *70.00*
b. Perf. 14 50.00 *55.00*
c. As "a," perf. 14 500.00 600.00

***Perf. 14***
**Wmk. 61**

6 A18 ½p green (V) 1.60 1.60
7 A35 1p carmine (Bl) .85 1.10
a. No period after "PENI" 9.00 *17.00*
b. Double surcharge 1,800. *2,000.*

***Perf. 11***
**Unwmk.**

8 A22 2½p blue (C) 2.50 *4.50*
a. No period after "PENI" 35.00 *55.00*
9 A22 2½p blue (V) 1.75 4.25
a. No period after "PENI" 30.00 55.00
b. Double surcharge 2,500.

The surcharge on the ½ & 1p stamps is printed in blocks of 60. Two stamps in each block have a space between the "U" and "E" of "NIUE" and one of the 1p stamps has a broken "E" like an "F."

### Blue Surcharge on Stamps of New Zealand, Types of 1898

e

f

g

h

**1903 Wmk. 61 *Perf. 11***

10 A23(e) 3p yellow brown 11.00 5.50
11 A26(f) 6p rose 15.00 12.50
13 A29(g) 1sh brown red 40.00 *50.00*
a. 1sh scarlet 40.00 *50.00*
b. 1sh orange red 50.00 *52.50*
c. As "b," surcharge "h" (error) 750.00
*Nos. 10-13 (3)* 66.00 *68.00*

Surcharged in Carmine or Blue on Stamps of New Zealand — j

**1911-12 *Perf. 14, 14x14½***

14 A41(j) ½p yellow grn (C) .60 .70
15 A41(f) 6p car rose (Bl) 2.50 *7.50*
16 A41(g) 1sh vermilion (Bl) 8.00 *50.00*
*Nos. 14-16 (3)* 11.10 *58.20*

**1915 *Perf. 14***

18 A22(d) 2½p dark blue (C) 26.00 *55.00*

Surcharged in Brown or Dark Blue on Stamps of New Zealand

**1917 *Perf. 14x15***

19 A42 1p carmine (Br) 24.00 6.25
a. No period after "PENI" 850.00

***Perf. 14x14½***

20 A45(e) 3p violet brn (Bl) 50.00 100.00
a. No period after "Pene" 850.00
b. Perf. 14x13½ 67.50 125.00
c. Vert. pair, #20 & 20b 190.00

New Zealand Stamps of 1909-19 Overprinted in Dark Blue or Red — k

**1917-20 Typo. *Perf. 14x15***

21 A43 ½p yellow grn (R) .80 *3.25*
22 A42 1p carmine (Bl) 11.00 *14.00*
23 A47 1½p gray black (R) 1.10 *2.50*
24 A47 1½p brown org (R) 1.00 *8.50*
25 A43 3p chocolate (Bl) 1.60 *40.00*

**Engr.**
***Perf. 14x14½***

26 A44 2½p dull blue (R) 1.50 *16.00*
a. Perf. 14x13½ 4.75 *19.00*
b. Vert. pair, #26-26a 19.00 *72.50*
27 A45 3p violet brown (Bl) 1.75 *2.25*
a. Perf. 14x13½ 3.50 2.25
b. Vert. pair, #27-27a 22.50 *50.00*
28 A45 6p car rose (Bl) 6.00 *26.00*
a. Perf. 14x13½ 11.00 *25.00*
b. Vert. pair, #28-28a 32.50 *125.00*
29 A45 1sh vermilion (Bl) 7.50 *30.00*
a. Perf. 14x13½ 17.00 *40.00*
b. Vert. pair, #29-29a 47.50 *135.00*
*Nos. 21-29 (9)* 32.25 *142.50*

### Same Overprint On Postal-Fiscal Stamps of New Zealand, 1906-15

***Perf. 14, 14½ and Compound***

**1918-23**

30 PF1 2sh blue (R) 18.00 *35.00*
31 PF1 2sh6p bn (Bl) ('23) 24.00 *55.00*
32 PF1 5sh green (R) 29.00 *57.50*
a. Perf. 14 115.00 *125.00*
b. Perf. 14½x14 ('29) 27.50 *67.50*
33 PF1 10sh red brn (Bl) ('23) 145.00 *185.00*
a. Perf. 14½x14 ('27) 100.00 *165.00*
34 PF2 £1 rose (Bl) ('23) 185.00 *275.00*
a. Perf. 14½x14 ('28) 170.00 *300.00*
*Nos. 30-34 (5)* 401.00 *607.50*

Nos. 32b, 33a and 34a come on thick paper and in different color varieties.

Landing of Captain Cook A16

Avarua Waterfront A17

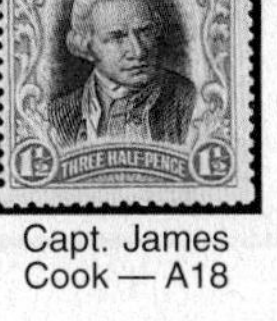

Capt. James Cook — A18

Coconut Palm — A19

Arorangi Village — A20

Avarua Harbor — A21

**Unwmk.**

**1920, Aug. 23 Engr. *Perf. 14***

35 A16 ½p yel grn & blk 4.25 *4.75*
36 A17 1p car & black 2.25 1.40
37 A18 1½p red & black 2.75 *18.00*
38 A19 3p pale blue & blk 1.90 *16.00*
39 A20 6p dp grn & red brn 5.25 *21.00*
a. Center inverted *1,000.*
40 A21 1sh blk brn & blk 5.25 *21.00*
*Nos. 35-40 (6)* 21.65 *82.15*

See Nos. 41-42. For surcharge see No. 48.

### Types of 1920 Issue and

Rarotongan Chief (Te Po) — A22

Avarua Harbor — A23

**1925-27 Wmk. 61**

41 A16 ½p yel grn & blk ('26) 2.75 *13.00*
42 A17 1p car & black 2.00 1.00
43 A22 2½p dk blue & blk ('27) 4.50 *16.00*
44 A23 4p dull vio & blk ('27) 8.00 *22.50*
*Nos. 41-44 (4)* 17.25 *52.50*

### New Zealand No. 182 Overprinted Type "k" in Red

**1927**

47 A56 2sh blue 18.00 *35.00*
a. 2sh dark blue 17.00 *50.00*

No. 37 Surcharged

**1931 Unwmk. *Perf. 14***

48 A18 2p on 1½p red & blk 5.25 1.10

### New Zealand Postal-Fiscal Stamps of 1931-32 Overprinted Type "k" in Blue or Red

**1931, Nov. 12 Wmk. 61**

49 PF5 2sh6p deep brown 5.00 13.00
50 PF5 5sh green (R) 40.00 *75.00*
51 PF5 10sh dark car 40.00 *110.00*
52 PF5 £1 pink ('32) 75.00 *350.00*
*Nos. 49-52 (4)* 160.00 *548.00*

See Nos. 86-89D, 116-119.

Landing of Captain Cook — A24

Capt. James Cook — A25

Polynesian Migratory Canoe — A26

Islanders Unloading Ship — A27

View of Avarua Harbor — A28

R.M.S. Monowai — A29

King George V — A30

***Perf. 13, 14 (4p, 1sh)***

**1932, Mar. 16 Engr. Unwmk.**

53 A24 ½p yel grn & blk 14.00 *25.00*
a. Perf. 13x14x13x13 275.00
54 A25 1p dp red & blk 1.10 .55
55 A26 2p org brn & blk 7.50 *4.50*
a. Perf. 14x13x13x13 150.00 *190.00*
56 A27 2½p indigo & blk 8.50 *80.00*
a. Center inverted 350.00
57 A28 4p Prus blue & blk 16.00 *60.00*
a. Perf. 13 15.00 *65.00*
58 A29 6p dp org & blk 2.75 2.25
59 A30 1sh dull vio & blk 3.75 *5.50*
*Nos. 53-59 (7)* 53.60 *177.80*

For types overprinted see Nos. 67-69.

**1933-36 Wmk. 61 *Perf. 14***

60 A24 ½p yel grn & blk .50 *3.50*
61 A25 1p deep red & blk .50 *2.25*
62 A26 2p brown & blk ('36) .50 *1.75*
63 A27 2½p indigo & blk .50 *4.75*
64 A28 4p Prus blue & blk 2.00 *4.25*
65 A29 6p org & blk ('36) .80 *.90*
66 A30 1sh dk vio & blk ('36) 9.00 *27.50*
*Nos. 60-66 (7)* 13.80 *44.90*

See Nos. 77-82.

### Silver Jubilee Issue

Types of 1932 Overprinted in Black or Red

**1935, May 7** *Perf. 14*

| No. | Type | Description | Unused | Used |
|---|---|---|---|---|
| 67 | A25 | 1p car & brown red | .80 | 3.50 |
| 68 | A27 | 2½p indigo & bl (R) | 4.25 | 13.00 |
| a. | | Vert. pair, imperf. horiz. | 275.00 | |
| 69 | A29 | 6p dull org & grn | 6.75 | 10.00 |
| | | *Nos. 67-69 (3)* | 11.80 | 26.50 |
| | | Set, never hinged | 20.00 | |

The vertical spacing of the overprint is wider on No. 69.

No. 68a is from proof sheets.

### Coronation Issue

New Zealand Stamps of 1937 Overprinted in Black

*Perf. 13½x13*

**1937, May 13** **Wmk. 253**

| No. | Type | Description | Unused | Used |
|---|---|---|---|---|
| 70 | A78 | 1p rose carmine | .25 | .25 |
| 71 | A78 | 2½p dark blue | .25 | 1.50 |
| 72 | A78 | 6p vermilion | .30 | .30 |
| | | *Nos. 70-72 (3)* | .80 | 2.05 |
| | | Set, never hinged | 1.25 | |

George VI — A31

Village Scene — A32

Coastal Scene with Canoe — A33

**1938, May 2** **Wmk. 61** *Perf. 14*

| No. | Type | Description | Unused | Used |
|---|---|---|---|---|
| 73 | A31 | 1sh dp violet & blk | 5.00 | 8.00 |
| 74 | A32 | 2sh dk red brown & blk | 6.50 | 17.00 |
| 75 | A33 | 3sh yel green & blue | 18.50 | 17.00 |
| | | *Nos. 73-75 (3)* | 30.00 | 42.00 |
| | | Set, never hinged | 55.00 | |

See Nos. 83-85.

Mt. Ikurangi behind Avarua — A34

*Perf. 13½x14*

**1940, Sept. 2** **Engr.** **Wmk. 253**

| No. | Type | Description | Unused | Used |
|---|---|---|---|---|
| 76 | A34 | 3p on 1½p rose vio & blk | .45 | .25 |
| | | Never hinged | .75 | |

Examples without surcharge are from printer's archives. Value, $250 unused.

See Cook Islands No. 115.

### Types of 1932-38

**1944-46** **Wmk. 253** *Perf. 14*

| No. | Type | Description | Unused | Used |
|---|---|---|---|---|
| 77 | A24 | ½p yel grn & blk | .40 | 2.25 |
| 78 | A25 | 1p dp red & blk ('45) | .40 | 1.25 |
| 79 | A26 | 2p org brn & blk ('46) | 3.75 | 6.00 |
| 80 | A27 | 2½p dk bl & blk ('45) | .50 | 1.00 |
| 81 | A28 | 4p Prus blue & blk | 2.75 | .90 |
| 82 | A29 | 6p dp orange & blk | 1.40 | 1.40 |
| 83 | A31 | 1sh dp vio & blk | .85 | 1.00 |
| 84 | A32 | 2sh brn car & blk ('45) | 8.50 | 3.75 |
| 85 | A33 | 3sh yel grn & bl ('45) | 11.00 | 8.50 |
| | | *Nos. 77-85 (9)* | 29.55 | 26.05 |
| | | Set, never hinged | 35.00 | |

New Zealand Postal-Fiscal Stamps Overprinted (narrow "E") in Blue or Red

**1941-45** **Wmk. 61** *Perf. 14*

| No. | Type | Description | Unused | Used |
|---|---|---|---|---|
| 86 | PF5 | 2sh6p brown | 65.00 | 100.00 |
| 87 | PF5 | 5sh green (R) | 140.00 | 300.00 |
| 88 | PF5 | 10sh rose | 85.00 | 250.00 |
| 89 | PF5 | £1 pink | 125.00 | 400.00 |
| | | *Nos. 86-89 (4)* | 415.00 | 1,050. |
| | | Set, never hinged | 750.00 | |

**Wmk. 253**

| No. | Type | Description | Unused | Used |
|---|---|---|---|---|
| 89A | PF5 | 2sh6p brown | 2.75 | 11.00 |
| 89B | PF5 | 5sh brt grn (R) | 5.50 | 15.00 |
| e. | | 5sh light yellow green, wmkd. sideways ('67) | 10.00 | 80.00 |
| 89C | PF5 | 10sh rose | 37.50 | 135.00 |
| 89D | PF5 | £1 pink | 400.00 | 80.00 |
| | | *Nos. 89A-89D (4)* | 445.75 | 241.00 |
| | | Set, never hinged | 125.00 | |

No. 89Be exists in both line and comb perf.

**Catalogue values for unused stamps in this section, from this point to the end of the section, are for Never Hinged items.**

### Peace Issue

New Zealand Nos. 248, 250, 254 and 255 Overprinted in Black or Blue

p

q

**1946, June 4** *Perf. 13x13½, 13½x13*

| No. | Type | Description | Unused | Used |
|---|---|---|---|---|
| 90 | A94 (p) | 1p emerald | .40 | .35 |
| 91 | A96 (q) | 2p rose violet (Bl) | .40 | .35 |
| 92 | A100 (p) | 6p org red & red brn | .40 | .75 |
| 93 | A101 (p) | 8p brn lake & blk (Bl) | .50 | .75 |
| | | *Nos. 90-93 (4)* | 1.70 | 2.20 |

Map of Niue — A35

H.M.S. Resolution — A36

Designs: 2p, Alofi landing. 3p, Thatched Dwelling. 4p, Arch at Hikutavake. 6p, Alofi bay. 9p, Fisherman. 1sh, Cave at Makefu. 2sh, Gathering bananas. 3sh, Matapa Chasm.

*Perf. 14x13½, 13½x14*

**1950, July 3** **Engr.** **Wmk. 253**

| No. | Type | Description | Unused | Used |
|---|---|---|---|---|
| 94 | A35 | ½p red orange & bl | .25 | 1.25 |
| 95 | A36 | 1p green & brown | 2.25 | 2.50 |
| 96 | A36 | 2p rose car & blk | 1.25 | 2.00 |
| 97 | A36 | 3p blue vio & blue | .25 | .25 |
| 98 | A36 | 4p brn vio & ol grn | .30 | .40 |
| 99 | A36 | 6p brn org & bl grn | .90 | 1.40 |
| 100 | A35 | 9p dk brn & brn org | .40 | 1.40 |
| 101 | A36 | 1sh black & purple | .45 | .60 |
| 102 | A35 | 2sh dp grn & brn org | 4.00 | 5.00 |
| 103 | A36 | 3sh black & dp blue | 4.75 | 5.00 |
| | | *Nos. 94-103 (10)* | 14.80 | 19.80 |

For surcharges see Nos. 106-115.

### Coronation Issue

Queen Elizabeth II — A36a

Westminster Abbey — A36b

**1953, May 24** **Photo.** *Perf. 14x14½*

| No. | Type | Description | Unused | Used |
|---|---|---|---|---|
| 104 | A36a | 3p brown | .60 | .60 |
| 105 | A36b | 6p slate black | 1.00 | 1.00 |

Nos. 94-103 Surcharged

*Perf. 14x13½, 13½x14*

**1967, July 10** **Engr.** **Wmk. 253**

| No. | Type | Description | Unused | Used |
|---|---|---|---|---|
| 106 | A35 | ½c on ½p red org & blue | .25 | .25 |
| 107 | A36 | 1c on 1p green & brn | .40 | .25 |
| 108 | A36 | 2c on 2p rose car & blk | .25 | .25 |
| 109 | A36 | 2½c on 3p bl vio & bl | .25 | .25 |
| 110 | A36 | 3c on 4p brn vio & ol grn | .25 | .25 |
| 111 | A36 | 5c on 6p brn org & grn | .25 | .25 |
| 112 | A35 | 8c on 9p dk brn & brn org | .25 | .25 |
| 113 | A36 | 10c on 1sh blk & pur | .25 | .25 |
| 114 | A35 | 20c on 2sh dp grn & brn org | .30 | 1.25 |
| 115 | A35 | 30c on 3sh blk & dp bl | .50 | 1.25 |
| | | *Nos. 106-115 (10)* | 2.95 | 4.50 |

The position of the numeral varies on each denomination. The surcharge on the ½c, 2½c, 8c, 10c and 20c contains one dot only.

New Zealand Arms — A37

**Wmk. 253**

**1967, July 10** **Typo.** *Perf. 14*

**Black Surcharge**

| No. | Type | Description | Unused | Used |
|---|---|---|---|---|
| 116 | A37 | 25c yellow brown | .50 | .45 |
| 117 | A37 | 50c green | .85 | .90 |
| 118 | A37 | $1 cerise | .55 | 1.75 |
| 119 | A37 | $2 pale pink | .85 | 3.00 |
| | | *Nos. 116-119 (4)* | 2.75 | 6.10 |

**1967** *Perf. 11*

| No. | Type | Description | Unused | Used |
|---|---|---|---|---|
| 116a | A37 | 25c | 8.25 | 13.00 |
| 117a | A37 | 50c | 9.50 | 15.00 |
| 118a | A37 | $1 | 12.00 | 15.00 |
| 119a | A37 | $2 | 15.00 | 20.00 |
| | | *Nos. 116a-119a (4)* | 44.75 | 63.00 |

The perf. 11 stamps were produced when a normal perforating machine broke down and 2,500 of each denomination were perforated on a treadle machine first used by the N.Z. Post Office in 1899.

### Christmas Issues

Adoration of the Shepherds, by Poussin — A37a

*Perf. 13½x14*

**1967, Oct. 3** **Photo.** **Wmk. 253**

| No. | Type | Description | Unused | Used |
|---|---|---|---|---|
| 120 | A37a | 2½c multicolored | .30 | .25 |

Nativity, by Federico Fiori — A37b

**1969, Oct. 1** **Photo.** **Wmk. 253**

| No. | Type | Description | Unused | Used |
|---|---|---|---|---|
| 121 | A37b | 2½c multicolored | .30 | .25 |

Pua — A38

Flowers (except 20c): 1c, Golden shower. 2c, Flamboyant. 2½c, Frangipani. 3c, Niue crocus. 5c, Hibiscus. 8c, Passion fruit. 10c, Kamapui. 20c, Queen Elizabeth II. 30c, Tapeu orchid.

*Perf. 12½x13*

**1969, Nov. 27** **Litho.** **Unwmk.**

| No. | Type | Description | Unused | Used |
|---|---|---|---|---|
| 122 | A38 | ½c green & multi | .25 | .25 |
| 123 | A38 | 1c orange & multi | .25 | .25 |
| 124 | A38 | 2c gray & multi | .25 | .25 |
| 125 | A38 | 2½c bister & multi | .25 | .25 |
| 126 | A38 | 3c blue & multi | .25 | .25 |
| 127 | A38 | 5c ver & multi | .25 | .25 |
| 128 | A38 | 8c violet & multi | .25 | .25 |
| 129 | A38 | 10c yellow & multi | .25 | .25 |
| 130 | A38 | 20c dk blue & multi | .75 | 1.50 |
| 131 | A38 | 30c olive grn & multi | 1.00 | 2.00 |
| | | *Nos. 122-131 (10)* | 3.75 | 5.50 |

See Nos. 678.

Edible Crab A39

*Perf. 13½x12½*

**1969, Aug. 19** **Litho.**

| No. | Type | Description | Unused | Used |
|---|---|---|---|---|
| 132 | A39 | 3c Kalahimu | .25 | .25 |
| 133 | A39 | 5c Kalavi | .25 | .25 |
| 134 | A39 | 30c Unga | .40 | .40 |
| | | *Nos. 132-134 (3)* | .90 | .90 |

### Christmas Issue

Adoration, by Correggio — A39a

**1970, Oct. 1** **Litho.** *Perf. 12½*

| No. | Type | Description | Unused | Used |
|---|---|---|---|---|
| 135 | A39a | 2½c multicolored | .30 | .25 |

Plane over Outrigger Canoe A40

Designs: 5c, Plane over ships in harbor. 8c, Civair plane over island.

**1970, Dec. 9** **Litho.** *Perf. 13½*

| No. | Type | Description | Unused | Used |
|---|---|---|---|---|
| 136 | A40 | 3c multicolored | .25 | .25 |
| 137 | A40 | 5c multicolored | .25 | .25 |
| 138 | A40 | 8c multicolored | .25 | .25 |
| | | *Nos. 136-138 (3)* | .75 | .75 |

Opening of Niue Airport.

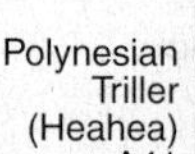

Polynesian Triller (Heahea) A41

Birds: 10c, Crimson-crowned fruit pigeon (kulukulu). 20c, Blue-crowned lory (henga).

**1971, June 23** **Litho.** *Perf. 13½x13*

| No. | Type | Description | Unused | Used |
|---|---|---|---|---|
| 139 | A41 | 5c multicolored | .25 | .25 |
| 140 | A41 | 10c multicolored | .50 | .25 |
| 141 | A41 | 20c multicolored | .85 | .25 |
| | | *Nos. 139-141 (3)* | 1.60 | .75 |

**Christmas Issue**

Holy Night, by Carlo Maratta — A41a

**1971, Oct. 6 Photo.** ***Perf. 13x13½***
**142** A41a 3c orange & multi .35 .25

People of Niue — A42

**1971, Nov. 17**
**143** A42 4c Boy .25 .25
**144** A42 6c Girl .25 .25
**145** A42 9c Man .25 .35
**146** A42 14c Woman .25 .70
*Nos. 143-146 (4)* 1.00 1.55

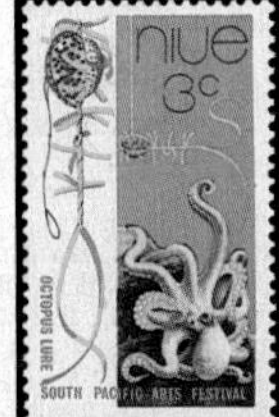


Octopus Lure and Octopus — A43

5c, Warrior and weapons. 10c, Sika (spear) throwing, horiz. 25c, Vivi dance, horiz.

**1972, May 3 Litho.** ***Perf. 13x13½***
**147** A43 3c blue & multi .25 .25
**148** A43 5c rose & multi .25 .25
**149** A43 10c blue & multi .25 .25
**150** A43 25c yellow & multi .25 .25
*Nos. 147-150 (4)* 1.00 1.00

So. Pacific Festival of Arts, Fiji, May 6-20.

Alofi Wharf A44

South Pacific Commission Emblem and: 5c, Health service. 6c, School children. 18c, Cattle and dwarf palms.

**1972, Sept. 6 Litho.** ***Perf. 13½x14***
**151** A44 4c blue & multi .25 .25
**152** A44 5c blue & multi .25 .25
**153** A44 6c blue & multi .25 .25
**154** A44 18c blue & multi .25 .25
*Nos. 151-154 (4)* 1.00 1.00

So. Pacific Commission, 25th anniv.

**Christmas Issue**

Madonna and Child, by Murillo — A44a

**1972, Oct. 4 Photo.** ***Perf. 11½***
**155** A44a 3c gray & multi .30 .25

Pempheris Oualensis A45

Designs: Various fish.

***Perf. 13½x13***
**1973, June 27 Litho. Unwmk.**
**156** A45 8c shown .35 .35
**157** A45 10c Cephalopholis .35 .35
**158** A45 15c Variola louti .40 .40
**159** A45 20c Etelis carbunculus .45 .45
*Nos. 156-159 (4)* 1.55 1.55

Flowers, by Jan Breughel — A46

Paintings of Flowers: 5c, by Hans Bollongier. 10c, by Rachel Ruysch.

**1973, Nov. 21 Litho.** ***Perf. 13½x13***
**160** A46 4c bister & multi .25 .25
**161** A46 5c orange brn & multi .25 .25
**162** A46 10c emerald & multi .25 .25
*Nos. 160-162 (3)* .75 .75

Christmas.

Capt. Cook and "Resolution" — A47

Capt. Cook and: 3c, Cook's landing place and ship. 8c, Map of Niue. 20c, Administration Building and flag of 1774.

**1974, June 20 Litho.** ***Perf. 13½x14***
**163** A47 2c multicolored .25 .25
**164** A47 3c multicolored .25 .25
**165** A47 8c multicolored .25 .30
**166** A47 20c multicolored .35 .55
*Nos. 163-166 (4)* 1.10 1.35

Bicentenary of Cook's landing on Niue.

King Fataaiki — A48

Annexation Day, Oct. 19, 1900 — A49

Village Meeting A50

Design: 10c, Legislative Assembly Building.

***Perf. 14x13½, 13½x14***
**1974, Oct. 19 Litho.**
**167** A48 4c multicolored .25 .25
**168** A49 8c multicolored .25 .25
**169** A50 10c multicolored .25 .25
**170** A50 20c multicolored .25 .25
*Nos. 167-170 (4)* 1.00 1.00

Referendum for Self-government, 9/3/74.

Decorated Bicycle — A51

Christmas: 10c, Decorated motorcycle. 20c, Going to church by truck.

**1974, Nov. 13 Litho.** ***Perf. 12½***
**171** A51 3c green & multi .25 .25
**172** A51 10c dull blue & multi .25 .25
**173** A51 20c brown & multi .25 .25
*Nos. 171-173 (3)* .75 .75

Children Going to Church A52

Children's Drawings: 5c, Child on bicycle trailing balloons. 10c, Balloons and gifts hanging from tree.

**1975, Oct. 29 Litho.** ***Perf. 14½***
**174** A52 4c multicolored .25 .25
**175** A52 5c multicolored .25 .25
**176** A52 10c multicolored .25 .25
*Nos. 174-176 (3)* .75 .75

Christmas.

Opening of Tourist Hotel A53

Design: 20c, Hotel, building and floor plan.

**1975, Nov. 19 Litho.** ***Perf. 14x13½***
**177** A53 8c multicolored .25 .25
**178** A53 20c multicolored .25 .25

Preparing Ground for Taro A54

2c, Planting taro (root vegetable). 3c, Banana harvest. 4c, Bush plantation. 5c, Shellfish gathering. 10c, Reef fishing. 20c, Luku (fern) harvest. 50c, Canoe fishing. $1, Husking coconuts. $2, Hunting uga (land crab).

**1976, Mar. 3 Litho.** ***Perf. 13½x14***
**179** A54 1c multicolored .25 .25
**180** A54 2c multicolored .25 .25
**181** A54 3c multicolored .25 .25
**182** A54 4c multicolored .25 .25
**183** A54 5c multicolored .25 .25
**184** A54 10c multicolored .25 .25
**185** A54 20c multicolored .25 .25
**186** A54 50c multicolored .25 .50
**187** A54 $1 multicolored .25 .75
**188** A54 $2 multicolored .75 1.00
*Nos. 179-188 (10)* 3.00 4.00

See #222-231. For surcharges see #203-210.

Water Tower, Girl Drawing Water — A55

15c, Teleprinter & Niue radio station. 20c, Instrument panel, generator & power station.

**1976, July 7 Litho.** ***Perf. 14x14½***
**189** A55 10c multicolored .25 .25
**190** A55 15c multicolored .25 .25
**191** A55 20c multicolored .25 .25
*Nos. 189-191 (3)* .75 .75

Technical achievements.

Christmas Tree (Flamboyant) and Administration Building — A56

Christmas: 15c, Avatele Church, interior.

**1976, Sept. 15 Litho.** ***Perf. 14½***
**192** A56 9c orange & multi .25 .25
**193** A56 15c orange & multi .25 .25

Elizabeth II, Coronation Portrait, and Westminster Abbey — A57

Design: $2, Coronation regalia.

**1977, June 7 Photo.** ***Perf. 13½***
**194** A57 $1 multicolored .50 .50
**195** A57 $2 multicolored 1.25 .75
*a.* Souvenir sheet of 2, #194-195 2.00 2.00

25th anniv. of reign of Elizabeth II. Nos. 194-195 each printed in sheets of 5 stamps and label showing Niue flag and Union Jack.

For surcharge see No. 213.

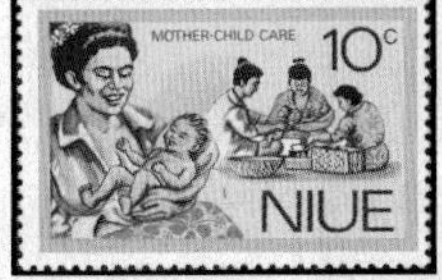


Mothers and Infants A58

Designs: 15c, Mobile school dental clinic. 20c, Elderly couple and home.

**1977, June 29 Litho.** ***Perf. 14½***
**196** A58 10c multicolored .25 .25
**197** A58 15c multicolored .25 .25
**198** A58 20c multicolored .25 .25
*Nos. 196-198 (3)* .75 .75

Personal (social) services.

For surcharges see Nos. 211-212.

Annunciation, by Rubens — A59

Rubens Paintings (details, Virgin and Child): 12c, Adoration of the Kings. 20c, Virgin with Garland. 35c, Holy Family.

**1977, Nov. 15 Photo.** ***Perf. 13x13½***
**199** A59 10c multicolored .25 .25
**200** A59 12c multicolored .25 .25
**201** A59 20c multicolored .35 .50
**202** A59 35c multicolored .40 .80
*a.* Souvenir sheet of 4, #199-202 1.75 1.75
*Nos. 199-202 (4)* 1.25 1.80

Christmas and 400th birth anniversary of Peter Paul Rubens (1577-1640). Nos. 199-202 each printed in sheets of 6 stamps.

**Stamps of 1976-77 Surcharged with New Value and 4 Bars in Black or Gold**
**Printing and Perforations as Before**

**1977, Nov. 15**

**203** A54 12c on 1c (#179) .45 .25
**204** A54 16c on 2c (#180) .50 .30
**205** A54 30c on 3c (#181) .50 .40
**206** A54 35c on 4c (#182) .50 .45
**207** A54 40c on 5c (#183) .50 .50
**208** A54 60c on 20c (#185) .50 .50
**209** A54 70c on $1 (#187) .50 .50
**210** A54 85c on $2 (#188) .50 .60
**211** A58 $1.10 on 10c (#196) .50 .60
**212** A58 $2.60 on 20c (#198) .85 .65
**213** A57 $3.20 on $2 (#195, G) 1.05 .75
*Nos. 203-213 (11)* 6.35 5.50

"An Inland View in Atooi," by John Webber — A60

Scenes in Hawaii, by John Webber: 16c, A View of Karakooa in Owyhee. 20c, An Offering Before Capt. Cook in the Sandwich Islands. 30c, Tereoboo, King of Owyhee, bringing presents (boats). 35c, Masked rowers in boat.

**1978, Jan. 18 Photo.** ***Perf. 13½***

**214** A60 12c gold & multi .70 .35
**215** A60 16c gold & multi .75 .40
**216** A60 20c gold & multi .75 .50
**217** A60 30c gold & multi .85 .60
**218** A60 35c gold & multi .90 .65
*a.* Souv. sheet, #214-218 + label 4.50 2.75
*Nos. 214-218 (5)* 3.95 2.50

Bicentenary of Capt. Cook's arrival in Hawaii. Nos. 214-218 printed in sheets of 5 stamps and one label showing flags of Hawaii and Niue.

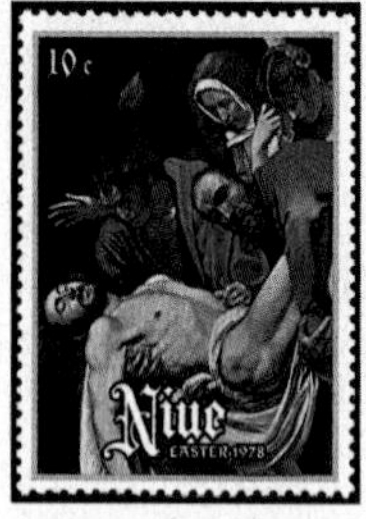


Descent from the Cross, by Caravaggio A61

Easter: 20c, Burial of Christ, by Bellini.

**1978, Mar. 15 Photo.** ***Perf. 13x13½***

**219** A61 10c multicolored .25 .25
**220** A61 20c multicolored .35 .25
*a.* Souv. sheet, #219-220, perf. 13½ 1.00 1.00

Nos. 219-220 issued in sheets of 8.
See Nos. B1-B2.

Souvenir Sheet

Elizabeth II — A62

**1978, June 26 Photo.** ***Perf. 13***

**221** A62 Sheet of 6 3.00 3.00
*a.* $1.10 Niue and UK flags .50 .75
*b.* $1.10 shown .50 .75
*c.* $1.10 Queen's New Zealand flag .50 .75
*d.* Souvenir sheet of 3 2.25 2.25

25th anniv. of coronation of Elizabeth II. No. 221 contains 2 horizontal se-tenant strips of Nos. 221a-221c, separated by horizontal gutter showing coronation coach. No. 221d contains a vertical se-tenant strip of Nos. 221a-221c.

**Type of 1977**

12c, Preparing ground for taro. 16c, Planting taro. 30c, Banana harvest. 35c, Bush plantation. 40c, Shellfish gathering. 60c, Reef fishing. 75c, Luku (fern) harvest. $1.10, Canoe fishing. $3.20, Husking coconuts. $4.20, Hunting uga (land crab).

**1978, Oct. 27 Litho.** ***Perf. 14***

**222** A54 12c multicolored .25 .25
**223** A54 16c multicolored .25 .25
**224** A54 30c multicolored .25 .25
**225** A54 35c multicolored .25 .25
**226** A54 40c multicolored .25 .25
**227** A54 60c multicolored .30 .35
**228** A54 75c multicolored .35 .40
**229** A54 $1.10 multicolored .45 .50
**230** A54 $3.20 multicolored 1.25 1.50
**231** A54 $4.20 multicolored 1.90 2.25
*Nos. 222-231 (10)* 5.50 6.25

Celebration of the Rosary, by Dürer — A63

Designs: 30c, Nativity, by Dürer. 35c, Adoration of the Kings, by Dürer.

**1978, Nov. 30 Photo.** ***Perf. 13***

**232** A63 20c multicolored .30 .30
**233** A63 30c multicolored .45 .45
**234** A63 35c multicolored .50 .50
*a.* Souv. sheet, #232-234 + label 1.60 1.60
*Nos. 232-234 (3)* 1.25 1.25

Christmas and 450th death anniversary of Albrecht Dürer (1471-1528). Nos. 232-234 each printed in sheets of 5 stamps and descriptive label.
See Nos. B3-B5.

Pietà, by Gregorio Fernandez — A64

Easter: 35c, Burial of Christ, by Pedro Roldan.

**1979, Apr. 2**

**235** A64 30c multicolored .35 .35
**236** A64 35c multicolored .40 .40
*a.* Souvenir sheet of 2, #235-236 1.50 1.50

See Nos. B6-B7.

Child, by Franz Hals — A65

IYC (Emblem and Details from Paintings): 16c, Nurse and Child. 20c, Child of the Duke of Osuna, by Goya. 30c, Daughter of Robert Strozzi, by Titian. 35c, Children Eating Fruit, by Murillo.

**1979, May 31 Photo.** ***Perf. 14***

**237** A65 16c multicolored .25 .25
**238** A65 20c multicolored .35 .35
**239** A65 30c multicolored .40 .40
**240** A65 35c multicolored .50 .50
*a.* Souvenir sheet of 4, #237-240 2.10 2.10
*Nos. 237-240 (4)* 1.50 1.50

See Nos. B8-B11.

Penny Black, Bath Mail Coach, Rowland Hill — A66

30c, Basel #3L1 & Alpine village coach. 35c, US #1 & 1st US transatlantic mail ship. 50c, France #3 & French railroad mail car, 1849. 60c, Bavaria #1 & Bavarian mail coach.

**1979, July 3 Photo.** ***Perf. 14***

**241** A66 20c Pair, #a.-b. .40 .40
**242** A66 30c Pair, #a.-b. .55 .55
**243** A66 35c Pair, #a.-b. .65 .65
**244** A66 50c Pair, #a.-b. 1.00 1.00
**245** A66 60c Pair, #a.-b. 1.10 1.10
*c.* Souv. sheet of 10, #241-245 + 2 labels 4.25 4.25
*Nos. 241-245 (5)* 3.70 3.70

Sir Rowland Hill (1795-1879), originator of penny postage.
For overprints and surcharges see Nos. 281-285, B16, B21, B26, B30, B33, B41.

Cook's Landing at Botany Bay A68

18th Century Paintings: 30c, Cook's Men during a Landing on Erromanga. 35c, Resolution and Discovery in Queen Charlotte's Sound. 75c, Death of Capt. Cook on Hawaii, by Johann Zoffany.

**1979, July 30 Photo.** ***Perf. 14***

**251** A68 20c multicolored .65 .30
**252** A68 30c multicolored .85 .40
**253** A68 35c multicolored 1.10 .50
**254** A68 75c multicolored 1.10 .90
*a.* Souv. sheet, #251-254, perf. 13½ 3.75 3.75
*Nos. 251-254 (4)* 3.70 2.10

200th death anniv. of Capt. James Cook.
For surcharges see Nos. B18, B23, B28, B36.

Apollo 11 Lift-off — A69

**1979, Sept. 27 Photo.** ***Perf. 13½***

**255** A69 30c shown .35 .35
**256** A69 35c Lunar module .40 .40
**257** A69 60c Splashdown .70 .70
*a.* Souvenir sheet of 3 1.90 1.90
*Nos. 255-257 (3)* 1.45 1.45

Apollo 11 moon landing, 10th anniversary. No. 257a contains Nos. 255-257 in changed colors.
For surcharges see Nos. B24, B29, B35.

Virgin and Child, by P. Serra — A70

Virgin and Child by: 25c, R. di Mur. 30c, S. diG. Sasseta. 50c, J. Huguet.

**1979, Nov. 29 Photo.** ***Perf. 13***

**258** A70 20c multicolored .25 .25
**259** A70 25c multicolored .25 .25
**260** A70 30c multicolored .25 .25
**261** A70 50c multicolored .25 .25
*a.* Souvenir sheet of 4, #258-261 1.40 1.40
*Nos. 258-261 (4)* 1.00 1.00

Christmas. See Nos. B12-B15. For surcharges see Nos. B19-B20, B25, B32.

Pietà, by Giovanni Bellini — A71

Easter (Pietà, Paintings by): 30c, Botticelli. 35c, Anthony Van Dyck.

**1980, Apr. 2 Photo.** ***Perf. 13***

**262** A71 25c multicolored .30 .30
**263** A71 30c multicolored .35 .35
**264** A71 35c multicolored .40 .40
*Nos. 262-264 (3)* 1.05 1.05

See Nos. B37-B40.

A72

#265a, Ceremonial Stool, New Guinea (shown). #265b, Ku-Tagwa plaque. #265c, Suspension hook. #266a, Platform post. #266b, Canoe ornament. #266c, Carved figure. #266d, Woman and child. #267a, God A'a, statue. #267b, Tangaroa, statue. #267c, Ivory pendant. #267d, Tapa cloth. #268a, Maori feather box. #268b, Hei-tiki. #268c, House post. #268d, God Ku, feather image.

**1980, July 30 Photo.** ***Perf. 13***

**265** A72 20c Strip of 4, #a.-d. .65 .65
**266** A72 25c Strip of 4, #a.-d. .80 .80
**267** A72 30c Strip of 4, #a.-d. .95 .95
**268** A72 35c Strip of 4, #a.-d. 1.10 1.10

**Souvenir Sheets of 4**

*e.* #265a, 266a, 267a, 268a 1.10 1.10
*f.* #265b, 266b, 267b, 268b 1.10 1.10
*g.* #265c, 266c, 267c, 268c 1.10 1.10
*h.* #265d, 266d, 267d, 268d 1.10 1.10
*Nos. 265-268 (4)* 3.50 3.50

3rd South Pacific Festival of Arts, Port Moresby, Papua New Guinea, June 30-July 12. Stamps in souvenir sheets have 2c surtax.
For surcharges see Nos. 626-629.

**Nos. 241-250, Overprinted in Black on Silver**

**1980, Aug. 22** ***Perf. 14***

**281** A66 20c Pair, #a.-b. .50 .50
**282** A66 30c Pair, #a.-b. .70 .70
**283** A66 35c Pair, #a.-b. .80 .80
**284** A66 50c Pair, #a.-b. 1.10 1.10
**285** A66 60c Pair, #a.-b. 1.40 1.40
*Nos. 281-285 (5)* 4.50 4.50

ZEAPEX '80, New Zealand International Stamp Exhibition, Auckland, Aug. 23-31.

Queen Mother Elizabeth, 80th Birthday — A73

**1980, Sept. 15 Photo. *Perf. 13x13½***

| | | | | |
|---|---|---|---|---|
| **291** | A73 | $1.10 multicolored | .90 | 1.40 |

**Souvenir Sheet**

| | | | | |
|---|---|---|---|---|
| **292** | A73 | $3 multicolored | 2.00 | 2.00 |

No. 291 issued in sheets of 5 and label showing coad of arms.

A74

#293a, 100-meter dash. #293b, Allen Wells, England. #294a, 400-Meter freestyle. #294b, Ines Diers, DDR. #295a, Soling class yachting. #295b, Denmark. #296a, Soccer. #296b, Czechoslovakia.

**1980, Oct. 30 Photo. *Perf. 14***

| | | | | |
|---|---|---|---|---|
| **293** | A74 | 20c Pair, #a.-b. | .45 | .45 |
| **294** | A74 | 25c Pair, #a.-b. | .50 | .50 |
| **295** | A74 | 30c Pair, #a.-b. | .60 | .60 |
| **296** | A74 | 35c Pair, #a.-b. | .70 | .70 |
| | | *Nos. 293-296 (4)* | 2.25 | 2.25 |

22nd Summer Olympic Games, Moscow, July 19-Aug. 3.

See No. B42.

Virgin and Child, by del Sarto — A76

Paintings of Virgin & Child, by Andrea del Sarto.

**1980, Nov. 28 Photo. *Perf. 13x13½***

| | | | | |
|---|---|---|---|---|
| **301** | A76 | 20c multicolored | .25 | .25 |
| **302** | A76 | 25c multicolored | .25 | .25 |
| **303** | A76 | 30c multicolored | .25 | .25 |
| **304** | A76 | 35c multicolored | .25 | .25 |
| *a.* | | Souvenir sheet of 4, #301-304 | 1.00 | 1.25 |
| | | *Nos. 301-304 (4)* | 1.00 | 1.00 |

Christmas and 450th death anniversary of Andrea del Sarto.

See Nos. B43-B46.

A77

Golden Shower Tree — A77a

#317a, Phalaenopsis sp. #317b, Moth Orchid. #318a, Euphorbia pulcherrima. #318b, Poinsettia. #319a, Thunbergia alata. #319b, Black-eyed Susan. #320a, Cochlospermum hibiscoides. #320b, Buttercup tree. #321a, Begonia sp. #321b, Begonia. #322a, Plumeria sp. #322b, Frangipani. #323a, Sterlitzia reginae. #323b, Bird of paradise. #324a, Hibiscus syriacus. #324b, Rose of Sharon. #325a, Nymphaea sp. #325b, Water lily. #326a, Tibouchina sp. #326b, Princess flower. #327a, Nelumbo sp. #327b, Lotus. #328a, Hybrid hibiscus. #328b, Yellow hibiscus.

**1981-82 Photo. *Perf. 13x13½***

| | | | | |
|---|---|---|---|---|
| **317** | A77 | 2c Pair, #a.-b. | .25 | .25 |
| **318** | A77 | 5c Pair, #a.-b. | .25 | .25 |
| **319** | A77 | 10c Pair, #a.-b. | .25 | .25 |
| **320** | A77 | 15c Pair, #a.-b. | .30 | .30 |
| **321** | A77 | 20c Pair, #a.-b. | .40 | .40 |
| **322** | A77 | 25c Pair, #a.-b. | .50 | .50 |
| **323** | A77 | 30c Pair, #a.-b. | .55 | .55 |
| **324** | A77 | 35c Pair, #a.-b. | .65 | .65 |
| **325** | A77 | 40c Pair, #a.-b. | .70 | .70 |
| **326** | A77 | 50c Pair, #a.-b. | 1.00 | 1.00 |
| **327** | A77 | 60c Pair, #a.-b. | 1.10 | 1.10 |
| **328** | A77 | 80c Pair, #a.-b. | 1.60 | 1.60 |

***Perf. 13½***

| | | | | |
|---|---|---|---|---|
| **329** | A77a | $1 shown | 1.00 | 1.00 |
| **330** | A77a | $2 Orchid var. | 2.00 | 2.00 |
| **331** | A77a | $3 Orchid sp. | 2.75 | 2.75 |
| **332** | A77a | $4 Poinsettia | 4.00 | 4.00 |
| **333** | A77a | $6 Hybrid hibiscus | 5.75 | 5.75 |
| **334** | A77a | $10 Hibiscus rosa-sinensis | 10.00 | 10.00 |
| | | *Nos. 317-334 (18)* | 33.05 | 33.05 |

Issued: 2c, 5c, 10c, 15c, 20c, 25c, Apr. 2; 30c, 35c, 40c, 50c, 60c, 80c, May 26; $1, $2, $3, Dec. 9, 1981; $4, $6, $10, Jan. 15, 1982.

For surcharges and overprints see Nos. 406-409, 413E, 594-595, O14, O16, O19.

Jesus Defiled, by El Greco A78

Easter (Paintings): 50c, Pieta, by Fernando Gallego. 60c, The Supper of Emaus, by Jacopo da Pontormo.

**1981, Apr. 10 *Perf. 14***

| | | | | |
|---|---|---|---|---|
| **337** | A78 | 35c multicolored | .40 | .40 |
| **338** | A78 | 50c multicolored | .65 | .65 |
| **339** | A78 | 60c multicolored | .75 | .75 |
| | | *Nos. 337-339 (3)* | 1.80 | 1.80 |

See Nos. B47-B50.

Prince Charles and Lady Diana — A79

**1981, June 26 Photo. *Perf. 14***

| | | | | |
|---|---|---|---|---|
| **340** | A79 | 75c Charles | .50 | .50 |
| **341** | A79 | 95c Lady Diana | .65 | .65 |
| **342** | A79 | $1.20 shown | .90 | .90 |
| *a.* | | Souvenir sheet of 3, #340-342 | 2.50 | 2.50 |
| | | *Nos. 340-342 (3)* | 2.05 | 2.05 |

Royal Wedding. Nos. 340-342 each printed in sheets of 5 plus label showing St. Paul's Cathedral.

For overprints and surcharges see Nos. 357-359, 410, 412, 455, 596-598, B52-B55.

1982 World Cup Soccer A80

No. 343: Players dribbling ball. No. 344, Players kicking ball (#a, b.), heading ball (#c.). No. 345, Players kicking ball (#a, b.), goalie (#c.)

**1981, Oct. 16 Photo. *Perf. 13***

| | | | | |
|---|---|---|---|---|
| **343** | | Strip of 3 | .80 | .80 |
| *a.-c.* | A80 | 30c any single | .25 | .25 |
| **344** | | Strip of 3 | 1.05 | 1.05 |
| *a.-c.* | A80 | 35c any single | .35 | .35 |
| **345** | | Strip of 3 | 1.20 | 1.20 |
| *a.-c.* | A80 | 40c any single | .40 | .40 |
| | | *Nos. 343-345 (3)* | 3.05 | 3.05 |

See No. B51.

Christmas 1981 — A81

Rembrandt Paintings: 20c, Holy Family with Angels, 1645. 35c, Presentation in the Temple, 1631. 50c, Virgin and Child in Temple, 1629. 60c, Holy Family, 1640.

**1981-82 Photo. *Perf. 14x13***

| | | | | |
|---|---|---|---|---|
| **346** | A81 | 20c multicolored | .35 | .35 |
| **347** | A81 | 35c multicolored | .80 | .80 |
| **348** | A81 | 50c multicolored | 1.10 | 1.10 |
| **349** | A81 | 60c multicolored | 1.25 | 1.25 |
| *a.* | | Souvenir sheet of 4, #346-349 | 3.50 | 3.50 |
| | | *Nos. 346-349 (4)* | 3.50 | 3.50 |

**Souvenir Sheets**

| | | | | |
|---|---|---|---|---|
| **350** | A81 | 80c + 5c like #346 | .80 | .80 |
| **351** | A81 | 80c + 5c like #347 | .80 | .80 |
| **352** | A81 | 80c + 5c like #348 | .80 | .80 |
| **353** | A81 | 80c + 5c like #349 | .80 | .80 |

Surtax was for school children.

Issued: #346-349, 12/11; others, 1/22/82.

21st Birthday of Princess Diana — A82

**1982, July 1 *Perf. 14***

| | | | | |
|---|---|---|---|---|
| **354** | A82 | 50c Charles | .50 | .50 |
| **355** | A82 | $1.25 Wedding | 1.25 | 1.25 |
| **356** | A82 | $2.50 Diana | 2.25 | 2.25 |
| *a.* | | Souvenir sheet of 3, #354-356 | 6.00 | 6.00 |
| | | *Nos. 354-356 (3)* | 4.00 | 4.00 |

Nos. 354-356 each printed in sheets of 5 plus label showing wedding day picture.

For overprints and surcharges see Nos. 359B-359D, 411, 413, 456.

**Nos. 340-342a Overprinted**

Type I

Type II

Type III

**1982, July 23 *Perf. 14***

| | | | | |
|---|---|---|---|---|
| **357** | A79 | 75c multi (I) | 1.40 | 1.40 |
| **357A** | A79 | 75c multi (II) | 1.40 | 1.40 |
| **358** | A79 | 95c multi (I) | 1.75 | 1.75 |
| **358A** | A79 | 95c multi (II) | 1.75 | 1.75 |
| **359** | A79 | $1.20 multi (I) | 2.25 | 2.25 |
| **359A** | A79 | $1.20 multi (II) | 2.25 | 2.25 |
| | | *Nos. 357-359A (6)* | 10.80 | 10.80 |

**Souvenir Sheet**

| | | | | |
|---|---|---|---|---|
| **359B** | A79 | Sheet of 3, #a.-c. | 7.50 | 7.50 |
| *a.* | | 75c multi (III) | 2.00 | 2.00 |
| *b.* | | 95c multi (III) | 2.00 | 2.00 |
| *c.* | | $1.20 multi (III) | 2.00 | 2.00 |

Nos. 357/357A, 358/358A and 359/359A were printed in small sheets containing three stamps overprinted Type I, two overprinted type II and one label.

Birthday Type of 1982 Inscribed in Silver

**1982 Photo. *Perf. 14***

| | | | | |
|---|---|---|---|---|
| **359C** | A82 | 50c like #354 | .70 | .70 |
| **359D** | A82 | $1.25 like #355 | 1.75 | 1.75 |
| **359E** | A82 | $2.50 like #356 | 3.25 | 3.25 |
| *a.* | | Souvenir sheet of 3 | 7.00 | 7.00 |
| | | *Nos. 359C-359E (3)* | 5.70 | 5.70 |

Christmas — A83

Princess Diana Holding Prince William and Paintings of Infants by: 40c, Bronzino (1502-1572). 52c, Murillo (1617-1682). 83c, Murillo, diff. $1.05, Boucher (1703-1770). Singles in No. 363a: 34x30mm, showing paintings only.

**1982, Dec. 3 Photo. *Perf. 13½x14½***

| | | | | |
|---|---|---|---|---|
| **360** | A83 | 40c multicolored | 1.20 | 1.20 |
| **361** | A83 | 52c multicolored | 1.40 | 1.40 |
| **362** | A83 | 83c multicolored | 2.40 | 2.40 |
| **363** | A83 | $1.05 multicolored | 3.50 | 3.50 |
| *a.* | | Souvenir sheet of 4, #364-367 | 6.75 | 6.75 |
| | | *Nos. 360-363 (4)* | 8.50 | 8.50 |

**Souvenir Sheets**

| | | | | |
|---|---|---|---|---|
| **364** | A83 | 80c + 5c like #360 | 2.40 | 2.40 |
| **365** | A83 | 80c + 5c like #361 | 2.40 | 2.40 |
| **366** | A83 | 80c + 5c like #362 | 2.40 | 2.40 |
| **367** | A83 | 80c + 5c like #363 | 2.40 | 2.40 |

Nos. 364-367 each contain one 30x42mm stamp showing Royal family. Surtax was for children's funds.

Commonwealth Day — A84

No. 368, Flag, Premier Robert R. Rex. No. 369, Resolution, Adventurer. No. 370, Passion flower. No. 371, Lime branch.

**1983, Mar. 14 Photo. *Perf. 13***

| | | | | |
|---|---|---|---|---|
| **368** | A84 | 70c multi | .75 | .75 |
| **369** | A84 | 70c multi | .75 | .75 |
| **370** | A84 | 70c multi | .75 | .75 |
| **371** | A84 | 70c multi | .75 | .75 |
| *a.* | | Block of 4, #368-371 | 3.00 | 3.00 |

For overprints see Nos. 484-487.

Scouting Year — A85

**1983, Apr. 28 Photo. *Perf. 13***

| | | | | |
|---|---|---|---|---|
| **372** | A85 | 40c Flag signals | .70 | .70 |
| **373** | A85 | 50c Tree planting | .80 | .80 |
| **374** | A85 | 83c Map reading | 1.50 | 1.50 |
| | | *Nos. 372-374 (3)* | 3.00 | 3.00 |

**Souvenir Sheet**

| | | | | |
|---|---|---|---|---|
| **375** | | Sheet of 3 | 3.00 | 3.00 |
| *a.* | A85 | 40c + 3c like 40c | .75 | .75 |
| *b.* | A85 | 50c + 3c like 50c | .80 | .80 |
| *c.* | A85 | 83c + 3c like 83c | 1.30 | 1.30 |

**Nos. 372-375 Overprinted in Black on Silver: "XV WORLD JAMBOREE CANADA"**

**1983, July 14** **Photo.**

**376** A85 40c multicolored .60 .60
**377** A85 50c multicolored .75 .75
**378** A85 83c multicolored 1.15 1.15
*Nos. 376-378 (3)* 2.50 2.50

**Souvenir Sheet**

**379** Sheet of 3 2.75 2.75
*a.* A85 40c + 3c multicolored .60 .60
*b.* A85 50c + 3c multicolored .70 .70
*c.* A85 83c + 3c multicolored 1.40 1.40

Save the Whales Campaign — A86

**1983, Aug. 15** ***Perf. 13x14***

**380** A86 12c Right whale .90 .50
**381** A86 25c Fin whale 1.30 .60
**382** A86 35c Sei whale 1.75 .95
**383** A86 40c Blue whale 2.00 1.10
**384** A86 58c Bowhead whale 2.25 1.25
**385** A86 70c Sperm whale 2.75 1.25
**386** A86 83c Humpback whale 3.00 1.75
**387** A86 $1.05 Lesser rorqual 3.75 1.90
**388** A86 $2.50 Gray whale 5.00 3.25
*Nos. 380-388 (9)* 22.70 12.55

Manned Flight Bicentenary — A87

25c, Montgolfier, 1783. 40c, Wright Bros. Flyer, 1903. 58c, Graf Zeppelin, 1928. 70c, Boeing 247, 1933. 83c, Apollo VIII, 1968. $1.05, Columbia space shuttle.

**1983, Oct. 14** **Photo.** ***Perf. 14***

**389** A87 25c multicolored .50 .50
**390** A87 40c multicolored .75 .75
**391** A87 58c multicolored 1.25 1.25
**392** A87 70c multicolored 1.75 1.75
**393** A87 83c multicolored 2.10 2.10
**394** A87 $1.05 multicolored 2.40 2.40
*a.* Souvenir sheet of 6 5.50 5.50
*Nos. 389-394 (6)* 8.75 8.75

No. 394a contains Nos. 389-394 inscribed "AIRMAIL."

Christmas A87a

Paintings by Raphael (1483-1520): 30c, Garvagh Madonna, National Gallery, London. 40c, Granduca Madonna, Pitti Gallery, Florence. 58c, Goldfinch Madonna, Uffizi Gallery, Florence. 70c, Holy Family of Francis I, Louvre, Paris. 83c, Holy Family with Saints, Alte Pinakothek, Munich.

**1983** **Photo.** ***Perf. 14***

**395** A87a 30c multicolored .60 .60
**396** A87a 40c multicolored .80 .80
**397** A87a 58c multicolored 1.20 1.20
**398** A87a 70c multicolored 1.30 1.30
**399** A87a 83c multicolored 1.60 1.60
*Nos. 395-399 (5)* 5.50 5.50

**Souvenir Sheets**

***Perf. 13½***

**400** Sheet of 5 4.00 4.00
*a.* A87a 30c + 3c like #395 .40 .40
*b.* A87a 40c + 3c like #396 .55 .55
*c.* A87a 58c + 3c like #397 .80 .80
*d.* A87a 70c + 3c like #398 .90 .90
*e.* A87a 83c + 3c like #399 1.10 1.10
**401** A87a 85c + 5c like #395 1.20 1.20
**402** A87a 85c + 5c like #396 1.20 1.20
**403** A87a 85c + 5c like #397 1.20 1.20
**404** A87a 85c + 5c like #398 1.20 1.20
**405** A87a 85c + 5c like #399 1.20 1.20

500th birth anniv. of Raphael.
Issued: #395-400, 11/25; #401-405, 12/29.

**Nos. 323, 326-328, 341, 355, 342, 356 and 331 Surcharged in Black or Gold with One or Two Bars**

**1983, Nov. 30** **Photo.**

**Pairs, #a.-b. (#406-409)**

**406** A77 52c on 30c 1.60 1.60
**407** A77 58c on 50c 1.75 1.75
**408** A77 70c on 60c 2.25 2.25
**409** A77 83c on 80c 2.75 2.75
**410** A79 $1.10 on 95c #341 1.60 1.60
**411** A82 $1.10 on $1.25 #355 (G) 1.60 1.60
**412** A79 $2.60 on $1.20 #342 4.00 4.00
**413** A82 $2.60 on $2.50 #356 (G) 4.00 4.00
**413A** A77a $3.70 on $3 #331 5.50 5.50
*Nos. 406-413A (9)* 25.05 25.05

World Communications Year — A88

**1984, Jan. 23** **Photo.** ***Perf. 13x13½***

**414** A88 40c Telegraph sender .45 .45
**415** A88 52c Early telephone .65 .65
**416** A88 83c Satellite 1.10 1.10
*a.* Souvenir sheet of 3, #414-416 2.00 2.00
*Nos. 414-416 (3)* 2.20 2.20

Moth Orchid — A89

Golden Shower Tree A90

25c, Poinsettia. 30c, Buttercup tree. 35c, Begonia. 40c, Frangipani. 52c, Bird of paradise. 58c, Rose of Sharon. 70c, Princess flower. 83c, Lotus. $1.05, Yellow hibiscus. $2.30, Orchid var. $3.90, Orchid sp. $5, Poinsettia, diff. $6.60, Hybrid hibiscus. $8.30, Hibiscus rosasinensis.

**1984** ***Perf. 13x13½***

**417** A89 12c shown .25 .25
**418** A89 25c multicolored .35 .35
**419** A89 30c multicolored .50 .50
**420** A89 35c multicolored .50 .50
**421** A89 40c multicolored .55 .55
**422** A89 52c multicolored .70 .70
**423** A89 58c multicolored .80 .80
**424** A89 70c multicolored 1.00 1.00
**425** A89 83c multicolored 1.10 1.10
**426** A89 $1.05 multicolored 1.60 1.60
**427** A90 $1.75 shown 1.60 1.60
**428** A90 $2.30 multicolored 2.25 2.25
**429** A90 $3.90 multicolored 3.50 3.50
**430** A90 $5 multicolored 4.50 4.50
**431** A90 $6.60 multicolored 6.00 6.00
**431A** A90 $8.30 multicolored 8.00 8.00
*Nos. 417-431A (16)* 33.20 33.20

Issued: #417-426, 2/20; #427-429, 5/10; others 6/18.
For overprints see #O1-O13, O15, O17-O18.

1984 Summer Olympics A91

Designs: Greek pottery designs, 3rd cent. BC. 30c, 70c vert.

**1984, Mar. 15** **Photo.** ***Perf. 14***

**432** A91 30c Discus .45 .45
**433** A91 35c Running .50 .50
**434** A91 40c Equestrian .55 .55
**435** A91 58c Boxing .80 .80
**436** A91 70c Javelin .95 .95
*Nos. 432-436 (5)* 3.25 3.25

For overprints and surcharges see #446-450, 480-483.

AUSIPEX '84, Australian Animals — A92

25c, Koala on gray branch. 35c, Koala sitting in curve of branch. 40c, Koala on green branch (yellow background). 58c, Koala on branch, arms stretched out in front. 70c, Koala on green branch (lt. blue green background). 83c, Kangaroo with joey, facing right. $1.05, Kangaroo with joey, facing left. $2.50, Kangaroo, tail in LR corner.

**1984** **Photo.** ***Perf. 14***

**437** A92 25c gold & multi .30 .30
**438** A92 35c gold & multi .40 .40
**439** A92 40c gold & multi .65 .65
**440** A92 58c gold & multi 1.00 1.00
**441** A92 70c gold & multi 1.30 1.30
**442** A92 83c gold & multi 1.50 1.50
**443** A92 $1.05 gold & multi 1.75 1.75
**444** A92 $2.50 gold & multi 4.00 4.00
*Nos. 437-444 (8)* 10.90 10.90

**Souvenir Sheets**

**445** Sheet of 2 + label 5.00 5.00
*a.* A92 $1.75 Wallaby 2.50 2.50
*b.* A92 $1.75 Koala, diff. 2.50 2.50
*c.* Sheet, #437-441, 445b, perf 13½ 4.50 4.50
*d.* Sheet, #442-444, 445a, perf 13½ 6.50 6.50

Nos. 442-444 airmail.
Issued: #437-444, Aug. 24; $445, Sept. 20.

**Nos. 432-436 Ovptd. with Event, Names of Gold Medalists, Country in Gold or Red**

**1984, Sept. 7** ***Perf. 14***

**446** A91 30c Danneberg .40 .40
**447** A91 35c Coe (R) .50 .50
**448** A91 40c Todd .55 .55
**449** A91 58c Biggs .80 .80
**450** A91 70c Haerkoenen 1.00 1.00
*Nos. 446-450 (5)* 3.25 3.25

10th Anniv. of Self Government — A93

**1984, Oct. 19** **Photo.** ***Perf. 13***

**451** A93 40c Niue flag .55 .55
**452** A93 58c Niue map 1.00 1.00
**453** A93 70c Ceremony 1.15 1.15
*a.* Souvenir sheet of 3, #451-453 2.50 2.50
*Nos. 451-453 (3)* 2.70 2.70

**Souvenir Sheet**

**454** A93 $2.50 like 70c 2.50 2.50

For overprints and surcharges see Nos. 655-660.

**Nos. 340, 354 Surcharged "Prince Henry / 15.9.84" and Bars and New Values in Red or Silver**

**1984, Oct. 22** **Photo.** ***Perf. 14***

**455** A79 $2 on 75c multi (R) 2.25 2.25
**456** A82 $2 on 50c multi (S) 2.25 2.25

Nos. 455-456 issued in sheets of 5 + label.

Christmas A94

Paintings: 40c, The Nativity, by A. Vaccaro. 58c, Virgin with Fly, anonymous. 70c, Adoration of the Shepherds, by B. Murillo. 83c, Flight into Egypt, by B. Murillo.

**1984, Oct. 19** **Photo.** ***Perf. 13x13½***

**457** A94 40c multicolored .55 .55
**458** A94 58c multicolored .80 .80
**459** A94 70c multicolored 1.00 1.00
**460** A94 83c multicolored 1.10 1.10
*Nos. 457-460 (4)* 3.45 3.45

**Souvenir Sheets**

**461** Sheet of 4 3.25 3.25
*a.* A94 40c + 5c Like 40c .55 .55
*b.* A94 58c + 5c Like 58c .70 .70
*c.* A94 70c + 5c Like 70c .90 .90
*d.* A94 83c + 5c Like 83c 1.00 1.00

***Perf. 13½***

**462** A94 95c + 10c Like 40c 1.25 1.25
**463** A94 95c + 10c Like 58c 1.25 1.25
**464** A94 95c + 10c Like 70c 1.25 1.25
**465** A94 95c + 10c Like 83c 1.25 1.25

Audubon Birth Bicentenary A95

Illustrations of North American bird species by artist/naturalist John J. Audubon: 40c, House wren. 70c, Veery. 83c, Grasshopper sparrow. $1.05, Henslow's sparrow. $2.50, Vesper sparrow.

**1985, Apr. 15** **Photo.** ***Perf. 14½***

**466** A95 40c multicolored 1.50 1.50
**467** A95 70c multicolored 2.00 2.00
**468** A95 83c multicolored 2.75 2.75
**469** A95 $1.05 multicolored 3.25 3.25
**470** A95 $2.50 multicolored 7.50 7.50
*Nos. 466-470 (5)* 17.00 17.00

**Souvenir Sheets**

***Perf. 14***

**471** A95 $1.75 like #466 2.50 2.50
**472** A95 $1.75 like #467 2.50 2.50
**473** A95 $1.75 like #468 2.50 2.50
**474** A95 $1.75 like #469 2.50 2.50
**475** A95 $1.75 like #470 2.50 2.50
*Nos. 471-475 (5)* 12.50 12.50

Queen Mother, 85th Birthday A96

Designs: 70c, Wearing mantle of the Order of the Garter. $1.15, With Queen Elizabeth II. $1.50, With Prince Charles. $3, Writing letter.

**1985, June 14** ***Perf. 13½x13***

**476** A96 70c multicolored 1.00 1.00
**477** A96 $1.15 multicolored 1.25 1.25
**478** A96 $1.50 multicolored 1.75 1.75
*a.* Souvenir sheet of 3 + label, #476-478 8.00 8.00
*Nos. 476-478 (3)* 4.00 4.00

**Souvenir Sheet**

***Perf. 13½***

**479** A96 $3 multicolored 4.25 4.25

Nos. 476-478 issued in sheets of 5 plus label. No. 479 contains one 39x36mm stamp. No. 478a issued 8/4/86, for 86th birthday.

**Nos. 432-433, 435-436 Overprinted "Mini South Pacific Games, Rarotonga" and Surcharged with Gold Bar and New Value in Black**

**1985, July 26** *Perf. 14*

**480** A91 52c on 95c multi .55 .55
**481** A91 83c on 58c multi 1.15 1.15
**482** A91 95c on 35c multi 1.30 1.30
**483** A91 $2 on 30c multi 2.50 2.50
*Nos. 480-483 (4)* 5.50 5.50

**Nos. 368-371 Overprinted with Conference Emblem and: "Pacific Islands Conference, Rarotonga"**

**1985, July 26** *Perf. 13½x13*

**484** A84 70c on #368 .75 .75
**485** A84 70c on #369 .75 .75
**486** A84 70c on #370 .75 .75
**487** A84 70c on #371 .75 .75
*a.* Block of 4, #484-487 3.00 3.00

A97

Paintings of children: 58c, Portrait of R. Strozzi's Daughter, by Titian. 70c, The Fifer, by Manet. $1.15, Portrait of a Young Girl, by Renoir. $1.50, Portrait of M. Berard, by Renoir.

**1985, Oct. 11** *Perf. 13*

**488** A97 58c multicolored 1.75 1.75
**489** A97 70c multicolored 2.00 2.00
**490** A97 $1.15 multicolored 3.50 3.50
**491** A97 $1.50 multicolored 4.50 4.50
*Nos. 488-491 (4)* 11.75 11.75

**Souvenir Sheets**

***Perf. 13x13½***

**492** A97 $1.75 + 10c like #488 5.00 5.00
**493** A97 $1.75 + 10c like #489 5.00 5.00
**494** A97 $1.75 + 10c like #490 5.00 5.00
**495** A97 $1.75 + 10c like #491 5.00 5.00

Intl. Youth Year.

A98

Christmas, Paintings (details) by Correggio: 58c, No. 500a, Virgin and Child. 85c, No. 500b, Adoration of the Magi. $1.05, No. 500c, Virgin and Child, diff. $1.45, No. 500d, Virgin and Child with St. Catherine.

**1985, Nov. 29** **Photo.** *Perf. 13x13½*

**496** A98 58c multicolored 1.25 1.25
**497** A98 85c multicolored 2.25 2.25
**498** A98 $1.05 multicolored 2.75 2.75
**499** A98 $1.45 multicolored 3.75 3.75
*Nos. 496-499 (4)* 10.00 10.00

**Souvenir Sheets**

**500** Sheet of 4 5.50 5.50
*a.-d.* A98 60c + 10c, any single 1.30 1.30

***Imperf***

**501** A98 65c like #496 1.25 1.25
**502** A98 95c like #497 1.75 1.75
**503** A98 $1.20 like #498 2.50 2.50
**504** A98 $1.75 like #499 3.50 3.50
*Nos. 500-504 (5)* 14.50 14.50

Nos. 501-504 each contain one 61x71mm stamp.

Halley's Comet — A99

The Constellations, fresco by Giovanni De Vecchi, Farnesio Palace, Caprarola, Italy.

**1986, Jan. 24** *Perf. 13½*

**505** A99 60c multicolored .90 .90
**506** A99 75c multicolored 1.10 1.00
**507** A99 $1.10 multicolored 1.50 1.50
**508** A99 $1.50 multicolored 2.40 2.40
*Nos. 505-508 (4)* 5.90 5.80

**Souvenir Sheet**

**509** Sheet of 4 8.00 8.00
*a.* A99 95c like #505 2.00 2.00
*b.* A99 95c 95c like #506 2.00 2.00
*c.* A99 95c like #507 2.00 2.00
*d.* A99 95c like #508 2.00 2.00

A100

Elizabeth II, 60th Birthday: $1.10, No. 513a, Elizabeth and Prince Philip at Windsor Castle. $1.50, No. 513b, At Balmoral. $2, No. 513c, Elizabeth at Buckingham Palace. $3, Elizabeth seated and Prince Philip.

**1986, Apr. 28** *Perf. 14½x13½*

**510** A100 $1.10 multicolored 1.00 1.00
**511** A100 $1.50 multicolored 1.50 1.50
**512** A100 $2 multicolored 2.00 2.00
*Nos. 510-512 (3)* 4.50 4.50

**Souvenir Sheets**

**513** Sheet of 3 2.75 2.75
*a.-c.* A100 75c any single .90 .90
**514** A100 $3 multicolored 3.50 3.50

For surcharges see Nos. 546-547.

A101

AMERIPEX '86: #515a, Washington, US #1. #515b, Jefferson, Roosevelt, Lincoln.

**1986, May 22** **Photo.** *Perf. 14*

**515** A101 $1 Pair, #a.-b. 7.75 7.75

A102

Paintings: $1, Statue under construction, 1883, by Victor Dargaud. $2.50, Unveiling the Statue of Liberty, 1886, by Edmund Morand (1829-1901).

**1986, July 4** *Perf. 13x13½*

**517** A102 $1 multicolored 2.25 2.25
**518** A102 $2.50 multicolored 5.50 5.50

**Souvenir Sheet**

**519** Sheet of 2 4.00 4.00
*a.* A102 $1.25 like #517 2.00 2.00
*b.* A102 $1.25 like #518 2.00 2.00

Statue of Liberty, cent.

Wedding of Prince Andrew and Sarah Ferguson — A103

Designs: $2.50, Portraits, Westminster Abbey. $5, Portraits.

**1986, July 23** *Perf. 13½x13*

**520** A103 $2.50 multicolored 4.00 4.00

**Souvenir Sheet**

**521** A103 $5 Portraits 8.25 8.25

No. 520 printed in sheets of 4. No. 521 contains one 45x32mm stamp.

STAMPEX '86, Adelaide, Aug. 4-10 — A104

Birds — 40c, Egretta alba, vert. 60c, Emblema picta. 75c, Aprosmictus scapularis, vert. 80c, Malurus lamberti. $1, Falco peregrinus, vert. $1.65, Halcyon azurea. $2.20, Melopsittacus undulatus, vert. $4.25,

***Perf. 13x13½, 13½x13***

**1986, Aug. 4** **Photo.**

**522** A104 40c multi 1.10 1.10
**523** A104 60c multi 1.60 1.60
**524** A104 75c multi 2.25 2.25
**525** A104 80c multi 2.50 2.50
**526** A104 $1 multi 3.00 3.00
**527** A104 $1.65 multi 4.75 4.75
**528** A104 $2.20 multi 7.00 7.00
**529** A104 $4.25 multi 13.00 13.00
*Nos. 522-529 (8)* 35.20 35.20

Christmas A105

Paintings in the Vatican Museum: 80c, No. 534a, Virgin and Child, by Perugino (1446-1523). $1.15, No. 534b, Virgin of St. N. dei Frari, by Titian. $1.80, No. 534c, Virgin with Milk, by Lorenzo di Credi (1459-1537). $2.60, $7.50, No. 534d, Foligno Madonna, by Raphael.

**1986, Nov. 14** **Litho.** *Perf. 14*

**530** A105 80c multi 1.60 1.60
**531** A105 $1.15 multi 2.25 2.25
**532** A105 $1.80 multi 4.00 4.00
**533** A105 $2.60 multi 6.00 6.00
*Nos. 530-533 (4)* 13.85 13.85

**Souvenir Sheets**

***Perf. 13½***

**534** Sheet of 4 11.00 11.00
*a.-d.* A105 $1.50 any single 2.75 2.75

***Perf. 14½x13½***

**535** A105 $7.50 multi 12.00 12.00

For surcharges see Nos. B56-B61.

**Souvenir Sheets**

Statue of Liberty, Cent. — A106

Photographs: No. 536a, Tall ship, bridge. No. 536b, Workmen, flame from torch. No. 536c, Workman, flame, diff. No. 536d, Ships, New York City. No. 536e, Tall ship, sailboat, bridge. No. 537a, Statue, front. No. 537b, Statue, left side. No. 537c, Torch dismantled. No. 537d, Statue, right side. No. 537e, Welder.

**1987, May 20**

**536** A106 Sheet of 5 + label 3.75 3.75
*a.-e.* 75c any single .75 .75
**537** A106 Sheet of 5 + label 3.75 3.75
*a.-e.* 75c any single, vert. .75 .75

Tennis Champions — A107

Olympic emblem, coin and: 80c, $1.15, $1.40, $1.80, Boris Becker. 85c, $1.05, $1.30, $1.75, Steffi Graf. Various action scenes.

**1987**

**538** A107 80c multi 2.50 2.50
**539** A107 85c multi 2.10 2.10
**540** A107 $1.05 multi 2.50 2.50
**541** A107 $1.15 multi 2.60 2.60
**542** A107 $1.30 multi 2.50 2.50
**543** A107 $1.40 multi 3.00 3.00
**544** A107 $1.75 multi 3.00 3.00
**545** A107 $1.80 multi 3.75 3.75
*Nos. 538-545 (8)* 21.95 21.95

Issued: 80c, $1.15, $1.40, $1.80, 9/25; others, 10/20.

For overprints see Nos. 560-563.

**Nos. 511-512 Surcharged "40th /WEDDING / ANNIV." with Denomination in Black on Gold**

***Perf. 14½x13½***

**1987, Nov. 20** **Photo.**

**546** A100 $4.85 on $1.50 #511 6.00 6.00
**547** A100 $4.85 on $2 #512 6.00 6.00

40th Wedding anniv. of Queen Elizabeth II and Prince Philip, Duke of Edinburgh.

Christmas — A108

Paintings (details) by Albrecht Durer (Angel with Lute on 80c, $1.05, $2.80): 80c, No. 551a, The Nativity. $1.05, No. 551b, Adoration of the Magi. $2.80, No. 551c, $7.50, Celebration of the Rosary.

**1987, Dec. 4** **Photo.** *Perf. 13½*

**548** A108 80c multi 1.75 1.75
**549** A108 $1.05 multi 2.25 2.25
**550** A108 $2.80 multi 5.00 5.00
*Nos. 548-550 (3)* 9.00 9.00

### Souvenir Sheets

**551** Sheet of 3 9.00 9.00
*a.-c.* A108 $1.30 any single 3.00 3.00
**552** A108 $7.50 multi 11.00 11.00

Size of Nos. 551a-551c: 49½x38½mm. No. 552 contains one 51x33mm stamp.

European Soccer Championships — A109

Highlights from Franz Beckenbauer's career: 20c, Match scene. 40c, German all-star team. 60c, Brussels, 1974. 80c, England, 1966. $1.05, Mexico, 1970. $1.30, Munich, 1974. $1.80, FC Bayern Munchen vs. Athletico Madrid.

**1988, June 20 Litho. *Perf. 14***

**553** A109 20c multi .40 .40
**554** A109 40c multi .80 .80
**555** A109 60c multi 1.25 1.25
**556** A109 80c multi 1.60 1.60
**557** A109 $1.05 multi 2.25 2.25
**558** A109 $1.30 multi 3.00 3.00
**559** A109 $1.80 multi 3.75 3.75
*Nos. 553-559 (7)* 13.05 13.05

### Nos. 539-540, 542 and 543 Ovptd.

*a.* "AUSTRALIA 24 JAN 88 / FRENCH OPEN 4 JUNE 88"
*b.* "WIMBLEDON 2 JULY 88 / U S OPEN 10 SEPT. 88"
*c.* "WOMEN'S TENNIS GRAND / SLAM: 10 SEPTEMBER 88"
*d.* "SEOUL OLYMPIC GAMES / GOLD MEDAL WINNER"

**1988, Oct. 14 Litho. *Perf. 13½x14***

**560** A107(a) 85c on No. 539 1.75 1.75
**561** A107(b) $1.05 on No. 540 2.25 2.25
**562** A107(c) $1.30 on No. 542 2.75 2.75
**563** A107(d) $1.75 on No. 543 3.75 3.75
*Nos. 560-563 (4)* 10.50 10.50

Steffi Graf, 1988 Olympic gold medalist; opportunities for youth in sports.

Christmas A110

Adoration of the Shepherds, by Rubens: 60c, Angels. 80c, Joseph and witness. $1.05, Madonna. $1.30, Christ child. $7.20, Entire painting.

**1988, Oct. 28 Photo. *Perf. 13½***

**564** A110 60c multi 1.40 1.40
**565** A110 80c multi 2.40 2.40
**566** A110 $1.05 multi 3.50 3.50
**567** A110 $1.30 multi 4.00 4.00
*Nos. 564-567 (4)* 11.30 11.30

### Souvenir Sheet

**568** A110 $7.20 multi 10.00 10.00

No. 568 contains one 40x50mm stamp.

First Moon Landing, 20th Anniv. A111

Apollo 11: #a, Mission emblem and astronaut. #b, Earth, Moon and simplified flight plan. #c, Olive branch, Apollo 1 mission emblem and astronaut on Moon. Printed in continuous design.

**1989, July 20 Photo. *Perf. 14***

**571** A111 $1.50 Strip of 3, #a.-c. 14.50 14.50

### Souvenir Sheet of 3

***Perf. 13½x13***

**572** A111 $1.15 #a.-c. 8.00 8.00

Christmas — A112

Details of Presentation in the Temple, 1631, by Rembrandt, Royal Cabinet of Paintings, The Hague: 70c, Priests. 80c, Madonna. $1.05, Joseph. $1.30, Christ child. $7.20, Entire painting.

**1989, Nov. 22 Photo. *Perf. 13x13½***

**573** A112 70c gold & multi 2.60 2.60
**574** A112 80c gold & multi 2.75 2.75
**575** A112 $1.05 gold & multi 3.50 3.50
**576** A112 $1.30 gold & multi 4.50 4.50
*Nos. 573-576 (4)* 13.35 13.35

### Souvenir Sheet

***Perf. 13½***

**577** A112 $7.20 gold & multi 13.50 13.50

No. 577 contains one 39x50mm stamp.

Emblem of the German Natl. Soccer Team and Signatures — A113

Former team captains: 80c, Fritz Walter. $1.15, Franz Beckenbauer. $1.40, Uwe Seeler.

**1990, Feb. 5 Photo. *Perf. 13½***

**578** A113 80c multicolored 2.25 2.25
**579** A113 $1.15 multicolored 2.60 2.60
**580** A113 $1.40 multicolored 4.50 4.50
**581** A113 $1.80 shown 5.25 5.25
*Nos. 578-581 (4)* 14.60 14.60

1990 World Cup Soccer Championships, Italy.

First Postage Stamp, 150th Anniv. — A114

Paintings by Rembrandt showing letters: 80c, No. 586d, Merchant Maarten Looten (1632). $1.05, No. 586c, Rembrandt's son Titus holding pen (1655). $1.30, No. 586b, The Shipbuilder and his Wife (1633). $1.80, No. 586a, Bathsheba with King David's letter (1654).

**1990, May 2 Photo. *Perf. 13½***

**582** A114 80c multicolored 2.25 2.25
**583** A114 $1.05 multicolored 3.00 3.00
**584** A114 $1.30 multicolored 4.50 4.50
**585** A114 $1.80 multicolored 6.00 6.00
*Nos. 582-585 (4)* 15.75 15.75

### Souvenir Sheet

**586** Sheet of 4 11.00 11.00
*a.-d.* A114 $1.50 any single 2.75 2.75

A115

**1990, July 23 *Perf. 13x13½***

**587** A115 $1.25 multicolored 5.00 5.00

### Souvenir Sheet

**588** A115 $7 multicolored 16.00 16.00

Queen Mother, 90th birthday.

A116

Christmas (Paintings): 70c, Adoration of the Magi by Bouts. 80c, Holy Family by Fra Bartolomeo. $1.05, The Nativity by Memling. $1.30, Adoration of the King by Pieter Bruegel, the Elder. $7.20, Virgin and Child Enthroned by Cosimo Tura.

**1990, Nov. 27 Litho. *Perf. 14***

**589** A116 70c multicolored 2.25 2.25
**590** A116 80c multicolored 3.00 3.00
**591** A116 $1.05 multicolored 3.50 3.50
**592** A116 $1.30 multicolored 4.25 4.25
*Nos. 589-592 (4)* 13.00 13.00

### Souvenir Sheet

**593** A116 $7.20 multicolored 13.00 13.00

### No. 334 Overprinted in Silver

**1990, Dec. 5 *Perf. 13x13½***

**594** A77a $10 multicolored 16.00 16.00

Birdpex '90, 20th Intl. Ornithological Congress, New Zealand.

### No. 333 Overprinted "SIXTY FIFTH BIRTHDAY QUEEN ELIZABETH II"

**1991, Apr. 22 Litho. *Perf. 13x13½***

**595** A77a $6 multicolored 8.00 8.00

### Nos. 340-342 Overprinted in Black or Silver

| TENTH ANNIVERSARY | TENTH ANNIVERSARY |
|---|---|
| Typo. | Litho. |

**1991, June 26 Photo. *Perf. 14***

**596** A79 75c on #340 (S) 1.50 1.50
*a.* Litho. overprint 1.50 1.50
**597** A79 95c on #341 2.25 2.25
*a.* Litho. overprint 2.25 2.25
**598** A79 $1.20 on #342 3.25 3.25
*a.* Litho. overprint 3.25 3.25
*Nos. 596-598 (3)* 7.00 7.00
*Nos. 596a-598a (3)* 7.00 7.00

Nos. 596-598 issued in miniature sheets of 5 with typo. overprint. Nos. 596a-598a issued in uncut panes of 4 miniature sheets of 5. Letters of typo. overprint are taller and thinner than litho. overprint.

Christmas — A117

Paintings: 20c, The Virgin and Child with Saints Jerome and Dominic, by Filippino Lippi. 50c, The Isenheim Altarpiece, The Virgin and Child, by Grunewald. $1, The Nativity, by Pittoni. $2, Adoration of the Kings, by Jan Brueghel, the Elder. $7, The Adoration of the Shepherds, by Reni.

**1991, Nov. 11 Litho. *Perf. 14***

**599** A117 20c multicolored .50 .50
**600** A117 50c multicolored 1.40 1.40
**601** A117 $1 multicolored 3.00 3.00
**602** A117 $2 multicolored 5.50 5.50
*Nos. 599-602 (4)* 10.40 10.40

### Souvenir Sheet

**603** A117 $7 multicolored 11.00 11.00

Birds — A118

20c, Banded rail. 50c, Red-tailed tropicbird. 70c, Purple swamphen. $1, Pacific pigeon. $1.50, White-collared kingfisher. $2, Blue-crowned lory. $3, Crimson-crowned fruit dove. $5, Barn owl. $7, Longtailed cockoo. $10, Reef heron. $15, Polynesian triller.

**1992-93 Litho. *Perf. 14x13½***

**604** A118 20c multicolored .30 .30
**605** A118 50c multicolored .70 .70
**606** A118 70c multicolored 1.00 1.00
**607** A118 $1 multicolored 1.50 1.50
**608** A118 $1.50 multicolored 2.00 2.00
**609** A118 $2 multicolored 2.75 2.75
**610** A118 $3 multicolored 4.25 4.25
**611** A118 $5 multicolored 6.50 6.50

***Perf. 13***

**Size: 51x38mm**

**612** A118 $7 multicolored 8.50 8.50

**Size: 49x35mm**

**613** A118 $10 multicolored 11.50 11.50
**614** A118 $15 multicolored 18.00 18.00
*Nos. 604-614 (11)* 57.00 57.00

Issued $1.50, $2, 3/20; $3, 4/16; $5, 5/15; $7, 3/26/93; $10, 4/16/93; $15, 8/10/93; others, 2/92.

For overprints & surcharges see Nos. O20-O25, 676-677.

This is an expanding set. Numbers may change.

Discovery of America, 500th Anniv. — A119

$2, Queen Isabella supports Columbus. $3, Columbus' fleet. $5, Columbus landing in America.

**1992 Litho. *Perf. 13***

**621** A119 $2 multicolored 2.55 2.55
**622** A119 $3 multicolored 4.50 4.50
**623** A119 $5 multicolored 7.50 7.50
*Nos. 621-623 (3)* 14.55 14.55

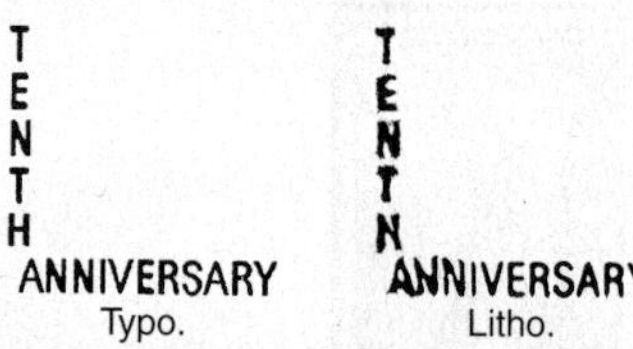

1992 Summer Olympics, Barcelona — A120

#624: a, $10 coin, tennis player. b, Flags, torch. c, Gymnast, $10 coin. $5, Water polo player.

**1992, July 22 Litho. *Perf. 13½x13***

**624** A120 $2.50 Strip of 3, #a.-c. 17.00 17.00

**Souvenir Sheet**

**625** A120 $5 multicolored 10.50 10.50

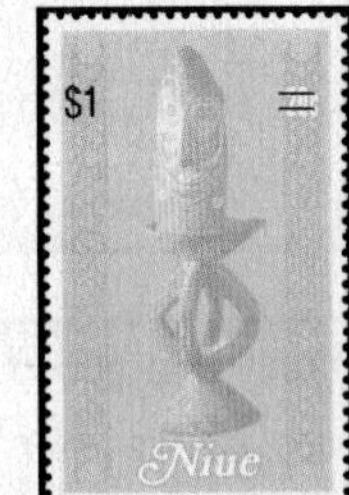


Nos. 265-268 Surcharged

**1992, Sept. 30 Photo. *Perf. 13***

**Strips of 4, #a.-d.**

**626** A72 $1 on 20c 4.75 4.75
**627** A72 $1 on 25c 4.75 4.75
**628** A72 $1 on 30c 4.75 4.75
**629** A72 $1 on 35c 4.75 4.75
*Nos. 626-629 (4)* 19.00 19.00

6th South Pacific Festival of the Arts.

Christmas A121

Design: Different details from St. Catherine's Mystic Marriage, by Hans Memling.

**1992, Nov. 18 Litho. *Perf. 13½***

**642** A121 20c multicolored .35 .35
**643** A121 50c multicolored 1.00 1.00
**644** A121 $1 multicolored 2.40 2.40
**645** A121 $2 multicolored 4.00 4.00
*Nos. 642-645 (4)* 7.75 7.75

**Souvenir Sheet**

**646** A121 $7 like #643 11.50 11.50

No. 646 contains one 39x48mm stamp.

Queen Elizabeth II's Accession to the Throne, 40th Anniv. — A122

Various portraits of Queen Elizabeth II.

**1992, Dec. 7 *Perf. 14***

**647** A122 70c multicolored .60 .60
**648** A122 $1 multicolored 1.75 1.75
**649** A122 $1.50 multicolored 3.50 3.50
**650** A122 $2 multicolored 4.25 4.25
*Nos. 647-650 (4)* 10.10 10.10

Dolphins A123

Designs: 20c, Rough-toothed dolphin. 50c, Fraser's dolphin. 75c, Pantropical spotted dolphin. $1, Risso's dolphin.

**1993, Jan. 13 Litho. *Perf. 14***

**651** A123 20c multicolored 1.25 .75
**652** A123 50c multicolored 3.50 1.50
**653** A123 75c multicolored 4.75 2.50
**654** A123 $1 multicolored 6.00 4.50
*Nos. 651-654 (4)* 15.50 9.25

World Wildlife Fund.

Nos. 451-453 Ovptd.

**1993, Mar. 15 Photo. *Perf. 13***

**655** A93 40c on #451 multi .65 .65
**656** A93 58c on #452 multi 1.25 1.25
**657** A93 70c on #453 multi 1.75 1.75

**Nos. 655-657 Surcharged**

**1993, Mar. 15**

**658** A93 $1 on 40c #655 3.25 3.25
**659** A93 $1 on 58c #656 3.25 3.25
**660** A93 $1 on 70c #657 3.25 3.25
*Nos. 655-660 (6)* 13.40 13.40

Queen Elizabeth II, 40th Anniv. of Coronation — A124

**1993, June 2 Litho. *Perf. 14***

**661** A124 $5 multicolored 10.50 10.50

Christmas A125

Details from Virgin of the Rosary, by Guido Reni: 20c, Infant Jesus. 70c, Cherubs. $1, Two men, one pointing upward. $1.50, Two men looking upward. $3, Madonna and child.

**1993, Oct. 29 Litho. *Perf. 14***

**662** A125 20c multicolored .30 .30
**663** A125 70c multicolored 1.20 1.20
**664** A125 $1 multicolored 1.75 1.75
**665** A125 $1.50 multicolored 3.25 3.25

**Size: 32x47mm**

***Perf. 13½***

**666** A125 $3 multicolored 6.00 6.00
*Nos. 662-666 (5)* 12.50 12.50

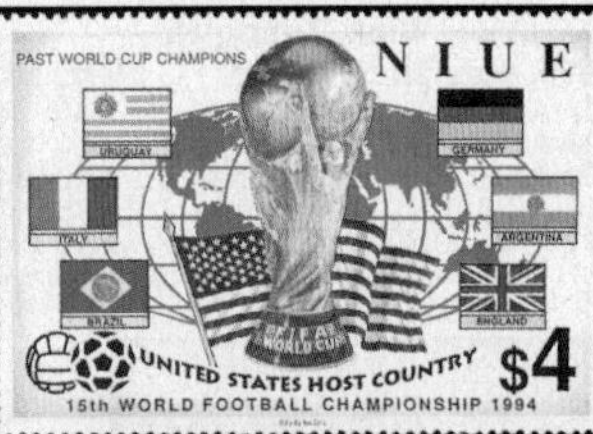


1994 World Cup Soccer Championships, U.S. — A126

**1994, June 17 Litho. *Perf. 14***

**667** A126 $4 multicolored 8.00 8.00

First Manned Moon Landing, 25th Anniv. — A127

Designs: a, Flight to Moon, astronaut opening solar wind experiment lunar surface. b, Astronaut holding flag. c, Astronaut standing by lunar experiment package.

**1994, July 20 Litho. *Perf. 14***

**668** A127 $2.50 Tryptic, #a.-c. 20.00 20.00

Christmas A128

Entire paintings or details: No. 669a, The Adoration of the Kings, by Jan Gossaert. b, Madonna & Child with Saints John & Catherine, by Titian. c, The Holy Family and Shepherd, by Titian. d, Virgin & Child with Saints, by Gerard David.

No. 670: a-b, Adoration of the Shepherds, by N. Poussin. c, Madonna & Child with Saints Joseph & John, by Sebastiano. d, Adoration of the Kings, by Veronese.

**1994, Nov. 28 Litho. *Perf. 14***

**669** A128 70c Block of 4, #a.-d. 4.50 4.50
**670** A128 $1 Block of 4, #a.-d. 7.00 7.00

Robert Louis Stevenson (1850-94), Writer — A129

a, Treasure Island. b, Dr. Jekyll and Mr. Hyde. c, Kidnapped. d, Stevenson, tomb, inscription.

**1994, Dec. 14 *Perf. 15x14***

**671** A129 $1.75 Block of 4, #a.-d. 15.00 15.00

Flowers — A130

**1996, May 10 Litho. *Perf. 14½x14***

**672** A130 70c Tapeu orchid .90 .90
**673** A130 $1 Frangipani 1.40 1.40
**674** A130 $1.20 Golden shower 1.60 1.60
**675** A130 $1.50 Pua 2.10 2.10
*Nos. 672-675 (4)* 6.00 6.00

Nos. 606, 608 Surcharged

**1996, Feb. 19 Litho. *Perf. 14x13½***

**676** A118 50c on 70c #606 11.50 8.50
**677** A118 $1 on $1.50 #608 13.50 10.50

**Flower Type of 1969 Redrawn**

Design: 20c, Hibiscus.

**1996, Aug. 22 Litho. *Rouletted 7***

**678** A38 20c red & green .45 .45

Yachting A131

**1996 Litho. *Perf. 14½***

**679** A131 70c Jackfish 1.00 1.00
**680** A131 $1 S/V Jennifer 1.40 1.40
**681** A131 $1.20 Mikeva 2.00 2.00
**682** A131 $2 Eye of the Wind 3.50 3.50
*Nos. 679-682 (4)* 7.90 7.90

**Souvenir Sheet**

***Perf. 14***

**683** A131 $1.50 Desert Star 2.50 2.50

Issued: Nos. 679-682, 9/30/96. No. 683, 10/96 (Taipei '96). No. 683 contains one 30x30mm stamp.

Coral A132

20c, Acropora gemmifera. 50c, Acropora nobilis. 70c, Goniopora lobata. $1, Stylaster. $1.20, Alveopora catalai. $1.50, Fungia scutaria. $2, Porites solida. $3, Millepora. $4, Pocillopora eydouxi. $5, Platygyra pini.

**1996, Dec. 20 Litho. *Perf. 14***

**684-693** A132 Set of 10 26.00 26.00

Souvenir Sheet

New Year 1997 (Year of the Ox) — A133

**1997, Feb. 10 Litho. *Perf. 13***

**694** A133 $1.50 multicolored 2.50 2.50

Hong Kong '97.

Humpback Whale — A134

20c, Whale in water. 50c, Killer whale. 70c, Minke whale. $1, Adult, young whale swimming upward. $1.20, Sperm whale. $1.50, Whale breaching.

**1997 Litho. *Perf. 14***

| | | | | |
|---|---|---|---|---|
| **695** | A134 | 20c multi | .40 | .40 |
| **696** | A134 | 50c multi, vert. | 1.05 | 1.05 |
| **697** | A134 | 70c multi, vert. | 1.40 | 1.40 |
| **698** | A134 | $1 multi, vert. | 2.25 | 2.25 |
| **699** | A134 | $1.20 multi, vert. | 2.60 | 2.60 |
| **700** | A134 | $1.50 multi, vert. | 3.50 | 3.50 |
| *a.* | | Souvenir sheet, #695, 698, 700 | 4.25 | 4.25 |
| | | *Nos. 695-700 (6)* | 11.20 | 11.20 |

Pacific '97 (#700a).
Issued: 20c, $1, $1.50, 5/29; others, 9/3.

Island Scenes — A135

Designs: a, Steps leading over island along inlet. b, Island, vegetagion, sky. c, Coral reef, undersea vegetation. d, Reef, vegetation, diff.

**1997, Apr. 18 Litho. *Perf. 13½x14***

**701** A135 $1 Block of 4, #a.-d. 5.50 5.50

Christmas A136

Bouquets of various flowers.

**1997, Nov. 26 Litho. *Perf. 14***

| | | | | |
|---|---|---|---|---|
| **702** | A136 | 20c deep plum & multi | .30 | .30 |
| **703** | A136 | 50c green & multi | .70 | .70 |
| **704** | A136 | 70c blue & multi | 1.00 | 1.00 |
| **705** | A136 | $1 red & multi | 1.50 | 1.50 |
| | | *Nos. 702-705 (4)* | 3.50 | 3.50 |

**Diana, Princess of Wales (1961-97)**

Common Design Type

Various portraits: a, 20c. b, 50c. c, $1. d, $2.

**1998, Apr. 29 Litho. *Perf. 14½x14***

**706** CD355 Sheet of 4, #a.-d. 5.50 5.50

No. 706 sold for $3.70 + 50c, with surtax from international sales being donated to the Princess of Wales Memorial fund and surtax from national sales being donated to designated local charity.

Diving A137

Designs: 20c, Two snorkeling beneath water's surface. 70c, One diver, coral. $1, Diving into underwater canyon, vert. $1.20, Two divers, coral. $1.50, Divers exploring underwater cavern.

**Wmk. Triangles**

**1998, May 20 Litho. *Perf. 14½***

| | | | | |
|---|---|---|---|---|
| **707** | A137 | 20c multicolored | .40 | .40 |
| **708** | A137 | 70c multicolored | 1.00 | 1.00 |
| **709** | A137 | $1 multicolored | 1.40 | 1.40 |
| **710** | A137 | $1.20 multicolored | 1.75 | 1.75 |
| **711** | A137 | $1.50 multicolored | 2.40 | 2.40 |
| | | *Nos. 707-711 (5)* | 6.95 | 6.95 |

Sea Birds A138

Designs: 20c, Pacific black duck. 70c, Fairy tern. $1, Great frigatebird, vert. $1.20, Lesser golden plover. $2, Brown noddy.

***Perf. 14½x14, 14x14½***

**Wmk. Triangles**

**1998, July 23 Litho.**

| | | | | |
|---|---|---|---|---|
| **712** | A138 | 20c multicolored | .55 | .55 |
| **713** | A138 | 70c multicolored | 1.20 | 1.20 |
| **714** | A138 | $1 multicolored | 2.10 | 2.10 |
| **715** | A138 | $1.20 multicolored | 2.40 | 2.40 |
| **716** | A138 | $2 multicolored | 3.50 | 3.50 |
| | | *Nos. 712-716 (5)* | 9.75 | 9.75 |

Shells A139

Two views of various shells from the Pacific Ocean.

***Perf. 14½***

**1998, Sept. 23 Litho. Unwmk.**

| | | | | |
|---|---|---|---|---|
| **717** | A139 | 20c multicolored | .50 | .50 |
| **718** | A139 | 70c multicolored | 1.15 | 1.15 |
| **719** | A139 | $1 multicolored | 2.40 | 2.40 |
| **720** | A139 | $5 multicolored | 7.50 | 7.50 |
| | | *Nos. 717-720 (4)* | 11.55 | 11.55 |

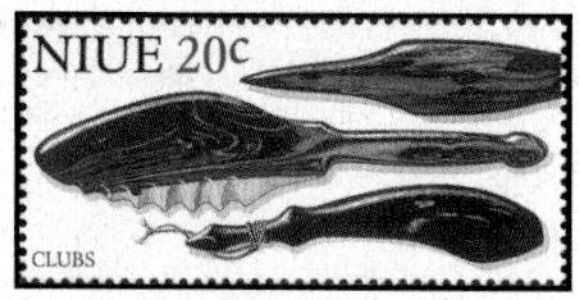

Ancient Weapons — A140

***Perf. 14x14½***

**1998, Nov. 18 Litho. Unwmk.**

| | | | | |
|---|---|---|---|---|
| **721** | A140 | 20c Clubs | .50 | .50 |
| **722** | A140 | $1.20 Spears | 1.50 | 1.50 |
| **723** | A140 | $1.50 Spears, diff. | 1.90 | 1.90 |
| **724** | A140 | $2 Throwing stones | 2.60 | 2.60 |
| | | *Nos. 721-724 (4)* | 6.50 | 6.50 |

Nos. 722-723 are each 60x23mm.

Maritime Heritage — A141

Designs: 70c, First migration of Niue Fekai. $1, Crew of Resolution discover Niue. $1.20, LMS John Williams. $1.50, Captain James Cook (1728-79).

**1999, Feb. 24 Litho. *Perf. 14½x14***

| | | | | |
|---|---|---|---|---|
| **725** | A141 | 70c bright violet blue | .90 | .90 |
| **726** | A141 | $1 bright violet blue | 1.40 | 1.40 |
| **727** | A141 | $1.20 bright violet blue | 1.75 | 1.75 |
| **728** | A141 | $1.50 bright violet blue | 2.10 | 2.10 |
| | | *Nos. 725-728 (4)* | 6.15 | 6.15 |

Nudibranchs A142

World Wide Fund for Nature: 20c, Risbecia tryoni. $1, Chromodoris lochi. $1.20, Chromodoris elizabethina. $1.50, Chromodoris bullocki.

**1999, Mar. 17 Litho. *Perf. 14½***

| | | | | |
|---|---|---|---|---|
| **729** | A142 | 20c multicolored | .40 | .40 |
| **730** | A142 | $1 multicolored | 1.40 | 1.40 |
| **731** | A142 | $1.20 multicolored | 1.50 | 1.50 |
| **732** | A142 | $1.50 multicolored | 2.25 | 2.25 |
| *a.* | | Souv. sheet, 2 ea #729-732 | 11.50 | 11.50 |
| | | *Nos. 729-732 (4)* | 5.55 | 5.55 |

Scenic Views A143

$1, Togo Chasm, vert. $1.20, Matapa Chasm, vert. $1.50, Tufukia. $2, Talava Arches.

**1999, June 16 Litho. *Perf. 14***

| | | | | |
|---|---|---|---|---|
| **734** | A143 | $1 multicolored | 1.40 | 1.40 |
| **735** | A143 | $1.20 multicolored | 1.50 | 1.50 |
| **736** | A143 | $1.50 multicolored | 1.90 | 1.90 |
| **737** | A143 | $2 multicolored | 2.75 | 2.75 |
| | | *Nos. 734-737 (4)* | 7.55 | 7.55 |

Woven Baskets A144

Various styles and patterns: #738a, 20c. #738b, $1. #739a, 70c. #739b, $3.

**1999, Sept. 18 Litho. *Perf. 12***

| | | | | |
|---|---|---|---|---|
| **738** | A144 | Pair, a.-b. | 2.00 | 2.00 |
| **739** | A144 | Pair, a.-b. | 4.00 | 4.00 |

Nos. 738b, 739b are each 45x35mm.

Souvenir Sheet

Self-Government, 25th Anniv. — A145

Designs: a, 20c, Natives, boats. b, $5, Fish, tree, diver, child.

**Litho. with Foil application**

**1999, Dec. 1 *Perf. 15x14¾***

**740** A145 Sheet of 2, #a.-b 6.00 6.00

Millennium — A146

a, 20c, Man in outrigger canoe. b, 70c, Women pointing up. c, $4, Swimmers, bird, fish.

**1999, Dec. 31 Litho. *Perf. 14¼x15***

**741** A146 Strip of 3, #a.-c. 6.50 6.50

Birds and Flora — A147

20c, Purple-capped fruit dove, mamane. $1, Purple swamphen, fig. $1.20, Barn owl, koa. $2, Blue-crowned lory, ohia lehua.

**2000, Apr. 5 Litho. *Perf. 13x13¼***

**742-745** A147 Set of 4 6.50 6.50

Royal Birthdays A148

Designs: $1.50, Queen Mother, 100th birthday, vert. $3, Prince William, 18th birthday, and Queen Mother.

**2000, May 22 *Perf. 13¼x13, 13x13¼***

**746-747** A148 Set of 2 4.50 4.50

2000 Summer Olympics, Sydney A149

Designs: 50c, Pole vault. 70c, Diving. $1, Hurdles. $3, Gymnastics.

***Perf. 13½x13¼***

**2000, Sept. 16 Litho.**

**748-751** A149 Set of 4 5.00 5.00

Dancers — A150

No. 752: a, Couple. b, Woman with red garments. c, Woman with white garments. d, Child with garments made of leaves.

**2000, Nov. 22 Litho. *Perf. 13¼x13***

| | | | | |
|---|---|---|---|---|
| **752** | | Horiz. strip of 4 | 5.00 | 5.00 |
| *a.* | A150 | 20c multi | .30 | .30 |
| *b.* | A150 | 70c multi | .65 | .65 |
| *c.* | A150 | $1.50 multi | 1.30 | 1.30 |
| *d.* | A150 | $3 multi | 2.75 | 2.75 |

Niue Postage Stamps, Cent. (in 2002) — A151

Designs: 70c, #1. $3, #34.

**2001, Jan. 31**

**753-754** A151 Set of 2 3.25 3.25

Butterflies A152

No. 755: a, Large green-banded blue. b, Leafwing. c, Cairns birdwing. d, Meadow argus.

**2001, Mar. 22** ***Perf. 13½x13¼***

**755** Horiz. strip of 4 4.00 4.00
*a.* A152 20c multi .25 .25
*b.* A152 70c multi .60 .60
*c.* A152 $1.50 multi 1.40 1.40
*d.* A152 $2 multi 1.75 1.75

Turtles A153

Designs: 50c, Green turtle hatching. $1, Hawksbill turtle. $3, Green turtle on beach.

**2001, May 10**

**756-758** A153 Set of 3 4.00 4.00

Coconut Crabs — A154

Crab: 20c, In water. 70c, On beach. $1.50, Climbing tree. $3, With coconut.

**2001, July 7** ***Perf. 14***

**759-762** A154 Set of 4 5.00 5.00

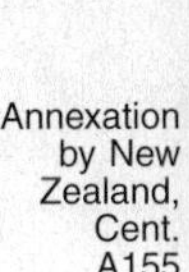
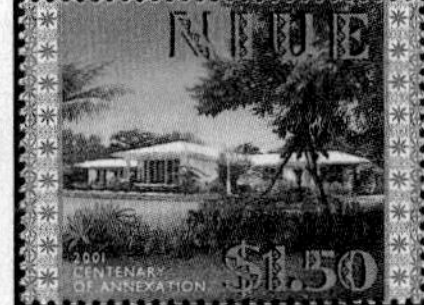


Annexation by New Zealand, Cent. A155

Designs: $1.50, Building. $2, Man and woman.

**2001, Oct. 19 Litho.** ***Perf. 13½x13¼***

**763-764** A155 Set of 2 3.25 3.25

Christmas — A156

Designs: 20c, Magi. 70c, Dove. $1, Angel. $2, Star.

**2001, Dec. 13** ***Perf. 13x13¼***

**765-768** A156 Set of 4 3.50 3.50
*768a* Horiz. strip, #765-768 3.50 3.50

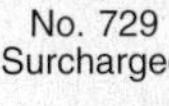
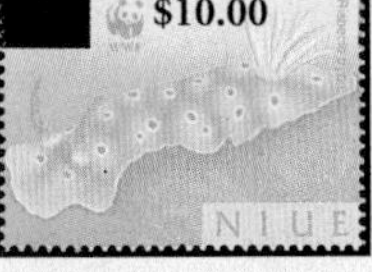


No. 729 Surcharged

**2002, July 7 Litho.** ***Perf. 14½***

**769** A142 $10 on 20c multi *75.00 65.00*

Worldwide Fund for Nature (WWF) — A156a

Various depictions of small giant clam.

**2002, Nov. 7 Litho.** ***Perf. 13¼x13***

**769A** Horiz. strip of 4 4.50 4.50
*b.* A156a 50c multi .60 .60
*c.* A156a 70c multi .75 .70
*d.* A156a $1 multi 1.10 1.10
*e.* A156a $1.50 multi 1.60 1.60
*f.* As #769Ab, without emblem — —
*g.* As #760Ac, without emblem — —
*h.* As #769Ad, without emblem — —
*i.* As #769Ae, without emblem — —
*j.* Souvenir sheet of 4, #769Af-769Ai — —

A limited quantity of No. 769Ab received a $10 surcharge.

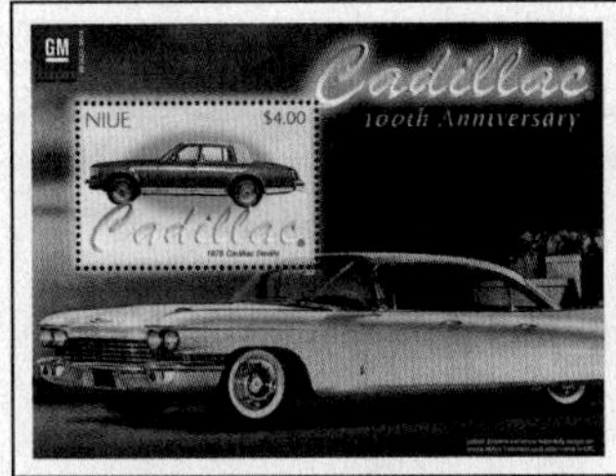


General Motors Automobiles — A157

No. 770, $1.50 — Cadillacs: a, 1953 Eldorado. b, 2002 Eldorado. c, 1967 Eldorado. d, 1961 Sedan de Ville.
No. 771, $1.50 — Corvettes: a, 1954 convertible. b, 1979. c, 1956 convertible. d, 1964 Stingray.
No. 772, $4, 1978 Cadillac Seville. No. 773, $4, 1979 Corvette.

**2003 Litho.** ***Perf. 14***

**Sheets of 4, #a-d**

**770-771** A157 Set of 2 24.00 24.00

**Souvenir Sheets**

**772-773** A157 Set of 2 22.00 22.00

Issued: Nos. 770, 772, 8/25; Nos. 771, 773, 9/2.

Coronation of Queen Elizabeth II, 50th Anniv. — A158

No. 774: a, Wearing crown as younger woman. b, Wearing tiara. c, Wearing crown as older woman.
$4, Wearing hat.

**2003, Sept. 2**

**774** A158 $1.50 Sheet of 3, #a-c 9.00 9.00

**Souvenir Sheet**

**775** A158 $4 multi 9.00 9.00

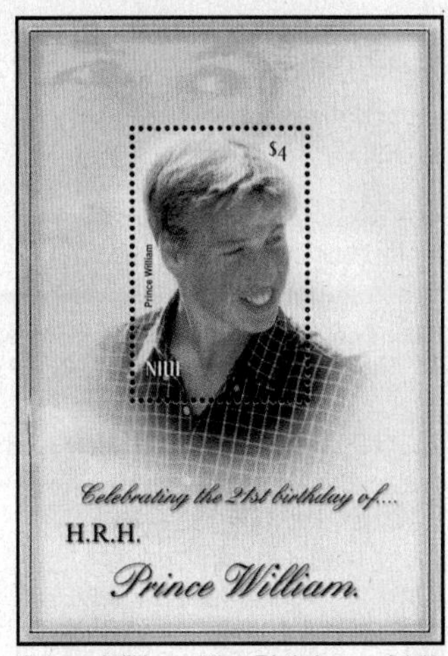


Prince William, 21st Birthday — A159

No. 776: a, Wearing blue checked tie. b, Wearing shirt and jacket. c, Wearing striped shirt and tie.
$4, Wearing shirt.

**2003, Sept. 2**

**776** A159 $1.50 Sheet of 3, #a-c 9.00 9.00

**Souvenir Sheet**

**777** A159 $4 multi 8.50 8.50

Tour de France Bicycle Race, Cent. — A160

No. 778: a, Nicholas Frantz, 1927. b, Frantz, 1928. c, Maurice de Waele, 1929. d, André Leducq, 1930.
$4, Leducq, 1930, diff.

**2003, Sept. 2** ***Perf. 13½x13¼***

**778** A160 $1.50 Sheet of 4, #a-d 10.50 10.50

**Souvenir Sheet**

**779** A160 $4 multi 8.75 8.75

Powered Flight, Cent. — A161

No. 780: a, Boeing 737-200. b, Boeing Stratocruiser. c, Boeing Model SA-307B. d, Douglas DC-2. e, Wright Flyer I. f, De Havilland D.H.4A.
$4, Boeing 767.

**2003, Sept. 2** ***Perf. 14***

**780** A161 80c Sheet of 6, #a-f 9.00 9.00

**Souvenir Sheet**

**781** A161 $4 multi 9.00 9.00

Birds, Butterflies and Fish — A162

No. 782, $1.50, vert. — Birds: a, Wrinkled hornbill. b, Toco toucan. c, Roseate spoonbill. d, Blue and gold macaw.
No. 783, $1.50 — Butterflies: a, Agrias beata. b, Papilio blumei. c, Cethosia bibbis. d, Cressida cressida.
No. 784, $1.50 — Fish: a, Garibaldi fish. b, Golden damselfish. c, Squarespot anthias. d, Orange-fin anemonefish.
No. 785, $3, Green-wing macaw. No. 786, $3, Blue morpho butterfly. No. 787, $3, Maculosus angelfish.

***Perf. 13½x13¼, 13¼x13½***

**2004, Aug. 16 Litho.**

**Sheets of 4, #a-d**

**782-784** A162 Set of 3 24.00 24.00

**Souvenir Sheets**

**785-787** A162 Set of 3 12.00 12.00

Miniature Sheet

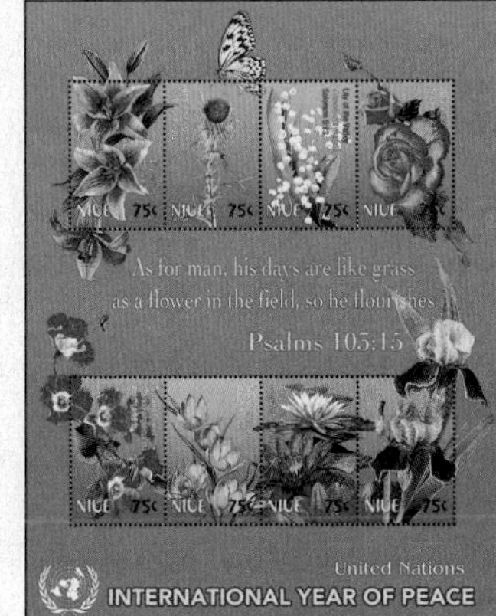


Intl. Year of Peace — A163

No. 788: a, Lily. b, Thistle. c, Lily of the valley. d, Rose. e, Garland flower. f, Crocus. g, Lotus. h, Iris.

**2004, Oct. 13** ***Perf. 13½x13¼***

**788** A163 75c Sheet of 8, #a-h 8.50 8.50

Miniature Sheet

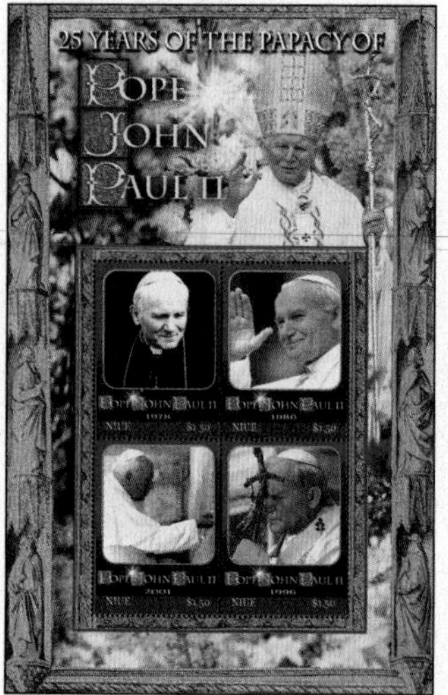

Election of Pope John Paul II, 25th Anniv. (in 2003) — A164

No. 789 — Pope in: a, 1978. b, 1986. c, 2001. d, 1996.

**2004, Oct. 13** ***Perf. 13¼***
**789** A164 $1.50 Sheet of 4, #a-d 8.50 8.50

D-Day, 60th Anniv. — A165

No. 790: a, Allied Air Forces begin bombing German coastal batteries. b, Allied naval guns pound Atlantic Wall. c, Paratroopers drop over Normandy. d, Allies advance and the Germans begin to surrender.
$3, Assault troops disembark on the shores of Normandy.

**2004, Oct. 13** ***Perf. 13¼x13½***
**790** A165 $1.50 Sheet of 4, #a-d 8.50 8.50

**Souvenir Sheet**

**791** A165 $3 multi 4.50 4.50

Locomotives, 200th Anniv. — A166

No. 792: a, 520 Class 4-8-4, Australia. b, FEF-2 Class 4-8-4, US. c, Royal Scot Class 4-6-0, Great Britain. d, A4 Class 4-6-2, Great Britain.
$3, Class GS-4 4-8-4, US.

**2004, Oct. 13**
**792** A166 $1.50 Sheet of 4, #a-d 8.50 8.50

**Souvenir Sheet**

**793** A166 $3 multi 4.50 4.50

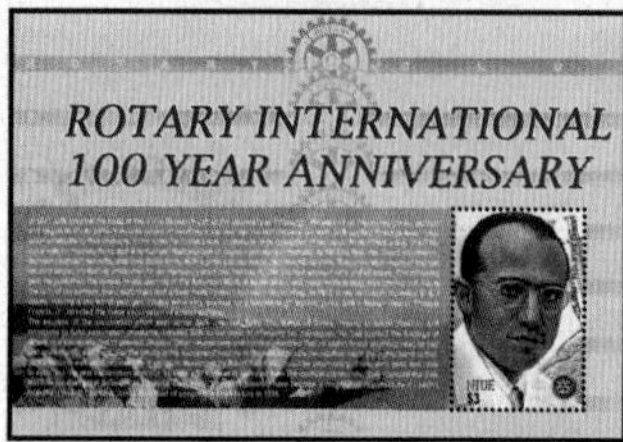

Pope John Paul II (1920-2005) — A167

**2005, Dec. 13** **Litho.** ***Perf. 13¼***
**794** A167 $2 multi 3.00 3.00

Printed in sheets of 4.

Rotary International, Cent. — A168

No. 795: a, Children. b, Paul P. Harris, Rotary founder. c, Carlo Ravizza, 1999-2000 Rotary International President.
$3, Dr. Jonas Salk, polio vaccine pioneer.

**2005, Dec. 22**
**795** A168 $1.50 Sheet of 3, #a-c 6.50 6.50

**Souvenir Sheet**

**796** A168 $3 multi 4.50 4.50

Pope Benedict XVI — A169

**2005, Dec. 27**
**797** A169 $1.50 multi 2.25 2.25

Printed in sheets of 4.

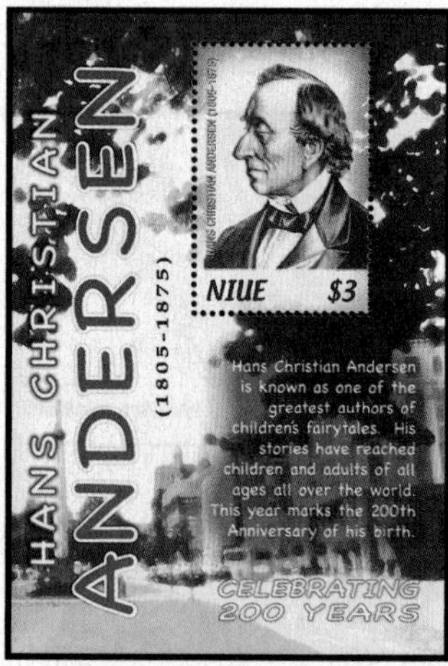

Hans Christian Andersen (1805-75), Author — A170

No. 798 — Andersen and country name and denomination in: a, Lilac. b, Ocher. c, Red.
$3, Andersen facing left.

**2005, Dec. 27**
**798** A170 $1.50 Sheet of 3, #a-c 6.50 6.50

**Souvenir Sheet**

**799** A170 $3 multi 4.50 4.50

World Cup Soccer Championships, 75th Anniv. — A171

No. 800: a, Frank Bauman. b, Marcus Babbel. c, Dietmar Hamann.
$3, Christian Worns.

**2005, Dec. 27**
**800** A171 $1.50 Sheet of 3, #a-c 6.50 6.50

**Souvenir Sheet**

**801** A171 $3 multi 4.50 4.50

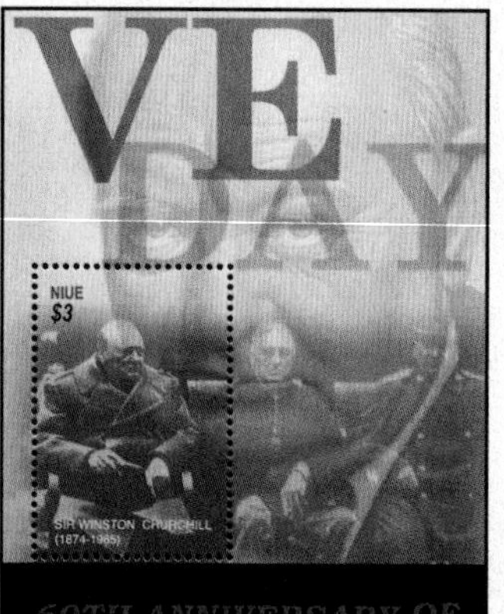

End of World War II, 60th Anniv. — A172

No. 802, horiz.: a, Entertaining the troops in the Pacific. b, USS Argonaut sailors reading letters from home. c, Japan surrenders on USS Missouri. d, A toast to peace. e, Entertainment at sea. f, Welcoming peace.
No. 803: a, D-Day invasion, Normandy, France. b, Lt. Meyrick Clifton-James, double for Field Marshal Bernard Montgomery. c, RAF Hawker Typhoon over French coast. d, Allied war cemetery, St. Laurent-sur-Mer, France.
No. 804, $3, Sir Winston Churchill. No. 805, $3, Pres. Franklin D. Roosevelt.

**2005, Dec. 27**
**802** A172 75c Sheet of 6, #a-f 6.75 6.75
**803** A172 $1.25 Sheet of 4, #a-d 7.50 7.50

**Souvenir Sheets**

**804-805** A172 Set of 2 9.00 9.00

Souvenir Sheets

National Basketball Association Players and Team Emblems — A173

No. 806, $4.50: a, LeBron James. b, Cleveland Cavaliers emblem.
No. 807, $4.50: a, Tim Duncan. b, San Antonio Spurs emblem.
No. 808, $4.50: a, Allen Iverson. b, Denver Nuggets emblem.
No. 809, $4.50: a, Kobe Bryant. b, Los Angeles Lakers emblem.
No. 810, $4.50: a, Tracy McGrady. b, Houston Rockets emblem.
No. 811, $4.50: a, Jermaine O'Neal. b, Indiana Pacers emblem.

**Litho. & Embossed**
**2007, Feb. 4** ***Imperf.***
**Without Gum**
**Sheets of 2, #a-b**
**806-811** A173 Set of 6 77.50 77.50

Miniature Sheet

Elvis Presley (1935-77) — A174

No. 812 — Presley: a, With hands resting on guitar. b, In green shirt, playing guitar. c, In brown red shirt, playing guitar. d, Holding guitar by neck.

**2007, Feb. 15** **Litho.** ***Perf. 12¾***
**812** A174 $1.50 Sheet of 4, #a-d 8.50 8.50

Miniature Sheets

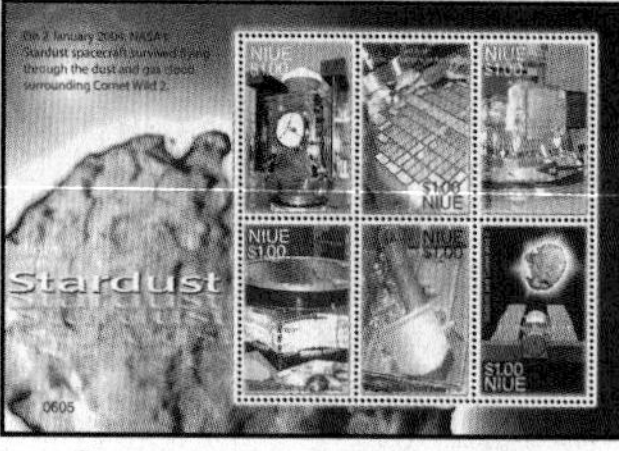

Space Achievements — A175

No. 813: a, Stardust probe at Kennedy Space Center. b, Stardust dust collector with aerogel. c, Stardust navigational camera. d, Stardust Whipple shield. e, Cometary and interstellar dust analyzer. f, Stardust and Comet Wild 2.
No. 814, horiz. — Artist's rendition of future projects: a, Astrobiology field laboratory. b, Deep-drill lander. c, Mars science laboratory. d, Phoenix lander.

**2007, Feb. 15**
**813** A175 $1 Sheet of 6, #a-f 8.50 8.50
**814** A175 $1.50 Sheet of 4, #a-d 8.50 8.50

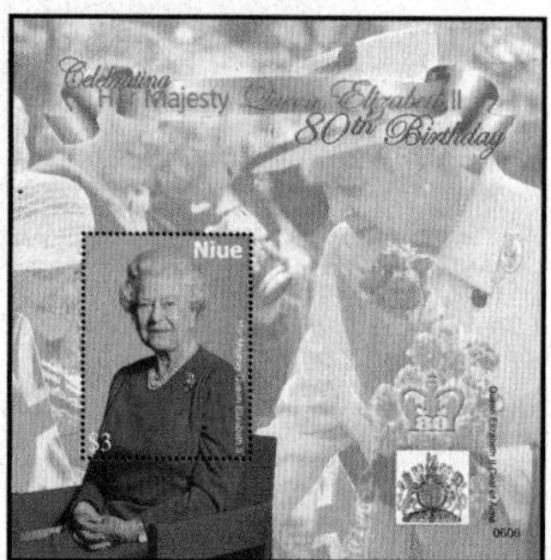

Queen Elizabeth II, 80th Birthday (in 2006) — A176

No. 815 — Dress color: a, Brown. b, Pink. c, Red. d, White.
$3, Purple.

**2007, Feb. 15** ***Perf. 12¼x12***
**815** A176 $1.50 Sheet of 4, #a-d 8.50 8.50

**Souvenir Sheet**
***Perf. 13¼***

**816** A176 $3 multi 4.50 4.50

Rembrandt (1606-69), Painter A177

Designs: 75c, Life Study of a Young Man Pulling a Rope. $1.25, Self-portrait. $1.50, Joseph Telling His Dreams. $2, The Blindness of Tobit.
$3, Christ in the Storm on the Lake of Galilee.

**2007, Feb. 15** *Perf. 12¼x12*
**817-820** A177 Set of 4 8.25 8.25

***Imperf***
**Size: 70x100mm**

**821** A177 $3 multi 4.75 4.75

Princess Diana (1961-97) — A178

No. 822 — Diana wearing: a, Purple dress. b, Tiara and black dress. c, Green dress, close-up. d, Purple dress, close-up. e, Tiara, close-up. f, Green dress.
$3, Diana with head on hand.

**2007, May 3** *Perf. 13½x13¼*
**822** A178 $1 Sheet of 6, #a-f 9.50 9.50

**Souvenir Sheet**

**823** A178 $3 multi 4.75 4.75

Local Attractions, Flora and Fauna — A179

Designs: 20c, Palaha Cave. 70c, White pua flower. $1, Talava Natural Arch. $1.20, Avaiki Pool. $1.50, Coral rock spears. $2, Humpback whale. $3, Spinner dolphins.

**2007, July 9** **Litho.** *Perf. 14x14¾*

| | | | | |
|---|---|---|---|---|
| **824** A179 | 20c multi | | .35 | .35 |
| **825** A179 | 70c multi | | 1.20 | 1.20 |
| **826** A179 | $1 multi | | 1.60 | 1.60 |
| **827** A179 | $1.20 multi | | 2.00 | 2.00 |
| **828** A179 | $1.50 multi | | 2.40 | 2.40 |
| **829** A179 | $2 multi | | 3.25 | 3.25 |
| **830** A179 | $3 multi | | 4.75 | 4.75 |
| | *Nos. 824-830 (7)* | | 15.55 | 15.55 |

Miniature Sheets

Concorde — A180

No. 831, $1: a, Concorde and hangar, blue tint. b, Concorde in air, normal tint. c, Concorde and hangar, red tint. d, Concorde in air, pink tint. e, Concorde and hangar, normal tint. f, Concorde in air, blue tint.
No. 832, $1: a, Concorde landing, yellow green frame. b, Concorde being towed, gray frame. c, Concorde landing, green gray frame. d, Concorde being towed, brown frame. e, Concorde landing, gray frame. f, Concorde being towed, blue frame.

**2007, July 21** *Perf. 13¼*
**Sheets of 6, #a-f**

**831-832** A180 Set of 2 19.00 19.00

Wedding of Queen Elizabeth II and Prince Philip, 60th Anniv. — A181

No. 833, vert.: a, Queen and Prince, "N" of "Niue" and denomination over white area, parts of flag in faded area between country name and denomination. b, Queen, "N" of "Niue" and denomination over white and blue areas. c, Queen, flower buds in faded area between country name and denomination. d, Queen and Prince, "N" of "Niue" and denomination over gray area, parts of flag in faded area between country name and denomination. e, Queen and Prince, country name and denomination over solid gray area. f, Queen, country name and denomination over solid gray area.
$3, Queen and Prince.

**2007, July 21** *Perf. 13¼*
**833** A181 $1 Sheet of 6, #a-f 9.25 9.25

**Souvenir Sheet**

**834** A181 $3 multi 4.25 4.25

Miniature Sheets

A182

Marilyn Monroe (1926-62), Actress — A183

Various portraits.

**2007, Aug. 21**
**835** A182 $1.50 Sheet of 4, #a-d 8.50 8.50
**836** A183 $1.50 Sheet of 4, #a-d 8.50 8.50

Jamestown, Virginia, 400th Anniv. — A184

No. 837: a, Marriage of John Rolfe to Pocahontas. b, First settlers reach Jamestown. c, Tobacco plant. d, Capt. John Smith. e, Jamestown Tercentenary Monument. f, Map of Jamestown.
$3, Queen Elizabeth II and Prince Philip at Jamestown.

**2007, Aug. 21**
**837** A184 $1 Sheet of 6, #a-f 9.00 9.00

**Souvenir Sheet**

**838** A184 $3 multi 4.50 4.50

Pope Benedict XVI — A185

**2007, Dec. 3** **Litho.** *Perf. 13¼*
**839** A185 70c multi 1.25 1.25

Printed in sheets of 8.

Miniature Sheet

Ferrari Automobiles, 60th Anniv. — A186

No. 840: a, 1949 166 FL. b, 1991 512 TR. c, 2003 Challenge Stradale. d, 1988 F1 87/88C. e, 2007 F2007. f, Building with Ferrari sign.

**2007, Dec. 10**
**840** A186 $1 Sheet of 6, #a-f 10.50 10.50

Tourism A187

Designs: 10c, Coconut palm. 20c, Tropical sunset. 30c, Humpback whale. 50c, Rainbow over rainforest. $1, Hio Beach. $1.20, Talava Arches. $1.40, Limu Pools. $1.70, Limestone caves. $2, Snorkeling in Limu Pools. $3, Panoramic coastline. $5, Liku Caves.

*Perf. 13½x13¼*
**2009, Sept. 14** **Litho.**

| | | | | |
|---|---|---|---|---|
| **841** A187 | 10c multi | | .25 | .25 |
| **842** A187 | 20c multi | | .30 | .30 |
| **843** A187 | 30c multi | | .45 | .45 |
| **844** A187 | 50c multi | | .75 | .75 |
| **845** A187 | $1 multi | | 1.50 | 1.50 |
| **846** A187 | $1.20 multi | | 1.75 | 1.75 |
| *a.* | Miniature sheet of 6, #841-846, perf. 14 | | 5.00 | 5.00 |
| **847** A187 | $1.40 multi | | 2.00 | 2.00 |
| **848** A187 | $1.70 multi | | 2.50 | 2.50 |
| **849** A187 | $2 multi | | 3.00 | 3.00 |
| **850** A187 | $3 multi | | 4.50 | 4.50 |
| **851** A187 | $5 multi | | 7.25 | 7.25 |
| *a.* | Miniature sheet of 5, #847-851, perf. 14 | | 19.50 | 19.50 |
| | *Nos. 841-851 (11)* | | 24.25 | 24.25 |

Christmas A188

Stained-glass window depicting: 30c, Man facing right, Ekalesia Millennium Hall. 80c, Dove, Lakepa Ekalesia Church. $1.20, Chalice and bread, Lakepa Ekalesia Church. $1.40, Man facing left, Ekalesia Millennium Hall.

*Perf. 13¼x13½*
**2009, Nov. 25** **Litho.**
**852-855** A188 Set of 4 5.50 5.50
*855a* Souvenir sheet, #852-855 5.50 5.50

Butterflies A189

Designs: $1.40, Hypolimnas bolina. $1.70, Junonia villida, vert. (22x26mm). $2.40, Hypolimnas antilope.

**2010, July 7** **Litho.** *Perf. 14*
**856-858** A189 Set of 3 8.00 8.00
*858a* Souvenir sheet of 3, #856-858 8.00 8.00

Christmas A190

Designs: a, Annunciation. b, Journey to Bethlehem. c, Nativity. d, Adoration of the Shepherds.

**2010, Oct. 20** *Perf. 13¼x13½*

| | | | |
|---|---|---|---|
| **859** | Horiz. strip of 4 | 12.00 | 12.00 |
| *a.* | A190 30c multicolored | .45 | .45 |
| *b.* | A190 $1.40 multicolored | 2.10 | 2.10 |
| *c.* | A190 $2 multicolored | 3.00 | 3.00 |
| *d.* | A190 $4 multicolored | 6.00 | 6.00 |

Whales A191

Designs: 80c, Whale's flukes. $1.20, Two whales raising heads out of water. $1.40, Calf breaching surface. $2, Mother and calf playing.

**2010, Nov. 17** **Litho.** *Perf. 14*
**860-863** A191 Set of 4 8.50 8.50
*863a* Souvenir sheet, #860-863 8.50 8.50

Wedding of Prince William and Catherine Middleton — A192

No. 864: a, $2.40, Catherine Middleton. b, $3.40, Prince William.

**2011, Mar. 23**

**864** A192 Horiz. pair, #a-b 9.25 9.25
*c.* Souvenir sheet, #864a-864b 9.25 9.25

Birds — A193

Designs: $1.70, Aplonis tabuensis. $2, Lalage maculosa, vert. (25x30mm). $2.40, Ptilinopus porphyraceus.

**2011, July 6**

**865-867** A193 Set of 3 10.50 10.50
*867a* Souvenir sheet of 3, #865-867 10.50 10.50

Christmas A194

Designs: 30c, Pacific sunset. $1.40, Matapa Chasm. $2, Coconut palms. $4, Centennial Church, Alofi.

**2011, Nov. 16** ***Perf. 13¼x13½***

**868-871** A194 Set of 4 12.00 12.00
*871a* Souvenir sheet of 4, #868-871 12.00 12.00

Shells A195

Designs: $1.20, Map cowrie. $1.40, Geography cone. $1.70, Partridge tun. $2, Tiger cowrie.

**2012, Apr. 11** ***Perf. 13½x13¼***

**872-875** A195 Set of 4 10.50 10.50
*875a* Souvenir sheet of 4, #872-875 10.50 10.50

Reign of Queen Elizabeth II, 60th Anniv. — A196

Hibiscus flowers and photograph of Queen Elizabeth II from: $2.40, 1953. $3.40, 2012.

**2012, May 23** ***Perf. 13¼x13½***

**876-877** A196 Set of 2 9.00 9.00
*877a* Souvenir sheet of 2, #876-877 9.00 9.00
*877b* Horiz. pair, #876-877 9.00 9.00

Worldwide Fund For Nature (WWF) A197

Various depictions of Giant sea fan: $1.20, $1.40, $1.70, $2.

**2012, Sept. 5** ***Perf. 13½x13¼***

**878-881** A197 Set of 4 10.50 10.50
*881a* Souvenir sheet of 4, #878-881 10.50 10.50

Christmas A198

Designs: 30c, Angel and infant Jesus. $1.40, Holy Family. $2, Magi. $4, Shepherds.

**2012, Nov. 21**

**882-885** A198 Set of 4 13.00 13.00

Niue Blue Butterfly A199

Designs: $1.20, Male underside. $1.40, Male upperside. $1.70, Female underside. $2, Female upperside.

**2013, Apr. 10** ***Perf. 13½***

**886-889** A199 Set of 4 10.50 10.50
*889a* Souvenir sheet of 4, #886-889 10.50 10.50

Coronation of Queen Elizabeth II, 60th Anniv. — A200

Designs: $2.40, Queen Elizabeth II. $3.40, Queen Elizabeth II, Prince Philip, Princess Margaret, Queen Mother.

**2013, May 8** ***Perf. 13¼x13½***

**890-891** A200 Set of 2 9.25 9.25
*891a* Souvenir sheet of 2, #890-891 9.25 9.25

Christmas A201

Designs: 30c, Dove. $1.40, Angel. $2, Star of Bethlehem. $4, Bells.

***Perf. 13¼x13¾***

**2013, Nov. 20** **Litho.**

**892-895** A201 Set of 4 13.00 13.00
*895a* Souvenir sheet of 4, #892-895 13.00 13.00

Traditional Dress A202

Designs: 30c, Pulou (hat). $1.40, Pipi (belt). $2, Tiputa (poncho). $4, Patutiti (skirt).

**2014, Apr. 23 Litho.** ***Perf. 13½x13¼***

**896-899** A202 Set of 4 13.50 13.50
*899a* Souvenir sheet of 4 #896-899 13.50 13.50

Fish A203

Designs: 30c, Whitemouth moray. $1.40, Orangefin anemonefish. $2, Fire dartfish. $4, Longnose butterflyfish.

***Perf. 13½x13¼***

**2014, June 18** **Litho.**

**900-903** A203 Set of 4 13.50 13.50
*903a* Souvenir sheet of 4 #900-903 13.50 13.50

Island Views — A204

Designs: 20c, Talava Arches. 30c, Mutalau. $1, Avaiki Caves. $1.20, Lakepa Village Church. $1.40, Golf course. $1.70, Huvalu Forest. $2, Tepa Point. $4, Togo Chasm.

**2014, Oct. 18 Litho.** ***Perf. 14x14¼***

| | | | | |
|---|---|---|---|---|
| **904** | A204 | 20c multi | .35 | .35 |
| **905** | A204 | 30c multi | .50 | .50 |
| **906** | A204 | $1 multi | 1.60 | 1.60 |
| **907** | A204 | $1.20 multi | 1.90 | 1.90 |
| **908** | A204 | $1.40 multi | 2.25 | 2.25 |
| **909** | A204 | $1.70 multi | 2.75 | 2.75 |
| **910** | A204 | $2 multi | 3.25 | 3.25 |
| **911** | A204 | $4 multi | 6.25 | 6.25 |
| | | *Nos. 904-911 (8)* | 18.85 | 18.85 |

Christmas A205

Various Christmas ornaments in: 30c Blue. $1.40, Red. $2, Green. $4, Purple.

***Perf. 13¼x13½***

**2014, Dec. 10** **Litho.**

**912-915** A205 Set of 4 12.00 12.00
*915a* Souvenir sheet of 4, #912-915 12.00 12.00

Haipo (Tapa Cloths) A206

Various haipo designs: 30c, $1.40, $2, $4.

**2015, Apr. 7 Litho.** ***Perf. 13½***

**916-919** A206 Set of 4 12.00 12.00
*919a* Souvenir sheet of 4, #916-919 12.00 12.00

Flora — A207

Designs: 30c, Hibiscus tiliaceus. $1.40, Fagraea Berteroana. $2, Alphitonia zizyphoides. $4, Cordyline fruticosa.

**2015, June 3 Litho.** ***Perf. 13½***

**920-923** A207 Set of 4 10.50 10.50
*923a* Souvenir sheet of 4, #920-923 10.50 10.50

Traditional Weapons — A208

Designs: 30c, Spear. $1.40, Club. $3, Spear, diff. $4, Club, diff.

**2015, Aug. 5 Litho.** ***Perf. 13½***

**924-927** A208 Set of 4 11.00 11.00
*927a* Souvenir sheet of 4, #924-927 11.00 11.00

Miniature Sheet

World War I, Cent. — A209

No. 928: a, 20c, Life in Niue, pre-war. b, 30c, Soldiers at Narrow Neck Camp, Auckland. c, $1, Troops departing for war from Auckland. d, $1.20, Badge of New Zealand Pioneer Battalion, map of Egypt. e, $1.40, Trench in Armentières, France. f, $1.70, New Zealand Convalescent Hospital, Hornchurch, England. g, $2, Soldiers and nurses recovering in Auckland. h, $4, War Memorial, Niue.

**2015, Oct. 13 Litho.** ***Perf. 14x14½***

**928** A209 Sheet of 8, #a-h 16.00 16.00

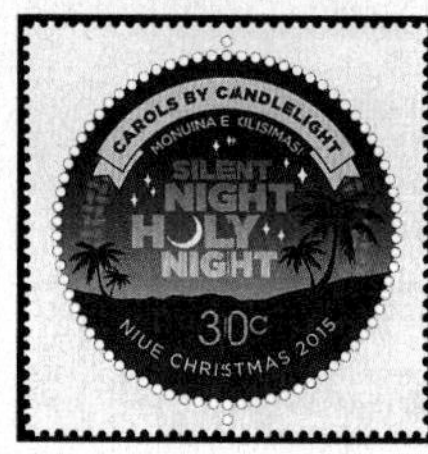


Christmas A210

Carols: 30c, Silent Night. $1.40, Joy to the World. $2, Away in the Manger. $4, Deck the Halls.

**2015, Nov. 25 Litho.** ***Perf. 14½***

**929-932** A210 Set of 4 10.50 10.50
*932a* Souvenir sheet of 4, #929-932 10.50 10.50

Queen Elizabeth II, 90th Birthday — A211

Queen Elizabeth II: $2.40, As young child. $3.40, In 2016.

**2016, May 4 Litho.** ***Perf. 13¼x13½***

**933-934** A211 Set of 2 8.00 8.00
*934a* Souvenir sheet of 2, #933-934 8.00 8.00

Humpback Whale — A212

Designs: 30c, Whale with flukes above water. $1.40, Two whales exhaling. $2, Whale with head above water. $4, Whale breaching surface of water.

**2016, Aug. 3 Litho. *Perf. 14x14¼***

| | | | | |
|---|---|---|---|---|
| **935-938** | A212 | Set of 4 | 11.50 | 11.50 |
| *938a* | | Souvenir sheet of 4, #935-938 | 11.50 | 11.50 |

Language Week — A213

Niuean phrases for: 30c, "Hello." $1.40, "How are you?" $2, "Nice to meet you." $4, "Goodbye."

**2016, Oct. 5 Litho. *Perf. 13¼x13½***

| | | | | |
|---|---|---|---|---|
| **939-942** | A213 | Set of 4 | 11.50 | 11.50 |
| *942a* | | Souvenir sheet of 4, #939-942 | 11.50 | 11.50 |

Christmas A214

Winning children's art in stamp design contest: 30c, Golden grouper, by Bailey Pasisi. $1.40, Family arriving for Christmas feast, by Bentley Poihenga. $2, Gift box, by Iva Tanevesi. $4, Family at Christmas, by Flornie R. Malinao.

**2016, Dec. 7 Litho. *Perf. 14x14¼***

| | | | | |
|---|---|---|---|---|
| **943-946** | A214 | Set of 4 | 11.00 | 11.00 |
| *946a* | | Souvenir sheet of 4, #943-946 | 11.00 | 11.00 |

Awarding of Knight Companion of the New Zealand Order of Merit to Niue Premier Sir Toke Talagi — A215

Designs: $2.40, Talagi and Niue flag. $3.40, Talagi.

**2017, Mar. 21 Litho. *Perf. 13½***

| | | | | |
|---|---|---|---|---|
| **947-948** | A215 | Set of 2 | 8.25 | 8.25 |

Reptiles A216

Designs: 30c, Mourning gecko. $1.40, Flat-tail sea snake. $2, Snake-eyed skink. $4, Pacific slender-toed gecko.

**2017, Apr. 5 Litho. *Perf. 13½***

| | | | | |
|---|---|---|---|---|
| **949-952** | A216 | Set of 4 | 11.00 | 11.00 |
| *952a* | | Souvenir sheet of 4, #949-952 | 11.00 | 11.00 |

Walkways — A217

Designs: 30c, Matapa Chasm. $1.40, Avaiki Cave. $2, Anapala Chasm. $4, Talava Arches.

**2017, July 12 Litho. *Perf. 13½***

| | | | | |
|---|---|---|---|---|
| **953-956** | A217 | Set of 4 | 11.50 | 11.50 |
| *956a* | | Souvenir sheet of 4, #953-956 | 11.50 | 11.50 |

Butterflyfish A218

Designs: 30c, Reticulate butterflyfish. $1.40, Bennett's butterflyfish. $2, Lined butterflyfish. $4, Acropora butterflyfish.

**2017, Sept. 20 Litho. *Perf. 13½***

| | | | | |
|---|---|---|---|---|
| **957-960** | A218 | Set of 4 | 11.00 | 11.00 |
| *960a* | | Souvenir sheet of 4, #957-960 | 11.00 | 11.00 |

70th Wedding Anniversary of Queen Elizabeth II and Prince Philip — A219

Photographs of Queen Elizabeth II and Prince Philip: 30c, On wedding day, 1947. $1.40, With their children, 1960. $2, On vacation, 1972. $4, With family of Duke and Duchess of Cambridge at Trooping the Colors ceremony, 2017.

**2017, Nov. 20 Litho. *Perf. 13¼***

| | | | | |
|---|---|---|---|---|
| **961-964** | A219 | Set of 4 | 10.50 | 10.50 |
| *964a* | | Souvenir sheet of 4, #961-964 | 10.50 | 10.50 |

Christmas A220

Flowers: 30c, Frangipani. $1.40, Guava. $2, Hibiscus. $4, Papaya.

**2017, Dec. 6 Litho. *Perf. 14x14¼***

| | | | | |
|---|---|---|---|---|
| **965-968** | A220 | Set of 4 | 11.00 | 11.00 |
| *968a* | | Souvenir sheet of 4, #965-968 | 11.00 | 11.00 |

Fruit Trees — A221

Designs: 30c, Lime. $1.40, Mango. $2, Avocado. $4, Coconut.

**2018, Mar. 7 Litho. *Perf. 13¼x13½***

| | | | | |
|---|---|---|---|---|
| **969-972** | A221 | Set of 4 | 11.50 | 11.50 |
| *972a* | | Souvenir sheet of 4, #969-972 | 11.50 | 11.50 |

---

## SEMI-POSTAL STAMPS

**Catalogue values for unused stamps in this section are for Never Hinged items.**

### Easter Type of 1978
Souvenir Sheets

Designs: No. B1, Descent from the Cross, by Caravaggio. No. B2, Burial of Christ, by Bellini. Sheets show paintings from which stamp designs were taken.

**1978, Mar. 15 Photo. *Perf. 13½***

| | | | | |
|---|---|---|---|---|
| **B1** | A61 | 70c + 5c multi | 1.00 | 1.00 |
| **B2** | A61 | 70c + 5c multi | 1.00 | 1.00 |

Surtax was for school children in Niue.

### Christmas Type of 1978
Souvenir Sheets

**1978, Nov. 30 Photo. *Perf. 13***

| | | | | |
|---|---|---|---|---|
| **B3** | A63 | 60c + 5c like #232 | .90 | .90 |
| **B4** | A63 | 60c + 5c like #233 | .90 | .90 |
| **B5** | A63 | 60c + 5c like #234 | .90 | .90 |
| | | *Nos. B3-B5 (3)* | 2.70 | 2.70 |

Surtax was for school children of Niue. The sheets show paintings from which designs of stamps were taken.

### Easter Type of 1979
Souvenir Sheets

**1979, Apr. 2**

| | | | | |
|---|---|---|---|---|
| **B6** | A64 | 70c + 5c like #235 | 1.10 | 1.10 |
| **B7** | A64 | 70c + 5c like #236 | 1.10 | 1.10 |

Surtax was for school children of Niue. The sheets show altarpiece from which designs of stamps were taken.

### IYC Type of 1979
Souvenir Sheets

**1979, May 31 Photo. *Perf. 13***

| | | | | |
|---|---|---|---|---|
| **B8** | A65 | 70c + 5c like #237 | .85 | .85 |
| **B9** | A65 | 70c + 5c like #238 | .85 | .85 |
| **B10** | A65 | 70c + 5c like #239 | .85 | .85 |
| **B11** | A65 | 70c + 5c like #240 | .85 | .85 |
| | | *Nos. B8-B11 (4)* | 3.40 | 3.40 |

Sheets show paintings from which designs of stamps were taken.

### Christmas Type of 1979
Souvenir Sheets

**1979, Nov. 29 Photo. *Perf. 13***

| | | | | |
|---|---|---|---|---|
| **B12** | A70 | 85c + 5c like #258 | .80 | .80 |
| **B13** | A70 | 85c + 5c like #259 | .80 | .80 |
| **B14** | A70 | 85c + 5c like #260 | .80 | .80 |
| **B15** | A70 | 85c + 5c like #261 | .80 | .80 |
| | | *Nos. B12-B15 (4)* | 3.20 | 3.20 |

Multicolored margins show entire paintings.

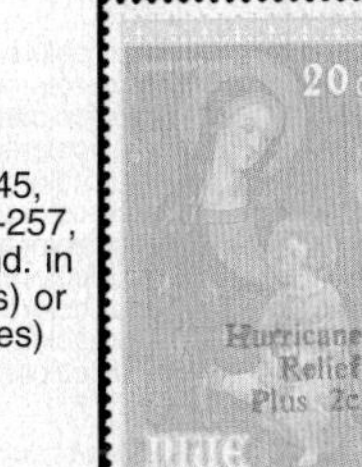

Nos. 241-245, 251-254, 255-257, 258-261 Srchd. in Black (2 lines) or Silver (3 lines)

**1980, Jan. 25 Photo. *Perf. 14, 13½***

| | | | | |
|---|---|---|---|---|
| **B16** | A66 | 20c + 2c pair | .55 | .55 |
| **B18** | A68 | 20c + 2c multi (S) | .30 | .30 |
| **B19** | A70 | 20c + 2c multi (S) | .30 | .30 |
| **B20** | A70 | 25c + 2c multi (S) | .40 | .40 |
| **B21** | A66 | 30c + 2c pair | .80 | .80 |
| **B23** | A68 | 30c + 2c multi (S) | .45 | .45 |
| **B24** | A69 | 30c + 2c multi (S) | .45 | .45 |
| **B25** | A70 | 30c + 2c multi (S) | .45 | .45 |
| **B26** | A66 | 35c + 2c pair | 1.00 | 1.00 |
| **B28** | A68 | 35c + 2c multi (S) | .55 | .55 |
| **B29** | A69 | 35c + 2c multi (S) | .55 | .55 |
| **B30** | A66 | 50c + 2c pair | 1.20 | 1.20 |
| **B32** | A70 | 50c + 2c multi (S) | .65 | .65 |
| **B33** | A66 | 60c + 2c pair | 1.40 | 1.40 |
| **B35** | A69 | 60c + 2c multi (S) | .80 | .80 |
| **B36** | A68 | 75c + 2c multi (S) | 1.00 | 1.00 |
| | | *Nos. B16-B36 (16)* | 10.85 | 10.85 |

### Easter Type of 1980
Souvenir Sheets

**1980, Apr. 2 Photo. *Perf. 13***

| | | | |
|---|---|---|---|
| **B37** | Sheet of 3 | 1.05 | 1.05 |
| *a.* | A71 25c + 2c like #262 | .30 | .30 |
| *b.* | A71 30c + 2c like #263 | .35 | .35 |
| *c.* | A71 35c + 2c like #264 | .40 | .40 |

**1980, Apr. 2**

| | | | | |
|---|---|---|---|---|
| **B38** | A71 | 85c + 5c like #262 | .75 | .75 |
| **B39** | A71 | 85c + 5c like #263 | .75 | .75 |
| **B40** | A71 | 85c + 5c like #264 | .75 | .75 |
| | | *Nos. B38-B40 (3)* | 2.25 | 2.25 |

Surtax was for hurricane relief.

### No. 245c Overprinted and Surcharged
Souvenir Sheet

**1980, Aug. 22 Photo. *Perf. 14***

| | | | |
|---|---|---|---|
| **B41** | Sheet of 10 | 5.00 | 5.00 |
| *a.* | A66 20c + 2c pair | .50 | .50 |
| *b.* | A66 30c + 2c pair | .65 | .65 |
| *c.* | A66 35c + 2c pair | .80 | .80 |
| *d.* | A66 50c + 2c pair | 1.25 | 1.25 |
| *e.* | A66 60c + 2c pair | 1.60 | 1.60 |

ZEAPEX '80, New Zealand Intl. Stamp Exhib., Auckland, Aug. 23-31.

### Nos. 293-296 Surcharged in Black
Souvenir Sheet

**1980, Oct. 30 Photo. *Perf. 14***

| | | | |
|---|---|---|---|
| **B42** | Sheet of 8, #a.-h. | 2.50 | 2.50 |

22nd Summer Olympic Games, Moscow, July 19-Aug. 3.

### Christmas Type of 1980
Souvenir Sheets

**1980, Nov. 28 Photo. *Perf. 13½x13***

| | | | | |
|---|---|---|---|---|
| **B43** | A76 | 80c + 5c like #301 | .75 | .75 |
| **B44** | A76 | 80c + 5c like #302 | .75 | .75 |
| **B45** | A76 | 80c + 5c like #303 | .75 | .75 |
| **B46** | A76 | 80c + 5c like #304 | .75 | .75 |
| | | *Nos. B43-B46 (4)* | 3.00 | 3.00 |

Nos. B43-B46 each contain one 31x39mm stamp.

### Easter Type of 1981
Souvenir Sheets

**1981, Apr. 10 Photo. *Perf. 13½***

| | | | |
|---|---|---|---|
| **B47** | Sheet of 3 | 1.75 | 1.75 |
| *a.* | A78 35c + 2c like #337 | .40 | .40 |
| *b.* | A78 50c + 2c like #338 | .50 | .50 |
| *c.* | A78 60c + 2c like #339 | .60 | .60 |
| **B48** | A78 80c + 5c like #337 | .75 | .75 |
| **B49** | A78 80c + 5c like #338 | .75 | .75 |
| **B50** | A78 80c + 5c like #339 | .75 | .75 |
| | *Nos. B47-B50 (4)* | 4.00 | 4.00 |

### Soccer Type of 1981

**1981, Oct. 16 Photo. *Perf. 13***

| | | | | |
|---|---|---|---|---|
| **B51** | A80 | Sheet of 9 | 3.25 | 3.25 |

#B51 contains #343-345 each with 3c surtax.

Nos. 340-342a Surcharged

**1981, Nov. 3 Photo. *Perf. 14***

**B52** A79 75c + 5c like #340 1.00 1.00
**B53** A79 95c + 5c like #341 1.25 1.25
**B54** A79 $1.20 + 5c like #342 1.50 1.50
*Nos. B52-B54 (3)* 3.75 3.75

**Souvenir Sheet**

**B55** Sheet of 3 4.50 4.50
*a.* A79 75c + 10c like #340 1.20 1.20
*b.* A79 95c + 10c like #341 1.40 1.40
*c.* A79 $1.20 + 10c like #342 1.75 1.75

Intl. Year of the Disabled. Surtax was for disabled.

Nos. 530-535 Surcharged in Black on Silver

**1986, Nov. 21 Litho. *Perf. 14***

**B56** A105 80c + 10c multi 2.75 2.75
**B57** A105 $1.15 + 10c multi 3.75 3.75
**B58** A105 $1.80 + 10c multi 5.50 5.50
**B59** A105 $2.60 + 10c multi 8.00 8.00
*Nos. B56-B59 (4)* 20.00 20.00

**Souvenir Sheets**

***Perf. 13½***

**B60** Sheet of 4 18.00 18.00
*a.-d.* A105 $1.50 + 10c on #534a-534d 4.50 4.50

***Perf. 14½x13½***

**B61** A105 $7.50 + 50c multi 18.00 18.00

No. B60 ovptd. "FIRST VISIT OF A POPE TO SOUTH PACIFIC" and "HIS HOLINESS POPE JOHN PAUL II" on margin. No. B61 ovptd. on margin only "Visit of Pope John Paul II, Nov 21-24 1986 / First Papal Visit to the South Pacific."

**Souvenir Sheets**

Aupex '97 Stamp Exhibition — SP1

**1997, June 9 Litho. *Perf. 14x15***

**B62** SP1 $2 +20c like #1 3.75 3.75

***Perf. 14½x15***

**B63** SP1 $2 +20c like #34 3.25 3.25

No. B63 contains one 31x60mm stamp.

**AIR POST STAMPS**

**Catalogue values for unused stamps in this section are for Never Hinged items.**

**Type of 1977**

Designs: 15c, Preparing ground for taro. 20c, Banana harvest. 23c, Bush plantation. 50c, Canoe fishing. 90c, Reef fishing. $1.35, Preparing ground for taro. $2.10, Shellfish gathering. $2.60, Luku harvest.

**1979 Litho. *Perf. 14***

**C1** A54 15c gold & multi .25 .25
**C2** A54 20c gold & multi .25 .25
**C3** A54 23c gold & multi .30 .30
**C4** A54 50c gold & multi .45 .45
**C5** A54 90c gold & multi .70 .70
**C6** A54 $1.35 gold & multi 1.10 1.10
**C7** A54 $2.10 gold & multi 1.75 1.75
**C8** A54 $2.60 gold & multi 2.25 2.25
**C9** A54 $5.10 like #187 4.25 4.25
**C10** A54 $6.35 like #188 5.50 5.50
*Nos. C1-C10 (10)* 16.80 16.80

Issue dates: Nos. C1-C5, Feb. 26. Nos. C6-C8, Mar. 30. C9-C10, May 28.

**OFFICIAL STAMPS**

**Catalogue values for unused stamps in this section are for Never Hinged items.**

Nos. 417-430, 332-334, 431-431A Ovptd. in Metallic Blue or Gold

***Perf. 13½, 13½x13, 13x13½, 13***

**1985-87 Photo.**

**O1** A89 12c multi .25 .25
**O2** A89 25c multi .25 .25
**O3** A89 30c multi .25 .25
**O4** A89 35c multi .25 .25
**O5** A89 40c multi .30 .30
**O6** A89 52c multi .40 .40
**O7** A89 58c multi .50 .50
**O8** A89 70c multi .55 .55
**O9** A89 83c multi .65 .65
**O10** A89 $1.05 multi .75 .75
**O11** A90 $1.75 multi 1.50 1.50
**O12** A90 $2.30 multi 2.50 2.50
**O13** A90 $3.90 multi 4.75 4.75
**O14** A77a $4 multi (G) 4.50 4.50
**O15** A90 $5 multi 5.50 5.50
**O16** A77a $6 multi ('87) (G) 10.00 10.00
**O17** A90 $6.60 multi ('86) 7.00 7.00
**O18** A90 $8.30 multi ('86) 9.00 9.00
**O19** A77a $10 multi ('87) (G) 16.00 16.00
*Nos. O1-O19 (19)* 64.90 64.90

Nos. 604-613 Ovptd. in Gold

**1993-94 Litho. *Perf. 14x13½***

**O20** A118 20c multicolored .30 .30
**O21** A118 50c multicolored .55 .55
**O22** A118 70c multicolored .80 .80
**O23** A118 $1 multicolored 1.25 1.25
**O24** A118 $1.50 multicolored 2.00 2.00
**O25** A118 $2 multicolored 3.50 3.50
**O26** A118 $3 multicolored 4.25 4.25
**O27** A118 $5 multicolored 6.50 6.50
**O28** A118 $7 multicolored 9.00 9.00
**O29** A118 $10 multicolored 13.00 13.00
**O30** A118 $15 multicolored 20.00 20.00
*Nos. O20-O30 (11)* 61.15 61.15

Nos. O20-O30 were not sold unused to local customers.

Issued: 20c-$2, 12/10/93; $3, $5, 4/27/94; $7, $10, 9/1/94; $15, 9/30/94.

# NORFOLK ISLAND

'nor-fək 'ī-lənd

LOCATION — Island in the south Pacific Ocean, 900 miles east of Australia
GOVT. — Territory of Australia
AREA — 13½ sq. mi.
POP. — 1,905 (1999 est.)

12 Pence = 1 Shilling
100 Cents = 1 Dollar (1966)

**Catalogue values for all unused stamps in this country are for Never Hinged items.**

**Watermark**

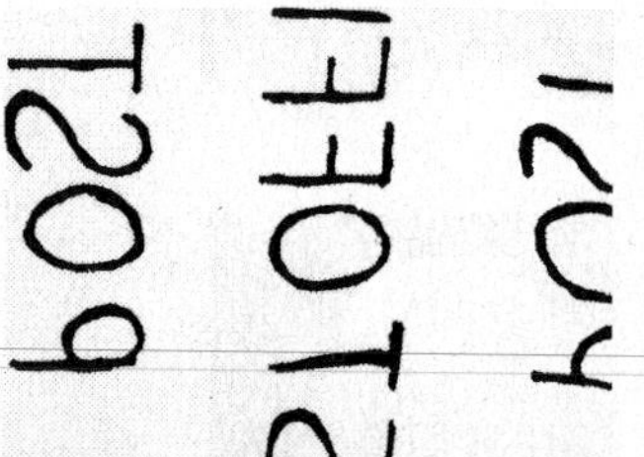

Wmk. 380 — "POST OFFICE"

View of Ball Bay — A1

**Unwmk.**

**1947, June 10 Engr. *Perf. 14***

**On Toned Paper**

**1** A1 ½p deep orange .50 .40
**2** A1 1p violet .45 .40
**3** A1 1½p bright green .50 .50
**4** A1 2p red violet .65 .45
**5** A1 2½p red .75 .35
**6** A1 3p brown orange .80 .45
**7** A1 4p rose lake 1.00 .45
**8** A1 5½p slate .75 .50
**9** A1 6p sepia .75 .45
**10** A1 9p lilac rose 1.25 .70
**11** A1 1sh gray green 1.00 .60
**12** A1 2sh olive bister 4.50 1.75
*Nos. 1-12 (12)* 12.90 7.00

Nos. 1-4 were reprinted in 1956-59 on white paper. Values, set: never hinged $125; used $200.

See Nos. 23-24.

The ½p, 1p, 1½p, 6p, and 1sh exist perf. 11 in different colors. These were not officially issued.

Warder's Tower — A2

Airfield — A3

Designs: 7½p, First Governor's Residence. 8½p, Barracks entrance. 10p, Salt House. 5sh, Bloody Bridge.

**1953, June 10 *Perf. 14½***

**13** A2 3½p rose brown 1.25 1.00
**14** A3 6½p dark green 2.50 3.50
**15** A3 7½p deep ultra 1.75 3.00
**16** A2 8½p chocolate 2.25 4.75
**17** A2 10p rose lilac 1.40 .75
**18** A3 5sh dark brown 32.50 9.00
*Nos. 13-18 (6)* 41.65 22.00

See Nos. 35, 40. For surcharges see Nos. 21-22, 27. For types surcharged see Nos. 26, 28.

Original Norfolk Seal and First Settlers — A4

**1956, June 8**

**19** A4 3p bluish green 1.00 .75
**20** A4 2sh violet 2.00 1.75

Cent. of the landing of the Pitcairn Islanders on Norfolk Island.

**Nos. 15 and 16 Surcharged with New Value and Bars**

**1958, July 1**

**21** A3 7p on 7½p dp ultra 1.00 *1.00*
**22** A2 8p on 8½p choc 1.25 *1.25*

**Ball Bay Type of 1947**

**1959, July 6 Engr. *Perf. 14***

**23** A1 3p green 11.50 8.00
**24** A1 2sh dark blue 13.50 10.00

A5

**Australia #332 Surcharged in Red**

**1959, Dec. 7**

**25** A5 5p on 4p dk gray blue 1.25 1.25

**No. 14 and Types of 1953 Surcharged with New Values and Bars**

**1960, Sept. 26 *Perf. 14½***

**26** A2 1sh1p on 3½p dk bl 4.00 2.75
**27** A3 2sh5p on 6½p dk grn 5.50 4.25
**28** A3 2sh8p on 7½p dk brn 7.25 5.75
*Nos. 26-28 (3)* 16.75 12.75

**Types of 1953 and**

Island Hibiscus — A6

Fairy Tern — A7

Red-Tailed Tropic Bird — A8

Designs: 2p, Lagunaria patersonii (flowers). 5p, Lantana. 8p, Red hibiscus. 9p, Cereus and Queen Elizabeth II. 10p, Salt House. 1sh1p, Fringed hibiscus. 2sh, Providence petrel, vert. 2sh5p, Passion flower. 2sh8p, Rose apple. 5sh, Bloody Bridge.

**1960-62 Unwmk. Engr. *Perf. 14½***

**29** A6 1p blue green .25 .25
**30** A6 2p gray grn & brt pink .25 .25
**31** A7 3p brt green ('61) .40 .25
**32** A6 5p lilac .85 .55
**33** A6 8p vermilion 1.50 1.10
**34** A6 9p ultramarine 1.50 1.10
**35** A2 10p pale pur & brn ('61) 2.60 1.25
**36** A6 1sh1p dark red ('61) 2.00 1.10
**37** A6 2sh sepia ('61) 2.00 1.25
**38** A6 2sh5p dk purple ('62) 2.00 1.25
**39** A6 2sh8p green & sal ('62) 3.25 1.50
**40** A3 5sh green & gray ('61) 4.75 2.10

***Perf. 14½x14***

**41** A8 10sh green ('61) 32.50 30.00
*Nos. 29-41 (13)* 53.85 41.95

See #585-586. For surcharges see #71-82.

Map of Norfolk Island — A9

**1960, Oct. 24 Engr. *Perf. 14***

**42** A9 2sh8p rose violet 14.00 12.00

Introduction of local government for Norfolk Island.

Open Bible and Candle — A9a

**1960, Nov. 21 *Perf. 14½***

**43** A9a 5p bright lilac rose 2.00 2.00

Christmas.

Page from Book of Hours, 15th Century A9b

**1961, Nov. 20** *Perf. 14½x14*

| | | | |
|---|---|---|---|
| **44** | A9b 5p slate blue | 1.00 | 1.00 |

Nos. 43-44 were issued to mark the beginning and the end of the 350th anniversary year of the publication of the King James translation of the Bible.

Madonna and Child — A9c

**1962, Nov. 19** *Perf. 14½*

| | | | |
|---|---|---|---|
| **45** | A9c 5p blue | 1.00 | 1.00 |

Christmas.

Overlooking Kingston — A10

Dreamfish — A11

Designs: 6p, Tweed trousers (fish). 8p, Kingston scene. 9p, "The Arches." 10p, Slaughter Bay. 11p, Trumpeter fish. 1sh, Po'ov (wrasse). 1sh6p, Queensland grouper. 2sh3p, Ophie (carangidae).

*Perf. 14½x14*

**1962-64** **Unwmk.** **Photo.**

| | | | | |
|---|---|---|---|---|
| **49** | A10 | 5p multi ('64) | .45 | .40 |
| **50** | A11 | 6p multi | .55 | .55 |
| **51** | A10 | 8p multi ('64) | .70 | .60 |
| **52** | A10 | 9p multi ('64) | 1.00 | .90 |
| **53** | A10 | 10p multi ('64) | 1.15 | 1.15 |
| **54** | A11 | 11p multi ('63) | 1.75 | 1.15 |
| **55** | A11 | 1sh olive, bl & pink | 2.00 | 1.60 |
| **57** | A11 | 1sh3p bl, mar & grn ('63) | 2.25 | 2.00 |
| **58** | A11 | 1sh6p bl, brn & lil ('63) | 2.50 | 2.50 |
| **60** | A11 | 2sh3p dl bl, yel & red ('63) | 3.00 | 2.75 |
| | | *Nos. 49-60 (10)* | 15.35 | 13.60 |

Star of Bethlehem — A11a

**1963, Nov. 11** **Engr.** *Perf. 14½*

| | | | |
|---|---|---|---|
| **65** | A11a 5p vermilion | .90 | .90 |

Christmas.

Symbolic Pine Tree — A12

**1964, July 1** **Photo.** *Perf. 13½x13*

| | | | |
|---|---|---|---|
| **66** | A12 5p orange, blk & red | .75 | .75 |
| **67** | A12 8p gray green, blk & red | 1.00 | 1.00 |

50th anniv. of Norfolk Island as an Australian Territory.

Child Looking at Nativity Scene — A12a

**1964, Nov. 9** *Perf. 13½*

| | | | |
|---|---|---|---|
| **68** | A12a 5p multicolored | .75 | .75 |

Christmas.

"Simpson and His Donkey" by Wallace Anderson — A12b

**1965, Apr. 14** **Photo.** *Perf. 13½x13*

| | | | |
|---|---|---|---|
| **69** | A12b 5p brt grn, sepia & blk | .55 | .45 |

ANZAC issue. See note after Australia No. 387.

Nativity — A12c

**1965, Oct. 25** **Unwmk.** *Perf. 13½*

| | | | |
|---|---|---|---|
| **70** | A12c 5p gold, blk, ultra & redsh brn | .40 | .40 |

Christmas. No. 70 is luminescent. See note after Australia No. 331.

**Nos. 29-33 and 35-41 Surcharged in Black on Overprinted Metallic Rectangles**

No. 74

Type IV

Two types of 1c on 1p:
I. Silver rectangle 4x5½mm.
II. Silver rectangle 5½x5¼mm.
Two types of $1 on 10sh:
III. Silver rectangle 7x6½mm.
IV. Silver rectangle 6x4mm.

*Perf. 14½, 14½x14*

**1966, Feb. 14** **Engr.**

| | | | | |
|---|---|---|---|---|
| **71** | A6 | 1c on 1p bl grn (I) | .25 | .25 |
| *a.* | | Type II | .30 | .30 |
| **72** | A6 | 2c on 2p gray grn & brt pink | .25 | .25 |
| **73** | A7 | 3c on 3p brt green | .35 | *.60* |
| **74** | A6 | 4c on 5p purple | .25 | .25 |
| **75** | A6 | 5c on 8p vermilion | .25 | .25 |
| **76** | A2 | 10c on 10p pale pur & brn | .70 | .25 |
| **77** | A6 | 15c on 1sh1p dark red | .30 | .40 |
| **78** | A6 | 20c on 2sh sepia | 2.75 | 2.25 |
| **79** | A6 | 25c on 2sh5p dk pur | 1.10 | .30 |
| **80** | A6 | 30c on 2sh8p grn & sal | .75 | .40 |
| **81** | A3 | 50c on 5sh grn & gray | 2.75 | .55 |
| **82** | A8 | $1 on 10sh green (III) | 2.50 | 2.00 |
| *a.* | | Type IV | 5.00 | 5.00 |
| | | *Nos. 71-82 (12)* | 12.20 | 7.75 |

Headstone Bridge — A13

**1966, June 27** **Photo.** *Perf. 14½*

| | | | |
|---|---|---|---|
| **88** | A13 7c shown | .25 | .25 |
| **89** | A13 9c Cemetery road | .40 | .40 |

St. Barnabas Chapel — A14

Design: 4c, Interior of St. Barnabas Chapel.

*Perf. 14x14½*

**1966, Aug. 23** **Photo.** **Unwmk.**

| | | | |
|---|---|---|---|
| **97** | A14 4c multicolored | .25 | .25 |
| **98** | A14 25c multicolored | .45 | .45 |

Centenary of the Melanesian Mission.

Star over Philip Island — A15

**1966, Oct. 24** **Photo.** *Perf. 14½*

| | | | |
|---|---|---|---|
| **99** | A15 4c violet, grn, blue & sil | .35 | .35 |

Christmas.

H.M.S. Resolution, 1774 — A16

Ships: 2c, La Boussole and Astrolabe, 1788. 3c, Brig Supply, 1788. 4c, Sirius, 1790. 5c, The Norfolk, 1798. 7c, Survey cutter Mermaid, 1825. 9c, The Lady Franklin, 1853. 10c The Morayshire, 1856. 15c, Southern Cross, 1866. 20c, The Pitcairn, 1891. 25c, Norfolk Island whaleboat, 1895. 30c, Cable ship Iris, 1907. 50c, The Resolution, 1926. $1, S.S. Morinda, 1931.

**1967-68** **Photo.** *Perf. 14x14½*

| | | | | |
|---|---|---|---|---|
| **100** | A16 | 1c multicolored | .25 | .25 |
| **101** | A16 | 2c multicolored | .25 | .25 |
| **102** | A16 | 3c multicolored | .25 | .25 |
| **103** | A16 | 4c multicolored | .40 | .25 |
| **104** | A16 | 5c multicolored | .25 | .25 |
| **105** | A16 | 7c multicolored | .25 | .25 |
| **106** | A16 | 9c multicolored | .30 | .25 |
| **107** | A16 | 10c multicolored | .40 | .35 |
| **108** | A16 | 15c multicolored | .60 | .55 |
| **109** | A16 | 20c multicolored | .90 | .80 |
| **110** | A16 | 25c multicolored | 1.40 | 1.25 |
| **111** | A16 | 30c multicolored | 1.75 | 1.50 |
| **112** | A16 | 50c multicolored | 2.25 | 2.00 |
| **113** | A16 | $1 multicolored | 3.50 | 3.25 |
| | | *Nos. 100-113 (14)* | 12.75 | 11.45 |

Issued: #100-103, 4/17; #104-107, 8/19; #108-110, 3/18/68; #111-113, 6/18/68.

Lions Intl., 50th Anniv. — A16a

**1967, June 7** **Photo.** *Perf. 13½*

| | | | |
|---|---|---|---|
| **114** | A16a 4c citron, blk & bl grn | .40 | .40 |

Printed on luminescent paper; see note after Australia No. 331.

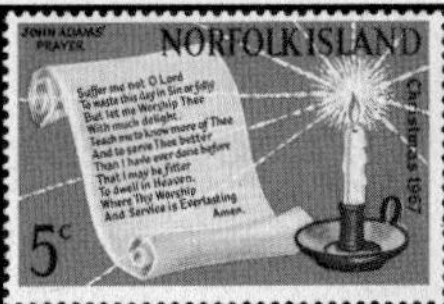


John Adams' Prayer A17

**1967, Oct. 16** **Photo.** *Perf. 14x14½*

| | | | |
|---|---|---|---|
| **115** | A17 5c brick red, blk & buff | .40 | .40 |

Christmas.

**Queen Elizabeth II Type of Australia, 1966-67**

Coil Stamps

***Perf. 15 Horizontally***

**1968-71** **Photo.** **Unwmk.**

| | | | | |
|---|---|---|---|---|
| **116** | A157 | 3c brn org, blk & buff | .25 | .25 |
| **117** | A157 | 4c blue grn, blk & buff | .25 | .25 |
| **118** | A157 | 5c brt purple, blk & buff | .25 | .25 |
| **118A** | A157 | 6c dk red, brn, blk & buff | .30 | .40 |
| | | *Nos. 116-118A (4)* | 1.05 | 1.15 |

Issued: 6c, 8/2/71; others, 8/5/68.

DC-4 Skymaster and Lancastrian Plane — A18

**1968, Sept. 25** *Perf. 14½x14*

| | | | |
|---|---|---|---|
| **119** | A18 5c dk car, sky bl & ind | .25 | .25 |
| **120** | A18 7c dk car, bl grn & sep | .25 | .25 |

21st anniv. of the Sydney to Norfolk Island air service by Qantas Airways.

Star and Hibiscus Wreath — A19

**Photo.; Silver Impressed (Star)**

**1968, Oct. 24** *Perf. 14½x14*

| | | | |
|---|---|---|---|
| **121** | A19 5c sky blue & multi | .35 | .35 |

Christmas.

Map of Pacific, Transit of Venus before Sun, Capt. Cook and Quadrant A20

**1969, June 3** **Photo.** *Perf. 14x14½*

| | | | |
|---|---|---|---|
| **122** | A20 10c brn, ol, pale brn & yel | .35 | .35 |

Bicent. of the observation at Tahiti by Capt. James Cook of the transit of the planet Venus across the sun.

Map of Van Diemen's Land and Norfolk Island A21

**1969, Sept. 29** *Perf. 14x14½*

| | | | |
|---|---|---|---|
| **123** | A21 5c multicolored | .25 | .25 |
| **124** | A21 30c multicolored | .50 | .50 |

125th anniv. of the annexation of Norfolk Island by Van Diemen's Land (Tasmania).

Nativity (Mother-of-Pearl carving) — A22

**1969, Oct. 27 Photo. *Perf. 14½x14***

| | | | | |
|---|---|---|---|---|
| **125** | A22 | 5c brown & multi | .35 | .35 |

Christmas.

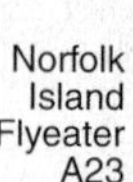

Norfolk Island Flyeater A23

Birds of Norfolk Island from Book by Gregory Mathews: 1c, Robins, vert. 2c, Norfolk Island whistlers (thickheads), vert. 4c, Long-tailed cuckoos. 5c, Red-fronted parakeet, vert. 7c, Long-tailed trillers, vert. 9c, Island thrush. 10c, Owl, vert. 15c, Norfolk Island pigeon (extinct; vert.). 20c, White-breasted white-eye. 25c, Norfolk Island parrots, vert. 30c, Gray fantail. 45c, Norfolk Island starlings. 50c, Crimson rosella, vert. $1, Sacred kingfisher.

***Perf. 14x14½, 14½x14***

**1970-71 Photo. Unwmk.**

| | | | | |
|---|---|---|---|---|
| **126** | A23 | 1c multicolored | .25 | .25 |
| **127** | A23 | 2c multicolored | .25 | .30 |
| **128** | A23 | 3c multicolored | .25 | .25 |
| **129** | A23 | 4c multicolored | .45 | .30 |
| **130** | A23 | 5c multicolored | 1.25 | .80 |
| **131** | A23 | 7c multicolored | .35 | .25 |
| **132** | A23 | 9c multicolored | .55 | .30 |
| **133** | A23 | 10c multicolored | 1.40 | 1.60 |
| **134** | A23 | 15c multicolored | 1.25 | .75 |
| **135** | A23 | 20c multicolored | 5.75 | 3.50 |
| **136** | A23 | 25c multicolored | 2.00 | 1.25 |
| **137** | A23 | 30c multicolored | 5.75 | 3.00 |
| **138** | A23 | 45c multicolored | 2.50 | 1.40 |
| **139** | A23 | 50c multicolored | 3.00 | 2.25 |
| **140** | A23 | $1 multicolored | 8.25 | 7.00 |
| | | *Nos. 126-140 (15)* | 33.25 | 23.20 |

Issued: 3c, 4c, 9c, 45c, 2/25; 1c, 7c, 10c, 25c, 7/22; 2c, 2c, 5c, 15c, 50c, 2/24/71; 20c, 30c, $1, 6/16/71.

Map of Australia, James Cook and Southern Cross A24

Design: 10c, "Endeavour" entering Botany Bay, Apr. 29, 1770, and aborigine with spear. The 1776 portrait of James Cook on the 5c is by John Webber.

**1970, Apr. 29 Photo. *Perf. 14x14½***

| | | | | |
|---|---|---|---|---|
| **141** | A24 | 5c multicolored | .25 | .25 |
| **142** | A24 | 10c multicolored | .25 | .25 |

200th anniv. of Cook's discovery and exploration of the eastern coast of Australia.

First Christmas, Sydney Bay, 1788 — A25

**1970, Oct. 15 Photo. *Perf. 14x14½***

| | | | | |
|---|---|---|---|---|
| **143** | A25 | 5c multicolored | .25 | .25 |

Christmas.

Bishop Patteson, Open Bible — A26

#145, Bible opened to Acts Chap. 7, martyrdom of St. Stephen, & knotted palm fronds. #146, Bishop Patteson, rose window of Melanesian Mission Chapel on Norfolk Island. #147, Cross erected at Nukapu where Patteson died & his arms.

**1971, Sept. 20**

| | | | | |
|---|---|---|---|---|
| **144** | A26 | 6c brown & multi | .25 | .25 |
| **145** | A26 | 6c brown & multi | .25 | .25 |
| *a.* | | Pair, #144-145 | .45 | .45 |
| **146** | A26 | 10c purple & multi | .25 | .25 |
| **147** | A26 | 10c purple & multi | .25 | .25 |
| *a.* | | Pair, #146-147 | .55 | .55 |
| | | *Nos. 144-147 (4)* | 1.00 | 1.00 |

Centenary of the death of Bishop John Coleridge Patteson (1827-1871), head of the Melanesian mission.

Rose Window, St. Barnabas Chapel, Norfolk Island — A27

**1971, Oct. 25 *Perf. 14x13½***

| | | | | |
|---|---|---|---|---|
| **148** | A27 | 6c dk vio blue & multi | .30 | .30 |

Christmas.

Map of South Pacific and Commission Flag — A28

**1972, Feb. 7 *Perf. 14x14½***

| | | | | |
|---|---|---|---|---|
| **149** | A28 | 7c multicolored | .35 | .35 |

So. Pacific Commission, 25th anniv.

Stained-glass Window — A29

**1972, Oct. 16 Photo. *Perf. 14x14½***

| | | | | |
|---|---|---|---|---|
| **150** | A29 | 7c dark olive & multi | .30 | .30 |

Christmas. The stained-glass window by Edward Coley Burne-Jones is in All Saints Church, Norfolk Island.

Cross, Church, Pines — A30

**1972, Nov. 20**

| | | | | |
|---|---|---|---|---|
| **151** | A30 | 12c multicolored | .30 | .30 |
| *a.* | | Purple omitted | *1,600.* | |

Centenary of All Saints Church, first built by Pitcairners on Norfolk Island.

"Resolution" in Antarctica — A31

**1973, Jan. 17 Photo. *Perf. 14½x14***

| | | | | |
|---|---|---|---|---|
| **152** | A31 | 35c multicolored | 3.25 | 3.25 |

200th anniv. of the 1st crossing of the Antarctic Circle by Cook, Jan. 17, 1773.

Sleeping Child, and Christmas Tree — A32

Christmas: 35c, Star over lagoon.

**1973, Oct. 22 Photo. *Perf. 14x14½***

| | | | | |
|---|---|---|---|---|
| **153** | A32 | 7c black & multi | .25 | .25 |
| **154** | A32 | 12c black & multi | .30 | .30 |
| **155** | A32 | 35c black & multi | 1.05 | 1.05 |
| | | *Nos. 153-155 (3)* | 1.60 | 1.60 |

Protestant Clergyman's House — A33

Designs: 2c, Royal Engineer Office. 3c, Double quarters for free overseers. 4c, Guard House. 5c, Pentagonal Gaol entrance. 7c, Pentagonal Gaol, aerial view. 8c, Convict barracks. 10c, Officers' quarters, New Military Barracks. 12c, New Military Barracks. 14c, Beach stores. 15c, Magazine. 20c, Old Military Barracks, entrance. 25c, Old Military Barracks. 30c, Old stores, Crankmill. 50c, Commissariat stores. $1, Government House.

**1973-75 Photo. *Perf. 14x14½***

| | | | | |
|---|---|---|---|---|
| **156** | A33 | 1c multicolored | .25 | .25 |
| **157** | A33 | 2c multicolored | .25 | .25 |
| **158** | A33 | 3c multicolored | .35 | *.70* |
| **159** | A33 | 4c multicolored | .25 | .25 |
| **160** | A33 | 5c multicolored | .25 | .25 |
| **161** | A33 | 7c multicolored | .35 | .35 |
| **162** | A33 | 8c multicolored | 1.40 | 1.40 |
| **163** | A33 | 10c multicolored | .50 | .50 |
| **164** | A33 | 12c multicolored | .50 | .40 |
| **165** | A33 | 14c multicolored | .50 | *.65* |
| **166** | A33 | 15c multicolored | 1.25 | .90 |
| **167** | A33 | 20c multicolored | .50 | .50 |
| **168** | A33 | 25c multicolored | 1.25 | 1.25 |
| **169** | A33 | 30c multicolored | .50 | .50 |
| **170** | A33 | 50c multicolored | .55 | *1.10* |
| **171** | A33 | $1 multicolored | 1.10 | *1.75* |
| | | *Nos. 156-171 (16)* | 9.75 | 11.00 |

Issued: 1c, 5c, 10c, 50c, 11/19/73; 2c, 7c, 12c, 30c, 5/1/74; 4c, 14c, 20c, $1, 7/12/74; 3c, 8c, 15c, 25c, 2/19/75.

Map of Norfolk Island A34

**1974, Feb. 8 Photo. *Perf. 14x14½***

| | | | | |
|---|---|---|---|---|
| **172** | A34 | 7c red lilac & multi | .35 | .35 |
| **173** | A34 | 25c dull blue & multi | 1.00 | 1.00 |

Visit of Queen Elizabeth II and the Duke of Edinburgh, Feb. 11-12.

Gipsy Moth over Norfolk Island A35

**1974, Mar. 28 Litho. *Perf. 14x14½***

| | | | | |
|---|---|---|---|---|
| **174** | A35 | 14c multicolored | 1.25 | 1.25 |

1st aircraft to visit Norfolk, Sir Francis Chichester's "Mme. Elijah," Mar. 28, 1931.

Capt. Cook — A36

Designs: 10c, "Resolution," by Henry Roberts. 14c, Norfolk Island pine, cone and seedling. 25c, Norfolk Island flax, by George Raper, 1790. Portrait of Cook on 7c by William Hodges, 1770.

**1974, Oct. 8 Litho. *Perf. 14***

| | | | | |
|---|---|---|---|---|
| **175** | A36 | 7c multicolored | .65 | .65 |
| **176** | A36 | 10c multicolored | 1.60 | 1.60 |
| **177** | A36 | 14c multicolored | 1.30 | 1.30 |
| **178** | A36 | 25c multicolored | 1.30 | 1.30 |
| | | *Nos. 175-178 (4)* | 4.85 | 4.85 |

Bicentenary of the discovery of Norfolk Island by Capt. James Cook.

Nativity — A37

**1974, Oct. 18 Photo. *Perf. 14***

| | | | | |
|---|---|---|---|---|
| **179** | A37 | 7c rose & multi | .25 | .25 |
| **180** | A37 | 30c violet & multi | 1.00 | 1.00 |

Christmas.

Norfolk Island Pine — A38

15c, Off-shore islands. 35c, Crimson rosella and sacred kingfisher. 40c, Map showing Norfolk's location. Stamps in shape of Norfolk Island.

**1974, Dec. 16 Litho. *Imperf.***

**Self-adhesive**

| | | | | |
|---|---|---|---|---|
| **181** | A38 | 10c brown & multi | .30 | .30 |
| **182** | A38 | 15c dk blue & multi | .40 | .40 |
| **183** | A38 | 35c dk purple & multi | 1.05 | 1.05 |
| **184** | A38 | 40c dk blue grn & multi | 1.25 | 2.10 |
| *a.* | | Souvenir sheet of 4 | 22.50 | 24.00 |
| | | *Nos. 181-184 (4)* | 3.00 | 3.85 |

Cent. of UPU. Stamps printed on peelable paper backing. No. 184a contains 4 imperf. stamps similar to Nos. 181-184 in reduced size on a background of map of Norfolk Island. Peelable paper backing shows beach scene on Norfolk Island.

Survey Cutter "Mermaid," 1825 — A39

Design: 35c, Kingston, 1835, after painting by Thomas Seller. Stamps outlined in shape of Norfolk Island map.

**1975, Aug. 18 Litho. *Imperf.***
**Self-adhesive**

| | | | | |
|---|---|---|---|---|
| **185** | A39 | 10c multicolored | .35 | .35 |
| **186** | A39 | 35c multicolored | .65 | .65 |

Sesquicentennial of 2nd settlement of Norfolk Island. Printed on peelable paper backing with green and black design and inscription.

Star over Norfolk Island Pine and Map — A40

**1975, Oct. 6 Photo. *Perf. 14½x14***

| | | | | |
|---|---|---|---|---|
| **187** | A40 | 10c lt blue & multi | .25 | .25 |
| **188** | A40 | 15c lt brown & multi | .40 | .40 |
| **189** | A40 | 35c lilac & multi | .55 | .55 |
| | | *Nos. 187-189 (3)* | 1.20 | 1.20 |

Christmas.

Brass Memorial Cross — A41

Design: 60c, Laying foundation stone, 1875, and chapel, 1975, horiz.

***Perf. 14½x14, 14x14½***

**1975, Nov. 24 Photo.**

| | | | | |
|---|---|---|---|---|
| **190** | A41 | 30c multicolored | .35 | .35 |
| **191** | A41 | 60c multicolored | .90 | .90 |

St. Barnabas Chapel, centenary.

Launching "Resolution" A42

Design: 45c, "Resolution" under sail.

**1975, Dec. 1 *Perf. 14x14½***

| | | | | |
|---|---|---|---|---|
| **192** | A42 | 25c multicolored | .40 | .40 |
| **193** | A42 | 45c multicolored | .85 | .85 |

50th anniversary of launching of schooner "Resolution."

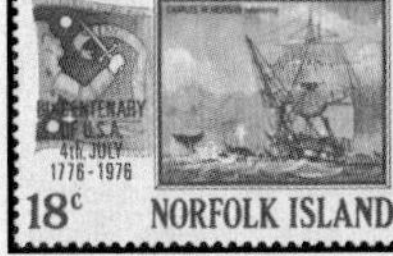


Bedford Flag, Charles W. Morgan Whaler A43

Designs: 25c, Grand Union Flag, church interior. 40c, 15-stari flag, 1795, and plane over island, WWII. 45c, 13-star flag and California quail.

**1976, July 5 Photo. *Perf. 14***

| | | | | |
|---|---|---|---|---|
| **194** | A43 | 18c multicolored | .30 | .35 |
| **195** | A43 | 25c multicolored | .30 | .30 |
| **196** | A43 | 40c multicolored | .65 | .75 |
| **197** | A43 | 45c multicolored | .75 | .85 |
| | | *Nos. 194-197 (4)* | 2.00 | 2.25 |

American Bicentennial.

Bird in Flight, Brilliant Sun — A44

**1976, Oct. 4 Photo. *Perf. 14***

| | | | | |
|---|---|---|---|---|
| **198** | A44 | 18c blue grn & multi | .30 | .30 |
| **199** | A44 | 25c dp blue & multi | .50 | .50 |
| **200** | A44 | 45c violet & multi | .80 | .80 |
| | | *Nos. 198-200 (3)* | 1.60 | 1.60 |

Christmas.

Bassaris Itea — A45

Butterflies and Moths: 2c, Utetheisa pulchelloides vaga. 3c, Agathia asterias jowettorum. 4c, Cynthia kershawi. 5c, Leucania loreyimima. 10c, Hypolimnas bolina nerina. 15c, Pyrrhorachis pyrrhogona. 16c, Austrocarea iocephala millsi. 17c, Pseudocoremia christiani. 18c, Cleora idiocrossa. 19c, Simplicia caeneusalis buffetti. 20c, Austrocidaria ralstonae. 30c, Hippotion scrofa. 40c, Papilio ilioneus. 50c, Tiracola plagiata. $1, Precis vililda. $2, Cepora perimale.

**1976-77 Photo. *Perf. 14***

| | | | | |
|---|---|---|---|---|
| **201** | A45 | 1c multicolored | .25 | *.40* |
| **202** | A45 | 2c multicolored | .25 | *.40* |
| **203** | A45 | 3c multicolored | .25 | .30 |
| **204** | A45 | 4c multicolored | .25 | .30 |
| **205** | A45 | 5c multicolored | .25 | *.70* |
| **206** | A45 | 10c multicolored | .25 | *.70* |
| **207** | A45 | 15c multicolored | .25 | .30 |
| **208** | A45 | 16c multicolored | .25 | .30 |
| **209** | A45 | 17c multicolored | .30 | .30 |
| **210** | A45 | 18c multicolored | .30 | .30 |
| **211** | A45 | 19c multicolored | .30 | .30 |
| **212** | A45 | 20c multicolored | .35 | .30 |
| **213** | A45 | 30c multicolored | .45 | *.60* |
| **214** | A45 | 40c multicolored | .50 | .35 |
| **215** | A45 | 50c multicolored | .65 | *.75* |
| **216** | A45 | $1 multicolored | .70 | *.75* |
| **217** | A45 | $2 multicolored | 1.10 | *1.30* |
| | | *Nos. 201-217 (17)* | 6.65 | *8.35* |

Issued: 1c, 5c, 10c, 16c, 18c, $1, 11/17; others, 1977.

View of Kingston A46

**1977, June 10**

| | | | | |
|---|---|---|---|---|
| **218** | A46 | 25c multicolored | .50 | .50 |

25th anniv. of reign of Elizabeth II.

Hibiscus and 19th Century Whaler's Lamp — A47

**1977, Oct. 4 Photo. *Perf. 14½***

| | | | | |
|---|---|---|---|---|
| **219** | A47 | 18c multicolored | .25 | .25 |
| **220** | A47 | 25c multicolored | .25 | .25 |
| **221** | A47 | 45c multicolored | .40 | .40 |
| | | *Nos. 219-221 (3)* | .90 | .90 |

Christmas.

Capt. Cook, by Nathaniel Dance — A48

Designs: 25c, Discovery of Northern Hawaiian Islands (Cook aboard ship), horiz. 80c, British flag and Island, horiz.

**1978, Jan. 18 Photo. *Perf. 14½***

| | | | | |
|---|---|---|---|---|
| **222** | A48 | 18c multicolored | .35 | .35 |
| **223** | A48 | 25c multicolored | .35 | .35 |
| **224** | A48 | 80c multicolored | .70 | .70 |
| | | *Nos. 222-224 (3)* | 1.40 | 1.40 |

Bicentenary of Capt. Cook's arrival in Hawaiian Islands.

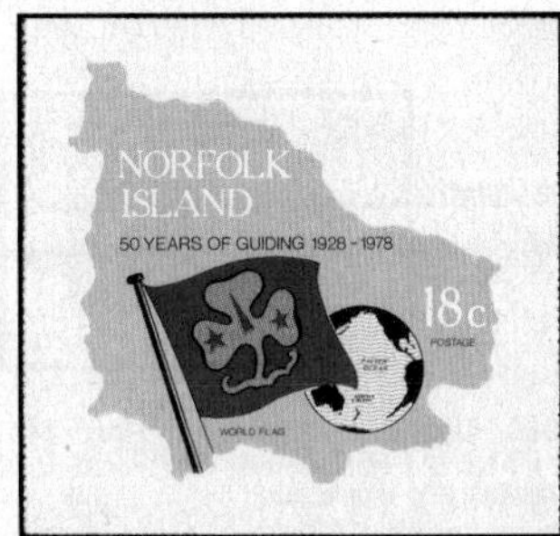


World Guides Flag and Globe — A49

Designs: 25c, Norfolk Guides' scarf badge and trefoil. 35c, Elizabeth II and trefoil. 45c, FAO Ceres medal with portrait of Lady Olive Baden-Powell, and trefoil. Stamps outlined in shape of Norfolk Island map.

**1978, Feb. 22 Litho. *Imperf.***
**Self-adhesive**

| | | | | |
|---|---|---|---|---|
| **225** | A49 | 18c lt ultra & multi | .30 | .30 |
| **226** | A49 | 25c yellow & multi | .30 | .30 |
| **227** | A49 | 35c lt green & multi | .40 | .40 |
| **228** | A49 | 45c yellow grn & multi | .50 | .50 |
| | | *Nos. 225-228 (4)* | 1.50 | 1.50 |

50th anniversary of Norfolk Island Girl Guides. Printed on peelable paper backing with green multiple pines and tourist publicity inscription.

St. Edward's Crown A50

Design: 70c, Coronation regalia.

**1978, June 29 Photo. *Perf. 14½***

| | | | | |
|---|---|---|---|---|
| **229** | A50 | 25c multicolored | .30 | .30 |
| **230** | A50 | 70c multicolored | .70 | .70 |

25th anniv. of coronation of Elizabeth II.

Norfolk Island Boy Scouts, 50th Anniv. — A51

Designs: 20c, Cliffs, Duncombe Bay, Scout Making Fire. 25c, Emily Bay, Philip and Nepean Islands from Kingston. 35c, Anson Bay, Cub and Boy Scouts. 45c, Sunset and Lord Baden-Powell. Stamps outlined in shape of Norfolk Island map.

**1978, Aug. 22 Litho. *Imperf.***
**Self-adhesive**

| | | | | |
|---|---|---|---|---|
| **231** | A51 | 20c multicolored | .40 | .40 |
| **232** | A51 | 25c multicolored | .45 | .45 |
| **233** | A51 | 35c multicolored | .65 | .65 |
| **234** | A51 | 45c multicolored | .70 | .70 |
| | | *Nos. 231-234 (4)* | 2.20 | 2.20 |

Printed on peelable paper backing with green multiple pines and tourist publicity inscription and picture.

Map of Bering Sea and Pacific Ocean, Routes of Discovery and Resolution — A52

Design: 90c, Discovery and Resolution trapped in ice, by John Webber.

**1978, Aug. 29 Photo. *Perf. 14½***

| | | | | |
|---|---|---|---|---|
| **235** | A52 | 25c multicolored | .40 | .40 |
| **236** | A52 | 90c multicolored | 1.00 | 1.00 |

Northernmost point of Cook's voyages.

Poinsettia and Bible — A53

Christmas: 30c, Native oak (flowers) and Bible. 55c, Hibiscus and Bible.

**1978, Oct. 3 Photo. *Perf. 14½***

| | | | | |
|---|---|---|---|---|
| **237** | A53 | 20c multicolored | .25 | .25 |
| **238** | A53 | 30c multicolored | .30 | .30 |
| **239** | A53 | 55c multicolored | .60 | .60 |
| | | *Nos. 237-239 (3)* | 1.15 | 1.15 |

Capt. Cook, View of Staithes A54

80c, Capt. Cook and view of Whitby harbor.

**1978, Oct. 27**

| | | | | |
|---|---|---|---|---|
| **240** | A54 | 20c multicolored | .40 | *.50* |
| **241** | A54 | 80c multicolored | 1.10 | *1.25* |

Resolution, Map of Asia and Australia — A55

Designs: No. 243, Map of Hawaii and Americas, Cook's route and statue. No. 244, Capt. Cook's death. No. 245, Ships off Hawaii.

**1979, Feb. 14 Photo. *Perf. 14½***

| | | | |
|---|---|---|---|
| **242** | 20c multicolored | .30 | .30 |
| **243** | 20c multicolored | .30 | .30 |
| *a.* | A55 Pair, #242-243 | .60 | .60 |
| **244** | 40c multicolored | .65 | .65 |
| **245** | 40c multicolored | .65 | .65 |
| *a.* | A55 Pair, #244-245 | 1.30 | 1.30 |
| | *Nos. 242-245 (4)* | 1.90 | 1.90 |

Bicentenary of Capt. Cook's death.

Rowland Hill and Tasmania No. 1 A56

Rowland Hill and: 30c, Great Britain No. 8. 55c, Norfolk Island No. 2.

**1979, Aug. 27** *Perf. 14x14½*

246 A56 20c multicolored .30 .30
247 A56 30c multicolored .30 .30
248 A56 55c multicolored .40 .40
a. Souvenir sheet of 1 1.00 1.00
*Nos. 246-248 (3)* 1.00 1.00

Sir Rowland Hill (1795-1879), originator of penny postage.

Legislative Assembly — A57

**1979, Aug. Photo.** *Perf. 14½x14*

249 A57 $1 multicolored .90 .90

First session of Legislative Assembly.

Map of Pacific Ocean, IYC Emblem A58

**1979, Sept. 25 Litho.** *Perf. 15*

250 A58 80c multicolored .75 .75

International Year of the Child.

Emily Bay Beach — A59

**1979, Oct. 2 Photo.** *Perf. 12½x13*

251 15c Beach .25 .25
252 20c Emily Bay .25 .25
253 30c Salt House .30 .30
a. Souv. sheet of 3, #251-253, perf. 14x14½ 1.25 1.25
b. A59 Strip of 3, #251-253 .80 .80

Christmas. #253b has continuous design.

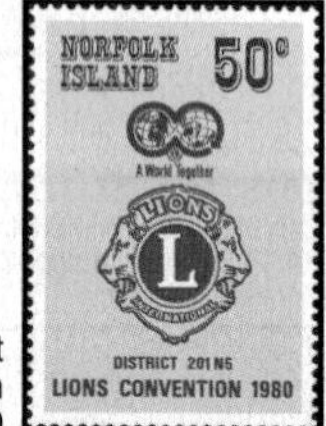


Lions District Convention 1980 — A60

**1980, Jan. 25 Litho.** *Perf. 15*

254 A60 50c multicolored .50 .50

Rotary International, 75th Anniversary — A61

**1980, Feb. 21**

255 A61 50c multicolored .55 .55
a. Black omitted *11,000.*

No. 255a is unique.

DH-60 "Gypsy Moth" A62

1c, Hawker Siddeley HS-748. 3c, Curtiss P-40 Kittyhawk. 4c, Chance Vought Corsair. 5c, Grumman Avenger. 15c, Douglas Dauntless. 20c, Cessna 172. 25c, Lockheed Hudson. 30c, Lockheed PV-1 Ventura. 40c, Avro York. 50c, DC-3. 60c, Avro 691 Lancastrian. 80c, DC-4. $1, Beechcraft Super King Air. $2, Fokker Friendship. $5, Lockheed C-130 Hercules.

**1980-81 Litho.** *Perf. 14½*

256 A62 1c multicolored .25 .25
257 A62 2c multicolored .25 .25
258 A62 3c multicolored .25 .25
259 A62 4c multicolored .25 .25
260 A62 5c multicolored .25 .25
261 A62 15c multicolored .25 .25
262 A62 20c multicolored .30 .30
262A A62 25c multicolored .40 .40
263 A62 30c multicolored .50 .50
264 A62 40c multicolored .60 .60
265 A62 50c multicolored .75 .75
266 A62 60c multicolored .85 .85
267 A62 80c multicolored 1.30 1.30
268 A62 $1 multicolored 1.50 1.50
269 A62 $2 multicolored 1.90 1.90
270 A62 $5 multicolored 5.00 5.00
*Nos. 256-270 (16)* 14.60 14.60

Issued: 2, 3, 20c, $5, 3/25; 4, 5, 15c, $2, 8/19; 30, 50, 60, 80c, 1/13/81; 1, 25, 40c, $1, 3/3/81.

Queen Mother Elizabeth, 80th Birthday A63

**1980, Aug. 4 Litho.** *Perf. 14½*

271 A63 22c multicolored .25 .25
272 A63 60c multicolored .65 .65

Red-tailed Tropic Birds — A64

22c, Adult and juvenile white terns. 35c, White-capped noddys. 60c, Two adult white terns.

**1980, Oct. 28 Litho.** *Perf. 14x14½*

273 A64 15c shown .25 .25
274 A64 22c multicolored .25 .25
275 A64 35c multicolored .40 .40
a. Strip of 3, #273-275 1.00 1.00
276 A64 60c multicolored .75 .75
*Nos. 273-276 (4)* 1.65 1.65

Christmas. No. 275a has continuous design.

Citizens Arriving at Norfolk Island A65

**1981, June 5 Litho.** *Perf. 14½*

277 A65 5c Departure .25 .25
278 A65 35c shown .40 .40
279 A65 60c Settlement .70 .70
a. Souvenir sheet of 3, #277-279 1.50 1.50
*Nos. 277-279 (3)* 1.35 1.35

Pitcairn migration to Norfolk Island, 125th anniv.

Common Design Types pictured following the introduction.

**Royal Wedding Issue**
Common Design Type

**1981, July 22 Litho.** *Perf. 14*

280 CD331 35c Bouquet .30 .30
281 CD331 55c Charles .50 .50
282 CD331 60c Couple .55 .55
*Nos. 280-282 (3)* 1.35 1.35

Nos. 280-282 each se-tenant with decorative label.

Uniting Church of Australia A66

24c, Seventh Day Adventist Church. 30c, Church of the Sacred Heart. $1, St. Barnabas Church.

**1981, Sept. 15 Litho.** *Perf. 14½*

283 A66 18c shown .25 .25
284 A66 24c multicolored .25 .25
285 A66 30c multicolored .25 .25
286 A66 $1 multicolored .90 .90
*Nos. 283-286 (4)* 1.65 1.65

Christmas.

White-breasted Silvereye — A67

**1981, Nov. 10 Litho.** *Perf. 14½*

287 Strip of 5 2.75 2.75
a.-e. A67 35c any single .50 .50

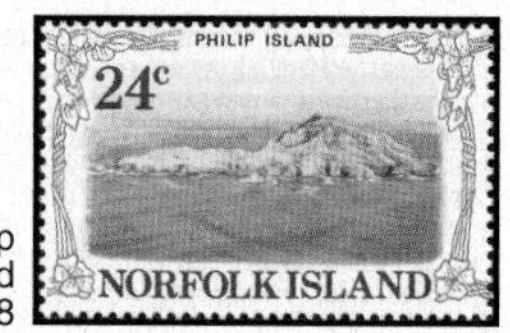


Philip Island A68

Views, Flora and Fauna: No. 288, Philip Isld. No. 289, Nepean Island.

**1982, Jan. 12 Litho.** *Perf. 14*

288 Strip of 5 1.25 1.25
a.-e. A68 24c any single .25 .25
289 Strip of 5 2.00 2.00
a.-e. A68 35c any single .40 .40

Sperm Whale A69

55c, Southern right whale. 80c, Humpback whale.

**1982, Feb. 23 Litho.** *Perf. 14½*

290 A69 24c shown .50 .50
291 A69 55c multicolored 1.00 1.00
292 A69 80c multicolored 1.75 1.75
*Nos. 290-292 (3)* 3.25 3.25

Shipwrecks — A70

**1982 Litho.** *Perf. 14½*

293 A70 24c Sirius, 1790 .55 .55
294 A70 27c Diocet, 1873 .60 .60
295 A70 35c Friendship, 1835 .95 .95
296 A70 40c Mary Hamilton, 1873 1.05 1.05
297 A70 55c Fairlie, 1840 1.25 1.25
298 A70 65c Warrigal, 1918 1.60 1.60
*Nos. 293-298 (6)* 6.00 6.00

Christmas and 40th Anniv. of Aircraft Landing A71

**1982, Sept. 7** *Perf. 14*

299 A71 27c Supplies drop .35 .35
300 A71 40c Landing .60 .60
301 A71 75c Sharing supplies 1.25 1.25
*Nos. 299-301 (3)* 2.20 2.20

A72

British Army Uniforms, Second Settlement, 1839-1848: 27c, Battalion Company Officer, 50th Regiment, 1835-1842. 40c, Light Company Officer, 58th Reg., 1845. 55c, Private, 80th Bat., 1838. 65c, Bat. Company Officer, 11th Reg., 1847.

**1982, Nov. 9** *Perf. 14½*

302 A72 27c multicolored .30 .30
303 A72 40c multicolored .50 .50
304 A72 55c multicolored .55 .55
305 A72 65c multicolored .70 .70
*Nos. 302-305 (4)* 2.05 2.05

Local Mushrooms — A73

Designs: 27c, Panaeolus papilonaceus. 40c, Coprinus domesticus. 55c, Marasmius niveus. 65c, Cymatoderma elegans.

**1983, Mar. 29 Litho.** *Perf. 14x13½*

306 A73 27c multicolored .35 .35
307 A73 40c multicolored .55 .55
308 A73 55c multicolored .70 .70
309 A73 65c multicolored .90 .90
*Nos. 306-309 (4)* 2.50 2.50

Manned Flight Bicentenary A74

10c, Beech 18, aerial mapping. 27c, Fokker F-28. 45c, DC4. 75c, Sikorsky helicopter.

**1983, July 12 Litho.** *Perf. 14½x14*

310 A74 10c multicolored .25 .25
311 A74 27c multicolored .30 .30
312 A74 45c multicolored .65 .65
313 A74 75c multicolored .95 .95
a. Souvenir sheet of 4, #310-313 2.50 2.50
*Nos. 310-313 (4)* 2.15 2.15

Christmas — A75

Stained-glass Windows by Edward Burne-Jones (1833-1898), St. Barnabas Chapel.

**1983, Oct. 4 Litho.** *Perf. 14*

314 A75 5c multicolored .25 .25
315 A75 24c multicolored .30 .30
316 A75 30c multicolored .35 .35
317 A75 45c multicolored .45 .45
318 A75 85c multicolored .90 .90
*Nos. 314-318 (5)* 2.25 2.25

World Communications Year — A76

ANZCAN Cable Station: 30c, Chantik, Cable laying Ship. 45c, Shore end. 75c, Cable Ship Mercury. 85c, Map of cable route.

**1983, Nov. 15 Litho. *Perf. 14½x14***

| | | | | |
|---|---|---|---|---|
| **319** | A76 30c multicolored | .30 | .30 |
| **320** | A76 45c multicolored | .50 | .50 |
| **321** | A76 75c multicolored | .90 | .90 |
| **322** | A76 85c multicolored | 1.00 | 1.00 |
| | *Nos. 319-322 (4)* | 2.70 | 2.70 |

Local Flowers — A77

1c, Myoporum obsurum. 2c, Ipomoea pes-caprae. 3c, Phreatia crassiuscula. 4c, Streblorrhiza speciosa. 5c, Rhopalostylis baueri. 10c, Alyxia gynopogon. 15c, Ungeria floribunda. 20c, Capparis nobilis. 25c, Lagunaria patersonia. 30c, Cordyline obtecta. 35c, Hibiscus insularis. 40c, Millettia australis. 50c, Jasminum volubile. $1, Passiflora aurantia. $3, Oberonia titania. $5, Araucaria heterophylla.

**1984 Litho. *Perf. 14***

| | | | |
|---|---|---|---|
| **323** | A77 1c multicolored | .25 | .25 |
| **324** | A77 2c multicolored | .25 | .25 |
| **325** | A77 3c multicolored | .25 | .25 |
| **326** | A77 4c multicolored | .25 | .25 |
| **327** | A77 5c multicolored | .25 | .25 |
| **328** | A77 10c multicolored | .25 | .25 |
| **329** | A77 15c multicolored | .25 | .25 |
| **330** | A77 20c multicolored | .25 | .25 |
| **331** | A77 25c multicolored | .25 | .25 |
| **332** | A77 30c multicolored | .35 | .35 |
| **333** | A77 35c multicolored | .40 | .40 |
| **334** | A77 40c multicolored | .45 | .45 |
| **335** | A77 50c multicolored | .55 | .55 |
| **336** | A77 $1 multicolored | 1.10 | 1.10 |
| **337** | A77 $3 multicolored | 3.50 | 3.50 |
| **338** | A77 $5 multicolored | 5.50 | 5.50 |
| | *Nos. 323-338 (16)* | 14.10 | 14.10 |

Issued: 2-3, 10, 20-25, 40-50c, $5, 1/10; others 3/27.

Reef Fish — A78

30c, Painted morwong. 45c, Black-spot goatfish. 75c, Ring-tailed surgeon fish. 85c, Three-striped butterfly fish.

***Perf. 13½x14***

**1984, Apr. 17 Litho. Wmk. 373**

| | | | |
|---|---|---|---|
| **339** | A78 30c multicolored | .40 | .40 |
| **340** | A78 45c multicolored | .55 | .55 |
| **341** | A78 75c multicolored | 1.00 | 1.00 |
| **342** | A78 85c multicolored | 1.10 | 1.10 |
| | *Nos. 339-342 (4)* | 3.05 | 3.05 |

Boobook Owl — A79

Designs: a, Laying eggs. b, Standing at treehole. c, Sitting on branch looking sideways. d, Looking head on. e, Flying.

**Wmk. 373**

**1984, July 17 Litho. *Perf. 14***

| | | | |
|---|---|---|---|
| **343** | Strip of 5 | 6.00 | 6.00 |
| *a.-e.* | A79 30c any single | 1.20 | 1.20 |

AUSIPEX '84 — A80

**1984, Sept. 18 Litho. *Perf. 14½***

| | | | |
|---|---|---|---|
| **344** | A80 30c Nos. 15 and 176 | .45 | .45 |
| **345** | A80 45c First day cover | .70 | .70 |
| **346** | A80 75c Presentation pack | 1.30 | 1.30 |
| *a.* | Souvenir sheet of 3, #344-346 | 6.00 | 6.00 |
| | *Nos. 344-346 (3)* | 2.45 | 2.45 |

Christmas — A81

5c, The Font. 24c, Church at Kingston, interior. 30c, Pastor and Mrs. Phelps. 45c, Phelps, Church of Chester. 85c, Phelps, Methodist Church, modern interior.

**1984, Oct. 9 Litho. *Perf. 13½***

| | | | |
|---|---|---|---|
| **347** | A81 5c multicolored | .25 | .25 |
| **348** | A81 24c multicolored | .30 | .30 |
| **349** | A81 30c multicolored | .35 | .35 |
| **350** | A81 45c multicolored | .55 | .55 |
| **351** | A81 85c multicolored | 1.05 | 1.05 |
| | *Nos. 347-351 (5)* | 2.50 | 2.50 |

Rev. George Hunn Nobbs, Death Cent. — A82

30c, As teacher. 45c, As minister. 75c, As chaplain. 85c, As community leader.

**1984, Nov. 6 Litho. *Perf. 14x15***

| | | | |
|---|---|---|---|
| **352** | A82 30c multicolored | .35 | .35 |
| **353** | A82 45c multicolored | .45 | .45 |
| **354** | A82 75c multicolored | .80 | .80 |
| **355** | A82 85c multicolored | 1.00 | 1.00 |
| | *Nos. 352-355 (4)* | 2.60 | 2.60 |

Whaling Ships — A83

**1985 Litho. *Perf. 13½x14***

| | | | |
|---|---|---|---|
| **356** | A83 5c Fanny Fisher | .25 | .25 |
| **357** | A83 15c Waterwitch | .30 | .30 |
| **358** | A83 20c Canton | .40 | .40 |
| **359** | A83 33c Costa Rica Packet | .60 | .60 |
| **360** | A83 50c Splendid | .90 | .90 |
| **361** | A83 60c Aladin | 1.50 | 1.50 |
| **362** | A83 80c California | 1.75 | 1.75 |
| **363** | A83 90c Onward | 2.25 | 2.25 |
| | *Nos. 356-363 (8)* | 7.95 | 7.95 |

Issued: 5c, 33c, 50c, 90c, 2/19; others 4/30.

**Queen Mother 85th Birthday**

Common Design Type

5c, Portrait, 1926. 33c, With Princess Anne. 50c, Photograph by N. Parkinson. 90c, Holding Prince Henry.

$1, With Princess Anne, Ascot Races.

***Perf. 14½x14***

**1985, June 6 Litho. Wmk. 384**

| | | | |
|---|---|---|---|
| **364** | CD336 5c multicolored | .25 | .25 |
| **365** | CD336 33c multicolored | .45 | .45 |
| **366** | CD336 50c multicolored | .60 | .60 |
| **367** | CD336 90c multicolored | 1.25 | 1.25 |
| | *Nos. 364-367 (4)* | 2.55 | 2.55 |

**Souvenir Sheet**

| | | | |
|---|---|---|---|
| **368** | CD336 $1 multicolored | 2.50 | 2.50 |

Intl. Youth Year — A84

Children's drawings.

**1985, July 9 Litho. *Perf. 13½x14***

| | | | |
|---|---|---|---|
| **369** | A84 33c Swimming | .60 | .60 |
| **370** | A84 50c Nature walk | 1.00 | 1.00 |

Girl, Prize-winning Cow — A85

Designs: 90c, Embroidery, jam-making, baking, animal husbandry.

**1985, Sept. 10 Litho. *Perf. 13½x14***

| | | | |
|---|---|---|---|
| **371** | A85 80c multicolored | 1.00 | 1.00 |
| **372** | A85 90c multicolored | 1.10 | 1.10 |
| *a.* | Souvenir sheet of 2, #371-372 | 3.00 | 3.00 |

Royal Norfolk Island Agricultural & Horticultural Show, 125th anniv.

Christmas — A86

27c, Three Shepherds. 33c, Journey to Bethlehem. 50c, Three Wise Men. 90c, Nativity.

**1985, Oct. 3 *Perf. 13½***

| | | | |
|---|---|---|---|
| **373** | A86 27c multicolored | .35 | .35 |
| **374** | A86 33c multicolored | .50 | .50 |
| **375** | A86 50c multicolored | .65 | .65 |
| **376** | A86 90c multicolored | 1.30 | 1.30 |
| | *Nos. 373-376 (4)* | 2.80 | 2.80 |

Marine Life — A87

5c, Long-spined sea urchin. 33c, Blue starfish. 55c, Eagle ray. 75c, Moray eel.

**1986, Jan. 14 *Perf. 13½x14***

| | | | |
|---|---|---|---|
| **377** | A87 5c multicolored | .25 | .25 |
| **378** | A87 33c multicolored | .50 | .50 |
| **379** | A87 55c multicolored | .85 | .85 |
| **380** | A87 75c multicolored | 1.20 | 1.20 |
| *a.* | Souvenir sheet of 4, #377-380 | 4.00 | 4.00 |
| | *Nos. 377-380 (4)* | 2.80 | 2.80 |

Halley's Comet — A88

Designs: a, Giotto space probe. b, Comet.

**1986, Mar. 11 *Perf. 15***

| | | | |
|---|---|---|---|
| **381** | A88 Pair | 3.25 | 3.25 |
| *a.-b.* | $1 any single | 1.60 | 1.60 |

Se-tenant in continuous design.

AMERIPEX '86 — A89

Designs: 33c, Isaac Robinson, US consul in Norfolk, 1887-1908, vert. 50c, Ford Model-T. 80c, Statue of Liberty.

**1986, May 22 Litho. *Perf. 13½***

| | | | |
|---|---|---|---|
| **382** | A89 33c multicolored | .45 | .45 |
| **383** | A89 50c multicolored | .70 | .70 |
| **384** | A89 80c multicolored | 1.10 | 1.10 |
| *a.* | Souvenir sheet of #382-384 | 2.75 | 2.75 |
| | *Nos. 382-384 (3)* | 2.25 | 2.25 |

Queen Elizabeth II, 60th Birthday — A90

Various portraits — 5c, As Princess. 33c, Contemporary photograph. 80c, Opening N.I. Golf Club. 90c, With Prince Philip.

**1986, June 12**

| | | | |
|---|---|---|---|
| **385** | A90 5c multicolored | .25 | .25 |
| **386** | A90 33c multicolored | .65 | .65 |
| **387** | A90 80c multicolored | 1.40 | 1.40 |
| **388** | A90 90c multicolored | 1.75 | 1.75 |
| | *Nos. 385-388 (4)* | 4.05 | 4.05 |

Christmas A91

**1986, Sept. 23 Litho. *Perf. 13½x14***

| | | | |
|---|---|---|---|
| **389** | A91 30c multicolored | .40 | .40 |
| **390** | A91 40c multicolored | .50 | .50 |
| **391** | A91 $1 multicolored | 1.30 | 1.30 |
| | *Nos. 389-391 (3)* | 2.20 | 2.20 |

Commission of Gov. Phillip, Bicent. — A92

36c, British prison, 1787. 55c, Transportation, Court of Assize. No. 394, Gov. meeting Home Society. No. 395, Gov. meeting Home Secretary. $1, Gov. Phillip, 1738-1814.

**1986 Litho. *Perf. 14x13½***
**392** A92 36c multicolored 1.00 .75
**393** A92 55c multicolored 1.75 1.15
**394** A92 90c multicolored 3.00 3.00
**395** A92 90c multicolored 3.00 3.00
**396** A92 $1 multicolored 4.00 4.00
*Nos. 392-396 (5)* 12.75 11.90

No. 395 was issued because No. 394 is incorrectly inscribed.
Issued: #395, Dec. 16; others, Oct. 14.
See #417-420, 426-436.

Commission of Gov. Phillip, Bicent. — A93

**1986, Dec. 16 *Perf. 13½***
**397** A93 36c Maori chief 1.25 1.25
**398** A93 36c Bananas, taro 1.25 1.25
**399** A93 36c Stone tools 1.25 1.25
**400** A93 36c Polynesian outrigger 1.25 1.25
*Nos. 397-400 (4)* 5.00 5.00

Pre-European occupation of the Island.

Island Scenery — A94

1c, Cockpit Creek Bridge. 2c, Cemetery Bay Beach. 3c, Guesthouse. 5c, Philip Island from Point Ross. 15c, Cattle grazing. 30c, Rock fishing. 37c, Old home. 40c, Shopping center. 50c, Emily Bay. 60c, Bloody Bridge. 80c, Pitcairner-style shop. 90c, Government House. $1, Melanesian Memorial Chapel. $2, Kingston convict settlement. $3, Ball Bay. $5, Northerly cliffs.

**1987-88 Litho. *Perf. 13½***
**401** A94 1c multicolored .25 *.35*
**402** A94 2c multicolored .25 *.35*
**403** A94 3c multicolored .25 *.35*
**404** A94 5c multicolored .25 *.35*
**405** A94 15c multicolored .25 *.35*
**406** A94 30c multicolored .45 *.65*
**407** A94 37c multicolored .55 *.75*
**408** A94 40c multicolored .60 *.85*
**409** A94 50c multicolored .75 *1.05*
**410** A94 60c multicolored .85 *1.20*
**411** A94 80c multicolored 1.10 *1.60*
**412** A94 90c multicolored 1.25 *1.75*
**413** A94 $1 multicolored 1.50 *2.25*
**414** A94 $2 multicolored 3.00 *4.25*
**415** A94 $3 multicolored 4.50 *6.50*
**416** A94 $5 multicolored 10.00 *14.50*
*Nos. 401-416 (16)* 25.80 *37.10*

Issued: 5c, 50c, 90c, $1, 2/17; 30c, 40c, 80c, $2, 4/17; 15c, 37c, 60c, $3, 7/27; 1c, 2c, 3c, $5, 5/17/88.

### Bicentennial Type of 1986

Designs: 5c, Loading supplies at Deptford, England, 1787. No. 418, First Fleet sailing from Spithead (buoy in water). No. 419, Sailing from Spithead (ship flying British merchant flag). $1, Convicts below deck.

**1987, May 13 Litho. *Perf. 14x13½***
**417** A92 5c multicolored .55 .55
**418** A92 55c multicolored 1.75 1.75
**419** A92 55c multicolored 1.75 1.75
*a.* Pair, #418-419 4.25 4.25
**420** A92 $1 multicolored 2.75 2.75
*Nos. 417-420 (4)* 6.80 6.80

No. 419a has a continuous design.

A96

World Wildlife Fund: Green parrot.

**1987, Sept. 16 Unwmk.**
**421** Strip of 4 *17.50 17.50*
*a.* A96 5c Parrot facing right *3.00 2.25*
*b.* A96 15c Parrot, chick, egg *3.50 1.75*
*c.* A96 36c Parrots *4.75 3.50*
*d.* A96 55c Parrot facing left *6.50 4.50*

Christmas A97

Children's party: 30c, Norfolk Island pine tree, restored convicts' settlement. 42c, Santa Claus, children opening packages. 58c, Santa, children, gifts in fire engine. 63c, Meal.

***Perf. 13½x14***
**1987, Oct. 13 Litho. Wmk. 384**
**422** A97 30c multicolored .45 .45
**423** A97 42c multicolored .65 .65
**424** A97 58c multicolored .85 .85
**425** A97 63c multicolored .95 .95
*Nos. 422-425 (4)* 2.90 2.90

### Bicentennial Type of 1986

Designs: 5c, Lt. Philip Gidley King. No. 427, La Perouse and Louis XVI of France. No. 428, Gov. Phillip sailing in ship's cutter from Botany Bay to Port Jackson. No. 429, Flag raising on Norfolk Is. 55c, Lt. King and search party exploring the island. 70c, Landfall, Sydney Bay. No. 432, L'Astrolabe and La Boussole off coast of Norfolk. No. 433, HMS Supply. No. 434, Wrecking of L'Astrolabe off the Solomon Isls. No. 435, First Fleet landing at Sydney Cove. No. 436, First settlement, Sydney Bay, 1788.

**1987-88 Litho. *Perf. 14x13½***
**426** A92 5c multicolored .25 .25
**427** A92 37c multicolored .85 .85
**428** A92 37c multicolored .85 .85
**429** A92 37c multicolored .85 .85
**430** A92 55c multicolored 1.75 1.75
**431** A92 70c multicolored 1.50 1.50
**432** A92 90c multicolored 2.75 2.75
**433** A92 90c multicolored 2.25 2.25
**434** A92 $1 multicolored 2.75 2.75
**435** A92 $1 multicolored 2.50 2.50
**436** A92 $1 multicolored 2.50 2.50
*Nos. 426-436 (11)* 18.80 18.80

Visit of Jean La Perouse (1741-88), French navigator, to Norfolk Is. (Nos. 427, 432, 434); arrival of the First Fleet at Sydney Cove (Nos. 428, 435); founding of Norfolk Is. (Nos. 426, 429-431, 433, 436).
Issued: #427, 432, 434, Dec. 8, 1987; #428, 435, Jan. 25, 1988; others, Mar. 4, 1988.

SYDPEX '88, July 30-Aug. 7 A98

Sydney-Norfolk transportation and communication links — No. 437, Air and sea transports, vert. No. 439, Telecommunications, vert.

***Perf. 14x13½ 13½x14***
**1988, July 30 Litho.**
**437** A98 37c multicolored .90 .90
**438** A98 37c shown .90 .90
**439** A98 37c multicolored .90 .90
*a.* Souvenir sheet of 3, #437-439 8.50 8.50
*Nos. 437-439 (3)* 2.70 2.70

No. 438 exists perf. 13½ within No. 439a.

Christmas — A99

**1988, Sept. 27 Litho. *Perf. 14x13½***
**440** A99 30c shown .45 .45
**441** A99 42c Flowers, diff. .65 .65
**442** A99 58c Trees, fish .95 .95
**443** A99 63c Trees, sailboats .95 .95
*Nos. 440-443 (4)* 3.00 3.00

Convict Era Georgian Architecture, c. 1825-1850 A100

Designs: 39c, Waterfront shop and boat shed. 55c, Royal Engineers' Building. 90c, Old military barracks. $1, Commissary and new barracks.

**1988, Dec. 6 Litho. *Perf. 13½x14***
**444** A100 39c multicolored .55 .55
**445** A100 55c multicolored .80 .80
**446** A100 90c multicolored 1.30 1.30
**447** A100 $1 multicolored 1.50 1.50
*Nos. 444-447 (4)* 4.15 4.15

Indigenous Insects A101

39c, Lamprima aenea. 55c, Insulascirtus nythos. 90c, Caedicia araucariae. $1, Thrincophora aridela.

***Perf. 13½x14***
**1989, Feb. 14 Litho. Unwmk.**
**448** A101 39c multicolored .85 .85
**449** A101 55c multicolored 1.15 1.15
**450** A101 90c multicolored 1.75 1.75
**451** A101 $1 multicolored 2.25 2.25
*Nos. 448-451 (4)* 6.00 6.00

Mutiny on the Bounty A102

Designs: 5c, *Bounty's* landfall, Adventure Bay, Tasmania. 39c, Mutineers and Polynesian maidens, c. 1790. 55c, Cumbria, Christian's home county. $1.10, Capt. Bligh and crewmen cast adrift.

***Perf. 13½***
**1989, Apr. 28 Litho. Unwmk.**
**452** A102 5c multicolored .70 .70
**453** A102 39c multicolored 2.40 2.40
**454** A102 55c multicolored 3.00 3.00
**455** A102 $1.10 multicolored 4.50 4.50
*Nos. 452-455 (4)* 10.60 10.60

### Souvenir Sheet

**456** Sheet of 3 + label (#453, 456a-456b) 8.25 8.25
*a.* A102 90c Isle of Man No. 393 3.25 3.25
*b.* A102 $1 Pitcairn Isls. No. 321d 3.50 3.50

See Isle of Man Nos. 389-394 and Pitcairn Isls. Nos. 320-322.

Self-Government, 10th Anniv. — A103

41c, Flag. 55c, Ballot box. $1, Norfolk Is. Act of 1979. $1.10, Norfolk Island crest.

***Perf. 14x13½***
**1989, Aug. 10 Litho. Unwmk.**
**457** A103 41c multicolored .95 .95
**458** A103 55c multicolored 1.05 1.05
**459** A103 $1 multicolored 2.25 2.25
**460** A103 $1.10 multicolored 2.40 2.40
*Nos. 457-460 (4)* 6.65 6.65

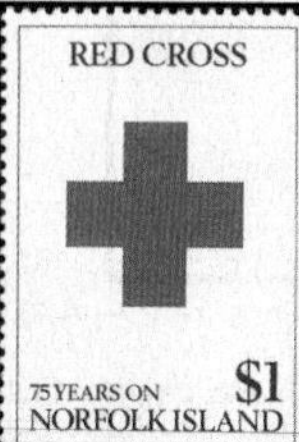

Natl. Red Cross, 75th Anniv. — A104

***Perf. 13½x13***
**1989, Sept. 25 Litho. Unwmk.**
**461** A104 $1 dk ultra & dk red 4.00 4.00

Bounty Hymns A105

Designs: 36c, "While nature was sinking in stillness to rest, The last beams of daylight show dim in the west." 60c, "There's a land that is fairer than day, And by faith we can see it afar." 75c, "Let the lower lights be burning, Send a gleam across the wave." 80c, "Oh, have you not heard of that beautiful stream That flows through our father's lands."

**1989, Oct. 9 *Perf. 13½x14***
**462** A105 36c multicolored .90 .90
**463** A105 60c multicolored 1.75 1.75
**464** A105 75c multicolored 2.60 2.60
**465** A105 80c multicolored 2.60 2.60
*Nos. 462-465 (4)* 7.85 7.85

Radio Australia, 50th Anniv. — A106

41c, Announcer John Royle. 65c, Sound waves on map. $1.10, Jacko, the laughing kookaburra.

**1989, Nov. 21 *Perf. 14x13½***
**466** A106 41c multicolored 1.50 1.50
**467** A106 65c multicolored 2.10 2.10
**468** A106 $1.10 multicolored 3.25 3.25
*Nos. 466-468 (3)* 6.85 6.85

A107

Settlement of Pitcairn (The Norfolk Islanders): 70c, The *Bounty* on fire. $1.10, Armorial ensign of Norfolk.

***Perf. 15x14½***
**1990, Jan. 23 Litho. Unwmk.**
**469** A107 70c multicolored 3.50 3.50
**470** A107 $1.10 multicolored 3.75 3.75

Salvage Team at Work A108

Designs: No. 471, HMS *Sirius* striking reef. No. 472, HMS *Supply* clearing reef. $1, Map of salvage sites, artifacts.

**1990, Mar. 19** *Perf. 14x13½*

**Size of Nos. 471-472: 40x27**

**471** A108 41c multicolored 2.00 2.00
**472** A108 41c multicolored 2.00 2.00
*a.* Pair, #471-472 4.50 4.50
**473** A108 65c shown 3.00 3.00
**474** A108 $1 multicolored 3.25 3.25
*Nos. 471-474 (4)* 10.25 10.25

Wreck of HMS *Sirius*, 200th anniv. No. 472a has continuous design.

Lightering Cargo Ashore, Kingston
A109

MV Ile de Lumiere
A110

45c, La Dunkerquoise. 50c, Dmitri Mendeleev. 65c, Pacific Rover. 75c, Norfolk Trader. 80c, Roseville. 90c, Kalia. $1, HMS Bounty. $2, HMAS Success. $5, HMAS Whyalia.

**1990-91** **Litho.** *Perf. 14x14½*

**479** A109 5c shown .30 .30
**480** A109 10c like #479 .30 .30

*Perf. 14½*

**481** A110 45c multicolored .70 .70
**482** A110 50c multicolored .80 .80
**483** A110 65c multicolored 1.05 1.05
**484** A110 70c shown 1.10 1.10
**485** A110 75c multicolored 1.20 1.20
**486** A110 80c multicolored 1.20 1.20
**487** A110 90c multicolored 1.40 1.40
**488** A110 $1 multicolored 1.60 1.60
**489** A110 $2 multicolored 3.25 3.25
**490** A110 $5 multicolored 8.25 8.25
*Nos. 479-490 (12)* 21.15 21.15

Issued: 5c, 10c, 70c, $2, 7/17/90; 45c, 50c, 65c, $5, 2/19/91; 75c, 80c, 90c, $1, 8/13/91.

Christmas — A111

38c, Island home. 43c, New post office. 65c, Sydney Bay, Kingston, horiz. 85c, Officers' Quarters, 1836, horiz.

**1990, Sept. 25** **Litho.** *Perf. 14½*

**491** A111 38c multicolored .90 .90
**492** A111 43c multicolored .95 .95
**493** A111 65c multicolored 2.10 2.10
**494** A111 85c multicolored 2.40 2.40
*Nos. 491-494 (4)* 6.35 6.35

A112

Designs: 70c, William Charles Wentworth (1790-1872), Australian politician. $1.20, Thursday October Christian (1790-1831).

**1990, Oct. 11** **Litho.** *Perf. 15x14½*

**495** A112 70c brown 1.50 1.50
**496** A112 $1.20 brown 2.25 2.25

Norfolk Island Robin
A113 A114

**1990, Dec. 3** **Litho.** *Perf. 14½*

**497** A113 65c multicolored 1.50 1.50
**498** A113 $1 shown 2.50 2.50
**499** A113 $1.20 multi, diff. 3.00 3.00
*Nos. 497-499 (3)* 7.00 7.00

**Souvenir Sheet**

**500** Sheet of 2 7.00 7.00
*a.* A114 $1 shown 3.00 3.00
*b.* A114 $1 Two robins 3.00 3.00

Birdpex '90, 20th Intl. Ornithological Congress, New Zealand.

Ham Radio — A115

**1991, Apr. 9** **Litho.** *Perf. 14½*

**501** A115 43c Island map 1.60 1.60
**502** A115 $1 World map 3.50 3.50
**503** A115 $1.20 Regional location 3.50 3.50
*Nos. 501-503 (3)* 8.60 8.60

Museum Displays
A116

43c, Ship's bow, Sirius Museum, vert. 70c, House Museum. $1, Carronade, Sirius Museum. $1.20, Pottery, Archaeology Museum, vert.

**1991, May 16** **Litho.** *Perf. 14½*

**504** A116 43c multicolored 1.20 1.20
**505** A116 70c multicolored 2.10 2.10
**506** A116 $1 multicolored 2.40 2.40
**507** A116 $1.20 multicolored 2.75 2.75
*Nos. 504-507 (4)* 8.45 8.45

Wreck of HMS Pandora, Aug. 28, 1791
A117

Design: $1.20, HMS Pandora searching for Bounty mutineers.

**1991, July 2** **Litho.** *Perf. 13½x14*

**508** A117 $1 shown 4.00 4.00
**509** A117 $1.20 multicolored 4.50 4.50

Christmas
A118

**1991, Sept. 23** **Litho.** *Perf. 14½*

**510** A118 38c multicolored .80 .80
**511** A118 43c multicolored 1.10 1.10
**512** A118 65c multicolored 1.75 1.75
**513** A118 85c multicolored 2.10 2.10
*Nos. 510-513 (4)* 5.75 5.75

Start of World War II in the Pacific, 50th Anniv.
A119

**1991, Dec. 9** **Litho.** *Perf. 14½*

**514** A119 43c Tank and soldier 1.60 1.60
**515** A119 70c B-17 2.75 2.75
**516** A119 $1 War ships 3.75 3.75
*Nos. 514-516 (3)* 8.10 8.10

Discovery of America, 500th Anniv. — A120

45c, Columbus' Coat of Arms. $1.05, Santa Maria. $1.20, Columbus at globe.

**1992, Feb. 11** **Litho.** *Perf. 14½*

**517** A120 45c multicolored .90 .90
**518** A120 $1.05 multicolored 2.25 2.25
**519** A120 $1.20 multicolored 2.75 2.75
*Nos. 517-519 (3)* 5.90 5.90

A121

Designs: No. 520, Map of Coral Sea Battle area. No. 521, Battle area, Midway. No. 522, HMAS Australia. No. 523, Catalina PBY5. No. 524, USS Yorktown. No. 525, Dauntless dive bomber.

**1992, May 4** **Litho.** *Perf. 14½*

**520** A121 45c multicolored 1.00 1.00
**521** A121 45c multicolored 1.00 1.00
**522** A121 70c multicolored 1.75 1.75
**523** A121 70c multicolored 1.75 1.75
**524** A121 $1.05 multicolored 2.75 2.75
**525** A121 $1.05 multicolored 2.75 2.75
*Nos. 520-525 (6)* 11.00 11.00

Battles of the Coral Sea and Midway, 50th anniv.

US Invasion of Guadalcanal, 50th Anniv.
A122

Designs: 45c, Troops landing on beach. 70c, Troops in battle. $1.05, Map, flags.

**1992, Aug. 6** **Litho.** *Perf. 14½*

**526** A122 45c multicolored 1.40 1.40
**527** A122 70c multicolored 2.25 2.25
**528** A122 $1.05 multicolored 4.00 4.00
*Nos. 526-528 (3)* 7.65 7.65

Christmas — A123

Scenes of Norfolk Island: 40c, Ball Bay, looking over Point Blackbourne. 45c, Headstone Creek. 75c, Ball Bay. $1.20, Rocky Point Reserve.

**1992, Oct. 29** **Litho.** *Perf. 15x14½*

**529** A123 40c multicolored .75 .75
**530** A123 45c multicolored .85 .85
**531** A123 75c multicolored 1.75 1.75
**532** A123 $1.20 multicolored 2.50 2.50
*Nos. 529-532 (4)* 5.85 5.85

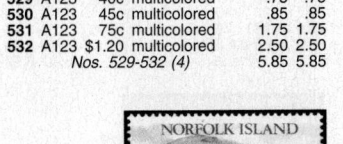

Tourism
A124

Tourist sites at Kingston: a, Boat shed, flaghouses. b, Old military barracks. c, All Saints Church. d, Officers quarters. e, Quality row.

**1993, Feb. 23** **Litho.** *Perf. 14½*

**533** A124 45c Strip of 5, #a.-e. 5.50 5.50

Emergency Services
A125

45c, Volunteer fire service. 70c, Rescue squad. 75c, St. John ambulance. $1.20, Police service.

**1993, May 18** **Litho.** *Perf. 14½*

**534** A125 45c multicolored 1.25 1.25
**535** A125 70c multicolored 1.50 1.50
**536** A125 75c multicolored 1.90 1.90
**537** A125 $1.20 multicolored 3.50 3.50
*Nos. 534-537 (4)* 8.15 8.15

Nudibranchs
A126

45c
NORFOLK ISLAND

No. 538, Phyllidia ocellata. No. 539, Glaucus atlanticus. 75c, Bornella sp. 85c, Glossodoris rubroannolata. 95c, Halgerda willeyi. $1.05, Chromodoris amoena.

**1993, July 7** **Litho.** *Perf. 14½*

**538** A126 45c multicolored 1.25 1.25
**539** A126 45c multicolored 1.50 1.50
**540** A126 75c multicolored 1.75 1.75
**541** A126 85c multicolored 2.00 2.00
**542** A126 95c multicolored 2.25 2.25
**543** A126 $1.05 multicolored 2.50 2.50
*Nos. 538-543 (6)* 11.25 11.25

No. 539 identified as "glauc."

A127

Designs: 70c, Maori patus. $1.20, First Maori map of New Zealand on paper, 1793.

**1993, Oct. 28** **Litho.** *Perf. 14½*

**544** A127 70c tan, buff & black 1.75 1.75
**545** A127 $1.20 tan, buff & black 3.25 3.25

Cultural contact with New Zealand, bicent.

A128

**1993, Oct. 28**

| | | | | |
|---|---|---|---|---|
| 546 | A128 | 40c blue & multi | .95 | .95 |
| 547 | A128 | 45c red & multi | 1.05 | 1.05 |
| 548 | A128 | 75c green & multi | 1.75 | 1.75 |
| 549 | A128 | $1.20 black & multi | 2.75 | 2.75 |
| | | *Nos. 546-549 (4)* | 6.50 | 6.50 |

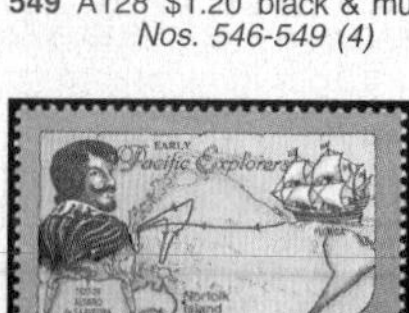


Early Pacific Explorers A129

Explorer, ship: 5c, Vasco Nunez de Balboa, Barbara. 10c, Ferdinand Magellan, Victoria. 20c, Juan Sebastian de Elcano, Victoria. 50c, Alvaro de Saavedra, Florida. 70c, Ruy Lopez de Villalobos, San Juan. 75c, Miguel Lopez de Legaspi, San Lesmes. 80c, Sir Frances Drake, Golden Hinde. 85c, Alvaro de Mendana, Santiago. 90c, Pedro Fernandes de Quiros, San Pedro Paulo. $1, Luis Baez de Torres, San Perico. $2, Abel Tasman, Heemskerk. $5, William Dampier, Cygnet. No. 562, Golden Hinde (Francis Drake).

**1994 Litho. *Perf. 14½***

| | | | | |
|---|---|---|---|---|
| 550 | A129 | 5c multicolored | .35 | .35 |
| 551 | A129 | 10c multicolored | .40 | .40 |
| 552 | A129 | 20c multicolored | .75 | .75 |
| 554 | A129 | 50c multicolored | 1.10 | 1.10 |
| 556 | A129 | 70c multicolored | 1.40 | 1.40 |
| 557 | A129 | 75c multicolored | 1.60 | 1.60 |
| 558 | A129 | 80c multicolored | 1.60 | 1.60 |
| 559 | A129 | 85c multicolored | 1.75 | 1.75 |
| 560 | A129 | 90c multicolored | 2.00 | 2.00 |
| 560A | A129 | $1 multicolored | 2.25 | 2.25 |
| 561 | A129 | $2 multicolored | 4.50 | 4.50 |
| 561A | A129 | $5 multicolored | 10.00 | 10.00 |
| | | *Nos. 550-561A (12)* | 27.70 | 27.70 |

**Souvenir Sheet**

***Perf. 13***

| | | | | |
|---|---|---|---|---|
| 562 | A129 | $1.20 multicolored | 4.75 | 4.75 |

No. 562 contains one 32x52mm stamp.

Issued: 50c, 70c, 75c, $2, No. 562, 2/8/94; 5c, 10c, 20c, $5, 5/3/94. 80c, 85c, 90c, $1, 7/26/94.

A130

Seabirds: a, Sooty tern. b, Red-tailed tropic bird. c, Australasian gannet. d, Wedge-tail shearwater. e, Masked booby.

**1994, Aug. 17 Litho. *Perf. 14½x14***

| | | | | |
|---|---|---|---|---|
| 565 | A130 | 45c Strip of 5, #a.-e. | 7.00 | 7.00 |
| | | Booklet, 2 #565 | 14.00 | |

A131

Christmas: 45c, Church, flowers, words from Pitcairn anthem. 75c, Stained glass windows, "To God be the glory." $1.20, Rainbow, ship, "Ship of Fame."

**1994, Oct. 27 Litho. *Die Cut***

**Self-Adhesive**

| | | | | |
|---|---|---|---|---|
| 566 | A131 | 45c multicolored | 1.50 | 1.50 |
| 567 | A131 | 75c multicolored | 1.75 | 1.75 |
| 568 | A131 | $1.20 multicolored | 3.00 | 3.00 |
| | | *Nos. 566-568 (3)* | 6.25 | 6.25 |

Vintage Cars — A132

45c, 1926 Chevrolet. 75c, 1928 Model A Ford. $1.05, 1929 Model A A/C Ford truck. $1.20, 1930 Model A Ford.

**1995, Feb. 7 Litho. *Perf. 14x14½***

| | | | | |
|---|---|---|---|---|
| 569 | A132 | 45c multicolored | .80 | .80 |
| 570 | A132 | 75c multicolored | 1.60 | 1.60 |
| 571 | A132 | $1.05 multicolored | 2.25 | 2.25 |
| 572 | A132 | $1.20 multicolored | 3.00 | 3.00 |
| | | *Nos. 569-572 (4)* | 7.65 | 7.65 |

Humpback Whales A133

***Perf. 14x14½, 14½x14***

**1995, May 9 Litho.**

| | | | | |
|---|---|---|---|---|
| 573 | A133 | 45c Tail fluke | 1.30 | 1.30 |
| 574 | A133 | 75c Mother & calf | 2.00 | 2.00 |
| 575 | A133 | $1.05 Breaching, vert. | 2.75 | 2.75 |
| | | *Nos. 573-575 (3)* | 6.05 | 6.05 |

**Souvenir Sheet**

***Perf. 14x14½***

| | | | | |
|---|---|---|---|---|
| 576 | A133 | $1.20 Bubble netting, vert. | 4.25 | 4.25 |
| a. | | Overprinted in gold & black | 4.00 | 4.00 |

No. 576 contains one 30x50mm stamp and is a continuous design.

Overprint in margin of No. 576a has "Selamat Hari Merdeka" and JAKARTA '95 exhibition emblem.

Butterfly Fish — A134

Chaetodon: 5c, pelewensis. 45c, plebeius. $1.20, tricinctus. $1.50, auriga.

**1995, June 15 Litho. *Perf. 14***

| | | | | |
|---|---|---|---|---|
| 577 | A134 | 5c multicolored | 1.10 | 1.10 |
| 578 | A134 | 45c multicolored | 1.75 | 1.75 |
| 579 | A134 | $1.20 multicolored | 3.50 | 3.50 |
| 580 | A134 | $1.50 multicolored | 4.00 | 4.00 |
| | | *Nos. 577-580 (4)* | 10.35 | 10.35 |

World War II Vehicles A135

Designs: 5c, 1942 Intl. 4x4 refueler. 45c, 1942 Ford 5 passenger sedan. $1.20, 1942 Ford 3-ton tipper. $2, D8 Caterpillar with scraper.

**1995, Aug. 8 Litho. *Perf. 14x15***

**Black Vignettes**

| | | | | |
|---|---|---|---|---|
| 581 | A135 | 5c brown & tan | .60 | .60 |
| 582 | A135 | 45c blue & red lil | 1.50 | 1.50 |
| 583 | A135 | $1.20 grn & org | 3.25 | 3.25 |
| 584 | A135 | $2 red & gray | 5.25 | 5.25 |
| | | *Nos. 581-584 (4)* | 10.60 | 10.60 |

**Island Flower Type of 1960**

**1995, Sept. 1 Litho. *Rouletted 7***

**Booklet Stamps**

| | | | | |
|---|---|---|---|---|
| 585 | A6 | 5c like No. 30 | .30 | .30 |
| a. | | Booklet pane of 18 + 3 labels | 5.50 | |
| 586 | A6 | 5c like No. 33 | .30 | .30 |
| a. | | Booklet pane of 18 + 3 labels | 5.50 | |
| | | Complete booklet, 1 each #585a-586a | 11.00 | |

A136

Victory in the Pacific Day, 50th Anniv. A136a

Designs: 5c, Fighter plane en route. 45c, Sgt. T.C. Derrick, VC, vert. 75c, Gen. MacArthur, vert. $1.05, Girls at victory party.

**1995, Sept. 1 Litho. *Perf. 12***

| | | | | |
|---|---|---|---|---|
| 587 | A136 | 5c multicolored | .40 | .40 |
| 588 | A136 | 45c multicolored | .95 | .95 |
| 589 | A136 | 75c multicolored | 1.60 | 1.60 |
| 590 | A136 | $1.05 multicolored | 2.50 | 2.50 |
| | | *Nos. 587-590 (4)* | 5.45 | 5.45 |

**Litho. & Embossed**

| | | | | |
|---|---|---|---|---|
| 591 | A136a | $10 Medals | 24.00 | 24.00 |

Singapore '95.

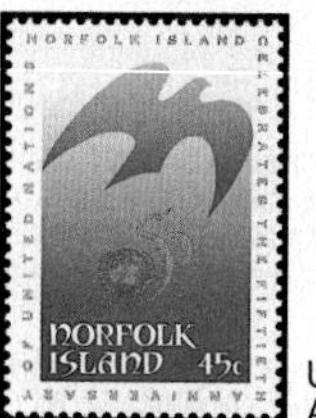


UN, 50th Anniv. — A137

45c, Dove. 75c, Christmas star. $1.05, Christmas candles. $1.20, Olive branch.

**1995, Nov. 7 Litho. *Perf. 14½x14***

| | | | | |
|---|---|---|---|---|
| 592 | A137 | 45c multicolored | .90 | .90 |
| 593 | A137 | 75c multicolored | 1.30 | 1.30 |
| 594 | A137 | $1.05 multicolored | 1.75 | 1.75 |
| 595 | A137 | $1.20 multicolored | 2.40 | 2.40 |
| | | *Nos. 592-595 (4)* | 6.35 | 6.35 |

Christmas (#593-594).

Skinks and Geckos A138

World Wildlife Fund: a, 5c, Skink crawling left. b, 45c, Skink crawling right. c, 5c, Gecko crawling right. d, 45c, Gecko crawling left, flower.

**1996, Feb. 7 Litho. *Perf. 14½x15***

| | | | | |
|---|---|---|---|---|
| 596 | A138 | Strip of 4, #a.-d. | 4.00 | 4.00 |

No. 596 was issued in sheets of 4 strips with stamps in each strip in different order.

Royal Australian Air Force, 75th Anniv. — A139

**1996, Apr. 22 Litho. *Perf. 14***

| | | | | |
|---|---|---|---|---|
| 597 | A139 | 45c Sopwith pup | .85 | .85 |
| 598 | A139 | 45c Wirraway | .85 | .85 |
| 599 | A139 | 75c F-111C | 1.40 | 1.40 |
| 600 | A139 | 85c F/A-18 Hornet | 1.60 | 1.60 |
| | | *Nos. 597-600 (4)* | 4.70 | 4.70 |

Souvenir Sheet

New Year 1996 (Year of the Rat) — A140

**1996, May 17 Litho. *Perf. 12***

| | | | | |
|---|---|---|---|---|
| 601 | A140 | $1 multicolored | 3.00 | 3.00 |
| a. | | With addl. inscription in sheet margin | 3.00 | 3.00 |

No. 601a is inscribed in sheet margin with China '96 exhibition emblem.

Shells — A141

Designs: No. 602, Argonauta nodosa. No. 603, Janthina janthina. No. 604, Naticarius oncus. No. 605, Cypraea caputserpentis.

**1996, July 2 Litho. *Perf. 14***

| | | | | |
|---|---|---|---|---|
| 602 | A141 | 45c multicolored | 1.00 | 1.00 |
| 603 | A141 | 45c multicolored | 1.00 | 1.00 |
| 604 | A141 | 45c multicolored | 1.00 | 1.00 |
| 605 | A141 | 45c multicolored | 1.00 | 1.00 |
| | | *Nos. 602-605 (4)* | 4.00 | 4.00 |

Tourism A142

**1996, Sept. 17 Litho. *Perf. 13½x14***

| | | | | |
|---|---|---|---|---|
| 606 | A142 | 45c Shopping | .85 | .85 |
| 607 | A142 | 75c Bounty day | 1.40 | 1.40 |
| 608 | A142 | $2.50 Horse riding | 4.50 | 4.50 |
| 609 | A142 | $3.70 Working the ship | 6.75 | 6.75 |
| | | *Nos. 606-609 (4)* | 13.50 | 13.50 |

A143

Christmas: Cow, star, Bible verse, and: No. 610, Nativity scene. No. 611, Boats, boathouses. 75c, House, trees. 85c, Flowers, fruits.

**1996, Nov. 5 Litho. *Perf. 15***

| | | | | |
|---|---|---|---|---|
| 610 | A143 | 45c multicolored | .75 | .75 |
| 611 | A143 | 45c multicolored | .75 | .75 |
| 612 | A143 | 75c multicolored | 1.25 | 1.25 |
| 613 | A143 | 85c multicolored | 1.40 | 1.40 |
| | | *Nos. 610-613 (4)* | 4.15 | 4.15 |

A144

No. 614, Natl. Arms. No. 615, Natl. Seal.

**1997, Jan. 22 Litho. *Roulette 7***

| | | | | |
|---|---|---|---|---|
| 614 | A144 | 5c yellow & green | .40 | .40 |
| a. | | Booklet pane of 10 | 4.00 | |
| 615 | A144 | 5c tan & brown | .40 | .40 |
| a. | | Booklet pane of 10 | 4.00 | |
| | | Complete booklet, 2 each #614a-615a | 8.00 | |

Souvenir Sheet

Beef Cattle — A145

**1997, Feb. 11** *Perf. 13½x13*

**616** A145 $1.20 multicolored 3.00 3.00
*a.* Inscribed in sheet margin 30.00 25.00

No. 616a is inscribed with Hong Kong '97 exhibition emblem.

Butterflies A146

Designs: 75c, Cepora perimale perimale. 90c, Danaus chrysippus petilia. $1, Danaus bamata bamata. $1.20, Danaus plexippus.

**1997, Mar. 28** *Perf. 14½*

**617** A146 75c multicolored 1.50 1.50
*a.* Black omitted, denomination and country name are missing 10,000.
**618** A146 90c multicolored 1.75 1.75
**619** A146 $1 multicolored 2.00 2.00
**620** A146 $1.20 multicolored 2.50 2.50
*Nos. 617-620 (4)* 7.75 7.75

On No. 617a the denomination and country name are missing.

Dolphins — A147

**1997, May 29** **Litho.** *Perf. 14*

**621** A147 45c Dusky dolphin 1.25 1.25
**622** A147 75c Common dolphin 2.50 2.50

**Souvenir Sheet**

**623** A147 $1.05 Dolphin, diff. 3.50 3.50
*a.* Inscribed in sheet margin 4.50 4.50

No. 623a is inscribed in sheet margin with PACIFIC 97 exhibition emblem.

First Norfolk Island Stamp, 50th Anniv. A148

Designs: $1, View of Ball Bay. $1.50, #4. $8, #12, view of Ball Bay.

**1997, June 10** *Perf. 12*

**624** A148 $1.00 multicolored 1.75 1.75
**625** A148 $1.50 multicolored 2.75 2.75
*a.* Pair, #624-625 4.50 4.50

**Size: 90x45mm**

**626** A148 $8 multicolored 13.00 13.00

Queen Elizabeth II & Prince Philip, 50th Wedding Anniv. — A149

Designs: 20c, Queen. No. 628, Prince guiding 4-in-hand team. No. 629, Prince in formal suit, hat. 50c, Queen riding in royal coach.

$1.50, Younger picture of Queen, Prince riding in carriage.

**1997, Aug. 12** **Litho.** *Perf. 14½*

**627** A149 20c multicolored .50 .50
**628** A149 25c multicolored .60 .60
*a.* Pair, #627-628 1.10 1.10
**629** A149 25c multicolored .60 .60
**630** A149 50c multicolored 1.30 1.30
*a.* Pair, #629-630 1.90 1.90

**Souvenir Sheet**

**631** A149 $1.50 multicolored 3.25 3.25

Souvenir Sheet

Return of Hong Kong to China — A150

**1997, Sept. 16** **Litho.** *Perf. 14*

**632** A150 45c Royal Yacht Britannia 2.00 2.00

Greetings Stamps — A151

**1997, Nov. 4** **Litho.** *Perf. 13x13½*

**633** A151 45c Christmas .75 .75
**634** A151 75c New Year's Eve 1.25 1.25
**635** A151 $1.20 Valentine's Day 2.00 2.00
*Nos. 633-635 (3)* 4.00 4.00

Souvenir Sheet

Oriental Pearl TV Tower, Shanghai — A152

**1997, Nov. 18** *Perf. 14½*

**636** A152 45c multicolored 1.50 1.50

Shanghai '97, Intl. Stamp & Coin Expo.

Souvenir Sheet

New Year 1998 (Year of the Tiger) — A153

**1998, Feb. 12** **Litho.** *Perf. 12*

**637** A153 45c multicolored 2.00 2.00

Paintings of Cats — A154

**1998, Feb. 26** *Perf. 14½*

**638** A154 45c "Pepper" .75 .75
**639** A154 45c "Tabitha" .75 .75
**640** A154 75c "Midnight" 1.25 1.25
**641** A154 $1.20 "Rainbow" 2.00 2.00
*Nos. 638-641 (4)* 4.75 4.75

Island Scenes, by Brent Hilder — A155

Designs: No. 642, Penal Settlement, 1825-56. No. 643, First settlement, 1788-1814.

**1998, Feb. 27** ***Rouletted 7***

**642** A155 5c blue & black .30 .30
*a.* Booklet pane of 10 3.00
**643** A155 5c blue green & black .30 .30
*a.* Booklet pane of 10 3.00
Complete booklet, 2 each 1642a-1643a 6.00

**Diana, Princess of Wales (1961-97)**

Common Design Type

#645: a, Wearing blue & white dress. b, Wearing pearl pendant earrings. c, In striped dress.

**1998, Apr. 28** **Litho.** *Perf. 14½x14*

**644** CD355 45c multicolored .75 .75

**Sheet of 4**

**645** CD355 45c #a.-c., #644 4.50 4.50

No. 644 sold for $1.80 + 45c, with surtax from international sales being donated to the Princess Diana Memorial fund and surtax from national sales being dontated to designated local charity.

Reef Fish — A156

Designs: 10c, Tweed trousers. 20c, Conspicuous angelfish. 30c, Moon wrasse. 45c, Wide-stiped clownfish. 50c, Raccoon butterfly fish. 70c, Artooti. 75c, Splendid hawkfish. 85c, Scorpion fish. 90c, Orange fairy basslet. $1, Sweetlip. $3, Moorish idol. $4, Gold ribbon soapfish.

$1.20, Shark.

**1998** **Litho.** *Perf. 14½*

**646** A156 10c multicolored .25 .25
**647** A156 20c multicolored .30 .30
**648** A156 30c multicolored .45 .45
**649** A156 45c multicolored .65 .65
**650** A156 50c multicolored .75 .75
**651** A156 70c multicolored 1.00 1.00
**652** A156 75c multicolored 1.10 1.10
**653** A156 85c multicolored 1.25 1.25
**654** A156 90c multicolored 1.25 1.25
**655** A156 $1 multicolored 1.50 1.50
**656** A156 $3 multicolored 4.50 4.50
**657** A156 $4 multicolored 6.00 6.00
*Nos. 646-657 (12)* 19.00 19.00

**Souvenir Sheet**

***Perf. 14x14½***

**658** A156 $1.20 multicolored 2.50 2.50

No. 658 contains 30x40mm stamp.

Issued: 10c, 30c, 50c, 75c, 90c, $1.20, $4, 5/5; others, 6/29.

16th Commonwealth Games, Kuala Lumpur — A157

Designs: 75c, Hammer throw, vert. 95c, Trap shooting. $1.05, Lawn bowling, vert.

85c, Flag bearer, vert.

**1998, July 23** **Litho.** *Perf. 14½*

**659** A157 75c black & red 1.00 1.00
**660** A157 95c black & violet blue 1.20 1.20
**661** A157 $1.05 black & red lilac 1.25 1.25
*Nos. 659-661 (3)* 3.45 3.45

**Souvenir Sheet**

**662** A157 85c black & greenish blue 1.60 1.60

The Norfolk, Bicent. A158

**1998, Sept. 24** **Litho.** *Perf. 13*

**663** A158 45c multicolored 2.25 2.25

**Souvenir Sheet**

**664** A158 $1.20 multicolored 4.50 4.50

Souvenir Sheet

Whales — A159

**1998, Oct. 23** **Litho.** *Perf. 13½x14*

**665** A159 $1.50 multicolored 4.25 4.25

See Namibia No. 919, South Africa No. 1095.

Christmas A160

Designs: 45c, "Peace on earth." 75c, "Joy to the World." $1.05, Doves, "A season of love." $1.20, Candle, "Light of the World."

**1998, Nov. 10** ***Perf. 13x13½***

**666** A160 45c multicolored .65 .65
**667** A160 75c multicolored 1.10 1.10
**668** A160 $1.05 multicolored 1.50 1.50
**669** A160 $1.20 multicolored 1.75 1.75
*Nos. 666-669 (4)* 5.00 5.00

Airplanes A161

No. 670, S23 Sandringham. No. 671, DC4 "Norfolk Trader."

**1999, Jan. 28 Litho.** ***Roulette 7***

**Booklet Stamps**

**670** A161 5c dk grn & lake .60 .60
*a.* Booklet pane of 10 5.00
**671** A161 5c lake & dk grn .60 .60
*a.* Booklet pane of 10 6.00
Complete booklet, 2 ea #670a-671a 12.00

Souvenir Sheet

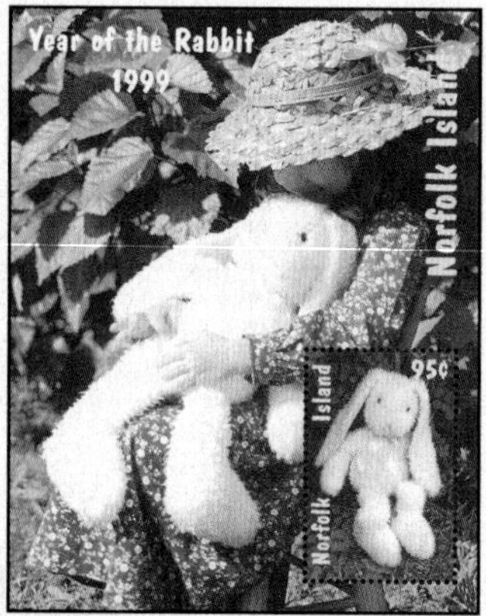


New Year 1999 (Year of the Rabbit) — A162

**1999, Feb. 9 Litho.** ***Perf. 14***

**672** A162 95c multicolored 2.25 2.25
*a.* With additional sheet margin inscription 4.50 4.50

No. 672a is inscribed in sheet margin with China '99 exhibition emblem. Issued: 8/23/99.

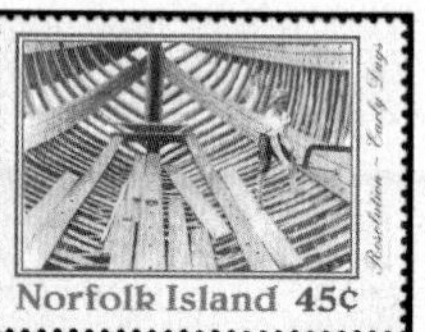


Trading Ship Resolution A163

Designs: No. 673, Under construction. No. 674, Launch day. No. 675, Emily Bay. No. 676, Cascade. No. 677, Docked at Auckland.

**1999, Mar. 19** ***Perf. 13x13½***

**Booklet Stamps**

**673** A163 45c multicolored 1.40 1.40
**674** A163 45c multicolored 1.40 1.40
**675** A163 45c multicolored 1.40 1.40
**676** A163 45c multicolored 1.40 1.40
**677** A163 45c multicolored 1.40 1.40
*a.* Booklet pane, #673-677 + label 7.00
Complete booklet, #677a 7.00

Australia '99, World Stamp Expo.

Souvenir Sheet

Pacific Black Duck — A164

**1999, Apr. 27 Litho.** ***Perf. 14***

**678** A164 $2.50 multicolored 6.00 6.00

IBRA '99, Intl. Philatelic Exhibition, Nuremberg, Germany.

Providence Petrel A165

**1999, May 27 Litho.** ***Perf. 14½***

**679** A165 75c In flight, vert. 2.40 2.40
**680** A165 $1.05 Up close 3.50 3.50
**681** A165 $1.20 Adult, young 3.75 3.75
*Nos. 679-681 (3)* 9.65 9.65

**Souvenir Sheet**

***Perf. 13***

**682** A165 $4.50 In flight 8.50 8.50

No. 682 contains one 35x51mm stamp. See No. 710.

Roses — A166

**1999, July 30 Litho.** ***Perf. 14½x14***

**683** A166 45c Cecile Brunner .85 .85
**684** A166 75c Green 1.25 1.25
**685** A166 $1.05 David Buffett 1.90 1.90
*Nos. 683-685 (3)* 4.00 4.00

**Souvenir Sheet**

**686** A166 $1.20 A Country Woman 2.25 2.25

Handicrafts — A167

Designs: a, 45c, Pottery. b, 45c, Woodcarving. c, 75c, Quilting. d, $1.05, Weaving.

**1999, Sept. 16** ***Perf. 14¼x14¾***

**687** A167 Strip of 4, #a.-d. 4.75 4.75

**Queen Mother's Century**

Common Design Type

Queen Mother: No. 688, Inspecting bomb damage at Buckingham Palace, 1940. No. 689, With royal family at Abergeldy Castle, 1955. 75c, With Queen Elizabeth, Prince William, 94th birthday. $1.20, As colonel-in-chief of King's Regiment.

$3, With Amy Johnson, pilot of 1930 flight to Australia.

**Wmk. 384**

**1999, Oct. 12 Litho.** ***Perf. 13½***

**688** CD358 45c multicolored .75 .75
**689** CD358 45c multicolored .75 .75
**690** CD358 75c multicolored 1.30 1.30
**691** CD358 $1.20 multicolored 2.00 2.00
*Nos. 688-691 (4)* 4.80 4.80

**Souvenir Sheet**

**692** CD358 $3 multicolored 5.50 5.50

Melanesian Mission, 150th Anniv. — A168

Christmas: a, 45c, Bishop George Augustus Selwyndd. b, 45c, Bishop John Coleridge Pateson. c, 75c, Text. d, $1.05, Stained glass. e, $1.20, Southern Cross.

**1999, Nov. 10 Litho.** ***Perf. 14***

**693** A168 Strip of 5, #a.-e. 9.00 9.00

See Solomon Islands No. 890.

Festivals A169

No. 694, Thanksgiving. No. 695, Country music festival.

**2000, Jan. 31 Litho.** ***Roulette 5¾***

**Booklet Stamps**

**694** A169 5c lav & blk .25 .25
**695** A169 5c blue & blk .25 .25
*a.* Booklet pane, 5 each #694-695 1.75
Complete booklet, 4 #695a 7.00

Souvenir Sheet

New Year 2000 (Year of the Dragon) — A170

**2000, Feb. 7 Litho.** ***Perf. 13¼***

**696** A170 $2 multi 3.25 3.25

Fowl — A171

Designs: 45c, Domestic goose. 75c, Pacific black duck. $1.05, Mallard drake. $1.20, Aylesbury duck.

**2000, Feb. 18 Litho.** ***Perf. 14¼***

**697** A171 45c multi 1.00 1.00
**698** A171 75c multi 1.50 1.50
**699** A171 $1.05 multi 2.00 2.00
**700** A171 $1.20 multi 2.50 2.50
*Nos. 697-700 (4)* 7.00 7.00

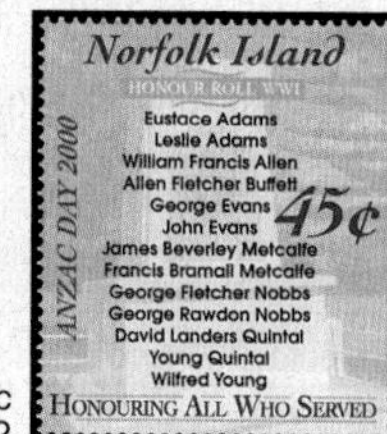


Anzac Day — A172

Monument and lists of war dead from: 45c, WWI. 75c, WWII and Korean War.

**2000, Apr. 25 Litho.** ***Perf. 14x14¾***

**701-702** A172 Set of 2 3.00 3.00

Souvenir Sheets

Whaler Project — A173

Designs: No. 703, shown. No. 704, As #703, with gold overprints for The Stamp Show 2000, London, and Crown Agents.

***Perf. 14¼, Imperf. (#704)***

**2000, May 1**

**703-704** A173 $4 Set of 2 17.50 17.50

Bounty Day — A174

Designs: 45c, Capt. William Bligh. 75c, Fletcher Christian.

**2000, June 8** ***Perf. 14¼***

**705-706** A174 Set of 2 4.00 4.00

Eighth Festival of Pacific Arts, New Caledonia — A175

Designs: 45c, Pot and broom.

No. 708: a, 75c, Turtle and shells. $1.05, Paintings. $1.20, Spear, mask. $2, Decorated gourds.

**2000, June 19** ***Die cut 9x9½***

**Self-Adhesive**

**707** A175 45c multi 1.75 1.75

**Souvenir Sheet**

***Perf. 13¾***

**Water-Activated Gum**

**708** A175 Sheet of 4, #a-d 8.75 8.75

No. 708 contains four 30x38mm stamps.

Souvenir Sheet

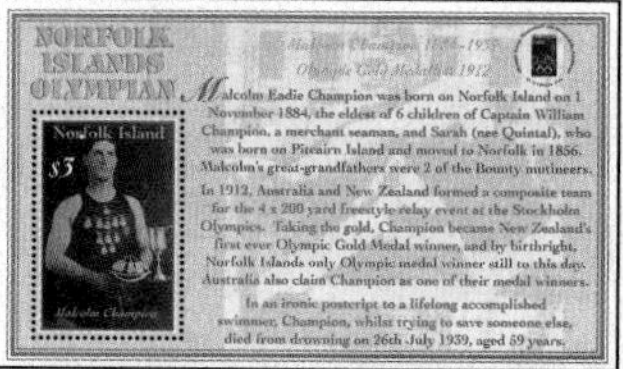


Malcolm Eadie Champion, 1912 Olympic Gold Medalist — A176

**2000, Sept. 15 Litho.** ***Perf. 14x14¼***

**709** A176 $3 multi 6.75 6.75

Olymphilex 2000 Stamp Exhibition, Sydney.

**Providence Petrel Type of 1999**

Souvenir Sheet

**2000, Oct. 5** ***Perf. 14½x14¾***

**710** Sheet of 2 #710a 7.50 7.50
*a.* A165 $1.20 Like #681, 32x22mm, with white frame 3.75 3.75

Canpex 2000 Stamp Exhibition, Christchurch, New Zealand.

Christmas A177

Words from "Silent Night" and: 45c, Sun. 75c, Candle. $1.05, Moon. $1.20, Stars.

**2000, Oct. 20** *Perf. 13¼x13*
**711-714** A177 Set of 4 9.00 9.00

Millennium A178

Children's art by: No. 715, 45c, Jessica Wong and Mardi Pye. No. 716, 45c, Roxanne Spreag. No. 717, 75c, Tara Grube. No. 718, 75c, Tom Greenwood.

**2000, Nov. 26** *Perf. 14¾x14½*
**715-718** A178 Set of 4 9.50 9.50

Green Parrot — A179

**2001, Jan. 26** *Rouletted 5½*
**Booklet Stamp**
**719** A179 5c green & red .25 .25
*a.* Booklet pane of 10 2.25
Booklet, 4 #719a 9.00

Tarler Bird — A180

Designs: $2.30, Norfolk island eel and tarler bird.

**2001, Feb. 1** *Perf. 13¼*
**720** A180 45c multi 1.75 1.75
***Imperf***
**Size: 110x70mm**
**721** A180 $2.30 multi 6.25 6.25

No. 720 issued in sheet of 5 + label. New Year 2001 (Year of the snake), Hong Kong 2001 Stamp Exhibition (#721).

Australian Federation, Cent. — A181

Pre-federation political cartoons from The Bulletin Magazine: No. 722, 45c, Promises, Promises! No. 723, 45c, The Gout of Federation. No. 724, 45c, The Political Garotters. No. 725, 45c, Tower of Babel. No. 726, 45c, Old Clothes. No. 727, 45c, The Federal Spirit. 75c, Australia Faces the Dawn. $1.05, The Federal Capital Question. $1.20, The Imperial Fowl Yard.

**2001, Mar. 12 Litho.** *Perf. 14x14¾*
**722-730** A181 Set of 9 8.50 8.50

Souvenir Sheet

2001 A Stamp Odyssey Stamp Show, Invercargill, New Zealand — A182

Blue portion of background at: a, Right. b, Left. c, Top.

**2001, Mar. 16** *Perf. 13*
**731** A182 75c Sheet of 3, #a-c, + 3 labels 4.50 4.50

Bounty Day — A183

**2001, June 8** *Rouletted 6*
**732** A183 5c green & black .25 .25
*a.* Booklet pane of 10 1.50
Booklet, 4 #732a 6.00

Tourism A184

Perfume bottle and: 45c, Jasminium simplicifolium. 75c, Woman's face in perfume bottle. $1.05, Woman with roses. $1.20, Taylors Road. $1.50, Couple shopping for perfume. $3, Woman and Norfolk pine trees.

**2001, June 9** *Perf. 13¼*
**733** A184 45c multi 1.00 1.00
**734** A184 75c multi 2.00 2.00
*a.* Booklet pane, #733-734 3.00 —
**735** A184 $1.05 multi 2.00 2.00
**736** A184 $1.20 multi 2.25 2.25
*a.* Booklet pane, #735-736 4.25 —
**737** A184 $1.50 multi 3.25 2.75
*a.* Booklet pane of 1 3.25 —
**Souvenir Sheet**
**738** A184 $3 multi 6.00 6.00
**Booklet Stamp**
**Size: 154x97mm**
***Microrouletted at Left***
**739** A184 $3 Like #738 6.00 6.00
*a.* Booklet pane of 1 6.00 —
Booklet, #734a, 736a, 737a, 739a 16.50

Nos. 733-739 are impregnated with jasmine perfume. No. 738 contains one 60x72mm stamp.

No. 739 has perfume bottle at LR, country name moved on one line at UL, and is impregnated with jasmine perfume. No. 739a has binding stub at left. Booklet sold for $10 and includes postal card.

For overprint see No. 824.

Boats A185

Designs: 45c, Whaler, vert. No. 741, $1, Rowers in boat. No. 742, $1, Motorboat, vert. $1.50, Men in cutter.

*Perf. 14½x14¼, 14¼x14½*
**2001, Aug. 1** **Litho.**
**740-743** A185 Set of 4 6.75 6.75
**Coil Stamp**
**Self-Adhesive**
***Die Cut Perf. 14¼x14¾***
**744** A185 45c multi 1.00 1.00

Peace Keepers in Japan — A186

No. 745: a, Australian soldiers playing cards. b, Soldiers with birthday cake.

No. 746: a, Soldiers on Christmas float. b, Soldiers controlling traffic.

**2001, Sept. 9** *Perf. 14½x14¾*
**745** Pair with central label 3.00 3.00
*a.* A186 45c multi .90 .90
*b.* A186 $1 multi 2.10 2.10
**746** Pair with central label 3.00 3.00
*a.* A186 45c multi .90 .90
*b.* A186 $1 multi 2.10 2.10

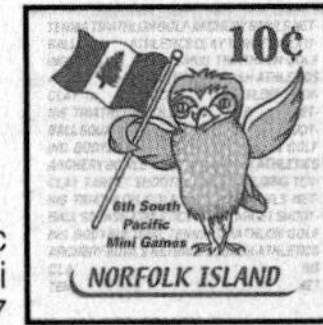
6th South Pacific Mini Games — A187

**2001, Oct. 1** *Rouletted 6*
**747** A187 10c green & brown .30 .30
*a.* Booklet pane of 10 3.00 —
Booklet, 2 #747a 6.00

Two souvenir sheets publicizing the 6th South Pacific Mini-Games, featuring four 45c and four $1 values, respectively, were scheduled for release but were withdrawn from sale upon arrival in Norfolk, when serious design errors were discovered. A small quantity had previously been sold by Crown Agents. Value for pair of sheets, $150.

Christmas A188

Christmas carols and flora: No. 748, 45c, Hark, the Herald Angels Sing, strawberry guava. No. 749, 45c, Deck the Halls, poinsettia. No., 750, $1, The First Noel, hibiscus. No. 751, $1, Joy to the World, Christmas croton. $1.50, We Wish You a Merry Christmas, Indian shot.

**2001, Oct. 26** *Perf. 12½*
**748-752** A188 Set of 5 9.00 9.00

Sacred Kingfisher — A189

**2002, Jan. 15 Litho.** *Rouletted 5¾*
**Booklet Stamp**
**753** A189 10c aqua & dk bl .25 .25
*a.* Booklet pane of 10 2.50 —
Booklet, 2 #753a 5.00

Cliff Ecology A190

Designs: 45c, Red-tailed tropicbird. No. 755, $1, White oak tree. No. 756, $1, White oak flower. $1.50, Eagle ray.

**2002, Jan. 21 Unwmk.** *Perf. 13*
**754-757** A190 Set of 4 9.00 9.00

**Reign Of Queen Elizabeth II, 50th Anniv. Issue**
Common Design Type

Designs: Nos. 758, 762a, 45c, Queen Mother with Princesses Elizabeth and Margaret, 1930. Nos. 759, 762b, 75c, Wearing scarf, 1977. Nos. 760, 762c, $1, Wearing crown, 1953. Nos. 761, 762d, $1.50, Wearing yellow hat, 2000. No. 762e, $3, 1955 portrait by Annigoni (38x50mm).

*Perf. 14¼x14½, 13¾ (#762e)*
**2002, Feb. 6 Litho. Wmk. 373**
**With Gold Frames**
**758** CD360 45c multicolored .90 .90
**759** CD360 75c multicolored 1.50 1.50
**760** CD360 $1 multicolored 2.10 2.10
**761** CD360 $1.50 multicolored 3.00 3.00
*Nos. 758-761 (4)* 7.50 7.50
**Souvenir Sheet**
**Without Gold Frames**
**762** CD360 Sheet of 5, #a-e 12.00 12.00

The Age of Steam — A191

*Perf. 14½x14¾*
**2002, Mar. 21 Litho. Unwmk.**
**763** A191 $4.50 multi 9.00 9.00

South Pacific Mini Games — A192

Designs: 50c, Track and field. $1.50, Tennis.

**2002, Mar. 21** *Perf. 13¾x14¼*
**764-765** A192 Set of 2 4.25 4.25

2002 Bounty Bowls Tournament A193

**2002, May 6** *Rouletted 6*
**Booklet Stamp**
**766** A193 10c multi .25 .25
*a.* Booklet pane of 10 2.00 —
Booklet, 2 #766a 4.00

Phillip Island Flowers — A194

Designs: 10c, Streblorrhiza speciocа. 20c, Plumbago zeylanica. 30c, Canavalia rosea. 40c, Ipomoea pes-caprae. 45c, Hibiscus insularis. 50c, Solanum laciniatum. 95c, Phormium tenax. $1, Lobelia anceps. $1.50, Carpobrotus glaucescens. $2, Abutilon julianae. $3, Wollastonia biflora. $5, Oxalis corniculata.

**2002** *Perf. 14½*
**767** A194 10c multi .25 .25
**768** A194 20c multi .35 .35
**769** A194 30c multi .50 .50
**770** A194 40c multi .65 .65
**771** A194 45c multi .70 .70
**772** A194 50c multi .80 .80
**773** A194 95c multi 1.75 1.75
**774** A194 $1 multi 2.00 2.00
**775** A194 $1.50 multi 2.75 2.75

**776** A194 $2 multi 3.75 3.75
**777** A194 $3 multi 5.50 5.50
**778** A194 $5 multi 9.00 9.00
*Nos. 767-778 (12)* 28.00 28.00

Issued: 20c, 40c, 45c, 95c, $2, $5, 5/21; others 9/18.

2002 Commonwealth Games, Manchester, England — A195

Designs: 10c, Track and field, vert. 45c, Cycling. $1, Lawn bowling, vert. $1.50, Shooting.

**2002, July 25**
**779-782** A195 Set of 4 7.25 7.25

Operation Cetacean — A196

No. 783: a, Sperm whale and calf. b, Sperm whale and squid.

**2002, Sept. 18** ***Perf. 14***
**783** A196 Horiz. pair with central label 8.00 8.00
*a.-b.* $1 Either single 4.00 4.00

See New Caledonia No. 906.

Christmas A197

White tern: No. 784, 45c, Hatchling. No. 785, 45c, Bird on egg in nest. $1, Pair in flight. $1.50, One in flight.

**2002, Nov. 12 Litho.** ***Perf. 14***
**784-787** A197 Set of 4 8.00 8.00

Horses on Norfolk Island A198

No. 788: a, Horses with riders near stable. b, Horses grazing. c, Show jumping. d, Horse racing. e, Horses pulling carriage.

**2003, Jan. 14**
**788** Horiz. strip of 5 8.00 8.00
*a.-c.* A198 45c Any single 1.00 1.00
*d.-e.* A198 75c Either single 2.25 2.25

Year of the horse (in 2002).

Island Scenes — A199

Photographs by Mary Butterfield: 50c, Buildings. 95c, Boat on beach. $1.10 Cattle grazing. $1.65 Tree near water.

**2003, Mar. 18** ***Perf. 14x14¼***
**789-792** A199 Set of 4 9.50 9.50

See Nos. 805-808.

Day Lilies — A200

No. 793: a, Southern Prize. b, Becky Stone. c, Cameroons. d, Chinese Autumn. e, Scarlet Orbit. f, Ocean Rain. g, Gingerbread man. h, Pink Corduroy. i, Elizabeth Hinrichsen. j, Simply Pretty.

**2003, June 10 Litho.** ***Perf. 14¼***
**793** Block of 10 9.50 9.50
*a.-j.* A200 50c Any single .95 .95
Complete booklet, #793 9.50

Island Views — A201

No. 794: a, Large trees at left, ocean. b, Beach. c, Rocks at shoreline. d, Cattle grazing.

**2003, July 21** ***Perf. 14***
**794** Horiz. strip of 4 + 4 labels 7.75 7.75
*a.-d.* A201 50c Any single + label 1.20 1.20

No. 794 was issued in sheets of five strips that had labels that could be personalized for an additional fee.

First Norfolk Island Writer's Festival — A202

No. 795: a, Maeve and Gil Hitch. b, Alice Buffett. c, Nan Smith. d, Archie Bigg. e, Colleen McCullough. f, Peter Clarke. g, Bob Tofts. h, Merval Hoare.

**2003, July 21** ***Perf. 14½***
**795** Block of 8 + 2 labels 6.75 6.75
*a.-d.* A202 10c Any single .30 .30
*e.-h.* A202 50c Any single .95 .95

Souvenir Sheet

Coronation of Queen Elizabeth II, 50th Anniv. — A203

No. 796: a, 10c, Queen wearing crown. b, $3, Queen wearing hat.

**2003, July 29** ***Perf. 14½***
**796** A203 Sheet of 2, #a-b 7.00 7.00

Christmas — A204

Designs: No. 797, 50c, Dove, rainbow, "Joy to the World." No. 798, 50c, Earth, "Peace on Earth." $1.10, Heart, "Give the gift of Love." $1.65, Candle, "Trust in Faith."

**2003, Oct. 21** ***Perf. 14¼x14***
**797-800** A204 Set of 4 9.00 9.00

Powered Flight, Cent. A205

Designs: 50c, Seaplane. $1.10, QANTAS airliner in flight. No. 803, $1.65, QANTAS airliner on ground.
No. 804, $1.65, Wright Flyer.

**2003, Dec. 2** ***Perf. 14x14¼***
**801-803** A205 Set of 3 10.00 10.00

**Souvenir Sheet**
***Perf. 14½x14***

**804** A205 $1.65 multi 6.50 6.50

No. 804 contains one 48x30mm stamp.
Limited quantities of No. 804 exist with an 85c surcharge and a 2004 Hong Kong Stamp Expo emblem in the margin. These were sold only at the exhibition. Value, mint never hinged or cto, $60.

**Island Scenes Type of 2003**

Designs: 50c, Houses, boat prow with foliage, vert. 95c, Waterfall, vert. $1.10, Cattle, vert. $1.65, Sea shore, vert.

**2004, Feb. 10 Litho.** ***Perf. 14¼x14***
**805-808** A199 Set of 4 10.00 10.00

Sharks — A206

Designs: 10c, Whale shark. 50c, Hammerhead shark. $1.10, Tiger shark. $1.65, Bronze whaler shark.

**2004, Apr. 6** ***Perf. 14¾***
**809-812** A206 Set of 4 11.00 11.00

Spiders A207

Designs: No. 813, 50c, Golden orb spider. No. 814, 50c, Community spider. $1, St. Andrew's cross spider. $1.65, Red-horned spider.
$1.50, Red-horned spider, diff.

**2004, June 1** ***Perf. 14½***
**813-816** A207 Set of 4 8.50 8.50

**Souvenir Sheet**
***Perf. 14½x14***

**817** A207 $1.50 multi 4.25 4.25

No. 817 contains one 47x40mm stamp.

Unloading of Ship Cargo — A208

Designs: 50c, Men climbing on cargo nets. $1.10, Small boat with men and cargo. No. 820, $1.65, Two small boats.
No. 821, $1.65, Two small boats at dock.

**2004, July 13 Litho.** ***Perf. 14¾***
**818-820** A208 Set of 3 7.25 7.25

**Souvenir Sheet**

**821** A208 $1.65 multi 4.25 4.25

Souvenir Sheet

Quota International, 25th Anniv. on Norfolk Island — A209

No. 822: a, 50c, Three children. b, $1.10, "We Care" on feet. c, $1.65, Child drawing "Quota" in sand.

**2004, Aug. 16** ***Perf. 14¼***
**822** A209 Sheet of 3, #a-c 7.25 7.25

Day Lilies A210

No. 823 — Hippeastrum varieties: a, Apple Blossom. b, Carnival. c, Cherry Blossom. d, Lilac Wonder. e, Millenium Star. f, Cocktail. g, Milady. h, Pacific Sunset. i, Geisha Girl. j, Lady Jane.

**2004, Aug. 16** ***Perf. 14½***
**823** Block of 10 12.00 12.00
*a.-j.* A210 50c Any single 1.20 1.20
Complete booklet, #823 12.50

**No. 738 Overprinted in Silver**

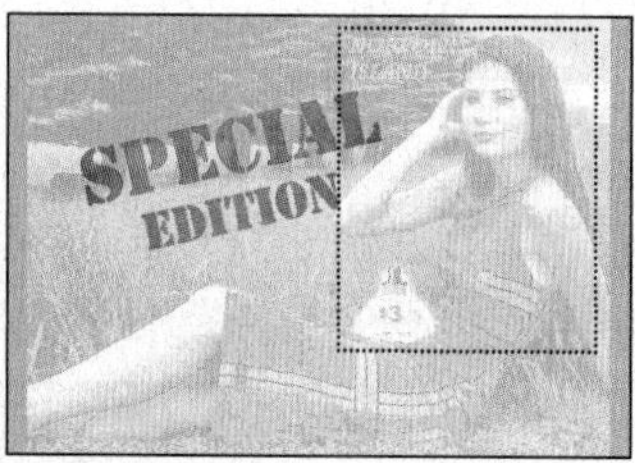


**Souvenir Sheet**

**2004, Aug. Litho.** ***Perf. 13¼***
**824** A184 $3 multi 7.50 7.50

No. 824 is impregnated with jasmine perfume.

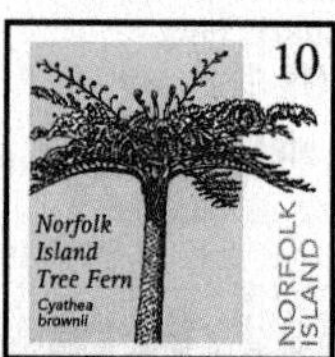


Flora — A211

Designs: No. 825, Norfolk Island tree fern. No. 826, Norfolk Island palm.

**2004, Sept. 28** ***Rouletted 6***

**Booklet Stamps**

**825** A211 10c bl grn & blk .40 .30
*a.* Booklet pane of 10 4.00 —
**826** A211 10c yel & blk .40 .25
*a.* Booklet pane of 10 4.00 —
Complete booklet, #825a, 826a 8.00

Christmas — A212

Norfolk pine and words from: No. 827, 50c, Silent Night. No. 828, 50c, 'Twas the Night

Before Christmas. $1.10, On the First Day of Christmas. $1.65, Oh, Holy Night.

**2004, Oct. 26** *Perf. 14¼*
**827-830** A212 Set of 4 7.50 7.50

Legislative Assembly, 25th Anniv. — A213

**2004, Dec. 14** *Perf. 14*
**831** A213 $5 multi 10.50 10.50

Worldwide Fund for Nature (WWF) — A214

Sacred kingfisher: No. 832, 50c, Two birds on tree branch. No. 833, 50c, Bird in flight with insect in beak. $1, Bird on branch. $2, Bird on branch, diff.

**2004, Dec. 14**
**832-835** A214 Set of 4 9.00 9.00
*835a* Miniature sheet, 2 each #832-835 17.50 17.50

Rotary International, Cent. A215

Emblem and: No. 836, 50c, Beach Carnival. No. 837, 50c, Tree planting, vert. $1.20, Paul Harris. $1.80, Rotary Youth Leadership Awards, vert.
$2, District 9910 ceremony.

**2005, Feb. 23** **Litho.** *Perf. 14½*
**836-839** A215 Set of 4 8.00 8.00

**Souvenir Sheet**

**840** A215 $2 multi 5.00 5.00

No. 840 contains one 40x30mm stamp.

Items From Norfolk Island Museum A216

Designs: No. 841, 50c, Teacup, 1856. No. 842, 50c, Salt cellar from HMAV Bounty, 1856. $1.10, Medicine cups, 1825-55. $1.65, Stoneware jar, 1825-55.

**2005, Apr. 5**
**841-844** A216 Set of 4 9.00 9.00

Pacific Explorers A217

Designs: 50c, Polynesian explorer, boat and fish. $1.20, Magellan's ship and bird. $1.80, Captain James Cook, ship and flower.
$2, Old map of world, horiz.

**2005, Apr. 21** *Perf. 14*
**845-847** A217 Set of 3 7.50 7.50

**Souvenir Sheet**
*Perf. 14¾*

**848** A217 $2 multi 5.00 5.00

Pacific Explorer 2005 World Stamp Expo, Sydney. No. 848 contains one 46x32mm stamp.

Old Houses A218

Designs: No. 849, 50c, Greenacres. No. 850, 50c, Branka House. $1.20, Ma Annas. $1.80, Naumai.

**2005, June 16** **Litho.** *Perf. 14½*
**849-852** A218 Set of 4 7.75 7.75

Sea Birds — A219

Designs: 10c, Red-tailed tropicbird. 50c, Australasian gannet. $1.50 Gray ternlet. $2, Masked booby. $5, White-necked petrel.
$4, Red-tailed tropicbird, horiz.

**2005, Aug. 9**
**853-857** A219 Set of 5 21.00 21.00

**Souvenir Sheet**

**858** A219 $4 multi 9.00 9.00

See Nos. 883-888. For surcharge, see No. 1044.

Hibiscus Varieties A220

No. 859: a, Marjory Brown. b, Aloha. c, Pulau Tree. d, Ann Miller. e, Surfrider. f, Philip Island. g, Rose of Sharon. h, D. J. O'Brien. i, Elaine's Pride. j, Castle White. k, Skeleton Hibiscus. l, Pink Sunset.

**2005, Aug. 30** *Perf. 14¼x14*
**859** Block of 12 12.00 12.00
*a.-l.* A220 50c Any single 1.00 1.00
Complete booklet, #859 12.00

Christmas — A221

Designs: 50c, Anson Bay. $1.20, Cascade Bay. $1.80, Ball Bay.

**2005, Oct. 25** **Litho.** *Perf. 14¼x14*
**860-862** A221 Set of 3 6.75 6.75

Jazz Festival — A222

Designs: 50c, Drummer. $1.20, Saxophonist. $1.80, Guitarist.

**2005, Dec. 6** *Perf. 14x14¼*
**863-865** A222 Set of 3 7.25 7.25

Queen's Baton Relay for 2006 Commonwealth Games — A223

No. 866: a, 50c, Baton relay runner, boat's prow. b, $1.50, Baton.

**2006, Jan. 16** **Litho.** *Perf. 14½x14¾*
**866** A223 Horiz. pair, #a-b 4.25 4.25

2006 Commonwealth Games, Melbourne — A224

Norfolk Island flag and: 50c, Shooting. $1.50, Lawn bowling. $2, Squash.

**2006, Mar. 14** **Litho.** *Perf. 14½*
**867-869** A224 Set of 3 7.25 7.25

Pitcairn Migration, 150th Anniv. — A225

Pitcairn Island history: No. 870, 50c, The Bounty at Portsmouth. No. 871, 50c, Collecting breadfruit at Tahiti. $1.20, The mutiny. $1.50, Burning of the Bounty at Pitcairn Island. $1.80, Pitcairners arrive at Norfolk Island, 1856.

**2006, May 4** *Perf. 14x14½*
**870-874** A225 Set of 5 11.00 11.00

Bounty Anniversary Day — A226

Designs: 10c, Re-enactment procession. 30c, Remembering old soldiers. No. 877, 50c, Honoring ancestors. No. 878, 50c, Community picnic. $4, Bounty Ball.

**2006, June 7**
**875-879** A226 Set of 5 10.50 10.50

See Pitcairn Islands No. 643.

Traditional Hat Making — A227

No. 880, 50c — Purple panel: a, Hat with flowers on brim. b, Hat with no flowers.
No. 881, 50c — Blue green panel: a, Hat with flowers on brim. b, Hat with feather at right.
No. 882, 50c — Green panel: a, Hat with flowers on brim. b, Hat with no flowers.

**2006, June 7** *Perf. 15¼x14¾*
**Horiz. Pairs, #a-b**
**880-882** A227 Set of 3 5.75 5.75

**Sea Birds Type of 2005**

Designs: 25c, White tern. 40c, Sooty tern. 70c, Black-winged petrel. $1, Black noddy. $3, Wedge-tailed shearwater.
$2.50, Sooty tern, diff.

**2006, Aug. 9** *Perf. 14½*
**883-887** A219 Set of 5 10.00 10.00

**Souvenir Sheet**

**888** A219 $2.50 multi 5.50 5.50

Dogs — A228

Dogs named: 10c, Wal. 50c, Axel. $1, Wag. $2.65, Gemma.

**2006, Sept. 12** *Perf. 14½*
**889-892** A228 Set of 4 9.00 9.00

Norfolk Island Central School, Middlegate, Cent. — A229

Designs: No. 893, $2, Sepia-toned photograph. No. 894, $2, Color photograph.

**2006, Oct. 3**
**893-894** A229 Set of 2 8.50 8.50

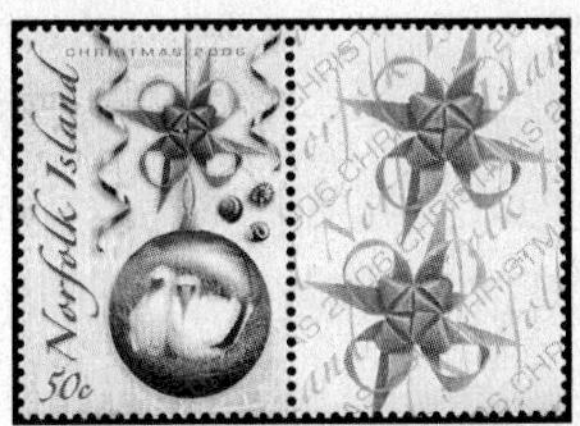


Christmas — A230

Ornaments showing: No. 895, 50c, Birds. No. 896, 50c, House. $1.20, Building. $1.80, Flower.

**2006, Nov. 21** **Litho.**
**Stamp + Label**
**895-898** A230 Set of 4 *15.00 15.00*

Weeds A231

Designs: No. 899, 50c, Ageratina riparia. No. 900, 50c, Lantana camara. $1.20, Ipomoea cairica. $1.80, Solanum mauritianum.

**2007, Feb. 6** *Perf. 14¼*
**899-902** A231 Set of 4 7.50 7.50

Adventure Sports A232

Designs: No. 903, 50c, Wind surfing. No. 904, 50c, Sea kayaking. $1.20, Mountain biking. $1.80, Surfing.

**2007, Apr. 3 Litho. *Perf. 14½***
**903-906** A232 Set of 4 8.00 8.00

**Souvenir Sheet**

Kentia Palm Seed Harvest — A233

No. 907: a, Ladder and trees, vert. b, Dog and buckets of seeds. c, Man pouring seeds into box. d, Seeds on tree, vert.

***Perf. 14 (14½ on Short Side Not Adjacent to Another Stamp)***

**2007, May 29**
**907** A233 50c Sheet of 4, #a-d, + central label 5.00 5.00

Ghosts — A234

Designs: 10c, Violinist, musical notes, building. 50c, Graveyard. $1, Female ghost on dock steps. $1.80, Ghosts on building steps.

**2007, June 26 *Perf. 14½***
**908-911** A234 Set of 4 7.50 7.50

Queen Victoria — A235

**2007, July 31 *Die Cut***

**Self-Adhesive**

**Booklet Stamp (10c)**

**912** A235 10c multi .40 .40
*a.* Booklet pane of 10 4.00

**Size: 21x28mm**

**913** A235 $5 multi 11.00 11.00

Queen Victoria Scholarship, 120th anniv.

13th South Pacific Games, Samoa — A236

Designs: 50c, Squash. $1, Golf. $1.20, Netball. $1.80, Running.
$2, Games emblem.

**2007, Aug. 28 *Perf. 14¼***
**914-917** A236 Set of 4 9.00 9.00

**Souvenir Sheet**

**918** A236 $2 multi 4.00 4.00

Closure of First Convict Settlement, Bicent. A237

Designs: 10c, HMS Sirius and Supply off Kingston. 50c, Shipping signal, Kingston. $1.20, First settlement, Kingston. $1.80, Ship Lady Nelson leaving for Tasmania.

**2007, Nov. 13**
**919-922** A237 Set of 4 7.75 7.75

Banyan Park Play Center A238

Children and slogans: 50c, "Friendship." $1, "Community." $1.20, "Play, learn, grow together." $1.80, "Read books."

**2007, Nov. 27 Litho. *Perf. 14x14¼***
**923-926** A238 Set of 4 8.75 8.75

Christmas A239

Items with Christmas lights: 50c, Christmas tree. $1.20, Building. $1.80, Rowboat.

**2007, Nov. 27**
**927-929** A239 Set of 3 6.75 6.75

Automobiles A240

Designs: 50c, 1965 Ford Falcon XP. $1, 1952 Chevrolet Styleline. $1.20, 1953 Pontiac Silver Arrow. $1.80, 1971 Rolls Royce Silver Shadow.

**2008, Feb. 5**
**930-933** A240 Set of 4 8.25 8.25

Norfolk Islanders With Pitcairn Islands Heritage — A241

Designs: 50c, Andre Nobbs. $1, Darlene Buffett. $1.20, Colin "Boonie" Lindsay Buffett. $1.80, Tania Grube.

**2008, Apr. 4 Litho. *Perf. 14½***
**934-937** A241 Set of 4 8.50 8.50

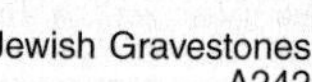

Jewish Gravestones A242

Gravestone of: 50c, Carl Hans Nathan Strauss. $1.20, Meta Kienhuize. $1.80, Johan Jacobus Kienhuize.
$2, Sally Kadesh.

**2008, May 14 *Perf. 14½***
**938-940** A242 Set of 3 6.75 6.75

**Souvenir Sheet**

***Perf. 13½***

**941** A242 $2 multi 4.00 4.00

2008 World Stamp Championship, Israel (#941). No. 941 contains one 30x40mm stamp.

Calves A243

Designs: 50c, Limousin Cross. $1, Murray Grey. $1.20, Poll Hereford. $1.80, Brahman Cross.

**2008, May 30 *Perf. 14¼***
**942-945** A243 Set of 4 8.75 8.75

St. John Ambulance, 25th Anniv. on Norfolk Island — A244

Designs: 30c, Past and present members. 40c, Re-enactment of treatment of accident victim at scene. 95c, Accident victim being placed in ambulance. $4, Accident victim entering hospital.

**2008, June 27 *Perf. 14½***
**946-949** A244 Set of 4 11.00 11.00

Ferns — A245

No. 950, 20c: a, Netted brakefern. b, Pteris zahlbruckneriana.
No. 951, 50c: a, Robinsonia. b, Asplenium australasicum.
No. 952, 80c: a, Hanging fork fern. b, Tmesipteris norfolkensis.
No. 953, $2: a, King fern. b, Marattia salicina.

**2008, Aug. 1 Litho. *Perf. 14¼***

**Horiz. Pairs, #a-b**

**950-953** A245 Set of 4 13.00 13.00

Ships Built On Norfolk Island — A246

Designs: 50c, Sloop Norfolk, 1798. $1.20, Schooner Resolution, 1925. $1.80, Schooner Endeavour, 1808.

**2008, Sept. 2**
**954-956** A246 Set of 3 5.75 5.75

A247

Designs: 25c, Prison buildings. 55c, Gate and prison buildings. $1.75, Graveyard. $2.50, Building and walls.

**2008, Oct. 27 Litho. *Perf. 14½***
**957-960** A247 Set of 4 7.00 7.00

Isles of Exile Conference, Norfolk Island.

A248

Christmas: 55c, Adoration of the Shepherds. $1.40, Madonna and Child. $2.05, Adoration of the Magi.

**2008, Nov. 7 *Perf. 14¼***
**961-963** A248 Set of 3 5.50 5.50

Mosaics A249

Designs: 5c, Fish. No. 965, 15c, Flower. 55c, Bird. $1.40, Tree.
No. 968, 15c, Turtle. No. 969, 15c, Starfish.

**2009, Feb. 16 *Perf. 14x14¼***
**964-967** A249 Set of 4 3.00 3.00

**Booklet Stamps**

**Self-Adhesive**

***Serpentine Die Cut 9½x10***

**968-969** A249 Set of 2 .75 .75
*969a* Booklet pane of 12, 6 each #968-969 4.50 4.50

Cattle Breeds A250

Designs: 15c, Shorthorn. 55c, South Devon. $1.40, Norfolk Blue. $2.05, Lincoln Red.
$5.00, Three calves.

**2009, Apr. 24 Litho. *Perf. 14x14¼***
**970-973** A250 Set of 4 6.00 6.00

**Souvenir Sheet**

***Perf. 14¼***

**974** A250 $5 multi 7.25 7.25

Mushrooms — A251

Designs: 15c, Gyrodon sp. 55c, Stereum ostrea. $1.40, Cymatoderma elegans. $2.05, Chlorophyllum molybdites.

**2009, May 29 Litho. *Perf. 14½x14***
**975-978** A251 Set of 4 6.75 6.75
*978a* Souvenir sheet, #975-978 6.75 6.75
*978b* As "a," overprinted with Intl. Stamp & Coin Expo emblem and text in sheet margin in gold 8.25 8.25

Issued: No. 978b, 11/7/10.

Endangered Wildlife — A252

Designs: No. 979, Bridled nailtail wallaby. No. 980, Norfolk Island green parrot. No. 981, Subarctic fur seal. No. 982, Christmas Island blue-tailed skink. No. 983, Green turtle.

**2009, Aug. 4 Litho. *Perf. 14¾x14***

**"Norfolk Island" Above Denomination**

| | | | | |
|---|---|---|---|---|
| **979** | A252 55c multi | | .95 | .95 |
| **980** | A252 55c multi | | .95 | .95 |
| **981** | A252 55c multi | | .95 | .95 |
| **982** | A252 55c multi | | .95 | .95 |
| **983** | A252 55c multi | | .95 | .95 |
| *a.* | Horiz. strip of 5, #979-983 | | 4.75 | 4.75 |
| | *Nos. 979-983 (5)* | | 4.75 | 4.75 |

**Miniature Sheet**

**984** A252 55c Sheet of 5, #980, Australia #3126, 3128-3130 5.25 5.25

See Australia Nos. 3126-3136. No. 984 is identical to Australia No. 3131. Australia No. 3127 is similar to No. 980, but has "Australia" above denomination.

Birds — A253

Designs: 15c, Gray fantail. 55c, Pacific robin, vert. $1.40, Golden whistler, vert. $2.05, Sacred kingfisher.

**2009, Aug. 19 *Perf. 14½***

| | | | | |
|---|---|---|---|---|
| **985** | A253 15c multi | | .25 | .25 |
| **986** | A253 55c multi | | .95 | .95 |
| | Complete booklet, 10 #986 | | 9.50 | |
| **987** | A253 $1.40 multi | | 2.40 | 2.40 |
| **988** | A253 $2.05 multi | | 3.50 | 3.50 |
| | *Nos. 985-988 (4)* | | 7.10 | 7.10 |

Self-government, 30th Anniv. — A254

**2009, Aug. 19 *Perf. 14***

**989** A254 $10 multi 17.00 17.00

Christmas A255

Stained-glass windows depicting: 15c, St. Matthew. 50c, Roses. $1.45, Christ in Glory. $2.10, Saint with Chalice.

**2009, Nov. 2 Litho. *Perf. 14¼***

**990-993** A255 Set of 4 7.75 7.75

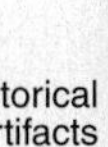

Historical Artifacts A256

Designs: 5c, China from second convict settlement, drawing of man and woman. 55c, Polynesian ivory fish hook, drawing of fishing boat. $1.10, Regimental badge, painting of soldiers. $1.45, Brass wall fitting from HMS Sirius shipwreck, drawing of shipwreck. $1.65, Bottles from convict settlement's Civil Hospital, drawing of treatment of an ill woman. $2.10, Bounty wedding ring, painting of the Bounty.

**2010, Feb. 22 Litho. *Perf. 14½***

| | | | | |
|---|---|---|---|---|
| **994** | A256 5c multi | | .25 | .25 |
| **995** | A256 55c multi | | 1.00 | 1.00 |
| **996** | A256 $1.10 multi | | 1.10 | 1.10 |
| **997** | A256 $1.45 multi | | 2.60 | 2.60 |
| **998** | A256 $1.65 multi | | 3.00 | 3.00 |
| **999** | A256 $2.10 multi | | 3.75 | 3.75 |
| | *Nos. 994-999 (6)* | | 11.70 | 11.70 |

See Nos. 1021-1026.

Cruise Ships A257

Designs: 55c, Pacific Jewel. $1.45, Pacific Sun. $1.65, Pacific Pearl. $1.75, Pacific Dawn. $2.10, RMS Strathaird.

**2010, Mar. 26 Litho. *Perf. 14x14½***

**1000-1004** A257 Set of 5 14.00 14.00

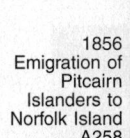

1856 Emigration of Pitcairn Islanders to Norfolk Island A258

Ship Morayshire and: 55c, Pitcairn Island girls on Norfolk Island, 1857. $1.10, Passengers aboard ship, 1856. $1.45, Pitcairn Island men on Norfolk Island, 1861. $2.75, Naomi and Jane Nobbs.

**2010, June 15 *Perf. 13½x13¼***

**1005-1008** A258 Set of 4 10.00 10.00

History of Whaling A259

Designs: No. 1009, 60c, Blessing of the fleet. No. 1010, 60c, Launching of boats. $1.20, Cliff top navigational fires. $3, Products made from whales.

**2010, Aug. 16 Litho. *Perf. 14x14¼***

**1009-1012** A259 Set of 4 10.00 10.00

Christmas A260

Parrots and: 15c, Bells. 55c, Conifer sprig. 60c, Gift. $1.30, Christmas ornament.

**2010, Oct. 18 Litho. *Perf. 13¼x13½***

**1013-1016** A260 Set of 4 5.25 5.25

2010 World Bowls Champion of Champions Lawn Bowling Tournament, Norfolk Island — A261

Designs: 60c, Woman holding trophy. $1.50, Man bowling. $2.20, Bowling balls.

**2010, Nov. 23 Litho. *Perf. 14***

**1017-1019** A261 Set of 3 8.75 8.75

**Souvenir Sheet**

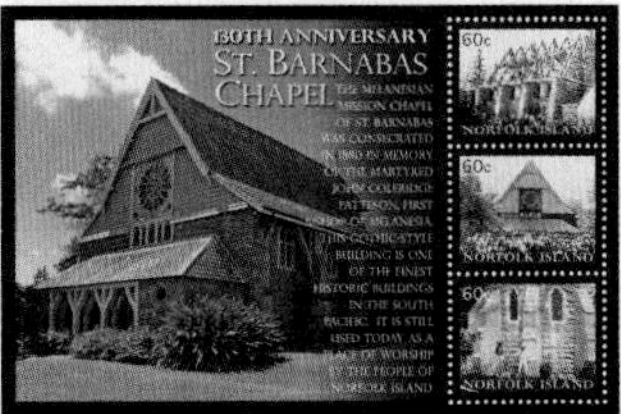


St. Barnabas Chapel, 130th Anniv. — A262

No. 1020: a, Chapel under construction. b, Congregation in front of chapel. c, Two men in front of chapel.

**2010, Dec. 7 *Perf. 14½x14***

**1020** A262 60c Sheet of 3, #a-c 3.75 3.75

**Historical Artifacts Type of 2010**

Designs: 15c, Women, iron. 60c, Thursday October Christian and his mug. $1.20, Soldiers, bone dominoes. $1.50, Soldier in front of Civil Hospital, clay pipe and ceramic shards. $1.80, Woman and child, doll and doll's head. $3, People at Melanesian Mission, wooden and shell hair items.

**2011, Feb. 22 *Perf. 14½***

| | | | | |
|---|---|---|---|---|
| **1021** | A256 15c multi | | .30 | .30 |
| **1022** | A256 60c multi | | 1.25 | 1.25 |
| **1023** | A256 $1.20 multi | | 2.50 | 2.50 |
| **1024** | A256 $1.50 multi | | 3.00 | 3.00 |
| **1025** | A256 $1.80 multi | | 3.75 | 3.75 |
| **1026** | A256 $3 multi | | 6.25 | 6.25 |
| | *Nos. 1021-1026 (6)* | | 17.05 | 17.05 |

Shells — A263

Designs: 15c, Cirostrema zelebori, Canarium labiatum. 60c, Janthina janthina, Spirula spirula. $1.50, Conus capitaneus, Conus ebraeus. $1.80, Cypraea vitellus, Cypraea caputserpentis. $3, Nerita atramentosa, Neritina turrita.

**2011, Apr. 21 Litho. *Perf. 14½***

**1027-1031** A263 Set of 5 15.00 15.00

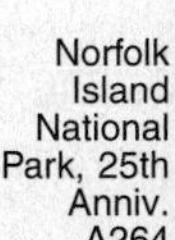

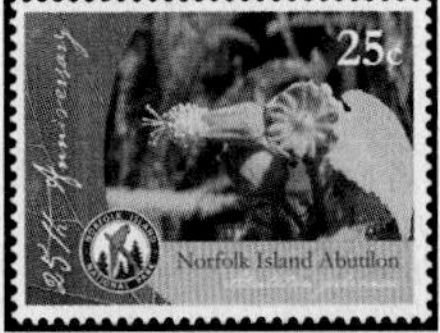


Norfolk Island National Park, 25th Anniv. A264

Park emblem and: 25c, Abutilon julianae. 60c, Hibiscus insularis. $1.55, Myoporum obscurum. $2.25, Meryta latifolia.

**2011, June 24 *Perf. 13½x13¼***

**1032-1035** A264 Set of 4 10.00 10.00

Kingston and Arthur's Vale UNESCO World Heritage Site — A265

No. 1036: a, Guard House, 1796-1826. b, Graveyard, 1790s-1825. c, Government House, 1804-28. d, Pier Store, 1825. e, Crank Mill, 1827. f, Bloody Bridge, 1835. g, Commissariat Store, 1835. h, Kingston Pier, 1839. i, No. 9 Quality Row, 1839. j, Flaghouses, 1840s. k, New Jail, 1847. l, Royal Engineers Office, 1851.

**2011, Aug. 1 *Die Cut Perf. 9¾x10***

**Self-Adhesive**

| | | | | |
|---|---|---|---|---|
| **1036** | Booklet pane of 12 | | 15.00 | |
| *a.-l.* | A265 60c Any single | | 1.25 | 1.25 |

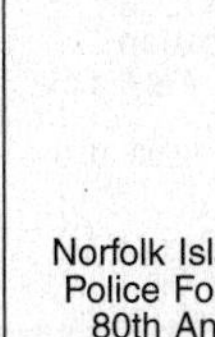

Norfolk Island Police Force, 80th Anniv. A266

Designs: 60c, Mounted policeman on Bounty Day, c. 1933. $1.55, 1970s police car. $2.25, Policeman observing ship.

**2011, Oct. 14 Litho. *Perf. 13x13¼***

**1037-1039** A266 Set of 3 9.25 9.25

Christmas A267

Various flowers: 15c, 55c, 60c, $1.35.

**2011, Oct. 14 *Perf. 14½***

**1040-1043** A267 Set of 4 5.50 5.50

No. 853 Surcharged in Brown and Black

**Methods and Perfs As Before**

**2012, Feb. 13**

**1044** A219 $4 on 10c #853 8.75 8.75

Iconic Activities A268

Designs: 60c, Collecting hi hi shells. 75c, Collecting whale bird eggs. $1.55, Fishing off the rocks. $2.75, Clifftop barbecue.

**2012, Apr. 10 Litho. *Die Cut***

**Self-Adhesive**

**1045-1048** A268 Set of 4 11.50 11.50

Souvenir Sheet

Reign of Queen Elizabeth II, 60th Anniv. — A269

No. 1049: a, Commemorative plaque on Queen Elizabeth Avenue. b, Beacon at Queen Elizabeth Lookout. c, Decorated pine tree at Government House.

**Litho. With Foil Application**

**2012, Aug. 20** ***Perf. 14½***
**1049** A269 $1.60 Sheet of 3, #a-c 10.00 10.00

Sunshine Club, 51st Anniv. A270

Designs: 60c, Baked goods. $1.60, Basket with bananas, flour and sugar. $1.65, Cook book and pie ingredients. $2.35, Hands.

**2012, Oct. 19** **Litho.** ***Perf. 14***
**1050-1053** A270 Set of 4 13.00 13.00

Christmas A271

Various pearl inlays from pews in St. Barnabas Chapel and lyrics from Christmas carols: 15c, 55c, $1.55, $2.35.

**2012, Nov. 1**
**1054-1057** A271 Set of 4 9.75 9.75

Airplanes Landing on Norfolk Island, 70th Anniv. — A272

No. 1058: a, Royal New Zealand Air Force Hudson Bomber. b, DC-3. c, Lancastrian. d, DC-4 Skymaster. e, Fokker F27 Friendship. f, Beechcraft Super King Air 200. g, Fokker F28 Fellowship. h, C-130 Hercules. i, BAe 146. j, Boeing 737-300. k, F/A-18 Hornet. l, Airbus A320.

***Serpentine Die Cut 9¾x10***

**2012, Dec. 24**
**1058** Booklet pane of 12 15.00
*a.-l.* A272 60c Any single 1.25 1.25

Bell, All Saints Church, Kingston — A273

**2013, Apr. 9** ***Perf. 14***
**1059** A273 $5 multi 10.50 10.50

Norfolk Island Country Music Festival, 20th Anniv. A274

Designs: 15c, Boots, Emily Bay Beach. 60c, Adam Harvey with guitar. $1.60, Guitar. $1.65, Dennis Marsh with guitar. $2.35, Street perfomer with guitar.

**2013, May 20**
**1060-1064** A274 Set of 5 12.00 12.00

Shorelines — A275

Designs: 15c, Ball Bay. 60c, Second Sands. 95c, Anson Bay. $1.20, Slaughter Bay. $1.70, Bumboras. $1.85, Emily Bay.

**2013, Sept. 30** **Litho.** ***Perf. 13½***

| | | | | |
|---|---|---|---|---|
| **1065** | A275 | 15c multi | .30 | .30 |
| **1066** | A275 | 60c multi | 1.10 | 1.10 |
| **1067** | A275 | 95c multi | 1.90 | 1.90 |
| **1068** | A275 | $1.20 multi | 2.25 | 2.25 |
| **1069** | A275 | $1.70 multi | 3.25 | 3.25 |
| **1070** | A275 | $1.85 multi | 3.50 | 3.50 |
| | | *Nos. 1065-1070 (6)* | 12.30 | 12.30 |

See Nos. 1079-1084.

Christmas A276

Locally-made Christmas ornamentation: 15c, Wreath. 55c, Christmas tree made of driftwood. $1.10, Bird made of driftwood. $1.65, Three stars.

**2013, Nov. 1** **Litho.** ***Perf. 14½***
**1071-1074** A276 Set of 4 6.50 6.50

Trans-Tasman Freestyle Motocross Challenge — A277

Flag of Norfolk Island and New Zealand motorcyclists performing stunts on motorcycle: 50c, Joe McNaughton. $1, McNaughton, diff. $1.50, McNaughton, diff. $1.60, Callum Shaw.

**2013, Dec. 18** **Litho.** ***Perf. 13½***
**1075-1078** A277 Set of 4 8.25 8.25

**Shorelines Type of 2013**

Designs: 5c, Cemetery Beach. 10c, Beefsteak. 25c, Crystal Pool. 70c, Cascade Bay. $1.75, Garnet Point. $2.60, Duncombe Bay.

**2014, May 7** **Litho.** ***Perf. 13½***

| | | | | |
|---|---|---|---|---|
| **1079** | A275 | 5c multi | .25 | .25 |
| **1080** | A275 | 10c multi | .25 | .25 |
| **1081** | A275 | 25c multi | .50 | .50 |
| **1082** | A275 | 70c multi | 1.40 | 1.40 |
| **1083** | A275 | $1.75 multi | 3.25 | 3.25 |
| **1084** | A275 | $2.60 multi | 4.75 | 4.75 |
| | | *Nos. 1079-1084 (6)* | 10.40 | 10.40 |

Wearable Art — A278

Designs: 15c, Fishing for the Groom, by Wayne Boniface. 70c, Pasta Bella, by Boniface. $1.40, Flora Abunda Metallica, by Tony Gazzard., $1.50, Romeo and Julieta, by Julie Paris. $3.50, Bamboo Princess Warrior, by Robyn Butterfield.

**2014, May 26** **Litho.** ***Perf. 14***
**1085-1089** A278 Set of 5 13.50 13.50

Norfolk Island Pine — A279

Norfolk Island Pine and: 20c, Cottesloe Beach, Western Australia. 70c, Old Military Barracks, Kingston, Norfolk Island.

**2014, July 22** **Litho.** ***Perf. 14x14¾***
**1090-1091** A279 Set of 2 1.75 1.75

See Australia Nos. 4145-4146.

Norfolk Island Quota International Club, 35th Anniv. — A280

Designs: 15c, Picnic table near Emily Bay. 70c, Telescope on Queen Elizabeth Lookout. $3.20, Family on bench overlooking ocean.

**2014, Aug. 15** **Litho.** ***Perf. 14***
**1092-1094** A280 Set of 3 7.50 7.50

Souvenir Sheet

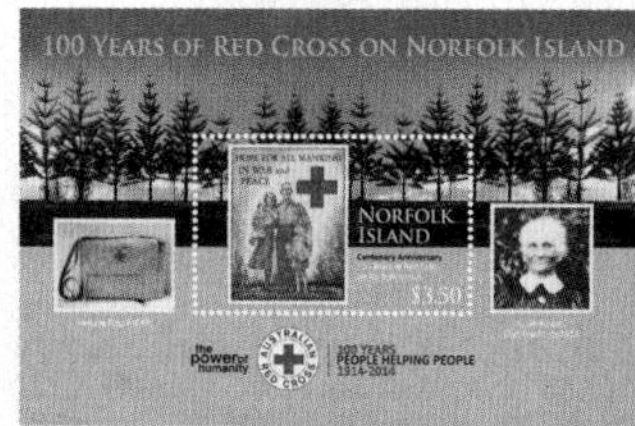


Red Cross on Norfolk Island, Cent. — A281

**2014, Sept. 29** **Litho.** ***Perf. 14***
**1095** A281 $3.50 multi 6.25 6.25

Tip of Norfolk Island Pine — A282

Developing Norfolk Island Pine Cone — A283

Norfolk Island Pine Seedling A284

Norfolk Island Pine Forest A285

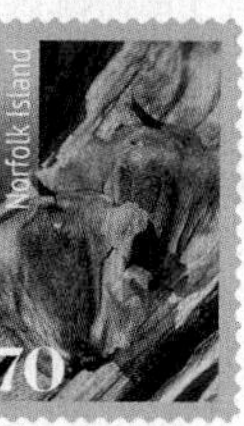

Norfolk Island Pine Seeds A286

Norfolk Island Pine Branches A287

Shed Norfolk Island Pine Needles — A288

Hollowed-out Norfolk Island Pine — A289

Norfolk Island Pines — A290

Norfolk Island Pine — A291

***Serpentine Die Cut 10¾x10***

**2014, Sept. 29** **Litho.**

**Self-Adhesive**

| | | | |
|---|---|---|---|
| **1096** | Booklet pane of 10 | 12.50 | |
| *a.* | A282 70c multi | 1.25 | 1.25 |
| *b.* | A283 70c multi | 1.25 | 1.25 |
| *c.* | A284 70c multi | 1.25 | 1.25 |
| *d.* | A285 70c multi | 1.25 | 1.25 |
| *e.* | A286 70c multi | 1.25 | 1.25 |
| *f.* | A287 70c multi | 1.25 | 1.25 |
| *g.* | A288 70c multi | 1.25 | 1.25 |
| *h.* | A289 70c multi | 1.25 | 1.25 |
| *i.* | A290 70c multi | 1.25 | 1.25 |
| *j.* | A291 70c multi | 1.25 | 1.25 |

See No. 1109.

Quilts — A292

Designs: 15c, Memory Quilt, by Julie South. 70c, Sampler Quilt, by Kay Greenbury, Raewyn Maxwell, Rowena Massicks and Barbara Solomon. $1.40, Sunset at Puppy's Point, by Greenbury. $1.50, Southern Cross Shared, by Greenbury. $3.50, Storm at Sea, by Massicks.

**2014, Oct. 17** **Litho.** ***Perf. 14½***
**1097-1101** A292 Set of 5 12.50 12.50

Christmas — A293

Fabric designs by Sue Pearson depicting: 15c, Breadfruit leaves. 65c, Passion fruit flowers. $1.70, Turtles. $1.80, Taro leaves. $2.55, Hibiscus flowers.

**2014, Nov. 3 Litho. *Perf. 14¼x14***
**1102-1106** A293 Set of 5 12.00 12.00

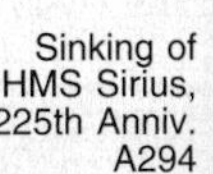

Sinking of HMS Sirius, 225th Anniv. A294

No. 1107: a, Diver at underwater memorial. b, HMS Sirius, painting by John Allcott. c, The Melancholy Loss of HMS Sirius, painting by George Rapet. d, Cross belt plate from HMS Sirius. e, Capt. John Hunter of the HMS Sirius. f, Anchor of HMS Sirius. g, HMS Sirius, painting by Francis J. Bayldon. h, Carronades of HMS Sirius. i, Bronze shackle from HMS Sirius. j, Pantograph from HMS Sirius.

***Serpentine Die Cut 10x10¾***
**2015, Mar. 19 Litho.**
**Self-Adhesive**

**1107** Booklet pane of 10 11.00
*a.-j.* A294 70c Any single 1.10 1.10

Souvenir Sheet

Battle of Gallipoli, Cent. — A295

**Litho. With Foil Application**
**2015, Apr. 24 *Perf. 13½***
**1108** A295 $5 multi 8.00 8.00

**Norfolk Island Pine Types of 2014**

Designs as before.

***Serpentine Die Cut 10¾x10***
**2015, June 1 Litho.**
**Self-Adhesive**

**1109** Booklet pane of 10 2.50
*a.* A282 15c multi .25 .25
*b.* A283 15c multi .25 .25
*c.* A284 15c multi .25 .25
*d.* A285 15c multi .25 .25
*e.* A286 15c multi .25 .25
*f.* A287 15c multi .25 .25
*g.* A288 15c multi .25 .25
*h.* A289 15c multi .25 .25
*i.* A290 15c multi .25 .25
*j.* A291 15c multi .25 .25

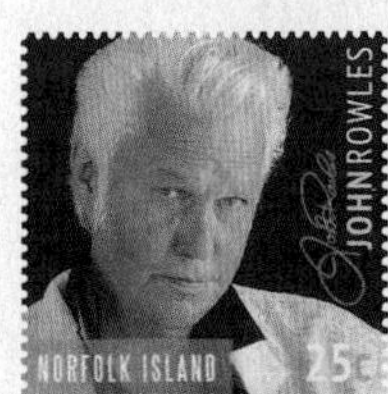

Celebrities at Christmas in July Festival A296

Designs: 25c, John Rowles, singer. 35c, Suzanne Prentice, singer. 45c, Normie Rowe, singer. $1.40, Glenn A. Baker, journalist and 2015 festival master of ceremonies. $1.95, Colleen McCullough (1937-2015), writer.

**2015, July 13 Litho. *Perf. 14¼x14***
**1110-1114** A296 Set of 5 6.50 6.50

Christmas A297

Ornaments made from plant fibers: 15c, Bird. 65c, Star. $1.30, Fish. $1.70, Rings around glass balls, candle. $2.55, Netting around glass ball.

**2015, Oct. 1 Litho. *Perf. 14½x14¾***
**1115-1119** A297 Set of 5 9.00 9.00

Norfolk's Ocean Challenge Canoe Races — A298

Various participants with panel color of: No. 1120, $1, Cerise. No. 1121, $1, Cobalt. $1.85, Green. $2.75, Gray blue.

**2016, Jan. 14 Litho. *Perf. 14x14½***
**1120-1123** A298 Set of 4 9.50 9.50

Phillip Island A299

Designs: 15c, Building. 20c, Building, diff. No. 1126, $1, Building, diff. No. 1127, $1, Man, woman and building. $1.85, Building, diff. $2, Tree near cliff.

**2016, Feb. 22 Litho. *Perf. 14½***
**1124-1129** A299 Set of 6 9.00 9.00

Souvenir Sheet

Landing of Pitcairn Islanders on Norfolk Island, 160th Anniv. — A300

**2016, June 7 Litho. *Perf. 13½***
**1130** A300 $5 multi 7.50 7.50

Sea Birds — A301

Designs: $1, Red-tailed tropicbird. $2, Masked booby.

**2016, Sept. 20 Litho. *Perf. 14x14¾***
**1131-1132** A301 Set of 2 4.75 4.75
*1132a* Souvenir sheet of 2, #1131-1132 4.75 4.75

Waterfalls — A302

Designs: $1, Cockpit Waterfall. $2, Cascade Creek Falls.

**2017, Jan. 17 Litho. *Perf. 14¾x14***
**1133-1134** A302 Set of 2 4.50 4.50
*1134a* Souvenir sheet of 2, #1133-1134 4.50 4.50

Flowers A303

Designs: $1, Hibiscus insularis. $2, Lagunaria patersonia.

**2017, July 18 Litho. *Perf. 14x14¾***
**1135-1136** A303 Set of 2 5.00 5.00
*1136a* Souvenir sheet of 2, #1135-1136 5.00 5.00

UNESCO World Heritage Sites on Norfolk Island — A304

Designs: $1, New Jail. $2, Prisoners Barracks.

**2017, Sept. 19 Litho. *Perf. 14¾x14***
**1137-1138** A304 Set of 2 4.75 4.75
*1138a* Souvenir sheet of 2, #1137-1138 4.75 4.75

Norfolk Island Golf Club — A305

**2018, Feb. 27 Litho. *Perf. 13¾x14***
**1139** A305 $5 multi 7.75 7.75
*a.* Souvenir sheet of 1 7.75 7.75

## NORTH BORNEO

'north 'bor-nē-,ō

LOCATION — Northeast part of island of Borneo, Malay archipelago
GOVT. — British colony
AREA — 29,388 sq. mi.
POP. — 470,000 (est. 1962)
CAPITAL — Jesselton

The British North Borneo Company administered North Borneo, under a royal charter granted in 1881, until 1946 when it became a British colony. Labuan (q.v.) became part of the new colony. As "Sabah," North Borneo joined with Singapore, Sarawak and Malaya to form the Federation of Malaysia on Sept. 16, 1963.

100 Cents = 1 Dollar

Quantities of most North Borneo stamps through 1912 have been canceled to order with an oval of bars. Values given for used stamps beginning with No. 6 are for those with this form of cancellation. Stamps from No. 6 through Nos. 159 and J31 that do not exist CTO have used values in italics. Stamps with dated town cancellations sell for much higher prices.

**Catalogue values for unused stamps in this country are for Never Hinged items, beginning with Scott 238.**

**North Borneo**

Coat of Arms — A1

**1883-84 Unwmk. Litho. *Perf. 12***
**1** A1 2c brown 47.50 *75.00*
*a.* Horiz. pair, imperf. btwn. 20,000.
**2** A1 4c rose ('84) 65.00 *70.00*
**3** A1 8c green ('84) 90.00 *60.00*
*Nos. 1-3 (3)* 202.50 *205.00*

For surcharges see Nos. 4, 19-21.

No. 1 Surcharged in Black

**4** A1 8c on 2c brown 500.00 *210.00*
*a.* Double surcharge *6,000.*

Coat of Arms with Supporters
A4 A5

*Perf. 14*

| | | | | |
|---|---|---|---|---|
| 6 | A4 50c violet | 225.00 | 40.00 |
| 7 | A5 $1 red | 185.00 | 19.00 |

**1886** *Perf. 14*

| | | | |
|---|---|---|---|
| 8 A1 ½c magenta | 120.00 | *200.00* |
| 9 A1 1c orange | *210.00* | *350.00* |
| a. Imperf., pair | 300.00 | |
| b. Vert. pair, imperf horiz. | 1,500. | |
| 10 A1 2c brown | 47.50 | 42.50 |
| a. Horiz. pair, imperf. between | 700.00 | |
| 11 A1 4c rose | 20.00 | *55.00* |
| a. Horiz. pair, imperf. between | — | 1,700. |
| 12 A1 8c green | 22.50 | *50.00* |
| a. Horiz. pair, imperf. between | *900.00* | |
| 13 A1 10c blue | 55.00 | *65.00* |
| a. Imperf., pair | 375.00 | |
| *Nos. 8-13 (6)* | 475.00 | *762.50* |

**Nos. 8, 11, 12 and 13 Surcharged or Overprinted in Black**

b

c

3
CENTS

d

**1886**

| | | |
|---|---|---|
| 14 A1 (b) ½c magenta | 225.00 | *325.00* |
| 15 A1 (c) 3c on 4c rose | 130.00 | *150.00* |
| 16 A1 (d) 3c on 4c rose | 1,800. | |
| 17 A1 (c) 5c on 8c green | 140.00 | *150.00* |
| a. Inverted surcharge | 2,750. | |
| 18 A1 (b) 10c blue | 300.00 | *375.00* |

**On Nos. 2 and 3**

*Perf. 12*

| | | |
|---|---|---|
| 19 A1 (c) 3c on 4c rose | 325.00 | *375.00* |
| 20 A1 (d) 3c on 4c rose | — | *16,000.* |
| a. Double surcharge, both types of "3" | | — |
| 21 A1 (c) 5c on 8c green | 325.00 | *375.00* |

**British North Borneo**

A9

**1886 Unwmk. Litho. *Perf. 12***

| | | |
|---|---|---|
| 22 A9 ½c lilac rose | 400.00 | *700.00* |
| 23 A9 1c orange | 250.00 | *400.00* |

*Perf. 14*

| | | |
|---|---|---|
| 25 A9 ½c rose | 4.75 | *21.00* |
| a. ½c lilac rose | *21.00* | *50.00* |
| b. Imperf., pair | 70.00 | |
| 26 A9 1c orange | 2.25 | *16.00* |
| a. Imperf., pair | 80.00 | |
| b. Vert. pair, imperf. btwn. | 425.00 | |
| 27 A9 2c brown | 2.25 | *16.00* |
| a. Imperf., pair | 50.00 | |
| 28 A9 4c rose | 6.50 | *19.00* |
| a. Cliché of 1c in plate of 4c | 350.00 | *1,300.* |
| b. Imperf., pair | 65.00 | |
| c. As "a," imperf. in pair with #28 | 7,500. | |
| d. Horiz. pair, imperf vert. | 425.00 | |
| 29 A9 8c green | 30.00 | *28.00* |
| a. Imperf., pair | 55.00 | *55.00* |
| 30 A9 10c blue | 15.00 | *45.00* |
| a. Imperf., pair | 55.00 | |
| b. Vert. pair, imperf btwn. | 425.00 | |
| *Nos. 25-30 (6)* | 60.75 | *145.00* |

For surcharges see Nos. 54-55.

A10 A11

A12 A13

| | | |
|---|---|---|
| 31 A10 25c slate blue | 475.00 | 25.00 |
| a. Imperf., pair | 475.00 | 50.00 |
| 32 A11 50c violet | 475.00 | 25.00 |
| a. Imperf., pair | 550.00 | 50.00 |
| 33 A12 $1 red | 400.00 | 24.00 |
| a. Imperf., pair | 600.00 | 50.00 |
| 34 A13 $2 sage green | 700.00 | 30.00 |
| a. Imperf., pair | 600.00 | 55.00 |
| *Nos. 31-34 (4)* | 2,050. | 104.00 |
| *Nos. 22-34 (12)* | 2,761. | *1,349.* |

See Nos. 44-47.

A14

**1887-92** *Perf. 14*

| | | |
|---|---|---|
| 35 A14 ½c rose | 1.50 | .60 |
| a. ½c magenta | 4.00 | *3.00* |
| 36 A14 1c orange | 6.50 | .50 |
| 37 A14 2c red brown | 7.50 | .50 |
| b. As "a," horiz. pair imperf. between | | *425.00* |
| 38 A14 3c violet | 2.75 | .50 |
| 39 A14 4c rose | 14.50 | .50 |
| a. Horiz. pair, imperf. vert. | | *250.00* |
| 40 A14 5c slate | 3.00 | .50 |
| 41 A14 6c lake ('92) | 20.00 | .50 |
| 42 A14 8c green | 32.50 | 1.00 |
| a. Horiz. pair, imperf. between | | |
| 43 A14 10c blue | 7.25 | .50 |
| *Nos. 35-43 (9)* | 95.50 | 5.10 |

Exist imperf. Value $20 each, unused, $4.50 used. Forgeries exist, perf. 11½.

For surcharges see Nos. 52-53, 56-57.

**Redrawn**

25c. The letters of "BRITISH NORTH BORNEO" are 2mm high instead of 1½mm.

50c. The club of the native at left does not touch the frame. The 0's of "50" are flat at top and bottom instead of being oval.

$1.00. The spear of the native at right does not touch the frame. There are 14 pearls at each side of the frame instead of 13.

$2.00. "BRITISH" is 11mm long instead of 12mm. There are only six oars at the side of the dhow.

**1888**

| | | |
|---|---|---|
| 44 A10 25c slate blue | 115.00 | .75 |
| b. Horiz. pair, imperf. between | | *300.00* |
| c. Imperf., pair | 500.00 | 22.50 |
| 45 A11 50c violet | 135.00 | .75 |
| a. Imperf., pair | 600.00 | 22.50 |
| 46 A12 $1 red | 67.50 | .75 |
| a. Imperf., pair | 450.00 | 22.50 |
| 47 A13 $2 sage green | 250.00 | 1.50 |
| a. Imperf., pair | 750.00 | 25.00 |
| *Nos. 44-47 (4)* | 567.50 | 3.75 |

For surcharges see Nos. 50-51, 58.

A15

A16

**1889**

| | | |
|---|---|---|
| 48 A15 $5 red violet | 400.00 | 9.00 |
| a. Imperf., pair | 1,100. | 80.00 |
| 49 A16 $10 brown | 400.00 | 12.50 |
| b. Imperf., pair | 1,300. | 90.00 |

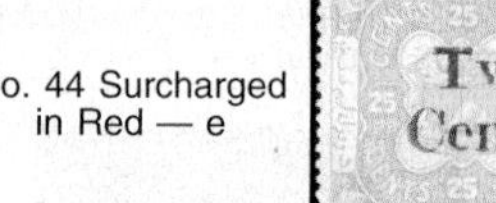
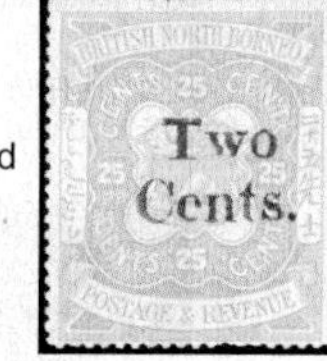


No. 44 Surcharged in Red — e

**1890**

| | | |
|---|---|---|
| 50 A10 2c on 25c slate blue | 87.50 | *100.00* |
| a. Inverted surcharge | 450.00 | *450.00* |
| b. With additional surcharge "2 cents" in black | | |
| 51 A10 8c on 25c slate blue | 135.00 | *145.00* |

Surcharged in Black On #42-43 — f

**1891-92**

| | | |
|---|---|---|
| 52 A14 6c on 8c green | 25.00 | *11.00* |
| a. "c" of "cents" inverted | 700.00 | *750.00* |
| b. "cetns" | 700.00 | *750.00* |
| c. Inverted surcharge | 500.00 | *500.00* |
| 53 A14 6c on 10c blue | 210.00 | *27.50* |

**On Nos. 29 and 30**

| | | |
|---|---|---|
| 54 A9 6c on 8c green | 9,000. | *4,750.* |
| 55 A9 6c on 10c blue | 67.50 | *22.50* |
| a. Inverted surcharge | 300.00 | *300.00* |
| b. Double surcharge | 1,500. | |
| c. Triple surcharge | 550.00 | |

**Nos. 39, 40 and 44 Surcharged in Red**

**1892**

| | | |
|---|---|---|
| 56 A14 1c on 4c rose | 27.50 | 15.00 |
| a. Double surcharge | 1,650. | |
| b. Surcharged on face & back | | *675.00* |
| 57 A14 1c on 5c slate | 8.00 | 6.50 |
| 58 A10 8c on 25c blue | 185.00 | *200.00* |
| *Nos. 56-58 (3)* | 220.50 | *221.50* |

**North Borneo**

Dyak Chief — A21

Malayan Sambar — A22

Malay Dhow — A26

Sago Palm — A23

Saltwater Crocodile — A27

Argus Pheasant A24

Mt. Kinabalu A28

Coat of Arms — A25

Coat of Arms with Supporters — A29

A30

A31

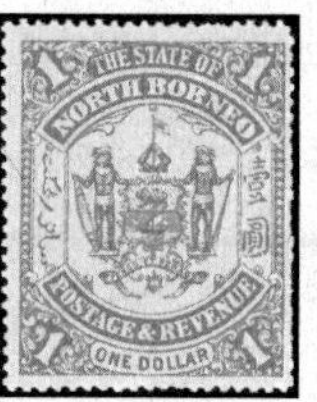

A32

A33

A34

A35

*Perf. 12 to 15 and Compound*

**1894 Engr. Unwmk.**

| | | |
|---|---|---|
| 59 A21 1c bis brn & blk | 1.40 | .50 |
| a. Vert. pair, imperf. btwn. | *950.00* | |

**60** A22 2c rose & black 5.50 .75
*a.* Horiz. pair, imperf. btwn. 950.00 950.00
*b.* Vert. pair, imperf. btwn. 950.00 950.00
**61** A23 3c vio & ol green 4.00 .55
*a.* Horiz. pair, imperf. btwn. — 850.00
*b.* Vert. pair, imperf. btwn. 1,350.
**62** A24 5c org red & blk 14.00 .75
*a.* Horiz. pair, imperf. btwn. 850.00
**63** A25 6c brn ol & blk 4.50 .60
**64** A26 8c lilac & black 6.50 .75
*a.* Vert. pair, imperf. btwn. 550.00 350.00
*b.* Horiz. pair, imperf. btwn. 750.00
**65** A27 12c ultra & black 47.50 3.00
*a.* 12c blue & black 30.00 2.75
**66** A28 18c green & black 30.00 2.00
**67** A29 24c claret & blue 25.00 2.00

**Litho.** *Perf. 14*

**68** A30 25c slate blue 10.00 1.00
*a.* Imperf., pair 60.00 12.00
**69** A31 50c violet 50.00 2.00
*a.* Imperf., pair 12.00
**70** A32 $1 red 14.50 1.25
*a.* Perf. 14x11 300.00
*b.* Imperf., pair 47.50 12.00
**71** A33 $2 gray green 27.50 2.75
*a.* Imperf., pair 18.00
**72** A34 $5 red violet 275.00 17.50
*a.* Imperf., pair 925.00 65.00
**73** A35 $10 brown 325.00 16.00
*a.* Imperf., pair 950.00 60.00
*Nos. 59-73 (15)* 840.40 51.40

For #68-70 in other colors see Labuan #63b-65b.

For surcharges & overprints see #74-78, 91-94, 97-102, 115-119, 130-135, 115-119, 150-151, 158-159, J1-J8. In other colors see Labuan #63-65, 93-95, 116-118, and 120.

No. 70 Surcharged in Black

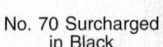

**1895, June**

**74** A32 4c on $1 red 7.00 1.25
*a.* Double surcharge 1,000.
**75** A32 10c on $1 red 27.50 .60
**76** A32 20c on $1 red 57.50 .60
**77** A32 30c on $1 red 52.50 2.00
**78** A32 40c on $1 red 65.00 2.00
*Nos. 74-78 (5)* 209.50 6.45

See No. 99.

A37

A38

A39

A40

A41

A42

A43

"Postal Revenue" — A44

No "Postal Revenue" — A45

***Perf. 13 to 16 and Compound***

**1897-1900** **Engr.**

**79** A37 1c bis brn & blk 12.00 .55
*a.* Horiz. pair, imperf. btwn. 600.00
**80** A38 2c dp rose & blk 25.00 .55
**81** A38 2c grn & blk ('00) 72.50 .60
**82** A39 3c lilac & ol green 36.00 .55
**83** A40 5c orange & black 125.00 .85
**84** A41 6c ol brown & blk 57.50 .50
**85** A42 8c brn lilac & blk 16.50 .75
**86** A43 12c blue & black 160.00 1.50
**87** A44 18c green & black 40.00 4.50
*a.* Vert. pair, imperf. btwn. 350.00
*b.* Horiz. pair, imperf. vert. 95.00
*c.* Imperf. pair 200.00
**88** A45 24c claret & blue 40.00 4.25
*Nos. 79-88 (10)* 584.50 14.60

For overprints and surcharges see Nos. 105-107, 109-112, 124-127, J9-J17, J20-J22, J24-J26, J28.

"Postage & Revenue"
A46 A47

**1897**

**89** A46 18c green & black 135.00 1.75
**90** A47 24c claret & blue 62.50 2.10

For surcharges & overprints see #95-96, 128-129, 113-114, J18-J19, J30-J31.

Stamps of 1894-97 Surcharged in Black

**1899**

**91** A40 4c on 5c org & blk 40.00 *12.50*
**92** A41 4c on 6c ol brn & blk 20.00 *25.00*
**93** A42 4c on 8c brn lil & blk 16.00 *13.00*
**94** A43 4c on 12c bl & blk 29.00 *15.00*
*a.* Horiz. pair, imperf. btwn. 850.00
*b.* Vert. pair, imperf. btwn. 950.00
**95** A46 4c on 18c grn & blk 16.00 *18.00*
**96** A47 4c on 24c cl & blue 25.00 *20.00*
*a.* Perf. 16 55.00 *55.00*
**97** A30 4c on 25c sl blue 6.00 *10.00*
**98** A31 4c on 50c violet 18.00 *18.00*
**99** A32 4c on $1 red 6.25 *14.00*
**100** A33 4c on $2 gray grn 6.25 *19.00*

**"CENTS" 8½mm below "4"**

**101** A34 4c on $5 red vio 7.25 *18.00*
*a.* Normal spacing 170.00 *250.00*
**102** A35 4c on $10 brown 7.25 *18.00*
*a.* Normal spacing 130.00 *250.00*
*Nos. 91-102 (12)* 197.00 *200.50*

No. 99 differs from No. 74 in the distance between "4" and "cents" which is 4¾mm on No. 99 and 3¾mm on No. 74.

Orangutan — A48

**1899-1900** **Engr.**

**103** A48 4c green & black 10.00 1.75
**104** A48 4c dp rose & blk ('00) 40.00 .75

For overprints see Nos. 108, J13, J23.

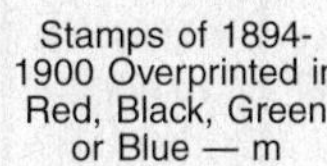
Stamps of 1894-1900 Overprinted in Red, Black, Green or Blue — m

**1901-05**

**105** A37 1c bis brn & blk (R) 4.00 .35
**106** A38 2c grn & blk (R) 3.50 .35
**107** A39 3c lil & ol grn (Bk) 2.00 .35
**108** A48 4c dp rose & blk (G) 10.00 .35
**109** A40 5c org & blk (G) 16.00 .35
**110** A41 6c ol brn & blk (R) 4.50 .75
**111** A42 8c brn & blk (Bl) 4.25 .55
*a.* Vert. pair, imperf. btwn. 425.00
**112** A43 12c blue & blk (R) 60.00 1.50
**113** A46 18c grn & blk (R) 15.00 1.40
**114** A47 24c red & blue (Bk) 18.00 1.75
**115** A30 25c slate blue (R) 3.00 .60
*a.* Inverted overprint 700.00
**116** A31 50c violet (R) 3.00 .70
**117** A32 $1 red (R) 20.00 3.75
**118** A32 $1 red (Bk) 10.00 2.75
*a.* Double overprint 425.00
**119** A33 $2 gray grn (R) 37.50 4.00
*a.* Double overprint 1,600.
*Nos. 105-119 (15)* 210.75 19.50

Nos. 110, 111 and 122 are known without period after "PROTECTORATE."

See Nos. 122-123, 150-151.

Bruang (Sun Bear) — A49

Railroad Train — A50

**1902** **Engr.**

**120** A49 10c slate & dk brn 130.00 3.25
*a.* Vertical pair, imperf. between 575.00
**121** A50 16c yel brn & grn 150.00 3.75

**Overprinted type "m" in Red or Black**

**122** A49 10c sl & dk brn (R) 75.00 1.10
*a.* Double overprint 900.00 350.00
**123** A50 16c yel brn & grn (Bk) 150.00 2.50
*Nos. 120-123 (4)* 505.00 10.60

For overprints see Nos. J27, J29.

Stamps of 1894-97 Surcharged in Black

**1904**

**124** A40 4c on 5c org & blk 50.00 14.00
**125** A41 4c on 6c ol brn & blk 8.00 14.00
*a.* Inverted surcharge 350.00
**126** A42 4c on 8c brn lil & blk 15.00 14.00
*a.* Inverted surcharge 350.00
**127** A43 4c on 12c blue & blk 40.00 14.00
**128** A46 4c on 18c grn & blk 16.00 14.00
**129** A47 4c on 24c cl & bl 20.00 14.00
**130** A30 4c on 25c sl blue 5.00 14.00
**131** A31 4c on 50c violet 5.50 14.00
**132** A32 4c on $1 red 7.00 14.00
**133** A33 4c on $2 gray grn 10.50 14.00
**134** A34 4c on $5 red vio 14.00 14.00
**135** A35 4c on $10 brown 14.00 14.00
*a.* Inverted surcharge 2,750.
*Nos. 124-135 (12)* 205.00 168.00

Malayan Tapir — A51

Traveler's Palm — A52

Railroad Station — A53

Meeting of the Assembly — A54

Elephant and Mahout
A55

Sumatran Rhinoceros
A56

Natives Plowing — A57

Wild Boar — A58

Palm Cockatoo
A59

Rhinoceros Hornbill
A60

Banteng (Wild Ox)
A61 A62

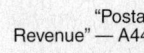

Cassowary
A63

**1909-22** **Unwmk.** **Engr.** ***Perf. 14***

**Center in Black**

**136** A51 1c chocolate 7.00 .30
*b.* Perf. 13½
*c.* Perf. 15 47.50 .40
**137** A52 2c green 1.00 .30
*b.* Perf. 15 3.25 .30
**138** A53 3c deep rose 3.25 .30
*b.* Perf. 15 42.50 .55
**139** A53 3c green ('22) 42.50 *.40*
**140** A54 4c dull red 2.75 .30
*b.* Perf. 13½ *11.00* *10.50*
*c.* Perf. 15 21.00 .40
**141** A55 5c yellow brn 16.00 .40
*b.* Perf. 15
**142** A56 6c olive green 13.00 .30
*b.* Perf. 15 80.00 1.00
**143** A57 8c rose 4.00 .60
*b.* Perf 15 *12.00*

**144** A58 10c blue 45.00 2.00
*b.* Perf. 13½ —
*c.* Perf. 15 70.00 *6.50*
**145** A59 12c deep blue 42.50 1.00
*c.* Perf. 15 *12.00*
**146** A60 16c red brown 26.00 1.25
*b.* Perf. 13½ 30.00 6.50
**147** A61 18c blue green 120.00 1.25
**148** A62 20c on 18c bl grn (R) 7.00 .55
*b.* Perf. 15 250.00 *75.00*
**149** A63 24c violet 28.00 1.75
*Nos. 136-149 (14)* 358.00 10.70

Issued: #139, 1922; others, July 1, 1909.
See #167-178. #136a-149a follow #162.
For surcharges and overprints see #160-162, 166, B1-B12, B14-B24, B31-B41, J32-J49.

### Nos. 72-73 Overprinted type "m" in Red

**1910**
**150** A34 $5 red violet 325.00 9.00
**151** A35 $10 brown 550.00 11.00
*a.* Double overprint
*b.* Inverted overprint 2,700. 450.00

A64

A65

**1911** **Engr.** ***Perf. 14***
**Center in Black**
**152** A64 25c yellow green 18.00 2.00
*a.* Perf. 15 19.00
*b.* Imperf., pair 55.00
**153** A64 50c slate blue 18.00 2.25
*a.* Perf. 15 24.00 *22.50*
*b.* Imperf., pair 90.00
**154** A64 $1 brown 18.00 4.00
*a.* Perf. 15 60.00 *8.00*
*c.* Imperf., pair 180.00
**155** A64 $2 dk violet 75.00 5.00
**156** A65 $5 claret 150.00 32.50
*a.* Perf. 13½ *150.00*
*b.* Imperf., pair 200.00
**157** A65 $10 vermilion 500.00 90.00
*a.* Imperf., pair 475.00
*Nos. 152-157 (6)* 779.00 *135.75*

See #179-184. #152c-153c follow #162.
For overprint and surcharges see Nos. B13, B25-B30, B42-B47.

Nos. 72-73 Overprinted in Red

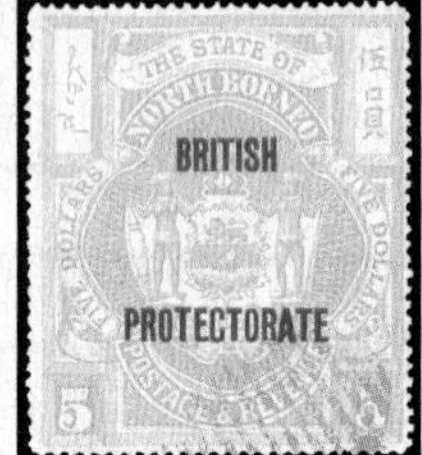


**1912**
**158** A34 $5 red violet 1,500. 9.25
**159** A35 $10 brown 1,800. 9.25

Nos. 158 and 159 were prepared for use but not regularly issued.

Nos. 138, 142 and 145 Surcharged in Black or Red

**1916** **Center in Black** ***Perf. 14***
**160** A53 2c on 3c dp rose 30.00 15.00
*a.* Inverted "S" 110.00 95.00
**161** A56 4c on 6c ol grn (R) 30.00 20.00
*a.* Inverted "S" 110.00 100.00
**162** A59 10c on 12c bl (R) 60.00 *70.00*
*a.* Inverted "S" 180.00 *190.00*
*Nos. 160-162 (3)* 120.00 105.00

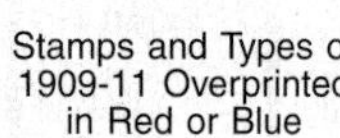
Stamps and Types of 1909-11 Overprinted in Red or Blue

**1922** **Center in Black**
*136a* A51 1c brown 20.00 *70.00*
*137a* A52 2c green 2.50 *25.00*
*138a* A53 3c deep rose (B) 16.00 *65.00*
*140a* A54 4c dull red (B) 3.75 *45.00*
*141a* A55 5c yel brown (B) 9.50 *65.00*
*142a* A56 6c olive green 9.50 *70.00*
*143a* A57 8c rose (B) 8.50 *42.50*
*144a* A58 10c gray blue 20.00 *65.00*
*145a* A59 12c deep blue 12.00 *45.00*
*146a* A60 16c red brown (B) 26.00 *75.00*
*148a* A62 20c on 18c bl grn 27.50 *90.00*
*149a* A63 24c violet 50.00 *75.00*
*152c* A64 25c yel green 12.00 *65.00*
*153c* A64 50c slate blue 17.50 *70.00*
*Nos. 136a-153c (14)* 234.75 *867.50*

Industrial fair, Singapore, 3/31-4/15/22.

No. 140 Surcharged in Black

**1923**
**166** A54 3c on 4c dull red & blk 2.75 *6.00*
*a.* Double surcharge *1,300.*

### Types of 1909-22 Issues

**1926-28** **Engr.** ***Perf. 12½***
**Center in Black**
**167** A51 1c chocolate 1.00 .70
**168** A52 2c lake .85 .60
**169** A53 3c green 3.00 .75
**170** A54 4c dull red .50 .25
**171** A55 5c yellow brown 6.00 3.50
**172** A56 6c yellow green 10.00 .90
**173** A57 8c rose 4.75 .50
**174** A58 10c bright blue 4.25 .90
**175** A59 12c deep blue 24.00 .80
**176** A60 16c orange brn 37.50 *225.00*
**177** A62 20c on 18c bl grn (R) 16.00 4.00
**178** A63 24c dull violet 60.00 *170.00*
**179** A64 25c yellow grn 16.00 5.50
**180** A64 50c slate blue 25.00 *14.00*
**181** A64 $1 brown 25.00 *500.00*
**182** A64 $2 dark violet 85.00 *650.00*
**183** A65 $5 deep rose 200.00 *1,300.*
**184** A65 $10 dull vermilion 550.00 *1,500.*
*Nos. 167-184 (18)* 1,069. *4,377.*

Murut — A66

Orangutan — A67

Dyak — A68

Mt. Kinabalu A69

Clouded Leopard A70

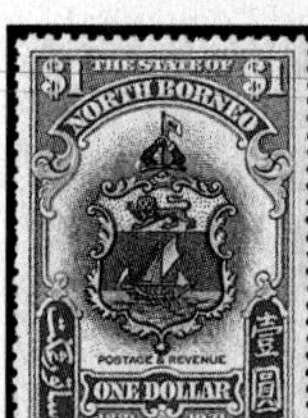
Coat of Arms — A71

Arms with Supporters and Motto A72

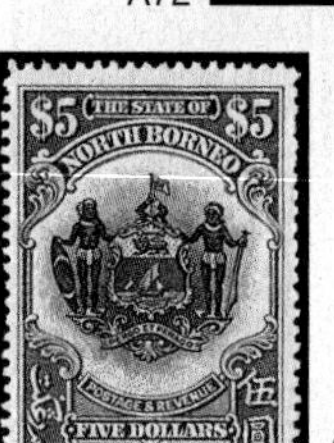
Arms with Supporters — A73

**1931, Jan. 1** **Engr.** ***Perf. 12½***
**Center in Black**
**185** A66 3c blue green 1.50 *1.50*
**186** A67 6c orange red 17.50 4.75
**187** A68 10c carmine 4.50 *13.00*
**188** A69 12c ultra 4.75 *8.00*
**189** A70 25c deep violet 40.00 35.00
**190** A71 $1 yellow green 27.50 *110.00*
**191** A72 $2 red brown 47.50 *110.00*
**192** A73 $5 red violet 160.00 *500.00*
*Nos. 185-192 (8)* 303.25 *782.25*

50th anniv. of the North Borneo Co.

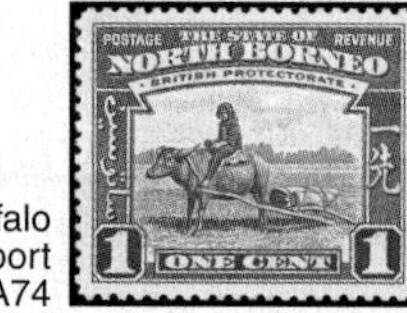
Buffalo Transport A74

Palm Cockatoo — A75

Murut — A76

Proboscis Monkey — A77

Bajaus — A78

Map of North Borneo and Surrounding Lands — A79

Orangutan — A80

Murut with Blowgun — A81

Dyak — A82

River Scene — A83

Proa — A84

Mt. Kinabalu — A85

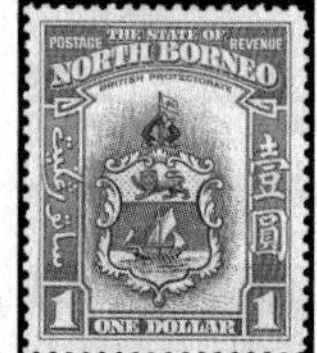
Coat of Arms — A86

Arms with Supporters A87

**1939, Jan. 1** ***Perf. 12½***
**193** A74 1c red brn & dk grn 2.75 2.25
**194** A75 2c Prus bl & red vio 3.25 2.25
**195** A76 3c dk grn & sl blue 3.50 2.50
**196** A77 4c rose vio & ol grn 8.50 .50
**197** A78 6c dp cl & dk blue 7.75 14.00
**198** A79 8c red 11.00 2.00
**199** A80 10c olive grn & vio 26.00 7.00
**200** A81 12c ultra & grn 27.50 8.00
**201** A82 15c bis brn & brt bl grn 21.00 13.00
**202** A83 20c ind & rose vio 14.50 7.00
**203** A84 25c dk brn & bl grn 21.00 15.00
**204** A85 50c purple & brn 22.50 14.00
**205** A86 $1 car & brown 72.50 22.50
**206** A86 $2 ol grn & pur 120.00 *150.00*
**207** A87 $5 blue & indigo 350.00 *375.00*
*Nos. 193-207 (15)* 711.75 635.00
Set, never hinged 1,200.

For overprints see #208-237, MR1-MR2, N1-N15, N16-N31.

Nos. 193 to 207 Overprinted in Black

**1945, Dec. 17 Unwmk. *Perf. 12½***

| No. | Type | Description | Unused | Used |
|---|---|---|---|---|
| **208** | A74 | 1c red brn & dk grn | 9.50 | 2.25 |
| **209** | A75 | 2c Prus bl & red vio | 10.00 | 2.00 |
| **210** | A76 | 3c dk grn & sl bl | .90 | 1.25 |
| **211** | A77 | 4c rose vio & ol grn | 12.00 | *16.00* |
| **212** | A78 | 6c dp cl & dk bl | .90 | 1.25 |
| **213** | A79 | 8c red | 2.10 | .75 |
| **214** | A80 | 10c ol green & vio | 2.10 | .40 |
| **215** | A81 | 12c ultra & green | 4.25 | 3.50 |
| **216** | A82 | 15c bis brn & brt bl grn | 1.20 | 1.10 |
| **217** | A83 | 20c ind & rose vio | 4.25 | 2.50 |
| **218** | A84 | 25c dk brn & bl grn | 4.75 | 1.50 |
| **219** | A85 | 50c purple & brn | 3.00 | 2.50 |
| **220** | A86 | $1 carmine & brn | 35.00 | *40.00* |
| **221** | A86 | $2 ol green & pur | 35.00 | *42.50* |
| *a.* | | Double overprint | 4,000. | |
| **222** | A87 | $5 blue & indigo | 18.00 | 18.00 |
| | | *Nos. 208-222 (15)* | 142.95 | 135.50 |
| | | Set, never hinged | 235.00 | |

"BMA" stands for British Military Administration.

Nos. 193 to 207 Ovptd. in Black or Carmine

**1947**

| No. | Type | Description | Unused | Used |
|---|---|---|---|---|
| **223** | A74 | 1c red brn & dk grn | .25 | 1.00 |
| **224** | A75 | 2c Prus bl & red vio | 1.25 | .80 |
| **225** | A76 | 3c dk grn & sl bl (C) | .25 | .80 |
| **226** | A77 | 4c rose vio & ol grn | .50 | .80 |
| **227** | A78 | 6c dp cl & dk bl (C) | .25 | .25 |
| **228** | A79 | 8c red | .25 | .25 |
| **229** | A80 | 10c olive grn & vio | 1.10 | .35 |
| **230** | A81 | 12c ultra & grn | 2.40 | 2.75 |
| **231** | A82 | 15c bis brn & brt bl grn | 1.75 | .30 |
| **232** | A83 | 20c ind & rose vio | 2.40 | .85 |
| **233** | A84 | 25c dk brn & bl grn | 2.40 | .50 |
| **234** | A85 | 50c purple & brn | 2.00 | .85 |
| **235** | A86 | $1 carmine & brn | 8.50 | 1.75 |
| **236** | A86 | $2 ol green & pur | 11.50 | *18.00* |
| **237** | A87 | $5 blue & ind (C) | 19.00 | *25.00* |
| | | *Nos. 223-237 (15)* | 53.80 | 54.25 |
| | | Set, never hinged | 80.00 | |

The bars obliterate "The State of" and "British Protectorate."

**Catalogue values for unused stamps in this section, from this point to the end of the section, are for Never Hinged items.**

### Silver Wedding Issue

Common Design Types

***Perf. 14x14½***

**1948, Nov. 1 Wmk. 4 Photo.**

**238** CD304 8c scarlet .30 *.75*

***Perf. 11½x11***

**Engraved; Name Typographed**

**239** CD305 $10 purple 35.00 *45.00*

Common Design Types pictured following the introduction.

### UPU Issue

Common Design Types

**Engr.; Name Typo. on 10c and 30c**

**1949, Oct. 10 *Perf. 13½, 11x11½***

| No. | Type | Description | Unused | Used |
|---|---|---|---|---|
| **240** | CD306 | 8c rose carmine | .65 | .25 |
| **241** | CD307 | 10c chocolate | 3.25 | 1.75 |
| **242** | CD308 | 30c deep orange | 1.50 | 1.75 |
| **243** | CD309 | 55c blue | 1.75 | *2.75* |
| | | *Nos. 240-243 (4)* | 7.15 | 6.50 |

Mount Kinabalu — A88

Coconut Grove — A89

Designs: 2c, Musician. 4c, Hemp drying. 5c, Cattle at Kota Belud. 8c, Map. 10c, Logging. 15c, Proa at Sandakan. 20c, Bajau Chief. 30c, Suluk Craft. 50c, Clock tower. $1, Bajau horsemen. $2, Murut with blowgun. $5, Net fishing. $10, Arms.

***Perf. 13½x14½, 14½x13½***

**1950, July 1 Photo.**

| No. | Type | Description | Unused | Used |
|---|---|---|---|---|
| **244** | A88 | 1c red brown | .25 | *1.25* |
| **245** | A88 | 2c blue | .25 | *.50* |
| **246** | A89 | 3c green | .25 | .25 |
| **247** | A89 | 4c red violet | .25 | .25 |
| **248** | A89 | 5c purple | .25 | .25 |
| **249** | A88 | 8c red | 1.25 | .85 |
| **250** | A88 | 10c violet brn | 1.75 | .25 |
| **251** | A88 | 15c brt ultra | 2.00 | .65 |
| **252** | A88 | 20c dk brown | 2.25 | .25 |
| **253** | A89 | 30c brown | 5.50 | .25 |
| **254** | A89 | 50c cer *(Jessleton)* | 1.75 | 4.75 |
| **255** | A89 | $1 red orange | 6.00 | 1.75 |
| **256** | A88 | $2 dark green | 15.00 | *20.00* |
| **257** | A88 | $5 emerald | 25.00 | *30.00* |
| **258** | A88 | $10 gray blue | 65.00 | *90.00* |
| | | *Nos. 244-258 (15)* | 126.75 | 151.25 |

### Redrawn

**1952, May 1 *Perf. 14½x13½***

**259** A89 50c cerise *(Jesselton)* 16.00 3.25

### Coronation Issue

Common Design Type

**1953, June 3 Engr. *Perf. 13½x13***

**260** CD312 10c carmine & black 2.00 1.00

### Types of 1950 with Portrait of Queen Elizabeth II

***Perf. 13½x14½, 14½x13½***

**1954-57 Photo.**

| No. | Type | Description | Unused | Used |
|---|---|---|---|---|
| **261** | A88 | 1c red brown | .25 | .30 |
| **262** | A88 | 2c brt blue ('56) | 1.25 | .25 |
| **263** | A89 | 3c green ('57) | 4.00 | 2.00 |
| **264** | A89 | 4c red violet ('55) | 1.75 | .25 |
| **265** | A89 | 5c purple | 1.00 | .25 |
| **266** | A88 | 8c red | 1.25 | .30 |
| **267** | A88 | 10c violet brown | .40 | .25 |
| **268** | A88 | 15c brt ultra ('55) | 1.00 | .25 |
| **269** | A88 | 20c dk brown | .50 | .25 |
| **270** | A89 | 30c brown | 3.25 | .25 |
| **271** | A89 | 50c cerise ('56) | 6.25 | .25 |
| **272** | A89 | $1 red orange ('55) | 7.50 | .25 |
| **273** | A88 | $2 dk green ('55) | 15.00 | 1.25 |
| **274** | A88 | $5 emerald ('57) | 12.50 | *32.50* |
| **275** | A88 | $10 gray blue ('57) | 27.50 | *35.00* |
| | | *Nos. 261-275 (15)* | 83.40 | 73.60 |

Issued: 10c, 3/1; 5c, 7/1; 20c, 30c, 8/3; 1c, 8c, 10/1; $1, 4/1/55; 4c, 15c, 5/16/55; $2, 10/1/55; 50c, 2/10/56; 2c, 6/1/56; 3c, $5, $10, 2/1/57.

In 1960, the 30c plate was remade, using a finer, smaller-dot (250) screen instead of the 200 screen. The background appears smoother. Value, $2.75 unused.

Borneo Railway, 1902 — A90

Comp. Arms — A91

15c, Proa (sailboat). 35c, Mount Kinabalu.

***Perf. 13x13½, 13½x13***

**1956, Nov. 1 Engr. Wmk. 4**

| No. | Type | Description | Unused | Used |
|---|---|---|---|---|
| **276** | A90 | 10c rose car & blk | 1.25 | .40 |
| **277** | A90 | 15c red brown & blk | .65 | .30 |
| **278** | A90 | 35c green & blk | .65 | 1.50 |
| **279** | A91 | $1 slate & blk | 1.50 | 2.50 |
| | | *Nos. 276-279 (4)* | 4.05 | 4.70 |

75th anniv. of the founding of the Chartered Company of North Borneo.

Malayan Sambar — A92

Orangutan — A93

Designs: 4c, Honey bear. 5c, Clouded leopard. 6c, Dusun woman with gong. 10c, Map of Borneo. 12c, Banteng (wild ox). 20c, Butterfly orchid. 25c, Rhinoceros. 30c, Murut with blowgun. 35c, Mount Kinabalu. 50c, Dusun with buffalo transport. 75c, Bajau horsemen. $2, Rhinoceros hornbill. $5, Crested wood partridge. $10, Coat of arms.

***Perf. 13x12½, 12½x13***

**1961, Feb. 1 Wmk. 314 Engr.**

| No. | Type | Description | Unused | Used |
|---|---|---|---|---|
| **280** | A92 | 1c lt red brn & grn | .25 | .25 |
| **281** | A92 | 4c orange & olive | .90 | .90 |
| **282** | A92 | 5c violet & sepia | .30 | .25 |
| **283** | A92 | 6c bluish grn & sl | .75 | .40 |
| **284** | A92 | 10c rose red & lt grn | 1.25 | .25 |
| **285** | A92 | 12c dull grn & brn | .50 | .25 |
| **286** | A92 | 20c ultra & bl grn | 4.00 | .25 |
| **287** | A92 | 25c rose red & gray | 1.25 | *1.50* |
| **288** | A92 | 30c gray ol & sep | 1.25 | .25 |
| **289** | A92 | 35c redsh brn & stl bl | 2.50 | 2.25 |
| **290** | A92 | 50c brn org & bl grn | 2.25 | .25 |
| **291** | A92 | 75c red vio & sl bl | 16.00 | .90 |
| **292** | A93 | $1 yel grn & brn | 14.00 | .80 |
| **293** | A93 | $2 slate & brown | 35.00 | 3.75 |
| **294** | A93 | $5 brn vio & grn | 37.50 | 22.50 |
| **295** | A93 | $10 blue & car | 50.00 | 50.00 |
| | | *Nos. 280-295 (16)* | 167.70 | 84.75 |

### Freedom from Hunger Issue

Common Design Type

**1963, June 4 Photo. *Perf. 14x14½***

**296** CD314 12c ultramarine 1.90 .75

## SEMI-POSTAL STAMPS

Nos. 136-138, 140-146, 148-149, 152 Ovptd. in Carmine or Vermilion

**1916 Unwmk. *Perf. 14***

**Center in Black**

| No. | Type | Description | Unused | Used |
|---|---|---|---|---|
| **B1** | A51 | 1c chocolate | 7.50 | *35.00* |
| **B2** | A52 | 2c green | 30.00 | *80.00* |
| *a.* | | Perf. 15 | 35.00 | *80.00* |
| **B3** | A53 | 3c deep rose | 27.50 | *50.00* |
| **B4** | A54 | 4c dull red | 7.25 | *32.50* |
| *a.* | | Perf. 15 | 275.00 | *180.00* |
| **B5** | A55 | 5c yellow brown | 50.00 | *55.00* |
| **B6** | A56 | 6c olive green | 70.00 | *75.00* |
| *a.* | | Perf. 15 | 225.00 | 225.00 |
| **B7** | A57 | 8c rose | 24.00 | *60.00* |
| **B8** | A58 | 10c brt blue | 55.00 | *70.00* |
| **B9** | A59 | 12c deep blue | 100.00 | *100.00* |
| **B10** | A60 | 16c red brown | 110.00 | *110.00* |
| **B11** | A62 | 20c on 18c bl grn | 55.00 | *100.00* |
| **B12** | A63 | 24c violet | 130.00 | *130.00* |

***Perf. 15***

| No. | Type | Description | Unused | Used |
|---|---|---|---|---|
| **B13** | A64 | 25c yellow green | 375.00 | *425.00* |
| | | *Nos. B1-B13 (13)* | 1,041. | *1,323.* |

All values exist with the vermilion overprint and all but the 4c with the carmine.

Of the total overprinting, a third was given to the National Philatelic War Fund Committee in London to be auctioned for the benefit of the wounded and veterans' survivors. The balance was lost en route from London to Sandakan when a submarine sank the ship. Very few were postally used.

Nos. 136-138, 140-146, 149, 152-157 Surcharged

**1918 Center in Black *Perf. 14***

| No. | Type | Description | Unused | Used |
|---|---|---|---|---|
| **B14** | A51 | 1c + 2c choc | 3.50 | *14.00* |
| **B15** | A52 | 2c + 2c green | 1.00 | *8.50* |
| **B16** | A53 | 3c + 2c dp rose | 14.00 | *19.00* |
| *a.* | | Perf. 15 | 30.00 | *65.00* |
| **B17** | A54 | 4c + 2c dull red | .70 | *5.00* |
| *a.* | | Inverted surcharge | 450.00 | |
| **B18** | A55 | 5c + 2c yel brn | 8.00 | *29.00* |
| **B19** | A56 | 6c + 2c olive grn | 5.00 | *29.00* |
| *a.* | | Perf. 15 | 225.00 | *250.00* |
| **B20** | A57 | 8c + 2c rose | 5.50 | *11.00* |
| **B21** | A58 | 10c + 2c brt blue | 8.00 | *27.50* |
| **B22** | A59 | 12c + 2c deep bl | 21.00 | *55.00* |
| *a.* | | Inverted surcharge | 700.00 | |
| **B23** | A60 | 16c + 2c red brn | 22.50 | *45.00* |
| **B24** | A63 | 24c + 2c violet | 22.50 | *45.00* |
| **B25** | A64 | 25c + 2c yel grn | 12.00 | *42.50* |
| **B26** | A64 | 50c + 2c sl blue | 14.00 | *42.50* |
| **B27** | A64 | $1 + 2c brown | 50.00 | *55.00* |
| **B28** | A64 | $2 + 2c dk vio | 75.00 | *95.00* |
| **B29** | A65 | $5 + 2c claret | 425.00 | *650.00* |
| **B30** | A65 | $10 + 2c ver | 475.00 | *700.00* |
| | | *Nos. B14-B30 (17)* | 1,163. | *1,873.* |

On Nos. B14-B24 the surcharge is 15mm high, on Nos. B25-B30 it is 19mm high.

Nos. 136-138, 140-146, 149, 152-157 Surcharged in Red

**1918 Center in Black**

| No. | Type | Description | Unused | Used |
|---|---|---|---|---|
| **B31** | A51 | 1c + 4c choc | .60 | *5.00* |
| **B32** | A52 | 2c + 4c green | .65 | *8.00* |
| **B33** | A53 | 3c + 4c dp rose | 1.00 | *3.75* |
| **B34** | A54 | 4c + 4c dull red | .40 | *4.75* |
| **B35** | A55 | 5c + 4c yel brn | 2.00 | *22.50* |
| **B36** | A56 | 6c + 4c olive grn | 2.00 | *12.00* |
| *a.* | | Vert. pair, imperf. btwn. | 2,500. | |
| **B37** | A57 | 8c + 4c rose | 1.25 | *9.50* |
| **B38** | A58 | 10c + 4c brt blue | 3.75 | *12.00* |
| **B39** | A59 | 12c + 4c dp blue | 14.00 | *14.00* |
| **B40** | A60 | 16c + 4c red brn | 8.00 | *16.00* |
| **B41** | A63 | 24c + 4c violet | 11.00 | *20.00* |
| **B42** | A64 | 25c + 4c yel grn | 9.00 | *50.00* |
| **B43** | A64 | 50c + 4c sl blue | 15.00 | *45.00* |
| *a.* | | Perf. 15 | 60.00 | |
| **B44** | A64 | $1 + 4c brown | 22.50 | *60.00* |
| *a.* | | Perf. 15 | *180.00* | |
| **B45** | A64 | $2 + 4c dk vio | 55.00 | *80.00* |
| **B46** | A65 | $5 + 4c claret | 300.00 | *400.00* |
| **B47** | A65 | $10 + 4c ver | 375.00 | *450.00* |
| | | *Nos. B31-B47 (17)* | 821.15 | *1,213.* |

## POSTAGE DUE STAMPS

Regular Issues Overprinted

**On Nos. 60 to 67**

**Reading Up Vert. (V), or Horiz. (H)**

**1895, Aug. 1 Unwmk. *Perf. 14, 15***

| No. | Type | Description | Unused | Used |
|---|---|---|---|---|
| **J1** | A22 | 2c rose & blk (V) | 30.00 | 2.50 |
| **J2** | A23 | 3c vio & ol grn (V) | 6.00 | 1.25 |
| **J3** | A24 | 5c org red & blk (V) | 60.00 | 3.25 |
| *a.* | | Period after "DUE" (V) | 275.00 | |
| **J4** | A25 | 6c ol brn & blk (V) | 20.00 | 2.75 |
| **J5** | A26 | 8c lilac & blk (H) | 50.00 | 3.00 |
| *a.* | | Double ovpt. (H) | | *400.00* |
| **J6** | A27 | 12c blue & blk (H) | 70.00 | 3.00 |
| *a.* | | Double overprint (H) | | *325.00* |
| **J7** | A28 | 18c green & blk (V) | 70.00 | 4.25 |
| *a.* | | Ovpt. reading down | 600.00 | *350.00* |
| *b.* | | Overprinted horizontally | 70.00 | 4.25 |
| *c.* | | Same as "b" inverted | 375.00 | *400.00* |
| **J8** | A29 | 24c claret & bl (H) | 40.00 | 4.00 |
| | | *Nos. J1-J8 (8)* | 346.00 | 24.00 |

**1897 On Nos. 80 and 85**

**J9** A38 2c dp rose & blk (V) 8.50 1.50
*a.* Overprinted horizontally 23.00 *15.00*
**J10** A42 8c brn lil & blk (H) 65.00 *80.00*
*a.* Period after "DUE" 30.00 *75.00*

**On Nos. 81-88 and 104 Vertically reading up**

**1901**

**J11** A38 2c green & blk 75.00 .70
*a.* Overprinted horizontally 225.00
**J12** A39 3c lilac & ol grn 32.00 .50
*a.* Period after "DUE" 70.00 *70.00*
**J13** A48 4c dp rose & blk 70.00 .50
**J14** A40 5c orange & blk 28.00 .90
*a.* Period after "DUE" 90.00
**J15** A41 6c olive brn & blk 7.00 .50
**J16** A42 8c brown & blk 9.00 .50
*a.* Overprinted horizontally 30.00
*b.* Period after "DUE" (H) 23.00 75.00
**J17** A43 12c blue & blk 150.00 4.00
**J18** A46 18c green & blk 80.00 4.00
**J19** A47 24c red & blue 50.00 2.50
*Nos. J11-J19 (9)* 501.00 14.10

**On Nos. 105-114, 122-123 Horizontally**

**1903-11** ***Perf. 14***

**J20** A37 1c bis brn & blk, period after "DUE" 4.50 55.00
*a.* Period omitted
**J21** A38 2c green & blk 27.50 .30
*a.* Ovpt. vert., perf. 16 550.00 *275.00*
*b.* Perf 15 (ovpt. horiz.) 55.00 *55.00*
**J22** A39 3c lilac & ol grn 7.00 .35
*a.* Ovpt. vert. 140.00 *140.00*
*b.* Perf. 15 (ovpt. horiz.) 50.00 *45.00*
**J23** A48 4c dp rose & blk, perf. 15 11.00 2.00
*a.* "Postage Due" double 550.00 170.00
*b.* Perf. 14 21.00 1.00
**J24** A40 5c orange & blk 45.00 .45
*a.* Ovpt. vert., perf. 15 250.00 *160.00*
*b.* Perf. 13½ (ovpt. horiz.)
*c.* Perf. 15 (ovpt. horiz.) 85.00 *35.00*
**J25** A41 6c olive brn & blk 24.00 .40
*a.* "Postage Due" double 750.00
*b.* "Postage Due" inverted 500.00 *125.00*
*c.* Perf. 16 90.00 *37.50*
**J26** A42 8c brown & blk 27.50 .50
*a.* Overprint vertical 200.00 *125.00*
**J27** A49 10c slate & brn 130.00 1.60
**J28** A43 12c blue & blk 42.50 3.75
**J29** A50 16c yel brn & grn 85.00 3.75
**J30** A46 18c green & blk 17.50 1.50
*a.* "Postage Due" double 500.00 *100.00*
**J31** A47 24c claret & blue 17.50 3.75
*a.* "Postage Due" double 350.00 *125.00*
*b.* Overprint vertical 325.00 *140.00*
*Nos. J20-J31 (12)* 439.00 73.35

**On Nos. 137 and 139-146**

**1921-31** ***Perf. 14, 15***

**J32** A52 2c green & blk 27.50 *80.00*
*a.* Perf. 13½ 11.00 *75.00*
**J33** A53 3c green & blk 5.25 *50.00*
**J34** A54 4c dull red & blk 1.25 1.25
**J35** A55 5c yel brn & blk 9.50 *30.00*
**J36** A56 6c olive grn & blk 17.00 17.00
**J37** A57 8c rose & blk 2.00 2.00
**J38** A58 10c blue & blk 16.00 *19.00*
*a.* Perf. 15 120.00 *200.00*
**J39** A59 12c dp vio & blk 70.00 55.00
**J40** A60 16c red brn & blk 26.00 65.00
*Nos. J32-J40 (9)* 174.50 319.25

**On Nos. 168 to 176**

**1926-28** ***Perf. 12½***

**J41** A52 2c lake & blk .75 *2.00*
**J42** A53 3c green & blk 10.00 *32.50*
**J43** A54 4c dull red & blk 3.25 *2.00*
**J44** A55 5c yel brown & blk 8.50 *90.00*
**J45** A56 6c yel green & blk 14.00 3.00
**J46** A57 8c rose & black 11.00 *22.50*
**J47** A58 10c brt blue & blk 12.00 *90.00*
**J48** A59 12c dp blue & blk 32.50 *160.00*
**J49** A60 16c org brn & blk 75.00 *225.00*
*Nos. J41-J49 (9)* 167.00 *627.00*

Crest of British North Borneo Company — D1

**1939, Jan. 1 Engr. *Perf. 12½***

**J50** D1 2c brown 4.25 *80.00*
**J51** D1 4c carmine 4.75 *110.00*
**J52** D1 6c dp rose violet 17.50 *150.00*
**J53** D1 8c dk blue green 22.50 *300.00*
**J54** D1 10c deep ultra 50.00 *450.00*
*Nos. J50-J54 (5)* 99.00 *1,090.*
Set, never hinged 160.00

## WAR TAX STAMPS

**Nos. 193-194 Overprinted**

No. MR1

No. MR2

**1941, Feb. 24 Unwmk. *Perf. 12½***

**MR1** A74 1c red brn & dk grn 2.75 4.50
**MR2** A75 2c Prus blue & red violet 11.00 4.75

For overprints see Nos. N15A-N15B.

## OCCUPATION STAMPS

**Issued under Japanese Occupation**

Nos. 193-207 Handstamped in Violet or Black

On Nos. N1-N15B, the violet overprint is attributed to Jesselton, the black to Sandakan. Nos. N1-N15 are generally found with violet overprint, Nos. N15A-N15B with black.

**1942 Unwmk. *Perf. 12½***

**N1** A74 1c 200.00 *250.00*
**N2** A75 2c 220.00 *300.00*
**N3** A76 3c 175.00 *300.00*
**N4** A77 4c 175.00 *300.00*
**N5** A78 6c 200.00 *355.00*
**N6** A79 8c 275.00 *210.00*
**N7** A80 10c 250.00 *360.00*
**N8** A81 12c 275.00 *525.00*
**N9** A82 15c 220.00 *525.00*
**N10** A83 20c 300.00 *650.00*
**N11** A84 25c 300.00 *700.00*
**N12** A85 50c 400.00 *775.00*
**N13** A86 $1 440.00 *925.00*
**N14** A86 $2 650.00 *1,250.*
**N15** A87 $5 775.00 *1,350.*
*Nos. N1-N15 (15)* 4,855. *8,775.*

For overprints see Nos. N22a, N31a.

**Same Overprint on Nos. MR1-MR2 in Black or Violet**

**1942**

**N15A** A74 1c *750.00 325.00*
**N15B** A75 2c *1,900. 650.00*

Nos. 193 to 207 Overprinted in Black

**1944, Sept. 30 Unwmk. *Perf. 12½***

**N16** A74 1c 8.25 13.00
**N17** A75 2c 8.25 10.00
*a.* On No. N2 300.00
**N18** A76 3c 8.25 11.00
*a.* On. No. N3 400.00
**N19** A77 4c 15.00 25.00
**N20** A78 6c 12.00 7.00
**N21** A79 8c 11.00 *18.50*
*a.* On No. N6 375.00
**N22** A80 10c 9.25 *14.50*
*a.* On No. N7 425.00
**N23** A81 12c 17.50 *14.50*
*a.* On No. N8 400.00
**N24** A82 15c 17.50 *17.50*
*a.* On No. N9 450.00
**N25** A83 20c 40.00 *60.00*
**N26** A84 25c 40.00 *60.00*
**N27** A85 50c 100.00 *130.00*
**N28** A86 $1 150.00 *150.00*
*Nos. N16-N28 (13)* 437.00 *531.00*

**Nos. N1 and 205 Surcharged in Black**

No. N30

No. N31

**1944, May**

**N30** A74 $2 on 1c *7,500. 5,000.*
**N31** A86 $5 on $1 7,000. 4,500.
*a.* On No. N13 10,000. 6,000.

Mt. Kinabalu OS1

Boat and Traveler's Palm OS2

**1943, Apr. 29 Litho.**

**N32** OS1 4c dull rose red 30.00 60.00
**N33** OS2 8c dark blue 25.00 55.00

Stamps of Japan, 1938-43, Overprinted in Black

1s, War factory girl. 2s, Gen. Maresuke Nogi. 3s, Power plant. 4s, Hyuga Monument and Mt. Fuji. 5s, Adm. Heihachiro Togo. 6s, Garambi Lighthouse, Formosa. 8s, Meiji Shrine, Tokyo. 10s, Palms and map of "Greater East Asia." 15s, Aviator saluting and Japanese flag. 20s, Mt. Fuji and cherry blossoms. 25s, Horyu Temple, Nara. 30s, Miyajima Torii, Itsukushima shrine. 50s, Golden Pavilion, Kyoto. 1y, Great Buddha, Kamakura. See Burma, Vol. 1, for illustrations of 2s, 3s, 5s, 8s, 20s and watermark. For others, see Japan.

**Wmk. Curved Wavy Lines (257)**

**1944, Sept. 30 *Perf. 13***

**N34** A144 1s orange brown 10.00 *35.00*
**N35** A84 2s vermilion 9.00 *30.00*
**N36** A85 3s green 10.00 *35.00*
**N37** A146 4s emerald 17.00 *27.50*
**N38** A86 5s brown lake 12.50 *30.00*
**N39** A88 6s orange 15.00 *32.50*
**N40** A90 8s dk purple & pale vio 11.00 *32.50*
**N41** A148 10s crim & dull rose 15.00 *35.00*
**N42** A150 15s dull blue 15.00 *32.50*
**N43** A94 20s ultra 100.00 *125.00*
**N44** A95 25s brown 80.00 *110.00*
**N45** A96 30s peacock blue 200.00 *200.00*
**N46** A97 50s olive 100.00 *100.00*
**N47** A98 1y lt brown 100.00 *120.00*
*Nos. N34-N47 (14)* 694.50 *945.00*

The overprint translates "North Borneo."

## OCCUPATION POSTAGE DUE STAMPS

Nos. J50-J51, J53 Handstamped in Black

**1942, Sept. 30**

**NJ1** D1 2c brown 600. —
**NJ2** D1 4c carmine 600. —
**NJ3** D1 8c dk blue green 600. —

# NORTHERN NIGERIA

'nor-thər n nī-'jir-ē-ə

LOCATION — Western Africa
GOVT. — British Protectorate
AREA — 281,703 sq. mi.
POP. — 11,866,250
CAPITAL — Zungeru

In 1914 Northern Nigeria united with Southern Nigeria to form the Colony and Protectorate of Nigeria.

12 Pence = 1 Shilling
20 Shillings = 1 Pound

Victoria — A1

Numerals of 5p and 6p, types A1 and A2, are in color on plain tablet.

**Wmk. Crown and C A (2)**

**1900, Mar. Typo. *Perf. 14***

**1** A1 ½p lilac & grn 8.75 *22.00*
**2** A1 1p lilac & rose 5.75 5.50
**3** A1 2p lilac & yel 16.00 *60.00*
**4** A1 2½p lilac & blue 13.00 *45.00*
**5** A1 5p lilac & brn 30.00 *70.00*
**6** A1 6p lilac & vio 30.00 *50.00*
**7** A1 1sh green & blk 32.50 *85.00*
**8** A1 2sh6p green & blue 180.00 *550.00*
**9** A1 10sh green & brn 325.00 *900.00*
*Nos. 1-9 (9)* 641.00 *1,788.*

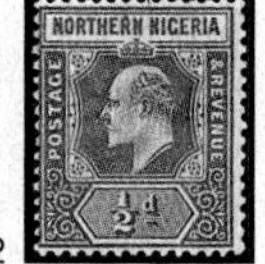

Edward VII — A2

**1902, July 1**

**10** A2 ½p violet & green 2.25 2.00
**11** A2 1p vio & car rose 5.00 1.00
**12** A2 2p violet & org 2.50 *3.00*
**13** A2 2½p violet & ultra 2.00 *13.00*
**14** A2 5p vio & org brn 7.00 *7.50*
**15** A2 6p violet & pur 20.00 *8.00*
**16** A2 1sh green & black 8.50 *8.50*
**17** A2 2sh6p green & ultra 19.00 *75.00*
**18** A2 10sh green & brown 55.00 *60.00*
*Nos. 10-18 (9)* 121.25 *178.00*

**1904, Apr. Wmk. 3**

**18A** A2 £25 green & car *60,000.*

No. 18A was available for postage but probably was used only for fiscal purposes.

**1905**

**19a** A2 ½p violet & grn 6.00 5.50
**20a** A2 1p violet & car rose 6.00 1.25
**21** A2 2p violet & org 19.00 *32.50*
**22** A2 2½p violet & ultra 7.25 *10.00*
**23** A2 5p violet & org brn 32.50 *85.00*
**24** A2 6p violet & pur 29.00 *65.00*
**25a** A2 1sh green & black 24.00 *55.00*
**26a** A2 2sh6p green & ultra 45.00 *60.00*
*Nos. 19a-26a (8)* 166.25 314.25

All values except the 2½p exist on ordinary and chalky papers. The less expensive values are given above. For detailed listings, see the *Scott Classic Specialized Catalogue of Stamps and Covers 1840-1940.*

**1910-11 Ordinary Paper**

**28** A2 ½p green 2.25 1.25
**29** A2 1p carmine 5.75 1.25
**30** A2 2p gray 9.50 *6.50*
**31** A2 2½p ultra 4.25 *11.00*

**Chalky Paper**

**32** A2 3p violet, *yel* 4.50 1.00
**33** A2 5p vio & ol grn 6.00 *19.00*
**34** A2 6p vio & red vio ('11) 6.00 *6.00*
*a.* 6p violet & deep violet 7.50 *28.00*
**35** A2 1sh black, *green* 5.25 .75
**36** A2 2sh6p blk & red, *bl* 19.00 *50.00*
**37** A2 5sh grn & red, *yel* 29.00 *75.00*
**38** A2 10sh grn & red, *grn* 55.00 *50.00*
*Nos. 28-38 (11)* 146.50 221.75

George V — A3

For description of dies I and II, see A pages in front section of catalogue.

**Die I**

**1912** **Ordinary Paper**

**40** A3 ½p green 4.50 1.00
**41** A3 1p carmine 4.50 .60
**42** A3 2p gray 6.75 *17.00*

**Chalky Paper**

**43** A3 3p violet, *yel* 2.25 1.25
**44** A3 4p blk & red, *yel* 1.25 *2.25*
**45** A3 5p vio & ol grn 4.50 *20.00*
**46** A3 6p vio & red vio 4.25 *4.50*
**47** A3 9p violet & scar 2.25 *12.00*
**48** A3 1sh blk, *green* 5.00 2.25
**49** A3 2sh6p blk & red, *bl* 10.00 *55.00*
**50** A3 5sh grn & red, *yel* 25.00 *90.00*
**51** A3 10sh grn & red, *grn* 45.00 *50.00*
**52** A3 £1 vio & blk, *red* 200.00 120.00
*Nos. 40-52 (13)* 315.25 *375.85*

Numerals of 3p, 4p, 5p and 6p, type A3, are in color on plain tablet.

Stamps of Northern Nigeria were replaced in 1914 by those of Nigeria.

# NORTHERN RHODESIA

'nor-thə,rn rō-'dē-zhē-,ə

LOCATION — In southern Africa, east of Angola and separated from Southern Rhodesia by the Zambezi River.
GOVT. — British Protectorate
AREA — 287,640 sq. mi.
POP. — 2,550,000 (est. 1962)
CAPITAL — Lusaka

Prior to April 1, 1924, Northern Rhodesia was administered by the British South Africa Company. It joined the Federation of Rhodesia and Nyasaland in 1953 and used its stamps in 1954-63. It resumed issuing its own stamps in December, 1963, after the Federation was dissolved. On Oct. 24, 1964, Northern Rhodesia became the independent republic of Zambia. See Rhodesia, Southern Rhodesia, Rhodesia and Nyasaland, Zambia.

12 Pence = 1 Shilling
20 Shillings = 1 Pound

**Catalogue values for unused stamps in this country are for Never Hinged items, beginning with Scott 46 in the regular postage section and Scott J5 in the postage due section.**

King George V
A1 A2

**1925-29** **Engr.** **Wmk. 4** ***Perf. 12½***

**1** A1 ½p dk green 1.75 .80
**2** A1 1p dk brown 1.75 .25
**3** A1 1½p carmine 4.25 .30
**4** A1 2p brown org 4.50 .25
**5** A1 3p ultra 4.50 1.30
**6** A1 4p dk violet 7.50 .50
**7** A1 6p gray 9.00 .40
**8** A1 8p rose lilac 9.00 *60.00*
**9** A1 10p olive grn 9.00 *50.00*
**10** A2 1sh black & org 4.75 2.25
**11** A2 2sh ultra & brn 32.50 *50.00*
**12** A2 2sh6p green & blk 26.00 *15.00*
**13** A2 3sh indigo & vio 50.00 28.00
**14** A2 5sh dk vio & gray 57.50 22.50
**15** A2 7sh6p blk & lil rose 200.00 *325.00*
**16** A2 10sh black & green 125.00 *100.00*
**17** A2 20sh rose lil & red 375.00 *400.00*
*Nos. 1-17 (17)* 922.00 *1,057.*

High values with revenue cancellations are inexpensive.

Issue dates: 3sh, 1929; others, Apr. 1.

Common Design Types pictured following the introduction.

**Silver Jubilee Issue**
Common Design Type

**1935, May 6** ***Perf. 13½x14***

**18** CD301 1p olive grn & ultra 1.50 1.50
**19** CD301 2p indigo & grn 2.75 2.00
**20** CD301 3p blue & brown 4.25 *9.00*
**21** CD301 6p brt vio & indigo 8.50 2.50
*Nos. 18-21 (4)* 17.00 15.00
Set, never hinged 26.00

**Coronation Issue**
Common Design Type

**1937, May 12** ***Perf. 11x11½***

**22** CD302 1½p dark carmine .25 .25
**23** CD302 2p yellow brown .30 *.75*
**24** CD302 3p deep ultra .40 *1.25*
*Nos. 22-24 (3)* .95 2.25
Set, never hinged 1.50

King George VI — A3

**1938-52** **Wmk. 4** ***Perf. 12½***

**Size: 19x24mm**

**25** A3 ½p green .25 .25
**26** A3 ½p dk brn ('51) 1.40 *1.50*
*a.* Perf. 12½x14 1.00 *6.00*
**27** A3 1p dk brown .25 .25
**28** A3 1p green ('51) .90 *2.25*
**29** A3 1½p carmine 27.50 .75
*a.* Horiz. pair, imperf. between *30,000.*
**30** A3 1½p brn org ('41) .30 .25
**31** A3 2p brown org 27.50 1.75
**32** A3 2p carmine ('41) 1.00 .50
**33** A3 2p rose lilac ('51) .40 *1.50*
**34** A3 3p ultra .45 .30
**35** A3 3p red ('51) .30 *3.00*
**36** A3 4p dk violet .30 .40
**37** A3 4½p dp blue ('52) 1.75 *12.00*
**38** A3 6p dark gray .30 .25
**39** A3 9p violet ('52) 1.75 *12.00*

**Size: 21½x26¾mm**

**40** A3 1sh blk & brn org 2.50 .60
**41** A3 2sh6p green & blk 8.00 7.00
**42** A3 3sh ind & dk vio 14.00 *16.00*
**43** A3 5sh violet & gray 14.50 *17.00*
**44** A3 10sh black & green 16.00 *32.50*
**45** A3 20sh rose lil & red 37.50 *75.00*
*Nos. 25-45 (21)* 156.85 *185.05*
Set, never hinged 275.00

**Catalogue values for unused stamps in this section, from this point to the end of the section, are for Never Hinged items.**

**Peace Issue**
Common Design Type

**1946, Nov. 26** **Engr.** ***Perf. 13½x14***

**46** CD303 1½p deep orange 1.00 *1.50*
*a.* Perf. 13½ 14.00 *13.00*
**47** CD303 2p carmine .25 *.50*

**Silver Wedding Issue**
Common Design Types

**1948, Dec. 1** **Photo.** ***Perf. 14x14½***

**48** CD304 1½p orange .30 .25

***Perf. 11½x11***

**Engr.**

**49** CD305 20sh rose brown 100.00 90.00

**UPU Issue**
Common Design Types
**Engr.; Name Typo. on 3p, 6p**
***Perf. 13½, 11x11½***

**1949, Oct. 10** **Wmk. 4**

**50** CD306 2p rose carmine .50 .50
**51** CD307 3p indigo 2.00 *3.00*
**52** CD308 6p gray 1.50 1.50
**53** CD309 1sh red orange 1.00 *1.50*
*Nos. 50-53 (4)* 5.00 *6.50*

Victoria Falls and Railway Bridge, Cecil Rhodes and Elizabeth II — A4

**1953, May 30** **Engr.** ***Perf. 12x11***

**54** A4 ½p brown .55 *1.25*
**55** A4 1p green .45 *1.25*
**56** A4 2p deep claret .80 .40
**57** A4 4½p deep blue .55 *4.00*
**58** A4 1sh gray & orange 1.25 *4.25*
*Nos. 54-58 (5)* 3.60 11.15

Cecil Rhodes (1853-1902).

Exhibition Seal — A5

**1953, May 30** ***Perf. 14x13½***

**59** A5 6p purple .70 *1.25*

Central African Rhodes Centenary Exhib.

**Coronation Issue**
Common Design Type

**1953, June 2** ***Perf. 13½x13***

**60** CD312 1½p orange & black .70 .25

Elizabeth II — A6

***Perf. 12½x13½***

**1953, Sept. 15** **Engr.**

**Size: 19x23mm**

**61** A6 ½p dark brown .65 .25
**62** A6 1p green .75 .25
**63** A6 1½p brown orange 1.25 .25
**64** A6 2p rose lilac 1.40 .25
**65** A6 3p red .80 .25
**66** A6 4p dark violet 1.25 *2.00*
**67** A6 4½p deep blue 1.50 *4.25*
**68** A6 6p dark gray 1.25 .40
**69** A6 9p violet 1.25 *4.25*

**Size: 21x27mm**

**70** A6 1sh black & brn org 1.00 .25
**71** A6 2sh6p green & blk 15.00 8.00
**72** A6 5sh violet & gray 16.00 *15.00*
**73** A6 10sh black & green 12.00 *32.50*
**74** A6 20sh rose lilac & red 30.00 *37.50*
*Nos. 61-74 (14)* 84.10 105.40

Coat of Arms — A7

**Size: 23x19mm**

***Perf. 14½***

**1963, Dec. 1** **Unwmk.** **Photo.**

**Arms in Black, Blue and Orange**

**75** A7 ½p violet & blk .70 *1.00*
*a.* Value omitted 1,100.
*b.* Orange (eagle) omitted 1,400.
**76** A7 1p blue & blk 1.50 .25
*a.* Value omitted 12.50
**77** A7 2p brown & blk .70 .25
**78** A7 3p orange & blk .25 .25
*a.* Bklt. pane of 4 1.00
*b.* Value omitted 120.00
*c.* Orange (eagle) omitted *1,200.* —
*d.* Value and orange (eagle) omitted 325.00
**79** A7 4p green & blk .70 .30
*a.* Value omitted 130.00
**80** A7 6p yel grn & blk 1.00 .25
*a.* Value omitted 800.00
**81** A7 9p ocher & blk .70 *1.60*
*a.* Value omitted 600.00
*b.* Value and orange (eagle) omitted 600.00
**82** A7 1sh dk gray & blk .50 .25
**83** A7 1sh3p brt red lil & blk 2.25 .25

***Perf. 13***

**Size: 27x23mm**

**84** A7 2sh dp org & blk 2.50 *5.25*
**85** A7 2sh6p maroon & blk 2.50 2.25
**86** A7 5sh dk car rose & blk 10.00 8.00
*a.* Value omitted *2,750.*
**87** A7 10sh brt pink & blk 17.00 *22.50*
**88** A7 20sh dk blue & blk 22.00 *40.00*
*a.* Value omitted 1,100.
*Nos. 75-88 (14)* 62.30 *82.40*

Stamps of Northern Rhodesia were replaced by those of Zambia, starting Oct. 24, 1964.

## POSTAGE DUE STAMPS

D1

**1929** **Typo.** **Wmk. 4** ***Perf. 14***

**J1** D1 1p black 3.00 *2.75*
*a.* Wmk. 4a (error) 7,000.
**J2** D1 2p black 8.00 *3.50*
*a.* Bisected, used as 1d, on cover *850.00*
**J3** D1 3p black 3.00 *27.50*
*a.* Crown in watermark missing 700.00
*b.* Wmk. 4a (error) 425.00
**J4** D1 4p black 11.00 *42.50*
*Nos. J1-J4 (4)* 25.00 *76.25*

**Catalogue values for unused stamps in this section, from this point to the end of the section, are for Never Hinged items.**

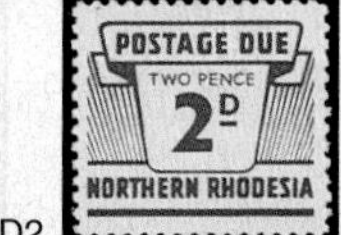

D2

**1964** **Unwmk.** **Litho.** ***Perf. 12½***

**J5** D2 1p orange 3.00 *5.50*
**J6** D2 2p dark blue 3.00 *4.50*
**J7** D2 3p rose claret 3.00 *7.50*
**J8** D2 4p violet blue 3.00 *13.00*
**J9** D2 6p purple 9.50 *10.00*
**J10** D2 1sh emerald 11.00 *30.00*
*Nos. J5-J10 (6)* 32.50 *70.50*

## NORTH INGERMANLAND

'north 'iŋ-gər-mən-ˌland

LOCATION — In Northern Russia lying between the River Neva and Finland
CAPITAL — Kirjasalo

In 1920 the residents of this territory revolted from Russian rule and set up a provisional government. The new State existed only a short period as the revolution was quickly quelled by Soviet troops.

100 Pennia = 1 Markka

Arms — A1

**Perf. 11½**

**1920, Mar. 21 Unwmk. Litho.**

1 A1 5p green 2.75 *3.50*
2 A1 10p rose red 2.75 *3.50*
b. Horiz. pair, imperf. btwn. 50.00
3 A1 25p bister 2.75 *3.50*
b. Horiz. pair, imperf. btwn. 50.00
c. Vert. pair, imperf. btwn. 50.00
4 A1 50p dark blue 2.50 *3.50*
5 A1 1m car & black 30.00 *42.50*
6 A1 5m lilac & black 175.00 160.00
7 A1 10m brown & blk 200.00 200.00
*Nos. 1-7 (7)* 415.75 *416.50*
Set, never hinged 1,100.

Well centered examples sell for twice the values shown.

**Imperf., Pairs**

*1a* A1 5p 45.00
*2a* A1 10p 100.00
*3a* A1 25p 50.00
*4a* A1 50p 50.00
*5a* A1 1m 65.00
*6a* A1 5m 200.00
*7a* A1 10m 350.00

Arms — A2

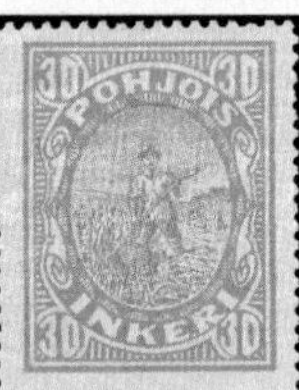
Peasant — A3

Plowing — A4

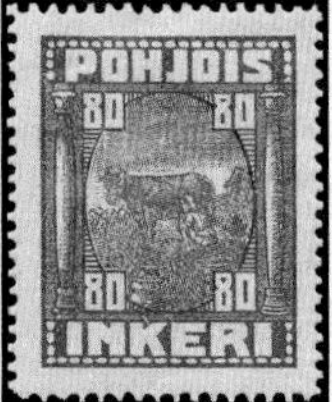
Milking — A5

Planting A6

Ruins of Church A7

Peasants Playing Zithers A8

**1920, Aug. 2**

8 A2 10p gray grn & ultra 3.50 *7.00*
9 A3 30p buff & gray grn 3.50 *7.00*
a. Horiz. pair, imperf. btwn. 100.00
10 A4 50p ultra & red brn 3.50 *7.00*
11 A5 80p claret & slate 3.50 *7.00*
12 A6 1m red & slate 20.00 *45.00*
13 A7 5m dk vio & dl rose 8.25 *18.00*
14 A8 10m brn & violet 8.25 *18.00*
a. Center inverted 1,000.
*Nos. 8-14 (7)* 50.50 *109.00*
Set, never hinged 120.00

Counterfeits abound.

Nos. 8-14 exist imperf. Value for set in pairs, $200.

## NORTH WEST PACIFIC ISLANDS

'north 'west pə-'si-fik 'ī-ləndz

LOCATION — Group of islands in the West Pacific Ocean including a part of New Guinea and adjacent islands of the Bismarck Archipelago
GOVT. — Australian military government
AREA — 96,160 sq. mi.
POP. — 636,563

Stamps of Australia were overprinted for use in the former German possessions of Nauru and German New Guinea which Australian troops had captured. Following the League of Nations' decision which placed these territories under mandate to Australia, these provisional issues were discontinued. See German New Guinea, New Britain, Nauru and New Guinea.

12 Pence = 1 Shilling
20 Shillings = 1 Pound

Stamps of Australia Overprinted — a

Type a: "P" of "PACIFIC" above "S" of "ISLANDS."

There are two varieties of the letter "S" in the Type "a" overprint. These occur in three combinations: a, both normal "S"; b, 1st "S" with small head and long bottom stroke, 2nd "S" normal; c, both "S" with small head and long bottom stroke.

DESIGN A1
Die I — The inside frameline has a break at left, even with the top of the letters of the denomination.
Die II — The frameline does not show a break.
Die IV — As Die III, with a break in the top outside frameline above the "ST" of "AUSTRALIA." The upper right inside frameline has an incomplete corner.
Dies are only indicated when there are more than one for any denomination.

**1915-16 Wmk. 8 *Perf. 12***

1 A1 2p gray 25.00 *75.00*
2 A1 2½p dark blue 5.00 *22.50*
3 A1 3p ol bis, die I 25.00 *65.00*
a. Die II 385.00 *600.00*
b. Pair, #3, 3a 825.00 *1,200.*
c. Pair, die I and die II 2,500.
4 A1 6p ultra 120.00 *130.00*
5 A1 9p violet 60.00 *72.50*
6 A1 1sh blue green 75.00 *77.50*
8 A1 5sh yel & gray ('16) 2,750. *3,850.*
9 A1 10sh pink & gray 170.00 *200.00*
Revenue cancel
10 A1 £1 ultra & brown *600.00 775.00*
*Nos. 1-6,8-10 (9)* *3,830. 5,268.*

For surcharge see No. 27.

**Wmk. Wide Crown and Narrow A (9)**
***Perf. 12, 14***

ONE PENNY
Die I — Normal die, having outside the oval band with "AUSTRALIA" a white line and a heavy colored line.
Die Ia — As die I with a small white spur below the right serif at foot of the "1" in left tablet.
Dies are only indicated when there are more than one for any denomination.

11 A4 ½p emerald 3.25 *10.00*
a. Double overprint
12 A4 1p car (Die I) 7.75 7.25
a. 1p carmine rose (Die I) 120.00 *150.00*
b. 1p carmine (Die Ia) 110.00 *145.00*
13 A1 2p gray 20.00 *50.00*
14 A1 2½p dk bl ('16) *30,000. 30,000.*
16 A4 4p orange 4.50 *17.50*
17 A4 5p org brown 3.25 *19.00*
18 A1 6p ultra 11.00 *13.00*
19 A1 9p violet 17.50 *24.00*
20 A1 1sh blue green 12.50 *27.50*
21 A1 2sh brown 110.00 *130.00*
22 A1 5sh yel & gray 82.50 *120.00*
*Nos. 11-13,16-22 (10)* 272.25 *418.25*

For surcharge see No. 28.

**1915-16 Wmk. 10 *Perf. 12***

23 A1 2p gray, die I 9.00 *32.50*
24 A1 3p ol bis, die I 7.00 *15.00*
a. Die II 125.00 *190.00*
b. Pair, #24, 24a 350.00
25 A1 2sh brown ('16) 45.00 *65.00*
26 A1 £1 ultra & brn ('16) 400.00 *525.00*
*Nos. 23-26 (4)* 461.00 *637.50*

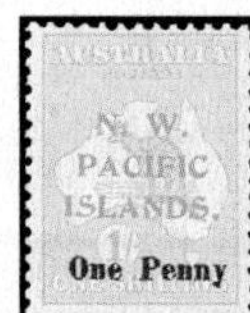

Nos. 6 and 17 Surcharged

**1918, May 23 Wmk. 8 *Perf. 12***

27 A1 1p on 1sh bl grn 125.00 100.00

**Wmk. 9 *Perf. 14***

28 A4 1p on 5p org brn 110.00 100.00

Stamps of Australia Overprinted — b

Type "b": "P" of "PACIFIC" above space between "I" and "S" of "ISLANDS."

**1918-23 Wmk. 10 *Perf. 12***

29 A1 2p gray 8.50 *30.00*
a. Die II 13.50 *57.50*
30 A1 2½p dk bl ('19) 6.50 *19.00*
a. "1" of fraction omitted *14,000. 16,500.*
31 A1 3p ol bis, die I 27.50 *30.00*
a. Die II 80.00 *100.00*
b. Pair, #31, 31a 500.00 *650.00*
32 A1 6p ultra ('19) 7.50 *16.50*
a. 6p chalky blue 50.00 *75.00*
33 A1 9p violet ('19) 11.50 *60.00*
34 A1 1sh bl grn ('18) 16.50 *37.50*
a. 1sh emerald green 7.00 *32.50*
35 A1 2sh brown 25.00 *42.50*
36 A1 5sh yel & gray ('19) 75.00 *80.00*
37 A1 10sh pink & gray ('19) 200.00 *275.00*
38 A1 £1 ultra & brn 4,500. *5,500.*
*Nos. 29-37 (9)* 378.00 *590.50*

**1919 Wmk. 11 *Perf. 14***

39 A4 ½p emerald 5.00 *6.00*

**1918-23 Wmk. 9**

40 A4 ½p emerald 2.00 *4.00*
41 A4 1p car red, die 1 4.25 1.75
a. 1p carmine red, die Ia 125.00 90.00
42 A4 1p scar, die I, rough paper 1,000. 675.00
a. 1p rose red, die Ia, rough paper 1,000. 675.00
43 A4 1p violet ('22) 2.75 *7.25*
44 A4 2p orange 8.75 2.75
45 A4 2p red ('22) 10.50 2.25
46 A4 4p yel org 4.00 *17.50*
47 A4 4p violet ('22) 22.50 *45.00*
a. "Four Penc" in thinner letters 900.00 *1,550.*
48 A4 4p light ultra ('22) 12.50 *65.00*
a. "Four Penc" in thinner letters 1,000. *2,000.*
49 A4 5p brown 4.25 *13.50*
*Nos. 40-41,43-49 (9)* 71.50 *159.00*

North West Pacific Islands stamps were largely used in New Britain. Some were used in Nauru. They were intended to serve the Bismarck Archipelago and other places.

# NORWAY

ˈnor-ˌwā

LOCATION — Western half of the Scandinavian Peninsula in northern Europe
GOVT. — Kingdom
AREA — 125,051 sq. mi.
POP. — 4,644,457 (2008 est.)
CAPITAL — Oslo

120 Skilling = 1 Specie Daler
100 Ore = 1 Krone (1877)

**Catalogue values for unused stamps in this country are for Never Hinged items, beginning with Scott 275 in the regular postage section, Scott B27 in the semi-postal section, and Scott O65 in the official section.**

### Watermarks

Wmk. 159 — Lion

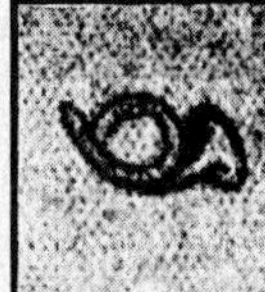
Wmk. 160 — Post Horn

Coat of Arms — A1

**Wmk. 159**

**1855, Jan. 1 Typo. *Imperf.***

| | | | | |
|---|---|---|---|---|
| 1 | A1 | 4s blue | *4,250.* | 175. |
| *a.* | | Double foot on right hind leg of lion | | 3,000. |

Only a few genuine unused examples of No. 1 exist. Stamps often offered have had pen-markings removed. The unused catalogue value is for a stamp without gum. Stamps with original gum sell for much more.

*No. 1 was reprinted in 1914 and 1924 unwatermarked. Lowest value reprint, $75.*

### ROULETTED REPRINTS

1963: No. 1, value $25; Nos. 2-5, 15, value each $15.

1966: Nos. 57, 70a, 100, 152, J1, O1. Value each $12.

1969: Nos. 69, 92, 107, 114, 128, J12. Value each $12.

King Oscar I — A2

**1856-57 Unwmk. *Perf. 13***

| | | | | |
|---|---|---|---|---|
| 2 | A2 | 2s yellow ('57) | 800.00 | 160.00 |
| 3 | A2 | 3s lilac ('57) | 550.00 | 120.00 |
| 4 | A2 | 4s blue | 450.00 | 20.00 |
| *a.* | | Imperf. | | *10,000.* |
| *b.* | | Half used as 2s on cover | | — |
| 5 | A2 | 8s dull lake | 1,450. | 75.00 |

*Nos. 2-5 were reprinted in 1914 and 1924, perf. 13½. Lowest valued reprint, $50 each.*

A3

**1863 Litho. *Perf. 14½x13½***

| | | | | |
|---|---|---|---|---|
| 6 | A3 | 2s yellow | 1,250. | 300.00 |
| 7 | A3 | 3s gray lilac | 850.00 | 600.00 |
| 8 | A3 | 4s blue | 275.00 | 18.00 |
| 9 | A3 | 8s rose | 1,200. | 80.00 |
| 10 | A3 | 24s brown | 55.00 | 65.00 |
| | | *Nos. 6-10 (5)* | 3,630. | 1,063. |

There are four types of the 2, 3, 8 and 24 skilling and eight types of the 4 skilling. See note on used value of No. 10 following No. 21.

No. 8 exists imperf. Value, unused $900.

A4

**1867-68 Typo.**

| | | | | |
|---|---|---|---|---|
| 11 | A4 | 1s black, coarse impression ('68) | 100.00 | 70.00 |
| 12 | A4 | 2s orange | 35.00 | *55.00* |
| *b.* | | Vert. pair, imperf between | *1,750.* | |
| 13 | A4 | 3s dl lil, coarse impression ('68) | 600.00 | 160.00 |
| 14 | A4 | 4s blue, thin paper | 175.00 | 15.00 |
| 15 | A4 | 8s car rose | 750.00 | 70.00 |
| *a.* | | 8s rose, clear impression | 1,900. | 550.00 |
| | | *Nos. 11-15 (5)* | 1,660. | 370.00 |

See note on used value of #12 following #21.

For surcharges see Nos. 59-61, 149.

*No. 15 was reprinted in 1914 and 1924, perf. 13½. Lowest valued reprint, $50.*

Post Horn and Crown — A5

**1872-75 Wmk. 160**

| | | | | |
|---|---|---|---|---|
| 16 | A5 | 1s yel grn ('75) | 13.50 | *25.00* |
| *a.* | | 1s deep green ('73) | 375.00 | 100.00 |
| *b.* | | "E.EN" | 25.00 | *75.00* |
| *d.* | | Vert. pair, imperf between | | — |
| 17 | A5 | 2s ultra ('74) | 20.00 | *40.00* |
| *a.* | | 2s Prussian blue ('74) | *17,000.* | *5,000.* |
| *b.* | | 2s gray blue | 15.00 | *30.00* |
| 18 | A5 | 3s rose | 85.00 | 35.00 |
| *a.* | | 3s carmine | 95.00 | 16.00 |
| *b.* | | 3s carmine, *bluish* thin paper | 450.00 | 50.00 |
| 19 | A5 | 4s lilac, thin paper ('75) | 19.00 | *30.00* |
| *a.* | | 4s dark violet, *bluish,* thin paper | 700.00 | 200.00 |
| *b.* | | 4s brown violet, *bluish,* thin paper ('73) | 700.00 | 250.00 |
| *c.* | | 4s violet, *white,* thick paper ('73) | 120.00 | 80.00 |
| 20 | A5 | 6s org brn ('75) | 675.00 | 90.00 |
| 21 | A5 | 7s red brn ('73) | 75.00 | 65.00 |
| | | *Nos. 16-21 (6)* | 887.50 | 285.00 |

In this issue there are 12 types each of Nos. 16, 17, 18 and 19; 12 types of No. 20 and 20 types of No. 21. The differences are in the words of value.

Nos. 10, 12, 16, 17, 19 and 21 were re-released in 1888 and used until March 31, 1908. Used values of these stamps are for examples canceled in this later period, usually with a two-ring cancellation. Examples bearing clear dated cancellations before 1888 are worth considerably more, as follows: No. 10 $165, No. 12 $70, No. 16 $60, No. 17 $100, No. 17b $450, No. 19 $90, No. 21 $100.

No. 21 exists imperf. Value, unused without gum $800.

No. 19 comes on thin and thick paper.

For surcharges see Nos. 62-63.

Post Horn — A6

King Oscar II — A7

### "NORGE" in Sans-serif Capitals, Ring of Post Horn Shaded

**1877-78**

| | | | | |
|---|---|---|---|---|
| 22 | A6 | 1o drab | 12.00 | *14.00* |
| 23 | A6 | 3o orange | 125.00 | 45.00 |
| 24 | A6 | 5o ultra | 40.00 | 18.00 |
| *a.* | | 5o dull blue | 800.00 | 125.00 |
| *b.* | | 5o bright blue | 300.00 | 70.00 |
| *c.* | | No period after "Postfrim" | 57.50 | 20.00 |
| *d.* | | Retouched plate | 200.00 | 25.00 |
| *e.* | | As "c," retouched plate | 225.00 | 27.50 |
| 25 | A6 | 10o rose | 120.00 | 4.50 |
| *b.* | | Retouched plate | 120.00 | 5.50 |
| 26 | A6 | 12o lt green | 150.00 | 30.00 |
| 27 | A6 | 20o orange brn | 450.00 | 20.00 |
| 28 | A6 | 25o lilac | 600.00 | 150.00 |
| 29 | A6 | 35o bl grn ('78) | 30.00 | 20.00 |
| *a.* | | Retouched plate | 250.00 | 110.00 |
| 30 | A6 | 50o maroon | 65.00 | 12.50 |
| 31 | A6 | 60o dk bl ('78) | 70.00 | 12.50 |
| 32 | A7 | 1k gray grn & grn ('78) | 45.00 | 12.50 |
| 33 | A7 | 1.50k ultra & bl ('78) | 100.00 | 50.00 |
| 34 | A7 | 2k rose & mar ('78) | 55.00 | 25.00 |
| | | *Nos. 22-34 (13)* | 1,862. | 414.00 |

There are 6 types each of Nos. 22, 26 and 28 to 34; 12 types each of Nos. 23, 24, 25 and 27. The differences are in the numerals.

A 2nd plate of the 5o ultramarine has 100 types, the 10o, 200 types.

The retouch on 5o, 10o and 35o shows as a thin white line between crown and post horn.

Post Horn — A8

### "NORGE" in Sans-serif Capitals, Ring of Horn Unshaded

**1882-93 Wmk. 160 *Perf. 14½x13½***

| | | | | |
|---|---|---|---|---|
| 35 | A8 | 1o blk brn ('86) | 25.00 | *30.00* |
| *a.* | | No period after "Postfrim" | 60.00 | 60.00 |
| *b.* | | Small "N" in "NORGE" | 60.00 | 60.00 |
| 36 | A8 | 1o gray ('93) | 15.00 | 15.00 |
| 37 | A8 | 2o brown ('90) | 8.00 | *10.00* |
| 38 | A8 | 3o yellow ('89) | 100.00 | 12.50 |
| *a.* | | 3o orange ('83) | 300.00 | 25.00 |
| *b.* | | Perf. 13½x12½ ('93) | 12,000. | 4,000. |
| 39 | A8 | 5o bl grn ('89) | 95.00 | 4.00 |
| *a.* | | 5o gray green ('86) | 120.00 | 6.00 |
| *b.* | | 5o emerald ('88) | 300.00 | 12.50 |
| *c.* | | 5o yellow green ('91) | 100.00 | 4.50 |
| *d.* | | Perf. 13½x12½ ('93) | *5,000.* | *1,200.* |
| 40 | A8 | 10o rose | 80.00 | 2.00 |
| *a.* | | 10o rose red ('86) | 80.00 | 2.00 |
| *b.* | | 10o carmine ('91) | 80.00 | 2.00 |
| *c.* | | As "b," imperf. ('91) | *3,000.* | *2,750.* |
| 41 | A8 | 12o green ('84) | 1,800. | 500.00 |
| 42 | A8 | 12o org brn ('84) | 50.00 | 35.00 |
| *a.* | | 12o bister brown ('83) | 100.00 | 70.00 |
| 43 | A8 | 20o brown | 200.00 | 25.00 |
| 44 | A8 | 20o blue ('86) | 125.00 | 3.50 |
| *a.* | | 20o ultramarine ('83) | 500.00 | 25.00 |
| *b.* | | No period after "Postfrim" ('85) | 700.00 | 30.00 |
| *c.* | | As "a," imperf. ('90) | *2,500.* | *3,000.* |
| *d.* | | 20o Prussian blue | 350.00 | 30.00 |
| 45 | A8 | 25o dull vio ('84) | 25.00 | 30.00 |

Dies vary from 20 to 21mm high. Numerous types exist due to different production methods, including separate handmade dies for value figures. Many shades exist.

No. 42 and 42a Surcharged in Black

**1888 *Perf. 14½x13½***

| | | | | |
|---|---|---|---|---|
| 46 | A8 | 2o on 12o org brn | 3.50 | *4.50* |
| *a.* | | 2o on 12o bister brown | 7.00 | 5.50 |

Post Horn — A10

### "NORGE" in Roman instead of Sans-serif capitals

***Perf. 14½x13½***

**1893-1908 Wmk. 160**

**Size: 16x20mm**

| | | | | |
|---|---|---|---|---|
| 47 | A10 | 1o gray ('99) | 4.50 | *5.00* |
| 48 | A10 | 2o pale brn ('99) | 3.25 | *3.00* |
| 49 | A10 | 3o orange yel | 2.75 | .40 |
| 50 | A10 | 5o dp green ('98) | 7.00 | .30 |
| *b.* | | Booklet pane of 6 | *800.00* | |
| 51 | A10 | 10o carmine ('98) | 16.00 | .30 |
| *b.* | | Booklet pane of 6 | *1,100.* | |
| *d.* | | 10o rose ('94) | 350.00 | 4.00 |
| *e.* | | Imperf | | *4,000.* |
| 52 | A10 | 15o brown ('08) | 65.00 | 16.00 |
| 53 | A10 | 20o dp ultra | 30.00 | .40 |
| *b.* | | Booklet pane of 6 | | |
| 54 | A10 | 25o red vio ('01) | 85.00 | 5.00 |
| 55 | A10 | 30o sl gray ('07) | 65.00 | 5.50 |
| 56 | A10 | 35o dk bl grn ('98) | 18.00 | 12.50 |
| 57 | A10 | 50o maroon ('94) | 75.00 | 3.00 |
| 58 | A10 | 60o dk blue ('00) | 85.00 | 16.00 |
| | | *Nos. 47-58 (12)* | 456.50 | 67.40 |

Two dies exist of 3, 10 and 20o.

See Nos. 74-95, 162-166, 187-191, 193, 307-309, 325-326, 416-419, 606, 709-714, 960-968, 1141-1145.

For overprints and surcharge see Nos. 99, 207-211, 220-224, 226, 329.

**1893-98 Wmk. 160 *Perf. 13½x12½***

| | | | | |
|---|---|---|---|---|
| *47a* | A10 | 1o gray ('95) | 25.00 | *45.00* |
| *49a* | A10 | 3o orange ('95) | 50.00 | 12.00 |
| *50a* | A10 | 5o green | 35.00 | 1.75 |
| *51a* | A10 | 10o carmine ('96) | 35.00 | 1.50 |
| *c.* | | 10o rose ('95) | 100.00 | 3.25 |
| *53a* | A10 | 20o dull ultra ('95) | 110.00 | 7.50 |
| *54a* | A10 | 25o red violet ('98) | 140.00 | 55.00 |
| *56a* | A10 | 35o dark blue green ('95) | 100.00 | 30.00 |
| *57a* | A10 | 50o maroon ('97) | 350.00 | 25.00 |
| | | *Nos. 47a-57a (8)* | 845.00 | 177.75 |

Two dies exist of each except 25 and 35o.

No. 12 Surcharged in Green, Blue or Carmine

**1905 Unwmk. *Perf. 14½x13½***

| | | | | |
|---|---|---|---|---|
| 59 | A4 | 1k on 2s org (G) | 57.50 | 50.00 |
| 60 | A4 | 1.50k on 2s org (Bl) | 100.00 | 85.00 |
| 61 | A4 | 2k on 2s org (C) | 110.00 | 100.00 |
| | | *Nos. 59-61 (3)* | 267.50 | 235.00 |

Used values are for stamps canceled after 1910. Stamps used before that sell for twice as much.

Nos. 19 and 21 Surcharged in Black

**1906-08 Wmk. 160 *Perf. 14½x13½***

**62** A5 15o on 4s lilac ('08) 8.50 8.50
*a.* 15o on 4s violet ('08) 20.00 17.50
**63** A5 30o on 7s red brn 16.00 12.00
*a.* Inverted overprint *10,000.*

Used values are for stamps canceled after 1914. Stamps used before that sell for twice as much.

King Haakon VII — A11

Die A

Die B

Die C

Die A — Background of ruled lines. The coils at the sides are ornamented with fine cross-lines and small dots. Stamps 20¼mm high.

Die B — Background of ruled lines. The coils are ornamented with large white dots and dashes. Stamps 21¼mm high.

Die C — Solid background. The coils are without ornamental marks. Stamps 20¾mm high.

**Die A**

**1907 Typo. *Perf. 14½x13½***

**64** A11 1k yellow grn 70.00 40.00
**65** A11 1.50k ultra 120.00 90.00
**66** A11 2k rose 185.00 125.00
*Nos. 64-66 (3)* 375.00 255.00

Used values are for stamps postmarked after 1910. Stamps postmarked before that sell for twice as much. Stamps postmarked after 1914 sell for one-half the values listed. See note after No. 180.

**1909-10 Die B**

**67** A11 1k green 225.00 130.00
**68** A11 1.50k ultra 260.00 *375.00*
**69** A11 2k rose 200.00 8.00
*Nos. 67-69 (3)* 685.00 *513.00*

Used values are for stamps canceled after 1914. Stamps used before that sell for twice as much.

**1911-18 Die C**

**70** A11 1k light green .90 .25
*a.* 1k dark green 90.00 3.50
**71** A11 1.50k ultra 3.50 1.00
**72** A11 2k rose ('15) 4.50 1.50
**73** A11 5k dk violet ('18) 6.00 6.00
*Nos. 70-73 (4)* 14.90 8.75
Set, never hinged 40.00

See note following No. 180.

**Post Horn Type Redrawn**

Original

Redrawn

In the redrawn stamps the white ring of the post horn is continuous instead of being broken by a spot of color below the crown. On the 3 and 30 ore the top of the figure "3" in the oval band is rounded instead of flattened.

**1910-29 *Perf. 14½x13½***

**74** A10 1o pale olive .40 *.75*
**75** A10 2o pale brown .40 *.50*
**76** A10 3o orange .40 *.50*
**77** A10 5o green 4.50 .25
*a.* Booklet pane of 6 175.00
Complete booklet, 4 #77a 3,200.
**78** A10 5o magenta ('22) .80 .25
**79** A10 7o green ('29) .80 .25
**80** A10 10o car rose 6.50 .25
*a.* Booklet pane of 6 100.00
Complete booklet, 2 #80a 500.00
**81** A10 10o green ('22) 8.00 .50
**82** A10 12o purple ('17) 1.00 1.50
**83** A10 15o brown 8.00 .50
*a.* Booklet pane of 6 25.00
Complete booklet, 2 #83a 90.00
**84** A10 15o indigo ('20) 9.00 .25
**85** A10 20o deep ultra 9.00 .25
*a.* Booklet pane of 6 400.00
Complete booklet, 2 #85a *4,000.*
**86** A10 20o ol grn ('21) 11.00 .30
**87** A10 25o red lilac 55.00 .50
**88** A10 25o car rose ('22) 9.00 .80
**89** A10 30o slate gray 12.00 .50
**90** A10 30o lt blue ('27) 10.00 8.00
**91** A10 35o dk olive ('20) 15.00 .50
**92** A10 40o ol grn ('17) 6.00 .50
**93** A10 40o dp ultra ('22) 30.00 .30
**94** A10 50o claret 25.00 .50
**95** A10 60o deep blue 30.00 .50
*Nos. 74-95 (22)* 251.80 18.15
Set, never hinged 1,500.

Constitutional Assembly of 1814 — A12

**1914, May 10 Engr. *Perf. 13½***

**96** A12 5o green 1.25 .75
**97** A12 10o car rose 3.00 .75
**98** A12 20o deep blue 10.00 12.00
*Nos. 96-98 (3)* 14.25 13.50
Set, never hinged 80.00

Norway's Constitution of May 17, 1814.

No. 87 Surcharged

**1922, Mar. 1 *Perf. 14½x13½***

**99** A10 5o on 25o red lilac 1.00 *1.50*
Never hinged 2.00

Lion Rampant — A13

**"NORGE" in Roman capitals, Line below "Ore"**

**1922-24 Typo. *Perf. 14½x13½***

**100** A13 10o dp grn ('24) 10.00 .60
**101** A13 20o dp vio 16.00 .25
**102** A13 25o scarlet ('24) 27.50 .75
**103** A13 45o blue ('24) 2.00 1.50
*Nos. 100-103 (4)* 55.50 3.10
Set, never hinged 250.00

For surcharge see No. 129.

Polar Bear and Airplane — A14

**1925, Apr. 1**

**104** A14 2o yellow brn 2.25 *3.50*
**105** A14 3o orange 4.50 *6.00*
**106** A14 5o magenta 12.00 *22.50*
**107** A14 10o yellow grn 16.00 *35.00*
**108** A14 15o dark blue 15.00 *32.50*
**109** A14 20o plum 25.00 *40.00*
**110** A14 25o scarlet 6.00 *8.00*
*Nos. 104-110 (7)* 80.75 147.50
Set, never hinged 180.00

Issued to help finance Roald Amundsen's attempted flight to the North Pole.

A15

**1925, Aug. 19**

**111** A15 10o yellow green 7.00 *15.00*
**112** A15 15o indigo 5.00 *9.00*
**113** A15 20o plum 7.00 *2.50*
**114** A15 45o dark blue 6.00 *9.00*
*Nos. 111-114 (4)* 25.00 35.50
Set, never hinged 100.00

Annexation of Spitsbergen (Svalbard). For surcharge see No. 130.

A16

**"NORGE" in Sans-serif Capitals, No Line below "Ore"**

**1926-34 Wmk. 160**

**Size: 16x19½mm**

**115** A16 10o yel grn .70 .25
**116** A16 14o dp org ('29) 2.25 3.00
**117** A16 15o olive brown .85 .25
**118** A16 20o plum 30.00 .40
**119** A16 20o scar ('27) 1.00 .25
*a.* Booklet pane of 6 80.00
Complete booklet, 2 #119a 375.00
**120** A16 25o red 12.00 3.00
**121** A16 25o org brn ('27) 1.25 .25
**122** A16 30o dull bl ('28) 1.25 .25
**123** A16 35o ol brn ('27) 75.00 .25
**124** A16 35o red vio ('34) 2.00 .25
**125** A16 40o dull blue 5.00 1.50
**126** A16 40o slate ('27) 2.00 .25
**127** A16 50o claret ('27) 2.00 .25
**128** A16 60o Prus bl ('27) 2.00 .25
*Nos. 115-128 (14)* 137.30 10.40
Set, never hinged 675.00

See Nos. 167-176, 192, 194-202A. For overprints and surcharges see Nos. 131, 212-219, 225, 227-234, 302-303.

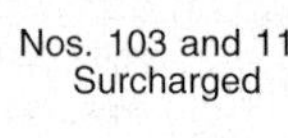


Nos. 103 and 114 Surcharged

**1927, June 13**

**129** A13 30o on 45o blue 13.00 3.00
**130** A15 30o on 45o dk blue 7.00 10.00
Set, never hinged 60.00

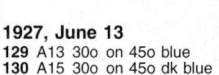

No. 120 Surcharged

**1928**

**131** A16 20o on 25o red 2.50 2.50
Never hinged 15.00

See Nos. 302-303.

Henrik Ibsen — A17

**1928, Mar. 20 Litho.**

**132** A17 10o yellow grn 10.00 5.00
**133** A17 15o chnt brown 4.00 4.50
**134** A17 20o carmine 3.50 .90
**135** A17 30o dp ultra 7.00 5.00
*Nos. 132-135 (4)* 24.50 15.40
Set, never hinged 85.00

Ibsen (1828-1906), dramatist.

**Postage Due Stamps of 1889-1923 Overprinted**

a

b

**1929, Jan.**

**136** D1 (a) 1o gray .90 *1.75*
**137** D1 (a) 4o lilac rose .60 .60
**138** D1 (a) 10o green 2.50 *5.00*
**139** D1 (b) 15o brown 3.50 *8.00*
**140** D1 (b) 20o dull vio 1.25 1.00
**141** D1 (b) 40o deep ultra 2.00 1.00
**142** D1 (b) 50o maroon 10.00 10.00
**143** D1 (a) 100o orange yel 4.25 *4.25*
**144** D1 (b) 200o dk violet 5.50 5.00
*Nos. 136-144 (9)* 30.50 36.60
Set, never hinged 75.00

Niels Henrik Abel — A18

**1929, Apr. 6 Litho. *Perf. 14½x13½***

**145** A18 10o green 3.50 1.00
**146** A18 15o red brown 3.50 2.50
**147** A18 20o rose red 1.25 .50
**148** A18 30o deep ultra 3.25 3.00
*Nos. 145-148 (4)* 11.50 7.00
Set, never hinged 50.00

Abel (1802-1829), mathematician.

No. 12 Surcharged

***Perf. 14½x13½***

**1929, July 1 Unwmk.**

**149** A4 14o on 2s orange 3.50 *8.00*
Never hinged 7.00

Saint Olaf A19

Trondheim Cathedral A20

Death of Olaf in Battle of Stiklestad A21

**Typo.; Litho. (15o)**

***Perf. 14½x13½***

**1930, Apr. 1 Wmk. 160**

**150** A19 10o yellow grn 14.00 .70
**151** A20 15o brn & blk 1.75 1.00
**152** A19 20o scarlet 1.25 .50

**Engr.**

***Perf. 13½***

**153** A21 30o deep blue 4.50 5.00
*Nos. 150-153 (4)* 21.50 7.20
Set, never hinged 90.00

King Olaf Haraldsson (995-1030), patron saint of Norway.

Björnson — A22

**1932, Dec. 8** *Perf. 14½x13½*
**154** A22 10o yellow grn 10.00 .75
**155** A22 15o black brn 1.50 1.50
**156** A22 20o rose red 1.00 .50
**157** A22 30o ultra 3.50 *4.50*
*Nos. 154-157 (4)* 16.00 7.25
Set, never hinged 60.00

Björnstjerne Björnson (1832-1910), novelist, poet and dramatist.

Holberg — A23

**1934, Nov. 23**
**158** A23 10o yellow grn 4.50 .90
**159** A23 15o brown 1.00 1.25
**160** A23 20o rose red 18.00 .50
**161** A23 30o ultra 4.00 4.50
*Nos. 158-161 (4)* 27.50 7.15
Set, never hinged 90.00

Ludvig Holberg (1684-1754), Danish man of letters.

**Types of 1893-1900, 1926-34**
**Second Redrawing**
***Perf. 13x13½***
**1937** **Wmk. 160** **Photo.**
**Size: 17x21mm**
**162** A10 1o olive .70 2.00
**163** A10 2o yellow brn .70 1.75
**164** A10 3o deep orange 1.75 *4.00*
**165** A10 5o rose lilac .55 .40
**166** A10 7o brt green .70 .40
**167** A16 10o brt green .45 .30
Complete booklet, 2 panes of 6 #167 675.00
**168** A16 14o dp orange 3.00 6.00
**169** A16 15o olive bis 1.75 .25
**170** A16 20o scarlet 1.25 .25
Complete booklet, 2 panes of 6 #170 1,250.
Complete booklet, panes of 6 ea of #165, 167, 170 500.00
**171** A16 25o dk org brn 6.00 .50
**172** A16 30o ultra 3.50 .50
**173** A16 35o brt vio 2.50 .25
**174** A16 40o dk slate grn 3.50 .25
**175** A16 50o deep claret 3.50 .75
**176** A16 60o Prussian bl 2.50 .25
*Nos. 162-176 (15)* 32.35 17.85
Set, never hinged 125.00

Nos. 162 to 166 have a solid background inside oval. Nos. 74, 75, 76, 78, 79 have background of vertical lines.

King Haakon VII — A24

**1937-38**
**177** A24 1k dark green .25 .25
**178** A24 1.50k sapphire ('38) 1.00 2.00
**179** A24 2k rose red ('38) 1.00 1.25
**180** A24 5k dl vio ('38) 9.00 *10.00*
*Nos. 177-180 (4)* 11.25 13.50
Set, never hinged 25.00

Nos. 64-66, 67-69, 70-73, 177-180 and B11-B14 were demonitized and banned on Sept. 30, 1940. Nos. 267, B19, B32-B34 and B38-B41 were demonetized on May 15, 1945. All of these stamps became valid again Sept. 1, 1981. Nos. 64-66, 67-69 and 70-73 rarely were used after 1981, and values represent stamps used in the earlier period. Values for Nos. B11-B14 used are for stamps used in the earlier period, and used examples in the later period are worth the same as mint stamps. Values for the other stamps used are for examples used in the later period, and stamps with dated cancellations prior to May 15, 1945 sell for more. False cancellations exist.

Reindeer — A25

Borgund Church — A26

Jolster in Sunnfiord A27

***Perf. 13x13½, 13½x13***
**1938, Apr. 20** **Wmk. 160**
**181** A25 15o olive brn 1.25 1.25
**182** A26 20o copper red 4.00 .55
**183** A27 30o brt ultra 4.00 2.50
*Nos. 181-183 (3)* 9.25 4.30
Set, never hinged 40.00

**1939, Jan. 16** **Unwmk.**
**184** A25 15o olive brn .50 .75
**185** A26 20o copper red .50 .25
**186** A27 30o brt ultra .50 .50
*Nos. 184-186 (3)* 1.50 1.50
Set, never hinged 3.00

**Types of 1937**
***Perf. 13x13½***
**1940-49** **Unwmk.** **Photo.**
**Size: 17x21mm**
**187** A10 1o olive grn ('41) .25 .25
**188** A10 2o yel brn ('41) .25 .25
**189** A10 3o dp org ('41) .25 .25
**190** A10 5o rose lilac ('41) .35 .25
**191** A10 7o brt green ('41) .40 .25
**192** A16 10o brt green .35 .25
Complete booklet, 2 panes of 6 #192 50.00
**193** A10 12o brt vio .80 2.00
**194** A16 14o dp org ('41) 1.50 4.00
**195** A16 15o olive bister .50 .25
**196** A16 20o red .45 .25
Complete booklet, 2 panes of 6 #196 60.00
Complete booklet, pane of 6 ea of #190, 192, 196 200.00
Complete booklet, pane of 10 ea of #190, 192, 196 125.00
**197** A16 25o dk org brn 1.25 .25
**197A** A16 25o scarlet ('46) .50 .25
Complete booklet, pane of 10 ea of #190, 192, 197A 110.00
Complete booklet, pane of 10 ea of #192, 195, 197A 100.00
**198** A16 30o brt ultra ('41) 1.75 .40
**198A** A16 30o gray ('49) 6.00 .25
**199** A16 35o brt vio ('41) 1.75 .25
**200** A16 40o dk sl grn ('41) 1.00 .25
**200A** A16 40o dp ultra ('46) 3.75 .40
**201** A16 50o dp claret ('41) 1.00 .25
**201A** A16 55o dp org ('46) 15.00 .40
**202** A16 60o Prus bl ('41) 1.25 .25
**202A** A16 80o dk org brn ('46) 14.00 .40
*Nos. 187-202A (21)* 52.35 11.35
Set, never hinged 150.00

Lion Rampant — A28

**1940** **Unwmk.** **Photo.** *Perf. 13x13½*
**203** A28 1k brt green 1.00 .25
**204** A28 1½k deep blue 1.75 .30
**205** A28 2k bright red 2.50 1.25
**206** A28 5k dull purple 7.00 *7.00*
*Nos. 203-206 (4)* 12.25 8.80
Set, never hinged 40.00

For overprints see Nos. 235-238.

Stamps of 1937-41, Types A10, A16, A28, Overprinted in Black

**1941** **Wmk. 160** *Perf. 13x13½*
**207** A10 1o olive .50 *9.00*
**208** A10 2o yellow brn .50 *12.00*
**209** A10 3o orange 2.50 *25.00*
**210** A10 5o rose lilac .50 *2.50*
**211** A10 7o brt green .50 *6.00*
**212** A16 10o brt green 7.50 *40.00*
**213** A16 14o dp orange 1.00 *22.50*
**214** A16 15o olive bis .30 *1.25*
**215** A16 30o ultra 3.00 *5.00*
**216** A16 35o brt violet 1.00 *1.00*
**217** A16 40o dk slate grn 7.50 *12.50*
**218** A16 50o dp claret 275.00 *750.00*
Never hinged 600.00
**219** A16 60o Prus blue 1.00 *2.50*
*Nos. 207-217,219 (12)* 25.80 *139.25*
Set, never hinged 55.00

The "V" overprint exists on Nos. 170-171, but these were not regularly issued.

**Unwmk.**
**220** A10 1o olive .35 *6.00*
**221** A10 2o yellow brn .35 *10.00*
**222** A10 3o deep orange .35 *7.50*
**223** A10 5o rose lilac .35 .50
**224** A10 7o brt green 1.25 *10.00*
**225** A16 10o brt green .35 .25
**226** A10 12o brt violet 1.10 *20.00*
**227** A16 15o olive bis 1.90 *25.00*
**228** A16 20o red .35 .25
*a.* Inverted overprint 1,250. 1,750.
**229** A16 25o dk orange brn .50 .40
**230** A16 30o brt ultra 1.50 *5.00*
**231** A16 35o brt violet 1.25 .70
**232** A16 40o dk slate grn .70 .90
**233** A16 50o dp claret 1.00 *3.50*
**234** A16 60o Prus blue 3.00 2.00
**235** A28 1k brt green 1.25 .75
**236** A28 1½k dp blue 3.75 *18.00*
**237** A28 2k bright red 12.00 *70.00*
**238** A28 5k dull purple 22.50 *150.00*

Lion Rampant with "V" — A29

**Coil Stamp**
**239** A29 10o brt green 1.25 *15.00*
*Nos. 220-239 (20)* 55.05 *345.75*
Set, never hinged 100.00

No. 239 has a white "V" incorporated into design, rather than an overprint. Nos. 207-239 were demonitized March 29, 1944. Used values are for stamps with postmarks dated prior to March 29, 1944. Forged cancellations exist.

Dream of Queen Ragnhild A30

Snorri Sturluson A32

Einar Tambarskjelve in Fight at Svolder — A31

Designs: 30o, King Olaf sailing in wedding procession to Landmerket. 50o, Syipdag's sons and followers going to Hall of Seven Kings. 60o, Before Battle of Stiklestad.

**1941** *Perf. 13½x13, 13x13½*
**240** A30 10o bright green .35 .50
**241** A31 15o olive brown .40 .75
**242** A32 20o dark red .35 .25
**243** A31 30o blue 1.75 *2.50*
**244** A31 50o dull violet 1.10 *2.00*
**245** A31 60o Prus blue 2.00 2.25
*Nos. 240-245 (6)* 5.95 8.25
Set, never hinged 20.00

700th anniversary of the death of Snorri Sturluson, writer and historian.

University of Oslo — A36

**1941, Sept. 2** *Perf. 13x13½*
**246** A36 1k dk olive grn 50.00 80.00
Never hinged 80.00

Centenary of cornerstone laying of University of Oslo building.

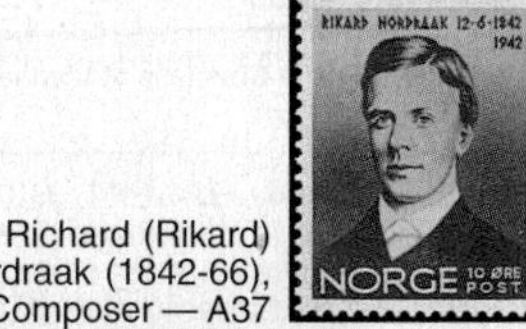
Richard (Rikard) Nordraak (1842-66), Composer — A37

"Broad Sails Go over the North Sea" A38

View of Coast and Lines of National Anthem A39

**1942, June 12** *Perf. 13*

| | | | |
|---|---|---|---|
| **247** A37 10o dp green | 1.75 | *4.00* |
| **248** A38 15o dp brown | 1.50 | *3.00* |
| **249** A37 20o rose red | 1.50 | *3.50* |
| **250** A39 30o sapphire | 1.50 | *3.00* |
| *Nos. 247-250 (4)* | 6.25 | 13.50 |
| Set, never hinged | 18.00 | |

Johan Herman Wessel (1742-1785), Author — A40

**1942, Oct. 6**

| | | |
|---|---|---|
| **251** A40 15o dull brown | .30 | .50 |
| **252** A40 20o henna | .30 | .50 |
| Set, never hinged | 1.00 | |

Designs of 1942 and 1855 Stamps of Norway A41

**1942, Oct. 12**

| | | |
|---|---|---|
| **253** A41 20o henna | .25 | 1.75 |
| **254** A41 30o sapphire | .35 | 2.75 |
| Set, never hinged | 1.25 | |

European Postal Congress at Vienna, October, 1942.

Nos. 253-254, B24-B27, B31 and B35-B37 were demonitized May 15, 1945. Used values are for stamps with postmarks dated prior to May 15, 1945. Forged cancellations exist.

Edvard Grieg (1843-1907), Composer — A42

**1943, June 15**

| | | |
|---|---|---|
| **255** A42 10o deep green | .25 | *.50* |
| **256** A42 20o henna | .25 | *.50* |
| **257** A42 40o grnsh black | .25 | *.50* |
| **258** A42 60o dk grnsh blue | .25 | *.50* |
| *Nos. 255-258 (4)* | 1.00 | 2.00 |
| Set, never hinged | 2.50 | |

Destroyer Sleipner — A43

5o, 10o, "Sleipner." 7o, 30o, Convoy under midnight sun. 15o, Plane and pilot. 20o, "We will win." 40o, Ski troops. 60o, King Haakon VII.

**1943-45 Unwmk. Engr.** *Perf. 12½*

| | | |
|---|---|---|
| **259** A43 5o rose vio ('45) | .25 | .25 |
| **260** A43 7o grnsh blk ('45) | .25 | .75 |
| **261** A43 10o dk blue grn | .25 | .25 |
| **262** A43 15o dk olive grn | .60 | *2.00* |
| **263** A43 20o rose red | .25 | .25 |
| **264** A43 30o dp ultra | .65 | *2.00* |
| **265** A43 40o olive black | 1.00 | *1.75* |
| **266** A43 60o dark blue | 1.00 | *1.75* |
| *Nos. 259-266 (8)* | 4.25 | *9.00* |
| Set, never hinged | 10.00 | |

Nos. 261-266 were used for correspondence carried on Norwegian ships until after the liberation of Norway, when they became regular postage stamps.

Nos. 261-266 exist with overprint "London 17-5-43" and serial number. Value for set, unused, $850; canceled $1,500.

Gran's Plane and Map of His North Sea Flight Route A49

**1944, July 30** *Perf. 13*

| | | |
|---|---|---|
| **267** A49 40o dk grnsh blue | .40 | .40 |
| Never hinged | .60 | |

20th anniv. of the 1st flight over the North Sea, made by Tryggve Gran on July 30, 1914.

Value for used stamp postmarked before May 15, 1945, $6. See note following No. 180.

New National Arms of 1943 — A50

**1945, Feb. 15 Typo.** *Perf. 13*

| | | |
|---|---|---|
| **268** A50 1½k dark blue | 1.25 | .60 |
| Never hinged | 4.00 | |

Henrik Wergeland — A51

**1945, July 12** **Photo.**

| | | |
|---|---|---|
| **269** A51 10o dk olive green | .30 | *.50* |
| **270** A51 15o dark brown | .85 | 1.25 |
| **271** A51 20o dark red | .25 | .30 |
| *Nos. 269-271 (3)* | 1.40 | 2.05 |
| Set, never hinged | 2.00 | |

Wergeland, poet & playwright, death cent.

Lion Rampant — A52

**1945, Dec. 19**

| | | |
|---|---|---|
| **272** A52 10o dk olive green | .50 | .50 |
| **273** A52 20o red | .50 | .50 |
| Set, never hinged | 3.50 | |

Norwegian Folklore Museum, 50th anniv.

Pilot and Mechanic — A53

**1946, Mar. 22 Engr.** *Perf. 12*

| | | |
|---|---|---|
| **274** A53 15o brown rose | .40 | *2.00* |
| Never hinged | 1.00 | |

Issued in honor of Little Norway, training center in Canada for Norwegian pilots.

**Catalogue values for unused stamps in this section, from this point to the end of the section, are for Never Hinged items.**

King Haakon VII — A54

**1946, June 7 Photo.** *Perf. 13*

| | | |
|---|---|---|
| **275** A54 1k bright green | 3.00 | .25 |
| **276** A54 1½k Prus blue | 7.50 | .25 |
| **277** A54 2k henna brown | 60.00 | .25 |
| **278** A54 5k violet | 50.00 | .50 |
| *Nos. 275-278 (4)* | 120.50 | 1.25 |

Hannibal Sehested — A55

Designs: 10o, Letter carrier, 1700. 15o, Adm. Peter W. Tordenskjold. 25o, Christian Magnus Falsen. 30o, Cleng Peerson and "Restaurationen." 40o, Post ship "Constitution." 45o, First Norwegian locomotive. 50o, Sven Foyn and whaler. 55o, Fridtjof Nansen and Roald Amundsen. 60o, Coronation of King Haakon VII and Queen Maud, 1906. 80o, Return of King Haakon, June 7, 1945.

**1947, Apr. 15 Photo.** *Perf. 13*

| | | |
|---|---|---|
| **279** A55 5o red lilac | .50 | .25 |
| **280** A55 10o green | .80 | .25 |
| **281** A55 15o brown | 1.50 | .25 |
| **282** A55 25o orange red | 1.25 | .25 |
| **283** A55 30o gray | 2.50 | .25 |
| **284** A55 40o blue | 8.00 | .25 |
| **285** A55 45o violet | 3.00 | .75 |
| **286** A55 50o orange brn | 5.50 | .35 |
| **287** A55 55o orange | 8.00 | .35 |
| **288** A55 60o slate gray | 8.00 | 2.00 |
| **289** A55 80o dk brown | 8.00 | .35 |
| *Nos. 279-289 (11)* | 47.05 | 5.30 |

Establishment of the Norwegian Post Office, 300th anniv.

Petter Dass — A66

**1947, July 1** **Unwmk.**

| | | |
|---|---|---|
| **290** A66 25o bright red | 2.00 | 1.75 |

300th birth anniv. of Petter Dass, poet.

King Haakon VII — A67

**1947, Aug. 2**

| | | |
|---|---|---|
| **291** A67 25o orange red | 1.00 | 1.00 |

75th birthday of King Haakon.

Axel Heiberg — A68

**1948, June 15**

| | | |
|---|---|---|
| **292** A68 25o deep carmine | 1.25 | .60 |
| **293** A68 80o dp red brown | 3.50 | .30 |

50th anniv. of the Norwegian Society of Forestry; birth cent. of Axel Heiberg, its founder.

Alexander L. Kielland — A69

**1949, May 9**

| | | |
|---|---|---|
| **295** A69 25o rose brown | 2.00 | .50 |
| **296** A69 40o greenish blue | 2.50 | .75 |
| **297** A69 80o orange brown | 3.00 | 1.00 |
| *Nos. 295-297 (3)* | 7.50 | 2.25 |

Birth cent. of Alexander L. Kielland, author.

Symbols of UPU Members A70

Stylized Pigeons and Globe A71

Symbolical of the UPU A72

**1949, Oct. 8** *Perf. 13*

| | | |
|---|---|---|
| **299** A70 10o dk green & blk | .75 | .60 |
| **300** A71 25o scarlet | .75 | .50 |
| **301** A72 40o dull blue | .90 | .75 |
| *Nos. 299-301 (3)* | 2.40 | 1.85 |

75th anniv. of the formation of the UPU.

**Nos. 196 and 200A Surcharged with New Value and Bar in Black**

**1949** *Perf. 13x13½*

| | | |
|---|---|---|
| **302** A16 25o on 20o red | .75 | .25 |
| **303** A16 45o on 40o dp ultra | 3.75 | .65 |

King Harald Haardraade and Oslo City Hall — A73

**1950, May 15 Photo.** *Perf. 13*

| | | |
|---|---|---|
| **304** A73 15o green | .90 | 1.00 |
| **305** A73 25o red | 1.00 | .50 |
| **306** A73 45o ultramarine | 1.00 | 1.00 |
| *Nos. 304-306 (3)* | 2.90 | 2.50 |

900th anniversary of Oslo.

**Redrawn Post Horn Type of 1937**

**1950-51 Photo.** *Perf. 13x13½*

**Size: 17x21mm**

| | | |
|---|---|---|
| **307** A10 10o grnsh gray | 1.00 | .25 |
| Complete booklet, pane of 10 #307 | 250.00 | |
| **308** A10 15o dark green | 2.50 | .50 |
| **309** A10 20o chnt brn ('51) | 5.00 | 3.00 |
| *Nos. 307-309 (3)* | 8.50 | 3.75 |

King Haakon VII — A74

**1950-51 Photo.** *Perf. 13x13½*

| | | |
|---|---|---|
| **310** A74 25o dk red ('50) | 1.00 | .25 |
| Complete booklet, pane of 10 ea of #307, 308, 310 | 85.00 | |
| **311** A74 30o gray | 10.00 | .75 |
| **312** A74 35o red brn | 20.00 | .35 |
| **313** A74 45o brt blue | 2.00 | 3.00 |
| **314** A74 50o olive brn | 6.00 | .25 |
| **315** A74 55o orange | 2.50 | 1.50 |

**316** A74 60o gray blue 18.00 .25
**317** A74 80o chnt brn 4.00 .40
*Nos. 310-317 (8)* 63.50 6.75

See Nos. 322-324, 345-352. For surcharge see No. 321.

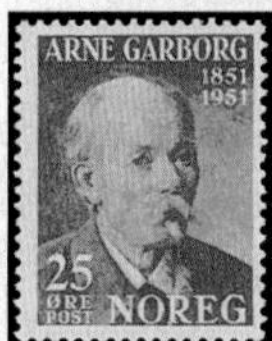

Arne Garborg — A75

**1951, Jan. 25** ***Perf. 13***
**318** A75 25o red 1.00 .50
**319** A75 45o dull blue 3.75 4.00
**320** A75 80o brown 3.75 2.00
*Nos. 318-320 (3)* 8.50 6.50

Birth cent. of Arne Garborg, poet.

**No. 310 Surcharged with New Value in Black**

**1951** ***Perf. 13x13½***
**321** A74 30o on 25o dk red 1.00 .30

**Haakon Type of 1950-51**

**1951-52** **Photo.**
**322** A74 25o gray 25.00 .25
**323** A74 30o dk red ('52) .90 .25
Complete booklet, pane of 10 ea of #307, 308, 323 225.00
Complete booklet, pane of 10 ea of #307, 325, 323 110.00
**324** A74 55o blue ('52) 2.50 .50
*Nos. 322-324 (3)* 28.40 1.00

**Redrawn Post Horn Type of 1937**

**1952, June 3** ***Perf. 13x13½***
**325** A10 15o org brn .70 .25
**326** A10 20o dark green .70 .25

King Haakon VII — A76

**1952, Aug. 3** **Unwmk.** ***Perf. 13***
**327** A76 30o red .50 .50
**328** A76 55o deep blue 1.50 1.50

80th birthday of King Haakon VII.

**No. 308 Surcharged with New Value**

**1952, Nov. 18** ***Perf. 13x13½***
**329** A10 20o on 15o dk grn .60 .25

Medieval Sculpture, Nidaros Cathedral — A77

**1953, July 15** ***Perf. 13***
**330** A77 30o henna brn 1.75 .75

800th anniv. of the creation of the Norwegian Archbishopric of Nidaros.

Train of 1854 and Horse-drawn Sled — A78

Designs: 30o, Diesel train. 55o, Engineer.

**1954, Apr. 30** **Photo.**
**331** A78 20o green 1.25 .60
**332** A78 30o red 1.50 .40
**333** A78 55o ultra 2.00 1.50
*Nos. 331-333 (3)* 4.75 2.50

Inauguration of the first Norwegian railway, cent.

Carsten T. Nielsen — A79

Designs: 30o, Government radio towers. 55o, Lineman and telegraph poles in snow.

**1954, Dec. 10**
**334** A79 20o ol grn & blk .60 .60
**335** A79 30o brt red .60 .40
**336** A79 55o blue 1.50 1.25
*Nos. 334-336 (3)* 2.70 2.25

Centenary (in 1955) of the inauguration of the first Norwegian public telegraph line.

Norway No. 1 — A80

Stamp Reproductions: 30o, Post horn type A5. 55o, Lion type A13.

**1955, Jan. 3** ***Perf. 13***
**337** A80 20o dp grn & gray bl .45 .45
**338** A80 30o red & carmine .40 .40
**339** A80 55o gray bl & dp bl .95 .50
*Nos. 337-339 (3)* 1.80 1.35

Centenary of Norway's first postage stamp.

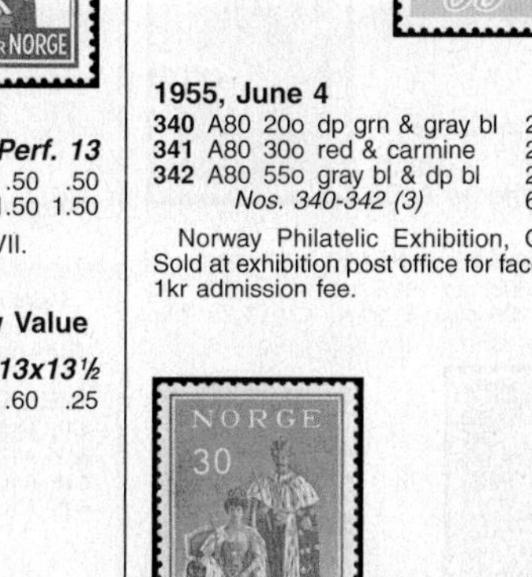

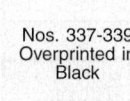

Nos. 337-339 Overprinted in Black

**1955, June 4**
**340** A80 20o dp grn & gray bl 20.00 20.00
**341** A80 30o red & carmine 20.00 20.00
**342** A80 55o gray bl & dp bl 20.00 20.00
*Nos. 340-342 (3)* 60.00 60.00

Norway Philatelic Exhibition, Oslo, 1955. Sold at exhibition post office for face value plus 1kr admission fee.

King Haakon VII and Queen Maud in Coronation Robes — A81

**1955, Nov. 25** **Photo.** ***Perf. 13***
**343** A81 30o rose red .40 .40
**344** A81 55o ultra .75 .75

Haakon's 50th anniv. as King of Norway.

**Haakon Type of 1950-51**

**1955-57** **Unwmk.** ***Perf. 13x13½***
**345** A74 25o dk grn ('56) 1.50 .25
**346** A74 35o brn red ('56) 6.00 .25
Complete booklet, pane of 10 ea of #307, 325, 346 100.00
**347** A74 40o pale pur 2.25 .25
Complete booklet, pane of 10 ea of #307, 325, 347 80.00
**348** A74 50o bister ('57) 6.00 .25
**349** A74 65o ultra ('56) 1.50 .40
**350** A74 70o brn ol ('56) 25.00 .25
**351** A74 75o mar ('57) 3.00 .25
**352** A74 90o dp org 2.00 .25
*Nos. 345-352 (8)* 47.25 2.15

**Northern Countries Issue**

Whooper Swans — A81a

**1956, Oct. 30** **Engr.** ***Perf. 12½***
**353** A81a 35o rose red .95 .60
**354** A81a 65o ultra .95 .85

Close bonds connecting the northern countries: Denmark, Finland, Iceland, Norway and Sweden.

Jan Mayen Island A82

Map of Spitsbergen — A83

Design: 65o, Map of South Pole with Queen Maud Land.

***Perf. 12½x13, 13x12½***

**1957, July 1** **Photo.** **Unwmk.**
**355** A82 25o slate green .75 .60
**356** A83 35o dk red & gray 1.00 .50
**357** A83 65o dk grn & bl 1.00 .70
*Nos. 355-357 (3)* 2.75 1.80

Intl. Geophysical Year, 1957-58.

King Haakon VII — A84

**1957, Aug. 3** ***Perf. 13***
**358** A84 35o dark red .80 .50
**359** A84 65o ultra 1.40 1.25

85th birthday of King Haakon VII.

King Olav V — A85

**1958-60** **Photo.** ***Perf. 13x13½***
**360** A85 25o emerald 1.50 .25
Complete booklet, pane of 4 of #360 150.00
**361** A85 30o purple ('59) 2.50 .25
**361A** A85 35o brown car ('60) 1.25 .25
**362** A85 40o dark red 1.25 .25
Complete booklet, pane of 10 of ea of #307, 325, 362 115.00
**363** A85 45o scarlet 1.90 .25
Complete booklet, pane of 10 of #363 75.00
Complete booklet, pane of 10 ea of #307, 325, 363 100.00
**364** A85 50o bister ('59) 8.50 .25
**365** A85 55o dk gray ('59) 2.25 1.00
**366** A85 65o blue 3.50 .50
**367** A85 80o org brn ('60) 14.00 1.00
**368** A85 85o olive brn ('59) 2.50 .25
**369** A85 90o orange ('59) 2.00 .25
*Nos. 360-369 (11)* 41.15 4.50

See Nos. 408-412.

King Olav V — A86

**1959, Jan. 12**
**370** A86 1k green 1.50 .25
**371** A86 1.50k dark blue 4.50 .25
**372** A86 2k crimson 4.50 .25
**373** A86 5k lilac 70.00 .25
**374** A86 10k dp orange 10.00 .25
*Nos. 370-374 (5)* 90.50 1.25

See Phosphorescence note following No. 430.

Asbjörn Kloster — A87

**1959, Feb. 2**
**375** A87 45o violet brown .70 .40

Centenary of the founding of the Norwegian Temperance Movement; Asbjörn Kloster, its founder.

Agricultural Society Medal — A88

**1959, May 26**
**376** A88 45o red & ocher .80 .75
**377** A88 90o blue & gray 2.50 2.50

150th anniversary of the Royal Agricultural Society of Norway.

Sower — A89

Design: 90o, Grain, vert.

**1959, Oct. 1** **Photo.** ***Perf. 13***
**378** A89 45o ocher & blk 1.00 .75
**379** A89 90o blue & blk 2.00 1.50

Agricultural College of Norway, cent.

Society Seal — A90

**1960, Feb. 26** **Unwmk.**
**380** A90 45o carmine .75 .50
**381** A90 90o dark blue 2.50 2.00

Bicentenary of the Royal Norwegian Society of Sciences, Trondheim.

Viking Ship A91

25o, Caravel & fish. 45o, Sailing ship & nautical knot. 55o, Freighter & oil derricks. 90o, Passenger ship & Statue of Liberty.

**1960, Aug. 27** ***Perf. 12½x13***

**382** A91 20o gray & blk 2.50 1.75
**383** A91 25o yel grn & blk 1.50 1.50
**384** A91 45o ver & blk 1.50 .40
**385** A91 55o ocher & blk 4.00 3.50
**386** A91 90o Prus bl & blk 5.00 2.50
*Nos. 382-386 (5)* 14.50 9.65

Norwegian shipping industry.

Common Design Types pictured following the introduction.

### Europa Issue
Common Design Type

**1960, Sept. 19** ***Perf. 13***
**Size: 27x21mm**

**387** CD3 90o blue 1.25 1.25

DC-8 Airliner — A91a

**1961, Feb. 24** **Photo.** ***Perf. 13***

**388** A91a 90o dark blue 1.00 1.00

Scandinavian Airlines System, SAS, 10th anniv.

Javelin Thrower — A92

**1961, Mar. 15**

**389** A92 20o shown 1.25 1.00
**390** A92 25o Skater 1.25 1.00
**391** A92 45o Ski jumper 1.00 .50
**392** A92 90o Sailboat 1.75 1.75
*Nos. 389-392 (4)* 5.25 4.25

Norwegian Sports Federation centenary.

Haakonshallen — A93

**1961, May 25** ***Perf. 12½x13***

**393** A93 45o maroon & gray 1.00 .50
**394** A93 1k gray green & gray 1.50 .50

700th anniv. of Haakonshallen, castle in Bergen.

Domus Media, Oslo University A94

**1961, Sept. 2** **Photo.** ***Perf. 12½x13***

**395** A94 45o dark red 1.00 .50
**396** A94 1.50k Prus blue 1.50 .50

150th anniversary of Oslo University.

Fridtjof Nansen — A95

**1961, Oct. 10** ***Perf. 13***

**397** A95 45o orange red & gray 1.25 .40
**398** A95 90o chlky blue & gray 2.00 1.75

Birth centenary of Fridtjof Nansen, explorer.

Roald Amundsen A96

Design: 90o, Explorers and tent at Pole.

**1961, Nov. 10** **Unwmk.** ***Perf. 13***

**399** A96 45o dl red brn & gray 1.50 .75
**400** A96 90o dk & lt blue 2.50 2.00

50th anniversary of Roald Amundsen's arrival at the South Pole.

Frederic Passy, Henri Dunant — A97

**1961, Dec. 9** **Photo.**

**401** A97 45o henna brown .50 .50
**402** A97 1k yellow green 1.75 .50

Winners of the first Nobel Peace prize. Frederic Passy, a founder of the Interparliamentary Union, and Henri Dunant, founder of the International Red Cross.

Vilhelm Bjerknes — A98

**1962, Mar. 14** ***Perf. 13***

**403** A98 45o dk red & gray .50 .40
**404** A98 1.50k dk blue & gray 1.25 .50

Vilhelm Bjerknes (1862-1951), physicist, mathematician, meteorologist, etc.

German Rumpler Taube over Oslo Fjord A99

**1962, June 1** **Photo.**

**405** A99 1.50k dl bl & blk 4.50 .85

50th anniversary of Norwegian aviation.

Fir Branch and Cone — A100

**1962, June 15**

**406** A100 45o salmon & blk .75 .75
**407** A100 1k pale grn & blk 8.00 .50

### Olav Type of 1958-60

**1962** **Unwmk.** ***Perf. 13x13½***

**408** A85 25o slate grn 1.75 .25
Complete booklet, pane of 4 of #408 150.00
Complete booklet, pane of 10 ea of #190, 307, 408 40.00
**409** A85 35o emerald 7.50 .25
**410** A85 40o gray 5.00 2.50
**411** A85 50o scarlet 11.50 .25
Complete booklet, pane of 10 of #411 200.00
**412** A85 60o violet 8.00 .75
*Nos. 408-412 (5)* 33.75 4.00

### Europa Issue
Common Design Type

**1962, Sept. 17** **Photo.** ***Perf. 13***
**Size: 37x21mm**

**414** CD5 50o dp rose & maroon .75 .50
**415** CD5 90o blue & dk blue 1.50 1.75

### Post Horn Type of 1893-1908 Redrawn and

Rock Carvings A101

Boatswain's Knot A102

Designs: 30o, 55o, 85o, Rye and fish. 65o, 80o, Stave church and northern lights.

**1962-63** **Engr.** ***Perf. 13x13½***

**416** A10 5o rose cl .25 .25
**417** A10 10o slate .25 .25
Complete booklet, pane of 10 of #417 40.00
**418** A10 15o orange brn .30 .25
**419** A10 20o green .25 .25
Complete booklet, pane of 4 ea of #416, 419 20.00
**420** A101 25o gray grn ('63) 1.50 .25
Complete booklet, pane of 4 of #420 25.00
Complete booklet, pane of 10 ea of #416, 417, 420 45.00
**421** A101 30o olive brn ('63) 5.00 5.00
**422** A102 35o brt green ('63) .30 .25
**423** A101 40o lake ('63) 3.50 .25
**424** A102 50o vermilion 4.75 .25
Complete booklet, pane of 10 of #424 100.00
**425** A101 55o orange brn ('63) .50 .55
**426** A102 60o dk grnsh gray ('63) 15.00 .25
**427** A102 65o dk blue ('63) 3.50 .35
Complete booklet, pane of 10 of #427 110.00
**428** A102 80o rose lake ('63) 2.50 2.50
**429** A101 85o sepia ('63) .50 .25
**430** A101 90o blue ('63) .30 .25
*Nos. 416-430 (15)* 38.40 11.15

Nos. 416-419 have been redrawn and are similar to 1910-29 issue, with vertical lines inside oval and horizontal lines in oval frame. See Nos. 462-470, 608-615.

**Phosphorescence**
Nos. 370-372, 416-419, 423, 425, 428, 430, 462, 466, O65-O68, O75, O78-O82, O83-O84 and O88 have been issued on both ordinary and phosphorescent paper.

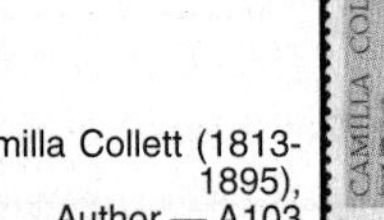

Camilla Collett (1813-1895), Author — A103

**1963, Jan. 23** **Photo.** ***Perf. 13***

**431** A103 50o red brn & tan 1.00 .50
**432** A103 90o slate & gray 1.75 1.25

Girl in Boat Loaded with Grain — A104

Still Life A105

**1963, Mar. 21** **Unwmk.** ***Perf. 13***

**433** A104 25o yellow brown .75 .75
**434** A104 35o dark green .75 .75
**435** A105 50o dark red .75 .50
**436** A105 90o dark blue 1.50 1.10
*Nos. 433-436 (4)* 3.75 3.10

FAO "Freedom from Hunger" campaign.

River Boat A106

Design: 90o, Northern sailboat.

**1963, May 20** **Unwmk.** ***Perf. 13***

**437** A106 50o brown red 1.50 1.00
**438** A106 90o blue 4.00 4.00

Tercentenary of regular postal service between Northern and Southern Norway.

Ivar Aasen — A107

**1963, Aug. 5** **Photo.**

**439** A107 50o dk red & gray .75 .50
**440** A107 90o dk blue & gray 2.50 1.75

150th birth anniv. of Ivar Aasen, poet and philologist.

### Europa Issue
Common Design Type

**1963, Sept. 14** **Unwmk.** ***Perf. 13***
**Size: 27x21½mm**

**441** CD6 50o dull rose & org 1.00 .50
**442** CD6 90o blue & yel grn 3.75 2.50

Patterned Fabric A108

**1963, Sept. 24**

**443** A108 25o olive & ol grn 1.00 1.00
**444** A108 35o Prus bl & dk bl 1.50 1.50
**445** A108 50o dk car rose & plum .85 .50
*Nos. 443-445 (3)* 3.35 3.00

Norwegian textile industry, 150th anniv.

"Loneliness" A109

Paintings by Edvard Munch (1863-1944): 25o, Self-portrait, vert. 35o, "Fertility." 90o, "Girls on Bridge," vert.

**1963, Dec. 12** **Litho.** ***Perf. 13***

**446** A109 25o black .50 .50
**447** A109 35o dark green .50 .50
**448** A109 50o deep claret .85 .50
**449** A109 90o gray bl & dk bl 1.25 1.25
*Nos. 446-449 (4)* 3.10 2.75

Eilert Sundt — A110

50o, Beehive, Workers' Society emblem.

**1964, Feb. 17** **Photo.**

**450** A110 25o dark green .75 .75
**451** A110 50o dk red brown .75 .25

Centenary of the Oslo Workers' Society.

Cato M. Guldberg and Peter Waage by Stinius Fredriksen
A111

**1964, Mar. 11 Unwmk. *Perf. 13***

**452** A111 35o olive green .90 .90
**453** A111 55o bister 2.00 1.75

Centenary of the presentation of the Law of Mass Action (chemistry) by Professors Cato M. Guldberg and Peter Waage in the Oslo Scientific Society.

Eidsvoll Building
A112

Design: 90o, Storting (Parliament House).

**1964, May 11 Photo.**

**454** A112 50o hn brn & blk 1.40 .50
**455** A112 90o Prus bl & dk bl 2.75 2.50

150th anniv. of Norway's constitution.

Church and Ships in Harbor
A113

**1964, Aug. 17 *Perf. 13***

**456** A113 25o dk sl grn & buff .75 .75
**457** A113 90o dk bl & gray 2.50 2.50

Centenary of the Norwegian Seamen's Mission, which operates 32 stations around the world.

**Europa Issue**
Common Design Type

**1964, Sept. 14 Photo. *Perf. 13***

**458** CD7 90o dark blue 4.50 4.50

Herman Anker and Olaus Arvesen
A114

**1964, Oct. 31 Litho. Unwmk.**

**459** A114 50o rose 1.00 .50
**460** A114 90o blue 3.25 3.25

Centenary of the founding of Norwegian schools of higher education (Folk High Schools).

**Types of Regular Issue, 1962-63**

Type I

Type II

Two types of 60o:
I — Four twists across bottom of knot.
II — Five twists.

Designs: 30o, 45o, Rye and fish. 40o, 100o, Rock carvings. 50o, 60o, 65o, 70o, Boatswain's knot.

**1964-70 Engr. *Perf. 13x13½***

**462** A101 30o dull green .40 .25
**463** A101 40o lt bl grn ('68) .30 .25
**464** A101 45o lt yel grn ('68) .75 .75
**465** A102 50o indigo ('68) .50 .25
**466** A102 60o brick red, II ('75) 2.50 .50
*a.* Type I 1.50 .30
Complete booklet, pane of 10 of #466a 90.00
**467** A102 65o lake ('68) .65 .25
Complete booklet, pane of 10 of #467 55.00

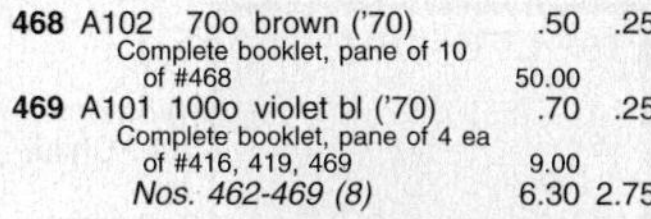

**468** A102 70o brown ('70) .50 .25
Complete booklet, pane of 10 of #468 50.00
**469** A101 100o violet bl ('70) .70 .25
Complete booklet, pane of 4 ea of #416, 419, 469 9.00
*Nos. 462-469 (8)* 6.30 2.75

See Phosphorescence note following #430.

**Coil Stamp**

**1965 *Perf. 13½ Horiz.***

**470** A101 30o dull green 5.00 3.50

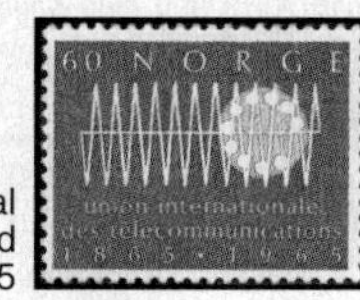


Telephone Dial and Waves — A115

Design: 90o, Television mast and antenna.

**1965, Apr. 1 Engr. *Perf. 13***

**471** A115 60o redsh brown .75 .50
**472** A115 90o slate 1.75 1.75

ITU, centenary.

Mountain Scene
A116

Design: 90o, Coastal view.

**1965, June 4 Unwmk. *Perf. 13***

**473** A116 60o brn blk & car 1.00 .60
**474** A116 90o slate bl & car 4.50 4.50

Centenary of the Norwegian Red Cross.

**Europa Issue**
Common Design Type

**1965, Sept. 25 Photo. *Perf. 13***
**Size: 27x21mm**

**475** CD8 60o brick red 1.25 .60
**476** CD8 90o blue 2.75 2.50

St. Sunniva and Buildings of Bergen — A117

90o, St. Sunniva and stylized view of Bergen.

**1965, Oct. 25 *Perf. 13***

**477** A117 30o dk green & blk .55 .50
**478** A117 90o blue & blk, horiz. 2.00 1.75

Bicentenary of Bergen's philharmonic society "Harmonien."

Rondane Mountains by Harold Sohlberg — A118

**1965, Nov. 29 Photo. *Perf. 13***

**484** A118 1.50k dark blue 3.00 .25

Rock Carving of Skier, Rodoy Island, c. 2000 B.C. — A120

Designs: 55o, Ski jumper. 60o, Cross country skier. 90o, Holmenkollen ski jump, vert.

**1966, Feb. 8 Engr. *Perf. 13***

**486** A120 40o sepia 1.50 1.50
**487** A120 55o dull green 2.00 2.00
**488** A120 60o dull red 1.00 .50
**489** A120 90o blue 2.00 2.00
*Nos. 486-489 (4)* 6.50 6.00

World Ski Championships, Oslo, Feb. 17-27.

Open Bible and Chrismon
A121

**1966, May 20 Photo. *Perf. 13***

**490** A121 60o dull red .75 .50
**491** A121 90o slate blue 1.50 1.50

150th anniv. of the Norwegian Bible Society.

Engine-turned Bank Note Design — A122

Bank of Norway — A123

**1966, June 14 Engr.**

**492** A122 30o green .85 .85
**493** A123 60o dk carmine rose .55 .25

150th anniversary of Bank of Norway.

Johan Sverdrup — A124

**1966, July 30 Photo. *Perf. 13***

**494** A124 30o green .50 .50
**495** A124 60o rose lake .50 .50

Johan Sverdrup (1816-92), Prime Minister of Norway (1884-89).

**Canceled to Order**

The Norwegian philatelic agency began in 1966 to sell commemorative and definitive issues canceled to order at face value.

**Europa Issue**
Common Design Type

**1966, Sept. 26 Engr. *Perf. 13***
**Size: 21x27mm**

**496** CD9 60o dark carmine 1.75 .50
**497** CD9 90o blue gray 3.25 2.50

Nitrogen Molecule in Test Tube — A125

Design: 55o, Wheat and laboratory bottle.

**1966, Oct. 29 Photo. *Perf. 13x12½***

**498** A125 40o bl & dp bl 1.75 1.75
**499** A125 55o red, org & lil rose 2.25 2.25

Centenary of the birth of Kristian Birkeland (1867-1917), and of Sam Eyde (1866-1940), who together developed the production of nitrates.

EFTA Emblem — A126

**1967, Jan. 16 Engr. *Perf. 13***

**500** A126 60o rose red .50 .35
**501** A126 90o dark blue 2.25 2.25

European Free Trade Association. Tariffs were abolished Dec. 31, 1966, among EFTA members: Austria, Denmark, Finland, Great Britain, Norway, Portugal, Sweden, Switzerland.

Sabers, Owl and Oak Leaves
A127

**1967, Feb. 16 Engr. *Perf. 13***

**502** A127 60o chocolate 1.00 1.00
**503** A127 90o black 4.00 4.00

Higher military training in Norway, 150th anniv.

**Europa Issue**
Common Design Type

**1967, May 2 Photo. *Perf. 13***
**Size: 21x27mm**

**504** CD10 60o magenta & plum 1.00 .50
**505** CD10 90o bl & dk vio bl 2.25 2.25

Johanne Dybwad, by Per Ung — A128

**1967, Aug. 2 Photo. *Perf. 13***

**506** A128 40o slate blue .55 .45
**507** A128 60o dk carmine rose .55 .45

Johanne Dybwad (1867-1950), actress.

Missionary L.O. Skrefsrud
A129

Ebenezer Church, Benagaria, Santal
A130

**1967, Sept. 26 Engr. *Perf. 13***

**508** A129 60o red brown .55 .45
**509** A130 90o blue gray 1.50 1.50

Norwegian Santal (India) mission, cent.

Mountaineers
A131

Designs: 60o, Mountain view. 90o, Glitretind mountain peak.

**1968, Jan. 22 Engr. *Perf. 13***

**510** A131 40o sepia 1.50 1.50
**511** A131 60o brown red 1.00 .30
**512** A131 90o slate blue 1.75 1.75
*Nos. 510-512 (3)* 4.25 3.55

Centenary of the Norwegian Mountain Touring Association.

Two Smiths
A132

**1968, Mar. 30 Photo. *Perf. 12½x13***
**513** A132 65o dk car rose & brn .45 .25
**514** A132 90o blue & brown 1.50 1.50

Issued to honor Norwegian craftsmen.

A. O. Vinje — A133

**1968, May 21 Engr. *Perf. 13***
**515** A133 50o sepia .75 .50
**516** A133 65o maroon .50 .25

Aasmund Olafsson Vinje (1818-1870), poet, journalist and language reformer.

Cross and Heart — A134

**1968, Sept. 16 Photo.**
**517** A134 40o brt grn & brn red 3.25 3.25
**518** A134 65o brn red & vio bl .65 .25

Centenary of the Norwegian Lutheran Home Mission Society.

Cathinka Guldberg — A135

**1968, Oct. 31 Engr. *Perf. 13***
**519** A135 50o bright blue .65 .45
**520** A135 65o dull red .65 .25

Nursing profession; centenary of Deaconess House in Oslo. Cathinka Guldberg was a pioneer of Norwegian nursing and the first deaconess.

Klas P. Arnoldson and Fredrik Bajer — A136

**1968, Dec. 10 Engr. *Perf. 13***
**521** A136 65o red brown .65 .30
**522** A136 90o dark blue 2.00 2.00

60th anniv. of the awarding of the Nobel Peace prize to Klas P. Arnoldson (1844-1916), Swedish writer and statesman, and to Fredrik Bajer (1837-1922), Danish writer and statesman.

**Nordic Cooperation Issue**

Five Ancient Ships — A136a

**1969, Feb. 28 Engr. *Perf. 13***
**523** A136a 65o red .35 .30
**524** A136a 90o blue 1.50 1.50

50th anniv. of the Nordic Society and centenary of postal cooperation among the northern countries. The design is taken from a coin found on the site of Birka, an ancient Swedish town.

See Demark Nos. 454-455, Finland No. 481, Iceland Nos. 404-405 and Sweden Nos. 808-810.

Ornament from Urnes Stave Church — A137

Traena Island
A138

**1969 Engr. *Perf. 13***
**526** A137 1.15k sepia 1.25 .50
**529** A138 3.50k bluish blk 2.00 .25

Issue dates: 1.15k, Jan. 23, 3.50k, June 18.

Plane, Train, Ship and Bus
A139

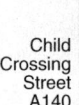

Child Crossing Street
A140

**1969, Mar. 24 Photo. *Perf. 13***
**531** A139 50o green 1.25 1.25
**532** A140 65o slate grn & dk red .75 .25

No. 531 for the centenary of the publication of "Rutebok of Norway" (Communications of Norway); No. 532 publicizes traffic safety.

**Europa Issue**
Common Design Type

**1969, Apr. 28 Size: 37x21mm**
**533** CD12 65o dk red & gray 1.00 .35
**534** CD12 90o chalky bl & gray 2.75 2.00

Johan Hjort — A141

Design: 90o, different emblem.

**1969, May 30 Engr. *Perf. 13***
**535** A141 40o brn & bl 1.50 1.25
**536** A141 90o bl & grn 2.50 2.25

Zoologist and oceanographer (1869-1948).

King Olav V — A142

**1969-83 Engr. *Perf. 13***
**537** A142 1k lt ol grn ('70) .65 .25
**538** A142 1.50k dk blue ('70) .85 .25
**539** A142 2k dk red ('70) .85 .25
**540** A142 5k vio bl ('70) 2.50 .25
**541** A142 10k org brn ('70) 5.00 .25
**542** A142 20k brown 12.00 .25
**543** A142 50k dk ol grn ('83) 22.00 1.00
*Nos. 537-543 (7)* 43.85 2.50

Man, Woman and Child, by Vigeland
A143

65o, Mother and Child, by Gustav Vigeland.

**1969, Sept. 8 Photo. *Perf. 13***
**545** A143 65o car rose & blk .50 .35
**546** A143 90o blue & black 1.50 1.50

Gustav Vigeland (1869-1943), sculptor.

People
A144

**1969, Oct. 10**
**547** A144 65o Punched card .75 .35
**548** A144 90o shown 1.50 1.50

1st Norwegian census, 200th anniv.

Queen Maud — A145

**1969, Nov. 26 Engr. *Perf. 13***
**549** A145 65o dk carmine .80 .40
**550** A145 90o violet blue 1.50 1.50

Queen Maud (1869-1938), wife of King Haakon VII.

Pulsatilla Vernalis — A146

European Nature Conservation Year: 40o, Wolf. 70o, Voringsfossen (waterfall). 100o, White-tailed sea eagle, horiz.

**1970, Apr. 10 Photo. *Perf. 13***
**551** A146 40o sep & pale bl 1.50 1.50
**552** A146 60o lt brn & gray 3.00 3.00
**553** A146 70o pale bl & brn 1.50 .60
**554** A146 100o pale bl & brn 2.50 2.50
*Nos. 551-554 (4)* 8.50 7.60

"V" for Victory — A147

Design: 100o, Convoy, horiz.

***Perf. 13x12½, 12½x13***
**1970, May 8 Photo.**
**555** A147 70o red & lilac 2.50 .65
**556** A147 100o vio bl & brt grn 2.50 2.25

Norway's liberation from the Germans, 25th anniv.

"Citizens" — A148

Designs: 70o, "The City and the Mountains." 100o, "Ships."

**1970, June 23 Engr. *Perf. 13***
**557** A148 40o green 2.50 2.00
**558** A148 70o rose claret 3.00 .50
**559** A148 100o violet blue 2.50 2.50
*Nos. 557-559 (3)* 8.00 5.00

City of Bergen, 900th anniversary.

Olive Wreath and Hands Upholding Globe — A149

**1970, Sept. 15 Engr. *Perf. 13***
**560** A149 70o dk car rose 3.00 .50
**561** A149 100o steel blue 2.00 1.75

25th anniversary of the United Nations.

Georg Ossian Sars (1837-1927) — A150

Portraits: 50o, Hans Strom (1726-1797). 70o, Johan Ernst Gunnerus (1718-1773). 100o, Michael Sars (1805-1869).

**1970, Oct. 15 Engr. *Perf. 13***
**562** A150 40o brown 1.75 1.75
**563** A150 50o dull purple 1.50 1.25
**564** A150 70o brown red 1.50 .50
**565** A150 100o bright blue 1.75 1.50
*Nos. 562-565 (4)* 6.50 5.00

Issued to honor Norwegian zoologists.

Central School of Gymnastics, Oslo, Cent. — A151

50o, Ball game, vert. 70o, Leapfrog.

**1970, Nov. 17 Photo. *Perf. 13***
**566** A151 50o dk blue, brn 1.00 .40
**567** A151 70o red, brn, blk 1.50 .25

Seal of Tonsberg
A152

**1971, Jan. 20 Photo. *Perf. 13***
**568** A152 70o dark red .85 .30
**569** A152 100o blue black 1.75 1.50

City of Tonsberg, 1,100th anniversary.

Parliament
A153

**1971, Feb. 23**
**570** A153 70o red brn & lil .75 .30
**571** A153 100o dk bl & sl grn 1.75 1.50

Centenary of annual sessions of Norwegian Parliament.

Hand, Heart and Eye A154

**1971, Mar. 26 Photo. *Perf. 13***
**572** A154 50o emerald & blk .75 .75
**573** A154 70o scarlet & blk .75 .30

Joint northern campaign for the benefit of refugees.

"Haugianerne" by Adolph Tiedemand — A155

**1971, Apr. 27 Photo. *Perf. 13***
**574** A155 60o dark gray .75 .75
**575** A155 70o brown .75 .35

Hans Nielsen Hauge (1771-1824), church reformer.

Worshippers Coming to Church — A156

Design: 70o, Building first church, vert.

**1971, May 21**
**576** A156 70o black & dk red .50 .35
**577** A156 1k black & blue 2.25 2.00

900th anniversary of the Bishopric of Oslo.

Roald Amundsen, Antarctic Treaty Emblem A157

**1971, June 23 Engr. *Perf. 13***
**578** A157 100o blue & org red 4.00 3.00

Antarctic Treaty pledging peaceful uses of and scientific cooperation in Antarctica, 10th anniv.

The Farmer and the Woman — A158

Designs: 50o, The Preacher and the King, horiz. 70o, The Troll and the Girl. Illustrations for legends and folk tales by Erik Werenskiold.

**1971, Nov. 17 Photo. *Perf. 13***
**579** A158 40o olive & blk 1.00 .50
**580** A158 50o blue & blk 1.00 .50
**581** A158 70o magenta & blk .85 .25
*Nos. 579-581 (3)* 2.85 1.25

Engine Turning A159

**1972, Apr. 10 Photo. *Perf. 13***
**582** A159 80o red & gold .80 .30
**583** A159 1.20k ultra & gold 1.50 1.25

Norwegian Savings Bank sesquicentennial.

Norway #18 — A160

**Engr. & Photo.**
**1972, May 6 *Perf. 12***
**584** A160 80o shown .75 .50
**585** A160 1k Norway #17 .75 .50
*a.* Souvenir sheet of 2, #584-585 6.00 10.00

Centenary of the post horn stamps. No. 585a sold for 2.50k.

Dragon's Head, Oseberg Viking Ship — A161

Ancient Artifacts: 50o, Horseman from Stone of Alstad. 60o, Horseman, wood carving, stave church, Hemsedal. 1.20k, Sword hilt, found at Lodingen.

**1972, June 7 Engr. *Perf. 13***
**586** A161 50o yellow grn .75 .75
**587** A161 60o brown 1.75 1.75
**588** A161 80o dull red 2.00 .45
**589** A161 1.20k ultra 1.75 1.75
*Nos. 586-589 (4)* 6.25 4.70

1,100th anniversary of unification.

King Haakon VII (1872-1957) — A162

**1972, Aug. 3 Engr. *Perf. 13***
**590** A162 80o brown orange 3.50 .35
**591** A162 1.20k Prussian bl 2.00 2.00

"Joy" — A163

Design: 1.20k, "Solidarity."

**1972, Aug. 15 Photo. *Perf. 13x13½***
**592** A163 80o brt magenta .75 .30
**593** A163 1.20k Prussian blue 1.75 1.50

2nd Intl. Youth Stamp Exhib., INTERJUNEX 72, Kristiansand, Aug. 25-Sept. 3.

**Nos. 592-593 Overprinted "INTERJUNEX 72"**

**1972, Aug. 25**
**594** A163 80o brt magenta 3.25 3.75
**595** A163 1.20k Prussian blue 3.25 3.75

Opening of INTERJUNEX 72. Sold at exhibition only together with 3k entrance ticket.

"Fram." — A164

Polar Exploration Ships: 60o, "Maud." 1.20k, "Gjoa."

**1972, Sept. 20 *Perf. 13½x13***
**596** A164 60o olive & green 1.75 1.25
**597** A164 80o red & black 3.50 .35
**598** A164 1.20k blue & red brn 2.50 2.00
*Nos. 596-598 (3)* 7.75 3.60

"Little Man" — A165

Illustrations for folk tales by Theodor Kittelsen (1857-1914): 60o, The Troll who wondered how old he was. 80o, The princess riding the polar bear.

**1972, Nov. 15 Litho. *Perf. 13½x13***
**599** A165 50o green & blk 1.00 .25
**600** A165 60o blue & blk 1.25 1.25
**601** A165 80o pink & blk 1.00 .25
*Nos. 599-601 (3)* 3.25 1.75

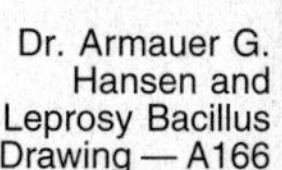

Dr. Armauer G. Hansen and Leprosy Bacillus Drawing — A166

Design: 1.40k, Dr. Hansen and leprosy bacillus, microscopic view.

**1973, Feb. 28 Engr. *Perf. 13x13½***
**602** A166 1k henna brn & bl .75 .25
**603** A166 1.40k dk bl & dp org 1.50 1.50

Centenary of the discovery of the Hansen bacillus, the cause of leprosy.

**Europa Issue**
Common Design Type

**1973, Apr. 30 Photo. *Perf. 12½x13***
**Size: 37x20mm**
**604** CD16 1k red, org & lil *4.00 .40*
**605** CD16 1.40k dk grn, grn & bl *2.25 2.00*

**Types of 1893 and 1962-63**

Designs: 75o, 85o, Rye and fish. 80o, 140o, Stave church. 100o, 110o, 120o, 125o, Rock carvings.

**1972-75 Engr. *Perf. 13x13½***
**606** A10 25o ultra ('74) .25 .25
Complete booklet, pane of 4 of #606 2.50
**608** A101 75o green ('73) .25 .25
**609** A102 80o red brown .50 .35
Complete booklet, pane of 10 of #609 65.00
**610** A101 85o bister ('74) .25 .25
**611** A101 100o red ('73) .75 .25
Complete booklet, pane of 10 of #611 50.00
**612** A101 110o rose car ('74) .50 .25
**613** A101 120o gray blue .75 .50
**614** A101 125o red ('75) .85 .25
Complete booklet, pane of 10 of #614 20.00
**615** A102 140o dk blue ('73) .75 .35
*Nos. 606-615 (9)* 4.85 2.70

**Nordic Cooperation Issue**

Nordic House, Reykjavik A167

**1973, June 26 Engr. *Perf. 12½***
**617** A167 1k multi 1.25 .40
**618** A167 1.40k multi 1.50 1.75

A century of postal cooperation among Denmark, Finland, Iceland, Norway and Sweden; Nordic Postal Conference, Reykjavik, Iceland.

King Olav V — A168

**1973, July 2 Engr. *Perf. 13***
**619** A168 1k car & org brn 1.50 .25
**620** A168 1.40k blue & org brn 1.75 1.75

70th birthday of King Olav V.

Jacob Aall — A169

**1973, Aug. 22 Engr. *Perf. 13***
**621** A169 1k deep claret .75 .25
**622** A169 1.40k dk blue gray 1.50 1.50

Jacob Aall (1773-1844), mill owner and industrial pioneer.

Blade Decoration — A170

Handicraft from Lapland: 1k, Textile pattern. 1.40k, Decoration made of tin.

**1973, Oct. 9 Photo. *Perf. 13x12½***
**623** A170 75o blk brn & buff .60 .60
**624** A170 1k dp car & buff 1.25 .30
**625** A170 1.40k blk & dl bl 1.50 1.50
*Nos. 623-625 (3)* 3.35 2.40

Viola Biflora — A171

70o, Veronica Fruticans. 1k, Phyllodoce corrulea.

**1973, Nov. 15 Litho. *Perf. 13***
**626** A171 65o shown .60 .50
**627** A171 70o multicolored .75 .75
**628** A171 1k multicolored .75 .25
*Nos. 626-628 (3)* 2.10 1.50

See Nos. 754-756, 770-771.

Surveyor in Northern Norway, 1907 — A172

1.40k, South Norway Mountains map, 1851.

**1973, Dec. 14 Engr. *Perf. 13***
**629** A172 1k red orange .50 .25
**630** A172 1.40k slate blue 1.50 1.50

Geographical Survey of Norway, bicent.

Lindesnes A173

Design: 1.40k, North Cape.

**1974, Apr. 25 Photo. *Perf. 13***
**631** A173 1k olive 1.50 .50
**632** A173 1.40k dark blue 3.00 3.00


Ferry in Hardanger Fjord, by A. Tidemand and H. Gude A174

Classical Norwegian paintings: 1.40k, Stugunoset from Filefjell, by Johan Christian Dahl.

**1974, May 21 Litho. *Perf. 13***

| | | | | |
|---|---|---|---|---|
| **633** | A174 | 1k multi | .75 | .25 |
| **634** | A174 | 1.40k multi | 1.50 | 1.50 |

Gulating Law Manuscript, 1325 A175

King Magnus VI Lagaböter A176

**1974, June 21 Engr.**

| | | | | |
|---|---|---|---|---|
| **635** | A175 | 1k red & brn | .75 | .25 |
| **636** | A176 | 1.40k ultra & brn | 1.75 | 1.75 |

700th anniv. of the National Code given by King Magnus VI Lagaböter (1238-80).

Saw Blade and Pines — A177

Design: 1k, Cog wheel and guard.

**1974, Aug. 12 Photo. *Perf. 13***

| | | | | |
|---|---|---|---|---|
| **637** | A177 | 85o grn, ol & dk grn | 2.50 | 2.50 |
| **638** | A177 | 1k org, plum & dk red | 1.75 | .40 |

Safe working conditions.

J.H.L. Vogt — A178

Geologists: 85o, V. M. Goldschmidt. 1k, Theodor Kjerulf. 1.40k, Waldemar C. Brogger.

**1974, Sept. 4 Engr. *Perf. 13***

| | | | | |
|---|---|---|---|---|
| **639** | A178 | 65o olive & red brn | .50 | .25 |
| **640** | A178 | 85o mag & red brn | 2.00 | 2.00 |
| **641** | A178 | 1k org & red brn | .75 | .25 |
| **642** | A178 | 1.40k blue & red brn | 1.50 | 1.50 |
| | | *Nos. 639-642 (4)* | 4.75 | 4.00 |

"Man's Work," Famous Buildings A179

Design: 1.40k, "Men, our brethren," people of various races.

**1974, Oct. 9 Photo. *Perf. 13***

| | | | | |
|---|---|---|---|---|
| **643** | A179 | 1k green & brn | 1.00 | .25 |
| **644** | A179 | 1.40k brn & grnsh bl | 1.50 | 1.50 |

Centenary of Universal Postal Union.

Horseback Rider A180

Flowers A181

**1974, Nov. 15 Litho. *Perf. 13***

| | | | | |
|---|---|---|---|---|
| **645** | A180 | 85o multicolored | .50 | .50 |
| **646** | A181 | 1k multicolored | .50 | .25 |

Norwegian folk art, rose paintings from furniture decorations.

Woman Skier, c. 1900 A182

**1975, Jan. 15 Litho. *Perf. 13***

| | | | | |
|---|---|---|---|---|
| **647** | A182 | 1k shown | 1.00 | .25 |
| **648** | A182 | 1.40k Telemark turn | 1.25 | 1.25 |

"Norway, homeland of skiing."

Women — A183

Design: Detail from wrought iron gates of Vigeland Park, Oslo.

**1975, Mar. 7 Litho. *Perf. 13***

| | | | | |
|---|---|---|---|---|
| **649** | A183 | 1.25k brt rose lil & dk bl | .65 | .25 |
| **650** | A183 | 1.40k bl & dk bl | 1.25 | 1.25 |

International Women's Year.

Nusfjord Fishing Harbor — A184

1.25k, Street in Stavanger. 1.40k, View of Roros.

**1975, Apr. 17 Litho. *Perf. 13***

| | | | | |
|---|---|---|---|---|
| **651** | A184 | 1k yellow green | 1.00 | .65 |
| **652** | A184 | 1.25k dull red | .75 | .25 |
| **653** | A184 | 1.40k blue | 1.50 | 1.50 |
| | | *Nos. 651-653 (3)* | 3.25 | 2.40 |

European Architectural Heritage Year.

Norwegian Krone, 1875 — A185

Ole Jacob Broch — A186

**1975, May 20 Engr. *Perf. 13***

| | | | | |
|---|---|---|---|---|
| **654** | A185 | 1.25k dark carmine | 1.00 | .25 |
| **655** | A186 | 1.40k blue | 1.25 | 1.25 |

Centenary of Monetary Convention of Norway, Sweden and Denmark (1.25k); and of Intl. Meter Convention, Paris, 1875. Ole Jacob Broch (1818-1889) was first director of Intl. Bureau of Weights and Measures.

Scouting in Summer A187

Design: 1.40k, Scouting in winter (skiers).

**1975, June 19 Litho. *Perf. 13***

| | | | | |
|---|---|---|---|---|
| **656** | A187 | 1.25k multicolored | 1.25 | .35 |
| **657** | A187 | 1.40k multicolored | 1.50 | 1.50 |

Nordjamb 75, 14th Boy Scout Jamboree, Lillehammer, July 29-Aug. 7.

Sod Hut and Settlers A188

Cleng Peerson and Letter from America, 1874 A189

**1975, July 4 Engr.**

| | | | | |
|---|---|---|---|---|
| **658** | A188 | 1.25k red brown | 1.00 | .25 |
| **659** | A189 | 1.40k bluish blk | 1.50 | 1.50 |

Sesquicentennial of Norwegian emigration to America.

Templet, Tempelfjord, Spitsbergen A190

Miners Leaving Coal Pit — A191

Design: 1.40k, Polar bear.

**1975, Aug. 14 Engr. *Perf. 13***

| | | | | |
|---|---|---|---|---|
| **660** | A190 | 1k olive black | 1.25 | 1.00 |
| **661** | A191 | 1.25k maroon | 1.25 | .25 |
| **662** | A191 | 1.40k Prus blue | 2.50 | 2.25 |
| | | *Nos. 660-662 (3)* | 5.00 | 3.50 |

50th anniversary of union of Spitsbergen (Svalbard) with Norway.

Microphone with Ear Phones — A192

Radio Tower and Houses — A193

Designs after children's drawings.

**1975, Oct. 9 Litho. *Perf. 13***

| | | | | |
|---|---|---|---|---|
| **663** | A192 | 1.25k multi | .60 | .25 |
| **664** | A193 | 1.40k multi | 1.10 | 1.10 |

50 years of broadcasting in Norway.

Annunciation A194

Nativity — A195

Painted vault of stave church of Al, 13th cent: 1k, Visitation. 1.40k, Adoration of the Kings.

**1975, Nov. 14**

| | | | | |
|---|---|---|---|---|
| **665** | A194 | 80o red & multi | .60 | .25 |
| **666** | A194 | 1k red & multi | .75 | .50 |
| **667** | A195 | 1.25k red & multi | .60 | .25 |
| **668** | A195 | 1.40k red & multi | 1.00 | 1.25 |
| | | *Nos. 665-668 (4)* | 2.95 | 2.25 |

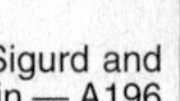

Sigurd and Regin — A196

**1976, Jan. 20 Engr. *Perf. 13***

| | | | | |
|---|---|---|---|---|
| **669** | A196 | 7.50k brown | 4.00 | .25 |

Norwegian folk tale, Sigurd the Dragonkiller. Design from portal of Hylestad stave church, 13th century.

Halling, Hallingdal Dance — A197

Folk Dances: 1k, Springar, Hordaland region. 1.25k, Gangar, Setesdal.

**1976, Feb. 25 Litho. *Perf. 13***

| | | | | |
|---|---|---|---|---|
| **670** | A197 | 80o black & multi | 1.00 | .75 |
| **671** | A197 | 1k black & multi | 1.00 | .75 |
| **672** | A197 | 1.25k black & multi | .75 | .25 |
| | | *Nos. 670-672 (3)* | 2.75 | 1.75 |

Silver Sugar Shaker, Stavanger, c. 1770 — A198

1.40k, Goblet, Nostetangen glass, c. 1770.

**1976, Mar. 25 Engr. *Perf. 13***

| | | | | |
|---|---|---|---|---|
| **673** | A198 | 1.25k multicolored | .85 | .40 |
| **674** | A198 | 1.40k multicolored | 1.00 | 1.25 |

Oslo Museum of Applied Art, centenary.

Ceramic Bowl Shaped Like Bishop's Mitre A199

Europa: 1.40k, Plate and CEPT emblem. Both designs after faience works from Herrebo Potteries, c. 1760.

**1976, May 3 Litho. *Perf. 13***

| | | | | |
|---|---|---|---|---|
| **675** | A199 | 1.25k rose mag & brn | *.75* | *.40* |
| **676** | A199 | 1.40k brt bl & vio bl | *1.25* | *1.25* |

The Pulpit, Lyse Fjord — A200

Gulleplet (Peak), Sogne Fjord — A201

***Perf. 13 on 3 Sides***

**1976, May 20 Litho.**

| | | | | |
|---|---|---|---|---|
| **677** | A200 | 1k multi | .60 | .25 |
| *a.* | | Booklet pane of 10 | 6.50 | |
| | | Complete booklet, #677a | 7.50 | |
| **678** | A201 | 1.25k multi | 1.00 | .25 |
| *a.* | | Booklet pane of 10 | 10.00 | |
| | | Complete booklet, #678a | 12.00 | |

Nos. 677-678 issued only in booklets.

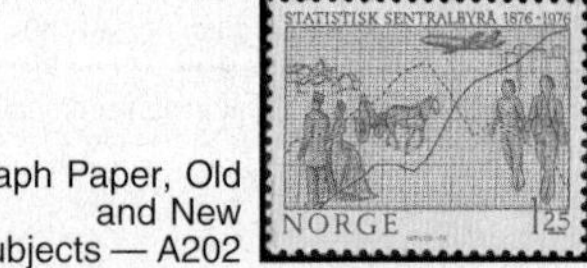

Graph Paper, Old and New Subjects — A202

Design: 2k, Graph of national product.

**1976, July 1 Engr. Perf. 13**

| | | | | |
|---|---|---|---|---|
| **679** | A202 | 1.25k red brown | .70 | .25 |
| **680** | A202 | 2k dark blue | 1.00 | .50 |

Central Bureau of Statistics, centenary.

Olav Duun on Dun Mountain A203

**1976, Sept. 10 Engr. Perf. 13**

| | | | | |
|---|---|---|---|---|
| **681** | A203 | 1.25k multi | .70 | .25 |
| **682** | A203 | 1.40k multi | 1.00 | 1.00 |

Olav Duun (1876-1939), novelist.

"Birches" by Th. Fearnley (1802-1842) A204

Design: 1.40k, "Gamle Furutraer" (trees), by L. Hertervig (1830-1902).

**1976, Oct. 8 Litho. Perf. 13**

| | | | | |
|---|---|---|---|---|
| **683** | A204 | 1.25k multi | .80 | .25 |
| **684** | A204 | 1.40k multi | 1.25 | 1.25 |

"April" — A205

"May" — A206

Baldishol Tapestry — A207

80o, 1k, Details from 13th cent. Baldishol tapestry, found in Baldishol stave church.

**1976, Nov. 5 Litho. Perf. 13**

| | | | | |
|---|---|---|---|---|
| **685** | A205 | 80o multi | .50 | .25 |
| **686** | A206 | 1k multi | .65 | .50 |
| **687** | A207 | 1.25k multi | .60 | .25 |
| | | *Nos. 685-687 (3)* | 1.75 | 1.00 |

Five Water Lilies — A208

**Photo. & Engr.**

**1977, Feb. 2 Perf. 12½**

| | | | | |
|---|---|---|---|---|
| **688** | A208 | 1.25k multi | .75 | .30 |
| **689** | A208 | 1.40k multi | .75 | 1.00 |

Nordic countries cooperation for protection of the environment and 25th Session of Nordic Council, Helsinki, Feb. 19.

Akershus Castle, Oslo — A209

Steinviksholm Fort, Asen Fjord — A210

Torungen Lighthouses, Arendal — A211

**1977, Feb. 24 Engr. Perf. 13**

| | | | | |
|---|---|---|---|---|
| **690** | A209 | 1.25k red | .70 | .25 |
| | | Complete booklet pane of 10 #690 | 12.00 | |
| | | Complete booklet pane of 8 #690 | 8.50 | |
| **691** | A210 | 1.30k olive brown | .75 | .25 |
| **692** | A211 | 1.80k blue | .85 | .25 |
| | | *Nos. 690-692 (3)* | 2.30 | .75 |

See Nos. 715-724, 772-774.

**Europa Issue**

Hamnoy, Lofoten, Fishing Village — A212

Huldre Falls, Loen — A213

***Perf. 13 on 3 Sides***

**1977, May 2 Litho.**

| | | | | |
|---|---|---|---|---|
| **693** | A212 | 1.25k multi | 1.00 | .25 |
| *a.* | | Booklet pane of 10 | 10.00 | |
| | | Complete booklet, #693a | 12.00 | |
| **694** | A213 | 1.80k multi | 1.00 | 1.00 |
| *a.* | | Booklet pane of 10 | 10.00 | |
| | | Complete booklet, #694a | 12.00 | |

Nos. 693-694 issued only in booklets.

Norwegian Trees — A214

**1977, June 1 Engr. Perf. 13**

| | | | | |
|---|---|---|---|---|
| **695** | A214 | 1k Spruce | .75 | .50 |
| **696** | A214 | 1.25k Fir | .75 | .25 |
| **697** | A214 | 1.80k Birch | 1.25 | 1.25 |
| | | *Nos. 695-697 (3)* | 2.75 | 2.00 |

"Constitutionen," Norway's 1st Steamship, at Arendal — A215

Designs: 1.25k, "Vesteraalen" off Bodo, 1893. 1.30k, "Kong Haakon," 1904 and "Dronningen," 1893, off Stavanger. 1.80k, "Nordstjernen" and "Harald Jarl" at pier, 1970.

**1977, June 22**

| | | | | |
|---|---|---|---|---|
| **698** | A215 | 1k brown | .60 | .25 |
| **699** | A215 | 1.25k red | 1.00 | .25 |
| **700** | A215 | 1.30k green | 2.00 | 1.75 |
| **701** | A215 | 1.80k blue | 1.50 | 1.25 |
| | | *Nos. 698-701 (4)* | 5.10 | 3.50 |

Norwegian ships serving coastal routes.

Fishermen and Boats — A216

Fish and Fishhooks A217

**1977, Sept. 22 Engr. Perf. 13**

| | | | | |
|---|---|---|---|---|
| **702** | A216 | 1.25k buff, lt brn & dk brn | 1.00 | .25 |
| **703** | A217 | 1.80k lt bl, bl & dk bl | 1.25 | 1.25 |

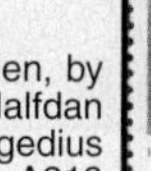

Men, by Halfdan Egedius A218

Landscape, by August Cappelen A219

**1977, Oct. 7 Litho. Perf. 13**

| | | | | |
|---|---|---|---|---|
| **704** | A218 | 1.25k multi | .60 | .25 |
| **705** | A219 | 1.80k multi | 1.25 | 1.25 |

Norwegian classical painting.

David with the Bells — A220

Christmas: 1k, Singing Friars. 1.25k, Virgin and Child, horiz. Designs from Bible of Bishop Aslak Bolt, 13th century.

**1977, Nov. 10 Litho. Perf. 13**

**Size: 21x27mm**

| | | | | |
|---|---|---|---|---|
| **706** | A220 | 80o multi | .50 | .25 |
| **707** | A220 | 1k multi | .50 | .35 |

**Size: 34x27mm**

| | | | | |
|---|---|---|---|---|
| **708** | A220 | 1.25k multi | .75 | .25 |
| | | *Nos. 706-708 (3)* | 1.75 | .85 |

**Post Horn Type of 1893 and Scenic Types of 1977**

Designs: 1k, Austrat Manor, 1650. 1.10k, Trondenes Chruch, early 13th Cent. 1.40k, Ruins of Hamar Cathedral, 12th Cent. 1.75k, Seamen's Hall, Stavern, 1926, vert. 2k, Tofte Estate, Dovre, 16-17th cent., vert. 2.25k, Oscarhall, Oslofijord, 1847, vert. 2.50k, Log house, Breiland, 1785. 2.75k, Damsgard Building, Lakesvag, 1770. 3k, Selje Monastery, 11th cent. 3.50k, Lighthouse, Lindesnes, 1655.

***Perf. 13x13½, 13½x13***

**1978-83 Engr.**

| | | | | |
|---|---|---|---|---|
| **709** | A10 | 40o olive | .30 | .25 |
| **710** | A10 | 50o dull purple | .30 | .25 |
| **711** | A10 | 60o vermilion | .30 | .25 |
| **712** | A10 | 70o orange | .50 | .30 |
| **713** | A10 | 80o red brown | .50 | .35 |
| **714** | A10 | 90o brown | .60 | .60 |
| **715** | A209 | 1k green | .50 | .25 |
| | | Complete booklet, pane of 4 ea #416, 419, 715 | 15.00 | |
| **716** | A209 | 1.10k rose mag | .75 | .25 |
| **717** | A209 | 1.40k dark purple | .90 | .30 |
| **718** | A211 | 1.75k green ('82) | .75 | .25 |
| **719** | A211 | 2k brown red ('82) | .75 | .25 |
| **720** | A211 | 2.25k dp vio ('82) | 1.00 | .50 |
| **721** | A209 | 2.50k brn red ('83) | 1.00 | .25 |
| **722** | A209 | 2.75k dp mag ('82) | 1.50 | 1.25 |
| **723** | A209 | 3k dk bl ('82) | 1.25 | .25 |
| **724** | A209 | 3.50k dp vio ('83) | 1.25 | .30 |
| | | *Nos. 709-724 (16)* | 12.15 | 5.85 |

See Nos. 772-774.

Peer Gynt, and Reindeer by Per Krogh — A222

Henrik Ibsen, by Erik Werenskiold, 1895 — A223

**1978, Mar. 10 Litho. Perf. 13**

| | | | | |
|---|---|---|---|---|
| **725** | A222 | 1.25k buff & blk | .80 | .25 |
| **726** | A223 | 1.80k multicolored | 1.25 | 1.00 |

Ibsen (1828-1906), poet and dramatist.

Heddal Stave Church, c. 1250 — A224

Europa: 1.80k, Borgund stave church.

**1978, May 2 Engr. Perf. 13**

| | | | | |
|---|---|---|---|---|
| **727** | A224 | 1.25k redsh brn & org | 1.25 | .45 |
| **728** | A224 | 1.80k sl grn & bl | 1.75 | 1.50 |

Lenangstindene and Jaegervasstindene — A225

1.25k, Gaustatoppen, mountain, Telemark.

***Perf. 13 on 3 Sides***

**1978, June 1 Litho.**

| | | | | |
|---|---|---|---|---|
| **729** | A225 | 1k multi | .55 | .40 |
| *a.* | | Booklet pane of 10 | 6.50 | |
| | | Complete booklet, #729a | 8.00 | |
| **730** | A225 | 1.25k multi | .70 | .25 |
| *a.* | | Booklet pane of 10 | 9.00 | |
| | | Complete booklet, #730a | 10.00 | |

Nos. 729-730 issued only in booklets.

Olav V Sailing A226

Design: 1.80k, King Olav delivering royal address in Parliament, vert.

**1978, June 30 Engr. Perf. 13**

| | | | | |
|---|---|---|---|---|
| **731** | A226 | 1.25k red brown | 1.25 | .25 |
| **732** | A226 | 1.80k violet blue | 1.25 | 1.25 |

75th birthday of King Olav V.

Norway No. 107 — A227

Stamps: b, #108. c, #109. d, #110. e, #111. f, #112. g, #113. h, #114.

***Perf. 13 on 3 Sides***

**1978, Sept. 19 Litho.**

| | | | |
|---|---|---|---|
| **733** | Booklet pane of 8 | 8.00 | 8.00 |
| *a.-h.* | A227 1.25k, any single | 1.00 | 1.00 |
| | Complete booklet, #733 | 8.00 | |

NORWEX '80 Philatelic Exhibition, Oslo, June 13-22, 1980. Booklet sold for 15k; the additional 5k went for financing the exhibition.

Willow Pipe Player A228

Musical Instruments: 1.25k, Norwegian violin. 1.80k, Norwegian zither. 7.50k, Ram's horn.

**1978, Oct. 6 Engr. Perf. 13**

| | | | | |
|---|---|---|---|---|
| **734** | A228 | 1k deep green | .35 | .25 |
| **735** | A228 | 1.25k dk rose car | .55 | .25 |
| **736** | A228 | 1.80k dk violet blue | 1.00 | 1.00 |
| **737** | A228 | 7.50k gray | 4.50 | .25 |
| | | *Nos. 734-737 (4)* | 6.40 | 1.75 |

Wooden Doll, 1830 — A229

Christmas: 1k, Toy town 1896-97. 1.25k, Wooden horse from Torpo in Hallingdal.

**1978, Nov. 10** **Litho.**

**738** A229 80o multi .50 .25
**739** A229 1k multi .50 .25
**740** A229 1.25k multi .70 .25
*Nos. 738-740 (3)* 1.70 .75

Ski Jump, Huseby Hill, c. 1900 — A230

1.25k, Crown Prince Olav, Holmenkollen ski jump competition, 1922. 1.80k, Cross-country race, Holmenkollen, 1976.

**1979, Mar. 2** **Engr.** ***Perf. 13***

**741** A230 1k green .75 .50
**742** A230 1.25k red 1.00 .25
**743** A230 1.80k blue 1.50 1.25
*Nos. 741-743 (3)* 3.25 2.00

Huseby Hills and Holmenkollen ski competitions, centenary.

Girl, by Mathias Stoltenberg A231

1.80k, Boy, by H. C. F. Hosenfelder.

**1979, Apr. 26** **Litho.** ***Perf. 13***

**744** A231 1.25k multi .75 .25
**745** A231 1.80k multi 1.00 1.00

International Year of the Child.

Road to Briksdal Glacier — A232

1.25k, Boat on Skjernoysund, near Mandal.

**1979, June 13** ***Perf. 13 on 3 Sides***

**746** A232 1k multi .60 .25
*a.* Booklet pane of 10 6.00
Complete booklet, #746a 7.00
**747** A232 1.25k multi .75 .25
*a.* Booklet pane of 10 7.50
Complete booklet, #747a 9.00

Nos. 746-747 issued only in booklets.

Johan Falkberget, by Harald Dal — A233

1.80k, "Ann-Magritt and the Hovi Bullock" (by Falkberget), monument by Kristofer Leirdal.

**1979, Sept. 4** **Engr.** ***Perf. 13***

**748** A233 1.25k deep claret .75 .25
**749** A233 1.80k Prus blue 1.10 1.00

Johan Falkberget (1879-1967), novelist.

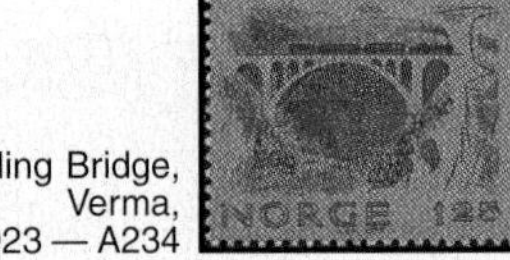

Kylling Bridge, Verma, 1923 — A234

Norwegian Engineering: 2k, Vessingsjo Dam, Nea, 1960. 10k, Stratfjord A, oil drilling platform in North Sea.

**1979, Oct. 5**

**750** A234 1.25k black & brown .60 .25
**751** A234 2k dk blue & blue 1.00 .40
**752** A234 10k brown & bister 5.00 .45
*Nos. 750-752 (3)* 6.60 1.10

Souvenir Sheet

Dornier Wal over Polar Map — A235

Arctic Aviation and Polar Maps: 2k, Dirigible Norge. 2.80k, Loening air yacht amphibian. 4k, Reidar Viking DC-7C.

**1979, Oct. 5** **Litho.** ***Perf. 13***

**753** Sheet of 4 7.00 7.00
*a.* A235 1.25k multi 1.50 1.50
*b.* A235 2k multi 1.50 1.50
*c.* A235 2.80k multi 1.50 1.50
*d.* A235 4k multi 1.50 1.50

Norwex '80 Intl. Phil. Exhib., Oslo, June 13-22, 1980. No. 753 sold for 15k.

**Mountain Flower Type of 1973**

80o, Ranunculus glacialis. 1k, Potentilla crantzii. 1.25k, Saxiflora oppositifolia.

**1979, Nov. 22** **Litho.** ***Perf. 13½***

**754** A171 80o multicolored .50 .25
**755** A171 1k multicolored .50 .25
**756** A171 1.25k multicolored .70 .25
*Nos. 754-756 (3)* 1.70 .75

Norwegian Christian Youth Assn. Centenary A237

180o, Emblems and doves.

**1980, Feb. 26** **Litho.** ***Perf. 13***

**757** A237 100o shown .70 .25
**758** A237 180o multicolored 1.00 1.00

Oyster Catcher — A238

***Perf. 13 on 3 Sides***

**1980, Apr. 18** **Litho.**

**759** A238 100o shown .35 .25
**760** A238 100o Mallard .35 .25
*a.* Bklt. pane, 5 #759, 5 #760 4.00
Complete booklet, #760a 5.00
**761** A238 125o Dipper .55 .25
**762** A238 125o Great tit .55 .25
*a.* Bklt. pane, 5 #761, 5 #762 5.50
Complete booklet, #762a 6.00
*Nos. 759-762 (4)* 1.80 1.00

Nos. 759-762 issued in booklets only. See Nos. 775-778, 800-801, 821-822.

Dish Antenna, Old Phone A239

National Telephone Service Centenary: 1.80k, Erecting telephone pole.

**1980, May 9** **Litho.** ***Perf. 13½***

**763** A239 1.25k multi .60 .25
**764** A239 1.80k multi 1.00 1.00

Souvenir Sheet

NORWEX '80 Stamp Exhibition — A240

**1980, June 13**

**765** A240 Sheet of 4 6.50 6.50
*a.* 1.25k Paddle Steamer "Bergen" 1.50 1.50
*b.* 2k Train, 1900 1.50 1.50
*c.* 2.80k Bus, 1940 1.50 1.50
*d.* 4k Boeing 737 1.50 1.50

NORWEX '80 Stamp Exhibition, Oslo, June 13-22. Sold for 15k.

**Nordic Cooperation Issue**

Vulcan as an Armourer, by Henrich Bech, 1761 — A241

Henrich Bech Cast Iron Stove Ornament: 1.80k, Hercules at a Burning Altar, 1769.

**1980, Sept. 9** **Engr.** ***Perf. 13***

**766** A241 1.25k dk vio brn .60 .25
**767** A241 1.80k dark blue 1.00 1.00

Self-Portrait, by Christian Skredsvig (1854-1924) A242

Paintings: 1.25k, Fire, by Nikolai Astrup.

**1980, Nov. 14** **Litho.** ***Perf. 13½x13***

**768** A242 1.25k multi .80 .25
**769** A242 1.80k multi 1.25 1.00

**Mountain Flower Type of 1973**

**1980, Nov. 14** ***Perf. 13***

**770** A171 80o Sorbus aucuparia .50 .25
**771** A171 1k Rosa canina .50 .25

**Scenic Type of 1977**

1.50k, Stavanger Cathedral, 13th cent. 1.70k, Rosenkrantz Tower, Bergen, 13th-16th cent. 2.20k, Church of Tromsdalen (Arctic Cathedral), 1965.

***Perf. 13x13½, 13½x13***

**1981, Feb. 26** **Engr.**

**772** A211 1.50k brown red .75 .25
**773** A211 1.70k olive green 1.00 .75
**774** A209 2.20k dark blue 1.25 .45
*Nos. 772-774 (3)* 3.00 1.45

**Bird Type of 1980**

***Perf. 13 on 3 Sides***

**1981, Feb. 26** **Litho.**

**775** A238 1.30k Anser erythropus .50 .50
**776** A238 1.30k Peregrine falcon .50 .50
*a.* Booklet pane of 10 (5 each) 5.50
Complete booklet, #776a 6.50
**777** A238 1.50k Black guillemot .65 .25
**778** A238 1.50k Puffin .65 .25
*a.* Booklet pane of 10 (5 each) 6.50
Complete booklet, #778a 7.50
*Nos. 775-778 (4)* 2.30 1.50

Nos. 775-778 issued in booklets. See Nos. 800-801, 821-822.

Nat'l Milk Producers Assn. Centenary A244

**1981, Mar. 24** **Litho.** ***Perf. 13x13½***

**779** A244 1.10k Cow .75 .25
**780** A244 1.50k Goat .75 .25

A245

Europa: 1.50k, The Mermaid, painted dish, Hol. 2.20k, The Proposal, painted box, Nes.

**1981, May 4** **Litho.** ***Perf. 13***

**781** A245 1.50k multi 1.00 .25
**782** A245 2.20k multi 1.25 .75

A246

Designs: 1.30k, Weighing anchor. 1.50k, Climbing rigging, vert. 2.20k, Training Ship Christian Radich.

**1981, May 4** **Engr.**

**783** A246 1.30k dk olive grn .75 .50
**784** A246 1.50k orange red .75 .25
**785** A246 2.20k dark blue 1.25 .75
*Nos. 783-785 (3)* 2.75 1.50

Paddle Steamer Skibladner, 1856, Mjosa Lake — A247

Lake Transportation: 1.30k, Victoria, 1882, Bandak Channel. 1.50k, Faemund II, 1905, Fermund Lake. 2.30k, Storegut, 1956, Tinnsjo Lake.

**1981, June 11** **Engr.** ***Perf. 13***

**786** A247 1.10k dark brown .75 .35
**787** A247 1.30k green 1.00 .50
**788** A247 1.50k red .75 .25
**789** A247 2.30k dark blue 1.25 .50
*Nos. 786-789 (4)* 3.75 1.60

Group Walking Arm in Arm — A248

**1981, Aug. 25** **Engr.**

**790** A248 1.50k shown .75 .25
**791** A248 2.20k Group, diff. 1.00 1.00

Intl. Year of the Disabled.

Paintings — A249

1.50k, Interior in Blue, by Harriet Backer (1845-1932). 1.70k, Peat Moor on Jaeren, by Kitty Lange Kielland (1843-1914).

**1981, Oct. 9** **Litho.** ***Perf. 13***

**792** A249 1.50k multi .75 .25
**793** A249 1.70k multi 1.00 .75

Tapestries — A250

1.10k, One of the Three Kings, Skjak, 1625. 1.30k, Adoration of the Infant Christ, tapestry, Skjak, 1625. 1.50k, The Marriage of Cana, Storen, 18th cent.

**1981, Nov. 25 Litho. *Perf. 13½***

**794** A250 1.10k multi .40 .25
**795** A250 1.30k multi .50 .50

**Size: 29x37mm**

**796** A250 1.50k multi .55 .25
*Nos. 794-796 (3)* 1.45 1.00

1921 Nobel Prize Winners A251

5k, Christian L. Lange (1869-1938) and Hjalmar Branting (1860-1925).

**1981, Nov. 25 Engr. *Perf. 13***

**797** A251 5k black 3.00 .40

World Skiing Championship, Oslo — A252

**1982, Feb. 16 *Perf. 13½***

**798** A252 2k Poles .75 .25
**799** A252 3k Skis 1.10 .60

**Bird Type of 1980**

***Perf. 13 on 3 Sides***

**1982, Apr. 1 Litho.**

**Booklet Stamps**

**800** A238 2k Blue-throat .75 .25
**801** A238 2k Robin .75 .25
*a.* Bklt. pane, 5 each #800-801 7.50
Complete booklet, #801a 8.50

Fight Against Tuberculosis A253

**1982, Apr. 1 *Perf. 13***

**802** A253 2k Nurse .50 .25
**803** A253 3k Microscope 1.00 .85

Jew's Harp — A254

**1982, May 3 Engr. *Perf. 13***

**804** A254 15k sepia 7.00 .35

Europa 1982 — A255

2k, Haakon VII, 1905. 3k, Prince Olav, King Haakon VII, 1945.

**1982, May 3**

**805** A255 2k brown red 2.50 .40
**806** A255 3k indigo 2.00 .75

Girls from Telemark, by Erik Werenskiold (1855-1938) A256

Design: 2k, Tone Veli at the Fence, by Henrik Sorensen (1882-1962), vert.

**1982, June 23 Litho. *Perf. 13***

**807** A256 1.75k multi .75 .50
**808** A256 2k multi .75 .25

Consecration Ceremony, Nidaros Cathedral, Trondheim A257

**1982, Sept. 2 Engr. *Perf. 13x13½***

**809** A257 3k blue 2.00 1.00

Reign of King Olav, 25th anniv.

Sigrid Undset (1882-1949), Writer, by A.C. Svarstad — A258

Painting: 1.75k, Bjornstjerne Bjornson (1832-1910), writer, by Erik Werenskiold, horiz.

**1982, Oct. 1 Litho. *Perf. 13***

**810** A258 1.75k multi 1.00 .50
**811** A258 2k multi 1.00 .25

A souvenir sheet containing Nos. 810-811 was prepared by the Norwegian Philatelic Association.

Graphical Union of Norway Centenary A259

**1982, Oct. 1**

**812** A259 2k "A" .75 .25
**813** A259 3k Type 1.25 .75

Fridtjof Nansen — A260

**1982, Nov. 15 Engr. *Perf. 13½x13***

**814** A260 3k dark blue 2.00 1.00

Fridtjof Nansen (1861-1930) polar explorer, 1922 Nobel Peace Prize winner.

Christmas — A261

Painting: Christmas Tradition, by Adolf Tidemand (1814-1876).

***Perf. 13 on 3 Sides***

**1982, Nov. 15 Litho.**

**815** A261 1.75k multi .50 .25
*a.* Booklet pane of 10 6.00
Complete booklet, #815a 6.75

Farm Dog — A262

**1983, Feb. 16 Litho. *Perf. 13x13½***

**816** A262 2k shown 1.25 .50
**817** A262 2.50k Elk hound 1.50 .25
**818** A262 3.50k Hunting dog 1.75 1.00
*Nos. 816-818 (3)* 4.50 1.75

Nordic Cooperation Issue — A263

**1983, Mar. 24 Litho. *Perf. 13***

**819** A263 2.50k Mountains 1.25 .25
**820** A263 3.50k Fjord 1.50 1.00

**Bird Type of 1980**

**1983, Apr. 14 *Perf. 13 on 3 Sides***

**821** A238 2.50k Goose 1.10 .25
**822** A238 2.50k Little auk 1.10 .25
*a.* Bklt. pane, 5 each #821-822 11.00
Complete booklet, #822a 12.00

Nos. 821-822 issued only in booklets.

Europa A264

Designs: 2.50k, Edvard Grieg (1843-1907), composer and his Piano Concerto in A-minor. 3.50k, Niels Henrik Abel (1802-1829), mathematician, by Gustav Vigeland, vert.

**1983, May 3 Engr. *Perf. 13***

**823** A264 2.50k red orange 2.25 .40
**824** A264 3.50k dk bl & grn 2.25 1.00

World Communications Year — A265

Symbolic arrow designs.

**1983, May 3 Litho.**

**825** A265 2.50k multi 1.25 .25
**826** A265 3.50k multi 1.25 .75

80th Birthday of King Olav V, July 2 — A266

**1983, June 22 Engr. *Perf. 13x13½***

**827** A266 5k green 3.00 .50

Jonas Lie (1833-1908), Writer — A267

**1983, Oct. 7 Engr. *Perf. 13½x13***

**828** A267 2.50k red 1.25 .25

Northern Ships — A268

**1983, Oct. 7 Litho.**

**829** A268 2k Nordlandsfemboring 1.25 .50
**830** A268 3k Nordlandsjekt 1.75 .75

Christmas 1983 — A269

Paintings: 2k, The Sleigh Ride by Axel Ender (1853-1920). 2.50k, The Guests are Arriving by Gustav Wenzel (1859-1927).

***Perf. 13 on 3 sides***

**1983, Nov. 17 Litho.**

**831** A269 2k multi 1.00 .25
*a.* Booklet pane of 10 10.00
Complete booklet, #831a 11.00
**832** A269 2.50k multi 1.10 .25
*a.* Booklet pane of 10 11.00
Complete booklet, #832a 12.00

Postal Services A270

**1984, Feb. 24 Litho. *Perf. 13½x13***

**833** A270 2k Counter service 1.00 .50
**834** A270 2.50k Sorting 1.10 .25
**835** A270 3.50k Delivery 1.75 1.00
*Nos. 833-835 (3)* 3.85 1.75

Freshwater Fishing — A271

**1984, Apr. 10 Engr. *Perf. 13***

**836** A271 2.50k shown 1.00 .25
**837** A271 3k Salmon fishing 1.50 .75
**838** A271 3.50k Ocean fishing 1.75 1.00
*Nos. 836-838 (3)* 4.25 2.00

Christopher Hansteen (1784-1873), Astronomer — A272

3.50k, Magnetic meridians, parallels, horiz.

**1984, Apr. 10**

**839** A272 3.50k multicolored 1.75 1.00
**840** A272 5k multicolored 2.50 .50

Europa (1959-84)
A273

**1984, June 4 Litho. *Perf. 13***

| | | | | |
|---|---|---|---|---|
| 841 | A273 | 2.50k multi | 2.00 | .40 |
| 842 | A273 | 3.50k multi | 2.00 | 1.20 |

Produce, Spices — A274

**1984, June 4 *Perf. 13***

| | | | | |
|---|---|---|---|---|
| 843 | A274 | 2k shown | 1.00 | .50 |
| 844 | A274 | 2.50k Flowers | 1.10 | .25 |

Horticultural Society centenary.

A275

**1984, June 4**

| | | | | |
|---|---|---|---|---|
| 845 | A275 | 2.50k Worker bees | 1.00 | .25 |
| 846 | A275 | 2.50k Rooster | 1.00 | .25 |

Centenaries: Beekeeping Society (No. 845); Poultry-breeding Society (No. 846).

A276

**1984, Oct. 5 Engr. *Perf. 13***

| | | | | |
|---|---|---|---|---|
| 847 | A276 | 2.50k lake | 1.40 | .25 |

Ludvig Holberg (1684-1754), writer, by J.M. Bernigeroth.

A277

**1984, Oct. 5 Litho. & Engr.**

| | | | | |
|---|---|---|---|---|
| 848 | A277 | 2.50k Children reading | .75 | .25 |
| 849 | A277 | 3.50k First edition | 1.25 | 1.00 |

Norwegian Weekly Press sesquicentennial.

A278

Illustrations from Children's Stories by Thorbjorn Egner: No. 850, Karius & Baktus. No. 851, Tree Shrew. No. 852, Cardamom Rovers. No. 853, Chief Constable Bastian.

***Perf. 13½x13 on 3 sides***

**1984, Nov. 15 Litho.**

**Booklet Stamps**

| | | | | |
|---|---|---|---|---|
| 850 | A278 | 2k multi | 1.75 | .50 |
| 851 | A278 | 2k multi | 1.75 | .50 |
| a. | | Bklt. pane, 5 each #850-851 | 17.50 | |
| | | Complete booklet, #851a | 24.00 | |
| 852 | A278 | 2.50k multi | 2.50 | .25 |
| 853 | A278 | 2.50k multi | 2.50 | .25 |
| a. | | Bklt. pane, 5 each #852-853 | 25.00 | |
| | | Complete booklet, #853a | 27.50 | |
| | | *Nos. 850-853 (4)* | 8.50 | 1.50 |

Parliament Centenary — A279

7.50k, Sverdrup Govt. parliament, 1884.

**1984, Nov. 15 Engr. *Perf. 13½x13***

| | | | | |
|---|---|---|---|---|
| 854 | A279 | 7.50k multicolored | 4.50 | 1.00 |

Antarctic Mountains
A280

2.50k, The Saw Blade. 3.50k, The Chopping Block.

**1985, Apr. 18 Litho. *Perf. 13***

| | | | | |
|---|---|---|---|---|
| 855 | A280 | 2.50k multi | 1.75 | .25 |
| 856 | A280 | 3.50k multi | 2.25 | 1.00 |

Liberation from the German Occupation Forces, 40th Anniv.
A281

**1985, May 8 Engr. *Perf. 13x13½***

| | | | | |
|---|---|---|---|---|
| 857 | A281 | 3.50k dk bl & red | 2.25 | 1.00 |

Norwegian Artillery
A282

Anniv.: 3k, Norwegian Artillery, 300th. 4k, Artillery Officers Training School, 200th.

**1985, May 22 Litho. *Perf. 13½x13***

| | | | | |
|---|---|---|---|---|
| 858 | A282 | 3k multi | 1.75 | 1.00 |
| 859 | A282 | 4k multi | 2.25 | .50 |

Kongsten Fort, 300th Anniv.
A283

**1985, May 22**

| | | | | |
|---|---|---|---|---|
| 860 | A283 | 2.50k multi | 1.50 | .25 |

Europa — A284

Designs: 2.50k, Torgeir Augundsson (1801-1872), fiddler. 3.50k, Ole Bull (1810-1880), composer, violinist.

**1985, June 19 Engr.**

| | | | | |
|---|---|---|---|---|
| 861 | A284 | 2.50k brown lake | 2.00 | .30 |
| 862 | A284 | 3.50k dark blue | 2.50 | 1.00 |

Intl. Youth Year — A285

Stone and bronze sculptures: 2k, Boy and Girl, detail, Vigeland Museum, Oslo. 3.50k, Fountain, detail, Vigeland Park, Oslo.

**1985, June 19 Litho.**

| | | | | |
|---|---|---|---|---|
| 863 | A285 | 2k multi | 1.00 | .50 |
| 864 | A285 | 3.50k multi | 2.25 | 1.25 |

Electrification of Norway, Cent. — A286

2.50k, Glomfjord Dam penstock. 4k, Linemen.

**1985, Sept. 6 Engr. *Perf. 13½x13***

| | | | | |
|---|---|---|---|---|
| 865 | A286 | 2.50k dp car & scar | 1.25 | .25 |
| 866 | A286 | 4k ultra & bl grn | 2.00 | .50 |

Public Libraries, 200th Anniv.
A287

Designs; 2.50k, Carl Deichman (1705-1780), Public Libraries System founder. 10k, Modern library interior, horiz.

**1985, Oct. 4**

| | | | | |
|---|---|---|---|---|
| 867 | A287 | 2.50k hn brn & yel brn | 1.50 | .25 |
| 868 | A287 | 10k dark green | 6.00 | .75 |

Ship Navigation
A288

2.50k, Dredger Berghavn, 1980. 5k, Sextant and chart, 1791.

**Lithographed & Engraved**

**1985, Nov. 14 *Perf. 13x13½***

| | | | | |
|---|---|---|---|---|
| 869 | A288 | 2.50k multicolored | 1.25 | .25 |
| 870 | A288 | 5k multicolored | 2.75 | .50 |

Port Authorities, 250th anniv., Hydrographic Services, bicent.

Christmas Wreath
A289

Bullfinches
A290

**Booklet Stamps**

***Perf. 13½ on 3 Sides***

**1985, Nov. 14 Litho.**

| | | | | |
|---|---|---|---|---|
| 871 | A289 | 2k multi | 2.00 | .25 |
| a. | | Booklet pane of 10 | 20.00 | |
| | | Complete booklet, #871a | 22.50 | |
| 872 | A290 | 2.50k multi | 2.00 | .25 |
| a. | | Booklet pane of 10 | 20.00 | |
| | | Complete booklet, #872a | 22.50 | |

World Biathlon Championships, Feb. 18-23 — A290a

3.50k, Shooting upright.

**1986, Feb. 18 *Perf. 13x13½***

| | | | | |
|---|---|---|---|---|
| 873 | A290a | 2.50k shown | 1.25 | .25 |
| 874 | A291 | 3.50k multicolored | 1.75 | 1.00 |

Ornaments
A291

Fauna
A292

**Litho. & Engr.**

**1986-90 *Perf. 13½x13***

| | | | | |
|---|---|---|---|---|
| 875 | A291 | 2.10k Sun | 1.00 | .25 |
| 876 | A291 | 2.30k Fish | 1.00 | .25 |
| 877 | A292 | 2.60k Fox | 1.25 | .25 |
| 878 | A291 | 2.70k Flowers, wheat | 1.25 | .25 |
| 879 | A292 | 2.90k Capercaillie | 1.50 | .25 |
| 880 | A292 | 3k Ermine | 1.50 | .25 |
| 881 | A292 | 3.20k Mute swan | 1.50 | .25 |
| 882 | A292 | 3.80k Reindeer | 2.00 | .25 |
| 883 | A291 | 4k Star | 1.50 | .30 |
| 883A | A292 | 4k Squirrel | 2.00 | .25 |
| 883B | A292 | 4.50k Beaver | 2.00 | .25 |
| | | *Nos. 875-883B (11)* | 16.50 | 2.80 |

Issued: 2.10k, #883, 2/18/86; 2.30k, 2.70k, 2/12/87; 2.90k, 3.80k, 2/18/88; 2.60k, 3k, #883A, 2/20/89; 3.20k, 4.50k, 2/23/90.

See Nos. 958-959.

Mushrooms — A293

No. 884, Cantharellus tubaeformis. No. 885, Rozites caperata. No. 886, Lepista nuda. No. 887, Lactarius deterrimus. No. 888, Cantharellus cibarius. No. 889, Suillus luteus.

**Booklet Stamps**

***Perf. 13½x13 on 3 Sides***

**1987-89 Litho.**

| | | | | |
|---|---|---|---|---|
| 884 | A293 | 2.70k multi | 1.50 | .25 |
| 885 | A293 | 2.70k multi | 1.50 | .25 |
| a. | | Bklt. pane, 5 #884, 5 #885 | 15.00 | |
| | | Complete booklet, #885a | 17.50 | |
| 886 | A293 | 2.90k multi | 1.50 | .25 |
| 887 | A293 | 2.90k multi | 1.50 | .25 |
| a. | | Bklt. pane, 5 #886, 5 #887 | 15.00 | |
| | | Complete booklet, #887a | 15.00 | |
| 888 | A293 | 3k multi | 1.25 | .25 |
| 889 | A293 | 3k multi | 1.25 | .25 |
| a. | | Bklt. pane, 5 #888, 5 #889 | 12.50 | |
| | | Complete booklet, #889a | 16.00 | |
| | | *Nos. 884-889 (6)* | 8.50 | 1.50 |

Issued: 2.70k, 5/8; 2.90k, 4/26/88; 3k, 2/20/89.

Natl. Federation of Craftsmen, Cent. — A294

**1986, Apr. 11 Engr.**

| | | | | |
|---|---|---|---|---|
| 890 | A294 | 2.50k Stone cutter | 1.00 | .25 |
| 891 | A294 | 7k Carpenter | 4.00 | 1.00 |

Europa
A295

**1986, Apr. 11 Litho. *Perf. 13***
**892** A295 2.50k Bird, industry 1.75 .40
**893** A295 3.50k Acid rain 2.25 1.25

Nordic Cooperation Issue A296

Sister towns.

**1986, May 27 *Perf. 13½x13***
**894** A296 2.50k Moss 1.25 .25
**895** A296 4k Alesund 2.00 .75

Famous Men — A297

Designs: 2.10k, Hans Poulson Egede (1686-1758), missionary, and map of Norway and Greenland. 2.50k, Herman Wildenvey (1886-1959), poet, and poem carved in Seaman's Commemoration Hall, Stavern. 3k, Tore Orjasaeter (1886-1968), poet, and antique cupboard, Skjak. 4k, Engebret Soot, engineer, and canal lock, Orje.

**Engr., Litho. & Engr. (#897)**
**1986, Oct. 17 *Perf. 13x13½***
**896** A297 2.10k multi 1.10 1.00
**897** A297 2.50k multi 1.25 .25
**898** A297 3k multi 1.50 .65
**899** A297 4k multi 2.00 .50
*Nos. 896-899 (4)* 5.85 2.40

Christmas — A298

Stained glass windows by Gabriel Kielland, Nidaros Cathedral, Trondheim: 2.10k, Olav Kyrre Founding The Diocese in Nidaros. 2.50k, The King and the Peasant at Sul.

***Perf. 13½ on 3 Sides***
**1986, Nov. 26 Litho.**
**Booklet Stamps**
**900** A298 2.10k multi 1.75 .40
*a.* Booklet pane of 10 17.50
Complete booklet, #900a 20.00
**901** A298 2.50k multi 1.75 .25
*a.* Booklet pane of 10 17.50
Complete booklet, #901a 20.00

Intl. Peace Year — A299

**Lithographed & Engraved**
**1986, Nov. 26 *Perf. 13½x13***
**902** A299 15k brt grn, org & lt bl 10.00 .75

A300

**1987, Feb. 12 Litho. *Perf. 13½***
**903** A300 3.50k red, yel & dk bl 1.75 1.00
**904** A300 4.50k bl, yel & grn 2.00 .50

Europa A301

Modern architecture: 2.70k, Wood. 4.50k, Glass and stone.

**1987, Apr. 3 Litho. *Perf. 13½x13***
**905** A301 2.70k multi 2.00 .40
**906** A301 4.50k multi 2.75 .75

Odelsting (Norwegian Assembly) Voting on Law Administering Local Councils, 150th Anniv. A302

**1987, Apr. 3 Engr. *Perf. 13x13½***
**907** A302 12k dark green 6.50 .55

**Miniature Sheet**

Red Crescent-Red Cross Rehabilitation Center, Mogadishu, Somalia — A303

**1987, May 8 Litho. *Perf. 13½x13***
**908** A303 4.50k multi 2.50 2.00

See Somalia Nos. 576-577.

Sandvig Collection, Maihaugen Open-air Museum A305

2.70k, Bjornstad Farm, Vaga. 3.50k, Horse and Rider, by Christen E. Listad.

**1987, June 10 Engr. *Perf. 13x13½***
**911** A305 2.70k multi 1.25 .30
**912** A305 3.50k multi 2.00 1.00

Churchyard, Inspiration for Valen's Churchyard by the Sea — A306

Fartein Valen (1887-1952), Composer — A306a

***Perf. 13x13½, 13½x13***
**1987, Aug. 25 Engr.**
**913** A306 2.30k emer grn & dark blue 1.25 1.00
**914** A306a 4.50k dark brown 2.00 .50

Tempest at Sea, by Christian Krogh (1852-1925) A307

Painting: 5k, The Farm, by Gerhard Munthe (1849-1929).

**1987, Oct. 9 Litho. *Perf. 13½x13***
**915** A307 2.70k multi 1.50 .30
**916** A307 5k multi 2.75 .50

Norwegian Horse Breeds A308

**Litho. & Engr.**
**1987, Nov. 12 *Perf. 13x13½***
**917** A308 2.30k Dales 1.25 1.00
**918** A308 2.70k Fjord 1.50 .30
**919** A308 4.50k Nordland 2.25 .60
*Nos. 917-919 (3)* 5.00 1.90

Christmas A309

2.30k, Children making tree ornaments. 2.70k, Baking gingersnaps.

**Booklet Stamps**
***Perf. 13½x13 on 3 sides***
**1987, Nov. 12 Litho.**
**920** A309 2.30k multi 1.40 .40
*a.* Booklet pane of 10 14.00
Complete booklet, #920a 16.00
**921** A309 2.70k multi 1.25 .25
*a.* Booklet pane of 10 12.50
Complete booklet, #921a 16.00

Salvation Army in Norway, Cent. A310

4.80k, Othilie Tonning, early Salvation Army worker in Norway.

**1988, Feb. 18 *Perf. 13½***
**922** A310 2.90k multi 1.50 .30
**923** A310 4.80k multi 2.50 1.00

European North-South Solidarity Campaign — A311

**1988, Apr. 26 *Perf. 13x13½***
**924** A311 25k multi 12.00 1.00

Defense Forces Activities A312

Defense Forces, 300th anniv.: 2.50k, Fortress construction. 2.90k, Army Signal Corps on duty. 4.60k, Pontoon bridge under construction, Corps of Engineers.

**1988, Apr. 26 Engr.**
**925** A312 2.50k dark green 1.40 .60
**926** A312 2.90k carmine lake 1.50 .30
**927** A312 4.60k dark blue 2.25 .50
*Nos. 925-927 (3)* 5.15 1.40

Europa A313

Transport: 2.90k, *Prinds Gustav* passing Lofoten Isls., 1st passenger steamer in northern Norway, sesquicent. 3.80k, Heroybrua Bridge, between Leinoy and Blankholm, 1976.

**Litho. & Engr.**
**1988, July 1 *Perf. 13x13½***
**928** A313 2.90k multi 2.50 .50
**929** A313 3.80k multi 2.75 1.75

85th Birthday of King Olav V — A314

Designs: No. 930, Portrait, c. 1988. No. 931a, Arrival in 1905 after Norway declared independence from Sweden. No. 931b, Olav in snowstorm at Holmenkollen.

**1988, July 1 Litho. *Perf. 13½x13***
**930** A314 2.90k multi 1.75 1.00

**Souvenir Sheet**
**931** Sheet of 3 7.00 5.50
*a.* A314 2.90k org red, black & ultra 1.75 1.50
*b.* A314 2.90k multi 1.75 1.50
*c.* A314 2.90k like No. 930, no date 1.75 1.50

Reign of King Christian IV (1577-1648), 400th Anniv. — A315

Designs: 10k, Reverse of a rixdaler struck in Christiania (Oslo), 1628, and excerpt of a mining decree issued by Christian IV.

**Litho. & Engr.**
**1988, Oct. 7 *Perf. 13½x13***
**932** A315 2.50k black & buff 1.75 .60
**933** A315 10k multi 7.00 .70

**Miniature Sheet**

Handball A316

Ball sports: b, Soccer. c, Basketball. d, Volleyball.

**1988, Oct. 7 Litho. *Perf. 13½x13***
**934** Sheet of 4 12.00 12.00
*a.-d.* A316 2.90k any single 3.00 3.00

Stamp Day. No. 934 sold for 15k.

Christmas — A317

Ludvig, a cartoon character created by Kjell Aukrust: No. 935, With ski pole. No. 936, Reading letter.

***Perf. 13½x13 on 3 sides***
**1988, Nov. 15 Litho.**
**Booklet Stamps**
**935** A317 2.90k multi 1.50 .25
**936** A317 2.90k multi 1.50 .25
*a.* Bklt. pane, 5 #935, 5 #936 15.00
Complete booklet, #936a 17.00

World Cross-Country Running Championships, Stavanger, Mar. 19 — A318

**1989, Feb. 20 Litho. *Perf. 13x13½***
**937** A318 5k multi 2.50 .30

Port City Bicentennials — A319

**Litho. & Engr.**
**1989, Apr. 20 *Perf. 13½x13***
**938** A319 3k Vardo 1.75 .30
**939** A319 4k Hammerfest 2.25 1.10

Nordic Cooperation Issue — A320

Folk costumes.

**1989, Apr. 20 Litho. *Perf. 13x13½***
**940** A320 3k Setesdal (woman) 1.50 .30
**941** A320 4k Kautokeino (man) 2.25 1.10

Europa 1989 — A321

Children's games: 3.70k, Building snowman. 5k, Cat's cradle.

**1989, June 7 Litho. *Perf. 13x13½***
**942** A321 3.70k multi 2.25 .75
**943** A321 5k multi 3.25 1.00

Public Primary Schools, 250th Anniv. — A322

3k, Child learning to write.

**Litho. & Engr.**
**1989, June 7 *Perf. 13½x13***
**944** A322 2.60k shown 1.50 .60

**Engr.**
**945** A322 3k multi 1.50 .30

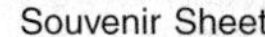

Souvenir Sheet

Winter Olympic Gold Medalists from Norway — A323

Portraits: a, Bjoerg Eva Jensen, women's 3000-meter speed skating, 1980. b, Eirik Kvalfoss, 10k biathlon, 1984. c, Tom Sandberg, combined cross-country and ski jumping, 1984. d, Women's Nordic ski team, 20k relay, 1984.

**1989, Oct. 6 Litho. *Perf. 13½x13***
**946** Sheet of 4 10.00 10.00
***a.-d.*** 4k any single 2.50 2.50

Sold for 20k to benefit Olympic sports promotion.

See Nos. 984, 997, 1021, 1035.

Souvenir Sheet

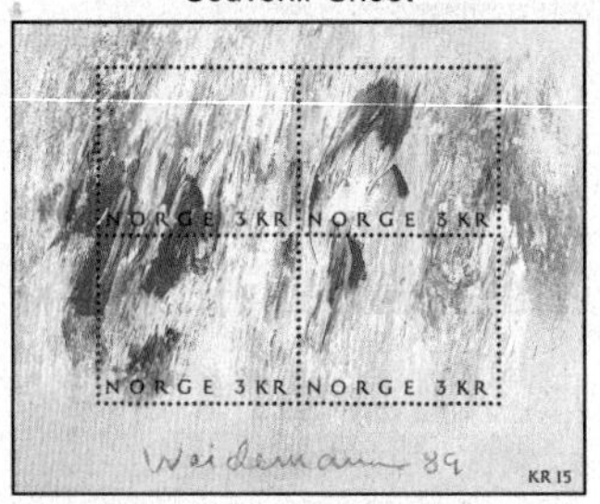


*Impression of the Countryside,* 1982, by Jakob Weidemann — A324

**1989, Oct. 6**
**947** A324 Sheet of 4 12.00 12.00
***a.-d.*** 3k any single 3.00 3.00

Stamp Day. Sold for 15k to benefit philatelic promotion.

Writers A325

3k, Arnulf Overland (1889-1968), poet. 25k, Hanna Winsnes (1789-1872), author.

**Litho. & Engr.**
**1989, Nov. 24 *Perf. 13x13½***
**948** A325 3k dk red & brt bl 1.25 .30
**949** A325 25k multicolored 12.00 1.25

Manors A326

**1989, Nov. 24 Engr. *Perf. 13***
**950** A326 3k Manor at Larvik 1.50 .30
**951** A326 3k Rosendal Barony 1.50 .30

Christmas Decorations — A327

***Perf. 13 on 3 sides***
**1989, Nov. 24 Litho.**
**Booklet Stamps**
**952** A327 3k Star 1.25 .25
**953** A327 3k Round ornament 1.25 .25
***a.*** Bklt. pane of 10, 5 #952, 5 #953 12.50
Complete booklet, #953a 15.00

Winter City Events, Tromso — A328

**1990, Feb. 23 Litho. *Perf. 13½***
**954** A328 5k multicolored 2.25 .35

**Fauna Type of 1988 and**

Scenes of Norway — A329

Designs: 4k, Cable cars. 4.50k, Goat Mountain. 5.50k, Top of the World outpost.

**1991-94 Litho. *Perf. 13***
**955** A329 4k multicolored 2.00 .60
**956** A329 4.50k multicolored 2.50 .60
**957** A329 5.50k multicolored 2.50 .50

**Litho. & Engr.**
**958** A292 5.50k Lynx 2.50 .25
**959** A292 6.40k Owl 2.50 .40
*Nos. 955-959 (5)* 12.00 2.35

Issued: #958-959, 2/21/91; #955-957, 4/19/94.

**Posthorn Type of 1893**

**1991-92 Engr. *Perf. 12½x13***
**960** A10 1k orange & black .75 .25
**961** A10 2k emerald & lake 1.00 .25
**962** A10 3k blue & green 1.25 .25
**963** A10 4k org & henna brn 1.50 .25
**964** A10 5k green & dark blue 2.00 .25
**965** A10 6k grn & red vio 2.25 .40
**966** A10 7k red brn & bl 2.50 .40
**967** A10 8k red vio & bl grn 3.25 .50
**968** A10 9k ultra & red brn 3.00 .50
*Nos. 960-968 (9)* 17.50 3.05

Issued: 1k-5k, 11/23/92; others, 11/22/91.

Orchids — A332

No. 970, Dactylorhiza fuchsii. No. 971, Epipactis atrorubens. No. 972, Cypripedium calceolus. No. 973, Ophrys insectifera.

***Perf. 13½x13 on 3 Sides***
**1990-92 Litho. Booklet Stamps**
**970** A332 3.20k multi 1.25 .25
**971** A332 3.20k multi 1.25 .25
***a.*** Bklt. pane, 5 #970, 5 #971 12.50
Complete booklet, #971a 14.00
**972** A332 3.30k multi 1.25 .25
**973** A332 3.30k multi 1.25 .25
***a.*** Bklt. pane, 5 each #972-973 13.00
Complete booklet, #973a 17.50
*Nos. 970-973 (4)* 5.00 1.00

Issued: #970-971, 2/23; #972-973, 2/21/92.

A334

German Invasion of Norway, 50th Anniv.: 3.20k, King Haakon VII's monogram, merchant navy, air force, Norwegian Home Guard and cannon Moses. 4k, Recapture of Narvik, May 28, 1940, by the Polish, British, Norwegian and French forces.

**1990, Apr. 9 Litho. *Perf. 13x13½***
**975** A334 3.20k shown 2.25 .25
**976** A334 4k multicolored 2.75 1.10

Souvenir Sheet

A335

Stamps on stamps: b, Norway #1.

**1990, Apr. 9 *Perf. 13½x13***
**977** Sheet of 2 9.00 9.00
***a.-b.*** A335 5k any single 4.00 4.00

Penny Black, 150th anniv. Sold for 15k.

A336

**1990, June 14 Litho. & Engr.**
**978** A336 3.20k Portrait 2.00 .25
**979** A336 5k Coat of arms 2.50 .50

Tordenskiold (Peter Wessel, 1690-1720), naval hero.

A337

Europa: Post offices.

**1990, June 14 Litho. *Perf. 13x13½***
**980** A337 3.20k Trondheim 2.50 .40
**981** A337 4k Longyearbyen 2.75 1.25

A338

2.70k, Svendsen. 15k, Monument by Fredriksen.

**1990, Oct. 5 Litho. & Engr. *Perf. 13***
**982** A338 2.70k multicolored 1.50 .75
**983** A338 15k multicolored 7.00 1.00

Johan Severin Svendsen (1840-1911), composer.

**Winter Olympic Type of 1989**
Souvenir Sheet

Gold medal winners: a, Thorleif Haug, skier, 1924. b, Sonja Henie, figure skater, 1928, 1932, 1936. c, Ivar Ballangrud, speed skater, 1928, 1936. d, Hjalmar Andersen, speed skater, 1952.

**1990, Oct. 5 Litho. *Perf. 13½x13***
**984** Sheet of 4 11.00 11.00
***a.-d.*** A323 4k any single 2.25 2.25

Sold for 20k to benefit Olympic sports promotion.

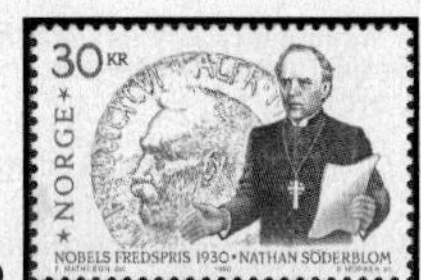

A339

**Litho & Engr.**

**1990, Nov. 23** *Perf. 13*
**985** A339 30k bl, brn & car rose 15.00 1.00

Lars Olof Jonathan Soderblom (1866-1931), 1930 Nobel Peace Prize winner.

A340

Christmas (Children's drawings): No. 987, Church, stars, and Christmas tree.

*Perf. 13 on 3 sides*

**1990, Nov. 23** **Litho.**
**986** A340 3.20k multicolored 1.25 .25
**987** A340 3.20k multicolored 1.25 .25
*a.* Bklt. pane, 5 each #986-987 12.50
Complete booklet, #987a 15.00

Ship Building Industry A341

**1991, Feb. 21** **Litho.** *Perf. 13½x13*
**988** A341 5k multicolored 2.50 .85

Europa — A342

3.20k, ERS-1. 4k, Andoya rocket range.

**1991, Apr. 16** **Litho.** *Perf. 13*
**989** A342 3.20k multi 3.75 .50
**990** A342 4k multi 3.50 1.25

City of Christiansand, 350th Anniv. — A343

**Litho. & Engr.**

**1991, Apr. 16** *Perf. 13*
**991** A343 3.20k Early view 1.50 .25
**992** A343 5.50k Modern view 2.75 .50

Lifeboat Service, Cent. — A344

Designs: 3.20k, Rescue boat, Skomvaer III, horiz. 27k, Sailboat Colin Archer.

**Litho & Engr.**

**1991, June 7** *Perf. 13*
**993** A344 3.20k multicolored 1.75 .25
**994** A344 27k multicolored 14.00 2.00

Tourism — A345

Designs: 3.20k, Fountain, Vigeland Park. 4k, Globe, North Cape.

**1991, June 7** **Litho.** *Perf. 13½x13*
**995** A345 3.20k multicolored 1.75 .25
**996** A345 4k multicolored 3.50 2.00

**Winter Olympic Type of 1989**
Souvenir Sheet

Gold medal winners: a, Birger Ruud, ski jumping. b, Johan Grottumsbraten, cross country skiing. c, Knut Johannesen, speed skating. d, Magnar Solberg, biathlon.

**1991, Oct. 11** **Litho.** *Perf. 13½x13*
**997** Sheet of 4 10.00 10.00
*a.-d.* A323 4k any single 2.50 2.50

Sold for 20k to benefit Olympic sports promotion.

A346

Natl. Stamp Day: a, Hands engraving. b, Magnifying glass above hands. c, View of hands through magnifying glass. d, Printed label being removed from plate.

**1991, Oct. 11** *Perf. 13x13½*
**Souvenir Sheet**
**998** Sheet of 4 12.00 12.00
*a.* A346 2.70k multicolored 2.50 2.50
*b.* A346 3.20k multicolored 2.50 2.50
*c.* A346 4k multicolored 2.50 2.50
*d.* A346 5k multicolored 2.50 2.50

Sold for 20k.

A347

Christmas: No. 1000, People with lantern.

*Perf. 13½x13 on 3 Sides*

**1991, Nov. 22** **Litho.**
**Booklet Stamps**
**999** A347 3.20k multicolored 1.25 .25
**1000** A347 3.20k multicolored 1.25 .25
*a.* Bklt. pane, 5 each #999-1000 12.50
Complete booklet, #1000a 14.00

Queen Sonja A348

King Harald A349

A349a

*Perf. 13x13½, 12½x13½ (6.50k)*

**1992-2002** **Litho. & Engr.**

| | | | | |
|---|---|---|---|---|
| **1004** | A348 | 2.80k multi | 1.75 | .25 |
| **1005** | A348 | 3k multi | 1.50 | .25 |
| **1007** | A349 | 3.30k multi | 2.00 | .25 |
| **1008** | A349 | 3.50k multi | 1.75 | .25 |
| **1009** | A349 | 4.50k carmine | 2.25 | .50 |
| **1011** | A349 | 5.50k multi | 2.25 | .25 |
| **1012** | A349 | 5.60k multi | 2.50 | .40 |
| **1014** | A349 | 6.50k green | 3.00 | .40 |
| **1015** | A349 | 6.60k multi | 3.25 | .50 |
| **1016** | A349 | 7.50k violet | 3.75 | 2.00 |
| **1016A** | A349 | 8.50k brown | 4.00 | 2.25 |

*Perf. 13½x13*

| | | | | |
|---|---|---|---|---|
| **1017** | A349a | 10k dark grn | 5.00 | .25 |
| *a.* | | Perf. 13½x13¾ | 4.00 | .75 |
| **1019** | A349a | 20k deep vio | 10.00 | .50 |
| *b.* | | Perf. 13½x13¾ | 8.50 | .75 |
| **1019A** | A349a | 30k dark blue | 12.00 | .50 |
| **1020** | A349a | 50k olive black | 17.00 | 1.00 |
| *a.* | | Perf. 13½x13¾ | 18.00 | 2.00 |
| | | *Nos. 1004-1020 (15)* | 72.00 | 9.55 |

Issued: 2.80k, 3.30k, 5.60k, 6.60k, 2/21/92; 50k, 6/12/92; 3k, 3.50k, 5.50k, 2/23/93; 10k, 20k, 6/17/93; 6.50k, 2/12/94; 30k, 11/18/94; 4.50k, 7.50k, 8.50k, 11/24/95; Nos. 1019b, 1020a, Dec. 2001. No. 1017a, 2002.

**Winter Olympic Type of 1989**
Souvenir Sheet

Gold Medal winners: a, Hallgeir Brenden, cross-country skiing. b, Arnfinn Bergmann, ski jumping. c, Stein Eriksen, giant slalom. d, Simon Slattvik, Nordic combined.

**1992, Feb. 21** **Litho.** *Perf. 13½x13*
**1021** Sheet of 4 9.00 9.00
*a.-d.* A323 4k any single 2.00 2.00

Sold for 20k to benefit Olympic sports promotion.

Expo '92, Seville A350

Designs: 3.30k, Norwegian pavilion, ship. 5.20k, Mountains, boat and fish.

**1992, Apr. 20** **Litho.** *Perf. 13x13½*
**1022** A350 3.30k multicolored 1.50 .25
**1023** A350 5.20k multicolored 2.25 .75

Discovery of America, 500th Anniv. A351

Europa: 3.30k, Sailing ship Restauration at sea, 1825. 4,20k, Stavangerfjord in New York Harbor, 1918.

**Litho. & Engr.**

**1992, Apr. 21** *Perf. 13x13½*
**1024** A351 3.30k multicolored 2.25 .30
**1025** A351 4.20k multicolored 2.75 1.00

Kristiansund, 250th Anniv. — A352

**Litho. & Engr.**

**1992, June 12** *Perf. 13*
**1026** A352 3.30k brn, bl & blk 1.50 .25
**1027** A352 3.30k View of Molde 1.50 .25

Molde, 250th anniv. (#1027).

Souvenir Sheet

Glass — A353

Stamp Day: a, Decorated vase. b, Carafe with gold design. c, Cut glass salad bowl. d, Decorated cup.

**1992, Oct. 9** **Litho.** *Perf. 13x13½*
**1028** A353 Sheet of 4 12.00 12.00
*a.* 2.80k multicolored 2.50 2.50
*b.* 3.30k multicolored 2.50 2.50
*c.* 4.20k multicolored 2.50 2.50
*d.* 5.20k multicolored 2.50 2.50

No. 1028 sold for 20k.

A354

Designs: 3.30k, Flags, buildings in Lillehammer. 4.20k, Flag.

**1992, Oct. 9** **Litho.** *Perf. 13x13½*
**1029** A354 3.30k multicolored 1.50 .25
**1030** A354 4.20k multicolored 2.50 .75

1994 Winter Olympics, Lillehammer.
See Nos. 1047-1048, 1053-1058.

A355

Christmas: No. 1031, Elves in front of mailbox. No. 1032, One elf holding other on shoulders to mail letters.

*Perf. 13 on 3 Sides*

**1992, Nov. 23** **Litho.**
**Booklet Stamps**
**1031** A355 3.30k multicolored 1.00 .25
**1032** A355 3.30k multicolored 1.00 .25
*b.* Booklet pane, 5 each #1031-1032 12.00
Complete booklet, #1032b 15.00

Butterflies — A356

Designs: No. 1033, Anthocharis cardamines. No. 1034, Aglais urticae.

*Perf. 13½x13 on 3 Sides*

**1993, Feb. 23** **Litho.**
**Booklet Stamps**
**1033** A356 3.50k multicolored 1.25 .25
**1034** A356 3.50k multicolored 1.25 .25
*b.* Booklet pane, 5 each #1033-1034 12.50
Complete booklet, #1034b 15.00

See Nos. 1051-1052.

**Winter Olympic Type of 1989**
Souvenir Sheet

1992 Gold Medal winners: a, Finn Christian Jagge, slalom. b, Bjorn Daehlie, cross-country skiing. c, Geir Karlstad, speed skating. d, Vegard Ulvang, cross-country skiing.

**1993, Feb. 23** *Perf. 13½x13*
**1035** Sheet of 4 9.00 9.00
*a.-d.* A323 4.50k any single 2.00 2.00

No. 1035 sold for 22k to benefit Olympic sports promotion.

Norden — A357

**1993, Apr. 23** **Litho.** *Perf. 13½x13*
**1036** A357 4k Canoe on lake 2.25 2.25
**1037** A357 4.50k River rafting 2.25 .50

Edvard Grieg A358

**Litho. & Engr.**

**1993, Apr. 23** *Perf. 13x13½*

**1038** A358 3.50k Portrait 1.75 .25
**1039** A358 5.50k Landscape 2.50 .50

1993 World Championships in Norway — A359

**1993, June 17 Litho.** *Perf. 13½x13*

**1040** A359 3.50k Team handball 1.50 .25
**1041** A359 5.50k Cycling 2.50 .50

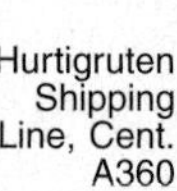

Hurtigruten Shipping Line, Cent. A360

3.50k, Richard With, ship. 4.50k, Ship, officers.

**Litho. & Engr.**

**1993, June 17** *Perf. 12½x13*

**1042** A360 3.50k multicolored 2.00 .25
**1043** A360 4.50k multicolored 2.25 .75

Worker's Organization, Cent. A361

**1993, Sept. 24 Engr.** *Perf. 13x13½*

**1044** A361 3.50k Johan Castberg 2.00 .40
**1045** A361 12k Betzy Kjelsberg 6.00 .75

Souvenir Sheet

Carvings — A362

Stamp Day: a, Spiral leaf scroll. b, Interlocking scroll. c, "1754" surrounded by scroll. d, Face with scroll above.

**1993, Sept. 24 Litho.** *Perf. 13½x13*

**1046** A362 Sheet of 4, #a.-d. 12.00 12.00
*a.* 3k multicolored 2.50 2.50
*b.* 3.50k multicolored 2.50 2.50
*c.* 4.50k multicolored 2.50 2.50
*d.* 5.50k multicolored 2.50 2.50

No. 1046 sold for 21k.
See No. 1069.

**1994 Winter Olympic Type of 1992**

#1047, Flags, cross country skiier. #1048, Flags, buildings in Lillehammer.

**1993, Nov. 27 Litho.** *Perf. 13x13½*

**1047** A354 3.50k multicolored 1.50 .25
**1048** A354 3.50k multicolored 1.50 .25
*a.* Pair, #1047-1048 3.25 2.00

No. 1048a has a continuous design.

Christmas — A363

Designs: No. 1049, Store Mangen Chapel. No. 1050, Church of Stamnes, Sandnes.

***Perf. 13½x13 on 3 Sides***

**1993, Nov. 27 Booklet Stamps**

**1049** A363 3.50k shown 1.25 .25
**1050** A363 3.50k multicolored 1.25 .25
*b.* Booklet pane, 5 each #1049-1050 12.50
Complete booklet, #1050b 15.00

**Butterfly Type of 1993**

No. 1051, Colias hecla. No. 1052, Clossiana freija.

***Perf. 13½x13 on 3 Sides***

**1994, Feb. 12 Litho.**

**Booklet Stamps**

**1051** A356 3.50k multi 1.25 .25
**1052** A356 3.50k multi 1.25 .25
*b.* Booklet pane, 5 each #1051-1052 12.50
Complete booklet, #1052b 15.00

**1994 Winter Olympic Type of 1992**

Designs: No. 1053, Stylized Norwegian flag, Olympic rings UR. No. 1054, Stylized Norwegian flag, Olympic rings, UL. No. 1055, Olympic rings, buildings in Lillehammer. No. 1056, Olympic rings, ski jump. 4.50k, Flags of Norway, Belgium, Greece, Switzerland, Sweden, Germany, United Kingdom. 5.50k, Flags of Australia, New Zealand, Brazil, Canada, US, Japan, Mexico, South Korea.

**1994, Feb. 12** *Perf. 13x13½*

**1053** A354 3.50k multicolored 1.50 .30
**1054** A354 3.50k multicolored 1.50 .30
**1055** A354 3.50k multicolored 1.50 .30
**1056** A354 3.50k multicolored 1.50 .30
*a.* Block of 4, #1053-1056 7.00 8.00
**1057** A354 4.50k multicolored 2.00 .60
**1058** A354 5.50k multicolored 2.25 .50
*Nos. 1053-1058 (6)* 10.25 2.30

1994 Paralympics A365

**1994, Mar. 10 Litho.** *Perf. 13*

**1059** A365 4.50k Skier 1.75 .60
**1060** A365 5.50k Skier, diff. 2.00 .50

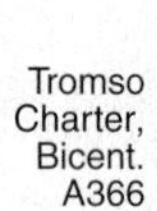

Tromso Charter, Bicent. A366

**Litho. & Engr.**

**1994, Apr. 19** *Perf. 13*

**1061** A366 3.50k Royal seal 1.75 .25
**1062** A366 4.50k Cathedral 2.25 .75

Norwegian Folk Museum, Cent. A367

Designs: 3k, Log buildings, Osterdal Valley. 3.50k, Sled, 1750.

**Litho. & Engr.**

**1994, June 14** *Perf. 12½x13*

**1063** A367 3k multicolored 1.50 .50
**1064** A367 3.50k multicolored 1.75 .25

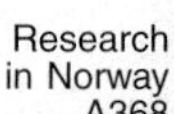

Research in Norway A368

Abstract designs with various formulas, microchips, glass flasks.

**1994, June 14 Litho.**

**1065** A368 4k multicolored 1.75 .60
**1066** A368 4.50k multicolored 2.25 .60

Electric Tram Lines, Cent. A369

3.50k, Early tram, map. 12k, Modern tram, map.

**Litho. & Engr.**

**1994, Sept. 23** *Perf. 13x13½*

**1067** A369 3.50k multi 1.75 .25
**1068** A369 12k multi 6.00 .60

**Stamp Day Type of 1993**

Ornamental broaches: a, Gold, embossed designs. b, Silver, embossed designs. c, Silver, circular designs. d, Gold, jeweled center.

**1994, Sept. 23 Litho.** *Perf. 13½x13*

**1069** Sheet of 4, #a.-d. 12.50 12.50
*a.* A362 3k multicolored 2.50 2.50
*b.* A362 3.50k multicolored 2.50 2.50
*c.* A362 4.50k multicolored 2.50 2.50
*d.* A362 5.50k multicolored 2.50 2.50

No. 1069 sold for 21k.

Christmas — A370

***Perf. 13½x13 on 3 Sides***

**1994, Nov. 18 Litho.**

**Booklet Stamps**

**1070** A370 3.50k Sled 1.50 .25
**1071** A370 3.50k Kick sled 1.50 .25
*a.* Booklet pane, 5 each 15.00
Complete booklet, #1071a 16.00

Berries — A371

No. 1086, Vaccinium vitis. No. 1087, Vaccinium myrtillus. No. 1088, Fragaria vesca. No. 1089, Rubus chamaemorus.

**Booklet Stamps**

**1995-96 Litho.** *Perf. 13½x13*

**1086** A371 3.50k multi 1.25 .25
**1087** A371 3.50k multi 1.25 .25
*a.* Bklt. pane, 4 ea #1086-1087 10.00
Complete booklet, #1087a 12.00
**1088** A371 3.50k multi 1.25 .25
**1089** A371 3.50k multi 1.25 .25
*a.* Bklt. pane, 4 ea #1088-1089 10.00
Complete booklet, #1089a 12.00
*Nos. 1086-1089 (4)* 5.00 1.00

Issued: #1086-1087, 2/23/95; #1088-1089, 2/22/96.

A372

Apothecary Shops, 400th Anniv.: 3.50k, Swan Pharmacy, Bergen. 25k, Apothecary's tools.

**Litho. & Engr.**

**1995, Feb. 23** *Perf. 13½x13*

**1090** A372 3.50k multicolored 1.75 .25
**1091** A372 25k multicolored 12.00 1.25

Tourism — A373

4k, Skudeneshavn Harbor. 4.50k, Torghatten mountain, Helgeland coastline.

**1995, May 8 Litho.** *Perf. 13½x13*

**Booklet Stamps**

**1092** A373 4k multicolored 1.50 .75
*a.* Booklet pane of 8 12.00
Complete booklet, #1092a 14.00
**1093** A373 4.50k multicolored 1.75 .75
*a.* Booklet pane of 8 14.00
Complete booklet, #1093a 16.00

Christianity in Norway A374

3.50k, Old Moster Church, c. 1100. 15k, Slettebakken Church, Bergen, 1970.

**Litho. & Engr.**

**1995, May 8** *Perf. 13x13½*

**1094** A374 3.50k multicolored 1.75 .25
**1095** A374 15k multicolored 7.00 1.00

End of World War II, 50th Anniv. A375

Designs: 3.50k, German commander saluting Terje Rollem in 1945, German forces marching down Karl Johans Gate from Royal Palace, 1940. 4.50k, King Haakon VII, Crown Prince leaving Norway in 1940, King saluting upon return in 1945. 5.50k, Children waving Norwegian flags, 1945.

**1995, May 8 Litho.** *Perf. 13½x13*

**1096** A375 3.50k multicolored 1.75 .25
**1097** A375 4.50k multicolored 2.25 .60
**1098** A375 5.50k multicolored 2.75 .50
*Nos. 1096-1098 (3)* 6.75 1.35

Kirsten Flagstad (1895-1962), Opera Singer — A376

Design: 5.50k, In Lohengrin.

**1995, June 26 Litho.** *Perf. 13*

**1099** A376 3.50k multicolored 2.00 .25
**1100** A376 5.50k multicolored 2.75 .60

Conciliation Boards, Bicent. A377

Designs: 7k, Three-man board between two people facing away from each other. 12k, Seated board member, two people talking to each other.

**1995, June 26** *Perf. 13½*

**1101** A377 7k multicolored 3.25 .60
**1102** A377 12k multicolored 5.00 .60

UN, 50th Anniv. A378

UN emblem and: 3.50k, Trygve Lie, Secretary General 1946-53. 5.50k, Woman drinking from clean water supply.

**Litho. & Engr.**

**1995, Sept. 22** *Perf. 13*

**1103** A378 3.50k multicolored 2.00 .25
**1104** A378 5.50k multicolored 2.75 .50

Norway Post, 350th Anniv. A379

No. 1105, Signature, portrait of Hannibal Sehested, letter post, 1647. No. 1106, Wax seal, registered letters, 1745. No. 1107, Christiania, etc. postmarks. No. 1108, Funds transfer, coins, canceled envelopes, 1883. No. 1109, "Norske Intelligenz-Seddeler," first newspaper, newspapers, magazines, 1660. No. 1110, Postmarks, label, parcel post, 1827. No. 1111, No. 1, Type A5, stamps, 1855. No. 1112, Savings book stamps, bank services, 1950.

**Booklet Stamps**

**1995, Sept. 22** **Litho.**

**1105** A379 3.50k multicolored 1.25 .50
**1106** A379 3.50k multicolored 1.25 .50
**1107** A379 3.50k multicolored 1.25 .50
**1108** A379 3.50k multicolored 1.25 .50
**1109** A379 3.50k multicolored 1.25 .50
**1110** A379 3.50k multicolored 1.25 .50
**1111** A379 3.50k multicolored 1.25 .50
*a.* Missing gray stamp at LR *12.50* 5.00
**1112** A379 3.50k multicolored 1.25 .50
*a.* Booklet pane, #1105-1112 12.50 18.00
Complete booklet, #1112a 15.00
*b.* Booklet pane, #1105-1110, #1111a, 1112 25.00 25.00
Complete booklet, #1112b 27.50

Christmas — A380

**Booklet Stamps**

***Perf. 13 on 3 Sides***

**1995, Nov. 24** **Litho.**

**1113** A380 3.50k Knitted cap 1.25 .25
**1114** A380 3.50k Knitted mitten 1.25 .25
*a.* Bklt. pane, 4 ea #1113-1114 10.00
Complete booklet, #1114a 12.00

Svalbard Islands A381

**1996, Feb. 22** **Litho.** *Perf. 13*

**1115** A381 10k Advent Bay 5.00 .75
**1116** A381 20k Polar bear 10.00 1.25

Olympic Games, Cent. — A382

Children's drawings: 3.50k, Cross country skier. 5.50k, Runner.

**1996, Apr. 18** **Litho.** *Perf. 13½*

**1117** A382 3.50k multicolored 1.75 .25
**1118** A382 5.50k multicolored 2.50 .50

Tourism — A383

4k, Besseggen. 4.50k, Urnes Stave Church. 5.50k, Alta Rock Carvings.

**1996, Apr. 18** ***Perf. 13 on 3 Sides***

**1119** A383 4k multi 1.25 .75
*a.* Booklet pane of 8 10.00
Complete booklet, #1119a 12.00
**1120** A383 4.50k multi 1.50 .75
*a.* Booklet pane of 8 12.00
Complete booklet, #1120a 14.00
**1121** A383 5.50k multi 1.75 .75
*a.* Booklet pane of 8 14.00
Complete booklet, #1121a 16.00
*Nos. 1119-1121 (3)* 4.50 2.25

See Nos. 1155-1157.

Railway Centennials — A384

**Litho. & Engr.**

**1996, June 19** *Perf. 13*

**1122** A384 3k Urskog-Holand 1.50 .50
**1123** A384 4.50k Setesdal 2.00 1.25

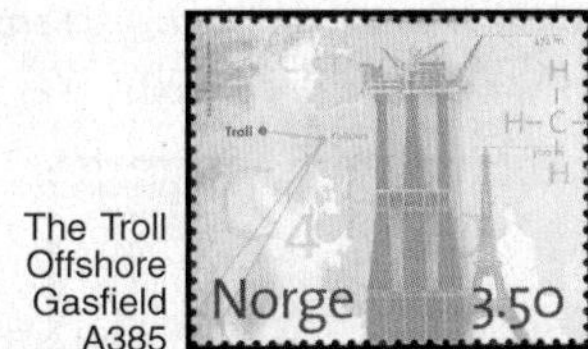


The Troll Offshore Gasfield A385

3.50k, Size of Troll platform compared to Eiffel Tower. 25k, Troll platform, map of gas pipelines.

**1996, June 19** **Litho.**

**1124** A385 3.50k multicolored 1.75 .25
**1125** A385 25k multicolored 11.00 1.25

Norway Post, 350th Anniv. A386

#1126, Postal courier on skis. #1127, Fjord boat, SS "Framnaes," 1920's. #1128, Mail truck, Oslo, 1920's. #1129, Early airmail service. #1130, Unloading mail, East Railroad Station, Oslo, 1950's. #1131, Using bicycle for rural mail delivery, 1970's. #1132, Customer, mail clerk, Elverum post office. #1133, Computer, globe, E-mail service.

**Booklet Stamps**

**1996, Sept. 20** **Litho.** *Perf. 13*

**1126** A386 3.50k multicolored 1.25 .85
**1127** A386 3.50k multicolored 1.25 .85
**1128** A386 3.50k multicolored 1.25 .85
**1129** A386 3.50k multicolored 1.25 .85
**1130** A386 3.50k multicolored 1.25 .85
**1131** A386 3.50k multicolored 1.25 .85
**1132** A386 3.50k multicolored 1.25 .85
**1133** A386 3.50k multicolored 1.25 .85
*a.* Booklet pane, #1126-1133 12.00 14.00
Complete booklet, #1133a 13.00

Motion Pictures, Cent. A387

Film strips showing: 3.50k, Leif Juster, Sean Connery, Liv Ullmann, The Olsen Gang Films, Il Temp Gigante. 5.50k, Wenche Foss, Jack Fjeldstad, Marilyn Monroe, murder, blood, shooting. 7k, Charlie Chaplin, Ottar Gladvedt, Laurel & Hardy, Marlene Dietrich.

**1996, Sept. 20**

**1134** A387 3.50k multicolored 1.50 .25
**1135** A387 5.50k multicolored 2.25 .50
**1136** A387 7k multicolored 2.75 .60
*Nos. 1134-1136 (3)* 6.50 1.35

A388

Christmas (Embroidered motif from Norwegian folk costume): Denomination at UL (#1137), UR (#1138).

***Perf. 13 on 3 Sides***

**1996, Nov. 21** **Litho.**

**1137** A388 3.50k multicolored 1.25 .25
**1138** A388 3.50k multicolored 1.25 .25
*a.* Bklt. pane, 4 ea #1137-1138 10.00
Complete booklet, #1138a 12.00

A389

Amalie Skram (1846-1905), Novelist: 3.50k, Portrait. 15k, Scene from performance of Skram's "People of Hellemyr."

**1996, Nov. 21** **Engr.**

**1139** A389 3.50k claret 1.75 .35
**1140** A389 15k claret & dk blue 6.50 1.50

**Posthorn Type of 1893 Redrawn**

**1997, Jan. 2** **Litho.** *Perf. 13x13½*

**Color of Oval**

**1141** A10 10o red .25 .25
**1142** A10 20o blue .25 .25
*a.* Perf. 13¾x13¼ .50 .50
**1143** A10 30o orange .25 .25
**1144** A10 40o gray .25 .25
**1145** A10 50o bl grn, bl grn numeral .25 .25
*Nos. 1141-1145 (5)* 1.25 1.25

Numerous design differences exist in the vertical shading lines, the size and shading of the posthorn, and in the corner wings.

See No. 1282A for stamp similar to No. 1145 but with blue numeral.

Issued: No. 1142a, Dec. 2000.

Insects — A390

**1997, Jan. 2** ***Perf. 13 on 3 Sides***

**1146** A390 3.70k Bumblebee 1.25 .25
**1147** A390 3.70k Ladybug 1.25 .25
*a.* Bklt. pane, 4 ea #1146-1147 10.00
Complete booklet 12.00

See Nos. 1180-1181.

Flowers — A391

3.20k, Red clover. 3.70k, Coltsfoot. 4.30k, Lily of the Valley. 5k, Harebell. 6k, Oxeye daisy.

**1997, Jan. 2** *Perf. 13*

**1148** A391 3.20k multi 1.25 .40
**1149** A391 3.70k multi 1.50 .35
**1150** A391 4.30k multi 2.00 .40
**1151** A391 5k multi 2.25 .45
**1152** A391 6k multi 2.50 .55
*Nos. 1148-1152 (5)* 9.50 2.15

See #1182-1187, 1210-1212, 1244-1247.

World Nordic Skiing Championships, Trondheim A392

3.70k, Ski jumping. 5k, Cross-country skiing.

**1997, Feb. 20**

**1153** A392 3.70k multi 1.75 .40
**1154** A392 5k multi 2.50 .60

**Tourism Type of 1996**

4.30k, Roros. 5k, Faerder Lighthouse. 6k, Nusfjord.

***Perf. 13 on 3 Sides***

**1997, Apr. 16** **Litho.**

**Booklet Stamps**

**1155** A383 4.30k multi 1.75 1.00
*a.* Booklet pane of 8 14.00
Complete booklet, #1155a 16.00
**1156** A383 5k multi 2.00 .75
*a.* Booklet pane of 8 16.00
Complete booklet, #1156a 18.00
**1157** A383 6k multi 2.25 .60
*a.* Booklet pane of 8 18.00
Complete booklet #1157a 20.00

King Harald, Queen Sonja, 60th Birthdays A393

No. 1159, King Harald, vert.

**1997, Apr. 16** **Litho.** *Perf. 13*

**1158** A393 3.70k shown 1.75 .40
**1159** A393 3.70k multi 1.75 .40

Norway Post, 350th Anniv. A394

Post-World War II development: No. 1160, Tools for construction, 1945. No. 1161, Kon-Tiki Expedition, 1947. No. 1162, Environmental protection, establishing national parks, 1962. No. 1163, Welfare, help for the elderly, 1967. No. 1164, Off-shore oil drilling, 1969. No. 1165, Grete Waitz, marathon winner, 1983. No. 1166, Askoy Bridge, 1992. No. 1167, Winter Olympic Games, Lillehammer, 1994.

**1997, Apr. 16** **Booklet Stamps**

**1160** A394 3.70k multicolored 1.25 .85
**1161** A394 3.70k multicolored 1.25 .85
**1162** A394 3.70k multicolored 1.25 .85
**1163** A394 3.70k multicolored 1.25 .85
**1164** A394 3.70k multicolored 1.25 .85
**1165** A394 3.70k multicolored 1.25 .85
**1166** A394 3.70k multicolored 1.25 .85
**1167** A394 3.70k multicolored 1.25 .85
*a.* Booklet pane, #1160-1167 12.00 14.00
Complete booklet, #1167a 14.00 12.00

City of Trondheim, Millenium A395

Stylized designs: 3.70k, New Trondheim. 12k, Ships entering harbor, King, early settlements in Old Nidaros.

**1997, June 6 Litho. *Perf. 13½x13***

**1168** A395 3.70k multicolored 2.00 .40
**1169** A395 12k multicolored 6.00 1.00

Einar Gerhardsen (1897-1987), Prime Minister — A396

Caricatures: 3.70k, In front on government buildings. 25k, Scenes of Norway.

**1997, June 6 *Perf. 13½***

**1170** A396 3.70k multicolored 2.00 .40
**1171** A396 25k multicolored 12.00 1.50

Junior Stamp Club — A397

Topics found on stamps: No. 1172, Insect, butterfly (silhouette of person's face), cartoon character, fish, flag, hand holding pen, heart, tiger, horn, boy with dog, globe. No. 1173, Flag, hand holding pen, tree, butterfly (silhouette of person's face), ladybug, cartoon character, antique postal vehicle, soccer ball, stylized bird, man on bicycle, lighthouse.

**1997, Sept. 29 Litho. *Perf. 13***

**1172** A397 3.70k multicolored 1.75 .40
**1173** A397 3.70k multicolored 1.75 .40

Harald Saeverud (1897-1992), Composer — A398

15k, Tarjei Vesaas (1897-1970), writer.

**Litho. & Engr.**

**1997, Sept. 19 *Perf. 13½x13***

**1174** A398 10k blue 5.50 1.00
**1175** A398 15k green 7.50 1.50

Petter Dass (1647-1706), Poet, Priest — A399

Designs: 3.20k, Dass standing in rowboat, verse. 3.70k, Dass, church on island of Alsten.

**Litho. & Engr.**

**1997, Nov. 26 *Perf. 13***

**1176** A399 3.20k multicolored 1.50 .75
**1177** A399 3.70k multicolored 1.75 .40

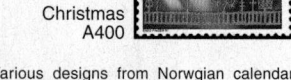

Christmas A400

Various designs from Norwgian calendar stick, medieval forerunner of modern day calendar.

***Serpentine Die Cut 13½ on 3 Sides***

**1997, Nov. 26 Litho.**

**Self-Adhesive**

**Booklet Stamps**

**1178** A400 3.70k yellow & multi 1.25 .30
**1179** A400 3.70k blue & multi 1.25 .30
*a.* Bklt. pane, 2 ea #1178-1179 6.00
Complete booklet, 2 #1179a 12.00

**Insect Type of 1997**

**1998, Jan. 2 *Perf. 13½ on 3 Sides***

**Booklet Stamps**

**1180** A390 3.80k Dragonfly 1.50 .25
**1181** A390 3.80k Grasshopper 1.50 .25
*a.* Bklt. pane, 4 ea #1180-1181 12.00
Complete booklet, #1181a 14.00

**Flower Type of 1997**

3.40k, Marsh marigold. 3.80k, Wild pansy. 4.50k, White clover. 5.50k, Hepatica. 7.50k, Pale pasqueflower. 13k, Purple saxifrage.

**1998, Jan. 2 Litho. *Perf. 13***

**1182** A391 3.40k multi 1.25 .25
**1183** A391 3.80k multi 1.50 .25
**1184** A391 4.50k multi 2.00 .40
**1185** A391 5.50k multi 2.25 .40
**1186** A391 7.50k multi 3.00 .50
**1187** A391 13k multi 5.00 .50
*Nos. 1182-1187 (6)* 15.00 2.30

Valentine's Day — A401

**1998, Feb. 9 *Die Cut Perf. 14x13***

**Self-Adhesive**

**1188** A401 3.80k multicolored 1.50 .50

No. 1188 was issued in sheets of 3 + 4 labels.

A402

Coastal Shipping: 3.80k, Mail boat, SS Hornelen. 4.50k, Catamaran, Kommandoren.

**Litho. & Engr.**

**1998, Apr. 20 *Perf. 13x13½***

**1189** A402 3.80k dark bl & grn 1.50 .30
**1190** A402 4.50k bl & dark grn 2.00 1.00

A403

Tourism: 3.80k, Holmenkollen ski jump, Oslo. 4.50k, Fisherman, city of Alesund. 5.50k, Summit of Hamaroyskaftet Mountain.

***Perf. 13 on 3 Sides***

**1998, Apr. 20 Litho.**

**1191** A403 3.80k multicolored 1.50 .25
*a.* Booklet pane of 8 12.00
Complete booklet, #1191a 12.00
**1192** A403 4.50k multicolored 1.75 1.00
*a.* Booklet pane of 8 14.00
Complete booklet, #1192a 14.00
**1193** A403 5.50k multicolored 2.00 .75
*a.* Booklet pane of 8 16.00
Complete booklet, #1193a 16.00
*Nos. 1191-1193 (3)* 5.25 2.00

Town of Egersund, Bicent. A404

Designs: 3.80k, Port, herring boats. 6k, Pottery, white stoneware.

**Litho. & Engr.**

**1998, Apr. 20 *Perf. 13***

**1194** A404 3.80k dk blue & pink 1.50 .30
**1195** A404 6k mag & dp bl 2.50 .60

Minerals — A405

**1998, June 18 Litho. *Perf. 13***

**1196** A405 3.40k Silver 1.50 .70
**1197** A405 5.20k Cobaltite 2.25 .75

Contemporary Art — A406

Designs: 6k, "Water Rider," painting by Frans Widerberg. 7.50k, "Red Moon," tapestry by Synnove Anker Aurdal. 13k, "King Haakon VII," sculpture by Nils Aas.

**1998, June 18**

**1198** A406 6k multicolored 2.40 .50
**1199** A406 7.50k multicolored 3.00 1.25
**1200** A406 13k multicolored 5.00 1.25
*Nos. 1198-1200 (3)* 10.40 3.00

Children's Games A407

**1998, Sept. 18 Litho. *Perf. 13***

**1201** A407 3.80k Hopscotch 1.50 .50
**1202** A407 5.50k Pitching coins 2.25 1.00

New Airport, Gardermoen — A408

**1998, Sept. 18 *Perf. 13½***

**1203** A408 3.80k DC-3 2.00 .50
**1204** A408 6k Boeing 737 3.00 .75
**1205** A408 24k New airport 10.00 1.50
*Nos. 1203-1205 (3)* 15.00 2.75

The Royal Palace A409

**1998, Nov. 20 Engr. *Perf. 13x13½***

**1206** A409 3.40k Royal Guard 1.50 1.00
**1207** A409 3.80k Facade 1.50 .50

Christmas A410

***Serpentine Die Cut 14x13 on 3 Sides***

**1998, Nov. 20 Photo.**

**Self-Adhesive**

**Booklet Stamps**

**1208** A410 3.80k red & multi 1.50 .30
**1209** A410 3.80k blue & multi 1.50 .30
*a.* Bklt. pane, 2 ea #1208-1209 6.00
Complete booklet, 2 #1209a 12.00

**Flower Type of 1997**

3.60k, Red campion. 4k, Wood anemone. 7k, Yellow wood violet.

**1999, Jan. 2 Litho. *Perf. 13***

**1210** A391 3.60k multi 1.50 .30
**1211** A391 4k multi 1.75 .25
**1212** A391 7k multi 2.75 .50
*Nos. 1210-1212 (3)* 6.00 1.05

Norwegian Inventions — A411

Designs: 3.60k, Cheese slicer, by Thor Bjorklund. 4k, Paper clip, by Johan Vaaler.

***Die Cut Perf. 13***

**1999, Jan. 2 Photo.**

**Self-Adhesive**

**1213** A411 3.60k blue & black 1.25 .25
**1214** A411 4k red & gray 1.50 .25

See No. 1260.

Salmon — A412

Cod — A413

***Die Cut Perf. 14x13***

**1999, Jan. 2 Litho. & Photo.**

**Self-Adhesive**

**Booklet Stamps**

**1215** A412 4k multicolored 1.25 .25
**1216** A413 4k multicolored 1.25 .25
*a.* Bklt. pane, 2 ea #1215-1216 5.00
Complete booklet, 2 #1216a 10.00

St. Valentine's Day — A414

**1999, Feb. 14 Litho. *Perf. 13x13½***

**1217** A414 4k multicolored 1.75 .50

A415

**Litho. & Engr.**

**1999, Apr. 12 *Perf. 13***

**1218** A415 4k multicolored 1.50 .50

Norwegian Confederation of Trade Unions, Cent.

A416

Tourism: 4k, Swans on lake. 5k, Hamar Cathedral. 6k, Man in traditional attire.

**1999, Apr. 12 Litho. *Perf. 13***

**Booklet Stamps**

**1219** A416 4k multicolored 1.25 .40
*a.* Booklet pane of 8 10.00
Complete booklet, #1219a 10.00
**1220** A416 5k multicolored 1.75 .50
*a.* Booklet pane of 8 14.00
Complete booklet, #1220a 14.00

**1221** A416 6k multicolored 2.00 .75
*a.* Booklet pane of 8 16.00
Complete booklet, #1221a 16.00

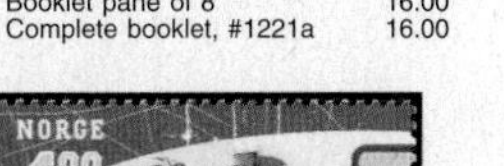

Ice Hockey World Championships — A417

Designs: 4k, Poland vs Norway, 1998 Class B Championships. 7k, Sweden vs Switzerland, 1998 Class A Championships.

**1999, Apr. 12** ***Perf. 13½***
**1222** A417 4k multicolored 1.50 .50
**1223** A417 7k multicolored 3.00 .75

Millennium Stamps A418

Events from 1000-1899: 4k, Family leaving Sejestad Station, emigration period, 1800's. 6k, Statue of St. Olav (995-1030), Christian III Bible, 1550, Christianization period. 14k, King Christian IV speciedaler, miners, union period, 1380-1814. 26k, Textile factory, paper mill on Aker River, Oslo, 1850's, industrialization period.

**Litho. & Engr.**

**1999, June 11** ***Perf. 12¾x13***
**1224** A418 4k multicolored 1.75 .50
**1225** A418 6k multicolored 2.75 .75
**1226** A418 14k multicolored 6.50 1.25
**1227** A418 26k multicolored 10.00 1.75
*Nos. 1224-1227 (4)* 21.00 4.25

Pictures of Everyday Life — A419

No. 1228, Carriage on ferry. No. 1229, Men with hammers. No. 1230, Pumping gasoline. No. 1231, Milking cow. No. 1232, Rakers. No. 1233, Skier. No. 1234, Boat captain. No. 1235, Soccer player.

**1999, Sept. 9** **Litho.** ***Perf. 13***
**1228** A419 4k multicolored 1.75 .50
**1229** A419 4k multicolored 1.75 .50
**1230** A419 4k multicolored 1.75 .50
**1231** A419 4k multicolored 1.75 .50
**1232** A419 4k multicolored 1.75 .50
**1233** A419 4k multicolored 1.75 .50
**1234** A419 4k multicolored 1.75 .50
**1235** A419 4k multicolored 1.75 .50
*a.* Souv. sheet of 8, #1228-1235 14.00 12.50

Children's Games — A420

**1999, Sept. 9** **Litho.** ***Perf. 13¼***
**1236** A420 4k Skateboarder 1.50 .50
**1237** A420 6k Roller skater 2.50 .75

National Theater, Cent. A421

Designs: 3.60k, Scene from "An Ideal Husband." 4k, Scene from "Peer Gynt."

**1999, Nov. 19** **Engr.** ***Perf. 12¾x13¼***
**1238** A421 3.60k claret & org yel 1.50 1.50
**1239** A421 4k dk bl & royal bl 1.25 .50

Christmas — A422

Designs: No. 1240, Mother, children at door. No. 1241, Mother, children at window.

***Die Cut Perf. 14x13 on 3 sides***

**1999, Nov. 19** **Litho.**

**Self-Adhesive**

**1240** A422 4k multi 1.50 .30
**1241** A422 4k multi 1.50 .30
*a.* Bklt. pane, 2 ea #1240-1241 5.00
Complete booklet, 2 #1241a 12.00

Millennium A423

Winners of photo competition: No. 1242, "Winter Night." No. 1243, "Sunset."

***Die Cut Perf. 13¼x13***

**1999, Dec. 31** **Litho. & Photo.**

**Self-Adhesive**

**1242** A423 4k multi 1.75 .50
**1243** A423 4k multi 1.75 .50
*a.* Bklt. pane of 2, #1242-1243 5.00
Complete booklet, #1243a 18.00
*b.* Bklt. pane, 2 ea #1242-1243 8.00
Complete booklet, 2 #1243b 16.00

One complete booklet containing No. 1243a was given free to each Norwegian household in January 2000.

**Flower Type of 1997**

Designs: 5.40k, Oeder's lousewort. 8k, White water lily. 14k, Globe flower. 25k, Melancholy thistle.

**2000, Feb. 9** **Litho.** ***Perf. 12¾x13¼***
**1244** A391 5.40k multi 2.00 .60
**1245** A391 8k multi 3.25 .75
**1246** A391 14k multi 5.00 1.00
**1247** A391 25k multi 10.00 1.25
*Nos. 1244-1247 (4)* 20.25 3.60

Love — A424

**2000, Feb. 9** ***Perf. 13x13¼***
**1248** A424 4k multi 1.50 .50

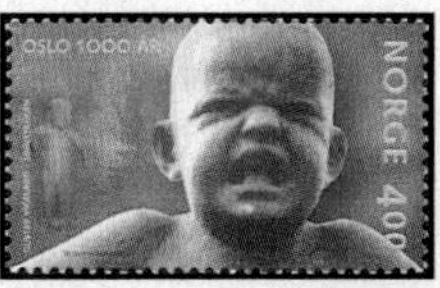

Oslo, 1000th Anniv. A425

4k, Angry Child sculpture, Frogner Park. 6k, Statue of King Christian IV, by C. L. Jacobsen. 8k, Oslo City Hall. 27k, Oslo Stock Exchange.

**2000, Apr. 7** **Litho.** ***Perf. 13¼***
**1249** A425 4k multi 1.75 .50
**1250** A425 6k multi 2.50 .75
**1251** A425 8k multi 3.50 1.00
**1252** A426 27k multi 11.00 1.50
*Nos. 1249-1252 (4)* 18.75 3.75

Fauna — A426

**2000, Apr. 7** ***Perf. 13¼ on 3 sides***

**Booklet Stamps**

**1253** A426 5k Golden eagle 1.75 .75
*a.* Booklet pane of 8 14.00
Booklet, #1253a 15.00
**1254** A426 6k Elk 2.00 .75
*a.* Booklet pane of 8 16.00
Booklet, #1254a 18.00
**1255** A426 7k Whale 2.25 .75
*a.* Booklet pane of 8 18.00
Complete booklet, #1255a 20.00
*Nos. 1253-1255 (3)* 6.00 2.25

Expo 2000, Hanover A427

Artwork of Marianne Heske: 4.20k, The Quiet Room. 6.30k, Power and Energy.

**2000, June 1** ***Perf. 13¼***
**1256** A427 4.20k multi 1.75 1.00
**1257** A427 6.30k multi 2.75 .50

Royal Norwegian Military Academy, 250th Anniv. — A428

**Litho. & Engr.**

**2000, June 2** ***Perf. 13x13¼***
**1258** A428 3.60k 1750 Cadets 1.75 2.00
**1259** A428 8k 2000 Cadets 3.25 1.00

**Inventions Type of 1999**

4.20k, Aerosol container, by Erik Rotheim.

***Die Cut Perf. 12¾***

**2000, June 2** **Photo.**

**Self-Adhesive**

**1260** A411 4.20k green & black 1.50 .25

Mackerel — A429

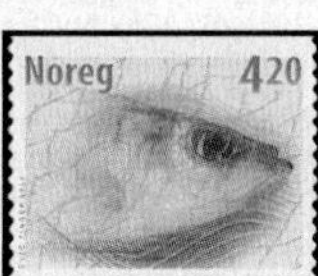

Herring — A430

***Die Cut Perf. 14x13 on 3 sides***

**2000, June 2** **Photo. & Litho.**

**Self-Adhesive**

**Booklet Stamps**

**1261** A429 4.20k multi 1.50 .25
**1262** A430 4.20k multi 1.50 .25
*a.* Booklet pane, 2 each #1261-1262 6.00
Complete booklet, 2#1262a 12.00

A431

**Litho. & Engr.**

**2000, Sept. 15** ***Perf. 13¼x13***
**1263** A431 5k multi 2.25 1.00

Lars Levi Laestadius (1800-61), botanist.

A432

Intl. Museum of Children's Art, Oslo: 4.20k, Astronaut, by May-Therese Vorland. 6.30k, Rocket, by Jann Fredrik Ronning.

***Perf. 13¼x13¾***

**2000, Sept. 15** **Litho.**
**1264** A432 4.20k multi 1.75 .50
**1265** A432 6.30k multi 2.50 .60

Skien, 1000th Anniv. — A433

Designs: 4.20k, Monument to loggers. 15k, Skien Church.

**2000, Sept. 15** ***Perf. 13¼x13***
**1266** A433 4.20k multi 1.75 .75
**1267** A433 15k multi 6.25 1.50

Church Altar Pieces A434

3.60k, Hamaroy Church. 4.20k, Ski Church.

**2000, Nov. 17** **Litho.** ***Perf. 13x13¼***
**1268** A434 3.60k multi 1.50 1.25
**1269** A434 4.20k multi 1.75 .75

Comic Strips — A435

Designs: No. 1270, Nils og Blamman, by Sigurd Winsnes and Ivar Mauritz-Hansen. No. 1271, Nr. 91 Stomperud, by Ernst Garvin and Torbjorn Wen.

***Die Cut Perf. 14x13 on 3 sides***

**2000, Nov. 17** **Photo. & Litho.**

**Booklet Stamps**

**Self-Adhesive**

**1270** A435 4.20k multi 1.50 .25
**1271** A435 4.20k multi 1.50 .25
*a.* Booklet pane, 2 each #1270-1271 6.00
Complete booklet, 2 #1271a 12.00

Rose Varieties A436

Designs: No. 1272, Sekel (green denomination). No. 1273, Namdal (brown denomination).

***Die Cut Perf.13¼ on 3 sides***

**2001, Jan. 2** **Photo.**

**Booklet Stamps**

**Self-Adhesive**

**1272** A436 4.50k multi 1.50 .25
**1273** A436 4.50k multi 1.50 .25
*a.* Booklet pane, 2 each #1272-1273 7.00
Complete booklet, 2 #1273a 14.00

See Nos. 1303-1304.

Crafts — A437

Designs: 4k, Mat of bound birch roots. 4.50k, Birch bark basket. 7k, Embroidered bunad.

**2001, Jan. 2** ***Die Cut Perf. 12¾***

**Coil Stamps**

**Self-Adhesive**

| | | | | | |
|---|---|---|---|---|---|
| 1274 | A437 | 4k | multi | 1.50 | .30 |
| 1275 | A437 | 4.50k | multi | 1.75 | .25 |
| 1276 | A437 | 7k | multi | 2.50 | .50 |
| | *Nos. 1274-1276 (3)* | | | 5.75 | 1.05 |

See Nos. 1305-1307, 1354.

Actors and Actresses A438

Designs: 4k, Aase Bye (1904-91). 4.50k, Per Aabel (1902-99). 5.50k, Alfred Maurstad (1896-1967). 7k, Lillebil Ibsen (1899-1989). 8k, Tore Segelcke (1901-79).

**2001, Jan. 2** **Litho.** ***Perf. 14x12¾***

| | | | | | |
|---|---|---|---|---|---|
| 1277 | A438 | 4k | brn & blk | 1.50 | .75 |
| 1278 | A438 | 4.50k | bl & blk | 2.00 | .50 |
| 1279 | A438 | 5.50k | gold & blk | 2.25 | .75 |
| 1280 | A438 | 7k | pur & blk | 2.75 | 1.00 |
| 1281 | A438 | 8k | bl gray & blk | 3.00 | 1.00 |
| | *Nos. 1277-1281 (5)* | | | 11.50 | 4.00 |

Ties That Bind, by Magne Furuholmen A439

**2001, Feb. 7** **Litho.** ***Perf. 14¾x14***

| | | | | | |
|---|---|---|---|---|---|
| 1282 | A439 | 4.50k | multi | 1.75 | .50 |

Redrawn Posthorn — A439a

**2001-06** **Litho.** ***Perf. 13¾x13¼***

**Color of Oval**

| | | | | | |
|---|---|---|---|---|---|
| 1282A | A439a | 50o | green, blue denomination | .25 | .25 |
| 1283 | A439a | 1k | green | .50 | .40 |
| a. | | | Horiz. rows of dots between vert. lines | 1.00 | .75 |
| 1284 | A439a | 2k | Prus blue | 1.00 | .75 |
| a. | | | Horiz. rows of dots between vert. lines | 1.00 | .75 |
| 1285 | A439a | 3k | blue | 1.00 | .50 |
| 1287 | A439a | 5k | purple | 3.00 | .75 |
| a. | | | Horiz. rows of dots between vert. lines | 3.00 | .25 |
| 1288 | A439a | 6k | purple | 2.00 | .45 |
| 1289 | A439a | 7k | brown | 2.50 | .90 |
| 1291 | A439a | 9k | orange brn | 4.50 | .75 |
| a. | | | Horiz. rows of dots between vert. lines | 4.00 | .75 |
| | *Nos. 1282A-1291 (8)* | | | 14.75 | 4.75 |

Numerous design differences exist between types A10 and A439a in the vertical shading lines, the size and shading of the posthorn and in the corner wings.

No. 1282A has no dots between vertical lines. Dots between vertical lines on Nos. 1283-1284, 1287-1288 and 1291 are arranged diagonally. Nos. 1285 and 1289 have horizontal rows of dots between vertical lines.

Issued: Nos.1283, 1284, 6k, 2/7/01; 50o, 3/01; 5k, 9k, 2/11/02; Nos. 1283a, 1284a, 1291a, 2003; 3k, 7k, 4/15/05; No. 1287a, 2006.

See No. 1145 for green 50o stamp with green denomination. See Nos. 1628-1630, 1661, 1690, 1723-1724, 1749-1752, 1783.

School Bands, Cent. A440

Designs: 4.50k, Tuba player. 9k, Drum majorette.

**2001, Apr. 20** **Litho.** ***Perf. 14¾x14***

| | | | | | |
|---|---|---|---|---|---|
| 1292 | A440 | 4.50k | multi | 1.75 | .50 |
| 1293 | A440 | 9k | multi | 3.50 | 1.50 |

Adventure Sports — A441

Designs: 4.50k, Kayaking. 7k, Rock climbing.

***Serpentine Die Cut 14x13 on 3 Sides***

**2001, Apr. 20** **Photo. & Litho.**

**Booklet Stamps**

**Self-Adhesive**

| | | | | | |
|---|---|---|---|---|---|
| 1294 | A441 | 4.50k | multi | 1.75 | .50 |
| a. | | | Booklet of 8 | 15.00 | |
| 1295 | A441 | 7k | multi | 2.50 | .75 |
| a. | | | Booklet of 8 | 20.00 | |

Norwegian Architecture A442

Designs: 5.50k, Bank of Norway, Oslo, by Christian Heinrich Grosch. 8.50k, Ivar Aasen Center, Orsta, by Sverre Fehn.

**2001, June 22** **Litho.** ***Perf. 14¾x14***

| | | | | | |
|---|---|---|---|---|---|
| 1296 | A442 | 5.50k | multi | 2.00 | .75 |
| 1297 | A442 | 8.50k | multi | 3.00 | 1.00 |

Actors and Actresses — A443

Designs: 5k, Lalla Carlsen (1889-1967). 5.50k, Leif Juster (1910-95). 7k, Kari Diesen (1914-87). 9k, Arvid Nilssen (1913-76). 10k, Einar Rose (1898-1979).

**2001, June 22** ***Perf. 13x14***

| | | | | | |
|---|---|---|---|---|---|
| 1298 | A443 | 5k | multi | 1.75 | 1.00 |
| 1299 | A443 | 5.50k | multi | 2.00 | .50 |
| 1300 | A443 | 7k | multi | 2.25 | 1.25 |
| 1301 | A443 | 9k | multi | 3.25 | 1.25 |
| 1302 | A443 | 10k | multi | 3.75 | 1.00 |
| | *Nos. 1298-1302 (5)* | | | 13.00 | 5.00 |

**Rose Type of 2001**

***Die Cut Perf. 13¼x13 on 3 Sides***

**2001, June 22** **Photo. & Litho.**

**Booklet Stamps**

**Self-Adhesive**

| | | | | | |
|---|---|---|---|---|---|
| 1303 | A436 | 5.50k | Red roses | 1.75 | .30 |
| 1304 | A436 | 5.50k | Pink roses | 1.75 | .30 |
| a. | | | Booklet pane, 2 each #1303-1304 | 7.00 | |
| | | | Booklet, 2 #1304a | 16.00 | |

Nos. 1303-1304 are impregnated with a rose scent.

Roses on No. 1303 have white centers. Compare with Illustration A460.

**Crafts Type of 2001**

Designs: 5k, Carved bird-shaped drinking vessel. 5.50k, Doll with crocheted clothing. 8.50k, Knitted cap.

***Die Cut Perf. 14½***

**2001, June 22** **Photo.**

**Coil Stamps**

**Self-Adhesive**

| | | | | | |
|---|---|---|---|---|---|
| 1305 | A437 | 5k | multi | 3.50 | 3.50 |
| 1306 | A437 | 5.50k | multi | 3.50 | 3.50 |
| 1307 | A437 | 8.50k | multi | 5.00 | 5.00 |
| | *Nos. 1305-1307 (3)* | | | 12.00 | 12.00 |

**2001, June 22** **Photo.**

**Coil Stamps**

**Self-Adhesive**

| | | | |
|---|---|---|---|
| *1305a* | Die cut perf. 12¾ | 1.75 | .30 |
| *1306a* | Die cut perf. 12¾ | 1.75 | .25 |
| *1307a* | Die cut perf. 12¾ | 3.00 | .50 |

Nobel Peace Prize, Cent. A444

Designs: No. 1308, 1991 winner Aung San Suu Kyi. No. 1309, 1993 winner Nelson Mandela. No. 1310, Alfred Nobel. No. 1311, 1901 winner Henri Dunant. No. 1312, 1922 winner Fridjof Nansen. No. 1313, 1990 winner, Mikhail S. Gorbachev. No. 1314, 1964 winner, Dr. Martin Luther King, Jr. No. 1315, 1992 winner Dr. Rigoberta Menchú Tum.

***Perf. 13¼x13¾***

**2001, Sept. 14** **Litho. & Engr.**

| | | | | | |
|---|---|---|---|---|---|
| 1308 | A444 | 5.50k | multi | 2.00 | .75 |
| 1309 | A444 | 5.50k | multi | 2.00 | .75 |
| a. | | | Vert. pair, #1308-1309 | 4.00 | 3.50 |
| 1310 | A444 | 7k | multi | 2.50 | 1.25 |
| a. | | | Souvenir sheet of 1 | 3.50 | 2.75 |
| 1311 | A444 | 7k | multi | 2.50 | 1.25 |
| a. | | | Vert. pair, #1310-1311 | 5.00 | 4.50 |
| 1312 | A444 | 9k | multi | 3.25 | 1.50 |
| 1313 | A444 | 9k | multi | 3.25 | 1.50 |
| a. | | | Vert. pair, #1312-1313 | 6.50 | 5.00 |
| 1314 | A444 | 10k | multi | 3.75 | 1.25 |
| 1315 | A444 | 10k | multi | 3.75 | 1.25 |
| a. | | | Vert. pair, #1314-1315 | 7.50 | 4.50 |
| | *Nos. 1308-1315 (8)* | | | 23.00 | 9.50 |

Pets — A445

**2001, Sept. 14** **Litho.** ***Perf. 14x13¼***

| | | | | | |
|---|---|---|---|---|---|
| 1316 | A445 | 5.50k | Kittens | 2.00 | .50 |
| 1317 | A445 | 7.50k | Goat | 3.00 | 1.25 |

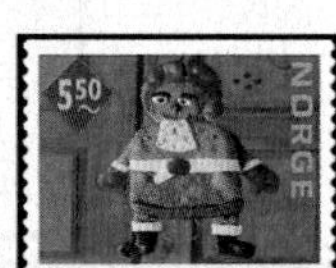

Aurora Borealis A446

**2001, Nov. 15**

| | | | | | |
|---|---|---|---|---|---|
| 1318 | A446 | 5k | Trees | 2.00 | 1.25 |
| 1319 | A446 | 5.50k | Reindeer | 2.25 | 1.00 |

Christmas A447

Gingerbread: No. 1320, Man. No. 1321, House.

***Serp. Die Cut 14x13 on 3 Sides***

**2001, Nov. 15** **Photo. & Litho.**

**Booklet Stamps**

**Self-Adhesive**

| | | | | | |
|---|---|---|---|---|---|
| 1320 | A447 | 5.50k | multi | 1.75 | .30 |
| 1321 | A447 | 5.50k | multi | 1.75 | .30 |
| a. | | | Booklet pane, 2 each #1320-1321 | 7.00 | |
| | | | Complete booklet, 2 #1321a | 14.00 | |

Actors and Actresses — A448

Designs: 5k, Tordis Maurstad (1901-97). 5.50k, Rolf Just Nilsen (1931-81). 7k, Lars Tvinde (1886-1973). 9k, Henry Gleditsch (1902-42). 10k, Norma Balean (1907-89).

**2002, Feb. 11** **Litho.** ***Perf. 13x14***

**Background Color**

| | | | | | |
|---|---|---|---|---|---|
| 1322 | A448 | 5k | rose lilac | 1.75 | 1.25 |
| 1323 | A448 | 5.50k | lilac | 2.00 | .50 |
| 1324 | A448 | 7k | beige | 2.50 | 1.25 |
| 1325 | A448 | 9k | light green | 3.25 | 1.50 |
| 1326 | A448 | 10k | dull rose | 3.50 | 1.50 |
| | *Nos. 1322-1326 (5)* | | | 13.00 | 6.00 |

Contemporary Sculpture — A449

Designs: 7.50k, Monument to Whaling, by Sivert Donali. 8.50k, Throw, by Kare Groven.

**2002, Apr. 12** **Litho.** ***Perf. 13¼x13¾***

| | | | | | |
|---|---|---|---|---|---|
| 1327 | A449 | 7.50k | multi | 2.50 | 1.50 |
| 1328 | A449 | 8.50k | multi | 2.75 | 1.25 |

Fairy Tales
A450 A451

Designs: No. 1329, Askeladden and the Good Helpers, by Ivo Caprino. No. 1330, Giant Troll on Karl Johan, by Theodor Kittelsen.

***Serpentine Die Cut 13x14 on 3 Sides***

**2002, Apr. 12** **Photo. & Litho.**

**Booklet Stamps**

**Self-Adhesive**

| | | | | | |
|---|---|---|---|---|---|
| 1329 | A450 | 5.50k | multi | 1.75 | .25 |
| a. | | | Booklet pane of 4 | 7.00 | |
| | | | Booklet, 2 #1329a | 14.00 | |
| 1330 | A451 | 9k | multi | 3.00 | 1.25 |
| a. | | | Booklet pane of 4 | 12.00 | |
| | | | Booklet, 2 #1330a | 24.00 | |

Norwegian Soccer Association, Cent. — A452

No. 1331: a, Boys playing soccer. b, Referee pointing, player. c, Girls playing soccer. d, Boy kicking ball.

**2002, Apr. 12** ***Die Cut Perf.***

**Self-Adhesive**

| | | | |
|---|---|---|---|
| 1331 | Booklet pane of 4 | 7.50 | |
| a.-d. | A452 5.50k Any single | 1.75 | .30 |
| | Booklet, 2 #1331 | 15.00 | |

The margins of the two panes in the booklet differ.

Niels Henrik Abel (1802-29), Mathematician — A453

Designs: 5.50k, Abel, formula and curves. 22k, Formula, front page of book by Abel, curve.

***Perf. 13¼x13¾***

**2002, June 5** **Litho. & Engr.**

| | | | | | |
|---|---|---|---|---|---|
| 1332 | A453 | 5.50k | multi | 2.00 | .75 |
| 1333 | A453 | 22k | multi | 8.00 | 2.25 |

For overprints, see No. 1346-1347.

City Charter Anniversaries — A454

Designs: No. 1334, Holmestrand, 250th anniv. No. 1335, Kongsberg, 200th anniv.

**2002, June 5** **Litho.**
**1334** A454 5.50k multi 2.00 .75
**1335** A454 5.50k multi 2.00 .75

Authors — A455

Designs: 11k, Johan Collett Muller Borgen (1902-79). 20k, Nordahl Grieg (1902-43).

**2002, June 5** ***Perf. 14¼x14***
**1336** A455 11k multi 4.00 1.50
**1337** A455 20k multi 7.50 2.25

Europa — A456

Designs: 5.50k, Clown juggling balls. 8.50k, Elephant, monkey on rocking horse.

**2002, Sept. 20** ***Perf. 14x14¾***
**1338** A456 5.50k multi 2.00 .75
**1339** A456 8.50k multi 3.00 1.25

Great Moments in Norwegian Soccer
A457

Players involved in: 5k, Victory against Germany in 1936 Olympics. No. 1341, Victory against Brazil in 1998 World Cup tournament. No. 1342, Victory of women's team against US in 2000 Olympics. 7k, Victory against Sweden, 1960. 9k, Victory against England, 1981. 10k, Rosenborg's victory against Milan, in Champions League tournament, 1996.

**2002, Sept. 20** ***Perf. 13¼x13¾***
**1340** A457 5k multi 1.75 .75
**1341** A457 5.50k multi 2.00 .50
**1342** A457 5.50k multi 2.00 .50
**1343** A457 7k multi 2.50 1.25
**1344** A457 9k multi 3.25 1.25
**1345** A457 10k multi 3.50 1.25
*a.* Souvenir sheet, #1340-1345 + 6 labels 15.00 15.00
*Nos. 1340-1345 (6)* 15.00 5.50

Norwegian Soccer Association, cent.

**Nos. 1332-1333 Overprinted**

***Perf. 13¼x13¾***
**2002, Oct. 10** **Litho. & Engr.**
**1346** A453 5.50k multi 6.00 6.00
**1347** A453 22k multi 13.00 13.00

Pastor Magnus B. Landstad (1802-80), Hymn Writer and Folk Song Collector
A458

Designs: 5k, Landstad on horse, front page of 1853 book of folk songs. 5.50k, Church's hymn board, front page of 1870 hymn book, portrait of Landstad.

**2002, Nov. 20**
**1348** A458 5k multi 1.75 1.00
**1349** A458 5.50k multi 2.00 .75

Christmas Ornaments
A459

***Die Cut Perf. 13½x13 on 3 Sides***
**2002, Nov. 20** **Photo.**
**Booklet Stamps**
**Self-Adhesive**
**1350** A459 5.50k Hearts 1.90 .30
**1351** A459 5.50k Star 1.90 .30
*a.* Booklet pane, 2 each #1350-1351 7.75
Booklet, 2 #1351a 15.50

**Rose Type of 2001 and**

Grand Prix Rose — A460

Design: No. 1353, Champagne roses (light yellow).

***Die Cut Perf. 13¼x13 on 3 Sides***
**2003, Feb. 10** **Photo. & Litho.**
**Booklet Stamps**
**Self-Adhseive**
**1352** A460 5.50k multi 2.25 .25
**1353** A436 5.50k multi 2.25 .25
*a.* Booklet pane, 2 each #1352-1353 9.00
Booklet, 2 #1353a 18.00

Roses on No. 1303 have white centers, while those on No. 1352 do not.

**Crafts Type of 2001**
**2003, Feb. 10** ***Die Cut Perf. 12¾***
**Self-Adhesive**
**1354** A437 5.50k Duodji knife handle 1.75 .25

Graphic Arts — A461

Designs: 5k, Nordmandens Krone, by Kaare Espolin Johnson. 8.50k, Bla Hester, by Else Hagen. 9k, Dirigent og Solist, by Niclas Gulbrandsen. 11k, Olympia, by Svein Strand. 22k, Still Life XVII, by Rigmor Hansen.

***Perf. 13¼x12¾***
**2003, Feb. 10** **Litho.**
**1355** A461 5k multi 1.75 1.00
**1356** A461 8.50k multi 3.00 1.50
**1357** A461 9k multi 3.25 1.75
**1358** A461 11k multi 4.00 1.50
**1359** A461 22k multi 8.00 2.00
*a.* Perf. 14x12¾ 8.00 2.25
*Nos. 1355-1359 (5)* 20.00 7.75

St. Valentine's Day — A462

Inscriptions beneath scratch-off heart: b, Elsker deg! c, Jusen kyss! d, Glad i dag! e, Klem fra meg! f, Du er sot! g, Min beste venn! h, Yndlings-bror. i, Yndlings-soster. j, Verdens beste far. k, Verdens beste mor.

**2003, Feb. 10** ***Perf. 14¾x14***
**1360** Sheet of 10 20.00 18.00
*a.* A462 5.50k Any single, unscrached 2.00 1.00
*b.-k.* A462 5.50k Any single, scratched .65

Unused value for No. 1360a is for stamp with attached selvage. Inscriptions are shown in selvage next to each stamp.

Fairy Tale Illustrations by Theodor Kittelsen (1857-1914)
A463 A464

***Serpentine Die Cut 13x14 on 3 Sides***
**2003, May 22** **Photo. & Litho.**
**Booklet Stamps**
**Self-Adhesive**
**1361** A463 5.50k Forest troll 1.90 .30
*a.* Booklet pane of 4 7.75
Complete booklet, 2 #1361a 15.50

***Serpentine Die Cut 14x13 on 3 Sides***
**1362** A464 9k Water sprite 3.00 1.25
*a.* Booklet pane of 4 12.00
Complete booklet, 2 #1362a 24.00

Bergen Intl. Music Festival, 50th Anniv.
A465

Musical score and: 5.50k, Violinist. 10k, Children.

**2003, May 22** **Litho.** ***Perf. 13¼x14***
**1363** A465 5.50k multi 2.00 1.00
**1364** A465 10k multi 3.75 2.00

Public Health Service, 400th Anniv.
A466

Designs: 5.50k, Heart transplant operation. 7k, Infant welfare clinic.

**2003, May 22**
**1365** A466 5.50k multi 2.00 1.00
**1366** A466 7k multi 2.50 1.75

Norwegian Refugee Council, 50th Anniv.
A467

Designs: 5.50k, Child with bread. 10k, Line of refugees.

**2003, June 20**
**1367** A467 5.50k multi 2.00 1.00
**1368** A467 10k multi 4.00 1.10

King Olav V (1903-91) — A468

Designs: 5.50k, As child, with parents. 8.50k, With Crown Princess Mãrtha. 11k, In uniform.

**Litho. & Engr.**
**2003, June 20** ***Perf. 14x13¼***
**1369** A468 5.50k multi 2.00 1.00
**1370** A468 8.50k multi 3.00 1.50
**1371** A468 11k multi 4.00 2.00
*a.* Souvenir sheet, #1369-1371 13.50 13.50
*Nos. 1369-1371 (3)* 9.00 4.50

Norwegian Nobel Laureates
A469

Designs: 11k, Bjornsterne Bjornson, Literature, 1903. 22k, Lars Onsager, Chemistry, 1968.

***Perf. 13¼x13¾***
**2003, Sept. 19** **Litho. & Engr.**
**1372** A469 11k multi 4.00 1.75
**1373** A469 22k multi 8.00 2.50

See nos. 1414-1415.

Europa — A470

Poster art: 8.50k, Dagbladet newspaper poster, by Per Krohg. 9k, Travel poster, by Knut Yran. 10k, 1985 North of Norway Music Festival poster, by Willibald Storn.

**2003, Sept. 19** **Litho.** ***Perf. 13¾***
**1374** A470 8.50k multi 3.00 1.75
**1375** A470 9k multi 3.25 1.75
**1376** A470 10k multi 3.75 1.75
*Nos. 1374-1376 (3)* 10.00 5.25

Special Occasions
A471

Designs: No. 1377, Baby, children's names. No. 1378, Children, birthday cake, toys. No. 1379, Man and woman at party, musical notes. No. 1380, Hands, Cupid. No. 1381, Lily.

***Die Cut Perf. 13x13½***
**2003, Sept. 19** **Photo.**
**Self-Adhesive**
**1377** A471 5.50k multi 2.00 1.00
**1378** A471 5.50k multi 2.00 1.00
**1379** A471 5.50k multi 2.00 1.00
**1380** A471 5.50k multi 2.00 1.00
**1381** A471 5.50k multi 2.00 1.00
*Nos. 1377-1381 (5)* 10.00 5.00

Graphic Arts — A472

Designs: 5k, Winter Landscape, woodcut by Terje Grostad. 5.50k, Goatherd and Goats, by Rolf Nesch.

***Perf. 13¾x12¾***
**2003, Nov. 21** **Litho.**
**1382** A472 5k multi 1.75 1.25
**1383** A472 5.50k multi 1.75 1.25

Christmas
A473

***Serpentine Die Cut 13¼x13 on 3 Sides***
**2003, Nov. 21** **Photo.**
**Booklet Stamps**
**Self-Adhesive**
**1384** A473 5.50k Santa Claus 1.75 .30
**1385** A473 5.50k Gift 1.75 .30
*a.* Booklet pane, 2 each #1384-1385 9.50
Complete booklet, 2 #1385a 20.00

Paintings — A474

Designs: 6k, Idyll, by Christian Skredsvig. 9.50k, Stetind in Fog, by Peder Balke. 10.50k, Worker's Protest, by Reidar Aulie.

**2004, Jan. 2 Litho. *Perf. 13x14***

| | | | | |
|---|---|---|---|---|
| **1386** A474 | 6k multi | 2.25 | .85 |
| **1387** A474 | 9.50k multi | 3.25 | 1.75 |
| **1388** A474 | 10.50k multi | 3.75 | 2.00 |
| | *Nos. 1386-1388 (3)* | 9.25 | 4.60 |

Marine Life — A475

Designs: 5.50k, Periphylla periphylla. 6k, Anarhichas lupus. 9k, Sepiola atlantica.

***Die Cut Perf. 15½x14¼***

**2004, Jan. 2 Photo.**

**Self-Adhesive**

| | | | |
|---|---|---|---|
| **1389** A475 5.50k multi | | 2.00 | .30 |
| **1390** A475 6k multi | | 2.25 | .25 |
| **1391** A475 9k multi | | 3.25 | .50 |
| | *Nos. 1389-1391 (3)* | 7.50 | 1.05 |

See Nos. 1440-1441.

"Person to Person" A476

Stylized: No. 1392, Man and woman. No. 1393, Globe.

***Serpentine Die Cut 13¼x13 on 3 Sides***

**2004, Jan. 2 Photo. & Litho.**

**Self-Adhesive**

**Booklet Stamps**

| | | |
|---|---|---|
| **1392** A476 6k multi | 2.00 | .25 |
| **1393** A476 6k multi | 2.00 | .25 |
| *a.* Booklet pane, 2 each #1392-1393 | 8.00 | |
| Complete booklet, 2 #1393a | 18.00 | |

Sunflower Heart — A477

**2004, Feb. 6 Litho. *Perf. 14x13¼***

| | | |
|---|---|---|
| **1394** A477 6k multi | 2.25 | .75 |

Printed in sheets of 6 stamps and 3 labels.

Europa A478

Designs: 6k, Bicyclist in Moskenes. 7.50k, Kayaker on Oslo Fjord. 9.50k, Hikers crossing Stygge Glacier.

***Die Cut Perf. 13½x13 on 3 Sides***

**2004, Mar. 26 Photo. & Litho.**

**Self-Adhesive**

**Booklet Stamps**

| | | |
|---|---|---|
| **1395** A478 6k multi | 2.00 | .50 |
| *a.* Booklet pane of 4 | 8.00 | |
| Complete booklet, 2 #1395a | 16.00 | |
| **1396** A478 7.50k multi | 2.50 | 1.00 |
| *a.* Booklet pane of 4 | 10.00 | |
| Complete booklet, 2 #1396a | 20.00 | |
| **1397** A478 9.50k multi | 3.25 | 1.25 |
| *a.* Booklet pane of 4 | 13.00 | |
| Complete booklet, 2 #1397a | 26.00 | |
| *Nos. 1395-1397 (3)* | 7.75 | 2.75 |

Otto Sverdrup (1854-1930), Arctic Explorer — A479

**Litho. & Engr.**

**2004, Mar. 26 *Perf. 13¼***

| | | |
|---|---|---|
| **1398** A479 6k shown | 2.25 | 1.25 |
| **1399** A479 9.50k Ship "Fram" | 3.50 | 2.10 |
| *a.* Souvenir sheet, #1398-1399 + label | 7.50 | 7.50 |

See Canada Nos. 2026-2027, Greenland No. 426.

Norse Mythology A480

Designs: 7.50k, Njord, god of wind, sea and fire and ship. 10.50k, Nanna, wife of Balder, Balder's horse, ship.

***Perf. 14¼x13¾***

**2004, Mar. 26 Litho.**

| | | |
|---|---|---|
| **1400** A480 7.50k multi | 2.75 | 1.75 |
| **1401** A480 10.50k multi | 4.00 | 2.25 |
| *a.* Souvenir sheet, #1400-1401 | 9.00 | 9.00 |

Souvenir Sheet

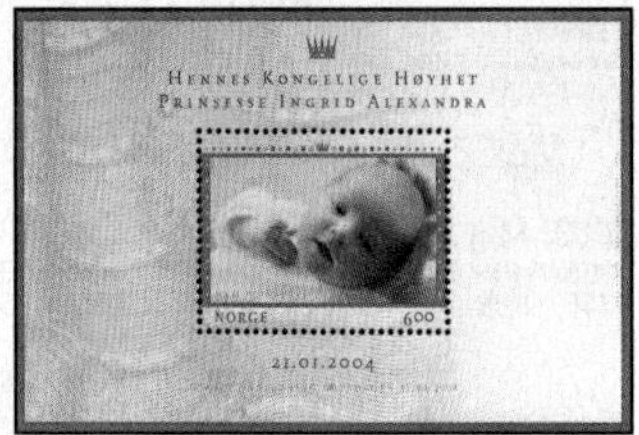

Birth of Princess Ingrid Alexandra — A481

**2004, Apr. 17 *Perf. 13¾***

| | | |
|---|---|---|
| **1402** A481 6k multi | 3.25 | 3.25 |

King Haakon IV Haakonson (1204-63) A482

Designs: 12k, Silhouette of King Haakon IV Haakonson, bows of Viking ships. 22k, Sword and Haakon's Hall, Bergen.

**2004, June 18 *Perf. 14¼x14¾***

| | | |
|---|---|---|
| **1403** A482 12k multi | 4.00 | 2.50 |
| **1404** A482 22k multi | 7.50 | 2.50 |

Railways in Norway, 150th Anniv. A483

Designs: 6k, Koppang Station. 7.50k, Dovre Station. 9.50k, Locomotive, Kylling Bridge. 10.50k, Airport Express train.

**2004, June 18 *Perf. 13¼***

| | | |
|---|---|---|
| **1405** A483 6k multi | 2.00 | .65 |
| **1406** A483 7.50k multi | 2.50 | 1.50 |
| **1407** A483 9.50k multi | 3.25 | 1.75 |
| **1408** A483 10.50k multi | 3.50 | 2.25 |
| *Nos. 1405-1408 (4)* | 11.25 | 6.15 |

A484

Children's Stamps — A485

**2004, Sept. 17 *Perf. 13¼x14***

| | | |
|---|---|---|
| **1409** A484 6k multi | 2.00 | .75 |
| **1410** A485 9k multi | 3.00 | 1.50 |

Oseberg Excavations, Cent. — A486

Designs: 7.50k, Archaeologists uncovering ship's stern, excavated containers. 9.50k, Textile fragment, ceremonial sleigh. 12k, Bed and rattle.

**Litho. & Engr.**

**2004, Sept. 17 *Perf. 13x13¼***

| | | |
|---|---|---|
| **1411** A486 7.50k multi | 2.50 | 1.75 |
| **1412** A486 9.50k multi | 3.25 | 1.75 |
| **1413** A486 12k multi | 4.00 | 1.75 |
| *Nos. 1411-1413 (3)* | 9.75 | 5.25 |

**Norwegian Nobel Laureates Type of 2003**

Designs: 5.50k, Odd Hassel, Chemistry, 1969. 6k, Christian Lous Lange, Peace, 1921.

***Perf. 13¼x13¾***

**2004, Nov. 19 Litho. & Engr.**

| | | |
|---|---|---|
| **1414** A469 5.50k multi | 1.90 | 1.40 |
| **1415** A469 6k multi | 2.00 | 1.00 |

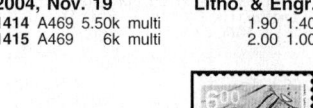

Christmas — A487

Winning art in UNICEF children's stamp design contest: No. 1416, Children and sun, by Hanne Soteland. No. 1417, Child on woman's lap, by Synne Amalie Lund Kallak.

***Serpentine Die Cut 13x13¼ on 3 Sides***

**2004, Nov. 19 Photo. & Litho.**

**Self-Adhesive**

**Booklet Stamps**

| | | |
|---|---|---|
| **1416** A487 6k multi | 2.00 | .30 |
| **1417** A487 6k multi | 2.00 | .30 |
| *a.* Booklet pane, 2 each #1416-1417 | 8.00 | |
| Complete booklet, 2 #1417a | 16.00 | |

Illustrations From "The Three Princesses in the Blue Hill," by Erik Werenskiold (1855-1936) A488

Designs: 7.50k, Princesses and guard. 9.50k, Baby in cradle.

**2005, Jan. 7 Litho. *Perf. 14¼x14***

| | | |
|---|---|---|
| **1418** A488 7.50k multi | 2.50 | 1.75 |
| **1419** A488 9.50k multi | 3.25 | 2.25 |

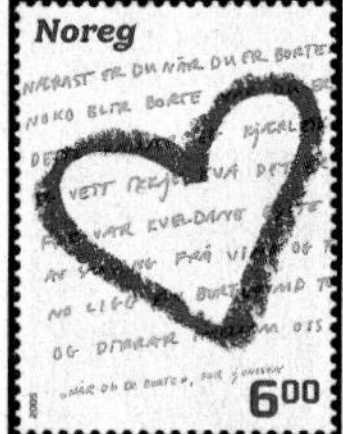

St. Valentine's Day — A489

**2005, Feb. 4 *Perf. 13¼x13¾***

| | | |
|---|---|---|
| **1420** A489 6k red & silver | 2.00 | 1.00 |

Church City Missions, 150th Anniv. A490

Designs: 5.50k, Soup kitchen. 6k, Ministers administering communion.

**2005, Feb. 4 *Perf. 13¾x14¼***

| | | |
|---|---|---|
| **1421** A490 5.50k multi | 1.75 | 1.25 |
| **1422** A490 6k multi | 2.00 | 1.00 |

Children's Mental Health Pioneers — A491

Designs: 12k, Nic Waal (1905-60), first Norwegian child psychiatrist. 22k, Aase Gruda Skard (1905-85), first Norwegian child psychologist.

**2005, Feb. 4 *Perf. 14¼x14¾***

| | | |
|---|---|---|
| **1423** A491 12k multi | 4.00 | 2.00 |
| **1424** A491 22k multi | 7.50 | 2.00 |

A492

Children's Drawings of Norway in 2105 — A493

**2005, Apr. 15 Litho. *Perf. 14x12¾***

| | | |
|---|---|---|
| **1425** A492 6k multi | 2.00 | 1.00 |
| **1426** A493 7.50k multi | 2.50 | 1.50 |

Tourism — A494

Designs: 6k, Geiranger Fjord. 9.50k, Kjofossen Waterfall, Flam. 10.50k, Polar bear, Svalbard.

*Die Cut Perf. 13x13¼ on 3 Sides*

**2005, Apr. 15 Photo. & Litho.**

**Booklet Stamps**

**Self-Adhesive**

**1427** A494 6k multi 2.00 .30
*a.* Booklet pane of 4 8.00
Complete booklet, 2 #1427a 17.00
**1428** A494 9.50k multi 3.25 1.50
*a.* Booklet pane of 4 13.00
Complete booklet, 2 #1428a 26.00
**1429** A494 10.50k multi 3.50 1.75
*a.* Booklet pane of 4 14.00
Complete booklet, 2 #1429a 28.00
*Nos. 1427-1429 (3)* 8.75 3.55

Dissolution of Union with Sweden, Cent. — A495

Designs: 6k, Norwegian Prime Minister Christian Michelsen, Norwegian negotiators and signatures. 7.50k, King Haakon VII, ships.

*Perf. 12½x12¾*

**2005, May 27 Litho. & Engr.**

**1430** A495 6k multi 2.00 1.00
**1431** A495 7.50k multi 2.50 1.25
*a.* Souvenir sheet, #1430-1431 5.00 6.00

See Sweden No. 2514.

Historic Events Since Dissolution of Union with Sweden A496

Designs: No. 1432, King Haakon VII taking oath of allegiance, 1905. No. 1433, Crown Prince Olav celebrating end of World War II, 1945. No. 1434, King Olav V at inauguration of Norwegian television broadcasting, 1960. No. 1435, Prime Minister Trygve Bratteli opening Ekofisk oil field, 1971. No. 1436, Victory of Norwegian World Cup soccer team over Brazil, 1998.

**2005, June 7 Litho. *Perf. 13¾***

**1432** A496 6k multi 2.00 1.00
**1433** A496 6k multi 2.00 1.00
**1434** A496 6k multi 2.00 1.00
**1435** A496 6k multi 2.00 1.00
**1436** A496 9k multi 3.00 1.50
*Nos. 1432-1436 (5)* 11.00 5.50

Tall Ships — A497

Designs: 6k, Christian Radich. 9.50k, Sorlandet. 10.50k, Statsraad Lehmkuhl.

**2005, June 7 *Perf. 13¾x13½***

**1437** A497 6k multi 2.00 1.00
**1438** A497 9.50k multi 3.25 1.75
**1439** A497 10.50k multi 3.50 2.40
*Nos. 1437-1439 (3)* 8.75 5.15

**Marine Life Type of 2004**

Designs: B, Orcinus orca. A, Urticina eques.

*Die Cut Perf. 15½x14¼*

**2005, Sept. 1 Photo.**

**Self-Adhesive**

**1440** A475 B multi 1.75 .30
**1441** A475 A multi 2.00 .30

No. 1440 sold for 5.50k and No. 1441 sold for 6k on day of issue.

Lighthouses A498

Designs: No. 1442, Jomfruland (white lighthouse). No. 1443, Tranoy (red and white lighthouse).

*Die Cut Perf. 13¼x13 on 3 Sides*

**2005, Sept. 1 Photo. & Litho.**

**Self-Adhesive**

**Booklet Stamps**

**1442** A498 A multi 2.00 .30
**1443** A498 A multi 2.00 .30
*a.* Booklet pane, 2 each #1442-1443 8.00
Complete booklet, 2 #1443a 17.00

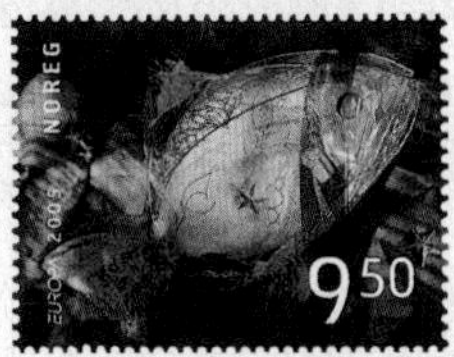

Europa A499

**2005, Sept. 16 Litho. *Perf. 14¾x14***

**1444** A499 9.50k Fish 3.25 2.25
**1445** A499 10.50k Table 3.50 2.00

Norwegian Telegraph Service, 150th Anniv. A500

Designs: 6k, Telegraph key and poles. 10.50k, Woman and symbols of modern communication.

*Perf. 13½x13¾*

**2005, Sept. 16 Litho. & Engr.**

**1446** A500 6k multi 2.00 1.40
**1447** A500 10.50k multi 3.50 2.00

Geological Society of Norway, Cent. — A501

Designs: 5.50k, Thortveitite and feldspar. 6k, Oil rig, ship, map of Norway, microfossil and stylized rock layers.

**2005, Sept. 16 Litho. *Perf. 13¾***

**1448** A501 5.50k multi 1.75 1.40
**1449** A501 6k multi 2.00 1.25

Norwegian Postage Stamps, 150th Anniv. — A502

Designs: A, Eye, vignette and spandrels of Norway #1. 12k, Norway #1, woman writing letter.

**Litho., Engr. & Silk Screened**

**2005, Nov. 17 *Perf. 14x14¼***

**1450** A502 A multi 2.00 1.00

**Souvenir Sheet**

**1451** Sheet, #1450, 1451a 6.50 6.50
*a.* A502 12k multi 4.50 4.00

No. 1450 sold for 6k on day of issue.

Royal House, Cent. — A503

Designs: No. 1452, Norwegian Prime Minister greeting King Haakon VII and Crown Prince Olav, 1905. No. 1453, Royal coat of arms, King Haakon VII, Queen Maud and Crown Prince Olav, 1945, King Harald V, Crown Prince Haakon, and Princess Ingrid Alexandra, 2004.

**2005, Nov. 18 Litho. *Perf. 14x13½***

**1452** A503 6k multi 2.00 1.00
**1453** A503 6k multi 2.50 1.00

Christmas — A504

Designs: No. 1454, Gingerbread Christmas tree. No. 1455, Oranges studded with cloves on bed of nuts.

*Serpentine Die Cut 13x13¼ on 3 Sides*

**2005, Nov. 19 Photo. & Litho.**

**Booklet Stamps**

**Self-Adhesive**

**1454** A504 A multi 2.00 .30
**1455** A504 A multi 2.00 .30
*a.* Booklet pane, 2 each #1454-1455 8.00
Complete booklet, 2, #1455a 16.00

Nos. 1454-1455 each sold for 6k on day of issue and are impregnated with a cinnamon scent.

Norwegian Language Society, Cent. — A505

**2006, Feb. 3 Litho. *Perf. 13¼x13¾***

**1456** A505 6k multi 2.00 1.40

St. Valentine's Day — A506

**2006, Feb. 3 *Perf. 13¾x14¼***

**1457** A506 A multi 2.00 1.00

Sold for 6k on day of issue.

2006 Winter Olympics, Turin — A507

Designs: 6k, Kari Traa, freestyle skier. 22k, Ole Einar Bjorndalen, biathlon.

**2006, Feb. 3 *Perf. 14¼x14¾***

**1458** A507 6k multi 2.00 1.00
**1459** A507 22k multi 7.50 2.00

Norwegian Lifesaving Society, Cent. — A508

Designs: 10k, Lifeguard carrying man. 10.50k, Child swimming.

**2006, Feb. 24 *Perf. 13¾***

**1460** A508 10k multi 3.50 2.50
**1461** A508 10.50k multi 3.50 2.75

Greetings A509

Designs: No. 1462, Baby and spoon. No. 1463, Birthday cake. No. 1464, Heart and wedding rings. No. 1465, Flower.

**2006, Feb. 24 *Die Cut Perf. 13¼***

**Self-Adhesive**

**1462** A509 A multi 2.00 1.00
**1463** A509 A multi 2.00 1.00
**1464** A509 A multi 2.00 1.00
**1465** A509 A multi 2.00 1.00
*Nos. 1462-1465 (4)* 8.00 4.00

Each stamp sold for 6k on day of issue. Each stamp was issued on a white paper backing with surrounding selvage and in coils on a translucent paper backing without surrounding selvage.

Polycera Quadrilineata A510

*Die Cut Perf. 15½x14½*

**2006, Mar. 29 Photo.**

**Coil Stamp**

**1466** A510 10k multi 3.50 .50

Wildlife A511

6.50k, Lynx. 8.50k, Capercaillie. 10k, Golden eagle. 10.50k, Arctic fox. 13k, Arctic hare.

**2006, Mar. 29 Litho. *Perf. 13¼x14***

**1467** A511 6.50k multi 2.25 .50
**1468** A511 8.50k multi 2.75 2.00
**1469** A511 10k multi 3.25 2.00
**1470** A511 10.50k multi 3.50 2.50
**1471** A511 13k multi 4.25 2.50
*Nos. 1467-1471 (5)* 16.00 9.50

See Nos. 1498-1499, 1531-1533, 1565-1567, 1600-1602, 1636-1637, 1726C-1728, 1756, 1763.

Souvenir Sheet

Norse Mythology — A512

No. 1472: a, Design on Sami shaman's drum. b, Carved door post from Hylestad Stave Church depicting dragon and dragon slayer.

**2006, Mar. 29** ***Perf. 14x14¼***

**1472** A512 Sheet of 2 7.50 8.00
*a.* A multi 2.75 2.75
*b.* 10.50k multi 3.25 3.25

No. 1472a sold for 6k on day of issue.

Norwegian Arctic Expeditions, Cent. — A513

Designs: 6.50k, Gunnar Isachsen and assistant surveying terrain. 8.50k, Coal cable car terminal, Store Norske Spitzbergen mines. 22k, Longyearbyen.

**Litho. & Engr.**

**2006, June 9** ***Perf. 13½x14***

**1473** A513 6.50k multi 2.25 .75
**1474** A513 8.50k multi 2.75 2.00

**Litho.**

**1475** A513 22k multi 7.00 4.25
*a.* Souvenir sheet, #1473-1475 12.50 12.50
*Nos. 1473-1475 (3)* 12.00 7.00

Tourism A514

Designs: No. 1476, Paddle steamer Skibladner. No. 1477, Maihaugen Museum, Lillehammer. No. 1478, Kirkeporten natural arch. No. 1479, North Cape. No. 1480, Bryggen UNESCO World Heritage Site. No. 1481, Storeseisundet Bridge on Atlantic Road.

***Die Cut Perf. 13¼x13½***

**2006, June 9** **Photo.**

**Self-Adhesive**

**Booklet Stamps**

**1476** A514 6.50k multi 2.25 .50
**1477** A514 6.50k multi 2.25 .50
*a.* Booklet pane, 5 each #1476-1477 22.50
**1478** A514 8.50k multi 2.75 2.00
**1479** A514 8.50k multi 2.75 2.00
*a.* Booklet pane, 5 each #1478-1479 27.50
**1480** A514 10.50k multi 3.50 2.50
**1481** A514 10.50k multi 3.50 2.50
*a.* Booklet pane, 5 each #1480-1481 35.00
*Nos. 1476-1481 (6)* 17.00 10.00

Consumer Cooperatives, Cent. — A515

**2006, June 9** **Litho.** ***Perf. 13½x14***

**1482** A515 6.50k multi 2.25 1.00

Personalized Stamp — A516

***Serpentine Die Cut 11¾ Syncopated***

**2006, Aug. 22** **Self-Adhesive**

**1483** A516 A multi 2.50 2.00

No. 1483 sold for 6.50k on the day of issue. The image shown is the generic image sold at face value. Stamps could be personalized, presumably for an extra fee.

Marine Life — A517

Designs: B, Strongylocentrotus droebachiensis. A, Labrus bimaculatus.

***Die Cut Perf. 15½x14½***

**2006, Sept. 15** **Photo.**

**Self-Adhesive**

**Coil Stamps**

**1484** A517 B multi 2.00 .50
**1485** A517 A multi 2.25 .30

On day of issue, No. 1484 sold for 6k; No. 1485 for 6.50k.

King's Guard, 150th Anniv. A518

Designs: 6.50k, King's Guard in dress uniforms. 13k, In field uniforms, with helicopter.

**2006, Sept. 15** **Litho.** ***Perf. 14x13¼***

**1486** A518 6.50k multi 2.25 1.25
**1487** A518 13k multi 4.50 3.00
*a.* Souvenir sheet, #1486-1487 7.00 7.00

Europa A519

Designs: 8.50k, Five children. 13k, Three children playing soccer.

**2006, Nov. 17** ***Perf. 13¾***

**1488** A519 8.50k multi 2.75 2.00
**1489** A519 13k multi 4.50 3.00

Christmas A520

Designs: No. 1490, Children and Christmas tree. No. 1491, Child and snowman.

***Die Cut Perf. 13¼x13½***

**2006, Nov. 17** **Photo. & Litho.**

**Self-Adhesive**

**Booklet Stamps**

**1490** A520 A multi 2.25 .50
**1491** A520 A multi 2.25 .50
*a.* Booklet pane, 5 each #1490-1491 22.50

On day of issue each stamp sold for 6.50k.

Personalized Stamp — A521

***Serpentine Die Cut 11¾ Syncopated***

**2006, Nov. 17** **Litho.**

**Self-Adhesive**

**1492** A521 A multi 2.50 2.10

No. 1492 sold for 6.50k on the day of issue. The image shown is the generic image sold at face value. Stamps could be personalized, presumably for an extra fee.

St. Valentine's Day — A522

**2007, Feb. 6** **Litho.** ***Perf. 13¼***

**1493** A522 A multi 2.25 1.50

Sold for 6.50k on day of issue. Values are for stamps with surrounding selvage.

Winter Rally Race Cars A523

Designs: No. 1494, Petter Solberg's Subaru Impreza. No. 1495, Henning Solberg's Peugeot 307. No. 1496, Thomas Schie's Ford Focus.

**Litho. With Foil Application**

**2007, Feb. 6** ***Perf. 13¼x13¾***

**1494** A523 A Innland multi 2.25 1.50
**1495** A523 A Europa multi 2.75 2.25
**1496** A523 A Verden multi 3.50 3.00
*a.* Souvenir sheet, #1494-1496 8.50 8.50
*Nos. 1494-1496 (3)* 8.50 6.75

On day of issue, No. 1494 sold for 6.50k; No. 1495, for 8.50k; No. 1496, for 10.50k.

King Harald V, 70th Birthday — A524

***Perf. 13¾x13¼***

**2007, Feb. 21** **Litho.**

**1497** A524 6.50k multi 2.25 1.50

**Wildlife Type of 2006**

**2007, Feb. 21** ***Perf. 13¼x13¾***

**1498** A511 12k Hedgehog 4.00 1.75
**1499** A511 22k Red squirrel 7.50 2.50

Souvenir Sheet

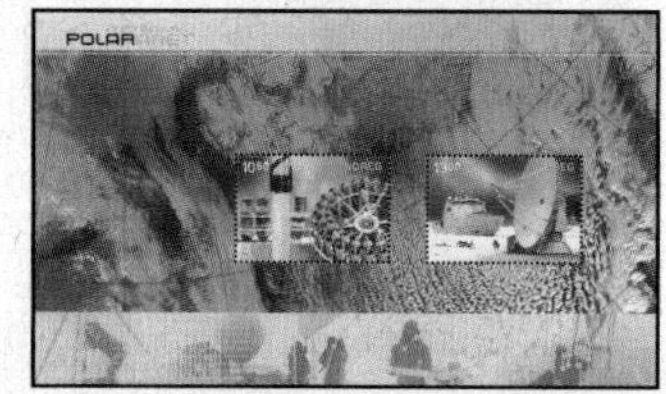

Intl. Polar Year — A526

No. 1500: a, Ice core, oceanographic equipment. b, K/V Svalbard, dish antenna.

**2007, Feb. 21**

**1500** A526 Sheet of 2 8.50 8.50
*a.* 10.50k multi 3.75 3.75
*b.* 13k multi 4.75 4.75

Porsgrunn, Bicent. — A527

**2007, Apr. 27**

**1501** A527 A Innland multi 2.40 1.50

Sold for 7k on day of issue.

Illustrations by Theodor Kittelsen (1857-1914) A528

Designs: No. 1502, An Attack (grasshoppers, mosquito, flower). No. 1503, Premature Delivery (frogs, hatched bird).

**2007, Apr. 27** ***Perf. 14x13½***

**1502** A528 A Europa multi 3.00 2.00
**1503** A528 A Verden multi 3.75 2.75

On day of issue, No. 1502 sold for 9k; No. 1503, for 11k.

Skydivers A529

Cyclists A530

Buildings, Roros A531

Bridge, Fredrikstad A532

Pilot House, Portor A533

Reine Harbor A534

***Die Cut Perf. 13¼x13¾***

**2007, Apr. 27**

**Self-Adhesive**

**Booklet Stamps**

**1504** A529 A Innland multi 2.40 .50
**1505** A530 A Innland multi 2.40 .50
*a.* Booklet pane, 5 each #1504-1505 24.00
**1506** A531 A Europa multi 3.00 1.00
**1507** A532 A Europa multi 3.00 1.00
*a.* Booklet pane, 5 each #1506-1507 30.00

| | | | |
|---|---|---|---|
| **1508** | A533 A Verden multi | 3.75 | 1.00 |
| **1509** | A534 A Verden multi | 3.75 | 1.00 |
| *a.* | Booklet pane, 5 each #1508-1509 | 37.50 | |
| | *Nos. 1504-1509 (6)* | 18.30 | 5.00 |

On day of issue, Nos. 1504-1505 each sold for 7k; Nos. 1506-1507 each sold for 9k; Nos. 1508-1509 each sold for 11k.

Marine Life — A535

Designs: No. 1510, Pandalus montagui. No. 1511, Homarus gammarus. No. 1512, Cancer pagurus. No. 1513, Galathea strigosa. 11k, Scomber scombrus.

**2007** ***Die Cut Perf. 15½x14½***

**Self-Adhesive**

**Coil Stamps**

| | | | |
|---|---|---|---|
| **1510** | A535 A Innland multi | 2.60 | .50 |
| **1511** | A535 A Innland multi | 2.60 | .50 |
| **1512** | A535 A Innland multi | 2.60 | .50 |
| **1513** | A535 A Innland multi | 2.60 | .50 |
| *a.* | Horiz. strip of 4, #1510-1513 | 10.50 | |
| **1514** | A535 11k multi | 3.75 | .90 |
| | *Nos. 1510-1514 (5)* | 14.15 | 2.90 |

Issued; Nos. 1510-1513, 9/21; No. 1514, 5/2. On day of issue, Nos. 1510-1513 each sold for 7k.

Europa A536

Designs: 9k, Scouts, knots. 11k, Hitch diagrams, camp gateway.

***Perf. 13¼x13¾***

**2007, May 11** **Litho. & Engr.**

| | | | |
|---|---|---|---|
| **1515** | A536 9k multi | 3.00 | 2.00 |
| **1516** | A536 11k multi | 3.75 | 2.50 |

Scouting, cent.

Building Anniversaries — A537

Designs: 14k, Church of Our Lady, Trondheim, 800th anniv. 23k, Vardohus Fortress, 700th anniv.

**2007, May 11**

| | | | |
|---|---|---|---|
| **1517** | A537 14k multi | 4.75 | 3.00 |
| **1518** | A537 23k multi | 7.75 | 5.00 |

Riksmaal Society, Cent. A538

**2007, June 15** **Litho.**

| | | | |
|---|---|---|---|
| **1519** | A538 7k multi | 2.40 | 1.25 |

Personalized Stamp — A539

***Serpentine Die Cut 11½ Syncopated***

**2007, June 15**

| | | | |
|---|---|---|---|
| **1520** | A539 A Innland multi | 2.75 | 2.75 |

No. 1520 sold for 7k on day of issue. The image shown is the generic image sold at face value. Stamps could be personalized, presumably for an extra fee.

Ona Lighthouse, Romsdal A540

Tungeneset Lighthouse, Ersfjorden A541

***Die Cut Perf. 13¼x13¾***

**2007, June 15**

| | | | |
|---|---|---|---|
| **1521** | A540 A Innland multi | 2.40 | .50 |
| **1522** | A541 A Innland multi | 2.40 | .50 |
| *a.* | Booklet pane, 5 each #1521-1522 | 24.00 | |

Nos. 1521-1522 each sold for 7k on day of issue.

Haldis Moren Vesaas (1907-95), Poet — A542

**Litho. With Foil Application**

**2007, Sept. 21** ***Perf. 14x13½***

| | | | |
|---|---|---|---|
| **1523** | A542 23k multi | 8.00 | 5.00 |

Mining Academy, Kongsberg, 250th Anniv. — A543

Norwegian Academy of Science and Letters, 150th Anniv. — A544

***Perf. 13¼x13¾***

**2007, Nov. 23** **Litho. & Engr.**

| | | | |
|---|---|---|---|
| **1524** | A543 14k multi | 4.50 | 3.50 |
| **1525** | A544 14k multi | 4.50 | 3.50 |

Personalized Stamp — A545

**Booklet Stamp**

***Serpentine Die Cut 10¼ Syncopated***

**2007, Nov. 23** **Self-Adhesive**

| | | | |
|---|---|---|---|
| **1526** | A545 A Innland multi | 2.60 | 2.25 |
| *a.* | Booklet pane of 8 | 21.00 | |

No. 1526 sold for 7k on day of issue. The image shown is the generic image sold at face value. Stamps could be personalized, presumably for an extra fee.

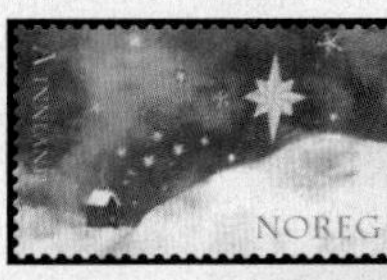

Christmas Star — A546

Adoration of the Magi — A547

***Die Cut Perf. 13¼x13¾***

**2007, Nov. 23** **Photo.**

**Self-Adhesive**

**Booklet Stamps**

| | | | |
|---|---|---|---|
| **1527** | A546 A Innland multi | 2.25 | .50 |
| **1528** | A547 A Innland multi | 2.25 | .50 |
| *a.* | Booklet pane, 5 each #1527-1528 | 22.50 | |

On day of issue, Nos. 1527-1528 each sold for 7k.

A548

St. Valentine's Day — A549

**2008, Feb. 8** **Litho.** ***Perf. 13¼x13¾***

| | | | |
|---|---|---|---|
| **1529** | A548 A Innland multi | 2.25 | 1.50 |
| **1530** | A549 A Europa multi | 3.00 | 2.00 |

On day of issue, Nos. 1529-1530 sold for 7k and 9k, respectively.

**Wildlife Type of 2006**

**2008, Feb. 21**

| | | | |
|---|---|---|---|
| **1531** | A511 11k Elk | 3.75 | 2.50 |
| **1532** | A511 14k Bear | 4.50 | 3.50 |
| **1533** | A511 23k Wolf | 8.00 | 5.00 |
| | *Nos. 1531-1533 (3)* | 16.25 | 11.00 |

Thorleif Haug, 1924 Olympic Cross-country Skiing Gold Medalist — A551

Espen Bredesen, 1994 Olympic Ski Jumping Gold Medalist A552

Children Skiing A553

Kjetil André Aamodt, 1992, 2002, and 2006 Olympic Alpine Skiing Gold Medalist A554

***Die Cut Perf. 15½x14½***

**2008, Mar. 14** **Photo.**

**Coil Stamps**

**Self-Adhesive**

| | | | |
|---|---|---|---|
| **1534** | A551 A Innland multi | 2.50 | .70 |
| **1535** | A552 A Innland multi | 2.50 | .70 |
| **1536** | A553 A Innland multi | 2.50 | .70 |
| **1537** | A554 A Innland multi | 2.50 | .70 |
| *a.* | Horiz. strip of 4, #1534-1537 | 10.00 | |

On day of issue, Nos. 1534-1537 each sold for 7k. Norwegian Ski Federation, cent.

Souvenir Sheet

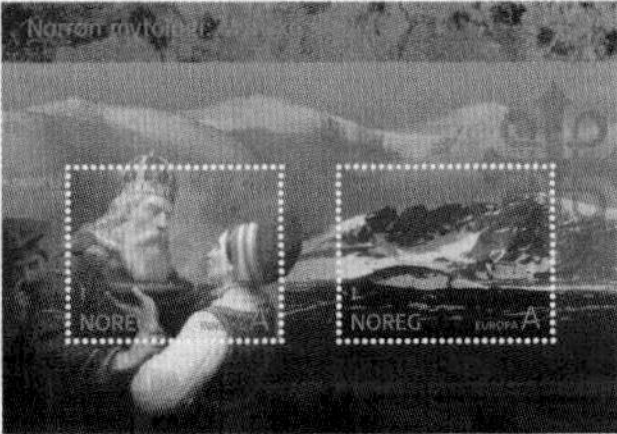

Norse Mythology — A555

No. 1538: a, Harald Fairhair meeting Snofrid. b, Snohetta Mountain.

**2008, Mar. 27** **Litho.** ***Perf. 14x14¼***

| | | | |
|---|---|---|---|
| **1538** | A555 Sheet of 2 | 6.00 | 6.00 |
| *a.* | A Innland multi | 2.50 | 2.50 |
| *b.* | A Europa multi | 3.50 | 3.50 |

On day of issue, No. 1538a sold for 7k, and No. 1538b sold for 9k.

Opera House, Oslo — A556

**Litho. With Foil Application**

**2008, Apr. 12** ***Perf. 14x13½***

| | | | |
|---|---|---|---|
| **1539** | A556 A Innland multi | 2.50 | 1.50 |

Sold for 7k on day of issue.

Famous Men — A557

Designs: No. 1540, Frederik Stang (1808-84), Interior Minister. No. 1541, Henrik Wergeland (1808-45), lyricist.

***Perf. 13¼x13¾***

**2008, Apr. 12** **Litho. & Engr.**

| | | | |
|---|---|---|---|
| **1540** | A557 A Innland multi | 2.50 | 1.50 |
| **1541** | A557 A Innland multi | 2.50 | 1.50 |

On day of issue, Nos. 1540-1541 each sold for 7k.

Oslo Harbor A558

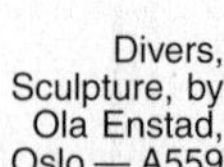

Divers, Sculpture, by Ola Enstad, Oslo — A559

The Blade, Sunnmore Alps — A560

Kjerag Boulder A561

Sailboat and Lyngor Lighthouse A562

Lyngor A563

*Die Cut Perf. 13¼x13¾*

**2008, Apr. 12 Photo.**

**Booklet Stamps**

**Self-Adhesive**

**1542** A558 A Innland multi 2.50 .70
**1543** A559 A Innland multi 2.50 .70
*a.* Booklet pane of 10, 5 each #1542-1543 25.00
**1544** A560 A Europa multi 3.00 2.50
**1545** A561 A Europa multi 3.00 2.50
*a.* Booklet pane of 10, 5 each #1544-1545 30.00
**1546** A562 A Varden multi 3.75 2.75
**1547** A563 A Varden multi 3.75 2.75
*a.* Booklet pane of 10, 5 each #1546-1547 37.50
*Nos. 1542-1547 (6)* 18.50 11.90

On day of issue, Nos. 1542-1543 each sold for 7k; Nos. 1544-1545, for 9k; Nos. 1546-1547, for 11k.

Stavanger, 2008 European Cultural Capital — A564

Designs: 7k, Dancer in a Cultural Landscape, photograph by Marcel Lelienhof. 14k, Swords in Rock, sculpture by Fritz Roed. 23k, Scene from musical, The Thousandth Heart, vert.

*Perf. 14x13½, 13½x14*

**2008, June 6 Litho.**

**1548** A564 7k multi 2.50 1.50
**1549** A564 14k multi 5.00 3.50
**1550** A564 23k multi 8.00 5.00
*a.* Souvenir sheet, #1548-1550 17.00 17.00
*Nos. 1548-1550 (3)* 15.50 10.00

No. 1550a issue 10/23. Nordia 2008 Philatelic Exhibition, Stavenger (#1550a).

Transportation Centenaries — A565

Designs: 7k, SS Boroysund. 9k, SS Oster. 25k, Automobile used on first bus route. 30k, Train on Thamshavn electric railroad line.

*Perf. 13¼x13¾*

**2008, June 6 Litho. & Engr.**

**1551** A565 7k ocher & green 2.50 1.50
**1552** A565 9k rose pink & blue 3.00 2.50
**1553** A565 25k lt bl & brown 8.50 5.50
**1554** A565 30k pur & green 10.00 6.50
*Nos. 1551-1554 (4)* 24.00 16.00

2008 Summer Olympics, Beijing A566

Designs: 9k, Andreas Thorkildsen, javelin thrower. 23k, Women's handball player, Gro Hammerseng.

**2008, Aug. 8 Litho.** ***Perf. 14¾x14¼***

**1555** A566 9k multi 3.00 2.25
**1556** A566 23k multi 8.00 5.00

Personalized Stamp — A567

No. 1558: a, Like No. 1557, but with line of post horns running through middle of top line of "E" in "Norge." b, "Bring."

*Serpentine Die Cut 11¾ Syncopated*

**2008, Sept. 5 Litho.**

**Self-Adhesive**

**1557** A567 A Innland multi 2.50 2.50

**Souvenir Sheet**

**1558** Sheet of 2 *32.50*
*a.* A567 A Innland red & gray *16.00 16.00*
*b.* A567 A Innland green & gray *16.00 16.00*

No. 1557 sold for 7k on day of issue. The image shown is the generic image sold at face value. Stamps could be personalized for an extra fee.

No. 1557 has line of post horn running through the right side of the top line of the "E" in "Norge."

About 375,000 examples of No. 1558 were distributed free of charge by Norway Post to the general public at post offices throught Norway and through their agents abroad in a campaign to promote the sale of personalized stamps. The sheet was never offered for sale by Norway Post or their agents. Nos. 1558a and 1558b each had a franking value of 7k, and could not be personalized.

Art — A568

Designs: No. 1559, In the Forecourt of the Revolution, by Arne Ekeland. No. 1560, Svalbard Motif, by Kare Tveter. No. 1561, Composition in Red, by Inger Sitter. No. 1562, From Sagorsk, c. 1985, by Terje Bergstad.

*Die Cut Perf. 15½x14½*

**2008, Oct. 24 Photo.**

**Coil Stamps**

**Self-Adhesive**

**1559** A568 A Innland multi 2.50 .70
**1560** A568 A Innland multi 2.50 .70
**1561** A568 A Innland multi 2.50 .70
**1562** A568 A Innland multi 2.50 .70
*a.* Horiz. strip of 4, #1559-1562 11.50 11.50
*Nos. 1559-1562 (4)* 10.00 2.80

On day of issue, Nos. 1559-1562 each sold for 7k.

Gnomes, Amperhaugen Farm, Stor-Elvdal A569

Gnome, Nordre Lien Farm, Stor-Elvdal A570

**Booklet Stamps**

*Die Cut Perf. 13¼x13¾*

**2008, Nov. 17 Self-Adhesive**

**1563** A569 A Innland multi 2.25 .50
**1564** A570 A Innland multi 2.25 .50
*a.* Booklet pane of 10, 5 each #1563-1564 22.50

Christmas. On day of issue, Nos. 1563-1564 each sold for 7k.

**Wildlife Type of 2006**

**2009, Jan. 2 Litho.** ***Perf. 13¼x13¾***

**1565** A511 11.50k Roe deer 4.00 2.50
**1566** A511 15.50k Reindeer 5.50 2.50
**1567** A511 25k Willow grouse 9.00 4.50
*Nos. 1565-1567 (3)* 18.50 9.50

Art — A572

Designs: B, Summer Night, a Tribute to E. M., by Kjell Nupen. 12k, Light at Whitsuntide, by Irma Salo Jaeger.

*Die Cut Perf. 15½x14½*

**2009, Jan. 2 Photo.**

**Coil Stamps**

**Self-Adhesive**

**1568** A572 B Innland multi 2.50 .75
**1569** A572 12k multi 4.00 1.00

No. 1568 sold for 7.50k on day of issue.

Souvenir Sheet

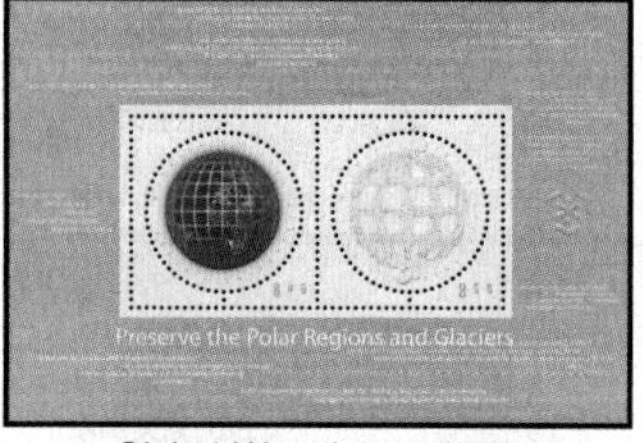


Global Warming — A573

No. 1570: a, Warm globe. b, Globe with melting ice at meridians.

**Litho. (#1570a), Litho and Embossed (#1570b)**

**2009, Feb. 20** ***Perf. 13½***

**1570** A573 Sheet of 2 6.00 6.00
*a.-b.* 8k Either single 2.75 2.75

Personalized Stamp — A574

*Serpentine Die Cut 10x10¼ Syncopated*

**2009, Mar. 2 Litho.**

**Booklet Stamp**

**Self-Adhesive**

**1571** A574 A Innland gray 2.75 2.25
*a.* Booklet pane of 8 22.00

No. 1571 sold for 8k on day of issue. The image shown is the generic image sold at face value. Stamps could be personalized for an extra fee.

National Anthem by Bjornestjerne Bjornson, 150th Anniv. — A575

**Litho. & Engr.**

**2009, Apr. 17** ***Perf. 13½x14***

**1572** A575 12k multi 4.00 3.25

Bergen Line Train in Mountains A576

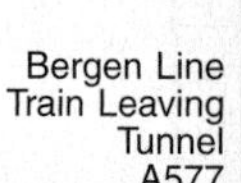

Bergen Line Train Leaving Tunnel A577

Stotta Fjord — A578

Rocky Shore, Revtangen A579

Aurora Borealis A580

Pot Rock, Vagsoy A581

*Die Cut Perf. 13¼x13½*

**2009, Apr. 17 Photo.**

**Booklet Stamps**

**Self-Adhesive**

**1573** A576 A Innland multi 3.00 1.25
**1574** A577 A Innland multi 3.00 1.25
*a.* Booklet pane of 10, 5 each #1573-1574 30.00
**1575** A578 A Europa multi 3.50 2.00
**1576** A579 A Europa multi 3.50 2.00
*a.* Booklet pane of 10, 5 each #1575-1576 35.00
**1577** A580 A Verden multi 4.00 2.50
**1578** A581 A Verden multi 4.00 2.50
*a.* Booklet pane of 10, 5 each #1577-1578 40.00
*Nos. 1573-1578 (6)* 21.00 11.50

On day of issue, Nos. 1573-1574 each sold for 8k, Nos. 1575-1576 each sold for 10k, and Nos. 1577-1578 each sold for 12k.

Royal Norwegian Society for Development, Bicent. — A582

*Perf. 13¼x13¾*

**2009, June 12** **Litho.**

**1579** A582 12k multi 4.00 3.25

Submarine Branch of Norwegian Navy, Cent. — A583

Designs: 14.50k, The Kobben. 15.50k, Ula Class submarine.

**Litho. & Engr.**

**2009, June 12** ***Perf. 13¼x14***

**1580** A583 14.50k multi 5.00 4.00
**1581** A583 15.50k multi 5.50 4.00

Norwegian Year of Cultural Heritage A584

Designs: No. 1582, Kurér radio, 1950. No. 1583, Telephone booth, 1932.

***Die Cut Perf. 15½x14½***

**2009, June 12** **Litho.**

**Coil Stamps**

**Self-Adhesive**

**1582** A584 A Innland multi 2.75 1.25
**1583** A584 A Innland multi 2.75 1.25
*a.* Horiz. pair, #1582-1583 5.50 5.50

On day of issue, Nos. 1582-1583 each sold for 8k.

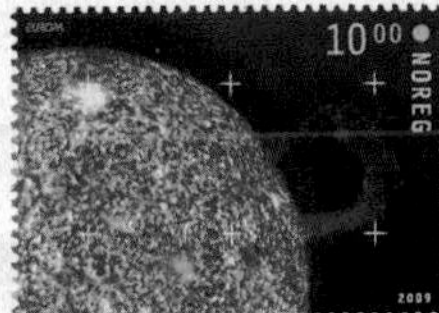

Europa A585

Designs: 10k, Solar explosion. 12k, Moon.

**2009, June 12** ***Perf. 14¼x13¾***

**1584** A585 10k multi 3.50 2.50
**1585** A585 12k multi 4.00 3.00
*a.* Souvenir sheet of 2, #1584-1585 9.00 9.00

Intl. Year of Astronomy.

Knut Hamsun (1859-1952), 1920 Nobel Literature Laureate A586

**Litho. & Engr.**

**2009, Aug. 4** ***Perf. 14¼***

**1586** A586 25k multi 9.00 5.00

Rock 'n' Roll Pioneers A587

Designs: No. 1587, Per "Elvis" Granberg (1941-80). No. 1588, Roald Stensby. No. 1589, Rocke-Pelle (Per Hartvig) (1938-80). No. 1590, Jan Rohde (1942-2005).

***Die Cut Perf. 15½x14½***

**2009. Aug. 21** **Photo.**

**Coil Stamps**

**Self-Adhesive**

**1587** A587 A Innland multi 2.75 1.25
**1588** A587 A Innland multi 2.75 1.25
**1589** A587 A Innland multi 2.75 1.25
**1590** A587 A Innland multi 2.75 1.25
*a.* Horiz. strip of 4, #1587-1590 11.00 11.00

On day of issue, Nos. 1587-1590 each sold for 8k.

Norwegian Shipowners' Association, Cent. — A588

***Perf. 13¾x13¼***

**2009, Sept. 15** **Litho.**

**1591** A588 15.50k multi 5.50 4.00

Norwegian Association of the Blind, Cent. — A589

**Litho. & Embossed**

**2009, Oct. 8** ***Perf. 13¼x14***

**1592** A589 8k red 3.00 2.50

Sculptures A590

Designs: No. 1593, Woman on a Man's Lap, by Gustav Vigeland. No. 1594, Crow, by Nils Aas. No. 1595, Birds in Flight, by Arnold Haukeland. No. 1596, Granite Head Lying on its Side, by Kristian Blystad.

***Die Cut Perf. 15½x14½***

**2009, Nov. 16** **Photo.**

**Coil Stamps**

**Self-Adhesive**

**1593** A590 A Innland multi 3.00 1.25
**1594** A590 A Innland multi 3.00 1.25
**1595** A590 A Innland multi 3.00 1.25
**1596** A590 A Innland multi 3.00 1.25
*a.* Horiz. strip of 4, #1593-1596 12.00
*Nos. 1593-1596 (4)* 12.00 5.00

Nos. 1593-1596 each sold for 8k on day of issue.

Christmas A591

Text and: No. 1597, Apple and snowflakes. No. 1598, Stars.

***Die Cut Perf. 13¼x13¾***

**2009, Nov. 16** **Photo.**

**Booklet Stamps**

**Self-Adhesive**

**1597** A591 A Innland multi 3.00 1.25
**1598** A591 A Innland multi 3.00 1.25
*a.* Booklet pane of 10, 5 each #1597-1598 30.00

Nos. 1597-1598 each sold for 8k on day of issue.

Man Drinking, Sculpture bu Per Palle Storm A592

***Die Cut Perf. 15½x14½***

**2010, Jan. 2** **Litho.**

**Coil Stamp**

**Self-Adhesive**

**1599** A592 13k multi 4.50 2.50

**Wildlife Type of 2006**

**2010, Jan. 2** ***Perf. 13¼x13¾***

**1600** A511 15k European otter 5.25 3.00
**1601** A511 16k Lemming 5.50 3.00
**1602** A511 26k Wolverine 9.00 4.50
*Nos. 1600-1602 (3)* 19.75 10.50

Famous Men — A595

Designs: No. 1603, Peter Andreas Munch (1810-63), historian, and illuminated text. No. 1604, Ole Bull (1810-80), violinist.

**2010, Feb. 5** ***Die Cut Perf. 15½x14½***

**Coil Stamps**

**Self-Adhesive**

**1603** A595 A Innland multi 3.00 1.25
**1604** A595 A Innland multi 3.00 1.25
*a.* Horiz. pair, #1603-1604 6.00

On day of issue, Nos. 1603-1604 each sold for 8.50k.

Souvenir Sheet

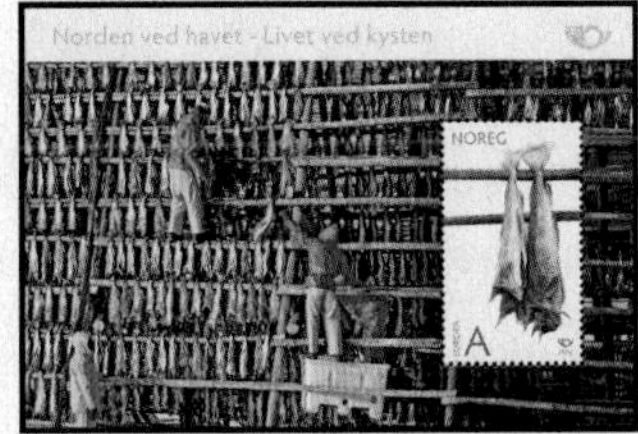

Dried Cod — A596

***Perf. 13¼x13¾***

**2010, Mar. 24** **Litho.**

**1605** A596 A Europa multi 4.50 4.50

No. 1605 sold for 11k on day of issue.

Personalized Stamp — A597

***Serpentine Die Cut 10x10¼ Syncopated***

**2010, Apr. 16** **Self-Adhesive**

**1606** A597 A Europa gray 3.75 3.75

No. 1606 sold for 11k on day of issue. The image shown is the generic image sold at face value. Stamps could be personalized for an additional fee.

Valdresflya Road A598

Gamle Strynefjellsvegen Road — A599

Sognefjellet Road A600

Trollstigen Road A601

Helgelandskysten Nord Road — A602

Lofoten National Tourist Road A603

**Booklet Stamps**

***Die Cut Perf. 13¼x13½***

**2010, Apr. 16** **Self-Adhesive**

**1607** A598 A Innland multi 3.00 3.00
**1608** A599 A Innland multi 3.00 3.00
*a.* Booklet pane of 10, 5 each #1607-1608 30.00
**1609** A600 A Europa multi 4.00 3.00
**1610** A601 A Europa multi 4.00 3.00
*a.* Booklet pane of 10, 5 each #1609-1610 40.00
**1611** A602 A Verda multi 4.50 4.50
**1612** A603 A Verda multi 4.50 4.50
*a.* Booklet pane of 10, 5 each #1611-1612 45.00
*Nos. 1607-1612 (6)* 23.00 21.00

On day of issue, Nos. 1607-1608 each sold for 8.50k, Nos. 1609-1610 each sold for 11k, and Nos. 1611-1612 each sold for 13k.

Norwegian Eurovision Song Contest Contestants A604

Designs: No. 1613, Bobbysocks, 1985 winner. No. 1614, Secret Garden, 1995 winner. No. 1615, Alexander Rybak, 2009 winner. No. 1616, Jahn Teigen, 1978 finalist.

**Coil Stamps**

***Die Cut Perf. 15½x14½***

**2010, May 18** **Self-Adhesive**

**1613** A604 A Innland multi 3.00 1.25
**1614** A604 A Innland multi 3.00 1.25
**1615** A604 A Innland multi 3.00 1.25
**1616** A604 A Innland multi 3.00 1.25
*a.* Horiz. strip of 4, #1613-1616 12.00
*Nos. 1613-1616 (4)* 12.00 5.00

On day of issue, Nos. 1613-1616 each sold for 8.50k.

Molde Jazz Festival, 50th Anniv. — A605

**2010, June 18** *Perf. 13¼x13¾*

1617 A605 13k gray & blue 4.50 3.50

Norwegian National Health Association, Cent. — A606

**2010, June 18** **Litho. & Engr.**

1618 A606 26k multi 9.00 6.75

A607

A608

A609

Television in Norway, 50th Anniv. A610

Designs: Nos. 1619a, 1620, Children's television characters Bjornen Teodor, Kometkameratene, Pompel & Pilt, Titten Tei. No. 1621, Comedy stars Trond Kirkvag, Robert Stoltenberg, Rolv Wesenlund and Trond-Viggo Torgersen. Nos. 1619b, 1622, Erik Diesen, Dan Borge Akero, Ivar Dyrhaug and Anne Grosvold. No. 1623, Arne Scheie, Ingrid Espelid Hovig, Erik Bye and Ragnhild Saelthun Fjortoft.

**2010, Aug. 20** **Litho.** *Perf. 13¼x13*

1619 Sheet of 2 7.00 7.00
*a.* A607 A Innland multi 3.00 3.00
*b.* A609 A Innland multi 3.00 3.00

**Coil Stamps**

**Self-Adhesive**

***Die Cut Perf. 15½x14½***

1620 A607 A Innland multi 3.00 1.25
1621 A608 A Innland multi 3.00 1.25
1622 A609 A Innland multi 3.00 1.25
1623 A610 A Innland multi 3.00 1.25
*a.* Horiz. strip of 4, #1620-1623 12.00
*Nos. 1620-1623 (4)* 12.00 5.00

On day of issue, Nos. 1619a-1619b, 1620-1623 each sold for 8.50k.

Norwegian Press Association, Norwegian Media Businesses Association, Cent. — A611

**2010, Sept. 15** *Perf. 13¼x13¾*

1624 A611 11k multi 4.00 3.00

Norwegian Seafarers' Union, Cent. — A612

**2010, Sept. 15** *Perf. 13¾x13¼*

1625 A612 16k multi 5.50 4.25

Norwegian University of Technology and Science, Cent. — A613

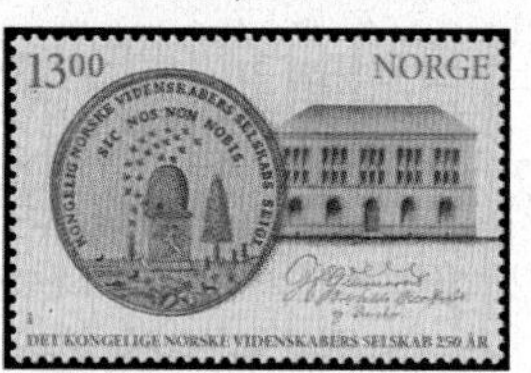

Royal Norwegian Society of Science and Letters, 250th Anniv. — A614

***Perf. 13¼x13¾***

**2010, Sept. 15** **Litho. & Engr.**

1626 A613 8.50k multi 3.00 2.25
1627 A614 13k multi 4.50 3.50

**Redrawn Posthorn Type of 2001-06**

***Perf. 13¾x13¼***

**2010, Nov. 15** **Litho.**

**Color of Oval**

1628 A439a 4k blue 1.40 1.00
1629 A439a 8k brown 2.75 2.00
1630 A439a 30k dull violet 10.00 6.00
*Nos. 1628-1630 (3)* 14.15 9.00

No. 1630 has a silver frame.

A615

Europa — A616

Illustrations from children's books by Anne-Cath. Vestly (1920-2008): A Innland, Marte and Grandma and Grandma and Morten. A Europa, The House in the Woods — A New Home.

**Litho. With Foil Application**

**2010, Nov. 15** *Perf. 13¼*

1631 A615 A Innland multi 3.00 2.25
1632 A616 A Europa multi 4.00 3.00

On day of issue, No. 1631 sold for 8.50k and No. 1632 sold for 11k.

Christmas A617

Designs from embroidered Christmas tablecloth: No. 1633, Straw billy goat. No. 1634, Candlesticks and mistletoe.

***Die Cut Perf. 13¼x13¾***

**2010, Nov. 15** **Litho.**

**Booklet Stamps**

**Self-Adhesive**

1633 A617 A Innland multi 3.00 1.25
1634 A617 A Innland multi 3.00 1.25
*a.* Booklet pane of 10, 5 each #1633-1634 30.00

On day of issue, Nos. 1633-1634 each sold for 8.50k.

Norwegian Sports Confederation, 150th Anniv. — A618

***Die Cut Perf. 15½x15***

**2011, Jan. 3** **Coil Stamp** **Litho.**

**Self-Adhesive**

1635 A618 14k multi 5.00 3.00

**Wildlife Type of 2006**

**2011, Jan. 3** **Litho.** *Perf. 13¼x13¾*

1636 A511 17k Polar bear 6.00 3.00
*a.* Perf. 14¼x13¾ 6.25 3.50
1637 A511 27k Musk ox 9.50 4.00

2011 World Nordic Skiing Championships, Oslo — A619

Designs: 9k, Holmenkollen ski jump. 12k, Skiers, Holmenkollen Ski Stadium.

**2011, Feb. 23** *Perf. 13½x13¼*

1638 A619 9k multi 3.25 2.50
1639 A619 12k multi 4.50 2.50
*a.* Souvenir sheet of 2, #1638-1639 9.00 9.00

Fridtjof Nansen (1861-1930), Explorer and Statesman — A620

**2011, Apr. 15** **Litho.** *Perf. 14x13¼*

1640 A620 12k multi 4.50 3.25

Amnesty International, 50th Anniv. A621

***Perf. 14¼x14½***

**2011, Apr. 15** **Litho. & Engr.**

1641 A621 A Innland multi 3.50 2.50

No. 1641 sold for 9k on day of issue.

Roald Amundsen Expedition to South Pole, Cent. — A622

Designs: 14k, Amundsen (1872-1928), men on expedition, Norwegian flag. 17k, Polar ship Fram and sled dogs.

**2011, Apr. 15** **Litho.** *Perf. 14x13¼*

1642 A622 14k multi 5.25 3.75
1643 A622 17k multi 6.50 4.50

Buildings A623

Designs: No. 1644, Global Seed Vault, Svalbard. No. 1645, Visitor's Center, Borgund. No. 1646, Preikestolen Mountain Lodge, Lysefjorden.

**Booklet Stamps**

***Die Cut Perf. 13¼x13½***

**2011, Apr. 15** **Self-Adhesive**

1644 A623 A Innland multi 3.50 1.25
*a.* Booklet pane of 10 35.00
1645 A623 A Europa multi 4.50 2.50
*a.* Booklet pane of 10 45.00
1646 A623 A Verden multi 5.25 2.25
*a.* Booklet pane of 10 52.50
*Nos. 1644-1646 (3)* 13.25 6.00

On day of issue, Nos. 1644-1646 sold for 9k, 12k and 14k, respectively.

Drammen, Bicent. — A624

**2011, May 20** *Perf. 14x13¼*

1647 A624 9k multi 3.50 2.50

Fire and Rescue Services, 150th Anniv. A625

Designs: 9k, Firemen and fire truck from Sagene Fire Station, Oslo. 27k, Firemen training.

**2011, June 3** *Perf. 13¼x13¾*

1648 A625 9k multi 3.50 2.50
1649 A625 27k multi 10.00 6.50

Europa — A626

Designs: 12k, Logging, Bjornsasen. 14k, Forest, Farrisvannet.

**2011, June 10** **Litho.**

**1650** A626 12k multi 4.50 3.25
**1651** A626 14k multi 5.25 3.75

Intl. Year of Forests.

University of Oslo, Bicent. — A627

**2011, Sept. 2** **Litho. & Engr.**

**1652** A627 9k ver & brn 3.25 2.50

Comic Strip Art — A628

Designs: 9k, Bird in nest, by John Arne Saeteroy. 14k, Hold Brillan (man opening envelope), by Cristopher Nielsen. 17k, Nemi (women with index finger and pinkie raised), by Lise Myhre. 20k, Pondus (soccer player), by Frode Overli.

**2011, Sept. 16** **Litho.**

**1653** A628 9k multi 3.25 2.50
**1654** A628 14k multi 5.00 3.75
**1655** A628 17k multi 6.00 4.50
**1656** A628 20k multi 7.00 5.50
*Nos. 1653-1656 (4)* 21.25 16.25

Female Singers A629

Designs: No. 1657, Wenche Myhre. No. 1658, Inger Lise Rypdal. No. 1659, Mari Boine. No. 1660, Sissel Kyrkjebo.

**Coil Stamps**

***Die Cut Perf. 15½x14½***

**2011, Sept. 16** **Self-Adhesive**

**1657** A629 A Innland multi 3.25 1.25
**1658** A629 A Innland multi 3.25 1.25
**1659** A629 A Innland multi 3.25 1.25
**1660** A629 A Innland multi 3.25 1.25
*a.* Horiz. coil strip of 4, #1657-1660 13.00
*Nos. 1657-1660 (4)* 13.00 5.00

On day of issue, Nos. 1657-1660 each sold for 9k.

**Redrawn Posthorn Type of 2001-06**

***Perf. 13¾x13¼***

**2011, Nov. 11** **Litho.**

**Color of Oval**

**1661** A439a 50k blue gray 18.00 9.00

No. 1661 has a silver frame.

Christmas — A630

Designs: No. 1662, Boy holding letter. No. 1663, Girl holding gifts.

***Die Cut Perf. 13½x13¼***

**2011, Nov. 11** **Litho.**

**Self-Adhesive**

**1662** A630 A Innland multi 3.25 1.25
**1663** A630 A Innland multi 3.25 1.25
*a.* Horiz. pair, #1662-1663, on tan backing paper 6.50
*b.* Booklet pane of 10, 5 each #1662-1663 32.50

On day of issue, Nos. 1662-1663 each sold for 9k. On No. 1663b, Nos. 1662 and 1663 are arranged in vertical pairs.

Personalized Stamp — A631

***Serpentine Die Cut 10x10¼***
***Syncopated***

**2012, Feb. 21** **Self-Adhesive**

**1664** A631 A Innland multi 3.50 3.50

No. 1664 sold for 9.50k on day of issue. The image shown is the generic image sold at face value. Stamps could be personalized for an additional fee.

75th Birthdays of King and Queen A632

Designs: 9.50k, Queen Sonja. 13k, King Harald V.

***Perf. 14¼x14½***

**2012, Feb. 21** **Litho. & Engr.**

**1665** A632 9.50k multi 3.50 2.75
**1666** A632 13k multi 4.75 3.50

A booklet containing booklet panes of 2 No. 1665, 2 No. 1666 and 1 each of Nos. 1665-1666 sold for 99k. Value $35.

Griffin From Roof Of National Gallery Oslo, Sculpture by Lars Utne — A633

Branntomt, by Hakon Stenstadvold A634

***Die Cut Perf. 15½x14½***

**2012, Feb. 21** **Litho.**

**Coil Stamps**

**Self-Adhesive**

**1667** A633 B Innland multi 3.25 1.25
**1668** A634 14k multi 5.00 3.00

No. 1667 sold for 9k on day of issue. An etiquette alternates with No. 1667 on rolls produced for sale to the public. On later printings, the etiquette is not present on the rolls.

Souvenir Sheet

Rescue Helicopter — A635

**2012, Mar. 21** ***Perf. 14x13½***

**1669** A635 A Europa multi 5.00 5.00

No. 1669 sold for 13k on day of issue.

Famous People A636

Designs: No. 1670, Sonja Henie (1912-69), figure skater. No. 1671, Close-up of Henie. No. 1672, Thorbjorn Egner (1912-90), writer of children's books. No. 1673, Egner's illustration of Kardemomme Town.

**Coil Stamps**

***Die Cut Perf. 15½x14½***

**2012, Apr. 13** **Self-Adhesive**

**1670** A636 A Innland multi 3.50 1.25
**1671** A636 A Innland multi 3.50 1.25
**1672** A636 A Innland multi 3.50 1.25
**1673** A636 A Innland multi 3.50 1.25
*a.* Horiz. strip of 4, #1670-1673 14.00
*Nos. 1670-1673 (4)* 14.00 5.00

On day of issue, Nos. 1670-1673 each sold for 9.50k. No. 1673a was made available with stamps on the strip in a different order and having a different distance between stamps.

Nidaros Cathedral, Trondheim A637

Abbey Ruins, Selja Island — A638

Pilgrims on Path Near Fokstugu A639

***Die Cut Perf. 13¼x13½***

**2012, Apr. 13** **Self-Adhesive**

**1674** A637 A Innland multi 3.50 1.25
*a.* Booklet pane of 10 on white backing paper 35.00
**1675** A638 A Europa multi 4.50 2.50
*a.* Booklet pane of 10 on white backing paper 45.00
**1676** A639 A Verden multi 5.25 3.00
*a.* Booklet pane of 10 on white backing paper 52.50
*Nos. 1674-1676 (3)* 13.25 6.75

Europa. On day of issue Nos. 1674-1676 each sold for 9.50k, 13k and 15k, respectively. Values for unused examples of Nos. 1674-1676 are for copies either on white backing paper (from booklet panes) or tan backing paper (single stamps).

Norwegian Aviation, Cent. — A640

Designs: 14k, Start (Rumpler Taube), first airplane of Navy Air Service. 15k, Douglas DC-3 Dakota. 27k, Glider.

**2012, May 18** **Litho.** ***Perf. 13¼***

**1677** A640 14k multi 4.75 4.75
**1678** A640 15k multi 5.00 5.00
**1679** A640 27k multi 9.00 9.00
*a.* Souvenir sheet of 3, #1677-1679 19.00 19.00
*Nos. 1677-1679 (3)* 18.75 18.75

Hadeland Glassworks, 250th Anniv. — A641

***Perf. 13¼x13¾***

**2012, June 15** **Litho. & Engr.**

**1680** A641 13k multi 4.25 4.25

Kavringen Lighthouse A642

Medfjordbaen Lighthouse A643

***Die Cut Perf. 13½x13¼***

**2012, June 15** **Litho.**

**Self-Adhesive**

**1681** A642 A Innland multi 3.25 3.25
**1682** A643 A Innland multi 3.25 3.25
*a.* Horiz. pair, #1681-1682, on tan backing paper 6.50
*b.* Booklet pane of 10, 5 each # 1681-1682 32.50

On day of issue, Nos. 1681-1682 each sold for 9.50k. On No. 1682b, Nos. 1681 and 1682 are arranged in vertical pairs.

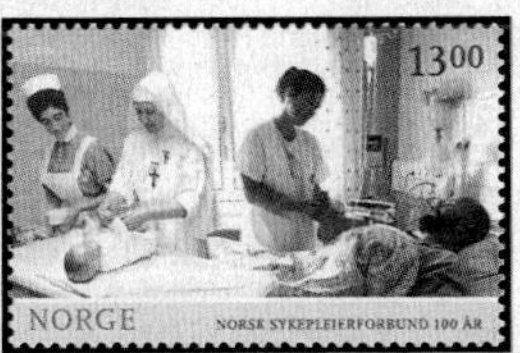

Norwegian Nurses Organization, Cent. — A644

**2012, Sept. 14** ***Perf. 13¼x13¾***

**1683** A644 13k multi 4.50 4.50

Famous Men — A645

Designs: 14k, Knud Knudsen (1812-95), linguist. 15k, Peter Christen Asbjornsen (1812-85) and Jorgen Moe (1813-82), collectors of Norwegian folklore.

**2012, Sept. 14** ***Perf. 14x13¼***

**1684** A645 14k multi 5.00 5.00
**1685** A645 15k multi 5.25 5.25

Popular Musicians A646

Designs: No. 1686, Sondre Lerche. No. 1687, Ole Paus. No. 1688, Age Aleksandersen. No. 1689, Morten Abel.

**Coil Stamps**

*Die Cut Perf. 15½x14½*

**2012, Sept. 14** **Self-Adhesive**

**1686** A646 A Innland multi 3.50 3.50
**1687** A646 A Innland multi 3.50 3.50
**1688** A646 A Innland multi 3.50 3.50
**1689** A646 A Innland multi 3.50 3.50
*a.* Horiz. strip of 4, #1686-1689 14.00
*Nos. 1686-1689 (4)* 14.00 14.00

**Redrawn Posthorn Type of 2001-06**

*Perf. 13¾x13¼*

**2012, Nov. 12** **Litho.**

**Color of Oval**

**1690** A439a 40k gray 14.00 14.00

No. 1690 has a silver frame.

Ruins of Hamar Cathedral A647

**2012, Nov. 12** **Litho.**

**1691** A647 15k multi 5.25 5.25

Directorate for Cultural Heritage, cent.

Santa Claus and Carpenter Andersen A648

Mrs. Claus and Children A649

*Die Cut Perf. 13¼x13¾*

**2012, Nov. 12** **Self-Adhesive**

**1692** A648 A Innland multi 3.50 3.50
**1693** A649 A Innland multi 3.50 3.50
*a.* Booklet pane of 10, 5 each #1692-1693, on white backing paper 35.00

Nos. 1692-1693 each sold for 9.50k on day of issue. Horizontal pairs of Nos. 1692-1693 are on white backing paper, which are from No. 1693a, and a tan backing paper, which were prepared for philatelic sale. The stamps on the tan backing paper were only made available as pairs, and were not available in coil rolls.

Fashion A650

Fashion designs by: No. 1694, Nina Skarras. No. 1695, Camilla Bruerberg.

**2013, Jan. 2** *Die Cut Perf. 15½x14½*

**Coil Stamps**

**Self-Adhesive**

**1694** A650 15k multi 5.50 5.50
**1695** A650 15k multi 5.50 5.50
*a.* Horiz. pair, #1694-1695 11.00

Paintings by Edvard Munch (1863-1944) — A651

Details from: 13k, Self-Portrait in Front of the House Wall, 1926. 15k, The Sick Child, 1898. 17k, Madonna, 1895. No. 1699, The Scream, 1893.
No. 1700, The Sun, 1911.

**2013, Feb. 15** *Perf. 14x13¼*

**1696** A651 13k multi 4.50 4.50
*a.* Booklet pane of 1 7.50 —
**1697** A651 15k multi 5.25 5.25
*a.* Booklet pane of 1 8.50 —
**1698** A651 17k multi 6.00 6.00
*a.* Booklet pane of 1 9.75 —
**1699** A651 20k multi 7.00 7.00
*a.* Booklet pane of 1 11.50 —
*Nos. 1696-1699 (4)* 22.75 22.75

**Souvenir Sheet**

**1700** A651 20k multi 7.00 7.00
*a.* Booklet pane of 1 11.50 —
Complete booklet, #1696a, 1697a, 1698a, 1699a, 1700a 49.00

Complete booklet sold for 139k.

Statue of King Karl Johan, by Brynjulv Bergslien A652

*Perf. 14¼x14½*

**2013, Apr. 19** **Litho. & Engr.**

**1701** A652 30k multi 10.50 10.50

King Karl Johan (1763-1844).

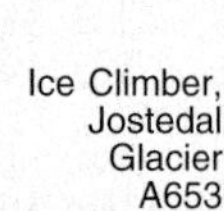

Ice Climber, Jostedal Glacier A653

Boya Glacier A654

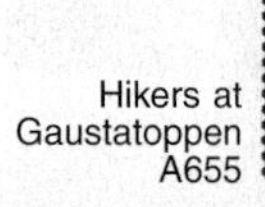

Hikers at Gaustatoppen A655

Hikers at Gaustatoppen A656

Rafters, Sjoa River — A657

Riverboarder, Sjoa River — A658

*Die Cut Perf. 13¼x13½*

**2013, Apr. 19** **Litho.**

**Booklet Stamps**

**Self-Adhesive**

**1702** A653 A Innland multi 3.25 3.25
**1703** A654 A Innland multi 3.25 3.25
*a.* Booklet pane of 10, 5 each #1702-1703 32.50
**1704** A655 A Europa multi 4.50 4.50
**1705** A656 A Europa multi 4.50 4.50
*a.* Booklet pane of 10, 5 each #1704-1705 45.00
**1706** A657 A Verden multi 5.25 5.25
**1707** A658 A Verden multi 5.25 5.25
*a.* Booklet pane of 10, 5 each #1706-1707 52.50
*Nos. 1702-1707 (6)* 26.00 26.00

On day of issue, Nos. 1702-1703 each sold for 9.50k, Nos. 1704-1705 each sold for 13k, and Nos. 1706-1707 each sold for 15k.

Norwegian Student Society, 200th Anniv. — A659

**2013, June 10** **Litho.** *Perf. 13¼*

**1708** A659 17k multi 6.00 6.00

Europa — A660

Postal vehicles: 13k, 1932 Harley-Davidson motorcycles and sidecars. 15k, Ford electric vans.

**2013, June 10** **Litho.** *Perf. 14x13½*

**1709** A660 13k multi 4.50 4.50
**1710** A660 15k multi 5.25 5.25

Crown Prince Haakon A661

Crown Princess Mette-Marit A662

Crown Prince Haakon, Crown Princess Mette-Marit and Their Children A663

King Harald V, Crown Prince Haakon, Princess Ingrid Alexandra A664

*Die Cut Perf. 15½x14½*

**2013, June 10** **Litho.**

**Coil Stamps**

**Self-Adhesive**

**1711** A661 A Innland multi 3.50 3.50
**1712** A662 A Innland multi 3.50 3.50
**1713** A663 A Innland multi 3.50 3.50
**1714** A664 A Innland multi 3.50 3.50
*a.* Horiz. strip of 4, #1711-1714 14.00
*Nos. 1711-1714 (4)* 14.00 14.00

Fortieth birthdays of Crown Prince Haakon and Crown Princess Mette-Marit. On day of issue, Nos. 1711-1714 each sold for 9.50k.

Woman Suffrage, Cent. — A665

Designs: 17k, Camilla Collett (1813-95), feminist writer, front page of *Amtmandens Døttre.* 30k, Anna Rogstad (1854-1938), first female in Parliament, Parliament Building.

*Perf. 13¼x13¾*

**2013, Sept. 9** **Litho. & Engr.**

**1715** A665 17k multi 5.75 5.75
**1716** A665 30k multi 10.00 10.00

National Language Year — A666

Designs: No. 1717, Lasse Kolstad (1922-2012), actor. No. 1718, Ivar Aasen (1813-96), writer and lexicographer.

*Die Cut Perf. 15½x14½*

**2013, Sept. 9** **Litho.**

**Coil Stamps**

**Self-Adhesive**

**1717** A666 A Innland multi 3.25 3.25
**1718** A666 A Innland multi 3.25 3.25
*a.* Horiz. pair, #1717-1718 6.50

Nos. 1717-1718 each sold for 9.50k on day of issue.

Rock Bands — A667

Designs: No. 1719, The Pussycats. No. 1720, DumDum Boys. No. 1721, Turbonegro. No. 1722, DeLillos.

*Die Cut Perf. 15½x14½*

**2013, Oct. 4** **Litho.**

**Coil Stamps**

**Self-Adhesive**

**1719** A667 A Innland multi 3.25 3.25
**1720** A667 A Innland multi 3.25 3.25
**1721** A667 A Innland multi 3.25 3.25
**1722** A667 A Innland multi 3.25 3.25
*a.* Horiz. strip of 4, #1719-1722 13.00
*Nos. 1719-1722 (4)* 13.00 13.00

Nos. 1719-1722 each sold for 9.50k on day of issue.

**Redrawn Posthorn Type of 2001-06**

*Perf. 13¾x13¼*

**2013, Nov. 11** **Litho.**

**Color of Oval**

**1723** A439a 10k brown 3.25 3.25
**1724** A439a 20k brown 6.50 6.50

Solan Gundersen A668

Nabonissen House A669

*Die Cut Perf. 13½x13¼*

**2013, Nov. 11** **Litho.**

**Self-Adhesive**

**1725** A668 A Innland multi 3.25 3.25
**1726** A669 A Innland multi 3.25 3.25
*a.* Horiz. pair, #1725-1726, on tan backing paper 6.50

| | | |
|---|---|---|
| *b.* | Bookleet pane of 10, 5 each #1725-1726, on white backing paper | 32.50 |

Christmas. Nos. 1725-1726 each sold for 9.50k on day of issue.

**Wildlife Type of 2006**

**2014 Litho. *Perf. 14¼x13¾***

**Self-Adhesive**

| | | | | |
|---|---|---|---|---|
| **1726C** | A511 16k Lemming | 5.25 | 5.25 |
| **1727** | A511 19k Red deer | 6.25 | 6.25 |
| **1728** | A511 35k Badger | 11.50 | 11.50 |
| | *Nos. 1726C-1728 (3)* | 23.00 | 23.00 |

Issued: Nos 1727-1728, 1/2; 1726C, 1/22.

Norwegian Church Abroad, 150th Anniv. — A670

***Die Cut Perf. 14½x15½***

**2014, Jan. 2 Litho.**

**Coil Stamp**

**Self-Adhesive**

| | | | |
|---|---|---|---|
| **1729** | A670 15k multi | 5.00 | 5.00 |

Marit Bjorgen A671

Tora Berger A672

Petter Northug A673

Aksel Lund Svindal A674

***Die Cut Perf. 13¼x13½***

**2014, Feb. 7 Litho.**

**Coil Stamps**

**Self-Adhesive**

| | | | |
|---|---|---|---|
| **1730** | A671 A Innland multi | 3.50 | 3.50 |
| **1731** | A672 A Innland multi | 3.50 | 3.50 |
| **1732** | A673 A Innland multi | 3.50 | 3.50 |
| **1733** | A674 A Innland multi | 3.50 | 3.50 |
| *a.* | Horiz. strip of 4, #1730-1733 | 14.00 | |
| | *Nos. 1730-1733 (4)* | 14.00 | 14.00 |

2014 Winter Olympics, Sochi, Russia. Nos. 1730-1733 each sold for 10k on day of issue.

Souvenir Sheet

Supply Ship MS Normand Arctic — A675

**2014, Mar. 17 Litho. *Perf. 14x13¼***

| | | | |
|---|---|---|---|
| **1734** | A675 A Europe multi | 4.50 | 4.50 |

No. 1734 sold for 13k on day of issue.

Viking Buckle, Longhouse and Woman in Viking Costume Sewing A676

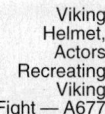

Viking Helmet, Actors Recreating Viking Fight — A677

Draken Harald Harfagre, Dragon Figurehead A678

***Die Cut Perf. 13¼x13½***

**2014, Apr. 28 Litho.**

**Self-Adhesive**

| | | | |
|---|---|---|---|
| **1735** | A676 A Innland multi | 3.50 | 3.50 |
| *a.* | Booklet pane of 10 | 35.00 | |
| **1736** | A677 A Europa multi | 4.50 | 4.50 |
| *a.* | Booklet pane of 10 | 45.00 | |
| **1737** | A678 A Verda multi | 5.50 | 5.50 |
| *a.* | Booklet pane of 10 | 55.00 | |
| | *Nos. 1735-1737 (3)* | 13.50 | 13.50 |

On day of issue, No. 1735 sold for 10k; No. 1736, for 13k; No. 1737, for 16k. Nos. 1735-1737 are on brownish translucent paper (single stamps for sale to collectors) and white translucent paper (stamps in booklet panes).

Thor Heyerdahl (1914-2002), Ethnographer A679

Kon-Tiki A680

Easter Island Moai — A681

Ra II — A682

**2014, Apr. 28 Litho. *Perf. 13¾x14***

**Booklet Stamps**

| | | | |
|---|---|---|---|
| **1737B** | A679 A Innland multi | 6.00 | 6.00 |
| *f.* | Booklet pane of 1 | 6.00 | — |
| **1737C** | A680 A Innland multi | 6.00 | 6.00 |
| *g.* | Booklet pane of 1 | 6.00 | — |
| **1737D** | A681 A Innland multi | 6.00 | 6.00 |
| *h.* | Booklet pane of 1 | 6.00 | — |
| **1737E** | A682 A Innland multi | 6.00 | 6.00 |
| *i.* | Booklet pane of 1 | 6.00 | — |
| *j.* | Booklet pane of 4, #1737B-1737E | 24.00 | — |
| | Complete booklet, #1737Bf, 1737Cg, 1737Dh, 1737Ei, 1737Ej | 48.00 | |
| | *Nos. 1737B-1737E (4)* | 24.00 | 24.00 |

**Coil Stamps**

**Self-Adhesive**

***Die Cut Perf. 13x13½***

| | | | |
|---|---|---|---|
| **1738** | A679 A Innland multi | 3.50 | 3.50 |
| **1739** | A680 A Innland multi | 3.50 | 3.50 |
| **1740** | A681 A Innland multi | 3.50 | 3.50 |
| **1741** | A682 A Innland multi | 3.50 | 3.50 |
| *a.* | Horiz. strip of 4, #1738-1741 | 14.00 | |
| | *Nos. 1738-1741 (4)* | 14.00 | 14.00 |

Nos. 1737B-1737E each had a franking value of 10k on day of issue. Complete booklet sold for 139k. Nos. 1738-1741 each sold for 10k on day of issue.

Norwegian Constitution, 200th Anniv. — A683

Designs: 13k, Constituent Assembly meeting at Eidsvoll, 1814. 16k, Prince Christian Frederik and 1814 Constitution. 19k, Lion statue at Parliament, May 17 parade. 30k, Hands forming heart, 1814 Constitution.

**Litho. & Engr.**

**2014, May 16 *Perf. 14x13¼***

| | | | |
|---|---|---|---|
| **1742** | A683 13k multi | 4.50 | 4.50 |
| **1743** | A683 16k multi | 5.50 | 5.50 |
| **1744** | A683 19k multi | 6.50 | 6.50 |
| **1745** | A683 30k multi | 10.00 | 10.00 |
| | *Nos. 1742-1745 (4)* | 26.50 | 26.50 |

Personalized Stamp — A684

***Serpentine Die Cut 10¼x10 Syncopated***

**2014, May 16 Litho.**

**Self-Adhesive**

| | | | |
|---|---|---|---|
| **1746** | A684 A Verden multi | 5.50 | 5.50 |

No. 1746 sold for 16k on day of issue. The image shown, depicting the Aurora Borealis, is the generic image sold at face value. Stamps could be personalized for an additional fee.

Alf Proysen (1914-70), Writer, and Radio — A685

Mrs. Pepperpot and Mouse A686

***Die Cut Perf. 15½x14½***

**2014, June 13 Coil Stamps Litho.**

**Self-Adhesive**

| | | | |
|---|---|---|---|
| **1747** | A685 A Innland multi | 3.25 | 3.25 |
| **1748** | A686 A Innland multi | 3.25 | 3.25 |
| *a.* | Horiz. pair, #1747-1748 | 6.50 | |

Nos. 1747-1748 each sold for 10k on day of issue.

**Redrawn Posthorn Type of 2001-06**

**2014-15 Litho. *Perf. 13¾x13¼***

**Self-Adhesive**

**Color of Oval**

| | | | |
|---|---|---|---|
| **1749** | A439a 1k green | .25 | .25 |
| **1750** | A439a 5k purple | 1.60 | 1.60 |
| **1751** | A439a 50k blue gray | 16.00 | 16.00 |
| **1752** | A439a 70k gray grn | 22.00 | 22.00 |
| | *Nos. 1749-1752 (4)* | 39.85 | 39.85 |

Issued: No. 1749, 1/7/15. No. 1750, 9/9; No. 1752, 9/12.

Norwegian Chess Federation, Cent. — A687

**Litho. & Engr.**

**2014, Aug. 1 *Perf. 13¼***

| | | | |
|---|---|---|---|
| **1753** | A687 15k multi | 4.75 | 4.75 |

Solvguttene Boys' Choir — A688

Characters From Production of *Putti Plutti Pott* — A689

***Die Cut Perf. 13¼x13½***

**2014, Nov. 10 Litho.**

**Self-Adhesive**

| | | | |
|---|---|---|---|
| **1754** | A688 A Innland multi | 3.00 | 3.00 |
| **1755** | A689 A Innland multi | 3.00 | 3.00 |
| *a.* | Horiz. pair, #1754-1755, on tan backing paper | 6.00 | |
| *b.* | Booklet pane of 10, 5 each #1754-1755 | 30.00 | |

Christmas. Nos. 1754-1755 both sold for 10k on day of issue.

**Wildlife Type of 2006**

Design: 31k, Eurasian eagle owl.

**2015, Jan. 2 Litho. *Perf. 14¼x13¾***

**Self-Adhesive**

| | | | |
|---|---|---|---|
| **1756** | A511 31k multicolored | 8.25 | 8.25 |

Birds — A690

Designs: No. 1757, Cyanistes caeruleus. No. 1758, Lophophanes cristatus.

***Die Cut Perf. 15½x14½***

**2015, Jan. 2 Litho. Coil Stamps**

**Self-Adhesive**

| | | | |
|---|---|---|---|
| **1757** | A690 16k multi | 4.25 | 4.25 |
| **1758** | A690 16k multi | 4.25 | 4.25 |
| *a.* | Horiz. pair, #1757-1758 | 8.50 | |

Norwegian Red Cross, 150th Anniv. A691

Designs: No. 1759, Rescue team members in snow. No. 1760, Visitor service representative meeting with elderly woman. No. 1761, Emergency aid worker with Philippine children. No. 1762, Attempt to create world's largest human cross, 2010.

***Die Cut Perf. 15½x14½***

**2015, Feb. 20 Litho.**

**Coil Stamps**

**Self-Adhesive**

| | | | |
|---|---|---|---|
| **1759** | A691 A Innland multi | 2.75 | 2.75 |
| **1760** | A691 A Innland multi | 2.75 | 2.75 |
| **1761** | A691 A Innland multi | 2.75 | 2.75 |
| **1762** | A691 A Innland multi | 2.75 | 2.75 |
| *a.* | Horiz. strip of 4, #1759-1762 | 11.00 | |
| | *Nos. 1759-1762 (4)* | 11.00 | 11.00 |

On day of issue, Nos. 1759-1762 each sold for 10.50k.

**Wildlife Type of 2006**

**2015, Mar. 4 Litho. *Perf. 14¼x13¾***

**Self-Adhesive**

| | | | |
|---|---|---|---|
| **1763** | A511 14k Bear | 3.75 | 3.75 |

Halden, 350th Anniv. — A692

**Litho. & Engr.**

**2015, Apr. 10** *Perf. 14½*

**1764** A692 20k multi 5.50 5.50

Photographs by Anders Beer Wilse (1865-1949) — A693

Design: A Innland, Street View of Oslo, 1924. 14k, Kyrkja Mountain, 1933. 16k, Three Large Cod, 1910.
20k, Setesdal on the Way to Church, 1934.

**2015, Apr. 16 Litho.** *Perf. 14x13½*

**1765** A693 A Innland multi 3.00 3.00
**1766** A693 14k multi 3.75 3.75
**1767** A693 16k multi 4.25 4.25
*Nos. 1765-1767 (3)* 11.00 11.00

**Souvenir Sheet**

**1768** A693 20k multi 5.50 5.50

No. 1765 sold for 10.50k on day of issue. No. 1768 contains one 70x30mm stamp. A booklet containing panes of 1 of each of Nos. 1765-1768 sold for 139k.

Europa A694

Old toys: 14k, Anne dolls. 17k Tomte Ford F-100 truck and firetruck.

**2015, June 5 Litho.** *Perf. 14¼x14½*

**1769** A694 14k multi 3.50 3.50
**1770** A694 17k multi 4.25 4.25

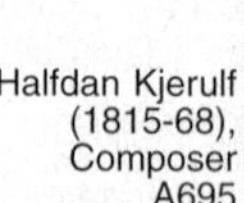

Halfdan Kjerulf (1815-68), Composer A695

Agnar Mykle (1915-94), Writer — A696

*Die Cut Perf. 15½x14½*

**2015, June 5** **Litho.**

**Coil Stamps**
**Self-Adhesive**

**1771** A695 A Innland multi 2.60 2.60
**1772** A696 A Innland multi 2.60 2.60
*a.* Horiz. pair, #1771-1772 5.20

Nos. 1771-1772 each sold for 10.50k on day of issue.

Lighthouses — A697

Designs: No. 1773, Kvitsoy Lighthouse. No. 1774, Slatteroy Lighthouse. No. 1775, Lindesnes Lighthouse. No. 1776, Kjeungskjaeret Lighthouse.

*Die Cut Perf. 13¾x13¼*

**2015, June 5** **Litho.**

**Self-Adhesive**

**1773** A697 A Europa multi 3.50 3.50
**1774** A697 A Europa multi 3.50 3.50
*a.* Booklet pane of 10, 5 each #1773-1774 35.00
**1775** A697 A Verda multi 4.25 4.25
**1776** A697 A Verda multi 4.25 4.25
*a.* Horiz. strip of 4, #1773-1776, on tan backing paper 15.50
*b.* Booklet pane of 10, 5 each #1773-1774 42.50
*Nos. 1773-1776 (4)* 15.50 15.50

On day of issue, Nos. 1773-1774 each sold for 14k and Nos. 1775-1776 each sold for 17k.

Bergen Philharmonic Orchestra, 250th Anniv. — A698

**2015, Aug. 20 Litho.** *Perf. 14x13½*

**1777** A698 31k multi 7.50 7.50

Supreme Court of Norway, 200th Anniv. — A699

**Litho. & Engr.**

**2015, Oct. 3** *Perf. 13½x14*

**1778** A699 20k multi 4.75 4.75

Birds — A700

Designs: No. 1779, Somateria spectabilis. No. 1780, Somateria mollissima. No. 1781, Motacilla alba. No. 1782, Oenanthe oenanthe.

*Die Cut Perf. 15½x14½*

**2015, Oct. 3** **Litho.**

**Coil Stamps**
**Self-Adhesive**

**1779** A700 B Innland 2.25 2.25
**1780** A700 B Innland 2.25 2.25
**1781** A700 A Innland 2.50 2.50
**1782** A700 A Innland 2.50 2.50
*a.* Horiz. strip of 4, #1779-1782 9.50
*Nos. 1779-1782 (4)* 9.50 9.50

On day of issue, Nos. 1779-1780 each sold for 9.50k and Nos. 1781-1782 each sold for 10.50k.

**Redrawn Posthorn Type of 2001-06**

*Perf. 13¾x13¼*

**2015, Nov. 13** **Litho.**

**Self-Adhesive**
**Color of Oval**

**1783** A439a 60k dull bl grn 14.00 14.00

A701

Christmas — A702

*Serpentine Die Cut 11*

**2015, Nov. 13** **Litho.**

**Booklet Stamps**
**Self-Adhesive**

**1784** A701 A Innland 2.50 2.50
**1785** A702 A Innland 2.50 2.50
*a.* Booklet pane of 8, 4 each #1784-1785 20.00

Reign of King Harald V, 25th Anniv. — A703

*Die Cut Perf. 14½x15½*

**2016, Jan. 11 Coil Stamp Litho.**

**Self-Adhesive**

**1786** A703 17k multi 4.00 4.00

Youth Winter Olympic Games, Lillehammer — A704

Designs: No. 1787, Skier. No. 1788, Person on mountain top.

*Die Cut Perf. 13½x13¼*

**2016, Jan. 11** **Litho.**

**Self-Adhesive**

**1787** A704 A Innland multi 2.50 2.50
**1788** A704 A Innland multi 2.50 2.50
*a.* Horiz. pair, #1787-1788, on tan backing paper 5.00
*b.* Booklet pane of 10, 5 each #1787-1788 25.00

World Biathlon Championships, Oslo — A705

Two competitors: 21k, Skiing. 33k, Shooting.

**Litho. With Foil Application**

**2016, Feb. 19** *Perf. 14x13½*

**1789** A705 21k multi 5.00 5.00
**1790** A705 33k multi 7.75 7.75

Cities A706

Designs: 11k, Harbor of Grimstad, statue of fisherman by Terje Vigen. 17k, Cannons of Nyholmd Skandse, Bodo, Bishop Mathias Bonsach Krogh, city founder. 18k, Cannons near Kragero, *Winter, Kragero,* by Edvard Munch. 21k, Waterfall, Sarpsborg, statue of St. Olav by Finn Eirik Modahl.

**2016, Apr. 15 Litho.** *Perf. 13½x13¾*

**1791** A706 11k multi 2.75 2.75
**1792** A706 17k multi 4.25 4.25
**1793** A706 18k multi 4.50 4.50
**1794** A706 21k multi 5.00 5.00
*Nos. 1791-1794 (4)* 16.50 16.50

Grimstad, 200th anniv.; Bodo, 200th anniv.; Kragero, 350th anniv.; Sarpsborg, 1000th anniv.

Nordic Food Culture — A707

Designs: No. 1795, Glazed langoustines, by Chef Espen Holmboe Bang. No. 1796, Beetroot barley risotto with Atlantic cod and kale, by Chef Freddy Storaker Bruu.

**2016, Apr. 15 Litho.** *Perf. 14x13½*

**1795** A707 14k multi 3.50 3.50
**1796** A707 14k multi 3.50 3.50
*a.* Souvenir sheet of 2, #1795-1796 7.00 7.00

A708

Europa A709

**2016, May 9 Litho.** *Perf. 13½x13¾*

**1797** A708 14k multi 3.50 3.50
**1798** A709 18k multi 4.50 4.50

Think Green Issue.

Norwegian Meteorological Institute, 150th Anniv. — A710

Clouds and: 17k, Lightning. 33k, Tree

**2016, June 10 Litho.** *Perf. 14x13½*

**1799** A710 17k multi 4.25 4.25
**1800** A710 33k multi 8.00 8.00

A booklet containing a pane of 1 of No. 1799 and a pane of 1 of No. 1800 sold for 149k and was printed in limited quantities.

Captain Sabertooth A711

Julius the Chimpanzee A712

*Die Cut Perf. 14½x15½*

**2016, June 10** **Litho.**

**Coil Stamps**
**Self-Adhesive**

**1801** A711 A Innland multi 2.75 2.75
**1802** A712 A Innland multi 2.75 2.75
*a.* Horiz. pair, #1801-1802 5.50

Kristiansand Zoo, 50th anniv. Nos. 1801-1802 each sold for 11k on day of issue.

Central Bank of Norway, 200th Anniv. — A713

Designs: 21k, 1819 Speciedaler coin, various banknotes. 50k, Bank headquarters, Oslo.

**Litho. & Engr.**

**2016, Oct. 1** ***Perf. 14x13½***

**1803** A713 21k multi 5.25 5.25
**1804** A713 50k multi 12.50 12.50

Lighthouses — A714

Designs: No. 1805, Sandvigodden Lighthouse. No. 1806, Sklinna Lighthouse.

***Die Cut Perf. 13¾x13¼***

**2016, Oct. 1** **Litho.**

**Self-Adhesive**

**1805** A714 A Innland multi 2.75 2.75
**1806** A714 A Innland multi 2.75 2.75
*a.* Horiz. pair on tan backing paper 5.50
*b.* Booklet pane of 10, 5 each #1805-1806 27.50

Nos. 1805-1806 each sold for 11k on day of issue.

Famous Men — A715

Designs: 20k, Tor Jonsson (1916-51), writer. 30k, Johan Sverdrup (1816-92), Prime Minister.

***Perf. 14¼x14½***

**2016, Nov. 11** **Litho. & Engr.**

**1807** A715 20k multi 4.75 4.75
**1808** A715 30k multi 7.25 7.25

A716

Christmas A717

***Die Cut Perf. 13¼x13½***

**2016, Nov. 11** **Litho.**

**Self-Adhesive**

**1809** A716 A Innland multi 2.60 2.60
**1810** A717 A Innland multi 2.60 2.60
*a.* Horiz. pair, #1809-1810, on tan backing paper 5.20
*b.* Booklet pane of 10, 5 each #1809-1810 26.00

On day of issue, Nos. 1809-1810 each sold for 11k.

Falcons A718

Designs: No. 1811, Falco columbarius. No. 1812, Falco subbuteo.

***Die Cut Perf. 15½x14¼***

**2017, Jan. 2** **Litho.**

**Coil Stamps**
**Self-Adhesive**

**1811** A718 20k multi 4.75 4.75
**1812** A718 20k multi 4.75 4.75
*a.* Horiz. pair, #1811-1812 9.50

Sami Culture A719

Sami flag and: No. 1813, Triangles (Sami Parliament). No. 1814, Elsa Laula Renberg (1877-1931), Sami politician.

***Die Cut Perf. 13½***

**2017, Feb. 6** **Litho.**

**Self-Adhesive**

**1813** A719 A Innland multi 3.25 3.25
**1814** A719 A Innland multi 3.25 3.25
*a.* Horiz. pair, #1813-1814, on tan backing paper 6.50
*b.* Booklet pane of 10, 5 each #1813-1814 32.50

On day of issue, Nos. 1813-1814 each sold for 13k.

Royalty — A720

80th birthday of: 23k, Queen Sonja. 36k, King Harald V.

**2017, Feb. 21** **Litho.** ***Perf. 13½x14***

**Self-Adhesive**

**1815** A720 23k gold & multi 5.50 5.50
**1816** A720 36k gold & multi 8.50 8.50

Viking Ship Excavated Near Tune and Drawing of Reconstructed Ship — A721

Viking Ship at Sea — A722

***Die Cut Perf. 15½x14½***

**2017, Apr. 21** **Litho.**

**Coil Stamps**
**Self-Adhesive**

**1817** A721 A Innland multi 3.00 3.00
**1818** A722 A Innland multi 3.00 3.00
*a.* Horiz. pair, #1817-1818 6.00

Nos. 1817-1818 each sold for 13k on day of issue.

National Archives, 200th Anniv. — A723

**2017, Apr. 21** **Litho.** ***Perf. 13¼***

**1819** A723 36k multi 8.50 8.50

Europa — A724

Designs: 17k, Akershus Castle. 21k, Royal Palace.

**2017, Apr. 21** **Litho.** ***Perf. 14x13¼***

**1820** A724 17k multi 4.00 4.00
**1821** A724 21k multi 5.00 5.00

Statue of King Frederik II, Frederikstad — A725

***Perf. 13¾x13¼***

**2017, June 16** **Litho.**

**1826** A725 23k multi 5.50 5.50

Frederikstad, 450th anniv.

International Cycling Union 2017 Road World Championships, Norway — A726

Designs: No. 1827, Six cyclists. No. 1828, Two cyclists, vert.

***Die Cut Perf. 13¼x13½***

**2017, June 16** **Litho.**

**Self-Adhesive**

**1827** A726 A Innland multi 3.25 3.25

***Die Cut Perf. 13½x13¼***

**1828** A726 A Innland multi 3.25 3.25
*a.* Pair, #1827-1828, on translucent paper without back printing 6.50
*b.* Booklet pane of 10, 5 each #1827-1828 32.50

On day of issue, Nos. 1827-1828 each sold for 13k.

Famous Men — A727

Designs: 23k: Marcus Thrane (1817-90), labor union leader, red flags and union newspaper. 30k, Eilert Sundt (1817-75), sociologist, buildings, and painting by Johannes Flintoe.

***Perf. 13¼x13¾***

**2017, June 16** **Litho. & Engr.**

**1829** A727 23k multi 5.50 5.50
**1830** A727 30k multi 7.25 7.25

Automobiles A728

Designs: Nos. 1831a, 1832, 1917 Mustad Giant. Nos. 1831b, 1833, 1921 Bjering. Nos. 1831c, 1834, 1956 Troll. Nos. 1831d, 1835, 1998 Think City A266.

**2017, Oct. 7** **Litho.** ***Perf. 13¼x13***

**Miniature Sheet**

**1831** Sheet of 4 13.00 13.00
*a.-d.* A728 A Innland Any single 3.25 3.25

**Coil Stamps**
**Self-Adhesive**

***Die Cut Perf. 15½x14½***

**1832** A728 A Innland multi 3.25 3.25
**1833** A728 A Innland multi 3.25 3.25
**1834** A728 A Innland multi 3.25 3.25
**1835** A728 A Innland multi 3.25 3.25
*a.* Horiz. strip of 4, #1832-1835 13.00
*Nos. 1832-1835 (4)* 13.00 13.00

On day of issue, Nos. 1831a-1831d, 1832-1835 each sold for 13k. A booklet containing four panes of one of Nos. 1831a-1831d sold for 169k.

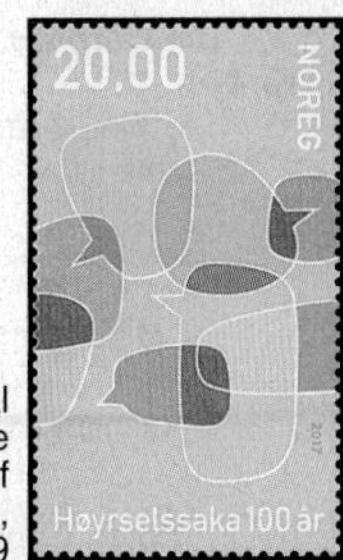

National Federation for the Deaf and Hard of Hearing, Cent. — A729

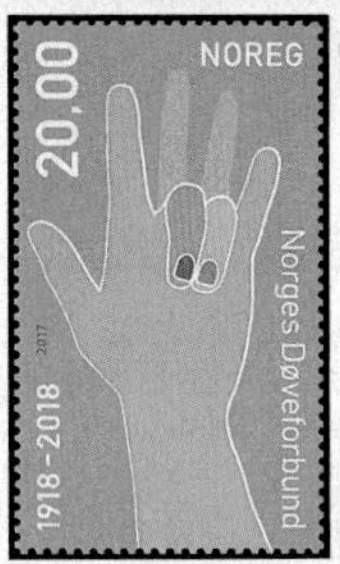

National Association of the Deaf, Cent. (in 2018) — A730

**2017, Nov. 10** **Litho.** ***Perf. 13¼x14***

**1836** A729 20k multi 5.00 5.00
**1837** A730 20k multi 5.00 5.00

A731

Christmas A732

***Die Cut Perf. 13¼x13½***

**2017, Nov. 10** **Litho.**

**Self-Adhesive**

**1838** A731 A Innland 3.25 3.25
**1839** A732 A Innland 3.25 3.25
*a.* Pair, #1838-1839, on translucent backing paper with numerals only or without printing on reverse 6.50
*b.* Booklet pane of 10, 5 each #1838-1839 32.50

On day of issue, Nos. 1838-1839 each sold for 13k.

Birds — A733

Designs: (14k), Strix nebulosa. 21k, Bubo scandiacus. 48k, Buteo lagopus.

***Die Cut Perf. 15½x14½***

**2018, Jan. 2** **Litho.**

**Coil Stamps**
**Self-Adhesive**

**1840** A733 (14k) multi 3.50 3.50
**1841** A733 21k multi 5.25 5.25
**1842** A733 48k multi 12.00 12.00
*a.* Horiz. strip of 3, #1840-1842 21.00
*Nos. 1840-1842 (3)* 20.75 20.75

No. 1840 is inscribed "Inland."

Wildlife of Bouvet Island — A734

Designs: 24k, Arctocephalus gazella. 38k, Pygoscelis antarcticus.

*Die Cut Perf. 13½x13¼*

**2018, Feb. 16** **Litho.**

**Self-Adhesive**

**1843** A734 24k multi 6.25 6.25
**1844** A734 38k multi 9.75 9.75
*a.* Pair, #1843-1844, on translucent backing paper without printing on back 16.00

## SEMI-POSTAL STAMPS

### North Cape Issue

North Cape — SP1

*Perf. 13½x14*

**1930, June 28** **Wmk. 160** **Photo.**

**Size: 33¼x21½mm**

**B1** SP1 15o + 25o blk brn 2.00 *6.00*
**B2** SP1 20o + 25o car 35.00 *80.00*
**B3** SP1 30o + 25o ultra 90.00 *110.00*
*Nos. B1-B3 (3)* 127.00 *196.00*
Set, never hinged 275.00

The surtax was given to the Tourist Association. See Nos. B9-B10, B28-B30, B54-B56, B59-B61.

Radium Hospital SP2

**1931, Apr. 1** ***Perf. 14½x13½***

**B4** SP2 20o + 10o carmine 16.00 10.00
Never hinged 65.00

The surtax aided the Norwegian Radium Hospital.

Fridtjof Nansen — SP3

**1935, Dec. 13** ***Perf. 13½***

**B5** SP3 10o + 10o green 3.50 *7.00*
**B6** SP3 15o + 10o red brn 10.00 *15.00*
**B7** SP3 20o + 10o crimson 5.00 4.50
**B8** SP3 30o + 10o brt ultra 12.00 *16.00*
*Nos. B5-B8 (4)* 30.50 42.50
Set, never hinged 55.00

The surtax aided the International Nansen Office for Refugees.

### North Cape Type of 1930

**1938, June 20** ***Perf. 13x13½***

**Size: 27x21mm**

**B9** SP1 20o + 25o brn car 3.50 *9.00*
**B10** SP1 30o + 25o dp ultra 13.50 32.50
Set, never hinged 27.50

Surtax given to the Tourist Assoc.

Queen Maud — SP4

*Perf. 13x13½*

**1939, July 24** **Photo.** **Unwmk.**

**B11** SP4 10o + 5o brt grn .40 10.00
**B12** SP4 15o + 5o red brn .40 10.00
**B13** SP4 20o + 5o scarlet .50 7.50
**B14** SP4 30o + 5o brt ultra .40 12.00
*Nos. B11-B14 (4)* 1.70 39.50
Set, never hinged 4.00

The surtax was used for charities.

Fridtjof Nansen — SP5

**1940, Oct. 21**

**B15** SP5 10o + 10o dk grn 3.50 4.50
**B16** SP5 15o + 10o henna brn 4.00 6.00
**B17** SP5 20o + 10o dark red .75 1.50
**B18** SP5 30o + 10o ultra 2.50 4.50
*Nos. B15-B18 (4)* 10.75 16.50
Set, never hinged 16.00

The surtax was used for war relief work.

SP6

Ancient Sailing Craft off Lofoten Islands.

**1941, May 16**

**B19** SP6 15o + 10o deep blue 1.75 .80
Never hinged 4.50

Haalogaland Exposition. Surtax for relief fund for families of lost fishermen.

Value for used stamp postmarked before May 15, 1945, $9.50. See note following No. 180.

---

Nos. 70-73, 177-180, 267, B19, B32-B34 and B38-B41 were demonetized from May 15, 1945 until Sept. 1, 1981. Used values are for stamps canceled after this period. Stamps with dated cancellations prior to May 15, 1945 sell for more. False cancellations exist.

---

Colin Archer and Lifeboat — SP7

Lifeboat — SP8

**1941, July 9** ***Perf. 13x13½, 13½x13***

**B20** SP7 10o + 10o yel grn 1.25 2.50
**B21** SP7 15o + 10o dk ol brn 1.75 3.50
**B22** SP8 20o + 10o brt red .50 .75
**B23** SP8 30o + 10o ultra 5.00 9.00
*Nos. B20-B23 (4)* 8.50 15.75
Set, never hinged 15.00

Norwegian Lifeboat Society, 50th anniv.

Legionary, Norwegian and Finnish Flags — SP9

**1941, Aug. 1** ***Perf. 13½x13***

**B24** SP9 20o + 80o scar ver 60.00 120.00
Never hinged 120.00

The surtax was for the Norwegian Legion.

Vidkun Quisling — SP10

**1942, Feb. 1**

**B25** SP10 20o + 30o henna 6.50 *25.00*
Never hinged 11.00

Overprinted in Red

**B26** SP10 20o + 30o henna 7.00 *30.00*
Never hinged 12.00

Inauguration of Quisling as prime minister.

**Catalogue values for unused stamps in this section, from this point to the end of the section, are for Never Hinged items.**

Vidkun Quisling — SP11

**1942, Sept. 26** ***Perf. 13***

**B27** SP11 20o + 30o henna .90 *9.00*

8th annual meeting of Nasjonal Samling, Quisling's party. The surtax aided relatives of soldiers killed in action.

### North Cape Type of 1930

**1943, Apr. 1** **Size: 27x21mm**

**B28** SP1 15o + 25o olive brn 2.00 2.00
**B29** SP1 20o + 25o dark car 3.50 3.50
**B30** SP1 30o + 25o chalky blue 3.50 3.50
*Nos. B28-B30 (3)* 9.00 9.00

The surtax aided the Tourist Association.

Frontier Guardsmen Emblem — SP12

**1943, Aug. 2** **Unwmk.**

**B31** SP12 20o + 30o henna .90 *9.00*

The surtax aided the Frontier Guardsmen (Norwegian Nazi Volunteers).

Fishing Village — SP13

Drying Grain — SP14

Barn in Winter — SP15

**1943, Nov. 10**

**B32** SP13 10o + 10o gray green 2.00 .60
**B33** SP14 20o + 10o henna 2.00 .60
**B34** SP15 40o + 10o grnsh blk 2.50 .60
*Nos. B32-B34 (3)* 6.50 1.80

The surtax was for winter relief.

Value, set postmarked before May 15, 1945, $15. See note following No. B19.

The Baroy Sinking — SP16

Sanct Svithun Aflame — SP17

Design: 20o+10o, "Irma" sinking.

**1944, May 20**

**B35** SP16 10o + 10o gray grn 2.50 *7.00*
**B36** SP17 15o + 10o dk olive 1.75 *7.00*
**B37** SP16 20o + 10o henna 1.75 *7.00*
*Nos. B35-B37 (3)* 6.00 *21.00*

The surtax aided victims of wartime ship sinkings, and their families.

Spinning SP19

Plowing SP20

Tree Felling — SP21

Child Care — SP22

**1944, Dec. 1**

**B38** SP19 5o + 10o deep mag 1.50 .40
**B39** SP20 10o + 10o dark yel grn 1.50 .40
**B40** SP21 15o + 10o chocolate 1.50 .40
**B41** SP22 20o + 10o henna 1.50 .40
*Nos. B38-B41 (4)* 6.00 1.60

The surtax was for National Welfare.

Value, set postmarked before May 15, 1945, $20. See note following No. B19.

Red Cross Nurse — SP23

**1945, Sept. 22**

**B42** SP23 20o + 10o red 1.00 *1.75*

80th anniv. of the founding of the Norwegian Red Cross. The surtax was for that institution.

For surcharge see No. B47.

Crown Prince Olav — SP24

**1946, Mar. 4** **Unwmk.**

**B43** SP24 10o + 10o ol grn .75 .60
**B44** SP24 15o + 10o ol brn .75 .60
**B45** SP24 20o + 10o dk red 1.00 .60
**B46** SP24 30o + 10o brt bl 2.50 2.50
*Nos. B43-B46 (4)* 5.00 4.30

The surtax was for war victims.

No. B42 Surcharged in Black

**1948, Dec. 1**
**B47** SP23 25o + 5o on 20o+10o 1.00 *1.75*

The surtax was for Red Cross relief work.

Child Picking Flowers — SP25

**1950, Aug. 15 Photo. *Perf. 13***
**B48** SP25 25o + 5o brt red 2.50 1.75
**B49** SP25 45o + 5o dp bl 9.00 10.00

The surtax was for poliomyelitis victims.

Skater — SP26

Winter Scene SP27

Design: 30o+10o, Ski jumper.

**1951, Oct. 1**
**B50** SP26 15o + 5o olive grn 2.75 3.50
**B51** SP26 30o + 10o red 4.00 4.50
**B52** SP27 55o + 20o blue 15.00 *16.00*
*Nos. B50-B52 (3)* 21.75 24.00

Olympic Winter Games, Oslo, 2/14-29/52.

Kneeling Woman — SP28

**1953, June 1 Photo. & Litho.**
**B53** SP28 30o + 10o red & cr 2.50 2.50

The surtax was for cancer research.

### North Cape Type of 1930

**1953, June 15 Photo.**
**Size: 27x21mm**
**B54** SP1 20o + 10o green 15.00 15.00
**B55** SP1 30o + 15o red 17.00 17.00
**B56** SP1 55o + 25o gray blue 20.00 20.00
*Nos. B54-B56 (3)* 52.00 52.00

The surtax aided the Tourist Association.

Crown Princess Martha — SP29

**1956, Mar. 28 *Perf. 13***
**B57** SP29 35o + 10o dark red 2.00 2.00
**B58** SP29 65o + 10o dark blue 5.00 5.00

The surtax was for the Crown Princess Martha Memorial Fund.

### North Cape Type of 1930

**1957, May 6 Size: 27x21mm**
**B59** SP1 25o + 10o green 8.50 8.50
**B60** SP1 35o + 15o red 10.00 12.00
**B61** SP1 65o + 25o gray blue 4.50 3.50
*Nos. B59-B61 (3)* 23.00 24.00

The surtax aided the Tourist Association.

White Anemone — SP30

Design: 90o+10o, Hepatica.

**1960, Jan. 12 Litho. *Perf. 13***
**B62** SP30 45o + 10o brt red & grn 4.00 4.00
**B63** SP30 90o + 10o bl, org & grn 12.00 *15.00*

The surtax was for anti-tuberculosis work.

Mother, Child, WRY Emblem — SP31

**1960, Apr. 7 Photo. Unwmk.**
**B64** SP31 45o + 25o rose & blk 8.00 9.00
**B65** SP31 90o + 25o bl & blk 16.00 20.00

World Refugee Year, July 1, 1959-June 30, 1960. The surtax was for aid to refugees.

Severed Chain and Dove SP32

Design: 60o+10o, Norwegian flags.

**1965, May 8 Photo. *Perf. 13***
**B66** SP32 30o + 10o grn, blk & tan .50 .50
**B67** SP32 60o + 10o red & dk bl .90 .75

20th anniversary of liberation from the Germans. The surtax was for war cripples.

Souvenir Sheet

Offshore Oil Drilling — SP33

Designs: a, Ekofisk Center. b, Treasure Scout drilling rig and Odin Viking supply vessel at Tromsoflaket, 1982. c, Statfjord C oil platform, 1984. d, Men working on deck of Neptune Nordraug.

**1985, Oct. 4 Litho. *Perf. 13½x13***
**B68** SP33 Sheet of 4 10.00 12.00
*a.-d.* 2k + 1k, any single 2.50 2.50

Stamp Day 1985. Surtax for philatelic promotion.

Souvenir Sheet

Paper Industry — SP34

Paper mill: a, Wood aging containers. b, Boiling plant. c, Paper-making machine. d, Paper dryer.

**1986, Oct. 17 Litho. *Perf. 13½***
**B69** SP34 Sheet of 4 14.00 16.00
*a.-d.* 2.50k + 1k, any single 3.50 3.50

Surtax for philatelic promotion. Nos. B69a-B69b and B69c-B69d printed in continuous designs.

Souvenir Sheet

Salmon Industry — SP35

Designs: a, Eggs and milt pressed out of fish by hand. b, Cultivation of eggs in tanks. c, Outdoor hatchery. d, Market.

**1987, Oct. 9 Litho. *Perf. 13½x13***
**B70** SP35 Sheet of 4 14.00 16.00
*a.* 2.30k +50o multi 3.50 3.50
*b.* 2.70k +50o multi 3.50 3.50
*c.* 3.50k +50o multi 3.50 3.50
*d.* 4.50k +50o multi 3.50 3.50

Souvenir Sheet

Norwegian Constituent Assembly, 200th Anniv. — SP36

No. B71: a, Prince Christian Frederik, Constitution of 1814. b, Parliament Lion sculpture, parade.

**2014, Nov. 21 Litho. *Perf. 14x13¼***
**B71** SP36 Sheet of 2 12.00 12.00
*a.* 16k multi 5.50 5.50
*b.* 19k multi 6.50 6.50

Nordia 2014 Stamp Exhibition, Oslo. No. B71 sold for 41k, with 6k defraying the costs of the exhibition.

## AIR POST STAMPS

Airplane over Akershus Castle — AP1

***Perf. 13½x14½***
**1927-34 Typo. Wmk. 160**
**C1** AP1 45o lt bl, strong frame line ('34) 4.50 *5.00*
Never hinged 20.00
*a.* Faint or broken frame line 25.00 9.00
Never hinged 150.00

Airplane over Akershus Castle — AP2

**1937, Aug. 18 Photo. *Perf. 13***
**C2** AP2 45o Prussian blue .90 .70
Never hinged 4.50

**1941, Nov. 10 Unwmk.**
**C3** AP2 45o indigo .50 .25
Never hinged 2.50

## POSTAGE DUE STAMPS

Numeral of Value — D1

**Inscribed "at betale"**

***Perf. 14½x13½***

**1889-1914 Typo. Wmk. 160**
**J1** D1 1o olive green ('15) 1.25 *2.50*
Never hinged 2.40
**J2** D1 4o magenta ('11) 2.00 2.00
Never hinged 12.00
**J3** D1 10o carmine rose ('99) 5.00 .90
Never hinged 15.00
*a.* 10o rose red ('89) 90.00 25.00
**J4** D1 15o brown ('14) 4.50 1.75
**J5** D1 20o ultra ('99) 3.50 .65
Never hinged 15.00
*a.* Perf. 13½x12½ ('95) 250.00 115.00
**J6** D1 50o maroon ('89) 6.50 4.00
Never hinged 30.00
*Nos. J1-J6 (6)* 22.75 11.80

See #J7-J12. For overprint see #136-144.

**1922-23 Inscribed "a betale"**
**J7** D1 4o lilac rose 11.00 18.00
Never hinged 35.00
**J8** D1 10o green 5.00 3.50
Never hinged 22.50
**J9** D1 20o dull violet 8.00 8.00
Never hinged 30.00
**J10** D1 40o deep ultra 12.00 1.50
Never hinged 40.00
**J11** D1 100o orange yel 35.00 17.00
Never hinged 150.00
**J12** D1 200o dark violet 75.00 30.00
Never hinged 160.00
*Nos. J7-J12 (6)* 146.00 78.00

## OFFICIAL STAMPS

Coat of Arms — O1

***Perf. 14½x13½***

**1926 Typo. Wmk. 160**
**O1** O1 5o rose lilac .75 *1.50*
**O2** O1 10o yellow green .50 .50
**O3** O1 15o indigo 2.00 *4.50*
**O4** O1 20o plum .50 .25
**O5** O1 30o slate 4.50 *10.00*
**O6** O1 40o deep blue 2.50 *2.00*
**O7** O1 60o Prussian blue 5.00 *10.00*
*Nos. O1-O7 (7)* 15.75 *28.75*
Set, never hinged 40.00

Official Stamp of 1926 Surcharged

**1929, July 1**
**O8** O1 2o on 5o magenta .60 *1.75*
Never hinged 2.00

Coat of Arms — O2

*Perf. 14½x13½*

**1933-34 Litho. Wmk. 160**

**Size: 35x19¼mm**

**O9** O2 2o ocher .60 *1.75*
**O10** O2 5o rose lilac 4.50 *7.00*
**O11** O2 7o orange 4.50 *10.00*
**O12** O2 10o green 30.00 1.25
**O13** O2 15o olive .60 *1.25*
**O14** O2 20o vermilion 30.00 .60
**O15** O2 25o yellow brn .60 *1.00*
**O16** O2 30o ultra .90 *1.25*
**O18** O2 40o slate 30.00 1.25
**O19** O2 60o blue 18.00 2.00
**O20** O2 70o olive brn 1.50 *4.00*
**O21** O2 100o violet 2.00 3.50
*Nos. O9-O16,O18-O21 (12)* 123.20 34.85
Same, never hinged 600.00

On the lithographed stamps, the lion's left leg is shaded.

**Typo.**

**Size: 34x18¾mm**

*O10a* O2 5o rose lilac 1.50 4.00
*O11a* O2 7o orange 8.00 *22.50*
*O12a* O2 10o green .70 .60
*O13a* O2 15o olive 6.00 *20.00*
*O14a* O2 20o vermilion .70 .50
**O17** O2 35o red violet ('34) .90 .90
*O18a* O2 40o slate 1.00 .90
*O19a* O2 60o blue 1.25 1.25
*Nos. O10a-O14a,O17,O18a-O19a (8)* 20.05 *50.65*
Same, never hinged 60.00

Coat of Arms — O3

**1937-38 Photo. *Perf. 13½x13***

**O22** O3 5o rose lilac ('38) .75 1.50
**O23** O3 7o dp orange .75 4.00
**O24** O3 10o brt green .40 .50
**O25** O3 15o olive bister .55 1.00
**O26** O3 20o carmine ('38) 2.50 5.00
**O27** O3 25o red brown ('38) 1.00 1.00
**O28** O3 30o ultra 1.00 1.00
**O29** O3 35o red vio ('38) 1.75 .60
**O30** O3 40o Prus grn ('38) 1.00 .60
**O31** O3 60o Prus bl ('38) 1.25 .60
**O32** O3 100o dk vio ('38) 2.00 1.50
*Nos. O22-O32 (11)* 12.95 *17.30*
Set, never hinged 35.00

See Nos. O33-O43, O55-O56. For surcharge see No. O57.

**1939-47 Unwmk.**

**O33** O3 5o dp red lil ('41) .25 .25
**O34** O3 7o dp orange ('41) .30 *1.50*
**O35** O3 10o brt green ('41) .25 .25
**O36** O3 15o olive ('45) .25 .25
**O37** O3 20o carmine .25 .25
**O38** O3 25o red brown 3.00 *20.00*
**O38A** O3 25o scarlet ('46) .25 .25
**O39** O3 30o ultra 2.75 2.75
**O39A** O3 30o dk gray ('47) .65 .55
**O40** O3 35o brt lilac ('41) .60 .50
**O41** O3 40o grnsh blk ('41) .55 .25
**O41A** O3 40o dp ultra ('46) 3.00 .25
**O42** O3 60o Prus blue ('41) .65 .50
**O43** O3 100o dk violet ('41) 1.00 .25
*Nos. O33-O43 (14)* 13.75 *27.80*
Set, never hinged 40.00

Norwegian Nazi Party Emblem — O4

**1942-44**

**O44** O4 5o magenta .25 *2.00*
**O45** O4 7o yellow org .25 *2.00*
**O46** O4 10o emerald .25 .25
**O47** O4 15o olive ('44) 1.50 *30.00*
**O48** O4 20o bright red .25 .25
**O49** O4 25o red brn ('43) 4.00 *40.00*
**O50** O4 30o brt ultra ('44) 3.00 *40.00*
**O51** O4 35o brt pur ('43) 3.00 *18.00*
**O52** O4 40o grnsh blk ('43) .25 .50
**O53** O4 60o indigo ('43) 2.25 *20.00*
**O54** O4 1k blue vio ('43) 2.25 *25.00*
*Nos. O44-O54 (11)* 17.25 *178.00*
Set, never hinged 30.00

**Type of 1937**

**1947, Nov. 1**

**O55** O3 50o deep magenta .70 .25
**O56** O3 200o orange 2.25 .65
Set, never hinged 5.00

No. O37 Surcharged in Black

**1949, Mar. 15**

**O57** O3 25o on 20o carmine .25 .50
Never hinged .75

Norway Coat of Arms — O5

**1951-52 Unwmk. Photo. *Perf. 13***

**O58** O5 5o rose lilac .75 .50
**O59** O5 10o dk gray .75 .25
**O60** O5 15o dp org brn ('52) 1.00 .90
**O61** O5 30o scarlet .35 .25
**O62** O5 35o red brn ('52) 1.25 .70
**O63** O5 60o blue gray .90 .25
**O64** O5 100o vio bl ('52) 1.25 .30
*Nos. O58-O64 (7)* 6.25 3.15
Set, never hinged 15.00

**Catalogue values for unused stamps in this section, from this point to the end of the section, are for Never Hinged items.**

Norway Coat of Arms — O6

**1955-61**

**O65** O6 5o rose lilac .25 .25
**O66** O6 10o slate .25 .25
**O67** O6 15o orange brn .65 2.75
**O68** O6 20o bl grn ('57) .65 .25
**O69** O6 25o emer ('59) .90 .25
**O70** O6 30o scarlet 4.00 .90
**O71** O6 35o brown red .70 .25
**O72** O6 40o blue lilac 1.50 .25
**O73** O6 45o scar ('58) 1.50 .25
**O74** O6 50o gldn brn ('57) 4.00 .25
**O75** O6 60o blue 16.00 .70
**O76** O6 70o brn olive ('56) 7.00 1.25
**O77** O6 75o maroon ('57) 25.00 18.00
**O78** O6 80o org brn ('58) 9.00 1.25
**O79** O6 90o org ('58) 1.25 .25
**O80** O6 1k vio ('57) 2.25 .25
**O81** O6 2k gray grn ('60) 4.00 .25
**O82** O6 5k red lil ('61) 9.00 .85
*Nos. O65-O82 (18)* 87.90 28.45

See Phosphorescence note after No. 430.

**1962-74 Photo.**

**O83** O6 30o green ('64) 2.00 .25
**O84** O6 40o ol grn ('68) 2.00 .50
**O85** O6 50o scarlet 2.50 .25
**O86** O6 50o slate ('69) .70 .25
**O87** O6 60o dk red ('64) 1.10 .25
**O87A** O6 60o grnsh bl ('72) 5.00 10.00
**O88** O6 65o dk red ('68) 1.75 .25
**O89** O6 70o dk red ('70) .50 .25
**O90** O6 75o lt grn ('73) 1.25 .75
**O90A** O6 80o red brn ('72) 1.25 .25
**O91** O6 85o ocher ('74) .95 2.00
**O92** O6 1k dp org ('73) .50 .25
**O93** O6 1.10k car lake ('74) 1.25 1.25
*Nos. O83-O93 (13)* 20.75 16.50

Shades exist of several values of type O6.
Nos O87A, O90A are on phosphored paper.

**1975-82 Litho.**

**O94** O6 5o rose lil ('80) .30 1.75
**O95** O6 10o bluish gray ('82) .30 3.00
**O96** O6 15o henna brn .90 4.00
**O97** O6 20o green ('82) 1.50 5.50
**O98** O6 25o yellow grn .40 .25
**O99** O6 40o ol grn ('79) 2.25 10.00
**O100** O6 50o grnsh gray ('76) 1.00 .25
**O101** O6 60o dk grnsh bl 2.25 10.00
**O102** O6 70o dk red ('82) 5.50 15.00
**O103** O6 80o red brn ('76) .60 .25
**O104** O6 1k vio ('80) 1.40 .50
**O105** O6 1.10k red ('80) 2.50 3.50
**O106** O6 1.25k dull red .60 .25
**O107** O6 1.30k lilac ('81) 2.00 2.25
**O108** O6 1.50k red ('81) .70 .25
**O109** O6 1.75k dl bl grn ('82) 2.25 2.00
**O110** O6 2k dk gray grn 1.00 .25
**O111** O6 2k cerise ('82) 1.40 .30
**O112** O6 3k purple ('82) 1.50 .50
**O113** O6 5k lt vio 40.00 3.50
**O114** O6 5k blue ('77) 2.50 .25
*Nos. O94-O114 (21)* 70.85 63.55

In lithographed set, shield's background is dotted; on photogravure stamps it is solid color.

Official stamps invalid as of Apr. 1, 1985.

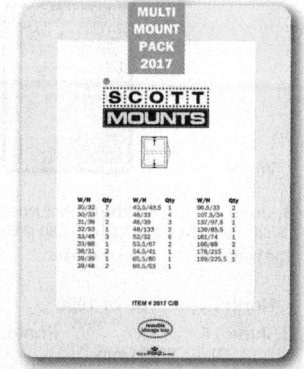

## NOSSI-BE

ˌno-sē-ˈbā

LOCATION — Island in the Indian Ocean, off the northwest coast of Madagascar
GOVT. — French Protectorate
AREA — 130 sq. mi.
POP. — 9,000 (approx. 1900)
CAPITAL — Hellville

In 1896 the island was placed under the authority of the Governor-General of Madagascar and postage stamps of Madagascar were placed in use.

100 Centimes = 1 Franc

**Stamps of French Colonies Surcharged in Blue**

a

b

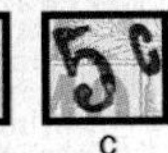
c

On the following issues the colors of the French Colonies stamps, type A9, are: 5c, green, *greenish*; 10c, black, *lavender*; 15c, blue; 20c, red, *green*; 30c, brown, *bister*; 40c, vermilion, *straw*; 75c, carmine, *rose*; 1fr, bronze green, *straw*.

**1889 Unwmk. *Imperf.***

1 A8(a) 25 on 40c red, *straw* 2,600. 1,100.
*a.* Double surcharge 3,400.
*b.* Inverted surcharge 3,750. 1,600.
2 A8(b) 25c on 40c red, *straw* 3,100. 2,000.
*a.* Double surcharge 5,500. 2,800.
*b.* Inverted surcharge 5,500. 2,800.
*c.* Pair, "a" and "c"

***Perf. 14x13½***

3 A9(b) 5c on 10c 3,750. 1,450.
*a.* Double surcharge 3,500.
*b.* Inverted surcharge 5,000. 3,100.
4 A9(b) 5c on 20c 4,000. 1,600.
*a.* Inverted surcharge 5,000. 3,100.
5 A9(c) 5c on 10c 3,100. 1,100.
*a.* Inverted surcharge 5,600.
6 A9(c) 5c on 20c 3,600. 2,400.
7 A9(a) 15 on 20c 2,800. 1,100.
*a.* Double surcharge 2,400.
*b.* Inverted surcharge 4,250. 1,750.
*c.* 15 on 30c (error) 32,000. 28,000.
8 A9(a) 25 on 30c 2,800. 950.
*a.* Double surcharge 2,200.
*b.* Inverted surcharge 3,600. 1,600.
9 A9(a) 25 on 40c 2,400. 1,100.
*a.* Double surcharge 2,000.
*b.* Inverted surcharge 3,600. 1,600.

d

e

f

**1890 Black Surcharge**

10 A9(d) 25c on 20c 425.00 300.00
11 A9(e) 0.25 on 20c 425.00 300.00
12 A9(f) 25 on 20c 1,000. 675.00
13 A9(d) 25c on 75c 425.00 300.00
14 A9(e) 0.25 on 75c 425.00 300.00
15 A9(f) 25 on 75c 1,000. 675.00
16 A9(d) 25c on 1fr 425.00 300.00
17 A9(e) 0.25 on 1fr 425.00 300.00
18 A9(f) 25 on 1fr 1,000. 675.00

The 25c on 20c with surcharge composed of "25 c." as in "d," "N S B" as in "e," and frame as in "f" is an essay.

**Surcharged or Overprinted in Black, Carmine, Vermilion or Blue**

j

k

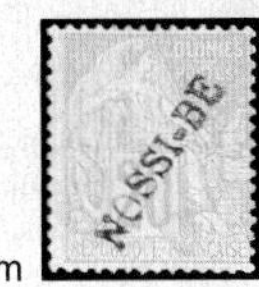
m

**1893**

23 A9(j) 25 on 20c (Bk) 52.50 45.00
24 A9(j) 50 on 10c (Bk) 67.50 47.50
*a.* Inverted surcharge 400.00 260.00
25 A9(j) 75 on 15c (Bk) 300.00 240.00
26 A9(j) 1fr on 5c (Bk) 150.00 110.00
*a.* Inverted surcharge 400.00 275.00
27 A9(k) 10c (C) 28.00 24.00
*a.* Inverted overprint 130.00 120.00
28 A9(k) 10c (V) 27.50 24.00
29 A9(k) 15c (Bk) 32.50 32.50
*a.* Inverted overprint 140.00 130.00
30 A9(k) 20c (Bk) 500.00 75.00
31 A9(m) 20c (Bl) 130.00 67.50
*a.* Inverted overprint 190.00 180.00

Counterfeits exist of surcharges and overprints of Nos. 1-31.

Navigation and Commerce — A14

**1894 Typo. *Perf. 14x13½***
**Name of Colony in Blue or Carmine**

32 A14 1c blk, *lil bl* 1.60 1.60
33 A14 2c brn, *buff* 2.00 2.00
34 A14 4c claret, *lav* 2.75 2.00
35 A14 5c grn, *greenish* 4.00 3.25
36 A14 10c blk, *lav* 9.50 6.50
37 A14 15c blue, quadrille paper 13.50 6.50
38 A14 20c red, *grn* 9.50 6.50
39 A14 25c blk, *rose* 16.00 9.50
40 A14 30c brn, *bister* 16.00 14.50
41 A14 40c red, *straw* 22.50 16.00
42 A14 50c carmine, *rose* 22.50 16.00
43 A14 75c dp vio, *orange* 37.50 37.50
44 A14 1fr brnz grn, *straw* 27.50 27.50
*Nos. 32-44 (13)* 184.85 149.35

Perf. 13½x14 stamps are counterfeits.

### POSTAGE DUE STAMPS

**Stamps of French Colonies Surcharged in Black**

n

o

**1891 Unwmk. *Perf. 14x13½***

J1 A9(n) 20 on 1c blk, *lil bl* 425.00 300.00
*a.* Inverted surcharge 925.00 675.00
*b.* Surcharged vertically 1,200. 1,400.
*c.* Surcharge on back 1,050. 1,050.
J2 A9(n) 30 on 2c brn, *buff* 400.00 300.00
*a.* Inverted surcharge 875.00 675.00
*b.* Surcharge on back 1,000. 1,200.
J3 A9(n) 50 on 30c brn, *bister* 120.00 105.00
*a.* Inverted surcharge 925.00 675.00
*b.* Surcharge on back 1,050. 1,300.
J4 A9(o) 35 on 4c cl, *lav* 450.00 325.00
*a.* Inverted surcharge 925.00 675.00
*b.* Surcharge on back 1,100. 1,300.
*c.* Pair, one without surcharge
J5 A9(o) 35 on 20c red, *green* 450.00 325.00
*a.* Inverted surcharge 925.00 675.00
J6 A9(o) 1fr on 35c vio, *orange* 325.00 240.00
*a.* Inverted surcharge 925.00 625.00

p

q

r

**1891**

J7 A9(p) 5c on 20c 225.00 225.00
J8 A9(q) 5c on 20c 275.00 275.00
*b.* In se-tenant pair with #J7 725.00
J9 A9(r) 0.10c on 5c 27.50 24.00
J10 A9(p) 10c on 15c 225.00 225.00
J11 A9(q) 10c on 15c 275.00 275.00
*b.* In se-tenant pair with #J10 725.00
J12 A9(p) 15c on 10c 200.00 200.00
J13 A9(q) 15c on 10c 210.00 210.00
*b.* In se-tenant pair with #J12 725.00
J14 A9(r) 0.15c on 20c 32.50 32.50
*a.* 25c on 20c (error) 40,000. 35,000.
J15 A9(p) 25c on 5c 180.00 180.00
J16 A9(q) 25c on 5c 200.00 200.00
*b.* In se-tenant pair with #J15 700.00
J17 A9(r) 0.25c on 75c 650.00 575.00

**Inverted Surcharge**

*J7a* A9(p) 5c on 20c 425.00 425.00
*J8a* A9(q) 5c on 20c 425.00 425.00
*J10a* A9(p) 10c on 15c 425.00 425.00
*J11a* A9(q) 10c on 15c 425.00 425.00
*J12a* A9(p) 15c on 10c 425.00 425.00
*J13a* A9(q) 15c on 10c 425.00 425.00
*J15a* A9(p) 25c on 5c 425.00 425.00
*J16a* A9(q) 25c on 5c 425.00 425.00
*J17a* A9(r) 0.25c on 75c 1,800. 1,500.

Stamps of Nossi-Be were superseded by those of Madagascar.
Counterfeits exist of surcharges on #J1-J17.

## NYASALAND PROTECTORATE

nī-ˈa-sə-ˌland prə-ˈtek-t̨ə-ˌrət

LOCATION — In southern Africa, bordering on Lake Nyasa
GOVT. — British Protectorate
AREA — 49,000 sq. mi.
POP. — 2,950,000 (est. 1962)
CAPITAL — Zomba

For previous issues, see British Central Africa.

Nyasaland joined the Federation of Rhodesia and Nyasaland in 1953, using its stamps until 1963. As the Federation began to dissolve in 1963, Nyasaland withdrew its postal services and issued provisional stamps. On July 6, 1964, Nyasaland became the independent state of Malawi.

12 Pence = 1 Shilling
20 Shillings = 1 Pound

**Catalogue values for unused stamps in this country are for Never Hinged items, beginning with Scott 68 in the regular postage section and Scott J1 in the postage due section.**

A1 King Edward VII — A2

**Wmk. Crown and C A (2)**
**1908, July 22 Typo. *Perf. 14***
**Chalky Paper**

1 A1 1sh black, *green* 7.00 *19.00*

**Wmk. Multiple Crown and C A (3)**
**Ordinary Paper**

2 A1 ½p green 2.00 2.25
3 A1 1p carmine 9.25 1.10

**Chalky Paper**

4 A1 3p violet, *yel* 1.75 *4.75*
5 A1 4p scar & blk, *yel* 2.25 *1.75*
6 A1 6p red vio & vio 7.00 *12.50*
7 A2 2sh6p car & blk, *bl* 75.00 *110.00*
8 A2 4sh black & car 110.00 *180.00*
9 A2 10sh red & grn, *grn* 200.00 *325.00*
10 A2 £1 blk & vio, *red* 650.00 *750.00*
11 A2 £10 ultra & lilac 12,000. *8,000.*
*Nos. 1-10 (10)* 1,064. 1,406.

A3 King George V — A4

**1913-19 Ordinary Paper**

12 A3 ½p green 1.75 *2.25*
13 A3 1p scarlet 8.25 1.00
*a.* 1p carmine 4.00 2.00
14 A3 2p gray 10.00 1.00
15 A3 2½p ultra 2.50 *9.00*

**Chalky Paper**

16 A3 3p violet, *yel* 6.00 4.50
17 A3 4p scar & blk, *yel* 2.00 *2.50*
18 A3 6p red vio & dull vio 5.00 *10.00*

| | | | | |
|---|---|---|---|---|
| **19** | A3 | 1sh black, *green* | 2.00 | *9.00* |
| *a.* | | 1sh black, *emerald* | 5.00 | *7.00* |
| *b.* | | 1sh blk, *bl grn*, olive back | 6.00 | 1.60 |
| **20** | A4 | 2sh6p red & blk, *bl* ('18) | 12.50 | *29.00* |
| **21** | A4 | 4sh blk & red ('18) | 50.00 | *90.00* |
| **22** | A4 | 10sh red & grn, *grn* | 130.00 | *160.00* |
| **23** | A4 | £1 blk & vio, *red* ('18) | 200.00 | 170.00 |
| **24** | A4 | £10 brt ultra & slate vio ('19) | *4,000.* | *2,000.* |
| | | Revenue cancel | | 275.00 |
| *a.* | | £10 pale ultra & dull vio ('14) | 8,000. | |
| | | Revenue cancel | | 300.00 |
| | | *Nos. 12-23 (12)* | 430.00 | *488.25* |

Stamps of Nyasaland Protectorate overprinted "N. F." are listed under German East Africa.

**1921-30 Wmk. 4 Ordinary Paper**

| | | | | |
|---|---|---|---|---|
| **25** | A3 | ½p green | 3.25 | .50 |
| **26** | A3 | 1p rose red | 3.75 | .50 |
| **27** | A3 | 1½p orange | 4.00 | *17.50* |
| **28** | A3 | 2p gray | 3.50 | .50 |

**Chalky Paper**

| | | | | |
|---|---|---|---|---|
| **29** | A3 | 3p violet, *yel* | 22.00 | 3.25 |
| **30** | A3 | 4p scar & blk, *yel* | 6.25 | *11.00* |
| **31** | A3 | 6p red vio & dl vio | 6.25 | 3.25 |
| **32** | A3 | 1sh blk, *grn* ('30) | 14.50 | 4.50 |
| **33** | A4 | 2sh ultra & dl vio, *bl* | 22.50 | 15.00 |
| **34** | A4 | 2sh6p red & blk, *bl* ('24) | 27.50 | 19.00 |
| **35** | A4 | 4sh black & car | 26.00 | *45.00* |
| **36** | A4 | 5sh red & grn, *yel* ('29) | 55.00 | 85.00 |
| **37** | A4 | 10sh red & grn, *emer* | 120.00 | *120.00* |
| | | *Nos. 25-37 (13)* | 314.50 | *325.00* |

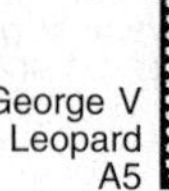

George V and Leopard
A5

**1934-35 Engr. *Perf. 12½***

| | | | | |
|---|---|---|---|---|
| **38** | A5 | ½p green | .75 | *1.25* |
| **39** | A5 | 1p dark brown | .75 | .75 |
| **40** | A5 | 1½p rose | .75 | *3.50* |
| **41** | A5 | 2p gray | 1.00 | *1.25* |
| **42** | A5 | 3p dark blue | 3.00 | 2.00 |
| **43** | A5 | 4p rose lilac ('35) | 7.25 | 4.00 |
| **44** | A5 | 6p dk violet | 3.50 | 1.00 |
| **45** | A5 | 9p olive bis ('35) | 8.50 | *16.00* |
| **46** | A5 | 1sh orange & blk | 24.00 | *15.00* |
| | | *Nos. 38-46 (9)* | 49.50 | *44.75* |

Common Design Types pictured following the introduction.

**Silver Jubilee Issue**

Common Design Type

**1935, May 6 *Perf. 11x12***

| | | | | |
|---|---|---|---|---|
| **47** | CD301 | 1p gray blk & ultra | 1.00 | *2.50* |
| **48** | CD301 | 2p indigo & grn | 2.75 | 2.75 |
| **49** | CD301 | 3p ultra & brn | 8.50 | *20.00* |
| **50** | CD301 | 1sh brown vio & ind | 27.50 | *55.00* |
| | | *Nos. 47-50 (4)* | 39.75 | *80.25* |
| | | Set, never hinged | 60.00 | |

**Coronation Issue**

Common Design Type

**1937, May 12 *Perf. 11x11½***

| | | | | |
|---|---|---|---|---|
| **51** | CD302 | ½p deep green | .25 | .30 |
| **52** | CD302 | 1p dark brown | .40 | .40 |
| **53** | CD302 | 2p gray black | .40 | .60 |
| | | *Nos. 51-53 (3)* | 1.05 | 1.30 |
| | | Set, never hinged | 1.75 | |

A6

King George VI — A7

**1938-44 Engr. *Perf. 12½***

| | | | | |
|---|---|---|---|---|
| **54** | A6 | ½p green | .25 | *2.00* |
| **54A** | A6 | ½p dk brown ('42) | .25 | *2.25* |
| **55** | A6 | 1p dark brown | 2.50 | *.35* |
| **55A** | A6 | 1p green ('42) | .25 | *1.75* |
| **56** | A6 | 1½p dark carmine | 5.00 | *6.00* |
| **56A** | A6 | 1½p gray ('42) | .25 | *5.75* |
| **57** | A6 | 2p gray | 5.00 | 1.25 |
| **57A** | A6 | 2p dark car ('42) | .25 | *2.00* |
| **58** | A6 | 3p blue | .60 | 1.00 |
| **59** | A6 | 4p rose lilac | 1.75 | 2.00 |
| **60** | A6 | 6p dark violet | 2.00 | 2.00 |
| **61** | A6 | 9p olive bister | 2.00 | *5.25* |
| **62** | A6 | 1sh orange & blk | 2.10 | *3.25* |

**Typo.**

***Perf. 14***

**Chalky Paper**

| | | | | |
|---|---|---|---|---|
| **63** | A7 | 2sh ultra & dl vio, *bl* | 7.00 | *17.50* |
| **64** | A7 | 2sh6p red & blk, *bl* | 9.00 | *24.00* |
| **65** | A7 | 5sh red & grn, *yel* | 35.00 | 30.00 |
| *a.* | | 5sh dk red & dp grn, *yel* ('44) | 55.00 | *140.00* |
| **66** | A7 | 10sh red & grn, *grn* | 35.00 | *70.00* |

**Wmk. 3**

| | | | | |
|---|---|---|---|---|
| **67** | A7 | £1 blk & vio, *red* | 30.00 | *52.50* |
| | | *Nos. 54-67 (18)* | 138.20 | *228.85* |
| | | Set, never hinged | 220.00 | |

**Catalogue values for unused stamps in this section, from this point to the end of the section, are for Never Hinged items.**

Canoe on Lake Nyasa — A8

Soldier of King's African Rifles — A9

Tea Estate, Mlanje Mountain
A10

Map and Coat of Arms — A11

Fishing Village, Lake Nyasa — A12

Tobacco Estate — A13

Arms of Nyasaland and George VI
A14

**1945, Sept. 1 Engr. *Perf. 12***

| | | | | |
|---|---|---|---|---|
| **68** | A8 | ½p brn vio & blk | .50 | .25 |
| **69** | A9 | 1p dp green & blk | .25 | .75 |
| **70** | A10 | 1½p gray grn & blk | .35 | .45 |
| **71** | A11 | 2p scarlet & blk | 1.50 | .90 |
| **72** | A12 | 3p blue & blk | .45 | .30 |
| **73** | A13 | 4p rose vio & blk | 2.50 | .80 |
| **74** | A10 | 6p violet & blk | 3.00 | .90 |
| **75** | A8 | 9p ol grn & blk | 4.50 | *3.00* |
| **76** | A11 | 1sh myr grn & ind | 3.75 | .55 |
| **77** | A12 | 2sh dl red brn & grn | 9.50 | 5.50 |
| **78** | A13 | 2sh6p ultra & green | 9.50 | 7.00 |
| **79** | A14 | 5sh ultra & lt vio | 7.00 | *6.50* |
| **80** | A11 | 10sh green & lake | 25.00 | 18.00 |
| **81** | A14 | 20sh black & scar | 29.00 | *35.00* |
| | | *Nos. 68-81 (14)* | 96.80 | 79.90 |

**Peace Issue**

Common Design Type

***Perf. 13½x14***

**1946, Dec. 16 Wmk. 4**

| | | | | |
|---|---|---|---|---|
| **82** | CD303 | 1p bright green | .25 | .25 |
| **83** | CD303 | 2p red orange | .25 | .25 |

A15

**1947, Oct. 20 *Perf. 12***

| | | | | |
|---|---|---|---|---|
| **84** | A15 | 1p emerald & org brn | .65 | .50 |

**Silver Wedding Issue**

Common Design Types

**1948, Dec. 15 Photo. *Perf. 14x14½***

| | | | | |
|---|---|---|---|---|
| **85** | CD304 | 1p dark green | .25 | .25 |

**Engr.; Name Typo.**

***Perf. 11½x11***

| | | | | |
|---|---|---|---|---|
| **86** | CD305 | 10sh purple | 18.00 | *30.00* |

**UPU Issue**

Common Design Types

**Engr.; Name Typo. on 3p, 6p**

***Perf. 13½, 11x11½***

**1949, Nov. 21 Wmk. 4**

| | | | | |
|---|---|---|---|---|
| **87** | CD306 | 1p blue green | .35 | .35 |
| **88** | CD307 | 3p Prus blue | 2.50 | 2.50 |
| **89** | CD308 | 6p rose violet | .85 | .85 |
| **90** | CD309 | 1sh violet blue | .35 | .35 |
| | | *Nos. 87-90 (4)* | 4.05 | 4.05 |

Arms of British Central Africa and Nyasaland Protectorate — A16

**1951, May 15 Engr. *Perf. 11x12***

**Arms in Black**

| | | | | |
|---|---|---|---|---|
| **91** | A16 | 2p rose | 1.25 | 1.25 |
| **92** | A16 | 3p blue | 1.25 | 1.25 |
| **93** | A16 | 6p purple | 1.50 | *2.25* |
| **94** | A16 | 5sh deep blue | 5.50 | *8.00* |
| | | *Nos. 91-94 (4)* | 9.50 | *12.75* |

60th anniv. of the Protectorate, originally British Central Africa.

Exhibition Seal — A17

**1953, May 30 *Perf. 14x13½***

| | | | | |
|---|---|---|---|---|
| **95** | A17 | 6p purple | .65 | .50 |

Central African Rhodes Cent. Exhib.

**Coronation Issue**

Common Design Type

**1953, June 2 *Perf. 13½x13***

| | | | | |
|---|---|---|---|---|
| **96** | CD312 | 2p orange & black | .75 | .75 |

**Types of 1945-47 with Portrait of Queen Elizabeth II and**

Grading Cotton
A18

**1953, Sept. 1 *Perf. 12***

| | | | | |
|---|---|---|---|---|
| **97** | A8 | ½p red brn & blk | .25 | *1.25* |
| *a.* | | Booklet pane of 4 | 3.75 | |
| *b.* | | Perf. 12x12½ ('54) | .25 | *1.25* |
| **98** | A15 | 1p emer & org brn | .65 | .25 |
| *a.* | | Booklet pane of 4 | 3.75 | |
| **99** | A10 | 1½p gray grn & blk | .25 | *1.75* |
| **100** | A11 | 2p orange & blk | .85 | .30 |
| *a.* | | Booklet pane of 4 | 4.25 | |
| *b.* | | Perf. 12x12½ ('54) | .40 | .30 |
| **101** | A18 | 2½p blk & brt grn | .30 | *.50* |
| **102** | A13 | 3p scarlet & blk | .30 | .30 |
| **103** | A12 | 4½p blue & blk | .90 | .45 |
| **104** | A10 | 6p violet & blk | 1.25 | 1.25 |
| *a.* | | Booklet pane of 4 | 11.50 | |
| *b.* | | Perf. 12x12½ ('54) | 2.00 | .90 |
| **105** | A8 | 9p olive & blk | 1.25 | *2.75* |
| **106** | A11 | 1sh myr grn & ind | 3.75 | .50 |
| **107** | A12 | 2sh rose brn & grn | 3.50 | *3.75* |
| **108** | A13 | 2sh6p ultra & grn | 4.25 | *6.75* |
| **109** | A14 | 5sh Prus bl & rose lil | 10.00 | 7.00 |
| **110** | A11 | 10sh green & lake | 11.00 | *17.50* |
| **111** | A14 | 20sh black & scar | 25.00 | *32.50* |
| | | *Nos. 97-111 (15)* | 63.50 | *76.80* |

Issue date: Nos. 97b, 100b, 104b, Mar. 8.

**Revenue Stamps Overprinted in Black**

Arms of Nyasaland
A19

***Perf. 11½x12***

**1963, Nov. 1 Engr. Unwmk.**

| | | | | |
|---|---|---|---|---|
| **112** | A19 | ½p on 1p blue | .30 | .30 |
| **113** | A19 | 1p green | .30 | .25 |
| **114** | A19 | 2p rose red | .30 | .30 |
| **115** | A19 | 3p dark blue | .30 | .25 |
| **116** | A19 | 6p rose lake | .30 | .25 |
| **117** | A19 | 9p on 1sh car rose | .40 | .40 |
| **118** | A19 | 1sh purple | .45 | 2.75 |
| **119** | A19 | 2sh6p black | 1.25 | *2.00* |
| **120** | A19 | 5sh brown | 3.00 | 3.50 |
| **121** | A19 | 10sh gray olive | 5.25 | *8.00* |
| **122** | A19 | £1 violet | 5.75 | *8.50* |
| | | *Nos. 112-122 (11)* | 17.60 | *26.50* |

Nos. 112, 117 have 3 bars over old value.

Mother and Child — A20

Designs: 1p, Chambo fish. 2p, Zebu bull. 3p, Peanuts. 4p, Fishermen in boat. 6p, Harvesting tea. 1sh, Lumber and tropical pine branch. 1sh3p, Tobacco industry. 2sh6p, Cotton industry. 5sh, Monkey Bay, Lake Nyasa. 10sh, Afzelia tree (pod mahogany). £1, Nyala antelope, vert.

***Perf. 14½***

**1964, Jan. 1 Unwmk. Photo.**

**Size: 23x19mm**

| | | | | |
|---|---|---|---|---|
| **123** | A20 | ½p lilac | .25 | *.35* |
| **124** | A20 | 1p green & blk | .25 | *.25* |
| **125** | A20 | 2p red brown | .25 | *.25* |
| **126** | A20 | 3p pale brn, brn red & grn | .25 | *.25* |
| **127** | A20 | 4p org yel & indigo | .30 | *.35* |

**Size: 41½x25mm, 25x41½mm**

| | | | | |
|---|---|---|---|---|
| **128** | A20 | 6p bl pur & brt yel grn | .70 | *.70* |
| **129** | A20 | 1sh yel brn & dk grn | .50 | .30 |
| **130** | A20 | 1sh3p red brn & olive | 3.75 | .30 |
| **131** | A20 | 2sh6p blue & brn | 3.25 | .50 |
| **132** | A20 | 5sh grn, bl, sep & yel | 1.50 | 1.50 |
| **133** | A20 | 10sh org brn grn & gray | 2.75 | *3.25* |
| **134** | A20 | £1 yel & dk brn | 8.00 | *11.00* |
| | | *Nos. 123-134 (12)* | 21.75 | 19.00 |

### POSTAGE DUE STAMPS

**Catalogue values for unused stamps in this section are for Never Hinged items.**

D1

*Perf. 14*

**1950, July 1 Wmk. 4 Typo.**

| No. | Type | Description | Unused | Used |
|---|---|---|---|---|
| J1 | D1 | 1p rose red | 4.00 | *32.50* |
| J2 | D1 | 2p ultramarine | 18.00 | *32.50* |
| J3 | D1 | 3p green | 15.00 | *8.00* |
| J4 | D1 | 4p claret | 29.50 | *60.00* |
| J5 | D1 | 6p ocher | 40.00 | *160.00* |
| | | *Nos. J1-J5 (5)* | 106.50 | *293.00* |

## NYASSA

nī-ˈa-sə

LOCATION — In the northern part of Mozambique in southeast Africa
AREA — 73,292 sq. mi.
POP. — 3,000,000 (estimated)
CAPITAL — Porto Amelia

The district formerly administered by the Nyassa Company is now a part of Mozambique.

1000 Reis = 1 Milreis
100 Centavos = 1 Escudo (1919)

Mozambique Nos. 24-35 Overprinted in Black

**1898 Unwmk. *Perf. 11½, 12½***

| No. | Type | Description | Unused | Used |
|---|---|---|---|---|
| 1 | A3 | 5r yellow | 3.00 | 1.50 |
| 2 | A3 | 10r redsh violet | 3.00 | 1.50 |
| 3 | A3 | 15r chocolate | 3.00 | 1.50 |
| 4 | A3 | 20r gray violet | 3.00 | 1.50 |
| 5 | A3 | 25r blue green | 3.00 | 1.50 |
| 6 | A3 | 50r light blue | 3.00 | 1.50 |
| *a.* | | Inverted overprint | | |
| *b.* | | Perf. 12½ | 6.00 | 3.50 |
| 7 | A3 | 75r rose | 4.00 | 2.00 |
| 8 | A3 | 80r yellow grn | 4.00 | 2.00 |
| 9 | A3 | 100r brown, *buff* | 4.00 | 2.00 |
| 10 | A3 | 150r car, *rose* | 6.50 | 4.00 |
| 11 | A3 | 200r dk blue, *blue* | 5.00 | 3.00 |
| 12 | A3 | 300r dk blue, *salmon* | 5.00 | 3.00 |
| | | *Nos. 1-12 (12)* | 46.50 | 25.00 |

*Reprints of Nos. 1, 5, 8, 9, 10 and 12 have white gum and clean-cut perforation 13½. Value of No. 9, $15; others $3 each.*

### Same Overprint on Mozambique Issue of 1898

**1898 *Perf. 11½***

| No. | Type | Description | Unused | Used |
|---|---|---|---|---|
| 13 | A4 | 2½r gray | 2.50 | .80 |
| 14 | A4 | 5r orange | 2.50 | .80 |
| 15 | A4 | 10r light green | 2.50 | .80 |
| 16 | A4 | 15r brown | 3.00 | 1.00 |
| 17 | A4 | 20r gray violet | 3.00 | 1.00 |
| 18 | A4 | 25r sea green | 3.00 | 1.00 |
| 19 | A4 | 50r blue | 3.00 | 1.00 |
| 20 | A4 | 75r rose | 2.75 | 1.00 |
| 21 | A4 | 80r violet | 3.50 | .80 |
| 22 | A4 | 100r dk bl, *bl* | 3.50 | .80 |
| 23 | A4 | 150r brown, *straw* | 3.50 | .80 |
| 24 | A4 | 200r red lilac, *pnksh* | 3.75 | 1.00 |
| 25 | A4 | 300r dk blue, *rose* | 4.00 | 1.00 |
| | | *Nos. 13-25 (13)* | 40.50 | 11.80 |

Giraffe — A5

Camels — A6

**1901 Engr. *Perf. 14***

| No. | Type | Description | Unused | Used |
|---|---|---|---|---|
| 26 | A5 | 2½r blk & red brn | 1.75 | .55 |
| 27 | A5 | 5r blk & violet | 1.75 | .55 |
| 28 | A5 | 10r blk & dp grn | 1.75 | .55 |
| 29 | A5 | 15r blk & org brn | 1.75 | .55 |
| 30 | A5 | 20r blk & org red | 1.75 | .70 |
| 31 | A5 | 25r blk & orange | 1.75 | .70 |
| 32 | A5 | 50r blk & dl bl | 1.75 | .70 |
| 33 | A6 | 75r blk & car lake | 2.00 | .70 |
| 34 | A6 | 80r blk & lilac | 2.00 | .90 |
| 35 | A6 | 100r blk & brn bis | 2.00 | .90 |
| 36 | A6 | 150r blk & dp org | 2.25 | 1.00 |
| 37 | A6 | 200r blk & grnsh bl | 2.50 | 1.00 |
| 38 | A6 | 300r blk & yel grn | 2.50 | 1.00 |
| | | *Nos. 26-38 (13)* | 25.50 | 9.80 |

Nos. 26 to 38 are known with inverted centers but are believed to be purely speculative and never regularly issued. Value $80 each.
Perf 13½, 14½, 15½ & compound also exist.
For overprints and surcharges see Nos. 39-50, 63-80.

Nos. 34, 36, 38 Surcharged

**1903**

| No. | Type | Description | Unused | Used |
|---|---|---|---|---|
| 39 | A6 | 65r on 80r | 1.00 | .75 |
| 40 | A6 | 115r on 150r | 1.00 | .75 |
| 41 | A6 | 130r on 300r | 1.00 | .75 |
| | | *Nos. 39-41 (3)* | 3.00 | 2.25 |

Nos. 29, 31 Overprinted

**1903**

| No. | Type | Description | Unused | Used |
|---|---|---|---|---|
| 42 | A5 | 15r black & org brn | 1.00 | .75 |
| 43 | A5 | 25r black & orange | 1.00 | .75 |

Nos. 34, 36, 38 Surcharged

**1903**

| No. | Type | Description | Unused | Used |
|---|---|---|---|---|
| 44 | A6 | 65r on 80r | 32.50 | 15.00 |
| 45 | A6 | 115r on 150r | 32.50 | 15.00 |
| 46 | A6 | 130r on 300r | 32.50 | 15.00 |
| | | *Nos. 44-46 (3)* | 97.50 | 45.00 |

Nos. 29, 31 Overprinted

**1903**

| No. | Type | Description | Unused | Used |
|---|---|---|---|---|
| 47 | A5 | 15r black & org brn | 500.00 | 100.00 |
| 48 | A5 | 25r black & orange | 150.00 | 100.00 |

Forgeries exist of Nos. 44-48.

Nos. 26, 35 Surcharged

**1910**

| No. | Type | Description | Unused | Used |
|---|---|---|---|---|
| 49 | A5 | 5r on 2½r | 1.00 | .75 |
| 50 | A6 | 50r on 100r | 1.00 | .75 |
| *a.* | | "50 REIS" omitted | 300.00 | |

*Reprints of Nos. 49-50, made in 1921, have 2mm space between surcharge lines, instead of 1½mm. Value, each 25 cents.*

Zebra — A7

Vasco da Gama's Flagship "San Gabriel" — A8

Designs: Nos. 51-53, Camels. Nos. 57-59, Giraffe and palms.

**1911 Red Overprint**

| No. | Type | Description | Unused | Used |
|---|---|---|---|---|
| 51 | A7 | 2½r blk & dl vio | 1.25 | .55 |
| 52 | A7 | 5r black | 1.25 | .55 |
| 53 | A7 | 10r blk & gray grn | 1.25 | .55 |
| 54 | A7 | 20r blk & car lake | 1.25 | .55 |
| 55 | A7 | 25r blk & vio brn | 1.25 | .55 |
| 56 | A7 | 50r blk & dp bl | 1.25 | .55 |
| 57 | A8 | 75r blk & brn | 1.25 | .55 |
| 58 | A8 | 100r blk & brn, *grn* | 1.25 | .55 |
| 59 | A8 | 200r blk & dp grn, *sal* | 1.40 | 1.00 |
| 60 | A8 | 300r blk, *blue* | 2.40 | 1.60 |
| 61 | A8 | 400r blk & dk brn | 3.00 | 2.00 |
| *a.* | | Pair, one without overprint | | |
| 62 | A8 | 500r ol & vio brn | 4.00 | 3.00 |
| | | *Nos. 51-62 (12)* | 20.80 | 12.00 |

Nos. 51-62 exist without overprint but were not issued in that condition. Value $7.50 each.
For surcharges see Nos. 81-105.

Stamps of 1901-03 Surcharged

**1918 On Nos. 26-38**

| No. | Type | Description | Unused | Used |
|---|---|---|---|---|
| 63 | A5 | ¼c on 2½r | 140.00 | 110.00 |
| 64 | A5 | ½c on 5r | 140.00 | 110.00 |
| 65 | A5 | 1c on 10r | 140.00 | 110.00 |
| 66 | A5 | 1½c on 15r | 2.10 | 1.10 |
| 67 | A5 | 2c on 20r | 1.25 | 1.00 |
| 68 | A5 | 3½c on 25r | 1.50 | 1.00 |
| 69 | A5 | 5c on 50r | 1.25 | 1.00 |
| 70 | A6 | 7½c on 75r | 1.25 | 1.00 |
| 71 | A6 | 8c on 80r | 1.25 | 1.00 |
| 72 | A6 | 10c on 100r | 1.25 | 1.00 |
| 73 | A6 | 15c on 150r | 2.10 | 2.00 |
| 74 | A6 | 20c on 200r | 2.00 | 2.00 |
| 75 | A6 | 30c on 300r | 3.25 | 2.40 |

**On Nos. 39-41**

| No. | Type | Description | Unused | Used |
|---|---|---|---|---|
| 76 | A6 | 40c on 65r on 80r | 18.00 | 16.50 |
| 77 | A6 | 50c on 115r on 150r | 3.00 | 2.00 |
| 78 | A6 | 1e on 130r on 300r | 5.00 | 2.00 |

**On Nos. 42-43**

| No. | Type | Description | Unused | Used |
|---|---|---|---|---|
| 79 | A5 | 1½c on 15r | 7.00 | 3.00 |
| 80 | A5 | 3½c on 25r | 2.00 | 1.00 |
| | | *Nos. 63-80 (18)* | 472.20 | 368.00 |

On Nos. 70-78 there is less space between "REPUBLICA" and the new value than on the other stamps of this issue.
On Nos. 76-78 the 1903 surcharge is canceled by a bar.
The surcharge exists inverted on #64, 66-70, 72, 76, 78-80, and double on #64, 67, 69.

Nos. 51-62 Surcharged in Black or Red

Numerals: The "1" (large or small) is thin, sharp-pointed, and has thin serifs. The "2" is italic, with the tail thin and only slightly wavy. The "3" has a flat top. The "4" is open at the top. The "7" has thin strokes.
Centavos: The letters are shaded, i.e., they are thicker in some parts than in others. The "t" has a thin cross bar ending in a downward stroke at the right. The "s" is flat at the bottom and wider than in the next group.

**1921 Lisbon Surcharges**

| No. | Type | Description | Unused | Used |
|---|---|---|---|---|
| 81 | A7 | ¼c on 2½r | 5.00 | 2.75 |
| 83 | A7 | ½c on 5r (R) | 5.00 | 2.75 |
| *a.* | | ½c on 2½r (R) (error) | 275.00 | 250.00 |
| 84 | A7 | 1c on 10r | 5.00 | 2.75 |
| *a.* | | Pair, one without surcharge | | |
| 85 | A8 | 1½c on 300r (R) | 5.00 | 2.75 |
| 86 | A7 | 2c on 20r | 5.00 | 2.75 |
| 87 | A7 | 2½c on 25r | 5.00 | 2.75 |
| 88 | A8 | 3c on 400r | 5.00 | 2.75 |
| *a.* | | "Republica" omitted | | |
| 89 | A7 | 5c on 50r | 5.00 | 2.75 |
| 90 | A8 | 7½c on 75r | 5.00 | 2.75 |
| 91 | A8 | 10c on 100r | 5.00 | 2.75 |
| 92 | A8 | 12c on 500r | 5.00 | 2.75 |
| 93 | A8 | 20c on 200r | 5.00 | 2.75 |
| | | *Nos. 81-93 (12)* | 60.00 | 33.00 |

The surcharge exists inverted on Nos. 83-85, 87-88 and 92, and double on Nos. 81, 83 and 86.
Forgeries exist of Nos. 81-93.

### London Surcharges

Numerals — The "1" has the vertical stroke and serifs thicker than in the Lisbon printing. The "2" is upright and has a strong wave in the tail. The small "2" is heavily shaded. The "3" has a rounded top. The "4" is closed at the top. The "7" has thick strokes.
Centavos — The letters are heavier than in the Lisbon printing and are of even thickness throughout. The "t" has a thick cross bar with scarcely any down stroke at the end. The "s" is rounded at the bottom and narrower than in the Lisbon printing.

| No. | Type | Description | Unused | Used |
|---|---|---|---|---|
| 94 | A7 | ¼c on 2½r | 1.50 | 1.25 |
| 95 | A7 | ½c on 5r (R) | 1.50 | 1.25 |
| 96 | A7 | 1c on 10r | 1.50 | 1.25 |
| 97 | A8 | 1½c on 300r (R) | 1.50 | 1.25 |
| 98 | A7 | 2c on 20r | 1.50 | 1.25 |
| 99 | A7 | 2½c on 25r | 1.50 | 1.25 |
| 100 | A8 | 3c on 400r | 1.50 | 1.25 |
| 101 | A7 | 5c on 50r | 1.50 | 1.25 |
| 102 | A8 | 7½c on 75r | 1.50 | 1.25 |
| *a.* | | Inverted surcharge | | |
| 103 | A8 | 10c on 100r | 1.50 | 1.25 |
| 104 | A8 | 12c on 500r | 1.50 | 1.25 |
| 105 | A8 | 20c on 200r | 1.50 | 1.25 |
| | | *Nos. 94-105 (12)* | 18.00 | 15.00 |

A9

Zebra and Warrior — A10

Designs: 2c-6c, Vasco da Gama. 7½c-20c, "San Gabriel." 2e-5e, Dhow and warrior.

***Perf. 12½, 13½-15 & Compound***

**1921-23 Engr.**

| No. | Type | Description | Unused | Used |
|---|---|---|---|---|
| 106 | A9 | ¼c claret | 1.25 | .70 |
| 107 | A9 | ½c steel blue | 1.25 | .70 |
| 108 | A9 | 1c grn & blk | 1.25 | .70 |
| 109 | A9 | 1½c blk & ocher | 1.25 | .70 |
| 110 | A9 | 2c red & blk | 1.25 | .70 |
| 111 | A9 | 2½c blk & ol grn | 1.25 | .70 |
| 112 | A9 | 4c blk & org | 1.25 | .70 |
| 113 | A9 | 5c ultra & blk | 1.25 | .70 |
| 114 | A9 | 6c blk & vio | 1.25 | .70 |
| 115 | A9 | 7½c blk & blk brn | 1.25 | .70 |
| 116 | A9 | 8c blk & ol grn | 1.25 | .70 |
| 117 | A9 | 10c blk & red brn | 1.25 | .70 |
| 118 | A9 | 15c blk & carmine | 1.25 | .70 |
| 119 | A9 | 20c blk & pale bl | 1.25 | .70 |
| 120 | A10 | 30c blk & bister | 1.25 | .70 |
| 121 | A10 | 40c blk & gray bl | 1.25 | .70 |
| 122 | A10 | 50c blk & green | 1.25 | .70 |
| 123 | A10 | 1e blk & red brn | 1.25 | .70 |
| 124 | A10 | 2e red brn & blk ('23) | 3.25 | 2.50 |
| 125 | A10 | 5e ultra & red brn ('23) | 3.00 | 2.25 |
| | | *Nos. 106-125 (20)* | 28.75 | 17.35 |

## POSTAGE DUE STAMPS

Giraffe — D1

½c, 1c, Giraffe. 2c, 3c, Zebra. 5c, 6c, 10c, "San Gabriel." 20c, 50c, Vasco da Gama.

**1924 Unwmk. Engr. *Perf. 14***

| | | | | |
|---|---|---|---|---|
| **J1** | D1 | ½c deep green | 1.00 | *1.75* |
| **J2** | D1 | 1c gray | 1.00 | *1.75* |
| **J3** | D1 | 2c red | 1.00 | *1.75* |
| **J4** | D1 | 3c red orange | 1.00 | *1.75* |
| **J5** | D1 | 5c dark brown | 1.00 | *1.75* |
| **J6** | D1 | 6c orange brown | 1.00 | *1.75* |
| **J7** | D1 | 10c brown violet | 1.00 | *1.75* |
| **J8** | D1 | 20c carmine | 1.00 | *1.75* |
| **J9** | D1 | 50c lilac gray | 1.00 | *1.75* |
| | | *Nos. J1-J9 (9)* | 9.00 | *15.75* |

Used values are for c-t-o copies.

## NEWSPAPER STAMP

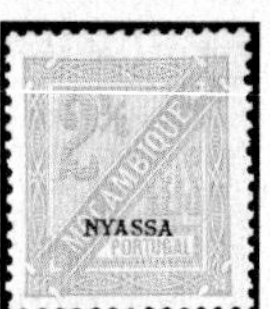

Mozambique No. P6 Ovptd. Like Nos. 1-25 in Black

**1898 Unwmk. *Perf. 13½***

| | | | | |
|---|---|---|---|---|
| **P1** | N3 | 2½r brown | 2.00 | 1.00 |

*Reprints have white gum and clean-cut perf. 13½. Value $1.*

## POSTAL TAX STAMPS

**Pombal Issue**

Mozambique Nos. RA1-RA3 Overprinted "NYASSA" in Red

**1925 Unwmk. *Perf. 12½***

| | | | | |
|---|---|---|---|---|
| **RA1** | CD28 | 15c brown & blk | 5.00 | 5.00 |
| **RA2** | CD29 | 15c brown & blk | 5.00 | 5.00 |
| **RA3** | CD30 | 15c brown & blk | 5.00 | 5.00 |
| | | *Nos. RA1-RA3 (3)* | 15.00 | 15.00 |

## POSTAL TAX DUE STAMPS

**Pombal Issue**

Mozambique Nos. RAJ1-RAJ3 Overprinted "NYASSA" in Red

**1925 Unwmk. *Perf. 12½***

| | | | | |
|---|---|---|---|---|
| **RAJ1** | CD28 | 30c brown & blk | 12.50 | 7.75 |
| **RAJ2** | CD29 | 30c brown & blk | 12.50 | 7.75 |
| **RAJ3** | CD30 | 30c brown & blk | 12.50 | 7.75 |
| | | *Nos. RAJ1-RAJ3 (3)* | 37.50 | 23.25 |

# OBOCK

'ō-,bäk

LOCATION — A seaport in eastern Africa on the Gulf of Aden, directly opposite Aden.

Obock was the point of entrance from which French Somaliland was formed. The port was acquired by the French in 1862 but was not actively occupied until 1884 when Sagallo and Tadjoura were ceded to France. In 1888 Djibouti was made into a port and the seat of government moved from Obock to the latter city. In 1902 the name Somali Coast was adopted on the postage stamps of Djibouti, these stamps superseding the individual issues of Obock.

100 Centimes = 1 Franc

Counterfeits exist of Nos. 1-31.

### Stamps of French Colonies Handstamped in Black

#1-11, J1-J4

#12-20, J5-J18

**1892 Unwmk. Perf. 14x13½**

| No. | Type | Description | Unused | Used |
|---|---|---|---|---|
| 1 | A9 | 1c blk, *lil bl* | 45.00 | 45.00 |
| 2 | A9 | 2c brn, *buff* | 45.00 | 45.00 |
| 3 | A9 | 4c claret, *lav* | 450.00 | *475.00* |
| 4 | A9 | 5c grn, *grnsh* | 40.00 | 32.50 |
| 5 | A9 | 10c blk, *lavender* | 80.00 | 47.50 |
| 6 | A9 | 15c blue | 72.50 | 50.00 |
| 7 | A9 | 25c blk, *rose* | 110.00 | 80.00 |
| 8 | A9 | 35c vio, *org* | 450.00 | 450.00 |
| 9 | A9 | 40c red, *straw* | 400.00 | *425.00* |
| 10 | A9 | 75c car, *rose* | 450.00 | *475.00* |
| 11 | A9 | 1fr brnz grn, *straw* | 500.00 | 550.00 |
| | | *Nos. 1-11 (11)* | 2,643. | 2,675. |

*No. 3 has been reprinted. On the reprints the second "O" of "OBOCK" is 4mm high instead of 3½mm. Value $32.50.*

**1892**

| No. | Type | Description | Unused | Used |
|---|---|---|---|---|
| 12 | A9 | 4c claret, *lav* | 27.50 | 27.50 |
| 13 | A9 | 5c grn, *grnsh* | 27.50 | 27.50 |
| 14 | A9 | 10c blk, *lavender* | 27.50 | 27.50 |
| 15 | A9 | 15c blue | 27.50 | 27.50 |
| 16 | A9 | 20c red, *grn* | 47.50 | 45.00 |
| 17 | A9 | 25c blk, *rose* | 35.00 | 27.50 |
| 18 | A9 | 40c red, *straw* | 60.00 | 52.50 |
| 19 | A9 | 75c car, *rose* | 325.00 | 275.00 |
| 20 | A9 | 1fr brnz grn, *straw* | 87.50 | 80.00 |
| | | *Nos. 12-20 (9)* | 665.00 | 590.00 |

Exists inverted or double on all denominations.

### Nos. 14, 15, 17, 20 with Additional Surcharge Handstamped in Red, Blue or Black

Nos, 21-30

No. 31

**1892**

| No. | Type | Description | Unused | Used |
|---|---|---|---|---|
| 21 | A9 | 1c on 25c blk, *rose* | 20.00 | 20.00 |
| 22 | A9 | 2c on 10c blk, *lav* | 72.50 | 60.00 |
| 23 | A9 | 2c on 15c blue | 22.50 | 20.00 |
| 24 | A9 | 4c on 15c bl (Bk) | 20.00 | 20.00 |
| 25 | A9 | 4c on 25c blk, *rose* (Bk) | 20.00 | 20.00 |
| 26 | A9 | 5c on 25c blk, *rose* | 27.50 | 27.50 |
| 27 | A9 | 20c on 10c blk, *lav* | 95.00 | 95.00 |
| 28 | A9 | 30c on 10c blk, *lav* | 120.00 | 110.00 |
| 29 | A9 | 35c on 25c blk, *rose* | 100.00 | 92.50 |
| *a.* | | "3" instead of "35" | 950.00 | 950.00 |
| 30 | A9 | 75c on 1fr brnz grn, *straw* | 110.00 | 110.00 |
| *b.* | | "57" instead of "75" | *8,750.* | *9,250.* |
| *c.* | | "55" instead of "75" | *8,750.* | *9,250.* |
| 31 | A9 | 5fr on 1fr brnz grn, *straw* (Bl) | 775.00 | 700.00 |
| | | *Nos. 21-31 (11)* | 1,383. | 1,275. |

Exists inverted on most denominations.

Navigation and Commerce — A4

### Obock in Red (1c, 5c, 15c, 25c, 75c, 1fr) or Blue

**1892 Typo. Perf. 14x13½**

| No. | Type | Description | Unused | Used |
|---|---|---|---|---|
| 32 | A4 | 1c blk, *lil bl* | 2.75 | 2.75 |
| 33 | A4 | 2c brn, *buff* | 2.00 | 2.00 |
| 34 | A4 | 4c claret, *lav* | 2.75 | 2.75 |
| 35 | A4 | 5c grn, *grnsh* | 6.25 | 4.00 |
| 36 | A4 | 10c blk, *lavender* | 8.00 | 5.25 |
| 37 | A4 | 15c bl, quadrille paper | 19.50 | 11.50 |
| 38 | A4 | 20c red, *grn* | 27.50 | 27.50 |
| 39 | A4 | 25c blk, *rose* | 27.50 | 24.00 |
| 40 | A4 | 30c brn, *bis* | 24.00 | 20.00 |
| 41 | A4 | 40c red, *straw* | 24.00 | 20.00 |
| 42 | A4 | 50c car, *rose* | 28.00 | 24.00 |
| 43 | A4 | 75c vio, *org* | 32.50 | 24.00 |
| *a.* | | Name double | 350.00 | 350.00 |
| *b.* | | Name inverted | *5,500.* | *5,500.* |
| 44 | A4 | 1fr brnz grn, *straw* | 47.50 | 40.00 |
| | | *Nos. 32-44 (13)* | 252.25 | 207.75 |

Perf. 13½x14 stamps are counterfeits.

Camel and Rider — A5

### Quadrille Lines Printed on Paper

**1893 Size: 32mm at base Imperf.**

| No. | Type | Description | Unused | Used |
|---|---|---|---|---|
| 44A | A5 | 2fr slate | 65.00 | 55.00 |

**Size: 45mm at base**

| No. | Type | Description | Unused | Used |
|---|---|---|---|---|
| 45 | A5 | 5fr red | 140.00 | 125.00 |

Somali Warriors A7

A8

**1894 Imperf.**

### Quadrille Lines Printed on Paper

| No. | Type | Description | Unused | Used |
|---|---|---|---|---|
| 46 | A7 | 1c blk & rose | 2.75 | 2.75 |
| 47 | A7 | 2c vio brn & grn | 2.75 | 2.75 |
| 48 | A7 | 4c brn vio & org | 2.75 | 2.75 |
| 49 | A7 | 5c bl grn & brn | 3.50 | 3.50 |
| 50 | A7 | 10c blk & grn | 9.50 | 8.00 |
| *a.* | | Half used as 5c on cover ('01) | | 350.00 |
| 51 | A7 | 15c bl & rose | 9.50 | 7.25 |
| 52 | A7 | 20c brn org & mar | 9.50 | 8.00 |
| *a.* | | Half used as 10c on cover ('01) | | 325.00 |
| 53 | A7 | 25c blk & bl | 10.50 | 6.50 |
| *a.* | | Right half used as 5c on cover ('01) | | 300.00 |
| *b.* | | Left half used as 2c on cover ('03) | | 300.00 |
| 54 | A7 | 30c bis & yel grn | 20.00 | 14.50 |
| *a.* | | Half used as 15c on cover ('01) | | 2,200. |
| 55 | A7 | 40c red & bl grn | 17.00 | 13.00 |
| 56 | A7 | 50c rose & bl | 15.00 | 12.00 |
| *a.* | | Half used as 25c on cover | | 3,400. |
| 57 | A7 | 75c gray lil & org | 20.00 | 13.00 |
| 58 | A7 | 1fr ol grn & mar | 17.00 | 10.50 |

**Size: 37mm at base**

| No. | Type | Description | Unused | Used |
|---|---|---|---|---|
| 60 | A8 | 2fr vio & org | 120.00 | 120.00 |

**Size: 42mm at base**

| No. | Type | Description | Unused | Used |
|---|---|---|---|---|
| 61 | A8 | 5fr rose & bl | 95.00 | 95.00 |

**Size: 46mm at base**

| No. | Type | Description | Unused | Used |
|---|---|---|---|---|
| 62 | A8 | 10fr org & red vio | 160.00 | 160.00 |
| 63 | A8 | 25fr brn & bl | 875.00 | 875.00 |
| 64 | A8 | 50fr red vio & grn | 1,000. | 1,000. |

Counterfeits exist of Nos. 63-64.

Stamps of Obock were replaced in 1901 by those of Somali Coast. The 5c on 75c, 5c on 25fr and 10c on 50fr of 1902 are listed under Somali Coast.

## POSTAGE DUE STAMPS

### Postage Due Stamps of French Colonies Handstamped Like #1-20

**1892 Unwmk. Imperf.**

| No. | Type | Description | Unused | Used |
|---|---|---|---|---|
| J1 | D1 | 5c black | *11,000.* | |
| J2 | D1 | 10c black | 240.00 | *275.00* |
| J3 | D1 | 30c black | 375.00 | *450.00* |
| J4 | D1 | 60c black | 475.00 | *550.00* |
| J5 | D1 | 1c black | 55.00 | 55.00 |
| J6 | D1 | 2c black | 45.00 | 45.00 |
| J7 | D1 | 3c black | 52.50 | 52.50 |
| J8 | D1 | 4c black | 45.00 | 45.00 |
| J9 | D1 | 5c black | 16.00 | 16.00 |
| J10 | D1 | 10c black | 35.00 | 35.00 |
| J11 | D1 | 15c black | 24.00 | 24.00 |
| J12 | D1 | 20c black | 32.50 | 32.50 |
| J13 | D1 | 30c black | 32.50 | 32.50 |
| J14 | D1 | 40c black | 60.00 | 60.00 |
| J15 | D1 | 60c black | 80.00 | 80.00 |
| J16 | D1 | 1fr brown | 225.00 | 225.00 |
| J17 | D1 | 2fr brown | 240.00 | 240.00 |
| J18 | D1 | 5fr brown | 525.00 | 525.00 |
| | | *Nos. J2-J18 (17)* | 2,558. | 2,743. |

### Overprint Inverted

| No. | Type | Description | Unused | Used |
|---|---|---|---|---|
| *J5a* | D1 | 1c black | *200.00* | *200.00* |
| *J6a* | D1 | 2c black | *200.00* | *200.00* |
| *J7a* | D1 | 3c black | *200.00* | *200.00* |
| *J8a* | D1 | 4c black | *200.00* | *200.00* |
| *J9a* | D1 | 5c black | *200.00* | *200.00* |
| *J10a* | D1 | 10c black | *250.00* | *250.00* |
| *J11a* | D1 | 15c black | *200.00* | *200.00* |
| *J15a* | D1 | 60c black | *275.00* | *275.00* |
| *J16a* | D1 | 1fr brown | *550.00* | *550.00* |
| *J17a* | D1 | 2fr brown | *550.00* | *550.00* |

### Double Overprint

| No. | Type | Description | Unused | Used |
|---|---|---|---|---|
| *J5b* | D1 | 1c black | *200.00* | *200.00* |
| *J6b* | D1 | 2c black | *200.00* | *200.00* |
| *J9b* | D1 | 5c black | *250.00* | *250.00* |
| *J10b* | D1 | 10c black | *300.00* | *300.00* |
| *J11b* | D1 | 15c black | *250.00* | *250.00* |
| *J12b* | D1 | 20c black | *250.00* | *250.00* |
| *J13b* | D1 | 30c black | *300.00* | *300.00* |

These handstamped overprints may be found double on some values. Counterfeits exist of Nos. J1-J18.

*No. J1 has been reprinted. The overprint on the original measures 12½x3¾mm and on the reprint 12x3¼mm. Value, $325.*

# OLTRE GIUBA

,ōl-trā-'jü-bə

## (Italian Jubaland)

LOCATION — A strip of land, 50 to 100 miles in width, west of and parallel to the Juba River in East Africa

GOVT. — Former Italian Protectorate

AREA — 33,000 sq. mi.

POP. — 12,000

CAPITAL — Kismayu

Oltre Giuba was ceded to Italy by Great Britain in 1924 and in 1926 was incorporated with Italian Somaliland. In 1936 it became part of Italian East Africa.

100 Centesimi = 1 Lira

### Watermark

Wmk. 140 — Crown

### Italian Stamps of 1901-26 Overprinted

On #1-15

On #16-20

**1925, July 29 Wmk. 140 Perf. 14**

| No. | Type | Description | Unused | Used |
|---|---|---|---|---|
| 1 | A42 | 1c brown | 5.50 | *30.00* |
| *a.* | | Inverted overprint | 475.00 | |
| 2 | A43 | 2c yel brown | 4.25 | *30.00* |
| 3 | A48 | 5c green | 4.25 | *12.50* |
| 4 | A48 | 10c claret | 4.25 | *12.50* |
| 5 | A48 | 15c slate | 4.25 | *17.50* |
| 6 | A50 | 20c brn orange | 4.25 | *17.50* |
| 7 | A49 | 25c blue | 4.25 | *17.50* |
| 8 | A49 | 30c org brown | 5.50 | *22.50* |
| 9 | A49 | 40c brown | 11.00 | *17.50* |
| 10 | A49 | 50c violet | 11.00 | *17.50* |
| 11 | A49 | 60c carmine | 11.00 | *22.50* |
| 12 | A46 | 1 l brn & green | 16.00 | 30.00 |
| 13 | A46 | 2 l dk grn & org | 85.00 | 60.00 |
| 14 | A46 | 5 l blue & rose | 110.00 | 87.50 |
| 15 | A51 | 10 l gray grn & red | 21.00 | *95.00* |
| | | *Nos. 1-15 (15)* | 301.50 | *490.00* |

**1925-26**

| No. | Type | Description | Unused | Used |
|---|---|---|---|---|
| 16 | A49 | 20c green | 7.00 | *17.50* |
| 17 | A49 | 30c gray | 10.00 | *22.50* |
| 18 | A46 | 75c dk red & rose | 42.50 | *95.00* |
| 19 | A46 | 1.25 l bl & ultra | 87.50 | *160.00* |
| 20 | A46 | 2.50 l dk grn & org | 120.00 | *275.00* |
| | | *Nos. 16-20 (5)* | 267.00 | *570.00* |

Issue years: #18-20, 1926; others 1925.

### Victor Emmanuel Issue

Italian Stamps of 1925 Overprinted

**1925-26 Unwmk. Perf. 11**

| No. | Type | Description | Unused | Used |
|---|---|---|---|---|
| 21 | A78 | 60c brown car | 1.60 | *16.00* |
| *a.* | | Perf. 13½ | *12,000.* | |
| 22 | A78 | 1 l dark blue | 1.60 | *25.00* |
| *a.* | | Perf. 13½ | 650.00 | *2,400.* |
| 23 | A78 | 1.25 l dk bl ('26) | 6.50 | *40.00* |
| *a.* | | Perf. 13½ | 6.50 | *40.00* |
| | | *Nos. 21-23 (3)* | 9.70 | *81.00* |

### Saint Francis of Assisi Issue

Italian Stamps and Type of 1926 Overprinted

**1926, Apr. 12 Wmk. 140 Perf. 14**

| No. | Type | Description | Unused | Used |
|---|---|---|---|---|
| 24 | A79 | 20c gray green | 2.50 | *45.00* |
| 25 | A80 | 40c dark violet | 2.50 | *45.00* |
| 26 | A81 | 60c red brown | 2.50 | *65.00* |

### Overprinted in Red

**Unwmk.**

| | | | | |
|---|---|---|---|---|
| **27** | A82 | 1.25 l dk bl, perf. 11 | 2.50 | *87.50* |
| **28** | A83 | 5 l + 2.50 l ol grn, perf. 13½ | 8.00 | *135.00* |
| | | *Nos. 24-28 (5)* | 18.00 | *377.50* |

Map of Oltre Giuba — A1

**1926, Apr. 21 Typo. Wmk. 140**

| | | | | |
|---|---|---|---|---|
| **29** | A1 | 5c yellow brown | 1.60 | *35.00* |
| **30** | A1 | 20c blue green | 1.60 | *35.00* |
| **31** | A1 | 25c olive brown | 1.60 | *35.00* |
| **32** | A1 | 40c dull red | 1.60 | *35.00* |
| **33** | A1 | 60c brown violet | 1.60 | *35.00* |
| **34** | A1 | 1 l blue | 1.60 | *35.00* |
| **35** | A1 | 2 l dark green | 1.60 | *35.00* |
| | | *Nos. 29-35 (7)* | 11.20 | *245.00* |

Oltre Giuba was incorporated with Italian Somaliland on July 1, 1926, and stamps inscribed "Oltre Giuba" were discontinued.

## SEMI-POSTAL STAMPS

Note preceding Italy semi-postals applies to No. 28.

### Colonial Institute Issue

"Peace" Substituting Spade for Sword — SP1

**Wmk. 140**

**1926, June 1 Typo. *Perf. 14***

| | | | | |
|---|---|---|---|---|
| **B1** | SP1 | 5c + 5c brown | 1.20 | *9.50* |
| **B2** | SP1 | 10c + 5c ol grn | 1.20 | *9.50* |
| **B3** | SP1 | 20c + 5c blue grn | 1.20 | *9.50* |
| **B4** | SP1 | 40c + 5c brn red | 1.20 | *9.50* |
| **B5** | SP1 | 60c + 5c orange | 1.20 | *9.50* |
| **B6** | SP1 | 1 l + 5c blue | 1.20 | *20.00* |
| | | *Nos. B1-B6 (6)* | 7.20 | *67.50* |

Surtax for Italian Colonial Institute.

## SPECIAL DELIVERY STAMPS

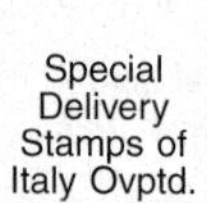

Special Delivery Stamps of Italy Ovptd.

**1926 Wmk. 140 *Perf. 14***

| | | | | |
|---|---|---|---|---|
| **E1** | SD1 | 70c dull red | 32.50 | *65.00* |
| **E2** | SD2 | 2.50 l blue & red | 67.50 | *180.00* |

## POSTAGE DUE STAMPS

### Italian Postage Due Stamps of 1870-1903 Ovptd. Like Nos. E1-E2

**1925, July 29 Wmk. 140 *Perf. 14***

| | | | | |
|---|---|---|---|---|
| **J1** | D3 | 5c buff & magenta | 24.00 | 24.00 |
| **J2** | D3 | 10c buff & magenta | 24.00 | 24.00 |
| **J3** | D3 | 20c buff & magenta | 24.00 | *40.00* |
| **J4** | D3 | 30c buff & magenta | 24.00 | *40.00* |
| **J5** | D3 | 40c buff & magenta | 24.00 | *45.00* |
| **J6** | D3 | 50c buff & magenta | 32.50 | *55.00* |
| **J7** | D3 | 60c buff & brown | 32.50 | *65.00* |
| **J8** | D3 | 1 l blue & magenta | 35.00 | *80.00* |
| **J9** | D3 | 2 l blue & magenta | 175.00 | *275.00* |
| **J10** | D3 | 5 l blue & magenta | 225.00 | 275.00 |
| | | *Nos. J1-J10 (10)* | 620.00 | *923.00* |

## PARCEL POST STAMPS

These stamps were used by affixing them to the waybill so that one half remained on it following the parcel, the other half staying on the receipt given the sender. Most used halves are right halves. Complete stamps were obtainable canceled, probably to order. Both unused and used values are for complete stamps.

### Italian Parcel Post Stamps of 1914-22 Overprinted

**1925, July 29 Wmk. 140 *Perf. 13½***

| | | | | |
|---|---|---|---|---|
| **Q1** | PP2 | 5c brown | 21.00 | *45.00* |
| **Q2** | PP2 | 10c blue | 17.50 | *45.00* |
| **Q3** | PP2 | 20c black | 17.50 | *45.00* |
| **Q4** | PP2 | 25c red | 17.50 | *45.00* |
| **Q5** | PP2 | 50c orange | 21.00 | *45.00* |
| **Q6** | PP2 | 1 l violet | 17.50 | *100.00* |
| *a.* | | Double overprint | 550.00 | |
| **Q7** | PP2 | 2 l green | 28.00 | *100.00* |
| **Q8** | PP2 | 3 l bister | 65.00 | *130.00* |
| **Q9** | PP2 | 4 l slate | 29.00 | *130.00* |
| **Q10** | PP2 | 10 l rose lilac | 95.00 | *225.00* |
| **Q11** | PP2 | 12 l red brown | 175.00 | *350.00* |
| **Q12** | PP2 | 15 l olive green | 160.00 | *350.00* |
| **Q13** | PP2 | 20 l brown violet | 160.00 | *350.00* |
| | | *Nos. Q1-Q13 (13)* | 824.00 | 1,960. |

**Halves Used**

| | |
|---|---|
| Q1-Q4 | 1.75 |
| Q5-Q7 | 3.00 |
| Q8-Q9 | 4.75 |
| Q10 | 9.25 |
| Q11 | 15.00 |
| Q12-Q13 | 10.00 |

# OMAN

'ō-,män

## Muscat and Oman

LOCATION — Southeastern corner of the Arabian Peninsula
GOVT. — Sultanate
AREA — 105,000 sq. mi.
POP. — 2,446,645 (1999 est.)
CAPITAL — Muscat

Nos. 16-93, the stamps with "value only" surcharges, were used not only in Muscat, but also in Dubai (Apr. 1, 1948 - Jan. 6, 1961), Qatar (Aug. 1950 - Mar. 31, 1957), and Abu Dhabi (Mar. 30, 1963 - Mar. 29, 1964). Occasionally they were also used in Bahrain and Kuwait.

The Sultanate of Muscat and Oman changed its name to Oman in 1970.

12 Pies = 1 Anna
16 Annas = 1 Rupee
100 Naye Paise = 1 Rupee (1957)
64 Baizas = 1 Rupee (1966)
1000 Baizas = 1 Rial Saidi (1970)

**Catalogue values for all unused stamps in this country are for Never Hinged items, beginning with No. 25.**

### Muscat

Stamps of India 1937-43 Overprinted in Black

On #1-13 the overprint is smaller — 13x6mm.

**Wmk. Multiple Stars (196)**

**1944, Nov. 20 *Perf. 13½x14***

| | | | | |
|---|---|---|---|---|
| **1** | A83 | 3p slate | .40 | *8.00* |
| **2** | A83 | ½a rose violet | .40 | *8.00* |
| **3** | A83 | 9p lt green | .40 | *8.00* |
| **4** | A83 | 1a carmine rose | .40 | *8.00* |
| **5** | A84 | 1½a dark purple | .40 | *8.00* |
| *a.* | | Double overprint | 300.00 | |
| **6** | A84 | 2a scarlet | .50 | *8.00* |
| **7** | A84 | 3a violet | 1.00 | *8.00* |
| **8** | A84 | 3½a ultra | 1.00 | *8.00* |
| **9** | A85 | 4a chocolate | 1.10 | *8.00* |
| **10** | A85 | 6a pck blue | 1.25 | *8.00* |
| **11** | A85 | 8a blue violet | 1.40 | *8.50* |
| **12** | A85 | 12a car lake | 1.50 | *8.50* |
| **13** | A81 | 14a rose violet | 2.75 | *13.50* |
| **14** | A82 | 1r brown & slate | 1.75 | *12.50* |
| **15** | A82 | 2r dk brn & dk vio | 5.00 | *20.00* |
| | | *Nos. 1-15 (15)* | 19.25 | *143.00* |

200th anniv. of Al Busaid Dynasty.

Used values for Nos. 1-15 are for stamps canceled with contemperaneous postmarks of the Indian postal administration. Examples with later British post office cancellations are worth much less.

### Great Britain, Nos. 258 to 263, 243, 248, 249A Surcharged

***Perf. 14½x14***

**1948, Apr. 1 Wmk. 251**

| | | | | |
|---|---|---|---|---|
| **16** | A101 | ½a on ½p green | 3.00 | *8.00* |
| **17** | A101 | 1a on 1p vermilion | 3.25 | *.30* |
| **18** | A101 | 1½a on 1½p lt red brn | 15.00 | *4.25* |
| **19** | A101 | 2a on 2p lt org | 2.25 | *3.50* |
| **20** | A101 | 2½a on 2½p ultra | 4.25 | *8.50* |
| **21** | A101 | 3a on 3p violet | 4.00 | *.25* |
| **22** | A102 | 6a on 6p rose lilac | 4.50 | *.25* |
| **23** | A103 | 1r on 1sh brown | 5.00 | *.75* |

**Wmk. 259 *Perf. 14***

| | | | | |
|---|---|---|---|---|
| **24** | A104 | 2r on 2sh6p yel grn | 14.00 | *52.50* |
| | | *Nos. 16-24 (9)* | 55.25 | *78.30* |

**Catalogue values for unused stamps in this section from this point to the end of the section are for Never Hinged items.**

### Silver Wedding Issue

Great Britain, Nos. 267 and 268, Surcharged with New Value in Black

***Perf. 14½x14, 14x14½***

**1948, Apr. 26 Wmk. 251**

| | | | | |
|---|---|---|---|---|
| **25** | A109 | 2½a on 2½p brt ultra | 3.50 | *5.00* |
| **26** | A110 | 15r on £1 dp chlky bl | 42.50 | *42.50* |

Three bars obliterate the original denomination on No. 26.

### Olympic Games Issue

Great Britain, Nos. 271 to 274, Surcharged with New Value in Black

**1948, July 29 *Perf. 14½x14***

| | | | | |
|---|---|---|---|---|
| **27** | A113 | 2½a on 2½p brt ultra | .75 | *2.75* |
| **28** | A114 | 3a on 3p dp violet | .85 | *2.75* |
| **29** | A115 | 6a on 6p red violet | .95 | *3.00* |
| **30** | A116 | 1r on 1sh dk brn | 2.25 | *4.25* |
| *a.* | | Double surcharge | 1,500. | |
| | | *Nos. 27-30 (4)* | 4.80 | 12.75 |

A square of dots obliterates the original denomination on Nos. 28-30.

### UPU Issue

Great Britain Nos. 276 to 279 Surcharged with New Value and Square of Dots in Black

**1949, Oct. 10 Photo.**

| | | | | |
|---|---|---|---|---|
| **31** | A117 | 2½a on 2½p brt ultra | .75 | *2.75* |
| **32** | A118 | 3a on 3p brt violet | .95 | *3.75* |
| **33** | A119 | 6a on 6p red violet | 1.10 | *2.50* |
| **34** | A120 | 1r on 1sh brown | 2.75 | *6.75* |
| | | *Nos. 31-34 (4)* | 5.55 | 15.75 |

### Great Britain Nos. 280-286 Surcharged with New Value in Black

**1951**

| | | | | |
|---|---|---|---|---|
| **35** | A101 | ½a on ½p lt org | 1.00 | *9.00* |
| **36** | A101 | 1a on 1p ultra | .60 | *7.50* |
| **37** | A101 | 1½a on 1½p green | 17.00 | *35.00* |
| **38** | A101 | 2a on 2p lt red brn | .85 | *8.00* |
| **39** | A101 | 2½a on 2½p vermilion | 1.50 | *16.00* |
| **40** | A102 | 4a on 4p ultra | 1.25 | *3.25* |

***Perf. 11x12***

**Wmk. 259**

| | | | | |
|---|---|---|---|---|
| **41** | A121 | 2r on 2sh6p green | 45.00 | 7.00 |
| | | *Nos. 35-41 (7)* | 67.20 | *85.75* |

Two types of surcharge on No. 41.

### Stamps of Great Britain, 1952-54, Srchd. with New Value in Black and Dark Blue

**1952-54 Wmk. 298 *Perf. 14½x14***

| | | | | |
|---|---|---|---|---|
| **42** | A126 | ½a on ½p red org ('53) | .35 | *2.00* |
| **43** | A126 | 1a on 1p ultra ('53) | .35 | *2.00* |
| **44** | A126 | 1½a on 1½p grn ('52) | .40 | *2.00* |
| **45** | A126 | 2a on 2p red brn ('53) | .50 | .25 |
| **46** | A127 | 2½a on 2½p scar ('52) | .35 | .25 |
| **47** | A127 | 3a on 3p dk pur (dk bl) | .50 | *1.00* |
| **48** | A128 | 4a on 4p ultra ('53) | 2.25 | *3.75* |
| **49** | A129 | 6a on 6p lilac rose | .60 | .45 |
| **50** | A132 | 12a on 1sh3p dk grn ('53) | 8.00 | .90 |
| **51** | A131 | 1r on 1sh6p dk bl ('53) | 3.00 | .75 |
| | | *Nos. 42-51 (10)* | 16.30 | 13.35 |

### Coronation Issue

Great Britain Nos. 313-316 Surcharged

**1953, June 10**

| | | | | |
|---|---|---|---|---|
| **52** | A134 | 2½a on 2½p scarlet | 2.50 | 3.00 |
| **53** | A135 | 4a on 4p brt ultra | 2.50 | 1.25 |
| **54** | A136 | 12a on 1sh3p dk grn | 4.50 | 1.25 |
| **55** | A137 | 1r on 1sh6p dk blue | 5.75 | 1.00 |
| | | *Nos. 52-55 (4)* | 15.25 | 6.50 |

Squares of dots obliterate the original denominations on Nos. 54-55.

### Great Britain Stamps of 1955-56 Surcharged

***Perf. 14½x14***

**1955-57 Wmk. 308 Photo.**

| | | | | |
|---|---|---|---|---|
| **56** | A126 | 1a on 1p ultra | .50 | *.60* |
| **56A** | A126 | 1½a on 1½p grn | 6,000. | *950.00* |
| **57** | A126 | 2a on 2p red brn | .85 | *2.00* |
| **58** | A127 | 2½a on 2½p scar | 1.00 | *3.00* |
| **59** | A127 | 3a on 3p dk pur | 1.10 | *7.50* |
| **60** | A128 | 4a on 4p ultra | 6.50 | *19.00* |
| **61** | A129 | 6a on 6p lilac rose | 1.40 | *6.50* |
| **62** | A131 | 1r on 1sh6p dk bl | 8.00 | *.50* |

**Engr. *Perf. 11x12***

| | | | | |
|---|---|---|---|---|
| **63** | A133 | 2r on 2sh6p dk brown | 8.00 | 1.50 |
| **64** | A133 | 5r on 5sh crimson | 14.00 | 3.50 |
| | | *Nos. 56,57-64 (9)* | 41.35 | *44.10* |

Surcharge on No. 63 exists in three types, on No. 64 in two types.

Issued: 2r, 9/23/55; 2a, 2½a, 6/8/56; 1r, 8/2/56; 4a, 12/9/56; 1½a, 1956; 3a, 2/3/57; 6a, 2/10/57; 5r, 3/1/57; 1a, 3/4/57.

### Great Britain Nos. 317-325, 328, 332 Surcharged

**1957, Apr. 1 *Perf. 14½x14***

| | | | | |
|---|---|---|---|---|
| **65** | A129 | 1np on 5p lt brown | .25 | *.90* |
| **66** | A126 | 3np on ½p red org | .35 | *2.00* |
| **67** | A126 | 6np on 1p ultra | .40 | *2.25* |
| **68** | A126 | 9np on 1½p green | .50 | *1.50* |
| **69** | A126 | 12np on 2p red brown | .55 | *1.75* |
| **70** | A127 | 15np on 2½p scar, I | .65 | .50 |
| *a.* | | Type II | .55 | *3.00* |
| **71** | A127 | 20np on 3p dk pur | .40 | .30 |
| **72** | A128 | 25np on 4p ultra | 1.00 | *6.00* |
| **73** | A129 | 40np on 6p lilac rose | .75 | .60 |
| **74** | A130 | 50np on 9p dp ol grn | 1.50 | 2.50 |
| **75** | A132 | 75np on 1sh3p dk grn | 3.00 | .75 |
| | | *Nos. 65-75 (11)* | 9.35 | *19.05* |

The arrangement of the surcharge varies on different values; there are three bars through value on No. 74.

### Jubilee Jamboree Issue

Great Britain Nos. 334-336 Surcharged with New Value and Square of Dots

***Perf. 14½x14***

**1957, Aug. 1 Wmk. 308**

| | | | | |
|---|---|---|---|---|
| **76** | A138 | 15np on 2½p scar | 1.40 | 1.50 |
| **77** | A138 | 25np on 4p ultra | 1.40 | 1.50 |
| **78** | A138 | 75np on 1sh3p dk grn | 1.75 | 1.50 |
| | | *Nos. 76-78 (3)* | 4.55 | 4.50 |

50th anniv. of the Boy Scout movement and the World Scout Jubilee Jamboree, Aug. 1-12.

### Great Britain Stamps of 1958-60 Surcharged

***Perf. 14½x14***

**1960-61 Wmk. 322 Photo.**

| | | | | |
|---|---|---|---|---|
| **79** | A129 | 1np on 5p lt brn | .25 | *.30* |
| **80** | A126 | 3np on ½p red org | 1.00 | *1.25* |
| **81** | A126 | 5np on 1p ultra | 1.75 | *3.00* |
| **82** | A126 | 6np on 1p ultra | 1.25 | 1.00 |
| **83** | A126 | 10np on 1½p green | 1.00 | *2.50* |
| **84** | A126 | 12np on 2p red brn | 3.00 | 3.00 |
| **85** | A127 | 15np on 2½p scar | .50 | .25 |
| **86** | A127 | 20np on 3p dk pur | .50 | .25 |
| **87** | A128 | 30np on 4½p hn brn | .75 | *1.10* |
| **88** | A129 | 40np on 6p lil rose | .85 | .30 |
| **89** | A130 | 50np on 9p dp ol grn | 1.50 | *2.25* |
| **90** | A132 | 75np on 1sh3p dk grn | 4.00 | 1.75 |

**91** A131 1r on 1sh6p dk blue 30.00 6.50
**92** A133 2r on 2sh6p dk brn 15.00 *37.50*
**93** A133 5r on 5sh crim 35.00 *55.00*
*Nos. 79-93 (15)* 96.35 *115.95*

Issued: 15np, 4/26; 3np, 6np, 12np, 6/21; 1np, 8/8; 20np, 40np, 9/28; 5np, 10np, 30np, 50np-5r, 4/8/61.

### Muscat and Oman

Crest — A1

View of Harbor — A2

Nakhal Fort — A3

BAIZAS

RUPEES

Crest and: 50b, Samail Fort. 1r, Sohar Fort. 2r, Nizwa Fort. 5r, Matrah Fort. 10r, Mirani Fort.

***Perf. 14½x14 (A1), 14x14½ (A2), 14x13½ (A3)***

**1966, Apr. 29 Photo. Unwmk.**

**94** A1 3b plum .25 .25
**95** A1 5b brown .25 .25
**96** A1 10b red brown .25 .25
**97** A2 15b black & violet 1.00 .25
**98** A2 20b black & ultra 1.50 .25
**99** A2 25b black & orange 2.25 .60
**100** A3 30b dk blue & lil rose 2.75 .65
**101** A3 50b red brn & brt grn 3.75 1.50
*a.* Value in "baizas" in Arabic 225.00 110.00
**102** A3 1r org & dk bl 7.50 1.75
**103** A3 2r grn & brn org 14.00 5.00
**104** A3 5r dp car & vio 30.00 17.00
**105** A3 10r dk vio & car rose 60.00 35.00
*Nos. 94-105 (12)* 123.50 62.75

No. 101 has value in rupees in Arabic.
See Nos. 110-121. For overprints & surcharges see Nos. 122-133C.

Mina al Fahal Harbor A4

Designs: 25b, Oil tanks. 40b, Oil installation in the desert. 1r, View of Arabian Peninsula from Gemini IV.

***Perf. 13½x13***

**1969, Jan. 1 Litho. Unwmk.**

**106** A4 20b multicolored 5.00 1.00
**107** A4 25b multicolored 7.00 1.50
**108** A4 40b multicolored 10.00 2.25
**109** A4 1r multicolored 26.00 6.75
*Nos. 106-109 (4)* 48.00 11.50

1st oil shipment from Muscat & Oman, July, 1967.

### Types of 1966

Designs: 50b, Nakhal Fort. 75b, Samail Fort. 100b, Sohar Fort. ¼r, Nizwa Fort. ½r, Matrah Fort. 1r, Mirani Fort.

***Perf. 14½x14 (A1), 14x14½ (A2), 14x13½ (A3)***

**1970, June 27 Photo. Unwmk.**

**110** A1 5b plum 1.00 .25
**111** A1 10b brown 2.00 .40
**112** A1 20b red brown 2.25 .45
**113** A2 25b black & vio 4.00 .60
**114** A2 30b black & ultra 5.00 1.00
**115** A2 40b black & org 6.00 1.25
**116** A3 50b dk blue & lil rose 8.00 1.50
**117** A3 75b red brn & brt grn 9.50 2.00
**118** A3 100b orange & dk bl 11.00 2.25
**119** A3 ¼r grn & brn org 27.50 6.75
**120** A3 ½r brn car & vio 50.00 19.00
**121** A3 1r dk vio & car rose 90.00 32.50
*Nos. 110-121 (12)* 216.25 67.95

### Sultanate of Oman

Nos. 110-121 Overprinted

a

b

c

5b, 10b 20b:
Type 1 — Lower bars 15¼mm long; letter "A" has low, thick crossbar.
Type 2 — Lower bars 14¾mm; "A" crossbar high, thin.

***Perf. 14½x14, 14x14½, 14x13½***

**1971, Jan. 16 Photo. Unwmk.**

**122** A1 (a) 5b plum 12.50 .60
*a.* Type 2 *60.00 25.00*
**123** A1 (a) 10b brown 35.00 17.50
*a.* Type 2 *65.00 30.00*
**124** A1 (a) 20b red brown 16.00 .80
*a.* Type 2 *70.00 30.00*
**125** A2 (b) 25b black & vio 2.25 .50
**126** A2 (b) 30b black & ultra 3.25 .80
**127** A2 (b) 40b black & org 4.00 1.00
**128** A3 (c) 50b dk bl & lil rose 5.50 1.25
**129** A3 (c) 75b red brn & brt grn 8.25 2.00
**130** A3 (c) 100b org & dk bl 11.00 3.50
**131** A3 (c) ¼r grn & brn org 27.50 8.50
**132** A3 (c) ½r brn car & vio 60.00 15.00
**133** A3 (c) 1r dk vio & car rose 130.00 30.00
*Nos. 122-133 (12)* 315.25 81.45

For surcharge see No. 133B.

### No. 94 Surcharged Type "a," Nos. 127, 102 Surcharged

***Perf. 14½x14, 14x14½, 14½x13½***

**1971-72**

**133A** A1 5b on 3b *170.00 22.50*
**133B** A2 25b on 40b *180.00 160.00*
**133C** A3 25b on 1r *190.00 160.00*
*Nos. 133A-133C (3) 540.00 342.50*

No. 133C surcharge resembles type "c" with "Sultanate of Oman" omitted and bars of criss-cross lines.
No. 133A exists with inverted surchagre and in pair, one with surcharge omitted. No. 133C exists with Arabic "2" or "5" omitted.
Issued: 5b, Nov; #133C, 6/6/7; #133B, 7/1/72.

Sultan Qaboos bin Said and New Buildings — A5

National Day: 40b, Sultan Qaboos and freedom symbols. 50b, Crest of Oman and health clinic. 100b, Crest of Oman, classrooms and school.

**1971, July 23 Litho.** ***Perf. 13½x14***

**134** A5 10b multicolored 3.25 .45
**135** A5 40b multicolored 12.00 .90
**136** A5 50b multicolored 15.00 1.50
**137** A5 100b multicolored 30.00 5.00
*Nos. 134-137 (4)* 60.25 7.85

Open Book A6

**1972, Jan. 3** ***Perf. 14x14½***

**138** A6 25b ap grn, dk bl & dk red 30.00 5.00

International Book Year, 1972.

View of Muscat, 1809 A7

Designs: 5, 10, 20, 25b, View of Matrah, 1809. 30, 40, 50, 75b, View of Shinas, 1809.

**Wmk. 314 Sideways**

**1972, July 23 Litho.** ***Perf. 14x14½***

**Size: 21x17mm**

**139** A7 5b tan & multi 1.00 .30
**140** A7 10b blue & multi 1.75 .30
**141** A7 20b gray grn & multi 2.00 .30
**142** A7 25b violet & multi 2.75 .30

***Perf. 14½x14***

**Size: 25x21mm**

**143** A7 30b tan & multi 3.50 .35
**144** A7 40b gray blue & multi 3.50 .40
**145** A7 50b rose brn & multi 4.50 .50
**146** A7 75b olive & multi 10.00 .90

***Perf. 14***

**Size: 41x25mm**

**147** A7 100b lilac & multi 13.50 1.50
**148** A7 ¼r green & multi 30.00 3.00
**149** A7 ½r bister & multi 57.50 9.50
**150** A7 1r dull bl grn & multi 90.00 19.00
*Nos. 139-150 (12)* 220.00 36.35

***Perf. 14x14½, 14½x14***

**1972-75 Wmk. 314 Upright**

*139a* A7 5b tan & multi ('75) .45 .25
*140a* A7 10b blue & multi ('75) 1.25 .35
*141a* A7 20b gray grn & multi ('75) 2.50 .65
*142a* A7 25b violet & multi ('75) 3.50 .90
*143a* A7 30b tan & multi 4.75 1.20
*144a* A7 40b blue & multi 7.50 1.50
*145a* A7 50b rose brn & multi 8.00 1.75
*146a* A7 75b olive & multi 13.50 5.00
*Nos. 139a-146a (8)* 41.45 11.60

Issue dates: Nov. 17, 1972, Sept. 11, 1975.

***Perf. 14x14½, 14½x14, 14***

**1976-82 Wmk. 373**

*139b* A7 5b tan & multi ('78) .80 .60
*140b* A7 10b blue & multi ('78) 1.25 .50
*141b* A7 20b gray grn & multi ('82) 2.00 .55
*142b* A7 25b vio & multi ('78) 2.50 .60
*143b* A7 30b tan & multi 3.00 .85
*144b* A7 40b blue & multi 4.00 1.25
*145b* A7 50b rose brn & multi 5.00 1.40
*146b* A7 75b olive & multi 8.75 1.60
*147b* A7 100b lilac & multi 9.00 2.25
*148a* A7 ¼r grn & multi ('78) 26.00 6.50
*149a* A7 ½r bister & multi 37.50 11.00
*150a* A7 1r dull bl grn & multi 90.00 22.50
*Nos. 139b-150a (12)* 189.80 49.60

Issued: 4/12/76; 1/27/78; 3/15/82.

Ministerial Complex — A8

**Litho.; Date Typo.**

**1973, Sept. 20 Unwmk.** ***Perf. 13***

**151** A8 25b emerald & multi 4.25 1.25
**152** A8 100b brown org & multi 15.00 3.00

Opening of ministerial complex.
Nos. 151-152 exist with date omitted and hyphen omitted.

Dhows — A9

***Perf. 12½x12***

**1973, Nov. 18 Litho. Wmk. 314**

**153** A9 15b shown 2.25 .55
**154** A9 50b Seeb Airport 10.00 2.25
**155** A9 65b Dhow and tanker 11.00 2.50
**156** A9 100b Camel rider 17.50 4.00
*Nos. 153-156 (4)* 40.75 9.30

National Day.

Port Qaboos — A10

**1974, July 30 Litho.** ***Perf. 13***

**157** A10 100b multicolored 18.00 5.00

Opening of Port Qaboos.

Open Book, Map of Arab World A11

100b, Hands reaching for book, vert.

**1974, Sept. 8 Wmk. 314** ***Perf. 14½***

**158** A11 25b multicolored 3.75 .55
**159** A11 100b multicolored 12.00 3.25

International Literacy Day, Sept. 8.

Sultan Qaboos, UPU and Arab Postal Union Emblems — A12

**1974, Oct. 29 Litho.** ***Perf. 13½***

**160** A12 100b multicolored 5.00 2.00

Centenary of Universal Postal Union.

Arab Scribe A13

**1975, May 8 Photo.** ***Perf. 13x14***

**161** A13 25b multicolored 12.00 3.00

Eradication of illiteracy.

New Harbor at Mina Raysoot — A14

Designs: 50b, Stadium and map of Oman. 75b, Water desalination plant. 100b, Oman color television station. 150b, Satellite earth station and map. 250b, Telephone, radar, cable and map.

*Perf. 14x13½*

**1975, Nov. 18 Litho. Wmk. 373**

| | | | | |
|---|---|---|---|---|
| 162 | A14 | 30b multicolored | 1.50 | .65 |
| 163 | A14 | 50b multicolored | 3.00 | .75 |
| 164 | A14 | 75b multicolored | 4.00 | 1.25 |
| 165 | A14 | 100b multicolored | 5.50 | 2.25 |
| 166 | A14 | 150b multicolored | 7.50 | 3.25 |
| 167 | A14 | 250b multicolored | 14.00 | 7.00 |
| | | *Nos. 162-167 (6)* | 35.50 | 15.15 |

National Day 1975.
For surcharges see Nos. 190A, 190C.

Mother with Child, Nurse, Globe, Red Crescent, IWY Emblem — A15

Design: 150b, Hand shielding mother and children, Omani flag, IWY emblem, vert.

*Perf. 13½x14, 14x13½*

**1975, Dec. 27 Litho.**

| | | | | |
|---|---|---|---|---|
| 168 | A15 | 75b citron & multi | 4.00 | 1.25 |
| 169 | A15 | 150b ultra & multi | 6.50 | 2.25 |

International Women's Year 1975.
For surcharge see No. 190B.

Sultan Presenting Colors and Opening Seeb-Nizwa Road — A16

National Day: 40b, Paratroopers bailing out from plane and mechanized harvester. 75b, Helicopter squadron and Victory Day procession. 150b, Army building road and Salalah television station.

**1976, Nov. 15 Litho. *Perf. 14½***

| | | | | |
|---|---|---|---|---|
| 173 | A16 | 25b multicolored | 1.25 | .25 |
| 174 | A16 | 40b multicolored | 3.50 | .50 |
| 175 | A16 | 75b multicolored | 7.00 | 1.50 |
| 176 | A16 | 150b multicolored | 8.75 | 2.50 |
| | | *Nos. 173-176 (4)* | 20.50 | 4.75 |

Great Bath at Mohenjo-Daro — A17

**1977, Jan. 6 Wmk. 373 *Perf. 13½***

| | | | | |
|---|---|---|---|---|
| 177 | A17 | 125b multicolored | 8.25 | 3.00 |

UNESCO campaign to save Mohenjo-Daro excavations in Pakistan.

APU Emblem, Members' Flags — A18

**1977, Apr. 4 Litho. *Perf. 12***

| | | | | |
|---|---|---|---|---|
| 178 | A18 | 30b emerald & multi | 3.50 | 1.00 |
| 179 | A18 | 75b blue & multi | 8.00 | 2.75 |

Arab Postal Union, 25th anniversary.

Coffeepots — A19

Designs: 75b, Earthenware. 100b, Stone tablet, Khor Rori, 100 B.C. 150b, Jewelry.

**1977, Nov. 18 Litho. *Perf. 13½***

| | | | | |
|---|---|---|---|---|
| 180 | A19 | 40b multicolored | 2.00 | .50 |
| 181 | A19 | 75b multicolored | 4.00 | 1.00 |
| 182 | A19 | 100b multicolored | 6.00 | 1.50 |
| 183 | A19 | 150b multicolored | 9.00 | 2.00 |
| | | *Nos. 180-183 (4)* | 21.00 | 5.00 |

National Day 1977.

Forts A20

**Wmk. 373**

**1978, Nov. 18 Litho. *Perf. 14***

| | | | | |
|---|---|---|---|---|
| 184 | A20 | 20b Jalali | 1.25 | .30 |
| 185 | A20 | 25b Nizwa | 1.50 | .40 |
| 186 | A20 | 40b Rostaq | 3.50 | .80 |
| 187 | A20 | 50b Sohar | 4.00 | .90 |
| 188 | A20 | 75b Bahla | 4.50 | 1.50 |
| 189 | A20 | 100b Jibrin | 7.50 | 2.00 |
| | | *Nos. 184-189 (6)* | 22.25 | 5.90 |

National Day 1978.

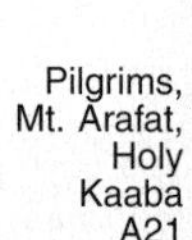

Pilgrims, Mt. Arafat, Holy Kaaba A21

**1978, Nov. 1 Litho. *Perf. 13½***

| | | | | |
|---|---|---|---|---|
| 190 | A21 | 40b multicolored | 7.25 | 2.50 |

Pilgrimage to Mecca.

**Nos. 166, 169 and 167 Surcharged**

*Perf. 14x13½*

**1978, July 30 Litho. Wmk. 373**

| | | | | |
|---|---|---|---|---|
| 190A | A14 | 40b on 150b | *450.00* | *450.00* |
| 190B | A15 | 50b on 150b | *475.00* | *475.00* |
| 190C | A14 | 75b on 250b | *2,250.* | *2,250.* |
| | | *Nos. 190A-190C (3)* | *3,175.* | *3,175.* |

World Map, Book, Symbols of Learning A22

**1979, Mar. 22 Litho. *Perf. 14x13½***

| | | | | |
|---|---|---|---|---|
| 191 | A22 | 40b multicolored | 2.75 | .60 |
| 192 | A22 | 100b multicolored | 5.50 | 1.50 |

Cultural achievements of the Arabs.

Girl on Swing, IYC Emblem A23

**1979, Oct. 28 Litho. *Perf. 14***

| | | | | |
|---|---|---|---|---|
| 193 | A23 | 40b multicolored | 6.00 | 2.50 |

International Year of the Child.

Gas Plant — A24

National Day: 75b, Fisheries.

**1979, Nov. 18 Photo. *Perf. 11½***

| | | | | |
|---|---|---|---|---|
| 194 | A24 | 25b multicolored | 3.50 | .85 |
| 195 | A24 | 75b multicolored | 9.00 | 2.75 |

Sultan on Horseback, Military Symbols — A25

Design: 100b, Soldier, parachutes, tank.

**1979, Dec. 11**

| | | | | |
|---|---|---|---|---|
| 196 | A25 | 40b multicolored | 8.50 | 1.75 |
| 197 | A25 | 100b multicolored | 14.00 | 4.00 |

Armed Forces Day.

Hegira (Pilgrimage Year) — A26

**1980, Nov. 9 Photo. *Perf. 11½***

| | | | | |
|---|---|---|---|---|
| 198 | A26 | 50b shown | 7.00 | 1.10 |
| 199 | A26 | 150b Hegira emblem | 11.00 | 3.75 |

Omani Women — A27

75b, Bab Alkabir. 100b, Corniche Highway. 250b, Polo match.

**1980, Nov. 18 Granite Paper**

| | | | | |
|---|---|---|---|---|
| 200 | A27 | 75b multi | 2.75 | 1.10 |
| 201 | A27 | 100b multi | 4.00 | 2.00 |
| 202 | A27 | 250b multi | 7.00 | 4.75 |
| 203 | A27 | 500b shown | 14.00 | 8.75 |
| | | *Nos. 200-203 (4)* | 27.75 | 16.60 |

10th National Day.
For surcharges see Nos. 212-213.

Sultan and Patrol Boat — A28

750b, Sultan, mounted troops.

**1980, Dec. 11 Granite Paper**

| | | | | |
|---|---|---|---|---|
| 204 | A28 | 150b shown | 6.00 | 3.00 |
| 205 | A28 | 750b multi | 32.50 | 15.00 |

Armed Forces Day.
For surcharges see Nos. 210-211.

Policewoman and Children Crossing Street — A29

100b, Marching band. 150b, Mounted police on beach. ½r, Headquarters.

**1981, Feb. 7 Litho. *Perf. 13½x14***

| | | | | |
|---|---|---|---|---|
| 206 | A29 | 50b shown | 4.00 | 1.00 |
| 207 | A29 | 100b multi | 5.00 | 2.00 |
| 208 | A29 | 150b multi | 6.00 | 3.00 |
| 209 | A29 | ½r multi | 15.00 | 9.50 |
| | | *Nos. 206-209 (4)* | 30.00 | 15.50 |

First National Police Day.

**Nos. 204-205, 200, 203 Surcharged in Black on Silver**

**1981, Apr. 8 Photo. *Perf. 11½***

| | | | | |
|---|---|---|---|---|
| 210 | A28 | 20b on 150b multi | 5.50 | 1.00 |
| 211 | A28 | 30b on 750b multi | 7.00 | 1.25 |
| 212 | A27 | 50b on 75b multi | 8.00 | 2.25 |
| 213 | A27 | 100b on 500b multi | 13.00 | 3.75 |
| | | *Nos. 210-213 (4)* | 33.50 | 8.25 |

Welfare of the Blind — A30

**1981, Oct. 14 Photo. *Perf. 11½***

| | | | | |
|---|---|---|---|---|
| 214 | A30 | 10b multicolored | 27.50 | 2.75 |

World Food Day — A31

**1981, Oct. 16 Photo. *Perf. 12***

| | | | | |
|---|---|---|---|---|
| 215 | A31 | 50b multicolored | 7.50 | 2.50 |

Hegira (Pilgrimage Year) — A32

**1981, Oct. 25 Litho. *Perf. 14½***

| | | | | |
|---|---|---|---|---|
| 216 | A32 | 50b multicolored | 8.25 | 3.25 |

11th Natl. Day — A32a

160b, Al-Razha match (sword vs. stick). 300b, Sultan, map, vert.

**1981, Nov. 18 Photo. *Perf. 12***

| | | | | |
|---|---|---|---|---|
| **216A** | A32a | 160b multicolored | 6.00 | 3.25 |
| **216B** | A32a | 300b multicolored | 10.00 | 5.00 |

Voyage of Sinbad A33

50b, Muscat Port, 1981. 100b, Dhow Shohar. 130b, Map. 200b, Muscat Harbor, 1650.

**1981, Nov. 23 Litho. *Perf. 14½x14***

| | | | | |
|---|---|---|---|---|
| **217** | A33 | 50b multicolored | 2.50 | 1.10 |
| **218** | A33 | 100b multicolored | 5.25 | 3.00 |
| **219** | A33 | 130b multicolored | 6.25 | 4.00 |
| **220** | A33 | 200b multicolored | 8.75 | 5.50 |
| *a.* | | Souvenir sheet of 4, #217-220 | 57.50 | 57.50 |
| | | *Nos. 217-220 (4)* | 22.75 | 13.60 |

Armed Forces Day — A34

**1981, Dec. 11 Photo. *Perf. 11½***

| | | | | |
|---|---|---|---|---|
| **221** | A34 | 100b Sultan, planes | 7.00 | 3.25 |
| **222** | A34 | 400b Patrol boats | 18.00 | 8.75 |

Natl. Police Day A35

**1982, Jan. 5 Litho. *Perf. 14½***

| | | | | |
|---|---|---|---|---|
| **223** | A35 | 50b Patrol launch | 3.75 | 1.50 |
| **224** | A35 | 100b Band, vert. | 6.50 | 3.00 |

Nerium Mascatense A36

Red-legged Partridge A37

10b, Dionysia mira. 20b, Teucrium mascatense. 25b, Geranium mascatense. 30b, Cymatium boschi, horiz. 40b, Acteon eloiseae, horiz. 50b, Cypraea teulerei, horiz. 75b, Cypraea pulchra, horiz. ¼r, Hoopoe. ½r, Tahr. 1r, Arabian oryx.

**1982, July 7 Photo. *Perf. 12½***
**Granite Paper**

| | | | | |
|---|---|---|---|---|
| **225** | A36 | 5b multicolored | .35 | .25 |
| **226** | A36 | 10b multicolored | .35 | .25 |
| **227** | A36 | 20b multicolored | .65 | .25 |
| **228** | A36 | 25b multicolored | .65 | .30 |
| **229** | A36 | 30b multicolored | 1.00 | .45 |
| **230** | A36 | 40b multicolored | 1.00 | .55 |
| **231** | A36 | 50b multicolored | 1.25 | .65 |
| **232** | A36 | 75b multicolored | 1.50 | .95 |
| **233** | A37 | 100b multicolored | 5.00 | 1.25 |
| **234** | A37 | ¼r multicolored | 11.50 | 5.75 |

**Size: 25x38mm**

| | | | | |
|---|---|---|---|---|
| **235** | A37 | ½r multicolored | 14.00 | 8.25 |
| **236** | A37 | 1r multicolored | 22.50 | 15.50 |
| | | *Nos. 225-236 (12)* | 59.75 | 34.40 |

2nd Municipalities Week (1981) — A38

**1982, Oct. 28 Litho. *Perf. 13½x14½***

| | | | | |
|---|---|---|---|---|
| **237** | A38 | 40b multicolored | 8.50 | 3.00 |

ITU Plenipotentiaries Conference, Nairobi, Sept. — A39

**1982, Nov. 6 *Perf. 14½x13½***

| | | | | |
|---|---|---|---|---|
| **238** | A39 | 100b multicolored | 12.00 | 4.00 |

12th Natl. Day A40

40b, State Consultative Council inaugural session. 100b, Oil refinery.

**1982, Nov. 18 *Perf. 12***

| | | | | |
|---|---|---|---|---|
| **239** | A40 | 40b multicolored | 5.00 | 2.00 |
| **240** | A40 | 100b multicolored | 9.50 | 3.50 |

Armed Forces Day — A41

**1982, Dec. 11 *Perf. 13½x14***

| | | | | |
|---|---|---|---|---|
| **241** | A41 | 50b Soldiers | 5.00 | 2.00 |
| **242** | A41 | 100b Mounted band | 9.50 | 4.00 |

Arab Palm Tree Day — A42

***Perf. 13½x14½***
**1982, Sept. 19 Litho.**

| | | | | |
|---|---|---|---|---|
| **243** | A42 | 40b Picking coconuts | 5.50 | 2.25 |
| **244** | A42 | 100b Dates | 11.00 | 3.50 |

Natl. Police Day — A43

**1983, Jan. 5 Litho. *Perf. 14x13½***

| | | | | |
|---|---|---|---|---|
| **245** | A43 | 50b multicolored | 8.50 | 2.50 |

World Communications Year — A44

**1983, May 17 *Perf. 13½x14***

| | | | | |
|---|---|---|---|---|
| **246** | A44 | 50b multicolored | 6.75 | 2.50 |

Bees — A45

Designs: a, Beehive. b, Bee, flower.

**1983, Aug. 15 Litho. *Perf. 13½***

| | | | | |
|---|---|---|---|---|
| **247** | A45 | Pair | 22.50 | 22.50 |
| *a.-b.* | | 50b any single | 5.00 | 3.25 |

Hegira (Pilgrimage Year) — A46

**1983, Sept. 14 Photo. *Perf. 13½***

| | | | | |
|---|---|---|---|---|
| **248** | A46 | 40b multicolored | 11.50 | 3.25 |

Youth Year — A47

***Perf. 12½x13½***
**1983, Nov. 15 Litho.**

| | | | | |
|---|---|---|---|---|
| **249** | A47 | 50b multicolored | 7.00 | 2.75 |

National Day 1983 — A48

50b, Sohar Copper Factory. 100b, Sultan Qaboos University.

**1983, Nov. 18 Litho. *Perf. 13½x14***

| | | | | |
|---|---|---|---|---|
| **250** | A48 | 50b multicolored | 5.25 | 2.25 |
| **251** | A48 | 100b multicolored | 9.25 | 4.50 |

Armed Forces Day A49

**1983, Dec. 11 Litho. *Perf. 13½x14***

| | | | | |
|---|---|---|---|---|
| **252** | A49 | 100b multicolored | 8.50 | 3.00 |

Police Day A50

**1984, Jan. 5 Litho. *Perf. 13½x14***

| | | | | |
|---|---|---|---|---|
| **253** | A50 | 100b multicolored | 11.00 | 3.50 |

7th Arabian Gulf Soccer Tournament, Muscat, Mar. 9-26 — A51

**1984, Mar. 9 Litho. *Perf. 13½***

| | | | | |
|---|---|---|---|---|
| **254** | A51 | 40b Players, cup, vert. | 3.50 | 1.60 |
| **255** | A51 | 50b Emblem | 5.75 | 2.50 |

Pilgrims at Stone-Throwing Ceremony — A52

**1984, Sept. 5 Litho. *Perf. 13½x14***

| | | | | |
|---|---|---|---|---|
| **256** | A52 | 50b multicolored | 7.50 | 2.75 |

Pilgrimage to Mecca.

National Day 1984 — A53

130b, Mail sorting, new p.o. 160b, Map, vert.

***Perf. 13½x14, 14x13½***
**1984, Nov. 18 Litho.**

| | | | | |
|---|---|---|---|---|
| **257** | A53 | 130b multicolored | 7.50 | 3.25 |
| **258** | A53 | 160b multicolored | 9.50 | 4.00 |

Inauguration of the new Central P.O., development of telecommunications.

16th Arab Scout Conference, Muscat — A54

No. 259, Setting-up camp. No. 260, Map reading. No. 261, Saluting natl. flag. No. 262, Scouts and girl guides.

**1984, Dec. 5 Litho. *Perf. 14½***
**259** A54 50b multicolored 2.25 .75
**260** A54 50b multicolored 2.25 .75
*a.* Pair, #259-260 9.50 9.50
**261** A54 130b multicolored 7.00 2.25
**262** A54 130b multicolored 7.00 2.25
*a.* Pair, #261-262 22.50 22.50
*Nos. 259-262 (4)* 18.50 6.00

Armed Forces Day A55

**1984, Dec. 11 *Perf. 13½x14***
**263** A55 100b multicolored 11.50 4.50

Police Day — A56

**1985, Jan. 5 *Perf. 14x13½***
**264** A56 100b multicolored 11.50 4.00

Hegira (Pilgrimage Year) — A57

50b, Al-Khaif Mosque, Mina.

**1985, Aug. 20 Litho. *Perf. 13½x14***
**265** A57 50b multicolored 6.75 2.00

Intl. Youth Year A58

50b, Emblems. 100b, Emblem, youth activities.

**1985, Sept. 22 Litho. *Perf. 13½x14***
**266** A58 50b multicolored 3.75 1.00
**267** A58 100b multicolored 6.75 2.25

Jabrin Palace Restoration — A59

**1985, Sept. 22 Litho. *Perf. 13½x14***
**268** A59 100b Interior 3.50 2.00
**269** A59 250b Restored ceiling 8.75 5.75

Intl. Symposium on Traditional Music — A60

**1985, Oct. 6 Litho. *Perf. 13½x14***
**270** A60 50b multicolored 6.50 2.00

UN Child Survival Campaign — A61

**1985, Oct. 25 Litho. *Perf. 13½x14***
**271** A61 50b multicolored 5.25 1.50

Flags, Map and Sultan Qaboos — A62

50b, Supreme Council, vert.

**1985, Nov. 3 Litho. *Perf. 12½***
**272** A62 40b shown 3.25 1.25
**273** A62 50b multi 4.25 1.50

6th Session of Arab Gulf States Supreme Council, Muscat.

Natl. Day 1985 — A63

Progress and development. 20b, Sultan Qaboos University. 50b, Date picking, plowing field. 100b, Port Qaboos Cement Factory. 200b, Post, transportation and communications. 250b, Sultan Qaboos, vert.

**1985, Nov. 18**
**274** A63 20b multicolored 1.10 1.00
**275** A63 50b multicolored 2.75 2.00
**276** A63 100b multicolored 5.00 3.00
**277** A63 200b multicolored 8.25 5.25
**278** A63 250b multicolored 9.75 6.00
*Nos. 274-278 (5)* 26.85 17.25

Armed Forces Day A64

**1985, Dec. 11 *Perf. 13½x14***
**279** A64 100b multicolored 10.50 2.25

Fish and Crustaceans A65

20b, Chaetodon collaris. 50b, Chaetodon melapterus. 100b, Chaetodon gardineri. 150b, Scomberomorus commerson. 200b, Panulirus homarus.

***Perf. 11½x12, 12x11½***
**1985, Dec. 15 Photo.**
**280** A65 20b multicolored .65 .25
**281** A65 50b multicolored 1.25 .45
**282** A65 100b multicolored 2.00 1.00
**283** A65 150b multicolored 3.00 2.10
**284** A65 200b multicolored 4.25 2.75
*Nos. 280-284 (5)* 11.15 6.55

Nos. 280-282, vert.

Frankincense Trees in Oman — A66

**1985, Dec. 15 Litho. *Perf. 13½x14***
**285** A66 100b multicolored 1.75 1.25
**286** A66 3r multicolored 47.50 32.50

Police Day A67

50b, Camel Corps, Muscat.

**1986, Jan. 5 Litho. *Perf. 13½x14***
**287** A67 50b multi 5.75 1.75

Statue of Liberty, Cent. A68

Maps and: 50b, Sultanah, voyage from Muscat to US 1840. 100b, Statue, Shabab Oman voyage from Oman to US, 1986, and fortress.

**1986, July 4 *Perf. 14½***
**288** A68 50b multicolored 4.75 1.75
**289** A68 100b multicolored 8.00 3.00
*a.* Souvenir sheet of 2, #288-289 32.50 22.50

No. 289a sold for 250b.

Pilgrimage to Mecca — A69

**1986, Aug. 9**
**290** A69 50b Holy Kaaba 4.75 1.50

17th Arab Scout Camp — A70

**1986, Aug. 20**
**291** A70 50b Erecting tent 3.50 1.25
**292** A70 100b Surveying 5.50 2.50

Sultan Qaboos Sports Complex Inauguration — A71

**1986, Oct. 18 Litho. *Perf. 14½***
**293** A71 100b multicolored 4.50 2.00

Intl. Peace Year A72

**1986, Oct. 24 *Perf. 13½x13***
**294** A72 130b multicolored 4.50 1.75

A73

A74

Natl. Day 1986 — A75

**1986, Nov. 18 *Perf. 14½***
**295** A73 50b mutlicolored 1.75 1.00
**296** A74 100b multicolored 4.25 2.10
***Perf. 13½x13***
**297** A75 130b multicolored 5.00 2.50
*Nos. 295-297 (3)* 11.00 5.60

Police Day A76

**1987, Jan. 5 *Perf. 13½x14***
**298** A76 50b multicolored 4.25 1.75

Second Arab Gulf Week for Social Work, Bahrain A77

**1987, Mar. 21 *Perf. 13½x13***
**299** A77 50b multicolored 3.50 1.25

Intl. Environment Day — A78

50b, Flamingos in flight. 130b, Irrigation canal, vert.

*Perf. 13½x13, 13x13½*

**1987, June 5** **Litho.**

| | | | |
|---|---|---|---|
| **300** A78 50b multi | | 3.00 | 1.00 |
| **301** A78 130b multi | | 5.00 | 1.50 |

Pilgrimage to Mecca A79

Stages of Pilgrimage (not in consecutive order): a, Pilgrims walking the tawaf, circling the Holy Kaaba 7 times. b, Tent City, Mina. c, Symbolic stoning of Satan. d, Pilgrims in Muzdalifah at dusk, picking up stones. e, Veneration of the prophet (pilgrims praying), Medina. f, Pilgrims wearing ihram, Pilgrim's Village, Jeddah.

**1987, July 29** **Litho.** ***Perf. 13½***

| | | |
|---|---|---|
| **302** Strip of 6 | 25.00 | 25.00 |
| *a.-f.* A79 50b any single | 1.75 | 1.25 |

Third Municipalities Month — A80

**1987, Oct. 1** ***Perf. 13x13½***

| | | |
|---|---|---|
| **303** A80 50b multicolored | 2.75 | 1.10 |

Natl. Day A81

Designs: 50b, Marine Biology and Fisheries Center. 130b, Royal Hospital.

**1987, Nov. 18** **Litho.** ***Perf. 13½x13***

| | | |
|---|---|---|
| **304** A81 50b multicolored | 1.25 | .75 |
| **305** A81 130b multicolored | 3.00 | 2.00 |

Royal Omani Amateur Radio Soc., 15th Anniv. — A82

**1987, Dec. 23** **Litho.** ***Perf. 13½x13***

| | | |
|---|---|---|
| **306** A82 130b multicolored | 4.20 | 1.75 |

Traditional Handicrafts — A83

**1988, June 1** **Photo.** ***Perf. 12x11½***

**Granite Paper**

| | | |
|---|---|---|
| **307** A83 50b Weaver | 1.25 | .75 |
| **308** A83 100b Potter | 2.00 | 1.00 |
| **309** A83 150b Halwa maker | 2.75 | 1.75 |
| **310** A83 200b Silversmith | 3.25 | 2.25 |
| *a.* Souvenir sheet of 4, #307-310 | 20.00 | 17.50 |
| *Nos. 307-310 (4)* | 9.25 | 5.75 |

No. 310a sold for 600b.

1988 Summer Olympics, Seoul — A84

**1988, Sept. 17** **Litho.** ***Perf. 14½***

| | | |
|---|---|---|
| **311** A84 100b Equestrian | 1.75 | 1.10 |
| **312** A84 100b Field hockey | 1.75 | 1.10 |
| **313** A84 100b Soccer | 1.75 | 1.10 |
| **314** A84 100b Running | 1.75 | 1.10 |
| **315** A84 100b Swimming | 1.75 | 1.10 |
| **316** A84 100b Shooting | 1.75 | 1.10 |
| *a.* Block of 6, #311-316 | 22.50 | 22.50 |
| *b.* Souvenir sheet of 6, #311-316 | 30.00 | 30.00 |

WHO, 40th Anniv. — A85

**1988, Nov. 1** **Litho.** ***Perf. 13½***

| | | |
|---|---|---|
| **317** A85 100b multicolored | 2.50 | 1.50 |

Natl. Day, Agriculture Year A86

**1988, Nov. 18** ***Perf. 14½x13½***

| | | |
|---|---|---|
| **318** A86 100b Tending crops | 1.75 | 1.25 |
| **319** A86 100b Animal husbandry | 1.75 | 1.25 |
| *a.* Pair, #318-319 | 5.25 | 5.25 |

No. 319a has a continuous design.

Women Wearing Regional Folk Costume — A87

Designs: 200b-1r, Men wearing regional folk costumes.

**1989** **Photo.** ***Perf. 11½x12***

**Granite Paper**

| | | |
|---|---|---|
| **320** A87 30b Dhahira | .75 | .25 |
| **321** A87 40b Eastern | 1.00 | .40 |
| **322** A87 50b Batinah | 1.25 | .55 |
| **323** A87 100b Interior | 2.00 | 1.00 |
| **324** A87 130b Southern | 2.50 | 2.25 |
| **325** A87 150b Muscat | 3.50 | 2.75 |
| *a.* Souvenir sheet of 6, #320-325 | 22.50 | 22.50 |
| **326** A87 200b Dhahira | 2.00 | 1.40 |
| **327** A87 ¼r Eastern | 2.50 | 1.60 |
| **328** A87 ½r Southern | 4.00 | 4.00 |
| **329** A87 1r Muscat | 8.50 | 6.75 |
| *a.* Souvenir sheet of 4, #326-329 | 35.00 | 32.50 |
| *Nos. 320-329 (10)* | 28.00 | 20.95 |

No. 325a sold for 700b, No. 329a for 2r. Issued: 30b-150b, 8/26; 200b-1r, 11/11.

National Day, Agriculture Year — A88

**1989, Nov. 18** ***Perf. 12½x13***

| | | |
|---|---|---|
| **330** A88 100b Fishing | 2.00 | 1.00 |
| **331** A88 100b Farming | 2.00 | 1.00 |
| *a.* Pair, #330-331 | 5.00 | 4.50 |

Printed se-tenant in a continuous design.

10th Session of Supreme Council of the Cooperation Council for Arab Gulf States — A89

No. 332, Flags, Omani crest. No. 333, Sultan Qaboos, council emblem.

**1989, Dec. 18** **Litho.** ***Perf. 13x12***

| | | |
|---|---|---|
| **332** A89 50b multi | 2.25 | .75 |
| **333** A89 50b multi | 2.25 | .75 |
| *a.* Pair, #332-333 | 5.00 | 4.00 |

No. 333a has a continuous design.

Gulf Investment Corp., 5th Anniv. (in 1989) — A90

**1990, Jan. 1** **Litho.** ***Perf. 13x12***

| | | |
|---|---|---|
| **334** A90 50b multicolored | 2.50 | 1.00 |
| **335** A90 130b multicolored | 3.25 | 1.75 |

Gulf Air, 40th Anniv. A91

**1990, Mar. 24** ***Perf. 13x13½***

| | | |
|---|---|---|
| **336** A91 80b multicolored | 6.00 | 2.00 |

Symposium on the Oman Ophiolite — A92

**1990, Apr. 22** **Photo.** ***Perf. 11½***

**Granite Paper**

| | | |
|---|---|---|
| **337** A92 80b shown | 1.75 | 1.00 |
| **338** A92 150b multicolored | 3.50 | 2.00 |

First Omani Envoy to the U.S., 150th Anniv. A93

**1990, Apr. 30** **Litho.** ***Perf. 13***

| | | |
|---|---|---|
| **339** A93 200b multicolored | 3.50 | 2.00 |

Sultan Qaboos Rose — A94

**1990, May 5** **Photo.** ***Perf. 11½***

**Granite Paper**

| | | |
|---|---|---|
| **340** A94 200b multicolored | 3.25 | 2.00 |

20th National Day A95

100b, Natl. Day emblem. 200b, Sultan Qaboos.

**Litho. & Embossed**

**1990, Nov. 18** ***Perf. 12x11½***

**Granite Paper**

| | | |
|---|---|---|
| **341** A95 100b gold, red & green | 1.50 | 1.00 |
| **342** A95 200b gold, green & red | 3.75 | 2.10 |
| *a.* Souvenir sheet of 2, #341-342 | 8.50 | 8.50 |

No. 342a sold for 500b.

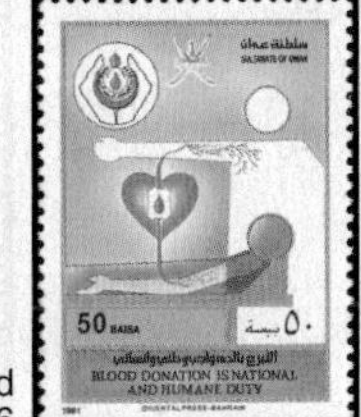
Blood Donors — A96

**1991, Apr. 22** **Litho.** ***Perf. 13½x13***

| | | |
|---|---|---|
| **343** A96 50b multicolored | .80 | .60 |
| **344** A96 200b multicolored | 4.25 | 2.00 |
| *a.* Pair, #343-344 | 25.00 | 25.00 |

National Day — A97

**1991, Nov. 18** **Photo.** ***Perf. 13½***

| | | |
|---|---|---|
| **345** A97 100b shown | 3.50 | 1.10 |
| **346** A97 200b Sultan Qaboos | 5.75 | 2.25 |
| *a.* Souvenir sheet of 2, #345-346 | 10.00 | 8.00 |

No. 346a sold for 400b.

Armed Forces Day
A98

**1991, Dec. 11 Litho. *Perf. 14½***
**347** A98 100b multicolored 3.50 1.25

A99

**1992, Jan. 29 Litho. *Perf. 13½x14***
**348** A99 100b multicolored 3.25 1.25
*a.* Sheet of 1, perf. 13x13½ 13.00 9.00

Inauguration of Omani-French Museum, Muscat. No. 348a sold for 300b.

A100

**1992, Mar. 23 Litho. *Perf. 14½***
**349** A100 200b multicolored 4.25 1.75

World Meteorological Day.

A101

**1992, June 5 Litho. *Perf. 13x13½***
**350** A101 100b multicolored 2.50 1.25

World Environment Day.

A102

**1992, Sept. 26 Litho. *Perf. 13½x14***
**351** A102 70b multicolored 2.50 .75

Welfare of Handicapped Children.

Sultan Qaboos Encyclopedia of Arab Names — A103

**1992, Oct. 10 *Perf. 14½***
**352** A103 100b gold & multi 2.50 1.25

National Day — A104

Sultan Qaboos and emblems of: 100b, Year of Industry. 200b, Majlis As'shura.

**1992, Nov. 18 Litho. *Perf. 14x13½***
**353** A104 100b multicolored 3.00 1.75
**354** A104 200b multicolored 4.25 2.50

Royal Oman Police Day
A105

**1993, Jan. 5 Litho. *Perf. 13½x14***
**355** A105 80b multicolored 3.25 1.10

1993 Census
A106

**1993, Sept. 4 Litho. *Perf. 14x13½***
**356** A106 100b multicolored 2.50 1.25

Royal Navy Day — A107

**1993, Nov. 3 Litho. *Perf. 13***
**357** A107 100b multicolored 3.25 1.50

23rd National Day
A108

**1993, Nov. 18 Photo. *Perf. 12***
**Granite Paper**
**358** A108 100b Year of Youth emblem 2.25 1.50
**359** A108 200b Sultan Qaboos 3.50 2.00

Scouting — A109

#360, Emblem of Scouts & Guides, Scout Headquarters. #361, Scout camp, Sultan Qaboos.

**1993, Nov. 20 Litho. *Perf. 13x13½***
**360** A109 100b multicolored 1.75 1.25
**361** A109 100b multicolored 1.75 1.25
*a.* Pair, #360-361 5.00 5.00

Scouting movement in Oman, 61st anniv. (#360). Installation of Sultan Qaboos as chief scout, 10th anniv. (#361).

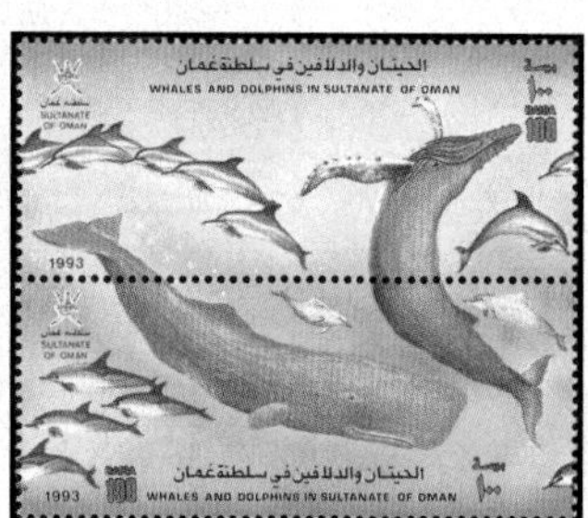
Whales and Dolphins — A110

#362, Dolphins, humpback whale. #363, Dolphins, sperm whale.

**1993, Dec. 8 *Perf. 14½***
**362** 100b multicolored 3.75 1.75
**363** 100b multicolored 3.75 1.75
*a.* A110 Pair, #362-363 12.00 12.00
*b.* Souvenir sheet of 2, #362-363 45.00 45.00

No. 363a has a continuous design. No. 363b sold for 400b and has a white border surrounding the stamps.

World Day for Water — A111

**1994, Mar. 22 Litho. *Perf. 13½***
**364** A111 50b multicolored 2.25 .75

Muscat Municipality, 70th Anniv. — A112

**1994, Apr. 16**
**365** A112 50b multicolored 2.50 1.00

Intl. Olympic Committee, Cent. — A113

**1994, Aug. 29 Litho. *Perf. 13½***
**366** A113 100b multicolored 16.00 8.25

Al Busaid Dynasty, 250th Anniv. — A114

Natl. arms or sultan, dates: a, 1744-75. b, 1775-79. c, 1779-92. d, 1792-1804. e, 1804-7. f, Sa'id ibn Sultan, 1807-56. g, 1856-65. h, 1866-68. i, 1868-71. j, Sultan, 1871-88. k, Sultan, 1888-1913. l, Sultan Taymur ibn Faysal, 1913-32. m, Sultan Qaboos, laurel tree. n, Sultan Sa'id ibn Taymur, 1932-70. o, Sultan Qaboos, 1970-.

200b, Sultan Qaboos atop family "tree," Arabic listing of former Sultans, years in power.

**Litho. & Embossed**

**1994, Dec. 28 *Perf. 11½***
**367** A114 50b Block of 15, #a.-o. *30.00 30.00*

**Litho. & Typo.**
***Imperf***
**Size: 140x110mm**

**367P** A114 200b gold & multi 7.00 5.50

Nos. 367f, 367j-367o contain portraits of sultans.

Open Parliament — A115

**1995, Jan. 7 Litho. *Perf. 14***
**Granite Paper**
**368** A115 50b silver & multi 2.25 1.00

24th National Day, Year of the Heritage — A116

**1994, Nov. 18 Litho. *Perf. 13½***
**369** A116 50b Emblem 1.00 .75
**370** A116 50b Sultan Qaboos 1.00 .75
*a.* Pair, #369-370 6.25 6.25

ICAO, 50th Anniv. A117

**1994, Dec. 7** *Perf. 13½x14*

**371** A117 100b multicolored 7.25 3.00

Arab League, 50th Anniv. — A118

**1995, Mar. 22 Litho.** *Perf. 13*

**372** A118 100b multicolored 2.50 1.00

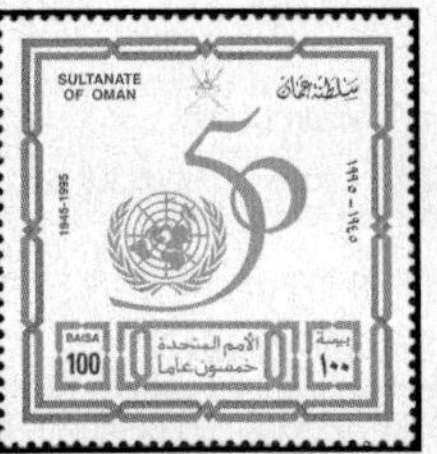

UN, 50th Anniv. A119

**1995, Sept. 2** *Perf. 13½*

**373** A119 100b multicolored 4.50 1.50

16th Session of Supreme Council of the Co-operative Council for Arab Gulf States A120

Designs: 100b, Emblem. 200b, Flags of Arab Gulf States, map, Sultan Qaboos.

**1995, Dec. 4** *Perf. 12*

**Granite Paper**

**374** A120 100b multicolored 2.00 .70
**375** A120 200b multicolored 4.00 1.25
*a.* Pair, #374-375 *30.00 20.00*

25th National Day A121

Portraits of Sultan Qaboos: 50b, In traditional attire. 100b, In military uniform.

**Litho. & Embossed**

**1995, Nov. 18** *Perf. 11½*

**Granite Paper**

**376** A121 50b multicolored 1.75 .80
**377** A121 100b multicolored 3.25 1.00
*a.* Souvenir sheet of 2, #376-377 7.75 5.75

No. 377a sold for 300b.

1996 Summer Olympic Games, Atlanta — A122

a, Shooting. b, Swimming. c, Cycling. d, Running.

**1996, July 19 Litho.** *Perf. 14½*

**378** A122 100b Strip of 4, #a.-d. 27.50 22.50

13th Arabian Gulf Cup Soccer Tournament — A123

**1996, Oct. 15** *Perf. 13½*

**379** A123 100b multicolored 2.00 1.00

UN Decade Against Drug Abuse — A124

**1996, June 26** *Perf. 13½x14*

**380** A124 100b multicolored 23.00 15.00

UNICEF, 50th Anniv. A125

**1996, Dec. 11 Litho.** *Perf. 14½*

**381** A125 100b multicolored 2.25 1.10

26th National Day — A126

Designs: No. 382, Sultan Qaboos waving, boats in harbor. No. 383, Boats in harbor, Sultan Qaboos.

**1996, Nov. 26** *Perf. 13½*

**382** 50b multicolored 1.50 .90
**383** 50b multicolored 1.50 .90
*a.* A126 Pair, #382-383 4.25 4.25

No. 383a is a continuous design.

Traditional Boats — A127

**1996, Apr. 15 Photo.** *Perf. 13½x14*

**384** A127 50b Ash'Shashah .30 .25
**385** A127 100b Al-Battil .65 .60
**386** A127 200b Al-Boum 1.25 1.10
**387** A127 250b Al-Badan 1.75 1.40
**388** A127 350b As'Sanbuq 2.50 2.00
**389** A127 450b Al-Galbout 3.25 2.50
**390** A127 650b Al-Baghlah 4.25 3.50
**391** A127 1r Al-Ghanjah 7.50 5.50
*Nos. 384-391 (8)* 21.45 16.85

**Souvenir Sheet**

***Imperf***

**392** A127 600b Designs of #384-391 10.00 8.00

No. 392 has simulated perfs. and individual stamps are defaced and not valid for postage.

Tourism — A128

a, Oasis fort among palm trees. b, Small waterfalls, trees. c, Highway, coastline, castle on hilltop. d, Lake, mountains. e, Ruins of ancient fort on cliff. f, Waterfall, mountain stream.

**1997 Litho.** *Perf. 13½x14*

**393** A128 100b Block of 6, #a.-f. 13.50 13.50

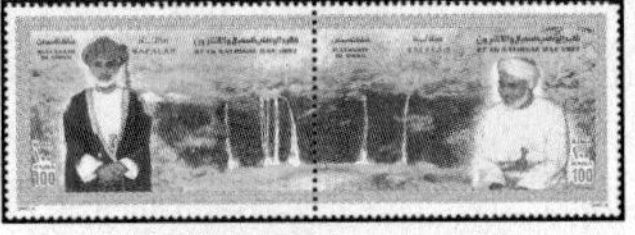

27th National Day — A129

Waterfall, Sultan Qaboos wearing: No. 394, Multicolored outfit. No. 395, Wearing white outfit.

**1997, Nov. 18 Litho.** *Perf. 13½*

**394** 100b multicolored 2.50 1.25
**395** 100b multicolored 2.50 1.25
*a.* A129 Pair, #394-395 8.00 8.00

Girl Guides in Oman, 25th Anniv. A130

**1997, Nov. 30** *Perf. 14½*

**396** A130 100b multicolored 2.75 1.50

Amateur Radio Society, 25th Anniv. — A131

**1997, Dec. 23** *Perf. 13½*

**397** A131 100b multicolored 3.75 2.00

Al-Khanjar Assaidi — A132

**1997 Granite Paper** *Perf. 11½*

**398** A132 50b red & multi .85 .70
**399** A132 50b green & multi .85 .70
**400** A132 100b purple & multi 2.25 1.50
**401** A132 200b brown & multi 3.25 2.25
*Nos. 398-401 (4)* 7.20 5.15

See No. 418.

Traffic Week A133

**1998** *Perf. 13½*

**402** A133 100b multicolored 8.00 4.00

Tourism — A134

Designs: a, Fort. b, Rocky mountainside, lake. c, City. d, Men raising swords, drummers. e, Stream running through countryside. f, Girls standing beside stream, trees.

**1998** *Perf. 13½x13*

**403** A134 100b Block of 6, #a.-f. 14.00 14.00

4th Arab Gulf Countries Philatelic Exhibition, Muscat — A135

**1998 Litho.** *Perf. 13½*

**404** A135 50b multicolored 2.00 .80

Sultan Qaboos, Recipient of Intl. Peace Award A136

**1998**

**405** A136 500b multicolored 21.00 14.00

28th National Day — A137

**1998** *Perf. 12½*

**406** A137 100b Sultan Qaboos 2.25 1.00
**407** A137 100b Emblem, map 2.25 1.00
*a.* Pair, #406-407 6.50 6.50
*b.* Souvenir sheet, #406-407 *40.00 40.00*

Opening of Raysut Port-Salalah Container Terminal — A138

**1998** ***Perf. 13x13½***
**408** A138 50b multicolored 5.50 2.25

World Stamp Day — A139

**1998** ***Perf. 13½***
**409** A139 100b multicolored 2.00 1.50

Royal Air Force of Oman, 40th Anniv. — A140

**1999 Litho.** ***Perf. 13½x13¾***
**410** A140 100b multicolored 4.00 1.75

Butterflies — A141

Designs: a, Danaus chrysippus. b, Papilio demoleus. c, Precis orithya. d, Precis hierta.

**1999 Litho.** ***Perf. 13¼***
**411** A141 100b Block of 4, #a.-d. *13.00 13.00*
*e.* Souvenir sheet of 4, #a.-d. *35.00 35.00*

See No. 421.

Marine Life — A142

Designs: a, Parupeneus macronema. b, Etrumeus teres. c, Epinephelus chlorostigma. d, Lethrinus lentjan. e, Lutjanus erythropterus. f, Acanthocybium solandri. g, Thunnus tongol. h, Pristipomoides filamentosus. i, Thunnus albacares. j, Penaeus indicus. k, Sepia pharaonis. l, Panulirus homarus.

**1999 Litho.** ***Perf. 13½x13***
**412** A142 100b Sheet of 12, #a.-l. 21.00 21.00

Wildlife — A143

Designs: a, Sand cat. b, Genet. c, Leopard. d, Sand fox. e, Caracal lynx. f, Hyena.

**1999 Litho.** ***Perf. 13½x13***
**413** 100b Block of 6, #a.-f. 11.50 11.50
*g.* A143 Souvenir sheet, #a.-f. *40.00 40.00*

UPU, 125th Anniv. A144

**1999** ***Perf. 11***
**414** A144 200b multi 2.75 2.25

29th National Day — A145

**1999 Litho.** ***Perf. 13½***
**415** 100b Sultan in black 2.25 1.25
**416** 100b Sultan in white 2.25 1.25
*a.* A145 Pair, #415-416 6.00 6.00

Souvenir Sheet

Millennium — A146

**Litho. & Embossed with Foil Application**

**2000, Jan. 1** ***Perf. 13¼***
**417** A146 500b multi 15.00 15.00

**Al-Khanjar Assaidi Type of 1997**

**2000, Feb. 12 Litho.** ***Perf. 11½***
**Granite Paper**
**418** A132 80b orange & multi 1.75 1.25

GCC Water Week — A147

**2000 Litho.** ***Perf. 13¼***
**419** A147 100b multi 2.00 1.10

Gulf Air, 50th Anniv. — A148

**2000** ***Perf. 13½***
**420** A148 100b multi 2.00 1.10

**Butterfly Type of 1999**

No. 421: a, Colotis danae. b, Anaphaeis aurota. c, Tarucus rosaceus. d, Lampides boeticus.

**2000 Litho.** ***Perf. 13½***
**421** Block of 4 12.00 12.00
*a.-d.* A141 100b Any single 2.50 1.25
*e.* Souvenir sheet, #421 *30.00 30.00*

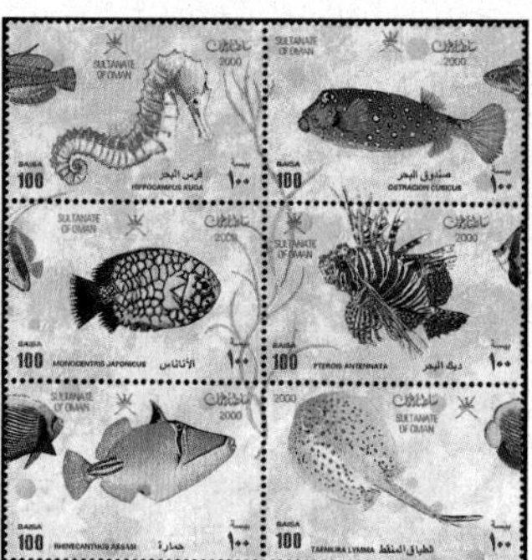

Fish — A148a

No. 421F: g, Hippocampus kuda. h, Ostracion cubicus. i, Monocentris japonicus. j, Pterois antennata. k, Phinecanthus assasi. l, Taenura lymma.

***Perf. 13½x13¾***
**2000, June 12 Litho.**
**421F** A148a 100b Block of 6, #g-l 22.50 17.50
*m.* Souvenir sheet, #421F 24.00 17.50

2000 Summer Olympics, Sydney — A149

Designs: a, Shooting. b, Emblem of Sydney Games. c, Running. d, Swimming.

**2000, Sept. 15** ***Perf. 13½x13¾***
**422** A149 100b Block of 4, #a-d 10.00 10.00
*e.* Souvenir sheet, #422 *32.50 32.50*

Coup by Sultan Qaboos, 30th Anniv. — A150

No. 423: a, Emblem, Sultan in blue hat. b, Emblem, Sultan seated. c, Emblem, Sultan in red beret. d, Emblem, Sultan in white hat. e, Emblem. f, Emblem, Sultan in black hat.

**Litho. & Embossed**

**2000, Nov. 18** ***Perf. 13½***
**423** Block of 6 17.50 14.00
*a.-f.* A150 100b Any single 2.25 1.25
*g.* Souvenir sheet, #423 16.00 16.00

Wildlife — A151

No. 424: a, Arabian tahr. b, Nubian ibex. c, Arabian oryx. d, Arabian gazelle.

**2000, July 23 Litho.** ***Perf. 13½x13***
**424** A151 100b Block of 4, #a-d 15.00 11.00
*e.* Souvenir sheet, #424 22.50 13.00

Souvenir Sheet

Environment Day — A152

**2001, Jan. 8 Litho.** ***Perf. 13¾x14¼***
**425** A152 200b multi 16.00 12.00

Souvenir Sheet

Palestinian Uprising in Jerusalem — A153

**Litho. & Embossed**

**2001, July 31** ***Perf. 13½x13***
**426** A153 100b multi 8.00 3.00

Al-Khanjar A'Suri — A154

***Perf. 14½x13¾***
**2001, Mar. 19 Litho.**
**427** A154 50b red & multi .75 .50
**428** A154 80b yel org & multi 1.25 1.00

**Size: 26x34mm**

***Perf. 13¼x13***

429 A154 100b blue & multi 1.50 1.25
430 A154 200b multi 3.00 2.50
*a.* Miniature sheet, #427-430 9.00 7.50

See Nos. 474-476.

Souvenir Sheets

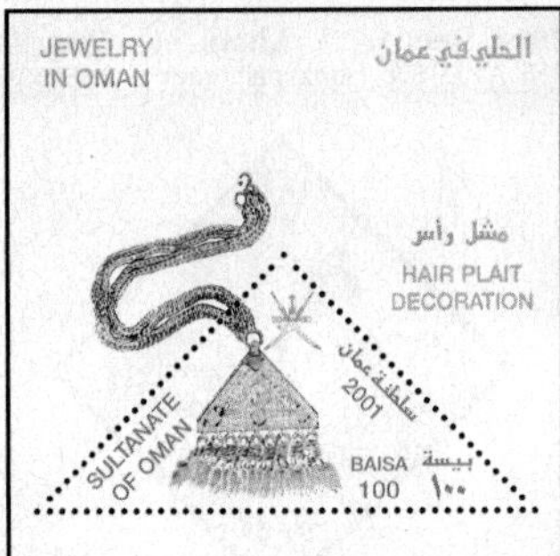


Jewelry — A155

**Litho., Typo. & Embossed**

**2001** ***Perf. 12¾x12½***

431 A155 100b Hair plait decoration 5.25 3.00

**Stamp Size: 62x27mm**

***Perf. 13¼x13¾***

432 A155 100b Pendant 5.25 3.00

**Stamp Size: 44x44mm**

***Perf. 12¾***

433 A155 100b Necklace 5.25 3.00

**Stamp Size: 38mm Diameter**

***Perf.***

434 A155 100b Mazrad 5.25 3.00
*Nos. 431-434 (4)* 21.00 12.00

Supreme Council of Arab Gulf Cooperation Council States, 22nd Session A156

Designs: 50b, Map. 100b, Sultan Qaboos.

**2001 Litho. & Typo.** ***Perf. 14x14¼***

435-436 A156 Set of 2 2.50 1.50

Year of Dialogue Among Civilizations A157

**2001 Litho.** ***Perf. 13¾x13¼***

437 A157 200b multi 6.50 3.25

Shells — A157a

No. 437A: b, Nassarius coronatus. c, Epitoneum pallasii d, Cerithium caeruleum. e, Cerithidea cingulata.

**2001 Litho.** ***Perf. 13¼***

437A A157a 100b Block of 4, #b-e 7.00 5.75

31st National Day — A158

No. 438: a, Map of Oman, tree. b, Sultan Qaboos.

**2001** ***Perf. 13¼***

438 A158 100b Horiz. pair, #a-b 4.75 4.75

Turtles — A159

No. 439: a, Olive Ridley. b, Green. c, Hawksbill. d, Loggerhead.

**2002, Aug. 12 Litho.** ***Perf. 13¼x13***

439 A159 100b Block of 4, #a-d 8.75 7.50
*e.* Souvenir sheet, #439a-439d 12.50 9.50

Sultan Qaboos Grand Mosque — A160

No. 440: a, Interior view of dome and chandelier. b, Exterior view of mosque and minaret. c, Exterior view of archway. d, Interior view of corner arches.

100b, Aerial view of mosque.

**Litho. With Foil Application**

**2002, May 25** ***Perf. 13¼***

440 A160 50b Block of 4, #a-d 6.00 4.75

**Size: 120x90mm**

***Imperf***

441 A160 100b multi 7.50 4.75

Souvenir Sheet

32nd National Day — A160a

Design: 100b, Sultan Qaboos, flowers in corners.

**Litho. With Foil Application**

**2002, Nov. 18** ***Perf. 13x13¼***

441A A160a 100b multi 5.25 3.00
441B A160a 200b shown 3.50 2.75

Birds — A161

No. 442: a, Streptopelia decaocto. b, Tchagra senegala. c, Ploceus galbula. d, Hieraaetus fasciatus. e, Pycnonotus xanthopygos. f, Bubo bubo. g, Eremalauda dunni. h, Burhinus capensis. i, Prinia gracilis. j, Francolinus pondicerianus. k, Onychognathus tristramii. l, Hoplopterus indicus. m, Corvus splendens. n, Chlamydotis undulata. o, Halcyon chloris. p, Pterocles coronatus.

**2002, Dec. 15** ***Perf. 13x13¼***

442 A161 50b Sheet of 16, #a-p 22.50 17.50

Early Intervention for Children With Special Needs — A161a

**2002, Oct. 30 Litho.** ***Perf. 13x13¼***

442Q A161a 100b multi 3.50 1.75

**Booklet Stamp**

**Self-Adhesive**

442R A161a 100b multi 4.00 2.00
*s.* Booklet pane of 10 40.00 —

Muscat Festival 2003 A162

**2003, Jan. 8** ***Perf. 14½***

443 A162 100b multi 2.00 1.00

Oman - People's Republic of China Diplomatic Relations, 25th Anniv. — A163

**2003, May 25 Litho.** ***Perf. 12***

444 A163 70b multi 2.50 1.25

Souvenir Sheets

A164

Arabian Horses — A165

**2003, Apr. 8** ***Perf. 13¼x12¾***

445 A164 100b shown 2.75 1.50
446 A165 100b shown 2.75 1.50
447 A165 100b White horse facing left 2.75 1.50
448 A165 100b Brown horse 2.75 1.50
*Nos. 445-448 (4)* 11.00 6.00

Census — A166

No. 449: a, Emblem, buildings. b, Emblem, blue circle.

**2003, Sept. 16 Litho.** ***Perf. 13***

449 A166 50b Horiz. pair, #a-b 2.10 1.00

Intl. Day of Peace — A167

**2003, Sept. 21** ***Perf. 13¼x12¾***

450 A167 200b multi 2.75 2.50

Organization of the Islamic Conference — A168

**Litho. & Embossed**

**2003, Sept. 25** *Perf. 13*
**451** A168 100b multi 2.25 1.75

Self-Employment and National Autonomous Development Program — A169

**2003, Oct. 6 Litho.** *Perf. 13¼*

**Souvenir Sheet**

**452** A169 100b multi 2.00 2.00

**Booklet Stamp**
**Self-Adhesive**

***Serpentine Die Cut 12½***

**453** A169 100b multi 1.60 1.10
*a.* Booklet pane of 4 6.50
Complete booklet, 3 #453a 19.50

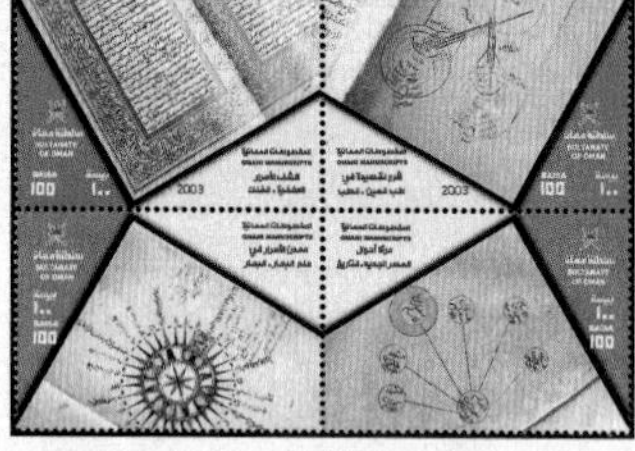

A170

Manuscripts — A171

No. 454: a, Denomination at lower left. b, Denomination at lower right. c, Denomination at left center. d, Denomination at right center.

No. 455: a, Illustrations of ships. b, Illustration of connected circles. c, Illustration of concentric circles. d, Text in large red circle.

**2003, Oct. 14 Litho.** *Perf. 13½x13¼*
**454** A170 100b Block of 4, #a-d 5.00 5.00

**Miniature Sheet**

**Litho. With Foil Application**

***Perf. 13¼***

**455** A171 50b Sheet of 4, #a-d 4.75 4.00

33rd National Day — A172

No. 456 — Sultan Qaboos and background color of: a, Light green. b, Light blue. c, Buff. d, Light red violet.

**Litho. & Embossed**

**2003, Nov. 18** *Perf. 13x13¼*
**456** A172 50b Block of 4, #a-d 3.50 3.50

Flowers — A173

No. 457: a, Anogeissus dhofarica. b, Tecomella undulata. c, Euryops pinifolius. d, Aloe dhufarensis. e, Cleome glaucescens. f, Cassia italica. g, Cibirhiza dhofarensis. h, Ipomoea nil. i, Viola cinerea. j, Dyschoriste dalyi. k, Calotropis procera. l, Lavandula dhofarensis. m, Teucrium mascatense. n, Capparis mucronifolia. o, Geranium mascatense. p, Convolvulus arvensis.

**2004, Jan. 24 Litho.** *Perf. 14½*
**457** Sheet of 16 11.50 11.50
*a.-p.* A173 50b Any single .60 .50

FIFA (Fédération Internationale de Football Association), Cent. — A174

**Litho. & Embossed**

**2004, May 21** *Perf. 13¾*
**458** A174 250b multi 4.25 3.75

Worldwide Fund for Nature (WWF) — A175

No. 459 — Arabian leopard: a, Front feet on mound. b, Pair of leopards. c, Rear feet on mound. d. Feet in depression.

**2004, June 5 Litho.** *Perf. 13¾x13½*
**459** A175 Horiz. strip of 4 5.00 5.00
*a.-d.* 50b Any single .85 .75

Corals A176

No. 460: a, Montipora. b, Porites. c, Acropora. d, Cycloseris.

**2004, Aug. 1** *Perf. 13¾*
**460** Horiz. strip of 4 7.00 7.00
*a.-d.* A176 100b Any single .90 .75

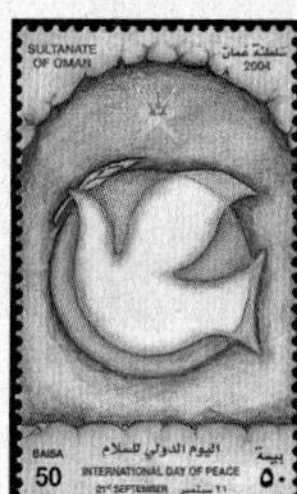


Intl. Day of Peace — A177

Designs: 50b, Dove and green circle. 100b, Doves and Earth.

**2004, Sept. 21** *Perf. 13½x13¾*
**461-462** A177 Set of 2 1.50 1.50

Souvenir Sheet

Intl. White Cane Day — A178

**2004 Litho.** *Perf. 14x13¼*
**463** A178 100b black 4.25 4.25

Braille text was applied by a thermographic process producing a shiny, raised effect.

34th National Day — A179

No. 464 — Sultan Qaboos with kaffiyah in: a, Red. b, Blue green. c, Gray and white. d, Black and white.

**Litho. & Embossed With Foil Application**

**2004, Nov. 18** *Perf. 13¾x13½*
**464** A179 100b Block of 4, #a-d 3.50 3.50

Water Supply Projects — A180

No. 465: a, Al Massarat. b, Ash'Sharqiyah.

**2004, Dec. 1 Litho.** *Perf. 14*
**465** A180 50b Horiz. pair, #a-b 3.25 3.25

10th Gulf Cooperation Council Stamp Exhibition — A181

**2004, Dec. 4** *Perf. 13½*
**466** A181 50b multi 1.75 1.75

**Self-Adhesive**
**Booklet Stamp**

***Serpentine Die Cut 12½***

**467** A181 50b multi 1.40 1.00
*a.* Booklet pane of 4 5.50
Complete booklet, 3 #467a 17.00

Civil Defense — A182

Designs: 50b, Civil defense workers, Omani people. 100b, Rescue workers in action.

**2005, May 14 Litho.** *Perf. 14*
**468-469** A182 Set of 2 2.10 2.10

World Blood Donor Day — A183

**2005, June 14 Litho.** *Perf. 13¾x14*
**470** A183 100b multi 1.50 1.50

Agricultural Census — A184

No. 471 — Census taker and: a, Herder and livestock. b, Farmer and crops.

**2005, July 18** *Perf. 14x13¼*
**471** A184 100b Horiz. pair, #a-b 3.25 3.25

World Summit on the Information Society, Tunis — A185

**2005, Nov. 16** ***Perf. 14***
**472** A185 100b multi 1.75 1.75

Miniature Sheet

35th National Day — A186

No. 473: a, Airplane, dish antennas. b, Helicopter, mounted soldiers. c, Sultan Qaboos. d, People in costumes. e, Military aircraft, ship, vehicle. f, Tower, highway. g, Tower, people at computers. h, Emblem of 35th National Day. i, Man at oasis. j, Petroleum facility.

**Litho., Litho. & Embossed With Foil Application (#473c)**

**2005, Nov. 18** ***Perf. 13¼x13½***
**473** A186 100b Sheet of 10, #a-j 14.00 14.00

**Al-Khanjar A'Suri Type of 2001**

**2005, Dec. 7 Litho.** ***Perf. 13¼x13***

**Size: 26x34mm**

**474** A154 250b bl grn & multi 1.40 1.40
**475** A154 300b red vio & multi 1.60 1.60
**476** A154 400b yel brn & multi 2.10 2.10
*Nos. 474-476 (3)* 5.10 5.10

A187

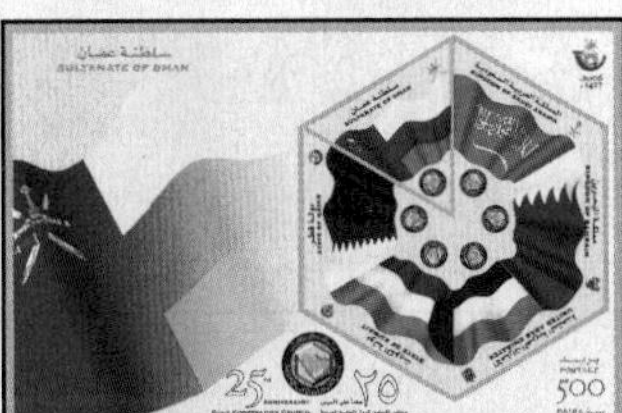

Gulf Cooperation Council, 25th Anniv. — A188

**Litho. With Foil Application**

**2006, May 25** ***Perf. 14***
**477** A187 100b multi 7.00 7.00

***Imperf***

**Size: 165x100mm**

**478** A188 500b multi 26.00 26.00

See Bahrain Nos. 628-629, Kuwait Nos. 1646-1647, Qatar Nos. 1007-1008, Saudi Arabia No. 1378, and United Arab Emirates Nos. 831-832.

Souvenir Sheet

Muscat, 2006 Capital of Arab Culture — A189

**2006, Aug. 26 Litho.** ***Perf. 14***
**479** A189 100b multi 3.00 3.00

Tourism — A190

No. 480: a, Man picking flowers, houses on mountain. b, Six men, building. c, Scuba diver, turtle on beach. d, Women with clothing on line, camels.

**2006, Sept. 27 Litho.** ***Perf. 14***
**480** A190 100b Block of 4, #a-d 6.00 6.00

Oman Post Emblem A191

Text in: 100b, Blue. 250b, White.

**Litho. With Foil Application**

**2006, Nov. 6** ***Perf. 13¾x13½***
**481-482** A191 Set of 2 4.75 4.75

36th National Day — A192

**2006, Nov. 18** ***Perf. 13x13½***
**483** A192 100b multi 1.50 1.50

Sultan Qaboos Prize for Cultural Innovation — A193

**2006, Dec. 24 Litho.** ***Perf. 13¼x13***
**484** A193 250b multi 4.00 4.00

Exportation of Crude Oil, 40th Anniv. — A194

No. 485: a, Oil tanker and oil storage facility. b, Oil storage facility and oil well.

**2007, July 27 Litho.** ***Perf. 13¾***
**485** A194 100b Horiz. pair, #a-b 1.75 1.75

Symposium on Agricultrual Development A195

**2007, Oct. 1 Litho.** ***Perf. 13¾x14***
**486** A195 100b multi 1.25 1.25

37th National Day — A196

**2008, Nov. 18** ***Perf. 13***
**487** A196 100b multi 2.00 2.00

Khasab Castle — A197

No. 488: a, Exterior of castle. b, Man behind table. c, People reading. d, Men and cannons near door.

**2007, Dec. 1** ***Perf. 13¼x13***
**488** A197 100b Block of 4, #a-d 2.75 2.75

Scouting, Cent., and Scouting in Oman, 75th Anniv. — A198

**2007, Dec. 20** ***Perf. 13¾x13¼***
**489** A198 250b multi 2.25 2.25

19th Arabian Gulf Cup Soccer Tournament — A199

**2008, Jan. 4 Litho.** ***Perf. 12¾x13¼***
**490** A199 100b multi .70 .70

38th National Day A200

**Litho. & Embossed With Foil Application**

**2008, Nov. 18** ***Perf. 13¾***
**491** A200 200b multi 1.40 1.40

Souvenir Sheet

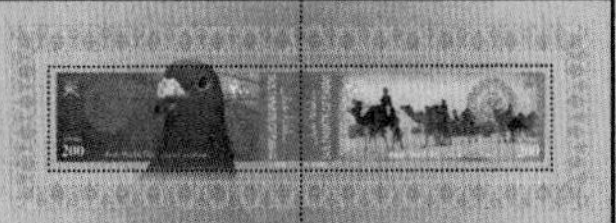

Arab Postal Day — A201

No. 492 — Emblem and: a, World map, pigeon. b, Camel caravan.

***Perf. 14½x13¾***

**2008, Dec. 21** **Litho.**
**492** A201 200b Sheet of 2, #a-b 4.00 4.00

Supreme Council of Gulf Cooperation Council, 29th Session — A202

Emblem and: 100b, Flags. 300b, Rulers of Council states.

**Litho. With Foil Application**

**2008, Dec. 29** ***Perf. 13¼x13***
**493** A202 100b multi 1.60 1.60

**Size: 162x81mm**

***Imperf***

**494** A202 300b multi 4.00 4.00

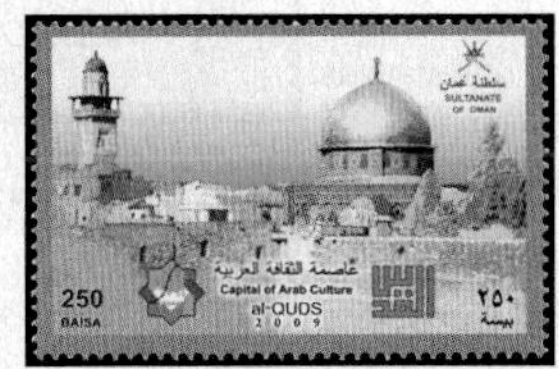

Jerusalem, 2009 Capital of Arab Culture — A203

**2009, Nov. 10 Litho.** ***Perf. 13¾***
**495** A203 250b multi 1.75 1.75

**Souvenir Sheet**
**With White Frame Around Stamp**

**496** A203 250b multi *9.00 9.00*

15th Gulf Cooperation Council Stamps Exhibition, Oman — A204

No. 497: a, Part of Bahrain flag at right. b, Part of Bahrain flag at left, part of United Arab Emirates flag at right. c, Part of United Arab Emirates flag at left. d, Part of Oman flag at right. e, Part of Oman flag at left, part of Saudi Arabia flag at right. f, Part of Saudi Arabia flag at left. g, Part of Kuwait flag at right. h, Part of Kuwait flag at left, part of Qatar flag at right. i, Part of Qatar flag at left.

50b, No flag in background.

**2009 Litho. *Perf. 13***

**497** Sheet of 9 + 6 labels 13.00 13.00
*a.-i.* A204 200b Any single 1.40 1.40

**Booklet Stamp**
**Self-Adhesive**
***Serpentine Die Cut 12¾***

**498** A204 50b multi .35 .35
*a.* Booklet pane of 12 4.25 4.25

39th National Day — A205

**Litho. & Embossed**

**2009, Nov. 18 *Perf. 13¼***

**499** A205 200b multi 1.40 1.40

Oman, Champions of 19th Arabian Gulf Cup Soccer Tournament A206

**2009, Dec. 19 Litho. *Perf. 13¼***

**500** A206 200b multi 1.40 1.40

Censuses A207

Emblem of: No. 502, 50b, Third census of Oman. No. 503, 50b, Joint Gulf Cooperation Council census.

**2010, Feb. 2 Litho. *Perf. 13¼***

**502-503** A207 Set of 2 .70 .70

Arab Water Day A209

**2010, Mar. 3 Litho. *Perf. 14¼***

**506** A209 100b multi .70 .70

A210

Expo 2010, Shanghai A211

**2010, May 1 *Perf. 12¾x13¼***

**Souvenir Sheet**

**507** A210 100b multi .70 .70

**Self-Adhesive**
***Serpentine Die Cut***

**508** A211 50b multi .35 .35

Souvenir Sheet

Jewel of Muscat — A212

**2010, July 3 *Perf. 13¾x13¼***

**509** A212 100b multi .70 .70

Miniature Sheet

Renaissance Day — A213

No. 510 — Sultan Qaboos in: a, Blue uniform. b, Brown uniform, red brown background. c, White uniform. d, Beige uniform. e, Brown uniform, gray brown background.

**Litho. & Embossed**

**2010, July 23 *Perf. 13¼***

**510** A213 50b Sheet of 5, #a-e 1.75 1.75

Souvenir Sheet

40th National Day — A214

No. 511 — Doves and: a, 100b, Map of Oman. b, 150b, Sultan Qaboos.

**2010, Oct. 18 *Perf.***

**511** A214 Sheet of 2, #a-b 1.75 1.75

Traffic Safety Day — A215

**2010, Oct. 18 Litho. *Perf. 13¼***

**Souvenir Sheet**

**512** A215 100b multi .70 .70

**Self-Adhesive**
***Serpentine Die Cut 13¼***

**513** A215 50b white & multi .35 .35

Miniature Sheet

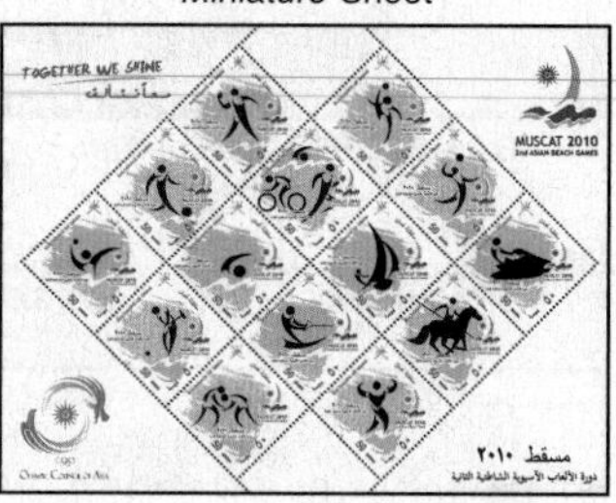

Second Asian Beach Games, Muscat — A216

No. 514: a, Handball. b, Sepak takraw (player kicking ball in air). c, Soccer player dribbling ball. d, Triathlon. e, Volleyball. f, Water polo. g, Swimming. h, Sailing. i, Jet skiing. j, Woodball (player with mallet and ball). k, Water skiing. l, Tent pegging (rider on horse). m, Kabbadi (two athletes wrestling). n, Body building.

**2010, Dec. 8 Litho. *Perf. 13¼***

**514** A216 50b Sheet of 14, #a-n 5.00 5.00

Miniature Sheet

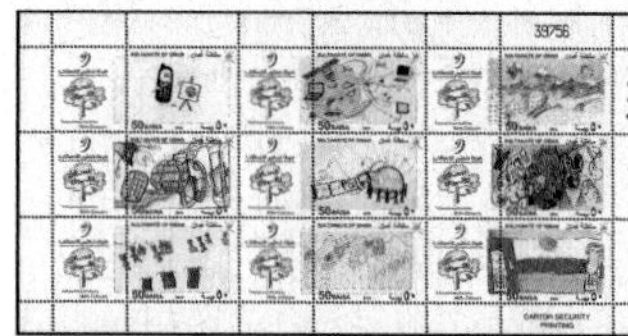

Children's Art — A217

No. 515: a, Cell phone with palette and brush painting Earth on easel. b, Satellite, satellite dish, electronic devices, scissors cutting cables. c, Car on road near buildings and mountains with satellite dishes. d, Cell phone, hand pointing at electronic options, telephone handset. e, Electronic devices, film strip, people circling Earth. f, Spider web, satellite dish, cell phones, antenna towers. g, Children and boxes with colored squares. h, Boy using cell phone. i, Flag of Oman, Sun, cell phones.

**2010, Dec. 19 *Perf. 14¼x14***

**515** A217 50b Sheet of 9, #a-i, + 9 labels 3.25 3.25

Sultan Qaboos University, 25th Anniv. — A218

Emblems, tower, and: 50b, Symbols of science and industry. 100b, Sultan Qaboos, horiz.

**2011, Nov. 9 *Perf. 13¾x13¼***

**516** A218 50b multi .25 .25

**Size: 90x65mm**
***Imperf***

**517** A218 100b multi .55 .55

41st National Day — A219

Sultan Qaboos, Royal Opera House, Muscat, and scenes from various productions: 50b, 100b, 150b.

**2011, Nov. 18**

**518-520** A219 Set of 3 1.60 1.60

Intl. Year of Chemistry A220

**2011, Dec. 27 *Perf. 14¼x14***

**521** A220 100b multi .55 .55

Friendship With Japan, 40th Anniv. — A221

**2012, May 7 *Perf. 14x13¼***

**522** A221 100b multi .70 .70

Frankincense and Incense Burner — A222

**2012, June 21 Litho. *Perf. 13¼x14***

**523** A222 250b multi 1.75 1.75

Salalah Tourism Festival. Portions of No. 523 have a scratch-and-sniff covering with a frankincese aroma.

Miniature Sheet

Muscat, 2012 Arab Tourism Capital — A223

No. 524: a, Old Muscat. b, Sultan Qaboos Grand Mosque. c, Matrah and port. d, Royal Opera House at night. e, Matrah Corniche with docked ships. f, Barr al Jissah Resort.

**2012, July 23 Litho. *Perf. 14¼x14***

**524** A223 50b Sheet of 6, #a-f, + 6 labels 2.10 2.10

Arab Postal Day A224

**Litho. & Embossed**

**2012, Aug. 3 *Perf. 13½***

**525** A224 100b multi .70 .70

Sultan Qaboos Sailing Trophy A225

**Litho. & Embossed With Foil Application**

**2012, Nov. 3** *Perf. 14x13½*
**526** A225 250b multi 1.75 1.75

42nd National Day — A226

Sultan Qaboos and various ships at Oman Drydock Company: 50b, 100b, 150b.

*Perf. 13½x13¼*

**2012, Nov. 18** **Litho.**
**527-529** A226 Set of 3 2.10 2.10

Miniature Sheets

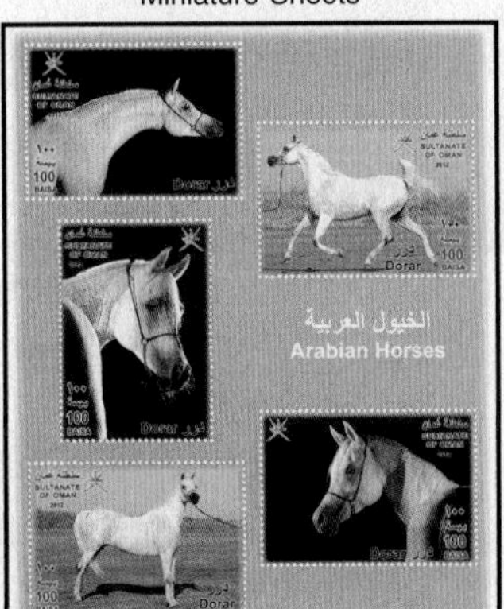
Arabian Horses — A227

No. 530, 100b — Horse named Dorar: a, Facing right, black background. b, Facing left, outdoors. c, Head, facing right, and hindquarters, black background, vert. d, Facing left, black background. e, Standing, facing right, outdoors.

No. 531, 100b — Horse named: a, Ajlad, standing and facing right. b, Psymamon, vert. c, Ajlad, head only, vert. d, Modheeah. e, Sadeed, vert.

**2012, Dec. 12** **Litho.** *Perf. 13¼*
**Sheets of 5, #a-e**
**530-531** A227 Set of 2 7.00 7.00

Girl Guides 20th Arab Regional Conference — A231

**2013, Aug. 24** **Litho.** *Perf. 14¼x14*
**538** A231 100b multi .70 .70

Oman Boy Scouts 16th Intl. Youth Gathering for Cultural Exchange — A232

**2013, Sept. 4** **Litho.** *Perf. 14¼x14*
**539** A232 200b multi 1.40 1.40

A233

Omani Women's Day — A234

**Litho. & Embossed**

**2013, Oct. 17** *Perf. 14*
**540** A233 100b multi .70 .70
**541** A234 100b multi .70 .70

Traffic Safety Day — A235

**2013, Oct. 18** **Litho.** *Perf. 14*
**542** A235 50b multi .35 .35

A236

A237

Sultan Qaboos — A238

**2013, Nov. 18** **Litho.** *Perf. 13½x13*
**543** A236 200b multi 1.40 1.40
**544** A237 200b multi 1.40 1.40
**545** A238 200b multi 1.40 1.40
*Nos. 543-545 (3)* 4.20 4.20

43rd National Day. Nos. 543-545 each were printed in sheets of 4.

Sultan's Armed Forces Museum, 25th Anniv. A239

Designs: 50b, Museum exterior. 100b, Sultan Qaboos in museum.

**2013, Dec. 11** **Litho.** *Perf. 13½*
**546-547** A239 Set of 2 1.10 1.10

Establishement of Omani Philatelic Association — A240

Designs: 100b, Association emblem. 150b, Cancels and canceler. 200b, Various Oman stamps.

**2014, May 21** **Litho.** *Perf. 13x13¼*
**548-550** A240 Set of 3 3.25 3.25
*550a* Souvenir sheet of 3, #548-550 3.25 3.25

Salalah Festival A241

Emblem and: 100b, People, raised hands, flag.
150b, Building, vert.

**2014, July 30** **Litho.** *Perf. 13¼*
**551** A241 100b multi .70 .70

**Souvenir Sheet**
***Perf. 13½x13***
**552** A241 150b multi 1.10 1.10

No. 552 contains one 30x40mm stamp.

Muscat Festival A242

**2014, Aug. 14** **Litho.** *Perf. 13x13½*
**553** A242 100b multi .70 .70

Souvenir Sheet

Tour of Oman Bicycle Race — A243

**2014, Aug. 14** **Litho.** *Perf. 13x13½*
**554** A243 250b multi 1.75 1.75

Architectural Details From Castles and Forts — A244

No. 555: a, Jabreen Castle. b, Nizwa Fort. c, Bahla Fort. d, Al Hazm Castle.

No. 556, 250b, Like #555a. No. 557, 250b, Like #555b. No. 558, 250b, Like #555c. No. 559, 250b, Like #555d.

**2014, Sept. 29** **Litho.** *Perf. 13½x13*
**555** A244 150b Sheet of 4, #a-d 4.25 4.25

**Souvenir Sheets**
**556-559** A244 Set of 4 7.00 7.00

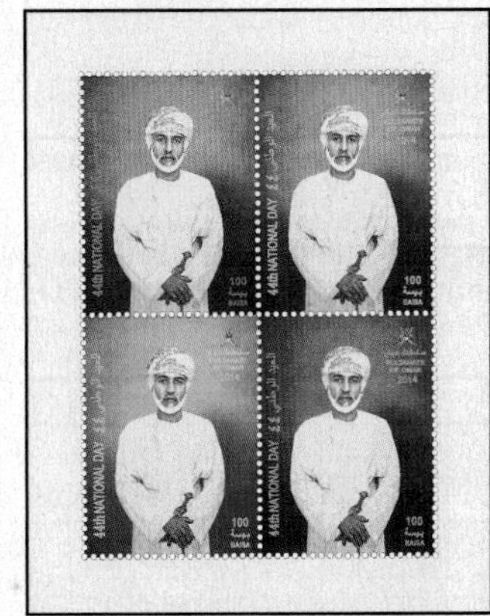
44th National Day — A245

No. 560 — Sultan Qaboos with background color of: a, Purple brown. b, Blue. c, Green. d, Purple.
200b, Sultan Qaboos, diff.

**2014, Nov. 18** **Litho.** *Perf. 13½x13*
**560** A245 100b Sheet of 4, #a-d 2.75 2.75

**Souvenir Sheet**
**Litho. With Foil Application**
***Imperf***
**561** A245 200b gold & multi 1.40 1.40

Souvenir Sheets

Souq Muttrah — A247

Designs: 200b, Entrance. 250b, Souq Muttrah, diff.

**2014, Dec. 12** **Litho.** *Perf. 14x14¼*
**563-564** A247 Set of 2 3.25 3.25

Miniature Sheet

Oman Post Mascot — A248

No. 565 — Inscription: a, Delivery items. b, Kids corner. c, Deposit boxes. d, Post boxes.

**2014, Dec. 14 Litho. *Perf. 13¼***

**565** A248 100b Sheet of 4, #a-d 2.75 2.75

Souvenir Sheets

Arabian and World Water Day — A250

Designs: No. 574, 200b, Falaj Al-Khatmeen. No. 575. 200b, Falaj Dares.

**2015, Mar. 3 Litho. *Perf. 14¼x14½***

**574-575** A250 Set of 2 2.75 2.75

Nizwa, Capital of Islamic Culture — A251

No. 576: a, Old door. b, Emblem, white backround. c, Siaal Mosque. d, Arrazha dance art. e, Emblem light brown background. f, Falaj Daris.

No. 577, 250b: a, Like #576e. b, Like #576a. c, Like #576c.

No. 578, 250b: a, Like #576d. b, Like #576b. c, Like #576f.

**2015, Mar. 15 Litho. *Perf. 13¼x13***

**576** A251 200b Sheet of 6, #a-f 8.50 8.50

**Souvenir Sheets of 3, #a-c**

**577-578** A251 Set of 2 10.50 10.50

Souvenir Sheets

Omani Postal Service, 50th Anniv. — A258

No. 585, 250b: a, Post office and mail sorters. b, Oman #105, 129, 137, horiz. c, Red pillar box.

No. 586, 250b: a, Mail trucks. b, Oman #99, horiz. c, Yellow mail box.

**Litho., Sheet Margin Litho. With Foil Application**

***Perf. 13¼x13 (vert. stamps), 13x13¼***

**2016, Apr. 30 Sheets of 3, #a-c**

**585-586** A258 Set of 2 10.50 10.50

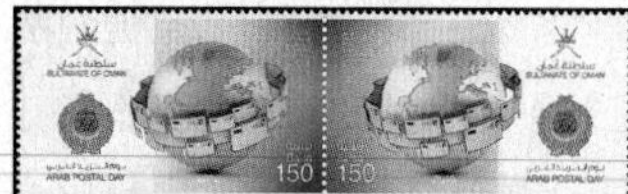

Arab Postal Day — A259

No. 587: a, Blue background, denomination at LR. b, Green background, denomination at LL.

**2016, Aug. 3 Litho. *Perf. 14***

**587** A259 150b Horiz. pair, #a-b 2.10 2.10

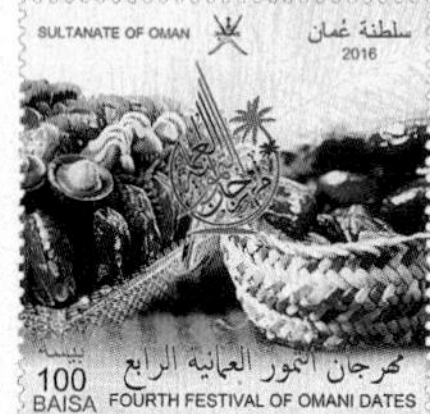


Fourth Festival of Omani Dates A260

**2016, Oct. 23 Litho. *Perf. 13***

**588** A260 100b multi .70 .70

National Oncology Center — A261

**2016, Nov. 2 Litho. *Perf. 13***

**589** A261 100b multi .70 .70

46th National Day — A262

**Litho. & Embossed With Foil Application**

**2016, Nov. 18 *Perf. 13x13¼***

**590** A262 300b multi 2.10 2.10

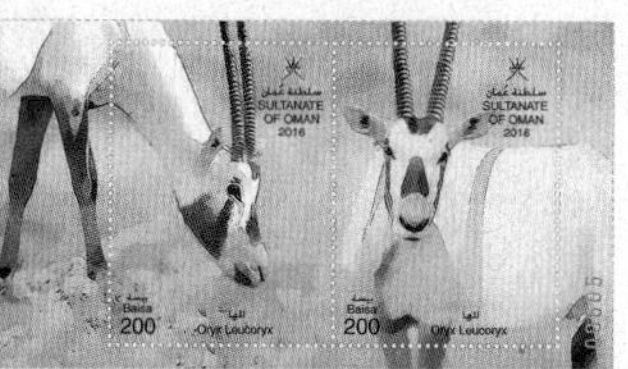

Wildlife — A263

No. 591, 200b — Oryx leucoryx with: a, Head down. b, Head up.

No. 592, 200b — Bubo ascalaphus: a, Feet visible. b, Feet not visible.

No. 593, 200b: a, Neophron pecnopterus. b, Alectoris chukar.

No. 594, 200b: a, Byblia ilithyia ilithyia. b, Hypolimnas misippus.

No. 595, 400b, Paraechinus aethiopicus, horiz. No. 596, 400b, Pterocles exustus, horiz.

**Litho. & Embossed**

**2016, Dec. 20 *Perf. 13***

**Sheets of 2, #a-b**

**591-594** A263 Set of 4 11.50 11.50

**Souvenir Sheets**

**595-596** A263 Set of 2 5.75 5.75

A264

A265

A266

A267

A268

A269

A270

A271

A272

Arches in Sultan Qaboos Grand Mosque A273

**2016, Dec. 21 Litho. *Perf. 13x13¼***

| | | | |
|---|---|---|---|
| **597** | Booklet pane of 5 | 7.00 | — |
| ***a.*** | A264 200b multi | 1.40 | 1.40 |
| ***b.*** | A265 200b multi | 1.40 | 1.40 |
| ***c.*** | A266 200b multi | 1.40 | 1.40 |
| ***d.*** | A267 200b multi | 1.40 | 1.40 |
| ***e.*** | A268 200b multi | 1.40 | 1.40 |
| | Complete booklet, #597 | 7.00 | |
| **598** | Booklet pane of 5 | 7.00 | — |
| ***a.*** | A269 200b multi | 1.40 | 1.40 |
| ***b.*** | A270 200b multi | 1.40 | 1.40 |
| ***c.*** | A271 200b multi | 1.40 | 1.40 |
| ***d.*** | A272 200b multi | 1.40 | 1.40 |
| ***e.*** | A273 200b multi | 1.40 | 1.40 |
| | Complete booklet, #598 | 7.00 | |

Souvenir Sheet

2nd International Military Sports Council World Cup Soccer Tournament, Muscat — A274

No. 599: a, Tournament emblem. b, Mascot.

**Litho. With Foil Application**

**2017, Jan. 15 *Perf. 13***

**599** A274 250b Sheet of 2, #a-b, + central label 3.50 3.50

Miniature Sheet

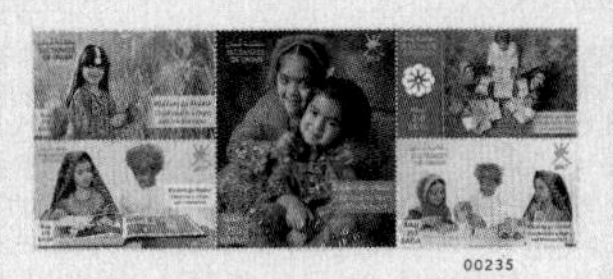

Children — A275

No. 600: a, Girl with magnifying glass (56x33mm). b, Two girls (56x66mm). c, Five children reading (56x33mm). d, Two children reading (56x33mm). e, Three children playing with toys (56x33mm).

**Litho. With Foil Application**

**2017, Apr. 3** ***Perf. 13½x13¼***

**600** A275 250b Sheet of 5, #a-e 8.75 8.75

**SEMI-POSTAL STAMP**

UNICEF Emblem, Girl with Book — SP1

**Wmk. 314**

**1971, Dec. 25** **Litho.** ***Perf. 14***

**B1** SP1 50b + 25b multicolored 42.50 6.50

25th anniv. of UNICEF.

**OFFICIAL STAMPS**

Official Stamps of India 1938-43 Overprinted in Black

***Perf. 13½x14***

**1944, Nov. 20** **Wmk. 196**

| | | | | |
|---|---|---|---|---|
| **O1** | O8 | 3p slate | .80 | *15.00* |
| **O2** | O8 | ½a dk rose violet | .80 | *15.00* |
| **O3** | O8 | 9p green | .80 | *15.00* |
| **O4** | O8 | 1a carmine rose | .80 | *15.00* |
| **O5** | O8 | 1½a dull purple | .80 | *15.00* |
| **O6** | O8 | 2a scarlet | .80 | *15.00* |
| **O7** | O8 | 2½a purple | 5.50 | *15.00* |
| **O8** | O8 | 4a dark brown | 2.00 | *15.00* |
| **O9** | O8 | 8a blue violet | 3.50 | *17.50* |
| **O10** | A82 | 1r brown & slate | 6.00 | *27.50* |
| | | *Nos. O1-O10 (10)* | 21.80 | *165.00* |

Al Busaid Dynasty, 200th anniv. On Nos. O1-O9 the overprint is smaller — 13x6mm.

Used values for Nos. O1-O10 are for stamps canceled with contemporaneous postmarks of the Indian postal administration. Examples with the later British post office cancellations are worth much less.

# ORANGE RIVER COLONY

'är-inj 'ri-vər 'kä-lə-nē

## (Orange Free State)

LOCATION — South Africa, north of the Cape of Good Hope between the Orange and Vaal Rivers

GOVT. — A former British Crown Colony

AREA — 49,647 sq. mi.

POP. — 528,174 (1911)

CAPITAL — Bloemfontein

Orange Free State was an independent republic, 1854-1900. Orange River Colony existed from May, 1900, to June, 1910, when it united with Cape of Good Hope, Natal and the Transvaal to form the Union of South Africa.

12 Pence = 1 Shilling

Values for unused stamps are for examples with original gum as defined in the catalogue introduction. Very fine examples of Nos. 1-60c will have perforations touching the design on one or more sides due to the narrow spacing of the stamps on the plates. Stamps with perfs clear of the design on all four sides are scarce and will command higher prices.

Een = 1
Twee = 2
Drie = 3
Vier = 4

**Issues of the Republic**

Orange Tree — A1

**1868-1900** **Unwmk.** **Typo.** ***Perf. 14***

| | | | | |
|---|---|---|---|---|
| **1** | A1 | ½p red brown ('83) | 8.25 | .75 |
| **2** | A1 | ½p orange ('97) | 3.00 | .60 |
| *a.* | | ½p yellow ('97) | 3.00 | .40 |
| **3** | A1 | 1p red brown | 22.50 | .50 |
| *a.* | | 1p pale brown | 32.50 | 2.50 |
| *b.* | | 1p deep brown | 32.50 | .60 |
| **4** | A1 | 1p violet ('94) | 5.00 | .35 |
| **5** | A1 | 2p violet ('83) | 20.00 | 1.50 |
| *a.* | | 2p pale mauve ('83-'84) | 23.00 | .50 |
| **6** | A1 | 3p ultra ('83) | 8.25 | 2.25 |
| **7** | A1 | 4p ultra ('78) | 6.25 | 4.50 |
| *a.* | | 4p pale blue ('78) | 26.00 | 5.25 |
| **8** | A1 | 6p car rose ('90) | 30.00 | 13.00 |
| *a.* | | 6p rose ('71) | 37.50 | 8.00 |
| *b.* | | 6p pale rose ('68) | 72.50 | 8.75 |
| *c.* | | 6p bright carmine ('94) | 18.50 | 2.25 |
| **9** | A1 | 6p ultramarine ('00) | 80.00 | |
| **10** | A1 | 1sh orange | 65.00 | 1.75 |
| *a.* | | 1sh orange buff | *110.00* | *7.25* |
| **11** | A1 | 1sh brown ('97) | 32.50 | 1.75 |
| **12** | A1 | 5sh green ('78) | 14.00 | *22.50* |
| | | *Nos. 1-8,10-12 (11)* | 214.75 | 49.45 |

No. 8b was not placed in use without surcharge.

For surcharges see #13-53, 44j-53c, 57-60.

No. 13

No. 8a Surcharged in Four Different Types

4 4 4 4
a b c d

**1877**

| | | | |
|---|---|---|---|
| **13** | (a) 4p on 6p rose | 450.00 | 65.00 |
| *a.* | Inverted surcharge | — | 600.00 |
| *b.* | Double surcharge, one inverted ("a" + "c" inverted) | | *4,250.* |
| *c.* | Double surcharge, one inverted ("a" inverted + "c" | | *6,000.* |
| **14** | (b) 4p on 6p rose | 1,450. | 225.00 |
| *a.* | Inverted surcharge | — | 1,250. |
| *b.* | Double surcharge, one inverted ("b" and "d") | — | |
| **15** | (c) 4p on 6p rose | 220.00 | 42.50 |
| *a.* | Inverted surcharge | — | 400.00 |
| **16** | (d) 4p on 6p rose | 325.00 | 50.00 |
| *a.* | Inverted surcharge | *1,500.* | 500.00 |
| *b.* | Double surcharge, one inverted ("d" and "c" inverted) | — | *4,250.* |
| *c.* | Double surcharge, one inverted ("d" inverted and "c") | — | *6,500.* |

No. 17

No. 12 Surcharged with Bar and

1d. 1d. 1d.
f g h

1d. 1d. 1d.
i k l

**1881**

**First Printing**

| | | | |
|---|---|---|---|
| **17** | (f) 1p on 5sh green | 120.00 | 32.50 |

**Second Printing**

| | | | |
|---|---|---|---|
| **18** | (g) 1p on 5sh green | 65.00 | 32.50 |
| *a.* | Inverted surcharge | — | *1,250.* |
| *b.* | Double surcharge | | *1,450.* |
| **19** | (h) 1p on 5sh green | 300.00 | 95.00 |
| *a.* | Inverted surcharge | — | *1,450.* |
| *b.* | Double surcharge | — | *1,650.* |
| **20** | (i) 1p on 5sh green | 100.00 | 32.50 |
| *a.* | Double surcharge | — | *1,325.* |
| *b.* | Inverted surcharge | *2,000.* | *1,000.* |
| **21** | (k) 1p on 5sh green | 600.00 | 275.00 |
| *a.* | Inverted surcharge | — | *2,500.* |
| *b.* | Double surcharge | | *2,500.* |

**Third Printing**

| | | | |
|---|---|---|---|
| **21C** | (l) 1p on 5sh green | 95.00 | 32.50 |
| *d.* | Inverted surcharge | — | *875.00* |
| *e.* | Double surcharge | | *900.00* |
| | *Nos. 17-21C (6)* | 1,280. | 500.00 |

No. 12 Surcharged

**1882**

| | | | | |
|---|---|---|---|---|
| **22** | A1 | ½p on 5sh green | 25.00 | 7.00 |
| *a.* | | Double surcharge | 550.00 | 400.00 |
| *b.* | | Inverted surcharge | *1,500.* | *1,000.* |

**No. 7 Surcharged with Thin Line and**

m

n

o

p

q

**1882**

| | | | |
|---|---|---|---|
| **23** | (m) 3p on 4p ultra | 100.00 | 35.00 |
| *a.* | Double surcharge | | 1,400. |
| **24** | (n) 3p on 4p ultra | 100.00 | 20.00 |
| *a.* | Double surcharge | | 1,400. |
| **25** | (o) 3p on 4p ultra | 55.00 | 25.00 |
| *a.* | Double surcharge | | 1,400. |
| **26** | (p) 3p on 4p ultra | 275.00 | 80.00 |
| *a.* | Double surcharge | | 3,500. |
| **27** | (q) 3p on 4p ultra | 100.00 | 24.00 |
| *a.* | Double surcharge | | 1,400. |
| | *Nos. 23-27 (5)* | 630.00 | 184.00 |

No. 6 Surcharged

**1888**

| | | | | |
|---|---|---|---|---|
| **28** | A1 | 2p on 3p ultra | 60.00 | 2.25 |
| *a.* | | Wide "2" at top | 77.50 | 10.00 |
| *b.* | | As No. 28, invtd. surch. | | 350.00 |
| *c.* | | As No. 28a, invtd. surch. | | 825.00 |
| *d.* | | Curved base on "2" | *1,450.* | *650.00* |

**Nos. 6 and 7 Surcharged**

r

s

t

**1890-91**

| | | | |
|---|---|---|---|
| **29** | (r) 1p on 3p ultra ('91) | 9.50 | 1.00 |
| *a.* | Double surcharge | 100.00 | 77.50 |
| *b.* | "1" and "d" wide apart | 170.00 | 135.00 |
| **30** | (r) 1p on 4p ultra | 45.00 | 12.50 |
| *a.* | Double surcharge | 170.00 | 135.00 |
| *b.* | Triple surcharge | | *3,250.* |
| **31** | (s) 1p on 3p ultra ('91) | 25.00 | 3.00 |
| *a.* | Double surcharge | 325.00 | 300.00 |
| **32** | (s) 1p on 4p ultra | 95.00 | 60.00 |
| *a.* | Double surcharge | 475.00 | 375.00 |
| **33** | (t) 1p on 4p ultra | *2,500.* | *675.00* |

No. 6 Surcharged

**1892**

| | | | | |
|---|---|---|---|---|
| **34** | A1 | 2½p on 3p ultra | 21.00 | .80 |
| *a.* | | Without period | 92.50 | 55.00 |

**No. 6 Surcharged**

v

w

x

y

z

**1896**

| | | | |
|---|---|---|---|
| **35** | (v) ½p on 3p ultra | 8.50 | 12.00 |
| *a.* | Double surcharge "v" and "y" | 15.50 | 15.50 |
| **36** | (w) ½p on 3p ultra | 14.50 | 3.00 |
| *a.* | Double surcharge "w" and "y" | 15.00 | 11.00 |
| **37** | (x) ½p on 3p ultra | 14.50 | 2.50 |
| **38** | (y) ½p on 3p ultra | 9.00 | 5.50 |
| *a.* | Double surcharge | 14.50 | 11.00 |
| *b.* | Triple surcharge | 77.50 | 77.50 |
| **39** | (z) ½p on 3p ultra | 14.50 | 2.50 |

**Surcharged as "v" but "1" with Straight Serif**

| | | | | |
|---|---|---|---|---|
| **40** | A1 | ½p on 3p ultra | 15.50 | *16.50* |
| *a.* | | Double surcharge, one type "y" | 75.00 | 75.00 |

**Surcharged as "z" but "1" with Straight Serif**

| | | | | |
|---|---|---|---|---|
| **41** | A1 | ½p on 3p ultra | 15.50 | 15.50 |
| *a.* | | Double surcharge, one type "y" | 75.00 | 75.00 |
| | | *Nos. 35-41 (7)* | 92.00 | 57.50 |

No. 6 Surcharged

**1896**

42 A1 ½p on 3p ultra 1.10 .65
*a.* No period after "Penny" 22.50 *35.00*
*b.* "Peuny" 22.50 *35.00*
*c.* Inverted surcharge 65.00 *72.50*
*d.* Double surch., one inverted 200.00 *225.00*
*e.* Without bar 10.00
*f.* With additional surcharge as on Nos. 35-41 37.50
*g.* As "a", inverted surcharge 2,250.
*h.* As "b", inverted surcharge 1,750.

No. 6 Surcharged

**1897**

43 A1 2½p on 3p ultra 10.50 .90
*a.* Roman "I" instead of "1" in "½" 185.00 100.00

### Issued under British Occupation

Nos. 2-8, 8a, 10-12 Surcharged or Overprinted

### Periods in "V.R.I." Level with Bottoms of Letters

**1900, Mar.-Apr. Unwmk. *Perf. 14***

44 A1 ½p on ½p org 5.00 *7.25*
*a.* No period after "V" 25.00 *35.00*
*b.* No period after "I" 175.00 175.00
*c.* "I" and period after "R" omitted 300.00 275.00
*f.* "½" omitted *210.00* *210.00*
*g.* Small "½" 65.00 65.00
*h.* Double surcharge 200.00
*i.* As "g," double surcharge 575.00
45 A1 1p on 1p violet 3.00 2.00
*a.* No period after "V" 20.00 18.50
*b.* "I" and period after "R" omitted 300.00 300.00
*d.* "1" of "1d" omitted 225.00 225.00
*e.* "d" omitted 425.00 425.00
*f.* "1d" omitted, "V.R.I." at top 475.00
45O A1 1p on 1p brown *675.00* *450.00*
*y.* No period after "V" *4,000.*
46 A1 2p on 2p violet 4.75 3.00
*a.* No period after "V" 22.00 24.00
*b.* No period after "R" 360.00 360.00
*c.* No period after "I" 360.00 360.00
47 A1 '2½' on 3p ultra 22.50 22.50
*a.* No period after "V" 105.00 105.00
*b.* Roman "I" in "½" 275.00 275.00
48 A1 3p on 3p ultra 3.25 4.75
*a.* No period after "V" 25.00 30.00
*b.* Dbl. surch. one diagonal 600.00
*c.* Pair, one with surcharge omitted 725.00
*j.* "3d" omitted 275.00 275.00
*k.* "V.R.I." omitted 275.00 275.00
49 A1 4p on 4p ultra 11.00 *18.50*
*a.* No period after "V" 72.50 *82.50*
50 A1 6p on 6p car rose 50.00 45.00
*a.* No period after "V" 275.00 300.00
*b.* "6" omitted 340.00 325.00
51 A1 6p on 6p ultra 16.00 7.50
*a.* No period after "V" 55.00 55.00
*c.* "6" omitted 95.00 *100.00*
*h.* "V.R.I." omitted 550.00 425.00
52 A1 1sh on 1sh brown 8.00 3.00
*a.* No period after "V" 55.00 35.00
*c.* "1" of "1s" omitted 165.00 155.00
*j.* "1s" omitted 225.00 220.00
*k.* "V.R.I." omitted 225.00 220.00
52G A1 1sh on 1sh org *4,100.* *2,750.*
53 A1 5sh on 5sh green 32.50 60.00
*a.* No period after "V" 300.00 *360.00*
*b.* "5" omitted 1,100. 1,100.

#47, 47c overprinted "V.R.I." on #43.

No. 45f ("1d" omitted) with "V.R.I." at bottom is a shift which sells for a fifth of the value of the listed item. Varieties such as "V.R.I." omitted, denomination omitted and pair, one without surcharge are also the result of shifts.

For surcharges see Nos. 57, 60.

Nos. 2, 4-12 Surcharged or Overprinted

### Periods in "V.R.I." Raised Above Bottoms of Letters

**1900-01**

*44j* A1 ½p on ½p orange .35 .25
*k.* Mixed periods 3.25 2.25
*l.* Pair, one with level periods 15.50 *20.00*
*m.* No period after "V" 4.00 *4.25*
*n.* No period after "I" 42.50 42.50
*o.* "V" omitted 675.00
*p.* Small "½" 20.00 *22.50*
*q.* "1" for "I" in "V.R.I." 10.00
*r.* Thick "V" 6.00 4.00
*45i* A1 1p on 1p violet .35 .25
*j.* Mixed periods 2.00 *2.50*
*k.* Pair, one with level periods 25.00 *25.00*
*l.* No period after "V" 6.00 *7.00*
*m.* No period after "R" 19.00 19.00
*n.* No period after "I" 19.00 19.00
*p.* Double surcharge 120.00 120.00
*q.* Inverted surcharge 425.00
*s.* Small "1" in "1d" 120.00 120.00
*t.* "1" for "I" in "V.R.I." 13.00
*u.* Thick "V" 7.50 .40
*v.* As "u," invtd. "1" for "I" in "V.R.I." 24.00 24.00
*w.* As "u," double surcharge 375.00 360.00
*z.* As "u," no period after "R" 50.00 *55.00*
*za.* Pair, one without surchage 275.00
*zb.* Stamp double impression, one inverted 2,750.
*46e* A1 2p on 2p violet 3.50 .35
*f.* Mixed periods 8.50 5.25
*g.* Pair, one with level periods 15.00 *15.00*
*h.* Inverted surcharge 360.00 360.00
*i.* Thick "V" 16.50 15.50
*j.* As "i," invtd. "1" for "I" in "V.R.I." 32.50 *35.00*
*47c* A1 '2½' on 3p ultra 250.00 250.00
*d.* Thick "V" 4,250.
*f.* As "d," Roman "I" on "½" —
*48d* A1 3p on 3p ultra 1.60 .35
*e.* Mixed periods 9.50 9.50
*f.* Pair, one with level periods 25.00 *25.00*
*g.* Double surcharge 440.00
*h.* Thick "V" 7.50 *17.50*
*i.* As "h," invtd. "1" for "I" in "V.R.I." 72.50 *85.00*
*l.* Double surcharge, one diagonal 450.00
*m.* As "l", thick "V" *600.00*
*n.* As "l", mixed periods *7,500.*
*o.* As "n", thick "V" —
*49b* A1 4p on 4p ultra 3.25 *3.75*
*c.* Mixed periods 11.00 *16.00*
*d.* Pair, one with level periods 24.00 *35.00*
*50c* A1 6p on 6p car rose 45.00 *55.00*
*d.* Mixed periods 160.00 *175.00*
*e.* Pair, one with level periods 300.00 *350.00*
*f.* Thick "V" *500.00* *525.00*
*51d* A1 6p on 6p ultra 1.10 .45
*e.* Mixed periods 10.50 *11.00*
*f.* Pair, one with level periods 25.00 *30.00*
*g.* Thick "V" 25.00 35.00
*i.* "6d" omitted 500.00
*52e* A1 1sh on 1sh brown 10.00 .50
*f.* Mixed periods 27.50 25.00
*h.* Pair, one with level periods 50.00 *55.00*
*i.* Thick "V" 32.50 11.00
*52j* A1 1sh on 1sh orange *1,500.* *1,500.*
*53c* A1 5sh on 5sh green 10.50 *15.00*
*d.* Mixed periods 400.00 400.00
*e.* Pair, one with level periods *1,600.*
*f.* "5" with short flag 65.00 *77.50*
*g.* Thick "V" 72.50 *60.00*

Stamps with mixed periods have one or two periods level with the bottoms of letters. One stamp in each pane had all periods level. Later settings had several stamps with thick "V." Forgeries of the scarcer varieties exist.

"V.R.I." stands for Victoria Regina Imperatrix. On No. 59, "E.R.I." stands for Edward Rex Imperator.

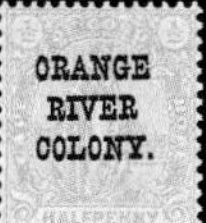

Cape of Good Hope Stamps of 1893-98 Overprinted

**1900 Wmk. 16**

54 A15 ½p green .65 .25
*a.* No period after "COLONY" 12.00 *25.00*
*b.* Double overprint 900.00 775.00
55 A13 2½p ultramarine 3.50 1.00
*a.* No period after "COLONY" 82.50 82.50

### Overprinted as in 1900

**1902, May**

56 A15 1p carmine rose 2.25 .25
*a.* No period after "COLONY" 25.00 *30.00*

### Nos. 51d, 53c, Surcharged and No. 8b Surcharged like No. 51 but Reading "E.R.I."

### Carmine or Vermilion and Black Surcharges

**1902 Unwmk.**

57 A1 4p on 6p on 6p ultra 1.60 2.25
*a.* Thick "V" 2.75 *8.25*
*b.* As "a," invtd. "1" instead of "I" 7.25 *18.50*
*c.* No period after "R" 42.50 *55.00*

### Black Surcharge

59 A1 6p on 6p ultra 6.00 *19.00*
*a.* Double surcharge, one invtd. — —

### Orange Surcharge

60 A1 1sh on 5sh on 5sh grn 10.50 *25.00*
*a.* Thick "V" 17.50 *55.00*
*b.* "5" with short flag 80.00 *95.00*
*c.* Double surcharge 1,100.
*Nos. 57-60 (3)* 18.10 *46.25*

"E.R.I." stands for Edward Rex Imperator.

King Edward VII — A8

**1903-04 Wmk. 2 Typo.**

61 A8 ½p yellow green 10.00 2.50
62 A8 1p carmine 8.50 .25
63 A8 2p chocolate 10.00 1.00
64 A8 2½p ultra 6.00 1.25
65 A8 3p violet 10.50 1.25
66 A8 4p olive grn & car 42.50 5.50
67 A8 6p violet & car 9.25 1.25
68 A8 1sh bister & car 50.00 3.00
69 A8 5sh red brn & bl ('04) 160.00 30.00
*Nos. 61-69 (9)* 306.75 46.00

Some of the above stamps are found with the overprint "C. S. A. R." for use by the Central South African Railway.

The "IOSTAGE" variety on the 4p is the result of filled in type.

Issue dates: 1p, Feb. 3. ½p, 2p, 2½p, 3p, 4p, 6p, 1sh, July 6. 5sh, Oct. 31.

**1907-08 Wmk. 3**

70 A8 ½p yellow green 16.50 1.10
71 A8 1p carmine 10.50 .35
72 A8 4p olive grn & car 5.00 5.25
73 A8 1sh bister & car 85.00 25.00
*Nos. 70-73 (4)* 117.00 31.70

The "IOSTAGE" variety on the 4p is the result of filled-in type.

Stamps of Orange River Colony were replaced by those of Union of South Africa.

### MILITARY STAMP

M1

**1899, Oct. 15 Unwmk. *Perf. 12***

M1 M1 black, *bister yellow* 50.00 60.00

No. M1 was provided to members of the Orange Free State army on active service during the Second Boer War. Soldiers' mail carried free was required to bear either No. M1 or be signed by the sender's unit commander. The stamps were used extensively from Oct. 1899 until the fall of Kroonstad in May 1900.

No. M1 was typeset and printed by Curling & Co., Bloemfontein, in sheets of 20 (5x4), with each row of five containing slightly different types.

Forgeries exist. The most common counterfeits either have 17 pearls, rather than 16, in the top and bottom frames, or omit the periods after "BRIEF" and "FRANKO."

## PAKISTAN

'pa-ki-ˌstan

LOCATION — In southern, central Asia
GOVT. — Republic
AREA — 307,293 sq. mi.
POP. — 130,579,571 (1998)
CAPITAL — Islamabad

Pakistan was formed August 14, 1947, when India was divided into the Dominions of the Union of India and Pakistan, with some princely states remaining independent. Pakistan became a republic on March 23, 1956.

Pakistan had two areas made up of all or part of several predominantly Moslem provinces in the northwest and northeast corners of pre-1947 India. West Pakistan consists of the entire provinces of Baluchistan, Sind (Scinde) and "Northwest Frontier," and 15 districts of the Punjab. East Pakistan, consisting of the Sylhet district in Assam and 14 districts in Bengal Province, became independent as Bangladesh in December 1971.

The state of Las Bela was incorporated into Pakistan.

12 Pies = 1 Anna
16 Annas = 1 Rupee
100 Paisa = 1 Rupee (1961)

**Catalogue values for all unused stamps in this country are for Never Hinged items.**

### Watermarks

Wmk. 274

Wmk. 351 — Crescent and Star Multiple

### Stamps of India, 1937-43, Overprinted in Black

Nos. 1-12

Nos. 13-19

***Perf. 13½x14***

**1947, Oct. 1 Wmk. 196**

1 A83 3p slate .25 .25
2 A83 ½a rose violet .25 .25
3 A83 9p lt green .25 .25
4 A83 1a car rose .25 .25
4A A84 1a3p bister ('49) 4.75 *5.75*
5 A84 1½a dk purple .25 .25
6 A84 2a scarlet .25 .40
7 A84 3a violet .25 .40
8 A84 3½a ultra 2.00 *3.00*
9 A85 4a chocolate .55 .30
10 A85 6a peacock blue 2.10 1.25
11 A85 8a blue violet .65 *.85*
12 A85 12a carmine lake 2.10 .40
13 A81 14a rose violet 5.75 3.50
14 A82 1r brn & slate 3.50 1.50
*a.* Inverted overprint 310.00
*b.* Pair, one without ovpt. 900.00
15 A82 2r dk brn & dk vio 6.50 3.25
16 A82 5r dp ultra & dk grn 8.00 5.00
17 A82 10r rose car & dk vio 10.00 6.50
18 A82 15r dk grn & dk brn 90.00 *110.00*

**19** A82 25r dk vio & bl vio 70.00 70.00
*Nos. 1-19 (20)* 207.65 213.35
Set, hinged 135.00

Provisional use of stamps of India with handstamped or printed "PAKISTAN" was authorized in 1947-49. Nos. 4A, 14a 14b exist only as provisional issues.

Used values are for postal cancels. Telegraph cancels (concentric circles) sell for much less.

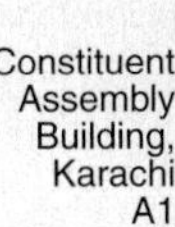

Constituent Assembly Building, Karachi A1

Crescent and Urdu Inscription — A2

Designs: 2½a, Karachi Airport entrance. 3a, Lahore Fort gateway.

**Unwmk.**

**1948, July 9 Engr. *Perf. 14***

**20** A1 1½a bright ultra 1.25 *2.00*
**21** A1 2½a green 1.25 .25
**22** A1 3a chocolate 1.25 .30

***Perf. 12***

**23** A2 1r red 1.25 .85
*a.* Perf. 14 6.00 *10.00*
*Nos. 20-23 (4)* 5.00 3.40

Pakistan's independence, Aug. 15, 1947.

Examples of No. 23a used on cover are unknown. Used examples of No. 23a are cto.

Scales, Star and Crescent A3

Star and Crescent A4

Karachi Airport Building A5

Karachi Port Authority Building — A6

Khyber Pass — A7

2½a, 3½a, 4a, Ghulan Muhammed Dam, Indus River, Sind. 1r, 2r, 5r, Salimullah Hostel.

***Perf. 12½, 14 (3a, 10a), 14x13½ (2½a, 3½a, 6a, 12a)***

**1948-57 Unwmk.**

**24** A3 3p org red, perf. 12½ .25 .25
*a.* Perf. 13½ ('54) 2.00 1.00
**25** A3 6p pur, perf. 12½ 1.25 .25
*a.* Perf. 13½ ('54) 4.00 3.50
**26** A3 9p dk grn, perf. 12½ .55 .25
*a.* Perf. 13½ ('54) 3.50 1.75
**27** A4 1a dark blue .25 .50
**28** A4 1½a gray green .25 .25
**29** A4 2a orange red 4.50 .70
**30** A6 2½a green 6.50 *5.00*
**31** A5 3a olive green 8.00 1.00
**32** A6 3½a violet blue 6.50 *4.00*
**33** A6 4a chocolate 1.25 .25
**34** A6 6a deep blue 2.00 .55
**35** A6 8a black 2.00 *1.25*
**36** A5 10a red 8.00 *8.00*
**37** A6 12a red 8.00 1.25

***Perf. 14***

**38** A5 1r ultra 19.00 .25
*a.* Perf. 13½ ('54) 25.00 7.00
**39** A5 2r dark brown 20.00 .80
*a.* Perf. 13½ ('54) 30.00 3.00

***Perf. 13½***

**40** A5 5r car ('54) 13.00 .40
*a.* Perf. 13½x14 17.00 2.25

***Perf. 13***

**41** A7 10r rose lilac ('51) 19.00 2.50
*a.* Perf. 14 14.00 *26.00*
*b.* Perf. 12 110.00 8.50
**42** A7 15r blue green ('57) 20.00 16.00
*a.* Perf. 14 20.00 *65.00*
*b.* Perf. 12 32.50 20.00

***Perf. 14***

**43** A7 25r purple 55.00 *67.50*
*a.* Perf. 13 ('54) 40.00 27.50
*b.* Perf. 12 32.50 *37.50*
*Nos. 24-43 (20)* 195.30 110.95
Set, hinged 100.00

Many compound perforations exist.

See No. 259, types A9-A11. For surcharges and overprints see Nos. 124, O14-O26, O35-O37, O41-O43A, O52, O63, O68.

Imperfs of Nos. 24-43 are from proof sheets improperly removed from the printer's archives.

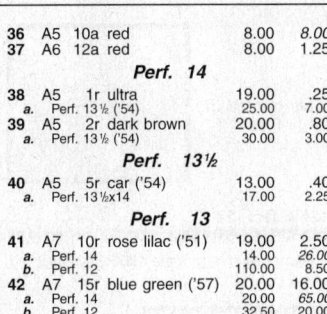

"Quaid-i-Azam" (Great Leader), "Mohammed Ali Jinnah" — A8

**1949, Sept. 11 Engr. *Perf. 13½x14***

**44** A8 1½a brown 1.75 1.00
**45** A8 3a dark green 2.25 1.25
**46** A8 10a blk *(English inscriptions)* 6.00 *6.00*
*Nos. 44-46 (3)* 10.00 8.25

1st anniv. of the death of Mohammed Ali Jinnah (1876-1948), Moslem lawyer, president of All-India Moslem League and first Governor General of Pakistan.

**Re-engraved (Crescents Reversed)**

A9

A10

A11

***Perf. 12½, 13½x14 (3a, 10a), 14x13½ (6a, 12a)***

**1949-53**

**47** A10 1a dk blue ('50) 2.50 .55
*a.* Perf. 13 ('52) 3.00 .25
**48** A10 1½a gray green 7.00 2.00
*a.* Perf. 13 ('53) 2.50 .25
**49** A10 2a orange red 2.50 .55
*a.* Perf. 13 ('53) 2.00 .25
**50** A9 3a olive green 7.50 1.00
**51** A11 6a deep blue ('50) 14.00 .50
**52** A11 8a black ('50) 6.00 1.10
**53** A9 10a red 7.50 1.25
**54** A11 12a red ('50) 27.50 .90
*Nos. 47-54 (8)* 74.50 7.85

For overprints see #O27-O31, O38-O40.

Vase and Plate — A12

Star and Crescent, Plane and Hour Glass — A13

Moslem Leaf Pattern — A14

Arch and Lamp of Learning A15

**1951, Aug. 14 Engr. *Perf. 13***

**55** A12 2½a dark red 1.90 1.25
**56** A13 3a dk rose lake 1.00 .25
**57** A12 3½a dp ultra (Urdu "⅓3") 1.25 *8.00*
**57A** A12 3½a dp ultra (Urdu "3½") ('56) 4.50 6.00
**58** A14 4a deep green 1.50 .25
**59** A14 6a red orange 1.50 .25
**60** A15 8a brown 4.50 .35
**61** A15 10a purple 2.25 .60
**62** A13 12a dk slate blue 2.00 .25
*Nos. 55-62 (9)* 20.40 17.20

Fourth anniversary of independence.

On No. 57, the characters of the Urdu denomination at right appears as "⅓3." On the reengraved No. 57A, they read "3½."

Issue date: Dec. 1956.

See Nos. 88, O32-O34.

For surcharges see Nos. 255, 257.

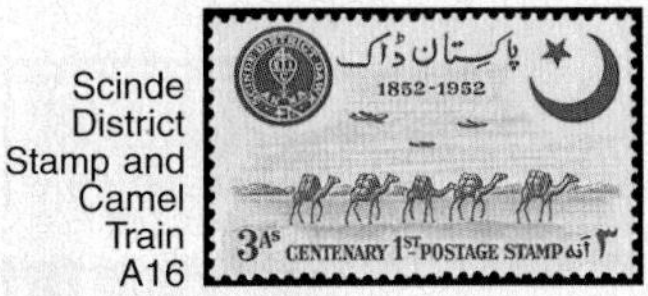
Scinde District Stamp and Camel Train A16

**1952, Aug. 14**

**63** A16 3a olive green, *citron* 1.00 .85
**64** A16 12a dark brown, *salmon* 1.75 .25

5th anniv. of Pakistan's Independence and the cent. of the 1st postage stamps in the Indo-Pakistan sub-continent.

Peak K-2, Karakoram Mountains A17

**1954, Dec. 25**

**65** A17 2a violet .50 .30

Conquest of K-2, world's 2nd highest mountain peak, in July 1954.

Kaghan Valley — A18

Gilgit Mountains A19

Tea Garden, East Pakistan A20

Designs: 1a, Badshahi Mosque, Lahore. 1½a, Emperor Jahangir's Mausoleum, Lahore. 1r, Cotton field. 2r, River craft and jute field.

**1954, Aug. 14 Engr.**

**66** A18 6p rose violet .25 .25
**67** A19 9p blue *5.00* 1.00
**68** A19 1a carmine rose .25 .25
**69** A18 1½a red .25 .25
**70** A20 14a dark green 5.00 .25
**71** A20 1r yellow green 11.00 .25
**72** A20 2r orange 3.00 .25
*Nos. 66-72 (7)* 24.75 2.50

Seventh anniversary of independence.

Nos. 66, 69 exist in booklet panes of 4 torn from sheets. Value of booklet, $9.

For overprints & surcharges see #77, 101, 123, 126, O44-O50, O53-O56, O60-O62, O67, O69-O71.

Karnaphuli Paper Mill, East Pakistan (Urdu "½2") — A21

6a, Textile mill. 8a, Jute mill. 12a, Sui gas plant.

**1955, Aug. 14 Unwmk. *Perf. 13***

**73** A21 2½a dk car (Urdu "½2") .50 *1.50*
**73A** A21 2½a dk car (Urdu "2½") ('56) 1.00 *1.50*
**74** A21 6a dark blue 1.50 .25
**75** A21 8a violet 4.00 .25
**76** A21 12a car lake & org 4.00 .25
*Nos. 73-76 (5)* 11.00 3.75

Eighth anniversary of independence.

On No. 73, the characters of the Urdu denomination at right appear as "½2." On the reengraved No. 73A, they read "2½."

Issue date: Dec. 1956.

See No. 87. For overprints and surcharges see Nos. 78, 102-103, 256, O51, O58-O59.

Nos. 69 and 76 Overprinted in Ultramarine

**1955, Oct. 24**

**77** A18 1½a red *3.75* *7.00*
**78** A21 12a car lake & org *1.50* *7.00*

UN, 10th anniv.

Beware of forgeries. Two settings exists, "United Nations", 1mm to left of normal "N" over "NI". Value set, $25.

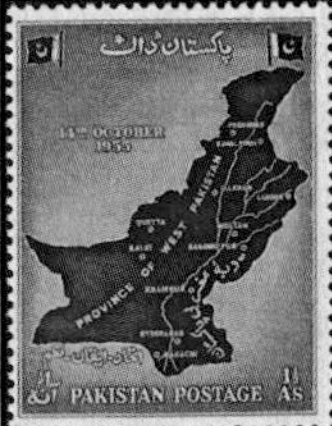
Map of West Pakistan — A22

**1955, Dec. 7 Unwmk. *Perf. 13½x13***

**79** A22 1½a dark green .65 .50
**80** A22 2a dark brown .60 .25
**81** A22 12a deep carmine 1.00 .50
*Nos. 79-81 (3)* 2.25 1.25

West Pakistan unification, Nov. 14, 1955.
Nos. 79-81 from the bottom (eighth) row of the sheet are 41.5mm tall instead of 40.5mm. Value, $4 each.

National Assembly A23

**1956, Mar. 23 Litho. *Perf. 13x12½***

**82** A23 2a green .75 .25

Proclamation of the Republic of Pakistan, Mar. 23, 1956.

Crescent and Star — A24

**1956, Aug. 14 Engr. *Perf. 13***

**83** A24 2a red .90 .25

Ninth anniversary of independence.
For surcharges and overprints see Nos. 127, O57, O72-O73.

Map of East Pakistan — A25

**1956, Oct. 15 *Perf. 13½x13***

**84** A25 1½a dark green .40 *1.50*
**85** A25 2a dark brown .50 .25
**86** A25 12a deep red .40 *1.25*
*Nos. 84-86 (3)* 1.30 3.00

1st Session at Dacca (East Pakistan) of the National Assembly of Pakistan.
Nos. 84-86 from the bottom (eighth) row of the sheet are 1mm taller. Value, $4 each.

**Redrawn Types of 1951, 1955 and**

Orange Tree — A26

***Perf. 13x13½, 13½x13***

**1957, Mar. 23 Engr.**

**87** A21 2½a dark carmine .25 .25
**88** A12 3½a bright blue .35 .25
**89** A26 10r dk green & orange .90 .40
*Nos. 87-89 (3)* 1.50 .90

Nos. 87-89 inscribed "Pakistan" in English, Urdu and Bengali. Denomination in English only.
Islamic Republic of Pakistan, 1st anniv.
See Nos. 95, 258, 475A. For surcharge and overprint see Nos. 159, O64.

Flag and Broken Chain — A27

**1957, May 10 Litho. *Perf. 13***

**90** A27 1½a green .50 .25
**91** A27 12a blue 1.25 .50

Cent. of the struggle for Independence (Indian Mutiny).
Examples of Nos. 90-91 exist that are 1mm taller than other stamps from the sheet. Value, $4 each.

Industrial Plants and Roses as Symbols of Progress A28

**1957, Aug. 14 Unwmk. *Perf. 13½***

**92** A28 1½a light ultra .25 .25
**93** A28 4a orange vermilion .50 *1.50*
**94** A28 12a red lilac 1.00 .50
*Nos. 92-94 (3)* 1.75 2.25

Tenth anniversary of independence.

**Type of 1957**

Design: 15r, Coconut Tree.

**1958, Mar. 23 Engr. *Perf. 13½x13***

**95** A26 15r rose lilac & red 2.50 1.50

Issued to commemorate the second anniversary of the Islamic Republic of Pakistan.

Verse of Iqbal Poem A29

**1958, Apr. 21 Photo. *Perf. 14½x14***
**Black Inscriptions**

**96** A29 1½a citron .50 .40
**97** A29 2a orange brown .50 .25
**98** A29 14a aqua *2.50* 1.50
*Nos. 96-98 (3)* 3.50 *2.15*

20th anniv. of the death of Mohammad Iqbal (1877-1938), Moslem poet and philosopher.

Globe and Book — A30

**1958, Dec. 10 Litho. *Perf. 13***

**99** A30 1½a Prus blue .25 .25
**100** A30 14a dark brown .50 *.25*

10th anniv. of the signing of the Universal Declaration of Human Rights.

Nos. 66 and 75 Overprinted

**1958, Dec. 28 Engr. *Perf. 13***

**101** A18 6p rose violet .25 .25
**102** A21 8a violet .40 .25

2nd National Boy Scout Jamboree held at Chittagong, Dec. 28-Jan. 4.
Numerous plate flaws exist for Nos. 101-102. Value: $2 each.

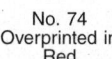

No. 74 Overprinted in Red

**1959, Oct. 27**

**103** A21 6a dark blue .80 .25

First anniversary of the 1958 Revolution.

Red Cross — A31

**Engr.; Cross Typo.**

**1959, Nov. 19 Unwmk. *Perf. 13***

**104** A31 2a green & red .30 .25
**105** A31 10a dk blue & red .60 .25

Armed Forces Emblem — A32

**1960, Jan. 10 Litho. *Perf. 13***

**106** A32 2a blue grn, red & ultra .40 .25
**107** A32 14a ultra & red .90 .25

Issued for Armed Forces Day.

Map Showing Disputed Areas A33

**1960, Mar. 23 Engr. Unwmk.**

**108** A33 6p purple .35 .25
**109** A33 2a copper red .55 .25
**110** A33 8a green 1.10 .25
**111** A33 1r blue 1.75 .25
*Nos. 108-111 (4)* 3.75 1.00

Publicizing the border dispute with India over Jammu and Kashmir, Junagarh and Manavadar.
For overprints and surcharges see Nos. 122, 125, 128, 178, O65-O66, O74-O75.

Uprooted Oak Emblem — A34

**1960, Apr. 7**

**112** A34 2a carmine rose .25 .25
**113** A34 10a green .25 *.25*

Issued to publicize World Refugee Year, July 1, 1959-June 30, 1960.

House, Field and Column (Allegory of Democratic Development) A35

**1960, Oct. 27 Photo. *Perf. 13***

**114** A35 2a brown, pink & grn .25 .25
*a.* Green & pink omitted 18.00
**115** A35 14a multicolored .50 *.75*

Revolution Day, Oct. 27, 1960.
No. 114a is easily counterfeited.

Punjab Agricultural College, Lyallpur A36

Design: 8a, College shield.

**1960, Oct. Engr. *Perf. 12½x14***

**116** A36 2a rose red & gray blue .25 .25
**117** A36 8a lilac & green .25 *.30*

50th anniv. of the Punjab Agricultural College, Lyallpur.

Caduceus, College Emblem — A37

**1960, Nov. 16 Photo. *Perf. 13½x13***

**118** A37 2a blue, yel & blk .50 .25
**119** A37 14a car rose, blk & emerald 1.75 1.00

King Edward Medical College, Lahore, cent.

Map of South-East Asia and Commission Emblem — A38

**1960, Dec. 5 Engr. *Perf. 13***

**120** A38 14a red orange .90 *.25*

Conf. of the Commission on Asian and Far Eastern Affairs of the Intl. Chamber of Commerce, Karachi, Dec. 5-9.

"Kim's Gun" and Scout Badge A39

***Perf. 12½x14***

**1960, Dec. 24 Unwmk.**

**121** A39 2a dk green, car & yel .75 .25

3rd Natl. Boy Scout Jamboree, Lahore, Dec. 24-31.

No. 110 Ovptd. in Red

**1961, Feb. 12**

**122** A33 8a green .95 .95

10th Lahore Stamp Exhibition, Feb. 12.

**New Currency**

Nos. 24, 68-69, 83, 108-109 Surcharged with New Value in Paisa

**1961 *Perf. 13***

**123** A18 1p on 1½a red .40 .25
**124** A3 2p on 3p orange red .25 .25
**125** A33 3p on 6p purple .25 .25
**126** A19 7p on 1a car rose .40 .25
**127** A24 13p on 2a red .40 .25
**128** A33 13p on 2a copper red .30 .25
*Nos. 123-128 (6)* 2.00 1.50

Various violet handstamped surcharges were applied to a variety of regular-issue stamps. Most of these repeat the denomination of the basic stamp and add the new value. Example: "8 Annas (50 Paisa)" on No. 75. Many errors exist from printer's waste.
For overprints see Nos. O74-O75.

Many errors exist from No. 123 onwards on stamps printed within Pakistan. These are generally printer's waste.

Khyber Pass — A40

Chota Sona Masjid Gate — A41

Design: 10p, 13p, 25p, 40p, 50p, 75p, 90p, Shalimar Gardens, Lahore.

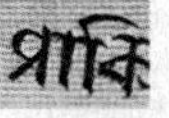
Type I

Type II

Two types of 1p, 2p and 5p:

I — First Bengali character beside "N" lacks appendage at left side of loop.

II — This character has a downward-pointing appendage at left side of loop, correcting "sh" to read "p".

On Nos. 129, 130, 132 the corrections were made individually on the plates, and each stamp may differ slightly. On No. 131a, the corrected letter is more clearly corrected, and the added appendage comes close to, almost touching, the leg of the first Bengali character.

**1961-63 Engr.** ***Perf. 13½x14***

| | | | | | |
|---|---|---|---|---|---|
| **129** | A40 | 1p | violet (II) | 1.00 | .25 |
| *a.* | | | Type I | 1.50 | .25 |
| **130** | A40 | 2p | rose red (II) | 1.00 | .25 |
| *a.* | | | Type I | 1.50 | .25 |
| **131** | A40 | 3p | magenta | .75 | .25 |
| *a.* | | | Retouched plate | 5.00 | 5.00 |
| **132** | A40 | 5p | ultra (II) | 4.50 | 1.00 |
| *a.* | | | Type I | 3.00 | .25 |
| **133** | A40 | 7p | emerald | 2.00 | .25 |
| **134** | A40 | 10p | brown | .25 | .25 |
| **135** | A40 | 13p | blue vio | .25 | .25 |
| **136** | A40 | 25p | dark blue ('62) | 5.00 | .25 |
| **137** | A40 | 40p | dull purple ('62) | .25 | .25 |
| **138** | A40 | 50p | dull green ('62) | .25 | .25 |
| **139** | A40 | 75p | dk carmine ('62) | .45 | .70 |
| **140** | A40 | 90p | lt olive grn ('62) | .70 | .70 |

***Perf. 13½x13***

| | | | | | |
|---|---|---|---|---|---|
| **141** | A41 | 1r | vermilion ('63) | 1.00 | .25 |
| **142** | A41 | 1.25r | purple | .75 | .75 |
| **143** | A41 | 2r | orange ('63) | 2.00 | .25 |
| **144** | A41 | 5r | green ('63) | 6.00 | 2.25 |
| | | | *Nos. 129-144 (16)* | 26.15 | 8.15 |

See #200-203. For surcharge and overprints see Nos. 184, O76-O82, O85-O93A.

**Designs Redrawn**

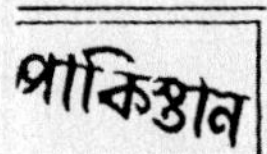
1961-62 Bengali Inscription

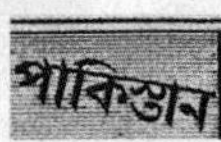
Redrawn Bengali Inscription

Bengali inscription redrawn with straight connecting line across top of characters. Shading of scenery differs, especially in Shalimar Gardens design where reflection is strengthened and trees at right are composed of horizontal lines instead of vertical lines and dots.

Designs as before; 15p, 20p, Shalimar Gardens.

**1963-70** ***Perf. 13½x14***

| | | | | | |
|---|---|---|---|---|---|
| *129b* | A40 | 1p | violet | .25 | .25 |
| *130b* | A40 | 2p | rose red ('64) | 1.75 | .25 |
| *131b* | A40 | 3p | magenta ('70) | 8.00 | 2.50 |
| *132b* | A40 | 5p | ultra | .25 | .25 |
| *133a* | A40 | 7p | emerald ('64) | 7.00 | 1.50 |
| *134a* | A40 | 10p | brown | .25 | .25 |
| *135a* | A40 | 13p | blue violet | .25 | .25 |
| **135B** | A40 | 15p | rose lilac ('64) | .25 | .25 |
| **135C** | A40 | 20p | dull green ('70) | .25 | .25 |
| *136a* | A40 | 25p | dark blue | 5.00 | .50 |
| *137a* | A40 | 40p | dull purple ('64) | .25 | .25 |
| *138a* | A40 | 50p | dull green ('64) | .25 | .25 |
| *139a* | A40 | 75p | dark carmine ('64) | 1.25 | .70 |
| *140a* | A40 | 90p | lt olive green ('64) | 4.00 | 1.00 |
| | | | *Nos. 129b-140a (14)* | 29.00 | 8.45 |

Many exists imperf.

For overprints see #174, O76b, O77b, O78a, O79b, O80a, O81a, O82a, O83-O84A, O85a, O86a.

Warsak Dam, Kabul River A42

**1961, July 1 Engr.** ***Perf. 12½x13½***

| | | | | | |
|---|---|---|---|---|---|
| **150** | A42 | 40p | black & lt ultra | .60 | .25 |

Dedication of hydroelectric Warsak Project.

Symbolic Flower — A43

**1961, Oct. 2 Unwmk.** ***Perf. 14***

| | | | | | |
|---|---|---|---|---|---|
| **151** | A43 | 13p | greenish blue | .50 | .25 |
| **152** | A43 | 90p | red lilac | 1.00 | .25 |

Issued for Children's Day.

Roses — A44

**1961, Nov. 4** ***Perf. 13½x13***

| | | | | | |
|---|---|---|---|---|---|
| **153** | A44 | 13p | deep green & ver | .40 | .25 |
| **154** | A44 | 90p | blue & vermilion | .90 | .90 |

Cooperative Day.

Police Crest and Traffic Policeman's Hand — A45

**1961, Nov. 30 Photo.** ***Perf. 13x12½***

| | | | | | |
|---|---|---|---|---|---|
| **155** | A45 | 13p | dk blue, sil & blk | .50 | .25 |
| **156** | A45 | 40p | red, silver & blk | 1.00 | .25 |

Centenary of the police force.

"Eagle Locomotive, 1861" — A46

Design: 50pa, Diesel Engine, 1961.

**1961, Dec. 31** ***Perf. 13½x14***

| | | | | | |
|---|---|---|---|---|---|
| **157** | A46 | 13p | yellow, green & blk | .75 | .80 |
| **158** | A46 | 50p | green, blk & yellow | 1.00 | 1.50 |

Centenary of Pakistan railroads.

**No. 87 Surcharged in Red with New Value, Boeing 720-B Jetliner and: "FIRST JET FLIGHT KARACHI-DACCA"**

**1962, Feb. 6 Engr.** ***Perf. 13***

| | | | | | |
|---|---|---|---|---|---|
| **159** | A21 | 13p | on 2½a dk carmine | 1.75 | 1.25 |

1st jet flight from Karachi to Dacca, Feb. 6, 1962.

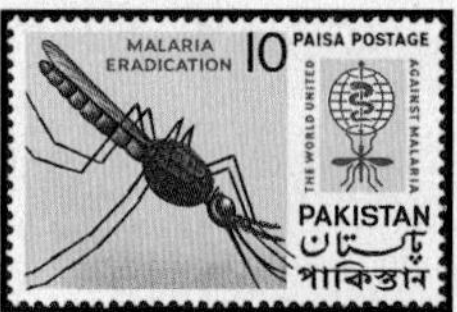

Mosquito and Malaria Eradication Emblem — A47

13p, Dagger pointing at mosquito, and emblem.

**1962, Apr. 7 Photo.** ***Perf. 13½x14***

| | | | | | |
|---|---|---|---|---|---|
| **160** | A47 | 10p | multicolored | .45 | .25 |
| **161** | A47 | 13p | multicolored | .45 | .25 |

WHO drive to eradicate malaria.

Map of Pakistan and Jasmine — A48

**1962, June 8 Unwmk.** ***Perf. 12***

| | | | | | |
|---|---|---|---|---|---|
| **162** | A48 | 40p | grn, yel grn & gray | 1.00 | .25 |

Introduction of new Pakistan Constitution.

Soccer A49

13p, Hockey & Olympic gold medal. 25p, Squash rackets & British squash rackets championship cup. 40p, Cricket & Ayub challenge cup.

**1962, Aug. 14 Engr.** ***Perf. 12½x13½***

| | | | | | |
|---|---|---|---|---|---|
| **163** | A49 | 7p | blue & black | .25 | .25 |
| **164** | A49 | 13p | green & black | .60 | 1.50 |
| **165** | A49 | 25p | lilac & black | .25 | .25 |
| **166** | A49 | 40p | brown org & blk | 2.00 | 2.25 |
| | | | *Nos. 163-166 (4)* | 3.10 | 4.25 |

Marble Fruit Dish and Clay Flask — A50

13p, Sporting goods. 25p, Camel skin lamp, brass jug. 40p, Wooden powder bowl, cane basket. 50p, Inlaid box, brassware.

**1962, Nov. 10** ***Perf. 13½x13***

| | | | | | |
|---|---|---|---|---|---|
| **167** | A50 | 7p | dark red | .25 | .25 |
| **168** | A50 | 13p | dark green | 1.50 | .75 |
| **169** | A50 | 25p | bright purple | .25 | .25 |
| **170** | A50 | 40p | yellow green | .25 | .25 |
| **171** | A50 | 50p | dull red | .25 | .25 |
| | | | *Nos. 167-171 (5)* | 2.50 | 1.75 |

Pakistan Intl. Industries Fair, Oct. 12-Nov. 20, publicizing Pakistan's small industries.

Children's Needs A51

**1962, Dec. 11 Photo.** ***Perf. 13½x14***

| | | | | | |
|---|---|---|---|---|---|
| **172** | A51 | 13p | blue, plum & blk | .35 | .25 |
| **173** | A51 | 40p | multicolored | .35 | .25 |

16th anniv. of UNICEF.

**No. 135a Overprinted in Red: "U.N. FORCE W. IRIAN"**

**1963, Feb. 15 Engr. Unwmk.**

| | | | | | |
|---|---|---|---|---|---|
| **174** | A40 | 13p | blue violet | .25 | .60 |

Issued to commemorate the dispatch of Pakistani troops to West New Guinea.

Camel, Bull, Dancing Horse and Drummer A52

**1963, Mar. 13 Photo.** ***Perf. 12***

| | | | | | |
|---|---|---|---|---|---|
| **175** | A52 | 13p | multicolored | .25 | .25 |

National Horse and Cattle Show, 1963.

Wheat and Tractor A53

Design: 50p, Hands and heap of rice.

**1963, Mar. 21 Engr.** ***Perf. 12½x13½***

| | | | | | |
|---|---|---|---|---|---|
| **176** | A53 | 13p | brown orange | 2.50 | .25 |
| **177** | A53 | 50p | brown | 4.00 | .55 |

FAO "Freedom from Hunger" campaign.

**No. 109 Surcharged with New Value and: "INTERNATIONAL/DACCA STAMP/EXHIBITION/1963"**

**1963, Mar. 23** ***Perf. 13***

| | | | | | |
|---|---|---|---|---|---|
| **178** | A33 | 13p | on 2a copper red | .50 | .50 |

International Stamp Exhibition at Dacca.

Centenary Emblem — A54

**Engr. and Typo.**

**1963, June 25** ***Perf. 13½x12½***

| | | | | | |
|---|---|---|---|---|---|
| **179** | A54 | 40p | dark gray & red | 1.50 | .25 |

International Red Cross, cent.

Paharpur Stupa A55

Designs: 13p, Cistern, Mohenjo-Daro, vert. 40p, Stupas, Taxila. 50pa, Stupas, Mainamati.

***Perf. 12½x13½, 13½x12½***

**1963, Sept. 16 Engr. Unwmk.**

| | | | | | |
|---|---|---|---|---|---|
| **180** | A55 | 7p | ultra | .60 | .25 |
| **181** | A55 | 13p | brown | .60 | .25 |
| **182** | A55 | 40p | carmine rose | 1.10 | .25 |
| **183** | A55 | 50p | dark violet | 1.40 | .65 |
| | | | *Nos. 180-183 (4)* | 3.70 | 1.40 |

**No. 131 Surcharged and Overprinted: "100 YEARS OF P.W.D. OCTOBER, 1963"**

**1963, Oct. 7** ***Perf. 13½x14***

| | | | | | |
|---|---|---|---|---|---|
| **184** | A40 | 13p | on 3pa magenta | .25 | .25 |

Centenary of Public Works Department.

Atatürk Mausoleum, Ankara A56

**1963, Nov. 10** ***Perf. 13x13½***
**185** A56 50p red .65 .25

25th anniv. of the death of Kemal Atatürk, pres. of Turkey.

Globe and UNESCO Emblem A57

**1963, Dec. 10 Photo.** ***Perf. 13½x14***
**186** A57 50p dk brn, vio blue & red .45 .25

15th anniv. of the Universal Declaration of Human Rights.

Multan Thermal Power Station A58

**1963, Dec. 25 Engr.** ***Perf. 12½x13½***
**187** A58 13p ultra .25 .25

Issued to mark the opening of the Multan Thermal Power Station.

**Type of 1961-63**
***Perf. 13½x13***

**1963-65 Engr. Wmk. 351**
**200** A41 1r vermilion .40 .25
**201** A41 1.25r purple ('64) 2.75 .30
**202** A41 2r orange 1.00 .25
**203** A41 5r green ('65) 6.75 .60
*Nos. 200-203 (4)* 10.90 1.40

For overprints see Nos. O92-O93A.

A59

13p, Temple of Thot, Dakka, and Queen Nefertari with Goddesses Hathor and Isis. 50p, Ramses II, Abu Simbel, and View of Nile.

***Perf. 13x13½***
**1964, Mar. 30 Unwmk.**
**204** A59 13p brick red & turq blue .60 .25
**205** A59 50p black & rose lilac 1.20 .25

UNESCO world campaign to save historic monuments in Nubia.

Pakistan Pavilion and Unisphere A60

1.25r, Pakistan pavilion, Unisphere, vert.

***Perf. 12½x14, 14x12½***
**1964, Apr. 22 Engr. Unwmk.**
**206** A60 13p ultramarine .25 .25
**207** A60 1.25r dp orange & ultra .40 .25

New York World's Fair, 1964-65.

Mausoleum of Shah Abdul Latif — A61

**1964, June 25** ***Perf. 13½x13***
**208** A61 50p magenta & ultra 1.00 .25

Bicentenary (?) of the death of Shah Abdul Latif of Bhit (1689-1752).

Examples of No. 208 exist that are 1mm taller than other stamps from the sheet. Value, $4.

Mausoleum of Jinnah — A62

Design: 15p, Mausoleum, horiz.

**1964, Sept. 11 Unwmk.** ***Perf. 13***
**209** A62 15p green .75 .25
**210** A62 50p greenish gray 1.50 .25

16th anniv. of the death of Mohammed Ali Jinnah (1876-1948), the Quaid-i-Azam (Great Leader), founder and president of Pakistan.

Bengali Alphabet on Slate and Slab with Urdu Alphabet A63

**1964, Oct. 5 Engr.**
**211** A63 15p brown .25 .25

Issued for Universal Children's Day.

West Pakistan University of Engineering and Technology — A64

**1964, Dec. 21** ***Perf. 12½x14***
**212** A64 15p henna brown .25 .25

1st convocation of the West Pakistan University of Engineering & Technology, Lahore, Dec. 1964.

Eyeglasses and Book — A65

***Perf. 13x13½***
**1965, Feb. 28 Litho. Unwmk.**
**213** A65 15p yellow & ultra .25 .25

Issued to publicize aid for the blind.

ITU Emblem, Telegraph Pole and Transmission Tower — A66

**1965, May 17 Engr.** ***Perf. 12½x14***
**214** A66 15p deep claret 1.90 .30

Cent. of the ITU.

ICY Emblem A67

**1965, June 26 Litho.** ***Perf. 13½***
**215** A67 15p blue & black .50 .25
**216** A67 50p yellow & green 1.50 .40

International Cooperation Year, 1965.

Hands Holding Book — A68

50p, Map & flags of Turkey, Iran & Pakistan.

***Perf. 13½x13, 13x12½***
**1965, July 21 Litho. Unwmk.**
**Size: 46x35mm**
**217** A68 15p org brn, dk brn & buff .25 .25
**Size: 54x30½mm**
**218** A68 50p multicolored 1.10 .25

1st anniv. of the signing of the Regional Cooperation for Development Pact by Turkey, Iran and Pakistan.

See Iran 1327-1328, Turkey 1648-1649.

Tanks, Army Emblem and Soldier — A69

Designs: 15p, Navy emblem, corvette No. O204 and officer. 50p, Air Force emblem, two F-104 Starfighters and pilot.

**1965, Dec. 25 Litho.** ***Perf. 13½x13***
**219** A69 7p multicolored 1.50 .25
**220** A69 15p multicolored 1.50 .25
**221** A69 50p multicolored 2.50 .30
*Nos. 219-221 (3)* 5.50 .80

Issued to honor the Pakistani armed forces.

Emblems of Pakistan Armed Forces — A70

**1966, Feb. 13 Litho.** ***Perf. 13½x13***
**222** A70 15p buff, grn & dk bl 1.00 .25

Issued for Armed Forces Day.

Atomic Reactor, Islamabad — A71

**Unwmk.**
**1966, Apr. 30 Engr.** ***Perf. 13***
**223** A71 15p black .25 .25

Pakistan's first atomic reactor.

Habib Bank Emblem A72

***Perf. 12½x13½***
**1966, Aug. 25 Litho. Unwmk.**
**224** A72 15p brown, org & dk grn .25 .25

25th anniversary of the Habib Bank.

Boy and Girl — A73

**1966, Oct. 3 Litho.** ***Perf. 13x13½***
**225** A73 15p multicolored .25 .25

Issued for Children's Day.

UNESCO Emblem A74

**1966, Nov. 24 Unwmk.** ***Perf. 14***
**226** A74 15p multicolored 1.00 .30

20th anniv. of UNESCO.

Secretariat Buildings, Islamabad, Flag and Pres. Mohammed Ayub Khan — A75

**1966, Nov. 29 Litho.** ***Perf. 13***
**227** A75 15p multicolored .30 .25
**228** A75 50p multicolored .60 .25

Publicizing the new capital, Islamabad.

Avicenna — A76

**1966, Dec. 3** ***Perf. 13½***
**229** A76 15p sal pink & slate grn .30 .25

Issued to publicize the Health Institute.

Mohammed Ali Jinnah — A77

Design: 50p, Different frame.

**Lithographed and Engraved**

**1966, Dec. 25 Unwmk.** ***Perf. 13***
**230** A77 15p orange, blk & bl .25 .25
**231** A77 50p lilac, blk & vio bl .35 .25

90th anniv. of the birth of Mohammed Ali Jinnah (1876-1948), 1st Governor General of Pakistan.

ITY Emblem — A78

**1967, Jan. 1** **Litho.**
**232** A78 15p bis brn, blue & blk .25 .25

International Tourist Year, 1967.

Red Crescent Emblem — A79

**1967, Jan. 10 Litho.** ***Perf. 13½***
**233** A79 15p brn, brn org & red .25 .25

Tuberculosis eradication campaign.

Scout Sign and Emblem A80

***Perf. 12½x13½***

**1967, Jan. 29** **Photo.**
**234** A80 15p dp plum & brn org .25 .25

4th National Pakistan Jamboree.
"Faisa" is a plate flaw, not an error. Value, unused or used, $5.

Justice Holding Scales — A81

**Unwmk.**

**1967, Feb. 17 Litho.** ***Perf. 13***
**235** A81 15p multicolored .25 .25

Centenary of High Court of West Pakistan.

Mohammad Iqbal — A82

**1967, Apr. 21 Litho.** ***Perf. 13***
**236** A82 15p red & brown .25 .25
**237** A82 1r dk green & brn .60 .25

90th anniv. of the birth of Mohammad Iqbal (1877-1938), poet and philosopher.

Flag of Valor — A83

**1967, May 15 Litho.** ***Perf. 13***
**238** A83 15p multicolored .25 .25

Flag of Valor awarded to the cities of Lahore, Sialkot and Sargodha.

Star and "20" — A84

**1967, Aug. 14 Photo. Unwmk.**
**239** A84 15p red & slate green .25 .25

20th anniversary of independence.

Rice Plant and Globe A85

Cotton Plant, Bale and Cloth — A86

Design: 50p, Raw jute, bale and cloth.

**1967, Sept. 26 Photo.** ***Perf. 13x13½***
**240** A85 10p dk blue & yellow .25 .25

***Perf. 13***
**241** A86 15p orange, bl grn & yel .25 .25
**242** A86 50p blue grn, brn & tan .25 .25
*Nos. 240-242 (3)* .75 .75

Issued to publicize major export products.

Toys — A87

**1967, Oct. 2 Litho.** ***Perf. 13***
**243** A87 15p multicolored .25 .25

Issued for International Children's Day.

Shah and Empress Farah of Iran — A88

**Lithographed and Engraved**

**1967, Oct. 26** ***Perf. 13***
**244** A88 50p yellow, blue & lilac 1.50 .25

Coronation of Shah Mohammed Riza Pahlavi and Empress Farah of Iran.

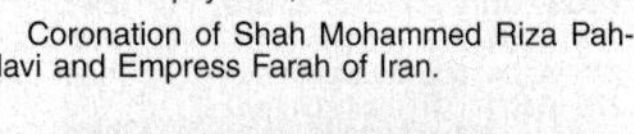

"Each for all, . . ." — A89

**1967, Nov. 4 Litho.** ***Perf. 13***
**245** A89 15p multicolored .25 .25

Cooperative Day, 1967.

Mangla Dam — A90

**1967, Nov. 23 Litho.** ***Perf. 13***
**246** A90 15p multicolored .25 .25

Indus Basin Project, harnessing the Indus River for flood control and irrigation.

"Fight Against Cancer" — A91

**1967, Dec. 26**
**247** A91 15p red & dk brown .70 .25

Issued to publicize the fight against cancer.

Human Rights Flame — A92

**1968, Jan. 31 Photo.** ***Perf. 14x12½***
**248** A92 15p Prus green & red .25 .25
**249** A92 50p yellow, silver & red .25 .25

International Human Rights Year 1968.

Agricultural University and Produce A93

**1968, Mar. 28 Litho.** ***Perf. 13½***
**250** A93 15p multicolored .25 .25

Issued to publicize the first convocation of the East Pakistan Agricultural University.

WHO Emblem — A94

**1968, Apr. 7 Photo.** ***Perf. 13½x12½***
**251** A94 15p emerald & orange .25 .25
**252** A94 50p orange & dk blue .25 .25

20th anniv. of WHO. "Pais" is a plate flaw, not an error. Value $2.

Kazi Nazrul Islam A95

**Lithographed and Engraved**

**1968, June 25 Unwmk.** ***Perf. 13***
**253** A95 15p dull yellow & brown .35 .25
**254** A95 50p rose & brown .65 .25

Kazi Nazrul Islam, poet and composer.

**Nos. 56, 61 and 74 Surcharged with New Value and Bars in Black or Red**

**1968, Sept. Engr.** ***Perf. 13***
**255** A13 4p on 3a dk rose lake 1.00 *1.75*
**256** A21 4p on 6a dk blue (R) 1.25 *1.75*
**257** A15 60p on 10a purple (R) 1.00 .35
*a.* Black surcharge 1.50 2.00
*Nos. 255-257 (3)* 3.25 3.85

**Types of 1948-57**

**1968 Wmk. 351 Engr.** ***Perf. 13***
**258** A26 10r dk grn & org 5.00 4.00
**259** A7 25r purple 6.00 6.00

Children with Hoops A96

**Unwmk.**

**1968, Oct. 7 Litho.** ***Perf. 13***
**260** A96 15p buff & multi .25 .25

Issued for International Children's Day.

Symbolic of Political Reforms — A97

Designs: 15p, Agricultural and industrial development. 50p, Defense. 60p, Scientific and cultural advancement.

**1968, Oct. 27 Litho. *Perf. 13***

**261** A97 10p multicolored .25 .25
**262** A97 15p multicolored .25 .25
**263** A97 50p multicolored 1.75 .35
**264** A97 60p multicolored .50 .35
*Nos. 261-264 (4)* 2.75 1.20

Development Decade, 1958-1968.

Chittagong Steel Mill — A98

**1969, Jan. 7 Unwmk. *Perf. 13***

**265** A98 15p lt gray grn, lt blue & blk .25 .25

Opening of Pakistan's first steel mill.

Family of Four A99

**1969, Jan. 14 Litho. *Perf. 13½***

**266** A99 15p lt blue & plum .25 .25

Issued to publicize family planning.

Hockey Player and Medal — A100

**1969, Jan. 30 Photo. *Perf. 13½***

**267** A100 15p green, lt bl, blk & gold 1.00 .30
**268** A100 1r grn, sal pink, blk & gold 2.25 .80

Pakistan's hockey victory at the 19th Olympic Games in Mexico.

Mirza Ghalib — A101

**1969, Feb. 15 Litho. *Perf. 13***

**269** A101 15p blue & multi .25 .25
**270** A101 50p multicolored .60 .25

Mirza Ghalib (Asad Ullab Beg Khan, 1797-1869), poet who modernized the Urdu language.

Dacca Railroad Station A102

**1969, Apr. 27 Litho. *Perf. 13***

**271** A102 15p yel, grn, blk & dl bl .60 .25

Opening of the new railroad station in Kamalpur area of Dacca.

ILO Emblem and Ornamental Border — A103

**1969, May 15 Litho. *Perf. 13½***

**272** A103 15p brt grn & ocher .25 .25
**273** A103 50p car rose & ocher .40 .25

50th anniv. of the ILO.

Lady on Balcony, Mogul Miniature, Pakistan A104

50p, Lady Serving Wine, Safavi miniature, Iran. 1r, Sultan Suleiman Receiving Sheik Abdul Latif, 16th cent. miniature, Turkey.

**1969, July 21 Litho. *Perf. 13***

**274** A104 20p multicolored .30 .25
**275** A104 50p multicolored .30 .25
**276** A104 1r multicolored .50 .25
*Nos. 274-276 (3)* 1.10 .75

5th anniv. of the signing of the Regional Cooperation for Development Pact by Turkey, Iran and Pakistan.

See Iran 1513-1515, Turkey 1813-1815.

Eastern Refinery, Chittagong A105

**1969, Sept. 14 Photo. *Perf. 13½***

**277** A105 20p yel, blk & vio bl .25 .25

Opening of the 1st oil refinery in East Pakistan.

Children Playing — A106

**1969, Oct. 6 *Perf. 13***

**278** A106 20p blue & multi .25 .25

Issued for Universal Children's Day.

Japanese Doll, Map of Dacca-Tokyo Pearl Route — A107

**1969, Nov. 1 Litho. *Perf. 13½x13***

**279** A107 20p multicolored .60 .25
**280** A107 50p ultra & multi .90 .30

Inauguration of the Pakistan International Airways' Dacca-Tokyo "Pearl Route."

Reflection of Light Diagram — A108

**1969, Nov. 4 *Perf. 13***

**281** A108 20p multicolored .25 .25

Alhazen (abu-Ali al Hasan ibn-al-Haytham, 965-1039), astronomer and optician.

Vickers Vimy and London-Darwin Route over Karachi — A109

**1969, Dec. 2 Photo. *Perf. 13½x13***

**282** A109 50p multicolored 1.10 .30

50th anniv. of the 1st England to Australia flight.

View of EXPO '70, Sun Tower, Flags of Pakistan, Iran and Turkey A110

**1970, Feb. 15 Litho. *Perf. 13***

**283** A110 50p multicolored .25 .25

Issued to publicize EXPO '70 International Exhibition, Osaka, Japan, Mar. 15-Sept. 13.

UPU Headquarters, Bern — A111

**1970, May 20 Litho. *Perf. 13½x13***

**284** A111 20p multicolored .25 .25
**285** A111 50p multicolored .25 .25

Opening of new UPU headquarters in Bern.

A souvenir sheet of 2 exists, inscribed "U.P.U. Day 9th Oct. 1971". It contains stamps similar to Nos. 284-285, imperf. Value, $25.

UN Headquarters, New York — A112

Design: 50p, UN emblem.

**1970, June 26**

**286** A112 20p green & multi .25 .25
**287** A112 50p violet & multi .25 .25

25th anniversary of the United Nations.

Education Year Emblem and Open Book — A113

**1970, July 6 Litho. *Perf. 13***

**288** A113 20p blue & multi .25 .25
**289** A113 50p orange & multi .25 .25

International Education Year, 1970.

Saiful Malook Lake, Pakistan A114

Designs: 50p, Seeyo-Se-Pol Bridge, Esfahan, Iran. 1r, View, Fethiye, Turkey.

**1970, July 21**

**290** A114 20p yellow & multi .25 .25
**291** A114 50p yellow & multi .35 .25
**292** A114 1r yellow & multi .35 .25
*Nos. 290-292 (3)* .95 .75

6th anniv. of the signing of the Regional Cooperation for Development Pact by Pakistan, Iran and Turkey.

See Iran 1558-1560, Turkey 1857-1859.

Asian Productivity Year Emblem — A115

**1970, Aug. 18 Photo. *Perf. 12½x14***

**293** A115 50p black, yel & grn .25 .25

Asian Productivity Year, 1970.

Dr. Maria Montessori A116

**1970, Aug. 31 Litho. *Perf. 13***

**294** A116 20p red & multi .25 .25
**295** A116 50p multicolored .25 .25

Maria Montessori (1870-1952) Italian educator and physician.

Tractor and Fertilizer Factory — A117

**1970, Sept. 12**

**296** A117 20p yel grn & brn org .25 .25

10th Regional Food and Agricultural Organization Conf. for the Near East in Islamabad.

Boy, Girl, Open Book — A118

**1970, Oct. 5 Photo. *Perf. 13***

**297** A118 20p multicolored .25 .25

Issued for Children's Day.

Flag and Inscription — A119

**1970, Dec. 7 Litho. *Perf. 13½x13***

**298** A119 20p violet & green .25 .25
**299** A119 20p brt pink & green .25 .25

No. 298 inscribed "Elections for National Assembly 7th Dec. 1970," No. 299 inscribed "Elections for Provincial Assemblies 17th Dec. 1970."

Emblem and Burning of Al Aqsa Mosque — A120

**1970, Dec. 26 *Perf. 13½x12½***

**300** A120 20p multicolored .25 .25

Islamic Conference of Foreign Ministers, Karachi, Dec. 26-28.

Coastal Embankment — A121

**1971, Feb. 25 Litho. *Perf. 13***

**301** A121 20p multicolored .25 .25

Development of coastal embankments in East Pakistan.

Men of Different Races — A122

**1971, Mar. 21 Litho. *Perf. 13***

**302** A122 20p multicolored .25 .25
**303** A122 50p lilac & multi .25 .25

Intl. Year against Racial Discrimination.

Cement Factory, Daudkhel — A123

**1971, July 1 Litho. *Perf. 13***

**304** A123 20p purple, blk & brn .25 .25

20th anniversary of Colombo Plan.

Badshahi Mosque, Lahore — A124

Designs: 10pa, Mosque of Selim, Edirne, Turkey. 50pa, Religious School, of Chaharbagh, Isfahan, Iran, vert.

**1971, July 21 Litho. *Perf. 13***

**305** A124 10p red & multi .25 .25
**306** A124 20p green & multi .25 .25
**307** A124 50p blue & multi .50 .30
*Nos. 305-307 (3)* 1.00 .80

7th anniversary of Regional Cooperation among Pakistan, Iran and Turkey.
See Iran 1599-1601, Turkey 1886-1888.

Electric Train and Boy with Toy Locomotive — A125

**1971, Oct. 4 Litho. *Perf. 13***

**308** A125 20p slate & multi 1.50 .50

Children's Day.

Messenger and Statue of Cyrus the Great — A126

**1971, Oct. 15**

**309** A126 10p green & multi .30 .25
**310** A126 20p blue & multi .50 .30
**311** A126 50p red & multi .90 .50
*Nos. 309-311 (3)* 1.70 1.05

2500th anniversary of the founding of the Persian Empire by Cyrus the Great.
A souvenir sheet of 3 contains stamps similar to Nos. 309-311, imperf. Value, $52.50.

Hockey Player and Cup — A127

**1971, Oct. 24**

**312** A127 20p red & multi 1.75 .50

First World Hockey Cup, Barcelona, Spain, Oct. 15-24.

Great Bath at Mohenjo-Daro — A128

**1971, Nov. 4**

**313** A128 20p dp org, dk brn & blk .25 .25

25th anniv. of UNESCO.

UNICEF Emblem A129

**1971, Dec. 11 Litho. *Perf. 13***

**314** A129 50p dull bl, org & grn .25 .25

25th anniv. of UNICEF.

King Hussein and Jordan Flag A130

**1971, Dec. 25**

**315** A130 20p blue & multi .25 .25

50th anniversary of the Hashemite Kingdom of Jordan.

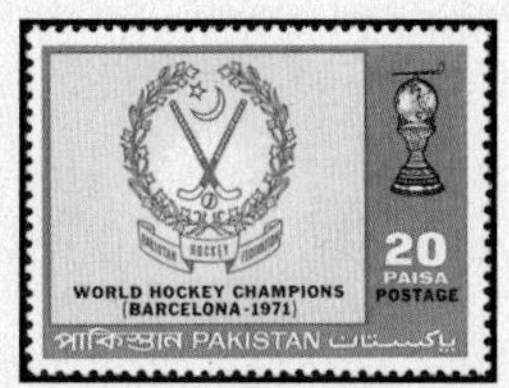


Pakistan Hockey Federation Emblem, and Cup — A131

**1971, Dec. 31**

**316** A131 20p yellow & multi 2.50 .75

Pakistan, world hockey champions, Barcelona, Oct. 1971.

Arab Scholars A132

**1972, Jan. 15 Litho. *Perf. 13½***

**317** A132 20p brown, blk & blue .25 .30

International Book Year 1972.

Angels and Grand Canal, Venice — A133

**1972, Feb. 5 *Perf. 13***

**318** A133 20p blue & multi .35 .35

UNESCO campaign to save Venice.

ECAFE Emblem A134

**1972, Mar. 28 Litho. *Perf. 13***

**319** A134 20p blue & multi .25 .30

Economic Commission for Asia and the Far East (ECAFE), 25th anniversary.

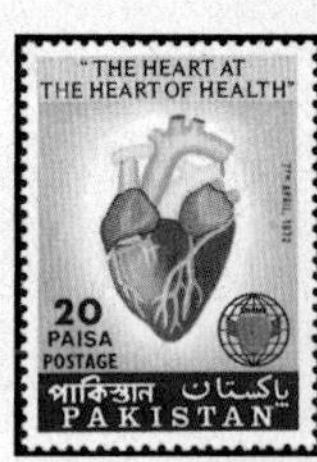


"Your Heart is your Health" — A135

**1972, Apr. 7 *Perf. 13x13½***

**320** A135 20p vio blue & multi .25 .30

World Health Day 1972.

"Only One Earth" A136

**1972, June 5 Litho. *Perf. 12½x14***

**321** A136 20p ultra & multi .25 .30

UN Conference on Human Environment, Stockholm, June 5-16.

Young Man, by Abdur Rehman Chughtai A137

Paintings: 10p, Fisherman, by Cevat Dereli (Turkey). 20p, Persian Woman, by Behzad.

**1972, July 21** **Litho.** ***Perf. 13***

| | | | | |
|---|---|---|---|---|
| **322** | A137 | 10p multicolored | .30 | .25 |
| **323** | A137 | 20p multicolored | .50 | .30 |
| **324** | A137 | 50p multicolored | 1.20 | .60 |
| | | *Nos. 322-324 (3)* | 2.00 | 1.15 |

Regional Cooperation for Development Pact among Pakistan, Turkey and Iran, 8th anniversary.

See Iran 1647-1649, Turkey 1912-1914.

Jinnah and Independence Memorial A138

"Land Reforms" — A139

Designs: Nos. 326-329, Principal reforms. 60pa, State Bank, Islamabad, meeting-place of National Assembly, horiz.

***Perf. 13 (A138), 13½x12½ (A139)***

**1972, Aug. 14**

| | | | | |
|---|---|---|---|---|
| **325** | A138 | 10p shown | .25 | .25 |
| **326** | A139 | 20p shown | .25 | .25 |
| **327** | A139 | 20p Labor reforms | .25 | .25 |
| **328** | A139 | 20p Education | .25 | .25 |
| **329** | A139 | 20p Health care | .25 | .25 |
| *a.* | | Vert. strip of 4, As #326-329 plus "labels" | 1.00 | 1.00 |
| **330** | A138 | 60p rose lilac & car | .35 | .30 |
| | | *Nos. 325-330 (6)* | 1.60 | 1.55 |

25th anniversary of independence. No. 329a contains designs of Nos. 326-329, each with a decorative label, separated by simulated perfs.

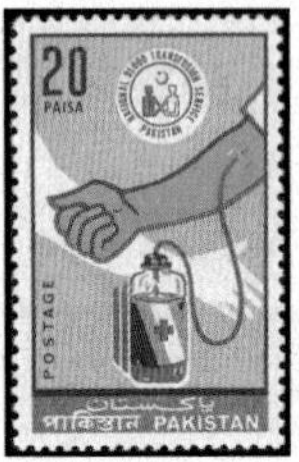


Blood Donor, Society Emblem — A140

**1972, Sept. 6** **Litho.** ***Perf. 14x12½***

| | | | | |
|---|---|---|---|---|
| **331** | A140 | 20p multicolored | .25 | .35 |

Pakistan National Blood Transfusion Service.

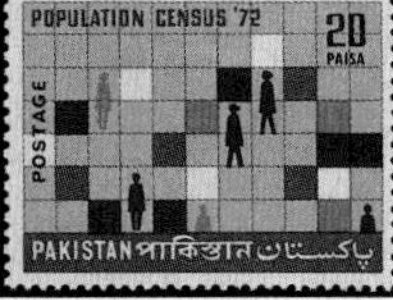


Census Chart A141

**1972, Sept. 16** **Litho.** ***Perf. 13½***

| | | | | |
|---|---|---|---|---|
| **332** | A141 | 20p multicolored | .25 | .25 |

Centenary of population census.

Children Leaving Slum for Modern City — A142

**1972, Oct. 2** **Litho.** ***Perf. 13***

| | | | | |
|---|---|---|---|---|
| **333** | A142 | 20p multicolored | .25 | .30 |

Children's Day.

Giant Book and Children A143

**1972, Oct. 23**

| | | | | |
|---|---|---|---|---|
| **334** | A143 | 20p purple & multi | .25 | .30 |

Education Week.

Nuclear Power Plant, Karachi A144

**1972, Nov. 28** **Litho.** ***Perf. 13***

| | | | | |
|---|---|---|---|---|
| **335** | A144 | 20p multicolored | .25 | .40 |

Pakistan's first nuclear power plant.

Copernicus in Observatory, by Jan Matejko — A145

**1973, Feb. 19** **Litho.** ***Perf. 13***

| | | | | |
|---|---|---|---|---|
| **336** | A145 | 20p multicolored | .60 | .30 |

Dancing Girl, Public Baths, Mohenjo-Daro — A146

**1973, Feb. 23** ***Perf. 13½x13***

| | | | | |
|---|---|---|---|---|
| **337** | A146 | 20p multicolored | .35 | .30 |

Mohenjo-Daro excavations, 50th anniv.

Radar, Lightning, WMO Emblem — A147

**1973, Mar. 23** **Litho.** ***Perf. 13***

| | | | | |
|---|---|---|---|---|
| **338** | A147 | 20p multicolored | .25 | .40 |

Cent. of intl. meteorological cooperation.

Prisoners of War — A148

**1973, Apr. 18**

| | | | | |
|---|---|---|---|---|
| **339** | A148 | 1.25r black & multi | 1.50 | *2.50* |

A plea for Pakistani prisoners of war in India.

National Assembly, Islamabad A149

**1973, Apr. 21** ***Perf. 12½x13½***

| | | | | |
|---|---|---|---|---|
| **340** | A149 | 20p green & multi | .55 | .55 |

Constitution Week.

State Bank and Emblem — A150

**1973, July 1** **Litho.** ***Perf. 13***

| | | | | |
|---|---|---|---|---|
| **341** | A150 | 20p multicolored | .25 | .25 |
| **342** | A150 | 1r multicolored | .30 | .35 |

State Bank of Pakistan, 25th anniversary.

Street, Mohenjo-Daro, Pakistan A151

Designs: 20p, Statue of man, Shahdad, Kerman, Persia, 4000 B.C. 1.25r, Head from mausoleum of King Antiochus I (69-34 B.C.), Turkey.

**1973, July 21** ***Perf. 13x13½***

| | | | | |
|---|---|---|---|---|
| **343** | A151 | 20p blue & multi | .25 | .25 |
| **344** | A151 | 60p emerald & multi | .65 | .35 |
| **345** | A151 | 1.25r red & multi | 1.00 | .75 |
| | | *Nos. 343-345 (3)* | 1.90 | 1.35 |

Regional Cooperation for Development Pact among Pakistan, Turkey and Iran, 9th anniversary.

See Iran 1714-1716, Turkey 1941-1943.

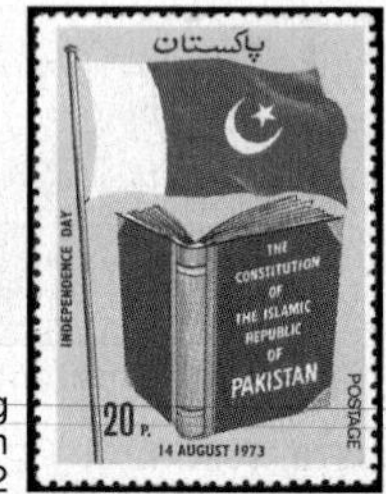


Pakistani Flag and Constitution A152

**1973, Aug. 14** **Litho.** ***Perf. 13***

| | | | | |
|---|---|---|---|---|
| **346** | A152 | 20p blue & multi | .25 | .25 |

Independence Day.

Mohammed Ali Jinnah — A153

**1973, Sept. 11** **Litho.** ***Perf. 13***

| | | | | |
|---|---|---|---|---|
| **347** | A153 | 20p emerald, yel & blk | .25 | .25 |

Mohammed Ali Jinnah (1876-1948), president of All-India Moslem League.

Wallago Attu — A154

Fish: 20p, Labeo rohita. 60p, Tilapia mossambica. 1r, Catla catla.

**1973, Sept. 24** **Litho.** ***Perf. 13½***

| | | | | |
|---|---|---|---|---|
| **348** | A154 | 10p multicolored | 1.10 | 1.10 |
| **349** | A154 | 20p multicolored | 1.25 | 1.25 |
| **350** | A154 | 60p multicolored | 1.40 | 1.40 |
| **351** | A154 | 1r ultra & multi | 1.40 | 1.40 |
| *a.* | | Strip of 4, #348-351 | 5.75 | 5.75 |

Book, Torch, Child and School — A155

**1973, Oct. 1**

| | | | | |
|---|---|---|---|---|
| **352** | A155 | 20p multicolored | .25 | .25 |

Universal Children's Day.

Sindhi Farmer and FAO Emblem A156

**1973, Oct. 15** **Litho.** ***Perf. 13***

| | | | | |
|---|---|---|---|---|
| **353** | A156 | 20p multicolored | .75 | .35 |

World Food Organization, 10th anniv.

Kemal Ataturk and Ankara — A157

**1973, Oct. 29**

**354** A157 50p multicolored .75 .40

50th anniversary of Turkish Republic.

Scout Pointing to Planet and Stars — A158

*Perf. 13½x12½*

**1973, Nov. 11** **Litho.**

**355** A158 20p dull blue & multi 2.00 .50

25th anniversary of Pakistani Boy Scouts and Silver Jubilee Jamboree.

Human Rights Flame, Sheltered Home — A159

**1973, Nov. 16**

**356** A159 20p multicolored .45 .40

25th anniversary of the Universal Declaration of Human Rights.

al-Biruni and Jhelum Observatory — A160

**1973, Nov. 26** **Litho.** ***Perf. 13***

**357** A160 20p multicolored .50 .25

**358** A160 1.25r multicolored 1.25 .50

International Congress on Millenary of abu-al-Rayhan al-Biruni, Nov. 26-Dec. 12.

Dr. A. G. Hansen A161

**1973, Dec. 29**

**359** A161 20p ultra & multi 1.20 .50

Centenary of the discovery by Dr. Armauer Gerhard Hansen of the Hansen bacillus, the cause of leprosy.

Family and WPY Emblem A162

**1974, Jan. 1** **Litho.** ***Perf. 13***

**360** A162 20p yellow & multi .30 .25

**361** A162 1.25r salmon & multi .30 .40

World Population Year 1974.

Summit Emblem and Ornament — A163

Emblem, Crescent and Rays A164

**1974, Feb. 22** ***Perf. 14x12½, 13***

**362** A163 20p multicolored .25 .25

**363** A164 65p multicolored .30 .40

*a.* Souvenir sheet of 2 2.00 3.25

Islamic Summit Meeting. No. 363a contains two stamps similar to Nos. 362-363 with simulated perforations.

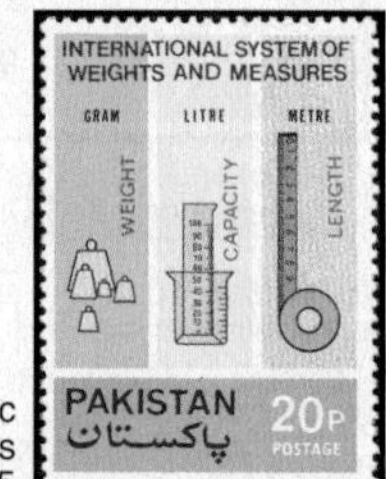


Metric Measures A165

**1974, July 1** **Litho.** ***Perf. 13***

**364** A165 20p multicolored .25 .30

Introduction of metric system.

Kashan Rug, Lahore A166

Designs: 60p, Persian rug, late 16th century. 1.25r, Anatolian rug, 15th century.

**1974, July 21**

**365** A166 20p multicolored .25 .25

**366** A166 60p multicolored .40 .50

**367** A166 1.25r multicolored .75 1.00

*Nos. 365-367 (3)* 1.40 1.75

10th anniversary of the Regional Cooperation for Development Pact among Pakistan, Iran and Turkey.

See Iran 1806-1808, Turkey 1979-1981.

Hands Protecting Sapling — A167

**1974, Aug. 9** **Litho.** ***Perf. 13***

**368** A167 20p multicolored .60 .60

Arbor Day.

Torch over Map of Africa with Namibia — A168

**1974, Aug. 26**

**369** A168 60p green & multi .55 .60

Namibia (South-West Africa) Day. See note after United Nations No. 241.

Map of Pakistan with Highways and Disputed Area — A169

**1974, Sept. 23**

**370** A169 20p multicolored 1.25 1.00

Highway system under construction.

Child and Students A170

**1974, Oct. 7** **Litho.** ***Perf. 13***

**371** A170 20p multicolored .40 .50

Universal Children's Day.

UPU Emblem — A171

2.25r, Jet, UPU emblem, mail coach.

**1974, Oct. 9** **Size: 24x36mm**

**372** A171 20p multicolored .25 .25

**Size: 29x41mm**

**373** A171 2.25r multicolored .55 .70

*a.* Souv. sheet of 2, #372-373, imperf. 1.50 1.50

Centenary of Universal Postal Union.

Liaqat Ali Khan — A172

**1974, Oct. 16** **Litho.** ***Perf. 13x13½***

**374** A172 20p black & red .45 .35

Liaqat Ali Khan, Prime Minister 1947-1951.

Mohammad Allama Iqbal — A173

**1974, Nov. 9** **Litho.** ***Perf. 13***

**375** A173 20p multicolored .45 .35

Mohammad Allama Iqbal (1877-1938), poet and philosopher.

Dr. Schweitzer on Ogowe River, 1915 — A174

**1975, Jan. 14** **Litho.** ***Perf. 13***

**376** A174 2.25r multicolored 4.50 *4.50*

Dr. Albert Schweitzer (1875-1965), medical missionary, birth centenary.

Tourism Year 75 Emblem A175

**1975, Jan. 15**

**377** A175 2.25r multicolored .60 .80

South Asia Tourism Year, 1975.

Flags of Participants, Memorial and Prime Minister Bhutto — A176

**1975, Feb. 22** **Litho.** ***Perf. 13***

**378** A176 20p lt blue & multi .25 .25

**379** A176 1r brt pink & multi 1.25 1.00

2nd Lahore Islamic Summit, Feb. 22, 1st anniv.

IWY Emblem and Woman Scientist — A177

Design: 2.25r, Old woman and girl learning to read and write.

**1975, June 15 Litho. *Perf. 13***

| | | | | |
|---|---|---|---|---|
| **380** | A177 | 20p multicolored | .25 | .25 |
| **381** | A177 | 2.25r multicolored | 1.40 | 1.75 |

International Women's Year 1975.

Globe with Dates, Arabic "X" — A178

**1975, July 14 Litho. *Perf. 13***

| | | | | |
|---|---|---|---|---|
| **382** | A178 | 20p multicolored | .75 | .60 |

International Congress of Mathematical Sciences, Karachi, July 14-20.

Camel Leather Vase, Pakistan A179

60p, Ceramic plate and RCD emblem, Iran, horiz. 1.25r, Porcelain vase, Turkey.

**1975, July 21**

| | | | | |
|---|---|---|---|---|
| **383** | A179 | 20p lilac & multi | .30 | .25 |
| **384** | A179 | 60p violet blk & multi | .60 | .75 |
| **385** | A179 | 1.25r blue & multi | 1.00 | 1.10 |
| | | *Nos. 383-385 (3)* | 1.90 | 2.10 |

Regional Cooperation for Development Pact among Turkey, Iran and Pakistan.

See Iran 1871-1873, Turkey 2006-2008.

Sapling, Trees and Ant — A180

**1975, Aug. 9 Litho. *Perf. 13x13½***

| | | | | |
|---|---|---|---|---|
| **386** | A180 | 20p multicolored | .45 | .45 |

Tree Planting Day.

Black Partridge A181

**1975, Sept. 30 Litho. *Perf. 13***

| | | | | |
|---|---|---|---|---|
| **387** | A181 | 20p blue & multi | 1.50 | .25 |
| **388** | A181 | 2.25r yellow & multi | 4.50 | 3.50 |

Wildlife Protection.

Universal Children's Day — A182

**1975, Oct. 6**

| | | | | |
|---|---|---|---|---|
| **389** | A182 | 20p multicolored | .45 | .50 |

Hazrat Amir Khusrau, Sitar and Tabla — A183

**1975, Oct. 24 Litho. *Perf. 14x12½***

| | | | | |
|---|---|---|---|---|
| **390** | A183 | 20p lt blue & multi | .25 | .50 |
| **391** | A183 | 2.25r pink & multi | 1.00 | 2.00 |

700th anniversary of Hazrat Amir Khusrau (1253-1325), musician who invented the sitar and tabla instruments.

Mohammad Iqbal — A184

**1975, Nov. 9 *Perf. 13***

| | | | | |
|---|---|---|---|---|
| **392** | A184 | 20p multicolored | .50 | .50 |

Mohammad Allama Iqbal (1877-1938), poet and philosopher, birth centenary.

Wild Sheep of the Punjab — A185

**1975, Dec. 31 Litho. *Perf. 13***

| | | | | |
|---|---|---|---|---|
| **393** | A185 | 20p multicolored | .35 | .25 |
| **394** | A185 | 3r multicolored | 2.00 | 1.75 |

Wildlife Protection. See Nos. 410-411.

Mohenjo-Daro and UNESCO Emblem A186

View of Mohenjo-Daro excavations.

**1976, Feb. 29 Litho. *Perf. 13***

| | | | | |
|---|---|---|---|---|
| **395** | A186 | 10p multicolored | .65 | .80 |
| **396** | A186 | 20p multicolored | .75 | .90 |
| **397** | A186 | 65p multicolored | .75 | .90 |
| **398** | A186 | 3r multicolored | .75 | .90 |
| **399** | A186 | 4r multicolored | .85 | 1.00 |
| *a.* | | Strip of 5, #395-399 | 4.00 | 4.00 |

UNESCO campaign to save Mohenjo-Daro excavations.

Dome and Minaret of Rauza-e-Mubarak Mausoleum — A187

**1976, Mar. 3 Photo. *Perf. 13½x14***

| | | | | |
|---|---|---|---|---|
| **400** | A187 | 20p blue & multi | .25 | .25 |
| **401** | A187 | 3r gray & multi | .75 | .70 |

International Congress on Seerat, the teachings of Mohammed, Mar. 3-15.

Alexander Graham Bell, 1876 Telephone and Dial — A188

**1976, Mar. 10 *Perf. 13***

| | | | | |
|---|---|---|---|---|
| **402** | A188 | 3r blue & multi | 1.50 | 2.00 |

Centenary of first telephone call by Alexander Graham Bell, Mar. 10, 1876.

College Emblem — A189

**1976, Mar. 15 Litho. *Perf. 13***

| | | | | |
|---|---|---|---|---|
| **403** | A189 | 20p multicolored | .45 | .45 |

Cent. of Natl. College of Arts, Lahore.

Peacock A190

**1976, Mar. 31 Litho. *Perf. 13***

| | | | | |
|---|---|---|---|---|
| **404** | A190 | 20p lt blue & multi | 1.00 | .40 |
| **405** | A190 | 3r pink & multi | 4.00 | 3.75 |

Wildlife protection.

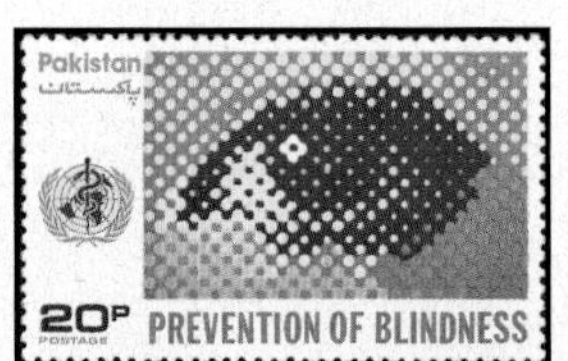

Eye and WHO Emblem — A191

**1976, Apr. 7**

| | | | | |
|---|---|---|---|---|
| **406** | A191 | 20p multicolored | 1.10 | .75 |

World Health Day: "Foresight prevents blindness."

Mohenjo-Daro, UNESCO Emblem, Bull (from Seal) — A192

**1976, May 31 Litho. *Perf. 13***

| | | | | |
|---|---|---|---|---|
| **407** | A192 | 20p multicolored | .45 | .40 |

UNESCO campaign to save Mohenjo-Daro excavations.

Jefferson Memorial, US Bicentennial Emblem — A193

Declaration of Independence, by John Trumbull — A194

**1976, July 4 *Perf. 13***

| | | | | |
|---|---|---|---|---|
| **408** | A193 | 90p multicolored | .75 | .50 |

***Perf. 13½x13***

| | | | | |
|---|---|---|---|---|
| **409** | A194 | 4r multicolored | 3.00 | *3.50* |

American Bicentennial.

**Wildlife Type of 1975**

Wildlife protection: 20p, 3r, Ibex.

**1976, July 12**

| | | | | |
|---|---|---|---|---|
| **410** | A185 | 20p multicolored | .35 | .35 |
| **411** | A185 | 3r multicolored | 1.40 | 2.00 |

Mohammed Ali Jinnah — A195

65p, Riza Shah Pahlavi. 90p, Kemal Ataturk.

**1976, July 21 Litho. *Perf. 14***

| | | | | |
|---|---|---|---|---|
| **412** | A195 | 20p multicolored | .70 | .50 |
| **413** | A195 | 65p multicolored | .70 | .50 |
| **414** | A195 | 90p multicolored | .70 | .50 |
| *a.* | | Strip of 3, #412-414 | 2.50 | 3.25 |

Regional Cooperation for Development Pact among Pakistan, Turkey and Iran, 12th anniversary.

See Iran 1903-1905, Turkey 2041-2043.

Ornament
A196

Jinnah and
Wazir Mansion
A197

Designs (Jinnah and): 40p, Sind Madressah (building). 50p, Minar Qarardad (minaret). 3r, Mausoleum.

**1976, Aug. 14 Litho. *Perf. 13½***

**415** A196 5p multicolored .25 .25
**416** A196 10p multicolored .25 .25
**417** A196 15p multicolored .25 .25
**418** A197 20p multicolored .25 .25
**419** A197 40p multicolored .25 .25
**420** A197 50p multicolored .25 .25
**421** A196 1r multicolored .35 .40
**422** A197 3r multicolored .50 .50
*a.* Block of 8, #415-422 3.50 3.50

Mohammed Ali Jinnah (1876-1948), first Governor General of Pakistan, birth centenary. Horizontal rows of types A196 and A197 alternate in sheet.

Mohenjo-Daro and UNESCO
Emblem — A198

**1976, Aug. 31 *Perf. 14***

**423** A198 65p multicolored .45 .50

UNESCO campaign to save Mohenjo-Daro excavations.

Racial Discrimination Emblem — A199

***Perf. 12½x13½***

**1976, Sept. 15 Litho.**

**424** A199 65p multicolored .45 .45

Fight against racial discrimination.

Child's Head, Symbols of Health,
Education and Food — A200

**1976, Oct. 4 *Perf. 13***

**425** A200 20p blue & multi .60 .45

Universal Children's Day.

Verse by
Allama
Iqbal
A201

**1976, Nov. 9 Litho. *Perf. 13***

**426** A201 20p multicolored .25 .30

Mohammed Allama Iqbal (1877-1938), poet and philosopher, birth centenary.

Scout Emblem,
Jinnah Giving
Salute — A202

**1976, Nov. 20**

**427** A202 20p multicolored 1.10 .45

Quaid-I-Azam Centenary Jamboree, Nov. 1976.

Children
Reading
A203

**1976, Dec. 15 Litho. *Perf. 13***

**428** A203 20p multicolored .60 .30

Books for children.

Mohammed Ali Jinnah — A204

**Lithographed and Embossed**

**1976, Dec. 25 *Perf. 12½***

**429** A204 10r gold & green 3.00 3.00

Mohammed Ali Jinnah (1876-1948), 1st Governor General of Pakistan.

An imperf presentation sheet of 1 exists. Value $100.

Farm Family
and Village,
Tractor,
Ambulance
A205

**1977, Apr. 14 Litho. *Perf. 13***

**430** A205 20p multicolored .45 .25

Social Welfare and Rural Development Year, 1976-77.

Terracotta Bullock Cart,
Pakistan — A206

Designs: 20p, Terra-cotta jug, Turkey. 90p, Decorated jug, Iran.

**1977, July 21 Litho. *Perf. 13***

**431** A206 20p ultra & multi .45 .25
**432** A206 65p blue green & multi .65 .35
**433** A206 90p lilac & multi 1.00 1.40
*Nos. 431-433 (3)* 2.10 2.00

Regional Cooperation for Development Pact among Pakistan, Turkey and Iran, 13th anniversary.

See Iran 1946-1948, Turkey 2053-2055.

Trees — A207

**1977, Aug. 9 Litho. *Perf. 13***

**434** A207 20p multicolored .25 .30

Tree planting program.

Desert
A208

**1977, Sept. 5 Litho. *Perf. 13***

**435** A208 65p multicolored .45 .30

UN Conference on Desertification, Nairobi, Kenya, Aug. 29-Sept. 9.

"Water for the
Children" — A209

**1977, Oct. 3 Litho. *Perf. 14x12½***

**436** A209 50p multicolored .45 .40

Universal Children's Day.

Aga Khan III — A210

**1977, Nov. 2 Litho. *Perf. 13***

**437** A210 2r multicolored .75 .75

Aga Khan III (1877-1957), spiritual ruler of Ismaeli sect, statesman, birth centenary.

Mohammad
Iqbal — A211

20p, Spirit appearing to Iqbal, painting by Behzad. 65p, Iqbal looking at Jamaluddin Afghani & Saeed Halim offering prayers, by Behzad. 1.25r, Verse in Urdu. 2.25r, Verse in Persian.

**1977, Nov. 9**

**438** A211 20p multicolored .60 .60
**439** A211 65p multicolored .60 .60
**440** A211 1.25r multicolored .70 .70
**441** A211 2.25r multicolored .75 .75
**442** A211 3r multicolored .85 .85
*a.* Strip of 5, #438-442 4.50 4.50

Mohammad Allama Iqbal (1877-1938), poet and philosopher, birth centenary.

Holy Kaaba,
Mecca
A212

**1977, Nov. 21 *Perf. 14***

**443** A212 65p green & multi .45 .30

1977 pilgrimage to Mecca.

Healthy and
Sick
Bodies — A213

**1977, Dec. 19 Litho. *Perf. 13***

**444** A213 65p blue green & multi .45 .30

World Rheumatism Year.

Woman from Rawalpindi-
Islamabad — A214

**1978, Feb. 5 Litho. *Perf. 12½x13½***

**445** A214 75p multicolored .45 .25

Indonesia-Pakistan Economic and Cultural Cooperation Organization.

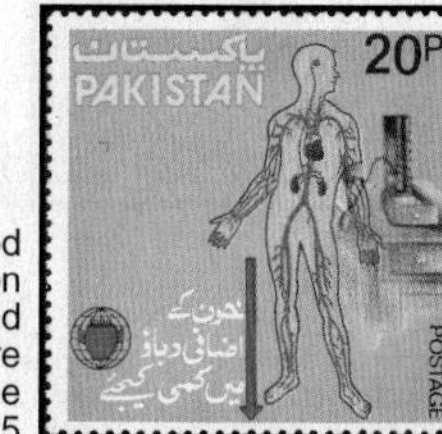


Blood
Circulation
and
Pressure
Gauge
A215

**1978, Apr. 20 Litho. *Perf. 13***

**446** A215 20p blue & multi .25 .25
**447** A215 2r yellow & multi .85 .75

Campaign against hypertension.

Henri
Dunant, Red
Cross, Red
Crescent
A216

**1978, May 8 *Perf. 14***

**448** A216 1r multicolored 1.00 .30

Henri Dunant (1828-1910), founder of Red Cross, 150th birth anniversary.

Red Roses, Pakistan — A217

90p, Pink roses, Iran. 2r, Yellow rose, Turkey.

**1978, July 21** **Litho.** ***Perf. 13½***

**449** A217 20p multicolored .35 .25
**450** A217 90p multicolored .50 .25
**451** A217 2r multicolored .75 .35
*a.* Strip of 3, #449-451 2.00 2.00

Regional Cooperation for Development Pact among Turkey, Iran and Pakistan.
See Iran 1984-1986, Turkey 2094-2096.

Hockey Stick and Ball, Championship Cup — A218

Fair Building, Fountain, Piazza Tourismo A219

**1978, Aug. 26** **Litho.** ***Perf. 13***

**452** A218 1r multicolored 1.25 .25
**453** A219 2r multicolored .50 .30

Riccione '78, 30th International Stamp Fair, Riccione, Italy, Aug. 26-28. No. 452 also commemorates Pakistan as World Hockey Cup Champion.

Globe and Cogwheels A220

**1978, Sept. 3**

**454** A220 75p multicolored .45 .25

UN Conference on Technical Cooperation among Developing Countries, Buenos Aires, Argentina, Sept. 1978.

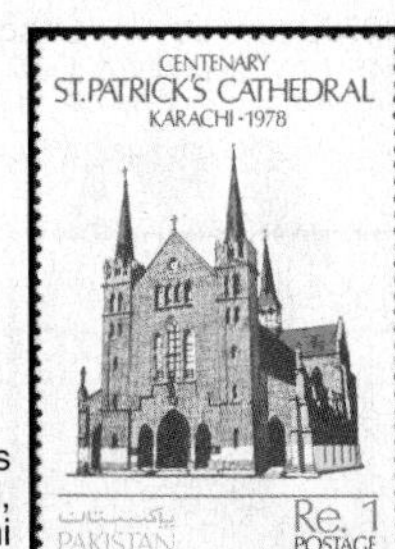


St. Patrick's Cathedral, Karachi A221

Design: 2r, Stained-glass window.

**1978, Sept. 29** **Litho.** ***Perf. 13***

**455** A221 1r multicolored .25 .25
**456** A221 2r multicolored .65 .25

St. Patrick's Cathedral, Karachi, centenary.

"Four Races" — A222

**1978, Nov. 20** **Litho.** ***Perf. 13***

**457** A222 1r multicolored .45 .25

Anti-Apartheid Year.

Maulana Jauhar — A223

**1978, Dec. 10** **Litho.** ***Perf. 13***

**458** A223 50p multicolored .55 .25

Maulana Muhammad Ali Jauhar, writer, journalist and patriot, birth centenary.

**Type of 1957 and**

Qarardad Monument — A224

Tractor — A225

Tomb of Ibrahim Khan Makli — A225a

**Engr.; Litho. (10p, 25p, 40p, 50p, 90p)**

**1978-81** ***Perf. 14***

**459** A224 2p dark green .25 .25
**460** A224 3p black .25 .25
**461** A224 5p violet blue .25 .25
**462** A225 10p lt blue & blue ('79) .25 .25
**463** A225 20p yel green ('79) .40 .25
**464** A225 25p rose car & grn ('79) .75 .25
**465** A225 40p carmine & blue .25 .25
**466** A225 50p bl grn & vio ('79) .25 .25
**467** A225 60p black .25 .25
**468** A225 75p dull red .50 .25
**469** A225 90p blue & carmine .25 .25

***Perf. 13½x13***

**Engr.** **Wmk. 351**

**470** A225a 1r olive ('80) .25 .25
**471** A225a 1.50r dp org ('79) .25 .25
**472** A225a 2r car rose ('79) .25 .25
**473** A225a 3r indigo ('80) .25 .25
**474** A225a 4r black ('81) .25 .25
**475** A225a 5r dk brn ('81) .25 .25
**475A** A26 15r rose lil & red ('79) 1.50 1.50
*Nos. 459-475A (18)* 6.65 5.75

Lithographed stamps, type A225, have bottom panel in solid color with colorless lettering and numerals 2mm high instead of 3mm.
For overprints see Nos. O94-O110.

Tornado Jet Fighter, de Havilland Rapide and Flyer A — A226

Wright Flyer A and: 1r, Phantom F4F jet fighter & Tristar airliner. 2r, Bell X15 fighter & TU-104 airliner. 2.25r, MiG fighter & Concorde.

**Unwmk.**

**1978, Dec. 24** **Litho.** ***Perf. 13***

**476** A226 65p multicolored 1.10 1.60
**477** A226 1r multicolored 1.20 1.90
**478** A226 2r multicolored 1.25 2.00
**479** A226 2.25r multicolored 1.25 2.00
*a.* Block of 4, #476-479 6.00 6.00

75th anniv. of 1st powered flight.

Koran Lighting the World and Mohammed's Tomb — A227

**1979, Feb. 10** **Litho.** ***Perf. 13***

**480** A227 20p multicolored .45 .25

Mohammed's birth anniversary.

Mother and Children A228

**1979, Feb. 25**

**481** A228 50p multicolored .75 .25

APWA Services, 30th anniversary.

Lophophorus Impejanus — A229

Pheasants: 25p, Lophura leucomelana. 40p, Puccrasia macrolopha. 1r, Catreus walichii.

**1979, June 17** **Litho.** ***Perf. 13***

**482** A229 20p multicolored 1.25 .60
**483** A229 25p multicolored 1.25 .75
**484** A229 40p multicolored 1.50 1.75
**485** A229 1r multicolored 3.00 2.00
*Nos. 482-485 (4)* 7.00 5.10

For overprint see No. 525.

At the Well, by Allah Baksh — A230

Paintings: 75p, Potters, by Kamalel Molk, Iran. 1.60r, Plowing, by Namik Ismail, Turkey.

**1979, July 21** **Litho.** ***Perf. 14x13***

**486** A230 40p multicolored .25 .25
**487** A230 75p multicolored .25 .25
**488** A230 1.60r multicolored .25 .25
*a.* Strip of 3, #486-488 .90 .90

Regional Cooperation for Development Pact among Pakistan, Iran and Turkey, 15th anniversary.
See Iran 2020-2022, Turkey 2112-2114.

Guj Embroidery — A231

Handicrafts: 1r, Enamel inlay brass plate. 1.50r, Baskets. 2r, Peacock, embroidered rug.

**1979, Aug. 23** **Litho.** ***Perf. 14x13***

**489** A231 40p multicolored .25 .25
**490** A231 1r multicolored .25 .25
**491** A231 1.50r multicolored .30 .30
**492** A231 2r multicolored .40 .35
*a.* Block of 4, #489-492 1.50 1.50

Children, IYC and SOS Emblems — A232

**1979, Sept. 10** **Litho.** ***Perf. 13***

**493** A232 50p multicolored .50 .30

SOS Children's Village, Lahore, opening.

Playground, IYC Emblem — A233

IYC Emblem and: Children's drawings.

**1979, Oct. 22** ***Perf. 14x12½***

**494** A233 40p multicolored .25 .25
**495** A233 75p multicolored .25 .25
**496** A233 1r multicolored .25 .30
**497** A233 1.50r multicolored .30 .30
*a.* Block of 4, #494-497 1.25 1.25

**Souvenir Sheet**

***Imperf***

**498** A233 2r multi, vert. 1.25 *2.10*

IYC. For overprints see #520-523.

Fight Against Cancer A234

**Unwmk.**

**1979, Nov. 12 Litho. *Perf. 14***
**499** A234 40p multicolored .75 .70

Pakistan Customs Service Centenary — A235

**1979, Dec. 10 *Perf. 13x13½***
**500** A235 1r multicolored .35 .25

"1378" is a plate flaw, not an error.

Tippu Sultan Shaheed — A236

15r, Syed Ahmad Khan. 25r, Altaf Hussain Hali.

**1979, Mar. 23 Wmk. 351 *Perf. 14***
**501** A236 10r shown .75 1.00
**502** A236 15r multicolored 1.00 1.50
**503** A236 25r multicolored 1.50 2.25
*a.* Strip of 3, #501-503 4.00 4.00

See No. 699.

A237

A238

Ornament — A239

***Perf. 12x11½, 11½x12***

**1980 Unwmk.**
**506** A237 10p dk grn & yel org .25 .25
**507** A237 15p dk grn & apple grn .25 .25
**508** A237 25p multicolored .25 .25
**509** A237 35p multicolored .25 .25
**510** A238 40p red & lt brown .25 .25
**511** A239 50p olive & vio bl .25 .25
**512** A239 80p black & yel grn .25 .30
*Nos. 506-512 (7)* 1.75 1.80

Issued: 25, 35, 50, 80p, 3/10; others, 1/15.
See Nos. O111-O117.

Pakistan International Airline, 25th Anniversary — A240

**1980, Jan. 10 Litho. *Perf. 13***
**516** A240 1r multicolored 2.00 1.00

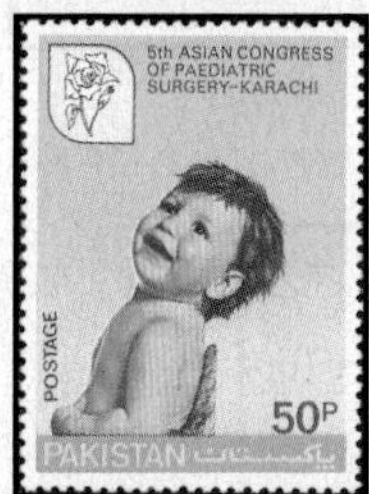


Infant, Rose — A241

**1980, Feb. 16 *Perf. 13***
**517** A241 50p multicolored 1.00 1.25

5th Asian Congress of Pediatric Surgery, Karachi, Feb. 16-19.

Conference Emblem A242

**1980, May 17 Litho. *Perf. 13***
**518** A242 1r multicolored .80 .50

11th Islamic Conference of Foreign Ministers, Islamabad, May 17-21.

Lighthouse, Oil Terminal, Map Showing Karachi Harbor — A243

**1980, July 15 *Perf. 13½***
**519** A243 1r multicolored 1.75 1.50

Karachi Port, cent. of independent management.

**Nos. 494-497 Overprinted in Red: RICCIONE 80**

**1980, Aug. 30 Litho. *Perf. 14x12½***
**520** A233 40p multicolored .30 *.50*
**521** A233 75p multicolored .40 *.60*
**522** A233 1r multicolored .45 *.65*
**523** A233 1.50r multicolored .60 *.75*
*a.* Block of 4, #520-523 2.00 *3.00*

RICCIONE 80 International Stamp Exhibition, Riccione, Italy, Aug. 30-Sept. 2.

Quetta Command and Staff College, 75th Anniversary A244

**1980, Sept. 18 Litho. *Perf. 13***
**524** A244 1r multicolored .25 .40

**No. 485 Overprinted: "World Tourism Conference/Manila 80"**

**1980, Sept. 27**
**525** A229 1r multicolored 1.00 .50

World Tourism Conf., Manila, Sept. 27.

Birth Centenary of Mohammed Shairani — A245

**1980, Oct. 5 Litho. *Perf. 13***
**526** A245 40p multicolored .45 .45

Aga Khan Architecture Award — A246

**1980, Oct. 23 Litho. *Perf. 13½***
**527** A246 2r multicolored .60 .55

Rising Sun A247

**1981, Mar. 7 Litho. *Perf. 13***
**Size: 30x41mm**
**528** A247 40p Hegira emblem .25 .40

**1980, Nov. 6 Litho. *Perf. 13***
**529** A247 40p shown .25 .25

***Perf. 14***
**Size: 33x33mm**
**530** A247 2r Moslem symbols .25 .35

***Perf. 13x13½***
**Size: 31x54mm**
**531** A247 3r Globe, hands holding Koran .25 .50
*Nos. 528-531 (4)* 1.00 1.50

**Souvenir Sheet**
***Imperf***
**532** A247 4r Candles .75 .75

Hegira (Pilgrimage Year).

Airmail Service, 50th Anniversary — A248

Postal History: No. 533, Postal card cent. No. 534, Money order service cent.

**1980-81 *Perf. 13***
**533** A248 40p multi, vert. .25 .35
**534** A248 40p multi, vert. .25 .35
**535** A248 1r multi .75 .25
*Nos. 533-535 (3)* 1.25 .95

Issued: #533, 12/27; #534, 12/20; #535, 2/15/81.

Heinrich von Stephan, UPU Emblem A249

**1981, Jan. 7 *Perf. 13½***
**536** A249 1r multicolored .45 .25

Von Stephan (1831-97), founder of UPU.

Conference Emblem, Afghan Refugee A250

Conference Emblem, Flags of Participants, Men — A251

Conference Emblem, Map of Afghanistan — A252

**1981, Mar. 29 Litho. *Perf. 13***
**537** A250 40p multicolored .25 .25
**538** A251 40p multicolored .25 .25
**539** A250 1r multicolored .50 .25
**540** A251 1r multicolored .50 .25
**541** A252 2r multicolored .65 .35
*Nos. 537-541 (5)* 2.15 1.35

Conference Emblem in Ornament A253

Conference Emblem, Flags of Participants
A254

**1981, Mar. 29** *Perf. 13½*

| | | | | |
|---|---|---|---|---|
| **542** | A253 | 40p multicolored | .25 | .25 |
| **543** | A254 | 40p multicolored | .25 | .25 |
| **544** | A253 | 85p multicolored | .25 | .25 |
| **545** | A254 | 85p multicolored | .25 | .25 |
| | | *Nos. 542-545 (4)* | 1.00 | 1.00 |

3rd Islamic Summit Conference, Makkah al-Mukarramah, Jan. 25-28.

Kemal Ataturk (1881-1938), First President of Turkey — A255

**1981, May 19** **Litho.** *Perf. 13x13½*

| | | | | |
|---|---|---|---|---|
| **546** | A255 | 1r multicolored | .60 | .25 |

Green Turtle
A256

**1981, June 20** **Litho.** *Perf. 12x11½*

| | | | | |
|---|---|---|---|---|
| **547** | A256 | 40p multicolored | 1.40 | .75 |

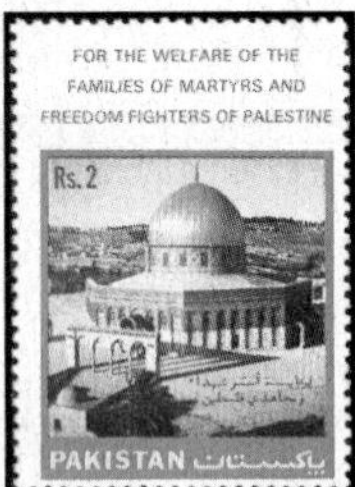


Palestinian Cooperation
A257

**1981, July 25** **Litho.** *Perf. 13*

| | | | | |
|---|---|---|---|---|
| **548** | A257 | 2r multicolored | .55 | .25 |

Mountain Ranges and Peaks — A258

Designs: No. 549, Malubiting West, range. No. 550, Peak. No. 551, Mt. Maramosh, range. No. 552, Mt. Maramosh, peak. No. 553, K6, range. No. 554, Peak. No. 555, K2, range. No. 556, Peak.

**1981, Aug. 20** *Perf. 14x13½*

| | | | |
|---|---|---|---|
| **549** | 40p multicolored | .45 | .30 |
| **550** | 40p multicolored | .45 | .30 |
| *a.* | A258 Pair, #549-550 | 1.00 | 1.00 |
| **551** | 1r multicolored | .65 | .50 |
| **552** | 1r multicolored | .65 | .50 |
| *a.* | A258 Pair, #551-552 | 1.50 | 1.50 |
| **553** | 1.50r multicolored | .80 | .60 |
| **554** | 1.50r multicolored | .80 | .60 |
| *a.* | A258 Pair, #553-554 | 1.75 | 1.75 |
| **555** | 2r multicolored | .80 | .80 |
| **556** | 2r multicolored | .80 | .80 |
| *a.* | A258 Pair, #555-556 | 1.75 | 1.75 |
| | *Nos. 549-556 (8)* | 5.40 | 4.40 |

Inauguration of Pakistan Steel Furnace No. 1, Karachi
A260

**1981, Aug. 31** *Perf. 13*

| | | | | |
|---|---|---|---|---|
| **557** | A260 | 40p multicolored | .25 | .25 |
| **558** | A260 | 2r multicolored | .60 | .75 |

Western Tragopan in Summer
A261

**1981, Sept. 15** **Litho.** *Perf. 14*

| | | | | |
|---|---|---|---|---|
| **559** | A261 | 40p shown | 2.25 | .75 |
| **560** | A261 | 2r Winter | 4.50 | 4.00 |

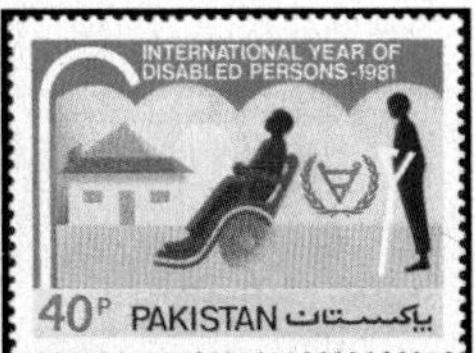


Intl. Year of the Disabled
A262

**1981, Dec. 12** **Litho.** *Perf. 13*

| | | | | |
|---|---|---|---|---|
| **561** | A262 | 40p multicolored | .25 | .30 |
| **562** | A262 | 2r multicolored | 1.25 | 1.00 |

World Cup Championship
A263

**1982, Jan. 31** **Litho.** *Perf. 13½x13*

| | | | | |
|---|---|---|---|---|
| **563** | A263 | 1r Cup, flags in arc | 2.00 | 1.00 |
| **564** | A263 | 1r shown | 2.00 | 1.00 |
| *a.* | | Pair, #563-564 | 4.50 | 4.50 |

Nos. 563-564 were printed with a vertical strip of labels, picturing different scenes, in the middle of each sheet, allowing for pairs with label between. Value, pair with label $4.

Camel Skin Lampshade
A264

**1982, Feb. 20** **Litho.** *Perf. 14*

| | | | | |
|---|---|---|---|---|
| **565** | A264 | 1r shown | .70 | .60 |
| **566** | A264 | 1r Hala pottery | .70 | .60 |

See Nos. 582-583.

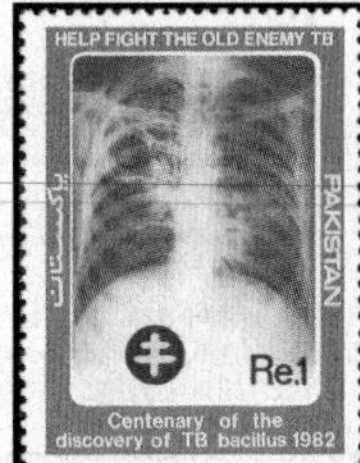


TB Bacillus Centenary
A265

**1982, Mar. 24**

| | | | | |
|---|---|---|---|---|
| **567** | A265 | 1r multicolored | 1.50 | 1.25 |

Blind Indus Dolphin
A266

**1982, Apr. 24** **Litho.** *Perf. 12x11½*

| | | | | |
|---|---|---|---|---|
| **568** | A266 | 40p Dolphin | 1.50 | .75 |
| **569** | A266 | 1r Dolphin, diff. | 3.50 | 1.50 |

Peaceful Uses of Outer Space — A267

**1982, June 7** **Litho.** *Perf. 13*

| | | | | |
|---|---|---|---|---|
| **570** | A267 | 1r multicolored | 2.00 | 1.10 |

No. 570 was printed with a vertical strip of labels, picturing different space satellites, in the middle of each sheet, allowing for pairs with label between. Value, pair with label $4.

50th Anniv. of Sukkur Barrage — A268

**1982, July 17** **Litho.** *Perf. 13*

| | | | | |
|---|---|---|---|---|
| **571** | A268 | 1r multicolored | .35 | .25 |

For overprint see No. 574.

Independence Day — A269

**1982, Aug. 14**

| | | | | |
|---|---|---|---|---|
| **572** | A269 | 40p Flag | .25 | .25 |
| **573** | A269 | 85p Map | .50 | .50 |

### No. 571 Overprinted "RICCIONE-82/1932-1982"

**1982, Aug. 28**

| | | | | |
|---|---|---|---|---|
| **574** | A268 | 1r multicolored | .25 | .25 |

RICCIONE '82 Intl. Stamp Exhibition, Riccione, Italy, Aug. 28-30.

University of the Punjab Centenary — A270

**1982, Oct. 14** **Litho.** *Perf. 13½*

| | | | | |
|---|---|---|---|---|
| **575** | A270 | 40p multicolored | 1.20 | .40 |

No. 575 was printed with a vertical strip of labels, picturing different university buildings, in the middle of each sheet, allowing for pairs with label between. Value, pair with label: $4.

Scouting Year — A271

**1982, Dec. 23** **Litho.** *Perf. 13*

| | | | | |
|---|---|---|---|---|
| **576** | A271 | 2r Emblem | .50 | .35 |

Quetta Natural Gas Pipeline Project
A272

**1983, Jan. 6** **Litho.** *Perf. 13*

| | | | | |
|---|---|---|---|---|
| **577** | A272 | 1r multicolored | .35 | .25 |

Common Peacock
A273

Designs: 50p, Common rose. 60p, Plain tiger. 1.50r, Lemon butterfly.

**1983, Feb. 15** **Litho.** *Perf. 14*

| | | | | |
|---|---|---|---|---|
| **578** | A273 | 40p shown | 1.25 | .25 |
| **579** | A273 | 50p multi | 1.50 | .25 |
| **580** | A273 | 60p multi | 1.75 | .55 |
| **581** | A273 | 1.50r multi | 2.50 | 2.25 |
| | | *Nos. 578-581 (4)* | 7.00 | 3.30 |

### Handicraft Type of 1982

Designs: No. 582, Straw mats. No. 583, Five-flower cloth design.

**1983, Mar. 9**

| | | | | |
|---|---|---|---|---|
| **582** | A264 | 1r multi | .25 | .25 |
| **583** | A264 | 1r multi | .25 | .25 |

Opening of Aga Khan University — A274

**1983, Mar. 16** *Perf. 13½*

| | | | | |
|---|---|---|---|---|
| **584** | A274 | 2r multicolored | 1.50 | 1.00 |

No. 584 was printed with a vertical strip of labels, picturing different university views, in the middle of each sheet, allowing for pairs with label between. Value, pair with label $4.

Yak Caravan, Zindiharam-Darkot Pass, Hindu Kush Mountains — A275

**1983, Apr. 28** **Litho.** ***Perf. 13***
**585** A275 1r multicolored 1.60 .50

Marsh Crocodile A276

**1983, May 19** ***Perf. 13½x14***
**586** A276 3r multicolored 3.75 1.60

**1983, June 20** **Litho.** ***Perf. 14***
**Size: 50x40mm**
**587** A276 1r Gazelle 3.25 1.60

36th Anniv. of Independence A277

**1983, Aug. 14** ***Perf. 13***
**588** A277 60p Star .25 .25
**589** A277 4r Torch .40 .40

25th Anniv. of Indonesia-Pakistan Economic and Cultural Cooperation Org. — A278

Weavings — No. 590, Pakistani (geometric). No. 591, Indonesian (figures).

**1983, Aug. 19** **Litho.** ***Perf. 13***
**590** A278 2r multicolored .30 .25
**591** A278 2r multicolored .30 .25

Siberian Cranes — A279

**1983, Sept. 8** ***Perf. 13½***
**592** A279 3r multicolored 4.00 3.00

World Communications Year — A280

**1983, Oct. 9** **Litho.** ***Perf. 13***
**593** A280 2r multicolored .35 .25
**Size: 33x33mm**
**594** A280 3r Symbol, diff. .30 .25

World Food Day A281

**1983, Oct. 24** **Litho.** ***Perf. 13***
**595** A281 3r Livestock 1.50 1.50
**596** A281 3r Fruit 1.50 1.50
**597** A281 3r Grain 1.50 1.50
**598** A281 3r Seafood 1.50 1.50
*a.* Strip of 4, #595-598 6.50 6.50

National Fertilizer Corp. — A282

**1983, Oct. 24** **Litho.** ***Perf. 13½***
**599** A282 60p multicolored .25 .25

View of Lahore City, 1852 — A283

**1983, Nov. 13** **Litho.** ***Perf. 13***
**600** Strip of 6 3.50 3.50
*a.-f.* A283 60p any single .50 .50

PAKPHILEX '83 Natl. Stamp Exhibition.

Yachting Victory in 9th Asian Games, 1982 — A284

**1983, Dec. 31** **Litho.** ***Perf. 13***
**601** A284 60p OK Dinghy 1.75 1.75
**602** A284 60p Enterprise 1.75 1.75

Snow Leopard — A285

**1984, Jan. 21** ***Perf. 14***
**603** A285 40p lt green & multi 2.00 1.00
**604** A285 1.60r blue & multi 5.00 5.00

Jehangir Khan (b. 1963), World Squash Champion A286

**1984, Mar. 17** **Litho.** ***Perf. 13***
**605** A286 3r multicolored 2.75 1.40

Pakistan Intl. Airway China Service, 20th Anniv. A287

**1984, Apr. 29** **Litho.** ***Perf. 13***
**606** A287 3r Jet 5.75 4.50

Glass Work, Lahore Fort — A288

Various glass panels.

**1984, May 31** **Litho.** ***Perf. 13***
**607** A288 1r green & multi .25 .25
**608** A288 1r purple & multi .25 .25
**609** A288 1r vermilion & multi .25 .25
**610** A288 1r brt blue & multi .25 .25
*Nos. 607-610 (4)* 1.00 1.00

Forts — A289

**1984-88** **Litho.** ***Perf. 11***
**613** A289 5p Kot Diji *.40* .25
**614** A289 10p Rohtas *.40* .25
**615** A289 15p Bala Hissar ('86) *.75* .25
**616** A289 20p Attock *1.50* .25
**617** A289 50p Hyderabad ('86) *1.50* .25
**618** A289 60p Lahore *1.25* .25
**619** A289 70p Sibi ('88) *1.50* .25
**620** A289 80p Ranikot ('86) *1.50* .25
*Nos. 613-620 (8)* *8.80* 2.00

Issued: 5p, 11/1; 10p, 9/25; 80p, 7/1.
For overprints see Nos. O118-O124.

Shah Rukn-i-Alam Tomb, Multan — A290

**1984, June 26** **Litho.** ***Perf. 13***
**624** A290 60p multicolored 3.00 1.40

Aga Khan Award for Architecture.

Asia-Pacific Broadcasting Union, 20th Anniv. — A290a

**1984, July 1** **Litho.** ***Perf. 13***
**625** A290a 3r multicolored .90 .50

1984 Summer Olympics, Los Angeles — A291

**1984, July 31**
**626** A291 3r Athletics 1.25 1.00
**627** A291 3r Boxing 1.25 1.00
**628** A291 3r Hockey 1.25 1.00
**629** A291 3r Yachting 1.25 1.00
**630** A291 3r Wrestling 1.25 1.00
*Nos. 626-630 (5)* 6.25 5.00

Issued in sheets of 10.

A press sheet containing sheets of 10 each of Nos. 626-630 was produced for limited sales overseas. Value, $100.

Independence, 37th Anniv. — A292

**1984, Aug. 14**
**631** A292 60p Jasmine .25 .25
**632** A292 4r Lighted torch .50 .45

Intl. Trade Fair, Sept. 1-21, Karachi A293

**1984, Sept. 1**
**633** A293 60p multicolored .60 .30

1984 Natl. Tourism Convention, Karachi, Nov. 5-8 — A293a

Shah Jahan Mosque: a, Main dome interior. b, Tile work. c, Entrance. d, Archways. e, Dome interior, diff.

**1984, Nov. 5** **Litho.** ***Perf. 13½***
**634** Strip of 5 3.00 3.00
*a.-e.* A293a 1r any single .50 .40

United Bank Limited, 25th Anniv. A294

**1984, Nov. 7**
**635** A294 60p multicolored .75 .60

UNCTAD, UN Conference on Trade and Development, 20th Anniv. — A294a

**1984, Dec. 24** ***Perf. 14½x14***
**636** A294a 60p multicolored .85 .35

Postal Life Insurance, Cent. — A295

**1984, Dec. 29** ***Perf. 13½x14***
**637** A295 60p multicolored .50 .25
**638** A295 1r multicolored .75 .25

UNESCO World Heritage Campaign — A296

No. 639, Unicorn, rock painting. No. 640, Unicorn seal, round.

**1984, Dec. 31**
**639** 2r multicolored 1.50 .80
**640** 2r multicolored 1.50 .80
*a.* A296 Pair, #639-640 3.50 3.50

Restoration of Mohenjo-Daro.

IYY, Girl Guides 75th Anniv. A297

**1985, Jan. 5** ***Perf. 13½***
**641** A297 60p Emblems 4.00 1.25

Smelting A298

Pouring Steel — A299

**1985, Jan. 15** ***Perf. 13***
**642** A298 60p multicolored .75 .30
**643** A299 1r multicolored 1.25 .40

Referendum Reinstating Pres. Zia — A300

**1985, Mar. 20 Litho.** ***Perf. 13***
**644** A300 60p Map, sunburst 1.25 .40

Minar-e-Qarardad-e-Pakistan Tower — A301

Ballot Box A302

1985 Elections.

**1985, Mar. 23**
**645** A301 1r multicolored .70 .25
**646** A302 1r multicolored .70 .25

Mountaineering — A303

40p, Mt. Rakaposhi, Karakoram. 2r, Mt. Nangaparbat, Western Himalayas.

**1985, May 27 Litho.** ***Perf. 14***
**647** A303 40p multicolored 2.00 .75
**648** A303 2r multicolored 4.25 5.50

Championship Pakistani Men's Field Hockey Team — A304

Design: 1984 Olympic gold medal, 1985 Dhaka Asia Cup, 1982 Bombay World Cup.

**1985, June 5 Litho.** ***Perf. 13***
**649** A304 1r multicolored 2.50 1.25

King Edward Medical College, Lahore, 125th Anniv. — A305

**1985, July 28 Litho.** ***Perf. 13***
**650** A305 3r multicolored 2.25 .80

Natl. Independence Day — A306

Designs: No. 651a, 37th Independence Day written in English. No. 651b, In Urdu.

**1985, Aug. 14**
**651** A306 Pair + 2 labels .75 .75
*a.-b.* 60p any single .35 .30

Printed in sheets of 4 stamps + 4 labels.

Sind Madressah-Tul-Islam, Karachi, Education Cent. — A307

**1985, Sept. 1**
**652** A307 2r multicolored 2.10 .80

Mosque, Jinnah Avenue, Karachi — A308

**1985, Sept. 14**
**653** A308 1r Mosque by day 1.00 .35
**654** A308 1r At night 1.00 .35

35th anniv. of the Jamia Masjid Pakistan Security Printing Corporation's miniature replica of the Badshahi Mosque, Lahore.

Lawrence College, Murree, 125th Anniv. — A309

**1985, Sept. 21**
**655** A309 3r multicolored 2.50 .75

UN, 40th Anniv. — A310

**1985, Oct. 24 Litho.** ***Perf. 14x14½***
**656** A310 1r UN building, sun .40 .25
**657** A310 2r Building emblem .60 .30

10th Natl. Scouting Jamboree, Lahore, Nov. 8-15 — A311

**1985, Nov. 8** ***Perf. 13***
**658** A311 60p multicolored 3.00 1.90

Islamabad and Capital Development Authority Emblem — A312

**1985, Nov. 30** ***Perf. 14½***
**659** A312 3r multicolored 2.10 .50

Islamabad, capital of Pakistan, 25th anniv.

Flags and Map of SAARC Nations A313

Flags as Flower Petals A314

**1985, Dec. 8** ***Perf. 13½, 13***
**660** A313 1r multicolored 2.50 3.50
**661** A314 2r multicolored 1.00 1.75

SAARC, South Asian Assoc. for Regional Cooperation.

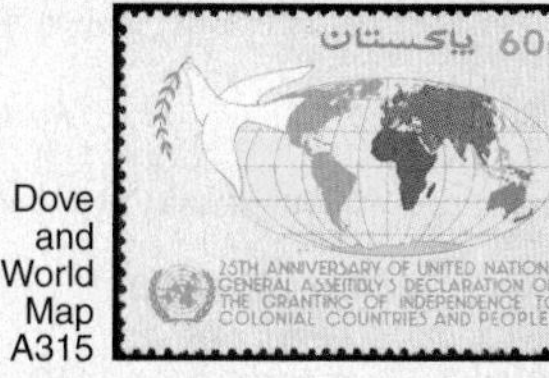
Dove and World Map A315

**1985, Dec. 14** ***Perf. 13***
**662** A315 60p multicolored 1.00 .60

UN Declaration on the Granting of Independence to Colonial Countries and Peoples, 25th Anniv.

Shaheen Falcon — A316

**1986, Jan. 20** ***Perf. 13½x14***
**663** A316 1.50r multicolored 5.00 4.00

Agricultural Development Bank, 25th Anniv. — A317

**1986, Feb. 18** **Litho.** ***Perf. 13***
**664** A317 60p multicolored 1.00 .40

Sadiq Egerton College, Bahawalpur, Cent. — A318

**1986, Apr. 25**
**665** A318 1r multicolored 3.50 1.00

A319

**1986, May 11** ***Perf. 13½***
**666** A319 1r multicolored 3.25 .85

Asian Productivity Organization, 25th anniv.

A320

**1986, Aug. 14** **Litho.** ***Perf. 14½x14***
**667** A320 80p "1947-1986" 1.50 .60
**668** A320 1r Urdu text, fireworks 1.50 .60

Independence Day, 39th anniv.

Intl. Literacy Day — A321

**1986, Sept. 8** ***Perf. 13***
**669** A321 1r Teacher, students 1.75 .60

A322

**1986, Oct. 28** **Litho.** ***Perf. 13½x13***
**670** A322 80p multicolored 2.50 .40

UN Child Survival Campaign.

Aitchison College, Lahore, Cent. — A323

**1986, Nov. 3** ***Perf. 13½***
**671** A323 2.50r multicolored 1.75 .60

Intl. Peace Year — A324

**1986, Nov. 20** ***Perf. 13***
**672** A324 4r multicolored .65 .55

4th Asian Cup Table Tennis Tournament, Karachi A325

**1986, Nov. 25** ***Perf. 14½***
**673** A325 2r multicolored 2.50 .50

Marcopolo Sheep — A326

**1986, Dec. 4** **Litho.** ***Perf. 14***
**674** A326 2r multicolored 3.25 2.50

See No. 698.

Eco Philex '86 — A327

Mosques: No. 675a, Selimiye, Turkey. No. 675b, Gawhar Shad, Iran. No. 675c, Grand Mosque, Pakistan.

**1986, Dec. 20** ***Perf. 13***
**675** Strip of 3 4.00 4.00
***a.-c.*** A327 3r any single 1.25 1.25

St. Patrick's School, Karachi, 125th Anniv. — A328

**1987, Jan. 29** **Litho.** ***Perf. 13***
**676** A328 5r multicolored 3.00 1.10

Savings Bank Week — A329

Birds, berries and: a, National defense. b, Education. c, Agriculture. d, Industry.

**1987, Feb. 21** **Litho.** ***Perf. 13***
**677** Block of 4 + 2 labels 5.00 5.00
***a.-d.*** A329 5r any single 1.00 .75

Parliament House Opening, Islamabad — A330

**1987, Mar. 23**
**678** A330 3r multicolored .60 .25

Fight Against Drug Abuse A331

**1987, June 30** **Litho.** ***Perf. 13***
**679** A331 1r multicolored .60 .25

Natl. Independence, 40th Anniv. — A332

Natl. flag and: 80p, Natl. anthem, written in Urdu. 3r, Jinnah's first natl. address, the Minar-e-Qarardad-e-Pakistan and natl. coat of arms.

**1987, Aug. 14** **Litho.** ***Perf. 13***
**680** A332 80p multicolored .75 .25
**681** A332 3r multicolored 2.00 .75

Miniature Sheet

Air Force, 40th Anniv. — A333

Aircraft: a, Tempest II. b, Hawker Fury. c, Super Marine Attacker. d, F86 Sabre. e, F104 Star Fighter. f, C130 Hercules. g, F6. h, Mirage III. i, A5. j, F16 Fighting Falcon.

**1987, Sept. 7** **Litho.** ***Perf. 13½***
**682** Sheet of 10 16.00 16.00
***a.-j.*** A333 3r any single 1.25 1.00

Tourism Convention 1987 — A334

Views along Karakoram Highway: a, Pasu Glacier. b, Apricot trees. c, Highway winding through hills. d, Khunjerab peak.

**1987, Oct. 1** ***Perf. 13***
**683** Block of 4 2.50 2.50
***a.-d.*** A334 1.50r any single .50 .25

Shah Abdul Latif Bhitai Mausoleum — A335

**1987, Oct. 8** *Perf. 13*
**684** A335 80p multicolored .25 .25

D.J. Sind Government Science College, Karachi, Cent. — A336

**1987, Nov. 7**
**685** A336 80p multicolored .25 .25

College of Physicians and Surgeons, 25th Anniv. — A337

**1987, Dec. 9** **Litho.** *Perf. 13*
**686** A337 1r multicolored 1.75 .60

Intl. Year of Shelter for the Homeless A338

**1987, Dec. 15**
**687** A338 3r multicolored .50 .35

Cathedral Church of the Resurrection, Lahore, Cent. — A339

**1987, Dec. 20**
**688** A339 3r multicolored .50 .25

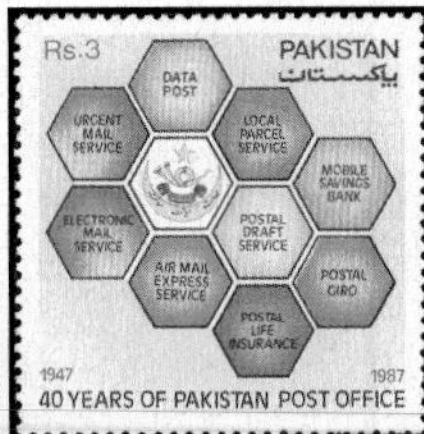


Natl. Postal Service, 40th Anniv. A340

**1987, Dec. 28**
**689** A340 3r multicolored .50 .25

Radio Pakistan A341

**1987, Dec. 31**
**690** A341 80p multicolored .25 .25

Jamshed Nusserwanjee Mehta (1886-1952), Mayor of Karachi, Member of the Sind Legislative Assembly — A342

**1988, Jan. 7**
**691** A342 3r multicolored .50 .35

World Leprosy Day — A343

**1988, Jan. 31**
**692** A343 3r multicolored .75 .25

World Health Organization, 40th Anniv. — A344

**1988, Apr. 7** **Litho.** *Perf. 13*
**693** A344 4r multicolored .75 .30

Intl. Red Cross and Red Crescent Organizations, 125th Annivs. — A345

**1988, May 8**
**694** A345 3r multicolored .70 .45

Independence Day, 41st Anniv. — A346

**1988, Aug. 14** **Litho.** *Perf. 13½*
**695** A346 80p multicolored .35 .25
**696** A346 4r multicolored .35 .35

Miniature Sheet

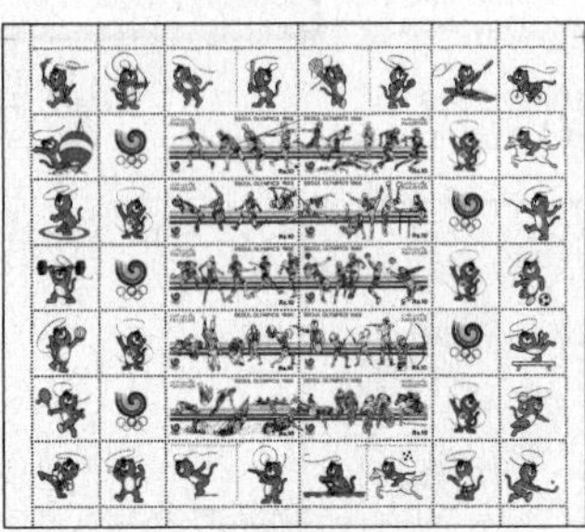

1988 Summer Olympics, Seoul — A347

Events: a, Discus, shot put, hammer throw, javelin. b, Relay, hurdles, running, walking. c, High jump, long jump, triple jump, pole vault. d, Gymnastic floor exercises, rings, parallel bars. e, Table tennis, tennis, field hockey, baseball. f, Volleyball, soccer, basketball, team handball. g, Wrestling, judo, boxing, weight lifting. h, Sport pistol, fencing, rifle shooting, archery. i, Swimming, diving, yachting, quadruple-sculling, kayaking. j, Equestrian jumping, cycling, steeplechase.

**1988, Sept. 17** **Litho.** *Perf. 13½x13*
**697** A347 Sheet of 10+32 labels 13.00 13.00
*a.-j.* 10r any single 1.00 1.00

Labels contained in No. 697 picture the Seoul Games character trademark or emblem. Size of No. 697: 251x214mm.

**Fauna Type of 1986**

2r, Suleman markhor, vert.

**1988, Oct. 29** **Litho.** *Perf. 14*
**698** A326 2r multi .85 .40

**Pioneers of Freedom Type of 1979**

3r, Maulana Hasrat Mohani.

**1989, Jan. 23** **Litho.** **Wmk. 351**
**699** A236 3r multi .45 .25

Islamia College, Peshawar, 75th Anniv. — A348

**1988, Dec. 22** **Unwmk.** *Perf. 13½*
**700** A348 3r multicolored .60 .25

SAARC Summit Conference, Islamabad — A349

Designs: 25r, Flags, symbols of commerce. 50r, Globe, communication and transportation. 75r, Bangladesh #69, Maldive Islands #1030, Bhutan #132, Pakistan #403, Ceylon #451, India #580, Nepal #437.

**1988, Dec. 29** *Perf. 13*
**701** A349 25r shown 1.50 1.50

No. 701 exists with attached label. Values: *$10* mint, *$20* used.

**Size: 33x33mm**
***Perf. 14***
**702** A349 50r multicolored 4.50 3.25

**Size: 52x28mm**
***Perf. 13½x13***
**703** A349 75r multicolored 3.50 *3.50*
*Nos. 701-703 (3)* 9.50 8.25

No. 703 exists with attached label. Value, strip of three with label $20.

Adasia '89, 16th Asian Advertising Congress, Lahore, Feb. 18-22 — A350

**1989, Feb. 18** **Litho.** *Perf. 13*
**704** Strip of 3 3.50 3.25
*a.* A350 1r deep rose lilac & multi .95 .65
*b.* A350 1r green & multi .95 .65
*c.* A350 1r bright vermilion & multi .95 .65

Printed in sheets of 9.

Pres. Zulfikar Ali Bhutto (1928-1979), Ousted by Military Coup and Executed A351

Portraits.

**1989, Apr. 4** **Litho.** *Perf. 13*
**705** A351 1r shown .25 .25
**706** A351 2r multi, diff. .40 .25

Submarine Operations, 25th Anniv. — A352

Submarines: a, *Agosta.* b, *Daphne.* c, *Fleet Snorkel.*

**1989, June 1** **Litho.** *Perf. 13½*
**707** Strip of 3 4.25 4.25
*a.-c.* A352 1r any single 1.25 1.25

*Oath of the Tennis Court,* by David — A353

**1989, June 24** **Litho.** *Perf. 13½*
**708** A353 7r multicolored 2.25 .80

French revolution, bicent.

Archaeological Heritage — A354

Terra cotta vessels excavated in Baluchistan: a, Pirak, c. 2200 B.C. b, Nindo Damb, c. 2300 B.C. c, Mehrgarh, c. 3600 B.C. d, Nausharo, c. 2600 B.C.

**1989, June 28** ***Perf. 14½x14***

**709** Block of 4 1.25 1.25
***a.-d.*** A354 1r any single .25 .25

Asia-Pacific Telecommunity, 10th Anniv. — A355

**1989, July 1** ***Perf. 13½x14***

**710** A355 3r multicolored .50 .25

Laying the Foundation Stone for the 1st Integrated Container Terminal, Port Qasim A356

**1989, Aug. 5** **Litho.** ***Perf. 14***

**711** A356 6r Ship in berth 3.25 3.25

Mohammad Ali Jinnah — A357

**Litho & Engr.**

**1989, Aug. 14** **Wmk. 351** ***Perf. 13***

| | | | | |
|---|---|---|---|---|
| **712** | A357 | 1r multicolored | .65 | .25 |
| **713** | A357 | 1.50r multicolored | .80 | .25 |
| **714** | A357 | 2r multicolored | .90 | .25 |
| **715** | A357 | 3r multicolored | 1.00 | .30 |
| **716** | A357 | 4r multicolored | 1.50 | .35 |
| **717** | A357 | 5r multicolored | 1.75 | .40 |
| | | *Nos. 712-717 (6)* | 6.60 | 1.80 |

Independence Day.

Nos. 712-717 exist overprinted "NATIONAL SEMINAR ON PHILATELY MULTAN 1992." These were available only at the seminar and were not sold in post offices. Value $125. Beware of forgeries.

Abdul Latif Bhitai Memorial A358

**1989, Sept. 16** **Litho.** **Unwmk.**

**718** A358 2r multicolored .60 .25

245th death and 300th birth annivs. of Shah Abdul Latif Bhitai.

World Wildlife Fund — A359

Himalayan black bears and WWF emblem: a, Bear on slope, emblem UR. b, Bear on slope, emblem UL. c, Bear on top of rock, emblem UR. d, Seated bear, emblem UL.

***Perf. 14x13½***

**1989, Oct. 7** **Litho.** **Unwmk.**

**719** A359 Block of 4 4.00 4.00
***a.-d.*** 4r, any single .75 .75

World Food Day — A360

**1989, Oct. 16** ***Perf. 14x12½***

**720** A360 1r multicolored .45 .30

Quilt and Bahishiti Darwaza (Heavenly Gate) — A361

**1989, Oct. 20** ***Perf. 13***

**721** A361 3r multicolored .50 .25

800th Birth anniv. of Baba Farid.

4th SAF Games, Islamabad A362

**1989, Oct. 20**

**722** A362 1r multicolored .45 .40

Pakistan Television, 25th Anniv. A363

**1989, Nov. 26** **Litho.** ***Perf. 13½***

**723** A363 3r multicolored .50 .25

SAARC Year Against Drug Abuse and Drug Trafficking A364

**1989, Dec. 8** ***Perf. 13***

**724** A364 7r multicolored 2.50 .85

Murray College, Sialkot, Cent. A365

**1989, Dec. 18** ***Perf. 14***

**725** A365 6r multicolored .60 .40

Government College, Lahore, 125th Anniv. — A366

**1989, Dec. 21** ***Perf. 13***

**726** A366 6r multicolored .60 .50

Center on Integrated Rural Development for Asia and the Pacific (CIRDAP), 10th Anniv. — A367

**1989, Dec. 31**

**727** A367 3r multicolored .60 .40

Organization of the Islamic Conference (OIC), 20th Anniv. — A368

**1990, Feb. 9** **Litho.** ***Perf. 13***

**728** A368 1r multicolored 1.40 .50

7th World Field Hockey Cup, Lahore, Feb. 12-23 — A369

**1990, Feb. 12** ***Perf. 14x13½***

**729** A369 2r multicolored 5.25 4.00

A370

Pakistan Resolution, 50th Anniv. — A371

Designs: a, Allama Mohammad Iqbal addressing the Allahabad Session of the All-India Muslim League and swearing-in of Liat Ali Khan as league secretary-general. b, Freedom fighter Maulana Mohammad Ali Jauhar at Muslim rally and Mohammed Ali Jinnah at microphone. c, Muslim woman holding flag and swearing-in of Mohammed Ali Jinnah as governor-general of Pakistan, Aug. 14, 1947. 7r, English and Urdu translations of the resolution, natl. flag and Minar-e-Qarardade Pakistan.

**1990, Mar. 23** **Litho.** ***Perf. 13***

**730** Strip of 3 3.00 3.00
***a.-c.*** A370 1r any single 1.00 .75

**Size: 90x45mm**

***Perf. 13½***

**731** A371 7r multicolored 2.00 2.00

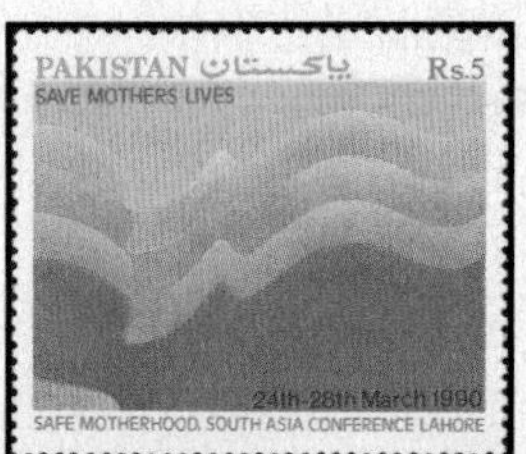

Safe Motherhood South Asia Conference, Lahore — A372

**1990, Mar. 24** ***Perf. 13½***

**732** A372 5r multicolored .75 .50

Calligraphic Painting of a Ghalib Verse, by Shakir Ali (1916-1975) — A373

**1990, Apr. 19** **Litho.** ***Perf. 13½x13***

**733** A373 1r multicolored 2.25 .65

See Nos. 757-758.

Badr-1 Satellite — A374

**1990, July 26 Litho. *Perf. 13***

**734** A374 3r multicolored 3.75 2.50

Pioneers of Freedom A375

No. 735: a, Allama Mohammad Iqbal (1877-1938). b, Mohammad Ali Jinnah (1876-1948). c, Sir Syed Ahmad Khan (1817-98). d, Nawab Salimullah (1884-1915). e, Mohtarma Fatima Jinnah (1893-1967). f, Aga Khan III (1877-1957). g, Nawab Mohammad Ismail Khan (1884-1958). h, Hussain Shaheed Suhrawardy (1893-1963). i, Syed Ameer Ali (1849-1928).

No. 736: a, Nawab Bahadur Yar Jung (1905-44). b, Khawaja Nazimuddin (1894-1964). c, Maulana Obaidullah Sindhi (1872-1944). d, Sahibzada Abdul Qaiyum Khan (c. 1863-1937). e, Begum Jahanara Shah Nawaz (1896-1979). f, Sir Ghulam Hussain Hidayatullah (1879-1948). g, Qazi Mohammad Isa (1913-76). h, Sir M. Shahnawaz Khan Mamdot (1883-1942). i, Pir Shaib of Manki Sharif (1923-60).

No. 737: a, Liaquat Ali Khan (1895-1951). b, Maulvi A.K. Fazl-Ul-Haq (1873-1962). c, Allama Shabbir Ahmad Usmani (1885-1949). d, Sardar Abdur Rab Nishtar (1899-1958). e, Bi Amma (c. 1850-1924). f, Sir Abdullah Haroon (1872-1942). g, Chaudhry Rahmat Ali (1897-1951). h, Raja Sahib of Mahmudabad (1914-73). i, Hassanally Effendi (1830-1895).

No. 737J: k, Maulana Zafar Ali Khan (1873-1956). l, Maulana Mohamed Ali Jauhar (1878-1931). m, Chaudhry Khaliquzzaman (1889-1973). n, Hameed Nizami (1915-62). o, Begum Ra'ana Liaquat Ali Khan (1905-90). p, Mirza Abol Hassan Ispahani (1902-81). q, Raja Ghazanfar Ali Khan (1895-1963). r, Malik Barkat Ali (1886-1946). s, Mir Jaffer Khan Jamali (c. 1911-67).

**1990-91 Litho. *Perf. 13***

**Miniature Sheets**

| | | | |
|---|---|---|---|
| **735** | Sheet of 9 | 3.50 | 3.50 |
| ***a.-i.*** | A375 1r any single | .40 | .25 |
| **736** | Sheet of 9 | 3.50 | 3.50 |
| ***a.-i.*** | A375 1r any single | .40 | .25 |
| **737** | Sheet of 9 | 3.50 | 3.50 |
| ***a.-i.*** | A375 1r any single | .40 | .25 |
| **737J** | Sheet of 9 ('91) | 6.00 | 6.00 |
| ***k.-s.*** | A375 1r any single | .40 | .25 |
| | *Nos. 735-737J (4)* | 16.50 | 16.50 |

Issued: #735-737, Aug. 19; #737J, 1991.

See Nos. 773, 792, 804, 859-860, 865, 875-876, 922-924.

Indonesia Pakistan Economic and Cultural Cooperation Organization, 1968-1990 — A376

**1990, Aug. 19**

**738** A376 7r multicolored 3.50 1.10

Intl. Literacy Year — A377

**1990, Sept. 8**

**739** A377 3r multicolored 1.25 .75

A378

**1990, Sept. 22**

**740** A378 2r multicolored 1.10 .40

Joint meeting of Royal College of Physicians, Edinburgh and College of Physicians and Surgeons, Pakistan.

World Summit for Children A379

**1990, Sept. 19**

**741** A379 7r multicolored .85 .50

Year of the Girl Child A380

**1990, Nov. 21 Litho. *Perf. 13½***

**742** A380 2r multicolored .75 .50

Security Papers Ltd., 25th Anniv. — A381

**1990, Dec. 8 *Perf. 13***

**743** A381 3r multicolored 4.50 1.50

Intl. Civil Defense Day — A382

**1991, Mar. 1 Litho. *Perf. 13***

**744** A382 7r multicolored 2.75 2.00

South & West Asia Postal Union — A383

**1991, Mar. 21**

**745** A383 5r multicolored 2.10 1.50

World Population Day — A384

**1991, July 11**

**746** A384 10r multicolored 2.50 1.50

Intl. Special Olympics A385

**1991, July 19**

**747** A385 7r multicolored 2.10 1.50

Habib Bank Limited, 50th Anniv. — A386

**1991, Aug. 25 Litho. *Perf. 13***

**748** A386 1r brt red & multi 1.25 .45

**749** A386 5r brt green & multi 4.50 3.25

St. Joseph's Convent School, Karachi — A387

**1991, Sept. 8**

**750** A387 5r multicolored 4.25 3.00

Emperor Sher Shah Suri (c. 1472-1545) A388

**1991, Oct. 5**

**751** A388 5r multicolored 1.75 1.75

**Souvenir Sheet**

**Size: 90x81mm**

***Imperf***

**752** A388 7r multicolored 2.00 2.00

Pakistani Scientific Expedition to Antarctica — A389

**1991, Oct. 28**

**753** A389 7r multicolored 3.50 2.50

Houbara Bustard — A390

**1991, Nov. 4**

**754** A390 7r multicolored 3.00 2.00

Asian Development Bank, 25th Anniv. — A391

**1991, Dec. 19 Litho. *Perf. 13***

**755** A391 7r multicolored 3.50 1.50

Hazrat Sultan Bahoo, 300th Death Anniv. A392

**1991, Dec. 22**

**756** A392 7r multicolored 2.10 1.10

**Painting Type of 1990**

Paintings and artists: No. 757, Village Life, by Allah Ustad Bux (1892-1978). No. 758, Miniature of Royal Procession, by Muhammad Haji Sharif (1889-1978).

**1991, Dec. 24**

**757** A373 1r multicolored 2.25 1.25

**758** A373 1r multicolored 2.25 1.25

American Express Travelers Cheques, 100th Anniv. — A393

**1991, Dec. 26** *Perf. 13½*
**759** A393 7r multicolored 2.50 1.50

Muslim Commercial Bank, First Year of Private Operation — A394

7r, City skyline, worker, cogwheels, computer operators.

**1992, Apr. 8** **Litho.** *Perf. 13*
**760** A394 1r multicolored .25 .25
**761** A394 7r multicolored 1.00 .65

Pakistan, 1992 World Cricket Champions — A395

World Cricket Cup and: 2r, Pakistani player, vert. 7r, Pakistan flag, fireworks, vert.

**1992, Apr. 27**
**762** A395 2r multicolored .75 .50
**763** A395 5r multicolored 1.75 1.10
**764** A395 7r multicolored 2.00 1.40
*Nos. 762-764 (3)* 4.50 3.00

Intl. Space Year — A396

Design: 2r, Globe, satellite.

**1992, June 7** **Litho.** *Perf. 13*
**771** A396 1r multicolored .35 .25
**772** A396 2r multicolored .55 .35

30th anniv. of first Pakistani rocket (#771).

**Pioneers of Freedom Type of 1990**

Designs: a, Syed Suleman Nadvi (1884-1953). b, Nawab Iftikhar Hussain Khan Mamdot (1906-1969). c, Maulana Muhammad Shibli Naumani (1857-1914).

**1992, Aug. 14** **Litho.** *Perf. 13*
**773** A375 1r Strip of 3, #a.-c. 4.50 3.75

World Population Day — A397

**1992, July 25**
**774** A397 6r multicolored 1.10 1.10

Medicinal Plants — A398

**1992, Nov. 22** **Litho.** *Perf. 13*
**775** A398 6r multicolored 3.75 3.50

See No. 791.

Extraordinary Session of Economic Cooperation Organization Council of Ministers, Islamabad — A399

**1992, Nov. 28**
**776** A399 7r multicolored 1.40 1.00

Intl. Conference on Nutrition, Rome A400

**1992, Dec. 5** *Perf. 14*
**777** A400 7r multicolored .85 .85

Islamic Cultural Heritage A401

**1992, Dec. 14** *Perf. 13*
**778** A401 7r Alhambra, Spain .60 .60

Islamic Scouts, Islamabad — A402

**1992, Aug. 23** *Perf. 14x12½*
**779** A402 6r 6th Jamboree .70 .60
**780** A402 6r 4th Conference .70 .60

Government Islamia College, Lahore, Cent. — A403

**1992, Nov. 1** *Perf. 13*
**781** A403 3r multicolored .60 .60

Industries A404

Designs: a, 10r, Surgical instruments. b, 15r, Leather goods. c, 25r, Sports equipment.

**1992, July 5** **Litho.** *Perf. 13½x13*
**782** A404 Strip of 3, #a.-c. 5.50 5.50

World Telecommunications Day — A405

**1993, May 17** **Litho.** *Perf. 13*
**783** A405 1r multicolored 1.50 .55

21st Islamic Foreign Ministers Conference A406

**1993, Apr. 25**
**784** A406 1r buff & multi .50 .50
**785** A406 6r green & multi 2.25 1.40

A407

Traditional costumes of provinces.

**1993, Mar. 10**
**786** A407 6r Sindh 1.50 1.00
**787** A407 6r North West Frontier 1.50 1.00
**788** A407 6r Baluchistan 1.50 1.00
**789** A407 6r Punjab 1.50 1.00
*Nos. 786-789 (4)* 6.00 4.00

A408

Birds: a, Gadwall. b, Common shelduck. c, Mallard. d, Greylag goose.

The order of the birds is different on each row. Therefore the arc of the rainbow is different on each of the 4 Gadwalls, etc.

**1992, Dec. 31** *Perf. 14x13*
**790** A408 5r Sheet of 16 10.00 *15.00*
*a.-d.* Any single .60 .60
*e.* Horiz. strip of 4, #a-d 2.00 *3.00*

**Medicinal Plants Type**

**1993, June 20** **Litho.** *Perf. 13*
**791** A398 6r Fennel, chemistry equipment 3.25 1.25

**Pioneers of Freedom Type of 1990**

Designs: a, Rais Ghulam Mohammad Bhurgri (1878-1924). b, Mir Ahmed Yar Khan, Khan of Kalat (1902-1977). c, Mohammad Abdul Latif Pir Sahib Zakori Sharif (1914-1978).

**1993, Aug. 14** **Litho.** *Perf. 13*
**792** A375 1r Strip of 3, #a.-c. 3.50 2.50

Gordon College, Rawalpindi, Cent. — A410

**1993, Sept. 1**
**793** A410 2r multicolored 1.50 1.00

Juniper Forests, Ziarat — A411

**1993, Sept. 30**
**794** A411 7r multicolored 7.50 3.00

See No. 827.

World Food Day — A412

**1993, Oct. 16** *Perf. 14*
**795** A412 6r multicolored 1.00 1.00

A413

**Wmk. 351**

**1993, Dec. 25** **Litho.** *Perf. 13½*
**796** A413 1r multicolored 1.50 .55

Wazir Mansion, birthplace of Muhammad Ali Jinnah.

A414

*Perf. 13x13½*

**1993, Oct. 28** **Unwmk.**
**797** A414 7r multicolored 1.50 1.00

Burn Hall Institutions, 50th anniv.

South & West Asia Postal Union — A415

**1993, Nov. 18** ***Perf. 13***
**798** A415 7r multicolored 2.00 1.00

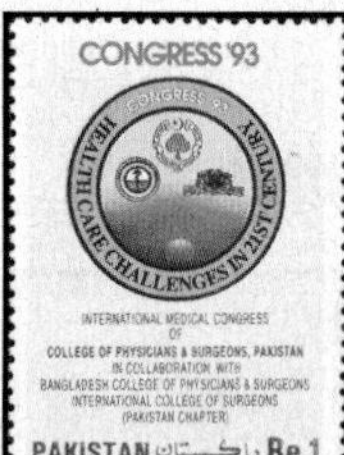

Pakistani College of Physicians & Surgeons, Intl. Medical Congress A416

**1993, Dec. 10**
**799** A416 1r multicolored 1.75 .65

ILO, 75th Anniv. A417

**1994, Apr. 11** **Litho.** ***Perf. 13***
**800** A417 7r multicolored 1.75 1.00

Bio-diversity — A418

a, Ratan jot, medicinal plant. b, Wetlands. c, Mahseer fish. d, Himalayan brown bear.

**1994, Apr. 20** **Litho.** ***Perf. 13½***
**801** A418 6r Strip or block of 4, #a.-d. 2.00 2.00

Intl. Year of the Family — A419

**1994, May 15** ***Perf. 13***
**802** A419 7r multicolored .75 .75

World Population Day — A420

**1994, July 11** **Litho.** ***Perf. 13***
**803** A420 7r multicolored .75 .75

**Pioneers of Freedom Type of 1990**
Miniature Sheet of 8

Designs: a, Nawab Mohsin-Ul-Mulk (1837-1907). b, Sir Shahnawaz Bhutto (1888-1957). c, Nawab Viqar-Ul-Mulk (1841-1917). d, Pir Ilahi Bux (1890-1975). e, Sheikh Sir Abdul Qadir (1874-1950). f, Dr. Sir Ziauddin Ahmed (1878-1947). g, Jam Mir Ghulam Qadir Khan (1920-88). h, Sardar Aurangzeb Khan (1899-1953).

**1994, Aug. 14** **Litho.** ***Perf. 13***
**804** A375 1r #a.-h. + label 3.25 3.25

A421

**1994, Oct. 2** ***Perf. 13x13½***
**805** A421 2r multicolored 1.50 .45

First Intl. Festival of Islamic Artisans.

Intl. Literacy Day — A422

**1994, Sept. 8**
**806** A422 7r multicolored .75 .75

Hyoscyamus Niger — A423

**1994** ***Perf. 13***
**807** A423 6r multicolored 1.00 .75

Mohammad Ali Jinnah — A424

**Litho. & Engr.**
**1994, Sept. 11** **Wmk. 351** ***Perf. 13***

| | | | | |
|---|---|---|---|---|
| **808** | A424 | 1r slate & multi | .35 | .25 |
| **809** | A424 | 2r claret & multi | .50 | .25 |
| **810** | A424 | 3r brt bl & multi | .65 | .25 |
| **811** | A424 | 4r emer & multi | .70 | .25 |
| **812** | A424 | 5r lake & multi | .75 | .25 |
| **813** | A424 | 7r blue & multi | 1.00 | .25 |
| **814** | A424 | 10r green & multi | .80 | .30 |
| **815** | A424 | 12r orange & multi | .90 | .60 |
| **816** | A424 | 15r violet & multi | 1.00 | .80 |
| **817** | A424 | 20r rose & multi | 1.10 | 1.00 |
| **818** | A424 | 25r brown & multi | 1.25 | 1.25 |
| **818A** | A424 | 28r blk & multi | | — |
| **819** | A424 | 30r olive brn & multi | 1.75 | 1.25 |
| | | *Nos. 808-819 (12)* | 10.75 | 6.70 |

Issued: 28r, 9/30/2011.

2nd SAARC & 12th Natl. Scout Jamboree, Quetta — A425

**1994, Sept. 22** **Litho.**
**820** A425 7r multicolored 1.00 .60

Publication of Ferdowsi's Book of Kings, 1000th Anniv. — A426

**1994, Oct. 27**
**821** A426 1r multicolored .50 .50

Indonesia-Pakistan Economic & Cultural Cooperation Organization — A427

**1994, Aug. 19**

| | | | | |
|---|---|---|---|---|
| **822** | A427 | 10r Hala pottery | 1.25 | .60 |
| **823** | A427 | 10r Lombok pottery | 1.25 | .60 |
| *a.* | | Pair, #822-823 | 4.25 | 4.25 |

See Indonesia Nos. 1585-1586.

Lahore Museum, Cent. — A428

**Wmk. 351**
**1994, Dec. 27** **Litho.** ***Perf. 13***
**824** A428 4r multicolored .60 .60

Pakistan, 1994 World Cup Field Hockey Champions A429

**1994, Dec. 31**
**825** A429 5r multicolored 1.00 .40

World Tourism Organization, 20th Anniv. — A430

**1995, Jan. 2**
**826** A430 4r multicolored 1.00 .30

**Juniper Forests Type of 1993**

**1995, Feb. 14** **Litho.** ***Perf. 13***
**827** A411 1r like #794 .75 .25

Third Economic Cooperation Organization Summit, Islamabad A431

**1995, Mar. 14** **Litho.** ***Perf. 14***
**828** A431 6r multicolored 1.60 1.10

Khushall Khan Khatak (1613-89) A432

**1995, Feb. 28** ***Perf. 13***
**829** A432 7r multicolored 2.50 2.25

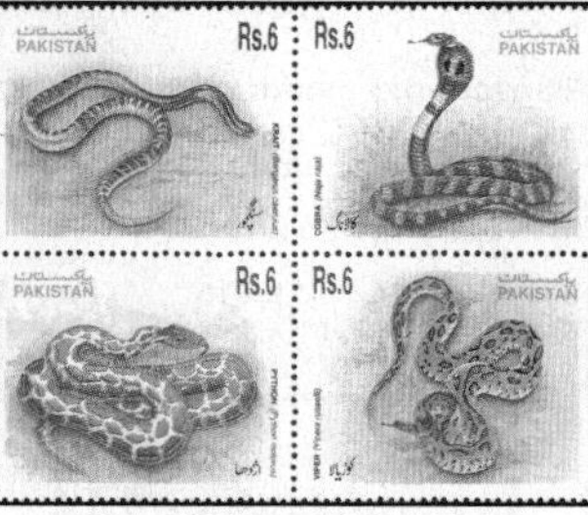

Earth Day A433

**Wmk. 351**
**1995, Apr. 20** **Litho.** ***Perf. 13***
**830** A433 6r multicolored .75 .75

Snakes — A434

a, Krait. b, Cobra. c, Python. d, Viper.

**1995, Apr. 15** **Unwmk.** ***Perf. 13½***
**831** A434 6r Block of 4, #a.-d. 4.00 4.00

Traditional Means of Transportation — A435

5r, Horse-drawn carriage.

**Wmk. 351**

**1995, May 22 Litho. *Perf. 13***
**832** A435 5r multicolored 1.00 .85

Louis Pasteur (1822-95) A436

**Wmk. 351**

**1995, Sept. 28 Litho. *Perf. 13***
**833** A436 5r multicolored .85 .80

UN, FAO, 50th Anniv. A437

**1995, Oct. 16**
**834** A437 1.25r multicolored 1.00 .25

Kinnaird College for Women, Lahore — A438

**1995, Nov. 3 *Perf. 14x13***
**835** A438 1.25r multicolored 1.00 .25

4th World Conference on Women, Beijing — A439

Women in various activities: a, Playing golf, in armed forces, repairing technical device. b, Graduates, student, chemist, computer operator, reading gauge. c, At sewing machine, working with textiles. d, Making rugs, police woman, laborers.

**1995, Sept. 15 *Perf. 13***
**836** A439 1.25r Strip of 4, #a.-d. 1.40 1.40

Presentation Convent School, Rawalpindi, Cent. A440

**Wmk. 351**

**1995, Sept. 8 Litho. *Perf. 13½***
**837** A440 1.25r multicolored .80 .45

A440a

Panel colors: 5p, Orange. 15p, Violet. 25p, Red. 75p, Red brown.

**1995-96 Litho. Unwmk. *Perf. 13½***
**837A-837D** A440a Set of 4 2.50 .60

Issued: 5p, 15p, 10/10/95; 25p, 9/28/95; 75p, 5/15/96.

Liaquat Ali Khan (1895-1951) — A441

**1995, Oct. 1 *Perf. 13***
**838** A441 1.25r multicolored 1.00 .40

1st Conference of Women Parliamentarians from Muslim Countries — A442

Designs: No. 839, Dr. Tansu Ciller, Prime Minister of Turkey. No. 840, Mohtarma Benazir Bhutto, Prime Minister of Pakistan.

**1995, Aug. 1 Unwmk.**
**839** A442 5r multicolored .90 .90
**840** A442 5r multicolored .90 .90
*a.* Pair, #839-840 2.00 *7.50*

Intl. Conference of Writers and Intellectuals A443

**Wmk. 351**

**1995, Nov. 30 Litho. *Perf. 14***
**841** A443 1.25r multicolored 1.00 .40

Allama Iqbal Open University, 20th Anniv. — A444

**1995, Dec. 16 *Perf. 13***
**842** A444 1.25r multicolored .45 .30

Butterflies — A445

Designs: a, Érasmie. b, Catogramme. c, Ixias. d, Héliconie.

**Wmk. 351**

**1995, Sept. 1 Litho. *Perf. 13½***
**843** A445 6r Strip of 4, #a.-d. 2.50 2.50

Fish — A446

Designs: a, Sardinella long. b, Tilapia mossambica. c, Salmo fario. d, Labeo rohita.

**1995, Sept. 1**
**844** A446 6r Strip of 4, #a.-d. 3.50 3.50

SAARC, 10th Anniv. — A447

**1995, Dec. 8 *Perf. 13***
**845** A447 1.25r multicolored .45 .40

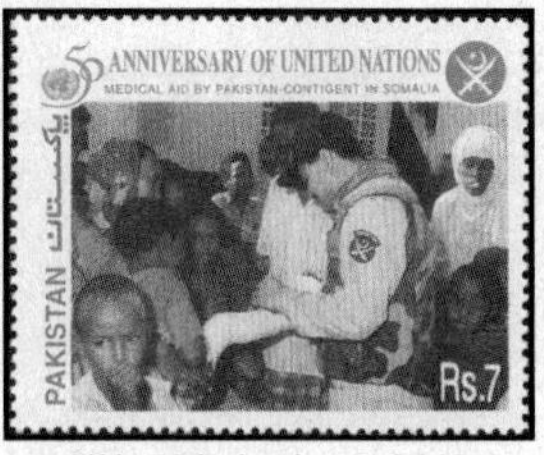


UN, 50th Anniv. — A448

**Wmk. 351**

**1995, Oct. 24 Litho. *Perf. 13½***
**846** A448 7r multicolored 1.25 1.25

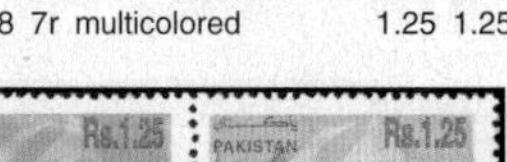

Karachi '95, Natl. Water Sports Gala — A449

Designs: a, Man on jet ski. b, Gondola race. c, Sailboard race. d, Man water skiing.

**1995, Dec. 14 *Perf. 14x13***
**847** A449 1.25r Block of 4, #a.-d. 1.50 1.50

University of Baluchistan, Quetta, 25th Anniv. — A452

**Wmk. 351**

**1995, Dec. 31 Litho. *Perf. 13***
**850** A452 1.25r multicolored .60 .55

Zulfikar Ali Bhutto (1928-79), Politician, President — A455

Designs: 1.25r, Bhutto, flag, crowd of people, vert. 8r, like No. 855

**Wmk. 351**

**1996, Apr. 4 Litho. *Perf. 13***
**855** A455 1.25r multicolored .75 .35
**856** A455 4r shown 2.25 1.10

**Size: 114x69mm**

***Imperf***

**857** A455 8r multicolored 2.50 2.50

Raja Aziz Bhatti Shaheed (1928-65) — A456

**Wmk. 351**

**1995, Sept. 5 Litho. *Perf. 13***
**858** A456 1.25r multicolored 1.75 .40

See Nos. 953, 983, 997, 1016.

**Pioneers of Freedom Type of 1990**

#859, Maulana Shaukat Ali (1873-1938). #860, Chaudhry Ghulam Abbas (1904-67).

**1995, Aug. 14 Unwmk. *Perf. 13***
**859** A375 1r green & brown .80 .50
**860** A375 1r green & brown .80 .50
*a.* Pair, #859-860 1.75 1.75

1996 Summer Olympic Games, Atlanta — A457

Design: 25r, #861-864 without denominations, simulated perfs, Olympic rings, "100," Atlanta '96 emblem.

**Wmk. 351**

**1996, Aug. 3 Litho. *Perf. 13***
**861** A457 5r Wrestling .70 .70
**862** A457 5r Boxing .70 .70
**863** A457 5r Pierre de Coubertin .70 .70
**864** A457 5r Field hockey .70 .70
*Nos. 861-864 (4)* 2.80 2.80

***Imperf***

**Size: 111x101mm**

**864A** A457 25r multicolored 3.00 3.00

**Pioneers of Freedom Type of 1990**

Allama Abdullah Yousuf Ali (1872-1953).

**Unwmk.**

**1996, Aug. 14 Litho. *Perf. 13***
**865** A375 1r green & brown .45 .40

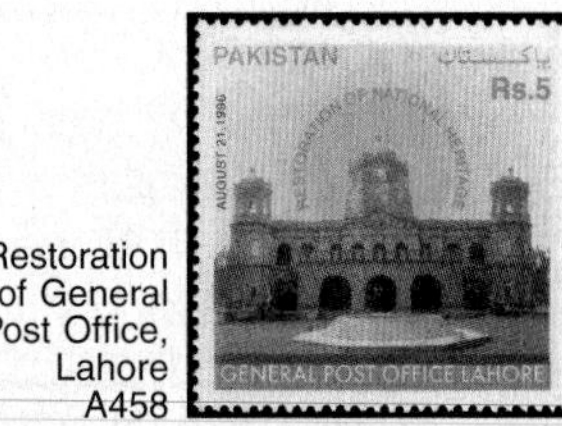


Restoration of General Post Office, Lahore A458

**1996, Aug. 21 Wmk. 351** ***Perf. 14***
**866** A458 5r multicolored .45 .45

Intl. Literacy Day A459

**1996, Sept. 8 Wmk. 351** ***Perf. 13***
**867** A459 2r multicolored .45 .40

Yarrow — A459a

**Wmk. 351**

**1996, Nov. 25 Litho.** ***Perf. 13***
**867A** A459a 3r multicolored 1.00 .65

Faiz Ahmed Faiz, Poet, 86th Birthday A460

**Unwmk.**

**1997, Feb. 13 Litho.** ***Perf. 13***
**868** A460 3r multicolored .80 .55

Tamerlane (1336-1405) A461

**Unwmk.**

**1997, Apr. 8 Litho.** ***Perf. 13***
**869** A461 3r multicolored .45 .40

Famous Men — A462

Designs: No. 870, Allama Mohammad Iqbal. No. 871, Jalal-Al-Din Moulana Rumi.

**1997, Apr. 21** ***Perf. 13½***
**870** A462 3r multicolored .25 .25
**871** A462 3r multicolored .25 .25

Compare with Iran 2726-2727.

Pakistani Independence, 50th Anniv. — A463

**1997, Mar. 23** ***Perf. 13***
**872** A463 2r multicolored .45 .45

Special Summit of Organization of Islamic Countries, Islamabad.

World Population Day — A464

**Unwmk.**

**1997, July 11 Litho.** ***Perf. 13***
**873** A464 2r multicolored .45 .40

Intl. Atomic Energy Agency-Pakistan Atomic Energy Commission Cooperation, 40th Anniv. — A465

**1997, July 29** ***Perf. 14***
**874** A465 2r multicolored .90 .40

**Pioneers of Freedom Type of 1990**

#875, Begum Salma Tassaduq Hussain (1908-95). #876, Mohammad Ayub Khuhro (1901-80).

**1997, Aug. 14 Litho.** ***Perf. 13***
**875** A375 1r green & brown .55 .55
**876** A375 1r green & brown .55 .55

Fruits of Pakistan A466

**1997, May 8**
**877** A466 2r Apples .45 .45

Independence, 50th Anniv. — A467

Designs: a, Allama Mohammad Iqbal. b, Mohammad Ali Jinnah. c, Liaquat Ali Khan. d, Mohtarma Fatima Jinnah.

**Block of 4 + 2 Labels**

**1997, Aug. 14**
**878** A467 3r gold & multi 2.50 .75

No. 878 exists with No. 878d unretouched. Value, $5 mint or used.

Lophophorus Impejanus A468

**Wmk. 351**

**1997, Oct. 29 Litho.** ***Perf. 13***
**879** A468 2r multicolored 2.50 .90

Lahore College for Women, 75th Anniv. — A469

**1997, Sept. 23**
**880** A469 3r multicolored 1.50 1.00

Intl. Day of the Disabled A470

**Unwmk.**

**1997, Dec. 3 Litho.** ***Perf. 13***
**881** A470 4r multicolored 1.40 .45

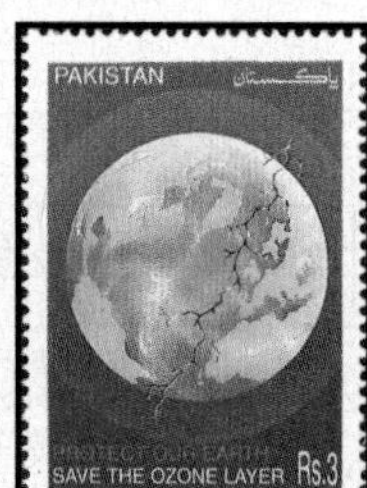

Protection of the Ozone Layer — A471

**1997, Nov. 15**
**882** A471 3r multicolored 1.60 1.00

Pakistan Motorway, 50th Anniv. A472

**1997, Nov. 26** ***Perf. 13½***
**883** A472 10r multicolored 2.25 2.25
*a.* Souvenir sheet of 1 2.50 2.50

No. 883a sold for 15r.

Karachi Grammar School, 150th Anniv. A473

**1997, Dec. 30 Litho.** ***Perf. 13½***
**884** A473 2r multicolored 1.10 1.10

Garlic A474

**1997, Oct. 22** ***Perf. 13***
**885** A474 2r multicolored 1.50 .25

Mirza Asad Ullah Khan Ghalib (1797-1869), Poet — A475

**1998, Feb. 15**
**886** A475 2r multicolored .50 .50

Pakistan Armed Forces, 50th Anniv. A476

**Wmk. 351**

**1997, Mar. 23 Litho.** ***Perf. 13½***
**887** A476 7r multicolored 1.00 1.00

Sir Syed Ahmad Khan (1817-98), Educator, Jurist, Author — A477

**1998, Mar. 27** *Perf. 14*
**888** A477 7r multicolored 1.00 1.00

27th Natl. Games, Peshawar A478

**Wmk. 351**

**1998, Apr. 22** **Litho.** *Perf. 13*
**889** A478 7r multicolored 1.00 1.00

Jimsonweed A479

**1998, Apr. 27**
**890** A479 2r multicolored 1.40 1.40

Faisalabad Government College, Cent. (in 1997) — A480

**1998, Aug. 14** **Litho.** *Perf. 13*
**891** A480 5r multicolored .70 .70

Pakistan Senate, 25th Anniv. A481

**1998, Aug. 6** *Perf. 13½*
**892** A481 2r green & multi .25 .25
**893** A481 5r blue & multi .80 .80

Mohammed Ali Jinnah — A482

**Litho. & Engr.**

**1998-2001** **Wmk. 351** *Perf. 14*

| | | | | |
|---|---|---|---|---|
| **893A** | A482 1r red & black | .25 | .25 |
| **894** | A482 2r dk bl & red | .25 | .25 |
| **895** | A482 3r slate grn & brn | .65 | .25 |
| **896** | A482 4r dp vio blk & org | .65 | .25 |
| **897** | A482 5r dp brn & grn | .90 | .65 |
| **898** | A482 6r dp grn & bl grn | 1.10 | .75 |
| **899** | A482 7r dp brn red & dp vio | 1.10 | .90 |
| | *Nos. 894-899 (6)* | 4.65 | 3.05 |

Nos. 894 issued 8/14/98. No. 893A, 2001(?).

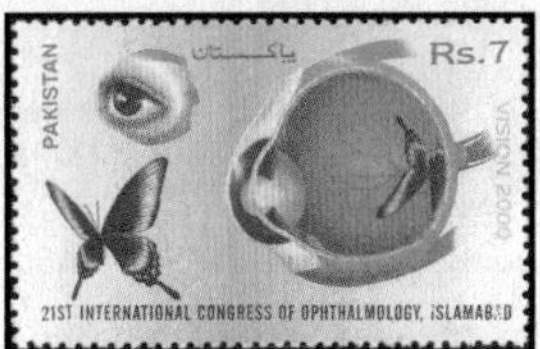


21st Intl. Congress of Ophthalmology, Islamabad — A483

**Wmk. 351**

**1998, Sept. 11** **Litho.** *Perf. 13*
**900** A483 7r multicolored 1.60 1.60

Syed Ahmed Shah Patrus Bukhari, Birth Cent. A484

**1998, Oct. 1**
**901** A484 5r multicolored 1.25 1.00

Philately in Pakistan, 50th Anniv. — A485

Various portions of stamps inside "50," #20-23.

**1998, Oct. 4**
**902** A485 6r multicolored .60 .60

World Food Day A486

**Wmk. 351**

**1998, Oct. 16** **Photo.** *Perf. 13*
**903** A486 6r multicolored .75 .75

Mohammad Ali Jinnah (1876-1948) A487

**Wmk. 351**

**1998, Sept. 11** **Photo.** *Perf. 13½*
**904** A487 15r multicolored 2.25 2.25
*a.* Souvenir sheet of 1, unwmk. 2.25 2.25

No. 904a sold for 20r.

Universal Declaration of Human Rights, 50th Anniv. A488

*Perf. 13x14*

**1998, Dec. 10** **Wmk. 351**
**905** A488 6r multicolored 1.40 1.00

Better Pakistan, 2010 A489

#906, Harvesting grain. #907, Health care. #908, Satellite dishes. #909, Airplane.

**1998, Nov. 27** **Unwmk.**

| | | | |
|---|---|---|---|
| **906** | A489 2r multicolored | .45 | .35 |
| **907** | A489 2r multicolored | .45 | .35 |
| **908** | A489 2r multicolored | .45 | .35 |
| **909** | A489 2r multicolored | .45 | .35 |
| | *Nos. 906-909 (4)* | 1.80 | 1.40 |

Dr. Abdus Salam, Scientist A490

**Unwmk.**

**1998, Nov. 21** **Litho.** *Perf. 13*
**910** A490 2r multicolored .75 .50

See No. 916.

National Flag March A491

**1998, Dec. 16** **Wmk. 351**
**911** A491 2r multicolored .45 .30

Intl. Year of the Ocean A492

**1998, Dec. 15** *Perf. 14*
**912** A492 5r multicolored 1.50 1.00

UNICEF in Pakistan, 50th Anniv. — A493

a, Distributing water. b, Child holding book. c, Girl. d, Child receiving oral vaccine.

**1998, Dec. 15**
**913** A493 2r Block of 4, #a.-d. 1.50 1.50

Kingdom of Saudi Arabia, Cent. — A494

*Perf. 13½*

**1999, Jan. 27** **Litho.** **Unwmk.**
**914** A494 2r Emblem on sand .50 .50
**915** A494 15r Emblem on carpet 1.50 1.50
*a.* Souvenir sheet of 1 2.75 2.75

No. 915a sold for 20r.

**Scientists of Pakistan Type**

Dr. Salimuz Zaman Siddiqui (1897-1994).

**1999, Apr. 14** *Perf. 13*
**916** A490 5r multicolored .60 .60

Pakistani Nuclear Test, 1st Anniv. — A495

**1999, May 28** **Litho.** *Perf. 13*
**917** A495 5r multicolored .60 .60

Completion of Data Darbar Mosque Complex — A496

**1999, May 31** **Litho.** *Perf. 13*
**918** A496 7r multicolored .80 .80

Fasting Buddha, c. 3-4 A.D. — A497

**1999, July 21** **Litho.** *Perf. 13½x13¾*
**919** A497 7r shown 1.00 1.00
**920** A497 7r Facing forward 1.00 1.00
*a.* Souv. sheet of 2, #919-920 3.00 3.00

No. 920a sold for 25r. China 1999 World Philatelic Exhibition (No. 920a).

Geneva Conventions, 50th Anniv. — A498

*Perf. 12¾x13¾*

**1999, Aug. 12 Litho.**

**921** A498 5r pink, black & red .60 .60

### Pioneers of Freedom Type of 1990

Designs: No. 922, Chaudhry Muhammad Ali (1905-80), 1st Secretary General. No. 923, Sir Adamjee Haji Dawood (1880-1948), banker. No. 924, Maulana Abdul Hamid Badayuni (1898-1970), religious scholar.

**1999, Aug. 14 Litho. *Perf. 13***

**922** A375 2r green & brown .45 .45
**923** A375 2r green & brown .45 .45
**924** A375 2r green & brown .45 .45
*Nos. 922-924 (3)* 1.35 1.35

Ustad Nusrat Fateh Ali Khan (1948-97), Singer — A499

**1999, Aug. 16**

**925** A499 2r multicolored .75 .75

Islamic Development Bank, 25th Anniv. (in 2000) — A500

**1999, Sept. 18**

**926** A500 5r multicolored 1.00 1.00

People's Republic of China, 50th Anniv. — A501

2r, Gate of Heavenly Peace. 15r, Arms, Mao Zedong, horiz.

**1999, Sept. 21**

**927** A501 2r multicolored .25 .25
**928** A501 15r multicolored 1.50 1.50

Ninth Asian Sailing Championship — A502

No. 929: a, Enterprise class. b, 470 class. c, Optimist class. d, Laser class. e, Mistral class.

**1999, Sept. 28 *Perf. 13½x13¼***

**929** A502 2r Strip of 5, #a.-e. 2.25 2.25

10th Asian Optimist Sailing Championships — A502a

**1999, Oct. 7 Litho. *Perf. 13¾x13½***

**929F** A502a 2r multi + label .80 .80

UPU, 125th Anniv. A503

**1999, Oct. 9 *Perf. 14¼***

**930** A503 10r multicolored 1.00 1.00

Hakim Mohammed Said (1920-98), Physician A504

**1999, Oct. 17 Litho. *Perf. 13***

**931** A504 5r multicolored .65 .65

National Bank of Pakistan, 50th Anniv. — A505

*Perf. 13¼x13¾*

**1999, Nov. 8 Litho. Wmk. 351**

**932** A505 5r multi .80 .80

Shell Oil in Pakistan, Cent. — A506

*Perf. 13¼x13*

**1999, Nov. 15 Wmk. 351**

**933** A506 4r multi .60 .60

Rights of the Child, 10th Anniv. — A507

*Perf. 13x13¼*

**1999, Nov. 20 Unwmk.**

**934** A507 2r multi .60 .60

Allam Iqbal Open University, Islamabad — A508

Designs: 2r, University crest, flasks, microphone, mortarboard, book, computer. 3r, Similar to 2r, crest in center. 5r, Crest, map, mortarboard, book.

**Unwmk.**

**1999, Nov. 20 Litho. *Perf. 13***

**935** A508 2r bl grn & multi .25 .25
**936** A508 3r multi .30 .30
**937** A508 5r multi 1.20 .75
*Nos. 935-937 (3)* 1.75 1.30

Shabbir Hassan Khan Josh Malihabadi (1898-1982), Poet — A509

**1999, Dec. 5**

**938** A509 5r multi .60 .60

Dr. Afzal Qadri (1912-74), Entomologist — A510

**1999, Dec. 6**

**939** A510 3r multi .60 .60

Ghulam Bari Aleeg (1907-49), Journalist A511

**1999, Dec. 10 Litho. *Perf. 13***

**940** A511 5r multi .60 .60

See No. 982.

Plantain — A512

**1999, Dec. 20**

**941** A512 5r multi 1.60 1.60

Eid-Ul-Fitr — A513

*Perf. 13¾x13½*

**1999, Dec. 24 Litho.**

**942** A513 2r green & multi .75 .75
**943** A513 15r blue & multi 2.25 2.25

SOS Children's Villages of Pakistan, 25th Anniv. — A514

**2000, Mar. 12 *Perf. 13***

**944** A514 2r multi .50 .50

International Cycling Union, Cent. — A515

**2000, Apr. 14 Litho. *Perf. 13¼***

**945** A515 2r multi 1.50 1.50

Convention on Human Rights and Dignity — A516

*Perf. 13¼*

**2000, Apr. 21 Litho. Unwmk.**

**946** A516 2r multi .50 .50

Edwardes College, Peshawar, Cent. — A517

**2000, Apr. 24 *Perf. 13½***

**947** A517 2r multi .50 .50

Mahomed Ali Habib (1904-59), Banker, Philantropist — A518

**2000, May 15 Litho. *Perf. 13***

**948** A518 2r multi .50 .50

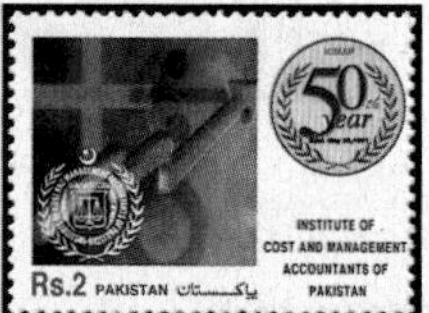

Institute of Cost and Management Accountants, 50th Anniv. — A519

Design: 2r, Arrow. 15r, Globe.

**2000, June 23 Litho. *Perf. 13***

**949** A519 2r multi .30 .30
**950** A519 15r multi 2.00 2.00

Ahmed E. H. Jaffer (1909-90), Politician A520

**2000, Aug. 9 Litho. *Perf. 13***
**951** A520 10r multi 1.25 1.25

Creation of Pakistan, 53rd Anniv. — A521

a, No tree. b, Tree in foreground. c, Tree behind people, cart. d, Tree in distance.

**2000, Aug. 14 Litho. *Perf. 13***
**952** A521 5r Strip of 4, #a-d 2.00 2.00

**Nishan-e-Haider Medal Type of 1995**

Nishan-e-haider gallantry award winners: a, Capt. Muhammad Sarwar Shaheed (1910-48). b, Maj. Tufail Muhammad (1914-58).

**2000, Sept. 6 Litho. *Perf. 13***
**953** A456 5r Pair, #a-b 2.00 2.00

2000 Summer Olympics, Sydney — A523

No. 954: a, Runners. b, Field hockey. c, Weight lifting. d, Cycling.

**2000, Sept. 20 *Perf. 14¼***
**954** A523 4r Block of 4, #a-d 2.25 2.25

Natl. College of Arts, 125th Anniv. A524

**2000, Oct. 28**
**955** A524 5r multi .45 .45

Creating the Future — A525

**2000, Nov. 4 *Perf. 13½x13¼***
**956** A525 5r multi 1.00 1.00

Intl. Defense Exhibition and Seminar — A526

**2000, Nov. 14 Litho. *Perf. 13***
**957** A526 7r multi 1.10 1.10

Licorice — A527

**2000, Nov. 28 Litho. *Perf. 13***
**958** A527 2r multi 2.00 2.00

Rotary Intl. Campaign Against Polio — A528

**2000, Dec. 13**
**959** A528 2r multi .75 .75

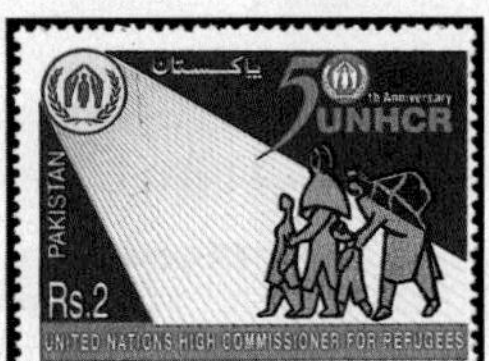

UN High Commissioner for Refugees, 50th Anniv. — A529

**2000, Dec. 14**
**960** A529 2r multi .45 .45

Poets — A530

Design: 2r, Hafeez Jalandhri (1900-82). 5r, Khawaja Ghulam Farid.

**2001 Litho. *Perf. 13***
**961** A530 2r multi .50 .50
**962** A530 5r multi 1.25 1.25

Issued: 2r, 1/14. 5r, 9/25.
See No. 986.

Habib Bank AG Zurich — A531

**2001, Mar. 20 Litho. *Perf. 13***
**963** A531 5r multi 1.75 1.25

Chashma Nuclear Power Plant A532

**2001, Mar. 29**
**964** A532 4r multi 1.40 1.25

9th SAF Games, Islamabad A533

Background colors: No. 965, 4r, Light blue. No. 966, 4r, Lilac.

**2001, Apr. 9 *Perf. 13½x13¼***
**965-966** A533 Set of 2 1.40 1.40

Pakistan-People's Rep. of China Diplomatic Relations, 50th Anniv. — A534

Designs: No. 967, Yugur and Hunza women, flags.
No. 968 — Paintings by Yao Youdou: a, Ma Gu's Birthday Offering. b, Two Pakistani Women Drawing Water.

**2001, May 12 *Perf. 13***
**967** A534 4r multi .25 .25
**968** A534 4r Horiz. pair, #a-b 1.50 1.50

Mohammed Ali Jinnah (1876-1948) A535

**2001, Aug. 14**
**969** A535 4r multi .90 .90

Sindh Festival A536

**Unwmk.**
**2001, Sept. 22 Litho. *Perf. 13***
**970** A536 4r multi .75 .75

Year of Dialogue Among Civilizations A537

**2001, Oct. 9 *Perf. 13½***
**971** A537 4r multi .75 .75

Turkmenistan, 10th Anniv. of Independence A538

**2001, Oct. 27 *Perf. 13***
**972** A538 5r multi .90 .90

Convent of Jesus and Mary, Lahore, 125th Anniv. — A539

**2001, Nov. 15 Wmk. 351**
**973** A539 4r multi 1.00 1.00

**Men of Letters Type of 1999**

Design: 4r, Dr. Ishtiaq Husain Qureshi (1903-81), historian.

**2001, Nov. 20 Unwmk.**
**974** A511 4r multi .75 .75

Birds — A540

No. 975: a, Blue throat. b, Hoopoe. c, Pin-tailed sandgrouse. d, Magpie robin.

**2001, Nov. 26 *Perf. 13¼x13***
**975** A540 4r Block of 4, #a-d 6.00 6.00

Pakistan — United Arab Emirates Friendship, 30th Anniv. — A541

Designs: 5r, Flags, handshake, vert. 30r, Sheik Zaid bin Sultan al Nahayan, Mohammed Ali Jinnah.

**2001, Dec. 2** *Perf. 13*
**976-977** A541 Set of 2 3.75 3.75

Nishtar Medical College, Multan, 50th Anniv. — A542

**2001, Dec. 20**
**978** A542 5r multi .75 .75

Quaid Year — A543

No. 979: a, Mohammed Ali Jinnah reviewing troops, 1948. b, Jinnah, soldiers, artillery gun, 1948.

No. 980, vert.: a, Jinnah taking oath as Governor General, 1947. b, Jinnah at opening ceremony of State Bank of Pakistan, 1948. c, Jinnah saluting at presentation of colors, 1948.

**2001, Dec. 25** *Perf. 13*
**979** Horiz. pair .80 .80
*a.-b.* A543 4r Any single .25 .25

**Size: 33x56mm**

***Perf. 13x13¼***

**980** Horiz. strip of 3 1.00 1.00
*a.-c.* A543 4r Any single .25 .25

Pakistan Ordnance Factories, 50th Anniv. — A544

**2001, Dec. 28** *Perf. 13¼x13½*
**981** A544 4r multi 1.00 1.00

**Men of Letters Type of 1999**

Design: 5r, Syed Imtiaz Ali Taj (1900-70), playwright.

**2001, Oct. 13** *Perf. 13*
**982** A511 5r multi .60 .60

**Nishan-e-Haider Type of 1995**

No. 983: a, Maj. Mohammad Akram Shaheed (1938-71). b, Maj. Shabbir Sharif Shaheeb (1943-71).

**2001, Sept. 6** *Perf. 13*
**983** Horiz. pair 1.50 1.50
*a.-b.* A456 4r Any single .75 .75

Peppermint A545

Design: 5r, Hyssop.

**2001-02 Litho. Wmk. 351** *Perf. 13*
**984** A545 4r multi 1.00 1.00
**985** A545 5r multi .80 .80

Issued: 4r, 11/12/01. 5r, 2/15/02.

**Poets Type of 2001**

Design: Samandar Khan Samandar (1901-90).

**2002, Jan. 17 Litho.** *Perf. 13*
**986** A530 5r multi .60 .60

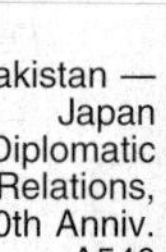

Pakistan — Japan Diplomatic Relations, 50th Anniv. A546

**2002, Apr. 28 Litho.** *Perf. 14*
**987** A546 5r multi .60 .60

Pakistan - Kyrgyzstan Diplomatic Relations, 10th Anniv. — A547

**2002, May 27** *Perf. 13¾x12¾*
**988** A547 5r multi .60 .60

Mangoes — A548

No. 989: a, Anwar Ratol. b, Dusheri. c, Chaunsa. d, Sindhri.

**2002, June 18**
**989** A548 4r Block of 4, #a-d 2.40 2.40

Independence, 55th Anniv. — A549

Famous people: No. 990, 4r, Noor-us-Sabah Begum (1908-78), Muslim leader and writer. No. 991, 4r, Prime Minister Ismail I. Chundrigar (1897-1960). No. 992, 4r, Habib Ibrahim Rahimtoola (1912-91), governmental minister. No. 993, 4r, Qazi Mureed Ahmed (1913-89), politician.

**2002, Aug. 14 Litho.** *Perf. 13¼x13*
**990-993** A549 Set of 4 2.40 2.40

World Summit on Sustainable Development, Johannesburg A550

Designs: No. 994, 4r, Children, Pakistani flag, dolphin, goat. No. 995, 4r, Water droplet, mountain (33x33mm).

**2002, Aug. 26** *Perf. 13¼, 14¼ (#995)*
**994-995** A550 Set of 2 1.00 1.00

Mohammad Aly Rangoonwala (1924-98), Philanthropist A551

**2002, Aug. 31** *Perf. 13*
**996** A551 4r multi .60 .60

**Nishan-e-Haidar type of 1995**

No. 997: a, Lance Naik Muhammad Mahfuz Shaheed (1944-71). b, Sawar Muhammad Hussain Shaheed (1949-71).

**2002, Sept. 6** *Perf. 13*
**997** Horiz. pair 1.25 1.25
*a.-b.* A456 4r Either single .25 .25

Muhammad Iqbal Year — A552

No. 998: a, Iqbal wearing hat. b, Iqbal without hat.

**Unwmk.**

**2002, Nov. 9 Litho.** *Perf. 13*
**998** A552 4r Horiz. pair, #a-b 1.60 1.60

Eid ul-Fitr — A553

***Perf. 13¾x14***

**2002, Nov. 14 Wmk. 351**
**999** A553 4r multi .60 .60

Shifa-ul-Mulk Hakim Muhammad Hassan Qarshi (1896-1974), Physician A554

**2002, Dec. 20 Unwmk.** *Perf. 13½*
**1000** A554 4r multi 1.00 1.00

Pakistan 2003 Natl. Philatelic Exhibition, Karachi — A555

**Wmk. 351**

**2003, Jan. 31 Litho.** *Perf. 13*
**1001** A555 4r multi + label 1.50 1.50

Pakistan Academy of Sciences, 50th Anniv. A556

**2003, Feb. 15 Unwmk.** *Perf. 14¼*
**1002** A556 4r multi .60 .60

North West Frontier Province, Cent. — A557

***Perf. 13½x13¼***

**2003, Mar. 23 Litho. Wmk. 351**
**1003** A557 4r multi .60 .60

Pakistan Council of Scientific and Industrial Research, 50th Anniv. — A558

**2003, Mar. 31** *Perf. 14x13¾*
**1004** A558 4r multi .60 .60

A. B. A. Haleem (1897-1975), Educator A559

**2003, Apr. 20** *Perf. 13½x13¼*
**1005** A559 2r multi .60 .60

Campaign Against Illegal Drugs — A560

**2003, Apr. 21** *Perf. 13*
**1006** A560 2r multi 1.00 1.00

Sir Syed Memorial, Islamabad A561

**2003, Apr. 30** *Perf. 13¼x13½*
**1007** A561 2r multi .60 .60

Rosa Damascena A562

***Perf. 13¼x12¾***

**2003, July 14 Unwmk.**
**1008** A562 2r multi 1.60 1.60

Mohtarma Fatima Jinnah (1893-1967), Presidential Candidate in 1964 — A563

**2003, July 31** **Litho.**
**1009** A563 4r multi .60 .60

Famous Men — A564

Designs: No. 1010, 2r, M. A. Rahim (1919-2003), labor leader. No. 1011, 2r, Abdul Rahman (1959-2002), slain postal worker.

**2003, Aug. 3** ***Perf. 12¾x13¼***
**1010-1011** A564 Set of 2 1.00 1.00

Famous Men — A565

Designs: No. 1012, 2r, Moulana Abdul Sattar Khan Niazi (1915-2001), politician. No. 1013, 2r, Muhammad Yousaf Khattak (1917-91), politician. No. 1014, 2r, Moulana Muhammad Ismail Zabeeh (1913-2001), political leader and journalist.

**2003, Apr. 14** ***Perf. 13¼x12¾***
**1012-1014** A565 Set of 3 1.75 1.75

UN Literacy Decade, 2003-12 — A566

**2003, Sept. 6**
**1015** A566 1r multi .60 .60

**Nishan-e-Haider Type of 1995**

**2003, Sept. 7** ***Perf. 14***
**1016** A456 2r Pilot Officer Rashid Minhas Shaheed 1.25 1.25

Pakistan Academy of Letters, 25th Anniv. — A567

**2003, Sept. 24** ***Perf. 13¼x12¾***
**1017** A567 2r multi .60 .60

Karakoram Highway, 25th Anniv. — A568

***Perf. 12¾x13***

**2003, Oct. 1** **Litho.** **Unwmk.**
**1018** A568 2r multi .60 .60

Pakistan Air Force Public School, Sargodha, 50th Anniv. — A569

***Perf. 13x13¼***

**2003, Oct. 10** **Litho.** **Wmk. 351**
**1019** A569 4r multi 1.25 1.25

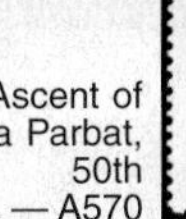

First Ascent of Nanga Parbat, 50th Anniv. — A570

***Perf. 12¾x13***

**2003, Oct. 6** **Litho.** **Unwmk.**
**1020** A570 2r multi 1.25 1.25

Exports — A571

No. 1021: a, Leather garments. b, Towels. c, Ready-made garments. d, Karachi Port Trust and Port Qasim. e, Fisheries. f, Yarn. g, Sporting goods. h, Fabrics. i, Furniture. j, Surgical instruments. k, Gems and jewelry. l, Leather goods. m, Information technology. n, Rice. o, Auto parts. p, Carpets. q, Marble and granite. r, Fruits. s, Cutlery. t, Engineering goods.

**2003, Oct. 20** ***Perf. 13x12¾***
**1021** Sheet of 20 6.00 6.00
*a.-t.* A571 1r Any single .35 .35

Intl. Day of the Disabled A572

**2003, Dec. 3** ***Perf. 12¾x13***
**1022** A572 2r multi 1.00 1.00

World Summit on the Information Society, Geneva, Switzerland A573

**2003, Dec. 10** ***Perf. 13x12¾***
**1023** A573 2r multi .60 .60

Submarines A574

Khalid Class (Agosta 90B) submarine and flag of: 1r, Pakistan Navy, vert. 2r, Pakistan.

**2003, Dec. 12** ***Perf. 13x12¾, 12¾x13***
**1024-1025** A574 Set of 2 3.00 3.00

Powered Flight, Cent. — A575

Designs: No. 1026, 2r, Pakistan Air Force's transition into jet age, 1956. No. 1027, 2r, Air Force in action at Siachen, 1988-90.

**2003, Dec. 17** ***Perf. 12¾x13***
**1026-1027** A575 Set of 2 1.75 1.75

12th South Asian Association for Regional Cooperation Summit, Islamabad A576

**2004, Jan. 4**
**1028** A576 4r multi .60 .60

Sadiq Public School, Bahawalpur, 50th Anniv. — A577

**2004, Jan. 28** **Litho.** ***Perf. 14***
**1029** A577 4r multi .60 .60

Ninth SAF Games, Islamabad — A578

No. 1030: a, Gold medal. b, Running. c, Squash (yellow and blue uniform). d, Boxing. e, Wrestling. f, Judo. g, Javelin. h, Soccer. i, Rowing. j, Shooting. k, Shot put. l, Badminton (white uniform). m, Weight lifting. n, Volleyball. o, Table tennis. p, Swimming.

**2004, Mar. 29** **Litho.** ***Perf. 13x12¾***
**1030** A578 2r Sheet of 16, #a-p 5.25 5.25

Pir Muhammad Karam Shah Al-Azhari (1918-98), Jurist — A579

**2004, Apr. 7**
**1031** A579 2r multi .60 .60

Cadet College, Hasan Abdal — A580

**2004, Apr. 8** ***Perf. 12¾x13***
**1032** A580 4r multi .60 .60

Central Library, Bahawalpur A581

**2004, Apr. 26** **Litho.** ***Perf. 13x12¾***
**1033** A581 2r multi .60 .60

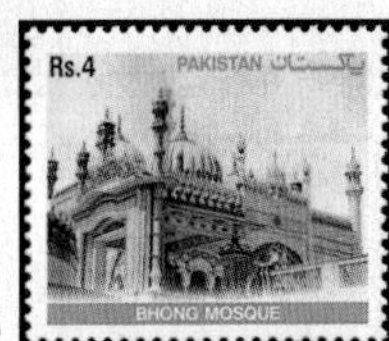

Mosque, Bhong — A582

**2004, May 12** ***Perf. 12¾x13***
**1034** A582 4r multi .60 .60

FIFA (Fédération Internationale de Football Association), Cent. — A583

No. 1035 — FIFA centenary emblem and: a, Player. b, Blue panel at bottom. c, Player, green panel at bottom.

**2004, May 21** ***Perf. 14***
**1035** A583 Horiz. strip of 3 2.40 2.40
*a.-c.* 5r Any single .70 .70

Silk Road — A584

Designs: No. 1036, 4r, Indus River near Chilas. No. 1037, 4r, Haramosh Peak near Gilgit, vert.

**2004, June 7** ***Perf. 12¾x13, 13x12¾***
**1036-1037** A584 Set of 2 1.00 1.00

Sui Southern Gas Company, 50th Anniv. — A585

**2004, July 24** **Litho.** ***Perf. 12¾x13***
**1038** A585 4r multi .60 .60

First Ascent of K2, 50th Anniv. — A586

**2004, July 31** ***Perf. 13x12¾***
**1039** A586 5r shown .60 .60

***Imperf***

**Size: 95x64mm**

**1040** A586 30r Tent, K2 2.75 2.75

2004 Summer Olympics, Athens — A587

No. 1041: a, Track. b, Boxing. c, Field hockey. d, Wrestling.

**2004, Aug. 13** ***Perf. 13x12¾***

**1041** A587 Horiz. strip of 4 2.40 2.40
*a.-d.* 5r Any single .60 .60

7 Lines of Text — A588

6½ Lines of Text — A589

6 Lines of Text — A590

6¾ Lines of Text — A591

**2004, Aug. 14**

**1042** Horiz. strip of 4 1.50 1.50
*a.* A588 5r multi .30 .30
*b.* A589 5r multi .30 .30
*c.* A590 5r multi .30 .30
*d.* A591 5r multi .30 .30

Independence, 57th anniv.

Maulvi Abdul Haq (1870-1961), Lexicographer A592

**2004, Aug. 16**

**1043** A592 4r multi .60 .60

Fourth Intl. Calligraphy and Calligraphic Art Exhibitiion and Competition, Lahore — A593

**2004, Oct. 1**

**1044** A593 5r multi .40 .40

Tropical Fish — A594

No. 1045: a, Neon tetra. b, Striped gourami. c, Black widow. d, Yellow dwarf cichlid. e, Tiger barb.

**2004, Oct. 9** ***Perf. 12½***

**1045** Horiz. strip of 5 2.75 2.75
*a.-e.* A594 2r Any single .50 .50

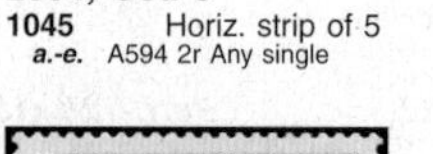

Japanese Economic Assistance, 50th Anniv. A595

Designs: No. 1046, 5r, Training for handicapped. No. 1047, 5r, Polio eradication. No. 1048, 5r, Ghazi Barotha hydroelectric power project. No. 1049, 5r, Kohat Friendship Tunnel. 30r, Vignettes of Nos. 1046-1049, Friendship Tunnel.

**2004, Nov. 8** **Litho.** ***Perf. 12¾x13***

**1046-1049** A595 Set of 4 3.00 3.00

***Imperf***

**1050** A595 multi 3.00 3.00

Year of Child Welfare and Rights — A596

**2004, Nov. 20** ***Perf. 12½***

**1051** A596 4r multi .45 .45

Allama Iqbal Open University, Islamabad, 30th Anniv. — A597

**2004, Dec. 6** ***Perf. 12¾x13***

**1052** A597 20r multi 1.50 1.50

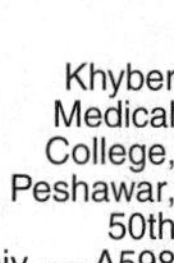

Khyber Medical College, Peshawar, 50th Anniv. — A598

**2004, Dec. 30**

**1053** A598 5r multi .60 .60

Prof. Ahmed Ali (1910-94), Writer — A599

**2005, Jan. 14** **Litho.** ***Perf. 13x12¾***

**1054** A599 5r multi .50 .50

Pakistan — Romania Friendship A600

Poets Mihai Eminescu and Allama Iqbal and: No. 1055, 5r, Flags of Romania and Pakistan. No. 1056, 5r, Flags, monument to Eminescu and Iqbal by Emil Ghitulescu, Islamabad.

**2005, Jan. 14**

**1055-1056** A600 Set of 2 1.40 1.40

Saadat Hasan Manto (1912-55), Writer — A601

**2005, Jan. 18** ***Perf. 13x12¾***

**1057** A601 5r multi .50 .50

A602

PAKISTAN AIR FORCE

Second to None

Rs.5

A603

A604

Pakistan Air Force, 50th Anniv. — A605

**2005, Mar. 23** **Litho.** ***Perf. 12¾x13***

**1058** A602 5r multi 1.00 1.00
**1059** A603 5r multi 1.00 1.00
**1060** A604 5r multi 1.00 1.00

***Perf. 13x12¾***

**1061** A605 5r multi 1.00 1.00
*Nos. 1058-1061 (4)* 4.00 4.00

Command and Staff College, Quetta, Cent. — A606

**2005, Apr. 2** ***Perf. 12¾x13***

**1062** A606 5r multi .50 .50

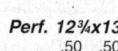

Turkish Grand National Assembly, 85th Anniv. — A607

No. 1063 — Assembly building and: a, Kemal Ataturk, Turkish flag. b, Ataturk, Mohammed Ali Jinnah, Turkish and Pakistani flags.

**2005, Apr. 23** ***Perf. 14***

**1063** A607 10r Horiz. pair, #a-b 2.00 2.00

Institute of Business Administration, Karachi, 50th Anniv. — A608

Various views of campus with country name at: No. 1064, 3r, Right. No. 1065, 3r, Bottom.

**2005, Apr. 30** ***Perf. 12¾x13***

**1064-1065** A608 Set of 2 1.00 1.00

Islamia High School, Quetta, 95th Anniv. — A609

**2005, May 25** ***Perf. 13x12¾***

**1066** A609 5r multi .50 .50

Akhtar Shairani (1905-48), Poet — A610

**2005, June 30**

**1067** A610 5r multi .50 .50

World Summit on Information Technology, Tunis, Tunisia — A611

**2005, July 15**

**1068** A611 5r multi .50 .50

Abdul Rehman Baba (1632-1707), Poet — A612

**2005, Aug. 4**

**1069** A612 5r multi .50 .50

Lahore Marathon A613

**2005, Sept. 10** ***Perf. 12¾x13***

**1070** A613 5r multi .50 .50

Mushrooms — A614

No. 1071: a, Lepiota procera. b, Tricholoma gambosum. c, Amanita caesarea. d, Cantharellus cibarius. e, Boletus luridus. f, Morchella vulgaris. g, Amanita vaginata. h, Agaricus arvensis. i, Coprinus comatus. j, Clitocybe geotropa.

**2005, Oct. 1 Litho. *Perf. 13¼x12¾***
**1071** A614 Block of 10 7.50 7.50
*a.-j.* 5r Any single .40 .40

Intl. Year of Sports and Physical Education A615

**2005, Nov. 5 *Perf. 14***
**1072** A615 5r multi .50 .50

South Asian Association for Regional Cooperation, 20th Anniv. — A616

**2005, Nov. 12 *Perf. 13¼x12¾***
**1073** A616 5r multi .50 .50

Khwaja Sarwar Hasan (1902-73), Diplomat — A617

**2005, Nov. 18 *Perf. 14***
**1074** A617 5r multi .50 .50

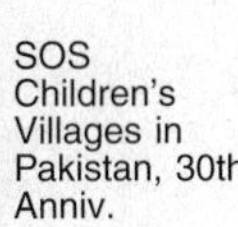

SOS Children's Villages in Pakistan, 30th Anniv. A618

**2005, Nov. 20 *Perf. 12¾x13¼***
**1075** A618 5r multi .50 .50

20th World Men's Team Squash Championships, Islamabad — A619

**2005, Dec. 8 Litho. *Perf. 14***
**1076** A619 5r multi .50 .50

Supreme Court, 50th Anniv. A620

Supreme Court Building: 4r, In daylight. 15r, At night.

**2006, Mar. 23**
**1077-1078** A620 Set of 2 2.75 2.75

Mohammed Ali Jinnah's 1948 Visit to Armored Corps Center — A621

Jinnah, soldiers and: No. 1079, 5r, Tanks. No. 1080, 5r, Flags, vert.

**2006, Apr. 14**
**1079-1080** A621 Set of 2 1.00 1.00

Begum Ra'na Liaquat Ali Khan (1905-90), Diplomat A622

**2006, June 13 *Perf. 13½***
**1081** A622 4r multi .60 .50

Sri Arjun Dev Jee (1563-1606), Sikh Guru — A623

**2006, June 16**
**1082** A623 5r multi .50 .50

Polo at Shandur Pass A624

**2006, July 1 *Perf. 14***
**1083** A624 5r multi 1.00 .75

Tourism — A625

No. 1084: a, Hanna Lake. b, Lake Payee. c, Lake Saiful Maluk. d, Lake Dudi Pat Sar.

**2006, July 20**
**1084** A625 5r Block of 4, #a-d 2.75 2.75

Miniature Sheet

Painters — A626

No. 1085: a, Shakir Ali (1916-75). b, Anna Molka Ahmed (1917-94). c, Sadequain (1930-87). d, Ali Imam (1924-2002). e, Zubeida Agha (1922-97). f, Laila Shahzada (1926-94). g, Ahmed Parvez (1926-79). h, Bashir Mirza (1941-2000). i, Zahoorul Akhlaque (1941-99). j, Askari Mian Irani (1940-2004).

**2006, Aug. 14 *Perf. 13x12¾***
**1085** A626 4r Sheet of 10, #a-j 2.50 2.50

Hamdard Services, Cent. — A627

**2006, Aug. 25 *Perf. 13¼x13***
**1086** A627 5r multi .60 .50

Oct. 8, 2005 Earthquake, 1st Anniv. — A628

**2006, Oct. 8 *Perf. 13½x13¾***
**1087** A628 5r multi .60 .50

Medicinal Plants A629

Designs: No. 1088, 5r, Aloe vera. No. 1089, 5r, Chamomile, vert.

***Perf. 13½x13¼, 13¼x13½***
**2006, Oct. 28**
**1088-1089** A629 Set of 2 1.00 1.00

Intl. Anti-Corruption Day — A630

**2006, Dec. 9 *Perf. 13***
**1090** A630 5r multi .60 .60

Baltit Fort Heritage Trust, 10th Anniv. A631

**2006, Dec. 20 *Perf. 13¼***
**1091** A631 15r multi 1.50 1.50

Miniature Sheet

Muslim League, Cent. — A632

No. 1092: a, Mohammed Ali Jinnah's letter requesting membership in Muslim League. b, Jinnah in sherwani and cap. c, Jinnah addressing Lucknow session. d, Jinnah and wife with youth and women's wing. e, Jinnah hoisting Muslim League flag. f, Jinnah addressing Lahore session. g, Crowd, flags and ballot box. h, Jinnah addressing first Constituent Assembly.

**Wmk. 351**

**2006, Dec. 28 Litho. *Perf. 13***
**1092** A632 4r Sheet of 8, #a-h 2.50 2.50

Karachi Municipal Corporation Building, 75th Anniv. A633

**2007, Jan. 16 *Perf. 14¼***
**1093** A633 10r multi .60 .60

Cadet College Petaro, 50th Anniv. A634

**Wmk. 351**

**2007, Feb. 28 Litho. *Perf. 14¼***
**1094** A634 10r multi .60 .60

Intl. Women's Day — A635

**2007, Mar. 8 *Perf. 13***
**1095** A635 10r multi .60 .60

Hugh Catchpole (1907-97), Educator A636

**2007, May 26**
**1096** A636 10r multi .60 .60

Pakistan Post Emblem A637

**2007, June 7** ***Perf. 14¼***
**1097** A637 4r multi .60 .60

First Public Appearance of JF-17 Thunder Airplane — A638

**2007, Sept. 6** ***Perf. 13***
**1098** A638 5r multi .60 .60

Completion of Term of National Assembly — A639

**2007, Nov. 15**
**1099** A639 15r multi 1.50 1.50

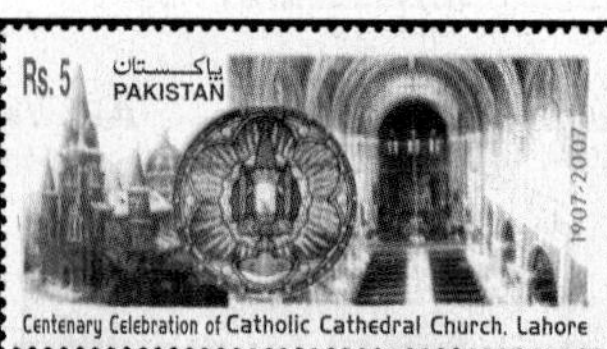


Catholic Cathedral, Lahore, Cent. — A640

**2007, Nov. 19**
**1100** A640 5r multi .60 .60

Third Meeting of Economic Cooperation Organization Postal Authorities, Tehran (in 2006) — A641

**Wmk. 351**

**2007, Sept. 22** **Litho.** ***Perf. 13***
**1101** A641 10r multi *6.00 10.00*

No. 1101 was withdrawn from sale a few weeks after issuance as it is inscribed "I. R. Iran" and lacks the "Pakistan" country name. It is additionally inscribed with a denomination in Iranian currency, and dated "2006" though issued in 2007. This stamp was not valid in Iran, as Iran issued a similar stamp, No. 2917, in 2006.

Pres. Zulfikar Ali Bhutto (1928-79) and Prime Minister Benazir Bhutto (1953-2007) — A642

**Wmk. 351**

**2008, Apr. 4** **Litho.** ***Perf. 13***
**1102** A642 4r multi .60 .60

***Imperf***

**Size: 106x71mm**

**1103** A642 20r multi 2.00 2.00

No. 1103 contains No. 1102 with simulated perforations.

Benazir Bhutto (1953-2007), Prime Minister — A643

Designs: 4r, Head. 5r, 20r, Bhutto waving.

**Wmk. 351**

**2008, June 21** **Litho.** ***Perf. 13***
**1104** A643 4r multi .60 .60

**Size: 34x57mm**

***Perf. 13x13¼***

**1105** A643 5r multi .60 .60

**Size: 67x99mm**

***Imperf***

**1106** A643 20r multi 1.40 1.40

No. 1106 has simulated perforations.

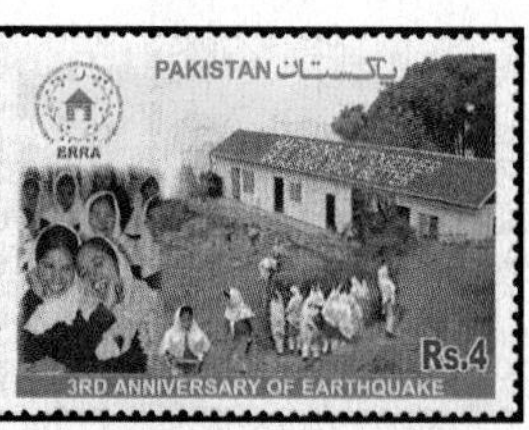


Oct. 8, 2005 Earthquake, 3rd Anniv. — A644

**2008, Oct. 8** ***Perf. 13***
**1107** A644 4r multi .60 .60

Selection of Benazir Bhutto for 2008 United Nations Human Rights Award A645

**Wmk. 351**

**2008, Dec. 10** **Litho.** ***Perf. 13***
**1108** A645 4r multi .60 .60

Assassination of Benazir Bhutto, 1st Anniv. — A646

**2008, Dec. 27** **Wmk. 351** ***Perf. 13***
**1109** A646 4r multi .60 .60

**Size: 98x67mm**

***Imperf***

**Unwmk.**

**1110** A646 20r multi 1.50 1.50

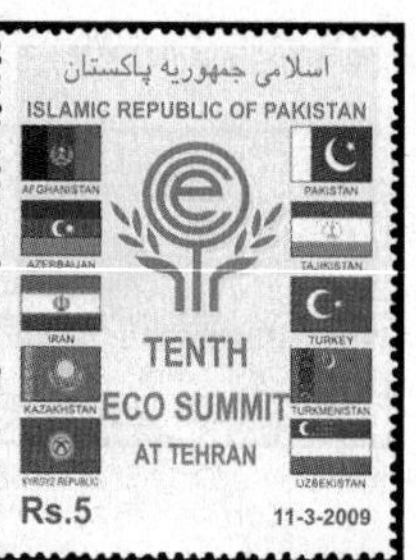


10th Economic Cooperation Organization Summit, Tehran — A647

***Perf. 13¼x13½***

**2009, Mar. 11** **Wmk. 351**
**1111** A647 5r multi .60 .60

Compare with Azerbaijan 895, Iran 2981.

Natl. Environment Year — A648

Designs: No. 1112, 5r, Deodar tree. No. 1113, 5r, Jasmine flower. No. 1114, 5r, Markhor. No. 1115, 5r, Chukar.

**2009, Mar. 23** ***Perf. 13***
**1112-1115** A648 Set of 4 1.50 1.50

Habib Public School, 50th Anniv. A649

**2009, Mar. 29**
**1116** A649 5r multi .50 .50

Bai Virbaiji Soparivala Parsi High School, Karachi, 150th Anniv. — A650

**2009, May 23** ***Perf. 13¼x13½***
**1117** A650 5r multi .60 .60

Karachi Chamber of Commerce and Industry Building, 75th Anniv. — A651

**Wmk. 351**

**2009, May 30** **Litho.** ***Perf. 13***
**1118** A651 4r multi .50 .50

Ahmad Nadeem Qasmi (1916-2006), Writer — A652

**2009, July 10**
**1119** A652 5r multi .50 .50

Minorities Week — A653

**Wmk. 351**

**2009, Aug. 11** **Litho.** ***Perf. 13***
**1120** A653 5r multi .60 .60

Independence Day — A654

**Wmk. 351**

**2009, Aug. 14** **Litho.** ***Perf. 13***
**1121** A654 5r multi .60 .60

Festival of Hazrat Musa Pak Shaheed A655

**2009, Aug. 15**
**1122** A655 5r multi .60 .60

"United For Peace" — A656

**2009, Aug. 16** ***Perf. 13½***
**1123** A656 5r multi .60 .60

Diplomatic Relations Between Pakistan and the Philippines, 60th Anniv. — A657

**Wmk. 351**
**2009, Sept. 9 Litho.** ***Perf. 13***
**1124** A657 5r multi .60 .60

People's Republic of China, 60th Anniv. — A658

**2009, Oct. 1**
**1125** A658 5r multi .50 .50

A659

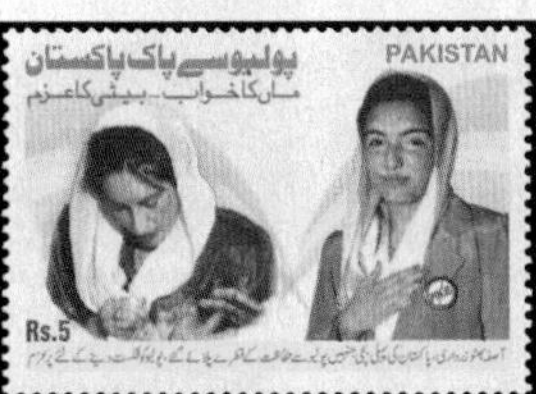

Polio-free Pakistan — A660

**2009, Oct. 10**
**1126** A659 5r multi .50 .50
**1127** A660 5r multi .50 .50

Seventh Natl. Finance Commission Award — A661

**Wmk. 351**
**2010, Jan. 11 Litho.** ***Perf. 13***
**1128** A661 8r multi .60 .60

Port of Gwardar — A662

**2010, Jan. 11**
**1129** A662 8r multi .60 .60

Navy Rifle Association 50th Anniv. Meet — A663

**Wmk. 351**
**2010, Feb. 13 Litho.** ***Perf. 13½***
**1130** A663 10r multi .60 .60

Awarding of Hilal-i-Eissar (Selflessness) Awards to Cities — A664

No. 1131 — Flag and: a, War Memorial, Nowshera. b, Islamia College, Peshawar. c, Judicial Complex, Swabi. d, Takht-e-Bahi, Mardan. e, Sugar mills, Charsadda.

**2010, Feb. 22** ***Perf. 13***
**1131** Vert. strip of 5 1.50 1.50
***a.-e.*** A664 5r Any single .30 .30

Overseas Investors Chamber of Commerce and Industry, 150th Anniv. — A665

**2010, Apr. 7** ***Perf. 13x13¼***
**1132** A665 8r multi .60 .60

2010 Youth Olympics, Singapore — A666

**Wmk. 351**
**2010, Aug. 14 Litho.** ***Perf. 13¼***
**1133** A666 8r multi .60 .60

Lawrence College, Murree Hills, 150th Anniv. — A667

No. 1134 — Crest of college and: a, Building and flagpoles. b, Building in brown. c, Aerial view of building. d, Building and plaza.

**2010, Oct. 7 Litho.** ***Perf. 13***
**1134** A667 Block of 4 + 2 central labels 1.75 1.75
***a.-d.*** 8r Any single .30 .30

Children's Art Competition — A668

**2010, Nov. 5**
**1135** A668 8r multi + label .60 .60

International Islamic University, Islamabad, 25th Anniv. — A669

***Perf. 13x13¼***
**2010, Dec. 15 Wmk. 351**
**1136** A669 8r multi .60 .60

Islamabad, 50th Anniv. — A670

**2010, Dec. 31** ***Perf. 13½***
**1137** A670 5r multi .60 .60

100 Millionth Cell Phone Subscribers of Pakistan Telecommunications Authority — A671

**2011, Jan. 19** ***Perf. 13x13¼***
**1138** A671 8r multi .60 .60

Sixth Population and Housing Census — A672

**2011, Feb. 10 Wmk. 351**
**1139** A672 10r multi .60 .60

Railways in Pakistan, 150th Anniv. — A673

**2011, May 13 Litho.**
**1140** A673 8r multi .60 .60

Diplomatic Relations Between Pakistan and People's Republic of China, 60th Anniv. — A674

No. 1141 — Flags of Pakistan and People's Republic of China and: a, Pakistan President Asif Ali Zardari and Chinese President Hu Jintao (handshake above baseline). b, Pakistan Prime Minister and Yousuf Raza Gilani and Chinese Premier Wen Jiabao (handshake touching baseline).

**2011, May 21** ***Perf. 13x13¼***
**1141** A674 8r Horiz. pair, #a-b 1.00 1.00

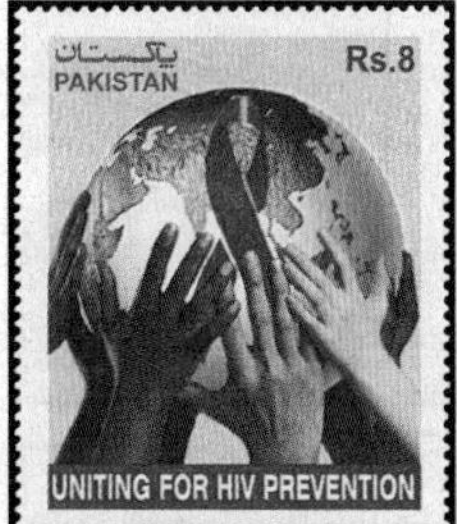

Campaign Against Human Immunodeficiency Virus — A675

***Perf. 13½x13¾***
**2011, June 8 Wmk. 351**
**1142** A675 8r multi .60 .60

Friendship Between Pakistan and Russia — A676

***Perf. 13x13¼***
**2011, June 10 Litho. Wmk. 351**
**1143** A676 8r multi .60 .60

A677

A678

A679

A680

A681

A682

A683

Works From Children's Art Competition at National Stamp Exhibition, Kurrachee — A684

**2011, June 24 Unwmk. *Perf. 13***

| | | | |
|---|---|---|---|
| **1144** | Sheet of 8 + 2 labels | 3.50 | 3.50 |
| *a.* | A677 8r multi | .40 | .40 |
| *b.* | A678 8r multi | .40 | .40 |
| *c.* | A679 8r multi | .40 | .40 |
| *d.* | A680 8r multi | .40 | .40 |
| *e.* | A681 8r multi | .40 | .40 |
| *f.* | A682 8r multi | .40 | .40 |
| *g.* | A683 8r multi | .40 | .40 |
| *h.* | A684 8r multi | .40 | .40 |

Institute of Chartered Accountants of Pakistan, 50th Anniv. — A685

***Perf. 13x13¼***

**2011, July 1 Wmk. 351**
**1145** A685 8r multi .60 .60

Dr. Syedna Mohammed Burhannudin Saheb, Religious Leader, 100th Birthday — A686

**2011, July 17**
**1146** A686 8r multi .60 .60

Dr. Burhanuddin Saheb was born in 1915. The centenary of his birth is based on the Islamic calendar.

Zarai Taraqiati Bank, Ltd., 50th Anniv. A687

**2011, Aug. 14 *Perf. 13***
**1147** A687 8r multi .60 .60

Frequency Allocation Board, 60th Anniv. — A688

**2011, Aug. 18 *Perf. 13x13¼***
**1148** A688 8r multi .60 .60

Towers in Pakistan and Iran — A689

No. 1149: a, Milad Tower, Tehran. b, Minar-e-Pakistan, Lahore.

**2011, Aug. 29 *Perf. 13***
**1149** A689 8r Horiz. pair, #a-b, + flanking label .60 .60

See Iran No. 3023.

Pakistan Space and Upper Atmosphere Research Commission, 50th Anniv. — A690

**2011, Sept. 16 Wmk. 351**
**1150** A690 8r multi .60 .60

Karachi Gymkhana, 125th Anniv. — A691

No. 1151: a, Building with archways, tree at right. b, Building, white pole at right. c, Building, two white poles and trees in front. d, Building, shelter with awning at left.

**2011, Sept. 23 *Perf. 13x13¼***
**1151** A691 8r Block of 4, #a-d 2.00 2.00

Campaign Against Breast Cancer — A692

**2011, Nov. 30 *Perf. 13***
**1152** A692 8r multi .60 .60

Diplomatic Relations Between Pakistan and Thailand, 60th Anniv. A693

**2011, Dec. 13 *Perf. 13¼x13***
**1153** A693 8r multi .60 .60

St. Patrick's High School, Karachi, 150th Anniv. A694

**2011, Dec. 31**
**1154** A694 8r multi .60 .60

100th Meeting of Federal Cabinet — A695

**2012, Jan. 18 *Perf. 13x13¼***
**1155** A695 8r multi .60 .60

Arfa Karim (1995-2012), World's Youngest Microsoft Certified Professional — A696

**2012, Feb. 2**
**1156** A696 8r multi .60 .60

Nur Khan (1923-2011), Air Marshal — A697

**2012, Feb. 22 *Perf. 13¾x13½***
**1157** A697 8r multi .60 .60

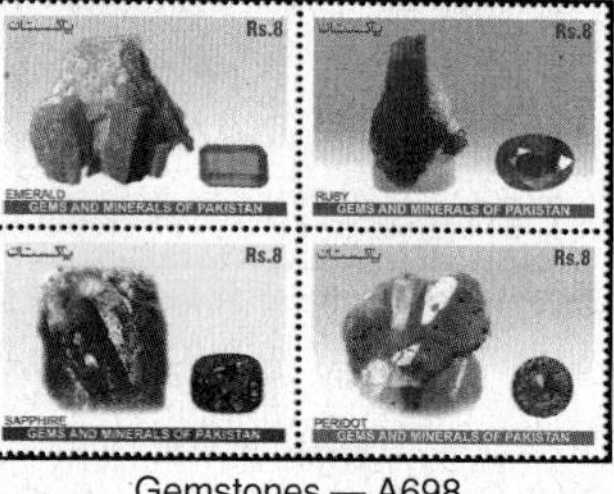
Gemstones — A698

No. 1158: a, Emerald. b, Ruby. c, Sapphire. d, Peridot.

**2012, Feb. 24 *Perf. 13***
**1158** A698 8r Block of 4, #a-d 2.00 2.00

Aitchison College, Lahore, 125th Anniv. — A699

**2012, Mar. 3**
**1159** A699 8r multi .60 .60

St. Joseph's Convent School, Karachi, 150th Anniv. — A700

**2012, Mar. 19 *Perf. 13¾x13½***
**1160** A700 8r multi .60 .60

Asian-Pacific Postal Union, 50th Anniv. — A701

**2012, Apr. 1 Wmk. 351 *Perf. 13***
**1161** A701 8r multi .60 .60

Government High School No. 1, Thana, Cent. — A702

**2012, Apr. 15** ***Perf. 13½***
**1162** A702 8r multi .60 .60

Martyr's Day — A703

**2012, Apr. 30** ***Perf. 13x13¼***
**1163** A703 8r multi .60 .60

State Visit of Thailand's King Bhumibol Adulyadej and Queen Sirikit to Pakistan, 50th Anniv. — A704

**2012, May 5** **Litho.**
**1164** A704 8r multi .60 .60

Campaign Against Thalassemia — A705

**2012, May 8** **Wmk. 351**
**1165** A705 8r multi .60 .60

World Environment Day — A706

No. 1166: a, Mountains and lake. b, Horses and riders. c, Arches at Shalimar Gardens, Lahore. d, Khyber Pass Gateway and flag.

**2012, June 5** ***Perf. 13x13¼***
**1166** A706 8r Block of 4, #a-d 1.50 1.50

United Nations Environment Program, 40th anniv.

Ayub Bridge, 50th Anniv. — A707

**2012, June 15**
**1167** A707 8r multi .60 .60

A708

A709

A710

A711

A712

A713

A714

Works From Children's Art Competition at 2012 National Stamp Exhibition, Kurrachee — A715

**2012, June 22** ***Perf. 13***
**1168** Sheet of 8 + 2 labels 3.50 3.50
*a.* A708 8r multi .40 .40
*b.* A709 8r multi .40 .40
*c.* A710 8r multi .40 .40
*d.* A711 8r multi .40 .40
*e.* A712 8r multi .40 .40
*f.* A713 8r multi .40 .40
*g.* A714 8r multi .40 .40
*h.* A715 8r multi .40 .40

Eid Greetings — A716

No. 1169: a, Yellow roses, pale orange frame. b, Rink roses, yellow frame. c, White roses, light blue frame. d, Yellow roses, light green frame.

**2012, Aug. 13**
**1169** A716 8r Block of 4, #a-d 1.50 1.50

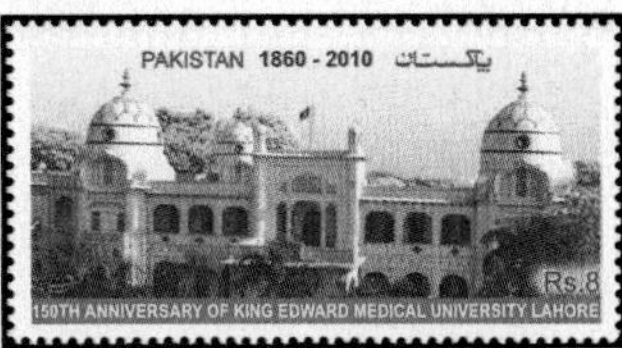


King Edward Medical University, Lahore, 150th Anniv. — A717

**2012, Aug. 28** ***Perf. 13x13¼***
**1170** A717 8r multi .60 .60

Pakistan No. 23, Abdur Rahman Chughtai (1897-1975), Painter — A718

**2012, Aug. 30** ***Perf. 13¼x13½***
**1171** A718 10r multi .60 .60

Independence, 65th anniv.

Sialkot Chamber of Commerce and Industry, 30th Anniv. — A719

**2012, Sept. 26** ***Perf. 13x13¼***
**1172** A719 8r multi .60 .60

Birds in Flight — A720

No. 1173: a, White storks. b, Shoveler ducks. c, Snow geese. d, Siberian cranes.

**2012, Sept. 27** **Wmk. 351**
**1173** A720 8r Block of 4, #a-d 1.50 1.50

A721

A722

A723

A724

Arabian Sea Coral Reefs — A724

**2012, Oct. 4** **Litho.**
**1174** Block of 4 2.00 2.00
*a.* A721 8r multi .50 .50
*b.* A722 8r multi .50 .50
*c.* A723 8r multi .50 .50
*d.* A724 8r multi .50 .50

Hameed Naseem (1920-98), Writer — A725

**2012, Oct. 19** ***Perf. 13***
**1175** A725 8r multi .60 .60

Men of Letters. See Nos. 1181-1183, 1185-1189, 1196, 1202, 1206, 1248.

University of Karachi Geography Department, 60th Anniv. — A726

**2012, Nov. 19** ***Perf. 13x13¼***
**1176** A726 15r multi .90 .90

National Investment Trust Limited, 50th Anniv. — A727

**2012, Nov. 21** **Wmk. 351**
**1177** A727 15r multi .90 .90

Muhammad Luthfullah Khan (1916-2012), Writer and Recordings Collector A728

**2012, Nov. 25** *Perf. 13*

**1178** A728 15r multi .90 .90

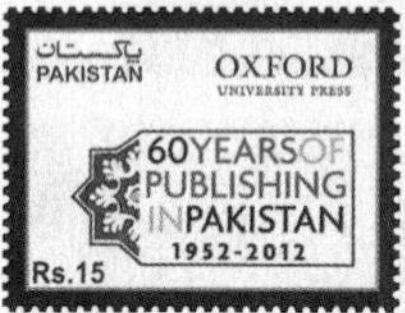


Publishing in Pakistan, 60th Anniv. A729

**2012, Dec. 15** *Perf. 13½x13¼*

**1179** A729 15r multi .30 .30

Commercial Operation of First Wind Farm Power Project in Pakistan — A730

**2012, Dec. 24** *Perf. 13x13¼*

**1180** A730 15r multi .90 .90

**Men of Letters Type of 2012**

Designs: No. 1181, Syed Nasir Raza Kazmi (1925-72), poet. No. 1182, Allama Muhammad Asad (1900-92), writer. No. 1183, Qudrat Ullah Shahab (1917-86), writer.

**2013**

**1181** A725 15r multi .60 .60
**1182** A725 15r multi .60 .60
**1183** A725 15r multi .60 .60
*Nos. 1181-1183 (3)* 1.80 1.80

Issued: No. 1181, 3/2; Nos. 1182, 1183, 3/23.

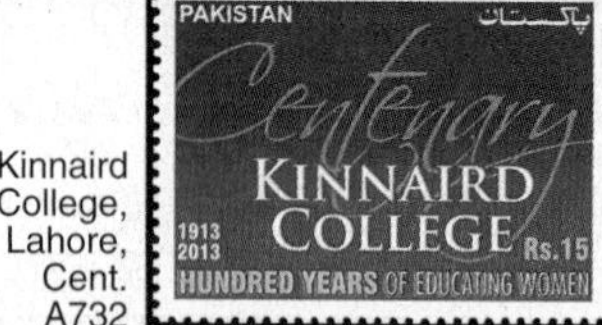


Kinnaird College, Lahore, Cent. A732

**2013, Apr. 11**

**1184** A732 15r multi .90 .90

**Men of Letters Type of 2012**

Design: No. 1185, Sufi Barkat Ali (1911-97), Muslim Sufi saint. No. 1186, Syed Zamir Jafri (1916-99), poet. No. 1187, Shafiq-ur-Rehman (1920-2000), writer. No. 1188, Mumtaz Mufti (1905-95), writer. No. 1189, Ishfaq Ahmed (1925-2004), writer.

**2013**

**1185** A725 8r multi .60 .60
**1186** A725 8r multi .60 .60
**1187** A725 8r multi .60 .60
**1188** A725 8r multi .60 .60
**1189** A725 8r multi .60 .60
*Nos. 1185-1189 (5)* 3.00 3.00

Issued: No. 1185, 4/27; No. 1186, 5/29; No. 1187, 6/6; Nos. 1188-1189, 6/12.

Sir Muhammad Iqbal (1877-1938), Poet — A733

**Wmk. 351**

**2013, Apr. 21** **Litho.** *Perf. 13½*

**1190** A733 15r multi .90 .90

Reopening of Pakistan Army Museum, Rawalpindi — A734

**2013, Apr. 30** *Perf. 13x13¼*

**1191** A734 15r multi .90 .90

2013 General Elections — A735

**2013, May 11**

**1192** A735 8r multi .60 .60

Recipients of Pakistan's Highest Military Medals — A736

No. 1193: a, Capt. Karnal Sher Khan Shaheed (1970-99), Nishan-e-Haider medal. b, Havildar Lalak Jan Shaheed (1967-99), Nishan-e-Haider medal. c, Naik Saif Ali Janjua Shaheed (1922-48), Hilal-i-Kashmir medal.

*Perf. 13½x13¼*

**2013, Apr. 30** **Litho.** **Wmk. 351**

**1193** A736 Horiz. strip of 3 1.50 1.50
*a.-c.* 8r Any single .50 .50

Sadiq Muhammad Khan Abbasi V (1904-66), Nawab of Bahawalpur A737

**Wmk. 351**

**2013, May 24** **Litho.** *Perf. 13*

**1194** A737 8r multi .60 .60

Islamia College, Peshawar, Cent. — A738

**2013, May 30**

**1195** A738 8r multi .60 .60

**Men of Letters Type of 2012**

Design: Ibn-e-Insha (1927-78), poet.

**2013, June 15**

**1196** A725 8r multi .50 .50

All-Pakistan Newspaper Society, 60th Anniv. — A739

**2013, June 20**

**1197** A739 8r multi .60 .60

Red-vented Bulbul A740

*Perf. 13½x13¼*

**2013, July 1** **Litho.** **Wmk. 351**

**1198** A740 8r multi .60 .60

Pir Meher Ali Shah (1859-1937), Sufi Scholar — A741

**Wmk. 351**

**2013, July 30** **Litho.** *Perf. 13*

**1199** A741 8r multi — —

Frigate PNS Aslat — A742

**Wmk. 351**

**2013, Sept. 3** **Litho.** *Perf. 13¼*

**1200** A742 10r multi .60 .60

Noor Jahan (1926-2000), Singer — A743

**Wmk. 351**

**2013, Sept. 21** **Litho.** *Perf. 13¼*

**1201** A743 8r multi .60 .60

**Men of Letters Type of 2012**

Design: Jon Elia (1931-2002), writer.

**Wmk. 351**

**2013, Nov. 8** **Litho.** *Perf. 13*

**1202** A725 8r multi .50 .50

Two Decades of Extended Cooperation with Economic Cooperation Organization A744

*Perf. 13¼x13*

**2013, Nov. 28** **Litho.** **Wmk. 351**

**1203** A744 25r multi .60 .60

Perveen Shakir (1952-94), Poet — A745

**Wmk. 351**

**2013, Dec. 26** **Litho.** *Perf. 13*

**1204** A745 10r multi .60 .60

Pakistan Bible Society, 150th Anniv. — A746

**Wmk. 351**

**2013, Dec. 28** **Litho.** *Perf. 13*

**1205** A746 8r multi .60 .60

**Men of Letters Type of 2012**

Design: Habib Jalib (1928-93), poet.

**Wmk. 351**

**2014, Mar. 12** **Litho.** *Perf. 13*

**1206** A725 15r multi .50 .50

Air Commodore Muhammad Mahmood Alam (1935-2013) — A747

*Perf. 13¾x13½*

**2014, Mar. 20 Litho. Wmk. 351**

**1207** A747 8r multi .60 .60

Hyder M. Habib (1931-2011), Banker — A748

**Wmk. 351**

**2014, Apr. 6 Litho. *Perf. 13***

**1208** A748 8r multi .60 .60

Forman Christian College, 150th Anniv. — A749

**Wmk. 351**

**2014, May 14 Litho. *Perf. 13***

**1209** A749 8r multi .25 .25

Pakistan Navy Submarine Force, 50th Anniv. — A750

**Wmk. 351**

**2014, June 1 Litho. *Perf. 13***

**1210** A750 10r multi .25 .25

Frontier Constabulary, Cent. — A751

**Wmk. 351**

**2014, July 11 Litho. *Perf. 13½***

**1211** A751 8r multi .25 .25

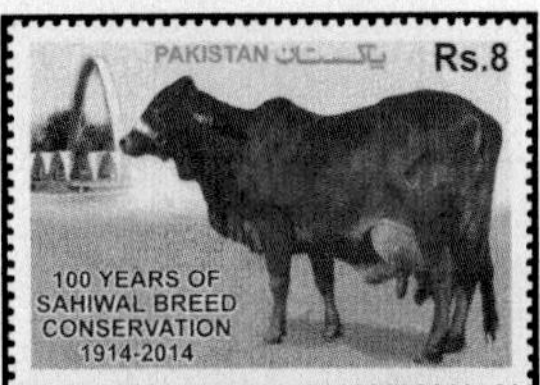


Sahiwal Cattle Conservation, Cent. — A752

*Perf. 13x13¼*

**2014, Aug. 5 Litho. Wmk. 351**

**1212** A752 8r multi .25 .25

A753

Pakistan 2025 Planning Program — A754

*Perf. 13½x13¼*

**2014, Aug. 11 Litho. Wmk. 351**

**1213** A753 8r multi .25 .25

*Perf. 13*

**1214** A754 10r multi .25 .25

Norman Borlaug (1914-2009), 1970 Nobel Peace Laureate — A755

*Perf. 13x13¼*

**2014, Dec. 4 Litho. Wmk. 351**

**1215** A755 8r multi .25 .25

Intl. Anti-Corruption Day — A756

*Perf. 13x13¼*

**2014, Dec. 9 Litho. Wmk. 351**

**1216** A756 8r multi .25 .25

Gems and Minerals A757

No. 1217: a, Apatite. b, Aquamarine. c, Black tourmaline. d, Garnet. e, Epidot. f, Vesuvianite. g, Topaz. h, Sphene.

*Perf. 13x13¼*

**2014, Dec. 11 Litho. Wmk. 351**

**1217** Block of 8 1.60 1.60

*a.-h.* A757 10r Any single .25 .25

14th National Scout Jamboree, Khairpur — A758

*Perf. 13x13¼*

**2014, Dec. 23 Litho. Wmk. 351**

**1218** A758 8r multi .25 .25

Artifacts of Ancient Civilizations — A759

No. 1219: a, Artifacts from Trypillia, Ukraine archaeological site, flag of Ukraine. b, Artifacts from Mohenjo-daro, Pakistan archaeological site, flag of Pakistan.

*Perf. 13¼x13*

**2014, Dec. 25 Litho. Wmk. 351**

**1219** A759 20r Horiz. pair, #a-b .80 .80

*c.* Souvenir sheet of 2, #1219a-1219b, imperf. 1.00 1.00

No. 1219c has simulated perforations and sold for 50r.

See Ukraine No. 997.

Moulana Altaf Hussain Hali (1837-1914), Poet — A760

*Perf. 13x13¼*

**2014, Dec. 31 Litho. Wmk. 351**

**1220** A760 8r multi .25 .25

First 100 Megawatt Solar Plant in Pakistan — A762

**Wmk. 351**

**2015, May 4 Litho. *Perf. 13½***

**1222** A762 8r multi .25 .25

Year of Pakistan-China Friendly Exchanges — A763

No. 1223: a, Flag of People's Republic of China and Pres. Xi Jinping. b, Great Wall of China. c, Karakoram Highway. d, Shalimar Garden, Pakistan. e, Flag of Pakistan and Prime Minister Nawaz Sharif.

**Wmk. 351**

**2015, Aug. 14 Litho. *Perf. 13***

**1223** Horiz. strip of 5 1.25 1.25

*a.-f.* A763 10r Any single .25 .25

A764

A765

A766

A767

A768

India-Pakistan War, 50th Anniv. — A769

*Perf. 13x13¼*

**2015, Sept. 7 Litho. Wmk. 351**

**1224** Block of 6 1.50 1.50

*a.* A764 10r multi .25 .25

*b.* A765 10r multi .25 .25

*c.* A766 10r multi .25 .25

*d.* A767 10r multi .25 .25

*e.* A768 10r multi .25 .25

*f.* A769 10r multi .25 .25

Cadet College, Kohat, 50th Anniv. — A770

**Wmk. 351**

**2015, Oct. 10 Litho. *Perf.***

**1225** A770 8r multi .25 .25

Urdu Language in Turkey, Cent. — A771

**Wmk. 351**

**2015, Oct. 12 Litho. *Perf. 13***

**1226** A771 10r multi .25 .25

Restoration of Murree General Post Office — A772

**Wmk. 351**

**2015, Nov. 4 Litho. *Perf. 13***

**1227** A772 8r multi .25 .25

Army Public School Massacre, 1st Anniv. — A773

**Wmk. 351**

**2015, Dec. 16 Litho. *Perf. 13***

**1228** A773 16r multi .30 .30

Reopening of Murree General Post Office — A774

**Wmk. 351**

**2015, Dec. 29 Litho. *Perf. 13***

**1229** A774 10r multi .25 .25

Safe Operation of First Pinstech Nuclear Reactor, 50th Anniv. — A775

***Perf. 14 Syncopated***

**2016, Feb. 10 Litho. Wmk. 351**

**1230** A775 50r multi 1.00 1.00

Water Conservation — A776

**Wmk. 351**

**2016, Mar. 22 Litho. *Perf. 13***

**1231** A776 8r multi .25 .25

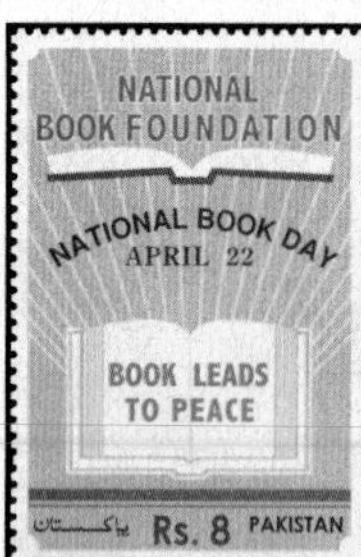


National Book Day — A777

**Wmk. 351**

**2016, Apr. 22 Litho. *Perf. 13***

**1232** A777 8r multi .25 .25

S. P Singha (1893-1948), Politician — A778

***Perf. 14 Syncopated***

**2016, Apr. 26 Litho. Wmk. 351**

**1233** A778 10r multi .25 .25

Diplomatic Relations Between Pakistan and People's Republic of China, 65th Anniv. — A779

**Wmk. 351**

**2016, May 21 Litho. *Perf. 13***

**1234** A779 8r multi .25 .25

Abdul Sattar Edhi (1928-2016), Philanthropist — A780

***Perf. 13¼x13½***

**2016, Aug. 14 Litho. Wmk. 351**

**1235** A780 20r multi .40 .40

Souvenir Sheet

Directorate General of Training and Research Building (Old Custom House), Karachi, Cent. — A781

No. 1236 — Various views of building with: a, Country name in white at left, "100" in red at bottom. b, Country name in black at right, "100" in blue at bottom. c, Country name in black at right, "100" in magenta at bottom.

**Wmk. 351**

**2016, Sept. 6 Litho. *Perf.***

**1236** A781 8r Sheet of 3, #a-c .50 .50

Habib Bank Limited, 75th Anniv. — A782

**Wmk. 351**

**2016, Sept. 23 Litho. *Perf. 13***

**1237** A782 8r multi .25 .25

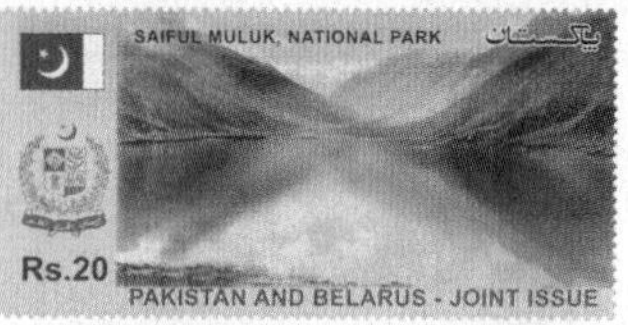


National Parks of Pakistan and Belarus — A783

No. 1238: a, Saiful Muluk National Park, flag and arms of Pakistan. b, Narachanski National Park, flag and arms of Belarus.

***Perf. 13¼x13½***

**2016, Oct. 5 Litho. Wmk. 351**

**1238** Horiz. pair .80 .80

*a.-b.* A783 20r Either single .40 .40

See Belarus No. 1014.

Diplomatic Relations Between Pakistan and Singapore, 50th Anniv. — A784

No. 1239: a, Vanda Miss Joaquim orchid, Merlion's head. b, Jasmine flower, flag of Pakistan.

**Wmk. 351**

**2016, Oct. 18 Litho. *Perf. 13***

**1239** A784 8r Horiz. pair, #a-b .30 .30

See Singapore Nos. 1800-1801.

Rotary Foundation, Cent. — A785

**Wmk. 351**

**2016, Nov. 20 Litho. *Perf. 13***

**1240** A785 8r multi .25 .25

Lahore High Court, 150th Anniv. — A786

**Wmk. 351**

**2016, Nov. 26 Litho. *Perf. 13***

**1241** A786 8r multi .25 .25

National Voter's Day A787

***Perf. 14 Syncopated***

**2016, Dec. 7 Litho. Wmk. 351**

**1242** A787 8r multi .25 .25

Dinshaw B. Avari (1902-88), Philanthropist A788

**Wmk. 351**

**2016, Dec. 18 Litho. *Perf. 13***

**1243** A788 8r multi .25 .25

A789

A790

A791

A792

A793

A794

A795

Works From Children's Art Competition at 2016 National Stamp Exhibition, Karachi — A796

**Wmk. 351**

**2016, Dec. 30 Litho. *Perf. 13***

| | | | |
|---|---|---|---|
| **1244** | Sheet of 8 + 2 labels | 2.00 | 2.00 |
| *a.* | A789 8r multi | .25 | .25 |
| *b.* | A790 8r multi | .25 | .25 |
| *c.* | A791 8r multi | .25 | .25 |
| *d.* | A792 8r multi | .25 | .25 |
| *e.* | A793 8r multi | .25 | .25 |
| *f.* | A794 8r multi | .25 | .25 |
| *g.* | A795 8r multi | .25 | .25 |
| *h.* | A796 8r multi | .25 | .25 |

International Year of Sustainable Tourism for Development

No. 1245 — United Nations World Tourism Organization emblem and mountains: a, Broad Peak. b, Gasherbrum I. c, Nangaparbat. d, K2.

***Perf. 13¼x13½***

**2017, Jan. 1 Litho. Wmk. 351**

| | | | |
|---|---|---|---|
| **1245** | Horiz. strip of 4, #a-d | 1.00 | 1.00 |
| *a.-d.* | A797 10r Any single | .25 | .25 |

A798

13th Econonic Cooperation Organization Summit, Islamabad — A799

***Perf. 14 Syncopated***

**2017, Mar. 6 Litho. Wmk. 351**

**1246** A798 8r multi .25 .25

***Perf. 13***

**1247** A799 8r multi .25 .25

**Men of Letters Type of 2012**

Design: Majeed Amjad (1914-74), poet.

**Wmk. 351**

**2017, June 29 Litho. *Perf. 13***

**1248** A725 8r multi .25 .25

Partnership Between Pakistan and Asian Development Bank, 50th Anniv. — A800

***Perf. 13¼x13½***

**2017, July 6 Litho. Wmk. 351**

**1249** A800 8r multi .25 .25

Maulana Mufti Mahmood (1919-80), Governmental Minister — A801

**Wmk. 351**

**2017, Oct. 14 Litho. *Perf. 13***

**1250** A801 8r multi .25 .25

Sir Syed Ahmed Khan (1817-98), Educator, Jurist, Philosopher A802

**Wmk. 351**

**2017, Oct. 17 Litho. *Perf. 13½***

| | | | |
|---|---|---|---|
| **1251** | A802 10r multi | .25 | .25 |
| *a.* | Souvenir sheet of 1, imperf. | .40 | .40 |

No. 1251a has simulated perforations, smaller-sized reproductions of Nos. 502, 735c, 888, and sold for 20r.

Government Islamia College, Lahore, 125th Anniv. — A803

**Wmk. 351**

**2017, Nov. 1 Litho. *Perf. 14***

**1252** A803 8r multi .25 .25

Pakistan Cricket Team, Winners of 2017 ICC Champions Trophy — A804

No. 1253: a, Team standing behind orange letters spelling "Champions." b, Trophy and stadium. c, Team on victory platform.

**Wmk. 351**

**2017, Nov. 2 Litho. *Perf. 13***

| | | | |
|---|---|---|---|
| **1253** | Horiz. strip of 3 | .75 | .75 |
| *a.-c.* | A804 10r Any single | .25 | .25 |
| *d.* | Souvenir sheet of 3, #1253a-1253c, imperf. | .95 | .95 |

No. 1253d sold for 50r and stamps have simulated perforations.

Souvenir Sheet

Diplomatic Relations Between Pakistan and Turkey, 70th Anniv. — A805

No. 1254: a, Mehmet Akif Ersoy (1873-1936), poet. b, Allama Muhammad Iqbal (1877-1938), poet.

***Perf. 13¼x13½***

**2017, Nov. 9 Litho. Wmk. 351**

**1254** A805 10r Sheet of 2, #a-b .40 .40

See Turkey No.

Pakistan Air Force's No. 6 Air Transport Support Squadron, 75th Anniv. — A806

**Wmk. 351**

**2017, Dec. 1 Litho. *Perf. 13***

**1255** A806 10r multi .25 .25

Souvenir Sheet

Dr. Ruth Katharina Martha Pfau (1929-2017), Nun and Physician to Lepers — A807

**Wmk. 351**

**2017, Dec. 3 Litho. *Perf.***

**1256** A807 8r brt pur, dp vio & multi .25 .25

Aga Khan IV, 60th Anniv. as Imam — A808

No. 1257 — Inscriptions: a, Providing clean drinking water. b, Early childhood development. c, Aga Khan University. d, Restoration of Shahi Hammam. e, Skills development. f, Aga Khan Medical Center.

**Wmk. 351**

**2017, Dec. 8 Litho. *Perf. 13***

**1257** A808 10r Block of 6, #a-f 1.10 1.10

## SEMI-POSTAL STAMPS

Earthquake Relief — SP1

**2005, Oct. 27 Litho. *Perf. 13¾x14***

**B1** SP1 4r +(8.50r) multi 1.50 1.50

Printed in sheets of 8 stamps +17 labels.

Child and Man at Refugee Camp — SP2

***Perf. 13x13½***

**2009, Aug. 1 Litho. Unwmk.**

**B2** SP2 5r +(7.50r) multi 2.50 2.50

Printed in sheets of eight stamps + 17 labels. Surtax for Prime Minister's Relief Fund for Swat Refugees.

## OFFICIAL STAMPS

Official Stamps of India, 1939-43, Overprinted in Black

**1947-49 Wmk. 196 *Perf. 13½x14***

| | | | | |
|---|---|---|---|---|
| **O1** | O8 | 3p slate | 1.50 | .50 |
| **O2** | O8 | ½a dk rose vio | .60 | .25 |
| **O3** | O8 | 9p green | 4.00 | 1.50 |
| **O4** | O8 | 1a carmine rose | .60 | .25 |
| **O4A** | O8 | 1a3p bister ('49) | *9.00* | *25.00* |
| **O5** | O8 | 1½a dull purple | .60 | .25 |
| **O6** | O8 | 2a scarlet | .60 | .40 |
| **O7** | O8 | 2½a purple | 7.00 | *11.00* |
| **O8** | O8 | 4a dk brown | 1.40 | *.50* |
| **O9** | O8 | 8a blue violet | 2.00 | *.75* |

India Nos. O100-O103 Overprinted in Black

| | | | | |
|---|---|---|---|---|
| **O10** | A82 | 1r brown & slate | 1.00 | *1.25* |
| **O11** | A82 | 2r dk brn & dk vio | 7.50 | 1.50 |
| **O12** | A82 | 5r dp ultra & dk grn | 30.00 | *55.00* |
| | | Telegraph cancel | | 7.50 |
| **O13** | A82 | 10r rose car & dk vio | 60.00 | *30.00* |
| | | Telegraph cancel | | *5.00* |
| | | *Nos. O1-O13 (14)* | 125.80 | 128.15 |
| | | Set, hinged | 90.00 | |

Regular Issue of 1948 Overprinted in Black or Carmine — a

"C" in "SERVICE" is nearly round.

***Perf. 12½, 13, 13½x14, 14x13½***

**1948, Aug. 14 Unwmk.**

| | | | | |
|---|---|---|---|---|
| **O14** | A3 | 3p orange red | .25 | .25 |
| **O15** | A3 | 6p purple (C) | .25 | .25 |
| **O16** | A3 | 9p dk green (C) | .25 | .25 |
| **O17** | A4 | 1a dk blue (C) | 4.25 | .25 |
| **O18** | A4 | 1½a gray grn (C) | 4.00 | .25 |
| **O19** | A4 | 2a orange red | 1.75 | .25 |
| **O20** | A5 | 3a olive green | 29.00 | 14.00 |
| **O21** | A6 | 4a chocolate | 1.25 | .25 |
| **O22** | A6 | 8a black (C) | 2.50 | *10.00* |
| **O23** | A5 | 1r ultra | 1.25 | .30 |
| **O24** | A5 | 2r dark brown | 17.50 | 10.00 |
| **O25** | A5 | 5r carmine | 50.00 | 20.00 |

O26 A7 10r rose lil, perf. 14x13½ 22.50 *60.00*
a. Perf. 12 25.00 *65.00*
b. Perf. 13 22.50 *70.00*
*Nos. O14-O26 (13)* 134.75 116.05
Set, hinged 72.50

Issued: No. O26a, 10/10/51; No. O26b, 1954(?).

**Nos. 47-50 and 52 Overprinted Type "a" in Black or Carmine**

**1949-50** ***Perf. 12½, 13½x14***
O27 A10 1a dark blue (C) 2.10 .25
O28 A10 1½a gray green (C) .65 .25
a. Inverted ovpt. 275.00 45.00
O29 A10 2a orange red 2.10 .25
O30 A9 3a olive grn ('49) 37.50 7.50
O31 A11 8a black (C) 57.50 25.00
*Nos. O27-O31 (5)* 99.85 33.25

No. O32

No. O33

No. O34

**Inscribed "SERVICE"**

**Unwmk.**

**1951, Aug. 14 Engr. *Perf. 13***
O32 A13 3a dark rose lake 9.25 *10.00*
O33 A14 4a deep green 2.40 .40
O34 A15 8a brown *10.00* 5.00
*Nos. O32-O34 (3)* 21.65 *15.40*

See Nos. 56, 58, 60.

Nos. 24-26, 47-49, 38-41 Overprinted in Black or Carmine — b

"C" in "SERVICE" is oval.

**1954**
O35 A3 3p orange red .25 .25
O36 A3 6p purple (C) .25 .25
O37 A3 9p dk green (C) .25 .25
O38 A10 1a dk blue (C) .25 .25
O39 A10 1½a gray grn (C) .25 .25
O40 A10 2a orange red .25 .25
O41 A5 1r ultra 12.00 5.00
O42 A5 2r dark brown 5.50 .25
O43 A5 5r carmine 42.50 26.00
O43A A7 10r rose lilac 37.50 *70.00*
*Nos. O35-O43A (10)* 99.00 *102.75*

**Nos. 66-72 Overprinted Type "b" in Carmine or Black**

**1954, Aug. 14**
O44 A18 6p rose violet (C) .25 *3.25*
O45 A19 9p blue (C) 1.75 *8.50*
O46 A19 1a carmine rose .25 *2.50*
O47 A18 1½a red .25 *2.50*
O48 A20 14a dk green (C) 1.25 *8.00*
O49 A20 1r yellow grn (C) 1.40 .25
O50 A20 2r orange 4.00 .25
*Nos. O44-O50 (7)* 9.15 *25.25*

**No. 75 Overprinted in Carmine Type "b" Overprint: 13x2½mm**

**1955, Aug. 14 Unwmk. *Perf. 13***
O51 A21 8a violet .75 .25

Nos. 24, 40, 66-72, 74-75, 83, 89 Overprinted in Black or Carmine — c

**1957-61**
O52 A3 3p org red ('58) .25 .25
O53 A18 6p rose vio (C) .25 .25
O54 A19 9p blue (C) ('58) .25 *.25*
O55 A19 1a carmine rose .25 .25
O56 A18 1½a red .25 .25
O57 A24 2a red ('58) .25 .25
O58 A21 6a dk bl (C) ('60) .25 .25
O59 A21 8a vio (C) ('58) .25 .25
O60 A20 14a dk grn (C) ('58) .50 *4.25*
O61 A20 1r yel grn (C) ('58) .50 .25
O62 A20 2r orange ('58) 5.50 .25
O63 A5 5r carmine ('58) 7.50 .25
O64 A26 10r dk grn & org (C) ('61) 7.00 *9.00*
*Nos. O52-O64 (13)* 23.00 16.00

For surcharges see Nos. O67-O73.

**Nos. 110-111 Overprinted Type "c"**

**1961, Apr.**
O65 A33 8a green .25 .25
O66 A33 1r blue .25 .25
a. Inverted overprint 7.50

**New Currency**

Nos. O52, O55-O57 Surcharged with New Value in Paisa

**1961**
O67 A18 1p on 1½a red .25 .25
a. Overprinted type "b" 5.00 1.75
O68 A3 2p on 3p orange red .25 .25
a. Overprinted type "b" 8.50 5.00
O69 A19 6p on 1a car rose
O70 A19 7p on 1a car rose .25 .25
a. Overprinted type "b" 9.50 *11.00*
O71 A18 9p on 1½a red
O72 A24 13p on 2a red ("PAISA") .25 .25
O73 A24 13p on 2a red ("Paisa")

Nos. O69, O71, O73 were locally overprinted at Mastung. On these stamps "paisa" is in lower case.

Forgeries of No. O69, O71 and O73 abound.

**Nos. 125, 128 Overprinted Type "c"**

**1961**
O74 A33 3p on 6p purple .25 .25
O75 A33 13p on 2a copper red .25 .25

Various violet handstamped surcharges were applied to several official stamps. Most of these repeat the denomination of the basic stamp and add the new value. Example: "4 ANNAS (25 Paisa)" on No. O33.

Nos. 129-135, 135B, 135C, 136a, 137-140a Overprinted in Carmine — d

**1961-78** ***Perf. 13½x14***
O76 A40 1p violet (II) .25 .25
a. Type I .40 .40
O77 A40 2p rose red (II) .25 .25
a. Type I .40 .40
O78 A40 3p magenta .25 .25
O79 A40 5p ultra (II) .25 .25
a. Type I .40 .40
O80 A40 7p emerald 5.00 5.00
O81 A40 10p brown .25 .25
O82 A40 13p blue violet .25 .25
O85 A40 40p dull pur ('62) .25 .25
O86 A40 50p dull grn ('62) .25 .25
O87 A40 75p dk car ('62) .25 .25
*Nos. O76-O87 (10)* 7.25 7.25

**1961-78 Designs Redrawn**
*O76b* A40 1p violet (#129b) ('63) .25 .25
*O77b* A40 2p rose red (#130b) ('64) .25 .25
*O78a* A40 3p mag (#131a) ('66) 3.00 3.00
*O78b* A40 3p mag (#131b) 3.00 1.00
*O79b* A40 5p ultra (#132b) ('63) .25 .25
*O80a* A40 7p emerald (#133a) 25.00 14.00
*O81a* A40 10p brown (#134a) ('64) .25 .25
*O82a* A40 13p blue vio (#135a) ('63) .25 .25
O83 A40 15p rose lil (#135B; '64) .25 .25
O84 A40 20p dl grn (#135C; '70) .25 .25
O84A A40 25p dk blue (#136a; '77) 4.50 1.00
*O85a* A40 40p dull purple (#137a) 20.00 8.00
*O86a* A40 50p dull grn (#138a) ('64) .25 .25
*O87a* A40 75p dark carmine (#139a) 15.00 7.50
O88 A40 90p lt ol grn (#140a; '78) 5.00 5.00
*Nos. O76b-O88 (14)* 74.50 40.50

**Nos. 141, 143-144 Overprinted Type "c" in Black or Carmine**

**1963, Jan. 7 Unwmk. *Perf. 13½x13***
O89 A41 1r vermilion .35 .25
O90 A41 2r orange 1.50 .25
O91 A41 5r green (C) 4.25 7.00
*Nos. O89-O91 (3)* 6.10 7.50

**Nos. 200, 202-203 Overprinted Type "c"**

**1968-? Wmk. 351 *Perf. 13½x13***
O92 A41 1r vermilion 3.75 1.00
O93 A41 2r orange 16.00 2.00
O93A A41 5r green (C) 29.00 8.00
*Nos. O92-O93A (3)* 48.75 11.00

**Nos. 459-468, 470-475 Overprinted Type "d" in Carmine or Black**

**1979-84**
O94 A224 2p dark green .25 *.30*
O95 A224 3p black .25 *.30*
O96 A224 5p violet blue .25 *.30*
O97 A225 10p grnsh blue .25 *.30*
O98 A225 20p yel grn ('81) .25 .25
O99 A225 25p rose car & grn ('81) .25 .25
O100 A225 40p car & bl .45 .25
O101 A225 50p bl grn & vio .25 .25
O102 A225 60p black 1.75 .25
O103 A225 75p dp orange 1.75 .25
O105 A225a 1r olive ('81) 4.00 .25
O106 A225a 1.50r dp orange .25 *.30*
O107 A225a 2r car rose .25 .25
O108 A225a 3r indigo ('81) .30 .30
O109 A225a 4r black ('84) 3.50 .50
O110 A225a 5r dk brn ('84) 3.50 .50
*Nos. O94-O110 (16)* 17.50 4.80

**Types A237-A239 Inscribed "SERVICE POSTAGE"**

No. O111

No. O115

No. O117

**1980 Litho. *Perf. 12x11½, 11½x12***
O111 A237 10p dk grn & yel org 1.40 .25
O112 A237 15p dk grn & ap grn 1.40 .25
O113 A237 25p dp vio & rose car .25 *1.00*
O114 A237 35p rose pink & brt yel grn .25 *7.50*
O115 A238 40p red & lt brn 1.40 .25
O116 A239 50p olive & vio bl .25 *.60*
O117 A239 80p blk & yel grn .40 *1.50*
*Nos. O111-O117 (7)* 5.35 *11.35*

Issued: 10p, 15p, 40p, 1/15; others, 3/10.

**Nos. 613-614, 616-620 Ovptd. "SERVICE" in Red**

**1984-87 Litho. *Perf. 11***
O118 A289 5p Kot Diji .25 .60
O119 A289 10p Rohtas .25 .25
O120 A289 20p Attock Fort .30 .40
O121 A289 50p Hyderabad .40 .40
O122 A289 60p Lahore ('86) .45 *.50*
O123 A289 70p Sibi .50 *.70*
O124 A289 80p Ranikot .55 *.70*
*Nos. O118-O124 (7)* 2.70 3.55

Issued: 10p, 9/25; 80p, 8/3/87.

**No. 712 Ovptd. "SERVICE"**

**Litho. & Engr.**

**1989, Dec. 24 *Perf. 13***
O124A A357 1r multicolored *5.00 5.00*

National Assembly, Islamabad — O1

**Wmk. 351**

**1991-99 Litho. *Perf. 13½***
O125 O1 1r green & red .25 .25
O126 O1 2r rose car & red .25 .25
O127 O1 3r ultra & red .35 .25
O128 O1 4r red brown & red .45 .25
O129 O1 5r rose lilac & red .50 .25
O130 O1 10r brown & red 1.25 .40
*Nos. O125-O130 (6)* 3.05 1.65

Issued: 10r, 2/6/99; others, 4/12/91.

**1999 Unwmk.**
O131 O1 2r rose car & red .40 .25

**National Assembly Type of 1991-99**

***Perf. 13¼x13½***

**2012 ? Litho. Wmk. 351**
O132 O1 8r claret & red .25 .25

## BAHAWALPUR

LOCATION — A State of Pakistan.
AREA — 17,494 sq. mi.
POP. — 1,341,209 (1941)
CAPITAL — Bahawalpur

Bahawalpur was an Indian princely state that was autonomous from Aug. 15-Oct. 3, 1947, when it united with Pakistan. These stamps had franking power solely within Bahawalpur.

Used values are for c-t-o or favor cancels.

India George VI stamps of 1937-40 and 1941-43 were overprinted for use in Bahawalpur during the brief period of that state's independence, following the creation of the separate dominions of India and Pakistan on Aug. 15, 1947. Stamps of Bahawalpur were replaced by stamps of Pakistan for external mail when the state united with Pakistan on Oct. 3, 1947. They continued to be used on internal mail until 1953.

**Stamps of India Used in Bahawalpur**

Overprinted in Red or Black

**1947, Aug. 15**
A1 A83 3p slate (R) 30.00
A2 A83 ½a rose vio 30.00
A3 A83 9p light grn (R) 30.00
A4 A83 1a car rose 30.00
A5 A84 1½a dark pur (R) 30.00
A6 A84 2a scarlet 30.00
a. Double overprint 3,500.
A7 A84 3a violet (R) 30.00
A8 A84 3½a ultramarine (R) 30.00
A9 A85 4a chocolate 30.00
A10 A85 6a peacock bl (R) 30.00
a. Double overprint 3,500.
A11 A85 8a blue vio (R) 30.00
A12 A85 12a carm lake 30.00
A13 A81 14a rose vio 75.00
A14 A82 1r brn & slate 35.00
a. Double overprint, one albino 400.00
A15 A82 2r dk brn & dk vio (R) 2,250.
A16 A82 5r dp ultra & dk grn (R) 2,250.
A17 A82 10r rose car & dk vio 2,250.

**Catalgoue values for unused stamps in this section, from this point to the end of the section are for Never Hinged items.**

Amir Muhammad Bahawal Khan I Abbasi — A1

***Perf. 12½x12***

**1947, Dec. 1 Wmk. 274 Engr.**
1 A1 ½a brt car rose & blk 4.00 *8.00*

Bicentenary of the ruling family.

Nawab Sadiq Muhammad Khan V Abbasi Bahadur — A2

Tombs of the Amirs — A3

Mosque, Sadiq Garh — A4

Fort Dirawar A5

Nur-Mahal Palace — A6

Palace, Sadiq Garh — A7

Nawab Sadiq Muhammad Khan V Abbasi Bahadur — A8

A9

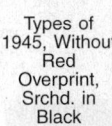

***Perf. 12½ (A2), 12x12½ (A3, A5, A6, A7), 12½x12 (A4, A8), 13x13½ (A9)***

**1948, Apr. 1 Engr. Wmk. 274**

| | | | | |
|---|---|---|---|---|
| **2** | A2 | 3p dp blue & blk | 2.00 | *11.00* |
| **3** | A2 | ½a lake & blk | 2.00 | *11.00* |
| **4** | A2 | 9p dk green & blk | 2.00 | *11.00* |
| **5** | A2 | 1a dp car & blk | 2.00 | *11.00* |
| **6** | A2 | 1½a violet & blk | 3.00 | *11.00* |
| **7** | A3 | 2a car & dp grn | 3.00 | *11.00* |
| **8** | A4 | 4a brn & org red | 3.00 | *11.00* |
| **9** | A5 | 6a dp bl & vio brn | 3.50 | *11.00* |
| **10** | A6 | 8a brt pur & car | 3.75 | *11.00* |
| **11** | A7 | 12a dp car & dk bl grn | 4.50 | *11.00* |
| **12** | A8 | 1r chocolate & vio | 25.00 | *35.00* |
| **13** | A8 | 2r dp mag & dk grn | 50.00 | *45.00* |
| **14** | A8 | 5r purple & black | 50.00 | *55.00* |
| **15** | A9 | 10r black & car | 45.00 | *65.00* |
| | | *Nos. 2-15 (14)* | 198.75 | *310.00* |

See #18-21. For overprints see #O17-O24.

Soldiers of 1848 and 1948 — A10

**1948, Oct. 15 Engr. *Perf. 11½***

| | | | | |
|---|---|---|---|---|
| **16** | A10 | 1½a dp car & blk | 1.75 | *8.00* |

Centenary of the Multan Campaign.

Amir Khan V and Mohammed Ali Jinnah — A11

**1948, Oct. 3 *Perf. 13x12½***

| | | | | |
|---|---|---|---|---|
| **17** | A11 | 1½a grn & car rose | 1.50 | *5.25* |

1st anniv. of the union of Bahawalpur with Pakistan.

**Types of 1948**

**1948 *Perf. 12x11½***

| | | | | |
|---|---|---|---|---|
| **18** | A8 | 1r orange & dp grn | 1.75 | *17.00* |
| **19** | A8 | 2r carmine & blk | 1.90 | *21.00* |
| **20** | A8 | 5r ultra & red brn | 2.25 | *37.50* |

***Perf. 13½***

| | | | | |
|---|---|---|---|---|
| **21** | A9 | 10r green & red brn | 2.75 | *50.00* |
| | | *Nos. 18-21 (4)* | 8.65 | *125.50* |

Panjnad Weir — A12

**1949, Mar. 3 *Perf. 14***

| | | | | |
|---|---|---|---|---|
| **22** | A12 | 3p shown | .25 | *8.00* |
| **23** | A12 | ½a Wheat | .25 | *8.00* |
| **24** | A12 | 9p Cotton | .25 | *8.00* |
| **25** | A12 | 1a Sahiwal Bull | .25 | *8.00* |
| | | *Nos. 22-25 (4)* | 1.00 | *32.00* |

25th anniv. of the acquisition of full ruling powers by Amir Khan V.

UPU Monument, Bern — A13

**1949, Oct. 10 *Perf. 13***

**Center in Black**

| | | | | |
|---|---|---|---|---|
| **26** | A13 | 9p green | .25 | *3.00* |
| **27** | A13 | 1a red violet | .25 | *3.00* |
| **28** | A13 | 1½a brown orange | .25 | *3.00* |
| **29** | A13 | 2½a blue | .25 | *3.00* |
| | | *Nos. 26-29 (4)* | 1.00 | *12.00* |

UPU, 75th anniv. Exist perf 17½x17; value, each $2. Exist imperf.

For overprints see Nos. O25-O28.

---

## OFFICIAL STAMPS

Two printings of Nos. O1-O10 exist. The first printing has brownish, streaky gum, and the second printing has clear, even gum.

Panjnad Weir — O1

Camel and Colt — O2

Antelopes O3

Pelicans O4

Juma Masjid Palace, Fort Derawar O5

Temple at Pattan Munara O6

**Red Overprint**

**Wmk. 274**

**1945, Jan. 1 Engr. *Perf. 14***

| | | | | |
|---|---|---|---|---|
| **O1** | O1 | ½a brt grn & blk | 4.50 | *12.50* |
| **O2** | O2 | 1a carmine & blk | 5.75 | *12.50* |
| **O3** | O3 | 2a violet & blk | 5.00 | *12.50* |
| **O4** | O4 | 4a olive & blk | 12.50 | *16.00* |
| **O5** | O5 | 8a brown & blk | 22.00 | 20.00 |
| **O6** | O6 | 1r orange & blk | 22.00 | 20.00 |
| | | *Nos. O1-O6 (6)* | 71.75 | *93.50* |

For types overprinted see Nos. O7-O9, O11-O13.

Types of 1945, Without Red Overprint, Srchd. in Black

**1945 Unwmk.**

| | | | | |
|---|---|---|---|---|
| **O7** | O5 | ½a on 8a lake & blk | *10.00* | *10.00* |
| **O8** | O6 | 1½a on 1r org & blk | 35.00 | *10.00* |
| **O9** | O1 | 1½a on 2r ultra & blk | 200.00 | 20.00 |
| | | *Nos. O7-O9 (3)* | 245.00 | 40.00 |

Camels — O7

**1945, Mar. 10 Red Overprint**

| | | | | |
|---|---|---|---|---|
| **O10** | O7 | 1a brown & black | 80.00 | *75.00* |

Types of 1945, Without Red Overprint, Ovptd. in Black

**1945**

| | | | | |
|---|---|---|---|---|
| **O11** | O1 | ½a carmine & black | 1.75 | *7.00* |
| **O12** | O2 | 1a carmine & black | 3.00 | *7.00* |
| **O13** | O3 | 2a orange & black | 5.25 | *7.00* |
| | | *Nos. O11-O13 (3)* | 10.00 | *21.00* |

Nawab Sadiq Muhammad Khan V Abbasi Bahadur — O8

**1945**

| | | | | |
|---|---|---|---|---|
| **O14** | O8 | 3p dp blue & blk | 4.50 | *8.00* |
| **O15** | O8 | 1½a dp violet & blk | 27.50 | 17.00 |

Flags of Allied Nations O9

**1946, May 1**

| | | | | |
|---|---|---|---|---|
| **O16** | O9 | 1½a emerald & gray | 5.50 | *7.00* |

Victory of Allied Nations in World War II.

Stamps of 1948 Overprinted in Carmine or Black

***Perf. 12½, 12½x12, 12x11½, 13½***

**1948 Wmk. 274**

| | | | | |
|---|---|---|---|---|
| **O17** | A2 | 3p dp bl & blk (C) | 1.00 | *15.00* |
| **O18** | A2 | 1a dp carmine & blk | 1.00 | *15.00* |
| **O19** | A3 | 2a car & dp grn | 1.00 | *15.00* |
| **O20** | A4 | 4a brown & org red | 1.00 | *15.00* |
| **O21** | A8 | 1r org & dp grn (C) | 1.00 | *15.00* |
| **O22** | A8 | 2r car & blk (C) | 1.00 | *15.00* |
| **O23** | A8 | 5r ultra & red brn (C) | 1.00 | *15.00* |
| **O24** | A9 | 10r grn & red brn (C) | 1.00 | *15.00* |
| | | *Nos. O17-O24 (8)* | 8.00 | *120.00* |

Same Ovpt. in Carmine on #26-29

**1949 Center in Black *Perf. 13, 18***

| | | | | |
|---|---|---|---|---|
| **O25** | A13 | 9p green | .25 | *7.50* |
| **O26** | A13 | 1a red violet | .25 | *7.50* |
| **O27** | A13 | 1½a brown orange | .25 | *7.50* |
| **O28** | A13 | 2½a blue | .25 | *7.50* |
| | | *Nos. O25-O28 (4)* | 1.00 | *30.00* |

75th anniv. of the UPU. Exist perf 17½x17; value, each *$10*. Exist imperf.

# PALAU

pə-'lau

LOCATION — Group of 100 islands in the West Pacific Ocean about 1,000 miles southeast of Manila
AREA — 179 sq. mi.
POP. — 18,467 (1999 est.)
CAPITAL — Melekeok

Palau, the western section of the Caroline Islands (Micronesia), was part of the US Trust Territory of the Pacific, established in 1947. By agreement with the USPS, the republic began issuing its own stamps in 1984, with the USPS continuing to carry the mail to and from the islands.

On Jan. 10, 1986 Palau became a Federation as a Sovereign State in Compact of Free Association with the US.

100 Cents = 1 Dollar

**Catalogue values for all unused stamps in this country are for Never Hinged items.**

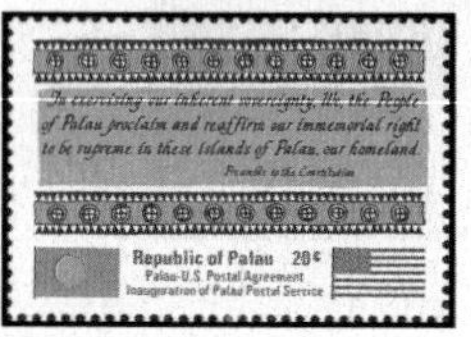

Inauguration of Postal Service — A1

**1983, Mar. 10 Litho. *Perf. 14***

1 A1 20c Constitution preamble .55 .55
2 A1 20c Hunters .55 .55
3 A1 20c Fish .55 .55
4 A1 20c Preamble, diff. .55 .55
*a.* Block of 4, #1-4 2.75 2.75

Palau Fruit Dove — A2

**1983, May 16 *Perf. 15***

5 A2 20c shown .45 .45
6 A2 20c Palau morningbird .45 .45
7 A2 20c Giant white-eye .45 .45
8 A2 20c Palau fantail .45 .45
*a.* Block of 4, #5-8 2.50 2.50

Sea Fan — A3

3c, Map cowrie. 5c, Jellyfish. 10c, Hawksbill turtle. 13c, Giant Clam. 20c, Parrotfish. 28c, Chambered Nautilus. 30c, Dappled sea cucumber. 37c, Sea Urchin. 50c, Starfish. $1, Squid. $2, Dugong. $5, Pink sponge.

**1983-84 Litho. *Perf. 13½x14***

9 A3 1c shown .25 .25
10 A3 3c multicolored .25 .25
11 A3 5c multicolored .25 .25
12 A3 10c multicolored .25 .25
13 A3 13c multicolored .25 .25
*a.* Booklet pane of 10 *10.00* —
*b.* Bklt. pane of 10 (5 #13, 5 #14) *12.00* —
14 A3 20c multicolored .35 .35
*b.* Booklet pane of 10 *11.00* —
15 A3 28c multicolored .45 .45
16 A3 30c multicolored .50 .50
17 A3 37c multicolored .55 .55
18 A3 50c multicolored .80 .80
19 A3 $1 multicolored 1.60 1.60

***Perf. 15x14***

20 A3 $2 multicolored 4.25 4.25
21 A3 $5 multicolored 10.50 10.50
*Nos. 9-21 (13)* 20.25 20.25

See Nos. 75-85.

Humpback Whale, World Wildlife Emblem — A4

**1983, Sept. 21 *Perf. 14***

24 A4 20c shown 1.25 1.25
25 A4 20c Blue whale 1.25 1.25
26 A4 20c Fin whale 1.25 1.25
27 A4 20c Great sperm whale 1.25 1.25
*a.* Block of 4, #24-27 6.50 6.50

Christmas 1983 — A5

Paintings by Charlie Gibbons, 1971 — No. 28, First Child ceremony. No. 29, Spearfishing from Red Canoe. No. 30, Traditional feast at the Bai. No. 31, Taro gardening. No. 32, Spearfishing at New Moon.

**1983, Oct. Litho. *Perf. 14½***

28 A5 20c multicolored .50 .50
29 A5 20c multicolored .50 .50
30 A5 20c multicolored .50 .50
31 A5 20c multicolored .50 .50
32 A5 20c multicolored .50 .50
*a.* Strip of 5, #28-32 2.75 2.75

A6

Capt. Wilson's Voyage, Bicentennial — A7

No. 33, Capt. Henry Wilson. No. 34, Approaching Pelew. No. 35, Englishman's Camp on Ulong. No. 36, Prince Lee Boo. No. 37, King Abba Thulle. No. 38, Mooring in Koror. No. 39, Village scene of Pelew Islands. No. 40, Ludee.

**1983, Dec. 14 *Perf. 14x15***

33 A6 20c multicolored .45 .45
34 A7 20c multicolored .45 .45
35 A7 20c multicolored .45 .45
36 A6 20c multicolored .45 .45
37 A6 20c multicolored .45 .45
38 A7 20c multicolored .45 .45
39 A7 20c multicolored .45 .45
40 A6 20c multicolored .45 .45
*a.* Block or strip of 8, #33-40 5.00 5.00

Local Seashells — A8

Shell paintings (dorsal and ventral) by Deborah Dudley Max.

**1984, Mar. 15 Litho. *Perf. 14***

41 A8 20c Triton trumpet, d. .45 .45
42 A8 20c Horned helmet, d. .45 .45
43 A8 20c Giant clam, d. .45 .45
44 A8 20c Laciniate conch, d. .45 .45
45 A8 20c Royal cloak scallop, d. .45 .45
46 A8 20c Triton trumpet, v. .45 .45
47 A8 20c Horned helmet, v. .45 .45
48 A8 20c Giant clam, v. .45 .45
49 A8 20c Laciniate conch, v. .45 .45
50 A8 20c Royal cloak scallop, v. .45 .45
*a.* Block of 10, #41-50 5.50 5.50

Explorer Ships A9

**1984, June 19 Litho. *Perf. 14***

51 A9 40c Oroolong, 1783 .85 .85
52 A9 40c Duff, 1797 .85 .85
53 A9 40c Peiho, 1908 .85 .85
54 A9 40c Albatross, 1885 .85 .85
*a.* Block of 4, #51-54 4.25 4.25

UPU Congress.

Ausipex '84 — A10

Fishing Methods: No. 55, Throw spear fishing. No. 56, Kite fishing. No. 57, Underwater spear fishing. No. 58, Net fishing.

**1984, Sept. 6 Litho. *Perf. 14***

55 A10 20c multicolored .40 .40
56 A10 20c multicolored .40 .40
57 A10 20c multicolored .40 .40
58 A10 20c multicolored .40 .40
*a.* Block of 4, #55-58 2.25 2.25

Christmas Flowers — A11

No. 59, Mountain Apple. No. 60, Beach Morning Glory. No. 61, Turmeric. No. 62, Plumeria.

**1984, Nov. 28 Litho. *Perf. 14***

59 A11 20c multicolored .40 .40
60 A11 20c multicolored .40 .40
61 A11 20c multicolored .40 .40
62 A11 20c multicolored .40 .40
*a.* Block of 4, #59-62 2.00 2.00

Audubon Bicentenary — A12

**1985, Feb. 6 Litho. *Perf. 14***

63 A12 22c Shearwater chick .85 .85
64 A12 22c Shearwater's head .85 .85
65 A12 22c Shearwater in flight .85 .85
66 A12 22c Swimming .85 .85
*a.* Block of 4, #63-66 4.50 4.50
*Nos. 63-66,C5 (5)* 4.50 4.50

Canoes and Rafts — A13

**1985, Mar. 27 Litho.**

67 22c Cargo canoe .55 .55
68 22c War canoe .55 .55
69 22c Bamboo raft .55 .55
70 22c Racing/sailing canoe .55 .55
*a.* A13 Block of 4, #67-70 2.25 2.25

**Marine Life Type of 1983**

14c, Trumpet triton. 22c, Bumphead parrotfish. 25c, Soft coral, damsel fish. 33c, Sea anemone, clownfish. 39c, Green sea turtle. 44c, Pacific sailfish. $10, Spinner dolphins.

**1985, June 11 Litho. *Perf. 14½x14***

75 A3 14c multicolored .30 .30
*a.* Booklet pane of 10 *8.50* —
76 A3 22c multicolored .55 .55
*a.* Booklet pane of 10 *10.50* —
*b.* Booklet pane, 5 14c, 5 22c *12.00* —
77 A3 25c multicolored .60 .60
79 A3 33c multicolored .80 .80
80 A3 39c multicolored .95 .95
81 A3 44c multicolored 1.10 1.10

***Perf. 15x14***

85 A3 $10 multicolored 19.00 19.00
*Nos. 75-85 (7)* 23.30 23.30

A14

IYY emblem and children of all nationalities joined in a circle.

**1985, July 15 Litho. *Perf. 14***

86 A14 44c multicolored .85 .85
87 A14 44c multicolored .85 .85
88 A14 44c multicolored .85 .85
89 A14 44c multicolored .85 .85
*a.* Block of 4, #86-89 3.75 3.75

No. 89a has a continuous design.

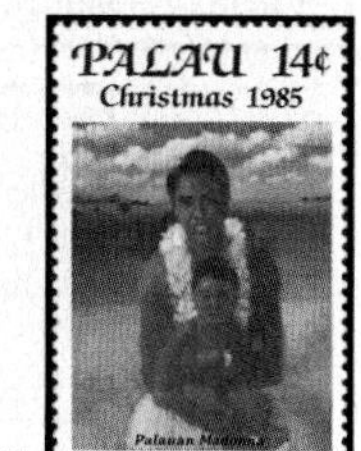

A15

Christmas: Island mothers and children.

**1985, Oct. 21 Litho. *Perf. 14***

90 A15 14c multicolored .35 .35
91 A15 22c multicolored .50 .50
92 A15 33c multicolored .80 .80
93 A15 44c multicolored 1.10 1.10
*Nos. 90-93 (4)* 2.75 2.75

**Souvenir Sheet**

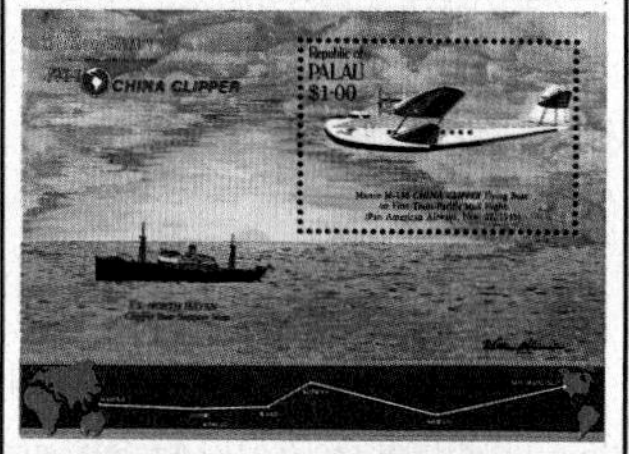

Pan American Airways Martin M-130 China Clipper — A16

**1985, Nov. 21 Litho. *Perf. 14***

94 A16 $1 multicolored 2.50 2.50

1st Trans-Pacific Mail Flight, Nov. 22, 1935. See Nos. C10-C13.

Return of Halley's Comet A17

Fictitious local sightings — No. 95, Kaeb canoe, 1758. No. 96, U.S.S. Vincennes, 1835. No. 97, S.M.S. Scharnhorst, 1910. No. 98, Yacht, 1986.

**1985, Dec. 21 Litho. *Perf. 14***

| | | | |
|---|---|---|---|
| **95** | A17 44c multicolored | .80 | .80 |
| **96** | A17 44c multicolored | .80 | .80 |
| **97** | A17 44c multicolored | .80 | .80 |
| **98** | A17 44c multicolored | .80 | .80 |
| *a.* | Block of 4, #95-98 | 4.00 | 4.00 |

Songbirds — A18

No. 99, Mangrove flycatcher. No. 100, Cardinal honeyeater. No. 101, Blue-faced parrotfinch. No. 102, Dusky and bridled white-eyes.

**1986, Feb. 24 Litho. *Perf. 14***

| | | | |
|---|---|---|---|
| **99** | A18 44c multicolored | .85 | .85 |
| **100** | A18 44c multicolored | .85 | .85 |
| **101** | A18 44c multicolored | .85 | .85 |
| **102** | A18 44c multicolored | .85 | .85 |
| *a.* | Block of 4, #99-102 | 4.00 | 4.00 |

World of Sea and Reef — A19

Designs: a, Spear fisherman. b, Native raft. c, Sailing canoes. d, Rock islands, sailfish. e, Inter-island boat, flying fish. f, Bonefish. g, Common jack. h, Mackerel. i, Sailfish. j, Barracuda. k, Triggerfish. l, Dolphinfish. m, Spear fisherman, grouper. n, Manta ray. o, Marlin. p, Parrotfish. q, Wrasse. r, Red snapper. s, Herring. t, Dugong. u, Surgeonfish. v, Leopard ray. w, Hawksbill turtle. x, Needlefish. y, Tuna. z, Octopus. aa, Clownfish. ab, Squid. ac, Grouper. ad, Moorish idol. ae, Queen conch, starfish. af, Squirrelfish. ag, Starfish, sting ray. ah, Lion fish. ai, Angel fish. aj, Butterfly fish. ak, Spiny lobster. al, Mangrove crab. am, Tridacna. an, Moray eel.

**1986, May 22 Litho. *Perf. 15x14***

| | | | |
|---|---|---|---|
| **103** | Sheet of 40 | *37.50* | |
| ***a.-an.*** | A19 14c any single | .75 | .50 |

AMERIPEX '86, Chicago, May 22-June 1

See Nos. 854, 1326.

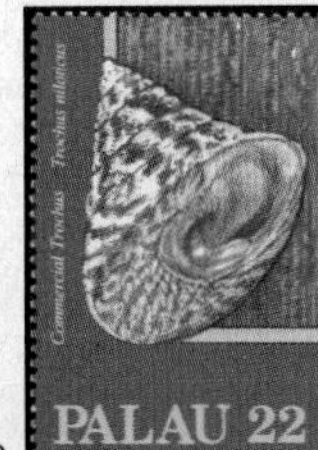

Seashells — A20

**1986, Aug. 1 Litho. *Perf. 14***

| | | | |
|---|---|---|---|
| **104** | A20 22c Commercial trochus | .55 | .55 |
| **105** | A20 22c Marble cone | .55 | .55 |
| **106** | A20 22c Fluted giant clam | .55 | .55 |
| **107** | A20 22c Bullmouth helmet | .55 | .55 |
| **108** | A20 22c Golden cowrie | .55 | .55 |
| *a.* | Strip of 5, #104-108 | 3.25 | 3.25 |

See Nos. 150-154, 191-195, 212-216.

Intl. Peace Year — A21

**1986, Sept. 19 Litho.**

| | | | |
|---|---|---|---|
| **109** | 22c Soldier's helmet | .75 | .75 |
| **110** | 22c Plane wreckage | .75 | .75 |
| **111** | 22c Woman playing guitar | .75 | .75 |
| **112** | 22c Airai vista | .75 | .75 |
| *a.* | A21 Block of 4, #109-112 | 3.50 | 3.50 |
| | *Nos. 109-112,C17 (5)* | 4.00 | 4.00 |

Reptiles A22

**1986, Oct. 28 Litho. *Perf. 14***

| | | | |
|---|---|---|---|
| **113** | A22 22c Gecko | .65 | .65 |
| **114** | A22 22c Emerald tree skink | .65 | .65 |
| **115** | A22 22c Estuarine crocodile | .65 | .65 |
| **116** | A22 22c Leatherback turtle | .65 | .65 |
| *a.* | Block of 4, #113-116 | 2.75 | 2.75 |

Christmas — A23

Joy to the World, carol by Isaac Watts and Handel: No. 117, Girl playing guitar, boys, goat. No. 118, Girl carrying bouquet, boys singing. No. 119, Palauan mother and child. No. 120, Children, baskets of fruit. No. 121, Girl, fairy tern. Nos. 117-121 printed in a continuous design.

**1986, Nov. 26 Litho.**

| | | | |
|---|---|---|---|
| **117** | A23 22c multicolored | .40 | .40 |
| **118** | A23 22c multicolored | .40 | .40 |
| **119** | A23 22c multicolored | .40 | .40 |
| **120** | A23 22c multicolored | .40 | .40 |
| **121** | A23 22c multicolored | .40 | .40 |
| *a.* | Strip of 5, #117-121 | 2.50 | 2.50 |

Butterflies — A23a

No. 121B, Tangadik, soursop. No. 121C, Dira amartal, sweet orange. No. 121D, Ilhuochel, swamp cabbage. No. 121E, Bauosech, fig.

**1987, Jan. 5 Litho. *Perf. 14***

| | | | |
|---|---|---|---|
| **121B** | A23a 44c multicolored | 1.00 | .90 |
| **121C** | A23a 44c multicolored | 1.00 | .90 |
| **121D** | A23a 44c multicolored | 1.00 | .90 |
| **121E** | A23a 44c multicolored | 1.00 | .90 |
| *f.* | Block of 4, #121B-121E | 4.50 | 4.50 |

See Nos. 183-186.

Fruit Bats — A24

**1987, Feb. 23 Litho.**

| | | | |
|---|---|---|---|
| **122** | 44c In flight | .85 | .85 |
| **123** | 44c Hanging | .85 | .85 |
| **124** | 44c Eating | .85 | .85 |
| **125** | 44c Head | .85 | .85 |
| *a.* | A24 Block of 4, #122-125 | 4.00 | 4.00 |

Indigenous Flowers — A25

1c, Ixora casei. 3c, Lumnitzera littorea. 5c, Sonneratia alba. 10c, Tristellateria australasiae. 14c, Bikkia palauensis. 15c, Limnophila aromatica. 22c, Bruguiera gymnorhiza. 25c, Fagraea ksid. 36c, Ophiorrhiza palauensis. 39c, Cerbera manghas. 44c, Sandera indica. 45c, Maesa canfieldiae. 50c, Dolichandrone spathacea. $1, Barringtonia racemosa. $2, Nepenthes mirabilis. $5, Dendrobium palawense. $10, Bouquet.

**1987-88 Litho. *Perf. 14***

| | | | |
|---|---|---|---|
| **126** | A25 1c multicolored | .25 | .25 |
| **127** | A25 3c multicolored | .25 | .25 |
| **128** | A25 5c multicolored | .25 | .25 |
| **129** | A25 10c multicolored | .25 | .25 |
| **130** | A25 14c multicolored | .25 | .25 |
| *a.* | Booklet pane of 10 | 4.00 | — |
| **131** | A25 15c multi ('88) | .25 | .25 |
| *a.* | Booklet pane of 10 ('88) | 3.25 | — |
| **132** | A25 22c multicolored | .40 | .40 |
| *a.* | Booklet pane of 10 | 6.50 | — |
| *b.* | Booklet pane, 5 each 14c, 22c | 6.50 | — |
| **133** | A25 25c multi ('88) | .50 | .50 |
| *a.* | Booklet pane of 10 ('88) | 5.00 | — |
| *b.* | Booklet pane, 5 each 15c, 25c ('88) | 5.00 | — |
| **134** | A25 36c multi ('88) | .65 | .65 |
| **135** | A25 39c multicolored | .70 | .70 |
| **136** | A25 44c multicolored | .85 | .85 |
| **137** | A25 45c multi ('88) | .90 | .90 |
| **138** | A25 50c multicolored | 1.00 | 1.00 |
| **139** | A25 $1 multicolored | 2.00 | 2.00 |
| **140** | A25 $2 multicolored | 4.25 | 4.00 |
| **141** | A25 $5 multicolored | 10.00 | 9.50 |

**Size: 49x28mm**

| | | | |
|---|---|---|---|
| **142** | A25 $10 multi ('88) | 17.00 | 16.00 |
| | *Nos. 126-142 (17)* | 39.75 | 38.00 |

Issued: 3/12; $10, 3/17; 15c, 25c, 36c, 45c, 7/1; #131a, 133a-133b, 7/5.

CAPEX '87 — A26

**1987, June 15 Litho. *Perf. 14***

| | | | |
|---|---|---|---|
| **146** | 22c Babeldaob Is. | .50 | .50 |
| **147** | 22c Floating Garden Isls. | .50 | .50 |
| **148** | 22c Rock Is. | .50 | .50 |
| **149** | 22c Koror | .50 | .50 |
| *a.* | A26 Block of 4, #146-149 | 2.25 | 2.25 |

**Seashells Type of 1986**

**1987, Aug. 25 Litho. *Perf. 14***

| | | | |
|---|---|---|---|
| **150** | A20 22c Black-striped triton | .55 | .55 |
| **151** | A20 22c Tapestry turban | .55 | .55 |
| **152** | A20 22c Adusta murex | .55 | .55 |
| **153** | A20 22c Little fox miter | .55 | .55 |
| **154** | A20 22c Cardinal miter | .55 | .55 |
| *a.* | Strip of 5, #150-154 | 3.00 | 3.00 |

US Constitution Bicentennial A27

Excerpts from Articles of the Palau and US Constitutions and Seals: No. 155, Art. VIII, Sec. 1, Palau. No. 156, Presidential seals. No. 157, Art. II, Sec. 1, US. No. 158, Art. IX, Sec. 1, Palau. No. 159, Legislative seals. No. 160, Art. I, Sec. 1, US. No. 161, Art X, Sec. 1, Palau. No. 162, Supreme Court seals. No. 163, Art. III, Sec. 1, US.

**1987, Sept. 17 Litho. *Perf. 14***

| | | | |
|---|---|---|---|
| **155** | A27 14c multicolored | .25 | .25 |
| **156** | A27 14c multicolored | .25 | .25 |
| **157** | A27 14c multicolored | .25 | .25 |
| *a.* | Triptych + label, #155-157 | .80 | .80 |
| **158** | A27 22c multicolored | .40 | .40 |
| **159** | A27 22c multicolored | .40 | .40 |
| **160** | A27 22c multicolored | .40 | .40 |
| *a.* | Triptych + label, #158-160 | 1.50 | 1.50 |
| **161** | A27 44c multicolored | .75 | .75 |
| **162** | A27 44c multicolored | .75 | .75 |
| **163** | A27 44c multicolored | .75 | .75 |
| *a.* | Triptych + label, #161-163 | 3.00 | 3.00 |
| | *Nos. 155-163 (9)* | 4.20 | 4.20 |

Nos. 156, 159 and 162 are each 28x42mm. Labels picture national flags.

Japanese Links to Palau — A28

Japanese stamps, period cancellations and installations: 14c, No. 257 and 1937 Datsun sedan used as mobile post office, near Ngerchelechuus Mountain. 22c, No. 347 and phosphate mine at Angaur. 33c, No. B1 and Japan Airways DC-2 over stone monuments at Badrulchau. 44c, No. 201 and Japanese post office, Koror. $1, Aviator's Grave, Japanese Cemetary, Peleliu, vert.

**1987, Oct. 16 Litho. *Perf. 14x13½***

| | | | |
|---|---|---|---|
| **164** | A28 14c multicolored | .30 | .30 |
| **165** | A28 22c multicolored | .45 | .45 |
| **166** | A28 33c multicolored | .65 | .65 |
| **167** | A28 44c multicolored | .85 | .85 |
| | *Nos. 164-167 (4)* | 2.25 | 2.25 |

**Souvenir Sheet**

***Perf. 13½x14***

| | | | |
|---|---|---|---|
| **168** | A28 $1 multicolored | 2.25 | 2.25 |

Christmas — A30

Verses from carol "I Saw Three Ships," Biblical characters, landscape and Palauans in outrigger canoes.

**1987, Nov. 24 Litho. *Perf. 14***

| | | | |
|---|---|---|---|
| **173** | A30 22c I saw... | .50 | .50 |
| **174** | A30 22c And what was... | .50 | .50 |
| **175** | A30 22c 'Twas Joseph... | .50 | .50 |
| **176** | A30 22c Saint Michael... | .50 | .50 |
| **177** | A30 22c And all the bells... | .50 | .50 |
| *a.* | Strip of 5, #173-177 | 3.00 | 3.00 |

Symbiotic Marine Species — A31

#178, Snapping shrimp, goby. #179, Mauve vase sponge, sponge crab. #180, Pope's damselfish, cleaner wrasse. #181, Clown anemone fish, sea anemone. #182, Four-color nudibranch, banded coral shrimp.

**1987, Dec. 15**

| | | | | |
|---|---|---|---|---|
| **178** | A31 22c multicolored | | .55 | .55 |
| **179** | A31 22c multicolored | | .55 | .55 |
| **180** | A31 22c multicolored | | .55 | .55 |
| **181** | A31 22c multicolored | | .55 | .55 |
| **182** | A31 22c multicolored | | .55 | .55 |
| *a.* | Strip of 5, #178-182 | | 3.25 | 3.25 |

### Butterflies and Flowers Type of 1987

Designs: No. 183, Dannaus plexippus, Tournefotia argentia. No. 184, Papilio machaon, Citrus reticulata. No. 185, Captopsilia, Crataeva speciosa. No. 186, Colias philodice, Crataeva speciosa.

**1988, Jan. 25**

| | | | |
|---|---|---|---|
| **183** | A23a 44c multicolored | .75 | .75 |
| **184** | A23a 44c multicolored | .75 | .75 |
| **185** | A23a 44c multicolored | .75 | .75 |
| **186** | A23a 44c multicolored | .75 | .75 |
| *a.* | Block of 4, #183-186 | 3.50 | 3.50 |

Ground-dwelling Birds — A32

**1988, Feb. 29 Litho. *Perf. 14***

| | | | |
|---|---|---|---|
| **187** | A32 44c Whimbrel | .75 | .75 |
| **188** | A32 44c Yellow bittern | .75 | .75 |
| **189** | A32 44c Rufous night-heron | .75 | .75 |
| **190** | A32 44c Banded rail | .75 | .75 |
| *a.* | Block of 4, #187-190 | 3.50 | 3.50 |

### Seashells Type of 1986

**1988, May 11 Litho. *Perf. 14***

| | | | |
|---|---|---|---|
| **191** | A20 25c Striped engina | .55 | .55 |
| **192** | A20 25c Ivory cone | .55 | .55 |
| **193** | A20 25c Plaited miter | .55 | .55 |
| **194** | A20 25c Episcopal miter | .55 | .55 |
| **195** | A20 25c Isabelle cowrie | .55 | .55 |
| *a.* | Strip of 5, #191-195 | 4.00 | 4.00 |

Souvenir Sheet

Postal Independence, 5th Anniv. — A33

FINLANDIA '88: a, Kaep (pre-European outrigger sailboat). b, Spanish colonial cruiser. c, German colonial cruiser SMS Cormoran, c. 1885. d, Japanese mailbox, WWII machine gun, Koror Museum. e, US Trust Territory ship, Malakal Harbor. f, Koror post office.

**1988, June 8 Litho. *Perf. 14***

| | | | |
|---|---|---|---|
| **196** | A33 Sheet of 6 | 3.00 | 3.00 |
| *a.-f.* | 25c multicolored | .45 | .45 |

Souvenir Sheet

US Possessions Phil. Soc., 10th Anniv. — A34

PRAGA '88: a, "Collect Palau Stamps," original artwork for No. 196f and head of a man. b, Soc. emblem. c, Nos. 1-4. d, China Clipper original artwork and covers. e, Man and boy studying covers. f, Girl at show cancel booth.

**1988, Aug. 26 Litho. *Perf. 14***

| | | | |
|---|---|---|---|
| **197** | A34 Sheet of 6 | 5.00 | 5.00 |
| *a.-f.* | 45c any single | .80 | .80 |

Christmas — A35

*Hark! The Herald Angels Sing:* No. 198, Angels playing the violin, singing and sitting. No. 199, 3 angels and 3 children. No. 200, Nativity. No. 201, 2 angels, birds. No. 202, 3 children and 2 angels playing horns. Se-tenant in a continuous design.

**1988, Nov. 7 Litho. *Perf. 14***

| | | | |
|---|---|---|---|
| **198** | A35 25c multicolored | .50 | .50 |
| **199** | A35 25c multicolored | .50 | .50 |
| **200** | A35 25c multicolored | .50 | .50 |
| **201** | A35 25c multicolored | .50 | .50 |
| **202** | A35 25c multicolored | .50 | .50 |
| *a.* | Strip of 5, #199-202 | 2.75 | 2.75 |

Miniature Sheet

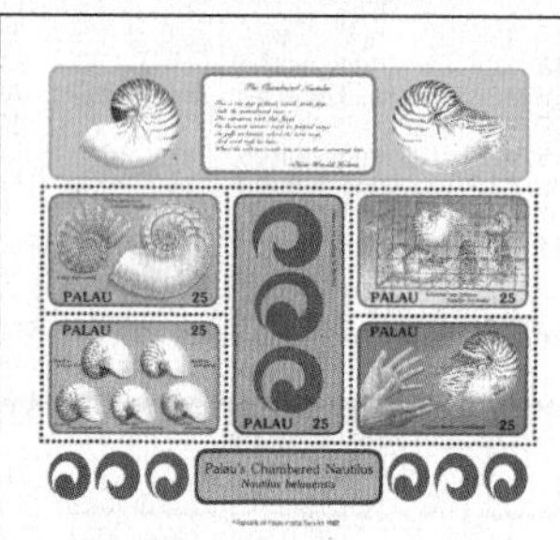

Chambered Nautilus — A36

Designs: a, Fossil and cross section. b, Palauan *bai* symbols for the nautilus. c, Specimens trapped for scientific study. d, *Nautilus belauensis, pompilius, macromphalus, stenomphalus* and *scrobiculatus.* e, Release of a tagged nautilus.

**1988, Dec. 23 Litho. *Perf. 14***

| | | | |
|---|---|---|---|
| **203** | A36 Sheet of 5 | 3.00 | 3.00 |
| *a.-e.* | 25c multicolored | .60 | .60 |

Endangered Birds of Palau — A37

No. 204, Nicobar pigeon. No. 205, Ground dove. No. 206, Micronesian megapode. No. 207, Owl.

**1989, Feb. 9 Litho. *Perf. 14***

| | | | |
|---|---|---|---|
| **204** | A37 45c multicolored | .85 | .85 |
| **205** | A37 45c multicolored | .85 | .85 |
| **206** | A37 45c multicolored | .85 | .85 |
| **207** | A37 45c multicolored | .85 | .85 |
| *a.* | Block of 4, #204-207 | 4.00 | 4.00 |

Exotic Mushrooms — A38

**1989, Mar. 16 Litho. *Perf. 14***

| | | | |
|---|---|---|---|
| **208** | A38 45c Gilled auricularia | .90 | .80 |
| **209** | A38 45c Rock mushroom | .90 | .80 |
| **210** | A38 45c Polyporous | .90 | .80 |
| **211** | A38 45c Veiled stinkhorn | .90 | .80 |
| *a.* | Block of 4, #208-211 | 4.00 | 4.00 |

### Seashells Type of 1986

No. 212, Robin redbreast triton. No. 213, Hebrew cone. No. 214, Tadpole triton. No. 215, Lettered cone. No. 216, Rugose miter.

**1989, Apr. 12 Litho. *Perf. 14x14½***

| | | | |
|---|---|---|---|
| **212** | A20 25c multicolored | .55 | .55 |
| **213** | A20 25c multicolored | .55 | .55 |
| **214** | A20 25c multicolored | .55 | .55 |
| **215** | A20 25c multicolored | .55 | .55 |
| **216** | A20 25c multicolored | .55 | .55 |
| *a.* | Strip of 5, #212-216 | 3.25 | 3.25 |

Souvenir Sheet

*A Little Bird, Amidst Chrysanthemums,* 1830s, by Hiroshige (1797-1858) — A39

**1989, May 17 Litho. *Perf. 14***

| | | | |
|---|---|---|---|
| **217** | A39 $1 multicolored | 2.25 | 2.25 |

Hirohito (1901-1989) and enthronement of Akihito as emperor of Japan.

Miniature Sheet

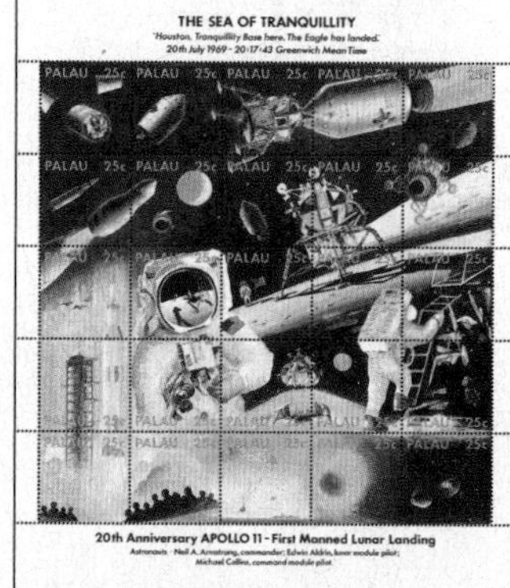

First Moon Landing, 20th Anniv. — A40

Apollo 11 mission: a, Third stage jettison. b, Lunar spacecraft. c, Module transposition *(Eagle).* d, *Columbia* module transposition (command module). e, *Columbia* module transposition (service module). f, Third stage burn. g, Vehicle entering orbit, Moon. h, *Columbia* and *Eagle.* i, *Eagle* on the Moon. j, *Eagle* in space. k, Three birds, Saturn V third stage, lunar spacecraft and escape tower. l, Astronaut's protective visor, pure oxygen system. m, Astronaut, American flag. n, Footsteps on lunar plain Sea of Tranquillity, pure oxygen system. o, Armstrong descending from *Eagle.* p, Mobile launch tower, Saturn V second stage. q, Space suit remote control unit and oxygen hoses. r, *Eagle* lift-off from Moon. s, Armstrong's first step on the Moon. t, Armstrong descending ladder, module transposition *(Eagle* and *Columbia).* u, Launch tower, spectators and Saturn V engines achieving thrust. v, Spectators, clouds of backwash. w, Parachute splashdown, U.S. Navy recovery ship and helicopter. x, Command module reentry. y, Jettison of service module prior to reentry.

**1989, July 20 Litho. *Perf. 14***

| | | | |
|---|---|---|---|
| **218** | A40 Sheet of 25 | 12.00 | 12.00 |
| *a.-y.* | 25c any single | .45 | .45 |

Buzz Aldrin Photographed on the Moon by Neil Armstrong — A41

**1989, July 20 *Perf. 13½x14***

| | | | |
|---|---|---|---|
| **219** | A41 $2.40 multicolored | 4.75 | 4.75 |

First Moon landing 20th anniv.

Literacy — A42

Imaginary characters and children reading: a, Youth astronaut. b, Boy riding dolphin. c, Cheshire cat in palm tree. d, Mother Goose. e, New York Yankee at bat. f, Girl reading. g, Boy reading. h, Mother reading to child. i, Girl holding flower and listening to story. j, Boy dressed in baseball uniform. Printed se-tenant in a continuous design.

**1989, Oct. 13 Litho. *Perf. 14***

| | | | |
|---|---|---|---|
| **220** | A42 Block of 10 | 4.75 | 4.75 |
| *a.-j.* | 25c any single | .40 | .40 |

No. 220 printed in sheets containing two blocks of ten with strip of 5 labels between. Inscribed labels contain book, butterflies and "Give Them / Books / Give Them / Wings." Value, sheet $15.

Miniature Sheet

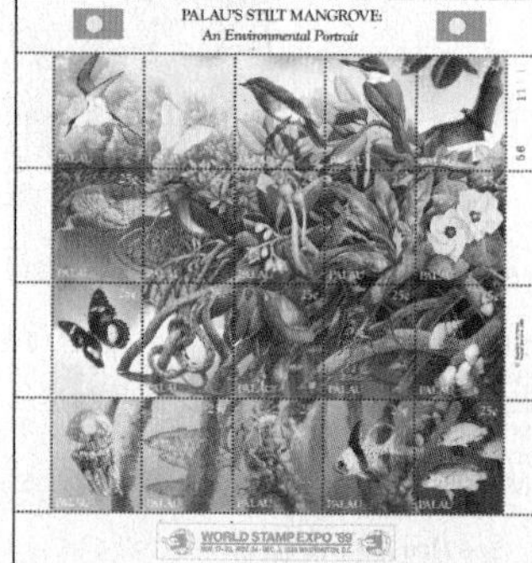

Stilt Mangrove Fauna — A43

World Stamp Expo '89: a, Bridled tern. b, Sulphur butterfly. c, Mangrove flycatcher. d, Collared kingfisher. e, Fruit bat. f, Estuarine crocodile. g, Rufous night-heron. h, Stilt mangrove. i, Bird's nest fern. j, Beach hibiscus tree. k, Common eggfly. l, Dog-faced water-snake. m, Jingle shell. n, Palau bark cricket. o, Periwinkle, mangrove oyster. p, Jellyfish. q, Striped mullet. r, Mussels, sea anemones, algae. s, Cardinalfish. t, Snapper.

**1989, Nov. 20 Litho. *Perf. 14½***
**221** A43 Block of 20 12.00 12.00
*a.-t.* 25c any single .55 .55

Christmas — A44

*Whence Comes this Rush of Wings?* a carol: No. 222, Dusky tern, Audubon's shearwater, angels, island. No. 223, Fruit pigeon, angel. No. 224, Madonna and Child, ground pigeons, fairy terns, rails, sandpipers. No. 225, Angel, blue-headed green finch, red flycatcher, honeyeater. No. 226, Angel, black-headed gulls. Printed se-tenant in a continuous design.

**1989, Dec. 18 Litho. *Perf. 14***
**222** A44 25c multicolored .55 .55
**223** A44 25c multicolored .55 .55
**224** A44 25c multicolored .55 .55
**225** A44 25c multicolored .55 .55
**226** A44 25c multicolored .55 .55
*a.* Strip of 5, #222-226 3.25 3.25

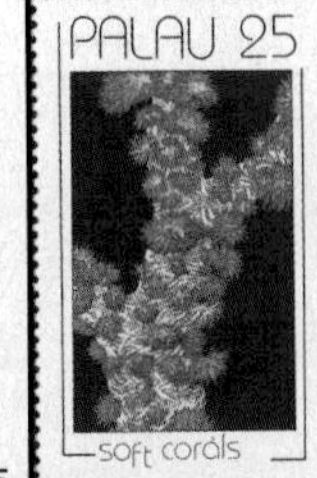


Soft Coral — A45

**1990, Jan. 3**
**227** A45 25c Pink coral .50 .50
**228** A45 25c Pink & violet coral .50 .50
**229** A45 25c Yellow coral .50 .50
**230** A45 25c Red coral .50 .50
*a.* Block of 4, #227-230 3.00 3.00

Birds of the Forest A46

**1990, Mar. 16**
**231** A46 45c Siberian rubythroat .85 .85
**232** A46 45c Palau bush-warbler .85 .85
**233** A46 45c Micronesian starling .85 .85
**234** A46 45c Cicadabird .85 .85
*a.* Block of 4, #231-234 4.00 4.00

Miniature Sheet

State Visit of Prince Lee Boo of Palau to England, 1784 — A47

Prince Lee Boo, Capt. Henry Wilson and: a, HMS *Victory* docked at Portsmouth. b, St. James's Palace, London. c, Rotherhithe Docks, London. d, Capt. Wilson's residence, Devon. e, Lunardi's Grand English Air Balloon. f, St. Paul's and the Thames. g, Lee Boo's tomb, St. Mary's Churchyard, Rotherhithe. h, St. Mary's Church. i, Memorial tablet, St. Mary's Church.

**1990, May 6 Litho. *Perf. 14***
**235** A47 Sheet of 9 4.50 4.50
*a.-i.* 25c any single .45 .45

Stamp World London '90.

Souvenir Sheet

Penny Black, 150th Anniv. — A48

**1990, May 6**
**236** A48 $1 Great Britain #1 2.00 2.00

Orchids — A49

No. 237, Corymborkis veratrifolia. No. 238, Malaxis setipes. No. 239, Dipodium freycinetianum. No. 240, Bulbophyllum micronesiacum. No. 241, Vanda teres and hookeriana.

**1990, June 7 *Perf. 14***
**237** A49 45c multicolored .90 .90
**238** A49 45c multicolored .90 .90
**239** A49 45c multicolored .90 .90
**240** A49 45c multicolored .90 .90
**241** A49 45c multicolored .90 .90
*a.* Strip of 5, #237-241 5.00 5.00

Butterflies and Flowers A50

No. 242, Wedelia strigulosa. No. 243, Erthrina variegata. No. 244, Clerodendrum inerme. No. 245, Vigna marina.

**1990, July 6 Litho. *Perf. 14***
**242** A50 45c multicolored .85 .85
**243** A50 45c multicolored .85 .85
**244** A50 45c multicolored .85 .85
**245** A50 45c multicolored .85 .85
*a.* Block of 4, #242-245 3.75 3.75

Miniature Sheet

Fairy Tern, Lesser Golden Plover, Sanderling A51

Lagoon life: b, Bidekill fisherman. c, Sailing yacht, insular halfbeaks. d, Palauan kaeps. e, White-tailed tropicbird. f, Spotted eagle ray. g, Great barracuda. h, Reef needlefish. i, Reef blacktip shark. j, Hawksbill turtle. k, Octopus. l, Batfish. m, Lionfish. n, Snowflake moray. o, Porcupine fish, sixfeeler threadfins. p, Blue sea star, regal angelfish, cleaner wrasse. q, Clown triggerfish. r, Spotted garden eel and orange fish. s, Blue-lined sea bream, blue-green chromis, sapphire damselfish. t, Orangespine unicornfish, white-tipped soldierfish. u, Slatepencil sea urchin, leopard sea cucumber. v, Partridge tun shell. w, Mandarinfish. x, Tiger cowrie. y, Feather starfish, orange-fin anemonefish.

**1990, Aug. 10 Litho. *Perf. 15x14½***
**246** A51 25c Sheet of 25, #a.-y. 12.50 12.50

Nos. 246a-246y inscribed on reverse.

Pacifica — A52

**1990, Aug. 24 Litho. *Perf. 14***
**247** 45c Mailship, 1890 1.50 1.50
**248** 45c US #803 on cover, forklift, plane 1.50 1.50
*a.* A52 Pair, #247-248 3.25 3.25

Christmas — A53

Here We Come A-Caroling: No. 250, Girl with music, poinsettias, doves. No. 251, Boys playing guitar, flute. No. 252, Family. No. 253, Three girls singing.

**1990, Nov. 28**
**249** A53 25c multicolored .50 .40
**250** A53 25c multicolored .50 .40
**251** A53 25c multicolored .50 .40
**252** A53 25c multicolored .50 .40
**253** A53 25c multicolored .50 .40
*a.* Strip of 5, #249-253 3.00 3.00

US Forces in Palau, 1944 A54

Designs: No. 254, B-24s over Peleliu. No. 255, LCI launching rockets. No. 256, First Marine Division launching offensive. No. 257, Soldier, children. No. 258, USS *Peleliu.*

**1990, Dec. 7**
**254** A54 45c multicolored 1.00 .85
**255** A54 45c multicolored 1.00 .85
**256** A54 45c multicolored 1.00 .85
**257** A54 45c multicolored 1.00 .85
*a.* Block of 4, #254-257 4.25 4.25

**Souvenir Sheet**
***Perf. 14x13½***

**258** A54 $1 multicolored 2.50 2.50

No. 258 contains one 51x38mm stamp.
See No. 339 for No. 258 with added inscription.

Coral — A55

**1991, Mar. 4 Litho. *Perf. 14***
**259** 30c Staghorn .65 .65
**260** 30c Velvet Leather .65 .65
**261** 30c Van Gogh's Cypress .65 .65
**262** 30c Violet Lace .65 .65
*a.* A55 Block of 4, #259-262 3.25 3.25

Miniature Sheet

Angaur, The Phosphate Island — A56

Designs: a, Virgin Mary Statue, Nkulangelul Point. b, Angaur kaep, German colonial postmark. c, Swordfish, Caroline Islands No. 13. d, Phosphate mine locomotive. e, Copra ship off Lighthouse Hill. f, Dolphins. g, Estuarine crocodile. h, Workers cycling to phosphate plant. i, Ship loading phosphate. j, Hammerhead shark, German overseer. k, Marshall Islands No. 15. l, SMS Scharnhorst. m, SMS Emden. n, Crab-eating macaque monkey. o, Great sperm whale. p, HMAS Sydney.

**1991, Mar. 14**
**263** A56 30c Sheet of 16, #a.-p. 10.00 10.00

Nos. 263b-263c, 263f-263g, 263j-263k, 263n-263o printed in continuous design showing map of island.

Birds — A57

1c, Palau bush-warbler. 4c, Common moorhen. 6c, Banded rail. 19c, Palau fantail. 20c, Mangrove flycatcher. 23c, Purple swamphen. 29c, Palau fruit dove. 35c, Great crested tern. 40c, Pacific reef heron. 45c, Micronesian pigeon. 50c, Great frigatebird. 52c, Little pied cormorant. 75c, Jungle night jar. 95c, Cattle egret. $1.34, Great sulphur-crested cockatoo. $2, Blue-faced parrotfinch. $5, Eclectus parrot. $10, Palau bush warbler.

***Perf. 14½x15, 13x13½***
**1991-92 Litho.**
**266** A57 1c multicolored .25 .25
**267** A57 4c multicolored .25 .25
**268** A57 6c multicolored .25 .25
**269** A57 19c multicolored .35 .30
*b.* Booklet pane, 10 #269 3.50 —
Complete booklet, #269b 3.75
**270** A57 20c multicolored .40 .30
**271** A57 23c multicolored .45 .35
**272** A57 29c multicolored .55 .45
*a.* Booklet pane, 5 each #269, #272 5.00 —
Complete booklet, #272a 5.25
*b.* Booklet pane, 10 #272 4.50 —
Complete booklet, #272b 4.50
**273** A57 35c multicolored .70 .55
**274** A57 40c multicolored .80 .60
**275** A57 45c multicolored .90 .70
**276** A57 50c multicolored 1.00 .80
**277** A57 52c multicolored 1.00 .90
**278** A57 75c multicolored 1.50 1.25
**279** A57 95c multicolored 2.00 1.50
**280** A57 $1.34 multicolored 2.25 2.00
**281** A57 $2 multicolored 3.25 3.00
**282** A57 $5 multicolored 8.00 7.75

**Size: 52x30mm**

**283** A57 $10 multicolored 16.00 15.00
*Nos. 266-283 (18)* 39.90 36.20

The 1, 6, 20, 52, 75c, $10 are perf. 14½x15.
Issued: 1, 6, 20, 52, 75c, $5, 4/6/92; $10, 9/10/92; #269b, 272a, 272b, 8/23/91; others, 4/18/91.

Miniature Sheet

Christianity in Palau, Cent. — A58

Designs: a, Pope Leo XIII, 1891. b, Ibedul Ilengelekei, High Chief of Koror, 1871-1911. c, Fr. Marino de la Hoz, Br. Emilio Villar, Fr. Elias

Fernandez. d, Fr. Edwin G. McManus (1908-1969), compiler of Palauan-English dictionary. e, Sacred Heart Church, Koror. f, Pope John Paul II.

**1991, Apr. 28** *Perf. 14½*
**288** A58 29c Sheet of 6, #a.-f. 3.50 3.50

Miniature Sheet

Marine Life A59

Designs: a, Pacific white-sided dolphin. b, Common dolphin. c, Rough-toothed dolphin. d, Bottlenose dolphin. e, Harbor porpoise. f, Killer whale. g, Spinner dolphin, yellowfin tuna. h, Dall's porpoise. i, Finless porpoise. j, Map of Palau, dolphin. k, Dusky dolphin. l, Southern right-whale dolphin. m, Striped dolphin. n, Fraser's dolphin. o, Peale's dolphin. p, Spectacled porpoise. q, Spotted dolphin. r, Hourglass dolphin. s, Risso's dolphin. t, Hector's dolphin.

**1991, May 24** **Litho.** *Perf. 14*
**289** A59 29c Sheet of 20, #a.-t. 13.50 13.50

Miniature Sheet

Operations Desert Shield / Desert Storm — A60

Designs: a, F-4G Wild Weasel fighter. b, F-117A Stealth fighter. c, AH-64A Apache helicopter. d, TOW missle launcher on M998 HMMWV. e, Pres. Bush. f, M2 Bradley fighting vehicle. g, Aircraft carrier USS Ranger. h, Corvette fast patrol boat. i, Battleship Wisconsin.
No. 291, Fairy tern, yellow ribbon.

**1991, July 2** **Litho.** *Perf. 14*
**290** A60 20c Sheet of 9, #a.-i. 3.75 3.75

**Size: 38x51mm**

**291** A60 $2.90 multicolored 5.25 5.25

**Souvenir Sheet**

**292** A60 $2.90 like #291 5.75 5.75

No. 291 has a white border around design. No. 292 printed in continuous design.

Republic of Palau, 10th Anniv. — A61

Designs: a, Palauan bai. b, Palauan bai interior, denomination UL. c, Same, denomination UR. d, Demi-god Chedechuul. e, Spider, denomination at UL. f, Money bird facing right. g, Money bird facing left. h, Spider, denomination at UR.

**1991, July 9** *Perf. 14½*
**293** A61 29c Sheet of 8, #a.-h. 5.00 5.00

See No. C21.

Miniature Sheet

Giant Clams — A62

Designs: a, Tridacna squamosa, Hippopus hippopus, Hippopus porcellanus, and Tridacna derasa. b, Tridacna gigas. c, Hatchery and tank culture. d, Diver, bottom-based clam nursery. e, Micronesian Mariculture Demonstration Center.

**1991, Sept. 17** **Litho.** *Perf. 14*
**294** A62 50c Sheet of 5, #a.-e. 5.00 5.00

No. 294e is 109x17mm and imperf on 3 sides, perf 14 at top.

Miniature Sheet

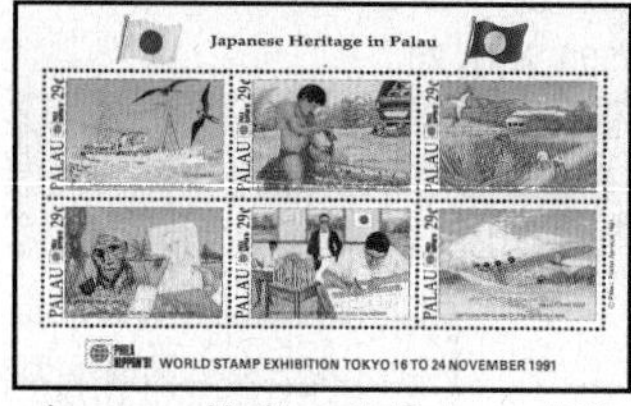

Japanese Heritage in Palau — A63

Designs: No. 295: a, Marine research. b, Traditional arts, carving story boards. c, Agricultural training. d, Archaeological research. e, Training in architecture and building. f, Air transportation. $1, Map, cancel from Japanese post office at Parao.

**1991, Nov. 19**
**295** A63 29c Sheet of 6, #a.-f. 3.50 3.50

**Souvenir Sheet**

**296** A63 $1 multicolored 3.00 3.00

Phila Nippon '91.

Miniature Sheet

Peace Corps in Palau, 25th Anniv. — A64

Children's drawings: No. 297a, Flag, doves, children, and islands. b, Airplane, people being greeted. c, Red Cross instruction. d, Fishing industry. e, Agricultural training. f, Classroom instruction.

**1991, Dec. 6** **Litho.** *Perf. 13½*
**297** A64 29c Sheet of 6, #a.-f. 3.75 3.75

Christmas — A65

Silent Night: No. 298: a, Silent night, holy night. b, All is calm, all is bright. c, Round yon virgin, mother and Child. d, Holy Infant, so tender and mild. e, Sleep in heavenly peace.

**1991, Nov. 14** *Perf. 14*
**298** A65 29c Strip of 5, #a.-e. 2.75 2.75

Miniature Sheet

World War II in the Pacific A66

Designs: No. 299a, Pearl Harbor attack begins. b, Battleship Nevada gets under way. c, USS Shaw explodes. d, Japanese aircraft carrier Akagi sunk. e, USS Wasp sunk off Guadalcanal. f, Battle of the Philippine Sea. g, US landing craft approach Saipan. h, US 1st Cavalry on Leyte. i, Battle of Bloody Nose Ridge, Peleliu. j, US troops land on Iwo Jima.

**1991, Dec. 6** *Perf. 14½x15*
**299** A66 29c Sheet of 10, #a.-j. 8.50 8.50

See No. C22.

A67

Butterflies: a, Troides criton. b, Alcides zodiaca. c, Papillio poboroi. d, Vindula arsinoe.

**1992, Jan. 20** **Litho.** *Perf. 14*
**300** A67 50c Block of 4, #a.-d. 4.00 4.00

A68

Shells: a, Common hairy triton. b, Eglantine cowrie. c, Sulcate swamp cerith. d, Black-spined murex. e, Black-mouth moon.

**1992, Mar. 11**
**301** A68 29c Strip of 5, #a.-e. 3.00 3.00

Miniature Sheet

Age of Discovery A69

Designs: a, Columbus. b, Magellan. c, Drake. d, Wind as shown on old maps.
Maps and: e, Compass rose. f, Dolphin, Drake's ship Golden Hinde. g, Corn, Santa Maria. h, Fish. i, Betel palm, cloves and black pepper. j, Victoria, shearwater and great crested tern. k, White-tailed tropicbird, bicolor parrotfish, pineapple and potatoes. l, Compass. m, Sea monster. n, Paddles and astrolabe. o, Parallel ruler, dividers and Inca gold treasures. p, Back staff.
Portraits: q, Wind, diff. r, Vespucci. s, Pizarro. t, Balboa.

**1992, May 25** **Litho.** *Perf. 14*
**302** A69 29c Sheet of 20, #a.-t. 12.00 12.00

Miniature Sheet

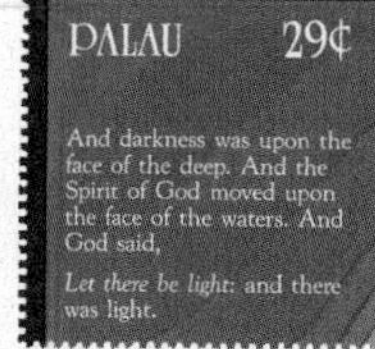

Biblical Creation of the World — A70

Designs: a, "And darkness was..." b, Sun's rays. c, Water, sun's rays. d, "...and it was good." e, "Let there be a..." f, Land forming. g, Water and land. h, "...and it was so." i, "Let the waters..." j, Tree branches. k, Shoreline. l, Shoreline, flowers, tree. m, "Let there be lights..." n, Comet, moon. o, Mountains. p, Sun, hillside. q, "Let the waters..." r, Birds. s, Fish, killer whale. t, Fish. u, "Let the earth..." v, Woman, man. w, Animals. x, "...and it was very good."

**1992, June 5** *Perf. 14½*
**303** A70 29c Sheet of 24, #a.-x. 14.00 14.00

Nos. 303a-303d, 303e-303h, 303i-303l, 303m-303p, 303q-303t, 303u-303x are blocks of 4.

Souvenir Sheets

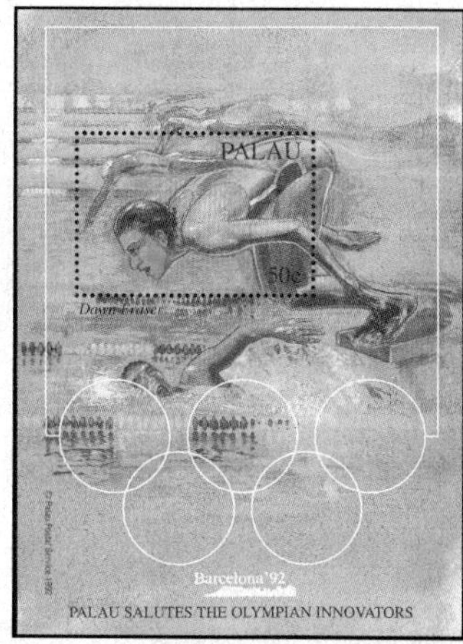

1992 Summer Olympics, Barcelona — A71

**1992, July 10** *Perf. 14*

| | | | | |
|---|---|---|---|---|
| **304** | A71 | 50c | Dawn Fraser | 1.00 1.00 |
| **305** | A71 | 50c | Olga Korbut | 1.00 1.00 |
| **306** | A71 | 50c | Bob Beamon | 1.00 1.00 |
| **307** | A71 | 50c | Carl Lewis | 1.00 1.00 |
| **308** | A71 | 50c | Dick Fosbury | 1.00 1.00 |
| **309** | A71 | 50c | Greg Louganis | 1.00 1.00 |
| | | | *Nos. 304-309 (6)* | 6.00 6.00 |

Miniature Sheet

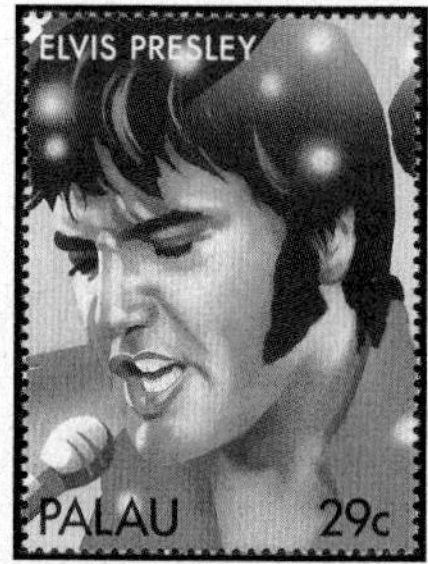

Elvis Presley A72

Various portraits.

**1992, Aug. 17** *Perf. 13½x14*
**310** A72 29c Sheet of 9, #a.-i. 7.00 7.00

See No. 350.

Christmas — A73

The Friendly Beasts carol depicting animals in Nativity Scene: No. 312a, "Thus Every Beast." b, "By Some Good Spell." c, "In The Stable Dark Was Glad to Tell." d, "Of The Gift He Gave Emanuel." e, "The Gift He Gave Emanuel."

**1992, Oct. 1 Litho.** ***Perf. 14***
**312** A73 29c Strip of 5, #a.-e. 3.00 3.00

Fauna A74

Designs: a, Dugong. b, Masked booby. c, Macaque. d, New Guinean crocodile.

**1993, July 9 Litho.** ***Perf. 14***
**313** A74 50c Block of 4, #a.-d. 4.00 4.00

Seafood A75

Designs: a, Giant crab. b, Scarlet shrimp. c, Smooth nylon shrimp. d, Armed nylon shrimp.

**1993, July 22**
**314** A75 29c Block of 4, #a.-d. 2.25 2.25

Sharks A76

Designs: a, Oceanic whitetip. b, Great hammerhead. c, Leopard. d, Reef black-tip.

**1993, Aug. 11 Litho.** ***Perf. 14½***
**315** A76 50c Block of 4, #a.-d. 4.00 4.00

Miniature Sheet

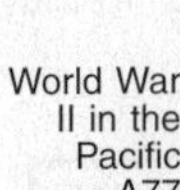

World War II in the Pacific A77

Actions in 1943: a, US takes Guadalcanal, Feb. b, Hospital ship Tranquility supports action. c, New Guineans join Allies in battle. d, US landings in New Georgia, June. e, USS California participates in every naval landing. f, Dauntless dive bombers over Wake Island, Oct. 6. g, US flamethrowers on Tarawa, Nov. h, US landings on Makin, Nov. i, B-25s bomb Simpson Harbor, Rabaul, Oct. 23. j, B-24s over Kwajalein, Dec. 8.

**1993, Sept. 23 Litho.** ***Perf. 14½x15***
**316** A77 29c Sheet of 10, #a.-j. + label 8.00 8.00

See Nos. 325-326.

Christmas — A78

Christmas carol, "We Wish You a Merry Christmas," with Palauan customs: a, Girl, goat. b, Goats, children holding leis, prow of canoe. c, Santa Claus. d, Children singing. e, Family with fruit, fish.

**1993, Oct. 22 Litho.** ***Perf. 14***
**317** A78 29c Strip of 5, #a.-e. 3.00 3.00

Miniature Sheet

Prehistoric and Legendary Sea Creatures — A79

**1993, Nov. 26 Litho.** ***Perf. 14***
**318** A79 29c Sheet of 25, #a.-y. 14.00 14.00

Miniature Sheet

Intl. Year of Indigenous People — A80

Paintings, by Charlie Gibbons: No. 319: a, After Child-birth Ceremony. b, Village in Early Palau.
Storyboard carving, by Ngiraibuuch: $2.90, Quarrying of Stone Money, vert.

**1993, Dec. 8** ***Perf. 14x13½***
**319** A80 29c Sheet, 2 ea #a.-b. 2.25 2.25

**Souvenir Sheet**
***Perf. 13½x14***

**320** A80 $2.90 multicolored 6.00 6.00

Miniature Sheet

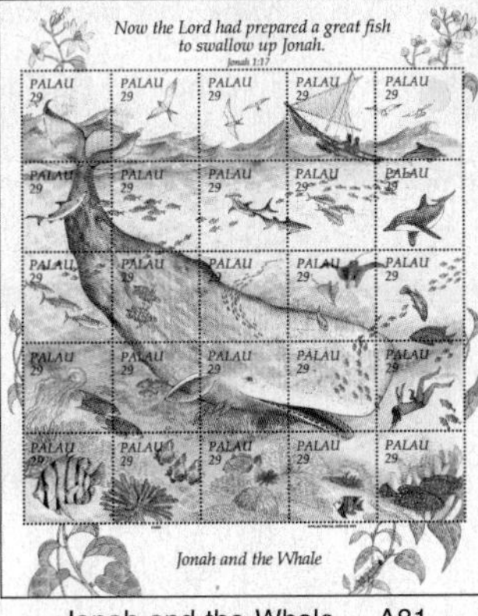

Jonah and the Whale — A81

**1993, Dec. 28 Litho.** ***Perf. 14***
**321** A81 29c Sheet of 25, #a.-y. 14.50 14.50

Hong Kong '94 A82

Rays: a, Manta (b). b, Spotted eagle (a). c, Coachwhip (d). d, Black spotted.

**1994, Feb. 18 Litho.** ***Perf. 14***
**322** A82 40c Block of 4, #a.-d. 3.00 3.00

Estuarine Crocodile A83

Designs: a, With mouth open. b, Hatchling. c, Crawling on river bottom. d, Swimming.

**1994, Mar. 14**
**323** A83 20c Block of 4, #a.-d. 3.50 3.50

World Wildlife Fund.

Large Seabirds — A84

a, Red-footed booby. b, Great frigatebird. c, Brown booby. d, Little pied cormorant.

**1994, Apr. 22 Litho.** ***Perf. 14***
**324** A84 50c Block of 4, #a.-d. 4.00 4.00

**World War II Type of 1993**
Miniature Sheets

Action in the Pacific, 1944: No. 325: a, US Marines capture Kwajalien, Feb. 1-7. b, Japanese enemy base at Truk destroyed, Feb. 17-18. c, SS-284 Tullibee participates in Operation Desecrate, March. d, US troops take Saipan, June 15-July 9. e, Great Marianas Turkey Shoot, June 19-20. f, Guam liberated, July-Aug. g, US troops take Peleliu, Sept. 15-Oct. 14. h, Angaur secured in fighting, Sept. 17-22. i, Gen. Douglas MacArthur returns to Philippines, Oct. 20. j, US Army Memorial, Palau, Nov. 27.

D-Day, Allied Invasion of Normandy, June 6, 1944: No. 326: a, C-47 transport aircraft dropping Allied paratroopers. b, Allied warships attack beach fortifications. c, Commandos attack from landing craft. d, Tanks land. e, Sherman flail tank beats path through minefields. f, Allied aircraft attack enemy reinforcements. g, Gliders deliver troops behind enemy lines. h, Pegasus Bridge, first French house liberated. i, Allied forces move inland to form bridgehead. j, View of beach at end of D-Day.

**1994, May Sheets of 10** ***Perf. 14½***
**325** A77 29c #a.-j. + label 8.50 8.50
**326** A77 50c #a.-j. + label 12.00 12.00

Pierre de Coubertin (1863-1937) — A85

Winter Olympic medalists: No. 328, Anne-Marie Moser, vert. No. 329, James Craig. No. 330, Katarina Witt. No. 331, Eric Heiden, vert. No. 332, Nancy Kerrigan. $2, Dan Jansen.

**1994, July 20 Litho.** ***Perf. 14***
**327** A85 29c multicolored .70 .70

**Souvenir Sheets**

**328** A85 50c multicolored 1.00 1.00
**329** A85 50c multicolored 1.00 1.00
**330** A85 $1 multicolored 2.00 2.00
**331** A85 $1 multicolored 2.00 2.00
**332** A85 $1 multicolored 2.00 2.00
**333** A85 $2 multicolored 4.00 4.00

Intl. Olympic Committee, cent.

Miniature Sheets

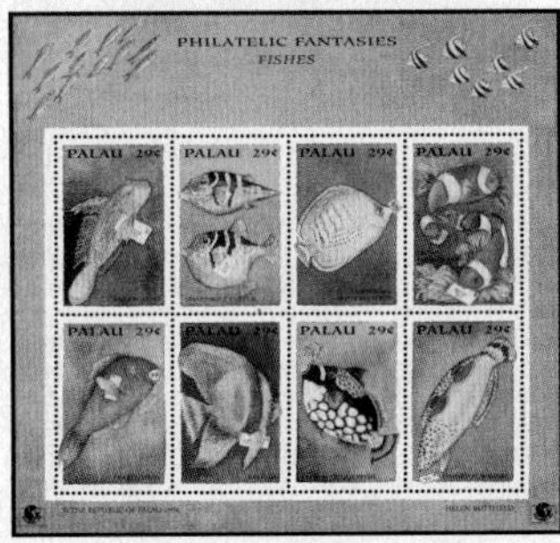

PHILAKOREA '94 — A86

Wildlife carrying letters: No. 334: a, Sailfin goby. b, Sharpnose puffer. c, Lightning butterflyfish. d, Clown anemonefish. e, Parrotfish. f, Batfish. g, Clown triggerfish. h, twinspot wrasse.

No. 335a, Palau fruit bat. b, Crocodile. c, Dugong. d, Banded sea snake. e, Bottle-nosed dophin. f, Hawksbill turtle. g, Octopus. h, Manta ray.

No. 336: a, Palau fantail. b, Banded crake. c, Island swiftlet. d, Micronesian kingfisher. e. Red-footed booby. f, Great frigatebird. g, Palau owl. h, Palau fruit dove.

**1994, Aug. 16 Litho.** ***Perf. 14***
**334** A86 29c Sheet of 8, #a.-h. 6.00 6.00
**335** A86 40c Sheet of 8, #a.-h. 8.00 8.00
**336** A86 50c Sheet of 8, #a.-h. 10.00 10.00

No. 336 is airmail.

Miniature Sheet

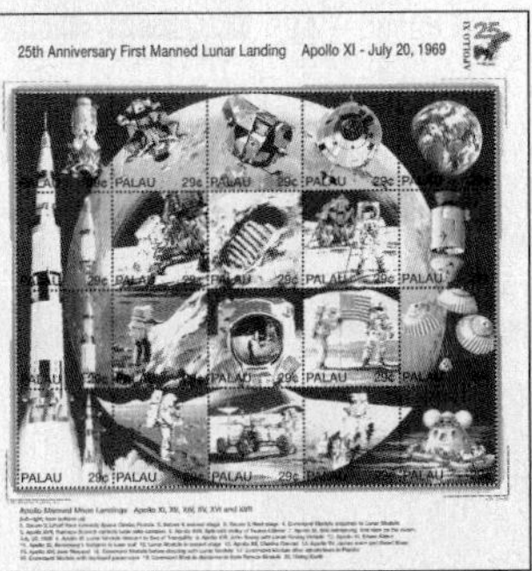

First Manned Moon Landing, 25th Anniv. — A87

Various scenes from Apollo moon missions.

**1994, July 20**
**337** A87 29c Sheet of 20, #a.-t. 12.00 12.00

Independence Day — A88

#338: b, Natl. seal. c, Pres. Kuniwo Nakamura, Palau, US Pres. Clinton. d, Palau, US flags. e, Musical notes of natl. anthem.

**1994, Oct. 1** ***Perf. 14***
**338** A88 29c Strip of 5, #a.-e. 2.75 2.75

No. 338c is 57x42mm.

**No. 258 with added text "50th ANNIVERSARY / INVASION OF PELELIU / SEPTEMBER 15, 1944"**

**1994** **Litho.** ***Perf. 14X13½***
**339** A54 $1 multicolored 2.50 2.50

Miniature Sheet

Disney Characters Visit Palau — A89

No. 340: a, Mickey, Minnie arriving. b, Goofy finding way to hotel. c, Donald enjoying beach. d, Minnie, Daisy learning the Ngloik. e, Minnie, Mickey sailing to Natural Bridge. f, Scrooge finding money in Babeldaob jungle. g, Goofy, Napoleon Wrasse. h, Minnie, Clam Garden. i, Grandma Duck weaving basket.

No. 341, Mickey exploring underwater shipwreck. No. 342, Donald visiting Airai Bai on Babeldaob. No. 343, Pluto, Mickey in boat, vert.

**1994, Oct. 14** ***Perf. 13½x14***
**340** A89 29c Sheet of 9, #a.-i. 6.00 6.00

**Souvenir Sheets**

**341-342** A89 $1 each 3.00 3.00

***Perf. 14x13½***

**343** A89 $2.90 multicolored 7.75 7.75

Miniature Sheet

Intl. Year of the Family — A90

Story of Tebruchel: a, With mother as infant. b, Father. c, As young man. d, Wife-to-be. e, Bringing home fish. f, Pregnant wife. g, Elderly mother. h, Elderly father. i, With first born. j, Wife seated. k, Caring for mother. l, Father, wife and baby.

**1994, Nov. 1** **Litho.** ***Perf. 14***
**344** A90 20c Sheet of 12, #a.-l. 4.75 4.75

Christmas — A91

O Little Town of Bethlehem: a, Magi, cherubs. b, Angel, shepherds, sheep. c, Angels, nativity. d, Angels hovering over town, shepherd, sheep. e, Cherubs, doves.

**1994, Nov. 23** **Litho.** ***Perf. 14***
**345** A91 29c Strip of 5, #a-e 3.00 3.00

No. 345 is a continuous design and is printed in sheets containing three strips. The bottom strip is printed with se-tenant labels.

Miniature Sheets

1994 World Cup Soccer Championships, US — A92

US coach, players: No. 346: a, Bora Milutinovic. b, Cle Kooiman. c, Ernie Stewart. d, Claudio Reyna. e, Thomas Dooley. f, Alexi Lalas. g, Dominic Kinnear. h, Frank Klopas. i, Paul Caligiuri. j, Marcelo Balboa. k, Cobi Jones. l, US flag, World Cup trohpy.

US players: No. 347a, Tony Meola. b, John Doyle. c, Eric Wynalda. d, Roy Wegerle. e, Fernando Clavijo. f, Hugo Perez. g, John Harkes. h, Mike Lapper. i, Mike Sorber. j, Brad Friedel. k, Tab Ramos. l, Joe-Max Moore.

No. 348: a, Babeto, Brazil. b, Romario, Brazil. c, Franco Baresi, Italy. d, Roberto Baggio, Italy. e, Andoni Zubizarreta, Spain. f, Oleg Salenko, Russia. g, Gheorghe Hagi, Romania. h, Dennis Bergkamp, Netherlands. i, Hristo Stoichkov, Bulgaria. j, Tomas Brolin, Sweden. k, Lothar Matthaus, Germany. l, Arrigo Sacchi, Italy, Carlos Alberto Parreira, Brazil, flags of Italy & Brazil, World Cup trophy.

**1994, Dec. 23**
**346** A92 29c Sheet of 12, #a.-l. 6.25 6.25
**347** A92 29c Sheet of 12, #a.-l. 6.25 6.25
**348** A92 50c Sheet of 12, #a.-l. 10.50 10.50

**Elvis Presley Type of 1992**

Miniature Sheet

Various portraits.

**1995, Feb. 28** **Litho.** ***Perf. 14***
**350** A72 32c Sheet of 9, #a.-i. 6.25 6.25

Fish — A93

1c, Cube trunkfish. 2c, Lionfish. 3c, Longjawed squirrelfish. 4c, Longnose filefish. 5c, Ornate butterflyfish. 10c, Yellow seahorse. 20c, Magenta dottyback. 32c, Reef lizardfish. 50c, Multibarred goatfish. 55c, Barred blenny. $1, Fingerprint sharpnose puffer. $2, Longnose hawkfish. $3, Mandarinfish. $5, Blue surgeonfish. $10, Coral grouper.

**1995, Apr. 3** **Litho.** ***Perf. 14½***

| | | | | |
|---|---|---|---|---|
| **351** | A93 | 1c multicolored | .25 | .25 |
| **352** | A93 | 2c multicolored | .25 | .25 |
| **353** | A93 | 3c multicolored | .25 | .25 |
| **354** | A93 | 4c multicolored | .25 | .25 |
| **355** | A93 | 5c multicolored | .25 | .25 |
| **356** | A93 | 10c multicolored | .25 | .25 |
| **357** | A93 | 20c multicolored | .35 | .30 |
| **358** | A93 | 32c multicolored | .50 | .45 |
| **359** | A93 | 50c multicolored | .85 | .70 |
| **360** | A93 | 55c multicolored | 1.00 | .75 |
| **361** | A93 | $1 multicolored | 1.75 | 1.50 |
| **362** | A93 | $2 multicolored | 3.50 | 3.00 |
| **363** | A93 | $3 multicolored | 5.00 | 4.50 |
| **364** | A93 | $5 multicolored | 8.50 | 7.75 |

**Size: 48x30mm**

| | | | | |
|---|---|---|---|---|
| **365** | A93 | $10 multicolored | 17.50 | 16.00 |
| | | *Nos. 351-365 (15)* | 40.45 | 36.45 |

**Booklet Stamps**

**Size: 18x21mm**

***Perf. 14x14½ Syncopated***

| | | | |
|---|---|---|---|
| **366** A93 20c multicolored | | .40 | .40 |
| *a.* | Booklet pane of 10 | 3.75 | |
| | Complete booklet, #366a | 4.00 | |
| **367** A93 32c multicolored | | .60 | .60 |
| *a.* | Booklet pane of 10 | 6.00 | |
| | Complete booklet, #367a | 6.25 | |
| *b.* | Booklet pane, 5 ea #366, 367 | 5.25 | |
| | Complete booklet, #367b | 5.50 | |

Miniature Sheet

Lost Fleet of the Rock Islands A94

Underwater scenes, silhouettes of Japanese ships sunk during Operation Desecrate, 1944: a, Unyu Maru 2. b, Wakatake. c, Teshio Maru. d, Raizan Maru. e, Chuyo Maru. f, Shinsei Maru. g, Urakami Maru. h, Ose Maru. i, Iro. j, Shosei Maru. k, Patrol boat 31. l, Kibi Maru. m, Amatsu Maru. n, Gozan Maru. o, Matuei Maru. p, Nagisan Maru. q, Akashi. r, Kamikazi Maru.

**1995, Mar. 30** **Litho.** ***Perf. 14***
**368** A94 32c Sheet of 18, #a.-r. 12.00 12.00

Miniature Sheet

Flying Dinosaurs A95

Designs: a, Pteranodon sternbergi. b, Pteranodon ingens (a, c). c, Pterodoctyls (b). d, Dorygnathus (e). e, Dimorphodon (f). f, Nyctosaurus (e, c). g, Pterodactylus kochi. h, Ornithodesmus (g, i). i, Diatryma (l). j, Archaeopteryx. k, Campylognathoides (l). l, Gallodactylus. m, Batrachognathus (j). n, Scaphognathus (j, k, m, o). o, Peteinosaurus (l). p, Ichthyorinis. q, Ctenochasma (m, p, r). r, Rhamphorhynchus (n, o, q).

**1995** **Litho.** ***Perf. 14***
**369** A95 32c Sheet of 18, #a.-r. 12.00 12.00

Earth Day, 25th anniv.

Miniature Sheet

Research & Experimental Jet Aircraft — A96

Designs: a, Fairey Delta 2. b, B-70 "Valkyrie." c, Douglas X-3 "Stilletto." d, Northrop/NASA HL-10. e, Bell XS-1. f, Tupolev Tu-144. g, Bell X-1. h, Boulton Paul P.111. i, EWR VJ 101C. j, Handley Page HP-115. k, Rolls Royce TMR "Flying Bedstead." l, North American X-15.

$2, BAC/Aerospatiale Concorde SST.

**1995** **Litho.** ***Perf. 14***
**370** A96 50c Sheet of 12, #a.-l. 12.00 12.00

**Souvenir Sheet**

**371** A96 $2 multicolored 3.75 3.75

No. 370 is airmail. No. 371 contains one 85x29mm stamp.

Miniature Sheet

Submersibles — A97

Designs: a, Scuba gear. b, Cousteau diving saucer. c, Jim suit. d, Beaver IV. e, Ben Franklin. f, USS Nautilus. g, Deep Rover. h, Beebe Bathysphere. i, Deep Star IV. j, DSRV. k, Aluminaut. l. Nautile. m, Cyana. n, FNRS Bathyscaphe. o, Alvin. p, Mir 1. q, Archimede. r, Trieste.

**1995, July 21** **Litho.** ***Perf. 14***
**372** A97 32c Sheet of 18, #a.-r. 12.00 12.00

Singapore '95 — A98

Designs: a, Dolphins, diver snorkeling, marine life. b, Turtle, diver, seabirds above. c, Fish, coral, crab. d, Coral, fish, diff.

**1995, Aug. 15** **Litho.** ***Perf. 13½***
**373** A98 32c Block of 4, #a.-d. 2.50 2.50

No. 373 is a continuous design and was issued in sheets of 24 stamps.

UN, FAO, 50th Anniv. A99

Designs: No. 374a, Outline of soldier's helmet, dove, peace. b, Outline of flame, Hedul Gibbons, human rights. c, Books, education. d, Outline of tractor, bananas, agriculture.

No. 375, Palau flag, bird, UN emblem. No. 376, Water being put on plants, UN emblem, vert.

**1995, Sept. 15** **Litho.** ***Perf. 14***
**374** A99 60c Block of 4, #a.-d. 4.75 4.75

**Souvenir Sheets**

**375** A99 $2 multicolored 4.00 4.00
**376** A99 $2 multicolored 4.00 4.00

Independence, 1st Anniv. — A100

Palau flag and: a, Fruit doves. b, Rock Islands. c, Map of islands. d, Orchid, hibiscus. 32c, Marine life.

**1995, Sept. 15** ***Perf. 14½***
**377** A100 20c Block of 4, #a.-d. 1.50 1.50
**378** A100 32c multicolored .65 .65

No. 377 was issued in sheets of 16 stamps. See US No. 2999.

Miniature Sheets

A101

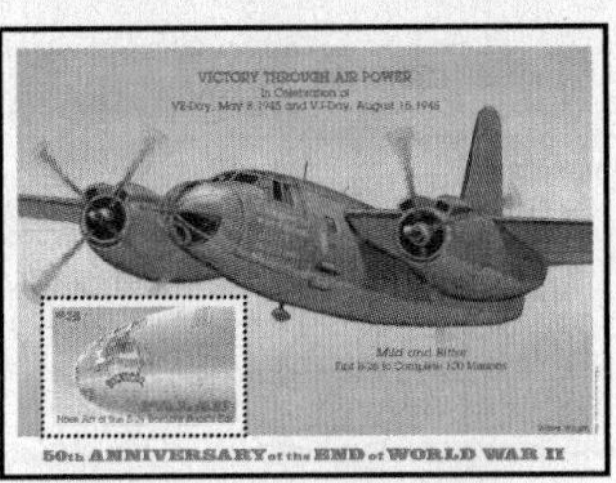

End of World War II, 50th Anniv. — A102

Paintings by Wm. F. Draper: No. 379a, Preparing Tin-Fish. b, Hellcats Take-off into Palau's Rising Sun. c, Dauntless Dive Bombers over Malakai Harbor. d, Planes Return from Palau. e, Communion Before Battle. f, The Landing. g, First Task Ashore. h, Fire Fighters Save Flak-torn Pilot.

Paintings by Tom Lea: No. 379i, Young Marine Headed for Peleliu. j, Peleliu. k, Last Rites. l, The Thousand-Yard Stare.

Portraits by Albert Murray, vert.: No. 380a, Adm. Chester W. Nimitz. b, Adm. William F. Halsey. c, Adm. Raymond A. Spruance. d, Vice Adm. Marc A. Mitscher. e, Gen. Holland M. Smith, USMC.

$3, Nose art of B-29 Bock's Car.

**1995, Oct. 18** ***Perf. 14x13½***

**379** A101 32c Sheet of 12, #a.-l 7.75 7.75

***Perf. 13½x14***

**380** A101 60c Sheet of 5, #a.-e. 7.50 7.50

**Souvenir Sheet**

***Perf. 14***

**381** A102 $3 multicolored 6.00 6.00

Christmas — A103

Native version of "We Three Kings of Orient Are:" a, Angel, animals. b, Two wise men. c, Joseph, Mary, Jesus in manger. d, Wise man, shepherd, animals. e, Girl with fruit, goat, shepherd.

**1995, Oct. 31** **Litho.** ***Perf. 14***

**382** A103 32c Strip of 5, #a.-e. 3.00 3.00

No. 382 is a continuous design and was issued in sheets of 15 stamps + 5 labels se-tenant with bottom row of sheet.

Miniature Sheet

Life Cycle of the Sea Turtle — A104

Small turtles, arrows representing routes during life cycle and: a, Large turtle. b, Upper half of turtle shell platter, Palau map. c, Rooster in tree, island scene. d, Native woman. e, Lower half of turtle shell platter, Palau map, island couple. f, Fossil, palm trees, native house

**1995, Nov. 15** **Litho.** ***Perf. 14***

**383** A104 32c Sheet of 12, 2 each, #a.-f. 9.50 9.50

John Lennon (1940-80) — A105

**1995, Dec. 8** **Litho.** ***Perf. 14***

**384** A105 32c multicolored 1.10 1.10

No. 384 was issued in sheets of 16.

Miniature Sheet

New Year 1996 (Year of the Rat) — A106

Stylized rats in parade: No. 385: a, One carrying flag, one playing horn. b, Three playing musical instruments. c, Two playing instruments. d, Family in front of house.

Mirror images, diff. colors: No. 386: a, Like #385c-385d. b, Like #385a-385b.

**1996, Feb. 2** **Litho.** ***Perf. 14***

**385** A106 10c Strip of 4, #a.-d. 1.75 1.75

**Miniature Sheet**

**386** A106 60c Sheet of 2, #a.-b. 2.25 2.25

No. 385 was issued in sheets of 2 + 4 labels like No. 386. Nos. 386a-386b are airmail and are each 56x43mm.

UNICEF, 50th Anniv. — A107

Three different children from Palau in traditional costumes, child in middle wearing: a, Red flowerd dress. b, Pink dress. c, Blue shorts. d, Red headpiece and shorts.

**1996, Mar. 12** **Litho.** ***Perf. 14***

**387** A107 32c Block of 4, #a.-d. 2.50 2.50

No. 387 was issued in sheets of 4.

Marine Life — A108

Letter spelling "Palau," and: a, "P," fairy basslet, vermiculate parrotfish. b, "A," yellow cardinalfish. c, "L," Marten's butterflyfish. d, "A," starry moray, slate pencil sea urchin. e, "U," cleaner wrasse, coral grouper.

**1996, Mar. 29** **Litho.** ***Perf. 14***

**388** A108 32c Strip of 5, #a.-e. 3.00 3.00

No. 388 was issued in miniature sheets of 3. China '96, Intl. Stamp Exhibition, Beijing.

Capex '96 A109

Circumnavigators of the earth: No. 389: a, Ferdinand Magellan, ship Victoria. b, Charles Wilkes, ship Vincennes. c, Joshua Slocum, oyster boat Spray. d, Ben Carlin, amphibious vehicle Half-Safe. e, Edward L. Beach, submarine USS Triton. f, Naomi James, yacht Express Crusader. g, Sir Ranulf Fiennes, polar vehicle. h, Rick Hansen, wheel chair. i, Robin Knox-Johnson, catamaran Enza New Zealand.

No. 390: a, Lowell Smith, Douglas World Cruisers. b, Ernst Lehmann, Graf Zeppelin. c, Wiley Post, Lockheed Vega Winnie Mae. d, Yuri Gagarin, spacecraft Vostok I. e, Jerrie Mock, Cessna 180 Spirit of Columbus. f, Ross Perot, Jr., Bell Longranger III, Spirit of Texas. g, Brooke Knapp, Gulfstream III, The American Dream. h, Jeana Yeager, Dick Rutan, airplane Voyager. i, Fred Lasby, piper Commanche.

Each $3: No. 391, Bob Martin, Mark Sullivan, Troy Bradley, Odyssey Gondola. No. 392, Sir Francis Chichester, yacht Gipsy Moth IV.

**1996, May 3** **Litho.** ***Perf. 14***

**389** A109 32c Sheet of 9, #a.-i. 5.50 5.50

**390** A109 60c Sheet of 9, #a.-i. 11.00 11.00

**Souvenir Sheets**

**391-392** A109 Set of 2 12.00 12.00

No. 390 is airmail.

Miniature Sheet

Disney Sweethearts — A110

1c, like #393a. 2c, #393c. 3c, #393d. 4c, like #393e. 5c, #393f. 6c, #393h.

#393: a, Simba, Nala, Timon. b, Bernard, Bianca, Mr. Chairman. c, Georgette, Tito, Oliver. d, Duchess, O'Malley, Marie. e, Bianca, Jake, Polly. f, Tod, Vixey, Copper. g, Robin Hood, Maiden Marian, Alan-a-Dale. h, Thumper, Flower, their sweethearts. i, Pongo, Perdita, puppies.

Each $2: #394, Lady, vert. #395, Bambi, Faline.

**1996, May 30** **Litho.** ***Perf. 14x13½***

**392A-392F** A110 Set of 6 1.00 1.00

**Sheet of 9**

**393** A110 60c #a.-i. 13.50 13.50

**Souvenir Sheets**

***Perf. 13½x14, 14x13½***

**394-395** A110 Set of 2 9.50 9.50

Jerusalem, 3000th Anniv. — A111

Biblical illustrations of the Old Testament appearing in "In Our Image," by Guy Rowe (1894-1969): a, Creation. b, Adam and Eve. c, Noah and his Wife. d, Abraham. e, Jacob's Blessing. f, Jacob Becomes Israel. g, Joseph and his Brethren. h, Moses and the Burning Bush. i, Moses and the Tablets. j, Balaam. k, Joshua. l, Gideon. m, Jephthah. n, Samson. o, Ruth and Naomi. p, Saul Anointed. q, Saul Denounced. r, David and Jonathan. s, David and Nathan. t, David Mourns. u, Solomon Praying. v, Solomon Judging. w, Elijah. x, Elisha. y, Job. z, Isaiah. aa, Jeremiah. ab, Ezekiel. ac, Nebuchadnezzar's Dream. ad, Amos.

**1996, June 15** **Litho.** ***Perf. 14***

**396** A111 20c Sheet of 30, #a.-ad. 12.00 12.00

For overprint see No. 461.

1996 Summer Olympics, Atlanta A112

No. 397, Fanny Blankers Koen, gold medalist, 1948, vert. No. 398, Bob Mathias, gold medalist, 1948, 1952, vert. No. 399, Torchbearer entering Wembley Stadium, 1948. No. 400, Olympic flag, flags of Palau and U.K. before entrance to Stadium, Olympia, Greece.

Athletes: No. 401: a, Hakeem Olajuwan, US. b, Pat McCormick, US. c, Jim Thorpe, US. d, Jesse Owens, US. e, Tatyana Gutsu, Unified Team. f, Michael Jordan, US. g, Fu Mingxia, China. h, Robert Zmelik, Czechoslovakia. i, Ivan Pedroso, Cuba. j, Nadia Comaneci, Romania. k, Jackie Joyner-Kersee, US. l, Michael Johnson, US. m, Kristin Otto, E. Germany. n, Vitali Scherbo, Unified Team. o, Johnny Weissmuller, US. p, Babe Didrikson, US. q, Eddie Tolan, US. r, Krisztina Egerszegi, Hungary. s, Sawao Kato, Japan. t, Alexander Popov, Unified Team.

**1996, June 17** **Litho.** ***Perf. 14***

**397** A112 40c multicolored .90 .90

**398** A112 40c multicolored .90 .90

*a.* Pair, #397-398 2.00 2.00

**399** A112 60c multicolored 1.40 1.40

**400** A112 60c multicolored 1.40 1.40

*a.* Pair, #399-400 3.00 3.00

**401** A112 32c Sheet of 20, #a.-t. 13.00 13.00

Nos. 398a, 400a were each issued in sheets of 20 stamps. No. 401 is a continuous design.

Birds Over Palau Lagoon A113

Designs: a, Lakkotsiang, female. b, Maladaob. c, Belochel (g). d, Lakkotsiang, male. e, Sechosech. f, Mechadelbedaoch (j). g, Laib. h, Cheloteachel. i, Deroech. j, Kerkirs. k, Dudek. l, Lakkotsiang. m, Bedaoch. n, Bedebedchaki. o, Sechou (gray Pacific reef-heron) (p). p, Kekereiderariik. q, Sechou (white Pacific reef-heron). r, Ochaieu. s, Oltirakladial. t, Omechederiibabad.

**1996, July 10**

**402** A113 50c Sheet of 20, #a.-t. 20.00 20.00

Aircraft A114

Stealth, surveillance, and electronic warfare: No. 403: a, Lockheed U-2. b, General Dynamics EF-111A. c, Lockheed YF-12A. d, Lockheed SR-71. e, Teledyne-Ryan-Tiere II Plus. f, Lockheed XST. g, Lockhood ER-2. h, Lockheed F-117A Nighthawk. i, Lockheed EC-130E. j, Ryan Firebee. k, Lockheed Martin/Boeing "Darkstar." l, Boeing E-3A Sentry.

No. 404: a, Northrop XB-35. b, Leduc O.21. c, Convair Model 118. d, Blohm Und Voss BV 141. e, Vought V-173. f, McDonnell XF-85 Goblin. g, North American F-82B Twin Mustang. h, Lockheed XFV-1. i, Northrop XP-79B. j, Saunders Roe SR/A1. k, Caspian Sea Monster. l, Grumman X-29.

No. 405, Northrop B-2A Stealth Bomber. No. 406, Martin Marietta X-24B.

**1996, Sept. 9** **Litho.** ***Perf. 14***

**403** A114 40c Sheet of 12, #a.-l. 10.00 10.00

**404** A114 60c Sheet of 12, #a.-l. 15.00 15.00

**Souvenir Sheets**

**405** A114 $3 multicolored 6.50 6.50
**406** A114 $3 multicolored 6.50 6.50

No. 404 is airmail. No. 406 contains one 85x28mm stamp.

Independence, 2nd Anniv. — A115

Paintings, by Koh Sekiguchi: No. 407, "In the Blue Shade of Trees-Palau (Kirie). No. 408 "The Birth of a New Nation (Kirie).

**1996, Oct. 1 Litho. *Perf. 14½***

**407** 20c multicolored .40 .40
**408** 20c multicolored .40 .40
***a.*** A115 Pair, #407-408 .80 .80

#408a issued in sheets of 16 stamps.

Christmas — A116

Christmas trees: a, Pandanus. b, Mangrove. c, Norfolk Island pine. d, Papaya. e, Casuarina.

**1996, Oct. 8 *Perf. 14***

**409** A116 32c Strip of 5, #a.-e. 3.25 3.25

No. 409 was issued in sheets of 3.

Voyage to Mars — A117

No. 410: a, Viking 1 (US) in Mars orbit. b, Mars Lander fires de-orbit engines. c, Viking 1 symbol (top). d, Viking 1 symbol (bottom). e, Martian moon phobos. f, Mariner 9 in Mars orbit. g, Viking lander enters Martian atmosphere. h, Parachute deploys for Mars landing, heat shield jettisons. i, Proposed manned mission to Mars, 21st cent., US-Russian spacecraft (top). j, US-Russian spacecraft (botton). k, Lander descent engines fire for Mars landing. l, Viking 1 lands on Mars, July 20, 1976.

Each $3: No. 411, NASA Mars rover. No. 412, NASA water probe on Mars. Illustration reduced.

**1996, Nov. 8 Litho. *Perf. 14x14½***

**410** A117 32c Sheet of 12, #a.-l. 7.75 7.75

**Souvenir Sheets**

**411-412** A117 Set of 2 12.00 12.00

No. 411 contains one 38x30mm stamp.

Souvenir Sheet

New Year 1997 (Year of the Ox) — A117a

**1997, Jan. 2 Litho. *Perf. 14***

**412A** A117a $2 multicolored 4.25 4.25

Souvenir Sheet

South Pacific Commission, 50th Anniv. — A118

**1997, Feb. 6 Litho. *Perf. 14***

**413** A118 $1 multicolored 2.00 2.00

Hong Kong '97 — A119

Flowers: 1c, Pemphis acidula. 2c, Sea lettuce. 3c, Tropical almond. 4c, Guettarda. 5c, Pacific coral bean. $3, Sea hibiscus.

No. 420: a, Black mangrove. b, Cordia. c, Lantern tree. d, Palau rock-island flower.

No. 421: a, Fish-poison tree. b, Indian mulberry. c, Pacific poison-apple. d, Ailanthus.

**1997, Feb. 12 *Perf. 14½, 13½ (#419)***

**414-419** A119 Set of 6 7.00 7.00
**420** A119 32c Block of 4, #a.-d. 2.50 2.50
**421** A119 50c Block of 4, #a.-d. 4.00 4.00

Size of No. 419 is 73x48mm.

Nos. 420-421 were each issued in sheets of 16 stamps.

Bicent. of the Parachute A120

Uses of parachute: No. 422: a, Apollo 15 Command Module landing safely. b, "Caterpillar Club" flyer ejecting safely over land. c. Skydiving team formation. d, Parasailing. e, Military parachute demonstration teams. f, Parachute behind dragster. g, Dropping cargo from C-130 aircraft. h, "Goldfish Club" flyer ejecting safely at sea.

No. 423: a, Demonstrating parachute control. b, A.J. Gernerin, first successful parachute descent, 1797. c, Slowing down world land-speed record breaking cars. d, Dropping spies behind enemy lines. e, C-130E demonstrating "LAPES." f, Parachutes used to slow down high performance aircraft. g, ARD parachutes. g, US Army parachutist flying Parafoil.

Each $2: No. 424 Training tower at Ft. Benning, Georgia. No. 425, "Funny Car" safety chute.

***Perf. 14½x14, 14x14½***

**1997, Mar. 13 Litho.**

**422** A120 32c Sheet of 8, #a.-h. 5.25 5.25
**423** A120 60c Sheet of 8, #a.-h. 9.75 9.75

**Souvenir Sheets**

***Perf. 14***

**424-425** A120 Set of 2 10.00 10.00

Nos. 422a-423a, 422b-423b, 422g-423g, 422h-423h are 20x48mm. No. 424 contains one 28x85mm, No. 425 one 57x42mm stamps.

No. 423 is airmail.

Postage Stamp Mega-Event, NYC, Mar. 1997 (#422-423).

Native Birds A121

a, Gray duck, banana tree. b, Red junglefowl, calamondin. c, Nicobar pigeon, fruited parinari tree. d, Cardinal honeyeater, wax apple tree. e, Yellow bittern, purple swamphen, giant taro, taro. f, Eclectus parrot, pangi football fruit tree. g, Micronesian pigeon, Rambutan. h, Micronesian starling, mango tree. i, Fruit bat, breadfruit tree. j, Collared kingfisher, coconut palm. k, Palau fruit dove, sweet orange tree. l, Chestnut mannikin, soursop tree.

**1997, Mar. 27 Litho. *Perf. 13½x14***

**426** A121 20c Sheet of 12, #a.-l. 5.00 5.00

UNESCO, 50th Anniv. — A122

Sites in Japan, vert: Nos. 427: a, c-h, Himeji-jo. b, Kyoto.

Sites in Germany: Nos. 428: a-b, Augustusburg Castle. c, Falkenlust Castle. d, Roman ruins, Trier. e, Historic house, Trier.

Each $2: No. 429, Forest, Shirakami-Sanchi, Japan. No. 430, Yakushima, Japan.

***Perf. 13½x14, 14x13½***

**1997, Apr. 7 Litho.**

**Sheets of 8 or 5 + Label**

**427** A122 32c #a.-h. 5.50 5.50
**428** A122 60c #a.-e. 6.25 6.25

**Souvenir Sheets**

**429-430** A122 Set of 2 8.75 8.75

A123

Paintings by Hiroshige (1797-1858): No. 431: a, Swallows and Peach Blossoms under a Full Moon. b, A Parrot on a Flowering Branch. c, Crane and Rising Sun. d, Cock, Umbrella, and Morning Glories. e, A Titmouse Hanging Head Downward on a Camellia Branch.

Each $2: No. 432, Falcon on a Pine Tree with the Rising Sun. No. 433, Kingfisher and Iris.

**1997, June 2 Litho. *Perf. 14***

**431** A123 32c Sheet of 5, #a.-e. 4.00 4.00

**Souvenir Sheets**

**432-433** A123 Set of 2 8.25 8.25

A124

Volcano Goddesses of the Pacific: a, Darago, Philippines. b, Fuji, Japan. c, Pele, Hawaii. d, Pare, Maori. e, Dzalarhons, Haida. f, Chuginadak, Aleuts.

**1997 Litho. *Perf. 14***

**434** A124 32c Sheet of 6, #a.-f. 4.50 4.50

PACIFIC 97.

Independence, 3rd Anniv. — A125

**1997, Oct. 1 Litho. *Perf. 14***

**435** A125 32c multicolored .65 .65

No. 435 was issued in sheets of 12.

Oceanographic Research — A126

Ships: No. 436: a, Albatross. b, Mabahiss. c, Atlantis II. d, Xarifa. e, Meteor. f, Egabras III. g, Discoverer. h, Kaiyo. i, Ocean Defender.

Each $2: No. 437, Jacques-Yves Cousteau (1910-97). No. 438, Cousteau, diff., vert. No. 439, Pete Seeger, vert.

**1997, Oct. 1 *Perf. 14x14½, 14½x14***

**436** A126 32c Sheet of 9, #a.-i. 6.00 6.00

**Souvenir Sheets**

**437-439** A126 Set of 3 13.00 13.00

Diana, Princess of Wales (1961-97) A127

**1997, Nov. 26 Litho. *Perf. 14***
**440** A127 60c multicolored 1.25 1.25

No. 440 was issued in sheets of 6.

Disney's "Let's Read" — A128

Various Disney characters: 1c, like #447i. 2c, like #447d. 3c, like #447c. 4c, like #447f. 5c, #447b. 10c, like #447h.

No. 447: a, "Exercise your right to read." b, "Reading is the ultimate luxury." c, "Share your knowledge." d, "Start them Young." e, "Reading is fundamental." f, "The insatiable reader." g, "Reading time is anytime." h, "Real men read." i, "I can read by myself."

No. 448, Daisy, "The library is for everyone," vert. No. 449, Mickey, "Books are magical."

**1997, Oct. 21 *Perf. 14x13½, 13½x14***
**441-446** A128 Set of 6 1.00 1.00

**Sheet of 9**

**447** A128 32c #a.-i. 5.75 5.75

**Souvenir Sheets**

**448** A128 $2 multicolored 4.50 4.50
**449** A128 $3 multicolored 6.50 6.50

Christmas — A129

Children singing Christmas carol, "Some Children See Him:" No. 450: a, Girl, boy in striped shirt. b, Boy, girl in pigtails. c, Girl, boy, Madonna and Child. d, Girl, two children. e, Boy, girl with long black hair.

**1997, Oct. 28 *Perf. 14***
**450** A129 32c Strip of 5, #a.-e. 3.25 3.25

No. 450 was issued in sheets of 3 strips, bottom strip printed se-tenant with 5 labels containing lyrics.

**Souvenir Sheets**

New Year 1998 (Year of the Tiger) — A130

Chinese toys in shape of tiger: No. 451, White background. No. 452, Green background.

**1998, Jan. 2 Litho. *Perf. 14***
**451** A130 50c multicolored 1.25 1.25
**452** A130 50c multicolored 1.25 1.25

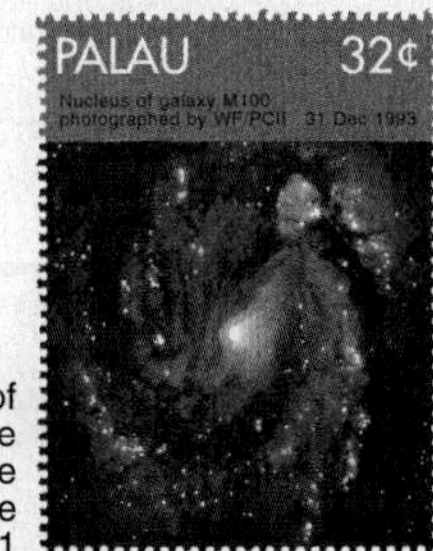


Repair of Hubble Space Telescope A131

No. 453: a, Photograph of nucleus of galaxy M100. b, Top of Hubble telescope with solar arrays folded. c, Astronaut riding robot arm. d, Astronaut anchored to robot arm. e, Astronaut in cargo space with Hubble mounted to shuttle Endeavor. f, Hubble released after repair.

Each $2: No. 454, Hubble cutaway, based on NASA schematic drawing. No. 455, Edwin Hubble (1889-1953), astronomer who proved existence of star systems beyond Milky Way. No. 456, Hubble Mission STS-82/Discovery.

**1998, Mar. 9 Litho. *Perf. 14***
**453** A131 32c Sheet of 6, #a.-f. 4.00 4.00

**Souvenir Sheets**

**454-456** A131 Set of 3 12.50 12.50

Mother Teresa (1910-97) — A132

Various portraits.

**1998, Mar. 12 Litho. *Perf. 14***
**457** A132 60c Sheet of 4, #a.-d. 5.00 5.00

Deep Sea Robots A133

No. 458: a, Ladybird ROV. b, Slocum Glider. c, Hornet. d, Scorpio. e, Odyssey AUV. f, Jamstec Survey System Launcher. g, Scarab. h, USN Torpedo Finder/Salvager. i, Jamstec Survey System Vehicle. j, Cetus Tether. k, Deep Sea ROV. l, ABE. m, OBSS. n, RCV 225G Swimming Eyeball. o, Japanese UROV. p, Benthos RPV. q, CURV. r, Smartie.

Each $2: No. 459, Jason Jr. inspecting Titanic. No. 460, Dolphin 3K.

**1998, Apr. 21**
**458** A133 32c Sheet of 18, #a.-r. 12.00 12.00

**Souvenir Sheets**

**459-460** A133 Set of 2 8.50 8.50

UNESCO Intl. Year of the Ocean.

No. 396 Ovptd. in Silver

**1998, May 13 Litho. *Perf. 14***
**461** A111 20c Sheet of 30, #a.-ad. 12.00 12.00

No. 461 is overprinted in sheet margin, "ISRAEL 98 — WORLD STAMP EXHIBITION / TEL AVIV 13-21 MAY 1998." Location of overprint varies.

Legend of Orachel — A134

#462: a, Bai (hut), people. b, Bai, lake. c, Bai, lake, person in canoe. d, Bird on branch over lake. e, Men rowing in canoe. f, Canoe, head of snake. g, Alligator under water. h, Fish, shark. i, Turtle, body of snake. j, Underwater bai, "gods". k, Snails, fish, Orachel swimming. l, Orachel's feet, coral, fish.

**1998, May 29 Litho. *Perf. 14***
**462** A134 40c Sheet of 12, #a.-l. 9.50 9.50

1998 World Cup Soccer Championships, France — A135

Players, color of shirt — #463: a, Yellow, black & red. b, Blue, white & red. c, Green & white. d, White, red & blue. e, Green & white (black shorts). f, White, red & black. g, Blue & yellow. h, Red & white.

$3, Pele.

**1998, June 5**
**463** A135 50c Sheet of 8, #a.-h. 8.00 8.00

**Souvenir Sheet**

**464** A135 $3 multicolored 6.00 6.00

4th Micronesian Games, Palau — A136

Designs: a, Spear fishing. b, Spear throwing. c, Swimming. d, Pouring milk from coconut. e, Logo of games. f, Climbing coconut trees. g, Canoeing. h, Husking coconut. i, Deep sea diving.

**1998, July 31 Litho. *Perf. 14***
**465** A136 32c Sheet of 9, #a.-i. 5.75 5.75

Rudolph The Red-Nosed Reindeer — A137

Christmas: a, Rudolph, two reindeer, girl. b, Two reindeer, girl holding flowers. c, Girl, two reindeer, boy. d, Two reindeer, girl smiling. e, Santa, children, Christmas gifts.

**1998, Sept. 15 Litho. *Perf. 14***
**466** A137 32c Strip of 5, #a.-e. 3.25 3.25

No. 466 is a continuous design and was issued in sheets of 15 stamps.

Disney/Pixar's "A Bug's Life" — A138

No. 467: a, Dot. b, Heimlich, Francis, Slim. c, Hopper. d, Princess Atta.

No. 468: Various scenes with Flik, Princess Atta.

No. 469, horiz.: a, Circus bugs. b, Slim, Francis, Heimlich. c, Manny. d, Francis.

No. 470: a, Slim, Flik. b, Heimlich, Slim, Francis performing. c, Manny, Flik. d, Gypsy, Manny, Rosie.

Each $2: No. 471, Gypsy. No. 472, Princess Atta, Flik, horiz. No. 473, Slim, Francis, Heimlich, horiz. No. 474, Francis, Slim, Flik, Heimlich, horiz.

***Perf. 13½x14, 14x13½***

**1998, Dec. 1 Litho. Sheets of 4**
**467** A138 20c #a.-d. 1.75 1.75
**468** A138 32c #a.-d. 2.75 2.75
**469** A138 50c #a.-d. 4.25 4.25
**470** A138 60c #a.-d. 5.25 5.25

**Souvenir Sheets**

**471-474** A138 Set of 4 18.00 18.00

Nos. 473-474 each contain one 76x51mm stamp.

John Glenn's Return to Space — A139

No. 475, Various photos of Project Mercury, Friendship 7 mission, 1962, each 60c.

No. 476, Various photos of Discovery Space Shuttle mission, 1998, each 60c.

Each $2: No. 477, Portrait, 1962. No. 478, Portrait, 1998.

**1999, Jan. 7 Litho. *Perf. 14***

**Sheets of 8, #a-h**

**475-476** A139 Set of 2 19.00 19.00

**Souvenir Sheets**

**477-478** A139 Set of 2 8.50 8.50

Nos. 477-478 each contain one 28x42mm stamp.

Environmentalists — A140

a, Rachel Carson. b, J.N. "Ding" Darling, US Duck stamp #RW1. c, David Brower. d, Jacques Cousteau. e, Roger Tory Peterson. f, Prince Philip. g, Joseph Wood Krutch. h, Aldo Leopold. i, Dian Fossey. j, US Vice-President Al Gore. k, David Attenborough. l, Paul McCready. m, Sting (Gordon Sumner). n, Paul Winter. o, Ian MacHarg. p, Denis Hayes.

**1999, Feb. 1 Litho. *Perf. 14½***

**479** A140 33c Sheet of 16, #a.-p. 10.50 10.50

No. 479i shows Dian Fossey's name misspelled "Diane."

MIR Space Station A141

No. 480: a, Soyuz Spacecraft, Science Module. b, Specktr Science Module. c, Space Shuttle, Spacelab Module. d, Kvant 2, Scientific and Air Lock Module. e, Kristall Technological Module. f, Space Shutle, Docking Module.

Each $2: No. 481, Astronaut Charles Precout, Cosmonaut Talgat Musabayev. No. 482, Cosmonaut Valeri Poliakov. No. 483, US Mission Specialist Shannon W. Lucid, Cosmonaut Yuri Y. Usachov. No. 484, Cosmonaut Anatoly Solovyov.

**1999, Feb. 18 Litho. *Perf. 14***

**480** A141 33c Sheet of 6, #a.-f. 3.75 3.75

**Souvenir Sheets**

**481-484** A141 Set of 4 16.00 16.00

Personalities — A142

1c, Haruo Remiliik. 2c, Lazarus Salil. 20c, Charlie W. Gibbons. 22c, Adm. Raymond A. Spruance. 33c, Kuniwo Nakamura. 50c, Adm. William F. Halsey. 55c, Col. Lewis "Chesty" Puller. 60c, Franklin D. Roosevelt. 77c, Harry S Truman. $3.20, Jimmy Carter.

**1999, Mar. 4 *Perf. 14x15***

| | | | | |
|---|---|---|---|---|
| **485** A142 | 1c | green | .25 | .25 |
| **486** A142 | 2c | purple | .25 | .25 |
| **487** A142 | 20c | violet | .40 | .40 |
| **488** A142 | 22c | bister | .45 | .45 |
| **489** A142 | 33c | red brown | .65 | .65 |
| **490** A142 | 50c | brown | 1.00 | 1.00 |
| **491** A142 | 55c | blue green | 1.10 | 1.10 |
| **492** A142 | 60c | orange | 1.25 | 1.25 |
| **493** A142 | 77c | yellow brown | 1.50 | 1.50 |
| **494** A142 | $3.20 | red violet | 6.50 | 6.50 |
| | | *Nos. 485-494 (10)* | 13.35 | 13.35 |

Nos. 485, 492 exist dated 2001.

Australia '99 World Stamp Expo A143

Endangered species — #495: a, Leatherback turtle. b, Kemp's ridley turtle. c, Green turtle. d, Marine iguana. e, Table mountain ghost frog. f, Spiny turtle. g, Hewitt's ghost frog. h, Geometric tortoise. i, Limestone salamander. j, Desert rain frog. k, Cape plantanna. l, Long-toed tree frog.

Each $2: No. 496, Marine crocodile. No. 497, Hawksbill turtle.

**1999, Mar. 19 Litho. *Perf. 13***

**495** A143 33c Sheet of 12, #a.-l. 8.00 8.00

**Souvenir Sheets**

**496-497** A143 Set of 2 8.00 8.00

IBRA '99, Nuremburg — A144

No. 498, Leipzig-Dresden Railway, Caroline Islands Type A4. No. 499, Gölsdorf 4-8-0, Caroline Islands #8, 10.

$2, Caroline Islands #1.

**1999, Apr. 27 Litho. *Perf. 14***

**498-499** A144 55c Set of 2 2.25 2.25

**Souvenir Sheet**

**500** A144 $2 multicolored 4.00 4.00

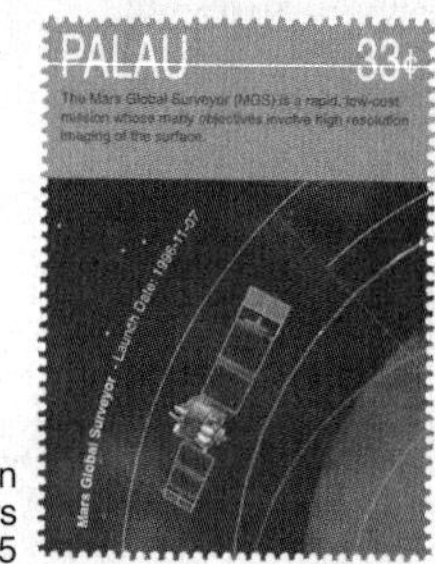

Exploration of Mars A145

No. 501: a, Mars Global Surveyor. b, Mars Climate Orbiter. c, Mars Polar Lander. d, Deep Space 2. e, Mars Surveyor 2001 Orbiter. f, Mars Surveyor 2001 Lander.

Each $2: No. 502, Mars Global Surveyor. No. 503, Mars Climate Orbiter. No. 504, Mars Polar Lander. No. 505, Mars Surveyor 2001 Lander.

**1999, May 10 Litho. *Perf. 14***

**501** A145 33c Sheet of 6, #a.-f. 4.00 4.00

**Souvenir Sheets**

**502-505** A145 Set of 4 16.00 16.00

Nos. 502-505 each contain one 38x50mm stamp.

See Nos. 507-511.

Earth Day — A146

Pacific insects: a, Banza Natida. b, Drosophila heteroneura. c, Nesomicromus vagus. d, Megalagrian leptodemus. e, Pseudopsectra cookearum. f, Ampheida neacaledonia. g, Pseudopsectra swezeyi. h, Deinacrida heteracantha. i, Beech forest butterfly. j, Hercules moth. k, Striped sphinx moth. l, Tussock butterfly. m. Elytrocheilus. n, Bush cricket. o, Longhorn beetle. p, Abathrus bicolor. q, Stylagymnusa subantartica. r, Moth butterfly. s, Paraconosoma naviculare. t, Ornithoptera priamus.

**1999, May 24**

**506** A146 33c Sheet of 20, #a.-t. 13.50 13.50

**Space Type**

International Space Station — #507: a, Launch 1R. b, Launch 14A. c, Launch 8A. d, Launch 1J. e, Launch 1E. f, Launch 16A.

Each $2: No. 508, Intl. Space Station. No. 509, Cmdr. Bob Cabana, Cosmonaut Sergei Krikalev. No. 510, Crew of Flight 2R, horiz. No. 511, X-38 Crew Return Vehicle, horiz.

**1999, June 12 Litho. *Perf. 14***

**507** A145 33c Sheet of 6, #a.-f. 4.00 4.00

**Souvenir Sheets**

**508-511** A145 Set of 4 16.00 16.00

20th Century Visionaries A147

Designs: a, William Gibson, "Cyberspace." b, Danny Hillis, Massively Parallel Processing. c, Steve Wozniak, Apple Computer. d, Steve Jobs, Apple Computer. e, Nolan Bushnell, Atari, Inc. f, John Warnock, Adobe, Inc. g, Ken Thompson, Unix. h, Al Shugart, Seagate Technologies. i, Rand & Robyn Miller, "MYST." j, Nicolas Negroponte, MIT Media Lab. k, Bill Gates, Microsoft, Inc. l, Arthur C. Clarke, Orbiting Communications Satellite. m, Marshall Mcluhan, "The Medium is the Message." n, Thomas Watson, Jr., IBM. o, Gordon Moore, Intel Corporation, "Moore's Law." p, James Gosling, Java. q, Sabeer Bhatia & Jack Smith, Hotmail.com. r, Esther Dyson, "Release 2.0." s, Jerry Yang, David Filo, Yahoo! t, Jeff Bezos, Amazon.com. u, Bob Kahn, TCP-IP. v, Jaron Lanter, "Virtual Reality." w, Andy Grove, Intel Corporation. x, Jim Clark, Silicon Graphics, Inc., Netscape Communications Corp. y, Bob Metcalfe, Ethernet, 3com.

**1999, June 30 Litho. *Perf. 14***

**512** A147 33c Sheet of 25, #a.-y. 17.00 17.00

Paintings by Hokusai (1760-1849) — A148

#513, each 33c: a, Women Divers. b, Bull and Parasol. c, Drawings of Women (partially nude). d, Drawings of Women (seated, facing forward). e, Japanese spaniel. f, Porters in Landscape.

#514, each 33c: a, Bacchanalian Revelry. b, Bacchanalian Revelry (two seated back to back). c, Drawings of Women (crawling). d, Drawings of Women (facing backward). e, Ox-Herd. f, Ox-Herd (man on bridge).

Each $2: No. 515, Mount Fuji in a Thunderstorm, vert. No. 516, At Swan Lake in Shinano.

**1999, July 20 *Perf. 14x13¾***

**Sheets of 6, #a-f**

**513-514** A148 Set of 2 8.00 8.00

**Souvenir Sheets**

**515-516** A148 Set of 2 8.00 8.00

Apollo 11, 30th Anniv. A149

No. 517: a, Lift-off, jettison of stages. b, Earth, moon, capsule. c, Astronaut on lunar module ladder. d, Lift-off. e, Planting flag on moon. f, Astronauts Collins, Armstrong and Aldrin.

Each $2: No. 518, Rocket on launch pad. No. 519, Astronaut on ladder, earth. No. 520, Lunar module above moon. No. 521, Capsule in ocean.

**1999, July 20 Litho. *Perf. 13½x14***

**517** A149 33c Sheet of 6, #a.-f. 4.00 4.00

**Souvenir Sheets**

**518-521** A149 Set of 4 16.00 16.00

Queen Mother (b. 1900) — A150

No. 522: a, In Australia, 1958. b, In 1960. c, In 1970. d, In 1987.

$2, Holding book, 1947.

**Gold Frames**

**522** A150 60c Sheet of 4, #a.-d., + label 4.75 4.75

**Souvenir Sheet**

***Perf. 13¾***

**523** A150 $2 black 4.00 4.00

No. 523 contains one 38x51mm stamp.

See Nos. 636-637.

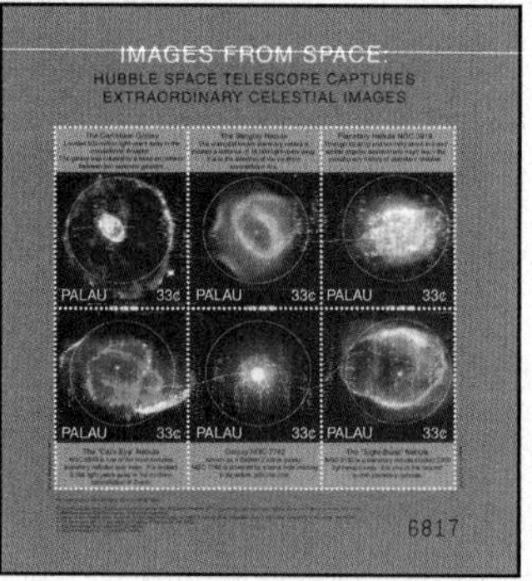


Hubble Space Telescope Images — A151

No. 524: a, Cartwheel Galaxy. b, Stingray Nebula. c, NGC 3918. d, Cat's Eye Nebula (NGC 6543). e, NGC 7742. f, Eight-burst Nebula (NGC 3132).

Each $2: No. 525, Eta Carinae. No. 526, Planetary nebula M2-9. No. 527, Supernova 1987-A. No. 528, Infrared aurora of Saturn.

**1999, Oct. 15 Litho. *Perf. 13¾***

**524** A151 33c Sheet of 6, #a.-f. 4.00 4.00

**Souvenir Sheets**

**525-528** A151 Set of 4 16.00 16.00

Christmas — A152

Birds and: a, Cows, chickens. b, Donkey, geese, rabbit. c, Infant, cat, lambs. d, Goats, geese. e, Donkey, rooster.

**1999, Nov. 15 *Perf. 14***

**529** A152 20c Strip of 5, #a.-e. 2.00 2.00

Love for Dogs — A153

No. 530: a, Keep safe. b, Show affection. c, A place of one's own. d, Communicate. e, Good food. f, Annual checkup. g, Teach rules.

h, Exercise & play. i, Let him help. j, Unconditional love.

Each $2: No. 531, Pleasure of your company. No. 532, Love is a gentle thing.

**1999, Nov. 23 Litho. *Perf. 14***

**530** A153 33c Sheet of 10, #a.-j. 6.75 6.75

**Souvenir Sheets**

**531-532** A153 Set of 2 8.00 8.00

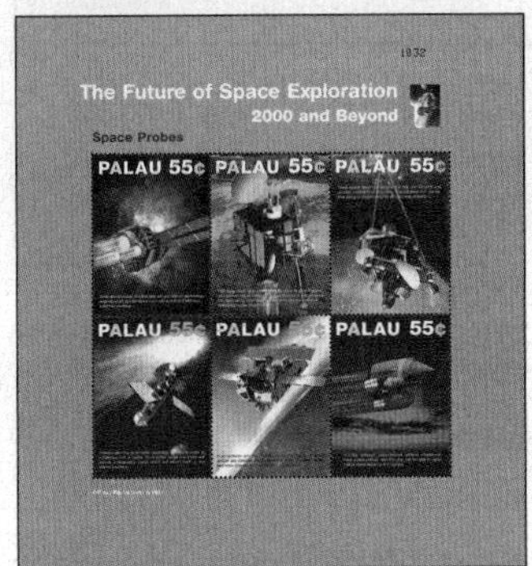

Futuristic Space Probes — A154

Text starting with — No. 533: a, Deep space probes like. . . b, This piggy-back. . . c, Deep space telescope. . . d, Mission planning. . . e, In accordance. . . f, Utilizing onboard. . .

Each $2: No. 534, This secondary. . . No. 535, Deep space probes are an integral. . . No. 536, Deep space probes are our. . . , horiz. No. 537, With the. . . , horiz.

**2000, Jan. 18 Litho. *Perf. 13¾***

**533** A154 55c Sheet of 6, #a.-f. 6.00 6.00

**Souvenir Sheets**

**534-537** A154 Set of 4 16.00 16.00

Millennium — A155

Highlights of 1800-50 — No. 538, each 20c: a, Brazilian Indians. b, Haiti slave revolt. c, Napoleon becomes Emperor of France. d, Shaka Zulu. e, "Frankenstein" written. f, Simon Bolivar. g, Photography invented. h, First water purification works built. i, First all-steam railway. j, Michael Faraday discovers electromagnetism. k, First use of anesthesia. l, Samuel Morse completes first telegraph line. m, Women's rights convention in Seneca Falls, NY. n, Birth of Karl Marx. o, Revolution in German Confederation. p, Charles Darwin's voyages on the "Beagle" (60x40mm). q, Beijing, China.

Highlights of 1980-89 — No. 539, each 20c; a, Lech Walesa organizes Polish shipyard workers. b, Voyager I photographs Saturn. c, Ronald Reagan elected US president. d, Identification of AIDS virus. e, Wedding of Prince Charles and Lady Diana Spencer. f, Compact discs go into production. g, Bhopal, India gas disaster. h, I. M. Pei's Pyramid entrance to the Louvre opens. i, Mikhail Gorbachev becomes leader of Soviet Union. j, Chernobyl nuclear disaster. k, Explosion of Space Shuttle "Challenger." l, Klaus Barbie convicted of crimes against humanity. m, Life of author Salman Rushdie threatened by Moslems. n, Benazir Bhutto becomes first woman prime minister of a Moslem state. o, Tiananmen Square revolt. p, Berlin Wall falls (60x40mm). q, World Wide Web.

**2000, Feb. 2 Litho. *Perf. 12¾x12½***

**Sheets of 17, #a.-q.**

**538-539** A155 Set of 2 14.00 14.00

Misspellings and historical inaccuracies abound on Nos. 538-539.

See No. 584.

New Year 2000 (Year of the Dragon) — A156

**2000, Feb. 5 *Perf. 13¾***

**540** A156 $2 multi 4.00 4.00

US Presidents — A157

**2000, Mar. 1 Litho. *Perf. 13½x13¼***

**541** A157 $1 Bill Clinton 2.00 2.00
**542** A157 $2 Ronald Reagan 4.00 4.00
**543** A157 $3 Gerald Ford 6.00 6.00
**544** A157 $5 George Bush 10.00 10.00

**Size: 40x24mm**

***Perf. 14¾x14***

**545** A157 $11.75 Kennedy 22.50 22.50
*Nos. 541-545 (5)* 44.50 44.50

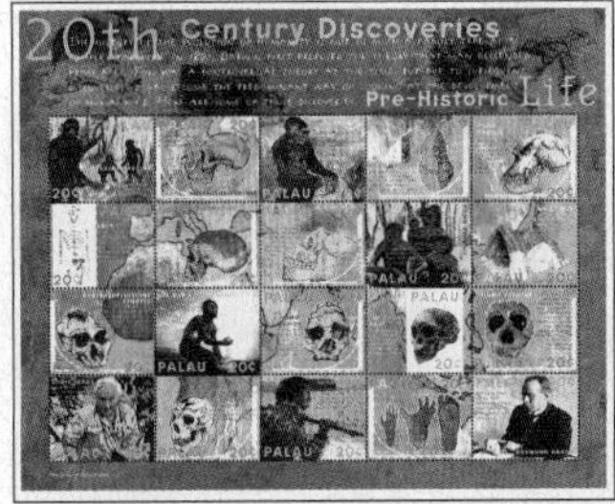

20th Century Discoveries About Prehistoric Life — A158

Designs: a, Australopithecines. b, Australopithecine skull. c, Homo habilis. d, Hand axe. e, Homo habilis skull. f, Lucy, Australopithecine skeleton. g, Archaic Homo sapiens skull. h, Diapithicine skull. i, Homo erectus. j, Wood hut. k, Australopithecine ethopsis skull. l, Dawn of mankind. m, Homo sapiens skull. n, Taung baby's skull. o, Homo erectus skull. p. Louis Leakey (1903-72), paleontologist. q, Neanderthal skull. r, Neandertahal. s, Evolution of the foot. t, Raymond Dart (1893-1988), paleontologist.

**2000, Mar. 15 *Perf. 14¼***

**546** A158 20c Sheet of 20, #a.-t. 8.00 8.00

Misspellings and historical inaccuracies are found on Nos. 546g, 546m, 546p, 546t and perhaps others.

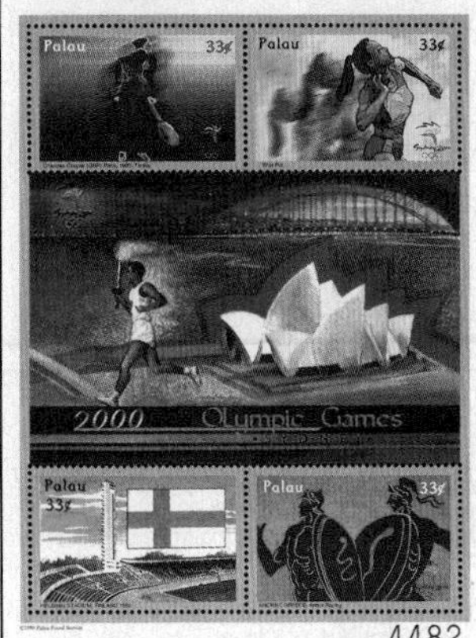

2000 Summer Olympics, Sydney — A159

Designs: a, Charlotte Cooper, tennis player at 1924 Olympics. b, Women's shot put. c, Helsinki Stadium, site of 1952 Olympics. d, Ancient Greek athletes.

**2000, Mar. 31 *Perf. 14***

**547** A159 33c Sheet of 4, #a.-d. 2.75 2.75

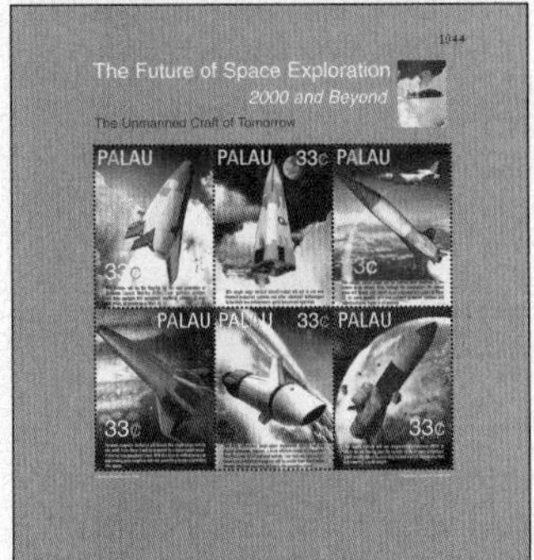

Future of Space Exploration — A160

Text starting with — No. 548: a, This vehicle will be. . . b, This single stage. . . c, This robotic rocket. . . d, Dynamic. . . e, This fully. . . f, This launch vehicle. . .

Each $2: No. 549, Increasingly, space travel. . . No. 550, Designed with projects. . ., horiz. No. 551, Design is currently. . ., horiz. No. 552, Inevitably, the future. . ., horiz.

**2000, Apr. 10 *Perf. 13¾***

**548** A160 33c Sheet of 6, #a.-f. 4.00 4.00

**Souvneir Sheets**

**549-552** A160 Set of 4 16.00 16.00

Birds — A161

No. 553: a, Slatey-legged crake. b, Micronesian kingfisher. c, Little pied cormorant. d, Pacific reed egret. e, Nicobar pigeon. f, Rufous night heron.

No. 554: a, Palau ground dove. b, Palau scops owl. c, Mangrove flycatcher. d, Palau bush warbler. e, Palau fantail. f, Morningbird.

Each $2: No. 555, Palau fruit dove, horiz. No. 556, Palau white-eye, horiz.

**2000, Apr. 14 Litho. *Perf. 14¼***

**553** A161 20c Sheet of 6, #a.-f. 2.40 2.40
**554** A161 33c Sheet of 6, #a.-f. 4.00 4.00

**Souvenir Sheets**

**555-556** A161 Set of 2 8.00 8.00

Visionaries of the 20th Century — A162

a, Booker T. Washington. b, Buckminster Fuller. c, Marie Curie. d, Walt Disney. e, F. D. Roosevelt. f, Henry Ford. g, Betty Friedan. h, Sigmund Freud. i, Mohandas Gandhi. j, Mikhail Gorbachev. k, Stephen Hawking. l, Martin Luther King, Jr. m, Toni Morrison. n, Georgia O'Keeffe. o, Rosa Parks. p, Carl Sagan. q, Jonas Salk. r, Sally Ride. s, Nikola Tesla. t, Wilbur and Orville Wright.

**2000, Apr. 28 Litho. *Perf. 14¼x14½***

**557** A162 33c Sheet of 20, #a.-t. 13.50 13.50

20th Century Science and Medicine Advances — A163

No. 558, each 33c: a, James D. Watson, 1962 Nobel laureate. b, Har Gobind Khorana and Robert Holley, 1968 Nobel laureates. c, Hamilton O. Smith and Werner Arber, 1978 Nobel laureates. d, Extraction fo DNA from cells. e, Richard J. Roberts, 1993 Nobel laureate.

No. 559, each 33c: a, Francis Crick, 1962 Nobel laureate. b, Marshall W. Nirenberg, 1968 Nobel laureate. c, Daniel Nathans, 1978 Nobel laureate. d, Harold E. Varmus and J. Michael Bishop, 1989 Nobel laureates. e, Phillip A. Sharp, 1993 Nobel laureate.

No. 560, each 33c: a, Maurice H. F. Wilkins, 1962 Nobel laureate. b, DNA strand. c, Frederick Sanger and Walter Gilbert, 1980 Nobel laureates. d, Kary B. Mullis, 1993 Nobel laureate. e, Two DNA strands.

No. 561, each 33c: a, Four sheep, test tube. b, Two DNA strands, diagram of DNA fragments. c, Paul Berg, 1980 Nobel laureate. d, Michael Smith, 1993 Nobel laureate. e, Deer, DNA strands.

Each $2: #562, Deer. #563, Dolly, 1st cloned sheep.

Illustration reduced.

**2000, May 10** ***Perf. 13¾***
**Sheets of 5, #a.-e.**

**558-561** A163 Set of 4 14.00 14.00

**Souvenir Sheets**

**562-563** A163 Set of 2 8.00 8.00

Nos. 562-563 each contain one 38x50mm stamp.

Marine Life — A164

No. 564, each 33c: a, Prawn. b, Deep sea angler. c, Rooster fish. d, Grenadier. e, Platyberix opalescens. f, Lantern fish.

No. 565, each 33c: a, Emperor angelfish. b, Nautilus. c, Moorish idol. d, Sea horse. e, Clown triggerfish. f, Clown fish.

Each $2: No. 566, Giant squid. No. 567, Manta ray.

**2000, May 10** **Litho.** ***Perf. 14***
**Sheets of 6, #a-f**

**564-565** A164 Set of 2 8.00 8.00

**Souvenir Sheets**

**566-567** A164 Set of 2 8.00 8.00

Millennium — A165

No. 568, horiz. — "2000," hourglass, and map of: a, North Pacific area. b, U.S. and Canada. c, Europe. d, South Pacific. e, South America. f, Southern Africa.

No. 569 — Clock face and: a, Sky. b, Building. c, Cove and lighthouse. d, Barn. e, Forest. f, Desert.

**2000, May 25** ***Perf. 13¾***

**568** A165 20c Sheet of 6, #a-f 2.40 2.40
**569** A165 55c Sheet of 6, #a-f 6.75 6.75

The Stamp Show 2000, London.

New and Recovering Species — A166

No. 570, each 33c: a, Aleutian Canada goose. b, Western gray kangaroo. c, Palau scops owl. d, Jocotoco antpitta. e, Orchid. f, Red lechwe.

No. 571, each 33c: a, Bald eagle. b, Small-whorled pogonia. c, Arctic peregrine falcon. d, Golden lion tamarin. e, American alligator. f, Brown pelican.

Each $2: No. 572, Leopard. No. 573, Lahontan cutthroat trout, horiz.

**2000, June 20** ***Perf. 14***
**Sheets of 6, #a-f**

**570-571** A166 Set of 2 8.00 8.00

**Souvenir Sheets**

**572-573** A166 Set of 2 8.00 8.00

Dinosaurs — A167

No. 574: a, Rhamphorhynchus. b, Ceratosaurus. c, Apatosaurus. d, Stegosaurus. e, Archaeopteryx. f, Allosaurus.

No. 575: a, Parasaurolophus. b, Pteranodon. c, Tyrannosaurus. d, Triceratops. e, Ankylosaurus. f, Velociraptor.

Each $2: No. 576, Jurassic era view. No. 577, Cretaceous era view.

**2000, June 20**

**574** A167 20c Sheet of 6, #a-f 2.40 2.40
**575** A167 33c Sheet of 6, #a-f 4.00 4.00

**Souvenir Sheets**

**576-577** A167 Set of 2 8.00 8.00

Queen Mother, 100th Birthday — A168

No. 578, 55c: a, With King George VI. b, Wearing brown hat.

No. 579, 55c: a, Wearing green hat. b, Wearing white hat.

**2000, Sept. 1** **Litho.** ***Perf. 14***
**Sheets of 4, 2 each #a-b**

**578-579** A168 Set of 2 9.00 9.00

**Souvenir Sheet**

**580** A168 $2 Wearing yellow hat 4.00 4.00

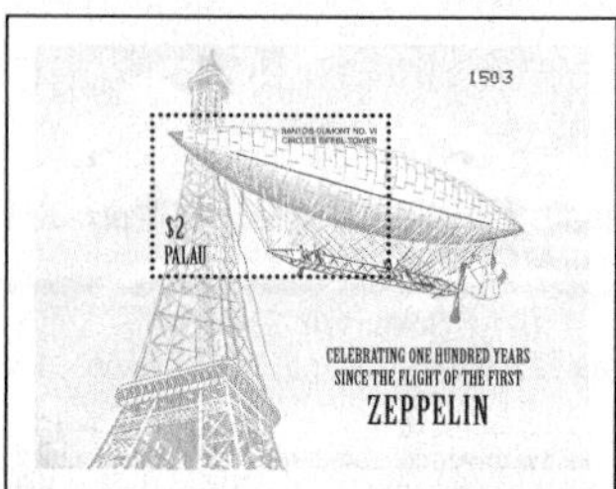


First Zeppelin Flight, Cent. — A169

No. 581: a, Le Jaune. b, Forlanini's Leonardo da Vinci. c, Baldwin's airship. d, Astra-Torres I. e, Parseval PL VII. f, Lebaudy's Liberte.

No. 582, $2, Santos-Dumont No. VI. No. 583, $2, Santos-Dumont Baladeuse No. 9.

**2000, Sept. 1**

**581** A169 55c Sheet of 6, #a-f 6.75 6.75

**Souvenir Sheets**

**582-583** A169 Set of 2 8.00 8.00

**Millennium Type of 2000**

Sheet of 17

Undersea History and Exploration: a, Viking diver. b, Arab diver Issa. c, Salvage diver. d, Diver. e, Diving bell. f, Turtle. g, Siebe helmet. h, C.S.S. Hunley. i, Argonaut. j, Photosphere. k, Helmet diver. l, Bathysphere. m, Coelacanth. n, WWII charioteers. o, Trieste. p, Alvin visits geothermal vents (60x40mm). q, Jim suit.

**2000, Oct. 16** ***Perf. 12¾x12½***

**584** A155 33c #a-q + label 13.00 13.00

Photomosaic of Pope John Paul II — A170

Various photos with religious themes.

**2000, Dec. 1** ***Perf. 13¾***

**585** A170 50c Sheet of 8, #a-h 8.00 8.00

Souvenir Sheets

New Year 2001 (Year of the Snake) — A171

Snake color: #586, Black. #587, Red.

**2000, Dec. 1** ***Perf. 14¼***

**586-587** A171 60c Set of 2 2.40 2.40

Pacific Ocean Marine Life — A172

No. 588: a, Scalloped hammerhead shark. b, Whitetip reef shark. c, Moon jellyfish. d, Lionfish. e, Seahorse. f, Spotted eagle ray.

**2000** ***Perf. 14½x14¼***

**588** A172 55c Sheet of 6, #a-f 6.75 6.75

Atlantic Ocean Fish — A173

No. 589, horiz.: a, Reef bass. b, White shark. c, Sharptail eel. d, Sailfish. e, Southern stingray. f, Ocean triggerfish.

#590, Short bigeye. #591, Gafftopsail catfish.

**2000** ***Perf. 13¾***

**589** A173 20c Sheet of 6, #a-f 2.40 2.40

**Souvenir Sheets**

**590-591** A173 $2 Set of 2 8.00 8.00

Pacific Arts Festival — A174

No. 592: a, Dancers, by S. Adelbai. b, Story Board Art, by D. Inabo. c, Traditional Money, by M. Takeshi. d, Clay Lamp and Bowl, by W. Watanabe. e, Meeting House, by Pasqual Tiakl. f, Outrigger Canoe, by S. Adelbai. g, Weaver, by M. Vitarelli. h, Rock Island Scene, by W. Marcil. i, Contemporary Music, by J. Imetuker.

**2000, Nov. 1** **Litho.** ***Perf. 14¼***

**592** A174 33c Sheet of 9, #a-i 6.00 6.00

National Museum, 45th Anniv. — A175

No. 593: a, Klilt; turtle shell bracelet. b, Sculpture by H. Hijikata. c, Turtle shell women's money. d, Cherecheroi, by T. Suzuki. e, Money jar, by B. Sylvester. f, Prince Lebu by Ichikawa. g, Beach at Lild, by H. Hijikata. h, Traditional mask. i, Taro platter, by T. Rebluud. j, Meresebang, by Ichikawa. k, Wood sculpture, by B. Sylvester. l, Birth Ceremony, by I. Kishigawa.

**2000, Nov. 1** ***Perf. 14x14¾***

**593** A175 33c Sheet of 12, #a-l 8.00 8.00

Butterflies A176

Designs: No. 594, 33c, Indian red admiral. No. 595, 33c, Fiery jewel. No. 596, 33c, Checkered swallowtail. No. 597, 33c, Yamfly.

No. 598, 33c: a, Large green-banded blue. b, Union Jack. c, Broad-bordered grass yellow. d, Striped blue crow. e, Red lacewing. f, Palmfly.

No. 599, 33c: a, Cairn's birdwing. b, Meadow argus. c, Orange albatross. d, Glasswing. e, Beak. f, Great eggfly.

No. 600, $2, Clipper. No. 601, $2, Blue triangle.

**2000, Dec. 15** ***Perf. 14***
**594-597** A176 Set of 4 2.75 2.75

**Sheets of 6, #a-f**

**598-599** A176 Set of 2 8.00 8.00

**Souvenir Sheets**

**600-601** A176 Set of 2 8.00 8.00

Flora and Fauna — A177

No. 602, 33c: a, Giant spiral ginger. b, Good luck plant. c, Ti tree, coconuts. d, Butterfly. e, Saltwater crocodile. f, Orchid.

No. 603, 33c: a, Little kingfisher. b, Mangrove snake. c, Bats, breadfruit. d, Giant tree frog. e, Giant centipede. f, Crab-eating macaque.

No. 604, $2, Soft coral, surgeonfish. No. 605, $2, Land crab, vert.

**2000, Dec. 29** ***Perf. 14x14¼, 14¼x14***

**Sheets of 6, #a-f**

**602-603** A177 Set of 2 8.00 8.00

**Souvenir Sheets**

**604-605** A177 Set of 2 8.00 8.00

### Personalities Type of 1999

Designs: 11c, Lazarus Salil. 70c, Gen. Douglas MacArthur. 80c, Adm. Chester W. Nimitz. $12.25, John F. Kennedy.

**2001** **Litho.** ***Perf. 14x14¾***

| | | | | |
|---|---|---|---|---|
| **606** | A142 | 11c purple | .25 | .25 |
| **607** | A142 | 70c lilac | 1.40 | 1.40 |
| **608** | A142 | 80c green | 1.60 | 1.60 |
| **609** | A142 | $12.25 red | 25.00 | 25.00 |
| | | *Nos. 606-609 (4)* | 28.25 | 28.25 |

Issued: Nos. 607-609, 6/10.

Phila Nippon '01, Japan — A178

No. 610, 60c: a, Ono no Komachi Washing the Copybook, by Kiyomitsu Torii. b, Woman Playing Samisen and Woman Reading al Letter, by School of Matabei Iwasa. c, The Actor Danjura Ichikawa V as a Samurai in a Wrestling Arena Striking a Pose on a Go Board, by Shunsho Katsukawa. d, Gentleman Entertained by Courtesans, by Kiyonaga Torii. e, Geisha at a Teahouse in Shinagawa, by Kiyonaga Torii.

No. 611, 60c: a, Preparing Sashimi, by Utamaro. b, Ichimatsu Sanogawa I as Sogo no Goro and Kikugoro Onoe as Kyo no Jiro in Umewakana Futaba Soga, by Toyonobu Ishikawa. c, Courtesan Adjusting Her Comb, by Dohan Kaigetsudo. d, The Actor Tomijuro Nakamura I in a Female Role Dancing, by Shunsho Katsukawa. e, Woman with Poem Card and Writing Brush, by Gakutei Yashima.

No. 612, Six panels of screen, Kitano Shrine in Kyoto, by unknown artist.

No. 613, $2, Raiko Attacks a Demon Kite, by Hokkei Totoya. No. 614, $2, Beauty Writing a Letter, by Doshin Kaigetsudo. No. 615, $2, Fireworks at Ikenohata, by Kiyochika Kobayashi.

**2001, Aug. 13** **Litho.** ***Perf. 14***

**Sheets of 5, #a-e**

**610-611** A178 Set of 2 12.00 12.00
**612** A178 60c Sheet of 6, #a-f 7.25 7.25

**Souvenir Sheets**

**613-615** A178 Set of 3 12.00 12.00

Moths — A179

Designs: 20c, Veined tiger moth. 21c, Basker moth. 80c, White-lined sphinx moth. $1, Isabella tiger moth.

No. 620, 34c: a, Cinnabar moth. b, Beautiful tiger moth. c, Great tiger moth. d, Provence burnet moth. e, Jersey tiger moth. f, Ornate moth.

No. 621, 70c: a, Hoop pine moth. b, King's bee hawk moth. c, Banded bagnest moth. d, Io moth. e, Tau emperor moth. f, Lime hawkmoth.

No. 622, $2, Spanish moon moth. No. 623, $2, Owl moth.

**2001, Oct. 15** **Litho.** ***Perf. 14***
**616-619** A179 Set of 4 4.50 4.50

**Sheets of 6, #a-f**

**620-621** A179 Set of 2 12.50 12.50

**Souvenir Sheets**

**622-623** A179 Set of 2 8.00 8.00

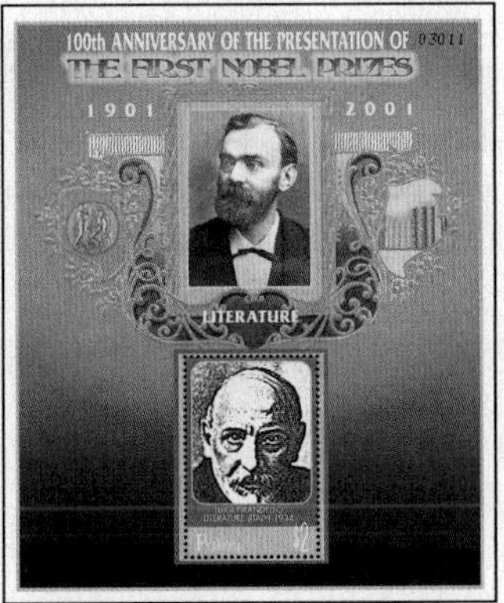


Nobel Prizes, Cent. — A180

Literature laureates — No. 624, 34c: a, Ivo Andric, 1961. b, Eyvind Johnson, 1974. c, Salvatore Quasimodo, 1959. d, Mikhail Sholokhov, 1965. e, Pablo Neruda, 1971. f, Saul Bellow, 1976.

No. 625, 70c: a, Boris Pasternak, 1958. b, Francois Mauriac, 1952. c, Frans Eemil Sillanpää, 1939. d, Roger Martin du Gard, 1937. e, Pearl Buck, 1938. f, André Gide, 1947.

No. 626, 80c: a, Karl Gjellerup, 1917. b, Anatole France, 1921. c, Sinclair Lewis, 1930. d, Jacinto Benavente, 1922. e, John Galsworthy, 1932. f, Erik. A. Karlfeldt, 1931.

No. 627, $2, Luigi Pirandello, 1934. No. 628, $2, Bertrand Russell, 1950. No. 629, Harry Martinson, 1974.

**2001, Oct. 30** **Sheets of 6, #a-f**
**624-626** A180 Set of 3 22.50 22.50

**Souvenir Sheets**

**627-629** A180 Set of 3 12.00 12.00

2002 World Cup Soccer Championships, Japan and Korea — A181

No. 630, 34c — World Cup posters from: a, 1950. b, 1954. c, 1958. d, 1962. e, 1966. f, 1970.

No. 631, 80c — World Cup posters from: a, 1978. b, 1982. c, 1986. d, 1990. e, 1994. f, 1998.

No. 632, $2, World Cup poster, 1930. No. 633, $2, Head and globe from World Cup trophy.

**2001, Nov. 29** ***Perf. 13¾x14¼***

**Sheets of 6, #a-f**

**630-631** A181 Set of 2 14.00 14.00

**Souvenir Sheets**

***Perf. 14½x14¼***

**632-633** A181 Set of 2 8.00 8.00

Christmas — A182

Denominations: 20c, 34c.

**2001, Nov. 29** ***Perf. 14***
**634-635** A182 Set of 2 1.10 1.10

### Queen Mother Type of 1999 Redrawn

No. 636: a, In Australia, 1958. b, In 1960. c, In 1970. d, In 1987.

$2, Holding book, 1947.

**2001, Dec. 13** ***Perf. 14***

**Yellow Orange Frames**

**636** A150 60c Sheet of 4, #a-d, + label 4.75 4.75

**Souvenir Sheet**

***Perf. 13¾***

**637** A150 $2 black 4.00 4.00

Queen Mother's 101st birthday. No. 637 contains one 38x51mm stamp that is slightly darker than that found on No. 523. Sheet margins of Nos. 636-637 lack embossing and gold arms and frames found on Nos. 522-523.

Pasturing Horses, by Han Kan — A183

**2001, Dec. 17** ***Perf. 14x14¾***
**638** A183 60c multi 1.25 1.25

New Year 2002 (Year of the Horse). Printed in sheets of 4.

Birds — A184

No. 639, 55c: a, Yellow-faced myna. b, Red-bellied pitta. c, Red-bearded bee-eater. d, Superb fruit dove. e, Coppersmith barbet. f, Diard's trogon.

No. 640, 60c: a, Spectacled monarch. b, Banded pitta. c, Rufous-backed kingfisher. d, Scarlet robin. e, Golden whistler. f, Jewel babbler.

No. 641, $2, Paradise flycatcher. No. 642, $2, Common kingfisher.

**2001, Dec. 26** ***Perf. 14***

**Sheets of 6, #a-f**

**639-640** A184 Set of 2 14.00 14.00

**Souvenir Sheets**

***Perf. 14¾***

**641-642** A184 Set of 2 8.00 8.00

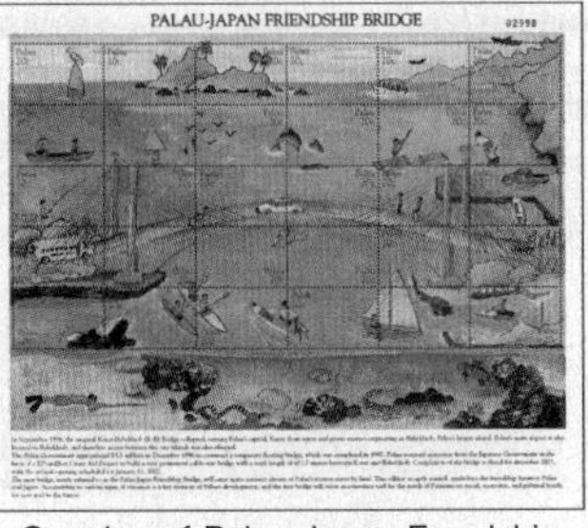


Opening of Palau-Japan Frendship Bridge — A185

No. 643, 20c; No. 644, 34c: a, Bird on orange rock. b, Island, one palm tree. c, Island, three palm trees. d, Rocks, boat prow. e, Boat, bat. f, Cove, foliage. g, Red boat with two people. h, Buoy, birds. i, Birds, dolphin's tail. j, Dolphins. k, Person on raft. l, Two people standing in water. m, Person with fishing pole in water. n, Bridge tower. o, Bicyclist, taxi. p, Front of taxi. q, People walking on bridge, bridge tower. r, Truck, boat. s, School bus. t, Base of bridge tower. u, Birds under bridge, oar. v, Birds under bridge. w, Base of bridge tower, tip of sail. x, Motorcyclist. y, Birds on black rock. z, Kayakers. aa, Kayak, boat. ab, Boat, sailboat. ac, Sailboat, jetty. ad, Jetski.

**2002, Jan. 11** ***Perf. 13***

**Sheets of 30, #a-ad**

**643-644** A185 Set of 2 32.50 32.50

United We Stand — A186

**2002, Jan. 24** ***Perf. 14***
**645** A186 $1 multi 2.00 2.00

Reign of Queen Elizabeth II, 50th Anniv. — A187

No. 646: a, In uniform. b, Wearing flowered hat. c, Prince Philip. d, Wearing tiara.
$2, Wearing white dress.

**2002, Feb. 6** ***Perf. 14¼***
**646** A187 80c Sheet of 4, #a-d 6.50 6.50

**Souvenir Sheet**

**647** A187 $2 multi 4.00 4.00

Birds — A188

Designs: 1c, Gray-backed white-eye. 2c, Great frigatebird. 3c, Eclectus parrot. 4c, Red-footed booby. 5c Cattle egret. 10c, Cardinal honeyeater. 11c, Blue-faced parrot-finch. 15c, Rufous fantail. 20c, White-faced storm petrel. 21c, Willie wagtail. 23c, Black-headed gull. 50c, Sanderling. 57c, White-tailed tropicbird. 70c, Rainbow lorikeet. 80c, Moorhen. $1, Buff-banded rail. $2, Beach thick-knee. $3, Common tern. $3.50, Ruddy turnstone. $3.95, White-collared kingfisher. $5, Sulphur-crested cockatoo. $10, Barn swallow.

**2002, Feb. 20** ***Perf. 14¼***

| | | | | |
|---|---|---|---|---|
| **648** | A188 | 1c multi | .25 | .25 |
| **649** | A188 | 2c multi | .25 | .25 |
| **650** | A188 | 3c multi | .25 | .25 |
| **651** | A188 | 4c multi | .25 | .25 |
| **652** | A188 | 5c multi | .25 | .25 |
| **653** | A188 | 10c multi | .25 | .25 |
| **654** | A188 | 11c multi | .25 | .25 |
| **655** | A188 | 15c multi | .30 | .30 |
| **656** | A188 | 20c multi | .40 | .40 |
| **657** | A188 | 21c multi | .40 | .40 |
| **658** | A188 | 23c multi | .45 | .45 |
| **659** | A188 | 50c multi | 1.00 | 1.00 |
| **660** | A188 | 57c multi | 1.10 | 1.10 |
| **661** | A188 | 70c multi | 1.40 | 1.40 |
| **662** | A188 | 80c multi | 1.60 | 1.60 |
| **663** | A188 | $1 multi | 2.00 | 2.00 |
| **664** | A188 | $2 multi | 4.00 | 4.00 |
| **665** | A188 | $3 multi | 6.00 | 6.00 |
| **666** | A188 | $3.50 multi | 7.00 | 7.00 |
| **667** | A188 | $3.95 multi | 8.00 | 8.00 |
| **668** | A188 | $5 multi | 10.00 | 10.00 |
| **669** | A188 | $10 multi | 20.00 | 20.00 |
| | *Nos. 648-669 (22)* | | 65.40 | 65.40 |

Flowers — A189

Designs: 20c, Euanthe sanderiana. 34c, Ophiorrhiza palauensis. No. 672, 60c, Cerbera manghas. 80c, Mendinilla pterocaula.
No. 674, 60c: a, Bruguiera gymnorhiza. b, Samadera indiccal. c, Maesa canfieldiae. d, Lumnitzera litorea. e, Dolichandrone palawense. f, Limnophila aromatica (red and white orchids).
No. 675, 60c: a, Sonneratia alba. b, Barringtonia racemosa. c, Ixora casei. d, Tristellateia australasiae. e, Nepenthes mirabilis. f, Limnophila aromatica (pink flowers).
No. 676, $2, Fagraea ksid. No. 677, $2, Cerbera manghas, horiz.

**2002, Mar. 4** ***Perf. 14***
**670-673** A189 Set of 4 4.00 4.00

**Sheets of 6, #a-f**

**674-675** A189 Set of 2 14.50 14.50

**Souvenir Sheets**

**676-677** A189 Set of 2 8.00 8.00

2002 Winter Olympics, Salt Lake City A190

Skier with: No. 678, $1, Blue pants. No. 679, $1, Yellow pants.

**2002, Mar. 18** ***Perf. 14¼***
**678-679** A190 Set of 2 4.00 4.00
*679a* Souvenir sheet, #678-679 4.00 4.00

Cats and Dogs — A191

No. 680, 50c, horiz.: a, Himalayan. b, Norwegian forest cat. c, Havana. d, Exotic shorthair. e, Persian. f, Maine coon cat.
No. 681, 50c, horiz.: a, Great Dane. b, Whippet. c, Bedlington terrier. d, Golden retriever. e, Papillon. f, Doberman pinscher.
No. 682, $2, British shorthair. No. 683, $2, Shetland sheepdog.

**2002, Mar. 18 Litho.** ***Perf. 14***

**Sheets of 6, #a-f**

**680-681** A191 Set of 2 12.00 12.00

**Souvenir Sheets**

**682-683** A191 Set of 2 8.00 8.00

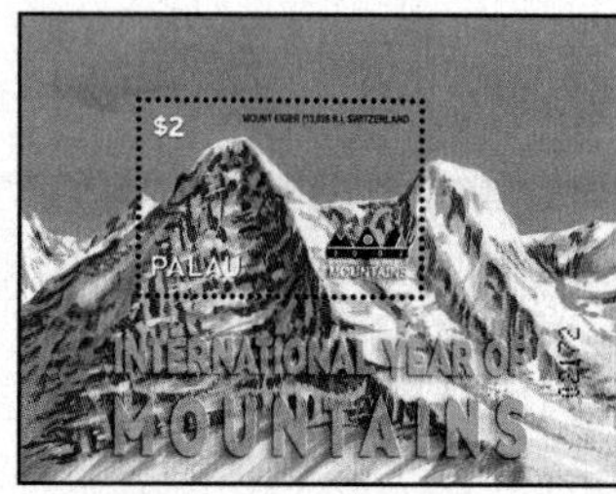


Intl. Year of Mountains — A192

No. 684: a, Mt. Fuji, Japan. b, Mt. Everest, Nepal and China. c, Mt. Owen, US. d, Mt. Huascarán, Peru.
$2, Mt. Eiger, Switzerland.

**2002, June 17 Litho.** ***Perf. 14***
**684** A192 80c Sheet of 4, #a-d 6.50 6.50

**Souvenir Sheet**

**685** A192 $2 multi 4.00 4.00

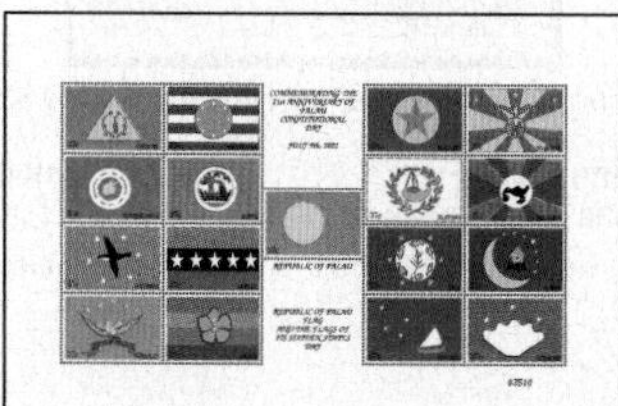

Flags of Palau and its States — A193

No. 686: a, Palau (no inscription). b, Kayangel. c, Ngarchelong. d, Ngaraard. e, Ngardmau. f, Ngaremlengui. g, Ngiwal. h, Ngatpang. i, Melekeor. j, Ngchesar. k, Aimeliik. l, Airai. m, Koror. n, Peleliu. o, Angaur. p, Sonsorol. q, Hatohobei.

**2002, July 9**
**686** A193 37c Sheet of 17, #a-q 13.00 13.00

All stamps on No. 686 lack country name.

**Winter Olympics Type of 2002 Redrawn with White Olympic Rings**

Skier with: No. 687, $1, Blue pants. No. 688, $1, Yellow pants.

**2002, July 29** ***Perf. 13½***
**687-688** A190 Set of 2 4.00 4.00
*688a* Souvenir sheet, #687-688 4.00 4.00

Intl. Year of Ecotourism — A194

No. 689: a, Divers, angelfish facing right. b, Ray. c, Sea cucumber. d, Emperor angelfish facing left. e, Sea turtle. f, Nautilus.
$2, Person in canoe.

**2002, Apr. 26** ***Perf. 14½x14¼***
**689** A194 60c Sheet of 6, #a-f 7.25 7.25

**Souvenir Sheet**

**690** A194 $2 multi 4.00 4.00

Japanese Art — A195

No. 691, vert. (38x50mm): a, The Actor Shuka Bando as Courtesan Shiraito, by Kunisada Utagawa. b, The Actor Danjuro Ichikawa VII as Sugawara no Michizane, by Kunisada Utagawa. c, The Actor Sojuro Sawamura III as Yuranosuke Oboshi, by Toyokuni Utagawa. d, The Actor Nizaemon Kataoka VII as Shihei Fujiwara, by Toyokuni Utagawa. e, Bust Portrait of the Actor Noshio Nakamura II, by Kunimasa Utagawa. f, The Actor Gon-Nosuke Kawarazaki as Daroku, by Kunichika Toyohara.
No. 692, 80c, vert. (27x88mm): a, Bush Clover Branch and Sweetfish, by Kuniyoshi Utagawa. b, Catfish, by Kuniyoshi Utagawa. c, Scene at Takanawa, by Eisen Keisai. d, Ochanomizu, by Keisai.
No. 693, 80c (50x38mm): a, Gaslight Hall, by Kiyochika Kobayashi. b, Cherry Blossoms at Night at Shin Yoshiwara, by Yasuji Inoue. c, Night Rain at Oyama, by Toyokuni Utagawa II. d, Kintai Bridge, by Keisai.
No. 694, $2, Okane, a Strong Woman of Omi, by Kuniyoshi Utagawa. No. 695, $2, Scene on the Banks of the Oumaya River, by Kuniyoshi Utagawa.

***Perf. 14¼, 13½ (#692)***

**2002, Sept. 23**
**691** A195 60c Sheet of 6, #a-f 7.25 7.25

**Sheets of 4, #a-d**

**692-693** A195 Set of 2 13.00 13.00

**Size: 105x85mm**

***Imperf***

**694-695** A195 Set of 2 8.00 8.00

Popeye — A196

No. 696, vert.: a, Wimpy. b, Swee'Pea. c, Popeye. d, Fish. e, Jeep. f, Brutus.
$2, Popeye golfing.

**2002, Oct. 7** ***Perf. 14***
**696** A196 60c Sheet of 6, #a-f 7.25 7.25

**Souvenir Sheet**

**697** A196 $2 multi 4.00 4.00

Elvis Presley (1935-77) — A197

No. 698: a, On horse. b, Holding guitar, wearing white jacket, no hat. c, Wearing black hat. d, With guitar with two necks. e, Holding guitar, wearing colored jacket, no hat. f, Wearing shirt.

**2002, Oct. 23**
**698** A197 37c Sheet of 6, #a-f 4.75 4.75

Christmas A198

Designs: 23c, Presentation of Jesus in the Temple, by Perugino, vert. 37c, Madonna and Child Enthroned Between Angels and Saints, by Domenico Ghirlandaio, vert. 60c, Maesta, by Simone Martini, vert. 80c, Sacred Conversation, by Giovanni Bellini. $1, Nativity, by Ghirlandaio.
$2, Sacred Conversation (detail), by Bellini.

**2002, Nov. 5**
**699-703** A198 Set of 5 6.00 6.00

**Souvenir Sheet**

**704** A198 $2 multi 4.00 4.00

The painting shown on No. 704 does not appear to be a detail of the painting shown on No. 702.

Teddy Bears, Cent. — A199

No. 705: a, Accountant bear. b, Computer programmer bear. c, Businesswoman bear. d, Lawyer bear.

**2002, Nov. 19**
**705** A199 60c Sheet of 4, #a-d 5.00 5.00

Queen Mother Elizabeth (1900-2002) — A200

No. 706: a, Holding bouquet. b, Wearing blue blouse and pearls. c, Wearing purple hat. d, Wearing tiara.
$2, Wearing flowered hat.

**2002, Dec. 30**
**706** A200 80c Sheet of 4, #a-d 6.50 6.50

**Souvenir Sheet**

**707** A200 $2 multi 4.00 4.00

20th World Scout Jamboree, Thailand (in 2002) — A201

No. 708, horiz.: a, Scout climbing rocks. b, Scout emblem, knife. c, Branches lashed together with rope. d, Cub scout (wearing cap). e, Knot. f, Boy scout (without cap).
$2 Lord Robert Baden-Powell.

**2003, Jan. 13** ***Perf. 14***
**708** A201 60c Sheet of 6, #a-f 7.25 7.25

**Souvenir Sheet**

**709** A201 $2 multi 4.00 4.00

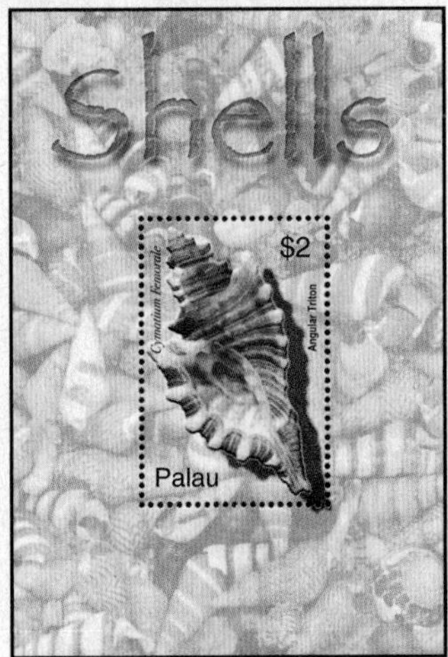


Shells — A202

No. 710: a, Leafy murex. b, Trumpet triton. c, Giant tun. d, Queen conch. e, Spotted tun. f, Emperor helmet.
$2, Angular triton.

**2003, Jan. 13**
**710** A202 60c Sheet of 6, #a-f 7.25 7.25

**Souvenir Sheet**

**711** A202 $2 multi 4.00 4.00

New Year 2003 (Year of the Ram) — A203

No. 712: a, Ram facing right. b, Ram facing forward. c, Ram facing left.

**2003, Jan. 27** ***Perf. 14¼x13¾***
**712** A203 37c Vert. strip of 3, #a-c 2.25 2.25
Sheet of 2 strips 4.50

No. 712 printed in sheets of 2 strips with slightly different backgrounds.

Pres. John F. Kennedy (1917-63) — A204

No. 713: a, Wearing cap. b, Facing left. c, Facing right. d, Holding ship's wheel.

**2003, Feb. 10** ***Perf. 14***
**713** A204 80c Sheet of 4, #a-d 6.50 6.50

**Bird Type of 2002 With Unserifed Numerals**

Designs: 26c, Golden whistler. 37c, Pale white-eye.

**2003, Mar. 1** ***Perf. 14¼x13¾***
**714** A188 26c multi .55 .55
**715** A188 37c multi .75 .75

Astronauts Killed in Space Shuttle Columbia Accident — A205

No. 716: a, Mission Specialist 1 David M. Brown. b, Commander Rick D. Husband. c, Mission Specialist 4 Laurel Blair Salton Clark. d, Mission Specialist 4 Kalpana Chawla. e, Payload Commander Michael P. Anderson. f, Pilot William C. McCool. g, Payload Specialist 4 Ilan Ramon.

**2003, Apr. 7** ***Perf. 13¼***
**716** A205 37c Sheet of 7, #a-g 5.25 5.25

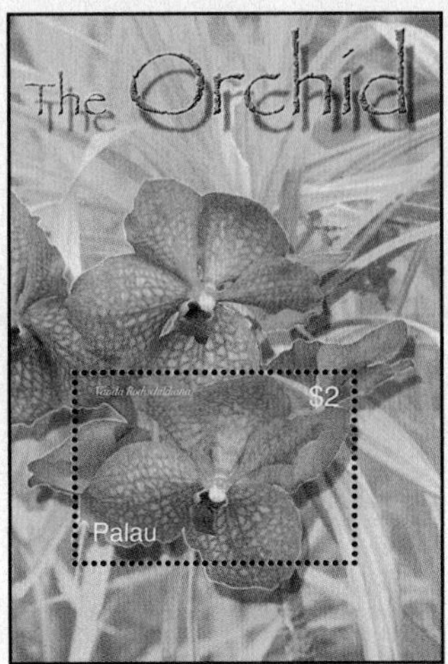


Orchids — A206

No. 717: a, Phalaenopsis grex. b, Cattleya loddigesii. c, Phalaenopsis joline. d, Dendrobium. e, Laelia anceps. f, Cymbidium Stanley Fouracre.
$2, Vanda rothschildiana.

**2003, Jan. 13** **Litho.** ***Perf. 14***
**717** A206 60c Sheet of 6, #a-f 7.25 7.25

**Souvenir Sheet**

**718** A206 $2 multi 4.00 4.00

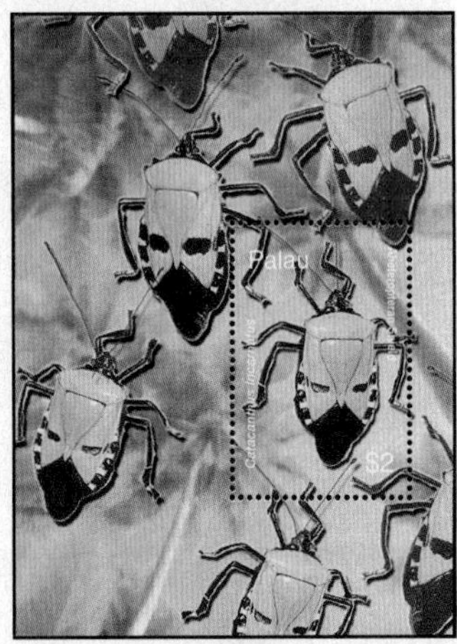


Insects — A207

No. 719: a, Giant water bug. b, Weevil. c, Blister beetle. d, Bess beetle. e, Metallic stag beetle. f, Violin beetle.
$2, Aheteropteran shield.

**2003, Jan. 13**
**719** A207 60c Sheet of 6, #a-f 7.25 7.25

**Souvenir Sheet**

**720** A207 $2 multi 4.00 4.00

First Non-stop Solo Transatlantic Flight, 75th Anniv. — A208

No. 721: a, Charles Lindbergh, Donald Hall and Spirit of St. Louis. b, Spirit of St. Louis, Apr. 28, 1927. c, Spirit of St. Louis towed from Curtiss Field, May 20, 1927. d, Spirit of St. Louis takes off, May 20, 1927. e, Arrival in Paris, May 21, 1927. f, New York ticker tape parade.

**2003, Feb. 10**
**721** A208 60c Sheet of 6, #a-f 7.25 7.25

Pres. Ronald Reagan — A209

Reagan with: a, Orange bandana. b, Red shirt. c, Blue shirt, head at left. d, Blue shirt, head at right.

**2003, Feb. 10**
**722** A209 80c Sheet of 4, #a-d 6.50 6.50

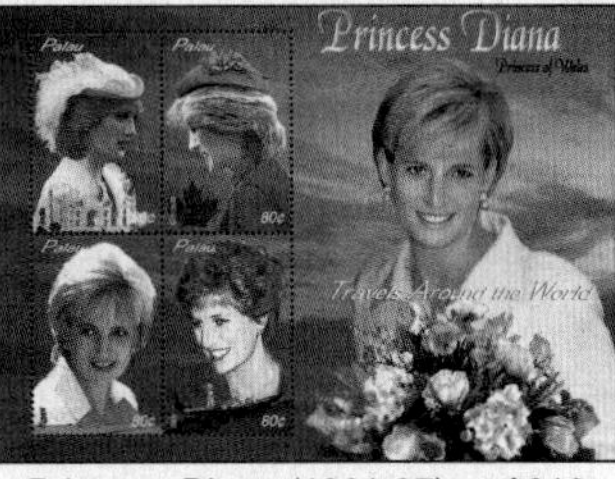


Princess Diana (1961-97) — A210

Diana and clothing worn in: a, India. b, Canada. c, Egypt. d, Italy.

**2003, Feb. 10**
**723** A210 80c Sheet of 4, #a-d 6.50 6.50

Coronation of Queen Elizabeth II, 50th Anniv. — A211

No. 724 — Queen with: a, Tiara. b, Pink dress. c, Hat.
$2, Tiara, diff.

**2003, May 13**
**724** A211 $1 Sheet of 3, #a-c 6.00 6.00

**Souvenir Sheet**

**725** A211 $2 multi 4.00 4.00

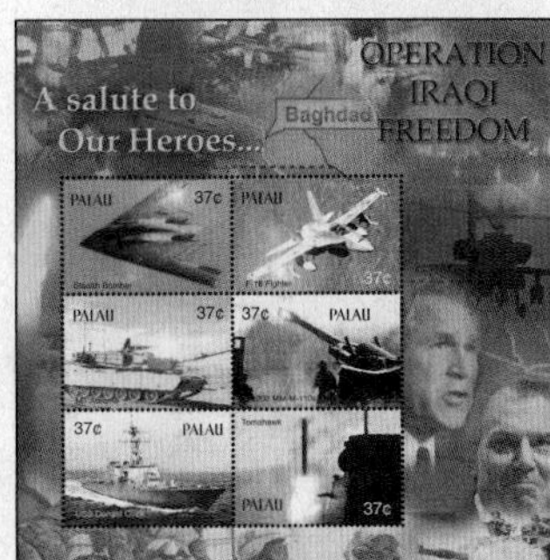


Operation Iraqi Freedom — A212

No. 726: a, Stealth bomber. b, F-18 fighter. c, MT Abrams tank. d, 203mm M-110s. e, USS Donald Cook. f, Tomahawk missile.

**2003, May 14**

**726** A212 37c Sheet of 6, #a-f 4.50 4.50

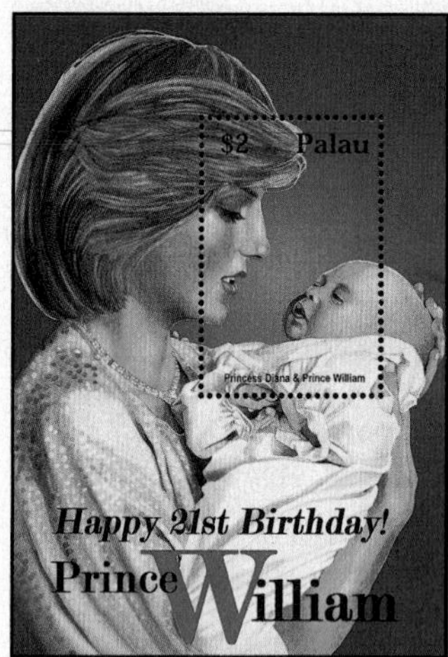


Prince William, 21st Birthday — A213

No. 727 — William: a, In yellow green shirt. b, As infant. c, In black sweater.
$2, As infant with Princess Diana.

**2003, June 21**

**727** A213 $1 Sheet of 3, #a-c 6.00 6.00

**Souvenir Sheet**

**728** A213 $2 multi 4.00 4.00

Tour de France Bicycle Race, Cent. — A214

No. 729: a, Henri Pelissier, 1923. b, Ottavio Bottecchia, 1924. c, Bottecchia, 1925. d, Lucien Buysse, 1926.
$2, Philippe Thys, 1920.

**2003, Aug. 23** ***Perf. 13¼***

**729** A214 60c Sheet of 4, #a-d 5.00 5.00

**Souvenir Sheet**

**730** A214 $2 multi 4.00 4.00

Powered Flight, Cent. — A215

No. 731: a, Fokker 70. b, Boeing 747-217B. c, Curtiss T-32 Condor. d, Vickers Viscount Type 761. e, Wright Flyer III. f, Avro Ten Achilles.
$2, Wright Flyer III, diff.

**2003, Aug. 25** ***Perf. 14***

**731** A215 55c Sheet of 6, #a-f 6.75 6.75

**Souvenir Sheet**

**732** A215 $2 multi 4.00 4.00

Paintings by James McNeill Whistler — A216

Designs: 37c, Blue and Silver: Trouville. 55c, The Last of Old Westminster. 60c, Wapping. $1, Cremorne Gardens, No. 2.
No. 737, vert.: a, Arrangement in Flesh Color and Black, Portrait of Theodore Duret. b, Arrangement in White and Black. c, Harmony in Pink and Gray, Portrait of Lady Meux. d, Arrangement in Black and Gold, Comte Robert de Montesquiou-Fezensac.
$2, Arrangement in Gray and Black No. 1, Portrait of Painter's Mother, vert.

***Perf. 14¼, 13¼ (#737)***

**2003, Sept. 22**

**733-736** A216 Set of 4 5.25 5.25
**737** A216 80c Sheet of 4, #a-d 6.50 6.50

**Souvenir Sheet**

**738** A216 $2 multi 4.00 4.00

No. 737 contains four 35x71mm stamps.

Circus Performers — A217

No. 739, 80c — Clowns: a, Apes. b, Mo Life. c, Gigi. d, "Buttons" McBride.
No. 740, 80c: a, Dogs. b, Olena Yaknenko. c, Mountain High. d, Chinese Circus.

**2003, Sept. 29** ***Perf. 14***

**Sheets of 4, #a-d**

**739-740** A217 Set of 2 13.00 13.00

Christmas A218

Designs: 37c, Madonna della Melagrana, by Botticelli. 60c, Madonna del Magnificat, by Botticelli. 80c, Madonna and Child with the Saints and the Angels, by Andrea del Sarto. $1, La Madonna del Roseto, by Botticelli.
$2, Madonna and Child with the Angels and Saints, by Domenico Ghirlandaio.

**2003, Dec. 1** ***Perf. 14¼***

**741-744** A218 Set of 4 5.75 5.75

**Souvenir Sheet**

**745** A218 $2 multi 4.00 4.00

Sea Turtles — A219

No. 746: a, Mating. b, Laying eggs at night. c, Hatching. d, Turtles going to sea. e, Growing up at sea. f, Returning to lay eggs.
$2, Head of sea turtle.

**2004, Feb. 6** ***Perf. 14***

**746** A219 60c Sheet of 6, #a-f 7.25 7.25

**Souvenir Sheet**

**747** A219 $2 multi 4.00 4.00

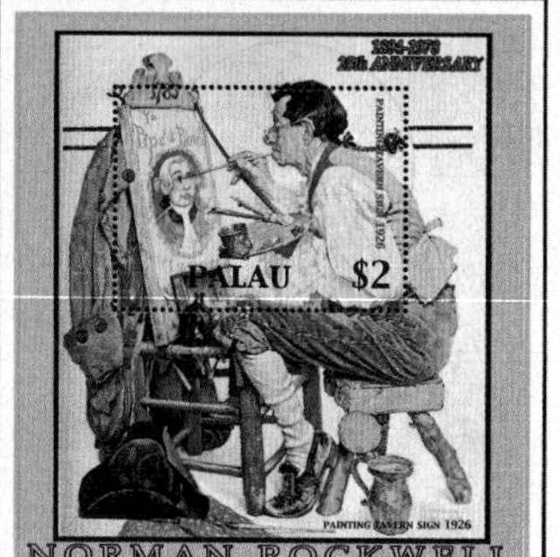


Paintings by Norman Rockwell — A220

No. 748, vert.: a, The Connoisseur. b, Artist Facing a Blank Canvas (Deadline). c, Art Critic. d, Stained Glass Artistry.
$2, Painting Tavern Sign.

**2004, Feb. 6 Litho.** ***Perf. 14¼***

**748** A220 80c Sheet of 4, #a-d 6.50 6.50

**Souvenir Sheet**

**749** A220 $2 multi 4.00 4.00

Paintings by Pablo Picasso — A221

No. 750: a, Dora Maar. b, The Yellow Sweater (Dora). c, Woman in Green (Dora). d, Woman in an Armchair (Dora).
$2, Woman Dressing Her Hair (Dora).

**2004, Feb. 16 Litho.** ***Perf. 14¼***

**750** A221 80c Sheet of 4, #a-d 6.50 6.50

***Imperf***

**751** A221 $2 multi 4.00 4.00

No. 750 contains four 37x50mm stamps.

Paintings in the Hermitage, St. Petersburg, Russia A222

Designs: 37c, Antonia Zarate, by Francisco de Goya. 55c, Portrait of a Lady, by Antonio Correggio. 80c, Portrait of Count Olivarez, by Diego Velázquez. $1, Portrait of a Young Man With a Lace Collar, by Rembrandt.
$2, Family Portrait, by Anthony Van Dyck.

**2004, Feb. 16 Litho.** ***Perf. 14¼***

**752-755** A222 Set of 4 5.50 5.50

**Size: 62x81mm**

***Imperf***

**756** A222 $2 multi 4.00 4.00

Marine Life — A223

No. 757: a, Coral hind. b, Sea octopus. c, Manta ray. d, Dugong. e, Marine crab. f, Grouper.
$2, Gray reef shark.

**2004, Feb. 16** ***Perf. 14¼***

**757** A223 55c Sheet of 6, #a-f 6.75 6.75

**Souvenir Sheet**

**758** A223 $2 multi 4.00 4.00

Minerals — A224

No. 759: a, Phosphate. b, Antimony. c, Limonite. d, Calcopyrite. e, Bauxite. f, Manganite.
$2, Gold.

**2004, Feb. 16**

**759** A224 55c Sheet of 6, #a-f 6.75 6.75

**Souvenir Sheet**

**760** A224 $2 multi 4.00 4.00

New Year 2004 (Year of the Monkey) A225

Green Bamboo and a White Ape, by Ren Yu: 50c, Detail. $1, Entire painting.

**2004, Mar. 9** *Perf. 13¼*
**761** A225 50c multi 1.00 1.00

**Souvenir Sheet**
***Perf. 13½x13¼***

**762** A225 $1 multi 2.00 2.00

No. 761 printed in sheets of 4. No. 762 contains one 27x83mm stamp.

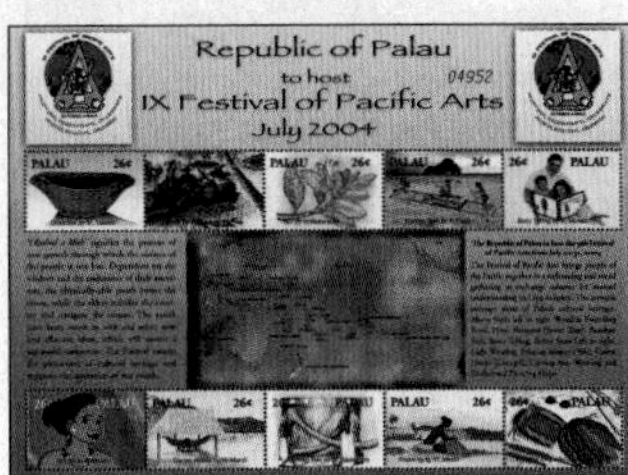


Ninth Festival of Pacific Arts — A226

No. 763, 26c: a, Oraschel, by M. Takeshi. b, Flute, by Sim Adelbai. c, Rur, by W. Watanabe. d, Bamboo Raft, by P. Tiakl. e, Story Telling, by K. Murret. f, Yek, by A. Imetuker. g, Canoe House, by W. Marsil. h, Carving Axe, by Watanabe. i, Weaving, by Marsil. j, Dancing Props, by Adelbai.

No. 764, 37c: a, Ongall, by Tiakl. b, Bai, by S. Weers. c, Taro Plant, by S. Smaserui. d, Toluk, by Watanabe. e, Medicinal Plants, by Smaserui. f, War Canoe, by Takeshi. g, Painting, by Adelbai. h, Pounding Taro, by Imetuker. h, Llengel, by Takeshi. i, Spear Technique, by Imetuker.

**2004, Apr. 13** *Perf. 13*
**Sheets of 10, #a-j**
**763-764** A226 Set of 2 13.00 13.00

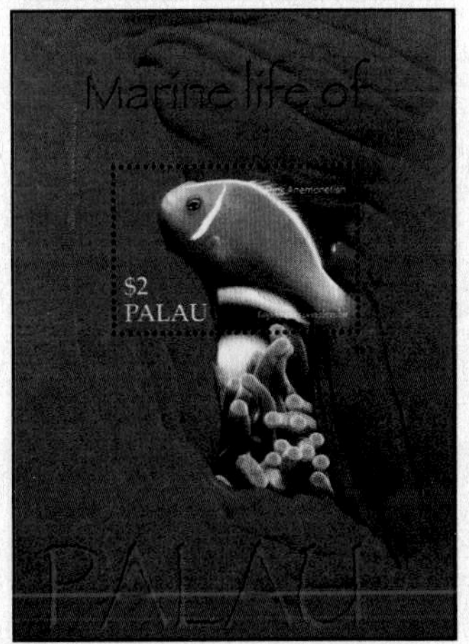


Marine Life — A227

No. 765, 26c: a, Cuttlefish. b, Long fin bannerfish. c, Red sponge, Medusa worm. d, Risbecia tryoni. e, Emperor angelfish. f, Chromodoris coi.

No. 766, 37c: a, Spotted eagle ray. b, Jellyfish. c, Nautilus. d, Gray reef shark. e, Tunicates. f, Manta ray.

No. 767, $2, Pink anemonefish. No. 768, $2, Dusky anemonefish.

**2004, May 20** *Perf. 14*
**Sheets of 6, #a-f**
**765-766** A227 Set of 2 7.75 7.75

**Souvenir Sheets**
**767-768** A227 Set of 2 8.00 8.00

No. 765 contains six labels.

Intl. Year of Peace — A228

No. 769, vert.: a, Mahatma Gandhi. b, Nelson Mandela. c, Dr. Martin Luther King, Jr. $2, Dove.

**2004, May 24** *Perf. 13½x13¼*
**769** A228 $3 Sheet of 3, #a-c 18.00 18.00

**Souvenir Sheet**
***Perf. 13¼x13½***

**770** A228 $2 multi 4.00 4.00

2004 Summer Olympics, Athens — A229

Designs: 37c, Athletes. 55c, Gold medals, Atlanta, 1996. 80c, Johannes Edström, Intl. Olympic Committee President, 1942-52, vert. $1, Women's soccer, Atlanta, 1996.

**2004, June 18** *Perf. 14¼*
**771-774** A229 Set of 4 5.50 5.50

Election of Pope John Paul, 25th Anniv. (in 2003) — A230

Pope John Paul II: a, With Mehmet Agca, 1983. b, Visiting Poland, 2002. c, At concert in Ischia, Italy, 2002. d, With Patriarch Zakka, 2003.

**2004, June 18**
**775** A230 80c Sheet of 4, #a-d 6.50 6.50

**Souvenir Sheet**

Deng Xiaoping (1904-97) Chinese Leader — A231

**2004, June 18**
**776** A231 $2 multi 4.00 4.00

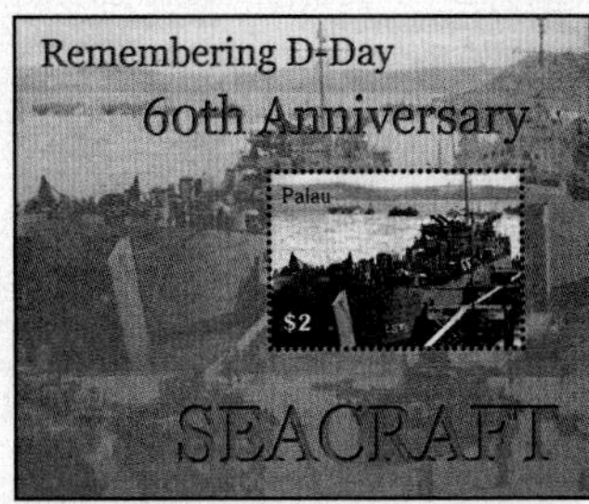


D-Day, 60th Anniv. — A232

No. 777: a, LCA 1377. b, Landing Craft, Infantry. c, LCVP. d, U-309. e, HMS Begonia. f, HMS Roberts.

$2, LSTs.

**2004, June 18**
**777** A232 50c Sheet of 6, #a-f 6.00 6.00

**Souvenir Sheet**
**778** A232 $2 multi 4.00 4.00

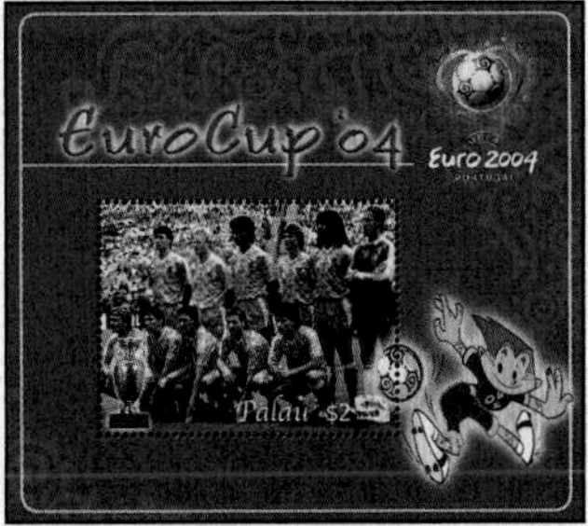


European Soccer Championships, Portugal — A233

No. 779, vert.: a, Rinus Michels. b, Rinat Dasaev. c, Marco Van Basten. d, Olympiastadion.

$2, 1988 Netherlands team.

**2004, June 18**
**779** A233 80c Sheet of 4, #a-d 6.50 6.50

**Souvenir Sheet**
**780** A233 $2 multi 4.00 4.00

No. 779 contains four 28x42mm stamps.

Babe Ruth (1895-1948), Baseball Player — A234

Ruth and: No. 781, 37c, Signed baseball. No. 782, 37c, World Series 100th anniversary emblem.

**2004, Sept. 3** *Perf. 13½x13¼*
**781-782** A234 Set of 2 1.50 1.50

Nos. 781-782 each printed in sheets of 8.

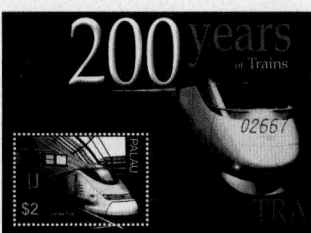

Trains, Bicent. — A235

No. 783: a, ATSF 315. b, Amtrak 464. c, Railway N52. d, SD 70 MAC Diesel-electric locomotive. No. 784, 50c: a, CS SO2002. b, P 36 N0032. c, SW-600. d, Gambier LNV 9703 4-4-0 NG.

No. 785, $2, CN5700 locomotive. No. 786, $2, Eurostar.

**2004, Sept. 27** *Perf. 13¼x13½*
**783** A235 26c Sheet of 4, #a-d 2.10 2.10
**784** A235 50c Sheet of 4, #a-d 4.00 4.00

**Souvenir Sheet**
**785** A235 $2 multi 4.00 4.00
**786** A235 $2 multi 4.00 4.00

Butterflies, Reptiles, Amphibians and Birds — A236

No. 787, 80c — Butterflies: a, Cethosia hypsea. b, Cethosia myrina. c, Charaxes durnfordi. d, Charaxes nitebis.

No. 788, 80c — Reptiles: a, Bull snake. b, Garter snake. c, Yellow-lipped sea snake. d, Yellow-bellied sea snake.

No. 789, 80c, vert. — Birds: a, Blue-faced parrot finch. b, Mangrove flycatcher. c, Palau swiftlet. d, Bridled white-eye.

No. 790, $2, Charaxes nitebis, diff. No. 791, $2, Glass frog. No. 792, $2, Dusky white-eye, vert.

**2004, Oct. 13** **Litho.** *Perf. 14*
**Sheets of 4, #a-d**
**787-789** A236 Set of 3 19.50 19.50

**Souvenir Sheets**
**790-792** A236 Set of 3 12.00 12.00



Dinosaurs — A237

No. 793, 26c, vert.: a, Kritosaurus. b, Triceratops. c, Hypselosaurus. d, Yingshanosaurus.

No. 794, 80c: a, Hadrosaurus. b, Pterodaustro. c, Agilisaurus. d, Amargasaurus.

No. 795, 80c, vert.: a, Corythosaurus. b, Dryosaurus. c, Euoplocephalus. d, Compsognathus.

No. 796, $2, Ornithomimus. No. 797, $2, Archaeopteryx. No. 798, $2, Deinonychus, vert.

**2004, Oct. 13** **Sheets of 4, #a-d**
**793-795** A237 Set of 3 15.00 15.00

**Souvenir Sheets**
**796-798** A237 Set of 3 12.00 12.00

FIFA (Fédération Internationale de Football Association), Cent. — A238

No. 799: a, Diego Maradona. b, David Seaman. c, Andreas Brehme. d, Paul Ince.
$2, Fernando Redondo.

**2004, Oct. 27** *Perf. 12¾x12½*
**799** A238 80c Sheet of 4, #a-d 6.50 6.50

**Souvenir Sheet**

**800** A238 $2 multi 4.00 4.00

National Basketball Association Players — A239

Designs: No. 801, 26c, Chris Bosh, Toronto Raptors. No. 802, 26c, Tim Duncan, San Antonio Spurs. No. 803, 26c, Kevin Garnett, Minnesota Timberwolves.

**2004, Nov. 3** *Perf. 14*
**801-803** A239 Set of 3 1.60 1.60

Each stamp printed in sheets of 12.

Christmas — A240

Paintings of Madonna and Child by: 37c, Quentin Metsys. 60c, Adolphe William Bouguereau. 80c, William Dyce. $1, Carlo Crivelli.
$2, Peter Paul Rubens, vert.

**2004, Dec. 23** *Perf. 14¼*
**804-807** A240 Set of 4 5.75 5.75

**Souvenir Sheet**

**808** A240 $2 multi 4.00 4.00

Miniature Sheet

Palau — Republic of China Diplomatic Relations, 5th Anniv. — A241

No. 809: a, Agricultural products. b, Republic of China Navy ship. c, Ngarachamayong Cultural Center. d, Palau National Museum.

**2004, Dec. 29** *Perf. 14*
**809** A241 80c Sheet of 4, #a-d 6.50 6.50

Souvenir Sheet

New Year 2005 (Year of the Rooster) — A242

No. 810: a, Rooster facing right, tail feathers at LL. b, Rooster facing left, tail feathers at LR. c, Rooster facing right, no tail feathers at LL. d, Rooster facing left, no tail feathers at LR.

**2005, Jan. 26** **Litho.** *Perf. 12½*
**810** A242 50c Sheet of 4, #a-d 4.00 4.00

Souvenir Sheet

Rotary International, Cent. — A243

No. 811: a, Rotary International emblem. b, Rotary Centennial bell. c, Flags of Rotary International, US, Great Britain, Canada, Germany, China and Italy. d, James Wheeler Davidson.

**2005, Apr. 4** *Perf. 14*
**811** A243 80c Sheet of 4, #a-d 6.50 6.50

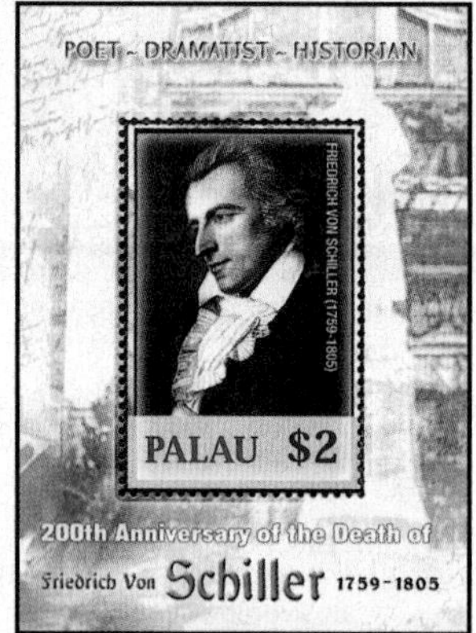

Friedrich von Schiller (1759-1805), Writer — A244

No. 812 — Schiller facing: a, Right (sepia tone). b, Right (color). c, Left (sepia tone).
$2, Facing left, diff.

**2005, Apr. 4**
**812** A244 $1 Sheet of 3, #a-c 6.00 6.00

**Souvenir Sheet**

**813** A244 $2 multi 4.00 4.00

Hans Christian Andersen (1805-75), Author — A245

No. 814, vert. — Book covers: a, Hans Christian Andersen Fairy Tales. b, Hans Christian Andersen's The Ugly Duckling. c, Tales of Hans Christian Andersen.
$2, The Little Match Girl.

**2005, Apr. 4**
**814** A245 $1 Sheet of 3, #a-c 6.00 6.00

**Souvenir Sheet**

**815** A245 $2 multi 4.00 4.00

Battle of Trafalgar, Bicent. — A246

Various ships in battle: 37c, 55c, 80c, $1.
$2, Admiral Horatio Nelson Wounded During Battle of Trafalgar.

**2005, Apr. 4** *Perf. 14¼*
**816-819** A246 Set of 4 5.50 5.50

**Souvenir Sheet**

**820** A246 $2 multi 4.00 4.00

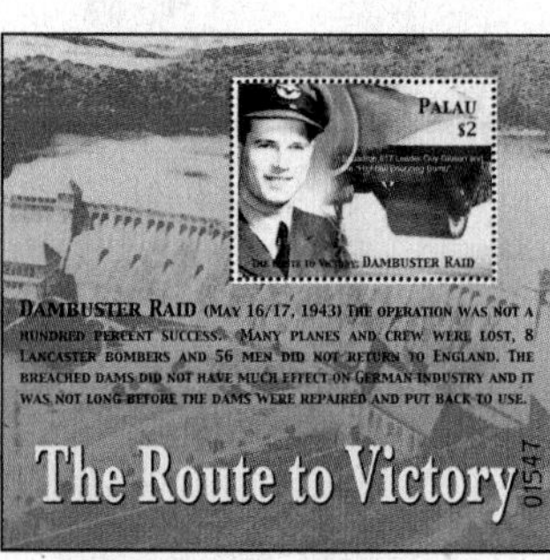

End of World War II, 60th Anniv. — A247

No. 821, 80c — Dambuster Raid: a, Pilots review routes prior to mission. b, Dambuster crew. c, Ground crews prepare Lancaster bomber. d, Bomber over Möhne Dam.
No. 822, 80c — Battle of Kursk: a, Russian tanks move forward. b, Tank commanders review maps. c, Russian and German armor clash. d, Destroyed German tank.
No. 823, $2, Squadron 617 leader Guy Gibson and "Highball Bouncing Bomb." No. 824, $2, Russian troops converge on destroyed German tank.

**2005, May 9** *Perf. 13½*

**Sheets of 4, #a-d**

**821-822** A247 Set of 2 13.00 13.00

**Souvenir Sheets**

**823-824** A247 Set of 2 8.00 8.00

Jules Verne (1828-1905), Writer — A248

No. 825, horiz.: a, 20,000 Leagues Under the Sea. b, Mysterious Island. c, Journey to the Center of the Earth.
$2, Around the World in 80 Days.

**2005, June 7** *Perf. 12¾*
**825** A248 $1 Sheet of 3, #a-c 6.00 6.00

**Souvenir Sheet**

**826** A248 $2 multi 4.00 4.00

Pope John Paul II (1920-2005) A249

**2005, June 27** *Perf. 13½x13¼*
**827** A249 $1 multi 2.00 2.00

A250

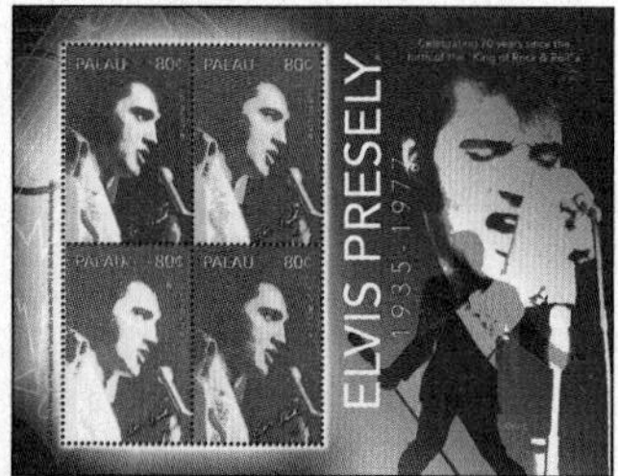

Elvis Presley (1935-77) — A251

No. 829 — Color of Presley: a, Blue. b, Green. c, Yellow. d, Orange.

**2005, July 2** *Perf. 14*
**828** A250 80c multi 1.60 1.60
**829** A251 80c Sheet of 4, #a-d 6.50 6.50

No. 828 printed in sheets of 4.

**Trains Type of 2004**

No. 830: a, Birney N62 Interurban. b, C62-2-103103. c, WR MO 2007. d, Atchison, Topeka & Santa Fe locomotive 314.
$2, Royal Hudson #2860, vert.

**2005** *Perf. 13¼x13½*
**830** A235 80c Sheet of 4, #a-d 6.50 6.50

**Souvenir Sheet**
*Perf. 13½x13¼*

**831** A235 $2 multi 4.00 4.00

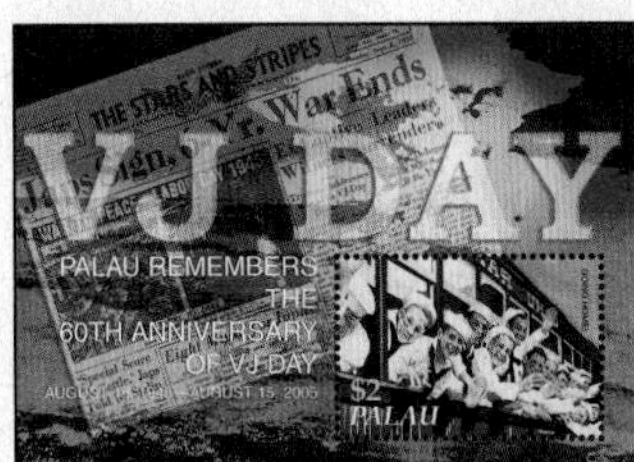

V-J Day, 60th Anniv. — A252

No. 832, vert.: a, Audie Murphy. b, John F. Kennedy. c, Fleet Admiral Chester W. Nimitz. d, Marines recapture Guam from the Japanese.
$2, Sailors going home.

**2005, June 7 Litho.** *Perf. 12¾*
**832** A252 80c Sheet of 4, #a-d 6.50 6.50

**Souvenir Sheet**

**833** A252 $2 multi 4.00 4.00

Miniature Sheet

Expo 2005, Aichi, Japan — A253

No. 834: a, Seagulls. b, The cosmos. c, Koala. d, Childbirth.

**2005, June 27** *Perf. 12*
**834** A253 80c Sheet of 4, #a-d 6.50 6.50

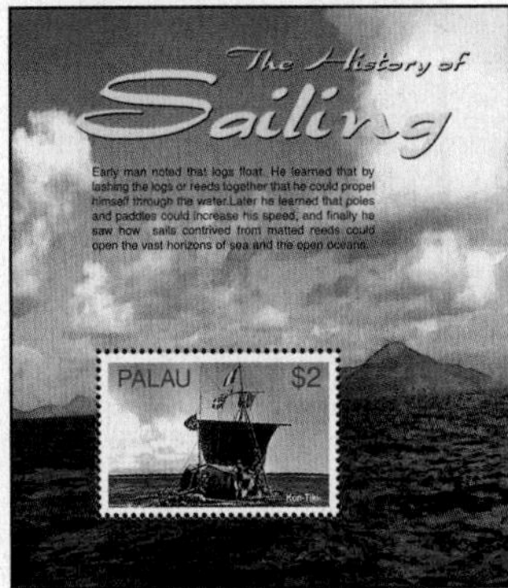

Sailing — A254

No. 835: a, Tepukei. b, Tainui. c, Palauan canoe. d, Yap outrigger.
$2, Kon-Tiki.

**2005, June 27** *Perf. 12¾*
**835** A254 80c Sheet of 4, #a-d 6.50 6.50

**Souvenir Sheet**

**836** A254 $2 multi 4.00 4.00

World Cup Soccer Championships, 75th Anniv. — A255

No. 837, $1 — Scene from final match of: a, 1954. b, 1966. c, 1974.
No. 838, $1: a, Scene from 2002 final match. b, Lothar Matthias. c, Gerd Muller.
No. 839, $2, Sepp Herberger. No. 840, $2, Franz Beckenbauer.

**2005, July 19** *Perf. 12*

**Sheets of 3, #a-c**

**837-838** A255 Set of 2 12.00 12.00

**Souvenir Sheets**

**839** A255 $2 multi 4.00 4.00

*Perf. 12¾*

**840** A255 $2 multi 4.00 4.00

No. 840 contains one 42x28mm stamp.

Vatican City No. 61 — A256

**2005, Aug. 9** *Perf. 13x13¼*
**841** A256 37c multi .75 .75

Printed in sheets of 12.

Miniature Sheet

Taipei 2005 Intl. Stamp Exhibition — A257

No. 842: a, Wildeve rose. b, Graham Thomas rose. c, Crocus rose. d, Tes of the d'Urbervilles rose.

**2005, Aug. 19** *Perf. 14*
**842** A257 80c Sheet of 4, #a-d 6.50 6.50

Miniature Sheet

Items from National Museum — A258

No. 843: a, Decorated bowl, light yellow background. b, Potsherds, dull rose background. c, Sculpture with three people, blue background. d, Model of native house, light yellow background. e, Lidded container with strings. f, Cannon. g, Drawing of man on ship. h, Drawing of native craftwork. i, Bird-shaped figurine. j, Decorated bowl, pink background.

**2005, Sept. 30**
**843** A258 37c Sheet of 10, #a-j 7.50 7.50

Pope Benedict XVI — A259

**2005, Nov. 21** *Perf. 13¾x13½*
**844** A259 80c multi 1.60 1.60

Printed in sheets of 4.

Christmas — A260

Paintings: 37c, Madonna and Child, by Daniel Seghers. 60c, Madonna and Child, by Raphael. 80c, The Rest on the Flight to Egypt, by Gerard David. $1, Granducci Madonna, by Raphael.
$2, Madonna and Child, by Bartolome Esteban Murillo.

**2005, Dec. 21** *Perf. 14*
**845-848** A260 Set of 4 5.75 5.75

**Souvenir Sheet**

**849** A260 $2 multi 4.00 4.00

New Year 2006 (Year of the Dog) A261

**2006, Jan. 3** *Perf. 13¼*
**850** A261 50c multi 1.00 1.00

Printed in sheets of 4.

Birds A262

Designs: 24c, Black oystercatcher. 39c, Great blue heron, vert.

**2006, Feb. 21 Litho.** *Perf. 12*
**851** A262 24c multi .50 .50
**852** A262 39c multi .80 .80

Worldwide Fund for Nature (WWF) — A263

No. 853 — Chambered nautilus: a, Two facing right. b, Two facing left. c, One, near coral. d, One, no coral.

**2006, Feb. 21** *Perf. 12¾*
**853** A263 63c Block of 4, #a-d 5.25 5.25
*e.* Sheet, 2 each #853a-853d 10.50 10.50

**World of Sea and Reef Type of 1986 Redrawn**

Miniature Sheet

No. 854: a, Spear fisherman. b, Native raft. c, Sailing canoes. d, Rock islands, sailfish. e, Inter-island boat, flying fish. f, Bonefish. g, Common jack. h, Mackerel. i, Sailfish. j, Barracuda. k, Triggerfish. l, Dolphinfish. m, Spear fisherman, grouper. n, Manta ray. o, Marlin. p, Parrotfish. q, Wrasse. r, Red snapper. s, Herring. t, Dugong. u, Surgeonfish. v, Leopard ray. w, Hawksbill turtle. x, Needlefish. y, Tuna. z, Octopus. aa, Clownfish, ab, Squid. ac, Grouper. ad, Moorish idol. ae, Queen conch. af, Squirrelfish. ag, Starfish, sting ray. ah, Lionfish. ai, Angelfish. aj, Butterflyfish. ak, Spiny lobster. al, Mangrove crab, am, Tridacna. an, Moray eel.

**2006, May 29 Litho.** *Perf. 13*
**854** Sheet of 40 14.50 14.50
*a.-an.* A19 18c Any single .35 .35

Washington 2006 World Philatelic Exhibition.

Souvenir Sheet

Wolfgang Amadeus Mozart (1756-91), Composer — A264

**2006, June 23** *Perf. 12¾*
**855** A264 $2 multi 4.00 4.00

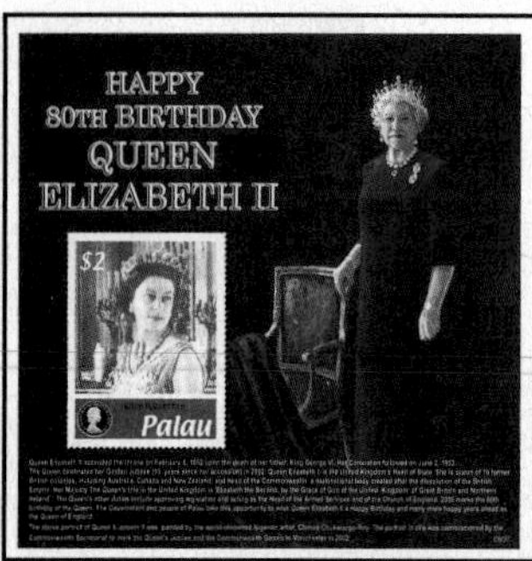

Queen Elizabeth II, 80th Birthday — A265

No. 856 — Queen wearing crown or tiara with background color of: a, Tan. b, Red. c, Blue. d, Lilac.
$2, Sepia photograph.

**2006, June 23** ***Perf. 14¼***
**856** A265 84c Sheet of 4, #a-d 6.75 6.75

**Souvenir Sheet**

**857** A265 $2 multi 4.00 4.00

Rembrandt (1606-69), Painter — A266

No. 858: a, Old Man in a Fur Hat. b, Head of a Man. c, An Old Man in a Cap. d, Portrait of an Old Man.
$2, Saskia With a Veil.

**2006, June 23** ***Perf. 13¼***
**858** A266 $1 Sheet of 4, #a-d 8.00 8.00

**Size: 70x100mm**

***Imperf***

**859** A266 $2 multi 4.00 4.00

No. 858 contains four 38x50mm stamps.

A267

Space Achievements — A268

No. 860 — Inscription, "International Space Station": a, At left. b, At UR, in white. c, At LL. d, AT UR, in black.
No. 861, 75c — Viking 1: a, Viking orbiting Mars. b, Simulation of Viking on Mars. c, Viking probe. d, Solar panels. e, Picture from Viking on Mars, parts of spacecraft at right. f, Picture from Viking on Mars, large rock at right.
No. 862, 75c, vert. — First flight of Space Shuttle Columbia: a, Shuttle on launch pad. b, Half of shuttle, denomination at UL. c, Half of shuttle, denomination at UR. d, Mission emblem. e, Astronaut Robert Crippen. f, Commander John Young.
No. 863, $2, Sputnik 1. No. 864, $2, Apollo 11. No. 865, $2, Space Shuttle Columbia lifting off.

**2006, July 10** ***Perf. 14¼***
**860** A267 $1 Sheet of 4, #a-d 8.00 8.00

**Sheets of 6, #a-f**

**861-862** A267 Set of 2 18.00 18.00

**Souvenir Sheets**

**863-865** A268 Set of 3 12.00 12.00

Souvenir Sheet

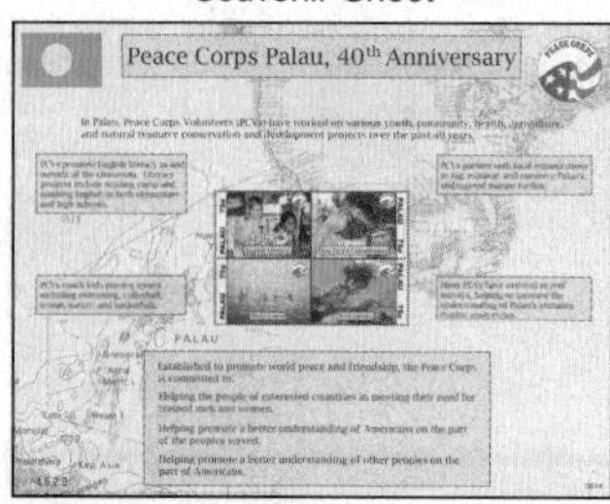

Peace Corps, 40th Anniv. — A269

No. 867: a, English literacy. b, Sea turtle conservation. c, Swim camp. d, Reef survey.

**2006, Nov. 6 Litho.** ***Perf. 14x14¾***
**867** A269 75c Sheet of 4, #a-d 6.00 6.00

Concorde — A270

No. 868, 75c: a, Concorde over New York City. b, Concorde over London
No. 869, 75c: a, Wheel. b, Nose.

**2006, Dec. 20** ***Perf. 13¼x13½***

**Pairs, #a-b**

**868-869** A270 Set of 2 6.00 6.00

Souvenir Sheet

Christmas — A271

No. 870 — Tree ornaments: a, Soldier. b, Santa Claus. c, Elf holding gift. d, Mice in sleigh.

**2006** ***Perf. 13¼***
**870** A271 84c Sheet of 4, #a-d 6.75 6.75

New Year 2007 (Year of the Pig) — A272

**2007, Jan. 3 Litho.** ***Perf. 13¼***
**871** A272 75c multi 1.50 1.50

Printed in sheets of 4.

Souvenir Sheet

Marilyn Monroe (1926-62), Actress — A273

Various drawings.

**2007, Feb. 15**
**872** A273 84c Sheet of 4, #a-d 6.75 6.75

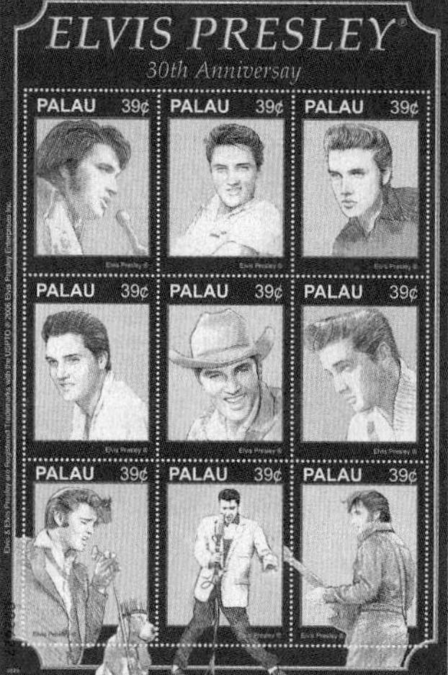

A274

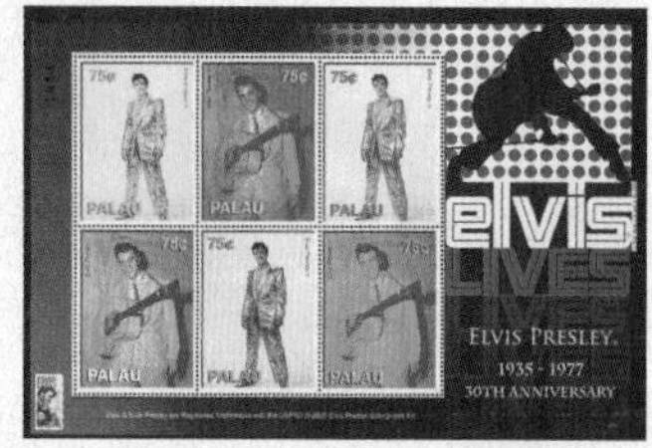

Elvis Presley (1935-77) — A275

No. 873 — Presley with: a, Microphone. b, Shirt with design on pocket. c, Dark shirt. d, White shirt. e, Hat. f, Sweater. g, Dog. h, Jacket and microphone. i, Guitar.
No. 874 — Presley with or without guitar and background color of: a, Yellow. b, Red violet. c, Pale green. d, Red. e, Pale blue. f, Orange.

**2007, Feb. 15** ***Perf. 13¼***
**873** A274 39c Sheet of 9, #a-i 7.25 7.25

***Perf. 14¼***

**874** A275 75c Sheet of 6, #a-f 9.00 9.00

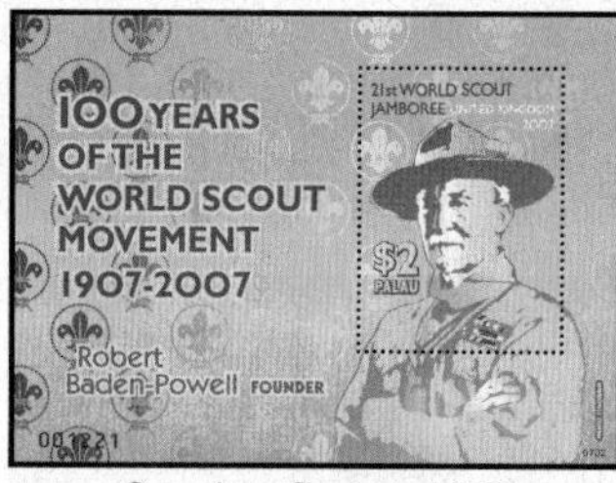

Scouting, Cent. — A276

No. 875, horiz. — Dove, Scouting flag, globe featuring Europe and frame color of: a, Purple. b, Bright pink. c, Green and blue.
$2, Lord Robert Baden-Powell.

**2007, Feb. 15** ***Perf. 13¼***
**875** A276 $1 Sheet of 3, #a-c 6.00 6.00

**Souvenir Sheet**

**876** A276 $2 multi 4.00 4.00

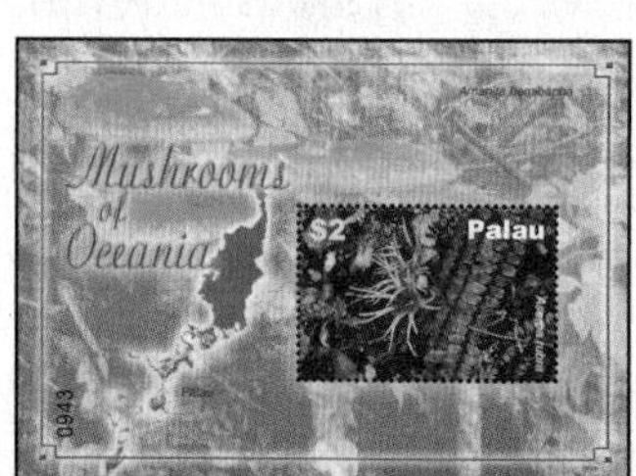

Mushrooms — A277

No. 877, vert.: a, Entoloma hochstetteri. b, Aseroe rubra. c, Omphalotus nidiformis. d, Amanita sp.
$2, Aseroe rubra, diff.

**2007, Feb. 15** ***Perf. 14¼x14***
**877** A277 $1 Sheet of 4, #a-d 8.00 8.00

**Souvenir Sheet**

***Perf. 14x14¼***

**878** A277 $2 multi 4.00 4.00

Helicopters, Cent. — A278

Designs: 10c, Bell 206B JetRanger III. 19c, McDonnell Douglas MD500D. 20c, McDonnell Douglas AH-64A Apache. 22c, Aérospatiale AS 332 Super Puma. 75c, Aérospatiale AS 355F-1 Twin Squirrel. 84c, MBB Eurocopter BO 105DBS/4. $1, Sikorsky MH-53J Pave Low III.
$2, Boeing Helicopters 234LR Chinook.

**2007, Feb. 26** ***Perf. 14x14¼***
**879-885** A278 Set of 7 6.75 6.75

**Souvenir Sheet**

**886** A278 $2 multi 4.00 4.00

Souvenir Sheet

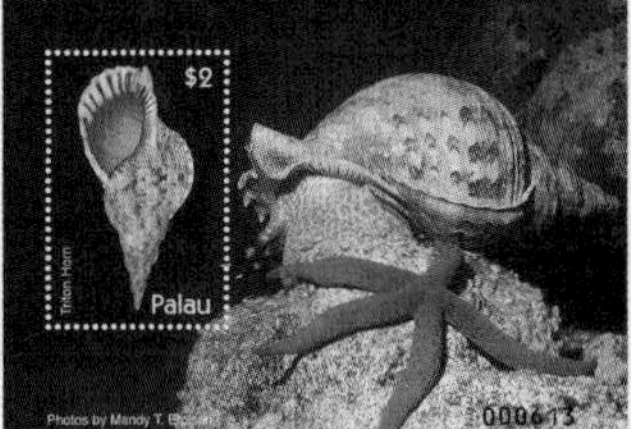


Triton Horn Shell — A279

**2007, Mar. 1** ***Perf. 13¼***
**887** A279 $2 multi 4.00 4.00

Miniature Sheets

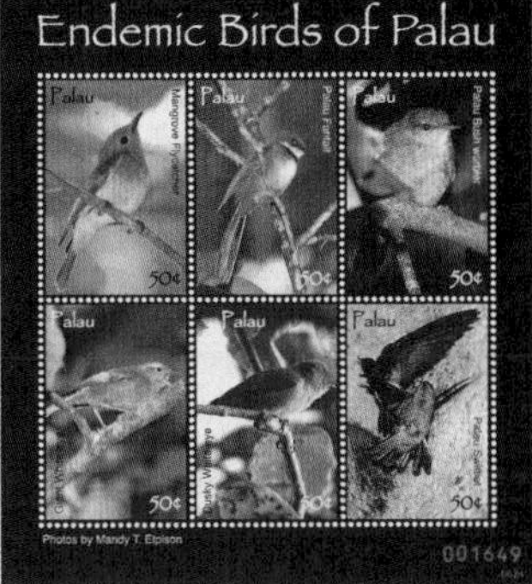


Birds — A280

No. 888, 50c: a, Mangrove flycatcher. b, Palau fantail. c, Palau bush warbler. d, Giant white-eye. e, Dusky white-eye. f, Palau swiftlet.
No. 889, 50c: a, Palau owl. b, Palau fruit dove. c, Palau ground dove. d, Morning bird. e, Palau megapode. f, Rusty-capped kingfisher.

**2007, Mar. 1** **Litho.**
**Sheets of 6, #a-f**
**888-889** A280 Set of 2 12.00 12.00

Wedding of Queen Elizabeth II and Prince Philip, 60th Anniv. A281

No. 890 — Photograph from: a, July 1947. b, November 1947.

**2007, May 1**
**890** A281 60c Pair, #a-b 2.40 2.40

Printed in sheets containing three of each stamp.

Souvenir Sheet

Crabs — A282

No. 891: a, Fiddler crab. b, Ghost crab. c, Coconut crab. d, Land crab.

**2007, May 16**
**891** A282 $1 Sheet of 4, #a-d 8.00 8.00

Flowers — A283

No. 892: a, Plumeria. b, Streptosolen jamesonii. c, Heliconia pseudoaemygdiana. d, Mananita.
$2, Spider lily.

**2007, May 16** ***Perf. 13¼***
**892** A283 $1 Sheet of 4, #a-d 8.00 8.00

**Souvenir Sheet**

**893** A283 $2 multi 4.00 4.00

Pope Benedict XVI — A284

**2007, June 20**
**894** A284 41c multi .85 .85

Printed in sheets of 8.

Princess Diana (1961-97) — A285

No. 895 — Diana with: a, Earring at right, white dress. b, Choker. c, Earring at right. d, Earring at left, country name in white.
$2, Wearing veiled hat.

**2007, June 20**
**895** A285 90c Sheet of 4, #a-d 7.25 7.25

**Souvenir Sheet**

**896** A285 $2 multi 4.00 4.00

Butterflies — A286

Designs: 2c, Troides amphrysus. 3c, Paraeronia boebera. 4c, Delias catisa. 5c, Chilasa clytia. 11c, Ornithoptera goliath. 15c, Graphium delesserii. 20c, Euploea sp. 23c, Papilio euchenor. 26c, Ornithoptera tithonus. 41c, Hypolimnas misippus. 45c, Delias meeki. 50c, Papilio ulysses autolycus. 75c, Ornithoptera croesus. 90c, Trogonoptera brookiana. $1, Idea lynceus. $2, Parantica weiskei. $3, Graphium weiskei. $4, Ornithoptera goliath titan. $5, Attacus lorquini. $10, Delias henningia voconia.

**2007, July 5** ***Perf. 12½x13½***

| | | | | |
|---|---|---|---|---|
| **897** | A286 | 2c multi | .25 | .25 |
| **898** | A286 | 3c multi | .25 | .25 |
| **899** | A286 | 4c multi | .25 | .25 |
| **900** | A286 | 5c multi | .25 | .25 |
| **901** | A286 | 11c multi | .25 | .25 |
| **902** | A286 | 15c multi | .30 | .30 |
| **903** | A286 | 20c multi | .40 | .40 |
| **904** | A286 | 23c multi | .50 | .50 |
| **905** | A286 | 26c multi | .55 | .55 |
| **906** | A286 | 41c multi | .85 | .85 |
| **907** | A286 | 45c multi | .90 | .90 |
| **908** | A286 | 50c multi | 1.00 | 1.00 |
| **909** | A286 | 75c multi | 1.50 | 1.50 |
| **910** | A286 | 90c multi | 1.90 | 1.90 |
| **911** | A286 | $1 multi | 2.00 | 2.00 |
| **912** | A286 | $2 multi | 4.00 | 4.00 |
| **913** | A286 | $3 multi | 6.00 | 6.00 |
| **914** | A286 | $4 multi | 8.00 | 8.00 |
| **915** | A286 | $5 multi | 10.00 | 10.00 |
| **916** | A286 | $10 multi | 20.00 | 20.00 |
| | | *Nos. 897-916 (20)* | 59.15 | 59.15 |

Miniature Sheet

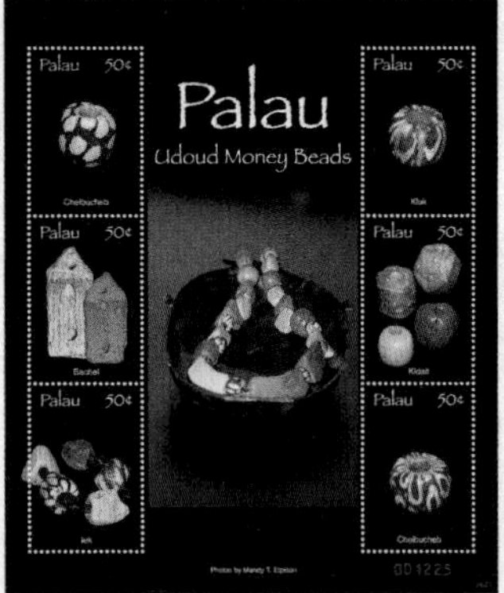


Udoud Money Beads — A287

No. 917: a, Black and white Chelbucheb. b, Kluk. c, Bachel. d, Kldait. e, Iek. f, Green and white Chelbucheb.

**2007, Mar. 1** **Litho.** ***Perf. 13¼***
**917** A287 50c Sheet of 6, #a-f 6.00 6.00

Miniature Sheet

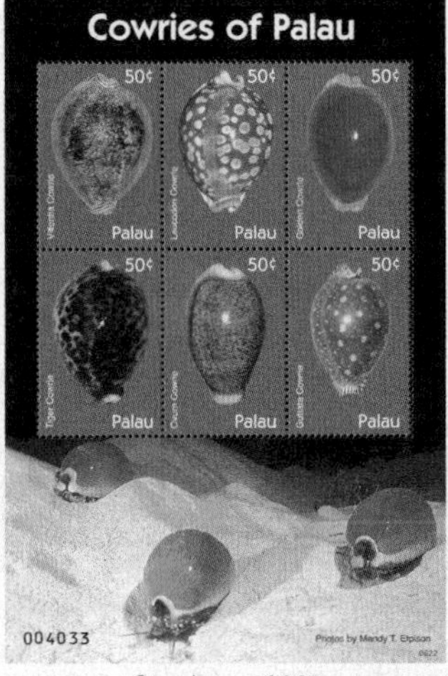


Cowries — A288

No. 918: a, Valentia cowrie. b, Leucodon cowrie. c, Golden cowrie. d, Tiger cowrie. e, Ovum cowrie. f, Guttata cowrie.

**2007, Mar. 1**
**918** A288 50c Sheet of 6, #a-f 6.00 6.00

Miniature Sheet

Children and Wildlife — A289

No. 919: a, Praying mantis. b, Boy holding lobster. c, Boy holding bat. d, Dolphins.

**2007, Mar. 1**
**919** A289 75c Sheet of 4, #a-d, + 4 labels 6.00 6.00

Birds of Southeast Asia — A290

No. 920: a, Red-billed leiothrix. b, Unidentified bird. c, Wahne's parotia. d, White-bellied yuhina.
$2, Wilson's bird-of-paradise.

**2007, May 16**
**920** A290 80c Sheet of 4, #a-d 6.50 6.50

**Souvenir Sheet**

**921** A290 $2 multi 4.00 4.00

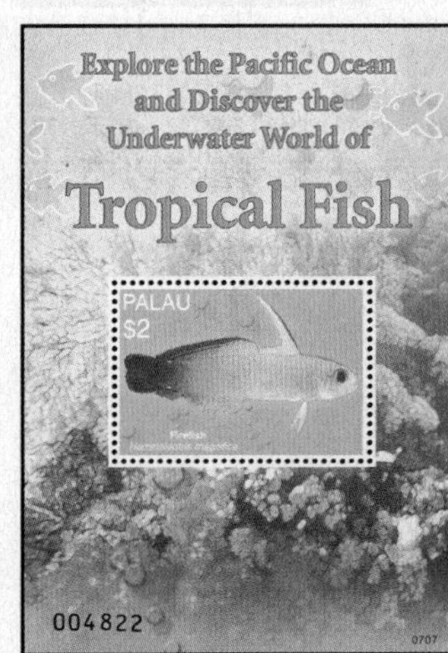


Tropical Fish — A291

No. 922: a, Boxfish. b, Copperband butterflyfish. c, Long-nosed hawkfish. d, Emperor angelfish.
$2, Firefish.

**2007, May 16**
**922** A291 80c Sheet of 4, #a-d 6.50 6.50

**Souvenir Sheet**

**923** A291 $2 multi 4.00 4.00

Miniature Sheet

Intl. Holocaust Remembrance Day — A292

No. 924 — United Nations diplomats and delegates: a, Eduardo J. Sevilla Somoza, Nicaragua. b, Aminu Bashir Wali, Nigeria. c, Stuart Beck, Palau. d, Ricardo Alberto Arias, Panama. e, Robert G. Aisi, Papua New Guinea. f, Eladio Loizaga, Paraguay. g, Jorge Voto-Bernales, Peru. h, Ban-Ki Moon, United Nations Secretary General.

**2007, Nov. 20**
**924** A292 50c Sheet of 8, #a-h 8.00 8.00

Christmas A293

Color of ornament: 22c, Red. 26c, Green. 41c, Blue. 90c, Yellow brown.

**2007, Nov. 20** **Litho.** ***Perf. 12***
**925-928** A293 Set of 4 3.75 3.75

32nd America's Cup Yacht Races A294

Various yachts.

**2007, Dec. 13** ***Perf. 13¼***

| | | | |
|---|---|---|---|
| **929** | Strip of 4 | 8.50 | 8.50 |
| *a.* | A294 26c multi | .50 | .50 |
| *b.* | A294 80c multi | 1.60 | 1.60 |
| *c.* | A294 $1.14 multi | 2.40 | 2.40 |
| *d.* | A294 $2 multi | 4.00 | 4.00 |

New Year 2008 (Year of the Rat) — A295

**2008, Jan. 2** ***Perf. 12***
**930** A295 50c multi 1.00 1.00

Printed in sheets of 4.

Miniature Sheet

Pres. John F. Kennedy (1917-63) — A296

No. 931: a, Crowd, Kennedy campaign poster. b, Kennedy shaking hands with crowd. c, Kennedy at lectern. d, Kennedy behind microphones, with hands showing.

**2008, Jan. 2** ***Perf. 14¼***
**931** A296 90c Sheet of 4, #a-d 7.25 7.25

2008 Summer Olympics, Beijing — A297

No. 932 — Items and athletes from 1908 London Olympics: a, Fencing poster. b, Program cover. c, Wyndham Halswelle, track gold medalist. d, Dorando Pietri, marathon runner.

**2008, Jan. 8**
**932** A297 50c Sheet of 4, #a-d 4.00 4.00

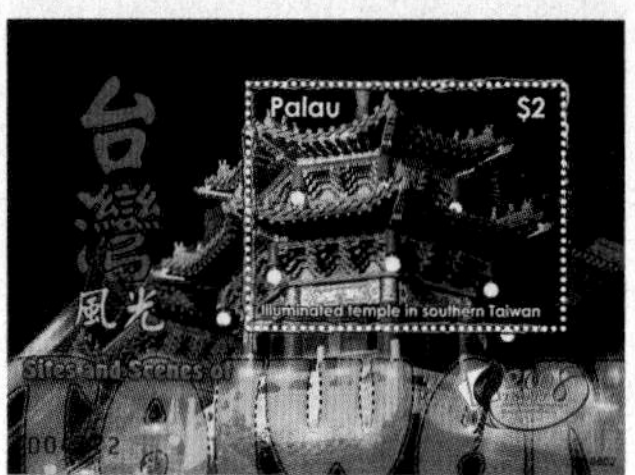

Taiwan Tourist Attractions — A298

No. 933: a, National Taiwan Democracy Memorial Hall. b, Chinese ornamental garden, Taipei. c, Taipei skyline. d, Eastern coast of Taiwan.

$2, Illuminated temple, Southern Taiwan.

**2008, Apr. 11** ***Perf. 11½***
**933** A298 50c Sheet of 4, #a-d 4.00 4.00

**Souvenir Sheet**

***Perf. 13¼***

**934** A298 $2 multi 4.00 4.00

2008 Taipei Intl. Stamp Exhibition. No. 933 contains four 40x30mm stamps.

2008 World Stamp Championships, Israel — A299

**2008, May 14** ***Imperf.***
**935** A299 $3 multi 6.00 6.00

Miniature Sheet

Sir Edmund Hillary (1919-2008), Mountaineer — A300

No. 936: a, Hillary and Prince Charles. b, Hillary. c, Hillary and Nepal Prime Minister Lokendra Bahadur Chand. d, Hillary with bird on shoulder.

**2008, May 28** ***Perf. 13¼***
**936** A300 90c Sheet of 4, #a-d 7.25 7.25

Miniature Sheet

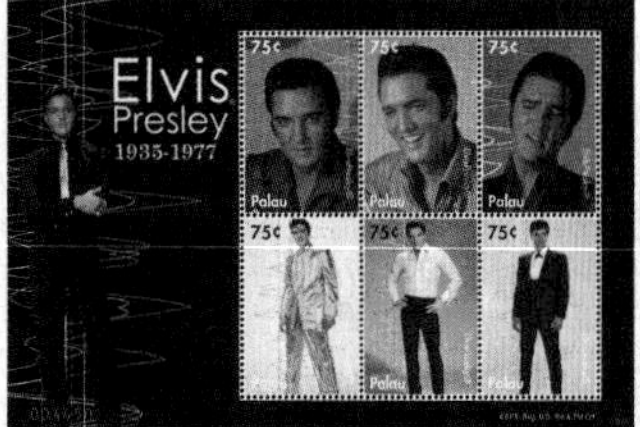

Elvis Presley (1935-77) — A301

No. 301 — Presley wearing: a, Gray shirt. b, Green shirt. c, Red shirt. d, Gold suit. e, White shirt, no jacket. f, White shirt, black suit.

**2008, June 12**
**937** A301 75c Sheet of 6, #a-f 9.00 9.00

Miniature Sheet

Visit to United States of Pope Benedict XVI — A302

No. 938 — Pope Benedict XVI and US flag faintly in background: a, Part of flag star on Pope's head (no frame line above denomination). b, Red stripe under "au" of "Palau." c, Red stripe under "P" of Palau. d, Red stripe under entire country name.

**2008, July 28**
**938** A302 90c Sheet of 4, #a-d 7.25 7.25

Miniature Sheets

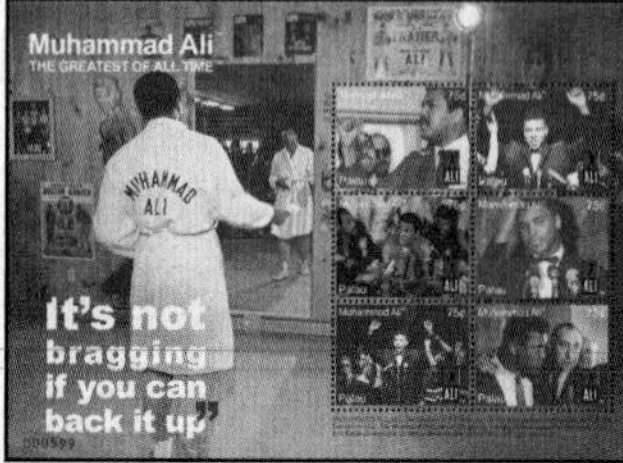

Muhammad Ali, Boxer — A303

No. 939 — Ali: a, In suit, clenching fist. b, Behind microphones, with both arms raised, with hands around his right forearm. c, Behind microphones, with towel around neck. d, Behind microphones, scratching head. e, Behind microphones, raising arms, with crowd. f, With hand of Howard Cosell on shoulder.

No. 940 — Ali: a, Pointing up, wearing short-sleeved shirt. b, Pointing to left, wearing suit. c, Making fist, in robe. d, Pointing to right, wearing suit.

**2008, Sept. 22** ***Perf. 11½x12***
**939** A303 75c Sheet of 6, #a-f 9.00 9.00

***Perf. 13¼***

**940** A303 94c Sheet of 4, #a-d 7.50 7.50

No. 940 contains four 50x37mm stamps.

Miniature Sheets

Space Exploration, 50th Anniv. (in 2007) — A304

No. 941, 75c — Mir Space Station: a, With black background. b, With Earth at bottom. c, Technical drawing. d, Above clouds. e, With Space Shuttle Atlantis. f, Against starry background.

No. 942, 75c: a, Pres. John F. Kennedy. b, Apollo 11 Command Module. c, Apollo 11 Lunar Module, Earth and Moon. d, Lunar Module and Moon. e, Kennedy, Astronaut John Glenn and Friendship 7 capsule. f, Edwin "Buzz" Aldrin on Moon.

No. 943, 94c: a, Technical drawing of R-7 launch vehicle. b, Sputnik 1, antennae at right. c, Technical drawing of Sputnik 1. d, Sputnik 1, antennae at left.

No. 944, 94c: a, Yuri Gagarin, first man in space, wearing medals. b, Technical drawing of Vostok rocket. c, Technical drawing of Vostok 1. d, Gagarin in space helmet.

**2008, Sept. 22** ***Perf. 13¼***

**Sheets of 6, #a-f**

**941-942** A304 Set of 2 18.00 18.00

**Sheets of 4, #a-d**

**943-944** A304 Set of 2 15.00 15.00

Miniature Sheets

Star Trek The Next Generation — A305

No. 945: a, Capt. Jean-Luc Picard. b, Lt. Commander Data. c, Commander William T. Riker. d, Counselor Deanna Troi. e, Lt. Commander Geordi La Forge. f, Lieutenant Worf.
No. 946: a, Wesley Crusher. b, Worf. c, Picard. d, Dr. Beverly Crusher.

**2008, Dec. 4** ***Perf. 11½***
**945** A305 75c Sheet of 6, #a-f 9.00 9.00

***Perf. 13¼***
**946** A305 94c Sheet of 4, #a-d 7.50 7.50

No. 946 contains four 37x50mm stamps.

Christmas A306

Designs: 22c, Angel holding candle. 26c, Angel with violin. 42c, Angel and conifer wreath. 94c, Angel in light display.

**2008, Dec. 11 Litho.** ***Perf. 14x14¾***
**947-950** A306 Set of 4 3.75 3.75

Inauguration of US Pres. Barack Obama — A307

No. 951, horiz. — Pres. Obama: a, Holding microphone. b, Smiling, denomination at LL. c, Smiling, denomination at UL. d, With index finger raised.
$2, Head of Pres. Obama.

**2009, Jan. 20** ***Perf. 11½x11¼***
**951** A307 94c Sheet of 4, #a-d 7.75 7.75

**Souvenir Sheet**
**952** A307 $2 multi 4.00 4.00

No. 951 contains four 40x30mm stamps.

New Year 2009 (Year of the Ox) — A308

No. 953 — Ox and Chinese characters in diamond in: a, Black. b, White.

**2009, Jan. 26** ***Perf. 12***
**953** A308 94c Horiz. pair, #a-b 4.00 4.00

Printed in sheets containing two pairs.

**Miniature Sheet**

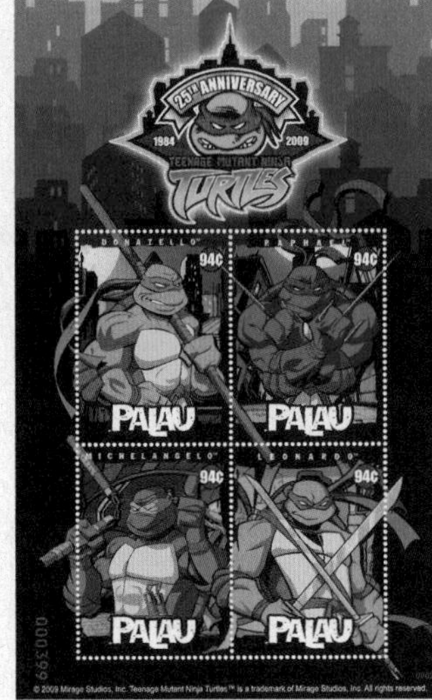


Teenage Mutant Ninja Turtles, 25th Anniv. — A309

No. 954: a, Donatello. b, Raphael. c, Michelangelo. d, Leonardo.

**2009, Feb. 25** ***Perf. 13¼***
**954** A309 94c Sheet of 4, #a-d 7.75 7.75

**Miniature Sheets**

A310

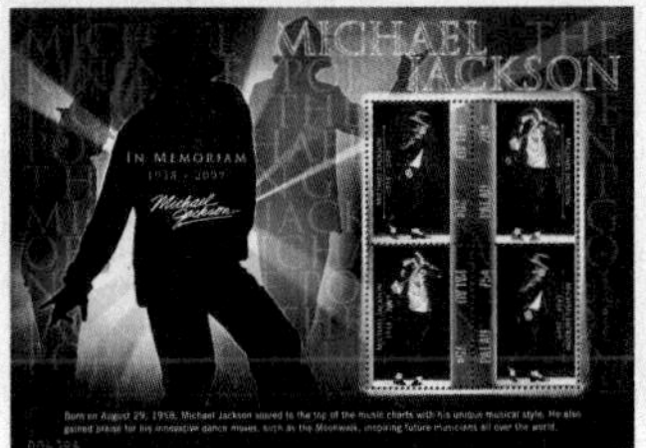


Michael Jackson (1958-2009), Singer — A311

No. 955 — Background color: a, Red (Jackson with mouth open). b, Green. c, Blue. d, Red (Jackson with mouth closed).
No. 956 — Jackson dancing with denomination at: a, 28c, Right. b, 28c, Left. c, 75c, Right. d, 75c, Left.

**2009, Sept. 3** ***Perf. 12x11½***
**955** A310 44c Sheet of 4, #a-d 3.75 3.75
**956** A311 Sheet of 4, #a-d 4.25 4.25

**Miniature Sheet**

Palau Pacific Resort, 25th Anniv. — A312

No. 957: a, Four beach umbrellas, shadow of palm trees. b, Palm trees near beach under cloudy skies. c, Resort at night. d, Lounge chairs on beach. e, Swimming pool. f, Palm tree, two beach umbrellas.

**2009, Oct. 5** ***Perf. 11½***
**957** A312 26c Sheet of 6, #a-f 3.25 3.25

Dolphins A313

Designs: 28c, Spinner dolphin. 44c, Hourglass dolphin. 98c, Costero. $1.05, Risso's dolphin.
No. 962: a, Heaviside's dolphin. b, Chilean dolphin. c, Dusky dolphin. d, Commerson's dolphin. e, Fraser's dolphin. f, Striped dolphin.

**2009, Oct. 13** ***Perf. 14¾x14***
**958-961** A313 Set of 4 5.50 5.50
**962** A313 75c Sheet of 6, #a-f 9.00 9.00

Shells A314

Designs: 28c, Morula musiva. 44c, Littoraria articulata. 98c, Architectonica perdix. $1.05, Scalptia crossei.
No. 967: a, Pugilina cochlidium. b, Epitonium scalare. c, Ellobium tornatelliforme. d, Polinices sebae. e, Cyclophorus siamensis. f, Acrosterigma maculosum.

**2009, Oct. 13**
**963-966** A314 Set of 4 5.50 5.50
**967** A314 75c Sheet of 6, #a-f 9.00 9.00

A315

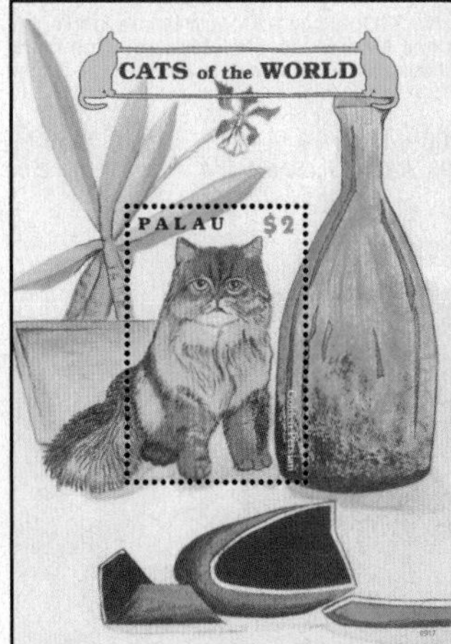


Cats — A316

No. 968: a, Devon Rex cream lynx point sirex. b, Ocicat chocolate. c, Asian chocolate smoke. d, Burmilla lilac shaded. e, Egyptian Mau bronze. f, Himalayan blue tortie point.

No. 969: a, Turkish Van and fireplace. b, Tiffany. c, Turkish Van, diff. d, Birman seal lynx point.
No. 970, $2, Golden Persian. No. 971, $2, Red silver tabby.

**2009, Oct. 13** ***Perf. 14***
**968** A315 75c Sheet of 6, #a-f 9.00 9.00
**969** A315 94c Sheet of 4, #a-d 7.75 7.75

**Souvenir Sheets**
**970-971** A316 Set of 2 8.00 8.00

**Miniature Sheet**

Fish — A317

No. 972: a, Two-spot snappers. b, Goggle-eye. c, Bluestreak cardinalfish. d, Bluefin trevally. e, Rainbow runners. f, Fire goby.

**2009, Oct. 13** ***Perf. 11½x11¼***
**972** A317 75c Sheet of 6, #a-f 9.00 9.00

**Miniature Sheet**

Pres. Abraham Lincoln (1809-65) — A318

No. 973 — Photographs of Lincoln: a, Hands showing, denomination in white. b, Hands not showing, denomination in white. c, Hands not showing, denomination in black. d, Hand showing, denomination in black.

**2009, Oct. 13** ***Perf. 11¼x11½***
**973** A318 44c Sheet of 4, #a-d 3.75 3.75

**Souvenir Sheet**

Visit of Pope Benedict XVI to Yad Vashem Holocaust Memorial, Israel — A319

No. 974 — Pope Benedict XVI: a, 98c, Looking at flame (30x40mm). b, $2, Praying in front of flowers (60x40mm).

**2009, Oct. 13**
**974** A319 Sheet of 3, #974b, 2 #974a 8.00 8.00

Souvenir Sheets

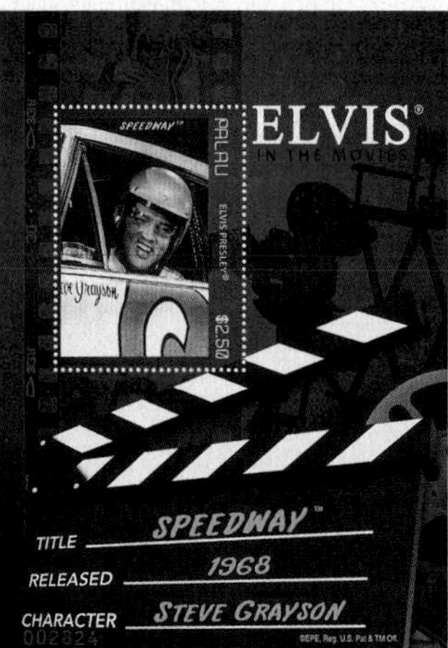


A320

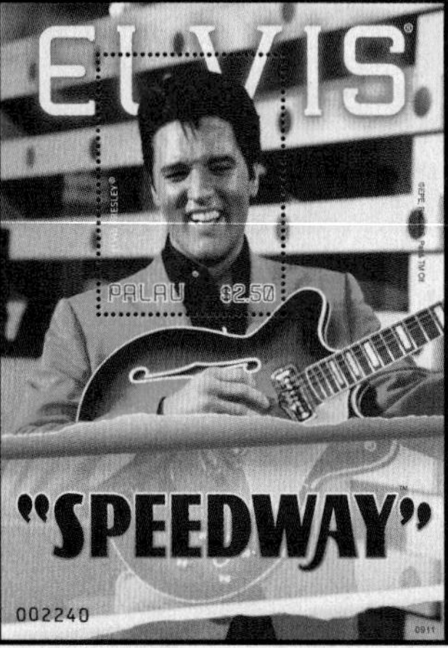


A321

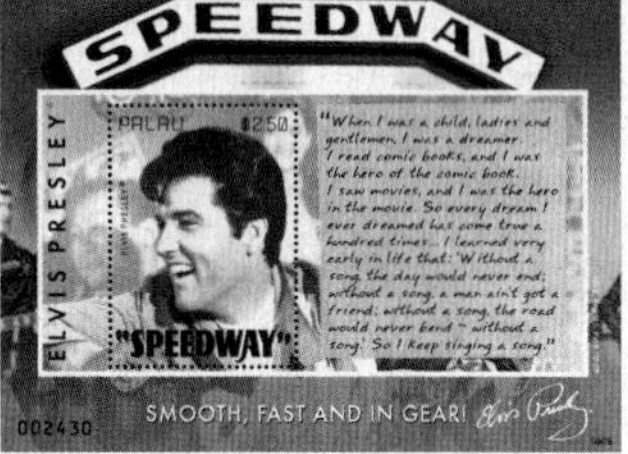


A322

Elvis Presley (1935-77) — A323

**2009, Oct. 13** *Perf. 13¼*

| | | | | |
|---|---|---|---|---|
| **975** | A320 | $2.50 multi | 5.00 | 5.00 |
| **976** | A321 | $2.50 multi | 5.00 | 5.00 |
| **977** | A322 | $2.50 multi | 5.00 | 5.00 |
| **978** | A323 | $2.50 multi | 5.00 | 5.00 |
| | | *Nos. 975-978 (4)* | 20.00 | 20.00 |

A324

Fish — A325

Designs: 1c, Giant trevally. 2c, Pink anemonefish. 3c, Gray reef shark. 4c, Leaf fish. 5c, Scissor-tailed fusiliers. 26c, Helfrich's dartfish. 44c, Bigscale soldierfish. $1, Peach anthias. $2, Spotted eagle ray. $3, African pompano. $4, Harlequin grouper. $5, Pyramid butterflyfish. $10, Longnose hawkfish.

**2009, Oct. 13** **Litho.** *Perf. 11¾x12¼*

| | | | | |
|---|---|---|---|---|
| **979** | A324 | 1c multi | .25 | .25 |
| **980** | A324 | 2c multi | .25 | .25 |
| **981** | A324 | 3c multi | .25 | .25 |
| **982** | A324 | 4c multi | .25 | .25 |
| **983** | A324 | 5c multi | .25 | .25 |
| **984** | A325 | 26c multi | .55 | .55 |
| **985** | A324 | 44c multi | .90 | .90 |
| **986** | A324 | $1 multi | 2.00 | 2.00 |
| **987** | A324 | $2 multi | 4.00 | 4.00 |
| **988** | A324 | $3 multi | 6.00 | 6.00 |
| **989** | A324 | $4 multi | 8.00 | 8.00 |
| **990** | A324 | $5 multi | 10.00 | 10.00 |
| **991** | A324 | $10 multi | 20.00 | 20.00 |
| | | *Nos. 979-991 (13)* | 52.70 | 52.70 |

Worldwide Fund for Nature (WWF) — A326

No. 992 — Red lionfish: a, Two fish. b, One fish facing forward, brown background. c, One fish facing right. d, One fish facing forward, blue background.

**2009, Nov. 9** **Litho.** *Perf. 13¼*

| | | | | |
|---|---|---|---|---|
| **992** | A326 | 53c Block of 4, #a-d | 4.25 | 4.25 |
| *a.* | | Sheet of 8, 2 each #992a-992d | 8.50 | 8.50 |

Miniature Sheet

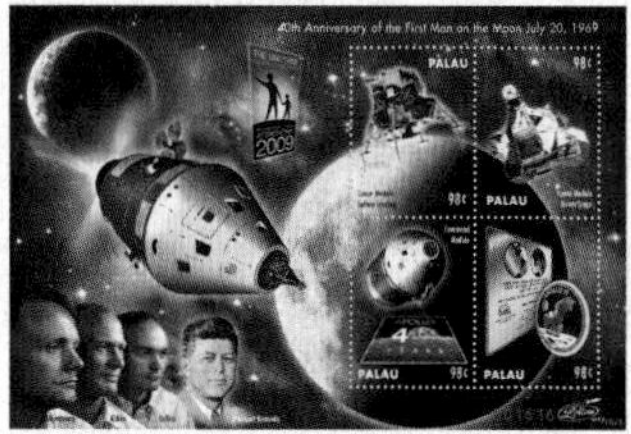

First Man on the Moon, 40th Anniv. — A327

No. 993: a, Lunar Module before landing. b, Lunar Module ascent stage. c, Command module. d, Mission patch and plaque left on Moon.

**2009, Dec. 10** *Perf. 12x11½*

| | | | | |
|---|---|---|---|---|
| **993** | A327 | 98c Sheet of 4, #a-d | 8.00 | 8.00 |

Intl. Year of Astronomy.

Christmas A328

Designs: 26c, Christmas ornaments and stocking on coral. 44c, Wreath and "Merry Christmas." 98c, Gingerbread house with flag of Palau. $2, Wreath and bell.

**2009, Dec. 10** *Perf. 14¼x14¾*

| | | | | |
|---|---|---|---|---|
| **994-997** | A328 | Set of 4 | 7.50 | 7.50 |

Miniature Sheet

Charles Darwin (1809-82), Naturalist — A329

No. 998: a, HMS Beagle. b, Captain Robert Fitzroy. c, Sextant of HMS Beagle. d, Diagram of HMS Beagle. e, Darwin. f, Darwin's report on the zoology of the voyage of the HMS Beagle.

**2010, Mar. 2** *Perf. 13¼*

| | | | | |
|---|---|---|---|---|
| **998** | A329 | 75c Sheet of 6, #a-f | 9.00 | 9.00 |

Reptiles and Amphibians — A330

Designs: 26c, Bufo marinus. 44c, Chelonia mydas. 98c, Lepidodactylus lugubris. $1.05, Varanus olivaceus.

No. 1003: a, Northern forest dragon. b, Common house gecko. c, Hawksbill turtle. d, Indopacific tree gecko. e, Amboina box turtle. f, Flying dragon.

**2010, Mar. 2** *Perf. 12*

| | | | | |
|---|---|---|---|---|
| **999-1002** | A330 | Set of 4 | 5.50 | 5.50 |
| **1003** | A330 | 75c Sheet of 6, #a-f | 9.00 | 9.00 |

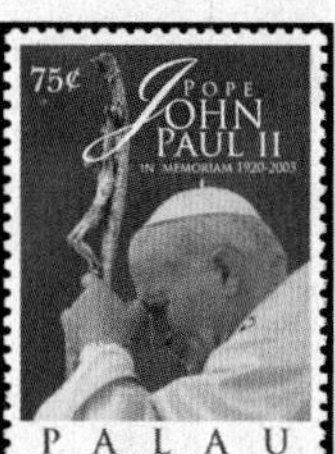


Pope John Paul II (1920-2005) A331

**2010, Apr. 22** *Perf. 12x11½*

| | | | | |
|---|---|---|---|---|
| **1004** | A331 | 75c multi | 1.50 | 1.50 |

Printed in sheets of 4. Compare with type A451.

Miniature Sheet

Pres. Abraham Lincoln (1809-65) — A332

No. 1005 — Lincoln: a, Without beard. b, With beard, no cowlick on forehead. c, With beard, cowlick on forehead, point of shirt above "M." d, With beard, cowlick on forehead, point of shirt above "LIN."

**2010, Apr. 22** *Perf. 11½*

| | | | | |
|---|---|---|---|---|
| **1005** | A332 | 75c Sheet of 4, #a-d | 6.00 | 6.00 |

Miniature Sheet

Elvis Presley (1935-77) — A333

No. 1005 — Presley: a, Facing backwards. b, Wearing sequined suit. c, With hand and microphone cord at left. d, Wearing suit with bordered lapels.

**2010, Apr. 22** *Perf. 11½*

| | | | | |
|---|---|---|---|---|
| **1006** | A333 | 75c Sheet of 4, #a-d | 6.00 | 6.00 |

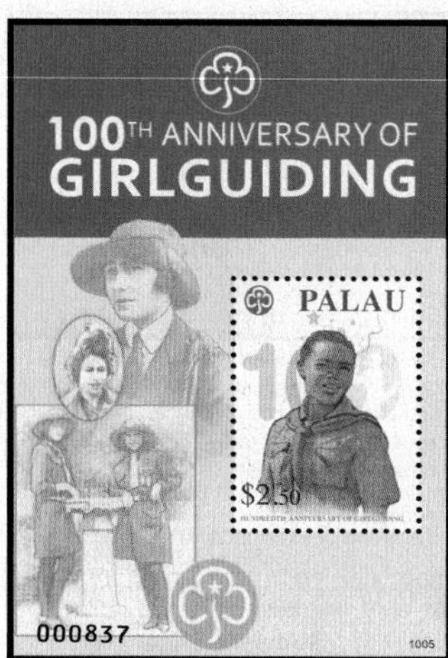


Girl Guides, Cent. — A334

No. 1007, horiz.: a, Two Girl Guides in blue uniforms. b, Two Girl Guides, one wearing cap. c, Girl Guide playing bongo drum. d, Four Girl Guides.

$2.50, Girl Guide in green uniform.

**2010, June 9** *Perf. 11½x12*

| | | | | |
|---|---|---|---|---|
| **1007** | A334 | 94c Sheet of 4, #a-d | 7.75 | 7.75 |

**Souvenir Sheet**

***Perf. 11½***

| | | | | |
|---|---|---|---|---|
| **1008** | A334 | $2.50 multi | 5.00 | 5.00 |

Souvenir Sheet

Governmental Buildings — A335

No. 1009: a, Executive Building. b, OEK Congress. c, Judiciary Building.

**2010, July 1** *Perf. 13½*

| | | | | |
|---|---|---|---|---|
| **1009** | A335 | $1 Sheet of 3, #a-c | 6.00 | 6.00 |

Princess Diana (1961-97) — A336

No. 1010 — Princess Diana wearing: a, Tiara. b, Blue violet gown.

**2010, Sept. 8** ***Perf. 12x11½***
**1010** A336 75c Pair, #a-b 3.00 3.00

Printed in sheets containing two pairs.

Miniature Sheet

Mother Teresa (1910-97), Humanitarian — A337

No. 1011 — Mother Teresa and: a, Blue sky behind name and country name. b, Blue sky behind country name, cloud behind name. c, Cloud behind country name, blue sky partly behind name. d, Blue sky partly behind country name, cloud behind name.

**2010, Sept. 8** ***Perf. 11½***
**1011** A337 94c Sheet of 4, #a-d 7.75 7.75

Henri Dunant (1828-1910), Founder of Red Cross — A338

No. 1012 Dunant and: a, Frédèric Passy. b, Czar Nicholas II, c, Henri Dufour. d, Bertha von Suttner.
$2.50, Obverse and reverse of Nobel medal.

**2010, Sept. 8** ***Perf. 11½x12***
**1012** A338 94c Sheet of 4, #a-d 7.75 7.75

**Souvenir Sheet**
***Perf. 11½***

**1013** A338 $2.50 multi 5.00 5.00

Paintings by Sandro Botticelli (1445-1510) — A339

No. 1014, vert.: a, Madonna and Child. b, Nastagio Degli Onesti. c, Calumny of Apelles. d, Primavera.
$2.50, Orazione Nell'Orto.

**2010, Sept. 8** ***Perf. 12x11½***
**1014** A339 94c Sheet of 4, #a-d 7.75 7.75

**Souvenir Sheet**
***Perf. 11½***

**1015** A339 $2.50 multi 5.00 5.00

Souvenir Sheet

Issuance of the Penny Black, 170th Anniv. — A340

No. 1016: a, Penny Black (Great Britain #1). b, Palau #2.

**2010, Sept. 8** ***Perf. 13¼***
**1016** A340 $2 Sheet of 2, #a-b 8.00 8.00

Christmas A341

Paintings: 26c, Adoration of the Magi, by Leonardo da Vinci. 44c, Adoration of the Shepherds, by Carlo Crivelli. 98c, Adoration of the Magi, by Hieronymus Bosch. $2, Adoration of the Magi, by Albrecht Altdorfer.

**2010, Sept. 8** ***Perf. 11½***
**1017-1020** A341 Set of 4 7.50 7.50

Miniature Sheets

2010 World Cup Soccer Championships, South Africa — A342

No. 1021, 61c: a, Gabriel Heinze. b, Philipp Lahm. c, Javier Mascherano. d, Mesut Dezil. e, Angel Di Maria. f, Lukas Podolski.
No. 1022, 61c: a, Antolin Alcaraz. b, Cesc Fabregas. c, Dario Veron. d, Carlos Puyol. e, Victor Caceres. f, Xabi Alonso.

**2010, Dec. 16** ***Perf. 12***

**Sheets of 6, #a-f**

**1021-1022** A342 Set of 2 15.00 15.00

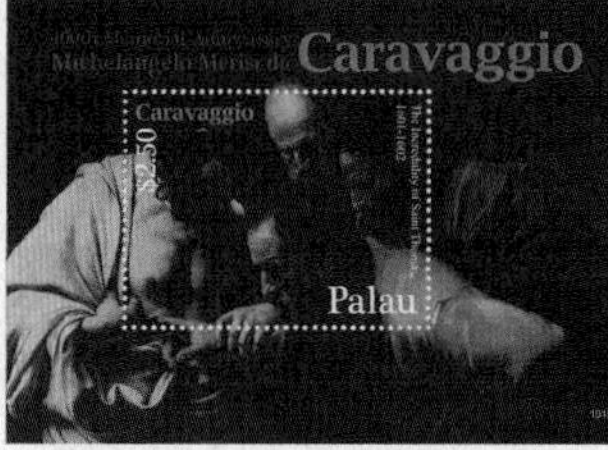


Paintings by Michelangelo Merisi da Caravaggio (1571-1610) — A343

No. 1023.: a, Supper at Emmaus. b, Ecce Homo. c, Omnia Vincit Amor. d, Flagellazione di Cristo.
$2.50, The Incredulity of Saint Thomas.

**2010, Dec. 16** ***Perf. 12***
**1023** A343 94c Sheet of 4, #a-d 7.75 7.75

**Souvenir Sheet**
***Perf. 12½***

**1024** A343 $2.50 multi 5.00 5.00

No. 1023 contains four 40x30mm stamps.

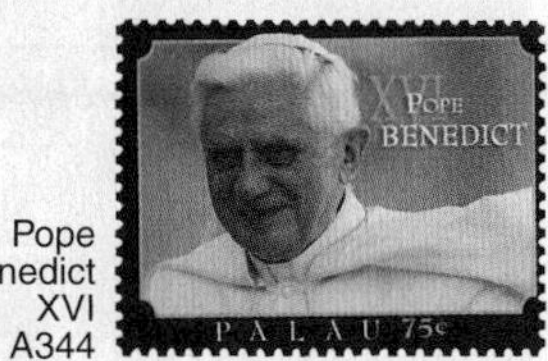


Pope Benedict XVI A344

**2010, Dec. 16** ***Perf. 12***
**1025** A344 75c multi 1.50 1.50

Printed in sheets of 4 with slight color differences in the background.

Miniature Sheets

Sharks — A346

Sea Turtles — A347

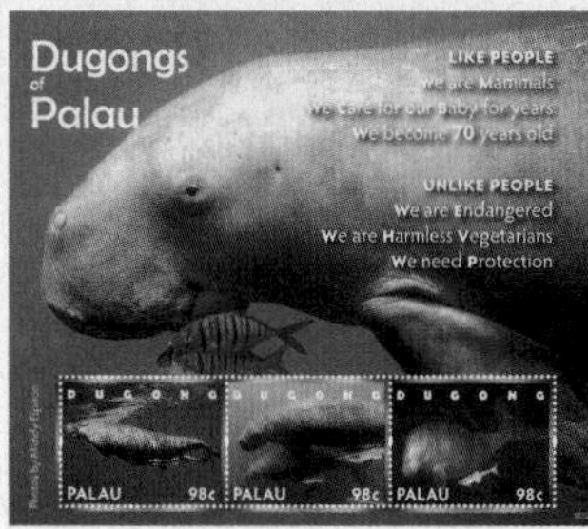


Dugongs — A348

No. 1027 — Shark with dorsal fin: a, Touching "R" in "Shark." b, Between "A" and "R" in "Shark." c, Touching "A" in "Shark."
No. 1028 — Sea turtle: a, Swimming left. b, At ocean floor. c, Swimming right.

No. 1029: a, Dugong at water's surface. b, Two dugongs. c, Dugong and fish.

***Perf. 13 Syncopated***

**2010, Dec. 21** **Litho.**
**1027** A346 98c Sheet of 3, #a-c 6.00 6.00
**1028** A347 98c Sheet of 3, #a-c 6.00 6.00
**1029** A348 98c Sheet of 3, #a-c 6.00 6.00
*Nos. 1027-1029 (3)* 18.00 18.00

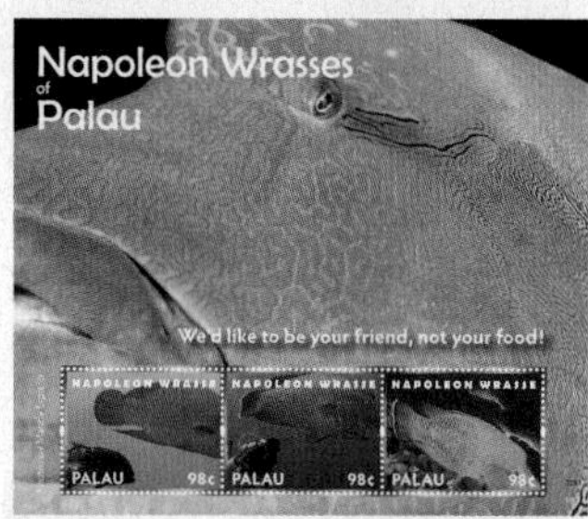

The top sheet, containing poorly cropped stamp images, was received by Palau postal officials but was never put on sale in Palau. The bottom sheet was sold by dealers, but was never received by Palau postal officials.

Miniature Sheet

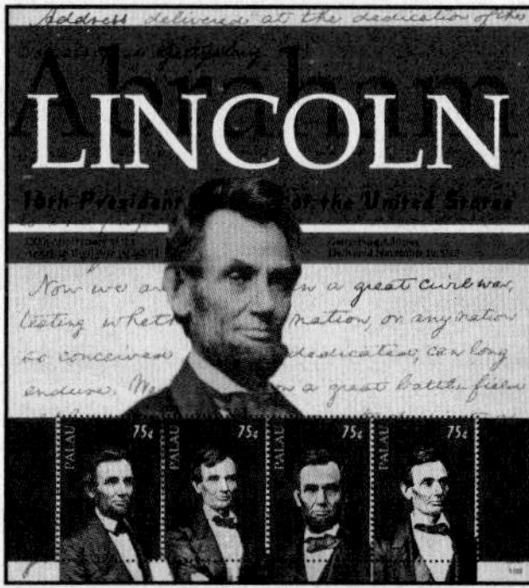


Pres. Abraham Lincoln (1809-65) — A349

Various photographs of Lincoln.

**2011, Mar. 11** ***Perf. 12***
**1030** A349 75c Sheet of 4, #a-d 6.00 6.00

Miniature Sheet

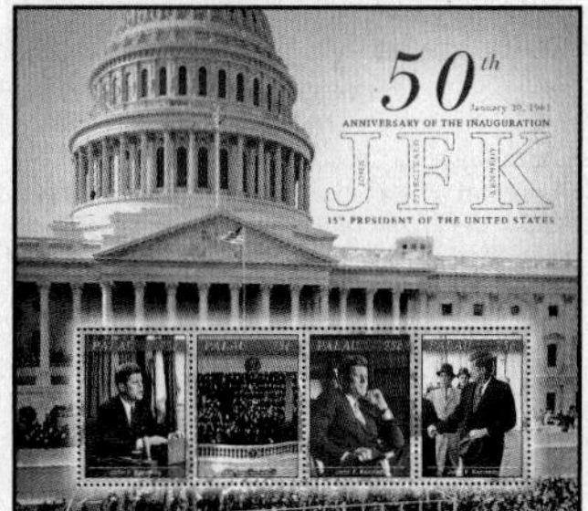


Inauguration of Pres. John F. Kennedy, 50th Anniv. — A350

No. 1031 — Kennedy: a, Behind microphone. b, At inauguration. c, In rocking chair. d, Shaking person's hand.

**2011, Mar. 11**

**1031** A350 75c Sheet of 4, #a-d 6.00 6.00

Miniature Sheet

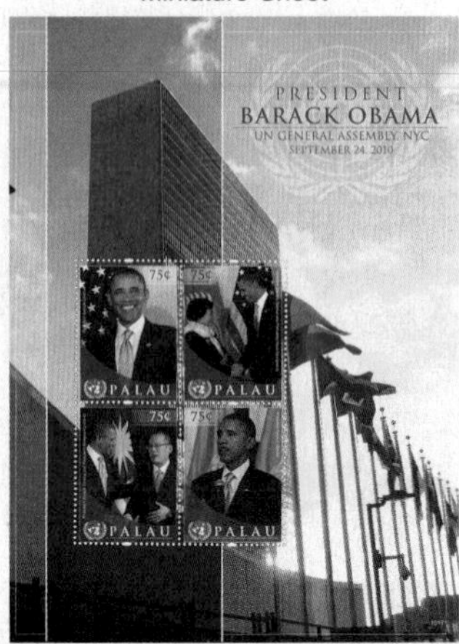


Pres. Barack Obama's Visit to the United Nations — A351

No. 1032 — Pres. Obama and: a, US flag. b, Kyrgyzstan Pres. Rosa Otunbaeva. c, Philippines Pres. Benigno Aquino III. d, United Nations flags.

**2011, Mar. 11** ***Perf. 13 Syncopated***

**1032** A351 75c Sheet of 4, #a-d 6.00 6.00

Indipex 2011 Intl. Philatelic Exhibition, New Delhi — A352

No. 1033: a, Bhagat Singh (1907-31), nationalist. b, Lal Bahadur Shastri (1904-66), Prime Minister. c, Subhas Chandra Bose (1897-1945), politician. d, Dr. Rajendra Prasad (1884-1963), politician. e, Jawaharlal Nehru (1889-1964), Prime Minister. f, Sardar Patel (1875-1950), Deputy Prime Minister.
$2.50, Mohandas K. Gandhi (1869-1948), independence leader.

**2011, Mar. 11** ***Perf. 12***

**1033** A352 50c Sheet of 6, #a-f 6.00 6.00

**Souvenir Sheet**

***Perf. 13 Syncopated***

**1034** A352 $2.50 multi 5.00 5.00

Whales — A353

No. 1035: a, Blainville's beaked whale. b, Shepherd's beaked whale. c, Cuvier's beaked whale. d, Baird's beaked whale. e, Stejneger's beaked whale. f, Ginkgo-toothed beaked whale.
$2.50, Pygmy sperm whale.

**2011, Mar. 11** ***Perf. 13 Syncopated***

**1035** A353 75c Sheet of 6, #a-f 9.00 9.00

**Souvenir Sheet**

**1036** A353 $2.50 multi 5.00 5.00

Visit to Spain of Pope Benedict XVI — A354

No. 1037: a, Pope Benedict XVI, Prince Felipe and Princess Letizia of Spain. b, Santiago de Compostela Cathedral. c, Pope Benedict XVI celebrating mass. d, King Juan Carlos and Queen Sofia of Spain.
$2.50, Pope Benedict XVI and Sagrada Familia Basilica, Barcelona, vert.

**2011, Mar. 11** **Litho.**

**1037** A354 94c Sheet of 4, #a-d 7.75 7.75

**Souvenir Sheet**

**1038** A354 $2.50 multi 5.00 5.00

Miniature Sheet

Pres. Ronald Reagan (1911-2004) — A355

No. 1039: a, Pres. Reagan at podium. b, Pres. Reagan with wife, Nancy. c, Pres. Reagan. d, Pres. Reagan with Soviet Union General Secretary Mikhail Gorbachev.

**2011, Apr. 5** ***Perf. 13 Syncopated***

**1039** A355 98c Sheet of 4, #a-d 8.00 8.00

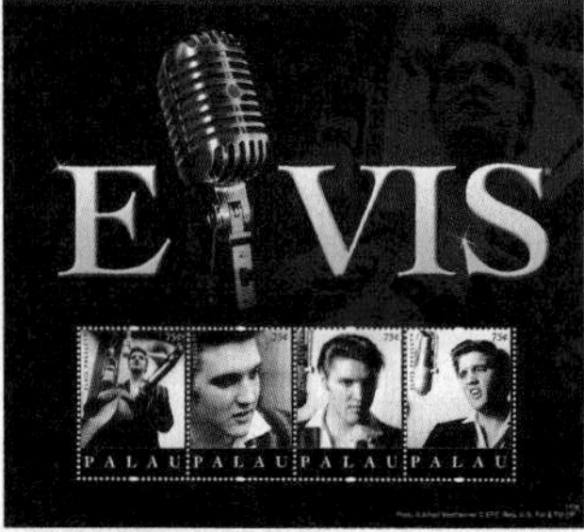


A356

A357

A358

A359

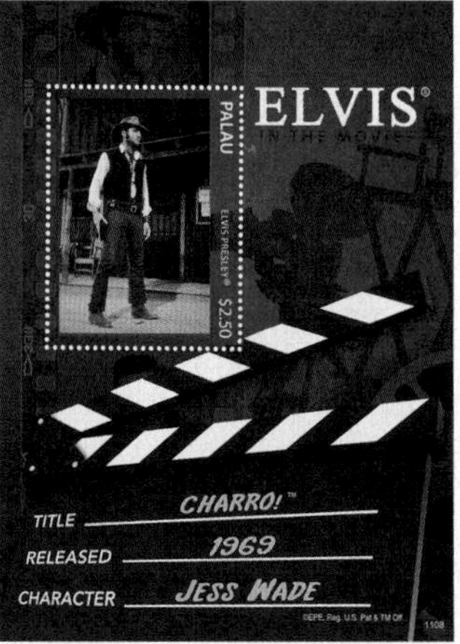


A360

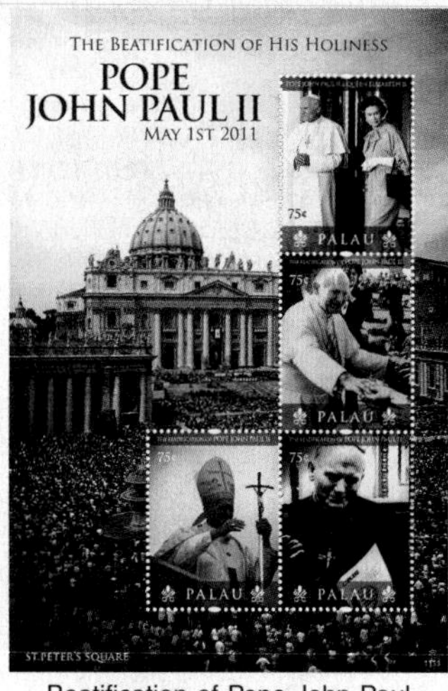


Elvis Presley (1935-77) — A361

No. 1040: a, Presley with guitar, two microphones. b, Presley facing right. c, Presley with closed mouth, microphone at left. d, Presley singing, microphone at left.
No. 1041 — Presley: a, With hand on ear. b, Microphone at left. c, Microphone at right, denomination in white. d, Microphone at right, denomination in black.

**2011** ***Perf. 13 Syncopated***

**1040** A356 75c Sheet of 4, #a-d 6.00 6.00

**1041** A357 75c Sheet of 4, #a-d 6.00 6.00

**Souvenir Sheets**

***Perf. 12¾***

**1042** A358 $2.50 multi 5.00 5.00
**1043** A359 $2.50 multi 5.00 5.00
**1044** A360 $2.50 multi 5.00 5.00
**1045** A361 $2.50 multi 5.00 5.00
*Nos. 1042-1045 (4)* 20.00 20.00

Issued: Nos. 1040-1041, 7/14; Nos. 1042-1045, 4/5.



Beatification of Pope John Paul II — A362

No. 1046 — Pope John Paul II: a, With Queen Elizabeth II. b, Greeting crowd. c, Wearing miter. d, Holding paper.
$2.50, Wearing miter, priests in background.

**2011, May 25** ***Perf. 13 Syncopated***

**1046** A362 75c Sheet of 4, #a-d 6.00 6.00

**Souvenir Sheet**

***Perf. 12¾***

**1047** A362 $2.50 multi 5.00 5.00

No. 1047 contains one 38x51mm stamp.

Wedding of Prince William and Catherine Middleton A363

Designs: 98c, Couple.
No. 1049, $2, Prince William. No. 1050, $2, Catherine Middleton.

**2011, June 17** ***Perf. 12x12½***

**1048** A363 98c multi 2.00 2.00

**Souvenir Sheets**

***Perf. 13½***

**1049-1050** A363 Set of 2 8.00 8.00

Nos. 1049-1050 each contain one 51x32mm triangular stamp.

Miniature Sheets

A364

Princess Diana (1961-97) — A365

No. 1051 — Princess Diana wearing: a, Black lace dress and choker on black ribbon. b, White dress. c, Pink hat. d, Black dress, no choker.

No. 1052 — Princess Diana wearing: a, Earring. b, Plaid jacket. c, Red Cross uniform. d, Black hat with veil.

**2011, July 6** ***Perf. 13 Syncopated***

**1051** A364 75c Sheet of 4, #a-d 6.00 6.00
**1052** A365 75c Sheet of 4, #a-d 6.00 6.00

Taro Festival — A366

No. 1053 — Taro plant and inscription: a, Dung er a terrekaki. b, Renged. c, Meuarch. d, Okelang. e, Metengal e ngas. f, Kirang. g, Rriu. h, Ngerbachel. i, Saikerei. j, Oiremech. k, Terebkul. l, Esuuch. m, Dungersuul. n, Ngesuas. o, Kerdeu. p, Terrekaki. q, Ngiroi-lang. r, Dilisior. s, Brak. t, Ulechem. u, Homusted. v, Besechel. w, Ungildil. x, Urungel. y, Ngatmadei. z, Dois. aa, Bsachel. ab, Ochab. ac, Kirang (redil). ad, Ngeruuch.

**2011, July 8** ***Perf. 12¾x13***

**1053** Sheet of 30 18.00 18.00
***a.-ad.*** A366 29c Any single .60 .60

Souvenir Sheet

Haruo I. Remeliik (1933-85), First President of Palau — A367

**2011, July 8** ***Perf. 13¼***

**1054** A367 $2 multi 4.00 4.00

Birds — A368

No. 1055, 98c: a, Black-headed gull. b, Red-tailed tropicbird. c, Intermediate egret. d, Yellow bittern.

No., 1056, 98c, vert.: a, Cattle egret. b, Red-footed booby. c, Australian pelican. d, Little pied cormorant.

No. 1057, $2, Greater crested tern. No. 1058, $2, Brown noddy, vert.

**2011, July 14** ***Perf. 13 Syncopated***

**Sheets of 4, #a-d**

**1055-1056** A368 Set of 2 16.00 16.00

**Souvenir Sheets**

**1057-1058** A368 Set of 2 8.00 8.00

Pres. Abraham Lincoln (1809-65) — A369

No. 1059 — Details from First Reading of the Emancipation Proclamation of President Lincoln, by Francis Bicknell Carpenter: a, Treasury Secretary Salmon P. Chase, Secretary of War Edwin M. Stanton. b, Lincoln. c, Secretary of the Navy Gideon Welles. d, Postmaster General Montgomery Blair, Interior Secretary, Caleb B. Smith, Secretary of State William H. Seward. e, Attorney General Edward Bates.
$2.50, Photograph of Lincoln.

**2011, July 27** ***Perf. 11½x11¾***

**1059** A369 60c Sheet of 5, #a-d 6.00 6.00

**Souvenir Sheet**

***Perf. 12x12½***

**1060** A369 $2.50 multi 5.00 5.00

No. 1060 contains one 30x80mm stamp.

Miniature Sheet

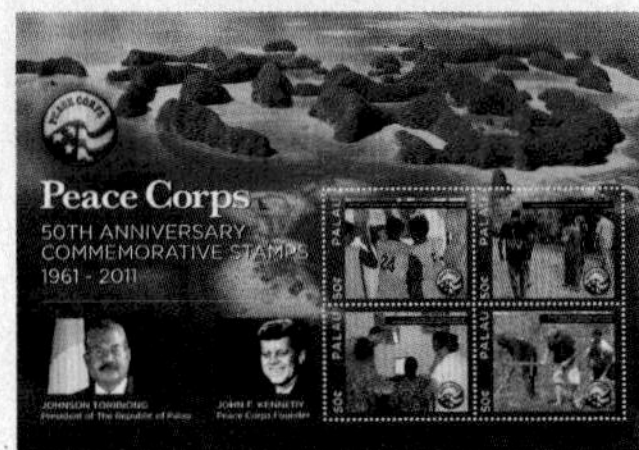


Peace Corps, 50th Anniv. — A370

No. 1061 — Peace Corps emblem and: a, Students and volunteer painting. b, Palauan host family and volunteers walking. c, Volunteer and teachers work on Internet project. d, Volunteers working in community garden.

**2011, Aug. 2** ***Perf. 13x13¼***

**1061** A370 50c Sheet of 4, #a-d 4.00 4.00

Sept. 11, 2001 Terrorist Attacks, 10th Anniv. — A371

No. 1062 — Firefighters, soldiers, U.S. flag and: a, Firefighter on rubble pile. b, Flags and flowers. c, Person looking at candlelight tribute. d, Tribute in light.
$2.50, World Trade Center and U.S flag.

**2011, Sept. 11** ***Perf. 12***

**1062** A371 75c Sheet of 4, #a-d 6.00 6.00

**Souvenir Sheet**

***Perf. 12¾***

**1063** A371 $2.50 multi 5.00 5.00

No. 1063 contains one 38x51mm stamp.

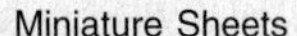

Miniature Sheets

A372

Women's World Cup Soccer Championships, Germany — A373

No. 1064: a, Nahomi Kawasumi. b, Japanese team members lifting trophy, "Team Japan" in black. c, Members of Japanese team. d, Yuki Nagasato.

No. 1065: a, Japan coach Norio Sasaki. b, Japanese team members lifting trophy, "Team Japan" in white. c, U.S. team. d, U.S. coach Pia Sundhage.

**2011, Sept. 21** ***Perf. 12x12½***

**1064** A372 98c Sheet of 4, #a-d 8.00 8.00
**1065** A373 98c Sheet of 4, #a-d 8.00 8.00

Pres. Barack Obama, 50th Birthday — A374

No. 1066 — Pres. Obama, White House, and one-quarter of Presidential Seal at: a, LR. b, LL. c, UR. d, UL.
$2.50, Pres. Obama.

**2011, Oct. 26** ***Perf. 13 Syncopated***

**1066** A374 98c Sheet of 4, #a-d 8.00 8.00

**Souvenir Sheet**

**1067** A374 $2.50 multi 5.00 5.00

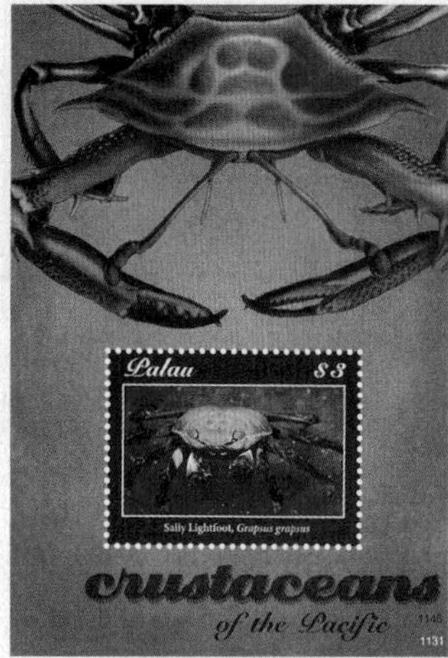


Crustaceans — A375

No. 1068, $1.25, vert.: a, Calcinus elegans. b, Dardanus pedunculatus. c, Odontodactylus scyllarus. d, Dardanus megistos.

No. 1069, $1.25, vert.: a, Birgus latro. b, Goneplax rhomboides. c, Bellia picta. d, Etisus dentatus.

No. 1070, $3, Grapsus grapsus. No. 1071, $3, Zebra mantis shrimp, vert.

**2011, Oct. 26** ***Perf. 12***

**Sheets of 4, #a-d**

**1068-1069** A375 Set of 2 20.00 20.00

**Souvenir Sheets**

**1070-1071** A375 Set of 2 12.00 12.00

No. 1071 contains one 30x50mm stamp.

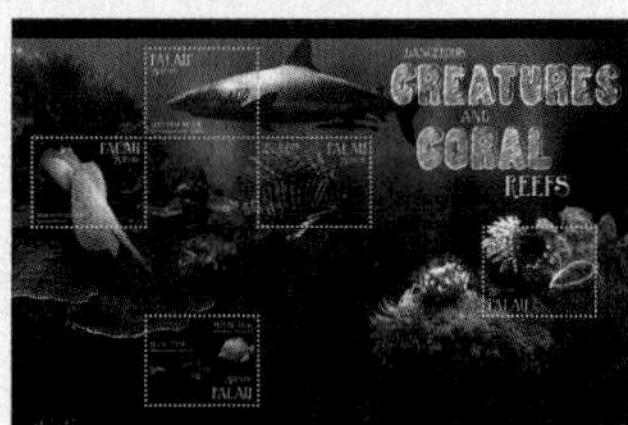


Marine Life — A376

No. 1072: a, Gray reef shark. b, Blue-spotted ray. c, Red lionfish. d, Feather duster worm. e, Regal tang, Yellow tang.

No. 1073: a, Pfeffer's flamboyant cuttlefish. b, Striped surgeonfish. c, Spiny sea urchin.

No. 1074, Box jellyfish, vert. No. 1075, Sawtooth barracuda.

**2011, Nov. 29** ***Perf. 11½x12***

**1072** A376 75c Sheet of 5, #a-e 7.50 7.50

***Perf. 12½x12***

**1073** A376 $1 Sheet of 3, #a-c 6.00 6.00

**Souvenir Sheets**

***Perf. 13½***

**1074** A376 $2.50 multi 5.00 5.00

***Perf.***

**1075** A376 $2.50 multi 5.00 5.00

No. 1074 contains one 38x51mm stamp. No. 1075 contains one 35mm diameter stamp.

Christmas — A377

Paintings: 22c, Landscape with the Flight into Egypt, by Annibale Carracci. 44c, Madonna and Saints, by Giovanni Bellini. 98c, Merode Altarpiece, by Robert Campin. $4.25, The Annunciation, by Matthias Grünewald.

**2012, Jan. 2** ***Perf. 14***

**1076-1079** A377 Set of 4 12.00 12.00

Lizards — A378

No. 1080, 98c: a, Snake-eyed skink. b, Solomon Islands skink. c, Vanuatu gecko. d, White-bellied skink.

No. 1081, 98c: a, Emerald tree skink. b, Common dwarf gecko. c, Mourning gecko. d, Moth skink.

No. 1082, $2.50, White-line gecko. No. 1083, $2.50, Mangrove monitor.

**2012, Jan. 2** ***Perf. 13 Syncopated***

**Sheets of 4, #a-d**

**1080-1081** A378 Set of 2 16.00 16.00

**Souvenir Sheets**

**1082-1083** A378 Set of 2 10.00 10.00

Miniature Sheet

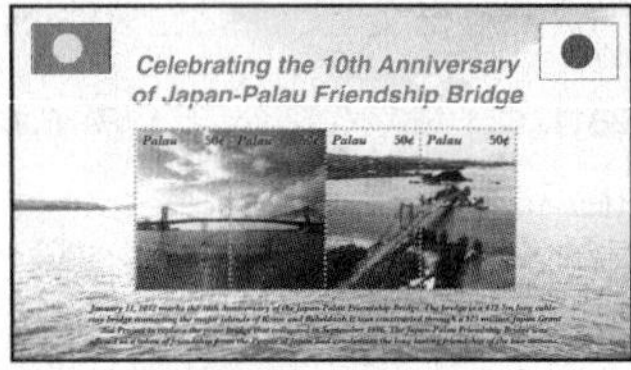


Japan-Palau Friendship Bridge, 10th Anniv. — A379

No. 1084: a, Side view of bridge, tower at left. b, Side view of bridge, tower at right. c, Aerial view of bridge, approach at bottom. d, Aerial view of bridge with road connecting other islands in distance.

**2012, Jan. 11** ***Perf. 12***

**1084** A379 50c Sheet of 4, #a-d 4.00 4.00

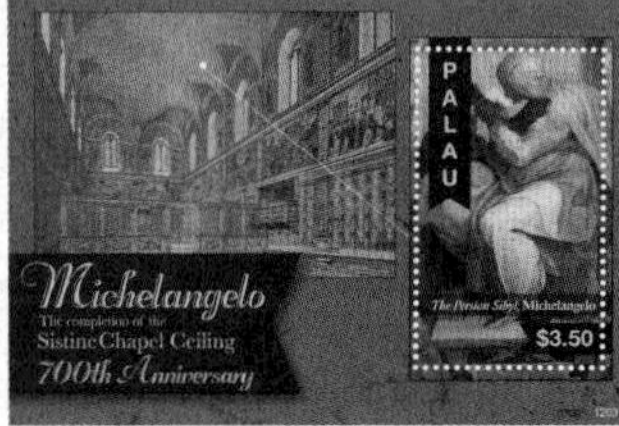


Painting of the Sistine Chapel Ceiling by Michelangelo, 500th Anniv. — A380

No. 1085, horiz.: a, Downfall of Adam and Eve. b, The Ignudi. c, The Prophet Jonah.

$3.50, The Persian Sibyl.

**2012, Jan. 24** ***Perf. 12***

**1085** A380 $1.25 Sheet of 3, #a-c 7.50 7.50

**Souvenir Sheet**

**1086** A380 $3.50 multi 7.00 7.00

Nos. 1085 and 1086 are erroneously inscribed "700th Anniversary."

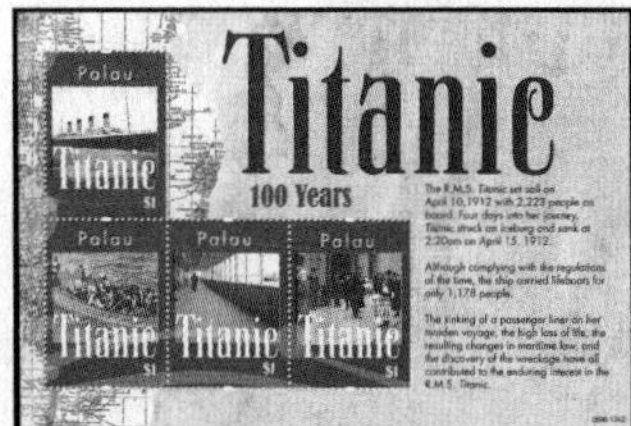


Sinking of the Titanic, Cent. — A381

No. 1087: a, Titanic at sea. b, Lifeboat. c, Man walking on deck. d, People reading newspapers reporting on the sinking.

$3, Titanic, diff.

**2012, Jan. 25** ***Perf. 13 Syncopated***

**1087** A381 $1 Sheet of 4, #a-d 8.00 8.00

**Souvenir Sheet**

**1088** A381 $3 multi 6.00 6.00

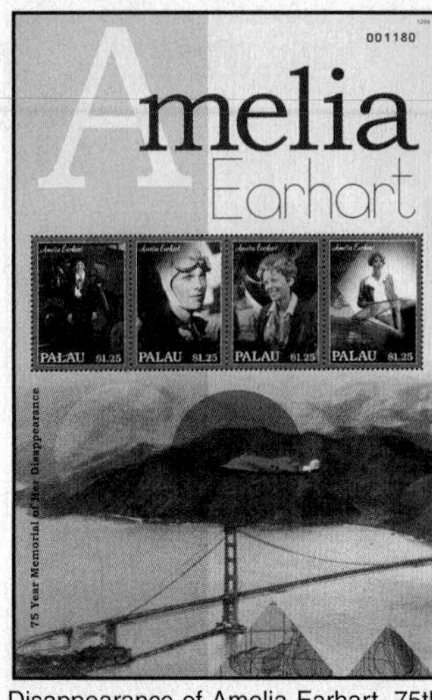


Disappearance of Amelia Earhart, 75th Anniv. — A382

No. 1089 — Earhart: a, Standing in front of airplane without helmet, hands visible. b, Wearing helmet and goggles. c, Standing in front of airplane without helmet, hands not visible. d, Standing in airplane cockpit without helmet.

No. 1090 — Earhart in helmet and goggles, airplane diagram, and text, "Amelia Earhart" in: a, White. b, Black.

**2012, Feb. 6** ***Perf. 13½***

**1089** A382 $1.25 Sheet of 4, #a-d 10.00 10.00

**Souvenir Sheet**

***Perf. 12x12½***

**1090** A382 $1.25 Sheet of 2, #a-b 5.00 5.00

Miniature Sheet

2012 Summer Olympics, London — A383

No. 1091: a, Tennis. b, Swimming. c, Weight lifting. d, Basketball.

**2012, Mar. 26** ***Perf. 13¼x13***

**1091** A383 80c Sheet of 4, #a-d 6.50 6.50

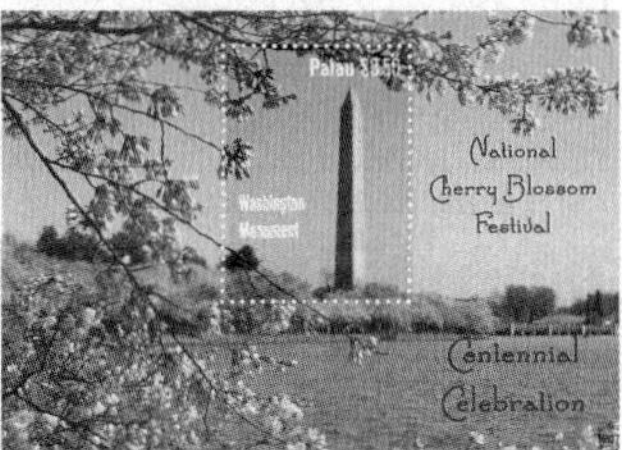


Cherry Trees in Bloom and Washington Monument — A384

No. 1092, horiz. — Blossoms of flowering trees: a, Washington hawthorn. b, Flowering dogwood. c, Callery pear. d, Crabapple. e, Magnolia. f, Eastern redbud.

**2012, Mar. 26** ***Perf. 12***

**1092** A384 $1 Sheet of 6, #a-f 12.00 12.00

**Souvenir Sheet**

**1093** A384 $3.50 shown 7.00 7.00

Miniature Sheets

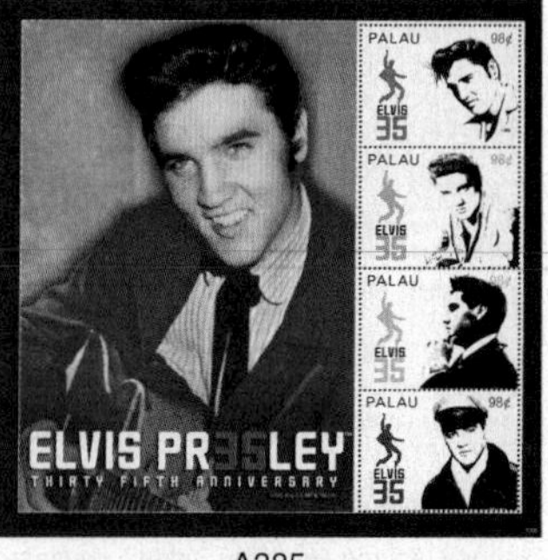


A385

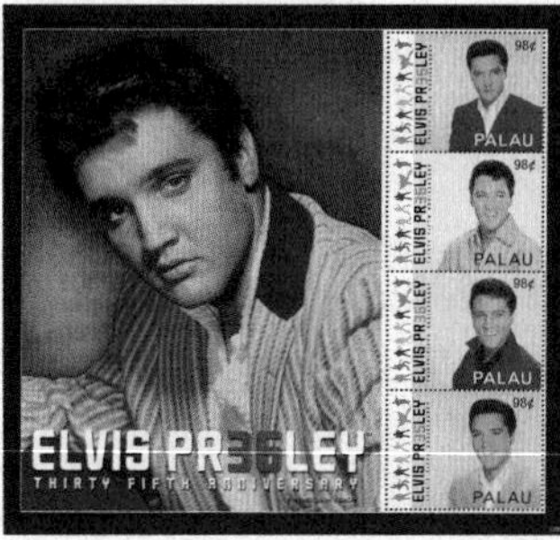


Elvis Presley (1935-77) — A386

No. 1094 — Color of "35" and silhouette: a, Red violet. b, Green. c, Yellow. d, Violet.

No. 1095 — Presley wearing: a, Red jacket, white shirt. b, Tan shirt. c, Red jacket, black shirt. d, Gray jacket, white shirt.

**2012, Apr. 11** ***Perf. 12½***

**1094** A385 98c Sheet of 4, #a-d 8.00 8.00

**1095** A386 98c Sheet of 4, #a-d 8.00 8.00

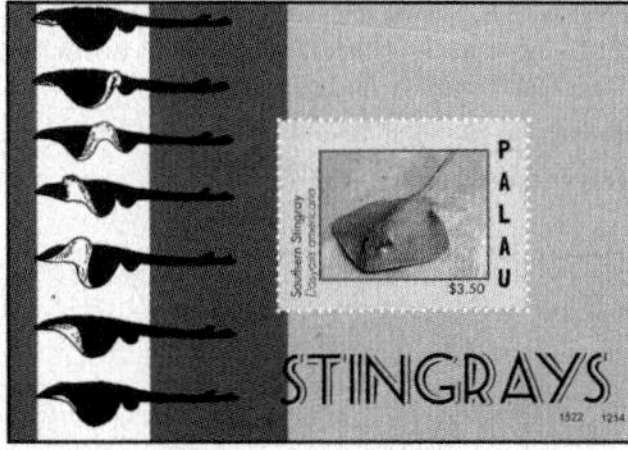


Stingrays — A387

No. 1096: a, Spotted eagle ray. b, Pacific electric ray. c, Blue-spotted stingray. d, Blotched fantail ray.

$3.50, Southern stingray.

**2012, May 7** ***Perf. 12***

**1096** A387 $1.25 Sheet of 4, #a-d 10.00 10.00

**Souvenir Sheet**

**1097** A387 $3.50 multi 7.00 7.00

Souvenir Sheets

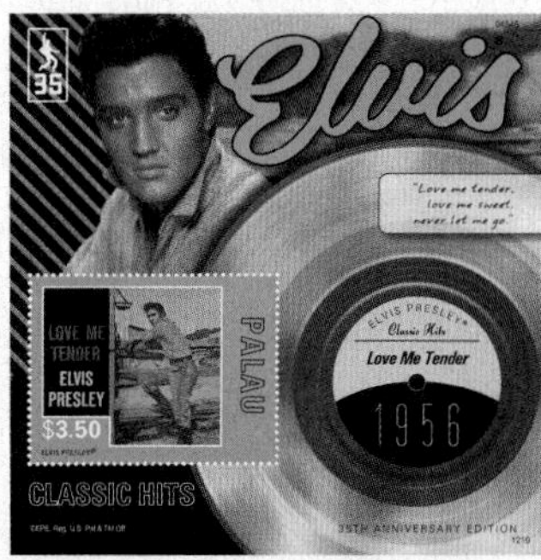


Elvis Presley (1935-77) — A388

Designs: No. 1098, $3.50, Presley on *Love Me Tender* record cover. No. 1099, $3.50, Presley on *Jailhouse Rock* album cover. No. 1100, $3.50, Presley on *Blue Hawaii* album cover. No. 1101, $3.50, Presley on *Just Tell Her Jim Said Hello/She's Not You* record cover. No. 1102, $3.50, Presley on *G.I. Blues* record cover.

**2012, May 14** ***Perf. 12½***

**1098-1102** A388 Set of 5 35.00 35.00

Miniature Sheet

Characters From *Peter Pan,* by Sir James M. Barrie (1860-1937) — A389

No. 1103: a, Peter Pan. b, Tiger Lily. c, Captain Hook. d, Wendy Darling.

**2012, June 7** ***Perf. 12***

**1103** A389 $1.25 Sheet of 4, #a-d 10.00 10.00

Miniature Sheet

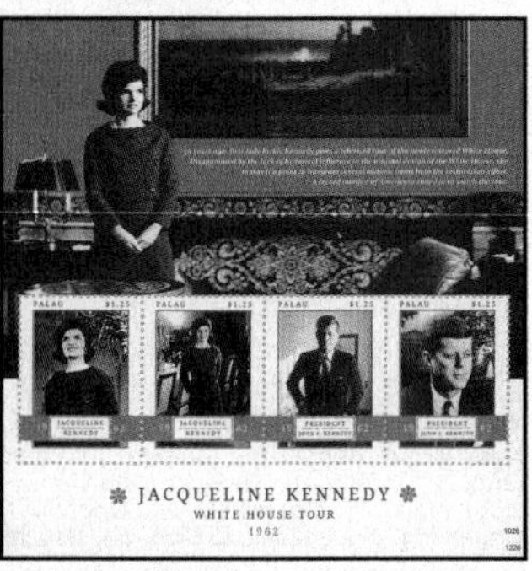


Televised Tour of the White House, 50th Anniv. — A390

No. 1104: a, Jacqueline Kennedy, chandelier. b, Jacqueline Kennedy, table and chairs. c, Pres. John F. Kennedy, picture frame. d, Pres. Kennedy, White House.

**2012, Aug. 28** **Litho.**

**1104** A390 $1.25 Sheet of 4, #a-d 10.00 10.00

Pope Benedict XVI, 85th Birthday — A391

No. 1105 — Pope Benedict wearing: a, Miter. b, Zucchetto.

**2012, Aug. 28** ***Perf. 14***

**1105** A391 $1.25 Horiz. pair, #a-b 5.00 5.00

Printed in sheets containing two pairs.

Miniature Sheets

End of Apollo Moon Missions, 40th Anniv. — A392

No. 1106, $1.25: a, Apollo 9. b, Apollo 7. c, Apollo 15. d, Apollo 12.

No. 1107, $1.25: a, Apollo 14. b, Apollo 17. c, Apollo 8. d, Apollo 11.

**2012, Aug. 28** ***Perf. 13 Syncopated***
**Sheets of 4, #a-d**

**1106-1107** A392 Set of 2 20.00 20.00

Paintings by Raphael — A393

No. 1108: a, Giuliano de' Medici. b, Saint Sebastian. c, Portrait of Julius II. d, Bindo Altoviti.
$3, St. Catherine of Alexandria.

**2012, Sept. 5** ***Perf. 12½***

**1108** A393 $1 Sheet of 4, #a-d 8.00 8.00

**Souvenir Sheet**

**1109** A393 $3 multi 6.00 6.00

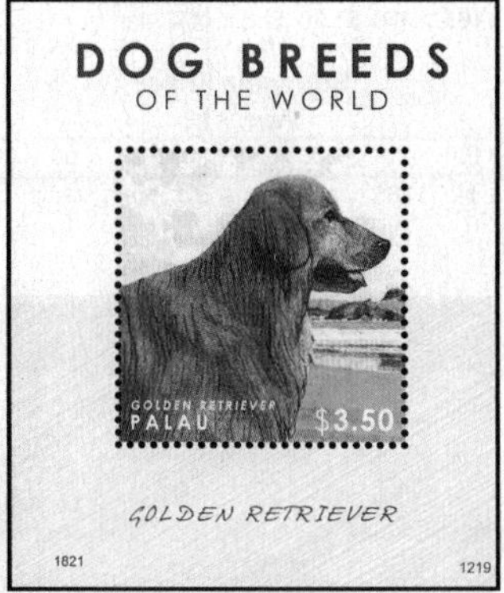


Dog Breeds — A394

No. 1110: a, Akita. b, Cane Corso. c, Collie. d, Rottweiler.
$3.50, Golden retriever.

**2012, Sept. 5** ***Perf. 13¾***

**1110** A394 $1.25 Sheet of 4, #a-d 10.00 10.00

**Souvenir Sheet**

**1111** A394 $3.50 multi 7.00 7.00

Souvenir Sheets

Famous Speeches — A395

Orators of famous speeches: No. 1112, $3.50, Pres. Theodore Roosevelt. No. 1113, $3.50, Mahatma Gandhi. No. 1114, $3.50, Pres. John F. Kennedy. No. 1115, $3.50, Dr. Martin Luther King, Jr.

**2012, Sept. 5** ***Perf. 12½***

**1112-1115** A395 Set of 4 28.00 28.00

Carnivorous Plants — A396

No. 1116: a, Pale butterwort. b, Corkscrew plant. c, Alice sundew. d, Zigzag bladderwort.
$3.50, King sundew, vert.

**2012, Nov. 28** ***Perf. 13¾***

**1116** A396 $1.20 Sheet of 4, #a-d 9.75 9.75

**Souvenir Sheet**
***Perf. 12½***

**1117** A396 $3.50 multi 7.00 7.00

No. 1117 contains one 38x51mm stamp.

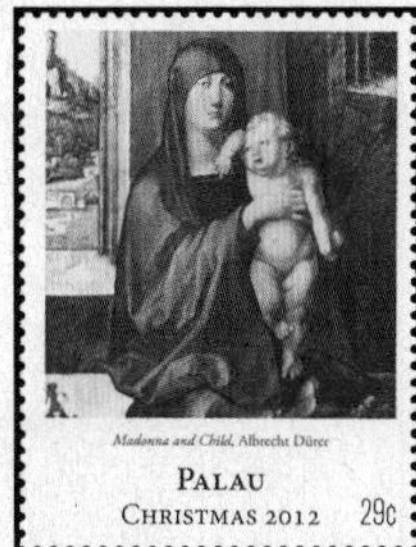


Christmas A397

Paintings by Albrecht Dürer: No. 1118, 29c, Madonna and Child. No. 1119, 29c, The Flight to Egypt. No. 1120, 45c, The Virgin and Child with St. Anne. No. 1121, 45c, Virgin and Child Holding a Half-eaten Pear. No. 1122, $1.05, Mother of Sorrows. No. 1123, $1.05, The Virgin Mary in Prayer.
$3.50, Jesus Boy with a Globe.

**2012, Dec. 24** ***Perf. 12½***

**1118-1123** A397 Set of 6 7.25 7.25

**Souvenir Sheet**

**1124** A397 $3.50 multi 7.00 7.00

The Hindenburg — A398

Designs: $1.20, Hindenburg. $3.50, Hindenburg, Chrysler Building, Eiffel Tower, Empire State Building, 40 Wall Street Building, vert.

**2012, Dec. 31** ***Perf. 12***

**1125** A398 $1.20 multi 2.40 2.40

**Souvenir Sheet**
***Perf. 12½***

**1126** A398 $3.50 multi 7.00 7.00

No. 1125 was printed in sheets of 4. No. 1126 contains one 38x51mm stamp.

World Radio Day — A399

No. 1127: a, Microphone. b, Antenna and waves. c, Table radio. d, Radio waves, diagram of ear canals.
$3.50, Solar system, radio wave, horiz.

**2013, Jan. 2** **Litho.** ***Perf. 13¾***

**1127** A399 $1.20 Sheet of 4, #a-d 9.75 9.75

**Souvenir Sheet**
***Perf. 12½***

**1128** A399 $3.50 multi 7.00 7.00

No. 1128 contains one 51x38mm stamp.

Paintings by Paul Signac (1863-1935) — A400

No. 1129: a, L'Orage (The Storm). b, The Pine, Saint Tropez. c, Portrait of Félix Fénéon.
$3.50, Femmes au Puits (Women at the Well).

**2013, Jan. 8** **Litho.** ***Perf. 12½***

**1129** A400 $1.50 Sheet of 3, #a-c 9.00 9.00

**Souvenir Sheet**

**1130** A400 $3.50 multi 7.00 7.00

Reign of Queen Elizabeth II, 60th Anniv. (in 2012) — A401

No. 1131 — Queen Elizabeth II: a, With Prince Philip. b, With dog. c, Waving. d, With Prince Charles.
$3.50, Queen Elizabeth II, vert.

**2013, Jan. 8** **Litho.** ***Perf. 13¾***

**1131** A401 $1.20 Sheet of 4, #a-d 9.75 9.75

**Souvenir Sheet**
***Perf. 12½***

**1132** A401 $3.50 multi 7.00 7.00

No. 1132 contains one 38x51mm stamp.

Shells — A402

No. 1133: a, Conus gloriamaris. b, Hydatina albocincta. c, Marginella strigata. d, Conus betulinus.
$3.50, Tellina pharaonis, horiz.

**2013, Mar. 20** **Litho.** ***Perf. 12***

**1133** A402 $1.20 Sheet of 4, #a-d 9.75 9.75

**Souvenir Sheet**

**1134** A402 $3.50 multi 7.00 7.00

Cat Breeds — A403

Cat Depictions From Other Cultures — A404

No. 1135, $1.20: a, Russian Blue. b, Turkish Angora. c, Norwegian forest cat. d, Siamese.
No. 1136, $1.20: a, Siberian. b, Oriental shorthair. c, Japanese bobtail. d, Chartreux.
No. 1137, $3.50, Egyptian goddess Bastet. No. 1138, $3.50, Japanese Maneki-neko figurine.

**2013, Mar. 20** **Litho.** ***Perf. 12***
**Sheets of 4, #a-d**

**1135-1136** A403 Set of 2 19.50 19.50

**Souvenir Sheets**
***Perf. 13¾***

**1137-1138** A404 Set of 2 14.00 14.00

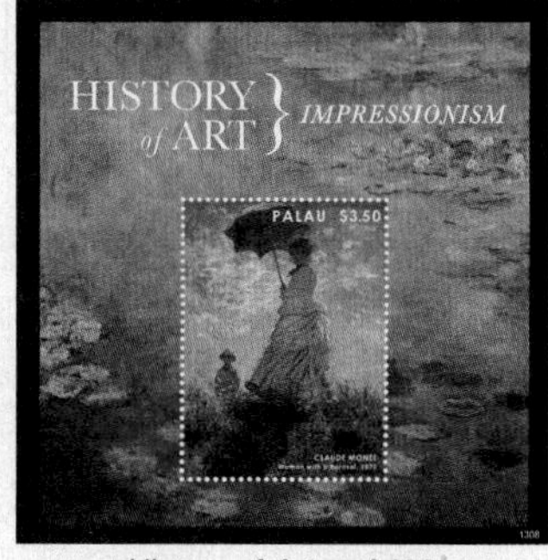


History of Art — A405

No. 1139, $1.50: a, Sunset at Ivry, by Armand Guillaumin. b, Landscape with Big Trees, by Camille Pissarro. c, A Box at the Theater, by Pierre-Auguste Renoir.
No. 1140, $1.50: a, Sunshine in the Blue Room, by Anna Ancher. b, Woman Washing Her Feet in a Brook, by Pissarro. c, Woman in the Bath, by Edgar Degas.
No. 1141, $3.50, Woman with a Parasol, by Claude Monet. No. 1142, $3.50, The Star, by Edgar Degas.

**2013, Apr. 4** **Litho.** ***Perf. 12½***
**Sheets of 3, #a-c**

**1139-1140** A405 Set of 2 18.00 18.00

**Souvenir Sheets**

**1141-1142** A405 Set of 2 14.00 14.00

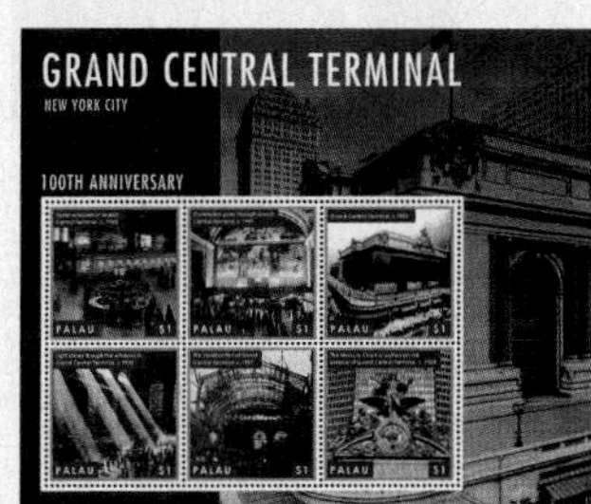


Grand Central Terminal, New York City, Cent. — A406

No. 1143: a, Ticket window, c. 1945. b, Commuters in station, c. 1941. c, Terminal exterior, c, 1920. d, Light shining through windows, c. 1930. e, Terminal under construction, c. 1907. f, Mercury Clock, c. 1988.
$3.50, Terminal exterior, horiz.

**2013, Apr. 29** **Litho.** ***Perf. 13¾***

**1143** A406 $1 Sheet of 6, #a-f 12.00 12.00

**Souvenir Sheet**

***Perf. 12½***

**1144** A406 $3.50 multi 7.00 7.00

No. 1144 contains one 51x38mm stamp.

A407

Pres. John F. Kennedy (1917-63) — A408

No. 1145 — Black-and-white images of Pres. Kennedy: a, Facing right, flag in background. b, Facing left, flag in background. c, With people in background. d, With door in background.

No. 1146 — Color images of Pres. Kennedy: a, Facing right, with woman's head in background. b, With black background. c, With tie pattern visible. d, Facing right, with indistinguishable light reflections in background.

No. 1147, $3.50, Pres. Kennedy, country name at LL in blue panel. No. 1148, $3.50, Pres. Kennedy pointing, country name at UL in blue panel.

***Perf. 13 Syncopated***

**2013, Apr. 29 Litho.**

**1145** A407 $1.20 Sheet of 4, #a-d 9.75 9.75

**1146** A408 $1.20 Sheet of 4, #a-d 9.75 9.75

**Souvenir Sheets**

**1147-1148** A408 Set of 2 14.00 14.00

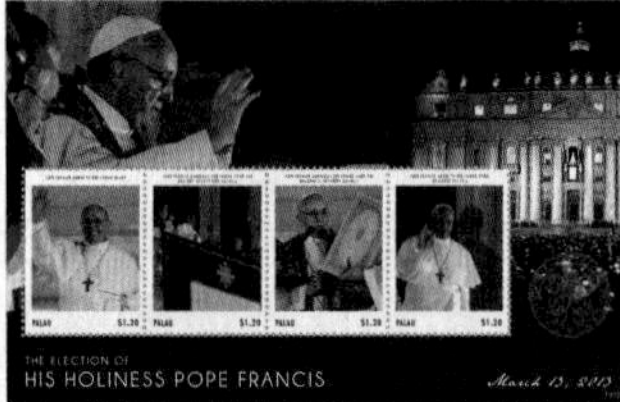

Election of Pope Francis — A409

No. 1150 — Pope Francis: a, Waving to crowd below (orange background). b, Addressing crowd from balcony of St. Peter's Basilica (with cardinals). c, Behind microphone, addressing crowd, with assistant holding Bible. d, Waving to crowd (shadow and wall in background).

$3.50, Pope Francis, diff.

**2013, June 3 Litho. *Perf. 12***

**1149** A409 $1.20 Sheet of 4, #a-d 9.75 9.75

**Souvenir Sheet**

***Perf. 12½***

**1150** A409 $3.50 multi 7.00 7.00

No. 1150 contains one 38x51mm stamp.

Lady Margaret Thatcher (1925-2013), British Prime Minister — A410

No. 1151 — Thatcher: a, Wearing black dress. b, With Pres. George H. W. Bush. c, Wearing gray striped dress. d, Wearing black dresss with whtie dots.

$3.50, Thatcher in doorway of bus.

**2013, June 3 Litho. *Perf. 12***

**1151** A410 $1.25 Sheet of 4, #a-d 10.00 10.00

**Souvenir Sheet**

***Perf. 12½***

**1152** A410 $3.50 multi 7.00 7.00

No. 1152 conatins one 38x51mm stamp.

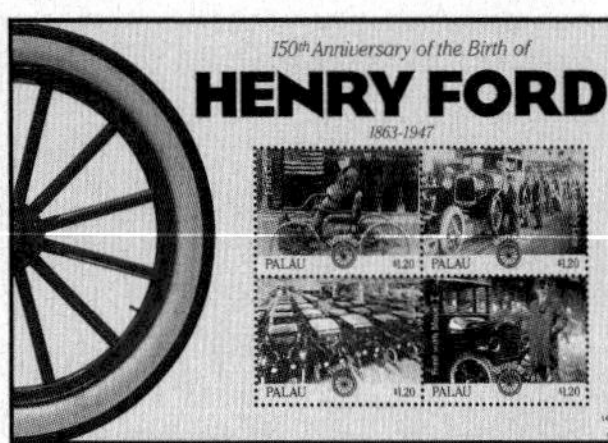

Henry Ford (1863-1947), Automobile Manufacturer — A411

No. 1153: a, Ford and first car. b, Assembly line. c, Parked Model T autombiles. d, Ford and Model T.

$3.50, Ford, vert.

**2013, June 25 Litho. *Perf. 12***

**1153** A411 $1.20 Sheet of 4, #a-d 9.75 9.75

**Souvenir Sheet**

**1154** A411 $3.50 multi 7.00 7.00

Tropical Fish — A412

No. 1155, $1.20: a, Australasian snapper. b, Tomato clownfish. c, Pennant coralfish. d, Yellow watchman goby.

No. 1156, $1.20: a, Pink-spotted shirmp goby. b, Ocellated dragonet. c, Common warehou. d, Gray moray.

No. 1157, $3.50, Blue-eyed triplefin. No. 1158, $3.50, Barred mudskipper.

**2013, June 25 Litho. *Perf. 12***

**Sheets of 4, #a-d**

**1155-1156** A412 Set of 2 19.50 19.50

**Souvenir Sheets**

**1157-1158** A412 Set of 2 14.00 14.00

Thailand 2013 World Stamp Exhibition, Bangkok — A413

No. 1159: a, Mondop Staircases. b, Floating market. c, Asian elephants. d, Buddhist temple.

$3.50, Sedge hats.

**2013, July 7 Litho. *Perf. 12***

**1159** A413 $1.20 Sheet of 4, #a-d 9.75 9.75

**Souvenir Sheet**

**1160** A413 $3.50 multi 7.00 7.00

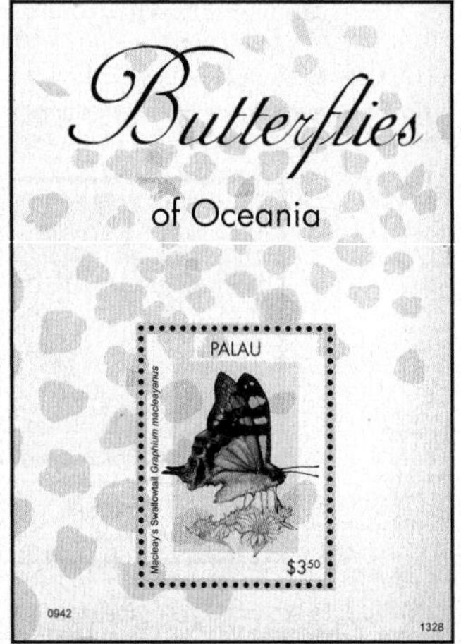

Butterflies — A414

No. 1161, horiz.: a, Tailed jay swallowtail. b, Old world swallowtail. c, Common albatross. d, Australian lurcher.

$3.50, Macleay's swallowtail.

**2013, Sept. 17 Litho. *Perf. 12***

**1161** A414 $1.20 Sheet of 4, #a-d 9.75 9.75

**Souvenir Sheet**

**1162** A414 $3.50 multi 7.00 7.00

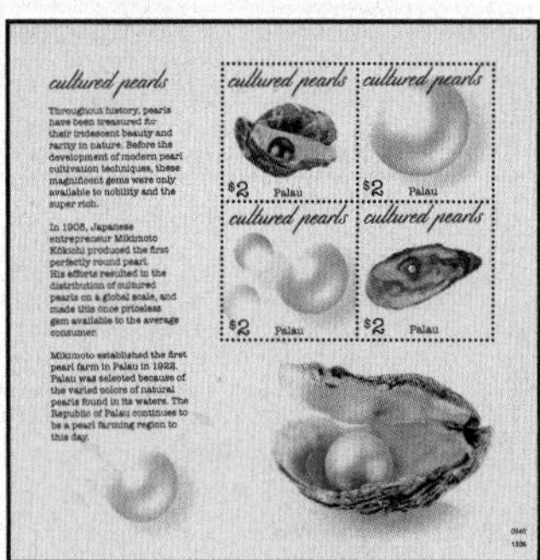

Cultured Pearls — A415

No. 1163: a, Large brown pearl in oyster shell, upper shell. b, Large white pearl. c, Three pearls. d, Small pearl in oyster shell.

$4, Pearl, tan background.

**2013, Sept. 17 Litho. *Perf. 13¾***

**1163** A415 $2 Sheet of 4, #a-d 16.00 16.00

**Souvenir Sheet**

**1164** A415 $4 multi 8.00 8.00

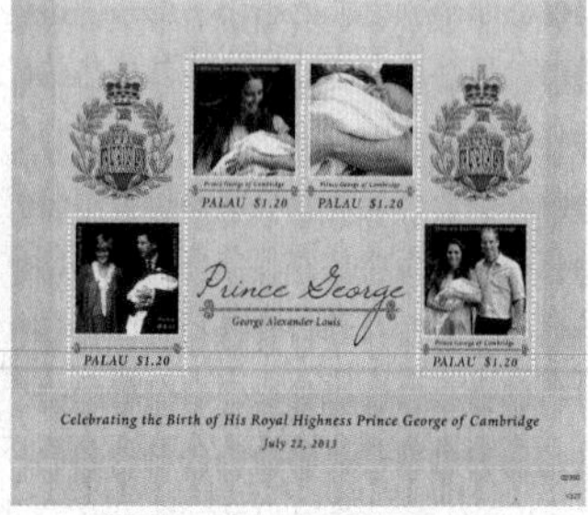

Birth of Prince George of Cambridge — A416

No. 1165: a, Duchess of Cambridge holding Prince George. b, Prince George, close-up. c, Prince Charles, Princess Diana, Prince William. d, Duke and Duchess of Cambridge with Prince George.

$3.50, Duke and Duchess of Cambridge with Prince George, diff.

**2013, Sept. 17 Litho. *Perf. 14***

**1165** A416 $1.20 Sheet of 4, #a-d 9.75 9.75

**Souvenir Sheet**

***Perf. 12***

**1166** A416 $3.50 multi 7.00 7.00

No. 1166 contains one 30x50mm stamp.

Miniature Sheets

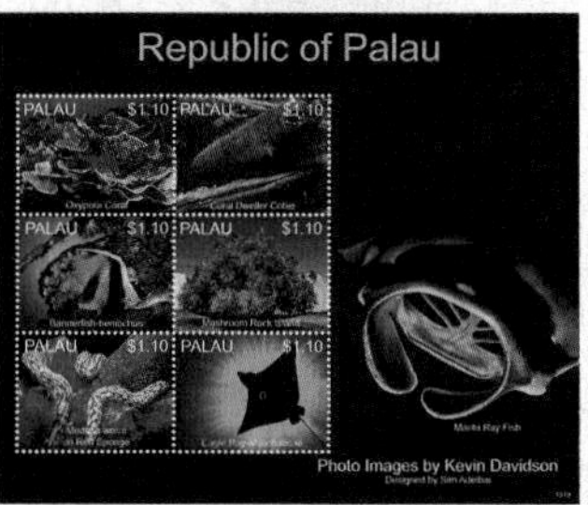

Photographs by Kevin Davidson — A417

No. 1167: a, Oxypora coral, country name at UL, reading across. b, Coral dweller cobie, country name at UL, reading across. c, Bannerfish. d, Mushroom Rock Island, country name at UL, reading across. e, Medusa worm on red sponge. f, Eagle ray, decimal point of denomination to right of ray, wing of ray just touching vertical line of first "1" in denomination.

No. 1168: a, Baby green turtles. b, Mandarin fish, country name at UL, reading across. c, Eagle ray, decimal point of denomination on ray. d, Pink anemone fish, country name at UL, reading across. e, Head of fish (incorrectly inscribed "Medusa worm on red sponge"). f, Masked angelfish.

No. 1169: a, Harlequin sweetlips. b, Nautilus. c, Eagle Ray, decimal point of denomination to right of ray, wing of ran not touching vertical line of first "1" in denomination. d, Red sea fan. e, Soft coral crab.

No. 1170: a, Oxypora coral, country name at left, reading up. b, Coral dweller cobie, country name at left, reading up. c, Pink anemone fish, country name at left, reading up. d, Mushroom Rock Island, country name at left, reading up. e, Mandarin fish, country name at left, reading up. f, Longnose hawkfish.

No. 1171, vert.: a, Three jellyfish. b, Starfish on red coral fan, country name at UL, reading across. c, Jellyfish and diver. d, Oxypora coral, country name at UL, reading across. e, Seahorse. f, Lionfish.

No. 1172, vert.: a, Coconut climber. b, Pink anemone fish, country name at UL, reading across. c, Cup coral, country name at UL, reading across. d, Humphead wrasse, e, Shark.

No. 1173, vert.: a, Cup coral, country name at UL, reading up. b, Manta ray. c, Rock Island. d, Red seahorse. e, Pink anemone fish, country name at UL, reading up. f, Starfish on red coral fan, country name at UL, reading up.

**2013, Oct. 1 Litho. *Perf. 12***

**1167** A417 $1.10 Sheet of 6, #a-f 13.50 13.50

**1168** A417 $1.10 Sheet of 6, #a-f 13.50 13.50

**1169** A417 $1.10 Sheet of 6, #a-e, 1168f 13.50 13.50

**1170** A417 $1.10 Sheet of 6, #a-f 13.50 13.50

**1171** A417 $1.10 Sheet of 6, #a-f 13.50 13.50

**1172** A417 $1.10 Sheet of 6, #a-e, 1171d 13.50 13.50
**1173** A417 $1.10 Sheet of 6, #a-f 13.50 13.50
*Nos. 1167-1173 (7)* 94.50 94.50

Souvenir Sheet

Elvis Presley (1935-77) — A418

**Litho., Margin Embossed With Foil Application**

**2013, Oct. 1** ***Imperf.***
**1174** A418 $10 multi 20.00 20.00

Coronation of Queen Elizabeth II, 60th Anniv. — A419

No. 1175 — Queen Elizabeth II: a, With Prince Philip. b, Wearing pink hat. c, Wearing white hat. d, Alone, wearing sash and tiara.
$3.50, Queen Elizabeth II in coach, vert.

**2013, Oct. 7** **Litho.** ***Perf. 14***
**1175** A419 $1.20 Sheet of 4, #a-d 9.75 9.75

**Souvenir Sheet**

**1176** A419 $3.50 multi 7.00 7.00

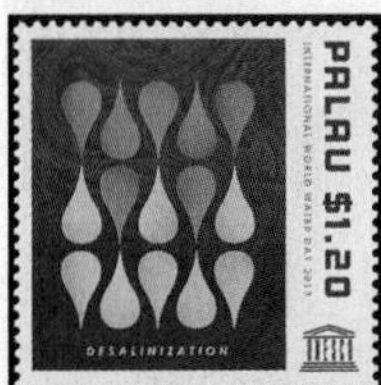


World Water Day — A420

Designs: $1.20, Water droplets. $3.50, Water droplet, vert.

**2013, Nov. 18** **Litho.** ***Perf. 13¾***
**1177** A420 $1.20 multi 2.40 2.40

**Souvenir Sheet**

***Perf. 12½***

**1178** A420 $3.50 multi 7.00 7.00

No. 1177 was printed in sheets of 4. No. 1178 contains one 38x51mm stamp.

Christmas A421

Paintings: 29c, Madonna Worshipping the Child and an Angel, by Biagio D'Antonio Tucci. 44c, Nativity, by unknown artist. $1.05, The Annunciation, by Simone Martini. $3.50, Virgin and Child, by Gentile da Fabriano.

**2013, Dec. 2** **Litho.** ***Perf. 12½***
**1179-1182** A421 Set of 4 11.00 11.00

A422

Nelson Mandela (1918-2013), President of South Africa — A423

No. 1183: a, Mandela and wife, Winnie, waving. b, Mandela as young man wearing traditional collar. c, Mandela in crowd, laughing.
No. 1184 — Mandela: a, wearing black and gray shirt. b, Wearing suit and tie, building in background. c, Holding microphone stand. d, Seated. e, Behind microphone, pointing. f, With raised fist.
No. 1185, $3.50, Mandela holding ballot, wearing shirt with pens in pocket, vert. No. 1186, $3.50, Mandela with arm raised, wearing patterned shirt, vert.

**2013, Dec. 15** **Litho.** ***Perf. 13¾***
**1183** A422 $1.20 Vert. strip of 3, #a-c 7.25 7.25
**1184** A423 $1.20 Sheet of 6, #a-f 14.50 14.50

**Souvenir Sheets**

***Perf. 12½***

**1185-1186** A423 Set of 2 14.00 14.00

No. 1183 was printed in sheet of 6 stamps containing two each of Nos. 1183a-1183c. Nos. 1185-1186 each contain on 38x51mm stamp.

Orchids — A424

No. 1187: Various Phalaenopsis orchids, as shown.
$3.50, Lady's slipper, horiz.

**2013, Dec. 18** **Litho.** ***Perf. 13¾***
**1187** A424 $1 Sheet of 6, #a-f 12.00 12.00

**Souvenir Sheet**

***Perf. 12½***

**1188** A424 $3.50 multi 7.00 7.00

No. 1188 contains one 51x38mm stamp.

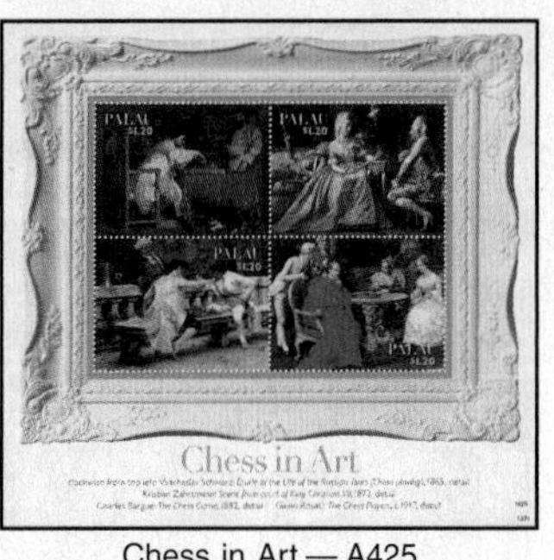


Chess in Art — A425

No. 1189: a, Etude of the Life of the Russian Tsars, by Vyacheslav Schwarz (players, table with green tablecloth). b, Scene from the Court of King Christian VII, by Kristian Zahrtmann (woman and man playing). c, The Chess Players, by Giulio Rosati (players on bench). d, The Chess Game, by Charles Bargue (woman and cardinal playing).
$3.50, Proposal, by Knut Ekwall, vert.

**2013, Dec. 23** **Litho.** ***Perf. 12½***
**1189** A425 $1.20 Sheet of 4, #a-d 9.75 9.75

**Souvenir Sheet**

**1190** A425 $3.50 multi 7.00 7.00

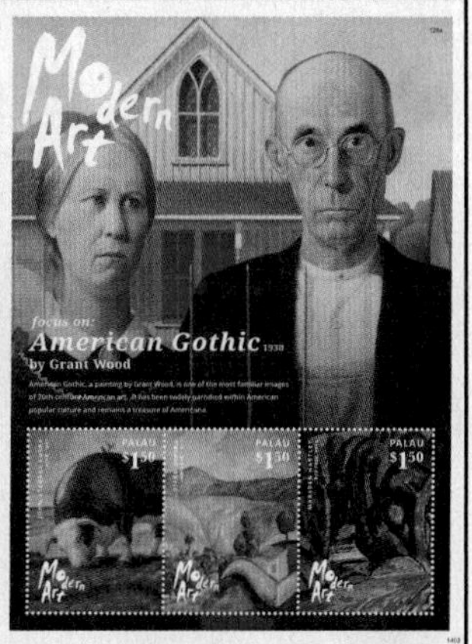


Modern Art — A426

No. 1191, $1.50 — Paintings: a, Ajax, by John Steuart Curry. b, Landscape, by Diego Rivera. c, Red Tree, by Marsden Hartley.
No. 1192, $1.50 — Photographs: a, Power Farming Displaces Tenants, by Dorothea Lange. b, Toward Los Angeles, California, by Lange. c, Power House Mechanic Working on Steam Pump, by Lewis Hine.
No. 1193, $3.50, Red Cavalry, by Kazimir Malevich. No. 1194, $3.50, The Alarm Clock, by Rivera.

**2014, Jan. 2** **Litho.** ***Perf. 12½***

**Sheets of 3, #a-c**

**1191-1192** A426 Set of 2 18.00 18.00

**Souvenir Sheets**

**1193-1194** A426 Set of 2 14.00 14.00

Shells — A427

No. 1195, $1.75: a, Chicoreus palma-rosae. b, Phalium glaucum. c, Conus generalis (blue background at top). d, Conus episcopus.
No. 1196, $1.75: a, Conus generalis (purple background at top). b, Harpa articularis. c, Strombus minimus. d, Strombus gibberulus.
No. 1197, $3.50: a, Chicoreus ramosus. b, Murex troscheli.
No. 1198, $3.50: a, Charonia tritonis. b, Syrinx aruanus.

**2014, Feb. 26** **Litho.** ***Perf. 12***

**Sheets of 4, #a-d**

**1195-1196** A427 Set of 2 28.00 28.00

**Souvenir Sheets of 2, #a-b**

***Perf. 12½***

**1197-1198** A427 Set of 2 28.00 28.00

Nos. 1197-1198 each contain two 38x51mm stamps.

Caroline Kennedy, United States Ambassador to Japan — A428

No. 1199 — Caroline Kennedy: a, Greeting Japanese students. b, With parents and brother. c, As young woman at graduation ceremony. d, As child, with father.
$4, Caroline Kennedy, vert.

**2014, Mar. 5** **Litho.** ***Perf. 13¾***
**1199** A428 $1.50 Sheet of 4, #a-d 12.00 12.00

**Souvenir Sheet**

***Perf. 12½***

**1200** A428 $4 multi 8.00 8.00

No. 1200 contains one 38x51mm stamp.

Miniature Sheets

Winter Sports — A429

No. 1201: a, Ice hockey. b, Speed skating. c, Bobsled. d, Figure skating.
No. 1202, horiz.: a, Freestyle skiing. b, Nordic combined skiing. c, Curling. d, Luge. f, Skeleton. g, Bobsled, diff.

**2014, Mar. 5 Litho. *Perf. 12½***

**1201** A429 $1.20 Sheet of 4, #a-d 9.75 9.75

***Perf. 14***

**1202** A429 $1.20 Sheet of 6, #a-f 14.50 14.50

No. 1202 contains six 40x30mm stamps.

Pope Francis — A430

No. 1203, $1.20: a, Pres. Horacio Cartes of Paraguay. b, Pope Francis (painting in backgound). c, Pres. Cartes and Pope Francis (painting in background). d, Pres. Cartes and Pope Francis (painting and table in background).
No. 1204, $1.20: a, Pres. Denis Sassou Nguesso of Congo Republic. b, Pope Francis (book shelves in background). c, Pres. Sassou Nguesso and Pope Francis (painting and chairs in background). d, Pres. Sassou Nguesso and Pope Francis (corner of room in background).
No. 1205, $2: a, Pope Francis hugging person. b, Pope Francis patting child's head.
No. 1206, $2: a, Pope Francis looking upwards. b, Pope Francis with hands together.

**2014, Mar. 10 Litho. *Perf. 12½***

**Sheets of 4, #a-d**

**1203-1204** A430 Set of 2 19.50 19.50

**Souvenir Sheets of 2, #a-b**

***Perf. 12***

**1205-1206** A430 Set of 2 16.00 16.00

Nos. 1205-1206 each contain two 30x40mm stamps.

World War I, Cent. — A431

No. 1207, $2.50: a, London Scottish Regiment drill. b, British Army recruits in training. c, New recruits with officers, London. d, British Army volunteers, Aldershot.
No. 1208, $2.50: a, Bergmann MP18 machine gun, Germany. b, Carl Gustav Mauser M96, Sweden. c, Browning 1917 A1 machine gun, Belgium. d, Fedorov Avtomat rifle, Russia.
No. 1209, $2: a, Herbert Henry Asquith, British Prime Minister. b, Winston Churcill, First Lord of the Admiralty.
No. 1210, $2: a, Luger P08, Germany. b, Model 1892 revolver, France.

**2014, Apr. 23 Litho. *Perf. 14***

**Sheets of 4, #a-d**

**1207-1208** A431 Set of 2 40.00 40.00

**Souvenir Sheets of 2, #a-b**

***Perf. 12½***

**1209-1210** A431 Set of 2 16.00 16.00

Nos. 1209-1210 each contain two 51x38mm stamps.

Miniature Sheet

South Korean Stamps — A432

No. 1211: a, South Korea #936 (1975 stamp). b, South Korea #1398 (1985 stamp). c, South Korea #1635 (1991 stamp). d, South Korea #704 (1970 stamp). e, South Korea #948 (1975 stamp). f, Never-used stamp of 1884. g, South Korea #861 (1973 stamp). h, South Korea #300 (1959 stamp).

**2014, May 12 Litho. *Perf. 12***

**1211** A432 $1 Sheet of 8, #a-h 16.00 16.00

Philakorea 2014 World Stamp Exhibition, Seoul.

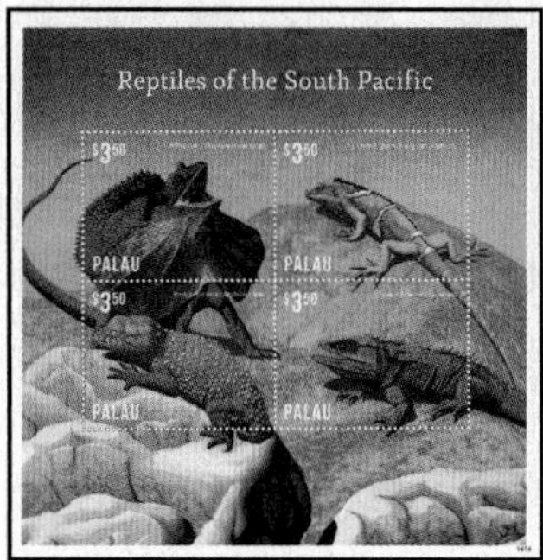


Reptiles — A433

No. 1212, $3.50: a, Frilled lizard. b, Fiji crested iguana. c, Knob-tailed gecko. d, Tuatara.
No. 1213, $3.50: a, Eastern brown snake (35x35mm). b, Children's python (35x35mm). c, Copperhead (35x70mm). d, Red-bellied black snake (35x35mm).
No. 1214, $3.50, Green sea turtle. No. 1215, $3.50, Saltwater crocodile.

***Perf. 12½, 13¾ (#1213)***

**2014, July 1 Litho.**

**Sheets of 4, #a-d**

**1212-1213** A433 Set of 2 56.00 56.00

**Souvenir Sheets**

**1214-1215** A433 Set of 2 14.00 14.00

Miniature Sheets

A434

Seagulls — A435

Various depictions of seagulls, as shown.

***Perf. 13 Syncopated***

**2014, July 21 Litho.**

**1216** A434 $1 Sheet of 6, #a-f 12.00 12.00
**1217** A435 $1 Sheet of 6, #a-f 12.00 12.00

Prince George of Cambridge — A436

No. 1218: a, Duke and Duchess of Cambridge, Prince George. b, Prince George. c, Duchess of Cambridge and Prince George.
No. 1219: a, Duke of Cambridge and Prince George. b, Prince George, diff.
No. 1220, $4, Prince George facing left, horiz. No. 1221, $4, Prince George facing right, horiz.

**2014, July 21 Litho. *Perf. 14***

**1218** A436 75c Horiz. strip of 3, #a-c 4.50 4.50
**1219** A436 $1 Pair, #a-b 4.00 4.00

**Souvenir Sheets**

**1220-1221** A436 Set of 2 16.00 16.00

No. 1218 was printed in sheets of 8 stamps containing 4 #1218b and 2 each #1218a and 1218c. No. 1219 was printed in sheets containing 3 pairs.

Miniature Sheet

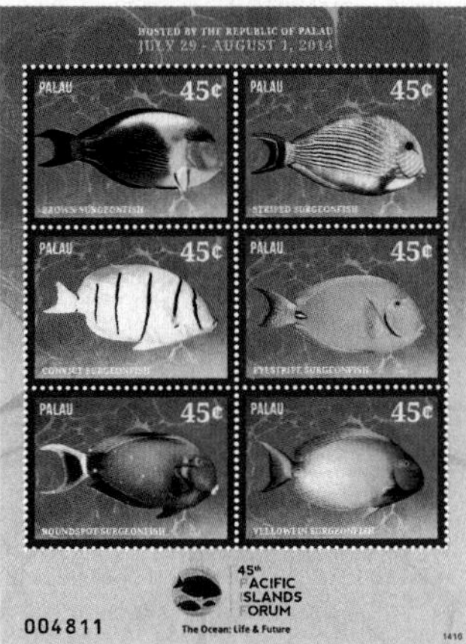


Fish — A437

No. 1222: a, Brown surgeonfish. b, Striped surgeonfish. c, Convict surgeonfish. d, Eyestripe surgeonfish. e, Roundspot surgeonfish. f, Yellowfin surgeonfish.

**2014, July 30 Litho. *Perf. 12½x13¼***

**1222** A437 45c Sheet of 6, #a-f 5.50 5.50

45th Pacific Islands Forum, Palau.

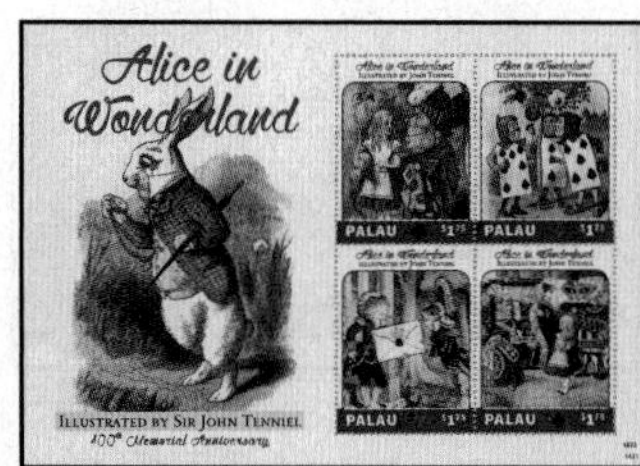


Illustrations for *Alice's Adventures in Wonderland,* by Sir John Tenniel (1820-1914) — A438

No. 1223, $1.75: a, Alice, Flamingo and Duchess (club in panel). b, Playing Cards painting rose bush (diamond in panel). c, Fish delivers letter to frog (heart in panel). d, Alice and the Queen of Hearts (spade in panel).
No. 1224, $1.75: a, Alice at tea party (club in panel). b, Alice and flowers (diamond in panel). c, Alice holding bottle (heart in panel). d, Alice and playing cards (spade in panel).
No. 1225, $2.50: a, King of Hearts (club in panel). b, Queen of Hearts (heart in panel).
No. 1226, $2.50: a, Knave of Hearts (spade in panel). b, Birds in powdered wigs (diamond in panel).

**2014, July 31 Litho. *Perf. 12½***

**Sheets of 4, #a-d**

**1223-1224** A438 Set of 2 28.00 28.00

**Souvenir Sheets of 2, #a-b**

**1225-1226** A438 Set of 2 20.00 20.00

Tourist Attractions in Russia — A439

No. 1227: a, Uzon Caldera. b, Mt. Elbrus. c, Trans-Siberian Railway.
No. 1228, vert.: a, Peter and Paul Cathedral, St. Petersburg. b, St. Sophia Cathedral, Vologda.

**2014, Aug. 14 Litho. *Perf. 12***

**1227** A439 $1.50 Sheet of 3, #a-c 9.00 9.00

**Souvenir Sheet**

**1228** A439 $2 Sheet of 2, #a-b 8.00 8.00

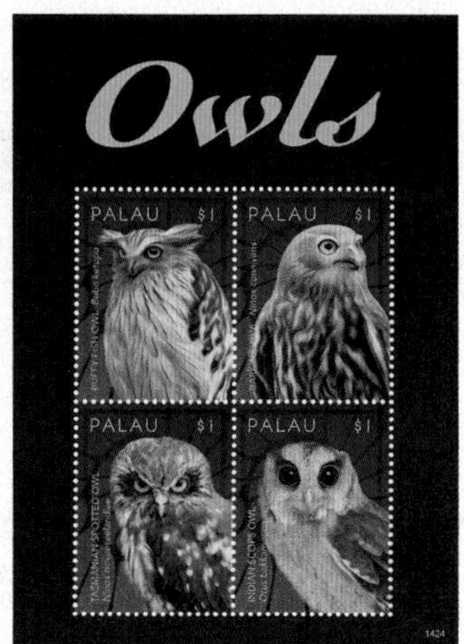


Owls — A440

No. 1229: a, Buffy fish owl. b, Barking owl. c, Tasmanian spotted owl. d, Indian scops owl. $3, Ural owl. $4, Short-eared owl.

**2014, Aug. 14 Litho. *Perf. 12***

**1229** A440 $1 Sheet of 4, #a-d 8.00 8.00

**Souvenir Sheets**

**1230** A440 $3 multi 6.00 6.00
**1231** A440 $4 multi 8.00 8.00

Marine Life — A441

Designs: 2c, Damselfish. 3c, Green sea turtle. 5c, Mailed butterflyfish. 10c, Ornate butterflyfish. 15c, Queen triggerfish. 20c, Reef manta ray. 75c, Yellow boxfish. $1, Palau nautilus.

**2014, Aug. 27 Litho. *Perf. 13¾***

**1232** A441 2c multi .25 .25
**1233** A441 3c multi .25 .25
**1234** A441 5c multi .25 .25
**1235** A441 10c multi .25 .25

**1236** A441 15c multi .30 .30
**1237** A441 20c multi .40 .40
**1238** A441 75c multi 1.50 1.50
**1239** A441 $1 multi 2.00 2.00
*Nos. 1232-1239 (8)* 5.20 5.20

Trains — A442

No. 1240: a, Golden Arrow. b, Orient Express. c. Royal Scot. d, Super Chief. $3.50, 20th Century Limited.

**2014, Sept. 3 Litho. *Perf. 12***
**1240** A442 $1.20 Sheet of 4, #a-d 9.75 9.75

**Souvenir Sheet**

**1241** A442 $3.50 multi 7.00 7.00

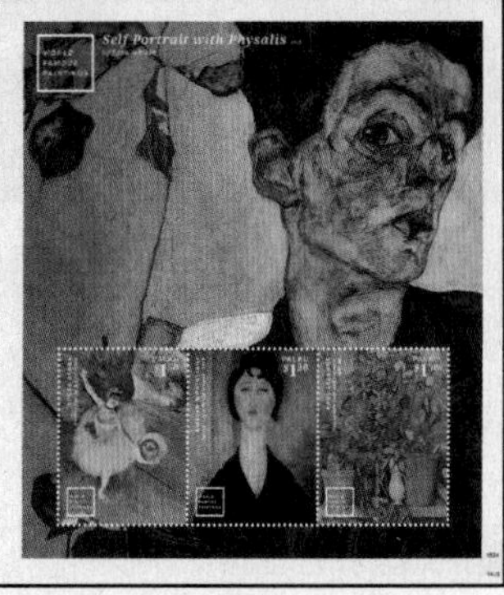

Paintings — A443

No. 1242, $1.50: a, Dancer Taking a Bow, by Edgar Degas. b, Portrait of a Young Woman, by Amedeo Modigliani. c, Terracotta Pots and Flowers, by Paul Cézanne.
No. 1243, $1.50: a, The Ballet Class, by Degas. b, Anxiety, by Edvard Munch. c, The Child's Bath, by Mary Cassatt.
No. 1244, $4, In the Kitchen, by Carl Larsson. No. 1245, $4, Farewell, by August Macke.

**2014, Sept. 3 Litho. *Perf. 12½***

**Sheets of 3, #a-c**

**1242-1243** A443 Set of 2 18.00 18.00

**Size: 100x100mm**

***Imperf***

**1244-1245** A443 Set of 2 16.00 16.00

Frogs and Toads — A444

No. 1246, $1.20: a, Rough-backed forest frog. b, Common tree frog. c, Luzon frog. d, Wrinkled ground frog.
No. 1247, $1.20: a, Taylor's wrinkled ground frog. b, Woodworth's wart frog. c, Pygmy forest frog. d, Kalinga narrowmouth toad.
No. 1248, $4, Luzon fanged frog. No. 1249, $4, Harlequin tree frog.

***Perf. 14, 12 (#1249)***

**2014, Sept. 15 Litho.**

**Sheets of 4, #a-d**

**1246-1247** A444 Set of 2 19.50 19.50

**Souvenir Sheets**

**1248-1249** A444 Set of 2 16.00 16.00

Miniature Sheets

Characters From *Downton Abbey* Television Series — A445

No. 1250, $1.20: a, Dowager Countess of Grantham. b, Earl of Grantham. c, Countess of Grantham. d, Lady Mary Crawley. e, Lady Edith Crawley.
No. 1251, $1.20: a, Thomas Barrow. b, Mr. Carson. c, Mrs. Hughes. d, Mrs. Patmore. e, Daisy Mason.

**2014, Nov. 11 Litho. *Perf. 14***

**Sheets of 5, #a-e**

**1250-1251** A445 Set of 2 24.00 24.00

Christmas A446

Paintings and details of paintings by Raphael: 34c, The Adoration of the Magi. 49c, The Adoration of the Magi, diff. $1.50, Ansidei Madonna. $3.50, Colonna Madonna.

**2014, Nov. 24 Litho. *Perf. 12½***
**1252-1255** A446 Set of 4 12.00 12.00

Worldwide Fund for Nature (WWF) — A447

Nos. 1256 and 1257 — Lagoon jellyfish: a, Near water's surface. b, Two jellyfish. c, Above seafloor. d, In sea cave.

**2014, Dec. 1 Litho. *Perf. 14***
**1256** A447 40c Block or horiz. strip of 4, #a-d 3.25 3.25
**1257** A447 90c Block or horiz. strip of 4, #a-d 7.25 7.25

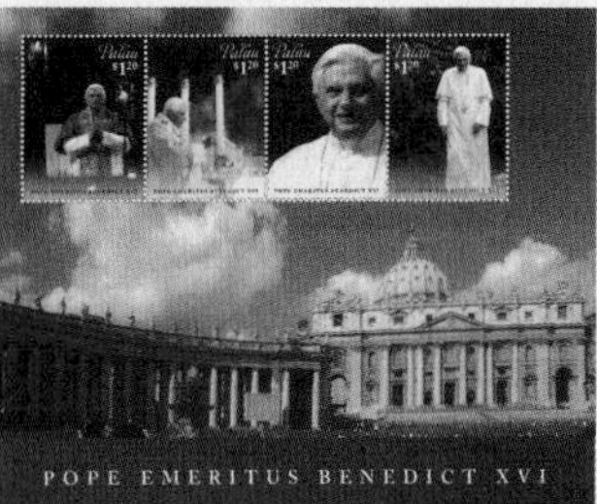


Pope Benedict XVI — A448

No. 1258 — Pope Benedict XVI: a, Wearing red vestments. b, Swinging censer. c, Close-up. d, Standing in front of bushes.
$4, Pope Benedict XVI in green vestments.

**2014, Dec. 16 Litho. *Perf. 14***
**1258** A448 $1.20 Sheet of 4, #a-d 9.75 9.75

**Souvenir Sheet**

**1259** A448 $4 multi 8.00 8.00

Dinosaurs — A449

No. 1260, $1.20: a, Nigersaurus. b, Iguanodon. c, Agustinia. d, Doliosauriscus.
No. 1261, $1.20: a, Ankylosaurus. b, Giganotosaurus. c, Diplodocus. d, Tyrannosaurus.
No. 1262, $4, Stegosaurus. No. 1263, $4, Gigantspinosaurus.

**2014, Dec. 22 Litho. *Perf. 12***

**Sheets of 4, #a-d**

**1260-1261** A449 Set of 2 19.50 19.50

**Souvenir Sheets**

**1262-1263** A449 Set of 2 16.00 16.00

No. 1261 contains four 50x30mm stamps.

Bubble Tea — A450

No. 1264 — Cup of tea with straw and inscription of: a, Pineapple. b, Taro. c, Strawberry. d, Mango. e, Avocado. f, Blueberry.
$4, Cup of tea with lid and straw.

**2015, Jan. 5 Litho. *Perf. 13¾***
**1264** A450 $1.20 Sheet of 6, #a-f 14.50 14.50

**Souvenir Sheet**

***Perf. 12***

**1265** A450 $4 multi 8.00 8.00

No. 1265 contains one 30x40mm stamp.
Asian International Stamp Exhibition, 30th Anniv.

Pope John Paul II (1920-2005) A451

**2015, Feb. 2 Litho. *Perf. 12***
**1266** A451 75c multi 1.50 1.50

Printed in sheets of 4. Compare with type A331.

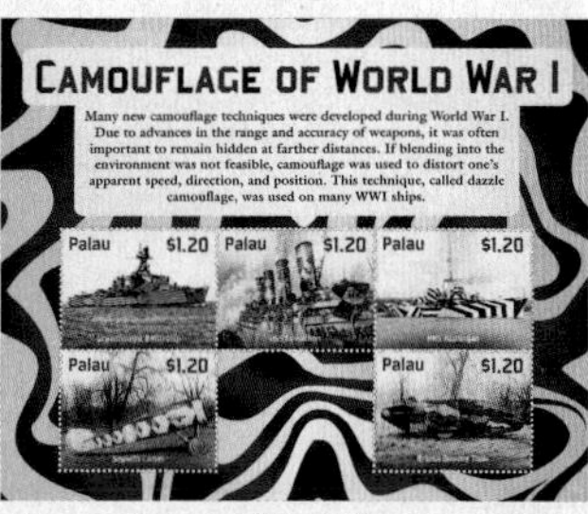


Camouflage of World War I — A452

No. 1267: a, Dreadnought Battleship. b, USS Leviathan. c, HMS Kildangan. d, Sopwith Camel airplane. e, British dummy tank.
$4, Soldier in tree-climbing camouflage.

**2015, Feb. 2 Litho. *Perf. 14***
**1267** A452 $1.20 Sheet of 5, #a-e 12.00 12.00

**Souvenir Sheet**

***Perf. 13¾***

**1268** A452 $4 multi 8.00 8.00

No. 1268 contains one 35x35mm stamp.

UNESCO World Heritage Sites — A453

No. 1269: a, Great Barrier Reef, Australia. b, Prambanan Temple Compounds, Indonesia. c, Rice Terraces of the Philippine Cordilleras, Philippines. d, Kinabalu Park, Malaysia. e, Komodo National Park, Indonesia.
$4, Rock Islands Southern Lagoon, Palau.

**2015, Mar. 9 Litho. *Perf. 14***
**1269** A453 $1.20 Sheet of 5, #a-e 12.00 12.00

**Souvenir Sheet**

***Perf. 13¾***

**1270** A453 $4 multi 8.00 8.00

No. 1270 contains one 70x35mm stamp.

Ships Involved in the 1940 Evacuation of Dunkirk — A454

No. 1271, 45c: a, Minnehaha, b, Cygnet. c, Rapid. d, Skylark. e, Wanda. f, Marchioness. g, Jovial. h, Fedalma II. i, Jane Hannah MacDonald. j, Massey Shaw. k, Mimosa. l, Aberdonia. m, Reda. n, Blue Bird. o, Dorian. p, White Heathe.

No. 1272, 45c: a, Cachalot. b, Fervant. c, Omega. d, Greater London. e, Jane Holland. f, Lucy Lavers. g, Tom Tit. h, Cyril and Lillian Bishop. i, Latona. j, Endeavour. k, Polly. l, Tigris. m, Eothen. n, Lazy Days. o, Wairakei II. p, Matoya.

**2015, May 25 Litho. *Perf. 14***

**Sheets of 16, #a-p, + Label**

**1271-1272** A454 Set of 2 29.00 29.00

Queen Elizabeth II, Longest-Reigning British Monarch — A455

No. 1273 — Queen Elizabeth II wearing: a, Dark green dress, light green hat and gloves. b, Pink dress and hat, black gloves. c, Green coat. b, Dark blue dress. c, White gown and tiara. d, Lilac dress.

$4, Queen Elizabeth II in white and blue dress with blue buttons and matching hat.

**2015, May 25 Litho. *Perf. 14***

**1273** A455 $1.20 Sheet of 6, #a-f 14.50 14.50

**Souvenir Sheet**

***Perf. 12***

**1274** A455 $4 multi 8.00 8.00

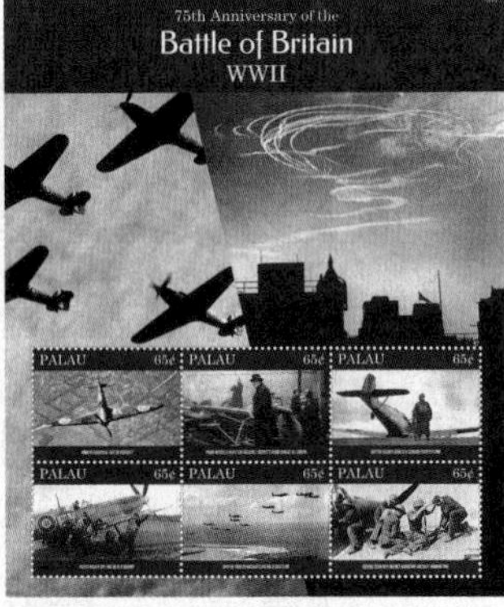


Battle of Britain, 75th Anniv. — A456

No. 1275: a, Hawker Hurricane. b, Prime Minister Winston Churchill inspects bomb damage in London. c, British soldier guards a German fighter plane. d, Pilots push a Spitfire onto a runway. e, Spitfires patrol a coastline. f, Ground crew replenishes Hurricane aircraft ammunition.

$4, Churchill and Queen Elizabeth inspect damage to Buckingham Palace.

**2015, June 1 Litho. *Perf. 12***

**1275** A456 65c Sheet of 6, #a-f 8.00 8.00

**Souvenir Sheet**

**1276** A456 $4 multi 8.00 8.00

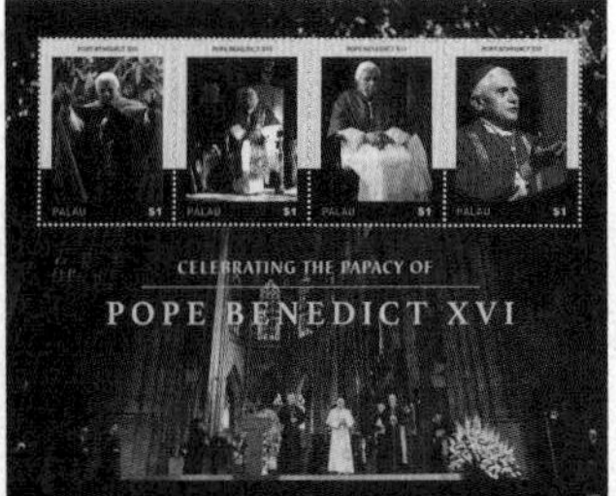


Pope Benedict XVI — A457

No. 1277 — Pope Benedict XVI: a, With arms raised. b, Seated next to bishop. c, Seated alone. d, With hand outstretched.

$3.50, Pope Benedict XVI wearing large crucifix.

**2015, June 8 Litho. *Perf. 12½***

**1277** A457 $1 Sheet of 4, #a-d 8.00 8.00

**Souvenir Sheet**

**1278** A457 $3.50 multi 7.00 7.00

Birds — A458

No. 1279: a, Eclectus parrot (30x40mm). b, Brahminy kite (60x40mm). c, Whiskered tern (30x40mm). d, Black-winged stilt (30x40mm). e, Collared kingfisher (60x40mm). f, Black kite (30x40mm).

$4, Sulphur-crested cockatoo, horiz.

**2015, June 15 Litho. *Perf. 12***

**1279** A458 65c Sheet of 6, #a-f 8.00 8.00

**Souvenir Sheet**

**1280** A458 $4 multi 8.00 8.00

No. 1280 contains one 40x30mm stamp.

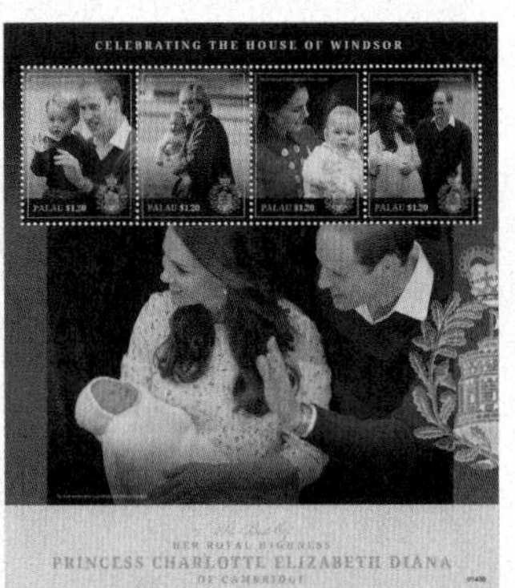


Birth of Princess Charlotte of Cambridge — A459

No. 1281: a, Duke of Cambridge and Prince George. b, Princess Diana and Prince William. c, Duchess of Cambridge and Prince George. d, Duke and Duchess of Cambridge, Princess Charlotte.

$4, Duchess of Cambridge holding Princess Charlotte.

**2015, July 13 Litho. *Perf. 12***

**1281** A459 $1.20 Sheet of 4, #a-d 9.75 9.75

**Souvenir Sheet**

**1282** A459 $4 multi 8.00 8.00

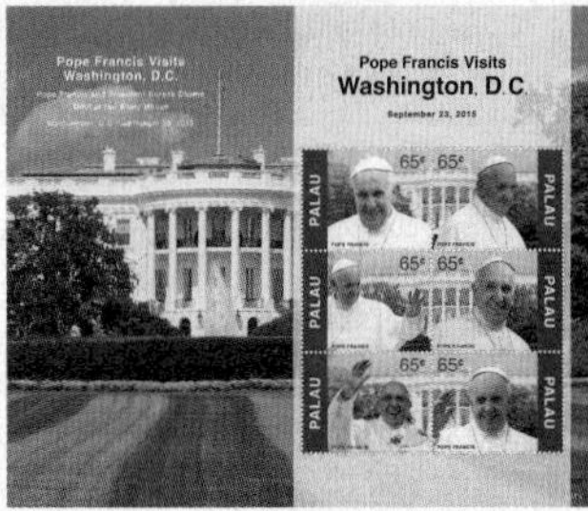


Visit of Pope Francis to Washington, D.C. — A460

No. 1283 — Pope Francis: a, Smiling, denomination at UR. b, Facing right, denomination at UL. c, Waving, hand at right, denomination at UR. d, Smiling, denomination at UL. e, Waving, hand at left, denomination at UR. f, Waving, hand at left, denomination at UL.

$4, Pope Francis with Pres. Barack Obama and wife, Michelle.

**2015, Nov. 25 Litho. *Perf. 14***

**1283** A460 65c Sheet of 6, #a-f 8.00 8.00

**Souvenir Sheet**

**1284** A460 $4 multi 8.00 8.00

No. 1284 contains one 80x30mm stamp.

Pres. Dwight D. Eisenhower (1890-1969) — A461

No. 1285 — Pres. Eisenhower: a, Wearing golf cap. b, With three men on golf course. c, Giving "V" for victory sign. d, Holding baseball. e, Waving to crowd from train. f, Wearing military uniform, standing in car.

$4, Pres. Eisenhower with wife, Mamie, horiz.

**2015, Dec. 7 Litho. *Perf. 14***

**1285** A461 65c Sheet of 6, #a-f 8.00 8.00

**Souvenir Sheet**

***Perf. 12½***

**1286** A461 $4 multi 8.00 8.00

No. 1286 contains one 51x38mm stamp.

Sir Winston Churchill (1874-1965), British Prime Minister — A462

No. 1287 — Churchill: a, Smoking cigar. b, Aiming submachine gun. c, With Pres. Franklin D. Roosevelt. d, Giving "V" for Victory sign.

$4, Churchill speaking in front of picture of Abraham Lincoln, horiz.

**2015, Dec. 7 Litho. *Perf. 12½***

**1287** A462 $1.20 Sheet of 4, #a-d 9.75 9.75

**Souvenir Sheet**

**1288** A462 $4 multi 8.00 8.00

William Shakespeare (1564-1616), Writer — A463

No. 1289: a, Portrait of Shakespeare. b, Statue of Shakespeare. c, Shakespeare's burial place, Stratford-upon-Avon, Great Britain. d, Shakespeare Memorial Theater, Stratford-upon-Avon. e, Shakespeare's birthplace, Stratford-upon-Avon. f, Globe Theater, London.

$4, Shakespeare's first folio, 1623, vert.

**2015, Dec. 7 Litho. *Perf. 14***

**1289** A463 65c Sheet of 6, #a-f 8.00 8.00

**Souvenir Sheet**

***Perf. 12***

**1290** A463 $4 multi 8.00 8.00

No. 1290 contains one 30x50mm stamp.

Christmas A464

Paintings by Bartolomé Esteban Murillo: 34c, The Annunciation. 49c, Virgin and Child in Glory. $1, Madonna and Child. $2, Virgin with Child.

**2015, Dec. 7 Litho. *Perf. 12½***

**1291-1294** A464 Set of 4 7.75 7.75

German Reunification, 25th Anniv. — A465

No. 1295 — Reichstag Building, Berlin: a, Side towers in red light. b, Side towers in yellow light. c, Side towers in purple light, statues near dome not visible. d, Side towers in purple light, statues near dome in blue light.

$4, Reichstag Building with columns in red and white light, vert.

**2015, Dec. 17 Litho. *Perf. 12***

**1295** A465 $1.20 Sheet of 4, #a-d 9.75 9.75

**Souvenir Sheet**

***Perf. 12½***

**1296** A465 $4 multi 8.00 8.00

No. 1296 contains one 38x51mm stamp.

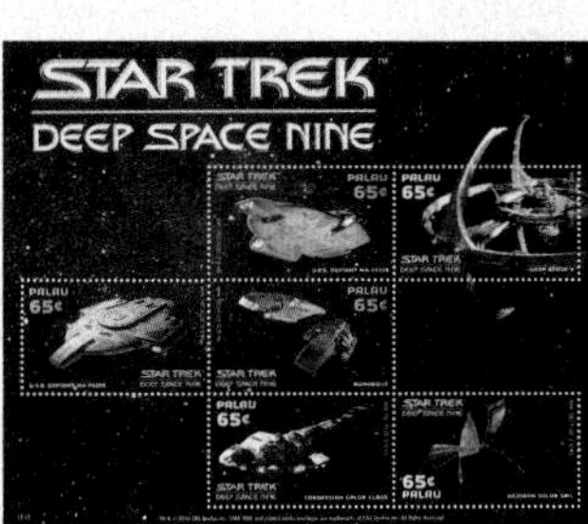


Spacecraft from *Star Trek Deep Space Nine* — A466

No. 1297: a, U.S.S. Defiant, denomination at UR. b, Deep Space 9. c, U.S.S. Defiant, denomination at UL. d, Runabout. e, Cardassian Galor Class. f, Bajoran Solar Sail.

$4, U.S.S. Defiant, diff.

**2015, Dec. 31 Litho. *Perf. 12***

**1297** A466 65c Sheet of 6, #a-f 8.00 8.00

**Souvenir Sheet**

***Perf. 14***

**1298** A466 $4 multi 8.00 8.00

No. 1298 contains one 80x30mm stamp.

Mollusks — A467

No. 1299: a, Palau nautilus, tentacles at left. b, Chambered nautilus, tentacles at left. c, Palau nautilus, tentacles at right. d, Chambered nautilus, tentacles at right.
$4, Palau nautilus, vert.

**2015, Dec. 31 Litho. *Perf. 14***

**1299** A467 $1.20 Sheet of 4, #a-d 9.75 9.75

**Souvenir Sheet**

***Perf. 12***

**1300** A467 $4 multi 8.00 8.00

Coral Reef Snakes — A468

No. 1301: a, Turtle-headed sea snake, name in white at top. b, Turtle-headed sea snake, name in black at bottom. c, Yellow-lipped sea krait, snake's body extending to right. d, Yellow-lipped sea krait, snake's body extending to left. e, Yellow-lipped sea krait and orange rock. f, Yellow-lipped sea krait, snake's body going through coral.
$4, Head of Yellow-lipped sea krait, horiz.

**2015, Dec. 31 Litho. *Perf.***

**1301** A468 65c Sheet of 6, #a-f 8.00 8.00

**Souvenir Sheet**

**1302** A468 $4 multi 8.00 8.00

No. 1302 contains one 44x33mm oval stamp.

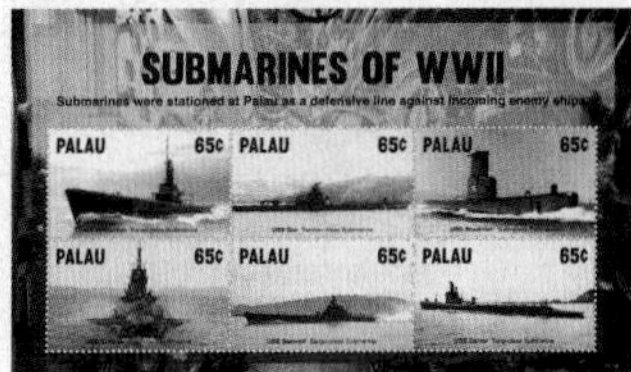


World War II Submarines — A469

No. 1303: a, USS Archerfish. b, USS Gar. c, USS Blackfish. d, USS Tullibee, e, USS Seawolf. f, USS Darter.
$4, USS Seal.

**2015, Dec. 31 Litho. *Perf. 12***

**1303** A469 65c Sheet of 6, #a-f 8.00 8.00

**Souvenir Sheet**

***Perf. 14***

**1304** A469 $4 multi 8.00 8.00

No. 1304 contains one 80x30mm stamp.

Flora — A470

No. 1305: a, Screw pine. b, Coral tree flowers. c, Bayhops. d, Breadfruit. e, Coconut palm. f, Beach naupaka.
$4, Mangrove flowers.

**2016, Feb. 2 Litho. *Perf.***

**1305** A470 65c Sheet of 6, #a-f 8.00 8.00

**Souvenir Sheet**

**1306** A470 $4 multi 8.00 8.00

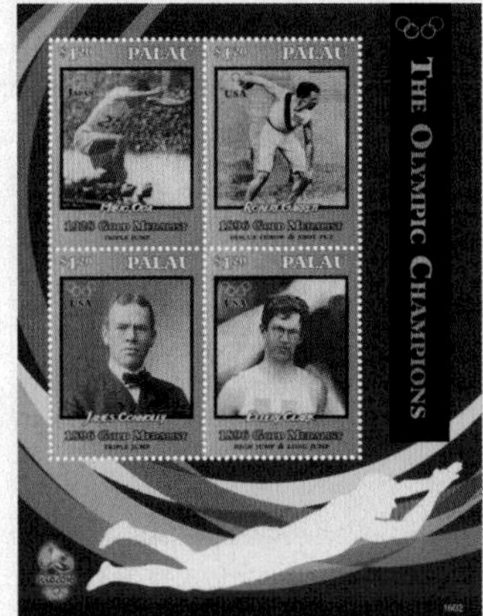


2016 Summer Olympics, Rio de Janeiro — A471

No. 1307 — Gold medalists: a, Mikio Oda, 1928 triple jump, Japan. b, Robert Garrett, 1896 discus and shot put, United States. c, James Connolly, 1896 triple jump, United States. d, Ellery Clark, 1896 high jump and long jump, United States.
$4, Yoshiyuki Tsuruta, 1928 200-meter breaststroke, Japan.

**2016, Mar. 8 Litho. *Perf. 14***

**1307** A471 $1.20 Sheet of 4, #a-d 9.75 9.75

**Souvenir Sheet**

***Perf. 12½***

**1308** A471 $4 multi 8.00 8.00

No. 1308 contains one 38x51mm stamp.

1888 Paintings of the Roulin Family by Vincent van Gogh (1853-90) — A472

No. 1309: a, Portrait of the Postman Joseph Roulin (Nov.-Dec.). b, Portrait of Madame Augustine Roulin. c, Portrait of Madame Augustine Roulin and Baby Marcelle. d, Young Man with a Cap (Armand Roulin). e, The Schoolboy with Uniform Cap (Camille Roulin). f, Portait of Marcelle Roulin.
$4, Portrait of the Postman Joseph Roulin (April).

**2016, Mar. 8 Litho. *Perf. 14***

**1309** A472 65c Sheet of 6, #a-f 8.00 8.00

**Souvenir Sheet**

***Perf. 12½***

**1310** A472 $4 multi 8.00 8.00

No. 1310 contains one 38x51mm stamp.

A473

Jimi Hendrix (1942-70), Rock Guitarist — A474

No. 1311 — Various photographs of Hendrix with frame color of: a, Magenta. b, Purple. c, Green. d, Greenish blue. e, Red orange. f, Yellow.
No. 1312 — Various photographs of Hendrix with frame color of: a, Red orange. b, Greenish blue. c, Yellow. d, Green. e, Magenta. f, Purple.
$4, Hendrix, greenish blue frame, vert.

**2016, Mar. 8 Litho. *Perf.***

**1311** A473 65c Sheet of 6, #a-f 8.00 8.00
**1312** A474 65c Sheet of 6, #a-f 8.00 8.00

**Souvenir Sheet**

***Perf. 12½***

**1313** A474 $4 multi 8.00 8.00

No. 1313 contains one 38x51mm stamp.

Souvenir Sheets

Elvis Presley (1935-77) — A475

Presley: No. 1314, $4, Donating blood to the Red Cross. No. 1315, $4, At recording session, vert. No. 1316, $4, At 1975 Tornado Victim Benefit Concert, vert. No. 1317, $4, Enjoying a moment of Army downtime, vert.

**2016, Mar. 8 Litho. *Perf. 14***

**1314-1317** A475 Set of 4 32.00 32.00

Queen Elizabeth II, 90th Birthday — A476

No. 1318 — Queen Elizabeth II: a, Waving, b, Wearing deep violet hat. c, Wearing pale yellow hat.
$5, Queen Elizabeth II wearing blue dress.

**2016, Apr. 1 Litho. *Perf. 12½***

**1318** A476 $1.50 Sheet of 3, #a-c 9.00 9.00

**Souvenir Sheet**

**1319** A476 $5 multi 10.00 10.00

World Stamp Show 2016, New York — A477

No. 1320: a, Gapstow Bridge, Central Park. b, Statue of Liberty. c, Grand Central Terminal. d, Manhattan Bridge.
$3, New York City skyline, horiz.

**2016, Apr. 19 Litho. *Perf. 12***

**1320** A477 $1.25 Sheet of 4, #a-d 10.00 10.00

**Souvenir Sheet**

***Perf. 14***

**1321** A477 $3 multi 6.00 6.00

No. 1321 contains one 160x60mm stamp.

Nancy Reagan (1921-2016), First Lady — A478

No. 1322 — Mrs. Reagan with: a, Pres. Ronald Reagan, Queen Elizabeth II and Prince Philip. b, Queen Elizabeth II. c, Princess Diana. d, Pres. Reagan, Pope John Paul II. e, British Prime Minister Margaret Thatcher. f, Pres. Reagan, Japanese Prime Minister Yasuhiro Nakasone and his wife, Tsutako.
No. 1323 — Mrs. Reagan with: a, Pres. Reagan, Vice-President George H.W. Bush and his wife, Barbara. b, Pres. George W. Bush and his wife, Laura. c, First ladies Rosalynn Carter, Barbara Bush, Betty Ford and Hillary Clinton. d, Pres. Barack Obama.
No. 1324, Mrs. Reagan as actress with picture having: a, White background. b, Black background.
$5, Mrs. Reagan seated, vert.

**2016, Apr. 19 Litho. *Perf. 14***

**1322** A478 $1 Sheet of 6, #a-f 12.00 12.00
**1323** A478 $1.20 Sheet of 4, #a-d 9.75 9.75

### Souvenir Sheets

*Perf. 13¾*

**1324** A478 $2.50 Sheet of 2, #a-b 10.00 10.00

*Perf. 12*

**1325** A478 $5 multi 10.00 10.00

No. 1324 contains two 50x50mm diamond-shaped stamps.

### World of Sea and Reef Type of 1986 Redrawn

Miniature Sheet

No. 1326: a, Spear fisherman. b, Native raft. c, Sailing canoes. d, Rock islands, sailfish. e, Inter-island boat, flying fish. f, Bonefish. g, Common jack. h, Mackerel. i, Sailfish. j, Barracuda. k, Triggerfish. l, Dolphinfish. m, Spear fisherman, grouper. n, Manta ray. o, Marlin. p, Parrotfish. q, Wrasse. r, Red snapper. s, Herring. t, Dugong. u, Surgeonfish. v, Leopard ray. w, Hawksbill turtle. x, Needlefish. y, Tuna. z, Octopus. aa, Clownfish. ab, Squid. ac, Grouper. ad, Moorish idol. ae, Queen conch, starfish. af, Squirrelfish. ag, Starfish, sting ray. ah, Lionfish. ai, Angelfish. aj, Butterflyfish. ak, Spiny lobster. al, Mangrove crab. am, Tridacna. an, Moray eel.

**2016, May 18 Litho. *Perf. 13¼***

**1326** Sheet of 40 38.00 38.00
*a.-an.* A19 47c Any single .95 .95

World Stamp Show 2016, New York. No. 1326 contains forty 26x21mm stamps.

Characters From *Star Trek* Television Series — A479

No. 1327: a, Capt. James T. Kirk. b, Mr. Spock. c, Scotty. d, Sulu. e, Dr. McCoy. f, Uhura.
$3, Kirk, Spock, McCoy, Uhura and Sulu.

**2016, Aug. 15 Litho. *Perf. 14***

**1327** A479 $1 Sheet of 6, #a-f 12.00 12.00

### Souvenir Sheet

*Perf. 12*

**1328** A479 $3 multi 6.00 6.00

No. 1328 contains one 40x60mm stamp.

Birds — A480

No. 1329: a, Dusky white-eye. b, Palau flycatcher. c, Palau fantail. d, Giant white-eye.
$5, Palau fruit dove, vert.

**2016, Sept. 22 Litho. *Perf. 12½***

**1329** A480 $1.50 Sheet of 4, #a-d 12.00 12.00

### Souvenir Sheet

**1330** A480 $5 multi 10.00 10.00

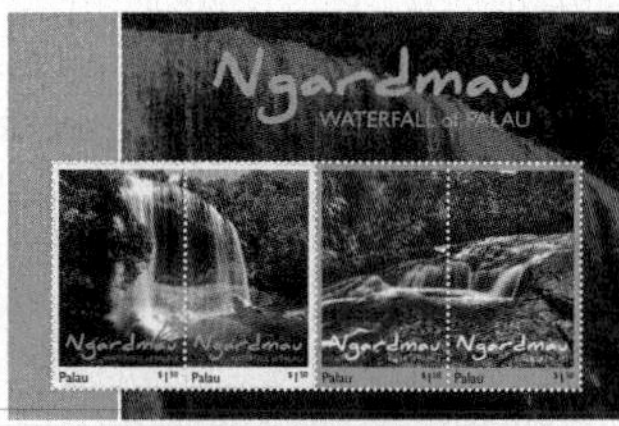


Ngardmau Waterfall — A481

No. 1331 — Waterfall with: a, White frame at left, top and bottom. b, White frame at right, top and bottom. c, Orange frame at left, top and bottom. d, Orange frame at right, top and bottom.
$5, Waterfall, diff.

**2016, Sept. 22 Litho. *Perf. 12***

**1331** A481 $1.50 Sheet of 4, #a-d 12.00 12.00

### Souvenir Sheet

**1332** A481 $5 multi 10.00 10.00

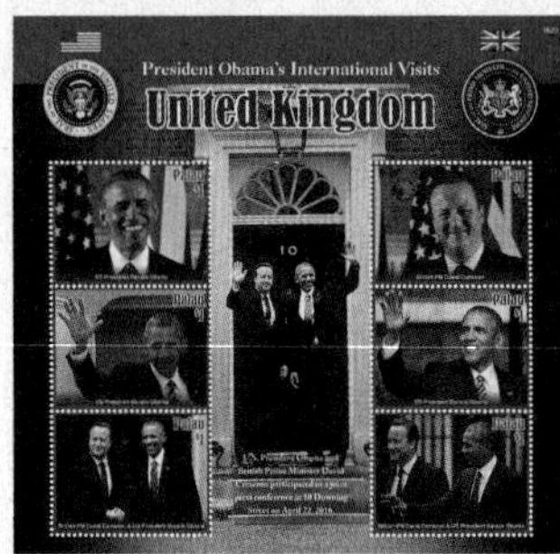


Visit of Pres. Barack Obama to the United Kingdom — A482

No. 1333: a, Pres. Obama, flags in background. b, British Prime Minister David Cameron, flags in background. c, Pres. Obama waving, open airplane door in background. d, Pres. Obama waving. e, Pres. Obama shaking hands with Cameron. f, Pres. Obama and Cameron, fence in background.
No. 1334: a, Pres. Obama shaking hands with Queen Elizabeth II (40x30mm). b, Queen Elizabeth II, Pres. Obama and his wife, Michelle (40x30mm). c, The Obamas with Prince Harry, Duke and Duchess of Cambridge (80x30mm).
No. 1335: a, Pres. Obama seated. b, Cameron seated.

**2016, Sept. 22 Litho. *Perf. 14***

**1333** A482 $1 Sheet of 6, #a-f 12.00 12.00
**1334** A482 $2 Sheet of 3, #a-c 12.00 12.00

### Souvenir Sheet

*Perf. 12*

**1335** A482 $2.50 Sheet of 2, #a-b 10.00 10.00

William Shakespeare (1564-1616), Writer — A483

No. 1336: a, 1873 engraving depicting scene from *As You Like It*. b, Line from *As You Like It*. c, Line from *Twelfth Night*. d, 1873 engraving depicting scene from *Twelfth Night*. e, 1873 engraving depicting scene from *King Richard II*. f, Line from *King Richard II*.

No. 1337 — 1870 engravings depicting scenes from: a, *Hamlet*. b, *The Winter's Tale*. c, *A Midsummer Night's Dream*. d, *Twelfth Night*.
$5, Shakespeare, vert.

**2016, Sept. 30 Litho. *Perf. 14***

**1336** A483 $1 Sheet of 6, #a-f 12.00 12.00

*Perf. 12½*

**1337** A483 $1.50 Sheet of 4, #a-d 12.00 12.00

### Souvenir Sheet

*Perf.*

**1338** A483 $5 multi 10.00 10.00

No. 1337 contains four 51x38mm stamps. No. 1338 contains one 33x43mm oval stamp.

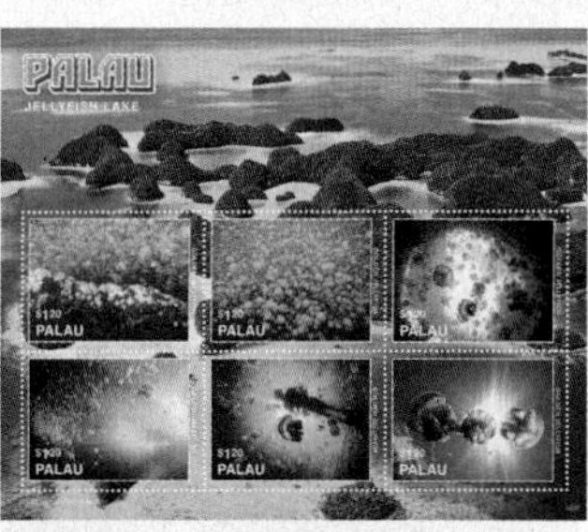


A484

A485

A486

Tourism — A487

No. 1339, $1.20: Various photographs of golden jellyfish in Jellyfish lake, as shown.
No. 1340, $1.20 — Giant clams: a, True giant clam. b, Bear claw giant clam. c, China giant clam. d, Smooth giant clam. e, Elongated giant clam. f, Fluted giant clam.
No. 1341, $1.25 — Abais: a, Koror Abai. b, Melekeok Abai. c, Aimeliik Abai. d, Airai Abai.
No. 1342, $1.50 — Rock Islands landscapes: a, Tutkalrenguis. b, Milky Way. c, Akasi Island. d, Arc Island.
No. 1343, $1.75 — Rays: a, Manta ray. b, Manta ray and diver. c, Devil ray. d, Two Manta rays.
No. 1344, $1.75 — Underwater World War II airplane wreckage: a, Jake float plane wing and engine. b, Jake float plane fuselage. c, Jake float plane propeller. d, Zero plane.

No. 1345, $1.50 — Protected species: a, Gray reef shark. b, Hawksbill turtle. c, Napoleon wrasse.
No. 1346, $1.75 — Crabs: a, Hermit crab. b, Land crab. c, Coconut crab.

**2016, Oct. 1 Litho. *Perf. 12½***

### Sheets of 6, #a-f

**1339-1340** A484 Set of 2 29.00 29.00

### Sheets of 4, #a-d

*Perf. 14*

**1341-1342** A485 Set of 2 22.00 22.00
**1343-1344** A486 Set of 2 28.00 28.00

### Sheets of 3, #a-c

**1345-1346** A487 Set of 2 19.50 19.50

Attack on Pearl Harbor, 75th Anniv. — A488

No. 1347: a, Sailor. b, U. S. Coast Guard poster. c, These Colors Won't Run poster. d, Avenge Pearl Harbor poster. e, American flag at half-staff. f, Remember Pearl Harbor recruitment poster.
No. 1348, horiz.: a, USS West Virginia. b, USS Arizona.

**2016, Dec. 30 Litho. *Perf. 14***

**1347** A488 $1.35 Sheet of 6, #a-f 16.50 16.50

### Souvenir Sheet

*Perf. 12*

**1348** A488 $3 Sheet of 2, #a-b 12.00 12.00

No. 1348 contains two 64x32mm triangular stamps.

Fish — A489

No. 1349: a, Orange-striped wrasse. b, Palauan deepwater cardinalfish. c, Aurora anthias. d, Dabra goby. e, Bullseye pygmy goby. f, Needlespine coral goby.
No. 1350: a, Giant pygmy goby. b, Deep blue chromis.

**2016, Dec. 30 Litho. *Perf. 12***

**1349** A489 $1 Sheet of 6, #a-f 12.00 12.00

### Souvenir Sheet

**1350** A489 $2.50 Sheet of 2, #a-b 10.00 10.00

Miniature Sheet

2016 Summer Olympics, Rio de Janeiro — A490

No. 1351 — Photographs of Palauan Olympic Team: a, 50c, Shawn Dingilius Wallace (30x40mm). b, 50c, Dirngulbau Ub Misech (30x40mm). c, 50c, Florian Temengil (30x40mm). d, 50c, Rodman Teltull (30x40mm). e, 50c, Marina Toribiong (30x40mm). f, $1, Olympic team following Palauan flagbearer (90x40mm). g, $1, Palauan athletes and Olympic rings (60x40mm).

**2016, Dec. 20 Litho. *Perf. 14***

**1351** A490 Sheet of 7, #a-g 9.00 9.00

Miniature Sheet

2016 Festival of the Pacific Arts — A491

No. 1352: a, 50c, Man and woman (30x40mm). b, 50c, Man and woman, large pole in background (30x40mm). c, 50c, Man dancing with spears (30x40mm). d, 50c, Man standing (30x40mm). e, 50c, Man kneeling, holding shell (30x40mm). f, 50c, Woman facing right (30x40mm). g, 50c, Women dancing (30x40mm). h, 50c, Two women, one with greenish blue skirt (30x40mm). i, $1, Festival participants in front of building (120x40mm). j, $1, Four women (60x40mm). k, $1, Male dancers holding spears (60x40mm).

**2016, Dec. 30 Litho. *Perf. 14***

**1352** A491 Sheet of 11, #a-k 14.00 14.00

Legends of the Wild West — A492

No. 1353: a, Bat Masterson. b, Annie Oakley. c, Kit Carson. d, Wild Bill Hickok. e, John Frémont. f, Wyatt Earp.

$5, Buffalo Bill Cody.

***Perf. 13¼x12½***

**2017, Feb. 28 Litho.**

**1353** A492 $1 Sheet of 6, #a-f 12.00 12.00

**Souvenir Sheet**

***Perf. 13¼***

**1354** A492 $5 multi 10.00 10.00

No. 1354 contains one 38x51mm stamp.

Miniature Sheets

A493

Princess Diana (1961-97) — A494

No. 1355 — Photograph of Princess Diana and flag of: a, $1, Saudi Arabia (30x40mm). b, $1, Hong Kong (30x40mm). c, $1, Italy (30x40mm). d, $1, Pakistan (30x40mm). e, $1, Egypt (30x40mm). f, $1, Nepal (30x40mm). g, $1.50, India (60x40mm).

No. 1356 — Princess Diana wearing: a, Black dress and pearl necklace. b, Purple dress. c, Black dress, no necklace. d, Yellow jacket.

**2017, Apr. 14 Litho. *Perf. 14***

**1355** A493 Sheet of 7, #a-g 15.00 15.00

***Perf.***

**1356** A494 $1.80 Sheet of 4, #a-d 14.50 14.50

Miniature Sheets

A495

Pres. John F. Kennedy (1917-63) — A496

No. 1357 — Pres. John F. Kennedy: a, As baby. b, As young boy, holding dog. c, In Navy uniform. d, On sailboat with wife, Jacqueline. e, With wife and children. f, Seated at desk.

No. 1358 — Pres. Kennedy with: a, His father, mother and siblings. b, Mother, Rose and sister, Eunice. c, Brother Joe, Jr., sisters Kathleen and Rosemary. d, Brothers Robert and Edward.

**2017, Apr. 14 Litho. *Perf. 14***

**1357** A495 $1.35 Sheet of 6, #a-f 16.50 16.50

***Perf. 12***

**1358** A496 $1.60 Sheet of 4, #a-d 13.00 13.00

Seals — A497

No. 1359: a, Baby harp seal. b, Australian sea lion. c, Harbor seal. d, Antarctic fur seal. e, Galapagos sea lion. f, Grey seal.

$4.50, New Zealand fur seal.

**2017, May 5 Litho. *Perf.***

**1359** A497 $1.25 Sheet of 6, #a-f 15.00 15.00

**Souvenir Sheet**

**1360** A497 $4.50 multi 9.00 9.00

Animals — A498

No. 1361: a, Waxy monkey frog. b, Persian leopard. c, Alexandrine parakeet. d, Yellow-bellied slider.

$4, Golden lion tamarin, vert.

**2017, May 15 Litho. *Perf. 12½x12¾***

**1361** A498 $2 Sheet of 4, #a-d 16.00 16.00

**Souvenir Sheet**

**1362** A498 $4 multi 8.00 8.00

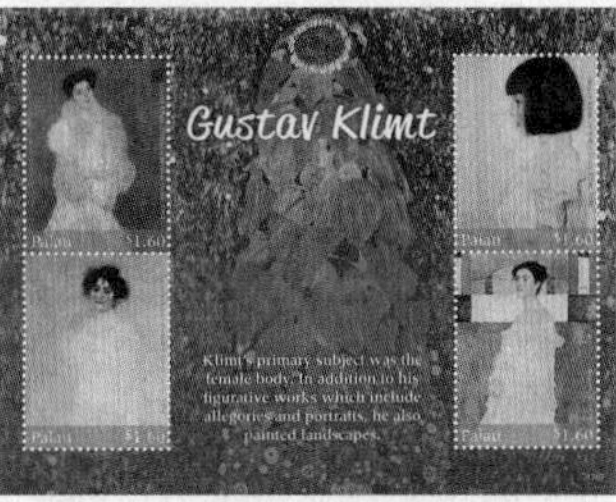


Paintings by Gustav Klimt (1862-1918) — A499

No. 1363: a, Portrait of Hermine Gallia. b, Portrait of Helene Klimt. c, Portrait of Serena Lederer. d, Margaret Stonborough-Wittgenstein.

$4, Adele Bloch-Bauer I (not named on stamp).

**2017, Oct. 19 Litho. *Perf. 12***

**1363** A499 $1.60 Sheet of 4, #a-d 13.00 13.00

**Souvenir Sheet**

***Perf. 12½***

**1364** A499 $4 multi 8.00 8.00

No. 1364 contains one 38x51mm stamp.

Souvenir Sheets

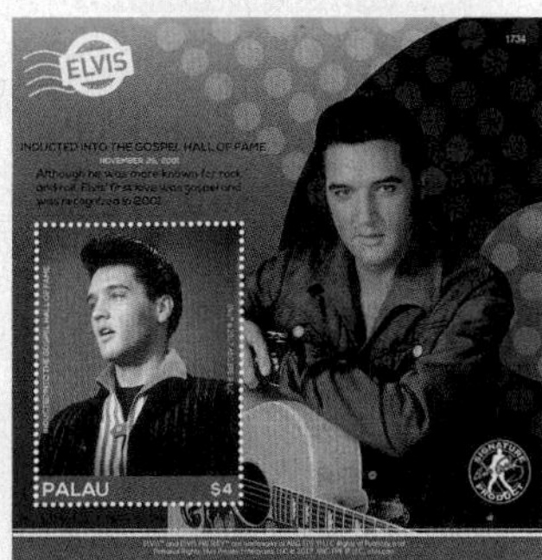


Elvis Presley (1935-77) — A500

Inscriptions: No. 1365, $4, Inducted into the Gospel Hall of Fame. No. 1366, $4, Joins Country Music Hall of Fame. No. 1367, $4, Receives W. C. Handy Award. No. 1368, $4, Inducted into the Rock 'n' Roll Hall of Fame.

**2017, Oct. 26 Litho. *Perf. 12½***

**1365-1368** A500 Set of 4 32.00 32.00

Miniature Sheet

Palau Community Action Agency, 50th Anniv. — A501

No. 1369 — Inscriptions: a, Agriculture. b, Apprentice Program. c, History. d, Small Business. e, Care for Environment. f, Fishing Industry. g, Pre-school Head Start. h, Health Screening. i, Nutrition Healthy Food. j, Play to Learn. k, Education. l, Local Produce Market. m, Local Medicine. n, Tourism & Community. o, Youth Programs.

**2017, Nov. 10 Litho. *Perf. 11***

**1369** A501 50c Sheet of 15, #a-o 15.00 15.00

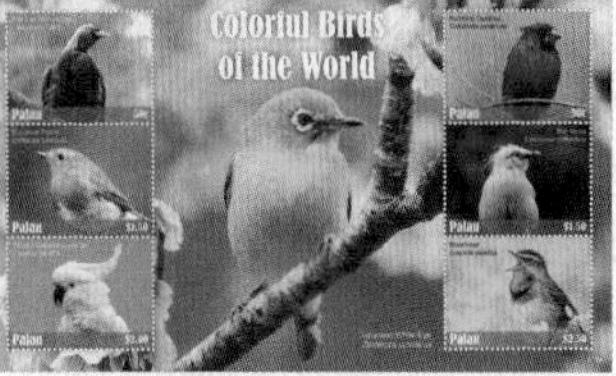


Birds — A502

No. 1370: a, 50c, Red bird-of-paradise. b, 50c, Northern cardinal. c, $1.50, European robin. d, $1.50, Bali myna. e, $2, Sulphur-crested cockatoo. f, $2.50, Bluethroat.

No. 1371: a, $1.25, Atlantic puffin. b, $2.25, Lilac-breasted roller. c, $3.25, Nicobar pigeon.

**2018, Jan. 24 Litho. *Perf. 14***

**1370** A502 Sheet of 6, #a-f 17.00 17.00

**Souvenir Sheet**

***Perf. 12***

**1371** A502 Sheet of 3, #a-c 13.50 13.50

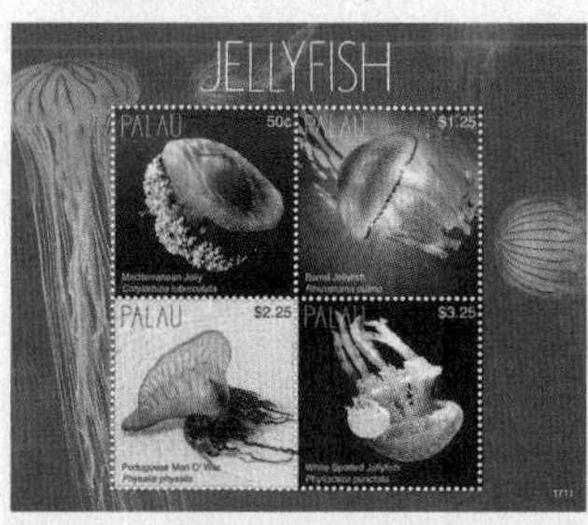


Jellyfish — A503

No. 1372: a, 50c, Mediterranean jelly. b, $1.25, Barrel jellyfish. c, $2.25, Portuguese man o' war. d, $3.25, White-spotted jellyfish.

No. 1373, vert.: a, Lion's mane jellyfish. b, Mediterranean jelly, turquoise blue background.

**2018, Jan. 24 Litho. *Perf. 13¾***

**1372** A503 Sheet of 4, #a-d 14.50 14.50

**Souvenir Sheet**

***Perf. 12¾x12½***

**1373** A503 $3 Sheet of 2, #a-b 12.00 12.00

No. 1373 contains two 38x51mm stamps.

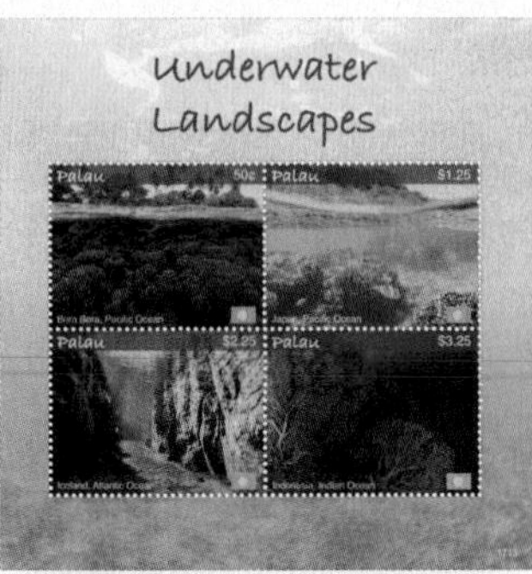


Underwater Landscapes — A504

No. 1374: a, 50c, Bora Bora, Pacific Ocean. b, $1.25, Japan, Pacific Ocean. c, $2.25, Iceland, Atlantic Ocean. d, $3.25, Indonesia, Indian Ocean.

No. 1375: a, Palau, Pacific Ocean. b, Maldives, Indian Ocean.

**2018, Jan. 24 Litho. *Perf. 14***

**1374** A504 Sheet of 4, #a-d 14.50 14.50

**Souvenir Sheet**

***Perf. 12½***

**1375** A504 $3 Sheet of 2, #a-b 12.00 12.00

No. 1375 contains two 51x38mm stamps.

Visit of Pres. Donald Trump to Japan — A505

No. 1376: a, First Lady Melania Trump. b, Pres. Donald Trump. c, Japanese Prime Minister Shinzo Abe. d, Akie Abe.

$4, Abe and Pres. Trump, horiz.

**2018, Jan. 24 Litho. *Perf. 12***

**1376** A505 $1.60 Sheet of 4, #a-d 13.00 13.00

**Souvenir Sheet**

***Perf. 12¾***

**1377** A505 $4 multi 8.00 8.00

No. 1376 contains one 51x38mm stamp.

Souvenir Sheet

Engagement of Prince Harry and Meghan Markle — A506

No. 1378 — Couple and background of: a, Grass. b, Brick wall.

**2018, Jan. 31 Litho. *Perf. 12***

**1378** A506 $3 Sheet of 2, #a-b 12.00 12.00

Miniature Sheet

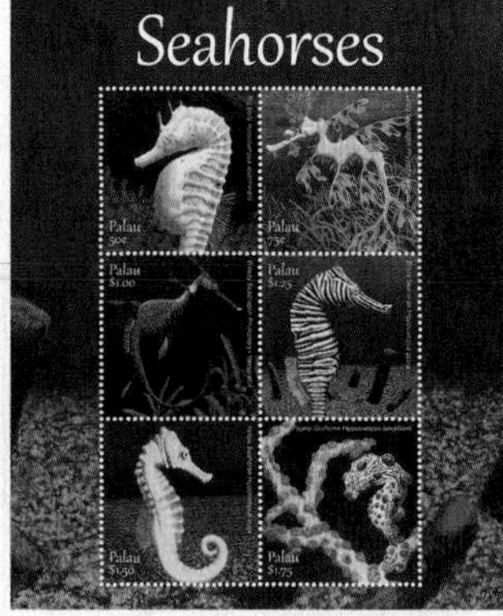


Seahorses — A507

No. 1379: a, 50c, Big belly seahorse. b, 75c, Leafy seadragon. c, $1, Weedy seadragon. d, $1.25, Zebra seahorse. e, $1.50, Yellow seahorse. f, $1.75, Pygmy seahorse.

**2018, Feb. 1 Litho. *Perf. 13¾***

**1379** A507 Sheet of 6, #a-f 13.50 13.50

**SEMI-POSTAL STAMPS**

Olympic Sports SP1

No. B1, Baseball glove, player. No. B2, Running shoe, athlete. No. B3, Goggles, swimmer. No. B4, Gold medal, diver.

**1988, Aug. 8 Litho. *Perf. 14***

| | | | |
|---|---|---|---|
| **B1** | SP1 25c +5c multi | .50 | .50 |
| **B2** | SP1 25c +5c multi | .50 | .50 |
| *a.* | Pair, #B1-B2 | 1.25 | 1.25 |
| **B3** | SP1 45c +5c multi | 1.25 | 1.25 |
| **B4** | SP1 45c +5c multi | 1.25 | 1.25 |
| *a.* | Pair, #B3-B4 | 2.75 | 2.75 |

**AIR POST STAMPS**

White-tailed Tropicbird — AP1

**1984, June 12 Litho. *Perf. 14***

| | | | |
|---|---|---|---|
| **C1** | AP1 40c shown | .75 | .75 |
| **C2** | AP1 40c Fairy tern | .75 | .75 |
| **C3** | AP1 40c Black noddy | .75 | .75 |
| **C4** | AP1 40c Black-naped tern | .75 | .75 |
| *a.* | Block of 4, #C1-C4 | 3.50 | 3.50 |

**Audubon Type of 1985**

**1985, Feb. 6 Litho. *Perf. 14***

**C5** A12 44c Audubon's Shearwater 1.10 1.10

Palau-Germany Political, Economic & Cultural Exchange Cent. — AP2

Germany Nos. 40, 65, Caroline Islands Nos. 19, 13 and: No. C6, German flag-raising at Palau, 1885. No. C7, Early German trading post in Angaur. No. C8, Abai architecture recorded by Prof. & Frau Kramer, 1908-1910. No. C9, S.M.S. Cormoran.

**1985, Sept. 19 Litho. *Perf. 14x13½***

| | | | |
|---|---|---|---|
| **C6** | AP2 44c multicolored | .95 | .95 |
| **C7** | AP2 44c multicolored | .95 | .95 |
| **C8** | AP2 44c multicolored | .95 | .95 |
| **C9** | AP2 44c multicolored | .95 | .95 |
| *a.* | Block of 4, #C6-C9 | 4.50 | 4.50 |

**Trans-Pacific Airmail Anniv. Type of 1985**

Aircraft: No. C10, 1951 Trans-Ocean Airways PBY-5A Catalina Amphibian. No. C11, 1968 Air Micronesia DC-6B Super Cloudmaster. No. C12, 1960 Trust Territory Airline SA-16 Albatross. No. C13, 1967 Pan American Douglas DC-4.

**1985, Nov. 21 Litho. *Perf. 14***

| | | | |
|---|---|---|---|
| **C10** | A16 44c multicolored | .85 | .85 |
| **C11** | A16 44c multicolored | .85 | .85 |
| **C12** | A16 44c multicolored | .85 | .85 |
| **C13** | A16 44c multicolored | .85 | .85 |
| *a.* | Block of 4, #C10-C13 | 3.75 | 3.75 |

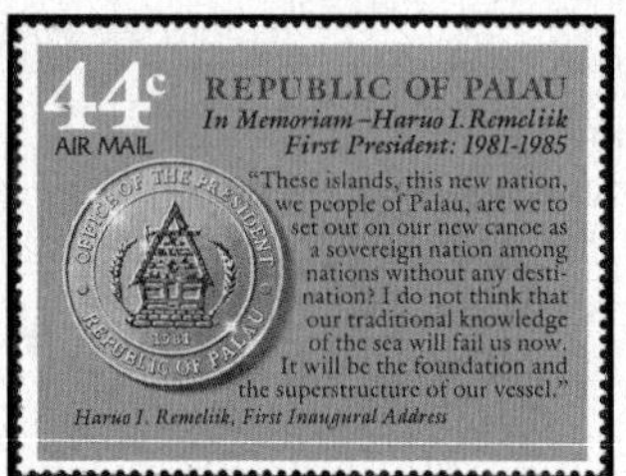


Haruo I. Remeliik (1933-1985), 1st President — AP3

Designs: No. C14, Presidential seal, excerpt from 1st inaugural address. No. C15, War canoe, address excerpt, diff. No. C16, Remeliik, US Pres. Reagan, excerpt from Reagan's speech, Pacific Basin Conference, Guam, 1984.

**1986, June 30 Litho. *Perf. 14***

| | | | |
|---|---|---|---|
| **C14** | AP3 44c multicolored | 1.10 | 1.10 |
| **C15** | AP3 44c multicolored | 1.10 | 1.10 |
| **C16** | AP3 44c multicolored | 1.10 | 1.10 |
| *a.* | Strip of 3, #C14-C16 | 3.75 | 3.75 |

Intl. Peace Year, Statue of Liberty Cent. — AP4

**1986, Sept. 19 Litho.**

**C17** AP4 44c multicolored 1.00 1.00

Aircraft — AP5

36c, Cessna 207 Skywagon. 39c, Embraer EMB-110 Bandeirante. 45c, Boeing 727.

**1989, May 17 Litho. *Perf. 14x14½***

| | | | |
|---|---|---|---|
| **C18** | AP5 36c multicolored | .65 | .65 |
| *a.* | Booklet pane of 10 | 7.00 | — |
| **C19** | AP5 39c multicolored | .85 | .85 |
| *a.* | Booklet pane of 10 | 7.50 | — |
| **C20** | AP5 45c multicolored | 1.00 | 1.00 |
| *a.* | Booklet pane of 10 | 8.25 | — |
| *b.* | Booklet pane, 5 each 36c, 45c | 8.50 | — |
| | *Nos. C18-C20 (3)* | 2.50 | 2.50 |

**Palauan Bai Type**

**1991, July 9 Litho. *Die Cut***

**Self-Adhesive**

**C21** A61 50c like #293a 1.50 1.50

**World War II in the Pacific Type**

Miniature Sheet

Aircraft: No. C22: a, Grumman TBF Avenger, US Navy. b, Curtiss P-40C, Chinese Air Force "Flying Tigers." c, Mitsubishi A6M Zero-Sen, Japan. d, Hawker Hurricane, Royal Air Force. e, Consolidated PBY Catalina, Royal Netherlands Indies Air Force. f, Curtiss Hawk 75, Netherlands Indies. g, Boeing B-17E, US Army Air Force. h, Brewster Buffalo, Royal Australian Air Force. i, Supermarine Walrus, Royal Navy. j, Curtiss P-40E, Royal New Zealand Air Force.

**1992, Sept. 10 Litho. *Perf. 14½x15***

**C22** A66 50c Sheet of 10, #a.-j. 11.00 11.00

Birds — AP6

a, Palau swiftlet. b, Barn swallow. c, Jungle nightjar. d, White-breasted woodswallow.

**1994, Mar. 24 Litho. *Perf. 14***

**C23** AP6 50c Block of 4, #a.-d. 4.00 4.00

No. C23 is printed in sheets of 16 stamps.

# PALESTINE

'pa-lə-ˌstīn

LOCATION — Western Asia bordering on the Mediterranean Sea
GOVT. — Former British Mandate
AREA — 10,429 sq. mi.
POP. — 1,605,816 (estimated)
CAPITAL — Jerusalem

Formerly a part of Turkey, Palestine was occupied by the Egyptian Expeditionary Forces of the British Army in World War I and was mandated to Great Britain in 1923. Mandate ended May 14, 1948.

10 Milliemes = 1 Piaster
1000 Milliemes = 1 Egyptian Pound
1000 Mils = 1 Palestine Pound (1928)

Jordan stamps overprinted with "Palestine" in English and Arabic are listed under Jordan.

### Watermark

Wmk. 33

### Issued under British Military Occupation

For use in Palestine, Transjordan, Lebanon, Syria and in parts of Cilicia and northeastern Egypt

A1

**Wmk. Crown and "GvR" (33)**

**1918, Feb. 10 Litho. *Rouletted 20***

| | | | | |
|---|---|---|---|---|
| 1 | A1 | 1pi deep blue | 190.00 | 105.00 |
| 2 | A1 | 1pi ultra | 2.50 | 2.50 |

Nos. 2 & 1 Surcharged in Black

**1918, Feb. 16**

| | | | | |
|---|---|---|---|---|
| 3 | A1 | 5m on 1pi ultra | 8.50 | 4.25 |
| *a.* | | 5m on 1pi gray blue | 110.00 | *600.00* |

Nos. 1 and 3a were issued without gum. No. 3a is on paper with a surface sheen.

**1918 Typo. *Perf. 15x14***

| | | | | |
|---|---|---|---|---|
| 4 | A1 | 1m dark brown | .35 | *.45* |
| 5 | A1 | 2m blue green | .35 | *.50* |
| 6 | A1 | 3m light brown | .50 | .40 |
| 7 | A1 | 4m scarlet | .40 | *.45* |
| 8 | A1 | 5m orange | .75 | .35 |
| 9 | A1 | 1pi indigo | .50 | .30 |
| 10 | A1 | 2pi olive green | 3.50 | 1.00 |
| 11 | A1 | 5pi plum | 3.75 | 2.50 |
| 12 | A1 | 9pi bister | 12.50 | 7.50 |
| 13 | A1 | 10pi ultramarine | 12.50 | 4.50 |
| 14 | A1 | 20pi gray | 18.50 | *20.00* |
| | | *Nos. 4-14 (11)* | 53.60 | 37.95 |

Many shades exist.

Nos. 4-11 exist with rough perforation.

Issued: 1m, 2m, 4m, 2pi, 5pi, 7/16; 5m, 9/25; 1pi, 11/9; 3m, 9pi, 10pi, 12/17; 20pi, 12/27.

Nos. 4-11 with overprint "O. P. D. A." (Ottoman Public Debt Administration) or "H.J.Z." (Hejaz-Jemen Railway) are revenue stamps; they exist postally used.

For overprints on stamps and types see #15-62 & Jordan #1-63, 73-90, 92-102, 130-144, J12-J23.

### Issued under British Administration

Overprinted at Jerusalem

Stamps and Type of 1918 Overprinted in Black or Silver

**1920, Sept. 1 Wmk. 33 *Perf. 15x14***

**Arabic Overprint 8mm long**

| | | | | |
|---|---|---|---|---|
| 15 | A1 | 1m dark brown | 10.00 | 2.25 |
| 16 | A1 | 2m bl grn, perf 14 | 4.50 | 1.75 |
| *d.* | | Perf 15x14 | 14.00 | 6.00 |
| 17 | A1 | 3m lt brown | 18.50 | 8.50 |
| *d.* | | Perf 14 | 140.00 | 70.00 |
| *e.* | | Inverted overprint | 550.00 | *700.00* |
| 18 | A1 | 4m scarlet | 5.25 | 1.75 |
| 19 | A1 | 5m org, perf 14 | 8.00 | .75 |
| *e.* | | Perf 15x14 | 27.50 | 10.00 |
| 20 | A1 | 1pi indigo (S) | 5.75 | 1.25 |
| 21 | A1 | 2pi olive green | 7.00 | 2.50 |
| 22 | A1 | 5pi plum | 27.50 | *30.00* |
| 23 | A1 | 9pi bister | 15.00 | *23.00* |
| 24 | A1 | 10pi ultra | 13.00 | *19.50* |
| 25 | A1 | 20pi gray | 35.00 | *50.00* |
| | | *Nos. 15-25 (11)* | 149.50 | 141.25 |

Forgeries exist of No. 17e.

Similar Ovpt., with Arabic Line 10mm Long, Arabic "S" and "T" Joined, ".." at Left Extends Above Other Letters

**1920-21 *Perf. 15x14***

| | | | | |
|---|---|---|---|---|
| *15a* | A1 | 1m dark brown | 2.75 | 1.20 |
| *e.* | | Perf. 14 | 875.00 | 975.00 |
| *g.* | | As "a," invtd. ovpt. | 450.00 | |
| *16a* | A1 | 2m blue green | 12.00 | 4.50 |
| *e.* | | "PALESTINE" omitted | *2,500.* | *1,500.* |
| *f.* | | Perf. 14 | 6.00 | 6.00 |
| *17a* | A1 | 3m light brown | 4.25 | 1.20 |
| *18a* | A1 | 4m scarlet | 6.25 | 1.60 |
| *b.* | | Perf. 14 | 95.00 | 125.00 |
| *19a* | A1 | 5m orange | 4.50 | .90 |
| *f.* | | Perf. 14 | 12.00 | 1.25 |
| *20a* | A1 | 1pi indigo, perf. 14 (S) ('21) | 67.50 | 2.00 |
| *d.* | | Perf. 15x14 | 575.00 | 40.00 |
| *21a* | A1 | 2pi olive green ('21) | 90.00 | 42.50 |
| *22a* | A1 | 5pi plum ('21) | 52.50 | 11.00 |
| *d.* | | Perf. 14 | 225.00 | *525.00* |
| | | *Nos. 15a-22a (8)* | 239.75 | 64.90 |

This overprint often looks grayish to grayish black. In the English line the letters are frequently uneven and damaged.

Similar Ovpt., with Arabic Line 10mm Long, Arabic "S" and "T" Separated and 6mm Between English and Hebrew Lines

**1920, Dec. 6**

| | | | | |
|---|---|---|---|---|
| *15b* | A1 | 1m dk brn, perf 14 | 62.50 | 37.50 |
| *17b* | A1 | 3m lt brn, perf 15x14 | 60.00 | 37.50 |
| *19b* | A1 | 5m orange, perf 14 | 475.00 | 37.50 |
| *d.* | | Perf. 15x14 | *16,000.* | *13,750.* |
| | | *Nos. 15b-19b (3)* | 597.50 | 112.50 |

**Overprinted as Before, 7½mm Between English and Hebrew Lines, ".." at Left Even With Other Letters**

**1921 *Perf. 15x14***

| | | | | |
|---|---|---|---|---|
| *15c* | A1 | 1m dark brown | 21.00 | 4.00 |
| *f.* | | 1m dull brown, perf 14 | | *2,300.* |
| *16c* | A1 | 2m blue green | 32.50 | 6.25 |
| *17c* | A1 | 3m light brown | 47.50 | 3.50 |
| *18c* | A1 | 4m scarlet | 50.00 | 4.00 |
| *19c* | A1 | 5m orange | 82.50 | 1.10 |
| *20c* | A1 | 1pi indigo (S) | 32.50 | 1.60 |
| *21c* | A1 | 2pi olive green | 26.50 | 7.00 |
| *22c* | A1 | 5pi plum | 29.00 | 9.25 |
| *23c* | A1 | 9pi bister | 75.00 | *125.00* |
| *24c* | A1 | 10pi ultra | 90.00 | 16.00 |
| *25c* | A1 | 20pi pale gray | 135.00 | 75.00 |
| *d.* | | Perf. 14 | *13,750.* | *2,900.* |
| | | *Nos. 15c-25c (11)* | 621.50 | *252.70* |

**Overprinted at London**

Stamps of 1918 Overprinted

**1921 *Perf. 15x14***

| | | | | |
|---|---|---|---|---|
| 37 | A1 | 1m dark brown | 2.25 | .35 |
| 38 | A1 | 2m blue green | 3.25 | .35 |
| 39 | A1 | 3m light brown | 3.50 | .35 |
| 40 | A1 | 4m scarlet | 4.00 | .70 |
| 41 | A1 | 5m orange | 3.75 | .35 |
| 42 | A1 | 1pi bright blue | 3.00 | .40 |
| 43 | A1 | 2pi olive green | 5.00 | .45 |
| 44 | A1 | 5pi plum | 12.50 | 5.75 |
| 45 | A1 | 9pi bister | 26.00 | 16.00 |
| 46 | A1 | 10pi ultra | 29.00 | *675.00* |
| 47 | A1 | 20pi gray | 85.00 | *1,600.* |
| | | *Nos. 37-47 (11)* | 140.00 | |
| | | *Nos. 37-45 (9)* | | 24.70 |

The 2nd character from left on bottom line that looks like quotation marks consists of long thin lines.

Deformed or damaged letters exist in all three lines of the overprint.

**Similar Overprint on Type of 1921**

**1922 Wmk. 4 *Perf. 14***

| | | | | |
|---|---|---|---|---|
| 48 | A1 | 1m dark brown | 2.50 | .35 |
| *a.* | | Inverted overprint | — | *13,750.* |
| *b.* | | Double overprint | 260.00 | 500.00 |
| 49 | A1 | 2m yellow | 3.25 | .35 |
| 50 | A1 | 3m Prus blue | 3.50 | .25 |
| 51 | A1 | 4m rose | 3.50 | .25 |
| 52 | A1 | 5m orange | 2.75 | .35 |
| 53 | A1 | 6m blue green | 3.00 | .35 |
| 54 | A1 | 7m yellow brown | 3.00 | .35 |
| 55 | A1 | 8m red | 3.00 | .35 |
| 56 | A1 | 1pi gray | 3.50 | .35 |
| 57 | A1 | 13m ultra | 4.00 | .25 |
| 58 | A1 | 2pi olive green | 4.00 | .40 |
| *a.* | | Inverted overprint | 350.00 | *575.00* |
| *b.* | | 2pi yellow bister | *140.00* | *7.50* |
| 59 | A1 | 5pi plum | 6.25 | 1.40 |
| *a.* | | Perf. 15x14 | 67.50 | 7.50 |

***Perf. 15x14***

| | | | | |
|---|---|---|---|---|
| 60 | A1 | 9pi bister | 10.00 | 10.00 |
| *a.* | | Perf. 14 | 1,150. | 275.00 |
| 61 | A1 | 10pi light blue | 8.50 | 4.25 |
| *a.* | | Perf. 14 | 95.00 | 17.50 |
| 62 | A1 | 20pi violet | 12.50 | 6.25 |
| *a.* | | Perf. 14 | 225.00 | 125.00 |
| | | *Nos. 48-62 (15)* | 73.25 | 25.50 |

The 2nd character from left on bottom line that looks like quotation marks consists of short thick lines.

The "E. F. F." for "E. E. F." on No. 61 is caused by damaged type.

Rachel's Tomb — A3

Mosque of Omar (Dome of the Rock) — A4

Citadel at Jerusalem A5

Tiberias and Sea of Galilee A6

**1927-42 Typo. *Perf. 13½x14½***

| | | | | |
|---|---|---|---|---|
| 63 | A3 | 2m Prus blue | 2.75 | .25 |
| 64 | A3 | 3m yellow green | 1.75 | .25 |
| 65 | A4 | 4m rose red | 9.00 | 1.60 |
| 66 | A4 | 4m violet brn ('32) | 3.25 | .25 |
| 67 | A5 | 5m brown org | 4.25 | .25 |
| *c.* | | Perf. 14½x14 (coil stamp) ('36) | 16.00 | *21.00* |
| 68 | A4 | 6m deep green | 1.50 | .25 |
| 69 | A5 | 7m deep red | 12.00 | .70 |
| 70 | A5 | 7m dk violet ('32) | 1.00 | .25 |
| 71 | A4 | 8m yellow brown | 18.50 | 7.00 |
| 72 | A4 | 8m scarlet ('32) | 1.50 | .25 |
| 73 | A3 | 10m deep gray | 2.25 | .25 |
| *a.* | | Perf. 14½x14 (coil stamp) ('38) | 23.50 | *27.50* |
| 74 | A4 | 13m ultra | 17.50 | .40 |
| 75 | A4 | 13m olive bister ('32) | 3.75 | .25 |
| 76 | A4 | 15m ultra ('32) | 5.75 | .25 |
| 77 | A5 | 20m olive green | 2.50 | .25 |

***Perf. 14***

| | | | | |
|---|---|---|---|---|
| 78 | A6 | 50m brown purple | 3.50 | .40 |
| 79 | A6 | 90m bister | 87.50 | *60.00* |
| 80 | A6 | 100m bright blue | 2.60 | .80 |
| 81 | A6 | 200m dk violet | 9.25 | 5.75 |
| 82 | A6 | 250m dp brown ('42) | 7.50 | 3.50 |
| 83 | A6 | 500m red ('42) | 9.00 | 3.50 |
| 84 | A6 | £1 gray black ('42) | 13.00 | 4.00 |
| | | *Nos. 63-84 (22)* | 219.60 | 90.40 |

Issued: 3m, #74, 6/1; 2m, 5m, 6m, 10m, #65, 69, 71, 77-81, 8/14; #70, 72, 6/1/32; #75, 15m, 8/1/32; #66, 11/1/32; #82-84, 1/15/42.

### POSTAGE DUE STAMPS

D1

**1923 Unwmk. Typo. *Perf. 11***

| | | | | |
|---|---|---|---|---|
| J1 | D1 | 1m bister brown | 27.50 | *40.00* |
| *b.* | | Horiz. pair, imperf. btwn. | 1,300. | *750.00* |
| J2 | D1 | 2m green | 22.50 | 11.50 |
| J3 | D1 | 4m red | 12.00 | *13.50* |
| J4 | D1 | 8m violet | 8.50 | *8.50* |
| *b.* | | Horiz. pair, imperf. btwn. | | *2,300.* |
| J5 | D1 | 13m dark blue | 7.50 | *8.50* |
| *a.* | | Horiz. pair, imperf. btwn. | 1,200. | |
| | | *Nos. J1-J5 (5)* | 78.00 | *82.00* |

Imperfs. of 1m, 2m, 8m, are from proof sheets.

Values for Nos. J1-J5 are for fine centered copies.

D2

**1924, Dec. 1 Wmk. 4**

| | | | | |
|---|---|---|---|---|
| J6 | D2 | 1m brown | 1.10 | 2.00 |
| J7 | D2 | 2m yellow | 4.00 | 1.75 |
| J8 | D2 | 4m green | 2.00 | 1.50 |
| J9 | D2 | 8m red | 3.00 | 1.00 |
| J10 | D2 | 13m ultramarine | 3.50 | 2.50 |
| J11 | D2 | 5pi violet | 15.00 | 1.75 |
| | | *Nos. J6-J11 (6)* | 28.60 | 10.50 |

D3

**1928-45 *Perf. 14***

| | | | | |
|---|---|---|---|---|
| J12 | D3 | 1m lt brown | 2.75 | 1.00 |
| *a.* | | Perf. 15x14 ('45) | 42.50 | 80.00 |
| J13 | D3 | 2m yellow | 3.75 | .70 |
| J14 | D3 | 4m green | 4.25 | 1.60 |
| *a.* | | 4m bluish grn, perf. 15x14 ('45) | 75.00 | *120.00* |
| J15 | D3 | 6m brown org ('33) | 19.00 | 5.00 |
| J16 | D3 | 8m red | 2.75 | 2.00 |
| J17 | D3 | 10m light gray | 2.00 | .70 |
| J18 | D3 | 13m ultra | 4.50 | 3.00 |
| J19 | D3 | 20m olive green | 4.50 | 1.25 |
| J20 | D3 | 50m violet | 5.00 | 2.50 |
| | | *Nos. J12-J20 (9)* | 48.50 | 17.75 |

The Hebrew word for "mil" appears below the numeral on all values but the 1m.

Issued: 6m, Oct. 1933; others, Feb. 1, 1928.

## PALESTINIAN AUTHORITY

'pa-lə-ˌs-ti-nē-ən 'o-thōr-itē

LOCATION — Areas of the West Bank and the Gaza Strip.
AREA — 2,410 sq. mi.
POP. — 2,825,000 (2000 est.)

1000 Fils (Mils) = 5 Israeli Shekels
1000 Fils = 1 Jordanian Dinar (Jan. 1, 1998)

**Catalogue values for all unused stamps in this country are for Never Hinged items.**

Hisham Palace, Jericho A1

5m, 10m, 20m, Hisham Palace. 30m, 40m, 50m, 75m, Mosque, Jerusalem. 125, 150m, 250m, 300m, 500m, Flag. 1000m, Dome of the Rock.

**1994** **Litho.** ***Perf. 14***
**1** A1 5m multicolored .25 .25
**2** A1 10m multicolored .25 .25
**3** A1 20m multicolored .25 .25
**4** A1 30m multicolored .25 .25
**5** A1 40m multicolored .25 .25
**6** A1 50m multicolored .30 .30
**7** A1 75m multicolored .35 .35
**8** A1 125m multicolored .60 .60
**9** A1 150m multicolored .90 .90
**10** A1 250m multicolored 1.25 1.25
**11** A1 300m multicolored 1.75 1.75

**Size: 51x29mm**

**12** A1 500m multicolored 2.50 2.50
**13** A1 1000m multicolored 4.00 4.00
*Nos. 1-13 (13)* 12.90 12.90

Issued: 125m-500m, 8/15; others, 9/1.

**Nos. 1-13 Surcharged "FILS" in English and Arabic in Black or Silver and with Black Bars Obliterating "Mils"**

**1995, Apr. 10** **Litho.** ***Perf. 14***
**14** A1 5f multicolored .25 .25
**15** A1 10f multicolored .25 .25
**16** A1 20f multicolored .25 .25
**17** A1 30f multicolored (S) .25 .25
**18** A1 40f multicolored (S) .25 .25
**19** A1 50f multicolored (S) .30 .30
**20** A1 75f multicolored (S) .35 .35
**21** A1 125f multicolored .50 .50
**22** A1 150f multicolored .65 .65
**23** A1 250f multicolored 1.10 1.10
**24** A1 300f multicolored 1.40 1.40

**Size: 51x29mm**

**25** A1 500f multicolored 2.25 2.25
**26** A1 1000f multicolored 4.00 4.00
*Nos. 14-26 (13)* 11.80 11.80

Palestine No. 63 — A2

350f, Palestine #67. 500f, Palestine #72.

**1995, May 17** **Litho.** ***Perf. 14***
**27** A2 150f multicolored 1.00 1.00
**28** A2 350f multicolored 1.60 1.60
**29** A2 500f multicolored 2.00 2.00
*Nos. 27-29 (3)* 4.60 4.60

Traditional Costumes — A3

Women wearing various costumes.

**1995, May 31**
**30** A3 250f multicolored .90 .90
**31** A3 300f multicolored 1.00 1.00
**32** A3 550f multicolored 2.00 2.00
**33** A3 900f multicolored 3.00 3.00
*Nos. 30-33 (4)* 6.90 6.90

Christmas — A4

Designs: 10f, Ancient view of Bethlehem. 20f, Modern view of Bethlehem. 50f, Entrance to grotto, Church of the Nativity. 100f, Yasser Arafat, Pope John Paul II. 1000f, Star of the Nativity, Church of the Nativity, Bethlehem.
10f, 20f, 100f, 1000f are horiz.

**1995, Dec. 18**
**34** A4 10f multicolored .25 .25
**35** A4 20f multicolored .25 .25
**36** A4 50f multicolored .25 .25
**37** A4 100f multicolored .60 .60
**38** A4 1000f multicolored 5.00 5.00
*Nos. 34-38 (5)* 6.35 6.35

Pres. Yasser Arafat — A5

**1996, Mar. 20**
**39** A5 10f red vio & bluish blk .25 .25
**40** A5 20f yellow & bluish black .25 .25
**41** A5 50f blue & bluish black .25 .25
**42** A5 100f apple grn & bluish blk .50 .50
**43** A5 1000f org & bluish blk 4.25 4.25
*Nos. 39-43 (5)* 5.50 5.50

1996 Intl. Philatelic Exhibitions — A6

Exhibition, site: 20f, CHINA '96, Summer Palace, Beijing. 50f, ISTANBUL '96, Hagia Sofia. 100f, ESSEN '96, Villa Hugel. 1000f, CAPEX '96, Toronto skyline.

**1996, May 18**
**44** A6 20f multicolored .25 .25
**45** A6 50f multicolored .30 .30
**46** A6 100f multicolored .45 .45
**47** A6 1000f multicolored 4.50 4.50
*a.* Sheet, 2 each #44-47 + 2 labels 13.00
*Nos. 44-47 (4)* 5.50 5.50

Souvenir Sheet

1st Palestinian Parliamentary & Presidential Elections — A7

**1996, May 20**
**48** A7 1250f multicolored 5.50 5.50

1996 Summer Olympic Games, Atlanta — A8

Designs: 30f, Boxing. 40f, Medal, 1896. 50f, Runners. 150f, Olympic flame. 1000f, Palestinian Olympic Committee emblem.

**1996, July 19** ***Perf. 13½***
**49** A8 30f multicolored .25 .25
**50** A8 40f multicolored .25 .25
**51** A8 50f multicolored .35 .35
**52** A8 150f multicolored .70 .70
*a.* Sheet of 3, #49, 51-52 5.50 5.50
**53** A8 1000f multicolored 4.25 4.25
*Nos. 49-53 (5)* 5.80 5.80

Flowers — A9

**1996, Nov. 22**
**54** A9 10f Poppy .25 .25
**55** A9 25f Hibiscus .25 .25
**56** A9 100f Thyme .50 .50
**57** A9 150f Lemon .70 .70
**58** A9 750f Orange 3.00 3.00
*Nos. 54-58 (5)* 4.70 4.70

**Souvenir Sheet**

**59** A9 1000f Olive 4.50 4.50

Souvenir Sheet

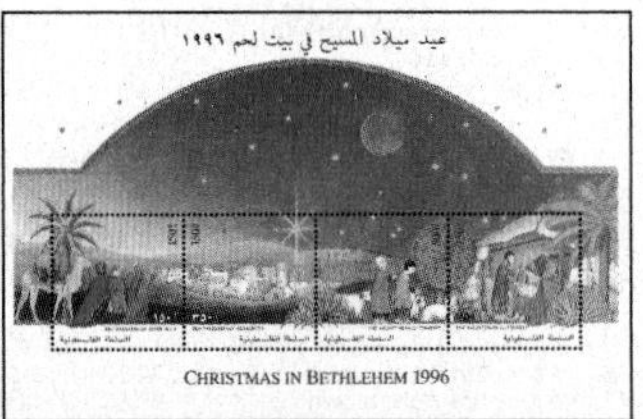

Christmas — A10

a, 150f, Magi. b, 350f, View of Bethlehem. c, 500f, Shepherds, sheep. d, 750f, Nativity scene.

**1996, Dec. 14** ***Perf. 14***
**60** A10 Sheet of 4, #a.-d. 6.50 6.50

Birds — A11

**1997, May 29**
**61** A11 25f Great tit .30 .30
**62** A11 75f Blue rock thrush .40 .40
**63** A11 150f Golden oriole .85 .85
**64** A11 350f Hoopoe 2.00 2.00
**65** A11 600f Peregrine falcon 2.75 2.75
*Nos. 61-65 (5)* 6.30 6.30

Historic Views — A12

**1997, June 19**
**66** A12 350f Gaza, 1839 1.50 1.50
**67** A12 600f Hebron, 1839 2.50 2.50

Souvenir Sheet

Return of Hong Kong to China — A13

**1997, July 1**
**68** A13 225f multicolored 2.40 2.40

Friends of Palestine — A14

#69, Portraits of Yasser Arafat, Hans-Jürgen Wischnewski. #70, Wischnewski shaking hands with Arafat. #71, Mother Teresa. #72, Mother Teresa with Arafat.

**1997** **Litho.** ***Perf. 14***
**69** A14 600f multicolored 1.75 1.75
**70** A14 600f multicolored 1.75 1.75
*a.* Pair, #69-70 4.50 4.50
**71** A14 600f multicolored 2.00 2.00
**72** A14 600f multicolored 2.00 2.00
*a.* Pair, #71-72 4.75 4.75
*Nos. 69-l72 (1)* 1.75 1.75

#70a, 72a were issued in sheets of 4 stamps.
Issued: #69-70, 7/24; #71-72, 12/17.

Christmas A15

**1997, Nov. 28**
**73** A15 350f multicolored 1.25 1.25
**74** A15 700f multicolored 2.25 2.25
*a.* Pair, #73-74 3.75 3.75

Mosaics from Floor of Byzantine Church, Jabalia-Gaza A16

50f, Rabbit, palm tree. 125f, Goat, rabbit, dog. 200f, Basket, fruit tree, jar. 400f, Lion.

**1998, June 22 Litho. *Perf. 13½***

| | | | | |
|---|---|---|---|---|
| 75 | A16 | 50f multicolored | .30 | .30 |
| 76 | A16 | 125f multicolored | .90 | .60 |
| 77 | A16 | 200f multicolored | 1.25 | 1.00 |
| 78 | A16 | 400f multicolored | 2.75 | 1.75 |
| | | *Nos. 75-78 (4)* | 5.20 | 3.65 |

Souvenir Sheet

Baal — A17

**1998, June 15 *Perf. 14***

| | | | | |
|---|---|---|---|---|
| 79 | A17 | 600f multicolored | 2.75 | 2.75 |

Medicinal Plants — A18

**1998, Sept. 30 Litho. *Perf. 14***

| | | | | |
|---|---|---|---|---|
| 80 | A18 | 40f Urginea maritima | .25 | .25 |
| 81 | A18 | 80f Silybum marianum | .30 | .30 |
| 82 | A18 | 500f Foeniculum vulgare | 1.50 | 1.50 |
| 83 | A18 | 800f Inula viscosa | 3.00 | 3.00 |
| | | *Nos. 80-83 (4)* | 5.05 | 5.05 |

Raptors A19

**1998, Nov. 12 Litho. *Perf. 14***

| | | | | |
|---|---|---|---|---|
| 84 | A19 | 20f Bonelli's eagle | .25 | .25 |
| 85 | A19 | 60f Hobby | .30 | .30 |
| 86 | A19 | 340f Verreaux's eagle | 1.75 | 1.75 |
| 87 | A19 | 600f Bateleur | 2.75 | 2.75 |
| 88 | A19 | 900f Buzzard | 3.75 | 3.75 |
| | | *Nos. 84-88 (5)* | 8.80 | 8.80 |

Souvenir Sheet

Granting of Additional Rights to Palestinian Authority's Observer to UN — A20

**1998, Nov. 12**

| | | | | |
|---|---|---|---|---|
| 89 | A20 | 700f multicolored | 3.00 | 3.00 |

Butterflies — A21

Designs: a, 100f, Papilio alexanor. b, 200f, Danaus chrysippus. c, 300f, Gonepteryx cleopatra. d, 400f, Melanargia titea.

**1998, Dec. 3**

| | | | | |
|---|---|---|---|---|
| 90 | A21 | Sheet of 4, #a.-d. | 4.50 | 4.50 |

Souvenir Sheet

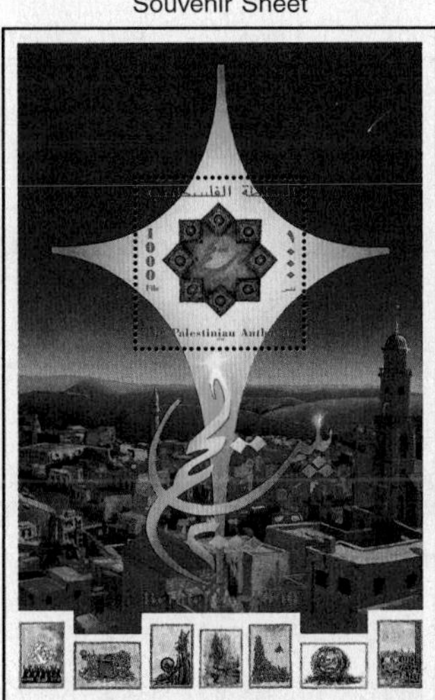

Christmas, Bethlehem 2000 — A22

**1998, Dec. 3**

| | | | | |
|---|---|---|---|---|
| 91 | A22 | 1000f multicolored | 4.25 | 4.25 |

Souvenir Sheet

Signing of Middle East Peace Agreement, Wye River Conference, Oct. 23, 1998 — A23

Palestinian Pres. Yasser Arafat and US Pres. Bill Clinton.

**1999 Litho. *Perf. 14***

| | | | | |
|---|---|---|---|---|
| 92 | A23 | 900f multicolored | 3.75 | 3.75 |

New Airport, Gaza A24

Designs: 80f, Control tower, vert. 300f, Airplane. 700f, Terminal building.

**1999**

| | | | | |
|---|---|---|---|---|
| 93 | A24 | 80f multicolored | .25 | .25 |
| 94 | A24 | 300f multicolored | .90 | .90 |
| 95 | A24 | 700f multicolored | 2.50 | 2.50 |
| | | *Nos. 93-95 (3)* | 3.65 | 3.65 |

Intl. Philatelic Exhibitions & UPU, 125th Anniv. — A25

a, 20f, Buildings, China 1999. b, 260f, Buildings, Germany, IBRA '99. c. 80f, High-rise buildings, Australia '99. d, 340f, Eiffel Tower, Philex France '99. e, 400f, Aerial view of countryside, denomination LR, UPU, 125th anniv. f, 400f, like #96e, denomination LL.

**1999**

| | | | | |
|---|---|---|---|---|
| 96 | A25 | Block of 6, #a.-f. | 6.75 | 6.75 |

Hebron — A26

a, 400f, Lettering in gold. b, 500f, Lettering in white.

**1999, Aug. 20 Litho. *Perf. 14***

| | | | | |
|---|---|---|---|---|
| 97 | A26 | Pair, #a.-b. | 4.00 | 4.00 |

Arabian Horses — A27

a, 25f. b, 75f. c, 150f. d, 350f. e, 800f.

**1999, Apr. 27**

| | | | | |
|---|---|---|---|---|
| 98 | A27 | Strip of 5, #a.-e. | 5.50 | 5.50 |

Souvenir Sheet

Palestinian Sunbird — A28

**1999 Litho. *Perf. 13¾***

| | | | | |
|---|---|---|---|---|
| 99 | A28 | 750f multi | 3.50 | 3.50 |

A29

Christmas, Bethlehem 2000 — A30

Giotto Paintings (Type A30): 200f, 280f, 2000f, The Nativity. 380f, 460f, The Adoration of the Magi. 560f, The Flight into Egypt. Inscription colors: Nos. 108a, 110a, Black. Nos. 109a, 111a, White. No. 112a, Yellow. Nos. 108b-112b have silver inscriptions and frames. No. 113, country name at lower left. No. 113A, country name at upper right, denomination at lower left.

**1999, Dec. 8 Litho. *Perf. 13¼x13***

**Background Color**

| | | | | |
|---|---|---|---|---|
| 100 | A29 | 60f black | .25 | .25 |
| 101 | A29 | 80f light blue | .25 | .25 |
| 102 | A29 | 100f dark gray | .35 | .35 |
| 103 | A29 | 280f lilac rose | .90 | .90 |
| 104 | A29 | 300f green | .95 | .95 |
| 105 | A29 | 400f red violet | 1.40 | 1.40 |
| 106 | A29 | 500f dark red | 1.60 | 1.60 |
| 107 | A29 | 560f light gray | 1.90 | 1.90 |

***Perf. 13¼***

| | | | | |
|---|---|---|---|---|
| 108 | A30 | 200f Pair, #a.-b | *2.50* | *2.50* |
| 109 | A30 | 280f Pair, #a.-b. | *2.75* | *2.75* |
| 110 | A30 | 380f Pair, #a.-b. | *3.25* | *3.25* |
| 111 | A30 | 460f Pair, #a.-b. | *4.25* | *4.25* |
| 112 | A30 | 560f Pair, #a.-b. | *7.00* | *7.00* |

**Litho. & Embossed Foil Application**

| | | | | |
|---|---|---|---|---|
| 113 | A30 | 2000f multi | 8.00 | 8.00 |
| 113A | A30 | 2000f multi, booklet pane of 1 | 8.00 | 8.00 |
| | | *Nos. 100-113 (14)* | *35.35* | *35.35* |

Nos. 108-112 each printed in sheets of 10 containing 9 "a" +1 "b." No. 113 printed in sheets of 4. Nos. 108a-112a also exist in sheets of 10.

Issued: No. 113A, 2000.

Easter — A31

Designs: 150f, Last Supper, by Giotto, white inscriptions. 200f, Last Supper, yellow inscriptions. 300f, Lamentation, by Giotto, white inscriptions. 350f, Lamentation, yellow inscriptions. 650f, Crucifix, by Giotto, orange frame.

No. 119, 2000f, Crucifix, gold frame, denomination and country name in orange. No. 119A, 2000f, denomination and country name in white.

**2000 Litho. *Perf. 13¼***
**114-118** A31 Set of 5 5.50 5.50

**Souvenir Sheet**

**Litho. & Embossed Foil Application**

**119** A31 2000f multi 8.50 8.50
**119A** A31 2000f multi, booklet pane of 1 9.50

See Nos. 140-144.

Christmas — A32

Madonna of the Star by Fra Angelico.

**Litho. & Embossed Foil Application**

**2000 *Perf. 13¼***
**120** A32 2000f Miniature sheet of 1 8.50 8.50
*a.* Booklet pane of 1 9.50 9.50
Complete booklet, #113A, 119A, 120a 28.50

See Nos. 134-139.

Holy Land Visit of Pope John Paul II — A33

Designs: 500f, Pope, Yasser Arafat holding hands. 600f, Pope with miter. 750f, Pope touching Arafat's shoulder. 800f, Pope, creche. 1000f, Pope, back of Arafat's head.

**2000 Litho. *Perf. 13¾***
**121-125** A33 Set of 5 12.00 12.00

Intl. Children's Year — A34

Designs: 50f, Landscape. 100f, Children. 350f, Domed buildings. 400f, Family.

**2000**
**126-129** A34 Set of 4 3.50 3.50

Pres. Arafat's Visit to Germany A35

Arafat and: 200f, German Chancellor Gerhard Schröder. 300f, German President Johannes Rau.

**2000 *Perf. 14x14¼***
**130-131** A35 Set of 2 2.75 2.75

Marine Life — A36

No. 132: a, Parrotfish. b, Mauve stinger. c, Ornate wrasse. d, Rainbow wrasse. e, Red starfish. f, Common octopus. g, Purple sea urchin. h, Striated hermit crab.

**2000 Litho. *Perf. 13¾***
**132** A36 700f Sheet of 8, #a-h 17.50 17.50

**Souvenir Sheet**

Blue Madonna — A37

**2000 *Perf. 14x13¾***
**133** A37 950f multi 3.25 3.25

**Christmas Type of 2000**

Designs: No. 134, 100f, No. 138, 500f, Nativity, by Gentile da Fabriano, horiz. No. 135, 150f, Adoration of the Magi, by Fabriano, horiz. No. 136, 250f, Immaculate Conception, by Fabriano, horiz. No. 137, 350f, No. 139, 1000f, Like #120.

**2000 Litho. *Perf. 13¼***
**134-139** A32 Set of 6 7.75 7.75

**Easter Type of 2000**

Designs: 150f, Christ Carrying Cross, by Fra Angelico, blue inscriptions. 200f, Christ Carrying Cross, white inscriptions. 300f, Removal of Christ from Cross, by Fra Angelico, yellow inscriptions. 350f, Removal of Christ from the Cross, white inscriptions.
2000f, Crucifix, by Giotto, vert.

**2001 Litho. *Perf. 13¼***
**140-143** A31 Set of 4 3.25 3.25

**Souvenir Sheet**

**Litho. & Embossed**

**144** A31 2000f gold & multi 7.50 7.50

A38

Palestinian Authority flag and flag of various organizations: 50f, 100f, 200f, 500f.

**2001 Litho. *Perf. 13¾***
**145-148** A38 Set of 4 2.75 2.75

**Souvenir Sheet**

Art by Ibrahim Hazimeh — A39

No. 149: a, 350f, Jerusalem After Rain. b, 550f, Mysticism. c, 850f, Ramallah. d, 900f, Remembrance.

**2001 *Perf. 14x13¾***
**149** A39 Sheet of 4, #a-d 9.00 9.00

Worldwide Fund for Nature (WWF) — A40

No. 150 — Houbara bustard, WWF emblem at: a, 350f, UR. b, 350f, LR. c, 750f, UL. d, 750f, LL.

**2001 Litho. *Perf. 13¾x14***
**150** A40 Block of 4, #a-d 11.50 11.50

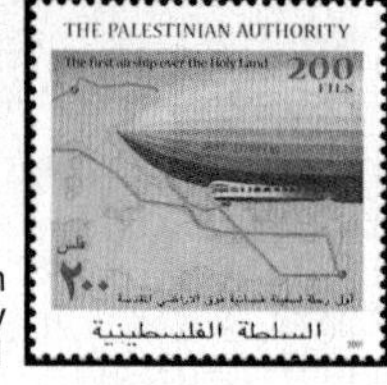


Graf Zeppelin Over Holy Land — A41

Zeppelin and: 200f, Map of voyage. 600f, Hills.

**2001 *Perf. 13¾***
**151-152** A41 Set of 2 3.00 3.00

Legends A42

Designs: 300f, Man with magic lamp, buildings. 450f, Eagle, snake, gemstones, man. 650f, Man and woman on flying horse. 800f, Man hiding behind tree.

**2001 *Perf. 13¾x14***
**153-156** A42 Set of 4 7.00 7.00

**Souvenir Sheet**

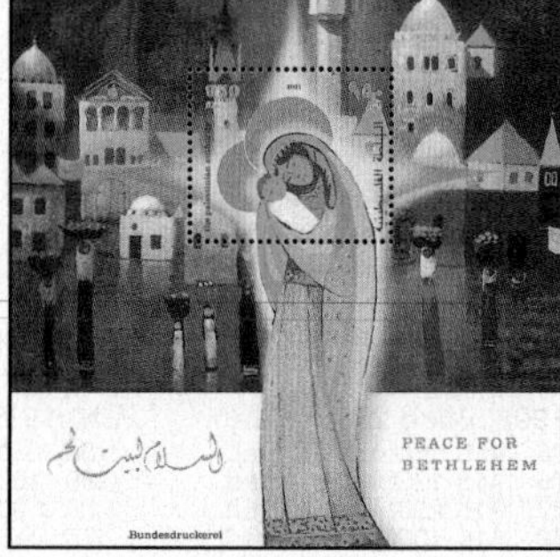


Peace for Bethlehem — A43

**2001 *Perf. 14x13¾***
**157** A43 950f multi 3.25 3.25

City Views — A44

Designs: 450f, Jerusalem. 650f, El-Eizariya. 850f, Nablus.

**2002 Litho. *Perf. 13¾***
**158-160** A44 Set of 3 7.25 7.25

Women's Traditional Clothing — A44a

Various costumes: 50f, 100f, 500f.

**2002, June Litho. *Perf. 14***
**160A-160C** A44a Set of 3 4.75 4.75

**Souvenir Sheet**

Christmas — A45

**2002, Dec. 20 *Perf. 14¼x14***
**161** A45 1000f multi 3.75 3.75

Succulent Plants — A46

Designs: 550f, Prickly pear. 600f, Big-horned euphorbia. 750f, Century plant.

**2003, May 10 Litho. *Perf. 13¾x14***
**162-164** A46 Set of 3 8.00 8.00
*164a* Souvenir sheet, #162-164 8.00 8.00

Trees — A47

Designs: 300f, Olive tree. 700f, Blessing tree.

**2003, July 12**
**165-166** A47 Set of 2 5.50 5.50

Universities — A48

Designs: 250f, Al-Azhar University, Gaza. 650f, Hebron University, Hebron. 800f, Arab American University, Jenin.

**2003, July 19**
**167-169** A48 Set of 3 7.75 7.75

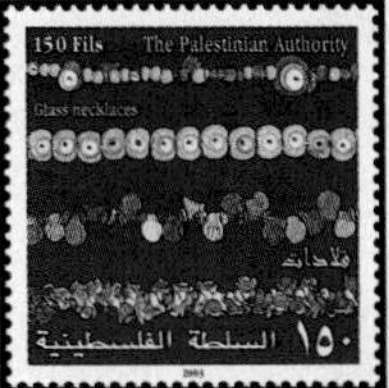


Handicrafts A49

Designs: 150f, Glass necklaces. 200f, Headdress. 450f, Embroidery. 500f, Costume embroidery. 950f, Head veil.

**2003, Oct. 11 Litho.** ***Perf. 13¾***
**170-174** A49 Set of 5 11.00 11.00

French President Jacques Chirac A50

No. 175 — Chirac and: a, 200f, Yasser Arafat, French flag. b, 450f, Palestinian flag.

**2004 Litho.** ***Perf. 14***
**175** A50 Pair, #a-b 5.25 5.25

Printed in sheets containing two each of Nos. 175a-175b

Souvenir Sheet

Worship of the Virgin Mary — A51

**2004**
**176** A51 1000f multi 5.25 5.25

Souvenir Sheet

Arab League, 60th Anniv. — A52

**2005 Litho.** ***Perf. 13¾***
**177** A52 750f multi *9.00 9.00*

Mahmoud Darwish (1941-2008), Poet — A53

Denominations: 150f, 250f, 350f, 400f.

**2008, July 29 Litho.** ***Perf. 13***
**178-181** A53 Set of 4 9.00 9.00

A54

Jericho, 10,000th Anniv. — A55

**2010, Dec. 26** ***Perf. 13¼x13***

**Background Color**

**182** A54 50f white .40 .40
**183** A55 150f pink 1.25 1.25
**184** A54 350f gray 2.75 2.75
**185** A55 1000f light green 7.75 7.75
*Nos. 182-185 (4)* 12.15 12.15

Christmas — A56

Color of panel above denomination: 100f, Red. 150f, Purple. 250f, Green. 500f, Blue.

**2010, Dec. 26**
**186-189** A56 Set of 4 7.50 7.50

Souvenir Sheet

Arab Postal Day — A57

No. 190 — Emblem and: a, 350f, Camel caravan. b, 500f, Pigeon and map.

**Litho. With Foil Application**

**2011, Mar. 17** ***Perf. 13¾x13¼***
**190** A57 Sheet of 2, #a-b 9.50 9.50

Ramadan A58

Designs: 50f, Dome of the Rock, crescent, arches, flag. 100f, Lantern, arabesque, flag. 250f, Lantern, crescent, arabesque, arch, flag. 500f, Dome of the Rock, crescent, flag.

No. 195, 1000f, Dome of the Rock, lantern, crescent. No. 196, 1000f, Flag, crescent, Arabic text.

**2011, Aug. 1 Litho.** ***Perf. 13x13¼***
**191-194** A58 Set of 4 8.25 8.25

**Souvenir Sheets**

***Perf. 13¼x14¼***

**195-196** A58 Set of 2 16.00 16.00

Nos. 195 and 196 each contain one 45x35mm stamp.

Yasser Arafat (1929-2004), President of the Palestinian Authority A59

Various photographs of Arafat: 50f, 100f, 150f, 5000f.

**2012, June 6 Litho.** ***Perf. 14¼***
**197-200** A59 Set of 4 21.00 21.00

A booklet containing five 250f, three 500f, three 750f, and four 1000f stamps, each depicting Arafat, sold for 20,000f.

Souvenir Sheet

Soccer Ball and Flag of Palestinian Authority — A60

**2012, June 6 Litho.** ***Perf. 13***
**201** A60 1000f multi 4.25 4.25

Recognition by FIFA of first home soccer match of Palestinian Authority team, 4th anniv. Compare with type A68.

Miniature Sheet

Governmental Ministries — A61

No. 202 — Ministry of: a, Transport. b, Public Works and Housing. c, Telecommunication and Information Technology. d, Finance. e, Interior.

**2012, June 6 Litho.** ***Perf. 13¼***
**202** A61 300f Sheet of 5, #a-e 7.25 7.25

Miniature Sheet

Fruit — A62

No. 203: a, 150f, Grapes. b, 300f, Oranges. c, 350f, Bananas. d, 450f, Dates.

**2012, June 6 Litho.** ***Perf. 14***
**203** A62 Sheet of 8, 2 each #a-d 12.00 12.00

The two examples of Nos. 203a-203d on the sheet have different frames, being placed in different areas on the marginal illustration depicting trees.

Arab Postal Day A63

Denominations: 150f, 250f, 350f, 1000f, 5000f.

**2012, Aug. 3 Litho.** ***Perf. 13¼***
**204-208** A63 Set of 5 30.00 30.00

Christmas — A64

Various depictions of Christmas trees: 20f, 250f, 600f.

1000f, Man praying.

**2012, Dec. 24 Litho.** ***Perf. 14***
**209-211** A64 Set of 3 3.75 3.75

**Souvenir Sheet**

**212** A64 1000f multi 4.25 4.25

Intl. Day of Civil Defense A65

Designs: 200f, Firemen in smoke. 250f, Firemen and fire truck. 500f, Firemen spraying water on building, ladder truck.

1000f, Firemen and fire truck, diff.

**2013 Litho. *Perf. 14***
**213-215** A65 Set of 3 4.50 4.50

**Souvenir Sheet**

**216** A65 1000f multi 5.00 5.00

Flora and Fauna — A66

Designs: 20f, White flower. 100f, Caracal. 200f, Bird. 480f, Poppies. 720f, Turtle. 1080f, Nubian ibex.

No. 223, 1000f, Daisies, horiz. No. 224, 1000f, Eagle, horiz.

**2013, June 3 Litho. *Perf. 14***
**217-222** A66 Set of 6 13.50 13.50

**Souvenir Sheets**

**223-224** A66 Set of 2 12.00 12.00

Police A67

Designs: 100f, Policeman directing traffic. 200f, Policemen inspecting plants. 250f, Policemen with pick and hoe.

500f, Policeman assisting elderly woman, vert.

**2013 Litho. *Perf. 14***
**225-227** A67 Set of 3 3.25 3.25

**Souvenir Sheet**

**228** A67 500f multi 3.00 3.00

**Souvenir Sheet**

Soccer Ball and Flag of Palestinian Authority — A68

**2013 Litho. *Perf. 13***
**229** A68 1000f multi 9.00 9.00

Recognition by FIFA of first home soccer match of Palestinian Authority team, 5th anniv. Compare with type A60.

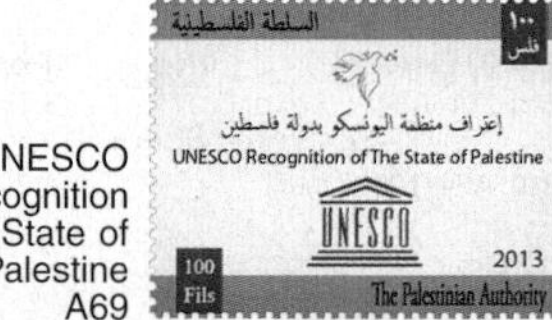

UNESCO Recognition of State of Palestine A69

Dove, text, UNESCO emblem and panel color of: 100f, Green. 200f, Red brown. 420f, Black.

1000f, Dove, text and UNESCO emblem on Palestinian Authority flag, vert.

**2013, Oct. 31 Litho. *Perf. 14***
**230-232** A69 Set of 3 4.25 4.25

**Souvenir Sheet**

**233** A69 1000f multi 5.75 5.75

Abdel Rahim Mahmoud (1913-48), Poet — A70

Background color: 80f, Apple green. 200f, Yellow orange. 500f, Gray.

1800f, Turquoise green background.

**2013, July 13 Litho. *Perf. 14***
**234-236** A70 Set of 3 4.50 4.50

**Souvenir Sheet**

**237** A70 1800f multi 10.00 10.00

Declaration of State of Palestine, 1st Anniv. — A71

No. 238: a, Folk dancers. b, Musical score. c, Woman and olive tree. d, Dove, Al-Aqsa Mosqu, Church of the Holy Sepulchre. e, Sunbird and anemone flowers.

1000f, Dove, Pres. Mahmoud Abbas speaking at United Nations.

**2013, Nov. 29 Litho. *Perf. 13¼***
**238** A71 200f Sheet of 5, #a-e 5.75 5.75

**Souvenir Sheet**

**239** A71 1000f multi 5.75 5.75

International Anti-Corruption Day — A72

Designs: 200f, Stop sign. 360f, Man refusing bribe. 420f, Money and gavel on balance. 720f, Hand.

1000f, "No" symbol over hand accepting bribe, horiz.

**2013, Dec. 9 Litho. *Perf. 14***
**240-243** A72 Set of 4 7.75 7.75

**Souvenir Sheet**

**244** A72 1000f multi 5.75 5.75

**Souvenir Sheet**

Mosques — A73

No. 245: a, Al-Aqsa Mosque, Jerusalem (one minaret). b, Sultan Ahmed Mosque, Istanbul (six minarets).

**2014, Apr. Litho. *Perf. 13½x13¾***
**245** A73 1000f Sheet of 2, #a-b 11.00 11.00

Joint issue between Palestine Authority and Turkey.

See Turkey No. 3371.

Palestinian Prisoners' Day — A74

Designs: 200f, Dove, chained hands, barbed wire. 360f, Prisoner holding prison bars. 600f, Blindfolded prisoner, barbed wire.

1200f, Maysara Abu Hamdiya (1948-2013), jailed Palestinian Liberation Organization fighter.

**2014, Apr. 17 Litho. *Perf. 14***
**246-248** A74 Set of 3 6.50 6.50

**Souvenir Sheet**

**249** A74 1200f multi 6.75 6.75

Palestinian Scouts, Cent. (in 2012) — A75

Emblem with panel color of: 120f, Red. 480f, Yellow. 720f, Green.

1500f, Scouting trefoil.

**2014, May 7 Litho. *Perf. 14***
**250-252** A75 Set of 3 7.00 7.00

**Souvenir Sheet**

**253** A75 1500f multi 8.00 8.00

Popular Resistence A76

Designs: 60f, Bab Al-Shams. 920f, Tents, flag of Palestinian Authority.

1500f, Tent, flag of Palestinian Authority, horiz.

**2014, May 15 Litho. *Perf. 14***
**254-255** A76 Set of 2 5.25 5.25

**Souvenir Sheet**

**256** A76 1500f multi 8.00 8.00

Visit of Pope Francis — A77

Pope Francis, Pres. Mahmoud Abbas, and Ecumenical Patriarch of Constantinople Bartholomew I and: 250f, People near doorway of Church of the Nativity, Jerusalem. 480f, Stylized key.

1500f, Pope Francis, Abbas, Patriarch Bartholomew I and Church of the Nativity, Jerusalem.

**2014, May 25 Litho. *Perf. 14***
**257-258** A77 Set of 2 4.00 4.00

**Souvenir Sheet**

**259** A77 1500f multi 8.00 8.00

Euromed Postal Emblem and Mediterranean Sea — A78

**2014, July 9 Litho. *Perf. 12¾x13¼***
**260** A78 500f multi 3.00 3.00

**Souvenir Sheet**

Arab Lawyers Union, 70th Anniv. — A79

**2014, Aug. 12 Litho. *Perf. 14***
**261** A79 1200f multi 6.25 6.25

A80

A81

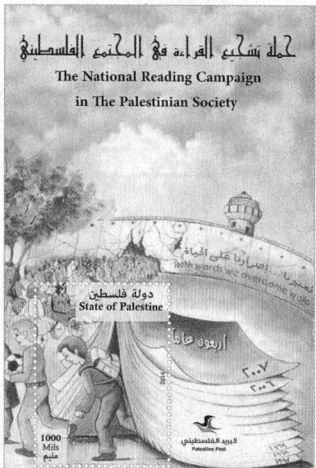

National Reading Campaign — A82

**2014, Oct. 22 Litho. *Perf. 14***
**262** A80 200f multi 1.00 1.00
**263** A81 250f multi 1.25 1.25

**Souvenir Sheet**

**264** A82 1000f multi 5.00 5.00

International Year of Solidarity With the Palestinian People — A83

Palestinians and flag with background color of: 200f, Buff. 420f, Rose lilac.
1800f, Palestinians, flag and houses of worship.

**2014, Nov. 29 Litho. *Perf. 14***
**265-266** A83 Set of 2 3.00 3.00

**Souvenir Sheet**

**267** A83 1800f multi 8.75 8.75

International Women's Day — A84

Images of various women: 250f, 600f.
1500f, Woman holding tree.

**2015, Mar. 8 Litho. *Perf. 14***
**268-269** A84 Set of 2 4.50 4.50

**Souvenir Sheet**

**270** A84 1500f multi 7.75 7.75

Miniature Sheet

Canonization of Saints — A85

No. 271: a, 500f, St. Marie Alphonsine Gattas (1843-1927). b, 500f, St. Mariam Baouardy (1846-78). c, 750f, Both saints. d, 750f, Pope Francis and Pres. Mahmoud Abbas.

**2015, May 17 Litho. *Perf. 14***
**271** A85 Sheet of 4, #a-d 13.00 13.00

Euromed Postal Emblem and Fishing Boat — A86

**2015, July 9 Litho. *Perf. 14***
**272** A86 500f multi 2.60 2.60

Jerusalem, Permanent Capital of Arab Culture — A87

Emblem and panel color of: 100f, Olive green. 200f, Red orange. 500f, Lilac.
1000f, Emblem and Jerusalem buildings.

**2015, Oct. 2 Litho. *Perf. 14***
**273-275** A87 Set of 3 4.25 4.25

**Souvenir Sheet**

**276** A87 1000f multi 5.25 5.25

Figs and Olives — A88

Designs: 480f, Figs, green and black olives. 920f, Fig leaf and olive branch.
1200f, Olives on tree and figs.

**2015, Oct. 10 Litho. *Perf. 14***
**277-278** A88 Set of 2 7.25 7.25

**Souvenir Sheet**

**279** A88 1200f multi 6.25 6.25

Islamic New Year — A89

Designs: 200f, Camel caravan in desert. 420f, Camels, mosque, Holy Ka'aba.
1500f, Camel, spider web, bird, palm tree.

**2015, Nov. 15 Litho. *Perf. 14***
**280-281** A89 Set of 2 3.25 3.25

**Souvenir Sheet**

**282** A89 1500f multi 7.75 7.75

Speeches by Palestinian Leaders at United Nations — A90

No. 283: a, 2012 speech by Pres. Mahmoud Abbas. b, 1974 speech by Yasser Arafat.
1500f, Like No. 283b.

**2015, Nov. 29 Litho. *Perf. 14***
**283** A90 750f Sheet of 2, #a-b 7.75 7.75

**Souvenir Sheet**

**284** A90 1500f multi 7.75 7.75

Grotto of the Nativity — A91

***Serpentine Die Cut 14x15***
**2016, Mar. 27 Litho.**

**Self-Adhesive**

**285** A91 250f multi 1.40 1.40

International Workers' Day — A92

Designs: 250f, Man holding large claw hammer. 920f, Man, pliers, mallet, wrench.
1500f, Man, crane, mortared bricks.

**2016, May 1 Litho. *Perf. 14***
**286-287** A92 Set of 2 6.00 6.00

**Souvenir Sheet**

**288** A92 1500f multi 7.75 7.75

Fish A93

No. 289: a, Gray mullet. b, Red mullet. c, Grouper. d, Malabar grouper. e, Sea bass. f, Meagre. g, Sardine. h, Mackerel. i, Blue runner. j, Albacore tuna.

**2016, July 3 Litho. *Perf. 12¾x13¼***
**289** Sheet of 10 26.00 26.00
*a.-j.* A93 500f Any single 2.60 2.60

Solomon's Pools A94

Various photographs of pools: 250f, 420f.
1500f, Pool at night, vert.

**2016, Aug. 8 Litho. *Perf. 14***
**290-291** A94 Set of 2 3.50 3.50

**Souvenir Sheet**

**292** A94 1500f multi 7.75 7.75

Water Rights — A95

No. 293: a, "No water no life." b, "Water is a human right."
No. 294, vert.: a, "Our water is our right." b, "Water for development."
1200f, "Water is life," vert.

**2016, Aug. 8 Litho. *Perf. 14***
**293** A95 420f Horiz. pair, #a-b 4.50 4.50
**294** A95 800f Vert. pair, #a-b 8.25 8.25

**Souvenir Sheet**

**295** A95 1200f multi 6.25 6.25

Arab Postal Day — A96

No. 296: a, 10f, Green background, denomination at LL. b, 480f, Blue background, denomination at LR.

**2016, Oct. 17 Litho. *Perf. 14***
**296** A96 Horiz. pair, #a-b 2.60 2.60

Flag Day — A97

Designs: 250f, Palestinian Authority flag at United Nations Headquarters. 420f, Woman, flag and tree.
1800f, Dove carrying flag over Jerusalem.

**Litho. With Foil Application**
**2016, Sept. 30 *Perf. 14***
**297-298** A97 Set of 2 3.50 3.50

**Souvenir Sheet**

**299** A97 1800f multi 9.25 9.25

Olive Tree — A98

**2016, Nov. 15 Litho. *Perf. 14***

**Background Color**

**300** A98 200f pale orange 1.00 1.00
**301** A98 1400f pale green 7.00 7.00
**302** A98 4500f white 22.00 22.00
*Nos. 300-302 (3)* 30.00 30.00

A99

Arabic Calligraphy Day — A100

Calligraphic designs with background color of: 250f, Dark brown. 420f, Grayish green.
No. 305: a, Calligraphic design with four dots at bottom, floral embellishment at UL and LL. b, Calligraphic design, diff. c, As "a," floral embellishment at UR and LR.

**2016, Dec. 18 Litho. *Perf. 13x13¼***
**303-304** A99 Set of 2 3.25 3.25

**Souvenir Sheet**

***Perf. 14***

**305** A100 600f Sheet of 3, #a-c 9.00 9.00

Fadwa Touqan (1917-2003), Poet — A101

Denominations: 150f, 500f.
1800f, Touqan, diff.

**2017, Mar. 1 Litho. *Perf. 14***
**306-307** A101 Set of 2 3.50 3.50

**Souvenir Sheet**

**308** A101 1800f multi 9.75 9.75

Faqqu'a Iris — A102

**2017, Apr. 5 Litho. *Perf. 14***
**309** A102 500f shown 2.75 2.75

**Souvenir Sheet**

**310** A102 1500f Irises 8.50 8.50

Miniature Sheet

Stones — A103

No. 311: a, 100f, Jerusalem stone. b, 200f, Nablus stone. c, 300f, Jenin stone. d, 400f, Ramallah stone. e, 500f, Hebron stone. f, 600f, Tulkarm stone. g, 700f, Bethlehem stone. h, 800f, Qalqilya stone.

**2017, June 1 Litho. *Perf. 14***
**311** A103 Sheet of 8, #a-h 20.00 20.00

Miniature Sheet

Dead Sea — A104

No. 312: a, 150f, No shoreline. b, 280f, Shoreline at UL and LL. c, 420f, Shoreline at top. d, 950f, Shoreline at top and left.

**2017, July 17 Litho. *Perf. 14***
**312** A104 Sheet of 4, #a-d 10.00 10.00

Dates — A105

Designs: 150f, Medjool dates. 200f, Berhi dates. 500f, Hayani dates.
1500f, Date palms.

**2017, Aug. 25 Litho. *Perf. 14***
**313-315** A105 Set of 3 4.75 4.75

**Souvenir Sheet**

**316** A105 1500f multi 8.50 8.50

World Post Day — A106

**2017, Oct. 9 Litho. *Perf. 14***
**317** A106 500f multi 2.75 2.75

Teachers' Day — A107

Teacher pointing to map, with background color of: 200f, Light blue. 400f, Red brown.
1500f, Buff.

**2017, Dec. 14 Litho. *Perf. 14***
**318-319** A107 Set of 2 3.50 3.50

**Souvenir Sheet**

**320** A107 1500f multi 8.50 8.50

## SEMI-POSTAL STAMPS

Souvenir Sheet

Gaza-Jericho Peace Agreement — SP1

**1994, Oct. 7 Litho. *Perf. 14***
**B1** SP1 750m +250m multi 5.75 5.75

For surcharge see No. B3.

Souvenir Sheet

Arab League, 50th Anniv. — SP2

Painting: View of Palestine, by Ibrahim Hazimeh.

**1995, Mar. 22 *Perf. 13½***
**B2** SP2 750f +250f multi 3.75 3.75

**No. B1 Surcharged "FILS" in English & Arabic and with Added Text at Left and Right**

**1995, Apr. 10 Litho. *Perf. 14***
**B3** SP1 750f +250f multi 7.00 7.00

Honoring 1994 Nobel Peace Prize winners Arafat, Rabin and Peres.

International Day of Persons With Disabilities — SP3

**2015, Dec. 3 Litho. *Perf. 14***
**B4** SP3 100f +100f multi 1.00 1.00

## OFFICIAL STAMPS

Natl. Arms — O1

**1994, Aug. 15 Litho. *Perf. 14***
**O1** O1 50m yellow .25 .25
**O2** O1 100m green blue .35 .35
**O3** O1 125m blue .50 .50
**O4** O1 200m orange .75 .75
**O5** O1 250m olive 1.00 1.00
**O6** O1 400m maroon 1.40 1.40
*Nos. O1-O6 (6)* 4.25 4.25

Nos. O1-O6 could also be used by the general public, and non-official-use covers are known.

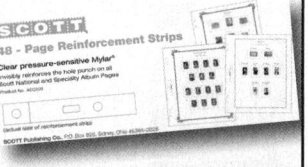

## PANAMA

ˈpa-nə-ˌmä

LOCATION — Central America between Costa Rica and Colombia
GOVT. — Republic
AREA — 30,134 sq. mi.
POP. — 2,778,526 (1999 est.)
CAPITAL — Panama

Formerly a department of the Republic of Colombia, Panama gained its independence in 1903. Dividing the country at its center is the Panama Canal.

100 Centavos = 1 Peso
100 Centesimos = 1 Balboa (1904)

**Catalogue values for unused stamps in this country are for Never Hinged items, beginning with Scott 350 in the regular postage section, Scott C82 in the airpost section, Scott CB1 in the airpost semi-postal section, and Scott RA21 in the postal tax section.**

### Watermarks

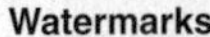

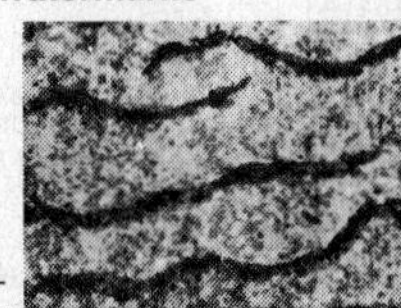

Wmk. 229 — Wavy Lines

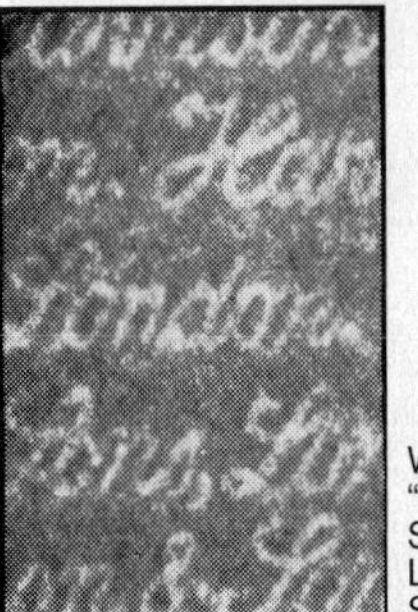

Wmk. 233 — "Harrison & Sons, London." in Script

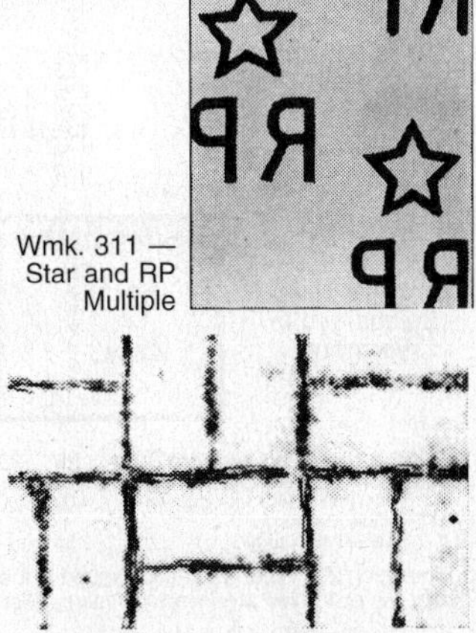

Wmk. 311 — Star and RP Multiple

Wmk. 334 — Rectangles

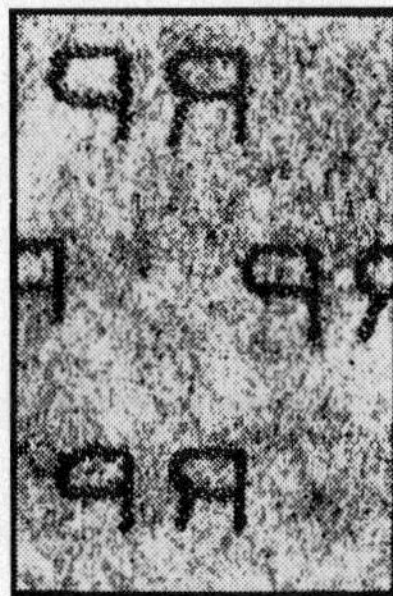

Wmk. 343 — RP Multiple

Wmk. 365 — Argentine Arms, Casa de Moneda de la Nacion & RA Multiple

Wmk. 377 — Interlocking Circles

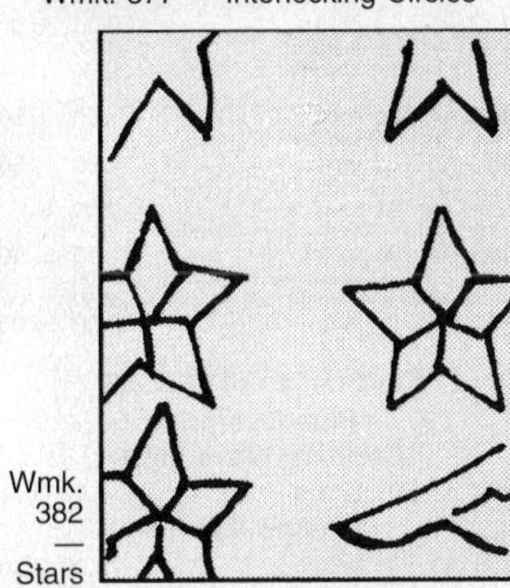

Wmk. 382 — Stars

Wmk. 382 may be a sheet watermark. It includes stars, wings with sun in middle and "Panama R de P."

### Issues of the Sovereign State of Panama Under Colombian Dominion

Valid only for domestic mail.

Coat of Arms
A1 A2

**1878 Unwmk. Litho. *Imperf.***

**Thin Wove Paper**

| No. | Type | Description | Unused | Used |
|---|---|---|---|---|
| 1 | A1 | 5c gray green | 25.00 | 30.00 |
| a. | | 5c yellow green | 25.00 | 30.00 |
| 2 | A1 | 10c blue | 60.00 | 60.00 |
| 3 | A1 | 20c rose red | 40.00 | 32.50 |
| | | *Nos. 1-3 (3)* | 125.00 | 122.50 |

**Very Thin Wove Paper**

| No. | Type | Description | Unused | Used |
|---|---|---|---|---|
| 4 | A2 | 50c buff | *1,500.* | |

All values of this issue are known rouletted unofficially.

**Medium Thick Paper**

| No. | Type | Description | Unused | Used |
|---|---|---|---|---|
| 5 | A1 | 5c blue green | 25.00 | 30.00 |
| 6 | A1 | 10c blue | 65.00 | 70.00 |
| 7 | A2 | 50c orange | 13.00 | |
| | | *Nos. 5-7 (3)* | 103.00 | 100.00 |

Nos. 5-7 were printed before Nos. 1-4, according to Panamanian archives.

Values for used Nos. 1-5 are for hand-stamped postal cancellations.

*These stamps have been reprinted in a number of shades, on thin to moderately thick, white or yellowish paper. They are without gum or with white, crackly gum. All values have been reprinted from new stones made from retouched dies. The marks of retouching are plainly to be seen in the sea and clouds. On the original 10c the shield in the upper left corner has two blank sections; on the reprints the design of this shield is completed. The impression of these reprints is frequently blurred.*

*Reprints of the 50c are rare. Beware of remainders of the 50c offered as reprints.*

### Issues of Colombia for use in the Department of Panama

Issued because of the use of different currency.

Map of Panama — A3

**1887-88 *Perf. 13½***

| No. | Type | Description | Unused | Used |
|---|---|---|---|---|
| 8 | A3 | 1c black, *green* | .90 | .80 |
| 9 | A3 | 2c black, *pink* ('88) | 1.60 | 1.25 |
| a. | | 2c black, *salmon* | 1.60 | |
| 10 | A3 | 5c black, *blue* | .90 | .35 |
| 11 | A3 | 10c black, *yellow* | .90 | .40 |
| a. | | Imperf., pair | | |
| 12 | A3 | 20c black, *lilac* | 1.00 | .50 |
| 13 | A3 | 50c brown ('88) | 2.00 | 1.00 |
| a. | | Imperf. | | |
| | | *Nos. 8-13 (6)* | 7.30 | 4.30 |

See No. 14. For surcharges and overprints see Nos. 24-30, 107-108, 115-116, 137-138.

**1892 Pelure Paper**

| No. | Type | Description | Unused | Used |
|---|---|---|---|---|
| 14 | A3 | 50c brown | 2.50 | 1.10 |

*The stamps of this issue have been reprinted on papers of slightly different colors from those of the originals.*

*These are: 1c yellow green, 2c deep rose, 5c bright blue, 10c straw, 20c violet.*

*The 50c is printed from a very worn stone, in a lighter brown than the originals. The series includes a 10c on lilac paper.*

*All these stamps are to be found perforated, imperforate, imperforate horizontally or imperforate vertically. At the same time that they were made, impressions were struck upon a variety of glazed and surface-colored papers.*

Map of Panama — A4

**Wove Paper**

**1892-96 Engr. *Perf. 12***

| No. | Type | Description | Unused | Used |
|---|---|---|---|---|
| 15 | A4 | 1c green | .25 | .25 |
| 16 | A4 | 2c rose | .40 | .25 |
| 17 | A4 | 5c blue | 1.50 | .50 |
| 18 | A4 | 10c orange | .35 | .25 |
| 19 | A4 | 20c violet ('95) | .50 | .35 |
| 20 | A4 | 50c bister brn ('96) | .50 | .40 |
| 21 | A4 | 1p lake ('96) | 6.50 | 4.00 |
| | | *Nos. 15-21 (7)* | 10.00 | 6.00 |

In 1903 Nos. 15-21 were used in Cauca and three other southern Colombia towns. Stamps canceled in these towns are worth much more.

For surcharges and overprints see Nos. 22-23, 51-106, 109-114, 129-136, 139, 151-161, 181-184, F12-F15, H4-H5.

### Nos. 16, 12-14 Surcharged

a

b

c

d

e

f

g

**1894 Black Surcharge**

| No. | Type | Description | Unused | Used |
|---|---|---|---|---|
| 22 | (a) | 1c on 2c rose | .50 | .40 |
| a. | | Inverted surcharge | 2.50 | 2.50 |
| b. | | Double surcharge | | |
| 23 | (b) | 1c on 2c rose | .40 | .50 |
| a. | | "CCNTAVO" | 2.50 | 2.50 |
| b. | | Inverted surcharge | 2.50 | 2.50 |
| c. | | Double surcharge | | |

**Red Surcharge**

| No. | Type | Description | Unused | Used |
|---|---|---|---|---|
| 24 | (c) | 5c on 20c black, *lil* | 2.50 | 1.50 |
| a. | | Inverted surcharge | 12.50 | 12.50 |
| b. | | Double surcharge | | |
| c. | | Without "HABILITADO" | | |
| 25 | (d) | 5c on 20c black, *lil* | 3.50 | 3.00 |
| a. | | "CCNTAVOS" | 7.50 | 7.50 |
| b. | | Inverted surcharge | 12.50 | 12.50 |
| c. | | Double surcharge | | |
| d. | | Without "HABILITADO" | | |
| 26 | (e) | 5c on 20c black, *lil* | 6.00 | 5.00 |
| a. | | Inverted surcharge | 12.50 | 12.50 |
| b. | | Double surcharge | | |
| 27 | (f) | 10c on 50c brown | 3.00 | 3.00 |
| a. | | "1894" omitted | | |
| b. | | Inverted surcharge | | |
| c. | | "CCNTAVOS" | 15.00 | |
| 28 | (g) | 10c on 50c brown | 12.50 | 12.50 |
| a. | | "CCNTAVOS" | 32.50 | |
| b. | | Inverted surcharge | | |

**Pelure Paper**

| No. | Type | Description | Unused | Used |
|---|---|---|---|---|
| 29 | (f) | 10c on 50c brown | 4.00 | 3.00 |
| a. | | "1894" omitted | 7.50 | |
| b. | | Inverted surcharge | 12.50 | 12.50 |
| c. | | Double surcharge | | |
| 30 | (g) | 10c on 50c brown | 10.00 | 10.00 |
| a. | | "CCNTAVOS" | | |
| b. | | Without "HABILITADO" | | |
| c. | | Inverted surcharge | 25.00 | 25.00 |
| d. | | Double surcharge | | |
| | | *Nos. 22-30 (9)* | 42.40 | 38.90 |

There are several settings of these surcharges. Usually the surcharge is about 15½mm high, but in one setting, it is only 13mm. All the types are to be found with a comma after "CENTAVOS." Nos. 24, 25, 26, 29 and 30 exist with the surcharge printed sideways. Nos. 23, 24 and 29 may be found with an inverted "A" instead of "V" in "CENTAVOS." There are also varieties caused by dropped or broken letters.

### Issues of the Republic Issued in the City of Panama

Stamps of 1892-96 Overprinted

**1903, Nov. 16 Rose Handstamp**

| No. | Type | Description | Unused | Used |
|---|---|---|---|---|
| 51 | A4 | 1c green | 2.00 | 1.50 |
| 52 | A4 | 2c rose | 5.00 | 3.00 |
| 53 | A4 | 5c blue | 2.00 | 1.25 |
| 54 | A4 | 10c yellow | 2.00 | 2.00 |
| 55 | A4 | 20c violet | 4.00 | 3.50 |
| 56 | A4 | 50c bister brn | 10.00 | 7.00 |
| 57 | A4 | 1p lake | 50.00 | 40.00 |
| | | *Nos. 51-57 (7)* | 75.00 | 58.25 |

**Blue Black Handstamp**

| No. | Type | Description | Unused | Used |
|---|---|---|---|---|
| 58 | A4 | 1c green | 2.00 | 1.25 |
| 59 | A4 | 2c rose | 1.00 | 1.00 |
| 60 | A4 | 5c blue | 7.00 | 6.00 |

**61** A4 10c yellow 5.00 3.50
**62** A4 20c violet 10.00 7.50
**63** A4 50c bister brn 10.00 7.50
**64** A4 1p lake 50.00 42.50
*Nos. 58-64 (7)* 85.00 69.25

The stamps of this issue are to be found with the handstamp placed horizontally, vertically or diagonally; inverted; double; double, one inverted; double, both inverted; in pairs, one without handstamp; etc.

This handstamp is known in brown rose on the 1, 5, 20 and 50c, in purple on the 1, 2, 50c and 1p, and in magenta on the 5, 10, 20 and 50c.

*Reprints were made in rose, black and other colors when the handstamp was nearly worn out, so that the "R" of "REPUBLICA" appears to be shorter than usual, and the bottom part of "LI" has been broken off. The "P" of "PANAMA" leans to the left and the tops of "NA" are broken. Many of these varieties are found inverted, double, etc.*

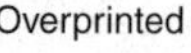
Overprinted

**Bar in Similar Color to Stamp**

**1903, Dec. 3** **Black Overprint**

**65** A4 2c rose 2.50 2.50
*a.* "PANAMA" 15mm long 3.50
*b.* Violet bar 5.00
**66** A4 5c blue 100.00
*a.* "PANAMA" 15mm long 100.00
**67** A4 10c yellow 2.50 2.50
*a.* "PANAMA" 15mm long 6.00
*b.* Horizontal overprint 17.50

**Gray Black Overprint**

**68** A4 2c rose 2.00 2.00
*a.* "PANAMA" 15mm long 2.50

**Carmine Overprint**

**69** A4 5c blue 2.50 2.50
*a.* "PANAMA" 15mm long 3.50
*b.* Bar only 75.00 75.00
*c.* Double overprint
**70** A4 20c violet 7.50 6.50
*a.* "PANAMA" 15mm long 10.00
*b.* Double overprint, one in black 150.00
*Nos. 65,67-70 (5)* 17.00 16.00

This overprint was set up to cover fifty stamps. "PANAMA" is normally 13mm long and 1¾mm high but, in two rows in each sheet, it measures 15 to 16mm.

This word may be found with one or more of the letters taller than usual; with one, two or three inverted "V's" instead of "A's"; with an inverted "Y" instead of "A"; an inverted "N"; an "A" with accent; and a fancy "P."

Owing to misplaced impressions, stamps exist with "PANAMA" once only, twice on one side, or three times.

Overprinted in Red

**1903, Dec.**

**71** A4 1c green .75 .60
*a.* "PANAMA" 15mm long 1.25
*b.* "PANAMA" reading down 3.00 .75
*c.* "PANAMA" reading up and down 3.00
*d.* Double overprint 8.00
**72** A4 2c rose .50 .40
*a.* "PANAMA" 15mm long 1.00
*b.* "PANAMA" reading down .75 .50
*c.* "PANAMA" reading up and down 4.00
*d.* Double overprint 8.00
**73** A4 20c violet 1.50 1.00
*a.* "PANAMA" 15mm long 2.25
*b.* "PANAMA" reading down
*c.* "PANAMA" reading up and down 8.00 8.00
*d.* Double overprint 18.00 18.00
**74** A4 50c bister brn 3.00 2.50
*a.* "PANAMA" 15mm long 5.00
*b.* "PANAMA" reading up and down 12.00 12.00
*c.* Double overprint 6.00 6.00
**75** A4 1p lake 6.00 4.50
*a.* "PANAMA" 15mm long 6.25
*b.* "PANAMA" reading up and down 15.00 15.00
*c.* Double overprint 15.00
*d.* Inverted overprint 25.00
*Nos. 71-75 (5)* 11.75 9.00

This setting appears to be a re-arrangement (or two very similar re-arrangements) of the previous overprint. The overprint covers fifty stamps. "PANAMA" usually reads upward but sheets of the 1, 2 and 20c exist with the word reading upward on one half the sheet and downward on the other half.

In one re-arrangement one stamp in fifty has the word reading in both directions. Nearly all the varieties of the previous overprint are repeated in this setting excepting the inverted "Y" and fancy "P." There are also additional varieties of large letters and "PANAMA" occasionally has an "A" missing or inverted. There are misplaced impressions, as the previous setting.

Overprinted in Red

**1904-05**

**76** A4 1c green .25 .25
*a.* Both words reading up 1.50
*b.* Both words reading down 2.75
*c.* Double overprint
*d.* Pair, one without overprint 15.00
*e.* "PANAAM" 20.00
*f.* Inverted "M" in "PANAMA" 5.00
**77** A4 2c rose .25 .25
*a.* Both words reading up 2.50
*b.* Both words reading down 2.50
*c.* Double overprint 10.00
*d.* Double overprint, one inverted 14.00
*e.* Inverted "M" in "PANAMA" 5.00
**78** A4 5c blue .30 .25
*a.* Both words reading up 3.00
*b.* Both words reading down 4.25
*c.* Inverted overprint 12.50
*d.* "PANAAM" 25.00
*e.* "PANANA" 8.00
*f.* "PAMANA" 5.00
*g.* Inverted "M" in "PANAMA" 5.00
*h.* Double overprint 20.00
**79** A4 10c yellow .30 .25
*a.* Both words reading up 5.00
*b.* Both words reading down 5.00
*c.* Double overprint 15.00
*d.* Inverted overprint 6.75
*e.* "PAMANA" 8.00
*f.* Inverted "M" in "PANAMA" 15.00
*g.* Red brown overprint 7.50 3.50
**80** A4 20c violet 2.00 1.00
*a.* Both words reading up 5.00
*b.* Both words reading down 10.00
**81** A4 50c bister brn 2.00 1.60
*a.* Both words reading up 10.50
*b.* Both words reading down 10.00
*c.* Double overprint
**82** A4 1p lake 5.00 5.00
*a.* Both words reading up 12.50
*b.* Both words reading down 12.50
*c.* Double overprint
*d.* Double overprint, one inverted 20.00
*e.* Inverted "M" in "PANAMA" 45.00
*Nos. 76-82 (7)* 10.10 8.60

This overprint is also set up to cover fifty stamps. One stamp in each fifty has "PANAMA" reading upward at both sides. Another has the word reading downward at both sides, a third has an inverted "V" in place of the last "A" and a fourth has a small thick "N." In a resetting all these varieties are corrected except the inverted "V." There are misplaced overprints as before.

Later printings show other varieties and have the bar 2½mm instead of 2mm wide. The colors of the various printings of Nos. 76-82 range from carmine to almost pink.

Experts consider the black overprint on the 50c to be speculative.

The 20c violet and 50c bister brown exist with bar 2½mm wide, including the error "PAMANA," but are not known to have been issued. Some examples have been canceled "to oblige."

**Issued in Colon**

Handstamped in Magenta or Violet

**1903-04** **On Stamps of 1892-96**

**101** A4 1c green .75 .75
**102** A4 2c rose .75 .75
**103** A4 5c blue 1.00 1.00
**104** A4 10c yellow 3.50 3.00
**105** A4 20c violet 8.00 6.50
**106** A4 1p lake 80.00 70.00

**On Stamps of 1887-92**

**Ordinary Wove Paper**

**107** A3 50c brown 25.00 20.00
*Nos. 101-107 (7)* 119.00 102.00

**Pelure Paper**

**108** A3 50c brown 70.00

Handstamped in Magenta, Violet or Red

**On Stamps of 1892-96**

**109** A4 1c green 5.50 5.00
**110** A4 2c rose 5.50 5.00
**111** A4 5c blue 5.50 5.00
**112** A4 10c yellow 8.25 7.00
**113** A4 20c violet 12.00 9.00
**114** A4 1p lake 70.00 60.00

**On Stamps of 1887-92**

**Ordinary Wove Paper**

**115** A3 50c brown 35.00 25.00
*Nos. 109-115 (7)* 141.75 116.00

**Pelure Paper**

**116** A3 50c brown 50.00 37.50

The first note after No. 64 applies also to Nos. 101-116.

The handstamps on Nos. 109-116 have been counterfeited.

Stamps with this overprint were a private speculation. They exist on cover. The overprint was to be used on postal cards.

Overprinted On Stamps Of 1892-96

**On Stamps of 1892-96**

**Carmine Overprint**

**129** A4 1c green .40 .40
*a.* Inverted overprint 6.00
*b.* Double overprint 2.25
*c.* Double overprint, one inverted 6.00
**130** A4 5c blue .50 .50

**Brown Overprint**

**131** A4 1c green 12.00
*a.* Double overprint, one inverted

**Black Overprint**

**132** A4 1c green 60.00 30.00
*a.* Vertical overprint 42.50
*b.* Inverted overprint 42.50
*c.* Double overprint, one inverted 42.50
**133** A4 2c rose .50 .50
*a.* Inverted overprint
**134** A4 10c yellow .50 .50
*a.* Inverted overprint 4.00
*b.* Double overprint 16.00
*c.* Double overprint, one inverted 6.00
**135** A4 20c violet .50 .50
*a.* Inverted overprint 4.00
*b.* Double overprint 5.50
**136** A4 1p lake 16.00 14.00

**On Stamps of 1887-88**

**Blue Overprint**

**Ordinary Wove Paper**

**137** A3 50c brown 3.00 3.00

**Pelure Paper**

**138** A3 50c brown 3.00 3.00
*a.* Double overprint 14.00

This overprint is set up to cover fifty stamps. In each fifty there are four stamps without accent on the last "a" of "Panama," one with accent on the "a" of "Republica" and one with a thick, upright "i."

Overprinted in Carmine

**On Stamp of 1892-96**

**139** A4 20c violet *200.00*
*a.* Double overprint

Unknown with genuine cancels.

**Issued in Bocas del Toro**

Stamps of 1892-96 Overprinted Handstamped in Violet

**1903-04**

**151** A4 1c green 20.00 14.00
**152** A4 2c rose 20.00 14.00
**153** A4 5c blue 25.00 16.00
**154** A4 10c yellow 15.00 8.25
**155** A4 20c violet 50.00 30.00
**156** A4 50c bister brn 100.00 55.00
**157** A4 1p lake 140.00 110.00
*Nos. 151-157 (7)* 370.00 247.25

The handstamp is known double and inverted. Counterfeits exist.

Handstamped in Violet

**158** A4 1c green *100.00*
**159** A4 2c rose *70.00*
**160** A4 5c blue *80.00*
**161** A4 10c yellow *100.00*
*Nos. 158-161 (4)* *350.00*

This handstamp was applied to these 4 stamps only by favor, experts state. Counterfeits are numerous. The 1p exists only as a counterfeit.

**General Issues**

A5

**1905, Feb. 4** **Engr.** ***Perf. 12***

**179** A5 1c green .60 .40
**180** A5 2c rose .80 .50

Panama's Declaration of Independence from the Colombian Republic, Nov. 3, 1903.

Surcharged in Vermilion on Stamps of 1892-96 Issue

**1906**

**181** A4 1c on 20c violet .25 .25
*a.* "Panrma" 2.25 2.25
*b.* "Pnnama" 2.25 2.25
*c.* "Pauama" 2.25 2.25
*d.* Inverted surcharge 4.00 4.00
*e.* Double surcharge 3.50 3.50
*f.* Double surcharge, one inverted

Stamps of 1892-96 Surcharged in Vermilion

**182** A4 2c on 50c bister brn .25 .25
*a.* 3rd "A" of "PANAMA" inverted 2.25 2.25
*b.* Both "PANAMA" reading down 4.00 4.00
*c.* Double surcharge
*d.* Inverted surcharge 2.50

The 2c on 20c violet was never issued to the public. All examples are inverted. Value, 75c.

**Carmine Surcharge**

**183** A4 5c on 1p lake .60 .40
*a.* Both "PANAMA" reading down 6.00 6.00
*b.* "5" omitted
*c.* Double surcharge
*d.* Inverted surcharge
*e.* 3rd "A" of "PANAMA" inverted 5.50 5.50

**On Stamp of 1903-04, No. 75**

**184** A4 5c on 1p lake .60 .40
*a.* "PANAMA" 15mm long
*b.* "PANAMA" reading up and down
*c.* Both "PANAMA" reading down
*d.* Inverted surcharge
*e.* Double surcharge
*f.* 3rd "A" of "PANAMA" inverted
*Nos. 181-184 (4)* 1.70 1.30

National Flag — A6

Vasco Núñez de Balboa — A7

Fernández de Córdoba — A8

Coat of Arms — A9

Justo Arosemena A10

Manuel J. Hurtado A11

José de Obaldía — A12

Tomás Herrera — A13

José de Fábrega — A14

**1906-07 Engr. *Perf. 11½***

| No. | Type | Description | Unused | Used |
|---|---|---|---|---|
| **185** | A6 | ½c orange & multi | .70 | .35 |
| **186** | A7 | 1c dk green & blk ('07) | .70 | .35 |
| **187** | A8 | 2c scarlet & blk | 1.00 | .35 |
| **188** | A9 | 2½c red orange | 1.00 | .35 |
| **189** | A10 | 5c blue & black | 1.75 | .35 |
| *a.* | | 5c ultramarine & black | 2.00 | .50 |
| **190** | A11 | 8c purple & blk | 1.50 | .65 |
| **191** | A12 | 10c violet & blk | 1.50 | .50 |
| **192** | A13 | 25c brown & blk | 3.50 | 1.10 |
| **193** | A14 | 50c black | 9.00 | 3.50 |
| | | *Nos. 185-193 (9)* | 20.65 | 7.50 |

Inverted centers exist of Nos. 185-187, 189, 189a, 190-193, Value, each $25. Nos. 185-193 exist imperf.

For surcharge see No. F29.

Issued: Nos. 185, 188-193, 11/20; No. 187, 9/1.

Map — A17

Balboa — A18

Córdoba — A19

Arms — A20

Arosemena A21

Obaldía A23

**1909-16 *Perf. 12***

| No. | Type | Description | Unused | Used |
|---|---|---|---|---|
| **195** | A17 | ½c org ('11) | 1.00 | .30 |
| **196** | A17 | ½c rose ('15) | .70 | .60 |
| **197** | A18 | 1c dk grn & blk | 1.00 | .50 |
| *a.* | | Inverted center | 7,500. | 7,500. |
| *b.* | | Booklet pane of 6 ('16) | *160.00* | |
| | | Complete booklet, 4 #197b | | — |
| **198** | A19 | 2c ver & blk | 1.00 | .30 |
| *a.* | | Booklet pane of 6 | *160.00* | |
| **199** | A20 | 2½c red orange | 1.50 | .30 |
| **200** | A21 | 5c blue & blk | 2.00 | .30 |
| *a.* | | Booklet pane of 6 ('16) | *350.00* | |
| **201** | A23 | 10c violet & blk | 3.75 | 1.10 |
| | | Complete booklet, panes of 6 (3x2) of #195 (3), 197 (3), 199 (2), 200, 201 ('11) | | — |
| | | *Nos. 195-201 (7)* | 10.95 | 3.40 |

Value for No. 197a used is for an off-center example with faults.

The panes contained in the booklet listed following No. 201 are marginal blocks of 6 (3x2), without gum, stapled within the booklet cover, with advertising paper interleaving. The complete booklet was sold for B1.50.

Nos. 197b and 198a are gummed panes of 6 (2x3), imperf on outside edges.

For overprints and surcharges see #H23, I4-I7.

Balboa Sighting Pacific Ocean, His Dog "Leoncico" at His Feet — A24

**1913, Sept. 1**

| No. | Type | Description | Unused | Used |
|---|---|---|---|---|
| **202** | A24 | 2½c dk grn & yel grn | 1.75 | .65 |

400th anniv. of Balboa's discovery of the Pacific Ocean.

**Panama-Pacific Exposition Issue**

Chorrera Falls — A25

Map of Panama Canal — A26

Balboa Taking Possession of the Pacific A27

Ruins of Cathedral of Old Panama A28

Palace of Arts — A29

Gatun Locks — A30

Culebra Cut — A31

Santo Domingo Monastery's Flat Arch — A32

**1915, Mar. 1 *Perf. 12***

| No. | Type | Description | Unused | Used |
|---|---|---|---|---|
| **204** | A25 | ½c ol grn & blk | .40 | .30 |
| **205** | A26 | 1c dk grn & blk | .95 | .30 |
| **206** | A27 | 2c car & blk | .75 | .30 |
| *a.* | | 2c ver & blk ('16) | .75 | .30 |
| **208** | A28 | 2½c scarlet & blk | .95 | .35 |
| **209** | A29 | 3c violet & blk | 1.60 | .55 |
| **210** | A30 | 5c blue & blk | 2.10 | .35 |
| *a.* | | Center inverted | 1,500. | 650.00 |
| **211** | A31 | 10c orange & blk | 2.10 | .70 |
| **212** | A32 | 20c brown & blk | 10.50 | 3.25 |
| *a.* | | Center inverted | 300.00 | — |
| | | *Nos. 204-212 (8)* | 19.35 | 6.10 |

For surcharges and overprints see Nos. 217, 233, E1-E2.

Manuel J. Hurtado — A33

**1916**

| No. | Type | Description | Unused | Used |
|---|---|---|---|---|
| **213** | A33 | 8c violet & blk | 9.00 | 4.25 |

For surcharge see No. F30.

S. S. Panama in Culebra Cut Aug. 11, 1914 A34

S. S. Panama in Culebra Cut Aug. 11, 1914 A35

S. S. Cristobal in Gatun Lock — A36

**1918, Aug. 23**

| No. | Type | Description | Unused | Used |
|---|---|---|---|---|
| **214** | A34 | 12c purple & blk | 15.00 | 5.75 |
| **215** | A35 | 15c brt blue & blk | 10.00 | 3.50 |
| **216** | A36 | 24c yellow brn & blk | 15.00 | 3.50 |
| | | *Nos. 214-216 (3)* | 40.00 | 12.75 |

No. 208 Surcharged in Dark Blue

**1919, Aug. 15**

| No. | Type | Description | Unused | Used |
|---|---|---|---|---|
| **217** | A28 | 2c on 2½c scar & blk | .35 | .35 |
| *a.* | | Inverted surcharge | 11.00 | 5.00 |
| *b.* | | Double surcharge | 15.00 | 6.00 |

City of Panama, 400th anniversary.

Dry Dock at Balboa A38

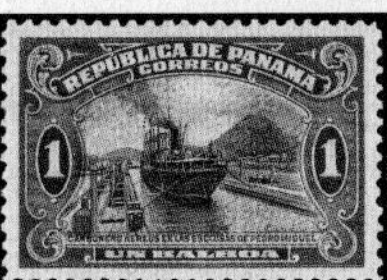
Ship in Pedro Miguel Lock — A39

**1920, Sept. 1 Engr.**

| No. | Type | Description | Unused | Used |
|---|---|---|---|---|
| **218** | A38 | 50c orange & blk | 30.00 | 22.50 |
| **219** | A39 | 1b dk violet & blk | 40.00 | 27.50 |

For overprint and surcharge see Nos. C6, C37.

Arms of Panama City — A40

José Vallarino — A41

"Land Gate" — A42

Simón Bolivar — A43

Statue of Cervantes — A44

Bolívar's Tribute — A45

Carlos de Ycaza — A46

Municipal Building in 1821 and 1921 — A47

Statue of Balboa — A48

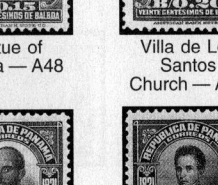

Villa de Los Santos Church — A49

Herrera — A50

Fábrega — A51

**1921, Nov.**

220 A40 ½c orange .80 .25
221 A41 1c green 1.00 .25
222 A42 2c carmine 1.25 .25
223 A43 2½c red 2.75 1.10
224 A44 3c dull violet 2.75 1.10
225 A45 5c blue 2.75 .35
226 A46 8c olive green 10.00 3.50
227 A47 10c violet 6.75 1.50
228 A48 15c lt blue 8.00 2.00
229 A49 20c olive brown 14.50 3.50
230 A50 24c black brown 14.50 4.25
231 A51 50c black 25.00 8.00
*Nos. 220-231 (12)* 90.05 26.05

Centenary of independence.
For overprints and surcharges see Nos. 264, 275-276, 299, 304, 308-310, C35.

Hurtado — A52

**1921, Nov. 28**

232 A52 2c dark green .65 .65

Manuel José Hurtado (1821-1887), president and folklore writer.
For overprints see Nos. 258, 301.

No. 208 Surcharged in Black

**1923**

233 A28 2c on 2½c scar & blk .45 .45
a. "1923" omitted 4.00
b. Bar over "CENTESIMOS" 4.00
c. Inverted surcharge 4.00
d. Double surcharge 4.00
e. Pair, one without surcharge 4.00

Two stamps in each sheet have a bar above "CENTESIMOS" (No. 233b).

Arms — A53

**1924, May** **Engr.**

234 A53 ½c orange .25 .25
235 A53 1c dark green .25 .25
236 A53 2c carmine .25 .25
237 A53 5c dark blue .45 .25
238 A53 10c dark violet .60 .25
239 A53 12c olive green .75 .40
240 A53 15c ultra .95 .40
241 A53 24c yellow brown 1.90 .60
242 A53 50c orange 4.50 1.10
243 A53 1b black 6.75 2.50
*Nos. 234-243 (10)* 16.65 6.25

For overprints & surcharges see Nos. 277, 321A, 331-338, 352, C19-C20, C68, RA5, RA10-RA22.

Bolívar — A54

Statue of Bolívar — A55

Bolívar Hall — A56

**1926, June 10** ***Perf. 12½***

244 A54 ½c orange .55 .25
245 A54 1c dark green .55 .25
246 A54 2c scarlet .70 .30
247 A54 4c gray .90 .35
248 A54 5c dark blue 1.40 .50
249 A55 8c lilac 2.25 .80
250 A55 10c dull violet 1.60 .80
251 A55 12c olive green 2.50 1.00
252 A55 15c ultra 3.25 1.25
253 A55 20c brown 6.75 1.60
254 A56 24c black violet 8.00 2.00
255 A56 50c black 13.50 5.00
*Nos. 244-255 (12)* 41.95 14.10

Bolivar Congress centennial.
For surcharges and overprints see Nos. 259-263, 266-267, 274, 298, 300, 302-303, 305-307, C33-C34, C36, C38-C39.

Lindbergh's Airplane, "The Spirit of St. Louis" — A57

Lindbergh's Airplane and Map of Panama — A58

**1928, Jan. 9** **Typo.** ***Rouletted 7***

256 A57 2c dk red & blk, *salmon* .40 .25
257 A58 5c dk blue, *grn* .60 .40

Visit of Colonel Charles A. Lindbergh to Central America by airplane.
No. 256 has black overprint.

No. 232 Overprinted in Red

**1928, Nov. 1** ***Perf. 12***

258 A52 2c dark green .25 .25

25th anniversary of the Republic.

No. 247 Surcharged in Black

**1930, Dec. 17** ***Perf. 12½, 13***

259 A54 1c on 4c gray .25 .25

Centenary of the death of Simón Bolívar, the Liberator.

Nos. 244-246 Overprinted in Red or Blue

**1932** ***Perf. 12½***

260 A54 ½c orange (R) .25 .25
261 A54 1c dark green (R) .35 .25
a. Double overprint 18.00
262 A54 2c scarlet (Bl) .35 .25

No. 252 Surcharged in Red

263 A55 10c on 15c ultra 1.00 .50
a. Double surcharge 55.00
*Nos. 260-263 (4)* 1.95 1.25

**No. 220 Overprinted as in 1932 in Black**

**1933, May 25** ***Perf. 12***

**Overprint 19mm Long**

264 A40 ½c orange .35 .25
a. Overprint 17mm long —

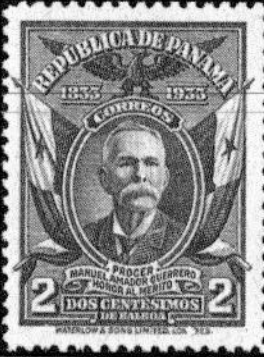

Dr. Manuel Amador Guerrero — A60

**1933, June 30** **Engr.** ***Perf. 12½***

265 A60 2c dark red .50 .25

Centenary of the birth of Dr. Manuel Amador Guerrero, founder of the Republic of Panama and its first President.

No. 251 Surcharged in Red

**1933**

266 A55 10c on 12c olive grn 1.25 .65

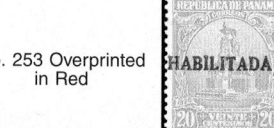

No. 253 Overprinted in Red

267 A55 20c brown 2.25 1.75

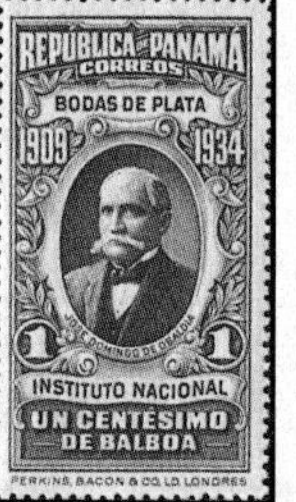

José Domingo de Obaldía — A61

Quotation from Emerson — A63

National Institute — A64

Designs: 2c, Eusebio A. Morales. 12c, Justo A. Facio. 15c, Pablo Arosemena.

**1934, July 24** **Engr.** ***Perf. 14***

268 A61 1c dark green 1.00 .50
269 A61 2c scarlet 1.00 .45
270 A63 5c dark blue 1.25 .80
271 A64 10c brown 3.25 1.50
272 A61 12c yellow green 6.50 2.00
273 A61 15c Prus blue 8.50 2.50
*Nos. 268-273 (6)* 21.50 7.75

25th anniv. of the Natl. Institute.

Nos. 248, 227 Overprinted in Black or Red

**1935-36** ***Perf. 12½, 12***

274 A54 5c dark blue .90 .30
275 A47 10c violet (R) ('36) 1.25 .60

No. 225 Surcharged in Red

**1936. Sept. 19** ***Perf. 11½***

276 A45 1c on 5c blue .40 .40
a. Lines of surcharge 1½mm btwn. 6.50

No. 241 Surcharged in Blue

**1936, Sept. 24** ***Perf. 12***

277 A53 2c on 24c yellow brn .60 .50
a. Double surcharge 20.00

Centenary of the birth of Pablo Arosemena, president of Panama in 1910-12. See Nos. C19-C20.

Panama Cathedral A67

Designs: ½c, Ruins of Custom House, Portobelo. 1c, Panama Tree. 2c, "La Pollera." 5c, Simon Bolivar. 10c, Cathedral Tower Ruins. Old Panama. 15c, Francisco Garcia y Santos, 20c, Madden Dam, Panama Canal. 25c, Columbus. 50c, Gaillard Cut. 1b, Panama Cathedral.

**1936, Dec. 1** **Engr.** ***Perf. 11½***

278 A67 ½c yellow org .55 .25
279 A67 1c blue green .55 .25
280 A67 2c carmine rose .55 .25
281 A67 5c blue .80 .50
282 A67 10c dk violet 1.75 .75
283 A67 15c turq blue 1.75 .75
284 A67 20c red 2.00 1.50
285 A67 25c black brn 3.50 2.00
286 A67 50c orange 7.75 5.00
287 A67 1b black 18.00 12.00
*Nos. 278-287,C21-C26 (16)* 62.70 40.00

4th Postal Congress of the Americas and Spain.

Stamps of 1936 Overprinted in Red or Blue

**1937, Mar. 9**

288 A67 ½c yellow org (R) .35 .30
a. Inverted overprint 25.00
289 A67 1c blue green (R) .45 .25
290 A67 2c car rose (Bl) .45 .25
291 A67 5c blue (R) .70 .25
292 A67 10c dk vio (R) 1.10 .35
293 A67 15c turq bl (R) 5.25 3.25
294 A67 20c red (Bl) 2.00 1.25
295 A67 25c black brn (R) 2.75 1.25
296 A67 50c orange (Bl) 9.00 6.00
297 A67 1b black (R) 14.50 10.00
*Nos. 288-297,C27-C32 (16)* 84.60 54.15

Stamps of 1921-26 Overprinted in Red or Blue

**1937, July** *Perf. 12, 12½*

**298** A54 ½c orange (R) 1.10 .80
*a.* Inverted overprint 30.00
**299** A41 1c green (R) .35 .25
*a.* Inverted overprint 30.00
**300** A54 1c dk green (R) .35 .25
**301** A52 2c dk green (R) .45 .35
**302** A54 2c scarlet (Bl) .55 .35

Stamps of 1921-26 Surcharged in Red

**303** A54 2c on 4c gray .70 .45
**304** A46 2c on 8c ol grn .70 .60
**305** A55 2c on 8c lilac .70 .45
**306** A55 2c on 10c dl vio .70 .50
**307** A55 2c on 12c ol grn .70 .45
**308** A48 2c on 15c lt blue .70 .60
**309** A50 2c on 24c blk brn .70 .75
**310** A51 2c on 50c black .70 .35
*Nos. 298-310 (13)* 8.40 6.15

Ricardo Arango A77

Juan A. Guizado A78

La Concordia Fire — A79

Modern Fire Fighting Equipment A80

Firemen's Monument A81

David H. Brandon A82

*Perf. 14x14½, 14½x14*

**1937, Nov. 25** **Photo.** **Wmk. 233**

**311** A77 ½c orange red 2.10 .35
**312** A78 1c green 2.10 .35
**313** A79 2c red 2.10 .25
**314** A80 5c brt blue 4.00 .50
**315** A81 10c purple 7.25 1.25
**316** A82 12c yellow grn 11.50 2.00
*Nos. 311-316,C40-C42 (9)* 49.30 7.05

50th anniversary of the Fire Department.

Old Panama Cathedral Tower and Statue of Liberty Enlightening the World, Flags of Panama and US — A83

**Engr. & Litho.**

**1938, Dec. 7** **Unwmk.** *Perf. 12½*

**Center in Black; Flags in Red and Ultramarine**

**317** A83 1c deep green .35 .25
**318** A83 2c carmine .55 .25
**319** A83 5c blue .80 .30
**320** A83 12c olive 1.40 .75
**321** A83 15c brt ultra 1.75 1.25
*Nos. 317-321,C49-C53 (10)* 22.45 15.35

150th anniv. of the US Constitution.

No. 236 Overprinted in Black

**1938, June 5** *Perf. 12*

**321A** A53 2c carmine .45 .25
*b.* Inverted overprint 22.50
*Nos. 321A,C53A-C53B (3)* 1.25 1.05

Opening of the Normal School at Santiago, Veraguas Province, June 5, 1938.

Gatun Lake — A84

Designs: 1c, Pedro Miguel Locks. 2c, Allegory. 5c, Culebra Cut. 10c, Ferryboat. 12c, Aerial View of Canal. 15c, Gen. William C. Gorgas. 50c, Dr. Manuel A. Guerrero. 1b, Woodrow Wilson.

**1939, Aug. 15** **Engr.** *Perf. 12½*

**322** A84 ½c yellow .35 .25
**323** A84 1c dp blue grn .55 .25
**324** A84 2c dull rose .65 .25
**325** A84 5c dull blue 1.00 .25
**326** A84 10c dk violet 1.10 .35
**327** A84 12c olive green 1.10 .50
**328** A84 15c ultra 1.10 .80
**329** A84 50c orange 2.75 1.60
**330** A84 1b dk brown 5.75 3.00
*Nos. 322-330,C54-C61 (17)* 34.35 14.45

25th anniversary of the opening of the Panama Canal. For surcharges see Nos. C64, G2.

Stamps of 1924 Overprinted in Black or Red

**1941, Jan. 2** *Perf. 12*

**331** A53 ½c orange .35 .25
**332** A53 1c dk grn (R) .35 .30
**333** A53 2c carmine .35 .25
**334** A53 5c dk bl (R) .55 .30
**335** A53 10c dk vio (R) .80 .50
**336** A53 15c ultra (R) 1.75 .65
**337** A53 50c dp org 6.25 3.50
**338** A53 1b blk (R) 14.50 6.00
*Nos. 331-338,C67-C71 (13)* 49.90 31.25

New Panama constitution, effective 1/241.

Black Overprint

**1942, Feb. 19** **Engr.**

**339** A93 10c purple 1.40 1.00

**Surcharged with New Value**

**340** A93 2c on 5c dk bl 1.75 .50
*Nos. 339-340,C72 (3)* 7.15 4.00

Flags of Panama and Costa Rica A94

**Engraved and Lithographed**

**1942, April 25**

**341** A94 2c rose red, dk bl & dp rose .30 .25

1st anniv. of the settlement of the Costa Rica-Panama border dispute. See No. C73.

National Emblems — A95

Farm Girl in Work Dress — A96

Cart Laden with Sugar Cane (Inscribed "ACARRERO DE CAÑA") — A97

Balboa Taking Possession of the Pacific A98

Golden Altar of San José — A99

San Blas Indian Woman and Child — A101

Santo Tomas Hospital A100

Modern Highway A102

**Engr.; Flag on ½c Litho.**

**1942, May 11**

**342** A95 ½c dl vio, bl & car .25 .25
**343** A96 1c dk green .25 .25
**344** A97 2c vermilion .25 .25
**345** A98 5c dp bl & blk .25 .25
**346** A99 10c car rose & org .65 .25
**347** A100 15c lt bl & blk 1.00 .50
**348** A101 50c org red & ol blk 2.50 1.00
**349** A102 1b black 3.50 1.00
*Nos. 342-349 (8)* 8.65 3.75

See Nos. 357, 365, 376-377, 380, 395, 409.

For surcharges and overprints see Nos. 366-370, 373-375, 378-379, 381, 387-388, 396, C129-C130, RA23.

**Catalogue values for unused stamps in this section, from this point to the end of the section, are for Never Hinged items.**

Flag of Panama — A103

Arms of Panama — A104

**Engraved; Flag on 2c Lithographed**

**1947, Apr. 7** **Unwmk.** *Perf. 12½*

**350** A103 2c car, bl & red .25 .25
**351** A104 5c deep blue .25 .25

Natl. Constitutional Assembly of 1945, 2nd anniv.

No. 241 Surcharged in Black

**1947, Oct. 29** *Perf. 12*

**352** A53 50c on 24c yel brn 2.00 1.50
*a.* "Habiitada" 2.00 2.00

Nos. C6C, C75, C74 and C87 Surcharged in Black or Carmine

**353** AP5 ½c on 8c gray blk .25 .25
*a.* "B/.0.0½ CORREOS" (transposed) 2.50 2.50
**354** AP34 ½c on 8c dk ol brn & blk (C) .25 .25
**355** AP34 1c on 7c rose car .25 .25
**356** AP42 2c on 8c vio .25 .25
*Nos. 352-356 (5)* 3.00 2.50

**Flag Type of 1942**

**1948** **Engr. and Litho.**

**357** A95 ½c car, org, bl & dp car .25 .25

Monument to Firemen of Colon — A105

American-La France Fire Engine — A106

20c, Firemen & hose cart. 25c, New Central Fire Station, Colon. 50c, Maximino Walker. 1b, J. J. A. Ducruet.

**1948, June 10** **Engr.**

**Center in Black**

**358** A105 5c dp car .65 .25
**359** A106 10c orange .90 .25
**360** A106 20c gray bl 1.75 .40
**361** A106 25c chocolate 1.75 .70

**362** A105 50c purple 3.50 .70
**363** A105 1b dp grn 5.00 1.50
*Nos. 358-363 (6)* 13.55 3.80

50th anniversary of the founding of the Colon Fire Department.
For overprint see No. C125.

Cervantes A107

**1948, Nov. 15 Unwmk. *Perf. 12½***
**364** A107 2c car & blk .80 .25
*Nos. 364,C105-C106 (3)* 2.25 .75

Miguel de Cervantes Saavedra, novelist, playwright and poet, 400th birth anniv.

**Oxcart Type of 1942 Redrawn**
Inscribed: "ACARREO DE CANA"

**1948 *Perf. 12***
**365** A97 2c vermilion .60 .25

**No. 365 Surcharged or Overprinted in Black**

**1949, May 26**
**366** A97 1c on 2c ver .25 .25
**367** A97 2c vermilion .25 .25
*a.* Inverted overprint 10.00 5.00
*Nos. 366-367,C108-C111 (6)* 3.90 3.90

Incorporation of Chiriqui Province, cent.

**Stamps and Types of 1942-48 Issues Overprinted in Black or Red**

**1949, Sept. 9 Engr.**
**368** A96 1c dk green .25 .25
**369** A97 2c ver (#365) .45 .25
**370** A98 5c blue (R) .70 .25
*Nos. 368-370,C114-C118 (8)* 8.70 4.55

75th anniv. of the UPU.
Overprint on No. 368 is slightly different and smaller, 15½x12mm.

Francisco Javier de Luna — A108

**1949, Dec. 7 *Perf. 12½***
**371** A108 2c car & blk .25 .25

200th anniversary of the founding of the University of San Javier. See No. C119.

Dr. Carlos J. Finlay — A109

**1950, Jan. 12 Unwmk. *Perf. 12***
**372** A109 2c car & gray blk .45 .25

Issued to honor Dr. Carlos J. Finlay (1833-1915), Cuban physician and biologist who found that a mosquito transmitted yellow fever. See No. C120.

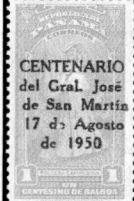

Nos. 343, 357 and 345, Overprinted or Surcharged in Carmine or Black

**1950, Aug. 17**
**373** A96 1c dk green .25 .25
**374** A95 2c on ½c car, org, bl & dp car (Bk) .25 .25
**375** A98 5c dp bl & blk .30 .25
*Nos. 373-375,C121-C125 (8)* 5.65 3.75

Gen. José de San Martin, death cent.
The overprint is in four lines on No. 375.

**Types of 1942**

**1950, Oct. 13 Engr.**
**376** A97 2c ver & blk .25 .25
**377** A98 5c blue .25 .25

No. 376 is inscribed "ACARREO DE CANA."

**Nos. 376 and 377 Overprinted in Green or Carmine**

**1951, Sept. 26**
**378** A97 2c ver & blk (G) .25 .25
*a.* Inverted overprint 20.00 20.00
*b.* First line omitted, second line repeated 20.00 20.00
**379** A98 5c blue (C) .45 .25
*a.* Inverted overprint 20.00 20.00

St. Jean-Baptiste de la Salle, 500th birth anniv.

**Altar Type of 1942**

**1952 Engr. *Perf. 12***
**380** A99 10c pur & org .75 .25

No. 357 Surcharged in Black

**1952, Oct. 29**
**381** A95 1c on ½c multi .25 .25

Queen Isabella I and Arms — A110

**1952, Oct. 20 Engr. *Perf. 12½***
**Center in Black**
**382** A110 1c green .45 .25
**383** A110 2c carmine .45 .25
**384** A110 5c dk bl .45 .25
**385** A110 10c purple .70 .25
*Nos. 382-385,C131-C136 (10)* 15.35 5.70

Queen Isabella I of Spain. 500th birth anniv.

**No. 380 and Type of 1942 Srchd. "B/ .0.01 1953" in Black or Carmine**

**1953 *Perf. 12***
**387** A99 1c on 10c pur & org .25 .25
**388** A100 1c on 15c black (C) .25 .25

Issued: No. 387, 4/22; No. 388, 9/4.
A similar surcharge on No. 346 was privately applied.

A111

A112

2c, Baptism of the Flag. 5c, Manuel Amador Guerrero & Senora de Amador. 12c, Santos Jorge A. & Jeronimo de la Ossa. 20c, Revolutionary Junta. 50c, Old city hall. 1b, Natl. coinage.

**1953, Nov. 2 Engr. *Perf. 12***
**389** A111 2c purple .45 .25
**390** A112 5c red orange .55 .25
**391** A112 12c dp red vio 1.25 .25
**392** A112 20c slate gray 2.25 .25
**393** A111 50c org yel 3.50 .60
**394** A112 1b blue 5.75 1.25
*Nos. 389-394 (6)* 13.75 2.85

Founding of the Republic of Panama, 50th anniv.
See #C140-C145. For surcharge see #413.

**Farm Girl Type of 1942**

**1954 Unwmk. *Perf. 12***
**395** A96 1c dp car rose .25 .25

Surcharged in Black

**396** A96 3c on 1c dp car rose .25 .25

Issued: No. 395, 4/21; No. 396, 6/21.

Monument to Gen. Tomas Herrera — A113

**1954, Dec. 4 Litho. *Perf. 12½***
**397** A113 3c purple .25 .25
*Nos. 397,C148-C149 (3)* 4.50 2.75

Gen. Tomas Herrera, death cent.

Tocumen International Airport A114

**1955, Apr. 16**
**398** A114 ½c org brn .45 .25

For surcharges see Nos. 411-412.

General Remon Cantera, 1908-1955 — A115

**1955, June 1**
**399** A115 3c lilac rose & blk .25 .25

See No. C153.

Victor de la Guardia y Ayala and Miguel Chiari A116

**1955, Sept. 12**
**400** A116 5c violet .35 .25

Centenary of province of Coclé.

Ferdinand de Lesseps — A117

First Excavation of Panama Canal A118

Design: 50c, Theodore Roosevelt.

**1955, Nov. 22**
**401** A117 3c rose brn, *rose* .55 .25
**402** A118 25c vio bl, *lt bl* 2.25 1.40
**403** A117 50c vio, *lt vio* 3.00 1.50
*Nos. 401-403,C155-C156 (5)* 11.15 5.90

Ferdinand de Lesseps, 150th birth anniv., French promoter connected with building of Panama Canal. 75th anniv. of the 1st French excavations.
Imperfs exist, but were not sold at any post office.

**Popes**

A set of twelve stamps picturing various Popes exists. Value, approximately $100.

Arms of Panama City — A119

*Perf. 12½*

**1956, Aug. 17 Litho. Unwmk.**

**404** A119 3c green .25 .25

Sixth Inter-American Congress of Municipalities, Panama City, Aug. 14-19, 1956.
For souvenir sheet see C182a.

Carlos A. Mendoza — A120

**1956, Oct. 31 Wmk. 311**

**405** A120 10c rose red & dp grn .35 .25

Pres. Carlos A. Mendoza, birth cent.

National Archives A121

**1956, Nov. 27**

**406** A121 15c shown .70 .25
**407** A121 25c Pres. Belisario Porras 1.00 .50
*Nos. 406-407,C183-C184 (4)* 2.40 1.25

Centenary of the birth of Pres. Belisario Porras. For surcharge see No. 446.

Pan-American Highway, Panama — A122

**1957, Aug. 1**

**408** A122 3c gray green .25 .25
*Nos. 408,C185-C187 (4)* 3.90 3.30

7th Pan-American Highway Congress.

**Hospital Type of 1942**
**Unwmk.**

**1957, Aug. 17 Engr. *Perf. 12***

**409** A100 15c black .50 .30

Manuel Espinosa Batista — A123

**Wmk. 311**

**1957, Sept. 12 Litho. *Perf. 12½***

**410** A123 5c grn & ultra .25 .25

Centenary of the birth of Manuel Espinosa B., independence leader.

**No. 398 Surcharged "1957" and New Value in Violet or Black**

**1957, Dec. 21 Unwmk.**

**411** A114 1c on ½c org brn (V) .25 .25
**412** A114 3c on ½c org brn .25 .25

**No. 391 Surcharged "1958," New Value and Dots**

**1958, June 6 Engr. *Perf. 12***

**413** A112 3c on 12c dp red vio .25 .25

Flags of 21 American Nations — A124

**Center yellow & black; flags in national colors**

*Perf. 12½*

**1958, Aug. 12 Litho. Unwmk.**

**414** A124 1c lt gray .25 .25
**415** A124 2c brt yel grn .25 .25
**416** A124 3c red org .25 .25
**417** A124 7c vio bl .25 .25
*Nos. 414-417,C203-C206 (8)* 4.45 3.70

Organization of American States, 10th anniv.

Brazilian Pavilion, Brussels Fair — A125

3c, Argentina. 5c, Venezuela. 10c, Great Britain.

**1958, Sept. 8 Wmk. 311**

**418** A125 1c org yel & emer .25 .25
**419** A125 3c lt bl & olive .25 .25
**420** A125 5c lt brn & slate .25 .25
**421** A125 10c aqua & redsh brn .25 .25
*Nos. 418-421,C207-C209 (7)* 3.55 3.30

World's Fair, Brussels, Apr. 17-Oct. 19.

Pope Pius XII as Young Man — A126

**Wmk. 311**

**1959, Jan. 21 Litho. *Perf. 12½***

**422** A126 3c orange brown .25 .25
*Nos. 422,C210-C212 (4)* 2.05 1.55

Pope Pius XII, 1876-1958. See #C212a.

UN Headquarters Building — A127

Design: 15c, Humanity looking into sun.

**1959, Apr. 14 Wmk. 311**

**423** A127 3c maroon & olive .25 .25
**424** A127 15c orange & emer .35 .25
*Nos. 423-424,C213-C217 (7)* 3.90 3.30

10th anniv. (in 1958) of the signing of the Universal Declaration of Human Rights.
For overprints see Nos. 425-426, C219-C221.

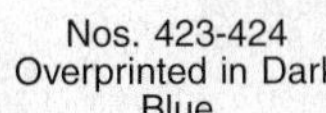
Nos. 423-424 Overprinted in Dark Blue

**1959, May 16**

**425** A127 3c maroon & olive .25 .25
**426** A127 15c orange & emer .35 .25
*Nos. 425-426,C218-C221 (6)* 3.80 3.15

Issued to commemorate the 8th Reunion of the Economic Commission for Latin America.

Eusebio A. Morales — A128

National Institute A129

**Wmk. 311**

**1959, Aug. 5 Litho. *Perf. 12½***

**427** A128 3c shown .25 .25
**428** A128 13c Abel Bravo .45 .25
**429** A129 21c shown .70 .25
*Nos. 427-429,C222-C223 (5)* 1.90 1.25

50th anniversary, National Institute.

Soccer — A130

**1959, Oct. 26**

**430** A130 1c shown .25 .25
**431** A130 3c Swimming .35 .25
**432** A130 20c Hurdling 1.75 .80
*Nos. 430-432,C224-C226 (6)* 6.15 3.05

3rd Pan American Games, Chicago, 8/27-9/7/59.
For overprint and surcharge see #C289, C349.

Fencing — A131

**Wmk. 343**

**1960, Sept. 23 Litho. *Perf. 12½***

**433** A131 3c shown .25 .25
**434** A131 5c Soccer .45 .25
*Nos. 433-434,C234-C237 (6)* 4.85 2.55

17th Olympic Games, Rome, 8/25-9/11.
For surcharges & overprints see #C249-C250, C254, C266-C270, C290, C298, C350, RA40.

Agricultural Products and Cattle A132

**1961, Mar. 3 Wmk. 311 *Perf. 12½***

**435** A132 3c blue green .25 .25

Issued to publicize the second agricultural and livestock census, Apr. 16, 1961.

Children's Hospital A133

**1961, May 2**

**436** A133 3c greenish blue .25 .25
*Nos. 436,C245-C247 (4)* 1.15 1.00

25th anniv. of the Lions Club of Panama. See #C245-C247.

Flags of Panama and Costa Rica A134

**1961, Oct. 2 Wmk. 343 *Perf. 12½***

**437** A134 3c car & bl .25 .25

Meeting of Presidents Mario Echandi of Costa Rica and Roberto F. Chiari of Panama at Paso Canoa, Apr. 21, 1961. See No. C251.

Arms of Colon — A135

**1962, Feb. 28 Litho. Wmk. 311**

**438** A135 3c car, yel & vio bl .25 .25

3rd Central American Municipal Assembly, Colon, May 13-17. See No. C255.

Mercury and Cogwheel — A136

**1962, Mar. 16 Wmk. 343**

**439** A136 3c red orange .25 .25

First industrial and commercial census.

Social Security Hospital A137

**1962, June 1 *Perf. 12½***

**440** A137 3c vermilion & gray .25 .25

Opening of the Social Security Hospital.
For surcharge see No. 445.

San Francisco de la Montana Church, Veraguas A138

Ruins of Old Panama Cathedral (1519-1671) A139

Designs: 3c, David Cathedral. 5c, Natá Church. 10c, Don Bosco Church. 15c, Church of the Virgin of Carmen. 20c, Colon Cathedral. 25c, Greek Orthodox Temple. 50c, Cathedral of Panama. 1b, Protestant Church of Colon.

**1960-64 Litho. Wmk. 343**

**Buildings in Black**

**441** A138 1c red & bl .25 .25
**441A** A139 2c red & yel .25 .25
**441B** A138 3c vio & yel .25 .25
**441C** A139 5c rose & lt grn .25 .25
**441D** A139 10c grn & yel .25 .25
**441E** A139 10c red & bl ('64) .25 .25
**441F** A139 15c ultra & lt grn .35 .25
**441G** A139 20c red & pink .55 .25
**441H** A138 25c grn & pink .65 .45
**441I** A139 50c ultra & pink 1.10 .60
**441J** A138 1b lilac & yel 2.75 1.60
*Nos. 441-441J (11)* 6.90 4.65

Freedom of religion in Panama.
Issued: #441E, 6/4/64; others, 7/29/60.
See #C256-C265; souvenir sheet #C264a.
For surcharges and overprints see Nos. 445A, 451, 467, C288, C296-C297, C299.

Bridge of the Americas during Construction — A140

**1962, Oct. 12** ***Perf. 12½***
**442** A140 3c carmine & gray .25 .25

Opening of the Bridge of the Americas (Thatcher Ferry Bridge), Oct. 12, 1962. See No. C273. For surcharge see No. 445B.

Fire Brigade Exercises, Inauguration of Aqueduct, 1906 — A141

Portraits of Fire Brigade Officials: 3c, Lt. Col. Luis Carlos Endara P., Col. Raul Arango N. and Major Ernesto Arosemena A. 5c, Guillermo Patterson Jr., David F. de Castro, Pres. T. Gabriel Duque, Telmo Rugliancich and Tomas Leblanc.

**1963, Jan. 22 Wmk. 311** ***Perf. 12½***
**443** A141 1c emer & blk .25 .25
**443A** A141 3c vio bl & blk .30 .25
**444** A141 5c mag & blk .50 .25
*Nos. 443-444,C279-C281 (6)* 2.75 1.75

75th anniversary (in 1962) of the Panamanian Fire Brigade.
For surcharge see No. 445C.

**Nos. 440, 441A, 442, 443A and 407 Surcharged "VALE" and New Value in Black or Red**

**1963 Wmk. 343** ***Perf. 12½***
**445** A137 4c on 3c ver & gray .25 .25
**445A** A138 4c on 3c vio & yel .25 .25
**445B** A140 4c on 3c car & gray .25 .25

**Wmk. 311**

**445C** A141 4c on 3c vio bl & blk .25 .25
**446** A121 10c on 25c dk car rose & bluish blk (R) .35 .25
*Nos. 445-446 (5)* 1.35 1.25

Issued: Nos. 445-445C, 8/30; No. 446, 10/9.

1964 Winter Olympics, Innsbruck — 141a

***Perf. 14x13½, 13½x14 (#447A, 447C)***
**1963, Dec. 20 Litho.**
**447** A141a ½c Mountains .25 .25
**447A** A141a 1c Speed skating .25 .25
**447B** A141a 3c like No. 447 .55 .25
**447C** A141a 4c like No. 447A .65 .25
**447D** A141a 5c Slalom skiing .80 .25
**447E** A141a 15c like No. 447D 1.50 .60
**447F** A141a 21c like No. 447D 2.75 1.00
**447G** A141a 31c like No. 447D 4.00 1.50
*h.* Souv. sheet of 2, #447F-447G, perf. 13½x14 18.00 10.00
*Nos. 447-447G (8)* 10.75 4.35

#447D-447G are airmail. #447Gh exists imperf., with background colors switched. Value, $17.50.

Pres. Francisco J. Orlich, Costa Rica — A142

Flags and Presidents: 2c, Luis A. Somoza, Nicaragua. 3c, Dr. Ramon Villeda M., Honduras. 4c, Roberto F. Chiari, Panama.

***Perf. 12½x12***
**1963, Dec. 18 Litho. Unwmk.**

**Portrait in Slate Green**

**448** A142 1c lt grn, red & ultra .25 .25
**448A** A142 2c lt bl, red & ultra .25 .25
**448B** A142 3c pale pink, red & ultra .25 .25
**448C** A142 4c rose, red & ultra .25 .25
*Nos. 448-448C,C292-C294 (7)* 3.30 2.70

Meeting of Central American Presidents with Pres. John F. Kennedy, San José, Mar. 18-20, 1963.

Vasco Nuñez de Balboa — A143

**1964, Jan. 22 Photo.** ***Perf. 13***
**449** A143 4c green, *pale rose* .25 .25

450th anniv. of Balboa's discovery of the Pacific Ocean. See No. C295.

**No. C231 Surcharged "Correos B/.0.10" in Red**

**Wmk. 311**

**1964, Feb. 25 Litho.** ***Perf. 12½***
**450** AP74 10c on 21c lt bl .30 .25

**Type of 1962 Overprinted "HABILITADA" in Red**

**1964, Oct. 20 Wmk. 343**
**451** A138 1b red, bl & blk 2.50 2.50

1964 Summer Olympics, Tokyo — A144

**1964, Mar. 4** ***Perf. 13½x14***
**452** A144 ½c shown .25 .25
**452A** A144 1c Torch bearer .25 .25

***Perf. 14x13½***

**452B** A144 5c Olympic stadium .30 .25
**452C** A144 10c like No. 452B .55 .30
**452D** A144 21c like No. 452B 1.10 .60
**452E** A144 50c like No. 452B 2.25 1.25
*f.* Souv. sheet of 1, perf. 13½x14 17.50 16.00
*Nos. 452-452E (6)* 4.70 2.90

Nos. 452B-452E are airmail. No. 452Ef exists imperf. with different colors. Value, $17.50.

Space Conquest — A145

½c, Projected Apollo spacecraft. 1c, Gemini, Agena spacecraft. 5c, Astronaut Walter M. Schirra. 10c, Astronaut L. Gordon Cooper. 21c, Schirra's Mercury capsule. 50c, Cooper's Mercury capsule.

**1964, Apr. 24** ***Perf. 14x14x13½***
**453** A145 ½c bl grn & multi .25 .25
**453A** A145 1c dk blue & multi .25 .25
**453B** A145 5c yel bis & multi .35 .35
**453C** A145 10c lil rose & multi .55 .45
**453D** A145 21c blue & multi 1.25 1.00
**453E** A145 50c violet & multi 5.75 5.00
*f.* Souvenir sheet of 1 22.50 22.50
*Nos. 453-453E (6)* 8.40 7.30

Nos. 453B-453E are airmail. No. 453Ef exists imperf. with different colors. Value, $22.50.

Aquatic Sports A146

***Perf. 14x13½, 13½x14***
**1964, Jun3. 17**
**454** A146 ½c Water skiing .25 .25
**454A** A146 1c Skin diving .25 .25
**454B** A146 5c Fishing .35 .25
**454C** A146 10c Sailing, vert. 1.75 .50
**454D** A146 21c Hydroplane racing 3.25 1.00
**454E** A146 31c Water polo 4.00 1.25
*f.* Souvenir sheet of 1 20.00 20.00
*Nos. 454-454E (6)* 9.85 3.50

Nos. 454B-454E are airmail.
Nos. 454-454Ef exist imperf in different colors. Value imperf, Nos. 454-454E $20. Value imperf, No. 454Ef $20.

Eleanor Roosevelt — A147

***Perf. 12x12½***
**1964, Oct. 9 Litho. Unwmk.**
**455** A147 4c car & blk, *grnsh* .30 .25

Issued to honor Eleanor Roosevelt (1884-1962). See Nos. C330-C330a.

Canceled to Order
Canceled sets of new issues have been sold by the government. Postally used examples are worth more.

1964 Winter Olympics, Innsbruck — A147a

Olympic medals and winners: ½c, Women's slalom. 1c, Men's 500-meter speed skating. 2c, Four-man bobsled. 3c, Women's figure skating. 4c, Ski jumping. 5c, 15km cross country skiing. 6c, 50km cross country skiing. 7c, Women's 3000-meter speed skating. 10c, Men's figure skating. 21c, Two-man bobsled. 31c, Men's downhill skiing.

**Litho. & Embossed**

***Perf. 13½x14***

**1964, Oct. 14 Unwmk.**
**456** A147a ½c bl grn & multi .25 .25
**456A** A147a 1c dk bl & multi .25 .25
**456B** A147a 2c brn vio & multi .25 .25
**456C** A147a 3c lil rose & multi .45 .25
**456D** A147a 4c brn lake & multi .70 .25
**456E** A147a 5c brt vio & multi .55 .30
**456F** A147a 6c grn bl & multi .70 .40
**456G** A147a 7c dp vio & multi 1.10 .65
**456H** A147a 10c emer grn & multi 1.75 1.00
**456I** A147a 21c ver & multi 2.00 1.10
**456J** A147a 31c ultra & multi 3.50 2.00
*k.* Souv. sheet of 3, #456H-456J 17.50 16.00
*Nos. 456-456J (11)* 11.50 6.70

Nos. 456E-456J are airmail.
No. 456Jk exists imperf. Value $17.50.
See Nos. 458-458J.

Satellites — A147b

Designs: ½c, Telstar 1. 1c, Transit 2A. 5c, OSO 1 Solar Observatory. 10c, Tiros 2 weather satellite. 21c, Weather station. 50c, Syncom 3.

**1964, Dec. 21** ***Perf. 14x14x13½***
**457** A147b ½c ver & multi .55 .25
**457A** A147b 1c vio & multi .55 .25
**457B** A147b 5c lil rose & multi .55 .40
**457C** A147b 10c blue & multi .70 .25
**457D** A147b 21c bl grn & multi 2.00 1.25

**457E** A147b 50c green & multi 3.00 1.75
*f.* Souvenir sheet of 1 17.50 16.00
*Nos. 457-457E (6)* 7.35 4.15

Nos. 457B-457E are airmail. No. 457Ef exists imperf in different colors. Value, $20.

For overprints see Nos. 489-489b.

### 1964 Olympic Medals Type

Summer Olympic Medals and Winners: ½c, Parallel bars. 1c, Dragon-class sailing. 2c, Individual show jumping. 3c, Two-man kayak. 4c, Team road race cycling. 5c, Individual dressage. 6c, Women's 800-meter run. 7c, 3000-meter steeplechase. 10c, Men's floor exercises. 21c, Decathlon. 31c, Men's 100-meter freestyle swimming.

**Litho. & Embossed**

**1964, Dec. 28** ***Perf. 13½x14***

**458** A147a ½c org & multi .25 .25
**458A** A147a 1c plum & multi .25 .25
**458B** A147a 2c bl grn & multi .25 .25
**458C** A147a 3c red brn & multi .25 .25
**458D** A147a 4c lilac rose & multi .30 .25
**458E** A147a 5c dull grn & multi .60 .25
**458F** A147a 6c blue & multi .70 .25
**458G** A147a 7c dk vio & multi .85 .30
**458H** A147a 10c ver & multi 1.25 .40
**458I** A147a 21c dl vio & multi 1.90 .65
**458J** A147a 31c dk bl grn & multi 3.25 1.00
*k.* Souv. sheet of 3, #458H-458J 22.50 17.50
*Nos. 458-458J (11)* 9.85 4.10

#458E-458J are airmail. #458Jk exists imperf. Value, $25.

John F. Kennedy & Cape Kennedy — A147c

Designs: 1c, Launching of Titan II rocket, Gemini capsule. 2c, Apollo lunar module. 3c, Proposed Apollo command and service modules. 5c, Gemini capsule atop Titan II rocket. 6c, Soviet cosmonauts Komarov, Yegorov, Feoktistov. 11c, Ranger VII. 31c, Lunar surface.

**1965, Feb. 25** **Litho.** ***Perf. 14***

**459** A147c ½c vio bl & multi .55 .25
**459A** A147c 1c blue & multi .55 .25
**459B** A147c 2c plum & multi .55 .25
**459C** A147c 3c ol grn & multi .70 .30
**459D** A147c 5c lilac rose & multi .70 .40
**459E** A147c 10c dull grn & multi 1.25 .70
**459F** A147c 11c brt vio & multi 2.00 1.10
**459G** A147c 31c grn & multi 3.50 2.00
*h.* Souvenir sheet of 1 20.00 20.00
*Nos. 459-459G (8)* 9.80 5.25

Nos. 459D-459G are airmail. No. 459Gh exists imperf. in different colors. Value, $20.

For overprints see Nos. 491-491b.

Atomic Power for Peace — A147d

Designs: ½c, Nuclear powered submarine *Nautilus.* 1c, Nuclear powered ship *Savannah.* 4c, First nuclear reactor, Calderhall, England. 6c, Nuclear powered icebreaker *Lenin.* 10c, Nuclear powered observatory. 21c, Nuclear powered space vehicle.

**1965, May 12**

**460** A147d ½c blue & multi
**460A** A147d 1c grn & multi
**460B** A147d 4c red & multi
**460C** A147d 6c dl bl grn & multi
**460D** A147d 10c blue grn & multi
**460E** A147d 21c dk vio & multi
*f.* Souv. sheet of 2, #460D-460E 12.50 12.50
Set, #460-460E 6.75 3.50

Nos. 460C-460E are airmail.

Nos. 460-460Ef exists imperf in different colors. Value imperf, Nos. 460-460E $12.50. Value imperf, No. 460Ef $12.50.

John F. Kennedy Memorial A147e

Kennedy and: ½c, PT109. 1c, Space capsule. 10c, UN emblem. 21c, Winston Churchill. 31c, Rocket launch at Cape Kennedy.

**1965, Aug. 23** ***Perf. 13½x13***

**461** A147e ½c multicolored
**461A** A147e 1c multicolored
**461B** A147e 10c + 5c, multi
**461C** A147e 21c + 10c, multi
**461D** A147e 31c + 15c, multi
*e.* Souv. sheet of 2, #461A, 461D, perf. 12½x12 20.00 20.00
Set, #461-461D 6.00 1.50

Nos. 461B-461D are airmail semipostal.

Nos. 461-461De exist imperf in different colors. Value $15.

For overprints see Nos. C367A-C367B.

Keel-billed Toucan A148

Song Birds: 2c, Scarlet macaw. 3c, Red-crowned woodpecker. 4c, Blue-gray tanager, horiz.

**1965, Oct. 27** **Unwmk.** ***Perf. 14***

**462** A148 1c brt pink & multi .65 .25
**462A** A148 2c multicolored .65 .25
**462B** A148 3c brt vio & multi 1.00 .25
**462C** A148 4c org yel & multi 1.00 .25
*Nos. 462-462C,C337-C338 (6)* 7.20 1.50

Snapper — A149

**1965, Dec. 7** **Litho.**

**463** A149 1c shown .35 .25
**463A** A149 2c Dorado .35 .25
*Nos. 463-463A,C339-C342 (6)* 3.95 1.60

Pope Paul VI, Visit to UN — A149a

Designs: ½c, Pope on Balcony of St. Peters, Vatican City. 1c, Pope Addressing UN General Assembly. 5c, Arms of Vatican City, Panama, UN emblem. 10c, Lyndon Johnson, Pope Paul VI, Francis Cardinal Spellman. 21c, Ecumenical Council, Vatican II. 31c, Earlybird satellite.

**1966 Apr. 4** ***Perf. 12x12½***

**464** A149a ½c multicolored
**464A** A149a 1c multicolored
**464B** A149a 5c multicolored
**464C** A149a 10c multicolored
**464D** A149a 21c multicolored
**464E** A149a 31c multicolored
*f.* Souv. sheet of 2, #464B, 464E, perf. 13x13½ 20.00 20.00
Set, #464-464E 8.00 3.00

Nos. 464B-464E are airmail. No. 464Ef exists imperf. with different margin color. Value $20.

For overprints see Nos. 490-490B.

Famous Men — A149b

Designs: ½c, William Shakespeare. 10c, Dante Alighieri. 31c, Richard Wagner.

**1966, May 26** ***Perf. 14***

**465** A149b ½c multicolored
**465A** A149b 10c multicolored
**465B** A149b 31c multicolored
*c.* Souv. sheet of 2, #465A-465B, perf. 13½x14 15.00 15.00
Set, #465-465B 6.75 3.25

Nos. 465A-465B are airmail. No. 465Bc exists imperf. with different margin color. Value $20.

Works by Famous Artists A149c

Paintings: ½c, Elizabeth Tucher by Durer. 10c, Madonna of the Rocky Grotto by Da Vinci. 31c, La Belle Jardiniere by Raphael.

**1966, May 26**

**466** A149c ½c multicolored
**466A** A149c 10c multicolored
**466B** A149c 31c multicolored
*c.* Souv. sheet of 2, #466-466B 15.00 15.00
Set, #466-465B 7.00 2.25

Nos. 466A-466B are airmail.

No. 466Bc exists imperf. with different margin color. Value $30.

### No. 441H Surcharged

**1966, June 27** **Wmk. 343** ***Perf. 12½***

**467** A138 13c on 25c grn & pink .40 .25

The "25c" has not been obliterated.

A149d

No. 468A, Uruguay, 1930, 1950. No. 468B, Italy, 1934, 1938. No. 468C, Brazil, 1958, 1962. No. 468D, Germany, 1954. No. 468E, Great Britain.

**1966, July 11** ***Perf. 14***

**468** A149d ½c multi
**468A** A149d .005b multi
**468B** A149d 10c multi
**468C** A149d 10c multi
**468D** A149d 21c multi
**468E** A149d 21c multi
*f.* Souv. sheet of 2, #468B, 468D 15.00 15.00
*g.* Souv. sheet of 2, #468, 468E, imperf. 12.50 11.00
Set, #468-465E 6.00 2.25

World Cup Soccer Championships, Great Britain. Nos. 468B-468E are airmail.

Nos. 468-468E exist imperf in different colors. Value, $22.50.

For overprints see Nos. 470-470g.

A149e

Italian Contributions to Space Research: ½c, Launch of Scout rocket, San Marco satellite. 1c, San Marco in orbit, horiz. 5c, Italian scientists, rocket. 10c, Arms of Panama, Italy, horiz. 21c, San Marco boosted into orbit, horiz.

***Perf. 12x12½, 12½x12***

**1966, Aug. 12**

**469** A149e ½c multicolored
**469A** A149e 1c multicolored
**469B** A149e 5c multicolored
**469C** A149e 10c multicolored
**469D** A149e 21c multicolored
*e.* Souv. sheet of 2, #469C-469D, imperf. 15.00 15.00
Set, #469-469D 7.25 4.00

Nos. 469B-469D are airmail.

Nos. 468-468g Ovptd.

**1966, Nov. 21** ***Perf. 14***

**470** A149d ½c on #468
**470A** A149d .005b on #468A
**470B** A149d 10c on #468B
**470C** A149d 10c on #468C
**470D** A149d 21c on #468D
**470E** A149d 21c on #468E
*f.* on #468Ef 30.00 30.00
*g.* on #468Eg, imperf. 30.00 30.00
Set, #470-470E 13.50 3.75

Nos. 470B-470E are airmail.

A149f

Religious Paintings A149g

Paintings: ½c, Coronation of Mary. 1c, Holy Family with Angel. 2c, Adoration of the Magi. 3c, Madonna and Child. No. 471D, The Annunciation. No. 471E, The Nativity. No. 471Fh, Madonna and Child.

**1966, Oct. 24** ***Perf. 11***

**Size of No. 471D: 32x34mm**

**471** A149f ½c Velazquez
**471A** A149f 1c Saraceni
**471B** A149g 2c Durer
**471C** A149f 3c Orazio
**471D** A149g 21c Rubens
**471E** A149f 21c Boticelli

**Souvenir Sheet**

***Perf. 14***

**471F** Sheet of 2
*g.* A149f 21c like No. 471E, black inscriptions 12.50 11.00
*h.* A149f 31c Mignard 18.00 18.00
Set, #471-471E 9.00 1.25

Nos. 471D-471F are airmail.

Nos. 471-471F exist imperf in different colors. Value imperf, Nos. 471-471E $10. Value imperf, No. 471F $17.50.

Sir Winston Churchill, British Satellites — A149h

Churchill and: 10c, Blue Streak, NATO emblem. 31c, Europa 1, rocket engine.

**1966, Nov. 25** ***Perf. 12x12½***

**472** A149h ½c shown
**472A** A149h 10c org & multi
**472B** A149h 31c dk bl & multi
*c.* Souv. sheet of 2, #472A-472B, perf. 13½x14 11.50 11.50
Set, #472-472B 6.25 2.00

Nos. 472A-472B are airmail.

No. 472Bc exists imperf in different colors. Value $12.50.

For overprints see Nos. 492-492B.

John F. Kennedy, 3rd Death Anniv. — A149i

10c, Kennedy, UN building. 31c, Kennedy, satellites & map.

**1966, Nov. 25** ***Perf. 14***

**473** A149i ½c shown
**473A** A149i 10c multi
**473B** A149i 31c multi
*c.* Souv. sheet of 2, #473A-473B 18.00 18.00
Set, #473-473B 5.75 2.00

Nos. 473A-473B are airmail.

No. 473Bc exists imperf in different colors. Value $17.50.

Jules Verne (1828-1905), French Space Explorations — A149j

Designs: ½c, Earth, A-1 satellite. 1c, Verne, submarine. 5c, Earth, FR-1 satellite. 10c, Verne, telescope. 21c, Verne, capsule heading toward Moon. 31c, D-1 satellite over Earth.

**1966, Dec. 28** ***Perf. 13½x14***

**474** A149j ½c bl & multi
**474A** A149j 1c bl grn & multi
**474B** A149j 5c ultra & multi
**474C** A149j 10c lil, blk & red
**474D** A149j 21c vio & multi
*f.* Souv. sheet of 2, #474C, 474D, imperf. 12.50 12.50
**474E** A149j 31c dl bl & multi
*g.* Souvenir sheet of 1 15.00 15.00
Set, #474-474E 8.50 2.00

Nos. 474B-474E are airmail.

Nos. 474-474Eg exist imperf in different colors. Value imperf. Nos. 474-474E $10. Value imperf, No. 474Eg $17.50.

Hen and Chicks A150

Domestic Animals: 3c, Rooster. 5c, Pig, horiz. 8c, Cow, horiz.

**1967, Feb. 3** **Unwmk.** ***Perf. 14***

**475** A150 1c multi .25 .25
**475A** A150 3c multi .25 .25
**475B** A150 5c multi .25 .25
**475C** A150 8c multi .25 .25
*Nos. 475-475C,C353-C356 (8)* 4.25 2.60

Easter A150a

Paintings: ½c, Christ at Calvary, by Giambattista Tiepolo. 1c, The Crucifixion, by Rubens. 5c, Pieta, by Sarto, horiz. 10c, Body of Christ, by Raphael Santi. 21c, The Arisen Christ, by Multscher. No. 476E, Christ Ascending into Heaven, by Grunewald. No. 476F, Christ on the Cross, by Van der Weyden. No. 476G, Madonna and Child, by Rubens.

**1967, Mar. 13** ***Perf. 14x13½, 13½x14***

**476** A150a ½c multi
**476A** A150a 1c multi
**476B** A150a 5c multi
**476C** A150a 10c multi
**476D** A150a 21c multi
**476E** A150a 31c multi
Set, #476-476E 7.50 3.00

**Souvenir Sheets**

***Perf. 12½x12x12½x13½***

**476F** A150a 31c multi 20.00 20.00

***Imperf***

**476G** A150a 31c multi 20.00 20.00

Nos. 476B-476G are airmail.

1968 Summer Olympics, Mexico City — A150b

Indian Ruins at: ½c, Teotihuacan. 1c, Tajin. 5c, Xochicalco. 10c, Monte Alban. 21c, Palenque. 31c, Chichen Itza.

**1967, Apr. 18** ***Perf. 12x12½***

**477** A150b ½c plum & multi
**477A** A150b 1c red lil & multi
**477B** A150b 5c blue & multi
**477C** A150b 10c ver & multi
**477D** A150b 21c grn bl & multi
**477E** A150b 31c grn & multi
Set, #477-477E 8.00 3.00

**Souvenir Sheet**

***Perf. 12x12½x14x12½***

**477F** A150a 31c multi 18.00 18.00

Nos. 477B-477E are airmail.

New World Anhinga A151

Birds: 1c, Quetzals. 3c, Turquoise-browed motmot. 4c, Double-collared aracari, horiz. 5c, Macaw. 13c, Belted kingfisher. 50c, Hummingbird.

**1967, July 20** ***Perf. 14***

**478** A151 ½c lt bl & multi 1.00 .25
**478A** A151 1c lt gray & multi 1.00 .25
**478B** A151 3c pink & multi 1.10 .25
**478C** A151 4c lt grn & multi 1.40 .25
**478D** A151 5c buff & multi 1.75 .25
**478E** A151 13c yel & multi 6.75 .75
*Nos. 478-478E (6)* 13.00 2.00

**Souvenir Sheet**

***Perf. 14½***

**478F** A151 50c Sheet of 1 15.00 15.00

No. 478A exists imperf. with blue background. Value $17.50.

Works of Famous Artists A151a

Paintings: No. 479, Maiden in the Doorway, by Rembrandt. No. 479A, Blueboy, by Gainsborough. No. 479B, The Promise of Louis XIII, by Ingres. No. 479C, St. George and the Dragon, by Raphael. No. 479D, The Blacksmith's Shop, by Velazquez, horiz. No. 479E, St. Hieronymus, by Durer. Nos. 479F-479K, Self-portraits.

***Perf. 14x13½, 13½x14***

**1967, Aug. 23**

**479** A151a 5c multi
**479A** A151a 5c multi
**479B** A151a 5c multi
**479C** A151a 21c multi
**479D** A151a 21c multi
**479E** A151a 21c multi
Set, #479-479E 7.25 2.00

**Souvenir Sheets**

***Various Compound Perfs.***

**479F** A151a 21c Gainsborough 8.50 5.00
**479G** A151a 21c Rembrandt 8.50 5.00
**479H** A151a 21c Ingres 8.50 5.00
**479I** A151a 21c Raphael 8.50 5.00
**479J** A151a 21c Velazquez 8.50 5.00
**479K** A151a 21c Durer 8.50 5.00

Nos. 479C-479K are airmail.

Red Deer, by Franz Marc — A152

Animal Paintings by Franz Marc: 3c, Tiger, vert. 5c, Monkeys. 8c, Blue Fox.

**1967, Sept. 1** ***Perf. 14***

**480** A152 1c multicolored .25 .25
**480A** A152 3c multicolored .25 .25
**480B** A152 5c multicolored .25 .25
**480C** A152 8c multicolored .25 .25
*Nos. 480-480C,C357-C360 (8)* 3.80 2.20

Paintings by Goya A152a

Designs: 2c, The Water Carrier. 3c, Count Floridablanca. 4c, Senora Francisca Sebasa y Garcia. 5c, St. Bernard and St. Robert. 8c, Self-portrait. 10c, Dona Isabel Cobos de Porcel. 13c, Clothed Maja, horiz. 21c, Don Manuel Osoria de Zuniga as a child. 50c, Cardinal Luis of Bourbon and Villabriga.

**1967, Oct. 17** ***Perf. 14x13½, 13½x14***

**481** A152a 2c multicolored
**481A** A152a 3c multicolored
**481B** A152a 4c multicolored
**481C** A152a 5c multicolored
**481D** A152a 8c multicolored
**481E** A152a 10c multicolored
**481F** A152a 13c multi, horiz.
**481G** A152a 21c multicolored
Set, #481-481G 9.00 2.25

**Souvenir Sheet**

**481H** A152a 50c multicolored 20.00 20.00

Nos. 481C-481H are airmail.

Life of Christ A152b

Paintings: No. 482, The Holy Family, by Michaelangelo. No. 482A, Christ Washing Feet, by Brown. 3c, Christ's Charge to Peter, by Rubens. 4c, Christ and the Money Changers in the Temple, by El Greco, horiz. No. 482D, Christ's Entry into Jerusalem, by Van Dyck, horiz. No. 482E, The Last Supper, by de Juanes.

No. 482Fl, Pastoral Adoration. No. 482Fm, The Holy Family. No. 482Gn, Christ with Mary and Martha. No. 482Go, Flight from Egypt. No. 482Hp, St. Thomas. No. 482Hq, The Tempest. No. 482Ir, The Transfiguration. No. 482Is, The Crucification.

No. 482J, The Baptism of Christ, by Guido Reni. No. 482K, Christ at the Sea of Galilee, by Tintoretto, horiz.

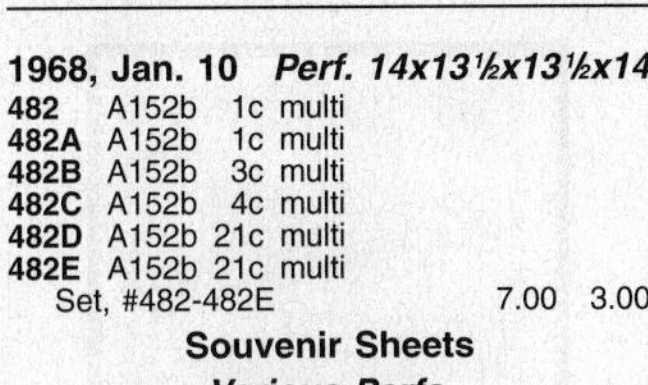

**1968, Jan. 10** ***Perf. 14x13½x13½x14***

**482** A152b 1c multi
**482A** A152b 1c multi
**482B** A152b 3c multi
**482C** A152b 4c multi
**482D** A152b 21c multi
**482E** A152b 21c multi
Set, #482-482E 7.00 3.00

**Souvenir Sheets**

***Various Perfs.***

**482F** Sheet of 2 13.50 13.50
*l.* A152b 1c Schongauer
*m.* A152b 21c Raphael
**482G** Sheet of 2 13.50 13.50
*n.* A152b 3c Tintoretto
*o.* A152b 21c Caravaggio
**482H** Sheet of 2 13.50 13.50
*p.* A152b 21c Anonymous, 12th cent.
*q.* A152b 31c multicolored
**482I** Sheet of 2 13.50 13.50
*r.* A152b 21c Raphael
*s.* A152b 31c Montanez
**482J** A152b 22c Sheet of 1 13.50 13.50
**482K** A152b 24c Sheet of 1 13.50 13.50

Nos. 482C-482K are airmail.
Nos. 482J-482K also exist imperf.

Butterflies — A152c

½c, Apodemia albinus. 1c, Caligo ilioneus, vert. 3c, Meso semia tenera. 4c, Pamphila epictetus. 5c, Entheus peleus. 13c, Tmetoglene drymo.
50c, Thymele chalco, vert.

**1968, Feb. 23** ***Perf. 14***

**483** A152c ½c multi
**483A** A152c 1c multi
**483B** A152c 3c multi
**483C** A152c 4c multi
**483D** A152c 5c multi
**483E** A152c 13c multi
Set, #483-483E 22.00 4.00

**Souvenir Sheet**

***Perf. 14½***

**483F** A152c 50c multi 15.00 15.00

Nos. 483D-483F are airmail.
No. 483F exists imperf with pink margin. Value $15.

10th Winter Olympics, Grenoble — A152d

½c, Emblem, vert. 1c, Ski jumper. 5c, Skier. 10c, Mountain climber. 21c, Speed skater. 31c, Two-man bobsled.

**1968, Feb. 2** ***Perf. 14x13½, 13½x14***

**484** A152d ½c multi
**484A** A152d 1c multi
**484B** A152d 5c multi
**484C** A152d 10c multi
**484D** A152d 21c multi
**484E** A152d 31c multi
Set, #484-484E 7.00 1.50

**Souvenir Sheets**

***Perf. 14***

**484F** Sheet of 2 16.00 16.00
*h.* A152d 10c Emblem, snow-flake
*i.* A152d 31c Figure skater
**484G** Sheet of 2 16.00 16.00
*j.* A152d 31c Biathlon
*k.* A152d 10c Skier on ski lift

Nos. 484B-484G are airmail.

Sailing Ships — A152e

Paintings by: ½c, Gamiero, vert. 1c, Lebreton. 3c, Anonymous Japanese. 4c, Le Roi. 5c, Van de Velde. 13c, Duncan. 50c, Anonymous Portuguese, vert.

**1968, May 7** ***Perf. 14***

**485** A152e ½c multicolored
**485A** A152e 1c multicolored
**485B** A152e 3c multicolored
**485C** A152e 4c multicolored
**485D** A152e 5c multicolored
**485E** A152e 13c multicolored
Set, #485-485E 7.50 2.00

**Souvenir Sheet**

***Perf. 14½***

**485F** A152e 50c multicolored 9.00 9.00

Nos. 485D-485E are airmail. No. 485F exists imperf. with light blue margin. Value $9.

Tropical Fish — A152f

½c, Balistipus undulatus. 1c, Holacanthus ciliaris. 3c, Chaetodon ephippium. 4c, Epinephelus elongatus. 5c, Anisotremus virginicus. 13c, Balistoides conspicillum.
50c, Raja texana, vert.

**1968, June 26** ***Perf. 14***

**486** A152f ½c multi
**486A** A152f 1c multi
**486B** A152f 3c multi
**486C** A152f 4c multi
**486D** A152f 5c multi
**486E** A152f 13c multi
Set, #486-486E 6.75 2.00

**Souvenir Sheet**

***Perf. 14½***

**486F** A152f 50c multi 15.00 15.00

Nos. 486D-486F are airmail. No. 486F exists imperf. with pink margin. Value $15.

Olympic Medals and Winners, Grenoble — A152g

Olympic Medals and Winners: 1c, Men's giant slalom. 2c, Women's downhill. 3c, Women's figure skating. 4c, 5000-meter speed skating. 5c, 10,000-meter speed skating. 6c, Women's slalom. 8c, Women's 1000-meter speed skating. 13c, Women's 1500-meter speed skating. 30c, Two-man bobsled. 70c, Nordic combined.

**Litho. & Embossed**

**1968, July 30** ***Perf. 13½x14***

**487** A152g 1c pink & multi
**487A** A152g 2c vio & multi
**487B** A152g 3c grn & multi
**487C** A152g 4c plum & multi
**487D** A152g 5c red brn & multi
**487E** A152g 6c brt vio & multi
**487F** A152g 8c Prus bl & multi
**487G** A152g 13c bl & multi
**487H** A152g 30c rose lil & multi
Set, #487-487H 6.75 2.00

**Souvenir Sheet**

**487I** A152g 70c red & multi 18.00 18.00

Nos. 487G-487H are airmail.

Miniature Sheet

Music — A152h

Paintings of Musicians, Instruments: 5c, Mandolin, by de la Hyre. 10c, Lute, by Caravaggio. 15c, Flute, by ter Brugghen. 20c, Chamber ensemble, by Tourmer. 25c, Violin, by Caravaggio. 30c, Piano, by Vermeer. 40c, Harp, by Memling.

**1968, Sept. 11 Litho.** ***Perf. 13½x14***

**488** A152h Sheet of 6 10.00 2.00
*a.* 5c multicolored
*b.* 10c multicolored
*c.* 15c multicolored
*d.* 20c multicolored
*e.* 25c multicolored
*f.* 30c multicolored

**Souvenir Sheet**

***Perf. 14***

**488A** A152h 40c multicolored 18.00 18.00

**Nos. 457, 457E Ovptd. in Black**

**1968, Oct. 17**

**489** A147b ½c on No. 457 2.50 .75
**489A** A147b 50c on No. 457E 2.50 .75
*b.* Souv. sheet of 1, on No. 457Ef 22.50 22.50

Nos. 489-489A exist with gold overprint. Overprint differs on No. 489Ab.

**Nos. 464, 464D & 464Ef Ovptd. in Black or Gold**

**1968, Oct. 18** ***Perf. 12x12½***

**490** A149a ½c on No. 464 6.75
**490A** A149a 21c on No. 464D 6.75

**Souvenir Sheet**

***Perf. 13x13½***

**490B** on No. 464Ef (G) 27.50 27.50

Nos. 490A-490B are airmail. No. 490B exists imperf. with different colored border. Value same as No. 490B. Overprint differs on No. 490B.

**Nos. 459, 459G-459Gh Ovptd. in Black**

**1968, Oct. 21** ***Perf. 14***

**491** A147c ½c on No. 459 6.75
**491A** A147c 31c on No. 459G 6.75
*b.* on souv. sheet, No. 459Gh 9.00 9.00

Nos. 491A-491Ab are airmail.
Nos. 491-491A exist overprinted in gold, and imperf., overprinted in gold. No. 491Ab exists imperf in different colors and black or gold overprints. Values, black $9, gold $90.

**Nos. 472-472A, 472Bc Overprinted in Black or Gold**

**1968, Oct. 22** ***Perf. 12x12½***

**492** A149h ½c (#472) 2.00
**492A** A149h 10c (#472A) 2.00

**Souvenir Sheet**

***Perf. 13½x14***

**492B** on No. 472Bc 13.50 13.50

Nos. 492A-492B are airmail.
No. 492B exists imperf in different colors.

Hunting on Horseback — A152i

Paintings and Tapestries: 1c, Koller. 3c, Courbet. 5c, Tischbein, the Elder. 10c, Gobelin, vert. 13c, Oudry. 30c, Rubens.

**1968, Oct. 29** ***Perf. 14***

**493** A152i 1c multicolored
**493A** A152i 3c multicolored
**493B** A152i 5c multicolored
**493C** A152i 10c multicolored
**493D** A152i 13c multicolored
**493E** A152i 30c multicolored
Set, #493-493E 5.75 2.00

Nos. 493D-493E are airmail.

Miniature Sheet

Famous Race Horses — A152j

Horse Paintings: a, 5c, Lexington, by Edward Troye. b, 10c, American Eclipse, by Alvan Fisher. c, 15c, Plenipotentiary, by Abraham Cooper. d, 20c, Gimcrack, by George Stubbs. e, 25c, Flying Childers, by James Seymour. f, 30c, Eclipse, by Stubbs.

**1968, Dec. 18** ***Perf. 13½x14***

**494** A152j Sheet of 6, #a.-f. 15.00 12.50

1968 Summer Olympics, Mexico City — A152k

Mexican art: 1c, Watermelons, by Diego Rivera. 2c, Women, by Jose Clemente Orozco. 3c, Flower Seller, by Miguel Covarrubias, vert. 4c, Nutall Codex, vert. 5c, Mayan statue, vert. 6c, Face sculpture, vert. 8c, Seated figure, vert. 13c. Ceramic angel, vert. 30c, Christ, by David Alfaro Siqueiros. 70c, Symbols of Summer Olympic events.

**1968, Dec. 23** ***Perf. 13½x14, 14x13½***

| | | | | |
|---|---|---|---|---|
| **495** | A152k | 1c multicolored | | |
| **495A** | A152k | 2c multicolored | | |
| **495B** | A152k | 3c multicolored | | |
| **495C** | A152k | 4c multicolored | | |
| **495D** | A152k | 5c multicolored | | |
| **495E** | A152k | 6c multicolored | | |
| **495F** | A152k | 8c multicolored | | |
| **495G** | A152k | 13c multicolored | | |
| **495H** | A152k | 30c multicolored | | |
| | Set, #495-495H | | 10.50 | 2.25 |

**Souvenir Sheet**

***Perf. 14***

| | | | | |
|---|---|---|---|---|
| **495I** | A152k | 70c multicolored | 16.00 | 16.00 |

Nos. 495G-495H are airmail.

First Visit of Pope Paul VI to Latin America A152l

Paintings: 1c, Madonna and Child, by Raphael. 2c, Madonna and Child, by Ferruzzi. 3c, Madonna and Child, by Bellini. 4c, The Annunciation, 17th cent. 5c, Madonna and Child, by Van Dyck. 6c, Madonna and Child, by Albani. 7c, Adoration of the Magi, by Master of the Viennese Schottenaltar. 8c, Adoration of the Magi, by Van Dyck. 10c, Holy Family, 16th cent.

50c, Madonna and Child, angel, by Del Sarto.

**1969, Aug. 5** ***Perf. 14***

| | | | | |
|---|---|---|---|---|
| **496** | A152l | 1c multi | | |
| **496A** | A152l | 2c multi | | |
| **496B** | A152l | 3c multi | | |
| **496C** | A152l | 4c multi | | |
| **496D** | A152l | 5c multi | | |
| **496E** | A152l | 6c multi | | |
| **496F** | A152l | 7c multi | | |
| **496G** | A152l | 8c multi | | |
| **496H** | A152l | 10c multi | | |
| | Set, #496-496H | | 10.00 | 2.75 |

**Souvenir Sheet**

***Perf. 14½***

| | | | | |
|---|---|---|---|---|
| **496I** | A152l | 50c multi | 15.00 | 7.50 |

Nos. 496E-496I are airmail.

Map of Americas and People — A153

5c, Map of Panama, People and Houses, horiz.

**1969, Aug. 14 Photo. Wmk. 350**

| | | | | |
|---|---|---|---|---|
| **500** | A153 | 5c violet blue | .25 | .25 |
| **501** | A153 | 10c bright rose lilac | .30 | .25 |

Issued to publicize the 1970 census.

Cogwheel A154

**1969, Aug. 14**

| | | | | |
|---|---|---|---|---|
| **502** | A154 | 13c yel & dk bl gray | .35 | .25 |

50th anniv. of Rotary Intl. of Panama.

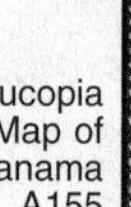

Cornucopia and Map of Panama A155

***Perf. 14½x15***

**1969, Oct. 10 Litho. Unwmk.**

| | | | | |
|---|---|---|---|---|
| **503** | A155 | 10c lt bl & multi | .35 | .25 |

1st anniv. of the October 11 Revolution.

Map of Panama and Ruins — A156

Natá Church — A157

Designs: 5c, Farmer, wife and mule. 13c, Hotel Continental. 20c, Church of the Virgin of Carmen. 21c, Gold altar, San José Church. 25c, Del Rey bridge. 30c, Dr. Justo Arosemena monument. 34c, Cathedral of Panama. 38c, Municipal Palace. 40c, French Plaza. 50c, Thatcher Ferry Bridge (Bridge of the Americas). 59c, National Theater.

***Perf. 14½x15, 15x14½***

**1969-70 Litho. Unwmk.**

| | | | | |
|---|---|---|---|---|
| **504** | A156 | 3c org & blk | .25 | .25 |
| **505** | A156 | 5c lt bl grn ('70) | .25 | .25 |
| **506** | A157 | 8c dl brn ('70) | .25 | .25 |
| **507** | A156 | 13c emer & blk | .35 | .25 |
| **508** | A157 | 20c vio brn ('70) | .50 | .25 |
| **509** | A157 | 21c yellow ('70) | .50 | .40 |
| **510** | A156 | 25c lt bl grn ('70) | .65 | .25 |
| **511** | A157 | 30c black ('70) | .80 | .40 |
| **512** | A156 | 34c org brn ('70) | 1.00 | .50 |
| **513** | A156 | 38c brt bl ('70) | 1.00 | .40 |
| **514** | A156 | 40c org yel ('70) | 1.25 | .60 |
| **515** | A156 | 50c brt rose lil & blk | 1.40 | .70 |
| **516** | A156 | 59c brt rose lil ('70) | 2.00 | .90 |
| | *Nos. 504-516 (13)* | | 10.20 | 5.40 |

Issued: Nos. 504, 507, 515, 10/10/69. Others, 1/28/70.

For surcharges see Nos. 541, 543, 545-547, RA78-RA80.

Stadium and Discus Thrower A158

Flor del Espiritu Santo — A159

**Wmk. 365**

**1970, Jan. 6 Litho.** ***Perf. 13½***

| | | | | |
|---|---|---|---|---|
| **517** | A158 | 1c ultra & multi | .25 | .25 |
| **518** | A158 | 2c ultra & multi | .25 | .25 |
| **519** | A158 | 3c ultra & multi | .25 | .25 |
| **520** | A158 | 5c ultra & multi | .25 | .25 |
| **521** | A158 | 10c ultra & multi | .30 | .25 |
| **522** | A158 | 13c ultra & multi | .35 | .25 |
| **523** | A159 | 13c pink & multi | .40 | .25 |
| **524** | A158 | 25c ultra & multi | .85 | .50 |
| **525** | A158 | 30c ultra & multi | 1.00 | .75 |
| | *Nos. 517-525,C368-C369 (11)* | | 6.15 | 4.05 |

11th Central American and Caribbean Games, Feb. 28-Mar. 14.

Office of Comptroller General, 1970 — A160

Designs: 5c, Alejandro Tapia and Martin Sosa, first Comptrollers, 1931-34, horiz. 8c, Comptroller's emblem. 13c, Office of Comptroller General, 1955-70, horiz.

**1971, Feb. 25 Litho. Wmk. 365**

| | | | | |
|---|---|---|---|---|
| **526** | A160 | 3c yel & multi | .25 | .25 |
| **527** | A160 | 5c brn, buff & gold | .25 | .25 |
| **528** | A160 | 8c gold & multi | .25 | .25 |
| **529** | A160 | 13c blk & multi | .25 | .25 |
| | *Nos. 526-529 (4)* | | 1.00 | 1.00 |

Comptroller General's Office, 40th anniv.

Indian Alligator Design A161

**1971, Aug. 18 Wmk. 343** ***Perf. 13½***

| | | | | |
|---|---|---|---|---|
| **530** | A161 | 8c multicolored | .80 | .25 |

SENAPI (Servicio Nacional de Artesania y Pequeñas Industrias), 5th anniv.

Education Year Emblem, Map of Panama A162

**1971, Aug. 19 Litho.**

| | | | | |
|---|---|---|---|---|
| **531** | A162 | 1b multicolored | 3.50 | 2.50 |

International Education Year, 1970.

For surcharge see No. 542.

Congress Emblem — A163

**1972, Aug. 25**

| | | | | |
|---|---|---|---|---|
| **532** | A163 | 25c multicolored | 1.00 | .60 |

9th Inter-American Conference of Saving and Loan Associations, Panama City, Jan. 23-29, 1971.

UPU Headquarters, Bern — A164

Design: 30c, UPU Monument, Bern, vert.

**1971, Dec. 14 Wmk. 343**

| | | | | |
|---|---|---|---|---|
| **533** | A164 | 8c multicolored | .25 | .25 |
| **534** | A164 | 30c multicolored | 1.00 | .60 |

Inauguration of Universal Postal Union Headquarters, Bern, Switzerland.

For surcharge see No. RA77.

Cow, Pig and Produce A165

**1971, Dec. 15**

| | | | | |
|---|---|---|---|---|
| **535** | A165 | 3c yel, brn & blk | .25 | .25 |

3rd agricultural census.

Map of Panama and "4-S" Emblem A166

**1971, Dec. 16**

| | | | | |
|---|---|---|---|---|
| **536** | A166 | 2c multicolored | .25 | .25 |

Rural youth 4-S program.

UNICEF Emblem, Children A167

**Wmk. 365**

**1972, Sept. 12 Litho.** ***Perf. 13½***

| | | | | |
|---|---|---|---|---|
| **537** | A167 | 1c yel & multi | .25 | .25 |
| | *Nos. 537,C390-C392 (4)* | | 2.00 | 1.30 |

25th anniv. (in 1971) of UNICEF. See No. C392a.

Tropical Fruits A168

**1972, Sept. 13**

| | | | | |
|---|---|---|---|---|
| **538** | A168 | 1c shown | .25 | .25 |
| **539** | A168 | 2c Isla de Noche | .25 | .25 |
| **540** | A168 | 3c Carnival float, vert. | .25 | .25 |
| | *Nos. 538-540,C393-C395 (6)* | | 2.05 | 1.70 |

Tourist publicity.

For surcharges see Nos. RA75-RA76.

Nos. 516, 531 and 511 Surcharged in Red

***Perf. 14½x15, 15x14½, 13½***
**Wmk. 343, Unwmkd.**

**1973, Mar. 15**

**541** A156 8c on 59c brt rose lil .25 .25
**542** A162 10c on 1b multi .25 .25
**543** A157 13c on 30c blk .25 .25
*Nos. 541-543,C402 (4)* 1.10 1.05

UN Security Council Meeting, Panama City, Mar. 15-21. Surcharges differ in size and are adjusted to fit shape of stamp.

José Daniel Crespo, Educator A169

**Wmk. 365**

**1973, June 20 Litho. *Perf. 13½***

**544** A169 3c lt bl & multi .25 .25
*Nos. 544,C403-C413 (12)* 7.95 4.35

For overprints and surcharges see Nos. C414-C416, C418-C421, RA81-RA82, RA84.

Nos. 511-512 and 509 Surcharged in Red

***Perf. 15x14½, 14½x15***

**1974, Nov. 11 Unwmk.**

**545** A157 5c on 30c blk .25 .25
**546** A156 10c on 34c org brn .25 .25
**547** A157 13c on 21c yel .25 .25
*Nos. 545-547,C417-C421 (8)* 2.00 2.00

Surcharge vertical on No. 546.

Bolivar, Bridge of the Americas, Men with Flag — A170

***Perf. 12½***

**1976, Mar. 30 Litho. Unwmk.**

**548** A170 6c multicolored .25 .25
*Nos. 548,C426-C428 (4)* 2.90 1.40

150th anniversary of Congress of Panama.

Evibacus Princeps A171

Marine life: 3c, Ptitosarcus sinuosus, vert. 4c, Acanthaster planci. 7c, Starfish. 1b, Mithrax spinossimus.

***Perf. 12½x13, 13x12½***

**1976, May 6 Litho. Wmk. 377**

**549** A171 2c multi .65 .25
**550** A171 3c multi .65 .25
**551** A171 4c multi .65 .25
**552** A171 7c multi .65 .25
*Nos. 549-552,C429-C430 (6)* 6.45 2.15

**Souvenir Sheet**

***Imperf***

**553** A171 1b multi 7.00

Bolivar from Bolivar Monument A172

Bolivar and Argentine Flag A173

Stamps of design A172 show details of Bolivar Monument, Panama City; design A173 shows head of Bolivar and flags of Latin American countries.

***Perf. 13½***

**1976, June 22 Unwmk. Litho.**

**554** A172 20c shown .50 .50
**555** A173 20c shown .50 .50
**556** A173 20c Bolivia .50 .50
**557** A173 20c Brazil .50 .50
**558** A173 20c Chile .50 .50
**559** A172 20c Battle scene .50 .50
**560** A173 20c Colombia .50 .50
**561** A173 20c Costa Rica .50 .50
**562** A173 20c Cuba .50 .50
**563** A173 20c Ecuador .50 .50
**564** A173 20c El Salvador .50 .50
**565** A173 20c Guatemala .50 .50
**566** A173 20c Guyana .50 .50
**567** A173 20c Haiti .50 .50
**568** A172 20c Assembly .50 .50
**569** A172 20c Liberated people .50 .50
**570** A173 20c Honduras .50 .50
**571** A173 20c Jamaica .50 .50
**572** A173 20c Mexico .50 .50
**573** A173 20c Nicaragua .50 .50
**574** A173 20c Panama .50 .50
**575** A173 20c Paraguay .50 .50
**576** A173 20c Peru .50 .50
**577** A173 20c Dominican Rep. .50 .50
**578** A172 20c Bolivar and flag bearer .50 .50
**579** A173 20c Surinam .50 .50
**580** A173 20c Trinidad-Tobago .50 .50
**581** A173 20c Uruguay .50 .50
**582** A173 20c Venezuela .50 .50
**583** A172 20c Indian delegation .50 .50
*a.* Sheet of 30, #554-583 25.00 25.00

**Souvenir Sheet**

**584** Sheet of 3 3.50 3.50
*a.* A172 30c Bolivar and flag bearer .65 .65
*b.* A172 30c Monument, top .65 .65
*c.* A172 40c Inscription tablet .80 .80

Amphictyonic Congress of Panama, sesquicentennial. No. 584 comes perf. and imperf. Values the same.

Nos. 554-583 amd 584 were overprinted to honor the 1980 Olympics. The overprinted sets were issued Nov. 27, 1980.

Nicanor Villalaz, Designer of Coat of Arms — A174

National Lottery Building, Panama City — A175

**1976, Nov. 12 Litho. *Perf. 12½***

**585** A174 5c dk blue .25 .25
**586** A175 6c multicolored .25 .25

Contadora Island — A176

**1976, Dec. 29 *Perf. 12½***

**587** A176 3c multicolored .25 .25

Pres. Carter and Gen. Omar Torrijos Signing Panama Canal Treaties — A177

Design: 23c, like No. 588. Design includes Alejandro Orfila, Secretary General of OAS.

**1978, Jan. 3 Litho. *Perf. 12***

**Size: 90x40mm**

**588** A177 50c Strip of 3 8.00 8.00
*a.* 3c multicolored .25 .25
*b.* 40c multicolored 1.00 1.00
*c.* 50c multicolored 1.25 *1.25*

***Perf. 14***

**Size: 36x26mm**

**589** A177 23c multicolored .45 .25

Signing of Panama Canal Treaties, Washington, DC, Sept. 7, 1977.

Pres. Carter and Gen. Torrijos Signing Treaties — A178

**1978, Nov. 13 Litho. *Perf. 12***

**590** A178 Strip of 3 7.00 7.00
*a.* 5c multi (30x40mm) .25 .25
*b.* 35c multi (30x40mm) 1.00 .35
*c.* 41c multi (45x40mm) 1.00 .40

**Size: 36x26mm**

**591** A178 3c Treaty signing .25 .25

Signing of Panama Canal Treaties ratification documents, Panama City, Panama, June 6, 1978.

World Commerce Zone, Colon A179

**1978, Nov. 13 Litho. *Perf. 12***

**592** A179 6c multicolored .25 .25

Free Zone of Colon, 30th anniversary.

Melvin Jones, Lions Emblem A180

**1978, Nov. 13**

**593** A180 50c multicolored 1.25 .75

Birth centenary of Melvin Jones, founder of Lions International.

Torrijos with Children, Ship, Flag A181

"75," Coat of Arms A182

Rotary Emblem, "75" A183

Gen. Torrijos and Pres. Carter, Flags, Ship A184

UPU Emblem, Globe — A185

Boy and Girl Inside Heart — A186

**1979, Oct. 1 Litho. *Perf. 14***

**594** A181 3c multicolored .25 .25
**595** A182 6c multicolored .25 .25
**596** A183 17c multicolored .35 .30
**597** A184 23c multicolored .45 .25
**598** A185 35c multicolored .70 .60
**599** A186 50c multicolored 1.00 .50
*Nos. 594-599 (6)* 3.00 2.15

Return of Canal Zone to Panama, Oct. 1 (3c, 23c); Natl. Bank, 75th anniv.; Rotary Intl., 75th anniv.; 18th UPU Cong., Rio, Sept.-Oct., 1979; Intl. Year of the Child.

Colon Station, St. Charles Hotel, Engraving A187

Postal Headquarters, Balboa, Inauguration — A188

Return of Canal Zone to Panama, Oct. 1, 1979 — A189

Census of the Americas A190

Panamanian Tourist and Convention Center Opening — A191

Inter-American Development Bank, 25th Anniversary — A192

Canal Centenary A193

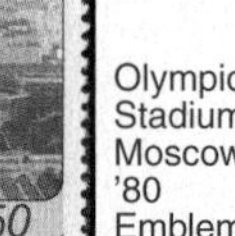


Olympic Stadium, Moscow '80 Emblem A194

**1980, May 21 Litho. *Perf. 12***

| | | | | |
|---|---|---|---|---|
| **600** | A187 | 1c rose violet | .25 | .25 |
| **601** | A188 | 3c multicolored | .25 | .25 |
| **602** | A189 | 6c multicolored | .25 | .25 |
| **603** | A190 | 17c multicolored | .35 | .25 |
| **604** | A191 | 23c multicolored | .45 | .25 |
| **605** | A192 | 35c multicolored | .70 | .30 |
| **606** | A193 | 41c pale rose & blk | .90 | .45 |
| **607** | A194 | 50c multicolored | 1.00 | .50 |
| | | *Nos. 600-607 (8)* | 4.15 | 2.50 |

Transpanamanian Railroad, 130th anniv. (1c); 22nd Summer Olympic Games, Moscow, July 19-Aug. 3 (50c).

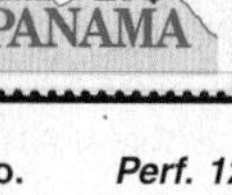


La Salle Congregation, 75th Anniv. (1979) — A195

**1981, May 15 Litho. *Perf. 12***

| | | | | |
|---|---|---|---|---|
| **608** | A195 | 17c multicolored | .50 | .25 |

Louis Braille — A196

**1981, May 15**

| | | | | |
|---|---|---|---|---|
| **609** | A196 | 23c multicolored | .45 | .25 |

Intl. Year of the Disabled.

Bull's Blood — A197

6c, Lory, vert. 41c, Hummingbird, vert. 50c, Toucan.

**1981, June 26 Litho. *Perf. 12***

| | | | | |
|---|---|---|---|---|
| **610** | A197 | 3c shown | 1.00 | .25 |
| **611** | A197 | 6c multicolored | 1.00 | .25 |
| **612** | A197 | 41c multicolored | 4.25 | .50 |
| **613** | A197 | 50c multicolored | 5.25 | .40 |
| | | *Nos. 610-613 (4)* | 11.50 | 1.40 |

Apparition of the Virgin to St. Catherine Laboure, 150th Anniv. — A198

**1981, June 26 Litho. *Perf. 12***

| | | | | |
|---|---|---|---|---|
| **614** | A198 | 35c multicolored | .90 | .35 |

Gen. Torrijos and Bayano Dam A199

**Wmk. 311**

**1982, Mar. 22 Litho. *Perf. 10½***

| | | | | |
|---|---|---|---|---|
| **615** | A199 | 17c multicolored | .35 | .25 |

78th Anniv. of Independence Soldiers Institute — A200

**1981, Mar. 17 Litho. *Perf. 10½***

| | | | | |
|---|---|---|---|---|
| **616** | A200 | 3c multicolored | .25 | .25 |

First Death Anniv. of Gen. Omar Torrijos Herrera A201

5c, Aerial view. 6c, Army camp. 50c, Felipillo Engineering Works.

**1982, May 14 Litho. *Perf. 10½***

| | | | | |
|---|---|---|---|---|
| **617** | A201 | 5c multicolored | .25 | .25 |
| **618** | A201 | 6c multicolored | .25 | .25 |
| **619** | A201 | 50c multicolored | 1.00 | .40 |
| | | *Nos. 617-619,C433-C434 (5)* | 3.60 | 1.70 |

Ricardo J. Alfaro (1882-1977), Statesman A202

**1982, Aug. 18 Wmk. 382**

| | | | | |
|---|---|---|---|---|
| **620** | A202 | 3c multicolored | .25 | .25 |

See Nos. C436-C437.

1982 World Cup A203

**1982, Dec. 27 Litho. *Perf. 10½***

| | | | | |
|---|---|---|---|---|
| **621** | A203 | 50c Italian team | 1.40 | .50 |

See Nos. C438-C440.

Expo Comer '83, Panama Intl. Commerce Exposition, Jan. 12-16 A204

**Wmk. 382**

**1983, Jan. 12 Litho. *Perf. 10½***

| | | | | |
|---|---|---|---|---|
| **622** | A204 | 17c multicolored | .40 | .30 |

Visit of Pope John Paul II — A205

Various portraits of the Pope. 35c airmail.

***Perf. 12x11***

**1983, Mar. 1 Litho. Wmk. 382**

| | | | | |
|---|---|---|---|---|
| **623** | A205 | 6c multicolored | .45 | .25 |
| **624** | A205 | 17c multicolored | .80 | .25 |
| **625** | A205 | 35c multicolored | 1.75 | .25 |
| | | *Nos. 623-625 (3)* | 3.00 | .75 |

Bank Emblem — A206

**1983, Mar. 18**

| | | | | |
|---|---|---|---|---|
| **626** | A206 | 50c multicolored | 1.25 | .40 |

24th Council Meeting of Inter-American Development Bank, Mar. 21-23.

Simon Bolivar (1783-1830) A207

**1983, July 25 Litho. *Perf. 12***

| | | | | |
|---|---|---|---|---|
| **627** | A207 | 50c multicolored | 1.25 | .50 |

**Souvenir Sheet**

***Imperf***

| | | | | |
|---|---|---|---|---|
| **628** | A207 | 1b like 50c | 4.00 | 1.25 |

World Communications Year — A208

**1983, Oct. 9 Litho. *Perf. 14***

| | | | | |
|---|---|---|---|---|
| **629** | A208 | 30c UPAE emblem | .80 | .25 |
| **630** | A208 | 40c WCY emblem | 1.00 | .35 |
| **631** | A208 | 50c UPU emblem | 1.25 | .45 |
| **632** | A208 | 60c Dove in flight | 1.60 | .55 |
| | | *Nos. 629-632 (4)* | 4.65 | 1.60 |

**Souvenir Sheet**

***Imperf***

| | | | | |
|---|---|---|---|---|
| **633** | A208 | 1b multicolored | 2.75 | 2.75 |

No. 633 contains designs of Nos. 629-632 without denominations.

Freedom of Worship A209

3c, Panama Mosque. 5c, Bahai Temple. 6c, St. Francis Church. 17c, Kol Shearit Israel Synagogue.

**1983, Oct. 21 Litho. *Perf. 11½***

| | | | | |
|---|---|---|---|---|
| **634** | A209 | 3c multicolored | .25 | .25 |
| **635** | A209 | 5c multicolored | .25 | .25 |
| **636** | A209 | 6c multicolored | .25 | .25 |
| **637** | A209 | 17c multicolored | .70 | .25 |
| | | *Nos. 634-637 (4)* | 1.45 | 1.00 |

No. 637 incorrectly inscribed.

Ricardo Miro (1883-1940), Poet — A210

Famous Men: 3c, Richard Newman (1883-1946), educator. 5c, Cristobal Rodriguez (1883-1943), politician. 6c, Alcibiades Arosemena (1883-1958), industrialist and financier. 35c, Cirilo Martinez (1883-1924), linguist.

**1983, Nov. 8** **Litho.** ***Perf. 14***
**638** A210 1c multicolored .25 .25
**639** A210 3c multicolored .25 .25
**640** A210 5c multicolored .25 .25
**641** A210 6c multicolored .25 .25
**642** A210 35c multicolored 1.00 .35
*Nos. 638-642 (5)* 2.00 1.35

The Prophet, by Alfredo Sinclair — A211

#643, Village House, by Juan Manuel Cedeno. #644, Large Nude, by Manuel Chong Neto. 3c, On Another Occasion, by Spiros Vamvas. 6c, Punta Chame Landscape, by Guillermo Trujillo. 28c, Neon Light, by Alfredo Sinclair. 41c, Highland Girls, by Al Sprague. 1b, Bright Morning, by Ignacio Mallol Pibernat. Nos. 643-647, 650 horiz.

**1983, Dec. 12** ***Perf. 12***
**643** A211 1c multicolored .25 .25
**644** A211 1c multicolored .25 .25
**645** A211 3c multicolored .25 .25
**646** A211 6c multicolored .25 .25
**647** A211 28c multicolored .70 .25
**648** A211 35c multicolored .90 .35
**649** A211 41c multicolored 1.00 .40
**650** A211 1b multicolored 2.75 1.00
*Nos. 643-650 (8)* 6.35 3.00

Double Cup, Indian Period A212

Pottery: 40c, Raised dish, Tonosi period. 50c, Jug with face, Canazas period, vert. 60c, Bowl, Conte, vert.

**1984, Jan. 16** **Litho.** ***Perf. 12***
**651** A212 30c multicolored 1.10 .25
**652** A212 40c multicolored 1.25 .30
**653** A212 50c multicolored 1.60 .40
**654** A212 60c multicolored 2.00 .55
*Nos. 651-654 (4)* 5.95 1.50

**Souvenir Sheet**

***Imperf***

**655** A212 1b like 30c 4.50 4.50

Pre-Olympics — A213

**1984, Mar. 15** **Litho.** ***Perf. 14***
**656** A213 19c Baseball .90 .35
**657** A213 19c Basketball, vert. .90 .35
**658** A213 19c Boxing .90 .35
**659** A213 19c Swimming, vert. .90 .35
*Nos. 656-659 (4)* 3.60 1.40

Roberto Duran — A214

**1984, June 14** **Litho.** ***Perf. 14***
**660** A214 26c multicolored .60 .25

1st Panamanian to hold 3 boxing championships.

1984 Olympic Games — A214a

**1984, July, 12** **Litho.** ***Perf. 14***
**660A** A214a 6c Shooting .25 .25
**660B** A214a 30c Weight lifting .90 .30
**660C** A214a 37c Wrestling 1.00 .40
**660D** A214a 1b Long jump 3.00 1.50
*Nos. 660A-660D (4)* 5.15 2.45

**Souvenir Sheet**

**660E** A214a 1b Running 4.75 4.75

Nos. 660B-660D are airmail. No. 660E contains one 45x45x64mm stamp.

Paintings — A215

Paintings by Panamanian artists: 1c, Woman Thinking, by Manuel Chong Neto. 3c, The Child, by Alfredo Sinclair. 6c, A Day in the Life of Rumalda, by Brooke Alfaro. 30c, Highlands People, by Al Sprague. 37c, Intermission during the Dance, by Roberto Sprague. 44c, Punta Chame Forest, by Guillermo Trujillo. 50c, The Blue Plaza, by Juan Manuel Cedeno. 1b, Ira, by Spiros Vamvas.

**1984, Sept. 17** **Litho.** ***Perf. 14***
**661** A215 1c multi .25 .25
**662** A215 3c multi, horiz. .25 .25
**663** A215 6c multi, horiz. .25 .25
**664** A215 30c multi .90 .30
**665** A215 37c multi, horiz. 1.00 .40
**666** A215 44c multi, horiz. 1.25 .50
**667** A215 50c multi, horiz. 1.50 .55
**668** A215 1b multi, horiz. 3.00 1.50
*Nos. 661-668 (8)* 8.40 4.00

Postal Sovereignty — A216

19c, Gen. Torrijos, canal.

**1984, Oct. 1** **Litho.** ***Perf. 12***
**669** A216 19c multicolored .80 .30

Fauna A217

3c, Manatee. 30c, Gato negro. 44c, Tigrillo congo. 50c, Puerco de monte. 1b, Perezoso de tres dedos, vert.

**1984, Dec. 5** **Engr.** ***Perf. 14***
**670** A217 3c black .25 .25
**671** A217 30c black 1.40 .50
**672** A217 44c black 2.00 .75
**673** A217 50c black 2.25 .90
*Nos. 670-673 (4)* 5.90 2.40

**Souvenir Sheet**

**674** A217 1b black 5.00 5.00

Nos. 671-673 are airmail.

Coins A218

***Perf. 11x12***

**1985, Jan. 17** **Litho.** **Wmk. 353**
**675** A218 3c 1935 1c .25 .25
**676** A218 3c 1904 10c .25 .25
**677** A218 6c 1916 5c .25 .25
**678** A218 30c 1904 50c 1.25 .50
**679** A218 37c 1962 half-balboa 1.60 .60
**680** A218 44c 1953 balboa 2.00 .70
*Nos. 675-680 (6)* 5.60 2.55

Nos. 678-680 are airmail.

**Contadora Type of 1985**

Souvenir Sheet

***Perf. 13½x13***

**1985, Oct. 1** **Litho.** **Unwmk.**
**680A** AP108 1b Dove, flags, map 4.50 4.50

Cargo Ship in Lock A219

**1985, Oct. 16** ***Perf. 14***
**681** A219 19c multicolored 1.10 .30

Panama Canal, 70th anniv. (1984).

UN 40th Anniv. A220

**1986, Jan. 17** **Litho.** ***Perf. 14***
**682** A220 23c multicolored .80 .35

Intl. Youth Year A221

**1986, Jan. 17**
**683** A221 30c multicolored .90 .35

Waiting Her Turn, by Al Sprague (b.1938) — A222

Oil paintings: 5c, Aerobics, by Guillermo Trujillo (b. 1927). 19c, Cardboard House, by Eduardo Augustine (b. 1954). 30c, Door to the Homeland, by Juan Manuel Cedeno (b. 1914). 36c, Supper for Three, by Brooke Alfaro (b. 1949). 42c, Tenderness, by Alfredo Sinclair (b. 1915). 50c, Woman and Character, by Manuel Chong Neto (b. 1927). 60c, Calla lillies, by Maigualida de Diaz (b. 1950).

**1986, Jan. 21**
**684** A222 3c multicolored .25 .25
**685** A222 5c multicolored .25 .25
**686** A222 19c multicolored .80 .30
**687** A222 30c multicolored 1.25 .50
**688** A222 36c multicolored 1.50 .55
**689** A222 42c multicolored 1.75 .65
**690** A222 50c multicolored 2.25 .80
**691** A222 60c multicolored 2.75 1.00
*Nos. 684-691 (8)* 10.80 4.30

Miss Universe Pageant A223

**1986, July 7** **Litho.** ***Perf. 12***
**692** A223 23c Atlapa Center .80 .30
**693** A223 60c Emblem, vert. 2.10 .80

Halley's Comet A224

30c, Old Panama Cathedral tower, vert.

**1986, Oct. 30** **Litho.** ***Perf. 13½***
**694** A224 23c multicolored .80 .35
**695** A224 30c multicolored 1.00 .35

**Size: 75x86mm**

***Imperf***

**695A** A224 1b multicolored 8.00

A225

1986 World Cup Soccer Championships, Mexico — Illustrations from Soccer History, by Sandoval and Meron: 23c, Argentina, winner. 30c, Fed. Rep. of Germany, 2nd. 37c, Argentina, Germany.

1b, Argentina, two players one with black shorts, one with blue shorts.

**1986, Oct. 30**
**696** A225 23c multicolored .90 .35
**697** A225 30c multicolored 1.00 .35
**698** A225 37c multicolored 1.25 .60
*Nos. 696-698 (3)* 3.15 1.30

**Souvenir Sheet**

**698A** A225 1b multicolored 4.00

A226

**1986, Nov. 21**
**699** A226 20c shown .65 .25
**700** A226 23c Montage of events .70 .35

15th Central American and Caribbean Games, Dominican Republic.

Christmas A227

**1986, Dec. 18** **Litho.**

| | | |
|---|---|---|
| 701 A227 23c shown | .70 | .30 |
| 702 A227 36c Green tree | 1.10 | .50 |
| 703 A227 42c Silver tree | 1.25 | .55 |
| *Nos. 701-703 (3)* | 3.05 | 1.35 |

Intl. Peace Year — A228

**1986, Dec. 30** ***Perf. 13½***

| | | |
|---|---|---|
| 704 A228 8c multicolored | .25 | .25 |
| 705 A228 19c multicolored | .65 | .25 |

Tropical Carnival, Feb.-Mar. A229

20c, Diablito Sucio mask. 35c, Sun.

**1987, Jan. 27** **Litho.** ***Perf. 13½***

| | | |
|---|---|---|
| 706 A229 20c multi | .65 | .30 |
| 707 A229 35c multi | 1.25 | .50 |

**Size: 74x84mm**

***Imperf***

| | | |
|---|---|---|
| 708 A229 1b like 35c | 3.25 | 1.50 |
| *Nos. 706-708 (3)* | 5.15 | 2.30 |

1st Panamanian Eye Bank — A230

**1987, Feb. 17** **Litho.** ***Perf. 14***

| | | |
|---|---|---|
| 709 A230 37c multicolored | 1.25 | .75 |

Panama Lions Club, 50th Anniv. (in 1985). Dated 1986.

Flowering Plants — A231

Birds A232

3c, Brownea macrophylla. 5c, Thraupis episcopus. 8c, Solandra grandiflora. 15c, Tyrannus melancholicus. 19c, Barleria micans. 23c, Pelecanus occidentalis. 30c, Cordia dentata. 36c, Columba cayennensis.

**1987, Mar. 5**

| | | |
|---|---|---|
| 710 A231 3c multicolored | .25 | .25 |
| 711 A232 5c multicolored | .25 | .25 |
| 712 A231 8c multicolored | .25 | .25 |
| 713 A232 15c multicolored | .55 | .25 |
| 714 A231 19c multicolored | .70 | .35 |
| 715 A232 23c multicolored | .80 | .35 |
| 716 A231 30c multicolored | 1.10 | .45 |
| 717 A232 36c multicolored | 1.50 | .55 |
| *Nos. 710-717 (8)* | 5.40 | 2.70 |

Dated 1986.

Monument and Octavio Mendez Pereira, Founder A233

**1987, Mar. 26** **Litho.** ***Perf. 14***

| | | |
|---|---|---|
| 718 A233 19c multicolored | .65 | .30 |

University of Panama, 50th anniv. (in 1985). Stamp dated "1986."

UNFAO, 40th Anniv. (in 1985) A234

**1987, Apr. 9** ***Perf. 13½***

| | | |
|---|---|---|
| 719 A234 10c blk, pale ol & yel org | .25 | .25 |
| 720 A234 45c blk, dk grn & yel grn | 1.50 | .70 |

Natl. Theater, 75th Anniv. A235

Baroque composers: 19c, Schutz (1585-1672). 37c, Bach. 60c, Handel. Nos. 721, 723-724 vert.

**1987, Apr. 28** ***Perf. 14***

| | | |
|---|---|---|
| 721 A235 19c multicolored | .55 | .30 |
| 722 A235 30c shown | .90 | .50 |
| 723 A235 37c multicolored | 1.00 | .60 |
| 724 A235 60c multicolored | 1.75 | 1.00 |
| *Nos. 721-724 (4)* | 4.20 | 2.40 |

A236

**1987, May 13** **Litho.** ***Perf. 14***

| | | |
|---|---|---|
| 725 A236 23c multicolored | .70 | .45 |

Inter-American Development Bank, 25th anniv.

Panama Fire Brigade, Cent. — A237

25c, Fire wagon, 1887, and modern ladder truck. 35c, Fireman carrying victim.

**1987, Nov. 28** **Litho.** ***Perf. 14***

| | | |
|---|---|---|
| 726 A237 25c multicolored | 1.25 | .40 |
| 727 A237 35c multicolored | 1.75 | .60 |

A238

**1987, Dec. 11**

| | | |
|---|---|---|
| 728 A238 15c Wrestling, horiz. | .70 | .25 |
| 729 A238 23c Tennis | 1.00 | .40 |
| 730 A238 30c Swimming, horiz. | 1.25 | .50 |
| 731 A238 41c Basketball | 1.75 | .70 |
| 732 A238 60c Cycling | 2.50 | 1.00 |
| *Nos. 728-732 (5)* | 7.20 | 2.85 |

**Souvenir Sheet**

| | | |
|---|---|---|
| 733 A238 1b Weight lifting | 3.75 | 3.75 |

10th Pan American Games, Indianapolis. For surcharges see Nos. 813, 817.

A239

Christmas (Religious paintings): 22c, Adoration of the Magi, by Albrecht Nentz (d. 1479). 35c, Virgin Adored by Angels, by Matthias Grunewald (d. 1528). 37c, The Virgin and Child, by Konrad Witz (c. 1400-1445).

**1987, Dec. 17**

| | | |
|---|---|---|
| 734 A239 22c multicolored | .70 | .35 |
| 735 A239 35c multicolored | 1.10 | .60 |
| 736 A239 37c multicolored | 1.10 | .60 |
| *Nos. 734-736 (3)* | 2.90 | 1.55 |

Intl. Year of Shelter for the Homeless A240

45c, by A. Sinclair. 50c, Woman, boy, girl, shack, housing in perspective by A. Pulido.

**1987, Dec. 29** ***Perf. 14***

| | | |
|---|---|---|
| 737 A240 45c multicolored | 1.25 | .75 |
| 738 A240 50c multicolored | 1.40 | .80 |

For surcharge see No. 814.

Reforestation Campaign — A241

**1988, Jan. 14** **Litho.** ***Perf. 14½x14***

| | | |
|---|---|---|
| 739 A241 35c dull grn & yel grn | 1.10 | .55 |
| 740 A241 40c red & pink | 1.25 | .70 |
| 741 A241 45c brn & lemon | 1.50 | .75 |
| *Nos. 739-741 (3)* | 3.85 | 2.00 |

Dated 1987. For surcharge see No. 816.

Say No to Drugs — A242

**1988, Jan. 14**

| | | |
|---|---|---|
| 742 A242 10c org lil rose | .25 | .25 |
| 743 A242 17c yel grn & lil rose | .65 | .30 |
| 744 A242 25c pink & sky blue | 1.00 | .40 |
| *Nos. 742-744 (3)* | 1.90 | .95 |

Child Survival Campaign A243

20c, Breast-feeding. 31c, Universal immunization. 45c, Growth and development, vert.

**1988, Feb. 29** **Litho.** ***Perf. 14***

| | | |
|---|---|---|
| 745 A243 20c multicolored | .65 | .35 |
| 746 A243 31c multicolored | 1.10 | .60 |
| 747 A243 45c multicolored | 1.75 | .90 |
| *Nos. 745-747 (3)* | 3.50 | 1.85 |

For surcharge see No. 816A.

Fish A244

7c, Myripristis jacobus. 35c, Pomacanthus paru. 60c, Holocanthus tricolor. 1b, Equetus punctatus.

**1988, Mar. 14**

| | | |
|---|---|---|
| 748 A244 7c multicolored | .25 | .25 |
| 749 A244 35c multicolored | 1.10 | .60 |
| 750 A244 60c multicolored | 2.00 | 1.00 |
| 751 A244 1b multicolored | 3.50 | 1.60 |
| *Nos. 748-751 (4)* | 6.85 | 3.45 |

The 7c actually shows the Holocanthus tricolor, the 60c the Myripristis jacobus. For surcharge see No. 819.

Girl Guides, 75th Anniv. — A245

**1988, Apr. 14**

| | | |
|---|---|---|
| 752 A245 35c multicolored | 1.00 | .60 |

Christmas A246

Paintings: 17c, *Virgin and Gift-givers.* 45c, *Virgin of the Rosary and St. Dominic.*

**1988, Dec. 29** **Litho.** ***Perf. 12***

| | | |
|---|---|---|
| 753 A246 17c multicolored | .65 | .30 |
| 754 A246 45c multicolored | 1.50 | .75 |

See No. C446.

St. John Bosco (1815-1888) A247

**1989, Jan. 31**

| | | |
|---|---|---|
| 755 A247 10c Portrait | .25 | .25 |
| 756 A247 20c Minor Basilica | .65 | .35 |

1988 Summer Olympics, Seoul A248

Athletes and medals.

**1989, Mar. 17 Litho. *Perf. 12***

**757** A248 17c Running .55 .30
**758** A248 25c Wrestling .80 .40
**759** A248 60c Weight lifting 2.00 1.00
*Nos. 757-759 (3)* 3.35 1.70

**Souvenir Sheet**

**760** A248 1b Swimming, vert. 3.75 3.75

See No. C447.

A249

1b, Emergency and rescue services.

**1989, Apr. 12 Litho. *Perf. 12***

**761** A249 40c red, blk & blue 1.25 .75
**762** A249 1b multicolored 3.25 1.75

Intl. Red Cross and Red Crescent organizations, 125th annivs.

America Issue: Pre-Columbian Artifacts — A250

20c, Monolith of Barriles. 35c, Vessel.

**1989, Oct. 12 Litho. *Perf. 12***

**767** A250 20c multi 1.25 .50
**768** A250 35c multi 2.75 1.25

French Revolution, Bicent. A251

**1989, Nov. 14 *Perf. 13½***

**769** A251 25c multicolored 1.10 .50
*Nos. 769,C450-C451 (3)* 4.95 2.00

Christmas — A252

17c, Holy family in Panamanian costume. 35c, Creche. 45c, Holy family, gift givers.

**1989, Dec. 1**

**770** A252 17c multicolored .70 .30
**771** A252 35c multicolored 1.50 .65
**772** A252 45c multicolored 2.00 .85
*Nos. 770-772 (3)* 4.20 1.80

Rogelio Sinán (b. 1902), Writer — A253

**1990, July 3**

**773** A253 23c brown & blue .70 .45

A254

**1990, Nov. 20 Litho. *Perf. 13½***

**774** A254 25c blue & black 1.00 .45
**775** A254 35c Experiment 1.25 .60
**776** A254 45c Beakers, test tubes, books 1.60 .75
*Nos. 774-776 (3)* 3.85 1.80

Dr. Guillermo Patterson, Jr., chemist.

Fruits A255

20c, Byrsonima crassifolia. 35c, Bactris gasipaes. 40c, Anacardium occidentale.

**1990, May 18 *Perf. 13½***

**777** A255 20c multicolored .55 .35
**778** A255 35c multicolored 1.10 .60
**779** A255 40c multicolored 1.50 .70
*Nos. 777-779 (3)* 3.15 1.65

Tortoises A256

35c, Pseudemys scripta. 45c, Lepidochelys olivacea. 60c, Geochelone carbonaria.

**1990, Sept. 11**

**780** A256 35c multicolored 1.40 .60
**781** A256 45c multicolored 1.75 .75
**782** A256 60c multicolored 2.50 1.00
*Nos. 780-782 (3)* 5.65 2.35

For surcharges see Nos. 815, 818.

Native American A257

**1990, Oct. 12**

**783** A257 20c shown 1.40 .40
**784** A257 35c Native, vert. 2.25 .85

Discovery of Isthmus of Panama, 490th Anniv. — A258

**1991, Nov. 19 Litho. *Perf. 12***

**785** A258 35c multicolored 1.75 1.25

St. Ignatius of Loyola, 500th Birth Anniv. — A259

No. 786, St. Ignatius of Loyola.

No. 786B: c, St. Ignatius' seal over map of Panama (horiz.); d, 5c stamp, Panama Scott No. C119 in black (horiz.).

**1991, Nov. 29**

**786** A259 20c multicolored .65 .30
*a.* Tete beche pair 1.25 1.25

**Souvenir Sheet**

**786B** Sheet of 2, #a.-b. — —
*c.* A259 25c multi — —
*d.* A259 25c multi — —

Society of Jesus, 450th anniv.

Christmas A260

**1991, Dec. 2**

**787** A260 35c Luke 2:14 1.10 .65
**788** A260 35c Nativity scene 1.10 .65
*a.* Pair, #787-788 2.25 2.25

Social Security Administration, 50th Anniv. — A261

Design: No. 790, Dr. Arnulfo Arias Madrid (1901-1988), Constitution of Panama, 1941.

**1991, Feb. 20 Litho. *Perf. 12***

**789** A261 10c multicolored .35 .25
**790** A261 10c multicolored .35 .25

Women's citizenship rights, 50th anniv. (No. 790).

Epiphany — A262

**1992, Feb. 5 Litho. *Perf. 12***

**791** A262 10c multicolored .50 .25
*a.* Tete beche pair 1.00 .30

New Life Housing Project — A263

**1992, Feb. 17**

**792** A263 5c multicolored .50 .25
*a.* Tete beche pair 1.00 .50

Border Treaty Between Panama and Costa Rica, 50th Anniv. — A264

a, 20c, Hands clasped. b, 40c, Map. c, 50c, Pres. Rafael A. Calderon, Costa Rica, Pres. Arnulfo Arias Madrid, Panama.

**1992, Feb. 20**

**793** A264 Strip of 3, #a.-c. 3.25 3.25

Causes of Hole in Ozone Layer — A265

**1992, Feb. 24**

**794** A265 40c multicolored 1.75 .70
*a.* Tete beche pair 3.50 3.50

Expocomer '92, Intl. Commercial Exposition — A266

**1992, Mar. 11**

**795** A266 10c multicolored .25 .25

A267

Margot Fonteyn (1919-91), ballerina: a, 35c, Wearing dress. b, 45c, In costume.

**1992, Mar. 13**

**796** A267 Pair, #a.-b. 4.50 4.50

A268

**1992, June 22 Litho. *Perf. 12***

**797** A268 10c multicolored .50 .25
*a.* Tete beche pair 1.00 .30

Maria Olimpia de Obaldia (1891-1985), poet.

1992 Summer Olympics, Barcelona — A269

**1992, June 22 Litho. *Perf. 12***

**798** A269 10c multicolored .50 .25
*a.* Tete-beche pair 1.00 .35

Zion Baptist Church, Bocas del Toro, 1892 — A270

**1992, Oct. 1 Litho. *Perf. 12***

**799** A270 20c multicolored .65 .35
*a.* Tete beche pair 1.25 1.25

Baptist Church in Panama, Cent.

Discovery of America, 500th Anniv. — A271

a, 20c, Columbus' fleet. b, 35c, Coming ashore.

**1992, Oct. 12**

**800** A271 Pair, #a.-b. 3.00 3.00

Endangered Wildlife — A272

a, 5c, Agouti paca. b, 10c, Harpia harpyja. c, 15c, Felis onca. d, 20c, Iguana iguana.

**1992, Sept. 23**

**801** A272 Strip of 4, #a.-d. 6.25 6.25

Expo '92, Seville — A273

**1992, Dec. 21 Litho. *Perf. 12***

**802** A273 10c multicolored .50 .25
*a.* Tete beche pair 1.00 .30

Worker's Health Year — A274

**1992, Dec. 21**

**803** A274 15c multicolored .45 .30
*a.* Tete beche pair 1.00 1.00

Unification of Europe — A275

**1992, Dec. 21 Litho. *Perf. 12***

**804** A275 10c multi + label .75 .25

Christmas — A276

a, 20c, Angel announcing birth of Christ. b, 35c, Mary and Joseph approaching city gate.

**1992, Dec. 21**

**805** A276 Pair, #a.-b. 1.75 1.75

Evangelism in America, 500th Anniv. (in 1992) — A277

**1993, Apr. 13 Litho. *Perf. 12***

**806** A277 10c multicolored .50 .25
*a.* Tete beche pair 1.00 .30

Natl. Day for the Disabled A278

**1993, May 10**

**807** A278 5c multicolored .50 .25
*a.* Tete beche pair 1.00 .50

Dr. Jose de la Cruz Herrera (1876-1961), Humanitarian A279

**1993, May 26**

**808** A279 5c multicolored .50 .25
*a.* Tete beche pair 1.00 .50

1992 Intl. Conference on Nutrition, Rome — A280

**1993, June 22 Litho. *Perf. 12***

**809** A280 10c multicolored .50 .25
*a.* Tete beche pair 1.00 .50

Columbus' Exploration of the Isthmus of Panama, 490th Anniv. — A281

**1994, June 2 Litho. *Perf. 12***

**810** A281 50c multicolored 1.50 .95
*a.* Tete beche pair + 2 labels 3.00 3.00

Dated 1993.

Greek Community in Panama, 50th Anniv. A282

Designs: 20c, Greek influences in Panama, Panamanian flag, vert. No. 812a, Parthenon. No. 812b, Greek Orthodox Church.

**1995, Feb. 16 Litho. *Perf. 12***

**811** A282 20c multicolored .45 .30

**Souvenir Sheet**

**812** A282 75c Sheet of 2, #a.-b. 4.00 2.50

Nos. 729, 731, 737, 741, 747, 750, 781-782 Surcharged

**1995 *Perfs., Etc. as Before***

| | | | | |
|---|---|---|---|---|
| **813** | A238 | 20c on 23c #729 | .75 | .35 |
| **814** | A240 | 25c on 45c #737 | 1.10 | .50 |
| **815** | A256 | 30c on 45c #781 | 1.25 | .65 |
| **816** | A241 | 35c on 45c #741 | 1.40 | .75 |
| **816A** | A243 | 35c on 45c No. 747 | 1.60 | .85 |
| **817** | A238 | 40c on 41c #731 | 1.90 | .90 |
| **818** | A256 | 50c on 60c #782 | 3.00 | 1.25 |
| **819** | A244 | 1b on 60c No. 750 | 5.00 | 2.50 |
| | | *Nos. 813-819 (8)* | 16.00 | 7.75 |

Issued: #816A, 819, 5/6; Others, 3/3.

First Settlement of Panama, 475th Anniv. (in 1994) — A283

Designs: 15c, Horse and wagon crossing bridge. 20c, Arms of first Panama City, vert. 25c, Model of an original cathedral. 35c, Ruins of cathedral, vert.

**1996, Oct. 11 Litho. *Perf. 14***

| | | | | |
|---|---|---|---|---|
| **820** | A283 | 15c beige, blk & brn | .45 | .30 |
| **821** | A283 | 20c multicolored | .65 | .40 |
| **822** | A283 | 25c beige, blk & brn | .80 | .45 |
| **823** | A283 | 35c beige, blk & brn | 1.25 | .70 |
| | | *Nos. 820-823 (4)* | 3.15 | 1.85 |

Endangered Species — A284

**1996, Oct. 18 Litho. *Perf. 14***

**824** A284 20c Tinamus major 1.25 .60

Mammals A285

a, Nasua narica. b, Tamandua mexicana. c, Cyclopes didactylus. d, Felis concolor.

**1996, Oct. 18**

**825** A285 25c Block of 4, #a.-d. 4.75 4.75

A286

**1996, Oct. 22 Litho. *Perf. 14***

**826** A286 40c multicolored 1.25 .75

Kiwanis Clubs of Panama, 25th anniv. (in 1993.)

A287

**1996, Oct. 15**

**827** A287 5b multicolored 15.00 9.50

Rotary Clubs of Panama, 75th anniv. (in 1994).

UN, 50th anniv. (in 1995) — A288

**1996, Oct. 21**

**828** A288 45c multicolored 1.40 .85

A289

Design: Ferdinand de Lesseps (1805-94), builder of Suez Canal.

**1996, Oct. 21**
**829** A289 35c multicolored 1.10 .70

Andrés Bello Covenant, 25th Anniv. (in 1995) — A290

**1996, Oct. 23**
**830** A290 35c multicolored 1.25 .70

Chinese Presence in Panama A291

**1996, June 10** *Perf. 14½*
**831** A291 60c multicolored 2.25 1.10

**Litho.**
***Imperf***
**Size: 80x68mm**

Patterns depicting four seasons: 1.50b, Invierno, Primavera, Verano, Otono.

**832** A291 1.50b multicolored 5.00 5.00

Radiology, Cent. (in 1995) — A292

**1996, Oct. 24 Litho.** *Perf. 14*
**833** A292 1b multicolored 3.00 1.90

University of Panama, 60th Anniv. A293

**1996, Oct. 14**
**834** A293 40c multicolored 1.25 .75

Christmas — A295

**1996, Oct. 24 Litho.** *Perf. 14*
**836** A295 35c multicolored 1.10 .70

Mail Train A296

**1996, Dec. 10 Litho.** *Perf. 14*
**837** A296 30c multicolored 2.00 .60

America issue.

Universal Congress of the Panama Canal — A297

No. 838: a, Pedro Miguel Locks. b, Miraflores Double Locks. 1.50b, Gatún Locks.

**1997, Sept. 9 Litho.** *Perf. 14½x14*
**838** A297 45c Pair, #a.-b. 2.75 2.75

***Imperf***

**839** A297 1.50b multicolored 5.00 5.00

Perforated portion of No. 839 is 76x31mm.

Torrijos-Carter Panama Canal Treaties, 20th Anniv. — A298

Designs: 20c, Painting, "Panama, More Than a Canal," by C. Gonzalez P. 30c, "Curtain of Our Flag," by A. Siever M., vert. 45c, "Huellas Perpetuas," by R. Marinez R. 50c, 1.50b, #588.

**1997, Sept. 9** *Perf. 14*
**840** A298 20c multicolored .65 .50
**841** A298 30c multicolored 1.00 .75
**842** A298 45c multicolored 1.40 1.10
**843** A298 50c multicolored 1.60 1.25
*Nos. 840-843 (4)* 4.65 3.60

***Imperf***

**844** A298 1.50b multicolored *5.00 5.00*

Perforated portion of No. 844 is 114x50mm.

India's Independence, 50th Anniv. — A299

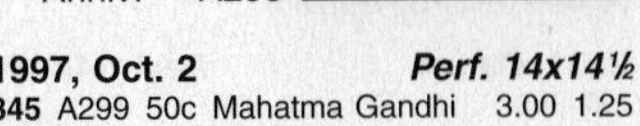

**1997, Oct. 2** *Perf. 14x14½*
**845** A299 50c Mahatma Gandhi 3.00 1.25

Crocodylus Acutus A300

World Wildlife Fund: a, Heading right. b, Looking left. c, One in distance, one up close. d, With mouth wide open.

**1997, Nov. 18** *Perf. 14½x14*
**846** A300 25c Block of 4, #a.-d. 5.50 5.50

Christmas A301

**1997, Nov. 18 Litho.** *Perf. 14x14½*
**847** A301 35c multicolored 1.75 .70

Colon Fire Brigade, Cent. A302

**1997, Nov. 21 Litho.** *Perf. 14½x14*
**848** A302 20c multicolored .65 .50

Frogs — A303

Designs: a, Eleutherodactylus biporcatus. b, Hyla colymba. c, Hyla rufitela. d, Nelsonphryne aterrima.

**1997, Nov. 21**
**849** A303 25c Block of 4, #a.-d. 3.25 3.25

National Costumes A304

**1997, Nov. 25**
**850** A304 20c multicolored 1.00 .75

America issue.

Colon Chamber of Commerce, Agriculture and Industry, 85th Anniv. — A305

**1997, Nov. 27** *Perf. 14x14½*
**851** A305 1b multicolored 3.25 2.50

Justo Arosemena, Lawyer, Politician, Death Cent. (in 1996) — A306

**1997, Nov. 27**
**852** A306 40c multicolored 1.25 1.00

Panamanian Aviation Co., 50th Anniv. — A307

Designs: a, Douglas DC-3. b, Martin-404. c, Avro HS-748. d, Electra L-168. e, Boeing B727-100. f, Boeing B737-200 Advanced.

**1997, Dec. 3** *Perf. 14½x14*
**853** A307 35c Block of 6, #a.-f. 6.75 6.75

Jerusalem, 3000th Anniv. — A308

20c, Jewish people at the Wailing Wall. 25c, Christians being led in worship at Church of the Holy Sepulchre. 60c, Muslims at the Dome of the Rock.

**1997, Dec. 29** *Perf. 14x14½*
**854** A308 20c multicolored .65 .50
**855** A308 25c multicolored .80 .65
**856** A308 60c multicolored 1.75 1.50
*Nos. 854-856 (3)* 3.20 2.65

***Imperf***

**857** A308 1.50b like #854-856 5.00 5.00

Perforated portion of No. 857 is 90x40mm.

Tourism A309

10c, Old center of town, Panama City. 20c, Soberania Park. 25c, Panama Canal. 35c, Panama Bay. 40c, Fort St. Jerónimo. 45c, Rafting on Chagres River. 60c, Beach, Kuna Yala Region.

***Perf. 14x14½, 14½x14***

**1998, July 7 Litho.**
**858** A309 10c multi, vert .25 .25
**859** A309 20c multi, vert .65 .40
**860** A309 25c multi .80 .50
**861** A309 35c multi 1.10 .70
**862** A309 40c multi 1.25 .80
**863** A309 45c multi 1.50 .90
**864** A309 60c multi 2.00 1.25
*Nos. 858-864 (7)* 7.55 4.80

Organization of American States (OAS), 50th Anniv. — A310

**1998, Apr. 30** *Perf. 14½x14*
**865** A310 40c multicolored 1.25 .80

Colón Free Trade Zone, 50th Anniv. — A311

*Perf. 14x14½*
**1998, Feb. 2 Litho. Unwmk.**
**866** A311 15c multi .70 .40

Protection of the Harpy Eagle — A312

Contest-winning art by students: a, Luis Mellilo. b, Jorvisis Jiménez. c, Samuel Castro. d, Jorge Ramos.

**1998, Jan. 20**
**867** A312 20c Block of 4, #a.-d. 4.50 4.50

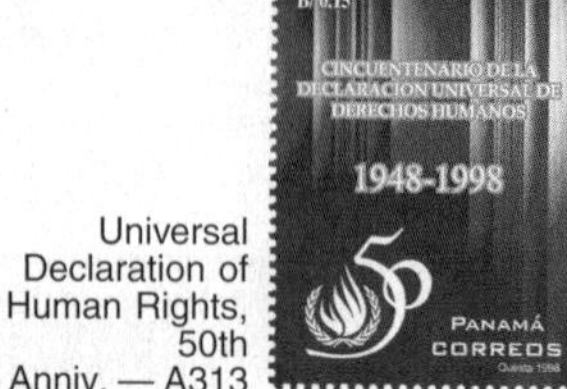
Universal Declaration of Human Rights, 50th Anniv. — A313

**1998, Feb. 10**
**868** A313 15c multi .70 .30

Panamanian Assoc. of Business Executives, 40th Anniv. — A314

**1998, Jan. 28** *Perf. 14½x14*
**869** A314 50c multi 2.25 1.00

Beetles — A315

Designs: a, Platyphora haroldi. b, Stilodes leoparda. c, Stilodes fuscolineata. d, Platyphora boucardi.

**1998, Feb. 10**
**870** A315 30c Block of 4, #a.-d. 6.75 6.75

Christmas — A316

**1998, Jan. 14 Litho.** *Perf. 14x14½*
**871** A316 40c multi 1.40 .80

Panama Pavilion, Expo '98, Lisbon A317

**1998, Jan. 14 Litho.** *Perf. 14½x14*
**872** A317 45c multi 1.60 .90

Panama Canal, 85th Anniv. (in 1999) — A318

No. 873: a, Canal builders and crane on train trestle. b, Partially built structures, construction equipment.

**2000, Sept. 7 Litho.** *Perf. 14½x14*
**873** A318 40c Pair, #a-b 4.00 4.00

**Souvenir Sheet**

**874** A318 1.50b Valley 7.50 7.50

No. 874 contains one label.

Reversion of Panama Canal to Panama (in 1999) A319

Various ships. Denominations: 20c, 35c, 40c, 45c.

**2000, Sept. 7** *Perf. 14½x14*
**875-878** A319 Set of 4 6.25 3.50

Pres. Arnulfo Arias Madrid (1901-88) — A320

No. 879: a, 20c, Arias as medical doctor, with people. b, 20c, Arias giving speech, holding glasses.

No. 880, a, 30c, Arias in 1941, 1951 and 1969, Panamanian flag. b, 30c, Arias giving speech, crowd.

**2001, Aug. 14 Litho.** *Perf. 13x13½*
**Horiz. pairs, #a-b**
**879-880** A320 Set of 2 4.50 4.50

Christmas — A321

**2001, Dec. 4 Litho.** *Perf. 14x14½*
**881** A321 35c multi .80 .70

Dated 1999.

Holy Year (in 2000) A322

**2001, Dec. 4** *Perf. 14½x14*
**882** A322 20c multi .90 .50

Dated 2000.

18th UPAEP Congress (in 2000) A323

**2001, Dec. 4**
**883** A323 5b multi 22.50 12.50

Dated 2000.

Dreaming of the Future — A324

Children's art by: No. 884, 20c, I. Guerra. No. 885, 20c, D. Ortega.
No. 886, horiz.: a, J. Aguilar P. b, S. Sittón.

**2001, Dec. 4** *Perf. 14x14½*
**884-885** A324 Set of 2 1.75 1.00

**Souvenir Sheet**
*Perf. 14½x14*

**886** A324 75c Sheet of 2, #a-b 6.75 6.75

Dated 2000.

Architecture of the 1990s — A325

Designs: No. 887, 35c, Los Delfines Condominium, by Edwin Brown. No. 888, 35c, Banco General Tower, by Carlos Medina.
No. 889, horiz.: a, Building with round sides, by Ricardo Moreno. b, Building with three peaked roofs, by Moreno.

**2001, Dec. 4** *Perf. 14x14½*
**887-888** A325 Set of 2 3.25 1.75

**Souvenir Sheet**
*Perf. 14½x14*

**889** A325 75c Sheet of 2, #a-b 6.75 6.75

Dated 2000.

Orchids A326

Designs: No. 890, 35c, Cattleya dowiana. No. 891, 35c, Psychopsis krameriana.
No. 892: a, Peristeria clata. b, Miltoniopsis roezlii.

**2001, Dec. 4** *Perf. 14½x14*
**890-891** A326 Set of 2 3.25 1.75

**Souvenir Sheet**

**892** A326 75c Sheet of 2, #a-b 6.75 6.75

Dated 2000.

San Fernando Hospital, 50th Anniv. (in 1999) A327

**2001, Dec. 21 Litho.** *Perf. 14½x14*
**893** A327 20c multi .90 .50

Dated 2000.

Pres. Mireya Moscoso A328

**2002, Mar. 25**
**894** A328 35c multi 1.60 .90

Dated 2000.

Independence From Spain, 180th Anniv. — A329

Details from mural by Roberto Lewis: No. 895, 15c, "180" at L. No. 896, 15c, "180" at R.

**2002, Apr. 30** *Perf. 13¼x13*
**895-896** A329 Set of 2 1.25 .70

Dated 2001.

Discovery of the Isthmus, 500th Anniv. A330

Designs: 50c, Natives, ship. 5b, Native, European, crucifix, ships.

**2002, Apr. 30** *Perf. 13x13¼*
**897-898** A330 Set of 2 21.00 12.00

Dated 2001. No. 898 is airmail.

America Issue — UNESCO World Heritage — A331

No. 899, 15c: a, Castle of San Lorenzo. b, Salón Bolivar, Panama City.

No. 900, 1.50b, horiz.: a, Cathedral, Panama City. b, Portobelo Fortifications.

**2002, May 30** ***Perf. 13¼x13, 13x13¼***
**Horiz. Pairs, #a-b**

| | | | |
|---|---|---|---|
| **899-900** A331 Set of 2 | 14.50 | 8.00 |

Dated 2001. No. 900 is airmail.

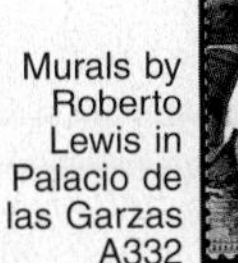

Murals by Roberto Lewis in Palacio de las Garzas A332

No. 901: a, Heron, flagbearer and natives. b, Battle with natives. c, Woman, horse, men. d, Heron, woman in dress, woman picking fruit.

**2002, June 19** ***Perf. 13x13¼***

| | | |
|---|---|---|
| **901** Horiz. strip of 4 | 1.60 | 1.60 |
| *a.-d.* A332 5c Any single | .40 | .25 |

Dated 2001.

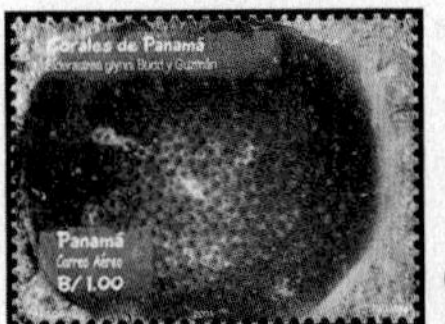

Corals A333

No. 902: a, Montastraea annularis. b, Pavona chiriquiensis.

1b, Siderastrea glynni. 2b, Pociliopora.

**2002, June 28**

| | | |
|---|---|---|
| **902** A333 10c Horiz. pair, #a-b | .70 | .40 |
| **903** A333 1b multi | 4.00 | 2.00 |
| **904** A333 2b multi | 8.00 | 4.00 |
| *Nos. 902-904 (3)* | 12.70 | 6.40 |

Dated 2001. Nos. 903-904 are airmail.

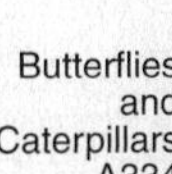

Butterflies and Caterpillars A334

Designs: No. 905, 10c, Ophioderes materna. No. 906, 10c, Rhuda focula. 1b, Morpho peleides. 2b, Tarchon felderi.

**2002, June 28** **Litho.** ***Perf. 13x13¼***

| | | |
|---|---|---|
| **905-908** A334 Set of 4 | 14.50 | 8.00 |

Dated 2001. Nos. 907-908 are airmail.

Christmas 2002 A335

**2003, June 16** **Litho.** ***Perf. 14***

| | | |
|---|---|---|
| **909** A335 15c multi | .60 | .60 |

Dated 2002.

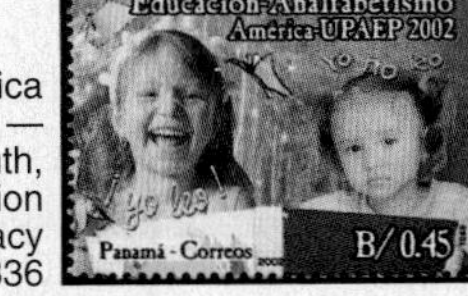

America Issue — Youth, Education and Literacy A336

**2003, June 23**

| | | |
|---|---|---|
| **910** A336 45c multi | 1.40 | .90 |

Dated 2002.

Clara González de Behringer, First Female Lawyer in Panama — A337

**2003, July 10** ***Perf. 13½x13***

| | | |
|---|---|---|
| **911** A337 30c multi | 1.00 | .60 |

Dated 2002.

Colón, 150th Anniv. (in 2002) — A338

**2003, July 17**

| | | |
|---|---|---|
| **912** A338 15c multi | .55 | .30 |

Dated 2002.

Luis C. Russell (b. 1902), Jazz Musician A339

**2003, Aug. 6** ***Perf. 14***

| | | |
|---|---|---|
| **913** A339 10c multi | .50 | .25 |

Dated 2002.

Artwork in the National Theater — A340

Designs: No. 914, 5c, Statue of Erato (holding lyre). No. 915, 5c, Statue of Melpomene (holding mask). 50c, Decoration on front of theater box, horiz. 60c, Theater facade and painting, horiz.

***Perf. 13½x13, 14 (50c), 13x13½ (60c)***
**2003, Aug. 12**

| | | |
|---|---|---|
| **914-917** A340 Set of 4 | 4.00 | 2.40 |

Dated 2002. Nos. 916-917 are airmail.

St. Josemaría Escrivá de Balaguer (1902-75) — A341

**2003, Aug. 13** ***Perf. 14***

| | | |
|---|---|---|
| **918** A341 10c multi | .50 | .25 |

Dated 2002.

Republic of Panama, Cent. A342

Designs: 5c, National arms. 10c, First national flag. No. 921a, Manuel Amador Guerrero, first president. No. 921b, Pres. Mireya Moscoso. 25c, Declaration of Independence. No. 923a, Sterculia apetala. No. 923b, Peristeria elata. 35c, Revolutionary junta. 45c, Flag, Constitution of 1904, Constituent Delegates.

**2003, Nov. 26** ***Perf. 12***

| | | |
|---|---|---|
| **919** A342 5c multi | .40 | .25 |
| **920** A342 10c multi | .50 | .25 |
| **921** A342 15c Horiz. pair, #a-b | 1.25 | .95 |
| **922** A342 25c multi | 1.20 | .80 |
| **923** A342 30c Horiz. pair, #a-b | 2.75 | 2.10 |
| **924** A342 35c multi | 1.60 | 1.10 |
| **925** A342 45c multi | 2.10 | 1.40 |
| *Nos. 919-925 (7)* | 9.80 | 6.85 |

Nos. 924-925 are airmail.

**Republic of Panama, Cent. Type of 2003 Redrawn**

**2003, Nov. 26** **Litho.** ***Perf. 12***

| | | |
|---|---|---|
| **925A** Souvenir booklet | 12.00 | |
| *b.* Booklet pane, #f-g | .80 | — |
| *c.* Booklet pane, #h-i | 1.60 | — |
| *d.* Booklet pane, #j, m | 3.50 | — |
| *e.* Booklet pane, #k-l | 3.50 | — |
| *f.* A342 5c Similar to #919 | .35 | .25 |
| *g.* A342 10c Similar to #920 | .35 | .25 |
| *h.* A342 15c Similar to #921a | .75 | .30 |
| *i.* A342 15c Similar to #921b | .75 | .30 |
| *j.* A342 25c Similar to #922 | 1.60 | .50 |
| *k.* A342 30c Similar to #923a | 1.60 | .60 |
| *l.* A342 30c Similar to #923b | 1.60 | .60 |
| *m.* A342 35c Similar to #924 | 1.60 | .70 |

The text "1903 — Centenario de lar República de Panamá - 2003" is inscribed across the se-tenant pair stamps in each booklet pane. Other differences in text are also on each of Nos. 925Af-925Am.

Christmas A343

**2003, Nov. 28**

| | | |
|---|---|---|
| **926** A343 10c multi | .50 | .50 |

Panama, 2003 Iberoamerican Cultural Capital — A344

**2003, Dec. 4**

| | | |
|---|---|---|
| **927** A344 5c multi | .50 | .25 |

For surcharges, see Nos. 945-948.

Pres. Mireya Moscoso A345

**2004, Aug. 10** **Litho.** ***Perf. 14½x14***

| | | |
|---|---|---|
| **928** A345 35c multi | 1.60 | 1.60 |

Compare with Type A328. Dated 2000.

A346

Publication of Don Quixote, by Miguel de Cervantes, 400th Anniv. (in 2005).

**2007, Apr. 23** **Litho.** ***Perf. 12***

| | | |
|---|---|---|
| **929** A346 45c multi | 1.40 | 1.40 |

St. Augustine High School, Panama, 50th Anniv. A347

**2007, May 7**

| | | |
|---|---|---|
| **930** A347 35c multi | 1.25 | 1.25 |

A348

A349

A350

Worldwide Fund for Nature (WWF) A351

**2007, June 27**

| | | |
|---|---|---|
| **931** Horiz. strip of 4 | 3.25 | 3.25 |
| *a.* A348 20c multi | .75 | .75 |
| *b.* A349 20c multi | .75 | .75 |
| *c.* A350 20c multi | .75 | .75 |
| *d.* A351 20c multi | .75 | .75 |

Popes — A352

No. 932: a, Pope John Paul II (1920-2005). b, Pope Benedict XVI.

***Imperf. x Perf. 12 on 1 Side***

**2007, June 29**

**932** A352 50c Horiz. pair, #a-b 3.25 3.25

Tourism A353

**2007, July 10** ***Perf. 12***

**933** A353 5c multi .50 .25

See Nos. 936-941.

Panama Canal Railway Company, 150th Anniv. (in 2005) A354

Designs: 20c, Emblem, Diesel and steam trains. 30c, Emblem, Diesel and steam trains, Diesel train in foreground.

**2007, Nov. 27 Litho.** ***Perf. 12***

**934-935** A354 Set of 2 1.00 1.00

**Tourism Type of 2007**

Designs: 15c, Devil's mask. 20c, Chorrera Waterfalls, vert. 25c, Sarigua National Park. 35c, Pottery from Barilles archaeological site. 45c, San Fernando Fort, Portobelo. 60c, Colonial era buildings, vert.

**2008, Feb. 27 Litho.** ***Perf. 12***

**936-941** A353 Set of 6 6.00 4.00

Dated 2007.

Carter-Torrijos Panama Canal Treaty, 30th Anniv. — A355

**2008, Nov. 11 Litho.** ***Perf. 14***

**942** A355 35c multi .70 .70

Souvenir Sheet

Various Airplanes of Copa Airlines — A356

**2010, July 30** ***Perf. 14 on 3 Sides***

**943** A356 1b multi 2.00 2.00

Copa Airlines, 60th anniv.

Miniature Sheet

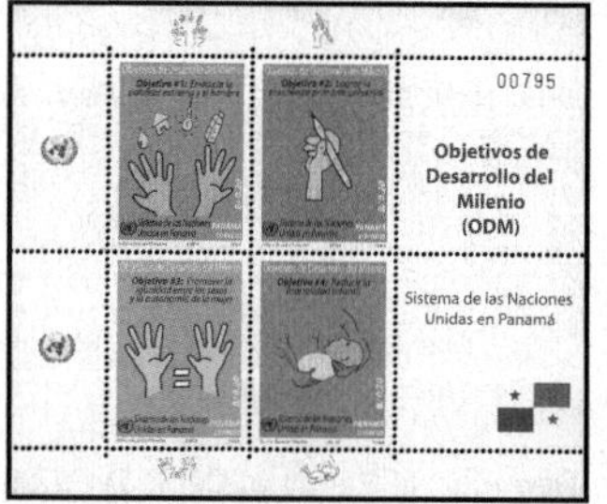

United Nations Millennium Objectives — A357

No. 944: a, Objective #1, Eradication of extreme poverty and hunger. b, Objective #2, Universal primary education. c, Objective #3, Promotion of equality of the sexes and women's rights. d, Objective #4, Reduction of infant mortality.

**2010, Aug. 18** ***Perf. 14***

**944** A357 20c Sheet of 4, #a-d — —

Dated 2008.

**No. 927 Surcharged in Black or Blue**

No. 945

No. 946

No. 947

No. 948

**Methods and Perfs. As Before**

**2014, June 1**

| | | | | |
|---|---|---|---|---|
| **945** | A344 10c on 5c #927 (Bl) | .25 | .25 |
| **946** | A344 20c on 5c #927 (Bl) | .40 | .40 |
| **947** | A344 25c on 5c #927 (Bl) | .50 | .50 |
| **948** | A344 35c on 5c #927 | .70 | .70 |
| | *Nos. 945-948 (4)* | 1.85 | 1.85 |

**Nos. 873, 902, 923 Surcharged in Black or Silver**

No. 949a

No. 949b

No. 950a

No. 950b

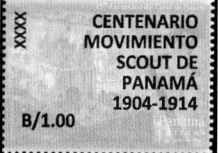

No. 951a

No. 951b

No. 952a

No. 952b

No. 953a

No. 953b

**Methods and Perfs As Before**

**2015, Dec. 1**

| | | | |
|---|---|---|---|
| **949** | Horiz. pair (S) | 4.00 | 4.00 |
| *a.* | A342 1b on 30c #923a (S) | 2.00 | 2.00 |
| *b.* | A342 1b on 30c #923b (S) | 2.00 | 2.00 |
| **950** | Horiz. pair | 4.00 | 4.00 |
| *a.* | A318 1b on 40c #873a | 2.00 | 2.00 |
| *b.* | A318 1b on 40c #873b | 2.00 | 2.00 |
| **951** | Horiz. pair | 8.00 | 8.00 |
| *a.* | A318 2b on 40c #873a | 4.00 | 4.00 |
| *b.* | A318 2b on 40c #873b | 4.00 | 4.00 |
| **952** | Horiz. pair (S) | 16.00 | 16.00 |
| *a.* | A342 4b on 30c #923a (S) | 8.00 | 8.00 |
| *b.* | A342 4b on 30c #923b (S) | 8.00 | 8.00 |
| **953** | Horiz. pair (S) | 20.00 | 20.00 |
| *a.* | A333 5b on 10c #902a (S) | 10.00 | 10.00 |
| *b.* | A333 5b on 10c #902b (S) | 10.00 | 10.00 |
| | *Nos. 949-953 (5)* | 52.00 | 52.00 |

Tourism A358

Designs: 20c, San Francisco de la Montaña Church, Veraguas Province. 25c, Centennial Bridge over Panama Canal. 35c, Presidential Palace, Panama City. 60c, Building, Mi Pueblito Afroantilliano Complex, Cerro Ancón. 1b, Beach, Guna Yala Province. 4b, Cinta Costera 1, Panama City. 10b, Royal Customs House, San Felipe Portobelo.

**2016 Litho.** ***Perf. 13x13¼***

**954-960** A358 Set of 7 33.00 33.00

## AIR POST STAMPS

Special Delivery Stamp No. E3 Srchd. in Dark Blue

**1929, Feb. 8 Unwmk.** ***Perf. 12½***

| | | | |
|---|---|---|---|
| **C1** | SD1 25c on 10c org | 1.00 | .80 |
| *a.* | Inverted surcharge | 22.50 | 22.50 |

Nos. E3-E4 Overprinted in Blue

**1929, May 22**

**C2** SD1 10c orange .50 .50
  *a.* Inverted overprint 20.00 17.50
  *b.* Double overprint 20.00 17.50

Some specialists claim the red overprint is a proof impression.

**With Additional Surcharge of New Value**

**C3** SD1 15c on 10c org .50 .50
**C4** SD1 25c on 20c dk brn 1.10 1.00
  *a.* Double surcharge 20.00 20.00
  *Nos. C2-C4 (3)* 2.10 2.00

No. E3 Surcharged in Blue

**1930, Jan. 25**

**C5** SD1 5c on 10c org .50 .50

No. 219 Overprinted in Red

**1930, Feb. 28** *Perf. 12*

**C6** A39 1b dk vio & blk 16.00 12.50

AP5

**1930-41 Engr. *Perf. 12***

**C6A** AP5 5c blue ('41) .25 .25
**C6B** AP5 7c rose car ('41) .25 .25
**C6C** AP5 8c gray blk ('41) .25 .25
**C7** AP5 15c dp grn .30 .25
**C8** AP5 20c rose .35 .25
**C9** AP5 25c deep blue .65 .65
  *Nos. C6A-C9 (6)* 2.05 1.90

Issued: Nos. C7-C9, 1/20; Nos. C6A-C6C, 7/1/41. See No. C112.

For surcharges and overprints see Nos. 353, C16-C16A, C53B, C69, C82-C83, C109, C122, C124.

Airplane over Map of Panama — AP6

**1930, Aug. 4** *Perf. 12½*

**C10** AP6 5c ultra .25 .25
**C11** AP6 10c orange .30 .25
**C12** AP6 30c dp vio 5.50 4.00
**C13** AP6 50c dp red 1.50 .50
**C14** AP6 1b black 5.50 4.00
  *Nos. C10-C14 (5)* 13.05 9.00

For surcharge and overprints see Nos. C53A, C70-C71, C115.

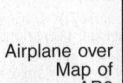

Amphibian AP7

**1931, Nov. 28 Typo.**

**Without Gum**

**C15** AP7 5c deep blue .80 1.00
  *a.* 5c gray blue .80 1.00
  *b.* Horiz. pair, imperf. btwn. 50.00

For the start of regular airmail service between Panama City and the western provinces, but valid only on Nov. 28-29 on mail carried by hydroplane "3 Noviembre."

Many sheets have a papermaker's watermark "DOLPHIN BOND" in double-lined capitals.

No. C9 Surcharged in Red 19mm long

**1932, Dec. 14** *Perf. 12*

**C16** AP5 20c on 25c dp bl 6.25 .70

**Surcharge 17mm long**

**C16A** AP5 20c on 25c dp bl 200.00 2.50

Special Delivery Stamp No. E4 Overprinted in Red or Black

**1934** *Perf. 12½*

**C17** SD1 20c dk brn 1.00 .50
**C17A** SD1 20c dk brn (Bk) 100.00 55.00

Issued: No. C17, 7/31.

Surcharged In Black

**1935, June**

**C18** SD1 10c on 20c dk brn .80 .50

**Same Surcharge with Small "10"**

**C18A** SD1 10c on 20c dk brn 40.00 5.00
  *b.* Horiz. pair, imperf. vert. 100.00

Nos. 234 and 242 Surcharged in Blue

**1936, Sept. 24**

**C19** A53 5c on ½c org 400.00 250.00
**C20** A53 5c on 50c org 1.00 .80
  *a.* Double surcharge 60.00 60.00

Centenary of the birth of President Pablo Arosemena.

It is claimed that No. C19 was not regularly issued. Counterfeits of No. C19 exist.

Urracá Monument AP8

Palace of Justice AP9

10c, Human Genius Uniting the Oceans. 20c, Panama City. 30c, Balboa Monument. 50c, Pedro Miguel Locks.

**1936, Dec. 1 Engr. *Perf. 12***

**C21** AP8 5c blue .65 .40
**C22** AP9 10c yel org .85 .60
**C23** AP9 20c red 3.00 1.50
**C24** AP8 30c dk vio 3.50 2.50
**C25** AP9 50c car rose 8.00 5.75
**C26** AP9 1b black 9.50 6.00
  *Nos. C21-C26 (6)* 25.50 16.75

4th Postal Congress of the Americas and Spain.

**Nos. C21-C26 Overprinted in Red or Blue**

**1937, Mar. 9**

**C27** AP8 5c blue (R) .55 .30
  *a.* Inverted overprint 50.00
**C28** AP9 10c yel org (Bl) .75 .45
**C29** AP9 20c red (Bl) 1.75 1.00
  *a.* Double overprint 50.00
**C30** AP8 30c dk vio (R) 4.50 3.25
**C31** AP8 50c car rose (Bl) 18.00 13.00
  *a.* Double overprint 175.00
**C32** AP9 1b black (R) 22.50 13.00
  *Nos. C27-C32 (6)* 48.05 31.00

Regular Stamps of 1921-26 Surcharged in Red

**1937, June 30** *Perf. 12, 12½*

**C33** A55 5c on 15c ultra .75 .75
**C34** A55 5c on 20c brn .75 .75
**C35** A47 10c on 10c vio 1.75 1.50

Regular Stamps of 1920-26 Surcharged in Red

**C36** A56 5c on 24c blk vio .75 .75
**C37** A39 5c on 1b dk vio & blk .75 .50
**C38** A56 10c on 50c blk 2.25 2.00
  *a.* Inverted surcharge 30.00

No. 248 Overprinted in Red

**C39** A54 5c dark blue .75 .75
  *a.* Double overprint 18.00
  *Nos. C33-C39 (7)* 7.75 7.00

Fire Dept. Badge AP14

Florencio Arosemena AP15

José Gabriel Duque — AP16

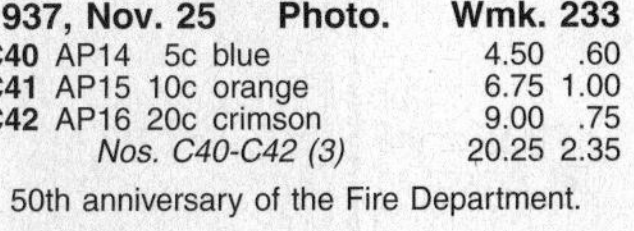

*Perf. 14x14½*

**1937, Nov. 25 Photo. Wmk. 233**

**C40** AP14 5c blue 4.50 .60
**C41** AP15 10c orange 6.75 1.00
**C42** AP16 20c crimson 9.00 .75
  *Nos. C40-C42 (3)* 20.25 2.35

50th anniversary of the Fire Department.

Basketball — AP17

Baseball AP18

**1938, Feb. 12** *Perf. 14x14½, 14½x14*

**C43** AP17 1c shown 2.25 .25
**C44** AP18 2c shown 2.25 .25
**C45** AP18 7c Swimming 3.00 .25
**C46** AP18 8c Boxing 3.00 .25
**C47** AP17 15c Soccer 5.00 1.25
  *a.* Souv. sheet of 5, #C43-C47 18.00 18.00
  *b.* As "a," No. C43 omitted 3,500.
  *Nos. C43-C47 (5)* 15.50 2.25

4th Central American Caribbean Games.

**US Constitution Type**

**Engr. & Litho.**

**1938, Dec. 7 Unwmk. *Perf. 12½***

**Center in Black, Flags in Red and Ultramarine**

**C49** A83 7c gray .35 .25
**C50** A83 8c brt ultra .55 .35
**C51** A83 15c red brn .70 .45
**C52** A83 50c orange 8.00 5.75
**C53** A83 1b black 8.00 5.75
  *Nos. C49-C53 (5)* 17.60 12.55

Nos. C12 and C7 Surcharged in Red

**1938, June 5** *Perf. 12½, 12*

**C53A** AP6 7c on 30c dp vio .40 .40
  *c.* Double surcharge 27.50
  *d.* Inverted surcharge 27.50
**C53B** AP5 8c on 15c dp grn .40 .40
  *e.* Inverted surcharge 22.50

Opening of the Normal School at Santiago, Veraguas Province, June 5, 1938. The 8c surcharge has no bars.

Belisario Porras AP23

Designs: 2c, William Howard Taft. 5c, Pedro J. Sosa. 10c, Lucien Bonaparte Wise. 15c, Armando Reclus. 20c, Gen. George W. Goethals. 50c, Ferdinand de Lesseps. 1b, Theodore Roosevelt.

**1939, Aug. 15 Engr.**

**C54** AP23 1c dl rose .40 .25
**C55** AP23 2c dp bl grn .40 .25
**C56** AP23 5c indigo .65 .25
**C57** AP23 10c dk vio .70 .25
**C58** AP23 15c ultra 1.60 .35
**C59** AP23 20c rose pink 4.00 1.40
**C60** AP23 50c dk brn 5.00 .70
**C61** AP23 1b black 7.25 3.75
  *Nos. C54-C61 (8)* 20.00 7.00

Opening of Panama Canal, 25th anniv.

For surcharges see Nos. C63, C65, G1, G3.

Flags of the 21 American Republics AP31

**1940, Apr. 15** **Unwmk.**
**C62** AP31 15c blue .40 .35

Pan American Union, 50th anniversary.
For surcharge see No. C66.

**Stamps of 1939-40 Surcharged in Black**

a 

b 

c 

d 

**1940, Aug. 12**

| | | | |
|---|---|---|---|
| **C63** | AP23 (a) 5c on 15c lt ultra | .25 | .25 |
| *a.* | "7 AEREO 7" on 15c | 60.00 | 60.00 |
| **C64** | A84 (b) 7c on 15c ultra | .40 | .25 |
| **C65** | AP23 (c) 7c on 20c rose pink | .40 | .25 |
| **C66** | AP31 (d) 8c on 15c blue | .40 | .25 |
| | *Nos. C63-C66 (4)* | 1.45 | 1.00 |

**Stamps of 1924-30 Overprinted in Black or Red**

e 

f

g

**1941, Jan. 2** ***Perf. 12½, 12***

| | | | |
|---|---|---|---|
| **C67** | SD1 (e) 7c on 10c org | 1.00 | 1.00 |
| **C68** | A53 (f) 15c on 24c yel brn (R) | 2.50 | 2.50 |
| **C69** | AP5 (g) 20c rose | 2.00 | 2.00 |
| **C70** | AP6 (g) 50c deep red | 6.00 | 4.00 |
| **C71** | AP6 (g) 1b black (R) | 13.50 | 10.00 |
| | *Nos. C67-C71 (5)* | 25.00 | 19.50 |

New constitution of Panama which became effective Jan. 2, 1941.

Liberty — AP32

**Black Overprint**

**1942, Feb. 19** **Engr.** ***Perf. 12***
**C72** AP32 20c chestnut brn 4.00 2.50

**Costa Rica - Panama Type**
**Engr. & Litho.**

**1942, Apr. 25** **Unwmk.**
**C73** A94 15c dp grn, dk bl & dp rose .70 .25

Swordfish AP34

J. D. Arosemena Normal School — AP35

Designs: 8c, Gate of Glory, Portobelo. 15c, Taboga Island, Balboa Harbor. 50c, Fire-house. 1b, Gold animal figure.

**1942, May 11** **Engr.** ***Perf. 12***

| | | | |
|---|---|---|---|
| **C74** | AP34 7c rose carmine | .90 | .25 |
| **C75** | AP34 8c dk ol brn & blk | .25 | .25 |
| **C76** | AP34 15c dark violet | .45 | .25 |
| **C77** | AP35 20c red brown | .65 | .25 |
| **C78** | AP34 50c olive green | 1.10 | .40 |
| **C79** | AP34 1b blk & org yel | 2.75 | .80 |
| | *Nos. C74-C79 (6)* | 6.10 | 2.20 |

See Nos. C96-C99, C113, C126. For surcharges and overprints see Nos. 354-355, C84-C86, C108, C110-C111, C114, C116, C118, C121, C123, C127-C128, C137.

Alejandro Meléndez G. — AP40

Design: 5b, Ernesto T. Lefevre.

**1943, Dec. 15**
**C80** AP40 3b dk olive gray 6.00 4.75
**C81** AP40 5b dark blue 9.00 7.50

For overprint & surcharge see #C117, C128A.

**Catalogue values for unused stamps in this section, from this point to the end of the section, are for Never Hinged items.**

Nos. C6C and C7 Surcharged in Carmine

**1947, Mar. 8** ***Perf. 12***
**C82** AP5 5c on 8c gray blk .25 .25
*a.* Double overprint 25.00 22.50
**C83** AP5 10c on 15c dp grn .55 .40

Nos. C74 to C76 Surcharged in Black or Carmine

| | | | |
|---|---|---|---|
| **C84** | AP34 5c on 7c rose car (Bk) | .25 | .25 |
| *a.* | Double surcharge | | 500.00 |
| *b.* | Pair, one without surcharge | 75.00 | |
| **C85** | AP34 5c on 8c dk ol brn & blk | .25 | .25 |
| **C86** | AP34 10c on 15c dk vio | .25 | .25 |
| *a.* | Double surcharge | 30.00 | 30.00 |
| | *Nos. C82-C86 (5)* | 1.55 | 1.40 |

National Theater — AP42

**1947, Apr. 7** **Engr.** **Unwmk.**
**C87** AP42 8c violet .40 .25

Natl. Constitutional Assembly of 1945, 2nd anniv.
For surcharge see No. 356.

Manuel Amador Guerrero AP43

Manuel Espinosa B. — AP44

5c, José Agustin Arango. 10c, Federico Boyd. 15c, Ricardo Arias. 50c, Carlos Constantino Arosemena. 1b, Nicanor de Obarrio. 2b, Tomas Arias.

**1948, Feb. 20** ***Perf. 12½***
**Center in Black**

| | | | |
|---|---|---|---|
| **C88** | AP43 3c blue | .45 | .25 |
| **C89** | AP43 5c brown | .45 | .25 |
| **C90** | AP43 10c orange | .45 | .25 |
| **C91** | AP43 15c deep claret | .45 | .25 |
| **C92** | AP44 20c deep carmine | .80 | .55 |
| **C93** | AP44 50c dark gray | 1.40 | .80 |
| **C94** | AP44 1b green | 4.50 | 2.50 |
| **C95** | AP44 2b yellow | 10.00 | 6.00 |
| | *Nos. C88-C95 (8)* | 18.50 | 10.85 |

Members of the Revolutionary Junta of 1903.

**Types of 1942**

**1948, June 14** ***Perf. 12***

| | | | |
|---|---|---|---|
| **C96** | AP34 2c carmine | .90 | .25 |
| **C97** | AP34 15c olive gray | .45 | .25 |
| **C98** | AP35 20c green | .45 | .25 |
| **C99** | AP34 50c rose carmine | 7.25 | 3.00 |
| | *Nos. C96-C99 (4)* | 9.05 | 3.75 |

Franklin D. Roosevelt and Juan D. Arosemena AP45

Four Freedoms AP46

Monument to F. D. Roosevelt — AP47

Map showing Boyd-Roosevelt Trans-Isthmian Highway — AP48

Franklin D. Roosevelt — AP49

**1948, Sept. 15** ***Perf. 12½***

| | | | |
|---|---|---|---|
| **C100** | AP45 5c dp car & blk | .25 | .25 |
| **C101** | AP46 10c yellow org | .35 | .30 |
| **C102** | AP47 20c dull green | .45 | .35 |
| **C103** | AP48 50c dp ultra & blk | .70 | .60 |
| **C104** | AP49 1b gray black | 1.75 | 1.25 |
| | *Nos. C100-C104 (5)* | 3.50 | 2.75 |

Franklin Delano Roosevelt (1882-1945).
For surcharges see Nos. RA28-RA29.

Monument to Cervantes AP50

10c, Don Quixote attacking windmill.

**1948, Nov. 15**
**C105** AP50 5c dk blue & blk .55 .25
**C106** AP50 10c purple & blk .90 .25

400th anniv. of the birth of Miguel de Cervantes Saavedra, novelist, playwright and poet.

No. C106 Ovptd. in Carmine

**1949, Jan. 18**
**C107** AP50 10c purple & blk .60 .40
*a.* Inverted overprint 50.00

José Gabriel Duque (1849-1918), newspaper publisher and philanthropist.

**Nos. C96, C6A, C97 and C99 Overprinted in Black or Red**

h

i

**1949, May 26**

| | | | |
|---|---|---|---|
| **C108** AP34(h) 2c carmine | .25 | .25 |
| *a.* Double overprint | 7.50 | 7.00 |
| *b.* Inverted surcharge | 20.00 | 20.00 |
| *c.* On No. C74 (error) | 70.00 | |
| **C109** AP5(i) 5c blue (R) | .25 | .25 |
| **C110** AP34(h) 15c ol gray (R) | .65 | .65 |
| **C111** AP34(h) 50c rose car | 2.25 | 2.25 |
| *Nos. C108-C111 (4)* | 3.35 | 3.35 |

Centenary of the incorporation of Chiriqui Province.

### Types of 1930-42

Design: 10c, Gate of Glory, Portobelo.

**1949, Aug. 3** *Perf. 12*

| | | |
|---|---|---|
| **C112** AP5 5c orange | .25 | .25 |
| **C113** AP34 10c dk blue & blk | .25 | .25 |

For surcharge see No. C137.

### Stamps of 1943-49 Overprinted or Surcharged in Black, Green or Red

**1949, Sept. 9**

| | | |
|---|---|---|
| **C114** AP34 2c carmine | .25 | .25 |
| *a.* Inverted overprint | 24.00 | |
| *b.* Double overprint | 32.50 | |
| *c.* Double overprint, one inverted | 37.50 | 35.00 |
| **C115** AP5 5c orange (G) | .90 | .35 |
| *a.* Inverted overprint | 12.50 | |
| *b.* Double overprint | 30.00 | 30.00 |
| *c.* Double ovpt., one inverted | 30.00 | 30.00 |
| **C116** AP34 10c dk bl & blk (R) | .90 | .40 |
| **C117** AP40 25c on 3b dk ol gray (R) | 1.25 | .70 |
| **C118** AP34 50c rose carmine | 4.00 | 2.10 |
| *Nos. C114-C118 (5)* | 7.30 | 3.75 |

75th anniv. of the UPU.

No. C115 has small overprint, 15½x12mm, like No. 368. Overprint on Nos. C114, C116 and C118 as illustrated. Surcharge on No. C117 is arranged vertically, 29x18mm.

University of San Javier AP51

**1949, Dec. 7** **Engr.** *Perf. 12½*

| | | |
|---|---|---|
| **C119** AP51 5c dk blue & blk | .35 | .25 |

See note after No. 371.

Mosquito — AP52

**1950, Jan. 12** *Perf. 12*

| | | |
|---|---|---|
| **C120** AP52 5c dp ultra & gray blk | 1.60 | .65 |

See note after No. 372.

Nos. C96, C112, C113 and C9 Overprinted in Black or Carmine (5 or 4 lines)

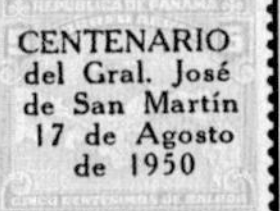


**1950, Aug. 17** **Unwmk.**

| | | |
|---|---|---|
| **C121** AP34 2c carmine | .55 | .25 |
| **C122** AP5 5c orange | .65 | .35 |
| **C123** AP34 10c dk bl & blk (C) | .65 | .40 |
| **C124** AP5 25c deep blue (C) | 1.00 | .75 |

### Same on No. 362, Overprinted "AEREO"

| | | |
|---|---|---|
| **C125** A105 50c pur & blk (C) | 2.00 | 1.25 |
| *Nos. C121-C125 (5)* | 4.85 | 3.00 |

Gen. José de San Martin, death cent.

### Firehouse Type of 1942

**1950, Oct. 30** **Engr.**

| | | |
|---|---|---|
| **C126** AP34 50c deep blue | 3.50 | 1.00 |

### Nos. C113 and C81 Surcharged in Carmine or Orange

**1952, Feb. 20**

| | | |
|---|---|---|
| **C127** AP34 2c on 10c | .25 | .25 |
| *a.* Pair, one without surch. | 375.00 | |
| **C128** AP34 5c on 10c (O) | .25 | .25 |
| *b.* Pair, one without surch. | 375.00 | |
| **C128A** AP40 1b on 5b | 29.00 | 20.00 |

The surcharge on No. C128A is arranged to fit stamp, with four bars covering value panel at bottom, instead of crosses.

### Nos. 376 and 380 Srchd. "AEREO 1952" and New Value in Carmine or Black

**1952, Aug. 1**

| | | |
|---|---|---|
| **C129** A97 5c on 2c ver & blk (C) | .25 | .25 |
| *a.* Inverted surcharge | 32.50 | |
| **C130** A99 25c on 10c pur & org | 1.00 | 1.00 |

### Isabella Type of Regular Issue

*Perf. 12½*

**1952, Oct. 20** **Unwmk.** **Engr.**

**Center in Black**

| | | |
|---|---|---|
| **C131** A110 4c red orange | .45 | .25 |
| **C132** A110 5c olive green | .45 | .25 |
| **C133** A110 10c orange | .65 | .25 |
| **C134** A110 25c gray blue | 1.75 | .30 |
| **C135** A110 50c chocolate | 2.50 | .65 |
| **C136** A110 1b black | 7.50 | 3.00 |
| *Nos. C131-C136 (6)* | 13.30 | 4.60 |

Queen Isabella I of Spain, 500th birth anniv.

### No. C113 Surcharged "5 1953" in Carmine

**1953, Apr. 22** *Perf. 12*

| | | |
|---|---|---|
| **C137** AP34 5c on 10c dk bl & blk | .35 | .25 |

Masthead of La Estrella — AP54

**1953, July 15**

| | | |
|---|---|---|
| **C138** AP54 5c rose carmine | .25 | .25 |
| **C139** AP54 10c blue | .45 | .25 |

Panama's 1st newspaper, La Estrella de Panama, cent.

For surcharges see Nos. C146-C147.

Act of Independence AP55

Senora de Remon and Pres. José A. Remon Cantera AP56

Designs: 7c, Pollera. 25c, National flower. 50c, Marcos A. Salazar, Esteban Huertas and Domingo Diaz A. 1b, Dancers.

**1953, Nov. 2**

| | | |
|---|---|---|
| **C140** AP55 2c deep ultra | .45 | .25 |
| **C141** AP56 5c deep green | .45 | .25 |
| **C142** AP56 7c gray | .55 | .25 |
| **C143** AP56 25c black | 3.50 | .65 |
| **C144** AP56 50c dark brown | 2.25 | .75 |
| **C145** AP56 1b red orange | 5.75 | 1.50 |
| *Nos. C140-C145 (6)* | 12.95 | 3.65 |

Founding of republic, 50th anniversary.

For overprints see Nos. C227-C229.

### Nos. C138-C139 Surcharged with New Value in Black or Red

**1953-54**

| | | |
|---|---|---|
| **C146** AP54 1c on 5c rose car ('54) | .25 | .25 |
| **C147** AP54 1c on 10c blue (R) | .25 | .25 |

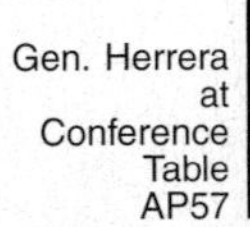

Gen. Herrera at Conference Table AP57

Design: 1b, Gen. Herrera leading troops.

**1954, Dec. 4** **Litho.** *Perf. 12½*

| | | |
|---|---|---|
| **C148** AP57 6c deep green | .25 | .25 |
| **C149** AP57 1b scarlet & blk | 4.00 | 2.25 |

Death of Gen. Tomas Herrera, cent.

For surcharge see No. C198.

Rotary Emblem and Map — AP58

**1955, Feb. 23**

| | | |
|---|---|---|
| **C150** AP58 6c rose violet | .25 | .25 |
| **C151** AP58 21c red | .70 | .35 |
| **C152** AP58 1b black | 5.50 | 2.50 |
| *a.* 1b violet black | 6.75 | 3.75 |
| *Nos. C150-C152 (3)* | 6.45 | 3.10 |

Rotary International, 50th anniv.

For surcharge see No. C154.

### Cantera Type

**1955, June 1**

| | | |
|---|---|---|
| **C153** A115 6c rose vio & blk | .25 | .25 |

Issued in tribute to Pres. José Antonio Remon Cantera, 1908-1955.

For surcharge see No. C188.

No. C151 Surcharged

**1955, Dec. 7**

| | | |
|---|---|---|
| **C154** AP58 15c on 21c red | .40 | .35 |

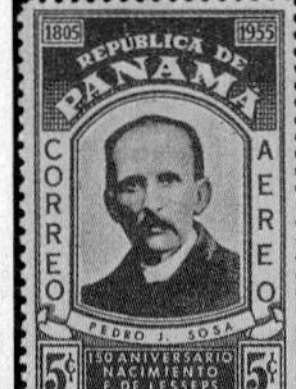


Pedro J. Sosa — AP60

First Barge Going through Canal and de Lesseps AP61

*Perf. 12½*

**1955, Nov. 22** **Unwmk.** **Litho.**

| | | |
|---|---|---|
| **C155** AP60 5c grn, *lt grn* | .35 | .25 |
| **C156** AP61 1b red lilac & blk | 5.00 | 2.50 |

150th anniversary of the birth of Ferdinand de Lesseps. Imperforates exist.

Pres. Dwight D. Eisenhower — AP62

Statue of Bolivar — AP63

Bolivar Hall AP64

Portraits-Presidents: C158, Pedro Aramburu, Argentina. C159, Dr. Victor Paz Estenssoro, Bolivia. C160, Dr. Juscelino Kubitschek O., Brazil. C161, Gen. Carlos Ibanez del Campo, Chile. C162, Gen. Gustavo Rojas Pinilla, Colombia. C163, Jose Figueres, Costa Rica. C164, Gen. Fulgencio Batista y Zaldivar, Cuba. C165, Gen. Hector B. Trujillo Molina, Dominican Rep. C166, José Maria Velasco Ibarra, Ecuador. C167, Col. Carlos Castillo Armas, Guatemala. C168, Gen. Paul E. Magloire, Haiti. C169, Julio Lozano Diaz, Honduras. C170, Adolfo Ruiz Cortines, Mexico. C171, Gen. Anastasio Somoza, Nicaragua. C172, Ricardo Arias Espinosa, Panama. C173, Gen. Alfredo Stroessner, Paraguay. C174, Gen. Manuel Odria, Peru. C175, Col. Oscar Osorio, El Salvador. C176, Dr. Alberto F. Zubiria, Uruguay. C177, Gen. Marcos Perez Jimenez, Venezuela. 1b, Simon Bolivar.

**1956, July 18**

| | | |
|---|---|---|
| **C157** AP62 6c rose car & vio bl | .45 | .35 |
| **C158** AP62 6c brt grnsh bl & blk | .45 | .25 |
| **C159** AP62 6c bister & blk | .45 | .25 |
| **C160** AP62 6c emerald & blk | .45 | .25 |
| **C161** AP62 6c lt grn & brn | .45 | .25 |
| **C162** AP62 6c yellow & grn | .45 | .25 |
| **C163** AP62 6c brt vio & grn | .45 | .25 |
| **C164** AP62 6c dl pur & vio bl | .45 | .25 |
| **C165** AP62 6c red lil & sl grn | .45 | .25 |
| **C166** AP62 6c citron & vio bl | .45 | .25 |
| **C167** AP62 6c ap grn & brn | .45 | .25 |
| **C168** AP62 6c brn & vio bl | .45 | .25 |
| **C169** AP62 6c brt car & grn | .45 | .25 |
| **C170** AP62 6c red & brn | .45 | .25 |
| **C171** AP62 6c lt bl & grn | .45 | .25 |
| **C172** AP62 6c vio bl & grn | .45 | .25 |
| **C173** AP62 6c orange & blk | .45 | .25 |
| **C174** AP62 6c bluish gray & brn | .45 | .25 |
| **C175** AP62 6c sal rose & blk | .45 | .25 |
| **C176** AP62 6c dk grn & vio bl | .45 | .25 |
| **C177** AP62 6c dk org brn & dk grn | .45 | .25 |
| **C178** AP63 20c dk bluish gray | 1.10 | .55 |
| **C179** AP64 50c green | 2.00 | 1.00 |
| **C180** AP63 1b brown | 5.00 | 1.75 |
| *Nos. C157-C180 (24)* | 17.55 | 8.65 |

Pan-American Conf., Panama City, July 21-22, 1956, and 130th anniv. of the 1st Pan-American Conf. Imperforates exist.

Ruins of First Town Council Building — AP65

Design: 50c, City Hall, Panama City.

**1956, Aug. 17**

**C181** AP65 25c red .65 .35
**C182** AP65 50c black 1.25 .90
*a.* Souv. sheet of 3, #404, C181-C182, imperf. 2.40 2.40

6th Inter-American Congress of Municipalities, Panama City, Aug. 14-19, 1956.
No. C182a sold for 85c.
For overprint see No. C187a.

Monument — AP66

St. Thomas Hospital AP67

**1956, Nov. 27 Wmk. 311**

**C183** AP66 5c green .25 .25
**C184** AP67 15c dk carmine .45 .25

Centenary of the birth of Pres. Belisario Porras.

Highway Construction AP68

20c, Road through jungle, Darien project. 1b, Map of Americas showing Pan-American Highway.

**Wmk. 311**

**1957, Aug. 1 Litho. *Perf. 12½***

**C185** AP68 10c black .25 .25
**C186** AP68 20c lt blue & blk .65 .55
**C187** AP68 1b green 2.75 2.25
*a.* AP65 Souvenir sheet of 3, unwmkd. 16.00 16.00
*Nos. C185-C187 (3)* 3.65 3.00

7th Pan-American Highway Congress.
No. C187a is No. C182a overprinted in black: "VII degree CONGRESSO INTERAMERICANO DE CARRETERAS 1957."

**No. C153 Surcharged "1957" and New Value**

**1957, Aug. 13 Unwmk.**

**C188** A115 10c on 6c rose vio & blk .25 .25

Remon Polyclinic — AP69

Customs House, Portobelo AP70

Buildings: #C191, Portobelo Castle. #C192, San Jeronimo Castle. #C193, Remon Hippodrome. #C194, Legislature. #C195, Interior & Treasury Department. #C196, El Panama Hotel. #C197, San Lorenzo Castle.

**Wmk. 311**

**1957, Nov. 1 Litho. *Perf. 12½***

**Design in Black**

**C189** AP69 10c lt blue .25 .25
**C190** AP70 10c lilac .25 .25
**C191** AP70 10c gray .25 .25
**C192** AP70 10c lilac rose .25 .25
**C193** AP70 10c ultra .25 .25
**C194** AP70 10c brown ol .25 .25
**C195** AP70 10c orange yel .25 .25
**C196** AP70 10c yellow grn .25 .25
**C197** AP70 1b red 2.25 1.60
*Nos. C189-C197 (9)* 4.25 3.60

**No. C148 Surcharged with New Value and "1958" in Red**

**1958, Feb. 11 Unwmk.**

**C198** AP57 5c on 6c dp grn .25 .25

United Nations Emblem — AP71

Flags of Panama and UN AP72

**1958, Mar. 5 Litho. Wmk. 311**

**C199** AP71 10c brt green .25 .25
**C200** AP71 21c lt ultra .45 .25
**C201** AP71 50c orange 1.10 .85
**C202** AP72 1b gray, ultra & car 2.25 1.60
*a.* Souv. sheet of 4, #C199-C202, imperf. 5.25 5.25
*Nos. C199-C202 (4)* 4.05 2.95

10th anniv. of the UN (in 1955).
The sheet also exists with the 10c and 50c omitted.

**OAS Type of Regular Issue, 1958**

Designs: 10c, 1b, Flags of 21 American Nations. 50c, Headquarters in Washington.

**1958, Aug. 12 Unwmk. *Perf. 12½***

**Center yellow and black; flags in national colors**

**C203** A124 5c lt blue .25 .25
**C204** A124 10c carmine rose .25 .25
**C205** A124 50c gray .70 .60
**C206** A124 1b black 2.25 1.60
*Nos. C203-C206 (4)* 3.45 2.60

**Type of Regular Issue**

Pavilions: 15c, Vatican City. 50c, United States. 1b, Belgium.

**1958, Sept. 8 Wmk. 311 *Perf. 12½***

**C207** A125 15c gray & lt vio .25 .25
**C208** A125 50c dk gray & org brn .70 .65
**C209** A125 1b brt vio & bluish grn 1.60 1.40
*a.* Souv. sheet of 7, #418-421, C207-C209 5.25 5.25
*Nos. C207-C209 (3)* 2.55 2.25

No. C209a sold for 2b.

**Pope Type of Regular Issue**

Portraits of Pius XII: 5c, As cardinal. 30c, Wearing papal tiara. 50c, Enthroned.

**1959, Jan. 21 Litho. Wmk. 311**

**C210** A126 5c violet .25 .25
**C211** A126 30c lilac rose .65 .40
**C212** A126 50c blue gray .90 .65
*a.* Souv. sheet of 4, #422, C210-C212, imperf. 2.25 2.25
*Nos. C210-C212 (3)* 1.80 1.25

#C212a is watermarked sideways and sold for 1b. The sheet also exists with 30c omitted. #C212a with C.E.P.A.L. overprint is listed as #C221a.

**Human Rights Issue Type**

Designs: 5c, Humanity looking into sun. 10c, 20c, Torch and UN emblem. 50c, UN Flag. 1b, UN Headquarters building.

**1959, Apr. 14 *Perf. 12½***

**C213** A127 5c emerald & bl .25 .25
**C214** A127 10c gray & org brn .25 .25
**C215** A127 20c brown & gray .25 .25
**C216** A127 50c green & ultra .80 .65
**C217** A127 1b red & blue 1.75 1.40
*Nos. C213-C217 (5)* 3.30 2.65

Nos. C213-C215, C212a Overprinted and C216 Surcharged in Red or Dark Blue

**1959, May 16**

**C218** A127 5c emer & bl (R) .25 .25
**C219** A127 10c gray & org brn (Bl) .25 .25
**C220** A127 20c brown & gray (R) .45 .25
**C221** A127 1b on 50c grn & ultra (R) 2.25 1.90
*a.* Souvenir sheet of 4 7.00 7.00
*Nos. C218-C221 (4)* 3.20 2.55

8th Reunion of the Economic Commission for Latin America.
This overprint also exists on Nos. C216-C217. These were disavowed by Panama's postmaster general.
No. C221a is No. C212a with two-line black overprint at top of sheet: "8a. REUNION DE LA C.E.P.A.L. MAYO 1959."

**Type of Regular Issue, 1959**

Portraits: 5c, Justo A. Facio, Rector. 10c, Ernesto de la Guardia, Jr., Pres. of Panama.

**Wmk. 311**

**1959, Aug. 5 Litho. *Perf. 12½***

**C222** A128 5c black .25 .25
**C223** A128 10c black .25 .25

**Type of Regular Issue, 1959**

**1959, Oct. 26 Wmk. 311 *Perf. 12½***

**C224** A130 5c Boxing .35 .25
**C225** A130 10c Baseball .70 .25
**C226** A130 50c Basketball 2.75 1.25
*Nos. C224-C226 (3)* 3.80 1.65

For surcharge see No. C349.

Nos. C143-C145 Overprinted in Vermilion, Red or Black

**Unwmk.**

**1960, Feb. 6 Engr. *Perf. 12***

**C227** AP56 25c black (V) .90 .25
**C228** AP56 50c dk brown (R) 1.25 .40
**C229** AP56 1b red orange 2.00 1.25
*Nos. C227-C229 (3)* 4.15 1.90

World Refugee Year, July 1, 1959-June 30, 1960.
The revenues from the sale of Nos. C227-C229 went to the United Nations Refugee Fund.

Administration Building, National University — AP74

Designs: 21c, Humanities building. 25c, Medical school. 30c, Dr. Octavio Mendez Pereria first rector of University.

**Wmk. 311**

**1960, Mar. 23 Litho. *Perf. 12½***

**C230** AP74 10c brt green .25 .25
**C231** AP74 21c lt blue .55 .25
**C232** AP74 25c ultra .80 .35
**C233** AP74 30c black 1.00 .40
*Nos. C230-C233 (4)* 2.60 1.25

National University, 25th anniv.
For surcharges see Nos. 450, C248, C253, C287, C291.

**Olympic Games Type**

5c, Basketball. 10c, Bicycling, horiz. 25c, Javelin thrower. 50c, Athlete with Olympic torch.

**1960, Sept. 22 Wmk. 343 *Perf. 12½***

**C234** A131 5c orange & red .25 .25
**C235** A131 10c ocher & blk .55 .25
**C236** A131 25c lt bl & dk bl 1.10 .55
**C237** A131 50c brown & blk 2.25 1.00
*a.* Souv. sheet of 2, #C236-C237 4.50 4.50
*Nos. C234-C237 (4)* 4.15 1.95

For surcharges see Nos. C249-C250, C254, C266-C270, C290, C350, RA40.

Citizens' Silhouettes AP75

10c, Heads and map of Central America.

**1960, Oct. 4 Litho. Wmk. 229**

**C238** AP75 5c black .25 .25
**C239** AP75 10c brown .25 .25

6th census of population and the 2nd census of dwellings (No. C238), Dec. 11, 1960, and the All America Census, 1960 (No. C239).

Boeing 707 Jet Liner AP76

**1960, Dec. 1 Wmk. 343 *Perf. 12½***

**C240** AP76 5c lt grnsh blue .25 .25
**C241** AP76 10c emerald .25 .25
**C242** AP76 20c red brown .45 .25
*Nos. C240-C242 (3)* .95 .75

1st jet service to Panama. For surcharge see No. RA41.

Souvenir Sheet

UN Emblem — AP77

**Wmk. 311**

**1961, Mar. 7 Litho. *Imperf.***

**C243** AP77 80c blk & car rose 2.25 2.25

15th anniv. (in 1960) of the UN.
Counterfeits without control number exist.

**No. C243 Overprinted in Blue with Large Uprooted Oak Emblem and "Ano de los Refugiados"**

**1961, June 2**

**C244** AP77 80c blk & car rose 2.50 2.50

World Refugee Year, July 1, 1959-June 30, 1960.

**Lions International Type**

Designs: 5c, Helen Keller School for the Blind. 10c, Children's summer camp. 21c, Arms of Panama and Lions emblem.

**1961, May 2 Wmk. 311 *Perf. 12½***

**C245** A133 5c black .25 .25
**C246** A133 10c emerald .25 .25
**C247** A133 21c ultra, yel & red .40 .25
*Nos. C245-C247 (3)* .90 .75

For overprints see Nos. C284-C286.

Nos. C230 and C236 Surcharged in Black or Red

**1961 Wmk. 311 (1c); Wmk. 343**

**C248** AP74 1c on 10c .25 .25
**C249** A131 1b on 25c (Bk) 2.10 2.00
**C250** A131 1b on 25c (R) 2.10 2.00
*Nos. C248-C250 (3)* 4.45 4.25

Issued: Nos. C248-C249, 7/6; No. C250, 9/5.

Pres. Roberto F. Chiari and Pres. Mario Echandi AP78

**Wmk. 343**

**1961, Oct. 2 Litho. *Perf. 12½***

**C251** AP78 1b black & gold 2.75 1.60

Meeting of the Presidents of Panama and Costa Rica at Paso Canoa, Apr. 21, 1961.

Dag Hammarskjold AP79

**1961, Dec. 27 *Perf. 12½***

**C252** AP79 10c black .25 .25

Dag Hammarskjold, UN Secretary General, 1953-61.

No. C230 Surcharged

**1962, Feb. 21 Wmk. 311**

**C253** AP74 15c on 10c brt grn .30 .25

No. C236 Surcharged

**Wmk. 343**

**C254** A131 1b on 25c 2.75 1.25

City Hall, Colon AP80

**1962, Feb. 28 Litho. Wmk. 311**

**C255** AP80 5c vio bl & blk .25 .25

Issued to publicize the third Central American Municipal Assembly, Colon, May 13-17.

**Church Type of Regular Issue, 1962**

Designs: 5c, Church of Christ the King. 7c, Church of San Miguel. 8c, Church of the Sanctuary. 10c, Saints Church. 15c, Church of St. Ann. 21c, Canal Zone Synagogue (Now used as USO Center). 25c, Panama Synagogue. 30c, Church of St. Francis. 50c, Protestant Church, Canal Zone. 1b, Catholic Church, Canal Zone.

**Wmk. 343**

**1962-64 Litho. *Perf. 12½***

**Buildings in Black**

**C256** A138 5c purple & buff .25 .25
**C257** A138 7c lil rose & brt pink .25 .25
**C258** A139 8c purple & bl .25 .25
**C259** A139 10c lilac & sal .25 .25
**C259A** A139 10c grn & dl red brn ('64) .25 .25
**C260** A139 15c red & buff .35 .25
**C261** A138 21c brown & blue .55 .40
**C262** A138 25c blue & pink .65 .35
**C263** A139 30c lil rose & bl .70 .40
**C264** A138 50c lilac & lt grn 1.10 .65
*a.* Souv. sheet of 4, #441H-441I, C262, C264, imperf. 5.75 5.75
**C265** A139 1b bl & sal 2.25 1.40
*Nos. C256-C265 (11)* 6.85 4.70

Freedom of religion in Panama. Issue dates: #C259A, 6/4/64; others, 7/20/62.

For overprints and surcharges see Nos. C288, C296-C297, C299.

Nos. C234, C236 Overprinted & Surcharged in Black, Green, Orange or Red

**1962, July 27 Wmk. 343 *Perf. 12½***

**C266** A131 5c org & red .25 .25
**C267** A131 10c on 25c (G) .65 .35
**C268** A131 15c on 25c (O) .80 .45
**C269** A131 20c on 25c (R) .90 .50
**C270** A131 25c lt bl & dk bl 1.00 .55
*Nos. C266-C270 (5)* 3.60 2.10

Ninth Central American and Caribbean Games, Kingston, Jamaica, Aug. 11-25.

Nos. CB1-CB2 Surcharged

**1962, May 3 Wmk. 311**

**C271** SPAP1 10c on 5c + 5c 1.40 .75
**C272** SPAP1 20c on 10c + 10c 2.10 1.50

**Type of Regular Issue, 1962**

Design: 10c, Canal bridge completed.

**1962, Oct. 12 Wmk. 343**

**C273** A140 10c blue & blk .25 .25

John H. Glenn, "Friendship 7" Capsule — AP81

Designs: 10c, "Friendship 7" capsule and globe, horiz. 31c, Capsule in space, horiz. 50c, Glenn with space helmet.

**1962, Oct. 19 Wmk. 311 *Perf. 12½***

**C274** AP81 5c rose red .25 .25
**C275** AP81 10c yellow .35 .25
**C276** AP81 31c blue 1.50 .80
**C277** AP81 50c emerald 1.75 1.00
*a.* Souv. sheet of 4, #C274-C277, imperf. 4.50 4.50
*Nos. C274-C277 (4)* 3.85 2.30

1st orbital flight of US astronaut Lt. Col. John H. Glenn, Jr., Feb. 20, 1962. No. C277a sold for 1b.

For surcharges see Nos. C290A-C290D, C367, CB4-CB7.

UPAE Emblem — AP82

**1963, Jan. 8 Litho. Wmk. 343**

**C278** AP82 10c multi .35 .25

50th anniversary of the founding of the Postal Union of the Americas and Spain, UPAE.

**Type of Regular Issue**

10c, Fire Engine "China", Plaza de Santa Ana. 15c, 14th Street team. 21c, Fire Brigade emblem.

**1963, Jan. 22 Wmk. 311 *Perf. 12½***

**C279** A141 10c orange & blk .35 .25
**C280** A141 15c lilac & blk .45 .25
**C281** A141 21c gold, red & ultra .90 .50
*Nos. C279-C281 (3)* 1.70 .90

"FAO" and Wheat Emblem — AP83

**1963, Mar. 21 Litho.**

**C282** AP83 10c green & red .35 .25
**C283** AP83 15c ultra & red .45 .25

FAO "Freedom from Hunger" campaign.

No. C245 Ovptd. in Yellow, Orange or Green

**1963, Apr. 18 Wmk. 311 *Perf. 12½***

**C284** A133 5c black (Y) .70 .25
**C285** A133 5c black (O) .70 .25
**C286** A133 5c black (G) .70 .25
*Nos. C284-C286 (3)* 2.10 .60

22nd Central American Lions Congress, Panama, Apr. 18-21.

No. C230 Surcharged

**1963, June 11**

**C287** AP74 4c on 10c brt grn .25 .25

Nos. 445 and 432 Overprinted Vertically

**1963 Wmk. 343 *Perf. 12½***

**C288** A139 10c green, yel & blk .25 .25

**Wmk. 311**

**C289** A130 20c emerald & red brn .65 .25

No. C234 Overprinted

**1963, Aug. 20 Wmk. 343**

**C290** A131 5c orange & red .25 .25

Freedom of Press Day, Aug. 20, 1963.

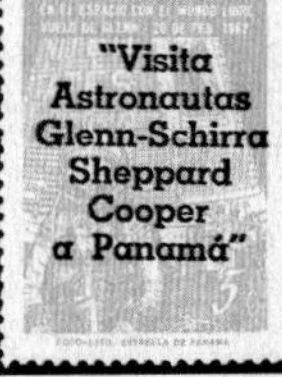


Nos. C274, C277a Overprinted or Surcharged — a

No. C274 Surcharged in Black — b

**Wmk. 311**

**1963, Aug. 22 Litho. *Perf. 12½***

**C290A** AP81(a) 5c on #C274 3.25
**C290B** AP81(a) 10c on 5c #C274 7.25
**C290C** AP81(b) 10c on 5c #C274 9.00

**Souvenir Sheet**

***Imperf.***

**C290D** AP81(a) Sheet of 4, #C277a 50.00

Overprint on No. C290D has names in capital letters and covers all four stamps.

No. C232 Surcharged in Red

**1963, Oct. 9 Wmk. 311 *Perf. 12½***

**C291** AP74 10c on 25c ultra .25 .25

**Type of Regular Issue, 1963**

Flags and Presidents: 5c, Julio A. Rivera, El Salvador. 10c, Miguel Ydigoras F., Guatemala. 21c, John F. Kennedy, US.

***Perf. 12½x12***

**1963, Dec. 18 Litho. Unwmk.**

**Portrait in Slate Green**

**C292** A142 5c yel, red & ultra .30 .25
**C293** A142 10c bl, red & ultra .50 .35
**C294** A142 21c org yel, red & ultra 1.50 1.10
*Nos. C292-C294 (3)* 2.30 1.70

**Balboa Type of Regular Issue, 1964**

**1964, Jan. 22 Photo. *Perf. 13***

**C295** A143 10c dk vio, *pale pink* .25 .25

No. C261 Srchd. in Red

**1964 Wmk. 343 Litho. *Perf. 12½***

**C296** A138 50c on 21c brn, bl & blk 1.00 .70

Type of 1962 Overprinted

C297 A139 1b emer, yel & blk 2.00 2.00

Issued. No. C296, 2/25; No. C297, 2/20.

Nos. 434 and 444 Surcharged

**1964 Wmk. 343 *Perf. 12½***

**C298** A131 10c on 5c bl grn & emer .25 .25
**C299** A139 10c on 5c rose, lt grn & blk .25 .25

Issued: No. C298, 4/6; No. C299, 3/30.

St. Patrick's Cathedral, New York — AP84

Cathedrals: #C301, St. Stephen's, Vienna. #C302, St. Sofia's, Sofia. #C303, Notre Dame, Paris. #C304, Cologne. #C305, St. Paul's, London. #C306, Metropolitan, Athens. #C307, St. Elizabeth's, Kosice, Czechoslovakia (inscr. Kassa, Hungary). #C308, New Delhi. #C309, Milan. #C310, Guadalupe Basilica. #C311, New Church, Delft, Netherlands. #C312, Lima. #C313, St. John's Poland. #C314, Lisbon. #C315, St. Basil's, Moscow. #C316, Toledo. #C317, Stockholm. #C318, Basel. #C319, St. George's Patriarchal Church, Istanbul. 1b, Panama City. 2b, St. Peter's Basilica, Rome.

**Unwmk.**
**1964, Feb. 17 Engr. *Perf. 12***
**Center in Black**

**C300** AP84 21c olive 1.40 .90
**C301** AP84 21c chocolate 1.40 .90
**C302** AP84 21c aqua 1.40 .90
**C303** AP84 21c red brown 1.40 .90
**C304** AP84 21c magenta 1.40 .90
**C305** AP84 21c red 1.40 .90
**C306** AP84 21c orange red 1.40 .90
**C307** AP84 21c blue 1.40 .90
**C308** AP84 21c brown 1.40 .90
**C309** AP84 21c green 1.40 .90
**C310** AP84 21c violet bl 1.40 .90
**C311** AP84 21c dk slate grn 1.40 .90
**C312** AP84 21c violet 1.40 .90
**C313** AP84 21c black 1.40 .90
**C314** AP84 21c emerald 1.40 .90
**C315** AP84 21c dp violet 1.40 .90
**C316** AP84 21c olive grn 1.40 .90
**C317** AP84 21c carmine rose 1.40 .90
**C318** AP84 21c Prus green 1.40 .90
**C319** AP84 21c dark brown 1.40 .90
**C320** AP84 1b dark blue 7.50 5.00
**C321** AP84 2b yellow green 14.50 9.00
*a.* Souv. sheet of 6 15.00 15.00
*Nos. C300-C321 (22)* 50.00 32.00

Vatican II, the 21st Ecumenical Council of the Roman Catholic Church.

No. C321a contains 6 imperf. stamps similar to Nos. C300, C303, C305, C315, C320 and C321. Size: 198x138mm. Sold for 3.85b.

For overprints, see Nos. C329C-C329i.

World's Fair, New York AP84a

5c, 10c, 15c, Various pavilions. 21c, Unisphere.

**1964, Sept. 14 Wmk. 311 *Perf. 12½***

**C322** AP84a 5c yellow & blk
**C323** AP84a 10c red & blk
**C324** AP84a 15c green & blk
**C325** AP84a 21c ultra & blk
Set, #C322-C325 7.25 3.00

**Souvenir Sheet**
***Perf. 12***

**C326** AP84a 21c ultra & blk 6.00 6.00

No. C326 contains one 49x35mm stamp. Exists imperf. Value, same as No. C326.

AP84b

Hammarskjold Memorial, UN Day: No. C327, C329a, Dag Hammarskjold. No. C328, C329b, UN emblem.

***Perf. 13½x14***
**1964, Sept. 1 Unwmk.**

**C327** AP84b 21c black & blue 1.00 .60
**C328** AP84b 21c black & blue 1.00 .60

**Souvenir Sheet**
***Imperf***

**C329** Sheet of 2 6.75 6.75
*a.-b.* AP84b 21c blk & grn, any single 1.25 1.25

Nos. C327-C328 exist imperf in black and green. Value $4.50.

Nos. C300//C321a Overprinted "1964"

**1964, Sept. 28**

**C329C** AP84 21c olive (#C300) 1.25 .75
**C329D** AP84 21c red (#C305) 1.25 .75
**C329E** AP84 21c grn (#C309) 1.25 .75
**C329F** AP84 21c dk brn (#C319) 1.25 .75
**C329G** AP84 1b dk blue (#C320) 4.50 3.25
**C329H** AP84 2b yel grn (#C321) 9.50 7.50
*i.* Souv. sheet of 6 (#C321a) 80.00 80.00
*Nos. C329C-C329H (6)* 19.00 13.75

Vatican II, the 21st Ecumenical Council of the Roman Catholic Church, Third Period.

On No. C329i, the original dates are obliterated by a bar, with "1964" and papal arms overprinted below.

The overprint is olive bister on the stamps, yellow on the souvenir sheet. The overprint also exists in yellow gold on the same six stamps and in olive bister on the souvenir sheet. Values: set, $400; souvenir sheet $325.

**Roosevelt Type of Regular Issue**
***Perf. 12x12½***
**1964, Oct. 9 Litho. Unwmk.**

**C330** A147 20c grn & blk, *buff* .40 .30
*a.* Souv. sheet of 2, #455, C330, imperf. .55 .55

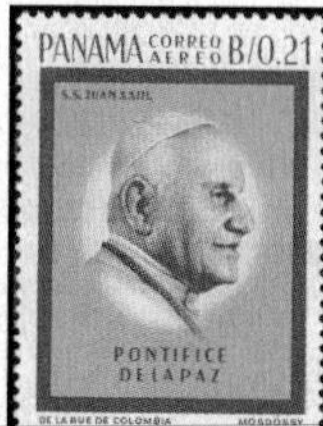


AP84c

**1964, Sept. 1 *Perf. 13½x14***

**C331** AP84c 21c shown .75 .50
**C332** AP84c 21c Papal coat of arms .75 .50
*a.* Souv. sheet of 2, #C331-C332 6.00 5.00

Pope John XXIII (1881-1963). Nos. C331-C332 exist imperf in different colors. Value $20.

Galileo, 400th Birth Anniv. — AP84d

21c, Galileo, studies of gravity.

**1965, May 12 *Perf. 14***

**C333** AP84d 10c blue & multi 2.00 .75
**C334** AP84d 21c green & multi 2.00 .75
*a.* Souv. sheet of 2, #C333-C334 15.00 15.00

Nos. C333-C334a exist imperf in different colors. Value, $11.

Alfred Nobel (1833-1896), Founder of Nobel Prize — AP84e

10c, Peace Medal, rev. 21c, Peace Medal, obv.

**1965, May 12 Litho. & Embossed**

**C335** AP84e 10c multi 2.25 .75
**C336** AP84e 21c multi 2.25 .75
*a.* Souv. sheet of 2, #C335-C336 15.00 15.00

Nos. C335-C336a exist imperf in different colors. Value, $4.50.

**Bird Type of Regular Issue, 1965**

Song Birds: 5c, Common troupial, horiz. 10c, Crimson-backed tanager, horiz.

**1965, Oct. 27 Unwmk. *Perf. 14***

**C337** A148 5c dp org & multi 1.40 .25
**C338** A148 10c brt blue & multi 2.50 .25
*a.* Souv. sheet of 6, #462-462C, C337-C338 22.50 22.50

No. C338a exists imperf. Value, $22.50.

**Fish Type of Regular Issue**

Designs: 8c, Shrimp. 12c, Hammerhead. 13c, Atlantic sailfish. 25c, Seahorse, vert.

**1965, Dec. 7 Litho.**

**C339** A149 8c multi .45 .25
**C340** A149 12c multi .70 .25
**C341** A149 13c multi .70 .25
**C342** A149 25c multi 1.40 .35
*Nos. C339-C342 (4)* 3.25 1.00

English Daisy and Emblem — AP85

Junior Chamber of Commerce Emblem and: #C344, Hibiscus. #C345, Orchid. #C346, Water lily. #C347, Gladiolus. #C348, Flor del Espiritu Santo.

**1966, Mar. 16**

**C343** AP85 30c brt pink & multi .90 .35
**C344** AP85 30c salmon & multi .90 .35
**C345** AP85 30c pale yel & multi .90 .35
**C346** AP85 40c lt grn & multi 1.25 .35
**C347** AP85 40c blue & multi 1.25 .35
**C348** AP85 40c pink & multi 1.25 .35
*Nos. C343-C348 (6)* 6.45 2.10

50th anniv. of the Junior Chamber of Commerce.

**Nos. C224 and C236 Surcharged**
**1966, June 27 Wmk. 311 *Perf. 12½***

**C349** A130 3c on 5c blk & red brn .25 .25

**Wmk. 343**

**C350** A131 13c on 25c lt & dk bl .35 .25

The old denominations are not obliterated on Nos. C349-C350.

ITU Cent. — AP85a

**1966, Aug. 12 *Perf. 13½x14***

**C351** AP85a 31c multicolored 4.50 —

**Souvenir Sheet**
***Perf. 14***

**C352** AP85a 31c multicolored 15.00 15.00

No. C352 exists imperf. with blue green background. Value $15.

**Animal Type of Regular Issue, 1967**

Domestic Animals: 10c, Pekingese dog. 13c, Zebu, horiz. 30c, Cat. 40c, Horse, horiz.

**1967, Feb. 3 Unwmk. *Perf. 14***

**C353** A150 10c multi .45 .25
**C354** A150 13c multi .55 .25
**C355** A150 30c multi 1.00 .50
**C356** A150 40c multi 1.25 .60
*Nos. C353-C356 (4)* 3.25 1.50

Young Hare, by Durer AP86

10c, St. Jerome and the Lion, by Albrecht Durer. 20c, Lady with the Ermine, by Leonardo Da Vinci. 30c, The Hunt, by Delacroix, horiz.

**1967, Sept. 1**

**C357** AP86 10c black, buff & car .35 .25
**C358** AP86 13c lt yellow & multi .55 .25
**C359** AP86 20c multicolored .80 .25
**C360** AP86 30c multicolored 1.10 .45
*Nos. C357-C360 (4)* 2.80 1.10

Panama-Mexico Friendship — AP86a

Designs: 1b, Pres. Gustavo Diaz Ordaz of Mexico and Pres. Marco A. Robles of Panama, horiz.

**1968, Jan. 20** *Perf. 14*

**C361** AP86a 50c shown 2.00 .60
**C361A** AP86a 1b multi 4.00 1.10
*b.* Souv. sheet of 2, #C361-C361A, imperf. 8.00 8.00

For overprints see Nos. C364-C364B.

Souvenir Sheet

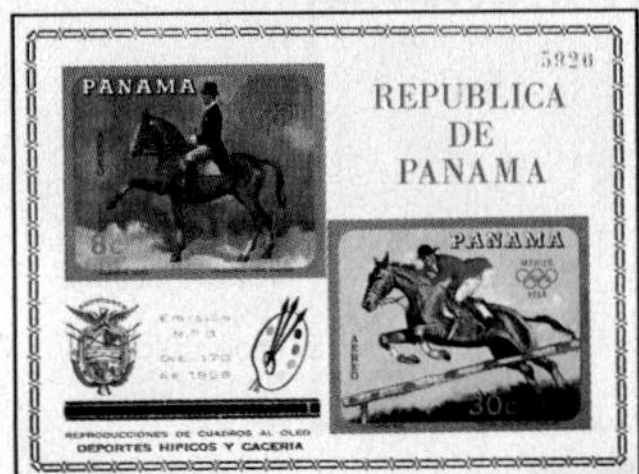

Olympic Equestrian Events — AP86b

**1968, Oct. 29** *Imperf.*

**C362** AP86b Sheet of 2 45.00 45.00
*a.* 8c Dressage 1.50 1.00
*b.* 30c Show jumping 5.00 3.50

Intl. Human Rights Year — AP86c

**1968, Dec. 18** *Perf. 14*

**C363** AP86c 40c multicolored 11.50 7.50
*a.* Miniature sheet of 1 30.00 30.00

**Nos. C361-C361b Ovptd. in Red or Black**

**1969, Jan. 31**

**C364** AP86a 50c on #C361 (R) 6.25 1.50
**C364A** AP86a 1b on #C361A (B) 6.25 1.50

**Souvenir Sheet**

**C364B** on #C361b (R) 11.50 11.50

Intl. Philatelic and Numismatic Expo.

Overprint larger on No. C364A, larger and in different arrangement on No. C364B.

Intl. Space Exploration — AP86d

Designs: a, France, Diadem I. b, Italy, San Marco II. c, Great Britain, UK 3. d, US, Saturn V/Apollo 7. e, US, Surveyor 7. f, Europe/US, Esro 2.

**1969, Mar. 14**

**C365** Sheet of 6 18.00 18.00
*a.* AP86d 5c multicolored .50 .25
*b.* AP86d 10c multicolored 1.00 .40
*c.* AP86d 15c multicolored 1.50 .50
*d.* AP86d 20c multicolored 2.00 .75
*e.* AP86d 25c multicolored 3.00 1.00
*f.* AP86d 30c multicolored 4.00 1.25

Satellite Transmission of Summer Olympics, Mexico, 1968 — AP86e

**1969, Mar. 14** *Perf. 14½*

**C366** AP86e 1b multi 3.00 1.00
*a.* Miniature sheet of 1 10.00 2.00

Nos. CB4, 461B & 461C Surcharged

**1969, Apr. 1** *Perf. 13½x13*

**C367** AP81 5c on 5c+5c 3.50 .50
**C367A** A147e 5c on 10c+5c 3.50 .50
**C367B** A147e 10c on 21c+10c 3.50 .50

**Games Type of Regular Issue and**

San Blas Indian Girl — AP87

Design: 13c, Bridge of the Americas.

**1970, Jan. 6** **Litho.** *Perf. 13½*

**C368** A158 13c multi 1.00 .30
**C369** AP87 30c multi 1.25 .75
*a.* "AEREO" omitted *50.00 50.00*

See notes after No. 525.

Juan D. Arosemena and Arosemena Stadium — AP88

Designs: 2c, 3c, 5c, like 1c. No. C374, Basketball. No. C375, New Panama Gymnasium. No. C376, Revolution Stadium. No. C377, Panamanian man and woman in Stadium. 30c, Stadium, eternal flame, arms of Mexico, Puerto Rico and Cuba.

**1970, Oct. 7** **Wmk. 365** *Perf. 13½*

**C370** AP88 1c pink & multi .25 .25
**C371** AP88 2c pink & multi .25 .25
**C372** AP88 3c pink & multi .25 .25
**C373** AP88 5c pink & multi .25 .25
**C374** AP88 13c lt blue & multi .45 .25
**C375** AP88 13c lilac & multi .45 .25
**C376** AP88 13c yellow & multi .45 .25
**C377** AP88 13c pink & multi .45 .25
**C378** AP88 30c yellow & multi 1.25 .50
*a.* Souv. sheet of 1, imperf. 2.00 2.00
*Nos. C370-C378 (9)* 4.05 2.50

11th Central American and Caribbean Games, Feb. 28-Mar. 14.

US astronauts Charles Conrad, Jr., Richard F. Gordon, Jr. and Alan L. Bean. — AP89

No. C379, Astronaut on Moon.

**1971, Aug. 20** **Wmk. 343** *Perf. 13½*

**C379** AP89 13c gold & multi .50 .35
**C380** AP89 13c lt green & multi .50 .35

Man's first landing on the moon, Apollo 11, July 20, 1969 (No. C379) and Apollo 12 moon mission, Nov. 14-24, 1969.

EXPO '70 Emblem and Pavilion AP90

**1971, Aug. 24** **Litho.**

**C381** AP90 10c pink & multi .25 .25

EXPO '70 International Exposition, Osaka, Japan, Mar. 15-Sept. 13.

Flag of Panama AP91

Design: 13c, Map of Panama superimposed on Western Hemisphere, and tourist year emblem.

**1971, Dec. 11** **Wmk. 343**

**C382** AP91 5c multi .25 .25
**C383** AP91 13c multi .25 .25

Proclamation of 1972 as Tourist Year of the Americas.

Mahatma Gandhi AP92

**1971, Dec. 17**

**C384** AP92 10c black & multi *60.00 25.00*

Centenary of the birth of Mohandas K. Gandhi (1869-1948), leader in India's fight for independence.

**Central American Independence Issue**

Flags of Central American States AP92a

**1971, Dec. 20**

**C385** AP92a 13c multi .35 .25

160th anniv. of Central America independence.

AP93

**1971, Dec. 21**

**C386** AP93 8c Panama #4 .25 .25

2nd National Philatelic and Numismatic Exposition, 1970.

AP94

**1972, Sept. 7** **Wmk. 365**

**C387** AP94 40c Natá Church .80 .60

450th anniversary of the founding of Natá.

For surcharges see Nos. C402, RA85.

Telecommunications Emblem — AP95

**1972, Sept. 8**

**C388** AP95 13c lt bl, dp bl & blk .40 .40

3rd World Telecommunications Day (in 1971).

Apollo 14 AP96

**1972, Sept. 11**

**C389** AP96 13c tan & multi .90 .50

Apollo 14 US moon mission, 1/1-2/9/71.

Shoeshine Boy Counting Coins — AP97

**1972, Sept. 12**

| | | | | |
|---|---|---|---|---|
| C390 | AP97 | 5c shown | .25 | .25 |
| C391 | AP97 | 8c Mother & Child | .25 | .25 |
| C392 | AP97 | 50c UNICEF emblem | 1.25 | .55 |
| a. | | Souv. sheet of 1, imperf. | 3.00 | 1.75 |
| | | *Nos. C390-C392 (3)* | 1.70 | 1.00 |

25th anniv. (in 1971) of the UNICEF.

San Blas Cloth, Cuna Indians AP98

8c, Beaded necklace, Guaymi Indians. 25c, View of Portobelo.

**1972, Sept. 13**

| | | | | |
|---|---|---|---|---|
| C393 | AP98 | 5c multicolored | .25 | .25 |
| C394 | AP98 | 8c multicolored | .25 | .25 |
| C395 | AP98 | 25c multicolored | .80 | .45 |
| a. | | Souv. sheet of 2, #C393, C395, imperf. | 3.50 | 3.50 |
| | | *Nos. C393-C395 (3)* | 1.25 | .85 |

Tourist publicity.

For surcharges see Nos. C417, RA83.

Baseball and Games' Emblem AP99

Games' Emblem and: 10c, Basketball, vert. 13c, Torch, vert. 25c, Boxing. 50c, Map and flag of Panama, Bolivar. 1b, Medals.

*Perf. 12½*

**1973, Feb. 10 Litho. Unwmk.**

| | | | | |
|---|---|---|---|---|
| C396 | AP99 | 8c rose red & yel | .25 | .25 |
| C397 | AP99 | 10c black & ultra | .25 | .25 |
| C398 | AP99 | 13c blue & multi | .35 | .25 |
| C399 | AP99 | 25c blk, yel grn & red | .70 | .25 |
| C400 | AP99 | 50c green & multi | 1.50 | .60 |
| C401 | AP99 | 1b multicolored | 3.00 | 1.00 |
| | | *Nos. C396-401 (1)* | .25 | .25 |

7th Bolivar Games, Panama City, 2/17-3/3.

### No. C387 Surcharged in Red Similar to No. 542

**1973, Mar. 15 Wmk. 365 *Perf. 13½***

| | | | | |
|---|---|---|---|---|
| C402 | AP94 | 13c on 40c multi | .35 | .30 |

UN Security Council Meeting, Panama City, Mar. 15-21.

### Portrait Type of Regular Issue 1973

Designs: 5c, Isabel Herrera Obaldia, educator. 8c, Nicolas Victoria Jaén, educator. 10c, Forest Scene, by Roberto Lewis. No. C406, Portrait of a Lady, by Manuel E. Amador. No. C407, Ricardo Miró, poet. 20c, Portrait, by Isaac Benitez. 21c, Manuel Amador Guerrero, statesman. 25c, Belisario Porras, statesman. 30c, Juan Demostenes Arosemena, statesman. 34c, Octavio Mendez Pereira, writer. 38c, Ricardo J. Alfaro, writer.

**1973, June 20 Litho. *Perf. 13½***

| | | | | |
|---|---|---|---|---|
| C403 | A169 | 5c pink & multi | .25 | .25 |
| C404 | A169 | 8c pink & multi | .25 | .25 |
| C405 | A169 | 10c gray & multi | .35 | .25 |
| C406 | A169 | 13c pink & multi | .55 | .25 |
| C407 | A169 | 13c pink & multi | .55 | .25 |
| C408 | A169 | 20c blue & multi | .70 | .40 |
| C409 | A169 | 21c yellow & multi | .80 | .40 |
| C410 | A169 | 25c pink & multi | .90 | .40 |
| C411 | A169 | 30c gray & multi | 1.00 | .45 |
| C412 | A169 | 34c lt blue & multi | 1.10 | .60 |
| C413 | A169 | 38c lt blue & multi | 1.25 | .60 |
| | | *Nos. C403-C413 (11)* | 7.65 | 3.85 |

Famous Panamanians.

For overprints and surcharges see Nos. C414-C416, C418-C421.

Nos. C403, C410, and C412 Overprinted in Black or Red

**1973, Sept. 14 Litho. *Perf. 13½***

| | | | | |
|---|---|---|---|---|
| C414 | A169 | 5c pink & multi | .25 | .25 |
| C415 | A169 | 25c pink & multi | .90 | .45 |
| C416 | A169 | 34c bl & multi (R) | 1.10 | .75 |
| | | *Nos. C414-C416 (3)* | 2.25 | 1.45 |

50th anniversary of the Isabel Herrera Obaldia Professional School.

### Nos. C395, C408, C413, C412 and C409 Surcharged in Red

**1974, Nov. 11 Litho. *Perf. 13½***

| | | | | |
|---|---|---|---|---|
| C417 | AP98 | 1c on 25c multi | .25 | .25 |
| C418 | A169 | 3c on 20c multi | .25 | .25 |
| C419 | A169 | 8c on 38c multi | .25 | .25 |
| C420 | A169 | 10c on 34c multi | .25 | .25 |
| C421 | A169 | 13c on 21c multi | .25 | .25 |
| | | *Nos. C417-C421 (5)* | 1.00 | 1.00 |

Women's Hands, Panama Map, UN and IWY Emblems AP100

*Perf. 12½*

**1975, May 6 Litho. Unwmk.**

| | | | | |
|---|---|---|---|---|
| C422 | AP100 | 17c blue & multi | .70 | .25 |
| a. | | Souv. sheet, typo., imperf., no gum | 1.50 | 1.50 |

International Women's Year 1975.

Victoria Sugar Plant, Sugar Cane, Map of Veraguas Province AP101

Designs: 17c, Bayano electrification project and map of Panama, horiz. 33c, Tocumen International Airport and map, horiz.

**1975, Oct. 9 Litho. *Perf. 12½***

| | | | | |
|---|---|---|---|---|
| C423 | AP101 | 17c bl, buff & blk | .70 | .30 |
| C424 | AP101 | 27c ultra & yel grn | 1.00 | .35 |
| C425 | AP101 | 33c bl & multi | 1.10 | .45 |
| | | *Nos. C423-C425 (3)* | 2.80 | 1.10 |

Oct. 11, 1968, Revolution, 7th anniv.

Bolivar Statue and Flags — AP102

Bolivar Hall, Panama City AP103

Design: 41c, Bolivar with flag of Panama, ruins of Old Panama City.

**1976, Mar.**

| | | | | |
|---|---|---|---|---|
| C426 | AP102 | 23c multi | .65 | .25 |
| C427 | AP103 | 35c multi | 1.00 | .30 |
| C428 | AP102 | 41c multi | 1.00 | .60 |
| | | *Nos. C426-C428 (3)* | 2.65 | 1.10 |

150th anniversary of Congress of Panama.

Issued: 23c, Mar. 5; others Mar. 30.

### Marine Life Type of 1976

Marine life: 17c, Diodon hystrix, vert. 27c, Pocillopora damicornis.

*Perf. 13x12½, 12½x13*

**1976, May 6 Litho. Wmk. 377**

| | | | | |
|---|---|---|---|---|
| C429 | A171 | 17c multi | 1.60 | .50 |
| C430 | A171 | 27c multi | 2.25 | .65 |

Cerro Colorado — AP104

**1976, Nov. 12 Litho. *Perf. 12½***

| | | | | |
|---|---|---|---|---|
| C431 | AP104 | 23c multi | .55 | .25 |

Cerro Colorado copper mines, Chiriqui Province.

Gen. Omar Torrijos Herrera (1929-1981) AP105

**1982, Feb. 13 Litho. *Perf. 10½***

| | | | | |
|---|---|---|---|---|
| C432 | AP105 | 23c multi | .65 | .25 |

### Torrijos Type of 1982

35c, Security Council reunion, 1973. 41c, Torrijos Airport.

**Wmk. 311**

**1982, May 14 Litho. *Perf. 10½***

| | | | | |
|---|---|---|---|---|
| C433 | A201 | 35c multicolored | 1.00 | .30 |
| C434 | A201 | 41c multicolored | 1.10 | .50 |

### Souvenir Sheet

*Imperf*

| | | | | |
|---|---|---|---|---|
| C435 | A201 | 23c like #C432 | 3.00 | 3.00 |

No. C435 sold for 1b.

### Alfaro Type of 1982

Photos by Luiz Gutierrez Cruz.

**1982, Aug. 18 Wmk. 382**

| | | | | |
|---|---|---|---|---|
| C436 | A202 | 17c multi | .45 | .25 |
| C437 | A202 | 23c multi | .65 | .25 |

### World Cup Type of 1982

**1982, Dec. 27 Litho. *Perf. 10½***

| | | | | |
|---|---|---|---|---|
| C438 | A203 | 23c Map | .70 | .25 |
| C439 | A203 | 35c Pele, vert. | 1.00 | .30 |
| C440 | A203 | 41c Cup, vert. | 1.25 | .40 |
| | | *Nos. C438-C440 (3)* | 2.95 | .95 |

1b imperf. souvenir sheet exists in design of 23c; black control number. Size; 85x75mm. Value $13.50.

Nicolas A. Solano (1882-1943), Tuberculosis Researcher AP106

**Wmk. 382 (Stars)**

**1983, Feb. 8 Litho. *Perf. 10½***

| | | | | |
|---|---|---|---|---|
| C441 | AP106 | 23c brown | .50 | .25 |

World Food Day — AP107

**1984, Oct. 16 Litho. *Perf. 12***

| | | | | |
|---|---|---|---|---|
| C442 | AP107 | 30c Hand grasping fork | 1.25 | .50 |

Contadora Group for Peace — AP108

**1985, Oct. 1 Litho. *Perf. 14***

| | | | | |
|---|---|---|---|---|
| C443 | AP108 | 10c multi | .45 | .25 |
| C444 | AP108 | 20c multi | .90 | .30 |
| C445 | AP108 | 30c multi | 1.25 | .50 |
| | | *Nos. C443-C445 (3)* | 2.60 | 1.05 |

See No. 680A.

### Christmas Type of 1988

**1988, Dec. 29 Litho. *Perf. 12***

| | | | | |
|---|---|---|---|---|
| C446 | A246 | 35c St. Joseph and the Infant | 1.10 | .40 |

### Olympics Type of 1989

**1989, Mar. 17 Litho. *Perf. 12***

| | | | | |
|---|---|---|---|---|
| C447 | A248 | 35c Boxing | 1.10 | .40 |

Opening of the Panama Canal, 75th Anniv. AP109

35c, Ancon in lock, 1914. 60c, Ship in lock, 1989.

**1989, Sept. 29 Litho. *Perf. 13½***

| | | | | |
|---|---|---|---|---|
| C448 | AP109 | 35c multicolored | 1.25 | .65 |
| C449 | AP109 | 60c multicolored | 2.00 | 1.10 |

### Revolution Type of 1989

**1989, Nov. 14 Litho.**

| | | | | |
|---|---|---|---|---|
| C450 | A251 | 35c Storming of the Bastille | 1.75 | .65 |
| C451 | A251 | 45c Anniv. emblem | 2.10 | .85 |

French revolution, bicent.

Christmas 2001 AP110

Designs: 60c, Man, woman, drums. 1b, Guitar, drum, candle. 2b, Pots, potted plant.

**2002, Apr. 30 Litho.** ***Perf. 13x13¼***

**C452-C454** AP110 Set of 3 14.50 14.50

Dated 2001.

La Salle Schools in Panama, Cent. (in 2002) AP111

**2003, May 15 Litho.** ***Perf. 13x13½***

**C455** AP111 5b multi 16.00 10.00

Dated 2002.

Natá, 480th Anniv. (in 2002) AP112

**2003, May 20**

**C456** AP112 1b multi 3.25 2.00

Dated 2002.

Trains AP113

Designs: 40c, Colón locomotive. 50c, Panama Railroad, vert.

***Perf. 13x13½, 14 (50c)***

**2003, July 17**

**C457-C458** AP113 Set of 2 4.00 2.50

Dated 2002.

Santa María de Belén, 500th Anniv. AP114

**2003, July 31** ***Perf. 14***

**C459** AP114 1.50b multi 5.00 3.00

Dated 2002.

Fourth Voyage of Christopher Columbus, 500th Anniv. (in 2002) AP115

**2003, July 31** ***Perf. 13x13½***

**C460** AP115 2b multi 6.75 4.00

Dated 2002.

Kuna Indians AP116

Designs: No. C461, 50c, Village, people in canoe, woman. No. C462, 50c, Man and woman, vert. No. C463, 60c, Woman sewing. No. C464, 60c, Dancers.
1.50b, Fish.

***Perf. 14 (#C461), 13½x13 (#C462), 13x13½***

**2003, Aug. 13**

**C461-C464** AP116 Set of 4 7.00 4.50

**Souvenir Sheet**

***Perf. 13½x14***

**C465** AP116 1.50b multi 7.50 5.75

Dated 2002. No. C465 contains one 50x45mm stamp.

Medicine in Panama AP117

Designs: No. C466, 50c, Santo Tomás de Villanueva Hospital, 300th anniv. No. C467, 50c, Gorgas Memorial Institute of Tropical and Preventative Medicine, 75th anniv.

**2003** ***Perf. 12***

**C466-C467** AP117 Set of 2 3.25 3.25

Issued: No. C466, 12/17; No. C467, 11/17.

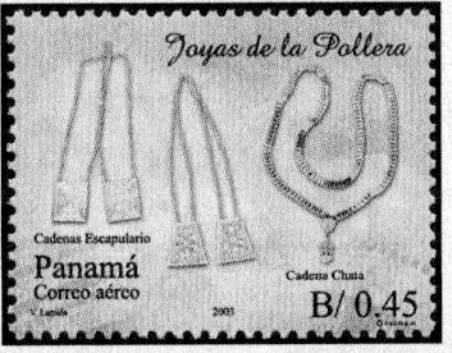

Jewelry AP118

Designs: 45c, Necklaces. 60c, Brooches.

**2003, Nov. 24**

**C468-C469** AP118 Set of 2 3.50 3.50

For surcharges, see Nos. C474-C475.

America Issue - Endangered Species — AP119

**2003, Nov. 26**

**C470** AP119 2b multi 6.25 6.25

La Estrella de Panama Newspaper, 150th Anniv. — AP120

**2003, Dec. 3**

**C471** AP120 40c multi 1.25 1.25

Scouting, Cent. AP121

**2010, Sept. 3 Litho.** ***Perf. 14***

**C472** AP121 20c multi .40 .40

Printed in sheets of 4.

Salesian Order in Panama, Cent. — AP122

**2010, Aug. 27**

**C473** AP122 20c multi .40 .40

**No. C468 Surcharged**

No. C474

Homenaje a
Gaceta del Gobierno
Independiente de Panamá
B/0.30

No. C475

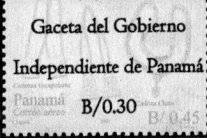

**Methods and Perfs. As Before**

**2014, June 1**

**C474** AP118 15c on 45c #C468 .30 .30

**C475** AP118 30c on 45c #C468 .60 .60

---

**AIR POST SEMI-POSTAL STAMPS**

**Catalogue values for unused stamps in this section are for Never Hinged items.**

"The World Against Malaria" — SPAP1

**Wmk. 311**

**1961, Dec. 20 Litho.** ***Perf. 12½***

**CB1** SPAP1 5c + 5c car rose .50 .50

**CB2** SPAP1 10c + 10c vio bl .50 .50

**CB3** SPAP1 15c + 15c dk grn .50 .50

*Nos. CB1-CB3 (3)* 1.50 1.50

WHO drive to eradicate malaria.
For surcharges see Nos. C271-C272.

Nos. C274-C276 Surcharged in Red

**Wmk. 311**

**1963, Mar. 4 Litho.** ***Perf. 12½***

**CB4** AP81 5c +5c on #C274 1.00 .75

**CB5** AP81 10c +10c on #C275 2.00 1.50

**CB6** AP81 15c +31c on #C276 2.00 1.50

Surcharge on No. CB4 differs to fit stamp. See No. CB7.

No. CB4 Surcharged in Black

**1963, Aug. 22**

**CB7** AP81 10c on 5c+5c 6.00 5.00

Intl. Red. Cross cent.

---

**SPECIAL DELIVERY STAMPS**

Nos. 211-212 Overprinted in Red

**1926 Unwmk.** ***Perf. 12***

**E1** A31 10c org & blk 7.50 3.25
- *a.* "EXRPESO" 40.00

**E2** A32 20c brn & blk 10.00 3.25
- *a.* "EXRPESO" 40.00
- *b.* Double overprint 35.00 35.00

Bicycle Messenger SD1

**1929, Feb. 8 Engr.** ***Perf. 12½***

**E3** SD1 10c orange 1.25 1.00

**E4** SD1 20c dk brn 4.75 2.50

For surcharges and overprints see Nos. C1-C5, C17-C18A, C67.

---

**REGISTRATION STAMPS**

**Issued under Colombian Dominion**

R1

**1888 Unwmk. Engr.** ***Perf. 13½***

**F1** R1 10c black, *gray* 8.00 5.25

*Imperforate and part-perforate copies without gum and those on surface-colored paper are reprints.*

Magenta, Violet or Blue Black Handstamped Overprint

**1898** ***Perf. 12***

**F2** A4 10c orange 7.00 6.50

The handstamp on No. F2 was also used as a postmark.

R3

**1900** **Litho.** ***Perf. 11***
**F3** R3 10c blk, *lt bl* 4.00 3.50

**1901**
**F4** R3 10c brown red 30.00 20.00

R4

**1902** **Blue Black Surcharge**
**F5** R4 20c on 10c brn red 20.00 16.00

### Issues of the Republic Issued in the City of Panama

Registration Stamps of Colombia Handstamped in Blue Black or Rose

**1903-04** ***Imperf.***
**F6** R9 20c red brn, *bl* 45.00 42.50
**F7** R9 20c blue, *blue* (R) 45.00 42.50

For surcharges and overprints see Nos. F8-F11, F16-F26.

*Reprints exist of Nos. F6 and F7; see note after No. 64.*

**With Additional Surcharge in Rose**

**F8** R9 10c on 20c red brn, *bl* 60.00 55.00
*b.* "10" in blue black 60.00 55.00
**F9** R9 10c on 20c bl, *bl* 60.00 45.00

**Handstamped in Rose**

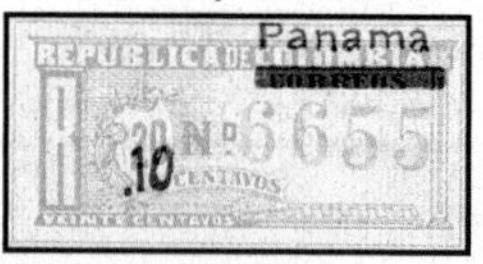

**F10** R9 10c on 20c red brn, *bl* 60.00 55.00
**F11** R9 10c on 20c blue, *blue* 45.00 42.50

**Issued in Colon**

Regular Issues Handstamped "R/COLON" in Circle (as on F2) Together with Other Overprints and Surcharges

Handstamped

**1903-04** ***Perf. 12***
**F12** A4 10c orange 3.00 2.50

Handstamped

**F13** A4 10c orange 22.50

Overprinted in Red

**F14** A4 10c orange 3.00 2.50

Overprinted in Black

**F15** A4 10c orange 7.50 5.00

The handstamps on Nos. F12 to F15 are in magenta, violet or red; various combinations of these colors are to be found. They are struck in various positions, including double, inverted, one handstamp omitted, etc.

**Colombia No. F13 Handstamped Like No. F12 in Violet**

***Imperf***

**F16** R9 20c red brn, *bl* 60.00 55.00

**Overprinted Like No. F15 in Black**

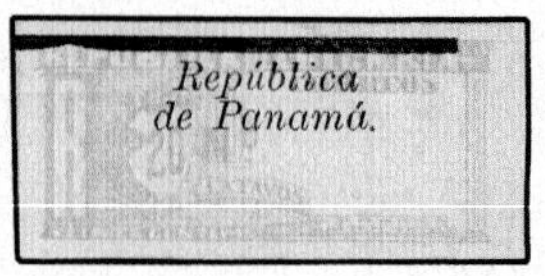

**F17** R9 20c red brn, *bl* 6.00 5.75

**No. F17 Surcharged in Manuscript**

**F18** R9 10c on 20c red brn, *bl* 60.00 55.00

No. F17 Surcharged in Purple **10**

**F19** R9 10c on 20c 82.50 80.00

**No. F17 Surcharged in Violet**

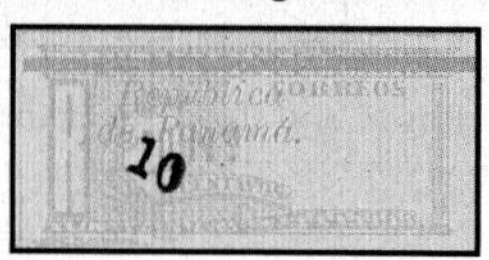

**F20** R9 10c on 20c 82.50 80.00

The varieties of the overprint which are described after No. 138 are also to be found on the Registration and Acknowledgment of Receipt stamps. It is probable that Nos. F17 to F20 inclusive owe their existence more to speculation than to postal necessity.

**Issued in Bocas del Toro**

Colombia Nos. F17 and F13 Handstamped in Violet

R DE PANAMA

**1903-04**
**F21** R9 20c blue, *blue* 125.00 125.00
**F22** R9 20c red brn, *bl* 125.00 125.00

**No. F21 Surcharged in Manuscript in Violet or Red**

**F23** R9 10c on 20c bl, *bl* 150.00 140.00

**Colombia Nos. F13, F17 Handstamped in Violet**

**Surcharged in Manuscript (a) "10" (b) "10cs" in Red**

**F25** R9 10 on 20c red brn, *bl* 70.00 65.00
**F26** R9 10cs on 20c bl, *bl* 55.00 50.00
*Nos. F21-F26 (5)* 525.00 505.00

No. F25 without surcharge is bogus, according to leading experts.

**General Issue**

R5

**1904, Aug. 1** **Engr.** ***Perf. 12***
**F27** R5 10c green 1.00 .50

**Nos. 190 and 213 Surcharged in Red**

#F29-F30

#F29b

**1916-17**
**F29** A11 5c on 8c pur & blk 3.00 2.25
*a.* "5" inverted 75.00
*b.* Large, round "5" 50.00
*c.* Inverted surcharge 12.50 11.00
*d.* Tête bêche surcharge
*e.* Pair, one without surcharge 10.00
**F30** A33 5c on 8c vio & blk 3.50 .80
*a.* Inverted surcharge 13.00 8.25
*b.* Tête bêche surcharge
*c.* Double surcharge 60.00

Issued: No. F29, 1/1/16; No. F30, 1/28/17.

Stamps similar to No. F30, overprinted in green were unauthorized.

## INSURED LETTER STAMPS

Stamps of 1939 Surcharged in Black

**1942, Nov. 14** **Unwmk.** ***Perf. 12½***
**G1** AP23 5c on 1b blk .50 .50
**G2** A84 10c on 1b dk brn .80 .80
**G3** AP23 25c on 50c dk brn 2.00 2.00
*Nos. G1-G3 (3)* 3.30 3.30

## ACKNOWLEDGMENT OF RECEIPT STAMPS

**Issued under Colombian Dominion**

Experts consider this handstamp-"A.R. / COLON / COLOMBIA"-to be a cancellation or a marking intended for a letter to receive special handling. It was applied at Colon to various stamps in 1897-1904 in different colored inks for philatelic sale. It exists on cover, usually with the bottom line removed by masking the handstamp.

Nos. 17-18 Handstamped in Rose

**1902**
**H4** A4 5c blue 5.00 5.00
**H5** A4 10c yellow 10.00 10.00

This handstamp was also used as a postmark.

### Issues of the Republic Issued in the City of Panama

Colombia No. H3 Handstamped in Rose

**1903-04** **Unwmk.** ***Imperf.***
**H9** AR2 10c blue, *blue* 10.00 8.00

*Reprints exist of No. H9, see note after No. 64.*

No. H9 Surcharged

**H10** AR2 5c on 10c bl, *bl* 5.00 5.00

Colombia No. H3 Handstamped in Rose

**H11** AR2 10c blue, *blue* 17.50 14.00

**Issued in Colon**

Handstamped in Magenta or Violet

***Imperf***

**H17** AR2 10c blue, *blue* 15.00 15.00

Handstamped

**H18** AR2 10c blue, *blue* 82.50 70.00

Overprinted in Black

**H19** AR2 10c blue, *blue* 11.00 8.00

**No. H19 Surcharged in Manuscript**

**H20** AR2 10c on 5c on 10c 100.00 82.50

**Issued in Bocas del Toro**

Colombia No. H3 Handstamped in Violet and Surcharged in Manuscript in Red Like Nos. F25-F26

**1904**
**H21** AR2 5c on 10c blue, *blue*

No. H21, unused, without surcharge is bogus.

### General Issue

AR3

**1904, Aug. 1** **Engr.** ***Perf. 12***
**H22** AR3 5c blue 1.00 .80

No. 199 Overprinted in Violet

**1916, Jan. 1**
**H23** A20 2½c red orange 1.00 .80
*a.* "R.A." for "A.R." 50.00
*b.* Double overprint 8.00
*c.* Inverted overprint 8.00

## LATE FEE STAMPS

### Issues of the Republic Issued in the City of Panama

Colombia No. I4 Handstamped in Rose or Blue Black

LF3

REPUBLICA DE PANAMA

**1903-04** **Unwmk.** ***Imperf.***
**I1** LF3 5c pur, *rose* 12.50 9.00
**I2** LF3 5c pur, *rose* (Bl Blk) 17.50 12.50

*Reprints exist of #I1-I2; see note after #64.*

### General Issue

LF4

**1904** **Engr.** ***Perf. 12***
**I3** LF4 2½c lake 1.00 .65

No. 199 Overprinted with Typewriter

**1910, Aug. 12**
**I4** A20 2½c red orange 125.00 100.00

Used only on Aug. 12-13. Counterfeits abound.

Handstamped

**1910**
**I5** A20 2½c red orange 60.00 50.00

Counterfeits abound.

No. 195 Surcharged in Green

**1917, Jan. 1**
**I6** A17 1c on ½c orange .80 .80
*a.* "UN CENTESIMO" inverted 50.00
*b.* Double surcharge 10.00
*c.* Inverted surcharge 6.50 6.50

No. 196 Surcharged in Green

**1921**
**I7** A17 1c on ½c rose 25.00 20.00

## POSTAGE DUE STAMPS

San Lorenzo Castle Gate, Mouth of Chagres River D1

Statue of Columbus D2

Pedro J. Sosa — D4

Design: 4c, Capitol, Panama City.

**Unwmk.**
**1915, Mar. 25** **Engr.** ***Perf. 12***
**J1** D1 1c olive brown 3.50 .75
**J2** D2 2c olive brown 5.25 .65
**J3** D1 4c olive brown 7.25 1.25
**J4** D4 10c olive brown 5.25 1.75
*Nos. J1-J4 (4)* 21.25 4.40

Type D1 was intended to show a gate of San Lorenzo Castle, Chagres, and is so inscribed.

D5

**1930, Dec. 30** ***Perf. 12½***
**J5** D5 1c emerald 1.00 .60
**J6** D5 2c dark red 1.00 .60
**J7** D5 4c dark blue 1.60 .80
**J8** D5 10c violet 1.60 .80
*Nos. J5-J8 (4)* 5.20 2.80

## POSTAL TAX STAMPS

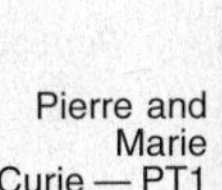

Pierre and Marie Curie — PT1

**Unwmk.**
**1939, June 15** **Engr.** ***Perf. 12***
**RA1** PT1 1c rose carmine .65 .25
**RA2** PT1 1c green .65 .25
**RA3** PT1 1c orange .65 .25
**RA4** PT1 1c blue .65 .25
*Nos. RA1-RA4 (4)* 2.60 1.00

See Nos. RA6-RA18, RA24-RA27, RA30.

Stamp of 1924 Overprinted in Black

**1940, Dec. 20**
**RA5** A53 1c dark green 1.40 .75

**1941, Jan. 30** **Inscribed 1940**
**RA6** PT1 1c rose carmine .65 .25
**RA7** PT1 1c green .65 .25
**RA8** PT1 1c orange .65 .25
**RA9** PT1 1c blue .65 .25
*Nos. RA6-RA9 (4)* 2.60 1.00

**1942** **Inscribed 1942**
**RA10** PT1 1c violet .40 .25

**1943** **Inscribed 1943**
**RA11** PT1 1c rose carmine .40 .25
**RA12** PT1 1c green .40 .25
**RA13** PT1 1c orange .40 .25
**RA14** PT1 1c blue .40 .25
*Nos. RA11-RA14 (4)* 1.60 1.00

**1945** **Inscribed 1945**
**RA15** PT1 1c rose carmine .90 .25
**RA16** PT1 1c green .90 .25
**RA17** PT1 1c orange .90 .25
**RA18** PT1 1c blue .90 .25
*Nos. RA15-RA18 (4)* 3.60 1.00

Nos. 234 and 235 Surcharged in Black or Red

**1946** **Unwmk.** ***Perf. 12***
**RA19** A53 1c on ½c orange .60 .25
**RA20** A53 1c on 1c dk grn (R) .60 .25

**Catalogue values for unused stamps in this section, from this point to the end of the section, are for Never Hinged items.**

### Same Surcharged in Black on Nos. 239 and 241

**1947, Apr. 7**
**RA21** A53 1c on 12c ol grn 1.00 .30
**RA22** A53 1c on 24c yel brn 1.00 .30

### Surcharged in Red on No. 342

**RA23** A95 1c on ½c dl vio, bl & car 1.00 .25

### Type of 1939 Inscribed 1947

**1947, July 21**
**RA24** PT1 1c rose carmine 1.25 .25
**RA25** PT1 1c green 1.25 .25
**RA26** PT1 1c orange 1.25 .25
**RA27** PT1 1c blue 1.25 .25
*Nos. RA24-RA27 (4)* 5.00 1.00

### Nos. C100 and C101 Surcharged in Black

a

b

**1949, Feb. 16** **Unwmk.** ***Perf. 12½***
**RA28** AP45 (a) 1c on 5c .65 .25
*a.* Inverted surcharge 15.00
**RA29** AP46 (b) 1c on 10c yel org .65 .25
*a.* Inverted surcharge —

### Type of 1939

**1949** **Inscribed 1949** ***Perf. 12***
**RA30** PT1 1c brown 2.00 .25

The tax from the sale of Nos. RA1-RA30 was used for the control of cancer.

Juan D. Arosemena Stadium PT2

Torch Emblem — PT3

No. RA33, Adan Gordon Olympic Swimming Pool.

**1951** **Unwmk.** **Engr.** ***Perf. 12½***
**RA31** PT2 1c carmine & blk 1.60 .25
**RA32** PT3 1c dk bl & blk 1.60 .25
**RA33** PT2 1c grn & blk 1.60 .25
*Nos. RA31-RA33 (3)* 4.80 .75

Issued: No. RA31, 2/21; No. RA32, 7/12; No. RA33, 12/13.

Discobolus — PT4

No. RA34, Turners' emblem.

**1952**
**RA34** PT3 1c org & blk 1.60 .25
**RA35** PT4 1c pur & blk 1.60 .25

Issued: No. RA34, 4/18; No. RA35, 9/10.

The tax from the sale of Nos. RA31-RA35 was used to promote physical education.

Boys Doing Farm Work PT5

**Wmk. 311**
**1958, Jan. 24** **Litho.** ***Perf. 12½***
**Size: 35x24mm**
**RA36** PT5 1c rose red & gray .25 .25

### Type of 1958 Inscribed 1959

**1959** **Size: 35x24mm**
**RA37** PT5 1c gray & emerald .25 .25
**RA38** PT5 1c vio bl & gray .25 .25

### Type of 1958 Inscribed 1960

**Wmk. 334**
**1960, July 20** **Litho.** ***Perf. 13½***
**Size: 32x23mm**
**RA39** PT5 1c carmine & gray .25 .25

**Nos. C235 and C241 Surcharged in Black or Red**

**1961, May 24 Wmk. 343 *Perf. 12½***

**RA40** A131 1c on 10c ocher & blk .25 .25
**RA41** AP76 1c on 10c emer (R) .25 .25

Girl at Sewing Machine PT6

**Wmk. 343**

**1961, Nov. 24 Litho. *Perf. 12½***

**RA42** PT6 1c brt vio .25 .25
**RA43** PT6 1c rose lilac .25 .25
**RA44** PT6 1c yellow .25 .25
**RA45** PT6 1c blue .25 .25
**RA46** PT6 1c emerald .25 .25
*Nos. RA42-RA46 (5)* 1.25 1.25

**1961, Dec. 1**

Design: Boy with hand saw.

**RA47** PT6 1c red lilac .25 .25
**RA48** PT6 1c rose .25 .25
**RA49** PT6 1c orange .25 .25
**RA50** PT6 1c blue .25 .25
**RA51** PT6 1c gray .25 .25
*Nos. RA47-RA51 (5)* 1.25 1.25

Boy Scout — PT7

Designs: Nos. RA57-RA61, Girl Scout.

**1964, Feb. 7 Wmk. 343**

**RA52** PT7 1c olive .25 .25
**RA53** PT7 1c gray .25 .25
**RA54** PT7 1c lilac .25 .25
**RA55** PT7 1c carmine rose .25 .25
**RA56** PT7 1c blue .25 .25
**RA57** PT7 1c bluish green .25 .25
**RA58** PT7 1c violet .25 .25
**RA59** PT7 1c orange .25 .25
**RA60** PT7 1c yellow .25 .25
**RA61** PT7 1c brn org .25 .25
*Nos. RA52-RA61 (10)* 2.50 2.50

The tax from Nos. RA36-RA61 was for youth rehabilitation.

Map of Panama, Flags — PT8

**1973, Jan. 22 Unwmk.**

**RA62** PT8 1c black .25 .25

7th Bolivar Sports Games, Feb. 17-Mar. 3, 1973. The tax was for a new post office in Panama City.

Post Office — PT9

Designs: No. RA63, Farm Cooperative. No. RA64, 5b silver coin. No. RA65, Victoriano Lorenzo. No. RA66, RA69, Cacique Urraca. No. RA67, RA70, Post Office.

**1973-75**

**RA63** PT9 1c brt yel grn & ver .45 .25
**RA64** PT9 1c gray & red .45 .25
**RA65** PT9 1c ocher & red .45 .25
**RA66** PT9 1c org & red .45 .25
**RA67** PT9 1c bl & red .45 .25
**RA68** PT9 1c blue ('74) .45 .25
**RA69** PT9 1c orange ('74) .45 .25
**RA70** PT9 1c vermilion ('75) .45 .25
*Nos. RA63-RA70 (8)* 3.60 2.00

Issued: No. RA63, 3/19; No. RA64, 6/4; No. RA65, 6/6; No. RA66, 8/16; No. RA67, 8/17; Nos. RA68-RA69, 4/9/74; No. RA70, 11/24/75.

The tax was for a new post office in Panama City.

Stamps of 1969-1973 Surcharged in Violet Blue, Yellow, Black or Carmine

**1975, Sept. 3**

**RA75** A168 1c on 1c (#538; VB) .25 .25
**RA76** A168 1c on 2c (#539; Y) .25 .25
**RA77** A164 1c on 30c (#534; B) .25 .25
**RA78** A157 1c on 30c (#511; B) .25 .25
**RA79** A156 1c on 40c (#514; B) .25 .25
**RA80** A156 1c on 50c (#515; B) .25 .25
**RA81** A169 1c on 20c (#C408; C) .25 .25
**RA82** A169 1c on 25c (#C410; B) .25 .25
**RA83** AP98 1c on 25c (#C395; B) .25 .25
**RA84** A169 1c on 30c (#C411; B) .25 .25
**RA85** AP94 1c on 40c (#C387; C) .25 .25
*Nos. RA75-RA85 (11)* 2.75 2.75

The tax was for a new post office in Panama City. Surcharge vertical, reading down on No. RA75 and up on Nos. RA76, RA78 and RA83. Nos. RA75-RA85 were obligatory on all mail.

PT10

No. RA86, Boys. No. RA87, Boy and chicks. RA88, Working in fields. RA89, Boys feeding piglet.

**1980, Dec. 3 Litho. *Perf. 12***

**RA86** PT10 2c multi .25 .25
**RA87** PT10 2c multi .25 .25
**RA88** PT10 2c multi .25 .25
**RA89** PT10 2c multi .25 .25
*a.* Souv. sheet of 4, #RA86-RA89 11.25
*b.* Block of 4, #RA86-RA89 1.00

Tax was for Children's Village (Christmas 1980). #RA89a sold for 1b.

PT11

**1981, Nov. 1 Litho. *Perf. 12***

**RA90** PT11 2c Boy, pony .25 .25
**RA91** PT11 2c Nativity .25 .25
**RA92** PT11 2c Tree .25 .25
**RA93** PT11 2c Church .25 .25
*a.* Block of 4, #RA90-RA93 1.00

**Souvenir Sheet**

**RA94** Sheet of 4 *12.50*
*a.-d.* PT11 2c, Children's drawings

Tax was for Children's Village. No. RA94 sold for 5b.

PT12

**1982, Nov. 1 Litho. *Perf. 13½x12½***

**RA95** PT12 2c Carpentry .25 .25
**RA96** PT12 2c Beekeeping .25 .25
*a.* Pair, #RA95-RA96 .20
**RA97** PT12 2c Pig farming, vert. .25 .25
**RA98** PT12 2c Gardening, vert. .25 .25
*a.* Pair, #RA97-RA98 .20

Tax was for Children's Village (Christmas 1982).

Two imperf souvenir sheets solf for 2B each. Value, each $16.

Children's Drawings PT13

No. RA99, Annunciation. No. RA100, Bethlehem and Star. No. RA101, Church and Houses. No. RA102, Flight into Egypt.

**1983, Nov. 1 Litho. *Perf. 14½***

**RA99** PT13 2c multicolored .25 .25
**RA100** PT13 2c multicolored .25 .25
**RA101** PT13 2c multicolored .25 .25
**RA102** PT13 2c multicolored .25 .25
*Nos. RA99-RA102 (4)* 1.00 1.00

Nos. RA100-RA102 are vert.

Souvenir sheets exist showing undenominated designs of Nos. RA99, RA101 and Nos. RA100, RA102 respectively. They sold for 2b each. Value $7.50 each.

Boy — PT14

**1984, Nov. 1 Litho. *Perf. 12x12½***

**RA103** PT14 2c White-collared shirt .25 .25
**RA104** PT14 2c T-shirt .25 .25
**RA105** PT14 2c Checked shirt .25 .25
**RA106** PT14 2c Scout uniform .25 .25
*a.* Block of 4, #RA103-RA106 1.00

Tax was for Children's Village. An imperf. souvenir sheet sold for 2b, with designs similar to Nos. RA103-RA106, exists. Value $7.50.

Christmas 1985 — PT15

Inscriptions: No. RA107, "Ciudad del Nino es . . . mi vida." No. RA108, "Feliz Navidad." No. RA109, "Feliz Ano Nuevo." No. RA110, "Gracias."

**1985, Dec. 10 Litho. *Perf. 13½x13***

**RA107** PT15 2c multi .25 .25
**RA108** PT15 2c multi .25 .25
**RA109** PT15 2c multi .25 .25
**RA110** PT15 2c multi .25 .25
*a.* Block of 4, #RA107-RA110 1.00

Tax for Children's Village. A souvenir sheet, perf. and imperf., sold for 2b, with designs of Nos. RA107-RA110. Value, each $14.

Children's Village, 20th Anniv. — PT16

Inscriptions and Embera, Cuna, Embera and Guaymies tribal folk figures: No. RA111, "1966-1986." No. RA112, "Ciudad del Nino es . . . mi vida." No. RA113, "20 anos de fundacion." No. RA114, "Gracias."

**1986, Nov. 1 Litho. *Perf. 13½***

**RA111** PT16 2c multi .40 .40
**RA112** PT16 2c multi .40 .40
**RA113** PT16 2c multi .40 .40
**RA114** PT16 2c multi .40 .40
*Nos. RA111-RA114 (4)* 1.60 1.60

Nos. RA111-RA114 obligatory on all mail through Nov., Dec. and Jan.; tax for Children's Village. Printed se-tenant. Sheets of 4 exist perf. and imperf. Sold for 2b. Sheet exists, perf and imperf, with one 58x68mm 2b stamp showing similar characters. Value $6.75 each.

# PAPUA NEW GUINEA

ˈpa-pyə-wə ˈnü ˈgi-nē

LOCATION — Eastern half of island of New Guinea, north of Australia
GOVT. — Independent state in British Commonwealth.
AREA — 185,136 sq. mi.
POP. — 4,705,126 (1999 est.)
CAPITAL — Port Moresby

In 1884 a British Protectorate was proclaimed over this part of the island, called "British New Guinea." In 1905 the administration was transferred to Australia and in 1906 the name was changed to Territory of Papua.

In 1949 the administration of Papua and New Guinea was unified, as the 1952 issue indicates. In 1972 the name was changed to Papua New Guinea. In 1973 came self-government, followed by independence on September 16, 1975.

Issues of 1925-39 for the mandated Territory of New Guinea are listed under New Guinea.

12 Pence = 1 Shilling
20 Shillings = 1 Pound
100 Cents = 1 Dollar (1966)
100 Toea = 1 Kina (1975)

**Catalogue values for unused stamps in this country are for Never Hinged items, beginning with Scott 122 in the regular postage section and Scott J1 in the postage due section.**

**Watermarks**

Wmk. 13 — Crown and Double-Lined A

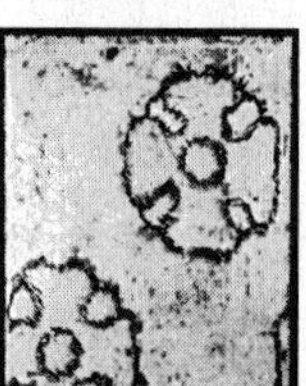

Wmk. 47 — Multiple Rosette

Wmk. 74 — Crown and Single-Lined A Sideways

Wmk. 228 — Small Crown and C of A Multiple

Wmk. 387

## British New Guinea

Lakatoi — A1

**Wmk. 47**

**1901, July 1 Engr. *Perf. 14***

**Center in Black**

| No. | Type | Description | Unused | Used |
|---|---|---|---|---|
| 1 | A1 | ½p yellow green | 24.00 | 6.00 |
| 2 | A1 | 1p carmine | 13.50 | 5.50 |
| 3 | A1 | 2p violet | 13.50 | 7.50 |
| 4 | A1 | 2½p ultra | 40.00 | 12.00 |
| 5 | A1 | 4p black brown | 45.00 | 40.00 |
| 6 | A1 | 6p dark green | 65.00 | 40.00 |
| 7 | A1 | 1sh orange | 65.00 | 75.00 |
| 8 | A1 | 2sh6p brown ('05) | 700.00 | 700.00 |
| | | *Nos. 1-8 (8)* | 966.00 | 886.00 |

The paper varies in thickness and the watermark is found in two positions, with the greater width of the rosette either horizontal or vertical.

For stamps inscribed "Papua New Guinea" see Nos. 1024-1029.

For overprints see Nos. 11-26.

## Papua

Stamps of British New Guinea, Overprinted

**Large Overprint**

**1906, Nov. 8 Wmk. 47 *Perf. 14***

**Center in Black**

| No. | Type | Description | Unused | Used |
|---|---|---|---|---|
| 11 | A1 | ½p yellow green | 12.00 | 25.00 |
| 12 | A1 | 1p carmine | 20.00 | 22.50 |
| 13 | A1 | 2p violet | 19.00 | 5.00 |
| 14 | A1 | 2½p ultra | 12.00 | 18.00 |
| 15 | A1 | 4p black brown | 250.00 | 160.00 |
| 16 | A1 | 6p dark green | 50.00 | 50.00 |
| 17 | A1 | 1sh orange | 30.00 | 50.00 |
| 18 | A1 | 2sh6p brown | 200.00 | 225.00 |
| | | *Nos. 11-18 (8)* | 593.00 | 555.50 |

Small Overprint

**1907 Center in Black**

| No. | Type | Description | Unused | Used |
|---|---|---|---|---|
| 19 | A1 | ½p yel grn | 24.00 | 29.00 |
| a. | | Double overprint | 3,500. | |
| 20 | A1 | 1p carmine | 12.00 | 7.50 |
| a. | | Vertical overprint, up | 8,250. | 4,500. |
| 21 | A1 | 2p violet | 8.00 | 4.00 |
| a. | | Double overprint | 4,250. | |
| 22 | A1 | 2½p ultra | 21.00 | 24.00 |
| a. | | Double overprint | | |
| 23 | A1 | 4p blk brn | 50.00 | 70.00 |
| 24 | A1 | 6p dk grn | 50.00 | 55.00 |
| a. | | Double overprint | 7,000. | 13,000. |
| 25 | A1 | 1sh orange | 55.00 | 60.00 |
| a. | | Double overprint | 21,000. | 14,000. |
| 26 | A1 | 2sh6p brown | 60.00 | 75.00 |
| b. | | Vert. ovpt., down | 8,500. | |
| d. | | Double horiz. ovpt. | | 4,500. |
| | | *Nos. 19-26 (8)* | 280.00 | 324.50 |

A2

Small "PAPUA"

***Perf. 11, 12½***

**1907-08 Litho. Wmk. 13**

**Center in Black**

| No. | Type | Description | Unused | Used |
|---|---|---|---|---|
| 28 | A2 | 1p carmine ('08) | 7.50 | 5.75 |
| 29 | A2 | 2p violet ('08) | 27.50 | 8.00 |
| 30 | A2 | 2½p ultra ('08) | 17.50 | 9.00 |
| 31 | A2 | 4p black brown | 9.00 | 9.00 |
| 32 | A2 | 6p dk green ('08) | 17.50 | 18.50 |
| 33 | A2 | 1sh orange ('08) | 57.50 | 25.00 |
| | | *Nos. 28-33 (6)* | 136.50 | 75.25 |

***Perf. 12½***

| No. | Type | Description | Unused | Used |
|---|---|---|---|---|
| 30a | A2 | 2½p | 180.00 | 190.00 |
| 31a | A2 | 4p | 13.00 | 13.00 |
| 33a | A2 | 1sh | 77.50 | 100.00 |
| | | *Nos. 30a-33a (3)* | 270.50 | 303.00 |

**1909-10 Wmk. Sideways**

**Center in Black**

| No. | Type | Description | Unused | Used |
|---|---|---|---|---|
| 34 | A2 | ½p yellow green | 5.50 | 6.50 |
| a. | | Perf. 11x12½ | 5,500. | 5,500. |
| b. | | Perf. 11 | 3.00 | 3.50 |
| 35 | A2 | 1p carmine | 10.00 | 14.00 |
| a. | | Perf. 11 | 11.00 | 9.25 |
| 36 | A2 | 2p violet ('10) | 10.00 | 15.00 |
| a. | | Perf. 11x12½ | 1,700. | |
| b. | | Perf. 11 | 27.50 | 10.50 |
| 37 | A2 | 2½p ultra ('10) | 7.00 | 26.00 |
| a. | | Perf. 12½ | 13.00 | 45.00 |
| 38 | A2 | 4p black brn ('10) | 6.50 | 12.00 |
| a. | | Perf. 11x12½ | 16,000. | |
| 39 | A2 | 6p dark green | 12.50 | 22.50 |
| a. | | Perf. 12½ | 5,500. | 14,000. |
| 40 | A2 | 1sh orange ('10) | 25.00 | 65.00 |
| a. | | Perf. 11 | 65.00 | 85.00 |
| | | *Nos. 34-40 (7)* | 76.50 | 161.00 |

One stamp in each sheet has a white line across the upper part of the picture which is termed the "rift in the clouds."

Large "PAPUA"

2sh6p:

Type I — The numerals are thin and irregular. The body of the "6" encloses a large spot of color. The dividing stroke is thick and uneven.

Type II — The numerals are thick and well formed. The "6" encloses a narrow oval of color. The dividing stroke is thin and sharp.

**1910 Wmk. 13**

**Center in Black**

| No. | Type | Description | Unused | Used |
|---|---|---|---|---|
| 41 | A2 | ½p yellow green | 6.00 | 14.00 |
| 42 | A2 | 1p carmine | 15.00 | 16.00 |
| 43 | A2 | 2p violet | 7.50 | 8.00 |
| 44 | A2 | 2½p blue violet | 13.00 | 22.50 |
| 45 | A2 | 4p black brown | 13.50 | 14.00 |
| 46 | A2 | 6p dark green | 11.00 | 13.00 |
| 47 | A2 | 1sh orange | 14.00 | 22.50 |
| 48 | A2 | 2sh6p brown, type II | 77.50 | 75.00 |
| a. | | Type I | 60.00 | 60.00 |
| | | *Nos. 41-48 (8)* | 157.50 | 185.00 |

**Wmk. Sideways**

| No. | Type | Description | Unused | Used |
|---|---|---|---|---|
| 49 | A2 | 2sh6p choc, type I | 85.00 | 100.00 |

**1911 Typo. Wmk. 74 *Perf. 12½***

| No. | Type | Description | Unused | Used |
|---|---|---|---|---|
| 50 | A2 | ½p yellow green | 1.25 | 4.00 |
| 51 | A2 | 1p lt red | 2.25 | 1.25 |
| 52 | A2 | 2p lt violet | 4.00 | 1.25 |
| 53 | A2 | 2½p ultra | 6.75 | 11.00 |
| 54 | A2 | 4p olive green | 3.50 | 14.00 |
| 55 | A2 | 6p orange brown | 5.00 | 6.50 |
| 56 | A2 | 1sh yellow | 14.00 | 20.00 |
| 57 | A2 | 2sh6p rose | 46.00 | 50.00 |
| | | *Nos. 50-57 (8)* | 82.75 | 108.00 |

For surcharges see Nos. 74-79.

**1915, June *Perf. 14***

| No. | Type | Description | Unused | Used |
|---|---|---|---|---|
| 59 | A2 | 1p light red | 22.50 | 3.00 |

A3

**1916-31**

| No. | Type | Description | Unused | Used |
|---|---|---|---|---|
| 60 | A3 | ½p pale yel grn & myr grn ('19) | 1.00 | 1.50 |
| 61 | A3 | 1p rose red & blk | 2.50 | 1.50 |
| 62 | A3 | 1½p yel brn & gray bl ('25) | 2.50 | 1.00 |
| 63 | A3 | 2p red vio & vio brn ('19) | 2.75 | 1.25 |
| 64 | A3 | 2p red brn & vio brn ('31) | 3.25 | 1.25 |
| a. | | 2p cop red & vio brn ('31) | 29.00 | 2.25 |
| 65 | A3 | 2½p ultra & dk grn ('19) | 5.75 | 15.00 |
| 66 | A3 | 3p emerald & blk | 4.75 | 3.00 |
| a. | | 3p dp bl grn & blk | 5.75 | 9.25 |
| 67 | A3 | 4p org & lt brn ('19) | 4.00 | 7.00 |
| 68 | A3 | 5p ol brn & sl ('31) | 5.50 | 18.00 |
| 69 | A3 | 6p vio & dl vio ('23) | 5.50 | 11.00 |
| 70 | A3 | 1sh ol grn & dk brn ('19) | 7.00 | 9.00 |
| 71 | A3 | 2sh6p rose & red brn ('19) | 27.50 | 47.50 |
| 72 | A3 | 5sh dp grn & blk | 55.00 | 60.00 |
| 73 | A3 | 10sh gray bl & grn ('25) | 175.00 | 200.00 |
| | | *Nos. 60-73 (14)* | 302.00 | 377.00 |

Type A3 is a redrawing of type A2.

The lines of the picture have been strengthened, making it much darker, especially the sky and water.

See Nos. 92-93. For surcharges & overprints see Nos. 88-91, O1-O10.

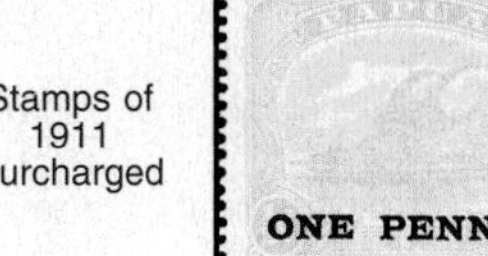



Stamps of 1911 Surcharged

**1917 *Perf. 12½***

| No. | Type | Description | Unused | Used |
|---|---|---|---|---|
| 74 | A2 | 1p on ½p yellow grn | 1.75 | 1.90 |
| 75 | A2 | 1p on 2p lt violet | 14.50 | 17.50 |
| 76 | A2 | 1p on 2½p ultra | 1.50 | 4.50 |
| 77 | A2 | 1p on 4p olive green | 2.10 | 5.25 |
| 78 | A2 | 1p on 6p org brn | 10.00 | 24.50 |
| 79 | A2 | 1p on 2sh6p rose | 4.00 | 7.00 |
| | | *Nos. 74-79 (6)* | 33.85 | 60.65 |

No. 62 Surcharged

**1931, Jan. 1 *Perf. 14***

| No. | Type | Description | Unused | Used |
|---|---|---|---|---|
| 88 | A3 | 2p on 1½p yellow brn & gray blue | 1.50 | 2.25 |

Nos. 70, 71 and 72 Surcharged in Black

**1931**

| No. | Type | Description | Unused | Used |
|---|---|---|---|---|
| 89 | A3 | 5p on 1sh #70 | 1.75 | 3.00 |
| 90 | A3 | 9p on 2sh6p #71 | 7.50 | 12.00 |
| 91 | A3 | 1sh3p on 5sh #72 | 7.50 | 14.00 |
| | | *Nos. 89-91 (3)* | 16.75 | 29.00 |

**Type of 1916 Issue**

**1932 Wmk. 228 *Perf. 11***

| No. | Type | Description | Unused | Used |
|---|---|---|---|---|
| 92 | A3 | 9p dp violet & gray | 9.50 | 37.50 |
| 93 | A3 | 1sh3p pale bluish grn & grayish vio | 14.50 | 37.50 |

For overprints see Nos. O11-O12.

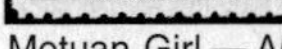

Motuan Girl — A5

Bird of Paradise and Boar's Tusk — A6

Mother and Child — A7

Papuan Motherhood — A8

Dubu (Ceremonial Platform) — A9

Fire Maker — A10

Designs: 1p, Steve, son of Oala. 1½p, Tree houses. 3p, Papuan dandy. 5p, Masked dancer. 9p, Shooting fish. 1sh3p, Lakatoi. 2sh, Delta art. 2sh6p, Pottery making. 5sh, Sgt.-Major Simoi. £1, Delta house.

**Unwmk.**

**1932, Nov. 14 Engr. *Perf. 11***

| No. | Type | Description | Unused | Used |
|---|---|---|---|---|
| 94 | A5 | ½p orange & blk | 4.50 | 4.00 |
| 95 | A5 | 1p yel grn & blk | 4.00 | .70 |
| 96 | A5 | 1½p red brn & blk | 4.50 | 9.25 |
| 97 | A6 | 2p light red | 12.50 | .35 |
| 98 | A5 | 3p blue & blk | 4.25 | 7.50 |
| 99 | A7 | 4p olive green | 12.00 | 12.00 |
| 100 | A5 | 5p grnsh sl & blk | 7.00 | 3.50 |
| 101 | A8 | 6p bister brown | 8.50 | 6.25 |
| 102 | A5 | 9p lilac & blk | 11.50 | 24.00 |
| 103 | A9 | 1sh bluish gray | 10.00 | 10.00 |
| 104 | A5 | 1sh3p brown & blk | 19.00 | 29.00 |
| 105 | A5 | 2sh bluish slate & blk | 19.00 | 26.00 |
| 106 | A5 | 2sh6p rose lilac & blk | 29.00 | 42.50 |
| 107 | A5 | 5sh olive & blk | 70.00 | 62.50 |
| 108 | A10 | 10sh gray lilac | 150.00 | 120.00 |
| 109 | A5 | £1 lt gray & black | 275.00 | 180.00 |
| | | *Nos. 94-109 (16)* | 640.75 | 537.55 |

For overprints see Nos. 114-117.

Hoisting Union Jack at Port Moresby A21

H. M. S. "Nelson" at Port Moresby A22

**1934, Nov. 6**

| No. | Type | Description | Unused | Used |
|---|---|---|---|---|
| 110 | A21 | 1p dull green | 3.00 | 3.50 |
| 111 | A22 | 2p red brown | 2.75 | 3.00 |
| 112 | A21 | 3p blue | 3.00 | 3.00 |
| 113 | A22 | 5p violet brown | 12.00 | 22.50 |
| | | *Nos. 110-113 (4)* | 20.75 | 32.00 |
| | | Set, never hinged | 27.50 | |

Declaration of British Protection, 50th anniv.

**Silver Jubilee Issue**

Stamps of 1932 Issue Overprinted in Black

a

b

**1935, July 9 Glazed Paper**

| No. | Type | Description | Unused | Used |
|---|---|---|---|---|
| 114 | A5(a) | 1p yellow grn & blk | 1.20 | 4.00 |
| 115 | A6(b) | 2p light red | 3.50 | 5.00 |
| 116 | A5(a) | 3p lt blue & blk | 2.25 | 4.00 |
| 117 | A5(a) | 5p grnsh slate & blk | 2.25 | 4.00 |
| | | *Nos. 114-117 (4)* | 9.20 | 17.00 |
| | | Set, never hinged | 16.50 | |

25th anniv. of the reign of George V.

### Coronation Issue

King George VI — A22a

**Unwmk.**

**1937, May 14 Engr. *Perf. 11***

**118** A22a 1p green .40 .25
**119** A22a 2p salmon rose .40 *1.50*
**120** A22a 3p blue .40 *1.50*
**121** A22a 5p brown violet .40 *2.00*
*Nos. 118-121 (4)* 1.60 *5.25*
Set, never hinged 2.50

**Catalogue values for unused stamps in this section, from this point to the end of the section, are for Never Hinged items.**

### Papua and New Guinea

Tree-climbing Kangaroo A23

Kiriwina Chief's House A24

Copra Making A25

Designs: 1p, Buka head-dress. 2p, Youth. 2½p, Bird of paradise. 3p, Policeman. 3½p, Chimbu headdress. 7½p, Kiriwina yam house. 1sh, Trading canoe. 1sh6p, Rubber tapping. 2sh, Shields and spears. 2sh6p, Plumed shepherd. 10sh, Map. £1, Spearing fish.

**Unwmk.**

**1952, Oct. 30 Engr. *Perf. 14***

**122** A23 ½p blue green .30 .25
**123** A23 1p chocolate .25 .25
**124** A23 2p deep ultra .75 .25
**125** A23 2½p orange 3.50 .60
**126** A23 3p dark green .85 .25
**127** A23 3½p dk carmine .85 .25
**128** A24 6½p vio brown 2.25 .25
**129** A24 7½p dp ultra 5.00 2.50
**130** A25 9p chocolate 4.75 .75
**131** A25 1sh yellow green 3.50 .25
**132** A24 1sh6p dark green 8.50 1.50
**133** A24 2sh deep blue 7.50 .25
**134** A25 2sh6p dk red brown 7.00 .75
**135** A25 10sh gray black 50.00 16.00
**136** A24 £1 chocolate 65.00 20.00
*Nos. 122-136 (15)* 160.00 44.10
Set, hinged 85.00

See #139-141. For surcharges & overprints see #137-138, 147, J1-J3, J5-J6.

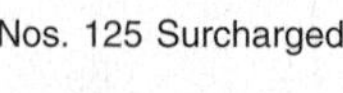

Nos. 125 Surcharged

Nos. 131 Surcharged

**1957, Jan. 29 *Perf. 14***

**137** A23 4p on 2½p orange .85 .35
**138** A25 7p on 1sh yellow green 1.75 .45

### Type of 1952 and

Klinki Plymill A26

Designs: 3½p, Chimbu headdress. 4p, 5p, Cacao. 8p, Klinki Plymill. 1sh7p, Cattle. 2sh5p, Cattle. 5sh, Coffee, vert.

**1958-60 Engr. *Perf. 14***

**139** A23 3½p black 7.00 2.00
**140** A23 4p vermilion 1.25 .25
**141** A23 5p green ('60) 1.50 .25
**142** A26 7p gray green 11.00 .25
**143** A26 8p dk ultra ('60) 2.50 2.00
**144** A26 1sh7p red brown 30.00 16.00
**145** A26 2sh5p vermilion ('60) 6.00 2.50
**146** A26 5sh gray olive & brn red 11.00 2.10
*Nos. 139-146 (8)* 70.25 25.35

Issued: June 2, 1958, Nov. 10, 1960.
For surcharge see No. J4.

**No. 122 Surcharged with New Value**

**1959, Dec. 1**

**147** A23 5p on ½p blue green .85 .25

Council Chamber and Frangipani Flowers A27

**1961, Apr. 10 Photo. *Perf. 14½x14***

**148** A27 5p green & yellow .80 .35
**149** A27 2sh3p grn & salmon 8.00 4.00

Reconstitution of the Legislative Council.

Woman's Head — A28

Red-plumed Bird of Paradise — A29

Port Moresby Harbor A30

Constable Ragas Amis Matia, Port Moresby A32

View of Rabaul, by Samuel Terarup Cham — A33

Woman Dancer A31

Elizabeth II A34

Designs: 3p, Man's head. 6p, Golden opossum. 2sh, Male dancer with drum. 2sh3p, Piaggio transport plane landing at Tapini.

***Perf. 14 (A28, A31, A32), 11½ (A29, A33), 14x13½ (A30), 14½ (A34)***

**1961-63 Engr. Unwmk.**

**153** A28 1p dk carmine .70 .25
**154** A28 3p bluish black .45 .25

**Photo.**

**155** A29 5p lt brn, red brn, blk & yel .50 .25
**156** A29 6p gray, ocher & slate .75 1.25

**Engr.**

**157** A30 8p green .30 .25
**158** A31 1sh gray green 4.75 .90
**159** A31 2sh rose lake 1.50 .45
**160** A30 2sh3p dark blue .90 .40
**161** A32 3sh green 2.25 2.00

**Photo.**

**162** A33 10sh multicolored 16.50 13.00
**163** A34 £1 brt grn, blk & gold 9.00 8.50
*Nos. 153-163 (11)* 37.60 27.50

The 5p and 6p are on granite paper.
Issued: 3sh, 9/5/62; 10sh, 2/13/63: 5p, 6p, 3/27/63; 8p, 2sh3p, 5/8/63; £1, 7/3/63; others, 7/26/61.

Malaria Eradication Emblem — A35

**1962, Apr. 7 Litho. *Perf. 14***

**164** A35 5p lt blue & maroon 1.25 .50
**165** A35 1sh lt brown & red 2.25 .75
**166** A35 2sh yellow green & blk 2.75 *3.25*
*Nos. 164-166 (3)* 6.25 4.50

WHO drive to eradicate malaria.

Map of Australia and South Pacific A36

**1962, July 9 Engr. Unwmk.**

**167** A36 5p dk red & lt grn 1.75 .30
**168** A36 1sh6p dk violet & yel 2.75 1.00
**169** A36 2sh6p green & lt blue 2.75 2.25
*Nos. 167-169 (3)* 7.25 3.55

5th So. Pacific Conf., Pago Pago, July 1962.

High Jump — A37

**1962, Oct. 24 Photo. *Perf. 11½***

**Size: 26x21mm**

**Granite Paper**

**171** A37 5p shown .50 .30
**172** A37 5p Javelin .50 .30

**Size: 32½x22½mm**

**173** A37 2sh3p runners 2.50 2.00
*Nos. 171-173 (3)* 3.50 2.60

British Empire and Commonwealth Games, Perth, Australia, Nov. 22-Dec. 1.
Nos. 171 and 172 printed in alternating horizontal rows in sheet.

Red Cross Centenary Emblem — A38

**1963, May 1 *Perf. 13½***

**174** A38 5p blue grn, gray & red .60 .25

Games Emblem — A38a

**1963, Aug. 14 Engr. *Perf. 13½x14***

**176** A38a 5p olive bister .25 .25
**177** A38a 1sh green .75 .25

So. Pacific Games, Suva, Aug. 29-Sept. 7.

Top of Wooden Shield — A39

Various Carved Heads.

***Perf. 11½***

**1964, Feb. 5 Unwmk. Photo.**

**Granite Paper**

**178** A39 11p multicolored .60 .25
**179** A39 2sh5p multicolored .65 *1.75*
**180** A39 2sh6p multicolored .75 .25
**181** A39 5sh multicolored .90 .25
*Nos. 178-181 (4)* 2.90 2.50

Casting Ballot — A40

**1964, Mar. 4 Unwmk. *Perf. 11½***

**Granite Paper**

**182** A40 5p dk brn & pale brn .25 .25
**183** A40 2sh3p dk brn & lt bl .80 .50

First Common Roll elections.

Territorial Health Services — A41

Designs: 5p, Patients at health center clinic. 8p, Dentist and school child patient. 1sh, Nurse holding infant. 1sh2p, Medical student using microscope.

**1964, Aug. 5 Engr. *Perf. 14***

**184** A41 5p violet .25 .25
**185** A41 8p green .25 .25
**186** A41 1sh deep ultra .25 .25
**187** A41 1sh2p rose brown .40 .40
*Nos. 184-187 (4)* 1.15 1.15

A42

Designs: 1p, Striped gardener bower birds. 3p, New Guinea regent bower birds. 5p, Blue birds of paradise. 6p, Lawes six-wired birds of paradise. 8p, Sickle-billed birds of paradise. 1sh, Emperor birds of paradise. 2sh, Brown sickle-billed bird of paradise. 2sh3p, Lesser bird of paradise. 3sh, Magnificent bird of paradise. 5sh, Twelve-wired bird of paradise. 10sh, Magnificent rifle birds.

**Birds in Natural Colors**
**Size: 21x26mm**

**1964-65 Unwmk. Photo. *Perf. 11½***

| No. | Type | Value | Description | Unused | Used |
|---|---|---|---|---|---|
| **188** | A42 | 1p | brt cit & dk brn | .55 | .25 |
| **189** | A42 | 3p | gray & dk brn | .65 | .25 |
| **190** | A42 | 5p | sal pink & blk | .70 | .25 |
| **191** | A42 | 6p | pale grn & sep | 1.05 | .25 |
| **192** | A42 | 8p | pale lil & dk brn | 1.50 | .35 |

**Size: 25x36mm**

| No. | Type | Value | Description | Unused | Used |
|---|---|---|---|---|---|
| **193** | A42 | 1sh | salmon & blk | 1.50 | .25 |
| **194** | A42 | 2sh | blue & dk brn | 1.05 | .40 |
| **195** | A42 | 2sh3p | lt grn & dk brn | 1.05 | 1.10 |
| **196** | A42 | 3sh | yel & dk brn | 1.05 | *1.50* |
| **197** | A42 | 5sh | lt ultra & dk brn | 11.00 | 2.25 |
| **198** | A42 | 10sh | gray & dk blue | 4.75 | *11.00* |
| | | | *Nos. 188-198 (11)* | 24.85 | 17.85 |

Issued: 6p, 8p, 1sh, 10sh, 10/28/64; others, 1/20/65.

Carved Crocodile's Head — A43

Designs: Wood carvings from Sepik River Region used as ship's prows and as objects of religious veneration.

**1965, Mar. 24 Photo. *Perf. 11½***

| No. | Type | Value | Description | Unused | Used |
|---|---|---|---|---|---|
| **199** | A43 | 4p | multicolored | .55 | .25 |
| **200** | A43 | 1sh2p | gray brn, bister & dk brn | 1.75 | 1.75 |
| **201** | A43 | 1sh6p | lil, dk brn & buff | .55 | .25 |
| **202** | A43 | 4sh | bl, dk vio & mar | .85 | .55 |
| | | | *Nos. 199-202 (4)* | 3.70 | 2.80 |

"Simpson and His Donkey" by Wallace Anderson — A43a

**1965, Apr. 14 *Perf. 13½x13***

| No. | Type | Value | Description | Unused | Used |
|---|---|---|---|---|---|
| **203** | A43a | 2sh3p | brt grn, sep & blk | .75 | .50 |

ANZAC issue. See note after Australia No. 387.

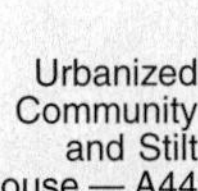

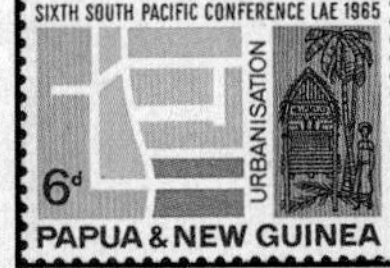


Urbanized Community and Stilt House — A44

Design: 1sh, Stilt house at left.

**1965, July 7 Photo. *Perf. 11½***

| No. | Type | Value | Description | Unused | Used |
|---|---|---|---|---|---|
| **204** | A44 | 6p | multicolored | .25 | .25 |
| **205** | A44 | 1sh | multicolored | .25 | .25 |

6th South Pacific Conf., Lae, July, 1965.

UN Emblem, Mother and Child A45

UN Emblem and: 1sh, Globe and orbit, vert. 2sh, Four globes in orbit, vert.

**1965, Oct. 13 Unwmk. *Perf. 11½***

| No. | Type | Value | Description | Unused | Used |
|---|---|---|---|---|---|
| **206** | A45 | 6p | brown, grnsh bl & dp bl | .25 | .25 |
| **207** | A45 | 1sh | dull pur, blue & org | .25 | .25 |
| **208** | A45 | 2sh | dp blue, pale grn & grn | .25 | .25 |
| | | | *Nos. 206-208 (3)* | .75 | .75 |

20th anniversary of the United Nations.

New Guinea Birdwing A46

Butterflies: 1c, Blue emperor, vert. 3c, White-banded map butterfly, vert. 4c, Mountain swallowtail, vert. 5c, Port Moresby terinos, vert. 12c, Blue crow. 15c, Euchenor butterfly. 20c, White-spotted parthenos. 25c, Orange Jezebel. 50c, New Guinea emperor. $1, Blue-spotted leaf-wing. $2, Paradise birdwing.

**1966 Photo. *Perf. 11½***
**Granite Paper**

| No. | Type | Value | Description | Unused | Used |
|---|---|---|---|---|---|
| **209** | A46 | 1c | sal, blk & aqua | .40 | *1.00* |
| **210** | A46 | 3c | gray grn, brn & org | .40 | *1.00* |
| **211** | A46 | 4c | multicolored | .40 | *1.00* |
| **212** | A46 | 5c | multicolored | .45 | .25 |
| **213** | A46 | 10c | multicolored | .55 | .30 |
| **214** | A46 | 12c | salmon & multi | 2.75 | 2.25 |
| **215** | A46 | 15c | pale vio, dk brn & buff | 1.75 | .80 |
| **216** | A46 | 20c | yel bister, dk brn & yel org | .65 | .25 |
| **217** | A46 | 25c | gray, blk & yel | 1.40 | 1.25 |
| **218** | A46 | 50c | multicolored | 12.00 | 2.00 |
| **219** | A46 | $1 | pale blue, dk brn & dp org | 3.50 | 2.75 |
| **220** | A46 | $2 | multicolored | 6.25 | *9.00* |
| | | | *Nos. 209-220 (12)* | 30.50 | *21.85* |

In 1967 Courvoisier made new plates for the $1 and $2. Stamps from these plates show many minor differences and slight variations in shade.

Issued: 12c, 10/10; others, 2/14.

Molala Harai and Paiva Streamer — A47

Myths of Elema People: 7c, Marai, the fisherman. 30c, Meavea Kivovia and the Black Cockatoo. 60c, Toivita Tapaivita (symbolic face decorations).

**1966, June 8 Photo. *Perf. 11½***
**Granite Paper**

| No. | Type | Value | Description | Unused | Used |
|---|---|---|---|---|---|
| **221** | A47 | 2c | black & carmine | .30 | .25 |
| **222** | A47 | 7c | blue, blk & yel | .30 | .25 |
| **223** | A47 | 30c | blk, yel grn & car | .35 | .25 |
| **224** | A47 | 60c | blk, org & car | .90 | .60 |
| | | | *Nos. 221-224 (4)* | 1.85 | 1.35 |

Discus — A48

**1966, Aug. 31 *Perf. 11½***
**Granite Paper**

| No. | Type | Value | Description | Unused | Used |
|---|---|---|---|---|---|
| **225** | A48 | 5c | shown | .25 | .25 |
| **226** | A48 | 10c | Soccer | .30 | .25 |
| **227** | A48 | 20c | Tennis | .40 | .35 |
| | | | *Nos. 225-227 (3)* | .95 | .85 |

Second South Pacific Games, Noumea, New Caledonia, Dec. 8-18.

d'Albertis' Creeper — A49

Flowers: 10c, Tecomanthe dendrophila. 20c, Rhododendron macgregoriae. 60c, Rhododendron konori.

**1966, Dec. 7 Photo. *Perf. 11½***

| No. | Type | Value | Description | Unused | Used |
|---|---|---|---|---|---|
| **228** | A49 | 5c | multicolored | .30 | .25 |
| **229** | A49 | 10c | multicolored | .30 | .25 |
| **230** | A49 | 20c | multicolored | .75 | .25 |
| **231** | A49 | 60c | multicolored | 1.90 | 1.50 |
| | | | *Nos. 228-231 (4)* | 3.25 | 2.25 |

Book and Pen ("Fine Arts") — A50

3c, "Surveying," transit, view finder, pencil. 4c, "Civil Engineering," buildings, compass. 5c, "Science," test tubes, chemical formula. 20c, "Justice," Justitia, scales.

**1967, Feb. 8 Photo. *Perf. 12½x12***

| No. | Type | Value | Description | Unused | Used |
|---|---|---|---|---|---|
| **232** | A50 | 1c | orange & multi | .25 | .25 |
| **233** | A50 | 3c | blue & multi | .25 | .25 |
| **234** | A50 | 4c | brown & multi | .25 | .25 |
| **235** | A50 | 5c | green & multi | .25 | .25 |
| **236** | A50 | 20c | pink & multi | .25 | .25 |
| | | | *Nos. 232-236 (5)* | 1.25 | 1.25 |

Issued to publicize the development of the University of Papua and New Guinea and the Institute of Higher Technical Education.

Leaf Beetle — A51

Beetles: 10c, Eupholus schoenherri. 20c, Sphingnotus albertisi. 25c, Cyphogastra albertisi.

**1967, Apr. 12 Unwmk. *Perf. 11½***

| No. | Type | Value | Description | Unused | Used |
|---|---|---|---|---|---|
| **237** | A51 | 5c | blue & multi | .40 | .25 |
| **238** | A51 | 10c | lt green & multi | .55 | .25 |
| **239** | A51 | 20c | rose & multi | .85 | .35 |
| **240** | A51 | 25c | yellow & multi | 1.20 | .45 |
| | | | *Nos. 237-240 (4)* | 3.00 | 1.30 |

Hydroelectric Power — A52

Designs: 10c, Pyrethrum (Chrysanthemum cinerariaefolium). 20c, Tea. 25c, like 5c.

**1967, June 28 Photo. *Perf. 12x12½***

| No. | Type | Value | Description | Unused | Used |
|---|---|---|---|---|---|
| **241** | A52 | 5c | multicolored | .25 | .25 |
| **242** | A52 | 10c | multicolored | .25 | .25 |
| **243** | A52 | 20c | multicolored | .35 | .25 |
| **244** | A52 | 25c | multicolored | .35 | .25 |
| | | | *Nos. 241-244 (4)* | 1.20 | 1.00 |

Completion of part of the Laloki River Hydroelectric Works near Port Moresby, and the Hydrological Decade (UNESCO), 1965-74.

Battle of Milne Bay — A53

Designs: 5c, Soldiers on Kokoda Trail, vert. 20c, The coast watchers. 50c, Battle of the Coral Sea.

**1967, Aug. 30 Unwmk. *Perf. 11½***

| No. | Type | Value | Description | Unused | Used |
|---|---|---|---|---|---|
| **245** | A53 | 2c | multicolored | .25 | *.45* |
| **246** | A53 | 5c | multicolored | .25 | .25 |
| **247** | A53 | 20c | multicolored | .35 | .25 |
| **248** | A53 | 50c | multicolored | .90 | .75 |
| | | | *Nos. 245-248 (4)* | 1.75 | 1.70 |

25th anniv. of the battles in the Pacific, which stopped the Japanese from occupying Papua and New Guinea.

Pesquet's Parrot — A54

Parrots: 5c, Fairy lory. 20c, Dusk-orange lory. 25c, Edward's fig parrot.

**1967, Nov. 29 Photo. *Perf. 12***

| No. | Type | Value | Description | Unused | Used |
|---|---|---|---|---|---|
| **249** | A54 | 5c | multicolored | .60 | .25 |
| **250** | A54 | 7c | multicolored | .75 | .90 |
| **251** | A54 | 20c | multicolored | 1.15 | .25 |
| **252** | A54 | 25c | multicolored | 1.40 | .25 |
| | | | *Nos. 249-252 (4)* | 3.90 | 1.65 |

Chimbu District Headdress — A55

Headdress from: 10c, Southern Highlands District, horiz. 20c, Western Highlands District. 60c, Chimbu District (different from 5c).

***Perf. 12x12½, 12½x12***
**1968, Feb. 21 Photo. Unwmk.**

| No. | Type | Value | Description | Unused | Used |
|---|---|---|---|---|---|
| **253** | A55 | 5c | multi | .25 | .25 |
| **254** | A55 | 10c | multi | .35 | .25 |
| **255** | A55 | 20c | multi, horiz. | .35 | .25 |
| **256** | A55 | 60c | multi | 1.10 | .80 |
| | | | *Nos. 253-256 (4)* | 2.05 | 1.55 |

Frogs — A56

**1968, Apr. 24 Photo. *Perf. 11½***

| No. | Type | Value | Description | Unused | Used |
|---|---|---|---|---|---|
| **257** | A56 | 5c | Tree | .60 | .45 |
| **258** | A56 | 10c | Tree, diff. | .60 | .25 |
| **259** | A56 | 15c | Swamp | .60 | .25 |
| **260** | A56 | 20c | Tree, diff. | .80 | .55 |
| | | | *Nos. 257-260 (4)* | 2.60 | 1.50 |

Human Rights Flame and Headdress A57

Symbolic Designs: 10c, Human Rights Flame surrounded by the world. 20c, 25c, "Universal Suffrage" in 2 abstract designs.

**1968, June 26 Litho. *Perf. 14x13***

| No. | Type | Value | Description | Unused | Used |
|---|---|---|---|---|---|
| **261** | A57 | 5c | black & multi | .25 | .25 |
| **262** | A57 | 10c | black & multi | .25 | .25 |
| **263** | A57 | 20c | black & multi | .30 | .30 |
| **264** | A57 | 25c | black & multi | .30 | .30 |
| | | | *Nos. 261-264 (4)* | 1.10 | 1.10 |

Issued for Human Rights Year, 1968, and to publicize free elections.

Sea Shells — A58

Designs: 1c, Ovula ovum. 3c, Strombus sinuatus. 4c, Conus litoglyphus. 5c, Conus marmoreus. 7c, Mitra mitra. 10c, Cymbiola rutila ruckeri. 12c, Phalium areola. 15c, Lambis scorpius. 20c, Tridacna squamosa. 25c, Lioconcha castrensis. 30c, Murex ramosus. 40c, Nautilus pompilius. 60c, Charonia tritonis. $1, Papustyla pulcherrima. $2, Conus gloriamaris, vert.

**1968-69 Photo. *Perf. 12½x12***

**Granite Paper**

**Size: 30x22½mm**

**265** A58 1c multicolored .25 .25
**266** A58 3c multicolored .40 *1.40*
**267** A58 4c multicolored .25 *1.40*
**268** A58 5c multicolored .35 .25
**269** A58 7c multicolored .45 .25
**270** A58 10c multicolored .60 .25
**271** A58 12c multicolored 1.75 *2.25*
**272** A58 15c multicolored 1.80 *1.25*
**273** A58 20c multicolored 1.00 .25

**Size: 30x25mm**

***Perf. 11***

**274** A58 25c multicolored 1.00 *1.75*
**275** A58 30c multicolored 1.00 *1.10*
**276** A58 40c multicolored 1.10 *1.40*
**277** A58 60c multicolored 1.00 .60
**278** A58 $1 multicolored 1.60 1.00

**Size: 25x30mm**

***Perf. 12x12½***

**279** A58 $2 multicolored 16.00 5.50
*Nos. 265-279 (15)* 28.55 18.90

Issued: 5c, 20c, 25c, 30c, 60c, 8/28/68; 3c, 10c, 15c, 40c, $1, 10/30/68; others, 1/29/69.

Legend of Tito-Iko — A59

Myths of Elema People: No. 281, 5c inscribed "Iko." No. 282, 10c inscribed "Luvuapo." No. 283, 10c inscribed "Miro."

***Nos. 280, 282: Perf. 12½x13½xRoul. 9xPerf. 13½***

***Nos. 281, 283: Roul. 9 x Perf. 13½x12½x13½***

**1969, Apr. 9 Litho. Unwmk.**

**280** 5c black, yellow & red .25 .25
**281** 5c black, yellow & red .25 .25
*a.* A59 Vert. pair, #280-281 .55 *.75*
**282** 10c black, gray & red .25 .25
**283** 10c black, gray & red .25 .25
*a.* Vert. pair, #282-283 .60 *.90*
*Nos. 280-283 (4)* 1.00 1.00

Nos. 281a, 283a have continuous designs, rouletted between.

Fireball Class Sailboat, Port Moresby Harbor — A60

Designs: 10c, Games' swimming pool, Boroko, horiz. 20c, Main Games area, Konedobu, horiz.

***Perf. 14x14½, 14½x14***

**1969, June 25 Engr.**

**284** A60 5c black .25 .25
**285** A60 10c bright violet .25 .25
**286** A60 20c green .40 .30
*Nos. 284-286 (3)* .90 .80

3rd S. Pacific Games, Port Moresby, Aug. 13-23.

Dendrobium Ostrinoglossum A61

Orchids: 10c, Dendrobium lawesii. 20c, Dendrobium pseudofrigidum. 30c, Dendrobium conanthum.

**1969, Aug. 27 Photo. *Perf. 11½***

**Granite Paper**

**287** A61 5c multicolored .70 .25
**288** A61 10c multicolored .80 .50
**289** A61 20c multicolored 1.00 .80
**290** A61 30c multicolored 1.10 .85
*Nos. 287-290 (4)* 3.60 2.40

Issued to publicize the 6th World Orchid Conference, Sydney, Australia, Sept. 1969.

Potter — A62

**1969, Sept. 24 Photo. *Perf. 11½***

**Granite Paper**

**291** A62 5c multicolored .35 .25

50th anniv. of the ILO.

Bird of Paradise — A63

**Coil Stamps**

**1969-71 *Perf. 14½ Horiz.***

**291A** A63 2c red, dp blue & blk .30 .25
**292** A63 5c orange & emerald .30 .25

Issue dates: 5c, Sept. 24, 2c, Apr. 1, 1971.

Seed Pod Rattle (Tareko) — A64

Musical Instruments: 10c, Hand drum (garamut). 25c, Pan pipes (iviliko). 30c, Hourglass drum (kundu).

**1969, Oct. 29 Photo. *Perf. 12½***

**293** A64 5c multicolored .25 .25
**294** A64 10c multicolored .25 .25
**295** A64 25c multicolored .40 .35
**296** A64 30c multicolored .80 .40
*Nos. 293-296 (4)* 1.70 1.25

Prehistoric Ambum Stone and Skull — A65

Designs: 10c, Masawa canoe of the Kula Circuit. 25c, Map of Papua and New Guinea made by Luis Valez de Torres, 1606. 30c, H.M.S. Basilisk, 1873.

**1970, Feb. 11 Photo. *Perf. 12½***

**297** A65 5c violet brown & multi .25 .25
**298** A65 10c ocher & multi .25 .25
**299** A65 25c org brn & multi .50 .35
**300** A65 30c olive green & multi 1.10 .40
*Nos. 297-300 (4)* 2.10 1.25

King of Saxony Bird of Paradise — A66

Birds of Paradise: 10c, King. 15c, Augusta Victoria. 25c, Multi-crested.

**1970, May 13 Photo. *Perf. 11½***

**301** A66 5c tan & multi .90 .25
**302** A66 10c multicolored 1.10 .60
**303** A66 15c lt blue & multi 1.50 1.00
**304** A66 25c multicolored 2.25 .75
*Nos. 301-304 (4)* 5.75 2.60

Canceled to Order

Starting in 1970 or earlier, the Philatelic Bureau at Port Moresby began to sell new issues canceled to order at face value.

Douglas DC-3 and Matupi Volcano — A67

Aircraft: No. 305, DC-6B and Mt. Wilhelm. No. 306, Lockheed Mark II Electra and Mt. Yule. No. 307, Boeing 727 and Mt. Giluwe. No. 308, Fokker F27 Friendship and Manam Island Volcano. 30c, Boeing 707 and Hombom's Bluff.

**1970, July 8 Photo. *Perf. 14½x14***

**305** A67 5c "TAA" on tail .30 .25
**306** A67 5c Striped tail .30 .25
**307** A67 5c "T" on tail .30 .25
**308** A67 5c Red tail .30 .25
*a.* Block of 4, #305-308 1.60 *2.00*
**309** A67 25c multicolored .75 .40
**310** A67 30c multicolored .75 .55
*Nos. 305-310 (6)* 2.70 1.95

Development of air service during the last 25 years between Australia and New Guinea.

Nicolaus N. de Miklouho-Maclay, Explorer, and Mask — A68

Designs: 10c, Bronislaw Kaspar Malinowski, anthropologist, and hut. 15c, Count Tommaso Salvadori, ornithologist, and cassowary. 20c, Friedrich R. Schlechter, botanist, and orchid.

**1970, Aug. 19 Photo. *Perf. 11½***

**311** A68 5c brown, blk & lilac .25 .25
**312** A68 10c multicolored .25 .25
**313** A68 15c dull lilac & multi .80 .35
**314** A68 20c slate & multi .80 .35
*Nos. 311-314 (4)* 2.10 1.20

42nd Cong. of the Australian and New Zealand Assoc. for the Advancement of Science, Port Moresby, Aug. 17-21.

Wogeo Island Food Bowl — A69

National Handicraft: 10c, Lime pot. 15c, Aibom sago storage pot. 30c, Manus Island bowl, horiz.

**1970, Oct. 28 Photo. *Perf. 12½***

**315** A69 5c multicolored .30 .25
**316** A69 10c multicolored .40 .25
**317** A69 15c multicolored .40 .25
**318** A69 30c multicolored .60 .50
*Nos. 315-318 (4)* 1.70 1.25

Eastern Highlands Round House — A70

Local Architecture: 7c, Milne Bay house. 10c, Purari Delta house. 40c, Sepik or Men's Spirit House.

**1971, Jan. 27 Photo. *Perf. 11½***

**319** A70 5c dark olive & multi .30 .25
**320** A70 7c Prus blue & multi .35 *.60*
**321** A70 10c deep org & multi .35 .25
**322** A70 40c brown & multi .80 .75
*Nos. 319-322 (4)* 1.80 1.85

Spotted Cuscus — A71

Animals: 10c, Brown and white striped possum. 15c, Feather-tailed possum. 25c, Spiny anteater, horiz. 30c, Good-fellow's tree-climbing kangaroo, horiz.

**1971, Mar. 31 Photo. *Perf. 11½***

**323** A71 5c blue green & multi .45 .25
**324** A71 10c multicolored .50 .25
**325** A71 15c multicolored .75 .90
**326** A71 25c dull yellow & multi 1.05 .90
**327** A71 30c olive & multi 1.05 .60
*Nos. 323-327 (5)* 3.80 2.90

Basketball A72

**1971, June 9 Litho. *Perf. 14***

**328** A72 7c shown .30 .25
**329** A72 14c Yachting .45 .25
**330** A72 21c Boxing .45 .30
**331** A72 28c Field events .45 .35
*Nos. 328-331 (4)* 1.65 1.15

Fourth South Pacific Games, Papeete, French Polynesia, Sept. 8-19.

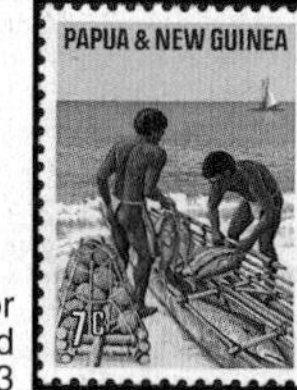

Bartering Fish for Coconuts and Taro — A73

Primary industries: 9c, Man stacking yams and taro. 14c, Market scene. 30c, Farm couple tending yams.

**1971, Aug. 18 Photo. *Perf. 11½***

**332** A73 7c multicolored .30 .25
**333** A73 9c multicolored .35 .25
**334** A73 14c multicolored .50 .25
**335** A73 30c multicolored .70 .50
*Nos. 332-335 (4)* 1.85 1.25

Siaa Dancer — A74

Designs: 9c, Urasena masked dancer. 20c, Two Siassi masked dancers, horiz. 28c, Three Siaa dancers, horiz.

**1971, Oct. 27 Photo. *Perf. 11½***

| | | | | |
|---|---|---|---|---|
| **336** | A74 | 7c orange & multi | .30 | .25 |
| **337** | A74 | 9c yel green & multi | .35 | .25 |
| **338** | A74 | 20c bister & multi | .90 | .80 |
| **339** | A74 | 28c multicolored | 1.25 | .95 |
| | | *Nos. 336-339 (4)* | 2.80 | 2.25 |

Papua New Guinea and Australia Arms — A75

#341, Papua New Guinea & Australia flags.

**1972, Jan. 26 *Perf. 12½x12***

| | | | | |
|---|---|---|---|---|
| **340** | A75 | 7c gray blue, org & blk | .30 | .30 |
| **341** | A75 | 7c gray blue, blk, red & yel | .30 | .30 |
| *a.* | | Pair, #340-341 | .75 | .75 |

Constitutional development for the 1972 House of Assembly elections.

Papua New Guinea Map, South Pacific Commission Emblem — A76

#343, Man's head, So. Pacific Commission flag.

**1972, Jan. 26**

| | | | | |
|---|---|---|---|---|
| **342** | A76 | 15c brt green & multi | .55 | .40 |
| **343** | A76 | 15c brt green & multi | .55 | .40 |
| *a.* | | Pair, #342-343 | 1.50 | 1.50 |

South Pacific Commission, 25th anniv.

Pitted-shelled Turtle — A77

Designs: 14c, Angle-headed agamid. 21c, Green python. 30c, Water monitor.

**1972, Mar. 15 Photo. *Perf. 11½***

| | | | | |
|---|---|---|---|---|
| **344** | A77 | 7c multicolored | .40 | .25 |
| **345** | A77 | 14c car rose & multi | 1.10 | 1.00 |
| **346** | A77 | 21c yellow & multi | 1.10 | 1.10 |
| **347** | A77 | 30c yel green & multi | 1.40 | 1.00 |
| | | *Nos. 344-347 (4)* | 4.00 | 3.35 |

Curtiss Seagull MF 6 and Ship — A78

14c, De Havilland 37 & porters from gold fields. 20c, Junkers G 31 & heavy machinery. 25c, Junkers F 13 & Lutheran mission church.

**1972, June 7 Granite Paper**

| | | | | |
|---|---|---|---|---|
| **348** | A78 | 7c dp yellow & multi | .25 | .25 |
| **349** | A78 | 14c dp orange & multi | .65 | 1.00 |
| **350** | A78 | 20c olive & multi | 1.10 | 1.00 |
| **351** | A78 | 25c multicolored | 1.25 | 1.00 |
| | | *Nos. 348-351 (4)* | 3.25 | 3.25 |

50th anniv. of aviation in Papua New Guinea.

National Day Unity Emblem — A79

Designs: 10c, Unity emblem and kundu (drum). 30c, Unity emblem and conch.

**1972, Aug. 16 *Perf. 12x12½***

| | | | | |
|---|---|---|---|---|
| **352** | A79 | 7c violet blue & multi | .30 | .25 |
| **353** | A79 | 10c orange & multi | .40 | .30 |
| **354** | A79 | 30c vermilion & multi | .60 | .55 |
| | | *Nos. 352-354 (3)* | 1.30 | 1.10 |

National Day, Sept. 15, 1972.

Rev. Copland King — A80

Pioneering Missionaries: No. 356, Pastor Ruatoka. No. 357, Bishop Stanislaus Henry Verjus. No. 358, Rev. Dr. Johannes Flierl.

**1972, Oct. 25 Photo. *Perf. 11½***

| | | | | |
|---|---|---|---|---|
| **355** | A80 | 7c dark blue & multi | .35 | .35 |
| **356** | A80 | 7c dark red & multi | .35 | .35 |
| **357** | A80 | 7c dark green & multi | .35 | .35 |
| **358** | A80 | 7c dark olive bister & multi | .35 | .35 |
| | | *Nos. 355-358 (4)* | 1.40 | 1.40 |

Christmas 1972.

Relay Station on Mt. Tomavatur — A81

**1973, Jan. 24 Photo. *Perf. 12½***

| | | | | |
|---|---|---|---|---|
| **359** | | 7c shown | .30 | .25 |
| **360** | | 7c Mt. Kerigomna | .30 | .25 |
| **361** | | 7c Sattelburg | .30 | .25 |
| **362** | | 7c Wideru | .30 | .25 |
| *a.* | A81 | Block of 4, #359-362 | 1.40 | 1.40 |
| | | Complete booklet, 3 each #359, 361, 2 each #360, 362 | | — |
| **363** | A81 | 9c Teleprinter | .35 | .25 |
| **364** | A81 | 30c Map of network | 1.25 | .85 |
| | | *Nos. 359-364 (6)* | 2.80 | 2.10 |

Telecommunications development 1968-1972. No. 362a has a unifying frame.

Queen Carol's Bird of Paradise — A82

Birds of Paradise: 14c, Goldie's. 21c, Ribbon-tailed astrapia. 28c, Princess Stephanie's.

**1973, Mar. 30 Photo. *Perf. 11½***

**Size: 22½x38mm**

| | | | | |
|---|---|---|---|---|
| **365** | A82 | 7c citron & multi | 1.00 | .45 |
| **366** | A82 | 14c dull green & multi | 2.50 | 1.25 |

**Size: 17x48mm**

| | | | | |
|---|---|---|---|---|
| **367** | A82 | 21c lemon & multi | 3.00 | 1.75 |
| **368** | A82 | 28c lt blue & multi | 4.00 | 2.50 |
| | | *Nos. 365-368 (4)* | 10.50 | 5.95 |

Wood Carver, Milne Bay — A83

Designs: 3c, Wig makers, Southern Highlands. 5c, Bagana Volcano, Bougainville. 6c, Pig Exchange, Western Highlands. 7c, Coastal village, Central District. 8c, Arawe mother, West New Britain. 9c, Fire dancers, East New Britain. 10c, Tifalmin hunter, West Sepik District. 14c, Crocodile hunters, Western District. 15c, Mt. Elimbari, Chimbu. 20c, Canoe racing, Manus District. 21c, Making sago, Gulf District. 25c, Council House, East Sepik. 28c, Menyamya bowmen, Morobe. 30c, Shark snaring, New Ireland. 40c, Fishing canoes, Madang. 60c, Women making tapa cloth, Northern District. $1, Asaro mudmen, Eastern Highlands. $2, Sing festival, Enga District.

**1973-74 Photo. *Perf. 11½***

**Granite Paper**

| | | | | |
|---|---|---|---|---|
| **369** | A83 | 1c multicolored | .25 | .25 |
| **370** | A83 | 3c multi ('74) | .35 | .25 |
| **371** | A83 | 5c multicolored | .75 | .25 |
| **372** | A83 | 6c multi ('74) | 1.00 | *2.00* |
| **373** | A83 | 7c multicolored | .30 | .25 |
| **374** | A83 | 8c multi ('74) | .35 | .30 |
| **375** | A83 | 9c multicolored | .40 | .25 |
| **376** | A83 | 10c multi ('74) | .60 | .25 |
| **377** | A83 | 14c multicolored | .45 | *.90* |
| **378** | A83 | 15c multicolored | .75 | .35 |
| **379** | A83 | 20c multi ('74) | 1.00 | .45 |
| **380** | A83 | 21c multicolored | .50 | *1.25* |
| **381** | A83 | 25c multicolored | .50 | *.60* |
| **382** | A83 | 28c multicolored | .50 | *1.25* |
| **383** | A83 | 30c multicolored | .60 | .60 |
| **385** | A83 | 40c multicolored | .50 | .50 |
| **386** | A83 | 60c multi ('74) | .60 | .75 |
| **387** | A83 | $1 multi ('74) | .85 | 1.50 |
| **388** | A83 | $2 multi ('74) | 3.50 | *6.50* |
| | | *Nos. 369-383,385-388 (19)* | 13.75 | 18.45 |

Issued: 1c, 7c, 9c, 15c, 25c, 40c, 6/13; 5c, 14c, 21c, 28c, 30c, Aug.; 3c, 8c, 10c, 20c, 60c, $1, 1/23/74.

Papua New Guinea No. 7 — A84

1c, Ger. New Guinea #1-2. 6c, Ger. New Guinea #17. 7c, New Britain #43. 25c, New Guinea #1. 30c, Papua New Guinea #108.

**Litho. (1c, 7c); Litho. & Engr. (others)**

**1973, Oct. 24 *Perf. 13½x14***

**Size: 54x31mm**

| | | | | |
|---|---|---|---|---|
| **389** | A84 | 1c gold, brn, grn & blk | .25 | .25 |
| **390** | A84 | 6c silver, blue & indigo | .30 | .25 |
| **391** | A84 | 7c gold, red, blk & buff | .30 | .25 |

***Perf. 14x14½***

**Size: 45x38mm**

| | | | | |
|---|---|---|---|---|
| **392** | A84 | 9c gold, org, blk & brn | .40 | .35 |
| **393** | A84 | 25c gold & orange | .75 | *.90* |
| **394** | A84 | 30c silver & dp lilac | .80 | *1.00* |
| | | *Nos. 389-394 (6)* | 2.80 | 3.00 |

75th anniv. of stamps in Papua New Guinea.

Masks — A85

**1973, Dec. 5 Photo. *Perf. 12½***

**Granite Paper**

| | | | | |
|---|---|---|---|---|
| **395** | A85 | 7c multicolored | .35 | .25 |
| **396** | A85 | 10c violet blue & multi | .65 | .65 |

Self-government.

Queen Elizabeth II A86

**1974, Feb. 22 Photo. *Perf. 14x14½***

| | | | | |
|---|---|---|---|---|
| **397** | A86 | 7c dp carmine & multi | .35 | .25 |
| **398** | A86 | 30c vio blue & multi | .90 | .90 |

Visit of Queen Elizabeth II and the Royal Family, Feb. 22-27.

Wreathed Hornbill — A87

Size of No. 400, 32½x48mm.

***Perf. 12, 11½ (10c)***

**1974, June 12 Photo.**

**Granite Paper**

| | | | | |
|---|---|---|---|---|
| **399** | A87 | 7c shown | 1.50 | .75 |
| **400** | A87 | 10c Great cassowary | 2.50 | *3.25* |
| **401** | A87 | 30c Kapul eagle | 5.50 | *7.50* |
| | | *Nos. 399-401 (3)* | 9.50 | *11.50* |

Dendrobium Bracteosum — A88

Orchids: 10c, Dendrobium anosmum. 20c, Dendrobium smillieae. 30c, Dendrobium insigne.

**1974, Nov. 20 Photo. *Perf. 11½***

**Granite Paper**

| | | | | |
|---|---|---|---|---|
| **402** | A88 | 7c dark green & multi | .95 | .25 |
| **403** | A88 | 10c dark blue & multi | .75 | .60 |
| **404** | A88 | 20c bister & multi | 1.25 | 1.25 |
| **405** | A88 | 30c green & multi | 1.60 | 1.60 |
| | | *Nos. 402-405 (4)* | 4.55 | 3.70 |

Motu Lakatoi A89

Traditional Canoes: 10c, Tami two-master morobe. 25c, Aramia racing canoe. 30c, Buka Island canoe.

**1975, Feb. 26 Photo. *Perf. 11½***

**Granite Paper**

| | | | | |
|---|---|---|---|---|
| **406** | A89 | 7c multicolored | .30 | .25 |
| **407** | A89 | 10c orange & multi | .50 | .50 |
| **408** | A89 | 25c apple green & multi | 1.00 | *2.00* |
| **409** | A89 | 30c citron & multi | 1.10 | *1.25* |
| | | *Nos. 406-409 (4)* | 2.90 | 4.00 |

Paradise Birdwing Butterfly, 1t Coin — A90

Ornate Butterfly Cod on 2t and Plateless Turtle on 5t — A91

New coinage: 10t, Cuscus on 10t. 20t, Cassowary on 20t. 1k, River crocodiles on 1k coin with center hole; obverse and reverse of 1k.

***Perf. 11, 11½ (A91)***

**1975, Apr. 21 Photo.**

**Granite Paper**

| | | | | |
|---|---|---|---|---|
| **410** | A90 | 1t green & multi | .25 | .25 |
| **411** | A91 | 7t brown & multi | .40 | .40 |
| **412** | A90 | 10t violet blue & multi | .40 | .40 |

**413** A90 20t carmine & multi .80 .80
**414** A91 1k dull blue & multi 2.40 2.40
*Nos. 410-414 (5)* 4.25 4.25

Ornithoptera Alexandrae — A92

Birdwing Butterflies: 10t, O. victoriae regis. 30t, O. allottei. 40t, O. chimaera.

**1975, June 11 Photo. *Perf. 11½***
**Granite Paper**

**415** A92 7t multicolored .40 .25
**416** A92 10t multicolored .50 .50
**417** A92 30t multicolored 1.60 1.60
**418** A92 40t multicolored 2.00 *3.25*
*Nos. 415-418 (4)* 4.50 5.60

Boxing and Games' Emblem — A93

**1975, Aug. 2 Photo. *Perf. 11½***
**Granite Paper**

**419** A93 7t shown .35 .25
**420** A93 20t Track and field .60 .45
**421** A93 25t Basketball .65 .60
**422** A93 30t Swimming .70 *.75*
*Nos. 419-422 (4)* 2.30 2.05

5th South Pacific Games, Guam, Aug. 1-10.

Map of South East Asia and Flag of PNG — A94

Design: 30t, Map of South East Asia and Papua New Guinea coat of arms.

**1975, Sept. 10 Photo. *Perf. 11½***
**Granite Paper**

**423** A94 7t red & multi .25 .25
**424** A94 30t blue & multi .65 .65
*a.* Souvenir sheet of 2, #423-424 1.40 1.40

Papua New Guinea independence, Sept. 16, 1975.

M. V. Bulolo A95

Ships of the 1930's: 15t, M.V. Macdhui. 25t, M.V. Malaita. 60t, S.S. Montoro.

**1976, Jan. 21 Photo. *Perf. 11½***
**Granite Paper**

**425** A95 7t multicolored .25 .25
**426** A95 15t multicolored .35 .30
**427** A95 25t multicolored .65 .50
**428** A95 60t multicolored 1.50 *2.00*
*Nos. 425-428 (4)* 2.75 3.05

Rorovana Carvings A96

Bougainville Art: 20t, Upe hats. 25t, Kapkaps (tortoise shell ornaments). 30t, Carved canoe paddles.

**1976, Mar. 17 Photo. *Perf. 11½***
**Granite Paper**

**429** A96 7t multicolored .30 .25
**430** A96 20t blue & multi .50 .45
**431** A96 25t dp orange & multi .60 *.90*
**432** A96 30t multicolored .75 *.75*
*Nos. 429-432 (4)* 2.15 2.35

Houses A97

**1976, June 9 Photo. *Perf. 11½***
**Granite Paper**

**433** A97 7t Rabaul .25 .25
**434** A97 15t Aramia .30 .25
**435** A97 30t Telefomin .65 .60
**436** A97 40t Tapini .70 *1.25*
*Nos. 433-436 (4)* 1.90 2.35

Boy Scouts and Scout Emblem A98

De Havilland Sea Plane, Map of Pacific — A99

Designs: 15t, Sea Scouts on outrigger canoe, Scout emblem. 60t, Plane on water.

**1976, Aug. 18 Photo. *Perf. 11½***
**Granite Paper**

**437** A98 7t multicolored .35 .25
**438** A99 10t lilac & multi .35 .25
**439** A98 15t multicolored .45 .45
**440** A99 60t multicolored 1.10 *1.75*
*Nos. 437-440 (4)* 2.25 2.70

50th anniversaries: Papua New Guinea Boy Scouts; 1st flight from Australia.

Father Ross and Mt. Hagen A100

**1976, Oct. 28 Photo. *Perf. 11½***
**Granite Paper**

**441** A100 7t multicolored .50 .25

Rev. Father William Ross (1896-1973), American missionary in New Guinea.

Clouded Rainbow Fish — A101

Tropical Fish: 15t, Imperial angelfish. 30t, Freckled rock cod. 40t, Threadfin butterflyfish.

**1976, Oct. 28 Granite Paper**

**442** A101 5t multicolored .25 .25
**443** A101 15t multicolored .70 .50
**444** A101 30t multicolored 1.40 .80
**445** A101 40t multicolored 1.90 1.90
*Nos. 442-445 (4)* 4.25 3.45

Kundiawa Man — A102

Mekeo Headdress A103

Headdresses: 5t, Masked dancer, East Sepik Province. 10t, Dancer, Koiari area. 15t, Hanuabada woman. 20t, Young woman, Orokaiva. 25t, Haus Tambaran dancer, East Sepik Province. 30t, Asaro Valley man. 35t, Garaina man, Morobe. 40t, Waghi Valley man. 50t, Trobriand dancer, Milne Bay. 1k, Wasara.

**Sizes: 25x30mm (1, 5, 20t), 26x26mm (10, 15, 25, 30, 50t), 23x38mm (35, 40t)**

***Perf. 12 (15, 25, 30t), 11½ (others)***

**1977-78 Photo.**

**446** A102 1t multicolored .25 .25
**447** A102 5t multicolored .25 .25
**448** A102 10t multicolored .30 .25
**449** A102 15t multicolored .30 .25
**450** A102 20t multicolored .55 .25
**451** A102 25t multicolored .35 .30
**452** A102 30t multicolored .40 .40
**453** A102 35t multicolored .65 .50
**454** A102 40t multicolored .60 .30
**455** A102 50t multicolored .85 *.90*

**Litho.**
***Perf. 14½x14***
**Size: 28x35½mm**

**456** A102 1k multicolored 1.50 *1.75*

***Perf. 14½x15***
**Size: 33x23mm**

**457** A103 2k multicolored 2.00 *3.25*
*Nos. 446-457 (12)* 8.00 8.65

Issued: #456-457, 1/12/77; #448, 450, 453, 455, 6/7/78; others, 3/29/78.

Elizabeth II and P.N.G. Arms A104

Designs: 7t, Queen and P.N.G. flag. 35t, Queen and map of P.N.G.

**1977, Mar. 16 Photo. *Perf. 15x14***

**462** A104 7t multicolored .35 .25
*a.* Silver omitted *500.00*
**463** A104 15t multicolored .45 .45
**464** A104 35t multicolored .75 *.90*
*Nos. 462-464 (3)* 1.55 1.60

25th anniv. of the reign of Elizabeth II.

Whitebreasted Ground Dove — A105

Protected Birds: 7t, Victoria crowned pigeon. 15t, Pheasant pigeon. 30t, Orange-fronted fruit dove. 50t, Banded imperial pigeon.

**1977, June 8 Photo. *Perf. 11½***
**Granite Paper**

**465** A105 5t multicolored .55 .25
**466** A105 7t multicolored .55 .25
**467** A105 15t multicolored .90 .85
**468** A105 30t multicolored 1.25 1.25
**469** A105 50t multicolored 1.75 *3.25*
*Nos. 465-469 (5)* 5.00 *5.85*

Girl Guides and Gold Badge A106

Designs (Girl Guides): 15t, Mapping and blue badge. 30t, Doing laundry in brook and red badge. 35t, Wearing grass skirts, cooking and green badge.

**1977, Aug. 10 Litho. *Perf. 14½***

**470** A106 7t multicolored .25 .25
**471** A106 15t multicolored .30 .25
**472** A106 30t multicolored .60 .60
**473** A106 35t multicolored .60 .60
*Nos. 470-473 (4)* 1.75 1.70

Papua New Guinea Girl Guides, 50th anniv.

Legend of Kari Marupi — A107

Myths of Elema People: 20t, Savoripi Clan. 30t, Oa-Laea. 35t, Oa-Iriarapo.

**1977, Oct. 19 Litho. *Perf. 13½***

**474** A107 7t black & multi .25 .25
**475** A107 20t black & multi .50 .35
**476** A107 30t black & multi .65 .65
**477** A107 35t black & multi .65 .65
*Nos. 474-477 (4)* 2.05 1.90

Blue-tailed Skink A108

Lizards: 15t, Green tree skink. 35t, Crocodile skink. 40t, New Guinea blue-tongued skink.

**1978, Jan. 25 Photo. *Perf. 11½***
**Granite Paper**

**478** A108 10t blue & multi .30 .25
**479** A108 15t lilac & multi .40 .25
**480** A108 35t olive & multi .60 *.75*
**481** A108 40t orange & multi .85 .85
*Nos. 478-481 (4)* 2.15 2.10

Roboastra Arika — A109

Sea Slugs: 15t, Chromodoris fidelis. 35t, Flabellina macassarana. 40t, Chromodoris trimarginata.

**1978, Aug. 29 Photo. *Perf. 11½***

**482** A109 10t multicolored .30 .25
**483** A109 15t multicolored .40 .40
**484** A109 35t multicolored .65 .65
**485** A109 40t multicolored .90 *1.15*
*Nos. 482-485 (4)* 2.25 2.45

Mandated New Guinea Constabulary A110

Constabulary and Badge: 10t, Royal Papua New Guinea. 20t, Armed British New Guinea. 25t, German New Guinea police. 30t, Royal Papua and New Guinea.

**1978, Oct. 26 Photo. *Perf. 14½x14***

**486** A110 10t multicolored .25 .25
**487** A110 15t multicolored .35 .35
**488** A110 20t multicolored .40 .40

489 A110 25t multicolored .45 .45
490 A110 30t multicolored .55 .55
*Nos. 486-490 (5)* 2.00 2.00

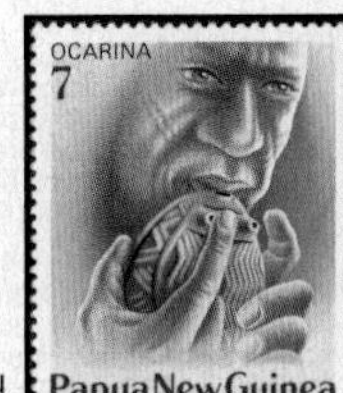

Ocarina, Chimbu Province — A111

Musical Instruments: 20t, Musical bow, New Britain, horiz. 28t, Launut, New Ireland. 35t, Nose flute, New Hanover, horiz.

***Perf. 14½x14, 14x14½***
**1979, Jan. 24 Litho.**
491 A111 7t multicolored .30 .25
492 A111 20t multicolored .40 .30
493 A111 28t multicolored .60 .60
494 A111 35t multicolored .70 .70
*Nos. 491-494 (4)* 2.00 1.85

Prow and Paddle, East New Britain — A112

Canoe Prows and Paddles: 21t, Sepik war canoe. 25t, Trobriand Islands. 40t, Milne Bay.

**1979, Mar. 28 Litho. *Perf. 14½***
495 A112 14t multicolored .30 .25
496 A112 21t multicolored .40 .25
497 A112 25t multicolored .55 .55
498 A112 40t multicolored .70 .70
*Nos. 495-498 (4)* 1.95 1.75

Belt of Shell Disks — A113

Traditional Currency: 15t, Tusk chest ornament. 25t, Shell armband. 35t, Shell necklace.

**1979, June 6 Litho. *Perf. 12½x12***
499 A113 7t multicolored .25 .25
500 A113 15t multicolored .35 .30
501 A113 25t multicolored .55 .55
502 A113 35t multicolored .65 .65
*Nos. 499-502 (4)* 1.80 1.75

Oenetus A114

Moths: 15t, Celerina vulgaris. 20t, Alcidis aurora, vert. 25t, Phyllodes conspicillator. 30t, Nyctalemon patroclus, vert.

**1979, Aug. 29 Photo. *Perf. 11½***
503 A114 7t multicolored .25 .25
504 A114 15t multicolored .40 .35
505 A114 20t multicolored .45 .45
506 A114 25t multicolored .50 *.75*
507 A114 30t multicolored .65 *.90*
*Nos. 503-507 (5)* 2.25 2.70

Baby in String Bag Scale — A115

IYC (Emblem and): 7t, Mother nursing baby. 30t, Boy playing with dog and ball. 60t, Girl in classroom.

**1979, Oct. 24 Litho. *Perf. 14x13½***
508 A115 7t multicolored .30 .25
509 A115 15t multicolored .35 .25
510 A115 30t multicolored .45 .45
511 A115 60t multicolored .80 .80
*Nos. 508-511 (4)* 1.90 1.75

Mail Sorting, Mail Truck A116

UPU Membership: 25t, Wartime mail delivery. 35t, UPU monument, airport and city. 40t, Hand canceling, letter carrier.

**1980, Jan. 23 Litho. *Perf. 13½x14***
512 A116 7t multicolored .30 .25
513 A116 25t multicolored .40 .30
514 A116 35t multicolored .50 .50
515 A116 40t multicolored .65 .65
*Nos. 512-515 (4)* 1.85 1.70

Male Dancer, Betrothal Ceremony — A117

Third South Pacific Arts Festival, Port Moresby (Minj Betrothal Ceremony Mural): a, One dancer, orange and yellow. b, Two dancers, red, yellow & blk. c, Two dancers side by side, orange, black. d, Two dancers, one in front of the other one. e, One dancer, yellow and red.

No. 516 has continuous design.

**1980, Mar. 26 Photo. *Perf. 11½***
**Granite Paper**
516 A117 Strip of 5 2.00 2.00
*a.-e.* 20t any single .30 .30

National Census — A118

**1980, June 4 Litho. *Perf. 14***
517 A118 7t shown .25 .25
518 A118 15t Population symbol .25 .25
519 A118 40t P. N. G. map .55 .55
520 A118 50t Faces .75 .75
*Nos. 517-520 (4)* 1.80 1.80

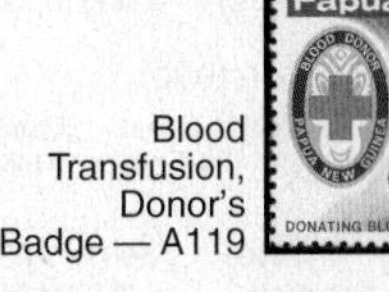

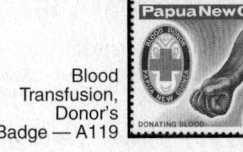

Blood Transfusion, Donor's Badge — A119

15t, Donating blood. 30t, Map of donation centers. 60t, Blood components and types.

**1980, Aug. 27 Litho. *Perf. 14½***
521 A119 7t shown .25 .25
522 A119 15t multicolored .25 .25
523 A119 30t multicolored .50 .50
524 A119 60t multicolored .85 .85
*Nos. 521-524 (4)* 1.85 1.85

Dugong A120

30t, Native spotted cat, vert. 35t, Tube-nosed bat, vert. 45t, Raffray's bandicoot.

**1980, Oct. 29 Photo. *Perf. 11½***
525 A120 7t shown .25 .25
526 A120 30t multicolored .60 .60
527 A120 35t multicolored .70 .70
528 A120 45t multicolored .95 .95
*Nos. 525-528 (4)* 2.50 2.50

Beach Kingfisher — A121

7t, Forest kingfisher. 20t, Sacred kingfisher. 25t, White-tailed paradise kingfisher. 60t, Blue-winged kookaburra.

**1981, Jan. 21 Photo. *Perf. 12***
**Granite Paper**
529 A121 3t shown .30 *.45*
530 A121 7t multicolored .30 .25
531 A121 20t multicolored .50 .50

**Size: 26x45½mm**
532 A121 25t multicolored .60 .60

**Size: 26x36mm**
533 A121 60t multicolored 1.60 *2.50*
*Nos. 529-533 (5)* 3.30 4.30

Mask — A122

**Coil Stamps**
***Perf. 14½ Horiz.***
**1981, Jan. 21 Photo.**
534 A122 2t shown .25 .25
535 A122 5t Hibiscus .25 .25

Defense Force Soldiers Firing Mortar — A123

15t, DC-3 military plane. 40t, Patrol boat Eitape. 50t, Medics treating civilians.

**1981, Mar. 25 Photo. *Perf. 13½x14***
536 A123 7t shown .25 .25
537 A123 15t multicolored .30 .25
538 A123 40t multicolored .65 .65
539 A123 50t multicolored .80 .80
*Nos. 536-539 (4)* 2.00 1.95

For surcharge see No. 615.

Missionary Aviation Fellowship Plane — A124

Planes of Missionary Organizations: 15t, Holy Ghost Society. 20t, Summer Institute of Linguistics. 30t, Lutheran Mission. 35t, Seventh Day Adventist.

**1981, June 17 Litho. *Perf. 14***
540 A124 10t multicolored .25 .25
541 A124 15t multicolored .30 .25
542 A124 20t multicolored .40 .30
543 A124 30t multicolored .50 .50
544 A124 35t multicolored .60 .60
*Nos. 540-544 (5)* 2.05 1.90

Scoop Net Fishing A125

**1981, Aug. 26**
545 A125 10t shown .25 .25
546 A125 15t Kite fishing .30 .30
547 A125 30t Rod fishing .55 .55
548 A125 60t Scissor net fishing 1.00 1.00
*Nos. 545-548 (4)* 2.10 2.10

Forcartia Buhleri A126

15t, Naninia citrina. 20t, Papuina adonis, papuina hermione. 30t, Papustyla hindei, papustyla novaepommeraniae. 40t, Rhynchotrochus strabo.

**1981, Oct. 28 Photo. *Perf. 12***
**Granite Paper**
549 A126 5t multicolored .25 .25
550 A126 15t multicolored .30 .30
551 A126 20t multicolored .40 .40
552 A126 30t multicolored .60 .60
553 A126 40t multicolored .75 .75
*Nos. 549-553 (5)* 2.30 2.30

75th Anniv. of Boy Scouts A127

15t, Lord Baden-Powell, flag raising. 25t, Leader, campfire. 35t, Scout, hut building. 50t, Percy Chatterton, first aid.

**1982, Jan. 20 Photo. *Perf. 11½***
**Granite Paper**
554 A127 15t multicolored .25 .25
555 A127 25t multicolored .45 .45
556 A127 35t multicolored .60 .60
557 A127 50t multicolored .90 .90
*Nos. 554-557 (4)* 2.20 2.20

Wanigela Pottery A128

10t, Boiken, East Sepik. 20t, Gumalu, Madang. 50t, Ramu Valley, Madang.

**1982, Mar. 24 Litho. *Perf. 14***
**Size: 29x29mm**
558 A128 10t multicolored .25 .25
559 A128 20t multicolored .40 .40

***Perf. 14½***
**Size: 36x23mm**
560 A128 40t shown .70 .70
561 A128 50t multicolored .90 .90
*Nos. 558-561 (4)* 2.25 2.25

Nutrition A129

**1982, May 5 Litho. *Perf. 14½x14***
562 A129 10t Mother, child .25 .25
563 A129 15t Protein .35 .35
564 A129 30t Fruits, vegetables .65 .65
565 A129 40t Carbohydrates .85 .85
*Nos. 562-565 (4)* 2.10 2.10

Coral
A130

1t, Stony Coral (Stylophora). 5t, Finger Coral (Acropora humilis). 15t, Lace Coral (Distichopora). 1k, Pulse Coral (Xenia).

**1982, July 21 Photo. *Perf. 11½***
**Granite Paper**

**566** A130 1t Stylophora sp. .35 .25
**567** A130 5t Acropora humilis .35 .25
**568** A130 15t Distichopora sp. .75 .40
**569** A130 1k Xenia sp. 3.75 2.75
*Nos. 566-569 (4)* 5.20 3.65

See Nos. 575-579, 588-591, 614.

Centenary of Catholic Church in Papua New Guinea — A131

a, Ship and Men, one dog. b, Men and three dogs. c, Men and tree.

**1982, Sept. 15 Photo. *Perf. 11½***

**570** A131 Strip of 3 1.00 1.00
***a.-c.*** 10t any single .30 .30

12th Commonwealth Games, Brisbane, Australia, Sept. 30-Oct. 9 — A132

**1982, Oct. 6 Litho. *Perf. 14½***

**571** A132 10t Running .25 .25
**572** A132 15t Boxing .25 .25
**573** A132 45t Shooting .90 .90
**574** A132 50t Lawn bowling 1.00 1.00
*Nos. 571-574 (4)* 2.40 2.40

**Coral Type of 1982**

3t, Cup Coral (Dendrophyllia). 10t, Carnation Tree Coral (Dendronephthya), orange coral, gray background. 30t, Carnation Tree Coral (Dendronephthya), red coral, blue green background. 40t, Black Coral (Antipathes). 3k, Lace Coral (Distichopora).

**1983, Jan. 12 Photo. *Perf. 11½***
**Granite Paper**

**575** A130 3t multi .70 *1.25*
**576** A130 10t multi .90 .90
**577** A130 30t multi 1.40 .90
**578** A130 40t multi 1.50 1.50
**579** A130 3k multi 6.50 6.50
*Nos. 575-579 (5)* 11.00 11.05

Nos. 575-579 vert.

Commonwealth Day — A133

10t, Flag, arms. 15t, Youth, recreation. 20t, Technical assistance. 50t, Export assistance.

**1983, Mar. 9 Litho. *Perf. 14***

**580** A133 10t multi .25 .25
**581** A133 15t multi .25 .25
**582** A133 20t multi .40 .40
**583** A133 50t multi .90 .90
*Nos. 580-583 (4)* 1.80 1.80

World Communications Year — A134

10t, Mail transport. 25t, Writing & receiving letter. 30t, Telephone calls. 60t, Family reunion.

**1983, Sept. 7 Litho. *Perf. 14***

**584** A134 10t multi .30 .25
**585** A134 25t multi .50 .40
**586** A134 30t multi .55 .45
**587** A134 60t multi 1.20 .95
*Nos. 584-587 (4)* 2.55 2.05

**Coral Type of 1982**

20t, Bamboo Coral (Isis). 25t, Small Polyp Stony Coral (Acropora). 35t, Elegant Hydrocoral (Stylaster elegans). 45t, Cup Coral (Turbinaria).

**1983, Nov. 9 Photo. *Perf. 11½***

**588** A130 20t multi 1.10 .70
**589** A130 25t multi .90 .90
**590** A130 35t multi 1.60 1.40
**591** A130 45t multi 2.50 1.75
*Nos. 588-591 (4)* 6.10 4.75

Nos. 588-591 vert.

Turtles
A135

5t, Chelonia depressa. 10t, Chelonia mydas. 15t, Eretkmochelys imbricata. 20t, Lepidochelys olivacea. 25t, Caretta caretta. 40t, Dermochelys coriacea.

**1984, Feb. 8 Photo.**
**Granite Paper**

**592** A135 5t multicolored .25 .25
**593** A135 10t multicolored .30 .30
**594** A135 15t multicolored .50 .50
**595** A135 20t multicolored .65 .60
**596** A135 25t multicolored 1.10 1.10
**597** A135 40t multicolored 1.30 1.30
*Nos. 592-597 (6)* 4.10 4.05

Papua-Australia Airmail Service, 50th Anniv. — A136

Mail planes — 20t, Avro X VH-UXX. 25t, DH86B VH-UYU Carmania. 40t, Westland Widgeon. 60t, Consolidated Catalina NC777.

**1984, May 9 Litho. *Perf. 14½x14***

**598** A136 20t multicolored .45 .45
**599** A136 25t multicolored .55 .55
**600** A136 40t multicolored 1.00 1.00
**601** A136 60t multicolored 1.40 1.40
*Nos. 598-601 (4)* 3.40 3.40

Parliament House Opening — A137

**1984, Aug. 7 Litho. *Perf. 13½x14***

**602** A137 10t multicolored .40 .40

Bird of Paradise
A138

**1984, Aug. 7 Photo. *Perf. 11½***
**Granite Paper**

**603** A138 5k multicolored 10.00 10.00

Ceremonial Shield — A139

**1984, Sept. 21**

**604** A139 10t Central Province .25 .25
**605** A139 20t West New Britain .55 .55
**606** A139 30t Madang .85 .85
**607** A139 50t East Sepik .90 .90
*Nos. 604-607 (4)* 2.55 2.55

See Nos. 677-680.

British New Guinea Proclamation Centenary — A140

**1984, Nov. 6 Litho. *Perf. 14½x14***

**608** A140 Pair .50 .50
***a.*** 10t Nelson, Port Moresby, 1884 .25 .25
***b.*** 10t Port Moresby, 1984 .25 .25
**609** A140 Pair 2.50 2.50
***a.*** 45t Rabaul, 1984 1.10 1.10
***b.*** 45t Elizabeth, Rabaul, 1884 1.10 1.10

Chimbu Gorge
A142

10t, Fergusson Island, vert. 25t, Sepik River, vert. 60t, Dali Beach, Vanimo.

**1985, Feb. 6 Photo. *Perf. 11½***

**610** A142 10t multicolored .25 .25
**611** A142 25t multicolored .70 .70
**612** A142 40t shown 1.15 1.15
**613** A142 60t multicolored 1.90 1.90
*Nos. 610-613 (4)* 4.00 4.00

**Coral Type of 1982**

12t, Carnation Tree Coral (Dendronephthya), orange coral, blue green background, vert.

**1985, May 29 Photo. *Perf. 11½***

**614** A130 12t multicolored 4.50 4.50

For surcharge see No. 686.

**No. 536 Surcharged**

**1985, Apr. 1 Litho. *Perf. 13½x14***

**615** A123 12t on 7t multi .75 *1.00*
***a.*** Inverted surcharge —

Ritual Structures
A143

Designs: 15t, Dubu platform, Central Province. 20t, Tamuniai house, West New Britain. 30t, Yam tower, Trobriand Island. 60t, Huli grave, Tari.

**1985, May 1 *Perf. 13x13½***

**616** A143 15t multicolored .45 .45
**617** A143 20t multicolored .65 .65
**618** A143 30t multicolored .95 .95
**619** A143 60t multicolored 1.50 1.50
*Nos. 616-619 (4)* 3.55 3.55

A set of four with designs similar to Nos. 616-619 and without the "t" in the denomination was prepared but not officially issued. A small number of sets found their way into the marketplace. Value, set $200.

Indigenous Birds of Prey — A144

**1985, Aug. 26 *Perf. 14x14½***

**620** 12t Accipiter brachyurus .75 .75
**621** 12t In flight .75 .75
***a.*** A144 Pair, #629-621 1.75 1.75
**622** 30t Megatriorchis doriae 1.25 1.25
**623** 30t In Flight 1.25 1.25
***a.*** A144 Pair, #622-623 3.00 3.00
**624** 60t Henicopernis longicauda 2.50 2.50
**625** 60t In flight 2.50 2.50
***a.*** A144 Pair, #624-625 6.00 6.00
*Nos. 620-625 (6)* 9.00 9.00

Flag and Gable of Parliament House, Port Moresby — A145

**1985, Sept. 11 *Perf. 14½x15***

**626** A145 12t multicolored .60 .60

Post Office Centenary
A146

Designs: 12t, No. 631a, 1901 Postal card, aerogramme, spectacles and inkwell. 30t, No. 631b, Queensland Type A15, No. 628. 40t, No. 631c, Plane and news clipping, 1885. 60t, No. 631d, 1892 German canceler, 1985 first day cancel.

**1985, Oct. 9 *Perf. 14½x14***

**627** A146 12t multicolored .70 .70
**628** A146 30t multicolored 1.75 1.75
**629** A146 40t multicolored 2.40 2.40
**630** A146 60t multicolored 3.00 3.00
*Nos. 627-630 (4)* 7.85 7.85

**Souvenir Sheet**

**631** Sheet of 4 9.00 9.00
***a.*** A146 12t multicolored .90 .90
***b.*** A146 30t multicolored 1.60 1.60
***c.*** A146 40t multicolored 2.00 2.00
***d.*** A146 60t multicolored 3.00 3.00

Nombowai Cave Carved Funerary Totems — A147

12t, Bird Rulowlaw, headman. 30t, Barn owl Raus, headman. 60t, Melerawuk. 80t, Cockerel, woman.

**1985, Nov. 13** ***Perf. 11½***

**632** A147 12t multicolored .70 .30
**633** A147 30t multicolored 1.40 .80
**634** A147 60t multicolored 2.25 2.25
**635** A147 80t multicolored 2.75 *3.75*
*Nos. 632-635 (4)* 7.10 7.10

Conch Shells — A148

15t, Cypraea valentia. 35t, Oliva buelowi. 45t, Oliva parkinsoni. 70t, Cypraea aurantium.

**1986, Feb. 12** ***Perf. 11½***

**636** A148 15t multicolored .80 .45
**637** A148 35t multicolored 1.90 1.50
**638** A148 45t multicolored 2.25 2.25
**639** A148 70t multicolored 3.00 *4.25*
*Nos. 636-639 (4)* 7.95 8.45

Common Design Types pictured following the introduction.

**Queen Elizabeth II 60th Birthday**
Common Design Type

Designs: 15t, In ATS officer's uniform, 1945. 35t, Silver wedding anniv. portrait by Patrick Lichfield, Balmoral, 1972. 50t, Inspecting troops, Port Moresby, 1982. 60t, Banquet aboard Britannia, state tour, 1982. 70t, Visiting Crown Agents' offices, 1983.

***Perf. 14½***

**1986, Apr. 21 Litho. Unwmk.**

**640** CD337 15t scar, blk & sil .30 .30
**641** CD337 35t ultra & multi .70 .70
**642** CD337 50t green & multi 1.00 1.00
**643** CD337 60t violet & multi 1.10 1.10
**644** CD337 70t rose vio & multi 1.40 1.40
*Nos. 640-644 (5)* 4.50 4.50

AMERIPEX '86
A149

Small birds — 15t, Pitta erythrogaster. 35t, Melanocharis striativentris. 45t, Rhipidura rufifrons. 70t, Poecilodryas placens, vert.

**1986, May 22 Photo.** ***Perf. 12½***
**Granite Paper**

**645** A149 15t multicolored 1.10 .70
**646** A149 35t multicolored 2.25 1.60
**647** A149 45t multicolored 2.50 2.10
**648** A149 70t multicolored 3.75 3.75
*Nos. 645-648 (4)* 9.60 8.15

Lutheran Church, Cent. — A150

15t, Monk, minister. 70t, Churches from 1886, 1986.

**1986, July 7 Litho.** ***Perf. 14x15***

**649** A150 15t multicolored .60 .55
**650** A150 70t multicolored 2.75 2.75

Indigenous Orchids — A151

15t, Dendrobium vexillarius. 35t, Dendrobium lineale. 45t, Dendrobium johnsoniae. 70t, Dendrobium cuthbertsonii.

**1986, Aug. 4 Litho.** ***Perf. 14***

**651** A151 15t multicolored 1.25 .75
**652** A151 35t multicolored 2.50 1.60
**653** A151 45t multicolored 2.75 2.10
**654** A151 70t multicolored 3.50 3.50
*Nos. 651-654 (4)* 10.00 7.95

Folk Dancers — A152

**1986, Nov. 12 Litho.** ***Perf. 14***

**655** A152 15t Maprik .95 .65
**656** A152 35t Kiriwina 1.75 1.50
**657** A152 45t Kundiawa 2.00 1.90
**658** A152 70t Fasu 3.50 *3.75*
*Nos. 655-658 (4)* 8.20 7.80

Fish
A153

17t, White-cap anemonefish. 30t, Black anemonefish. 35t, Tomato clownfish. 70t, Spine-cheek anemonefish.

**Unwmk.**

**1987, Apr. 15 Litho.** ***Perf. 15***

**659** A153 17t multicolored 1.00 .35
**660** A153 30t multicolored 1.50 1.75
**661** A153 35t multicolored 2.00 1.40
**662** A153 70t multicolored 3.00 *4.00*
*Nos. 659-662 (4)* 7.50 7.50

For surcharges see Nos. 720, 823, 868.

Ships — A154

1t, La Boudeuse, 1768. 5t, Roebuck, 1700. 10t, Swallow, 1767. 15t, Fly, 1845. 17t, like No. 666. 20t, Rattlesnake, 1849. 30t, Vitiaz, 1871. 35t, San Pedrico, Zabre, 1606. 40t, L'Astrolabe, 1827. 45t, Neva, 1876. 60t, Caravel of Jorge De Meneses, 1526. 70t, Eendracht, 1616. 1k, Blanche, 1872. 2k, Merrie England, 1889. 3k, Samoa, 1884.

**1987-88 Photo. Unwmk.** ***Perf. 11½***
**Granite Paper**

**663** A154 1t multicolored .55 *1.25*
**664** A154 5t multicolored 1.10 *1.50*
**665** A154 10t multicolored 1.40 1.40
**666** A154 15t multicolored 2.00 1.00
**667** A154 17t multicolored 2.00 .75
**668** A154 20t multicolored 2.00 1.00
**669** A154 30t multicolored 2.00 2.00
**670** A154 35t multicolored .75 *.90*
**671** A154 40t multicolored 2.25 2.25
**672** A154 45t multicolored .90 .90
**673** A154 60t multicolored 2.75 2.75
**674** A154 70t multicolored 2.25 2.25
**675** A154 1k multicolored 2.75 2.75
**676** A154 2k multicolored 4.25 4.25
**676A** A154 3k multicolored 5.25 *7.50*
*Nos. 663-676A (15)* 32.20 32.45

Issued: 5, 35, 45, 70t, 2k, 6/15/87; 15, 20, 40, 60t, 2/17/88; 17t, 1k, 3/1/88; 1, 10, 30t, 3k, 11/16/88.

See Nos. 960-963. For surcharge see No. 824.

**Shield Type of 1984**

War shields — 15t, Elema shield, Gulf Province, c. 1880. 35t, East Sepik Province. 45t, Simbai region, Madang Province. 70t, Telefomin region, West Sepik.

***Perf. 11½x12***

**1987, Aug. 19 Photo. Unwmk.**

**677** A139 15t multicolored .30 .30
**678** A139 35t multicolored .70 .70
**679** A139 45t multicolored .90 .90
**680** A139 70t multicolored 1.40 1.40
*Nos. 677-680 (4)* 3.30 3.30

Starfish
A156

17t, Protoreaster nodosus. 35t, Gomophia egeriae. 45t, Choriaster granulatus. 70t, Neoferdina ocellata.

**1987, Sept. 30 Litho.** ***Perf. 14***

**682** A156 17t multicolored .75 .40
**683** A156 35t multicolored 1.50 .90
**684** A156 45t multicolored 1.75 1.10
**685** A156 70t multicolored 2.25 *3.50*
*Nos. 682-685 (4)* 6.25 5.90

No. 614 Surcharged

**1987, Sept. 23 Photo.** ***Perf. 11½***
**Granite Paper**

**686** A130 15t on 12t multi 1.60 1.25

Aircraft
A157

Designs: 15t, Cessna Stationair 6, Rabaraba Airstrip. 35t, Britten-Norman Islander over Hombrum Bluff. 45t, DHC Twin Otter over the Highlands. 70t, Fokker F28 over Madang.

**Unwmk.**

**1987, Nov. 11 Litho.** ***Perf. 14***

**687** A157 15t multicolored 1.25 .45
**688** A157 35t multicolored 1.75 1.00
**689** A157 45t multicolored 2.00 1.25
**690** A157 70t multicolored 3.00 *4.25*
*Nos. 687-690 (4)* 8.00 6.95

Royal Papua New Guinea Police Force, Cent. — A158

Historic and modern aspects of the force: 17t, Motorcycle constable and pre-independence officer wearing a lap-lap. 35t, Sir William McGregor, Armed Native Constabulary founder, 1890, and recruit. 45t, Badges. 70t, Albert Hahl, German official credited with founding the island's police movement in 1888, and badge, early officer.

***Perf. 14x15***

**1988, June 15 Litho. Unwmk.**

**691** A158 17t multicolored .60 .45
**692** A158 35t multicolored 1.10 .85
**693** A158 45t multicolored 1.40 1.10
**694** A158 70t multicolored 2.00 2.00
*Nos. 691-694 (4)* 5.10 4.40

Sydney Opera House and a Lakatoi (ship) — A159

Fireworks and Globes — A160

**1988, July 30 Litho.** ***Perf. 13½***

**695** A159 35t multicolored .90 .90
**696** A160 Pair 2.00 2.00
*a.-b.* 35t any single .90 .90
*c.* Souvenir sheet of 2, #a.-b. 2.75 2.75

SYDPEX '88, Australia (No. 695); Australia bicentennial (No. 696).

World Wildlife Fund
A161

Metamorphosis of a Queen Alexandra's birdwing butterfly — 5t, Courtship. 17t, Ovi-positioning and larvae, vert. 25t, Emergence from pupa, vert. 35t, Adult male on leaf.

**1988, Sept. 19** ***Perf. 14½***

**697** A161 5t multicolored *2.50 2.00*
**698** A161 17t multicolored *3.75 1.25*
**699** A161 25t multicolored *4.25 3.50*
**700** A161 35t multicolored *5.50 4.50*
*Nos. 697-700 (4)* *16.00 11.25*

1988 Summer Olympics, Seoul
A162

**1988, Sept. 19 Litho.** ***Perf. 13½***

**701** A162 17t Running .75 .75
**702** A162 45t Weight lifting 1.50 1.50

Rhododendrons
A163

**Wmk. 387**

**1989, Jan. 25 Litho.** ***Perf. 14***

**703** A163 3t R. zoelleri .25 .25
**704** A163 20t R. cruttwellii .65 .65
**705** A163 60t R. superbum 1.60 1.60
**706** A163 70t R. christianae 2.00 2.00
*Nos. 703-706 (4)* 4.50 4.50

Intl. Letter Writing Week — A164

**1989, Mar. 22** ***Perf. 14½***

**707** A164 20t Writing letter .40 .40
**708** A164 35t Mailing letter .70 .60
**709** A164 60t Stamping letter 1.15 1.15
**710** A164 70t Reading letter 1.35 1.35
*Nos. 707-710 (4)* 3.60 3.50

Thatched Dwellings — A165

20t, Buka Is., 1880s. 35t, Koiari tree houses. 60t, Lauan, New Ireland, 1890s. 70t, Basilaki, Milne Bay Province, 1930s.

**1989, May 17 Wmk. 387 *Perf. 15***

| | | | | |
|---|---|---|---|---|
| **711** | A165 | 20t multicolored | .45 | .40 |
| **712** | A165 | 35t multicolored | .95 | .75 |
| **713** | A165 | 60t multicolored | 1.50 | 1.50 |
| **714** | A165 | 70t multicolored | 1.75 | 1.75 |
| | | *Nos. 711-714 (4)* | 4.65 | 4.40 |

Small Birds — A166

No. 715, Oreocharis arfaki female, shown. No. 716, Male. No. 717, Ifrita kowaldi. No. 718, Poecilodryas albonotata. No. 719, Sericornis nouhuysi.

**1989, July 12 Unwmk. *Perf. 14½***

| | | | | |
|---|---|---|---|---|
| **715** | A166 | 20t multicolored | 1.40 | 1.40 |
| **716** | A166 | 20t multicolored | 1.40 | 1.40 |
| *a.* | | Pair, #715-716 | 3.25 | 3.25 |
| **717** | A166 | 35t multicolored | 1.90 | 1.40 |
| **718** | A166 | 45t multicolored | 1.90 | 1.60 |
| **719** | A166 | 70t multicolored | 2.75 | 2.75 |
| | | *Nos. 715-719 (5)* | 9.35 | 8.55 |

**No. 659 Surcharged**

**1989, July 12 Unwmk. *Perf. 15***

| | | | | |
|---|---|---|---|---|
| **720** | A153 | 20t on 17t multi | 1.00 | 1.00 |
| *a.* | | Double surcharge | | 180.00 |

Traditional Dance — A167

Designs: 20t, Motumotu, Gulf Province. 35t, Baining, East New Britain Province. 60t, Vailala River, Gulf Province. 70t, Timbunke, East Sepik Province.

***Perf. 14x14½***

**1989, Sept. 6 Litho. Wmk. 387**

| | | | | |
|---|---|---|---|---|
| **721** | A167 | 20t multicolored | .80 | .65 |
| **722** | A167 | 35t multicolored | 1.40 | 1.10 |
| **723** | A167 | 60t multicolored | 2.40 | 2.40 |
| **724** | A167 | 70t multicolored | 2.75 | 2.75 |
| | | *Nos. 721-724 (4)* | 7.35 | 6.90 |

For surcharge see No. 860.

Christmas A168

Designs: 20t, Hibiscus, church and symbol from a gulf gope board, Kavaumai. 35t, Rhododendron, madonna and child, and mask, Murik Lakes region. 60t, D'Albertis creeper, candle, and shield from Oksapmin, West Sepik highlands. 70t, Pacific frangipani, peace dove and flute mask from Chungrebu, a Rao village in Ramu.

***Perf. 14x14½***

**1989, Nov. 8 Litho. Unwmk.**

| | | | | |
|---|---|---|---|---|
| **725** | A168 | 20t multicolored | .55 | .50 |
| **726** | A168 | 35t multicolored | .85 | .85 |
| **727** | A168 | 60t multicolored | 1.75 | 1.75 |
| **728** | A168 | 70t multicolored | 1.90 | 1.90 |
| | | *Nos. 725-728 (4)* | 5.05 | 5.00 |

Waterfalls — A169

**Unwmk.**

**1990, Feb. 1 Litho. *Perf. 14***

| | | | | |
|---|---|---|---|---|
| **729** | A169 | 20t Guni Falls | .75 | .55 |
| **730** | A169 | 35t Rouna Falls | 1.10 | .90 |
| **731** | A169 | 60t Ambua Falls | 2.10 | 2.10 |
| **732** | A169 | 70t Wawoi Falls | 2.40 | 2.40 |
| | | *Nos. 729-732 (4)* | 6.35 | 5.95 |

For surcharges see Nos. 866, 870.

Natl. Census A170

20t, Three youths, form. 70t, Man, woman, child, form.

**1990, May 2 *Perf. 14½x15***

| | | | | |
|---|---|---|---|---|
| **733** | A170 | 20t multicolored | .60 | .60 |
| **734** | A170 | 70t multicolored | 2.50 | 2.50 |

For surcharge see No. 869.

Gogodala Dance Masks — A171

**1990, July 11 Litho. *Perf. 13½***

| | | | | |
|---|---|---|---|---|
| **735** | A171 | 20t shown | 1.25 | .50 |
| **736** | A171 | 35t multi, diff. | 1.75 | .90 |
| **737** | A171 | 60t multi, diff. | 2.75 | *4.00* |
| **738** | A171 | 70t multi, diff. | 3.00 | *4.00* |
| | | *Nos. 735-738 (4)* | 8.75 | 9.40 |

For surcharges see Nos. 867, 871.

Waitangi Treaty, 150th Anniv. — A172

Designs: 20t, Dwarf Cassowary, Great Spotted Kiwi. No. 740, Double Wattled Cassowary, Brown Kiwi. No. 741, Sepik mask and Maori carving.

**1990, Aug. 24 Litho. *Perf. 14½***

| | | | | |
|---|---|---|---|---|
| **739** | A172 | 20t multicolored | 1.25 | .90 |
| **740** | A172 | 35t multicolored | 1.75 | .90 |
| **741** | A172 | 35t multicolored | 2.10 | 1.40 |
| | | *Nos. 739-741 (3)* | 5.10 | 3.20 |

No. 741 for World Stamp Exhibition, New Zealand 1990.

For surcharges see Nos. 862-863.

Birds A173

20t, Whimbrel. 35t, Sharp-tailed sandpiper. 60t, Ruddy turnstone. 70t, Terek sandpiper.

**1990, Sept. 26 Litho. *Perf. 14***

| | | | | |
|---|---|---|---|---|
| **742** | A173 | 20t multi | 1.25 | .70 |
| **743** | A173 | 35t multi | 1.90 | 1.10 |
| **744** | A173 | 60t multi | 3.00 | *4.00* |
| **745** | A173 | 70t multi | 3.75 | *4.00* |
| | | *Nos. 742-745 (4)* | 9.90 | 9.80 |

Musical Instruments A174

**1990, Oct. 31 Litho. *Perf. 13***

| | | | | |
|---|---|---|---|---|
| **746** | A174 | 20t Jew's harp | .90 | .75 |
| **747** | A174 | 35t Musical bow | 1.40 | 1.25 |
| **748** | A174 | 60t Wantoat drum | 2.75 | 2.75 |
| **749** | A174 | 70t Gogodala rattle | 3.00 | 3.00 |
| | | *Nos. 746-749 (4)* | 8.05 | 7.75 |

For surcharge see No. 861.

Snail Shells A174a

Designs: 21t, Rhynchotrochus weigmani. 40t, Forcartia globula, Canefriula azonata. 50t, Planispira deaniana. 80t, Papuina chancel, Papuina xanthocheila.

**1991, Mar. 6 Litho. *Perf. 14x14½***

| | | | | |
|---|---|---|---|---|
| **750** | A174a | 21t multicolored | 1.00 | .65 |
| **751** | A174a | 40t multicolored | 1.60 | 1.10 |
| **752** | A174a | 50t multicolored | 2.25 | 2.25 |
| **753** | A174a | 80t multicolored | 3.25 | 3.25 |
| | | *Nos. 750-753 (4)* | 8.10 | 7.25 |

For surcharge see No. 864.

A175

A176

1t, Ptiloris magnificus. 5t, Loria loriae. 10t, Cnemophilus macgregorii. 20t, Parotia wahnesi. 21t, Manucodia chalybata. 30t, Paradisaea decora. 40t, Loboparadisea sericea. 45t, Cicinnurus regius. 50t, Paradigalla brevicauda. 60t, Parotia carolae. 90t, Paradisaea guilielmi. 1k, Diphyllodes magnificus. 2k, Lophorina superba. 5k, Phonygammus keraudrenii. 10k, Paradisaea minor.

**1991-94 Litho. *Perf. 14½***

| | | | | |
|---|---|---|---|---|
| **755** | A175 | 1t multicolored | .25 | .25 |
| **756** | A175 | 5t multicolored | .25 | .25 |
| **757** | A175 | 10t multicolored | .25 | .25 |
| **758** | A175 | 20t multicolored | .45 | .45 |
| **759** | A175 | 21t multicolored | .50 | .50 |
| **760** | A175 | 30t multicolored | .70 | .70 |
| **761** | A175 | 40t multicolored | .90 | .90 |
| **762** | A175 | 45t multicolored | 2.25 | 1.10 |
| **763** | A175 | 50t multicolored | 1.25 | 1.25 |
| **764** | A175 | 60t multicolored | 3.75 | 1.40 |
| **765** | A175 | 90t multicolored | 3.75 | 2.10 |
| **766** | A175 | 1k multicolored | 2.25 | 2.25 |
| **767** | A175 | 2k multicolored | 4.10 | 4.50 |
| *a.* | | Strip of 4, #761, 763, 766-767 + label | 9.00 | 9.00 |
| **768** | A175 | 5k multicolored | 10.00 | 10.00 |

***Perf. 13***

| | | | | |
|---|---|---|---|---|
| **769** | A176 | 10k multicolored | 20.00 | 20.00 |
| | | *Nos. 755-769 (15)* | 50.65 | 45.90 |

No. 767a for Hong Kong '94 and sold for 4k.

Stamps in No. 767a do not have "1992 BIRD OF PARADISE" at bottom of design.

Issued: 21t, 45t, 60t, 90t, 3/25/92; 5t, 40t, 50t, 1k, 2k, 9/2/92; 1t, 10t, 20t, 30t, 5k, 1993; 10k, 5/1/91; No. 767a, 2/18/94.

For surcharges see #878A, 878C.

Large T — A176a

**1993 Litho. *Perf. 14½***

| | | | | |
|---|---|---|---|---|
| **770A** | A176a | 21T like #759 | 1.50 | .75 |
| **770B** | A176a | 45T like #762 | 3.00 | 1.60 |
| **770C** | A176a | 60T like #764 | 3.50 | 3.50 |
| **770D** | A176a | 90T like #765 | 4.25 | *5.25* |
| | | *Nos. 770A-770D (4)* | 12.25 | 11.10 |

Originally scheduled for release on Feb. 19, 1992, #770A-770D were withdrawn when the denomination was found to have an upper case "T." Corrected versions with a lower case "T" are #759, 762, 764-765. A quantity of the original stamps appeared in the market and to prevent speculation in these items, the Postal Administration of Papua New Guinea released the stamps with the upper case "T."

For surcharges see #878B, 878D.

1991 South Pacific Games A177

**1991, June 26 Litho. *Perf. 13***

| | | | | |
|---|---|---|---|---|
| **771** | A177 | 21t Cricket | 2.50 | .80 |
| **772** | A177 | 40t Running | 2.10 | 1.60 |
| **773** | A177 | 50t Baseball | 2.50 | 2.50 |
| **774** | A177 | 80t Rugby | 4.75 | *6.00* |
| | | *Nos. 771-774 (4)* | 11.85 | 10.90 |

Anglican Church in Papua New Guinea, Cent. A178

Churches: 21t, Cathedral of St. Peter & St. Paul, Dogura. 40t, Kaieta Shrine, Anglican landing site. 80t, First thatched chapel, modawa tree.

**1991, Aug. 7 Litho. *Perf. 14½***

| | | | | |
|---|---|---|---|---|
| **775** | A178 | 21t multicolored | 1.00 | .70 |
| **776** | A178 | 40t multicolored | 2.00 | 2.00 |
| **777** | A178 | 80t multicolored | 3.50 | 3.50 |
| | | *Nos. 775-777 (3)* | 6.50 | 6.20 |

Traditional Headdresses A179

Designs: 21t, Rambutso, Manus Province. 40t, Marawaka, Eastern Highlands. 50t, Tufi, Oro Province. 80t, Sina Sina, Simbu Province.

**1991, Oct. 16 Litho. Perf. 13**

| | | | | |
|---|---|---|---|---|
| **778** | A179 21t multicolored | .95 | .60 |
| **779** | A179 40t multicolored | 1.75 | 1.75 |
| **780** | A179 50t multicolored | 2.00 | 2.00 |
| **781** | A179 80t multicolored | 2.75 | *4.25* |
| | *Nos. 778-781 (4)* | 7.45 | 8.60 |

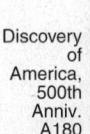

Discovery of America, 500th Anniv. A180

**1992, Apr. 15 Litho. Perf. 14**

| | | | |
|---|---|---|---|
| **782** | A180 21t Nina | .70 | .50 |
| **783** | A180 45t Pinta | 1.75 | 1.10 |
| **784** | A180 60t Santa Maria | 2.10 | 2.10 |
| **785** | A180 90t Columbus, ships | 3.00 | *3.50* |
| *a.* | Souvenir sheet of 2, #784-785 | 7.00 | 7.00 |
| | *Nos. 782-785 (4)* | 7.55 | 7.20 |

World Columbian Stamp Expo '92, Chicago. Issue date: No. 785a, June 3.

A181

Papuan Gulf Artifacts: 21t, Canoe prow shield, Bamu. 45t. Skull rack, Kerewa. 60t, Ancestral figure, Era River. 90t, Gope (spirit) board, Urama.

**1992, June 3 Litho. Perf. 14**

| | | | |
|---|---|---|---|
| **786** | A181 21t multicolored | .75 | .55 |
| **787** | A181 45t multicolored | 1.50 | 1.25 |
| **788** | A181 60t multicolored | 1.75 | 1.60 |
| **789** | A181 90t multicolored | 2.75 | 2.75 |
| | *Nos. 786-789 (4)* | 6.75 | 6.15 |

A182

Soldiers from: 21t, Papuan Infantry Battalion. 45t, Australian Militia. 60t, Japanese Nankai Force. 90t, US Army.

**1992, July 22 Litho. Perf. 14**

| | | | |
|---|---|---|---|
| **790** | A182 21t multicolored | .95 | .60 |
| **791** | A182 45t multicolored | 1.90 | 1.25 |
| **792** | A182 60t multicolored | 2.75 | 2.10 |
| **793** | A182 90t multicolored | 3.50 | 3.50 |
| | *Nos. 790-793 (4)* | 9.10 | 7.45 |

World War II, 50th anniv.

Flowering Trees — A183

21t, Hibiscus tiliaceus. 45t, Castanospermum australe. 60t, Cordia subcordata. 90t, Acacia auriculiformis.

**1992, Oct. 28 Litho. Perf. 14**

| | | | |
|---|---|---|---|
| **794** | A183 21t multicolored | 1.00 | .60 |
| **795** | A183 45t multicolored | 2.10 | 1.25 |
| **796** | A183 60t multicolored | 3.50 | 2.40 |
| **797** | A183 90t multicolored | 4.25 | 4.25 |
| | *Nos. 794-797 (4)* | 10.85 | 8.50 |

Mammals A184

21t, Myoictis melas. 45t, Microperoryctes longicauda. 60t, Mallomys rothschildi. 90t, Pseudocheirus forbesi.

**1993, Apr. 7 Litho. Perf. 14**

| | | | |
|---|---|---|---|
| **798** | A184 21t multicolored | .70 | .50 |
| **799** | A184 45t multicolored | 1.30 | 1.20 |
| **800** | A184 60t multicolored | 1.90 | 1.90 |
| **801** | A184 90t multicolored | 2.60 | 2.60 |
| | *Nos. 798-801 (4)* | 6.50 | 6.20 |

Small Birds — A185

21t, Clytomyias insignis. 45t, Pitta superba. 60t, Rhagologus leucostigma. 90t, Toxorhamphus poliopterus.

**1993, June 9 Litho. Perf. 14**

| | | | |
|---|---|---|---|
| **802** | A185 21t multicolored | .85 | .50 |
| **803** | A185 45t multicolored | 1.40 | 1.10 |
| **804** | A185 60t multicolored | 2.00 | 2.00 |
| **805** | A185 90t multicolored | 2.75 | 2.75 |
| | *Nos. 802-805 (4)* | 7.00 | 6.35 |

**Nos. 802-805 Redrawn with Taipei '93 emblem in Blue and Yellow**

**1993, Aug. 13 Litho. Perf. 14**

| | | | |
|---|---|---|---|
| **806** | A185 21t multicolored | 1.10 | .45 |
| **807** | A185 45t multicolored | 2.10 | 1.15 |
| **808** | A185 60t multicolored | 2.40 | 2.40 |
| **809** | A185 90t multicolored | 2.75 | *4.50* |
| | *Nos. 806-809 (4)* | 8.35 | 8.50 |

Freshwater Fish A186

Designs: 21t, Iriatherina werneri. 45t, Tateurndina ocellicauda. 60t, Melanotaenia affinis. 90t, Pseudomugil connieae.

**1993, Sept. 29 Litho. Perf. 14x14½**

| | | | |
|---|---|---|---|
| **810** | A186 21t multicolored | 1.10 | .70 |
| **811** | A186 45t multicolored | 2.10 | 1.40 |
| **812** | A186 60t multicolored | 2.50 | 2.50 |
| **813** | A186 90t multicolored | 3.50 | 3.50 |
| | *Nos. 810-813 (4)* | 9.20 | 8.10 |

For surcharges see Nos. 876-878.

Air Niugini, 20th Anniv. A187

**1993, Oct. 27 Perf. 14**

| | | | |
|---|---|---|---|
| **814** | A187 21t DC3 | 1.10 | .65 |
| **815** | A187 45t F27 | 2.50 | 1.25 |
| **816** | A187 60t Dash 7 | 3.00 | 3.00 |
| **817** | A187 90t Airbus A310-300 | 3.50 | *4.75* |
| | *Nos. 814-817 (4)* | 10.10 | 9.65 |

Souvenir Sheet

Paradisaea Rudolphi — A188

**1993, Sept. 29 Litho. Perf. 14**

| | | | |
|---|---|---|---|
| **818** | A188 2k multicolored | 11.50 | 11.50 |

Bangkok '93.

Huon Tree Kangaroo — A189

21t, Domesticated joey. 45t, Adult male. 60t, Female, joey in pouch. 90t, Adolescent.

**1994, Jan. 19 Litho. Perf. 14½**

| | | | |
|---|---|---|---|
| **819** | A189 21t multicolored | .75 | .65 |
| **820** | A189 45t multicolored | 1.60 | 1.25 |
| **821** | A189 60t multicolored | 2.25 | 2.25 |
| **822** | A189 90t multicolored | 3.25 | *3.75* |
| | *Nos. 819-822 (4)* | 7.85 | 7.90 |

**No. 661 Surcharged**

No. 671 Surcharged

**Perfs. and Printing Methods as Before**

**1994, Mar. 23**

| | | | |
|---|---|---|---|
| **823** | A153 21t on 35t multi | *15.00* | .80 |
| **824** | A154 1.20k on 40t multi | *4.50* | 1.75 |

No. 824 exists with double surcharge. Other varieties may exist.

Artifacts — A190

Designs: 1t, Hagen ceremonial axe, Western Highlands. 2t, Telefomin war shield, West Sepik. 20t, Head mask, Gulf of Papua. 21t, Kanganaman stool, East Sepik. 45t, Trobriand lime gourd, Milne Bay. 60t, Yuat River flute stopper, East Sepik. 90t, Tami island dish, Morobe. 1k, Kundu drum, Ramu River estuary. 5k, Gogodala dance mask, Western Province. 10k, Malanggan mask, New Ireland.

**1994-95 Litho. Perf. 14½**

| | | | |
|---|---|---|---|
| **825** | A190 1t multicolored | .25 | .25 |
| **826** | A190 2t multicolored | .25 | .25 |
| **828** | A190 20t multicolored | .35 | .35 |
| **829** | A190 21t multicolored | .35 | .35 |
| **833** | A190 45t multicolored | .80 | .80 |
| **835** | A190 60t multicolored | 1.10 | 1.10 |
| **836** | A190 90t multicolored | 1.65 | 1.65 |
| **837** | A190 1k multicolored | 5.00 | 3.00 |
| **839** | A190 5k multicolored | 9.00 | 9.00 |
| **840** | A190 10k multicolored | 15.00 | 15.00 |
| | *Nos. 825-840 (10)* | 33.75 | 31.75 |

Issued: 21, 45, 60, 90t, 3/23; 1, 2, 20t, 5k, 6/29/94; 1k, 10k, 4/12/95.

This is an expanding set. Numbers may change.

Classic Cars A191

**1994, May 11 Litho. Perf. 14**

| | | | |
|---|---|---|---|
| **841** | A191 21t Model T Ford | .80 | .65 |
| **842** | A191 45t Chevrolet 490 | 1.50 | 1.15 |
| **843** | A191 60t Baby Austin | 2.25 | 2.25 |
| **844** | A191 90t Willys Jeep | 3.00 | 3.00 |
| | *Nos. 841-844 (4)* | 7.55 | 7.05 |

PHILAKOREA '94 — A192

Tree kangaroos: 90t, Dendrolagus inustus. 1.20k, Dendrolagus dorianus.

**1994, Aug. 10 Litho. Perf. 14**

| | | | |
|---|---|---|---|
| **845** | A192 Sheet of 2, #a.-b. | 8.00 | 8.00 |

Moths A193

Designs: 21t, Daphnis hypothous pallescens. 45t, Tanaorhinus unipuncta. 60t, Neodiphthera sciron. 90t, Parotis maginata.

**1994, Oct. 26 Litho. Perf. 14**

| | | | |
|---|---|---|---|
| **846** | A193 21t multicolored | .60 | .50 |
| **847** | A193 45t multicolored | 1.50 | 1.00 |
| **848** | A193 60t multicolored | 1.75 | 1.75 |
| **849** | A193 90t multicolored | 3.00 | 3.00 |
| | *Nos. 846-849 (4)* | 6.85 | 6.25 |

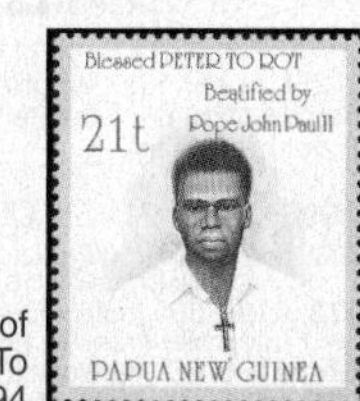

Beatification of Peter To Rot — A194

No. 850, Peter To Rot. No. 851, Pope John Paul II.

**1995, Jan. 11 Litho. Perf. 14**

| | | | |
|---|---|---|---|
| **850** | A194 21t multi | .80 | .80 |
| **851** | A194 1k on 90t multi | 4.50 | 4.50 |
| *a.* | Pair, #850-851 + label | 6.50 | 6.50 |

No. 851 was not issued without surcharge. For surcharge see No. 1008.

Tourism A195

#852, Cruising. #853, Handicrafts. #854, Jet. #855, Resorts. #856, Trekking adventure. #857, White-water rafting. #858, Boat, diver. #859, Divers, sunken plane.

**1995, Jan. 11**

| | | | | |
|---|---|---|---|---|
| 852 | A195 | 21t multicolored | .80 | .80 |
| 853 | A195 | 21t multicolored | .80 | .80 |
| a. | | Pair, #852-853 | 2.25 | 2.25 |
| 854 | A195 | 50t on 45t multi | 2.00 | 2.00 |
| 855 | A195 | 50t on 45t multi | 2.00 | 2.00 |
| a. | | Pair, #854-855 | 5.00 | 5.00 |
| 856 | A195 | 65t on 60t multi | 2.60 | 2.60 |
| a. | | "65t" omitted | 37.50 | |
| 857 | A195 | 65t on 60t multi | 2.60 | 2.60 |
| a. | | Pair, #856-857 | 6.00 | 6.00 |
| 858 | A195 | 1k on 90t multi | 4.00 | 4.00 |
| 859 | A195 | 1k on 90t multi | 4.00 | 4.00 |
| a. | | Pair, #858-859 | 9.25 | 9.25 |
| | | *Nos. 852-859 (8)* | 18.80 | 18.80 |

Nos. 854-859 were not issued without surcharge.

**Nos. 662, 722, 730, 732, 734, 736, 738, 740-741, 747, 753, 762, 765, 770B, 770D Surcharged**

Thick "t" in Surcharge

**1994** ***Perfs., Etc. as Before***

| | | | | |
|---|---|---|---|---|
| 860 | A167 | 5t on 35t #722 | 5.75 | 1.00 |
| 861 | A174 | 5t on 35t #747 | *27.50* | *17.50* |
| 862 | A172 | 10t on 35t #740 | *24.00* | *16.00* |
| 863 | A172 | 10t on 35t #741 | *17.50* | *6.50* |
| 864 | A174a | 21t on 80t #753 | *75.00* | *3.50* |
| 866 | A169 | 50t on 35t #730 | *35.00* | *17.50* |
| 867 | A171 | 50t on 35t #736 | *80.00* | *50.00* |
| a. | | Inverted surcharge | 650.00 | |
| 868 | A153 | 65t on 70t #662 | 4.00 | 1.75 |
| 869 | A170 | 65t on 70t #734 | 4.00 | 1.75 |
| 870 | A169 | 1k on 70t #732 | *20.00* | *6.50* |
| 871 | A171 | 1k on 70t #738 | 27.50 | 2.50 |
| | | *Nos. 860-871 (11)* | *320.25* | *124.50* |

Size, style and location of surcharge varies.

No. 861 exists in pair, one without surcharge. Other varieties exist.

Issued: #862, 8/23/94; #864, 8/28/94; #861, 863, 864, 10/3/94; #860, 871, 10/6/94; #866-868, 869-870, 11/28/94.

Mushrooms A196

25t, Lentinus umbrinus. 50t, Amanita hemibapha. 65t, Boletellus emodensis. 1k, Ramaria zippellii.

**1995, June 21** **Litho.** ***Perf. 14***

| | | | | |
|---|---|---|---|---|
| 872 | A196 | 25t multicolored | .80 | .60 |
| | | Complete booklet, 10 #872 | 15.00 | |
| 873 | A196 | 50t multicolored | 1.50 | 1.50 |
| | | Complete booklet, 10 #873 | 22.50 | |
| 874 | A196 | 65t multicolored | 1.90 | 1.90 |
| 875 | A196 | 1k multicolored | 3.00 | 3.00 |
| | | *Nos. 872-875 (4)* | 7.20 | 7.00 |

**1996** **Litho.** ***Perf. 12***

| | | | | |
|---|---|---|---|---|
| 875A | A196 | 25t like #872 | 2.25 | 2.25 |

No. 875A has a taller vignette, a smaller typeface for the description, denomination, and country name and does not have a date inscription like #872.

**Nos. 876-878 Surcharged Thick "t"**
**Nos. 878A-878D Surcharged Thin "t"**

Thin "t" in Srch.

See illustration above #860.

**1995** **Litho.** ***Perf. 14x14½***

| | | | | |
|---|---|---|---|---|
| 876 | A186 | 21t on 45t #811 | 1.00 | .35 |
| 877 | A186 | 21t on 60t #812 | 3.00 | 1.75 |
| 878 | A186 | 21t on 90t #813 | 1.00 | .70 |
| 878A | A175 | 21t on 45t #762 | 4.00 | .70 |
| 878B | A176a | 21t on 45T #770B | 11.00 | 1.75 |
| 878C | A175 | 21t on 90t #765 | 4.00 | .70 |
| 878D | A176a | 21t on 90T #770D | 11.00 | 1.75 |
| | | *Nos. 876-878D (7)* | 35.00 | 7.70 |

Nos. 878A-878D exist with thick surcharge. This printing of 3200 each does not seem to have seen much, if any, public sale. Value, $10 to $150 each.

Nos. 878A, 878C dated 1993. Nos. 878B, 878D dated 1992. Nos. 878A, 878C exist dated 1992.

Issued: Nos. 876-878, 6/20; Nos. 878A-878B, 5/16; No. 878C, 3/27; No. 878D, 4/25.

Independence, 20th Anniv. — A197

Designs: 50t, 1k, "20" emblem.

**1995, Aug. 30** ***Perf. 14***

| | | | | |
|---|---|---|---|---|
| 879 | A197 | 21t shown | .65 | .65 |
| 880 | A197 | 50t blue & multi | 1.40 | 1.40 |
| 881 | A197 | 1k green & multi | 2.75 | 2.75 |
| | | *Nos. 879-881 (3)* | 4.80 | 4.80 |

Souvenir Sheet

Singapore '95 — A198

Orchids: a, 21t, Dendrobium rigidifolium. b, 45t, Dendrobium convolutum. c, 60t, Dendrobium spectabile. d, 90t, Dendrobium tapiniense.

**1995, Aug. 30** **Litho.** ***Perf. 14***

| | | | | |
|---|---|---|---|---|
| 882 | A198 | Sheet of 4, #a.-d. | 6.00 | 6.00 |

No. 882 sold for 3k.

Souvenir Sheet

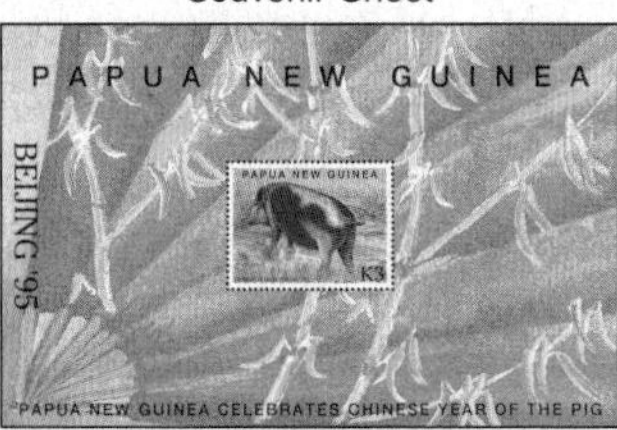


New Year 1995 (Year of the Boar) — A199

**1995, Sept. 14**

| | | | | |
|---|---|---|---|---|
| 883 | A199 | 3k multicolored | 7.50 | 7.50 |

Beijing '95.

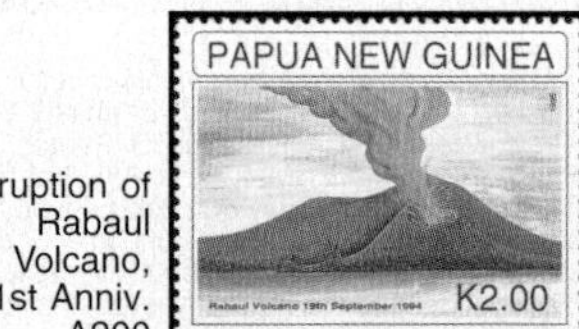


Eruption of Rabaul Volcano, 1st Anniv. A200

**1995, Sept. 19**

| | | | | |
|---|---|---|---|---|
| 884 | A200 | 2k multicolored | 4.00 | 4.00 |

Crabs A201

**1995, Oct. 25** **Litho.** ***Perf. 14***

| | | | | |
|---|---|---|---|---|
| 885 | A201 | 21t Zosimus aeneus | .70 | .55 |
| 886 | A201 | 50t Cardisoma carnifex | 1.40 | 1.40 |
| 887 | A201 | 65t Uca tetragonon | 1.90 | 1.90 |
| 888 | A201 | 1k Eriphia sebana | 2.75 | 2.75 |
| | | *Nos. 885-888 (4)* | 6.75 | 6.60 |

For surcharge see #939B.

Parrots — A202

Designs: 25t, Psittrichas fulgidas. 50t, Trichoglossus haemotodus. 65t, Alisterus chloropterus. 1k, Aprosmictus erythropterus.

**1996, Jan. 17** **Litho.** ***Perf. 12***

| | | | | |
|---|---|---|---|---|
| 889 | A202 | 25t multicolored | 1.75 | .60 |
| 890 | A202 | 50t multicolored | 2.50 | 1.05 |
| 891 | A202 | 65t multicolored | 3.00 | 2.25 |
| 892 | A202 | 1k multicolored | 3.75 | 3.75 |
| | | *Nos. 889-892 (4)* | 11.00 | 7.65 |

Beetles — A203

Designs: 25t, Lagriomorpha indigacea. 50t, Eupholus geoffroyi. 65t, Promechus pulcher. 1k, Callistola pulchra.

**1996, Mar. 20** **Litho.** ***Perf. 12***

| | | | | |
|---|---|---|---|---|
| 893 | A203 | 25t multicolored | .65 | .65 |
| 894 | A203 | 50t multicolored | 1.30 | 1.30 |
| 895 | A203 | 65t multicolored | 1.70 | 1.70 |
| 896 | A203 | 1k multicolored | 2.60 | 2.60 |
| | | *Nos. 893-896 (4)* | 6.25 | 6.25 |

Souvenir Sheet

Zhongshan Memorial Hall, Guangzhou, China — A204

**1996, Apr. 22** **Litho.** ***Perf. 14***

| | | | | |
|---|---|---|---|---|
| 897 | A204 | 70t multicolored | 2.50 | 2.50 |

CHINA '96, 9th Asian Intl. Philatelic Exhibition.

1996 Summer Olympics, Atlanta A205

**1996, July 24** **Litho.** ***Perf. 12***

| | | | | |
|---|---|---|---|---|
| 898 | A205 | 25t Shooting | .45 | .45 |
| 899 | A205 | 50t Track | .85 | .85 |
| 900 | A205 | 65t Weight lifting | 1.50 | 1.50 |
| 901 | A205 | 1k Boxing | 2.10 | 2.10 |
| | | *Nos. 898-901 (4)* | 4.90 | 4.90 |

Olymphilex '96.

Radio, Cent. A206

25t, Air traffic control. 50t, Commercial broadcasting. 65t, Gerehu earth station. 1k, 1st transmission in Papua New Guinea.

**1996, Sept. 11** **Litho.** ***Perf. 12***

| | | | | |
|---|---|---|---|---|
| 902 | A206 | 25t multicolored | .40 | .40 |
| 903 | A206 | 50t multicolored | .85 | .85 |
| 904 | A206 | 65t multicolored | 1.10 | 1.10 |
| 905 | A206 | 1k multicolored | 1.60 | 1.60 |
| | | *Nos. 902-905 (4)* | 3.95 | 3.95 |

Souvenir Sheet

Taipei '96, 10th Asian Intl. Philatelic Exhibition — A207

a, Dr. Sun Yat-sen (1866-1925). b, Dr. John Guise (1914-91).

**1996, Oct. 16** **Litho.** ***Perf. 14***

| | | | | |
|---|---|---|---|---|
| 906 | A207 | 65t Sheet of 2, #a.-b. | 4.50 | 4.50 |

Flowers A208

Designs: 1t, Hibiscus rosa-sinensis. 5t, Bougainvillea spectabilis. 65t, Plumeria rubra. 1k, Mucuna novo-guineensis.

**1996, Nov. 27** **Litho.** ***Perf. 14***

| | | | | |
|---|---|---|---|---|
| 907 | A208 | 1t multicolored | .40 | .25 |
| 908 | A208 | 5t multicolored | .40 | .25 |
| 909 | A208 | 65t multicolored | 1.40 | 1.40 |
| 910 | A208 | 1k multicolored | 2.10 | 2.10 |
| | | *Nos. 907-910 (4)* | 4.30 | 4.00 |

Souvenir Sheet

Oxen and Natl. Flag — A209

**1997, Feb. 3** **Litho.** ***Perf. 14***

| | | | | |
|---|---|---|---|---|
| 911 | A209 | 1.50k multicolored | 3.75 | 3.75 |

Hong Kong '97.

Boat Prows A210

**1997, Mar. 19 Litho. *Perf. 14½x14***

**912** A210 25t Gogodala .35 .35
**913** A210 50t East New Britain .75 .75
**914** A210 65t Trobriand Island 1.10 1.10
**915** A210 1k Walomo 1.60 1.60
*Nos. 912-915 (4)* 3.80 3.80

Queen Elizabeth II and Prince Philip, 50th Wedding Anniv. — A211

#916, Princess Anne, polo players. #917, Queen up close. #918, Prince in riding attire. #919, Queen, another person riding horses. #920, Grandsons riding horses, Prince waving. #921, Queen waving, riding pony.
2k, Queen, Prince riding in open carriage.

**1997, June 25 Litho. *Perf. 13½***

**916** A211 25t multicolored .50 .50
**917** A211 25t multicolored .50 .50
*a.* Pair, #916-917 1.25 1.25
**918** A211 50t multicolored 1.00 1.00
**919** A211 50t multicolored 1.00 1.00
*a.* Pair, #918-919 2.50 2.50
**920** A211 1k multicolored 1.75 1.75
**921** A211 1k multicolored 1.75 1.75
*a.* Pair, #920-921 4.00 4.00
*Nos. 916-921 (6)* 6.50 6.50

**Souvenir Sheet**

**922** A211 2k multicolored 3.75 3.75

Souvenir Sheet

Air Niugini, First Flight, Port Moresby-Osaka — A212

**1997, July 19 Litho. *Perf. 12***

**923** A212 3k multicolored 6.00 6.00

1997 Pacific Year of Coral Reef A213

Designs: 25t, Pocillopora woodjonesi. 50t, Subergorgia mollis. 65t, Oxypora glabra. 1k, Turbinaria reinformis.

**1997, Aug. 27 Litho. *Perf. 12***

**924** A213 25t multicolored .50 .50
**925** A213 50t multicolored 1.00 1.00
**926** A213 65t multicolored 1.50 1.50
**927** A213 1k multicolored 1.90 1.90
*Nos. 924-927 (4)* 4.90 4.90

Flowers — A214

Designs: 10t, Thunbergia fragrans. 20t, Caesalpinia pulcherrima. 25t, Hoya. 30t, Heliconia. 50t, Amomum goliathensis.

**1997, Nov. 26 Litho. *Perf. 12***

**928** A214 10t multicolored .60 .40
**929** A214 20t multicolored .80 .70
**930** A214 25t multicolored 1.00 .90
**931** A214 30t multicolored 1.25 1.25
**932** A214 50t multicolored 2.00 1.40
*Nos. 928-932 (5)* 5.65 4.65

Birds A215

Designs: 25t, Tyto tenebricosa. 50t, Aepypodius arfakianus. 65t, Accipiter poliocephalus. 1k, Zonerodius heliosylus.

**1998, Jan. 28 Litho. *Perf. 12***

**933** A215 25t multicolored 1.40 .75
**934** A215 50t multicolored 1.75 1.40
**935** A215 65t multicolored 2.75 2.75
**936** A215 1k multicolored 3.75 *4.25*
*Nos. 933-936 (4)* 9.65 9.15

**Diana, Princess of Wales (1961-97)**
Common Design Type

Designs: a, In beige colored dress. b, In violet dress with lace collar. c, Wearing plaid jacket. d, Holding flowers.

**1998, Apr. 29 Litho. *Perf. 14½x14***

**937** CD355 1k Sheet of 4, #a.-d. 6.50 6.50

No. 937 sold for 4k + 50t with surtax from international sales being donated to the Princess Diana Memorial fund and surtax from national sales being donated to designated local charity.

Mother Teresa (1910-97) A216

**1998, Apr. 29 *Perf. 14½***

**938** A216 65t With child 1.25 1.25
**939** A216 1k shown 1.90 1.90
*a.* Pair, #938-939 4.00 4.00

No. 887 Surcharged

**1998, May 28 Litho. *Perf. 14***

**939B** A201 25t on 65t multi 1.10 1.10

Moths A217

25t, Daphnis hypothous pallescens. 50t, Theretra polistratus. 65t, Psilogramma casurina. 1k, Meganoton hyloicoides.

**1998, June 17 Litho. *Perf. 14***

**940** A217 25t multicolored .55 .55
**941** A217 50t multicolored .90 .90
**942** A217 65t multicolored 1.40 1.40
**943** A217 1k multicolored 1.90 1.90
*Nos. 940-943 (4)* 4.75 4.75

A218

First Orchid Spectacular '98: 25t, Coelogyne fragrans. 50t, Den. cuthbertsonii. 65t, Den. vexillarius. 1k, Den. finisterrae.

**1998, Sept. 15 Litho. *Perf. 14***

**944** A218 25t multicolored .60 .60
**945** A218 50t multicolored 1.00 1.00
**946** A218 65t multicolored 1.50 1.50
**947** A218 1k multicolored 2.25 2.25
*Nos. 944-947 (4)* 5.35 5.35

A219

Sea Kayaking World Cup, Manus Island: 25t, Couple in kayak. 50t, Competitor running through Loniu Caves. 65t, Man standing in boat with sail, man seated in kayak. 1k, Competitor in kayak, bird of paradise silhouette.

**1998, Oct. 5 Litho. *Perf. 14***

**948** A219 25t multicolored .60 .60
**949** A219 50t multicolored 1.00 1.00
**950** A219 65t multicolored 1.50 1.50
**951** A219 1k multicolored 2.25 2.25
*Nos. 948-951 (4)* 5.35 5.35

1998 Commonwealth Games, Kuala Lumpur — A220

**1998, Sept. 30 Litho. *Perf. 14***

**952** A220 25t Weight lifting .40 .40
**953** A220 50t Lawn bowls .70 .70
**954** A220 65t Rugby .95 .95
**955** A220 1k Squash 1.40 1.40
*Nos. 952-955 (4)* 3.45 3.45

Christmas A221

Designs: 25t, Infant in manger. 50t, Mother breastfeeding infant. 65t, "Wise men" in traditional masks, headdresses looking at infant. 1k, Map of Papua New Guinea.

**1998, Nov. 18 Litho. *Perf. 14***

**956** A221 25t multicolored .35 .35
**957** A221 50t multicolored .70 .70
**958** A221 65t multicolored .95 .95
**959** A221 1k multicolored 1.60 1.60
*Nos. 956-959 (4)* 3.60 3.60

Australia '99, World Stamp Expo — A222

Ships: 25t, "Boudeuse," 1768. 50t, "Neva," 1876. 65t, "Merrir England," 1889. 1k, "Samoa," 1884.
#964: a, 5t, Rattlesnake, 1849. b, 10t, Swallow, 1767. c, 15t, Roebeck, 1700. d, 20t, Blanche, 1872. e, 30t, Vitiaz, 1871. f, 40t, San Pedrico and Eabre, 1606. g, 60t, Jorge de Menesis, 1526. h, 1.20k, L'Astrolabe, 1827.

**1999, Mar. 17**

**960** A222 25t multicolored .30 .30
**961** A222 50t multicolored .65 .65
**962** A222 65t multicolored 1.05 1.05
**963** A222 1k multicolored 1.25 1.25
*Nos. 960-963 (4)* 3.25 3.25

**Sheet of 8**

**964** A222 #a.-h. 5.50 5.50

No. 964a is incorrectly inscribed "Simpson Blanche '1872."

IBRA '99, World Philatelic Exhibition, Nuremberg — A223

Exhibition emblem and: a, German New Guinea #17. b, German New Guinea #1, #2.

**1999 Litho. *Perf. 14***

**965** A223 1k Pair, #a.-b. 3.00 3.00

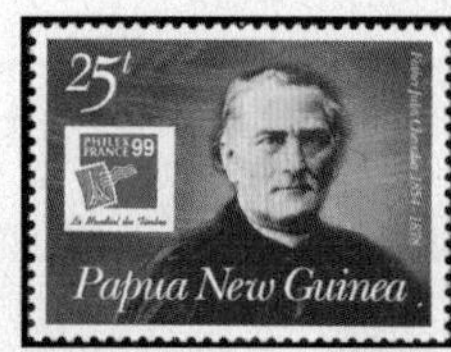


Millennium A224

Map and: 25t, Stopwatch, computer keyboard. 50t, Concentric circles. 65t, Internet page, computer user. 1k, Computers, satellite dish.

**1999 Litho. *Perf. 12¾***

**966** A224 25t multicolored .45 .25
**967** A224 50t multicolored .65 .40
**968** A224 65t multicolored 1.10 .90
**969** A224 1k multicolored 1.60 *1.75*
*Nos. 966-969 (4)* 3.80 3.30

For surcharge see No. 1010.

PhilexFrance '99 — A225

Frenchmen with historical ties to Papua New Guinea: 25t, Father Jules Chevalier. 50t, Bishop Alain-Marie. 65t, Chevalier D'Entrecasteaux. 1k, Count de Bougainville.

**1999, Mar. 2 Litho. *Perf. 12¾***

**970** A225 25t multicolored .30 .25
**971** A225 50t multicolored .55 .55
**972** A225 65t multicolored .85 .85
**973** A225 1k multicolored 1.25 *1.40*
*Nos. 970-973 (4)* 2.95 3.05

For surcharge see No. 1011.

Hiri Moale Festival A226

Designs: 25t, Clay pots, native. 50t, Hanenamo, native. 65t, Lakatoi, native. #977, 1k, Sorcerer, native.
No. 978: a, Sorcerer. b, Clay pots. c, Lakatoi.

**1999, Sept. 8 *Perf. 12¾***

**974** A226 25t multicolored .35 .30
**975** A226 50t multicolored .55 .55
**976** A226 65t multicolored .85 .85
**977** A226 1k multicolored 1.25 1.25
*Nos. 974-977 (4)* 3.00 2.95

**Souvenir Sheet**

**978** A226 1k Sheet of 3, #a.-c. 3.50 3.50

For surcharge see No. 1012.

Souvenir Sheet

Year of the Rabbit (in 1999) — A227

Color of rabbit: a, Gray. b, Tan. c, White. d, Pink.

**2000, Apr. 21 Litho. *Perf. 12¾***
**979** A227 65t Sheet of 4, #a-d 3.75 3.75

Queen Mother, 100th Birthday A228

Various photos. Color of frame: 25t, Yellow. 50t, Lilac. 65t, Green. 1k, Dull orange.

**2000, Aug. 4 *Perf. 14***
**980-983** A228 Set of 4 3.25 3.25

Shells A229

Designs: 25t, Turbo petholatus. 50t, Charonia tritonis. 65t, Cassis cornuta. 1k, Ovula ovum.

**2000, Feb. 23 Litho. *Perf. 14***
**984-987** A229 Set of 4 3.75 3.75

Independence, 25th Anniv. — A230

Designs: 25t, Shell. 50t, Bird of Paradise. 65t, Ring. 1k, Coat of arms.

**2000, June 21 *Perf. 14***
**Stamps with se-tenant label**
**988-991** A230 Set of 4 3.75 3.75
*991a* Souvenir sheet, #988-991, no labels 3.75 3.75

Strips with two stamps alternating with two different labels exist for Nos. 989 and 990.

2000 Summer Olympics, Sydney A231

Designs: 25t, Running. 50t, Swimming. 65t, Boxing. 1k, Weight lifting.

**2000, July 12**
**992-995** A231 Set of 4 3.50 3.50

For surcharge see No. 1009.

Souvenir Sheet

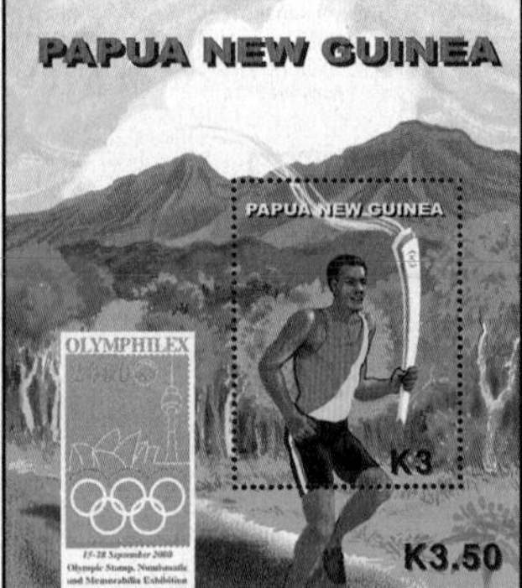

Olymphilex 2000, Sydney — A232

**2000, July 12 *Perf. 14¼***
**996** A232 3k multi 3.75 3.75

Sold for 3.50k.

Birds A233

Designs: 35t, Comb-crested jacana. 70t, Masked lapwing. 90t, White ibis. 1.40k, Black-tailed godwit.

**2001, Mar. 21 Litho. *Perf. 14***
**997-1000** A233 Set of 4 5.00 5.00

Mission Aviation Fellowship, 50th Anniv. in Papua New Guinea — A234

Designs: 35t, Cessna 170, pig, bird, Bibles. 70t, Harry Hartwig (1916-51), Auster Autocar. 90t, Pilot and Cessna 260. 1.40k, Twin Otter and plane mechanics.

**2001, Oct. 17 *Perf. 13¼x13¾***
**1001-1004** A234 Set of 4 4.50 4.50

A235

Designs: 10t, Flags, world map. 50t, Dragon, bird of paradise. 2k, Tien An Men Square, Papua New Guinea Parliament Building.

**2001, Oct. 12 Litho. *Perf. 12***
**1005-1007** A235 Set of 3 4.75 4.75

Papua New Guinea and People's Republic of China Diplomatic Relations, 25th Anniv.

Nos. 850, 968, 972, 976 and 992 Srchd.

**Methods and Perfs As Before**

**2001, Dec. 1**
**1008** A194 50t on 21t #850 2.50 1.25
*a.* Horiz. pair, 1008, 851 + central label 6.00 4.00
**1009** A231 50t on 25t #992 1.00 .50
*a.* Obliterator present, missing new denomination —
**1010** A224 50t on 65t #968 1.00 .50
**1011** A225 2.65k on 65t #972 4.00 4.00
**1012** A226 2.65k on 65t #976 4.00 4.00
*Nos. 1008-1012 (5)* 12.50 10.25

Provincial Flags A236

**2001, Dec. 12 Litho. *Perf. 14***
**1013** A236 10t Enga .45 .25
**1014** A236 15t Simbu .45 .25
**1015** A236 20t Manus .45 .25
**1016** A236 50t Central 1.10 .40
**1017** A236 2k New Ireland 3.50 2.25
**1018** A236 5k Sandaun 4.75 4.75
*Nos. 1013-1018 (6)* 10.70 8.15

For surcharge see No. 1113.

**Reign Of Queen Elizabeth II, 50th Anniv. Issue**
Common Design Type

Designs: Nos. 1019, 1023a, 1.25k, Princess Elizabeth with Queen Mother and Princess Margaret, 1941. Nos. 1020, 1023b, 1.45k, Wearing tiara, 1975. Nos. 1021, 1023c, 2k, With Princes Philip and Charles, 1951. Nos. 1022, 1023d, 2.65k, Wearing red hat. No. 1023e, 5k, 1955 portrait by Annigoni (38x50mm).

***Perf. 14¼x14½, 13¾ (#1023e)***
**2002, Feb. 6 Litho. Wmk. 373**
**With Gold Frames**
**1019** CD360 1.25k multicolored 1.20 1.20
**1020** CD360 1.45k multicolored 1.40 1.40
**1021** CD360 2k multicolored 1.90 1.90
**1022** CD360 2.65k multicolored 2.50 2.50
*Nos. 1019-1022 (4)* 7.00 7.00

**Souvenir Sheet**
**Without Gold Frames**
**1023** CD360 Sheet of 5, #a-e 7.50 7.50

**Lakatoi Type of 1901 Inscribed "Papua New Guinea"**

Frame colors: 5t, Red. 15t, Brown violet. 20t, Light blue. 1.25k, Brown. 1.45k, Green. 10k, Orange.

***Perf. 14½x14***
**2002, June 5 Litho. Unwmk.**
**Center in Brown Black**
**1024-1029** A1 Set of 6 13.00 13.00
*a.* Souvenir sheet, #1024-1029 15.00 15.00

British New Guinea stamps, cent. (in 2001).

Orchids — A237

Designs: 5t, Cadetia taylori. 30t, Dendrobium anosmum. 45t, Dendrobium bigibbum. 1.25k, Dendrobium cuthbertsonii. 1.45k, Sprianthes sinensis. 2.65k, Thelymitra carnea.
No. 1036, horiz.: a, Dendrobium bracteosum. b, Calochilus campestris. c, Anastomus oscitans. d, Thelymitra carnea, diff. e, Dendrobium macrophyllum. f, Dendrobium johnsoniae.
7k, Bulbophyllum graveolens, horiz.

**2002, Aug. 28 *Perf. 14***
**1030-1035** A237 Set of 6 8.00 8.00
**1036** A237 2k Sheet of 6, #a-f 12.00 12.00

**Souvenir Sheet**
**1037** A237 7k multi 9.00 9.00

Protected Butterflies A238

Designs: No. 1038, 50t, Ornithoptera chimaera. No. 1039, 50t, Ornithoptera goliath. 1.25k, Ornithoptera meridionalis. 1.45k, Ornithoptera paradisea. 2.65k, Ornithoptera victoriae. 5k, Ornithoptera alexandrae.

**2002, Oct. 16**
**1038-1043** A238 Set of 6 15.00 15.00

Queen Mother Elizabeth (1900-2002) — A239

No. 1044, horiz.: a, With Queen Elizabeth II (28x23mm). b, With Elizabeth and two other women (28x23mm). c, With pearl necklace visible at left (26x29mm). d, Color photograph (40x29mm). e, With pearl necklace visible at right (26x29mm). f, With man in top hat at right (28x23mm). g, With King George VI (28x23mm).
No. 1045, blue shading in UR of stamps : a, 3k, As child. b, 3k, Wearing black hat.
No. 1046, blue shading in UL of stamps: a, 3k, Wearing white hat. b, 3k, Wearing hat and brooch.

***Perf. 13¼x14¼ (#1044d), Compound x 14¼ (#1044c, 1044e) 13¼x10¾***
**2002**
**1044** A239 2k Sheet of 7, #a-g 14.00 14.00

**Souvenir Sheets**
***Perf. 14¾***
**1045-1046** A239 Set of 2 14.00 14.00

A240

United We Stand A241

**2002, Nov. 20 Litho. *Perf. 14***
**1047** A240 50t multi 1.25 1.25
**1048** A241 50t multi 1.25 1.25

No. 1048 was printed in sheets of 4.

Intl. Year of Mountains A242

Designs: 50t, Mt. Wilhelm, Papua New Guinea. 1.25k, Matterhorn, Switzerland. 1.45k, Mt. Fuji, Japan. 2.65k, Massif des Aravis, France.

**2002, Nov. 20**
**1049-1052** A242 Set of 4 6.50 6.50

Clay Pots — A243

Designs: 65t, Sago storage pot. 1k, Smoking pot. 1.50k, Water jar. 2.50k, Water jar, diff. 4k, Ridge pot.

**2003, Jan. 22**
**1053-1057** A243 Set of 5 9.50 9.50

20th World Scout Jamboree, Thailand — A244

Designs: 50t, Group of scouts. 1.25k, Two scouts seated. 1.45k, Scouts on tower. 2.65k, Two scouts standing.

**2003, Feb. 12**
**1058-1061** A244 Set of 4 8.50 8.50

A245

Various portraits of Queen Elizabeth II with background colors of: No. 1062, 65t, Purple. No. 1063, 65t, Olive green. 1.50k, Dark blue. No. 1065, 2k, Red. 2.50k, Dull green. 4k, Orange.

No. 1068, 2k — Yellow orange background with Queen: a, Without hat. b, Wearing crown and sash. c, Wearing hat with blue flowers. d, Wearing tiara. e, Wearing red dress. f, Wearing black hat.

8k, Wearing black robe, gray green background.

**2003, Apr. 30** **Litho.** ***Perf. 14***
**1062-1067** A245 Set of 6 9.50 9.50
**1068** A245 2k Sheet of 6, #a-f 10.00 10.00

**Souvenir Sheet**

**1069** A245 8k multi 7.00 7.00

Coronation of Queen Elizabeth, 50th anniv.

A246

Prince William: No. 1070, 65t, Wearing colored sports shirt. No. 1071, 65t, Wearing white shirt. 1.50k, As child. No. 1073, 2k, Wearing suit and tie, gray green background. 2.50k, Wearing plaid shirt. 4k, On polo pony.

No. 1076, 2k — Lilac background: a, As toddler. b, Wearing sunglasses. c, Wearing suit and tie (full face). d, Wearing suit and tie (profile). e, Wearing deep blue shirt. f, Wearing yellow shirt with black collar.

8k, Wearing suit and tie, gray green background, diff.

**2003, June 18**
**1070-1075** A246 Set of 6 8.50 8.50
**1076** A246 2k Sheet of 6, #a-f 9.50 9.50

**Souvenir Sheet**

**1077** A246 8k multi 7.00 7.00

Prince William, 21st birthday.

Coastal Villages A247

Designs: No. 1078, 65t, Gabagaba. No. 1079, 65t, Wanigela (Koki). 1.50k, Tubuserea. 2k, Hanuabada. 2.50k, Barakau. 4k, Porebada.

**2003, July 24**
**1078-1083** A247 Set of 6 9.50 9.50

For surcharges see Nos. 1114-1115.

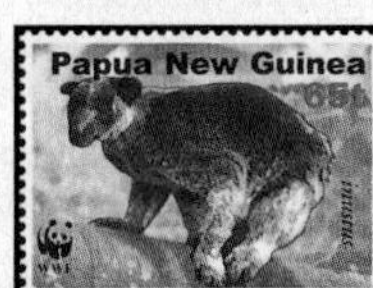

Powered Flight, Cent. A248

Designs: 65t, Orville Wright circles plane over Fort Myer, Va., 1908. 1.50k, Orville Wright pilots "Baby Grand" Belmont, 1910. No. 1086, 2.50k, Wilbur Wright holding anemometer, Pau, France, 1909. 4k, Wilbur Wright pilots Model A, Pau, France, 1909.

No. 1088, 2.50k — 1903 photos from Kitty Hawk: a, Untried airplane outside hangar. b, Rollout of airplane from hangar. c, Preparing airplane for takeoff. d, Airplane takes off.

10k, Airplane takes off, diff.

**2003, Aug. 27**
**1084-1087** A248 Set of 4 8.00 8.00
**1088** A248 Sheet of 4, #a-d 9.00 9.00

**Souvenir Sheet**

**1089** A248 10k multi 9.00 9.00

Worldwide Fund for Nature (WWF) A249

Tree kangaroos: Nos. 1090a, 1091a, Dendrolagus inustus. Nos. 1090b, 1091b, Dendrolagus matschiei. Nos. 1090c, 1091c, Dendrolagus dorianus. Nos. 1090d, 1091d, Dendrolagus goodfellowi.

**2003, Oct. 15** ***Perf. 14½x14¾***

**With White Frames**

**1090** Horiz. strip of 4 8.00 8.00
*a.* A249 65t multi .75 .75
*b.* A249 1.50k multi 1.40 1.40
*c.* A249 2.50k multi 2.25 2.25
*d.* A249 4k multi 3.25 3.25

**Without White Frames**

**1091** Sheet, 2 each #a-d 14.00 14.00
*a.* A249 65t multi .65 .65
*b.* A249 1.50k multi 1.25 1.25
*c.* A249 2.50k multi 2.00 2.00
*d.* A249 4k multi 2.75 2.75

Endangered Dolphins — A250

Designs: No. 1092, 65t, Humpback dolphin. No. 1093, 65t, Bottlenose dolphins. No. 1094, 1.50k, Bottlenose dolphin, with frame line. 2k, Irrawaddy dolphin. 2.50k, Humpback dolphin and fishermen. 4k, Irrawaddy dolphin and diver.

No. 1098, 1.50k: a, Humpback dolphin and sailboat. b, Bottlenose dolphin, without frame line. c, Bottlenose dolphins, diff. d, Irrawaddy dolphin and diver, diff. e, Irrawady dolphin, diff. f, Humpback dolphin underwater.

**2003, Nov. 19** ***Perf. 13½***
**1092-1097** A250 Set of 6 10.00 10.00
**1098** A250 1.50k Sheet of 6, #a-f 8.00 8.00

For surcharges see Nos. 1116-1117.

Freshwater Fish — A251

Designs: No. 1099, 70t, Lake Wanam rainbowfish. No. 1100, 70t, Kokoda mogurnda. 1k, Sepik grunter. 2.70k, Papuan black bass. 4.60k, Lake Tebera rainbowfish. 20k, Wichmann's mouth almighty.

**2004, Jan. 30** ***Perf. 14¼***
**1099-1104** A251 Set of 6 25.00 25.00
Complete booklet, 10 #1099 6.00
Complete booklet, 10 #1100 6.00

For surcharges see Nos. 1154-1155.

Dinosaurs A252

Designs: 70t, Ankylosaurus. 1k, Oviraptor. 2k, Tyrannosaurus. 2.65k, Gigantosaurus. 2.70k, Centrosaurus. 4.60k, Carcharodontosaurus.

No. 1111: a, Edmontonia. b, Struthiomimus. c, Psittacosaurus. d, Gastonia. e, Shunosaurus. f, Iguanodon.

7k, Afrovenator.

**2004, Feb. 25** ***Perf. 14***
**1105-1110** A252 Set of 6 11.00 11.00
**1111** A252 1.50k Sheet of 6, #a-f 8.75 8.75

**Souvenir Sheet**

**1112** A252 7k multi 6.25 6.25

**Nos. 1015, 1078, 1079, 1092 and 1093 Surcharged**

a

b

**Methods and Perfs As Before**

**2004**
**1113** A236(a) 5t on 20t #1015 .65 .65
**1114** A247(b) 70t on 65t #1078 1.25 1.25
**1115** A247(b) 70t on 65t #1079 1.50 1.50
**1116** A250(a) 70t on 65t #1092 1.50 1.50
**1117** A250(a) 70t on 65t #1093 1.25 1.25
*Nos. 1113-1117 (5)* 6.15 6.15

Issued: Nos. 1114-1115, 1/20; others, 6/2.

Orchids A253

Designs: 70t, Phalaenopsis amabilis. 1k, Phaius tankervilleae. No. 1120, 2k, Bulbophyllum macranthum. 2.65k, Dendrobium rhodostictum. 2.70k, Diplocaulobium ridleyanum. 4.60k, Spathoglottis papuana.

No. 1124, 2k: a, Dendrobium cruttwellii. b, Dendrobium coeloglossum. c, Dendrobium alaticaulinum. d, Dendrobium obtusisepalum. e, Dendrobium johnsoniae. f, Dendrobium insigne.

7k, Dendrobium biggibum.

**2004, May 19** **Litho.** ***Perf. 14***
**1118-1123** A253 Set of 6 11.00 11.00
**1124** A253 2k Sheet of 6, #a-f 10.50 10.50

**Souvenir Sheet**

**1125** A253 7k multi 6.50 6.50

Headdresses — A254

Province of headdress: No. 1126, 70t, Simbu. No. 1127, 70t, East Sepik. 2.65k, Southern Highlands. 2.70k, Western Highlands. 4.60k, Eastern Highlands. 5k, Central.

**2004, June 2**
**1126-1131** A254 Set of 6 14.00 14.00
Complete booklet, 10 #1126 6.00
Complete booklet, 10 #1127 6.00

For surcharges see Nos. 1156-1157.

2004 Summer Olympics, Athens — A255

Designs: 70t, Swimming. 2.65k, Weight lifting, vert. 2.70k, Torch race, vert. 4.60k, Poster for 1952 Helsinki Olympics, vert.

**2004, Aug. 11** ***Perf. 13¼***
**1132-1135** A255 Set of 4 10.50 10.50

National Soccer Team — A256

Various players in action: 70t, 2.65k, 2.70k, 4.60k.

**2004, Sept. 8** ***Perf. 14¼***
**1136-1139** A256 Set of 4 12.00 12.00

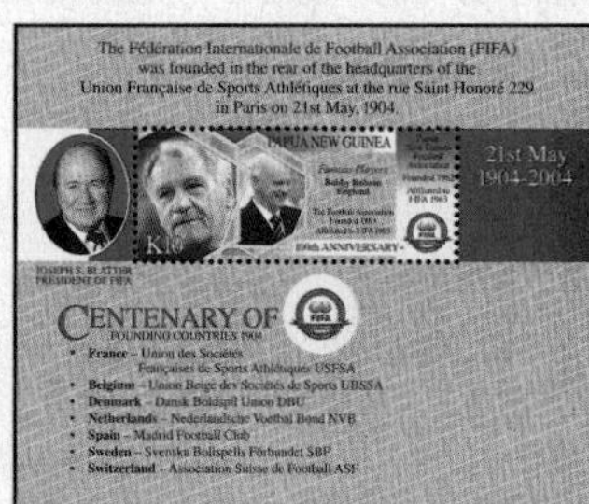

FIFA (Fédération Internationale de Football Association), Cent. — A257

No. 1140: a, Bruno Conti. b, Oliver Kahn. c, Mario Kempes. d, Bobby Moore.

10k, Bobby Robson.

**2004, Sept. 8** ***Perf. 13¼x13½***
**1140** A257 2.50k Sheet of 4, #a-d 12.00 12.00

**Souvenir Sheet**

**1141** A257 10k multi 10.00 10.00

Provincial Flags A258

Province: No. 1142, 70t, East New Britain. No. 1143, 70t, Madang. 2.65k, Eastern Highlands. 2.70k, Morobe. 4.60k, Milne Bay. 10k, East Sepik.

**2004, Oct. 20** *Perf. 14*
**1142-1147** A258 Set of 6 20.00 20.00

Shells A259

Designs: No. 1148, 70t, Phalium areola. No. 1149, 70t, Conus auratus. 2.65k, Oliva miniacea. 2.70k, Lambis chiragra. 4.60k, Conus suratensis. 10k, Architectonica perspectiva.

**2004, Nov. 17**
**1148-1153** A259 Set of 6 18.00 18.00

For surcharges see Nos. 1223-1224.

**Nos. 1099, 1100, 1126, 1127 Surcharged**

**Methods and Perfs as Before**

**2005, Jan. 3**
**1154** A251 75t on 70t #1099 1.10 1.10
**1155** A251 75t on 70t #1100 1.10 1.10
**1156** A254 75t on 70t #1126 1.10 1.10
**1157** A254 75t on 70t #1127 1.10 1.10
*Nos. 1154-1157 (4)* 4.40 4.40

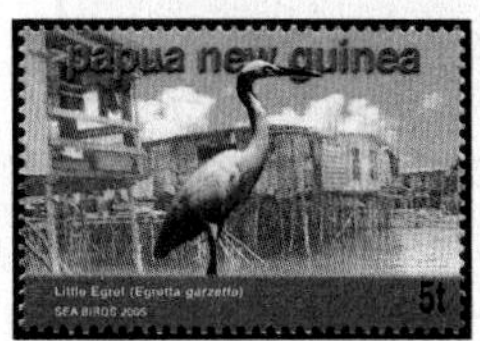
Birds A260

Designs: 5t, Little egret. No. 1159, 75t, White-faced heron. No. 1160, 75t, Nankeen night heron. 3k, Crested tern. 3.10k, Bar-tailed godwit. 5.20k, Little pied heron.

**2005, Jan. 26** **Litho.** *Perf. 14*
**1158-1163** A260 Set of 6 10.50 10.50

Rotary International, Cent. — A261

Designs: 75t, Mobilizing communities in the fight against HIV and AIDS. 3k, Barefoot child, PolioPlus and Rotary centennial emblems. 3.10k, Co-founders of first Rotary Club. 5.20k, Chicago skyline.

No. 1168, vert.: a, Silvester Schiele (1870-1945), first Rotary President. b, Paul Harris, founder. c, Children.

10k, Emblem and globe, vert.

**2005, Feb. 23** **Litho.** *Perf. 14*
**1164-1167** A261 Set of 4 9.00 9.00
**1168** A261 4k Sheet of 3, #a-c 9.00 9.00

**Souvenir Sheet**

**1169** A261 10k multi 7.50 7.50

Frangipani Varieties — A262

Designs: No. 1170, 75t, Evergreen. No. 1171, 75t, Lady in Pink. 1k, Carmine Flush. 3k, Cultivar acutifolia. 3.10k, American Beauty. 5.20k, Golden Kiss.

**2005, Apr. 6** *Perf. 12¾*
**1170-1175** A262 Set of 6 10.50 10.50

Mushrooms A263

Designs: No. 1176, 75t, Gymnopilus spectabilis. No. 1177, 75t, Melanogaster ambiguus. 3.10k, Microporus xanthopus. 5.20k, Psilocybe subcubensis.

No. 1180: a, Amanita muscaria. b, Amanita rubescens. c, Suillus luteus. d, Stropharia cubensis. e, Aseroes rubra. f, Psilocybe aucklandii.

10k, Mycena pura.

**2005, May 18**
**1176-1179** A263 Set of 4 7.50 7.50
**1180** A263 2k Sheet of 6, #a-f 9.50 9.50

**Souvenir Sheet**

**1181** A263 10k multi 7.50 7.50

Beetles A264

Designs: No. 1182, 75t, Promechus pulcher. No. 1183, 75t, Callistola pulchra. 1k, Lagriomorpha indigacea. 3k, Hellerhinus papuanus. 3.10k, Aphorina australis. 5.20k, Bothricara pulchella.

**2005, June 29** *Perf. 14*
**1182-1187** A264 Set of 6 10.00 10.00

**Souvenir Sheet**

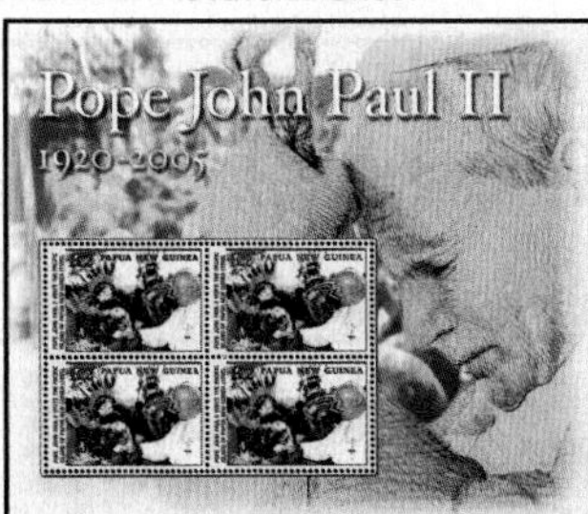
Pope John Paul II (1920-2005) — A265

No. 1188 — Denomination and country name in: a, Blue. b, Green. c, Orange. d, Red violet.

**2005, Aug. 10** **Litho.** *Perf. 12¾*
**1188** A265 2k Sheet of 4, #a-d 6.50 6.50

Provincial Flags A266

Province: No. 1189, 75t, Gulf. No. 1190, 75t, Southern Highlands. 1k, North Solomons. 3k, Oro. 3.10k, Western Highlands. 5.20k, Western.

**2005, Sept. 21** *Perf. 14*
**1189-1194** A266 Set of 6 10.00 10.00

Cats and Dogs — A267

Designs: No. 1195, 75t, Somali Rudy cat. No. 1196, 75t, Balinese Seal Lynx Point cat. 3k, Sphynx Brown Mackerel Tabby and White cat. 3.10k, Korat Blue cat. 5.20k, Bengal Brown Spotted Tabby cat.

No. 1200: a, Yorkshire terrier. b, Basenji. c, Neapolitan mastiff. d, Poodle.

10k, Boston terrier, horiz.

**2005, Nov. 2** *Perf. 12¾*
**1195-1199** A267 Set of 5 10.00 10.00
**1200** A267 2.50k Sheet of 4, #a-d 8.00 8.00

**Souvenir Sheet**

**1201** A267 10k multi 8.00 8.00

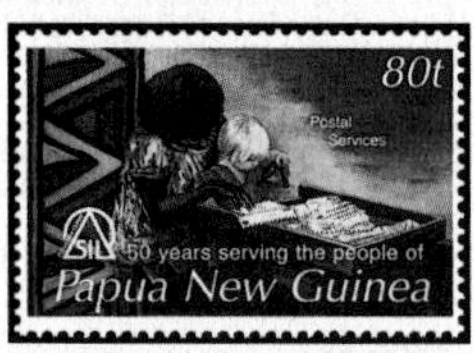
Summer Institute of Languages in Papua New Guinea, 50th Anniv. — A268

Designs: No. 1202, 80t, Postal services. No. 1203, 80t, Literacy. 1k, Jim Dean, first director. 3.20k, Tokples preschools. 3.25k, Aviation. 5.35k, Community development.

**2006, Jan. 4** **Litho.** *Perf. 13¼*
**1202-1207** A268 Set of 6 15.00 15.00

**Miniature Sheets**

Queen Elizabeth II, 80th Birthday — A269

No. 1208, 2.50k: a, Wearing polka dot dress. b, Engraving in brown from Canadian bank note. c, Engraving in blue from banknote. d, With Queen Mother.

No. 1209: a, 80t, With Pres. Bill Clinton. b, 3.20k, Dancing with Pres. Gerald Ford. c, 3.25k, With Pres. Ronald Reagan. d, 5.35k, With Pres. George W. Bush.

**2006, Feb. 22** **Litho.** *Perf. 13½*
**Sheets of 4, #a-d**
**1208-1209** A269 Set of 2 17.00 17.00

Contemporary Art — A270

Designs: 5t, Shown. No. 1211, 80t, One head. No. 1212, 80t, Two heads. 3.20k, Man wearing headdress. 3.25k, Man and woman. 5.35k, Man with beads and man with painted face.

**2006, Apr. 12** *Perf. 13¼x13½*
**1210-1215** A270 Set of 6 11.00 11.00

**Miniature Sheet**

2006 World Cup Soccer Championships, Germany — A271

No. 1216 — Player and uniform from: a, 80t, England. b, 3.20k, Germany. c, 3.25k, Argentina. d, 5.35k, Australia.

**2006, May 17** *Perf. 12*
**1216** A271 Sheet of 4, #a-d 10.00 10.00

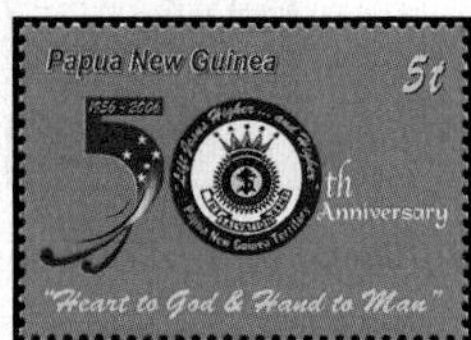
Salvation Army in Papua New Guinea, 50th Anniv. A272

Designs: 5t, Salvation Army emblem. 80t, Emblem, flags of Papua New Guinea and Salvation Army Papua New Guinea Territory. 1k, Lt. Ian Cutmore and Senior Major Keith Baker. 3.20k, Colonels, Andrew and Julie Kalai. 3.25k, Kei Geno. 5.35k, Lt. Dorothy Elphick holding baby.

**2006, June 14** *Perf. 13¼*
**1217-1222** A272 Set of 6 10.00 10.00

**Nos. 1148-1149 Surcharged**

**2006, July 5** **Litho.** *Perf. 14*
**1223** A259 80t on 70t #1148 .85 .85
**1224** A259 80t on 70t #1149 .85 .85

Butterflies A273

Designs: 80t, Delias iltis. 3.20k, Ornithoptera paradisea. 3.25k, Taenaris catops. 5.35k, Papilio ulysses autolycus.

**2006, Aug. 30** *Perf. 13¼*
**1225-1228** A273 Set of 4 11.00 11.00

Snakes
A274

Designs: 5t, Black whip snake. 80t, Papuan taipan. 2k, Smooth-scaled death adder. 3.20k, Papuan black snake. 3.25k, New Guinea small-eyed snake. 5.35k, Eastern brown snake.

**2006, Sept. 13** ***Perf. 14¼x14***
**1229-1234** A274 Set of 6 12.00 12.00

A275

Elvis Presley (1935-77) — A276

Designs: 80t, Wearing white jacket and pants. 3.20k, Wearing red shirt. 3.25k, Wearing white jacket and black bow tie. 5.35k, With guitar.

No. 1239 — Record covers: a, 80t, 50,000 Elvis Fans Can't Be Wrong. b, 3.20k, Elvis Country. c, 3.25k, His Hand in Mine. d, 5.35k, King Creole.

10k, Holding teddy bears.

***Perf. 13½, 13¼ (#1239)***
**2006, Nov. 15** **Litho.**
**1235-1238** A275 Set of 4 10.00 10.00
**1239** A276 Sheet of 4, #a-d 9.00 9.00

**Souvenir Sheet**

**1240** A275 10k multi 8.75 8.75

Tropical Fruits
A277

Designs: 5t, Mangos. No. 1242, 85t, Watermelons. No. 1243, 85t, Pineapples. No. 1244, 3.35t, Guavas. No. 1245, 3.35t, Pawpaws (papaya). 5.35t, Lemons.

**2007, Jan. 2** ***Perf. 14x14¼***
**1241-1246** A277 Set of 6 10.00 10.00

Endangered Turtles — A278

Designs: 10t, Hawksbill turtle. 35t, Flatback turtle. No. 1249, 85t, Loggerhead turtle. No. 1250, 3k, Leatherback turtle (blue violet panel). No. 1251, 3.35k, Green turtle (emerald panel). No. 1252, 5.35k, Olive Ridley turtle (tan panel).

No. 1253: a, 85t, Flatback turtle, diff. b, 3k, Leatherback turtle, diff. (olive green panel). c, 3.35k, Green turtle, diff. (olive green panel). d, 5.35k, Olive Ridley turtle, diff. (emerald panel).

**2007, Mar. 23** **Litho.** ***Perf. 13¼***
**1247-1252** A278 Set of 6 12.00 12.00

**Souvenir Sheet**

**1253** A278 Sheet of 4, #a-d 12.00 12.00

Scouting, Cent.
A279

Designs: 10t, Scouts standing at attention. 85t, Scouts carrying flag. 3.35k, Scouts and leaders at campsite. 5.35k, Scouts and leader.

10k, Lord Robert Baden-Powell, vert.

**2007, May 23** **Litho.** ***Perf. 14x14¼***
**1254-1257** A279 Set of 4 8.00 8.00
*1257a* Souvenir sheet, #1254-1257 6.50 6.50

**Souvenir Sheet**

**1257B** A279 10k multi 6.75 6.75

Law, Justice, Health and Education
A280

Inscriptions: 5t, "A Just, Safe & Secure Society for All." 30t, "Prosperity Through self-reliance." 85t, "HIV/AIDS." 3k, "Crime Reduction." 3.35k, "Infant Care & Child Immunization." 5.35k, "Minimizing Illiteracy."

**2007, July 25** ***Perf. 13¼***
**1258-1263** A280 Set of 6 8.75 8.75

A281

A282

A283

A284

A285

A286

A287

A288

A289

A290

A291

Orchids — A292

**2007, Aug. 3** **Litho.** ***Perf. 14***
**1264** Sheet of 12 +12 labels 12.00 12.00
*a.* A281 1k multi + label 1.00 1.00
*b.* A282 1k multi + label 1.00 1.00
*c.* A283 1k multi + label 1.00 1.00
*d.* A284 1k multi + label 1.00 1.00
*e.* A285 1k multi + label 1.00 1.00
*f.* A286 1k multi + label 1.00 1.00
*g.* A287 1k multi + label 1.00 1.00
*h.* A288 1k multi + label 1.00 1.00
*i.* A289 1k multi + label 1.00 1.00
*j.* A290 1k multi + label 1.00 1.00
*k.* A291 1k multi + label 1.00 1.00
*l.* A292 1k multi + label 1.00 1.00

Labels could not be personalized.

Dendrobium Conanthum, Dendrobium Lasianthera — A293

Dendrobium Conanthum — A294

Dendrobium Lasianthera "May River Red" — A295

Dendrobium Wulaiense — A296

**2007, Aug. 21** **Litho.** ***Perf. 14***
**1265** A293 85t multi + label .60 .60
**1266** A294 3k multi + label 2.10 2.10
**1267** A295 3.35k multi + label 2.40 2.40
**1268** A296 5.35k multi + label 3.75 3.75
*Nos. 1265-1268 (4)* 8.85 8.85

Nos. 1265-1268 were each issued in sheets of 20 + 20 labels. The labels illustrated are generic labels. Labels could be personalized for an additional fee.

Rotary International in Papua New Guinea, 50th Anniv. — A297

Inscriptions: 85t, Rotary's humanitarian service. 3.35k, Rotary against malaria. 5k, Rotary clubs in Papua New Guinea. 5.35k, Donations in kind.

**2007, Sept. 5** **Litho.** ***Perf. 13¼***
**1269-1272** A297 Set of 4 10.00 10.00
*1272a* Souvenir sheet, #1269-1272 10.00 10.00

A298

Wedding of Queen Elizabeth II and Prince Philip, 60th Anniv. — A299

No. 1273: a, Couple, pink background. b, Queen, pink background. c, Queen, lilac background. d, Couple, lilac background. e, Couple, pale yellow background. f, Queen, pale yellow background.

**2007, Oct. 31 Litho. *Perf. 14***

**1273** A298 2k Sheet of 6, #a-f 8.50 8.50

**Souvenir Sheet**

**1274** A299 10k multi 7.25 7.25

A300

Princess Diana (1961-97) — A301

No. 1275 — Photographs of Diana from: a, 85t, 1965. b, 2.45k, 1971. c, 3.35k, 1981. d, 5.35k, 1983.

**2007, Oct. 31**

**1275** A300 Sheet of 4, #a-d 8.50 8.50

**Souvenir Sheet**

**1276** A301 10k multi 7.00 7.00

St. John Ambulance in Papua New Guinea, 50th Anniv. — A302

Inscriptions: 5t, St. John Health Service. 20t, St. John Blood Service. 85t, St. John Blind Service. 1k, St. John Ambulance Service. 3.35k, St. John Volunteer Service. 5.35k, Order of St. John.

**2007, Nov. 30 *Perf. 14¼***

**1277-1282** A302 Set of 6 8.00 8.00

*1282a* Miniature sheet, #1277-1282 8.00 8.00

Contemporary Art — A303

Designs: 5t, Oro Gagara. 30t, Western Province tribesman. 85t, Sorcerer. 3k, Hewa wigman. 3.35k, Pigs Into Python Legend. 5.35k, Tolai masks.

**2007, Dec. 12**

**1283-1288** A303 Set of 6 9.50 9.50

*1288a* Miniature sheet, #1283-1288 9.50 9.50

Protected Birds A304

Designs: 10t, Papuan hornbill. 50t, Osprey. 85t, New Guinea harpy eagle. 3k, Victoria crowned pigeon.

No. 1293: a, 1k, Palm cockatoo. b, 5.35k, Great white egret.

10k, Like #1293a.

**2008, Jan. 25 Litho. *Perf. 14x14¼***

**1289-1292** A304 Set of 4 4.00 4.00

**1293** A304 Sheet of 6, #1289-1292, 1293a, 1293b 9.00 9.00

**Souvenir Sheet**

**1294** A304 10k multi 8.50 8.50

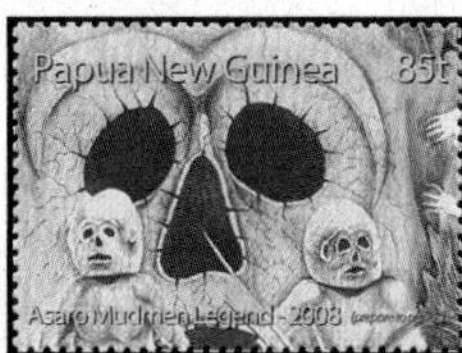

Asaro Mudmen Legend A305

Designs: 85t, Two Mudmen, large skull. 3k, Three Mudmen scouting for enemies in forest. 3.35k, Mudmen attacking enemies. 5.35k, Retreat of enemies.

10k, Similar to 85t.

**2008, Feb. 27 *Perf. 13¼***

**1295-1298** A305 Set of 4 9.50 9.50

*1298a* Miniature sheet, #1295-1298 9.50 9.50

**Souvenir Sheet**

**1299** A305 10k multi 8.00 8.00

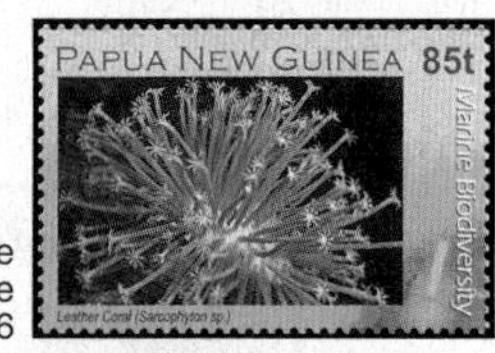

Marine Life A306

Designs: No. 1300, 85t, Leather coral. No. 1301, 3k, Kunei's chromodoris. No. 1302, 3.35k, Scorpion spider snail. No. 1303, 5.35k, Veined sponge.

No. 1304: a, 85t, Radiant sea urchin. b, 3k, Varicose. c, 3.35k, Sea squirt. d, 5.35k, Heffernan's sea star.

10k, White grape coral.

**2008, Mar. 21 *Perf. 14x14¼***

**1300-1303** A306 Set of 4 12.00 12.00

**1304** A306 Sheet of 4, #a-d 15.00 15.00

**Souvenir Sheet**

**1305** A306 10k multi 10.00 10.00

Miniature Sheet

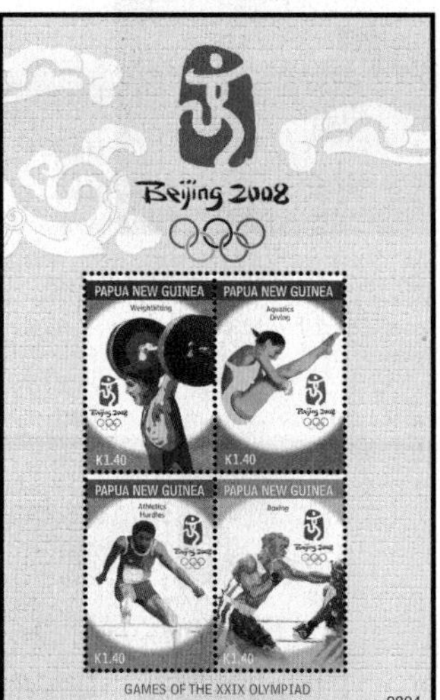

2008 Summer Olympics, Beijing — A307

No. 1306: a, Weight lifting. b, Diving. c, Hurdles. d, Boxing.

**2008, Apr. 16 *Perf. 12¾***

**1306** A307 1.40k Sheet of 4, #a-d 4.50 4.50

Papua New Guinea Partnership With European Union, 30th Anniv. — A308

Flags of Papua New Guinea and European Union, bird of paradise, circle of stars and background color of: Nos. 1307, 1311a, 85t, Gray. Nos. 1308, 1311b, 3k, Yellow. Nos. 1309, 1311c, 3.35k, Rose pink. Nos. 1310, 1311d, 5.35k, Light blue.

10k, Gray, without blue panel at bottom.

**2008, May 9 *Perf. 13x13¼***

**Stamps With Blue Panel With Bold White Drawings**

**1307-1310** A308 Set of 4 10.00 10.00

**Stamps With Blue Panel With Faint White Drawings**

**1311** A308 Sheet of 4, #a-d 10.00 10.00

**Souvenir Sheet**

**1312** A308 10k multi 8.00 8.00

Art by Timothy Akis (1944-84) — A309

Designs: No. 1313, 85t, Long Hair. No. 1314, 3k, Alone. No. 1315, 3.35k, Woman with Cassowary and Child. No. 1316, 5.35k, Man Shooting Cassowary.

No. 1317: a, 85t, Five Men in Their Gardens (top half). b, 3k, The Crocodile Woman and Two Headed Man (top half). c, 3.35k, As "a," bottom half. d, 5.35k, As "b," bottom half.

10k, Flying Fox.

**2008, June 25 Litho. *Perf. 14¼x14***

**1313-1316** A309 Set of 4 9.75 9.75

**1317** A309 Sheet of 4, #a-d 9.75 9.75

**Souvenir Sheet**

**1318** A309 10k multi 7.75 7.75

Headdresses A310

Headdresses of: No. 1319, 85t, Central Province (person showing shoulder). No. 1320, 3k, Western Highlands Province. No. 1321, 3.35k, Oro Province. No. 1322, 5.35k, Western Highlands Province, diff.

No. 1323: a, 85t, Central Province (headdress with yellow side tassels). b, 3k, Central Province, diff. c, 3.35k, Southern Highlands Province, diff. d, 5.35k, Oro Province, diff.

10k, Central Province, diff.

**2008, July 31**

**1319-1322** A310 Set of 4 10.00 10.00

**1323** A310 Sheet of 4, #a-d 10.00 10.00

**Souvenir Sheet**

**1324** A310 10k multi 8.00 8.00

Marilyn Monroe (1926-62), Actress — A311

No. 1325, horiz. — Various photographs of Monroe: a, 85t. b, 3k. c, 3.35k. d, 5.35k

10k, Monroe in automobile.

**2008, Aug. 6 Litho. *Perf. 13¼***

**1325** A311 Sheet of 4, #a-d 9.50 9.50

**Souvenir Sheet**

**1326** A311 10k multi 7.50 7.50

Birds of Paradise — A312

Designs: No. 1327, 85t, Paradisaea guilielmi. No. 1328, 3k, Parotia lawesi. No. 1329, 3.35k, Epimachus meyeri. No. 1330, 5.35k, Diphyllodes magnificus.

No. 1331: a, 85t, Astrapia stephaniae. b, 3k, Cnemophilus macgregorii. c, 3.35k, Pteridophora alberti. d, 5.35k, Astrapia meyeri.

10k, Cicinnurus regius.

**2008, Sept. 3 Litho. *Perf. 14¼x14***

**1327-1330** A312 Set of 4 10.00 10.00
**1331** A312 Sheet of 4, #a-d 11.00 11.00

**Souvenir Sheet**

**1332** A312 10k multi 8.00 8.00

Gold Mining A313

Designs: No. 1333, 85t, Tunnel drilling. No. 1334, 3k, Logistics. No. 1335, 3.35k, Refinery. No. 1336, 5.35k, Gold bars.

No. 1337: a, 85t, Open pit mining. b, 3k, Conveyor belt. c, 3.35k, Plant site. d, 5.35k, Refinery.

10k, Gold bar.

**2008, Oct. 31 *Perf. 14¼***

**1333-1336** A313 Set of 4 10.00 10.00
**1337** A313 Sheet of 4, #a-d 10.00 10.00

**Souvenir Sheet**

**1338** A313 10k multi 8.00 8.00

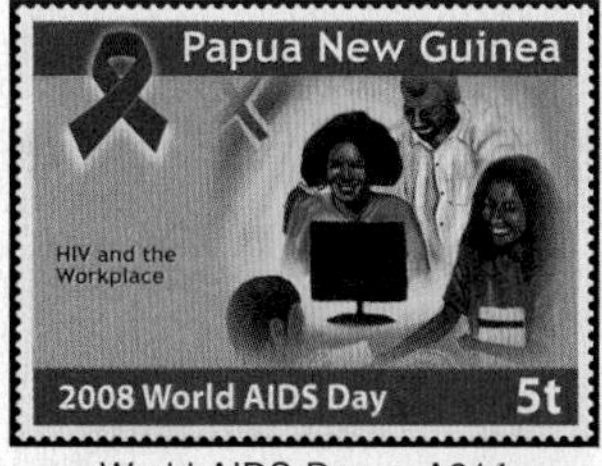


World AIDS Day — A314

Red ribbon and inscription: 5t, HIV and the workplace. 10t, Voluntary counseling and testing. 50t, Role of men and women. Nos. 1342, 1348a, 85t, Education. 1k, 10k, Eradicating stigma and discrimination. 2k, Living with the virus. Nos. 1345, 1348b, 3k, Care, support and the role of family. Nos. 1346, 1348c, 3.70k, Building leadership. Nos. 1347, 1348d, 6k, Health and nutrition.

**2008, Dec. 1 Litho. *Perf. 14¼***

**1339-1347** A314 Set of 9 14.00 14.00
**1348** A314 Sheet of 4, #a-d 13.00 13.00

**Souvenir Sheet**

**1349** A314 10k multi 9.00 9.00

No. 1348 contains four 42x28 stamps; No. 1349 contains one 42x28mm stamp.

Christmas — A315

Designs: No. 1350, 85t, Holy Family. No. 1351, 3k, Santa Claus on reindeer. No. 1352, 3.35k, Book and candle. No. 1353, 5.35k, Bell and book.

No. 1354: a, 85t, Journey to Bethlehem. b, 3k, Silent night. c, 3.35k, Behold that star. d, 5.35k, Three wise men.

10k, Gift and map of Papua New Guinea.

**2008, Dec. 3 *Perf. 14¼***

**1350-1353** A315 Set of 4 9.75 9.75
**1354** A315 Sheet of 4, #a-d 9.75 9.75

**Souvenir Sheet**

**1355** A315 10k multi 8.00 8.00

Plants A316

Designs: No. 1356, 85t, Bixa. No. 1357, 3k, Perfume tree. No. 1358, 3.70k, Beach kalofilum. No. 1359, 6k, Macaranga.

No. 1360: a, 85t, Native frangipani. b, 3k, Ten cent flower. c, 3.70k, Beach terminali. d, 6k, Red beech.

10k, Beach convolvulus (morning glory).

**2009, Jan. 14 *Perf. 14¼***

**1356-1359** A316 Set of 4 10.00 10.00
**1360** A316 Sheet of 4, #a-d 10.00 10.00

**Souvenir Sheet**

**1361** A316 10k multi 7.75 7.75

For surcharges, see Nos. 1732K, 1732V, 1732W.

Worldwide Fund for Nature (WWF) — A317

Designs: No. 1362, 85t, Albericus siegfriedi. No. 1363, 3k, Cophixalus nubicola. No. 1364, 3.70k, Nyctimystes pulcher. No. 1365, 6k, Sphenophryne cornuta.

No. 1366: a, 85t, Litoria sauroni. b, 3k, Litoria prora. c, 3.70k, Litoria multiplica. d, 6k, Litoria pronimia.

10k, Oreophryne sp.

**2009, Feb. 18 Litho. *Perf. 13¼***

**1362-1365** A317 Set of 4 10.00 10.00
**1366** A317 Sheet of 4, #a-d 10.00 10.00

**Souvenir Sheet**

**1367** A317 10k multi 7.50 7.50

Art by David Lasisi — A318

Designs: No. 1368, 85t, Chota. No. 1369, 3k, Stability. No. 1370, 3.70k, Taumimir. No. 1371, 6k, The Moieties.

No. 1372: a, 85t, Like a Log Being Adrifted. b, 3k, Lasisi. c, 3.70k, Lupa. d, 6k, In Memory of Marker Craftsman.

10k, Trapped by Cobweb of Stinging Pain.

**2008, Mar. 11 *Perf. 13½***

**1368-1371** A318 Set of 4 9.50 9.50
**1372** A318 Sheet of 4, #a-d 9.50 9.50

**Souvenir Sheet**

**1373** A318 10k multi 7.00 7.00

A319

China 2009 World Stamp Exhibition, Luoyang — A320

**2009, Apr. 10 *Perf. 12¾x12½***

**1374** A319 1k multi .90 .90

**Souvenir Sheet**

**1375** A320 6k multi 5.00 5.00

Chinese Antiquities A321

Designs: Nos. 1376, 1382a, 5t, Vessel with design of deities, animals and masks. Nos. 1377, 1382b, 10t, Evening in the Peach and Plum Garden, by Li Bai. Nos. 1378, 1382c, 85t, Reliquary with Buddhist figures. Nos. 1379, 1382d, 3k, Brick relief figure. Nos. 1380, 1382e, 3.70k, Round tray with scroll designs. Nos. 1381, 1382f, 6k, Plate in the shape of two peach halves with design of two foxes.

**2009, Apr. 10 *Perf. 14¼x14¾***

**With Inscription "World Stamp Exhibition / China 2009" At Left**

**1376-1381** A321 Set of 6 9.50 9.50

**Stamps Without Inscription "World Stamp Exhibition / China 2009" At Left**

**1382** A321 Sheet of 6, #a-f 9.50 9.50

Assets of Coral Triangle A322

Designs: No. 1383, 85t, Fish. No. 1384, 3k, Marine turtle (blue green frame). No. 1385, 3.70k, Mangroves. No. 1386, 6k, Coral reefs.

No. 1387: a, 85t, Dolphins. b, 3k, Marine turtle (no frame). c, 3.70k, Reef fish. d, 6k, Killer whale.

10k, Grouper.

**2009, May 22 Litho. *Perf. 14½x14¼***

**1383-1386** A322 Set of 4 10.00 10.00
**1387** A322 Sheet of 4, #a-d 10.00 10.00

**Souvenir Sheet**

**1388** A322 10k multi 7.50 7.50

Kokoda Trail A323

Designs: No. 1389, 85t, Guides assisting a trekker. No. 1390, 3k, Crossing Vabuyavi River. No. 1391, 3.70k, Waterfall near Abuari. No. 1392, 6k, Crossing Lake Myola 1.

No. 1393: a, 85t, Crossing Emune River. b, 3k, Entering Imita Ridge. c, 3.70k, Crossing Alo Creek. d, 6k, Templeton's Crossing No. 2.

10k, Golden Staircase, Imita Ridge.

**2009, June 23 *Perf. 14¼***

**1389-1392** A323 Set of 4 10.50 10.50
**1393** A323 Sheet of 4, #a-d 10.50 10.50

**Souvenir Sheet**

**1394** A323 10k multi 7.75 7.75

Bats A324

Designs: No. 1395, 85t, Black-bellied bat. No. 1396, 3k, Least blossom bat. No. 1397, 3.70k, Sanborn's broad-nosed bat. No. 1398, 6k, Mantled mastiff bat.

No. 1399: a, 85t, Trident leaf-nosed bat. b, 3k, Flower-faced bat. c, 3.70k, Eastern horseshoe bat. d, 6k, Greater tube-nosed bat.

10k, Bougainville's fruit bat.

**2009, July 15**

**1395-1398** A324 Set of 4 10.50 10.50
**1399** A324 Sheet of 4, #a-d 10.50 10.50

**Souvenir Sheet**

**1400** A324 10k multi 7.75 7.75

For surcharge, see No. 1732I.

Intl. Day of Non-violence A325

Doves and: No. 1401, 85t, Abraham Lincoln. No. 1402, 3k, Princess Diana. No. 1403, 3.70k, Nelson Mandela. No. 1404, 6k, Barack Obama.

No. 1405: a, 85t, Obama. b, 3k, Dr. Martin Luther King, Jr. c, 3.70k, Mohandas K. Gandhi. d, 6k, Princess Diana.

10k, Obama, diff.

**2009, Aug. 6 *Perf. 13¼***

**1401-1404** A325 Set of 4 10.50 10.50
**1405** A325 Sheet of 4, #a-d 10.50 10.50

**Souvenir Sheet**

**1406** A325 10k multi 7.75 7.75

No. 1406 contains one 38x51mm stamp.

Volcanoes — A326

Designs: No. 1407, 85t, Mount Vulcan. No. 1408, 3k, Mount Tavurvur. No. 1409, 3.70k, Mount Bagana. No. 1410, 6k, Manam Island.

No. 1411: a, 85t, Mount Tavurvur, diff. b, 3k, Manam Island, diff. c, 3.70k, Mount Tavurvur, diff. d, 6k, Mount Ulawun.

10k, Mount Tavurvur, diff.

**2009, Sept. 9 *Perf. 14¼***

**1407-1410** A326 Set of 4 10.50 10.50
**1411** A326 Sheet of 4, #a-d 10.50 10.50

**Souvenir Sheet**

**1412** A326 10k multi 7.75 7.75

Palm Oil Production — A327

Designs: No. 1413, 85t, Oil palm fruitlets. No. 1414, 3k, Oil palm nursery. No. 1415, 3.70k, Oil palm bunches. No. 1416, 6k, Fruit collection.

No. 1417: a, 85t, Irrigation. b, 3k, Oil palm bunches. c, 3.70k, Loose fruits. d, 6k, Mill.

10k, Oil palm fruitlets in hand.

**2009, Oct. 7 Litho. *Perf. 14¼***

**1413-1416** A327 Set of 4 10.50 10.50

**1417** A327 Sheet of 4, #a-d 10.50 10.50

**Souvenir Sheet**

**1418** A327 10k multi 7.75 7.75

For surcharge, see No. 1732P.

Canoes — A328

Canoe from: No. 1419, 85t, Mortlock Island. No. 1420, 3k, Manus Province. No. 1421, 3.70k, Bilbil. No. 1422, 6k, Central Province.

No. 1423: a, 85t, Kimbe. b, 3k, Vuvulu Island. c, 3.70k, Suau Island. d, 6k, Mailu.

10k, Gogodala.

**2009, Nov. 4 Litho. *Perf. 12¾***

**1419-1422** A328 Set of 4 10.50 10.50

**1423** A328 Sheet of 4, #a-d 10.50 10.50

**Souvenir Sheet**

**1424** A328 10k multi 7.50 7.50

Traditional Dances — A329

Designs: No. 1425, 1k, Engagement dance, Western Highlands Province. No. 1426, 3k, Bride price dance, Central Province. No. 1427, 4.65k, Engagement dance, Manus Province. No. 1428, 6.30k, Trobriand love dance, Milne Bay Province.

No. 1429: a, 1k, Courtship dance, Chimbu Province. b, 3k, Engagement dance, Enga Province. c, 4.65k, Engagement Dance, Central Province. d, 6.30k, Womanhood dance, Central Province.

10k, Trobriand love dance, Milne Bay Province, diff.

**2009, Dec. 2 *Perf. 14¼***

**1425-1428** A329 Set of 4 11.50 11.50

**1429** A329 Sheet of 4, #a-d 11.50 11.50

**Souvenir Sheet**

**1430** A329 10k multi 7.50 7.50

Pioneer Art A330

Paintings by Jakupa Ako: No. 1431, 1k, Fish Man. No. 1432, 3k, Story Board. No. 1433, 4.65k, Hunting Trip. No. 1434, 6.30k, Warrior.

No. 1435: a, 1k, Bird Art. b, 3k, Bird Eating. c, 4.65k, Bird Nest. d, 6.30k, Marsupial.

10k, Spirit Mask.

**2010, Jan. 1 *Perf. 14¼***

**1431-1434** A330 Set of 4 11.00 11.00

**1435** A330 Sheet of 4, #a-d 11.00 11.00

**Souvenir Sheet**

**1436** A330 10k multi 7.50 7.50

Beche-de-Mer Industry — A331

Edible sea cucumbers: No. 1437, 1k, Chalkfish. No. 1438, 3k, Elephant trunk fish. No. 1439, 4.65k, Curryfish. No. 1440, 6.30k, Tigerfish.

No. 1441: a, 1k, Surf redfish. b, 3k, Lollyfish. c, 4.65k, Brown sandfish. d, 6.30k, Sandfish.

10k, Pinkfish.

**2010, Feb. 8 Litho. *Perf. 14x14¼***

**1437-1440** A331 Set of 4 11.00 11.00

**1441** A331 Sheet of 4, #a-d 11.00 11.00

**Souvenir Sheet**

**1442** A331 10k multi 7.50 7.50

For surcharge, see No. 1732M.

Carteret Atoll A332

Designs: No. 1443, 1k, Huene Island divided. No. 1444, 3k, Upsurge of water through man-made barriers. No. 1445, 4.65k, Salt water intrusion No. 1446, 6.30k, Tree killed by salt water.

No. 1447: a, 1k, Dwindling island. b, 3k, Tree killed by salt water, diff. c, 4.65k, Storm surge and erosion. d, 6.30k, Man-made barriers.

10k, Divided atolls.

**2010, Mar. 18**

**1443-1446** A332 Set of 4 11.50 11.50

**1447** A332 Sheet of 4, #a-d 11.50 11.50

**Souvenir Sheet**

**1448** A332 10k multi 7.75 7.75

Girl Guides, Cent. A333

Designs: No. 1449, 1k, Guides learning cooking for badge work, 1970. No. 1450, 3k, Guide creating a wash bowl for badge work. No. 1451, 4.65k, Trainer teaching knot tying. No. 1452, 6.30k, Brownies displaying badge work.

No. 1453: a, 1k, Lady Kala Olewale, Second Papua New Guinea Chief Commissioner. b, 3k, Lady Christian Chartterton, founder of Papua New Guinea Girl Guides. c, 4.65k, Princess Anne visiting Papua New Guinea Girl Guides. d, 6.30k, Enny Moaitz, First Papua New Guinea Chief Commissioner.

10k, Lady Olave Baden-Powell.

**2010, Apr. 10 Litho. *Perf. 14x14¼***

**1449-1452** A333 Set of 4 11.00 11.00

**1453** A333 Sheet of 4, #a-d 11.00 11.00

**Souvenir Sheet**

**1454** A333 10k multi 7.50 7.50

For surcharges, see Nos. 1732O, 1732R.

Kokoda Campaigns, 68th Anniv. — A334

No. 1455: a, Soldiers in battle. b, Injured Australian soldier, Papuan natives. c, Tourists at Kokoda.

No. 1456: a, Veterans at Kokoda Campaign Memorial, Isurava. b, Veterans of Kokoda Campaign, Papuan houses.

**2010, Apr. 20 Litho. *Perf. 14¾x14***

**1455** A334 Horiz. strip of 3 2.40 2.40

*a.-c.* 1k Any single .80 .80

**1456** A334 Horiz. pair 7.50 7.50

*a.-b.* 4.65k Either single 3.75 3.75

*c.* Souvenir sheet, #1455a-1455c, 1456a-1456b 10.00 10.00

See Australia Nos. 3244-3252.

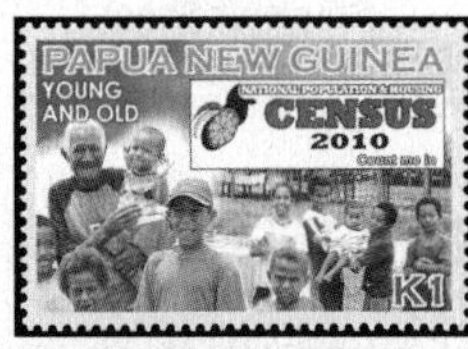


National Population and Housing Census — A335

Inscriptions: No. 1457, 1k, Young and old. No. 1458, 1k, Youths. No. 1459, 3k, Infants. No. 1460, 3k, Villagers.

No. 1461: a, 1k, School kids. b, 1k, Elderly men. c, 3k, Elderly women. d, 3k, All walks of life.

**2010, May 3 *Perf. 14x14¼***

**1457-1460** A335 Set of 4 6.00 6.00

**1461** A335 Sheet of 4, #a-d 6.00 6.00

For surcharge, see No. 1732Q.

Expo 2010, Shanghai — A336

Designs: 1k, Summer Palace, Wenchang Tower. No. 1463, 3k, Dancer, Shanghai Intl. Culture and Art Festival. 4.65k, Oriental Pearl Tower, Pudong, Shanghai. 6.30k, Male Chinese acrobatic performers.

No. 1466: a, 5t, Like 1k. b, 10t, Like #1463. c, 85t, Like 4.65k. d, 3k, Female Chinese acrobatic performers. e, 3.70k, Like 6.30k. f, 6k, Ancient Chinese building.

10k, Tower, Suzhou.

**2010, May 21 *Perf. 11¼x11½***

**1462-1465** A336 Set of 4 11.00 11.00

**1466** A336 Sheet of 6, #a-f 10.00 10.00

**Souvenir Sheet**

**1467** A336 10k multi 9.00 9.00

Sport Fishing — A337

Inscriptions: No. 1468, 1k, Female angler. No. 1469, 3k, Team effort. No. 1470, 4.65k, 25kg Sailfish. No. 1471, 6.30k, 10kg Barramundi.

No. 1472: a, 1k, Game fishing boat. b, 3k, Male angler. c, 4.65k, 14kg Wahoo. d, 6.30k, 11kg Barramundi.

10k, Irene Robinson's world record catch blue fin trevally (92.6kg) on a 4kg line.

**2010, June 11 *Perf. 13½***

**1468-1471** A337 Set of 4 11.00 11.00

**1472** A337 Sheet of 4, #a-d 11.00 11.00

**Souvenir Sheet**

**1473** A337 10k multi 7.25 7.25

Coffee A338

Designs: 15t, Coffee tree with cherries. No. 1475, 1k, Budding beans. No. 1476, 4.65k, Green coffee cherries. No. 1477, 6.30k, Red coffee cherries.

No. 1478: a, 1k, Man harvesting cherries. b, 3k, Fermentation. c, 4.65k, Drying parchment. d, 6.30k, Man holding green coffee beans.

10k, Green and red coffee cherries.

**2010, July 7 Litho. *Perf. 14¼***

**1474-1477** A338 Set of 4 9.00 9.00

**1478** A338 Sheet of 4, #a-d 11.00 11.00

**Souvenir Sheet**

**1479** A338 10k multi 7.25 7.25

Bowerbirds A339

Designs: 5t, Macgregor's gardener bowerbird. No. 1481, 1k, Flame bowerbird. No. 1482, 4.65k, Archbold's bowerbird. No. 1483, 6.30k, Adelbert regent bowerbird.

No. 1484: a, 1k, Pair of Flame bowerbirds. b, 3k, Yellow-fronted gardener bowerbird. c, 4.65k, Vogelkop gardener bowerbird. d, 6.30k, Lauterbach's bowerbird.

10k, Head of Flame bowerbird.

**2010, Aug. 4**

**1480-1483** A339 Set of 4 9.00 9.00

**1484** A339 Sheet of 4, #a-d 11.50 11.50

**Souvenir Sheet**

**1485** A339 10k multi 7.50 7.50

2010 Commonwealth Games, Delhi — A340

Designs: No. 1486, 1k, Rugby sevens. No. 1487, 3k, Boxing. No. 1488, 4.65k, Netball. No. 1489, 6.30k, Hurdles.

No. 1490: a, 1k, Weight lifting. b, 3k, Swimming. c, 4.65k, Lawn bowling. d, 6.30k, Sprinting.

10k, Tennis.

**2010, Sept. 3 *Perf. 13½***

**1486-1489** A340 Set of 4 11.50 11.50

**1490** A340 Sheet of 4, #a-d 11.50 11.50

**Souvenir Sheet**

**1491** A340 10k multi 7.75 7.75

Orchids A341

Designs: No. 1492, 1k, Dendrobium lasianthera May River Red. No. 1493, 3k, Dendrobium violaceoflavens J.J. Smith. No. 1494, 4.65k, Dendrobium mirbelianum var. Vanimo. No. 1495, 6.30k, Dendrobium helix.

No. 1496: a, 1k, Dendrobium nindii W. Hill. b, 3k, Dendrobium sp. off. D. gouldii Reichb. f. c, 4.65k, Dendrobium gouldii Reichb. f. var. Bougainville White. d, 6.30k, Dendrobium discolor var. pink Bensbach.
10k, Dendrobium lasianthera var. Sepik Blue.

**2010, Sept. 28** ***Perf. 14¼***
**1492-1495** A341 Set of 4 11.50 11.50
**1496** A341 Sheet of 4, #a-d 11.50 11.50

**Souvenir Sheet**

**1497** A341 10k multi 7.75 7.75

For surcharge, see No. 1732L.

Mother Teresa (1910-97) A342

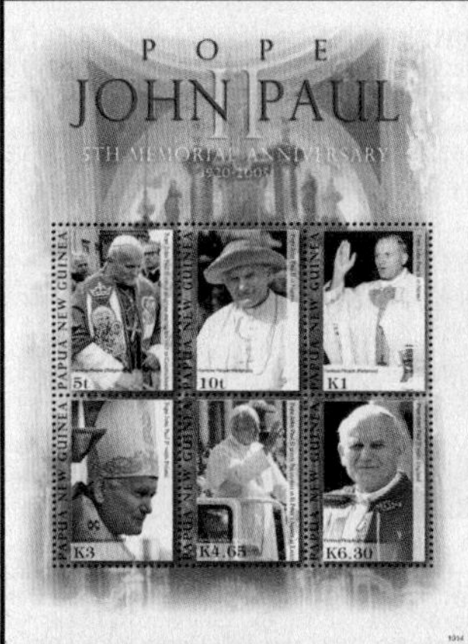

Pope John Paul II (1920-2005) — A343

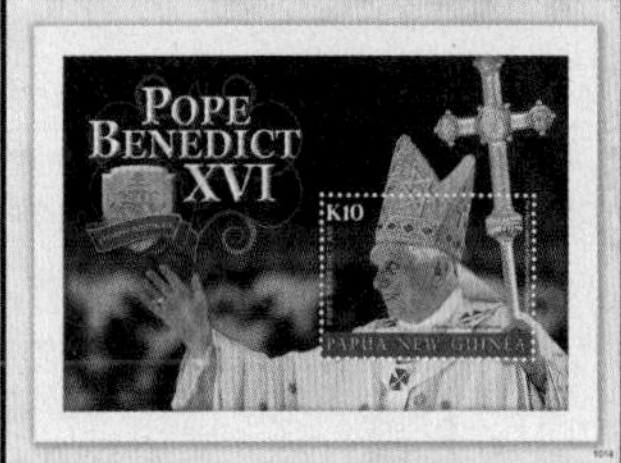

Pope Benedict XVI — A344

Photographs of Mother Teresa from: 1k, 1997. 3k, 1971. 4.65k, 1988. 6.30k, 1984.
No. 1502 — Photographs of Pope John Paul II: a, 5t, Meeting with pilgrims at Czestochowa. b, 10t, In Nigeria. c, 1k, In Poland, as young man (without miter). d, 3k, In Poland (wearing miter). e, 4.65k, Greeting crowds in St. Peter's Square. f, 6.30k, In England.

**2010, Oct. 13** ***Perf. 12***
**1498-1501** A342 Set of 4 12.00 12.00
**1502** A343 Sheet of 6, #a-f 12.00 12.00

**Souvenir Sheet**

**1503** A344 10k multi 8.00 8.00

Spiders A345

Designs: No. 1504, 1k, Nephila pilipes. No. 1505, 3k, Argiope aemula. No. 1506, 4.65k, Gasterocantha (blue violet color at UL). No. 1507, 6.30k, Cyrtophora moluccensis.
No. 1508: a, 1k, Leucauge celebesiana. b, 3k, Holconia. c, 4.65k, Gasterocantha (red background color at UL). d, 6.30k, Ocrisiona.
10k, Nephila pilipes, diff.

**2010, Nov. 3** **Litho.** ***Perf. 14½***
**1504-1507** A345 Set of 4 12.00 12.00
**1508** A345 Sheet of 4, #a-d 12.00 12.00

**Souvenir Sheet**

**1509** A345 10k multi 8.00 8.00

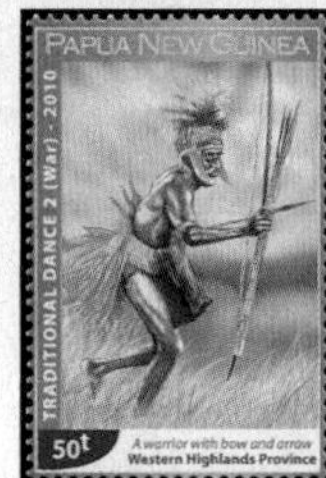

War Dances — A346

Designs: 50t, Warrior with bow and arrow, Western Highlands Province. 1.05k, Simbu warrior with spear, Chimbu Province. 5k, Warrior with spear and shield, Western Highlands Province. 7k, Mudman with bow and arrow, Eastern Highlands Province.
10k, Tasman Island knife dancer, North Solomons Province.

**2010, Dec. 1** **Litho.** ***Perf. 14¼x14***
**1510-1513** A346 Set of 4 11.00 11.00

**Souvenir Sheet**

**1514** A346 10k multi 8.00 8.00

Monitor Lizards A347

Designs: No. 1515, 1.05k, Emerald tree monitor. No. 1516, 5k, Papuan argus monitor. No. 1517, 5k, Papuan monitor. 7k, Blue-tailed monitor.
No. 1519: a, 1.05k, Blue-tailed monitor, diff. b, 2k, Spotted tree monitor. c, 5k, Mangrove monitor. d, 5k, Peach-throat monitor.
No. 1520, Papuan argus monitor with tongue extended.

**2011, Jan. 5** **Litho.** ***Perf. 14x14¼***
**1515-1518** A347 Set of 4 14.50 14.50
**1519** A347 Sheet of 4, #a-d 10.50 10.50

**Souvenir Sheet**

**1520** A347 5k multi 4.00 4.00

Chinese Zodiac Animals A348

Designs: No. 1521, 5t, Dragon. No. 1522, 50t, Tiger. No. 1523, 1.05k, Horse. 2k, Monkey. No. 1525, 5k, Snake. No. 1526, 5k, Dog.
No. 1527: a, 5t, Ox. b, 50t, Rooster. c, 55t, Sheep. d, 1.05k, Rat. e, 5k, Boar. f, 7k, Rabbit.

**2011, Feb. 8** ***Perf. 13 Syncopated***
**1521-1526** A348 Set of 6 11.00 11.00
**1527** A348 Sheet of 6 #a-f 11.00 11.00

Paintings by Mathias Kauage (1944-2003) — A349

Designs: No. 1528, 1.05k, Pailet Draivim Balus (Pilot Flying an Airplane). No. 1529, 5k, Fes Misineri (First Missionary). No. 1530, 5k, Pailet i Trein Long Draivim Balus (Trainee Pilot at Training). No. 1531, 7k, Eia Bas (Airbus).
No. 1532 — Details from Eia Bas Bilong Eiu Gini (Air New Guinea's Airbus): a, 1.05k, Wing at top. b, 5k, Bird at top. c, 5k, Wing at bottom. 7k, Rear wheel.
10k, Barasut Man (Parachute Man).

**2011, Mar. 18** **Litho.** ***Perf. 13¼***
**1528-1531** A349 Set of 4 14.50 14.50
**1532** A349 Sheet of 4, #a-d 14.50 14.50

**Souvenir Sheet**

**1533** A349 10k multi 8.00 8.00

Fish A350

Designs: No. 1534, 1.05k, Cephalopholis miniata. No. 1535, 1.05k, Cromileptes altivelis. 5k, Plectropomus areolatus. 7k, Epinephelus lanceolatus.
10k, Epinephelus polyphekadion.

**2011, Apr. 6** ***Perf. 14¼***
**1534-1537** A350 Set of 4 11.50 11.50

**Souvenir Sheet**

**1538** A350 10k multi 8.00 8.00

American Civil War, 150th Anniv. A351

Designs: 1k, Pres. Abraham Lincoln, text "With malice toward none, with charity for all." No. 1540, 1.05k, Lincoln, text "Of the people, by the people, for the people." No. 1541, 5k, Slave and banner. No. 1542, 7k, Lincoln, Confederate States Pres. Jefferson Davis, US and Confederate flags, eagle, banner.
No. 1543: a, 5t, The Peacemakers, painting by George P. A. Healy. b, 50t, Battle of Fort Sumter. c, 55t, Lincoln and his Cabinet. d, 1.05k, Lincoln, Generals Ulysses S. Grant and Robert E. Lee. e, 5k, Lincoln, slave, text "If slavery is not wrong, nothing is wrong." f, 7k, Battle of Gettysburg.
10k, Lincoln, text "A house divided cannot stand."

**2011, Apr. 20** ***Perf. 12***
**1539-1542** A351 Set of 4 12.00 12.00

***13 Syncopated***

**1543** A351 Sheet of 6, #a-f 12.00 12.00

**Souvenir Sheet**

**1544** A351 10k multi 8.50 8.50

Butterflies A352

Designs: No. 1545, 1.05k, Orange birdwing. No. 1546, 1.05k, Green birdwing. 5k, Blue birdwing. 7k, Goliath birdwing.
10k, Pair of Queen Alexandra's birdwings.

**2011, May 3** **Litho.** ***Perf. 14x14¼***
**1545-1548** A352 Set of 4 12.00 12.00

**Souvenir Sheet**

**1549** A352 10k multi 8.50 8.50

Pineapples — A353

Pineapple slices and: No. 1550, 1.05k, African Queen pineapples sliced. No. 1551, 1.05k, African Queen and Hawaiian pineapples sliced. No. 1552, 5k, One Hawaiian and Two African Queen pineapples, one basket. No. 1553, 7k, One Hawaiian and two African Queen pineapples, two baskets.
No. 1554 — Popular pineapple varieties found in Papua New Guinea: a, 10t. b, 2k. c, 5k. d, 7k.
10k, African pineapple species cut.

**2011, May 25** ***Perf. 14x14¼***
**1550-1553** A353 Set of 4 12.00 12.00
**1554** A353 Sheet of 4, #a-d 12.00 12.00

**Souvenir Sheet**

**1555** A353 10k multi 8.25 8.25

Nos. 1550-1555 are impregnated with a pineapple scent.

Urban Safety and Crime Prevention A354

Designs: 5t, National Capital District Commission emblem. No. 1557, 1.05k, No guns emblem. No. 1558, 5k, Meri SEIF Ples emblem. No. 1559, 7k, UN-Habitat certificate of recognition.
No. 1560: a, 1.05k, Shelter for women and children. b, 1.05k, Krismas SEIF Kempan members. c, 5k, Meri SEIF Ples members. d, 7k, Port Moresby Chamber of Commerce and Industry emblem.
10k, National Capital District Commission emblem, diff.

**2011, June 15** ***Perf. 14¼x14***
**1556-1559** A354 Set of 4 11.50 11.50
**1560** A354 Sheet of 4, #a-d 12.00 12.00

**Souvenir Sheet**

**1561** A354 10k multi 8.75 8.75

For surcharge, see No. 1732J.

Cacao Production — A355

Designs: 5t, Harvesting cocoa pods. No. 1563, 1.05k, Breaking cocoa pod. No. 1564, 5k, Drying cocoa. No. 1565, 7k, Exporting cocoa bags.
No. 1566: a, 1.05k, Cocoa seedling. b, 1.05k, Cocoa flower. c, 5k, Pruning cocoa treas. d, 7k, Cocoa pods.
10k, Exporting cocoa bags, diff.

**2011, July 7** ***Perf. 14x14¼***
**1562-1565** A355 Set of 4 11.50 11.50
**1566** A355 Sheet of 4, #a-d 12.00 12.00

**Souvenir Sheet**

**1567** A355 10k multi 8.75 8.75

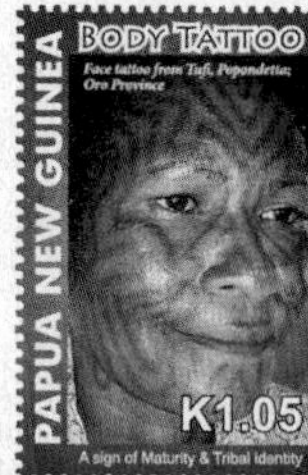

Tattoos — A356

Designs: No. 1568, 1.05k, Face tattoo from Tufi. No. 1569, 1.05k, Face tattoo from Nondugl-Banz. No. 1570, 5k, Face tattoo from Asaro. No. 1571, 7k, Face tattoo from Kudjip.
No. 1572: a, 1.05k, Arm tattoo from Kairuku. b, 1.05k, Chest tattoo from Gumine. c, 5k, Leg tattoo from South Whagi. d, 7k, Minei tribe arm tattoo, Manus.
10k, Face tattoo from Tufi, diff.

**2011, Aug. 4** ***Perf. 14¼x14***
**1568-1571** A356 Set of 4 13.00 13.00
**1572** A356 Sheet of 4, #a-d 13.00 13.00

**Souvenir Sheet**

**1573** A356 10k multi 9.00 9.00

Southern Cassowaries
A357

Designs: No. 1574, 1.05k, Two newly-weaned chicks feeding. No. 1575, 1.05k, One weaned chick feeding. No. 1576, 5k, Adult feeding. No. 1577, 7k, Heads of two adults.

No. 1578: a, 1.05k, Head and shoulder of adult. b, 1.05k, Back rump of adult. c, 5k, Full view of chick. d, 7k, Legs of adult.

10k, Cassowary in natural habitat.

**2011, Aug. 25**

**1574-1577** A357 Set of 4 13.00 13.00
**1578** A357 Sheet of 4, #a-d 13.00 13.00

**Souvenir Sheet**

**1579** A357 10k multi 9.25 9.25

Waterfalls
A358

Designs: No. 1580, 1.05k, Kesesoru Falls. No. 1581, 1.05k, Mageni Falls aerial view. No. 1582, 5k, Mageni Falls outlet. No. 1583, 7k, Waghi Falls.

No. 1584: a, 1.05k, Sogeri Falls. b, 1.05k, Beaver Falls. c, 5k, Wawoi Falls. d, 7k, Remote Island Falls.

10k, Ambua Falls.

**2011, Sept. 22** ***Perf. 14x14¼***

**1580-1583** A358 Set of 4 13.00 13.00
**1584** A358 Sheet of 4, #a-d 13.00 13.00

**Souvenir Sheet**

**1585** A358 10k multi 9.25 9.25

Wedding of Prince William and Catherine Middleton
A359

Badge of the House of Windsor and: No. 1586, 1.05k, Catherine Middleton (at right). No. 1587, 1.05k, Middleton and sister, Pippa. No. 1588, 5k, Prince William. No. 1589, 7k, Couple.

No. 1590 — Badge of the House of Windsor and: a, 1.05k, Middleton (at left). b, 1.05k, Couple waving. c, 5k, Couple holding hands. d, 7k, Prince William, diff.

10k, Couple and badge of the House of Windsor.

**2011, Oct. 19** ***Perf. 12, 14 (#1590)***

**1586-1589** A359 Set of 4 13.50 13.50
**1590** A359 Sheet of 4, #a-d 13.50 13.50

**Souvenir Sheet**

**1591** A359 10k multi 9.50 9.50

World War II Relics
A360

Designs: No. 1592, 1.05k, American B-17E 41-2446. No. 1593, 1.05k, Japanese Ki-21 Sally. No. 1594, 5k, American P-38F 12647-S. No. 1595, 7k, American B17E 41-9234.

No. 1596: a, 1.05k, Japanese 95 Ha Go tank. b, 1.05k, Australian Hudson A16-91. c, 5k, New Zealand PV-1 Ventura NZ4613 Tail 13. d, 7k, Japanese 120mm dual purpose gun.

10k, American B-17F "Black Jack."

**2011, Nov. 16** ***Perf. 13¼***

**1592-1595** A360 Set of 4 13.50 13.50
**1596** A360 Sheet of 4, #a-d 13.50 13.50

**Souvenir Sheet**

**1597** A360 10k multi 9.50 9.50

Victory Dancers — A361

Designs: No. 1598, 1.05k, Kiriwina woman. No. 1599, 1.05k, Oro man. No. 1600, 5k, Kandep woman. No. 1601, 7k, Siasi man.

No. 1602: a, 1.05k, Kerowagi man. b, 1.05k, Tolai man. c, 5k, Rigo man. d, 7k, Huli man.

10k, Baining fire dancer.

**2011, Dec. 1** ***Perf. 14¼x14***

**1598-1601** A361 Set of 4 13.50 13.50
**1602** A361 Sheet of 4, #a-d 13.50 13.50

**Souvenir Sheet**

**1603** A361 10k multi 9.50 9.50

For surcharge, see No. 1732S.

Fish
A362

Designs: No. 1604, 1.20k, Emperor angelfish. No. 1605, 1.20k, Yellow-mask angelfish. No. 1606, 6k, Meyer's butterflyfish. No. 1607, 8k, Barrier Reef anemonefish.

No. 1608: a, 1.20k, Clown anemonefish. b, 1.20k, Clown triggerfish. c, 6k, Clark's anemonefish. d, 8k, Spotfin lionfish.

10k, Bearded scorpionfish.

**2012, Jan. 5** ***Perf. 14x14¼***

**1604-1607** A362 Set of 4 15.50 15.50
**1608** A362 Sheet of 4, #a-d 15.50 15.50

**Souvenir Sheet**

**1609** A362 10k multi 9.25 9.25

A363

A364



A365

A366

Paintings by Philip Yobale (1968-2009) — A367

Designs: No. 1610, Fish Berserk. No. 1611, Facing Faces. No. 1612, Regiana Bird of Paradise and Its Four Captors. No. 1613, Face Without Eye.

No. 1614 — Untitled works with: a, 1.20k, Faces. b, 1.20k, Head with headband. c, 6k, Eye at UL. d, 8k, Mask at UR.

10k, On-looking Eyes.

**2012, Feb. 22** ***Perf. 14¼x14***

**1610** A363 1.20k multi 1.10 1.10
**1611** A364 1.20k multi 1.10 1.10
**1612** A365 6k multi 5.75 5.75
**1613** A366 8k multi 7.50 7.50
*Nos. 1610-1613 (4)* 15.45 15.45
**1614** A367 Sheet of 4, #a-d 15.50 15.50

**Souvenir Sheet**

**1615** A367 10k multi 9.50 9.50

Blessed Peter To Rot (1912-45), Christian Martyr — A368

Designs: No. 1616, 1.20k, Beatification ceremony, 1995. No. 1617, 1.20k, To Rot baptizing child. No. 1618, 6k, Beatification ceremony, diff. No. 1619, 8k, To Rot giving holy communion.

No. 1620: a, 1.20k, To Rot in Taliligap Catechist School. b, 1.20k, To Rot officiating a marriage. c, 6k, To Rot leading worship and devotion. d, 8k, Murder of To Rot in cell in Japanese concentration camp.

10k, Statue of To Rot.

**2012, Mar. 14** ***Perf. 14x14¼***

**1616-1619** A368 Set of 4 16.50 16.50

***Perf. 14***

**1620** A368 Sheet of 4, #a-d 16.50 16.50

**Souvenir Sheet**

**1621** A368 10k multi 10.00 10.00

Traditional Clay Cooking Pots — A369

Cooking pots from: No. 1622, 1.20k, Central Province. No. 1623, 1.20k, Mapang Province. No. 1624, 6k, Autonomous Region of Bougainville. No. 1625, 8k, East Sepik Province.

No. 1626: a, 1.20k, Milne Bay Province (brown pot). b, 1.20k, Milne Bay Province (black pot). c, 6k, East Sepik Province, diff. d, 8k, Manus Province.

10k, West Sepik Province.

**2012, Apr. 11** ***Perf. 14x14¼***

**1622-1625** A369 Set of 4 15.50 15.50

***Perf. 14***

**1626** A369 Sheet of 4, #a-d 15.50 15.50

**Souvenir Sheet**

**1627** A369 10k multi 9.50 9.50

For surcharges, see Nos. 1732A 1732B.

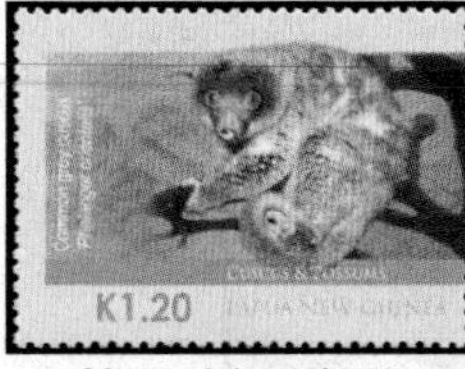


Marsupials — A370

Designs: No. 1628, 1.20k, Common gray cuscus. No. 1629, 1.20k, Common spotted cuscus. No. 1630, 6k, Black spotted cuscus. No. 1631, 8k, Woodlark cuscus.

No. 1632: a, 1.20k, Sugar glider. b, 1.20k, Feather-tail possum. c, 6k, Striped possum. d, 8k, Northern glider.

10k, Common spotted cuscus, diff.

**2012, May 7** ***Perf. 13¼***

**1628-1631** A370 Set of 4 15.50 15.50
**1632** A370 Sheet of 4, #a-d 15.50 15.50

**Souvenir Sheet**

**1633** A370 10k multi 9.50 9.50

For surcharges, see Nos. 1732C, 1732D.

Sports Legends
A371

Designs: No. 1634, 1.20k, Iamo Launa, track and field. No. 1635, 1.20k, Martin Beni, boxer. No. 1636, 6k, Stanley Nandex, kick boxer. No. 1637, 8k, Will Genia, rugby player.

No. 1638: a, 1.20k, Tau John, track. b, 1.20k, Iwila Jacobs, weight lifter. c, 6k, Takale Tuna, track. d, 8k, John Aba, boxer.

10k, Genia, diff.

**2012, June 18**

**1634-1637** A371 Set of 4 15.50 15.50
**1638** A371 Sheet of 4, #a-d 15.50 15.50

**Souvenir Sheet**

**1639** A371 10k multi 9.50 9.50

For surcharge, see No. 1732E.

Orchids
A372

Designs: No. 1640, 1.20k, Dendrobium macrophyllum. No. 1641, 1.20k, Dendrobium williamsianum. No. 1642, 6k, Pink Dendrobium bracteosum. No. 1643, 8k, Phalaenopsis amabilis.

No. 1644: a, 1.20k, White Dendrobium bracteosum. b, 1.20k, Dendrobium bifalce. c, 6k, Dendrobium strepsiceros. d, 8k, Vanda hindsii.

10k, Dendrobium spectabile.

**2012, July 2** ***Perf. 14x14¼***

**1640-1643** A372 Set of 4 15.50 15.50

***Perf. 14***

**1644** A372 Sheet of 4, #a-d 15.50 15.50

**Souvenir Sheet**

**1645** A372 10k multi 9.50 9.50

For surcharges, see Nos. 1732F, 1732G.

2012 Summer Olympics, London — A373

No. 1646: a, 50t, Weight lifting. b, 55t, Swimming. c, 1k, Relay race.
5k, Boxing.

**2012, July 27** *Perf. 12*
**1646** A373 Sheet of 3, #a-c 2.00 2.00
**Souvenir Sheet**
**1647** A373 5k multi 4.75 4.75

New Year 2012 (Year of the Snake) — A374

Flags of Papua New Guinea and People's Republic of China and snake with background color of: No. 1648, 1.20k, Pink. No. 1649, 1.20k, Blue. No. 1650, 6k, Yellow orange. No. 1651, 8k, Green.
No. 1652: a, 1.20k, Green. b, 1.20k, Yellow orange. c, 6k, Pink. d, 8k, Blue.
10k, Yellow.

**2012, Aug. 1** *Perf. 14, 12 (#1652)*
**1648-1651** A374 Set of 4 15.50 15.50
**1652** A374 Sheet of 4, #a-d 15.50 15.50
**Souvenir Sheet**
**1653** A374 10k multi 9.50 9.50

Traditional Costumes — A375

Designs: No. 1654, 1.20k, Man from Telefomin, Sandaun Province. No. 1655, 1.20k, Woman from Pomio, East New Britain Province. No. 1656, 6k, Women from Hanuabada, National Capital District. No. 1657, 8k, Woman and child from Duna, Southern Highlands Province.
No. 1658: a, 1.20k, Bride from Mendi, Southern Highlands Province. b, 1.20k, Woman from Tari, Southern Highlands Province. c, 6k, Family from Trobriand Islands, Milne Bay Province. d, 8k, Women from Mukawa, Milne Bay Province.
10k, Woman from Popondetta, Oro Province.

**2012, Sept. 5** *Perf. 14¼*
**1654-1657** A375 Set of 4 15.50 15.50
**1658** A375 Sheet of 4, #a-d 15.50 15.50
**Souvenir Sheet**
**1659** A375 10k multi 9.50 9.50

For surcharge, see No. 1732H.

Reign of Queen Elizabeth II, 60th Anniv. A376

Profile of Queen Elizabeth II, Diamond Jubilee emblem, and: 25t, Duchess of Cornwall and Prince of Wales. 50t, Prince of Wales. 1k, Prince of Wales, Duchess of Cornwall, Queen Elizabeth II and Prince Philip. 1.25k, Prince of Wales with sword. 6k, Queen Elizabeth II and Prince of Wales. 8k, Queen Elizabeth II and Prince Philip.
10k, Queen Elizabeth II, vert.

**2012, Nov. 4** *Perf. 14¼*
**1660-1665** A376 Set of 6 16.50 16.50
**Souvenir Sheet**
**1666** A376 10k multi 9.75 9.75

Public Transportation — A377

Designs: No. 1667, 1.30k, Passenger truck. No. 1668, 1.30k, Banana boat. No. 1669, 6k, Remote service airplane. No. 1670, 8.70k, Trading canoe.
No. 1671: a, 1.30k, Taxi. b, 1.30k, Passenger bus. c, 6k, Domestic and international airplane. d, 8k, Ship.
10k, Dugout canoe.

**2013, Jan. 2** *Perf. 13¾x13¼*
**1667-1670** A377 Set of 4 17.00 17.00
**1671** A377 Sheet of 4, #a-d 17.00 17.00
**Souvenir Sheet**
**1672** A377 10k multi 9.75 9.75



Sculptures by Gigmai Kundun — A378

Designs: No. 1673, 1.30k, Hiri Trade Canoe (Lakatoi). No. 1674, 1.30k, Kundu Slit Gong. No. 1675, 6k, Hiri Moale Queen. No. 1676, 8.70k, Bird of Paradise.
No. 1677: a, 1.30k, Follow the Leader. b, 1.30k, Walking Together. c, 6k, Relieving Education Burden. d, 8k, Inherited Believe System.
10k, Indo-Pacific Lionfish (Pterois).

**2013, Feb. 20** *Perf. 12*
**1673-1676** A378 Set of 4 16.50 16.50
**1677** A378 Sheet of 4, #a-d 16.50 16.50
**Souvenir Sheet**
**1678** A378 10k multi 9.50 9.50

---

In 2012, Papua New Guinea postal officials permitted customers who wished to purchase personalized stamps to work with them in designing the stamps and labels, instead of only providing the image for the attached label, as had been done with previous personalized stamp issues. Some of the items produced by customers are known to lack the country name on the stamp and label. These stamps are known to have a number of different denominations. Beyond Nos. 1264-1268, Papua New Guinea postal officials have not provided any information on other personalizable stamps that are available to any customer.

---

Pres. John F. Kennedy (1917-63) A379

Designs: No. 1679, 1.30k, Pres. Kennedy seated. No. 1680, 1.30k, Pres. Kennedy, wife, Jacqueline, and Vice-president Lyndon B. Johnson. No. 1681, 6k, Pres. Kennedy in limousine. No. 1682, 8.70k, Honor guard holding flag over Pres. Kennedy's casket.
No. 1683: a, 1.30k, Pres. Kennedy and flag. b, 1.30k, Pres. Kennedy and wife at Love Field, Dallas, Texas. c, 6k, Flag-draped coffin of Pres. Kennedy. d, 8.70k, Johnson being sworn in as President.
10k, Pres. Kennedy, vert.

**2013, Mar. 13** **Litho.** *Perf. 14*
**1679-1682** A379 Set of 4 16.00 16.00
**1683** A379 Sheet of 4, #a-d 16.00 16.00
**Souvenir Sheet**
*Perf. 12*
**1684** A379 10k multi 9.25 9.25

Root Crops A380

Designs: No. 1685, 1.30k, Cassava. No. 1686, 1.30k, Chinese taro. No. 1687, 6k, Sweet potatoes. No. 1688, 8.70k, Taro.
No. 1689: a, 1.30k, Five-leaflet yam. b, 1.30k, Lesser yam. c, 6k, Greater yam. d, 8.70k, Nummularia yam.
10k, Queensland arrowroot.

**2013, Apr. 10** **Litho.** *Perf. 12*
**1685-1688** A380 Set of 4 16.00 16.00
**1689** A380 Sheet of 4, #a-d 16.00 16.00
**Souvenir Sheet**
**1690** A380 10k multi 9.25 9.25

Orchids A381

Designs: No. 1691, 1.30k, Dendrobium gouldii. No. 1692, 1.30k, Dendrobium lineale. No. 1693, 6k, Dendrobium mirbelianum. No. 1694, 8.70k, Dendrobium sp. aff. D. cochiliodes.
No. 1695: a, 1.30k, Dendrobium sp. aff. D. gouldii. b, 1.30k, Dendrobium sp. aff. D. conanthum. c, 6k, Dendrobium lineale, diff. d, 8.70k, Dendrobium carronii.
10k, Dendrobium mussauense.

**2013, May 24** **Litho.** *Perf. 12*
**1691-1694** A381 Set of 4 15.50 15.50
**1695** A381 Sheet of 4, #a-d 15.50 15.50
**Souvenir Sheet**
**1696** A381 10k multi 9.00 9.00

Spacecraft and Space Stations A382

Designs: No. 1697, 1.30k, Skylab. No. 1698, 1.30k, Salyut 6 Space Station. No. 1699, 6k, Spacehab. No. 1700, 8.70k, Mir Space Station.
No. 1701: a, 1.30k, Skylab, diff. b, 1.30k, Salyut 6 Space Station, diff. c, 6k, Space shuttle re-entering atmosphere. d, 8.70k, Mir Space Station, diff.
10k, Space shuttle as seen from International Space Station window.

**2013, July 15** **Litho.** *Perf. 14*
**1697-1700** A382 Set of 4 15.50 15.50
*Perf. 12*
**1701** A382 Sheet of 4, #a-d 15.50 15.50
**Souvenir Sheet**
**1702** A382 10k multi 9.00 9.00

Launch of the International Space Station, 15th anniv.

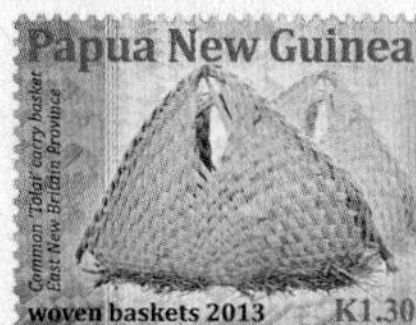


Woven Baskets A383

Designs: No. 1703, 1.30k, Common "Tolai" carry basket, East New Britain Province. No. 1704, 1.30k, Pepeni (yam basket), Kitava Island, Milne Bay Province. No. 1705, 6k, Carry basket, Milne Bay Province. No. 1706, 8.70k, Carry baskets, Ialibu, Southern Highlands Province.
No. 1707: a, 1.30k, Common Sepik basket, East Sepik Province. b, 1.30k, Carry basket, Milne Bay Province, diff. c, 6k, Carry basket, Gulf Province. d, 8.70k, Manus carry basket, Manus Province.
10k, Temporary palm leaf basket, Coastal and Island Provinces.

**2013, Aug. 9** **Litho.** *Perf. 12*
**1703-1706** A383 Set of 4 15.00 15.00
**1707** A383 Sheet of 4, #a-d 15.00 15.00
**Souvenir Sheet**
**1708** A383 10k multi 8.75 8.75

Coconuts A384

Designs: 4k, Green coconuts. No. 1710, 6k, Coconut husking. No. 1711, 8.70k, Coconut juice. 12k, Coconut meat.
No. 1713: a, 1k, Dry coconut. b, 1.30k, Inner shell. c, 6k, Meat. d, 8.70k, Apple.
10k, Inner shell.

**2013, Aug. 21** **Litho.** *Perf. 12*
**1709-1712** A384 Set of 4 25.00 25.00
**1713** A384 Sheet of 4, #a-d 14.00 14.00
**Souvenir Sheet**
**1714** A384 10k multi 8.25 8.25

Birth of Prince George of Cambridge A385

Designs (inscribed "22nd of July 2013" at top: No. 1715, 1.30k, Duke and Duchess of Cambridge, Prince George. No. 1716, 1.30k, Duke of Cambridge, Prince George. No. 1717, 6k, Duchess of Cambridge, Prince George. No. 1718, 8.70k, Duke and Duchess of Cambridge, Prince George, diff.
No. 1719 (stamps without "22nd of July 2013" inscription at top): a, 1.30k, Like #1715. b, 1.30k, Like #1716. c, 6k, Like #1717. d, 8.70k, Like #1718.
10k, Prince George in arms of Duchess of Cambridge.

*Perf. 13¼x12½*
**2013, Sept. 11** **Litho.**
**1715-1718** A385 Set of 4 14.00 14.00
*Perf. 12x12½*
**1719** A385 Sheet of 4, #a-d 14.00 14.00
**Souvenir Sheet**
**1720** A385 10k multi 8.25 8.25

Cooking Methods A386

Designs: No. 1721, 1.30k, Boiling. No. 1722, 1.30k, Drying. No. 1723, 6k, Drying, diff. No. 1724, 8.70k, Roasting.
No. 1725: a, 1.30k, Dug out mumu pit. b, 1.30k, Stones being heated in mumu pit. c, 6k, Food placed in mumu pit. d, 8.70k, Covered mumu pit.
10k, Hot stones steaming in pot.

**2013, Nov. 6** **Litho.** *Perf. 12*
**1721-1724** A386 Set of 4 13.50 13.50
**1725** A386 Sheet of 4, #a-d 13.50 13.50
**Souvenir Sheet**
**1726** A386 10k multi 7.75 7.75

New Year 2014 (Year of the Horse) A387

Various horses with background colors of: No. 1727, 1.70k, Grayish lilac. No. 1728, 1.70k, Tan. No. 1729, 6k, Red. No. 1730, 8.70k, Blue violet.

No. 1731 — Various horses with background colors of: a, 1.30k, Violet. b, 1.30k, Olive bister. c, 6k, Grayish lilac. d, 8.70k, Blue green.

10k, Horse with greenish gray background.

**2014, Jan. 2 Litho. *Perf. 12***

**1727-1730** A387 Set of 4 14.50 14.50
**1731** A387 Sheet of 4, #a-d 14.00 14.00

**Souvenir Sheet**

**1732** A387 10k multi 8.00 8.00

For surcharges, see Nos. 1733-1734.

### Nos. 1358, 1395, 1416, 1440, 1451, 1452, 1460, 1494, 1495, 1512, 1557, 1601, 1622, 1623, 1628, 1629, 1634, 1640, 1641, 1654, 1655 Surcharged in Black or Black and Red

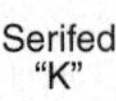
Serifed "K"

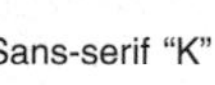
Sans-serif "K"

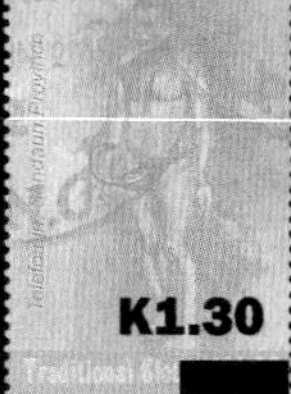

### Methods and Perfs. As Before

**2014, Jan.**

**Serifed "K" Surcharges**

**1732A** A369 1.30k on 1.20k #1622 —
**1732B** A369 1.30k on 1.20k #1623 — —
**1732C** A370 1.30k on 1.20k #1628 — —
**1732D** A370 1.30k on 1.20k #1629 —
**1732E** A371 1.30k on 1.20k #1634 — —
**1732F** A372 1.30k on 1.20k #1640 (Bk&R) — —
**1732G** A372 1.30k on 1.20k #1641 — —

**Sans-serif "K" Surcharges**

**1732H** A375 1.30k on 1.20k #1654 —
**1732I** A324 15k on 85t #1395 — —
**1732J** A354 15k on 1.05k #1557 — —
**1732K** A316 15k on 3.70k #1358 —
**1732L** A341 25k on 4.65k #1494 — —
**1732M** A331 25k on 6.30k #1440 — —
**1732N** A341 25k on 6.30k #1495 — —
**1732O** A333 40k on 4.65k #1451 — —
**1732P** A327 40k on 6k #1416 — —
**1732Q** A335 90k on 3k #1460 — —
**1732R** A333 90k on 6.30k #1452 — —
**1732S** A361 90k on 7k #1601 — —

Obliterators and sizes of surcharges vary.

### Nos. 1356, 1358, 1512, 1601 With Sans-Serif Surcharge Like No. 1732H

### No. 1641 With Serifed Surcharge in Black and Red Like No. 1732A

**2014 Method and Perf. As Before**

**1732X** A372 1.30k on 1.20k #1641 (Bk&R) —

### No. 1655 With Sans-Serif Surcharge Like No. 1732H

**2014 Method and Perf. As Before**

**1732Y** A375 1.30k on 1.20k #1655 —

### Nos. 1727-1728 Surcharged in Black and Red

**2014, Feb. 12 Litho. *Perf. 12***

**1733** A387 5k on 1.70k #1727 4.50 4.50
**1734** A387 5k on 1.70k #1728 4.50 4.50

Nelson Mandela (1918-2013), President of South Africa — A388

Various photographs of Mandela (stamps with white frames): No. 1735, 1.30k. No. 1736, 3k. No. 1737, 6k. No. 1738, 8k.

No. 1739 — Various photographs of Mandela (stamps with green frames): a, 1.30k. b, 3k. c, 6k. d, 8k.

10k, Mandela, diff. (stamp without frame).

**2014, Mar. 31 Litho. *Perf. 12***

**1735-1738** A388 Set of 4 13.50 13.50
**1739** A388 Sheet of 4, #a-d 13.50 13.50

**Souvenir Sheet**

**1740** A388 10k multi 7.25 7.25

Spirit of Hela Liquified Natural Gas Tanker A389

Various photographs of Spirit of Hela with side panel color of: 1.30k, Pale green, 3k, Beige. 6k, Light blue green. 8k, Lilac.

10k, Spirit of Hela, light blue panel.

**2014, Apr. 7 Litho. *Perf. 13½***

**1741-1744** A389 Set of 4 13.00 13.00
*1744a* Souvenir sheet of 4, #1741-1744 13.00 13.00

**Souvenir Sheet**

**1745** A389 10k multi 7.25 7.25

World War I, Cent. — A390

Designs: No. 1746, 1.30k, Russian soldier. No. 1747, 5k, American bugler. No. 1748, 6k, French airplanes. No. 1749, 8k, German observation balloon.

No. 1750: a, 1.30k, French lancers. b, 5k, British Army. c, 6k, American National Guard. 8k, French battleship.

10k, British soldier.

**2014, Apr. 24 Litho. *Perf. 13¼x12½***

**1746-1749** A390 Set of 4 14.50 14.50

***Perf. 12x12½***

**1750** A390 Sheet of 4, #a-d 14.50 14.50

**Souvenir Sheet**

**1751** A390 10k multi 7.25 7.25

Pope Francis — A391

Coat of arms of Pope Francis and various photographs with frame color of: No. 1752, 1.30k, Red violet. No. 1753, 5k, Green. No. 1754, 6k, Blue. No. 1755, 8k, Vermilion.

No. 1756 — Coat of arms of Pope Francis and photographs with bister frame: a, 1.30k, Photo like #1753. b, 5k, Photo like #1754. c, 6k, Photo like #1755. d, 8k, Photo like #1752

10k, Pope Francis, coat of arms.

**2014, July 28 Litho. *Perf. 13¼x12½***

**1752-1755** A391 Set of 4 16.00 16.00

***Perf. 12x12½***

**1756** A391 Sheet of 4, #a-d 16.00 16.00

**Souvenir Sheet**

**1757** A391 10k multi 8.00 8.00

Artifacts — A392

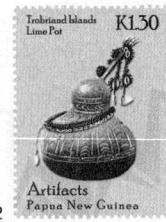

Designs: No. 1758, 1.30k, Trobriand Islands lime pot. No. 1759, 5k, Manus Island bowl. No. 1760, 6k, Wogeo Island food bowl. No. 1761, 8k, Sepik Region pan pipes.

No. 1762, horiz. — Various Sepik River canoe prows: a, 1.30k. b, 5k. c, 6k. d, 8k.

10k, Kiriwina lime pot.

***Perf. 13¼x13¾, 13¾x13¼ (#1762)***

**2014, Aug. 28 Litho.**

**1758-1761** A392 Set of 4 16.50 16.50
**1762** A392 Sheet of 4, #a-d 16.50 16.50

**Souvenir Sheet**

**1763** A392 10k multi 8.25 8.25

Bank of Papua New Guinea, 40th Anniv. A393

Bank building, 40th anniv. emblem and bank governors: No. 1764, 1.30k, Loi M. Bakani. No. 1765, 4k, Sir Mekere Morauta. No. 1766, 6k, Sir Henry ToRobert. No. 1767, 8k, Sir Wilson Kamit.

No. 1768 — 40th anniv. emblem and: a, 1.30k, Bank building, bank governor John Vulupindi. b, 4k, Bank building, bank governor Koiari Tarata. c, 6k, Bank building. d, 8k, Bank building, bank governor Morea Vele.

10k, 40th anniv. emblem, native costume, vert.

**Litho. With Foil Application**

**2014, Sept. 15 *Perf. 13¾x13¼***

**1764-1767** A393 Set of 4 15.50 15.50
**1768** A393 Sheet of 4, #a-d 15.50 15.50

**Souvenir Sheet**

***Perf. 13¼x13¾***

**1769** A393 10k multi 8.00 8.00

A394

A395

A396

New Year 2015 (Year of the Ram) — A397

No. 1774: a, 1.35k, Ram in circle. b, 1.35k, Ram in rectangle. c, 6.20k, Ram on pot. d, 8.95, Ram in circle, flowers at top.

10k, Ram and Chinese characters.

**2015, Jan. 5 Litho. *Perf. 13¼x12½***

**1770** A394 1.35k multi 1.00 1.00
**1771** A395 1.35k multi 1.00 1.00
**1772** A396 6.20k multi 4.75 4.75
**1773** A397 8.95k multi 6.75 6.75
*Nos. 1770-1773 (4)* 13.50 13.50

**Miniature Sheet**

**1774** A397 Sheet of 4, #a-d 13.50 13.50

**Souvenir Sheet**

**1775** A397 10k multi 7.75 7.75

Traditional Paintings — A398

Designs: No. 1776, 1.35k, Arawe Mother and Child. No. 1777, 1.35k, Motuan Village Totem Pole. No. 1778, 6.20k, Baining Fire Dancers. No. 1779, 8.95k, Crocodile Hunters.

No. 1780: a, 1.35k, Mount Elimbari. b, 1.35k, Wig Makers. c, 6.20k, Tifalmin Hunter. d, 8.95k, Wood Carver.

10k, Like No. 1777.

**2015, Mar. 9 Litho. *Perf. 14½x14***

**1776-1779** A398 Set of 4 13.50 13.50
**1780** A398 Sheet of 4, #a-d 13.50 13.50

**Souvenir Sheet**

**1781** A398 10k multi 7.50 7.50

Christian Leaders' Training College, 50th Anniv. — A399

Designs: No. 1782, 1.35k, College founder Dr. Gilbert J. McArthur and student leader, Jezreel Flora. No. 1783, 1.35k, Students of 1967. No. 1784, 6.20k, Graduates. No. 1785, 8.95k, Aerial view of Banz Campus.

No. 1786: a, 1.35k, Banz Campus, 1965. b, 1.35k, Banz Campus, 2015. c, 6.20k, Port Moresby Campus. d, 8.95k, Lae Campus.
10k, Graduation ceremony.

**Litho. With Foil Application**

**2015, Mar. 30** ***Perf. 14½x14***

**1782-1785** A399 Set of 4 13.50 13.50
**1786** A399 Sheet of 4, #a-d 13.50 13.50

**Souvenir Sheet**

**1787** A399 10k multi 7.50 7.50

Traditional Headdresses — A400

Headdress from: No. 1788, 1.35k, Central Province. No. 1789, 1.35k, Eastern Highlands Province. 6.20k, Central Province, diff. 8.95k, East Sepik Province.
10k, Headdress from Simbu Province.

**2015, June 22 Litho.** ***Perf. 14¼x14***

**1788-1791** A400 Set of 4 13.00 13.00
*1791a* Souvenir sheet of 4, #1788-1791 13.00 13.00

**Souvenir Sheet**

**1792** A400 10k multi 7.25 7.25

2015 Pacific Games, Port Moresby — A401

Emblem, mascot and: No. 1793, 1.35k, Dika Toua, weight lifting. No. 1794, 1.35k, Toea Wisil, running. No. 1795, 6.20k, Ryan Pini, swimming. No. 1796, 8.95k, Jack Biyufa, body building.
No. 1797: a, 1.35k, Abigail Tere Apisah, tennis. b, 1.35k, Betty Burua, running. c, 6.20k, Linda Pulsan, powerlifting. d, 8.95k, Steven Kari, weight lifting.
10k, Emblem and mascot.

**2015, June 22 Litho.** ***Perf. 14¼x14***

**1793-1796** A401 Set of 4 13.00 13.00
**1797** A401 Sheet of 4, #a-d 13.00 13.00

**Souvenir Sheet**

**1798** A401 10k multi 7.25 7.25

Queen Elizabeth II, Longest Reigning British Monarch — A402

Designs: No. 1799, 1.35k, Princesses Elizabeth and Margaret as children. No. 1800, 1.35k, Color photograph of Queen Elizabeth II. 6.20k, Queen Elizabeth II wearing crown. 8.95k, Queen Elizabeth II and Prince Philip.
10k, Queen Elizabeth II wearing crown, diff.

**2015, July 6 Litho.** ***Perf. 14***

**1799-1802** A402 Set of 4 13.00 13.00
*1802a* Souvenir sheet of 4, #1799-1802, perf. 12 13.00 13.00

**Souvenir Sheet**

***Perf. 12***

**1803** A402 10k multi 7.25 7.25

Birth of Princess Charlotte of Cambridge A403

Designs: No. 1804, 1.35k, Princess Charlotte in arms of Duchess of Cambridge. No. 1805, 1.35k, Duke and Duchess of Cambridge, Princess Charlotte. 6.20k, Duke and Duchess of Cambridge, Princess Charlotte, diff. 8.95k, Duke and Duchess of Cambridge, Princess Charlotte, diff.
10k, Duchess of Cambridge holding Princess Charlotte.

**2015, Aug. 3 Litho.** ***Perf. 14***

**1804-1807** A403 Set of 4 13.00 13.00
*1807a* Souvenir sheet of 4, #1804-1807 13.00 13.00

**Souvenir Sheet**

**1808** A403 10k multi 7.25 7.25

Singapore 2015 Intl. Stamp Exhibition — A404

Designs: No. 1809, 3.75k, Bird of paradise. No. 1810, 3.75k, Merlion.
No. 1811: a, Bird of paradise. b, Merlion.

**2015, Aug. 14 Litho.** ***Perf. 12***

**1809-1810** A404 Set of 2 5.25 5.25

**Embossed With Foil Application, Litho. Sheet Margin**

**Souvenir Sheet**

**1811** A404 20k Sheet of 2, #a-b 28.00 28.00

Nos. 1809-1810 were each printed in sheets of 4.

University of Papua New Guinea, 50th Anniv. A405

Designs: No. 1812, 1.35k, Cockatoo sculpture. No. 1813, 1.35k, University Chapel. 6.20k, Michael Somare Library. 8.95k, Graduation day.
10k, Sir John Gunther (1910-84), first university vice-chancellor.

**2015, Oct. 19 Litho.** ***Perf. 14x14¼***

**1812-1815** A405 Set of 4 12.50 12.50
*1815a* Souvenir sheet of 4, #1812-1815 12.50 12.50

**Souvenir Sheet**

**1816** A405 10k multi 6.75 6.75

Papuan Hornbills A406

Designs: No. 1817, 1.45k, Two hornbills in flight, orange pink background. No. 1818, 6.60k, Hornbill, lilac background. No. 1819, 15k, Two hornbills on perches, light green background. No. 1820, 25k, Two hornbills in flight, gray background.
No. 1821 — Stamps with pink background: a, 1.45k, Like #1817. b, 6.60k, Like #1818. c, 15k, Like #1819. d, 25k, Like #1820.
10k, Two hornbills on perches, light green background.

**2016, Jan. 4 Litho.** ***Perf. 12***

**1817-1820** A406 Set of 4 32.00 32.00
**1821** A406 Sheet of 4, #a-d 32.00 32.00

**Souvenir Sheet**

**1822** A406 10k multi 6.75 6.75

New Year 2016 (Year of the Monkey) A407

Monkey: No. 1823, 1.45k, Walking to left, green and orange background. No. 1824, 1.45k, Leaping with one arm raised, yellow and purple background. No. 1825, 3.30k, Sitting, purple and red background. No. 1826, 6.60k, Leaping with both arms raised, blue and green background.
No. 1827 — Orange and purple background, monkey: a, 1.45k, Running to right. b, 1.45k, Holding peach. c, 3.30k, Sitting. d, 6.60k, Walking to left.
10k, Monkey leaping with one arm raised.

**2016, Mar. 30 Litho.** ***Perf. 13½***

**1823-1826** A407 Set of 4 8.50 8.50
**1827** A407 Sheet of 4, #a-d 8.50 8.50

**Souvenir Sheet**

**1828** A407 10k multi 6.50 6.50

No. 1827 contains four 30x40mm stamps.

Coins and Banknotes A408

Bank of Papua New Guinea Governor Loi M. Bakani, standard and colored 2015 Pacific Games coins, and: No. 1829, 1.45k, Detail of 10-kina Pacific Games banknote at UR, denomination in bright purple. No. 1830, 1.45k, Detail of 20-kina Pacific Games banknote at UR, denomination in violet. No. 1831, 3.30k, Detail of standard 2015 Pacific Games coin at UR, denomination in brown purple. No. 1832, 6.60k, Detail of colored 2015 Pacific Games coin at UR, denomination in deep green.
No. 1833 — Bakani, standard and colored 2015 Pacific Games coin, detail of 2015 Independence Anniversary banknote, red denomination, and at upper right: a, 1.45k, Butterfly. b, 1.45k, Opossum. c, 3.30k, Cassowary. d. 6.60k, Turtle.
No. 1834, 5k — Bakani, standard and colored 2015 Pacific Games coin, detail of 2015 Independence Anniversary banknote, red denomination, and at upper right: a, Turtle. b, Cassowary.

**2016, May 19 Litho.** ***Perf. 13¾x13¼***

**1829-1832** A408 Set of 4 8.25 8.25
**1833** A408 Sheet of 4, #a-d 8.25 8.25

**Souvenir Sheet**

**1834** A408 5k Sheet of 2, #a-b 6.50 6.50

A409

A410

A411



Traditional Salt Making of Keri Tribe — A412

No. 1839 — Two men with: a, 1.45k, One holding hatchet, one pouring water. b, 2k, One holding sticks, one pointing at salt block. c, 4k, One holding water containers, one pouring water on salt block. d, 6.60k, One pointing at other, salt block and flowers on fabric.
10k, Man holding salt block.

**2016, Oct. 28 Litho.** ***Perf. 14½x14***

**1835** A409 1.45k multi .95 .95
**1836** A410 2k multi 1.25 1.25
**1837** A411 4k multi 2.50 2.50
**1838** A412 6.60k multi 4.25 4.25
*Nos. 1835-1838 (4)* 8.95 8.95

**Miniature Sheet**

**1839** A412 Sheet of 4, #a-d 9.00 9.00

**Souvenir Sheet**

**1840** A412 10k multi 6.50 6.50

Tunas A413

Designs: No. 1841, 1.45k, Yellowfin tuna. No. 1842, 2k, Bluefin tuna. No. 1843, 5k, Skipjack tuna. No. 1844, 6.60k, Albacore tuna.
No. 1845: a, 1.45k, Like #1842. b, 2k, Like #1844. c, 5k, Like #1841. d, 6.60k, Like #1843.
10k, Bluefin tuna, diff.

**2016, Oct. 29 Litho.** ***Perf. 14x14¼***

**1841-1844** A413 Set of 4 9.50 9.50
**1845** A413 Sheet of 4, #a-d 9.50 9.50

**Souvenir Sheet**

**1846** A413 10k multi 6.50 6.50

Worldwide Fund for Nature (WWF) — A414

No. 1847 — Various photographs of pig-nosed turtle with denomination in: a, 1.45k, Green. b, 3.80k, Yellow, c, 3.80k, Green. d, 6.60k, Green.

**2016, Nov. 4 Litho. *Perf. 14***

**1847** A414 Block or horiz. strip of 4, #a-d 10.00 10.00
*e.* Miniature sheet of 8, 2 each #1847a-1847d 20.00 20.00

Women's Under-20 World Cup Soccer Championships, Papua New Guinea — A415

Emblem, mascot and: 75t, Woman kicking ball. 1.50k, Goaltender reaching for ball. 3.40k, Flags and woman kicking ball. 5k, Athletic shoes and ball.
10k, Two women chasing ball.

**2016, Dec. 23 Litho. *Perf. 12***

**1848-1851** A415 Set of 4 6.75 6.75
*1851a* Souvenir sheet of 4, #1848-1851 6.75 6.75

**Souvenir Sheet**

**1852** A415 10k multi 6.50 6.50

New Year 2017 (Year of the Rooster) A416

Rooster facing: No. 1853, 1.50k, Right, both feet on ground. No. 1854, 2k, Left, one leg raised. No. 1855, 3.40k, Right, one leg raised. No. 1856, 6.80k, Left, both feet on ground.
No. 1857 — Two roosters: a, 1.50k. b, 2k, c, 3.40k. d, 6.80k.
13k, Two roosters, diff.

**2017, June 23 Litho. *Perf. 12***

**1853-1856** A416 Set of 4 8.75 8.75
**1857** A416 Sheet of 4, #a-d 8.75 8.75

**Souvenir Sheet**

**1858** A416 13k multi 8.25 8.25

No. 1857 contains four 30x40mm stamps. No. 1858 contains one 30x60mm stamp.

Faces of People From Southern Region — A417

Designs: No. 1859, 1.50k, Michael Hota, Motuan. No. 1860, 3.40k, Ruthie Masihada, Trobriand Islander. No. 1861, 5k, Madlyn Hera, Kairukuan. No. 1862, 6.80k, Rosemary Patrick, Motuan.
No. 1863: a, 1.50k, Hota, diff. b, 3.40k, Masihada, diff. c, 5k, Hera, diff. d, 6.80k, Patrick, diff.
13k, Pamela Lougaha, Tufian.

**2017, June 26 Litho. *Perf. 12***

**1859-1862** A417 Set of 4 10.50 10.50
**1863** A417 Sheet of 4, #a-d 10.50 10.50

**Souvenir Sheet**

**1864** A417 13k multi 8.25 8.25

No. 1863 contains four 30x40mm stamps.

A418

Princess Diana (1961-97) — A419

No. 1865 — Princess Diana wearing: a, Tiara. b, White hat.
No. 1866 — Princess Diana wearing a, Dark green hat. b, White hat, diff.

**2017, June 28 Litho. *Perf. 14***

**1865** A418 5k Pair, #a-b 6.25 6.25
**1866** A419 8k Horiz. pair, #a-b 10.00 10.00

No. 1865 was printed in sheets containing three each of Nos. 1865a-1865b. No. 1866 was printed in sheets containing two pairs.

Shells — A420

Designs: No. 1867, 75t, Tulip shells used for necklace. No. 1868, 1.50k, Conch shell used for communication. No. 1869, 3.40k, Cypraeidae shells used for traditional attire. No. 1870, 6.80k, Nassarius shells used for currency.
No. 1871: a, 75t, Man blowing into conch shell. b, 1.50k, Traditional costume made of Cypraeidae shells. c, 3.40k, Nassarius shell ring. d, 6.80k, Necklace made of shells.
13k, Papustyla pulcherrima used in Manus Province emblem.

**2017, Aug. 17 Litho. *Perf. 14***

**1867-1870** A420 Set of 4 7.75 7.75
**1871** A420 Sheet of 4, #a-d 7.75 7.75

**Souvenir Sheet**

**1872** A420 13k multi 8.25 8.25

New Year 2018 (Year of the Dog) — A421

No. 1873: a, Chinese character for "dog." b, Dog.
18k, Dog, horiz.

**2017, Aug. 18 Litho. *Perf. 14***

**1873** A421 5k Pair, #a-b 6.25 6.25

**Souvenir Sheet**

**1874** A421 18k multi 11.50 11.50

Birds — A422

Designs: No. 1875, 75t, Slaty-mantled goshawk. No. 1876, 1.50k, New Britain goshawk. No. 1877, 3.40k, Brown-collared brush turkey. No. 1878, 6.80k, Black honey buzzard.
No. 1879: a, 75t, Little eagle. b, 1.50k, Black-billed brush turkey. c, 3.40k, Magnificent ground pigeon. d, 6.80k, Collared sparrowhawk.

**2017, Aug. 24 Litho. *Perf. 14***

**1875-1878** A422 Set of 4 7.75 7.75
**1879** A422 Sheet of 4, #a-d 7.75 7.75

Bananas — A423

Designs: No. 1881, 75t, Buka. No. 1882, 1.50k, Goum. No. 1883, 3.40k, Itonia. No. 1884, 6.80k, Arawa.
No. 1885: a, 75t, Baby banana. b, 1.50k, Duma. c, 3.40k, Bubun. d, 6.80k, Abaus.
13k, Kalapua.

***Perf. 13¼x13½***

**2017, Aug. 28 Litho.**

**1881-1884** A423 Set of 4 7.75 7.75
**1885** A423 Sheet of 4, #a-d 7.75 7.75

**Souvenir Sheet**

**1886** A423 13k multi 8.25 8.25

Protestant Reformation, 500th Anniv. — A424

Martin Luther (1483-1546), Refomation 500th anniv. emblem, and emblem of Evangelical Lutheran Church of Papua New Guinea, and: No. 1887, 1.50k, Stained-glass window. No. 1888, 2k, Painting. No. 1889, 5k, Luther nailing 95 Theses on church door. No. 1890, 6.80k, Luther.
No. 1891, vert. — Head of Luther in: a, 1.50k, Bister. b, 2k, Dull ultramarine. c, 5k, Olive gray. d, 6.80k, Dull blue.
13k, Luther and Papua New Guinea church.

**2017, Oct. 25 Litho. *Perf. 13¼x13½***

**1887-1890** A424 Set of 4 9.50 9.50
**1891** A424 Sheet of 4, #a-d 9.50 9.50

**Souvenir Sheet**

**1892** A424 13k multi 8.25 8.25

No. 1891 contains four 30x40mm stamps.

Christmas — A425

Inscriptions: No. 1893, 75t, Hailareva soa (natives and hut). No. 1894, 1.50k, Bolmahogu wai (woman and infant). No. 1895, 3.40k, Abona lukara na kinakava (candles). No. 1896, 6.80k, Tamwasawasi towatanawa (natives carrying baskets).
No. 1897: a, 75t, Awogu amozin orande (Nativity scene). b, 1.50k, Lang nahpwen (natives carrying baskets). c, 3.40k, Abona lukara na kinakava (infant Jesus). d, 6.80k, Numan enem (three men wearing headdresses).
13k, Shondha gavo andha (Santa Claus).

***Perf. 13¼x13½***

**2017, Nov. 11 Litho.**

**1893-1896** A425 Set of 4 7.75 7.75

***Perf. 13½x13¼***

**1897** A425 Sheet of 4, #a-d 7.75 7.75

**Souvenir Sheet**

**1898** A425 13k multi 8.25 8.25

No. 1897 contains four 40x30mm stamps. No. 1898 contains one 40x30mm stamp.

Battle of Kokoda, 75th Anniv. — A426

Designs: No. 1899, 75t, Soldier assisting wounded soldier. No. 1900, 1.50k, Four Papuan natives carrying wounded soldier. No. 1901, 3.40k, Papuan soldiers. No. 1902, 6.80k, Papuan native assisting wounded soldier.
No. 1903, horiz.: a, 75t, Soldier assisting wounded soldier, Papuan natives carrying medical supplies. b, 1.50k, Soldiers on hike. c, 3.40k, Eleven Papuan natives carrying wounded soldier. d, 6.80k, Papuan natives carrying medical supplies.
13k, Veterans embracing.

***Perf. 13¼x13½, 13½x13¼ (#1903)***

**2017, Nov. 18 Litho.**

**1899-1902** A426 Set of 4 7.75 7.75
**1903** A426 Sheet of 4, #a-d 7.75 7.75

**Souvenir Sheet**

**1904** A426 13k multi 8.25 8.25

Papua New Guinea's Chairmanship of Asia-Pacific Economic Cooperation Area — A427

Inscription at left: 75t, People. 1.50k, Planet. No. 1907, 3.40k, Peace. No. 1908, 3.40k, Prosperity. No. 1909, 6.80k, Partnership. No. 1910, 6.80k, APEC.

No. 1911: a, 75t, Woman and child. b, 1.50k, Building and flags. c, 3.40k, Airplane, ship and dump truck. d, 6.80k, People and workers.

No. 1912, 20k, Map with lines leading to Papua New Guinea. No. 1913, 20k, Emblem of Papua New Guinea.

***Perf. 13¼x13½, 13½x13¼ (#1911)***

**2017, Dec. 4 Litho.**

| | | | | |
|---|---|---|---|---|
| **1905-1910** | A427 | Set of 6 | 14.00 | 14.00 |
| **1911** | A427 | Sheet of 4, #a-d | 7.75 | 7.75 |

**Souvenir Sheets**

| | | | | |
|---|---|---|---|---|
| **1912-1913** | A427 | Set of 2 | 25.00 | 25.00 |

No. 1911 contains four 40x30mm stamps.

First Voyage of Capt. James Cook, 250th Anniv. — A429

No. 1916: a, Capt. James Cook (1728-79). b, Captain Cook Memorial, Kurnell, New South Wales, Australia. c, The Bark, Earl of Pembroke, Later Endeavour, Leaving Whitby Harbor in 1768, by Thomas Luny. d, Map of Botany Bay, 1770. e, Statue of Captain Cook, Cooktown, Queensland, Australia. f, Landing of Captain Cook at Botany Bay, 1770, by E. Phillips Fox.

20k, Map of first voyage, horiz.

**2018, Feb. 15 Litho. *Perf. 14***

| | | | | |
|---|---|---|---|---|
| **1916** | A429 | 6.90k Sheet of 6, #a-f | 26.00 | 26.00 |

**Souvenir Sheet**

| | | | | |
|---|---|---|---|---|
| **1917** | A429 | 20k multi | 12.50 | 12.50 |

## AIR POST STAMPS

Regular Issue of 1916 Overprinted

**1929 Wmk. 74 *Perf. 14***

| | | | | |
|---|---|---|---|---|
| **C1** | A3 | 3p blue grn & dk gray | 3.50 | *20.00* |
| *b.* | | Vert. pair, one without ovpt. | *6,000.* | |
| *c.* | | Horiz. pair, one without ovpt. | *6,500.* | |
| *d.* | | 3p blue grn & sepia blk | 57.50 | *75.00* |
| *e.* | | Overprint on back, vert. | *5,000.* | |

No. C1 exists on white and on yellowish paper, No. C1d on yellowish paper only.

Regular Issues of 1916-23 Overprinted in Red

**1930, Sept. 15 Wmk. 74**

| | | | | |
|---|---|---|---|---|
| **C2** | A3 | 3p blue grn & blk | 2.00 | *11.00* |
| *a.* | | Yellowish paper | 3,800. | *5,600.* |
| *b.* | | Double overprint | 1,500. | |
| **C3** | A3 | 6p violet & dull vio | 8.00 | *12.00* |
| *a.* | | Yellowish paper | 5.00 | *15.00* |
| **C4** | A3 | 1sh ol grn & ol brn | 6.00 | *17.50* |
| *a.* | | Inverted overprint | *15,500.* | |
| *b.* | | Yellowish paper | 10.00 | 26.00 |
| | | *Nos. C2-C4 (3)* | 16.00 | *40.50* |

Port Moresby AP1

**Unwmk.**

**1938, Sept. 6 Engr. *Perf. 11***

| | | | | |
|---|---|---|---|---|
| **C5** | AP1 | 2p carmine | 2.75 | 3.25 |
| **C6** | AP1 | 3p ultra | 2.75 | 2.50 |
| **C7** | AP1 | 5p dark green | 2.75 | *3.50* |
| **C8** | AP1 | 8p red brown | 6.50 | *21.00* |
| **C9** | AP1 | 1sh violet | 17.50 | 22.50 |
| | | *Nos. C5-C9 (5)* | 32.25 | *52.75* |
| | | Set, never hinged | 65.00 | |

Papua as a British possession, 50th anniv.

Papuans Poling Rafts — AP2

**1939-41**

| | | | | |
|---|---|---|---|---|
| **C10** | AP2 | 2p carmine | 3.00 | 6.00 |
| **C11** | AP2 | 3p ultra | 3.00 | *11.00* |
| **C12** | AP2 | 5p dark green | 3.00 | 2.25 |
| **C13** | AP2 | 8p red brown | 7.50 | 3.25 |
| **C14** | AP2 | 1sh violet | 9.00 | 9.00 |
| **C15** | AP2 | 1sh6p lt olive ('41) | 27.50 | *40.00* |
| | | *Nos. C10-C15 (6)* | 53.00 | *71.50* |
| | | Set, never hinged | 90.00 | |

## POSTAGE DUE STAMPS

**Catalogue values for unused stamps in this section are for Never Hinged items.**

Nos. 128, 122, 129, 139 and 125 Surcharged in Black, Blue, Red or Orange

**1960 Unwmk. Engr. *Perf. 14***

| | | | | |
|---|---|---|---|---|
| **J1** | A24 | 1p on 6½p | 7.00 | *7.00* |
| **J2** | A23 | 3p on ½p (Bl) | 8.25 | 5.00 |
| *a.* | | Double surcharge | 600.00 | |
| **J3** | A24 | 6p on 7½p (R) | 25.00 | 12.00 |
| *a.* | | Double surcharge | 600.00 | |
| **J4** | A23 | 1sh3p on 3½p (O) | 9.50 | *7.50* |
| **J5** | A23 | 3sh on 2½p | 25.00 | 15.00 |
| | | *Nos. J1-J5 (5)* | 74.75 | 46.50 |

No. 129 Surcharged in Red

| | | | | |
|---|---|---|---|---|
| **J6** | A24 | 6p on 7½p | 1,100. | 775. |
| *a.* | | Double surcharge | 4,000. | 2,200. |

Surcharge forgeries exist.

D1

***Perf. 13½x14***

**1960, June 2 Litho. Wmk. 228**

| | | | | |
|---|---|---|---|---|
| **J7** | D1 | 1p orange | .50 | .55 |
| **J8** | D1 | 3p ocher | .55 | .55 |
| **J9** | D1 | 6p light ultra | .55 | .35 |
| **J10** | D1 | 9p vermilion | .55 | 1.25 |
| **J11** | D1 | 1sh emerald | .55 | .30 |
| **J12** | D1 | 1sh3p bright violet | .80 | 1.40 |
| **J13** | D1 | 1sh6p light blue | 4.00 | 4.00 |
| **J14** | D1 | 3sh yellow | 3.50 | .70 |
| | | *Nos. J7-J14 (8)* | 11.00 | 9.10 |

## OFFICIAL STAMPS

Nos. 60-63, 66-71, 92-93 Overprinted

**1931 Wmk. 74 *Perf. 14½***

| | | | | |
|---|---|---|---|---|
| **O1** | A3 | ½p #60 | 2.50 | *5.50* |
| **O2** | A3 | 1p #61 | 5.00 | *13.00* |
| **O3** | A3 | 1½p #62 | 2.00 | *14.00* |
| **O4** | A3 | 2p #63 | 4.50 | *14.00* |
| **O5** | A3 | 3p #66 | 3.00 | *25.00* |
| **O6** | A3 | 4p #67 | 3.00 | *21.00* |
| **O7** | A3 | 5p #68 | 7.00 | *42.50* |
| **O8** | A3 | 6p #69 | 5.00 | *9.75* |
| **O9** | A3 | 1sh #70 | 11.00 | *35.00* |
| **O10** | A3 | 2sh6p #71 | 47.50 | *97.50* |

**1932 Wmk. 228 *Perf. 11½***

| | | | | |
|---|---|---|---|---|
| **O11** | A3 | 9p #92 | 37.50 | *55.00* |
| **O12** | A3 | 1sh3p #93 | 37.50 | *55.00* |
| | | *Nos. O1-O12 (12)* | 165.50 | *387.25* |

# PARAGUAY

'par-ə-,gwī

LOCATION — South America, bounded by Bolivia, Brazil and Argentina
GOVT. — Republic
AREA — 157,042 sq. mi.
POP. — 5,434,095 (1999 est.)
CAPITAL — Asuncion

10 Reales = 100 Centavos = 1 Peso
100 Centimos = 1 Guarani (1944)

**Catalogue values for unused stamps in this country are for Never Hinged items, beginning with Scott 430 in the regular postage section, Scott B11 in the semi-postal section, and Scott C154 in the airpost section.**

**Watermarks**

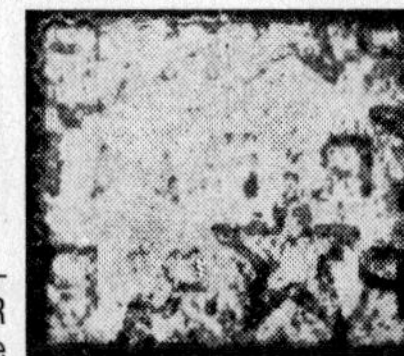

Wmk. 319 — Stars and R P Multiple

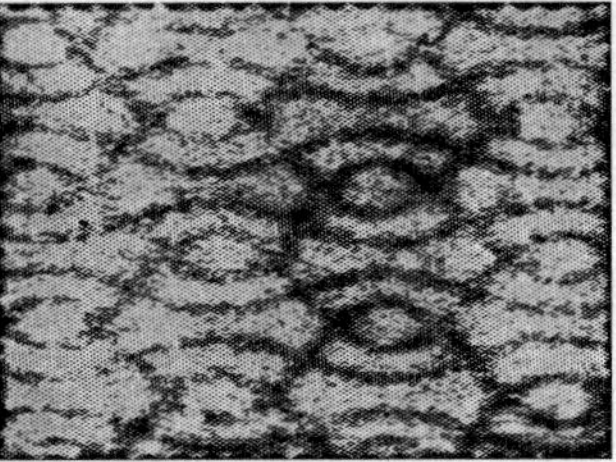

Wmk. 320 — Interlacing Lines

Wmk. 347 — RP Multiple

Vigilant Lion Supporting Liberty Cap
A1 A2

A3

**1870, Aug. Unwmk. Litho. *Imperf.***

| | | | | |
|---|---|---|---|---|
| **1** | A1 | 1r rose | 6.00 | *10.00* |
| **2** | A2 | 2r blue | 120.00 | *120.00* |
| **3** | A3 | 3r black | 230.00 | *250.00* |
| | | *Nos. 1-3 (3)* | 356.00 | *380.00* |

*Counterfeits of 2r in blue and other colors are on thicker paper than originals. They show a colored dot in upper part of "S" of "DOS" in upper right corner.*

For surcharges see Nos. 4-9, 19.

Handstamp Surcharged

**1878 Black Surcharge**

| | | | | |
|---|---|---|---|---|
| **4** | A1 | 5c on 1r rose | 100. | *120.* |
| **5** | A2 | 5c on 2r blue | 450. | 400. |
| **5E** | A3 | 5c on 3r black | 550. | 550. |
| | | *Nos. 4-5E (3)* | 1,100. | 1,070. |

**Blue Surcharge**

| | | | | |
|---|---|---|---|---|
| **5F** | A1 | 5c on 1r rose | 100. | *120.* |
| **5H** | A2 | 5c on 2r blue | *1,200.* | *1,200.* |
| **6** | A3 | 5c on 3r black | 675. | 650. |
| | | *Nos. 5F-6 (3)* | *1,975.* | *1,970.* |

The surcharge may be found inverted, double, sideways and omitted.

Remainders of Nos. 4 and 5F were placed on sale at Post Offices during 1892. Covers dated 1892 are worth about $7,500.

*The originals are surcharged in dull black or dull blue. The reprints are in intense black and bright blue. The reprint surcharges are over-inked and show numerous breaks in the handstamp.*

Handstamp Surcharged

**Black Surcharge**

7 A2 5c on 2r blue 450.00 375.00
8 A3 5c on 3r black 575.00 550.00

**Blue Surcharge**

9 A3 5c on 3r black 550.00 550.00
*a.* Dbl. surch., large & small "5" —
*Nos. 7-9 (3)* 1,575. 1,475.

The surcharge on Nos. 7, 8 and 9 is usually placed sideways. It may be found double or inverted on Nos. 8 and 9.

Nos. 4 to 9 have been extensively counterfeited.

Two examples recorded of No. 9a, one without gum, the other with full but disturbed original gum.

A4

**1879 Litho. *Perf. 12½***

**Thin Paper**

10 A4 5r orange .70
11 A4 10r red brown .80
*a.* Imperf.
*b.* Horiz. pair, imperf. vert. 60.00

Nos. 10 and 11 were never placed in use.
For surcharges see Nos. 17-18.

A4a

**1879-81 Thin Paper**

12 A4a 5c orange brown 2.50 2.50
13 A4a 10c blue grn ('81) 3.50 3.50
*a.* Imperf., pair 50.00 *60.00*

*Reprints of Nos. 10-13 are imperf., perf. 11½, 12, 12½ or 14. They have yellowish gum and the 10c is deep green.*

A5

A6

A7

**1881, Aug. Litho. *Perf. 11½-13½***

14 A5 1c blue .80 .70
*a.* Imperf., pair —
*b.* Horiz. pair, imperf. btwn. —
15 A6 2c rose red .80 *.70*
*a.* 2c dull orange red 1.00 .90
*b.* Imperf., pair —
*c.* Horiz. pair, imperf. vert. 25.00 25.00
*d.* Vert. pair, imperf. horiz. 25.00 25.00
16 A7 4c brown .80 *.70*
*a.* Imperf., pair —
*b.* Horiz. pair, imperf. vert. 25.00 25.00
*c.* Vert. pair, imperf. horiz. 25.00 25.00

**No. 11 Handstamped Surcharge in Black or Gray**

**1881, July *Perf. 12½***

17 A4 1c on 10c blue grn 16.00 15.00
18 A4 2c on 10c blue grn 16.00 15.00

Gray handstamps sell for 10 times more than black as many specialists consider the black to be reprints.

No. 1 Handstamped Surcharge in Black

**1884, May 8 *Imperf.***

19 A1 1c on 1r rose 10.00 8.00

The surcharges on Nos. 17-19 exist double, inverted and in pairs with one omitted. Counterfeits exist.

Seal of the Treasury — A11

**1884, Aug. 3 Litho. *Perf. 12½***

20 A11 1c green 1.00 .80
21 A11 2c rose pink, thin paper 1.00 .80

***Perf. 11½***

22 A11 5c pale blue, yellowish paper 1.00 .80
*Nos. 20-22 (3)* 3.00 2.40

There are two types of each value differing mostly in the shape of the numerals. In addition, there are numerous small flaws in the lithographic transfers.

For overprints see Nos. O1, O8, O15.

**Imperf., Pairs**

*20a* A11 1c green 12.50
*21a* A11 2c rose red 16.00
*22a* A11 5c blue 16.00
*Nos. 20a-22a (3)* 44.50

Seal of the Treasury — A12

***Perf. 11½, 11½x12, 12½x11½***

**1887 Typo.**

23 A12 1c green .30 .25
24 A12 2c rose .30 .25
25 A12 5c blue .50 .35
26 A12 7c brown .90 .50
27 A12 10c lilac .60 .35
28 A12 15c orange .60 .35
29 A12 20c pink .60 .35
*Nos. 23-29 (7)* 3.80 2.40

See #42-45. For surcharges & overprints see #46, 49-50, 71-72, 167-170A, O20-O41, O49.

Symbols of Liberty from Coat of Arms — A13

**1889, Feb. Litho. *Perf. 11½***

30 A13 15c red violet 2.50 2.00
*a.* Imperf., pair 10.00 8.00

For overprints see Nos. O16-O19.

Overprint Handstamped in Violet

**1892, Oct. 12 *Perf. 12x12½***

31 A15 10c violet blue 10.00 5.00

Discovery of America by Columbus, 400th anniversary. Overprint reads: "1492 / 12 DE OCTUBRE / 1892." Sold only on day of issue.

Cirilo A. Rivarola — A15

Designs: 2c, Salvador Jovellanos. 4c, Juan B. Gil. 5c, Higinio Uriarte. 10c, Cándido Bareiro. 14c, Gen. Bernardino Caballero. 20c, Gen. Patricio Escobar. 30c, Juan G. González.

**1892-96 Litho. *Perf. 12x12½***

32 A15 1c gray (centavos) .25 .25
33 A15 1c gray (centavo) ('96) .25 .25
34 A15 2c green .25 .25
*a.* Chalky paper ('96) .25 .25
35 A15 4c carmine .25 .25
*a.* Chalky paper ('96) .25 .25
36 A15 5c violet ('93) .25 .25
*a.* Chalky paper ('96) .25 .25
37 A15 10c vio bl (punched) ('93) .25 .25
Unpunched ('96) 5.00
38 A15 10c dull blue ('96) .25 .25
39 A15 14c yellow brown .75 .50
40 A15 20c red ('93) 1.25 .50
41 A15 30c light green 2.00 .80
*Nos. 32-41 (10)* 5.75 3.55

The 10c violet blue (No. 37) was, until 1896, issued punched with a circular hole in order to prevent it being fraudulently overprinted as No. 31.

Nos. 33 and 38 are on chalky paper.
For surcharge see No. 70.

**Seal Type of 1887**

**1892 Typo.**

42 A12 40c slate blue 3.00 1.25
43 A12 60c yellow 1.50 .50
44 A12 80c light blue 1.40 .50
45 A12 1p olive green 1.40 .50
*Nos. 42-45 (4)* 7.30 2.75

For surcharges see Nos. 71-72.

No. 26 Surcharged in Black

**1895, Aug. 1 *Perf. 11½x12***

46 A12 5c on 7c brown .75 .75

Telegraph Stamps Surcharged

**1896, Apr. Engr. *Perf. 11½***

**Denomination in Black**

47 5c on 2c brown & gray .90 .60
*a.* Inverted surcharge 10.00 10.00
48 5c on 4c yellow & gray .90 .60
*a.* Inverted surcharge 7.50 7.50

Nos. 28, 42 Surcharged

**1898-99 Typo.**

49 A12 10c on 15c org ('99) .75 .45
*a.* Inverted surcharge 17.50 17.50
*b.* Double surcharge 11.00 11.00
50 A12 10c on 40c slate bl .35 .25

Surcharge on No. 49 has small "c."

**Telegraph Stamps Surcharged**

**1900, May 14 Engr. *Perf. 11½***

50A 5c on 30c grn, gray & blk 2.75 1.50
50B 10c on 50c dl vio, gray & blk 6.00 3.75

The basic telegraph stamps are like those used for Nos. 47-48, but the surcharges on Nos. 50A-50B consist of "5 5" and "10 10" above a blackout rectangle covering the engraved denominations.

A 40c red, bluish gray and black telegraph stamp (basic type of A24) was used provisionally in August, 1900, for postage. Value, postally used, $5.

Seal of the Treasury — A25

**1900, Sept. Engr. *Perf. 11½, 12***

51 A25 2c gray .40 .30
52 A25 3c orange brown .40 .30
53 A25 5c dark green .40 .30
54 A25 8c dark brown .40 .30
55 A25 10c carmine rose 1.00 .30
56 A25 24c deep blue 1.20 .30
*Nos. 51-56 (6)* 3.80 1.80

See Nos. 57-67. For surcharges see Nos. 69, 74, 76, 156-157.

**Small Figures**

**1901, Apr. Litho. *Perf. 11½***

57 A25 2c rose .25 .25
58 A25 5c violet brown .25 .25
59 A25 40c blue .85 .30
*Nos. 57-59 (3)* 1.35 .80

**1901-02 Larger Figures**

60 A25 1c gray green ('02) .30 .30
61 A25 2c gray .30 .30
*a.* Half used as 1c on cover 10.00
62 A25 4c pale blue .30 .30
63 A25 5c violet .30 .30
64 A25 8c gray brown ('02) .30 .30
65 A25 10c rose red ('02) .75 .30
66 A25 28c orange ('02) 1.50 .30
67 A25 40c blue .75 .30
*Nos. 60-67 (8)* 4.50 2.40

For surcharges see Nos. 74, 76.

J. B. Egusquiza — A26

**Chalky Paper**

**1901, Sept. 24 Typo. *Perf. 12x12½***

68 A26 1p slate .30 .25

For surcharge see No. 73.

No. 56 Surcharged in Red

**1902, Aug.**

69 A25 20c on 24c dp blue .50 .40
*a.* Inverted surcharge 6.25

Counterfeit surcharges exist.

**Nos. 39, 43-44 Surcharged**

**1902, Dec. 22** *Perf. 12x12½*

| | | | | |
|---|---|---|---|---|
| 70 | A15 | 1c on 14c yellow brn | .25 | .25 |
| *a.* | | No period after "cent" | .90 | .75 |
| *b.* | | Comma after "cent" | .65 | .50 |
| *c.* | | Accent over "Un" | .65 | .50 |

**1903** *Perf. 11½*

| | | | | |
|---|---|---|---|---|
| 71 | A12 | 5c on 60c yellow | .35 | .30 |
| 72 | A12 | 5c on 80c lt blue | .30 | .30 |

**Nos. 68, 64, 66 Surcharged**

No. 73

No. 74

No. 76

**1902-03** *Perf. 12*

| | | | | |
|---|---|---|---|---|
| 73 | A26 | 1c on 1p slate ('03) | .40 | .40 |
| *a.* | | No period after "cent" | 3.25 | 3.00 |

*Perf. 11½*

| | | | | |
|---|---|---|---|---|
| 74 | A25 | 5c on 8c gray brown | .50 | .40 |
| *a.* | | No period after "cent" | 1.75 | 1.50 |
| *b.* | | Double surcharge | 7.00 | 6.00 |
| 76 | A25 | 5c on 28c orange | .50 | .40 |
| *a.* | | No period after "cent" | 1.75 | 1.50 |
| *b.* | | Comma after "cent" | .80 | .60 |
| | | *Nos. 73-76 (3)* | 1.40 | 1.20 |

The surcharge on Nos. 73 and 74 is found reading both upward and downward.

Sentinel Lion with Right Paw Ready to Strike for "Peace and Justice" — A32

*Perf. 11½*

**1903, Feb. 28** **Litho.** **Unwmk.**

| | | | | |
|---|---|---|---|---|
| 77 | A32 | 1c gray | .30 | .30 |
| 78 | A32 | 2c blue green | .45 | .30 |
| 79 | A32 | 5c blue | .60 | .30 |
| 80 | A32 | 10c orange brown | .75 | .30 |
| 81 | A32 | 20c carmine | .75 | .30 |
| 82 | A32 | 30c deep blue | .90 | .30 |
| 83 | A32 | 60c purple | 2.10 | 1.00 |
| | | *Nos. 77-83 (7)* | 5.85 | 2.80 |

For surcharges and overprints see Nos. 139-140, 166, O50-O56.

Sentinel Lion with Right Paw Ready to Strike for "Peace and Justice" — A33

**1903, Sept.**

| | | | | |
|---|---|---|---|---|
| 84 | A33 | 1c yellow green | .30 | .30 |
| 85 | A33 | 2c red orange | .30 | .30 |
| 86 | A33 | 5c dark blue | .45 | .30 |
| 87 | A33 | 10c purple | .45 | .30 |
| 88 | A33 | 20c dark green | 5.00 | .45 |
| 89 | A33 | 30c ultramarine | 1.50 | .30 |
| 90 | A33 | 60c ocher | 1.75 | .75 |
| | | *Nos. 84-90 (7)* | 9.75 | 2.70 |

Nos. 84-90 exist imperf. Value for pairs, $3 each for 1c-20c, $4 for 30c, $5 for 60c.

The three-line overprint "Gobierno provisorio Ago. 1904" is fraudulent.

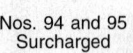

Sentinel Lion at Rest — A35

*Perf. 11½, 12, 11½x12*

**1905-10** **Engr.**

**Dated "1904"**

| | | | | |
|---|---|---|---|---|
| 91 | A35 | 1c orange | .30 | .25 |
| 92 | A35 | 1c vermilion ('07) | .30 | .25 |
| 93 | A35 | 1c grnsh bl ('07) | .30 | .25 |
| 94 | A35 | 2c vermilion ('06) | .30 | .25 |
| 95 | A35 | 2c olive grn ('07) | 60.00 | |
| 96 | A35 | 2c car rose ('08) | .45 | .25 |
| 97 | A35 | 5c dark blue | .30 | .25 |
| 98 | A35 | 5c slate blue ('06) | .30 | .25 |
| 99 | A35 | 5c yellow ('06) | .30 | .25 |
| 100 | A35 | 10c bister ('06) | .30 | .25 |
| 101 | A35 | 10c emerald ('07) | .30 | .25 |
| 102 | A35 | 10c dp ultra ('08) | .30 | .25 |
| 103 | A35 | 20c violet ('06) | .45 | .25 |
| 104 | A35 | 20c bister ('07) | .45 | .25 |
| 105 | A35 | 20c apple grn ('07) | .45 | .25 |
| 106 | A35 | 30c turq bl ('06) | .65 | .25 |
| 107 | A35 | 30c blue gray ('07) | .65 | .25 |
| 108 | A35 | 30c dull lilac ('08) | .90 | .25 |
| 109 | A35 | 60c chocolate ('07) | .60 | .25 |
| 110 | A35 | 60c org brn ('07) | 5.25 | 1.60 |
| 111 | A35 | 60c salmon pink ('10) | 5.25 | 1.60 |
| | | *Nos. 91-111 (21)* | 78.10 | |
| | | *Nos. 91-94,96-111 (20)* | 18.10 | 7.70 |

All but Nos. 92 and 104 exist imperf. Value for pair, $10 each, except No. 95 at $35.00 and Nos. 109-111 at $15.00 each pair.

For surcharges and overprints see Nos. 129-130, 146-155, 174-190, 266.

Sentinel Lion at Rest — A36

**1904, Aug.** **Litho.** *Perf. 11½*

| | | | | |
|---|---|---|---|---|
| 112 | A36 | 10c light blue | .50 | .40 |
| *a.* | | Imperf., pair | 6.00 | |

No. 112 Surcharged in Black

**1904, Dec.**

| | | | | |
|---|---|---|---|---|
| 113 | A36 | 30c on 10c light blue | .80 | .50 |

Peace between a successful revolutionary party and the government previously in power.

Governmental Palace, Asunción — A37

**Dated "1904"**
**Center in Black**

**1906-10** **Engr.** *Perf. 11½, 12*

| | | | | |
|---|---|---|---|---|
| 114 | A37 | 1p bright rose | 2.50 | 1.50 |
| 115 | A37 | 1p brown org ('07) | 1.00 | .50 |
| 116 | A37 | 1p ol gray ('07) | 1.00 | .50 |
| 117 | A37 | 2p turquoise ('07) | .50 | .40 |
| 118 | A37 | 2p lake ('09) | .50 | .40 |
| 119 | A37 | 2p brn org ('10) | .60 | .40 |
| 120 | A37 | 5p red ('07) | 1.50 | 1.00 |
| 121 | A37 | 5p ol grn ('10) | 1.50 | 1.00 |
| 122 | A37 | 5p dull bl ('10) | 1.50 | 1.00 |
| 123 | A37 | 10p brown org ('07) | 1.40 | 1.00 |
| 124 | A37 | 10p dp blue ('10) | 1.40 | 1.00 |
| 125 | A37 | 10p choc ('10) | 1.50 | 1.00 |
| 126 | A37 | 20p olive grn ('07) | 3.50 | 3.25 |
| 127 | A37 | 20p violet ('10) | 3.50 | 3.25 |
| 128 | A37 | 20p yellow ('10) | 3.50 | 3.25 |
| | | *Nos. 114-128 (15)* | 25.40 | 19.45 |

Nos. 94 and 95 Surcharged

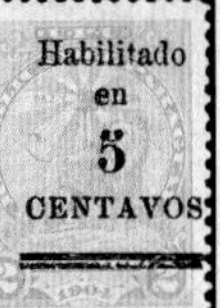


**1907**

| | | | | |
|---|---|---|---|---|
| 129 | A35 | 5c on 2c vermilion | .45 | .30 |
| *a.* | | "5" omitted | 1.50 | 1.50 |
| *b.* | | Inverted surcharge | 5.25 | 5.25 |
| *c.* | | Double surcharge | | |
| *d.* | | Double surcharge, one inverted | 1.50 | 1.50 |
| *e.* | | Double surcharge, both invtd. | 9.00 | 9.00 |
| 130 | A35 | 5c on 2c olive grn | .60 | .30 |
| *a.* | | "5" omitted | 1.50 | 1.50 |
| *b.* | | Inverted surcharge | 1.50 | 1.50 |
| *c.* | | Double surcharge | 3.00 | 3.00 |
| *d.* | | Bar omitted | 3.00 | 3.00 |

Official Stamps of 1906-08 Surcharged



**1908**

| | | | | |
|---|---|---|---|---|
| 131 | O17 | 5c on 10c bister | .45 | .30 |
| *a.* | | Double surcharge | 4.50 | 4.50 |
| 132 | O17 | 5c on 10c violet | .45 | .30 |
| *a.* | | Inverted surcharge | 3.50 | 3.50 |
| 133 | O17 | 5c on 20c emerald | .45 | .30 |
| 134 | O17 | 5c on 20c violet | .45 | .30 |
| *a.* | | Inverted surcharge | 3.50 | 3.50 |
| 135 | O17 | 5c on 30c slate bl | 1.50 | 1.00 |
| 136 | O17 | 5c on 30c turq bl | 1.50 | 1.00 |
| *a.* | | Inverted surcharge | | |
| *b.* | | Double surcharge | 9.00 | 9.00 |
| 137 | O17 | 5c on 60c choc | .45 | .30 |
| *a.* | | Double surcharge | 9.00 | 9.00 |
| 138 | O17 | 5c on 60c red brown | .90 | .30 |
| *a.* | | Inverted surcharge | 1.60 | 1.60 |
| | | *Nos. 131-138 (8)* | 6.15 | 3.80 |

**Same Surcharge on Official Stamps of 1903**

| | | | | |
|---|---|---|---|---|
| 139 | A32 | 5c on 30c dp blue | 3.75 | 3.25 |
| 140 | A32 | 5c on 60c purple | 1.50 | .90 |
| *a.* | | Double surcharge | 7.50 | 7.50 |

Official Stamps of 1906-08 Overprinted



| | | | | |
|---|---|---|---|---|
| 141 | O17 | 5c deep blue | .40 | .40 |
| *a.* | | Inverted overprint | 3.00 | 3.00 |
| *b.* | | Bar omitted | 9.00 | 9.00 |
| *c.* | | Double overprint | 4.00 | 4.00 |
| 142 | O17 | 5c slate blue | .50 | .40 |
| *a.* | | Inverted overprint | 4.00 | 4.00 |
| *b.* | | Double overprint | 3.50 | 3.50 |
| *c.* | | Bar omitted | 9.00 | 9.00 |
| 143 | O17 | 5c greenish blue | .40 | .40 |
| *a.* | | Inverted overprint | 2.50 | 2.50 |
| *b.* | | Bar omitted | 7.50 | 7.50 |
| 144 | O18 | 1p brown org & blk | .50 | .50 |
| *a.* | | Double overprint | 2.00 | 2.00 |
| *b.* | | Double overprint, one inverted | 2.50 | 2.50 |
| *c.* | | Triple overprint, two inverted | 4.50 | 4.50 |
| 145 | O18 | 1p brt rose & blk | .90 | .70 |
| *a.* | | Bar omitted | | |
| | | *Nos. 141-145 (5)* | 2.70 | 2.40 |

Regular Issues of 1906-08 Surcharged

**1908**

| | | | | |
|---|---|---|---|---|
| 146 | A35 | 5c on 1c grnsh bl | .30 | .30 |
| *a.* | | Inverted surcharge | 1.50 | 1.50 |
| *b.* | | Double surcharge | 2.25 | 2.25 |
| *c.* | | "5" omitted | 2.25 | 2.25 |
| 147 | A35 | 5c on 2c car rose | .30 | .30 |
| *a.* | | Inverted surcharge | 2.50 | 2.50 |
| *b.* | | "5" omitted | 3.00 | 3.00 |
| *c.* | | Double surcharge | 5.25 | 5.25 |
| *d.* | | Double surcharge, one invtd. | | |
| 148 | A35 | 5c on 60c org brn | .30 | .30 |
| *a.* | | Inverted surcharge | 3.75 | 3.75 |
| *b.* | | "5" omitted | 1.50 | 1.50 |
| 149 | A35 | 5c on 60c sal pink | .30 | .30 |
| *a.* | | Double surcharge | .75 | .75 |
| *b.* | | Double surcharge, one invtd. | 5.25 | 5.25 |
| 150 | A35 | 5c on 60c choc | .30 | .30 |
| *a.* | | Inverted surcharge | 7.50 | 7.50 |
| 151 | A35 | 20c on 1c grnsh bl | .30 | .30 |
| *a.* | | Inverted surcharge | 2.25 | 2.25 |
| 152 | A35 | 20c on 2c ver | 9.00 | 7.50 |
| 153 | A35 | 20c on 2c car rose | 5.25 | 4.50 |
| *a.* | | Inverted surcharge | 19.00 | |
| 154 | A35 | 20c on 30c dl lil | .30 | .30 |
| *a.* | | Inverted surcharge | 2.25 | 2.25 |
| *b.* | | Double surcharge | | |
| 155 | A35 | 20c on 30c turq bl | 2.25 | 2.25 |
| | | *Nos. 146-155 (10)* | 18.60 | 16.35 |

**Same Surcharge on Regular Issue of 1901-02**

| | | | | |
|---|---|---|---|---|
| 156 | A25 | 5c on 28c org | 1.90 | 1.60 |
| 157 | A25 | 5c on 40c dk bl | .60 | .45 |
| *a.* | | Inverted surcharge | 6.00 | 6.00 |

**Same Surcharge on Official Stamps of 1908**

| | | | | |
|---|---|---|---|---|
| 158 | O17 | 5c on 10c emer | .40 | .40 |
| *a.* | | Double surcharge | 14.00 | |
| 159 | O17 | 5c on 10c red lil | .40 | .40 |
| *a.* | | Double surcharge | 4.00 | 4.00 |
| *b.* | | "5" omitted | 3.00 | 3.00 |
| 160 | O17 | 5c on 20c bis | .80 | .60 |
| *a.* | | Double surcharge | 2.50 | 2.50 |
| 161 | O17 | 5c on 20c sal pink | .80 | .60 |
| *a.* | | "5" omitted | 3.50 | 3.50 |
| 162 | O17 | 5c on 30c bl gray | .40 | .40 |
| 163 | O17 | 5c on 30c yel | .40 | .40 |
| *a.* | | "5" omitted | 3.00 | 3.00 |
| *b.* | | Inverted surcharge | 2.50 | 2.50 |
| 164 | O17 | 5c on 60c org brn | .40 | .40 |
| *a.* | | Double surcharge | 12.00 | 12.00 |
| 165 | O17 | 5c on 60c dp ultra | .40 | .40 |
| *a.* | | Inverted surcharge | 5.00 | 5.00 |
| *b.* | | "5" omitted | 3.00 | |
| | | *Nos. 158-165 (8)* | 4.00 | 3.60 |

**Same Surcharge on No. O52**

| | | | | |
|---|---|---|---|---|
| 166 | A32 | 20c on 5c blue | 2.50 | 2.00 |
| *a.* | | Inverted surcharge | 6.00 | 7.50 |

Stamp of 1887 Surcharged

**1908** **On Stamp of 1887**

| | | | | |
|---|---|---|---|---|
| 167 | A12 | 20c on 2c car | 6.50 | 3.00 |
| *a.* | | Inverted surcharge | 22.50 | |

**On Official Stamps of 1892**

| | | | | |
|---|---|---|---|---|
| 168 | A12 | 5c on 15c org | 7.50 | 5.25 |
| 169 | A12 | 5c on 20c pink | 120.00 | 95.00 |
| 170 | A12 | 5c on 50c gray | 52.50 | 37.50 |
| 170A | A12 | 20c on 5c blue | 4.50 | 3.75 |
| *b.* | | Inverted surcharge | 25.00 | 25.00 |
| | | *Nos. 167-170A (5)* | 191.00 | 144.50 |

Nos. 151, 152, 153, 155, 167, 170A, while duly authorized, all appear to have been sold to a single individual, and although they paid postage, it is doubtful whether they can be considered as ever having been placed on sale to the public.

Nos. O82-O84 Surcharged (Date in Red)

**1908-09**

| | | | | |
|---|---|---|---|---|
| 171 | O18 | 1c on 1p brt rose & blk | .50 | .50 |
| 172 | O18 | 1c on 1p lake & blk | .50 | .50 |
| 173 | O18 | 1c on 1p brn org & blk ('09) | 5.00 | 5.00 |
| | | *Nos. 171-173 (3)* | 6.00 | 6.00 |

Varieties of surcharge on Nos. 171-173 include: "CETTAVO"; date omitted, double or inverted; third line double or omitted.

Types of 1905-1910 Overprinted

**1908, Mar. 5** *Perf. 11½*

| | | | | |
|---|---|---|---|---|
| 174 | A35 | 1c emerald | .30 | .30 |
| 175 | A35 | 5c yellow | .30 | .30 |
| 176 | A35 | 10c lilac brown | .30 | .30 |
| 177 | A35 | 20c yellow orange | .30 | .30 |
| 178 | A35 | 30c red | .40 | .30 |
| 179 | A35 | 60c magenta | .30 | .30 |
| 180 | A37 | 1p light blue | .30 | .30 |
| | | *Nos. 174-180 (7)* | 2.20 | 2.10 |

Overprinted

**1909, Sept.**

**181** A35 1c blue gray .40 .40
**182** A35 1c scarlet .40 .40
**183** A35 5c dark green .40 .40
**184** A35 5c deep orange .40 .40
**185** A35 10c rose .40 .40
**186** A35 10c bister brown .40 .40
**187** A35 20c yellow .40 .40
**188** A35 20c violet .40 .40
**189** A35 30c orange brown .60 .40
**190** A35 30c dull blue .60 .40
*Nos. 181-190 (10)* 4.40 4.00

Counterfeits exist.

Coat of Arms above Numeral of Value — A38

**1910-21** **Litho.** ***Perf. 11½***

**191** A38 1c brown .40 .25
**192** A38 5c bright violet .40 .25
*a.* Pair, imperf. between 2.00 2.00
**193** A38 5c blue grn ('19) .40 .25
**194** A38 5c lt blue ('21) .40 .25
**195** A38 10c yellow green .40 .25
**196** A38 10c dp vio ('19) .40 .25
**197** A38 10c red ('21) .40 .25
**198** A38 20c red .40 .25
**199** A38 50c car rose .60 .25
**200** A38 75c deep blue .40 .25
*a.* Diag. half perforated ('11) .40 .25
*Nos. 191-200 (10)* 4.20 2.50

Nos. 191-200 exist imperforate.
No. 200a was authorized for use as 20c.
For surcharges see Nos. 208, 241, 261, 265.

"The Republic" — A39

**1911** **Engr.**

**201** A39 1c olive grn & blk .30 .30
**202** A39 2c dk blue & blk .45 .30
**203** A39 5c carmine & indigo .45 .30
**204** A39 10c dp blue & brn .45 .30
**205** A39 20c olive grn & ind .60 .30
**206** A39 50c lilac & indigo .75 .30
**207** A39 75c ol grn & red lil .75 .30
*Nos. 201-207 (7)* 3.75 2.10

Centenary of National Independence.
The 1c, 2c, 10c and 50c exist imperf. Value for pairs, $2.25 each.

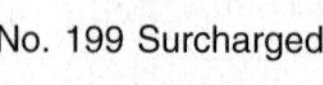

No. 199 Surcharged

**1912**

**208** A38 20c on 50c car rose .30 .30
*a.* Inverted surcharge 1.90 1.90
*b.* Double surcharge 1.90 1.90
*c.* Bar omitted 2.50 2.50

National Coat of Arms — A40

**1913** **Engr.** ***Perf. 11½***

**209** A40 1c gray .30 .25
**210** A40 2c orange .30 .25
**211** A40 5c lilac .30 .25
**212** A40 10c green .30 .25
**213** A40 20c dull red .30 .25
**214** A40 40c rose .30 .25
**215** A40 75c deep blue .30 .25
**216** A40 80c yellow .30 .25
**217** A40 1p light blue .45 .25
**218** A40 1.25p pale blue .45 .25
**219** A40 3p greenish blue .45 .25
*Nos. 209-219 (11)* 3.75 2.75

For surcharges see Nos. 225, 230-231, 237, 242, 253, 262-263, L3-L4.

Nos. J7-J10 Overprinted

**1918**

**220** D2 5c yellow brown .25 .25
**221** D2 10c yellow brown .25 .25
**222** D2 20c yellow brown .25 .25
**223** D2 40c yellow brown .25 .25

Nos. J10 and 214 Surcharged

**224** D2 5c on 40c yellow brn .25 .25
**225** A40 30c on 40c rose .25 .25
*Nos. 220-225 (6)* 1.50 1.50

Nos. 220-225 exist with surcharge inverted, double and double with one inverted.
The surcharge "Habilitado-1918-5 cents 5" on the 1c gray official stamps of 1914, is bogus.

No. J11 Overprinted

**1920**

**229** D2 1p yellow brown .25 .25
*a.* Inverted overprint .65 .65
*e.* As "g," "AABILITADO" .75 .75
*f.* As "g," "1929" for "1920" .75 .75
*g.* Overprint lines 8mm apart .25 .25

Nos. 216 and 219 Surcharged

**230** A40 50c on 80c yellow .25 .25
**231** A40 1.75p on 3p grnsh bl .75 .65

**Same Surcharge on No. J12**

**232** D2 1p on 1.50p yel brn .25 .25
*Nos. 229-232 (4)* 1.50 1.40

Nos. 229-232 exist with various surcharge errors, including inverted, double, double inverted and double with one inverted. Those that were issued are listed.

Parliament Building A41

**1920** **Litho.** ***Perf. 11½***

**233** A41 50c red & black .35 .30
*a.* "CORRLOS" 5.00 5.00
**234** A41 1p lt blue & blk 1.00 .45
**235** A41 1.75p dk blue & blk .30 .30
**236** A41 3p orange & blk 1.50 .30
*Nos. 233-236 (4)* 3.15 1.35

50th anniv. of the Constitution.
All values exist imperforate and Nos. 233, 235 and 236 with center inverted. It is doubtful that any of these varieties were regularly issued.

No. 215 Surcharged

**1920**

**237** A40 50c on 75c deep blue .60 .40

Nos. 200, 215 Surcharged

**1921**

**241** A38 50c on 75c deep blue .40 .40
**242** A40 50c on 75c deep blue .40 .40

A42

**1922, Feb. 8** **Litho.** ***Perf. 11½***

**243** A42 50c car & dk blue .40 .40
*a.* Imperf. pair 2.00
*b.* Center inverted 25.00 25.00
**244** A42 1p dk blue & brn .40 .40
*a.* Imperf. pair 2.00
*b.* Center inverted 30.00 30.00
*c.* As "b," imperf. pair *110.00*

For overprints see Nos. L1-L2.

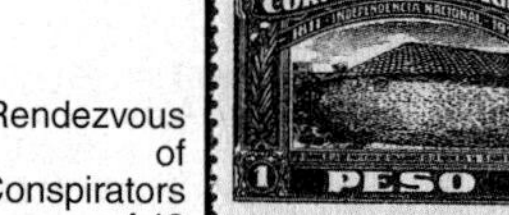

Rendezvous of Conspirators A43

**1922-23**

**245** A43 1p deep blue .40 .40
**246** A43 1p scar & dk bl ('23) .40 .40
**247** A43 1p red vio & gray ('23) .40 .40
**248** A43 1p org & gray ('23) .40 .40
**249** A43 5p dark violet 1.20 .40
**250** A43 5p dk bl & org brn ('23) 1.20 .40
**251** A43 5p dl red & lt bl ('23) 1.20 .40
**252** A43 5p emer & blk ('23) 1.20 .40
*Nos. 245-252 (8)* 6.40 3.20

National Independence.

**No. 218 Surcharged "Habilitado en $1:-1924" in Red**

**1924**

**253** A40 1p on 1.25p pale blue .40 .40

This stamp was for use in Asunción. Nos. L3 to L5 were for use in the interior, as is indicated by the "C" in the surcharge.

Map of Paraguay — A44

**1924** **Litho.** ***Perf. 11½***

**254** A44 1p dark blue .40 .40
**255** A44 2p carmine rose .40 .40
**256** A44 4p light blue .40 .40
*a.* Perf. 12 .80 .40
*Nos. 254-256 (3)* 1.20 1.20

#254-256 exist imperf. Value $3 each pair.
For surcharges and overprint see Nos. 267, C5, C15-C16, C54-C55, L7.

Gen. José E. Díaz — A45

**1925-26** ***Perf. 11½, 12***

**257** A45 50c red .25 .25
**258** A45 1p dark blue .25 .25
**259** A45 1p emerald ('26) .25 .25
*Nos. 257-259 (3)* .75 .75

#257-258 exist imperf. Value $1 each pair.
For overprints see Nos. L6, L8, L10.

Columbus — A46

**1925** ***Perf. 11½***

**260** A46 1p blue .50 .40
*a.* Imperf., pair 3.00

For overprint see No. L9.

Nos. 194, 214-215, J12 Surcharged in Black or Red

**1926**

**261** A38 1c on 5c lt blue .25 .25
**262** A40 7c on 40c rose .25 .25
**263** A40 15c on 75c dp bl (R) .25 .25
**264** D2 1.50p on 1.50p yel brn .25 .25
*Nos. 261-264 (4)* 1.00 1.00

**Nos. 194, 179 and 256 Surcharged "Habilitado" and New Values**

**1927**

**265** A38 2c on 5c lt blue .25 .25
**266** A35 50c on 60c magenta .25 .25
*a.* Inverted surcharge 2.00
**267** A44 1.50p on 4p lt blue .25 .25

**Official Stamp of 1914 Surcharged "Habilitado" and New Value**

**268** O19 50c on 75c dp bl .25 .25
*Nos. 265-268 (4)* 1.00 1.00

National Emblem — A47

Pedro Juan Caballero — A48

Map of Paraguay — A49

Fulgencio Yegros — A50

Ignacio Iturbe — A51

Oratory of the Virgin, Asunción — A52

*Perf. 12, 11, 11½, 11x12*

**1927-38** **Typo.**

| | | | | |
|---|---|---|---|---|
| **269** | A47 | 1c lt red ('31) | .25 | .25 |
| **270** | A47 | 2c org red ('30) | .25 | .25 |
| **271** | A47 | 7c lilac | .25 | .25 |
| **272** | A47 | 7c emerald ('29) | .25 | .25 |
| **273** | A47 | 10c gray grn ('28) | .25 | .25 |
| *a.* | | 10c light green ('31) | .25 | .25 |
| **274** | A47 | 10c lil rose ('30) | .25 | .25 |
| **275** | A47 | 10c light bl ('35) | .25 | .25 |
| **276** | A47 | 20c dull bl ('28) | .25 | .25 |
| **277** | A47 | 20c lil brn ('30) | .25 | .25 |
| **278** | A47 | 20c lt vio ('31) | .25 | .25 |
| **279** | A47 | 20c rose ('35) | .25 | .25 |
| **280** | A47 | 50c ultramarine | .25 | .25 |
| **281** | A47 | 50c dl red ('28) | .25 | .25 |
| **282** | A47 | 50c orange ('30) | .25 | .25 |
| **283** | A47 | 50c gray ('31) | .25 | .25 |
| **284** | A47 | 50c brn vio ('34) | .25 | .25 |
| **285** | A47 | 50c rose ('36) | .25 | .25 |
| **286** | A47 | 70c ultra ('28) | .25 | .25 |
| **287** | A48 | 1p emerald | .25 | .25 |
| **288** | A48 | 1p org red ('30) | .25 | .25 |
| **289** | A48 | 1p brn org ('34) | .25 | .25 |
| **290** | A49 | 1.50p brown | .25 | .25 |
| **291** | A49 | 1.50p lilac ('28) | .25 | .25 |
| **292** | A49 | 1.50p rose red ('32) | .25 | .25 |
| **293** | A50 | 2.50p bister | .25 | .25 |
| **294** | A51 | 3p gray | .25 | .25 |
| **295** | A51 | 3p rose red ('36) | .25 | .25 |
| **296** | A51 | 3p brt vio ('36) | .25 | .25 |
| **297** | A52 | 5p chocolate | .25 | .25 |
| **298** | A52 | 5p violet ('36) | .25 | .25 |
| **299** | A52 | 5p pale org ('38) | .25 | .25 |
| **300** | A49 | 20p red ('29) | 7.00 | 5.50 |
| **301** | A49 | 20p emerald ('29) | 7.00 | 5.50 |
| **302** | A49 | 20p vio brn ('29) | 7.00 | 5.50 |
| | | *Nos. 269-302 (34)* | 28.75 | 24.25 |

No. 281 is also known perf. 10½x11½.

Papermaker's watermarks are sometimes found on No. 271 ("GLORIA BOND" in double-lined circle) and No. 280 ("Extra Vencedor Bond" or "ADBANCE/M M C").

For surcharges and overprints see Nos. 312, C4, C6, C13-C14, C17-C18, C25-C32, C34-C35, L11-L30, O94-O96, O98.

Arms of Juan de Salazar de Espinosa — A53

**1928, Aug. 15** *Perf. 12*

| | | | | |
|---|---|---|---|---|
| **303** | A53 | 10p violet brown | 3.00 | 2.00 |

Juan de Salazar de Espinosa, founder of Asunción.

A papermaker's watermark ("INDIAN BOND EXTRA STRONG S.&C") is sometimes found on Nos 303, 305-307.

Columbus — A54

**1928** **Litho.**

| | | | | |
|---|---|---|---|---|
| **304** | A54 | 10p ultra | 2.40 | 1.50 |
| **305** | A54 | 10p vermilion | 2.40 | 1.50 |
| **306** | A54 | 10p deep red | 2.40 | 1.50 |
| | | *Nos. 304-306 (3)* | 7.20 | 4.50 |

For surcharge and overprint see Nos. C33, L37.

President Rutherford B. Hayes of US and Villa Occidental — A55

**1928, Nov. 20** *Perf. 12*

| | | | | |
|---|---|---|---|---|
| **307** | A55 | 10p gray brown | 10.00 | 3.50 |
| **308** | A55 | 10p red brown | 10.00 | 3.50 |

50th anniv. of the Hayes' Chaco decision.

Portraits of Archbishop Bogarin — A56

**1930, Aug. 15**

| | | | | |
|---|---|---|---|---|
| **309** | A56 | 1.50p lake | 2.00 | 1.50 |
| **310** | A56 | 1.50p turq blue | 2.00 | 1.50 |
| **311** | A56 | 1.50p dull vio | 2.00 | 1.50 |
| | | *Nos. 309-311 (3)* | 6.00 | 4.50 |

Archbishop Juan Sinforiano Bogarin, first archbishop of Paraguay.

For overprints see Nos. 321-322.

No. 272 Surcharged

**1930**

| | | | | |
|---|---|---|---|---|
| **312** | A47 | 5c on 7c emer | .25 | .25 |

A57

**1930-39** **Typo.** *Perf. 11½, 12*

| | | | | |
|---|---|---|---|---|
| **313** | A57 | 10p brown | 1.00 | .40 |
| **314** | A57 | 10p brn red, *bl* ('31) | 1.00 | .40 |
| **315** | A57 | 10p dk bl, *pink* ('32) | 1.00 | .40 |
| **316** | A57 | 10p gray brn ('36) | .80 | .40 |
| **317** | A57 | 10p gray ('37) | .80 | .40 |
| **318** | A57 | 10p blue ('39) | .40 | .40 |
| | | *Nos. 313-318 (6)* | 5.00 | 2.40 |

1st Paraguayan postage stamp, 60th anniv.

For overprint see No. L31.

Gunboat "Humaitá" — A58

**1931** *Perf. 12*

| | | | | |
|---|---|---|---|---|
| **319** | A58 | 1.50p purple | .80 | .50 |
| | | *Nos. 319,C39-C53 (16)* | 25.75 | 18.05 |

Constitution, 60th anniv.

For overprint see No. L33.

View of San Bernardino — A59

**1931, Aug.**

| | | | | |
|---|---|---|---|---|
| **320** | A59 | 1p light green | .50 | .40 |

Founding of San Bernardino, 50th anniv.

For overprint see No. L32.

**Nos. 309-310 Overprinted in Blue or Red**

**1931, Dec. 31**

| | | | | |
|---|---|---|---|---|
| **321** | A56 | 1.50p lake (Bl) | 3.00 | 3.00 |
| **322** | A56 | 1.50p turq blue (R) | 3.00 | 3.00 |

Map of the Gran Chaco — A60

**1932-35** **Typo.** *Perf. 12*

| | | | | |
|---|---|---|---|---|
| **323** | A60 | 1.50p deep violet | .40 | .40 |
| **324** | A60 | 1.50p rose ('35) | .40 | .40 |

For overprints see Nos. L34-L36, O97.

**Nos. C74-C78 Surcharged**

**1933** **Litho.**

| | | | | |
|---|---|---|---|---|
| **325** | AP18 | 50c on 4p ultra | .50 | .40 |
| **326** | AP18 | 1p on 8p red | 1.00 | .80 |
| **327** | AP18 | 1.50p on 12p bl grn | 1.00 | .80 |
| **328** | AP18 | 2p on 16p dk vio | 1.00 | .80 |
| **329** | AP18 | 5p on 20p org brn | 2.25 | 1.75 |
| | | *Nos. 325-329 (5)* | 5.75 | 4.55 |

**Flag of the Race Issue**

Flag with Three Crosses: Caravels of Columbus — A61

**1933, Oct. 10** **Litho.** *Perf. 11*

| | | | | |
|---|---|---|---|---|
| **330** | A61 | 10c multicolored | .50 | .40 |
| **331** | A61 | 20c multicolored | .75 | .40 |
| **332** | A61 | 50c multicolored | .75 | .40 |
| **333** | A61 | 1p multicolored | .75 | .40 |
| **334** | A61 | 1.50p multicolored | .75 | .40 |
| **335** | A61 | 2p multicolored | .90 | .50 |
| **336** | A61 | 5p multicolored | 1.40 | 1.00 |
| **337** | A61 | 10p multicolored | 1.75 | 1.00 |
| | | *Nos. 330-337 (8)* | 7.55 | 4.50 |

441st anniv. of the sailing of Christopher Columbus from the port of Palos, Aug. 3, 1492, on his first voyage to the New World.

Nos. 332, 334 and 335 exist with Maltese crosses omitted.

Monstrance — A62

**1937, Aug.** **Unwmk.** *Perf. 11½*

| | | | | |
|---|---|---|---|---|
| **338** | A62 | 1p dk blue, yel & red | .40 | .40 |
| **339** | A62 | 3p dk blue, yel & red | .40 | .40 |
| **340** | A62 | 10p dk blue, yel & red | .40 | .40 |
| | | *Nos. 338-340 (3)* | 1.20 | 1.20 |

1st Natl. Eucharistic Congress, Asuncion.

Arms of Asunción — A63

**1937, Aug.**

| | | | | |
|---|---|---|---|---|
| **341** | A63 | 50c violet & buff | .60 | .40 |
| **342** | A63 | 1p bis & lt grn | .60 | .40 |
| **343** | A63 | 3p red & lt bl | .60 | .40 |
| **344** | A63 | 10p car rose & buff | .60 | .40 |
| **345** | A63 | 20p blue & drab | .60 | .40 |
| | | *Nos. 341-345 (5)* | 3.00 | 2.00 |

Founding of Asuncion, 400th anniv.

Oratory of the Virgin, Asunción — A64

**1938-39** **Typo.** *Perf. 11, 12*

| | | | | |
|---|---|---|---|---|
| **346** | A64 | 5p olive green | .60 | .40 |
| **347** | A64 | 5p pale rose ('39) | .60 | .40 |
| **348** | A64 | 11p violet brown | .80 | .50 |
| | | *Nos. 346-348 (3)* | 2.00 | 1.30 |

Founding of Asuncion, 400th anniv.

Carlos Antonio Lopez — A65

José Eduvigis Diaz — A66

**1939** *Perf. 12*

| | | | | |
|---|---|---|---|---|
| **349** | A65 | 2p lt ultra & pale brn | .90 | .60 |
| **350** | A66 | 2p lt ultra & brn | .90 | .60 |

Reburial of ashes of Pres. Carlos Antonio Lopez (1790-1862) and Gen. José Eduvigis Diaz in the National Pantheon, Asuncion.

Pres. Patricio Escobar and Ramon Zubizarreta A67

Design: 5p, Pres. Bernardino Caballero and Senator José S. Decoud.

**1939-40** **Litho.** *Perf. 11½*

**Heads in Black**

| | | | | |
|---|---|---|---|---|
| **351** | A67 | 50c dull org ('40) | .60 | .60 |
| **352** | A67 | 1p lt violet ('40) | .60 | .60 |
| **353** | A67 | 2p red brown ('40) | .60 | .60 |
| **354** | A67 | 5p lt ultra | .75 | .60 |
| | | *Nos. 351-354,C122-C123,O99-O104 (12)* | 27.55 | 26.20 |

Founding of the University of Asuncion, 50th anniv.

Varieties of this issue include inverted heads (50c, 1p, 2p); doubled heads; Caballero and Decoud heads in 50c frame: imperforates and part-perforates. Examples with inverted heads were not officially issued.

Coats of Arms — A69

Flags of Paraguay, United States — A70

Designs: 1p, Pres. Baldomir, flags of Paraguay, Uruguay. 2p, Pres. Benavides, flags of Paraguay, Peru. 5p, Pres. Alessandri, flags of Paraguay, Chile. 6p, Pres. Vargas, flags of Paraguay, Brazil. 10p, Pres. Ortiz, flags of Paraguay, Argentina.

**1939 Engr.; Flags Litho. *Perf. 12***
**Flags in National Colors**

| | | | | |
|---|---|---|---|---|
| **355** | A69 | 50c violet blue | .30 | .30 |
| **356** | A70 | 1p olive | .30 | .30 |
| **357** | A70 | 2p blue green | .30 | .30 |
| **358** | A70 | 3p sepia | .35 | .35 |
| **359** | A70 | 5p orange | .30 | .30 |
| **360** | A70 | 6p dull violet | .75 | .60 |
| **361** | A70 | 10p bister brn | .60 | .35 |
| | | *Nos. 355-361,C113-C121 (16)* | 42.30 | 28.25 |

First Buenos Aires Peace Conference.
For overprint and surcharge, see Nos. 387, B10.

Coats of Arms of New York and Asunción A76

**1939, Nov. 30**

| | | | | |
|---|---|---|---|---|
| **362** | A76 | 5p scarlet | .80 | .80 |
| **363** | A76 | 10p deep blue | 1.20 | .80 |
| **364** | A76 | 11p dk blue grn | 1.20 | 1.20 |
| **365** | A76 | 22p olive blk | 2.00 | 1.60 |
| | | *Nos. 362-365,C124-C126 (7)* | 33.95 | 31.40 |

New York World's Fair.

Paraguayan Soldier — A77

Cowboys — A79

Paraguayan Woman — A78

Plowing — A80

View of Paraguay River — A81

Oxcart A82

Pasture A83

Pireretá Falls — A84

**1940, Jan. 1 Photo. *Perf. 12½***

| | | | | |
|---|---|---|---|---|
| **366** | A77 | 50c deep orange | .40 | .25 |
| **367** | A78 | 1p brt red violet | .40 | .25 |
| **368** | A79 | 3p bright green | .40 | .25 |
| **369** | A80 | 5p chestnut | .40 | .25 |
| **370** | A81 | 10p magenta | .40 | .25 |
| **371** | A82 | 20p violet | 1.00 | .30 |
| **372** | A83 | 50p cobalt blue | 2.00 | .45 |
| **373** | A84 | 100p black | 4.00 | 1.40 |
| | | *Nos. 366-373 (8)* | 9.00 | 3.40 |

Second Buenos Aires Peace Conference.
For surcharge see No. 386.

Map of the Americas — A85

**1940, May Engr. *Perf. 12***

| | | | | |
|---|---|---|---|---|
| **374** | A85 | 50c red orange | .30 | .25 |
| **375** | A85 | 1p green | .30 | .25 |
| **376** | A85 | 5p dark blue | .50 | .25 |
| **377** | A85 | 10p brown | 1.00 | .50 |
| | | *Nos. 374-377,C127-C130 (8)* | 12.20 | 9.20 |

Pan American Union, 50th anniversary.

Reproduction of Type A1 — A86

Sir Rowland Hill — A87

Designs: 6p, Type A2. 10p, Type A3.

**1940, Aug. 15 Photo. *Perf. 13½***

| | | | | |
|---|---|---|---|---|
| **378** | A86 | 1p aqua & brt red vio | .50 | .25 |
| **379** | A87 | 5p dp yel grn & red brn | .65 | .30 |
| **380** | A86 | 6p org brn & ultra | 1.50 | .65 |
| **381** | A86 | 10p ver & black | 1.50 | 1.00 |
| | | *Nos. 378-381 (4)* | 4.15 | 2.20 |

Postage stamp centenary.

Dr. José Francia
A90 A91

**1940, Sept. 20 Engr. *Perf. 12***

| | | | | |
|---|---|---|---|---|
| **382** | A90 | 50c carmine rose | .30 | .25 |
| **383** | A91 | 50c plum | .30 | .25 |
| **384** | A90 | 1p bright green | .30 | .25 |
| **385** | A91 | 5p deep blue | .30 | .25 |
| | | *Nos. 382-385 (4)* | 1.20 | 1.00 |

Centenary of the death of Dr. Jose Francia (1766-1840), dictator of Paraguay, 1814-1840.

No. 366 Surcharged in Black

**1940, Sept. 7 *Perf. 12½***

| | | | | |
|---|---|---|---|---|
| **386** | A77 | 5p on 50c dp org | .40 | .25 |

In honor of Pres. Jose F. Estigarribia who died in a plane crash Sept. 7, 1940.

No. 360 Overprinted in Black

**1941, Aug. *Perf. 12***

| | | | | |
|---|---|---|---|---|
| **387** | A70 | 6p multi | .40 | .40 |

Visit to Paraguay of Pres. Vargas of Brazil.

Nos. C113-C115 Overprinted in Blue or Red

**1942, Jan. 17 *Perf. 12½***

| | | | | |
|---|---|---|---|---|
| **388** | A69 | 1p multi (Bl) | .30 | .25 |
| **389** | A69 | 3p multi (R) | .30 | .25 |
| **390** | A70 | 5p multi (R) | .30 | .25 |
| | | *Nos. 388-390 (3)* | .90 | .75 |

Coat of Arms — A92

**1942-43 Litho. *Perf. 11, 12, 11x12***

| | | | | |
|---|---|---|---|---|
| **391** | A92 | 1p light green | .50 | .25 |
| **392** | A92 | 1p orange ('43) | .50 | .25 |
| **393** | A92 | 7p light blue | .50 | .25 |
| **394** | A92 | 7p yel brn ('43) | .50 | .25 |
| | | *Nos. 391-394 (4)* | 2.00 | 1.00 |

Values are for examples perforated 11. Stamps perforated 12 and 11x12 are worth more. Nos. 391-394 exist imperf.

The Indian Francisco — A93

Domingo Martinez de Irala and His Vision A94

Arms of Irala — A95

**1942, Aug. 15 Engr. *Perf. 12***

| | | | | |
|---|---|---|---|---|
| **395** | A93 | 2p green | .75 | .30 |
| **396** | A94 | 5p rose | .75 | .30 |
| **397** | A95 | 7p sapphire | .75 | .30 |
| | | *Nos. 395-397,C131-C133 (6)* | 10.75 | 5.90 |

400th anniversary of Asuncion.

Pres. Higinio Morinigo, Scenes of Industry & Agriculture — A96

**1943, Aug. 15 Unwmk.**

| | | | | |
|---|---|---|---|---|
| **398** | A96 | 7p blue | .25 | .25 |

For surcharges see Nos. 404, 428.

Christopher Columbus — A97

**1943, Aug. 15**

| | | | | |
|---|---|---|---|---|
| **399** | A97 | 50c violet | .25 | .25 |
| **400** | A97 | 1p gray brn | .25 | .25 |
| **401** | A97 | 5p dark grn | .50 | .25 |
| **402** | A97 | 7p brt ultra | .25 | .25 |
| | | *Nos. 399-402 (4)* | 1.25 | 1.00 |

Discovery of America, 450th anniv.
For surcharges see Nos. 405, 429.

No. 296 Surcharged in Black

**1944 *Perf. 12, 11, 11½, 11x12***

| | | | | |
|---|---|---|---|---|
| **403** | A51 | 1c on 3p brt vio | .50 | .25 |

Nos. 398 and 402 Surcharged in Red

**1944 *Perf. 12***

| | | | | |
|---|---|---|---|---|
| **404** | A96 | 5c on 7p blue | .50 | .25 |
| **405** | A97 | 5c on 7p brt ultra | .50 | .25 |

> Imperforates
> Starting with No. 406, many Paraguayan stamps exist imperf.

Primitive Postal Service among Indians — A98

Ruins of Humaitá Church — A99

Locomotive of early Paraguayan Railroad — A100

Marshal Francisco S. Lopez — A101

Early Merchant Ship — A102

Port of Asunción — A103

Birthplace of Paraguay's Liberation — A104

Monument to Heroes of Itororó — A105

**1944-45 Unwmk. Engr. *Perf. 12½***

| | | | | |
|---|---|---|---|---|
| **406** | A98 | 1c black | .25 | .25 |
| **407** | A99 | 2c copper brn ('45) | .25 | .25 |
| **408** | A100 | 5c light olive | 1.00 | .25 |
| **409** | A101 | 7c light blue ('45) | .40 | .25 |
| **410** | A102 | 10c green ('45) | .50 | .25 |
| **411** | A103 | 15c dark blue ('45) | .50 | .30 |
| **412** | A104 | 50c black brown | .65 | .40 |
| **413** | A105 | 1g dk rose car ('45) | 1.90 | 1.00 |
| | | *Nos. 406-413 (8)* | 5.45 | 2.95 |
| | | *Nos. 406-413,C134-C146 (21)* | 26.65 | 14.50 |

See #435, 437, 439, 441, C158-C162.
For surcharges see #414, 427.

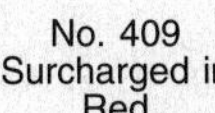

No. 409 Surcharged in Red

**1945**

| | | | | |
|---|---|---|---|---|
| **414** | A101 | 5c on 7c light blue | .50 | .25 |

Handshake, Map and Flags of Paraguay and Panama A106

Designs: 3c, Venezuela Flag. 5c, Colombia Flag. 2g, Peru Flag.

**Engr.; Flags Litho. in Natl. Colors**
**1945, Aug. 15 Unwmk. *Perf. 12½***

| | | | | |
|---|---|---|---|---|
| **415** | A106 | 1c dark green | .25 | .25 |
| **416** | A106 | 3c lake | .25 | .25 |
| **417** | A106 | 5c blue blk | .25 | .25 |
| **418** | A106 | 2g brown | 1.10 | .75 |
| | | *Nos. 415-418,C147-C153 (11)* | 21.40 | 21.05 |

Goodwill visits of Pres. Higinio Morinigo during 1943.

Nos. B6 to B9 Surcharged in Black

**1945 Engr. *Perf. 12***

| | | | | |
|---|---|---|---|---|
| **419** | SP4 | 2c on 7p + 3p red brn | .40 | .40 |
| **420** | SP4 | 2c on 7p + 3p purple | .40 | .40 |
| **421** | SP4 | 2c on 7p + 3p car rose | .40 | .40 |
| **422** | SP4 | 2c on 7p + 3p saph | .40 | .40 |
| **423** | SP4 | 5c on 7p + 3p red brn | .40 | .40 |
| **424** | SP4 | 5c on 7p + 3p purple | .40 | .40 |
| **425** | SP4 | 5c on 7p + 3p car rose | .40 | .40 |
| **426** | SP4 | 5c on 7p + 3p saph | .40 | .40 |
| | | *Nos. 419-426 (8)* | 3.20 | 3.20 |

**Similar Surcharge in Red on Nos. 409, 398 and 402**

***Perf. 12½, 12***

| | | | | |
|---|---|---|---|---|
| **427** | A101 | 5c on 7c lt blue | .40 | .40 |
| **428** | A96 | 5c on 7p blue | .40 | .40 |
| **429** | A97 | 5c on 7p brt ultra | .40 | .40 |
| | | *Nos. 427-429 (3)* | 1.20 | 1.20 |

Nos. 427-429 exist with black surcharge.

**Catalogue values for unused stamps in this section, from this point to the end of the section, are for Never Hinged items.**

Coat of Arms ("U.P.U." at bottom) — A110

**1946 Litho. *Perf. 11, 12***

| | | | | |
|---|---|---|---|---|
| **430** | A110 | 5c gray | .40 | .25 |

See Nos. 459-463, 478-480, 498-506, 525-536, 646-658.
For overprints see Nos. 464-466.

**Nos. B6 to B9 Surcharged "1946" and New Value in Black**

**1946 *Perf. 12***

| | | | | |
|---|---|---|---|---|
| **431** | SP4 | 5c on 7p + 3p red brn | 2.00 | 1.50 |
| **432** | SP4 | 5c on 7p + 3p purple | 2.00 | 1.50 |
| **433** | SP4 | 5c on 7p + 3p car rose | 2.00 | 1.50 |
| **434** | SP4 | 5c on 7p + 3p saph | 2.00 | 1.50 |
| | | *Nos. 431-434 (4)* | 8.00 | 6.00 |

**Types of 1944-45 and**

First Telegraph in South America A111

Monument to Antequera A112

Colonial Jesuit Altar — A113

**1946, Sept. 21 Engr. *Perf. 12½***

| | | | | |
|---|---|---|---|---|
| **435** | A102 | 1c rose car | .40 | .40 |
| **436** | A111 | 2c purple | .40 | .40 |
| **437** | A98 | 5c ultra | .40 | .40 |
| **438** | A112 | 10c org yel | .40 | .40 |
| **439** | A105 | 15c brn olive | .40 | .40 |
| **440** | A113 | 50c deep grn | .70 | .40 |
| **441** | A104 | 1g brt ultra | 1.25 | .80 |
| | | *Nos. 435-441 (7)* | 3.95 | 3.20 |

See Nos. C135-C138, C143, C172.

Marshal Francisco Solano Lopez — A114

**1947, May 15 *Perf. 12***

| | | | | |
|---|---|---|---|---|
| **442** | A114 | 1c purple | .30 | .25 |
| **443** | A114 | 2c org red | .30 | .25 |
| **444** | A114 | 5c green | .30 | .25 |
| **445** | A114 | 15c ultra | .30 | .25 |
| **446** | A114 | 50c dark grn | 1.00 | .65 |
| | | *Nos. 442-446,C163-C167 (10)* | 11.25 | 10.70 |

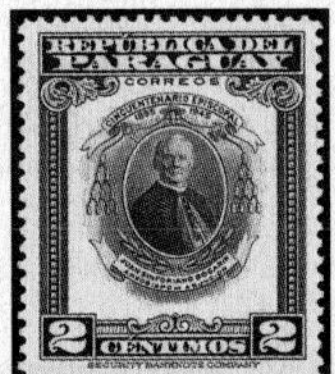

Juan Sinforiano Bogarin, Archbishop of Asunción — A115

Archbishopric Coat of Arms — A116

Projected Monument of the Sacred Heart of Jesus — A117

Vision of Projected Monument A118

**1948, Jan. 6 Engr. *Perf. 12½***

| | | | | |
|---|---|---|---|---|
| **447** | A115 | 2c dark blue | .40 | .25 |
| **448** | A116 | 5c deep car | .40 | .25 |
| **449** | A117 | 10c gray blk | .40 | .25 |
| **450** | A118 | 15c green | .70 | .25 |
| | | *Nos. 447-450,C168-C175 (12)* | 19.10 | 10.00 |

Archbishopric of Asunción, 50th anniv.
See Nos. C168-C171, C173-C175.

"Political Enlightenment" A119

**1948, Sept. 11 Engr. & Litho.**

| | | | | |
|---|---|---|---|---|
| **451** | A119 | 5c car red | .30 | .30 |
| **452** | A119 | 15c red org | .30 | .30 |
| | | *Nos. 451-452,C176-C177 (4)* | 9.50 | 9.50 |

Issued to honor the Barefeet, a political group.
See Nos. C176-C177.

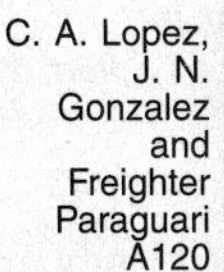

C. A. Lopez, J. N. Gonzalez and Freighter Paraguari A120

**Centers in Carmine, Black, Ultramarine and Blue**

**1949 Litho.**

| | | | | |
|---|---|---|---|---|
| **453** | A120 | 2c orange | .25 | .25 |
| **454** | A120 | 5c blue vio | .25 | .25 |
| **455** | A120 | 10c black | .25 | .25 |
| **456** | A120 | 15c violet | .25 | .25 |
| **457** | A120 | 50c blue grn | .25 | .25 |
| **458** | A120 | 1g dull vio brn | .30 | .25 |
| | | *Nos. 453-458 (6)* | 1.55 | 1.50 |

Paraguay's merchant fleet centenary.

**Arms Type of 1946**

**1950 Unwmk. *Perf. 10***

| | | | | |
|---|---|---|---|---|
| **459** | A110 | 5c red | .50 | .25 |
| **460** | A110 | 10c blue | .50 | .25 |
| **461** | A110 | 50c rose lilac | .75 | .25 |
| **462** | A110 | 1g pale violet | .75 | .25 |

**1951 Coarse Impression**

| | | | | |
|---|---|---|---|---|
| **463** | A110 | 30c green | .75 | .25 |
| | | *Nos. 459-463 (5)* | 3.25 | 1.25 |

**Nos. 459, 460 and 463 Overprinted in Various Colors**

**1951, Apr. 18**

| | | | | |
|---|---|---|---|---|
| **464** | A110 | 5c red (Bk), block | 1.00 | 1.00 |
| **465** | A110 | 10c blue (R), block | 2.00 | 2.00 |
| **466** | A110 | 30c green (V), block | 3.00 | 3.00 |
| | | *Nos. 464-466 (3)* | 6.00 | 6.00 |

1st Economic Cong. of Paraguay, 4/18/51.

Columbus Lighthouse — A121

**1952, Feb. 11 *Perf. 10***

| | | | | |
|---|---|---|---|---|
| **467** | A121 | 2c org brn | .40 | .25 |
| **468** | A121 | 5c light ultra | .40 | .25 |
| **469** | A121 | 10c rose | .40 | .25 |
| **470** | A121 | 15c light blue | .40 | .25 |
| **471** | A121 | 20c lilac | .40 | .25 |

| No. | Type | Description | Unused | Used |
|---|---|---|---|---|
| **472** | A121 | 50c orange | .40 | .25 |
| **473** | A121 | 1g bluish grn | .40 | .25 |
| | | *Nos. 467-473 (7)* | 2.80 | 1.75 |

Silvio Pettirossi, Aviator — A122

**1954, Mar. Litho. *Perf. 10***

| No. | Type | Description | Unused | Used |
|---|---|---|---|---|
| **474** | A122 | 5c blue | .55 | .25 |
| **475** | A122 | 20c rose pink | .55 | .25 |
| **476** | A122 | 50c vio brn | .55 | .25 |
| **477** | A122 | 60c lt vio | .55 | .25 |
| | | *Nos. 474-477,C201-C204 (8)* | 4.40 | 2.00 |

### Arms Type of 1946

**1954 *Perf. 11***

| No. | Type | Description | Unused | Used |
|---|---|---|---|---|
| **478** | A110 | 10c vermilion | 2.00 | .25 |

***Perf. 10***

| No. | Type | Description | Unused | Used |
|---|---|---|---|---|
| **478A** | A110 | 10c ver, redrawn | .75 | .25 |
| **479** | A110 | 10g orange | 5.00 | 2.00 |
| **480** | A110 | 50g vio brn | 9.00 | 7.00 |
| | | *Nos. 478-480 (4)* | 16.75 | 9.50 |

No. 478A measures 20½x24mm, has 5 frame lines at left and 6 at right. No. 478 measures 20x24½mm, has 6 frame lines at left and 5 at right.

Three National Heroes — A123

**1954, Aug. 15 Litho. *Perf. 10***

| No. | Type | Description | Unused | Used |
|---|---|---|---|---|
| **481** | A123 | 5c light vio | .25 | .25 |
| **482** | A123 | 20c light blue | .25 | .25 |
| **483** | A123 | 50c rose pink | .25 | .25 |
| **484** | A123 | 1g org brn | .25 | .25 |
| **485** | A123 | 2g blue grn | .35 | .25 |
| | | *Nos. 481-485,C216-C220 (10)* | 17.35 | 10.10 |

Marshal Francisco S. Lopez, Pres. Carlos A. Lopez and Gen. Bernardino Caballero.

Pres. Alfredo Stroessner and Pres. Juan D. Peron — A124

### Photo. & Litho.

**1955, Apr. Wmk. 90 *Perf. 13x13½***

| No. | Type | Description | Unused | Used |
|---|---|---|---|---|
| **486** | A124 | 5c multicolored | .25 | .25 |
| **487** | A124 | 10c multicolored | .25 | .25 |
| **488** | A124 | 50c multicolored | .25 | .25 |
| **489** | A124 | 1.30g multicolored | .25 | .25 |
| **490** | A124 | 2.20g multicolored | .35 | .25 |
| | | *Nos. 486-490,C221-C224 (9)* | 3.75 | 4.45 |

Visit of Pres. Juan D. Peron of Argentina.

Jesuit Ruins, Trinidad Belfry A125

Santa Maria Cornice — A126

Jesuit Ruins: 20c, Corridor at Trinidad. 2.50g, Tower of Santa Rosa. 5g, San Cosme gate. 15g, Church of Jesus. 25g, Niche at Trinidad.

***Perf. 12½x12, 12x12½***

**1955, June 19 Engr. Unwmk.**

| No. | Type | Description | Unused | Used |
|---|---|---|---|---|
| **491** | A125 | 5c org yel | .40 | .25 |
| **492** | A125 | 20c olive bister | .40 | .25 |
| **493** | A126 | 50c lt red brn | .40 | .25 |
| **494** | A126 | 2.50g olive | .40 | .25 |
| **495** | A125 | 5g yel brn | .40 | .25 |
| **496** | A125 | 15g blue grn | .40 | .25 |
| **497** | A126 | 25g deep grn | .90 | .25 |
| | | *Nos. 491-497,C225-C232 (15)* | 7.25 | 3.80 |

25th anniv. of the priesthood of Monsignor Rodriguez.

For surcharges see Nos. 545-551.

### Arms Type of 1946

***Perf. 10, 11 (No. 500)***

**1956-58 Litho. Unwmk.**

| No. | Type | Description | Unused | Used |
|---|---|---|---|---|
| **498** | A110 | 5c brown ('57) | 1.00 | .50 |
| **499** | A110 | 30c red brn ('57) | 2.00 | .50 |
| **500** | A110 | 45c gray olive | 3.00 | .50 |
| **500A** | A110 | 90c lt vio bl | 5.00 | .75 |
| **501** | A110 | 2g ocher | 5.00 | .25 |
| **502** | A110 | 2.20g lil rose | 2.00 | .25 |
| **503** | A110 | 3g ol bis ('58) | 3.00 | .25 |
| **503A** | A110 | 4.20g emer ('57) | 6.00 | .25 |
| **504** | A110 | 5g ver ('57) | 10.00 | 5.00 |
| **505** | A110 | 10g lt grn ('57) | 10.00 | 5.00 |
| **506** | A110 | 20g blue ('57) | 10.00 | 5.00 |
| | | *Nos. 498-506 (11)* | 57.00 | 18.25 |

No. 500A exists with four-line, carmine overprint: "DIA N. UNIDAS 24 Octubre 1945-1956". It was not regularly issued and no decree authorizing it is known.

Soldiers, Angel and Asuncion Cathedral — A127

Nos. 513-519, Soldier & nurse in medallion & flags.

***Perf. 13½***

**1957, June 12 Photo. Unwmk.**

**Granite Paper**

**Flags in Red and Blue**

| No. | Type | Description | Unused | Used |
|---|---|---|---|---|
| **508** | A127 | 5c bl grn | .25 | .25 |
| **509** | A127 | 10c carmine | .25 | .25 |
| **510** | A127 | 15c ultra | .25 | .25 |
| **511** | A127 | 20c dp claret | .25 | .25 |
| **512** | A127 | 25c gray blk | .25 | .25 |
| **513** | A127 | 30c lt blue | .25 | .25 |
| **514** | A127 | 40c gray blk | .25 | .25 |
| **515** | A127 | 50c dark car | .25 | .25 |
| **516** | A127 | 1g bluish grn | .25 | .25 |
| **517** | A127 | 1.30g ultra | .25 | .25 |
| **518** | A127 | 1.50g dp claret | .25 | .25 |
| **519** | A127 | 2g brt grn | .25 | .25 |
| | | *Nos. 508-519 (12)* | 3.00 | 3.00 |

Heroes of the Chaco war. See #C233-C245.

Statue of St. Ignatius (Guarani Carving) — A128

Blessed Roque Gonzales and St. Ignatius A129

A129a

1.50g, St. Ignatius and San Ignacio Monastery.

**Wmk. 319**

**1958, Mar. 15 Litho. *Perf. 11***

| No. | Type | Description | Unused | Used |
|---|---|---|---|---|
| **520** | A128 | 50c dk red brn | .80 | *1.25* |
| **521** | A129 | 50c lt bl grn | .80 | *1.25* |
| **522** | A129a | 1.50g brt vio | .80 | *1.25* |
| **523** | A128 | 3g light bl | .80 | .50 |
| **524** | A129 | 6.25g rose car | .80 | .25 |
| | | *Nos. 520-524 (5)* | 4.00 | 4.50 |

St. Ignatius of Loyola (1491-1556).

See Nos. 935-942.

On designs A129a text under Paraguay is different from those of design A185b (Nos. 939-942).

### Arms Type of 1946

**1958-64 Litho. *Perf. 10, 11***

| No. | Type | Description | Unused | Used |
|---|---|---|---|---|
| **525** | A110 | 45c gray olive | 2.00 | 1.00 |
| **526** | A110 | 50c rose vio | 1.25 | 1.00 |
| **527** | A110 | 70c lt brn ('59) | 2.00 | 1.00 |
| **527A** | A110 | 90c vio blue | 2.00 | 1.00 |
| **528** | A110 | 1g violet | 1.00 | .50 |
| **529** | A110 | 1.50g lilac ('59) | 1.50 | 1.00 |
| **529A** | A110 | 2g bister ('64) | 5.00 | 3.00 |
| **530** | A110 | 3g ol bis ('59) | 5.00 | 3.00 |
| **531** | A110 | 4.50g lt ultra ('59) | 2.00 | 2.00 |
| **531A** | A110 | 5g rose red ('59) | 1.00 | 1.00 |
| **531B** | A110 | 10g bl grn ('59) | 2.00 | 1.00 |
| **532** | A110 | 12.45g yel green | 3.00 | 3.00 |
| **533** | A110 | 15g dl orange | 10.00 | 2.00 |
| **534** | A110 | 30g citron | 3.00 | 2.00 |
| **535** | A110 | 50g brown red | 2.00 | 1.00 |
| **536** | A110 | 100g gray vio | 3.00 | 2.00 |
| | | *Nos. 525-536 (16)* | 45.75 | 25.50 |

Pres. Alfredo Stroessner A130

**Wmk. 320**

**1958, Aug. 15 Litho. *Perf. 13½***

**Center in Slate**

| No. | Type | Description | Unused | Used |
|---|---|---|---|---|
| **537** | A130 | 10c sal pink | .25 | *.30* |
| **538** | A130 | 15c violet | .25 | *.30* |
| **539** | A130 | 25c yel grn | .25 | *.30* |
| **540** | A130 | 30c light fawn | .25 | *.30* |
| **541** | A130 | 50c rose car | .30 | .30 |
| **542** | A130 | 75c light ultra | .30 | .30 |
| **543** | A130 | 5g lt bl grn | .50 | .50 |
| **544** | A130 | 10g brown | 1.00 | .50 |
| | | *Nos. 537-544,C246-C251 (14)* | 24.10 | 17.80 |

Re-election of President General Alfredo Stroessner.

Nos. 491-497 Srchd. in Red

***Perf. 12½x12, 12x12½***

**1959, May 14 Engr. Unwmk.**

| No. | Type | Description | Unused | Used |
|---|---|---|---|---|
| **545** | A125 | 1.50g on 5c org yel | .25 | *.50* |
| **546** | A125 | 1.50g on 20c ol bis | .25 | *.50* |
| **547** | A126 | 1.50g on 50c lt red brn | .25 | *.50* |
| **548** | A126 | 3g on 2.50g ol | .25 | *.50* |
| **549** | A125 | 6.25g on 5g yel brn | .25 | *.50* |
| **550** | A125 | 20g on 15g bl grn | .70 | *.80* |
| **551** | A126 | 30g on 25g dp grn | 1.00 | *1.00* |
| | | *Nos. 545-551,C252-C259 (15)* | 15.45 | 12.30 |

The surcharge is made to fit the stamps. Counterfeits of surcharge exist.

Goalkeeper Catching Soccer Ball — A131

**1960, Mar. 18 Photo. *Perf. 12½***

| No. | Type | Description | Unused | Used |
|---|---|---|---|---|
| **556** | A131 | 30c brt red & bl grn | .30 | .30 |
| **557** | A131 | 50c plum & dk bl | .30 | .30 |
| **558** | A131 | 75c ol grn & org | .30 | .30 |
| **559** | A131 | 1.50g dk vio & bl grn | .30 | .30 |
| | | *Nos. 556-559,C262-C264 (7)* | 2.25 | 2.25 |

Olympic Games of 1960.

WRY Emblem — A132

**1960, Apr. 7 Litho. *Perf. 11***

| No. | Type | Description | Unused | Used |
|---|---|---|---|---|
| **560** | A132 | 25c sal & yel grn | .60 | .25 |
| **561** | A132 | 50c lt yel grn & red org | .60 | .25 |
| **562** | A132 | 70c lt brn & lil rose | .75 | .25 |
| **563** | A132 | 1.50g lt bl & ultra | .75 | .25 |
| **564** | A132 | 3g gray & bis brn | 1.40 | .45 |
| | | *Nos. 560-564,C265-C268 (9)* | 9.90 | 4.75 |

World Refugee Year, July 1, 1959-June 30, 1960 (1st issue).

UN Emblem and Dove — A133

UN Declaration of Human Rights: 3g, Hand holding scales. 6g, Hands breaking chains. 20g, Flame.

**1960, Apr. 21 *Perf. 12½x13***

| No. | Type | Description | Unused | Used |
|---|---|---|---|---|
| **565** | A133 | 1g dk car & bl | .30 | .25 |
| **566** | A133 | 3g blue & org | .30 | .25 |
| **567** | A133 | 6g gray grn & sal | .40 | .25 |
| **568** | A133 | 20g ver & yel | .55 | .25 |
| | | *Nos. 565-568,C269-C271 (7)* | 2.75 | 2.20 |

Miniature sheets exist, perf. and imperf., containing one each of Nos. 565-568, all printed in purple and orange. Values: perf. $4; imperf. $15.

Flags of UN and Paraguay and UN Emblem A134

***Perf. 13x13½***

**1960, Oct. 24 Photo. Unwmk.**

| No. | Type | Description | Unused | Used |
|---|---|---|---|---|
| **569** | A134 | 30c lt bl, red & bl | .30 | .30 |
| **570** | A134 | 75c yel, red & bl | .30 | .30 |
| **571** | A134 | 90c pale lil, red & bl | .30 | .30 |
| | | *Nos. 569-571,C272-C273 (5)* | 1.70 | 1.50 |

15th anniversary of the United Nations.

International Bridge, Arms of Brazil, Paraguay — A135

**1961, Jan. 26 Litho. *Perf. 14***

**572** A135 15c green .50 .50
**573** A135 30c dull blue .50 .50
**574** A135 50c orange .50 .50
**575** A135 75c vio blue .50 .50
**576** A135 1g violet .50 .50
*Nos. 572-576,C274-C277 (9)* 6.75 6.75

Inauguration of the International Bridge between Paraguay and Brazil.

Truck Carrying Logs — A136

90c, 2g, Logs on river barge. 1g, 5g, Radio tower.

**Unwmk.**

**1961, Apr. 10 Photo. *Perf. 13***

**577** A136 25c yel grn & rose car .25 .25
**578** A136 90c blue & yel .25 .25
**579** A136 1g car rose & org .25 .25
**580** A136 2g ol grn & sal .25 .25
**581** A136 5g lilac & emer .25 .25
*Nos. 577-581,C278-C281 (9)* 4.05 3.70

Paraguay's progress, "Paraguay en Marcha."

P. J. Caballero, José G. R. Francia, F. Yegros, Revolutionary Leaders — A137

**1961, May 16 Litho. *Perf. 14½***

**582** A137 30c green .40 .25
**583** A137 50c lil rose .40 .25
**584** A137 90c violet .40 .25
**585** A137 1.50g Prus bl .40 .25
**586** A137 3g olive bis .40 .25
**587** A137 4g ultra .40 .25
**588** A137 5g brown .40 .25
*Nos. 582-588,C282-C287 (13)* 9.95 7.90

150th anniv. of Independence (1st issue).

"Chaco Peace" — A138

**1961, June 12 *Perf. 14x14½***

**589** A138 25c vermilion .40 .40
**590** A138 30c green .40 .40
**591** A138 50c red brn .40 .40
**592** A138 1g bright vio .40 .40
**593** A138 2g dk bl gray .40 .40
*Nos. 589-593,C288-C290 (8)* 7.80 7.10

Chaco Peace; 150th anniv. of Independence (2nd issue).

Puma — A139

**1961, Aug. 16 Unwmk. *Perf. 14***

**594** A139 75c dull vio 1.00 1.00
**595** A139 1.50g brown 1.00 1.00
**596** A139 4.50g green 1.00 1.00
**597** A139 10g Prus blue 1.00 1.00
*Nos. 594-597,C291-C293 (7)* 15.50 13.00

150th anniv. of Independence (3rd issue).

University Seal — A140

**1961, Sept. 18 *Perf. 14x14½***

**598** A140 15c ultra .30 .30
**599** A140 25c dk red .30 .30
**600** A140 75c bl grn .30 .30
**601** A140 1g orange .30 .30
*Nos. 598-601,C294-C296 (7)* 3.20 2.80

Founding of the Catholic University in Asuncion; 150th anniv. of Independence (4th issue).

Hotel Guarani A141

**1961, Oct. 14 Litho. *Perf. 15***

**602** A141 50c slate bl .50 *1.00*
**603** A141 1g green .50 *1.00*
**604** A141 4.50g lilac .50 *1.00*
*Nos. 602-604,C297-C300 (7)* 11.00 10.25

Opening of the Hotel Guarani; 150th anniv. of Independence (5th issue).

Tennis Racket and Balls in Flag Colors — A142

**1961, Oct. 16 Litho. *Perf. 11***

**605** A142 35c multi .25 .25
**606** A142 75c multi .25 .25
**607** A142 1.50g multi .25 .25
**608** A142 2.25g multi .25 .25
**609** A142 4g multi .25 .25
*Nos. 605-609 (5)* 1.25 1.25

28th South American Tennis Championships, Asuncion, Oct. 15-23 (1st issue). Some specialists question the status of this issue. See Nos. C301-C303.

Imperforates exist in changed colors as well as two imperf. souvenir sheets with stamps in changed colors. Values: stamps, set $25; souvenir sheets, pair $40.

Alan B. Shepard, First US Astronaut A143

18.15g, 36g, 50g, Shepard, Saturn, horiz.

**1961, Dec. 22 Litho. *Perf. 11***

**610** A143 10c blue & brown .25 .25
**611** A143 25c blue & car rose .25 .25
**612** A143 50c blue & yel org .25 .25
**613** A143 75c blue & green .25 .25
**614** A143 18.15g green & blue *10.50* *6.50*
**615** A143 36g org & blue *10.50* *6.50*
**616** A143 50g car rose & blue *14.00* *9.75*
*a.* Souvenir sheet of 1 37.50
*Nos. 610-616 (7)* 36.00 23.75

Nos. 614-616a are airmail.

Also exist imperf in different colors. Value, set $36, souvenir sheet $210.

Uprooted Oak Emblem — A145

**1961, Dec. 30 Unwmk. *Perf. 11***

**619** A145 10c ultra & lt bl .25 .25
**620** A145 25c maroon & org .25 .25
**621** A145 50c car rose & pink .25 .25
**622** A145 75c dk bl & yel grn .25 .25
*Nos. 619-622 (4)* 1.00 1.00

World Refugee Year, 1959-60 (2nd issue). Imperforates in changed colors and souvenir sheets exist. Values: imperf. set of 7, $5; souvenir sheet, perf. or imperf., each $15. Some specialists question the status of this issue.

See Nos. C307-C309.

Europa A146

Design: 20g, 50g, Dove.

**1961, Dec. 31**

**623** A146 50c multicolored .35 .35
**624** A146 75c multicolored .35 .35
**625** A146 1g multicolored .35 .35
**626** A146 1.50g multicolored .35 .35
**627** A146 4.50g multicolored .80 .75
*a.* Souvenir sheet of 5, #623-627 21.00
**628** A146 20g multicolored 21.00
**629** A146 50g multicolored 25.00
*a.* Souvenir sheet of 1 90.00
*Nos. 623-629 (7)* 48.20 2.15

Nos. 628-629 are airmail.

Imperforates in changed colors exist. Values: set, $30; souvenir sheets, pair, $90.

Tennis Player — A147

**1962, Jan. 5 *Perf. 15x14½***

**630** A147 35c Prussian bl .60 .25
**631** A147 75c dark vio .60 .25
**632** A147 1.50g red brn .60 .25
**633** A147 2.25g emerald .60 .25
**634** A147 4g carmine 2.00 .25
**635** A147 12.45g red lil 2.00 .25
**636** A147 20g bl grn 2.00 .40
**637** A147 50g org brn 2.00 .65
*Nos. 630-637 (8)* 10.40 2.55

28th South American Tennis Championships, 1961 (2nd issue) and the 150th anniv. of Independence (6th issue).

Nos. 634-637 are airmail.

Scout Bugler — A148

Lord Baden-Powell A148a

**1962, Feb. 6 *Perf. 11***

**Olive Green Center**

**638** A148 10c dp magenta .25 .25
**639** A148 20c red orange .25 .25
**640** A148 25c dk brown .25 .25
**641** A148 30c emerald .25 .25
**642** A148 50c indigo .25 .25
**643** A148a 12.45g car rose & bl .85 .85
**644** A148a 36g car rose & emer 2.40 2.40
**645** A148a 50g car rose & org yel 3.25 3.25
*Nos. 638-645 (8)* 7.75 7.75

Issued to honor the Boy Scouts. Imperfs in changed colors exist and imperf souvenir sheets exist. Value, set $22, souvenir sheet $95. Some specialists question the status of this issue.

Nos. 643-645 are airmail.

**Arms Type of 1946**

**1962-68 Litho. Wmk. 347**

**646** A110 50c steel bl ('63) 3.00 2.00
**647** A110 70c dull lil ('63) 3.00 2.00
**648** A110 1.50g violet ('63) 3.00 1.00
**649** A110 3g dp bl ('68) 5.00 2.00
**650** A110 4.50g redsh brn ('67) 5.00 1.00
**651** A110 5g lilac ('64) 5.00 2.00
**652** A110 10g car rose ('63) 10.00 3.00
**653** A110 12.45g ultra 7.00 3.00
**654** A110 15.45g org ver 10.00 2.00
**655** A110 18.15g lilac 10.00 2.00
**656** A110 20g lt brn ('63) 10.00 2.00
**657** A110 50g dl red brn ('67) 10.00 3.00
**658** A110 100g bl gray ('63) 3.00 2.00
*Nos. 646-658 (13)* 84.00 27.00

Map and Laurel Branch — A149

Design: 20g, 50g, Hands holding globe.

***Perf. 14x14½***

**1962, Apr. 14 Unwmk.**

**659** A149 50c ocher .30 .30
**660** A149 75c vio blue .30 .30
**661** A149 1g purple .30 .30
**662** A149 1.50g brt grn .30 .30
**663** A149 4.50g vermilion .30 .30
**664** A149 20g lil rose .30 .30
**665** A149 50g orange .90 .90
*Nos. 659-665 (7)* 2.70 2.70

Day of the Americas; 150th anniv. of Independence (7th issue).

Nos. 664-665 are airmail.

UN Emblem A150

Design: #670-673, UN Headquarters, NYC.

**1962, Apr. 23 *Perf. 15***

**666** A150 50c bister brn .40 .25
**667** A150 75c dp claret .40 .25
**668** A150 1g Prussian bl .40 .25
**669** A150 2g orange brn 2.00 .25
**670** A150 12.45g dl vio 2.00 .35
**671** A150 18.15g ol grn 2.00 .65

**672** A150 23.40g brn red 2.00 .95
**673** A150 30g carmine 2.00 1.10
*Nos. 666-673 (8)* 11.20 4.05

UN; Independence, 150th anniv. (8th issue). Nos. 670-673 are airmail.

Malaria Eradication Emblem and Mosquito A151

Design: 75c, 1g, 1.50g, Microscope, anopheles mosquito and eggs. 3g, 4g, Malaria eradication emblem. 12.45g, 18.15g, 36g, Mosquito, UN emblem and microscope.

***Perf. 14x13½***

**1962, May 23** **Wmk. 346**

**674** A151 30c pink, ultra & blk .30 .30
**675** A151 50c bis, grn & blk .30 .30
**676** A151 75c rose red, blk & bis .30 .30
**677** A151 1g brt grn, blk & bis .30 .30
**678** A151 1.50g dl red brn, blk & bis .30 .30
**679** A151 3g bl, red & blk .30 .30
**680** A151 4g grn, red & blk .30 .30
**681** A151 12.45g ol bis, grn & blk .30 .30
**682** A151 18.15g rose lil, red & blk .60 .45
**683** A151 36g rose red, vio bl & blk 1.50 1.10
*Nos. 674-683 (10)* 4.50 3.95

WHO drive to eradicate malaria.

Imperforates exist in changed colors. Value, $10. Also, two souvenir sheets exist, one containing one copy of No. 683, the other an imperf 36g in blue, red & black. Value, each $20.

Some specialists question the status of this issue.

Nos. 679-683 are airmail.

Stadium — A152

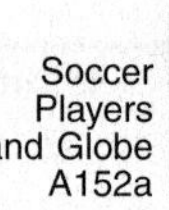

Soccer Players and Globe A152a

***Perf. 13½x14***

**1962, July 28** **Litho.** **Wmk. 346**

**684** A152 15c yel & dk brn .25 .25
**685** A152 25c brt grn & dk brn .25 .25
**686** A152 30c lt vio & dk brn .25 .25
**687** A152 40c dl org & dk brn .25 .25
**688** A152 50c brt yel grn & dk brn .25 .25
**689** A152a 12.45g brt rose, blk & vio .70 .35
**690** A152a 18.15g lt red brn, blk & vio 1.00 .45
**691** A152a 36g gray grn, blk & brn 2.25 .80
*Nos. 684-691 (8)* 5.20 2.85

World Soccer Championships, Chile, May 30-June 17.

Imperfs exist. Value $10. A souvenir sheet containing one No. 691 exists, both perforated and imperf. Value, $24 and $60, respectively.

Some specialists question the status of this issue.

Nos. 689-691 are airmail.

Freighter A153

Ship's Wheel — A153a

Designs: Various merchantmen. 44g, Like 12.45g with diagonal colorless band in background.

***Perf. 14½x15***

**1962, July 31** **Unwmk.**

**692** A153 30c bister brn .25 .25
**693** A153 90c slate bl .25 .25
**694** A153 1.50g brown red .25 .25
**695** A153 2g green .25 .25
**696** A153 4.20g vio blue .30 .25

***Perf. 15x14½***

**697** A153a 12.45g dk red 5.00 .25
**698** A153a 44g blue 5.00 .35
*Nos. 692-698 (7)* 11.30 1.85

Issued to honor the merchant marine.

Nos. 697-698 are airmail.

Friendship 7 over South America — A154

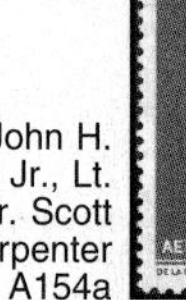

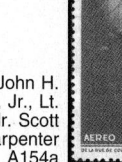

Lt. Col. John H. Glenn, Jr., Lt. Cmdr. Scott Carpenter A154a

***Perf. 13½x14***

**1962, Sept. 4** **Litho.** **Wmk. 346**

**699** A154 15c dk bl & bis .55 .45
**700** A154 25c vio brn & bis .55 .45
**701** A154 30c dk sl grn & bis .55 .45
**702** A154 40c dk gray & bis .55 .45
**703** A154 50c dk vio & bis .55 .45
**704** A154a 12.45g car lake & gray .55 .45
**705** A154a 18.15g red lil & gray .55 .45
**706** A154a 36g dl cl & gray .95 .80
*Nos. 699-706 (8)* 4.80 3.95

U.S. manned space flights. A souvenir sheet containing one No. 706 exists. Value $20.

Imperfs. in changed colors exist. Values: set, $14; souvenir sheet $60. Some specialists question the status of this issue.

Nos. 704-706 are airmail.

Discus Thrower — A155

Olympic flame &: 12.45g, Melbourne, 1956. 18.15g, Rome, 1960. 36g, Tokyo, 1964.

**1962, Oct. 1** **Litho.**

**707** A155 15c blk & yel .75 .25
**708** A155 25c blk & lt grn .75 .25
**709** A155 30c blk & pink .75 .25
**710** A155 40c blk & pale vio .75 .25
**711** A155 50c blk & lt bl .75 .25
**712** A155 12.45g brt grn, lt grn & choc .85 .75
**713** A155 18.15g ol brn, yel & choc .85 .75
**714** A155 36g rose red, pink & choc 1.50 1.00
*Nos. 707-714 (8)* 6.95 3.75

Olympic Games from Amsterdam 1928 to Tokyo 1964. Each stamp is inscribed with date and place of various Olympic Games. A souvenir sheet containing one No. 714 exists. Value $12.

Imperfs. in changed colors exist. Values: set, $27.50; souvenir sheet $125.

Some specialists question the status of this issue.

Nos. 712-714 are airmail.

Peace Dove and Cross A156

Dove Symbolizing Holy Ghost — A156a

***Perf. 14½***

**1962, Oct. 11** **Litho.** **Unwmk.**

**715** A156 50c olive .25 .25
**716** A156 70c dark blue .25 .25
**717** A156 1.50g bister .25 .25
**718** A156 2g violet .25 .25
**719** A156 3g brick red .25 .25
**720** A156a 5g vio bl 1.00 .25
**721** A156a 10g brt grn 1.00 .25
**722** A156a 12.45g lake 1.00 .25
**723** A156a 18.15g orange 1.00 .30
**724** A156a 23.40g violet 1.00 .40
**725** A156a 36g rose red 1.00 .50
*Nos. 715-725 (11)* 7.25 3.20

Vatican II, the 21st Ecumenical Council of the Roman Catholic Church, which opened Oct. 11, 1962.

Nos. 720-725 are airmail.

Europa A157

**1962, Dec. 17** ***Perf. 11***

**726** A157 4g yel, red & brn .50 .50
**727** A157 36g multi, diff. 10.00 3.00
*a.* Souvenir sheet of 2, #726-727 *25.00*
*Nos. 726-727 (2)* 10.50 3.50

No. 727 is airmail.

Exist imperf. in changed colors. Values: set, $45; souvenir sheet, $70.

Solar System A158

12.45g, 36g, 50g, Inner planets, Jupiter & rocket.

***Perf. 14x13½***

**1962, Dec. 17** **Wmk. 346**

**728** A158 10c org & purple .35 .35
**729** A158 20c org & brn vio .35 .35
**730** A158 25c org & dk vio .35 .35
**731** A158 30c org & ultra .35 .35
**732** A158 50c org & dull green .35 .35
**733** A158 12.45g org & brown 2.25 1.25
**734** A158 36g org & blue 4.25 2.00
**735** A158 50g org & green 8.50 4.25
*a.* Souvenir sheet of 1 17.50
*Nos. 728-735 (8)* 16.75 9.25

Nos. 733-735 are airmail.

Exist imperf. in changed colors. Values: set, $25; souvenir sheet, $80.

---

The following stamps exist imperf. in different colors: Nos. 736-743a, 744-751a, 752-759a, 760-766a, 775-782a, 783-790a, 791-798a, 799-805a, 806-813a, 814-821a, 828-835a, 836-843, 841a, 850-857a, 858-865a, 871-878, 876a, 887-894a, 895-902, 900a, 903-910a, 911-918a, 919-926a, 927-934a, 943-950a, 951-958a, 959-966a, 978-985a, 986-993a, 994-1001a, 1002-1003, 1003d, 1004-1007a, 1051-1059, B12-B19.

---

Pierre de Coubertin (1836-1937), Founder of Modern Olympic Games — A159

Summer Olympic Games sites and: 15c, Athens, 1896. 25c, Paris, 1900. 30c, St. Louis, 1904. 40c, London, 1908. 50c, Stockholm, 1912. 12.45g, No games, 1916. 18.15g, Antwerp, 1920. 36g, Paris, 1924.

12.45g, 18.15g, 36g, Torch bearer & stadium.

***Perf. 14x13½***

**1963, Feb. 16** **Wmk. 346**

**736** A159 15c multicolored .25 .25
**737** A159 25c multicolored .25 .25
**738** A159 30c multicolored .25 .25
**739** A159 40c multicolored .25 .25
**740** A159 50c multicolored .25 .25
**741** A159 12.45g multicolored 3.50 3.50
**742** A159 18.15g multicolored 3.50 3.50
**743** A159 36g multicolored 4.50 4.50
*a.* Souvenir sheet of 1 45.00
*Nos. 736-743 (8)* 12.75 12.75

Nos. 741-743a are airmail.

Exist imperf. in changed colors. Values: set, $30; souvenir sheet $150.

Walter M. Schirra, US Astronaut — A160

Design: 12.45g, 36g, 50g, Schirra.

**1963, Mar. 16** ***Perf. 13½x14***

**744** A160 10c brn org & blk .25 .25
**745** A160 20c car & blk .25 .25
**746** A160 25c lake & blk .25 .25
**747** A160 30c ver & blk .25 .25
**748** A160 50c mag & blk .25 .25
**749** A160 12.45g bl blk & lake 4.25 4.25
**750** A160 36g dl gray vio & lake 4.25 4.25
**751** A160 50g dk grn bl & lake 5.25 5.25
*a.* Souvenir sheet of 1 15.00
*Nos. 744-751 (8)* 15.00 15.00

Nos. 749-751a are airmail.

Exist imperf. in changed colors. Values: set, $25; souvenir sheet, $125.

Winter Olympics A161

Games sites and: 10c, Chamonix, 1924. 20c, St. Moritz, 1928. 25c, Lake Placid, 1932. 30c, Garmisch-Partenkirchen, 1936. 50c, St. Moritz, 1948. 12.45g, Oslo, 1952. 36g, Cortina d'Ampezzo, 1956. 50g, Squaw Valley, 1960. 12.45g, 36g, 50g, Snowflake.

**1963, May 16** *Perf. 14x13½*

**752** A161 10c multicolored .25 .25
**753** A161 20c multicolored .25 .25
**754** A161 25c multicolored .25 .25
**755** A161 30c multicolored .25 .25
**756** A161 50c multicolored .25 .25
**757** A161 12.45g multicolored 3.75 3.75
**758** A161 36g multicolored 3.75 3.75
**759** A161 50g multicolored 4.50 4.50
*a.* Souvenir sheet of 1 13.00 13.00
*Nos. 752-759 (8)* 13.25 13.25

Nos. 757-759a are airmail.
Exist imperf. in changed colors. Values: set, $17.50; souvenir sheet, $140.

Freedom from Hunger A162

**1963, May 31** *Perf. 13½x14, 14x13½*

**760** A162 10c yel grn & brn .25 .25
**761** A162 25c lt bl & brn .25 .25
**762** A162 50c lt grn bl & brn .25 .25
**763** A162 75c lt lil & brn .25 .25
**764** A162 18.15g yel org & brn 2.00 1.75
**765** A162 36g lt bl grn & brn 2.00 1.75
**766** A162 50g bis & brn 2.00 1.75
*a.* Souvenir sheet of 1 17.00
*Nos. 760-766 (7)* 7.00 6.25

Nos. 760-763 are vert. Nos. 764-766a are airmail.
Exist imperf. in changed colors. Values: set, $17; souvenir sheet, $22.50.

Pres. Alfredo Stroessner A163

**1963, Aug. 6** **Wmk. 347** *Perf. 11*

**767** A163 50c ol gray & sep 1.00 *2.50*
**768** A163 75c buff & sepia 1.00 *2.50*
**769** A163 1.50g lt lil & sep 1.00 *2.50*
**770** A163 3g emer & sepia 1.00 1.00
**771** A163 12.45g pink & claret 5.00 1.00
**772** A163 18.15g pink & grn 5.00 1.00
**773** A163 36g pink & vio 5.00 1.00
*Nos. 767-773 (7)* 19.00 11.50

Third presidential term of Alfredo Stroessner. A 36g imperf. souvenir sheet exists.
Nos. 771-773 are airmail.

---

MUESTRA

Some illustrated stamps show the word "MUESTRA" ("SPECIMEN"). This overprint is not on the actual stamps. The editors would like to borrow examples without the overprint so that replacement illustrations can be made.

---

Souvenir Sheet

Dag Hammarskjold, UN Secretary General — A164

**1963, Aug. 21** **Unwmk.** *Imperf.*

**774** A164 2g Sheet of 2 25.00 25.00

Project Mercury Flight of L. Gordon Cooper A165

12.45g, 18.15g, 50g, L. Gordon Cooper, vert.

*Perf. 14x13½, 13½x14*

**1963, Aug. 23** **Litho.** **Wmk. 346**

**775** A165 15c brn & orange .25 .25
**776** A165 25c brn & blue .25 .25
**777** A165 30c brn & violet .25 .25
**778** A165 40c brn & green .25 .25
**779** A165 50c brn & red vio .25 .25
**780** A165 12.45g brn & bl grn 3.50 2.50
**781** A165 18.15g brn & blue 3.50 2.50
**782** A165 50g brn & pink 3.50 2.50
*a.* Souvenir sheet of 1 25.00
*Nos. 775-782 (8)* 11.75 8.75

Nos. 780-782 are airmail.
Exist imperf. in changed colors. Values: set, $22.50; souvenir sheet, $30.

1964 Winter Olympics, Innsbruck A166

Design: 12.45g, 18.15g, 50g, Innsbruck Games emblem, vert.

*Perf. 14x13½, 13½x14*

**1963, Oct. 28** **Unwmk.**

**783** A166 15c choc & red .25 .25
**784** A166 25c gray grn & red .25 .25
**785** A166 30c plum & red .25 .25
**786** A166 40c sl grn & red .25 .25
**787** A166 50c dp bl & red .25 .25
**788** A166 12.45g sep & red 3.75 1.75
**789** A166 18.15g grn bl & red 3.75 1.75
**790** A166 50g tan & red 3.75 1.75
*a.* Souvenir sheet of 1 19.00
*Nos. 783-790 (8)* 12.50 6.50

Nos. 788-790 are airmail.
Exist imperf. in changed colors. Values: set, $25; souvenir sheet, $25.

1964 Summer Olympics, Tokyo — A167

12.45g, 18.15g, 50g, Tokyo games emblem.

**1964, Jan. 8** *Perf. 13½x14*

**791** A167 15c blue & red .25 .25
**792** A167 25c org & red .25 .25
**793** A167 30c tan & red .25 .25
**794** A167 40c vio brn & red .25 .25
**795** A167 50c grn bl & red .25 .25
**796** A167 12.45g vio & red 2.00 1.60
**797** A167 18.15g brn & red 2.00 1.60
**798** A167 50g grn bl & red 2.00 1.60
*a.* Souvenir sheet of 1 25.00
*Nos. 791-798 (8)* 7.25 6.05

Nos. 796-798 are airmail.
Exist imperf. in changed colors. Values: set, $20; souvenir sheet, $37.50.

Intl. Red Cross, Cent. A168

Designs: 10c, Helicopter. 25c, Space ambulance. 30c, Red Cross symbol, vert. 50c, Clara Barton, founder of American Red Cross, vert. 18.15g, Jean Henri Dunant, founder of Intl. Red Cross, vert. 36g, Red Cross space hospital, space ambulance. 50g, Plane, ship, ambulance, vert.

**1964, Feb. 4** *Perf. 14x13½, 13½x14*

**799** A168 10c vio brn & red .25 .25
**800** A168 25c bl grn & red .25 .25
**801** A168 30c dk bl & red .25 .25
**802** A168 50c ol blk & red .25 .25
**803** A168 18.15g choc, red, & pink 1.60 .80
**804** A168 36g grn bl & red 2.25 1.10
**805** A168 50g vio & red 3.50 2.00
*a.* Souvenir sheet of 1 14.00 11.00
*Nos. 799-805 (7)* 8.35 4.90

Nos. 803-805 are airmail.
Exist imperf. in changed colors. Values: set, $50; souvenir sheet, $20.

Space Research A169

15c, 25c, 30c, Gemini spacecraft rendezvous with Agena rocket. 40c, 50c, Future Apollo and Lunar Modules, vert. 12.45g, 18.15g, 50g, Telstar communications satellite, Olympic rings, vert.

**1964, Mar. 11**

**806** A169 15c vio & tan .25 .25
**807** A169 25c grn & tan .25 .25
**808** A169 30c bl & tan .25 .25
**809** A169 40c brt bl & red .25 .25
**810** A169 50c sl grn & red .25 .25
**811** A169 12.45g dk bl & tan 3.00 2.00
**812** A169 18.15g dk grn bl & tan 3.00 2.00
**813** A169 50g dp vio & tan 3.00 2.00
*a.* Souvenir sheet of 1 25.00 19.00
*Nos. 806-813 (8)* 10.25 7.25

1964 Summer Olympic Games, Tokyo (Nos. 811-813a). Nos. 811-813a are airmail.
Exist imperf. in changed colors. Values: set, $25; souvenir sheet, $17.

Rockets and Satellites A170

15c, 25c, Apollo command module mock-up. 30c, Tiros 7 weather satellite, vert. 40c, 50c, Ranger 6. 12.45g, 18.15g, 50g, Saturn I lift-off, vert.

**1964, Apr. 25**

**814** A170 15c brn & tan .25 .25
**815** A170 25c vio & tan .25 .25
**816** A170 30c Prus bl & lake .25 .25
**817** A170 40c ver & tan .25 .25
**818** A170 50c ultra & tan .25 .25
**819** A170 12.45g grn bl & choc 1.40 .85
**820** A170 18.15g bl & choc 2.25 1.60
**821** A170 50g lil rose & choc 3.50 2.50
*a.* Souvenir sheet of 1 12.00
*Nos. 814-821 (8)* 8.40 6.20

Nos. 819-821a are airmail.
Exist imperf. in changed colors. Values: set, $15; souvenir sheet, $17.

Popes Paul VI, John XXIII and St. Peter's, Rome A171

Design: 12.45g, 18.15g, 36g, Asuncion Cathedral, Popes Paul VI and John XXIII.

**1964, May 23** **Wmk. 347**

**822** A171 1.50g claret & org .25 .25
**823** A171 3g claret & dk grn .25 .25
**824** A171 4g claret & bister .25 .25
**825** A171 12.45g sl grn & lem 1.00 1.00
**826** A171 18.15g pur & lem 1.00 1.00
**827** A171 36g vio bl & lem 2.00 2.00
*Nos. 822-827 (6)* 4.75 4.75

National holiday of St. Maria Auxiliadora (Our Lady of Perpetual Help).
Nos. 825-827 are airmail.

United Nations A172

Designs: 15c, John F. Kennedy. 25c, 12.45g, Pope Paul VI and Patriarch Atenagoras. 30c, Eleanor Roosevelt, Chairman of UN Commission on Human Rights. 40c, Relay, Syncom and Telstar satellites. 50c, Echo 2 satellite. 18.15g, U Thant, UN Sec. Gen. 50g, Rocket, flags of Europe, vert.

*Perf. 14x13½, 14 (15c, 25c, 12.45g)*

**1964, July 30** **Unwmk.**

**Size: 35x35mm (#830, 834), 40x29mm (#831-832, 835)**

**828** A172 15c blk & brn .25 .25
**829** A172 25c blk, bl & red .25 .25
**830** A172 30c blk & ver .25 .25
**831** A172 40c dk bl & sep .25 .25
**832** A172 50c vio & car .25 .25
**833** A172 12.45g blk, grn & red .75 .75
**834** A172 18.15g blk & grn .75 .75

*Perf. 13½x14*

**835** A172 50g multicolored 1.75 1.75
*a.* Souvenir sheet of 1 32.50
*Nos. 828-835 (8)* 4.50 4.50

Nos. 833-835a are airmail.
Exist imperf. in changed colors. Values: set, $15; souvenir sheet, $32.50.

Space Achievements — A173

Designs: 10c, 30c, Ranger 7, Moon, vert. 15c, 12.45+6g, Wernher von Braun looking through periscope, vert. 20c, 20+10g, John F. Kennedy, rockets, vert. 40c, 18.15+9g, Rockets, von Braun.

**1964, Sept. 12** *Perf. 12½x12*

**836** A173 10c bl & blk .25 .25
**837** A173 15c yel grn & brt pink .25 .25
**838** A173 20c yel org & bl .25 .25
**839** A173 30c mag & blk .25 .25
**840** A173 40c yel org, bl & blk .25 .25
**841** A173 12.45g +6g red & bl 2.40 1.60
*a.* Souvenir sheet of 2, #840-841 24.00
**842** A173 18.15g +9g grn bl, brn & blk 2.40 1.60
**843** A173 20g +10g red & bl 3.25 2.40
*Nos. 836-843 (8)* 9.30 6.85

Nos. 841-843 are airmail.
Exist imperf. in changed colors. Values: set, $22.50; souvenir sheet, $37.50.

Coats of Arms of Paraguay and France A174

Designs: 3g, 12.45g, 36g, Presidents Stroessner and de Gaulle. 18.15g, Coats of Arms of Paraguay and France.

**1964, Oct. 6** **Wmk. 347**

**844** A174 1.50g brown .30 .30
**845** A174 3g ultramarine .30 .30
**846** A174 4g gray .30 .30
**847** A174 12.45g lilac .40 .40
**848** A174 18.15g bl grn .60 .60
**849** A174 36g magenta 2.50 1.75
*Nos. 844-849 (6)* 4.40 3.65

Visit of Pres. Charles de Gaulle of France.
Nos. 847-849 are airmail.

Boy Scout Jamborees — A175

Boy Scout Emblem — A175a

Designs: 10c, Argentina, 1961. 15c, Peru, canceled. 20c, Chile, 1959. 30c, Brazil, 1954. 50c, Uruguay, 1957. 12.45g, Brazil, 1960. 18.15g, Venezuela, 1964. 36g, Brazil, 1963.

15c, 18.15g, Lord Robert Baden-Powell (1857-1941), Boy Scouts founder.

**1965, Jan. 15 Unwmk. *Perf. 14***

| No. | Type | Denomination | Description | Unused | Used |
|---|---|---|---|---|---|
| **850** | A175 | 10c | multicolored | .25 | .25 |
| **851** | A175 | 15c | multicolored | .25 | .25 |
| **852** | A175a | 20c | multicolored | .25 | .25 |
| **853** | A175a | 30c | multicolored | .25 | .25 |
| **854** | A175 | 50c | multicolored | .25 | .25 |
| **855** | A175a | 12.45g | multicolored | 1.50 | 1.50 |
| **856** | A175 | 18.15g | multicolored | 1.60 | 1.40 |
| **857** | A175 | 36g | multicolored | 3.00 | 2.50 |
| *a.* | | | Souvenir sheet of 1, perf. 12x12½ | 17.00 | |
| | | | *Nos. 850-857 (8)* | 7.35 | 6.65 |

Nos. 855-857a are airmail.

Exist imperf. in changed colors. Values: set, $9; souvenir sheet, $22.50.

A176

Olympic and Paraguayan Medals: 25c, John F. Kennedy. 30c, Medal of Peace and Justice, reverse. 40c, Gens. Stroessner and DeGaulle, profiles. 50c, 18.15g, DeGaulle and Stroessner, in uniform. 12.45g, Medal of Peace and Justice, obverse.

**Litho. & Embossed**

**1965, Mar. 30 *Perf. 13½x13***

| No. | Type | Denomination | Description | Unused | Used |
|---|---|---|---|---|---|
| **858** | A176 | 15c | multicolored | .25 | .25 |
| **859** | A176 | 25c | multicolored | .25 | .25 |
| **860** | A176 | 30c | multicolored | .25 | .25 |

***Perf. 12½x12***

| No. | Type | Denomination | Description | Unused | Used |
|---|---|---|---|---|---|
| **861** | A176 | 40c | multicolored | .25 | .25 |
| **862** | A176 | 50c | multicolored | .25 | .25 |
| **863** | A176 | 12.45g | multicolored | 2.25 | 1.50 |
| **864** | A176 | 18.15g | multicolored | 2.75 | 1.75 |
| **865** | A176 | 50g | multicolored | 4.25 | 1.75 |
| *a.* | | | Souv. sheet of 1, perf. 13½x13 | 35.00 | |
| | | | *Nos. 858-865 (8)* | 10.50 | 6.25 |

Nos. 863-865a are airmail. Medal on No. 865a is gold foil.

Exist imperf. in changed colors. Values: set, $20; souvenir sheet, $60.

Overprinted in Black — A177

Design: Map of Americas.

**1965, Apr. 26 Wmk. 347 *Perf. 11***

| No. | Type | Denomination | Description | Unused | Used |
|---|---|---|---|---|---|
| **866** | A177 | 1.50g | dull grn | .40 | .40 |
| **867** | A177 | 3g | car red | .40 | .40 |
| **868** | A177 | 4g | dark blue | .40 | .40 |
| **869** | A177 | 12.45g | brn & blk | .40 | .40 |
| **870** | A177 | 36g | brt lil & blk | 1.00 | .70 |
| | | | *Nos. 866-870 (5)* | 2.60 | 2.30 |

Centenary of National Epic. Not issued without overprint.

Nos. 869-870 are airmail.

Scientists — A178

**Unwmk.**

**1965, June 5 Litho. *Perf. 14***

| No. | Type | Denomination | Description | Unused | Used |
|---|---|---|---|---|---|
| **871** | A178 | 10c | Newton | .25 | .25 |
| **872** | A178 | 15c | Copernicus | .25 | .25 |
| **873** | A178 | 20c | Galileo | .25 | .25 |
| **874** | A178 | 30c | like #871 | .25 | .25 |
| **875** | A178 | 40c | Einstein | .25 | .25 |
| **876** | A178 | 12.45g | +6g like #873 | 1.00 | .50 |
| *a.* | | | Souvenir sheet of 2, #875-876 | 12.50 | |
| **877** | A178 | 18.15g | +9g like #875 | 1.50 | 1.00 |
| **878** | A178 | 20g | +10g like #872 | 1.75 | 1.50 |
| | | | *Nos. 871-878 (8)* | 5.50 | 4.25 |

Nos. 876-878 are airmail.

Exist imperf. in changed colors. Values: set, $12; souvenir sheet, $12.50.

Cattleya Warscewiczii A179

Ceibo Tree — A179a

**1965, June 28 Unwmk. *Perf. 14½***

| No. | Type | Denomination | Description | Unused | Used |
|---|---|---|---|---|---|
| **879** | A179 | 20c | purple | .25 | .25 |
| **880** | A179 | 30c | blue | .25 | .25 |
| **881** | A179 | 90c | bright mag | .25 | .25 |
| **882** | A179 | 1.50g | green | .25 | .25 |
| **883** | A179a | 3g | brn red | 1.40 | .90 |
| **884** | A179a | 4g | green | 1.75 | .90 |
| **885** | A179 | 4.50g | orange | 1.75 | .90 |
| **886** | A179a | 66g | brn org | 3.50 | 1.40 |
| | | | *Nos. 879-886 (8)* | 9.40 | 5.10 |

150th anniv. of Independence (1811-1961).

Nos. 883-884, 886 are airmail.

John F. Kennedy and Winston Churchill — A180

Designs: 15c, Kennedy, PT 109. 25c, Kennedy family. 30c, 12.45g, Churchill, Parliament building. 40c, Kennedy, Alliance for Progress emblem. 50c, 18.15g, Kennedy, rocket launch at Cape Canaveral. 50g, John Glenn, Kennedy, Lyndon Johnson examining Friendship 7.

**1965, Sept. 4 *Perf. 12x12½***

| No. | Type | Denomination | Description | Unused | Used |
|---|---|---|---|---|---|
| **887** | A180 | 15c | bl & brn | .25 | .25 |
| **888** | A180 | 25c | red & brn | .25 | .25 |
| **889** | A180 | 30c | vio & blk | .25 | .25 |
| **890** | A180 | 40c | org & sep | .25 | .25 |
| **891** | A180 | 50c | bl grn & sep | .25 | .25 |
| **892** | A180 | 12.45g | yel & blk | 1.40 | .75 |
| **893** | A180 | 18.15g | car & blk | 2.00 | 1.20 |
| **894** | A180 | 50g | grn & blk | 3.50 | 1.75 |
| *a.* | | | Souvenir sheet of 1 | 20.00 | |
| | | | *Nos. 887-894 (8)* | 8.15 | 4.95 |

Nos. 892-894a are airmail.

Exist imperf. in changed colors. Values: set, $20; souvenir sheet, $20.

ITU, Cent. — A181

Satellites: 10c, 40c, Ranger 7 transmitting to Earth. 15c, 20g+10g, Syncom, Olympic rings. 20c, 18.15g+9g, Early Bird. 30c, 12.45g+6g, Relay, Syncom, Telstar, Echo 2.

**1965, Sept. 30**

| No. | Type | Denomination | Description | Unused | Used |
|---|---|---|---|---|---|
| **895** | A181 | 10c | dull bl & sep | .25 | .25 |
| **896** | A181 | 15c | lilac & sepia | .25 | .25 |
| **897** | A181 | 20c | ol grn & sep | .25 | .25 |
| **898** | A181 | 30c | blue & sepia | .25 | .25 |
| **899** | A181 | 40c | grn & sep | .25 | .25 |
| **900** | A181 | 12.45g | +6g ver & sep | 1.20 | .50 |
| *a.* | | | Souvenir sheet of 2, #899-900 | 22.50 | |
| **901** | A181 | 18.15g | +9g org & sep | 1.75 | .75 |
| **902** | A181 | 20g | +10g vio & sep | 3.00 | 1.25 |
| | | | *Nos. 895-902 (8)* | 7.20 | 3.75 |

Nos. 900-902 are airmail.

Exist imperf. in changed colors. Values: set, $17.50; souvenir sheet, $27.50.

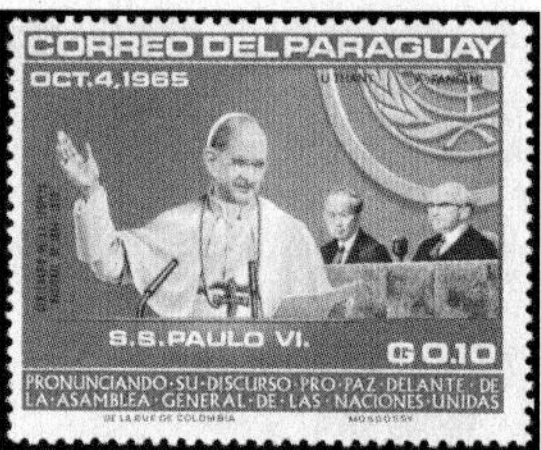

Pope Paul VI, Visit to UN A182

Designs: 10c, 50c, Pope Paul VI, U Thant, A. Fanfani. 15c, 12.45g, Pope Paul VI, Lyndon B. Johnson. 20c, 36g, Early Bird satellite, globe, papal arms. 30c, 18.15g, Pope Paul VI, Unisphere.

**1965, Nov. 19**

| No. | Type | Denomination | Description | Unused | Used |
|---|---|---|---|---|---|
| **903** | A182 | 10c | multicolored | .25 | .25 |
| **904** | A182 | 15c | multicolored | .25 | .25 |
| **905** | A182 | 20c | multicolored | .25 | .25 |
| **906** | A182 | 30c | multicolored | .25 | .25 |
| **907** | A182 | 50c | multicolored | .25 | .25 |
| **908** | A182 | 12.45g | multicolored | .75 | .50 |
| **909** | A182 | 18.15g | multicolored | 1.25 | 1.25 |
| **910** | A182 | 36g | multicolored | 2.50 | 1.75 |
| *a.* | | | Souvenir sheet of 1 | 22.50 | |
| | | | *Nos. 903-910 (8)* | 5.75 | 4.75 |

Nos. 908-910a are airmail.

Exist imperf. in changed colors. Values: set, $25; souvenir sheet, $32.50.

Astronauts and Space Exploration — A183

15c, 50g, Edward White walking in space, 6/3/65. 25c, 18.15g, Gemini 7 & 8 docking, 12/16-18/65. 30c, Virgil I. Grissom, John W. Young, 3/23/65. 40c, 50c, Edward White, James McDivitt, 6/3/65. 12.45g, Photographs of lunar surface.

**1966, Feb. 19 *Perf. 14***

| No. | Type | Denomination | Description | Unused | Used |
|---|---|---|---|---|---|
| **911** | A183 | 15c | multicolored | .25 | .25 |
| **912** | A183 | 25c | multicolored | .25 | .25 |
| **913** | A183 | 30c | multicolored | .25 | .25 |
| **914** | A183 | 40c | multicolored | .25 | .25 |
| **915** | A183 | 50c | multicolored | .25 | .25 |
| **916** | A183 | 12.45g | multicolored | 1.10 | 1.10 |
| **917** | A183 | 18.15g | multicolored | 1.90 | 1.90 |
| **918** | A183 | 50g | multicolored | 3.25 | 3.25 |
| *a.* | | | Souvenir sheet of 1 | 25.00 | |
| | | | *Nos. 911-918 (8)* | 7.50 | 7.50 |

Nos. 916-918a are airmail.

Exist imperf. in changed colors. Values: set, $12; souvenir sheet, $25.

Events of 1965 — A184

10c, Meeting of Pope Paul VI & Cardinal Spellman, 10/4/65. 15c, Intl. Phil. Exposition, Vienna. 20c, OAS, 75th anniv. 30c, 36g, Intl. Quiet Sun Year, 1964-65. 50c, 18.15g, Saturn rockets at NY World's Fair. 12.45g, UN Intl. Cooperation Year.

**1966, Mar. 9**

| No. | Type | Denomination | Description | Unused | Used |
|---|---|---|---|---|---|
| **919** | A184 | 10c | multicolored | .25 | .25 |
| **920** | A184 | 15c | multicolored | .25 | .25 |
| **921** | A184 | 20c | multicolored | .25 | .25 |
| **922** | A184 | 30c | multicolored | .25 | .25 |
| **923** | A184 | 50c | multicolored | .25 | .25 |
| **924** | A184 | 12.45g | multicolored | 1.10 | .75 |
| **925** | A184 | 18.15g | multicolored | 1.90 | 1.50 |
| **926** | A184 | 36g | multicolored | 3.75 | 1.25 |
| *a.* | | | Souvenir sheet of 1 | 20.00 | |
| | | | *Nos. 919-926 (8)* | 8.00 | 4.75 |

Nos. 924-926a are airmail.

Exist imperf. in changed colors. Values: set, $25; souvenir sheet, $25.

1968 Summer Olympics, Mexico City — A185

15c, God of Death. 20c, Aztec calendar stone. 50c, Zapotec deity.

***Perf. 12½x12 (Nos. 927, 929, 931, 933), 13½x13***

**1966, Apr. 1**

| No. | Type | Denomination | Description | Unused | Used |
|---|---|---|---|---|---|
| **927** | A185 | 10c | shown | .25 | .25 |
| **928** | A185 | 15c | multi | .25 | .25 |
| **929** | A185 | 20c | multi | .25 | .25 |
| **930** | A185 | 30c | like No. 928 | .25 | .25 |
| **931** | A185 | 50c | multi | .25 | .25 |
| **932** | A185 | 12.45g | like No. 931 | 1.25 | .75 |
| **933** | A185 | 18.15g | like No. 927 | 1.90 | 1.25 |
| **934** | A185 | 36g | like No. 929 | 4.50 | 3.00 |
| *a.* | | | Souvenir sheet of 1 | 15.00 | |
| | | | *Nos. 927-934 (8)* | 8.90 | 6.25 |

Nos. 932-934a are airmail.

Exist imperf. in changed colors. Values: set, $15; souvenir sheet, $30.

A185a

St. Ignatius and San Ignacio Monastery A185b

**1966, Apr. 20 Wmk. 347 *Perf. 11***

| | | | | |
|---|---|---|---|---|
| **935** | A185a | 15c ultramarine | 1.00 | .50 |
| **936** | A185a | 25c ultramarine | 1.00 | .50 |
| **937** | A185a | 75c ultramarine | 1.00 | .50 |
| **938** | A185a | 90c ultramarine | 1.00 | .50 |
| **939** | A185b | 3g brown | 1.00 | .50 |
| **940** | A185b | 12.45g sepia | 1.00 | .50 |
| **941** | A185b | 18.15g sepia | 1.00 | .50 |
| **942** | A185b | 23.40g sepia | 1.00 | .50 |
| | | *Nos. 935-942 (8)* | 8.00 | 4.00 |

350th anniv. of the founding of San Ignacio Guazu Monastery.

Nos. 939-942 are airmail.

On designs A185b text under Paraguay is different from that of design A129a (No. 522)

A186

A186a

German Contributors in Space Research — A186b

Designs: 10c, 36g, Paraguay #835, C97, Germany #C40. 15c, 50c, 18.15g, 3rd stage of Europa 1 rocket. 20c, 12.45g, Hermann Oberth, jet propulsion engineer. 30c, Reinhold K. Tiling, builder of 1st German rocket, 1931, vert.

***Perf. 12x12½ (Nos. 943, 950), 12½x12 (Nos. 945, 947, 949), 13½x13***

**1966, May 16 Unwmk.**

| | | | | |
|---|---|---|---|---|
| **943** | A186 | 10c multicolored | .25 | .25 |
| **944** | A186a | 15c multicolored | .25 | .25 |
| **945** | A186b | 20c multicolored | .25 | .25 |
| **946** | A186b | 30c multicolored | .25 | .25 |
| **947** | A186a | 50c multicolored | .25 | .25 |
| **948** | A186b | 12.45g multicolored | 1.50 | .50 |
| **949** | A186a | 18.15g multicolored | 1.90 | 1.00 |
| **950** | A186 | 36g multicolored | 3.75 | 2.25 |
| *a.* | | Souvenir sheet of 1, perf. 12x13½x13x13½ | 35.00 | |
| | | *Nos. 943-950 (8)* | 8.40 | 5.00 |

Nos. 948-950a are airmail.

Exist imperf. in changed colors. Values: set, $25; souvenir sheet, $50.

Writers — A187

**1966, June 11 *Perf. 12x12½***

| | | | | |
|---|---|---|---|---|
| **951** | A187 | 10c Dante | .25 | .25 |
| **952** | A187 | 15c Moliere | .25 | .25 |
| **953** | A187 | 20c Goethe | .25 | .25 |
| **954** | A187 | 30c Shakespeare | .25 | .25 |
| **955** | A187 | 50c like #952 | .25 | .25 |
| **956** | A187 | 12.45g like #953 | 1.90 | 1.50 |
| **957** | A187 | 18.15g like #954 | 2.25 | 1.50 |
| **958** | A187 | 36g like #951 | 3.75 | 1.50 |
| *a.* | | Souvenir sheet of 1, perf. 13½x14 | 14.00 | |
| | | *Nos. 951-958 (8)* | 9.15 | 5.75 |

Nos. 956-958a are airmail.

Exist imperf. in changed colors. Values: set, $12; souvenir sheet, $20.

Italian Contributors in Space Research — A188

10c, 36g, Italian satellite, San Marco 1. 15c, 18.15g, Drafting machine, Leonardo Da Vinci. 20c, 12.45g, Map, Italo Balbo (1896-1940), aviator. 30c, 50c, Floating launch & control facility, satellite.

**1966, July 11**

| | | | | |
|---|---|---|---|---|
| **959** | A188 | 10c multicolored | .25 | .25 |
| **960** | A188 | 15c multicolored | .25 | .25 |
| **961** | A188 | 20c multicolored | .25 | .25 |
| **962** | A188 | 30c multicolored | .25 | .25 |
| **963** | A188 | 50c multicolored | .25 | .25 |
| **964** | A188 | 12.45g multicolored | 1.50 | .50 |
| **965** | A188 | 18.15g multicolored | 2.60 | .50 |
| **966** | A188 | 36g multicolored | 4.50 | 3.00 |
| *a.* | | Souvenir sheet of 1, perf. 13x13½ | 15.00 | |
| | | *Nos. 959-966 (8)* | 9.85 | 5.25 |

Nos. 964-966a are airmail.

Exist imperf. in changed colors. Values: set, $20; souvenir sheet, $20.

Rubén Dario — A189

"Paraguay de Fuego" by Dario — A189a

**1966, July 16 Wmk. 347**

| | | | | |
|---|---|---|---|---|
| **967** | A189 | 50c ultramarine | .50 | .40 |
| **968** | A189 | 70c bister brn | .50 | .40 |
| **969** | A189 | 1.50g rose car | .50 | .40 |
| **970** | A189 | 3g violet | .50 | .40 |
| **971** | A189 | 4g greenish bl | .50 | .40 |
| **972** | A189 | 5g black | .50 | .40 |
| **973** | A189a | 12.45g blue | 1.50 | .40 |
| **974** | A189a | 18.15g red lil | 1.50 | .40 |
| **975** | A189a | 23.40g org brn | 1.50 | .40 |
| **976** | A189a | 36g brt grn | 1.50 | .90 |
| **977** | A189a | 50g rose car | 1.50 | 1.20 |
| | | *Nos. 967-977 (11)* | 10.50 | 5.70 |

50th death anniv. of Ruben Dario (pen name of Felix Rubén Garcia Sarmiento, 1867-1916), Nicaraguan poet, newspaper correspondent and diplomat.

Nos. 973-977 are airmail.

Space Missions — A190

10c, Gemini 8. 15c, Gemini 9. 20c, Surveyor 1 on moon. 30c, Gemini 10.

**1966, Aug. 25 Unwmk.**

| | | | | |
|---|---|---|---|---|
| **978** | A190 | 10c multi | .25 | .25 |
| **979** | A190 | 15c multi | .25 | .25 |
| **980** | A190 | 20c multi | .25 | .25 |
| **981** | A190 | 30c multi | .25 | .25 |
| **982** | A190 | 50c like #981 | .25 | .25 |
| **983** | A190 | 12.45g like #980 | 2.25 | 1.25 |
| **984** | A190 | 18.15g like #979 | 2.25 | 1.25 |
| **985** | A190 | 36g like #978 | 12.50 | 6.00 |
| *a.* | | Souvenir sheet of 1, perf. 13x13½ | 20.00 | |
| | | *Nos. 978-985 (8)* | 18.25 | 9.75 |

Nos. 983-985a are airmail.

Exist imperf. in changed colors. Values: set, $25; souvenir sheet, $25.

1968 Winter Olympics, Grenoble — A191

**1966, Sept. 30 *Perf. 14***

| | | | | |
|---|---|---|---|---|
| **986** | A191 | 10c Figure skating | .25 | .25 |
| **987** | A191 | 15c Downhill skiing | .25 | .25 |
| **988** | A191 | 20c Speed skating | .25 | .25 |
| **989** | A191 | 30c 2-man luge | .25 | .25 |
| **990** | A191 | 50c like #989 | .25 | .25 |
| **991** | A191 | 12.45g like #988 | 1.00 | .50 |
| **992** | A191 | 18.15g like #987 | 1.25 | .50 |
| **993** | A191 | 36g like #986 | 2.50 | 2.50 |
| *a.* | | Souvenir sheet of 1 | 15.00 | |
| | | *Nos. 986-993 (8)* | 6.00 | 4.75 |

Nos. 987, 992, World Skiing Championships, Portillo, Chile, 1966. Nos. 991-993a are airmail.

Exist imperf. in changed colors. Values: set, $12.50; souvenir sheet, $27.50.

Pres. John F. Kennedy, 3rd Death Anniv. — A192

10c, Echo 1 & 2. 15c, Telstar 1 & 2. 20c, Relay 1 & 2. 30c, Syncom 1, 2 & 3, Early Bird.

***Perf. 12x12½, 13½x14 (#997-998, 1001)***

**1966, Nov. 7**

| | | | | |
|---|---|---|---|---|
| **994** | A192 | 10c multi | .25 | .25 |
| **995** | A192 | 15c multi | .25 | .25 |
| **996** | A192 | 20c multi | .25 | .25 |
| **997** | A192 | 30c multi | .25 | .25 |
| **998** | A192 | 50c like #997 | .25 | .25 |
| **999** | A192 | 12.45g like #996 | 1.25 | .50 |
| **1000** | A192 | 18.15g like #995 | 1.50 | .50 |
| **1001** | A192 | 36g like #994 | 5.00 | 3.50 |
| *a.* | | Souvenir sheet of 1, perf. 13x14x13½x14 | 20.00 | |
| | | *Nos. 994-1001 (8)* | 9.00 | 5.75 |

Nos. 999-1001a are airmail.

Exist imperf. in changed colors. Values: set, $20; souvenir sheet, $24.

Paintings A193

Portraits of women by: No. 1002a, 10c, De Largilliere. b, 15c, Rubens. c, 20c, Titian. d, 30c, Hans Holbein. e, 50c, Sanchez Coello.

Paintings: No. 1003a, 12.45g, Mars and Venus with United by Love by Veronese. b, 18.15g, Allegory of Prudence, Peace and Abundance by Vouet. c, 36g, Madonna and Child by Andres Montegna.

**1966, Dec. 10 *Perf. 14x13½***

| | | | | |
|---|---|---|---|---|
| **1002** | A193 | Strip of 5, #a.-e. | 1.25 | 1.25 |
| **1003** | A193 | Strip of 3, #a.-c. | 4.50 | 4.50 |
| *d.* | | Souvenir sheet of 1, #1003c | 16.00 | |
| | | *Nos. 1002-1003 (2)* | 5.75 | 5.75 |

Nos. 1003a-1003d are airmail. No. 1003d has green pattern in border and is perf. 12½x12.

Exist imperf. in changed colors. Values: set, $15; souvenir sheet, $16.

Holy Week Paintings A194

Life of Christ by: No. 1004a, 10c, Raphael. b, 15c, Rubens. c, 20c, Da Ponte. d, 30c, El Greco. e, 50c, Murillo, horiz.

12.45g, G. Reni. 18.15g, Tintoretto. 36g, Da Vinci, horiz.

**1967, Feb. 28 *Perf. 14x13½, 13½x14***

| | | | | |
|---|---|---|---|---|
| **1004** | A194 | Strip of 5, #a.-e. | 1.25 | 1.25 |
| **1005** | A194 | 12.45g multicolored | .55 | .50 |
| **1006** | A194 | 18.15g multicolored | .55 | .50 |
| **1007** | A194 | 36g multicolored | 5.75 | 5.00 |
| *a.* | | Souvenir sheet of 1 | 15.00 | |
| | | *Nos. 1004-1007 (4)* | 8.10 | 7.25 |

Nos. 1005-1007a are airmail. No. 1007a has salmon pattern in border and contains one 60x40mm, perf. 14 stamp.

Exist imperf. in changed colors. Values: set, $15; souvenir sheet, $15.

Birth of Christ by Barocci A195

16th Cent. Paintings: 12.45g, Madonna and Child by Caravaggio. 18.15g, Mary of the Holy Family (detail) by El Greco. 36g, Assumption of the Virgin by Vasco Fernandes.

**1967, Mar. 10 *Perf. 14½***

| | | | | |
|---|---|---|---|---|
| **1008** | A195 | 10c lt bl & multi | .25 | .25 |
| **1009** | A195 | 15c lt grn & multi | .25 | .25 |
| **1010** | A195 | 20c lt brn & multi | .25 | .25 |
| **1011** | A195 | 30c lil & multi | .25 | .25 |
| **1012** | A195 | 50c pink & multi | .25 | .25 |
| **1013** | A195 | 12.45g lt bl grn & multi | .50 | .50 |
| **1014** | A195 | 18.15g brt pink & multi | .50 | .50 |
| **1015** | A195 | 36g lt vio & multi | 6.00 | 4.00 |
| *a.* | | Souv. sheet of 1, sep & multi | 17.00 | |
| | | *Nos. 1008-1015 (8)* | 8.25 | 6.25 |

Nos. 1013-1015a are airmail.

Exist imperf. with changed borders. Values: set, $15; souvenir sheet, $17.

Globe and Lions Emblem — A196

Medical Laboratory "Health" A196a

Designs: 1.50g, 3g, Melvin Jones. 4g, 5g, Lions' Headquarters, Chicago. 12.45g, 18.15g, Library "Education."

**1967, May 9 Litho. Wmk. 347**

**1016** A196 50c light vio 1.00 .50
**1017** A196 70c blue 1.00 .50
**1018** A196 1.50g ultra 1.00 .50
**1019** A196 3g brown 1.00 .50
**1020** A196 4g Prus grn 1.00 .50
**1021** A196 5g ol gray 2.00 .50
**1022** A196a 12.45g dk brn 2.00 .50
**1023** A196a 18.15g violet 2.00 .50
**1024** A196a 23.40g rose cl 2.00 .50
**1025** A196a 36g Prus blue 2.00 .50
**1026** A196a 50g rose car 2.00 .50
*Nos. 1016-1026 (11)* 17.00 5.50

50th anniversary of Lions International.
Nos. 1022-1026 are airmail.

Vase of Flowers by Chardin A197

Still Life Paintings by: No. 1027b, 15c, Fontanesi, horiz. c, 20c, Cezanne. d, 30c, Van Gogh. e, 50c, Renoir.

Paintings: 12.45g, Cha-U-Kao at the Moulin Rouge by Toulouse-Lautrec. 18.15g, Gabrielle with Jean Renoir by Renoir. 36g, Patience Escalier, Shepherd of Provence by Van Gogh.

**1967, May 16** ***Perf. 12½x12***

**1027** A197 Strip of 5, #a.-e. 1.25 1.25
**1028** A197 12.45g multicolored .50 .50
**1029** A197 18.15g multicolored .50 .50
**1030** A197 36g multicolored 4.00 4.00
*a.* Souvenir sheet of 1, perf. 14x12x14x13½ 20.00
*Nos. 1027-1030 (4)* 6.25 6.25

Nos. 1028-1030a are airmail. No. 1030a has a green pattern in border.
Exist imperf. with changed borders. Values: set, $10; souvenir sheet, $22.50.

Famous Paintings — A198

10c, Jan Steen. 15c, Frans Hals, vert. 20c, Jordaens. 25c, Rembrandt. 30c, de Marees, vert. 50c, Quentin, vert. 12.45g, Nicolaes Maes, vert. 18.15g, Vigee-Lebrun, vert. 36g, Rubens, vert.
50g, G. B. Tiepolo.

**1967, July 16** ***Perf. 12x12½***

**1031** A198 10c multicolored .25 .25

***Perf. 14x13½, 13½x14***

**1032** A198 15c multicolored .25 .25
**1033** A198 20c multicolored .25 .25
**1034** A198 25c multicolored .25 .25
**1035** A198 30c multicolored .25 .25
**1036** A198 50c multicolored .25 .25
**1037** A198 12.45g multicolored .60 .50
**1038** A198 18.15g multicolored .60 .50
**1039** A198 36g multicolored 6.00 4.00
*Nos. 1031-1039 (9)* 8.70 6.50

**Souvenir Sheet**

***Perf. 12x12½***

**1040** A198 50g multicolored 10.00

Nos. 1037-1039 are airmail. An imperf. souvenir sheet of 3, Nos. 1037-1039 exists with dark green pattern in border. Value $15.

John F. Kennedy, 50th Birth Anniv. A199

Kennedy and: 10c, Recovery of Alan Shepard's capsule, Lyndon Johnson, Mrs. Kennedy. 15c, John Glenn. 20c, Mr. and Mrs. M. Scott Carpenter. 25c, Rocket 2nd stage, Wernher Von Braun. 30c, Cape Canaveral, Walter Schirra. 50c, Syncom 2 satellite, horiz. 12.45g, Launch of Atlas rocket. 18.15g, Theorized lunar landing, horiz. 36g, Portrait of Kennedy by Torres. 50g, Apollo lift-off, horiz.

***Perf. 14x13½, 13½x14***

**1967, Aug. 19**

**1041** A199 10c multicolored .25 .25
**1042** A199 15c multicolored .25 .25
**1043** A199 20c multicolored .25 .25
**1044** A199 25c multicolored .25 .25
**1045** A199 30c multicolored .25 .25
**1046** A199 50c multicolored .25 .25
**1047** A199 12.45g multicolored 1.50 .75
**1048** A199 18.15g multicolored 2.00 1.00
**1049** A199 36g multicolored 7.50 4.00
*Nos. 1041-1049 (9)* 12.50 7.25

**Souvenir Sheet**

**1050** A199 50g multicolored 22.50

Nos. 1047-1050 are airmail. An imperf. souvenir sheet of 3 containing Nos. 1047-1049 exists with violet border. Value $30.

Sculptures A200

10c, Head of athlete. 15c, Myron's Discobolus. 20c, Apollo of Belvedere. 25c, Artemis. 30c, Venus De Milo. 50c, Winged Victory of Samothrace. 12.45g, Laocoon Group. 18.15g, Moses. 50g, Pieta.

**1967, Oct. 16** ***Perf. 14x13½***

**1051** A200 10c multicolored .25 .25
**1052** A200 15c multicolored .25 .25
**1053** A200 20c multicolored .25 .25
**1054** A200 25c multicolored .25 .25
**1055** A200 30c multicolored .25 .25
**1056** A200 50c multicolored .25 .25
**1057** A200 12.45g multicolored .75 .40
**1058** A200 18.15g multicolored 1.10 .40
**1059** A200 50g multicolored 5.00 3.00
*Nos. 1051-1059 (9)* 8.35 5.30

Nos. 1057-1059 are airmail.
Exist imperf. in changed colors. Value, set $8.

Mexican Art — A201

Designs: 10c, Bowl, Veracruz. 15c, Knobbed vessel, Colima. 20c, Mixtec jaguar pitcher. 25c, Head, Veracruz. 30c, Statue of seated woman, Teotihuacan. 50c, Vessel depicting a woman, Aztec. 12.45g, Mixtec bowl, horiz. 18.15g, Three-legged vessel, Teotihuacan, horiz. 36g, Golden mask, Teotihuacan, horiz. 50g, The Culture of the Totonac by Diego Rivera, 1950, horiz.

**1967, Nov. 29** ***Perf. 14x13½***

**1060** A201 10c multicolored .25 .25
**1061** A201 15c multicolored .25 .25
**1062** A201 20c multicolored .25 .25
**1063** A201 25c multicolored .25 .25
**1064** A201 30c multicolored .25 .25
**1065** A201 50c multicolored .25 .25

***Perf. 13½x14***

**1066** A201 12.45g multicolored 1.25 .60
**1067** A201 18.15g multicolored 1.50 .60
**1068** A201 36g multicolored 7.50 6.00
*Nos. 1060-1068 (9)* 11.75 8.70

**Souvenir Sheet**

***Perf. 14***

**1069** A201 50g multicolored 19.00

1968 Summer Olympics, Mexico City (#1065-1069).
Nos. 1066-1069 are airmail. An imperf. souvenir sheet of 3 containing #1066-1068 exists with green pattern in border. Value $30.

Paintings of the Madonna and Child A202

**1968, Jan. 27** ***Perf. 14x13½,13½x14***

**1070** A202 10c Bellini .25 .25
**1071** A202 15c Raphael .25 .25
**1072** A202 20c Corregio .25 .25
**1073** A202 25c Luini .25 .25
**1074** A202 30c Bronzino .25 .25
**1075** A202 50c Van Dyck .25 .25
**1076** A202 12.45g Vignon, horiz. .60 .40
**1077** A202 18.15g de Ribera .60 .40
**1078** A202 36g Botticelli 6.25 3.00
*Nos. 1070-1078 (9)* 8.95 5.30

Nos. 1076-1078 are airmail and also exist as imperf. souvenir sheet of 3 with olive brown pattern in border. Value $37.50.

Paintings of Winter Scenes — A203

1968 Winter Olympics Emblem A204

10c, Pissarro. 15c, Utrillo, vert. 20c, Monet. 25c, Breitner, vert. 30c, Sisley. 50c, Brueghel, vert. 12.45g, Avercampe, vert. 18.15g, Brueghel, diff. 36g, P. Limbourg & brothers, vert.

**1968, Apr. 23** ***Perf. 13½x14, 14x13½***

**1079** A203 10c multi .25 .25
**1080** A203 15c multi .25 .25
**1081** A203 20c multi .25 .25
**1082** A203 25c multi .25 .25
**1083** A203 30c multi .25 .25
**1084** A203 50c multi .25 .25
**1085** A203 12.45g multi .75 .40
**1086** A203 18.15g multi 1.10 .40
**1087** A203 36g multi 3.75 2.00
*Nos. 1079-1087 (9)* 7.10 4.30

**Souvenir Sheet**

**1088** Sheet of 2 25.00
*a.* A204 50g multicolored

Nos. 1087-1088, 1088a are airmail. No. 1088 contains #1088a and #1087 with red pattern.

Paraguayan Stamps, Cent. (in 1970) — A205

***Perf. 13½x14, 14x13½***

**1968, June 3 Litho.**

**1089** A205 10c #1, 4 .25 .25
**1090** A205 15c #C21, 310, vert. .25 .25
**1091** A205 20c #203, C140 .25 .25
**1092** A205 25c #C72, C61, vert. .25 .25
**1093** A205 30c #638, 711 .25 .25
**1094** A205 50c #406, C38, vert. .25 .25
**1095** A205 12.45g #B2, B7 .90 .45
**1096** A205 18.15g #C10, C11, vert. .90 .45
**1097** A205 36g #828, C76, 616 9.00 4.50
*Nos. 1089-1097 (9)* 12.30 6.90

**Souvenir Sheet**

***Perf. 14***

**1098** Sheet of 2 25.00 25.00
*a.* A205 50g #929 & #379

Nos. 1095-1098a are airmail. No. 1098 contains No. 1098a and No. 1097 with light brown pattern in border.

Paintings A206

#1099-1106, paintings of children. #1107-1108, paintings of sailboats at sea.

**1968, July 9** ***Perf. 14x13½, 13½x14***

**1099** A206 10c Russell .25 .25
**1100** A206 15c Velazquez .25 .25
**1101** A206 20c Romney .25 .25
**1102** A206 25c Lawrence .25 .25
**1103** A206 30c Caravaggio .25 .25
**1104** A206 50c Gentileschi .25 .25

| No. | Type | Value | Description | Unused | Used |
|---|---|---|---|---|---|
| 1105 | A206 | 12.45g | Renoir | .65 | .45 |
| 1106 | A206 | 18.15g | Copley | .65 | .45 |
| 1107 | A206 | 36g | Sessions, horiz. | 6.75 | 3.00 |
| | | | *Nos. 1099-1107 (9)* | 9.55 | 5.40 |

**Souvenir Sheet**

***Perf. 14***

**1108** Sheet of 2 15.00 15.00
***a.*** A206 50g Currier & Ives, horiz.

1968 Summer Olympics, Mexico City (Nos. 1107-1108).

Nos. 1106-1108a are airmail. No. 1108 contains No. 1108a and No. 1107 with a red pattern in border.

A207

WHO Emblem — A207a

**1968, Aug. 12 Wmk. 347 *Perf. 11***

| No. | Type | Value | Description | Unused | Used |
|---|---|---|---|---|---|
| 1109 | A207 | 3g | bluish grn | .50 | .40 |
| 1110 | A207 | 4g | brt pink | .50 | .40 |
| 1111 | A207 | 5g | bister brn | .50 | .40 |
| 1112 | A207 | 10g | violet | .50 | .40 |
| 1113 | A207a | 36g | blk brn | 2.00 | .40 |
| 1114 | A207a | 50g | rose claret | 2.00 | .50 |
| 1115 | A207a | 100g | brt bl | 2.00 | 1.20 |
| | | | *Nos. 1109-1115 (7)* | 8.00 | 3.70 |

WHO, 20th anniv.; cent. of the natl. epic. Nos. 1113-1115 are airmail.

39th Intl. Eucharistic Congress A208

Paintings of life of Christ by various artists (except No. 1125a).

***Perf. 14x13½***

**1968, Sept. 25 Litho. Unwmk.**

| No. | Type | Value | Description | Unused | Used |
|---|---|---|---|---|---|
| 1116 | A208 | 10c | Caravaggio | .25 | .25 |
| 1117 | A208 | 15c | El Greco | .25 | .25 |
| 1118 | A208 | 20c | Del Sarto | .25 | .25 |
| 1119 | A208 | 25c | Van der Weyden | .25 | .25 |
| 1120 | A208 | 30c | De Patinier | .25 | .25 |
| 1121 | A208 | 50c | Plockhorst | .25 | .25 |
| 1122 | A208 | 12.45g | Bronzino | .75 | .40 |
| 1123 | A208 | 18.15g | Raphael | .75 | .40 |
| 1124 | A208 | 36g | Correggio | 8.00 | 3.00 |
| | | | *Nos. 1116-1124 (9)* | 11.00 | 5.30 |

**Souvenir Sheet**

***Perf. 14***

**1125** Sheet of 2 15.00
***a.*** A208 36g Pope Paul VI
***b.*** A208 50g Tiepolo

Pope Paul VI's visit to South America (No. 1125). Nos. 1122-1125b are airmail.

Events of 1968 — A209

Designs: 10c, Mexican 25p Olympic coin. 15c, Rentry of Echo 1 satellite. 20c, Visit of Pope Paul VI to Fatima, Portugal. 25c, Dr. Christian Barnard, 1st heart transplant. 30c, Martin Luther King, assasination. 50c, Pres. Alfredo Stroessner laying wreath at grave of Pres. Kennedy, vert. 12.45g, Pres. Stroessner, Pres. Lyndon B. Johnson. 18.15g, John F. Kennedy, Abraham Lincoln, Robert Kennedy. 50g, Summer Olympics, Mexico City, satellite transmissions, vert.

**1968, Dec. 21 *Perf. 13½x14, 14x13½***

| No. | Type | Value | Description | Unused | Used |
|---|---|---|---|---|---|
| 1126 | A209 | 10c | multicolored | .25 | .25 |
| 1127 | A209 | 15c | multicolored | .25 | .25 |
| 1128 | A209 | 20c | multicolored | .25 | .25 |
| 1129 | A209 | 25c | multicolored | .25 | .25 |
| 1130 | A209 | 30c | multicolored | .25 | .25 |
| 1131 | A209 | 50c | multicolored | .25 | .25 |
| 1132 | A209 | 12.45g | multicolored | 1.10 | .40 |
| 1133 | A209 | 18.15g | multicolored | 1.50 | .40 |
| 1134 | A209 | 50g | multicolored | 7.50 | 3.00 |
| | | | *Nos. 1126-1134 (9)* | 11.60 | 5.30 |

Nos. 1132-1134 are airmail. Set exists imperf. in sheets of 3 in changed colors. Value, set of 3 sheets $35.

1968 Summer Olympics, Mexico City A210

Olympic Stadium A210a

Gold Medal Winners: 10c, Felipe Munoz, Mexico, 200-meter breast stroke. 15c, Daniel Rebillard, France, 4000-meter cycling. 20c, David Hemery, England, 400-meter hurdles. 25c, Bob Seagren, US, pole vault. 30c, Francisco Rodriguez, Venezuela, light flyweight boxing. 50c, Bjorn Ferm, Sweden, modern pentathlon. 12.45g, Klaus Dibiasi, Italy, platform diving. 50g, Ingrid Becker, West Germany, fencing, women's pentathlon.

**1969, Feb. 13 *Perf. 14x13½***

| No. | Type | Value | Description | Unused | Used |
|---|---|---|---|---|---|
| 1135 | A210 | 10c | multicolored | .25 | .25 |
| 1136 | A210 | 15c | multicolored | .25 | .25 |
| 1137 | A210 | 20c | multicolored | .25 | .25 |
| 1138 | A210 | 25c | multicolored | .25 | .25 |
| 1139 | A210 | 30c | multicolored | .25 | .25 |
| 1140 | A210 | 50c | multicolored | .25 | .25 |
| 1141 | A210 | 12.45g | multicolored | .70 | .30 |
| 1142 | A210a | 18.15g | multicolored | 1.00 | .40 |
| 1143 | A210 | 50g | multicolored | 5.50 | 3.00 |
| | | | *Nos. 1135-1143 (9)* | 8.70 | 5.20 |

Nos. 1141-1143 are airmail. Set exists imperf. in sheets of 3 in changed colors. Value, set of 3 sheets $30.

Space Missions — A211

Designs: 10c, Apollo 7, John F. Kennedy. 15c, Apollo 8, Kennedy. 20c, Apollo 8, Kennedy, diff. 25c, Study of solar flares, ITU emblem. 30c, Canary Bird satellite. 50c, ESRO satellite. 12.45g, Wernher von Braun, rocket launch. 18.15g, Global satellite coverage, ITU emblem. 50g, Otto Lilienthal, Graf Zeppelin, Hermann Oberth, evolution of flight.

**1969, Mar. 10 *Perf. 13½x14***

| No. | Type | Value | Description | Unused | Used |
|---|---|---|---|---|---|
| 1144 | A211 | 10c | multicolored | .25 | .25 |
| 1145 | A211 | 15c | multicolored | .25 | .25 |
| 1146 | A211 | 20c | multicolored | .25 | .25 |
| 1147 | A211 | 25c | multicolored | .25 | .25 |
| 1148 | A211 | 30c | multicolored | .25 | .25 |
| 1149 | A211 | 50c | multicolored | .25 | .25 |
| 1150 | A211 | 12.45g | multicolored | .60 | .40 |
| 1151 | A211 | 18.15g | multicolored | .90 | .40 |
| 1152 | A211 | 50g | multicolored | 3.25 | 2.00 |
| | | | *Nos. 1144-1152 (9)* | 6.25 | 4.30 |

Nos. 1150-1152 are airmail. Set exists imperf. in sheets of 3 in changed colors. Value, set of 3 sheets $50.

"World United in Peace" — A212

**1969, June 28 Wmk. 347 *Perf. 11***

| No. | Type | Value | Description | Unused | Used |
|---|---|---|---|---|---|
| 1153 | A212 | 50c | rose | .50 | .50 |
| 1154 | A212 | 70c | ultra | .50 | .50 |
| 1155 | A212 | 1.50g | light brn | .50 | .50 |
| 1156 | A212 | 3g | lil rose | .50 | .50 |
| 1157 | A212 | 4g | emerald | .75 | .50 |
| 1158 | A212 | 5g | violet | .90 | .50 |
| 1159 | A212 | 10g | brt lilac | 2.50 | .50 |
| | | | *Nos. 1153-1159 (7)* | 6.15 | 3.50 |

Peace Week.

Birds A213

Designs: 10c, Pteroglossus viridis. 15c, Phytotoma rutila. 20c, Porphyrula martinica. 25c, Oxyrunchus cristatus. 30c, Spizaetus ornatus. 50c, Phoenicopterus ruber. 75c, Amazona ochrocephala. 12.45g, Ara ararauna, Ara macao. 18.15g, Colibri coruscans.

***Perf. 13½x14, 14x13½***

**1969, July 9 Unwmk.**

| No. | Type | Value | Description | Unused | Used |
|---|---|---|---|---|---|
| 1160 | A213 | 10c | multicolored | .90 | .25 |
| 1161 | A213 | 15c | multicolored | .90 | .25 |
| 1162 | A213 | 20c | multicolored | .90 | .25 |
| 1163 | A213 | 25c | multicolored | .90 | .25 |
| 1164 | A213 | 30c | multicolored | .90 | .25 |
| 1165 | A213 | 50c | multicolored | .90 | .25 |
| 1166 | A213 | 75c | multicolored | .90 | .25 |
| 1167 | A213 | 12.45g | multicolored | 2.75 | .50 |
| 1168 | A213 | 18.15g | multicolored | 6.50 | 1.00 |
| | | | *Nos. 1160-1168 (9)* | 15.55 | 3.25 |

Nos. 1167-1168 are airmail. Nos. 1161, 1164-1168 are vert.

Fauna — A214

**1969, July 9**

| No. | Type | Value | Description | Unused | Used |
|---|---|---|---|---|---|
| 1169 | A214 | 10c | Porcupine | .25 | .25 |
| 1170 | A214 | 15c | Lemur, vert. | .25 | .25 |
| 1171 | A214 | 20c | 3-toed sloth, vert. | .25 | .25 |
| 1172 | A214 | 25c | Puma | .25 | .25 |
| 1173 | A214 | 30c | Alligator | .25 | .25 |
| 1174 | A214 | 50c | Jaguar | .25 | .25 |
| 1175 | A214 | 75c | Anteater | .25 | .25 |
| 1176 | A214 | 12.45g | Tapir | .50 | .25 |
| 1177 | A214 | 18.15g | Capybara | 1.50 | 1.00 |
| | | | *Nos. 1169-1177 (9)* | 3.75 | 3.00 |

Nos. 1176-1177 are airmail.

Olympic Soccer Champions, 1900-1968 A215

Designs: 10c, Great Britain, Paris, 1900. 15c, Canada, St. Louis, 1904. 20c, Great Britain, London, 1908 and Stockholm, 1912. 25c, Belgium, Antwerp, 1920. 30c, Uruguay, Paris, 1924 and Amsterdam, 1928. 50c, Italy, Berlin, 1936. 75c, Sweden, London, 1948; USSR, Melbourne, 1956. 12.45g, Yugoslavia, Rome, 1960. 18.15g, Hungary, Helsinki, 1952, Tokyo, 1964 and Mexico, 1968.

No. 1187, Soccer ball, Mexico 1968 emblem. No. 1188, Soccer player and ball.

**1969, Nov. 26 *Perf. 14***

| No. | Type | Value | Description | Unused | Used |
|---|---|---|---|---|---|
| 1178 | A215 | 10c | multicolored | .25 | .25 |
| 1179 | A215 | 15c | multicolored | .25 | .25 |
| 1180 | A215 | 20c | multicolored | .25 | .25 |
| 1181 | A215 | 25c | multicolored | .25 | .25 |
| 1182 | A215 | 30c | multicolored | .25 | .25 |
| 1183 | A215 | 50c | multicolored | .25 | .25 |
| 1184 | A215 | 75c | multicolored | .25 | .25 |
| 1185 | A215 | 12.45g | multicolored | .70 | .40 |
| 1186 | A215 | 18.15g | multicolored | 6.75 | 2.50 |
| | | | *Nos. 1178-1186 (9)* | 9.20 | 4.65 |

**Souvenir Sheet**

| No. | Type | Value | Description | Unused | Used |
|---|---|---|---|---|---|
| 1187 | A215 | 23.40g | multicolored | 7.50 | 7.50 |
| 1188 | A215 | 23.40g | multi | 15.00 | 15.00 |

Nos. 1185-1188 are airmail. No. 1187 contains one 49x60mm stamp. No. 1188 contains one 50x61mm stamp.

A216

World Cup or South American Soccer Champions: 10c, Paraguay, 1953. 15c, Uruguay, 1930. 20c, Italy, 1934. 25c, Italy, 1938. 30c, Uruguay, 1950. 50c, Germany, 1954, horiz. 75c, Brazil, 1958. 12.45g, Brazil, 1962. 18.15g, England, 1966. No. 1198, Trophy. No. 1199, Soccer player, satellite.

**1969, Nov. 26 *Perf. 14***

| No. | Type | Value | Description | Unused | Used |
|---|---|---|---|---|---|
| 1189 | A216 | 10c | multicolored | .25 | .25 |
| 1190 | A216 | 15c | multicolored | .25 | .25 |
| 1191 | A216 | 20c | multicolored | .25 | .25 |
| 1192 | A216 | 25c | multicolored | .25 | .25 |
| 1193 | A216 | 30c | multicolored | .25 | .25 |
| 1194 | A216 | 50c | multicolored | .30 | .25 |
| 1195 | A216 | 75c | multicolored | .45 | .25 |
| 1196 | A216 | 12.45g | multicolored | 2.00 | .25 |
| 1197 | A216 | 18.15g | multicolored | 4.50 | 1.50 |
| | | | *Nos. 1189-1197 (9)* | 8.50 | 3.50 |

**Souvenir Sheets**

***Perf. 13½, Imperf(#1199)***

| No. | Type | Value | Description | Unused | Used |
|---|---|---|---|---|---|
| 1198 | A216 | 23.40g | multicolored | 27.50 | 27.50 |
| 1199 | A216 | 23.40g | multicolored | 15.00 | 15.00 |

Nos. 1196-1199 are airmail. No. 1198 contains one 50x60mm stamp. No. 1199 contains one 45x57mm stamp.

Paintings by Francisco de Goya (1746-1828) — A217

Designs: 10c, Miguel de Lardibazal. 15c, Francisca Sabasa y Gracia. 20c, Don Manuel Osorio. 25c, Young Women with a Letter. 30c, The Water Carrier. 50c, Truth, Time and History. 75c, The Forge. 12.45g, The Spell. 18.15g, Duke of Wellington on Horseback. 23.40g, "La Maja Desnuda."

**1969, Nov. 29 Litho. *Perf. 14x13½***

**1200** A217 10c multicolored .25 .25
**1201** A217 15c multicolored .25 .25
**1202** A217 20c multicolored .25 .25
**1203** A217 25c multicolored .25 .25
**1204** A217 30c multicolored .25 .25
**1205** A217 50c multicolored .25 .25
**1206** A217 75c multicolored .30 .25
**1207** A217 12.45g multicolored 2.00 .60
**1208** A217 18.15g multicolored 4.50 1.25
*Nos. 1200-1208 (9)* 8.30 3.60

**Souvenir Sheet**

***Perf. 14***

**1209** A217 23.40g multicolored 20.00 20.00

Nos. 1207-1209 are airmail.

Christmas A218

Various paintings of The Nativity or Madonna and Child: 10c, Master Bertram. 15c, Procaccini. 20c, Di Crediti. 25c, De Flemalle. 30c, Correggio. 50c, Borgianni. 75c, Botticelli. 12.45g, El Greco. 18.15g, De Morales.
23.40g, Isenheimer Altar.

**1969, Nov. 29 *Perf. 14x13½***

**1210** A218 10c multi .25 .25
**1211** A218 15c multi .25 .25
**1212** A218 20c multi .25 .25
**1213** A218 25c multi .25 .25
**1214** A218 30c multi .25 .25
**1215** A218 50c multi .25 .25
**1216** A218 75c multi .25 .25
**1217** A218 12.45g multi 1.50 .60
**1218** A218 18.15g multi 3.25 1.50
*Nos. 1210-1218 (9)* 6.50 3.85

**Souvenir Sheet**

***Perf. 13½***

**1219** A218 23.40g multi 12.00 12.00

Nos. 1217-1219 are airmail.

Souvenir Sheet

European Space Program — A219

No. 1220, ESRO 1B. No. 1221, Ernst Stuhlinger.

**1969, Nov. 29 Litho. *Perf. 14***

**1220** A219 23.40g multi 15.00 15.00

***Imperf***

**1221** A219 23.40g multi 20.00 20.00

Francisco Solano — A220

**1970, Mar. 1 Wmk. 347 *Perf. 11***

**1222** A220 1g bis brn 1.00 1.00
**1223** A220 2g violet 1.00 1.00
**1224** A220 3g brt pink 1.00 .50
**1225** A220 4g rose claret 1.00 1.00
**1226** A220 5g blue 1.00 1.00
**1227** A220 10g bright grn 1.00 .75
**1228** A220 15g lt Prus bl 1.00 *2.00*
**1229** A220 20g org brn 1.00 *2.00*
**1230** A220 30g gray grn 1.00 1.00
**1231** A220 40g gray brn 1.00 3.00
*Nos. 1222-1231 (10)* 10.00 13.25

Marshal Francisco Solano Lopez (1827-1870), President of Paraguay. Nos. 1228-1231 are airmail.

1st Moon Landing, Apollo 11 — A221

Designs: 10c, Wernher von Braun, lift-off. 15c, Eagle and Columbia in lunar orbit. 20c, Deployment of lunar module. 25c, Landing on Moon. 30c, First steps on lunar surface. 50c, Gathering lunar soil. 75c, Lift-off from Moon. 12.45g, Rendevouz of Eagle and Columbia. 18.15g, Pres. Kennedy, von Braun, splashdown. No. 1241, Gold medal of Armstrong, Aldrin and Collins. No. 1242, Moon landing medal, Kennedy, von Braun. No. 1243, Apollo 12 astronauts Charles Conrad and Alan Bean on moon, and Dr. Kurt Debus.

**1970, Mar. 11 Unwmk. *Perf. 14***

**1232** A221 10c multicolored .25 .25
**1233** A221 15c multicolored .25 .25
**1234** A221 20c multicolored .25 .25
**1235** A221 25c multicolored .25 .25
**1236** A221 30c multicolored .25 .25
**1237** A221 50c multicolored .25 .25
**1238** A221 75c multicolored .25 .25
**1239** A221 12.45g multicolored 1.50 .60
**1240** A221 18.15g multicolored 3.00 1.25
*Nos. 1232-1240 (9)* 6.25 3.60

**Souvenir Sheets**

**1241** A221 23.40g multicolored 14.00 11.00

***Imperf***

**1242** A221 23.40g multicolored 17.00 15.00
**1243** A221 23.40g multicolored 14.00 11.00

Nos. 1239-1243 are airmail. Nos. 1241-1242 contain one 50x60mm stamp, No. 1243 one 60x50mm stamp.

Easter — A222

Designs: 10c, 15c, 20c, 25c, 30c, 50c, 75c, Stations of the Cross. 12.45g, Christ appears to soldiers, vert. 18.15g, Christ appears to disciples, vert. 23.40g, The sad Madonna, vert.

**1970, Mar. 11**

**1244** A222 10c multicolored .25 .25
**1245** A222 15c multicolored .25 .25
**1246** A222 20c multicolored .25 .25
**1247** A222 25c multicolored .25 .25
**1248** A222 30c multicolored .25 .25
**1249** A222 50c multicolored .25 .25
**1250** A222 75c multicolored .30 .25
**1251** A222 12.45g multicolored 1.25 .50
**1252** A222 18.15g multicolored 3.25 1.50
*Nos. 1244-1252 (9)* 6.30 3.75

**Souvenir Sheet**

***Perf. 13½***

**1253** A222 23.40g multicolored 10.00

Nos. 1251-1253 are airmail. No. 1253 contains one 50x60mm stamp.

Paraguay No. 2 — A223

Designs (First Issue of Paraguay): 2g, 10g, #1. 3g, #3. 5g, #2. 15g, #3. 30g, #2. 36g, #1.

**1970, Aug. 15 Litho. Wmk. 347**

**1254** A223 1g car rose 1.00 1.00
**1255** A223 2g ultra 1.00 1.00
**1256** A223 3g org brn 1.00 1.00
**1257** A223 5g violet 1.00 1.00
**1258** A223 10g lilac 1.00 1.00
**1259** A223 15g vio brn 2.00 2.00
**1260** A223 30g dp grn 2.00 2.00
**1261** A223 36g brt pink 2.00 2.00
*Nos. 1254-1261 (8)* 11.00 11.00

Centenary of stamps of Paraguay. #1259-1261 are airmail.

1972 Summer Olympics, Munich A224

No. 1262: a, 10c, Discus. b, 15c, Cycling. c, 20c, Men's hurdles. d, 25c, Fencing. e, 30c, Swimming, horiz.
50c, Shotput. 75c, Sailing. 12.45, Women's hurdles, horiz. 18.15g, Equestrian, horiz. No. 1267, Flags, Olympic coins. No. 1268, Frauenkirche Church, Munich. No. 1269, Olympic Village, Munich, horiz.

**1970, Sept. 28 Unwmk. *Perf. 14***

**1262** A224 Strip of 5, #a.-e. 1.25 1.25
**1263** A224 50c multicolored .25 .25
**1264** A224 75c multicolored .30 .25
**1265** A224 12.45g multicolored 1.40 .45
**1266** A224 18.15g multicolored 3.50 1.25
*Nos. 1262-1266 (5)* 6.70 3.45

**Souvenir Sheets**

***Perf. 13½***

**1267** A224 23.40g multicolored 12.50

***Imperf***

**1268** A224 23.40g multicolored 60.00
**1269** A224 23.40g multicolored 20.00 20.00

Nos. 1265-1269 are airmail. Nos. 1267-1269 each contain one 50x60mm stamp.

Paintings, Pinakothek, Munich, 1972 A225

Nudes by: No. 1270a, 10c, Cranach. b, 15c, Baldung. c, 20c, Tintoretto. d, 25c, Rubens. e, 30c, Boucher, horiz. 50c, Baldung, diff. 75c, Cranach, diff.
12.45g, Self-portrait, Durer. 18.15g, Alterpiece, Altdorfer. 23.40g, Madonna and Child.

**1970, Sept. 28 *Perf. 14***

**1270** A225 Strip of 5, #a.-e. 1.75 1.25
**1271** A225 50c multicolored .40 .25
**1272** A225 75c multicolored .40 .25
**1273** A225 12.45g multicolored 1.75 .50
**1274** A225 18.15g multicolored 2.25 1.50
*Nos. 1270-1274 (5)* 6.55 3.75

**Souvenir Sheet**

***Perf. 13½***

**1275** A225 23.40g multicolored 20.00 20.00

Nos. 1273-1275 are airmail. No. 1275 contains one 50x60mm stamp.

Apollo Space Program — A226

No. 1276: a, 10c, Ignition, Saturn 5. b, 15c, Apollo 1 mission emblem, vert. c, 20c, Apollo 7, Oct. 1968. d, 25c, Apollo 8, Dec. 1968. e, 30c, Apollo 9, Mar. 1969.
50c, Apollo 10, May 1969. 75c, Apollo 11, July 1969. 12.45g, Apollo 12, Nov. 1969. 18.15g, Apollo 13, Apr. 1970. No. 1281, Lunar landing sites. No. 1282, Wernher von Braun, rockets. No. 1283, James A. Lovell, John L. Swigert, Fred W. Haise.

**1970, Oct. 19 *Perf. 14***

**1276** A226 Strip of 5, #a.-e. 1.25 1.25
**1277** A226 50c multicolored .25 .25
**1278** A226 75c multicolored .25 .25
**1279** A226 12.45g multicolored 1.00 .50
**1280** A226 18.15g multicolored 3.50 1.50
*Nos. 1276-1280 (5)* 6.25 3.75

**Souvenir Sheets**

***Perf. 13½***

**1281** A226 23.40g multicolored 10.00

***Imperf***

**1282** A226 23.40g multicolored 50.00
**1283** A226 23.40g multicolored 20.00

Nos. 1279-1283 are airmail. Nos. 1281-1283 each contain one 60x50mm stamp.

**1970, Oct. 19 *Perf. 14***

Future Space Projects: No. 1284a, 10c, Space station, 2000. b, 15c, Lunar station, vert. c, 20c, Space transport. d, 25c, Lunar rover. e, 30c, Skylab.
50c, Space station, 1971. 75c, Lunar vehicle. 12.45g, Lunar vehicle, diff., vert. 18.15g, Vehicle rising above lunar surface. 23.40g, Moon stations, transport.

**1284** A226 Strip of 5, #a.-e. 1.25 1.25
**1285** A226 50c multicolored .25 .25
**1286** A226 75c multicolored .25 .25
**1287** A226 12.45g multicolored 1.25 .50
**1288** A226 18.15g multicolored 2.50 1.00
*Nos. 1284-1288 (5)* 5.50 3.25

**Souvenir Sheet**

***Perf. 13½***

**1289** A226 23.40g multicolored 12.50 12.50

Nos. 1287-1289 are airmail. No. 1289 contains one 50x60mm stamp. For overprints see Nos. 2288-2290, C653.

EXPO '70, Osaka, Japan A228

Paintings from National Museum, Tokyo: No. 1288a, 10c, Buddha. b, 15c, Fire, people. c, 20c, Demon, Ogata Korin. d, 25c, Japanese play, Hishikawa Moronobu. e, 30c, Birds.
50c, Woman, Utamaro. 75c, Samurai, Wantabe Kazan. 12.45c, Women Beneath Tree, Kano Hideroi. 18.15g, Courtesans, Torrii Kiyonaga. 50g, View of Mt. Fuji, Hokusai, horiz. No. 1296, Courtesan, Kaigetsudo Ando. No. 1297, Emblem of Expo '70. No. 1298, Emblem of 1972 Winter Olympics, Sapporo.

**1970, Nov. 26** **Litho.** ***Perf. 14***

**1290** A228 Strip of 5, #a.-e. 1.25 1.25
**1291** A228 50c multicolored .25 .25
**1292** A228 75c multicolored .25 .25
**1293** A228 12.45g multicolored .50 .50
**1294** A228 18.15g multicolored .60 .60
**1295** A228 50g multicolored 3.50 1.50
*Nos. 1290-1295 (6)* 6.35 4.35

**Souvenir Sheets**

***Perf. 13½***

**1296** A228 20g multicolored 10.00
**1297** A228 20g multicolored 17.50
**1298** A228 20g multicolored 30.00

Nos. 1293-1298 are airmail. Nos. 1296-1298 each contain one 50x60mm stamp.

Flower Paintings A229

Artists: No. 1299a, 10c, Von Jawlensky. b, 15c, Purrmann. c, 20c, De Vlaminck. d, 25c, Monet. e, 30c, Renoir.
50c, Van Gogh. 75, Cezanne. 12.45g, Van Huysum. 18.15g, Ruysch. 50g, Walscappelle. 20g, Bosschaert.

**1970, Nov. 26** ***Perf. 14***

**1299** A229 Strip of 5, #a.-e. 1.25 1.25
**1300** A229 50c multicolored .25 .25
**1301** A229 75c multicolored .25 .25
**1302** A229 12.45g multicolored .90 .40
**1303** A229 18.15g multicolored 1.20 .40
**1304** A229 50g multicolored 2.50 1.00
*Nos. 1299-1304 (6)* 6.35 3.55

**Souvenir Sheet**

***Perf. 13½***

**1305** A229 20g multicolored 7.50 7.50

Nos. 1302-1305 are airmail. No. 1305 contains one 50x60mm stamp.

Paintings from The Prado, Madrid — A230

Nudes by: No. 1306a, 10c, Titian. b, 15c, Velazquez. c, 20c, Van Dyck. d, 25c, Tintoretto. e, 30c, Rubens.
50c, Venus and Sleeping Adonis, Veronese. 75c, Adam and Eve, Titian. 12.45g, The Holy Family, Goya. 18.15g, Shepherd Boy, Murillo. 50g, The Holy Family, El Greco.

**1970, Dec. 16** ***Perf. 14***

**1306** A230 Strip of 5, #a.-e. 1.25 1.25
**1307** A230 50c multicolored .25 .25
**1308** A230 75c multicolored .25 .25
**1309** A230 12.45g multicolored .50 .25
**1310** A230 18.15g multicolored .50 .25
**1311** A230 50g multicolored 2.50 1.50
*Nos. 1306-1311 (6)* 5.25 3.75

Nos. 1309-1311 are airmail. Nos. 1307-1311 are vert.

**1970, Dec. 16**

Paintings by Albrecht Durer (1471-1528): No. 1312a, 10c, Adam and Eve. b, 15c, St. Jerome in the Wilderness. c, 20c, St. Eustachius and George. d, 25c, Piper and drummer. e, 30c, Lucretia's Suicide.
50c, Oswald Krel. 75c, Stag Beetle. 12.45g, Paul and Mark. 18.15g, Lot's Flight. 50g, Nativity.

**1312** A230 Strip of 5, #a.-e. 1.25 1.25
**1313** A230 50c multicolored .25 .25
**1314** A230 75c multicolored .25 .25
**1315** A230 12.45g multicolored .60 .40
**1316** A230 18.15g multicolored 1.20 .40
**1317** A230 50g multicolored 3.50 1.25
*Nos. 1312-1317 (6)* 7.05 3.80

Nos. 1315-1317 are airmail. See No. 1273.

Christmas A232

Paintings: No. 1318a, 10c, The Annunciation, Van der Weyden. b, 15c, The Madonna, Zeitblom. c, 20c, The Nativity, Von Soest. d, 25c, Adoration of the Magi, Mayno. e, 30c, Adoration of the Magi, Da Fabriano.
50c, Flight From Egypt, Masters of Martyrdom. 75c, Presentation of Christ, Memling. 12.45g, The Holy Family, Poussin, horiz. 18.15g, The Holy Family, Rubens. 20g, Adoration of the Magi, Giorgione, horiz. 50g, Madonna and Child, Batoni.

**1971, Mar. 23**

**1318** A232 Strip of 5, #a.-e. 1.25 1.25
**1319** A232 50c multicolored .25 .25
**1320** A232 75c multicolored .25 .25
**1321** A232 12.45g multicolored .60 .40
**1322** A232 18.15g multicolored 1.25 .40
**1323** A232 50g multicolored 3.50 1.25
*Nos. 1318-1323 (6)* 7.10 3.80

**Souvenir Sheet**

***Perf. 13½***

**1324** A232 20g multicolored 10.00 10.00

Nos. 1321-1324 are airmail. No. 1324 contains one 60x50mm stamp.

1972 Summer Olympics, Munich A233

Olympic decathlon gold medalists: No. 1325a, 10c, Hugo Wieslander, Stockholm 1912. b, 15c, Helge Lovland, Antwerp 1920. c, 20c, Harold M. Osborn, Paris 1924. d, 25c, Paavo Yrjola, Amsterdam 1928. e, 30c, James Bausch, Los Angeles 1932.
50c, Glenn Morris, Berlin 1936. 75c, Bob Mathias, London 1948, Helsinki 1952. 12.45g, Milton Campbell, Melbourne 1956. 18.15g, Rafer Johnson, Rome 1960. 50g, Willi Holdorf, Tokyo 1964. No. 1331, Bill Toomey, Mexico City 1968.
No. 1332, Pole vaulter, Munich, 1972.

**1971, Mar. 23** ***Perf. 14***

**1325** A233 Strip of 5, #a.-e. 1.25 1.25
**1326** A233 50c multicolored .25 .25
**1327** A233 75c multicolored .25 .25
**1328** A233 12.45g multicolored .60 .40
**1329** A233 18.15g multicolored 1.25 .40
**1330** A233 50g multicolored 3.50 1.25
*Nos. 1325-1330 (6)* 7.10 3.80

**Souvenir Sheets**

***Perf. 13½***

**1331** A233 20g multicolored 12.00 8.00
**1332** A233 20g multicolored 12.00 8.00

Nos. 1328-1332 are airmail. Nos. 1331-1332 each contain one 50x60mm stamp.

Art — A234

Paintings by: No. 1333a, 10c, Van Dyck. b, 15c, Titian. c, 20c, Van Dyck, diff. d, 25c, Walter. e, 30c, Orsi.
50c, 17th cent. Japanese artist, horiz. 75c, David. 12.45g, Huguet. 18.15g, Perugino. 20g, Van Eyck. 50g, Witz.

**1971, Mar. 26** ***Perf. 14***

**1333** A234 Strip of 5, #a.-e. 1.25 1.25
**1334** A234 50c multicolored .25 .25
**1335** A234 75c multicolored .25 .25
**1336** A234 12.45g multicolored .75 .40
**1337** A234 18.15g multicolored 1.25 .40
**1338** A234 50g multicolored 3.00 1.25
*Nos. 1333-1338 (6)* 6.75 3.80

**Souvenir Sheet**

***Perf. 13½***

**1339** A234 20g multicolored 15.00 15.00

Nos. 1336-1339 are airmail. No. 1339 contains one 50x60mm stamp.

**Paintings from the Louvre, Paris**

Portraits of women by: No. 1340a, 10c, De la Tour. b, 15c, Boucher. c, 20c, Delacroix. d, 25c, 16th cent. French artist. e, 30c, Ingres.
50c, Ingres, horiz. 75c, Watteau, horiz. 12.45g, 2nd cent. artist. 18.15g, Renoir. 20g, Mona Lisa, Da Vinci. 50g, Liberty Guiding the People, Delacroix.

**1971, Mar. 26** ***Perf. 14***

**1340** A234 Strip of 5, #a.-e. 1.25 1.25
**1341** A234 50c multicolored .25 .25
**1342** A234 75c multicolored .25 .25
**1343** A234 12.45g multicolored .60 .40
**1344** A234 18.15g multicolored .75 .40
**1345** A234 50g multicolored 2.00 1.00
*Nos. 1340-1345 (6)* 5.10 3.55

**Souvenir Sheet**

***Perf. 13½***

**1346** A234 20g multicolored 9.00 9.00

Nos. 1343-1346 are airmail. No. 1346 contains one 50x60mm stamp.

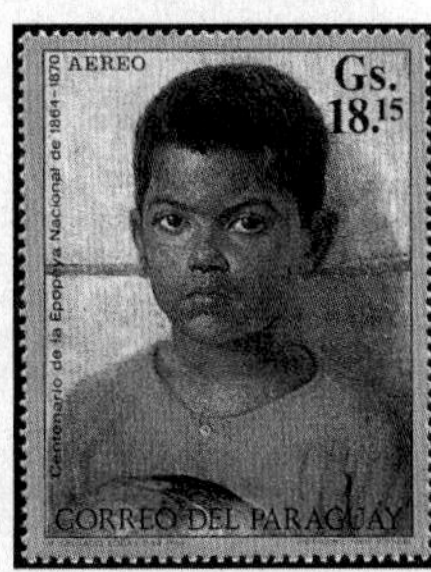


Paintings A236

Artist: No. 1347a, 10c, Botticelli. b, 15c, Titian. c, 20c, Raphael. d, 25c, Pellegrini. e, 30c, Caracci.
50c, Titian, horiz. 75c, Ricci, horiz. 12.45g, Courtines. 18.15g, Rodas. 50g, Murillo.

**1971, Mar. 29** ***Perf. 14***

**1347** A236 Strip of 5, #a.-e. 1.25 1.25
**1348** A236 50c multicolored .25 .25
**1349** A236 75c multicolored .25 .25
**1350** A236 12.45g multicolored .75 .40
**1351** A236 18.15g multicolored 1.25 .40
**1352** A236 50g multicolored 3.00 1.00
*Nos. 1347-1352 (6)* 6.75 3.55

Nos. 1350-1352 are airmail.

Hunting Scenes — A237

Different Paintings by: No. 1353a, 10c, Gozzoli, vert. b, 15c, Velazquez, vert. c, 20c, Brun. d, 25c, Fontainebleau School, 1550, vert. e, 30c, Uccello, vert.
50c, P. De Vos. 75c, Vernet. 12.45g, 18.15g, 50g, Alken & Sutherland. No. 1359, Paul & Derveaux. No. 1360, Degas.

**1971, Mar. 29**

**1353** A237 Strip of 5, #a.-e. 1.25 1.25
**1354** A237 50c multicolored .25 .25
**1355** A237 75c multicolored .25 .25
**1356** A237 12.45g multicolored .60 .40
**1357** A237 18.15g multicolored .75 .40
**1358** A237 50g multicolored 3.00 1.00
*Nos. 1353-1358 (6)* 6.10 3.55

**Souvenir Sheets**

***Perf. 13½***

**1359** A237 20g multicolored 10.00 10.00
**1360** A237 20g multicolored 10.00 10.00

Nos. 1356-1360 are airmail. Nos. 1359-1360 each contain one 60x50mm stamp.

Philatokyo '71 — A238

Designs: Nos. 1361a-1361e, 10c, 15c, 20c, 25c, 30c, Different flowers, Gukei. 50c, Birds, Lu Chi. 75c, Flowers, Sakai Hoitsu. 12.45g, Man and Woman, Utamaro. 18.15g, Tea Ceremony, from Tea museum. 50g, Bathers, Utamaro. No. 1367, Woman, Kamakura Period. No. 1368, Japan #1, #821, #904, #1023.

**1971, Apr. 7** ***Perf. 14***

**1361** A238 Strip of 5, #a.-e. 1.25 1.25
**1362** A238 50c multicolored .25 .25
**1363** A238 75c multicolored .25 .25
**1364** A238 12.45g multicolored .65 .40
**1365** A238 18.15g multicolored .65 .40
**1366** A238 50g multicolored 3.50 1.00
*Nos. 1361-1366 (6)* 6.55 3.55

**Souvenir Sheets**

***Perf. 13½***

**1367** A238 20g multicolored 12.50 12.50
**1368** A238 20g multicolored 12.50 12.50

Nos. 1364-1368 are airmail. Nos. 1367-1368 each contain one 50x60mm stamp.
See Nos. 1375-1376.

1972 Winter Olympics, Sapporo A239

Paintings of women by: No. 1369a, 10c, Harunobu. b, 15c, Hosoda. c, 20c, Harunobu, diff. d, 25c, Uemura Shoen. e, 30c, Ketao.
50c, Three Women, Torii. 75c, Old Man, Kakizahi. 12.45g, 2-man bobsled. 18.15g, Ice sculptures, horiz. 50g, Mt. Fuji, Hokusai, horiz. No. 1375, Skier, horiz. No. 1376, Sapporo Olympic emblems.

**1971, Apr.** ***Perf. 14***

**1369** A239 Strip of 5, #a.-e. 1.25 1.25
**1370** A239 50c multicolored .25 .25
**1371** A239 75c multicolored .25 .25
**1372** A239 12.45g multicolored .60 .40
**1373** A239 18.15g multicolored 1.25 .40
**1374** A239 50g multicolored 3.50 1.00
*Nos. 1369-1374 (6)* 7.10 3.55

**Souvenir Sheets**

***Perf. 14½***

**1375** A239 20g multicolored 14.00 14.00

***Perf. 13½***

**1376** A239 20g multicolored 20.00 20.00

Nos. 1372-1376 are airmail. No. 1375 contains one 35x25mm stamp with PhilaTokyo 71 emblem. No. 1376 contains one 50x60mm stamp.
For Japanese painting stamps with white border and Winter Olympics emblem see #1409-1410.

UNESCO and Paraguay Emblems, Globe, Teacher and Pupil A240

**Wmk. 347**

**1971, May 18 Litho. *Perf. 11***

| | | | | |
|---|---|---|---|---|
| **1377** | A240 | 3g ultra | 1.00 | 1.00 |
| **1378** | A240 | 5g lilac | 1.00 | 1.00 |
| **1379** | A240 | 10g emerald | 1.00 | 1.00 |
| **1380** | A240 | 20g claret | 2.00 | 2.00 |
| **1381** | A240 | 25g brt pink | 2.00 | 2.00 |
| **1382** | A240 | 30g brown | 2.00 | 2.00 |
| **1383** | A240 | 50g gray olive | 2.00 | 2.00 |
| | | *Nos. 1377-1383 (7)* | 11.00 | 11.00 |

International Education Year.
Nos. 1380-1383 are airmail.

Paintings, Berlin-Dahlem Museum — A241

Artists: 10c, Caravaggio. No. 1385: a, 15c, b, 20c, Di Cosimo. 25c, Cranach. 30c, Veneziano. 50g, Holbein. 75c, Baldung. 12.45g, Cranach, diff. 18.15g, Durer. 50g, Schongauer.

**1971, Dec. 24 Unwmk. *Perf. 14***

| | | | | |
|---|---|---|---|---|
| **1384** | A241 | 10c multicolored | .25 | .25 |
| **1385** | A241 | Pair, #a.-b. | .25 | .25 |
| **1386** | A241 | 25c multicolored | .25 | .25 |
| **1387** | A241 | 30c multicolored | .25 | .25 |
| **1388** | A241 | 50c multicolored | .25 | .25 |
| **1389** | A241 | 75c multicolored | .25 | .25 |
| **1390** | A241 | 12.45g multicolored | .90 | .40 |
| **1391** | A241 | 18.15g multicolored | .90 | .40 |
| **1392** | A241 | 50g multicolored | 3.50 | 1.00 |
| | | *Nos. 1384-1392 (9)* | 6.80 | 3.30 |

Nos. 1390-1392 are airmail. No. 1385 has continuous design.

Napoleon I, 150th Death Anniv. A242

Paintings: No. 1393a, 10c, Desiree Clary, Gerin. b, 15c, Josephine de Beauharnais, Gros. c, 20c, Maria Luisa, Gerard. d, 25c, Juliette Recamier, Gerard. e, 30c, Maria Walewska, Gerard.

50c, Victoria Kraus, unknown artist, horiz. 75c, Napoleon on Horseback, Chabord. 12.45g, Trafalgar, A. Mayer, horiz. 18.15g, Napoleon Leading Army, Gautherot, horiz. 50g, Napoleon's tomb.

**1971, Dec. 24**

| | | | | |
|---|---|---|---|---|
| **1393** | A242 | Strip of 5, #a.-e. | 1.25 | 1.25 |
| **1394** | A242 | 50c multicolored | .25 | .25 |
| **1395** | A242 | 75c multicolored | .25 | .25 |
| **1396** | A242 | 12.45g multicolored | .75 | .40 |
| **1397** | A242 | 18.15g multicolored | .90 | .40 |
| **1398** | A242 | 50g multicolored | 3.50 | 1.00 |
| | | *Nos. 1393-1398 (6)* | 6.90 | 3.55 |

Nos. 1396-1398 are airmail.

Locomotives — A243

Designs: No. 1399a, 10c, Trevithick, Great Britain, 1804. b, 15c, Blenkinsops, 1812. c, 20c, G. Stephenson #1, 1825. d, 25c, Marc Seguin, France, 1829. e, 30c, "Adler," Germany, 1835.

50c, Sampierdarena #1, Italy, 1854. 75c, Paraguay #1, 1861. 12.45g, "Munich," Germany, 1841. 18.15g, US, 1875. 20g, Japanese locomotives, 1872-1972. 50g, Mikado D-50, Japan, 1923.

**1972, Jan. 6**

| | | | | |
|---|---|---|---|---|
| **1399** | A243 | Strip of 5, #a.-e. | 1.25 | 1.25 |
| **1400** | A243 | 50c multicolored | .25 | .25 |
| **1401** | A243 | 75c multicolored | .25 | .25 |
| **1402** | A243 | 12.45g multicolored | .90 | .40 |
| **1403** | A243 | 18.15g multicolored | .90 | .40 |
| **1404** | A243 | 50g multicolored | 3.50 | .90 |
| | | *Nos. 1399-1404 (6)* | 7.05 | 3.45 |

**Souvenir Sheet**

***Perf. 13½***

| | | | | |
|---|---|---|---|---|
| **1405** | A243 | 20g multicolored | 30.00 | 30.00 |

Nos. 1402-1405 are airmail. No. 1405 contains one 60x50mm stamp.
See Nos. 1476-1480.

1972 Winter Olympics, Sapporo — A244

Designs: Nos. 1406a, 10c, Hockey player. b, 15c, Jean-Claude Killy. c, 20c, Gaby Seyfert. d, 25c, 4-Man bobsled. e, 30c, Luge.

50c, Ski jumping, horiz. 75c, Slalom skiing, horiz. 12.45g, Painting, Kuniyoshi. 18.15g, Winter Scene, Hiroshige, horiz. 50g, Ski lift, man in traditional dress.

**1972, Jan. 6 *Perf. 14***

| | | | | |
|---|---|---|---|---|
| **1406** | A244 | Strip of 5, #a.-e. | 1.25 | 1.25 |
| **1407** | A244 | 50c multicolored | .25 | .25 |
| **1408** | A244 | 75c multicolored | .25 | .25 |
| **1409** | A244 | 12.45g multicolored | 1.25 | .40 |
| **1410** | A244 | 18.15g multicolored | 1.25 | .40 |
| **1411** | A244 | 50g multicolored | 4.75 | 1.25 |
| | | *Nos. 1406-1411 (6)* | 9.00 | 3.80 |

**Souvenir Sheet**

***Perf. 13½***

| | | | | |
|---|---|---|---|---|
| **1412** | A244 | 20g Skier | 14.00 | 14.00 |
| **1413** | A244 | 20g Flags | 20.00 | 20.00 |

Nos. 1409-1413 are airmail. Nos. 1412-1413 each contain one 50x60mm stamp. For overprint see Nos. 2295-2297. For Winter Olympic stamps with gold border, see Nos. 1372-1373.

UNICEF, 25th Anniv. (in 1971) — A245

**1972, Jan. 24 Granite Paper**

| | | | | |
|---|---|---|---|---|
| **1414** | A245 | 1g red brn | 1.00 | 1.00 |
| **1415** | A245 | 2g ultra | 1.00 | 1.00 |
| **1416** | A245 | 3g lil rose | 1.00 | 1.00 |
| **1417** | A245 | 4g violet | 1.00 | 1.00 |
| **1418** | A245 | 5g emerald | 1.00 | 1.00 |
| **1419** | A245 | 10g claret | 2.00 | *3.00* |
| **1420** | A245 | 20g brt bl | 2.00 | *3.00* |
| **1421** | A245 | 25g lt ol | 2.00 | *3.00* |
| **1422** | A245 | 30g dk brn | 2.00 | *3.00* |
| | | *Nos. 1414-1422 (9)* | 13.00 | 17.00 |

Nos. 1420-1422 are airmail.

Race Cars A246

No. 1423: a, 10c, Ferrari. b, 15c, B.R.M. c, 20c, Brabham. d, 25c, March. e, 30c, Honda.

50c, Matra-Simca MS 650. 75c, Porsche. 12.45g, Maserati-8 CTF, 1938. 18.15g, Bugatti 35B, 1929. 20g, Lotus 72 Ford. 50g, Mercedes, 1924.

**1972, Mar. 20 Unwmk. *Perf. 14***

| | | | | |
|---|---|---|---|---|
| **1423** | A246 | Strip of 5, #a.-e. | 2.25 | 1.25 |
| **1424** | A246 | 50c multicolored | .35 | .25 |
| **1425** | A246 | 75c multicolored | .35 | .25 |
| **1426** | A246 | 12.45g multicolored | 1.00 | .45 |
| **1427** | A246 | 18.15g multicolored | 1.00 | .45 |
| **1428** | A246 | 50g multicolored | 5.25 | 5.25 |
| | | *Nos. 1423-1428 (6)* | 10.20 | 7.90 |

**Souvenir Sheet**

***Perf. 13½***

| | | | | |
|---|---|---|---|---|
| **1429** | A246 | 20g multicolored | 22.50 | |

Nos. 1426-1429 are airmail. No. 1429 contains one 60x50mm stamp.

Sailing Ships — A247

Paintings: No. 1430a, 10c, Holbein. b, 15c, Nagasaki print. c, 20c, Intrepid, Roux. d, 25c, Portuguese ship, unknown artist. e, 30c, Mount Vernon, US, 1798, Corne.

50c, Van Eertvelt, vert. 75c, Santa Maria, Van Eertvelt, vert. 12.45g, Royal Prince, 1679, Van Beecq. 18.15g, Van Bree. 50g, Book of Arms, 1497, vert.

**1972, Mar. 29 *Perf. 14***

| | | | | |
|---|---|---|---|---|
| **1430** | A247 | Strip of 5, #a.-e. | 1.25 | 1.25 |
| **1431** | A247 | 50c multicolored | .30 | .25 |
| **1432** | A247 | 75c multicolored | .40 | .25 |
| **1433** | A247 | 12.45g multicolored | 1.00 | .35 |
| **1434** | A247 | 18.15g multicolored | 1.40 | .40 |
| **1435** | A247 | 50g multicolored | 3.00 | .75 |
| | | *Nos. 1430-1435 (6)* | 7.35 | 3.25 |

Nos. 1433-1435 are airmail.

Paintings in Vienna Museum A248

Nudes by: No. 1436a, 10c, Rubens. b, 15c, Bellini. c, 20c, Carracci. d, 25c, Cagnacci. e, 30c, Spranger.

50c, Mandolin Player, Strozzi. 75c, Woman in Red Hat, Cranach the elder. 12.45g, Adam and Eve, Coxcie. 18.15g, Legionary on Horseback, Poussin. 50g, Madonna and Child, Bronzino.

**1972, May 22**

| | | | | |
|---|---|---|---|---|
| **1436** | A248 | Strip of 5, #a.-e. | 1.25 | 1.25 |
| **1437** | A248 | 50c multicolored | .25 | .25 |
| **1438** | A248 | 75c multicolored | .25 | .25 |
| **1439** | A248 | 12.45g multicolored | .70 | .40 |
| **1440** | A248 | 18.15g multicolored | .70 | .40 |
| **1441** | A248 | 50g multicolored | 2.75 | 1.25 |
| | | *Nos. 1436-1441 (6)* | 5.90 | 3.80 |

Nos. 1439-1441 are airmail.

Paintings in Asuncion Museum A249

No. 1442: a, 10c, Man in Straw Hat, Holden Jara. b, 15c, Portrait, Tintoretto. c, 20c, Indians, Holden Jara. d, 25c, Nude, Bouchard. e, 30c, Italian School.

50c, Reclining Nude, Berisso, horiz. 75c, Carracci, horiz. 12.45g, Reclining Nude, Schiaffino, horiz. 18.15g, Reclining Nude, Lostow, horiz. 50g, Madonna and Child, 17th cent. Italian School.

**1972, May 22**

| | | | | |
|---|---|---|---|---|
| **1442** | A249 | Strip of 5, #a.-e. | 1.25 | 1.25 |
| **1443** | A249 | 50c multicolored | .25 | .25 |
| **1444** | A249 | 75c multicolored | .25 | .25 |
| **1445** | A249 | 12.45g multicolored | .70 | .40 |
| **1446** | A249 | 18.15g multicolored | .70 | .40 |
| **1447** | A249 | 50g multicolored | 2.75 | 1.25 |
| | | *Nos. 1442-1447 (6)* | 5.90 | 3.80 |

Nos. 1445-1447 are airmail.

Presidential Summit — A250

No. 1448: a, 10c, Map of South America. b, 15c, Brazil natl. arms. c, 20c, Argentina natl. arms. d, 25c, Bolivia natl. arms. e, 30c, Paraguay natl. arms.

50c, Pres. Emilio Garrastazu, Brazil. 75c, Pres. Alejandro Lanusse, Argentina. 12.45g, Pres. Hugo Banzer Suarez, Bolivia. 18.15, Pres. Stroessner, Paraguay, horiz. 23.40g, Flags.

**1972, Nov. 18**

| | | | | |
|---|---|---|---|---|
| **1448** | A250 | Strip of 5, #a.-e. | 1.25 | 1.25 |
| **1449** | A250 | 50c multicolored | .25 | .25 |
| **1450** | A250 | 75c multicolored | .25 | .25 |
| **1451** | A250 | 12.45g multicolored | 1.40 | .25 |
| **1452** | A250 | 18.15g multicolored | 1.75 | .30 |
| | | *Nos. 1448-1452 (5)* | 4.90 | 2.30 |

**Souvenir Sheet**

***Perf. 13½***

| | | | | |
|---|---|---|---|---|
| **1453** | A250 | 23.40g multicolored | 2.50 | |

Nos. 1451-1453 are airmail. No. 1453 contains one 50x60mm stamp. For overprint see No. 2144.

Pres. Stroessner's Visit to Japan — A251

No. 1454: a, 10c, Departure of first Japanese mission to US & Europe, 1871. b, 15c, First railroad, Tokyo-Yokahama, 1872. c, 20c,

Samurai. d, 25c, Geishas. e, 30c, Cranes, Hiroshige.

50c, Honda race car. 75c, Pres. Stroessner, Emperor Hirohito, Mt. Fuji, bullet train, horiz. 12.45g, Rocket. 18.15g, Stroessner, Hirohito, horiz. No. 1459, Mounted samurai, Masanobu, 1740. No. 1460, Hirohito's speech, state dinner, horiz. No. 1461, Delegations at Tokyo airport, horiz.

**1972, Nov. 18** ***Perf. 14***

| | | | | |
|---|---|---|---|---|
| **1454** | A251 | Strip of 5, #a.-e. | 1.25 | 1.25 |
| **1455** | A251 | 50c multicolored | .25 | .25 |
| **1456** | A251 | 75c multicolored | .25 | .25 |
| **1457** | A251 | 12.45g multicolored | 2.00 | 2.00 |
| **1458** | A251 | 18.15g multicolored | 2.50 | 2.50 |
| | | *Nos. 1454-1458 (5)* | 6.25 | 6.25 |

**Souvenir Sheets**

***Perf. 13½***

| | | | | |
|---|---|---|---|---|
| **1459** | A251 | 23.40g multicolored | 7.50 | 7.50 |
| **1460** | A251 | 23.40g multicolored | 17.50 | 17.50 |

***Imperf***

| | | | | |
|---|---|---|---|---|
| **1461** | A251 | 23.40g multicolored | 15.00 | 15.00 |

Nos. 1457-1461 are airmail. Nos. 1459-1460 each contain one 50x60mm stamp. No. 1461 contains one 85x42mm stamp with simulated perforations. For overprints see Nos. 2192-2194, 2267.

Wildlife A252

Paintings — #1462: a, 10c, Cranes, Botke. b, 15c, Tiger, Utamaro. c, 20c, Horses, Arenys. d, 25c, Pheasant, Dietzsch. e, 30c, Monkey, Brueghel, the Elder. All vert.

50c, Deer, Marc. 75c, Crab, Durer. 12.45g, Rooster, Jakuchu, vert. 18.15g, Swan, Asselyn.

**1972, Nov. 18** ***Perf. 14***

| | | | | |
|---|---|---|---|---|
| **1462** | A252 | Strip of 5, #a.-e. | 1.25 | 1.25 |
| **1463** | A252 | 50c multicolored | .25 | .25 |
| **1464** | A252 | 75c multicolored | .25 | .25 |
| **1465** | A252 | 12.45g multicolored | 1.50 | .75 |
| **1466** | A252 | 18.15g multicolored | 1.75 | 1.00 |
| | | *Nos. 1462-1466 (5)* | 5.00 | 3.50 |

Nos. 1465-1466 are airmail.

Acaray Dam A253

Designs: 2g, Francisco Solano Lopez monument. 3g, Friendship Bridge. 5g, Tebicuary River Bridge. 10g, Hotel Guarani. 20g, Bus and car on highway. 25g, Hospital of Institute for Social Service. 50g, "Presidente Stroessner" of state merchant marine. 100g, "Electra C" of Paraguayan airlines.

***Perf. 13½x13***

**1972, Nov. 16** **Wmk. 347**

**Granite Paper**

| | | | | |
|---|---|---|---|---|
| **1467** | A253 | 1g sepia | 2.00 | 1.00 |
| **1468** | A253 | 2g brown | 2.00 | 1.00 |
| **1469** | A253 | 3g brt ultra | 2.00 | 1.00 |
| **1470** | A253 | 5g brt pink | 2.00 | 1.00 |
| **1471** | A253 | 10g dl grn | 3.00 | 2.00 |
| **1472** | A253 | 20g rose car | 3.00 | 2.00 |
| **1473** | A253 | 25g gray | 3.00 | 2.00 |
| **1474** | A253 | 50g violet | 3.00 | 2.00 |
| **1475** | A253 | 100g brt lil | 3.00 | 2.00 |
| | | *Nos. 1467-1475 (9)* | 23.00 | 14.00 |

Tourism Year of the Americas.
Nos. 1472-1475 are airmail.

**Locomotives Type**

No. 1476: a, 10c, Stephenson's Rocket, 1829. b, 15c, First Swiss railroad, 1847. c, 20c, 1st Spanish locomotive, 1848. d, 2c, Norris, US, 1850. e, 30c, Ansaldo, Italy, 1859.

50c, Badenia, Germany, 1863. 75c, 1st Japanese locomotive, 1895. 12.45g, P.L.M., France, 1924. 18.15g, Stephenson's Northumbrian.

**1972, Nov. 25** **Unwmk.** ***Perf. 14***

| | | | | |
|---|---|---|---|---|
| **1476** | A243 | Strip of 5, #a.-e. | 1.25 | 1.25 |
| **1477** | A243 | 50c multicolored | .25 | .25 |
| **1478** | A243 | 75c multicolored | .25 | .25 |
| **1479** | A243 | 12.45g multicolored | 3.50 | .40 |
| **1480** | A243 | 18.15g multicolored | 5.00 | 1.00 |
| | | *Nos. 1476-1480 (5)* | 10.25 | 3.15 |

Nos. 1479-1480 are airmail.

South American Wildlife — A254

No. 1481: a, 10c, Tetradactyla. b, 15c, Nasua socialis. c, 20c, Priodontes giganteus. d, 25c, Blastocerus dichotomus. e, 30c, Felis pardalis.

50c, Aotes, vert. 75c, Rhea americana. 12.45g, Desmodus rotundus. 18.15g, Urocyon cinereo-argenteus.

**1972, Nov. 25**

| | | | | |
|---|---|---|---|---|
| **1481** | A254 | Strip of 5, #a.-e. | 1.25 | 1.25 |
| **1482** | A254 | 50c multicolored | .35 | .25 |
| **1483** | A254 | 75c multicolored | .35 | .25 |
| **1484** | A254 | 12.45g multicolored | 3.75 | .75 |
| **1485** | A254 | 18.15g multicolored | 5.00 | 1.25 |
| | | *Nos. 1481-1485 (5)* | 10.70 | 3.75 |

Nos. 1484-1485 are airmail.

OAS Emblem A255

***Perf. 13x13½***

**1973** **Litho.** **Wmk. 347**

**Granite Paper**

| | | | | |
|---|---|---|---|---|
| **1486** | A255 | 1g multi | 1.00 | 1.00 |
| **1487** | A255 | 2g multi | 1.00 | 1.00 |
| **1488** | A255 | 3g multi | 1.00 | 1.00 |
| **1489** | A255 | 4g multi | 1.00 | 1.00 |
| **1490** | A255 | 5g multi | 1.00 | 1.00 |
| **1491** | A255 | 10g multi | 1.00 | 1.00 |
| **1492** | A255 | 20g multi | 2.00 | 1.00 |
| **1493** | A255 | 25g multi | 2.00 | 1.00 |
| **1494** | A255 | 50g multi | 3.00 | 1.00 |
| **1495** | A255 | 100g multi | 5.00 | 1.00 |
| | | *Nos. 1486-1495 (10)* | 18.00 | 10.00 |

Org. of American States, 25th anniv.
Nos. 1492-1495 are airmail.

Paintings in Florence Museum A256

Artists: No. 1496: a, 10c, Cranach, the Elder. b, 15c, Caravaggio. c, 20c, Fiorentino. d, 25c, Di Credi. e, 30c, Liss. f, 50c, Da Vinci. g, 75c, Botticelli.

No. 1497: a, 5g, Titian, horiz. b, 10g, Del Piombo, horiz. c, 20g, Di Michelino, horiz.

**1973, Mar. 13** **Unwmk.** ***Perf. 14***

| | | | | |
|---|---|---|---|---|
| **1496** | A256 | Strip of 7, #a.-g. | 1.75 | 1.00 |
| **1497** | A256 | Strip of 3, #a.-c. | 3.75 | 2.50 |
| | | *Nos. 1496-1497 (2)* | 5.50 | 3.50 |

No. 1497 is airmail.

Butterflies — A257

#1498: a, 10c, Catagramma patazza. b, 15c, Agrias narcissus. c, 20c, Papilio zagreus. d, 25c, Heliconius chestertoni. e, 30c, Metamorphadido. f, 50c, Catagramma astarte. g, 75c, Papilio brasiliensis.

No. 1499a, 5g, Agrias sardanapalus. b, 10g, Callithea saphhira. c, 20g, Jemadia hospita.

**1973, Mar. 13**

| | | | | |
|---|---|---|---|---|
| **1498** | A257 | Strip of 7, #a.-g. | 1.75 | 1.00 |
| **1499** | A257 | Strip of 3, #a.-c. | 6.25 | 3.50 |
| | | *Nos. 1498-1499 (2)* | 8.00 | 4.50 |

No. 1499 is airmail.

Cats A258

Faces of Cats: No. 1500: a, 10c, b, 15c. c, 20c, d, 25c, e, 30c. f, 50c. g, 75c.

No. 1501a, 5g, Cat under rose bush, by Desportes. b, 10g, Two cats, by Marc, horiz. c, 20g, Man with cat, by Rousseau.

**1973, June 29**

| | | | | |
|---|---|---|---|---|
| **1500** | A258 | Strip of 7, #a.-g. | 1.75 | 1.00 |
| **1501** | A258 | Strip of 3, #a.-c. | 7.25 | 3.50 |
| | | *Nos. 1500-1501 (2)* | 9.00 | 4.50 |

No. 1500 is airmail. For other cat designs, see type A287.

Flemish Paintings A259

Nudes by: No. 1502: a, 10c, Spranger. b, 15c, Jordaens. c, 20c, de Clerck. d, 25c, Spranger, diff. e, 30c, Goltzius. f, 50c, Rubens. g, 75c, Vase of flowers, J. Brueghel.

No. 1503a, 5g, Nude, de Clerck, horiz. b, 10g, Woman with mandolin, de Vos. c, 20g, Men, horses, Rubens, horiz.

**1973, June 29** **Litho.** ***Perf. 14***

| | | | | |
|---|---|---|---|---|
| **1502** | A259 | Strip of 7, #a.-g. | 1.75 | 1.00 |
| **1503** | A259 | Strip of 3, #a.-c. | 4.25 | 3.00 |
| | | *Nos. 1502-1503 (2)* | 6.00 | 4.00 |

No. 1503 is airmail.

Hand Holding Letter — A260

**Wmk. 347**

**1973, July 10** **Litho.** ***Perf. 11***

| | | | | |
|---|---|---|---|---|
| **1504** | A260 | 2g lil rose & blk | 5.00 | 1.50 |

No. 1504 was issued originally as a nonobligatory stamp to benefit mailmen, but its status was changed to regular postage.

EXPOPAR 73, Paraguayan Industrial Exhib. — A261

**1973, Aug. 11** ***Perf. 13x13½***

**Granite Paper**

| | | | | |
|---|---|---|---|---|
| **1505** | A261 | 1g org brn | 2.00 | 2.00 |
| **1506** | A261 | 2g vermilion | 2.00 | 2.00 |
| **1507** | A261 | 3g blue | 2.00 | 2.00 |
| **1508** | A261 | 4g emerald | 2.00 | 2.00 |
| **1509** | A261 | 5g lilac | 2.00 | 2.00 |
| **1510** | A261 | 20g lilac rose | 7.50 | 3.00 |
| **1511** | A261 | 25g rose claret | 7.50 | 3.00 |
| | | *Nos. 1505-1511 (7)* | 25.00 | 16.00 |

Nos. 1510-1511 are airmail.

1974 World Cup Soccer Championships, Munich — A262

No. 1512: a, 10c, Uruguay vs. Paraguay. b, 15c, Crerand, England and Eusebio, Portugal. c, 20c, Bobby Charlton, England. d, 25c, Franz Beckenbauer, Germany. e, 30c, Erler, Germany and McNab, England. f, 50c, Pele, Brazil and Willi Schulz, Germany. g, 75c, Arsenio Erico, Paraguay.

5g, Brian Labone, Gerd Mueller, Bobby Moore. No. 1514a, 10g, Luigi Riva, Italy. No. 1514b, 20g, World Cup medals. No. 1515, World Cup trophy. 25g, Player scoring goal.

**1973** **Litho.** **Unwmk.** ***Perf. 14***

| | | | | |
|---|---|---|---|---|
| **1512** | A262 | Strip of 7, #a.-g. | 1.75 | 1.00 |
| **1513** | A262 | 5g multicolored | 5.00 | 1.50 |
| **1514** | A262 | Pair, #a.-b. | 2.25 | 1.00 |
| | | *Nos. 1512-1514 (3)* | 9.00 | 3.50 |

**Souvenir Sheets**

***Perf. 13½***

| | | | | |
|---|---|---|---|---|
| **1515** | A262 | 25g multicolored | 25.00 | 25.00 |
| **1516** | A262 | 25g multicolored | 22.50 | 22.50 |

Nos. 1513-1516 are airmail. Issue dates: Nos. 1512-1514, 1516, Oct. 8. No. 1515, June 29. For overprint see No. 2131.

Paintings A263

Details from paintings, artist: No. 1517a, 10c, Lion of St. Mark, Carpaccio. b, 15c, Venus and Mars, Pittoni. c, 20c, Rape of Europa, Veronese. d, 25c, Susannah and the Elders, Tintoretto. e, 30c, Euphrosyne, Amigoni. f, 50c, Allegory of Moderation, Veronese. g, 75c, Ariadne, Tintoretto.

5g, Pallas and Mars, Tintoretto. No. 1519a, 10g, Portrait of Woman in Fur Hat, G.D. Tiepolo. b, 20g, Dialectic of Industry, Veronese.

**1973, Oct. 8** ***Perf. 14***

| | | | | |
|---|---|---|---|---|
| **1517** | A263 | Strip of 7, #a.-g. | 1.75 | 1.00 |
| **1518** | A263 | 5g multicolored | 2.50 | .75 |
| **1519** | A263 | Pair, #a.-b. | 3.00 | 1.25 |
| | | *Nos. 1517-1519 (3)* | 7.25 | 3.00 |

Nos. 1518-1519 are airmail.

Birds A264

No. 1520: a, 10c, Tersina viridis. b, 15c, Pipile cumanensis. c, 20c, Pyrocephalus rubinus. d, 25c, Andigena laminirostris. e, 30c, Xipholena punicea. f, 50c, Tangara chilensis. g, 75, Polytmus guainumbi.

5g, Onychorhynchus mexicanus, vert. No. 1522a, 10g, Rhinocrypta lanceolata, vert. b, 20g, Trogon collaris, vert. 25g, Colibri florisuga mellivora, vert.

**1973, Nov. 14**

**1520** A264 Strip of 7, #a.-g. 1.10 1.10
**1521** A264 5g multicolored 3.00 1.50
**1522** A264 Pair, #a.-b. 2.00 .50
*Nos. 1520-1522 (3)* 6.10 3.10

**Souvenir Sheet**

***Perf. 13½***

**1523** A264 25g multicolored 10.00 10.00

Nos. 1521-1523 are airmail. No. 1523 contains one 50x60mm stamp.

Space Exploration — A265

No. 1524a, 10c, Apollo 11. b, 15c, Apollo 12. c, 20c, Apollo 13. d, 25c, Apollo 14. e, 30c, Apollo 15. f, 50c, Apollo 16. g, 75c, Apollo 17.

5g, Skylab. No. 1526a, 10g, Space shuttle. b, 20g, Apollo-Soyuz mission. No. 1527, Pioneer 11, Jupiter. No. 1528, Pioneer 10, Jupiter, vert.

**1973, Nov. 14** ***Perf. 14***

**1524** A265 Strip of 7, #a.-g. 1.10 1.10
**1525** A265 5g multicolored 3.50 1.50
**1526** A265 Pair, #a.-b. 1.40 1.00
*Nos. 1524-1526 (3)* 6.00 3.60

**Souvenir Sheet**

***Perf. 14½***

**1527** A265 25g multicolored 17.00 12.00

***Perf. 13½***

**1528** A265 25g multicolored 15.00 10.00

#1525-1528 are airmail. #1527 contains on 35x25mm stamp, #1528 one 50x60mm stamp.

Souvenir Sheet

Women of Avignon, Pablo Picasso — A266

**1973, Nov. 14** ***Perf. 13½***

**1529** A266 25g multicolored 11.00 11.00

Traditional Costumes A267

No. 1530: a, 25c, Indian girl. b, 50c, Bottle dance costume. c, 75c, Dancer balancing vase on head. d, 1g, Dancer with flowers. e, 1.50g, Weavers. f, 1.75g, Man, woman in dance costumes. g, 2.25g, Musicians in folk dress, horiz.

**1973, Dec. 30** ***Perf. 14***

**1530** A267 Strip of 7, #a.-g. 2.00 1.00

Flowers A268

Designs: No. 1531a, 10c Passion flower. b, 20c, Dahlia. c, 25c, Bird of paradise. d, 30c, Freesia. e, 40c, Anthurium. f, 50c, Water lily. g, 75c, Orchid.

**1973, Dec. 31**

**1531** A268 Strip of 7, #a.-g. 6.00 2.50

Roses A269

Designs: No. 1532a, 10c, Hybrid perpetual. b, 15c, Tea scented. c, 20c, Japanese rose. d, 25c, Bouquet of roses and flowers. e, 30c, Rose of Provence. f, 50c, Hundred petals rose. g, 75c, Bouquet of roses, dragonfly.

**1974, Feb. 2**

**1532** A269 Strip of 7, #a.-g. 7.00 3.00

Paintings in Gulbenkian Museum A270

Designs and artists: No. 1533a, 10c, Cupid and Three Graces, Boucher. b, 15c, Bath of Venus, Burne-Jones. c, 20c, Mirror of Venus, Burne-Jones. d, 25c, Two Women, Natoire. e, 30c, Fighting Cockerels, de Vos. f, 50c, Portrait of a Young Girl, Bugiardini. g, 75c, Madonna and Child, J. Gossaert.

5g, Outing on Beach at Enoshima, Utamaro. No. 1535: a, 10g, Woman with Harp, Lawrence. b, 20g, Centaurs Embracing, Rubens.

**1974, Feb. 4**

**1533** A270 Strip of 7, #a.-g. 1.10 1.10
**1534** A270 5g multicolored 2.50 1.75
**1535** A270 Pair, #a.-b. 3.50 3.50
*Nos. 1533-1535 (3)* 7.10 6.35

Nos. 1534-1535 are airmail.

UPU Cent. A271

Horse-drawn mail coaches: No. 1536a, 10c, London. b, 15c, France. c, 20c, England. d, 25c, Bavaria. e, 30c, Painting by C.C. Henderson. f, 50c, Austria, vert. g, 75c, Zurich, vert.

5g, Hot air balloon, Apollo spacecraft, airplane, Graf Zeppelin. No. 1538a, 10g, Steam locomotive. b, 20g, Ocean liner, sailing ship. No. 1539, Airship, balloon. No. 1540, Mail coach crossing river.

**1974, Mar. 20** ***Perf. 14***

**1536** A271 Strip of 7, #a.-g. 1.25 1.25
**1537** A271 5g multicolored 1.40 .65
**1538** A271 Pair, #a.-b. 5.50 3.50
*Nos. 1536-1538 (3)* 8.15 5.40

**Souvenir Sheets**

***Perf. 14½***

**1539** A271 15g multicolored 25.00 25.00

***Perf. 13½***

**1540** A271 15g multicolored 25.00 25.00

Nos. 1537-1540 are airmail. No. 1539 contains one 50x35mm stamp, No. 1540 one 60x50mm stamp. Nos. 1539-1540 each include a 5g surtax for a monument to Francisco Solano Lopez. For overprint see No. 2127.

Paintings — A272

Details from works, artist: No. 1541a, 10c, Adam and Eve, Mabuse. b, 15c, Portrait, Piero di Cosimo. c, 20c, Bathsheba in her Bath, Cornelisz. d, 25c, Toilet of Venus, Boucher. e, 30c, The Bathers, Renoir. f, 50c, Lot and his Daughters, Dix. g, 75c, Bouquet of Flowers, van Kessel.

5g, King's Pet Horse, Seele. No. 1543a, 10g, Woman with Paintbrushes, Batoni. b, 20g, Three Musicians, Flemish master.

**1974, Mar. 20**

**1541** A272 Strip of 7, #a.-g. 1.25 1.25
**1542** A272 5g multicolored 1.40 .40
**1543** A272 Pair, #a.-b. 6.50 3.00
*Nos. 1541-1543 (3)* 9.15 4.65

Nos. 1542-1543 are airmail.

Sailing Ships — A272a

Designs: No. 1544a, 5c, Ship, map. b, 10c, English ship. c, 15c, Dutch ship. d, 20c, Whaling ships. e, 25c, Spanish ship. f, 35c, USS Constitution. g, 40c, English frigate. h, 50c, "Fanny," 1832.

**1974, Sept. 13** ***Perf. 14½***

**1544** A272a Strip of 8, #a.-h. 3.00 1.00

Strip price includes a 50c surtax.

Paintings in Borghese Gallery, Rome A273

Details from works and artists: No. 1545a, 5c, Portrait, Romano. b, 10c, Boy Carrying Fruit, Caravaggio. c, 15c, A Sybil, Domenichino. d, 20c, Nude, Titian. e, 25c, The Danae, Correggio. f, 35c, Nude, Savoldo. g, 40c, Nude, da Vinci. h, 50c, Nude, Rubens. 15g, Christ Child, Piero di Cosimo.

**1975, Jan. 15** ***Perf. 14***

**1545** A273 Strip of 8, #a.-h. 3.00 1.50

**Souvenir Sheet**

***Perf. 14½***

**1546** A273 15g multicolored 10.00 5.00

No. 1546 is airmail and price includes a 5g surtax used for a monument to Francisco Solano Lopez.

Christmas A274

Paintings, artists: No. 1547a, 5c, The Annunciation, della Robbia. b, 10c, The Nativity, G. David. c, 15c, Madonna and Child, Memling. d, 20c, Adoration of the Shepherds, Giorgione. e, 25c, Adoration of the Magi, French school, 1400. f, Madonna and Child with Saints, 35c, Pulzone. g, 40c, Madonna and Child, van Orley. h, 50c, Flight From Egypt, Pacher.

15g, Adoration of the Magi, Raphael.

**1975, Jan. 17** ***Perf. 14***

**1547** A274 Strip of 8, #a.-h. 3.00 1.50

**Souvenir Sheet**

***Perf. 14½***

**1548** A274 15g multicolored 10.00 5.00

No. 1548 is airmail and price includes a 5g surtax for a monument to Francisco Solano Lopez.

"U.P.U.," Pantheon, Carrier Pigeon, Globe — A275

**1975, Feb. Wmk. 347** ***Perf. 13½x13***

**1549** A275 1g blk & lilac .25 .25
**1550** A275 2g blk & rose red .25 .25
**1551** A275 3g blk & ultra .25 .25
**1552** A275 5g blk & blue .25 .25
**1553** A275 10g blk & lil rose .50 .25
**1554** A275 20g blk & brn 1.50 .25
**1555** A275 25g blk & emer 1.50 .25
*Nos. 1549-1555 (7)* 4.50 1.75

Centenary of Universal Postal Union. Nos. 1554-1555 are airmail.

Paintings in National Gallery, London A276

Details from paintings, artist: 5c, The Rokeby Venus, Velazquez, horiz. 10c, The Range of Love, Watteau. 15c, Venus (The School of Love), Correggio. 20c, Mrs. Sarah Siddons, Gainsborough. 25c, Cupid Complaining to Venus, L. Cranach the Elder. 35c, Portrait, Lotto. 40c, Nude, Rembrandt. 50c, Origin of the Milky Way, Tintoretto. 15g, Rider and Hounds, Pisanello.

**1975, Apr. 25 Unwmk. *Perf. 14***

**1556** A276 5c multicolored .25 .25
**1557** A276 10c multicolored .30 .25
**1558** A276 15c multicolored .40 .25
**1559** A276 20c multicolored .45 .25
**1560** A276 25c multicolored .50 .25
**1561** A276 35c multicolored .65 .25
**1562** A276 40c multicolored .70 .25
**1563** A276 50c multicolored .80 .25
*Nos. 1556-1563 (8)* 4.05 2.00

**Souvenir Sheet**

***Perf. 13½***

**1564** A276 15g multicolored 10.00 10.00

No. 1564 is airmail, contains one 50x60mm stamp and price includes a 5g surtax for a monument to Francisco Solano Lopez.

Dogs A277

**1975, June 7 *Perf. 14***

**1565** A277 5c Boxer .25 .25
**1566** A277 10c Poodle .25 .25
**1567** A277 15c Basset hound .25 .25
**1568** A277 20c Collie .25 .25
**1569** A277 25c Chihuahua .35 .25
**1570** A277 35c German shepherd .50 .25
**1571** A277 40c Pekinese .55 .25
**1572** A277 50c Chow .70 .25
*Nos. 1565-1572 (8)* 3.10 2.00

**Souvenir Sheet**

***Perf. 13½***

**1573** A277 15g Fox hound, horse 15.00 8.00

No. 1573 is airmail, contains one 39x57mm stamp and price includes a 5g surtax for a monument to Francisco Solano Lopez.

South American Fauna — A278

Designs: No. 1574a, 5c, Piranha (Pirana). b, 10c, Anaconda. c, 15c, Turtle (Tortuga). d, 20c, Iguana. e, 25c, Mono, vert. f, 35c, Mara. g, 40c, Marmota, vert. h, 50c, Peccary.

**1975, Aug. 20 Litho. *Perf. 14***

**1574** A278 Strip of 8, #a.-h. 3.00 1.50

**Souvenir Sheet**

***Perf. 13½***

**1575** A278 15g Aguara guazu 10.00 7.50

No. 1575 is airmail, contains and one 60x50mm stamp, and price includes a 5g surtax for a monument to Francisco Solano Lopez.
For overprints see Nos. 2197.

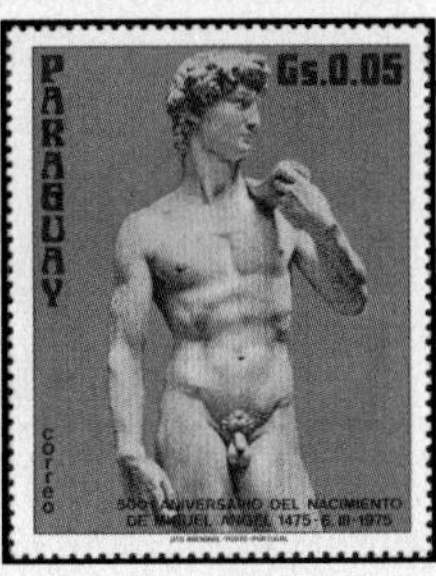


Michelangelo (1475-1564), Italian Sculptor and Painter — A279

No. 1583: Statues, a, 5c, David. b, 10c, Aurora.
Paintings, c, 15c, Original Sin. d, 20c, The Banishment. e, 25c, The Deluge. f, 35c, Eve. g, 40c, Mary with Jesus and John. h, 50c, Judgement Day.
4g, Adam Receiving Life from God, horiz. No. 1585a, 5g, Libyan Sybil. b, 10g, Delphic Sybil. No. 1586, God Creating the Heaven and the Earth, horiz. No. 1587, The Holy Family.

**1975, Aug. 23 Litho. *Perf. 14***

**1583** A279 Strip of 8, #a.-h. 1.50 1.50
**1584** A279 4g multicolored 4.00 2.75
**1585** A279 Pair, #a.-b. 1.00 .75

**Souvenir Sheets**

***Perf. 12***

**1586** A279 15g multicolored 15.00 7.50

***Perf. 13½***

**1587** A279 15g multicolored 15.00 12.00

Nos. 1586-1587 sold for 20g with surtax for a monument to Francisco Solano Lopez. Nos. 1584-1587 are airmail.

Winter Olympics, Innsbruck, 1976 — A280

No. 1596, Luge. No. 1599, 4-Man bobsled.
No. 1597a, 2g, Slalom skier. b, 3g, Cross country skier. c, 4g, Pair figure skating. d, 5g, Hockey.
No. 1598a, 10g, Speed skater. b, 15g, Downhill skier.
No. 1600, Ski jumper. No. 1601, Woman figure skater.

**1975, Aug. 27 Litho. *Perf. 14***

**1596** A280 1g multi .25 .25
**1597** A280 Strip of 4, #a.-d. 2.00 1.00
**1598** A280 Pair, #a.-b. 2.50 .80
**1599** A280 20g multi 3.00 1.50
*Nos. 1596-1599 (4)* 7.75 3.55

**Souvenir Sheet**

***Perf. 13½***

**1600** A280 25g multi 22.50 22.50
**1601** A280 25g multi 14.00 14.00

Nos. 1596, 1598-1601 are horiz. Nos. 1598-1601 are airmail. Nos. 1600-1601 each contain one 60x50mm stamp.

Summer Olympics, Montreal, 1976 — A281

No. 1606: a, 1g, Weightlifting. b, 2g, Kayak. c, 3g, Hildegard Flack, 800 meter run. d, Lasse Viren, 5,000 meter run.
No. 1607: a, 5g, Dieter Kottysch, boxing. b, 10g, Lynne Evans, archery. c, 15g, Akinori Nakayama, balance rings. 20g, Heide Rosendahl, broad jump. No. 1609, Decathlon. No. 1610, Liselott Linsenhoff, dressage, horiz.

**1975, Aug. 28 *Perf. 14***

**1606** A281 Strip of 4, #a.-d. .80 .80
**1607** A281 Strip of 3, #a.-c. 3.25 1.00
**1608** A281 20g multicolored 4.00 1.50
*Nos. 1606-1608 (3)* 8.05 3.30

**Souvenir Sheets**

***Perf. 14½***

**1609** A281 25g multicolored 15.00 15.00
**1610** A281 25g multicolored 15.00 15.00

Nos. 1607b-1610 are airmail.

US, Bicent. — A282

Ships: 5c, Sachem, vert. 10c, Reprisal, Lexington. 15c, Wasp. 20c, Mosquito, Spy. 25c, Providence, vert. 35c, Yankee Hero, Milford. 40c, Cabot, vert. 50c, Hornet, vert.
15g, Montgomery.

**Unwmk.**

**1975, Oct. 20 Litho. *Perf. 14***

**1616** A282 5c multicolored .25 .25
**1617** A282 10c multicolored .35 .25
**1618** A282 15c multicolored .35 .25
**1619** A282 20c multicolored .35 .25
**1620** A282 25c multicolored .35 .25
**1621** A282 35c multicolored .50 .25
**1622** A282 40c multicolored .55 .25
**1623** A282 50c multicolored .75 .30
*Nos. 1616-1623 (8)* 3.45 2.05

**Souvenir Sheet**

**1624** A282 15g multicolored 15.00 15.00

No. 1624 is airmail and contains one 50x70mm stamp.

US, Bicent. — A283

Details from paintings, artists: No. 1625a, 5c, The Collector, Kahill. b, 10c, Morning Interlude, Brackman, vert. c, 15c, White Cloud, Catlin, vert. d, 20c, Man From Kentucky, Benton, vert. e, 25c, The Emigrants, Remington. f, 35c, Spirit of '76, Willard, vert. g, John Paul Jones capturing Serapis, unknown artist. h, 50c, Declaration of Independence, Trumbull. 15g, George Washington, Stuart and Thomas Jefferson, Peale.

**1975, Nov. 20 *Perf. 14***

**1625** A283 Strip of 8, #a.-h. 4.00 1.50

**Souvenir Sheet**

***Perf. 13½***

**1625A** A283 15g multicolored 15.00 15.00

No. 1625A is airmail, contains one 60x50mm stamp and price includes a 5g surtax for a monument to Francisco Solano Lopez.

Institute of Higher Education — A284

***Perf. 13½x13***

**1976, Mar. 16 Litho. Wmk. 347**

**1626** A284 5g vio, blk & red 1.10 .50
**1627** A284 10g ultra, blk & red 2.00 1.50
**1628** A284 30g brn, blk & red 2.00 1.50
*Nos. 1626-1628 (3)* 5.10 3.50

Inauguration of Institute of Higher Education, Sept. 23, 1974.
No. 1628 is airmail.

Rotary Intl., 70th Anniv. — A285

**1976, Mar. 16 *Perf. 13x13½***

**1629** A285 3g blk, bl & citron 1.00 .75
**1630** A285 4g car, bl & citron 1.00 .75
**1631** A285 25g emer, bl & lemon 3.00 2.00
*Nos. 1629-1631 (3)* 5.00 3.50

No. 1631 is airmail.

IWY Emblem, Woman's Head — A286

**1976, Mar. 16**

**1632** A286 1g ultra & brn 1.00 .75
**1633** A286 2g car & brn 1.00 .75
**1634** A286 20g grn & brn 3.00 2.00
*Nos. 1632-1634 (3)* 5.00 3.50

Intl Women's Year (1975).
No. 1634 is airmail.

Cats A287

Various cats: No. 1635a, 5c. b, 10c. c, 15c. d, 20c. e, 25c. f, 35c. g, 40c. h, 50c. 15g.

**1976, Apr. 2 Unwmk. *Perf. 14***

**1635** A287 Strip of 8, #a.-h. 3.00 1.00

**Souvenir Sheet**

***Perf. 13½***

**1636** A287 15g multicolored 15.00 5.00

No. 1636 is airmail, contains one 50x60mm stamp and price includes a 5g surtax for a monument to Francisco Solano Lopez.
See Nos. 2132-2133, 2201-2202, 2274-2275. For overprint see No. 2212.

Railroads, 150th Anniv. (in 1975) — A288

Locomotives: 1g, Planet, England, 1830. 2g, Koloss, Austria, 1844. 3g, Tarasque, France,

1846. 4g, Lawrence, Canada, 1853. 5g, Carlsruhe, Germany, 1854. 10g, Great Sagua, US, 1856. 15g, Berga, Spain. 20g, Encarnacion, Paraguay. 25g, English locomotive, 1825.

**1976, Apr. 2** *Perf. 13x13½*

**1637** A288 1g multicolored .25 .25
**1638** A288 2g multicolored .25 .25
**1639** A288 3g multicolored .25 .25
**1640** A288 4g multicolored .25 .25
**1641** A288 5g multicolored .25 .25
**1642** A288 10g multicolored 1.50 .40
**1643** A288 15g multicolored 2.40 .60
**1644** A288 20g multicolored 3.00 1.00
*Nos. 1637-1644 (8)* 8.15 3.25

**Souvenir Sheet**

**1645** A288 25g multicolored 32.50 32.50

Nos. 1642-1645 are airmail. No. 1645 contains one 40x27mm stamp.

Painting by Spanish Artists — A289

Paintings: 1g, The Naked Maja by Goya. 2g, Nude by J. de Torres. 3g, Nude holding oranges by de Torres, vert. 4g, Woman playing piano by Z. Velazquez, vert. 5g, Knight on white horse by Esquivel, vert. 10g, The Shepherd by Murillo, vert. 15g, The Immaculate Conception by Antolinez, vert. 20g, Nude by Zuloaga. 25g, Prince Baltasar Carlos on Horseback by D. Velasquez.

**1976, Apr. 2** *Perf. 13x13½,13½x13*

**1646** A289 1g multicolored .25 .25
**1647** A289 2g multicolored .25 .25
**1648** A289 3g multicolored .25 .25
**1649** A289 4g multicolored .25 .25
**1650** A289 5g multicolored .30 .25
**1651** A289 10g multicolored .75 .40
**1652** A289 15g multicolored 1.10 .50
**1653** A289 20g multicolored 1.50 .60
*Nos. 1646-1653 (8)* 4.65 2.75

**Souvenir Sheet**

**1654** A289 25g multicolored 9.00 5.00

Nos. 1651-1654 are airmail. No. 1654 contains one 58x82mm stamp.

Butterflies — A290

No. 1655: a, 5c, Prepona praeneste. b, 10c, Prepona proschion. c, 15c, Pereute leucodrosime. d, 20c, Agrias amydon. e, 25c, Morpho aegea gynandromorphe. f, 35c, Pseudatteria leopardina. g, 40c, Morpho helena. h, 50c, Morpho hecuba.

**1976, May 12** **Unwmk.** *Perf. 14*

**1655** A290 Strip of 8, #a.-h. 5.00 1.50

Farm Animals — A291

**1976, June 15**

**1656** A291 1g Rooster, vert. .25 .25
**1657** A291 2g Hen, vert. .35 .25
**1658** A291 3g Turkey, vert. .35 .25
**1659** A291 4g Sow .40 .25
**1660** A291 5g Donkeys .50 .25
**1661** A291 10g Brahma cattle .55 .35
**1662** A291 15g Holstein cow .65 .35
**1663** A291 20g Horse .80 .50
*Nos. 1656-1663 (8)* 3.85 2.45

Nos. 1661-1663 are airmail.

US and US Post Office, Bicent. — A292

Designs: 1g, Pony Express rider. 2g, Stagecoach. 3g, Steam locomotive, vert. 4g, American steamship, Savannah. 5g, Curtiss Jenny biplane. 10g, Mail bus. 15g, Mail car, rocket train. 20g, First official missile mail, vert. No. 1672, First flight cover, official missile mail. No. 1673, US #C76 tied to cover by moon landing cancel.

**1976, June 18**

**1664** A292 1g multicolored .25 .25
**1665** A292 2g multicolored .35 .25
**1666** A292 3g multicolored .40 .25
**1667** A292 4g multicolored .50 .25
**1668** A292 5g multicolored .65 .25
**1669** A292 10g multicolored .85 .50
**1670** A292 15g multicolored 1.60 .70
**1671** A292 20g multicolored 2.50 1.00
*Nos. 1664-1671 (8)* 7.10 3.45

**Souvenir Sheets**

*Perf. 14½*

**1672** A292 25g multicolored 15.00 15.00
**1673** A292 25g multicolored 15.00 15.00

Nos. 1669-1673 are airmail and each contain one 50x40mm stamp.

Mythological Characters — A293

Details from paintings, artists: No. 1674a, 1g, Jupiter, Ingres. b, 2g, Saturn, Rubens. c, 3g, Neptune, Tiepolo. d, 4g, Uranus and Aphrodite, Medina, horiz. e, 5g, Pluto and Prosperpine, Giordano, horiz. f, 10g, Venus, Ingres. g, 15g, Mercury, de la Hyre. 20g, Mars and Venus, Veronese.

25g, Viking Orbiter descending to Mars, horiz.

**1976, July 18** *Perf. 14*

**1674** A293 Strip of 7, #a.-g. 4.50 3.00
**1675** A293 20g multicolored 2.50 1.50
*Nos. 1674-1675 (2)* 7.00 4.50

**Souvenir Sheet**

*Perf. 14½*

**1676** A293 25g multicolored 40.00 40.00

Nos. 1674f-1674g, 1675-1676 are airmail.

Sailing Ships — A294

Paintings: No. 1677a, 1g, Venice frigate of the Spanish Armada, vert. b, 2g, Swedish war ship, Vasa, 1628, vert. c, 3g, Spanish galleon being attacked by pirates by Puget. d, 4g, Combat by Dawson. e, 5g, European boat in Japan, vert. f, 10g, Elizabeth Grange in Liverpool by Walters. g, 15g, Prussen, 1903, by Holst. 20g, Grand Duchess Elizabeth, 1902, by Bohrdt.

**1976, July 15** *Perf. 14*

**1677** A294 Strip of 7, #a.-g. 4.00 2.50
**1678** A294 20g multicolored 2.00 .50
*Nos. 1677-1678 (2)* 6.00 3.00

Nos. 1677f-1678 are airmail.

German Sailing Ships — A295

Ship, artist: 1g, Bunte Kuh, 1402, Zeeden. 2g, Arms of Hamburg, 1667, Wichman, vert. 3g, Kaiser Leopold, 1667, Wichman, vert. 4g, Deutschland, 1848, Pollack, vert. 5g, Humboldt, 1851, Fedeler. 10g, Borussia, 1855, Seitz. 15g, Gorch Fock, 1958, Stroh, vert. 20g, Grand Duchess Elizabeth, 1902, Bohrdt. 25g, SS Pamir, Zeytline, vert.

**Unwmk.**

**1976, Aug. 20** **Litho.** *Perf. 14*

**1685** A295 1g multicolored .35 .25
**1686** A295 2g multicolored .50 .25
**1687** A295 3g multicolored .65 .25
**1688** A295 4g multicolored .80 .25
**1689** A295 5g multicolored .90 .30
**1690** A295 10g multicolored 1.00 .45
**1691** A295 15g multicolored 1.75 .80
**1692** A295 20g multicolored 2.25 1.00
*Nos. 1685-1692 (8)* 8.20 3.55

**Souvenir Sheet**

*Perf. 14½*

**1693** A295 25g multicolored 14.00 14.00

Intl. German Naval Exposition, Hamburg; NORDPOSTA '76 (No. 1693). Nos. 1690-1693 are airmail.

US Bicentennial — A296

Western Paintings by: No. 1694a, 1g, E. C. Ward. b, 2g, William Robinson Leigh. c, 3g, A. J. Miller. d, 4g, Charles Russell. e, 5g, Frederic Remington. f, 10g, Remington, horiz. g, 15g, Carl Bodmer.

No. 1695, A. J. Miller. No. 1696, US #1, 2, 245, C76.

**Unwmk.**

**1976, Sept. 9** **Litho.** *Perf. 14*

**1694** A296 Strip of 7, #a.-g. 5.25 2.00
**1695** A296 20g multicolored 2.75 1.00
*Nos. 1694-1695 (2)* 8.00 3.00

**Souvenir Sheet**

*Perf. 13x13½*

**1696** A296 25g multicolored 40.00 40.00

Nos. 1694f-1694g, 1695-1696 are airmail. No. 1696 contains one 65x55mm stamp.

1976 Summer Olympics, Montreal — A297

Gold Medal Winners: No. 1703a, 1g, Nadia Comaneci, Romania, gymnastics, vert. b, 2g, Kornelia Ender, East Germany, swimming. c, 3g, Luann Ryan, US, archery, vert. d, 4g, Jennifer Chandler, US, diving. e, 5g, Shirley Babashoff, US, swimming. f, 10g, Christine Stuckelberger, Switzerland, equestrian. g, 15g, Japan, volleyball, vert.

20g, Annegret Richter, W. Germany, running, vert. No. 1705, Bruce Jenner, US, decathlon. No. 1706, Alwin Schockemohle, equestrian. No. 1707, Medals list, vert.

**Unwmk.**

**1976, Dec. 18** **Litho.** *Perf. 14*

**1703** A297 Strip of 7, #a.-g. 5.00 2.00
**1704** A297 20g multicolored 2.00 .75
*Nos. 1703-1704 (2)* 7.00 2.75

**Souvenir Sheets**

*Perf. 14½*

**1705** A297 25g multicolored 25.00 25.00
**1706** A297 25g multicolored 25.00 25.00
**1707** A297 25g multicolored 25.00 25.00

Nos. 1703f-1703g, 1705-1707 are airmail. Nos. 1705-1706 each contain one 50x40mm stamp. No. 1707 contains one 50x70mm stamp.

Titian, 500th Birth Anniv. A298

Details from paintings: No. 1708a, 1g, Venus and Adonis. b, 2g, Diana and Callisto. c, 3g, Perseus and Andromeda. d, 4g, Venus of the Mirror. e, 5g, Venus Sleeping, horiz. f, 10g, Bacchanal, horiz. g, 15g, Venus, Cupid and the Lute Player, horiz. 20g, Venus and the Organist, horiz.

**1976, Dec. 18** *Perf. 14*

**1708** A298 Strip of 7, #a.-g. 6.00 2.50
**1709** A298 20g multicolored 2.00 1.00
*Nos. 1708-1709 (2)* 8.00 3.50

No. 1708f-1708g, 1709 are airmail.

Peter Paul Rubens, 400th Birth Anniv. A299

Paintings: No. 1710a, 1g, Adam and Eve. b, 2g, Tiger and Lion Hunt. c, 3g, Bathsheba Receiving David's Letter. d, 4g, Susanna in the Bath. e, 5g, Perseus and Andromeda. f, 10g, Andromeda Chained to the Rock. g, 15g, Shivering Venus. 20g, St. George Slaying the Dragon. 25g, Birth of the Milky Way, horiz.

**1977, Feb. 18**

**1710** A299 Strip of 7, #a.-g. 5.50 2.00
**1711** A299 20g multicolored 2.50 1.00
*Nos. 1710-1711 (2)* 8.00 3.00

**Souvenir Sheet**

*Perf. 14½*

**1712** A299 25g multicolored 30.00 30.00

Nos. 1710f-1710g, 1711-1712 are airmail.

US, Bicent. — A300

Space exploration: No. 1713a, 1g, John Glenn, Mercury 7. b, 2g, Pres. Kennedy, Apollo 11. c, 3g, Wernher von Braun, Apollo 17. d, 4g, Mercury, Venus, Mariner 10. e, 5g, Jupiter, Saturn, Pioneer 10/11. f, 10g, Viking, Mars. g, 15g, Viking A on Mars. 20g, Viking B on Mars. No. 1715, Future space projects on Mars, vert. No. 1716, Future land rover on Mars.

**1976, Mar. 3** *Perf. 14*

| | | | | |
|---|---|---|---|---|
| **1713** | A300 | Strip of 7, #a.-g. | 4.00 | 2.00 |
| **1714** | A300 | 20g multicolored | 2.00 | 1.20 |
| | | *Nos. 1713-1714 (2)* | 6.00 | 3.20 |

**Souvenir Sheets**

*Perf. 13½*

| | | | | |
|---|---|---|---|---|
| **1715** | A300 | 25g multicolored | 25.00 | 25.00 |
| **1716** | A300 | 25g multicolored | 20.00 | 20.00 |

Nos. 1713f-1713g, 1714-1716 are airmail. No. 1715 contains one 50x60mm stamp, No. 1716 one 60x50mm stamp.

Olympic History A301

Designs: 1g, Spiridon Louis, marathon 1896, Athens, Pierre de Coubertin. 2g, Giuseppe Delfino, fencing 1960, Rome, Pope John XXIII. 3g, Jean Claude Killy, skiing 1968, Grenoble, Charles de Gaulle. 4g, Ricardo Delgado, boxing 1968, Mexico City, G. Diaz Ordaz. 5g, Hayata, gymnastics 1964, Tokyo, Emperor Hirohito. 10g, Klaus Wolfermann, javelin 1972, Munich, Avery Brundage. 15g, Michel Vaillancourt, equestrian 1976, Montreal, Queen Elizabeth II. 20g, Franz Klammer, skiing 1976, Innsbruck, Austrian national arms.

25g, Emblems of 1896 Athens games and 1976 Montreal games.

**1977, June 7** *Perf. 14*

| | | | | |
|---|---|---|---|---|
| **1717** | A301 | 1g multicolored | .25 | .25 |
| **1718** | A301 | 2g multicolored | .25 | .25 |
| **1719** | A301 | 3g multicolored | .40 | .25 |
| **1720** | A301 | 4g multicolored | .60 | .25 |
| **1721** | A301 | 5g multicolored | .80 | .40 |
| **1722** | A301 | 10g multicolored | 1.00 | .50 |
| **1723** | A301 | 15g multicolored | 1.20 | .50 |
| **1724** | A301 | 20g multicolored | 2.00 | 1.00 |
| | | *Nos. 1717-1724 (8)* | 6.50 | 3.40 |

**Souvenir Sheet**

*Perf. 13½*

| | | | | |
|---|---|---|---|---|
| **1725** | A301 | 25g multicolored | 22.50 | 15.00 |

Nos. 1722-1725 are airmail. No. 1725 contains one 49x60mm stamp.

LUPOSTA '77, Intl. Stamp Exibition, Berlin A302

Graf Zeppelin 1st South America flight and: 1g, German girls in traditional costumes. 2g, Bull fighter, Seville. 3g, Dancer, Rio de Janeiro. 4g, Gaucho breaking bronco, Uruguay. 5g, Like #1530b. 10g, Argentinian gaucho. 15g, Ceremonial indian costume, Bolivia. 20g, Indian on horse, US.

No. 1734, Zeppelin over sailing ship. No. 1735, Ferdinand Von Zeppelin, zeppelin over Berlin, horiz.

**1977, June 9** *Perf. 14*

| | | | | |
|---|---|---|---|---|
| **1726** | A302 | 1g multicolored | .25 | .25 |
| **1727** | A302 | 2g multicolored | .25 | .25 |
| **1728** | A302 | 3g multicolored | .30 | .25 |
| **1729** | A302 | 4g multicolored | .50 | .25 |
| **1730** | A302 | 5g multicolored | .65 | .30 |
| **1731** | A302 | 10g multicolored | .80 | .40 |
| **1732** | A302 | 15g multicolored | 1.00 | .45 |
| **1733** | A302 | 20g multicolored | 1.60 | .75 |
| | | *Nos. 1726-1733 (8)* | 5.35 | 2.90 |

**Souvenir Sheets**

*Perf. 13½*

| | | | | |
|---|---|---|---|---|
| **1734** | A302 | 25g multicolored | 50.00 | 50.00 |
| **1735** | A302 | 25g multicolored | 20.00 | 20.00 |

#1731-1735 are airmail. #1734 contains one 49x60mm stamp, #1735 one 60x49mm stamp.

Mburucuya Flowers A303

Weaver with Spider Web Lace — A304

Designs: 1g, Ostrich feather panel. 2g, Black palms. 20g, Rose tabebuia. 25g, Woman holding ceramic pot.

*Perf. 13x13½*

**1977** **Litho.** **Wmk. 347**

| | | | | |
|---|---|---|---|---|
| **1736** | A304 | 1g multicolored | 2.00 | 1.50 |
| **1737** | A303 | 2g multicolored | 2.00 | 1.50 |
| **1738** | A303 | 3g multicolored | 2.00 | 1.50 |
| **1739** | A304 | 5g multicolored | 2.00 | 1.50 |
| **1740** | A303 | 20g multicolored | 3.00 | 2.00 |
| **1741** | A304 | 25g multicolored | 3.00 | 2.50 |
| | | *Nos. 1736-1741 (6)* | 14.00 | 10.50 |

Issued: 2g, 3g, 20g, 4/25; 1g, 5g, 25g, 6/27.
Nos. 1740-1741 are airmail.

Aviation History — A305

Designs: No. 1742a, 1g, Orville and Wilbur Wright, Wright Flyer, 1903. b, 2g, Alberto Santos-Dumont, Canard, 1906. c, 3g, Louis Bleriot, Bleriot 11, 1909. d, 4g, Otto Lilienthal, Glider, 1891. e, 5g, Igor Sikorsky, Avion le Grande, 1913. f, 10g, Juan de la Cierva, Autogiro. g, 15g, Silvio Pettirossi, Deperdussin acrobatic plane. No. 1743, Concorde jet. No. 1744, Lindbergh, Spirit of St. Louis, Statue of Liberty, Eiffel Tower. No. 1745, Design of flying machine by da Vinci.

**1977, July 18** **Unwmk.** *Perf. 14*

| | | | | |
|---|---|---|---|---|
| **1742** | A305 | Strip of 7, #a.-g. | 5.00 | 2.25 |
| **1743** | A305 | 20g multicolored | 2.50 | 1.25 |
| | | *Nos. 1742-1743 (2)* | 7.50 | 3.50 |

**Souvenir Sheet**

*Perf. 14½*

| | | | | |
|---|---|---|---|---|
| **1744** | A305 | 25g multicolored | 25.00 | 25.00 |
| **1745** | A305 | 25g multicolored | 27.50 | 27.50 |

Nos. 1742f-1745 are airmail. No. 1745 contains one label.

Francisco Solano Lopez — A306

*Perf. 13x13½*

**1977, July 24** **Litho.** **Wmk. 347**

| | | | | |
|---|---|---|---|---|
| **1752** | A306 | 10g brown | 1.50 | *2.00* |
| **1753** | A306 | 50g dk vio | 3.00 | 1.50 |
| **1754** | A306 | 100g green | 5.00 | 3.00 |
| | | *Nos. 1752-1754 (3)* | 9.50 | 6.50 |

Marshal Francisco Solano Lopez (1827-1870), President of Paraguay.
Nos. 1753-1754 are airmail.

Paintings — A307

Paintings by: No. 1755a, 1g, Gabrielle Rainer Istvanffy. b, 2g, L. C. Hoffmeister. c, 3g, Frans Floris. d, 4g, Gerard de Lairesse. e, 5g, David Teniers I. f, 10g, Jacopo Zucchi. g, 15g, Pierre Paul Prudhon. 20g, Francois Boucher. 25g, Ingres. 5g-25g vert.

**1977, July 25** *Perf. 14*

| | | | | |
|---|---|---|---|---|
| **1755** | A307 | Strip of 7, #a.-g. | 3.75 | 1.25 |
| **1756** | A307 | 20g multicolored | 1.25 | .50 |
| | | *Nos. 1755-1756 (2)* | 5.00 | 1.75 |

**Souvenir Sheet**

*Perf. 14½*

| | | | | |
|---|---|---|---|---|
| **1757** | A307 | 25g multicolored | 15.00 | 15.00 |

Nos. 1755f-1757 are airmail.

German Sailing Ships — A308

Designs: No. 1764a, 1g, De Beurs van Amsterdam. b, 2g, Katharina von Blankenese. c, 3g, Cuxhaven. d, 4g, Rhein. e, 5g, Churprinz and Marian. f, 10g, Bark of Bremen, vert. g, 15g, Elbe II, vert. 20g, Karacke. 25g, Admiral Karpeanger.

**Unwmk.**

**1977, Aug. 27** **Litho.** *Perf. 14*

| | | | | |
|---|---|---|---|---|
| **1764** | A308 | Strip of 7, #a.-g. | 4.75 | 2.00 |
| **1765** | A308 | 20g multicolored | 2.25 | 1.25 |
| | | *Nos. 1764-1765 (2)* | 7.00 | 3.25 |

**Souvenir Sheet**

*Perf. 13½*

| | | | | |
|---|---|---|---|---|
| **1766** | A308 | 25g multicolored | 12.00 | 12.00 |

Nos. 1764f-1766 are airmail. No. 1766 contains one 40x30mm stamp.

Nobel Laureates for Literature — A309

Authors and scenes from books: No. 1773a, 1g, John Steinbeck, Grapes of Wrath, vert. b, 2g, Ernest Hemingway, Death in the Afternoon. c, 3g, Pearl S. Buck, The Good Earth, vert. d, 4g, George Bernard Shaw, Pygmalion, vert. e, 5g, Maurice Maeterlinck, Joan of Arc, vert. f, 10g, Rudyard Kipling, The Jungle Book. g, Henryk Sienkiewicz, Quo Vadis. 20g, C. Theodor Mommsen, History of Rome. 25g, Nobel prize medal.

**1977, Sept. 5** *Perf. 14*

| | | | | |
|---|---|---|---|---|
| **1773** | A309 | Strip of 7, #a.-g. | 5.25 | 2.00 |
| **1774** | A309 | 20g multicolored | 2.75 | 1.25 |
| | | *Nos. 1773-1774 (2)* | 8.00 | 3.25 |

**Souvenir Sheet**

*Perf. 14½*

| | | | | |
|---|---|---|---|---|
| **1775** | A309 | 25g multicolored | 35.00 | 35.00 |

Nos. 1773f-1775 are airmail.

1978 World Cup Soccer Championships, Argentina — A310

Posters and World Cup Champions: No. 1782a, 1g, Uruguay, 1930. b, 2g, Italy, 1934. c, 3g, Italy, 1938. d, 4g, Uruguay, 1950. e, 5g, Germany, 1954. f, 10g, Soccer player by Fritz Genkinger. g, 15g, Soccer player, orange shirt by Genkinger.

No. 1783a, 1g, Brazil, 1958. b, 2g, Brazil, 1962. c, 3g, England, 1966. d, 4g, Brazil, 1970. e, 5g, Germany, 1974. f, 10g, Player #4 by Genkinger. g, 15g, Player #1 by Genkinger, horiz.

No. 1784, World Cup Trophy. No. 1785, German players, Argentina '78. No. 1786, The Loser, by Genkinger. No. 1787, The Defender, (player #11) by Genkinger.

**1977, Oct. 28** **Unwmk.** *Perf. 14*

| | | | | |
|---|---|---|---|---|
| **1782** | A310 | Strip of 7, #a.-g. | 5.50 | 2.25 |
| **1783** | A310 | Strip of 7, #a.-g. | 5.25 | 2.25 |
| **1784** | A310 | 20g multicolored | 1.60 | .65 |
| **1785** | A310 | 20g multicolored | 1.60 | .65 |
| | | *Nos. 1782-1785 (4)* | 13.95 | 5.80 |

**Souvenir Sheets**

*Perf. 14½*

| | | | | |
|---|---|---|---|---|
| **1786** | A310 | 25g red & multi | 30.00 | 30.00 |
| **1787** | A310 | 25g black & multi | 30.00 | 30.00 |

Nos. 1782f-1782g, 1783f-1783g, 1784-1787 are airmail.

Peter Paul Rubens, 400th Birth Anniv. A312

Details from paintings: No. 1788a, 1g, Rubens and Isabella Brant under Honeysuckle Bower. b, 2g, Judgment of Paris. c, 3g, Union of Earth and Water. d, 4g, Daughters of Kekrops Discovering Erichthonius. e, 5g, Holy Family with the Lamb. f, 10c, Adoration of the Magi. g, 15c, Philip II on Horseback.

20g, Education of Marie de Medici, horiz. 25g, Triumph of Eucharist Over False Gods.

**1978, Jan. 19** **Unwmk.** *Perf. 14*

| | | | | |
|---|---|---|---|---|
| **1788** | A312 | Strip of 7, #a.-g. | 5.00 | 2.50 |
| **1789** | A312 | 20g multicolored | 2.75 | 1.40 |
| | | *Nos. 1788-1789 (2)* | 7.75 | 3.90 |

**Souvenir Sheet**

*Perf. 14½*

| | | | | |
|---|---|---|---|---|
| **1790** | A312 | 25g multi, gold | 12.00 | 12.00 |
| **1790A** | A312 | 25g multi, silver | 17.50 | 17.50 |

Nos. 1788f-1788g, 1789-1790 are airmail. No. 1790 contains one 50x70mm stamp and exists inscribed in gold or silver.

1978 World Chess Championships, Argentina — A313

Paintings of chess players: No. 1791a, 1g, De Cremone. b, 2g, L. van Leyden. c, 3g, H. Muehlich. d, 4g, Arabian artist. e, 5g, Benjamin Franklin playing chess, E. H. May. f, 10g, G. Cruikshank. g, 15g, 17th cent. tapestry. 20g, Napoleon playing chess on St. Helena. 25g, Illustration from chess book, Shah Name.

**1978, Jan. 23** *Perf. 14*

**1791** A313 Strip of 7, #a.-g. 20.00 7.50
**1792** A313 20g multicolored 10.00 3.50
*Nos. 1791-1792 (2)* 30.00 11.00

**Souvenir Sheet**

*Perf. 14½*

**1793** A313 25g multicolored 40.00 40.00

Nos. 1791f-1791g, 1792-1793 are airmail. No. 1793 contains one 50x40mm stamp.

Jacob Jordaens, 300th Death Anniv. A314

Paintings: No. 1794a, 3g, Satyr and the Nymphs. b, 4g, Satyr with Peasant. c, 5g, Allegory of Fertility. d, 6g, Upbringing of Jupiter. e, 7g, Holy Family. f, 8g, Adoration of the Shepherds. g, 20g, Jordaens with his family. 10g, Meleagro with Atalanta, horiz. No. 1796, Feast for a King, horiz. No. 1797, Holy Family with Shepherds.

**1978, Jan. 25** *Perf. 14*

**1794** A314 Strip of 7, #a.-g. 8.50 2.75
**1795** A314 10g multicolored 2.00 .75
**1796** A314 25g multicolored 4.00 1.40
*Nos. 1794-1796 (3)* 14.50 4.90

**Souvenir Sheet**

*Perf. 14½*

**1797** A314 25g multicolored 14.00 14.00

Nos. 1795-1797 are airmail. No. 1797 contains one 50x70mm stamp.

Albrecht Durer, 450th Death Anniv. A315

Monograms and details from paintings: No. 1804a, 3g, Temptation of the Idler. b, 4g, Adam and Eve. c, 5g, Satyr Family. d, 6g, Eve. e, 7g, Adam. f, 8g, Portrait of a Young Man. g, 20g, Squirrels and Acorn. 10g, Madonna and Child. No. 1806, Brotherhood of the Rosary (Lute-playing Angel). No. 1807, Soldier on Horseback with a Lance.

**1978, Mar. 10** *Perf. 14*

**1804** A315 Strip of 7, #a.-g. 5.00 2.25
**1805** A315 10g multicolored 1.60 .50
**1806** A315 25g multicolored 3.25 1.20
*Nos. 1804-1806 (3)* 9.85 3.95

**Souvenir Sheet**

*Perf. 13½*

**1807** A315 25g blk, buff & sil 25.00 25.00

Nos. 1805-1807 are airmail. No. 1807 contains one 30x40mm stamp.

Francisco de Goya, 150th Death Anniv. A316

Paintings: No. 1814a, 3g, Allegory of the Town of Madrid. b, 4g, The Clothed Maja. c, 5g, The Parasol. d, 6g, Dona Isabel Cobos de Porcel. e, 7g, The Drinker. f, 8g, The 2nd of May 1908. g, 20g, General Jose Palafox on Horseback. 10g, Savages Murdering a Woman. 25g, The Naked Maja, horiz.

**1978, May 11** *Perf. 14*

**1814** A316 Strip of 7, #a.-g. 5.00 1.60
**1815** A316 10g multicolored 1.25 .40
**1816** A316 25g multicolored 2.00 .80
*Nos. 1814-1816 (3)* 8.25 2.80

Nos. 1815-1816 are airmail.

Future Space Projects — A317

Various futuristic space vehicles and imaginary creatures: No. 1816a, 3g. b, 4g. c, 5g. d, 6g. e, 7g. f, 8g. g, 20g.

**1978, May 16**

**1817** A317 Strip of 7, #a.-g. 4.50 2.25
**1818** A317 10g multicolored 1.00 .50
**1819** A317 25g multi, diff. 2.50 1.00
*Nos. 1817-1819 (3)* 8.00 3.75

Nos. 1818-1819 are airmail.

Racing Cars — A318

No. 1820: a, 3g, Tyrell Formula I. b, 4g, Lotus Formula 1, 1978. c, 5g, McLaren Formula 1. d, 6g, Brabham Alfa Romeo Formula 1. e, 7g, Renault Turbo Formula 1. f, 8g, Wolf Formula 1. g, 20g, Porsche 935. 10g, Bugatti. 25g, Mercedes Benz W196, Stirling Moss, driver. No. 1823, Ferrari 312T.

**1978, June 28** *Perf. 14*

**1820** A318 Strip of 7, #a.-g. 3.75 1.90
**1821** A318 10g multicolored .60 .25
**1822** A318 25g multicolored 1.60 .80
*Nos. 1820-1822 (3)* 5.95 2.95

**Souvenir Sheet**

*Perf. 14½*

**1823** A318 25g multicolored 16.00 16.00

Nos. 1821-1823 are airmail. No. 1823 contains one 50x35mm stamp.

Paintings by Peter Paul Rubens A319

3g, Holy Family with a Basket. 4g, Amor Cutting a Bow. 5g, Adam & Eve in Paradise. 6g, Crown of Fruit, horiz. 7g, Kidnapping of Ganymede. 8g, The Hunting of Crocodile & Hippopotamus. 10g, The Reception of Marie de Medici at Marseilles. 20g, Two Satyrs. 25g, Felicity of the Regency.

**1978, June 30** *Perf. 14*

**1824** A319 3g multicolored .30 .25
**1825** A319 4g multicolored .50 .25
**1826** A319 5g multicolored .65 .25
**1827** A319 6g multicolored .70 .25
**1828** A319 7g multicolored .85 .30
**1829** A319 8g multicolored 1.00 .40
**1830** A319 10g multicolored 2.40 .80
**1831** A319 20g multicolored 3.50 1.10
**1832** A319 25g multicolored 4.75 1.60
*Nos. 1824-1832 (9)* 14.65 5.20

Nos. 1830, 1832 are airmail.

National College A320

*Perf. 13½x13*

**1978** **Litho.** **Wmk. 347**

**1833** A320 3g claret 2.00 2.00
**1834** A320 4g violet blue 2.00 2.00
**1835** A320 5g lilac 2.00 2.00
**1836** A320 20g brown 2.00 2.00
**1837** A320 25g violet black 3.00 2.00
**1838** A320 30g bright green 3.00 2.00
*Nos. 1833-1838 (6)* 14.00 12.00

Centenary of National College in Asuncion. Nos. 1836-1838 are airmail.

José Estigarribia, Bugler, Flag of Paraguay A321

**1978** **Litho.** *Perf. 13x13½*

**1839** A321 3g multi 3.00 2.00
**1840** A321 5g multi 3.00 2.00
**1841** A321 10g multi 3.00 2.00
**1842** A321 20g multi 5.00 3.00
**1843** A321 25g multi 5.00 3.00
**1844** A321 30g multi 5.00 3.00
*Nos. 1839-1844 (6)* 24.00 15.00

Induction of Jose Felix Estigarribia (1888-1940), general and president of Paraguay, into Salon de Bronce (National Heroes' Hall of Fame).

Nos. 1842-1844 are airmail.

Queen Elizabeth II Coronation, 25th Anniv. A322

Flowers and: 3g, Barbados #234. 4g, Tristan da Cunha #13. 5g, Bahamas #157. 6g, Seychelles #172. 7g, Solomon Islands #88. 8g, Cayman Islands #150. 10g, New Hebrides #77. 20g, St. Lucia #156. 25g, St. Helena #139.

No. 1854, Solomon Islands #368a-368c, Gilbert Islands #312a-312c. No. 1855, Great Britain #313-316.

**1978, July 25** **Unwmk.** *Perf. 14*

**1845** A322 3g multicolored .30 .25
**1846** A322 4g multicolored .50 .25
**1847** A322 5g multicolored .65 .25
**1848** A322 6g multicolored .70 .25
**1849** A322 7g multicolored .85 .30
**1850** A322 8g multicolored 1.00 .40
**1851** A322 10g multicolored 2.40 .80
**1852** A322 20g multicolored 3.50 1.20
**1853** A322 25g multicolored 4.75 1.60
*Nos. 1845-1853 (9)* 14.65 5.30

**Souvenir Sheets**

*Perf. 13½*

**1854** A322 25g multicolored 25.00 25.00
**1855** A322 25g multicolored 25.00 25.00

Nos. 1851, 1853-1855 are airmail. Nos. 1854-1855 each contain one 60x40mm stamp.

Intl. Philatelic Exhibitions A323

Various paintings, ship, nudes, etc. for: No. 1856a, 3g, Nordposta '78. b, 4g, Riccione '78. c, 5g, Uruguay '79. d, 6g, ESSEN '78. e, 7g, ESPAMER '79. f, 8g, London '80. g, 20g, PRAGA '78. 10g, EUROPA '78. No. 1858, Eurphila '78.

No. 1859, Francisco de Pinedo, map of his flight.

**1978, July 19** *Perf. 14*

**1856** A323 Strip of 7, #a.-g. 6.00 1.25
**1857** A323 10g multicolored 1.40 .40
**1858** A323 25g multicolored 2.10 .70
*Nos. 1856-1858 (3)* 9.50 2.35

**Souvenir Sheet**

*Perf. 13½x13*

**1859** A323 25g multicolored 25.00 25.00

No. 1859 for Riccione '78 and Eurphila '78 and contains one 54x34mm stamp. Nos. 1857-1859 are airmail. Nos. 1856b-1858 are vert.

Intl. Year of the Child A324

Grimm's Snow White and the Seven Dwarfs: No. 1866a, 3g, Queen pricking her finger. b, 4g, Queen and mirror. c, 5g, Man with dagger, Snow White. d, 6g, Snow White in forest. e, 7g, Snow White asleep, seven dwarfs. f, 8g, Snow White dancing with dwarfs. g, 20g, Snow White being offered apple. 10g, Snow White in repose. 25g, Snow White, Prince Charming on horseback.

**1978, Oct. 26**

**1866** A324 Strip of 7, #a.-g. 4.50 2.25
**1867** A324 10g multicolored 1.00 .50
**1868** A324 25g multicolored 2.40 1.00
*Nos. 1866-1868 (3)* 7.90 3.75

Nos. 1867-1868 are airmail.
See Nos. 1893-1896, 1916-1919.

Mounted South American Soldiers A325

No. 1869a, 3g, Gen. Jose Felix Bogado (1771-1829). b, 4g, Colonel, First Volunteer Regiment, 1806. c, 5g, Colonel wearing dress uniform, 1860. d, 6g, Soldier, 1864-1870. e, 7g, Dragoon, 1865. f, 8g, Lancer. g, 20g, Soldier, 1865. 10g, Gen. Bernardo O'Higgins, 200th birth anniv. 25g, Jose de San Martin, 200th birth anniv.

**1978, Oct. 31**

**1869** A325 Strip of 7, #a.-g. 4.25 1.75
**1870** A325 10g multicolored .70 .25
**1871** A325 25g multicolored 2.00 .45
*Nos. 1869-1871 (3)* 6.95 2.45

Nos. 1870-1871 are airmail.

1978 World Cup Soccer Championships, Argentina — A326

Soccer Players: No. 1872a, 3g, Paraguay, vert. b, 4g, Austria, Sweden. c, 5g, Argentina, Poland. d, 6g, Italy, Brazil. e, 7g, Netherlands, Austria. f, 8g, Scotland, Peru. g, 20g, Germany, Italy. 10g, Argentina, Holland. 25g, Germany, Tunisia.
No. 1875, Stadium.

**1979, Jan. 9** ***Perf. 14***

**1872** A326 Strip of 7, #a.-g. 5.00 2.00
**1873** A326 10g multicolored .70 .25
**1874** A326 25g multicolored 2.00 .50
*Nos. 1872-1874 (3)* 7.70 2.75

**Souvenir Sheet**

***Perf. 13½***

**1875** A326 25g multicolored 40.00 40.00

Nos. 1873-1875 are airmail. No. 1875 contains one 60x40mm stamp.
For overprint see No. C610.

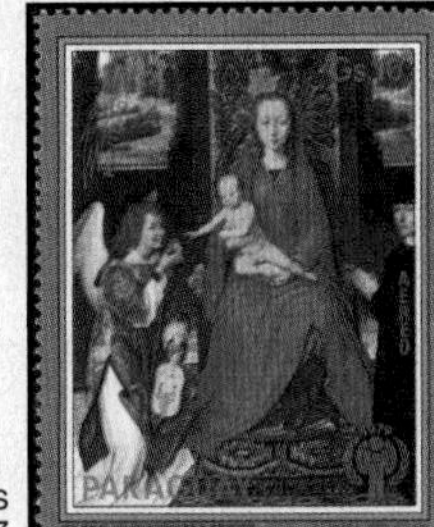
Christmas A327

Paintings of the Nativity and Madonna and Child by: No. 1876a, 3g, Giorgione, horiz. b, 4g, Titian. c, 5g, Titian, diff. d, 6g, Raphael. e, 7g, Schongauer. f, 8g, Muratti. g, 20g, Van Oost. 10g, Memling. No. 1878, Rubens.
No. 1879, Madonna and Child Surrounded by a Garland and Boy Angels, Rubens.

**1979, Jan. 10** **Litho.** ***Perf. 14***

**1876** A327 Strip of 7, #a.-g. 3.50 1.40
**1877** A327 10g multicolored .70 .25
**1878** A327 25g multicolored 1.40 .50
*Nos. 1876-1878 (3)* 5.60 2.15

**Souvenir Sheet**

**Photo. & Engr.**

***Perf. 12***

**1879** A327 25g multicolored 60.00 60.00

Nos. 1877-1879 are airmail.

First Powered Flight, 75th Anniv. (in 1978) — A328

Airplanes: No. 1880a, 3g, Eole, C. Ader, 1890. b, 4g, Flyer III, Wright Brothers. c, 5g, Voisin, Henri Farman, 1908. d, 6g, Curtiss, Eugene Ely, 1910. e, 7g, Etrich-Taube A11. f, 8g, Fokker EIII. g, 20g, Albatros C, 1915. 10g, Boeing 747 carrying space shuttle. No. 1882, Boeing 707. No. 1883, Zeppelin flight commemorative cancels.

**1979, Apr. 24** **Litho.** ***Perf. 14***

**1880** A328 Strip of 7, #a.-g. 5.50 1.40
**1881** A328 10g multicolored .85 .25
**1882** A328 25g multicolored 2.00 .50
*Nos. 1880-1882 (3)* 8.35 2.15

**Souvenir Sheet**

***Perf. 14½***

**1883** A328 25g blue & black 45.00 45.00

Nos. 1881-1883 are airmail. Nos. 1880-1883 incorrectly commemorate 75th anniv. of ICAO. No. 1883 contains one 50x40mm stamp.

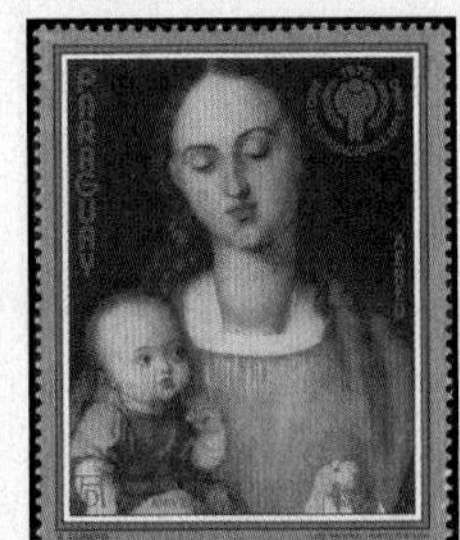
Albrecht Durer, 450th Death Anniv. (in 1978) A329

Paintings: No. 1884a, 3g, Virgin with the Dove. b, 4g, Virgin Praying. c, 5g, Mater Dolorosa. d, 6g, Virgin with a Carnation. e, 7g, Madonna and Sleeping Child. f, 8g, Virgin Before the Archway. g, 20g, Flight Into Egypt. No. 1885, Madonna of the Haller family. No. 1886, Virgin with a Pear.
No. 1887, Lamentation Over the Dead Christ for Albrecht Glimm. No. 1888, Space station, horiz., with Northern Hemisphere of Celestial Globe in margin.

**1979, Apr. 28** ***Perf. 14***

**1884** A329 Strip of 7, #a.-g. 3.75 2.00
**1885** A329 10g multicolored .85 .50
**1886** A329 25g multicolored 2.50 1.00
*Nos. 1884-1886 (3)* 7.10 3.50

**Souvenir Sheets**

***Perf. 13½***

**1887** A329 25g multicolored 17.00 17.00
**1888** A329 25g multicolored 25.00 25.00

Intl. Year of the Child (#1885-1886).
Nos. 1885-1886, 1888 are airmail. No. 1887 contains one 30x40mm stamp, No. 1888 one 40x30mm stamp.

Sir Rowland Hill, Death Cent. — A330

Hill and: No. 1889a, 3g, Newfoundland #C1, vert. b, 4g, France #C14. c, 5g, Spain #B106. d, 6g, Similar to Ecuador #C2, vert. e, 7g, US #C3a. f, 8g, Gelber Hund inverted overprint, vert. g, 20g, Switzerland #C20a.
10g, Privately issued Zeppelin stamp. No. 1891, Paraguay #C82, #C96, vert. No. 1892, Italy #C49. No. 1892A, France #C3-C4.

**1979, June 11** ***Perf. 14***

**1889** A330 Strip of 7, #a.-g. 4.50 1.50
**1890** A330 10g multicolored 1.20 .50
**1891** A330 25g multicolored 3.50 1.20
*Nos. 1889-1891 (3)* 9.20 3.20

**Souvenir Sheet**

***Perf. 13½x13***

**1892** A330 25g multicolored 25.00 25.00

***Perf. 14½***

**1892A** A330 25g multicolored 17.50 17.50

Issue dates: No. 1892A, Aug. 28. Others, June 11. Nos. 1890-1892A are airmail.

**Grimm's Fairy Tales Type of 1978**

Cinderella: No. 1893a, 3g, Two stepsisters watch Cinderella cleaning. b, 4g, Cinderella, father, stepsisters. c, 5g, Cinderella with birds while working. d, 6g, Finding dress. e, 7g, Going to ball. f, 8g, Dancing with prince. g, 20g, Losing slipper leaving ball.
10g, Prince Charming trying slipper on Cinderella's foot. No. 1895, Couple riding to castle. No. 1896, Couple entering ballroom.

**1979, June 24** ***Perf. 14***

**1893** A324 Strip of 7, #a.-g. 4.25 2.25
**1894** A324 10g multicolored 1.00 .55
**1895** A324 25g multicolored 2.75 1.20
*Nos. 1893-1895 (3)* 8.00 4.00

**Souvenir Sheet**

***Perf. 13½***

**1896** A324 25g multicolored 15.00 15.00

Intl. Year of the Child.

Congress Emblem A331

**1979, Aug.** **Litho.** ***Perf. 13x13½***

**1897** A331 10g red, blue & black 5.00 2.00
**1898** A331 50g red, blue & black 5.00 2.00

22nd Latin-American Tourism Congress, Asuncion. No. 1898 is airmail.

1980 Winter Olympics, Lake Placid — A332

#1899: a, 3g, Monica Scheftschik, luge. b, 4g, E. Deufl, Austria, downhill skiing. c, 5g, G. Thoeni, Italy, slalom skiing. d, 6g, Canada Two-man bobsled. e, 7g, Germany vs. Finland, ice hockey. f, 8g, Hoenl, Russia, ski jump. g, 20g, Dianne De Leeuw, Netherlands, figure skating, vert.
10g, Hanni Wenzel, Liechtenstein, slalom skiing. No. 1901, Frommelt, Liechtenstein, slalom skiing, vert. No. 1902, Kulakova, Russia, cross country skier. No. 1903, Dorothy Hamill, US, figure skating, vert. No. 1904, Brigitte Totschnig, skier.

**1979** **Unwmk.** ***Perf. 14***

**1899** A332 Strip of 7, #a.-g. 4.25 2.25
**1900** A332 10g multicolored 1.00 .55
**1901** A332 25g multicolored 2.75 1.20
*Nos. 1899-1901 (3)* 8.00 4.00

**Souvenir Sheets**

***Perf. 13½***

**1902** A332 25g multicolored 17.50 17.50
**1903** A332 25g multicolored 17.50 17.50
**1904** A332 25g multicolored 45.00 45.00

#1900-1904 are airmail. #1902-1903 each contain one 40x30mm stamp, #1904, one 25x36mm stamp.
Issued: #1899-1902, 8/22; #1903, 6/11; #1904, 4/24.

Sailing Ships — A333

No. 1905: a, 3g, Caravel, vert. b, 4g, Warship. c, 5g, Warship, by Jan van Beeck. d, 6g, H.M.S. Britannia, vert. e, 7g, Salamis, vert. f, 8g, Ariel, vert. g, 20g, Warship, by Robert Salmon.

**1979, Aug. 28** ***Perf. 14***

**1905** A333 Strip of 7, #a.-g. 4.50 2.00
**1906** A333 10g Lisette .70 .25
**1907** A333 25g Holstein, vert. 2.00 .50
*Nos. 1905-1907 (3)* 7.20 2.75

Nos. 1906-1907 are airmail.

Intl. Year of the Child A334

Various kittens: No. 1908a, 3g. b, 4g. c, 5g. d, 6g. e, 7g. f, 8g. g, 20g.

**1979, Nov. 29** ***Perf. 14***

**1908** A334 Strip of 7, #a.-g. 4.75 1.25
**1909** A334 10g multicolored 1.90 .25
**1910** A334 25g multicolored 1.60 .45
*Nos. 1908-1910 (3)* 8.25 1.95

Nos. 1909-1910 are airmail.

**Grimm's Fairy Tales Type of 1978**

Little Red Riding Hood: No. 1916a, 3g, Leaving with basket. b, 4g, Meets wolf. c, 5g, Picks flowers. d, 6g, Wolf puts on Granny's gown. e, 7g, Wolf in bed. f, 8g, Hunter arrives. g, 20g, Saved by the hunter.
10g, Hunter enters house. No. 1918, Hunter leaves. No. 1919, Overall scene.

**1979, Dec. 4** ***Perf. 14***

**1916** A324 Strip of 7, #a.-g. 4.25 2.25
**1917** A324 10g multicolored 1.00 .55
**1918** A324 25g multicolored 2.75 1.20
*Nos. 1916-1918 (3)* 8.00 4.00

**Souvenir Sheet**

***Perf. 14½***

**1919** A324 25g multicolored 20.00 20.00

Intl. Year of the Child. No. 1919 contains one 50x70mm stamp.

Greek Athletes A335

Paintings on Greek vases: No. 1926a, 3g, 3 runners. b, 4g, 2 runners. c, 5g, Throwing contest. d, 6g, Discus. e, 7g, Wrestlers. f, 8g, Wrestlers, diff. g, 20g, 2 runners, diff.
10g, Horse and rider, horiz. 25g, 4 warriors with shields, horiz.

**1979, Dec. 20** ***Perf. 14***

**1926** A335 Strip of 7, #a.-g. 4.00 1.60
**1927** A335 10g multicolored .65 .25
**1928** A335 25g multicolored 1.60 .55
*Nos. 1926-1928 (3)* 6.25 2.40

Nos. 1927-1928 are airmail.

Electric Trains — A336

No. 1929: a, 3g, First electric locomotive, Siemens, 1879, vert. b, 4g, Switzerland, 1897. c, 5g, Model E71 28, Germany. d, 6g, Mountain train, Switzerland. e, 7g, Electric locomotive used in Benelux countries. f, 8g, Locomotive "Rheinpfeil," Germany. g, 20g, Model BB-9004, France.

10g, 200-Km/hour train, Germany. 25g, Japanese bullet train.

**1979, Dec. 24 Litho. *Perf. 14***

| | | | | |
|---|---|---|---|---|
| **1929** | A336 | Strip of 7, #a.-g. | 5.00 | 2.00 |
| **1930** | A336 | 10g multicolored | 3.00 | 1.10 |
| **1931** | A336 | 25g multicolored | 3.00 | 1.10 |
| | | *Nos. 1929-1931 (3)* | 11.00 | 4.20 |

Nos. 1930-1931 are airmail.

Sir Rowland Hill, Death Cent. — A337

Hill and: No. 1938a, 3g, Spad S XIII, 1917-18. b, 4g, P-51 D Mustang, 1944-45. c, 5g, Mitsubishi A6M6c Zero-Sen, 1944. d, 6g, Depperdussin float plane, 1913. e, 7g, Savoia Marchetti SM 7911, 1936. f, 8g, Messerschmitt Me 262B, 1942-45. g, 20g, Nieuport 24bis, 1917-18.

10g, Zeppelin LZ 104-/l59, 1917. No. 1940, Fokker Dr-1 Caza, 1917. No. 1941, Vickers Supermarine "Spitfire" Mk.IX, 1942-45.

**1980, Apr. 8 *Perf. 14***

| | | | | |
|---|---|---|---|---|
| **1938** | A337 | Strip of 7, #a.-g. | 5.00 | 2.00 |
| **1939** | A337 | 10g multicolored | .90 | .55 |
| **1940** | A337 | 25g multicolored | 3.00 | 1.10 |
| | | *Nos. 1938-1940 (3)* | 8.90 | 3.65 |

**Souvenir Sheet**

***Perf. 13½***

| | | | | |
|---|---|---|---|---|
| **1941** | A337 | 25g multicolored | 20.00 | 20.00 |

Incorrectly commemorates 75th anniv. of ICAO. Nos. 1939-1941 are airmail. No. 1941 contains one 37x27mm stamp.

Sir Rowland Hill, Paraguayan Stamps — A338

Hill and: No. 1948a, 3g, #1. b, 4g, #5. c, 5g, #6. d, 6g, #379. e, 7g, #381. f, 8g, #C384. g, 20g, #C389.

10g, #C83, horiz. No. 1950, #C92, horiz. No. 1951, #C54, horiz. No. 1952, #C1, horiz.

**1980, Apr. 14 Litho. *Perf. 14***

| | | | | |
|---|---|---|---|---|
| **1948** | A338 | Strip of 7, #a.-g. | 5.25 | 2.50 |
| **1949** | A338 | 10g multicolored | 1.10 | .60 |
| **1950** | A338 | 25g multicolored | 3.50 | 1.40 |
| | | *Nos. 1948-1950 (3)* | 9.85 | 4.50 |

**Souvenir Sheets**

***Perf. 14½***

| | | | | |
|---|---|---|---|---|
| **1951** | A338 | 25g multicolored | 25.00 | 22.50 |
| **1952** | A338 | 25g multicolored | 25.00 | 22.50 |

#1949-1952 are airmail. #1951 contains one 50x40mm stamp. #1952 one 50x35mm stamp.

1980 Winter Olympics, Lake Placid A339

No. 1953: a, 3g, Thomas Wassberg, Sweden, cross country skiing. b, 4g, Scharer & Benz, Switzerland, 2-man bobsled. c, 5g, Annemarie Moser-Proll, Austria, women's downhill skiing. d, 6g, Hockey team, US. e, 7g, Leonhard Stock, Austria, men's downhill skiing. f, 8g, Anton (Toni) Innauer, Austria, ski jump. g, 20g, Christa Kinshofer, Germany, slalom skiing.

10g, Ingemar Stenmark, slalom, Sweden. No. 1955, Robin Cousins, figure skating, Great Britain. No. 1956, Eric Heiden, speed skating, US, horiz.

**1980, June 4 *Perf. 14***

| | | | | |
|---|---|---|---|---|
| **1953** | A339 | Strip of 7, #a.-g. | 5.25 | 3.00 |
| **1954** | A339 | 10g multi, horiz. | 1.10 | .60 |
| **1955** | A339 | 25g multi, horiz. | 3.50 | 1.40 |
| | | *Nos. 1953-1955 (3)* | 9.85 | 5.00 |

**Souvenir Sheet**

***Perf. 13½***

| | | | | |
|---|---|---|---|---|
| **1956** | A339 | 25g multicolored | 17.50 | 17.50 |

Nos. 1954-1956 are airmail. No. 1956 contains one 60x49mm stamp.

Composers and Paintings of Young Ballerinas A340

Paintings of ballerinas by Cydney or Degas and: No. 1957a, 3g, Gioacchino Rossini. b, 4g, Johann Strauss, the younger. c, 5g, Debussy. d, 6g, Beethoven. e, 7g, Chopin. f, 8g, Richard Wagner. g, 20g, Johann Sebastian Bach, horiz. 10g, Robert Stoltz. 25g, Verdi.

**1980, July 1 *Perf. 14***

| | | | | |
|---|---|---|---|---|
| **1957** | A340 | Strip of 7, #a.-g. | 4.75 | 2.50 |
| **1958** | A340 | 10g multicolored | 1.10 | .60 |
| **1959** | A340 | 25g multicolored | 3.25 | 1.40 |
| | | *Nos. 1957-1959 (3)* | 9.10 | 4.50 |

Birth and death dates are incorrectly inscribed on 4g, 8g, 10g. No. 1957f is incorrectly inscribed "Adolph" Wagner. Nos. 1958-1959 are airmail. For overprints see Nos. 1998-1999.

Pilar City Bicentennial — A341

***Perf. 13½x13***

**1980, July 17 Litho. Wmk. 347**

| | | | | |
|---|---|---|---|---|
| **1966** | A341 | 5g multi | 5.00 | 2.00 |
| **1967** | A341 | 25g multi | 5.00 | 2.00 |

No. 1967 is airmail.

Christmas, Intl. Year of the Child A342

No. 1968: a, 3g, Christmas tree. b, 4g, Santa filling stockings. c, 5g, Nativity scene. d, 6g, Adoration of the Magi. e, 7g, Three children, presents. f, 8g, Children, dove, fruit. g, 20g, Children playing with toys. 10g, Madonna and Child, horiz. No. 1970, Children blowing bubbles, horiz. No. 1971, Five children, horiz.

**1980, Aug. 4 Unwmk. *Perf. 14***

| | | | | |
|---|---|---|---|---|
| **1968** | A342 | Strip of 7, #a.-g. | 4.25 | 2.00 |
| **1969** | A342 | 10g multicolored | .65 | .25 |
| **1970** | A342 | 25g multicolored | 1.20 | .55 |
| | | *Nos. 1968-1970 (3)* | 6.10 | 2.80 |

**Souvenir Sheet**

| | | | | |
|---|---|---|---|---|
| **1971** | A342 | 25g multicolored | 17.50 | 17.50 |

Nos. 1969-1970 are airmail.

Ships A343

Emblems and ships: No. 1972a, 3g, ESPAMER '80, Spanish Armada. b, 4g, NORWEX '80, Viking longboat. c, 5g, RICCIONE '80, Battle of Lepanto. d, 6g, ESSEN '80, Great Harry of Cruickshank. e, 7g, US Bicentennial, Mount Vernon. f, 8g, LONDON '80, H.M.S. Victory. g, 20g, ESSEN '80, Hamburg III, vert. 10g, ESSEN '80, Gorch Fock. 25g, vert. PHILATOKYO '81, Nippon Maru, horiz.

**1980, Sept. 15 *Perf. 14***

| | | | | |
|---|---|---|---|---|
| **1972** | A343 | Strip of 7, #a.-g. | 4.75 | 2.25 |
| **1973** | A343 | 10g multicolored | 1.20 | .55 |
| **1974** | A343 | 25g multicolored | 3.25 | 1.40 |
| | | *Nos. 1972-1974 (3)* | 9.20 | 4.20 |

Nos. 1973-1974 are airmail. For overprint see No. 2278.

Souvenir Sheet

King Juan Carlos — A344

**1980, Sept. 19 *Perf. 14½***

| | | | | |
|---|---|---|---|---|
| **1975** | A344 | 25g multicolored | 15.00 | 15.00 |

Paraguay Airlines Boeing 707 Service Inauguration — A345

***Perf. 13½x13***

**1980, Sept. 17 Litho. Wmk. 347**

| | | | | |
|---|---|---|---|---|
| **1976** | A345 | 20g multi | 2.50 | 1.50 |
| **1977** | A345 | 100g multi | 2.50 | 1.50 |

No. 1977 is airmail.

A346

World Cup Soccer Championships, Spain — A346a

Various soccer players, winning country: No. 1978a, 3g, Uruguay 1930, 1950. b, 4g, Italy 1934, 1938. c, 5g, Germany 1954, 1974. d, 6g, Brazil 1958, 1962, 1970. e, 7g, England, 1966. f, 8g, Argentina, 1978. g, 20g, Espana '82 emblem.

10g, World Cup trophy, flags. 25g, Soccer player from Uruguay.

**1980, Dec. 10 Unwmk. *Perf. 14***

| | | | | |
|---|---|---|---|---|
| **1978** | A346 | Strip of 7, #a.-g. | 5.25 | 1.75 |
| **1979** | A346 | 10g multicolored | 1.60 | .50 |
| **1980** | A346 | 25g multicolored | 5.25 | 1.75 |
| | | *Nos. 1978-1980 (3)* | 12.10 | 4.00 |

**Souvenir Sheet**

***Perf. 14½***

| | | | | |
|---|---|---|---|---|
| **1981** | A346a | 25g Sheet of 1 + 2 labels | 19.00 | 19.00 |

Nos. 1979-1981 are airmail.

1980 World Chess Championships, Mexico — A347

Illustrations from The Book of Chess: No. 1982a, 3g, Two men, chess board. b, 4g, Circular chess board, players. c, 5g, Four-person chess match. d, 6g, King Alfonso X of Castile and Leon. e, 7g, Two players, chess board, horiz. f, 8g, Two veiled women, chess board, horiz. g, 20g, Two women in robes, chess board, horiz.

10g, Crusader knights, chess board, horiz. 25g, Three players, chess board, horiz.

**1980, Dec. 15 Litho. *Perf. 14***

| | | | | |
|---|---|---|---|---|
| **1982** | A347 | Strip of 7, #a.-g. | 9.50 | 2.50 |
| **1983** | A347 | 10g multicolored | 1.75 | .35 |
| **1984** | A347 | 25g multicolored | 2.10 | .70 |
| | | *Nos. 1982-1984 (3)* | 13.35 | 3.55 |

Nos. 1983-1984 are airmail.

See Nos. C506-C510. Compare with illustration AP199.

1980 Winter Olympics, Lake Placid A348

Olympic scenes, gold medalists: No. 1985a, 25c, Lighting Olympic flame. b, 50c, Hockey team, US. c, 1g, Eric Heiden, US, speed skating. d, 2g, Robin Cousins, Great Britain, figure skating. e, 3g, Thomas Wassberg, Sweden, cross country skiing. f, 4g, Annie Borckinck, Netherlands, speed skating. g, 5g, Gold, silver, and bronze medals.

No. 1986, Irene Epple, silver medal, slalom, Germany. 10g, Ingemar Stenmark, slalom, giant slalom, Sweden. 30g, Annemarie Moser-Proll, downhill, Austria. 25g, Baron Pierre de Coubertin.

**1981, Feb. 4 Litho. *Perf. 14***

| | | | | |
|---|---|---|---|---|
| **1985** | A348 | Strip of 7, #a.-g. | 3.00 | 1.90 |
| **1986** | A348 | 5g multicolored | .80 | .35 |
| **1987** | A348 | 10g multicolored | 1.10 | .50 |
| **1988** | A348 | 30g multicolored | 2.40 | 1.00 |
| | | *Nos. 1985-1988 (4)* | 7.30 | 3.75 |

**Souvenir Sheet**

***Perf. 13½***

| | | | | |
|---|---|---|---|---|
| **1988A** | A348 | 25g multicolored | 16.00 | 16.00 |

No. 1985 exists in strips of 4 and 3. Nos. 1986-1988A are airmail. No. 1988A contains one 30x40mm stamp.

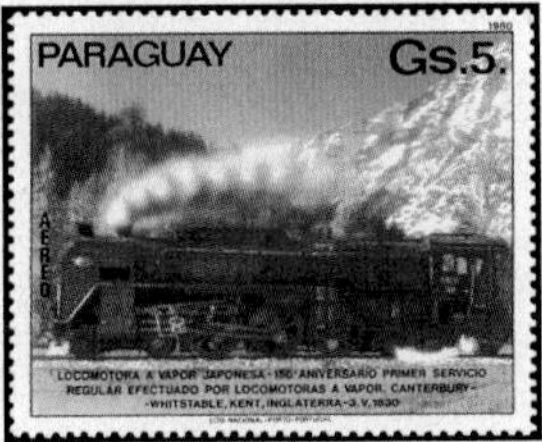


Locomotives — A349

No. 1989, 25c, Electric model 242, Germany. b, 50c, Electric, London-Midlands-Lancashire, England. c, 1g, Electric, Switzerland. d, 2g, Diesel-electric, Montreal-Vancouver, Canada. e, 3g, Electric, Austria. f, 4g, Electric inter-urban, Lyons-St. Etienne, France, vert. g, 5g, First steam locomotive in Paraguay.

No. 1991, Steam locomotive, Japan. 10g, Stephenson's steam engine, 1830 England. No. 1993, Crocodile locomotive, Switzerland. 30g, Stephenson's Rocket, 1829, England, vert.

**1981, Feb. 9 Litho. *Perf. 14***

| | | | | |
|---|---|---|---|---|
| **1989** | A349 | Strip of 7, #a.-g. | 2.10 | 1.10 |
| **1990** | A349 | 5g multicolored | 1.00 | .35 |
| **1991** | A349 | 10g multicolored | 1.75 | .65 |
| **1992** | A349 | 30g multicolored | 5.50 | 2.00 |
| | | *Nos. 1989-1992 (4)* | 10.35 | 4.10 |

**Souvenir Sheet**

***Perf. 13½x13***

| | | | | |
|---|---|---|---|---|
| **1993** | A349 | 25g multicolored | 25.00 | 25.00 |

Electric railroads, cent. (#1989a-1989f), steam-powered railway service, 150th anniv. (#1989g, 1990-1991), Liverpool-Manchester Railway, 150th anniv. (#1992). Swiss Railways, 75th anniv. (#1993).

Nos. 1990-1993 are airmail. No. 1993 contains one 54x34mm stamp.

Intl. Year of the Child A350

Portraits of children with assorted flowers: No. 1994a, 10g. b, 25g. c, 50g. d, 100g. e, 200g. f, 300g. g, 400g.

**1981, Apr. 13 Litho. *Perf. 14***

| | | | | |
|---|---|---|---|---|
| **1994** | A350 | Strip of 7, #a.-g. | 16.00 | 8.25 |
| **1995** | A350 | 75g multicolored | 1.50 | .70 |
| **1996** | A350 | 500g multicolored | 8.00 | 4.00 |
| **1997** | A350 | 1000g multicolored | 16.00 | 8.00 |
| | | *Nos. 1994-1997 (4)* | 41.50 | 20.95 |

Nos. 1995-1997 are airmail.

**Nos. 1957b and 1958 Overprinted in Red**

**1981, May 22**

| | | | | |
|---|---|---|---|---|
| **1998** | A340 | 4g on #1957b | 1.00 | .60 |
| **1999** | A340 | 10g on #1958 | 2.00 | 1.00 |

No. 1999 is airmail.

The following stamps were issued in sheets of 8 with 1 label: Nos. 2001, 2013, 2037, 2044, 2047, 2055, 2140.

The following stamp was issued in sheets of 10 with 2 labels: No. 1994a.

The following stamps were issued in sheets of 6 with 3 labels: Nos. 2017, 2029, 2035, 2104, 2145.

The following stamps were issued in sheets of 3 with 6 labels: 2079, 2143.

The following stamps were issued in sheets of 5 with 4 labels: Nos. 2050-2051, 2057, 2059, 2061, 2067, 2069, 2077, 2082, 2089, 2092, 2107, 2117, 2120, 2121, 2123, 2125, 2129, 2135, 2138, 2142, 2146, 2148, 2151, 2160, 2163, 2165, 2169, 2172, 2176, 2179, 2182, 2190, 2196, 2202, 2204, 2214, 2222, 2224, 2232, 2244, 2246, 2248, 2261, 2263, 2265, 2271, 2273, 2275, 2277.

The following stamps were issued in sheets of 4 with 5 labels: Nos. 2307, 2310, 2313, 2316, 2324, 2329.

Royal Wedding of Prince Charles and Lady Diana Spencer — A351

Prince Charles, sailing ships: No. 2000a, 25c, Royal George. b, 50c, Great Britain. c, 1g, Taeping. d, 2g, Star of India. e, 3g, Torrens. f, 4g, Loch Etive. No. 2001, Medway.

No. 2002, Charles, flags, and Concorde. 10g, Flags, flowers, Diana, Charles. 25g, Charles, Diana, flowers, vert. 30g, Coats of arms, flags.

**1981, June 27**

| | | | | |
|---|---|---|---|---|
| **2000** | A351 | Strip of 6, #a.-f. | 4.25 | 1.40 |
| **2001** | A351 | 5g multicolored | 1.40 | .35 |
| **2002** | A351 | 5g multicolored | .85 | .45 |
| **2003** | A351 | 10g multicolored | 2.75 | .75 |
| **2004** | A351 | 30g multicolored | 4.50 | 2.25 |
| | | *Nos. 2000-2004 (5)* | 13.75 | 5.20 |

**Souvenir Sheet**

***Perf. 13½***

| | | | | |
|---|---|---|---|---|
| **2005** | A351 | 25g multicolored | 17.50 | 17.50 |

Nos. 2002-2005 are airmail. No. 2005 contains one 50x60mm stamp. For overprint see No. 2253.

No. 2005 has an orange margin. It also exists with gray margin. Same value.

Traditional Costumes and Itaipu Dam A352

Women in various traditional costumes: a, 10g. b, 25g. c, 50g. d, 100g. e, 200g. f, 300g. g, 400g, President Stroessner, Itaipu Dam.

**1981, June 30 *Perf. 14***

| | | | | |
|---|---|---|---|---|
| **2006** | A352 | Strip of 7, #a.-g. | 25.00 | 8.00 |

For overprints see No. 2281.

UPU Membership Centenary — A353

**1981, Aug. 18 Litho. *Perf. 13½x13***

| | | | | |
|---|---|---|---|---|
| **2007** | A353 | 5g rose lake & blk | 2.00 | 1.00 |
| **2008** | A353 | 10g lil & blk | 2.00 | 1.00 |
| **2009** | A353 | 20g grn & blk | 2.00 | 1.00 |
| **2010** | A353 | 25g lt red brn & blk | 2.00 | 1.00 |
| **2011** | A353 | 50g bl & blk | 3.00 | 2.00 |
| | | *Nos. 2007-2011 (5)* | 11.00 | 6.00 |

Peter Paul Rubens, Paintings A354

Details from paintings: No. 2012: a, 25c, Madonna Surrounded by Saints. b, 50c, Judgment of Paris. c, 1g, Duke of Buckingham Conducted to the Temple of Virtus. d, 2g, Minerva Protecting Peace from Mars. e, 3g, Henry IV Receiving the Portrait of Marie de Medici. f, 4g, Triumph of Juliers. 5g, Madonna and Child Reigning Among Saints (Cherubs).

**1981, July 9 Litho. *Perf. 14***

| | | | | |
|---|---|---|---|---|
| **2012** | A354 | Strip of 6, #a.-f. | 2.25 | .75 |
| **2013** | A354 | 5g multicolored | .65 | .25 |
| | | *Nos. 2012-2013 (2)* | 2.90 | 1.00 |

Jean Auguste-Dominique Ingres (1780-1867), Painter — A355

Details from paintings: No. 2014: a, 25c, c, 1g, d, 2g, f, 4g, The Turkish Bath. b, 50c, The Water Pitcher. e, 3g, Oedipus and the Sphinx. g, 5g, The Bathing Beauty.

**1981, Oct. 13**

| | | | | |
|---|---|---|---|---|
| **2014** | A355 | Strip of 7, #a.-g. | 2.50 | 1.50 |

A horiz. strip of 5 containing Nos. 2014a-2014e exists.

No. 2014f and 2014g exist in sheet of 8 (four each) plus label.

For overprints see No. 2045.

Pablo Picasso, Birth Cent. — A356

Designs: No. 2015: a, 25c, Women Running on the Beach. b, 50c, Family on the Beach.

No. 2016: a, 1g, Still-life. b, 2g, Bullfighter. c, 3g, Children Drawing. d, 4g, Seated Woman. 5g, Paul as Clown.

**1981, Oct. 19**

| | | | | |
|---|---|---|---|---|
| **2015** | A356 | Pair, #a.-b. | .50 | .50 |
| **2016** | A356 | Strip of 4, #a.-d. | 5.00 | 1.50 |
| **2017** | A356 | 5g multicolored | 1.25 | .40 |
| | | *Nos. 2015-2017 (3)* | 6.75 | 2.40 |

**Nos. 2015-2016 Ovptd. in Silver**

**1981, Oct. 22**

| | | | | |
|---|---|---|---|---|
| **2018** | A356 | on #2015a-2015b | .50 | .50 |
| **2019** | A356 | on #2016a-2016d | 1.90 | 1.00 |
| | | *Nos. 2018-2019 (2)* | 2.40 | 1.50 |

Philatelia '81, Frankfurt.

**Nos. 2015-2016 Ovptd. in Gold**

**1981, Oct. 25**

| | | | | |
|---|---|---|---|---|
| **2020** | A356 | on #2015a-2015b | .50 | .50 |
| **2021** | A356 | on #2016a-2016d | 1.90 | 1.00 |
| | | *Nos. 2020-2021 (2)* | 2.40 | 1.50 |

Espamer '81 Philatelic Exhibition.

Royal Wedding of Prince Charles and Lady Diana A357

Designs: No. 2022a-2022c, 25c, 50c, 1g, Diana, Charles, flowers. d, 2g, Couple. e, 3g, Couple leaving church. f, 4g, Couple, Queen Elizabeth II waving from balcony. 2022G, 5g, Diana. No. 2023, Wedding party, horiz. 10g, Riding in royal coach, horiz. 30g, Yeomen of the guard, horiz.

**1981, Dec. 4 Litho. *Perf. 14***

| | | | | |
|---|---|---|---|---|
| **2022** | A357 | Strip of 6, #a.-f. | 1.50 | 1.50 |
| **2022G** | A357 | 5g multicolored | .25 | .25 |
| **2023** | A357 | 5g multicolored | 2.25 | .70 |
| **2024** | A357 | 10g multicolored | 4.25 | 1.40 |
| **2025** | A357 | 30g multicolored | 13.00 | 4.50 |
| | | *Nos. 2022-2025 (5)* | 21.25 | 8.35 |

### Souvenir Sheets

***Perf. 14½***

**2026** A357 25g like #2022d 30.00 30.00
**2027** A357 25g Wedding portrait 30.00 30.00

No. 2022g exists in sheets of 8 plus label. Nos. 2023-2027 are airmail. Nos. 2026-2027 contain one each 50x70mm stamp.

Christmas A358

Designs: No. 2028a, 25c, Jack-in-the-box. b, 50c, Jesus and angel. c, 1g, Santa, angels. d, 2g, Angels lighting candle. e, 3g, Christmas plant. f, 4g, Nativity scene. 5g, Children singing by Christmas tree.

**1981, Dec. 17** ***Perf. 14***
**2028** A358 Strip of 6, #a.-f. 4.00 1.00

**Size: 28x45mm**

***Perf. 13½***

**2029** A358 5g multicolored 2.00 .55

Intl. Year of the Child (Nos. 2028-2029). For overprints see No. 2042.

Intl. Year of the Child A359

Story of Puss 'n Boots: No. 2030a, 25c, Boy, Puss. b, 50c, Puss, rabbits.
1g, Puss, king. 2g, Prince, princess, king. 3g, Giant ogre, Puss. 4g, Puss chasing mouse. 5g, Princess, prince, Puss.

**1982, Apr. 16** **Litho.** ***Perf. 14***
**2030** A359 Pair, #a.-b. .50 .50
**2031** A359 1g multicolored .25 .25
**2032** A359 2g multicolored .50 .25
**2033** A359 3g multicolored .70 .25
**2034** A359 4g multicolored 1.20 .25
**2035** A359 5g multicolored 4.50 1.50
*Nos. 2030-2035 (6)* 7.65 3.00

Nos. 2031-2034 printed se-tenant with label.

Scouting, 75th Anniv. and Lord Baden-Powell, 125th Birth Anniv. — A360

No. 2036: a, 25c, Tetradactyla, Scout hand salute. b, 50c, Nandu (rhea), Cub Scout and trefoil. c, 1g, Peccary, Wolf's head totem. d, 2g, Coatimundi, emblem on buckle. e, 3g, Mara, Scouting's Intl. Communications emblem. f, 4g, Deer, boy scout.
No. 2037, Aotes, Den mother, Cub Scout. No. 2038, Ocelot, scouts cooking. 10g, Collie, boy scout. 30g, Armadillo, two scouts planting tree. 25g, Lord Robert Baden-Powell, founder of Boy Scouts.

**1982, Apr. 21**
**2036** A360 Strip of 6, #a.-f. 1.75 1.00
**2037** A360 5g multicolored 1.40 .40
**2038** A360 5g multicolored 1.40 .40
**2039** A360 10g multicolored 2.00 .45
**2040** A360 30g multicolored 2.50 .40
*Nos. 2036-2040 (5)* 9.05 2.65

### Souvenir Sheet

***Perf. 14½***

**2041** A360 25g multicolored 12.50 12.50

Nos. 2038-2041 are airmail. For overprint see No. 2140.

### No. 2028 Overprinted with ESSEN 82 Emblem

**1982, Apr. 28** ***Perf. 14***
**2042** A358 on #2028a-2028f 2.50 1.75

Essen '82 Intl. Philatelic Exhibition.

Cats and Kittens — A361

Various cats or kittens: No. 2043a, 25c. b, 50c. c, 1g. d, 2g. e, 3g. f, 4g.

**1982, June 7** ***Perf. 14***
**2043** A361 Strip of 6, #a.-f. 2.00 1.00
**2044** A361 5g multi, vert. .75 .35
*Nos. 2043-2044 (2)* 2.75 1.35

For overprints see Nos. 2054-2055.

### Nos. 2014a-2014e Ovptd. PHILEXFRANCE 82 Emblem ans "PARIS 11-21.6.82" in Blue

**1982, June 11**
**2045** A355 Strip of 5, #a.-e. 2.00 1.00

Philexfrance '82 Intl. Philatelic Exhibition. Size of overprint varies.

World Cup Soccer Championships, Spain — A362

Designs: 2046a, 25c, Brazilian team. b, 50c, Chilean team. c, 1g, Honduran team. d, 2g, Peruvian team. e, 3g, Salvadoran team. f, 4g, Globe as soccer ball, flags of Latin American finalists. No. 2047, Ball of flags. No. 2048, Austrian team. No. 2049, Players from Brazil, Austria. No. 2050, Spanish team. No. 2051, Two players from Argentina, Brazil, vert. No. 2052, W. German team. No. 2053, Players from Argentina, Brazil. No. 2053A, World Cup trophy, world map on soccer balls. No. 2053B, Players from W. Germany, Mexico, vert.

**1982** **Litho.** ***Perf. 14***
**2046** A362 Strip of 6, #a.-f. 3.75 1.25
**2047** A362 5g multicolored .35 .25
**2048** A362 5g multicolored 1.95 1.40
**2049** A362 5g multicolored 3.25 1.00
**2050** A362 10g multicolored .90 .25
**2051** A362 10g multicolored .50 .50
**2052** A362 30g multicolored 2.25 .25
**2053** A362 30g multicolored .25 .25
*Nos. 2046-2053 (8)* 13.20 5.15

### Souvenir Sheets

***Perf. 14½***

**2053A** A362 25g multicolored 14.00 14.00
**2053B** A362 25g multicolored 14.00 14.00

Issued: #2049, 2051, 2053, 2053A, 4/19; others, 6/13.
Nos. 2047 exists in sheets of 8 plus label. Nos. 2048-2053B are airmail.
For overprints see Nos. 2086, 2286, C593.

### Nos. 2043-2044 Overprinted in Silver With PHILATECIA 82 and Intl. Year of the Child Emblems

**1982, Sept. 12** ***Perf. 14***
**2054** A361 Strip of 5, #a.-e. 2.25 1.25
**2055** A361 5g on #2044 .90 .40
*Nos. 2054-2055 (2)* 3.15 1.65

Philatelia '82, Hanover, Germany and Intl. Year of the Child.

Raphael, 500th Birth Anniv. A363

Details from paintings: No. 2056a, 25c, Adam and Eve (The Fall). b, 50c, Creation of Eve. c, 1g, Portrait of a Young Woman (La Fornarina). d, 2g The Three Graces. e, 3g, f, 4g, Cupid and the Three Graces. 5g. Leda and the Swan.

**1982, Sept. 27**
**2056** A363 Strip of 6, #a.-f. 4.00 1.50
**2057** A363 5g multicolored 3.00 1.00
*Nos. 2056-2057 (2)* 7.00 2.50

Nos. 2056e-2056f have continuous design.

Christmas A364

Entire works or details from paintings by Raphael: No. 2058a, 25c, The Belvedere Madonna. b, 50c, The Ansidei Madonna. c, 1g, La Belle Jardiniere. d, 2g, The Aldobrandini (Garvagh) Madonna. e, 3g, Madonna of the Goldfinch. f, 4g, The Alba Madonna. No. 2059, Madonna of the Grand Duke. No. 2060, Madonna of the Linen Window. 10g, The Alba Madonna, diff. 25g, The Holy Family with St. Elizabeth and the Infant St. John and Two Angels. 30g, The Canigiani Holy Family.

**1982** ***Perf. 14, 13x13½ (#2061)***
**2058** A364 Strip of 6, #a.-f. 3.50 1.50
**2059** A364 5g multicolored 1.40 .50
**2060** A364 5g multicolored 3.25 1.00
**2061** A364 10g multicolored 1.50 .50
**2062** A364 30g multicolored .75 .25
*Nos. 2058-2062 (5)* 10.40 3.75

### Souvenir Sheet

***Perf. 14½***

**2063** A364 25g multicolored 15.00 15.00

Issued: #2058-2059, 9/30; others, 12/17.
Nos. 2058a-2058f and 2059 exist perf. 13. Nos. 2060-2063 are airmail and have silver lettering. For overprint see No. 2087.

Life of Christ, by Albrecht Durer A365

Details from paintings: No. 2064a, 25c, The Flight into Egypt. b, 50c, Christ Among the Doctors. c, 1g, Christ Carrying the Cross. d, 2g, Nailing of Christ to the Cross. e, 3g, Christ on the Cross. f, 4g, Lamentation Over the Dead Christ. 5g, The Circumcision of Christ.

**1982, Dec. 14** ***Perf. 14***
**2064** A365 Strip of 6, #a.-f. 5.50 2.75

***Perf. 13x13½***

**2065** A365 5g multicolored 2.50 .75
*Nos. 2064-2065 (2)* 8.00 3.50

For overprint see No. 2094.

South American Locomotives — A366

Locomotives from: No. 2066a, 25c, Argentina. b, 50c, Uruguay. c, 1g, Ecuador. d, 2g, Bolivia. e, 3g, Peru. f, 4g, Brazil. 5g, Paraguay.

**1983, Jan. 17** **Litho.** ***Perf. 14***
**2066** A366 Strip of 6, #a.-f. 2.50 1.00
**2067** A366 5g multicolored 2.00 .75
*Nos. 2066-2067 (2)* 4.50 1.75

For overprint see No. 2093.

Race Cars A367

No. 2068: a, 25c, ATS-Ford D 06. b, 50c, Ferrari 126 C 2. c, 1g, Brabham-BMW BT 50. d, 2g, Renault RE 30 B. e, 3g, Porsche 956. f, 4g, Talbot-Ligier-Matra JS 19. 5g, Mercedes Benz C-111.

**1983, Jan. 19** ***Perf. 14***
**2068** A367 Strip of 6, #a.-f. 3.25 1.00

***Perf. 13½x13***

**2069** A367 5g multicolored 1.50 .50
*Nos. 2068-2069 (2)* 4.75 1.50

For overprint see No. 2118.

Itaipua Dam, Pres. Stroessner — A368

**1983, Jan. 22** **Litho.** **Wmk. 347**
**2070** A368 3g multi 2.00 1.00
**2071** A368 5g multi 2.00 1.00
**2072** A368 10g multi 2.00 1.00
**2073** A368 20g multi 2.00 1.00
**2074** A368 25g multi 2.00 1.00
**2075** A368 50g multi 2.00 1.00
*Nos. 2070-2075 (6)* 12.00 6.00

25th anniv. of Stroessner City. Nos. 2073-2075 airmail.

1984 Winter Olympics, Sarajevo — A369

Ice skaters: No. 2076a, 25c, Marika Kilius, Hans-Jurgens Baumler, Germany, 1964. b, 50c, Tai Babilonia, Randy Gardner, US, 1976. c, 1g, Anett Poetzsch, E. Germany, 1980, vert. d, 2g, Tina Riegel, Andreas Nischwitz, Germany, 1980, vert. e, Dagmar Lurz, Germany, 1980, vert. f, 4g, Trixi Schuba, Austria, 1972, vert. 5g, Peggy Fleming, US, 1968, vert.

*Perf. 13½x13, 13x13½*

**1983, Feb. 23** **Unwmk.**
**2076** A369 Strip of 6, #a.-f. 1.40 1.00
**2077** A369 5g multicolored 2.10 .75
*Nos. 2076-2077 (2)* 3.50 1.75

For overprints see Nos. 2177, 2266.

Pope John Paul II A370

#2078: a, 25c, Virgin of Caacupe. b, 50c, Cathedral of Caacupe. c, 1g, Cathedral of Asuncion. d, 2g, Pope holding crucifix. e, 3g, Our Lady of the Assumption. f, 4g, Pope giving blessing. 5g, Pope with hands clasped. 25g, Madonna & child.

**1983, June 11** **Litho.** ***Perf. 14***
**2078** A370 Strip of 6, #a.-f. 3.75 2.00
**2079** A370 5g multicolored 1.75 .80
*Nos. 2078-2079 (2)* 5.50 2.80

**Souvenir Sheet**

***Perf. 14½***

**2080** A370 25g multicolored 14.00 14.00

No. 2080 is airmail. For overprint see No. 2143.

Antique Automobiles — A371

No. 2081: a, 25c, Bordino Steamcoach, 1854. b, 50c, Panhard & Levassor, 1892. c, 1g, Benz Velo, 1894. d, 2g, Peugeot-Daimler, 1894. e, 3g, 1st car with patented Lutzmann system, 1898. f, 4g, Benz Victory, 1891-92. No. 2082, Ceirano 5CV. No. 2083, Mercedes Simplex PS 32 Turismo, 1902. 10g, Stae Electric, 1909. 25g, Benz Velocipede, 1885. 30g, Rolls Royce Silver Ghost, 1913.

**1983, July 18** ***Perf. 14***
**2081** A371 Strip of 6, #a.-f. 1.75 1.25
**2082** A371 5g multicolored 1.10 .40
**2083** A371 5g multicolored 4.00 1.10
**2084** A371 10g multicolored .75 .25
**2085** A371 30g multicolored 1.50 .25
*Nos. 2081-2085 (5)* 9.10 3.25

**Souvenir Sheet**

***Perf. 14½***

**2085A** A371 25g Sheet of 1 + label 14.00 14.00

Nos. 2083-2085A are airmail.

**No. 2046 Ovptd. in Red, No. 2058 Ovptd. in Black with "52o CONGRESO F.I.P." and Brasiliana 83 Emblem**

**1983, July 27** ***Perf. 14***
**2086** A362 Strip of 6, #a.-f. 5.00 5.00
**2087** A364 Strip of 6, #a.-f. 5.00 5.00

Brasiliana '83, Rio de Janiero and 52nd FIP Congress. No. 2087 exists perf. 13.

Aircraft Carriers — A372

Carriers and airplanes: No. 2088a, 25c, 25 de Mayo, A-4Q Sky Hawk, Argentina. b, 50c, Minas Gerais, Brazil. c, 1g, Akagi, A6M3 Zero, Japan. d, 2g, Guiseppe Miraglia, Italy. e, 3g, Enterprise, S-3A Viking, US. f, 4g, Dedalo, AV-8A Matador, Spain. No. 2089, 5g, Schwabenland, Dornier DO-18, Germany.
No aircraft on Nos. 2088b, 2088d.
25g, US astronauts Donn Eisele, Walter Schirra & Walt Cunningham, Earth & Apollo 7.

**1983, Aug. 29** ***Perf. 14***
**2088** A372 Strip of 6, #a.-f. 3.50 1.50
**2089** A372 5g multicolored 1.50 .75
*Nos. 2088-2089 (2)* 5.00 2.25

**Souvenir Sheet**

***Perf. 13½***

**2090** A372 25g multicolored 15.00 15.00

No. 2090 is airmail and contains one 55x45mm stamp.

Birds A373

#2091: a, 25c, Pulsatrix perspicillata. b, 50c, Ortalis ruficauda. c, 1g, Chloroceryle amazona. d, 2g, Trogon violaceus. e, 3g, Pezites militaris. f, 4g, Bucco capensis. 5g, Cyanerpes cyaneus.

**1983, Oct. 22** ***Perf. 14***
**2091** A373 Strip of 6, #a.-f. 4.25 1.00

***Perf. 13***

**2092** A373 5g multicolored 1.75 .40
*Nos. 2091-2092 (2)* 6.00 1.40

**No. 2066 Ovptd. for PHILATELICA 83 in Silver**

**1983, Oct. 28**
**2093** A366 Strip of 6, #a.-f. 3.00 2.00

Philatelia '83, Dusseldorf, Germany.

**No. 2064 Overprinted in Silver for EXFIVIA - 83**

**1983, Nov. 5**
**2094** A365 Strip of 6, #a.-f. 4.50 2.00

Exfivia '83 Philatelic Exhibition, La Paz, Bolivia.

Re-election of President Stroessner — A374

10g, Passion flower, vert. 25g, Miltonia phalaenopsis, vert. 50g, Natl. arms, Chaco soldier. 75g, Acaray hydroelectric dam. 100g, Itaipu hydroelectric dam. 200g, Pres. Alfredo Stroessner, vert.

**1983, Nov. 24** ***Perf. 14***
**2095** A374 10g multicolored .25 .25
**2096** A374 25g multicolored .40 .25
**2097** A374 50g multicolored .80 .25
**2098** A374 75g multicolored .65 .25

***Perf. 13***

**2099** A374 100g multicolored .80 .25
**2100** A374 200g multicolored 1.60 .80
*Nos. 2095-2100 (6)* 4.50 2.05

Nos. 2099-2100 are airmail. No. 2096 exists perf 13. For overprint see No. C577.

Montgolfier Brothers' 1st Flight, Bicent. — A375

No. 2101: a, 25c, Santos-Dumont's Biplane, 1906. b, 50c, Airship. c, 1g, Paulhan's biplane over Juvisy. d, 2g, Zeppelin LZ-3, 1907. e, 3g, Biplane of Henri Farman. f, 4g, Graf Zeppelin over Friedrichshafen. 5g, Lebaudy's dirigible. 25g, Detail of painting, Great Week of Aviation at Betheny, 1910.

**1984, Jan. 7** ***Perf. 13***
**2101** A375 Strip of 6, #a.-f. 2.25 1.25

***Perf. 14***

**2104** A375 5g multicolored 3.75 .75
*Nos. 2101-2104 (2)* 6.00 2.00

**Souvenir Sheet**

***Perf. 13½***

**2105** A375 25g multicolored 15.00 15.00

No. 2105 is airmail and contains one 75x55mm stamp. For overprint see No. 2145.

Dogs A376

#2106: a, 25c, German Shepherd. b, 50c, Great Dane, vert. c, 1g, Poodle, vert. d, 2g, Saint Bernard. e, 3g, Greyhound. f, 4g, Dachshund. 5g, Boxer.

**1984, Jan. 11** **Litho.** ***Perf. 14***
**2106** A376 Strip of 6, #a.-f. 3.00 1.25
**2107** A376 5g multicolored 1.50 .50
*Nos. 2106-2107 (2)* 4.50 1.75

Animals, Anniversaries — A377

**1984, Jan. 24** ***Perf. 13***
**2108** A377 10g Puma .25 .25
**2109** A377 25g Alligator .65 .25
**2110** A377 50g Jaguar 1.25 .40
**2111** A377 75g Peccary 1.90 .60
**2112** A377 100g Simon Bolivar, vert. 2.90 .90
**2113** A377 200g Girl scout, vert. 5.50 1.75
*Nos. 2108-2113 (6)* 12.45 4.15

Simon Bolivar, birth bicent. and Girl Scouts of Paraguay, 76th anniv.
Nos. 2112-2113 are airmail.

Christmas A378

Designs: No. 2114a, 25c, Pope John Paul II. b, 50c, Christmas tree. c, 1g, Children. d, 2g, Nativity Scene. e, 3g, Three Kings. f, 4g, Madonna and Child. No. 2115, Madonna and Child by Raphael.

**1984, Mar. 23** ***Perf. 13x13½***
**2114** A378 Strip of 6, #a.-f. 7.50 1.50
**2115** A378 5g multicolored 3.50 1.00
*Nos. 2114-2115 (2)* 11.00 2.50

Troubadour Knights A379

Illustrations of medieval miniatures: No. 2116a, 25c, Ulrich von Liechtenstein. b, 50c, Ulrich von Gutenberg. c, 1g, Der Putter. d, 2g, Walther von Metz. e, 3g, Hartman von Aue. f, 4g, Lutok von Seuen. 5g, Werner von Teufen.

**1984, Mar. 27** ***Perf. 14***
**2116** A379 Strip of 6, #a.-f. 3.50 1.25

***Perf. 13***

**2117** A379 5g multicolored 2.00 .75
*Nos. 2116-2117 (2)* 5.50 2.00

For overprint see No. 2121.

**No. 2068 Ovptd. in Silver with ESSEN 84 Emblem**

**1984, May 10**
**2118** A367 Strip of 6, #a.-f. 2.50 1.25

Essen '84 Intl. Philatelic Exhibition.

Endangered Animals — A380

#2119: a, 25c, Priodontes giganteus. b, 50c, Catagonus wagneri. c, 1g, Felis pardalis. d, 2g, Chrysocyon brachyurus. e, 3g, Burmeisteria retusa. f, 4g, Myrmecophaga tridactyla. 5g, Caiman crocodilus.

**1984, June 16** ***Perf. 14***
**2119** A380 Strip of 6, #a.-f. 4.50 2.00

***Perf. 13***

**2120** A380 5g multicolored 2.00 .50
*Nos. 2119-2120 (2)* 6.50 2.50

A canceled-to-order perf. 13 strip of seven stamps containing Nos. 2119a-2119g and 2120 exists. For overprint see No. 2129.

**No. 2117 Ovptd. in Silver with Emblems, etc., for U.P.U. 19th World Congress, Hamburg**

**1984, June 19** ***Perf. 13***
**2121** A379 5g on #2117 2.50 1.25

UPU Congress, Hamburg '84 — A381

Sailing ships: No. 2122a, 25c, Admiral of Hamburg. b, 50c, Neptune. c, 1g, Archimedes. d, 2g, Passat. e, 3g, Finkenwerder cutter off Heligoland. f, 4g, Four-masted ship. 5g, Deutschland.

**1984, June 19** *Perf. 13*
**2122** A381 Strip of 6, #a.-f. 4.50 1.50
**2123** A381 5g multicolored 1.75 .50
*Nos. 2122-2123 (2)* 6.25 2.00

For overprints see Nos. 2146, 2279-2280.

British Locomotives — A382

No. 2124: a, 25c, Pegasus 097, 1868. b, 50c, Pegasus 097, diff. c, 1g, Cornwall, 1847. d, 2g, Cornwall, 1847, diff. e, 3g, Patrick Stirling #1, 1870. f, 4g, Patrick Stirling #1, 1870, diff. 5g, Stepney Brighton Terrier, 1872.

**1984, June 20** *Perf. 14*
**2124** A382 Strip of 6, #a.-f. 4.25 1.50
*Perf. 13*
**2125** A382 5g multicolored 1.75 .50
*Nos. 2124-2125 (2)* 6.00 2.00

**No. C486 Overprinted in Blue on Silver with UN emblem and "40o Aniversario de la / Fundacion de las / Naciones Unidas 26.6.1944"**

**1984, Aug. 1** **Litho.** *Perf. 14½*
**2126** AP161 25g on No. C486 15.00 15.00

**No. 1536 Ovptd. in Orange (#a.-d.) or Silver (#e.-g.)**

and

A383

**1984, Aug. 21** *Perf. 14*
**2127** A271 Strip of 7, #a.-g. 8.00 1.75

**Souvenir Sheet**
*Perf. 14½*
**2128** A383 25g multicolored 14.00 14.00

Ausipex '84 Intl. Philatelic Exhibition, Melbourne, Australia. No. 2128 is airmail.

**Nos. 2120 and C551 Ovptd. in Black and Red**

**1984** *Perf. 13*
**2129** A380 5g on #2120 2.00 2.00
*Perf. 14*
**2130** AP178 30g on #C551 4.00 4.00

Issued: #2129, Sept. 20; #2130, Aug. 30. No. 2130 is airmail.

**No. 1512 Ovptd. "VER STUTTGART CAMPEON NACIONAL DE FUTBOL DE ALEMANIA 1984" and Emblem**

**1984, Sept. 5** *Perf. 14*
**2131** A263 Strip of 7, #a.-g. 2.50 1.25

VFB Stuttgart, 1984 German Soccer Champions.

**Cat Type of 1976**

Various cats: No. 2132: a, 25c. b, 50c. c, 1g. d, 2g. e, 3g. f, 4g.

**1984, Sept. 10** *Perf. 13x13½*
**2132** A287 Strip of 6, #a.-f. 3.00 1.50
**2133** A287 5g multicolored 2.50 .75
*Nos. 2132-2133 (2)* 5.50 2.25

1984 Summer Olympics, Los Angeles — A384

Gold medalists: No. 2134a, 25c Michael Gross, W. Germany, swimming. b, 50c, Peter Vidmar, US, gymnastics. c, 1g, Fredy Schmidtke, W. Germany, cycling. d, 2g, Philippe Boisse, France, fencing. e, 3g, Ulrike Meyfarth, W. Germany, women's high jump. f, 4g, Games emblem. 5g, Mary Lou Retton, US, women's all-around gymnastics, vert. 30g, Rolf Milser, W. Germany, weight lifting, vert.

**1985, Jan. 16** **Litho.** *Perf. 13*
**2134** A384 Strip of 6, #a.-f. 2.00 1.25
**2135** A384 5g multicolored 3.00 .75
*Nos. 2134-2135 (2)* 5.00 2.00

**Souvenir Sheet**
*Perf. 13½*
**2136** A384 30g multicolored 15.00 15.00

No. 2136 is airmail and contains one 50x60mm stamp. For overprints see Nos. 2174, 2199, 2200. Compare with type A399.

Mushrooms A385

#2137: a, 25c, Boletus luteus. b, 50c, Agaricus campester. c, 1g, Pholiota spectabilis. d, 2g, Tricholoma terreum. e, 3g, Laccaria laccata. f, 4g, Amanita phalloides. 5g, Scleroderna verrucosum.

**1985, Jan. 19** *Perf. 14*
**2137** A385 Strip of 6, #a.-f. 9.00 3.00
**2138** A385 5g multicolored 8.00 3.00
*Nos. 2137-2138 (2)* 17.00 6.00

See Nos. 2166-2167.

World Wildlife Fund — A386

Endangered or extinct species: No. 2139a, 25c, Capybara. b, 50c, Mono titi, vert. c, 1g, Rana cornuda adornada. d, 2g, Priodontes giganteus, digging. e, 3g, Priodontes giganteus, by water. f, 4g, Myrmecophaga tridactyla. g, 5g, Myrmecophaga tridactyla, with young.

**1985, Mar. 13** *Perf. 14*
**2139** A386 Strip of 7, #a.-g. 47.50 10.00

See No. 2252.

**No. 2037 Ovptd. in Red with ISRAPHIL Emblem**

**1985, Apr. 10**
**2140** A360 5g on No. 2037 2.00 1.00

Israel '85 Intl. Philatelic Exhibition.

John James Audubon, Birth Bicent. A387

Birds: No. 2141a, 25c, Piranga flava. b, 50c, Polyborus plancus. c, 1g, Chiroxiphia caudata. d, 2g, Xolmis irupero. e, 3g, Phloeoceastes leucopogon. f, 4g, Thraupis bonariensis. 5g, Parula pitiayumi, horiz.

**1985, Apr. 18** *Perf. 13*
**2141** A387 Strip of 6, #a.-f. 3.75 1.25
**2142** A387 5g multicolored 1.75 .50
*Nos. 2141-2142 (2)* 5.50 1.75

**No. 2079 Ovptd. in Silver with Italia '85 Emblem**

**1985, May 20** *Perf. 14*
**2143** A370 5g on #2079 4.00 1.50

Italia '85 Intl. Philatelic Exhibition.

No. 1448e Ovptd. in Red on Silver

**1985, June 12**
**2144** A250 30c on #1448e 1.50 .75

**No. 2104 Ovptd. in Silver and Blue with LUPO 85 Congress Emblem**

**1985, July 5**
**2145** A375 5g on No. 2104 1.00 .50

LUPO '85, Lucerne, Switzerland.

**No. 2123 Ovptd. in Silver and Blue with MOPHILA 85 Emblem and "HAMBURGO 11-12. 9. 85"**

**1985, July 5** *Perf. 13*
**2146** A381 5g on #2123 1.00 .50

Mophila '85 Intl. Philatelic Exhibition, Hamburg.

Intl. Youth Year A388

Scenes from Tom Sawyer and Huckleberry Finn: No. 2147a, 25c, Mississippi riverboat. b, 50c, Finn. c, 1g, Finn and friends by campfire. d, 2g, Finn and Joe, sinking riverboat. e, 3g, Finn, friends, riverboat. f, 4g, Cemetery. 5g, Finn, Sawyer. 25g, Raft, riverboat.

**1985, Aug. 5** *Perf. 13½x13*
**2147** A388 Strip of 6, #a.-f. 3.50 1.50
**2148** A388 5g multicolored 3.00 .75
*Nos. 2147-2148 (2)* 6.50 2.25

**Souvenir Sheet**
*Perf. 14½*
**2149** A388 25g multicolored 12.00 12.00

No. 2149 is airmail. For overprint see No. C612.

German Railroads, 150th Anniv. — A389

Locomotives: No. 2150a, 25c, T3, 1883. b, 50c, T18, 1912. c, 1g, T16, 1914. d, 2g, #01 118, Historic Trains Society, Frankfurt. e, 3g, #05 001 Express, Nuremberg Transit Museum. f, 4g, #10 002 Express, 1957. 5g, Der Adler, 1835.

25g, Painting of 1st German Train, Dec. 7, 1835.

**1985, Aug. 8** *Perf. 14*
**2150** A389 Strip of 6, #a.-f. 4.50 1.50
*Perf. 13*
**2151** A389 5g multicolored 1.75 .50
*Nos. 2150-2151 (2)* 6.25 2.00

**Souvenir Sheet**
*Perf. 13½*
**2152** A389 25g multicolored 14.00 14.00

No. 2152 is airmail and contains one 75x53mm stamp. For overprint see No. 2165.

Development Projects — A390

Pres. Stroessner and: 10g, Soldier, map, vert. 25g, Model of Yaci Reta Hydroelectric Project. 50g, Itaipu Dam. 75g, Merchantman Lago Ipoa. 100g, 1975 Coin, vert. 200g, Asuncion Intl. Airport.

**1985, Sept. 17** **Litho.** *Perf. 13*
**2153** A390 10g multicolored .25 .25
**2154** A390 25g multicolored .25 .25
**2155** A390 50g multicolored .50 .25
**2156** A390 75g multicolored .75 .25

**2157** A390 100g multicolored 1.00 .25
**2158** A390 200g multicolored 2.00 .50
*Nos. 2153-2158 (6)* 4.75 1.75

Chaco Peace Agreement, 50th Anniv. (#2153, 2157). Nos. 2157-2158 are airmail. For overprints see Nos. 2254-2259.

Nudes by Peter Paul Rubens A391

Details from paintings: No. 2159a, 25c, b, 50c, Venus in the Forge of Vulcan. c, 1g, Cimon and Iphigenia, horiz. d, 2g, The Horrors of War. e, 3g, Apotheosis of Henry IV and the Proclamation of the Regency. f, 4g, The Reception of Marie de Medici at Marseilles. 5g, Union of Earth and Water. 25g, Nature Attended by the Three Graces.

**1985, Oct. 18** ***Perf. 14***
**2159** A391 Strip of 6, #a.-f. 4.50 1.50

***Perf. 13x13½***

**2160** A391 5g multicolored 2.00 .50
*Nos. 2159-2160 (2)* 6.50 2.00

**Souvenir Sheet**

***Perf. 14***

**2161** A391 25g multicolored 17.50 15.00

No. 2161 is airmail.

**1986, Jan. 16** ***Perf. 14***

Nudes by Titian: details from paintings. No. 2162a, 25c, Venus, an Organist, Cupid and a Little Dog. b, 50c, c, 1g, Diana and Actaeon. d, 2g, Danae. e, 3g, Nymph and a Shepherd. f, 4g, Venus of Urbino. 5g, Cupid Blindfolded by Venus, vert. 25g, Diana and Callisto, vert.

**2162** A391 Strip of 6, #a.-f. 6.00 2.00

***Perf. 13***

**2163** A391 5g multicolored 2.50 1.00
*Nos. 2162-2163 (2)* 8.50 3.00

**Souvenir Sheet**

***Perf. 13½***

**2164** A391 25g multicolored 15.00 15.00

No. 2164 is airmail and contains one 50x60mm stamp.

**Nos. 2150 Ovptd. in Red**

**1986, Feb. 25** ***Perf. 14***
**2165** A389 Strip of 6, #a.-f. 2.00 1.00

Essen '86 Intl. Philatelic Exhibition.

**Mushrooms Type of 1985**

Designs: No. 2166a, 25g, Lepiota procera. b, 50c, Tricholoma albo-brunneum. c, 1g, Clavaria. d, 2g, Volvaria. e, 3g, Licoperdon perlatum. f, 4g, Dictyophora duplicata. 5g, Polyporus rubrum.

**1986, Mar. 17** ***Perf. 14***
**2166** A385 Strip of 6, #a.-f. 6.00 1.50

***Perf. 13***

**2167** A385 5g multicolored 2.50 .50
*Nos. 2166-2167 (2)* 8.50 2.00

Automobile, Cent. — A393

No. 2168: a, 25c, Wolseley, 1904. b, 50c, Peugeot, 1892. c, 1g, Panhard, 1895. d, 2g, Cadillac, 1903. e, 3g, Fiat, 1902. f, 4g, Stanley Steamer, 1898. 5g, Carl Benz Velocipede, 1885. 25g, Carl Benz (1844-1929), automotive engineer.

**1986, Apr. 28 Litho.** ***Perf. 13½x13***
**2168** A393 Strip of 6, #a.-f. 2.75 1.50
**2169** A393 5g multicolored 3.25 1.25
*Nos. 2168-2169 (2)* 6.00 2.75

**Souvenir Sheet**

***Perf. 13½***

**2170** A393 25g multicolored 15.00 15.00

No. 2170 is airmail and contains one 30x40mm stamp.

World Cup Soccer Championships, Mexico City — A394

Various match scenes, Paraguay vs.: No. 2171a, 25c, b, 50c, US, 1930. c, 1g, d, 2g, Belgium, 1930. e, 3g, Bolivia, 1985. f, 4g, Brazil, 1985.
5g, Natl. Team, 1986. 25g, Player, vert.

**1986, Mar. 12** ***Perf. 13½x13***
**2171** A394 Strip of 6, #a.-f. 3.25 1.50
**2172** A394 5g multicolored 3.75 1.00
*Nos. 2171-2172 (2)* 7.00 2.50

**Souvenir Sheet**

***Perf. 14½***

**2173** A394 25g multicolored 15.00 15.00

No. 2173 is airmail. For overprints see Nos. 2283, 2287.

**No. 2135 Ovptd. in Silver "JUEGOS / PANAMERICANOS / INDIANAPOLIS / 1987"**

**1986, June 9** ***Perf. 13***
**2174** A384 5g on No. 2135 2.50 1.25

1987 Pan American Games, Indianapolis.

Maybach Automobiles — A395

#2175: a, 25c, W-6, 1930-36. b, 50c, SW-38 convertible. c, 1g, SW-38 hardtop, 1938. d, 2g, W-6/DSG, 1933. e, 3g, Zeppelin DS-8, 1931. f, 4g, Zeppelin DS-8, 1936. 5g, Zeppelin DS-8 aerodynamic cabriolet, 1936.

**1986, June 19** ***Perf. 13½x13***
**2175** A395 Strip of 6, #a.-f. 2.25 1.25
**2176** A395 5g multicolored 3.75 1.25
*Nos. 2175-2176 (2)* 6.00 2.50

**No. 2077 Overprinted in Bright Blue with Olympic Rings and "CALGARY 1988"**

**1986, July 9** ***Perf. 13***
**2177** A369 5g on #2077 2.50 1.25

1988 Winter Olympics, Calgary.

Statue of Liberty, Cent. — A396

Passenger liners: No. 2178a, 25c, City of Paris, England, 1867. b, 50c, Mauretania, England. c, 1g, Normandie, France, 1932. d, 2g, Queen Mary, England, 1938. e, 3g, Kaiser Wilhelm the Great II, Germany, 1897. f, 4g, United States, US, 1952. 5g, Bremen, Germany, 1928. 25g, Sailing ship Gorch Fock, Germany, 1976, vert.

**1986, July 25** ***Perf. 13***
**2178** A396 Strip of 6, #a.-f. 2.50 1.50
**2179** A396 5g multicolored 2.50 .60
*Nos. 2178-2179 (2)* 5.00 2.10

**Souvenir Sheet**

***Perf. 14½***

**2180** A396 25g multicolored 13.00 13.00

No. 2180 is airmail and contains one 50x70mm stamp.

**Dog Type of 1984**

#2181: a, 25c, German shepherd. b, 50c, Icelandic shepherd. c, 1g, Collie. d, 2g, Boxer. e, 3g, Scottish terrier. f, 4g, Welsh springer spaniel. 5g, Painting of Labrador retriever by Ellen Krebs, vert.

**1986, Aug. 28** ***Perf. 13x13½***
**2181** A376 Strip of 6, #a.-f. 2.50 1.00

***Perf. 13½x13***

**2182** A376 5g multicolored 1.50 .50
*Nos. 2181-2182 (2)* 4.00 1.50

Paraguay Official Stamps, Cent. — A397

#2183-2185, #O1. #2186-2188, #O4.

**1986, Aug. 28 Litho.** ***Perf. 13x13½***
**2183** A397 5g multi 1.50 1.50
**2184** A397 15g multi 1.50 1.50
**2185** A397 40g multi 1.50 1.50
**2186** A397 65g multi 1.50 1.50
**2187** A397 100g multi 1.50 1.50
**2188** A397 150g multi 1.50 1.50
*Nos. 2183-2188 (6)* 9.00 9.00

Nos. 2186-2188 are airmail.

Tennis Players A398

Designs: No. 2189a, Victor Pecci, Paraguay. b, 50c, Jimmy Connors, US. c, 1g, Gabriela Sabatini, Argentina. d, 2g, Boris Becker, W. Germany. e, 3g, Claudia Kohde, E. Germany. f, 4g, Sweden, 1985 Davis Cup team champions, horiz. 5g, Steffi Graf, W. Germany. 25g, 1986 Wimbledon champions Martina Navratilova and Boris Becker, horiz.

***Perf. 13x13½, 13½x13***

**1986, Sept. 17** **Unwmk.**
**2189** A398 Strip of 6, #a.-f. 3.00 1.25
**2190** A398 5g multicolored 1.50 .50
*Nos. 2189-2190 (2)* 4.50 1.75

**Souvenir Sheet**

***Perf. 13½***

**2191** A398 25g multicolored 12.00 12.00

No. 2191 is airmail and contains one 75x55mm stamp. For overprints see No. 2229.

**Nos. 1454-1456 Ovptd. in Red or Silver (#2192c, 2192d): "Homenage a la visita de Sus Altezas Imperiales los Principees Hitachi --28.9-3.10.86"**

**1986, Sept. 28** ***Perf. 14***
**2192** A251 Strip of 5, #a.-e. 1.50 1.00
**2193** A251 50c on #1455 .60 .50
**2194** A251 75c on #1456 .90 .75
*Nos. 2192-2194 (3)* 3.00 2.25

1988 Summer Olympics, Seoul A399

Athletes, 1984 Olympic medalists: No. 2195a, 25c, Runner. b, 50c, Boxer. c, 1g, Joaquim Cruz, Brazil, 800-meter run. d, 2g, Mary Lou Retton, US, individual all-around gymnastics. e, 3g, Carlos Lopes, Portugal, marathon. f, 4g, Fredy Schmidtke, W. Germany, 1000-meter cycling, horiz. 5g, Joe Fargis, US, equestrian, horiz.

**1986, Oct. 29** ***Perf. 13x13½, 13½x13***
**2195** A399 Strip of 6, #a.-f. 1.75 1.25
**2196** A399 5g multicolored 2.50 1.75
*Nos. 2195-2196 (2)* 4.25 3.00

For overprints see Nos. 2227-2228, 2230.

**Nos. 1574c-1574g Ovptd. in Silver, Ship Type of 1983 Ovptd. in Red**

**1987, Mar. 20** **Litho.** ***Perf. 14***
**2197** A278 Strip of 5, #a.-e. 3.50 3.00
**2198** AP176 10g multicolored 1.50 1.50
*Nos. 2197-2198 (2)* 5.00 4.50

500th Anniv. of the discovery of America and the 12th Spanish-American Stamp & Coin Show, Madrid.

**Olympics Type of 1985 Overprinted in Silver with Olympic Rings and 500th Anniv. of the Discovery of America Emblems and "BARCELONA 92 / Sede de las Olimpiadas en el ano del 500o Aniversario del Descubrimiento de America"**

Designs like Nos. 2134a-2134f.

**1987, Apr. 24** ***Perf. 14***
**2199** A384 Strip of 6, #a.-f. 8.00 8.00

1992 Summer Olympics, Barcelona and discovery of America, 500th anniv. in 1992.

**No. 2135 Overprinted in Silver "ROMA / OLYMPHILEX" / Olympic Rings / "SEOUL / CALGARY / 1988"**

**1987, Apr. 30** ***Perf. 13***
**2200** A384 5g on No. 2135 2.50 2.50

Olymphilex '87 Intl. Philatelic Exhibition, Rome.

**Cat Type of 1976**

Various cats and kittens: No. 2201: a, 1g. b, 2g. c, 3g. d, 5g. 60g, Black cat.

**1987, May 22** *Perf. 13x13½*

| | | | | |
|---|---|---|---|---|
| **2201** | A287 | Strip of 4, #a.-d. | 1.60 | .75 |
| **2202** | A287 | 60g multicolored | 1.10 | .95 |
| | | *Nos. 2201-2202 (2)* | 2.70 | 1.70 |

No. 2202 also exists perf. 14. For overprint see No. 2212.

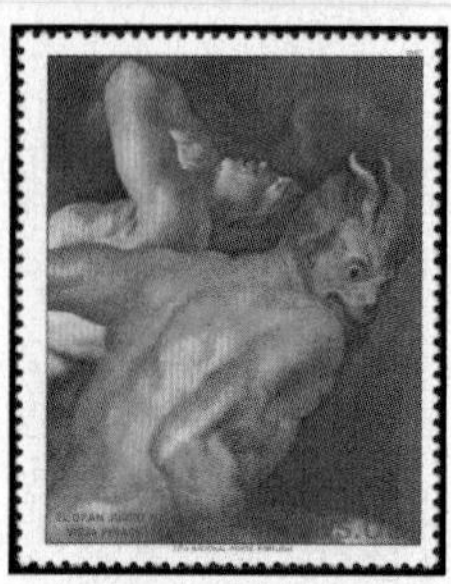

Paintings by Rubens A400

No. 2203: a, 1g, The Four Corners of the World, horiz. b, 2g, Jupiter and Calisto. c, 3g, Susanna and the Elders. d, 5g, Marriage of Henry IV and Marie de Medici in Lyon.
60g, The Last Judgment. 100g, The Holy Family with St. Elizabeth and John the Baptist. No. 2205A, War and Peace.

**1987 Litho.** *Perf. 13x13½, 13½x13*

| | | | | |
|---|---|---|---|---|
| **2203** | A400 | Strip of 4, #a.-d. | 1.50 | 1.00 |
| **2204** | A400 | 60g multicolored | 2.00 | 1.50 |
| | | *Nos. 2203-2204 (2)* | 3.50 | 2.50 |

**Souvenir Sheets**

| | | | | |
|---|---|---|---|---|
| **2205** | A400 | 100g multicolored | 14.00 | 14.00 |
| **2205A** | A400 | 100g multicolored | 14.00 | 14.00 |

Christmas 1986 (#2205).
Issued: #2204, May 25; #2205, May 26.
Nos. 2205-2205A are airmail and contain one 54x68mm stamp.

Places and Events — A401

10g, ACEPAR Industrial Plant. 25g, Franciscan monk, native, vert. 50g, Yaguaron Church altar, vert. 75g, Founding of Asuncion, 450th anniv. 100g, Paraguay Airlines passenger jet. 200g, Pres. Stoessner, vert.

**1987, June 2 Litho.** *Perf. 13*

| | | | | |
|---|---|---|---|---|
| **2206** | A401 | 10g multicolored | .25 | .25 |
| **2207** | A401 | 25g multicolored | .25 | .25 |
| **2208** | A401 | 50g multicolored | .25 | .25 |
| **2209** | A401 | 75g multicolored | .50 | .25 |
| **2210** | A401 | 100g multicolored | .75 | .30 |
| **2211** | A401 | 200g multicolored | 1.00 | .50 |
| | | *Nos. 2206-2211 (6)* | 3.00 | 1.80 |

Nos. 2210-2211 are airmail. For overprints see Nos. 2225-2226, C685, C722.

No. 2201 Ovptd. in Blue

**1987, June 12** *Perf. 13x13½*

| | | | | |
|---|---|---|---|---|
| **2212** | A287 | Strip of 4, #a.-d. | 1.50 | 1.50 |

Discovery of America, 500th Anniv. (in 1992) — A402

Discovery of America anniv. emblem and ships: No. 2213a, 1g, Spanish galleon, 17th cent. b, 2g, Victoria, 1st to circumnavigate the globe, 1519-22. c, 3g, San Hermenegildo. 5g, San Martin, c.1582. 60g, Santa Maria, c.1492, vert.

**1987, Sept. 9** *Perf. 14*

| | | | | |
|---|---|---|---|---|
| **2213** | A402 | Strip of 4, #a.-d. | 4.50 | 1.50 |

*Perf. 13x13½*

| | | | | |
|---|---|---|---|---|
| **2214** | A402 | 60g multicolored | 1.60 | 1.60 |
| | | *Nos. 2213-2214 (2)* | 6.10 | 3.10 |

Colorado Party, Cent. — A403

Bernardino Caballero (founder), President Stroessner and: 5g, 10g, 25g, Three-lane highway. 150g, 170g, 200g, Power lines.

*Perf. 13½x13*

**1987, Sept. 11** **Wmk. 347**

| | | | | |
|---|---|---|---|---|
| **2215** | A403 | 5g multi | 3.00 | 2.00 |
| **2216** | A403 | 10g multi | 3.00 | 2.00 |
| **2217** | A403 | 25g multi | 3.00 | 2.00 |
| **2218** | A403 | 150g multi | 3.00 | 2.00 |
| **2219** | A403 | 170g multi | 3.00 | 2.00 |
| **2220** | A403 | 200g multi | 3.00 | 2.00 |
| | | *Nos. 2215-2220 (6)* | 18.00 | 12.00 |

Nos. 2218-2220 are airmail.

Berlin, 750th Anniv. — A404

Berlin Stamps and Coins: No. 2221: a, 1g, #9NB145. b, 2g, #9NB154. c, 3g, #9N57, vert. d, 5g, #9N170, vert. 60g, 1987 Commemorative coin, vert.

*Perf. 13½x13, 13½x13*

**1987, Sept. 12** **Unwmk.**

| | | | | |
|---|---|---|---|---|
| **2221** | A404 | Strip of 4, #a.-d. | 6.50 | 2.00 |
| **2222** | A404 | 60g multicolored | 3.50 | 3.00 |
| | | *Nos. 2221-2222 (2)* | 10.00 | 5.00 |

For overprints see Nos. 2239, 2294.

Race Cars A405

No. 2223: a, 1g, Audi Sport Quattro. b, 2g, Lancia Delta S 4. c, 3g, Fiat 131. d, 5g, Porsche 911 4x4. 60g, Lancia Rally.

**1987, Sept. 27** *Perf. 13*

| | | | | |
|---|---|---|---|---|
| **2223** | A405 | Strip of 4, #a.-d. | 1.50 | 1.00 |

*Perf. 14*

| | | | | |
|---|---|---|---|---|
| **2224** | A405 | 60g multicolored | 1.50 | 1.00 |
| | | *Nos. 2223-2224 (2)* | 3.00 | 2.00 |

**Nos. 2209-2210 Ovptd. in Blue**

**1987, Sept. 30** *Perf. 13*

| | | | | |
|---|---|---|---|---|
| **2225** | A401 | 75g on #2209 | .70 | .70 |
| **2226** | A401 | 100g on #2210 | .80 | .80 |
| | | *Nos. 2225-2226 (2)* | 1.50 | 1.50 |

EXFIVIA '87 Intl. Philatelic Exhibition, LaPaz, Bolivia. No. 2226 is airmail. No. 2225 surcharge is in dark blue; and No. 2226 surcharge is bright blue.

**Nos. 2195d-2195f, 2196 Overprinted in Black or Silver**

**1987, Oct. 1** *Perf. 13½x13*

| | | | | |
|---|---|---|---|---|
| **2227** | A399 | Strip of 3, #a.-c. | 3.00 | 3.00 |
| **2228** | A399 | 5g on No. 2196 (S) | 2.00 | 2.00 |
| | | *Nos. 2227-2228 (2)* | 5.00 | 5.00 |

Olymphilex '87 Intl. Phil. Exhib., Seoul.

**No. 2189 Ovptd. with Emblem and "PHILATELIA '87," etc.**

**1987, Oct. 15** *Perf. 13x13½, 13½x13*

| | | | | |
|---|---|---|---|---|
| **2229** | A398 | Strip of 6, #a.-f. | 3.00 | 3.00 |

PHILATELIA '87 Intl. Phil. Exhib., Cologne. Size and configuration of overprint varies.

**Nos. 2195a-2195b Ovptd. in Bright Blue for EXFILNA '87 and BARCELONA 92**

**1987, Oct. 24** *Perf. 13x13½*

| | | | | |
|---|---|---|---|---|
| **2230** | A399 | Pair, #a.-b. | 4.00 | 4.00 |

Exfilna '87 Intl. Philatelic Exhibition.

Ship Paintings — A406

No. 2231: a, 1g, San Juan Nepomuceno. b, 2g, San Eugenio. c, 3g, San Telmo. d, 5g, San Carlos. 60g, Spanish galleon, 16th cent. 100g, One of Columbus' ships.

**1987 Litho.** *Perf. 14*

| | | | | |
|---|---|---|---|---|
| **2231** | A406 | Strip of 4, #a.-d. | 7.00 | 2.50 |

*Perf. 13x13½*

| | | | | |
|---|---|---|---|---|
| **2232** | A406 | 60g multicolored | 3.00 | 1.50 |
| | | *Nos. 2231-2232 (2)* | 10.00 | 4.00 |

**Souvenir Sheet**

*Perf. 13½*

| | | | | |
|---|---|---|---|---|
| **2233** | A406 | 100g multicolored | 13.00 | 13.00 |

Discovery of America, 500th anniv. in 1992 (#2233). Issue dates: Nos. 2231-2232, Dec. 10. No. 2233, Dec. 12.

No. 2233 is airmail and contains one 54x75mm stamp.

1988 Winter Olympics, Calgary — A407

#2237: a, 5g, Joel Gaspoz. b, 60g, Peter Mueller.

**1987, Dec. 31** *Perf. 14*

| | | | | |
|---|---|---|---|---|
| **2234** | A407 | 1g Maria Walliser | 3.50 | 1.25 |
| **2235** | A407 | 2g Erika Hess | 3.50 | 1.25 |
| **2236** | A407 | 3g Pirmin Zurbriggen | 3.50 | 1.25 |
| | | *Nos. 2234-2236 (3)* | 10.50 | 3.75 |

**Miniature Sheet**

*Perf. 13½x13*

| | | | | |
|---|---|---|---|---|
| **2237** | A407 | Sheet of 4 each #2237a, 2237b+label | 20.00 | 20.00 |

**Souvenir Sheet**

*Perf. 14½*

| | | | | |
|---|---|---|---|---|
| **2238** | A407 | 100g Walliser, Zurbriggen | 12.00 | 12.00 |

No. 2238 is airmail. For overprints see Nos. 2240-2242.

**No. 2221 Ovptd. in Silver "AEROPEX 88 / ADELAIDE"**

**1988, Jan. 29** *Perf. 13*

| | | | | |
|---|---|---|---|---|
| **2239** | A404 | Strip of 4, #a.-d. | 8.00 | 4.00 |

Aeropex '88, Adelaide, Australia.

**Nos. 2234-2236 Ovptd. in Gold with Olympic Rings and "OLYMPEX / CALGARY 1988"**

**1988, Feb. 13** *Perf. 14*

| | | | | |
|---|---|---|---|---|
| **2240** | A407 | 1g on #2234 | .75 | .75 |
| **2241** | A407 | 2g on #2235 | 1.50 | 1.50 |
| **2242** | A407 | 3g on #2236 | 2.00 | 2.00 |
| | | *Nos. 2240-2242 (3)* | 4.25 | 4.25 |

Olympex '88, Calgary. Size and configuration of overprint varies.

1988 Summer Olympics, Seoul — A408

Equestrians: No. 2243a, 1g, Josef Neckermann, W. Germany, on Venetia. b, 2g, Henri Chammartin, Switzerland. c, 3g, Christine Stueckelberger, Switzerland, on Granat. d, 5g, Liselott Linsenhoff, W. Germany, on Piaff. 60g, Hans-Guenter Winkler, W. Germany.

**1988, Mar. 7** *Perf. 13*

| | | | | |
|---|---|---|---|---|
| **2243** | A408 | Strip of 4, #a.-d. | 5.50 | 2.00 |

*Perf. 13½x13*

| | | | | |
|---|---|---|---|---|
| **2244** | A408 | 60g multicolored | 2.50 | 2.00 |
| | | *Nos. 2243-2244 (2)* | 8.00 | 4.00 |

For overprint see No. 2291.

Berlin, 750th Anniv. — A409

Paintings: No. 2245a, 1g, Virgin and Child, by Jan Gossaert. b, 2g, Virgin and Child, by Rubens. c, 3g, Virgin and Child, by Hans Memling. d, 5g, Madonna, by Albrecht Durer. 60g, Adoration of the Shepherds, by Martin Schongauer.

**1988, Apr. 8** *Perf. 13*

**2245** A409 Strip of 4, #a.-d. 6.50 2.00
**2246** A409 60g multicolored 3.50 3.00
*Nos. 2245-2246 (2)* 10.00 5.00

Christmas 1987. See Nos. C727-C731.

Visit of Pope John Paul II A410

Religious art: No. 2247a, 1g, Pope John Paul II, hands clasped. b, 2g, Statue of the Virgin. c, 3g, Czestochowa Madonna. d, 5g, Our Lady of Caacupe. Nos. 2247a-2247d are vert.

**1988, Apr. 11** *Perf. 13*

**2247** A410 Strip of 4, #a.-d. 2.50 1.00
**2248** A410 60g multicolored 1.50 1.00
*Nos. 2247-2248 (2)* 4.00 2.00

Visit of Pope John Paul II — A411

Rosette window and crucifix.

**1988, May 5** **Litho.** *Perf. 13x13½*

**2249** A411 10g blue & blk 2.00 .75
**2250** A411 20g blue & blk 2.00 .75
**2251** A411 50g blue & blk 2.00 .75
*Nos. 2249-2251 (3)* 6.00 2.25

### World Wildlife Fund Type of 1985

Endangered Animals: No. 2252a, 1g, like #2139g. b, 2g, like #2139f. c, 3g, like #2139d. d, 5g, like #2139e.

**1988, June 14** **Unwmk.** *Perf. 14*

**2252** A386 Strip of 4, #a.-d. 10.00 2.00

Nos. 2252a-2252d have denomination and border in blue.

### Nos. 2000a-2000d Ovptd. in Gold with Emblem and "Bicentenario de / AUSTRALIA / 1788-1988"

**1988, June 17**

**2253** A351 Strip of 4, #a.-d. 3.50 3.50

Australia, bicent.

### Types of 1985 Overprinted in 2 or 4 Lines in Gold "NUEVO PERIODO PRESIDENCIAL CONSTITUCIONAL 1988-1993"

**1988, Aug. 12** *Perf. 14*

**2254** A390 10g like #2153 .25 .25
**2255** A390 25g like #2154 .25 .25
**2256** A390 50g like #2155 .40 .40
**2257** A390 75g like #2156 .75 .75
**2258** A390 100g like #2157 .90 .90
**2259** A390 200g like #2158 1.50 1.50
*Nos. 2254-2259 (6)* 4.05 4.05

Pres. Stroessner's new term in office. Nos. 2258-2259 are airmail.

Olympic Tennis, Seoul — A412

Designs: No. 2260a, 1g, Steffi Graf, W. Germany. b, 2g, Olympic gold medal, horiz. c, 3g, Boris Becker, W. Germany. d, 5g, Emilio Sanchez, Spain. 60g, Steffi Graf, diff.

**1988, Aug. 16** *Perf. 13*

**2260** A412 Strip of 4, #a.-d. 10.00 3.25
**2261** A412 60g multicolored 2.50 2.50
*Nos. 2260-2261 (2)* 12.50 5.75

1992 Summer Olympics, Barcelona — A413

Olympic medalists from Spain: No. 2262a, 1g, Ricardo Zamora, soccer, Antwerp, 1920, vert. b, 2g, Equestrian team, Amsterdam, 1928. c, 3g, Angel Leon, shooting, Helsinki, 1952. d, 5g, Kayak team, Montreal, 1976. 60g, Francisco Fernandez Ochoa, slalom, Sapporo, 1972, vert. 100g, Olympic Stadium, Barcelona, vert.

**1989, Jan. 5** *Perf. 14*

**2262** A413 Strip of 4, #a.-d. 6.00 3.25

*Perf. 13*

**2263** A413 60g multicolored 1.50 1.25
*Nos. 2262-2263 (2)* 7.50 4.50

**Souvenir Sheet**

*Perf. 13½*

**2264** A413 100g multicolored 12.00 12.00

Discovery of America 500th anniv. (in 1992). No. 2264 is airmail and contains one 50x60mm stamp. For overprint see No. 2293.

Columbus Space Station A414

**1989, Jan. 7** **Litho.** *Perf. 13x13½*

**2265** A414 60g multicolored 4.00 2.00

Discovery of America 500th anniv. (in 1992). Printed in sheets of 4 + 5 labels.

### No. 2076 Overprinted in Silver, Red and Blue with Olympic Rings, "1992" and Emblem

**1989, Jan. 10** *Perf. 13½x13, 13x13½*

**2266** A369 Strip of 6, #a.-f. 5.00 5.00

1992 Winter Olympics, Albertville. Location and configuration of overprint varies.

### No. 1454 Ovptd. in Silver "HOMENAJE AL EMPERADOR HIROITO DE JAPON 29.IV,1901-6.1.1989"

**1989, Feb. 8** *Perf. 14*

**2267** A251 Strip of 5, #a.-e. 3.00 3.00

Death of Emperor Hirohito of Japan.

Formula 1 Drivers, Race Cars — A415

No. 2268: a, 1g, Stirling Moss, Mercedes W196. b, 2g, Emerson Fittipaldi, Lotus. c, 3g, Nelson Piquet, Lotus. d, 5g, Niki Lauda, Ferrari 312 B. 60g, Juan Manuel Fangio, Maserati 250F.

**1989, Mar. 6** *Perf. 13*

**2268** A415 Strip of 4, #a.-d. 6.50 2.00
**2269** A415 60g multicolored 2.50 2.50
*Nos. 2268-2269 (2)* 9.00 4.50

Paintings by Titian A416

No. 2270: a, 1g, Bacchus and Ariadne (Bacchus). b, 2g, Bacchus and Ariadne (tutelary spirit). c, 3g, Death of Actaeon. d, 5g, Portrait of a Young Woman with a Fur Cape. 60g, Concert in a Field. 100g, Holy Family with Donor.

**1989, Apr. 17** *Perf. 13x13½*

**2270** A416 Strip of 4, #a.-d. 5.50 1.75
**2271** A416 60g multicolored 2.50 .75
*Nos. 2270-2271 (2)* 8.00 2.50

**Souvenir Sheet**

*Perf. 13½*

**2271A** A416 100g multicolored 12.00 12.00

No. 2271A is airmail and contains one 60x49mm stamp. Issue date: May 27.

1994 Winter Olympics, Lillehammer — A417

Athletes: No. 2272a, 1g, Torbjorn Lokken, 1987 Nordic combined world champion. b, 2g, Atle Skardal, skier, Norway. c, 3g, Geir Karlstad, Norway, world 10,000-meter speed skating champion, 1987. d, 5g, Franck Piccard, France, 1988 Olympic medalist, skiing. 60g, Roger Ruud, ski jumper, Norway.

**1989, May 23** *Perf. 13½x13*

**2272** A417 Strip of 4, #a.-d. 12.00 4.00
**2273** A417 60g multicolored 5.50 3.50
*Nos. 2272-2273 (2)* 17.50 7.50

### Cat Type of 1976

Various cats: #2274a, 1g. b, 2g. c, 3g. d, 5g.

**1989, May 25** *Perf. 13*

**2274** A287 Strip of 4, #a.-d. 6.50 2.00
**2275** A287 60g Siamese 2.00 2.00
*Nos. 2274-2275 (2)* 8.50 4.00

Federal Republic of Germany, 40th Anniv. — A418

Famous men and automobiles: No. 2276a, 1g, Konrad Adenauer, chancellor, 1949-1963, Mercedes. b, 2g, Ludwig Erhard, chancellor, 1963-1966, Volkswagen Beetle. c, 3g, Felix Wankel, engine designer, 1963 NSU Spider. d, 5g, Franz Josef Strauss, President of Bavarian Cabinet, BMW 502. 60g, Pres. Richard von Weizsacker and Dr. Josef Neckermann.

**1989, May 27** *Perf. 13½x13*

**2276** A418 Strip of 4, #a.-d. 8.00 2.50
**2277** A418 60g multicolored 3.00 3.00
*Nos. 2276-2277 (2)* 11.00 5.50

For overprints see No. 2369.

### Ship Type of 1980 Overprinted with Discovery of America, 500th Anniv. Emblem in Red on Silver

**1989, May 29** *Perf. 14½*

**Miniature Sheet**

**2278** A343 Sheet of 7+label, like #1972 18.00 18.00

Discovery of America 500th anniv. (in 1992).

### No. 2122a Overprinted with Hamburg Emblem and Nos. 2122b-2122f, 2123 Ovptd. with Diff. Emblem in Red on Silver

**1989, May 30** **Litho.** *Perf. 13½x13*

**2279** A381 Strip of 6, #a.-f. 12.00 12.00
**2280** A381 5g on #2123 3.00 3.00
*Nos. 2279-2280 (2)* 15.00 15.00

City of Hamburg, 800th anniv.

### Nos. 2006a-2006b Ovptd. "BRASILIANA / 89"

**1989, July 5** *Perf. 14*

**2281** A352 Pair, #a.-b. 4.00 2.00

### No. 2171 Overprinted in Metallic Red and Silver with FIFA and Italia 90 Emblems and "PARAGUAY PARTICIPO EN 13 CAMPEONATOS MUNDIALES"

**1989, Sept. 14** **Litho.** *Perf. 13½x13*

**2283** A394 Strip of 6, #a.-f. 4.00 4.00

Size and configuration of overprint varies.

### Nos. C738, C753 Ovptd. in metallic red with Italia '90 emblem & "SUDAMERICA-GRUPO 2 / PARAGUAY-COLOMBIA / PARAGUAY-ECUADOR / COLOMBIA-PARAGUAY / ECUADOR-PARAGUAY" and in metallic red on silver with FIFA emblem

**1989, Sept. 14** **Litho.** *Perf. 13*

**2284** AP228 25g on #C738 7.50 3.50
**2285** AP232 25g on #C753 7.50 3.50
*Nos. 2284-2285 (2)* 15.00 7.00

### Nos. 2046, 2172 Overprinted in Metallic Red on Silver at top: "PARAGUAY CLASIFICADO EN 1930, 1950, 1958 Y 1986" and Emblems or "ITALIA '90". Overprinted Silver on stamps and Blue on Silver on side margins

**1989, Sept. 15** **Litho.** *Perf. 14*

**2286** A362 Strip of 6, #a.-f. 15.00 4.50

*Perf. 13½x13*

**2287** A394 5g multicolored 5.00 3.00
*Nos. 2286-2287 (2)* 20.00 7.50

1990 World Cup Soccer Championships, Italy. Location and size of overprint varies.

### Nos. 1284-1286 Ovptd. in Gold "...BIEN ESTUVIMOS EN LA LUNA AHORA NECESITAMOS LOS MEDIOS PARA LLEGAR A LOS PLANETAS" Wernher von Braun's Signature and UN and Space Emblems

**1989, Sept. 16** *Perf. 14*

**2288** A226 Strip of 5, #a.-e. 5.50 5.50
**2289** A226 50c multicolored 2.50 2.50
**2290** A226 75c multicolored 4.00 4.00
*Nos. 2288-2290 (3)* 12.00 12.00

Location, size and configuration of overprint varies.

### Nos. 2243, C764 Overprinted in Silver or Gold with Emblem and "ATENAS 100 ANOS DE LOS JUEGOS OLIMPICOS 1896-1996"

**1989, Sept. 18** *Perf. 13*

**2291** A408 Strip of 4, #a.-d. 3.00 3.00
**2292** AP233 25g on #C764 (G) 7.00 7.00
*Nos. 2291-2292 (2)* 10.00 10.00

1992 Summer Olympics Barcelona, Spain. Size and location of overprint varies.

**Nos. 2262a-2262d Ovptd. in Silver with Heads of Steffi Graf or Boris Becker and: "WIMBLEDON 1988 / SEUL 1988 / WIMBLEDON 1989 / EL TENIS NUEVAMENTE EN / LAS OLIMPIADAS 1988-1992" or Similar**

**1989, Sept. 19** *Perf. 14*

**2293** A413 Strip of 4, #a.-d. 8.00 8.00

Addition of tennis as an Olympic sport in 1992. Size and configuration of overprint varies.

**No. 2221 Ovptd. in Gold and Blue "PRIMER AEROPUERTO PARA / /COHETES, BERLIN 1930 OBERTH, / NEBEL, RITTER, VON BRAUN" space emblem and "PROF. DR. HERMANN / OBERTH 95o ANIV. / NACIMIENTO 25.6.1989"**

*Perf. 13½x13, 13x13½*

**1989, Sept. 20**

**2294** A404 Strip of 4, #a.-d. 18.00 6.00

Dr. Hermann Oberth, rocket scientist, 95th birth anniv. Overprint size, etc, varies.

**Nos. 1406-1408 Ovptd. in Metallic Red and Silver with Emblems and "OLIMPIADAS / DE INVIERNO / ALBERTVILLE 1992" in 2 or 3 Lines**

**1989, Sept. 21** *Perf. 14*

**2295** A244 Strip of 5, #a.-e. 9.00 3.00
**2296** A244 50c multicolored 4.50 2.50
**2297** A244 75c multicolored 6.50 4.00
*Nos. 2295-2297 (3)* 20.00 9.50

1992 Winter Olympics, Albertville. Size and configuration of overprint varies.

Nos. 2251, C724 Overprinted

*Perf. 13½, 13½x13*

**1989, Oct. 9** **Litho.** **Wmk. 347**

**2298** A411 50g on #2251 10.00 7.50
**2299** AP226 120g on #C724 10.00 8.00

Parafil '89, Paraguay-Argentina philatelic exhibition.

Birds Facing Extinction — A419

50g, Ara chloroptera. 100g, Mergus octosetaceus. 300g, Rhea americana. 500g, Ramphastos toco. 1000g, Crax fasciolata. 2000g, Ara ararauna.

*Perf. 13½x13*

**1989, Dec. 19** **Litho.** **Wmk. 347**

**2300** A419 50g multicolored .30 .30
**2301** A419 100g multicolored .30 .30
**2302** A419 300g multicolored .75 .75
**2303** A419 500g multicolored 1.20 1.20
**2304** A419 1000g multicolored 2.25 2.25
**2305** A419 2000g multicolored 4.25 4.25
*Nos. 2300-2305 (6)* 9.05 9.05

Nos. 2302-2305 airmail. Nos. 2300 & 2305 vert. Frames and typestyles vary greatly. Watermark on 50g, 100g, 300g is 8mm high.

1992 Summer Olympics, Barcelona — A420

Athletes: No. 2306a, 1g, A. Fichtel and S. Bau, W. Germany, foils, 1988. b, 2g, Spanish basketball team, 1984. c, 3g, Jackie Joyner-Kersee, heptathalon and long jump, 1988, horiz. d, 5g, L. Beerbaum, W. Germany, show jumping, team, 1988. 60g, W. Brinkmann, W. Germany, show jumping, team, 1988. 100g, Emilio Sanchez, tennis.

**Unwmk.**

**1989, Dec. 26** **Litho.** *Perf. 14*

**2306** A420 Strip of 4, #a.-d. 6.00 2.00

*Perf. 13*

**2307** A420 60g multicolored 6.50 3.50
*Nos. 2306-2307 (2)* 12.50 5.50

**Souvenir Sheet**

*Perf. 13½*

**2308** A420 100g multicolored 20.00 15.00

No. 2308 is airmail and contains one 47x57mm stamp.

World Cup Soccer Championships, Italy — A421

1986 World Cup soccer players in various positions: No. 2309a, 1g, England vs. Paraguay. b, 2g, Spain vs. Denmark. c, 3g, France vs. Italy. d, 5g, Germany vs. Morocco. 60g, Mexico vs. Paraguay. 100g, Germany vs. Argentina.

**1989, Dec. 29** *Perf. 14*

**2309** A421 Strip of 4, #a.-d. 8.50 2.50

*Perf. 13½*

**2310** A421 60g multicolored 5.50 2.50
*Nos. 2309-2310 (2)* 14.00 5.00

**Souvenir Sheet**

*Perf. 14½*

**2311** A421 100g multicolored 20.00 15.00

No. 2311 is airmail and contains one 40x50mm stamp.
For overprints see Nos. 2355-2356.

1992 Summer Olympics, Barcelona — A422

Barcelona '92, proposed Athens '96 emblems and: No. 2312a, 1g, Greece #128. b, 2g, Greece #126, vert. c, 3g, Greece #127, vert. d, 5g, Greece #123, vert. 60g, Paraguay #736. 100g, Horse and rider, vert.

**1990, Jan. 4** *Perf. 13½x13, 13x13½*

**2312** A422 Strip of 4, #a.-d. 6.00 2.00
**2313** A422 60g multicolored 11.00 4.00
*Nos. 2312-2313 (2)* 17.00 6.00

**Souvenir Sheet**

*Perf. 13½*

**2314** A422 100g multicolored 15.00 15.00

No. 2314 is airmail and contains one 50x60mm stamp and exists with either white or yellow border, same value. Stamps inscribed 1989.
For overprints see No. 2357.

Swiss Confederation, 700th Anniv. — A423

No. 2315: a, 3g, Monument to William Tell. b, 5g, Manship Globe, UN Headquarters, Geneva.
60g, 15th cent. messenger, Bern.
No. 2317, 1st Swiss steam locomotive, horiz. No. 2318, Jean Henri Dunant, founder of the Red Cross, horiz.

**1990, Jan. 25** *Perf. 14*

**2315** A423 Pair, #a.-b. 5.50 2.00

*Perf. 13*

**2316** A423 60g multicolored 5.00 3.50
*Nos. 2315-2316 (2)* 10.50 5.50

**Souvenir Sheets**

*Perf. 14½*

**2317** A423 100g multicolored 25.00 25.00
**2318** A423 100g multicolored 20.00 20.00

Nos. 2317-2318 are airmail. For overprints see Nos. 2352-2354.

Wood Carving — A424

Discovery of America, 500th anniv. emblem &: #2319: a, 1g, 1st cathechism in Guarani. b, 2g, shown. #2319 has continuous design.

**1990, Jan. 26** *Perf. 14*

**2319** A424 Pair, #a.-b. + label 4.00 1.40

Organization of American States, Cent. — A425

*Perf. 13½x13*

**1990, Feb. 9** **Litho.** **Wmk. 347**

**2320** A425 50g multicolored .30 .30
**2321** A425 100g multicolored .45 .35
**2322** A425 200g Map of Paraguay .90 .65
*Nos. 2320-2322 (3)* 1.65 1.30

1992 Winter Olympics, Albertville — A426

Calgary 1988 skiers: No. 2323a, 1g, Alberto Tomba, Italy, slalom and giant slalom. b, 2g, Vreni Schneider, Switzerland, women's slalom and giant slalom, vert. c, 3g, Luc Alphand, France, skier, vert. d, 5g, Matti Nykaenen, Finland, ski-jumping.
60g, Marina Kiehl, W. Germany, women's downhill. 100g, Frank Piccard, France, super giant slalom.

**1990, Mar. 7** **Unwmk.** *Perf. 14*

**2323** A426 Strip of 4, #a.-d. 5.75 2.25

*Perf. 13*

**2324** A426 60g multicolored 2.25 2.25
*Nos. 2323-2324 (2)* 8.00 4.50

**Souvenir Sheet**

*Perf. 14½*

**2325** A426 100g multicolored 15.00 15.00

No. 2325 is airmail, contains one 40x50mm stamp and exists with either white or yellow border.

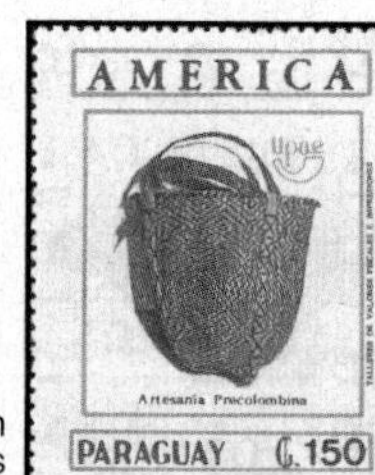


Pre-Columbian Art, Customs — A427

UPAE Emblem and: 150g, Pre-Columbian basket. 500g, Aboriginal ceremony.

**1990, Mar. 8** **Wmk. 347** *Perf. 13*

**2326** A427 150g multicolored 1.50 1.10
**2327** A427 500g multicolored 3.75 2.25

No. 2327 is airmail.
For overprints see Nos. 2345-2346.

First Postage Stamp, 150th Anniv. — A428

Penny Black, Mail Transportation 500th anniv. emblem and: No. 2328a, 1g, Penny Black on cover. b, 2g, Mauritius #1-2 on cover. c, 3g, Baden #4b on cover. d, 5g, Roman States #4 on cover. 60g, Paraguay #C38 and four #C54 on cover.

**1990, Mar. 12** **Unwmk.** *Perf. 14*

**2328** A428 Strip of 4, #a.-d. 5.50 2.25

*Perf. 13½x13*

**2329** A428 60g multicolored 2.25 2.25

Postal Union of the Americas and Spain (UPAE) A429

**1990, July 2** *Perf. 13x13½*

**2330** A429 200g Map, flags .90 .45
**2331** A429 250g Paraguay #1 1.10 .50
**2332** A429 350g FDC of #2326-2327, horiz. 2.40 .65
*Nos. 2330-2332 (3)* 4.40 1.60

National University, Cent. (in 1989) — A430

**1990, Sept. 8**

| | | | | |
|---|---|---|---|---|
| **2333** | A430 | 300g Future site | 1.25 | 1.00 |
| **2334** | A430 | 400g Present site | 1.60 | 1.25 |
| **2335** | A430 | 600g Old site | 2.50 | 2.00 |
| | | *Nos. 2333-2335 (3)* | 5.35 | 4.25 |

Franciscan Churches — A431

*Perf. 13½x13*

**1990, Sept. 25 Litho. Wmk. 347**

| | | | | |
|---|---|---|---|---|
| **2336** | A431 | 50g Guarambare | .30 | .30 |
| **2337** | A431 | 100g Yaguaron | .45 | .35 |
| **2338** | A431 | 200g Ita | .90 | .65 |
| | | *Nos. 2336-2338 (3)* | 1.65 | 1.30 |

For overprints see Nos. 2366-2368.

Democracy in Paraguay — A432

Designs: 100g, State and Catholic Church, vert. 200g, Human rights, vert. 300g, Freedom of the Press, vert. 500g, Return of the exiles. 3000g, People and democracy.

*Perf. 13½x13, 13x13½*

**1990, Oct. 5 Litho. Wmk. 347**

| | | | | |
|---|---|---|---|---|
| **2339** | A432 | 50g multicolored | .30 | .30 |
| **2340** | A432 | 100g multicolored | .30 | .30 |
| **2341** | A432 | 200g multicolored | .60 | .50 |
| **2342** | A432 | 300g multicolored | .90 | .80 |
| **2343** | A432 | 500g multicolored | 11.00 | 1.40 |
| **2344** | A432 | 3000g multicolored | 8.00 | 7.50 |
| | | *Nos. 2339-2344 (6)* | 21.10 | 10.80 |

Nos. 2343-2344 are airmail.

Nos. 2326-2327 Overprinted in Magenta

**1990 Litho. Wmk. 347 *Perf. 13***

| | | | | |
|---|---|---|---|---|
| **2345** | A427 | 150g multicolored | 1.25 | .60 |
| **2346** | A427 | 500g multicolored | 4.00 | 1.90 |

No. 2346 is airmail.

UN Development Program, 40th Anniv. — A433

Designs: 50m, Human Rights, sculpture by Hugo Pistilli. 100m, United Nations, sculpture by Hermann Guggiari. 150m, Miguel de Cervantes Literature Award, won by Augusto Roa Bastos.

**1990, Oct. 26**

| | | | | |
|---|---|---|---|---|
| **2347** | A433 | 50g lilac & multi | .45 | .30 |
| **2348** | A433 | 100g gray & multi | .65 | .35 |
| **2349** | A433 | 150g green & multi | 1.00 | .60 |
| | | *Nos. 2347-2349 (3)* | 2.10 | 1.25 |

America A434

50g, Paraguay River banks. 250g, Chaco land.

*Perf. 13½x13*

**1990, Oct. 31 Wmk. 347**

| | | | | |
|---|---|---|---|---|
| **2350** | A434 | 50g multicolored | 10.00 | 5.00 |
| **2351** | A434 | 250g multicolored | 20.00 | 10.00 |

No. 2351 is airmail.

Nos. 2315-2316, 2318 Ovptd. in Metallic Red and Silver

**Unwmk.**

**1991, Apr. 2 Litho. *Perf. 14***

| | | | | |
|---|---|---|---|---|
| **2352** | A423 | Pair, #a.-b. | 4.00 | 4.00 |

***Perf. 13***

| | | | | |
|---|---|---|---|---|
| **2353** | A423 | 60g on #2316 | 3.50 | 3.50 |
| | | *Nos. 2352-2353 (2)* | 7.50 | 7.50 |

**Souvenir Sheet**

***Perf. 14½***

| | | | | |
|---|---|---|---|---|
| **2354** | A423 | 100g on #2318 | 17.00 | 17.00 |

Swiss Confederation, 700th anniv. and Red Cross, 125th anniv. No. 2354 is airmail. No. 2352 exists perf. 13. Location of overprint varies.

Nos. 2309-2310 Ovptd. in Silver

**1991, Apr. 4 *Perf. 14***

| | | | | |
|---|---|---|---|---|
| **2355** | A421 | Strip of 4, #a.-d. | 6.25 | 6.25 |

***Perf. 13x13½***

| | | | | |
|---|---|---|---|---|
| **2356** | A421 | 60g on #2310 | 3.75 | 3.75 |
| | | *Nos. 2355-2356 (2)* | 10.00 | 10.00 |

1994 World Cup Soccer Championships. Location of overprint varies.

Nos. 2312, C822, C766 Ovptd. in Silver

**1991, Apr. 4 *Perf. 13***

| | | | | |
|---|---|---|---|---|
| **2357** | A422 | Strip of 4, #a.-d. | 7.00 | 5.00 |
| **2358** | AP246 | 25g on #C822 | 4.50 | 3.00 |

***Perf. 13x13½***

| | | | | |
|---|---|---|---|---|
| **2359** | AP233 | 30g on #C766 | 6.00 | 4.00 |

Participation of reunified Germany in 1992 Summer Olympics. Nos. 2358-2359 are airmail. Location of overprint varies.

Professors A435

Designs: 50g, Julio Manuel Morales, gynecologist. 100g, Carlos Gatti, clinician. 200g, Gustavo Gonzalez, geologist. 300g, Juan Max Boettner, physician and musician. 350g, Juan Boggino, pathologist. 500g, Andres Barbero, physician, founder of Paraguayan Red Cross.

*Perf. 13x13½*

**1991, Apr. 5 Wmk. 347**

| | | | | |
|---|---|---|---|---|
| **2360** | A435 | 50g multicolored | .30 | .30 |
| **2361** | A435 | 100g multicolored | .30 | .30 |
| **2362** | A435 | 200g multicolored | .60 | .50 |
| **2363** | A435 | 300g multicolored | .90 | .80 |
| **2364** | A435 | 350g multicolored | 1.00 | .90 |
| **2365** | A435 | 500g multicolored | 1.50 | 1.40 |
| | | *Nos. 2360-2365 (6)* | 4.60 | 4.20 |

Nos. 2364-2365 are airmail.

**Nos. 2336-2338 Ovptd. in Black and Red**

**1991 Wmk. 347 *Perf. 13½x13***

| | | | | |
|---|---|---|---|---|
| **2366** | A431 | 50g on #2336 | .50 | .50 |
| **2367** | A431 | 100g on #2337 | .60 | .60 |
| **2368** | A431 | 200g on #2338 | .90 | .90 |
| | | *Nos. 2366-2368 (3)* | 2.00 | 2.00 |

Espamer '91 Philatelic Exhibition.

**Nos. 2276a-2276b Ovptd. in Silver**

**Nos. 2276c-2276d Ovptd. in Silver**

**1991 Unwmk. *Perf. 13***

| | | | | |
|---|---|---|---|---|
| **2369** | A418 | Strip of 4, #a.-d. | 5.25 | 5.00 |

Writers and Muscians — A436

Designs: 50g, Ruy Diaz de Guzman, historian. 100g, Maria Talavera, war correspondent, vert. 150g, Augusto Roa Bastos, writer, vert. 200g, Jose Asuncion Flores, composer, vert. 250g, Felix Perez Cardozo, harpist. 300g, Juan Carlos Moreno Gonzalez, composer.

*Perf. 13½x13,13x13½*

**1991, Aug. 27 Litho. Wmk. 347**

| | | | | |
|---|---|---|---|---|
| **2373** | A436 | 50g multicolored | .30 | .30 |
| **2374** | A436 | 100g multicolored | .35 | .35 |
| **2375** | A436 | 150g multicolored | .60 | .50 |
| **2376** | A436 | 200g multicolored | .75 | .65 |
| **2377** | A436 | 250g multicolored | .90 | .80 |
| **2378** | A436 | 300g multicolored | 1.10 | 1.00 |
| | | *Nos. 2373-2378 (6)* | 4.00 | 3.60 |

Nos. 2376-2378 are airmail.

America A437

100g, War of Tavare. 300g, Arrival of Spanish explorer Domingo Martinez de Irala in Paraguay.

*Perf. 13x13½*

**1991, Oct. 9 Litho. Wmk. 347**

| | | | | |
|---|---|---|---|---|
| **2379** | A437 | 100g multicolored | 1.50 | .35 |
| **2380** | A437 | 300g multicolored | 1.75 | .90 |

No. 2380 is airmail.

Paintings A438

Designs: 50g, Compass of Life, by Alfredo Moraes. 100g, The Lighted Alley, by Michael Burt. 150g, Earring, by Lucy Yegros. 200g, Migrant Workers, by Hugo Bogado Barrios. 250g, Passengers Without a Ship, by Bernardo Ismachoviez. 300g, Native Guarani, by Lotte Schulz.

*Perf. 13x13½*

**1991, Nov. 12 Litho. Wmk. 347**

| | | | | |
|---|---|---|---|---|
| **2381** | A438 | 50g multicolored | .30 | .30 |
| **2382** | A438 | 100g multicolored | .35 | .35 |
| **2383** | A438 | 150g multicolored | .60 | .50 |
| **2384** | A438 | 200g multicolored | .75 | .65 |

**2385** A438 250g multicolored .90 .80
**2386** A438 300g multicolored 1.10 1.00
*Nos. 2381-2386 (6)* 4.00 3.60

Nos. 2384-2386 are airmail.

Endangered Species — A439

***Perf. 13x13½, 13½x13***

**1992, Jan. 28 Litho. Wmk. 347**

**2387** A439 50g Catagonus wagneri, vert. .30 .30
**2388** A439 100g Felis pardalis .35 .35
**2389** A439 150g Tapirus terrestri .60 .50
**2390** A439 200g Chrysocyon brachyurus .75 .65
*Nos. 2387-2390 (4)* 2.00 1.80

Tile Designs of Christianized Indians A440

***Perf. 13x13½***

**1992, Mar. 2 Litho. Wmk. 347**

**2391** A440 50g Geometric .35 .30
**2392** A440 100g Church .35 .30
**2393** A440 150g Missionary ship .50 .35
**2394** A440 200g Plant .65 .50
*Nos. 2391-2394 (4)* 1.85 1.45

Discovery of America, 500th anniv.

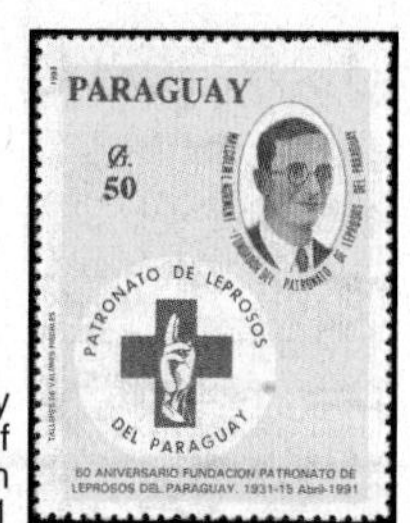


Leprosy Society of Paraguay, 60th Anniv. — A441

Designs: 50g, Society emblem, Malcolm L. Norment, founder. 250g, Gerhard Henrik Armauer Hansen (1841-1912), discoverer of leprosy bacillus.

***Perf. 13x13½***

**1992, Apr. 28 Litho. Wmk. 347**

**2395** A441 50g multicolored .30 .30
**2396** A441 250g multicolored .90 .80

Earth Summit, Rio de Janeiro A442

Earth Summit emblem, St. Francis of Assisi, and: 50g, Hands holding symbols of clean environment. 100g, Butterfly, industrial pollution. 250g, Globe, calls for environmental protection.

**1992, June 9**

**2397** A442 50g multicolored .30 .30
**2398** A442 100g multicolored .35 .35
**2399** A442 250g multicolored .80 .80
*Nos. 2397-2399 (3)* 1.45 1.45

For overprints see Nos. 2422-2424.

Natl. Census A443

**1992. July 30 *Perf. 13½x13, 13x13½***

**2400** A443 50g Economic activity .30 .30
**2401** A443 200g Houses, vert. .65 .65
**2402** A443 250g Population, vert. .90 .80
**2403** A443 300g Education 1.10 1.00
*Nos. 2400-2403 (4)* 2.95 2.75

1992 Summer Olympics, Barcelona — A444

**1992, Sept. 1 *Perf. 13x13½, 13½x13***

**2404** A444 50g Soccer, vert. .30 .30
**2405** A444 100g Tennis, vert. .35 .35
**2406** A444 150g Running, vert. .60 .50
**2407** A444 200g Swimming .75 .60
**2408** A444 250g Judo, vert. .90 .80
**2409** A444 350g Fencing 1.25 1.10
*Nos. 2404-2409 (6)* 4.15 3.65

Evangelism in Paraguay, 500th Anniv. — A445

Designs: 50g, Friar Luis Bolanos. 100g, Friar Juan de San Bernardo. 150g, San Roque Gonzalez de Santa Cruz. 200g, Father Amancio Gonzalez. 250g, Monsignor Juan Sinforiano Bogarin, vert.

***Rough Perf. 13½x13, 13x13½***

**1992, Oct. 9 Unwmk.**

**2410** A445 50g multicolored .30 .30
**2411** A445 100g multicolored .35 .35
**2412** A445 150g multicolored .60 .50
**2413** A445 200g multicolored .75 .65
**2414** A445 250g multicolored .90 .80
*Nos. 2410-2414 (5)* 2.90 2.60

For overprints see Nos. 2419-2421.

America A446

Designs: 150g, Columbus, fleet arriving in New World. 350g, Columbus, vert.

***Rough Perf. 13½x13, 13x13½***

**1992, Oct. 12**

**2415** A446 150g multicolored 1.00 .50
**2416** A446 350g multicolored 1.50 1.10

No. 2416 is airmail.

**Ovptd. "PARAFIL 92" in Blue**

**1992, Nov. 9**

**2417** A446 150g multicolored 1.00 .50
**2418** A446 350g multicolored 1.50 1.10

No. 2418 is airmail.

**Nos. 2410-2412 Ovptd. in Green**

**1992, Nov. 6 *Rough Perf. 13½x13***

**2419** A445 50g multicolored .30 .30
**2420** A445 100g multicolored .35 .35
**2421** A445 150g multicolored .60 .50
*Nos. 2419-2421 (3)* 1.25 1.15

Nos. 2397-2399 Ovptd. in Blue

***Perf. 13x13½***

**1992, Oct. 24 Wmk. 347**

**2422** A442 50g multicolored .30 .30
**2423** A442 100g multicolored .35 .35
**2424** A442 250g multicolored .85 .85
*Nos. 2422-2424 (3)* 1.50 1.50

Inter-American Institute for Cooperation in Agriculture, 50th Anniv. — A447

Designs: 50g, Field workers. 100g, Test tubes, cattle in pasture. 200g, Hands holding flower. 250g, Cows, corn, city.

***Perf. 13x13½***

**1992, Nov. 27 Unwmk.**

**2425** A447 50g multicolored .50 .30
**2426** A447 100g multicolored .60 .35
**2427** A447 200g multicolored .90 .75
**2428** A447 250g multicolored 1.25 .90
*Nos. 2425-2428 (4)* 3.25 2.30

For overprints see Nos. 2461-2462.

Notary College of Paraguay, Cent. — A448

Designs: 50g, Yolanda Bado de Artecona. 100g, Jose Ramon Silva. 150g, Abelardo Brugada Valpy. 200g, Tomas Varela. 250g, Jose Livio Lezcano. 300g, Francisco I. Fernandez.

**1992, Nov. 29 *Rough Perf. 13½x13***

**2429** A448 50g multicolored .30 .30
**2430** A448 100g multicolored .35 .35
**2431** A448 150g multicolored .60 .60
**2432** A448 200g multicolored .75 .75
**2433** A448 250g multicolored .90 .90
**2434** A448 300g multicolored 1.00 1.00
*Nos. 2429-2434 (6)* 3.90 3.90

Opening of Lopez Palace, Cent. A449

Paintings of palace by: 50g, Michael Burt. 100g, Esperanza Gill. 200g, Emili Aparici. 250g, Hugo Bogado Barrios, vert.

**1993, Mar. 9 *Perf. 13½x13, 13x13½***

**2435** A449 50g multicolored .30 .30
**2436** A449 100g multicolored .35 .35
**2437** A449 200g multicolored .75 .75
**2438** A449 250g multicolored .90 .90
*Nos. 2435-2438 (4)* 2.30 2.30

For overprints see Nos. 2453-2456.

Treaty of Asuncion, 1st Anniv. — A450

***Rough Perf. 13x13½***

**1993, Mar. 10 Wmk. 347**

**2439** A450 50g Flags, map .50 .30
**2440** A450 350g Flags, globe 1.50 1.25

Santa Isabel Leprosy Assoc., 50th Anniv. — A451

Various flowers.

***Perf. 13x13½***

**1993, May 24 Unwmk.**

**2441** A451 50g multicolored .30 .30
**2442** A451 200g multicolored .75 .75
**2443** A451 250g multicolored .90 .90
**2444** A451 350g multicolored 1.25 1.25
*Nos. 2441-2444 (4)* 3.20 3.20

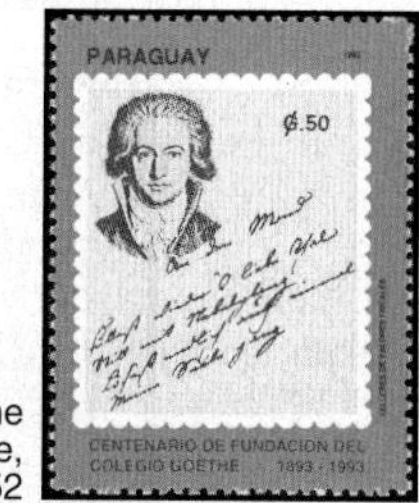


Goethe College, Cent. — A452

Designs: 50g, Goethe, by Johann Heinrich Lips, inscription. 100g, Goethe (close-up), by Johann Heinrich Wilhelm Tischbein.

**1993, June 18**

**2445** A452 50g multicolored .30 .30
**2446** A452 200g multicolored .75 .75

For overprints see Nos. 2451-2452.

World Friendship Crusade, 35th Anniv. — A453

Designs: 50g, Stylized globe. 100g, Map, Dr. Ramon Artemio Bracho. 200g, Children. 250g, Two people embracing.

**1993, July 1**

**2447** A453 50g multicolored .40 .30
**2448** A453 100g multicolored .40 .35
**2449** A453 200g multicolored .80 .75
**2450** A453 250g multicolored 1.00 .90
*Nos. 2447-2450 (4)* 2.60 2.30

For overprint see No. 2486.

**Nos. 2445-2446 Ovptd. "BRASILIANA 93"**

**1993, July 12**

**2451** A452 50g multicolored .30 .30
**2452** A452 200g multicolored .85 .85

**Nos. 2435-2438 Ovptd.**

***Perf. 13½x13, 13x13½***

**1993, Aug. 13**

**2453** A449 50g multicolored .30 .30
**2454** A449 100g multicolored .40 .35
**2455** A449 200g multicolored .80 .75
**2456** A449 250g multicolored 1.00 .90
*Nos. 2453-2456 (4)* 2.50 2.30

Size of overprint varies.

Church of the Incarnation, Cent. — A454

Design: 50g, Side view of church, vert.

**Unwmk.**

**1993, Oct. 8** **Litho.** ***Perf. 13***

**2457** A454 50g multicolored .30 .30
**2458** A454 350g multicolored 1.20 .60

Endangered Animals — A455

America: 50g, Myrmecophaga tridactyla. 250g, Speothos venaticus.

**1993, Oct. 27**

**2459** A455 50g multicolored 2.50 .60
**2460** A455 250g multicolored 1.50 .75

No. 2459 is airmail.

Nos. 2426-2427 Ovptd.

**1993, Nov. 16** ***Perf. 13x13½***

**2461** A447 100g multicolored .30 .30
**2462** A447 200g multicolored .60 .30

Christmas A456

**1993, Nov. 24**

**2463** A456 50g shown .30 .30
**2464** A456 250g Stars, wise men .70 .30

Scouting in Paraguay, 80th Anniv. A457

50g, Girl scouts watching scout instuctor. 100g, Boy scouts learning crafts. 200g, Lord Robert Baden-Powell. 250g, Girl scout with flag.

**1993, Dec. 30**

**2465** A457 50g multicolored .30 .30
**2466** A457 100g multicolored .30 .30
**2467** A457 200g multicolored .60 .30
**2468** A457 250g multicolored .80 .50
*Nos. 2465-2468 (4)* 2.00 1.40

First Lawyers to Graduate from Natl. University of Ascuncion, Cent. — A458

50g, Cecilio Baez. 100g, Benigno Riquelme, vert. 250g, Emeterio Gonzalez. 500g, J. Gaspar Villamayor.

**1994, Apr. 8** ***Perf. 13***

**2469** A458 50g multicolored .40 .30
**2470** A458 100g multicolored .50 .30
**2471** A458 250g multicolored .60 .45
**2472** A458 500g multicolored 1.00 .75
*Nos. 2469-2472 (4)* 2.50 1.80

Phoenix Sports Corporation, 50th Anniv. — A459

Designs: 50g, Basketball player, vert. 200g, Soccer players, vert. 250g, Pedro Andrias Garcia Arias, founder, tennis player.

**1994, May 20** **Litho.** ***Perf. 13***

**2473** A459 50g multicolored .30 .30
**2474** A459 200g multicolored .35 .35
**2475** A459 250g multicolored .50 .45
*Nos. 2473-2475 (3)* 1.15 1.10

1994 World Cup Soccer Championships, U.S. — A460

Various soccer plays.

**1994, June 2**

**2476** A460 250g multicolored .50 .45
**2477** A460 500g multicolored 1.00 .75
**2478** A460 1000g multicolored 1.75 1.50
*Nos. 2476-2478 (3)* 3.25 2.70

For overprints see Nos. 2483-2485.

Intl. Olympic Committee, Cent. — A461

350g, Runner. 400g, Lighting Olympic flame.

**Unwmk.**

**1994, June 23** **Litho.** ***Perf. 13***

**2479** A461 350g multicolored .60 .60
**2480** A461 400g multicolored .65 .65

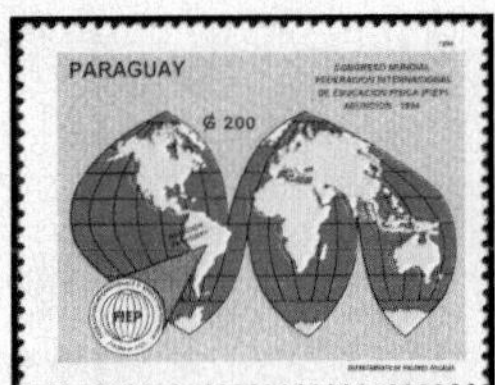


World Congress on Physical Education, Asuncion — A462

Designs: 1000g, Stylized family running to break finish line, vert.

***Perf. 13½x13, 13x13½***

**1994, July 19** **Litho.**

**2481** A462 200g multicolored .60 .45
**2482** A462 1000g multicolored 2.75 2.25

Nos. 2476-2478 Ovptd.

**1994, Aug. 2** ***Perf. 13***

**2483** A460 250g multicolored .65 .65
**2484** A460 500g multicolored 1.40 1.40
**2485** A460 1000g multicolored 2.75 2.25
*Nos. 2483-2485 (3)* 4.80 4.30

No. 2448 Ovptd.

**1994, Aug. 3** ***Perf. 13x13½***

**2486** A453 100g multicolored .50 .30

Agustin Pio Barrios Mangore (1885-1944), Musician A463

250g, In tuxedo. 500g, In traditional costume.

**1994, Aug. 5** ***Perf. 13x13½***

**2487** A463 250g multi .60 .50
**2488** A463 500g multi 1.25 1.00

Paraguayan Police, 151st Anniv. — A464

50g, 1913 Guardsman on horseback. 250g, Pedro Nolasco Fernandez, 1st capital police chief; Carlos Bernadino Cacabelos, 1st commissioner.

**1994, Aug. 26** ***Perf. 13x13½***

**2489** A464 50g multicolored .30 .30
**2490** A464 250g multicolored .65 .60

For overprint see Nos. 2569-2570.

Parafil '94 A465

Birds: 100g, Ciconia maquari. 150g, Paroaria capitata. 400g, Chloroceryle americana, vert. 500g, Jabiru mycteria, vert.

**1994, Sept. 9** ***Perf. 13***

**2491** A465 100g multicolored .50 .30
**2492** A465 150g multicolored .75 .40
**2493** A465 400g multicolored 1.90 .90
**2494** A465 500g multicolored 2.75 1.10
*Nos. 2491-2494 (4)* 5.90 2.70

Solar Eclipse A466

Designs: 50g, Eclipse, Copernicus. 200g, Sundial, Johannes Kepler.

**Unwmk.**

**1994, Sept. 23 Litho.** ***Perf. 13***

**2495** A466 50g multicolored .30 .30
**2496** A466 200g multicolored .60 .45

America Issue A467

100g, Derelict locomotive. 1000g, Motorcycle.

**1994, Oct. 11** ***Perf. 13½***

**2497** A467 100g multicolored .60 .45
**2498** A467 1000g multicolored 4.50 3.00

Intl. Year of the Family — A468

**1994, Oct. 25** ***Perf. 13x13½***

**2499** A468 50g Mother, child .40 .30
**2500** A468 250g Family faces .80 .60

Christmas — A469

Ceramic figures: 150g, Nativity. 700g, Joseph, infant Jesus, Mary, vert.

**1994, Nov. 4** ***Perf. 13½***

**2501** A469 150g multicolored .45 .35
**2502** A469 700g multicolored 2.10 1.60

Paraguayan Red Cross, 75th Anniv. — A470

Black Red Cross — A470a

Designs: 150g, Boy Scouts, Jean-Henri Dunant. 700g, Soldiers, paramedics, Dr. Andres Barbero.

**1994, Nov. 25** ***Perf. 13½x13***

**2503** A470 150g multi .60 .45
**2503A** A470a 500g multi 200.00
**2504** A470 700g multi 3.00 2.40

When it was discovered that No. 2503A contained a black cross instead of a red cross it was withdrawn.

San Jose College, 90th Anniv. — A471

Pope John Paul II and: 200g, Eternal flame. 250g, College entrance.

**1994, Dec. 4**

**2505** A471 200g multicolored .60 .45
**2506** A471 250g multicolored .75 .60

Louis Pasteur (1822-95) A472

**1995, Mar. 24 Litho.** ***Perf. 13½***

**2507** A472 1000g multicolored 3.00 2.10

Fight Against AIDS — A473

**1995, May 4**

**2508** A473 500g Faces 1.50 .75
**2509** A473 1000g shown 3.00 1.50

FAO, 50th Anniv. A474

**1995, June 23**

**2510** A474 950g Bread, pitcher 2.10 1.50
**2511** A474 2000g Watermelon 4.50 3.00

Fifth Neotropical Ornithological Congress — A475

100g, Parula pitiayumi. 200g, Chirroxiphia caudata. 600g, Icterus icterus. 1000g, Carduelis magellanica.

**1995, July 6**

**2512** A475 100g multicolored .60 .45
**2513** A475 200g multicolored .75 .45
**2514** A475 600g multicolored 2.75 1.20
**2515** A475 1000g multicolored 3.00 2.10
*Nos. 2512-2515 (4)* 7.10 4.20

Fifth Intl. Symposium on Municipalities, Ecology & Tourism A476

Designs: 1150g, Rio Monday rapids. 1300g, Areguá Railroad Station.

**1995, Aug. 4 Litho.** ***Perf. 13½***

**2516** A476 1150g multicolored 1.90 1.25
**2517** A476 1300g multicolored 2.10 1.40

Volleyball, Cent. — A477

600g, Ball, net. 1000g, Hands, ball, net.

**1995, Sept. 28**

**2518** A477 300g shown .55 .30
**2519** A477 600g multi 1.10 .60
**2520** A477 1000g multi 1.60 1.00
*Nos. 2518-2520 (3)* 3.25 1.90

America Issue A478

Preserve the environment: 950g, Macizo Monument, Achay. 2000g, Tinfunique Reserve, Chaco, vert.

**1995, Oct. 12**

**2521** A478 950g multicolored 3.00 1.00
**2522** A478 2000g multicolored 5.00 2.10

UN, 50th Anniv. — A479

Designs: 200g, Flags above olive branch. 3000g, UN emblem, stick figures.

**1995, Oct. 20**

**2523** A479 200g multicolored .30 .30
**2524** A479 3000g multicolored 4.50 3.00

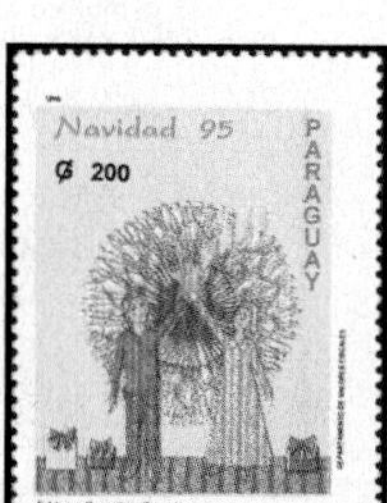


Christmas A480

**1995, Nov. 7**

**2525** A480 200g shown .50 .30
**2526** A480 1000g Nativity 2.00 1.00

Jose Marti (1853-95) — A481

Designs: 200g, Hedychium coronarium, Marti, vert. 1000g, Hedychium coronarium, map & flag of Cuba, Marti.

**1995, Dec. 19 Litho.** ***Perf. 13½***

**2527** A481 200g multicolored .50 .30
**2528** A481 1000g multicolored 2.50 1.10

Lion's Clubs of South America & the Caribbean, 25th Anniv. — A482

**1996, Jan. 11**

**2529** A482 200g Railway station .40 .30
**2530** A482 1000g Viola House 1.75 1.10

Orchids A483

Designs: 100g, Cattleya nobilior. 200g, Oncidium varicosum. 1000g, Oncidium jonesianum, vert. 1150g, Sophronitis cernua.

***Perf. 13½x13, 13x13½***

**1996, Apr. 22** **Litho.**

**2531** A483 100g multicolored .50 .45
**2532** A483 200g multicolored .50 .45
**2533** A483 1000g multicolored 2.25 1.20
**2534** A483 1150g multicolored 2.50 1.40
*Nos. 2531-2534 (4)* 5.75 3.50

1996 Summer Olympic Games, Atlanta A484

**1996, June 6** ***Perf. 13½x13***

**2535** A484 500g Diving 1.00 .45
**2536** A484 1000g Running 2.00 .90

Founding of Society of Salesian Fathers in Paraguay, Cent. — A485

Pope John Paul II, St. John Bosco (1815-88), and: 200g, Men, boys from Salesian Order, natl. flag. 300g, Madonna and Child, vert. 1000g, Map of Paraguay, man following light.

**1996, July 22** ***Perf. 13½x13, 13x13½***

**2537** A485 200g multicolored .40 .30
**2538** A485 300g multicolored .50 .30
**2539** A485 1000g multicolored 1.60 .90
*Nos. 2537-2539 (3)* 2.50 1.50

UNICEF, 50th Anniv. — A486

Children's paintings: 1000g, Outdoor scene, by S. Báez, 1300g, Four groups of children, by C. Pérez.

**1996, Sept. 27** *Perf. 13½x13*
**2540** A486 1000g multicolored 2.25 .90
**2541** A486 1300g multicolored 2.50 1.25

Visit of Pope John Paul II to Caacupe, Site of Apparition of the Virgin — A487

Design: 200g, Pope John Paul II, church, Virgin of Caacupe, vert.

**1996, Oct. 4** *Perf. 13x13½, 13½x13*
**2542** A487 200g multicolored .35 .35
**2543** A487 1300g multicolored 2.10 1.50

Traditional Costumes A488

America issue: 500g, Woman in costume. 1000g, Woman, man, in costumes.

**1996, Oct. 11** *Perf. 13x13½*
**2544** A488 500g multicolored 1.25 .45
**2545** A488 1000g multicolored 3.00 .90

UN Year for Eradication of Poverty — A489

**1996, Oct. 17** *Perf. 13½x13, 13x13½*
**2546** A489 1000g Food products 1.60 .90
**2547** A489 1150g Boy, fruit, vert. 1.75 1.10

Christmas A490

Madonna and Child, by: 200g, Koki Ruíz. 1000g, Hernán Miranda.

**1996, Nov. 7** *Perf. 13x13½*
**2548** A490 200g multicolored .75 .30
**2549** A490 1000g multicolored 1.75 .90

Butterflies A491

Designs: 200g, Eryphanis automedon. 500g, Dryadula phaetusa. 1000g, Vanessa myrinna. 1150g, Heliconius ethilla.

**1997, Mar. 5** **Litho.** *Perf. 13x13½*
**2550** A491 200g multicolored .60 .30
**2551** A491 500g multicolored 1.75 .45
**2552** A491 1000g multicolored 3.00 .80
**2553** A491 1150g multicolored 3.50 .95
*Nos. 2550-2553 (4)* 8.85 2.50

Official Buildings — A492

200g, 1st Legistlature. 1000g, Postal Headquarters.

**1997, May 5** *Perf. 13½x13*
**2554** A492 200g multicolored .75 .30
**2555** A492 1000g multicolored 1.75 .90

1997, Year of Jesus Christ — A493

1000g, Crucifix, Pope John Paul II.

**1997, June 10** *Perf. 13x13½*
**2556** A493 1000g multi 2.00 .75

11th Summit of the Rio Group Chiefs of State, Asunción — A494

**1997, Aug. 23** *Perf. 13½x13*
**2557** A494 1000g multicolored 2.00 1.00

Environmental and Climate Change — A495

Flowers: 300g, Opunita elata. 500g, Bromelia balansae, 1000g, Monvillea kroenlaini.

*Perf. 13½x13, 13x13½*
**1997, Aug. 25**
**2558** A495 300g multi .60 .30
**2559** A495 500g multi, vert. .80 .50
**2560** A495 1000g multi 1.75 1.00
*Nos. 2558-2560 (3)* 3.15 1.80

1st Philatelic Exposition of MERCOSUR Countries, Chile and Bolivia — A496

Fauna: 200g, Felis tigrina. 1000g, Alouatta caraya, vert. 1150g, Agouti paca.

*Perf. 13½x13, 13x13½*
**1997, Aug. 29**
**2561** A496 200g multicolored .50 .25
**2562** A496 1000g multicolored 2.00 1.00
**2563** A496 1150g multicolored 2.25 1.10
*Nos. 2561-2563 (3)* 4.75 2.35

MERCOSUR (Common Market of Latin America) A497

**1997, Sept. 26** *Perf. 13x13½*
**2564** A497 1000g multicolored 2.00 .90

See Argentina #1975, Bolivia #1019, Brazil #2646, Urugray #1681.

America Issue — A498

Life of a postman: 1000g, Postman, letters going around the world, vert. 1150g, Window with six panes showing weather conditions, different roads, postman.

**1997, Oct. 10** *Perf. 13x13½, 13½x13*
**2565** A498 1000g multicolored 2.50 1.00
**2566** A498 1150g multicolored 2.50 1.25

Natl. Council on Sports, 50th Anniv. — A499

200g, Neri Kennedy throwing javelin. 1000g, Ramón Milciades Giménez Gaona throwing discus.

**1997, Oct. 16** *Perf. 13x13½*
**2567** A499 200g multicolored .50 .30
**2568** A499 1000g multicolored 2.00 1.10

Nos. 2489-2490 Ovptd. in Red

**1997, Nov. 14**
**2569** A464 50g multicolored 1.00 .45
**2570** A464 250g multicolored 3.50 2.00

Christmas A500

Paintings of Madonna and Child: 200g, By Olga Blinder. 1000g, By Hermán Miranda.

**1997, Nov. 17**
**2571** A500 200g multicolored .50 .30
**2572** A500 1000g multicolored 2.00 1.00

UN Fund for Children of the World with AIDS — A501

Children's paintings: 500g, Boy. 1000g, Girl.

**1997, Dec. 5**
**2573** A501 500g multicolored 1.00 .45
**2574** A501 1000g multicolored 1.75 .90

Rotary Club of Asunción, 70th Anniv. — A502

**1997, Dec. 11**
**2575** A502 1150g multicolored 2.00 1.00

1998 World Cup Soccer Championships, France — A503

200g, Julio César Romero, vert. 500g, Carlos Gamarra, vert. 1000g, 1998 Paraguayan team.

**1998, Jan. 22** **Litho.** *Perf. 13*
**2576** A503 200g multicolored .30 .25
**2577** A503 500g multicolored .90 .45
**2578** A503 1000g multicolored 1.80 .90
*Nos. 2576-2578 (3)* 3.00 1.60

Fish
A504

Designs: 200g, Tetrogonopterus argenteus. 300g, Pseudoplatystoma coruscans. 500g, Salminus brasiliensis. 1000g, Acestrorhynchus altus.

**1998, Apr. 17 Litho.** ***Perf. 13⅓***

| | | | | |
|---|---|---|---|---|
| **2579** | A504 | 200g multicolored | .70 | .30 |
| **2580** | A504 | 300g multicolored | .90 | .30 |
| **2581** | A504 | 500g multicolored | 1.25 | .45 |
| **2582** | A504 | 1000g multicolored | 2.75 | .90 |
| | | *Nos. 2579-2582 (4)* | 5.60 | 1.95 |

Contemporary Paintings — A505

200g, Hands, geometric shape, by Carlos Colombino. 300g, Mother nursing infant, by Félix Toranzos. 400g, Flowers, by Edith Giménez. 1000g, Woman lifting tray of food, by Ricardo Migliorisi.

**1998, June 5**

| | | | | |
|---|---|---|---|---|
| **2583** | A505 | 200g multi, vert. | .30 | .25 |
| **2584** | A505 | 300g multi, vert. | .60 | .30 |
| **2585** | A505 | 400g multi, vert. | .70 | .30 |
| **2586** | A505 | 1000g multi | 1.60 | .75 |
| | | *Nos. 2583-2586 (4)* | 3.20 | 1.60 |

Mushrooms
A506

400g, Boletus edulis. 600g, Macrolepiota procera. 1000g, Geastrum triplex.

**1998, June 26**

| | | | | |
|---|---|---|---|---|
| **2587** | A506 | 400g multicolored | .75 | .30 |
| **2588** | A506 | 600g multicolored | 1.00 | .50 |
| **2589** | A506 | 1000g multicolored | 1.75 | .90 |
| | | *Nos. 2587-2589 (3)* | 3.50 | 1.70 |

Organization of American States (OAS), 50th Anniv. — A507

Designs: 500g, Home of Carlos A. López, botantical and zoological gardens, Asunción. 1000g, Palmerola Villa, Areguá.

**1998, July 16**

| | | | | |
|---|---|---|---|---|
| **2590** | A507 | 500g multicolored | 1.00 | .40 |
| **2591** | A507 | 1000g multicolored | 2.00 | .90 |

Episcopacy of Hernando de Trejo y Sanabria, 400th Anniv. — A508

Pope John Paul II and: 400g, Sacrarium doors, Caazapá Church, vert. 1700g, Statue of St. Francis of Assisi, Atyrá Church.

***Perf. 13x13½, 13½x13***

**1998, Sept. 5 Litho.**

| | | | | |
|---|---|---|---|---|
| **2592** | A508 | 400g multi | 1.00 | .40 |
| **2593** | A508 | 1700g multi | 3.00 | 1.75 |

Ruins of Jesuit Mission Church
A509

**1998, Sept. 16 Litho.** ***Perf. 13½x13***

| | | | | |
|---|---|---|---|---|
| **2594** | A509 | 5000g multicolored | 8.00 | 5.00 |

Flowers
A510

Designs: 100g, Acacia caven. 600g, Cordia trichotoma. 1900g, Glandularia sp.

**1998, Sept. 16 Litho.** ***Perf. 13x13½***

| | | | | |
|---|---|---|---|---|
| **2595** | A510 | 100g multi | .30 | .25 |
| **2596** | A510 | 600g multi | 1.20 | .50 |
| **2597** | A510 | 1900g multi | 3.25 | 1.75 |
| | | *Nos. 2595-2597 (3)* | 4.75 | 2.50 |

America Issue
A511

Famous women and buildings: 1600g, Serafina Davalos (1883-1957), first woman lawyer, National College building. 1700g, Adela Speratti (1865-1902), director of Normal School.

**1998, Oct. 12 Litho.** ***Perf. 13½x13***

| | | | | |
|---|---|---|---|---|
| **2598** | A511 | 1600g multi | 3.50 | 1.50 |
| **2599** | A511 | 1700g multi | 4.00 | 1.75 |

Universal Declaration of Human Rights, 50th Anniv. — A512

Artwork by: 500g, Carlos Colombino. 1000g, Jose Filártiga.

**1998, Oct. 23** ***Perf. 13x13½***

| | | | | |
|---|---|---|---|---|
| **2600** | A512 | 500g multi | 1.00 | .50 |
| **2601** | A512 | 1000g multi | 1.90 | 1.00 |

Christmas Creche Figures — A513

***Perf. 13½x13, 13x13½***

**1998, Sept. 16 Litho.**

| | | | | |
|---|---|---|---|---|
| **2602** | A513 | 300g shown | 1.00 | .25 |
| **2603** | A513 | 1600g Stable, vert. | 3.00 | 1.75 |

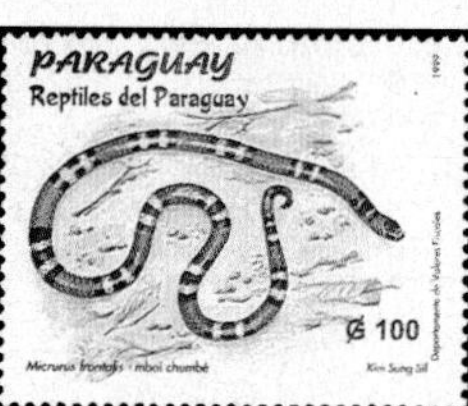

Reptiles
A514

Designs: 100g, Micrurus frontalis. 300g, Ameiva ameiva. 1600g, Geochelone carbonaria. 1700g, Caiman yacare.

**1999, May 13 Litho.** ***Perf. 13½x13***

| | | | | |
|---|---|---|---|---|
| **2604-2607** | A514 | Set of 4 | 6.00 | 4.00 |

Paintings — A515

Paintings by: 500g, Ignacio Nuñez Soler. 1600g, Modesto Delgado Rodas. 1700g, Jaime Bestard.

**1999, June 23 Litho.** ***Perf. 13½x13***

| | | | | |
|---|---|---|---|---|
| **2608** | A515 | 500g multi | .65 | .40 |
| **2609** | A515 | 1600g multi | 2.00 | 1.40 |
| **2610** | A515 | 1700g multi | 2.25 | 1.40 |
| | | *Nos. 2608-2610 (3)* | 4.90 | 3.20 |

America Soccer Cup
A516

Designs: 300g, Carlos Humberto Paredes, vert. 500g, South American Soccer Confederation Building, Luque. 1900g, Feliciano Cáceres Stadium, Luque.

***Perf. 13x13½, 13½x13***

**1999, June 24**

| | | | | |
|---|---|---|---|---|
| **2611** | A516 | 300g multi | .40 | .25 |
| **2612** | A516 | 500g multi | .70 | .35 |
| **2613** | A516 | 1900g multi | 2.75 | 1.50 |
| | | *Nos. 2611-2613 (3)* | 3.85 | 2.10 |

SOS Children's Villages, 50th Anniv. — A517

**1999, July 16** ***Perf. 13½x13, 13x13½***

| | | | | |
|---|---|---|---|---|
| **2614** | A517 | 1700g Toucan | 2.50 | 1.10 |
| **2615** | A517 | 1900g Toucan, vert. | 3.50 | 1.40 |

Protests of Assassination of Vice-President Luis Maria Argaña — A518

Designs: 100g, Protest at Governmental Palace. 500g, Argaña, vert. 1500g, Protest at National Congress.

**1999, Aug. 26**

| | | | | |
|---|---|---|---|---|
| **2616** | A518 | 100g multi | .25 | .25 |
| **2617** | A518 | 500g multi | .70 | .40 |
| **2618** | A518 | 1500g multi | 1.90 | 1.25 |
| | | *Nos. 2616-2618 (3)* | 2.85 | 1.90 |

Medicinal Plants — A519

Designs: 600g, Cochlospermum regium. 700g, Borago officinalis. 1700g, Passiflora cincinnata.

**1999, Sept. 8** ***Perf. 13x13½***

| | | | | |
|---|---|---|---|---|
| **2619** | A519 | 600g multi | .75 | .35 |
| **2620** | A519 | 700g multi | .75 | .45 |
| **2621** | A519 | 1700g multi | 2.00 | 1.00 |
| | | *Nos. 2619-2621 (3)* | 3.50 | 1.80 |

America Issue, A New Millennium Without Arms — A520

Various artworks by Ricardo Migliorisi.

***Perf. 13½x13, 13x13½***

**1999, Oct. 12 Litho.**

| | | | | |
|---|---|---|---|---|
| **2622** | A520 | 1500g multi | 2.00 | 1.10 |
| **2623** | A520 | 3000g multi, vert. | 3.50 | 2.25 |

Intl. Year of the Elderly
A521

Artwork by: 1000g, Olga Blinder. 1900g, Maria de los Reyes Omella Herrero, vert.

***Perf. 13½x13, 13x13½***

**1999, Oct. 20 Litho.**

| | | | | |
|---|---|---|---|---|
| **2624-2625** | A521 | Set of 2 | 3.50 | 2.00 |

Christmas
A522

Artwork by: 300g, Manuel Viedma. 1600g, Federico Ordiñana.

**1999, Nov. 11 Litho.** ***Perf. 13x13½***

**2626** A522 300g multi .75 .25
**2627** A522 1600g multi 2.25 1.00

City of Pedro Juan Caballero, Cent. — A523

Flowers: 1000g, Tabebuia impetiginosa. 1600g, Tabebuia pulcherrima, vert.

***Perf. 13½x13, 13x13½***

**1999, Dec. 1 Litho.**

**2628** A523 1000g multi 1.25 .70
**2629** A523 1600g multi 1.75 1.00

Inter-American Development Bank, 40th Anniv. — A524

Designs: 600g, Oratory of Our Lady of Asuncion and Pantheon of Heroes, Asuncion. 700g, Governmental Palace.

**1999, Dec. 6** ***Perf. 13½x13***

**2630** A524 600g multi 1.00 .35
**2631** A524 700g multi 1.25 .45

Intl. Women's Day — A525

Carmen Casco de Lara Castro and sculpture: 400g, Conjunction, by Domingo Rivarola. 2000g, Violation, by Gustavo Beckelmann.

**2000, Apr. 7 Litho.** ***Perf. 13x13½***

**2632-2633** A525 Set of 2 3.00 3.00

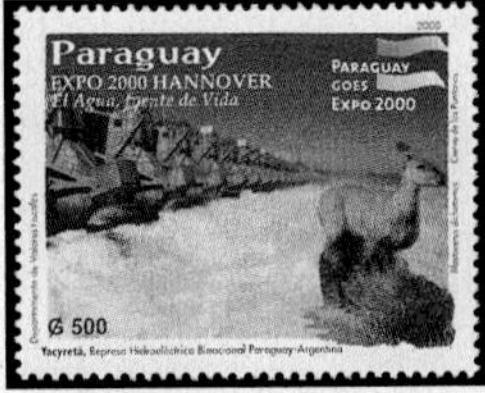


Expo 2000, Hanover A526

Designs: 500g, Yacyreta Dam and deer. 2500g, Itaipú Dam, tapir.

**2000, May 5** ***Perf. 13½x13***

**2634-2635** A526 Set of 2 4.00 3.50

Salesians in Paraguay, Cent. — A527

Madonna and Child, Pope John Paul II and: 600g, Salesians, vert. 2000g, College building.

***Perf. 13x13½, 13½x13***

**2000, May 19 Litho.**

**2636-2637** A527 Set of 2 3.00 3.00

2000 Summer Olympics, Sydney — A528

Designs: 2500g, Soccer, vert. 3000g, Runner Francisco Rojas Soto.

**2000, July 28** ***Perf. 13x13½, 13½x13***

**2638-2639** A528 Set of 2 7.50 7.50

Rights of the Child A529

Designs: 1500g, Child between hands, vert. 1700g, Handprints.

***Perf. 13x13½, 13½x13***

**2000, Aug. 16**

**2640-2641** A529 Set of 2 4.50 4.50

Fire Fighters A530

Designs: 100g, Fire fighters, white truck, vert. 200g, Fire fighter in old uniform, emblem, vert. 1500g, Fire fighters at fire. 1600g, Fire fighters, yellow truck.

***Perf. 13x13½, 13½x13***

**2000, Sept. 28**

**2642-2645** A530 Set of 4 5.00 4.50

Roads and Flowers — A531

Designs: 500g, Paved road between San Bernardino and Altos, Rosa banksiae. 3000g, Gaspar Rodriguez de Francia Highway, Calliandra brevicaulis.

**2000, Oct. 5 Litho.** ***Perf. 13½x13¼***

**2646-2647** A531 Set of 2 5.00 5.00

America Issue, Fight Against AIDS — A532

Designs: 1500g, Signs with arrows. 2500g, Tic-tac-toe game.

**2000, Oct. 19** ***Perf. 13x13½***

**2648-2649** A532 Set of 2 5.50 5.50

Intl. Year of Culture and Peace A533

Sculptures by: 500g, Hugo Pistilli. 2000g, Herman Guggiari.

**2000, Oct. 27 Litho.** ***Perf. 13¼x13½***

**2650-2651** A533 Set of 2 3.25 3.25

Christmas A534

Designs: 100g, Holy Family, sculpture by Hugo Pistilli. 500g, Poem by José Luis Appleyard. 2000g, Creche figures, horiz.

***Perf. 13x13½, 13½x13***

**2000, Nov. 17 Litho.**

**2652-2654** A534 Set of 3 3.50 3.50

Artisan's Crafts — A535

Designs: 200g, Campesina Woman, by Behage. 1500g, Cattle horns, by Quintin Velazquez, horiz. 2000g, Silver filigree orchid, by Quirino Torres.

***Perf. 13¼x13½, 13½x13¼***

**2000, Nov. 28 Litho.**

**2655-2657** A535 Set of 3 5.25 5.25

Guarania Music, 75th Anniv. — A536

Designs: 100g, José Asunción Flores (1904-72), composer. 1500g, Violin. 2500g, Trombone.

**2000, Dec. 20** ***Perf. 13¼x13½***

**2658-2660** A536 Set of 3 5.00 5.00

Signing of Asunción Treaty, 10th Anniv. A537

Designs: 500g, Delegates signing treaty. 2500g, Map of South America with signatory nations colored, vert.

***Perf. 13½x13¼, 13¼x13½***

**2001, June 20**

**2661-2662** A537 Set of 2 3.50 3.50

Cacti — A538

Designs: 2000g, Opuntia sp. 2500g, Cereus stenogonus.

**2001, June 29** ***Perf. 13¼x13½***

**2663-2664** A538 Set of 2 6.00 6.00

Second Paz del Chaco Philatelic Exhibition.

Under 20 Soccer Championships, Argentina — A539

Designs: 2000g, Players. 2500g, Players, diff., vert.

***Perf. 13½x13¼, 13¼x13½***

**2001, June 29**

**2665-2666** A539 Set of 2 6.00 6.00

Cattle A540

Designs: 200g, Holando-Argentino. 500g, Nelore. 1500g, Pampa Chaqueño.

**2001, July 20** ***Perf. 13½x13¼***

**2667-2669** A540 Set of 3 3.50 3.50

Engravings — A541

Woodcuts by: No. 2670, 500g, Josefina Plá. No. 2671, 500g, Leonor Cecotto, vert. 1500g, Jacinto Rivero. 2000g, Livio Abramo.

***Perf. 13½x13¼, 13¼x13½***

**2001, Aug. 28**

**2670-2673** A541 Set of 4 6.00 6.00

Mythological Heavens of the Guarani — A542

Designs: 100g, Eichu (Pleiades). 600g, Mborevi Rape (Milky Way). 1600g, Jagua Ho'u Jasy (lunar eclipse).

**2001, Sept. 24** ***Perf. 13½x13¼***
**2674-2676** A542 Set of 3 3.25 3.25

America Issue — UNESCO World Heritage Sites — A543

No. 2677: a, 500g, St. Ignatius of Loyola, Jesuit Mission Ruins, Trinidad. b, 2000g, Jesuit Mission Ruins.

**2001, Oct. 9** ***Perf. 13¼x13½***
**2677** A543 Horiz. pair, #a-b, + 2 flanking labels 3.50 3.50

World Teachers' Day — A544

Designs: 200g, Children studying, school blackboard, J. Inocencio Lezcano (1889-1935), educator. 1600g, Symbols of education, Ramón I. Cardozo (1876-1943), educator.

**2001, Oct. 9** ***Perf. 13½x13¼***
**2678-2679** A544 Set of 2 2.50 2.50

Year of Dialogue Among Civilizations — A545

**2001, Oct. 23** ***Perf. 13¼x13½***
**2680** A545 3000g multi + 2 flanking labels 4.25 4.25

Christmas — A546

Nativity scenes by: 700g, Gladys and Maria de Feliciangeli. 4000g, Mercedes Servin.

**2001, Nov. 29** ***Perf. 13½x13¼***
**2681-2682** A546 Set of 2 5.00 5.00

No to Terrorism A547

Designs: 700g, Statue of Liberty, World Trade Center, vert. 5000g, Flags of Paraguay and U.S., chain becoming doves.

***Perf. 13¼x13½, 13½x13¼***

**2001, Dec. 19** **Litho.**
**2683-2684** A547 Set of 2 8.50 8.50

Passiflora Caerulea A548

**2001, Dec. 21** ***Perf. 13¼x13½***
**2685** A548 4000g multi 4.50 4.00

Paraguayan, Bolivian, and Argentinian Scout Jamboree, Boquerón Province A549

**2002, Jan. 24**
**2686** A549 6000g multi 9.50 9.50

El Mbiguá Social Club, Asunción, Cent. — A550

**2002, May 3** ***Perf. 13½x13¼***
**2687** A550 700g multi 1.10 1.10

Juan de Salazar Spanish Cultural Center, 25th Anniv. — A551

Jesuit wood carvings, 18th cent.: 2500g, Pieta. 5000g, St. Michael Archangel.

**2002, May 7** ***Perf. 13¼x13½***
**2688-2689** A551 Set of 2 11.00 11.00

2002 World Cup Soccer Championships, Japan and Korea — A552

Designs: 3000g, Paraguay team. 5000g, Players in action, vert.

***Perf. 13½x13¼, 13¼x13½***

**2002, May 18**
**2690-2691** A552 Set of 2 12.00 12.00

For overprint see No. 2705.

Arrival of Mennonites in Paraguay, 75th Anniv. — A553

Cross, plow, Menno Simons (1496-1561), Religious Leader, and: 2000g, Mennonite Church, Filadelfia. 4000g, Mennonite Church, Loma Plata.

**2002, June 25** ***Perf. 13½x13¼***
**2692-2693** A553 Set of 2 7.50 7.50

Horses A554

Designs: 700g, Criollo. 1000g, Cuarto de Milla (quarterhorse). 6000g, Arabian.

**2002, July 12**
**2694-2696** A554 Set of 3 9.50 9.50

Olimpia Soccer Team, Cent. — A555

**2002, July 24**
**2697** A555 700g multi + 2 flanking labels 2.00 2.00

Pan-American Health Organization, Cent. — A556

Medicinal plants: 4000g, Stevia rebaudiana bertoni. 5000g, Ilex paraguayensis.

**2002, Sept. 16** ***Perf. 13¼x13½***
**2698-2699** A556 Set of 2 13.00 13.00

International Forum on Postal Service Modernization and Reform — A557

Forum emblem and statues by Serafin Marsal: 1000g, Campesina. 4000g, Quygua-vera.

**2002, Sept. 30** ***Perf. 13½x13¼***
**2700-2701** A557 Set of 2 7.00 7.00

Paraguay — Republic of China Diplomatic Relations, 45th Anniv. — A558

**2002, Oct. 10** ***Perf. 13¼x13½***
**2702** A558 4000g multi + 2 flanking labels 6.00 6.00

America Issue — Youth, Education and Literacy — A559

Designs: 3000g, Classroom. 6000g, Children playing.

**2002, Oct. 12** ***Perf. 13½x13¼***
**2703-2704** A559 Set of 2 12.00 12.00

**No. 2690 Overprinted**

**2002**
**2705** A552 3000g on #2690 4.00 4.00

Christmas — A560

Various creche figures: a, 1000g. b, 4000g. c, 700g.

**2002, Dec. 2** **Litho.** ***Perf. 13¼***
**2706** A560 Horiz. strip of 3, #a-c 7.00 7.00

Church, Areguá — A561

**2002, Dec. 18**
**2707** A561 4000g multi 4.50 4.50

District of San Antonio, Cent. — A562

**2003, Apr. 21** **Litho.** ***Perf. 13¼***
**2708** A562 700g multi .50 .50

Josefina Plá (1903-99), Artist — A563

Designs: 700g, Plate. 6000g, Carving.

**2003, May 30** **Litho.** ***Perf. 13¼***
**2709-2710** A563 Set of 2 5.00 5.00

Parrots — A564

Designs: 1000g, Amazona aestiva. 2000g, Myiopsitta monachus. 4000g, Aratinga leucophtalmus.

**2003, June 9**
**2711-2713** A564 Set of 3 6.50 6.50

Paraguay Philatelic Center, 90th anniv. (#2711), Paz del Chaco Bi-national Philatelic Exhibition (#2712), PARAFIL Bi-national Philatelic Exhibition (#2713).

Legislative Palace — A565

**2003, June 24** ***Perf. 13½x13¼***
**2714** A565 4000g multi + label 3.50 3.50

Printed in sheets of 12 stamps and 18 labels.

Pontificate of Pope John Paul II, 25th Anniv. — A566

**2003, June 27** ***Perf. 13¼***
**2715** A566 6000g multi + label 3.50 3.50

Farm Animals A567

Designs: 1000g, Pig. 3000g, Sheep. 8000g, Goat.

**2003, July 18**
**2716-2718** A567 Set of 3 8.50 8.50

Foods A568

Designs: 700g, Peanuts, honey and nougat. 2000g, Sopa Paraguaya. 3000g, Chipá.

**2003, July 25**
**2719-2721** A568 Set of 3 4.00 4.00

Folk Artists A569

Designs: 700g, Julio Correa (1890-1953), playwright. 1000g, Emiliano Rivarola Fernández (1894-1949), singer. 2000g, Manuel Ortiz Guerrero (1894-1933), poet.

**2003, Sept. 12**
**2722-2724** A569 Set of 3 2.75 2.75

Dances A570

Designs: 700g, Golondriana. 3000g, Polka. 4000g, Galopera.

**2003, Sept. 23**
**2725-2727** A570 Set of 3 5.50 5.50

Guaraní Soccer Team, Cent. — A571

**2003, Oct. 9**
**2728** A571 700g multi + label .50 .50

Native Clothing A572

Designs: 4000g, Sixty-strip poncho, Para'i. 5000g, Shirt, Ao Poí.

**2003, Oct. 22**
**2729-2730** A572 Set of 2 6.00 6.00

Christmas A573

Designs: 700g, Journey to Egypt. 1000g, Adoration of the Shepherds. 4000g, Nativity.

**2003, Nov. 12**
**2731-2733** A573 Set of 3 4.00 4.00

Indoor Soccer World Cup Championships, Paraguay — A574

No. 2734 — Various players: a, 4000g. b, 5000g.

**2003, Nov. 14**
**2734** A574 Horiz. pair, #a-b 5.50 5.50

Printed in sheets with two columns of five pairs separated by a column of labels.

### No. 2734 Overprinted "PARAGUAY / CAMPEON MUNDIAL" in Silver

No. 2734C: d, On #2734a. e, On #2734b.

**2003** **Litho.** ***Perf. 13¼***
**2734C** A574 Horiz. pair, #d-e 5.50 5.50

America Issue - Flowers A575

Designs: 1000g, Cordia bordasii. No. 2736, 5000g, Bulnesia sarmientoi. No. 2737, 5000g, Chorisia insignis.

**2003, Nov. 26**
**2735-2737** A575 Set of 3 7.50 7.50

For overprints see Nos. 2797-2798.

Comics by Robin Wood — A576

Designs: 1000g, Anahí. 3000g, Nippur de Lagash. 5000g, Dago.

**2004, May 24** **Litho.** ***Perf. 13¼***
**2738-2740** A576 Set of 3 7.00 7.00

National Soccer Team, Cent. — A577

**2004, June 25**
**2741** A577 700g multi + label .50 .50

San José College, Cent. — A578

**2004, July 2** **Litho.** ***Perf. 13¼***
**2742** A578 700g multi .65 .65

Pablo Neruda (1904-73), Poet — A579

**2004, July 6** **Litho.** ***Perf. 13¼***
**2743** A579 5000g multi 3.50 3.50

World of the Guaranís — A580

Designs: 700g, Monday Waterfalls. 6000g, Entrance to Ciudad de Tobati.

**2004, July 7**
**2744-2745** A580 Set of 2 4.00 4.00

Nos. 2744 and 2745 were issued in sheets of 15 stamps and 10 labels.

Independence House — A581

Dr. Carlos Pussineri and: 700g, Mural by José Laterza Parodi. 5000g, Independence House.

**2004, Aug. 13** **Litho.** ***Perf. 13¼***
**2746-2747** A581 Set of 2 4.00 4.00

José Asunción Flores (1904-72), Composer A582

**2004, Aug. 24** **Litho.** ***Perf. 13¼***
**2748** A582 5000g multi 3.50 3.50

Museo del Barro, 25th Anniv. A583

Designs: 2000g, Painting by Enrique Careaga. 3000g, Anthropomorphic jug, vert. 4000g, Christ of the Column, vert.

**2004, Aug. 26**
**2749-2751** A583 Set of 3 6.00 6.00

For overprint see No. 2799.

Paraguayan Railroads, 150th Anniv. — A584

Designs: 2000g, Locomotive No. 151, Camello. 3000g, Locomotive No. 104, El Coqueto, horiz.
6000g, Locomotiove No. 10, Sapucai, horiz.

**2004, Sept. 22** *Perf. 13¼*
**2752-2753** A584 Set of 2 3.00 3.00

**Souvenir Sheet**

***Rouletted 5¼***

**2754** A584 6000g multi 5.00 5.00

No. 2754 contains one 50x40mm stamp.

America Issue — Environmental Protection — A585

Designs: No. 2755, Procnias nudicollis. No. 2756, Ceratophrys cranwelli.

**2004, Oct. 11 Litho.** *Perf. 13¼*
**2755** A585 6000g multi 3.50 3.50

**Souvenir Sheet**

***Rouletted 5¼***

**2756** A585 6000g multi 5.00 5.00

Water Conservation — A586

Designs: 3000g, Felis pardalis, storks, telephone poles. 4000g, Myrmecophaga tridactyla, Hydrochoerus hydrochaeris, Chauna torquata.

**2004, Oct. 22**
**2757-2758** A586 Set of 2 7.00 7.00

Crops — A587

Designs: 2000g, Corn. 4000g, Cotton. 6000g, Soybeans.

**2004, Oct. 22 Litho.** *Perf. 13¼*
**2759-2761** A587 Set of 3 6.50 6.50

Christmas — A588

Paintings by Ricardo Migliorisi: 3000g, Madonna and Child. 5000g, Angel, vert.

**2004, Nov. 12**
**2762-2763** A588 Set of 2 5.50 5.50

Latin American Parliament, 40th Anniv. — A589

**2004, Nov. 16**
**2764** A589 4000g multi + label 2.50 2.50

For overprint, see No. 3006.

Itaipú Dam, 30th Anniv. A590

Designs: 4000g, Dam and spillway. 5000g, Aerial view of dam, vert.

**2004, Dec. 10 Litho.** *Perf. 13¼*
**2765-2766** A590 Set of 2 5.00 5.00

Rotary International, Cent. — A591

Jesuit Mission ruins, Trinidad: 3000g, Building ruins. 4000g, Religious statue, vert.

**2005, Feb. 23 Litho.** *Perf. 13¼*
**2767-2768** A591 Set of 2 4.50 4.50

Castelvi House, Asunción, 200th Anniv. — A592

**2005, Mar. 14**
**2769** A592 5000g multi 3.00 3.00

Herminio Giménez (1905-91), Conductor — A593

**2005, Apr. 22**
**2770** A593 700g multi .50 .50

Cabildo Cultural Center, Asunción, 1st Anniv. — A594

**2005, May 19**
**2771** A594 1000g multi .70 .70

Fernheim Colony, 75th Anniv. — A595

Designs: 5000g, Pioneer's Monument. 6000g, Cross, cactus, oxcart.

**2005, June 15** *Perf. 13¼*
**2772** A595 5000g multi 3.50 3.50

**Souvenir Sheet**

***Rouletted 5¼***

**2773** A595 6000g multi 3.50 3.50

Libertad Soccer Team, Cent. — A596

Illustration reduced.

**2005, July 20** *Perf. 13¼*
**2774** A596 700g multi + label .50 .50

Publication of Don Quixote, 400th Anniv. A597

**2005, July 26**
**2775** A597 8000g multi 5.00 5.00

Writers A598

Designs: 3000g, Herib Campos Cervera (1905-53), poet. 5000g, Gabriel Casaccia (1907-80), novelist.

**2005, July 27**
**2776-2777** A598 Set of 2 5.00 5.00

Pope John Paul II (1920-2005) A599

**2005, Aug. 18**
**2778** A599 2000g multi 2.00 2.00

Truth and Justice A600

**2005, Aug. 23**
**2779** A600 8000g multi 4.50 4.50

America Issue, Fight Against Poverty A601

Designs: 5000g, Women selling vegetables. 6000g, Cobbler.

**2005, Aug. 31**
**2780-2781** A601 Set of 2 6.50 6.50

Dogs and Cats A602

Designs: No. 2782, 2000g, Samoyed. No. 2783, 2000g, Three European cats. No. 2784, 3000g, Doberman pinscher. No. 2785, 3000g, White European cat.

**2005, Oct. 7**
**2782-2785** A602 Set of 4 6.00 6.00

Anthropologists — A603

Designs: 1000g, Branislava Susnik, bracelet. 2000g, Miguel Chase-Sardi, poncho. 8000g, León Cadogan, basket.

**2005, Oct. 26**
**2786-2788** A603 Set of 3 6.50 6.50

Intl. Year of Sports and Physical Education — A604

Designs: 5000g, Lucy Aguero throwing hammer and javelin. 6000g, Golfer Carlos Franco.

**2005, Nov. 9** ***Perf. 13¼***
**2789** A604 5000g multi 3.00 3.00

**Souvenir Sheet**
***Rouletted 5¼***
**2790** A604 6000g multi 5.00 5.00

Christmas A605

Designs: 700g, Angels, people celebrating Christmas, rooftops. 5000g, Nativity scene.

**2005, Nov. 22** ***Perf. 13¼***
**2791-2792** A605 Set of 2 3.50 3.50

Yacyreta Dam — A606

Various views of dam: 3000g, 5000g.

**2005, Nov. 28**
**2793-2794** A606 Set of 2 4.75 4.75

Ministry of Defense, 150th Anniv. A607

Designs: 700g, Monument to the Residents, by Javier Báez Rolón. 1000g, Defense Ministry Building, Marshal Francisco Solano López.

**2005, Dec. 21**
**2795-2796** A607 Set of 2 1.25 1.25

**Nos. 2736-2737 Overprinted**

**2005, Dec. 28** ***Perf. 13¼***
**2797** A575 5000g On #2736 3.00 3.00
**2798** A575 5000g On #2737 3.00 3.00

No. 2751 Overprinted

**2005, Dec. 28** ***Perf. 13¼***
**2799** A583 4000g On #2751 2.40 2.40

Paraguay — Germany Chamber of Commerce and Industry, 50th Anniv. — A608

**2006, Mar. 14**
**2800** A608 8000g multi 5.00 5.00

2006 World Cup Soccer Championships, Germany — A609

Emblem and: 3000g, Paraguayan team. 5000g, World Cup.

**2006, May 17** **Litho.** ***Perf. 13¼***
**2801-2802** A609 Set of 2 5.00 5.00

French Alliance of Asuncion, 50th Anniv. — A610

**2006, June 20**
**2803** A610 8000g multi + label 5.00 5.00

Cervantes Club, 50th Anniv. A611

**2006, June 27**
**2804** A611 700g multi .60 .60

Paraguayan Soccer Association, Cent. — A612

**2006, Aug. 1**
**2805** A612 1000g multi .75 .75

National Commerce School, Cent. — A613

**2006, Sept. 7**
**2806** A613 700g multi .65 .65

Japanese Emigration to Paraguay, 70th Anniv. — A614

Flags of Paraguay and Japan and butterflies: 1000g, Junonia evarete. 2000g, Anartia jatrophae. 3000g, Agraulis vanillae. 6000g, Danaus plexippus.

**2006, Sept. 8** ***Perf. 13¼***
**2807-2809** A614 Set of 3 4.00 4.00

**Souvenir Sheet**
***Rouletted 5¼***
**2810** A614 6000g multi 5.00 5.00

No. 2810 contains one 50x40mm stamp.

OPEC Intl. Development Fund, 30th Anniv. — A615

**2006, Sept. 18** ***Perf. 13¼***
**2811** A615 8000g multi 5.00 5.00

Tuparenda Shrine, 25th Anniv. — A616

**2006, Oct. 9**
**2812** A616 700g multi .50 .50

America Issue, Energy Conservation — A617

Designs: 5000g, Windmills. 6000g, Solar collector.

**2006, Oct. 11**
**2813-2814** A617 Set of 2 6.50 6.50

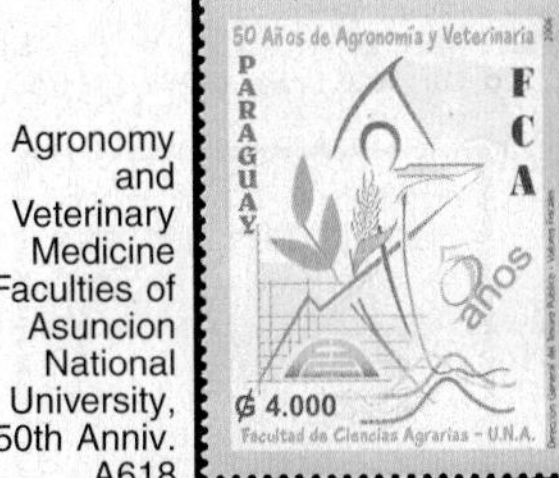

Agronomy and Veterinary Medicine Faculties of Asuncion National University, 50th Anniv. A618

Designs: No. 2815, 4000g, Symbols of agronomy. No. 2816, 4000g, Livestock.

**2006, Oct. 20**
**2815-2816** A618 Set of 2 5.00 5.00

South American Soccer Confederation, 90th Anniv. — A619

**2006, Nov. 6**
**2817** A619 8000g multi 5.00 5.00

Musical Instruments A620

Designs: 5000g, Harp. 6000g, Guitar.

**2006, Nov. 10**
**2818-2819** A620 Set of 2 6.50 6.50

Christmas
A621

Designs: 4000g, Our Lady of Asuncion Cathedral. 6000g, Holy Trinity Church, horiz.

**2006, Nov. 17**
**2820-2821** A621 Set of 2 6.00 6.00

First Lieutenant Adolfo Rojas Silva (1906-27), Military Hero — A622

Designs: 4000g, Rojas Silva and hut. 6000g, Rojas Silva, vert.

**2007, Feb. 27** **Litho.**
**2822-2823** A622 Set of 2 6.50 6.50

B'nai B'rith of Paraguay, 50th Anniv. — A623

**2007, Mar. 29** ***Perf. 13¼***
**2824** A623 8000g multi 5.00 5.00

Junior Chamber International Conference, Asuncion — A624

**2007, Apr. 18**
**2825** A624 8000g multi 5.00 5.00

World Tobacco-Free Day — A625

Emblem and: 5000g, Person wearing gas mask. 6000g, Map of Paraguay with umbrella, vert.

**2007, May 30**
**2826-2827** A625 Set of 2 6.50 6.50

Arlequin Theater, Asuncion, 25th Anniv. A626

**2007, June 11**
**2828** A626 700g multi .60 .60

Paz del Chaco 07 Philatelic Exhibition, Asuncion — A627

Exhibition emblem and: 700g, Felis pardalis. 8000g, Chaco War postman riding cow.

**2007, June 11**
**2829-2830** A627 Set of 2 5.00 5.00

Diplomatic Relations Between Paraguay and South Korea, 45th Anniv. — A628

Flags of Paraguay and South Korea and: 1000g, Open horse-drawn wagon. 2000g, Covered horse-drawn carriage. 3000g, Ox cart, vert.
6000g, Mugungfa flower.

**2007, June 15** ***Perf. 13¼***
**2831-2833** A628 Set of 3 3.50 3.50

**Souvenir Sheet**
***Rouletted 7¼***

**2834** A628 6000g multi 5.00 5.00

No. 2834 contains one 50x40mm stamp.

Friendship Between Paraguay and Republic of China, 50th Anniv. — A628a

**2007, July 8** ***Perf. 13¼***
**2834A** A628a 7000g multi + 2 flanking labels 4.25 4.25

Diplomatic Relations Between Paraguay and Indonesia, 25th Anniv. — A629

**2007, July 9**
**2835** A629 11,000g multi 6.50 6.50

Official Veterinary Service, 40th Anniv. A630

Designs: 5000g, Prize-winning cow. 7000g, Veterinarian inspecting cow, cattle herd, prize-winning cow, horiz.

**2007, June 11**
**2836-2837** A630 Set of 2 7.00 7.00

Peace Corps in Paraguay, 40th Anniv. A631

**2007, Sept. 19**
**2838** A631 7000g multi 4.50 4.50

Scouting, Cent. — A632

Designs: 700g, Scouts near campfire. 6000g, Lord Robert Baden-Powell, female Scouts.

**2007, Oct. 11**
**2839-2840** A632 Set of 2 4.00 4.00

Institute of Fine Arts, 50th Anniv. A633

Designs: 4000g, Pendants, by Engelberto Giménez Legal. 8000g, Sculpture by Hugo Pistilli, vert.

**2007, Nov. 20**
**2841-2842** A633 Set of 2 7.00 7.00

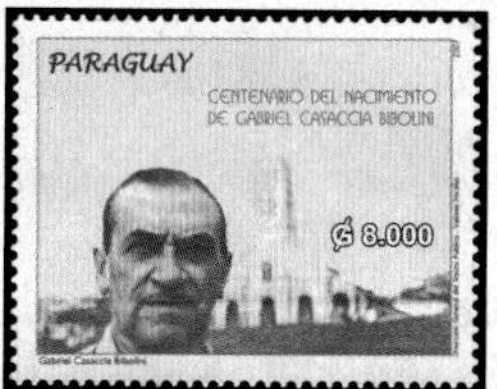

Gabriel Casaccia Bibolini (1907-80), Writer — A634

**2007, Nov. 23**
**2843** A634 8000g multi 5.00 5.00

Marco Aguayo Foundation, 15th Anniv. — A635

Designs: 1000g, Dr. Marco Aguayo (1956-92), red ribbon. 8000g, Red ribbon and geometrical design.

**2007, Dec. 11**
**2844-2845** A635 Set of 2 5.50 5.50

Dr. Nicolas Leoz Stadium — A636

**2007, Oct. 22**
**2846** A636 700g multi 1.00 1.00

Gen. Martin T. McMahon (1838-1906), US Minister to Paraguay A637

**2007, Sept. 19**
**2847** A637 700g multi .50 .50

Intl. Day of Deserts and Desertification (in 2006) — A638

**2007, Nov. 28**
**2848** A638 7000g multi 4.00 4.00

Parks and Reserves — A639

Designs: 3000g, Nú Guazú Park, Luque. 6000g, Monkey.

**2007, Nov. 27** ***Perf. 13¼***
**2849** A639 3000g multi 1.90 1.90

**Souvenir Sheet**
***Rouletted 7¼***

**2850** A639 6000g multi 4.00 4.00

No. 2850 contains one 50x40mm stamp.

America Issue, Education for All — A640

Teachers and school children in class: 5000g, 6000g.

**2007, Sept. 3** ***Perf. 13¼***
**2851-2852** A640 Set of 2 6.50 6.50

Architecture A641

Designs: 6000g, Nautilus Building, by Genaro Pindú. 7000g, Museo del Barro, by Carlos Colombino.

**2007, Sept. 3**
**2853-2854** A641 Set of 2 8.00 8.00

Christmas — A642

Designs: 700g, Coconut flower. 8000g, Creche figures.

**2007, Nov. 29** **Litho.** ***Perf. 13¼***
**2855-2856** A642 Set of 2 5.00 5.00

Paraguayan Atheneum, 125th Anniv. — A643

**2008, July 28**
**2857** A643 700g multi .60 .60

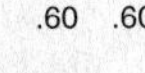

America Issue, Traditional Celebrations — A644

**2008, July 30**
**2858** A644 11,000g multi 7.50 7.50

Nasta Publicity Agency, 40th Anniv. A645

Designs: 700g, Flower. 5000g, Flower, vert.

**2008, Apr. 1**
**2859-2860** A645 Set of 2 3.50 3.50

Scouting in Paraguay, 70th Anniv. — A646

Designs: 3000g, Three scouts, tent. 4000g, Scout troop.

**2008, Oct. 11**
**2861-2862** A646 Set of 2 4.75 4.75

Asuncion Rotary Club, 80th Anniv. A647

Rotary International emblem and: 2000g, Stylized gearwheels. 8000g, Forest path, horiz.

**2008, Apr. 4**
**2863-2864** A647 Set of 2 6.50 6.50

Birds — A648

Designs: 5000g, Coryphospingus cucullatus. 6000g, Pitangus sulphuratus.

**2008, July 28**
**2865-2866** A648 Set of 2 7.50 7.50

Christmas A649

Paintings: 700g, Madonna and Child, by unknown artist. 5000g, Madonna and Child, by José Laterza Parodi.

**2008, Oct. 9**
**2867-2868** A649 Set of 2 4.00 4.00

Carter-Torrijos Treaty, 30th Anniv. (in 2007) — A650

Designs: 700g, Signing ceremony. 7000g, Panamanian General Omar Torrijos, U.S. President Jimmy Carter, ship in Panama Canal.

**2008, Aug. 5**
**2869-2870** A650 Set of 2 5.00 5.00

City of Coronel Oviedo, 250th Anniv. A651

Cotton boll and: 3000g, Cathedral. 7000g, Road.

**2008, Oct. 28**
**2871-2872** A651 Set of 2 7.00 7.00

Arbitration Decision of Pres. Rutherford B. Hayes in Chaco Land Dispute in Favor of Paraguay, 130th Anniv. — A652

**2008, Nov. 10** **Litho.** ***Perf. 13¼***
**2873** A652 1000g multi .75 .75

SOS Children's Village, Asuncion, 25th Anniv. — A653

SOS Children's Village emblem and: 2000g, Children and flower. 7000g, Red, white and blue ribbon.

**2008, Nov. 18** **Litho.** ***Perf. 13¼***
**2874-2875** A653 Set of 2 6.50 6.50

Year of the Harp — A654

**2008, Oct. 20** ***Perf. 13¼x13½***
**2876** A654 5000g multi 3.50 3.50

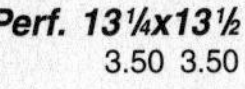

Schoenstatt Movement in Paraguay, 50th Anniv. — A655

**2009, Oct. 18** ***Perf. 13¼***
**2877** A655 3000g multi 1.90 1.90

Christmas A656

Designs: 800g, Our Lady of Caacupé. 5000g, Our Lady of Asunción.

**2009, Dec. 1**
**2878-2879** A656 Set of 2 3.75 3.75

Dr. José Segundo Decoud (1848-1909), Politician and Journalist — A657

**2009, Dec. 3**
**2880** A657 7000g multi 5.00 5.00

Exports A658

Designs: 2000g, Nelore cow. 5000g, Stevia rebaudiana.

**2009, Dec. 18**
**2881-2882** A658 Set of 2 4.50 4.50

Arsenio Erico (1915-77), Soccer Player — A659

Erico: 700g, Kicking soccer ball. 1000g, Holding four soccer balls, vert.

**2009, Dec. 22**
**2883-2884** A659 Set of 2 1.20 1.20

Ceryle Torquata — A660

**2009**
**2885** A660 7000g multi 3.00 3.00

Charles Darwin (1809-82), naturalist. Printed in sheets of 15 + 10 labels.

Diplomatic Relations Between Paraguay and Russia, Cent. — A661

**2009**
**2886** A661 7000g multi 3.00 3.00

Printed in sheets of 15 + 10 labels.

America Issue, Children's Games A662

Children: 4000g, Spinning top. 7000g, Playing marbles, horiz.

**2010, Jan. 2**
**2887-2888** A662 Set of 2 7.50 7.50

Independence, Bicent. — A663

Designs: 700g, Governor's House. 2000g, Painting by Jaime Bestard.

**2010, Feb. 23**
**2889-2890** A663 Set of 2 2.10 2.10

Astronomy Aided By Telescopes, 400th Anniv. A664

**2010, Mar. 3**
**2891** A664 2500g multi 1.90 1.90

Printed in sheets of 15 + 10 labels.

2010 World Cup Soccer Championships, South Africa — A665

Designs: 700g, Paraguayan players. 6000g, Team, crowd holding Paraguayan flags.

**2010, July 2 Litho. *Perf. 13¼***
**2892** A665 700g multi + label — —
**2893** A665 6000g multi — —

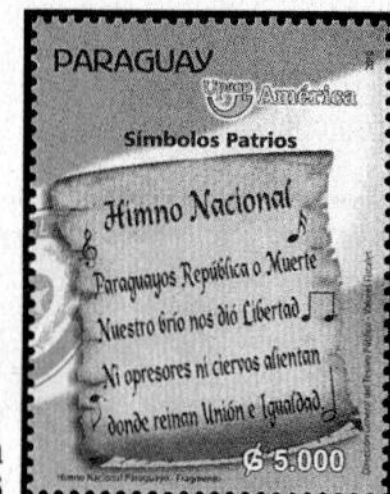

America Issue — A666

National symbols: 5000g, National anthem. 6000g, Flag and emblems, horiz.

**2010, Oct. 9 Litho. *Perf. 13¼***
**2894-2895** A666 Set of 2 7.00 7.00

Christmas — A667

Designs: 700g, Magi following Star of Bethlehem. 6000g, Nativity, vert. 11,000g, Journey to Bethlehem.

**2010, Nov. 19**
**2896-2898** A667 Set of 3 11.50 11.50

Road Safety Day A668

**2010**
**2899** A668 700g multi .60 .60

Famous Paraguayan Buildings — A669

Designs: 700g, Venancio López Palace. 2000g, Residencia Patri.

**2010, Dec. 17**
**2900-2901** A669 Set of 2 1.75 1.75

2010 Youth Olymmpics, Singapore — A670

Emblem and: 2000g, Diego Galeano Harrison, tennis player. 5000g, Paraguayan athletes.

**2010, Dec. 31**
**2902-2903** A670 Set of 2 5.00 5.00

Decade for Culture of Peace A671

Designs: 2000g, Hand below rose. 6000g, Hand holding rose.

**2010, Dec. 31**
**2904-2905** A671 Set of 2 5.25 5.25

Postal Union of the Americas, Spain and Portugal (UPAEP), Cent. — A672

Designs: 6000g, Map of South and Central America, Spain and Portugal with flags. 11,000g, Building and flags, horiz.

**2011, Mar. 18**
**2906-2907** A672 Set of 2 11.00 11.00

Dated 2010.

National Development Bank, 50th Anniv. — A673

**2011, Apr. 12 *Perf. 13¼***
**2908** A673 700g multi + label .60 .60

Republic of China, Cent. — A674

No. 2909: a, National Pantheon of Heroes, Paraguay. b, Pantheon of the Martyrs of the National Revolution, Taiwan.

**2011, Apr. 24 Litho.**
**2909** A674 6000g Horiz. pair, #a-b, + central label 8.50 8.50

Asunción Buildings A675

No. 2910: a, Asunción, Cathedral. b, Train station. c, Governmental Palace. d, Municipal Theater. e, Town Hall (Cabildo).
11,000g, Independence House, horiz.

**2011, May 6 *Perf. 13¼***
**2910** Horiz. strip of 5 + flanking label 3.50 3.50
***a.-e.*** A675 1000g Any single .65 .65

**Souvenir Sheet**

***Rouletted***

**2911** A675 11,000g multi 7.75 7.75

Marie Curie (1867-1934), Chemist and Physicist — A676

**2011, May 9 *Perf. 13¼***
**2912** A676 2000g multi + label 1.75 1.75

Intl. Year of Chemistry.

Campaign Against Violence Towards Women — A677

**2011, Apr. 29 Litho. *Perf. 13¼***
**2913** A677 700g multi + label .60 .60

**Souvenir Sheet**

Beatification of Pope John Paul II — A678

**2011, May 9 Litho. *Rouletted 1¼***
**2914** A678 10,000g multi 7.25 7.25

Masons in Paraguay, 140th Anniv. — A679

**2011, May 25 Litho. *Perf. 13¼***
**2915** A679 11,000g multi + label 8.00 8.00

Intl. Friendship Day — A680

**2011, Nov. 8 Litho.** ***Perf. 13¼***
**2916** A680 700g multi + label .60 .60

Radio Cáritas, 75th Anniv. — A681

**2011, Nov. 21 Litho.** ***Perf. 13¼***
**2917** A681 700g multi + label .55 .55

San José Academy, Cent. — A682

**2011, Nov. 29 Litho.** ***Perf. 13¼***
**2918** A682 700g multi + label .55 .55

America Issue — A683

No. 2919: a, 5000g, Red mailbox. b, 6000g, Green mailbox.

**2011, Dec. 13 Litho.** ***Perf. 13¼***
**2919** A683 Horiz. pair, #a-b 8.25 8.25

Campaign Against AIDS, 30th Anniv. — A684

**2011, Dec. 13 Litho.** ***Perf. 13¼***
**2920** A684 1000g multi + label .85 .85

Intl. Year of Forests A685

Designs: 5000g, Animals and forest. 6000g, Trees and map of North and South America.

**2011, Dec. 13 Litho.** ***Perf. 13¼***
**2921** A685 5000g multi 4.00 4.00

**Souvenir Sheet**

***Rouletted 4***

**2922** A685 6000g multi 4.75 4.75

Actors and Actresses — A686

Designs: 2000g, Map of Paraguay, Perlita Fernández (1951-2002), César Alvarez Blanco (1927-2003), Máxima Lugo (1925-91), José Olitte (1937-2000). 6000g, Edda de los Rios (1942-2007).

**2011, Dec. 13 Litho.** ***Perf. 13¼***
**2923** A686 2000g multi + label 1.60 1.60

**Souvenir Sheet**

***Rouletted 5***

**2924** A686 6000g multi 4.75 4.75

A687

Christmas A688

Designs: 700g, Star of Bethlehem and Magi. 5000g, Star of Bethlehem and manger. 11,000g, Holy Family and lambs.

**2011, Dec. 13 Litho.** ***Perf. 13¼***
**2925** A687 700g multi .50 .50
**2926** A687 5000g multi 3.25 3.25
**2927** A688 11,000g multi 6.50 6.50
*Nos. 2925-2927 (3)* 10.25 10.25

Campaign Against Terrorism — A689

No. 2928 — Handprint in: a, 2000g, Black. b, 5000g, White.

**2011, Dec. 30 Litho.** ***Perf. 13¼***
**2928** A689 Horiz. pair, #a-b 5.50 5.50

A690

2011 Copa America Soccer Tournament, Argentina — A691

**2011, Dec. 30 Litho.** ***Perf. 13¼***
**2929** A690 700g multi + label .55 .55
**2930** A691 6000g multi 4.75 4.75

José Luis Chilavert, Soccer Player, Estaban Casarino, Squash Player, Olegario Farrés, Shooter, Juan Carlos Giménez, Boxer — A692

Benjamin Hockin Brusquetti, Swimmer — A693

**2011, Dec. 30 Litho.** ***Perf. 13¼***
**2931** A692 700g multi + label .55 .55

**Souvenir Sheet**

***Rouletted 5x6***

**2932** A693 6000g multi 4.75 4.75

**Miniature Sheet**

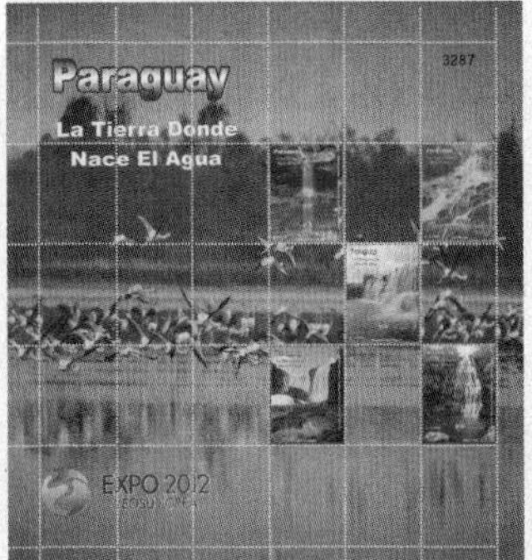


Expo 2012, Yeosu, South Korea — A694

No. 2933, 2000g — Expo 2012 emblem and: a, Small waterfall in Ybycuí National Park. b, Karapa Waterfall. c, Large waterfall in Ybycuí National Park. d, Monday Waterfall. e, Cristal Waterfall,

**2012, May 28 Litho.** ***Perf. 13¼***
**2933** A694 2000g Sheet of 5, #a-e, + 25 labels 7.75 7.75

**Souvenir Sheet**

National Police Band, Cent. — A695

**2012, June 1 Litho.** ***Rouletted 5***
**2934** A695 7000g multi 5.50 5.50

Myths and Legends — A696

No. 2935 — Guarani monsters: a, Teju Jagua. b, Moñai. c, Jasy Jatere. d, Luisón. e, Kurupi. f, Ao Ao. g, Mbói Tui.
7000p, Kerana, horiz.

**2012, June 7 Litho.** ***Perf. 13¼***
**2935** A696 1000g Sheet of 7, #a-g, + 23 labels 5.50 5.50

**Souvenir Sheet**

***Rouletted 5***

**2936** A696 7000g multi 5.50 5.50

America Issue.

**Souvenir Sheets**

Korean and Paraguayan Dancers — A697

Paraguayan Dancers — A698

Korean Dancers — A699

**2012, June 26 Litho. *Rouletted 5***

**2937** A697 2000g multi 1.75 1.75
**2938** A698 2000g multi 1.75 1.75
**2939** A699 2000g multi 1.75 1.75
*Nos. 2937-2939 (3)* 5.25 5.25

Diplomatic relations between Paraguay and South Korea, 50th anniv.

Authentic Radical Liberal Party, 125th Anniv. — A700

Party flag and: 2000g, Anodorhynchus hyacinthinus. 16,000g, Morpho peleides.

**2012, July 14 Litho. *Perf. 13¼***

**Stamp + Label**

**2940-2941** A700 Set of 2 14.00 14.00

2012 Summer Olympics, London A701

No. 2942 — Paraguayan flag, emblem of Paraguayan Olympic Committee and: a, Judo. b, Javelin. c, Running. d, Tennis. e, Table tennis. f, Rowing and swimming.

No. 2943, 4000g, Paraguayan flag, emblem of Paraguayan Olympic Committee, Marcelo Aguirre, table tennis player, and Benjamin Hockin Busquetti, swimmer. No. 2944, 4000g, Paraguayan flag, emblem of Paraguayan Olympic Committee and various athletes.

**2012, Aug. 9 Litho. *Perf. 13¼***

**2942** Horiz. strip of 6 5.50 5.50
*a.-f.* A701 1000g Any single .90 .90

**Souvenir Sheets**

***Rouletted 5***

**2943-2944** A701 Set of 2 7.50 7.50

Paraguayan Academy of History, 75th Anniv. — A702

No. 2945 — Academy emblem, building and: a, Ruy Díaz de Guzmán (c. 1558-1692), conquistador and historian. b, Dr. Manuel Domínguez (1868-1935), Vice-President of Paraguay and writer. c, Dr. Fulgencio R. Moreno (1872-1933), historian. d, Dr. Efraím Cardozo (1906-73), historian. e, Dr. Rafael E. Velázquez (1926-94), historian.

**2012, Aug. 10 Litho. *Perf. 13¼***

**2945** Horiz. strip of 5 5.50 5.50
*a.-e.* A702 1400g Any single 1.10 1.10

Souvenir Sheet

Asunción, 475th Anniv. — A703

**2012, Aug. 14 Litho. *Rouletted 5***

**2946** A703 10,000g multi 7.00 7.00

Souvenir Sheet

Locomotive — A704

**2012, Aug. 14 Litho. *Rouletted 5***

**2947** A704 8000g multi 6.00 6.00

Carlos Antonio López (1792-1862), first President of Paraguay.

National University of Asunción Economic Sciences Faculty, 75th Anniv. — A705

**2012, Aug. 22 Litho. *Perf. 13¼***

**2948** A705 1400g multi 1.10 1.10

Technical Planning Ministry, 50th Anniv. — A706

**2012, Sept. 17 Litho. *Perf. 13¼***

**2949** A706 8000g multi + label 6.00 6.00

Cerro Porteño Basketball Team — A707

Cerro Porteño Soccer Team — A708

**2012, Oct. 1 Litho. *Perf. 13¼***

**2950** A707 1000g multi .80 .80
**2951** A708 6000g multi + label 4.25 4.25

Cerro Porteño Sports Club, cent.

Independence of Slovakia, 20th Anniv. — A709

**2012, Nov. 13 Litho. *Perf. 13¼***

**2952** A709 11,000g multi + label 8.25 8.25

No. 2952 was printed in sheets of 10 stamps + 15 labels.

First National Eucharistic Congress, 75th Anniv. — A710

**2012, Nov. 19 Litho. *Perf. 13¼***

**2953** A710 3000g multi + label 2.25 2.25

Ardea Alba — A711

**2012, Nov. 20 Litho. *Perf. 13¼***

**2954** A711 1400g multi + label 1.10 1.10

Completion of new dam near Encarnacion. No. 2954 was printed in sheets containing 10 stamps + 15 labels.

Radio Nanduti, 50th Anniv. — A712

**2012, Nov. 29 Litho. *Perf. 13¼***

**2955** A712 1400g multi + label 1.10 1.10

United Nations Environmental Program, 40th Anniv. — A713

Designs: 3000g, Butorides striatus. 16,000g, Platalea ajaja.

**2012, Dec. 18 Litho. *Perf. 13¼***

**2956** A713 3000g multi 2.25 2.25

**Souvenir Sheet**

***Rouletted 5***

**2957** A713 16,000g multi 12.00 12.00

Christmas — A714

No. 2958 — Various creche figures: a, 1000g. b, 5000g. c, 11,000g.

**2012, Dec. 18 Litho. *Perf. 13¼***

**2958** A714 Vert. strip of 3, #a-c 13.00 13.00

National Library, 125th Anniv. A715

**2012, Dec. 27 Litho. *Perf. 13¼***

**2959** A715 1400g multi 1.10 1.10

Alternative Energy Sources A716

No. 2960: a, Wind energy (wind turbines). b, Solar energy (solar collector). c, Biodiesel (jatropha tree). d, Biomass (hay roll). e, Biodiesel (corn).

3000g, Biodiesel (sunflower), horiz.

**2012, Dec. 27 Litho. *Perf. 13¼***

**2960** Horiz. strip of 5 6.00 6.00
*a.-e.* A716 1500g Any single 1.20 1.20

**Souvenir Sheet**

***Rouletted 5***

**2961** A716 3000g multi 2.25 2.25

First Tramway in Paraguay, Cent. — A717

No. 2962: a, Van following tram. b, Motorcyclist and tram.

7000p, Line 5 tram, vert.

**2013, Aug. 19 Litho. *Perf. 13¼***

**2962** Horiz. pair + central label 1.90 1.90
*a.-b.* A717 2000g Either single .95 .95

**Souvenir Sheet**

***Rouletted 5***

**2963** A717 7000g multi 3.25 3.25

Paraguayan-Japanese Center, Asuncion — A718

No. 2964: a, Building exterior and flags. b, Cherry blossoms.

**2013, Aug. 19 Litho. *Perf. 13¼***

**2964** Horiz. pair + central label 8.75 8.75
*a.* A718 1400g multi 1.00 1.00
*b.* A718 11,000g multi 7.75 7.75

Birds — A719

No. 2965: a, Dendrocygna viduata. b, Amazona aestiva. c, Chlorostilbon aureoventris. d, Jabiru mycteria. e, Zenaida auriculata. f, Athene cunicularia. g, Aramides ypecaha. h, Dendrocygna autumnalis. i, Caracara plancus. j, Vanellus chilensis.

**2013, Aug. 19 Litho. *Perf. 13¼***

**2965** Block of 10 15.00 15.00
*a.-j.* A719 2000g Any single 1.50 1.50

Mammals — A720

No. 2966: a, Lycalopex gymnocercus. b, Myrmecophaga tridactyla. c, Cebus apella paraguayanus. d, Tayassu pecari. e, Nasua nasua.
6000g, Panthera onca, vert.

**2013, Aug. 19 Litho. *Perf. 13¼***

**2966** Horiz. strip of 5 10.00 10.00
*a.-e.* A720 3000g Any single 2.00 2.00

**Souvenir Sheet**

***Rouletted 5***

**2967** A720 6000g multi 4.50 4.50

Scouting in Paraguay, Cent. — A721

No. 2968: a, Group of Scouts. b, Scouts running.

**2013, Aug. 23 Litho. *Perf. 13¼***

**2968** Horiz. pair + central label 9.50 9.50
*a.* A721 5000g multi 3.75 3.75
*b.* A721 8000g multi 5.75 5.75

Rubio Nú Soccer Team, Cent. A722

Designs: 1400g, Six palyers celebrating. 6000g, Team photograph.

**2013, Aug. 24 Litho. *Perf. 13¼***

**2969-2970** A722 Set of 2 5.50 5.50

Flowers A723

No. 2971 — Inscriptions at LL: a, Azahar. b, Aguape. c, Agosto Poty. d, Chivato Poty. e, Santa Lucia. f, Ceibo.
No. 2972, 10,000g, Samu'u (yellow flower), horiz. No. 2973, 10,000g, Mburucuja (blue flower), horiz.

**2013, Sept. 17 Litho. *Perf. 13¼***

**2971** Horiz. strip of 6 21.00 21.00
*a.-f.* A723 5000g Any single 3.50 3.50

**Souvenir Sheets**

***Rouletted 5***

**2972-2973** A723 Set of 2 16.00 16.00

Agustín Barboza (1913-98), Musician A724

Barboza: 1400g, Holding neck of guitar. 4000g, Playing guitar.

**2013, Oct. 9 Litho. *Perf. 13¼***

**2974-2975** A724 Set of 2 4.00 4.00

Campaign Against Discrimination A725

Paintings by Juan de Dios Valdez depicting: 5000g, Old man. 10,000g, Old woman.

**2013, Oct. 9 Litho. *Perf. 13¼***

**2976** A725 5000g multi 3.50 3.50

**Souvenir Sheet**

***Rouletted 5***

**2977** A725 10,000g multi 7.00 7.00

America Issue.

Republic of Paraguay, 200th Anniv. — A726

200th Anniv. emblem and: 1000g, Map of Asuncion, 1809. 8000g, Consuls Fulgencio Yegros (1780-1821) and Dr. José Gaspar de Francia (1766-1840), vert.

**2013, Oct. 12 Litho. *Perf. 13¼***

**2978** A726 1000g multi + label .75 .75

**Souvenir Sheet**

***Rouletted 5***

**2979** A726 8000g multi 5.75 5.75

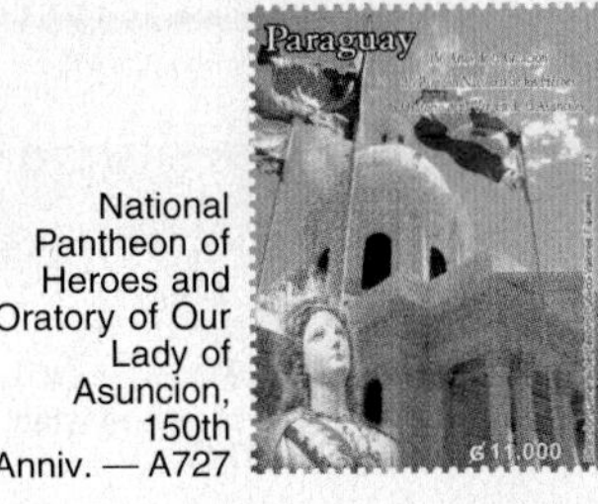

National Pantheon of Heroes and Oratory of Our Lady of Asuncion, 150th Anniv. — A727

Design: 6000g Building's dome and flags, horiz.

**2013, Nov. 1 Litho. *Perf. 13¼***

**2980** A727 11,000g multi 8.00 8.00

**Souvenir Sheet**

***Rouletted 5***

**2981** A727 6000p multi 2.75 2.75

Paraguayan Atheneum, 130th Anniv. — A728

**2013, Dec. 5 Litho. *Perf. 13¼***

**2982** A728 1400g multi 1.00 1.00

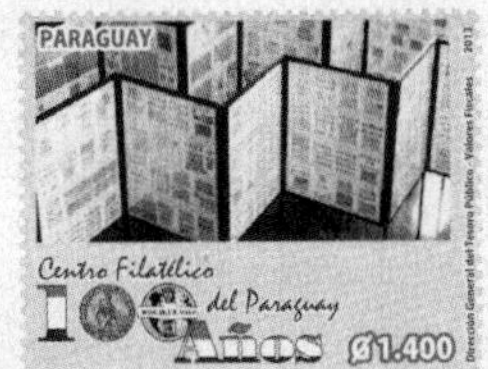

Philatelic Center of Paraguay, Cent. — A729

**2013, Dec. 6 Litho. *Perf. 13¼***

**2983** A729 1400g multi 1.00 1.00

Christmas A730

Designs: 3000g, Virgin Mary and St. Joseph. 8000g, Holy Family creche figurines. 16,000g, Creche figurines, horiz.

**2013, Dec. 6 Litho. *Perf. 13¼***

**2984-2986** A730 Set of 3 19.00 19.00

Paraguayan postal officials declared as "illegal" two blocks of nine stamps and two souvenir sheets of four dated 2013 and inscribed "Winter War."

Encarnación, 400th Anniv. (in 2015) — A731

Designs: 3000g, Mirador San José, Virgin of Itacuá. 11,000g, Woman in Carnaval costume, vert.

**2014, Feb. 6 Litho. *Perf. 13¼***

**2987** A731 3000g multi 2.10 2.10

**Souvenir Sheet**

***Rouletted 5***

**2988** A731 11,000g multi 8.00 8.00

Asuncion Tennis Club, Cent. — A732

**2014, Mar. 4 Litho. *Perf. 13¼***

**2989** A732 1400g multi 1.00 1.00

Villeta, 300th Anniv. — A733

**2014, Mar. 5 Litho. *Perf. 13¼***

**2990** A733 1400g multi + label 1.00 1.00

Campaign Against Violence Towards Women A734

**2014, Mar. 7 Litho. *Perf. 13¼***

**2991** A734 700g multi .50 .50

Vice-President Domingo F. Sánchez National College, 50th Anniv. — A735

**2014, Mar. 28 Litho. *Perf. 13¼***

**2992** A735 1400g multi 1.00 1.00

Jorge Castro, Singer — A736

Castro: 1400g, On horse. 5000g, With orchestra.

**2014, Apr. 25 Litho. *Perf. 13¼***
**2993** A736 1400g multi 1.00 1.00

**Souvenir Sheet**
***Rouletted 5***

**2994** A736 5000g multi 3.50 3.50

Cabildo Cultural Center, Asuncion, 10th Anniv. — A737

**2014, May 13 Litho. *Perf. 13¼***
**2995** A737 1400g multi 1.00 1.00

Itaipu Dam and Speothos Venaticus — A738

**2014, May 20 Litho. *Perf. 13¼***
**2996** A738 16,000g multi 11.00 11.00

Itaipu Binacional, 40th anniv.

44th General Assembly of the Organization of American States, Asuncion — A739

**2014, June 5 Litho. *Perf. 13¼***
**2997** A739 5000g multi + label 3.50 3.50

Pope Francis and Map of South America A740

**2014, June 27 Litho. *Perf. 13¼***
**2998** A740 9000g multi 6.00 6.00

Gen. José Gervasio Artigas (1764-1850), National Hero of Uruguay — A741

**2014, July 18 Litho. *Perf. 13¼***
**2999** A741 4000g multi + label 2.75 2.75

Salvador Cabañas and Emblem of 12 de Octubre Soccer Team — A742

**2014, Aug. 8 Litho. *Perf. 13¼***
**3000** A742 1400g multi + label 1.00 1.00

12 de Octubre Soccer Team, cent.

Apostolic Movement of Schoenstatt, Cent. — A743

**2014, Oct. 6 Litho. *Perf. 13¼***
**3001** A743 3000g multi + label 2.00 2.00

Paraguayan Presidents A744

Designs: 1400g, José Félix Estigarribia (1888-1940). 4000g, Bernardino Caballero (1839-1912)

**2014, Oct. 9 Litho. *Perf. 13¼***
**3002-3003** A744 Set of 2 3.75 3.75

America issue.

Telecommunications in Paraguay, 150th Anniv. — A745

**2014, Oct. 9 Litho. *Perf. 13¼***
**3004** A745 9000g multi + label 6.00 6.00

Asuncion Zoo and Botanical Gardens, Cent. — A746

No. 3005: a, Ara ararauna. b, Rhea americana.

**2014, Oct. 15 Litho. *Perf. 13¼***
**3005** Horiz. pair + central label 9.00 9.00
*a.* A746 3000g multi 2.00 2.00
*b.* A746 10,000g multi 7.00 7.00

**No. 2764 Overprinted**

**Method and Perf. As Before**
**2014, Oct. 16**
**3006** A589 4000g multi + label 2.75 2.75

Latin American Parliament, 50th anniv.

Asuncion, Green Capital — A747

**2014, Nov. 6 Litho. *Perf. 13¼***
**3007** A747 1400g multi + label 1.00 1.00

Carlos Miguel Jiménez (1914-70), Musician — A748

**2014, Nov. 10 Litho. *Perf. 13¼***
**3008** A748 2000g black + label 1.75 1.75

Silvio Pettirossi (1887-1916), Aviator — A749

No. 3009: a, Pettirossi, airplane inverted in flight, note written by Pettirossi. b, Pettirossi in airplace cockpit.

**2014, Nov. 17 Litho. *Perf. 13¼***
**3009** Horiz. pair + central label 8.00 8.00
*a.* A749 2500g multi 1.75 1.75
*b.* A749 9000g multi 6.25 6.25

Spanish Academy, 300th Anniv. — A750

Designs: No. 3010, Flowers. No. 3011, Emblem of Paraguayan Spanish Language Academy.

**2014, Nov. 21 Litho. *Perf. 13¼***
**3010** A750 11,000g multi 8.00 8.00

**Souvenir Sheet**
***Rouletted 5***

**3011** A750 11,000g multi 8.00 8.00

Christmas A751

Designs: 1400g, Star, pottery, angel. 5000g, Star, pottery, melons, grapes.

**2014, Dec. 5 Litho. *Perf. 13¼***
**3012-3013** A751 Set of 2 4.50 4.50

Campaign Against Discrimination — A752

Designs: 1000g, Three empty chairs of different heights. 10,000g, Handicapped child with other children.

**2015, Jan. 7 Litho. *Perf. 13¼***
**3014-3015** A752 Set of 2 7.50 7.50

Dated 2014.

Visit of United Nations Secretary General Ban Ki-moon — A753

**2015, Feb. 25 Litho. *Perf. 13¼***
**3016** A753 10,000g multi + label 7.00 7.00

Encarnación, 400th Anniv. — A754

No. 3017: a, Municipal Building, horse-drawn carriage. b, San Roque González de Santa Cruz Basilica, St. Roque González de Santa Cruz (1576-1628).

**2015, Mar. 25 Litho. *Perf. 13¼***
**3017** Horiz. pair + central label 6.00 6.00
*a.* A754 1000g multi .50 .50
*b.* A754 10,000g multi 5.50 5.50

Lorenzo Prieto, Record-Setting Bicyclist — A755

**2015, Apr. 24 Litho. *Perf. 13¼***
**3018** A755 2000g multi + label 1.40 1.40

Efrén Echeverría, Guitarist — A756

**2015, Apr. 24 Litho. *Perf. 13¼***
**3019** A756 5000g multi + label 3.25 3.25

Secretary of Social Action, 20th Anniv. — A757

**2015, May 7 Litho. *Perf. 13¼***
**3020** A757 10,000g multi + label 5.50 5.50

Instruments of the Recycled Orchestra of Catuera — A758

**2015, May 25 Litho. *Perf. 13¼***
**3021** A758 5000g Trumpet 2.75 2.75

**Souvenir Sheet**
***Rouletted 5***

**3022** A758 2000g Saxophone, vert. .80 .80

Santa Teresa de Jesus College, Cent. — A759

**2015, May 25 Litho. *Perf. 13¼***
**3023** A759 13,000g multi + label 7.25 7.25

Animals — A760

No. 3024: a, 1000g, Azara's night monkey (ka'i pyhare). b, 1400g, Geoffroy's cat (gato montés). c, 3000g, Capybara (carpincho).
No. 3025, 3000g, Blue-fronted Amazons (loro hablador).

**2015, June 12 Litho. *Perf. 13¼***
**3024** A760 Block of 3, #a-c, + label 3.00 3.00

**Souvenir Sheet**
***Rouletted 5***

**3025** A760 3000g multi 2.40 2.40

Junior Chamber International in Paragauy, cent.

Visit of Pope Francis to Paraguay — A762

Designs: 5000g, Pope Francis, map and flag of Paraguay.
6000g, Pope Francis, church.

**2015, July 6 Litho. *Perf. 13¼***
**3027** A762 5000g multi + label 2.75 2.75

**Souvenir Sheet**
***Rouletted 8***

**3028** A762 6000g multi 3.50 3.50

See Nos. 3032-3033.

St. John Bosco (1815-88) — A763

**2015, Aug. 12 Litho. *Perf. 13¼***
**3029** A763 2000g multi + label 1.40 1.40

Postal Headquarters — A764

No. 3030 — Postal Headquarters in: a, 5000g, Guatemala (denomination at left). b, 10,000g, Paraguay (denomination at right).

**2015, Aug. 13 Litho. *Perf. 13¼***
**3030** A764 Horiz. pair, #a-b 6.50 6.50

See Guatemala No. 708.

Luis Alberto del Paraná (1926-74) and Los Paraguayos, Musical Group — A765

No. 3031: a, 2000g, Three band members. b, 5000g, Del Paraná.

**2015, Sept. 15 Litho. *Perf. 13¼***
**3031** A765 Horiz. pair, #a-b, + flanking label 1.40 1.40

**Visit of Pope Francis Type of 2015**

**2015, Oct. 27 Litho. *Perf. 13¼***

**Stamp + Label**

**3032** A762 6000g Like #3027 2.25 2.25

**Souvenir Sheet**
***Rouletted 8***

**3033** A762 5000g Like #3028 1.90 1.90

Paraguay, Land of Water — A766

**2015, Nov. 4 Litho. *Perf. 13¼***
**3034** A766 4000g multi + label 1.75 1.75

Campaign Against Human Trafficking — A767

No. 3035: a, 5000g, Woman bound in ropes. b, 11,000g, Silhouettes of two people.

**2015, Nov. 9 Litho. *Perf. 13¼***
**3035** A767 Horiz. pair, #a-b 7.25 7.25

America Issue.

Children's Drawing of Farm — A768

**2015, Nov. 20 Litho. *Perf. 13¼***
**3036** A768 2500g multi + label 1.10 1.10

**Miniature Sheet**

Tourism Ambassadors of Paraguay — A769

No. 3037: a, Roque Santa Cruz, soccer player. b, Ismael Ledesma playing harp. c, Daiana Ferreira, guitarist. d, Luis Szarán, orchestra conductor. e, Arnaldo André, actor.

**2015, Dec. 3 Litho. *Perf. 13¼***
**3037** A769 2000g Sheet of 5, #a-e, + 7 labels 4.50 4.50

**Souvenir Sheet**

Christmas — A770

No. 3038 — Altar of Corn, by Koki Ruiz, and: a, 2000g, Pope Francis at pulpit. b, 12,000g, Statue of Madonna and Child.

**2015, Dec. 3 Litho. *Perf. 13¼***
**3038** A770 Sheet of 2, #a-b, + 2 labels 6.25 6.25

Canonization of St. Emilie de Villeneuve (1811-54) — A771

**2016, May 26 Litho. *Perf. 13¼***
**3039** A771 2500g multi + label .90 .90

Campaign Against Child Abuse and Sexual Violence — A772

**2016, May 31 Litho. *Perf. 13¼***
**3040** A772 9000g multi + label 3.25 3.25

**Souvenir Sheet**

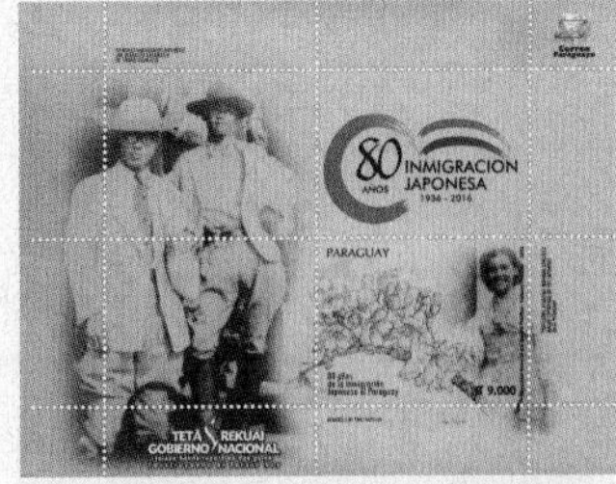
Japanese Immigration to Paraguay, 80th Anniv. — A773

**2016, May 31 Litho. *Perf. 13¼***
**3041** A773 9000g multi + 3 labels 3.25 3.25

College of Accounting, Cent. — A774

**2016, June 10 Litho. *Perf. 13¼***
**3042** A774 1400g multi + label .50 .50

International Day of Responsible Gambling A775

**2016, June 15 Litho. *Perf. 13¼***
**3043** A775 2500g multi .90 .90

Diplomatic Relations Between Paraguay and Israel — A776

No. 3044 — Flags of Paraguay and Israel and: a, 6000g, Bare-throated bellbird. b, 10,000g, Hoopoes.

**2016, June 20 Litho. *Perf. 13¼***
**3044** A776 Horiz. pair, #a-b 5.75 5.75

Hotel Guarani, Asuncion A777

**2016, June 27 Litho. *Perf. 13¼***
**3045** A777 10,000g multi 3.75 3.75

Employment of Prisoners — A778

**2016, June 27 Litho.** ***Perf. 13¼***
**3046** Horiz. pair + central label 4.75 4.75
*a.* A778 3000g Embroiderer 1.00 1.00
*b.* A778 10,000g Polisher 3.75 3.75

Miniature Sheet

Tourism Ambassadors — A779

No. 3047: a, Nelson Sanabria, racer in Dakar Rally. b, Chiara D'Odorico, pianist. c, Koki Ruiz, artist. d, José Mongelos, opera singer.

**2016, June 27 Litho.** ***Perf. 13¼***
**3047** A779 2000g Sheet of 4, #a-d, + 6 labels 3.00 3.00

Demetrio Ortiz (1916-75), Musician — A780

**2016, June 30 Litho.** ***Perf. 13¼***
**3048** A780 10,000g multi + label 3.75 3.75

Social Security Week — A781

**2016, July 20 Litho.** ***Perf. 13¼***
**3049** A781 2000g multi + label .75 .75

Paraguayan Customs Broker Center, 90th Anniv. — A782

**2016, July 28 Litho.** ***Perf. 13¼***
**3050** A782 1400g multi + label .50 .50

Souvenir Sheet

Paraguayan Olympic Committee Emblem — A783

**2016, July 29 Litho.** ***Rouletted 8***
**3051** A783 4000g multi 1.50 1.50

Famous People A784

No. 3052: a, Doña Máxima Lugo (1925-91), actress. b, Pedro Sosa Melgarejo (Carlos Sosa) (1926-89), composer.

**2016, Aug. 22 Litho.** ***Perf. 13¼***
**3052** Horiz. pair + central label 1.60 1.60
*a.* A784 1400g multi .50 .50
*b.* A784 3000g multi 1.10 1.10

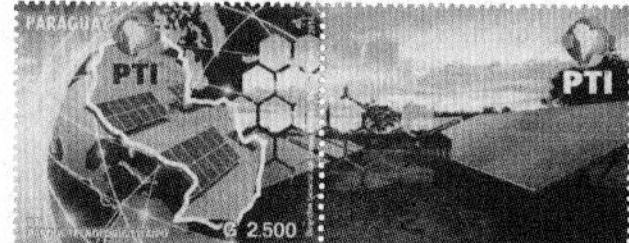

Itaipú Technological Park — A785

**2016, Nov. 28 Litho.** ***Perf. 13¼***
**3053** A785 2500g multi + label .85 .85

Christmas — A786

No. 3054: a, 3000g, Flight into Egypt. b, 10,000g, Nativity.

**2016, Dec. 1 Litho.** ***Perf. 13¼***
**3054** A786 Horiz. pair, #a-b, + central label 4.50 4.50

Paraguayan Industrial Union, Cent. — A787

**2016, Dec. 6 Litho.** ***Perf. 13¼***
**3055** A787 9000g multi 3.25 3.25

Miniature Sheet

39th Dakar Rally — A788

No. 3056: a, 1400g, Wheels of rally vehicle. b, 2000g, Vehicle number and visor of driver. c, 2500g, Nelson Sanabria on vehicle. d, 3000g, Map of Paraguayan portion of rally, flag of Paraguay.

**2016, Dec. 13 Litho.** ***Perf. 13¼***
**3056** A788 Sheet of 4, #a-d, + 12 labels 3.25 3.25

Souvenir Sheet

Annual Meeting of Governors of the Interamerican Development Bank, Paraguay — A789

No. 3057: a, 1400g, Palacio Alegre, Asunción. b, 2000g, Grain field. c, 3000g, Paraguayan coins and banknotes.

**2017, Mar. 13 Litho.** ***Perf. 13¼***
**3057** A789 Sheet of 3, #a-c, + label 2.25 2.25

Miniature Sheet

Flowers and Butterflies — A790

No. 3058: a, 700g, Cereus forbesii. b, 700g, Harrisia bonplandii. c, 1000g, Agraulis vanillae. d, 1400g, Male Euryades duponcheli. e, 2000g, Female Euryades duponcheli. f, 2500g, Echinopsis rhodotricha.

**2017, Mar. 28 Litho.** ***Perf. 13¼***
**3058** A790 Sheet of 6, #a-f, + 2 labels 3.00 3.00

Mother's Day A791

No. 3059: a, 1400g, Family in archway. b, 2000g, Family making meal.

**2017, May 15 Litho.** ***Perf. 13¼***
**3059** A791 Pair, #a-b 1.25 1.25

Miniature Sheet

Russian Immigrants to Paraguay — A792

No. 3060: a, 1000g, First Russian immigrants. b, 1400g, Sergio Bobrovsky and Sergio Conradi. c, 2000g, Tala Ern de Retivoff and Agripina Voitenko. d, 2500g, Nicolás Ern and Stephan Vysokolan. e, 3000g, Oreliev de Serebriakoff and Boris Kassianoff. f, 5000g, Dr. Arturo Weiss and Dr. Constantino Gramatchicoff. g, 6000g, Gen. Juan Belaieff and Paraguayans.

**2017, June 5 Litho.** ***Perf. 13¼***
**3060** A792 Sheet of 7, #a-g, + 9 labels 7.50 7.50

Pres. Horacio Cartes and Patriarch Kirill of Moscow A793

Chamaemelum Nobile — A794

**2017, June 8 Litho.** ***Perf. 13¼***
**3061** Horiz. pair + central label 5.50 5.50
*a.* A793 6000g multi 2.25 2.25
*b.* A794 9000g multi 3.25 3.25

Visit of Patriarch Kirill to Paraguay.

Souvenir Sheet

Augusto Roa Bastos (1917-2005), Writer — A795

**2017, June 13 Litho.** ***Perf. 13¼***
**3062** A795 13,000g multi + 3 labels 4.75 4.75

Peace Corps in Paraguay, 50th Anniv. — A796

**2017, June 19 Litho.** ***Perf. 13¼***
**3063** A796 10,000g multi + label 3.75 3.75

Institute of Fine Arts, 60th Anniv. — A797

**2017, July 5 Litho. *Perf. 13¼***
**3064** A797 5000g multi + label 1.90 1.90

Diplomatic Relations Between Paraguay and Republic of China, 60th Anniv. — A798

No. 3065: a, 1000g, Presidential Palace, Taipei, Republic of China. b, 3000g, López Presidential Palace, Asunción.

**2017, July 12 Litho. *Perf. 13¼***
**3065** Horiz. pair + central label 1.50 1.50
*a.* A798 1000g multi .35 .35
*b.* A798 3000g multi 1.10 1.10

Souvenir Sheet

Asunción, 480th Anniv. — A799

**2017, Aug. 11 Litho. *Perf. 13¼***
**3066** A799 1400g multi + 3 labels .50 .50

Souvenir Sheet

Quemil Yambay, Guitarist — A800

**2017, Aug. 22 Litho. *Perf. 13¼***
**3067** A800 5000g multi + 3 labels 1.75 1.75

Souvenir Sheet

National Radio of Paraguay, 75th Anniv. — A801

**2017, Aug. 30 Litho. *Perf. 13¼***
**3068** A801 1400g multi + 3 labels .50 .50

Flower and Cactus A802

Hummingbird and Cactus Flower — A803

**2017, Sept. 29 Litho. *Perf. 13¼***
**3069** Horiz. pair + central label 1.50 1.50
*a.* A802 1000g multi .35 .35
*b.* A803 3000g multi 1.10 1.10

National Secretary of Youth.

International Year of Sustainable Tourism for Development — A804

Designs: 2500g, Jesuit Mission of Santísima Trinidad UNESCO World Heritage Site. 3000p, Ypacaraí Lake.

**2017, Oct. 9 Litho. *Perf. 13¼***
**3070** A804 2500g multi + label .90 .90

**Souvenir Sheet**
***Rouletted 5***

**3071** A804 3000g multi 1.10 1.10

Souvenir Sheet

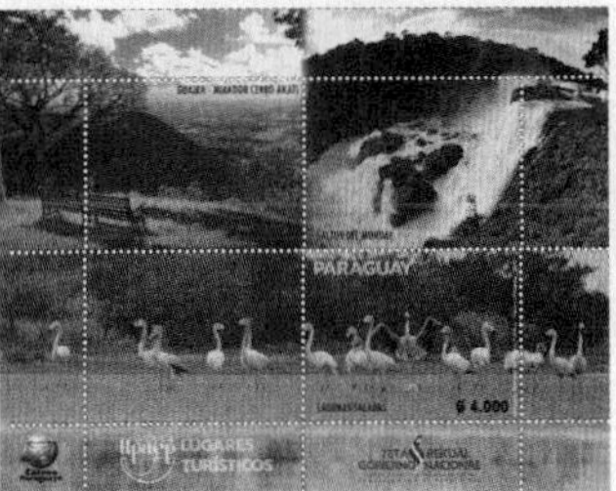


Laguna Salada — A805

**2017, Oct. 9 Litho. *Perf. 13¼***
**3072** A805 4000g multi + 3 labels 1.40 1.40

America issue.

## SEMI-POSTAL STAMPS

Red Cross Nurse SP1

**Unwmk.**

**1930, July 22 Typo. *Perf. 12***
**B1** SP1 1.50p + 50c gray violet 2.00 1.20
**B2** SP1 1.50p + 50c deep rose 2.00 1.20
**B3** SP1 1.50p + 50c dark blue 2.00 1.20
*Nos. B1-B3 (3)* 6.00 3.60

The surtax was for the benefit of the Red Cross Society of Paraguay.

College of Agriculture — SP2

**1930**
**B4** SP2 1.50p + 50c blue, *pale pink* .60 .50

Surtax for the Agricultural Institute.

The sheet of No. B4 has a papermaker's watermark: "Vencedor Bond."

A 1.50p+50c red on pale yellow was prepared but not regularly issued. Value, 40 cents.

Red Cross Headquarters SP3

**1932**
**B5** SP3 50c + 50c rose .60 .60

Our Lady of Asunción — SP4

**1941 Engr.**
**B6** SP4 7p + 3p red brown .40 .35
**B7** SP4 7p + 3p purple .40 .35
**B8** SP4 7p + 3p carmine rose .40 .35
**B9** SP4 7p + 3p sapphire .40 .35
*Nos. B6-B9 (4)* 1.60 1.40

For surcharges see Nos. 419-426, 431-434.

No. 361 Surcharged in Black

**1944**
**B10** A70 10c on 10p multicolored .70 .50

The surtax was for the victims of the San Juan earthquake in Argentina.

**Catalogue values for unused stamps in this section, from this point to the end of the section, are for Never Hinged items.**

**No. C169 Surcharged in Carmine "AYUDA AL ECUADOR 5 + 5"**

**1949 Unwmk. *Perf. 12½***
**B11** A117 5c + 5c on 30c dk blue .30 .30

Surtax for the victims of the Ecuador earthquake.

38th Intl. Eucharistic Congress, Bombay — SP5

Various coins and coat of arms.

**Litho. & Engr.**

**1964, Dec. 11 *Perf. 12x12½***
**B12** SP5 20g +10g multi 6.50 6.50
**B13** SP5 30g +15g multi 6.50 6.50
**B14** SP5 50g +25g multi 6.50 6.50
**B15** SP5 100g +50g multi 6.50 6.50
*a.* Souvenir sheet of 4, #B12-B15 26.00 26.00
*Nos. B12-B15 (4)* 26.00 26.00

Buildings and Coats of Arms of Popes John XXIII & Paul VI — SP6

#B16, Dome of St. Peters. #B17, Site of Saint Peter's tomb. #B18, Saint Peter's Plaza. #B19,Taj Mahal.

**1964, Dec. 12**
**B16** SP6 20g +10g multi 6.50 6.50
**B17** SP6 30g +15g multi 6.50 6.50
**B18** SP6 50g +25g multi 6.50 6.50
**B19** SP6 100g +50g multi 6.50 6.50
*a.* Souvenir sheet of 4, #B16-B19 140.00 140.00
*Nos. B16-B19 (4)* 26.00 26.00

## AIR POST STAMPS

Official Stamps of 1913 Surcharged

**1929, Jan. 1 Unwmk. *Perf. 11½***
**C1** O19 2.85p on 5c lilac 2.25 1.50
**C2** O19 5.65p on 10c grn 1.25 1.50
**C3** O19 11.30p on 50c rose 2.00 1.25
*Nos. C1-C3 (3)* 5.50 4.25

Counterfeits of surcharge exist.

Regular Issues of 1924-27 Surcharged

**1929, Feb. 26 *Perf. 12***
**C4** A51 3.40p on 3p gray 4.50 4.00
*a.* Surch. "Correo / en $3.40 / Habilitado / Aereo" 8.75
*b.* Double surcharge 8.75
*c.* "Aéro" instead of "Aéreo"
**C5** A44 6.80p on 4p lt bl 4.50 3.25
*a.* Surch. "Correo / Aereo / en $6.80 / Habilitado" 8.75
**C6** A52 17p on 5p choc 4.50 3.25
*a.* Surch. "Correo / Habilitado / Habilitado / en 17p" 4.50
*b.* Double surcharge 25.00 25.00
*Nos. C4-C6 (3)* 13.50 10.50

Wings
AP1

Pigeon with Letter
AP2

Airplanes — AP3

**1929-31 Typo. Perf. 12**

**C7** AP1 2.85p gray green 1.75 1.25
*a.* Imperf., pair 37.50
**C8** AP1 2.85p turq grn ('31) .50 .50
**C9** AP2 5.65p brown 2.00 1.25
**C10** AP2 5.65p scar ('31) 1.00 .50
**C11** AP3 11.30p chocolate 1.75 1.25
*a.* Imperf., pair 37.50
**C12** AP3 11.30p dp blue ('31) .50 .50
*Nos. C7-C12 (6)* 7.50 5.25

Sheets of these stamps sometimes show portions of a papermaker's watermark "Indian Bond C. Extra Strong."

Excellent counterfeits are plentiful.

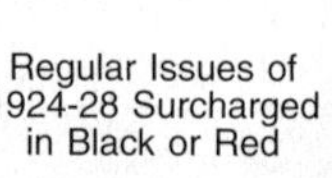
Regular Issues of 1924-28 Surcharged in Black or Red

**1929 Perf. 11½, 12**

**C13** A47 95c on 7c lilac .35 .30
**C14** A47 1.90p on 20c dull bl .35 .30
**C15** A44 3.40p on 4p lt bl (R) .45 .30
*a.* Double surcharge 3.00
**C16** A44 4.75p on 4p lt bl (R) .90 .75
*a.* Double surcharge 3.00
**C17** A51 6.80p on 3p gray 1.00 .90
*a.* Double surcharge 4.50
**C18** A52 17p on 5p choc 3.00 3.00
*a.* Horiz. pair, imperf. between 37.50
*Nos. C13-C18 (6)* 6.05 5.55

Six stamps in the sheet of No. C17 have the "$" and numerals thinner and narrower than the normal type.

Airplane and Arms — AP4

Cathedral of Asunción
AP5

Airplane and Globe — AP6

**1930 Perf. 12**

**C19** AP4 95c dp red, *pink* 1.50 .90
**C20** AP4 95c dk bl, *blue* 1.50 .90
**C21** AP5 1.90p lt red, *pink* 1.50 .90
**C22** AP5 1.90p violet, *blue* 1.50 .90
**C23** AP6 6.80p blk, *lt bl* 1.50 .90
**C24** AP6 6.80p green, *pink* 1.50 .90
*Nos. C19-C24 (6)* 9.00 5.40

Sheets of Nos. C19-C24 have a papermaker's watermark: "Extra Vencedor Bond."

Counterfeits exist.

Stamps and Types of 1927-28 Overprinted in Red

**1930**

**C25** A47 10c olive green .60 .40
*a.* Double overprint 6.00
**C26** A47 20c dull blue .60 .40
*a.* "CORREO CORREO" instead of "CORREO AEREO" 5.00
*b.* "AEREO AEREO" instead of "CORREO AEREO" 5.00
**C27** A48 1p emerald 1.40 1.40
**C28** A51 3p gray 1.40 1.40
*Nos. C25-C28 (4)* 4.00 3.60

Counterfeits of Nos. C26a and C26b exist.

**Nos. 273, 282, 286, 288, 300, 302, 305 Surcharged in Red or Black**

#C29-C30, C32

#C31

#C33

#C34-C35

**1930 Red or Black Surcharge**

**C29** A47 5c on 10c gray grn (R) .50 .50
*a.* "AEREO" omitted 30.00
**C30** A47 5c on 70c ultra (R) .50 .50
*a.* Vert. pair, imperf. between 40.00
**C31** A48 20c on 1p org red .60 .50
*a.* "CORREO" double 6.00 6.00
*b.* "AEREO" double 6.00 6.00
**C32** A47 40c on 50c org (R) .60 .50
*a.* "AEREO" omitted 9.00 9.00
*b.* "CORREO" double 6.00 6.00
*c.* "AEREO" double 6.00 6.00
**C33** A54 6p on 10p red 2.50 2.00
**C34** A49 10p on 20p red 10.00 10.00
**C35** A49 10p on 20p vio brn 10.00 10.00
*Nos. C29-C35 (7)* 24.70 24.00

Declaration of Independence
AP11

**1930, May 14 Typo.**

**C36** AP11 2.85p dark blue .70 .50
**C37** AP11 3.40p dark green .70 .40
**C38** AP11 4.75p deep lake .70 .40
*Nos. C36-C38 (3)* 2.10 1.30

Natl. Independence Day, May 14, 1811.

**Gunboat Type**

Gunboat "Paraguay."

**1931-39 Perf. 11½, 12**

**C39** A58 1p claret .60 .60
**C40** A58 1p dk blue ('36) .60 .60
**C41** A58 2p orange .60 .60
**C42** A58 2p dk brn ('36) .60 .60
**C43** A58 3p turq green .75 .75
**C44** A58 3p lt ultra ('36) .90 .75
**C45** A58 3p brt rose ('39) .60 .60
**C46** A58 6p dk green 1.20 .90
**C47** A58 6p violet ('36) 1.40 .90
**C48** A58 6p dull bl ('39) 1.20 .75
**C49** A58 10p vermilion 3.00 1.75
**C50** A58 10p bluish grn ('35) 4.50 3.00
**C51** A58 10p yel brn ('36) 3.25 2.25
**C52** A58 10p dk blue ('36) 2.75 1.50
**C53** A58 10p lt pink ('39) 3.00 2.00
*Nos. C39-C53 (15)* 24.95 17.55

1st constitution of Paraguay as a Republic and the arrival of the "Paraguay" and "Humaita."

Counterfeits of #C39-C53 are plentiful.

Regular Issue of 1924 Surcharged

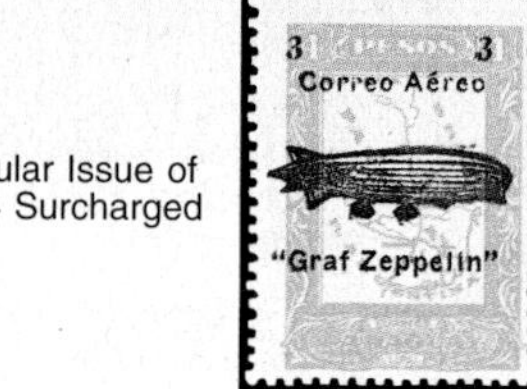


**1931, Aug. 22**

**C54** A44 3p on 4p lt bl 17.50 17.50

Overprinted

**C55** A44 4p lt blue 15.00 15.00

On Nos. C54-C55 the Zeppelin is handstamped. The rest of the surcharge or overprint is typographed.

War Memorial
AP13

Orange Tree and Yerba Mate — AP14

Yerba Mate — AP15

Palms — AP16

Eagle — AP17

**1931-36 Litho.**

**C56** AP13 5c lt blue .25 .40
*a.* Horiz. pair, imperf. btwn. 6.25
**C57** AP13 5c dp grn ('33) .25 .40
**C58** AP13 5c lt red ('33) .30 .40
**C59** AP13 5c violet ('35) .25 .40
**C60** AP14 10c dp violet .25 .40
**C61** AP14 10c brn lake ('33) .25 .40
**C62** AP14 10c yel brn ('33) .25 .40
**C63** AP14 10c ultra ('35) .25 .40
*a.* Imperf., pair 5.50
**C64** AP15 20c red .25 .40
**C65** AP15 20c dl blue ('33) .30 .40
**C66** AP15 20c emer ('33) .25 .40
**C67** AP15 20c yel brn ('35) .25 .40
*a.* Imperf., pair 3.75
**C68** AP16 40c dp green .25 .40
**C69** AP16 40c slate bl ('35) .25 .40
**C70** AP16 40c red ('36) .30 .40
**C71** AP17 80c dull blue .25 .40
**C72** AP17 80c dl grn ('33) .50 .40
**C73** AP17 80c scar ('33) .30 .40
*Nos. C56-C73 (18)* 4.95 7.20

Airship "Graf Zeppelin" — AP18

**1932, Apr. Litho.**

**C74** AP18 4p ultra 3.75 3.75
*a.* Imperf., pair 35.00
**C75** AP18 8p red 6.25 5.00
**C76** AP18 12p blue grn 5.00 5.00
**C77** AP18 16p dk violet 8.75 6.25
**C78** AP18 20p orange brn 8.75 6.25
*Nos. C74-C78 (5)* 32.50 26.25

For surcharges see Nos. 325-329.

"Graf Zeppelin" over Brazilian Terrain
AP19

"Graf Zeppelin" over Atlantic — AP20

**1933, May 5**

**C79** AP19 4.50p dp blue 4.00 3.00
**C80** AP19 9p dp rose 7.00 5.00
*a.* Horiz. pair, imperf. between 150.00
**C81** AP19 13.50p blue grn 8.00 6.00
**C82** AP20 22.50p bis brn 18.00 14.00
**C83** AP20 45p dull vio 24.00 24.00
*Nos. C79-C83 (5)* 61.00 52.00

Excellent counterfeits are plentiful.

For overprints see Nos. C88-C97.

Posts and Telegraph Building, Asunción — AP21

**1934-37 Perf. 11½**

**C84** AP21 33.75p ultra 6.00 5.25
**C85** AP21 33.75p car ('35) 6.00 5.25
*a.* 33.75p rose ('37) 5.25 4.50
**C86** AP21 33.75p emerald ('36) 7.50 6.00
**C87** AP21 33.75p bis brn ('36) 2.25 2.25
*Nos. C84-C87 (4)* 21.75 18.75

Excellent counterfeits exist.

For surcharge see No. C107.

Nos. C79-C83 Overprinted in Black

**1934, May 26**

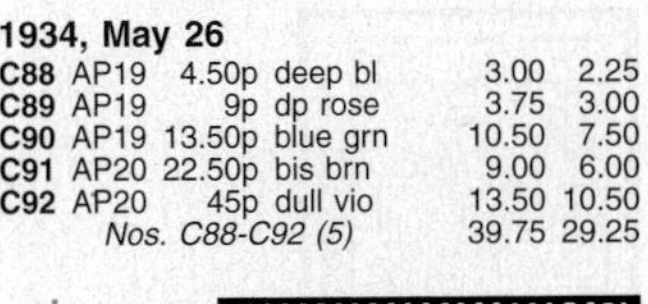

| | | | | | |
|---|---|---|---|---|---|
| **C88** | AP19 | 4.50p | deep bl | 3.00 | 2.25 |
| **C89** | AP19 | 9p | dp rose | 3.75 | 3.00 |
| **C90** | AP19 | 13.50p | blue grn | 10.50 | 7.50 |
| **C91** | AP20 | 22.50p | bis brn | 9.00 | 6.00 |
| **C92** | AP20 | 45p | dull vio | 13.50 | 10.50 |
| | | *Nos. C88-C92 (5)* | | 39.75 | 29.25 |

Types of 1933 Issue Overprinted in Black

**1935**

| | | | | | |
|---|---|---|---|---|---|
| **C93** | AP19 | 4.50p | rose red | 3.50 | 2.50 |
| **C94** | AP19 | 9p | lt green | 4.50 | 3.00 |
| **C95** | AP19 | 13.50p | brown | 9.50 | 7.00 |
| **C96** | AP20 | 22.50p | violet | 7.50 | 5.50 |
| **C97** | AP20 | 45p | blue | 22.50 | 13.00 |
| | | *Nos. C93-C97 (5)* | | 47.50 | 31.00 |

Tobacco Plant — AP22

**1935-39** **Typo.**

| | | | | | |
|---|---|---|---|---|---|
| **C98** | AP22 | 17p | lt brown | 12.50 | 12.50 |
| **C99** | AP22 | 17p | carmine | 21.00 | 21.00 |
| **C100** | AP22 | 17p | dark blue | 15.00 | 15.00 |
| **C101** | AP22 | 17p | pale yel grn ('39) | 8.00 | 8.00 |
| | | *Nos. C98-C101 (4)* | | 56.50 | 56.50 |

Excellent counterfeits are plentiful.

Church of Incarnation AP23

**1935-38**

| | | | | | |
|---|---|---|---|---|---|
| **C102** | AP23 | 102p | carmine | 7.50 | 5.00 |
| **C103** | AP23 | 102p | blue | 7.50 | 5.00 |
| **C103A** | AP23 | 102p | indigo ('36) | 4.50 | 4.50 |
| **C104** | AP23 | 102p | yellow brn | 5.50 | 4.75 |
| *a.* | | | Imperf., pair | 30.00 | |
| **C105** | AP23 | 102p | violet ('37) | 2.50 | 2.50 |
| **C106** | AP23 | 102p | brn org ('38) | 2.25 | 2.25 |
| | | *Nos. C102-C106 (6)* | | 29.75 | 24.00 |

Excellent counterfeits are plentiful.
For surcharges see Nos. C108-C109.

**Types of 1934-35 Surcharged in Red**

**1937, Aug. 1**

| | | | | | |
|---|---|---|---|---|---|
| **C107** | AP21 | 24p | on 33.75p sl bl | 1.00 | .70 |
| **C108** | AP23 | 65p | on 102p ol bis | 2.50 | 1.75 |
| **C109** | AP23 | 84p | on 102p bl grn | 2.50 | 1.50 |
| | | *Nos. C107-C109 (3)* | | 6.00 | 3.95 |

Plane over Asunción AP24

**1939, Aug. 3 Typo.** ***Perf. 10½, 11½***

| | | | | | |
|---|---|---|---|---|---|
| **C110** | AP24 | 3.40p | yel green | 1.00 | 1.00 |
| **C111** | AP24 | 3.40p | orange brn | .60 | .50 |
| **C112** | AP24 | 3.40p | indigo | .60 | .50 |
| | | *Nos. C110-C112 (3)* | | 2.20 | 2.00 |

**Buenos Aires Peace Conference Type and**

Map of Paraguay with New Chaco Boundary AP28

Designs: 1p, Flags of Paraguay and Bolivia. 3p, Coats of Arms. 5p, Pres. Ortiz of Argentina, flags of Paraguay, Argentina. 10p, Pres. Vargas, Brazil. 30p, Pres. Alessandri, Chile. 50p, US Eagle and Shield. 100p, Pres. Benavides, Peru. 200p, Pres. Baldomir, Uruguay.

**Engr.; Flags Litho.**

**1939, Nov.** ***Perf. 12½***

**Flags in National Colors**

| | | | | | |
|---|---|---|---|---|---|
| **C113** | A69 | 1p | red brown | .60 | .60 |
| **C114** | A69 | 3p | dark blue | .60 | .60 |
| **C115** | A70 | 5p | olive blk | .60 | .60 |
| **C116** | A70 | 10p | violet | .60 | .60 |
| **C117** | A70 | 30p | orange | .60 | .60 |
| **C118** | A70 | 50p | black brn | .60 | .60 |
| **C119** | A70 | 100p | brt green | 1.25 | .90 |
| **C120** | A70 | 200p | green | 6.75 | 3.75 |
| **C121** | AP28 | 500p | black | 27.50 | 17.50 |
| | | *Nos. C113-C121 (9)* | | 39.40 | 25.75 |

For overprints see Nos. 388-390.

**University of Asuncion Type**

Pres. Bernardino Caballero and Senator José S. Decoud.

**1939, Sept. Litho.** ***Perf. 12***

| | | | | | |
|---|---|---|---|---|---|
| **C122** | A67 | 28p | rose & blk | 10.00 | 10.00 |
| **C123** | A67 | 90p | yel grn & blk | 12.00 | 12.00 |

Map with Asunción to New York Air Route — AP35

**1939, Nov. 30** **Engr.**

| | | | | | |
|---|---|---|---|---|---|
| **C124** | AP35 | 30p | brown | 7.75 | 6.00 |
| **C125** | AP35 | 80p | orange | 9.00 | 9.00 |
| **C126** | AP35 | 90p | purple | 12.00 | 12.00 |
| | | *Nos. C124-C126 (3)* | | 28.75 | 27.00 |

New York World's Fair.

**Pan American Union Type**

**1940, May** ***Perf. 12***

| | | | | | |
|---|---|---|---|---|---|
| **C127** | A85 | 20p | rose car | .60 | .60 |
| **C128** | A85 | 70p | violet bl | 1.25 | .60 |
| **C129** | A85 | 100p | Prus grn | 1.50 | 1.50 |
| **C130** | A85 | 500p | dk violet | 6.75 | 5.25 |
| | | *Nos. C127-C130 (4)* | | 10.10 | 7.95 |

**Asuncion 400th Anniv. Type**

**1942, Aug. 15**

| | | | | | |
|---|---|---|---|---|---|
| **C131** | A93 | 20p | deep plum | 1.00 | .40 |
| **C132** | A94 | 70p | fawn | 2.00 | 1.10 |
| **C133** | A95 | 500p | olive gray | 5.50 | 3.50 |
| | | *Nos. C131-C133 (3)* | | 8.50 | 5.00 |

Imperforates

Starting with No. C134, many Paraguayan air mail stamps exist imperforate.

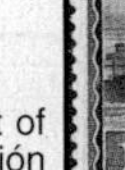

Port of Asunción AP40

First Telegraph in South America AP41

Early Merchant Ship — AP42

Birthplace of Paraguay's Liberation AP43

Monument to Antequera AP44

Locomotive of First Paraguayan Railroad AP45

Monument to Heroes of Itororó — AP46

Primitive Postal Service among Indians — AP48

Government House AP47

Colonial Jesuit Altar — AP49

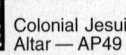

Ruins of Humaitá Church — AP50

Oratory of the Virgin — AP51

Marshal Francisco S. Lopez — AP52

**1944-45 Unwmk.** ***Perf. 12½***

| | | | | | |
|---|---|---|---|---|---|
| **C134** | AP40 | 1c | blue | .40 | .25 |
| **C135** | AP41 | 2c | green | .40 | .25 |
| **C136** | AP42 | 3c | brown vio | .40 | .25 |
| **C137** | AP43 | 5c | brt bl grn | .40 | .25 |
| **C138** | AP44 | 10c | dk violet | .40 | .25 |
| **C139** | AP45 | 20c | dk brown | .40 | .25 |
| **C140** | AP46 | 30c | lt blue | .40 | .25 |
| **C141** | AP47 | 40c | olive | .40 | .25 |
| **C142** | AP48 | 70c | brown red | .50 | .30 |
| **C143** | AP49 | 1g | orange yel | 1.50 | .60 |
| **C144** | AP50 | 2g | copper brn | 2.00 | .90 |
| **C145** | AP51 | 5g | black brn | 4.00 | 2.75 |
| **C146** | AP52 | 10g | indigo | 10.00 | 5.00 |
| | | *Nos. C134-C146 (13)* | | 21.20 | 11.15 |

See Nos. C158-C162. For surcharges see Nos. C154-C157.

**Flags Type**

20c, Ecuador. 40c, Bolivia. 70c, Mexico. 1g, Chile. 2g, Brazil. 5g, Argentina. 10g, US.

**Engr.; Flags Litho. in Natl. Colors**

**1945, Aug. 15**

| | | | | | |
|---|---|---|---|---|---|
| **C147** | A106 | 20c | orange | .60 | .60 |
| **C148** | A106 | 40c | olive | .60 | .60 |
| **C149** | A106 | 70c | lake | .60 | .60 |
| **C150** | A106 | 1g | slate bl | 1.00 | 1.00 |
| **C151** | A106 | 2g | blue vio | 1.50 | 1.50 |
| **C152** | A106 | 5g | green | 4.25 | 4.25 |
| **C153** | A106 | 10g | brown | 11.00 | 11.00 |
| | | *Nos. C147-C153 (7)* | | 19.55 | 19.55 |

Sizes: Nos. C147-C151, 30x26mm; 5g, 32x28mm; 10g, 33x30mm.

**Catalogue values for unused stamps in this section, from this point to the end of the section, are for Never Hinged items.**

**Nos. C139-C142 Surcharged "1946" and New Value in Black**

**1946 Engr.** ***Perf. 12½***

| | | | | | |
|---|---|---|---|---|---|
| **C154** | AP45 | 5c | on 20c dk brn | .80 | .80 |
| **C155** | AP46 | 5c | on 30c lt blue | .80 | .80 |
| **C156** | AP47 | 5c | on 40c olive | .80 | .80 |
| **C157** | AP48 | 5c | on 70c brn red | .80 | .80 |
| | | *Nos. C154-C157 (4)* | | 3.20 | 3.20 |

**Types of 1944-45**

**1946, Sept. 21** **Engr.**

| | | | | | |
|---|---|---|---|---|---|
| **C158** | AP50 | 10c | dp car | .40 | .40 |
| **C159** | AP40 | 20c | emerald | .40 | .40 |
| **C160** | AP47 | 1g | brown org | .70 | .70 |
| **C161** | AP52 | 5g | purple | 2.00 | 2.00 |
| **C162** | AP51 | 10g | rose car | 10.00 | 10.00 |
| | | *Nos. C158-C162 (5)* | | 13.50 | 13.50 |

**Marshal Francisco Solano Lopez Type**

**1947, May. 15** ***Perf. 12***

| | | | | | |
|---|---|---|---|---|---|
| **C163** | A114 | 32c | car lake | .30 | .30 |
| **C164** | A114 | 64c | orange brn | .45 | .45 |
| **C165** | A114 | 1g | Prus green | .90 | .90 |
| **C166** | A114 | 5g | Prus grn & brn vio | 2.40 | 2.40 |

**C167** A114 10g dk car rose & dk yel grn 5.00 5.00
*Nos. C163-C167 (5)* 9.05 9.05

### Archbishopric of Asunción Types

**1948, Jan. 6 Unwmk. *Perf. 12½***

**Size: 25½x31mm**

**C168** A116 20c gray blk .40 .25
**C169** A117 30c dark blue .40 .25
**C170** A118 40c lilac .70 .35
**C171** A115 70c orange red .90 .45
**C172** A112 1g brown red .90 .45
**C173** A118 2g red 1.90 1.25

**Size: 25½x34mm**

**C174** A115 5g brt car & dk bl 4.50 2.25
**C175** A116 10g dk grn & brn 7.50 3.75
*Nos. C168-C175 (8)* 17.20 8.90

For surcharges see Nos. B11, C178.

### Type of Regular Issue of 1948 Inscribed "AEREO"

**1948, Sept. 11 Engr. & Litho.**

**C176** A119 69c dk grn 1.40 1.40
**C177** A119 5g dk blue 7.50 7.50

The Barefeet, a political group.

No. C171 Surcharged in Black

**1949, June 29**

**C178** A115 5c on 70c org red .30 .25

Archbishop Juan Sinforiano Bogarin (1863-1949).

Symbols of UPU — AP65

**1950, Sept. 4 Engr. *Perf. 13½x13***

**C179** AP65 20c green & violet .60 .25
**C180** AP65 30c rose vio & brn .90 .40
**C181** AP65 50c gray & green 1.20 .50
**C182** AP65 1g blue & brown 1.50 .65
**C183** AP65 5g rose & black 3.50 1.00
*Nos. C179-C183 (5)* 7.70 2.80

UPU, 75th anniv. (in 1949).

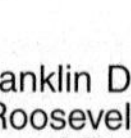

Franklin D. Roosevelt AP66

**Engr.; Flags Litho.**

**1950, Oct. 2 *Perf. 12½***

**Flags in Carmine & Violet Blue**

**C184** AP66 20c red .30 .25
**C185** AP66 30c black .30 .25
**C186** AP66 50c claret .30 .25
**C187** AP66 1g dk gray grn .40 .25
**C188** AP66 5g deep blue .50 .40
*Nos. C184-C188 (5)* 1.80 1.40

Franklin D. Roosevelt (1882-1945).

Urn Containing Remains of Columbus AP67

**1952, Feb. 11 Litho. *Perf. 10***

**C189** AP67 10c ultra .40 .25
**C190** AP67 20c green .40 .25
**C191** AP67 30c lilac .40 .25
**C192** AP67 40c rose .40 .25
**C193** AP67 50c bister brn .40 .25
**C194** AP67 1g blue .40 .25
**C195** AP67 2g orange .40 .25
**C196** AP67 5g red brown .60 .30
*Nos. C189-C196 (8)* 3.40 2.05

Queen Isabella I — AP68

**1952, Oct. 12**

**C197** AP68 1g vio blue .30 .25
**C198** AP68 2g chocolate .40 .30
**C199** AP68 5g dull green .80 .50
**C200** AP68 10g lilac rose 1.60 1.00
*Nos. C197-C200 (4)* 3.10 2.05

500th birth anniv. of Queen Isabella I of Spain (in 1951).

### Pettirossi Type

**1954, Mar.**

**C201** A122 40c brown .55 .25
**C202** A122 55c green .55 .25
**C203** A122 80c ultra .55 .25
**C204** A122 1.30g gray blue .55 .25
*Nos. C201-C204 (4)* 2.20 1.00

Church of San Roque AP70

**1954, June 20 Engr. *Perf. 12x13***

**C205** AP70 20c carmine .30 .25
**C206** AP70 30c brown vio .30 .25
**C207** AP70 50c ultra .30 .25
**C208** AP70 1g red brn & bl grn .35 .25
**C209** AP70 1g red brn & lil rose .35 .25
**C210** AP70 1g red brn & blk .35 .25
**C211** AP70 1g red brn & org .35 .25
*a.* Min. sheet of 4, #C208-C211, perf. 12x12½ 14.00 7.00
**C212** AP70 5g dk red brn & vio .70 .30
**C213** AP70 5g dk red brn & ol grn .70 .30
**C214** AP70 5g dk red brn & org yel .70 .30
**C215** AP70 5g dk red brn & yel org .70 .30
*a.* Min. sheet of 4, #C212-C215, perf. 12x12½ 14.00 7.00
*Nos. C205-C215 (11)* 5.10 2.95

Centenary (in 1953) of the establishment of the Church of San Roque, Asuncion.

Nos. C211a and C215a issued without gum.

### Heroes Type

**Unwmk.**

**1954, Aug. 15 Litho. *Perf. 10***

**C216** A123 5g violet .50 .25
**C217** A123 10g olive green 1.00 .40
**C218** A123 20g gray brown 1.75 .70
**C219** A123 50g vermilion 2.75 1.75
**C220** A123 100g blue 10.00 5.75
*Nos. C216-C220 (5)* 16.00 8.85

### Peron Visit Type

**Photo. & Litho.**

**1955, Apr. Wmk. 90 *Perf. 13x13½***

**Frames & Flags in Blue & Carmine**

**C221** A124 60c ol grn & cream .60 .80
**C222** A124 2g bl grn & cream .60 .80
**C223** A124 3g brn org & cream .60 .80
**C224** A124 4.10g brt rose pink & cr .60 .80
*Nos. C221-C224 (4)* 2.40 3.20

### Monsignor Rodriguez Type

Jesuit Ruins: 3g, Corridor at Trinidad. 6g, Tower of Santa Rosa. 10g, San Cosme gate. 20g, Church of Jesus. 30g, Niche at Trinidad. 50g, Sacristy at Trinidad.

***Perf. 12½x12, 12x12½***

**1955, June 19 Engr. Unwmk.**

**C225** A125 2g aqua .40 .25
**C226** A125 3g olive grn .40 .25
**C227** A126 4g lt blue grn .40 .25
**C228** A126 6g brown .40 .25
**C229** A125 10g rose .40 .25
**C230** A125 20g brown ol .40 .25
**C231** A126 30g dk green .70 .25
**C232** A126 50g dp aqua .85 .30
*Nos. C225-C232 (8)* 3.95 2.05

For surcharges see Nos. C252-C259.

Soldier and Flags — AP75

"Republic" and Soldier — AP76

**1957, June 12 Photo. *Perf. 13½***

**Granite Paper**

**Flags in Red and Blue**

**C233** AP75 10c ultra .25 .25
**C234** AP75 15c dp claret .25 .25
**C235** AP75 20c red .25 .25
**C236** AP75 25c light blue .25 .25
**C237** AP75 50c bluish grn .25 .25
**C238** AP75 1g rose car .30 .25
**C239** AP76 1.30g dp claret .30 .25
**C240** AP76 1.50p light blue .30 .25
**C241** AP76 2g emerald .30 .25
**C242** AP76 4.10g red .30 .25
**C243** AP76 5g gray black .30 .25
**C244** AP76 10g bluish grn .35 .25
**C245** AP76 25g ultra .30 .25
*Nos. C233-C245 (13)* 3.70 3.25

Heroes of the Chaco war.

### Stroessner Type of Regular Issue

**1958, Aug. 16 Litho. Wmk. 320**

**Center in Slate**

**C246** A130 12g rose lilac 1.00 1.00
**C247** A130 18g orange 1.25 1.00
**C248** A130 23g orange brn 1.25 1.00
**C249** A130 36g emerald 2.50 2.00
**C250** A130 50g citron 5.00 4.00
**C251** A130 65g gray 10.00 6.00
*Nos. C246-C251 (6)* 21.00 15.00

Re-election of Pres. General Alfredo Stroessner.

### Nos. C225-C232 Surcharged like #545-551 in Red

***Perf. 12½x12, 12x12½***

**1959, May 26 Engr. Unwmk.**

**C252** A125 4g on 2g aqua .50 *1.00*
**C253** A125 12.45g on 3g ol grn .50 .50
**C254** A126 18.15g on 6g brown .70 .50
**C255** A125 23.40g on 10g rose .80 .50
**C256** A125 34.80g on 20g brn ol 1.00 1.00
**C257** A126 36g on 4g lt bl grn 2.00 1.00
**C258** A126 43.95g on 30g dk grn 2.00 1.00
**C259** A126 100g on 50g deep aqua 5.00 2.50
*Nos. C252-C259 (8)* 12.50 8.00

The surcharge is made to fit the stamps. Counterfeits of surcharge exist.

UN Emblem AP77

**Unwmk.**

**1959, Aug. 27 Typo. *Perf. 11***

**C260** AP77 5g ocher & ultra 1.00 .80

Visit of Dag Hammarskjold, Secretary General of the UN, Aug. 27-29.

Map and UN Emblem — AP78

**1959, Oct. 24 Litho. *Perf. 10***

**C261** AP78 12.45g blue & salmon .50 .25

United Nations Day, Oct. 24, 1959.

### Olympic Games Type of Regular Issue

Design: Basketball.

**1960, Mar. 18 Photo. *Perf. 12½***

**C262** A131 12.45g red & dk bl .30 .30
**C263** A131 18.15g lilac & gray ol .30 .30
**C264** A131 36g bl grn & rose car .45 .45
*Nos. C262-C264 (3)* 1.05 1.05

The Paraguayan Philatelic Agency reported as spurious the imperf. souvenir sheet reproducing one of No. C264. Value, $10.

Uprooted Oak Emblem — AP79

**1960, Apr. 7 Litho. *Perf. 11***

**C265** AP79 4g green & pink .70 .40
**C266** AP79 12.45g bl & yel grn 1.25 .65
**C267** AP79 18.15g car & ocher 1.75 .75
**C268** AP79 23.40g red org & bl 2.10 1.50
*Nos. C265-C268 (4)* 5.80 3.30

World Refugee Year, July 1, 1959-June 30, 1960 (1st issue).

### Human Rights Type of Regular Issue, 1960

Designs: 40g, UN Emblem. 60g, Hands holding scales. 100g, Flame.

**1960, Apr. 21 *Perf. 12½x13***

**C269** A133 40g dk ultra & red .25 .25
**C270** A133 60g grnsh bl & org .30 .30
**C271** A133 100g dk ultra & red .65 .65
*Nos. C269-C271 (3)* 1.20 1.20

An imperf. miniature sheet exists, containing one each of Nos. C269-C271, all printed in green and vermilion. Value, $15.

### UN Type of Regular Issue

***Perf. 13x13½***

**1960, Oct. 24 Photo. Unwmk.**

**C272** A134 3g orange, red & bl .40 .30
**C273** A134 4g pale grn, red & bl .40 .30

International Bridge, Paraguay-Brazil AP80

**1961, Jan. 26 Litho. *Perf. 14***

**C274** AP80 3g carmine .50 .50
**C275** AP80 12.45g brown lake .75 .75
**C276** AP80 18.15g Prus grn 1.00 1.00
**C277** AP80 36g dk blue 2.00 2.00
*a.* Souv. sheet of 4, #C274-C277, imperf. 15.00 15.00
*Nos. C274-C277 (4)* 4.25 4.25

Inauguration of the International Bridge between Paraguay and Brazil.

### "Paraguay en Marcha" Type of 1961

12.45g, Truck carrying logs. 18.15g, Logs on river barge. 22g, Radio tower. 36g, Jet plane.

**1961, Apr. 10 Photo. *Perf. 13***

| | | | | |
|---|---|---|---|---|
| **C278** | A136 | 12.45g yel & vio bl | .45 | .35 |
| **C279** | A136 | 18.15g pur & ocher | .60 | .50 |
| **C280** | A136 | 22g ultra & ocher | .65 | .60 |
| **C281** | A136 | 36g brt grn & yel | 1.10 | 1.00 |
| | | *Nos. C278-C281 (4)* | 2.80 | 2.45 |

Declaration of Independence — AP81

**1961, May 16 Litho. *Perf. 14½***

| | | | | |
|---|---|---|---|---|
| **C282** | AP81 | 12.45g dl red brn | .60 | .40 |
| **C283** | AP81 | 18.15g dk blue | .70 | .60 |
| **C284** | AP81 | 23.40g green | 1.00 | .90 |
| **C285** | AP81 | 30g lilac | 1.25 | 1.00 |
| **C286** | AP81 | 36g rose | 1.60 | 1.50 |
| **C287** | AP81 | 44g olive | 2.00 | 1.75 |
| | | *Nos. C282-C287 (6)* | 7.15 | 6.15 |

150th anniv. of Independence (1st issue).

"Paraguay" and Clasped Hands — AP82

**1961, June 12 *Perf. 14x14½***

| | | | | |
|---|---|---|---|---|
| **C288** | AP82 | 3g vio blue | .60 | .50 |
| **C289** | AP82 | 4g rose claret | .70 | .60 |
| **C290** | AP82 | 100g gray green | 4.50 | 4.00 |
| | | *Nos. C288-C290 (3)* | 5.80 | 5.10 |

Chaco Peace; 150th anniv. of Independence (2nd issue).

South American Tapir — AP83

**1961, Aug. 16 Unwmk. *Perf. 14***

| | | | | |
|---|---|---|---|---|
| **C291** | AP83 | 12.45g claret | 3.00 | 2.00 |
| **C292** | AP83 | 18.15g ultra | 3.00 | 2.50 |
| **C293** | AP83 | 34.80g red brown | 5.50 | 4.50 |
| | | *Nos. C291-C293 (3)* | 11.50 | 9.00 |

150th anniv. of Independence (3rd issue).

### Catholic University Type of 1961

**1961, Sept. 18 *Perf. 14x14½***

| | | | | |
|---|---|---|---|---|
| **C294** | A140 | 3g bister brn | .50 | .40 |
| **C295** | A140 | 12.45g lilac rose | .50 | .40 |
| **C296** | A140 | 36g blue | 1.00 | .80 |
| | | *Nos. C294-C296 (3)* | 2.00 | 1.60 |

### Hotel Guarani Type of 1961

Design: Hotel Guarani, different view.

**1961, Oct. 14 Litho. *Perf. 15***

| | | | | |
|---|---|---|---|---|
| **C297** | A141 | 3g dull red brn | 1.75 | 1.75 |
| **C298** | A141 | 4g ultra | 1.75 | 1.75 |
| **C299** | A141 | 18.15g orange | 2.00 | 1.75 |
| **C300** | A141 | 36g rose car | 4.00 | 2.00 |
| | | *Nos. C297-C300 (4)* | 9.50 | 7.25 |

### Tennis Type

**1961, Oct. 16 Unwmk. *Perf. 11***

| | | | | |
|---|---|---|---|---|
| **C301** | A142 | 12.45g multi | .65 | .65 |
| **C302** | A142 | 20g multi | 1.25 | 1.25 |
| **C303** | A142 | 50g multi | 3.00 | 3.00 |
| | | *Nos. C301-C303 (3)* | 4.90 | 4.90 |

Some specialists question the status of this issue.

Two imperf. souvenir sheets exist containing four 12.45g stamps each in a different color with simulated perforations and black marginal inscription.

### WRY Type

Design: Oak emblem rooted in ground, wavy-lined frame.

**1961, Dec. 30**

| | | | | |
|---|---|---|---|---|
| **C307** | A145 | 18.15g brn & red | .50 | .50 |
| **C308** | A145 | 36g car & emer | 1.25 | 1.25 |
| **C309** | A145 | 50g emer & org | 1.60 | 1.60 |
| | | *Nos. C307-C309 (3)* | 3.35 | 3.35 |

Imperforates in changed colors and souvenir sheets exist. Some specialists question the status of this issue.

Pres. Alfredo Stroessner and Prince Philip AP84

**1962, Mar. 9 Litho.**

**Portraits in Ultramarine**

| | | | | |
|---|---|---|---|---|
| **C310** | AP84 | 12.45g grn & buff | 3.00 | 2.00 |
| **C311** | AP84 | 18.15g red & pink | 3.00 | 2.00 |
| **C312** | AP84 | 36g brn & yel | 3.00 | 2.00 |
| | | *Nos. C310-C312 (3)* | 9.00 | 6.00 |

Visit of Prince Philip, Duke of Edinburgh, perf. and imperf. souvenir sheets exist. Values: each $5.

Illustrations AP85-AP89, AP92-AP94, AP96-AP97, AP99-AP105, AP107-AP110, AP113-AP115, AP117, AP123, AP127a, AP132-AP133, AP136, AP138, AP140, AP142, AP144-AP145, AP149-AP150, AP152-AP153, AP156, AP158-AP159, AP165, AP167, AP171, AP180, AP183-AP184, AP187, AP196, AP202, AP205, AP208, AP211, AP221-AP222, AP224-AP225, AP229, AP234-AP235, AP237 and AP240 are reduced.

Souvenir Sheet

Abraham Lincoln (1809-1865), 16th President of U.S. — AP85

**1963, Aug. 21 Litho. *Imperf.***

| | | | | |
|---|---|---|---|---|
| **C313** | AP85 | 36g gray & vio brn | 10.00 | 10.00 |

Souvenir Sheet

1960 Summer Olympics, Rome — AP86

**1963, Aug. 21 Litho. & Engr.**

| | | | | |
|---|---|---|---|---|
| **C314** | AP86 | 50g lt bl, vio brn & sep | 50.00 | 50.00 |

MUESTRA

Illustrations may show the word "MUESTRA." This means specimen and is not on the actual stamps.

Souvenir Sheet

Cattleya Cigas — AP87

**1963, Aug. 21 Litho.**

| | | | | |
|---|---|---|---|---|
| **C315** | AP87 | 66g multicolored | 60.00 | 60.00 |

Souvenir Sheet

Pres. Alfredo Stroessner — AP88

**1964, Nov. 3**

| | | | | |
|---|---|---|---|---|
| **C316** | AP88 | 36g multicolored | 8.00 | 7.00 |

Souvenir Sheet

Saturn V Rocket, Pres. John F. Kennedy — AP89

**1968, Jan. 27 *Perf. 14***

| | | | | |
|---|---|---|---|---|
| **C317** | AP89 | 50g multicolored | 20.00 | 20.00 |

Pres. Kennedy, 4th death anniv. (in 1967).

Torch, Book, Houses — AP90

**1969, June 28 Wmk. 347 *Perf. 11***

| | | | | |
|---|---|---|---|---|
| **C318** | AP90 | 36g blue | 2.00 | 1.00 |
| **C319** | AP90 | 50g bister brn | 4.00 | 2.00 |
| **C320** | AP90 | 100g rose car | 6.00 | 3.00 |
| | | *Nos. C318-C320 (3)* | 12.00 | 6.00 |

National drive for teachers' homes.

Souvenir Sheets

U.S. Space Program — AP91

John F. Kennedy, Wernher von Braun, moon and: No. C321, Apollo 11 en route to moon. No. C322, Saturn V lift-off. No. C323, Apollo 9. No. C324, Apollo 10.

**1969, July 9 *Perf. 14***

| | | | | |
|---|---|---|---|---|
| **C321** | AP91 | 23.40g multi | 15.00 | 15.00 |
| **C322** | AP91 | 23.40g multi | 22.50 | 22.50 |

***Imperf***

| | | | | |
|---|---|---|---|---|
| **C323** | AP91 | 23.40g multi | 22.50 | 22.50 |
| **C324** | AP91 | 23.40g multi | 27.50 | 27.50 |

Nos. C323-C324 each contain one 56x46mm stamp.

Souvenir Sheets

Events and Anniversaries — AP92

#C325, Apollo 14. #C326, Dwight D. Eisenhower, 1st death anniv. #C327, Napoleon Bonaparte, birth bicent. #C328, Brazil, winners of Jules Rimet World Cup Soccer Trophy.

**1970, Dec. 16 *Perf. 13½***

| | | | | |
|---|---|---|---|---|
| **C325** | AP92 | 20g multicolored | 22.50 | 22.50 |
| **C326** | AP92 | 20g multicolored | 12.00 | 12.00 |
| **C327** | AP92 | 20g multicolored | 15.00 | 15.00 |
| **C328** | AP92 | 20g multicolored | 15.00 | 15.00 |
| | | *Nos. C325-C328 (4)* | 64.50 | 64.50 |

Souvenir Sheets

Paraguayan Postage Stamps, Cent. — AP93

No. C329, Marshal Francisco Solano Lopez, Pres. Alfredo Stroessner, Paraguay #1. No. C330, #3, 1014, 1242. No. C331, #1243, C8, C74.

**1971, Mar. 23**

**C329** AP93 20g multicolored 7.50 7.50
**C330** AP93 20g multicolored 14.00 14.00
**C331** AP93 20g multicolored 14.00 14.00
*Nos. C329-C331 (3)* 35.50 35.50

Issued: #C329, 3/23; #C330-C331, 3/29.

Souvenir Sheets

Emblems of Apollo Space Missions — AP94

Designs: No. C332, Apollo 7, 8, 9, & 10. No. C333, Apollo 11, 12, 13, & 14.

**1971, Mar. 26**

**C332** AP94 20g multicolored 13.00 13.00
**C333** AP94 20g multicolored 13.00 13.00

Souvenir Sheet

Charles de Gaulle — AP95

**1971, Dec. 24** ***Perf. 14***

**C334** AP95 20g multicolored 17.50 17.50

Souvenir Sheet

Taras Shevchenko (1814-1861), Ukrainian Poet — AP96

**1971, Dec. 24** ***Perf. 13½***

**C335** AP96 20g multicolored 7.50 7.50

Souvenir Sheets

Johannes Kepler (1571-1630), German Astronomer — AP97

Kepler and: No. C336, Apollo lunar module over moon. No. C337, Astronaut walking in space.

**1971, Dec. 24**

**C336** AP97 20g multicolored 17.00 17.00
**C337** AP97 20g multicolored 17.00 17.00

Souvenir Sheet

10 years of U.S. Space Program — AP98

**1972, Jan. 6** ***Perf. 13½***

**C338** AP98 20g multicolored 17.00 17.00

Souvenir Sheet

Apollo 16 Moon Mission — AP99

**1972, Mar. 29** **Litho.** ***Perf. 13½***

**C339** AP99 20g multicolored 17.00 17.00

Souvenir Sheets

History of the Olympics — AP100

Designs: No. C340, Pierre de Coubertin (1863-1937), founder of modern Olympics. No. C341, Skier, Garmisch-Partenkirchen, 1936. No. C342, Olympic flame, Sapporo, 1972. No. C343, French, Olympic flags. No. C344, Javelin thrower, Paris, 1924. No. C345, Equestrian event.

**1972, Mar. 29** ***Perf. 14½***

**C340** AP100 20g multicolored 15.00 12.00
**C341** AP100 20g multicolored 15.00 12.00
**C342** AP100 20g multicolored 15.00 15.00
**C343** AP100 20g multicolored 15.00 15.00
**C344** AP100 20g multicolored 15.00 15.00
**C345** AP100 20g multicolored 15.00 15.00
*Nos. C340-C345 (6)* 90.00 84.00

Souvenir Sheet

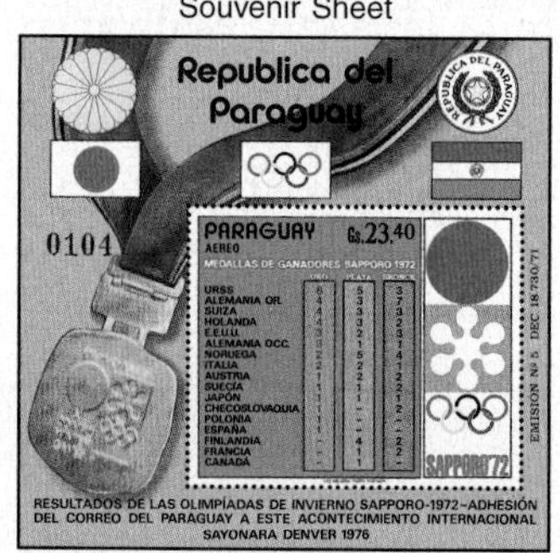

Medal Totals, 1972 Winter Olympics, Sapporo — AP101

**1972, Nov. 18** ***Perf. 13½***

**C346** AP101 23.40g multi 15.00 15.00

Souvenir Sheets

French Contributions to Aviation and Space Exploration — AP102

Georges Pompidou, Charles de Gaulle and: No. C347, Concorde. No. C348, Satellite D2A, Mirage G 8 jets.

**1972, Nov. 25**

**C347** AP102 23.40g multi 50.00 50.00
**C348** AP102 23.40g multi 45.00 45.00

Souvenir Sheets

Summer Olympic Gold Medals, 1896-1972 — AP103

No. C349, 9 medals, 1896-1932, vert. No. C350, 8 medals, 1936-1972.

**1972, Nov. 25**

**C349** AP103 23.40g multi 15.00 15.00
**C350** AP103 23.40g multi 15.00 15.00

Souvenir Sheet

Adoration of the Shepherds by Murillo — AP104

**1972, Nov. 25**

**C351** AP104 23.40g multi 15.00 15.00

Christmas.

Souvenir Sheet

Apollo 17 Moon Mission — AP105

**1973, Mar. 13**

**C352** AP105 25g multicolored 20.00 20.00

Souvenir Sheet

Medal Totals, 1972 Summer Olympics, Munich — AP106

**1973, Mar. 15** ***Perf. 13½***

**C353** AP106 25g multicolored 25.00 25.00

Souvenir Sheets

The Holy Family by Peter Paul Rubens — AP107

Design: No. C355, In the Forest at Pierrefonds by Alfred de Dreux.

**1973, Mar. 15**

**C354** AP107 25g multicolored 20.00 20.00
**C355** AP107 25g multicolored 15.00 15.00

Souvenir Sheet

German Championship Soccer Team F.C. Bayern, Bavaria #2 — AP108

**1973, June 29** ***Imperf.***

**C356** AP108 25g multicolored 15.00 15.00

IBRA '73 Intl. Philatelic Exhibition, Munich,

Souvenir Sheet

Copernicus, 500th Birth Anniv. and Space Exploration — AP109

#C357, Lunar surface, Apollo 11. #C358, Copernicus, position of Earth at soltices and equinoxes, vert. #C359, Skylab space laboratory.

**1973, June 29** ***Perf. 13½***

**C357** AP109 25g multicolored 30.00 30.00
**C358** AP109 25g multicolored 30.00 30.00
**C359** AP109 25g multicolored 20.00 20.00
*Nos. C357-C359 (3)* 80.00 80.00

Souvenir Sheets

Exploration of Mars — AP110

**1973, Oct. 8**

**C360** AP110 25g Mariner 9 20.00 20.00
**C361** AP110 25g Viking probe, horiz. 30.00 30.00

Pres. Stroessner's Visit to Europe and Morocco — AP111

Designs: No. C362a, 5g, Arms of Paraguay, Spain, Canary Islands. b, 10g, Gen. Franco, Stroessner, vert. c, 25g, Arms of Paraguay, Germany. d, 50g, Stroessner, Giovanni Leone, Italy, vert. No. C363, Itaipu Dam between Paraguay and Brazil.

**1973, Dec. 30** ***Perf. 14***

**C362** AP111 Strip of 4, #a.-d. 2.00 1.25
**C363** AP111 150g multicolored 2.50 1.75
*Nos. C362-C363 (2)* 4.50 3.00

**Souvenir Sheet**

***Imperf***

**C364** AP111 100g Country flags 15.00 15.00

No. C364 contains one 60x50mm stamp. See Nos. C375-C376.

1974 World Cup Soccer Championships, Munich — AP112

Abstract paintings of soccer players: No. C366a, 10g, Player seated on globe. b, 20g, Player as viewed from under foot. No. C367, Player kicking ball. No. C368, Goalie catching ball, horiz.

**1974, Jan. 31** ***Perf. 14***

**C365** AP112 5g shown 10.00 3.50
**C366** AP112 Pair, #a.-b. 2.00 1.00
*Nos. C365-C366 (2)* 12.00 4.50

**Souvenir Sheets**

***Perf. 13½***

**C367** AP112 25g multicolored 15.00 15.00
**C368** AP112 25g multicolored 15.00 15.00

Nos. C367-C368 each contain one 50x60mm stamp.

Souvenir Sheets

Tourism Year — AP113

Design: No. C370, Painting, Birth of Christ by Louis le Nain (1593-1648), horiz.

**1974, Feb. 4** ***Perf. 13½***

**C369** AP113 25g multicolored 12.00 12.00
**C370** AP113 25g multicolored 7.00 7.00

Christmas (No. C370).

Souvenir Sheets

Events and Anniversaries — AP114

No. C371, Rocket lift-off. No. C372, Solar system, horiz. No. C373, Skylab 2 astronauts, horiz. No. C374, Olympic Flame.

**1974, Mar. 20**

**C371** AP114 25g multicolored 20.00 20.00
**C372** AP114 25g multicolored 20.00 20.00
**C373** AP114 25g multicolored 12.00 12.00
**C374** AP114 25g multicolored 12.00 12.00
*Nos. C371-C374 (4)* 64.00 64.00

UPU centennial (#C371-C372). 1976 Olympic Games (#C374).

**President Stroessner Type of 1973**

100g, Stroessner, Georges Pompidou. 200g, Stroessner and Pope Paul VI.

**1974, Apr. 25** ***Perf. 14***

**C375** AP111 100g multicolored 2.00 1.00

**Souvenir Sheet**

***Perf. 13½***

**C376** AP111 200g multicolored 5.00 5.00

No. C376 contains one 60x50mm stamp.

Souvenir Sheet

Lufthansa Airlines Intercontinental Routes, 40th Anniv. — AP115

**1974, July 13** ***Perf. 13½***

**C377** AP115 15g multicolored 15.00 15.00

No. C377 face value was 15g plus 5g extra for a monument to Francisco Solano Lopez.

Souvenir Sheet

Hermann Oberth, 80th Anniv. of Birth — AP115a

**1974, July 13** **Litho.** ***Perf. 13½***

**C378** AP115a 15g multi 25.00 25.00

No. C378 face value was 15g plus 5g extra for a monument to Francisco Solano Lopez.

1974 World Cup Soccer Championships, West Germany — AP116

**1974, July 13** ***Perf. 14***

**C379** AP116 4g Goalie 10.00 5.00
**C380** AP116 5g Soccer ball 2.50 1.10
**C381** AP116 10g shown 3.50 1.50
*Nos. C379-C381 (3)* 16.00 7.60

**Souvenir Sheet**

***Perf. 13½***

**C382** AP116 15g Soccer ball, diff. 22.50 22.50

No. C382 contains one 53x46mm stamp. No. C382 face value was 15g plus 5g extra for a monument for Francisco Solano Lopez.

Souvenir Sheet

First Balloon Flight over English Channel — AP117

**1974, Sept. 13** ***Imperf.***

**C383** AP117 15g multicolored 24.00 24.00

No. C383 face value was 15g plus 5g extra for a monument for Francisco Solano Lopez.

Anniversaries and Events — AP118

Designs: 4g, US #C76 on covers that went to Moon. No. C385a, 5g, Pres. Pinochet of Chile. No. C385b, 10g, Pres. Stroessner's visit to South Africa. No. C386, Mariner 10 over Mercury, horiz.

**1974, Dec. 2** ***Perf. 14***

**C384** AP118 4g multicolored 5.00 5.00
**C385** AP118 Pair #a.-b. 1.25 1.00
*Nos. C384-C385 (2)* 6.25 6.00

**Souvenir Sheets**

***Perf. 13½***

**C386** AP118 15g multicolored 15.00 15.00

Nos. C386 contains one 60x50mm stamp, Face value was 15g plus 5g extra for a monument to Francisco Solano Lopez. Compare No. C386 with No. C392.

Anniversaries and Events — AP119

Designs: 4g, UPU, cent. 5g, 17th Congress, UPU, Lausanne. 10g, Intl. Philatelic Exposition, Montevideo, Uruguay. No. C392, Mariner 10 orbiting Mercury, horiz. No. C393, Figure skater, horiz. No. C394, Innsbruck Olympic emblem.

**1974, Dec. 7** ***Perf. 14***

**C389** AP119 4g multicolored 3.00 2.00
**C390** AP119 5g multicolored 1.10 .75
**C391** AP119 10g multicolored 1.10 .75
*Nos. C389-C391 (3)* 5.20 3.50

**Souvenir Sheets**

***Perf. 13½***

**C392** AP119 15g bl & multi 15.00 15.00
**C393** AP119 15g multicolored 15.00 15.00
**C394** AP119 15g multicolored 15.00 15.00

UPU centennial (#C389). Nos. C392-C394 each contain one 60x50mm stamp and face value was 15g plus 5g extra for a monument to Francisco Solano Lopez.

German World Cup Soccer Champions — AP120

4g, Holding World Cup trophy, vert. 5g, Team on field. 10g, Argentina '78 emblem, vert.

No. C398, Players holding trophy, vert. No. C399, Hemispheres, emblems of 1974 and 1978 World Cup championships.

**1974, Dec. 20** ***Perf. 14***

**C395** AP120 4g multicolored 5.00 3.25
**C396** AP120 5g multicolored .75 .35
**C397** AP120 10g multicolored 1.50 .35
*Nos. C395-C397 (3)* 7.25 3.95

**Souvenir Sheets**

***Perf. 13½***

**C398** AP120 15g multicolored 20.00 20.00
**C399** AP120 15g multicolored 20.00 20.00

No. C398 contains one 50x60mm stamp, and No. C399 contains one 60x50mm stamp. Face value of each sheet was 15g plus 5g extra for a monument to Francisco Solano Lopez.

**Souvenir Sheet**

Apollo-Soyuz — AP121

**1974, Dec. 20** ***Perf. 13½***

**C400** AP121 15g multicolored 17.50 17.50

Expo '75 — AP122

4g, Ryukyumurasaki, vert. 5g, Hibiscus. 10g, Ancient sailing ship.

15g, Expo emblem, vert.

**1975, Feb. 24** ***Perf. 14***

**C401** AP122 4g multicolored 3.00 1.10
**C402** AP122 5g multicolored .75 .25
**C403** AP122 10g multicolored 1.50 .25
*Nos. C401-C403 (3)* 5.25 1.60

**Souvenir Sheet**

***Perf. 14½***

**C404** AP122 15g multicolored 10.00 10.00

No. C404 face value was 15g plus 5g extra for a monument to Francisco Solano Lopez.

**Souvenir Sheets**

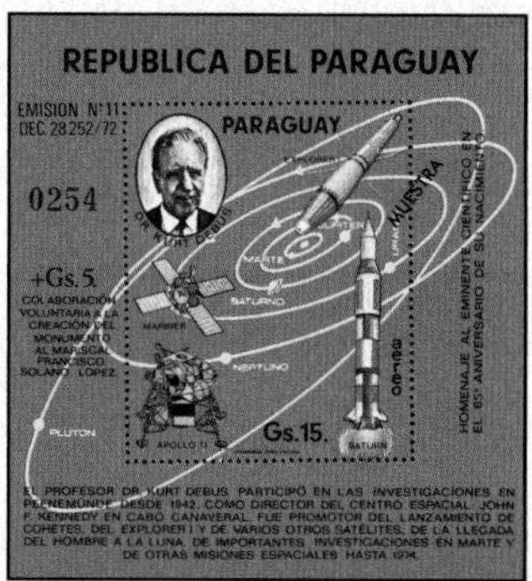


Anniversaries and Events — AP123

Designs: No. C405, Dr. Kurt Debus, space scientist, 65th birth anniv. No. C406, 1976 Summer Olympics, Montreal, horiz.

**1975, Feb. 24** ***Perf. 13½***

**C405** AP123 15g multicolored 17.00 17.00
**C406** AP123 15g multicolored 17.00 17.00

Nos. C405-C406 face value was 15g plus 5g extra for a monument to Francisco Solano Lopez.

GEOS Satellite AP124

No. C408a, 5g, ESPANA 75. b, 10g, Mother and Child, Murillo.

No. C409, Spain #1139, 1838, C167, charity stamp. No. C410, Zeppelin, plane, satellites. No. C411, Jupiter.

**1975, Aug. 21** ***Perf. 14***

**C407** AP124 4g shown 3.00 1.90
**C408** AP124 Pair, #1.-b. 2.25 .50
*Nos. C407-C408 (2)* 5.25 2.40

**Souvenir Sheet**

***Perf. 13½***

**C409** AP124 15g multicolored 30.00 30.00
**C410** AP124 15g multicolored 40.00 40.00

***Perf. 14½***

**C411** AP124 15g multicolored 15.00 15.00

Nos. C409-C411 face value was 15g plus 5g extra for a monument to Francisco Solano Lopez.

Size of stamps: No. C409, 45x55mm; C410, 55x45mm; C411, 32x22mm.

**Souvenir Sheets**

Anniversaries and Events — AP125

#C413, UN emblem, Intl. Women's Year, vert. #C414, Helios space satellite.

**1975, Aug. 26** ***Perf. 13½***

**C413** AP125 15g multicolored 15.00 15.00
**C414** AP125 15g multicolored 15.00 15.00

Nos. C413-C414 face value was 15g plus 5g extra for a monument to Francisco Solano Lopez.

Anniversaries and Events — AP125a

Designs: 4g, First Zeppelin flight, 75th anniv. 5g, Emblem of 1978 World Cup Soccer Championships, Argentina, vert. 10g, Emblem of Nordposta 75, statue.

**1975, Oct. 13** **Litho.** ***Perf. 14***

**C415-C417** AP125a Set of 3 6.00 3.00

**Souvenir Sheets**

Anniversaries and Events — AP126

No. C418, Zeppelin, boats. No. C419, Soccer, Intelsat IV, vert. No. C420, Viking Mars landing.

**1975, Oct. 13** ***Perf. 13½***

**C418** AP126 15g multicolored 17.50 17.50
**C419** AP126 15g multicolored 17.50 17.50
**C420** AP126 15g multicolored 17.50 17.50
*Nos. C418-C420 (3)* 52.50 52.50

Nos. C418-C420 face value was 15g plus 5g extra for a monument to Francisco Solano Lopez.

United States, Bicent. — AP127

#C421: a, 4g, Lunar rover. b, 5g, Ford Elite, 1975. c, 10g, Ford, 1896. No. C422, Airplanes and spacecraft. No. C423, Arms of Paraguay & US.

**1975, Nov. 28** **Litho.** ***Perf. 14***

**C421** AP127 Strip of 3, #a.-c. 6.00 3.00

**Souvenir Sheets**

***Perf. 13½***

**C422** AP127 15g multicolored 22.50 22.50
**C423** AP127 15g multicolored 22.50 22.50

Nos. C422-C423 each contain one 60x50mm stamp and face value was 15g plus 5g surtax for a monument to Francisco Solano Lopez.

**Souvenir Sheet**

La Musique by Francois Boucher — AP127a

**1975, Nov. 28** ***Perf. 13½***

**C424** AP127a 15g multicolored 7.50 7.50

No. C424 face value was 15g plus 5g extra for a monument to Francisco Solano Lopez.

Anniversaries and Events — AP128

Designs: 4g, Flight of Concorde jet. 5g, JU 52/3M, Lufthansa Airlines, 50th anniv. 10g, EXFILMO '75 and ESPAMER '75. No. C428, Concorde, diff. No. C429, Dr. Albert Schweitzer, missionary and Konrad Adenauer, German statesman. No. C430, Ferdinand Porsche, auto designer, birth cent., vert.

**1975, Dec. 20** ***Perf. 14***

**C425** AP128 4g multicolored 4.00 2.50
**C426** AP128 5g multicolored .40 .40
**C427** AP128 10g multicolored .40 .40
*Nos. C425-C427 (3)* 4.80 3.30

**Souvenir Sheets**

***Perf. 13½***

**C428** AP128 15g multicolored 27.50 25.00
**C429** AP128 15g multicolored 15.00 12.00
**C430** AP128 15g multicolored 40.00 40.00

Nos. C428-C430 face value was 15g plus 5g extra for a monument to Francisco Solano Lopez. No. C428 contains one 54x34mm stamp, No. C429 one 60x50mm stamp, No. C430 one 30x40mm stamp.

Anniversaries and Events — AP129

Details: 4g, The Transfiguration by Raphael, vert. 5g, Nativity by Del Mayno. 10g, Nativity by Vignon. No. C434, Detail from Adoration of the Shepherds by Ghirlandaio. No. C435, Austria, 1000th anniv., Leopold I, natl. arms, vert. No. C436, Sepp Herberger and Helmut Schon, coaches for German soccer team.

**1976, Feb. 2 Litho. *Perf. 14***

**C431** AP129 4g multicolored 4.00 2.00
**C432** AP129 5g multicolored .80 .40
**C433** AP129 10g multicolored .80 .40
*Nos. C431-C433 (3)* 5.60 2.80

**Souvenir Sheets**

***Perf. 13½***

**C434** AP129 15g multicolored 10.00 10.00
**C435** AP129 15g multicolored 40.00 40.00

***Perf. 13½x13***

**C436** AP129 15g multicolored 75.00 75.00

Nos. C434-C436 face value was 15g plus 5g extra for a monument to Francisco Solano Lopez. No. C434 contains one 40x30mm stamp, No. C435 one 30x40mm stamp, No. C436 one 54x34mm stamp.

Souvenir Sheet

Apollo-Soyuz — AP130

**1976, Apr. 2 *Perf. 13½x13***

**C437** AP130 25g multicolored 17.00 17.00

Souvenir Sheet

Lufthansa, 50th Anniv. — AP131

**1976, Apr. 7 *Perf. 13½x13***

**C438** AP131 25g multicolored 14.00 14.00

Souvenir Sheet

Interphil '76 — AP132

**1976, May 12 *Perf. 13½***

**C439** AP132 15g multicolored 9.00 9.00

No. C439 face value was 15g plus 5g extra for a monument to Francisco Solano Lopez.

Souvenir Sheets

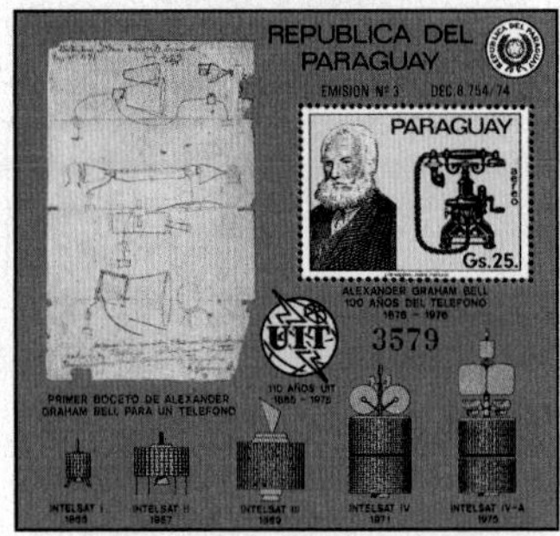

Anniversaries and Events — AP133

Designs: No. C440, Alexander Graham Bell, telephone cent. No. C441, Gold, silver, and bronze medals, 1976 Winter Olympics, Innsbruck. No. C442, Gold medalist Rosi Mittermaier, downhill and slalom, vert. No. C443, Viking probe on Mars. No. C444, UN Postal Administration, 25th anniv. and UPU, cent., vert. No. C445, Prof. Hermannm Oberth, Wernher von Braun. No. C446, Madonna and Child by Durer, vert.

**1976 *Perf. 13½***

**C440** AP133 25g multi 30.00 30.00
**C441** AP133 25g multi 17.50 17.50
**C442** AP133 25g multi 125.00 125.00

***Perf. 14½***

**C443** AP133 25g multi 15.00 15.00
**C444** AP133 25g multi 30.00 30.00
**C445** AP133 25g multi 60.00 60.00
**C446** AP133 25g multi 60.00 60.00
*Nos. C440-C446 (7)* 337.50 337.50

No. C442 contains one 35x54mm stamp, No. C443 one 46x36mm stamp, No. C444 one 25x35mm stamp.

Issued: #C440-C441, 6/15; #C443, 7/8; #C442, C444, 7/15; #C445, 8/20; #C446, 9/9.

Souvenir Sheet

UN Offices in Geneva #22, UN #42 — AP136

**1976, Dec. 18 *Perf. 13½***

**C447** AP136 25g multicolored 14.00 14.00

UN Postal Administration, 25th anniv. and telephone, cent.

Souvenir Sheet

Ludwig van Beethoven (1770-1827) — AP137

**1977, Feb. 28 Litho. *Perf. 14¼***

**C448** AP137 25g multi 6.00 6.00

Souvenir Sheet

Alfred Nobel, 80th Death Anniv. and First Nobel Prize, 75th Anniv. — AP138

**1977, June 7 *Perf. 13½***

**C449** AP138 25g multicolored 22.50 22.50

Souvenir Sheet

Coronation of Queen Elizabeth II, 25th Anniv. — AP139

**1977, July 25 *Perf. 14½***

**C450** AP139 25g multicolored 20.00 20.00

Souvenir Sheet

Uruguay '77 Intl. Philatelic Exhibition — AP140

**1977, Aug. 27 Litho. *Perf. 13½***

**C451** AP140 25g multicolored 14.00 14.00

Souvenir Sheets

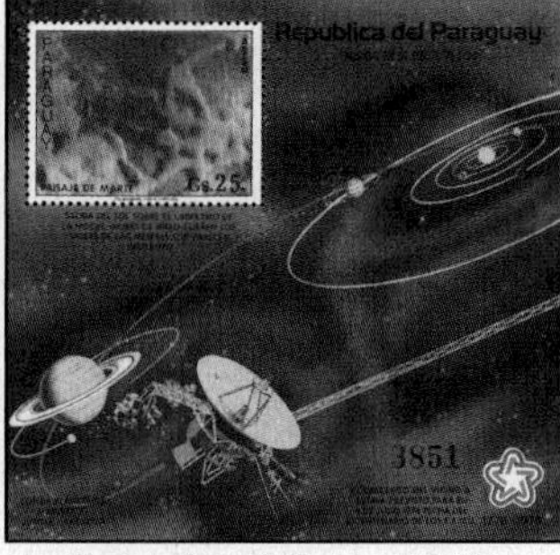

Exploration of Mars — AP141

No. C452, Martian craters. No. C453, Wernher von Braun. No. C454, Projected Martian lander.

**1977, Sept. 5 *Perf. 13½***

**C452** AP141 25g multicolored 35.00 35.00

***Perf. 14¼x14½***

**1977, Nov. 28 Litho.**

**C453** AP141 25g multicolored 40.00 40.00

**1977, Oct. 28 Litho. *Perf. 13½***

**C454** AP141 25g multicolored 60.00 60.00

Souvenir Sheet

Sepp Herberger, German Soccer Team Coach — AP142

**1978, Jan. 23 Litho. *Perf. 13½***

**C455** AP142 25g multicolored 35.00 35.00

Souvenir Sheet

Austria #B331, Canada #681, US #716, Russia #B66 — AP143

**1978, Mar. 10 Litho. *Perf. 14½***

**C456** AP143 25g multicolored 25.00 25.00

Inner perforations are simulated.

Souvenir Sheet

Alfred Nobel — AP144

**1978, Mar. 15 Litho. *Perf. 13½***
**C457** AP144 25g multicolored 35.00 35.00

Souvenir Sheets

Anniversaries and Events — AP145

Designs: No. C458, Queen Elizabeth II wearing St. Edward's Crown, holding orb and scepter. No. C459, Queen Elizabeth II presenting World Cup Trophy to English team captain. No. C460, Flags of nations participating in 1978 World Cup Soccer Championships. No. C461, Soccer action. No. C462, Argentina, 1978 World Cup Champions.

**1978 *Perf. 14½, 13½ (#C461)***

| | | | | |
|---|---|---|---|---|
| **C458** | AP145 25g multi | | 15.00 | 15.00 |
| **C459** | AP145 25g multi | | 25.00 | 25.00 |
| **C460** | AP145 25g multi | | 30.00 | 30.00 |
| **C461** | AP145 25g multi | | 25.00 | 25.00 |
| **C462** | AP145 25g multi | | 25.00 | 25.00 |
| | *Nos. C458-C462 (5)* | | 120.00 | 120.00 |

Coronation of Queen Elizabeth II, 25th Anniv. (#C458-C459). 1978 World Cup Soccer Championships, Argentina (#C460-C462).

No. C460 contains one 70x50mm stamp, No. C461 one 39x57mm stamp.

Issued: #C458, 5/11; #C459-C460, 5/16; #C461, 6/30; #C462, 10/26.

Souvenir Sheet

Jean-Henri Dunant, 150th Birth Anniv. — AP146

**1978, June 28 *Perf. 14½***
**C463** AP146 25g multicolored 20.00 20.00

Souvenir Sheet

Capt. James Cook, 250th Birth Anniv. — AP147

**1978, July 19 *Perf. 13½***
**C464** AP147 25g multicolored 15.00 15.00

Discovery of Hawaii, Death of Capt. Cook, bicentennial; Hawaii Statehood, 20th anniv.

Aregua Satellite Communication Station — AP148

Coat of Arms — AP148a

Pres. Alfredo Stroessner — AP148b

**1978, Aug. 15 Litho. *Perf. 14***

| | | | | |
|---|---|---|---|---|
| **C465** | AP148 | 75g multi | 1.60 | .30 |
| **C466** | AP148a | 500g multi | 6.50 | 2.00 |
| **C467** | AP148b | 1000g multi | 12.00 | 4.00 |
| | *Nos. C465-C467 (3)* | | 20.10 | 6.30 |

Souvenir Sheet

Adoration of the Magi by Albrecht Durer — AP149

**1978, Oct. 31 *Perf. 13½***
**C468** AP149 25g multicolored 15.00 15.00

Souvenir Sheet

Prof. Hermann Oberth, 85th Birth Anniv. — AP150

**1979, Aug. 28 *Perf. 14½***
**C469** AP150 25g multicolored 20.00 20.00

Souvenir Sheet

World Cup Soccer Championships — AP151

**1979, Nov. 29**
**C470** AP151 25g multicolored 25.00 25.00

Souvenir Sheet

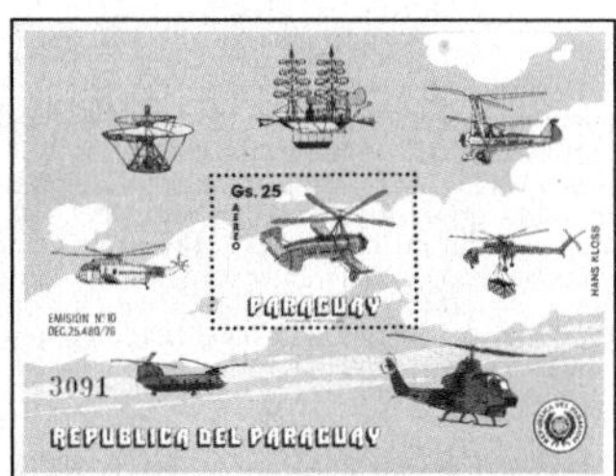

Helicopters — AP152

**1979, Nov. 29 Litho. *Perf. 13½***
**C471** AP152 25g multicolored 20.00 20.00

Souvenir Sheet

1980 Summer Olympics, Moscow — AP153

**1979, Dec. 20 *Perf. 14½***
**C472** AP153 25g Two-man canoe 30.00 30.00

Souvenir Sheet

1982 World Cup Soccer Championships, Spain — AP154

**1979, Dec. 24 Litho. *Perf. 13x13½***
**C473** AP154 25g Sheet of 1 + label 25.00 25.00

Souvenir Sheet

Maybach DS-8 "Zeppelin" — AP155

**1980, Apr. 8 *Perf. 14½***
**C474** AP155 25g multicolored 30.00 30.00

Wilhelm Maybach, 50th death anniv. Karl Maybach, 100th birth anniv.

Souvenir Sheet

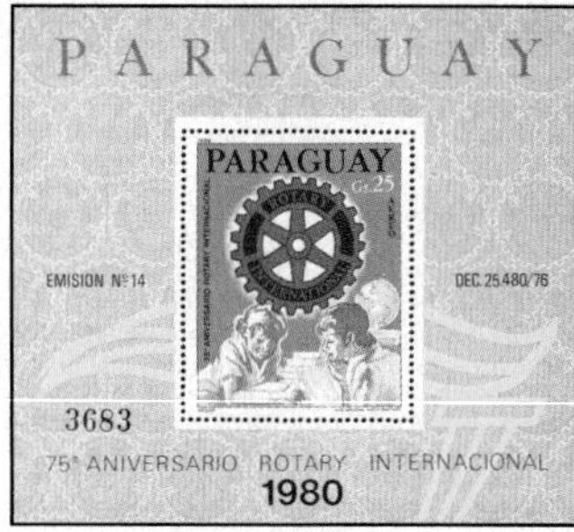


Rotary Intl., 75th Anniv. — AP156

**1980, July 1 Litho. *Perf. 14½***
**C475** AP156 25g multicolored 20.00 20.00

**Apollo 11 Type of 1970**

Souvenir Sheet

Design: 1st steps on lunar surface.

**1980, July 30 *Perf. 13½***
**Size: 36x26mm**
**C476** A221 25g multicolored 17.50 17.50

Souvenir Sheet

Virgin Surrounded by Animals by Albrecht Durer — AP158

**Photo. & Engr.**
**1980, Sept. 24 *Perf. 12***
**C477** AP158 25g multi 125.00 125.00

Souvenir Sheet

1980 Olympic Games — AP159

**1980, Dec. 15 Litho. *Perf. 14***

**C478** AP159 25g multi 20.00 20.00

Metropolitan Seminary Centenary — AP160

**1981, Mar. 26 Litho. Wmk. 347**

**C479** AP160 5g ultra 1.50 1.00
**C480** AP160 10g red brn 1.50 1.00
**C481** AP160 25g green 1.50 1.00
**C482** AP160 50g gray 3.00 1.00
*Nos. C479-C482 (4)* 7.50 4.00

Anniversaries and Events — AP161

5g, George Washington, 250th birth anniv. (in 1982). 10g, Queen Mother Elizabeth, 80th birthday (in 1980). 30g, Phila Tokyo '81.

No. C486, Emperor Hirohito, 80th birthday. No. C487, Washington Crossing the Delaware.

**1981, July 10 Unwmk. *Perf. 14***

**C483** AP161 5g multicolored 6.50 2.25
**C484** AP161 10g multicolored 1.25 .45
**C485** AP161 30g multicolored 1.50 .55
*Nos. C483-C485 (3)* 9.25 3.25

**Souvenir Sheets**

***Perf. 14½***

**C486** AP161 25g multicolored 17.50 17.50
**C487** AP161 25g multicolored 17.50 17.50

No. C484 issued in sheets of 8 plus label. For overprints see Nos. 2126, C590-C591, C611.

First Space Shuttle Mission — AP162

Pres. Ronald Reagan and: 5g, Columbia in Earth orbit. 10g, Astronauts John Young and Robert Crippen. 30g, Columbia landing.

George Washington and: No. C491, Columbia re-entering atmosphere. No. C492, Columbia inverted above Earth.

**1981, Oct. 9 *Perf. 14***

**C488** AP162 5g multicolored 6.50 3.25
**C489** AP162 10g multicolored 1.25 .80
**C490** AP162 30g multicolored 2.00 1.00
*Nos. C488-C490 (3)* 9.75 5.05

**Souvenir Sheets**

***Perf. 13½***

**C491** AP162 25g multicolored 17.50 17.50
**C492** AP162 25g multicolored 17.50 17.50

Nos. C491-C492 each contain one 60x50mm stamp. Inauguration of Pres. Reagan, George Washington, 250th birth anniv. (in 1982) (#C491-C492).

World Cup Soccer, Spain, 1982
AP163

**1981, Oct. 15 *Perf. 14***

**Color of Shirts**

**C493** AP163 5g yellow, green 4.00 2.00
**C494** AP163 10g blue, white 1.10 .50
**C495** AP163 30g white & blk, org .60 .30
*Nos. C493-C495 (3)* 5.70 2.80

**Souvenir Sheet**

***Perf. 14½***

**C496** AP163 25g Goalie 17.50 17.50

No. C494 exists in sheets of 5 plus 4 labels.

Christmas
AP164

Paintings: 5g, Virgin with the Child by Stefan Lochner. 10g, Our Lady of Caacupe. 25g, Altar of the Virgin by Albrecht Durer. 30g, Virgin and Child by Matthias Grunewald.

**1981, Dec. 21 *Perf. 14***

**C497** AP164 5g multicolored 1.25 .40
**C498** AP164 10g multicolored 2.50 .85
**C499** AP164 30g multicolored 6.75 2.10
*Nos. C497-C499 (3)* 10.50 3.35

**Souvenir Sheet**

***Perf. 13½***

**C500** AP164 25g multicolored 20.00

No. C500 contains one 54x75mm stamp.

Souvenir Sheet

Graf Zeppelin's First Flight to South America, 50th Anniv. — AP165

**1981, Dec. 28 *Perf. 14½***

**C501** AP165 25g multicolored 24.00 24.00

Mother Maria Mazzarello (1837-1881), Co-Founder of Daughters of Mary
AP166

***Perf. 13x13½***

**1981, Dec. 30 Litho. Wmk. 347**

**C502** AP166 20g blk & grn 1.00 1.00
**C503** AP166 25g blk & red brn 1.00 1.00
**C504** AP166 50g blk & gray vio 1.00 1.00
*Nos. C502-C504 (3)* 3.00 3.00

Souvenir Sheet

The Magus (Dr. Faust) by Rembrandt — AP167

**Litho. & Typo.**

**1982, Apr. 23 Unwmk. *Perf. 14½***

**C505** AP167 25g blk, buff & gold 20.00 20.00

Johann Wolfgang von Goethe, 150th death anniv.

---

The following stamps were issued 4 each in sheets of 8 with 1 label: Nos. C590-C591, C669-C670, C677-C678, C682-C683, C690-C691, C699-C700, C718-C719, C747-C748.

The following stamps were issued in sheets of 4 with 5 labels: Nos. C765-C766, C774, C779-C780, C785, C803, C813, C818, C823.

The following stamps were issued in sheets of 3 with 6 labels: Nos. C739, C754.

The following stamps were issued in sheets of 5 with 4 labels: Nos. C507, C512, C515, C519, C524, C529, C535, C539, C542, C548, C550, C559, C569, C572, C579, C582, C585, C588, C596, C598, C615, C622, C626, C634, C642, C647, C650, C656, C705, C711, C731, C791, C798, C808.

The following stamp was issued in sheets of 7 with 2 labels: No. C660.

---

**World Chess Championships Type of 1980**

Illustrations from The Book of Chess: 5g, The Game of the Virgins. 10g, Two gothic ladies. 30g, Chess game at apothecary shop.

No. C509, Christians and Jews preparing to play in garden. No. C510, Indian prince introducing chess to Persia.

**1982, June 10 Litho. *Perf. 14***

**C506** A347 5g multicolored 3.50 1.10
**C507** A347 10g multicolored 1.60 .55
**C508** A347 30g multicolored .80 .25
*Nos. C506-C508 (3)* 5.90 1.90

**Souvenir Sheets**

***Perf. 13½***

**C509** A347 25g multicolored 15.00 15.00

***Perf. 14½***

**C510** A347 25g multicolored 20.00 20.00

No. C509 contains one 50x60mm stamp, No. C510 one 50x70mm stamp. For overprint see No. C665.

Italy, Winners of 1982 World Cup Soccer Championships — AP168

Players: 5g, Klaus Fischer, Germany. 10g, Altobelli holding World Cup Trophy. 25g, Forster, Altobelli, horiz. 30g, Fischer, Gordillo.

**1982, Oct. 20 *Perf. 14***

**C511** AP168 5g multicolored 5.50 1.20
**C512** AP168 10g multicolored 1.60 .55
**C513** AP168 30g multicolored .80 .25
*Nos. C511-C513 (3)* 7.90 2.00

**Souvenir Sheet**

**C513A** AP168 25g multicolored 14.00 14.00

Christmas — AP169

Paintings by Peter Paul Rubens: 5g, The Massacre of the Innocents. 10g, The Nativity, vert. 25g, The Madonna Adored by Four Penitents and Saints. 30g, The Flight to Egypt.

**1982, Oct. 23**

**C514** AP169 5g multicolored 3.50 1.20
**C515** AP169 10g multicolored 1.60 .55
**C516** AP169 30g multicolored .80 .25
*Nos. C514-C516 (3)* 5.90 2.00

**Souvenir Sheet**

***Perf. 14½***

**C517** AP169 25g multicolored 14.00 14.00

No. C517 contains one 50x70mm stamp.

The Sampling Officials of the Draper's Guild by Rembrandt — AP170

Details from Rembrandt Paintings: 10g, Self portrait, vert. 25g, Night Watch, vert. 30g, Self portrait, diff., vert.

**1983, Jan. 21 *Perf. 14, 13 (10g)***

**C518** AP170 5g multicolored 3.50 1.20
**C519** AP170 10g multicolored 1.60 .55
**C520** AP170 30g multicolored .80 .25
*Nos. C518-C520 (3)* 5.90 2.00

**Souvenir Sheet**

***Perf. 13½***

**C521** AP170 25g multicolored 15.00 15.00

No. C521 contains one 50x60mm stamp.

Souvenir Sheet

1982 World Cup Soccer Championships, Spain — AP171

**1983, Jan. 21** ***Perf. 13½***

**C522** AP171 25g Fuji blimp 16.00 16.00

German Rocket Scientists — AP172

Designs: 5g, Dr. Walter R. Dornberger, V2 rocket ascending. 10g, Nebel, Ritter, Oberth, Riedel, and Von Braun examining rocket mock-up. 30g, Dr. A. F. Staats, Cyrus B research rocket.

No. C526, Dr. Eugen Sanger, rocket design. No. C527, Fritz Von Opel, Opel-Sander rocket plane. No. C528, Friedrich Schmiedl, first rocket used for mail delivery.

**1983** ***Perf. 14***

**C523** AP172 5g multicolored 4.00 1.25
**C524** AP172 10g multicolored 1.75 .60
**C525** AP172 30g multicolored .80 .25
*Nos. C523-C525 (3)* 6.55 2.10

**Souvenir Sheets**

***Perf. 14½***

**C526** AP172 25g multicolored 35.00 35.00
**C527** AP172 25g multicolored 35.00 35.00
**C528** AP172 25g multicolored 35.00 35.00

Issued: No. C528, Apr. 13; others, Jan. 24.

First Manned Flight, 200th Anniv. AP173

Balloons: 5g, Montgolfier brothers, 1783. 10g, Baron von Lutgendorf's, 1786. 30g, Adorne's, 1784.

No. C532, Montgolfier brothers, diff. No. C533, Profiles of Montgolfier Brothers. No. C534, Bicentennial emblem, nova.

**1983** ***Perf. 14, 13 (10g)***

**C529** AP173 5g multicolored 4.00 1.25
**C530** AP173 10g multicolored 2.50 .65
**C531** AP173 30g multicolored 1.60 .25
*Nos. C529-C531 (3)* 8.10 2.15

**Souvenir Sheets**

***Perf. 13½***

**C532** AP173 25g multicolored 17.00 17.00
**C533** AP173 25g multicolored 17.00 17.00
**C534** AP173 25g multicolored 17.00 17.00

Nos. C532-C533 each contain one 50x60mm stamp, No. C534 one 30x40mm stamp.

Issued: #C529-C533, 2/25; #C534, 10/19.

1984 Summer Olympics, Los Angeles AP174

1932 Gold medalists: 5g, Wilson Charles, US, 100-meter dash. 10g, Ellen Preis, Austria, fencing. 25g, Rudolf Ismayr, Germany, weight lifting. 30g, John Anderson, US, discus.

**1983, June 13** ***Perf. 14***

**C535** AP174 5g multicolored .80 .30
**C536** AP174 10g multicolored 1.25 .40
**C537** AP174 30g multicolored 3.25 .55
*Nos. C535-C537 (3)* 5.30 1.25

**Souvenir Sheet**

***Perf. 14½***

**C538** AP174 25g Sheet of 1 + label 20.00 20.00

No. C535 incorrectly credits Charles with gold medal.

Flowers AP175

**1983, Aug. 31** ***Perf. 14***

**C539** AP175 5g Episcia reptans 1.60 .40
**C540** AP175 10g Lilium .80 .25
**C541** AP175 30g Heliconia 1.60 .25
*Nos. C539-C541 (3)* 4.00 .90

Intl. Maritime Organization, 25th Anniv. — AP176

5g, Brigantine Undine. 10g, Training ship Sofia, 1881, horiz. 30g, Training ship Stein, 1879.

No. C545, Santa Maria. No. C546, Santa Maria and Telstar communications satellite.

***Perf. 14, 13½x13 (10g)***

**1983, Oct. 24** **Litho.**

**C542** AP176 5g multicolored 2.50 .55
**C543** AP176 10g multicolored 1.25 .40
**C544** AP176 30g multicolored 1.50 .25
*Nos. C542-C544 (3)* 5.25 1.20

**Souvenir Sheets**

***Perf. 14½***

**C545** AP176 25g multicolored 20.00 15.00

***Perf. 13½***

**C546** AP176 25g multicolored 20.00 15.00

No. C546 contains one 90x57mm stamp. Discovery of America, 490th Anniv. (in 1982) (#C545-C546). For overprint see No. 2198.

Space Achievements — AP177

Designs: 5g, Space shuttle Challenger. 10g, Pioneer 10, vert. 30g, Herschel's telescope, Cerro Tololo Obervatory, Chile, vert.

**1984, Jan. 9** ***Perf. 14***

**C547** AP177 5g multicolored 2.75 .90
**C548** AP177 10g multicolored 2.75 .90
**C549** AP177 30g multicolored .95 .35
*Nos. C547-C549 (3)* 6.45 2.15

Summer Olympics, Los Angeles AP178

5g, 400-meter hurdles. 10g, Small bore rifle, horiz. 25g, Equestrian, Christine Stuckleberger. 30g, 100-meter dash.

**1984, Jan.** ***Perf. 14***

**C550** AP178 5g multicolored 2.75 .80
**C551** AP178 10g multicolored 2.75 .55
**C552** AP178 30g multicolored 1.20 .25
*Nos. C550-C552 (3)* 6.70 1.60

**Souvenir Sheet**

***Perf. 14½***

**C553** AP178 25g multicolored 25.00 25.00

For overprint see No. 2130.

1984 Winter Olympics, Sarajevo AP179

No. C554, Steve Podborski, downhill. No. C555, Olympic Flag. No. C556, Gaetan Boucher, speed skating.

***Perf. 14, 13x13½ (10g)***

**1984, Mar. 24**

**C554** AP179 5g multicolored 2.40 .55
**C555** AP179 10g multicolored 1.60 .40
**C556** AP179 30g multicolored 1.60 .25
*Nos. C554-C556 (3)* 5.60 1.20

No. C555 printed se-tenant with label.

Souvenir Sheets

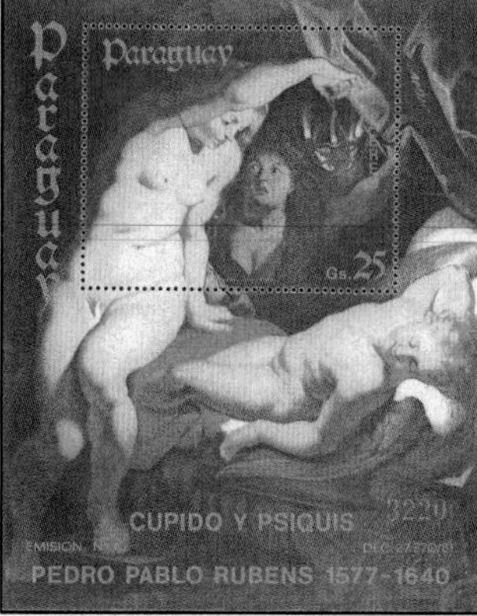

Cupid and Psyche by Peter Paul Rubens — AP180

Design: No. C558, Satyr and Maenad (copy of Rubens' Bacchanal) by Jean-Antoine Watteau (1684-1721).

**1984, Mar. 26** ***Perf. 13½***

**C557** AP180 25g multicolored 15.00 15.00
**C558** AP180 25g multicolored 17.00 17.00

No. C558 contains one 78x57mm stamp.

1982, 1986 World Cup Soccer Championships, Spain, Mexico City — AP181

Soccer players: 5g, Tardelli, Breitner. 10g, Zamora, Stielke. 30g, Walter Schachner, player on ground.

No. C562, Player from Paraguay. No. C563, World Cup Trophy, Spanish, Mexican characters, horiz.

**1984, Mar. 29** ***Perf. 14, 13 (10g)***

**C559** AP181 5g multicolored 2.40 .55
**C560** AP181 10g multicolored 1.50 .55
**C561** AP181 30g multicolored 1.50 .25
*Nos. C559-C561 (3)* 5.40 1.35

**Souvenir Sheets**

***Perf. 14½***

**C562** AP181 25g multicolored 15.00 15.00
**C563** AP181 25g multicolored 15.00 15.00

Souvenir Sheet

ESPANA '84 — AP182

**1984, Mar. 31**

**C564** AP182 25g multicolored 20.00 20.00

No. C564 has one stamp and a label.

Souvenir Sheets

ESPANA '84 — AP183

No. C565, Holy Family of the Lamb by Raphael. No. C566, Adoration of the Magi by Rubens.

**1984, Apr. 16** ***Perf. 13½***

**C565** AP183 25g multicolored 15.00 12.00
**C566** AP183 25g multicolored 15.00 12.00

Souvenir Sheet

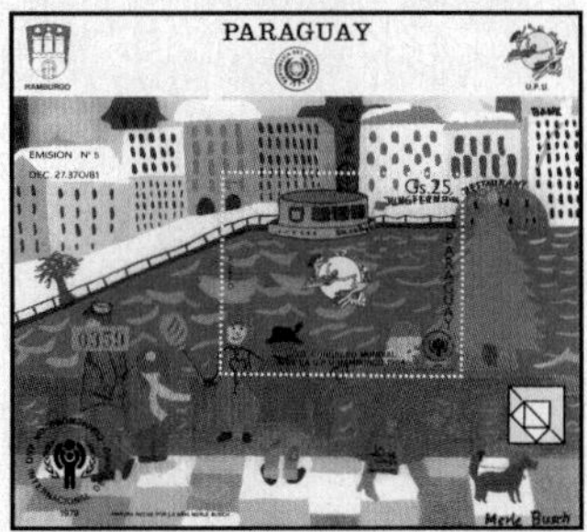


19th UPU Congress — AP184

**1984, June 9**

**C567** AP184 25g multicolored 15.00 12.00

Intl. Chess Federation, 60th Anniv. AP185

10g, Woman holding chess piece. 30g, Bishop, knight.

***Perf. 14, 13x13½ (10g)***

**1984, June 18**

**C568** AP185 5g shown 3.75 1.20
**C569** AP185 10g multicolored 3.00 .80
**C570** AP185 30g multicolored 2.25 .25
*Nos. C568-C570 (3)* 9.00 2.25

First Europe to South America Airmail Flight by Lufthansa, 50th Anniv. — AP186

Designs: 5g, Lockheed Superconstellation. 10g, Dornier Wal. 30g, Boeing 707.

***Perf. 14, 13½x13 (10g)***

**1984, June 22**

**C571** AP186 5g multicolored 2.75 .75
**C572** AP186 10g multicolored 1.50 .30
**C573** AP186 30g multicolored 1.10 .25
*Nos. C571-C573 (3)* 5.35 1.30

For overprint see No. C592.

Souvenir Sheets

First Moon Landing, 15th Anniv. — AP187

No. C574, Apollo 11 lunar module. No. C575, Prof. Hermann Oberth.

**1984, June 23** ***Perf. 14½***

**C574** AP187 25g multicolored 35.00 35.00
**C575** AP187 25g multicolored 35.00 35.00

Hermann Oberth, 90th Birthday (#C575).

Souvenir Sheet

The Holy Family with John the Baptist — AP188

**Photo. & Engr.**

**1984, Aug. 3** ***Perf. 14***

**C576** AP188 20g multicolored 45.00 45.00

Raphael, 500th birth anniv. (in 1983).

**No. 2099 Overprinted ANIVERSARIO GOBIERNO CONSTRUCTIVO Y DE LA PAZ DEL PRESIDENTE CONSTITUCIONAL GRAL. DE EJERCITO ALFREDO STROESSNER 15 / 8 / 1964 in Red**

**1984, Aug. 15** ***Perf. 13***

**C577** A374 100g on No. 2099 1.50 1.50

1984 Winter Olympics, Sarajevo — AP189

Gold medalists: 5g, Max Julen, giant slalom, Switzerland. 10g, Hans Stanggassinger, Franz Wembacher, luge, West Germany. 30g, Peter Angerer, biathlon, Germany.

***Perf. 14, 13½x13 (10g)***

**1984, Sept. 12**

**C578** AP189 5g multicolored 2.75 .80
**C579** AP189 10g multicolored 3.50 1.20
**C580** AP189 30g multicolored 1.25 .25
*Nos. C578-C580 (3)* 7.50 2.25

For overprint see No. C596.

Motorcycles, Cent. — AP190

5g, Reitwagen, Daimler-Maybach, 1885. 10g, BMW, 1980. 30g, Opel, 1930.

**1984, Nov. 9** ***Perf. 14, 13½x13 (10g)***

**C581** AP190 5g multicolored 2.50 .50
**C582** AP190 10g multicolored 1.90 .60
**C583** AP190 30g multicolored 1.10 .25
*Nos. C581-C583 (3)* 5.50 1.35

Christmas AP191

10g, Girl playing guitar. 30g, Girl, candle, basket.

**1985, Jan. 18** ***Perf. 13***

**C584** AP191 5g shown 1.90 .45
**C585** AP191 10g multicolored 1.10 .30
**C586** AP191 30g multicolored .80 .25
*Nos. C584-C586 (3)* 3.80 1.00

1986 World Cup Soccer Championships, Mexico — AP192

Various soccer players.

**1985, Jan. 21** ***Perf. 13x13½, 13½x13***

**Color of Shirt**

**C587** AP192 5g red & white 2.25 .80
**C588** AP192 10g white & black, horiz. 1.50 .40
**C589** AP192 30g blue 1.50 .25
*Nos. C587-C589 (3)* 5.25 1.45

**No. C484 Ovptd. in Silver**

No. C590, INTERPEX / 1985. No. C591, STAMPEX / 1985.

**1985, Feb. 6** ***Perf. 14***

**C590** AP161 10g multicolored 1.50 .75
**C591** AP161 10g multicolored 1.50 .75

**No. C572 Ovptd. in Vermilion**

**1985, Feb. 16** ***Perf. 13½x13***

**C592** AP186 10g on No. C572 4.00 1.50

**No. 2053A Ovptd. "FINAL / ALEMANIA 1 : 3 ITALIA"**

**1985, Mar. 7** ***Perf. 14½***

**C593** A362 25g multicolored 14.00 14.00

Souvenir Sheets

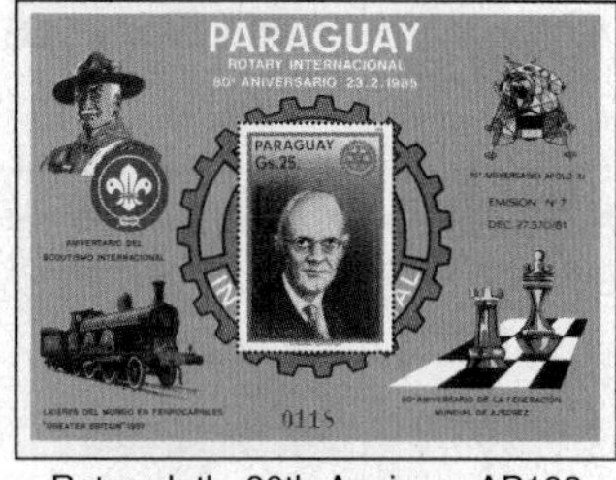


Rotary Intl., 80th Anniv. — AP193

Designs: No. C594, Paul Harris, founder of Rotary Intl. No. C595, Rotary Intl. Headquarters, Evanston, IL, horiz.

**1985, Mar. 11**

**C594** AP193 25g multicolored 30.00 30.00
**C595** AP193 25g multicolored 30.00 30.00

**No. C579 Ovptd. "OLYMPHILEX 85" in Black and Olympic Rings in Silver**

**1985, Mar. 18** ***Perf. 13½x13***

**C596** AP189 10g on No. C579 3.00 1.50

Music Year AP194

Designs: 5g, Agustin Barrios (1885-1944), musician, vert. 10g, Johann Sebastian Bach, composer, score. 30g, Folk musicians.

***Perf. 14, 13½x13 (10g)***

**1985, Apr. 16**

**C597** AP194 5g multicolored 1.75 .75
**C598** AP194 10g multicolored 1.00 .70
**C599** AP194 30g multicolored 1.25 .55
*Nos. C597-C599 (3)* 4.00 2.00

1st Paraguayan Locomotive, 1861 — AP195

10g, Transrapid 06, Germany. 30g, TGV, France.

**1985, Apr. 20** ***Perf. 14***

**C600** AP195 5g shown 10.00 3.50
*a.* Horiz. Pair 40.00 *40.00*

**C601** AP195 10g multi 2.50 .75
**C602** AP195 30g multi 2.50 .75
*Nos. C600-C602 (3)* 15.00 5.00

Souvenir Sheet

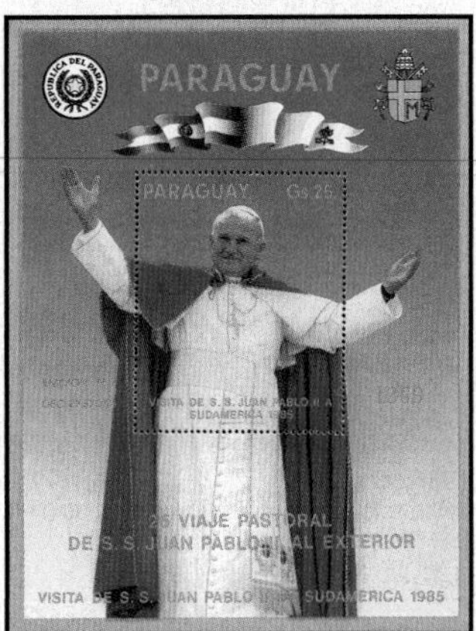


Visit of Pope John Paul II to South America — AP196

**1985, Apr. 22 Litho.** *Perf. 13½*
**C603** AP196 25g silver & multi 17.00 17.00

No. C603 also exists with gold inscriptions.

Inter-American Development Bank, 25th Anniv. — AP197

**1985, Apr. 25 Litho. Wmk. 347**
**C604** AP197 3g dl red brn, org & yel 1.00 1.00
**C605** AP197 5g vio, org & yel 1.00 1.00
**C606** AP197 10g rose vio, org & yel 1.00 1.00
**C607** AP197 50g sep, org & yel 1.00 1.00
**C608** AP197 65g bl, org & yel 1.00 1.00
**C609** AP197 95g pale bl grn, org & yel 1.00 1.00
*Nos. C604-C609 (6)* 6.00 6.00

**No. 1875 Ovptd. in Black**

**1985, May 24 Unwmk.** *Perf. 13½*
**C610** A326 25g on No. 1875 12.00 12.00

**No. C485 Ovptd. in Dark Blue with Emblem and: "Expo '85/TSUKUBA"**

**1985, July 5** *Perf. 14*
**C611** AP161 30g on No. C485 3.00 1.50

**No. 2149 Overprinted in Dark Blue**

**1985, Aug. 5** *Perf. 14½*
**C612** A388 25g on No. 2149 12.00 12.00

Jean-Henri Dunant, Founder of Red Cross, 75th Death Anniv. — AP198

Dunant and: 5g, Enclosed ambulance. 10g, Nobel Peace Prize, Red Cross emblem. 30g, Open ambulance with passengers.

**1985, Aug. 6** *Perf. 13*
**C614** AP198 5g multicolored 5.25 1.60
**C615** AP198 10g multicolored 4.75 1.60
**C616** AP198 30g multicolored 2.00 .60
*Nos. C614-C616 (3)* 12.00 3.80

World Chess Congress, Austria — AP199

5g, The Turk, copper engraving, Book of Chess by Racknitz, 1789. 10g, King seated, playing chess, Book of Chess, 14th cent. 25g, Margrave Otto von Brandenburg playing chess with his wife, Great Manuscript of Heidelberg Songs, 13th cent. 30g, Three men playing chess, Book of Chess, 14th cent.

**1985, Aug. 9 Litho.** *Perf. 13*
**C617** AP199 5g multicolored 6.25 2.10
**C618** AP199 10g multicolored 1.50 .50
**C619** AP199 30g multicolored 1.50 .50
*Nos. C617-C619 (3)* 9.25 3.10

**Souvenir Sheet**

***Perf. 13½***

**C620** AP199 25g multicolored 25.00 25.00

No. C620 contains one 60x50mm stamp.

Discovery of America 500th Anniv. AP200

Explorers, ships: 5g, Marco Polo and ship. 10g, Vicente Yanez Pinzon, Nina, horiz. 25g, Christopher Columbus, Santa Maria. 30g, James Cook, Endeavor.

***Perf. 14, 13½x13 (10g)***

**1985, Oct. 19 Litho.**
**C621** AP200 5g multicolored 2.50 .60
**C622** AP200 10g multicolored .85 .40
**C623** AP200 30g multicolored 1.25 .45
*Nos. C621-C623 (3)* 4.60 1.45

**Souvenir Sheet**

***Perf. 14½***

**C624** AP200 25g multicolored 22.00 22.00

Year of Cook's death is incorrect on No. C623. For overprint see No. C756.

ITALIA '85 — AP201

Nudes (details): 5g, La Fortuna, by Guido Reni, vert. 10g, The Triumph of Galatea, by Raphael. 30g, Sleeping Venus, by Il Giorgione.
25g, The Birth of Venus, by Botticelli, vert.

**1985, Dec. 3** *Perf. 14*
**C625** AP201 5g multicolored 4.50 1.50
**C626** AP201 10g multicolored 2.00 .60
**C627** AP201 30g multicolored 1.75 .40
*Nos. C625-C627 (3)* 8.25 2.50

**Souvenir Sheet**

***Perf. 13½***

**C628** AP201 25g multicolored 35.00 35.00

No. C628 contains one 49x60mm stamp.

Souvenir Sheet

Maimonides, Philosopher, 850th Birth Anniv. — AP202

**1985, Dec. 31** *Perf. 13½*
**C629** AP202 25g multicolored 22.50 22.50

UN, 40th Anniv. AP203

**1986, Feb. 27 Wmk. 392**
**C630** AP203 5g bl & sepia 1.00 1.00
**C631** AP203 10g bl & gray 1.00 1.00
**C632** AP203 50g bl & grysh brn 1.00 1.00
*Nos. C630-C632 (3)* 3.00 3.00

For overprint see No. C726.

AMERIPEX '86 AP204

Discovery of America 500th anniv. emblem and: 5g, Spain #424. 10g, US #233. 25g, Spain #426, horiz. 30g, Spain #421.

***Perf. 14, 13½x13 (10g)***

**1986, Mar. 19 Unwmk.**
**C633** AP204 5g multicolored 5.00 1.75
**C634** AP204 10g multicolored 2.00 .70
**C635** AP204 30g multicolored 1.75 .60
*Nos. C633-C635 (3)* 8.75 3.05

**Souvenir Sheet**

***Perf. 13½***

**C636** AP204 25g multicolored 12.00 *12.00*

No. C636 contains one 60x40mm stamp. For overprint see No. C755.

Souvenir Sheet

1984 Olympic Gold Medalist, Dr. Reiner Klimke on Ahlerich — AP205

**1986, Mar. 20** *Perf. 14½*
**C637** AP205 25g multicolored 20.00 20.00

Tennis Players AP206

Designs: 5g, Martina Navratilova, US. 10g, Boris Becker, W. Germany. 30g, Victor Pecci, Paraguay.

**1986, Mar. 26** *Perf. 14, 13 (10g)*
**C638** AP206 5g multicolored 4.25 1.25
**C639** AP206 10g multicolored 2.25 .55
**C640** AP206 30g multicolored .50 .25
*Nos. C638-C640 (3)* 7.00 2.05

Nos. C638-C640 exist with red inscriptions, perf. 13. For overprints see Nos. C672-C673.

Halley's Comet — AP207

5g, Bayeux Tapestry, c. 1066, showing comet. 10g, Edmond Halley, comet. 25g, Comet, Giotto probe. 30g, Rocket lifting off, Giotto probe, vert.

***Perf. 14, 13½x13 (10g)***

**1986, Apr. 30**

**C641** AP207 5g multicolored 5.50 2.00
**C642** AP207 10g multicolored 3.50 1.10
**C643** AP207 30g multicolored 2.50 .65
*Nos. C641-C643 (3)* 11.50 3.75

**Souvenir Sheet**

***Perf. 14½***

**C644** AP207 25g multicolored 20.00 20.00

Souvenir Sheet

Madonna by Albrecht Durer — AP208

**1986, June 4 Typo. *Rough Perf. 11***

**Self-Adhesive**

**C645** AP208 25g black & red 20.00 20.00

No. C645 was printed on cedar.

Locomotives — AP209

5g, #3038. 10g, Canadian Pacific A1E, 1887. 30g, 1D1 #483, 1925.

**1986, June 23 Litho. *Perf. 13***

**C646** AP209 5g multi 2.25 .50
**C647** AP209 10g multi 1.50 .50
**C648** AP209 30g multi 2.25 .50
*Nos. C646-C648 (3)* 6.00 1.50

1986 World Cup Soccer Championships — AP210

Paraguay vs.: 5g, Colombia. 10g, Chile. 30g, Chile, diff.
25g, Paraguay Natl. team.

***Perf. 13, 13½x13 (10g)***

**1986, June 24**

**C649** AP210 5g multicolored 2.25 .50
**C650** AP210 10g multicolored 1.50 .50
**C651** AP210 30g multicolored 2.50 .45
*Nos. C649-C651 (3)* 6.25 1.45

**Souvenir Sheet**

***Perf. 14½***

**C652** AP210 25g multicolored 13.00 13.00

No. C652 contains one 81x75mm stamp. For overprints see Nos. C693-C695.

**No. 1289 Ovptd. in Silver on Dark Blue with Mercury Capsule and "MERCURY / 5-V-1961 / 25 Anos Primer / Astronauta / Americano / Alan B. Shepard / 1986"**

**1986, July 11 *Perf. 13½***

**C653** A226 23.40g on No. 1289 13.00 13.00

Souvenir Sheet

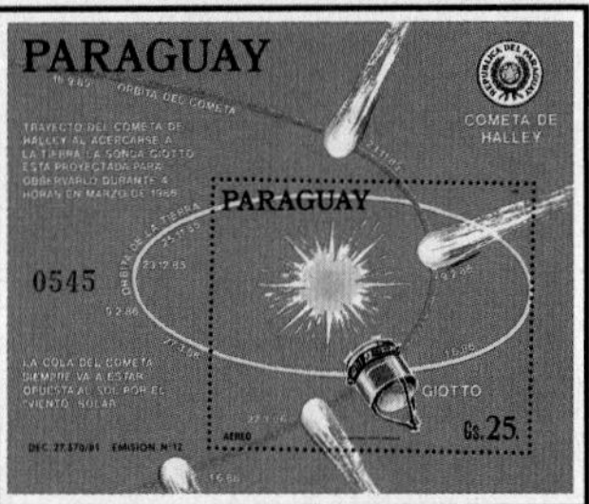


Trajectory Diagram of Halley's Comet, Giotto Probe — AP211

**1986, July 28**

**C654** AP211 25g multicolored 15.00 15.00

German Railroads, 150th Anniv. — AP212

5g, VT 10 501DB, 1954. 10g, 1st Electric, 1879. 30g, Hydraulic diesel, class 218.
25g, Christening of the 1st German Train, 1835, by E. Schilling & B. Goldschmitt.

**1986, Sept. 1 *Perf. 13½x13***

**C655** AP212 5g multicolored 4.50 1.50
**C656** AP212 10g multicolored 1.75 .50
**C657** AP212 30g multicolored 2.00 2.00
*Nos. C655-C657 (3)* 8.25 4.00

**Souvenir Sheet**

***Perf. 13½***

**C658** AP212 25g multicolored 18.00 18.00

No. C658 contains one 54x75mm stamp.

Intl. Peace Year AP213

Details from The Consequences of War by Rubens: 5g, Two women. 10g, Woman nursing child. 30g, Two men.

**1986, Oct. 27 *Perf. 13***

**C659** AP213 5g multicolored 5.00 1.75
**C660** AP213 10g multicolored 2.60 2.60
**C661** AP213 30g multicolored 1.75 .40
*Nos. C659-C661 (3)* 9.35 4.75

Japanese Emigrants in Paraguay, 50th Anniv. — AP214

5g, La Colemna Vineyard. 10g, Cherry, lapacho flowers. 20g, Integration monument, vert.

**1986, Nov. 6 *Perf. 13½x13, 13x13½***

**C662** AP214 5g multicolored 2.00 2.00
**C663** AP214 10g multicolored 2.00 2.00
**C664** AP214 20g multicolored 2.00 2.00
*Nos. C662-C664 (3)* 6.00 6.00

**No. C507 Ovptd. in Silver "XXVII-DUBAI / Olimpiada de / Ajedrez - 1986"**

**1986, Dec. 30 Unwmk. *Perf. 14***

**C665** A347 10g on No. C507 6.00 2.00

1986 World Cup Soccer Championships, Mexico — AP214a

Match scenes — 5g, England vs. Paraguay. 10g, Larios catching ball. 20g, Trejo, Ferreira. 25g, Torales, Flores, Romero. 30g, Mendoza. 100g, Romero.

**1987, Feb. 19 *Perf. 14***

**C666** AP214a 5g multicolored .60 .25
**C667** AP214a 10g multicolored 4.50 1.50
**C668** AP214a 20g multicolored 1.25 .40

***Perf. 13½x13***

**C669** AP214a 25g multicolored 1.20 1.20
**C670** AP214a 30g multicolored 1.50 1.50
*Nos. C666-C670 (5)* 9.05 4.85

**Souvenir Sheet**

***Perf. 14½***

**C671** AP214a 100g multi 15.00 13.00

Nos. C669-C670 are horiz. No. C671 contains one 40x50mm stamp.

**Nos. C639-C640 Ovptd. in Silver including Olympic Rings and "NUEVAMENTE EL / TENIS EN LAS / OLYMPIADAS 1988 / SEOUL COREA"**

**1987, Apr. 15 *Perf. 13***

**C672** AP206 10g on No. C639 *4.50 3.00*
**C673** AP206 30g on No. C640 *4.50 3.00*

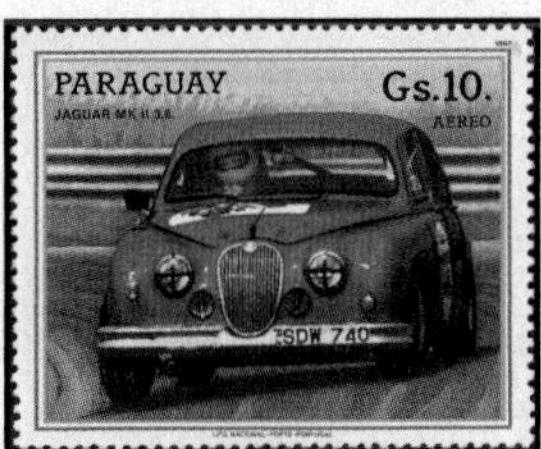


Automobiles — AP215

5g, Mercedes 300 SEL 6.3. 10g, Jaguar Mk II 3.8. 20g, BMW 635 CSI. 25g, Alfa Romeo GTA. 30g, BMW 1800 Tisa.

**1987, May 29 Litho. *Perf. 13½***

**C674** AP215 5g multicolored .60 .25
**C675** AP215 10g multicolored 4.50 1.50
**C676** AP215 20g multicolored 1.25 .40
**C677** AP215 25g multicolored 1.50 1.50
**C678** AP215 30g multicolored 1.50 1.50
*Nos. C674-C678 (5)* 9.35 5.15

1988 Winter Olympics, Calgary — AP216

Gold medalists or Olympic competitors: 5g, Michela Figini, Switzerland, downhill, 1984, vert. 10g, Hanni Wenzel, Liechtenstein, slalom and giant slalom, 1980. 20g, 4-Man bobsled, Switzerland, 1956, 1972. 25g, Markus Wasmeier, downhill. 30g, Ingemar Stenmark, Sweden, slalom and giant slalom, 1980. 100g, Pirmin Zurbriggen, Switzerland, vert. (downhill, 1988).

**1987, Sept. 10 *Perf. 14***

**C679** AP216 5g multicolored .75 .25
**C680** AP216 10g multicolored 4.50 1.40
**C681** AP216 20g multicolored 1.50 .40

***Perf. 13½x13***

**C682** AP216 25g multicolored 1.40 1.10
**C683** AP216 30g multicolored 1.60 1.40
*Nos. C679-C683 (5)* 9.75 4.55

**Souvenir Sheet**

***Perf. 13½***

**C684** AP216 100g multicolored 14.00 14.00

No. C684 contains one 45x57mm stamp.

**Nos. 2211 and C467 Ovptd. in Red on Silver "11.IX.1887 - 1987 / Centenario de la fundacion de / la A.N.R. (Partido Colarado) / Bernardino Caballero Fundador / General de Ejercito / D. Alfredo Stroessner Continuador"**

**1987, Sept. 11 *Perf. 13, 14***

**C685** A401 200g on No. 2211 .50 .50
**C686** AP148 1000g on No. C467 2.75 2.75
*Nos. C685-C686 (2)* 3.25 3.25

1988 Summer Olympics, Seoul — AP217

Medalists and competitors: 5g, Sabine Everts, West Germany, javelin. 10g, Carl Lewis, US, 100 and 200-meter run, 1984. 20g, Darrell Pace, US, archery, 1976, 1984. 25g, Juergen Hingsen, West Germany, decathlon, 1984. 30g, Claudia Losch, West Germany, shot put, 1984. 100g, Fredy Schmidtke, West Germany, cycling, 1984.

**1987, Sept. 22 *Perf. 14***

**C687** AP217 5g multi .50 .25
**C688** AP217 10g multi, vert. 2.00 .55
**C689** AP217 20g multi 1.20 .40

***Perf. 13½x13***

**C690** AP217 25g multi, vert. 1.10 1.10
**C691** AP217 30g multi, vert. 1.40 1.40
*Nos. C687-C691 (5)* 6.20 3.70

**Souvenir Sheet**

***Perf. 14½***

**C692** AP217 100g multi, vert. 13.00 13.00

**Nos. C650-C652 Ovptd. in Violet or Blue (#C694) with Soccer Ball and "ZURICH 10.VI.87 / Lanzamiento ITALIA '90 / Italia 3 - Argentina 1"**

***Perf. 13½x13, 13***

**1987, Oct. 19 Litho.**

**C693** AP210 10g on No. C650 2.00 2.00
**C694** AP210 30g on No. C651 3.00 3.00
*Nos. C693-C694 (2)* 5.00 5.00

**Souvenir Sheet**

***Perf. 14½***

**C695** AP210 25g on No. C652 12.00 12.00

Paintings by Rubens AP218

Details from: 5g, The Virtuous Hero Crowned. 10g, The Brazen Serpent, 1635. 20g, Judith with the Head of Holofernes, 1617. 25g, Assembly of the Gods of Olympus. 30g, Venus, Cupid, Bacchus and Ceres.

**1987, Dec. 14** ***Perf. 13***

**C696** AP218 5g multicolored .80 .25
**C697** AP218 10g multicolored 4.50 1.60
**C698** AP218 20g multicolored 1.40 .40

***Perf. 13x13½***

**C699** AP218 25g multicolored 1.10 1.10
**C700** AP218 30g multicolored 1.25 1.25
*Nos. C696-C700 (5)* 9.05 4.60

Christmas AP219

Details from paintings: 5g, Virgin and Child with St. Joseph and St. John the Baptist, anonymous. 10g, Madonna and Child under the Veil with St. Joseph and St. John, by Marco da Siena. 20g, Sacred Conversation with the Donors, by Titian. 25g, The Brotherhood of the Rosary, by Durer. 30g, Madonna with Standing Child, by Rubens. 100g, Madonna and Child, engraving by Albrecht Durer.

**1987** **Litho.** ***Perf. 14***

**C701** AP219 5g multicolored .40 .25
**C702** AP219 10g multicolored 1.40 .55
**C703** AP219 20g multicolored .80 .25
**C704** AP219 25g multicolored 1.20 .40

***Perf. 13x13½***

**C705** AP219 30g multicolored 2.00 2.00
*Nos. C701-C705 (5)* 5.80 3.45

**Souvenir Sheet**

***Perf. 14½***

**C706** AP219 100g multi 20.00 20.00

Issued: #C701-C705, 12/16; #C706, 12/17.

Austrian Railways, Sesquicentennial — AP220

Locomotives: 5g, Steam #3669, 1899. 10g, Steam #GZ 44074. 20g, Steam, diff. 25g, Diesel-electric. 30g, Austria No. 1067. 100g, Steam, vert.

**1988, Jan. 2** ***Perf. 14***

**C707** AP220 5g multicolored .75 .25
**C708** AP220 10g multicolored 3.25 1.00
**C709** AP220 20g multicolored 1.00 .30
**C710** AP220 25g multicolored 1.75 .45

***Perf. 13½x13***

**C711** AP220 30g multicolored 2.75 2.75
*Nos. C707-C711 (5)* 9.50 4.75

**Souvenir Sheet**

***Perf. 13½***

**C712** AP220 100g multicolored 25.00 25.00

No. C712 contains one 50x60mm stamp.

Souvenir Sheet

Christmas — AP221

**1988, Jan. 4** ***Perf. 13½***

**C713** AP221 100g Madonna, by Rubens 20.00 20.00

Souvenir Sheet

1988 Summer Olympics, Seoul — AP222

**1988, Jan. 18** ***Perf. 14½***

**C714** AP222 100g gold & multi 12.00 12.00

Exists with silver lettering and frame. Same value.

Colonization of Space — AP223

5g, NASA-ESA space station. 10g, Europace module Columbus docked at space station. 20g, NASA space sation. 25g, Ring section of space station, vert. 30g, Space station living quarters in central core, vert.

**1988, Mar. 9** **Litho.** ***Perf. 13½x13***

**C715** AP223 5g multicolored .55 .25
**C716** AP223 10g multicolored 2.60 .90
**C717** AP223 20g multicolored 1.00 .35

***Perf. 13x13½***

**C718** AP223 25g multicolored 1.40 .50
**C719** AP223 30g multicolored 2.25 2.25
*Nos. C715-C719 (5)* 7.80 4.25

Souvenir Sheet

Berlin, 750th Anniv. — AP224

**1988, Mar. 10** **Litho.** ***Perf. 14½***

**C720** AP224 100g multicolored 25.00 25.00

LUPOSTA '87.

Souvenir Sheet

Apollo 15 Launch, 1971 — AP225

**1988, Apr. 12**

**C721** AP225 100g multicolored 20.00 20.00

**No. 2210 Ovptd. in Metallic Red**

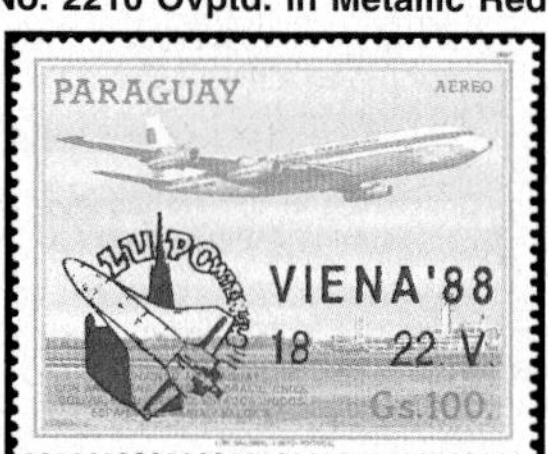


**1988, Apr. 28** ***Perf. 13***

**C722** A401 100g on No. 2210 2.00 2.00

Caacupe Basilica and Pope John Paul II — AP226

***Perf. 13½x13***

**1988, May 5** **Litho.** **Wmk. 347**

**C723** AP226 100g multi 2.00 2.00
**C724** AP226 120g multi 2.00 2.00
**C725** AP226 150g multi 2.00 2.00
*Nos. C723-C725 (3)* 6.00 6.00

Visit of Pope John Paul II.

No. C631 Overprinted

***Perf. 13x13½***

**1988, June 15** **Wmk. 392**

**C726** AP203 10g blue & gray .40 .25

Paraguay Philatelic Center, 75th Anniv.

**Berlin, 750th Anniv. Paintings Type of 1988**

5g, Venus and Cupid, 1742, by Francois Boucher. 10g, Perseus Liberates Andromeda, 1662, by Rubens. 20g, Venus and the Organist by Titian. 25g, Leda and the Swan by Correggio. 30g, St. Cecilia by Rubens.

**1988, June 15** **Unwmk.** ***Perf. 13***

**C727** A409 5g multi, horiz. *.35 .25*
**C728** A409 10g multi, horiz. *.75 .35*
**C729** A409 20g multi, horiz. *1.10 .50*
**C730** A409 25g multi, horiz. *1.60 .80*

***Perf. 13x13½***

**C731** A409 30g multicolored *2.50 2.50*
*Nos. C727-C731 (5)* 6.30 4.40

Founding of "New Germany" and 1st Cultivation of Herbal Tea, Cent. — AP227

90g, Cauldron, vert. 105g, Farm workers carrying crop.

***Perf. 13x13½, 13½x13***

**1988, June 18** **Litho.** **Wmk. 347**

**C732** AP227 90g multi 3.00 2.50
**C733** AP227 105g multi 3.00 2.50
**C734** AP227 120g like 105g 3.00 2.50
*Nos. C732-C734 (3)* 9.00 7.50

1990 World Cup Soccer Championships, Italy — AP228

5g, Machine slogan cancel from Montevideo, May 21, 1930. 10g, Italy #324, vert. 20g, France #349. 25g, Brazil #696, vert. 30g, Paraguayan commemorative cancel for ITALIA 1990.

**1988, Aug. 1** **Unwmk.** ***Perf. 13***

**C735** AP228 5g multicolored .85 .25
**C736** AP228 10g multicolored 2.60 .90
**C737** AP228 20g multicolored 1.60 .50
**C738** AP228 25g multicolored 1.40 .95

***Perf. 13½x13***

**C739** AP228 30g multicolored 1.60 1.20
*Nos. C735-C739 (5)* 8.05 3.80

For overprint see No. 2284.

Souvenir Sheet

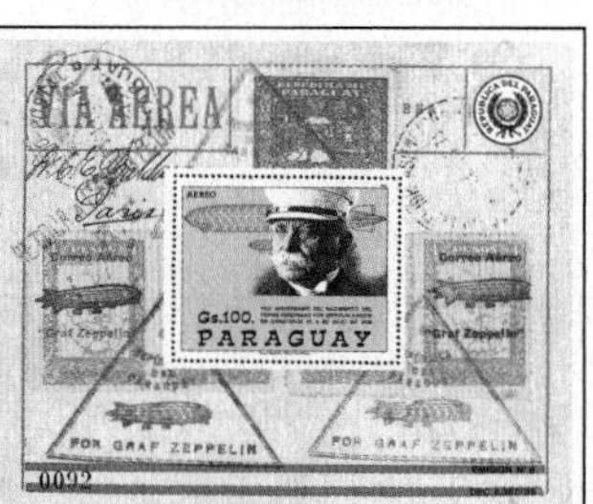


Count Ferdinand von Zeppelin, Airship Designer, Birth Sesquicentennial — AP229

**1988, Aug. 3** ***Perf. 14½***

**C740** AP229 100g multicolored 20.00 20.00

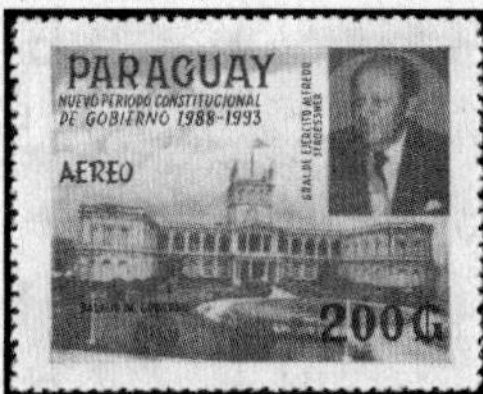


Government Palace and Pres. Stroessner — AP230

**Wmk. 347**

**1988, Aug. 5 Litho. *Perf. 13½***

| | | | | |
|---|---|---|---|---|
| **C741** | AP230 | 200g multi | .60 | .50 |
| **C742** | AP230 | 500g multi | 1.40 | 1.40 |
| **C743** | AP230 | 1000g multi | 2.50 | 2.50 |
| | | *Nos. C741-C743 (3)* | 4.50 | 4.40 |

Pres. Stroessner's new term in office, 1988-1993. Size of letters in watermark on 200g, 1000g: 5mm. On 500g, 10mm.

1988 Winter Olympics, Calgary — AP231

Gold medalists: 5g, Hubert Strolz, Austria, Alpine combined. 10g, Alberto Tomba, Italy, giant slalom and slalom. 20g, Franck Piccard, France, super giant slalom. 25g, Thomas Muller, Hans-Peter Pohl and Hubert Schwarz, Federal Republic of Germany, Nordic combined team, vert. 30g, Vreni Schneider, Switzerland, giant slalom and slalom, vert. 100g, Marina Kiehl, Federal Republic of Germany, downhill, vert.

***Perf. 13½x13***

**1988, Sept. 2 Unwmk.**

| | | | | |
|---|---|---|---|---|
| **C744** | AP231 | 5g multicolored | .85 | .25 |
| **C745** | AP231 | 10g multicolored | 2.60 | .90 |
| **C746** | AP231 | 20g multicolored | 1.60 | .50 |

***Perf. 13x13½***

| | | | | |
|---|---|---|---|---|
| **C747** | AP231 | 25g multicolored | 1.40 | .95 |
| **C748** | AP231 | 30g multicolored | 1.60 | 1.20 |
| | | *Nos. C744-C748 (5)* | 8.05 | 3.80 |

**Souvenir Sheet**

***Perf. 14½***

| | | | | |
|---|---|---|---|---|
| **C749** | AP231 | 100g multicolored | 13.00 | 13.00 |

1990 World Cup Soccer Championships, Italy — AP232

Designs: 5g, Mexico #C350. 10g, Germany #1146. 20g, Argentina #1147, vert. 25g, Spain #2211. 30g, Italy #1742.

**1988, Oct. 4 *Perf. 13***

| | | | | |
|---|---|---|---|---|
| **C750** | AP232 | 5g multicolored | .55 | .25 |
| **C751** | AP232 | 10g multicolored | 2.50 | .85 |
| **C752** | AP232 | 20g multicolored | .95 | .30 |
| **C753** | AP232 | 25g multicolored | 1.40 | .50 |

***Perf. 14***

| | | | | |
|---|---|---|---|---|
| **C754** | AP232 | 30g multicolored | 1.60 | 1.20 |
| | | *Nos. C750-C754 (5)* | 7.00 | 3.10 |

For overprint see No. 2285.

No. C635 Ovptd. in Metallic Red

**1988, Nov. 25 *Perf. 14***

| | | | | |
|---|---|---|---|---|
| **C755** | AP204 | 30g on No. C635 | 4.00 | 4.00 |

No. C623 Ovptd. in Gold

**1988, Nov. 25 *Perf. 14***

| | | | | |
|---|---|---|---|---|
| **C756** | AP200 | 30g on No. C623 | 2.00 | 2.00 |

1988 Summer Olympics, Seoul — AP233

Gold medalists: No. C757, Nicole Uphoff, individual dressage. No. C758, Anja Fichtel, Sabine Bau, Zita Funkenhauser, Anette Kluge and Christine Weber, team foil. No. C759, Silvia Sperber, smallbore standard rifle. No. C760, Mathias Baumann, Claus Erhorn, Thies Kaspareit and Ralph Ehrenbrink, equestrian team 3-day event. No. C761, Anja Fichtel, individual foil, vert. No. C762, Franke Sloothaak, Ludger Beerbaum, Wolfgang Brinkmann and Dirk Hafemeister, equestrian team jumping. No. C763, Arnd Schmitt, individual epee, vert. No. C764, Jose Luis Doreste, Finn class yachting. No. C765, Steffi Graf, tennis. No. C766, Michael Gross, 200-meter butterfly, vert. No. C767, West Germany, coxed eights. No. C768, Nicole Uphoff, Monica Theodorescu, Ann Kathrin Linsenhoff and Reiner Klimke, team dressage.

**1989 *Perf. 13***

| | | | | |
|---|---|---|---|---|
| **C757** | AP233 | 5g multicolored | .55 | .25 |
| **C758** | AP233 | 5g multicolored | .55 | .25 |
| **C759** | AP233 | 10g multicolored | 2.60 | .25 |
| **C760** | AP233 | 10g multicolored | 2.60 | .25 |
| **C761** | AP233 | 20g multicolored | .95 | .40 |
| **C762** | AP233 | 20g multicolored | .95 | .40 |
| **C763** | AP233 | 25g multicolored | 1.40 | .60 |
| **C764** | AP233 | 25g multicolored | 1.40 | .60 |

***Perf. 13½x13***

| | | | | |
|---|---|---|---|---|
| **C765** | AP233 | 30g multicolored | 2.60 | 2.60 |
| **C766** | AP233 | 30g multicolored | 2.60 | 2.60 |
| | | *Nos. C757-C766 (10)* | 16.20 | 8.20 |

**Souvenir Sheets**

***Perf. 14½***

| | | | | |
|---|---|---|---|---|
| **C767** | AP233 | 100g multicolored | 10.00 | 10.00 |
| **C768** | AP233 | 100g multicolored | 10.00 | 10.00 |

Nos. C767-C768 each contain one 80x50mm stamp.

Issue dates: Nos. C757, C759, C761, C763, C765, and C767, Mar. 3. Others, Mar. 20.

For overprints see Nos. 2292, 2359.

Souvenir Sheet

Intl. Red Cross, 125th Anniv. (in 1988) — AP234

**1989, Apr. 17 Litho. *Perf. 13½***

| | | | | |
|---|---|---|---|---|
| **C769** | AP234 | 100g #803 in changed colors | 10.00 | 10.00 |

No. C769 has perforated label picturing Nobel medal.

**Olympics Type of 1989**

1988 Winter Olympic medalists or competitors: 5g, Pirmin Zurbriggen, Peter Mueller, Switzerland, and Franck Piccard, France, Alpine skiing. 10g, Sigrid Wolf, Austria, super giant slalom, vert. 20g, Czechoslovakia vs. West Germany, hockey, vert. 25g, Piccard, skiing, vert. 30g, Piccard, wearing medal, vert.

**1989, Apr. 17 *Perf. 13½x13***

| | | | | |
|---|---|---|---|---|
| **C770** | AP233 | 5g multicolored | .80 | .25 |

***Perf. 13x13½***

| | | | | |
|---|---|---|---|---|
| **C771** | AP233 | 10g multicolored | 1.60 | .55 |
| **C772** | AP233 | 20g multicolored | 1.20 | .40 |
| **C773** | AP233 | 25g multicolored | 1.40 | .50 |
| **C774** | AP233 | 30g multicolored | 2.60 | 2.60 |
| | | *Nos. C770-C774 (5)* | 7.60 | 4.30 |

Souvenir Sheet

1990 World Cup Soccer Championships, Italy — AP235

**1989, Apr. 21 *Perf. 14½***

| | | | | |
|---|---|---|---|---|
| **C775** | AP235 | 100g Sheet of 1 + label | 10.00 | 10.00 |

1st Moon Landing, 20th Anniv. — AP236

Designs: 5g, Wernher von Braun, Apollo 11 launch, vert. 10g, Michael Collins, lunar module on moon. 20g, Neil Armstrong, astronaut on lunar module ladder, vert. 25g, Buzz Aldrin, solar wind experiment, vert. 30g, Kurt Debus, splashdown of Columbia command module, vert.

**1989, May 24 *Perf. 13***

| | | | | |
|---|---|---|---|---|
| **C776** | AP236 | 5g multicolored | .55 | .25 |
| **C777** | AP236 | 10g multicolored | 4.00 | 1.40 |
| **C778** | AP236 | 20g multicolored | 2.40 | .80 |
| **C779** | AP236 | 25g multicolored | 1.40 | 1.40 |
| **C780** | AP236 | 30g multicolored | 1.60 | 1.60 |
| | | *Nos. C776-C780 (5)* | 9.95 | 5.45 |

Souvenir Sheet

Luis Alberto del Parana and the Paraguayans — AP237

**1989, May 25 *Perf. 14½***

| | | | | |
|---|---|---|---|---|
| **C780A** | AP237 | 100g multi | 30.00 | 30.00 |

A clear plastic phonograph record is affixed to the souvenir sheet.

Hamburg, 800th Anniv. — AP238

Hamburg anniv. emblem, SAIL '89 emblem, and: 5g, Galleon and Icarus, woodcut by Pieter Brueghel. 10g, Windjammer, vert. 20g, Bark in full sail. 25g, Old Hamburg by A.E. Schliecker, vert. 30g, Commemorative coin issued by Federal Republic of Germany. 100g, Hamburg, 13th cent. illuminated manuscript, vert.

**1989, May 26 *Perf. 13½x13, 13x13½***

| | | | | |
|---|---|---|---|---|
| **C781** | AP238 | 5g multicolored | .80 | .25 |
| **C782** | AP238 | 10g multicolored | 3.50 | 1.10 |
| **C783** | AP238 | 20g multicolored | 1.20 | .40 |
| **C784** | AP238 | 25g multicolored | 1.60 | .50 |
| **C785** | AP238 | 30g multicolored | 3.00 | 3.00 |
| | | *Nos. C781-C785 (5)* | 10.10 | 5.25 |

**Souvenir Sheet**

***Perf. 14½***

| | | | | |
|---|---|---|---|---|
| **C786** | AP238 | 100g multicolored | 20.00 | 20.00 |

No. C786 contains one 40x50mm stamp.

French Revolution, Bicent. — AP239

Details from paintings: 5g, Esther Adorns Herself for her Presentation to King Ahasuerus, by Theodore Chasseriau, vert. 10g, Olympia, by Manet, vert. 20g, The Drunker Erigone with a Panther, by Louis A. Reisener. 25g, Anniv. emblem and natl. coats of arms. 30g, Liberty Leading the People, by Delacroix, vert. 100g, The Education of Maria de Medici, by Rubens, vert.

**1989, May 27 *Perf. 13x13½, 13½x13***

| | | | | |
|---|---|---|---|---|
| **C787** | AP239 | 5g multicolored | .80 | .25 |
| **C788** | AP239 | 10g multicolored | 3.50 | 1.20 |
| **C789** | AP239 | 20g multicolored | 1.20 | .40 |
| **C790** | AP239 | 25g multicolored | 1.60 | .50 |
| **C791** | AP239 | 30g multicolored | 2.40 | 2.40 |
| | | *Nos. C787-C791 (5)* | 9.50 | 4.75 |

**Souvenir Sheet**

***Perf. 14½***

| | | | | |
|---|---|---|---|---|
| **C792** | AP239 | 100g multicolored | 14.00 | 14.00 |

Souvenir Sheet

Railway Zeppelin, 1931 — AP240

**1989, May 27 Litho. *Perf. 13½***
**C793** AP240 100g multicolored 18.00 18.00

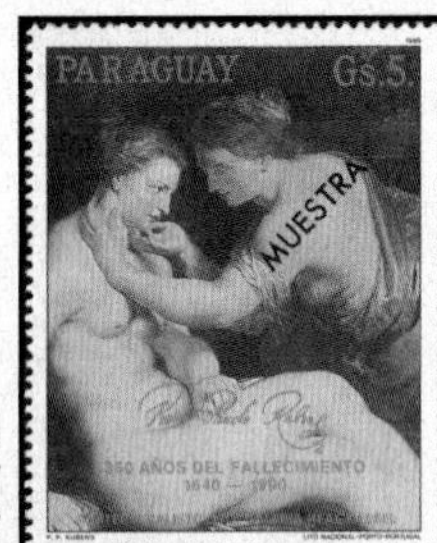


Jupiter and Calisto by Rubens AP241

Details from paintings by Rubens: 10g, Boreas Abducting Oreithyia (1619-20). 20g, Fortuna (1625). 25g, Mars with Venus and Cupid (1625). 30g, Virgin with Child (1620).

**1989, Dec. 27 Litho. *Perf. 14***
**C794** AP241 5g multicolored .50 .25
**C795** AP241 10g multicolored .80 .25
**C796** AP241 20g multicolored 1.75 .55
**C797** AP241 25g multicolored 2.25 .75

***Perf. 13***
**C798** AP241 30g multicolored 2.10 2.10
*Nos. C794-C798 (5)* 7.40 3.90

Death of Rubens, 350th anniversary.

Penny Black, 150th Anniv. AP242

Penny Black, 500 years of postal services emblem, Stamp World '90 emblem and: 5g, Brazil #1. 10g, British Guiana #2. 20g, Chile #1. 25g, Uruguay #1. 30g, Paraguay #1.

**1989, Dec. 30 *Perf. 14***
**C799** AP242 5g multicolored .40 .25
**C800** AP242 10g multicolored .80 .25
**C801** AP242 20g multicolored 1.60 .50
**C802** AP242 25g multicolored 2.00 .65

***Perf. 13***
**C803** AP242 30g multicolored 2.75 2.75
*Nos. C799-C803 (5)* 7.55 4.40

Animals AP243

Designs: 5g, Martucha. 10g, Mara. 20g, Lobo de crin. 25g, Rana cornuda tintorera, horiz. 30g, Jaguar, horiz. Inscribed 1989.

**1990, Jan. 8 *Perf. 13x13½, 13½x13***
**C804** AP243 5g multicolored .75 .25
**C805** AP243 10g multicolored 1.60 .50
**C806** AP243 20g multicolored 2.00 .65
**C807** AP243 25g multicolored 2.60 .90
**C808** AP243 30g multicolored 2.75 1.75
*Nos. C804-C808 (5)* 9.70 4.05

Columbus' Fleet AP244

Discovery of America 500th anniversary emblem and: 10g, Olympic rings, stylized basketball player, horiz. 20g, Medieval nave, Expo '92 emblem. 25g, Four-masted barkentine, Expo '92 emblem, horiz. 30g, Similar to Spain Scott 2571, Expo '92 emblem.

**1990, Jan. 27 *Perf. 14***
**C809** AP244 5g multicolored .55 .25
**C810** AP244 10g multicolored 1.10 .35
**C811** AP244 20g multicolored 1.20 .40
**C812** AP244 25g multicolored 1.40 .55

***Perf. 13½x13***
**C813** AP244 30g multicolored 1.75 1.75
*Nos. C809-C813 (5)* 6.00 3.30

Postal Transportation, 500th Anniv. — AP245

500th Anniv. Emblem and: 5g, 10g, 20g, 25g, Penny Black and various post coaches, 10g, vert. 30g, Post coach.

**1990, Mar. 9 *Perf. 13½x13, 13x13½***
**C814** AP245 5g multicolored .50 .25
**C815** AP245 10g multicolored .90 .35
**C816** AP245 20g multicolored 2.00 .65
**C817** AP245 25g multicolored 2.60 .85
**C818** AP245 30g multicolored 3.50 3.50
*Nos. C814-C818 (5)* 9.50 5.60

Fort and City of Arco by Durer — AP246

Paintings by Albrecht Durer, postal transportation 500th anniversary emblem and: 10g, Trent Castle. 20g, North Innsbruck. 25g, Fort yard of Innsbruck, vert. 30g, Virgin of the Animals. No. C824, Madonna and Child, vert. No. C825, Postrider, vert.

**1990, Mar. 14 *Perf. 14***
**C819** AP246 5g multicolored .50 .25
**C820** AP246 10g multicolored .95 .35
**C821** AP246 20g multicolored 2.00 .65
**C822** AP246 25g multicolored 2.75 1.00

***Perf. 13***
**C823** AP246 30g multicolored 3.75 3.75
*Nos. C819-C823 (5)* 9.95 6.00

**Souvenir Sheets**

***Perf. 14½***
**C824** AP246 100g multicolored 17.00 17.00
**C825** AP246 100g multicolored 17.00 17.00

Nos. C824-C825 each contain one 40x50mm stamp.
For overprint see No. 2358.

AP247

**Wmk. 347**

**1986-88? Photo. *Perf. 11***
**C826** AP247 40g red lilac 1.00 .85
**C827** AP247 60g brt grn ('88) 1.50 1.25

## POSTAGE DUE STAMPS

D1

**1904 Unwmk. Litho. *Perf. 11½***
**J1** D1 2c green 1.00 *2.00*
**J2** D1 4c green 1.00 *2.00*
**J3** D1 10c green 1.00 *2.00*
**J4** D1 20c green 1.00 *2.00*
*Nos. J1-J4 (4)* 4.00 8.00

D2

**1913 Engr.**
**J5** D2 1c yellow brown 1.00 1.00
**J6** D2 2c yellow brown 1.00 1.00
**J7** D2 5c yellow brown 1.00 1.00
**J8** D2 10c yellow brown 1.00 1.00
**J9** D2 20c yellow brown 1.00 1.00
**J10** D2 40c yellow brown 1.00 1.00
**J11** D2 1p yellow brown 1.00 1.00
**J12** D2 1.50p yellow brown 1.00 1.00
*Nos. J5-J12 (8)* 8.00 8.00

For overprints and surcharges see Nos. 220-224, 229, 232, 264, L5.

## INTERIOR OFFICE ISSUES

The "C" signifies "Campana" (rural). These stamps were sold by Postal Agents in country districts, who received a commission on their sales. These stamps were available for postage in the interior but not in Asunción or abroad.

Nos. 243-244 Overprinted in Red

**1922**
**L1** A42 50c car & dk bl .50 .50
**L2** A42 1p dk bl & brn .50 .50

The overprint on Nos. L2 exists double or inverted. Counterfeits exist. Double or inverted overprints on No. L1 and all overprints in black are counterfeit.

Nos. 215, 218, J12 Surcharged

**1924**
**L3** A40 50c on 75c deep bl .50 .50
**L4** A40 1p on 1.25p pale bl .50 .50
**L5** D2 1p on 1.50p yel brn .50 .50
*Nos. L3-L5 (3)* 1.50 1.50

Nos. L3-L4 exist imperf.

Nos. 254, 257-260 Overprinted in Black or Red

**1924-26**
**L6** A45 50c red ('25) 1.00 1.00
**L7** A44 1p dk blue (R) 1.00 1.00
**L8** A45 1p dk bl (R) ('25) 1.00 1.00
**L9** A46 1p blue (R) ('25) 1.00 1.00
**L10** A45 1p emerald ('26) 2.00 .75
*Nos. L6-L10 (5)* 6.00 4.75

Nos. L6, L8-L9 exist imperf. Value $2.50 each pair.

**Same Overprint on Stamps and Type of 1927-36 in Red or Black**

**1927-39**
**L11** A47 50c ultra (R) .50 .50
**L12** A47 50c dl red ('28) .50 .50
**L13** A47 50c orange ('29) .50 .50
**L14** A47 50c lt bl ('30) .50 .50
**L15** A47 50c gray (R) ('31) .50 .50
**L16** A47 50c bluish grn (R) ('33) .50 .50
**L17** A47 50c vio (R) ('34) .50 .50
**L18** A48 1p emerald .50 .50
**L19** A48 1p org red ('29) .50 .50
**L20** A48 1p lil brn ('31) .50 .50
**L21** A48 1p dk bl (R) ('33) .50 .50
**L22** A48 1p brt vio (R) ('35) .50 .50
**L23** A49 1.50p brown .50 .50
*a.* Double overprint 3.00
**L24** A49 1.50p lilac ('28) .50 .50
**L25** A49 1.50p dull bl (R) .50 .50
**L26** A50 2.50p bister ('28) .50 .50
**L27** A50 2.50p vio (R) ('36) .50 .50
**L28** A51 3p gray (R) .50 .50
**L29** A51 3p rose red ('39) .50 .50
**L30** A52 5p vio (R) ('36) .50 .50
**L31** A57 10p gray brn (R) ('36) 5.00 3.00
*Nos. L11-L31 (21)* 15.00 13.00

**Types of 1931-35 and No. 305 Overprinted in Black or Red**

**1931-36**
**L32** A59 1p light red 2.00 1.00
**L33** A58 1.50p dp bl (R) 1.00 .75
**L34** A60 1.50p bis brn ('32) 2.00 1.00
**L35** A60 1.50p grn (R) ('34) 2.00 1.00
**L36** A60 1.50p bl (R) ('36) 2.00 1.00
**L37** A54 10p vermilion 8.00 2.50
*Nos. L32-L37 (6)* 17.00 7.25

## OFFICIAL STAMPS

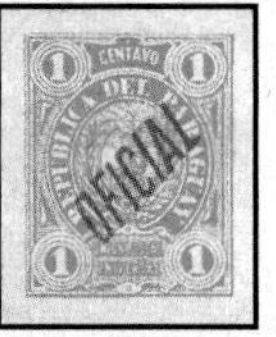


O1 O2

O3 O4

O5

O6

O7

**Unwmk.**

**1886, Aug. 20 — Litho. — *Imperf.***

O1 O1 1c orange 7.00 7.00
O2 O2 2c violet 7.00 7.00
O3 O3 5c red 7.00 7.00
O4 O4 7c green 7.00 7.00
O5 O5 10c brown 7.00 7.00
O6 O6 15c slate blue 7.00 7.00
*a.* Wavy lines on face of stamp
*b.* "OFICIAL" omitted 1.25
O7 O7 20c claret 7.00 7.00
*Nos. O1-O7 (7)* 49.00 49.00

Nos. O1 to O7 have the date and various control marks and letters printed on the back of each stamp in blue and black.

The overprints exist inverted on all values.

*Nos. O1 to O7 have been reprinted from new stones made from slightly retouched dies.*

Types of 1886 With Overprint

**1886 — *Perf. 11½***

O8 O1 1c dark green 1.50 1.50
O9 O2 2c scarlet 1.50 1.50
O10 O3 5c dull blue 1.50 1.50
O11 O4 7c orange 1.50 1.50
O12 O5 10c lake 1.50 1.50
O13 O6 15c brown 1.50 1.50
O14 O7 20c blue 1.50 1.50
*Nos. O8-O14 (7)* 10.50 10.50

The overprint exists inverted on all values. Value, each $1.50.

No. 20 Overprinted

**1886, Sept. 1**

O15 A11 1c dark green 4.00 4.00

Types of 1889 Regular Issue Surcharged

**Handstamped Surcharge in Black**

**1889 — *Imperf.***

O16 A13 3c on 15c violet 3.75 2.75
O17 A13 5c on 15c red brn 3.75 2.25

***Perf. 11½***

O18 A13 1c on 15c maroon 4.00 2.25
O19 A13 2c on 15c maroon 4.00 2.25
*Nos. O16-O19 (4)* 15.50 9.50

Counterfeits of Nos. O16-O19 abound.

Regular Issue of 1887 Handstamp Overprinted in Violet

***Perf. 11½-12½ & Compounds***

**1890 — Typo.**

O20 A12 1c green .35 .30
O21 A12 2c rose red .35 .30
O22 A12 5c blue .35 .30
O23 A12 7c brown 10.00 8.00
O24 A12 10c lilac .35 .35
O25 A12 15c orange .75 .45
O26 A12 20c pink .65 .45
*Nos. O20-O26 (7)* 12.80 10.15

Nos. O20-O26 exist with double overprint and all but the 20c with inverted overprint.

Nos. O20-O22, O24-O26 exist with blue overprint. The status is questioned. Value, set $15.

Stamps and Type of 1887 Regular Issue Overprinted in Black

**1892**

O33 A12 1c green .30 .30
O34 A12 2c rose red .30 .30
O35 A12 5c blue .30 .30
O36 A12 7c brown 4.00 1.75
O37 A12 10c lilac 1.25 .55
O38 A12 15c orange .35 .30
O39 A12 20c pink .65 .35
O40 A12 50c gray .75 .35
*Nos. O33-O40 (8)* 7.90 4.20

No. 26 Overprinted

**1893**

O41 A12 7c brown 17.50 8.00

Counterfeits of No. O41 exist.

O16

**1901, Feb. — Engr. — *Perf. 11½, 12½***

O42 O16 1c dull blue .75 .50
O43 O16 2c rose red .75 .50
O44 O16 4c dark brown .75 .50
O45 O16 5c dark green .75 .50
O46 O16 8c orange brn .75 .50
O47 O16 10c car rose 2.50 1.00
O48 O16 20c deep blue 2.50 1.00
*Nos. O42-O48 (7)* 8.75 4.50

A 12c deep green, type O16, was prepared but not issued.

No. 45 Overprinted

**1902 — *Perf. 12x12½***

O49 A12 1p olive grn 2.00 2.00
*a.* Inverted overprint 10.00

Counterfeits of No. O49a exist.

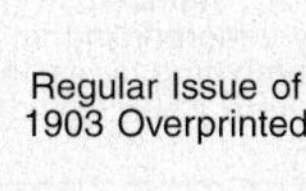
Regular Issue of 1903 Overprinted

**1903 — *Perf. 11½***

O50 A32 1c gray .90 .35
O51 A32 2c blue green .90 .35
O52 A32 5c blue .90 .35
O53 A32 10c orange brn .90 .35
O54 A32 20c carmine .90 .35
O55 A32 30c deep blue .90 .35
O56 A32 60c purple .90 .35
*Nos. O50-O56 (7)* 6.30 2.45

O17

**1905-08 — Engr. — *Perf. 11½, 12***

O57 O17 1c gray grn .50 .30
O58 O17 1c ol grn ('05) .90 .30
O59 O17 1c brn org ('06) .80 .30
O60 O17 1c ver ('08) .50 .30
O61 O17 2c brown org .35 .30
O62 O17 2c gray grn ('05) .35 .30
O63 O17 2c red ('06) 2.00 .75
O64 O17 2c gray ('08) 1.00 .50
O65 O17 5c deep bl ('06) .50 .35
O66 O17 5c gray bl ('08) 4.00 2.00
O67 O17 5c grnsh bl ('08) 2.00 1.50
O68 O17 10c violet ('06) .35 .50
O69 O17 20c violet ('08) 2.00 1.25
*Nos. O57-O69 (13)* 15.25 8.65

O18

**1908**

O70 O17 10c bister 10.50
O71 O17 10c emerald 10.50
O72 O17 10c red lilac 13.50
O73 O17 20c bister 9.00
O74 O17 20c salmon pink 10.50
O75 O17 20c green 10.50
O76 O17 30c turquoise bl 10.50
O77 O17 30c blue gray 10.50
O78 O17 30c yellow 4.50
O79 O17 60c chocolate 12.00
O80 O17 60c orange brn 15.00
O81 O17 60c deep ultra 12.00
O82 O18 1p brt rose & blk 72.50
O83 O18 1p lake & blk 72.50
O84 O18 1p brn org & blk 75.00
*Nos. O70-O84 (15)* 349.00

Nos. O70-O84 were not issued, but were surcharged or overprinted for use as regular postage stamps. See Nos. 131-138, 141-145, 158-165, 171-173.

O19

**1913 — *Perf. 11½***

O85 O19 1c gray .30 .35
O86 O19 2c orange .30 .35
O87 O19 5c lilac .30 .35
O88 O19 10c green .30 .35
O89 O19 20c dull red .30 .35
O90 O19 50c rose .30 .35
O91 O19 75c deep blue .30 .35
O92 O19 1p dull blue 1.00 .50
O93 O19 2p yellow 1.00 .50
*Nos. O85-O93 (9)* 4.10 3.45

For surcharges see Nos. 268, C1-C3.

Type of Regular Issue of 1927-38 Overprinted in Red

**1935**

O94 A47 10c light ultra .35 .30
O95 A47 50c violet .35 .30
O96 A48 1p orange .35 .30
O97 A60 1.50p green .35 .30
O98 A50 2.50p violet .35 .30
*Nos. O94-O98 (5)* 1.75 1.50

Overprint is diagonal on 1.50p.

**University of Asunción Type**

**1940 — Litho. — *Perf. 12***

O99 A67 50c red brn & blk .50 .30
O100 A67 1p rose pink & blk .50 .30
O101 A67 2p lt bl grn & blk .50 .30
O102 A67 5p ultra & blk .50 .30
O103 A67 10p lt vio & blk .50 .30
O104 A67 50p dp org & blk .50 .30
*Nos. O99-O104 (6)* 3.00 1.80

## PENRHYN ISLAND

pen-'rin 'ī-lənd

(Tongareva)

AREA — 3 sq. mi.
POP. — 395 (1926)

Stamps of Cook Islands were used in Penrhyn from 1932 until 1973.

12 Pence = 1 Shilling

**Catalogue values for unused stamps in this country are for Never Hinged items, beginning with Scott 35 in the regular postage section, Scott B1 in the semi-postal section and Scott O1 in the officials section.**

### Watermarks

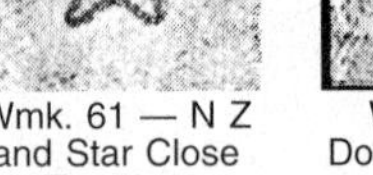

Wmk. 61 — N Z and Star Close Together

Wmk. 63 — Double-lined N Z and Star

On watermark 61 the margins of the sheets are watermarked "NEW ZEALAND POSTAGE" and parts of the double-lined letters of these words are frequently found on the stamps. It occasionally happens that a stamp shows no watermark whatever.

### Stamps of New Zealand Surcharged in Carmine, Vermilion, Brown or Blue

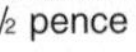

½ pence

1 pence

2½ pence

**1902** **Wmk. 63** ***Perf. 14***

1 A18 ½p green (C) 1.00 *14.00*
a. No period after "ISLAND" 175.00 *325.00*
2 A35 1p carmine (Br) 3.75 *27.50*
a. Perf. 11 *1,000.* *1,200.*
b. Perf. 11x14 *1,200.* *1,400.*

**Wmk. 61** ***Perf. 14***

5 A18 ½p green (V) 4.75 *16.00*
a. No period after "ISLAND" 180.00 *375.00*
6 A35 1p carmine (Bl) 1.50 *9.50*
a. No period after "ISLAND" 60.00 *170.00*
b. Perf. 11x14 *15,000.* *8,500.*

**Unwmk.** ***Perf. 11***

8 A22 2½p blue (C) 14.50 14.50
a. "½" and "PENI" 2mm apart 30.00 *35.00*
9 A22 2½p blue (V) 14.50 13.00
a. "½" and "PENI" 2mm apart 30.00 *35.00*
*Nos. 1-9 (6)* 40.00 *94.50*

Stamps with compound perfs. also exist perf. 11 or 14 on one or more sides.

d

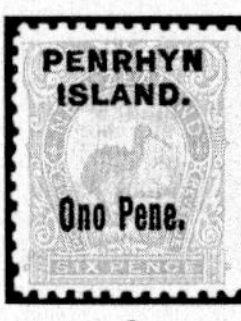


e

f

**1903** **Wmk. 61**

10 A23(d) 3p yel brn (Bl) 11.50 *42.50*
11 A26(e) 6p rose (Bl) 17.50 *50.00*
12 A29(f) 1sh org red (Bl) 67.50 *67.50*
a. 1sh bright red (Bl) 47.50 *47.50*
b. 1sh brown red (Bl) 65.00 *65.00*
*Nos. 10-12 (3)* 96.50 *160.00*

**1914-15** ***Perf. 14, 14x14½***

13 A41(a) ½p yel grn (C) 1.10 *12.00*
a. No period after "ISLAND" 29.00 *110.00*
b. No period after "PENI" 110.00 *350.00*
14 A41(a) ½p yel grn (V) ('15) 1.10 *9.25*
a. No period after "ISLAND" 11.50 *65.00*
b. No period after "PENI" 55.00 *190.00*
15 A41(e) 6p car rose (Bl) 27.50 *82.50*
16 A41(f) 1sh ver (Bl) 50.00 *110.00*
*Nos. 13-16 (4)* 79.70 *213.75*

New Zealand Stamps of 1915-19 Overprinted in Red or Dark Blue

***Perf. 14x13½, 14x14½***

**1917-20** **Typo.**

17 A43 ½p yel grn (R) ('20) 1.10 *2.25*
18 A47 1½p gray black (R) 7.50 *27.50*
19 A47 1½p brn org (R) ('19) 1.10 *27.50*
20 A43 3p choc (Bl) ('19) 4.25 *45.00*

**Engr.**

21 A44 2½p dull bl (R) ('20) 2.25 *10.00*
22 A45 3p vio brn (Bl) ('18) 12.00 *80.00*
23 A45 6p car rose (Bl) ('18) 5.75 *21.00*
24 A45 1sh vermilion (Bl) 14.00 *37.50*
*Nos. 17-24 (8)* 47.95 *250.75*

Landing of Capt. Cook A10

Avarua Waterfront A11

Capt. James Cook — A12

Coconut Palm — A13

Arorangi Village, Rarotonga — A14

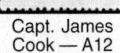

Avarua Harbor — A15

**1920** **Unwmk.** ***Perf. 14***

25 A10 ½p emerald & blk 1.25 *23.00*
a. Center inverted 1,000.
26 A11 1p red & black 2.00 *19.00*
a. Center inverted 1,000.
27 A12 1½p violet & blk 7.75 *24.00*
28 A13 3p red org & blk 3.25 *15.00*
29 A14 6p dk brn & red brn 4.00 *24.00*
30 A15 1sh dull bl & blk 12.00 *32.50*
*Nos. 25-30 (6)* 30.25 *137.50*

Rarotongan Chief (Te Po) — A16

**1927** **Engr.** **Wmk. 61**

31 A16 2½p blue & red brn 19.00 *50.00*

**Types of 1920 Issue**

**1928-29**

33 A10 ½p yellow grn & blk 6.50 *26.00*
34 A11 1p carmine rose & blk 6.50 *25.00*

## PENRHYN

Northern Cook Islands

POP. — 606 (1996).

The Northern Cook Islands include six besides Penrhyn that are inhabited: Nassau, Palmerston (Avarua), Manihiki (Humphrey), Rakahanga (Reirson), Pukapuka (Danger) and Suwarrow (Anchorage).

100 Cents = 1 Dollar

**Catalogue values for unused stamps in this section are for Never Hinged items.**

Cook Islands Nos. 200-201, 203, 205-208, 211-212, 215-217 Overprinted

**1973** **Photo.** **Unwmk.** ***Perf. 14x13½***

35 A34 1c gold & multi .25 .25
36 A34 2c gold & multi .25 .25
37 A34 3c gold & multi .25 .25
38 A34 4c gold & multi .25 .25
a. Overprinted on #204 38.00 38.00
39 A34 5c gold & multi .25 .25
40 A34 6c gold & multi .25 .35
41 A34 8c gold & multi .25 .45
42 A34 15c gold & multi .35 .60
43 A34 20c gold & multi 1.25 1.00
44 A34 50c gold & multi .90 2.00
45 A35 $1 gold & multi .90 2.25
46 A35 $2 gold & multi .90 4.50
*Nos. 35-46 (12)* 6.05 12.40

Nos. 45-46 are overprinted "Penrhyn" only. Overprint exists with broken "E" or "O."

Issued with and without fluorescent security underprinting.

Issued: #35-45, Oct. 24; #46, Nov. 14.

**Cook Islands Nos. 369-371 Overprinted in Silver: "PENRHYN / NORTHERN"**

**1973, Nov. 14** **Photo.** ***Perf. 14***

47 A60 25c Princess Anne .35 .25
48 A60 30c Mark Phillips .35 .25
49 A60 50c Princess and Mark Phillips .35 .25
*Nos. 47-49 (3)* 1.05 .75

Wedding of Princess Anne and Capt. Mark Phillips.

Fluorescence

Starting with No. 50, stamps carry a "fluorescent security underprinting" in a multiple pattern combining a sailing ship, "Penrhyn Northern Cook Islands" and stars.

Ostracion A17

Aerial View of Penrhyn Atoll — A18

Designs: ½c-$1, Various fish of Penrhyn. $5, Map showing Penrhyn's location.

**1974-75** **Photo.** ***Perf. 13½x14***

50 A17 ½c multicolored .25 .25
51 A17 1c multicolored .25 .25
52 A17 2c multicolored .25 .25
53 A17 3c multicolored .25 .25
54 A17 4c multicolored .25 .25
55 A17 5c multicolored .25 .25
56 A17 8c multicolored .25 .25
57 A17 10c multicolored .25 .25
58 A17 20c multicolored .75 .40
59 A17 25c multicolored .80 .45
60 A17 60c multicolored 2.00 1.10
61 A17 $1 multicolored 3.25 1.75
62 A18 $2 multicolored 6.50 *10.00*
63 A18 $5 multicolored 8.50 3.50
*Nos. 50-63 (14)* 23.80 19.20

Issued: $2, 2/12/75; $5, 3/12/75; others 8/15/74.

For surcharges and overprints see Nos. 72, 352-353, O1-O12.

Map of Penrhyn and Nos. 1-2 — A19

UPU, cent.: 50c, UPU emblem, map of Penrhyn and Nos. 27-28.

**1974, Sept. 27** ***Perf. 13***

64 A19 25c violet & multi .30 .30
65 A19 50c slate grn & multi .60 .60

Adoration of the Kings, by Memling — A20

Christmas: 10c, Adoration of the Shepherds, by Hugo van der Goes. 25c, Adoration of the Kings, by Rubens. 30c, Holy Family, by Orazio Borgianni.

**1974, Oct. 30**

66 A20 5c multicolored .25 .25
67 A20 10c multicolored .25 .25
68 A20 25c multicolored .30 .30
69 A20 30c multicolored .40 .40
*Nos. 66-69 (4)* 1.20 1.20

Churchill Giving "V" Sign — A21

**1974, Nov. 30** **Photo.**

70 A21 30c shown .35 *.80*
71 A21 50c Portrait .45 *.90*

Winston Churchill (1874-1965).

### No. 63 Overprinted

**1975, July 24** ***Perf. 13½x13***
**72** A18 $5 multicolored 2.25 2.75

Safe splashdown of Apollo space capsule.

Madonna, by Dirk Bouts — A22

Madonna Paintings: 15c, by Leonardo da Vinci. 35c, by Raphael.

**1975, Nov. 21** **Photo.** ***Perf. 14½x13***
**73** A22 7c gold & multi .45 .25
**74** A22 15c gold & multi .75 .30
**75** A22 35c gold & multi 1.10 .45
*Nos. 73-75 (3)* 2.30 1.00

Christmas 1975.

Pietà, by Michelangelo A23

**1976, Mar. 19** **Photo.** ***Perf. 14x13***
**76** A23 15c gold & dark brown .25 .25
**77** A23 20c gold & deep purple .40 .30
**78** A23 35c gold & dark green .55 .35
*a.* Souvenir sheet of 3, #76-78 1.60 1.60
*Nos. 76-78 (3)* 1.20 .90

Easter and for the 500th birth anniv. of Michelangelo Buonarroti (1475-1564), Italian sculptor, painter and architect.

The Spirit of '76, by Archibald M. Willard — A24

No. 79, Washington Crossing the Delaware, by Emmanuel Leutze.

**1976, May 20** **Photo.** ***Perf. 13½***
**79** A24 Strip of 3 1.00 1.00
*a.* 30c Boatsman .30 .30
*b.* 30c Washington .30 .30
*c.* 30c Men in boat .30 .30
**80** A24 Strip of 3 2.00 2.00
*a.* 50c Drummer boy .50 .50
*b.* 50c Old drummer .50 .50
*c.* 50c Fifer .50 .50
*d.* Souvenir sheet, #79-80 3.25 3.25

American Bicentennial. Nos. 79-80 printed in sheets of 15, 5 strips of 3 and 3-part corner labels.

For overprint see No. O13.

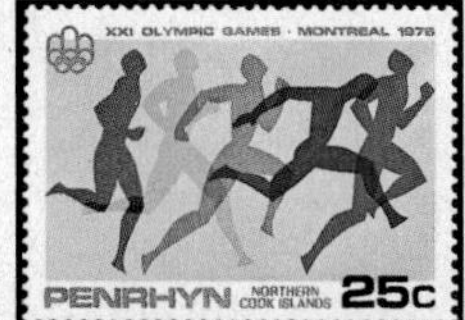
Running A25

Montreal Olympic Games Emblem and: 30c, Long jump. 75c, Javelin.

**1976, July 9** **Photo.** ***Perf. 13½***
**81** A25 25c multicolored .30 .25
**82** A25 30c multicolored .35 .30
**83** A25 75c multicolored .75 .50
*a.* Souvenir sheet of 3, #81-83, perf. 14½x13½ 1.40 1.40
*Nos. 81-83 (3)* 1.40 1.05

21st Olympic Games, Montreal, Canada, July 17-Aug. 1. Nos. 81-83 printed in sheets of 6 (2x3).

Flight into Egypt, by Dürer A26

Etchings by Albrecht Dürer: 15c, Adoration of the Shepherds. 35c, Adoration of the Kings.

**1976, Oct. 20** **Photo.** ***Perf. 13x13½***
**84** A26 7c silver & dk brown .25 .25
**85** A26 15c silver & slate grn .25 .25
**86** A26 35c silver & purple .45 .35
*Nos. 84-86 (3)* .95 .85

Christmas. Nos. 84-86 printed in sheets of 8 (2x4) with decorative border.

Elizabeth II and Westminster Abbey — A27

$1, Elizabeth II & Prince Philip. $2, Elizabeth II.

**1977, Mar. 24** **Photo.** ***Perf. 13½x13***
**87** A27 50c silver & multi .25 .25
**88** A27 $1 silver & multi .30 .30
**89** A27 $2 silver & multi .45 .45
*a.* Souvenir sheet of 3, #87-89 1.25 1.25
*Nos. 87-89 (3)* 1.00 1.00

25th anniversary of reign of Queen Elizabeth II. Nos. 87-89 issued in sheets of 4.

For overprints see Nos. O14-O15.

Annunciation A28

Designs: 15c, Announcement to Shepherds. 35c, Nativity. Designs from "The Bible in Images," by Julius Schnorr von Carolsfeld (1794-1872).

**1977, Sept. 23** **Photo.** ***Perf. 13½***
**90** A28 7c multicolored .25 .25
**91** A28 15c multicolored .65 .65
**92** A28 35c multicolored 1.10 1.10
*Nos. 90-92 (3)* 2.00 2.00

Christmas. Issued in sheets of 6.

A29

No. 93a, Red Sickle-bill (I'wii). No. 93b, Chief's Feather Cloak. No. 94a, Crimson creeper (apapane). No. 94b, Feathered head of Hawaiian god. No. 95a, Hawaiian gallinule (alae). No. 95b, Chief's regalia: feather cape, staff (kahili) and helmet. No. 96a, Yellow-tufted bee-eater (o'o). No. 96b, Scarlet feathered image (head).

Birds are extinct; their feathers were used for artifacts shown.

**1978, Jan. 19** **Photo.** ***Perf. 12½x13***
**93** A29 20c Pair, #a.-b. 1.40 .70
**94** A29 30c Pair, #a.-b. 1.75 .90
**95** A29 35c Pair, #a.-b. 1.90 1.00
**96** A29 75c Pair, #a.-b. 3.00 1.60
*c.* Souv. sheet, #93a, 94a, 95a, 96a 4.25 4.25
*d.* Souv. sheet, #93b, 94b, 95b, 96b 4.25 4.25
*Nos. 93-96 (4)* 8.05 4.20

Bicentenary of Capt. Cook's arrival in Hawaii. Printed in sheets of 8 (4x2).

A31

Rubens' Paintings: 10c, St. Veronica by Rubens. 15c, Crucifixion. 35c, Descent from the Cross.

**1978, Mar. 10** **Photo.** ***Perf. 13½x13***
**Size: 25x36mm**
**101** A31 10c multicolored .25 .25
**102** A31 15c multicolored .25 .25
**103** A31 35c multicolored .50 .50
*a.* Souvenir sheet of 3 1.10 1.10
*Nos. 101-103 (3)* 1.00 1.00

Easter and 400th birth anniv. of Peter Paul Rubens (1577-1640). Nos. 101-103 issued in sheets of 6. No. 103a contains one each of Nos. 101-103 (27x36mm).

Miniature Sheet

A32

**1978, May 24** **Photo.** ***Perf. 13***
**104** A32 Sheet of 6 1.75 1.75
*a.* 90c Arms of United Kingdom .35 .25
*b.* 90c shown .35 .25
*c.* 90c Arms of New Zealand .35 .25
*d.* Souvenir sheet of 3, #104a-104c 1.40 1.40

25th anniv. of coronation of Elizabeth II.

No. 104 contains 2 horizontal se-tenant strips of Nos. 104a-104c, separated by horizontal gutter showing coronation.

A33

Paintings by Dürer: 30c, Virgin and Child. 35c, Virgin and Child with St. Anne.

**1978, Nov. 29** **Photo.** ***Perf. 14x13½***
**105** A33 30c multicolored .60 .60
**106** A33 35c multicolored .65 .65
*a.* Souvenir sheet of 2, #105-106 1.25 1.25

Christmas and 450th death anniv. of Albrecht Dürer (1471-1528), German painter. Nos. 105-106 issued in sheets of 6.

A34

#107a, Penrhyn #64-65. #107b, Rowland Hill, Penny Black. #108a, Penrhyn #104b. #108b, Hill portrait.

**1979, Sept. 26** **Photo.** ***Perf. 14***
**107** A34 75c Pair, #a.-b. 1.00 1.00
**108** A34 90c Pair, #a.-b. 1.25 1.25
*c.* Souvenir sheet of 4, #107-108 2.25 2.25

Sir Rowland Hill (1795-1879), originator of penny postage. Issued in sheets of 8.

Max and Moritz, IYC Emblem — A35

IYC: Scenes from Max and Moritz, by Wilhelm Busch (1832-1908).

**1979, Nov. 20** **Photo.** ***Perf. 13x12½***
**111** Sheet of 4 1.00
*a.* A35 12c shown .25
*b.* A35 12c Looking down chimney .25
*c.* A35 12c With stolen chickens .25
*d.* A35 12c Woman and dog, empty pan .25
**112** Sheet of 4 1.00
*a.* A35 15c Sawing bridge .25
*b.* A35 15c Man falling into water .25
*c.* A35 15c Broken bridge .25
*d.* A35 15c Running away .25
**113** Sheet of 4 1.00
*a.* A35 20c Baker .25
*b.* A35 20c Sneaking into bakery .25
*c.* A35 20c Falling into dough .25
*d.* A35 20c Baked into breads .25
*Nos. 111-113 (3)* 3.00

Sheets come with full labels at top and bottom showing text from stories or trimmed with text removed. Values of 3 sheets with full labels $11.

A36

Easter (15th Century Prayerbook Illustrations): 12c, Jesus Carrying the Cross. 20c, Crucifixion, by William Vreland. 35c, Descent from the Cross.

**1980, Mar. 28** **Photo.** ***Perf. 13x13½***
**114** A36 12c multicolored .25 .25
**115** A36 20c multicolored .25 .25
**116** A36 35c multicolored .40 .40
*a.* Souvenir sheet of 3, #114-116 .75 .75
*Nos. 114-116 (3)* .90 .90

See Nos. B4-B6.

A37

**1980, Sept. 17 Photo. *Perf. 13***

**117** A37 $1 multicolored 1.10 1.10

**Souvenir Sheet**

**118** A37 $2.50 multicolored 2.10 2.10

Queen Mother Elizabeth, 80th birthday.

A38

Platform diving: #119a, Falk Hoffman, DDR. #119b, Martina Jaschke.

Archery: #120a, Tomi Polkolainen. #120b, Kete Losaberidse.

Soccer: #121a, Czechoslovakia, gold. #121b, DDR, silver.

Running: #122a, Barbel Wockel. #122b, Pietro Mennea.

**1980, Nov. 14 Photo. *Perf. 13½***

**119** A38 10c Pair, #a.-b. .25 .25
**120** A38 20c Pair, #a.-b. .45 .45
**121** A38 30c Pair, #a.-b. .70 .70
**122** A38 50c Pair, #a.-b. 1.10 1.10
*Nos. 119-122 (4)* 2.50 2.50

**Souvenir Sheet**

**123** A38 Sheet of 8 2.50 2.50

22nd Summer Olympic Games, Moscow, July 19-Aug, 3.

No. 123 contains #119-122 with gold borders and white lettering at top and bottom.

A39

Christmas (15th Century Virgin and Child Paintings by): 20c, Virgin and Child, by Luis Dalmau. 35c, Serra brothers. 50c, Master of the Porciuncula.

**1980, Dec. 5 Photo. *Perf. 13***

**127** A39 20c multicolored .25 .25
**128** A39 35c multicolored .30 .30
**129** A39 50c multicolored .45 .45
*a.* Souvenir sheet of 3, #127-129 2.40 2.40
*Nos. 127-129 (3)* 1.00 1.00

See Nos. B7-B9.

A40

A41

Cutty Sark, 1869 A42

#160a, 165a, Amatasi. #160b, 165b, Ndrua. #160c, 165c, Waka. #160d, 165d, Tongiaki. #161a, 166a, Va'a teu'ua. #161b, 166b, Victoria, 1500. #161c, 166c, Golden Hinde, 1560. #161d, 166d, Boudeuse, 1760. #162a, 167a, Bounty, 1787. #162b, 167b, Astrolabe, 1811. #162c, 167c, Star of India, 1861. #162d, 167d, Great Rep., 1853. #163a, 168a, Balcutha, 1886. #163b, 168b, Coonatto, 1863. #163c, 168c, Antiope, 1866. #163d, 168d, Teaping, 1863. #164a, 169a, Preussen, 1902. #164b, 169b, Pamir, 1921. #164c, 169c, Cap Hornier, 1910. #164d, 169d, Patriarch, 1869.

**1981 Photo. *Perf. 14***

**160** A40 1c Block of 4, #a.-d. .30 .30
**161** A40 3c Block of 4, #a.-d. .50 .50
**162** A40 4c Block of 4, #a.-d. .65 .65
**163** A40 6c Block of 4, #a.-d. 1.00 1.00
**164** A40 10c Block of 4, #a.-d. 1.25 1.25

***Perf. 13½x14½***

**165** A41 15c Block of 4, #a.-d. 1.40 1.40
**166** A41 20c Block of 4, #a.-d. 1.60 1.60
**167** A41 30c Block of 4, #a.-d. 2.75 2.75
**168** A41 50c Block of 4, #a.-d. 4.50 4.50
**169** A41 $1 Block of 4, #a.-d. 11.00 11.00

***Perf. 13½***

**170** A42 $2 shown 5.00 5.00
**171** A42 $4 Mermerus, 1872 10.00 10.00
**172** A42 $6 Resolution, Discovery, 1776 17.00 17.00
*Nos. 160-172 (13)* 56.95 56.95

Issued: 1c-10c, Feb. 16; 15c-50c, Mar. 16; $1, May 15; $2, $4, June 26; $6, Sept. 21.

For surcharges and overprints see Nos. 241-243, 251, 254, 395, O35, O37, O39.

Christ with Crown of Thorns, by Titian — A44

Easter: 30c, Jesus at the Grove, by Paolo Veronese. 50c, Pieta, by Van Dyck.

**1981, Apr. 5 *Perf. 14***

**173** A44 30c multicolored .40 .30
**174** A44 40c multicolored .60 .45
**175** A44 50c multicolored .75 .60
*a.* Souv. sheet, #173-175, perf 13½ 3.00 3.00
*Nos. 173-175 (3)* 1.75 1.35

See Nos. B10-B12.

A45

Designs: Portraits of Prince Charles.

**1981, July 10 Photo. *Perf. 14***

**176** A45 40c multicolored .25 .25
**177** A45 50c multicolored .25 .25
**178** A45 60c multicolored .25 .25
**179** A45 70c multicolored .30 .30
**180** A45 80c multicolored .35 .35
*a.* Souv. sheet of 5, #176-180+label 2.00 2.00
*Nos. 176-180 (5)* 1.40 1.40

Royal wedding. Nos. 176-180 each issued in sheets of 5 plus label showing couple.

For overprints and surcharges see Nos. 195-199, 244-245, 248, 299-300, B13-B18.

1982 World Cup Soccer — A46

Shirts: No. 181: a, Red. b, Striped. c, Blue. No. 182: a, Blue. b, Red. c, Striped. No. 183: a, Orange. b, Purple. c, Black.

**1981, Dec. 7 Photo. *Perf. 13***

**181** A46 15c Strip of 3, #a.-c. 1.00 1.00
**182** A46 35c Strip of 3, #a.-c. 1.75 1.75
**183** A46 50c Strip of 3, #a.-c. 2.75 2.75
*Nos. 181-183 (3)* 5.50 5.50

See No. B19.

Christmas — A47

Dürer Engravings: 30c, Virgin on a Crescent, 1508. 40c, Virgin at the Fence, 1503. 50c, Holy Virgin and Child, 1505.

**1981, Dec. 15 Photo. *Perf. 13x13½***

**184** A47 30c multicolored .75 .75
**185** A47 40c multicolored 1.25 1.25
**186** A47 50c multicolored 1.50 1.50
*a.* Souvenir sheet of 3 3.25 3.25
*Nos. 184-186 (3)* 3.50 3.50

**Souvenir Sheets**

***Perf. 14x13½***

**187** A47 70c + 5c like #184 1.10 1.10
**188** A47 70c + 5c like #185 1.10 1.10
**189** A47 70c + 5c like #186 1.10 1.10

No. 186a contains Nos. 184-186 each with 2c surcharge. Nos. 187-189 each contain one 25x40mm stamp. Surtaxes were for childrens' charities.

21st Birthday of Princess Diana — A48

Designs: Portraits of Diana.

**1982, July 1 Photo. *Perf. 14***

**190** A48 30c multicolored .75 .75
**191** A48 50c multicolored 1.00 1.00
**192** A48 70c multicolored 1.25 1.25
**193** A48 80c multicolored 1.50 1.50
**194** A48 $1.40 multicolored 3.25 3.25
*a.* Souv. sheet, #190-194 + label 7.75 7.75
*Nos. 190-194 (5)* 7.75 7.75

For new inscriptions, overprints and surcharges, see Nos. 200-204, 246-247, 249-250, 301-302.

**Nos. 176-180a Overprinted**

**1982, July 30**

**195** A45 40c multicolored .45 .45
**196** A45 50c multicolored .60 .60
**197** A45 60c multicolored .65 .65
**198** A45 70c multicolored .75 .75
**199** A45 80c multicolored .80 .80
*a.* Souv. sheet, #195-199 + label 6.00 6.00
*Nos. 195-199 (5)* 3.25 3.25

**Nos. 190-194a Inscribed in Silver**

**1982 Photo. *Perf. 14***

**200** A48 30c Pair, #a.-b. .70 .70
**201** A48 50c Pair, #a.-b. .90 .90
**202** A48 70c Pair, #a.-b. 1.60 1.60
**203** A48 80c Pair, #a.-b. 1.75 1.75
**204** A48 $1.40 Pair, #a.-b. 3.00 3.00
*c.* Souv. sheet, #200a, 201a, 202a, 203a, 204a + label 6.50 6.50
*Nos. 200-204 (5)* 7.95 7.95

Miniature sheets of each denomination were issued containing 2 "21 JUNE 1982...," 3 "COMMEMORATING...," and a label. Value, set of 5 sheets, $21.

Se-tenant pairs come with or without label.

For surcharges see Nos. 247, 250, 253.

A49

Christmas — Virgin and Child Paintings: 35c, Joos Van Cleve (1485-1540). 48c, Filippino Lippi (1457-1504). 60c, Cima Da Conegliano (1459-1517).

**1982, Dec. 10 Photo. *Perf. 14***

**205** A49 35c multicolored .50 .50
**206** A49 48c multicolored .70 .70
**207** A49 60c multicolored .80 .80
*a.* Souvenir sheet of 3 3.00 3.00
*Nos. 205-207 (3)* 2.00 2.00

**Souvenir Sheets**

**208** A49 70c + 5c like 35c 1.60 1.60
**209** A49 70c + 5c like 48c 1.60 1.60
**210** A49 70c + 5c like 60c 1.60 1.60

Nos. 205-207 were printed in sheets of five plus label. No. 207a contains Nos. 205-207 each with 2c surcharge. Nos. 208-210 each contain one stamp, perf. 13½. Surtaxes were for childrens' charities.

A50

#a, Red coral. #b, Aerial view. #c, Eleanor Roosevelt, grass skirt. #d, Map.

**1983, Mar. 14** *Perf. 13½x13*
**211** A50 60c Block of 4, #a.-d. 2.25 2.25

Commonwealth day.
For surcharges see No. O27-O30.

Scouting Year A51

Emblem and various tropical flowers.

**1983, Apr. 5** *Perf. 13½x14½*
**215** A51 36c multicolored 1.75 .75
**216** A51 48c multicolored 2.25 1.00
**217** A51 60c multicolored 2.50 1.25
*Nos. 215-217 (3)* 6.50 3.00

**Souvenir Sheet**

**218** A51 $2 multicolored 3.50 3.50

**Nos. 215-218 Overprinted: "XV / WORLD JAMBOREE / CANADA / 1983"**

**1983, July 8 Photo.** *Perf. 13½x14½*
**219** A51 36c multicolored 1.60 .65
**220** A51 48c multicolored 2.10 1.25
**221** A51 60c multicolored 2.50 1.25
*Nos. 219-221 (3)* 6.20 3.15

**Souvenir Sheet**

**222** A51 $2 multicolored 3.50 3.50

15th World Boy Scout Jamboree.

Save the Whales Campaign A52

Various whale hunting scenes.

**1983, July 29 Photo.** *Perf. 13*
**223** A52 8c multicolored .80 .70
**224** A52 15c multicolored 1.20 1.00
**225** A52 35c multicolored 2.40 1.40
**226** A52 60c multicolored 3.75 2.00
**227** A52 $1 multicolored 5.75 2.75
*Nos. 223-227 (5)* 13.90 7.85

World Communications Year — A53

Designs: Cable laying Vessels.

**1983, Sept. Photo.** *Perf. 13*
**228** A53 36c multicolored 1.00 .50
**229** A53 48c multicolored 1.25 .70
**230** A53 60c multicolored 1.50 .90
*Nos. 228-230 (3)* 3.75 2.10

**Souvenir Sheet**

**231** Sheet of 3 2.75 2.75
*a.* A53 36c + 3c like No. 228 .65 .65
*b.* A53 48c + 3c like No. 229 .85 .85
*c.* A53 60c + 3c like No. 230 1.00 1.00

Surtax was for local charities.

**Nos. 164, 166-167, 170, 172, 178-180, 192-194, 202-204 Surcharged**

**Blocks of 4, #a.-d. (#241-243)**
**Pairs, #a.-b. (#247, 250, 253)**

*Perf. 14, 13½x14½, 13½*

**1983** **Photo.**
**241** A40 18c on 10c #164 4.00 4.00
**242** A41 36c on 20c #166 5.00 5.00
**243** A41 36c on 30c #167 5.00 5.00
**244** A45 48c on 60c multi 1.25 1.25
**245** A45 72c on 70c multi 1.75 1.75
**246** A48 72c on 70c #192 1.75 1.75
**247** A48 72c on 70c #202 4.00 3.75
**248** A45 96c on 80c multi 3.50 2.25
**249** A48 96c on 80c #193 3.75 2.25
**250** A48 96c on 80c #203 4.75 4.00
**251** A42 $1.20 on $2 multi 5.00 3.00
**252** A48 $1.20 on $1.40 #194 4.00 3.00
**253** A48 $1.20 on $1.40 #204 7.00 5.00
**254** A42 $5.60 on $6 multi 21.00 15.00
*Nos. 241-254 (14)* 71.75 57.00

Issued: #241-243, 245, 251, Sept. 26; #244, 246, 249, 252, 254, Oct. 28; others Dec. 1.

First Manned Balloon Flight, 200th Anniv. — A54

Designs: 36c, Airship, Sir George Cayley (1773-1857). 48c, Man-powered airship, Dupuy de Lome (1818-1885). 60c, Brazilian Aviation Pioneer, Alberto Santos Dumont (1873-1932). 96c, Practical Airship, Paul Lebaudy (1858-1937). $1.32, L-Z 127 Graf Zeppelin.

**1983, Oct. 31 Litho.** *Perf. 13*
**255** A54 36c multicolored 1.00 1.00
**256** A54 48c multicolored 1.50 1.50
**257** A54 60c multicolored 1.75 1.75
**258** A54 96c multicolored 2.25 2.25
**259** A54 $1.32 multicolored 3.50 3.50
*a.* Souvenir sheet of 5, #255-259 9.00 9.00
*Nos. 255-259 (5)* 10.00 10.00

Nos. 255-259 se-tenant with labels. Sheets of 5 for each value exist.

Nos. 255-259 are misspelled "ISLANS." For correcting overprints see Nos. 287-291.

Christmas A55

Raphael Paintings: 36c, Madonna in the Meadow. 42c, Tempi Madonna. 48c, Small Cowper Madonna. 60c, Madonna Della Tenda.

**1983, Nov. 30 Photo.** *Perf. 13x13½*
**260** A55 36c multicolored .75 .45
**261** A55 42c multicolored 1.00 .55
**262** A55 48c multicolored 1.25 .60
**263** A55 60c multicolored 1.50 .80
*a.* Souvenir sheet of 4 4.50 4.50
*Nos. 260-263 (4)* 4.50 2.40

**Souvenir Sheets**

*Perf. 13½*

**264** A55 75c + 5c like #260 1.20 1.20
**265** A55 75c + 5c like #261 1.20 1.20
**266** A55 75c + 5c like #262 1.20 1.20
**267** A55 75c + 5c like #263 1.20 1.20

No. 263a contains Nos. 260-263 each with 3c surcharge. Nos. 264-267 each contain one 29x41mm stamp. Issued Dec. 28. Surtaxes were for children's charities.

Waka Canoe — A56

4c, Amatasi fishing boat. 5c, Ndrua canoe. 8c, Tongiaki canoe. 10c, Victoria, 1500. 18c, Golden Hind, 1560. 20c, Boudeuse, 1760. 30c, Bounty, 1787. 36c, Astrolabe, 1811. 48c, Great Republic, 1853. 50c, Star of India, 1861. 60c, Coonatto, 1863. 72c, Antiope, 1866. 80c, Balcutha, 1886. 96c, Cap Hornier, 1910. $1.20, Pamir, 1921. $3, Mermerus, 1872. $5, Cutty Sark, 1869. $9.60, Resolution, Discovery.

**1984 Photo.** *Perf. 14½*
**268** A56 2c multicolored .25 .25
**269** A56 4c multicolored .25 .25
**270** A56 5c multicolored .25 .25
**271** A56 8c multicolored .25 .25
**272** A56 10c multicolored .40 .40
**273** A56 18c multicolored 1.00 .55
**274** A56 20c multicolored .65 .65
**275** A56 30c multicolored 1.25 .90
**276** A56 36c multicolored 1.10 1.10
**277** A56 48c multicolored 1.50 1.50
**278** A56 50c multicolored 1.60 1.60
**279** A56 60c multicolored 1.75 1.75
**280** A56 72c multicolored 2.25 2.25
**281** A56 80c multicolored 2.50 2.50
**282** A56 96c multicolored 3.25 3.25
**283** A56 $1.20 multicolored 1.60 1.60

*Perf. 13*

**Size: 42x34mm**

**284** A56 $3 multicolored 6.25 6.25
**285** A56 $5 multicolored 10.00 10.00
**286** A56 $9.60 multicolored 20.00 20.00
*Nos. 268-286 (19)* 56.10 55.30

Issue dates: Nos. 268-277, Feb. 8. Nos. 278-283, Mar. 23. Nos. 284-286 June 15.

For overprints and surcharges see Nos. O16-O26, O31-O34, O36, O38, O40.

**Nos. 255-259a Overprinted**

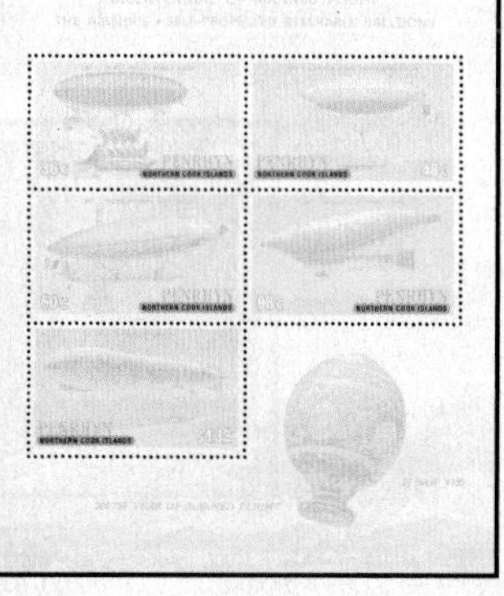

**1984 Litho.** *Perf. 13*
**287** A54 36c multicolored .85 .85
**288** A54 48c multicolored 1.10 1.10
**289** A54 60c multicolored 1.40 1.40
**290** A54 96c multicolored 2.25 2.25
**291** A54 $1.32 multicolored 3.00 3.00
*a.* Souvenir sheet of 5, #287-291 7.50 *8.75*
*Nos. 287-291 (5)* 8.60 8.60

1984 Los Angeles Summer Olympic Games A57

35c, Olympic flag. 60c, Torch, flags. $1.80, Classic runners, Memorial Coliseum.

**1984, July 20 Photo.** *Perf. 13½x13*
**292** A57 35c multicolored .45 .45
**293** A57 60c multicolored .80 .80
**294** A57 $1.80 multicolored 2.00 2.00
*Nos. 292-294 (3)* 3.25 3.25

**Souvenir Sheet**

**295** Sheet of 3 + label 3.00 3.00
*a.* A57 35c + 5c like #292 .35 .35
*b.* A57 60c + 5c like #293 .50 .50
*c.* A57 $1.80 + 5c like #294 1.75 1.75

Surtax for amateur sports.

AUSIPEX '84 — A57a

60c, Nos. 161c, 107b, 180, 104b. $1.20, Map of South Pacific.

**1984, Sept. 20**
**296** A57a 60c multicolored .85 .85
**297** A57a $1.20 multicolored 1.75 1.75

**Souvenir Sheet**

**298** Sheet of 2 3.00 3.00
*a.* A57a 96c like #296 1.50 1.50
*b.* A57a 96c like #297 1.50 1.50

For surcharge see No. 345.

**Nos. 176-177, 190-191 Ovptd. "Birth of/Prince Henry/15 Sept. 1984" and Surcharged in Black or Gold**

**1984, Oct. 18** *Perf. 14*
**299** A45 $2 on 40c 1.75 1.75
**300** A45 $2 on 50c 1.75 1.75
**301** A48 $2 on 30c 1.75 1.75
**302** A48 $2 on 50c 1.75 1.75
*Nos. 299-302 (4)* 7.00 7.00

Nos. 209-302 printed in sheets of 5 plus one label each picturing a portrait of the royal couple or an heraldic griffin.

Christmas 1984 — A58

Paintings: 36c, Virgin and Child, by Giovanni Bellini. 48c, Virgin and Child, by Lorenzo di Credi. 60c, Virgin and Child, by Palma, the Older. 96c, Virgin and Child, by Raphael.

**1984, Nov. 15 Photo.** *Perf. 13x13½*
**303** A58 36c multicolored .55 .55
**304** A58 48c multicolored .90 .90
**305** A58 60c multicolored 1.00 1.00
**306** A58 96c multicolored 1.75 1.75
*a.* Souvenir sheet of 4 4.25 4.25
*Nos. 303-306 (4)* 4.20 4.20

**Souvenir Sheets**

**307** A58 96c + 10c like #303 1.60 1.60
**308** A58 96c + 10c like #304 1.60 1.60
**309** A58 96c + 10c like #305 1.60 1.60
**310** A58 96c + 10c like #306 1.60 1.60

No. 306a contains Nos. 303-306, each with 5c surcharge. Nos. 307-310 issued Dec. 10. Surtax for children's charities.

Audubon Bicentenary — A59

20c, Harlequin duck. 55c, Sage grouse. 65c, Solitary sandpiper. 75c, Red-backed sandpiper.

**1985, Apr. 9 Photo. *Perf. 13***

**311** A59 20c multi 1.50 1.50
**312** A59 55c multi 4.00 4.00
**313** A59 65c multi 4.75 4.75
**314** A59 75c multi 5.25 5.25
*Nos. 311-314 (4)* 15.50 15.50

**Souvenir Sheets**

***Perf. 13½x13***

**315** A59 95c Like #311 3.00 2.00
**316** A59 95c Like #312 3.00 2.00
**317** A59 95c Like #313 3.00 2.00
**318** A59 95c Like #314 3.00 2.00

For surcharges see Nos. 391-394.

Queen Mother, 85th Birthday — A60

75c, Photograph, 1921. 95c, New mother, 1926. $1.20, Coronation day, 1937. $2.80, 70th birthday.
$5, Portrait, c. 1980.

**1985, June 24 Photo. *Perf. 13x13½***

**319** A60 75c multicolored .55 *.65*
**320** A60 95c multicolored .70 *.80*
**321** A60 $1.20 multicolored 1.00 *1.00*
**322** A60 $2.80 multicolored 2.25 *2.50*
*a.* Souvenir sheet of 4, #319-322 15.00 15.00
*Nos. 319-322 (4)* 4.50 *4.95*

**Souvenir Sheet**

**323** A60 $5 multicolored 3.75 3.75

No. 322a issued on 8/4/86, for 86th birthday.

Intl. Youth Year — A61

Grimm Brothers' fairy tales: 75c, House in the Wood. 95c, Snow White and Rose Red. $1.15, Goose Girl.

**1985, Sept. 10 *Perf. 13x13½***

**324** A61 75c multicolored 2.25 2.25
**325** A61 95c multicolored 3.25 3.25
**326** A61 $1.15 multicolored 4.50 4.50
*Nos. 324-326 (3)* 10.00 10.00

Christmas 1985 A62

Paintings (details) by Murillo: 75c, No. 330a, The Annunciation. $1.15, No. 330b, Adoration of the Shepherds. $1.80, No. 330c, The Holy Family.

**1985, Nov. 25 Photo. *Perf. 14***

**327** A62 75c multicolored 1.50 1.50
**328** A62 $1.15 multicolored 2.25 2.25
**329** A62 $1.80 multicolored 3.75 3.75
*Nos. 327-329 (3)* 7.50 7.50

**Souvenir Sheets**

***Perf. 13½***

**330** Sheet of 3 4.25 4.25
*a.-c.* A62 95c any single 1.30 1.30
**331** A62 $1.20 like #327 1.75 1.75
**332** A62 $1.45 like #328 2.00 2.00
**333** A62 $2.75 like #329 3.25 3.25

Halley's Comet — A63

Fire and Ice, by Camille Rendal. Nos. 334-335 se-tenant in continuous design.

**1986, Feb. 4 *Perf. 13½x13***

**334** A63 $1.50 Comet head 3.50 3.50
**335** A63 $1.50 Comet tail 3.50 3.50
*a.* Pair, #334-335 7.00 7.00

**Size: 109x43mm**

***Imperf***

**336** A63 $3 multicolored 6.00 6.00
*Nos. 334-336 (3)* 13.00 13.00

Elizabeth II, 60th Birthday A64

**1986, Apr. 21 *Perf. 14***

**337** A64 95c Age 3 1.25 1.25
**338** A64 $1.45 Wearing crown 1.60 1.60

**Size: 60x34mm**

***Perf. 13½x13***

**339** A64 $2.50 Both portraits 2.75 2.75
*Nos. 337-339 (3)* 5.60 5.60

A65

Statue of Liberty, Cent.: 95c, Statue, scaffolding. $1.75 Removing copper facade. $3, Restored statue on Liberty Island.

**1986, June 27 Photo. *Perf. 13½***

**340** A65 95c multicolored .85 .85
**341** A65 $1.75 multicolored 1.75 1.75
**342** A65 $3 multicolored 3.00 3.00
*Nos. 340-342 (3)* 5.60 5.60

A66

**1986, July 23 *Perf. 13x13½***

**343** A66 $2.50 Portraits 3.00 3.00
**344** A66 $3.50 Profiles 3.75 3.75

Wedding of Prince Andrew and Sarah Ferguson. Nos. 343-344 each printed in sheets of 4 plus 2 center decorative labels.

**No. 298 Surcharged with Gold Circle, Bar, New Value in Black and Exhibition Emblem in Gold and Black**

**1986, Aug. 4**

**345** Sheet of 2 8.75 8.75
*a.* A57a $2 on 96c #298a 4.25 4.25
*b.* A57a $2 on 96c #298b 4.25 4.25

STAMPEX '86, Adelaide, Aug. 4-10.

Christmas A67

Engravings by Rembrandt: 65c, No. 349a, Adoration of the Shepherds. $1.75, No. 349b, Virgin and Child. $2.50, No. 349c, The Holy Family.

**1986, Nov. 20 Litho. *Perf. 13x13½***

**346** A67 65c multicolored 2.50 2.50
**347** A67 $1.75 multicolored 3.50 3.50
**348** A67 $2.50 multicolored 5.00 5.00
*Nos. 346-348 (3)* 11.00 11.00

**Souvenir Sheet**

***Perf. 13½x13***

**349** Sheet of 3 13.00 13.00
*a.-c.* A67 $1.50 any single 4.00 4.00

Corrected inscription is black on silver.
For surcharges see Nos. B20-B23.

Souvenir Sheets

Statue of Liberty, Cent. — A68

Photographs: No. 350a, Workmen, crown. No. 350b, Ellis Is., aerial view. No. 350c, Immigration building, Ellis Is. No. 350d, Buildings, opposite side of Ellis Is. No. 350e, Workmen inside torch structure. No. 351a, Liberty's head and torch. No. 351b, Torch. No. 351c, Workmen on scaffold. No. 351d, Statue, full figure. No. 351e, Workmen beside statue. Nos. 351a-351e vert.

**1987, Apr. 15 Litho. *Perf. 14***

**350** A68 Sheet of 5 + label 5.75 5.75
*a.-e.* 65c any single 1.05 1.05
**351** A68 Sheet of 5 + label 5.75 5.75
*a.-e.* 65c any single 1.05 1.05

**Nos. 62-63 Ovptd. "Fortieth Royal Wedding / Anniversary 1947-87" in Lilac Rose**

**1987, Nov. 20 Photo. *Perf. 13½x14***

**352** A18 $2 multicolored 2.00 2.00
**353** A18 $5 multicolored 5.50 5.50

Christmas A69

Paintings (details) by Raphael: 95c, No. 357a, The Garvagh Madonna, the National Gallery, London. $1.60, No. 357b, The Alba Madonna, the National Gallery of Art, Washington. $2.25, No. 357c, $4.80, The Madonna of the Fish, Prado Museum, Madrid.

**1987, Dec. 11 Photo. *Perf. 13½***

**354** A69 95c multicolored 2.40 2.40
**355** A69 $1.60 multicolored 3.00 3.00
**356** A69 $2.25 multicolored 4.75 4.75
*Nos. 354-356 (3)* 10.15 10.15

**Souvenir Sheets**

**357** Sheet of 3 + label 16.00 16.00
*a.-c.* A69 $1.15 any single 4.75 4.75
**358** A69 $4.80 multicolored 16.00 16.00

No. 358 contains one 31x39mm stamp.

1988 Summer Olympics, Seoul — A70

Events and: 55c, $1.25, Seoul Games emblem. 95c, Obverse of a $50 silver coin issued in 1987 to commemorate the participation of Cook Islands athletes in the Olympics for the 1st time. $1.50, Coin reverse.

***Perf. 13½x13, 13x13½***

**1988, July 29 Photo.**

**359** A70 55c Running 1.20 1.20
**360** A70 95c High jump, vert. 2.40 2.40
**361** A70 $1.25 Shot put 2.75 2.75
**362** A70 $1.50 Tennis, vert. 4.50 4.50
*Nos. 359-362 (4)* 10.85 10.85

**Souvenir Sheet**

**363** Sheet of 2 10.00 10.00
*a.* A70 $2.50 like 95c 4.75 4.75
*b.* A70 $2.50 like $1.50 4.75 4.75

**Nos. 359-363 Ovptd. for Olympic Gold Medalists**

*a.* "CARL LEWIS / UNITED STATES / 100 METERS"
*b.* "LOUISE RITTER / UNITED STATES / HIGH JUMP"
*c.* "ULF TIMMERMANN / EAST GERMANY / SHOT-PUT"
*d.* "STEFFI GRAF / WEST GERMANY / WOMEN'S TENNIS"
*e.* "JACKIE / JOYNER-KERSEE / United States / Heptathlon"
*f.* "STEFFI GRAF / West Germany / Women's Tennis / MILOSLAV MECIR / Czechoslovakia / Men's Tennis"

***Perf. 13½x13, 13x13½***

**1988, Oct. 14 Photo.**

**364** A70(a) 55c on No. 359 1.20 1.20
**365** A70(b) 95c on No. 360 2.40 2.40
**366** A70(c) $1.25 on No. 361 2.75 2.75
**367** A70(d) $1.50 on No. 362 4.50 4.50
*Nos. 364-367 (4)* 10.85 10.85

**Souvenir Sheet**

**368** Sheet of 2 10.00 10.00
*a.* A70(e) $2.50 on No. 363a 4.75 4.75
*b.* A70(f) $2.50 on No. 363b 4.75 4.75

Christmas A71

*Virgin and Child* paintings by Titian.

**1988, Nov. 9 *Perf. 13x13½***

**369** A71 70c multicolored 1.40 1.40
**370** A71 85c multi, diff. 1.75 1.75
**371** A71 95c multi, diff. 2.25 2.25
**372** A71 $1.25 multi, diff. 2.50 2.50
*Nos. 369-372 (4)* 7.90 7.90

**Souvenir Sheet**

***Perf. 13***

**373** A71 $6.40 multi, diff. 10.00 10.00

No. 373 contains one diamond-shaped stamp, size: 55x55mm.

1st Moon Landing, 20th Anniv. A72

Apollo 11 mission emblem, US flag and: 55c, First step on the Moon. 75c, Astronaut carrying equipment. 95c, Conducting experiment. $1.25, Crew members Armstrong, Collins and Aldrin. $1.75, Armstrong and Aldrin aboard lunar module.

**1989, July 24 Photo. *Perf. 14***

| | | | |
|---|---|---|---|
| **374-378** | A72 Set of 5 | 12.00 | 12.00 |

Christmas A73

Details from *The Nativity*, by Albrecht Durer, 1498, center panel of the Paumgartner altarpiece: 55c, Madonna. 70c, Christ child, cherubs. 85c, Joseph. $1.25, Attendants. $6.40, Entire painting.

**1989, Nov. 17 Photo. *Perf. 13x13½***

| | | | |
|---|---|---|---|
| **379-382** | A73 Set of 4 | 6.25 | 6.25 |

**Souvenir Sheet**

| | | | |
|---|---|---|---|
| **383** | A73 $6.40 multicolored | 10.00 | 10.00 |

No. 383 contains one 31x50mm stamp.

Queen Mother, 90th Birthday — A74

**1990, July 24 Photo. *Perf. 13½***

| | | | |
|---|---|---|---|
| **384** | A74 $2.25 multicolored | 3.50 | 3.50 |

**Souvenir Sheet**

| | | | |
|---|---|---|---|
| **385** | A74 $7.50 multicolored | 17.00 | 17.00 |

Christmas — A75

Paintings: 55c, Adoration of the Magi by Veronese. 70c, Virgin and Child by Quentin Metsys. 85c, Virgin and Child Jesus by Van Der Goes. $1.50, Adoration of the Kings by Jan Gossaert. $6.40, Virgin and Child with Saints Francis, John the Baptist, Zenobius and Lucy by Domenico Veneziano.

**1990, Nov. 26 Litho. *Perf. 14***

| | | | |
|---|---|---|---|
| **386-389** | A75 Set of 4 | 9.50 | 9.50 |

**Souvenir Sheet**

| | | | |
|---|---|---|---|
| **390** | A75 $6.40 multicolored | 11.00 | 11.00 |

**Nos. 311-314 Surcharged in Red or Black**

**1990, Dec. 5 Photo. *Perf. 13***

| | | | |
|---|---|---|---|
| **391** | A59 $1.50 on 20c (R) | 2.75 | 2.75 |
| **392** | A59 $1.50 on 55c | 2.75 | 2.75 |
| **393** | A59 $1.50 on 65c | 2.75 | 2.75 |
| **394** | A59 $1.50 on 75c (R) | 2.75 | 2.75 |
| | *Nos. 391-394 (4)* | 11.00 | 11.00 |

Birdpex '90, 20th Intl. Ornithological Cong., New Zealand. Surcharge appears in various locations.

**No. 172 Overprinted "COMMEMORATING 65th BIRTHDAY OF H.M. QUEEN ELIZABETH II"**

**1991, Apr. 22 Photo. *Perf. 13½***

| | | | |
|---|---|---|---|
| **395** | A42 $6 multicolored | 13.00 | 13.00 |

Christmas A76

Paintings: 55c, Virgin and Child with Saints, by Gerard David. 85c, The Nativity, by Tintoretto. $1.15, Mystic Nativity, by Botticelli. $1.85, Adoration of the Shepherds, by Murillo. $6.40, Madonna of the Chair, by Raphael.

**1991, Nov. 11 Litho. *Perf. 14***

| | | | |
|---|---|---|---|
| **396-399** | A76 Set of 4 | 9.25 | 9.25 |

**Souvenir Sheet**

| | | | |
|---|---|---|---|
| **400** | A76 $6.40 multicolored | 16.00 | 16.00 |

1992 Summer Olympics, Barcelona — A77

**1992, July 27 Litho. *Perf. 14***

| | | | |
|---|---|---|---|
| **401** | A77 75c Runners | 2.25 | 2.25 |
| **402** | A77 95c Boxing | 2.60 | 2.60 |
| **403** | A77 $1.15 Swimming | 3.00 | 3.00 |
| **404** | A77 $1.50 Wrestling | 3.25 | 3.25 |
| | *Nos. 401-404 (4)* | 11.10 | 11.10 |

6th Festival of Pacific Arts, Rarotonga — A78

Festival poster and: $1.15, Marquesan canoe. $1.75, Statue of Tangaroa. $1.95, Manihiki canoe.

**1992, Oct. 16 Litho. *Perf. 14x15***

| | | | |
|---|---|---|---|
| **405** | A78 $1.15 multicolored | 2.75 | 2.75 |
| **406** | A78 $1.75 multicolored | 3.25 | 3.25 |
| **407** | A78 $1.95 multicolored | 3.75 | 3.75 |
| | *Nos. 405-407 (3)* | 9.75 | 9.75 |

For overprints see Nos. 455-457.

**Overprinted "ROYAL VISIT"**

**1992, Oct. 16**

| | | | |
|---|---|---|---|
| **408** | A78 $1.15 on #405 | 3.00 | 3.00 |
| **409** | A78 $1.75 on #406 | 3.75 | 3.75 |
| **410** | A78 $1.95 on #407 | 4.25 | 4.25 |
| | *Nos. 408-410 (3)* | 11.00 | 11.00 |

Christmas A79

Paintings by Ambrogio Bergognone: 55c, $6.40, Virgin with Child and Saints. 85c, Virgin on Throne. $1.05, Virgin on Carpet. $1.85, Virgin of the Milk.

**1992, Nov. 18 Litho. *Perf. 13½***

| | | | |
|---|---|---|---|
| **411-414** | A79 Set of 4 | 8.25 | 8.25 |

**Souvenir Sheet**

| | | | |
|---|---|---|---|
| **415** | A79 $6.40 multicolored | 11.50 | 11.50 |

No. 415 contains one 38x48mm stamp.

Discovery of America, 500th Anniv. — A80

Designs: $1.15, Vicente Yanez Pinzon, Nina. $1.35, Martin Alonso Pinzon, Pinta. $1.75, Columbus, Santa Maria.

**1992, Dec. 4 *Perf. 15x14***

| | | | |
|---|---|---|---|
| **416** | A80 $1.15 multicolored | 2.75 | 2.75 |
| **417** | A80 $1.35 multicolored | 3.00 | 3.00 |
| **418** | A80 $1.75 multicolored | 4.25 | 4.25 |
| | *Nos. 416-418 (3)* | 10.00 | 10.00 |

Coronation of Queen Elizabeth II, 40th Anniv. — A81

**1993, June 4 Litho. *Perf. 14x14½***

| | | | |
|---|---|---|---|
| **419** | A81 $6 multicolored | 9.50 | 9.50 |

Marine Life — A82

Marine Life — A82a

5c, Helmet shell. 10c, Daisy coral. 15c, Hydroid coral. 20c, Feather star. 25c, Sea star. 30c, Nudibranch. 50c, Smooth sea star. 70c, Black pearl oyster. 80c, Pyjama nudibranch. 85c, Prickly sea cucumber. 90c, Organ pipe coral. $1, Aeolid nudibranch. $2, Textile cone shell.

**1993-98 Litho. *Perf. 14***

| | | | | |
|---|---|---|---|---|
| **420** | A82 | 5c multi | .25 | .25 |
| **421** | A82 | 10c multi | .25 | .25 |
| **422** | A82 | 15c multi | .25 | .25 |
| **423** | A82 | 20c multi | .25 | .25 |
| **424** | A82 | 25c multi | .30 | .30 |
| **425** | A82 | 30c multi | .35 | .35 |
| **426** | A82 | 50c multi | .55 | .55 |
| **427** | A82 | 70c multi | .85 | .80 |
| **428** | A82 | 80c multi | .95 | .90 |
| **429** | A82 | 85c multi | 1.05 | .95 |
| **430** | A82 | 90c multi | 1.05 | 1.00 |
| **431** | A82 | $1 multi | 1.25 | 1.10 |
| **432** | A82 | $2 multi | 3.50 | 2.25 |
| **433** | A82a | $3 pink & multi | 5.00 | 3.25 |
| **434** | A82a | $5 lilac & multi | 8.50 | 5.50 |
| | | ***Perf. 14x13½*** | | |
| **435** | A82a | $8 blue & multi | 12.00 | 11.00 |
| **435A** | A82a | $10 grn & multi | 13.00 | 12.00 |
| | | *Nos. 420-435A (17)* | 49.35 | 40.95 |

For overprints see #O41-O53.

Issued: 80c, 85c, 90c, $1, $2, 12/3/93; $3, $5, 11/21/94; $8, 11/17/97; $10, 10/1/98; others, 10/18/93.

Christmas — A83

Details from Virgin on Throne with Child, by Cosimo Tura: 55c, Madonna and Child. 85c, Musicians. $1.05, Musicians, diff. $1.95, Woman. $4.50, Entire painting.

**1993, Nov. 2 Litho. *Perf. 14***

| | | | |
|---|---|---|---|
| **436** | A83 55c multicolored | 1.40 | 1.40 |
| **437** | A83 85c multicolored | 2.10 | 2.10 |
| **438** | A83 $1.05 multicolored | 2.50 | 2.50 |
| **439** | A83 $1.95 multicolored | 3.75 | 3.75 |

**Size: 32x47mm**

***Perf. 13½***

| | | | |
|---|---|---|---|
| **440** | A83 $4.50 multicolored | 6.25 | 6.25 |
| | *Nos. 436-440 (5)* | 16.00 | 16.00 |

First Manned Moon Landing, 25th Anniv. A84

**1994, July 20 Litho. *Perf. 14***

| | | | |
|---|---|---|---|
| **441** | A84 $3.25 multicolored | 10.00 | 10.00 |

Christmas — A85

Details or entire paintings: No. 442a, Virgin and Child with Saints Paul & Jerome, by Vivarini. b, The Virgin and Child with St. John, by B. Luini. c, The Virgin and Child with Saints Jerome & Dominic, by F. Lippi. d, Adoration of Shepherds, by Murillo.

No. 443a, Adoration of the Kings, by Reni. b, Madonna & Child with the Infant Baptist, by Raphael. c, Adoration of the Kings, by Reni, diff. d, Virgin and Child, by Bergognone.

**1994, Nov. 30 Litho. *Perf. 14***

| | | | |
|---|---|---|---|
| **442** | A85 90c Block of 4, #a.-d. | 5.75 | 5.75 |
| **443** | A85 $1 Block of 4, #a.-d. | 6.25 | 6.25 |

End of World War II, 50th Anniv. — A86

Designs: a, Battleships on fire, Pearl Harbor, Dec. 7, 1941. b, B-29 bomber Enola Gay, A-bomb cloud, Aug. 1945.

**1995, Sept. 4 Litho. *Perf. 13***

| | | | |
|---|---|---|---|
| **444** | A86 $3.75 Pair, #a.-b. | 22.00 | 22.00 |

Queen Mother, 95th Birthday A87

**1995, Sept. 14 Litho. *Perf. 13½***

**445** A87 $4.50 multicolored 12.00 12.00

No. 445 was issued in sheets of 4.

UN, 50th Anniv. — A88

**1995, Oct. 20 Litho. *Perf. 13½***

**446** A88 $4 multicolored 5.75 5.75

No. 446 was issued in sheets of 4.

1995, Year of the Sea Turtle — A89

No. 447: a, Loggerhead. b, Hawksbill.
No. 448: a, Olive ridley. b, Green.

**1995, Dec. 7 Litho. *Perf. 13½***

**447** A89 $1.15 Pair, #a.-b. 4.75 4.75
**448** A89 $1.65 Pair, #a.-b. 7.25 7.25

Queen Elizabeth II, 70th Birthday A90

**1996, June 20 Litho. *Perf. 14***

**449** A90 $4.25 multicolored 7.50 7.50

No. 449 was issued in sheets of 4.

1996 Summer Olympic Games, Atlanta A91

**1996, July 12 Litho. *Perf. 14***

**450** A91 $5 multicolored 10.00 10.00

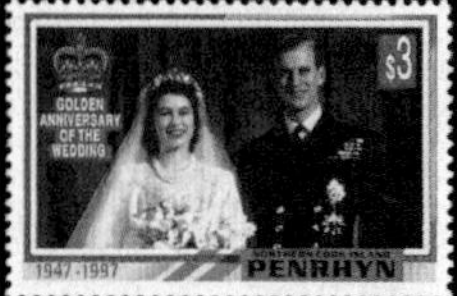

Queen Elizabeth II and Prince Philip, 50th Wedding Anniv. A92

**1997, Nov. 20 Litho. *Perf. 14***

**451** A92 $3 multicolored 4.50 4.50

**Souvenir Sheet**

**452** A92 $4 multicolored 5.50 5.50

No. 452 is a continuous design.

Diana, Princess of Wales (1961-97) — A93

**1998, May 7 Litho. *Perf. 14***

**453** A93 $1.50 multicolored 3.00 3.00

**Souvenir Sheet**

**454** A93 $3.75 like #453 6.00 6.00

No. 453 was issued in sheets of 5 + label. For surcharge see #B24.

**Nos. 405-407 Ovptd. "KIA ORANA / THIRD MILLENNIUM"**

**Methods and Perfs as before**

**1999, Dec. 31**

**455** A78 $1.15 multi 1.30 1.30
**456** A78 $1.75 multi 2.10 2.10
**457** A78 $1.95 multi 2.60 2.60
*Nos. 455-457 (3)* 6.00 6.00

Queen Mother, 100th Birthday — A94

No. 458: a, With King George VI. b, With Princess Elizabeth. c, With King George VI, Princesses Elizabeth and Margaret. d, With Princesses.

**2000, Oct. 20 Litho. *Perf. 14***

**458** A94 $2.50 Sheet of 4, #a-d 11.00 11.00

**Souvenir Sheet**

**459** A94 $10 Portrait 11.00 11.00

2000 Summer Olympics, Sydney — A95

No. 460, horiz.: a, Ancient javelin. b, Javelin. c, Ancient discus. d, Discus.

**2000, Dec. 14**

**460** A95 $2.75 Sheet of 4, #a-d 11.50 11.50

**Souvenir Sheet**

**461** A95 $3.50 Torch relay 5.00 5.00

Worldwide Fund for Nature (WWF) A96

Various photos of ocean sunfish: 80c, 90c, $1.15, $1.95.

**2003, Feb. 24**

**462-465** A96 Set of 4 6.50 6.50

Each printed in sheets of 4.

United We Stand — A97

**2003, Sept. 30**

**466** A97 $1.50 multicolored 2.00 2.00

Printed in sheets of 4.

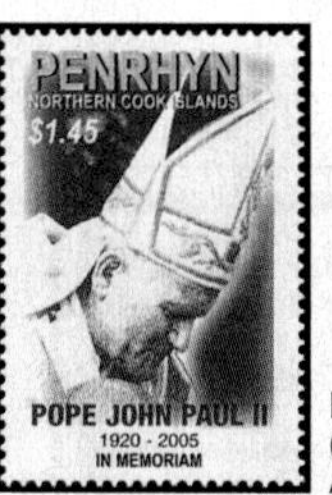

Pope John Paul II (1920-2005) A98

**2005, Nov. 11**

**467** A98 $1.45 multicolored 2.75 2.75

Printed in sheets of 5 + label.

Worldwide Fund for Nature (WWF) — A99

Pacific reef egret: 80c, Male and female. 90c, Bird at water's edge. $1.15, Bird in flight. $1.95, Adult and chicks.

**2008, Oct. 16 *Perf. 13½***

**468-471** A99 Set of 4 5.75 5.75

Nos. 468-471 each were printed in sheets of 4.

Worldwide Fund for Nature — A100

Striped dolphin: 80c, Breaching. 90c Pair underwater. $1.10, Breaching, diff. $1.20, Pod breaching.

**2010, Dec. 9 *Perf. 14***

**472-475** A100 Set of 4 6.00 6.00

Nos. 472-475 each were printed in sheets of 4.

A101

Engagement of Prince William and Catherine Middleton — A102

Designs: Nos. 476, 479a, 481, Prince. Nos. 477, 479b, 482, Middleton.

No. 478: a, Prince in military uniform. b, Prince playing polo. c, Middleton, fence. d, Prince, man and woman in background. e, Middleton, woman in background. f, Couple, Prince at left. g, Middleton with black hat. h, Prince. i, Couple, Middleton at left. j, Hands of couple, engagement ring.

$8.10, Couple, Prince in uniform at left.

**2011, Jan. 14 *Perf. 14***

**476** A101 $2 multi 3.25 3.25
**477** A101 $2 multi 3.25 3.25

**Miniature Sheets**

**478** A102 50c Sheet of 10, #a-j 7.75 7.75

***Perf. 13¾x13½***

**479** A101 $2 Sheet of 2, #a-b 6.25 6.25

**Souvenir Sheets**

***Perf. 14¼***

**480** A101 $8.10 multi 12.50 12.50
**481** A101 $11 multi 17.00 17.00
**482** A101 $11 multi 17.00 17.00
*Nos. 480-482 (3)* 46.50 46.50

No. 479 contains two 28x44mm stamps. Nos. 480-482 each contain one 38x50mm stamp.

A103

Peonies — A104

**2011, Apr. 8 Litho. *Perf. 13¼***
**483** A103 $1.10 multi 1.75 1.75

### Souvenir Sheet
***Perf. 14¾x14***
**484** A104 $7.20 multi 11.50 11.50

### Miniature Sheets

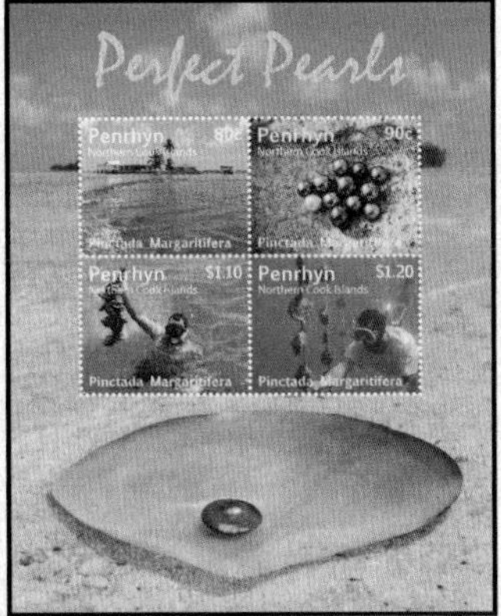

Pearl Industry — A105

No. 485 — Inscription "Pinctada Margaritifera" and: a, 80c, Buildings near shore. b, 90c, Pearls. c, $1.10, Diver at surface holding string of oysters. d, $1.20, Diver tending string of oysters underwater.

No. 486 — Inscription "Pearl Industry" and: a, 20c, Shark. b, 30c, Diver at surface. c, 50c, Pearls, diff. d, $1, Pearl in tongs. e, $2, Pearl oysters.

**2011, May 5 *Perf. 13¾***
**485** A105 Sheet of 4, #a-d 6.50 6.50
**486** A105 Sheet of 5, #a-e 6.50 6.50

Tourism A106

Designs: 10c, Birds flying over ocean. 20c, Ray. 30c, Buildings on shore. 40c, Rocky coastline. 50c, Road in forest. 60c, Sharks. 70c, Aerial view of island. 80c, Clouds over ocean. 90c, Palm trees near shore. $1, Sharks, diff. $1.10, Saab 340 airplane, aerial view of island. $1.20, Pearls. $1.50, Sea turtle. $2, Aerial view of island, diff. $3, Sun and clouds above island.

**2011, May 6 *Perf. 14***

| | | | | |
|---|---|---|---|---|
| **487** | A106 | 10c multi | .25 | .25 |
| **488** | A106 | 20c multi | .35 | .35 |
| **489** | A106 | 30c multi | .50 | .50 |
| **490** | A106 | 40c multi | .65 | .65 |
| **491** | A106 | 50c multi | .80 | .80 |
| **492** | A106 | 60c multi | .95 | .95 |
| **493** | A106 | 70c multi | 1.10 | 1.10 |
| **494** | A106 | 80c multi | 1.25 | 1.25 |
| **495** | A106 | 90c multi | 1.50 | 1.50 |
| **496** | A106 | $1 multi | 1.60 | 1.60 |
| **497** | A106 | $1.10 multi | 1.75 | 1.75 |
| **498** | A106 | $1.20 multi | 1.90 | 1.90 |
| **499** | A106 | $1.50 multi | 2.40 | 2.40 |
| **500** | A106 | $2 multi | 3.25 | 3.25 |
| **501** | A106 | $3 multi | 4.75 | 4.75 |
| *a.* | | Miniature sheet of 15, #487-501 | 23.00 | 23.00 |
| | | *Nos. 487-501 (15)* | 23.00 | 23.00 |

### Souvenir Sheet

Wedding of Prince William and Catherine Middleton — A107

No. 502 — Couple in wedding procession: a, $1. b, $1.20.

**2011, July 15 *Perf. 15x14¼***
**502** A107 Sheet of 2, #a-b 3.75 3.75

Christmas A108

No. 503: a, Partridge in a pear tree. b, Two turtle doves. c, Three French hens. d, Four calling birds.

**2011, Dec. 24 *Perf. 13¼***

| | | | |
|---|---|---|---|
| **503** | Horiz. strip of 4 | 6.00 | 6.00 |
| *a.* | A108 30c multi | .50 | .50 |
| *b.* | A108 50c multi | .80 | .80 |
| *c.* | A108 90c multi | 1.40 | 1.40 |
| *d.* | A108 $2 multi | 3.25 | 3.25 |
| *e.* | Souvenir sheet of 4, #503a-503d | 6.00 | 6.00 |

Beatification of Pope John Paul II — A109

No. 504: a, $1.20, Pope Benedict XVI. b, $5, Pope John Paul II.

**2012, Jan. 10 *Perf. 13¾***
**504** A109 Horiz. pair, #a-b 10.50 10.50

Christ Taking Leave of His Mother, by Correggio A110

Deposition, by Correggio A111

The Martyrdom of Four Saints, by Correggio A112

Mystic Marriage of St. Catherine and St. Sebastian, by Correggio A113

Nativity, by Correggio, c. 1510 A114

The Nativity of Christ, by Correggio, c. 1529-30 A115

***Perf. 14¾x14¼***
**2012, Nov. 16 Litho.**

### Stamps With White Frames

| | | | |
|---|---|---|---|
| **505** | Horiz. pair | 2.80 | 2.80 |
| *a.* | A110 80c multi | 1.40 | 1.40 |
| *b.* | A111 80c multi | 1.40 | 1.40 |
| **506** | Horiz. pair | 3.00 | 3.00 |
| *a.* | A112 90c multi | 1.50 | 1.50 |
| *b.* | A113 90c multi | 1.50 | 1.50 |
| **507** | Horiz. pair | 10.00 | 10.00 |
| *a.* | A114 $3 multi | 5.00 | 5.00 |
| *b.* | A115 $3 multi | 5.00 | 5.00 |
| | *Nos. 505-507 (3)* | 15.80 | 15.80 |

### Miniature Sheet
### Stamps With Colored Frames

| | | | |
|---|---|---|---|
| **508** | Sheet of 6 | 16.00 | 16.00 |
| *a.* | A110 80c multi | 1.40 | 1.40 |
| *b.* | A111 80c multi | 1.40 | 1.40 |
| *c.* | A112 90c multi | 1.50 | 1.50 |
| *d.* | A113 90c multi | 1.50 | 1.50 |
| *e.* | A114 $3 multi | 5.00 | 5.00 |
| *f.* | A115 $3 multi | 5.00 | 5.00 |

Fish — A116

Nos. 509 and 512: a, 80c, Myripristis hexagonia. b, 90c, Scarus psittacus. c, $1.10, Zanclus cornutus. d, $1.20, Acanthurus guttatus.

Nos. 510 and 513: a, $2, Pygoplites diacanthus. b, $2.25, Chaetodon flavirostris. c, $4, Pseudanthias pleurotaenia. d, $5, Chaetodon ornatissimus.

Nos. 511 and 514: a, $6, Chaetodon melanotus. b, $8, Gymnothorax rueppellii. c, $10, Synchiropus ocellatus. d, $20, Kyphosus sandwichensis.

**2012, Nov. 27 Litho. *Perf. 14***

### Stamps With White Frames

| | | | | |
|---|---|---|---|---|
| **509** | A116 | Block of 4, #a-d | 6.75 | 6.75 |
| **510** | A116 | Block of 4, #a-d | 22.00 | 22.00 |
| **511** | A116 | Block of 4, #a-d | 72.50 | 72.50 |
| | | *Nos. 509-511 (3)* | 101.25 | 101.25 |

### Stamps Without White Frames

| | | | | |
|---|---|---|---|---|
| **512** | A116 | Sheet of 4, #a-d | 6.75 | 6.75 |
| **513** | A116 | Sheet of 4, #a-d | 22.00 | 22.00 |
| **514** | A116 | Sheet of 4, #a-d | 72.50 | 72.50 |
| *e.* | | Sheet of 12, #512a-512d, 513a-513d, 514a-514d | 102.00 | 102.00 |
| | | *Nos. 512-514 (3)* | 101.25 | 101.25 |

Personalizable Stamp — A117

**2012, Dec. 21 Litho. *Perf. 14x14¾***
**515** A117 $4 multi 6.75 6.75

### Miniature Sheet

New Year 2013 (Year of the Snake) — A118

No. 516 — Various snakes with background color of: a, Blue. b, Bright rose. c, Green. d, Yellow.

***Perf. 14¾x14¼***
**2013, Feb. 21 Litho.**
**516** A118 $1.20 Sheet of 4, #a-d 8.00 8.00

### Souvenir Sheet

Duchess of Cambridge — A119

No. 517 — Various photographs of pregnant Duchess of Cambridge: a, $1.30. b, $1.50. c, $1.70.

**2013, Aug. 1 Litho. *Perf. 13¾x13½***
**517** A119 Sheet of 3, #a-c 7.25 7.25

Birth of Prince George of Cambridge.

Souvenir Sheet

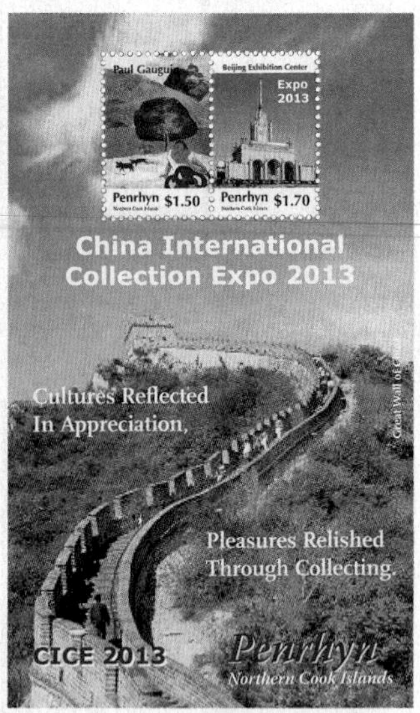


China International Collection Expo 2013, Beijing — A120

No. 518: a, $1.50, Painting by Paul Gauguin. b, $1.70, Beijing Exhibition Center.

**2013, Sept. 26 Litho. *Perf. 12***

**518** A120 Sheet of 2, #a-b 5.50 5.50

Pres. John F. Kennedy (1917-63) A121

Designs: $2, Photograph of Kennedy. $3, Photograph of Kennedy and crowd, quote from Kennedy.

**2013, Nov. 8 Litho. *Perf. 14x14¼***

**519-520** A121 Set of 2 8.25 8.25

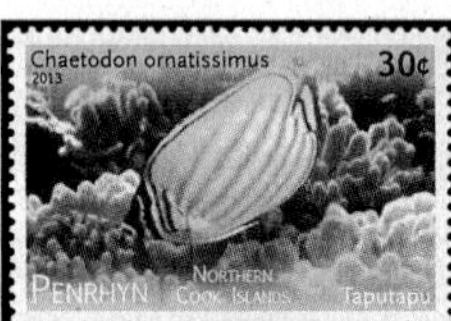


Fish A122

Designs: 30c, Chaetodon ornatissimus. 50c, Kyphosus pacificus. $1, Acanthurus guttatus. $1.30, Chaetodon flavirostris. $1.50, Myripristis murdjan. $1.70, Pygoplites diacanthus. $2.40, Zanclus cornutus. $2.50, Scarus psittacus. $3, Rhinomuraena quaesita. $4.50, Synchiropus ocellatus. $7.50, Gymnothorax rueppelliae. $12.90, Hoplolatilus starcki.

**2013, Nov. 11 Litho. *Perf. 14***

**Stamps With White Frames**

| | | | | |
|---|---|---|---|---|
| **521** | A122 | 30c multi | .50 | .50 |
| **522** | A122 | 50c multi | .85 | .85 |
| **523** | A122 | $1 multi | 1.75 | 1.75 |
| **524** | A122 | $1.30 multi | 2.25 | 2.25 |
| **525** | A122 | $1.50 multi | 2.50 | 2.50 |
| **526** | A122 | $1.70 multi | 2.75 | 2.75 |
| **527** | A122 | $2.40 multi | 4.00 | 4.00 |
| **528** | A122 | $2.50 multi | 4.25 | 4.25 |
| **529** | A122 | $3 multi | 5.00 | 5.00 |
| **530** | A122 | $4.50 multi | 7.50 | 7.50 |
| **531** | A122 | $7.50 multi | 12.50 | 12.50 |
| **532** | A122 | $12.90 multi | 21.50 | 21.50 |
| | | *Nos. 521-532 (12)* | 65.35 | 65.35 |

**Stamps Without White Frames**

| | | | |
|---|---|---|---|
| **533** | Sheet of 12 | 66.00 | 66.00 |
| *a.* | A122 30c multi | .50 | .50 |
| *b.* | A122 50c multi | .85 | .85 |
| *c.* | A122 $1 multi | 1.75 | 1.75 |
| *d.* | A122 $1.30 multi | 2.25 | 2.25 |
| *e.* | A122 $1.50 multi | 2.50 | 2.50 |
| *f.* | A122 $1.70 multi | 2.75 | 2.75 |
| *g.* | A122 $2.40 multi | 4.00 | 4.00 |
| *h.* | A122 $2.50 multi | 4.25 | 4.25 |
| *i.* | A122 $3 multi | 5.00 | 5.00 |
| *j.* | A122 $4.50 multi | 7.50 | 7.50 |
| *k.* | A122 $7.50 multi | 12.50 | 12.50 |
| *l.* | A122 $12.90 multi | 21.50 | 21.50 |

Christmas — A123

Paintings by: $1, Peter Paul Rubens. $1.30, Albrecht Dürer.

No. 536 — Paintings by: a, $2, Sandro Botticelli. b, $2.40, William Brassey Hole. c, $2.60, Gerard van Honthorst.

**2013, Nov. 18 Litho. *Perf. 13¼***

**534-535** A123 Set of 2 3.75 3.75

**Souvenir Sheet**

**536** A123 Sheet of 3, #a-c 11.50 11.50

Miniature Sheet

New Year 2014 (Year of the Horse) — A124

No. 537 — Background color: a, $1, Yellow. b, $1.30, Red. c, $1.50, Blue. d, $1.70, Green.

**2014, Jan. 10 Litho. *Perf. 13¾***

**537** A124 Sheet of 4, #a-d 9.00 9.00

Easter — A125

No. 538 — Religious paintings by: a, 50c, Peter Paul Rubens. b, $1, Lambert Lombard. c, $1.30, Titian. d, $1.50, Paolo Veronese. e, $1.70, Raphael.

$9.50, Painting by Dirck Bouts.

**2014, Apr. 9 Litho. *Perf. 13¼***

**538** A125 Sheet of 5, #a-e, + label 10.50 10.50

**Souvenir Sheet**

**539** A125 $9.50 multi 16.50 16.50

Worldwide Fund for Nature (WWF) A126

Pacific green turtle: Nos. 540, 544a, $1, On beach. Nos. 541, 544b, $1.70, Swimming. Nos. 542, 544c, $2, Swimming, diff. Nos. 543, 544d, $2.40, Pair on seafloor.

$7.50, Turtle swimming, diff.

***Perf. 14¾x14¼***

**2014, Nov. 28 Litho.**

**Stamps With White Frames**

**540-543** A126 Set of 4 11.00 11.00

**Stamps Without White Frames**

**544** A126 Strip of 4, #a-d 11.00 11.00

**Souvenir Sheet**

**545** A126 $7.50 multi 12.00 12.00

Souvenir Sheet

Christmas — A127

No. 546 — Religious paintings by: a, Antonio da Correggio. b, Piero della Francesca. c, Sandro Botticelli.

***Perf. 14¾x14¼***

**2014, Dec. 14 Litho.**

**546** A127 $1.50 Sheet of 3, #a-c 7.00 7.00

Souvenir Sheet

New Year 2015 (Year of the Sheep) — A128

No. 547: a, $3.80, Red sheep. b, $4.10, Green sheep.

**2015, Jan. 5 Litho. *Perf. 13½***

**547** A128 Sheet of 2, #a-b 11.50 11.50

Miniature Sheet

Easter — A129

No. 548 — Details from religious paintings by: a, Peter Paul Rubens. b, Edouard Manet. c, Carl Heinrich Bloch. d, Jacopo Tintoretto.

**2015, Mar. 31 Litho. *Perf. 14***

**548** A129 $2 Sheet of 4, #a-d 12.50 12.50

Souvenir Sheet

Birth of Princess Charlotte of Cambridge — A130

No. 549: a, Duke and Duchess of Cambridge, Princess Charlotte. b, Duke of Cambridge holding Prince George.

***Perf. 14¾x14¼***

**2015, June 23 Litho.**

**549** A130 $4.50 Sheet of 2, #a-b 12.00 12.00

New Year 2016 (Year of the Monkey) A131

Monkey with: $2.60, Both arms raised. $3, One arm raised.

No. 552 — Monkey with: a, $3.80, Both arms raised. b, $4.10, One arm raised.

**2015, Sept. 25 Litho. *Perf. 13¼***

**550-551** A131 Set of 2 7.25 7.25

**Souvenir Sheet**

**552** A131 Sheet of 2, #a-b 10.50 10.50

No. 552 contains two 50x50mm diamond-shaped stamps.

Miniature Sheet

Queen Elizabeth II, Longest-Reigning British Monarch — A132

No. 553 — Various photographs of Queen Elizabeth II: a, $1.30. b, $1.50. c, $1.70. d, $2.

**2015, Nov. 20 Litho. *Perf. 14***

**553** A132 Sheet of 4, #a-d 8.75 8.75

Souvenir Sheet

Christmas — A133

No. 554 — Nativity, by Gerard David (details): a, Virgin Mary. b, Infant Jesus and animals. c, St. Joseph.

**2015, Dec. 9 Litho. *Perf. 13¼***

**554** A133 $1 Sheet of 3, #a-c 4.25 4.25

Souvenir Sheet

Queen Elizabeth II, 90th Birthday — A134

No. 555 — Queen Elizabeth II wearing: a, Gown. b, Hat and coat.

**2016, May 10 Litho. *Perf. 13¼***
**555** A134 $3 Sheet of 2, #a-b 8.25 8.25

Marae Moana Marine Park — A135

Designs: 30c, Blue whale. 50c, Brown booby. 80c, Gray reef shark. $1, Emblem of Marae Moana Marine Park. $1.10, Humphead wrasse. $1.30, Scalloped hammerhead shark. $1.50, Hawksbill turtle. $1.70 False killer whale. $2, Brown noddy. $2.40, Blue shark. $2.50, Shortfin mako shark.

**2016, May 27 Litho. *Perf. 14x14¾***

| | | | | |
|---|---|---|---|---|
| **556** | A135 | 30c multi | .40 | .40 |
| **557** | A135 | 50c multi | .70 | .70 |
| **558** | A135 | 80c multi | 1.10 | 1.10 |
| **559** | A135 | $1 multi | 1.40 | 1.40 |
| **560** | A135 | $1.10 multi | 1.50 | 1.50 |
| **561** | A135 | $1.30 multi | 1.75 | 1.75 |
| **562** | A135 | $1.50 multi | 2.10 | 2.10 |
| **563** | A135 | $1.70 multi | 2.40 | 2.40 |
| **564** | A135 | $2 multi | 2.75 | 2.75 |
| **565** | A135 | $2.40 multi | 3.25 | 3.25 |
| **566** | A135 | $2.50 multi | 3.50 | 3.50 |
| | | *Nos. 556-566 (11)* | 20.85 | 20.85 |

New Year 2017 (Year of the Rooster) A136

Rooster facing: $2.30, Right. $4.50, Left.

**2016, Aug. 10 Litho. *Perf. 13¼***
**567-568** A136 Set of 2 10.00 10.00
*568a* Souvenir sheet of 2, #567-568 10.00 10.00

Christmas — A137

No. 569 — Stained-glass windows depicting: a, 50c, Madonna and Child, farm animals. b, 50c, Madonna and Child. c, $1, Madonna and Child. d, $1, Nativity with farm animals.

**2016, Dec. 19 Litho. *Perf. 13¼***
**569** A137 Block of 4, #a-d 4.25 4.25

Miniature Sheet

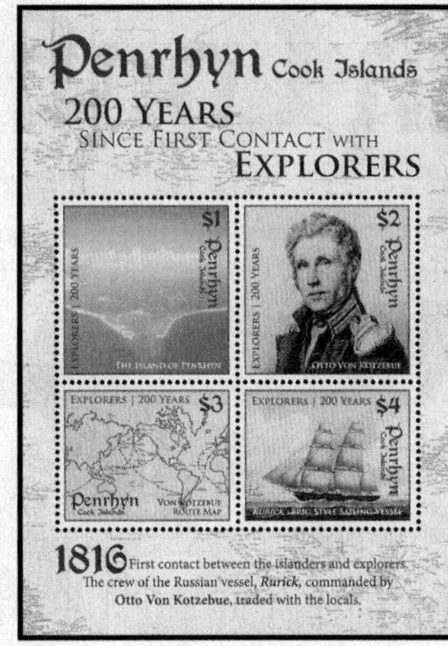

First Contact of Explorers with Penrhyn Islanders, 200th Anniv. — A138

No. 570: a, $1, Aerial view of Penrhyn Island (36x36mm). b, $2, Otto von Kotzebue (1787-1846), explorer (36x36mm). c, $3, Map of Kotzebue's route (36x29mm). d, $4, Kotzebue's ship, Rurick (36x29mm).

**2016, Dec. 28 Litho. *Perf. 13¼***
**570** A138 Sheet of 4, #a-d 14.00 14.00

Miniature Sheet

Easter — A139

No. 571 — Paintings of the Resurrection of Jesus by: a, Caravaggio. b, Mikhail Vasilyevich Nesterov. c, Rembrandt. d, Tintoretto.

**2017, Apr. 12 Litho. *Perf. 13***
**571** A139 $1 Sheet of 4, #a-d 5.50 5.50

Miniature Sheet

Pres. John F. Kennedy (1917-63) — A140

No. 572: a, $1, Pres. Kennedy and wife, Jacqueline at ceremony awarding medal to Alan B. Shepard, Jr. b, $1, Pres. Kennedy giving address at Rice University. c, $2.50, Nuclear weapon test on Bikini Atoll and radioactivity symbol. d, $2.50, Pres. Kennedy speaking after signing Nuclear Test Ban Treaty.

**2017, July 3 Litho. *Perf. 13***
**572** A140 Sheet of 4, #a-d 10.50 10.50

Miniature Sheet

Reign of Queen Elizabeth II, 65th Anniv. — A141

No. 573 — Queen Elizabeth II: a, Wearing coat with fur collar. b, Wearing tiara. c, Wearing maroon hat. d, Standing with military officer.

**2017, July 17 Litho. *Perf. 13***
**573** A141 $2.50 Sheet of 4, #a-d 15.00 15.00

New Year 2018 (Year of the Dog) — A142

Dog facing: $3, Right. $3.80, Left.

**2017, Nov. 1 Litho. *Perf. 13¼***
**574-575** A142 Set of 2 9.50 9.50
*575a* Souvenir sheet of 2, #574-575 9.50 9.50

Worldwide Fund for Nature (WWF) A143

Photographs of Bennett's butterflyfish: Nos. 576, 580a, $1, With three other fish. Nos. 577, 580b, $1.70, Nose facing UL corner. Nos. 578, 580c, $2, Nose facing LR corner. Nos. 579, 580d, $2.40, facing left.

**2017, Nov. 6 Litho. *Perf. 13x13¼***

**Stamps With White Frames**

**576-579** A143 Set of 4 9.75 9.75

**Stamps Without White Frames**

**580** A143 Block or horiz. strip of 4, #a-d 9.75 9.75

No. 580 was printed in sheets containing two each of Nos. 580a-580d.

Christmas — A144

No. 581: a, $1, Seahorse. b, $1, Sailboat. c, $2.40, Bird. d, $2.40, Shell.

**2017, Dec. 5 Litho. *Perf. 12½***
**581** A144 Block of 4, #a-d 9.75 9.75

## SEMI-POSTAL STAMPS

**Catalogue values for unused stamps in this section are for Never Hinged items.**

### Easter Type of 1978
Souvenir Sheets

Rubens Paintings: No. B1, like #101. No. B2, like #102. No. B3, like #103.

**1978, Apr. 17 Photo. *Perf. 13½x13***

| | | | | |
|---|---|---|---|---|
| **B1** | A31 | 60c + 5c multi | .50 | .50 |
| **B2** | A31 | 60c + 5c multi | .50 | .50 |
| **B3** | A31 | 60c + 5c multi | .50 | .50 |
| | | *Nos. B1-B3 (3)* | 1.50 | 1.50 |

Surtax was for school children.

### Easter Type of 1980
Souvenir Sheets

**1980, Mar. 28 Photo. *Perf. 13x13½***

| | | | | |
|---|---|---|---|---|
| **B4** | A36 | 70c + 5c like #114 | .45 | .45 |
| **B5** | A36 | 70c + 5c like #115 | .45 | .45 |
| **B6** | A36 | 70c + 5c like #116 | .45 | .45 |
| | | *Nos. B4-B6 (3)* | 1.35 | 1.35 |

Surtax was for local charities.

### Christmas Type of 1980
Souvenir Sheets

**1980, Dec. 5 Photo. *Perf. 13***

| | | | | |
|---|---|---|---|---|
| **B7** | A39 | 70c + 5c like #127 | 1.00 | 1.00 |
| **B8** | A39 | 70c + 5c like #128 | 1.00 | 1.00 |
| **B9** | A39 | 70c + 5c like #129 | 1.00 | 1.00 |
| | | *Nos. B7-B9 (3)* | 3.00 | 3.00 |

Surtax was for local charities.

### Easter Type of 1981
Souvenir Sheets

**1981, Apr. 5 Photo. *Perf. 13½***

| | | | | |
|---|---|---|---|---|
| **B10** | A44 | 70c + 5c like #173 | 1.00 | 1.00 |
| **B11** | A44 | 70c + 5c like #174 | 1.00 | 1.00 |
| **B12** | A44 | 70c + 5c like #175 | 1.00 | 1.00 |
| | | *Nos. B10-B12 (3)* | 3.00 | 3.00 |

Surtax was for local charities.

### Nos. 176-180a Surcharged

**1981, Nov. 30 Photo. *Perf. 14***

| | | | | |
|---|---|---|---|---|
| **B13** | A45 | 40c + 5c like #176 | .25 | .25 |
| **B14** | A45 | 50c + 5c like #177 | .25 | .25 |
| **B15** | A45 | 60c + 5c like #178 | .25 | .25 |
| **B16** | A45 | 70c + 5c like #179 | .30 | .30 |
| **B17** | A45 | 80c + 5c like #180 | .30 | .30 |
| | | *Nos. B13-B17 (5)* | 1.35 | 1.35 |

**Souvenir Sheet**

| | | | | |
|---|---|---|---|---|
| **B18** | | Sheet of 5 | 1.50 | 1.50 |
| *a.* | A45 | 40c + 10c like #176 | .25 | .25 |
| *b.* | A45 | 50c + 10c like #177 | .25 | .25 |
| *c.* | A45 | 60c + 10c like #178 | .25 | .25 |
| *d.* | A45 | 70c + 10c like #179 | .25 | .25 |
| *e.* | A45 | 80c + 10c like #180 | .25 | .25 |

Intl. Year of the Disabled. Surtax was for the disabled.

### Soccer Type of 1981

**1981, Dec. 7 *Perf. 13***
**B19** A46 Sheet of 9 5.75 4.75

No. B19 contains Nos. 181-183. Surtax was for local sports.

### Nos. 346-349 Surcharged ".SOUTH PACIFIC PAPAL VISIT . 21 TO 24 NOVEMBER 1986" in Metallic Blue

**1986, Nov. 24 Litho. *Perf. 13x13½***

| | | | | |
|---|---|---|---|---|
| **B20** | A67 | 65c + 10c multi | 4.50 | 4.50 |
| **B21** | A67 | $1.75 + 10c multi | 6.50 | 6.50 |
| **B22** | A67 | $2.50 + 10c multi | 8.00 | 8.00 |
| | | *Nos. B20-B22 (3)* | 19.00 | 19.00 |

**Souvenir Sheet**

***Perf. 13½x13***

| | | | | |
|---|---|---|---|---|
| **B23** | | Sheet of 3 | 23.00 | 23.00 |
| *a.-c.* | A67 | $1.50 + 10c on #349a-349c | 7.00 | 7.00 |

No. B23 inscribed "COMMEMORATING FIRST PAPAL VISIT TO SOUTH PACIFIC / VISIT OF POPE JOHN PAUL II . NOVEMBER 1986."

**No. 454 Surcharged "CHILDREN'S CHARITIES" in Silver**
Souvenir Sheet

| **1998, Nov. 19** | **Litho.** | ***Perf. 14*** | | |
|---|---|---|---|---|
| **B24** | A93 $3.75 +$1 multi | | 6.00 | 6.00 |

**OFFICIAL STAMPS**

**Catalogue values for unused stamps in this section are for Never Hinged items.**

**Nos. 51-60, 80, 88-89 Overprinted or Surcharged in Black, Silver or Gold**

***Perf. 13½x14, 13½, 13½x13***

| **1978, Nov. 14** | | | **Photo.** | |
|---|---|---|---|---|
| **O1** | A17 | 1c multi | .25 | .25 |
| **O2** | A17 | 2c multi | .25 | .25 |
| **O3** | A17 | 3c multi | .30 | .25 |
| **O4** | A17 | 4c multi | .30 | .25 |
| **O5** | A17 | 5c multi | .40 | .25 |
| **O6** | A17 | 8c multi | .45 | .25 |
| **O7** | A17 | 10c multi | .50 | .25 |
| **O8** | A17 | 15c on 60c multi | .55 | .35 |
| **O9** | A17 | 18c on 60c multi | .60 | .35 |
| **O10** | A17 | 20c multi | .60 | .35 |
| **O11** | A17 | 25c multi (S) | .65 | .40 |
| **O12** | A17 | 30c on 60c multi | .70 | .60 |
| **O13** | A24 | Strip of 3, multi | 4.25 | 2.75 |
| *a.* | | 50c, No. 80a (G) | 1.25 | .80 |
| *b.* | | 50c, No. 80b (G) | 1.25 | .80 |
| *c.* | | 50c, No. 80c (G) | 1.25 | .80 |
| **O14** | A27 | $1 multi (S) | 2.75 | .65 |
| **O15** | A27 | $2 multi (G) | 5.25 | .70 |
| | | *Nos. O1-O15 (15)* | 17.80 | 7.90 |

Overprint on No. O14 diagonal.

**Nos. 268-276, 278, 277, 211-214, 280, 282, 281, 283, 170, 284, 171, 285, 172, 286 Surcharged with Bar and New Value or Ovptd. "O.H.M.S." in Silver or Metallic Red**

| **1985-87** | **Photo.** | ***Perfs. as before*** | | |
|---|---|---|---|---|
| **O16** | A56 | 2c multi | .25 | .25 |
| **O17** | A56 | 4c multi | .25 | .25 |
| **O18** | A56 | 5c multi | .25 | .25 |
| **O19** | A56 | 8c multi | .25 | .25 |
| **O20** | A56 | 10c multi | .25 | .25 |
| **O21** | A56 | 18c multi | .25 | .25 |
| **O22** | A56 | 20c multi | .25 | .25 |
| **O23** | A56 | 30c multi | .25 | .25 |
| **O24** | A56 | 40c on 36c | .35 | .35 |
| **O25** | A56 | 50c multi | .40 | .40 |
| **O26** | A56 | 55c on 48c | .45 | .45 |
| **O27** | A50 | 65c on 60c #211a | .55 | .55 |
| **O28** | A50 | 65c on 60c #211b | .55 | .55 |
| **O29** | A50 | 65c on 60c #211c | .55 | .55 |
| **O30** | A50 | 65c on 60c #211d | .55 | .55 |
| **O31** | A56 | 75c on 72c | 1.05 | .65 |
| **O32** | A56 | 75c on 96c | 1.05 | .65 |
| **O33** | A56 | 80c multi | 1.05 | .65 |
| **O34** | A56 | $1.20 multi | 1.25 | .85 |
| **O35** | A42 | $2 multi (R) | 1.75 | 1.25 |
| **O36** | A56 | $3 multi | 3.50 | 2.10 |
| **O37** | A42 | $4 multi (R) | 4.00 | 3.50 |
| **O38** | A56 | $5 multi | 6.50 | 4.00 |
| **O39** | A42 | $6 multi (R) | 9.25 | 6.50 |
| **O40** | A56 | $9.60 multi | 12.00 | 10.00 |
| | | *Nos. O16-O40 (25)* | 46.80 | 35.55 |

Issued: #O16-O30, 8/15; #O31-O37, 4/29/86; #O38-O40, 11/2/87.

**Nos. 420-432 Ovptd. "O.H.M.S." in Silver**

| **1998** | **Litho.** | ***Perf. 14*** | | |
|---|---|---|---|---|
| **O41** | A82 | 5c multicolored | .30 | .30 |
| **O42** | A82 | 10c multicolored | .30 | .30 |
| **O43** | A82 | 15c multicolored | .30 | .30 |
| **O44** | A82 | 20c multicolored | .30 | .30 |
| **O45** | A82 | 25c multicolored | .30 | .30 |
| **O46** | A82 | 30c multicolored | .40 | .40 |
| **O47** | A82 | 50c multicolored | .55 | .55 |
| **O48** | A82 | 70c multicolored | .70 | .70 |
| **O49** | A82 | 80c multicolored | .95 | .95 |
| **O50** | A82 | 85c multicolored | 1.10 | 1.10 |
| **O51** | A82 | 90c multicolored | 1.20 | 1.20 |
| **O52** | A82 | $1 multicolored | 1.30 | 1.30 |
| **O53** | A82 | $2 multicolored | 4.00 | 4.00 |
| | | *Nos. O41-O53 (13)* | 11.70 | 11.70 |

Nos. O41-O52 were not sold unused to local customers.
Issued: $2, 9/30; others, 7/20.

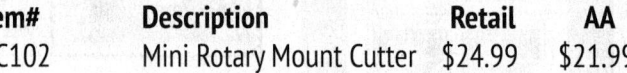

# PERU

pə-'rü

LOCATION — West coast of South America
GOVT. — Republic
AREA — 496,093 sq. mi.
POP. — 24,800,768 (1998 est.)
CAPITAL — Lima

8 Reales = 1 Peso (1857)
100 Centimos = 8 Dineros = 4 Pesetas = 1 Peso (1858)
100 Centavos = 1 Sol (1874)
100 Centimos = 1 Inti (1985)
100 Centimos = 1 Sol (1991)

**Catalogue values for unused stamps in this country are for Never Hinged items, beginning with Scott 426 in the regular postage section, Scott B1 in the semi-postal section, Scott C78 in the airpost section, Scott CB1 in the airpost semi-postal section, and Scott RA31 in the postal tax section.**

**Watermark**

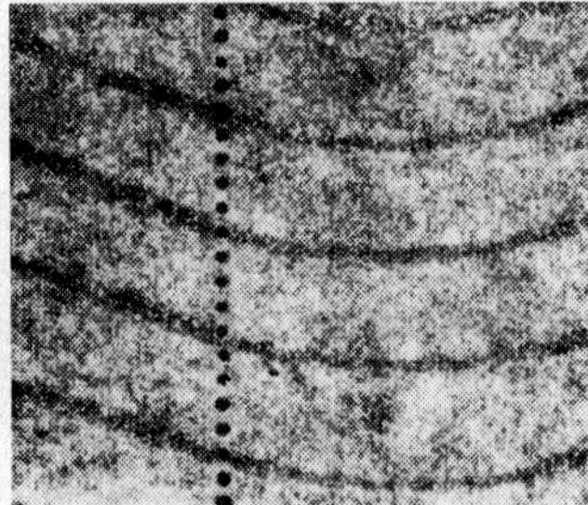

Wmk. 346 — Parallel Curved Lines

**ISSUES OF THE REPUBLIC**

Sail and Steamship — A1

Design: 2r, Ship sails eastward.

**Unwmk.**

**1857, Dec. 1 — Engr. — *Imperf.***

1 A1 1r blue, *blue* 1,700. 2,250.
2 A1 2r brn red, *blue* 1,900. 3,000.

The Pacific Steam Navigation Co. gave a quantity of these stamps to the Peruvian government so that a trial of prepayment of postage by stamps might be made.

Stamps of 1 and 2 reales, printed in various colors on white paper, laid and wove, were prepared for the Pacific Steam Navigation Co. but never put in use. Value $50 each on wove paper, $400 each on laid paper.

Coat of Arms
A2 A3

A4

**Wavy Lines in Spandrels**

**1858, Mar. 1 — Litho.**

3 A2 1d deep blue 275.00 47.50
4 A3 1p rose red 1,100. 160.00
5 A4 ½ peso rose red *6,500.* *4,750.*
6 A4 ½ peso buff *2,750.* 375.00
*a.* ½ peso orange yellow *2,750.* 375.00

A5 A6

**Large Letters**

**1858, Dec. — Double-lined Frame**

7 A5 1d slate blue 450.00 45.00
8 A6 1p red 450.00 65.00

A7 A8

**1860-61**

**Zigzag Lines in Spandrels**

9 A7 1d blue 175.00 10.50
*a.* 1d Prussian blue 175.00 20.00
*b.* Cornucopia on white ground 375.00 80.00
*c.* Zigzag lines broken at angles 225.00 22.50
10 A8 1p rose 450.00 42.50
*a.* 1p brick red 450.00 42.50
*b.* Cornucopia on white ground 450.00 42.50

**Retouched, 10 lines instead of 9 in left label**

11 A8 1p rose 250.00 27.50
*a.* Pelure paper 425.00 32.50
*Nos. 9-11 (3)* 875.00 80.50

A9 A10

**1862-63 — Embossed**

12 A9 1d red 14.50 4.50
*a.* Arms embossed sideways 550.00 150.00
*b.* Thick paper 120.00 37.50
*c.* Diag. half used on cover 350.00
13 A10 1p brown ('63) 120.00 37.50
*a.* Diag. half used on cover 1,000.

Counterfeits of Nos. 13 and 15 exist.

A11

**1868-72**

14 A11 1d green 19.00 3.75
*a.* Arms embossed inverted *2,250.* *1,200.*
*b.* Diag. half used on cover *2,000.*
15 A10 1p orange ('72) 150.00 55.00
*a.* Diag. half used on cover *1,100.*

Nos. 12-15, 19 and 20 were printed in horizontal strips. Stamps may be found printed on two strips of paper where the strips were joined by overlapping.

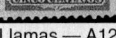

Llamas — A12 A13

A14

**1866-67 — Engr. — *Perf. 12***

16 A12 5c green 10.50 .95
17 A13 10c vermilion 15.00 2.25
18 A14 20c brown 40.00 7.00
*a.* Diagonal half used on cover 675.00
*Nos. 16-18 (3)* 65.50 10.20

See Nos. 109, 111, 113.

Locomotive and Arms — A15

**1871, Apr. — Embossed — *Imperf.***

19 A15 5c scarlet 125.00 42.50
*a.* 5c pale red 125.00 42.50

20th anniv. of the first railway in South America, linking Lima and Callao.

The so-called varieties "ALLAO" and "CALLA" are due to over-inking.

Llama — A16

**1873, Mar. — *Rouletted Horiz.***

20 A16 2c dk ultra 50.00 *325.00*

Counterfeits are plentiful.

Sun God of the Incas — A17

Coat of Arms
A18 A19

A20 A21

A22 A23

**Embossed with Grill**

**1874-84 — Engr. — *Perf. 12***

21 A17 1c orange ('79) .90 .65
22 A18 2c dk violet 1.25 .95
23 A19 5c blue ('77) 1.40 .45
24 A19 5c ultra ('79) 13.00 3.25
25 A20 10c green ('76) .45 .30
*a.* Imperf., pair 35.00
26 A20 10c slate ('84) 2.00 .45
*a.* Diag. half used as 5c on cover —
27 A21 20c brown red 3.50 1.10
28 A22 50c green 15.00 4.25
29 A23 1s rose 2.40 2.40
*Nos. 21-29 (9)* 39.90 13.80

No. 25a lacks the grill.

No. 26 with overprint "DE OFICIO" is said to have been used to frank mail of Gen. A. A. Caceres during the civil war against Gen. Miguel Iglesias, provisional president. Experts question its status.

**1880**

30 A17 1c green 2.50
31 A18 2c rose 2.50

Nos. 30 and 31 were prepared for use but not issued without overprint.

See Nos. 104-108, 110, 112, 114-115.

For overprints see Nos. 32-103, 116-128, J32-J33, O2-O22, N11-N23, 1N1-1N9, 3N11-3N20, 5N1, 6N1-6N2, 7N1-7N2, 8N7, 8N10-8N11, 9N1-9N3, 10N3-10N8, 10N10-10N11, 11N1-11N5, 12N1-12N3, 13N1, 14N1-14N16, 15N5-15N8, 15N13-15N18, 16N1-16N22.

Stamps of 1874-80 Overprinted in Red, Blue or Black

**1880, Jan. 5**

32 A17 1c green (R) .90 .65
*a.* Inverted overprint 10.00 10.00
*b.* Double overprint 13.50 13.50
33 A18 2c rose (Bl) 1.75 1.10
*a.* Inverted overprint 10.00 10.00
*b.* Double overprint 14.00 12.00
34 A18 2c rose (Bk) 75.00 60.00
*a.* Inverted overprint
*b.* Double overprint
35 A19 5c ultra (R) 3.50 1.75
*a.* Inverted overprint 10.00 10.00
*b.* Double overprint 14.00 14.00
36 A22 50c green (R) 45.00 27.50
*a.* Inverted overprint 45.00 45.00
*b.* Double overprint 55.00 55.00
37 A23 1s rose (Bl) 70.00 50.00
*a.* Inverted overprint 110.00 110.00
*b.* Double overprint 110.00 110.00
*Nos. 32-37 (6)* 196.15 141.00

Stamps of 1874-80 Overprinted in Red or Blue

**1881, Jan. 28**

38 A17 1c green (R) 1.25 .95
*a.* Inverted overprint 8.25 8.25
*b.* Double overprint 14.00 14.00
39 A18 2c rose (Bl) 24.00 15.00
*a.* Inverted overprint 17.50 15.00
*b.* Double overprint 25.00 20.00
40 A19 5c ultra (R) 2.75 1.25
*a.* Inverted overprint 14.00 14.00
*b.* Double overprint 20.00 20.00
41 A22 50c green (R) 750.00 425.00
*a.* Inverted overprint 850.00
42 A23 1s rose (Bl) 140.00 90.00
*a.* Inverted overprint 175.00

*Reprints of Nos. 38 to 42 were made in 1884. In the overprint the word "PLATA" is 3mm high instead of 2½mm. The cross bars of the letters "A" of that word are set higher than on the original stamps. The 5c is printed in blue instead of ultramarine.*

For stamps of 1874-80 overprinted with Chilean arms or small UPU "horseshoe," see Nos. N11-N23.

Stamps of 1874-79 Handstamped in Black or Blue

**1883**

65 A17 1c orange (Bk) 1.25 1.10
66 A17 1c orange (Bl) 50.00 50.00
68 A19 5c ultra (Bk) 13.00 7.00
69 A20 10c green (Bk) 1.25 1.10
70 A20 10c green (Bl) 5.00 4.00
71 A22 50c green (Bk) 7.00 4.25
73 A23 1s rose (Bk) 10.00 8.00
*Nos. 65-73 (7)* 87.50 75.45
*Nos. 65,68-73 (6)* 37.50 25.45

This overprint is found in 11 types.

The 1c green, 2c dark violet and 20c brown red, overprinted with triangle, are fancy varieties made for sale to collectors and never placed in regular use.

### Overprinted Triangle and "Union Postal Universal Peru" in Oval

**1883**

**77** A22 50c grn (R & Bk) 210.00 110.00
**78** A23 1s rose (Bl & Bk) 250.00 160.00

The 1c green, 2c rose and 5c ultramarine, over printed with triangle and "U. P. U. Peru" oval, were never placed in regular use.

### Overprinted Triangle and "Union Postal Universal Lima" in Oval

**1883**

**79** A17 1c grn (R & Bl) 70.00 70.00
**80** A17 1c grn (R & Bk) 7.00 7.00
*a.* Oval overprint inverted
*b.* Double overprint of oval
**81** A18 2c rose (Bl & Bk) 7.00 7.00
**82** A19 5c ultra (R & Bk) 11.00 10.00
**83** A19 5c ultra (R & Bl) 17.00 10.00
**84** A22 50c grn (R & Bk) 250.00 150.00
**85** A23 1s rose (Bl & Bk) 275.00 275.00
*Nos. 79-85 (7)* 637.00 529.00

Some authorities question the status of No. 79.

*Nos. 80, 81, 84, and 85 were reprinted in 1884. They have the second type of oval overprint with "PLATA" 3mm high.*

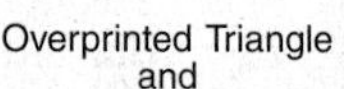

Overprinted Triangle and

**86** A17 1c grn (Bk & Bk) 1.75 1.25
*a.* Horseshoe inverted 10.00
**87** A17 1c grn (Bl & Bk) 5.00 3.50
**88** A18 2c ver (Bk & Bk) 1.75 1.25
**89** A19 5c bl (Bk & Bk) 2.25 1.60
**90** A19 5c bl (Bl & Bk) 12.00 10.50
**91** A19 5c bl (R & Bk) *1,500. 1,100.*

### Overprinted Horseshoe Alone

**1883, Oct. 23**

**95** A17 1c green 2.25 2.25
**96** A18 2c vermilion 2.25 *6.50*
*a.* Double overprint
**97** A19 5c blue 3.50 3.50
**98** A19 5c ultra 20.00 15.00
**99** A22 50c rose 57.50 57.50
**100** A23 1s ultra 55.00 22.50
*Nos. 95-100 (6)* 140.50 107.25

The 2c dark violet overprinted with the above design in red and triangle in black also the 1c green overprinted with the same combination plus the horseshoe in black, are fancy varieties made for sale to collectors.

No. 23 Overprinted in Black

**1884, Apr. 28**

**103** A19 5c blue .65 .40
*a.* Double overprint 5.00 5.00

Stamps of 1c and 2c with the above overprint, also with the above and "U. P. U. LIMA" oval in blue or "CORREOS LIMA" in a double-lined circle in red, were made to sell to collectors and were never placed in use.

### Without Overprint or Grill

**1886-95**

**104** A17 1c dull violet .90 .30
**105** A17 1c vermilion ('95) .65 .30
**106** A18 2c green 1.25 .30
**107** A18 2c dp ultra ('95) .55 .30
**108** A19 5c orange 1.00 .45
**109** A12 5c claret ('95) 2.25 .85
**110** A20 10c slate .65 .30
**111** A13 10c orange ('95) 1.00 .55
**112** A21 20c blue 8.75 1.10
**113** A14 20c dp ultra ('95) 10.50 2.25
**114** A22 50c red 2.75 1.10
**115** A23 1s brown 2.25 .85
*Nos. 104-115 (12)* 32.50 8.65

### Overprinted Horseshoe in Black and Triangle in Rose Red

**1889**

**116** A17 1c green .75 .75
*a.* Horseshoe inverted 7.50

### Nos. 30 and 25 Overprinted "Union Postal Universal Lima" in Oval in Red

**1889, Sept. 1**

**117** A17 1c green 2.00 1.60
**117A** A20 10c green 2.00 2.00

The overprint on Nos. 117 and 117A is of the second type with "PLATA" 3mm high.

### Stamps of 1874-80 Overprinted in Black

Pres. Remigio Morales Bermúdez

**1894, Oct. 23**

**118** A17 1c orange 1.00 .65
*a.* Inverted overprint 7.00 7.00
*b.* Double overprint 7.00 7.00
**119** A17 1c green .65 .55
*a.* Inverted overprint 3.50 3.50
*b.* Dbl. inverted ovpt. 5.00 5.00
**120** A18 2c violet .65 .55
*a.* Diagonal half used as 1c
*b.* Inverted overprint 7.00 7.00
*c.* Double overprint 7.00 7.00
**121** A18 2c rose .65 .55
*a.* Double overprint 7.00 7.00
*b.* Inverted overprint 9.75 7.00
**122** A19 5c blue 4.50 2.75
**122A** A19 5c ultra 7.25 3.50
*b.* Inverted overprint 10.00 10.00
**123** A20 10c green .65 .55
*a.* Inverted overprint 7.00 7.00
**124** A22 50c green 2.40 2.00
*a.* Inverted overprint 10.00 10.00
*Nos. 118-124 (8)* 17.75 11.10

Same, with Additional Ovpt. of Horseshoe

**125** A18 2c vermilion .55 .45
*a.* Head inverted 2.50 2.50
*b.* Head double 5.00 5.00
**126** A19 5c blue 1.75 .85
*a.* Head inverted 7.00 7.00
**127** A22 50c rose 70.00 42.50
*a.* Head double 55.00 45.00
*b.* Head inverted 75.00 60.00
**128** A23 1s ultra 175.00 150.00
*a.* Both overprints inverted 200.00 110.00
*b.* Head double 200.00 110.00
*Nos. 125-128 (4)* 247.30 193.80

A23a

### Vermilion Surcharge

**1895** ***Perf. 11½***

**129** A23a 5c on 5c grn 18.00 13.00
**130** A23a 10c on 10c ver 13.00 10.00
**131** A23a 20c on 20c brn 14.00 10.00
**132** A23a 50c on 50c ultra 18.00 13.00
**133** A23a 1s on 1s red brn 18.00 13.00
*Nos. 129-133 (5)* 81.00 59.00

Nos 129-133 were used only in Tumbes. The basic stamps were prepared by revolutionaries in northern Peru.

A23b

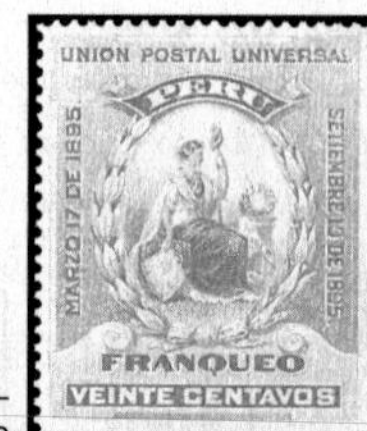
"Liberty" — A23c

**1895, Sept. 8** **Engr.**

**134** A23b 1c gray violet 1.90 1.10
**135** A23b 2c green 1.90 1.10
**136** A23b 5c yellow 1.90 1.10
**137** A23b 10c ultra 1.90 1.10
**138** A23c 20c orange 1.90 1.25
**139** A23c 50c dark blue 10.00 7.00
**140** A23c 1s car lake 55.00 35.00
*Nos. 134-140 (7)* 74.50 47.65

Success of the revolution against the government of General Caceres and of the election of President Pierola.

Manco Capac, Founder of Inca Dynasty — A24

Francisco Pizarro Conqueror of the Inca Empire — A25

General José de La Mar — A26

**1896-1900**

**141** A24 1c ultra .90 .30
*a.* 1c blue (error) 70.00 60.00
**142** A24 1c yel grn ('98) .90 .30
**143** A24 2c blue .90 .30
**144** A24 2c scar ('99) .90 .30
**145** A25 5c indigo 1.25 .30
**146** A25 5c green ('97) 1.25 .30
**147** A25 5c grnsh bl ('99) .90 .55
**148** A25 10c yellow 1.75 .45
**149** A25 10c gray blk ('00) 1.75 .30
**150** A25 20c orange 3.50 .45
**151** A26 50c car rose 8.75 1.60
**152** A26 1s orange red 13.00 1.60
**153** A26 2s claret 3.50 1.25
*Nos. 141-153 (13)* 39.25 8.00

The 5c in black is a chemical changeling.

For surcharges and overprints see Nos. 187-188, E1, O23-O26.

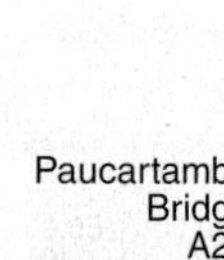

Paucartambo Bridge A27

Post and Telegraph Building, Lima — A28

Pres. Nicolás de Piérola — A29

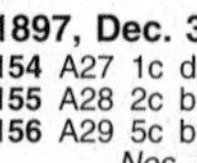

**1897, Dec. 31**

**154** A27 1c dp ultra 1.25 .60
**155** A28 2c brown 1.25 .40
**156** A29 5c bright rose 1.75 .60
*Nos. 154-156 (3)* 4.25 1.60

Opening of new P.O. in Lima.

No. J1 Overprinted in Black

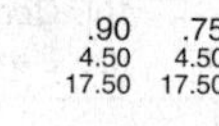

**1897, Nov. 8**

**157** D1 1c bister .90 .75
*a.* Inverted overprint 4.50 4.50
*b.* Double overprint 17.50 17.50

A31

**1899**

**158** A31 5s orange red 2.75 2.75
**159** A31 10s blue green 850.00 600.00

For surcharge see No. J36.

Pres. Eduardo de Romaña — A32

**1900** **Frame Litho., Center Engr.**

**160** A32 22c yel grn & blk 13.00 1.40

Admiral Miguel L. Grau — A33

2c, Col. Francisco Bolognesi. 5c, Pres. Romaña.

**1901, Jan.**

**161** A33 1c green & blk 1.75 .75
**162** A33 2c red & black 1.75 .75
**163** A33 5c dull vio & blk 1.75 .75
*Nos. 161-163 (3)* 5.25 2.25

Advent of 20th century.

A34

**1902** **Engr.**

**164** A34 22c green .55 .30

Municipal Hygiene Institute Lima — A35

**1905**

**165** A35 12c dp blue & blk 1.75 .50

For surcharges see Nos. 166-167, 186, 189.

Same Surcharged in Red or Violet

**1907**

| | | | | |
|---|---|---|---|---|
| **166** | A35 | 1c on 12c (R) | .35 | .30 |
| *a.* | | Inverted surcharge | 8.00 | 8.00 |
| *b.* | | Double surcharge | 8.00 | 8.00 |
| **167** | A35 | 2c on 12c (V) | .65 | .45 |
| *a.* | | Double surcharge | 8.00 | 8.00 |
| *b.* | | Inverted surcharge | 8.00 | 8.00 |

Monument of Bolognesi — A36

Admiral Grau — A37

Llama — A38

Statue of Bolivar — A39

City Hall, Lima, formerly an Exhibition Building — A40

School of Medicine, Lima — A41

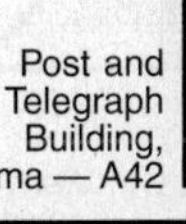

Post and Telegraph Building, Lima — A42

Grandstand at Santa Beatrix Race Track — A43

Columbus Monument — A44

**1907**

| | | | | |
|---|---|---|---|---|
| **168** | A36 | 1c yel grn & blk | .55 | .30 |
| **169** | A37 | 2c red & violet | .55 | .30 |
| **170** | A38 | 4c olive green | 9.25 | 1.25 |
| **171** | A39 | 5c blue & blk | 1.00 | .30 |
| **172** | A40 | 10c red brn & blk | 1.75 | .45 |
| **173** | A41 | 20c dk grn & blk | 40.00 | .75 |
| **174** | A42 | 50c black | 40.00 | 1.60 |
| **175** | A43 | 1s purple & grn | 200.00 | 3.75 |
| **176** | A44 | 2s dp bl & blk | 200.00 | 160.00 |
| | | *Nos. 168-176 (9)* | 493.10 | 168.70 |

For surcharges and overprint see #190-195, E2.

Manco Capac A45

Columbus A46

Pizarro A47

San Martin A48

Bolívar A49

La Mar A50

Ramón Castilla A51

Grau A52

Bolognesi — A53

**1909**

| | | | | |
|---|---|---|---|---|
| **177** | A45 | 1c gray | .35 | .25 |
| **178** | A46 | 2c green | .35 | .25 |
| **179** | A47 | 4c vermilion | .45 | .30 |
| **180** | A48 | 5c violet | .35 | .25 |
| **181** | A49 | 10c deep blue | .75 | .30 |
| **182** | A50 | 12c pale blue | 1.75 | .30 |
| **183** | A51 | 20c brown red | 1.90 | .45 |
| **184** | A52 | 50c yellow | 8.25 | .55 |
| **185** | A53 | 1s brn red & blk | 17.00 | .65 |
| | | *Nos. 177-185 (9)* | 31.15 | 3.30 |

See types A54, A78-A80, A81-A89.

For surcharges and overprint see Nos. 196-200, 208, E3.

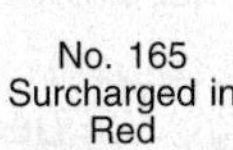

No. 165 Surcharged in Red

**1913, Jan.**

| | | | | |
|---|---|---|---|---|
| **186** | A35 | 8c on 12c dp bl & blk | .90 | .35 |

### Stamps of 1899-1908 Surcharged in Red

a

b

c

**1915** — **On Nos. 142, 149**

| | | | | |
|---|---|---|---|---|
| **187** | A24(a) | 1c on 1c | 27.50 | 22.50 |
| *a.* | | Inverted surcharge | 32.50 | 37.50 |
| **188** | A25(a) | 1c on 10c | 1.75 | 1.25 |
| *a.* | | Inverted surcharge | 4.50 | 4.50 |

**On No. 165**

| | | | | |
|---|---|---|---|---|
| **189** | A35(c) | 2c on 12c | .45 | .30 |
| *a.* | | Inverted surcharge | 7.75 | 7.75 |

**On Nos. 168-170, 172-174**

| | | | | |
|---|---|---|---|---|
| **190** | A36(a) | 1c on 1c | 1.10 | 1.10 |
| *a.* | | Inverted surcharge | 3.50 | 3.50 |
| **191** | A37(a) | 1c on 2c | 1.75 | 1.60 |
| *a.* | | Inverted surcharge | 4.50 | 4.50 |
| **192** | A38(b) | 1c on 4c | 3.25 | 2.75 |
| *a.* | | Inverted surcharge | 10.50 | 10.50 |
| **193** | A40(b) | 1c on 10c | 1.75 | 1.25 |
| *a.* | | Inverted surcharge | 3.75 | 3.75 |
| **193C** | A40(c) | 2c on 10c | 175.00 | 125.00 |
| *b.* | | Inverted surcharge | *175.00* | |
| **194** | A41(c) | 2c on 20c | 22.50 | 21.00 |
| *a.* | | Inverted surcharge | 45.00 | 45.00 |
| **195** | A42(c) | 2c on 50c | 3.25 | 3.25 |
| *a.* | | Inverted surcharge | 13.00 | 13.00 |
| | | *Nos. 187-195 (10)* | 238.30 | 180.00 |

### Nos. 182-184, 179, 185 Surcharged in Red, Green or Violet

d

e

f

**1916**

| | | | | |
|---|---|---|---|---|
| **196** | A50(d) | 1c on 12c (R) | .35 | .25 |
| *a.* | | Double surcharge | 5.00 | 5.00 |
| *b.* | | Green surcharge | 7.50 | 7.50 |
| **197** | A51(d) | 1c on 20c (G) | .35 | .25 |
| **198** | A52(d) | 1c on 50c (G) | .35 | .25 |
| *a.* | | Inverted surcharge | 5.00 | 5.00 |
| **199** | A47(e) | 2c on 4c (V) | .35 | .25 |
| *a.* | | Green surcharge | 1.60 | 1.25 |
| **200** | A53(f) | 10c on 1s (G) | 1.10 | .25 |
| *a.* | | "VALF" | 10.50 | 10.50 |
| | | *Nos. 196-200 (5)* | 2.50 | 1.25 |

### Official Stamps of 1909-14 Ovptd. or Srchd. in Green or Red

g

h

**1916**

| | | | | |
|---|---|---|---|---|
| **201** | O1(g) | 1c red (G) | .25 | .25 |
| **202** | O1(h) | 2c on 50c ol grn (R) | .35 | .25 |
| **203** | O1(g) | 10c bis brn (G) | .35 | .25 |

**Postage Due Stamps of 1909 Surcharged in Violet-Black**

| | | | | |
|---|---|---|---|---|
| **204** | D7 | 2c on 1c brown | .65 | .65 |
| **205** | D7 | 2c on 5c brown | .25 | .25 |
| **206** | D7 | 2c on 10c brown | .25 | .25 |
| **207** | D7 | 2c on 50c brown | .25 | .25 |
| | | *Nos. 201-207 (7)* | 2.35 | 2.15 |

Many examples of Nos. 187 to 207 have a number of pin holes. It is stated that these holes were made at the time the surcharges were printed.

The varieties listed of the 1915 and 1916 issues were sold to the public at post offices. Many other varieties which were previously listed are now known to have been delivered to one speculator or to have been privately printed by him from the surcharging plates which he had acquired.

No. 179 Surcharged in Black

**1917**

| | | | | |
|---|---|---|---|---|
| **208** | A47 | 1c on 4c ver | .55 | .55 |
| *a.* | | Double surcharge | 8.25 | 8.25 |
| *b.* | | Inverted surcharge | 8.25 | 8.25 |

San Martin — A54

Columbus at Salamanca — A62

Funeral of Atahualpa — A63

Battle of Arica, "Arica, the Last Cartridge" A64

Designs: 2c, Bolívar. 4c, José Gálvez. 5c, Manuel Pardo. 8c, Grau. 10c, Bolognesi. 12c, Castilla. 20c, General Cáceres.

**1918** — **Centers in Black** — **Engr.**

| | | | | |
|---|---|---|---|---|
| **209** | A54 | 1c orange | .35 | .25 |
| **210** | A54 | 2c green | .35 | .25 |
| **211** | A54 | 4c lake | .45 | .30 |
| **212** | A54 | 5c dp ultra | .45 | .30 |
| **213** | A54 | 8c red brn | 1.25 | .45 |
| **214** | A54 | 10c grnsh bl | .55 | .30 |
| **215** | A54 | 12c dl vio | 1.75 | .30 |
| **216** | A54 | 20c ol grn | 2.10 | .30 |
| **217** | A62 | 50c vio brn | 8.25 | .55 |
| **218** | A63 | 1s greenish bl | 21.00 | .75 |
| **219** | A64 | 2s deep ultra | 35.00 | 1.10 |
| | | *Nos. 209-219 (11)* | 71.50 | 4.85 |

For surcharges see Nos. 232-233, 255-256.

Augusto B. Leguía — A65

**1919, Dec.** — **Litho.**

| | | | | |
|---|---|---|---|---|
| **220** | A65 | 5c bl & blk | .35 | .30 |
| *a.* | | Imperf. | .35 | .35 |
| *b.* | | Center inverted | 15.00 | 15.00 |
| **221** | A65 | 5c brn & blk | .35 | .30 |
| *a.* | | Imperf. | .35 | .35 |
| *b.* | | Center inverted | 15.00 | 15.00 |

Constitution of 1919.

San Martín — A66

Thomas Cochrane — A70

Oath of Independence — A69

Designs: 2c, Field Marshal Arenales. 4c, Field Marshal Las Heras. 10c, Martin Jorge Guisse. 12c, Vidal. 20c, Leguia. 50c, San Martin monument. 1s, San Martin and Leguia.

**1921, July 28** — **Engr.; 7c Litho.**

| | | | | |
|---|---|---|---|---|
| **222** | A66 | 1c ol brn & red brn | .45 | .25 |
| *a.* | | Center inverted | 600.00 | 600.00 |
| **223** | A66 | 2c green | .55 | .30 |
| **224** | A66 | 4c car rose | 1.90 | .90 |
| **225** | A69 | 5c ol brn | .60 | .25 |

| No. | Type | Description | Unused | Used |
|---|---|---|---|---|
| 226 | A70 | 7c violet | 1.90 | .65 |
| 227 | A66 | 10c ultra | 1.90 | .65 |
| 228 | A66 | 12c blk & slate | 4.50 | .90 |
| 229 | A66 | 20c car & gray blk | 4.50 | 1.10 |
| 230 | A66 | 50c vio brn & dl vio | 13.00 | 3.75 |
| 231 | A69 | 1s car rose & yel grn | 19.00 | 8.00 |
| | | *Nos. 222-231 (10)* | 48.30 | 16.75 |

Centenary of Independence.

### Nos. 213, 212 Surcharged in Black or Red Brown

**1923-24**

| No. | Type | Description | Unused | Used |
|---|---|---|---|---|
| 232 | A54 | 5c on 8c No. 213 | .75 | .55 |
| 233 | A54 | 4c on 5c (RB) ('24) | .55 | .25 |
| *a.* | | Inverted surcharge | 5.00 | 5.00 |
| *b.* | | Double surcharge, one inverted | 6.00 | 6.00 |

A78

A79

Simón Bolívar — A80

***Perf. 14, 14x14½, 14½, 13½***

**1924 Engr.; Photo. (4c, 5c)**

| No. | Type | Description | Unused | Used |
|---|---|---|---|---|
| 234 | A78 | 2c olive grn | .40 | .25 |
| 235 | A79 | 4c yellow grn | .65 | .25 |
| 236 | A79 | 5c black | 2.25 | .25 |
| 237 | A80 | 10c carmine | .80 | .25 |
| 238 | A78 | 20c ultra | 2.25 | .30 |
| 239 | A78 | 50c dull violet | 5.50 | 1.10 |
| 240 | A78 | 1s yellow brn | 13.00 | 4.25 |
| 241 | A78 | 2s dull blue | 35.00 | 18.00 |
| | | *Nos. 234-241 (8)* | 59.85 | 24.65 |

Centenary of the Battle of Ayacucho which ended Spanish power in South America.

No. 237 exists imperf.

José Tejada Rivadeneyra A81

Mariano Melgar A82

Iturregui A83

Leguía A84

José de La Mar — A85

Monument of José Olaya — A86

Statue of María Bellido — A87

De Saco — A88

José Leguía — A89

**1924-29 Engr. *Perf. 12***

**Size: 18½x23mm**

| No. | Type | Description | Unused | Used |
|---|---|---|---|---|
| 242 | A81 | 2c olive gray | .35 | .25 |
| 243 | A82 | 4c dk grn | .35 | .25 |
| 244 | A83 | 8c black | 3.25 | 3.25 |
| 245 | A84 | 10c org red | .35 | .25 |
| 245A | A85 | 15c dp bl ('28) | 1.00 | .30 |
| 246 | A86 | 20c blue | 1.75 | .30 |
| 247 | A86 | 20c yel ('29) | 2.75 | .30 |
| 248 | A87 | 50c violet | 8.25 | .45 |
| 249 | A88 | 1s bis brn | 15.00 | 1.60 |
| 250 | A89 | 2s ultra | 40.00 | 8.00 |
| | | *Nos. 242-250 (10)* | 73.05 | 14.95 |

See Nos. 258, 260, 276-282.

For surcharges and overprint see Nos. 251-253, 257-260, 262, 268-271, C1.

### No. 246 Surcharged in Red

a b

**1925**

| No. | Type | Description | Unused | Used |
|---|---|---|---|---|
| 251 | A86(a) | 2c on 20c blue | *550.00* | *550.00* |
| 252 | A86(b) | 2c on 20c blue | 1.75 | 1.10 |
| *a.* | | Inverted surcharge | 50.00 | 50.00 |
| *b.* | | Double surch., one inverted | 50.00 | 50.00 |

No. 245 Overprinted

**1925**

| No. | Type | Description | Unused | Used |
|---|---|---|---|---|
| 253 | A84 | 10c org red | 1.75 | 1.75 |
| *a.* | | Inverted overprint | 21.00 | 21.00 |

This stamp was for exclusive use on letters from the plebiscite provinces of Tacna and Arica, and posted on the Peruvian transport "Ucayali" anchored in the port of Arica.

### No. 213 Surcharged

a

b

**1929**

| No. | Type | Description | Unused | Used |
|---|---|---|---|---|
| 255 | A54(a) | 2c on 8c | 1.25 | 1.25 |
| 256 | A54(b) | 2c on 8c | 1.25 | 1.25 |

No. 247 Surcharged

Habilitada 15 cts. 1929

| No. | Type | Description | Unused | Used |
|---|---|---|---|---|
| 257 | A86 | 15c on 20c yellow | 1.25 | 1.25 |
| *a.* | | Inverted surcharge | 13.00 | 13.00 |
| | | *Nos. 255-257 (3)* | 3.75 | 3.75 |

### Types of 1924 Coil Stamps

**1929 *Perf. 14 Horizontally***

| No. | Type | Description | Unused | Used |
|---|---|---|---|---|
| 258 | A81 | 2c olive gray | 65.00 | 40.00 |
| 260 | A84 | 10c orange red | 70.00 | 37.50 |

Postal Tax Stamp of 1928 Overprinted

**1930 *Perf. 12***

| No. | Type | Description | Unused | Used |
|---|---|---|---|---|
| 261 | PT6 | 2c dark violet | .55 | .55 |
| *a.* | | Inverted overprint | 3.25 | 3.25 |

No. 247 Surcharged

| No. | Type | Description | Unused | Used |
|---|---|---|---|---|
| 262 | A86 | 2c on 20c yellow | .55 | .55 |

Air Post Stamp of 1928 Surcharged

| No. | Type | Description | Unused | Used |
|---|---|---|---|---|
| 263 | AP1 | 2c on 50c dk grn | .55 | .55 |
| *a.* | | "Habitada" | 2.10 | 2.10 |

Coat of Arms — A91

Lima Cathedral A92

10c, Children's Hospital. 50c, Madonna & Child.

***Perf. 12x11½, 11½x12***

**1930, July 5 Litho.**

| No. | Type | Description | Unused | Used |
|---|---|---|---|---|
| 264 | A91 | 2c green | 1.75 | .95 |
| 265 | A92 | 5c scarlet | 3.75 | 2.10 |
| 266 | A92 | 10c dark blue | 2.25 | 1.60 |
| 267 | A91 | 50c bister brown | 30.00 | 19.00 |
| | | *Nos. 264-267 (4)* | 37.75 | 23.65 |

6th Pan American Congress for Child Welfare. By error the stamps are inscribed "Seventh Congress."

Type of 1924 Overprinted in Black, Green or Blue

**1930, Dec. 22 Photo. *Perf. 15x14***

**Size: 18¼x22mm**

| No. | Type | Description | Unused | Used |
|---|---|---|---|---|
| 268 | A84 | 10c orange red (Bk) | 1.00 | .80 |
| *a.* | | Inverted overprint | 14.00 | 14.00 |
| *b.* | | Without overprint | 8.50 | 8.50 |
| *c.* | | Double surcharge | 7.00 | 7.00 |

### Same with Additional Surcharge of Numerals in Each Corner

| No. | Type | Description | Unused | Used |
|---|---|---|---|---|
| 269 | A84 | 2c on 10c org red (G) | .35 | .25 |
| *a.* | | Inverted surcharge | 17.00 | |
| 270 | A84 | 4c on 10c org red (G) | .35 | .25 |
| *a.* | | Double surcharge | 12.50 | 12.50 |

**Engr.**

***Perf. 12***

**Size: 19x23½mm**

| No. | Type | Description | Unused | Used |
|---|---|---|---|---|
| 271 | A84 | 15c on 10c org red (Bl) | .35 | .25 |
| *a.* | | Inverted surcharge | 14.00 | 14.00 |
| *b.* | | Double surcharge | 14.00 | 14.00 |
| | | *Nos. 268-271 (4)* | 2.05 | 1.55 |

Bolívar — A95

**1930, Dec. 16 Litho.**

| No. | Type | Description | Unused | Used |
|---|---|---|---|---|
| 272 | A95 | 2c buff | .55 | .55 |
| 273 | A95 | 4c red | .90 | .75 |
| 274 | A95 | 10c blue green | .45 | .30 |
| 275 | A95 | 15c slate gray | .90 | .90 |
| | | *Nos. 272-275 (4)* | 2.80 | 2.50 |

Death cent. of General Simón Bolivar.

For surcharges see Nos. RA14-RA16.

### Types of 1924-29 Issues

Size: 18x22mm

**1931 Photo. *Perf. 15x14***

| No. | Type | Description | Unused | Used |
|---|---|---|---|---|
| 276 | A81 | 2c olive green | .45 | .30 |
| 277 | A82 | 4c dark green | .45 | .30 |
| 279 | A85 | 15c deep blue | 1.25 | .30 |
| 280 | A86 | 20c yellow | 2.10 | .30 |
| 281 | A87 | 50c violet | 2.10 | .45 |
| 282 | A88 | 1s olive brown | 3.25 | .55 |
| | | *Nos. 276-282 (6)* | 9.60 | 2.20 |

Pizarro — A96

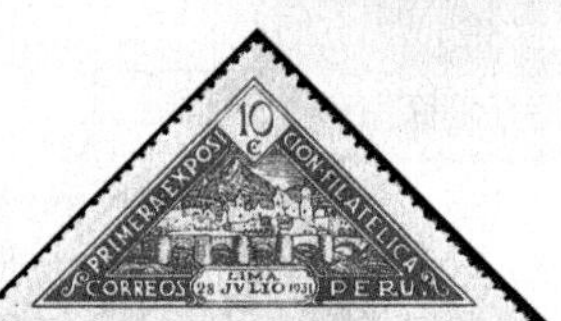

Old Stone Bridge, Lima — A97

**1931, July 28 Litho. *Perf. 11***

| No. | Type | Description | Unused | Used |
|---|---|---|---|---|
| 283 | A96 | 2c slate blue | 2.10 | 1.75 |
| 284 | A96 | 4c deep brown | 2.10 | 1.75 |
| 285 | A96 | 15c dark green | 2.10 | 1.75 |
| 286 | A97 | 10c rose red | 2.10 | 1.75 |
| 287 | A97 | 10c mag & lt grn | 2.10 | 1.75 |
| 288 | A97 | 15c yel & bl gray | 2.10 | 1.75 |
| 289 | A97 | 15c dk slate & red | 2.10 | 1.75 |
| | | *Nos. 283-289 (7)* | 14.70 | 12.25 |

1st Peruvian Phil. Exhib., Lima, July, 1931.

Manco Capac A99

Oil Refinery A100

Sugar Cane Field A102

Picking Cotton A103

Guano Deposits A104

Mining A105

Llamas — A106

**1931-32** *Perf. 11, 11x11½*

| | | | | | |
|---|---|---|---|---|---|
| **292** | A99 | 2c olive black | .35 | .25 |
| **293** | A100 | 4c dark green | .65 | .30 |
| **295** | A102 | 10c red orange | 1.75 | .25 |
| *a.* | | Vertical pair, imperf. between | 30.00 | |
| **296** | A103 | 15c turq blue | 2.00 | .30 |
| **297** | A104 | 20c yellow | 8.25 | .30 |
| **298** | A105 | 50c gray lilac | 8.25 | .30 |
| **299** | A106 | 1s brown olive | 20.00 | 1.40 |
| | | *Nos. 292-299 (7)* | 41.25 | 3.10 |

Arms of Piura — A107

**1932, July 28** *Perf. 11½x12*

| | | | | |
|---|---|---|---|---|
| **300** | A107 | 10c dark blue | 8.25 | 8.00 |
| **301** | A107 | 15c deep violet | 8.25 | 8.00 |
| | | *Nos. 300-301,C3 (3)* | 42.50 | 38.50 |

400th anniv. of the founding of the city of Piura. On sale one day. Counterfeits exist.

See No. C7.

Parakas A108

Chimu A109

Inca — A110

**1932, Oct. 15** *Perf. 11½, 12, 11½x12*

| | | | | |
|---|---|---|---|---|
| **302** | A108 | 10c dk vio | .35 | .25 |
| **303** | A109 | 15c brn red | .65 | .30 |
| **304** | A110 | 50c dk brn | 1.50 | .30 |
| | | *Nos. 302-304 (3)* | 2.50 | .85 |

4th cent. of the Spanish conquest of Peru.

Arequipa and El Misti — A111

President Luis M. Sánchez Cerro — A112

Monument to Simón Bolívar at Lima — A115

**1932-34** **Photo.** *Perf. 13½*

| | | | | |
|---|---|---|---|---|
| **305** | A111 | 2c black | .25 | .25 |
| **306** | A111 | 2c blue blk | .25 | .25 |
| **307** | A111 | 2c grn ('34) | .25 | .25 |
| **308** | A111 | 4c dk brn | .25 | .25 |
| **309** | A111 | 4c org ('34) | .25 | .25 |
| **310** | A112 | 10c vermilion | 27.50 | 16.00 |
| **311** | A115 | 15c ultra | .60 | .25 |
| **312** | A115 | 15c mag ('34) | .60 | .25 |
| **313** | A115 | 20c red brn | 1.25 | .25 |
| **314** | A115 | 20c vio ('34) | 1.25 | .25 |
| **315** | A115 | 50c dk grn ('33) | 1.25 | .25 |
| **316** | A115 | 1s dp org | 11.00 | 1.60 |
| **317** | A115 | 1s org brn | 12.00 | 1.10 |
| | | *Nos. 305-317 (13)* | 56.70 | 21.20 |

For overprint see No. RA24.

Statue of Liberty — A116

**1934**

| | | | | |
|---|---|---|---|---|
| **318** | A116 | 10c rose | .75 | .25 |

Pizarro — A117

The Inca — A119

Coronation of Huascar — A118

**1934-35** *Perf. 13*

| | | | | |
|---|---|---|---|---|
| **319** | A117 | 10c crimson | .40 | .25 |
| **320** | A117 | 15c ultra | 1.10 | .25 |
| **321** | A118 | 20c deep bl ('35) | 2.00 | .25 |
| **322** | A118 | 50c dp red brn | 1.60 | .25 |
| **323** | A119 | 1s dark vio | 11.00 | 1.10 |
| | | *Nos. 319-323 (5)* | 16.10 | 2.10 |

For surcharges and overprint see Nos. 354-355, J54, O32.

Pizarro and the Thirteen A120

Belle of Lima — A122

Francisco Pizarro — A123

4c, Lima Cathedral. 1s, Veiled woman of Lima.

**1935, Jan. 18** *Perf. 13½*

| | | | | |
|---|---|---|---|---|
| **324** | A120 | 2c brown | .55 | .30 |
| **325** | A120 | 4c violet | .60 | .45 |
| **326** | A122 | 10c rose red | .60 | .30 |
| **327** | A123 | 15c ultra | 1.10 | .75 |
| **328** | A120 | 20c slate gray | 2.25 | .95 |
| **329** | A122 | 50c olive grn | 3.25 | 1.90 |
| **330** | A122 | 1s Prus bl | 6.00 | 3.75 |
| **331** | A123 | 2s org brn | 14.50 | 10.00 |
| | | *Nos. 324-331,C6-C12 (15)* | 91.05 | 60.50 |

Founding of Lima, 4th cent.

View of Ica — A125

Lake Huacachina, Health Resort — A126

Grapes — A127

Cotton Boll — A128

Zuniga y Velazco and Philip IV — A129

Supreme God of the Nazcas — A130

**Engr.; Photo. (10c)**

**1935, Jan. 17** *Perf. 12½*

| | | | | |
|---|---|---|---|---|
| **332** | A125 | 4c gray blue | .45 | 1.25 |
| **333** | A126 | 5c dark car | .45 | 1.25 |
| **334** | A127 | 10c magenta | 6.50 | 3.25 |
| **335** | A126 | 20c green | 2.25 | 2.25 |
| **336** | A128 | 35c dark car | 11.00 | 8.00 |
| **337** | A129 | 50c org & brn | 7.75 | 7.00 |
| **338** | A130 | 1s pur & red | 22.50 | 17.00 |
| | | *Nos. 332-338 (7)* | 50.90 | 40.00 |

Founding of the City of Ica, 300th anniv.

Pizarro and the Thirteen — A131

**1935-36** **Photo.** *Perf. 13½*

| | | | | |
|---|---|---|---|---|
| **339** | A131 | 2c dp claret | .25 | .25 |
| **340** | A131 | 4c bl grn ('36) | .25 | .25 |

For surcharge and overprints see Nos. 353, J53, RA25-RA26.

"San Cristóbal," First Peruvian Warship — A132

Naval College at Punta A133

Independence Square, Callao — A134

Aerial View of Callao A135

Plan of Walls of Callao in 1746 A137

Grand Marshal José de La Mar — A138

Packetboat "Sacramento" — A139

Viceroy José Antonio Manso de Velasco — A140

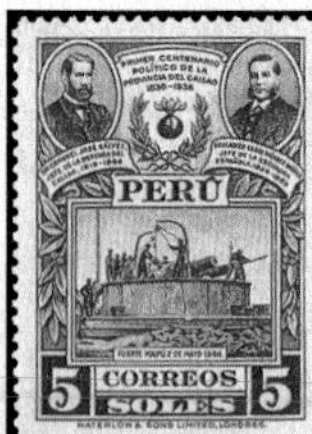
Fort Maipú — A141

Plan of Fort Real Felipe A142

Design: 15c, Docks and Custom House.

**1936, Aug. 27 Photo. *Perf. 12½***

| | | | | |
|---|---|---|---|---|
| **341** | A132 | 2c black | .75 | .30 |
| **342** | A133 | 4c bl grn | .75 | .30 |
| **343** | A134 | 5c yel brn | .75 | .30 |
| **344** | A135 | 10c bl gray | .75 | .30 |
| **345** | A135 | 15c green | .75 | .30 |
| **346** | A137 | 20c dk brn | 1.00 | .30 |
| **347** | A138 | 50c purple | 1.90 | .55 |
| **348** | A139 | 1s olive grn | 12.00 | 1.75 |
| | | **Engr.** | | |
| **349** | A140 | 2s violet | 20.00 | 9.00 |
| **350** | A141 | 5s carmine | 27.50 | 19.00 |
| **351** | A142 | 10s red org & brn | 65.00 | 55.00 |
| | | *Nos. 341-351,C13 (12)* | 134.40 | 88.85 |

Province of Callao founding, cent.

Nos. 340, 321 and 323 Surcharged in Black

**1936 *Perf. 13½, 13***

| | | | | |
|---|---|---|---|---|
| **353** | A131 | 2c on 4c bl grn | .35 | .25 |
| *a.* | | "0.20" for "0.02" | 4.25 | 4.25 |
| **354** | A118 | 10c on 20c dp bl | .35 | .25 |
| *a.* | | Double surcharge | 4.25 | 4.25 |
| *b.* | | Inverted surcharge | 4.25 | 4.25 |
| **355** | A119 | 10c on 1s dk vio | .55 | .55 |
| | | *Nos. 353-355 (3)* | 1.25 | 1.05 |

Many varieties of the surcharge are found on these stamps: no period after "S," no period after "Cts," period after "2," "S" omitted, various broken letters, etc.

The surcharge on No. 355 is horizontal.

Peruvian Cormorants (Guano Deposits) — A143

Oil Well at Talara — A144

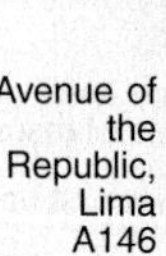

Avenue of the Republic, Lima A146

San Marcos University at Lima A148

Post Office, Lima — A149

Viceroy Manuel de Amat y Junyent — A150

Designs: 10c, "El Chasqui" (Inca Courier). 20c, Municipal Palace and Museum of Natural History. 5s, Joseph A. de Pando y Riva. 10s, Dr. José Dávila Condemarin.

**1936-37 Photo. *Perf. 12½***

| | | | | |
|---|---|---|---|---|
| **356** | A143 | 2c lt brn | .75 | .30 |
| **357** | A143 | 2c grn ('37) | 1.00 | .30 |
| **358** | A144 | 4c blk brn | .75 | .30 |
| **359** | A144 | 4c int blk ('37) | .45 | .30 |
| **360** | A143 | 10c crimson | .45 | .30 |
| **361** | A143 | 10c ver ('37) | .35 | .30 |
| **362** | A146 | 15c ultra | .90 | .30 |
| **363** | A146 | 15c brt bl ('37) | .45 | .30 |
| **364** | A146 | 20c black | .90 | .30 |
| **365** | A146 | 20c blk brn ('37) | .35 | .30 |
| **366** | A148 | 50c org yel | 3.25 | .85 |
| **367** | A148 | 50c dk gray vio ('37) | 1.00 | .30 |
| **368** | A149 | 1s brn vio | 6.50 | 1.10 |
| **369** | A149 | 1s ultra ('37) | 1.90 | .30 |
| | | **Engr.** | | |
| **370** | A150 | 2s ultra | 13.00 | 2.75 |
| **371** | A150 | 2s dk vio ('37) | 4.50 | .85 |
| **372** | A150 | 5s slate bl | 13.00 | 2.75 |
| **373** | A150 | 10s dk vio & brn | 75.00 | 37.50 |
| | | *Nos. 356-373 (18)* | 124.50 | 49.40 |

No. 370 Surcharged in Black

**1937**

| | | | | |
|---|---|---|---|---|
| **374** | A150 | 1s on 2s ultra | 3.25 | 3.25 |

Children's Holiday Center, Ancón — A153

Chavin Pottery — A154

Highway Map of Peru — A155

Archaeological Museum, Lima — A156

Industrial Bank of Peru — A157

Worker's Houses, Lima — A158

Toribio de Luzuriaga A159

Historic Fig Tree A160

Idol from Temple of Chavin — A161

Mt. Huascarán — A162

**Imprint: "Waterlow & Sons Limited, Londres"**

**1938, July 1 Photo. *Perf. 12½, 13***

| | | | | |
|---|---|---|---|---|
| **375** | A153 | 2c emerald | .25 | .25 |
| **376** | A154 | 4c org brn | .25 | .25 |
| **377** | A155 | 10c scarlet | .35 | .25 |
| **378** | A156 | 15c ultra | .40 | .25 |
| **379** | A157 | 20c magenta | .25 | .25 |
| **380** | A158 | 50c greenish blue | .50 | .25 |
| **381** | A159 | 1s dp claret | 1.60 | .25 |
| **382** | A160 | 2s green | 6.50 | .25 |
| | | **Engr.** | | |
| **383** | A161 | 5s dl vio & brn | 13.00 | .75 |
| **384** | A162 | 10s blk & ultra | 27.50 | 1.25 |
| | | *Nos. 375-384 (10)* | 50.60 | 4.00 |

See Nos. 410-418, 426-433, 438-441.

For surcharges see Nos. 388, 406, 419, 445-446A, 456, 758.

Palace Square A163

Lima Coat of Arms A164

Government Palace — A165

**1938, Dec. 9 Photo. *Perf. 12½***

| | | | | |
|---|---|---|---|---|
| **385** | A163 | 10c slate green | .65 | .45 |
| | | **Engraved and Lithographed** | | |
| **386** | A164 | 15c blk, gold, red & bl | 1.10 | .55 |
| | | **Photo.** | | |
| **387** | A165 | 1s olive | 2.75 | 1.60 |
| | | *Nos. 385-387,C62-C64 (6)* | 9.30 | 5.90 |

8th Pan-American Conf., Lima, Dec. 1938.

No. 377 Surcharged in Black

**1940 *Perf. 13***

| | | | | |
|---|---|---|---|---|
| **388** | A155 | 5c on 10c scarlet | .25 | .25 |
| *a.* | | Inverted surcharge | | |

National Radio Station A166

**Black Overprint**

**1941 Litho. *Perf. 12***

| | | | | |
|---|---|---|---|---|
| **389** | A166 | 50c dull yel | 3.25 | .25 |
| **390** | A166 | 1s violet | 3.25 | .30 |
| **391** | A166 | 2s dl gray grn | 5.25 | .85 |
| **392** | A166 | 5s fawn | 30.00 | 8.50 |
| **393** | A166 | 10s rose vio | 45.00 | 7.00 |
| | | *Nos. 389-393 (5)* | 86.75 | 16.90 |

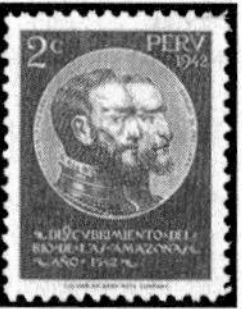
Gonzalo Pizarro and Orellana A167

Francisco de Orellana A168

Francisco Pizarro — A169

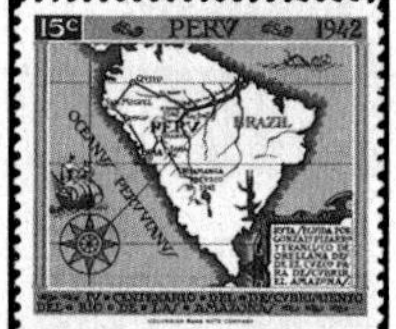
Map of South America with Amazon as Spaniards Knew It in 1542 — A170

Gonzalo Pizarro A171

Discovery of the Amazon River A172

**1943, Feb. *Perf. 12½***

| | | | | |
|---|---|---|---|---|
| **394** | A167 | 2c crimson | .35 | .25 |
| **395** | A168 | 4c slate | .35 | .25 |
| **396** | A169 | 10c yel brn | .35 | .25 |
| **397** | A170 | 15c vio blue | .65 | .30 |
| **398** | A171 | 20c yel olive | .35 | .30 |
| **399** | A172 | 25c dull org | 3.00 | .55 |
| **400** | A168 | 30c dp magenta | .45 | .30 |
| **401** | A170 | 50c blue grn | .55 | .45 |
| **402** | A167 | 70c violet | 2.75 | 1.25 |
| **403** | A171 | 80c lt bl | 2.75 | 1.25 |
| **404** | A172 | 1s cocoa brn | 5.50 | .75 |
| **405** | A169 | 5s intense blk | 11.00 | 5.00 |
| | | *Nos. 394-405 (12)* | 28.05 | 10.90 |

400th anniv. of the discovery of the Amazon River by Francisco de Orellana in 1542.

No. 377 Surcharged in Black

**1943** *Perf. 13*

**406** A155 10c on 10c scar .25 .25

Samuel Finley Breese Morse — A173

**1944** *Perf. 12½*

**407** A173 15c light blue .35 .30
**408** A173 30c olive gray 1.00 .30

Centenary of invention of the telegraph.

### Types of 1938

Imprint: "Columbian Bank Note Co."

**1945-47** **Litho.** *Perf. 12½*

**410** A153 2c green .25 .25
**411** A154 4c org brn ('46) .25 .25
**412** A156 15c ultra .25 .25
**413** A157 20c magenta 2.40 .25
**414** A158 50c grnsh bl .25 .25
**415** A159 1s vio brn .25 .25
**416** A160 2s dl grn 1.00 .25
**417** A161 5s dl vio & brn 6.00 .50
**418** A162 10s blk & ultra ('47) 7.50 .75
*Nos. 410-418 (9)* 18.15 3.00

No. 415 Surcharged in Black

**1946**

**419** A159 20c on 1s vio brn .50 .25
*a.* Surcharge reading down 8.25 8.25

A174

A175

A176

A177

A178

### Black Overprint

*Perf. 12½*

**1947, Apr. 15** **Litho.** **Unwmk.**

**420** A174 15c blk & car .30 .25
**421** A175 1s olive brn .60 .35
**422** A176 1.35s yel grn .60 .45
**423** A177 3s Prus blue 1.10 .75
**424** A178 5s dull grn 2.25 1.60
*Nos. 420-424 (5)* 4.85 3.40

1st National Tourism Congress, Lima. The basic stamps were prepared, but not issued, for the 5th Pan American Highway Congress of 1944.

**Catalogue values for unused stamps in this section, from this point to the end of the section, are for Never Hinged items.**

### Types of 1938

Imprint: "Waterlow & Sons Limited, Londres."

*Perf. 13x13½, 13½x13*

**1949-51** **Photo.**

**426** A154 4c chocolate .35 .25
**427** A156 15c aquamarine .35 .25
**428** A157 20c blue vio .35 .25
**429** A158 50c red brn .45 .25
**430** A159 1s blk brn .90 .30
**431** A160 2s ultra 1.90 .30

**Engr.**

*Perf. 12½*

**432** A161 5s ultra & red brn ('50) 1.90 .65
**433** A162 10s dk bl grn & blk ('51) 5.50 1.25
*Nos. 426-433 (8)* 11.70 3.50

Monument to Admiral Miguel L. Grau — A179

**1949, June 6** *Perf. 12½*

**434** A179 10c ultra & bl grn .35 .25

### Types of 1938

Imprint: "Inst. de Grav. Paris."

**1951** *Perf. 12½x12, 12x12½*

**438** A156 15c peacock grn .35 .25
**439** A157 20c violet .35 .25
**440** A158 50c org brn .35 .25
**441** A159 1s dark brn .90 .25
*Nos. 438-441 (4)* 1.95 1.00

Nos. 375 and 438 Surcharged in Black

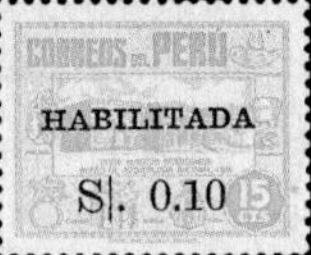


**1951-52** *Perf. 12½, 12½x12*

**445** A153 1c on 2c .25 .25
**446** A156 10c on 15c .25 .25
**446A** A156 10c on 15c ('52) .25 .25
*Nos. 445-446A (3)* .75 .75

On No. 446A "Sl. 0.10" is in smaller type measuring 11½mm. See No. 456.

Nos. 445-446A exist with surcharge double.

Water Promenade A180

Post Boy — A181

Designs: 4c, 50c, 1s, 2s, Various buildings, Lima. 20c, Post Office Street, Lima. 5s, Lake Llangamuco, Ancachs. 10s, Ruins of Machu-Picchu.

### Black Overprint: "V Congreso Panamericano de Carreteras 1951"

**1951, Oct. 13** **Unwmk.** *Perf. 12*

**447** A180 2c dk grn .35 .25
**448** A180 4c brt red .35 .25
**449** A181 15c gray .35 .25
**450** A181 20c ol brn .35 .25
**451** A180 50c dp plum .45 .25
**452** A180 1s blue .55 .30
**453** A180 2s deep blue .90 .30
**454** A180 5s brn lake 2.25 2.10
**455** A181 10s chocolate 4.00 2.10
*Nos. 447-455 (9)* 9.55 6.05

5th Pan-American Congress of Highways, 1951.

No. 438 Surcharged in Black

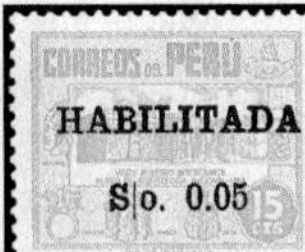


**1952** **Unwmk.** *Perf. 12½x12*

**456** A156 5c on 15c pck grn .25 .25

Engineering School A182

Vicuña — A183

Contour Farming, Cuzco A184

Designs: 2c, Tourist Hotel, Tacna. 5c, Fishing boat and principal fish. 10c, Matarani. 15c, Locomotive No. 80 and coaches. 30c, Ministry of Public Health and Social Assistance. 1s, Paramonga fortress. 2s, Monument to Native Farmer.

**Imprint: "Thomas De La Rue & Co. Ltd."**

*Perf. 13, 12 (A184)*

**1952-53** **Litho.** **Unwmk.**

**457** A182 2c red lil ('53) .25 .25
**458** A182 5c green .25 .25
**459** A182 10c yel grn ('53) .25 .25
**460** A182 15c gray ('53) .25 .25
**461** A183 20c red brn ('53) .65 .25
**462** A182 25c rose red .25 .25
**463** A182 30c indigo ('53) .25 .25
**464** A184 50c green ('53) .75 .25
**465** A184 1s brown .55 .25
**466** A184 2s Prus grn ('53) 1.10 .25
*Nos. 457-466 (10)* 4.55 2.50

See Nos. 468-478, 483-488, 497-501, C184-C185, C209.

For surcharges see Nos. C434, C437, C440-C441, C454, C494.

Gen. Marcos Perez Jimenez — A185

**1956, July 25** **Engr.** *Perf. 13½x13*

**467** A185 25c brown .25 .25

Visit of Gen. Marcos Perez Jimenez, Pres. of Venezuela, June 1955.

### Types of 1952-53

Imprint: "Thomas De La Rue & Co. Ltd."

Designs as before.

**1957-59** **Litho.** *Perf. 13, 12*

**468** A182 15c brown ('59) .65 .25
**469** A182 25c green ('59) .65 .25
**470** A182 30c brown red .35 .25
**471** A184 50c dull pur .55 .25
**472** A184 1s lt vio bl .60 .25
**473** A184 2s gray ('58) 1.10 .25
*Nos. 468-473 (6)* 3.90 1.50

### Types of 1952-53

Imprint: "Joh. Enschedé en Zonen-Holland"

Designs as before.

*Perf. 12½x13½, 13½x12½, 14x13*

**1960** **Litho.** **Unwmk.**

**474** A183 20c lt red brn .25 .25
**475** A182 30c lilac rose .25 .25
**476** A184 50c rose vio .25 .25
**477** A184 1s lt vio bl .55 .25
**478** A184 2s gray 1.00 .30
*Nos. 474-478 (5)* 2.30 1.30

#475 measures 33x22mm, #470 32x22½mm.

Symbols of the Eucharist — A186

**1960, Aug. 10** **Photo.** *Perf. 11½*

**479** A186 50c Cross and "JHS" .25 .25
**480** A186 1s shown .55 .50

Nos. 479-480 were intended for voluntary use to help finance the 6th National Eucharistic Congress at Piura, Aug. 25-28, 1960. Authorized for payment of postage on day of issue only, Aug. 10, but through misunderstanding within the Peruvian postal service they were accepted for payment of postage by some post offices until late in December. Reauthorized for postal use, they were again sold and used, starting in July, 1962. See Nos. RA37-RA38.

Trumpeting Angels — A187

**1961, Dec. 20** **Litho.** *Perf. 10½*

**481** A187 20c bright blue .55 .30

Christmas. Valid for postage for one day, Dec. 20. Used thereafter as a voluntary seal to benefit a fund for postal employees.

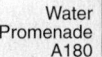

Centenary Cedar, Main Square, Pomabamba — A188

**Unwmk.**

**1962, Sept. 7 Engr. *Perf. 13***

| | | | |
|---|---|---|---|
| **482** A188 1s red & green | .55 | .30 |

Cent. (in 1961) of Pomabamba province.

### Types of 1952-53

Designs: 20c, Vicuña. 30c, Port of Matarani. 40c, Gunboat. 50c, Contour farming. 60c, Tourist hotel, Tacna. 1s, Paramonga, Inca fortress.

**Imprint: "Thomas De La Rue & Co. Ltd."**

***Perf. 13x13½, 13½x13, 12 (A184)***

**1962, Nov. 19 Litho. Wmk. 346**

| | | |
|---|---|---|
| **483** A183 20c rose claret | .25 | .25 |
| **484** A182 30c dark blue | .25 | .25 |
| **485** AP49 40c orange | .25 | .25 |
| **486** A184 50c lt bluish grn | .25 | .25 |
| **487** A182 60c grnsh blk | .55 | .25 |
| **488** A184 1s rose | .80 | .25 |
| *Nos. 483-488 (6)* | 2.35 | 1.50 |

Wheat Emblem and Symbol of Agriculture, Industry A189

**1963, July 23 Unwmk. *Perf. 12½***

| | | |
|---|---|---|
| **489** A189 1s red org & ocher | .25 | .25 |

FAO "Freedom from Hunger" campaign. See No. C190.

Alliance for Progress Emblem — A190

**1964, June 22 Litho. *Perf. 12x12½***

| | | |
|---|---|---|
| **490** A190 40c multi | .25 | .25 |
| *Nos. 490,C192-C193 (3)* | 1.25 | 1.10 |

Alliance for Progress. See note after US No. 1234.

Pacific Fair Emblem — A191

**1965, Oct. 30 Litho. *Perf. 12x12½***

| | | |
|---|---|---|
| **491** A191 1.50s multi | .35 | .25 |
| **492** A191 2.50s multi | .35 | .25 |
| **493** A191 3.50s multi | .60 | .30 |
| *Nos. 491-493 (3)* | 1.30 | .80 |

4th Intl. Pacific Fair, Lima, Oct. 30-Nov. 14.

Santa Claus and Letter A192

**1965, Nov. 2 *Perf. 11***

| | | |
|---|---|---|
| **494** A192 20c red & blk | .25 | .25 |
| **495** A192 50c grn & blk | .45 | .30 |
| **496** A192 1s bl & blk | .80 | .55 |
| *Nos. 494-496 (3)* | 1.50 | 1.10 |

Christmas. Valid for postage for one day, Nov. 2. Used Nov. 3, 1965-Jan. 31, 1966, as voluntary seals for the benefit of a fund for postal employees. See #522-524. For surcharges see #641-643.

### Types of 1952-62

20c, Vicuña. 30c, Port of Matarani. 40c, Gunboat. 50c, Contour farming. 1s, Paramonga, Inca fortress.

**Imprint: "I.N.A."**

***Perf. 12, 13½x14 (A184)***

**1966, Aug. 8 Litho. Unwmk.**

| | | |
|---|---|---|
| **497** A183 20c brn red | .35 | .30 |
| **498** A182 30c dk bl | .35 | .30 |
| **499** AP49 40c orange | .35 | .30 |
| **500** A184 50c gray grn | .35 | .30 |
| **501** A184 1s rose | .35 | .30 |
| *Nos. 497-501 (5)* | 1.75 | 1.50 |

### Postal Tax Stamps Nos. RA40, RA43 Surcharged

a

b

***Perf. 14x14½, 12½x12***

**1966, May 9 Litho.**

| | | |
|---|---|---|
| **501A** PT11 (a) 10c on 2c lt brn | .25 | .25 |
| **501B** PT14 (b) 10c on 3c lt car | .25 | .25 |

Map of Peru, Cordillera Central and Pelton Wheel A193

**1966, Nov. 24 Photo. *Perf. 13½x14***

| | | |
|---|---|---|
| **502** A193 70c bl, blk & vio bl | .35 | .25 |

Opening of the Huinco Hydroelectric Center. See No. C205.

Inca Window and Sun — A194

***Perf. 13½x14***

**1967, Apr. 18 Photo. Unwmk.**

| | | |
|---|---|---|
| **503** A194 90c dp lil rose, blk & gold | .35 | .25 |

6-year building program. See No. C212.

Pacific Fair Emblem — A195

**1967, Oct. 9 Photo. *Perf. 12***

| | | |
|---|---|---|
| **504** A195 1s gold, dk grn & blk | .30 | .25 |

5th Intl. Pacific Fair, Lima, Oct. 27-Nov. 12. See No. C216.

Gold Alligator, Mochica Culture A196

Designs (gold sculptures of the pre-Inca Yunca tribes): 2.60s, Bird, vert. 3.60s, Lizard. 4.60s, Bird, vert. 5.60s, Jaguar.

### Sculptures in Gold Yellow and Brown

**1968, Aug. 16 Photo. *Perf. 12***

| | | |
|---|---|---|
| **505** A196 1.90s dp magenta | 1.50 | .45 |
| **506** A196 2.60s black | 2.00 | .55 |
| **507** A196 3.60s dp magenta | 2.50 | .65 |
| **508** A196 4.60s black | 3.50 | .65 |
| **509** A196 5.60s dp magenta | 4.50 | .95 |
| *Nos. 505-509 (5)* | 14.00 | 3.25 |

See Nos. B1-B5. For surcharge see No. 685.

Indian and Wheat — A197

Designs: 3s, 4s, Farmer digging in field.

### Black Surcharge

**1969, Mar. 3 Litho. *Perf. 11***

| | | |
|---|---|---|
| **510** A197 2.50s on 90c brn & yel | .25 | .25 |
| **511** A197 3s on 90c lil & brn | .40 | .25 |
| **512** A197 4s on 90c rose & grn | .55 | .30 |
| *Nos. 510-512,C232-C233 (5)* | 2.50 | 1.50 |

Agrarian Reform Law.

#510-512 were not issued without surcharge.

Flag, Worker Holding Oil Rig and Map A198

**1969, Apr. 9 Litho. *Perf. 12***

| | | |
|---|---|---|
| **513** A198 2.50s multi | .35 | .25 |
| **514** A198 3s gray & multi | .35 | .25 |
| **515** A198 4s lil & multi | .65 | .30 |
| **516** A198 5.50s lt bl & multi | 1.00 | .30 |
| *Nos. 513-516 (4)* | 2.35 | 1.10 |

Nationalization of the Brea Parinas oilfields, Oct. 9, 1968.

Kon Tiki Raft. Globe and Jet — A199

**1969, June 17 Litho. *Perf. 11***

| | | |
|---|---|---|
| **517** A199 2.50s dp bl & multi | .55 | .30 |
| *Nos. 517,C238-C241 (5)* | 2.85 | 2.10 |

1st Peruvian Airlines (APSA) flight to Europe.

Capt. José A. Quiñones Gonzales (1914-41), Military Aviator — A200

**1969, July 23 Litho. *Perf. 11***

| | | |
|---|---|---|
| **518** A200 20s red & multi | 2.75 | 1.25 |

See No. C243.

Freed Andean Farmer A201

**1969, Aug. 28 Litho. *Perf. 11***

| | | |
|---|---|---|
| **519** A201 2.50s dk bl, lt bl & red | .25 | .25 |
| *Nos. 519,C246-C247 (3)* | 1.15 | .95 |

Enactment of the Agrarian Reform Law of June 24, 1969.

Adm. Miguel Grau A202

**1969, Oct. 8 Litho. *Perf. 11***

| | | |
|---|---|---|
| **520** A202 50s dk bl & multi | 5.50 | 3.25 |

Issued for Navy Day.

Flags and "6" — A203

**1969, Nov. 14**

| | | |
|---|---|---|
| **521** A203 2.50s gray & multi | .55 | .30 |
| *Nos. 521,C251-C252 (3)* | 1.65 | .80 |

6th Intl. Pacific Trade Fair, Lima, Nov. 14-30.

### Santa Claus Type of 1965

Design: Santa Claus and letter inscribed "FELIZ NAVIDAD Y PROSPERO AÑO NUEVO."

**1969, Dec. 1 Litho. *Perf. 11***

| | | |
|---|---|---|
| **522** A192 20c red & blk | .35 | .25 |
| **523** A192 20c org & blk | .35 | .25 |
| **524** A192 20c brn & blk | .35 | .25 |
| *Nos. 522-524 (3)* | 1.05 | .75 |

Christmas. Valid for postage for one day, Dec. 1, 1969. Used after that date as postal tax stamps.

Gen. Francisco Bolognesi and Soldier — A204

**1969, Dec. 9**

| | | |
|---|---|---|
| **525** A204 1.20s lt ultra, blk & gold | .40 | .25 |

Army Day, Dec. 9. See No. C253.

Puma-shaped Jug, Vicus Culture — A205

**1970, Feb. 23 Litho. *Perf. 11***

| | | |
|---|---|---|
| **526** A205 2.50s buff, blk & brn | .75 | .25 |
| *Nos. 526,C281-C284 (5)* | 8.45 | 2.80 |

Ministry of Transport and Communications A206

**1970, Apr. 1 Litho. *Perf. 11***

**527** A206 40c org & gray .30 .25
**528** A206 40c gray & lt gray .30 .25
**529** A206 40c brick red & gray .30 .25
**530** A206 40c brt pink & gray .30 .25
**531** A206 40c org brn & gray .30 .25
*Nos. 527-531 (5)* 1.50 1.25

Ministry of Transport and Communications, 1st anniv.

Anchovy A207

Fish: No. 533, Pacific hake.

**1970, Apr. 30 Litho. *Perf. 11***

**532** A207 2.50s vio bl & multi 2.00 .30
**533** A207 2.50s vio bl & multi 2.00 .30
***a.*** Strip of 5, #532-533, C285-C287 11.00 11.00

Composite Head; Soldier and Farmer A208

**1970, June 24 Litho. *Perf. 11***

**534** A208 2.50s gold & multi .55 .45
*Nos. 534,C290-C291 (3)* 2.20 .95

"United people and army building a new Peru."

Cadets, Chorrillos College, and Arms — A209

Coat of Arms and: No. 536, Cadets of La Punta Naval College. No. 537, Cadets of Las Palmas Air Force College.

**1970, July 27 Litho. *Perf. 11***

**535** A209 2.50s blk & multi .90 .30
**536** A209 2.50s blk & multi .90 .30
**537** A209 2.50s blk & multi .90 .30
***a.*** Strip of 3, #535-537 5.00 4.50

Peru's military colleges.

Courtyard, Puruchuco Fortress, Lima — A210

**1970, Aug. 6**

**538** A210 2.50s multi .80 .25
*Nos. 538,C294-C297 (5)* 6.10 1.85

Issued for tourist publicity.

Nativity, Cuzco School A211

Christmas paintings: 1.50s, Adoration of the Kings, Cuzco School. 1.80s, Adoration of the Shepherds, Peruvian School.

**1970, Dec. 23 Litho. *Perf. 11***

**539** A211 1.20s multi .30 .25
**540** A211 1.50s multi .35 .25
**541** A211 1.80s multi .40 .25
*Nos. 539-541 (3)* 1.05 .75

St. Rosa of Lima — A212

**1971, Apr. 12 Litho. *Perf. 11***

**542** A212 2.50s multi .35 .25

300th anniv. of the canonization of St. Rosa of Lima (1586-1617), first saint born in the Americas.

Tiahuanacoide Cloth — A213

Design: 2.50s, Chancay cloth.

**1971, Apr. 19**

**543** A213 1.20s bl & multi .30 .25
**544** A213 2.50s yel & multi .55 .25
*Nos. 543-544,C306-C308 (5)* 4.65 2.05

Nazca Sculpture, 5th Century, and Seriolella A214

**1971, June 7 Litho. *Perf. 11***

**545** A214 1.50s multi .50 .25
*Nos. 545,C309-C312 (5)* 4.75 2.40

Publicity for 200-mile zone of sovereignty of the high seas.

Mateo Garcia Pumacahua A215

#547, Mariano Melgar. #548, Micaela Bastidas. #549, Jose Faustino Sanchez Carrion. #550, Francisco Antonio de Zela. #551, Jose Baquijano y Carrillo. #552, Martin Jorge Guise.

**1971**

**546** A215 1.20s ver & blk .25 .25
**547** A215 1.20s gray & multi .25 .25
**548** A215 1.50s dk bl & multi .25 .25
**549** A215 2s dk bl & multi .25 .25
**550** A215 2.50s ultra & multi .35 .25
**551** A215 2.50s gray & multi .35 .25
**552** A215 2.50s dk bl & multi .35 .25
*Nos. 546-552,C313-C325 (20)* 8.20 5.80

150th anniv. of independence, and to honor the heroes of the struggle for independence.

Issue dates: Nos. 546, 550, May 10; Nos. 547, 551, July 5; Nos. 548-549, 552, July 27.

Gongora Portentosa A216

Designs: Various Peruvian orchids.

**1971, Sept. 27 *Perf. 13½x13***

**553** A216 1.50s pink & multi .90 .25
**554** A216 2s pink & multi 1.10 .25
**555** A216 2.50s pink & multi 1.10 .25
**556** A216 3s pink & multi 1.25 .25
**557** A216 3.50s pink & multi 2.25 .25
*Nos. 553-557 (5)* 6.60 1.25

"Progress of Liberation," by Teodoro Nuñez Ureta A217

3.50s, Detail from painting by Nuñez Ureta.

**1971, Nov. 4 *Perf. 13x13½***

**558** A217 1.20s multi .25 .25
**559** A217 3.50s multi .55 .25
*Nos. 558-559,C331 (3)* 7.30 2.75

2nd Ministerial meeting of the "Group of 77."

Plaza de Armas, Lima, 1843 A218

3.50s, Plaza de Armas, Lima, 1971.

**1971, Nov. 6**

**560** A218 3s pale grn & blk .65 .30
**561** A218 3.50s lt brick red & blk .65 .30

3rd Annual Intl. Stamp Exhibition, EXFILIMA '71, Lima, Nov. 6-14.

Army Coat of Arms — A219

**1971, Dec. 9 Litho. *Perf. 13½x13***

**562** A219 8.50s multi 1.25 .55

Sesquicentennial of Peruvian Army.

Flight into Egypt A220

Old Stone Sculptures of Huamanga: 2.50s, Three Kings. 3s, Nativity.

**1971, Dec. 18 *Perf. 13x13½***

**563** A220 1.80s multi .35 .30
**564** A220 2.50s multi .55 .30
**565** A220 3s gray & multi .65 .30
*Nos. 563-565 (3)* 1.55 .90

Christmas. See Nos. 597-599.

Fisherman, by J. M. Ugarte Elespuru — A221

Paintings by Peruvian Workers: 4s, Threshing Grain in Cajamarca, by Camilo Blas. 6s, Huanca Highlanders, by José Sabogal.

**1971, Dec. 30 *Perf. 13½x13***

**566** A221 3.50s blk & multi 1.10 .25
**567** A221 4s blk & multi 1.10 .25
**568** A221 6s blk & multi 1.60 .25
*Nos. 566-568 (3)* 3.80 .75

To publicize the revolution and change of order.

Gold Statuette, Chimu, c. 1500 — A222

Ancient Jewelry: 4s, Gold drummer, Chimu. 4.50s, Quartz figurine, Lambayeque culture, 5th century. 5.40s, Gold necklace and pendant, Mochiqua, 4th century. 6s, Gold insect, Lambayeque culture, 14th century.

**1972, Jan. 31 Litho. *Perf. 13½x13***

**569** A222 3.90s red, blk & ocher .55 .25
**570** A222 4s red, blk & ocher .55 .25
**571** A222 4.50s brt bl, blk & ocher 1.25 .25
**572** A222 5.40s red, blk & ocher 1.25 .25
**573** A222 6s red, blk & ocher 1.90 .25
*Nos. 569-573 (5)* 5.50 1.25

Popeye Catalufa A223

Fish: 1.50s, Guadara. 2.50s, Jack mackerel.

**1972, Mar. 20** *Perf. 13x13½*

**574** A223 1.20s lt bl & multi .60 .25
**575** A223 1.50s lt bl & multi .60 .25
**576** A223 2.50s lt bl & multi 1.25 .25
*Nos. 574-576,C333-C334 (5)* 5.95 2.25

Seated Warrior, Mochica — A224

Painted pottery jugs of Mochica culture, 5th cent.: 1.50s, Helmeted head. 2s, Kneeling deer. 2.50s, Helmeted head. 3s, Kneeling warrior.

**1972, May 8** *Perf. 13½x13*

**Emerald Background**

**577** A224 1.20s multi .60 .25
**578** A224 1.50s multi .75 .25
**579** A224 2s multi 1.25 .25
**580** A224 2.50s multi 1.25 .25
**581** A224 3s multi 1.90 .25
*Nos. 577-581 (5)* 5.75 1.25

"Bringing in the Harvest" (July) — A225

Monthly woodcuts from Calendario Incaico.

**1972-73** **Litho.** *Perf. 13½x13*

**Black Vignette & Inscriptions**

**582** A225 2.50s red brn *(July)* 1.90 .30
**583** A225 3s grn *(Aug.)* 1.90 .30
**584** A225 2.50s rose *(Sept.)* 1.90 .30
**585** A225 3s lt bl *(Oct.)* 1.90 .30
**586** A225 2.50s org *(Nov.)* 1.90 .30
**587** A225 3s lil *(Dec.)* 1.90 .30
**588** A225 2.50s brn *(Jan.)* ('73) 1.90 .30
**589** A225 3s pale grn *(Feb.)* ('73) 1.90 .30
**590** A225 2.50s bl *(Mar.)* ('73) 1.90 .30
**591** A225 3s org *(Apr.)* ('73) 1.90 .30
**592** A225 2.50s lil rose *(May)* ('73) 1.90 .30
**593** A225 3s yel & blk *(June)* ('73) 1.90 .30
*Nos. 582-593 (12)* 22.80 3.60

400th anniv. of publication of the Calendario Incaico by Felipe Guaman Poma de Ayala.

Family Tilling Field — A226

Sovereignty of the Sea (Inca Frieze) — A227

Oil Derricks — A228

*Perf. 13½x13, 13x13½*

**1972, Oct. 31** **Litho.**

**594** A226 2s multi .50 .30
**595** A227 2.50s multi .50 .30
**596** A228 3s gray & multi .50 .30
*Nos. 594-596 (3)* 1.50 .90

4th anniversaries of land reforms and the nationalization of the oil industry and 15th anniv. of the claim to a 200-mile zone of sovereignty of the sea.

**Christmas Type of 1971**

Sculptures from Huamanga, 17-18th cent.: 1.50s, Holy Family, wood, vert. 2s, Holy Family with lambs, stone. 2.50s, Holy Family in stable, stone, vert.

**1972, Nov. 30**

**597** A220 1.50s buff & multi .35 .25
**598** A220 2s buff & multi .35 .25
**599** A220 2.50s buff & multi .35 .25
*Nos. 597-599 (3)* 1.05 .75

Morning Glory — A228a

2.50s, Amaryllis. 3s, Liabum excelsum. 3.50s, Bletia (orchid). 5s, Cantua buxifolia.

**1972, Dec. 29** **Litho.** *Perf. 13*

**600** A228a 1.50s shown .55 .25
**601** A228a 2.50s multi .65 .25
**602** A228a 3s multi .90 .25
**603** A228a 3.50s multi 1.10 .25
**604** A228a 5s multi 1.75 .55
*Nos. 600-604 (5)* 4.95 1.55

Mayor on Horseback, by Fierro — A229

Paintings by Francisco Pancho Fierro (1803-1879): 2s, Man and Woman, 1830. 2.50s, Padre Abregu Riding Mule. 3.50s, Dancing Couple. 4.50s, Bullfighter Estevan Arredondo on Horseback.

**1973, Aug. 13** **Litho.** *Perf. 13*

**605** A229 1.50s salmon & multi .30 .25
**606** A229 2s salmon & multi .50 .25
**607** A229 2.50s salmon & multi .70 .25
**608** A229 3.50s salmon & multi 1.00 .25
**609** A229 4.50s salmon & multi 1.25 .60
*Nos. 605-609 (5)* 3.75 1.60

Presentation in the Temple — A230

Christmas Paintings of the Cuzqueña School: 2s, Holy Family, vert. 2.50s, Adoration of the Kings.

*Perf. 13x13½, 13½x13*

**1973, Nov. 30** **Litho.**

**610** A230 1.50s multi .25 .25
**611** A230 2s multi .35 .25
**612** A230 2.50s multi .40 .30
*Nos. 610-612 (3)* 1.00 .80

Peru No. 20 — A231

**1974, Mar. 1** **Litho.** *Perf. 13*

**613** A231 6s gray & dk bl .90 .40

Peruvian Philatelic Assoc., 25th anniv.

Non-ferrous Smelting Plant, La Oroya A232

Colombia Bridge, San Martin A233

Designs: 8s, 10s, Different views, Santiago Antunez Dam, Tayacaja.

**1974** **Litho.** *Perf. 13x13½*

**614** A232 1.50s blue .25 .25
**615** A233 2s multi .25 .25
**616** A232 3s rose claret .55 .25
**617** A232 4.50s green .90 .45
**618** A233 8s multi 1.10 .55
**619** A233 10s multi 1.10 .55
*Nos. 614-619 (6)* 4.15 2.30

"Peru Determines its Destiny."

Issued: 2s, 8s, 10s, 7/1; 1.50s, 3s, 4.50s, 12/6.

Battle of Junin, by Felix Yañez A234

2s, 3s, Battle of Ayacucho, by Felix Yañez.

**1974** **Litho.** *Perf. 13x13½*

**620** A234 1.50s multi .25 .25
**621** A234 2s multi .25 .25
**622** A234 2.50s multi .35 .30
**623** A234 3s multi .35 .30
*Nos. 620-623 (4)* 1.20 1.10

Sesquicentennial of the Battles of Junin and Ayacucho.

Issued: 1.50s, 2.50s, Aug. 6; 2s, 3s, Oct. 9.

See Nos. C400-C404.

Indian Madonna — A235

**1974, Dec. 20** **Litho.** *Perf. 13½x13*

**624** A235 1.50s multi .25 .25

Christmas. See No. C417.

Maria Parado de Bellido A236

International Women's Year Emblem — A237

IWY Emblem, Peruvian Colors and: 2s, Micaela Bastidas. 2.50s, Juana Alarco de Dammert.

*Perf. 13x13½, 13½x13*

**1975, Sept. 8** **Litho.**

**625** A236 1.50s bl grn, red & blk .25 .25
**626** A237 2s blk & red .35 .25
**627** A236 2.50s pink, blk & red .35 .25
**628** A237 3s red, blk & ultra .65 .25
*Nos. 625-628 (4)* 1.60 1.00

International Women's Year.

St. Juan Macias — A238

**1975, Nov. 14** *Perf. 13½x13*

**629** A238 5s blk & multi .55 .25

Canonization of Juan Macias in 1975.

Louis Braille A239

**1976, Mar. 2** **Litho.** *Perf. 13x13½*

**630** A239 4.50s gray, red & blk .55 .45

Sesquicentennial of the invention of Braille system of writing for the blind by Louis Braille (1809-1852).

Peruvian Flag A240

**1976, Aug. 29** **Litho.** *Perf. 13x13½*

**631** A240 5s gray, blk & red .35 .25

Revolutionary Government, phase II, 1st anniv.

St. Francis, by El Greco — A241

**1976, Dec. 9 Litho. *Perf. 13½x13***
**632** A241 5s gold, buff & brn .75 .25

St. Francis of Assisi, 750th death anniv.

Indian Mother — A242

**1976, Dec. 23**
**633** A242 4s multi .65 .25

Christmas.

Chasqui Messenger A243

**1977 Litho. *Perf. 13½x13***
**634** A243 6s grnsh bl & blk .55 .25
**635** A243 8s red & blk .55 .25
**636** A243 10s ultra & blk .55 .50
**637** A243 12s lt grn & blk .55 .50
*Nos. 634-637,C465-C467 (7)* 8.45 4.10

For surcharge see No. C502.

"X" over Flags — A244

**1977, Nov. 25 Litho. *Perf. 13½x13***
**638** A244 10s multi .35 .25

10th Intl. Pacific Fair, Lima, Nov. 16-27.

Republican Guard Badge — A245

**1977, Dec. 1**
**639** A245 12s multi .55 .30

58th anniversary of Republican Guard.

Indian Nativity — A246

**1977, Dec. 23**
**640** A246 8s multi .45 .35

Christmas. See No. C484.

**Nos. 495, 494, 496 Surcharged with New Value and Bar in Red, Dark Blue or Black: "FRANQUEO / 10.00 / RD-0161-77"**

**1977, Dec. *Perf. 11***
**641** A192 10s on 50c (R) .45 .30
**642** A192 20s on 20c (DB) .90 .55
**643** A192 30s on 1s (B) 1.25 .75
*Nos. 641-643 (3)* 2.60 1.60

Inca Head — A247

**1978 Litho. *Perf. 13½x13***
**644** A247 6s bright green .25 .25
**645** A247 10s red .25 .25
**646** A247 16s red brown .45 .30
*Nos. 644-646,C486-C489 (7)* 6.60 4.30

For surcharges see Nos. C498-C499, C501.

Flags of Germany, Argentina, Austria, Brazil A248

Argentina '78 Emblem and Flags of Participants: No. 648, 652, Hungary, Iran, Italy, Mexico. No. 649, 653, Scotland, Spain, France, Netherlands. No. 650, 654, Peru, Poland, Sweden and Tunisia. No. 651, like No. 647.

**1978 Litho. *Perf. 13x13½***
**647** A248 10s blue & multi .65 .30
**648** A248 10s blue & multi .65 .30
**649** A248 10s blue & multi .65 .30
**650** A248 10s blue & multi .65 .30
*a.* Block of 4, #647-650 3.00 3.00
**651** A248 16s blue & multi .65 .40
**652** A248 16s blue & multi .65 .40
**653** A248 16s blue & multi .65 .40
**654** A248 16s blue & multi .65 .40
*a.* Block of 4, #651-654 4.00 4.00
*Nos. 647-654 (8)* 5.20 2.80

11th World Soccer Cup Championship, Argentina, June 1-25.
Issued: #647-650, 6/28; #651-654, 12/4.

Thomas Faucett, Planes of 1928, 1978 A249

**1978, Oct. 19 Litho. *Perf. 13***
**655** A249 40s multicolored .90 .50

Faucett Aviation, 50th anniversary.

Nazca Bowl, Huaco A250

**1978-79 Litho. *Perf. 13x13½***
**656** A250 16s violet bl ('79) .45 .25
**657** A250 20s green ('79) .45 .25
**658** A250 25s lt green ('79) .55 .55
**659** A250 35s rose red ('79) .90 .30
**660** A250 45s dk brown 1.10 .55
**661** A250 50s black 1.25 .65
**662** A250 55s car rose ('79) 1.25 .65
**663** A250 70s lilac rose ('79) 1.50 1.10
**664** A250 75s blue 1.75 1.00
**665** A250 80s salmon ('79) 1.75 1.00
**667** A250 200s brt vio ('79) 4.25 3.25
*Nos. 656-667 (11)* 15.20 9.55

For surcharges see Nos. 715, 731.

Peruvian Nativity — A252

**1978, Dec. 28 Litho. *Perf. 13½x13***
**672** A252 16s multicolored .55 .50

Ministry of Education, Lima — A253

**1979, Jan. 4**
**673** A253 16s multicolored .45 .35

National Education Program.

**Nos. RA40, B1-B5 and 509 Surcharged in Various Colors**

a

SOBRE TASA OFICIAL S/. 3.00

b

Habilitado R.D. N° 0118 S/. 35.00

c

**1978, July-Aug.**
**674** PT11(a) 2s on 2c (O) .25 .25
**675** PT11(b) 3s on 2c (Bk) .25 .25
**676** PT11(a) 4s on 2c (G) .25 .25
**677** PT11(a) 5s on 2c (V) .25 .25
**678** PT11(b) 6s on 2c (DBl) .25 .25
**679** SP1 20s on 1.90s + 90c (G) 1.25 1.25
**680** SP1 30s on 2.60s + 1.30s (Bl) 1.25 1.25
**681** PT11(c) 35s on 2c (C) 1.60 1.60
**682** PT11(c) 50s on 2c (LtBl) 5.50 5.50
**683** SP1 55s on 3.60s + 1.80s (VBl) 1.75 1.75
**684** SP1 65s on 4.60s + 2.30s (Go) 1.75 1.75
**685** A196 80s on 5.60s (VBl) 1.40 1.40
**686** SP1 85s on 20s + 10s (Bk) 2.75 2.75
*Nos. 674-686 (13)* 18.50 18.50

Surcharge on Nos. 679-680, 683-684, 686 includes heavy bar over old denomination.

Battle of Iquique A254

Heroes' Crypt — A255

Col. Francisco Bolognesi A256

War of the Pacific: No. 688, Col. Jose J. Inclan. No. 689, Corvette Union running Arica blockade. No. 690, Battle of Angamos, Aguirre, Miguel Grau (1838-1879), Perre. No. 690A, Lt. Col. Pedro Ruiz Gallo. 85s, Marshal Andres A. Caceres. No. 692, Naval Battle of Angamos. No. 693, Battle of Tarapaca. 115s, Adm. Miguel Grau. No. 697, Col. Bolognesi's Reply, by Angeles de la Cruz. No. 698, Col. Alfonso Ugarte on horseback.

***Perf. 13½x13, 13x13½***

**1979-80 Litho.**
**687** A254 14s multicolored .35 .35
**688** A256 25s multicolored .55 .25
**689** A254 25s multicolored .90 .35
**690** A254 25s multicolored .90 .35
**690A** A256 25s multi ('80) .45 .25
**691** A256 85s multicolored .90 .65
**692** A254 100s multicolored 1.00 .65
**693** A254 100s multicolored 1.10 .65
**694** A256 115s multicolored 2.00 1.10
**695** A255 200s multicolored 11.00 7.00
**696** A256 200s multicolored 2.00 1.60
**697** A254 200s multicolored 2.00 1.60
**698** A254 200s multicolored 2.75 1.60
*Nos. 687-698 (13)* 25.90 16.40

For surcharges see Nos. 713, 732.

Peruvian Red Cross, Cent. A257

**1979, May 4 *Perf. 13x13½***
**699** A257 16s multicolored .40 .40

Billiard Balls — A258

**1979, June 4 *Perf. 13½x13***
**700** A258 34s multicolored .50 .25

For surcharge see No. 714.

Arms of Cuzco — A259

**1979, June 24**
**701** A259 50s multicolored 1.20 .35

Inca Sun Festival, Cuzco.

Peru Colors, Tacna Monument A260

**1979, Aug. 28 Litho. *Perf. 13½x13***
**702** A260 16s multicolored .55 .35

Return of Tacna Province to Peru, 50th anniv.
For surcharge see No. 712.

Telecom 79 — A261

**1979, Sept. 20**
**703** A261 15s multicolored .35 .35

3rd World Telecommunications Exhibition, Geneva, Sept. 20-26.

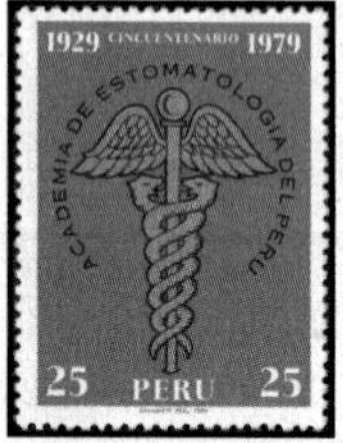

Caduceus A262

**1979, Nov. 13**
**704** A262 25s multicolored .55 .35

Stomatology Academy of Peru, 50th anniv.; 4th Intl. Congress.

World Map, "11," Fair Emblem A263

**1979, Nov. 24**
**705** A263 55s multicolored .65 .45

11th Pacific Intl. Trade Fair, Lima, 11/14-25.

Gold Jewelry — A264

**1979, Dec. 19 *Perf. 13½x13***
**706** A264 85s multicolored 2.75 1.25

Larco Herrera Archaeological Museum.

Christmas A265

**1979, Dec. 27 Litho. *Perf. 13x13½***
**707** A265 25s multicolored .55 .35

Queen Sofia and King Juan Carlos I, Visit to Peru A266

**1979, Feb. 7 Litho. *Perf. 13x13½***
**708** A266 75s multicolored .90 .25

**No. RA40 Surcharged in Black, Green or Blue**

No. 709

No. 710

No. 711

**1979, Oct. 8**
**709** PT11 7s on 2c brown .40 .40
**710** PT11 9s on 2c brown (G) .40 .40
**711** PT11 15s on 2c brown (B) .40 .40
*Nos. 709-711 (3)* 1.20 1.20

**Nos. 702, 687, 700, 663 Surcharged**
***Perf. 13½x13, 13x13½***

**1980, Apr. 14 Litho.**
**712** A260 20s on 16s multi .40 .40
**713** A254 25s on 14s multi .50 .40
**714** A258 65s on 34s multi .90 .70
**715** A250 80s on 70s lilac rose 1.25 .50
*Nos. 712-715,C501-C502 (6)* 4.20 2.95

Liberty Holding Arms of Peru — A267

Civic duties: 15s, Respect the Constitution. 20s, Honor country. 25s, Vote. 30s, Military service. 35s, Pay taxes. 45s, Contribute to national progress. 50s, Respect rights.

**1980 Litho.**
**716** A267 15s greenish blue .30 .30
**717** A267 20s salmon pink .30 .30
**718** A267 25s ultra .30 .30
**719** A267 30s lilac rose .30 .30
**720** A267 35s black .50 .35
**721** A267 45s light blue green .55 .50
**722** A267 50s brown 1.00 .50
*Nos. 716-722 (7)* 3.25 2.55

Chimu Cult Cup — A268

**1980, July 9 Litho.**
**723** A268 35s multicolored 1.50 .80

Map of Peru and Liberty — A269

Return to Civilian Government — A270

***Perf. 13½x13, 13x13½***
**1980, Sept. 9 Litho.**
**724** A269 25s multicolored .50 .40
**725** A270 35s multicolored .75 .40

For surcharge see No. 730.

Machu Picchu A271

**1980, Nov. 10 Litho. *Perf. 13x13½***
**726** A271 25s multicolored 2.00 2.00

World Tourism Conf., Manila, Sept. 27.

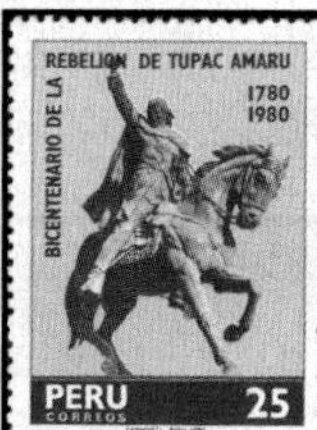

Tupac Amaru Rebellion Bicent. — A272

**1980, Dec. 22 Litho. *Perf. 13½x13***
**727** A272 25s multicolored .45 .35

Christmas A273

**1980, Dec. 31 Litho. *Perf. 13***
**728** A273 15s multicolored .65 .55

150th Death Anniv. of Simon Bolivar (in 1980) — A274

**1981, Jan. 28 Litho. *Perf. 13½x13***
**729** A274 40s multicolored .50 .25

**Nos. 725, 667, 694 Surcharged**

**1981 Litho. *Perf. 13x13½***
**730** A270 25s on 35s multi .30 .25
**731** A250 85s on 200s brt violet 1.10 .80
**732** A256 100s on 115s multi 1.25 .95
*Nos. 730-732 (3)* 2.65 2.00

Return to Constitutional Government, July 28, 1980 — A275

**1981, Mar. 26 Litho. *Perf. 13½x13***
**733** A275 25s multicolored .60 .40

For surcharges see Nos. 736-737, 737C.

Tupac Amaru and Micaela Bastidas, Bronze Sculptures, by Miguel Baca-Rossi A276

**1981, May 18 Litho. *Perf. 13x13½***
**734** A276 60s multicolored .70 .50

Rebellion of Tupac Amaru and Micaela Bastidas, bicentenary.

**Nos. 733, RA41 and Voluntary Postal Tax Stamps of 1965 Surcharged in Black, Dull Brown or Lake and**

Cross, Unleavened Bread, Wheat A276a

Chalice, Host A276b

***Perf. 13½x13, Rouletted 11 (#735, 737B), 11½ (#737A)***
**1981 Litho., Photo. (#737A-737B)**
**735** PT17 40s on 10c #RA41 .30 .25
**736** A275 40s on 25s #733 .90 .55
**737** A275 130s on 25s #733 (DB) .90 .55
**737A** A276a 140s on 50c brn, yel & red .55 .40
**737B** A276b 140s on 1s multi .55 .40
**737C** A275 140s on 25s #733 (L) .90 .55
*Nos. 735-737C (6)* 4.10 2.70

Issued: #735, Apr. 12; #736, 737, 737C, Apr. 6; #737A, Apr. 15; #737B, Apr. 28.

Carved Stone Head, Pallasca Tribe A277

#739, 742, 749 Pottery vase, Inca, vert. #740, Head, diff., vert. #743, 749A-749B, Huaco idol (fish), Nazca. 100s, Pallasca, vert. 140s, Puma.

*Perf. 13½x13, 13x13½*

**1981-82** **Litho.**

| | | | | |
|---|---|---|---|---|
| **738** | A277 | 30s dp rose lilac | .60 | .60 |
| **739** | A277 | 40s orange ('82) | .70 | .25 |
| **740** | A277 | 40s ultra | .70 | .25 |
| **742** | A277 | 80s brown ('82) | 2.00 | 1.50 |
| **743** | A277 | 80s red ('82) | 2.00 | 1.40 |
| **745** | A277 | 100s lilac rose | 1.75 | 1.50 |
| **748** | A277 | 140s lt blue grn | 2.50 | 2.10 |
| **749** | A277 | 180s green ('82) | 4.50 | 3.75 |
| **749A** | A277 | 240s grnsh blue ('82) | 2.75 | 2.10 |
| **749B** | A277 | 280s violet ('82) | 3.75 | 2.75 |
| | | *Nos. 738-749B (10)* | 21.25 | 16.20 |

For surcharges see #789, 798-799, 1026.

A278

**1981, May 31** *Perf. 13½x13*
**750** A278 130s multicolored .90 .90

Postal and Philatelic Museum, 50th anniv.

A279

**1981, Oct. 7** **Litho.** *Perf. 13½x13*
**751** A279 30s purple & gray .40 .40

1979 Constitution Assembly President Victor Raul Haya de la Torre.

Inca Messenger, by Guaman Poma (1526-1613) A280

**1981** **Litho.** *Perf. 12*

| | | | | |
|---|---|---|---|---|
| **752** | A280 | 30s lilac & blk | 1.25 | 1.00 |
| **753** | A280 | 40s vermilion & blk | 1.00 | 2.00 |
| **754** | A280 | 130s brt yel grn & blk | 2.50 | 2.00 |
| **755** | A280 | 140s brt blue & blk | 2.50 | 2.50 |
| **756** | A280 | 200s yel brn & blk | 4.50 | 4.50 |
| | | *Nos. 752-756 (5)* | 11.75 | 12.00 |

Christmas. Issue dates: 30s, 40s, 200s, Dec. 21; others, Dec. 31.

Intl. Year of the Disabled A280a

**1981** **Litho.** *Perf. 13½x13*
**756A** A280a 100s multicolored 1.25 .85

**Nos. 377, C130, C143, J56, O33, RA36, RA39, RA40, RA42, RA43 Surcharged in Brown, Black, Orange, Red, Green or Blue**

**1982**

| | | | | |
|---|---|---|---|---|
| **757** | PT11 | 10s on 2c (#RA40, Br) | .40 | .40 |
| **758** | A155 | 10s on 10c (#377) | .30 | .30 |
| **758A** | AP60 | 40s on 1.25s (#C143) | .30 | .30 |
| **758B** | PT15 | 70s on 5c (#RA36, R) | .40 | .40 |
| **759** | D7 | 80s on 10c (#J56) | .30 | .30 |
| **760** | O1 | 80s on 10c (#O33) | .30 | .30 |
| **761** | PT14 | 80s on 3c (#RA43, O) | .30 | .30 |
| **762** | PT17 | 100s on 10c (#RA42, R) | .40 | .40 |
| **763** | AP57 | 100s on 2.20s (#C130, R) | .50 | .50 |
| **764** | PT14 | 150s on 3c (#RA39, G) | .60 | .60 |
| **765** | PT14 | 180s on 3c (#RA43, R) | .60 | .60 |
| **766** | PT14 | 200s on 3c (#RA43, Bl) | .70 | .70 |
| **767** | AP60 | 240s on 1.25s (#C143, R) | 1.25 | 1.25 |
| **768** | PT15 | 280s on 5c (#RA36) | 1.10 | 1.10 |
| | | *Nos. 757-768 (14)* | 7.45 | 7.45 |

Nos. 758A, 763, 767 airmail. Nos. 759 and 760 surcharged "Habilitado / Franq. Postal / 80 Soles".

Jorge Basadre (1903-1980), Historian — A281

Julio C. Tello (1882-1947), Archaeologist — A282

*Perf. 13½x13, 13x13½*

**1982, Oct. 13** **Litho.**
**769** A281 100s pale green & blk .40 .30
**770** A282 200s lt green & dk bl .80 .55

9th Women's World Volleyball Championship, Sept. 12-26 — A283

**1982, Oct. 18** *Perf. 12*
**771** A283 80s black & red .30 .25

For surcharge see No. 791.

Rights of the Disabled — A284

**1982, Oct. 22**
**772** A284 200s blue & red .90 .30

Brena Campaign Centenary A285

70s, Andres Caceres medallion.

**1982, Oct. 26** *Perf. 13x13½*
**773** A285 70s multi .30 .25

For surcharge see No. 790.

1982 World Cup — A286

**1982, Nov. 2** *Perf. 12*
**774** A286 80s multicolored .80 .30

For surcharge see No. 800.

16th Intl. Congress of Latin Notaries, Lima, June — A287

**1982, Nov. 6**
**775** A287 500s Emblem 1.25 .85

Handicrafts Year A288

**1982, Nov. 24** *Perf. 13x13½*
**776** A288 200s Clay bull figurine .60 .30

Christmas A289

**1982** *Perf. 13½x13*
**777** A289 280s Holy Family .70 .70

For surcharge see No. 797.

Pedro Vilcapaza A290

**1982, Dec. 2** *Perf. 13½x13*
**778** A290 240s black & lt brn .65 .50

Death centenary of Indian leader against Spanish during Andes Rebellion.
For surcharges see Nos. 792.

Jose Davila Condemarin (1799-1882), Minister of Posts (1849-76) — A291

**1982, Dec. 10** *Perf. 13x13½*
**779** A291 150s blue & blk .40 .35

10th Anniv. of Intl. Potato Study Center, Lima A292

**1982, Dec. 27** *Perf. 13x13½*
**780** A292 240s multicolored .65 .45

For surcharge see No. 793.

450th Anniv. of City of San Miguel de Piura A293

**1982, Dec. 31** *Perf. 13x13½*
**781** A293 280s Arms .90 .65

For surcharge see No. 795.

TB Bacillus Centenary A294

**1983, Jan. 18** *Perf. 12*
**782** A294 240s Microscope, slide .70 .70

For surcharge see No. 794.

St. Teresa of Jesus of Avila (1515-1582), by Jose Espinoza de los Monteros, 1682 — A295

**1983, Mar. 1**
**783** A295 100s multicolored .30 .25

10th Anniv. of State Security Service A296

**1983, Mar. 8**
**784** A296 100s blue & orange .30 .25

Horseman's Ornamental Silver Shoe, 19th Cent. A297

**1983, Mar. 18**

**785** A297 250s multicolored .65 .45

30th Anniv. of Santiago Declaration A298

**1983, Mar. 25**

**786** A298 280s Map 1.00 .60

For surcharge see No. 796.

25th Anniv. of Lima-Bogota Airmail Service — A299

**1983, Apr. 8**

**787** A299 150s Jet .60 .25

75th Anniv. of Lima and Callao State Lotteries — A300

**1983, Apr. 26**

**788** A300 100s multicolored .30 .25

### Nos. 739, 773, 771, 778, 780, 782, 781, 786, 777, 749, 774 Srchd. in Black or Green

**1983** **Litho.**

| | | | | |
|---|---|---|---|---|
| **789** | A277 100s on 40s orange | 1.25 | .25 |
| **790** | A285 100s on 70s multi | 1.25 | .25 |
| **791** | A283 100s on 80s blk & red | 1.25 | .25 |
| **792** | A290 100s on 240s multi | 1.25 | .25 |
| **793** | A292 100s on 240s multi | 1.25 | .25 |
| **794** | A294 100s on 240s ol grn | 1.25 | .25 |
| **795** | A293 150s on 280s multi (G) | 1.50 | .50 |
| **796** | A298 150s on 280s multi | 1.50 | .50 |
| **797** | A289 200s on 280s multi | 2.25 | .60 |
| **798** | A277 300s on 180s green | 3.50 | 1.00 |
| **799** | A277 400s on 180s green | 4.50 | 1.25 |
| **800** | A286 500s on 80s multi | 1.25 | 1.25 |
| | *Nos. 789-800 (12)* | 22.00 | 6.60 |

Military Ships A301

150s, Cruiser Almirante Grau, 1907. 350s, Submarine Ferre, 1913.

**1983, May 2** ***Perf. 12***

**801** A301 150s multicolored .75 .25
**802** A301 350s multicolored 2.00 .50

Simon Bolivar Birth Bicentenary A302

**1983, Dec. 13** **Litho.** ***Perf. 14***

**803** A302 100s black & lt bl .70 .25

Christmas A303

**1983, Dec. 16**

**804** A303 100s Virgin and Child 1.00 .25

25th Anniv. of Intl. Pacific Fair — A304

**1983**

**805** A304 350s multicolored .90 .50

World Communications Year (in 1983) — A305

**1984, Jan. 27** **Litho.** ***Perf. 14***

**806** A305 700s multicolored 2.00 1.00

Col. Leoncio Prado (1853-83) A306

**1984, Feb. 3** **Litho.** ***Perf. 14***

**807** A306 150s ol & ol brn .60 .25

Postal Building A307

Pottery — A308

Shipbuilding and Repair — A309

Arms of City of Callao — A310

Peruvian Flora — A311

Peruvian Fauna — A312

50s, Ministry of Posts, Lima. 100s, Water jar. 150s, Llama. 200s, Painted vase. 300s, Mixed cargo ship. 400s, Arms of Cajamarca. 500s, Arms of Ayacucho. 700s, Canna edulis ker. 1000s, Lagothrix flavicauda.

**1984** **Litho.** ***Perf. 14***

| | | | | |
|---|---|---|---|---|
| **808** | A307 50s multi | .25 | .25 |
| **809** | A308 100s multi | .70 | .25 |
| **810** | A308 150s multi | .70 | .25 |
| **811** | A308 200s multi | .70 | .25 |
| **812** | A309 250s shown | .70 | .25 |
| **813** | A309 300s multi | 1.00 | .25 |
| **814** | A310 350s shown | .55 | .25 |
| **815** | A310 400s multi | 1.25 | .25 |
| **816** | A310 500s multi | 1.60 | .25 |
| **817** | A311 700s multi | 1.00 | .40 |
| **818** | A312 1000s multi | 2.00 | .60 |
| | *Nos. 808-818 (11)* | 10.45 | 3.25 |

Issued: 50s, 8/29; 100s-200s, 5/9; 250s-300s, 2/22; 350s, 4/23; 400s, 6/21; 500s, 6/22; 700s, 9/12; 1000s, 7/3.

See Nos. 844-853, 880-885.

A313

Designs: 50s, Hipolito Unanue (1758-1833). 200s, Ricardo Palma (1833-1919), Writer.

**1984** **Litho.** ***Perf. 14***

**819** A313 50s dull green .50 .30
**820** A313 200s purple .50 .30

Issue dates: 50s, Nov. 14; 200s, Mar. 20.

See No. 828.

1984 Summer Olympics — A315

**1984, Mar. 30**

**821** A315 500s Shooting .80 .40
**822** A315 750s Hurdles 1.20 .60

Independence Declaration Act — A316

**1984, July 18** **Litho.** ***Perf. 14***

**823** A316 350s Signing document .50 .25

Admiral Grau — A317

Naval Battle — A318

**1984, Oct. 8** **Litho.** ***Perf. 12½***

**824** Block of 4 4.00 3.00

- *a.* A317 600s Knight of the Seas, by Pablo Muniz .90 .25
- *b.* A318 600s Battle of Angamos .90 .25
- *c.* A317 600s Congressional seat .90 .25
- *d.* A318 600s Battle of Iquique .90 .25

Admiral Miguel Grau, 150th birth anniv.

Peruvian Naval Vessels A319

250s, Destroyer Almirante Guise, 1934. 400s, Gunboat America, 1905.

**1984, Dec.** **Litho.** ***Perf. 14***

**825** A319 250s multicolored .75 .25
**826** A319 400s multicolored .75 .25

Christmas
A320

**1984, Dec. 11 Litho.** ***Perf. 13x13½***

**827** A320 1000s multi .70 .50

### Famous Peruvians Type of 1984

**1984, Dec. 14 Litho.** ***Perf. 14***

**828** A313 100s brown lake .40 .25

Victor Andres Belaunde (1883-1967), Pres. of UN General Assembly, 1959-60.

450th Anniv., Founding of Cuzco — A322

**1984, Dec. 20 Litho.** ***Perf. 13½x13***

**829** A322 1000s Street scene .80 .40

15th Pacific Intl. Fair, Lima
A323

**1984, Dec. 28 Litho.** ***Perf. 13x13½***

**830** A323 1000s Llama .80 .40

450th Anniv., Lima — A324

The Foundation of Lima, by Francisco Gamarra

**1985, Jan. 17 Litho.** ***Perf. 13½x13***

**831** A324 1500s multicolored 3.00 .50

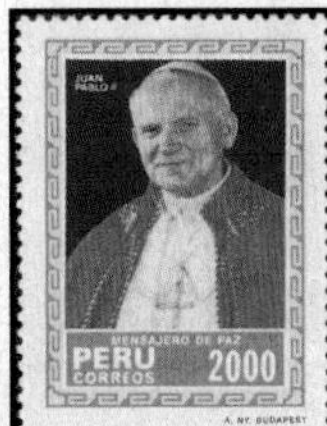


Visit of Pope John Paul II — A325

**1985, Jan. 31 Litho.** ***Perf. 13½x13***

**832** A325 2000s Portrait 2.50 .40

Microwave Tower — A326

**1985, Feb. 28 Litho.** ***Perf. 13½x13***

**833** A326 1100s multi 1.00 .30

ENTEL Peru, Natl. Telecommunications Org., 15th anniv.

Jose Carlos Mariategui (1894-1924), Author — A327

Designs: 500s, Francisco Garcia Calderon (1832-1905), president. No. 838, Oscar Miro Quesada (1884-1981), jurist. No. 839, Cesar Vallejo (1892-1938), author. No. 840, Jose Santos Chocano (1875-1934), poet.

**1985-86 Photo.** ***Perf. 13½x13***

| | | | | |
|---|---|---|---|---|
| **836** | A327 500s lt olive grn | .50 | .25 |
| **837** | A327 800s dull red | .50 | .25 |
| **838** | A327 800s dk olive grn | .50 | .25 |
| **839** | A327 800s Prus blue ('86) | .50 | .25 |
| **840** | A327 800s dk red brn ('86) | .50 | .25 |
| | *Nos. 836-840 (5)* | 2.50 | 1.25 |

See Nos. 901-905.

American Air Forces Cooperation System, 25th Anniv. — A328

**1985, Apr. 16**

**842** A328 400s Member flags, emblem .50 .25

Jose A. Quinones Gonzales (1914-1941), Air Force Captain — A329

**1985, Apr. 22** ***Perf. 13x13½***

**843** A329 1000s Portrait, bomber 1.10 .45

### Types of 1984

Design: 200s, Entrance arch and arcade, Central PO admin. building, vert. No. 845, Spotted Robles Moqo bisque vase, Pacheco, Ica. No. 846, Huaura bisque cat. No. 847, Robles Moqo bisque llama head. No. 848, Huancavelica city arms. No. 849, Huanuco city arms. No. 850, Puno city arms. No. 851, Llama wool industry. No. 852, Hymenocallis amancaes. No. 853, Penguins, Antarctic landscape.

**1985-86 Litho.** ***Perf. 13½x13***

| | | | | |
|---|---|---|---|---|
| **844** | A307 | 200s slate blue | .60 | .60 |
| **845** | A308 | 500s bister brn | .35 | .30 |
| **846** | A308 | 500s dull yellow brn | .35 | .30 |
| **847** | A308 | 500s black brn | .35 | .30 |
| **848** | A310 | 700s brt org yel | .80 | .70 |
| **849** | A310 | 700s brt bl ('86) | .80 | .70 |
| **850** | A310 | 900s brown ('86) | 1.10 | .70 |
| **851** | A309 | 1100s multicolored | .80 | .50 |
| **852** | A311 | 1100s multicolored | .80 | .50 |
| **853** | A312 | 1500s multicolored | 1.10 | .60 |
| | | *Nos. 844-853 (10)* | 7.05 | 5.20 |

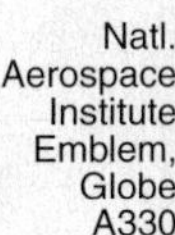

Natl. Aerospace Institute Emblem, Globe
A330

**1985, May 24** ***Perf. 13x13½***

**858** A330 900s ultra .70 .25

14th Inter-American Air Defense Day.

Founding of Constitution City — A333

**1985, July Litho.** ***Perf. 13½x13***

**859** A333 300s Map, flag, crucifix .70 .35

Natl. Radio Society, 55th Anniv.
A334

**1985, July 24** ***Perf. 13x13½***

**860** A334 1300s bl & brt org 1.00 .35

San Francisco Convent Church — A335

**1985, Oct. 12** ***Perf. 13½x13***

**861** A335 1300s multicolored .60 .25

Doctrina Christiana Frontispiece, 1585, Lima — A336

**1985, Oct. 23**

**862** A336 300s pale buff & blk .70 .25

1st printed book in South America, 400th anniv.

Intl. Civil Aviation Org., 40th Anniv.
A337

1100s, 1920 Curtis Jenny.

**1985, Oct. 31** ***Perf. 13x13½***

**863** A337 1100s multicolored .80 .35

Christmas
A338

2.50i, Virgin and child, 17th cent.

**1985, Dec. 30 Litho.** ***Perf. 13½x13***

**864** A338 2.50i multi 1.00 .25

Postman, Child — A338a

**1985, Dec. 30 Litho.** ***Perf. 13½x13***

**864A** A338a 2.50i multi .65 .35

Christmas charity for children's and postal workers' funds.

Founding of Trujillo, 450th Anniv. — A339

**1986, Mar. 5 Litho.** ***Perf. 13½x13***

**865** A339 3i City arms 1.00 .35

Restoration of Chan Chan Ruins, Trujillo Province
A340

**1986, Apr. 5 Litho.** ***Perf. 13x13½***

**866** A340 50c Bas-relief 1.00 .30

Saint Rose of Lima, Birth Quadricent.
A341

**1986, Apr. 30 Litho.** ***Perf. 13½x13***

**867** A341 7i multicolored 2.50 1.25

16th Intl. Pacific Fair — A342

1i, Natl. products symbols.

**1986, May 20**

**868** A342 1i multicolored .70 .40

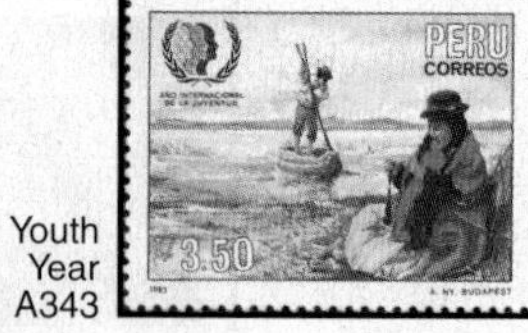
Intl. Youth Year A343

**1986, May 23** *Perf. 13x13½*
**869** A343 3.50i multicolored .65 .45

A344

**1986, June 27 Litho.** *Perf. 13½x13*
**870** A344 50c brown .50 .45

Pedro Vilcapaza (1740-81), independence hero.

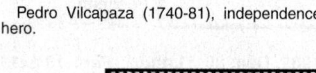

UN, 40th Anniv. A345

**1986, Aug. 8 Litho.** *Perf. 13x13½*
**871** A345 3.50i multi 1.10 .75

A346

**1986, Aug. 11** *Perf. 13½x13*
**872** A346 50c grysh brown .50 .25

Fernando and Justo Albujar Fayaque, Manuel Guarniz Lopez, natl. heroes.

Peruvian Navy A347

**1986, Aug. 19** *Perf. 13x13½*
**873** A347 1.50i R-1, 1926 .75 .35
**874** A347 2.50i Abtao, 1954 1.40 .35

### Flora and Fauna Type of 1984

No. 880, Tropaeolum majus. No. 881, Datura candida. No. 884, Canis ludus. No. 885, Penelope albipennis.

**1986 Litho.** *Perf. 13½x13*
**880** A311 80c multicolored .45 .45
**881** A311 80c multicolored .45 .45
**884** A312 2i multicolored 1.10 1.00
**885** A312 2i multicolored 1.25 1.10
*Nos. 880-885 (4)* 3.25 3.00

Canchis Province Folk Costumes A348

**1986, Aug. 26 Litho.** *Perf. 13½x13*
**890** A348 3i multicolored 1.10 .75

Tourism Day A349

**1986, Aug. 29** *Perf. 13x13½*
**891** A349 4i Sacsayhuaman 1.60 1.00

**1986, Oct. 12 Litho.** *Perf. 13x13½*
**891A** A349 4i Intihuatana, Cuzco 2.25 1.75

Interamerican Development Bank, 25th Anniv. — A350

**1986, Sept. 4**
**892** A350 1i multicolored .45 .45

Beatification of Sr. Ana de Los Angeles — A351

6i, Sr. Ana, Pope John Paul II.

**1986, Sept. 15**
**893** A351 6i multicolored 3.00 1.50

Jorge Chavez (1887-1910), Aviator, and Bleriot XI 1M — A352

**1986, Sept. 23** *Perf. 13½x13*
**894** A352 5i multicolored 1.50 .75

Chavez's flight over the Alps, 75th anniv.

VAN '86 — A353

**1986, Sept. 26**
**895** A353 50c light blue .40 .40

Ministry of Health vaccination campaign, Sept. 27-28, Oct. 25-26, Nov. 22-23.

Natl. Journalism Day — A354

**1986, Oct. 1**
**896** A354 1.50i multi .50 .25

Peruvian Navy A355

No. 897, Brigantine Gamarra, 1848. No. 898, Monitor Manco Capac, 1880.

**1986, Oct. 7 Litho.** *Perf. 13x13½*
**897** A355 1i multicolored .80 .35
**898** A355 1i multicolored .80 .35

Institute of Higher Military Studies, 35th Anniv. A356

**1986, Oct. 31 Litho.** *Perf. 13x13½*
**899** A356 1i multicolored .40 .25

Boy, Girl — A357

**1986, Nov. 3** *Perf. 13½x13*
**900** A357 2.50i red, brn & blk .70 .50

Christmas charity for children and postal workers' funds.

### Famous Peruvians Type of 1985

No. 901, Daniel A .Carrión. No. 902, José Gálvez Barrenechea. No. 904, José de la Riva Agüero. No. 905, Raúl Porras Barrenechea.

**1986-87**
**901** A327 50c blackish brown .45 .35
**902** A327 50c red brown .45 .35
**904** A327 80c brown .55 .45
**905** A327 80c orange brown .45 .35
*Nos. 901-905 (4)* 1.90 1.50

Issued: No. 901, 5/16/86; No. 902, 11/19/86; No. 904, 10/22/87; No. 905, 11/9/87.

Christmas A358

**1986, Dec. 3**
**908** A358 5i St. Joseph and Child 2.00 1.00

SENATI, 25th Anniv. — A359

**1986, Dec. 19** *Perf. 13½x13*
**909** A359 4i multicolored 1.10 .75

Shipibo Tribal Costumes A360

**1987, Apr. 24 Litho.** *Perf. 13½x13*
**910** A360 3i multicolored 1.00 .50

World Food Day — A361

**1987, May 26**
**911** A361 50c multicolored .60 .25

Preservation of the Nazca Lines — A362

Design: Nazca Lines and Dr. Maria Reiche (b. 1903), archaeologist.

**1987, June 13 Litho.** *Perf. 13x13½*
**912** A362 8i multicolored 3.00 1.25

A363

**1987, July 15 Litho.** *Perf. 13½x13*
**913** A363 50c violet .55 .25

Mariano Santos (1850-1900), "The Hero of Tarapaca," 1879, Chilean war. Dated 1986.

A364

**1987, July 19** *Perf. 13x13½*
**914** A364 3i multicolored .80 .50

Natl. Horse Club, 50th anniv. Dated 1986.

A365

**1987, Aug 13** ***Perf. 13½x13***
**915** A365 2i multicolored .70 .35

Gen. Felipe Santiago Salaverry (1806-1836), revolution leader. Dated 1986.

Colca's Canyon — A366

**1987, Sept. 8** **Litho.** ***Perf. 13½x13***
**916** A366 6i multicolored 1.00 .60

10th Natl. Philatelic Exposition, Arequipa. Dated 1986.

AMIFIL '87 — A367

**1987, Sept. 10**
**917** A367 1i Nos. 1-2 .45 .45

Dated 1986.

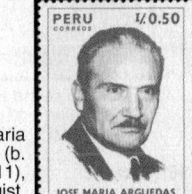

Jose Maria Arguedas (b. 1911), Anthropologist, Author — A368

**1987, Sept. 19**
**918** A368 50c brown .45 .45

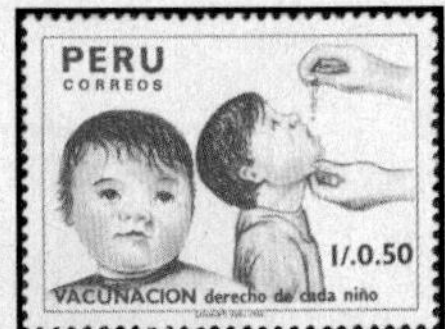


Arequipa Chamber of Commerce & Industry A369

**1987, Sept. 23** ***Perf. 13x13½***
**919** A369 2i multicolored .45 .30

Vaccinate Every Child Campaign A370

**1987, Sept. 30** **Litho.** ***Perf. 13x13½***
**920** A370 50c brown purple .45 .45

Argentina, Winner of the 1986 World Cup Soccer Championships — A371

**1987, Nov. 18**
**921** A371 4i multicolored .90 .45

Restoration of Chan Chan Ruins, Trujillo Province A372

Chimu culture (11th-15th cent.) bas-relief.

**1987, Nov. 27**
**922** A372 50c multicolored 1.10 .55

See No. 936.

Halley's Comet A373

4i, Comet, Giotto satellite.

**1987, Dec. 7**
**923** A373 4i multicolored 1.50 1.10

Jorge Chavez Dartnell (1887-1910), Aviator — A374

**1987, Dec. 15** ***Perf. 13½x13***
**924** A374 2i yel bis, claret brn & gold .60 .25

Founding of Lima, 450th Anniv. (in 1985) — A375

**1987, Dec. 18** **Litho.** ***Perf. 13½x13***
**925** A375 2.50i Osambela Palace .60 .25

Dated 1985.

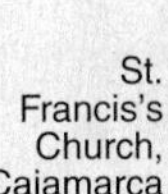

Discovery of the Ruins at Machu Picchu, 75th Anniv. (in 1986) A376

**1987, Dec.** ***Perf. 13x13½***
**926** A376 9i multicolored 3.25 2.00

Dated 1986.

St. Francis's Church, Cajamarca A377

**1988, Jan. 23** **Litho.** ***Perf. 13x13½***
**927** A377 2i multicolored .55 .25

Cultural Heritage. Dated 1986.

Participation of Peruvian Athletes in the Olympics, 50th Anniv. — A378

Design: Athletes on parade, poster publicizing the 1936 Berlin Games.

**1988, Mar. 1** **Litho.** ***Perf. 13½x13***
**928** A378 1.50i multicolored .65 .25

Dated 1986.

Ministry of Education, 150th Anniv. A379

**1988, Mar. 10** ***Perf. 13x13½***
**929** A379 1i multicolored .70 .30

Coronation of the Virgin of the Evangelization by Pope John Paul II — A380

**1988, Mar. 14** **Litho.** ***Perf. 13x13½***
**930** A380 10i multicolored 1.25 .60

Dated 1986.

Rotary Intl. Involvement in Anti-Polio Campaign A381

**1988, Mar. 16**
**931** A381 2i org, gold & dark blue .55 .55



Postman, Cathedral A382

**1988, Apr. 29** **Litho.** ***Perf. 13½x13***
**932** A382 9i brt blue 1.00 .60

Christmas charity for children and postal workers' funds.

Meeting of 8 Latin-American Presidents, Acapulco, 1st Anniv. — A383

**1988, May 4** ***Perf. 13x13½***
**933** A383 9i multicolored 1.25 .75

St. John Bosco (1815-1888), Educator — A384

**1988, June 1** ***Perf. 13½x13***
**934** A384 5i multicolored .45 .45

1st Peruvian Scientific Expedition to the Antarctic A385

7i, Ship Humboldt, globe.

**1988, June 2** ***Perf. 13x13½***
**935** A385 7i multicolored .65 .55

Restoration of Chan-Chan Ruins, Trujillo Province A386

**1988, June 7**
**936** A386 4i Bas-relief .55 .25

Cesar Vallejo (1892-1938), Poet — A387

**1988, June 15** ***Perf. 13½x13***
**937** A387 25i buff, blk & brn 1.25 .55

Journalists' Fund — A388

**1988, July 12** **Litho.** ***Perf. 13½x13***
**938** A388 4i buff & deep ultra .45 .45

Type A44 — A389

**1988, Sept. 1 Litho.** ***Perf. 13½x13***
**939** A389 20i blk, lt pink & ultra .50 .50

EXFILIMA '88, discovery of America 500th anniv.

17th Intl. Pacific Fair A390

**1988, Sept. 6** ***Perf. 13x13½***
**940** A390 4i multicolored 1.00 1.00

Painting by Jose Sabogal (1888-1956) — A391

**1988, Sept. 7**
**941** A391 12i multicolored .45 .45

Peru Kennel Club Emblem, Dogs — A392

**1988, Sept. 9** ***Perf. 13½x13***
**942** A392 20i multicolored 1.60 .90

CANINE '88 Intl. Dog Show, Lima.

Alfonso de Silva (1902-1934), Composer, and Score to Esplendido de Flores — A393

**1988, Sept. 27 Litho.** ***Perf. 13x13½***
**943** A393 20i multicolored .65 .30

2nd State Visit of Pope John Paul II — A394

**1988, Oct. 10** ***Perf. 13½x13***
**944** A394 50i multicolored .75 .30

1988 Summer Olympics, Seoul — A395

**1988, Nov. 10 Litho.** ***Perf. 13½x13***
**945** A395 25i Women's volleyball 1.00 .35

Women's Volleyball Championships (1982) — A396

**Surcharged in Red**

**1988, Nov. 16** ***Perf. 12***
**946** A396 95i on 300s multi 1.40 .70

No. 946 not issued without overprint.
Christmas charity for children's and postal workers' funds.

Chavin Culture Ceramic Vase — A397

**Surcharged in Henna or Black**

**1988 Litho.** ***Perf. 12***
**947** A397 40i on 100s red brn 1.50 1.10
**948** A397 80i on 10s blk 2.25 1.10

Nos. 947-948 not issued without surcharge.
Issue dates: 40i, Dec. 15. 80i, Dec. 22.

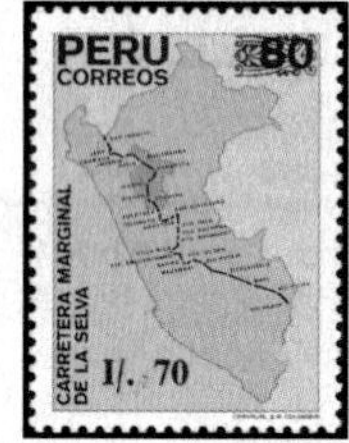
Rain Forest Border Highway — A398

**Surcharged in Black**

**1989, Jan. 27 Litho.** ***Perf. 12***
**949** A398 70i on 80s multi .60 .45

Not issued without surcharge.

Codex of the Indian Kings, 1681 — A399

**Surcharged in Olive Brown**

**1989, Feb. 10**
**950** A399 230i on 300s multi 1.25 .60

Not issued without surcharge.

Credit Bank of Peru, Cent. A400

500i, Huari Culture weaving.

**1989, Apr. 9 Litho.** ***Perf. 13x13½***
**951** A400 500i multicolored 1.50 .75

Postal Services A401

**1989, Apr. 20** ***Perf. 13***
**952** A401 50i SESPO, vert. .45 .35
**953** A401 100i CAN .55 .40

*El Comercio*, 150th Anniv. — A402

**1989, May 15**
**954** A402 600i multicolored 1.00 .50

Garcilaso de la Vega (1539-1616), Historian Called "The Inca" — A403

**1989, July 11 Litho.** ***Perf. 12½***
**955** A403 300i multicolored .60 .30

Express Mail Service A404

**1989, July 12**
**956** A404 100i dark red, org & dark blue .45 .35

Federation Emblem and Roca — A405

**1989, Aug. 29 Litho.** ***Perf. 13***
**957** A405 100i multicolored .45 .35

Luis Loli Roca (1925-1988), founder of the Federation of Peruvian Newspaper Publishers.

Restoration of Chan Chan Ruins, Trujillo Province A406

Chimu culture (11th-15th cent.) bas-relief.

**1989, Sept. 17** ***Perf. 12½***
**958** A406 400i multicolored 2.50 1.10

Geographical Society of Lima, Cent. — A407

**1989, Sept. 18** ***Perf. 13***
**959** A407 600i Early map of So. America 2.50 1.25

Founders of Independence Soc. — A408

**1989, Sept. 28 Litho.** ***Perf. 12½***
**960** A408 300i multicolored .60 .35

3rd Meeting of the Presidential Consultation and Planning Board — A409

**1989, Oct. 12** ***Perf. 13***
**961** A409 1300i Huacachina Lake 2.50 1.25

For surcharge see No. 1027.

Children Mailing Letters — A410

**1989, Nov. 29 Litho.** ***Perf. 12½***
**962** A410 1200i multicolored .65 .25

Christmas charity for children's and postal workers' funds.

Cacti A411

No. 963, Loxanthocereus acanthurus. No. 964, Corryocactus huincoensis. No. 965, Haageocereus clavispinus. No. 966,

Trichocereus pervianus. No. 967, Matucana cereoides.

**1989, Dec. 21 Litho. *Perf. 13***

| | | | | |
|---|---|---|---|---|
| **963** | A411 | 500i multicolored | .70 | .25 |
| **964** | A411 | 500i multicolored | .70 | .25 |
| **965** | A411 | 500i multicolored | .70 | .25 |
| **966** | A411 | 500i multicolored | .70 | .25 |
| **967** | A411 | 500i multicolored | .70 | .25 |
| | | *Nos. 963-967 (5)* | 3.50 | 1.25 |

Nos. 965-967 vert. For surcharges see Nos. 1028-1031

America Issue — A412

UPAE emblem and pre-Columbian medicine jars.

**1989, Dec. 28 *Perf. 12½***

| | | | | |
|---|---|---|---|---|
| **968** | A412 | 5000i shown | 7.00 | 2.50 |
| **969** | A412 | 5000i multi, diff. | 7.00 | 2.50 |

Belen Church, Cajamarca A413

**1990, Feb. 1 Litho. *Perf. 12½***

| | | | | |
|---|---|---|---|---|
| **970** | A413 | 600i multicolored | 1.60 | .25 |

Historic patrimony of Cajamarca and culture of the Americas.

Huascaran Natl. Park — A414

No. 971, Llanganuco Lagoons. No. 972, Mountain climber, Andes, vert. No. 973, Alpamayo mountain. No. 974, Puya raimondi, vert. No. 975, Condor and Quenual. No. 976, El Huascaran.

**1990, Feb. 4 *Perf. 13***

| | | | | |
|---|---|---|---|---|
| **971** | A414 | 900i multicolored | .60 | .25 |
| **972** | A414 | 900i multicolored | .60 | .25 |
| **973** | A414 | 1000i multicolored | .65 | .25 |
| **974** | A414 | 1000i multicolored | .65 | .25 |
| **975** | A414 | 1100i multicolored | .80 | .25 |
| **976** | A414 | 1100i multicolored | .80 | .25 |
| | | *Nos. 971-976 (6)* | 4.10 | 1.50 |

Pope and Icon of the Virgin — A415

**1990, Feb. 6 *Perf. 12½***

| | | | | |
|---|---|---|---|---|
| **977** | A415 | 1250i multicolored | 1.25 | .35 |

Visit of Pope John Paul II. For surcharge see No. 1039.

Butterflies — A416

No. 978, Amydon. No. 979, Agrias beata, female. No. 980, Sardanapalus, male. No. 981, Sardanapalus, female. No. 982, Agrias beata, male.

**1990, Feb. 11 *Perf. 13***

| | | | | |
|---|---|---|---|---|
| **978** | A416 | 1000i multi | 1.75 | .25 |
| **979** | A416 | 1000i multi | 1.75 | .25 |
| **980** | A416 | 1000i multi | 1.75 | .25 |
| **981** | A416 | 1000i multi | 1.75 | .25 |
| **982** | A416 | 1000i multi | 1.75 | .25 |
| | | *Nos. 978-982 (5)* | 8.75 | 1.25 |

For surcharges see Nos. 1033-1037.

A417

Victor Raul Haya de La Torre and Seat of Government.

**1990, Feb. 24 *Perf. 12½***

| | | | | |
|---|---|---|---|---|
| **983** | A417 | 2100i multicolored | .90 | .40 |

Return to constitutional government, 10th anniv.

A418

**1990, May 24 Litho. *Perf. 12½***

| | | | | |
|---|---|---|---|---|
| **984** | A418 | 300i multicolored | .60 | .35 |

Peruvian Philatelic Assoc., 40th anniv. Dated 1989. For surcharge see No. 1038.

Prenfil '88 A419

**1990, May 29**

| | | | | |
|---|---|---|---|---|
| **985** | A419 | 300i multicolored | .35 | .25 |

World Exposition of Stamp & Literature Printers, Buenos Aires. Dated 1989. For surcharge see No. 1032.

French Revolution, Bicentennial A420

#986, Liberty. #987, Storming the Bastille. #988, Lafayette celebrating the Republic. #989, Rousseau & symbols of the Revolution.

**1990, June 5**

| | | | | |
|---|---|---|---|---|
| **986** | A420 | 2000i multicolored | .85 | .45 |
| **987** | A420 | 2000i multicolored | .85 | .45 |
| **988** | A420 | 2000i multicolored | .85 | .45 |
| **989** | A420 | 2000i shown | .85 | .45 |
| *a.* | | Strip of 4, #986-989 + label | 5.50 | 5.50 |

Dated 1989.

Arequipa, 450th Anniv. — A421

**1990, Aug. 15 Litho. *Perf. 13***

| | | | | |
|---|---|---|---|---|
| **990** | A421 | 50,000i multi | .90 | .45 |

Lighthouse A422

Design: 230,000i, Hospital ship Morona.

**Surcharged in Black**

**1990, Sept. 19 *Perf. 12½***

| | | | | |
|---|---|---|---|---|
| **991** | A422 | 110,000i on 200i blue | 1.50 | .75 |
| **992** | A422 | 230,000i on 400i blue | 3.00 | 1.50 |

Not issued without surcharge. No. 991 exists with albino surcharge.

A423

110,000i, Torch bearer. 280,000i, Shooting. 290,000i, Running, horiz. 300,000i, Soccer. 560,000i, Swimming, horiz. 580,000i, Equestrian. 600,000i, Sailing. 620,000i, Tennis.

**1990-91 Litho. *Perf. 13***

| | | | | |
|---|---|---|---|---|
| **993** | A423 | 110,000i multi | 1.00 | .50 |
| **994** | A423 | 280,000i multi | 2.25 | 1.10 |
| **995** | A423 | 290,000i multi | 2.25 | 1.10 |
| **996** | A423 | 300,000i multi | 2.50 | 1.25 |
| **997** | A423 | 560,000i multi | 3.50 | 1.75 |
| **998** | A423 | 580,000i multi | 4.00 | 2.00 |
| **999** | A423 | 600,000i multi | 4.25 | 2.00 |
| **1000** | A423 | 620,000i multi | 4.25 | 2.00 |
| | | *Nos. 993-1000 (8)* | 24.00 | 11.70 |

4th South American Games, Lima. Issue dates: #993-996, Oct. 19. #997-1000, Feb. 5, 1991.

A424

**1990, Nov. 22 Litho. *Die Cut***

**Self-Adhesive**

| | | | | |
|---|---|---|---|---|
| **1001** | A424 | 250,000i No. 1 | 2.50 | 1.25 |
| **1002** | A424 | 350,000i No. 2 | 3.50 | 1.75 |

Pacific Steam Navigation Co., 150th anniv.

Postal Workers' Christmas Fund — A425

**1990, Dec. 7 Litho. *Perf. 12½***

| | | | | |
|---|---|---|---|---|
| **1003** | A425 | 310,000i multi | 3.00 | 1.40 |

Maria Jesus Castaneda de Pardo, First Woman President of Peruvian Red Cross A426

**1991, May 15 Litho. *Perf. 12½***

| | | | | |
|---|---|---|---|---|
| **1004** | A426 | .15im on 2500i red & blk | 1.10 | .60 |

Dated 1990. Not issued without surcharge.

2nd Peruvian Scientific Expedition to Antarctica — A427

.40im, Penguins, man. .45im, Peruvian research station, skua. .50im, Whale, map, research station.

**1991, June 20**

| | | | | |
|---|---|---|---|---|
| **1005** | A427 | .40im on 50,000i | 3.50 | 1.60 |
| **1006** | A427 | .45im on 80,000i | 3.75 | 1.75 |
| **1007** | A427 | .50im on 100,000i | 4.75 | 2.10 |
| | | *Nos. 1005-1007 (3)* | 12.00 | 5.45 |

Not issued without surcharge.

A428

St. Anthony Natl. Univ., Cuzco, 300th Anniv.: 10c, Siphoonandra ellipitica. 20c, Don Manuel de Mollinedo y Angulo, founder. 1s, University coat of arms.

**1991, Sept. 26 Litho. *Perf. 13½x13***

| | | | | |
|---|---|---|---|---|
| **1008** | A428 | 10c multicolored | .40 | .25 |
| **1009** | A428 | 20c multicolored | .80 | .40 |
| **1010** | A428 | 1s multicolored | 4.00 | 2.00 |
| | | *Nos. 1008-1010 (3)* | 5.20 | 2.65 |

A429

Paintings: No. 1011, Madonna and child. No. 1012, Madonna with lambs and angels.

**1991, Dec. 3 Litho. *Perf. 13½x13***
**1011** A429 70c multicolored 3.50 1.75
**1012** A429 70c multicolored 3.50 1.75

Postal Workers' Christmas fund.

America Issue A430

No. 1013, Mangrove swamp. No. 1014, Gera waterfall, vert.

**1991, Dec. 23 *Perf. 13***
**1013** A430 .50im multi 2.50 1.50
**1014** A430 .50im multi 2.50 1.50

Dated 1990.

Sir Rowland Hill and Penny Black A431

**1992, Jan. 15 Litho. *Perf. 13***
**1015** A431 .40im gray, blk & bl 1.75 .70

Penny Black, 150th anniv. (in 1990).

A432

**1992, Jan. 28**
**1016** A432 .30im multicolored 1.10 .50

Our Lady of Guadalupe College, 150th anniv. (in 1990)

Entre Nous Society, 80th Anniv. — A433

**1992, Jan. 30 *Perf. 13½x13***
**1017** A433 10c multicolored .35 .25

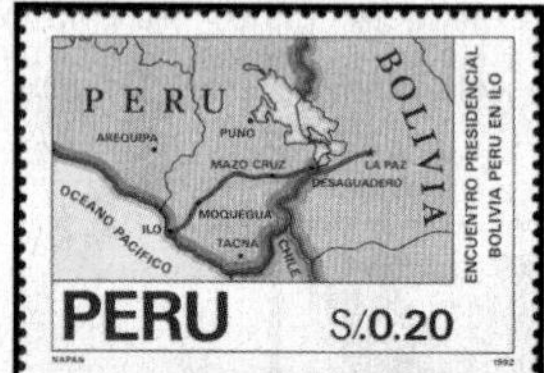

Peru-Bolivia Port Access Agreement — A434

**1992, Feb. 25 Litho. *Perf. 12½***
**1018** A434 20c multicolored .80 .40

Restoration of Chan-Chan Ruins — A435

**1992, Mar. 17**
**1019** A435 .15im multicolored 1.25 .60

Dated 1990.

Antonio Raimondi, Naturalist and Publisher, Death Cent. — A436

**1992, Mar. 31**
**1020** A436 .30im multicolored 1.40 .75

Dated 1990.

Newspaper "Diario de Lima", Bicent. (in 1990) — A437

**1992, May 22 Litho. *Perf. 13***
**1021** A437 .35im pale yel & black 1.10 .55

Dated 1990.

Mariano Melgar (1790-1815), Poet — A438

**1992, Aug. 5 Litho. *Perf. 12½x13***
**1022** A438 60c multicolored 2.25 1.10

8 Reales, 1568, First Peruvian Coinage A439

**1992, Aug. 7 *Perf. 13x12½***
**1023** A439 70c multicolored 2.00 1.00

Catholic Univeristy of Peru, 75th Anniv. — A440

**1992, Aug. 18 *Perf. 12½***
**1024** A440 90c black & tan 2.75 1.25

Pan-American Health Organization, 90th Anniv. — A441

**1992, Dec. 2 Litho. *Die Cut***
**Self-Adhesive**
**1025** A441 3s multicolored 6.00 4.50

Nos. 749, 961 Surcharged

***Perf. 13½x13, 13***
**1992, Nov. 18 Litho.**
**1026** A277 50c on 180s #749 1.00 .60
**1027** A409 1s on 1300i #961 2.50 1.40

**Nos. 963, 965-967, 977-982, & 984-985 Surcharged**

***Perfs. as Before***
**1992, Dec. 24 Litho.**

| | | | | |
|---|---|---|---|---|
| **1028** | A411 | 40c on 500i #963 | 15.00 | 6.00 |
| **1029** | A411 | 40c on 500i #965 | 15.00 | 6.00 |
| **1030** | A411 | 40c on 500i #966 | 15.00 | 6.00 |
| **1031** | A411 | 40c on 500i #967 | 15.00 | 6.00 |
| **1032** | A419 | 50c on 300i #985 | 15.00 | 6.00 |
| **1033** | A416 | 50c on 1000i #978 | 15.00 | 6.00 |
| **1034** | A416 | 50c on 1000i #979 | 15.00 | 6.00 |
| **1035** | A416 | 50c on 1000i #980 | 15.00 | 6.00 |
| **1036** | A416 | 50c on 1000i #981 | 20.00 | 6.00 |
| **1037** | A416 | 50c on 1000i #982 | 20.00 | 6.00 |
| **1038** | A418 | 1s on 300i #984 | 30.00 | 6.00 |
| **1039** | A415 | 1s on 1250i #977 | 30.00 | 6.00 |
| | | *Nos. 1028-1039 (12)* | 220.00 | 72.00 |

Virgin with a Spindle, by Urbina — A442

**1993, Feb. 10 Litho. *Die Cut***
**Self-Adhesive**
**1040** A442 80c multicolored 2.50 1.25

Sican Culture A443

Various artifacts.

**1993, Feb. 10 Self-Adhesive**
**1041** A443 2s multicolored 4.50 2.25
**1042** A443 5s multi, vert. 10.50 6.50

Evangelization in Peru, 500th Anniv. — A444

**1993, Feb. 12 Self-Adhesive**
**1043** A444 1s multicolored 3.00 1.40

Fruit Sellers, by Angel Chavez — A445

Dancers, by Monica Rojas — A446

**1993, Feb. 12 Self-Adhesive**
**1044** A445 1.50s multicolored 4.00 1.75
**1045** A446 1.50s multicolored 4.00 1.75

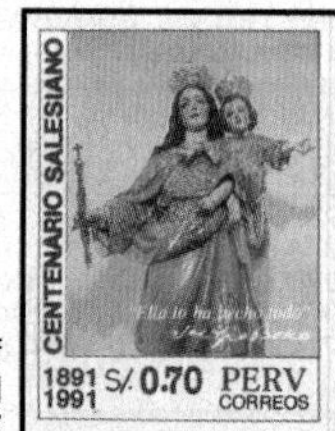

Statue of Madonna and Child — A447

**1993, Feb. 24 Litho. *Die Cut***
**Self-Adhesive**
**1046** A447 70c multicolored 1.90 .95

Salesian Brothers in Peru, cent. (in 1991).

America Issue — A448

UPAEP: No. 1047a, 90c, Francisco Pizarro, sailing ship. b, 1s, Sailing ship, map of northwest coast of South America.

**1993, Mar. 19 *Perf. 12½***
**1047** A448 Pair, #a.-b. 5.00 2.50

Sipan Gold Head — A449

**1993, Apr. 1**
**1048** A449 50c multicolored 10.00 10.00

Beatification of Josemaria Escriva, 1st Anniv. — A450

**1993, July 7 Litho. *Die Cut***
**Self-Adhesive**
**1049** A450 30c multicolored 1.00 .50

Peru-Japan Treaty of Peace and Trade, 120th Anniv. — A451

Designs: 1.50s, Flowers. 1.70s, Peruvian, Japanese children, mountains.

**1993, Aug. 21 Litho. *Perf. 11***
**1050** A451 1.50s multicolored 3.25 1.60
**1051** A451 1.70s multicolored 3.50 1.75

Sea Lions — A452

**1993, Sept. 20 Litho. *Perf. 11***
**1052** A452 90c shown 2.00 1.00
**1053** A452 1s Parrot, vert. 2.40 1.25

Amifil '93 (#1052). Brasiliana '93 (#1053).

A453

**1993, Nov. 9 Litho. *Die Cut***
**Self-Adhesive**
**1054** A453 50c olive brown 2.00 1.00

Honorio Delgado, Physician and Author, Birth Cent. (in 1992).

A454

**1993, Nov. 12 Self-Adhesive**
**1055** A454 80c orange brown 2.75 1.00

Rosalia De LaValle De Morales Macedo, Social Reformer, Birth Cent.

A455

Sculptures depicting Peruvian ethnic groups.

**1993, Nov. 22 Self-Adhesive**
**1056** A455 2s Quechua 10.00 5.00
**1057** A455 3.50s Orejon 12.00 5.00

Intl. Pacific Fair, Lima — A456

**1993, Nov. 25 Litho. *Perf. 11***
**1058** A456 1.50s multicolored 5.50 2.50

Christmas — A457

Design: 1s, Madonna of Loreto.

**1993, Nov. 30 *Perf. 11***
**1059** A457 1s multicolored 3.00 1.50

Cultural Artifacts — A458

2.50s, Sican artifacts. 4s, Sican mask. 10s, Chancay ceramic statue, vert. 20s, Chancay textile.

**Self-Adhesive**

**1993, Nov. 30 *Die Cut***
**1060** A458 2.50s multicolored 10.00 6.00
**1061** A458 4s multicolored 12.50 8.75
**1062** A458 10s multicolored 35.00 20.00
**1063** A458 20s multicolored 72.50 40.00
*Nos. 1060-1063 (4)* 130.00 74.75

See Nos. 1079-1082.

Prevention of AIDS — A459

**1993, Dec. 1 Litho. *Perf. 11***
**1064** A459 1.50s multicolored 4.25 2.50

A460

**1994, Mar. 4 Litho. *Die Cut***
**Self-Adhesive**
**1065** A460 1s multicolored 2.75 1.40

Natl. Council on Science and Technology (Concytec), 25th Anniv. Dated 1993.

A461

20c, 30c, 40c, 50c, Bridge of Huaman Poma de Ayala.

**1994 Self-Adhesive**
**1066** A461 20c blue .85 .40
**1067** A461 40c orange 1.60 .80
**1068** A461 50c purple 2.25 1.10
*Nos. 1066-1068 (3)* 4.70 2.30

**Litho.**
***Perf. 12x11***
**1073** A461 30c brown 1.10 .55
**1074** A461 40c black 1.75 .85
**1075** A461 50c vermilion 2.00 1.00
*Nos. 1073-1075 (3)* 4.85 2.40

Issued: Nos. 1066-1068, 3/11/94; Nos. 1073-1075, 5/13/94.

**Cultural Artifacts Type of 1993**

No. 1079, Engraved silver container, vert. No. 1080, Engraved medallion. No. 1081, Carved bull, Pucara. No. 1082, Plate with fish designs.

**1994, Mar. 25 Self-Adhesive**
**1079** A458 1.50s multicolored 4.00 2.00
**1080** A458 1.50s multicolored 4.00 2.00
**1081** A458 3s multicolored 7.00 3.50
**1082** A458 3s multicolored 7.00 3.50
*Nos. 1079-1082 (4)* 22.00 11.00

Dated 1993.

Sipan Artifacts A464

3s, Peanut-shaped beads. 5s, Mask, vert.

**1994, May 19 Litho. *Perf. 11***
**1083** A464 3s multi 9.00 4.50
**1084** A464 5s multi 15.00 7.50

El Brujo Archaelogical Site, Trujillo — A465

**1994, Nov. 3 Litho. *Perf. 14***
**1085** A465 70c multicolored 1.75 .85

Christmas A466

Ceramic figures: 1.80s, Christ child. 2s, Nativity scene. Dated 1994.

**1995, Mar. 17 Litho. *Perf. 13x13½***
**1086** A466 1.80s multicolored 4.00 2.00
**1087** A466 2s multicolored 4.25 2.10

1994 World Cup Soccer Championships, U.S. — A467

**1995, Mar. 20 *Perf. 13½x13***
**1088** A467 60c shown 1.00 .55
**1089** A467 4.80s Mascot, flags 8.00 4.25

Dated 1994.

Ministry of Transportation, 25th Anniv. — A468

**1995, Mar. 22 *Perf. 13x13½***
**1090** A468 20c multicolored .35 .30

Dated 1994.

Cultural Artifacts A469

Mochican art: 40c, Pitcher with figures beneath blanket. 80c, Jeweled medallion. 90c, Figure holding severed head.

**1995, Mar. 27 *Perf. 14***
**1091** A469 40c multicolored 1.10 .55
**1092** A469 80c multicolored 2.00 .90
**1093** A469 90c multicolored 2.25 1.10
*Nos. 1091-1093 (3)* 5.35 2.55

Dated 1994.

Juan Parra del Riego, Birth Cent. — A470

No. 1095, Jose Carlos Mariategui, birth cent.

**1995, Mar. 28 *Perf. 14***
**1094** A470 90c multicolored 3.00 1.40

***Perf. 13½x13***
**1095** A470 90c multicolored 3.00 1.40

Dated 1994.

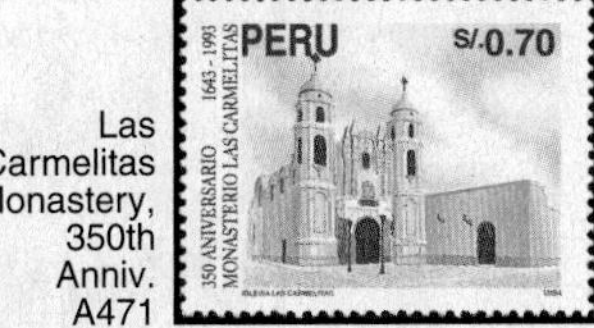

Las Carmelitas Monastery, 350th Anniv. A471

**1995, Mar. 31 Litho. *Perf. 13***
**1096** A471 70c multicolored 2.00 1.00

Dated 1994.

Peru's Volunteer Fireman's Assoc. A472

Fire trucks: 50c, Early steam ladder. 90c, Modern aerial ladder.

**1995, Apr. 12** ***Perf. 14***
**1097** A472 50c multicolored 1.50 .75
**1098** A472 90c multicolored 2.50 1.25

Dated 1994.

Musical Instruments A473

**1995, Apr. 10** **Litho.** ***Perf. 13½x13***
**1099** A473 20c Cello .60 .30
**1100** A473 40c Drum 1.10 .55

Union Club, Fountain, Plaza of Arms A474

Design: 1s, Santo Domingo Convent, Lima.

**1995, Apr. 19** **Litho.** ***Perf. 14***
**1101** A474 90c multicolored 4.00 2.00
**1102** A474 1s multicolored 4.50 2.25

Cultural history of Lima.

Ethnic Groups — A475

**1995, Apr. 26** ***Perf. 13½x13***
**1103** A475 1s Bora girl 2.75 1.40
**1104** A475 1.80s Aguaruna man 4.75 2.40

World Food Program, 30th Anniv. A476

**1995, May 3** ***Perf. 13x13½***
**1105** A476 1.80s multicolored 4.75 2.40

Solanum Ambosinum A477

Design: 2s, Mochica ceramic representation of papa flower.

**1995, May 8** ***Perf. 13½x13***
**1106** A477 1.80s multicolored 4.75 2.40
**1107** A477 2s multicolored 5.25 2.50

Reed Boat, Lake Titicaca — A478

**1995, May 12**
**1108** A478 2s multicolored 5.50 2.75

Fauna A479

1s, American owl, vert. 1.80s, Jaguar.

**1995, May 18** ***Perf. 13½x13, 13x13½***
**1109** A479 1s multi 2.75 1.40
**1110** A479 1.80s multi 4.75 2.40

Andes Development Corporation, 25th Anniv. — A480

**1995, Aug. 29** **Litho.** ***Perf. 14***
**1111** A480 5s multicolored 12.50 6.25

World Tourism Day A481

**1995, Sept. 27** ***Perf. 13x13½***
**1112** A481 5.40s multicolored 17.50 8.75

Dated 1994.

World Post Day A482

1.80s, Antique mail box.

**1995, Oct. 9** ***Perf. 14***
**1113** A482 1.80s multi 4.50 2.25

Dated 1994.

America Issue A483

1.50s, Landing of Columbus. 1.70s, Guanaco, vert. 1.80s, Early mail cart. 2s, Postal trucks.

***Perf. 13½x14, 14x13½ (#1115)***

**1995, Oct. 12**
**1114** A483 1.50s multi 3.50 1.75
**1115** A483 1.70s multi 4.00 2.00
**1116** A483 1.80s multi 4.00 2.00
**1117** A483 2s multi 4.50 2.25
*Nos. 1114-1117 (4)* 16.00 8.00

No. 1116-1117 are dated 1994.

UN, 50th Anniv. A484

Design: 90c, Peruvian delegates, 1945.

**1995, Oct. 28** ***Perf. 14***
**1118** A484 90c multicolored 2.25 1.10

Entries, Lima Cathedrals A485

Designs: 30c, St. Apolonia. 70c, St. Louis, side entry to St. Francis.

**1995, Oct. 20**
**1119** A485 30c multicolored .75 .40
**1120** A485 70c multicolored 1.75 .90

Dated 1994.

Artifacts from Art Museums A486

Carvings and sculptures: No. 1121, St. James on horseback, 19th cent. No. 1122, Church. 40c, Woman on pedestal. 50c, Archangel.

**1995, Oct. 31** ***Perf. 14½x14***
**1121** A486 20c multicolored .70 .40
**1122** A486 20c multicolored .70 .40
**1123** A486 40c multicolored 1.25 .70
**1124** A486 50c multicolored 1.75 .80
*Nos. 1121-1124 (4)* 4.40 2.30

Dated 1994.

Scouting — A487

Designs: a, 80c, Lady Olave Baden-Powell. b, 1s, Lord Robert Baden-Powell.

**1995, Nov. 9** **Litho.** ***Perf. 13½x13***
**1125** A487 Pair, #a.-b. 4.00 2.00

Dated 1994.

Folk Dances — A488

1,80s, Festejo. 2s, Marinera limeña, horiz.

**1995, Nov. 16** ***Perf. 14***
**1126** A488 1.80s multicolored 3.75 1.75
**1127** A488 2s multicolored 4.25 2.10

Dated 1994.

Biodiversity A489

50c, Manu Natl. Park. 90c, Anolis punctatus, horiz.

**1995, Nov. 23**
**1128** A489 50c multicolored 4.00 2.00
**1129** A489 90c multicolored 7.00 3.50

Dated 1994.

Electricity for Development A490

20c, Toma de Huinco. 40c, Antacoto Lake.

**1995, Nov. 27**
**1130** A490 20c multicolored .45 .25
**1131** A490 40c multicolored .90 .45

Dated 1994.

Peruvian Saints — A491

90c, St. Toribio de Mogrovejo. 1s, St. Francisco Solano.

**1995, Dec. 4**
**1132** A491 90c multicolored 1.90 .90
**1133** A491 1s multicolored 2.10 1.00

Dated 1994.

FAO, 50th Anniv. A492

**1996, Apr. 24** **Litho.** ***Perf. 14***
**1134** A492 60c multicolored 1.25 .75

Christmas 1995 A493

Local crafts: 30c, Nativity scene with folding panels, vert. 70c, Carved statues of three Magi.

**1996, May 2**
**1135** A493 30c multicolored .60 .30
**1136** A493 70c multicolored 1.60 .80

America Issue A494

Designs: 30c, Rock formations of Lachay. 70c, Coastal black crocodile.

**1996, May 9**
**1137** A494 30c multicolored 1.25 .60
**1138** A494 70c multicolored 2.50 1.10

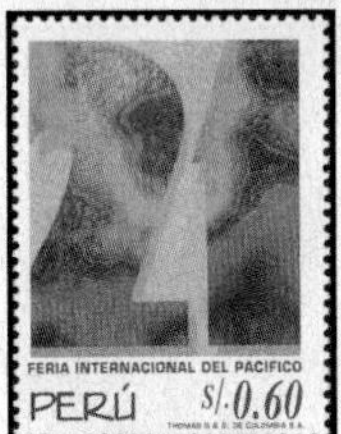
Intl. Pacific Fair — A495

**1996, May 16**
**1139** A495 60c multicolored 1.25 .75

1992 Summer Olympic Games, Barcelona A496

a, 40c Shooting. b, 40c Tennis. c, 60c Swimming. d, 60c Weight lifting.

**1996, June 10** **Litho.** ***Perf. 12½***
**1140** A496 Block of 4, #a.-d. 5.00 2.50

Dated 1992.
For surcharges see #1220-1223.

Expo '92, Seville A497

**1996, June 17**
**1141** A497 1.50s multicolored 5.75 3.50

Dated 1992.

Cesar Vallejo (1892-1938), Writer — A498

**1996, June 25**
**1142** A498 50c black & gray 1.60 .95

Dated 1992.

Lima, City of Culture — A499

**1996, July 1**
**1143** A499 30c brown & tan .80 .40

Dated 1992.
For surcharge see No. 1219.

Kon-Tiki Expedition, 50th Anniv. A500

**1997, Apr. 28** **Litho.** ***Perf. 12½***
**1144** A500 3.30s multicolored 5.50 4.00

Beginning with No. 1145, most stamps have colored lines printed on the back creating a granite paper effect.

UNICEF, 50th Anniv. (in 1996) A501

**1997, Aug. 7** **Litho.** ***Perf. 13½x14***
**1145** A501 1.80s multicolored 3.50 2.50

Mochica Pottery — A502

Designs: 20c, Owl. 30c, Ornamental container. 50c, Goose jar. 1s, Two monkeys on jar. 1.30s, Duck pitcher. 1.50s, Cat pitcher.

**1997, Aug. 18** **Litho.** ***Perf. 14½***

| | | | | | |
|---|---|---|---|---|---|
| **1146** | A502 | 20c | green | .60 | .30 |
| **1147** | A502 | 30c | lilac | .95 | .45 |
| **1148** | A502 | 50c | black | 1.50 | .75 |
| **1149** | A502 | 1s | red brown | 3.00 | 2.10 |
| **1150** | A502 | 1.30s | red | 4.00 | 3.00 |
| **1151** | A502 | 1.50s | brown | 4.75 | 3.50 |
| | | | *Nos. 1146-1151 (6)* | 14.80 | 10.10 |

See Nos. 1179-1183, 1211-1214.

1996 Summer Olympics, Atlanta — A503

a, Shooting. b, Gymnastics. c, Boxing. d, Soccer.

**1997, Aug. 25** ***Perf. 14x13½***
**1152** A503 2.70s Strip of 4, #a.-d. 16.00 12.00

College of Biology, 25th Anniv. — A504

**1997, Aug. 26**
**1153** A504 5s multicolored 7.25 5.50

Scouting, 90th Anniv. — A505

**1997, Aug. 29**
**1154** A505 6.80s multicolored 10.00 7.75

8th Intl. Conference Against Corruption, Lima A506

**1997, Sept. 7** ***Perf. 13½x14***
**1155** A506 2.70s multicolored 3.50 2.50

Montreal Protocol on Substances that Deplete Ozone Layer, 10th Anniv. — A507

**1997, Sept. 16** ***Perf. 14x13½***
**1156** A507 6.80s multicolored 13.50 9.50

Lord of Sipan Artifacts A508

Designs: 2.70s, Animal figure with large hands, feet. 3.30s, Medallion with warrior figure, vert.
10s, Tomb of Lord of Sipan, vert.

**1997, Sept. 22** **Litho.** ***Perf. 13½x14***
**1157** A508 2.70s multicolored 5.25 4.00
**1158** A508 3.30s multicolored 6.50 4.75

**Souvenir Sheet**

**1159** A508 10s multicolored 18.00 13.50

Peruvian Indians — A509

**1997, Oct. 12** **Litho.** ***Perf. 14x13½***
**1160** A509 2.70s Man 5.50 3.75
**1161** A509 2.70s Woman 5.50 3.75

America Issue. Nos. 1160-1161 are dated 1996.

Heinrich von Stephan (1831-97) A510

**1997, Oct. 9**
**1162** A510 10s multicolored 19.00 13.50

America Issue — A511

No. 1163, Early post carrier. No. 1164, Modern letter carrier.

**1997, Oct. 12**
**1163** A511 2.70s multicolored 6.50 3.75
**1164** A511 2.70s multicolored 6.50 3.75

13th Bolivar Games — A512

a, Tennis. b, Soccer. c, Basketball. d, Shot put.

**1997, Oct. 17** **Litho.** ***Perf. 14x13½***
**1165** A512 2.70s Block of 4, #a.-d. 22.50 15.75

Marshal Ramon Castilla (1797-1867) A513

**1997, Oct. 17**
**1166** A513 1.80s multicolored 4.00 3.00

Treaty of Tlatelolco Banning Nuclear Weapons in Latin America, 30th Anniv. — A514

**1997, Nov. 3**
**1167** A514 20s multicolored 37.50 29.00

Manu Natl. Park — A515

Birds: a, Kingfisher. b, Woodpecker. c, Crossbill. d, Eagle. e, Jabiru. f, Owl.

**1997, Oct. 24** **Sheet of 6**
**1168** A515 3.30s #a.-f. + label 40.00 27.50

8th Peruvian Antarctic Scientific Expedition A516

**1997, Nov. 10**
**1169** A516 6s multicolored 12.00 8.25

Christmas A517

**1997, Nov. 26**
**1170** A517 2.70s multicolored 5.00 3.75

Hipolito Unanue Agreement, 25th Anniv. — A518

**1997, Dec. 18 Litho.** ***Perf. 14x13½***
**1171** A518 1s multicolored 2.00 1.25

**Souvenir Sheet**

Peruvian Gold Libra, Cent. — A519

**1997, Dec. 18**
**1172** A519 10s multicolored 25.00 18.00

Dept. of Post and Telegraph, Cent. — A520

**1997, Dec. 31**
**1173** A520 1s multicolored 1.75 1.25

Organization of American States (OAS), 50th Anniv. — A521

**1998, Apr. 30 Litho.** ***Perf. 14x13½***
**1174** A521 2.70s multicolored 5.25 5.25

Chorrillos Military School, Cent. A522

**1998, Apr. 29** ***Perf. 13½x14***
**1175** A522 2.70s multicolored 5.25 5.25

Tourism — A523

**1998, June 22 Litho.** ***Perf. 14x13½***
**1176** A523 5s multicolored 9.00 9.00

Peruvian Horse — A524

**1998, June 5**
**1177** A524 2.70s pale vio & vio 5.75 5.75

1998 World Cup Soccer Championships, France — A525

a, 2.70s, Goalie. b, 3.30s, Two players. 10s, Player kicking ball.

**1998, June 26**
**1178** A525 Pair, #a.-b. 10.00 10.00

**Souvenir Sheet**

***Perf. 13½x14***

**1178C** A525 10s multicolored 18.00 18.00

**Mochica Pottery Type of 1997**

1s, like #1149. 1.30s, like #1146. 1.50s, like #1151. 2.70s, like #1148. 3.30s, like #1150.

**1998, June 19 Litho.** ***Perf. 14½***

| | | | | |
|---|---|---|---|---|
| **1179** | A502 | 1s slate | 3.00 | 3.00 |
| **1180** | A502 | 1.30s violet | 3.75 | 3.75 |
| **1181** | A502 | 1.50s pale blue | 4.50 | 4.50 |
| **1182** | A502 | 2.70s bister | 8.25 | 8.25 |
| **1183** | A502 | 3.30s black brown | 9.50 | 9.50 |
| | | *Nos. 1179-1183 (5)* | 29.00 | 29.00 |

Aero Peru, 25th Anniv. A526

1.50s, Cuzco Cathedral. 2.70s, Airplane.

**1998, May 22** ***Perf. 13½x14***
**1184** A526 1.50s multicolored 2.75 2.75
**1185** A526 2.70s multicolored 5.25 5.25

Restoration of the Cathedral of Lima, Cent. — A527

**1998, June 15** ***Perf. 14x13½***
**1186** A527 2.70s multicolored 5.00 5.00

Inca Rulers — A528

No. 1187, Lloque Yupanqui. No. 1188, Sinchi Roca. No. 1189, Manco Capac.

**1998, July 17 Litho.** ***Perf. 14x13½***

| | | | | |
|---|---|---|---|---|
| **1187** | A528 | 2.70s multicolored | 7.00 | 7.00 |
| **1188** | A528 | 2.70s multicolored | 7.00 | 7.00 |
| **1189** | A528 | 9.70s multicolored | 22.50 | 22.50 |
| | | *Nos. 1187-1189 (3)* | 36.50 | 36.50 |

See Nos. 1225-1228.

Intl. Year of the Ocean A529

**1998, Aug. 8** ***Perf. 13½x14***
**1190** A529 6.80s multicolored 13.00 13.00

Natl. Symphony Orchestra, 60th Anniv. — A530

**1998, Aug. 11** ***Perf. 14x13½***
**1191** A530 2.70s multicolored 5.00 5.00

Mother Teresa (1910-97) A531

**1998, Sept. 5**
**1192** A531 2.70s multicolored 6.00 6.00

Peruvian Children's Foundation A532

**1998, Sept. 17**
**1193** A532 8.80s multicolored 16.00 16.00

**Souvenir Sheet**

Heroes of the Cenepa River — A533

**1998, June 5**
**1194** A533 10s multicolored 18.00 18.00

**Souvenir Sheet**

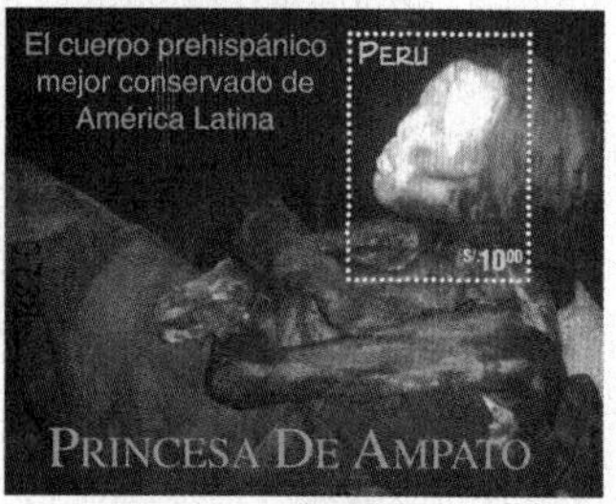


Princess De Ampato — A534

**1998, Sept. 8**
**1195** A534 10s multicolored 18.00 18.00

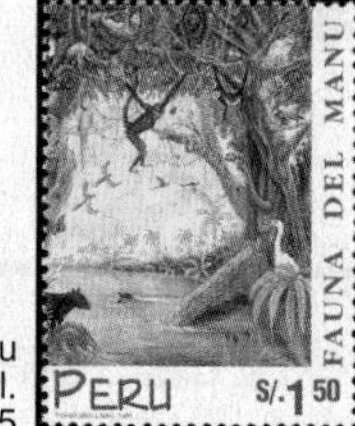


Fauna of Manu Natl. Park — A535

**1998, Sept. 27 Litho.** ***Perf. 14x13½***
**1196** A535 1.50s multicolored 3.50 3.50

America Issue — A536

**1998, Oct. 12**
**1197** A536 2.70s Chabuca 5.00 5.00

Stamp Day — A537

**1998, Oct. 9**
**1198** A537 6.80s No. 3 11.00 11.00

Frogs — A538

No. 1199: a, Agalychnis craspedopus. b, Ceratophrys cornuta. c, Epipedobates macero. d, Phyllomedusa vaillanti. e, Dendrobates biolat. f, Hemiphractus proboscideus.

**1998, Oct. 23 Litho. *Perf. 14x13½***
**1199** A538 3.30s Block of 6, #a.-f. + label *32.50 32.50*

Christmas A539

**1998, Nov. 16 *Perf. 13½x14***
**1200** A539 3.30s multicolored 3.75 3.75

Universal Declaration of Human Rights, 50th Anniv. A540

**1998, Dec. 10 Litho. *Perf. 13½x14***
**1201** A540 5s multicolored 5.00 5.00

Peru-Ecuador Peace Treaty — A541

**1998, Nov. 26 Litho. *Perf. 13½x14***
**1202** A541 2.70s multicolored 3.75 3.75

Brasilia '98.

19th World Scout Jamboree, Chile — A542

Designs: a, Scouting emblem, stylized tents. b, Emblem, tents, "SIEMPRE LISTO."

**1999, Jan. 5 Litho. *Perf. 14x13½***
**1203** A542 5s Pair, #a.-b. 10.00 10.00

Peruvian Philatelic Assoc., 50th Anniv. — A543

**1999, Jan. 10**
**1204** A543 2.70s No. 19 2.75 2.75

Paintings by Pancho Fierro (1809-79) — A544

Designs: 2.70s, Once Upon Time in a Shaded Grove. 3.30s, Sound of the Devil.

**1999, Jan. 16**
**1205** A544 2.70s multicolored 2.50 2.50
**1206** A544 3.30s multicolored 3.25 3.25

Regional Dance — A545

**1999, Feb. 10 Litho. *Perf. 14x13½***
**1207** A545 3.30s multicolored 3.25 3.25

CENDAF, 25th Anniv. A546

**1999, Mar. 1 *Perf. 13½x14***
**1208** A546 1.80s multicolored 1.90 1.90

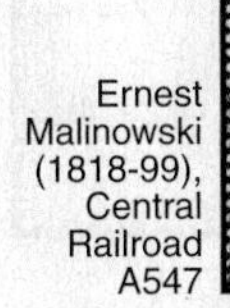

Ernest Malinowski (1818-99), Central Railroad A547

**1999, Mar. 3**
**1209** A547 5s multicolored 5.00 5.00

Peruvian Foundation for Children's Heart Disease A548

**1999, Mar. 6**
**1210** A548 2.70s multicolored 2.75 2.75

**Mochica Pottery Type of 1997**

Designs: 1s, like #1151. 1.50s, like #1148. 1.80s, like #1146. 2s, like #1150.

**1999, Feb. 16 Litho. *Perf. 14½***
**1211** A502 1s lake .95 .95
**1212** A502 1.50s dark blue blk 1.75 1.75
**1213** A502 1.80s brown 1.90 1.90
**1214** A502 2s orange 2.10 2.10
*Nos. 1211-1214 (4)* 6.70 6.70

Fauna of the Peruvian Rain Forest — A549

**1999, Apr. 23 *Perf. 14x13½***
**1215** A549 5s multicolored 5.50 5.50

Souvenir Sheet

Fauna of Manu Natl. Park — A550

**1999, Apr. 23 *Perf. 13½x14***
**1216** A550 10s multicolored 13.00 13.00

Milpo Mining Co., 50th Anniv. A551

**1999, Apr. 6 *Perf. 13½x14***
**1217** A551 1.50s multicolored 1.60 1.60

See note after No. 1145.

Japanese Immigration to Peru, Cent. — A552

**1999, Apr. 3 *Perf. 14x13½***
**1218** A552 6.80s multicolored 7.00 7.00

**Nos. 1140, 1143 Surcharged in Black, Brown, Dark Blue, Red or Green**

**1999 Litho. *Perf. 12½***
**1219** A499 2.40s on 30c (Br) multi 2.50 2.50

**Blocks of 4**

**1220** A496 1s on each value, #a.-d. 4.25 4.25
**1221** A496 1.50s on each value, #a.-d. 6.00 6.00
**1222** A496 2.70s on each value, #a.-d. 11.50 11.50
**1223** A496 3.30s on each value, #a.-d. 13.00 13.00

Size and location of surcharge varies.

Antarctic Treaty, 40th Anniv. A553

**1999, May 24 *Perf. 13½x14***
**1224** A553 6.80s multicolored 8.50 8.50

**Inca Rulers Type of 1998**

No. 1225, Capac Yupanqui. No. 1226, Yahuar Huaca. No. 1227, Inca Roca. No. 1228, Maita Capac.

**1999, June 24 Litho. *Perf. 14x13½***
**1225** A528 3.30s multi 3.25 3.25
**1226** A528 3.30s multi 3.25 3.25
**1227** A528 3.30s multi 3.25 3.25
**1228** A528 3.30s multi 3.25 3.25
*Nos. 1225-1228 (4)* 13.00 13.00

Souvenir Sheet

Nazca Lines — A554

**1999, June 8**
**1229** A554 10s multicolored 10.00 10.00

Margin shows Maria Reiche (1903-98), expert in Nazca Lines.

Minerals A555

Designs: 2.70s, Galena. 3.30s, Scheelite. 5s, Virgotrigonia peterseni.

**1999, July 3 *Perf. 13½x14***
**1230** A555 2.70s multicolored 2.50 2.50
**1231** A555 3.30s multicolored 3.25 3.25
**1232** A555 5s multicolored 5.25 5.25
*Nos. 1230-1232 (3)* 11.00 11.00

See Nos. 1339-1341.

Virgin of Carmen — A556

**1999, July 16 *Perf. 14x13½***
**1233** A556 3.30s multicolored 4.50 4.50

Santa Catalina Monastery, Arequipa — A557

**1999, Aug. 15 Litho. *Perf. 14x13½***
**1234** A557 2.70s multicolored 2.75 2.75

Chinese Immigration to Peru, 150th Anniv. A558

**1999 Litho. *Perf. 13½x14***
**1235** A558 1.50s red & black 2.75 2.75

Peruvian Medical Society, 25th Anniv. — A559

**1999 Litho. *Perf. 14x13½***
**1236** A559 1.50s multicolored 1.60 1.60

UPU, 125th Anniv. A560

**1999, Oct. 9 Litho. *Perf. 13½x14***
**1237** A560 3.30s multicolored 3.25 3.25

**America Issue**

A New Millennium Without Arms A561

2.70s, Earth, sunflower, vert.

**1999, Oct. 12 *Perf. 14x13½, 13½x14***
**1238** A561 2.70s multi 2.50 2.50
**1239** A561 3.30s shown 3.25 3.25

Señor de los Milagros Religious Procession A562

**1999, Oct. 18 *Perf. 14x13½***
**1240** A562 1s Incense burner 1.10 1.10
**1241** A562 1.50s Procession 1.50 1.50

Inter-American Development Bank, 40th Anniv. — A563

**1999, Oct. 22 *Perf. 13½x14***
**1242** A563 1.50s multicolored 1.50 1.50

Butterflies — A564

Designs: a, Pterourus zagreus chrysomelus. b, Asterope buckleyi. c, Parides chabrias. d, Mimoides pausanias. e, Nessaea obrina. f, Pterourus zagreus zagreus.

**Block of 6 + Label**

**1999, Oct. 23 *Perf. 14x13½***
**1243** A564 3.30s #a.-f. 22.00 22.00

Border Disputes Settled by Brasilia Peace Accords A565

Maps of regions from: No. 1244, Cusumasa Bumbuiza to Yaupi Santiago. No. 1245, Lagatococha to Güeppi, vert. No. 1246, Cunhuime Sur to 20 de Noviembre, vert.

**1999, Oct. 26 *Perf. 13½x14, 14x13½***
**1244** A565 1s multicolored 1.00 1.00
**1245** A565 1s multicolored 1.00 1.00
**1246** A565 1s multicolored 1.00 1.00
*Nos. 1244-1246 (3)* 3.00 3.00

See Nos. 1282-1286.

Peruvian Postal Services, 5th Anniv. — A566

**1999, Nov. 22 *Perf. 14x13½***
**1247** A566 2.70s multicolored 2.75 2.75

Christmas A567

**1999, Dec. 1 Litho. *Perf. 14x13½***
**1248** A567 2.70s multicolored 3.75 3.75

Ricardo Bentín Mujica (1899-1979), Businessman — A568

**1999, Dec. 29 Litho. *Perf. 13½x14***
**1249** A568 2.70s multicolored 2.75 2.75

Souvenir Sheet

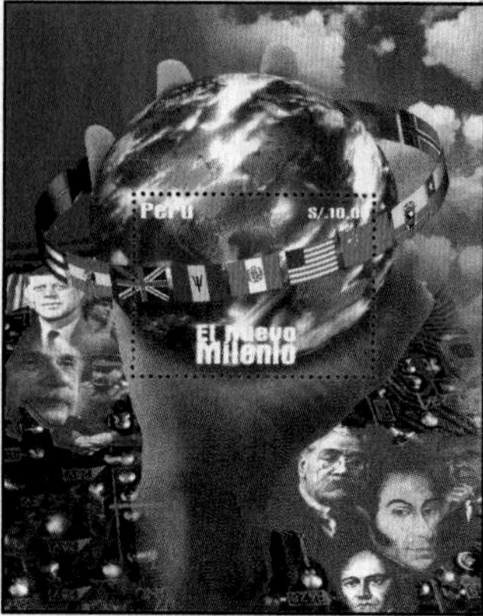

Millennium — A569

**2000, Jan. 1**
**1250** A569 10s multicolored 11.00 11.00

Ricardo Cillóniz Oberti, Businessman A570

**2000, Jan. 17 *Perf. 14x13½***
**1251** A570 1.50s multicolored 1.50 1.50

Printed se-tenant with label.

Alpaca Wool Industry — A571

a, Alpacas at right. b, Alpacas at left.

**2000, Jan. 27 Litho. *Perf. 14x13½***
**1252** A571 1.50s Pair, #a.-b. 3.25 3.25

Nuclear Energy Institute — A572

**2000, Feb. 4**
**1253** A572 4s multicolored 4.00 4.00

Retamas S.A. Gold Mine — A573

Miner, mine and buildings: a, Text in white. b, Text in blue violet.

**2000, Feb. 7**
**1254** A573 1s Pair, #a.-b. 2.00 2.00

Comptroller General, 70th Anniv. A574

**2000, Feb. 28 *Perf. 13½x14***
**1255** A574 3.30s multicolored 3.25 3.25

Emilio Guimoye, Field of Flowers A575

**2000, Mar. 19 Litho. *Perf. 13½x14***
**Granite Paper**
**1256** A575 1.50s multicolored 1.75 1.75

1999 Natl. Scholastic Games — A576

**2000, May 3 *Perf. 14x13½***
**Granite Paper**
**1257** A576 1.80s multi + label 2.25 2.25

Machu Picchu A577

**2000, July 20 *Perf. 13½x14***
**Granite Paper**
**1258** A577 1.30s multicolored 2.00 2.00

Campaign Against Domestic Violence A578

**2000, Aug. 22 Litho. *Perf. 13½x14***
**Granite Paper**
**1259** A578 3.80s multicolored 4.50 4.50

Holy Year 2000
A579

**2000, Aug. 23** **Granite Paper**

**1260** A579 3.20s multicolored 3.50 3.50

Children's Drawing Contest Winners
A580

Designs: No. 1261, 3.20s, Lake Yarinacocha, by Mari Trini Ramos Vargas. No. 1262, 3.20s, Ahuashiyacu Falls, by Susan Hidalgo Bacalla, vert. 3.80s, Arequipa Countryside, by Anibal Lajo Yañez.

*Perf. 13½x14, 14x13½*

**2000, Aug. 25** **Granite Paper**

**1261-1263** A580 Set of 3 12.00 12.00

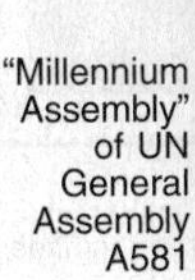

"Millennium Assembly" of UN General Assembly
A581

**2000, Aug. 28** *Perf. 13½x14*

**Granite Paper**

**1264** A581 3.20s multi 3.50 3.50

Gen. José de San Martín (1777-1850) — A582

**2000, Sept. 1** **Granite Paper**

**1265** A582 3.80s multi 4.00 4.00

Ormeño Bus Co., 30th Anniv. — A583

No. 1266: a, 1s, Bus and map of South America. b, 2.70s, Bus and map of North America.

**2000, Sept. 3** *Perf. 14x13½*

**Granite Paper**

**1266** A583 Pair, #a-b 5.00 5.00

Intl. Cycling Union, Cent.
A584

**2000, Sept. 11** *Perf. 13½x14*

**Granite Paper**

**1267** A584 3.20s multi 4.00 4.00

World Meteorological Organization, 50th Anniv. — A585

**2000, Sept. 13** **Granite Paper**

**1268** A585 1.50s multi 1.75 1.75

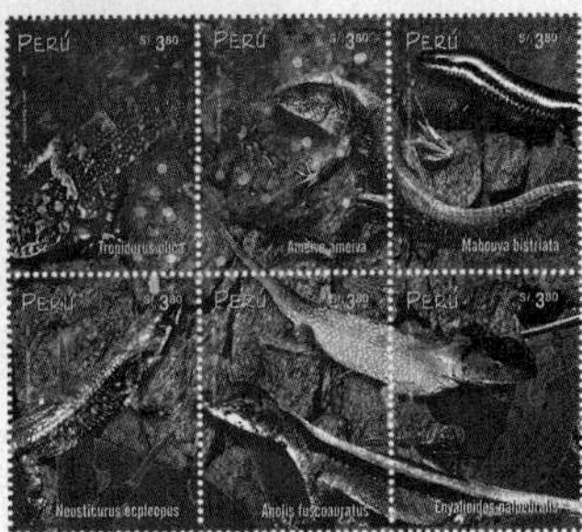

Lizards of Manu Natl. Park — A586

No. 1269: a, Tropidurus plica. b, Ameiva ameiva. c, Mabouya bistriata. d, Neusticurus ecpleopus. e, Anolis fuscoauratus. f, Enyalioides palpebralis.

**2000, Sept. 15** *Perf. 14x13½*

**Granite Paper**

**1269** A586 3.80s Block of 6, #a-f 26.50 26.50

Matucana Madisoniorum — A587

**2000, Sept. 18** *Perf. 13½x14*

**Granite Paper**

**1270** A587 3.80s multi 4.50 4.50

Carlos Noriega, First Peruvian Astronaut
A588

**2000, Sept. 20** **Granite Paper**

**1271** A588 3.80s multi 4.50 4.50

Toribio Rodríguez de Mendoza (1750-1825), Theologian
A589

**2000, Sept. 21** *Perf. 14x13½*

**Granite Paper**

**1272** A589 3.20s multi 4.00 4.00

Ucayali Province, Cent.
A590

**2000, Sept. 25** *Perf. 13½x14*

**Granite Paper**

**1273** A590 3.20s multi 4.00 4.00

Pisco Wine
A591

**2000, Sept. 27** **Granite Paper**

**1274** A591 3.80s multi 4.50 4.50

Latin American Integration Association, 20th Anniv. — A592

**2000, Sept. 29** *Perf. 14x13½*

**Granite Paper**

**1275** A592 10.20s multi 12.50 12.50

Peruvian Journalists Federation, 50th Anniv. — A593

**2000, Sept. 30** **Granite Paper**

**1276** A593 1.50s multi 2.10 2.10

Sexi Petrified Forest
A594

**2000, Oct. 3** *Perf. 13½x14*

**Granite Paper**

**1277** A594 1.50s multi 2.25 2.25

America Issue, Campaign Against AIDS
A595

**2000, Oct. 12** **Granite Paper**

**1278** A595 3.80s multi 5.00 5.00

Supreme Court
A596

**2000, Oct. 16** **Granite Paper**

**1279** A596 1.50s multi 1.75 1.75

Salvation Army in Peru, 90th Anniv. — A597

**2000, Nov. 3** *Perf. 14x13½*

**Granite Paper**

**1280** A597 1.50s multi 2.10 2.10

Peruvian Cancer League's Fight Against Cancer, 50th Anniv.
A598

**2000, Nov. 9** *Perf. 13½x14*

**Granite Paper**

**1281** A598 1.50s multi 2.00 2.00

**Border Map Type of 1999**

Flags and maps of border separating Peru and: 1.10s, Chile, vert. 1.50s, Brazil, vert. 2.10s, Colombia. 3.20s, Ecuador. 3.80s, Bolivia, vert.

*Perf. 14x13½, 13½x14*

**2000, Nov. 27** **Granite Paper**

**1282-1286** A565 Set of 5 14.50 14.50

Railroads in Peru, 150th Anniv.
A599

**2000, Nov. 27** *Perf. 13½x14*

**Granite Paper**

**1287** A599 1.50s multi 1.75 1.75

Luis Alberto Sanchez (1900-94), Politician — A600

**2000, Nov. 27** *Perf. 14x13½*

**Granite Paper**

**1288** A600 3.20s multi 4.00 4.00

National Congress
A601

**2000, Dec. 7** *Perf. 13½x14*

**Granite Paper**

**1289** A601 3.80s multi 4.50 4.50

Caretas Magazine, 50th Anniv.
A602

**2000, Dec. 15** **Granite Paper**

**1290** A602 3.20s multi 4.00 4.00

Cacti A603

Designs: 1.10s, Haageocereus acranthus, vert. 1.50s, Cleistocactus xylorhizus, vert. No. 1293, 2.10s, Mila caespitosa, vert. No. 1294, 2.10s, Haageocereus setosus, vert. 3.20s, Opuntia pachypus. 3.80s, Haageocereus tenuis.

*Perf. 13½x13¾, 13¾x13½*

**2001, Aug. 24** **Litho.**
**1291-1296** A603 Set of 6 16.00 16.00

San Marcos University, 450th Anniv. — A604

**2001, Sept. 4** *Perf. 13½x13¾*
**1297** A604 1.50s multi 1.75 1.75

Alianza Lima Soccer Team, Cent. — A605

No. 1298: a, Players. b, Players, ball.

**2001, Sept. 6**
**1298** A605 3.20s Horiz. pair, #a-b 7.50 7.50

Anti-Drug Campaign — A606

**2001, Sept. 7** *Perf. 13¾x13½*
**1299** A606 1.10s multi 1.50 1.50

Gen. Roque Sáenz Peña (1851-1914), Pres. of Argentina — A607

**2001, Sept. 7**
**1300** A607 3.80s multi 4.50 4.50

Lurín River Valley A608

**2001, Sept. 10**
**1301** A608 1.10s multi 1.25 1.25

Amphipoda Hyalella — A609

**2001, Sept. 10**
**1302** A609 1.80s multi 2.50 2.50

Postal and Philatelic Museum, 70th Anniv. — A610

**2001, Oct. 9** *Perf. 13½x13¾*
**1303** A610 3.20s multi 3.75 3.75

9th Iberoamerican Summit of Heads of State — A611

Country names and: a, 1.10s, Rectangle. b, 2.70s, Angled line.

**2002, Mar. 6** **Litho.** *Perf. 14x13½*
**1304** A611 Horiz. pair, #a-b 4.50 4.50

Dated 2001.

Peru — Costa Rica Diplomatic Relations, 150th Anniv. — A612

Flags, handshake and: a, 1.10s, Ruins. b, 2.70s, Grassland.

**2002, Mar. 12**
**1305** A612 Horiz. pair, #a-b 4.50 4.50

Dated 2001.

World Conference Against Racism, Durban, South Africa A613

**2002, Mar. 13** *Perf. 13½x14*
**1306** A613 3.80s multi 4.50 4.50

Dated 2001.

Intl. Day of Indigenous People — A614

**2002, Mar. 13** *Perf. 14x13½*
**1307** A614 5.80s multi 6.75 6.75

Dated 2001.

Intl. Organization for Migration, 50th Anniv. — A615

**2002, Apr. 2**
**1308** A615 3.80s multi 4.50 4.50

Dated 2001.

Pan-American Health Organization, Cent. — A616

**2002, Apr. 8** *Perf. 13½x14*
**1309** A616 3.20s multi 3.75 3.75

Dated 2001.

La Molina Agricultural University, Cent. — A617

Arms and: a, 1.10s, Sepia photograph of building. b, 2.70s, Color photograph of building.

**2002, Apr. 16** *Perf. 14x13½*
**1310** A617 Horiz. pair, #a-b 5.00 5.00

Dated 2001.

Pisco Distilling A618

Designs: 3.20s, Alembics. 3.80s, Jugs.

10s, La Fiesta de la Chicha y el Pisco, by José Sabogal.

**2002, Apr. 18** *Perf. 13½x14*
**1311-1312** A618 Set of 2 8.00 8.00

**Souvenir Sheet**

**1313** A618 10s multi 12.00 12.00

Dated 2001.

Orchids — A619

Designs: 1.50s, Stanhopea sp. 3.20s, Chloraea pavoni. 3.80s, Psychopsis sp.

**2002, Apr. 30** *Perf. 14x13½*
**1314-1316** A619 Set of 3 10.00 10.00

Dated 2001.

Flowers of Tuber Plants A620

Designs: 1.10s, Solanum stenotomum. 1.50s, Ipomoea batatas. 2.10s, Ipomoea purpurea.

**2002, May 7** *Perf. 13½x14*
**1317-1319** A620 Set of 3 5.25 5.25

America Issue — UNESCO World Heritage Sites — A621

Balconies of Lima buildings: 2.70s, Palacio de Osambela. 5.80s, Palacio de Torre Tagle.

**2002, May 14** **Litho.** *Perf. 14x13½*
**1320-1321** A621 Set of 2 10.00 10.00

Dated 2001.

Year of Dialogue Among Civilizations A622

Designs: 1.50s, Flower. 1.80s, shown.

**2002, May 16**
**1322-1323** A622 Set of 2 4.25 4.25

Dated 2001.

Paracas National Reserve A623

Designs: 1.10s, Sula dactilatra, vert. 1.50s, Sula variegata. 3.20s, Haematopus palliatus. 3.80s, Grapsus grapsus.

**2002, May 21** ***Perf. 14x13½, 13½x14***
**1324-1327** A623 Set of 4 11.00 11.00

Dated 2001.

Souvenir Sheet

Endangered Animals — A624

**2002, May 22** ***Perf. 13½x14***
**1328** A624 8s multi 10.00 10.00

Dated 2001.

Scouting in Peru, 90th Anniv. — A625

No. 1329: a, Lord Robert Baden-Powell. b, Juan Luis Rospigliosi.
10.20s, First Peruvian Scouts.

**2002, June 4** ***Perf. 14x13½***
**1329** A625 3.20s Horiz. pair, #a-b 7.50 7.50

**Souvenir Sheet**

**1330** A625 10.20s multi 12.00 12.00

Dated 2001.

Folk Dances — A626

Designs: 2.10s, Zamacueca. 2.70s, Alcatraz.

**2002, June 4**
**1331-1332** A626 Set of 2 5.50 5.50

Dated 2001.

International Express Service A627

**2002, June 10** ***Perf. 13½x14***
**1333** A627 20s multi 22.50 22.50

Dated 2001.

Inca Rulers — A628

Designs: 1.50s, Viracocha. 2.70s, Pachacutec. 3.20s, Inca Yupanqui. 3.80s, Tupac Inca Yupanqui.

**2002, June 24** **Litho.** ***Perf. 14x13½***
**1334-1337** A628 Set of 4 13.50 13.50

Dated 2001.

Primates — A629

No. 1338: a, Aotus nancymaea. b, Pithecia irrorata. c, Pithecia aequatorialis. d, Cebus albifrons. e, Saimiri boliviensis. f, Aotus vociferans.

**2002, June 25**
**1338** A629 3.80s Block of 6, #a-f 26.50 26.50

Dated 2001.

**Minerals Type of 1999**

Designs: 1.80s, Chalcopyrite. No. 1340, 3.20s, Sphalerite. No. 1341, 3.20s, Pyrargyrite.

**2002, July 3** ***Perf. 13½x14***
**1339-1341** A555 Set of 3 9.00 9.00

Dated 2001.

Pre-Columbian Artifacts — A630

Designs: 1.50s, Crab-like man, Sipán. 3.20s, Warrior, Sicán. 3.80s, Gold breastplate, Kuntur Wasi, horiz.
10.20s, Pinchudo, Gran Pajatén, horiz.

**2002, July 3** ***Perf. 14x13½, 13½x14***
**1342-1344** A630 Set of 3 10.00 10.00

**Souvenir Sheet**

**1345** A630 10.20s multi 12.00 12.00

Dated 2001.

Admiral Miguel Grau A631

**2002, July 23** ***Perf. 13½x14***
**1346** A631 3.80s multi 4.50 4.50

Dated 2001.

Peruvian — Spanish Business Meeting A632

**2002, Aug. 7**
**1347** A632 3.80s multi 4.50 4.50

Dated 2001.

National Fisheries Society, 50th Anniv. A633

***Perf. 13½x13¾***

**2002, Nov. 12** **Litho.**
**1348** A633 3.20s multi 3.75 3.75
*a.* Tete beche pair 7.50 7.50

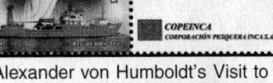

Alexander von Humboldt's Visit to Peru, Bicent. — A634

**2002, Nov. 20** ***Perf. 13¾x13½***
**1349** A634 3.20s multi + label 3.75 3.75
*a.* Tete beche strip, 2 #1349 +2 central labels 8.00 8.00

Peru - Bolivia Integration for Development — A635

**2002, Nov. 29** ***Perf. 13½x14***
**1350** A635 3.20s multi 3.75 3.75

Natl. Commission on Andean and Amazonian Peoples A636

**2002, Dec. 12**
**1351** A636 1.50s multi 1.75 1.75

Hydrography and Navigation Dept., Cent. — A637

**2003, June 13** **Litho.** ***Perf. 14x13½***
**1352** A637 1.10s multi 1.50 1.50

Manuela Ramos Movement, 25th Anniv. — A638

**2003, July 1**
**1353** A638 3.80s multi 4.00 4.00

Radioprogramas del Peru Network, 40th Anniv. — A639

**2003, Oct. 1** **Litho.** ***Perf. 13½x14***
**1354** A639 4s multi 4.00 4.00

Pres. Fernando Belaunde Terry (1912-2002) A640

**2003, Oct. 7** ***Perf. 14x13½***
**1355** A640 1.60s multi 1.60 1.60

Canonization of St. Josemaría Escrivá de Balaguer — A641

**2003, Oct. 11** ***Perf. 13½x14***
**1356** A641 1.20s multi 1.60 1.60

Sister Teresa de la Cruz Candamo (1875-1953), Founder of Canonesas de la Cruz — A642

**2003, Nov. 3**
**1357** A642 4s multi 4.50 4.50

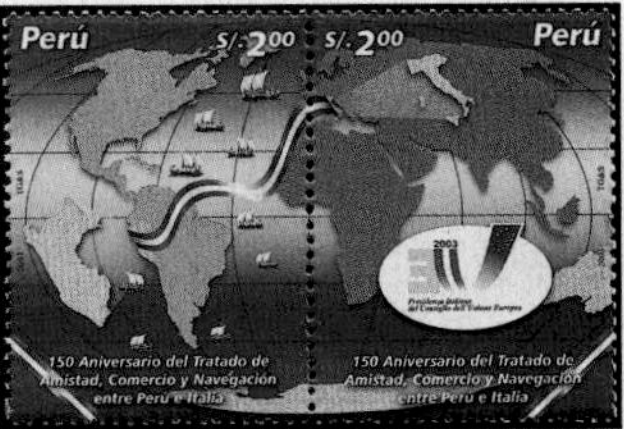

Treaty of Friendship, Commerce and Navigation Between Peru and Italy, 150th Anniv. — A643

No. 1358: a, Maps of Peru and Western Hemisphere. b, Map of Italy and Eastern Hemisphere.

**2003, Nov. 13** ***Perf. 14x13½***
**1358** A643 2s Horiz. pair, #a-b 4.25 4.25

Water Snake Bilingual Education Project — A644

No. 1359: a, Head of snake, project emblem. b, Tail of snake, children's drawing.

**2003, Nov. 28**
**1359** A644 2s Horiz. pair, #a-b 4.25 4.25

UNESCO Associated Schools Project Network, 50th Anniv. A645

**2003, Nov.** ***Perf. 13½x14***
**1360** A645 1.20s multi 1.50 1.50

America Issue - Fauna — A646

No. 1361: a, Four Rupicola peruviana and butterfly. b, One Rupicola peruviana.

**2003, Dec. 1** ***Perf. 14x13½***
**1361** A646 2s Horiz. pair, #a-b 4.50 4.50

Peru — Panama Diplomatic Relations, Cent. — A647

**2003, Dec. 12**
**1362** A647 4r multi 4.50 4.50

Powered Flight, Cent. — A648

**2003, Dec. 17** ***Perf. 13½x14***
**1363** A648 4.80s multi + label 4.50 4.50

Cajón A649

**2003, Dec. 18**
**1364** A649 4.80s multi 4.50 4.50

Chess A650

**2004, Jan. 5**
**1365** A650 1.20s multi 1.50 1.50

Dated 2003.

National Rehabilitation Institute — A651

**2004, Jan. 5**
**1366** A651 1.20s multi 2.10 2.10

Dated 2003.

Swimming A652

**2004, Jan. 5** ***Perf. 14x13½***
**1367** A652 1.20s multi 1.00 1.00

Dated 2003.

National Civil Defense System, 30th Anniv. (in 2002) — A653

**2004, Jan. 14**
**1368** A653 4.80s multi 4.75 4.75

Dated 2002.

Christmas 2003 A654

**2004, Jan. 14** ***Perf. 13½x14***
**1369** A654 4.80s multi 3.75 3.75

Dated 2002.

Cebiche A655

**2004, Jan. 14**
**1370** A655 4.80s multi 4.75 4.75

Dated 2003.

Viceroys — A656

No. 1371: a, 1.20s, Antonio de Mendoza (1495-1552). b, 1.20s, Andres Hurtado de Mendoza (1500-61). c, 1.20s, Diego Lopez de Zúñiga y Velasco (d. 1564). d, 4.80s, Blasco Nuñez de Vela (d. 1546).

**2004, Jan. 14** ***Perf. 14x13½***
**1371** A656 Block of 4, #a-d 8.00 8.00

Dated 2003.

Minerals A657

Designs: 1.20s, Orpiment. 4.80s, Rhodochrosite.

**2004, Jan. 21** ***Perf. 13½x14***
**1372-1373** A657 Set of 2 4.75 4.75

Dated 2002.

Peruvian Saints A658

Designs: No. 1374, 4.80s, St. Rose of Lima (1586-1617). No. 1375, 4.80s, St. Martin de Porres (1579-1639), vert.

**2004, Jan. 21** ***Perf. 13½x14, 14x13½***
**1374-1375** A658 Set of 2 7.00 7.00

Dated 2002.

Orchids A659

Designs: 1.20s, Chaubardia heteroclita, vert. 2.20s, Cochleanther amazonica, vert. 4.80s, Sobralia sp.

**2004, Jan. 21** ***Perf. 14x13½, 13½x14***
**1376-1378** A659 Set of 3 6.50 6.50

Dated 2002.

Jorge Basadre (1903-80), Historian — A660

**2004, Jan. 30** **Engr.** ***Perf. 14x13½***
**1379** A660 4.80s blue 4.00 4.00

Dated 2003.

Trains A661

Designs: 1.20s, Locomotive and train station. 4.80s, Train on Galeras Bridge.

**2004, Jan. 30** **Litho.** ***Perf. 13½x14***
**1380-1381** A661 Set of 2 5.00 5.00

Dated 2002.

Endangered Species — A662

Designs: No. 1382, 1.80s, Londra felina. No. 1383, 1.80s, Ara couloni, vert.

**2004, Jan. 30** ***Perf. 13½x14, 14x13½***
**1382-1383** A662 Set of 2 3.75 3.75

Dated 2002.

Fire Fighting A663

Designs: No. 1384, 2.20s, Firefighters with hose. No. 1385, 2.20s, Fire truck.

**2004, Jan. 30** ***Perf. 13½x14***
**1384-1385** A663 Set of 2 6.00 6.00

Dated 2002.

Incan Emperors A664

Designs: No. 1386, 1.20s, Huáscar (d. 1533). No. 1387, 1.20s, Atahualpa (d. 1533). 4.80s, Huayna Cápac (d. 1525).

**2004, Jan. 30** ***Perf. 14x13½***
**1386-1388** A664 Set of 3 6.00 6.00

Dated 2002.

Rubén Vargas Ugarte, Historian A665

**2004, Feb. 4** ***Perf. 13½x14***
**1389** A665 4.80s multi 4.00 4.00

Dated 2002.

2002 World Cup Soccer Championships, Japan and Korea — A666

**2004, Feb. 4**
**1390** A666 4.80s multi 4.00 4.00

Dated 2002.

National Stadium, 50th Anniv. (in 2002) A667

**2004, Feb. 4**
**1391** A667 4.80s multi 4.00 4.00

Dated 2002.

National Day of Biological Diversity, May 22, 2002 A668

**2004, Feb. 4**
**1392** A668 4.80s multi 4.00 4.00

Dated 2002.

World Population Day A669

**2004, Feb. 4**
**1393** A669 4.80s multi 4.00 4.00

Dated 2002.

José Jiménez Borja (1901-82), Writer — A670

**2004, Feb. 4** ***Perf. 14x13½***
**1394** A670 4.80s multi 4.00 4.00

Dated 2002.

Cacti — A671

Designs: No. 1395, 1.20s, Eriosyce islayensis. No. 1395, 1.20s, Matucana haynei. 4.80s, Pigmaeocereus bylesianus.

**2004, Feb. 4**
**1395-1397** A671 Set of 3 9.00 9.00

Dated 2002.

Antarctic Fauna A672

Designs: No. 1398, 1.80s, Leucocarbo atriceps. No. 1399, 1.80s, Pygosceles papua, vert. No. 1400, 1.80s, Asteroidea sp., vert.

**2004, Feb. 4** ***Perf. 13½x14, 14x13½***
**1398-1400** A672 Set of 3 6.00 6.00

Dated 2002.

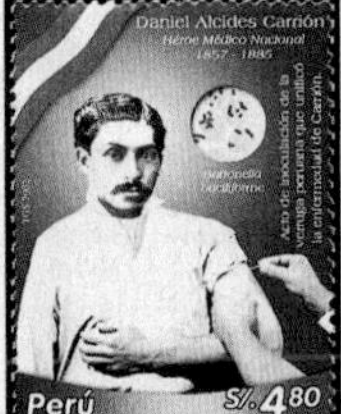


Pisco Sour A673

**2004, Feb. 10** ***Perf. 13½x14***
**1401** A673 4.80s multi 4.25 4.25

Daniel Alcides Carrión (1857-1885), Medical Martyr — A674

**2004, Feb. 19 Litho.** ***Perf. 14x13½***
**1402** A674 4.80s multi 4.25 4.25

Dated 2002.

Souvenir Sheet

Foundation of Jauja, by Wenceslao Hinostroza — A675

**2004, Feb. 20** ***Perf. 13½x14***
**1403** A675 7s multi 6.00 6.00

Dated 2002.

Animals — A676

**2004, Feb. 23** ***Perf. 14x14½***
**1404** A676 20c Alpaca .30 .25
**1405** A676 30c Vicuna .30 .25
**1406** A676 40c Guanaco .40 .25
**1407** A676 50c Llama .50 .30
*Nos. 1404-1407 (4)* 1.50 1.05

Dated 2002.

Vipers — A677

No. 1408: a, Bothrops roedingeri. b, Micrurus lemniscatus. c, Bothrops atrox. d, Bothrops microphtalmus. e, Micrurus surinamensis. f, Bothrops barnetti.

**2004, Feb. 23** ***Perf. 14x13½***
**1408** A677 1.80s Block of 6, #a-f, + label 10.00 10.00

Dated 2003.

Souvenir Sheet

Intl. Year of Mountains (in 2002) — A678

**2004, Feb. 23** ***Perf. 13½x14***
**1409** A678 7s multi 6.00 6.00

Dated 2002.

Royal Tombs of Sipán Museum A679

**2004, Feb. 24**
**1410** A679 4.80s multi 3.75 3.75

Dated 2003.

Lighthouses — A680

No. 1411: a, Punta Capones Lighthouse. b, Chincha Islands Lighthouse.

**2004, Feb. 26** ***Perf. 14x13½***
**1411** A680 2s Horiz. pair, #a-b 7.00 7.00

Dated 2003.

Volunteer Firefighters of Peru, 130th Anniv. — A681

**2004, Mar. 2**
**1412** A681 4.80s multi 6.00 6.00

Miniature Sheet

Fish — A682

No. 1413: a, Trachurus murphyi. b, Mugil cephalus. c, Engraulis ringens. d, Odontesthes regia regia. e, Merluccius gayi peruanus.

**2004, Mar. 3** ***Perf. 13½x14***
**1413** A682 1.60s Sheet of 5, #a-e 7.50 7.50

Dated 2002.

Souvenir Sheet

Arequipa Department — A683

No. 1414: a, Cathedral tower. b, Misti Volcano, horiz.

***Perf. 14x13½, 13½x14 (#1414b)***

**2004, Mar. 18**
**1414** A683 4s Sheet of 2, #a-b 6.50 6.50

Dated 2002.

Machu Picchu — A684

No. 1415: a, 1.20s, Sundial. b, 1.20s, Temple of the Three Windows. c, 1.20s, Waterfall, Huayna Picchu. d, 4.80s, Aerial view of Machu Picchu.

**2004, Mar. 20** ***Perf. 14x13½***
**1415** A684 Block of 4, #a-d 7.50 7.50

Dated 2003.

Medicinal Plants A685

Designs: No. 1416, 4.80s, Uncaria tomentosa. No. 1417, 4.80s, Myrciaria dubia. No. 1418, 4.80s, Lepidium meyenii.

**2004, Mar. 26** ***Perf. 13½x14***
**1416-1418** A685 Set of 3 10.00 10.00

Annual Assembly of Governors of the Inter-American Development Bank — A686

**2004, Mar. 29**
**1419** A686 4.80s multi 4.00 4.00

Dogs — A687

No. 1420: a, Italian Volpino. b, Peruvian hairless dog. c, Beauceron. d, Italian Spinone.

**2004, Apr. 2** ***Perf. 14x13½***
**1420** A687 4.80s Block of 4, #a-d 15.00 15.00

Dated 2003.

Dances — A688

Designs: No. 1421, 1.20s, Huaylash. No. 1422, 1.20s, Huayno.

**2004**
**1421-1422** A688 Set of 2 2.25 2.25

Issued: No. 1421, 4/16; No. 1422, 5/28. Dated 2003.

Preparation for "El Niño" — A689

**2004, Apr. 21** ***Perf. 13½x14***
**1423** A689 4.80s multi 4.00 4.00

Dated 2002.

Tourism A690

Designs: No. 1424, 4.80s, Lake Paca, Jauja. No. 1425, 4.80s, Ballestas Islands, Ica, vert. No. 1426, 4.80s, Inca Baths, Cajamarca, vert. No. 1427, 4.80s, Huanchaco, Trujillo, vert.

**2004** ***Perf. 13½x14, 14x13½***
**1424-1427** A690 Set of 4 17.00 17.00

Issued: No. 1424, 4/22; No. 1425, 4/29; No. 1426, 5/6; No. 1427, 6/10. Dated 2002 (#1425-1427) or 2003 (#1424).

Santiago Apostol Temple, Puno A691

**2004, July 2** ***Perf. 13½x14***
**1428** A691 1.80s multi 1.75 1.75

Dated 2003.

America Issue — Youth, Education and Literacy — A692

Designs: 1.20s, Children, stylized flower. 4.80s, Computer operator, horiz.

**2004, July 5** ***Perf. 14x13½, 13½x14***
**1429-1430** A692 Set of 2 4.00 4.00

Dated 2002 (#1429) or 2003 (#1430).

Souvenir Sheet

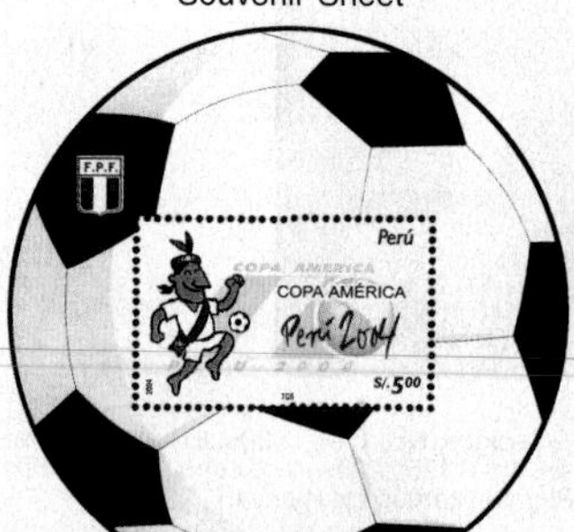

2004 Copa America Soccer Tournament, Peru — A693

**2004, July 9** ***Perf. 14x14½***
**1431** A693 5s multi 5.00 5.00

Horses — A694

No. 1432: a, 1.20s, White horse. b, 1.20s, Black horse, rider with raised hand. c, 1.20s, Black horse, rider with white poncho. d, 4.80s, Horse's head.

**2004, Aug. 6** ***Perf. 14x13½***
**1432** A694 Block of 4, #a-d, + label 6.50 6.50

Dated 2002.

Miniature Sheet

Worldwide Fund for Nature (WWF) — A695

No. 1433 — Pteronura brasiliensis: a, 30c. Looking. b, 50c, With mouth open. c, 1.50s, Eating. d, 1.50s, Sleeping.

**2004, Oct. 15** **Litho.**
**1433** A695 Sheet of 4, #a-d 4.00 4.00

America Issue — Environmental Protection — A696

**2004, Oct. 25** ***Perf. 13½x14***
**1434** A696 4.50s multi 3.25 3.25

Railroads A697

Designs: 5s, Modern train on bridge, 1870 train on bridge. 10s, Train on Infiernillo Bridge, horiz.

**2004, Oct. 29** ***Perf. 14x13½***
**1435** A697 5s multi 4.00 4.00

**Souvenir Sheet**

***Perf. 13½x14***

**1436** A697 10s multi 7.50 7.50

Peruvian Song Day, 60th Anniv. A698

**2004, Oct. 31** ***Perf. 13½x14***
**1437** A698 5s multi 4.00 4.00

FIFA (Fédération Internationale de Football Association), Cent. — A699

**2004, Nov. 2**
**1438** A699 5s multi 4.00 4.00

Election of Pope John Paul II, 25th Anniv. (in 2003) A700

**2004, Nov. 2**
**1439** A700 5s multi 4.00 4.00

Canonization of Mother Teresa — A701

**2004, Nov. 2** ***Perf. 14x13½***
**1440** A701 5s multi 4.00 4.00

Miniature Sheet

Musicians — A702

No. 1441: a, Juan Diego Flórez. b, Susana Baca. c, Gianmarco. d, Eva Ayllón, horiz. e, Libido, horiz.

***Perf. 14x13½, 14x14x13½x14 (#1441d, 1441e)***

**2004, Nov. 12**
**1441** A702 2s Sheet of 5, #a-e 7.50 7.50

Flora Tristan Women's Center, 25th Anniv. — A703

**2004, Nov. 9** **Litho.** ***Perf. 14***
**1442** A703 5s multi 4.00 4.00

Exporter's Day — A704

**2004, Nov. 9**
**1443** A704 5s multi 4.00 4.00

Latin American Parliament, 40th Anniv. — A705

No. 1444: a, Parliament emblem. b, Andrés Townsend Escurra, first President of Latin American Parliament, and flags.

**2004, Nov. 16** ***Perf. 13½x14***
**1444** A705 2.50s Horiz. pair, #a-b 4.00 4.00

Lima Bar Association, 200th Anniv. — A706

**2004, Nov. 17**
**1445** A706 5s multi 4.00 4.00

Serpost, 10th Anniv. A707

**2004, Nov. 22**
**1446** A707 5s multi 4.00 4.00

Jungle River Fauna A708

Designs: 2s, Serrasalmus. 4.50s, Pontoporia blainvillei. 5s, Arapaima gigas, vert.

***Perf. 13½x14, 14x13½***

**2004, Nov. 30**
**1447-1449** A708 Set of 3 9.00 9.00

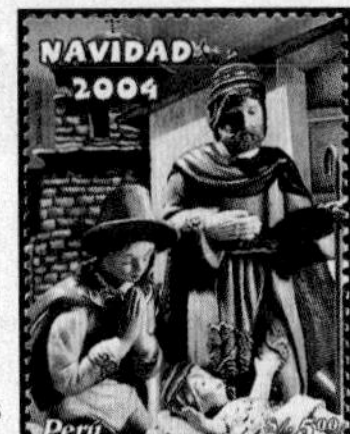

Christmas A709

**2004, Dec. 2** ***Perf. 14x13½***
**1450** A709 5s multi 4.00 4.00

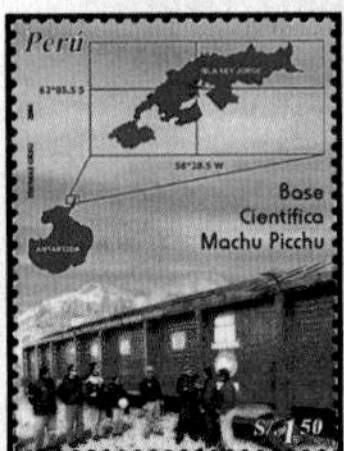

Antarctica A710

Designs: 1.50s, Machu Picchu Scientific Base, King George Island. 2s, Megaptera novaeangliae, horiz. 4.50s, Orcinus orca, horiz.

**2004, Dec. 3** ***Perf. 14x13½, 13½x14***
**1451-1453** A710 Set of 3 6.00 6.00

Prehistoric Animals — A711

No. 1454: a, 1.80s, Drawings of Smilodon neogaeus and Toxodon platensis Owen. 3.20s, Fossils, depiction of body of Toxodon platensis.

**2004, Dec. 6** ***Perf. 14x13½***
**1454** A711 Horiz. pair, #a-b 4.00 4.00

Mochica Ceramics — A712

Various ceramic pieces with background colors of: No. 1455, 4.50s, Dark blue. No. 1456, 4.50s, Red violet. 5s, Blue, horiz.

**2004, Dec. 6** ***Perf. 14x14½, 14½x14***
**1455-1457** A712 Set of 3 10.00 10.00

Third Meeting of South American Presidents A713

**2004, Dec. 8** ***Perf. 14x13½***
**1458** A713 5s multi 4.00 4.00

Lima Museum of Art, 50th Anniv. — A714

**2004, Dec. 9** **Litho.**
**1459** A714 5s multi 4.00 4.00

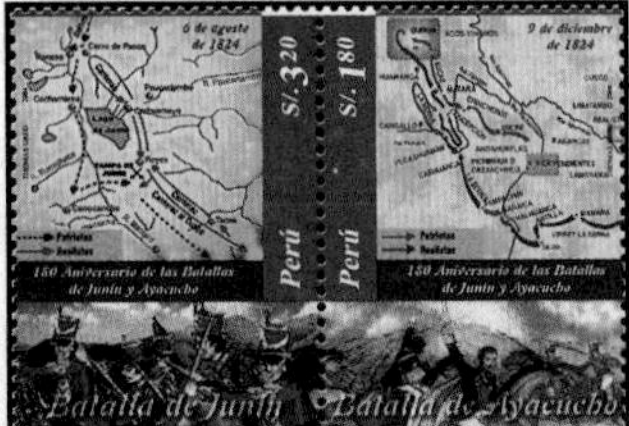

Battles, 180th Anniv. — A715

No. 1460: a, 1.80s, Map and scene of Battle of Ayacucho. b, 3.20s, Map and scene of Battle of Junín.

**2004, Dec. 9**
**1460** A715 Horiz. pair, #a-b 4.00 4.00

Lighthouses — A716

No. 1461: a, Pijuayal Lighthouse, Amazon River. b, Suana Lighhouse, Lake Titicaca.

**2004, Dec. 10**
**1461** A716 4.50s Horiz. pair, #a-b 7.00 7.00

Souvenir Sheet

Sacred City of Caral — A717

**2004, Dec. 15** ***Perf. 13½x14***
**1462** A717 10s multi 7.50 7.50

Parque de las Leyendes, 40th Anniv. — A718

No. 1463: a, Cantua buxifolia. b, Puma concolor.

**2005, Jan. 14** ***Perf. 14x13½***
**1463** A718 5s Horiz. pair, #a-b 7.50 7.50

Dated 2004.

Championship Trophies Won By Cienciano Soccer Team — A719

**2005, Jan. 22**
**1464** A719 5s multi 4.00 4.00

Dated 2004.

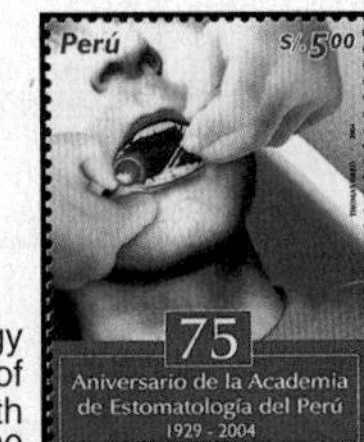

Stomatology Academy of Peru, 75th Anniv. — A720

**2005, Jan. 24**
**1465** A720 5s multi 4.00 4.00

Dated 2004.

National Health Crusade — A721

**2005, Feb. 2** ***Perf. 14***
**1466** A721 2s multi + label 1.50 1.50

Dated 2004.

Houses of Worship A722

Designs: 4.50s, San Cristóbal Church, Huamanga. 5s, Huancayo Cathedral.

**2005, Feb. 7** **Litho.** ***Perf. 13½x14***
**1467-1468** A722 Set of 2 7.00 7.00

Abolition of Slavery, 150th Anniv. A723

**2005, Feb. 25** **Engr.**
**1469** A723 5s claret 4.00 4.00

Armed Forces — A724

No. 1470: a, 1.80s, Army tank. b, 1.80s, Navy submarine. c, 1.80s, Air Force Mirage jets. d, 3.20s, Air Force Sukhoi jet. e, 3.20s, Army soldiers. f, 3.20s, Navy frigate.

**2005, Feb. 28** **Litho.**
**1470** A724 Block of 6, #a-f, + label 10.00 10.00

Fruit A725

Designs: No. 1471, 4.50s, Eugenia stipitata. No. 1472, 4.50s, Mauritia flexuosa. 5s, Solanum sessiflorum dunal, vert.

**2005, Mar. 4** ***Perf. 13½x14, 14x13½***
**1471-1473** A725 Set of 3 10.00 10.00

Opera Singer Luis Alva Talledo, Founder of Prolirica A726

**2005, Mar. 10** ***Perf. 13½x14***
**1474** A726 1.50s multi 1.10 1.10

Allpahuayo Reserve Wildlife — A727

No. 1475: a, Hormiguero norteño de cola castaña. b, Tiranuelo de Mishana. c, Rana arboricola. d, Sacha runa.

**2005, Mar. 21** ***Perf. 14x13½***
**1475** A727 4.50s Block of 4, #a-d, + label 13.00 13.00

Paintings — A728

No. 1476 — Unidentified paintings by: a, Pancho Fierro. b, Ignacio Moreno. c, Daniel Hernández. d, Camilo Blas. e, Ricardo Grau. f, Fernando de Szyszlo.

**2005, Apr. 4**
**1476** A728 2s Block of 6, #a-f, + label 9.00 9.00

Science of Antonio Raimondo — A729

No. 1477: a, 1.80s, Sculptures, Chavín de Huántar. b, 3.20s, Bird and bat. c, 4.50s, Stanophea. d, 5s, Fossil of N. C. Roemoceras Subplanum Hyatt.

**2005, Apr. 18**
**1477** A729 Block of 4, #a-d, + label 11.00 11.00

Souvenir Sheet

Penelope Albipennis — A730

**2005, May 2**
**1478** A730 10s multi 8.00 8.00

Architecture — A731

Designs: a, 4.50s, Government Palace. b, 4.50s, Italian Art Museum. c, 5s, Larco Mar. d, 5s, Mega Plaza.

**2005, May 18** ***Perf. 13½x14***
**1479** A731 Block of 4, #a-d, + label 14.00 14.00

Postal Money Orders A732

**2005, May 30**
**1480** A732 5s multi 4.00 4.00

Pope John Paul II (1920-2005) — A733

**2005, Nov. 24** **Litho.** ***Perf. 13½***
**1481** A733 1.80s multi 1.75 1.75

Souvenir Sheet

Europa Stamps, 50th Anniv. (in 2006) — A734

No. 1482: a, Mochica headdress and Spain #1526. b, Chimú ceremonial jewelry and Spain #941. c, Mochica earrings and Spain #1567. d, Mochica headdress and Spain #1607.

**2005, Nov. 24** **Litho.** ***Perf. 14***
**1482** A734 2s Sheet of 4, #a-d 6.00 6.00

Miniature Sheet

Naval Victories — A735

No. 1483: a, Battle of Punta Malpelo. b, Battle of Callao. c, Sinking of the Covadonga. d, Battle of Abtao. e, Battle of Iquique. f, Battle of Pedrera.

**2005, Dec. 21** **Litho.** ***Perf. 13½x14***
**1483** A735 2s Sheet of 6, #a-f 8.50 8.50

Medical College of Peru, 35th Anniv. A736

**2005, Dec. 29**
**1484** A736 5.50s multi 4.00 4.00

Christmas 2005 A737

**2006, Jan. 9**
**1485** A737 5.50s multi 4.00 4.00

Dated 2005.

Eighth Cultural Patrimony Colloquium, Cuzco — A738

**2006, Jan. 9** ***Perf. 14x13½***
**1486** A738 5.50s multi 4.00 4.00

Dated 2005.

Sister Ana de los Angeles Monteagudo (1602-86) — A739

**2006, Jan. 10** ***Perf. 13½x14***
**1487** A739 5.50s multi 4.00 4.00

Dated 2005.

Publication of Don Quixote, 400th Anniv. (in 2005) A740

**2006, Jan. 11**
**1488** A740 5s multi 4.00 4.00

Dated 2005.

Pope Benedict XVI — A741

No. 1489: a, Profile. b, With arms raised.

**2006, Jan. 11** ***Perf. 14x13½***
**1489** A741 2.50s Horiz. pair, #a-b 4.00 4.00

Dated 2005.

Rotary International, Cent. (in 2005) — A742

**2006, Jan. 13** ***Perf. 13½x14***
**1490** A742 5.50s multi 4.00 4.00

Dated 2005.

America Issue, Fight Against Poverty — A743

**2006, Jan. 16** ***Perf. 14x13½***
**1491** A743 5.50s multi 4.00 4.00

Dated 2005.

Natl. Academy of History, Cent. (in 2005) A744

**2006, Jan. 20** ***Perf. 13½x14***
**1492** A744 5.50s multi 4.00 4.00

Dated 2005.

St. Peter's Church, Lima — A745

No. 1493: a, Exterior. b, Interior.

**2006, Jan. 20** ***Perf. 14x13½***
**1493** A745 2.50s Horiz. pair, #a-b 3.50 3.50

Dated 2005.

Volcanoes — A746

No. 1494: a, Pichupichu. b, Chachani. c, Misti.

**2006, Jan. 20**
**1494** A746 Horiz. strip of 3 5.00 5.00
***a.-c.*** 2.50s Any single 1.60 1.60

Dated 2005.

YMCA in Peru, 85th Anniv. (in 2005) — A747

**2006, Jan. 23** **Litho.**
**1495** A747 5.50s multi 4.00 4.00

Dated 2005.

Dr. Julio C. Tello (1880-1947), Anthropologist and Archaeologist — A748

**2006, Jan. 26** ***Perf. 13½x14***
**1496** A748 5s multi 3.50 3.50

Dated 2005.

Cáritas, 50th Anniv. (in 2005) A749

**2006, Jan. 28**
**1497** A749 5.50s multi 4.00 4.00

Dated 2005.

Comptroller General, 75th Anniv. (in 2005) — A750

**2006, Feb. 6** ***Perf. 14x13½***
**1498** A750 5.50s multi 4.00 4.00

Dated 2005.

Creation of Cajamarca Department, 150th Anniv. (in 2005) — A751

**2006, Feb. 11** ***Perf. 13½x14***
**1499** A751 6s multi 4.25 4.25

Dated 2005.

Traditional Foods — A752

No. 1500: a, Chupe de camarones. b, Juane. c, Arroz con pato (duck and rice). d, Rocoto relleno.

**2006, Feb. 16**
**1500** A752 2s Block of 4, #a-d, + label 5.50 5.50

Dated 2005.

Butterflies — A753

No. 1501: a, Heliconius sara. b, Morpho achilles. c, Dryas iulia. d, Caligo eurilochus.

**2006, Feb. 17**
**1501** A753 2s Block of 4, #a-d, + label 6.00 6.00

Dated 2005.

12th Panamerican Scout Jamboree, Argentina — A754

No. 1502: a, Scout in foreground. b, Flag in foreground.

**2006, Feb. 20** ***Perf. 14x13½***
**1502** A754 2s Horiz. pair, #a-b 2.75 2.75

Dated 2005.

Pre-Columbian Cultures — A755

Artifacts of: No. 1503, 6s, Paracas culture, c. 500. No. 1504, 6s, Chavin culture, c. 1200.

**2006, Feb. 22** ***Perf. 13½x14***
**1503-1504** A755 Set of 2 7.50 7.50

Dated 2005.

See also Nos. 1602-1603, 1648-1649, 1700-1701, 1740-1741, 1774-1775.

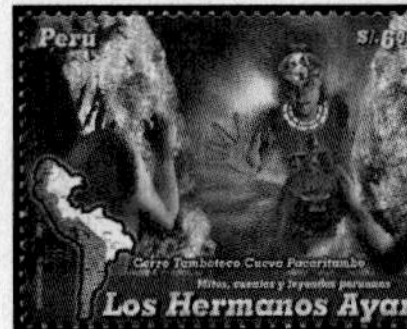


Legend of the Ayar Brothers, Incan Creation Myth A756

**2006, Feb. 24**
**1505** A756 6s multi 4.00 4.00

Dated 2005.

National Symbols — A757

No. 1506: a, Flag. b, Coat of arms. c, National anthem.

**2006, Feb. 27** ***Perf. 14x13½***
**1506** A757 Horiz. strip of 3 4.00 4.00
***a.-c.*** 2s Any single 1.25 1.25

Dated 2005.

Fruit A758

Designs: No. 1507, 6s, Pouteria lucuma. No. 1508, 6s, Annona cherimola.

**2006, Mar. 1** ***Perf. 13½x14***
**1507-1508** A758 Set of 2 8.00 8.00

Dated 2005.

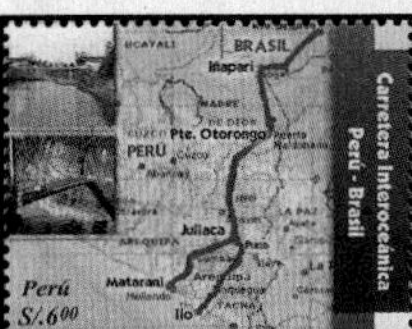


Peru to Brazil Interoceanic Highway A759

**2006, Mar. 3**
**1509** A759 6s multi 4.00 4.00

Dated 2005.

Writers — A760

Designs: No. 1510, 6s, Mario Vargas Llosa. No. 1511, 6s, Alfredo Bryce Echenique.

**2006, Mar. 28** **Engr.** ***Perf. 14x13½***
**1510-1511** A760 Set of 2 8.00 8.00

Dated 2005.

Health Ministry, 70th Anniv. (in 2005) A761

**2006, Apr. 7** **Litho.** ***Perf. 13½x14***
**1512** A761 6s multi 4.00 4.00

Dated 2005.

Latin American Integration Association, 25th Anniv. (in 2005) A762

**2006, Apr. 7**
**1513** A762 6s multi 4.00 4.00

Dated 2005.

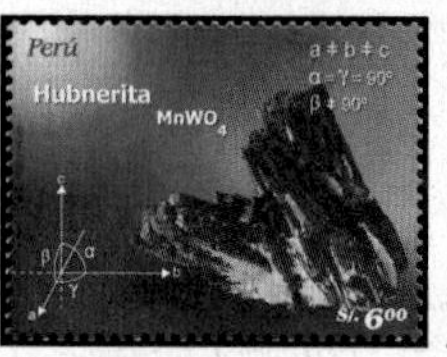


Hubnerite A763

**2006, Apr. 28**
**1514** A763 6s multi 4.00 4.00

Compare with type A657.

Purple Corn Chicha Beverage A764

**2006, Apr. 28**
**1515** A764 6s multi 4.00 4.00

Fauna of Lake Titicaca — A765

No. 1516: a, Orestias spp. b, Plegadis ridgwayi. c, Phoenicoparrus andinus. d, Telmatobius culeus.

**2006, May 2** ***Perf. 14x13½***
**1516** A765 5.50s Block of 4, #a-d, + label 14.50 14.50

Parrots — A766

No. 1517: a, Pionopsitta barrabandi. b, Tovit huetii. c, Pionites melanocephala. d, Ara severa. e, Amazona festiva. f, Ara ararauna.

**2006, May 5**
**1517** A766 5.50s Block of 6, #a-f, + label 22.50 22.50

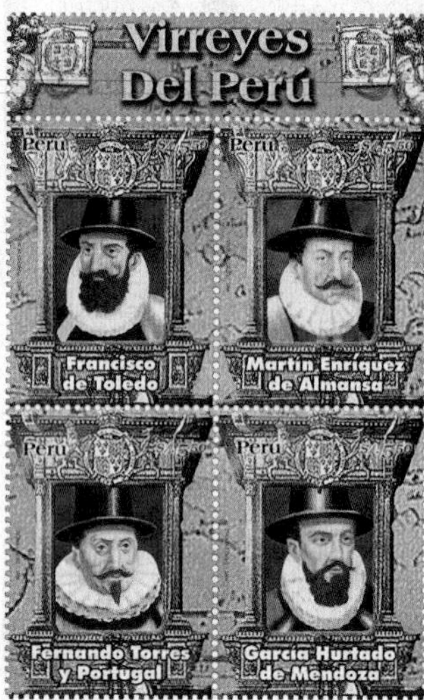


Viceroys of Peru — A767

No. 1518: a, Francisco de Toledo (1515-82). b, Martín Enríquez de Almansa (c. 1525-83). c, Fernando Torres y Portugal. d, García Hurtado de Mendoza (1535-1609).

**2006, May 8**
**1518** A767 5.50s Block of 4, #a-d, + label 14.50 14.50

See Nos. 1569, 1575, 1622, 1681, 1737, 1776, 1858. Compare with type A1063.

Souvenir Sheet

Lighthouses — A768

No. 1519: a, Isla Lobos de Tierra Lighthouse. b, Isla Blanca Lighthouse.

**2006, May 10**
**1519** A768 6s Sheet of 2, #a-b 8.00 8.00

Birds A769

Designs: No. 1520, 6s, Perlita de Iquitos. No. 1521, 6s, Tortolita moteada (turtledove). No. 1522, 6s, Ganse Andino (Andean geese), vert.

**2006, May 15** ***Perf. 13½x14, 14x13½***
**1520-1522** A769 Set of 3 12.00 12.00

El Peruano Newspaper, 180th Anniv. — A770

**2006, May 16** ***Perf. 13½x14***
**1523** A770 6s multi 4.00 4.00

Surfing — A771

No. 1524: a, Surfers on waves. b, Sofía Mulanovich, 2004 Surfing World Champion.

**2006, May 16** ***Perf. 14x13½***
**1524** A771 5.50s Horiz. pair, #a-b 7.50 7.50

Souvenir Sheet

Lima-Callao Railway, 150th Anniv. — A772

**2006, May 16** ***Perf. 13½x14***
**1525** A772 6s multi 4.00 4.00

Miniature Sheet

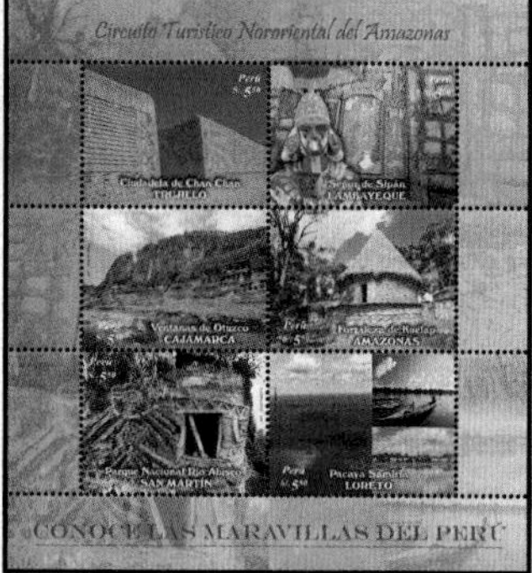


Tourism — A773

No. 1526: a, Chan Chan. b, Sipán man. c, Ventanas de Otuzco. d, Kuelap Fort. e, Río Abiseo Natl. Park. f, Pacaya Samiria.

**2006, May 17**
**1526** A773 5.50s Sheet of 6, #a-f 22.50 22.50

Miniature Sheet

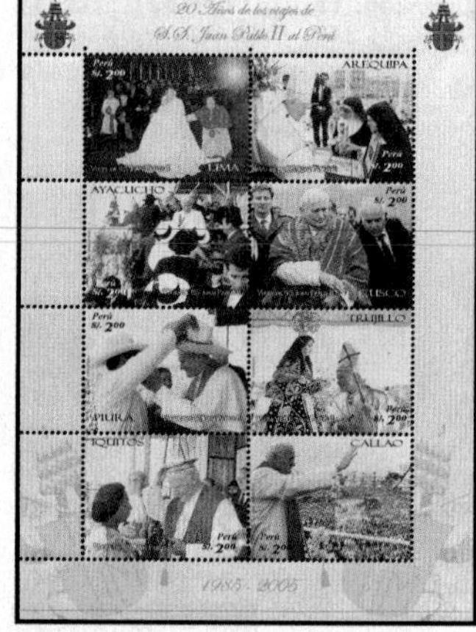

Visit of Pope John Paul II to Peru, 20th Anniv. — A774

No. 1527 — Pope in: a, Lima. b, Arequipa. c, Ayacucho. d, Cuzco. e, Piura. f, Trujillo. g, Iquitos. h, Callao.

**2006, May 19**
**1527** A774 2s Sheet of 8, #a-h 10.50 10.50

Peruvian Air Force — A775

No. 1528: a, Air Force emblem. b, Airplanes and pilot.

**2006, May 22**
**1528** A775 6s Horiz. pair, #a-b 8.00 8.00

Carnival Participants A776

Participants in carnivals from: No. 1529, 6s, Cajamarca. No. 1530, 6s, Arequipa. No. 1531, 6s, Puno.

**2006, May 22** ***Perf. 14x13½***
**1529-1531** A776 Set of 3 12.00 12.00

Precursors of Independence — A777

No. 1532: a, Micaela Bastidas. b, Plaza Mayor, Cuzco.

**2006, May 31**
**1532** A777 2s Horiz. pair, #a-b 2.75 2.75

Intl. Year of Deserts and Desertification — A778

**2006, Dec. 22 Litho.** ***Perf. 13½x14***
**1533** A778 2s multi 1.50 1.50

Christmas A779

**2006, Dec. 22**
**1534** A779 2s multi 1.50 1.50

Wolfgang Amadeus Mozart (1756-91), Composer A780

**2006, Dec. 22**
**1535** A780 5.50s multi 3.75 3.75

2006 World Cup Soccer Championships, Germany — A781

**2006, Dec. 22** ***Perf. 14x13½***
**1536** A781 8.50s multi 5.75 5.75

Christopher Columbus (1451-1506), Explorer — A782

**2006, Dec. 27** ***Perf. 13½x14***
**1537** A782 6s multi 4.00 4.00

First International Philatelic Exhibition in Peru, 75th Anniv. — A783

**Litho. With Foil Application**

**2006, Dec. 29** ***Perf. 13½x14***
**1538** A783 8.50s #286 5.75 5.75

America Issue, Energy Conservation — A784

No. 1539: a, 3s, Solar panels. b, 5.50s, Natural gas.

**2006, Dec. 29 Litho.** ***Perf. 14x13½***
**1539** A784 Horiz. pair, #a-b 5.75 5.75

Diplomatic Relations Between Peru and People's Republic of China, 35th Anniv. — A785

No. 1540: a, Giant panda. b, Guanaco. c, Machu Picchu. d, Great Wall of China.

**2006, Dec. 29**
**1540** A785 2s Block of 4, #a-d, + label 5.25 5.25

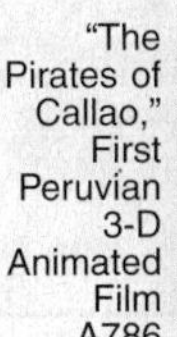

"The Pirates of Callao," First Peruvian 3-D Animated Film A786

Parrot and: No. 1541, 2s, Boy with sword. No. 1542, 2s, Captain with sword.

**Litho. With Foil Application**

**2007, Jan. 5** ***Perf. 13½x14***
**1541-1542** A786 Set of 2 2.75 2.75

Dated 2006.

Peruvian Art A787

Designs: No. 1543, 2.20s, Sculpture of horse by Victor Delfin. No. 1544, 2.20s, Painting by Fernando de Szyszlo.

**2007, Jan. 9 Litho.**
**1543-1544** A787 Set of 2 3.00 3.00

Dated 2006.

Souvenir Sheet

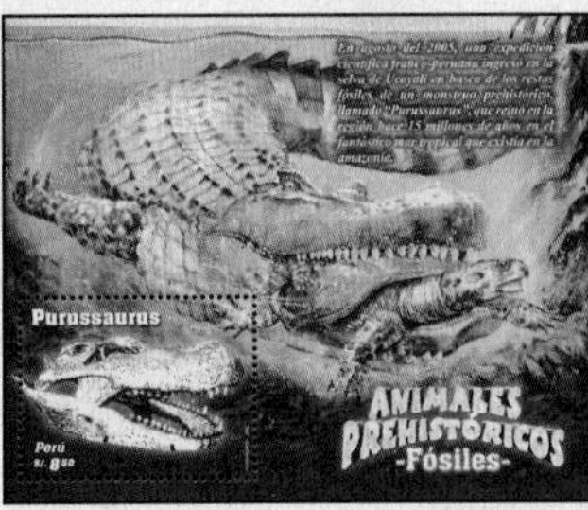


Purussaurus Fossil — A788

**Litho. (Foil Application on Sheet Margin)**

**2007, Jan. 16**
**1545** A788 8.50s multi 5.75 5.75

Dated 2006.

Flutes A789

Designs: No. 1546, 5.50s, Antara. No. 1547, 5.50s, Quena. No. 1548, 5.50s, Zampoña.

**2007, Jan. 23 Litho.**
**1546-1548** A789 Set of 3 11.00 11.00

Dated 2006.

St. Toribio de Mogrovejo (1538-1606), Founder of First Seminary in Americas A790

**2007, Jan. 27 Engr.** ***Perf. 14x13½***
**1549** A790 2s chocolate 1.40 1.40

Dated 2006.

Miniature Sheet

Religious Festivals — A791

No. 1550: a, Señor de los Milagros. b, Virgen de las Mercedes. c, Virgen de la Candelaria. d, Señor de Muruhuay.

**2007, Jan. 30 Litho.**
**1550** A791 5.50s Sheet of 4, #a-d 14.50 14.50

Dated 2006.

Peruvian Film, "Dragones Destino de Fuego" — A792

Designs: No. 1551, 2s, Flying dragons. No. 1552, 2s, Head of dragon.

**Litho. With Foil Application**

**2007, Feb. 5**
**1551-1552** A792 Set of 2 2.75 2.75

Dated 2006.

National Board of Elections, 75th Anniv. (in 2006) — A793

**2007, Feb. 13 Engr.**
**1553** A793 2.20s brown 1.50 1.50

Dated 2006.

Desserts — A794

No. 1554: a, Suspiro de limeña. b, Picarones. c, Mazamorra morada.

**2007, Mar. 12 Litho.** ***Perf. 13½x14***
**1554** A794 Horiz. strip of 3 5.00 5.00
***a.-c.*** 2.50s Any single 1.60 1.60

Dated 2006.

Dogs — A795

No. 1555: a, Perro sin pelo (hairless dog). b, Dachshund. c, Samoyed. d, Siberian husky.

**2007, Mar. 26 Litho.** ***Perf. 13½x14***
**1555** A795 6s Block of 4, #a-d, + label 16.00 16.00

Dated 2006.

Miniature Sheet

Architecture of the Viceregal Era in Lima — A796

No. 1556: a, St. Augustine Church. b, Sacristy of St. Francis. c, St. Apollonia Gate. d, Metropolitan Cathedral

**2007, Apr. 2 Litho. *Perf. 14x13½***
**1556** A796 5.50s Sheet of 4, #a-d 14.50 14.50

Dated 2006.

Incan Temples A797

Designs: No. 1557, 6s, Tambo Colorado, Ica. No. 1558, 6s, Pachacamac, Lima. No. 1559, 6s, Tambo Machay, Cusco.

**2007, Apr. 23 Litho. *Perf. 13½x14***
**1557-1559** A797 Set of 3 12.00 12.00

Dated 2006.

Felipe Pinglo Alva (1899-1936), Composer — A798

No. 1560: a, Photographs of Pinglo Alva and buildings. b, Guitar, photograph of Pinglo Alva.

**2007, May 7 *Perf. 14x13½***
**1560** A798 3s Horiz. pair, #a-b 4.00 4.00

Dated 2006.

Pre-Columbian Cultures — A799

Artifacts and maps of: No. 1561, 6s, Vicús culture, 500 B.C. No. 1562, 6s, Salinar culture, 200 B.C.

**2007, May 21 *Perf. 13½x14***
**1561-1562** A799 Set of 2 8.00 8.00

Dated 2006.

Dances and Costumes — A800

No. 1563: a, Danza de los Negritos. b, Danza de las Tijeras. c, Danza Cápac Colla. d, Danza La Diablada.

**2007, June 4 *Perf. 14x13½***
**1563** A800 2.50s Block of 4, #a-d, + label 6.75 6.75

Dated 2006.

Exports A801

Designs: No. 1564, 6s, Alpaca yarn. No. 1565, 6s, Mangos. No. 1566, 6s, Asparagus.

**2007, June 18 *Perf. 13½x14***
**1564-1566** A801 Set of 3 12.00 12.00

Dated 2006.

Adventure Sports — A802

No. 1567: a, Rafting. b, Cycling. c, Rock climbing.

**2007, July 2**
**1567** A802 Horiz. strip of 3 12.00 12.00
*a.-c.* 6s Any single 4.00 4.00

Dated 2006.

Miniature Sheet

First Peruvian Congress, 185th Anniv. — A803

No. 1568: a, Exposition Palace. b, Painting of Francisco González Gamarra. c, Tribunal of the Inquisition Building. d, Statue of Simón Bolívar. e, Legislative Palace at night. f, Pasos Perdidos Hall. g, Stained-glass window. h, Legislative Palace sculpture.

**Litho., Foil Application on Margin and Label**

**2007, July 12 *Perf. 14x13½***
**1568** A803 2.50s Sheet of 8, #a-h, + central label 13.50 13.50

**Viceroys Type of 2006**

No. 1569: a, Luis de Velasco (c. 1534-1617). b, Gaspar de Zuniga y Acevedo (1560-1606). c, Juan de Mendoza y Luna (1571-1628). d, Francisco de Borja y Aragon (1581-1658).

**2007, July 16 Litho.**
**1569** A767 6s Block of 4, #a-d, + label 16.00 16.00

Giuseppe Garibaldi (1807-82), Italian Leader A804

**2007, July 26 *Perf. 13½x14***
**1570** A804 6s multi 4.00 4.00

Scouting, Cent. — A805

No. 1571: a, Scouting emblem, pictures of Scouts. b, Lord Robert Baden-Powell blowing kudu horn, flags.

**2007, July 30 *Perf. 14x13½***
**1571** A805 3s Horiz. pair, #a-b 4.00 4.00

Endangered Animals — A806

No. 1572: a, 3s, Oncifelis colocolo. b, 3s, Lontra felina. c, 6s, Harpia harpyja. d, 6s, Odocoileus virginianus.

**2007, July 30 *Perf. 13½x14***
**1572** A806 Block of 4, #a-d, + label 12.00 12.00

Medicinal Plants — A807

No. 1573: a, Bixa orellana. b, Cestrum auriculatum. c, Brugmansia suaveolens. d, Anacardium occidentale. e, Caesalpinia spinosa. f, Croton lechleri.

**2007, Aug. 6 Litho.**
**1573** A807 2.50s Block of 6, #a-f, + label 10.00 10.00

Raul Maria Pereira, Architect, and Postal Headquarters, Lima — A808

**2007, Aug. 10**
**1574** A808 2s multi 1.50 1.50

See Portugal No. 2940.

**Viceroys Type of 2006**

No. 1575: a, Diego Fernández de Cordoba (1578-1630). b, Luis Jerónimo de Cabrera (1589-1647). c, Pedro de Toledo y Leiva (c. 1585-1654). d, Garcia Sarmiento de Sotomayor (c. 1595-1659).

**2007, Aug. 20 *Perf. 14x13½***
**1575** A767 6s Block of 4, #a-d, + label 16.00 16.00

Souvenir Sheet

Riva-Agüero Institute, 60th Anniv. — A809

**2007, Sept. 10**
**1576** A809 10.50s multi 7.00 7.00

Peruvian National Police Band, Cent. (in 2006) A810

Band: 2s, On steps of building. 8.50s, In parade.

**2007, Sept. 15 *Perf. 13½x14***
**1577-1578** A810 Set of 2 7.00 7.00

Birds A811

Designs: No. 1579, 5.50s, Coeraba flaveola. No. 1580, 5.50s, Mimus longicaudatus. No. 1581, 5.50s, Pyrocephalus rubinus. No. 1582, 5.50s, Sarcoramphus papa.

**Litho. With Foil Application**

**2007, Sept. 15**
**1579-1582** A811 Set of 4 15.00 15.00

Grand Masonic Lodge of Peru, 125th Anniv. — A812

**2007, Sept. 17 Litho. *Perf. 14x13½***
**1583** A812 6.50s multi 4.50 4.50

Souvenir Sheet

Joint Command of the Armed Forces, 50th Anniv. — A813

**2007, Sept. 24** ***Perf. 13½x14***
**1584** A813 14s multi 9.50 9.50

Children's Art A814

Winning pictures in children's art contest: No. 1585, 2s, River Scene, by Juana Chuquipiondo Mesía. No. 1586, 2s, Crane on Stump, by Rubén Saavedra Cobeñas, vert.

***Perf. 13½x14, 14x13½***
**2007, Sept. 28**
**1585-1586** A814 Set of 2 2.75 2.75

Miniature Sheet

Automobiles — A815

No. 1587: a, 1935 Auburn Speedster 851 SC. b, 1903 Clément Brass Phaeton 9 CV. c, 1926 Dodge Special Pickup truck. d, 1928 Stutz BB Sedan Convertible Victoria. e, 1936 Pierce Arrow 1603 Touring D 700.

**2007, Sept. 28** ***Perf. 13½x14***
**1587** A815 3s Sheet of 5, #a-e 10.00 10.00

Santa Clara Monastery, Cusco, 450th Anniv. — A816

**2007, Oct. 1** ***Perf. 14x13½***
**1588** A816 5.50s multi 3.75 3.75

Cats — A817

No. 1589: a, Angora. b, Persian. c, Bengal. d, Siamese.

**2007, Oct. 1** **Litho.**
**1589** A817 6s Block of 4, #a-d, + label 16.00 16.00

Miniature Sheet

Insects — A818

No. 1590: a, Macrodontia cervicornis. b, Dynastes hercules. c, Titanus giganteus. d, Megasoma sp.

**2007, Oct. 1** ***Perf. 13½x14***
**1590** A818 5.50s Sheet of 4, #a-d 15.00 15.00

First Peruvian Nautical Academy, 350th Anniv. A819

**2007, Oct. 8**
**1591** A819 5.50s multi 3.75 3.75

America Issue, Education for All — A820

Designs: No. 1592, 5.50s, Two boys reading. No. 1593, 5.50s, Two girls reading.

**2007, Oct. 9** ***Perf. 14x13½***
**1592-1593** A820 Set of 2 7.50 7.50

Daniel Alcides Carrión (1857-85), Describer of Carrion's Disease A821

**2007, Oct. 13** **Engr.** ***Perf. 13½x14***
**1594** A821 3s brown 2.00 2.00

Miniature Sheet

Mushrooms — A822

No. 1595: a, Dyctiophora indusiata. b, Sepultaria arenicola. c, Marasmius haematocephalus. d, Marasmiellus volvatus.

**Litho., Foil Application in Margin**
**2007, Oct. 15** ***Perf. 14x13½***
**1595** A822 2.50s Sheet of 4, #a-d 6.75 6.75

Peru No. 18 Volunteer Fire Brigade, Cent. — A823

No. 1596 — Fire trucks: a, 1908 Merry Weather. b, 1969 Mack.

**2007, Nov. 4** **Litho.** ***Perf. 13½x14***
**1596** A823 3s Horiz. pair, #a-b 4.50 4.50

Víctor Raúl Haya de la Torre (1895-1979), Politician — A824

**2007, Aug. 16** **Engr.** ***Perf. 14x13½***
**1597** A824 3s claret 2.10 2.10

Souvenir Sheet

Megatherium Fossils — A825

**2007, Sept. 28** **Litho.**
**1598** A825 10s multi 7.25 7.25

Miniature Sheet

Bush Dog — A826

No. 1599: a, 2s, Two dogs. b, 2s, One dog. c, 5.50s, One dog, facing right. d, 5.50s, One dog, facing left.

**2007, Oct. 19** ***Perf. 13½x14***
**1599** A826 Sheet of 4, #a-d 11.00 11.00

Souvenir Sheet

Real Felipe Fort, Callao — A827

**2007, Oct. 29**
**1600** A827 6s multi 4.50 4.50

Familia Serrana, by Camilo Blas (1910-85) — A828

**2007, Nov. 5** ***Perf. 14x13½***
**1601** A828 6s multi 4.50 4.50

**Pre-Columbian Cultures Type of 2006**

Artifacts of: 6s, Nasca culture, A.D. 600. 7s, Mochica culture, 700 B.C.-A.D. 200.

**2007, Nov. 12** ***Perf. 13½x14***
**1602-1603** A755 Set of 2 9.50 9.50

Souvenir Sheet

Cahuachi Archaeological Site — A829

**2007, Nov. 12**
**1604** A829 14.50s multi 10.50 10.50

Founders of Independence Society, 150th Anniv. — A830

**2007, Dec. 1**
**1605** A830 6s multi 4.50 4.50

Christmas A831

**2007, Dec. 1** ***Perf. 14x13½***
**1606** A831 6.50s multi 5.00 5.00

First Peruvian Postage Stamps, 150th Anniv. — A832

No. 1607: a, Peru #1. b, Peru #2.

**2007, Dec. 1**
**1607** A832 2.50s Horiz. pair, #a-b 3.75 3.75

Altars in Lima Churches A833

Altar from: 6s, Carmelite Church. 8.50s, Lima Cathedral.

**2007, Dec. 1**
**1608-1609** A833 Set of 2 10.50 10.50

Asia-Pacific Economic Cooperation Forum — A834

**2007, Dec. 3**
**1610** A834 6s multi 4.50 4.50

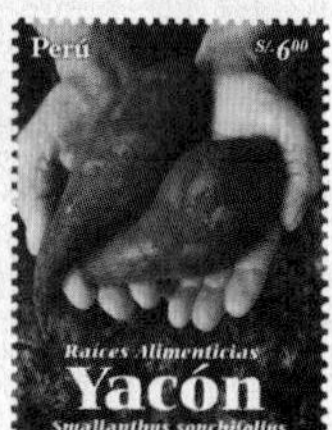

Roots — A835

Designs: No. 1611, 6s, Smallanthus sonchifolius. No. 1612, 6s, Manihot esculenta.

**2007, Dec. 17**
**1611-1612** A835 Set of 2 8.50 8.50

Launch of First Peruvian Rocket, 1st Anniv. — A836

No. 1613 — Emblem of National Space Commission and: a, Pedro Paulet Mostajo (1874-1945), aeronautical pioneer and Paulet I rocket in flight. b, Paulet I rocket on launch pad and civil ensign.

**Litho., Litho. With Foil Application (#1613b)**

**2007, Dec. 27** ***Perf. 13½x14***
**1613** A836 3s Horiz. pair, #a-b 4.50 4.50

Souvenir Sheet

First Peruvian Scientific Expedition to the Antarctic, 20th Anniv. — A837

No. 1614: a, Ship "Humboldt." b, Expedition members, horiz.

***Perf. 13½x14, 14x13½ (#1614b)***
**Litho. With Foil Application**

**2008, Feb. 22**
**1614** A837 10s Sheet of 2, #a-b 14.00 14.00

Arms Stamps of 1858, 150th Anniv. — A838

Designs: No. 1615, 5.50s, Peru #3. No. 1616, 5.50s, Peru #4. No. 1617, 5.50s, Peru #6.

**2008, Mar. 10 Litho.** ***Perf. 14x13½***
**1615-1617** A838 Set of 3 12.50 12.50

Santa Rosa de Santa María Monastery, 300th Anniv. A839

**2008, June 3** ***Perf. 13½x14***
**1618** A839 5.50s multi 4.00 4.00

Lima Philharmonic Society, Cent. — A840

No. 1619 — Emblem and: a, Violin. b, Musicians.

**2008, June 8** ***Perf. 14x13½***
**1619** A840 3s Horiz. pair, #a-b 4.25 4.25

Lima General Cemetery, Bicent. A841

Designs: No. 1620, 6.50s, Statue of angel and cross. No. 1621, 6.50s, Statue of praying woman, vert.

***Perf. 13½x14, 14x13½***

**2008, June 17**
**1620-1621** A841 Set of 2 8.75 8.75

**Viceroys Type of 2006**

No. 1622: a, Luis Enríquez de Guzmán (c. 1605-61). b, Diego de Benavides y de la Cueva (1607-66). c, Pedro Antonio Fernandez de Castro (1634-72). d, Baltasar de la Cueva Enríquez (1626-86).

**2008, June 24** ***Perf. 14x13½***
**1622** A767 6s Block of 4, #a-d, + label 16.50 16.50

ExportaFacil Package Service — A842

**2008, June 24**
**1623** A842 10s multi 6.75 6.75

America Issue — A843

No. 1624: a, Inti Raymi (Festival of the Sun), Cuzco. b, Grape Harvest Festival, Ica.

**2008, June 24** ***Perf. 13½x14***
**1624** A843 6.50s Horiz. pair, #a-b 8.75 8.75

Latin American, Caribbean and European Union Heads of State Summit, Lima — A844

**2008, July 1** ***Perf. 14x13½***
**1625** A844 6.50s red & black 4.50 4.50

2008 Summer Olympics, Beijing — A845

No. 1626 — Olympic mascots and places in Peru: a, Beibei, Máncora. b, Jingjing, Lima Cathedral. c, Yingying, Machu Picchu. d, Nini, Tambopata.

**2008, July 1** ***Perf. 13½x14***
**1626** A845 1.40s Block of 4, #a-d, + label 4.00 4.00

Latin American and European Parliamentary Summit, Lima — A846

**2008, July 2**
**1627** A846 6.50s multi 4.50 4.50

Aurelio Miró Quesada Sosa (1907-98), Lawyer and Writer A847

**2008, July 3**
**1628** A847 2.50s multi 1.75 1.75

National Literacy Program A848

**2008, July 4**
**1629** A848 2.50s multi 1.75 1.75

**Exports Type of 2007**

Designs: No. 1630, 5.50s, Olives (aceituna). No. 1631, 5.50s, Cotton (algodón). No. 1632, 5.50s, Avocados (palta).

**2008, July 8**
**1630-1632** A801 Set of 3 12.00 12.00

Miniature Sheet

River Fish — A849

No. 1633: a, Phractocephalus hemioliopterus. b, Mylossoma duriventre. c, Piaractus braphypomus. d, Ageneiosus ucayalensis. e, Brycon melanopterus.

**2008, July 18**
**1633** A849 3s Sheet of 5, #a-e 11.00 11.00

A850

A851

A852

Judgment Day Paintings, Lima Cathedral A853

**2008, Aug. 5**

| | | | | |
|---|---|---|---|---|
| **1634** | A850 6.50s multi | 4.50 | 4.50 |
| **1635** | A851 6.50s multi | 4.50 | 4.50 |
| **1636** | A852 6.50s multi | 4.50 | 4.50 |
| **1637** | A853 6.50s multi | 4.50 | 4.50 |
| | *Nos. 1634-1637 (4)* | 18.00 | 18.00 |

Edwin Vásquez Cam (1922-93), First Peruvian Olympic Gold Medalist A854

**2008, Aug. 6**

**1638** A854 6s multi 4.25 4.25

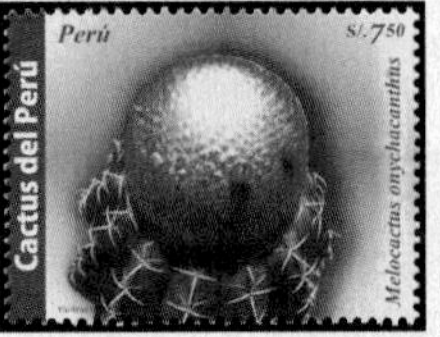

Cacti A855

Designs: No. 1639, 7.50s, Melocactus onychacanthus. No. 1640, 7.50s, Matucana oreodoxa. No. 1641, 7.50s, Espostoa mirabilis.

**2008, Aug. 13**

**1639-1641** A855 Set of 3 15.50 15.50

Dr. Javier Arias Stella, Pathologist A856

**2008, Aug. 22** ***Perf. 14x13½***

**1642** A856 2s multi 1.40 1.40

Miniature Sheet

Seven Wonders of the Modern World — A857

No. 1643: a, 2.50s, Petra, Jordan. b, 2.50s, Machu Picchu, Peru. c, 2.50s, Great Wall of China. d, 2.50s, Statue of Christ the Redeemer, Brazil. e, 7.50s, Chichén Itzá, Mexico. f, 10s, Roman Colosseum, Italy. g, 10.50s, Taj Mahal, India.

**2008, July 7 Litho.** ***Perf. 13½x14***

**1643** A857 Sheet of 7, #a-g 27.00 27.00

Intl. Year of the Potato A858

**Litho. With Foil Application**

**2008, Sept. 3**

**1644** A858 5.50s multi 3.75 3.75

Orchids — A859

Designs: No. 1645, 7s, Cattleya rex. No. 1646, 7s, Cattleya máxima.

**2008, Sept. 3 Litho.** ***Perf. 14x13½***

**1645-1646** A859 Set of 2 9.50 9.50

Souvenir Sheet

Crypt of the Heroes, Cent. — A860

**2008, Sept. 8**

**1647** A860 10.50s multi 7.00 7.00

**Pre-Columbian Cultures Type of 2006**

Artifacts of: 2s, Tiahuanaco culture, 100 B.C.-A.D. 1200. 6s, Recuay culture, A.D. 1-600.

**2008, Sept. 10** ***Perf. 13½x14***

**1648-1649** A755 Set of 2 5.50 5.50

Performing Arts Productions A861

Designs: No. 1650, 6.50s, Play *Na Catita.* No. 1651, 6.50s, Ballet *Huatyacuri.*

**Litho. with Foil Application**

**2008, Sept. 21** ***Perf. 14x13½***

**1650-1651** A861 Set of 2 8.75 8.75

Nos. 1650-1651 exist imperf.

National University of Trujillo Medical School, 50th Anniv. — A862

**2008, Oct. 3 Litho.**

**1652** A862 6s multi 4.00 4.00

Miniature Sheet

Spiders — A863

No. 1653: a, Micrathena sp. b, Lycosinae sp. c, Salticidae. d, Aglaoctenus castaneus.

**2008, Oct. 3** ***Perf. 13½x14***

**1653** A863 2s Sheet of 4, #a-d 5.50 5.50

Souvenir Sheet

1822 José de San Martín Currency — A864

No. 1654: a, 2-real note. b, 1-peso coin.

**Litho. & Engr. (Foil Application in Margin)**

**2008, Oct. 13**

**1654** A864 8.50s Sheet of 2, #a-b 11.00 11.00

Souvenir Sheet

Choquequirao Ruins — A865

**2008, Oct. 21 Litho.** ***Perf. 14x13½***

**1655** A865 10.50s multi 7.00 7.00

Museum of the Inquisition and Congress, Lima, 40th Anniv. — A866

No. 1656: a, Museum building (old National Senate Building). b, Inquisitors.

**2008, Oct. 28**

**1656** A866 6s Horiz. pair, #a-b 8.00 8.00

Traffic Policeman and Road Signs A867

**2008, Oct. 29** ***Perf. 13½x14***

**1657** A867 6.50s multi 4.25 4.25

Campaign for obeying traffic signs. No. 1657 exists imperf.

Edgardo Rebagliati National Hospital, 50th Anniv. A868

**2008, Nov. 3**

**1658** A868 2s multi 1.40 1.40

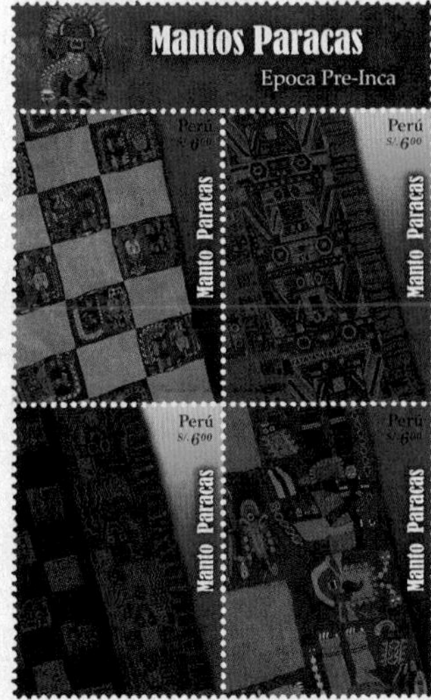

Paracas Mantles — A869

No. 1659: a, Unbordered mantle with white and illustrated squares. b, Fringed mantle with hexagons in design. c, Fringed mantle with black squares. d, Mantle with illustrated border.

**2008, Nov. 5** ***Perf. 14x13½***

**1659** A869 6s Block of 4 #a-d, + label 15.50 15.50

Xenoglaux Loweryi A870

**2008, Nov. 19** ***Perf. 13½x14***

**1660** A870 7.50s multi 5.00 5.00

Campaign Against Drug Abuse A871

Winning art in children's stamp design contest depicting: No. 1661, 2s, Boys and Hand, by Diego Gutierrez. No. 1662, 2s, Crossed bones and marijuana leaves, by Carolina Luna Polo, vert.

***Perf. 13½x14, 14x13½***

**2008, Nov. 21**
**1661-1662** A871 Set of 2 2.60 2.60

Christmas A872

**2008, Dec. 1** ***Perf. 13½x14***
**1663** A872 8.50s multi 5.50 5.50

Free Trade Agreement Between Peru and United States, 1st Anniv. A873

**2008, Dec. 4**
**1664** A873 6s multi 4.00 4.00

Jerónimo de Loayza Gonzáles (1498-1575), First Archbishop of Lima — A874

**2008, Dec. 10**
**1665** A874 2s multi 1.40 1.40

Souvenir Sheet

Inca God Wiracocha — A875

No. 1666 — Wiracocha: a, Breathing. b, With arm extended. c, Walking.

**2008, Dec. 10**
**1666** A875 2.50s Sheet of 3, #a-c 5.00 5.00

Miniature Sheet

Intl. Polar Year — A876

No. 1667: a, Iceberg. b, Raising of Peruvian flag. c, Map of Antarctica, International Polar Year emblem. d, Quelcayya Glacier, Peru.

**2009, Jan. 15**
**1667** A876 2.20s Sheet of 4, #a-d 5.50 5.50

College of Administrators, 30th Anniv. — A877

**2009, Feb. 11** **Litho.** ***Perf. 13½x14***
**1668** A877 6.50s multi 4.00 4.00

Intl. Heliophysical Year — A878

**Litho. With Foil Application**

**2009, Mar. 9** ***Perf. 14x13½***
**1669** A878 5.50s multi 3.50 3.50

Intl. Heliophysical Year was in 2007-08. The Intl. Year of Astronomy was in 2009.

Lighthouses A879

Designs: No. 1670, 6.50s, La Marina Lighthouse. No. 1671, 6.50s, Muelle Dársena Lighthouse and boat.

**2009, Mar. 9** **Litho.**
**1670-1671** A879 Set of 2 8.50 8.50

A880

Sunflowers A881

**2009, Mar. 13** ***Perf. 13½x14***
**1672** A880 2.50s multi 1.60 1.60
**1673** A881 2.50s multi 1.60 1.60

Honesty A882

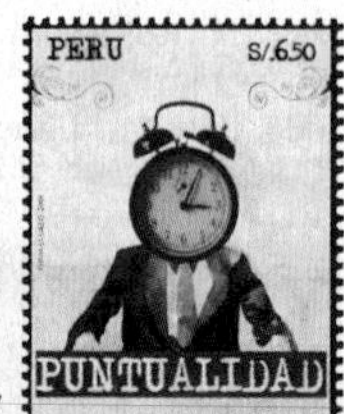


Punctuality A883

**2009, Mar. 16** ***Perf. 13½x14***
**1674** A882 6.50s multi 4.25 4.25

***Perf. 14x13½***

**1675** A883 6.50s multi 4.25 4.25

Intl. Meteorology Day — A884

**2009, Mar. 23** ***Perf. 14x13½***
**1676** A884 2s multi 1.40 1.40

Canyons — A885

No. 1677: a, Colca Canyon. b, Cotahuasi Canyon. c, Pato Canyon.

**2009, Mar. 23**
**1677** A885 2s Horiz. strip of 3, #a-c, + label 4.00 4.00

Parachuting — A886

No. 1678 — Skydivers with denomination in: a, UL. b, LR.

**2009, Mar. 31** ***Perf. 13½x14***
**1678** A886 7s Horiz. pair, #a-b 9.00 9.00

New Year 2009 (Year of the Ox) — A887

No. 1679 — Ring of Zodiac animals and: a, Rider on ox. b, Head of ox.

**2009, Apr. 8** **Litho.**
**1679** A887 2.50s Horiz. pair, #a-b 3.25 3.25

Earth Day A888

**2009, Apr. 22**
**1680** A888 5.50s multi 3.75 3.75

**Viceroys Type of 2006**

No. 1681: a, Melchor de Liñán y Cisneros (1629-1708). b, Melchor de Navarra y Rocafull (1626-91). c, Melchor Portocarrero Lasso de la Vega (1636-1705). d, Manuel de Oms y de Santa Pau (1651-1710).

**2009, Apr. 23** ***Perf. 14x13½***
**1681** A767 6s Block of 4 #a-d, + label 16.00 16.00

National University of Central Peru, Huancayo, 50th Anniv. — A889

**2009, Apr. 30**
**1682** A889 2s multi 1.40 1.40

Royal Commentaries of the Incas, 400th Anniv. — A890

Designs: No. 1683, 2s, Royal Commentaries of the Incas, book, by Garcellaso de la Vega. No. 1684, 2s, De la Vega (1539-1616), historian.

**2009, Apr. 30**
**1683-1684** A890 Set of 2 2.75 2.75

America Issue, Children's Games — A891

Designs: No. 1685, 10.50s, Boy flying kite. No. 1686, 10.50s, Children playing ronda.

**2009, Apr. 30** **Litho.**
**1685-1686** A891 Set of 2 14.00 14.00

Endangered Animals — A892

No. 1687: a, Blastocerus dichotomus. b, Pelecanoides garnotii. c, Podocnemis expansa. d, Crax unicornis.

**2009, May 4** ***Perf. 13½x14***
**1687** A892 7.50s Block of 4, #a-d, + label 20.00 20.00

Souvenir Sheet

"Libertad Parada" Coin — A893

No. 1688: a, Obverse (arms). b, Reverse (Liberty), vert.

***Perf. 13½x14 (#1688a), 14x13½ (#1688b)***

**2009, May 8**
**1688** A893 3s Sheet of 2, #a-b 4.00 4.00

Folk Art — A894

Designs: No. 1689, 6.50s, Retable, Ayacucho (Retablo Ayacuchano). No. 1690, 6.50s, Native clothing, Cusco (Muñequería Cusqueña). No. 1691, 6.50s, Decorated bull, Pucará (Torito de Pucará).

**2009, May 11** ***Perf. 14x13½***
**1689-1691** A894 Set of 3 13.50 13.50

Crustaceans — A895

No. 1692: a, Farfantepenaeus californiensis. b, Sicyonia aliaffnis. c, Ucides occidentalis. d, Palinurus elephas.

**2009, May 15** ***Perf. 13½x14***
**1692** A895 10s Block of 4, #a-d, + label 27.00 27.00

Souvenir Sheet

Peruvian Hairless Dog — A896

**2009, May 15** ***Perf. 14x13½***
**1693** A896 7s multi 4.75 4.75

Santiago de Surco Municipality, 80th Anniv. — A897

**2009, May 21** **Litho.**
**1694** A897 5.50s multi 3.75 3.75

Submarines — A898

No. 1695: a, BAP Pisagua. b, BAP Arica.

**2009, May 22** ***Perf. 13½x14***
**1695** A898 2.50s Vert. pair, #a-b 3.50 3.50

Cuzco as UNESCO World Heritage Site, 25th Anniv. (in 2008) A899

**Litho. With Foil Application**

**2009, May 24**
**1696** A899 2.50s multi 1.75 1.75

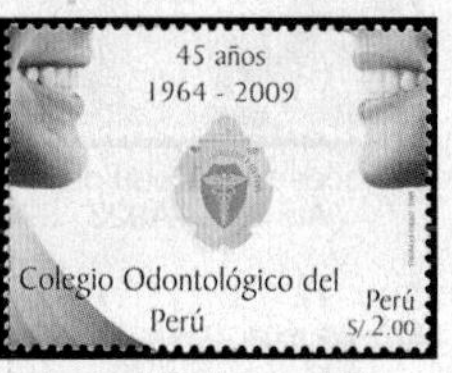

Odontological College of Peru, 45th Anniv. — A900

**2009, May 29** **Litho.**
**1697** A900 2s multi 1.40 1.40

Campaign Against Rabies A901

**2009, June 25** **Litho.** ***Perf. 13½x14***
**1698** A901 5.50s multi 3.75 3.75

Louis Braille (1809-52), Educator of the Blind — A902

No. 1699: a, Braille. b, Braille text.

**Litho. & Engr.**

**2009, June 30** ***Perf. 14x13½***
**1699** A902 2.20s Horiz. pair, #a-b 3.00 3.00

**Pre-Columbian Cultures Type of 2006**

Designs: No. 1700, 2s, Huari culture, 550-900. No. 1701, 2s, Chimú culture, 1000-1400.

**2009, July 3** **Litho.** ***Perf. 13½x14***
**1700-1701** A755 Set of 2 2.75 2.75

Ciro Alegría (1909-67), Journalist and Politician — A903

**2009, July 8** ***Perf. 14x13½***
**1702** A903 2.50s multi 1.75 1.75

Peruvian Tourist Attractions A904

Designs: No. 1703, 2.50s, Amazon River, Loretio Region. No. 1704, 2.50s, Boat on Lake Titicaca, Puno Region. No. 1705, 7.50s, Cumbemayo Archaeological Site, Cajamarca Region.

**2009** ***Perf. 13½x14***
**1703-1705** A904 Set of 3 8.50 8.50

Issued: Nos. 1703-1704, 7/17; No. 1705, 7/10.

Peruvian Philatelic Association, 60th Anniv. — A905

**2009, July 21** ***Perf. 14x13½***
**1706** A905 2s multi 1.40 1.40

Víctor Raúl Haya de la Torre (1895-1975), Politician — A906

**2009, Aug. 2** **Litho.** ***Perf. 13½x14***
**1707** A906 2s multi 1.40 1.40

Miniature Sheet

Peruvian Cuisine — A907

No. 1708: a, Tacacho con cecina. b, Ocopa. c, Cebiche de conchas negras. d, Picante de papa con cuy frito. e, Frejoles con cabrito.

**2009, Aug. 3**
**1708** A907 3s Sheet of 5, #a-e 10.50 10.50

Miniature Sheet

Incan Roads — A908

No. 1709: a, 6s, Inca Bridge, Qeswachaka. b, 6s, Inca Road, Wanacaure. c, 6s, Escalerayoc Sector, Lima. d, 7.50s, Quebrada Huarautambo, Pasco.

**2009, Aug. 6**
**1709** A908 Sheet of 4, #a-d 17.50 17.50

**Exports Type of 2007**

Designs: No. 1710, 2.50s, Guinea pig. No. 1711, 2.50s, Coffee.

**2009, Aug. 19**
**1710-1711** A801 Set of 2 3.50 3.50

Souvenir Sheet

Baguatherium Jaureguii Fossil — A909

**2009, Aug. 26** ***Perf. 14x13½***
**1712** A909 7s multi 4.75 4.75

Miniature Sheet

Mollusks — A910

No. 1713: a, Megalobulimus popelairianus. b, Megalobulimus capillaccus. c, Scutalus versicolor. d, Scutalus proteus.

**2009, Aug. 31** ***Perf. 13½x14***
**1713** A910 6.50s Sheet of 4, #a-d 18.00 18.00

Free Trade Treaty Between Peru and People's Republic of China A911

**2009, Sept. 10 Litho.** ***Perf. 13½x14***
**1714** A911 7.50s multi 5.25 5.25

Chinese Immigration to Peru, 160th Anniv. A912

**2009, Oct. 12**
**1715** A912 8.50s multi 6.00 6.00

Natl. Museum of Archaeology, Anthropology and History of Peru — A913

**2009, Oct. 13** ***Perf. 14x13½***
**1716** A913 5.50s multi 4.00 4.00

Miniature Sheet

Birds — A914

No. 1717: a, Actitis macularia. b, Glaucidium brasilianum. c, Numenius phaeopus. d, Egretta caerulea.

**2009, Nov. 9** ***Perf. 13½x14***
**1717** A914 6s Sheet of 4, #a-d 17.00 17.00

Luciano Pavarotti (1935-2007), Singer — A915

**2009, Nov. 12**
**1718** A915 10.50s multi 7.50 7.50

Children's Art — A916

Winning art in children's environmental protection stamp design contest: No. 1719, 2s, Orchid, parrot and hand, by Ahmed Lonia Heredia Pérez. No. 1720, 2s, Children, flora and fauna, by Scarie Estefany Rojas Reátegui.

**2009, Nov. 22** ***Perf. 14x13½***
**1719-1720** A916 Set of 2 3.00 3.00

Christmas A917

**2009, Nov. 30** ***Perf. 13½x14***
**1721** A917 2.20s multi 1.60 1.60

Souvenir Sheet

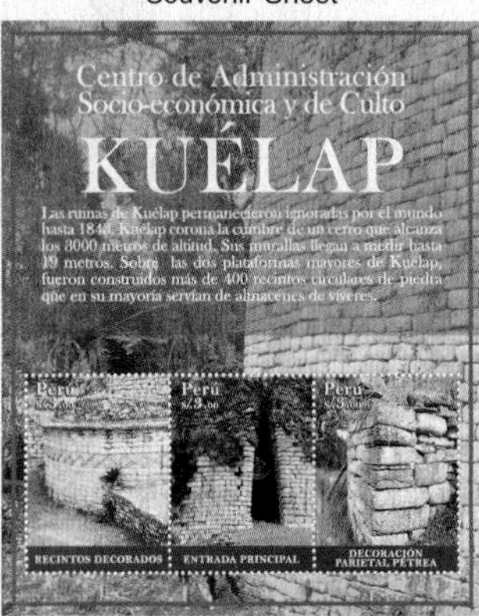

Kuélap Archaeological Site — A918

No. 1722: a, Decorated enclosures (Recintos decorados). b, Principal entrance (Entrada principal). c, Decorated stone walls (Decoración parietal petrea).

**2010, June 7 Litho.** ***Perf. 14x13½***
**1722** A918 3s Sheet of 3, #a-c 6.50 6.50

Central Station for Lima Metropolitan Bus Line — A919

No. 1723: a, Road over tunnel. b, Bus.

**2010, June 22** ***Perf. 13½x14***
**1723** A919 2.20s Horiz. pair, #a-b 3.25 3.25

Javier Pérez de Cuéllar, Fifth Secretary-General of the United Nations, 90th Birthday — A920

**2010, Aug. 9**
**1724** A920 50c multi .35 .35

St. Francis Solano (1549-1610) A921

**2010, Aug. 12** ***Perf. 14x13½***
**1725** A921 40c multi .30 .30

Gustavo Pons Muzzo (1916-2008), Historian — A922

**2010, Aug. 12**
**1726** A922 50c multi .35 .35

Archdiocese of Arequipa, 400th Anniv. — A923

**2010, Aug. 12** ***Perf. 13½x14***
**1727** A923 2s multi 1.50 1.50

Dogs — A924

No. 1728: a, Samoyed. b, Siberian husky.

**2010, Aug. 12** ***Perf. 14x13½***
**1728** A924 30c Horiz. pair, #a-b .45 .45

Rebeca Carrión Cachot, Archaeologist, 50th Anniv. of Death — A925

**2010, Aug. 13** **Litho.**
**1729** A925 40c multi .30 .30

Afro-Peruvian Culture Day — A926

No, 1730: a, Musical instruments. b, National Afro-Peruvian Museum, Lima.

**2010, Aug. 13** ***Perf. 13½x14***
**1730** A926 10c Horiz. pair, #a-b .25 .25

Miniature Sheet

2010 World Cup Soccer Championships, South Africa — A927

No. 1731: a, Mascot. b, Emblem. c, World Cup trophy. d, Soccer player and ball.

**2010, Aug. 13** ***Perf. 14x13½***
**1731** A927 10s Sheet of 4, #a-d 29.00 29.00

Tourist Sites in Lima — A928

Designs: No. 1732, 3s, Magic Fountains. No. 1733, 3s, Lake, Huascar Park.

**2010, Aug. 21**
**1732-1733** A928 Set of 2 4.50 4.50

Souvenir Sheet

"Seated Liberty" Coin — A929

**2010, Aug. 21** ***Perf. 14x13½***
**1734** A929 3s multi 2.25 2.25

Mushrooms — A930

No. 1735: a, Suillus luteus. b, Pleurotus cornucopiae.

**2010, Aug. 24** **Litho.**
**1735** A930 6s Horiz. pair, #a-b 8.75 8.75

New Year 2010 (Year of the Tiger) A931

No. 1736: a, Tiger at left. b, Tiger at right.

**2010, Aug. 26** ***Perf. 13½x14***
**1736** A931 20c Vert. pair, #a-b .30 .30

**Viceroys Type of 2006**

No. 1737: a, Diego Ladrón de Guevara Orozco y Calderon (1641-1718). b, Carmine Nicolao Caracciolo (1671-1726). c, Diego Morcillo Rubio de Auñón (1642-1730). d, José de Armendariz (1670-1740).

**2010, Sept. 1** ***Perf. 14x13½***
**1737** A767 3s Block of 4, #a-d, + label 8.75 8.75

Jorge Chavez (1887-1910), Pilot — A932

**Litho. & Engr.**

**2010, Sept. 3** ***Perf. 13½x14***
**1738** A932 2s multi 1.50 1.50

Centenary of Chavez's flight over Alps, after which he crash-landed and later died.

Souvenir Sheet

Stone Heads of the Chavin Culture — A933

**2010, Sept. 3** **Litho.** ***Perf. 14x13½***
**1739** A933 10s multi 7.25 7.25

**Pre-Columbian Cultures Type of 2006**

Artifacts of: No. 1740, 50c, Chincha culture, c. 1000. No. 1741, 50c, Chancay culture, c. 1000.

**2010, Sept. 7** ***Perf. 13½x14***
**1740-1741** A755 Set of 2 .75 .75

Volunteer Fire Brigades in Peru, 150th Anniv. — A934

No. 1742: a, 1860 Merryweather fire carriage. b, Pierce Contender fire truck.

**2010, Sept. 9**
**1742** A934 6s Horiz. pair, #a-b 8.75 8.75

Club Alianza Lima Soccer Team A935

**2010, Sept. 10**
**1743** A935 3s multi 2.25 2.25

Miniature Sheet

Orchids — A936

No. 1744: a, Anguloa virginalis. b, Masdevallia pernix. c, Stanhopea marizaiana. d, Telipogon campoverdei.

**2010, Sept. 16** **Litho.**
**1744** A936 3s Sheet of 4, #a-d 8.75 8.75

Colegio Nacional Iquitos Soccer Team A937

**2010, Sept. 17**
**1745** A937 3s multi 2.25 2.25

Frédéric Chopin (1810-49), Composer A938

**2010, Sept. 21** **Litho. & Engr.**
**1746** A938 3s multi 2.25 2.25

Windsurfing — A939

**Litho. With Foil Application**

**2010, Sept. 21**
**1747** A939 3s multi 2.25 2.25

Souvenir Sheet

Thalassocnus Littoralis — A940

**2010, Sept. 21** **Litho.**
**1748** A940 10s multi 7.25 7.25

Melgar Soccer Team A941

**2010, Sept. 24**
**1749** A941 3s multi 2.25 2.25

America Issue, National Symbols — A942

Peruvian: No. 1750, 5s, Arms. No. 1751, 5s, Flag.

**2010, Oct. 5** ***Perf. 14x13½***
**1750-1751** A942 Set of 2 7.25 7.25

Ollantaytambo Archaeological Site — A943

**2010, Oct. 29** ***Perf. 13½x14***
**1752** A943 5s multi 3.75 3.75

Christmas A944

**2010, Nov. 2**
**1753** A944 10s multi 7.25 7.25

Children's Art — A945

Winning art in children's art contest by: No. 1754, 2s, Jimena P. Vega Gonzáles, 1st place. No. 1755, 2s, Bettina Paz Pinto, 2nd place.

**2010, Nov. 22** ***Perf. 14x13½***
**1754-1755** A945 Set of 2 3.00 3.00

Folk Art — A946

Designs: No. 1756, 2s, Virgin of Pino, statue by Antonio Olave Palomino. No. 1757, 2s, San Marcos, retable by Jesús Urbano Rojas. No. 1758, 2s, Procession of St. Peter, carving by Fidel Barrientos Bustos.

**2010, Nov. 25** **Litho.**
**1756-1758** A946 Set of 3 4.25 4.25

Ninth Lions International Forum of Latin America and the Caribbean, Lima — A947

**2011, Jan. 15**
**1759** A947 7.80s multi 5.75 5.75

José María Arguedas (1911-69), Writer A948

**2011, Jan. 31** ***Perf. 13½x14***
**1760** A948 6.60s multi 4.75 4.75

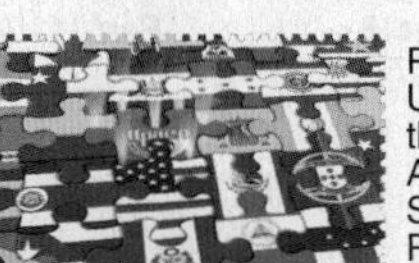


Postal Union of the Americas, Spain and Portugal (UPAEP), Cent. A949

**2011, Mar. 23**
**1761** A949 2s multi 1.50 1.50

Transportation Infrastructure — A950

Designs: 5s, Southern Pier, Port of Callao. 5.20s, Southern Interoceanic Highway.

**2011, May 16** **Litho.**
**1762-1763** A950 Set of 2 7.50 7.50

Scouting in Peru, Cent. — A951

Peruvian and Scouting flags and: No. 1764, 6.40s, Boy Scout. No. 1765, 6.40s, Girl Scout.

**2011, May 25** ***Perf. 14x13½***
**1764-1765** A951 Set of 2 9.25 9.25

Jicamarca Radio Observatory, 50th Anniv. — A952

**2011, June 7** ***Perf. 13½x14***
**1766** A952 6.60s multi 4.75 4.75

Awarding of 2010 Nobel Prize for Literature to Mario Vargas Llosa — A953

**2011, June 8** ***Perf. 14x13½***
**1767** A953 7.80s multi 5.75 5.75

Peruvian Submarine Force, Cent. — A954

No. 1768 — Emblem of Submarine Force, various submarines with denomination at: a, UR. b, UL.

**2011, June 9** ***Perf. 13½x14***
**1768** A954 7.20s Horiz. pair, #a-b 10.50 10.50

Javier Pulgar Vidal (1911-2003), Geographer A955

**2011, June 13** ***Perf. 14x13½***
**1769** A955 2.40s multi 1.75 1.75

Campaign Against HIV and AIDS — A956

No. 1770 — Text, AIDS ribbon and: a, Man. b, Woman.

**2011, June 13** ***Perf. 13½x14***
**1770** A956 5.50s Horiz. pair, #a-b 8.00 8.00

First Call for Peruvian Independence by Francisco Antonio de Zela y Arizaga, Bicent. — A957

No. 1771: a, Painting of Zela. b, Statue of Zela.

**2011, June 20** **Litho.**
**1771** A957 7.20s Horiz. pair, #a-b 10.50 10.50

Amazonia National University of Peru, 50th Anniv. — A958

**2011, June 23** ***Perf. 14x13½***
**1772** A958 2.70s multi 2,00 2.00

National Theater, Lima A959

**2011, June 23** ***Perf. 13½x14***
**1773** A959 5s multi 3.75 3.75

### Pre-Columbian Cultures Type of 2006

Artifacts of: No. 1774, 6.40s, Chachapoya culture, 700-1500. No. 1775, 6.40s, Inca culture, 1400-1572.

**2011, June 24** ***Perf. 13½x14***
**1774-1775** A755 Set of 2 9.50 9.50

### Viceroys Type of 2006

No. 1776: a, José Antonio de Mendoza Caamano y Sotomayor (1667-1746). b, José Antonio Manso de Velasco (1688-1767). c, Manuel de Amat y Junyent (1707-82). d, Manuel Guirior (1708-88).

**2011, July 1** ***Perf. 14x13½***
**1776** A767 7.80s Block of 4, #a-d, + label 23.00 23.00

Motocross Racing — A960

**2011, July 5** **Litho.**
**1777** A960 7.80s multi 5.75 5.75

Dances A961

Designs: No. 1778, 9s, Tijeras (scissors) dance. No. 1779, 9s, Huaconada.

**2011, July 5** ***Perf. 13½x14***
**1778-1779** A961 Set of 2 13.50 13.50

Year of the Rabbit — A962

No. 1780: a, Rabbit. b, Chinese character for "rabbit."

**2011, July 5** ***Perf. 14x13½***
**1780** A962 5.50s Horiz. pair, #a-b 8.00 8.00

Souvenir Sheet

Discovery of Machu Picchu, Cent. — A963

**2011, July 5**
**1781** A963 7.80s multi 5.75 5.75

Electric Trains — A964

No. 1782: a, One train. b, Two trains.

**2011, July 16** **Litho.**
**1782** A964 5.50s Horiz. pair, #a-b 8.00 8.00

Maxillaria Pyhalae — A965

**2011, July 19**
**1783** A965 10.50s multi 7.75 7.75

Governmental Palace and Presidents of Peru — A966

No. 1784: a, Government Palace, 18th cent. b, Marshal José de La Mar (1778-1830). c, Gen. Agustín Gamarra (1785-1841). d, Gen. Luis José de Orbegoso (1795-1847). e, Gen. Felipe Santiago Salaverry (1805-36). f, Marshal Andrés de Santa Cruz (1792-1865). g, Manuel Menéndez (1793-1847). h, Gen. Juan Crisóstomo Torrico (1808-75). i, Justo Figuerola (1771-1854). j, Government Palace, 20th cent. k, Gen. Manuel Ignacio de Vivanco (1806-73). l, Gen. Ramón Castilla (1797-1867). m, Gen. José Rufino Echenique (1808-87). n, Gen. Miguel de San Roman (1802-63). o, Gen. Juan Antonio Pezet (1809-79). p, Gen. Mariano Ignacio Prado (1826-1901). q, Col. José Balta (1814-72). r, Manuel Pardo y Lavalle (1834-78). s, Gen. Luis La Puerta (1811-96). t, Nicolás de Piérola (1839-1913). u, Francisco García Calderón (1834-1905). v, Admiral Lizardo Montero (1832-1905). w, Gen. Miguel Iglesias (1830-1909). x, Gold Room, Government Palace. y, Grand Hall, Government Palace. z, Flag and arms of Peru, Government Palace. aa, Túpac Amaru Room, Government Palace. ab, Gen. Andrés A. Cáceres (1836-1923). ac, Col. Remigio Morales Bermúdez (1836-94). ad, Eduardo López de Romaña (1847-1912). ae, Manuel Candamo (1841-1904). af, José Pardo Barreda (1864-1947). ag, Augusto B. Leguía (1863-1932). ah, Guillermo Billinghurst (1851-1915). ai, Gen. Oscar R. Benavides (1876-1945). aj, Lieutenant Colonel Luis M. Sánchez Cerro (1889-1933). ak, Manuel Prado y Ugarteche (1889-1967). al, José Luis Bustamente y Rivero (1894-1989). am, Gen. Manuel A. Odria (1897-1974). an, Gen. Ricardo Pérez Godoy (1905-82). ao, Honor Guard, Government Palace. ap, Gen. Nicolás Lindley (1908-95). aq, Fernando Belaunde Terry (1912-2002). ar, Gen. Juan Velasco Alvarado (1910-77). as, Gen. Francisco Morales Bermúdez. at, Alan García Pérez. au, Alberto Fujimori. av, Valentín Paniagua (1936-2006). aw, Alejandro Toledo Manrique. ax, Government Palace, 21st cent.

**2011, July 25** ***Perf. 14x13½***
**1784** A966 Sheet of 50 87.50 87.50
*a.-ax.* 2.40s Any single 1.75 1.75

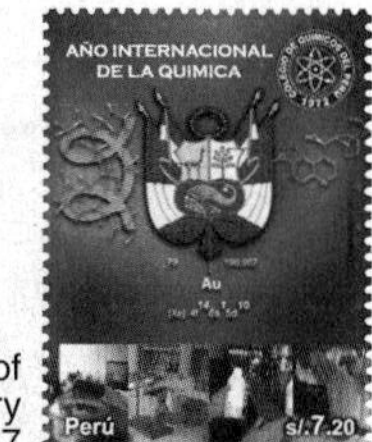


Intl. Year of Chemistry A967

**2011, Aug. 1** **Litho.**
**1785** A967 7.20s multi 5.25 5.25

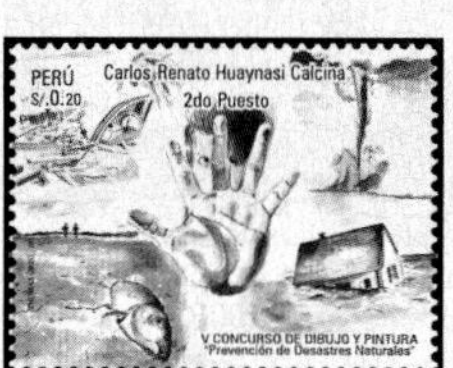


Children's Art A968

Winning art in children's prevention of natural disasters stamp design contest: 20c, Overturned boat, hand, tornado, dead fish and flooded house, by Carlos Renato Huaynasi Calcina. 2.40s, Children at school, by Sherley Breshley Suclupe Calderon.

**2011, Aug. 18** ***Perf. 13½x14***
**1786-1787** A968 Set of 2 1.90 1.90

National Archives, 150th Anniv. A969

**2011, Aug. 19**
**1788** A969 5.80s multi 4.25 4.25

Miniature Sheet

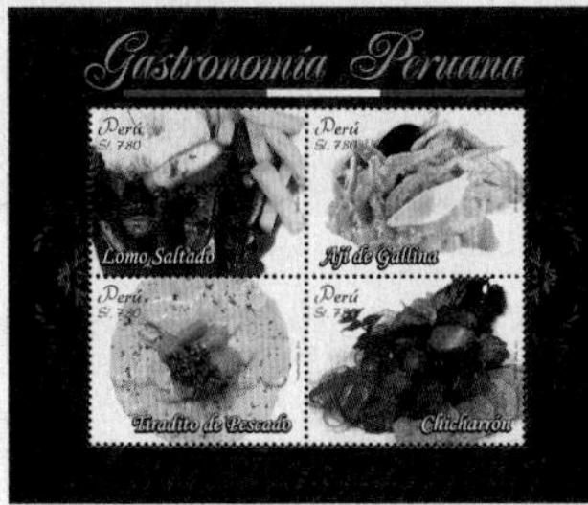
Peruvian Cuisine — A970

No. 1789: a, Lomo Saltado (beef with onions, tomatoes, rice and fried potatoes). b, Ají de Gallina (creamed chicken with chili peppers). c, Tiradito de Pescado (raw fish in spicy sauce). d, Chicharrón (fried pork rinds).

**2011, Aug. 25**
**1789** A970 7.80s Sheet of 4, #a-d 23.00 23.00

Statue of St. Sebastian, Patron Saint of Chepén — A971

**2011, Aug. 30** ***Perf. 14x13½***
**1790** A971 2s multi 1.50 1.50

Clorinda Matto de Turner (1852-1909), Writer — A972

**2011, Sept. 9** ***Perf. 13½x14***
**1791** A972 3.60s multi 2.75 2.75

1838 South Peru Gold 8-Escudo Coin — A973

No. 1792: a, Reverse. b, Obverse.

**2011, Sept. 12** ***Perf. 14x13½***
**1792** A973 5.80s Horiz. pair, #a-b 8.50 8.50

Cayetano Heredia University, 50th Anniv. A974

**2011, Sept. 22** ***Perf. 13½x14***
**1793** A974 3.60s multi 2.75 2.75

First Airplane Flight in Peru by Juan Bielovucic Cavalie, Cent. A975

**2011, Sept. 23** **Litho. & Engr.**
**1794** A975 7.20p multi 5.25 5.25

Miniature Sheet

Primates — A976

No. 1795: a, Lagothrix flavicauda. b, Callicebus oenanthe. c, Aotus miconax. d, Cacajao calvus.

**2011, Oct. 10** **Litho.** ***Perf. 14x13½***
**1795** A976 7.80s Sheet of 4, #a-d 23.00 23.00

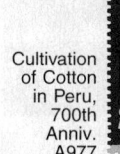

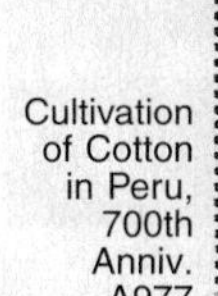

Cultivation of Cotton in Peru, 700th Anniv. A977

Gossypium barbadense with panel at bottom in: No. 1796, 8.50s, Blue. No. 1797, 8.50s, Red brown.

**2011, Oc. 11** ***Perf. 13½x14***
**1796-1797** A977 Set of 2 12.50 12.50

Souvenir Sheet

Fossils of Livyatan Melvillei — A978

**Litho. (With Foil Application in Sheet Margin)**

**2011, Oct. 17** ***Perf. 14x13½***
**1798** A978 10s multi 7.50 7.50

Franz Liszt (1811-86), Composer A979

**Litho. & Engr.**

**2011, Oct. 22** ***Perf. 14x13½***
**1799** A979 5.80s multi 4.25 4.25

Endangered Birds — A980

Designs: No. 1800, 10s, Loddigesia mirabilis. No. 1801, 10s, Cinclodes palliatus.

**2011, Oct. 28** **Litho.** ***Perf. 13½x14***
**1800-1801** A980 Set of 2 15.00 15.00

Christmas A981

**2011, Nov. 1**
**1802** A981 5.50s multi 4.25 4.25

America Issue — A982

Designs: No. 1803, 10s, Lion's head mailbox. No. 1804, 10s, Red rectangular mailbox.

**2011, Nov. 2** ***Perf. 14x13½***
**1803-1804** A982 Set of 2 15.00 15.00

Martín Chambi (1891-1973), Photographer A983

**2011, Nov. 4**
**1805** A983 5.20s multi 4.00 4.00

Peruvian Coffee A984

**2011, Nov. 10** ***Perf. 13½x14***
**1806** A984 6.60s multi 5.00 5.00

Summit of South American and Arab Countries A985

**2011, Dec. 2** ***Perf. 14x13½***
**1807** A985 8.40s multi 6.25 6.25

Diplomatic Relations Between Peru and Australia, 50th Anniv. — A986

No. 1808: a, Sloth (oso perezoso). b, Koala.

**2013, Mar. 1**
**1808** A986 3.30s Horiz. pair, #a-b 5.25 5.25

Diplomatic Relations Between Peru and India, 50th Anniv. — A987

No. 1809: a, Machu Picchu, Peru. b, Taj Mahal, India.

**2013, Mar. 19**
**1809** A987 3.60s Horiz. pair, #a-b 5.75 5.75

Diplomatic Relations Between Peru and South Korea, 50th Anniv. — A988

No. 1810: a, 2.50s, Machu Picchu, Peru. b, 3s, Seongsan Ilchulbong, South Korea.

**2013, Apr. 1** ***Perf. 13½x14***
**1810** A988 Horiz. pair, #a-b 4.25 4.25

See South Korea No. 2399.

Service and Maintenance for Peru Air Force, 80th Anniv. — A989

**2013, June 13 Litho.** ***Perf. 14x13½***
**1811** A989 5.50s multi 4.00 4.00

World Record Black Marlin Catch, 60th Anniv. — A990

Designs: No. 1812, 2.50s, Alfred C. Glassell, Jr. and 1,560-pound black marlin. No. 1813, 2.50s, Fishing boat "Miss Texas," horiz.

***Perf. 14x13½, 13½x14***
**2013, Aug. 2 Litho.**
**Stamps + Label**
**1812-1813** A990 Set of 2 3.75 3.75

New Year 2013 (Year of the Dragon) — A991

No. 1814: a, Chinese Zodiac wheel and Chinese character for "dragon." b, Dragon figurine.

**2013, Aug. 15 Litho.** ***Perf. 14x13½***
**1814** A991 6s Horiz. pair, #a-b 8.75 8.75

Diplomatic Relations Between Peru and Japan, 140th Anniv. — A992

No. 1815: a, Machu Picchu, Peru. b, Kinkaku-ji, Japan.

**2013, Aug. 21 Litho.** ***Perf. 14x13½***
**1815** A992 6s Horiz. pair, #a-b 8.75 8.75

Santa Teresa Convent, Arequipa — A993

**2013, Aug. 23 Litho.** ***Perf. 14x13½***
**1816** A993 6s multi 4.50 4.50

Anthropomorphic Monoliths, Ancash Archaeological Park and Museum — A994

**2013, Aug. 28 Litho.** ***Perf. 13½***
**1817** A994 6s multi 4.50 4.50

Benavidesite — A995

**2013, Aug. 29 Litho.** ***Perf. 13½x14***
**1818** A995 8s multi 5.75 5.75

Federico Villareal National University, 50th Anniv. A996

**2013, Sept. 5** ***Perf. 13½x14***
**1819** A996 4s multi 3.00 3.00

Souvenir Sheet

Inkayacu Paracasensis and Its Fossilized Remains — A997

**Litho. (With Foil Application in Sheet Margin)**
**2013, Sept. 12** ***Perf. 14x13½***
**1820** A997 10s multi 7.25 7.25

Diocese of Cuzco, 475th Anniv. — A998

**2013, Sept. 13 Litho.** ***Perf. 14x13½***
**1821** A998 4s multi 3.00 3.00

Intl. Year of Quinoa A999

**2013, Sept. 27 Litho.** ***Perf. 13½x14***
**1822** A999 5.50s multi 4.00 4.00

Souvenir Sheet

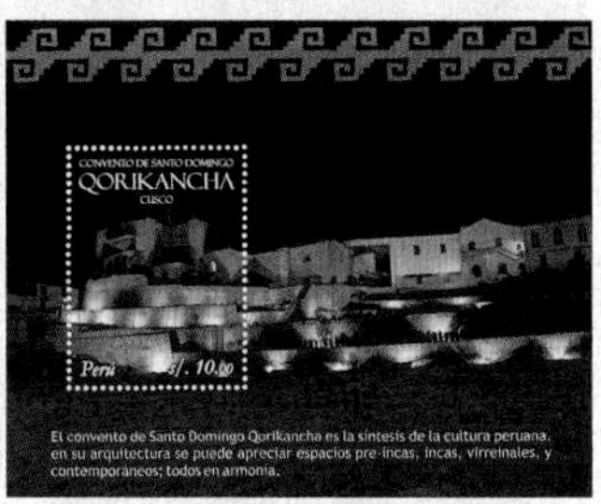

Santo Domingo Convent and Qorikancha Incan Temple, Cuzco — A1000

**2013, Sept. 27 Litho.** ***Perf. 14x13½***
**1823** A1000 10s multi 7.25 7.25

Souvenir Sheet

Temples of the Sun and Moon Archaeological Sites — A1001

**2013, Sept. 27 Litho.** ***Perf. 13½x14***
**1824** A1001 10s multi 7.25 7.25

Souvenir Sheet

Five-Peseta Coin of Peru From 1880 — A1002

No. 1825: a, Reverse (head of Ceres). b, Obverse (coat of arms).

**2013, Oct. 1 Litho.** ***Perf. 14x13½***
**1825** A1002 5s Sheet of 2, #a-b 7.25 7.25

Souvenir Sheet

1863 Centavo Coins — A1003

No. 1826 — Reverse of: a, One-centavo coin. b, Two-centavo coin.

**2013, Oct. 1 Litho.** ***Perf. 14x13½***
**1826** A1003 6s Sheet of 2, #a-b 8.75 8.75

Museum of Natural History, Lima, 95th Anniv. — A1004

**2013, Oct. 4 Litho.** ***Perf. 14x13½***
**1827** A1004 4s multi 3.00 3.00

Souvenir Sheet

Chahuaytiri Rock Paintings — A1005

**2013, Oct. 11 Litho.** ***Perf. 14x13½***
**1828** A1005 10s multi 7.25 7.25

Souvenir Sheet

Canaanimys Maquiensis and Its Fossilized Remains — A1006

**Litho. (With Foil Application in Sheet Margin)**
**2013, Oct. 12** ***Perf. 14x13½***
**1829** A1006 10s multi 7.25 7.25

Miniature Sheet

Eagles — A1007

No. 1830: a, Harpia harpyja. b, Morphus guianensis. c, Spizaetus ornatus. d, Spizaetus isidori.

**Litho. (With Foil Application in Sheet Margin)**

**2013, Oct. 14** *Perf. 14x13½*
**1830** A1007 3s Sheet of 4, #a-d 8.75 8.75

Miniature Sheet

Butterflies — A1008

No. 1831: a, Hypanartia splendida. b, Isanthrene flavizonata. c, Protesilaus glaucolaus. d, Histioea peruana.

**2013, Oct. 24 Litho.** *Perf. 13½x14*
**1831** A1008 4s Sheet of 4, #a-d 11.50 11.50

Miniature Sheet

Hummingbirds — A1009

No. 1832: a, Heliangelus regalis. b, Myrtis fanny. c, Taphrolesbia griseiventris. d, Rhodopis vesper.

**2013, Oct. 31 Litho.** *Perf. 13½x14*
**1832** A1009 5s Sheet of 4, #a-d 14.50 14.50

Canonization of St. Martin de Porres, 50th Anniv. (in 2012) — A1010

**2013, Nov. 4 Litho.** *Perf. 13½x14*
**1833** A1010 4s multi 3.00 3.00

Diplomatic Relations Between Peru and Russia, 45th Anniv. — A1011

No. 1834: a, Machu Picchu, Peru. b, Kizhi Pogost, Russia.

**2013, Nov. 4 Litho.** *Perf. 13½x14*
**1834** A1011 6s Horiz. pair, #a-b 8.75 8.75

America Issue — A1012

No. 1835: a, Animals and corn stalk from Myth of the Garden of Gold. b, Sun God from Myth of the Garden of Gold. c, Eyes of 14 people, face paint above 5th eye on top row. d, Eyes of 14 people, face paint below 3rd and 4th eyes on bottom row.

**2013, Nov. 4 Litho.** *Perf. 13½x14*
**1835** A1012 4s Block of 4, #a-d, + label 11.50 11.50

Souvenir Sheet

Boat Dock on Amazon River — A1013

**2013, Nov. 11 Litho.** *Perf. 13½x14*
**1836** A1013 8s multi 5.75 5.75

Miniature Sheet

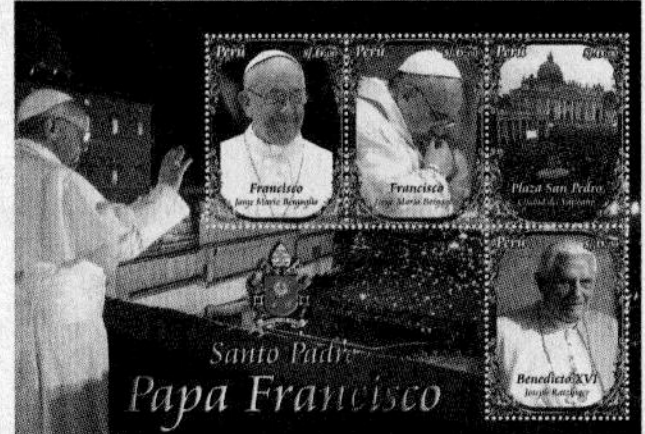

Election of Pope Francis — A1014

No. 1837: a, Pope Francis, hands not visible. b, Pope Francis, hand visible. c, St. Peter's Square. d, Pope Benedict XVI.

**2013, Nov. 13 Litho.** *Perf. 14x13½*
**1837** A1014 6s Sheet of 4, #a-d 17.50 17.50

Souvenir Sheet

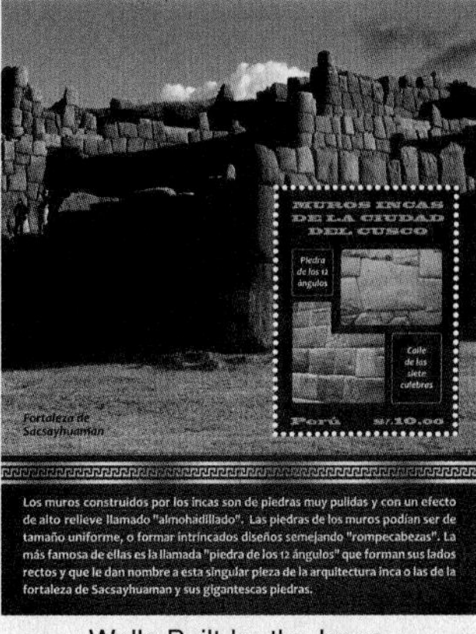

Walls Built by the Incas, Cuzco — A1015

**2013, Nov. 13 Litho.** *Perf. 14x13½*
**1838** A1015 10s multi 7.25 7.25

A1016

Winning Designs in 6th Children's Art Contest — A1017

**2013, Dec. 2 Litho.** *Perf. 13½x14*
**1839** A1016 4s multi 3.00 3.00

*Perf. 14x13½*

**1840** A1017 4s multi 3.00 3.00

A1018

Winning Designs in 7th Children's Art Contest A1019

**2013, Dec. 6 Litho.** *Perf. 13½x14*
**1841** A1018 4s multi 3.00 3.00
**1842** A1019 4s multi 3.00 3.00

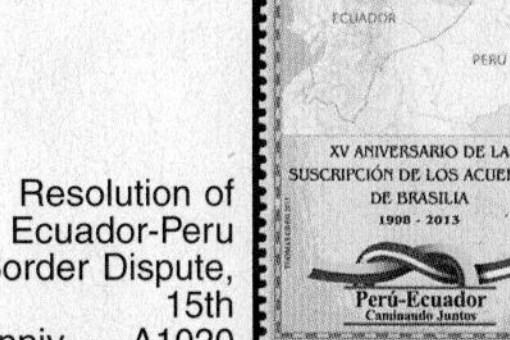

Resolution of Ecuador-Peru Border Dispute, 15th Anniv. — A1020

**2014, Jan. 30 Litho.** *Perf. 14x13½*
**1843** A1020 8s multi 5.75 5.75

Commercial Accords Between Peru, Colombia and the European Union — A1021

**2014, Feb. 28 Litho.** *Perf. 14x13½*
**1844** A1021 9.50s multi 6.75 6.75

Captain José Abelardo Quiñones Gonzales (1914-41), Military Hero A1022

**2014, Apr. 8 Litho.** *Perf. 13½x14*
**1845** A1022 3.80s multi 2.75 2.75

Miguel Grau Seminario (1834-79), Admiral — A1023

**2014, July 23 Litho.** *Perf. 14x13½*
**1846** A1023 6s multi 4.25 4.25

Peruvian Institute of the Sea, 50th Anniv. A1024

**2014, Sept. 5 Litho.** *Perf. 13½x14*
**1847** A1024 3.80s multi 2.60 2.60

Caballito de Totoro (Traditional Reed Watercraft) A1025

**2014, Sept. 17 Litho.** *Perf. 14x13½*
**1848** A1025 7s multi 5.00 5.00

Tambomachay Temple Archaeological Site — A1026

**2014, Sept. 19 Litho.** *Perf. 14x13½*
**1849** A1026 6s multi 4.25 4.25

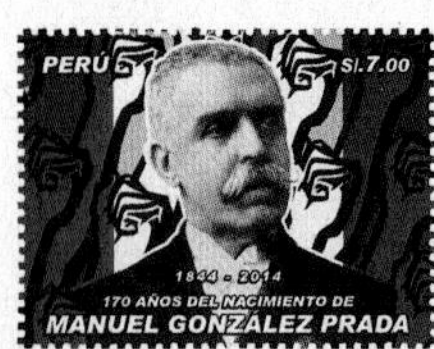

Manuel González Prada (1844-1918), Literary Critic — A1027

**2014, Sept. 22 Litho. *Perf. 13½x14***
**1850** A1027 7s multi 5.00 5.00

Kotosh Temple Archaeological Site — A1028

**2014, Sept. 24 Litho. *Perf. 14x13½***
**1851** A1028 6s multi 4.25 4.25

2014 Canonization of Popes — A1029

Designs: No. 1852, 7s, Pope John XXIII. No. 1853, 7s, Pope John Paul II.

**2014, Sept. 26 Litho. *Perf. 14x13½***
**1852-1853** A1029 Set of 2 9.75 9.75

Musical Instruments A1030

Designs: No. 1854, 6s, Botella silbadora. No. 1855, 6s, Antara (pan flute).

**2014, Sept. 30 Litho. *Perf. 13½x14***
**1854-1855** A1030 Set of 2 8.25 8.25

Souvenir Sheet

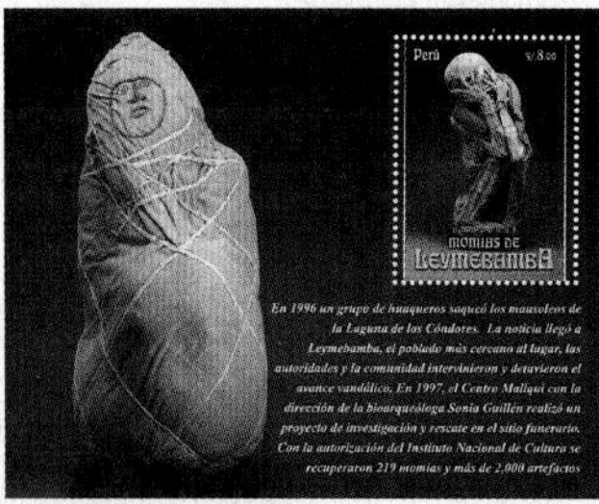

Leymebamba Mummy — A1031

**2014, Sept. 30 Litho. *Perf. 14x13½***
**1856** A1031 8s multi 5.50 5.50

William Shakespeare (1564-1616), Writer — A1032

**2014, Oct. 3 Litho. *Perf. 14x13½***
**1857** A1032 6s multi 4.25 4.25

**Viceroys Type of 2006**

No. 1858: a, Agustín de Jáuregui y Aldecoa (1711-84). b, Teodoro de Croix (1730-92). c, Francisco Gil de Taboada y Lemus (1736-1809). d, Ambrosio O'Higgins (1720-1801).

**2014, Oct. 7 Litho. *Perf. 14x13½***
**1858** A767 6.50s Block of 4, #a-d, + label 18.00 18.00

Souvenir Sheet

Forensic Facial Reconstruction of the Priestess of Chornancap — A1033

**2014, Oct. 13 Litho. *Perf. 14x13½***
**1859** A1033 8s multi 5.50 5.50

Dances A1034

Designs: No. 1860, 8s, La Wuallata. No. 1861, 8s, Carnaval Cusqueño.

**2014, Oct. 17 Litho. *Perf. 13½x14***
**1860-1861** A1034 Set of 2 11.00 11.00

Miniature Sheet

Birds — A1035

No. 1862: a, Crotophag sulcirostris. b, Xenospingus concolor. c, Burhinus superciliaris. d, Glaucidium peruanum.

**2014, Oct. 17 Litho. *Perf. 13½x14***
**1862** A1035 9s Sheet of 4, #a-d 24.50 24.50

Miniature Sheet

Trees — A1036

No. 1863: a, Swietenia macrophylla. b, Cedrela fissilis. c, Ceiba pentandra. d, Prosopis pallida.

**2014, Oct. 20 Litho. *Perf. 14x13½***
**1863** A1036 9.50s Sheet of 4, #a-d 26.00 26.00

Iquitos, 150th Anniv. A1037

**2014, Oct. 23 Litho. *Perf. 13½x14***
**1864** A1037 6s multi 4.25 4.25

Barranco District, 140th Anniv. — A1038

**2014, Oct. 26 Litho. *Perf. 14x13½***
**1865** A1038 7s multi 4.75 4.75

Miniature Sheet

Mammals — A1039

No. 1866: a, Panthera onca. b, Dinomys branickii. c, Tapirus pinchaque. d, Leopardus jacobitus.

**2014, Nov. 3 Litho. *Perf. 14x13½***
**1866** A1039 11s Sheet of 4, #a-d 30.00 30.00

The inscription on No. 1866d is incorrect. The stamp shows Leopardus colocolo.

Souvenir Sheet

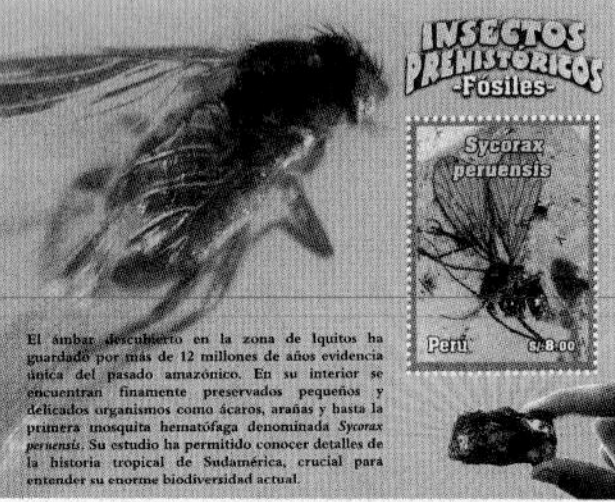

Sycorax Peruensis Preserved in Amber — A1040

**Litho. (With Foil Application in Sheet Margin)**

**2014, Nov. 5 *Perf. 14x13½***
**1867** A1040 8s multi 5.50 5.50

Minerals A1041

Designs: 6s, Quartz (Cuarzo). 8s, Jasper (Jaspe).

**2014, Nov. 10 Litho. *Perf. 13½x14***
**1868-1869** A1041 Set of 2 9.50 9.50

Christmas A1042

**2014, Nov. 14 Litho. *Perf. 14x13½***
**1870** A1042 6s multi 4.25 4.25

Parque de las Leyendas Zoo, 50th Anniv. — A1043

No. 1871: a, Cebuella pygmaea. b, Ateles belzebuth.

**2014, Nov. 17 Litho. *Perf. 14x13½***
**1871** A1043 9.50s Horiz. pair, #a-b 13.00 13.00

Serpost (Peruvian Postal Service), 20th Anniv. A1044

**2014, Nov. 22 Litho. *Perf. 13½x14***
**1872** A1044 6s multi 4.25 4.25

Miniature Sheet

2014 World Cup Soccer Championships, Brazil — A1045

No. 1873: a, Mascot Fuleco. b, Emblem. c, Soccer player and ball. d, World Cup Trophy.

**2014, Nov. 28 Litho.** ***Perf. 13½x14***
**1873** A1045 3.80s Sheet of 4, #a-d 10.50 10.50

Pancho Fierro (1807-79), Painter — A1046

No. 1874 — Paintings: a, El Soldado y la Rabona. b, Fraile de la Buena Muerte. c, El Notario Público. d, La Hermana de la Caridad.

**2014, Dec. 1 Litho.** ***Perf. 14x13½***
**1874** A1046 10s Sheet of 4, #a-d 27.50 27.50

Famous Men — A1047

Designs: No. 1875, 9s, Mariano Melgar (1790-1815), poet. No. 1876, 9s, José Olaya Balandra (1782-1823), hero in War of Independence.

**2014, Dec. 3 Litho.** ***Perf. 14x13½***
**1875-1876** A1047 Set of 2 12.00 12.00

America Issue.

Chinese Zodiac Animals — A1048

No. 1877: a, Snake. b, Horse.

**2014, Dec. 5 Litho.** ***Perf. 14x13½***
**1877** A1048 6.50s Horiz. pair, #a-b 8.75 8.75

Souvenir Sheet

1898 Gold Libra Coin — A1049

No. 1878: a, Obverse (Anverso). b, Reverse (Reverso).

**2014, Dec. 9 Litho.** ***Perf. 14x13½***
**1878** A1049 10s multi 13.50 13.50

Battle of Ayacucho, 190th Anniv. A1050

**2014, Dec. 9 Litho.** ***Perf. 13½x14***
**1879** A1050 7s multi 4.75 4.75

Archbiship Loayza National Hospital, 90th Anniv. A1051

**2014, Dec. 10 Litho.** ***Perf. 13½x14***
**1880** A1051 3.80s multi 2.60 2.60

Miniature Sheet

Carriages — A1052

No. 1881: a, Front view of covered carriage. b, Open-air carriage with red seats. c, Side view of covered carriage. d, Open-air carriage with white seats.

**2014, Dec. 15 Litho.** ***Perf. 13½x14***
**1881** A1052 11s Sheet of 4, #a-d 30.00 30.00

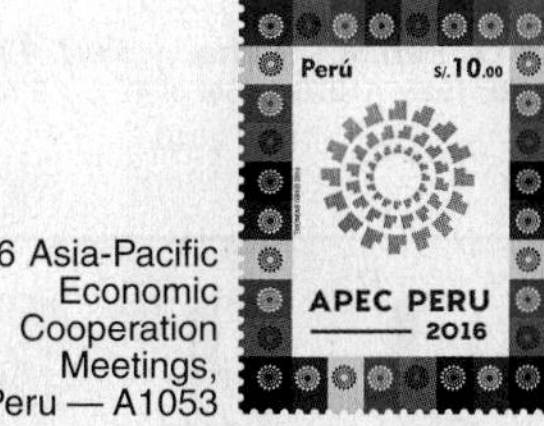

2016 Asia-Pacific Economic Cooperation Meetings, Peru — A1053

**2016, Nov. 17 Litho.** ***Perf. 14x13½***
**1882** A1053 10s multi 6.00 6.00

Diplomatic Relations Between Peru and People's Republic of China, 45th Anniv. — A1054

No. 1883 — Flags of Peru and People's Republic of China and: a, Machu Picchu. b, Temple of Heaven, Beijing.

**2016, Nov. 17 Litho.** ***Perf. 14x13½***
**1883** A1054 4s Horiz. pair, #a-b 4.75 4.75

Diplomatic Relations Between Peru and Malaysia, 30th Anniv. — A1055

No. 1884 — Flags of Peru and Malaysia, handshake and: a, Mt. Kinabalu, Malaysia. b, Machu Picchu.

**2016, Nov. 17 Litho.** ***Perf. 14x13½***
**1884** A1055 9s Horiz. pair, #a-b 10.50 10.50

Christmas A1056

**2016, Nov. 17 Litho.** ***Perf. 14x13½***
**1885** A1056 6.50s multi 4.00 4.00

Colonel Francisco Bolognesi Cervantes (1816-80), Hero in War of the Pacific — A1057

**2016, Dec. 19 Litho.** ***Perf. 14x13½***
**1886** A1057 8s multi 4.75 4.75

Cajamarca, 30th Anniv. on Organization of American States Cultural and Historical Heritage List — A1058

No. 1887: a, Cerro Santa Apolonia. b, Santa Catalina Cathedral.

**2016, Dec. 21 Litho.** ***Perf. 13½x14***
**1887** A1058 3s Horiz. pair, #a-b 3.50 3.50

Banco de la Nación, 50th Anniv. A1059

**2016, Dec. 22 Litho.** ***Perf. 13½x14***
**1888** A1059 10s multi 6.00 6.00

Dr. Carlos Monge Medrano (1884-1970), Founder of National Institute of Andean Biology — A1060

**2016, Dec. 23 Litho.** ***Perf. 13½x14***
**1889** A1060 10s multi 6.00 6.00

National Institute of Andean Biology, 85th anniv.

Office of the National Prosecutor, 35th Anniv. — A1061

**2016, Dec. 26 Litho.** ***Perf. 14x13½***
**1890** A1061 10s multi 6.00 6.00

World Autism Awareness Day A1062

**2016, Dec. 28 Litho.** ***Perf. 13½x14***
**1891** A1062 10s multi 6.00 6.00

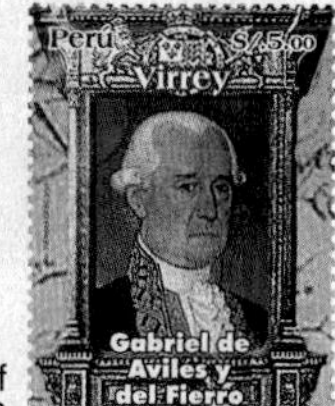

Viceroys of Peru — A1063

Designs: No. 1892, 5s, Gabriel de Avilés y del Fierro (c. 1735-1810). No. 1893, 5s, José Fernando de Abascal y Sousa (1743-1821). No. 1894, 5s, Joaquín de la Pezuela (1761-1830). No. 1895, 5s, José de la Serna e Hinojosa (1770-1832).

**2017, Jan. 2 Litho.** ***Perf. 14x13½***
**1892-1895** A1063 Set of 4 12.00 12.00

Dated 2016. Compare with type A767.

Pre-Hispanic Musical Instruments — A1064

Designs: No. 1896, 6.50s, Huayllaquepa de Punkurí. No. 1897, 6.50s, Antara de Caña de Caral.

**2017, Jan. 4 Litho. *Perf. 13½x14***
**1896-1897** A1064 Set of 2 8.00 8.00
Dated 2016.

Dominican Order, 800th Anniv. (in 2016) — A1065

**2017, Jan. 6 Litho. *Perf. 14x13½***
**1898** A1065 10s multi 6.25 6.25
Dated 2016.

Flora A1066

Designs: No. 1899, 4s, Rhizophora mangle. No. 1900, 4s, Azorella compacta. No. 1901, 4s, Cinchona pubescens. No. 1902, 4s, Puya raimondii.

**2017, Jan. 6 Litho. *Perf. 13½x14***
**1899-1902** A1066 Set of 4 9.75 9.75
Dated 2016.

Pelagornis and Its Fossilized Remains A1067

**2017, Jan. 10 Litho. *Perf. 13½x14***
**1903** A1067 10s multi 6.25 6.25
Dated 2016.

Cuzco School Paintings A1068

Designs: No. 1904, 6.50s, San Cristobal. No. 1905, 6.50s, Patrón Santiago. No. 1906, 6.50s, Paso de las Ordenes Religiosas. No. 1907, 6.50s, El Obispo Mollinedo Llevando la Custodia.

**2017, Jan. 12 Litho. *Perf. 13½x14***
**1904-1907** A1068 Set of 4 16.00 16.00
Dated 2016.

1879 20-Centavo Coin — A1069

Designs: No. 1908, 10s, Obverse (anverso). No. 1909, 10s, Reverse (reverso).

**2017, Jan. 16 Litho. *Perf. 14x13½***
**1908-1909** A1069 Set of 2 12.50 12.50

National Institute of Health, 120th Anniv. (in 2016) A1070

**2017, Jan. 17 Litho. *Perf. 13½x14***
**1910** A1070 10s multi 6.25 6.25
Dated 2016.

Chess — A1071

No. 1911: a, Black bishop (alfil). b, White pawn (peón).

**2017, Jan. 19 Litho. *Perf. 14x13½***
**1911** A1071 4s Horiz. pair, #a-b 5.00 5.00
Dated 2016.

Campaign Against Human Trafficking A1072

Designs: No. 1912, 9s, Photographs of people in blue heart. No. 1913, 9s, Raised hands and map, vert.

***Perf. 13½x14, 14x13½***
**2017, Jan. 23 Litho.**
**1912-1913** A1072 Set of 2 11.00 11.00
America Issue. Dated 2016.

Pisco Sour Drink, Cent. (in 2016) — A1073

No. 1914: a, Pisco Sour in glass, Pisco Sour bottle. b, Grapes and glass of Pisco Sour.

**2017, Jan. 26 Litho. *Perf. 14x13½***
**1914** A1073 9s Horiz. pair, #a-b 11.00 11.00
Dated 2016.

New Year 2015 (Year of the Goat) — A1074

No. 1915: a, Ring of Chinese Zodiac animals, Chinese character for "goat." b, Goat.

**2017, Jan. 27 Litho. *Perf. 14x13½***
**1915** A1074 6.50s Horiz. pair, #a-b 8.00 8.00
Dated 2016.

New Year 2016 (Year of the Monkey) — A1075

No. 1916: a, Monkeys. b, Ring of Chinese Zodiac animals, Chinese character for "monkey."

**2017, Jan. 27 Litho. *Perf. 14x13½***
**1916** A1075 6.50s Horiz. pair, #a-b 8.00 8.00
Dated 2016.

Fish A1076

Designs: No. 1917, 6.50s, Piaractus brachypomus. No. 1918, 6.50s, Anisotremus interruptus. No. 1919, 6.50s, Lebiasina bimaculata. No. 1920, 6.50s, Panaque schaeferi.

**2017, Feb. 1 Litho. *Perf. 13½x14***
**1917-1920** A1076 Set of 4 16.00 16.00
Dated 2016.

Poisonous Frogs A1077

Designs: No. 1921, 8s, Excidobates mysteriosus. No. 1922, 8s, Ameerega parvula. No. 1923, 8s, Ranitomeya fantastica. No. 1924, 8s, Ameerega pongoensis.

**2017, Feb. 6 Litho. *Perf. 13½x14***
**1921-1924** A1077 Set of 4 19.50 19.50
Dated 2016.

Peruvian-Chinese Food — A1078

Flags of People's Republic of China and Peru and: No. 1925, 3s, Sopa wantan (wonton soup). No. 1926, 3s, Arroz chaufa (rice). No. 1927, 3s, Chi Jau Cuy (guinea pig). No. 1928, 3s, Tallarín Saltado Taipa (noodles and vegetables).

**2017, Feb. 8 Litho. *Perf. 13½x14***
**1925-1928** A1078 Set of 4 7.50 7.50
Dated 2016.

Independence of Peru, 200th Anniv. (in 2021) — A1079

No. 1929 — Heroes: a, Juan José Crespo (1747-1812), leader of Huánuco Rebellion. b, Francisco de Zela (1768-1819), leader of Tacna Revolution. c, Mateo Pumacahua (1740-1815), leader of Cuzco Rebellion.

**2017, Feb. 10 Litho. *Perf. 14x13½***
**1929** A1079 3s Horiz. strip of 3, #a-c 5.50 5.50
Dated 2016.

Awajún Man — A1080

**2017, Feb. 13 Litho. *Perf. 14x13½***
**1930** A1080 5s multi 3.25 3.25
Dated 2016.

Vultur Gryphus — A1081

Podocnemis Unifilis A1082

**2017, June Litho. *Perf. 14x13½***
**1931** A1081 5s multi 3.25 3.25
***Perf. 13½x14***
**1932** A1082 5s multi 3.25 3.25
Dated 2016.

National Institute for the Defense of Competition and Protection of Intellectual Property (INDECOPI), 25th Anniv. — A1083

**2017, Nov. 21 Litho. *Perf. 13x13¼***
**1933** A1083 6.50s multi 4.00 4.00

Miniature Sheet

Visit to Peru of Pope Francis in 2018 — A1084

No. 1934 — Pope Francis: a, In map of Peru. b, Waving, bright green panel, arms of Puerto Maldonado. c, Waving, blue panel, arms of Trujillo. d, Touching child, orange panel, arms of Lima.

**2017, Nov. 29 Litho. *Perf. 13¼x13***
**1934** A1084 4s Sheet of 4, #a-d 10.00 10.00

Apparition of the Virgin Mary at Fatima, Portugal, Cent. (in 2017) A1085

**2018, Jan. 5 Litho. *Perf. 13x13¼***
**1935** A1085 3s multi 1.90 1.90

Dated 2017.

Holy Cross of Motupe — A1086

**2018, Jan. 8 Litho. *Perf. 13¼x13***
**1936** A1086 6.50s multi 4.00 4.00

Christmas. Dated 2017.

St. Rose of Lima (1586-1617) — A1087

No. 1937: a, Religious statue, roses. b, St. Rose of Lima, drawing of Lima.

**2018, Jan. 10 Litho. *Perf. 13x13¼***
**1937** A1087 6.50s Horiz. pair, #a-b 8.25 8.25

Dated 2017.

Pontifical Catholic University of Peru, Cent. (in 2017) — A1088

No. 1938: a, Star. b, Ship.

**2018, Jan. 10 Litho. *Perf. 13¼x13***
**1938** A1088 4s Horiz. pair, #a-b 5.00 5.00

Dated 2017.

Lima Central Post Office, 120th Anniv. A1089

**2018, Jan. 11 Litho. *Perf. 13x13¼***
**1939** A1089 2s multi 1.25 1.25

Dated 2017.

International Decade for People of African Descent — A1090

**2018, Jan. 12 Litho. *Perf. 13¼x13***
**1940** A1090 2s multi 1.25 1.25

Dated 2017.

Pampa Galeras-Bárbara D'Achille National Reserve, 50th Anniv. — A1091

**2018, Jan. 13 Litho. *Perf. 13x13¼***
**1941** A1091 2s multi 1.25 1.25

Dated 2017.

Winning Art in "Healthy Sentiments and Values" Stamp Design Contest A1092

**2018, Jan. 13 Litho. *Perf. 13x13¼***
**1942** A1092 2s multi 1.25 1.25

America issue. Dated 2017.

Inti Raymi Festival, 50th Anniv. (in 2017) — A1093

**2018, Jan. 15 Litho. *Perf. 13¼x13***
**1943** A1093 3s multi 1.90 1.90

Dated 2017.

Souvenir Sheet

International Year of Sustainable Tourism for Development — A1094

No. 1944: a, Amazilia viridicauda. b, Pipreola pulchra.

**2018, Jan. 15 Litho. *Perf. 13¼x13***
**1944** A1094 8s Sheet of 2, #a-b 10.00 10.00

Dated 2017.

A1095

Sipán Royal Jewelry — A1096

**2018, Jan. 16 Litho. *Perf. 13x13¼***
**1945** A1095 6.50s multi 4.00 4.00

***Perf. 13¼x13***
**1946** A1096 6.50s multi 4.00 4.00

Dated 2017.

Miniature Sheet

Ancash Tourism — A1097

No. 1947: a, Sechin Archaeological Site, Casma. b, Jancapampa, Pomabamba. c, Hatun Machay, Recuay. d, Yayno Archaeological Site, Pomabamba.

**2018, Jan. 18 Litho. *Perf. 13x13¼***
**1947** A1097 3s Sheet of 4, #a-d 7.50 7.50

Dated 2017.

Steatornis Caripensis A1098

Hippocamelus Antisensis A1099

**2018, Jan. 19 Litho. *Perf. 13x13¼***
**1948** A1098 9s multi 5.75 5.75

***Perf. 13¼x13***
**1949** A1099 9s multi 5.75 5.75

Dated 2017.

Souvenir Sheet

Insects — A1100

No. 1950: a, Sicophion yana. b, Ancognatha corcuerai.

**2018, Jan. 22 Litho. *Perf. 13¼x13***
**1950** A1100 9s Sheet of 2, #a-b 11.50 11.50

Dated 2017.

Miniature Sheet

Cuzco School Paintings — A1101

No. 1951: a, Virgen de Belén. b, La Ultima Cena. c, San Sebastián. d, Procesión de San Pedro.

**2018, Jan. 26 Litho. *Perf. 13x13¼***
**1951** A1101 6.50s Sheet of 4, #a-d 16.00 16.00

Dated 2017.

Souvenir Sheet

Minerals — A1102

No. 1952: a, Plata (silver). b, Oro (gold).

**2018, Jan. 29 Litho. *Perf. 13x13¼***
**1952** A1102 10s Sheet of 2, #a-b 12.50 12.50

Dated 2017.

Outdoor Activities in Apurímac Region — A1103

No. 1953: a, Cyclist on Cerro Quisapata. b, Kayaker on Rio Pachachaca.

**2018, Jan. 31 Litho. *Perf. 13x13¼***
**1953** A1103 10s Horiz. pair, #a-b 12.50 12.50

Dated 2017.

## SEMI-POSTAL STAMPS

**Catalogue values for unused stamps in this section are for Never Hinged items.**

Gold Funerary Mask SP1

Designs: 2.60s+1.30s, Ceremonial knife, vert. 3.60s+1.80s, Ceremonial vessel. 4.60s+2.30s, Goblet with precious stones, vert. 20s+10s, Earplug.

*Perf. 12x12½, 12½x12*

**1966, Aug. 16 Photo. Unwmk.**

| | | | | |
|---|---|---|---|---|
| **B1** | SP1 1.90s + 90c multi | 1.10 | .90 |
| **B2** | SP1 2.60s + 1.30s multi | 1.25 | 1.10 |
| **B3** | SP1 3.60s + 1.80s multi | 2.00 | 1.75 |
| **B4** | SP1 4.60s + 2.30s multi | 2.75 | 2.25 |
| **B5** | SP1 20s + 10s multi | 10.00 | 9.00 |
| | *Nos. B1-B5 (5)* | 17.10 | 15.00 |

The designs show gold objects of the 12th-13th centuries Chimu culture. The surtax was for tourist publicity.

For surcharges see Nos. 679-680, 683-684, 686.

## AIR POST STAMPS

No. 248 Overprinted in Black

**1927, Dec. 10 Unwmk. *Perf. 12***

| | | | | |
|---|---|---|---|---|
| **C1** | A87 50c violet | 50.00 | 26.00 |
| *a.* | Inverted overprint | 500.00 | — |

Two types of overprint: first printing, dull black ink; second printing, shiny black ink. Values are the same. No. C1a occurs in the first printing.

Counterfeits exist.

President Augusto Bernardino Leguía — AP1

**1928, Jan. 12 Engr.**

| | | | |
|---|---|---|---|
| **C2** | AP1 50c dark green | 1.10 | .55 |

For surcharge see No. 263.

### Coat of Arms of Piura Type

**1932, July 28 Litho.**

| | | | |
|---|---|---|---|
| **C3** | A107 50c scarlet | 26.00 | 22.50 |

Counterfeits exist.

Airplane in Flight — AP3

**1934, Feb. Engr. *Perf. 12½***

| | | | |
|---|---|---|---|
| **C4** | AP3 2s blue | 6.50 | .60 |
| **C5** | AP3 5s brown | 15.00 | 1.25 |

For surcharges see Nos. C14-C15.

Funeral of Atahualpa AP4

Palace of Torre-Tagle AP7

Designs: 35c, Mt. San Cristobal. 50c, Avenue of Barefoot Friars. 10s, Pizarro and the Thirteen.

**1935, Jan. 18 Photo. *Perf. 13½***

| | | | |
|---|---|---|---|
| **C6** | AP4 5c emerald | .35 | .25 |
| **C7** | AP4 35c brown | .45 | .45 |
| **C8** | AP4 50c orange yel | .90 | .75 |
| **C9** | AP4 1s plum | 1.75 | 1.25 |
| **C10** | AP7 2s red orange | 2.75 | 2.40 |
| **C11** | AP4 5s dp claret | 11.00 | 7.00 |
| **C12** | AP4 10s dk blue | 45.00 | 30.00 |
| | *Nos. C6-C12 (7)* | 62.20 | 42.10 |

4th centenary of founding of Lima.

Nos. C6-C12 overprinted "Radio Nacional" are revenue stamps.

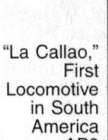

"La Callao," First Locomotive in South America AP9

**1936, Aug. 27 *Perf. 12½***

| | | | |
|---|---|---|---|
| **C13** | AP9 35c gray black | 3.25 | 1.75 |

Founding of the Province of Callao, cent.

**Nos. C4-C5 Surcharged "Habilitado" and New Value, like Nos. 353-355**

**1936, Nov. 4**

| | | | |
|---|---|---|---|
| **C14** | AP3 5c on 2s blue | .55 | .30 |
| **C15** | AP3 25c on 5s brown | 1.10 | .55 |
| *a.* | Double surcharge | 14.00 | 14.00 |
| *b.* | No period btwn. "O" & "25 Cts" | 1.60 | 1.60 |
| *c.* | Inverted surcharge | 21.00 | |

There are many broken letters in this setting.

Mines of Peru AP10

Jorge Chávez AP14

Aerial View of Peruvian Coast AP16

View of the "Sierra" — AP17

St. Rosa of Lima — AP22

Designs: 5c, La Mar Park, Lima. 15c, Mail Steamer "Inca" on Lake Titicaca. 20c, Native Queña (flute) Player and Llama. 30c, Ram at Model Farm, Puno. 1s, Train in Mountains. 1.50s, Jorge Chavez Aviation School. 2s, Transport Plane. 5s, Aerial View of Virgin Forests.

**1936-37 Photo. *Perf. 12½***

| | | | | |
|---|---|---|---|---|
| **C16** | AP10 | 5c brt green | .35 | .25 |
| **C17** | AP10 | 5c emer ('37) | .35 | .25 |
| **C18** | AP10 | 15c lt ultra | .55 | .25 |
| **C19** | AP10 | 15c blue ('37) | .35 | .25 |
| **C20** | AP10 | 20c gray blk | 1.50 | .25 |
| **C21** | AP10 | 20c pale ol grn ('37) | 1.00 | .30 |
| **C22** | AP14 | 25c mag ('37) | .45 | .25 |
| **C23** | AP10 | 30c henna brn | 4.75 | 1.10 |
| **C24** | AP10 | 30c dk ol brn ('37) | 1.50 | .25 |
| **C25** | AP14 | 35c brown | 2.75 | 2.25 |
| **C26** | AP10 | 50c yellow | .45 | .30 |
| **C27** | AP10 | 50c brn vio ('37) | .65 | .25 |
| **C28** | AP16 | 70c Prus grn | 5.50 | 5.00 |
| **C29** | AP16 | 70c pck grn ('37) | 1.00 | .85 |
| **C30** | AP17 | 80c brn blk | 6.50 | 5.00 |
| **C31** | AP17 | 80c ol blk ('37) | 1.25 | .55 |
| **C32** | AP10 | 1s ultra | 4.75 | .45 |
| **C33** | AP10 | 1s red brn ('37) | 2.40 | .30 |
| **C34** | AP14 | 1.50s red brn | 7.75 | 6.00 |
| **C35** | AP14 | 1.50s org yel ('37) | 4.75 | .45 |

**Engr.**

| | | | | |
|---|---|---|---|---|
| **C36** | AP10 | 2s deep blue | 13.00 | 7.75 |
| **C37** | AP10 | 2s yel grn ('37) | 9.25 | .80 |
| **C38** | AP16 | 5s green | 17.00 | 3.75 |
| **C39** | AP22 | 10s car & brn | 125.00 | 110.00 |
| | | *Nos. C16-C39 (24)* | 212.80 | 146.85 |

Nos. C23, C25, C28, C30, C36 Surcharged in Black or Red

**1936, June 26**

| | | | |
|---|---|---|---|
| **C40** | AP10 15c on 30c hn brn | .65 | .45 |
| **C41** | AP14 15c on 35c brown | .65 | .45 |
| **C42** | AP16 15c on 70c Prus grn | 4.50 | 3.50 |
| **C43** | AP17 25c on 80c brn blk (R) | 4.50 | 3.50 |
| **C44** | AP10 1s on 2s dp bl | 7.75 | 6.50 |
| | *Nos. C40-C44 (5)* | 18.05 | 14.40 |

Surcharge on No. C43 is vertical, reading down.

First Flight in Peru, 1911 — AP23

Jorge Chávez — AP24

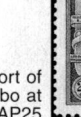

Airport of Limatambo at Lima — AP25

Map of Aviation Lines from Peru — AP26

Designs: 10c, Juan Bielovucic (1889-?) flying over Lima race course, Jan. 14, 1911. 15c, Jorge Chavez-Dartnell (1887-1910), French-born Peruvian aviator who flew from Brixen to Domodossola in the Alps and died of plane-crash injuries.

**1937, Sept. 15 Engr. *Perf. 12***

| | | | |
|---|---|---|---|
| **C45** | AP23 10c violet | .65 | .25 |
| **C46** | AP24 15c dk green | .90 | .25 |
| **C47** | AP25 25c gray brn | .65 | .25 |
| **C48** | AP26 1s black | 3.00 | 2.10 |
| | *Nos. C45-C48 (4)* | 5.20 | 2.85 |

Inter-American Technical Conference of Aviation, Sept. 1937.

Government Restaurant at Callao — AP27

Monument on the Plains of Junin — AP28

Rear Admiral Manuel Villar — AP29

View of Tarma — AP30

Dam, Ica River — AP31

View of Iquitos AP32

Highway and Railroad Passing AP33

Mountain Road — AP34

Plaza San Martín, Lima — AP35

National Radio of Peru AP36

Stele from Chavin Temple AP37

Ministry of Public Works, Lima — AP38

Crypt of the Heroes, Lima — AP39

**Imprint: "Waterlow & Sons Limited, Londres."**

**1938, July 1 Photo. *Perf. 12½, 13***

| | | | | |
|---|---|---|---|---|
| **C49** | AP27 | 5c violet brn | .25 | .25 |
| **C50** | AP28 | 15c dk brown | .25 | .25 |
| **C51** | AP29 | 20c dp magenta | .55 | .30 |
| **C52** | AP30 | 25c dp green | .25 | .25 |
| **C53** | AP31 | 30c orange | .25 | .25 |
| **C54** | AP32 | 50c green | .45 | .30 |
| **C55** | AP33 | 70c slate bl | .65 | .30 |
| **C56** | AP34 | 80c olive | 1.25 | .30 |
| **C57** | AP35 | 1s slate grn | 10.00 | 4.25 |
| **C58** | AP36 | 1.50s purple | 2.25 | .30 |

**Engr.**

| | | | | |
|---|---|---|---|---|
| **C59** | AP37 | 2s ind & org brn | 3.75 | .95 |
| **C60** | AP38 | 5s brown | 18.00 | 1.75 |
| **C61** | AP39 | 10s ol grn & ind | 70.00 | 37.50 |
| | | *Nos. C49-C61 (13)* | 107.90 | 46.95 |

See Nos. C73-C75, C89-C93, C103.
For surcharges see Nos. C65, C76-C77, C82-C88, C108.

Torre-Tagle Palace — AP40

National Congress Building — AP41

Manuel Ferreyros, José Gregorio Paz Soldán and Antonio Arenas — AP42

**1938, Dec. 9 Photo. *Perf. 12½***

| | | | | |
|---|---|---|---|---|
| **C62** | AP40 | 25c brt ultra | .90 | .65 |
| **C63** | AP41 | 1.50s brown vio | 2.40 | 1.90 |
| **C64** | AP42 | 2s black | 1.50 | .75 |
| | | *Nos. C62-C64 (3)* | 4.80 | 3.30 |

8th Pan-American Conference at Lima.

No. C52 Surcharged in Black

**1942 *Perf. 13***

| | | | | |
|---|---|---|---|---|
| **C65** | AP30 | 15c on 25c dp grn | 1.75 | .25 |

**Types of 1938**

Imprint: "Columbian Bank Note Co."

**1945-46 Unwmk. Litho. *Perf. 12½***

| | | | | |
|---|---|---|---|---|
| **C73** | AP27 | 5c violet brown | .25 | .25 |
| **C74** | AP31 | 30c orange | .25 | .25 |
| **C75** | AP36 | 1.50s purple ('46) | .35 | .30 |
| | | *Nos. C73-C75 (3)* | .85 | .80 |

Nos. C73 and C54 Overprinted in Black

**1947, Sept. 25 *Perf. 12½, 13***

| | | | | |
|---|---|---|---|---|
| **C76** | AP27 | 5c violet brown | .25 | .25 |
| **C77** | AP32 | 50c green | .25 | .30 |

1st Peru Intl. Airways flight from Lima to New York City, Sept. 27-28, 1947.

**Catalogue values for unused stamps in this section, from this point to the end of the section, are for Never Hinged items.**

Peru-Great Britain Air Route — AP43

Designs: 5s, Discus thrower. 10s, Rifleman.

**1948, July 29 Photo. *Perf. 12½***

| | | | | |
|---|---|---|---|---|
| **C78** | AP43 | 1s blue | 4.00 | 2.75 |

Basketball Players — AP44

**Carmine Overprint, "AEREO"**

| | | | | |
|---|---|---|---|---|
| **C79** | AP44 | 2s red brown | 5.50 | 3.50 |
| **C80** | AP44 | 5s yellow green | 9.25 | 5.75 |
| **C81** | AP44 | 10s yellow | 11.00 | 7.00 |
| *a.* | | Souv. sheet, #C78-C81, perf 13 | 50.00 | 50.00 |
| | | *Nos. C78-C81 (4)* | 29.75 | 19.00 |

Peru's participation in the 1948 Olympic Games held at Wembley, England, during July and August. Postally valid for four days, July 29-Aug. 1, 1948. Proceeds went to the Olympic Committee.

A surtax of 2 soles on No. C81a was for the Children's Hospital.

Remainders of Nos. C78-C81 and C81a were overprinted "Melbourne 1956" and placed on sale Nov. 19, 1956, at all post offices as "voluntary stamps" with no postal validity. Clerks were permitted to postmark them to please collectors, and proceeds were to help pay the cost of sending Peruvian athletes to Australia. On April 14, 1957, postal authorities declared these stamps valid for one day, April 15, 1957. The overprint was applied to 10,000 sets and 21,000 souvenir sheets. Value, set, $22.50; sheet, $17.50.

No. C55 Surcharged in Red

**1948, Dec. *Perf. 13***

| | | | | |
|---|---|---|---|---|
| **C82** | AP33 | 10c on 70c slate blue | .35 | .25 |
| **C83** | AP33 | 20c on 70c slate blue | .35 | .25 |
| **C84** | AP33 | 55c on 70c slate blue | .35 | .25 |
| | | *Nos. C82-C84 (3)* | 1.05 | .75 |

Nos. C52, C55 and C56 Surcharged in Black

**1949, Mar. 25**

| | | | | |
|---|---|---|---|---|
| **C85** | AP30 | 5c on 25c dp grn | .25 | .25 |
| **C86** | AP30 | 10c on 25c dp grn | .25 | .25 |
| **C87** | AP33 | 15c on 70c slate bl | .35 | .25 |
| **C88** | AP34 | 30c on 80c olive | 1.10 | .65 |
| | | *Nos. C85-C88 (4)* | 1.95 | 1.40 |

The surcharge reads up, on No. C87.

**Types of 1938**

Imprint: "Waterlow & Sons Limited, Londres."

***Perf. 13x13½, 13½x13***

**1949-50 Photo.**

| | | | | |
|---|---|---|---|---|
| **C89** | AP27 | 5c olive bister | .25 | .25 |
| **C90** | AP31 | 30c red | .25 | .25 |
| **C91** | AP33 | 70c blue | .45 | .25 |
| **C92** | AP34 | 80c cerise | 1.25 | .45 |
| **C93** | AP36 | 1.50s vio brn ('50) | .90 | .55 |
| | | *Nos. C89-C93 (5)* | 3.10 | 1.75 |

**Overprinted "U. P. U. 1874-1949" in Red or Black**

Air View, Reserva Park, Lima — AP45

Flags of the Americas and Spain AP46

Designs: 30c, National flag. 55c, Huancayo Hotel. 95c, Blanca-Ancash Cordillera. 1.50s, Arequipa Hotel. 2s, Coal chute and dock, Chimbote. 5s, Town hall, Miraflores. 10s, Hall of National Congress, Lima.

**1951, Apr. 2 Engr. *Perf. 12***

| | | | | |
|---|---|---|---|---|
| **C94** | AP45 | 5c blue grn | .25 | .25 |
| **C95** | AP45 | 30c black & car | .25 | .25 |
| *a.* | | Inverted overprint | | |
| **C96** | AP45 | 55c yel grn (Bk) | .25 | .25 |
| **C97** | AP45 | 95c dk green | .25 | .25 |
| **C98** | AP45 | 1.50s dp car (Bk) | .35 | .30 |
| **C99** | AP45 | 2s deep blue | .35 | .30 |
| **C100** | AP45 | 5s rose car (Bk) | 4.00 | 3.25 |
| **C101** | AP45 | 10s purple | 5.25 | 4.50 |
| **C102** | AP46 | 20s dk brn & ultra | 8.75 | 7.00 |
| | | *Nos. C94-C102 (9)* | 19.70 | 16.35 |

UPU, 75th anniv. (in 1949).

Nos. C94-C102 exist without overprint, but were not regularly issued. Value, set, $225.

**Type of 1938**

Imprint: "Inst. de Grav. Paris."

**1951, May Engr. *Perf. 12½x12***

| | | | | |
|---|---|---|---|---|
| **C103** | AP27 | 5c olive bister | .25 | .25 |

Type of 1938 Surcharged in Black

**1951**

| | | | | |
|---|---|---|---|---|
| **C108** | AP31 | 25c on 30c rose red | .25 | .25 |

Thomas de San Martin y Contreras and Jerónimo de Aliaga y Ramirez — AP47

San Marcos University — AP48

Designs: 50c, Church and convent of Santo Domingo. 1.20s, P. de Peralta Barnuevo, T. de San Martin y Contreras and J. Baquijano y Carrillo de Cordova. 2s, T. Rodriguez de Mendoza, J. Hipolito Unanue y Pavon and J. Cayetano Heredia y Garcia. 5s, Arms of the University, 1571 and 1735.

***Perf. 11½x12½***

**1951, Dec. 10 Litho.**

| | | | | |
|---|---|---|---|---|
| **C109** | AP47 | 30c gray | .45 | .45 |
| **C110** | AP48 | 40c ultra | .45 | .45 |
| **C111** | AP48 | 50c car rose | .45 | .45 |
| **C112** | AP47 | 1.20s emerald | .45 | .45 |
| **C113** | AP47 | 2s slate | 1.40 | .45 |
| **C114** | AP47 | 5s multicolored | 3.00 | .45 |
| | | *Nos. C109-C114 (6)* | 6.20 | 2.70 |

400th anniv. of the founding of San Marcos University.

River Gunboat Marañon AP49

Peruvian Cormorants — AP50

National Airport, Lima AP51

Tobacco Plant AP52

Manco Capac Monument AP54

Garcilaso de la Vega AP53

Designs: 1.50s, Housing Unit No. 3. 2.20s, Inca Solar Observatory.

**Imprint: "Thomas De La Rue & Co. Ltd."**

**1953-60 Unwmk.** ***Perf. 13, 12***

**C115** AP49 40c yellow grn .25 .25
*a.* 40c blue green ('57) .25 .25
**C116** AP50 75c dk brown 1.50 .30
**C116A** AP50 80c pale brn red ('60) .70 .25
**C117** AP51 1.25s blue .35 .25
**C118** AP49 1.50s cerise .45 .30
**C119** AP51 2.20s dk blue 2.25 .45
**C120** AP52 3s brown 1.90 .65
**C121** AP53 5s bister 1.50 .30
**C122** AP54 10s dull vio brn 3.75 .85
*Nos. C115-C122 (9)* 12.65 3.60

See #C158-C162, C182-C183, C186-C189, C210-C211.

For surcharges see #C420-C422, C429-C433, C435-C436, C438, C442-C443, C445-C450, C455, C471-C474, C476, C478-C479, C495.

Queen Isabella I — AP55

Fleet of Columbus — AP56

***Perf. 12½x11½, 11½x12½***

**1953, June 18 Engr. Unwmk.**

**C123** AP55 40c dp carmine .25 .25
**C124** AP56 1.25s emerald .65 .25
**C125** AP55 2.15s dp plum 1.10 .60
**C126** AP56 2.20s black 1.50 .65
*Nos. C123-C126 (4)* 3.50 1.75

500th birth anniv. (in 1951) of Queen Isabella I of Spain.

For surcharge see No. C475.

Arms of Lima and Bordeaux AP57

Designs: 50c, Eiffel Tower and Cathedral of Lima. 1.25s, Admiral Dupetit-Thouars and frigate "La Victorieuse." 2.20s, Presidents Coty and Prado and exposition hall.

**1957, Sept. 16** ***Perf. 13***

**C127** AP57 40c claret, grn & ultra .25 .25
**C128** AP57 50c grn, blk & hn brn .25 .25
**C129** AP57 1.25s bl, ind & dk grn .55 .45
**C130** AP57 2.20s bluish blk, bl & red brn .90 .90
*Nos. C127-C130 (4)* 1.95 1.85

French Exposition, Lima, Sept. 15-Oct. 1.

For surcharges see Nos. 763, C503-C505.

Pre-Stamp Postal Markings — AP58

10c, 1r Stamp of 1857. 15c, 2r Stamp of 1857. 25c, 1d Stamp of 1860. 30c, 1p Stamp of 1858. 40c, ½p Stamp of 1858. 1.25s, José Davila Condemarin. 2.20s, Ramon Castilla. 5s, Pres. Manuel Prado. 10s, Shield of Lima containing stamps.

***Perf. 12½x13***

**1957, Dec. 1 Engr. Unwmk.**

**C131** AP58 5c silver & blk .25 .25
**C132** AP58 10c lil rose & bl .25 .25
**C133** AP58 15c grn & red brn .25 .25
**C134** AP58 25c org yel & bl .25 .25
**C135** AP58 30c vio brn & org brn .25 .25
**C136** AP58 40c black & bis .25 .25
**C137** AP58 1.25s dk bl & dk brn .75 .55
**C138** AP58 2.20s red & sl bl 1.10 .75
**C139** AP58 5s lil rose & mar 2.40 1.50
**C140** AP58 10s ol grn & lil 4.50 2.50
*Nos. C131-C140 (10)* 10.25 6.80

Centenary of Peruvian postage stamps. No. C140 issued to publicize the Peruvian Centenary Phil. Exhib. (PEREX).

Carlos Paz Soldan — AP59

Port of Callao and Pres. Manuel Prado AP60

Design: 1s, Ramon Castilla.

***Perf. 14x13½, 13½x14***

**1958, Apr. 7 Litho. Wmk. 116**

**C141** AP59 40c brn & pale rose .30 .30
**C142** AP59 1s grn & lt grn .35 .30
**C143** AP60 1.25s dull pur & ind .55 .30
*Nos. C141-C143 (3)* 1.20 .90

Centenary of the telegraph connection between Lima and Callao and the centenary of the political province of Callao.

For surcharges see Nos. 758A, 767.

Flags of France and Peru — AP61

Cathedral of Lima and Lady AP62

1.50s, Horseback rider & mall in Lima. 2.50s, Map of Peru showing national products.

***Perf. 12½x13, 13x12½***

**1958, May 20 Engr. Unwmk.**

**C144** AP61 50c dl vio, bl & car .25 .25
**C145** AP62 65c multi .25 .25
**C146** AP62 1.50s bl, brn vio & ol .35 .25
**C147** AP61 2.50s sl grn, grnsh bl & claret .65 .30
*Nos. C144-C147 (4)* 1.50 1.05

Peruvian Exhib. in Paris, May 20-July 10.

Bro. Martin de Porres Velasquez AP63

First Royal School of Medicine (Now Ministry of Government and Police) — AP64

Designs: 1.20s, Daniel Alcides Carrion Garcia. 1.50s, Jose Hipolito Unanue Pavon.

***Perf. 13x13½, 13½x13***

**1958, July 24 Litho. Unwmk.**

**C148** AP63 60c multi .25 .25
**C149** AP63 1.20s multi .25 .25
**C150** AP63 1.50s multi .25 .25
**C151** AP64 2.20s black .65 .65
*Nos. C148-C151 (4)* 1.40 1.40

Daniel A. Carrion (1857-85), medical martyr.

Gen. Ignacio Alvarez Thomas AP65

**1958, Nov. 13** ***Perf. 13x12½***

**C152** AP65 1.10s brn lake, bis & ver .30 .30
**C153** AP65 1.20s blk, bis & ver .55 .55

General Thomas (1787-1857), fighter for South American independence.

"Justice" and Emblem — AP66

**1958, Nov. 13**

**Star in Blue and Olive Bister**

**C154** AP66 80c emerald .25 .25
**C155** AP66 1.10s red orange .25 .25
**C156** AP66 1.20s ultra .35 .25
**C157** AP66 1.50s lilac rose .35 .25
*Nos. C154-C157 (4)* 1.20 1.00

Lima Bar Assoc., 150th anniv.

**Types of 1953-57**

Designs: 80c, Peruvian cormorants. 3.80s, Inca Solar Observatory.

**Imprint: "Joh. Enschedé en Zonen-Holland"**

***Perf. 12½x14, 14x13, 13x14***

**1959, Dec. 9 Unwmk.**

**C158** AP50 80c brown red .35 .25
**C159** AP52 3s lt green 1.10 .45
**C160** AP51 3.80s orange 2.25 .55
**C161** AP53 5s brown 1.10 .55
**C162** AP54 10s orange ver 2.25 .65
*Nos. C158-C162 (5)* 7.05 2.45

WRY Emblem, Dove, Rainbow and Farmer — AP67

**1960, Apr. 7 Litho.** ***Perf. 14x13***

**C163** AP67 80c multi .55 .55
**C164** AP67 4.30s multi 1.00 1.00
*a.* Souv. sheet of 2, #C163-C164, imperf. 15.00 15.00

World Refugee Year, 7/1/59-6/30/60. No. C164a sold for 15s.

Peruvian Cormorant Over Ocean — AP68

**1960, May 30** ***Perf. 14x13½***

**C165** AP68 1s multi 3.75 1.75

Intl. Pacific Fair, Lima, 1959.

Lima Coin of 1659 AP69

**1961, Jan. 19 Unwmk.** ***Perf. 13x14***

**C166** AP69 1s org brn & gray .55 .45
**C167** AP69 2s Prus bl & gray .55 .45

1st National Numismatic Exposition, Lima, 1959; 300th anniv. of the first dated coin (1659) minted at Lima.

The Earth AP70

**1961, Mar. 8 Litho.** ***Perf. 13½x14***

**C168** AP70 1s multicolored 1.40 .65

International Geophysical Year.

Frigate Amazonas AP71

**1961, Mar. 8 Engr.** ***Perf. 13½***

**C169** AP71 50c brown & grn .30 .30
**C170** AP71 80c dl vio & red org .35 .30
**C171** AP71 1s green & sepia .55 .30
*Nos. C169-C171 (3)* 1.20 .90

Centenary (in 1958) of the trip around the world by the Peruvian frigate Amazonas.

---

Machu Picchu Sheet

A souvenir sheet was issued Sept. 11, 1961, to commemorate the 50th anniversary of the discovery of the ruins of Machu Picchu, ancient Inca city in the Andes, by Hiram Bingham. It contains two bi-colored imperf. airmail stamps, 5s and 10s, lithographed in a single design picturing the mountaintop ruins. The sheet was valid for one day and was sold in a restricted manner. Value $20.

Olympic Torch, Laurel and Globe — AP72

**1961, Dec. 13 Unwmk. *Perf. 13***

**C172** AP72 5s gray & ultra .90 .60
**C173** AP72 10s gray & car 2.00 1.25
*a.* Souv. sheet of 2, #C172-C173, imperf. 4.25 4.25

17th Olympic Games, Rome, 8/25-9/11/60.

Fair Emblem and Llama — AP73

**1962, Jan. Litho. *Perf. 10½x11***

**C174** AP73 1s multi .35 .25

2nd International Pacific Fair, Lima, 1961.

Map Showing Disputed Border, Peru-Ecuador — AP74

**1962, May 25 *Perf. 10½***

**Gray Background**

**C175** AP74 1.30s blk, red & car rose .35 .25
**C176** AP74 1.50s blk, red & emer .35 .25
**C177** AP74 2.50s blk, red & dk bl .70 .70
*Nos. C175-C177 (3)* 1.40 1.20

Settlement of the border dispute with Ecuador by the Protocol of Rio de Janeiro, 20th anniv.

Cahuide and Cuauhtémoc — AP75

2s, Tupac Amaru (Jose G. Condorcanqui) & Miguel Hidalgo. 3s, Pres. Manuel Prado & Pres. Adolfo Lopez Mateos of Mexico.

**1962, May 25 Engr. *Perf. 13***

**C178** AP75 1s dk car rose, red & brt grn .25 .25
**C179** AP75 2s grn, red & brt grn .45 .30
**C180** AP75 3s brn, red & brt grn .70 .50
*Nos. C178-C180 (3)* 1.40 1.05

Exhibition of Peruvian art treasures in Mexico.

Agriculture, Industry and Archaeology AP76

**1962, Sept. 7 Litho. *Perf. 14x13½***

**C181** AP76 1s black & gray .35 .25

Cent. (in 1961) of Pallasca Ancash province.

**Types of 1953-60**

1.30s, Guanayes. 1.50s, Housing Unit No. 3. 1.80s, Locomotive No. 80 (like #460). 2s, Monument to Native Farmer. 3s, Tobacco plant. 4.30s, Inca Solar Observatory. 5s, Garcilaso de la Vega. 10s, Inca Monument.

**Imprint: "Thomas De La Rue & Co. Ltd."**

**1962-63 Wmk. 346 Litho. *Perf. 13***

**C182** AP50 1.30s pale yellow .75 .25
**C183** AP49 1.50s claret .55 .25
**C184** A182 1.80s dark blue .55 .25

***Perf. 12***

**C185** A184 2s emerald ('63) .55 .25
**C186** AP52 3s lilac rose .60 .25
**C187** AP51 4.30s orange 1.25 .45
**C188** AP53 5s citron 1.25 .75

***Perf. 13½x14***

**C189** AP54 10s vio bl ('63) 2.75 .90
*Nos. C182-C189 (8)* 8.25 3.35

For surcharges see Nos. C429, C432, C446, C449, C473.

**Freedom from Hunger Type**

**1963, July 23 Unwmk. *Perf. 12½***

**C190** A189 4.30s lt grn & ocher 1.40 1.10

Jorge Chávez and Wing — AP77

**1964, Feb. 20 Engr. *Perf. 13***

**C191** AP77 5s org brn, dk brn & bl .90 .45

1st crossing of the Alps by air (Sept. 23, 1910) by the Peruvian aviator Jorge Chávez, 50th anniv.

**Alliance for Progress Type**

Design: 1.30s, Same, horizontal.

***Perf. 12½x12, 12x12½***

**1964, June 22 Litho.**

**C192** A190 1.30s multi .25 .25
**C193** A190 3s multi .75 .60

Fair Poster — AP78

**1965, Jan. 15 Unwmk. *Perf. 14½***

**C194** AP78 1s multi .25 .25

3rd International Pacific Fair, Lima 1963.

Basket, Globe, Pennant — AP79

**1965, Apr. 19 *Perf. 12x12½***

**C195** AP79 1.30s violet & red .75 .60
**C196** AP79 4.30s bis brn & red 1.75 1.40

4th Women's Intl. Basketball Championship.
For surcharge see No. C493.

St. Martin de Porres — AP80

Designs: 1.80s, St. Martin's miracle: dog, cat and mouse feeding from same dish. 4.30s, St. Martin with cherubim in Heaven.

**1965, Oct. 29 Litho. *Perf. 11***

**C197** AP80 1.30s gray & multi .35 .25
**C198** AP80 1.80s gray & multi .45 .25
**C199** AP80 4.30s gray & multi .95 .95
*Nos. C197-C199 (3)* 1.75 1.45

Canonization of St. Martin de Porres Velasquez (1579-1639), on May 6, 1962.
For surcharges see Nos. C439, C496 and footnote below No. RA57.

Victory Monument, Lima, and Battle Scene — AP81

Designs: 3.60s, Monument and Callao Fortress. 4.60s, Monument and José Galvez.

**1966, May 2 Photo. *Perf. 14x13½***

**C200** AP81 1.90s multicolored .65 .50
**C201** AP81 3.60s brn, yel & bis .75 .75
**C202** AP81 4.60s multicolored 1.25 1.00
*Nos. C200-C202 (3)* 2.65 2.25

Centenary of Peru's naval victory over the Spanish Armada at Callao, May, 1866.

Civil Guard Emblem AP82

1.90s, Various activities of Civil Guard.

**1966, Aug. 30 Photo. *Perf. 13½x14***

**C203** AP82 90c multicolored .25 .25
**C204** AP82 1.90s dp lil rose, gold & blk .55 .25

Centenary of the Civil Guard.

**Hydroelectric Center Type**

**1966, Nov. 24 Photo. *Perf. 13½x14***

**C205** A193 1.90s lil, blk & vio bl .35 .25

Sun Symbol, Ancient Carving — AP83

Designs: 3.60s, Map of Peru and spiral, horiz. 4.60s, Globe with map of Peru.

***Perf. 14x13½, 13½x14***

**1967, Feb. 16 Litho.**

**C206** AP83 2.60s red org & blk .35 .25
**C207** AP83 3.60s dp blue & blk .45 .45
**C208** AP83 4.60s tan & multi .55 .55
*Nos. C206-C208 (3)* 1.35 1.25

Photography exhibition "Peru Before the World" which opened simultaneously in Lima, Madrid, Santiago de Chile and Washington, Sept. 27, 1966.
For surcharges see #C444, C470, C492.

**Types of 1953-60**

2.60s, Monument to Native Farmer. 3.60s, Tobacco plant. 4.60s, Inca Solar Observatory.

**Imprint: "I.N.A."**

**1967, Jan. *Perf. 13½x14, 14x13½***

**C209** A184 2.60s brt green 1.00 .30
**C210** AP52 3.60s lilac rose 1.40 .45
**C211** AP51 4.60s orange 1.50 .90
*Nos. C209-C211 (3)* 3.90 1.65

For surcharges see Nos. C433, C436-C438, C440-C442, C445, C447-C450, C454-C455, C471-C472, C474, C476, C478.

**Window and Sun Type of Regular Issue**

**1967, Apr. 18 Photo. *Perf. 13½x14***

**C212** A194 1.90s yel brn, blk & gold .45 .30

St. Rosa of Lima by Angelino Medoro — AP84

St. Rosa Painted by: 2.60s, Carlo Maratta. 3.60s, Cuzquena School, 17th century.

**1967, Aug. 30 Photo. *Perf. 13½***

**Black, Gold & Multi**

**C213** AP84 1.90s .65 .25
**C214** AP84 2.60s 1.10 .30
**C215** AP84 3.60s 1.25 .55
*Nos. C213-C215 (3)* 3.00 1.10

350th death anniv. of St. Rosa of Lima.
For surcharge see No. C477.

**Fair Type of Regular Issue**

**1967, Oct. 27 Photo. *Perf. 12***

**C216** A195 1s gold, brt red lil & blk .35 .25

Lions Emblem — AP85

**1967, Dec. 29 Litho. *Perf. 14x13½***

**C217** AP85 1.60s brt bl & vio bl, *grysh* .60 .30

50th anniversary of Lions International.

Decorated Jug, Nazca Culture — AP86

Painted pottery jugs of pre-Inca Nazca culture: 2.60s, Falcon. 3.60s, Round jug decorated with grain-eating bird. 4.60s, Two-headed snake. 5.60s, Marine bird.

**1968, June 4 Photo. *Perf. 12***

**C218** AP86 1.90s multi .65 .30
**C219** AP86 2.60s multi .75 .35
**C220** AP86 3.60s black & multi .75 .35

**C221** AP86 4.60s brown & multi 1.10 .55

**C222** AP86 5.60s gray & multi 2.25 1.10

*Nos. C218-C222 (5)* 5.50 2.65

For surcharges see #C451-C453, C497, C500.

Antarqui, Inca Messenger AP87

Design: 5.60s, Alpaca and jet liner.

**1968, Sept. 2 Litho. *Perf. 12***

**C223** AP87 3.60s multi .55 .45

**C224** AP87 5.60s red, blk & brn .75 .65

12th anniv. of Peruvian Airlines (APSA). For surcharges see Nos. C480-C482.

Human Rights Flame — AP88

**1968, Sept. 5 Photo. *Perf. 14x13½***

**C225** AP88 6.50s brn, red & grn .55 .30

International Human Rights Year.

Discobolus and Mexico Olympics Emblem AP89

**1968, Oct. 19 Photo. *Perf. 13½***

**C226** AP89 2.30s yel, brn & dk bl .35 .25

**C227** AP89 3.50s yel grn, sl bl & red .35 .25

**C228** AP89 5s brt pink, blk & ultra .35 .30

**C229** AP89 6.50s lt bl, mag & brn .55 .40

**C230** AP89 8s lil, ultra & car .55 .40

**C231** AP89 9s org, vio & grn .55 .40

*Nos. C226-C231 (6)* 2.70 2.00

19th Olympic Games, Mexico City, 10/12-27.

Hand, Corn and Field AP90

**1969, Mar. 3 Litho. *Perf. 11***

**C232** AP90 5.50s on 1.90s grn & yel .55 .30

**C233** AP90 6.50s on 1.90s bl, grn & yel .75 .40

Agrarian Reform Law. Not issued without surcharge.

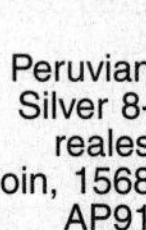

Peruvian Silver 8-reales Coin, 1568 AP91

**1969, Mar. 17 Litho. *Perf. 12***

**C234** AP91 5s yellow, gray & blk .55 .45

**C235** AP91 5s bl grn, gray & blk .55 .45

400th anniv. of the first Peruvian coinage.

Ramon Castilla Monument AP92

Design: 10s, Pres. Ramon Castilla.

**1969, May 30 Photo. *Perf. 13½***
**Size: 27x40mm**

**C236** AP92 5s emerald & indigo .55 .30

***Perf. 12***
**Size: 21x37mm**

**C237** AP92 10s plum & brn 1.25 .65

Ramon Castilla (1797-1867), president of Peru (1845-1851 and 1855-1862), on the occasion of the unveiling of the monument in Lima.

### Airline Type of Regular Issue

**1969, June 17 Litho. *Perf. 11***

**C238** A199 3s org & multi .45 .45

**C239** A199 4s multi .55 .45

**C240** A199 5.50s ver & multi .65 .45

**C241** A199 6.50s vio & multi .65 .45

*Nos. C238-C241 (4)* 2.30 1.80

First Peruvian Airlines (APSA) flight to Europe.

Radar Antenna, Satellite and Earth — AP93

**1969, July 14 Litho. *Perf. 11***

**C242** AP93 20s multi 2.25 1.10

*a.* Souv. sheet 3.50 3.50

Opening of the Lurin satellite earth station near Lima.

No. C242a contains one imperf. stamp with simulated perforations similar to No. C242.

### Gonzales Type of Regular Issue inscribed "AEREO"

**1969, July 23 Litho. *Perf. 11***

**C243** A200 20s red & multi 2.50 1.25

WHO Emblem AP94

**1969, Aug. 14 Photo. *Perf. 12***

**C244** AP94 5s gray, red brn, gold & blk .35 .30

**C245** AP94 6.50s dl org, gray bl, gold & blk .45 .30

WHO, 20th anniv.

### Agrarian Reform Type of Regular Issue

**1969, Aug. 28 Litho. *Perf. 11***

**C246** A201 3s lil & blk .35 .35

**C247** A201 4s brn & buff .55 .35

Garcilaso de la Vega — AP95

Designs: 2.40s, De la Vega's coat of arms. 3.50s, Title page of "Commemtarios Reales que tratan del origen de los Yncas," Lisbon, 1609.

**1969, Sept. 18 Litho. *Perf. 12x12½***

**C248** AP95 2.40s emer, sil & blk .30 .30

**C249** AP95 3.50s ultra, buff & blk .35 .30

**C250** AP95 5s sil, yel, blk & brn .55 .30

*a.* Souv. sheet of 3, #C248-C250, imperf. 2.25 2.25

*Nos. C248-C250 (3)* 1.20 .90

Garcilaso de la Vega, called "Inca" (1539-1616), historian of Peru.

### Fair Type of Regular Issue, 1969

**1969, Nov. 14 Litho. *Perf. 11***

**C251** A203 3s bis & multi .30 .25

**C252** A203 4s multi .80 .25

### Bolognesi Type of Regular Issue

**1969, Dec. 9 Litho. *Perf. 11***

**C253** A204 50s lt brn, blk & gold 4.00 1.90

Arms of Amazonas — AP96

**1970, Jan. 6 Litho. *Perf. 11***

**C254** AP96 10s multi 1.25 1.00

ILO Emblem AP97

**1970, Jan. 16**

**C278** AP97 3s dk vio bl & lt ultra .35 .25

ILO, 50th anniv.

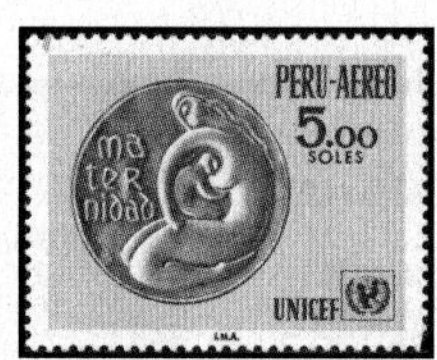


Motherhood and UNICEF Emblem AP98

**1970, Jan. 16 Photo. *Perf. 13½x14***

**C279** AP98 5s yel, gray & blk .45 .30

**C280** AP98 6.50s brt pink, gray & blk .65 .40

### Vicus Culture Type of Regular Issue

Ceramics of Vicus Culture, 6th-8th Centuries: 3s, Squatting warrior. 4s, Jug. 5.50s, Twin jugs. 6.50s, Woman and jug.

**1970, Feb. 23 Litho. *Perf. 11***

**C281** A205 3s buff, blk & brn 1.10 .30

**C282** A205 4s buff, blk & brn 1.10 .30

**C283** A205 5.50s buff, blk & brn 2.25 .85

**C284** A205 6.50s buff, blk & brn 3.25 1.10

*a.* Vert. strip, #526, C281-C284 10.00 10.00

*Nos. C281-C284 (4)* 7.70 2.55

### Fish Type of Regular Issue

**1970, Apr. 30 Litho. *Perf. 11***

**C285** A207 3s Swordfish 2.10 1.40

**C286** A207 3s Yellowfin tuna 2.10 1.40

**C287** A207 5.50s Wolf fish 2.10 2.10

*Nos. C285-C287 (3)* 6.30 4.90

Telephone — AP99

**1970, June 12 Litho. *Perf. 11***

**C288** AP99 5s multi .55 .25

**C289** AP99 10s multi 1.10 .55

Nationalization of the Peruvian telephone system, Mar. 25, 1970.

### Soldier-Farmer Type of Regular Issue

**1970, June 24 Litho. *Perf. 11***

**C290** A208 3s gold & multi .55 .25

**C291** A208 5.50s gold & multi 1.10 .25

UN Headquarters, NY — AP100

**1970 June 26**

**C292** AP100 3s vio bl & lt bl .35 .25

25th anniversary of United Nations.

Rotary Club Emblem — AP101

**1970, July 18**

**C293** AP101 10s blk, red & gold 1.25 .80

Rotary Club of Lima, 50th anniversary.

### Tourist Type of Regular Issue

3s, Ruins of Sun Fortress, Trujillo. 4s, Sacsayhuaman Arch, Cuzco. 5.50s, Arch & Lake Titicaca, Puno. 10s, Machu Picchu, Cuzco.

**1970, Aug. 6 Litho. *Perf. 11***

**C294** A210 3s multi .80 .25

**C295** A210 4s multi, vert. 1.00 .25

**C296** A210 5.50s multi, vert. 1.50 .35

**C297** A210 10s multi, vert. 2.00 .75

*a.* Souvenir sheet of 5 5.50 5.50

*Nos. C294-C297 (4)* 5.30 1.60

No. C297a contains 5 imperf. stamps similar to Nos. 538, C294-C297 with simulated perforations.

Procession, Lord of Miracles — AP102

4s, Cockfight, by T. Nuñez Ureta. 5.50s, Altar of Church of the Nazarene, vert. 6.50s, Procession, by J. Vinatea Reinoso. 8s, Procession, by José Sabogal, vert.

**1970, Nov. 30 Litho. *Perf. 11***

**C298** AP102 3s blk & multi .35 .35

**C299** AP102 4s blk & multi .35 .35

**C300** AP102 5.50s blk & multi .65 .40

**C301** AP102 6.50s blk & multi .75 .50

**C302** AP102 8s blk & multi 1.10 .60

*Nos. C298-C302 (5)* 3.20 2.20

October Festival in Lima.

"Tight Embrace" (from ancient monolith) AP103

**1971, Feb. 8 Litho. *Perf. 11***

| | | | | |
|---|---|---|---|---|
| **C303** | AP103 | 4s ol gray, yel & red | .55 | .30 |
| **C304** | AP103 | 5.50s dk bl, pink & red | .55 | .30 |
| **C305** | AP103 | 6.50s sl, buff & red | .55 | .30 |
| | | *Nos. C303-C305 (3)* | 1.65 | .90 |

Issued to express Peru's gratitude to the world for aid after the Ancash earthquake, May 31, 1970.

### Textile Type of Regular Issue

Designs: 3s, Chancay tapestry, vert. 4s, Chancay lace. 5.50s, Paracas cloth, vert.

**1971, Apr. 19 Litho. *Perf. 11***

| | | | | |
|---|---|---|---|---|
| **C306** | A213 | 3s multi | 1.10 | .50 |
| **C307** | A213 | 4s grn & multi | 1.10 | .50 |
| **C308** | A213 | 5.50s multi | 1.60 | .55 |
| | | *Nos. C306-C308 (3)* | 3.80 | 1.55 |

### Fish Type of Regular Issue

Fish Sculptures and Fish: 3.50s, Chimu Inca culture, 14th century and Chilean sardine. 4s, Mochica culture, 5th century, and engraulis ringens. 5.50s, Chimu culture, 13th century, and merluccios peruanos. 8.50s, Nazca culture, 3rd century, and brevoortis maculatachilcae.

**1971, June 7 Litho. *Perf. 11***

| | | | | |
|---|---|---|---|---|
| **C309** | A214 | 3.50s multi | .65 | .25 |
| **C310** | A214 | 4s multi | .75 | .25 |
| **C311** | A214 | 5.50s multi | 1.10 | .55 |
| **C312** | A214 | 8.50s multi | 1.75 | 1.10 |
| | | *Nos. C309-C312 (4)* | 4.25 | 2.15 |

### Independence Type of 1971

Paintings: No. C313, Toribio Rodriguez de Mendoza. No. C314, José de la Riva Aguero. No. C315, Francisco Vidal. 3.50s, José de San Martin. No. C317, Juan P. Viscardo y Guzman. No. C318, Hipolito Unanue. 4.50s, Liberation Monument, Paracas. No. C320, José G. Condorcanqui-Tupac Amaru. No. C321, Francisco J. de Luna Pizarro. 6s, March of the Numancia Battalion, horiz. 7.50s, Peace Tower, monument for Alvarez de Arenales, horiz. 9s, Liberators' Monument, Lima, horiz. 10s, Independence Proclamation in Lima, horiz.

**1971 Litho. *Perf. 11***

| | | | | |
|---|---|---|---|---|
| **C313** | A215 | 3s brt mag & blk | .25 | .25 |
| **C314** | A215 | 3s gray & multi | .25 | .25 |
| **C315** | A215 | 3s dk bl & multi | .25 | .25 |
| **C316** | A215 | 3.50s dk bl & multi | .35 | .25 |
| **C317** | A215 | 4s emer & blk | .35 | .25 |
| **C318** | A215 | 4s gray & multi | .35 | .25 |
| **C319** | A215 | 4.50s dk bl & multi | .35 | .25 |
| **C320** | A215 | 5.50s brn & blk | .55 | .25 |
| **C321** | A215 | 5.50s gray & multi | .55 | .25 |
| **C322** | A215 | 6s dk bl & multi | .65 | .30 |
| **C323** | A215 | 7.50s dk bl & multi | .75 | .50 |
| **C324** | A215 | 9s dk bl & multi | .75 | .50 |
| **C325** | A215 | 10s dk bl & multi | .75 | .50 |
| | | *Nos. C313-C325 (13)* | 6.15 | 4.05 |

150th anniversary of independence, and to honor the heroes of the struggle for independence. Sizes: 6s, 10s, 45x35mm, 7.50s, 9s, 41x39mm. Others 31x49mm.

Issued: #C313, C317, C320, 5/10; #C314, C318, C321, 7/5; others 7/27.

Ricardo Palma — AP104

**1971, Aug. 27 *Perf. 13***

| | | | | |
|---|---|---|---|---|
| **C326** | AP104 | 7.50s ol bis & blk | 1.10 | .55 |

Sesquicentennial of National Library. Ricardo Palma (1884-1912) was a writer and director of the library.

Weight Lifter — AP105

**1971, Sept. 15**

| | | | | |
|---|---|---|---|---|
| **C327** | AP105 | 7.50s brt bl & blk | 1.10 | .55 |

25th World Weight Lifting Championships, Lima.

Flag, Family, Soldier's Head — AP106

**1971, Oct. 4**

| | | | | |
|---|---|---|---|---|
| **C328** | AP106 | 7.50s blk, lt bl & red | .90 | .30 |
| *a.* | | Souv. sheet of 1, imperf. | 2.50 | 2.50 |

3rd anniv. of the revolution of the armed forces.

"Sacramento" — AP107

**1971, Oct. 8**

| | | | | |
|---|---|---|---|---|
| **C329** | AP107 | 7.50s lt bl & dk bl | 1.10 | .55 |

Sesquicentennial of Peruvian Navy.

Peruvian Order of the Sun AP108

**1971, Oct. 8**

| | | | | |
|---|---|---|---|---|
| **C330** | AP108 | 7.50s multi | .60 | .30 |

Sequicentennial of the Peruvian Order of the Sun.

### Liberation Type of Regular Issue

Design: 50s, Detail from painting "Progress of Liberation," by Teodoro Nuñez Ureta.

**1971, Nov. 4 Litho. *Perf. 13x13½***

| | | | | |
|---|---|---|---|---|
| **C331** | A217 | 50s multi | 6.50 | 2.25 |

2nd Ministerial meeting of the "Group of 77."

Fair Emblem AP109

**1971, Nov. 12 *Perf. 13***

| | | | | |
|---|---|---|---|---|
| **C332** | AP109 | 4.50s multi | .55 | .25 |

7th Pacific International Trade Fair.

### Fish Type of Regular Issue

3s, Pontinus furcirhinus dubius. 5.50s, Hogfish.

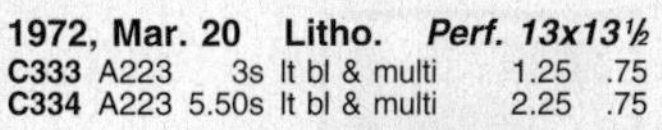
**1972, Mar. 20 Litho. *Perf. 13x13½***

| | | | | |
|---|---|---|---|---|
| **C333** | A223 | 3s lt bl & multi | 1.25 | .75 |
| **C334** | A223 | 5.50s lt bl & multi | 2.25 | .75 |

Teacher and Children, by Teodoro Nuñez Ureta AP110

**1972, Apr. 10 Litho. *Perf. 13x13½***

| | | | | |
|---|---|---|---|---|
| **C335** | AP110 | 6.50s multi | .60 | .30 |

Enactment of Education Reform Law.

White-tailed Trogon — AP111

2.50s, Amazonian umbrella bird. 3s, Peruvian cock-of-the-rock. 6.50s, Cuvier's toucan. 8.50s, Blue-crowned motmot.

**1972, June 19 Litho. *Perf. 13½x13***

| | | | | |
|---|---|---|---|---|
| **C336** | AP111 | 2s multi | 2.40 | 1.75 |
| **C337** | AP111 | 2.50s multi | 2.40 | 1.75 |
| **C338** | AP111 | 3s multi | 2.75 | 1.75 |
| **C339** | AP111 | 6.50s multi | 5.00 | 1.75 |
| **C340** | AP111 | 8.50s multi | 7.50 | 1.75 |
| | | *Nos. C336-C340 (5)* | 20.05 | 8.75 |

Quipu and Map of Americas AP112

**1972, Aug. 21**

| | | | | |
|---|---|---|---|---|
| **C341** | AP112 | 5s blk & multi | 1.00 | .50 |

4th Interamerican Philatelic Exhibition, EXFILBRA, Rio de Janeiro, Aug. 26-Sept. 2.

Inca Runner, Olympic Rings — AP113

**1972, Aug. 28**

| | | | | |
|---|---|---|---|---|
| **C342** | AP113 | 8s buff & multi | 1.10 | .55 |

20th Olympic Games, Munich, 8/26-9/11.

Woman of Catacaos, Piura — AP114

Regional Costumes: 2s, Tupe (Yauyos) woman of Lima. 4s, Indian with bow and arrow, from Conibo, Loreto. 4.50s, Man with calabash, Cajamarca. 5s, Moche woman, Trujillo. 6.50s, Man and woman of Ocongate, Cuzco. 8s, Chucupana woman, Ayacucho. 8.50s, Cotuncha woman, Junin. 10s, Woman of Puno dancing "Pandilla."

**1972-73 Design AP114**

| | | | |
|---|---|---|---|
| **C343** | 2s blk & multi | .45 | .45 |
| **C344** | 3.50s blk & multi | 1.25 | .70 |
| **C345** | 4s blk & multi | 1.50 | .80 |
| **C346** | 4.50s blk & multi | .90 | .90 |
| **C346A** | 5s blk & multi | .90 | .90 |
| **C347** | 6.50s blk & multi | 2.25 | 1.10 |
| **C347A** | 8s blk & multi | 1.75 | 1.40 |
| **C347B** | 8.50s blk & multi | 1.75 | 1.50 |
| **C348** | 10s blk & multi | 1.75 | 1.75 |
| | *Nos. C343-C348 (9)* | 12.50 | 9.50 |

Issued: 3.50s, 4s, 6.50s, 9/29/72; 2s, 4.50s, 10s, 4/30/73; 5s, 8s, 8.50s, 10/15/73.

Funerary Tower, Sillustani, Puno — AP115

Archaeological Monuments: 1.50s, Stone of the 12 angles, Cuzco. 3.50s, Ruins of Chavin, Ancash. 5s, Wall and gate, Chavin, Ancash. 8s, Ruins of Machu Picchu.

***Perf. 13½x13, 13x13½***

**1972, Oct. 16 Litho.**

| | | | | |
|---|---|---|---|---|
| **C349** | AP115 | 1.50s multi | .50 | .25 |
| **C350** | AP115 | 3.50s multi, horiz. | .75 | .25 |
| **C351** | AP115 | 4s multi | .75 | .25 |
| **C352** | AP115 | 5s multi, horiz. | 1.10 | .40 |
| **C353** | AP115 | 8s multi, horiz. | 1.75 | .55 |
| | | *Nos. C349-C353 (5)* | 4.85 | 1.70 |

AP116

Inca ponchos, various textile designs.

**1973, Jan. 29 Litho. *Perf. 13½x13***

| | | | | |
|---|---|---|---|---|
| **C354** | AP116 | 2s multi | .55 | .50 |
| **C355** | AP116 | 3.50s multi | .75 | .50 |
| **C356** | AP116 | 4s multi | .75 | .50 |
| **C357** | AP116 | 5s multi | .75 | .55 |
| **C358** | AP116 | 8s multi | 1.90 | .55 |
| | | *Nos. C354-C358 (5)* | 4.70 | 2.60 |

AP117

Antique Jewelry: 1.50s, Goblets and Ring, Mochica, 10th cent. 2.50s, Golden hands and arms, Lambayeque, 12th cent. 4s, Gold male statuette, Mochica, 8th ceny. 5s, Two gold brooches, Nazca, 8th cent. 8s, Flayed puma, Mochica, 8th cent.

**1973, Mar. 19 Litho. *Perf. 13½x13***

| | | | | |
|---|---|---|---|---|
| **C359** | AP117 | 1.50s multi | 1.10 | .80 |
| **C360** | AP117 | 2.50s multi | 1.10 | .80 |
| **C361** | AP117 | 4s multi | 1.10 | .80 |
| **C362** | AP117 | 5s multi | 1.50 | 1.25 |
| **C363** | AP117 | 8s multi | 2.75 | .80 |
| | | *Nos. C359-C363 (5)* | 7.55 | 4.45 |

Andean Condor — AP118

Protected Animals: 5s, Vicuña. 8s, Spectacled bear.

**1973, Apr. 16 Litho. *Perf. 13½x13***

**C364** AP118 4s blk & multi .55 .25
**C365** AP118 5s blk & multi .75 .40
**C366** AP118 8s blk & multi 1.60 .70
*Nos. C364-C366 (3)* 2.90 1.35

See Nos. C372-C376, C411-C412.

Indian Guide, by José Sabogal — AP119

Peruvian Paintings: 8.50s, Portrait of a Lady, by Daniel Hernandez. 20s, Man Holding Figurine, by Francisco Laso.

**1973, May 7 Litho. *Perf. 13½x13***

**C367** AP119 1.50s multi .40 .40
**C368** AP119 8.50s multi .80 .60
**C369** AP119 20s multi 2.50 1.10
*Nos. C367-C369 (3)* 3.70 2.10

Basket and World Map AP120

**1973, May 26 *Perf. 13x13½***

**C370** AP120 5s green .65 .30
**C371** AP120 20s lil rose 2.50 1.00

1st International Basketball Festival.

Darwin's Rhea — AP121

3.50s, Giant otter. 6s, Greater flamingo. 8.50s, Bush dog, horiz. 10s, Chinchilla, horiz.

**1973, Sept. 3 Litho. *Perf. 13½x13***

**C372** AP121 2.50s shown 1.75 1.00
**C373** AP121 3.50s multi 2.75 1.25
**C374** AP121 6s multi 3.50 1.25
**C375** AP121 8.50s multi 3.50 1.75
**C376** AP121 10s multi 4.50 2.50
*Nos. C372-C376 (5)* 16.00 7.75

Protected animals.

Orchid — AP122

Designs: Various orchids.

**1973, Sept. 27**

**C377** AP122 1.50s blk & multi 1.00 .75
**C378** AP122 2.50s blk & multi 1.75 .75
**C379** AP122 3s blk & multi 2.00 .75
**C380** AP122 3.50s blk & multi 2.25 .75
**C381** AP122 8s blk & multi 5.00 .75
*Nos. C377-C381 (5)* 12.00 3.75

Pacific Fair Emblem — AP123

**1973, Nov. 14 Litho. *Perf. 13½x13***

**C382** AP123 8s blk, red & gray 1.10 .45

8th International Pacific Fair, Lima.

Cargo Ship ILO AP124

Designs: 2.50s, Boats of Pescaperu fishing organization. 8s, Jet and seagull.

**1973, Dec. 14 Litho. *Perf. 13***

**C383** AP124 1.50s multi .25 .25
**C384** AP124 2.50s multi .40 .30
**C385** AP124 8s multi 1.25 .30
*Nos. C383-C385 (3)* 1.90 .85

Issued to promote government enterprises.

Lima Monument AP125

**1973, Nov. 27 *Perf. 13***

**C386** AP125 8.50s red & multi 1.10 .35

50th anniversary of Air Force Academy. Monument honors Jorge Chavez, Peruvian aviator.

Bridge at Yananacu, by Enrique Camino Brant AP126

Paintings: 10s, Peruvian Birds, by Teodoro Nuñez Ureta, vert. 50s, Boats of Totora, by Jorge Vinatea Reinoso.

**1973, Dec. 28 *Perf. 13x13½, 13½x13***

**C387** AP126 8s multi 1.10 .30
**C388** AP126 10s multi 1.75 .65
**C389** AP126 50s multi 7.00 3.25
*Nos. C387-C389 (3)* 9.85 4.20

Moral House, Arequipa AP127

2.50s, El Misti Mountain, Arequipa. 5s, Puya Raymondi (cacti), vert. 6s, Huascaran Mountain. 8s, Lake Querococha. Views on 5s, 6s, 8s are views in White Cordilleras Range, Ancash Province.

**1974, Feb. 11**

**C390** AP127 1.50s multi .25 .25
**C391** AP127 2.50s multi .50 .25
**C392** AP127 5s multi .75 .25
**C393** AP127 6s multi 1.10 .25
**C394** AP127 8s multi 1.75 .65
*Nos. C390-C394 (5)* 4.35 1.65

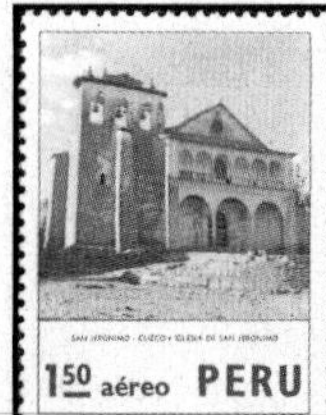

San Jeronimo's, Cuzco — AP128

Churches of Peru: 3.50s, Cajamarca Cathedral. 5s, San Pedro's, Zepita-Puno, horiz. 6s, Cuzco Cathedral. 8.50s, Santo Domingo, Cuzco.

**1974, May 6**

**C395** AP128 1.50s multi .75 .30
**C396** AP128 3.50s multi .75 .30
**C397** AP128 5s multi 1.25 .30
**C398** AP128 6s multi 1.25 .40
**C399** AP128 8.50s multi 2.10 .50
*Nos. C395-C399 (5)* 6.10 1.80

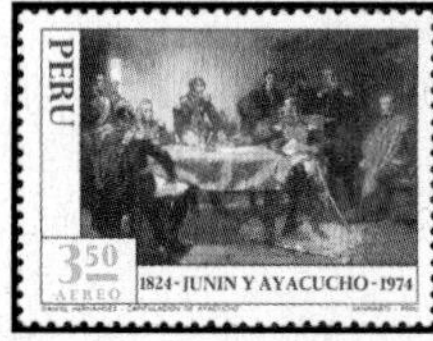

Surrender at Ayacucho, by Daniel Hernandez AP129

Designs: 6s, Battle of Junin, by Felix Yañex. 7.50s, Battle of Ayachucho, by Felix Yañez.

**1974 Litho. *Perf. 13x13½***

**C400** AP129 3.50s multi .55 .25
**C401** AP129 6s multi .90 .30
**C402** AP129 7.50s multi .90 .30
**C403** AP129 8.50s multi 1.10 .30
**C404** AP129 10s multi 1.25 .60
*Nos. C400-C404 (5)* 4.70 1.75

Sesquicentennial of the Battles of Junin and Ayacucho and of the surrender at Ayacucho. Issued: 7.50s, 8/6; 6s, 10/9; others, 12/9.

Chavin Stone, Ancash AP130

Machu Picchu, Cuzco AP131

#C407, C409, Different bas-reliefs from Chavin Stone. #C408, Baths of Tampumacchay, Cuzco. #C410, Ruins of Kencco, Cuzco.

**1974, Mar. 25 *Perf. 13½x13, 13x13½***

**C405** AP130 3s multi 1.10 .25
**C406** AP131 3s multi .75 .25
**C407** AP130 5s multi 2.00 .65
**C408** AP131 5s multi .85 .25
**C409** AP130 10s multi 2.00 .65
**C410** AP131 10s multi 1.75 .25
*Nos. C405-C410 (6)* 8.45 2.30

Cacajao Rubicundus AP132

**1974, Oct. 21 *Perf. 13½x13***

**C411** AP132 8s multi 1.10 .45
**C412** AP132 20s multi 2.75 1.10

Protected animals.

Inca Gold Mask AP133

**1974, Nov. 8 *Perf. 13x13½***

**C413** AP133 8s yel & multi 1.90 .60

8th World Mining Congress, Lima.

Chalan, Horseman's Cloak — AP134

**1974, Nov. 11 Litho. *Perf. 13½x13***

**C414** AP134 5s multi .55 .25
**C415** AP134 8.50s multi 1.10 .55

Pedro Paulet and Aerial Torpedo AP135

**1974, Nov. 28 Litho. *Perf. 13x13½***

**C416** AP135 8s bl & vio .75 .35

UPU, cent. Pedro Paulet, inventor of the mail-carrying aerial torpedo.

**Christmas Type of 1974**

Design: 6.50s, Indian Nativity scene.

**1974, Dec. 20 *Perf. 13½x13***

**C417** A235 6.50s multi .55 .30


Andean Village, Map of South American West Coast AP136

**1974, Dec. 30**

**C418** AP136 6.50s multi .65 .40

Meeting of Communications Ministers of Andean Pact countries.

Map of Peru, Modern Buildings, UN Emblem — AP137

**1975, Mar. 12 Litho. *Perf. 13½x13***

**C419** AP137 6s blk, gray & red .55 .45

2nd United Nations Industrial Development Organization Conference, Lima.

**Nos. C187, C211 and C160 Surcharged with New Value and Heavy Bar in Dark Blue**

**Wmk. 346**

**1975, April Litho. *Perf. 12***

**C420** AP51 2s on 4.30s org .45 .25

***Perf. 13½x14, 13x14***

**Unwmk.**

**C421** AP51 2.50s on 4.60s org .55 .25
**C422** AP51 5s on 3.80s org .60 .40
*Nos. C420-C422 (3)* 1.60 .90

World Map and Peruvian Colors AP138

**1975, Aug. 25 Litho. *Perf. 13x13½***
**C423** AP138 6.50s lt bl, vio bl & red 1.10 .30

Conference of Foreign Ministers of Nonaligned Countries.

Map of Peru and Flight Route AP139

**1975, Oct. 23 Litho. *Perf. 13x13½***
**C424** AP139 8s red, pink & blk 1.00 .30

AeroPeru's first flights: Lima-Rio de Janeiro, Lima-Los Angeles.

Fair Poster — AP140

**1975, Nov. 21 Litho. *Perf. 13½x13***
**C425** AP140 6s blk, bis & red .75 .30

9th International Pacific Fair, Lima, 1975.

Col. Francisco Bolognesi AP141

**1975, Dec. 23 Litho. *Perf. 13½x13***
**C426** AP141 20s multi 2.75 1.10

160th birth anniv. of Col. Bolognesi.

Indian Mother and Child — AP142

**1976, Feb. 23 Litho. *Perf. 13½x13***
**C427** AP142 6s gray & multi .75 .30

Christmas 1975.

Inca Messenger, UPAE Emblem — AP143

**1976, Mar. 19 Litho. *Perf. 13½x13***
**C428** AP143 5s red, blk & tan .75 .30

11th Congress of the Postal Union of the Americas and Spain, UPAE.

### Nos. C187, C211, C160, C209, C210 Surcharged in Dark Blue or Violet Blue (No Bar)

| **1976** | | | **As Before** | |
|---|---|---|---|---|
| **C429** | AP51 | 2s on 4.30s org | .25 | .25 |
| **C430** | AP51 | 3.50s on 4.60s org | .25 | .25 |
| **C431** | AP51 | 4.50s on 3.80s org | .25 | .25 |
| **C432** | AP51 | 5s on 4.30s org | .35 | .25 |
| **C433** | AP51 | 6s on 4.60s org | .55 | .25 |
| **C434** | A184 | 10s on 2.60s brt grn | .65 | .40 |
| **C435** | AP52 | 50s on 3.60s lil rose (VB) | 3.75 | 3.00 |
| | | *Nos. C429-C435 (7)* | 6.05 | 4.65 |

### Stamps of 1962-67 Surcharged with New Value and Heavy Bar in Black, Red, Green, Dark Blue or Orange

| **1976-77** | | | **As Before** | |
|---|---|---|---|---|
| **C436** | AP52 | 1.50s on 3.60s (Bk) #C210 | .35 | .25 |
| **C437** | A184 | 2s on 2.60s (R) #C209 ('77) | .35 | .25 |
| **C438** | AP52 | 2s on 3.60s (G) #C210 | .35 | .25 |
| **C439** | AP80 | 2s on 4.30s (Bk) #C199 | .35 | .25 |
| **C440** | A184 | 3s on 2.60s (Bk) #C209 ('77) | .35 | .25 |
| **C441** | A184 | 4s on 2.60s (DBl) #C209 | .45 | .30 |
| **C442** | AP52 | 4s on 3.60s (DBl) #C210 ('77) | .45 | .30 |
| **C443** | AP51 | 5s on 4.30s (R) #C187 | .65 | .30 |
| **C444** | AP83 | 6s on 4.60s (Bk) #C208 ('77) | .65 | .30 |
| **C445** | AP51 | 6s on 4.60s (DBl) #C211 ('77) | .65 | .30 |
| **C446** | AP51 | 7s on 4.30s (Bk) #C187 ('77) | .45 | .30 |
| **C447** | AP52 | 7.50s on 3.60s (DBl) #C210 | .75 | .40 |
| **C448** | AP52 | 8s on 3.60s (O) #C210 | 1.00 | .30 |
| **C449** | AP51 | 10s on 4.30s (Bk) #C187 ('77) | .55 | .30 |
| **C450** | AP51 | 10s on 4.60s (DBl) #C211 | 1.10 | .30 |
| **C451** | AP86 | 24s on 3.60s (Bk) #C220 ('77) | 2.75 | .95 |
| **C452** | AP86 | 28s on 4.60s (Bk) #C221 ('77) | 2.25 | 1.10 |
| **C453** | AP86 | 32s on 5.60s (Bk) #C222 ('77) | 2.25 | 1.10 |
| **C454** | A184 | 50s on 2.60s (O) #C209 ('77) | 5.00 | 1.75 |
| **C455** | AP52 | 50s on 3.60s (G) #C210 | 4.00 | 2.25 |
| | | *Nos. C436-C455 (20)* | 24.70 | 11.50 |

AP144

Map of Tacna and Tarata Provinces.

**1976, Aug. 28 Litho. *Perf. 13½x13***
**C456** AP144 10s multi .75 .30

Re-incorporation of Tacna Province into Peru, 47th anniversary.

AP145

Investigative Police badge.

**1976, Sept. 15 Litho. *Perf. 13½x13***
**C457** AP145 20s multi 1.25 .70

Investigative Police of Peru, 54th anniv.

Declaration of Bogota — AP146

**1976, Sept. 22**
**C458** AP146 10s multi .75 .30

Declaration of Bogota for cooperation and world peace, 10th anniversary.

AP147

Pal Losonczi and map of Hungary.

**1976, Nov. 2 Litho. *Perf. 13½x13***
**C459** AP147 7s ultra & blk .75 .30

Visit of Pres. Pal Losonczi of Hungary, Oct. 1976.

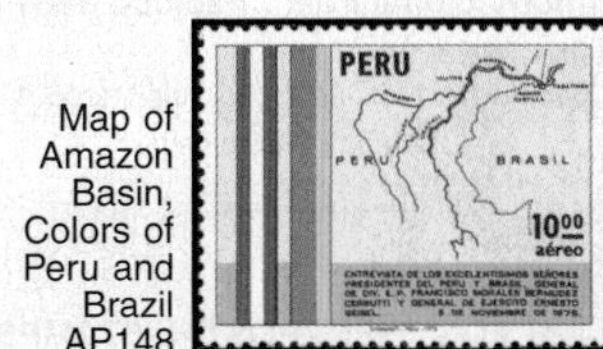

Map of Amazon Basin, Colors of Peru and Brazil AP148

**1976, Dec. 16 Litho. *Perf. 13***
**C460** AP148 10s bl & multi .75 .30

Visit of Gen. Ernesto Geisel, president of Brazil, Nov. 5, 1976.

Liberation Monument, Lima AP149

**1977, Mar. 9 Litho. *Perf. 13x13½***
**C461** AP149 20s red buff & blk 1.60 .65

Army Day.

Map of Peru and Venezuela, South America AP150

**1977, Mar. 14**
**C462** AP150 12s buff & multi 1.10 .55

Meeting of Pres. Francisco Morales Bermudez Cerrutti of Peru and Pres. Carlos Andres Perez of Venezuela, Dec. 1976.

Electronic Tree — AP151

**1977, May 30 Litho. *Perf. 13½x13***
**C463** AP151 20s gray, red & blk 2.10 .75

World Telecommunications Day.

Map of Peru, Refinery, Tanker — AP152

**1977, July 13 Litho. *Perf. 13½x13***
**C464** AP152 14s multi .75 .45

Development of Bayovar oil complex.

### Messenger Type of 1977

| **1977** | **Litho.** | ***Perf. 13½x13*** | | |
|---|---|---|---|---|
| **C465** | A243 | 24s mag & blk | 1.75 | .75 |
| **C466** | A243 | 28s bl & blk | 2.75 | .75 |
| **C467** | A243 | 32s rose brn & blk | 1.75 | 1.10 |
| | | *Nos. C465-C467 (3)* | 6.25 | 2.60 |

For surcharge see No. C502.

Arms of Arequipa AP153

**1977, Sept. 3 Litho. *Perf. 13½x13***
**C468** AP153 10s multi .35 .25

Gold of Peru Exhibition, Arequipa 1977.

Gen. Jorge Rafael Videla — AP154

**1977, Oct. 8 Litho. *Perf. 13½x13***
**C469** AP154 36s multi 1.10 .40

Visit of Jorge Rafael Videla, president of Argentina.

### Stamps of 1953-67 Surcharged with New Value and Heavy Bar in Black, Dark Blue or Green

**1977** **As Before**

**C470** AP83 2s on 3.60s #C207 .35 .25
**C471** AP51 2s on 4.60s (DB) #C211 .35 .25
**C472** AP51 4s on 4.60s (DB) #C211 .45 .25
**C473** AP51 5s on 4.30s #C187 .55 .40
**C474** AP52 5s on 3.60s #C210 .35 .25
**C475** AP55 10s on 2.15s #C125 .75 .30
**C476** AP52 10s on 3.60s (DB) #C210 1.25 .45
**C477** AP84 10s on 3.60s #C215 1.10 .45
**C478** AP52 20s on 3.60s (DB) #C210 1.10 .55
**C479** AP51 100s on 3.80s (G) #C160 5.00 3.00
*Nos. C470-C479 (10)* 11.25 6.15

### Nos. C223-C224 Surcharged with New Value, Heavy Bars and: "FRANQUEO"

**1977** **Litho.** ***Perf. 12***

**C480** AP87 6s on 3.60s multi 1.10 .65
**C481** AP87 8s on 3.60s multi 1.40 .90
**C482** AP87 10s on 5.60s multi 1.40 1.00
*Nos. C480-C482 (3)* 3.90 2.55

Adm. Miguel Grau — AP155

**1977, Dec. 15** **Litho.** ***Perf. 13½x13***

**C483** AP155 28s multi .75 .45

Navy Day. Miguel Grau (1838-1879), Peruvian naval commander.

### Christmas Type of 1977

**1977, Dec. 23**

**C484** A246 20s Indian Nativity .70 .35

Andrés Bello, Flag and Map of Participants AP156

**1978, Jan. 12** **Litho.** ***Perf. 13***

**C485** AP156 30s multi .60 .35

8th Meeting of Education Ministers honoring Andrés Bello, Lima.

### Inca Type of 1978

**1978** **Litho.** ***Perf. 13½x13***

**C486** A247 24s dp rose lil .65 .45
**C487** A247 30s salmon .75 .45
**C488** A247 65s brt bl 1.75 1.00
**C489** A247 95s dk bl 2.50 1.60
*Nos. C486-C489 (4)* 5.65 3.50

For surcharge see No. C501.

Antenna, ITU Emblem AP157

**1978, July 3** **Litho.** ***Perf. 13x13½***

**C490** AP157 50s gray & multi 1.25 1.25

10th World Telecommunications Day.

San Martin, Flag Colors of Peru and Argentina AP158

**1978, Sept. 4** **Litho.** ***Perf. 13½x13***

**C491** AP158 30s multi .75 .75

Gen. José de San Martin (1778-1850), soldier and statesman, protector of Peru.

### Stamps of 1965-67 Surcharged "Habilitado / R.D. No. O118" and New Value in Red, Green, Violet Blue or Black

**1978** **Litho.**

**C492** AP83 34s on 4.60s multi (R) #C208 .55 .40
**C493** AP79 40s on 4.30s multi (G) #C196 .65 .50
**C494** A184 70s on 2.60s brt grn (VB) #C209 1.10 .85
**C495** AP52 110s on 3.60s lil rose (Bk) #C210 2.25 1.10
**C496** AP80 265s on 4.30s gray & multi (Bk) #C199 4.00 3.25
*Nos. C492-C496 (5)* 8.55 6.10

### Stamps and Type of 1968-78 Surcharged in Violet Blue, Black or Red

**1978** **Litho.**

**C497** AP86 25s on 4.60s (VB) #C221 .55 .50
**C498** A247 45s on 28s dk grn (Bk) 1.10 .55
**C499** A247 75s on 28s dk grn (R) 1.75 1.10
**C500** AP86 105s on 5.60s (R) #C222 2.50 1.75
*Nos. C497-C500 (4)* 5.90 3.90

Nos. C498-C499 not issued without surcharge.

### Nos. C486, C467 Surcharged

**1980, Apr. 14** **Litho.** ***Perf. 13½x13***

**C501** A247 35s on 24s dp rose lil .55 .45
**C502** A243 45s on 32s rose brn & blk .60 .50

### No. C130 Surcharged in Black

**1981, Nov.** **Engr.** ***Perf. 13***

**C503** AP57 30s on 2.20s multi .50 .45
**C504** AP57 40s on 2.20s multi .50 .40

### No. C130 Surcharged and Overprinted in Green: "12 Feria / Internacional / del / Pacifico 1981"

**1981, Nov. 30**

**C505** AP57 140s on 2.20s multi 2.00 1.25

12th Intl. Pacific Fair.

---

## AIR POST SEMI-POSTAL STAMPS

**Catalogue values for unused stamps in this section are for Never Hinged items.**

Chavin Griffin SPAP1

1.50s+1s, Bird. 3s+2.50s, Cat. 4.30s+3s, Mythological figure, vert. 6s+ 4s, Chavin god, vert.

***Perf. 12½x12, 12x12½***

**1963, Apr. 18** **Litho.** **Wmk. 346**

**Design in Gray and Brown**

**CB1** SPAP1 1s + 50c sal pink .35 .35
**CB2** SPAP1 1.50s + 1s blue .55 .55
**CB3** SPAP1 3s + 2.50s lt grn .85 .85
**CB4** SPAP1 4.30s + 3s green 1.60 1.60
**CB5** SPAP1 6s + 4s citron 2.00 2.00
*Nos. CB1-CB5 (5)* 5.35 5.35

The designs are from ceramics found by archaeological excavations of the 14th century Chavin culture. The surtax was for the excavations fund.

Henri Dunant and Centenary Emblem SPAP2

***Perf. 12½x12***

**1964, Jan. 29** **Unwmk.**

**CB6** SPAP2 1.30s + 70c multi .55 .55
**CB7** SPAP2 4.30s + 1.70s multi 1.10 1.10

Centenary of International Red Cross.

---

## SPECIAL DELIVERY STAMPS

No. 149 Overprinted in Black

**1908** **Unwmk.** ***Perf. 12***

**E1** A25 10c gray black 25.00 19.00

No. 172 Overprinted in Violet

**1909**

**E2** A40 10c red brn & blk 40.00 22.50

No. 181 Handstamped in Violet

**1910**

**E3** A49 10c deep blue 24.00 20.00

Two handstamps were used to make No. E2. Impressions from them measure 22½x6½mm and 24x6½mm.

Counterfeits exist of Nos. E1-3.

---

## POSTAGE DUE STAMPS

Coat of Arms — D1

Steamship and Llama
D2 D3

D4

D5

### With Grill

**1874-79** **Unwmk.** **Engr.** ***Perf. 12***

**J1** D1 1c bister ('79) .45 .30
**J2** D2 5c vermilion .55 .30
**J3** D3 10c orange .65 .30
**J4** D4 20c blue 1.10 .55
**J5** D5 50c brown 17.00 6.50
*Nos. J1-J5 (5)* 19.75 7.95

A 2c green exists, but was not regularly issued.

For overprints and surcharges see Nos. 157, J6-J31, J37-J38, 8N14-8N15, 14N18.

**1902-07** **Without Grill**

*J1a* D1 1c bister .35
*J2a* D2 5c vermilion .55
*J3a* D3 10c orange .55
*J4a* D4 20c blue .65
*Nos. J1a-J4a (4)* 2.10

Nos. J1-J5 Overprinted in Blue or Red

**1881** **"PLATA" 2½mm High**

**J6** D1 1c bis (Bl) 6.00 5.00
**J7** D2 5c ver (Bl) 12.00 11.00
- *a.* Double overprint
- *b.* Inverted overprint 24.00 24.00

**J8** D3 10c org (Bl) 12.00 11.00
- *a.* Inverted overprint 24.00 24.00

**J9** D4 20c bl (R) 45.00 32.50
**J10** D5 50c brn (Bl) 100.00 90.00
*Nos. J6-J10 (5)* 175.00 149.50

*In the reprints of this overprint "PLATA" is 3mm high instead of 2½mm. Besides being struck in the regular colors it was also applied to the 1, 5, 10 and 50c in red and the 20c in blue.*

Overprinted in Red

**1881**

**J11** D1 1c bister 9.00 9.00
**J12** D2 5c vermilion 11.00 10.00
**J13** D3 10c orange 13.00 13.00
**J14** D4 20c blue 55.00 37.50
**J15** D5 50c brown 125.00 125.00
*Nos. J11-J15 (5)* 213.00 194.50

*Originals of Nos. J11 to J15 are overprinted in brick-red, oily ink; reprints in thicker, bright red ink. The 5c exists with reprinted overprint in blue.*

### Overprinted "Union Postal Universal Lima Plata" in Oval in first named color and Triangle in second named color

**1883**

**J16** D1 1c bis (Bl & Bk) 9.00 6.50
**J17** D1 1c bis (Bk & Bl) 13.00 13.00
**J18** D2 5c ver (Bl & Bk) 13.00 13.00
**J19** D3 10c org (Bl & Bk) 13.00 13.00
**J20** D4 20c bl (R & Bk) *850.00 850.00*
**J21** D5 50c brn (Bl & Bk) 60.00 60.00

*Reprints of Nos. J16 to J21 have the oval overprint with "PLATA" 3mm. high. The 1c also exists with the oval overprint in red.*

Overprinted in Black

**1884**

**J22** D1 1c bister .90 .90
**J23** D2 5c vermilion .90 .90
**J24** D3 10c orange .90 .90
**J25** D4 20c blue 1.90 .90
**J26** D5 50c brown 5.50 1.75
*Nos. J22-J26 (5)* 10.10 5.35

The triangular overprint is found in 11 types.

### Overprinted "Lima Correos" in Circle in Red and Triangle in Black

**1884**

**J27** D1 1c bister 42.50 42.50

*Reprints of No. J27 have the overprint in bright red. At the time they were made the overprint was also printed on the 5, 10, 20 and 50c Postage Due stamps.*

*Postage Due stamps overprinted with Sun and "CORREOS LIMA" (as shown above No. 103), alone or in combination with the "U. P. U. LIMA" oval or "LIMA CORREOS" in double-lined circle, are fancy varieties made to sell to collectors and never placed in use.*

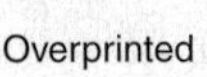
Overprinted

**1896-97**

**J28** D1 1c bister .65 .55
*a.* Double overprint
**J29** D2 5c vermilion .75 .45
*a.* Double overprint
*b.* Inverted overprint
**J30** D3 10c orange 1.00 .65
*a.* Inverted overprint
**J31** D4 20c blue 1.25 .85
*a.* Double overprint
**J32** A22 50c red ('97) 1.25 .85
**J33** A23 1s brown ('97) 1.90 1.25
*a.* Double overprint
*b.* Inverted overprint
*Nos. J28-J33 (6)* 6.80 4.60

Liberty — D6

**1899** **Engr.**

**J34** D6 5s yel grn 1.90 *10.50*
**J35** D6 10s dl vio 1,700. 1,700.

For surcharge see No. J39.

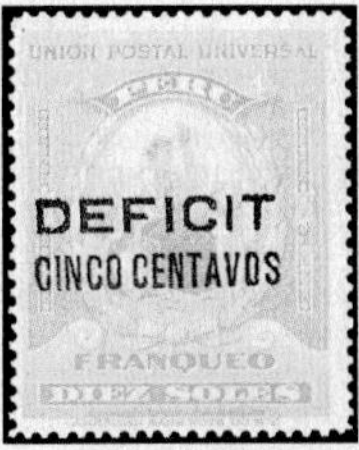

No. J36 No. J37

**1902** **On No. 159**

**J36** A31 5c on 10s bl grn 1.90 1.50
*a.* Double surcharge 20.00 20.00

**On No. J4**

**J37** D4 1c on 20c blue 1.10 .75
*a.* "DEFICIT" omitted 15.00 3.50
*b.* "DEFICIT" double 15.00 3.50
*c.* "UN CENTAVO" double 15.00 3.50
*d.* "UN CENTAVO" omitted 18.00 10.00

### Surcharged Vertically

**J38** D4 5c on 20c blue 2.75 1.75

No. J35 Surcharged Diagonally

**J39** D6 1c on 10s dull vio .75 .75
*Nos. J36-J39 (4)* 6.50 4.75

D7

**1909** **Engr.** ***Perf. 12***

**J40** D7 1c red brown .90 .30
**J41** D7 5c red brown .90 .30
**J42** D7 10c red brown 1.10 .45
**J43** D7 50c red brown 1.75 .45
*Nos. J40-J43 (4)* 4.65 1.50

**1921** **Size: 18¼x22mm**

**J44** D7 1c violet brown .45 .30
**J45** D7 2c violet brown .45 .30
**J46** D7 5c violet brown .65 .30
**J47** D7 10c violet brown .90 .45
**J48** D7 50c violet brown 2.75 1.25
**J49** D7 1s violet brown 13.00 5.25
**J50** D7 2s violet brown 22.50 6.50
*Nos. J44-J50 (7)* 40.70 14.35

Nos. J49 and J50 have the circle at the center replaced by a shield containing "S/.", in addition to the numeral.

In 1929 during a shortage of regular postage stamps, some of the Postage Due stamps of 1921 were used instead.

See Nos. J50A-J52, J55-J56. For surcharges see Nos. 204-207, 757.

### Type of 1909-22

**Size: 18¾x23mm**

**J50A** D7 2c violet brown 1.25 .30
**J50B** D7 10c violet brown 1.75 .45

### Type of 1909-22 Issues

**1932** **Photo.** ***Perf. 14½x14***

**J51** D7 2c violet brown 1.25 .45
**J52** D7 10c violet brown 1.25 .45

Regular Stamps of 1934-35 Overprinted in Black

**1935** ***Perf. 13***

**J53** A131 2c deep claret 1.25 .50
**J54** A117 10c crimson 1.25 .50

### Type of 1909-32

Size: 19x23mm

Imprint: "Waterlow & Sons, Limited, Londres."

**1936** **Engr.** ***Perf. 12½***

**J55** D7 2c light brown .45 .45
**J56** D7 10c gray green .90 .90

## OFFICIAL STAMPS

Regular Issue of 1886 Overprinted in Red

**1890, Feb. 2**

**O2** A17 1c dl vio 2.40 2.40
*a.* Double overprint 14.00 14.00
**O3** A18 2c green 2.40 2.40
*a.* Double overprint
*b.* Inverted overprint 14.00 14.00
**O4** A19 5c orange 3.50 2.75
*a.* Inverted overprint 14.00 14.00
*b.* Double overprint 14.00 14.00
**O5** A20 10c slate 2.00 1.25
*a.* Double overprint 14.00 14.00
*b.* Inverted overprint 14.00 14.00
**O6** A21 20c blue 5.50 3.50
*a.* Double overprint 14.00 14.00
*b.* Inverted overprint 14.00 14.00
**O7** A22 50c red 7.25 3.25
*a.* Inverted overprint 20.00
*b.* Double overprint
**O8** A23 1s brown 9.00 8.00
*a.* Double overprint 27.50 27.50
*b.* Inverted overprint 27.50 27.50
*Nos. O2-O8 (7)* 32.05 23.55

### Nos. 118-124 (Bermudez Ovpt.) Overprinted Type "a" in Red

**1894, Oct.**

**O9** A17 1c green 2.40 2.40
*a.* "Gobierno" and head invtd. 11.00 9.25
*b.* Dbl. ovpt. of "Gobierno"
**O10** A17 1c orange 40.00 32.50
**O11** A18 2c rose 2.40 2.40
*a.* Overprinted head inverted 17.00 17.00
*b.* Both overprints inverted
**O12** A18 2c violet 2.40 2.40
*a.* "Gobierno" double
**O13** A19 5c ultra 40.00 32.50
*a.* Both overprints inverted
**O14** A19 5c blue 19.00 16.00
**O15** A20 10c green 6.00 6.00
**O16** A22 50c green 9.00 9.00
*Nos. O9-O16 (8)* 121.20 103.20

### Nos. 125-126 ("Horseshoe" Ovpt.) Overprinted Type "a" in Red

**O17** A18 2c vermilion 3.50 3.50
**O18** A19 5c blue 3.50 3.50

### Nos. 105, 107, 109, 113 Overprinted Type "a" in Red

**1895, May**

**O19** A17 1c vermilion 13.00 13.00
**O20** A18 2c dp ultra 13.00 13.00
**O21** A12 5c claret 11.00 11.00
**O22** A14 20c dp ultra 11.00 11.00
*Nos. O19-O22 (4)* 48.00 48.00

Nos. O2-O22 have been extensively counterfeited.

Nos. 141, 148, 149, 151 Overprinted in Black

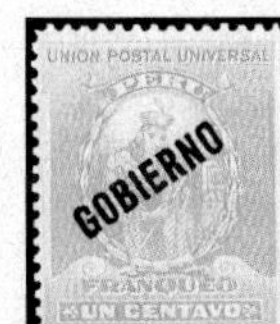


**1896-1901**

**O23** A24 1c ultra .35 .30
**O24** A25 10c yellow 1.00 .50
*a.* Double overprint 22.50
**O25** A25 10c gray blk ('01) .35 .30
**O26** A26 50c brt rose 5.00 5.00
*Nos. O23-O26 (4)* 6.70 6.10

O1

**1909-14** **Engr.** ***Perf. 12***

**Size: 18½x22mm**

**O27** O1 1c red .55 .30
*a.* 1c brown red .55 .30
**O28** O1 1c orange ('14) .90 .65
**O29** O1 10c bis brn ('14) .35 .30
*a.* 10c violet brown .90 .45
**O30** O1 50c ol grn ('14) 1.25 .65
*a.* 50c blue green 2.00 .65

**Size: 18¾x23½mm**

**O30B** O1 10c vio brn .90 .30
*Nos. O27-O30B (5)* 3.95 2.20

See Nos. O31, O33-O34. For overprints and surcharge see Nos. 201-203, 760.

**1933** **Photo.** ***Perf. 15x14***

**O31** O1 10c violet brown 1.25 .45

No. 319 Overprinted in Black

**1935** **Unwmk.** ***Perf. 13***

**O32** A117 10c crimson .35 .25

### Type of 1909-33

Imprint: "Waterlow & Sons, Limited, Londres."

**1936** **Engr.** ***Perf. 12½***

**Size: 19x23mm**

**O33** O1 10c light brown .25 .25
**O34** O1 50c gray green .65 .65

## PARCEL POST STAMPS

PP1

PP2

PP3

**1897** **Typeset** **Unwmk.** ***Perf. 12***

**Q1** PP1 1c dull lilac 4.00 3.50
**Q2** PP2 2c bister 5.50 3.75
*a.* 2c olive 5.50 3.75
*b.* 2c yellow 5.50 3.75
*c.* Laid paper 65.00 65.00
**Q3** PP3 5c dk bl 19.00 10.50
*a.* Tête bêche pair *375.00*
**Q4** PP3 10c vio brn 24.00 18.00
**Q5** PP3 20c rose red 29.00 22.50
**Q6** PP3 50c bl grn 85.00 75.00
*Nos. Q1-Q6 (6)* 166.50 133.25

Surcharged in Black

**1903-04**

**Q7** PP3 1c on 20c rose red 12.00 10.00
**Q8** PP3 1c on 50c bl grn 12.00 10.00
**Q9** PP3 5c on 10c vio brn 80.00 65.00
*a.* Inverted surcharge 125.00 110.00
*b.* Double surcharge
*Nos. Q7-Q9 (3)* 104.00 85.00

## POSTAL TAX STAMPS

### Plebiscite Issues

These stamps were not used in Tacna and Arica (which were under Chilean occupation) but were used in Peru to pay a supplementary tax on letters, etc.

It was intended that the money derived from the sale of these stamps should be used to help defray the expenses of the plebiscite.

Morro Arica — PT1

Adm. Grau and Col. Bolognesi Reviewing Troops — PT2

Bolognesi Monument PT3

**1925-26 Unwmk. Litho. *Perf. 12***

**RA1** PT1 5c dp bl 2.75 .75
**RA2** PT1 5c rose red 1.40 .55
**RA3** PT1 5c yel grn 1.25 .55
**RA4** PT2 10c brown 5.50 *22.50*
**RA5** PT3 50c bl grn 35.00 17.00
*Nos. RA1-RA5 (5)* 45.90 41.35

PT4

**1926**

**RA6** PT4 2c orange 1.10 .30

PT5

**1927-28**

**RA7** PT5 2c dp org 1.10 .30
**RA8** PT5 2c red brn 1.10 .30
**RA9** PT5 2c dk bl 1.10 .30
**RA10** PT5 2c gray vio 1.10 .30
**RA11** PT5 2c bl grn ('28) 1.10 .30
**RA12** PT5 20c red 5.50 1.75
*Nos. RA7-RA12 (6)* 11.00 3.25

PT6

**1928 Engr.**

**RA13** PT6 2c dk vio .55 .25

The use of the Plebiscite stamps was discontinued July 26, 1929, after the settlement of the Tacna-Arica controversy with Chile.

For overprint see No. 261.

### Unemployment Fund Issues

These stamps were required in addition to the ordinary postage, on every letter or piece of postal matter. The money obtained by their sale was to assist the unemployed.

Nos. 273-275 Surcharged

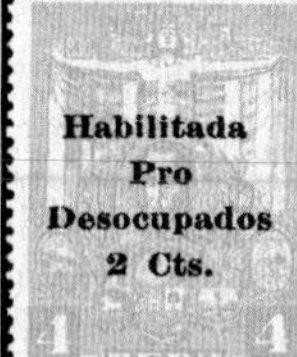

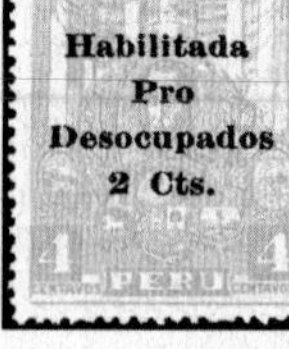



**1931**

**RA14** A95 2c on 4c red 1.75 .75
*a.* Inverted surcharge 4.25 4.25
**RA15** A95 2c on 10c bl grn .75 .75
*a.* Inverted surcharge 4.25 4.25
**RA16** A95 2c on 15c sl gray .75 .75
*a.* Inverted surcharge 4.25 4.25
*Nos. RA14-RA16 (3)* 3.25 2.25

"Labor" — PT7

Two types of Nos. RA17-RA18:
I — Imprint 15mm.
II — Imprint 13¾mm.

***Perf. 12x11½, 11½x12***

**1931-32 Litho.**

**RA17** PT7 2c emer (I) .25 .25
*a.* Type II .25
**RA18** PT7 2c rose car (I) ('32) .25 .25
*a.* Type II .25

Blacksmith — PT8

**1932-34**

**RA19** PT8 2c dp gray .25 .25
**RA20** PT8 2c pur ('34) .35 .25

Monument of 2nd of May — PT9

***Perf. 13, 13½, 13x13½***

**1933-35 Photo.**

**RA21** PT9 2c bl vio .25 .25
**RA22** PT9 2c org ('34) .25 .25
**RA23** PT9 2c brn vio ('35) .25 .25
*Nos. RA21-RA23 (3)* .75 .75

For overprint see No. RA27.

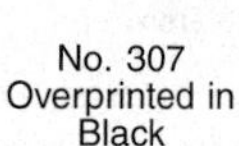

No. 307 Overprinted in Black

**1934 *Perf. 13½***

**RA24** A111 2c green .25 .25
*a.* Inverted overprint 2.25 2.00

No. 339 Overprinted in Black

**1935**

**RA25** A131 2c deep claret .25 .25

### No. 339 Overprinted Type "a" in Black

**1936 Unwmk. *Perf. 13½***

**RA26** A131 2c deep claret .25 .25

No. RA23 Overprinted in Black

**1936 *Perf. 13x13½***

**RA27** PT9 2c brn vio .25 .25
*a.* Double overprint 3.50
*b.* Overprint reading down 3.50
*c.* Overprint double, reading down 3.50

St. Rosa of Lima — PT10

**1937 Engr. *Perf. 12***

**RA28** PT10 2c car rose .25 .25

Nos. RA27 and RA28 represented a tax to help erect a church.

"Protection" by John Q. A. Ward — PT11

**Imprint: "American Bank Note Company"**

**1938 Litho.**

**RA29** PT11 2c brown .35 .25

The tax was to help the unemployed. See Nos. RA30, RA34, RA40.

**Type of 1938 Redrawn**

Imprint: "Columbian Bank Note Company."

**1943 *Perf. 12½***

**RA30** PT11 2c dl claret brn .35 .25

See note above #RA14. See #RA34, RA40.

**Catalogue values for unused stamps in this section, from this point to the end of the section, are for Never Hinged items.**

PT12 PT13

**Black Surcharge**

**1949 *Perf. 12½, 12***

**RA31** PT12 3c on 4c vio bl 1.10 .25
**RA32** PT13 3c on 10c blue 1.10 .25

The tax was for an education fund.

Symbolical of Education — PT14

**1950 Typo. *Perf. 14***
**Size: 16½x21mm**

**RA33** PT14 3c dp car .25 .25

See Nos. RA35, RA39, RA43

For surcharges see Nos. 501B, 761, 764-766, RA45-RA48, RA58.

**Type of 1938**

Imprint: "Thomas De La Rue & Co. Ltd."

**1951 Litho.**

**RA34** PT11 2c lt redsh brn .25 .25

**Type of 1950**

Imprint: "Thomas De La Rue & Company, Limited."

**1952 Unwmk. *Perf. 14, 13***
**Size: 16½x21½mm**

**RA35** PT14 3c brn car .25 .25

Emblem of Congress — PT15

**1954 *Rouletted 13***

**RA36** PT15 5c bl & red .35 .25

The tax was to help finance the National Marian Eucharistic Congress.

For surcharges see Nos. 758B, 768.

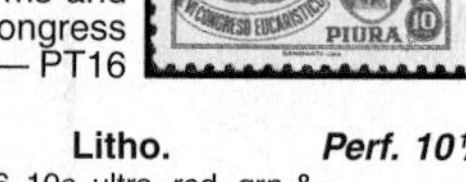

Piura Arms and Congress Emblem — PT16

**1960 Litho. *Perf. 10½***

**RA37** PT16 10c ultra, red, grn & yel .25 .25
*a.* Green ribbon inverted
**RA38** PT16 10c ultra & red .35 .25

Nos. RA37-RA38 were used to help finance the 6th National Eucharistic Congress, Piura, Aug. 25-28. Obligatory on all domestic mail until Dec. 31, 1960. Both stamps exist imperf.

**Type of 1950**

Imprint: "Bundesdruckerei Berlin"

**1961 Size: 17½x22½mm *Perf. 14***

**RA39** PT14 3c dp car .25 .25

**Type of 1938**

Imprint: "Harrison and Sons Ltd"

**1962, Apr. Litho. *Perf. 14x14½***

**RA40** PT11 2c lt brn .25 .25

For surcharges see Nos. 501A, 674-678, 681-682, 709-711, 757.

Symbol of Eucharist — PT17

**1962, May 8 *Rouletted 11***

**RA41** PT17 10c bl & org .25 .25

Issued to raise funds for the Seventh National Eucharistic Congress, Huancayo, 1964. Obligatory on all domestic mail.

See No. RA42. For surcharges and overprint see Nos. 735, 762, RA44.

**1962 Imprint: "Iberia"**

**RA42** PT17 10c bl & org .25 .25

**Type of 1950**
**Imprint: "Thomas de La Rue"**
**Size: 18x22mm**

**1965, Apr. Litho. *Perf. 12½x12***

**RA43** PT14 3c light carmine .25 .25

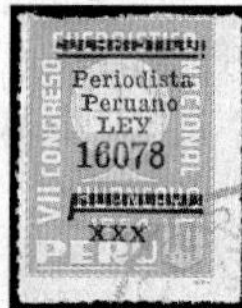



Type of 1962 Overprinted in Red

**Imprint: "Iberia"**

**1966, July 2 Litho.** ***Pin Perf.***

**RA44** PT17 10c vio & org .25 .25

### No. RA43 Surcharged in Green or Black

b

c

d

**1966-67** ***Perf. 12½x12***

**RA45** PT14 (b) 10c on 3c (G) 1.25 .25
**RA46** PT14 (c) 10c on 3c (Bk) 1.25 .25
**RA47** PT14 (c) 10c on 3c (G) .35 .25
**RA48** PT14 (d) 10c on 3c (G) .35 .25
*Nos. RA45-RA48 (4)* 3.20 1.00

The surtax of Nos. RA44-RA48 was for the Peruvian Journalists' Fund.

Pen Made of Newspaper — PT18

**1967, Dec. Litho.** ***Perf. 11***

**RA49** PT18 10c dk red & blk .25 .25

The surtax was for the Peruvian Journalists' fund.

For surcharges see Nos. RA56-RA57.

Temple at Chan-Chan — PT19

Designs: No. RA51, Side view of temple. Nos. RA52-RA55, Various stone bas-reliefs from Chan-Chan.

**1967, Dec. 27**

**RA50** PT19 20c bl & multi .25 .25
**RA51** PT19 20c lil rose & multi .25 .25
**RA52** PT19 20c brt bl & blk .25 .25
**RA53** PT19 20c emer & blk .25 .25
**RA54** PT19 20c sep & blk .25 .25
**RA55** PT19 20c lil rose & blk .25 .25
*Nos. RA50-RA55 (6)* 1.50 1.50

The surtax was for the excavations at Chan-Chan, northern coast of Peru. (Mochica-Chimu pre-Inca period).

### Type of 1967 Surcharged in Red: "VEINTE / CENTAVOS / R.S. 16-8-68"

Designs: No. RA56, Handshake. No. RA57, Globe and pen.

**1968, Oct. Litho.** ***Perf. 11***

**RA56** PT18 20c on 50c multi .90 .90
**RA57** PT18 20c on 1s multi .90 .90

Nos. RA56-RA57 without surcharge were not obligatory tax stamps.

No. C199 surcharged "PRO NAVIDAD/ Veinte Centavos/R.S. 5-11-68" was not a compulsory postal tax stamp.

### No. RA43 Srchd. Similar to Type "c"

**1968, Oct.** ***Perf. 12½x12***

**RA58** PT14 20c on 3c lt car .25 .25

Surcharge lacks quotation marks and 4th line reads: Ley 17050.

---

## OCCUPATION STAMPS

### Issued under Chilean Occupation

Stamps formerly listed as Nos. N1-N10 are regular issues of Chile canceled in Peru.

Stamps of Peru, 1874-80, Overprinted in Red, Blue or Black

**1881-82** ***Perf. 12***

**N11** A17 1c org (Bl) .50 1.00
*a.* Inverted overprint
**N12** A18 2c dk vio (Bk) .50 4.00
*a.* Inverted overprint 16.50
*b.* Double overprint 22.50
**N13** A18 2c rose (Bk) 1.60 *18.00*
*a.* Inverted overprint
**N14** A19 5c bl (R) 55.00 62.50
*a.* Inverted overprint
**N15** A19 5c ultra (R) 90.00 100.00
**N16** A20 10c grn (R) .50 *1.60*
*a.* Inverted overprint 6.50 6.50
*b.* Double overprint 12.00 12.00
**N17** A21 20c brn red (Bl) 80.00 125.00
*Nos. N11-N17 (7)* 228.10 312.10

*Reprints of No. N17 have the overprint in bright blue; on the originals it is in dull ultramarine. Nos. N11 and N12 exist with reprinted overprint in red or yellow. There are numerous counterfeits with the overprint in both correct and fancy colors.*

Same, with Additional Overprint in Black

**1882**

**N19** A17 1c grn (R) .50 .80
*a.* Arms inverted 8.25 10.00
*b.* Arms double 5.50 6.50
*c.* Horseshoe inverted 12.00 13.50
**N20** A19 5c bl (R) .80 .80
*a.* Arms inverted 13.50 15.00
*b.* Arms double 13.50 15.00
**N21** A22 50c rose (Bk) 1.60 2.00
*a.* Arms inverted 10.00
**N22** A22 50c rose (Bl) 1.60 2.75
**N23** A23 1s ultra (R) 3.25 4.50
*a.* Arms inverted 13.50
*b.* Horseshoe inverted 16.50
*c.* Arms and horseshoe inverted 20.00
*d.* Arms double 13.50
*Nos. N19-N23 (5)* 7.75 10.85

---

## PROVISIONAL ISSUES

### Stamps Issued in Various Cities of Peru during the Chilean Occupation of Lima and Callao

During the Chilean-Peruvian War which took place in 1879 to 1882, the Chilean forces occupied the two largest cities in Peru, Lima & Callao. As these cities were the source of supply of postage stamps, Peruvians in other sections of the country were left without stamps and were forced to the expedient of making provisional issues from whatever material was at hand. Many of these were former canceling devices made over for this purpose. Counterfeits exist of many of the overprinted stamps.

### ANCACHS

(See Note under "Provisional Issues")

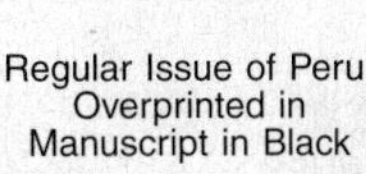

Regular Issue of Peru, Overprinted in Manuscript in Black

**1884 Unwmk.** ***Perf. 12***

**1N1** A19 5c blue 57.50 55.00

Regular Issues of Peru, Overprinted in Black

**1N2** A19 5c blue 18.00 16.50

Regular Issues of Peru, Overprinted in Black

**1N3** A19 5c blue 90.00 82.50
**1N4** A20 10c green 55.00 40.00
**1N5** A20 10c slate 55.00 35.00

### Same, with Additional Overprint "FRANCA"

**1N6** A20 10c green 82.50 42.50

Overprinted

**1N7** A19 5c blue 30.00 25.00
**1N8** A20 10c green 30.00 25.00

### Same, with Additional Overprint "FRANCA"

**1N9** A20 10c green

Revenue Stamp of Peru, 1878-79, Ovptd. in Black "CORREO FISCAL" and/or "FRANCA" — A1

**1N10** A1 10c yellow 37.50 37.50

---

### APURIMAC

(See Note under "Provisional Issues")

### Provisional Issue of Arequipa Overprinted in Black

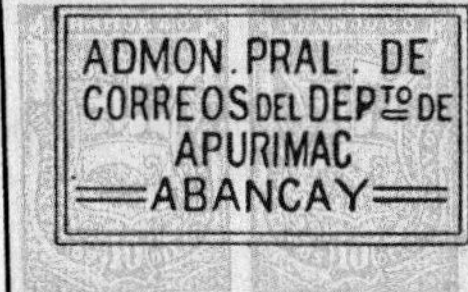


### Overprint Covers Two Stamps

**1885 Unwmk.** ***Imperf.***

**2N1** A6 10c gray 100.00 90.00

Some experts question the status of No. 2N1.

---

### AREQUIPA

(See Note under "Provisional Issues")

Coat of Arms
A1 A2

### Overprint ("PROVISIONAL 1881-1882") in Black

**1881, Jan. Unwmk.** ***Imperf.***

**3N1** A1 10c blue 2.50 3.50
*a.* 10c ultramarine 2.50 4.00
*b.* Double overprint 12.00 13.50
*c.* Overprinted on back of stamp 8.25 10.00
**3N2** A2 25c rose 2.50 6.00
*a.* "2" in upper left corner invtd. 8.25
*b.* "Cevtavos" 8.25 10.00
*c.* Double overprint 12.00 13.50

The overprint also exists on 5s yellow.

The overprints "1883" in large figures or "Habilitado 1883" are fraudulent.

For overprints see Nos. 3N3, 4N1, 8N1, 10N1, 15N1-15N3.

With Additional Overprint Handstamped in Red

**1881, Feb.**

**3N3** A1 10c blue 3.50 3.50
*a.* 10c ultramarine 13.50 11.50

A4

**1883** **Litho.**

**3N7** A4 10c dull rose 3.50 5.00
*a.* 10c vermilion 3.50 5.00

### Overprinted in Blue like No. 3N3

**3N9** A4 10c vermilion 5.00 4.00
*a.* 10c dull rose 5.00 4.00

See No. 3N10. For overprints see Nos. 8N2, 8N9, 10N2, 15N4.

*Reprints of No. 3N9 are in different colors from the originals, orange, bright red, etc. They are printed in sheets of 20 instead of 25.*

### Redrawn

**3N10** A4 10c brick red (Bl) 160.00

The redrawn stamp has small triangles without arabesques in the lower spandrels. The palm branch at left of the shield and other parts of the design have been redrawn.

### Same Overprint in Black, Violet or Magenta On Regular Issues of Peru

**1884 Embossed with Grill** ***Perf. 12***

**3N11** A17 1c org (Bk, V or M) 6.50 6.50
**3N12** A18 2c dk vio (Bk) 6.50 6.50
**3N13** A19 5c bl (Bk, V or M) 2.00 1.40
*a.* 5c ultramarine (Bk or M) 8.25 6.50
**3N15** A20 10c sl (Bk) 3.50 2.50
**3N16** A21 20c brn red (Bk, V or M) 25.00 25.00
**3N18** A22 50c grn (Bk or V) 25.00 25.00
**3N20** A23 1s rose (Bk or V) 35.00 35.00
*Nos. 3N11-3N20 (7)* 103.50 101.90

A5

A6

Rear Admiral M. L. Grau
A7

Col. Francisco Bolognesi
A8

### Same Overprint as on Previous Issues

**1885** ***Imperf.***

**3N22** A5 5c olive (Bk) 5.25 5.25
**3N23** A6 10c gray (Bk) 5.25 4.75
**3N25** A7 5c blue (Bk) 5.25 4.75
**3N26** A8 10c olive (Bk) 5.25 3.25
*Nos. 3N22-3N26 (4)* 21.00 18.00

For overprints see Nos. 2N1, 8N5-8N6, 8N12-8N13, 10N9, 10N12, 15N10-15N12.

*These stamps have been reprinted without overprint; they exist however with forged overprint. Originals are on thicker paper with distinct mesh, reprints on paper without mesh.*

**Without Overprint**

*3N22a* A5 5c olive 5.25 5.25
*3N23a* A6 10c gray 4.00 3.25
*3N25a* A7 5c blue 4.00 3.25
*3N26a* A8 10c olive 4.00 3.25
*Nos. 3N22a-3N26a (4)* 17.25 15.00

## AYACUCHO

(See Note under "Provisional Issues")

Provisional Issue of Arequipa Overprinted in Black

**1881 Unwmk. *Imperf.***
**4N1** A1 10c blue 150.00 125.00
*a.* 10c ultramarine 150.00 125.00

## CHACHAPOYAS

(See Note under "Provisional Issues")

Regular Issue of Peru Overprinted in Black

**1884 Unwmk. *Perf. 12***
**5N1** A19 5c ultra 190.00 160.00

## CHALA

(See Note under "Provisional Issues")

Regular Issues of Peru Overprinted in Black

**1884 Unwmk. *Perf. 12***
**6N1** A19 5c blue 17.00 13.00
**6N2** A20 10c slate 22.50 16.00

## CHICLAYO

(See Note under "Provisional Issues")

Regular Issue of Peru Overprinted in Black

**1884 Unwmk. *Perf. 12***
**7N1** A19 5c blue 29.00 18.00

Same, Overprinted **FRANCA**

**7N2** A19 5c blue 65.00 37.50

## CUZCO

(See Note under "Provisional Issues")

Provisional Issues of Arequipa Overprinted in Black

**1881-85 Unwmk. *Imperf.***
**8N1** A1 10c blue 125.00 110.00
**8N2** A4 10c red 125.00 110.00

**Overprinted "CUZCO" in an oval of dots**

**8N5** A5 5c olive 200.00 175.00
**8N6** A6 10c gray 200.00 175.00

**Regular Issue of Peru Overprinted in Black "CUZCO" in a Circle**

***Perf. 12***

**8N7** A19 5c blue 50.00 50.00

Provisional Issues of Arequipa Overprinted in Black

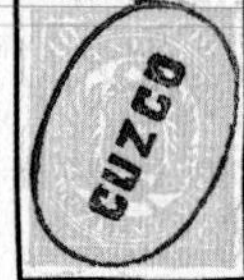


**1883 *Imperf.***
**8N9** A4 10c red 18.00 18.00

**Same Overprint in Black on Regular Issues of Peru**

**1884 *Perf. 12***
**8N10** A19 5c blue 29.00 18.00
**8N11** A20 10c slate 29.00 18.00

**Same Overprint in Black on Provisional Issues of Arequipa**

***Imperf***

**8N12** A5 5c olive 27.50 27.50
**8N13** A6 10c gray 8.00 8.00

Postage Due Stamps of Peru Surcharged in Black

***Perf. 12***

**8N14** D1 10c on 1c bis 200.00 175.00
**8N15** D3 10c on 10c org 200.00 175.00

## HUACHO

(See Note under "Provisional Issues")

Regular Issues of Peru Overprinted in Black

**1884 Unwmk. *Perf. 12***
**9N1** A19 5c blue 16.00 16.00
**9N2** A20 10c green 13.00 13.00
**9N3** A20 10c slate 27.50 27.50
*Nos. 9N1-9N3 (3)* 56.50 56.50

## MOQUEGUA

(See Note under "Provisional Issues")

Provisional Issues of Arequipa Overprinted in Violet

Overprint 27mm wide.

**1881-83 Unwmk. *Imperf.***
**10N1** A1 10c blue 75.00 70.00
**10N2** A4 10c red ('83) 75.00 70.00

**Same Overprint on Regular Issues of Peru in Violet**

**1884 *Perf. 12***
**10N3** A17 1c orange 75.00 70.00
**10N4** A19 5c blue 55.00 35.00

**Red Overprint**

**10N5** A19 5c blue 65.00 55.00

**Same Overprint in Violet on Provisional Issues of Peru of 1880**

***Perf. 12***

**10N6** A17 1c grn (R) 12.00 9.75
**10N7** A18 2c rose (Bl) 15.00 15.00
**10N8** A19 5c bl (R) 30.00 30.00

**Same Overprint in Violet on Provisional Issue of Arequipa**

**1885 *Imperf.***
**10N9** A6 10c gray 85.00 42.50

Regular Issues of Peru Overprinted in Violet

**10N10** A19 5c blue 200.00 125.00
**10N11** A20 10c slate 85.00 42.50

Same Overprint in Violet on Provisional Issue of Arequipa

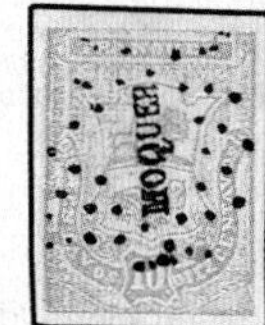

***Imperf***

**10N12** A6 10c gray 125.00 110.00

## PAITA

(See Note under "Provisional Issues")

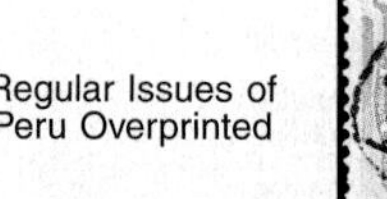
Regular Issues of Peru Overprinted

**Black Overprint**

**1884 Unwmk. *Perf. 12***
**11N1** A19 5c blue 40.00 40.00
*a.* 5c ultramarine 40.00 40.00
**11N2** A20 10c green 27.50 27.50
**11N3** A20 10c slate 40.00 40.00

**Red Overprint**

**11N4** A19 5c blue 40.00 40.00

Overprint lacks ornaments on #11N4-11N5.

**Violet Overprint Letters 5½mm High**

**11N5** A19 5c ultra 40.00 40.00
*a.* 5c blue

## PASCO

(See Note under "Provisional Issues")

Regular Issues of Peru Overprinted in Magenta or Black

**1884 Unwmk. *Perf. 12***
**12N1** A19 5c blue (M) 27.50 12.50
*a.* 5c ultramarine (M) 42.50 22.50
**12N2** A20 10c green (Bk) 65.00 55.00
**12N3** A20 10c slate (Bk) 125.00 90.00
*Nos. 12N1-12N3 (3)* 217.50 157.50

## PISCO

(See Note under "Provisional Issues")

Regular Issue of Peru Overprinted in Black

**1884 Unwmk. *Perf. 12***
**13N1** A19 5c blue 350.00 275.00

## PIURA

(See Note under "Provisional Issues")

Regular Issues of Peru Overprinted in Black

**1884 Unwmk. *Perf. 12***
**14N1** A19 5c blue 35.00 21.00
*a.* 5c ultramarine 45.00 27.50
**14N2** A21 20c brn red 150.00 150.00
**14N3** A22 50c green 350.00 350.00

**Same Overprint in Black on Provisional Issues of Peru of 1881**

**14N4** A17 1c grn (R) 35.00 35.00
**14N5** A18 2c rose (Bl) 55.00 55.00
**14N6** A19 5c ultra (R) 70.00 70.00

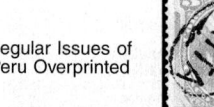

Regular Issues of Peru Overprinted in Violet, Black or Blue **PIURA**

**14N7** A19 5c bl (V) 27.50 18.00
*a.* 5c ultramarine (V) 27.50 18.00
*b.* 5c ultramarine (Bk) 27.50 18.00
**14N8** A21 20c brn red (Bk) 150.00 150.00
**14N9** A21 20c brn red (Bl) 150.00 150.00

**Same Overprint in Black on Provisional Issues of Peru of 1881**

**14N10** A17 1c grn (R) 35.00 35.00
**14N11** A19 5c bl (R) 42.50 42.50
*a.* 5c ultramarine (R) 70.00 70.00

Regular Issues of Peru Overprinted in Black

**14N13** A19 5c blue 7.25 6.50
**14N14** A21 20c brn red 150.00 150.00

Regular Issues of Peru Overprinted in Black

**14N15** A19 5c ultra 110.00 100.00
**14N16** A21 20c brn red 250.00 225.00

**Same Overprint on Postage Due Stamp of Peru**

**14N18** D3 10c orange 125.00 125.00

## PUNO

(See Note under "Provisional Issues")

Provisional Issue of Arequipa Overprinted in Violet or Blue

Diameter of outer circle 20½mm, PUNO 11½mm wide, M 3½mm wide.

Other types of this overprint are fraudulent.

| 1882-83 | Unwmk. | | *Imperf.* |
|---|---|---|---|
| **15N1** A1 10c blue (V) | | 29.00 | 29.00 |
| *a.* 10c ultramarine (V) | | 35.00 | 35.00 |
| **15N3** A2 25c red (V) | | 45.00 | 35.00 |
| **15N4** A4 10c dl rose (Bl) | | 29.00 | 29.00 |
| *a.* 10c vermilion (Bl) | | 29.00 | 29.00 |

The overprint also exists on 5s yellow of Arequipa.

Same Overprint in Magenta on Regular Issues of Peru

| 1884 | | *Perf. 12* |
|---|---|---|
| **15N5** A17 1c orange | 19.00 | 15.00 |
| **15N6** A18 2c violet | 65.00 | 65.00 |
| **15N7** A19 5c blue | 10.00 | 10.00 |

**Violet Overprint**

| | | |
|---|---|---|
| **15N8** A19 5c blue | 10.00 | 10.00 |
| *a.* 5c ultramarine | 20.00 | 20.00 |

**Same Overprint in Black on Provisional Issues of Arequipa**

| 1885 | | *Imperf.* |
|---|---|---|
| **15N10** A5 5c olive | 16.00 | 13.50 |
| **15N11** A6 10c gray | 10.00 | 10.00 |
| **15N12** A8 10c olive | 19.00 | 19.00 |

Regular Issues of Peru Overprinted in Magenta

| 1884 | | *Perf. 12* |
|---|---|---|
| **15N13** A17 1c orange | 21.00 | 21.00 |
| **15N14** A18 2c violet | 24.00 | 21.00 |
| **15N15** A19 5c blue | 10.00 | 10.00 |
| *a.* 5c ultramarine | 20.00 | 20.00 |
| **15N16** A20 10c green | 29.00 | 22.50 |
| **15N17** A21 20c brn red | 150.00 | 150.00 |
| **15N18** A22 50c green | | |

## YCA

(See Note under "Provisional Issues")

Regular Issues of Peru Overprinted in Violet

| 1884 | Unwmk. | | *Perf. 12* |
|---|---|---|---|
| **16N1** A17 1c orange | | 70.00 | 70.00 |
| **16N3** A19 5c blue | | 22.50 | 18.00 |

**Black Overprint**

| | | |
|---|---|---|
| **16N5** A19 5c blue | 19.00 | 9.00 |

**Magenta Overprint**

| | | |
|---|---|---|
| **16N6** A19 5c blue | 19.00 | 9.00 |
| **16N7** A20 10c slate | 55.00 | 55.00 |

Regular Issues of Peru Overprinted in Black

| | | |
|---|---|---|
| **16N12** A19 5c blue | 275.00 | 225.00 |
| **16N13** A21 20c brown | 350.00 | 275.00 |

Regular Issues of Peru Overprinted in Carmine

| | | |
|---|---|---|
| **16N14** A19 5c blue | 275.00 | 225.00 |
| **16N15** A20 10c slate | 350.00 | 275.00 |

Same, with Additional Overprint

| | | |
|---|---|---|
| **16N21** A19 5c blue | 275.00 | 275.00 |
| **16N22** A21 20c brn red | 475.00 | 450.00 |

Various other stamps exist with the overprints "YCA" and "YCA VAPOR" but they are not known to have been issued. Some of them were made to fill a dealer's order and others are reprints or merely cancellations.

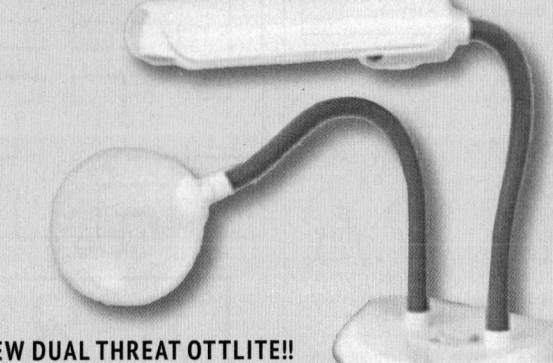

## PHILIPPINES

ˌfi-lə-ˈpēnz

LOCATION — Group of about 7,100 islands and islets in the Malay Archipelago, north of Borneo, in the North Pacific Ocean
GOVT. — Republic
AREA — 115,830 sq. mi.
POP. — 68,614,536 (1995)
CAPITAL — Manila

The islands were ceded to the United States by Spain in 1898. On November 15, 1935, they were given their independence, subject to a transition period. The Japanese occupation from 1942 to early 1945 delayed independence until July 4, 1946. On that date the Commonwealth became the Republic of the Philippines.

20 Cuartos = 1 Real
100 Centavos de Peso = 1 Peso (1864)
100 Centimos de Escudo = 1 Escudo (1871)
100 Centimos de Peseta = 1 Peseta (1872)
1000 Milesimas de Peso = 100 Centimos or Centavos = 1 Peso (1878)
100 Cents = 1 Dollar (1899)
100 Centavos = 1 Peso (1906)
100 Centavos (Sentimos) = 1 Peso (Piso) (1946)

**Catalogue values for unused stamps in this country are for Never Hinged items, beginning with Scott 500 in the regular postage section, Scott B1 in the semi-postal section, Scott C64 in the air post section, Scott E11 in the special delivery section, Scott J23 in the postage due section, and Scott O50 in the officials section.**

### Watermarks

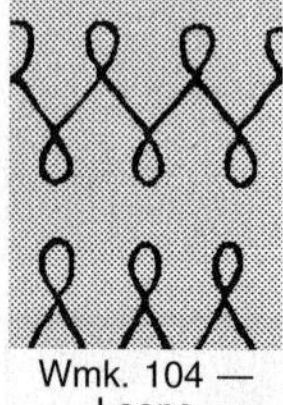
Wmk. 104 — Loops

Wmk. 257 — Curved Wavy Lines

Watermark 104: loops from different watermark rows may or may not be directly opposite each other.

Wmk. 190PI — Single-lined PIPS

Wmk. 191PI — Double-lined PIPS

Watermark 191 has double-lined USPS.

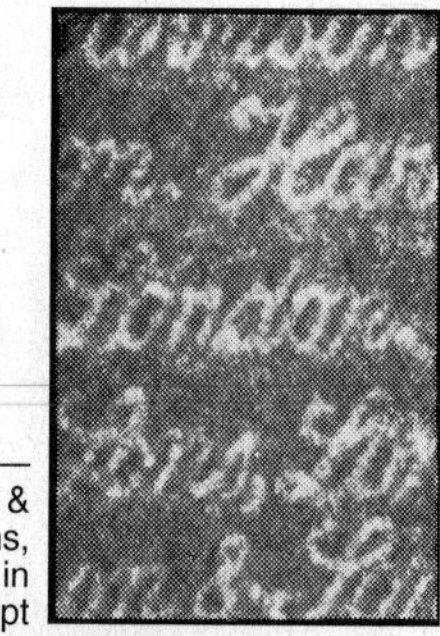
Wmk. 233 — "Harrison & Sons, London." in Script

Wmk. 372 — "RPKK" Multiple

Watermark 372 comes in two types: Type I - 24mm high Type II - 19mm high Type II was printed by the Japanese on white paper with white gum.

Wmk. 385

Wmk. 389

Wmk. 391 — Natl. Crest, Rising Sun and Eagle, with inscr. "REPUBLIKA / NG / PILIPINAS," "KAWANIHAN / NG / KOREO"

### Issued under Spanish Dominion

The stamps of Philippine Islands punched with a round hole were used on telegraph receipts or had been withdrawn from use and punched to indicate that they were no longer available for postage. In this condition they sell for less, as compared to postally used copies.

Many color varieties exist of Nos. 1-88. Only major varieties are listed.

Queen Isabella II
A1 A2

**1854 Unwmk. Engr. *Imperf.***

| | | | | |
|---|---|---|---|---|
| 1 | A1 | 5c orange | 4,000. | 350. |
| 2 | A1 | 10c carmine | 700. | 250. |
| *d.* | | 10c carmine, half used as 5c on cover | | 50,000. |
| 4 | A2 | 1r blue | 1,000. | 300. |
| *a.* | | 1r slate blue | 800. | 300. |
| 5 | A2 | 2r slate green | 1,000. | 250. |

Forty plate varieties of each value. Many color varieties exist.

A 10c black exists. This is a proof or an unissued trial color. Value about $8,000.

For overprints see Nos. 24A-25A.

A3

**1855 Litho.**

| | | | | |
|---|---|---|---|---|
| 6 | A3 | 5c pale red | 1,600. | 500. |

Four varieties.

A3a

**Redrawn**

| | | | | |
|---|---|---|---|---|
| 7 | A3a | 5c vermilion | *7,000.* | *1,100.* |

In the redrawn stamp the inner circle is smaller and is not broken by the labels at top and bottom. Only one variety.

Queen Isabella II — A4

**Blue Paper**

**1856 Typo. Wmk. 104**

| | | | | |
|---|---|---|---|---|
| 8 | A4 | 1r green | 100.00 | *75.00* |
| 9 | A4 | 2r carmine | 400.00 | 200.00 |

Nos. 8 and 9 used can be distinguished from Cuba Nos. 2 and 3 only by the cancellations.

For overprints, see Nos. 26-27.

Queen Isabella II — A5

**Dot After "CORREOS"**

**1859, Jan. 1 Litho. Unwmk.**

| | | | | |
|---|---|---|---|---|
| 10 | A5 | 5c vermilion | 15.00 | 8.00 |
| *a.* | | 5c scarlet | 24.00 | 12.00 |
| *b.* | | 5c orange | 32.50 | 17.50 |
| 11 | A5 | 10c lilac rose | 17.00 | *35.00* |

Four varieties of each value, repeated in the sheet.

For overprint see No. 28.

Dot after CORREOS
A6 A7

**1861-62**

| | | | | |
|---|---|---|---|---|
| 12 | A6 | 5c vermilion | 40.00 | 40.00 |
| 13 | A7 | 5c dull red ('62) | 190.00 | 95.00 |

No. 12, one variety only, repeated in the sheet.

For overprint see No. 29.

Colon after CORREOS — A8

A8a

A9

**1863**

| | | | | |
|---|---|---|---|---|
| 14 | A8 | 5c vermilion | 13.50 | 8.25 |
| 15 | A8 | 10c carmine | 37.50 | *250.00* |
| 16 | A8 | 1r violet | 850.00 | *3,000.* |
| 17 | A8 | 2r blue | 650.00 | *2,000.* |
| 18 | A8a | 1r gray grn | 500.00 | 140.00 |
| 20 | A9 | 1r green | 200.00 | 60.00 |
| | | *Nos. 14-20 (6)* | 2,251. | 5,458. |

No. 18 has "CORREOS" 10½mm long, the point of the bust is rounded and is about 1mm from the circle which contains 94 pearls.

No. 20 has "CORREOS" 11mm long, and the bust ends in a sharp point which nearly touches the circle of 76 pearls.

For overprints see Nos. 30-34.

A10

**1864 Typo.**

| | | | | |
|---|---|---|---|---|
| 21 | A10 | 3⅛c blk, *yellow* | 4.75 | 2.00 |
| 22 | A10 | 6⅝c grn, *rose* | 6.75 | 2.00 |
| 23 | A10 | 12⅘c blue, *sal* | 9.00 | 1.75 |
| 24 | A10 | 25c red, *buff* | 12.00 | 3.75 |
| | | *Nos. 21-24 (4)* | 32.50 | 9.50 |

For overprints see Nos. 35-38.

Preceding Issues Handstamped

**1868-74**

| | | | | |
|---|---|---|---|---|
| 24A | A1 | 5c orange ('74) | *8,000.* | *6,750.* |
| 25 | A2 | 1r sl bl ('74) | *2,800.* | *1,050.* |
| 25A | A2 | 2r grn ('74) | *9,000.* | *8,000.* |
| 26 | A4 | 1r grn, *bl* ('73) | 180.00 | 80.00 |
| 27 | A4 | 2r car, *bl* ('73) | 325.00 | 225.00 |
| 27A | A5 | 5c vermilion ('74) | *8,000.* | *10,000.* |
| 28 | A5 | 10c rose ('74) | 80.00 | 45.00 |
| 29 | A7 | 5c dull red ('73) | 250.00 | 175.00 |
| 30 | A8 | 5c ver ('72) | 115.00 | 35.00 |
| 30A | A8 | 10c car ('72) | *6,000.* | — |
| 31 | A8 | 1r vio ('72) | 700.00 | 600.00 |
| 32 | A8 | 2r bl ('72) | 500.00 | 425.00 |
| 33 | A8a | 1r gray grn ('71) | 175.00 | 85.00 |
| 34 | A9 | 1r grn ('71) | 50.00 | 30.00 |
| 35 | A10 | 3⅛c blk, *yellow* | 9.50 | 4.75 |
| 36 | A10 | 6⅝c grn, *rose* | 9.50 | 4.75 |
| 37 | A10 | 12⅘c bl, *salmon* | 27.50 | 12.00 |
| 38 | A10 | 25c red, *buff* | 29.00 | 15.00 |

Reprints exist of #24A-38. These have crisp, sharp letters and usually have a broken first "A" of "HABILITADO."

Imperforates

Imperforates of designs A11-A16 probably are from proof or trial sheets.

"Spain" — A11

**1871 Typo. *Perf. 14***

**39** A11 5c blue 95.00 9.25
**40** A11 10c deep green 15.00 6.00
**41** A11 20c brown 110.00 50.00
**42** A11 40c rose 170.00 60.00
*Nos. 39-42 (4)* 390.00 125.25

King Amadeo — A12

**1872**

**43** A12 12c rose 20.00 5.50
**44** A12 16c blue 190.00 37.50
**45** A12 25c gray lilac 13.50 5.50
**46** A12 62c violet 40.00 9.75
**47** A12 1p25c yellow brn 85.00 42.50
*Nos. 43-47 (5)* 348.50 100.75

A 12c in deep blue and a 62c in rose exist but were not issued. Value $30 each.

"Peace" — A13

**1874**

**48** A13 12c gray lilac 22.50 5.50
**49** A13 25c ultra 8.25 2.75
**50** A13 62c rose 65.00 5.50
**51** A13 1p25c brown 300.00 82.50
*Nos. 48-51 (4)* 395.75 96.25

King Alfonso XII — A14

**1875-77**

**52** A14 2c rose 3.50 .95
**53** A14 2c dk blue ('77) 260.00 100.00
**54** A14 6c orange ('77) 14.00 *16.00*
**55** A14 10c blue ('77) 4.50 .85
**56** A14 12c lilac ('76 4.50 .85
**57** A14 20c vio brn ('76 20.00 5.00
**58** A14 25c dp green ('76 25.00 5.00
*Nos. 52-58 (7)* 331.50 128.65

Imperforates of type A14 are from proof or trial sheets.

Nos. 52, 63 Handstamp Surcharged in Black or Blue

**1877-79**

**59** A14 12c on 2c rose (Bk) 85.00 22.50
*a.* Surcharge inverted *600.00 375.00*
*b.* Surcharge double *475.00 350.00*
**60** A16 12c on 25m blk (Bk) ('79) 105.00 47.50
*a.* Surcharge inverted *875.00 650.00*
**61** A16 12c on 25m blk (Bl) ('79) 350.00 225.00
*Nos. 59-61 (3)* 540.00 295.00

Forgeries of Nos. 59-61 exist.

A16

**1878-79 Typo.**

**62** A16 25m black 3.50 .45
**63** A16 25m green ('79) 67.50 *62.50*
**64** A16 50m dull lilac 34.00 10.00
**65** A16 0.0625 (62½m) gray 65.00 15.00
**66** A16 100m car ('79) 110.00 37.50
**67** A16 100m yel grn ('79) 10.00 2.75
**68** A16 125m blue 6.00 .50
**69** A16 200m rose ('79) 37.50 5.75
**70** A16 200m vio rose ('79) 350.00 *900.00*
**71** A16 250m bister ('79) 13.00 2.75
*Nos. 62-71 (10)* 696.50 *1,037.*

Imperforates of type A16 are from proof or trial sheets.

For surcharges see Nos. 60-61, 72-75.

### Stamps of 1878-79 Surcharged

a

b

**1879**

**72** A16 (a) 2c on 25m grn 55.00 11.00
*b.* Inverted surcharge 425.00 325.00
**73** A16 (a) 8c on 100m car 52.50 6.50
*a.* "COREROS" 150.00 80.00
*b.* Surcharge double *400.00* —
**74** A16 (b) 2c on 25m grn 300.00 57.50
**75** A16 (b) 8c on 100m car 400.00 57.50
*Nos. 72-75 (4)* 807.50 132.50

A19

Original state: The medallion is surrounded by a heavy line of color of nearly even thickness, touching the line below "Filipinas"; the opening in the hair above the temple is narrow and pointed.

1st retouch: The line around the medallion is thin, except at the upper right, and does not touch the horizontal line above it; the opening in the hair is slightly wider and rounded; the lock of hair above the forehead is shaped like a broad "V" and ends in a point; there is a faint white line below it, which is not found on the original. The shape of the hair and the width of the white line vary.

2nd retouch: The lock of hair is less pointed; the white line is much broader.

**1880-86 Typo.**

**76** A19 2c carmine .90 *.80*
**77** A19 2½c brown 8.00 1.90
**78** A19 2 4/8c ultra ('82) 1.25 2.25
**79** A19 2 4/8c ultra, 1st retouch ('83) .90 1.90
**80** A19 2 4/8c ultra, 2nd retouch ('86) 10.50 4.25
**81** A19 5c gray blue ('82) .90 *1.90*
**82** A19 6 2/8c dp grn ('82) 7.00 11.00
**83** A19 8c yellow brn 36.00 6.25
**84** A19 10c green 400.00 500.00
**85** A19 10c brn lil ('82) 3.75 *4.25*
**86** A19 12 4/8c brt rose ('82) 1.90 1.90
**87** A19 20c bis brn ('82) 3.50 1.75
**88** A19 25c dk brn ('82) 4.75 1.90
*Nos. 76-88 (13)* 479.35 540.05

See #137-139. For surcharges see #89-108, 110-111.

Surcharges exist double or inverted on many of Nos. 89-136. Several different surcharge types exist. There are many forgeries of the surcharges.

### Stamps and Type of 1880-86 Handstamp Surcharged in Black, Green or Red

c

d

e

f

**Design A19**

**1881-88 Black Surcharge**

**89** (c) 2c on 2½c 4.25 2.25
**91** (f) 10c on 2 4/8c (#80) ('87) 6.25 2.10
**92** (d) 20c on 8c brn ('83) 10.00 3.25
**93** (d) 1r on 2c ('83) 190.00 *325.00*
**94** (d) 2r on 2 4/8c (#78; '83) 6.25 2.10
*a.* On No. 79 57.50 *100.00*
*b.* On No. 80 110.00 *200.00*

Most used examples of No. 93 are hole punched. Postally used examples are rare.

**Green Surcharge**

**95** (e) 8c on 2c ('83) 11.00 2.25
**95A** (d+e) 8c on 1r on 2c ('83) 200.00 *275.00*
**96** (d) 10c on 2c ('83) 5.50 2.25
**97** (d) 1r on 2c ('83) 190.00 *225.00*
**98** (d) 1r on 5c gray bl ('83) 8.00 3.25
**99** (d) 1r on 8c brn ('83) 10.00 3.25

**Red Surcharge**

**100** (f) 1c on 2 4/8c (#79; '87) 1.25 *2.00*
**101** (f) 1c on 2 4/8c (#80; '87) 3.50 3.00
**102** (d) 16c on 2 4/8c (#78; '83) 10.00 3.25
**103** (d) 1r on 2c ('83) 6.25 3.25
On cover 550.00
**104** (d) 1r on 5c bl gray ('83) 12.00 5.25

### Handstamp Surcharged in Magenta

g

h

**1887**

**105** A19 (g) 8c on 2 4/8c (#79) 1.25 .90
**106** A19 (g) 8c on 2 4/8c (#80) 3.50 2.00

**1888**

**107** A19 (h) 2 4/8c on 1c gray grn 1.75 1.00
**108** A19 (h) 2 4/8c on 5c bl gray 1.90 .90
**109** N1 (h) 2 4/8c on 1/8c grn 1.90 1.40
**110** A19 (h) 2 4/8c on 50m bis 1.90 .80
**111** A19 (h) 2 4/8c on 10c grn 1.75 .65
*Nos. 107-111 (5)* 9.20 4.75

No. 109 is surcharged on a newspaper stamp of 1886-89 and has the inscriptions shown on cut N1.

### On Revenue Stamps

R1

R2

R3(d)

Handstamp Surcharged in Black, Yellow, Green, Red, Blue or Magenta

j

k

m

**1881-88 Black Surcharge**

**112** R1(c) 2c on 10c bis 50.00 12.50
**113** R1(j) 2 4/8c on 10c bis 12.00 1.75
**114** R1(j) 2 4/8c on 2r bl 200.00 140.00
**115** R1(j) 8c on 10c bis *450.00 6,000.*
**116** R1(j) 8c on 2r bl 8.50 2.10
**118** R1(d) 1r on 12 4/8c gray bl ('83) 7.75 3.75
**119** R1(d) 1r on 10c bis ('82) 11.50 4.00

**Yellow Surcharge**

**120** R2(e) 2c on 200m grn ('82) 6.25 *8.00*
**121** R1(d) 16c on 2r bl ('83) 6.00 *7.00*

**Green Surcharge**

**122** R1(d) 1r on 10c bis ('83) 11.50 4.00

**Red Surcharge**

**123** R1(d+e) 2r on 8c on 2r blue 55.00 35.00
*a.* On 8c on 2r blue (d+d) 80.00 75.00
**124** R1(d) 1r on 12 4/8c gray bl ('83) 16.50 13.00
**125** R1(k) 6 2/8c on 12 4/8c gray bl ('85) 5.00 *24.00*
**126** R3(d) 1r on 10p bis ('83) 95.00 23.00
**127** R1(m) 1r green 350.00 *700.00*
**127A** R1(m) 2r blue 900.00 *1,150.*
**127B** R1(d) 1r on 1r grn ('83) 700.00 *800.00*
**128** R2(d) 1r on 1p grn ('83) 150.00 65.00
**129** R2(d) 1r on 200m grn ('83) 600.00 *800.00*
**129A** R1(d) 2r on 2r blue *900.00 900.00*

The surcharge on No. 129A is pale red.

### Blue Surcharge

129B R1(m) 10c bister ('81) 700.00 —

### Magenta Surcharge

130 R2(h) 2 4/8c on 200m grn ('88) 4.25 2.10
131 R2(h) 2 4/8c on 20c brn ('88) 12.50 5.75

### On Telegraph Stamps

T1

T2

### Surcharged in Red, or Black

**1883-88**

132 T1(d) 2r on 250m ultra (R) 7.75 3.00
133 T1(d) 20c on 250m ultra *750.00* 375.00
134 T1(d) 2r on 250m ultra 10.00 4.75
135 T1(d) 1r on 20c on 250m ultra (R & Bk) 9.25 3.75

### Magenta Surcharge

136 T2(h) 2 4/8c on 1c bis ('88) .95 .90

Most, if not all, used stamps of No. 133 are hole-punched. Used value is for examples with hole punches.

### Type of 1880-86 Redrawn

**1887-89**

137 A19 50m bister .65 *6.00*
138 A19 1c gray grn ('88) .65 *5.00*
a. 1c yellow green ('89) .70 *6.00*
139 A19 6c yel brn ('88) 10.00 *47.50*
*Nos. 137-139 (3)* 11.30 *58.50*

King Alfonso XIII — A36

**1890-97** **Typo.**

140 A36 1c violet ('92) 1.00 .75
141 A36 1c rose ('94) 17.50 *40.00*
142 A36 1c bl grn ('96) 2.25 1.00
143 A36 1c claret ('97) 16.00 10.00
144 A36 2c claret ('94) .25 .25
145 A36 2c violet ('92) .25 .25
146 A36 2c dk brn ('94) .25 *3.50*
147 A36 2c ultra ('96) .35 .35
148 A36 2c gray brn ('96) .85 *2.25*
149 A36 2 4/8c dull blue .55 .30
150 A36 2 4/8c ol gray ('92) .30 *1.40*
151 A36 5c dark blue .50 *1.40*
152 A36 5c slate green .85 *1.40*
153 A36 5c green ('92) .80 .55
155 A36 5c vio brn ('96) 9.50 4.00
156 A36 5c blue grn ('96) 6.00 3.00
157 A36 6c brown vio ('92) .30 *1.40*
158 A36 6c red orange ('94) .95 2.25
159 A36 6c car rose ('96) 6.00 4.00
160 A36 8c yellow grn .30 .30
161 A36 8c ultra ('92) .75 .30
162 A36 8c red brn ('94) .85 .30
163 A36 10c blue grn 1.75 1.25
164 A36 10c pale cl ('91) 1.60 .40
165 A36 10c claret ('94) .75 .40
166 A36 10c yel brn ('96) .85 .30
167 A36 12 4/8c yellow grn .30 .25
168 A36 12 4/8c org ('92) .85 .25
169 A36 15c red brn ('92) .85 .30
170 A36 15c rose ('94) 2.10 .75
171 A36 15c bl grn ('96) 2.60 2.10
172 A36 20c pale vermilion 30.00 *45.00*
174 A36 20c gray brn ('92) 2.75 .45
175 A36 20c dk vio ('94) 15.00 8.00
176 A36 20c org ('96) 4.50 2.25
177 A36 25c brown 9.50 2.00
178 A36 25c dull bl ('91) 2.50 .50
179 A36 40c dk vio ('97) 13.50 *35.00*
180 A36 80c claret ('97) 30.00 40.00
*Nos. 140-180 (39)* 185.75 218.15

Many of Nos. 140-180 exist imperf and in different colors. These are considered to be proofs. Only major varieties are listed. Color varieties of most issues exist.

Stamps of Previous Issues Handstamp Surcharged in Blue, Red, Black or Violet

**1897** **Blue Surcharge**

181 A36 5c on 5c green 2.00 *5.00*
182 A36 15c on 15c red brn 5.50 3.00
183 A36 20c on 20c gray brn 12.00 *12.00*

### Red Surcharge

185 A36 5c on 5c green 4.50 4.75

### Black Surcharge

187 A36 5c on 5c green 100.00 *300.00*
188 A36 15c on 15c rose 5.50 3.00
189 A36 20c on 20c dk vio 35.00 18.00
190 A36 20c on 25c brown 25.00 *40.00*

### Violet Surcharge

191 A36 15c on 15c rose *15.00* *30.00*
*Nos. 181-191 (9)* 204.50 415.75

Inverted, double and other variations of this surcharge exist.

The 5c on 5c blue gray (#81a) was released during US Administration. The surcharge is a mixture of red and black inks.

*Impressions in violet black are believed to be reprints. The following varieties are known: 5c on 2 4/8c olive gray, 5c on 5c blue green, 5c on 25c brown, 15c on 15c rose, 15c on 15c red brown, 15c on 25c brown, 20c on 20c gray brown, 20c on 20c dark violet, 20c on 25c brown. Value: each $40. These surcharges are to be found double, inverted, etc.*

King Alfonso XIII — A39

**1898** **Typo.**

192 A39 1m orange brown .25 *1.25*
193 A39 2m orange brown .25 *1.75*
194 A39 3m orange brown .25 *1.75*
195 A39 4m orange brown 13.00 *40.00*
196 A39 5m orange brown .25 *2.75*
197 A39 1c black violet .25 .60
198 A39 2c dk bl grn .25 .60
199 A39 3c dk brown .25 .60
200 A39 4c orange 20.00 *40.00*
201 A39 5c car rose .25 .60
202 A39 6c dk blue 1.15 *1.75*
203 A39 8c gray brown .60 .35
204 A39 10c vermilion 2.75 1.25
205 A39 15c dull ol grn 2.25 1.10
206 A39 20c maroon 2.50 1.60
207 A39 40c violet 1.25 *1.75*
208 A39 60c black 6.00 4.00
209 A39 80c red brown 8.00 7.00
210 A39 1p yellow green 20.00 *10.00*
211 A39 2p slate blue 40.00 *12.00*
*Nos. 192-211 (20)* 119.50 *130.70*

Nos. 192-211 exist imperf. Value, set $2,000.

### Issued under U.S. Administration

Regular Issues of the United States Overprinted in Black

**1899-1901** **Unwmk.** ***Perf. 12***

### On U.S. Stamp No. 260

212 A96 50c orange 300. 225.
Never hinged 775.

### On U.S. Stamps Nos. 279, 279B, 279Bd, 279Bj, 279Bf, 279Bc, 268, 281, 282C, 283, 284, 275, 275a

### Wmk. Double-lined USPS (191)

213 A87 1c yellow green 3.50 .60
Never hinged 10.00
a. Inverted overprint *77,500.*
214 A88 2c red, type IV 1.75 .60
Never hinged 4.25
a. 2c orange red, type IV, ('01) 1.75 .60
Never hinged 4.25
b. Bklt. pane of 6, red, type IV ('00) 200.00 *300.00*
Never hinged 450.00
c. 2c reddish carmine, type IV 2.50 1.00
Never hinged 6.00
d. 2c rose carmine, type IV 3.00 1.10
Never hinged 7.25
215 A89 3c purple 9.00 1.25
Never hinged 21.50
216 A91 5c blue 9.00 1.00
Never hinged 21.50
a. Inverted overprint *6,500.*

No. 216a is valued in the grade of fine.

217 A94 10c brown, type I 35.00 4.00
Never hinged 80.00
217A A94 10c orange brown, type II 125.00 27.50
Never hinged 325.00

No. 217A was overprinted on U.S. No. 283a, vertical watermark.

218 A95 15c olive green 40.00 8.00
Never hinged 95.00
219 A96 50c orange 125.00 37.50
Never hinged 300.00
a. 50c red orange 250.00 55.00
Never hinged 600.00
*Nos. 213-219 (8)* 348.25 80.45

### Regular Issue
### Same Overprint in Black On U.S. Stamps Nos. 280b, 282 and 272

**1901, Aug. 30**

220 A90 4c orange brown 35.00 5.00
Never hinged 80.00
221 A92 6c lake 40.00 7.00
Never hinged 95.00
222 A93 8c violet brown 40.00 7.50
Never hinged 95.00
*Nos. 220-222 (3)* 115.00 19.50

### Same Overprint in Red On U.S. Stamps Nos. 276, 276A, 277a and 278

223 A97 $1 black, type I 300.00 200.00
Never hinged 1,000.
223A A97 $1 black, type II 2,000. 750.00
Never hinged 5,000.
224 A98 $2 dark blue 350.00 325.00
Never hinged 1,150.
225 A99 $5 dark green 600.00 *900.00*
Never hinged 1,600.

### Regular Issue
### Same Overprint in Black On U.S. Stamps Nos. 300 to 310 and Shades

**1903-04**

226 A115 1c blue green 7.00 .40
Never hinged 15.50
227 A116 2c carmine 9.00 1.10
Never hinged 20.00
228 A117 3c bright violet 67.50 12.50
Never hinged 150.00
229 A118 4c brown 80.00 22.50
Never hinged 175.00
a. 4c orange brown 80.00 20.00
Never hinged 175.00
230 A119 5c blue 17.50 1.00
Never hinged 40.00
231 A120 6c brownish lake 85.00 22.50
Never hinged 190.00
232 A121 8c violet black 50.00 15.00
Never hinged 125.00
233 A122 10c pale red brown 35.00 2.25
Never hinged 80.00
a. 10c red brown 35.00 3.00
Never hinged 80.00
b. Pair, one without overprint *1,500.*
234 A123 13c purple black 35.00 17.50
Never hinged 80.00
a. 13c brown violet 35.00 17.50
Never hinged 80.00
235 A124 15c olive green 60.00 15.00
Never hinged 135.00
236 A125 50c orange 125.00 35.00
Never hinged 275.00
*Nos. 226-236 (11)* 571.00 144.75
Set, never hinged 1,285.

### Same Overprint in Red On U.S. Stamps Nos. 311, 312 and 313

237 A126 $1 black 300.00 200.00
Never hinged 800.00
238 A127 $2 dark blue 550.00 *800.00*
Never hinged 1,500.
239 A128 $5 dark green 800.00 *2,750.*
Never hinged 2,000.

### Same Overprint in Black On U.S. Stamp Nos. 319 and 319c

240 A129 2c carmine 8.00 2.25
Never hinged 17.50
a. Booklet pane of 6 *2,000.*
b. 2c scarlet 8.00 2.75
Never hinged 19.00
c. As "b," booklet pane of 6 —

José Rizal — A40

Designs: 4c, McKinley. 6c, Ferdinand Magellan. 8c, Miguel Lopez de Legaspi. 10c, Gen. Henry W. Lawton. 12c, Lincoln. 16c, Adm. William T. Sampson. 20c, Washington. 26c, Francisco Carriedo. 30c, Franklin. 1p-10p, Arms of City of Manila.

### Wmk. Double-lined PIPS (191PI)

**1906, Sept. 8** ***Perf. 12***

241 A40 2c deep green .40 .25
Never hinged 1.00
a. 2c yellow green ('10) .60 .25
Never hinged 1.50
b. Booklet pane of 6 750.00 *800.00*
Never hinged *1,500.*
242 A40 4c carmine .50 .25
Never hinged 1.25
a. 4c carmine lake ('10) 1.00 .25
Never hinged 2.50
b. Booklet pane of 6 *650.00* *700.00*
Never hinged *1,250.*
243 A40 6c violet 2.50 .25
Never hinged 6.25
244 A40 8c brown 4.50 .90
Never hinged 11.00
245 A40 10c blue 3.50 .30
Never hinged 8.75
a. 10c dark blue 3.50 .30
Never hinged 8.75
246 A40 12c brown lake 9.00 2.50
Never hinged 22.50
247 A40 16c violet black 6.00 .35
Never hinged 15.00
248 A40 20c orange brown 7.00 .35
Never hinged 17.50
249 A40 26c vio brn 11.00 3.00
Never hinged 27.50
250 A40 30c olive green 6.50 1.75
Never hinged 16.00
251 A40 1p orange 55.00 17.50
Never hinged 130.00
252 A40 2p black 50.00 1.75
Never hinged 130.00
253 A40 4p dark blue 160.00 20.00
Never hinged 375.00
254 A40 10p dark green 225.00 80.00
Never hinged 575.00
*Nos. 241-254 (14)* 540.90 129.15
Set, never hinged 1,316.

**1909-13** **Change of Colors**

255 A40 12c red orange 11.00 3.00
Never hinged 27.50
256 A40 16c olive green 6.00 .75
Never hinged 15.00
257 A40 20c yellow 9.00 1.25
Never hinged 22.50
258 A40 26c blue green 3.50 1.25
Never hinged 8.75
259 A40 30c ultramarine 13.00 3.50
Never hinged 32.50
260 A40 1p pale violet 45.00 5.00
Never hinged 110.00
260A A40 2p violet brown ('13) 100.00 12.00
Never hinged 250.00
*Nos. 255-260A (7)* 187.50 26.75
Set, never hinged 466.25

### Wmk. Single-lined PIPS (190PI)

**1911**

261 A40 2c green .75 .25
Never hinged 1.80
a. Booklet pane of 6 *800.00* *900.00*
Never hinged *1,400.*
262 A40 4c carmine lake 3.00 .25
Never hinged 6.75
a. 4c carmine — —
b. Booklet pane of 6 *600.00* *700.00*
Never hinged *1,100.*
263 A40 6c deep violet 3.00 .25
Never hinged 6.75
264 A40 8c brown 9.50 .50
Never hinged 21.50
265 A40 10c blue 4.00 .25
Never hinged 9.00
266 A40 12c orange 4.00 .45
Never hinged 9.00
267 A40 16c olive green 4.50 .40
Never hinged 10.00
a. 16c pale olive green 4.50 .50
Never hinged 10.00
268 A40 20c yellow 3.50 .25
Never hinged 7.75
a. 20c orange 4.00 .30
Never hinged 9.00
269 A40 26c blue green 6.00 .30
Never hinged 13.50
270 A40 30c ultramarine 6.00 .50
Never hinged 13.50
271 A40 1p pale violet 27.50 .60
Never hinged 62.50
272 A40 2p violet brown 45.00 1.00
Never hinged 100.00
273 A40 4p deep blue 550.00 110.00
Never hinged 1,100.
274 A40 10p deep green 200.00 30.00
Never hinged 400.00
*Nos. 261-274 (14)* 866.75 145.00
Set, never hinged 1,862.

**1914**

275 A40 30c gray 12.00 .50
Never hinged 27.50

**1914** ***Perf. 10***

276 A40 2c green 3.00 .25
Never hinged 7.00
a. Booklet pane of 6 *750.00* *800.00*
Never hinged *1,250.*
277 A40 4c carmine 4.00 .30
Never hinged 9.00
a. Booklet pane of 6 *750.00*
Never hinged *1,300.*
278 A40 6c light violet 45.00 9.50
Never hinged 100.00
a. 6c deep violet 50.00 6.25
Never hinged 110.00
279 A40 8c brown 55.00 10.50
Never hinged 125.00
280 A40 10c dark blue 30.00 .25
Never hinged 67.50
281 A40 16c olive green 100.00 5.00
Never hinged 225.00
282 A40 20c orange 40.00 1.00
Never hinged 85.00
283 A40 30c gray 60.00 4.50
Never hinged 130.00

284 A40 1p pale violet 150.00 3.75
Never hinged 350.00
*Nos. 276-284 (9)* 487.00 35.05
Set, never hinged 1,020.

### Wmk. Single-lined PIPS (190PI)

**1918** *Perf. 11*

285 A40 2c green 21.00 4.25
Never hinged 40.00
a. Booklet pane of 6 *750.00 800.00*
Never hinged *1,300.*
286 A40 4c carmine 26.00 6.00
Never hinged 55.00
a. Booklet pane of 6 *1,350. 2,000.*
287 A40 6c deep violet 40.00 6.00
Never hinged 90.00
287A A40 8c light brown 220.00 25.00
Never hinged 400.00
288 A40 10c dark blue 60.00 3.00
Never hinged 140.00
289 A40 16c olive green 110.00 10.00
Never hinged 250.00
289A A40 20c orange 175.00 12.00
Never hinged 400.00
289C A40 30c gray 95.00 18.00
Never hinged 215.00
289D A40 1p pale violet 100.00 25.00
Never hinged 225.00
*Nos. 285-289D (9)* 847.00 109.25
Set, never hinged 1,815.

**1917 Unwmk.** *Perf. 11*

290 A40 2c yellow green .25 .25
Never hinged .55
Never hinged 25.00
a. 2c dark green .30 .25
Never hinged .65
b. Vert. pair, imperf. horiz. *2,000.*
c. Horiz. pair, imperf. between *1,500.* —
d. Vertical pair, imperf. btwn. *1,750. 1,000.*
e. Booklet pane of 6 27.50 *30.00*
Never hinged 60.00
291 A40 4c carmine .30 .25
Never hinged .65
a. 4c light rose .30 .25
Never hinged .65
b. Booklet pane of 6 20.00 *22.50*
Never hinged 35.00
292 A40 6c deep violet .35 .25
Never hinged .70
a. 6c lilac .40 .25
Never hinged .80
b. 6c red violet .40 .25
Never hinged .70
c. Booklet pane of 6 *550.00 800.00*
Never hinged *900.00*
293 A40 8c yellow brown .30 .25
Never hinged .50
a. 8c orange brown .30 .25
Never hinged .50
294 A40 10c deep blue .30 .25
Never hinged .65
295 A40 12c red orange .35 .25
Never hinged .75
296 A40 16c light olive green 65.00 .25
Never hinged 130.00
a. 16c olive bister 65.00 .50
Never hinged 130.00
297 A40 20c orange yellow .35 .25
Never hinged .75
298 A40 26c green .50 .45
Never hinged 1.10
a. 26c blue green .60 .25
Never hinged 1.35
299 A40 30c gray .55 .25
Never hinged 1.35
300 A40 1p pale violet 40.00 1.00
Never hinged 90.00
a. 1p red lilac 40.00 1.00
Never hinged 90.00
b. 1p pale rose lilac 40.00 1.10
Never hinged 90.00
301 A40 2p violet brown 35.00 1.00
Never hinged 77.50
302 A40 4p blue 32.50 .50
Never hinged 72.50
a. 4p dark blue 35.00 .55
Never hinged 77.50
*Nos. 290-302 (13)* 175.75 5.20
Set, never hinged 377.00

**1923-26**

Design: 16c, Adm. George Dewey.

303 A40 16c olive bister 1.00 .25
Never hinged 2.25
a. 16c olive green 1.25 .25
Never hinged 2.75
304 A40 10p dp grn ('26) 50.00 20.00
Never hinged 110.00

Legislative Palace A42

**1926, Dec. 20** *Perf. 12*

319 A42 2c green & black .50 .25
Never hinged 1.25
a. Horiz. pair, imperf. between *300.00*
b. Vert. pair, imperf. between *575.00*
320 A42 4c car & blk .55 .40
Never hinged 1.20
a. Horiz. pair, imperf. between *325.00*
b. Vert. pair, imperf. between *600.00*
321 A42 16c ol grn & blk 1.00 .65
Never hinged 2.25
a. Horiz. pair, imperf. between *350.00*
b. Vert. pair, imperf. between *625.00*
c. Double impression of center *675.00*
322 A42 18c lt brn & blk 1.10 .50
Never hinged 2.50
a. Double impression of center *1,250.*
b. Vertical pair, imperf. between *675.00*
323 A42 20c orange & black 2.00 1.00
Never hinged 4.50
a. 20c orange & brown *600.00* —
b. As No. 323, imperf., pair *575.00 575.00*
c. As "a," imperf., pair *1,750.*
d. Vert. pair, imperf. between *700.00*
324 A42 24c gray & black 1.00 .55
Never hinged 2.25
a. Vert. pair, imperf. between *700.00*
325 A42 1p rose lil & blk 47.50 50.00
Never hinged 70.00
a. Vert. pair, imperf. between *700.00*
*Nos. 319-325 (7)* 53.65 53.35
Set, never hinged 83.95

Opening of the Legislative Palace.
No. 322a is valued in the grade of fine.
For overprints, see Nos. O1-O4.

### Rizal Type of 1906 Coil Stamp

**1928** *Perf. 11 Vertically*

326 A40 2c green 7.50 *12.50*
Never hinged 19.00

### Types of 1906-1923

**1925-31** *Imperf.*

340 A40 2c yel green ('31) .50 .50
Never hinged .90
a. 2c green ('25) .80 .75
Never hinged 1.80
341 A40 4c car rose ('31) .50 *1.00*
Never hinged 1.00
a. 4c carmine ('25) 1.20 1.00
Never hinged 2.75
342 A40 6c violet ('31) 3.00 3.75
Never hinged 5.00
a. 6c deep violet ('25) 12.00 8.00
Never hinged 26.00
343 A40 8c brown ('31) 2.00 *5.00*
Never hinged 4.00
a. 8c yellow brown ('25) 13.00 8.00
Never hinged 26.00
344 A40 10c blue ('31) 5.00 *7.50*
Never hinged 12.00
a. 10c deep blue ('25) 45.00 20.00
Never hinged 100.00
345 A40 12c dp orange ('31) 8.00 10.00
Never hinged 15.00
a. 12c red orange ('25) 60.00 35.00
Never hinged 135.00
346 A40 16c olive green 6.00 7.50
Never hinged 11.00
a. 16c bister green ('25) 42.50 18.00
Never hinged 100.00
347 A40 20c dp yel org ('31) 5.00 *7.50*
Never hinged 11.00
a. 20c yellow orange ('25) 45.00 20.00
Never hinged 100.00
348 A40 26c green ('31) 6.00 *9.00*
Never hinged 11.00
a. 26c blue green ('25) 45.00 25.00
Never hinged 110.00
349 A40 30c light gray ('31) 8.00 10.00
Never hinged 16.00
a. 30c gray ('25) 45.00 25.00
Never hinged 110.00
350 A40 1p light violet ('31) 10.00 *15.00*
Never hinged 20.00
a. 1p violet ('25) 200.00 100.00
Never hinged 425.00
351 A40 2p brn vio ('31) 30.00 *45.00*
Never hinged 80.00
a. 2p violet brown ('25) 400.00 400.00
Never hinged 675.00
352 A40 4p blue ('31) 80.00 90.00
Never hinged 150.00
a. 4p deep blue ('25) 2,200. 1,100.
Never hinged 3,500.
353 A40 10p green ('31) 175.00 *225.00*
Never hinged 300.00
a. 10p deep green ('25) 2,750. *2,950.*
Never hinged 4,250.
*Nos. 340-353 (14)* 339.00 436.75
Set, never hinged 636.90
*Nos. 340a-353a (14)* 5,860. 4,711.

Nos. 340a-353a were the original post office issue. These were reprinted twice in 1931 for sale to collectors (Nos. 340-353).

Mount Mayon, Luzon A43

Post Office, Manila A44

Pier No. 7, Manila Bay — A45

(See footnote) — A46

Rice Planting A47

Rice Terraces A48

Baguio Zigzag A49

**1932, May 3** *Perf. 11*

354 A43 2c yellow green .75 .30
Never hinged 1.25
355 A44 4c rose carmine .75 .30
Never hinged 1.25
356 A45 12c orange .90 .75
Never hinged 1.30
357 A46 18c red orange 45.00 15.00
Never hinged 72.50
358 A47 20c yellow 1.00 .75
Never hinged 1.60
359 A48 24c deep violet 1.60 1.00
Never hinged 2.75
360 A49 32c olive brown 1.60 1.00
Never hinged 2.75
*Nos. 354-360 (7)* 51.60 19.10
Set, never hinged 83.40

The 18c vignette was intended to show Pagsanjan Falls in Laguna, central Luzon, and is so labeled. Through error the stamp pictures Vernal Falls in Yosemite National Park, California.

For overprints see #C29-C35, C47-C51, C63.

Nos. 302, 302a Surcharged in Orange or Red

**1932**

368 A40 1p on 4p blue (O) 6.00 1.00
Never hinged 9.75
a. 1p on 4p dark blue (O) 6.00 1.00
Never hinged 9.25
P# block of 10, Impt. 140.00
Never hinged 175.00
369 A40 2p on 4p dark blue (R) 9.00 1.50
Never hinged 15.00
P# block of 10, Impt. 160.00
Never hinged 200.00
a. 2p on 4p blue (R) 9.00 1.00
Never hinged 15.00

### Far Eastern Championship

Issued in commemoration of the Tenth Far Eastern Championship Games.

Baseball Players A50

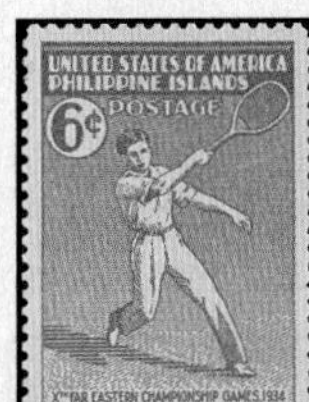
Tennis Player — A51

Basketball Players — A52

**1934, Apr. 14** *Perf. 11½*

380 A50 2c yellow brown 1.50 .80
Never hinged 2.25
381 A51 6c ultramarine .25 .25
Never hinged .30
a. Vertical pair, imperf. between *700.00*
Never hinged *1,100.*
382 A52 16c violet brown .50 .50
Never hinged .75
a. Vert. pair, imperf. horiz. *950.00*
Never hinged *1,500.*
*Nos. 380-382 (3)* 2.25 1.55
Set, never hinged 3.30

José Rizal — A53

Woman and Carabao A54

La Filipina — A55

Pearl Fishing A56

Fort Santiago A57

Salt Spring — A58

Magellan's Landing, 1521 — A59

"Juan de la Cruz" — A60

Rice Terraces A61

"Blood Compact," 1565 — A62

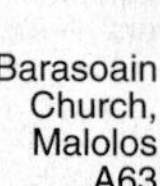

Barasoain Church, Malolos A63

Battle of Manila Bay, 1898 A64

Montalban Gorge A65

George Washington A66

**1935, Feb. 15** *Perf. 11*

383 A53 2c rose .25 .25
Never hinged .25
384 A54 4c yellow green .25 .25
Never hinged .25
385 A55 6c dark brown .25 .25
Never hinged .35
386 A56 8c violet .25 .25
Never hinged .35
387 A57 10c rose carmine .30 .25
Never hinged .45
388 A58 12c black .35 .25
Never hinged .50
389 A59 16c dark blue .35 .25
Never hinged .55
390 A60 20c light olive green .35 .25
Never hinged .45
391 A61 26c indigo .40 .40
Never hinged .60
392 A62 30c orange red .40 .40
Never hinged .60
393 A63 1p red org & blk 2.00 1.25
Never hinged 3.00
394 A64 2p bis brn & blk 12.00 2.00
Never hinged 16.00
395 A65 4p blue & black 12.00 4.00
Never hinged 16.00
396 A66 5p green & black 25.00 5.00
Never hinged 50.00
*Nos. 383-396 (14)* 54.15 15.05
Set, never hinged 74.45

For overprints & surcharges see Nos. 411-424, 433-446, 449, 463-466, 468, 472-474, 478-484, 485-494, C52-C53, O15-O36, O38, O40-O43, N2-N9, N28, NO2-NO6.

**Issues of the Commonwealth**

Issued to commemorate the inauguration of the Philippine Commonwealth, Nov. 15, 1935.

The Temples of Human Progress — A67

**1935, Nov. 15**

397 A67 2c carmine rose .25 .25
Never hinged .35
398 A67 6c deep violet .25 .25
Never hinged .35
399 A67 16c blue .25 .25
Never hinged .40
400 A67 36c yellow green .40 .30
Never hinged .65
401 A67 50c brown .70 .55
Never hinged 1.00
*Nos. 397-401 (5)* 1.85 1.60
Set, never hinged 2.75

**Jose Rizal Issue**

75th anniversary of the birth of Jose Rizal (1861-1896), national hero of the Filipinos.

Jose Rizal — A68

**1936, June 19** *Perf. 12*

402 A68 2c yellow brown .25 .25
Never hinged .25
403 A68 6c slate blue .25 .25
Never hinged .25
a. Imperf. vertically, pair *1,000.*
Never hinged *1,500.*
404 A68 36c red brown .50 *.70*
Never hinged .75
*Nos. 402-404 (3)* 1.00 1.20
Set, never hinged 1.25

**Commonwealth Anniversary Issue**

Issued in commemoration of the first anniversary of the Commonwealth.

President Manuel L. Quezon — A69

**1936, Nov. 15** *Perf. 11*

408 A69 2c orange brown .25 .25
Never hinged .30
409 A69 6c yellow green .25 .25
Never hinged .30
410 A69 12c ultramarine .25 .25
Never hinged .30
*Nos. 408-410 (3)* .75 .75
Set, never hinged .90

**Stamps of 1935 Overprinted in Black**

a

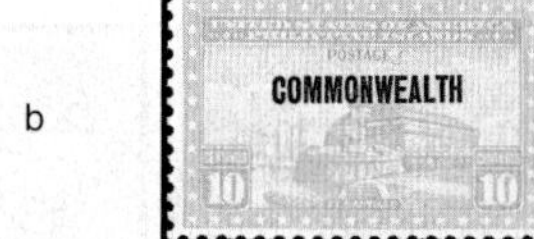
b

**1936-37**

411 A53(a) 2c rose .25 .25
Never hinged .25
a. Bklt. pane of 6 ('37) 2.50 2.00
Never hinged 4.00
b. Hyphen omitted 125.00 100.00
412 A54(b) 4c yel grn ('37) .45 *4.00*
Never hinged .70
P# block of 6 35.00
Never hinged 45.00
413 A55(a) 6c dark brown .25 .25
Never hinged .25
414 A56(b) 8c violet ('37) .25 .25
Never hinged .35
415 A57(b) 10c rose carmine .25 .25
Never hinged .25
a. "COMMONWEALT" 20.00 —
Never hinged 30.00
416 A58(b) 12c black ('37) .25 .25
Never hinged .30
417 A59(b) 16c dark blue .25 .25
Never hinged .40
418 A60(a) 20c lt ol grn ('37) .90 .40
Never hinged 1.50
419 A61(b) 26c indigo ('37) .80 .35
Never hinged 1.40
420 A62(b) 30c orange red .45 .25
Never hinged .75
421 A63(b) 1p red org & blk .90 .25
Never hinged 1.50
422 A64(b) 2p bis brn & blk ('37) 12.50 4.00
Never hinged 21.00
423 A65(b) 4p bl & blk ('37) 45.00 8.00
Never hinged 72.50
424 A66(b) 5p grn & blk ('37) 12.50 *25.00*
Never hinged 21.00
*Nos. 411-424 (14)* 75.00 43.75
Set, never hinged 122.15

**Eucharistic Congress Issue**

Issued to commemorate the 33rd International Eucharistic Congress held at Manila, Feb. 3-7, 1937.

Map of Philippines — A70

**1937, Feb. 3**

425 A70 2c yellow green .25 .25
Never hinged .25
426 A70 6c light brown .25 .25
Never hinged .25
427 A70 12c sapphire .25 .25
Never hinged .25
428 A70 20c deep orange .30 .25
Never hinged .50
429 A70 36c deep violet .55 .40
Never hinged .80
430 A70 50c carmine .70 .35
Never hinged 1.10
*Nos. 425-430 (6)* 2.30 1.75
Set, never hinged 3.15

Arms of Manila — A71

**1937, Aug. 27**

431 A71 10p gray 5.00 2.00
Never hinged 7.25
P# block of 6 67.50
Never hinged 85.00
432 A71 20p henna brown 4.00 1.40
Never hinged 6.50

**Stamps of 1935 Overprinted in Black**

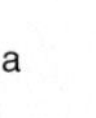

a

b

**1938-40**

433 A53(a) 2c rose ('39) .25 .25
Never hinged .25
P# block of 6 8.00
Never hinged 10.00
a. Booklet pane of 6 3.50 3.50
Never hinged 5.50
b. As "a," lower left-hand stamp overprinted "WEALTH COMMON-" *2,500.*
Never hinged *4,000.*
c. Hyphen omitted 100.00 50.00
434 A54(b) 4c yel grn ('40) 3.00 *30.00*
Never hinged 4.75
P# block of 6 35.00
Never hinged 45.00
435 A55(a) 6c dk brn ('39) .25 .25
Never hinged .40
a. 6c golden brown .25 .25
Never hinged .40
P# block of 6 5.50
Never hinged 7.00
436 A56(b) 8c violet ('39) .25 *1.75*
Never hinged .25
P# block of 6 8.00
Never hinged 10.00
a. "COMMONWEALT" (LR 31) 90.00
Never hinged 140.00
437 A57(b) 10c rose car ('39) .25 .25
Never hinged .25
P# block of 6 8.00
Never hinged 10.00
a. "COMMONWEALT" (LR 31) 65.00 —
Never hinged 100.00
438 A58(b) 12c black ('40) .25 *1.00*
Never hinged .25
P# block of 6 8.00
Never hinged 10.00
439 A59(b) 16c dark blue .25 .25
Never hinged .25
P# block of 6 16.00
Never hinged 20.00
440 A60(a) 20c lt ol grn ('39) .25 .25
Never hinged .25
P# block of 6 12.00
Never hinged 15.00
441 A61(b) 26c indigo ('40) 1.00 *2.50*
Never hinged 1.50
P# block of 6 16.00
Never hinged 20.00
442 A62(b) 30c org red ('39) 3.00 .70
Never hinged 5.00
P# block of 6 22.50
Never hinged 35.00
443 A63(b) 1p red org & blk .60 .25
Never hinged 1.00
444 A64(b) 2p bis brn & blk ('39) 10.00 1.00
Never hinged 15.00
P# block of 4 87.50
Never hinged 110.00
445 A65(b) 4p bl & blk ('40) 175.00 250.00
Never hinged 350.00
446 A66(b) 5p grn & blk ('40) 20.00 8.00
Never hinged 35.00
P# block of 4 200.00
Never hinged 250.00
*Nos. 433-446 (14)* 214.35 *296.45*
Set, never hinged 414.15

Overprint "b" measures 18½x1¾mm.

No. 433b occurs in booklet pane, No. 433a, position 5; all examples are straight-edged, left and bottom.

**First Foreign Trade Week Issue Nos. 384, 298a and 432 Surcharged in Red, Violet or Black**

a

b

c

**1939, July 5**

449 A54(a) 2c on 4c yel grn (R) .25 .25
Never hinged .35
450 A40(b) 6c on 26c blue grn (V) .25 .50
Never hinged .35
a. 6c on 26c green 3.00 1.00
Never hinged 5.00
451 A71(c) 50c on 20p henna brn (Bk) 1.25 1.00
Never hinged 2.00 5.00
*Nos. 449-451 (3)* 1.75 1.75
Set, never hinged 2.70

**Commonwealth 4th Anniversary Issue (#452-460)**

Triumphal Arch — A72

**1939, Nov. 15**

452 A72 2c yellow green .25 .25
Never hinged .25
453 A72 6c carmine .25 .25
Never hinged .25
454 A72 12c bright blue .25 .25
Never hinged .25
*Nos. 452-454 (3)* .75 .75
Set, never hinged .75

For overprints see Nos. 469, 476.

Malacañan Palace A73

**1939, Nov. 15**

455 A73 2c green .25 .25
Never hinged .25
456 A73 6c orange .25 .25
Never hinged .25

457 A73 12c carmine .25 .25
Never hinged .25
*Nos. 455-457 (3)* .75 .75
Set, never hinged .75

For overprint, see No. 470.

Pres. Quezon Taking Oath of Office — A74

**1940, Feb. 8**

458 A74 2c dark orange .25 .25
Never hinged .25
459 A74 6c dark green .25 .25
Never hinged .25
460 A74 12c purple .25 .25
Never hinged .30
*Nos. 458-460 (3)* .75 .75
Set, never hinged .80

For overprints, see Nos. 471, 477.

José Rizal — A75

ROTARY PRESS PRINTING

**1941, Apr. 14** ***Perf. 11x10½***

**Size: 19x22½mm**

461 A75 2c apple green .25 .50
Never hinged .25

FLAT PLATE PRINTING

**1941, Nov. 14** ***Perf. 11***

**Size: 18¾x22¼mm**

462 A75 2c pale apple green 1.00 —
Never hinged 1.25
a. Booklet pane of 6 6.00 —
Never hinged 7.50

No. 461 was issued only in sheets. No. 462 was issued only in booklet panes on Nov. 14, 1941, just before the war, and only a few used stamps and covers exist. All examples have one or two straight edges. Mint booklets reappeared after the war. In August 1942, the booklet pane was reprinted in a darker shade (apple green). However, the apple green panes were available only to U.S. collectors during the war years, so no war-period used stamps from the Philippines exist. Value of apple green booklet pane, never hinged, $6.

For type A75 overprinted, see Nos. 464, O37, O39, N1 and NO1.

Philippine Stamps of 1935-41, Handstamped in Violet

**1944** ***Perf. 11, 11x10½***

463 A53 2c rose (On 411) *1,250.* *650.00*
a. Booklet pane of 6 *12,500.*
463B A53 2c rose (On 433) *2,000.* *1,750.*
464 A75 2c apple grn (On 461) 12.50 10.00
Never hinged 22.50
a. Pair, one without ovpt. — —
465 A54 4c yel grn (On 384) 47.50 *50.00*
Never hinged 80.00
466 A55 6c dk brn (On 385) *3,250.* *2,000.*
467 A69 6c yel grn (On 409) 300.00 *150.00*
Never hinged *525.00*
468 A55 6c dk brn (On 413) *4,750.* *825.00*
469 A72 6c car (On 453) *350.00* *125.00*
470 A73 6c org (On 456) *1,750.* *725.00*
471 A74 6c dk grn (On 459) *275.00* *225.00*
472 A56 8c vio (On 436) 17.50 *30.00*
Never hinged 30.00
473 A57 10c car rose (On 415) *350.00* *150.00*
474 A57 10c car rose (On 437) *275.00* *200.00*
Never hinged *475.00*
475 A69 12c ultra (On 410) *1,100.* *400.00*
476 A72 12c brt bl (On 454) *7,000.* *2,500.*
477 A74 12c pur (On 460) *500.00* *275.00*
478 A59 16c dk bl (On 389) *3,000.* —
479 A59 16c dk bl (On 417) *1,500.* *1,000.*
480 A59 16c dk bl (On 439) *500.00* *200.00*
481 A60 20c lt ol grn (On 440) 140.00 35.00
Never hinged 230.00
482 A62 30c org red (On 420) *450.00* *1,500.*
483 A62 30c org red (On 442) *800.00* *375.00*
484 A63 1p red org & blk (On 443) *6,250.* *4,500.*

Nos. 463-484 are valued in the grade of fine to very fine.

No. 463 comes only from the booklet pane. All examples have one or two straight edges.

**Types of 1935-37 Overprinted**

a

b

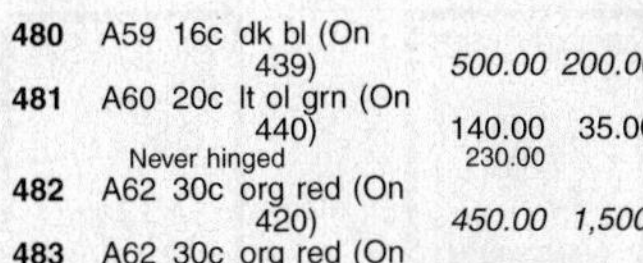

Nos. 431-432 Overprinted in Black — c

**1945** ***Perf. 11***

485 A53(a) 2c rose .25 .25
Never hinged .25
486 A54(b) 4c yellow green .25 .25
Never hinged .25
487 A55(a) 6c golden brown .25 .25
Never hinged .25
488 A56(b) 8c violet .25 .25
Never hinged .25
489 A57(b) 10c rose carmine .25 .25
Never hinged .25
490 A58(b) 12c black .25 .25
Never hinged .25
491 A59(b) 16c dark blue .25 .25
Never hinged .30
492 A60(a) 20c lt olive green .30 .25
Never hinged .40
493 A62(b) 30c orange red .50 .35
Never hinged .75
494 A63(b) 1p red orange & black 1.10 .25
Never hinged 1.60
495 A71(c) 10p gray 55.00 13.50
Never hinged 90.00
496 A71(c) 20p henna brown 50.00 15.00
Never hinged 75.00
*Nos. 485-496 (12)* 108.65 31.10
Set, never hinged 169.55

José Rizal — A76

**1946, May 28** ***Perf. 11x10½***

497 A76 2c sepia .25 .25
Never hinged .25

For overprints see Nos. 503, O44.

**Catalogue values for unused stamps in this section, from this point to the end of the section, are for Never Hinged items.**

**Republic**

Philippine Girl Holding Flag of the Republic — A77

**Unwmk.**

**1946, July 4** **Engr.** ***Perf. 11***

500 A77 2c carmine .50 .25
501 A77 6c green .50 .25
502 A77 12c blue 1.25 .40
*Nos. 500-502 (3)* 2.25 .90

Philippine independence, July 4, 1946.

No. 497 Overprinted in Brown

**1946, Dec. 30** ***Perf. 11x10½***

503 A76 2c sepia .40 .25

50th anniv. of the execution of José Rizal.

Rizal Monument A78

Bonifacio Monument A79

Jones Bridge — A80

Santa Lucia Gate — A81

Mayon Volcano — A82

Avenue of Palms — A83

**1947** **Engr.** ***Perf. 12***

504 A78 4c black brown .40 .25
505 A79 10c red orange .40 .25
506 A80 12c deep blue .40 .25
507 A81 16c slate gray 3.00 .60
508 A82 20c red brown 3.00 .25
509 A83 50c dull green 3.00 .35
510 A83 1p violet 3.00 .35
*Nos. 504-510 (7)* 13.20 2.30

Issued: Nos. 505 & 508, 3/23; Nos. 506-07, 509, 6/19; Nos. 504 & 510, 8/1.

For surcharges see Nos. 613-614, 809. For overprints see Nos. 609, O50-O52, O54-O55.

Manuel L. Quezon — A84

**1947, May 1** **Typo.**

511 A84 1c green .40 .25
a. Vert. pair, imperf. between 50.00

See No. 515.

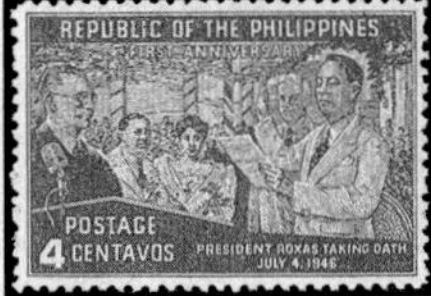
Pres. Manuel A. Roxas Taking Oath of Office A85

**1947, July 4** **Unwmk.** ***Perf. 12½***

512 A85 4c carmine rose .50 .25
513 A85 6c dk green .75 .45
514 A85 16c purple 1.25 .85
*Nos. 512-514 (3)* 2.50 1.55

First anniversary of republic.

**Quezon Type**
Souvenir Sheet

**1947, Nov. 28** ***Imperf.***

515 Sheet of 4 1.75 1.25
a. A84 1c bright green .25 .25

United Nations Emblem A87

**1947, Nov. 24** ***Perf. 12½***

516 A87 4c dk car & pink 2.40 1.40
a. Imperf. 6.00 3.75
517 A87 6c pur & pale vio 2.40 1.40
a. Imperf. 5.50 3.75
518 A87 12c dp bl & pale bl 3.50 2.10
a. Imperf. 6.00 3.75
*Nos. 516-518 (3)* 8.30 4.90
*Nos. 516a-518a (3)* 17.50 11.25

Conference of the Economic Commission in Asia and the Far East, held at Baguio.

Gen. Douglas MacArthur — A88

**1948, Feb. 3** **Engr.** ***Perf. 12***

519 A88 4c purple .90 .50
520 A88 6c rose car 1.25 .50
521 A88 16c brt ultra 1.60 .75
*Nos. 519-521 (3)* 3.75 1.75

Threshing Rice — A89

**1948, Feb. 23** **Typo.** ***Perf. 12½***

522 A89 2c grn & pale yel grn 1.00 .40
523 A89 6c brown & cream 1.75 .40
524 A89 18c dp bl & pale bl 3.25 1.25
*Nos. 522-524 (3)* 6.00 2.05

Conf. of the FAO held at Baguio. Nos. 522 and 524 exist imperf. Value, set $125.

See No. C67.

Manuel A. Roxas — A90

**1948, July 15** **Engr.** ***Perf. 12***

525 A90 2c black .30 .25
526 A90 4c black .45 .25

Issued in tribute to President Manuel A. Roxas who died April 15, 1948.

José Rizal — A91

**1948, June 19** **Unwmk.**

527 A91 2c bright green .40 .25
a. Booklet pane of 6 ('44) 4.00 3.00

For surcharges see Nos. 550, O56. For overprint see No. O53.

Scout Saluting — A92

**1948, Oct. 31 Typo. *Imperf.***
**528** A92 2c chocolate & green 1.25 .55
*a.* Perf. 11½ 1.75 1.40
**529** A92 4c chocolate & pink 1.50 .70
*a.* Perf. 11½ 2.50 2.00

Boy Scouts of the Philippines, 25th anniv.
Nos. 528 and 529 exist part perforate.

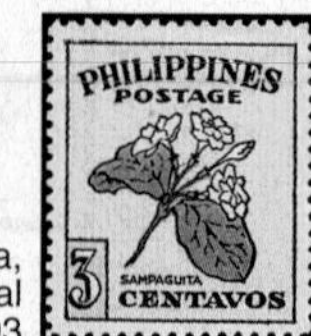


Sampaguita, National Flower — A93

**1948, Dec. 8 *Perf. 12½***
**530** A93 3c blk, pale grn & grn .60 .30

UPU Monument, Bern A94

**Unwmk.**

**1949, Oct. 9 Engr. *Perf. 12***
**531** A94 4c green .70 .25
**532** A94 6c dull violet .50 .25
**533** A94 18c blue gray .50 .25
*Nos. 531-533 (3)* 1.70 .75

**Souvenir Sheet**

***Imperf***

**534** Sheet of 3 3.00 2.00
*a.* A94 4c green .70 .35
*b.* A94 6c dull violet .70 .35
*c.* A94 18c blue .70 .60

75th anniv. of the UPU.
In 1960 an unofficial, 3-line overprint ("President D. D. Eisenhower /Visit to the Philippines/June 14-16, 1960") was privately applied to No. 534.
For surcharge & overprint see #806, 901.

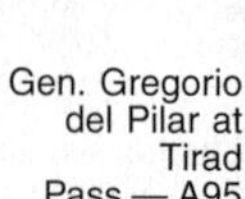

Gen. Gregorio del Pilar at Tirad Pass — A95

**1949, Dec. 2 *Perf. 12***
**535** A95 2c red brown .40 .25
**536** A95 4c green .60 .25

50th anniversary of the death of Gen. Gregorio P. del Pilar and fifty-two of his men at Tirad Pass.

Globe — A96

**1950, Mar. 1**
**537** A96 2c purple .40 .25
**538** A96 6c dk green .50 .25
**539** A96 18c dp blue .60 .25
*Nos. 537-539,C68-C69 (5)* 5.50 1.85

5th World Cong. of the Junior Chamber of Commerce, Manila, Mar. 1-8, 1950.
For surcharge see No. 825.

Red Lauan Tree — A97

**1950, Apr. 14**
**540** A97 2c green .60 .25
**541** A97 4c purple .75 .25

50th anniversary of the Bureau of Forestry.

F. D. Roosevelt with his Stamps — A98

**1950, May 22**
**542** A98 4c dark brown 1.40 .25
**543** A98 6c carmine rose .65 .45
**544** A98 18c blue .65 .45
*Nos. 542-544 (3)* 2.70 1.15

Honoring Franklin D. Roosevelt and for the 25th anniv. of the Philatelic Association of the Philippines. See No. C70.

Lions Club Emblem — A99

**1950, June 4 Engr.**
**545** A99 2c orange 1.00 .30
**546** A99 4c violet 1.00 .35
*Nos. 545-546,C71-C72 (4)* 5.75 1.70

Convention of the Lions Club, Manila, June 1950.

Pres. Elpidio Quirino Taking Oath A100

**1950, July 4 Unwmk. *Perf. 12***
**547** A100 2c car rose .30 .25
**548** A100 4c magenta .30 .25
**549** A100 6c blue green .50 .25
*Nos. 547-549 (3)* 1.10 .75

Republic of the Philippines, 4th anniv.

**No. 527 Surcharged in Black**

**1950, Sept. 20**
**550** A91 1c on 2c bright green .60 .25

Dove over Globe — A101

**1950, Oct. 23**
**551** A101 5c green .80 .25
**552** A101 6c rose carmine .60 .25
**553** A101 18c ultra .60 .35
*Nos. 551-553 (3)* 2.00 .85

Baguio Conference of 1950.
For surcharge see No. 828.

Headman of Barangay Inspecting Harvest A102

**1951, Mar. 31 Litho. *Perf. 12½***
**554** A102 5c dull green 1.00 .25
**555** A102 6c red brown .50 .25
**556** A102 18c violet blue .50 .30
*Nos. 554-556 (3)* 2.00 .80

The government's Peace Fund campaign.

**Imperf., Pairs**

*554a* A102 5c dull green 4.00 2.00
*555a* A102 6c red brown 2.00 .90
*556a* A102 18c violet blue 1.50 .75
*Nos. 554a-556a (3)* 7.50 3.65

Arms of Manila A103

Arms of Cebu A104

Arms of Zamboanga A105

Arms of Iloilo A106

**Various Frames**

**1951 Engr. *Perf. 12***
**557** A103 5c purple 1.50 .25
**558** A103 6c gray 1.00 .25
**559** A103 18c bright ultra .70 .40

**Various Frames**

**560** A104 5c crimson rose 1.50 .25
**561** A104 6c bister brown .50 .25
**562** A104 18c violet 1.20 .40

**Various Frames**

**563** A105 5c blue green 1.60 .25
**564** A105 6c red brown 1.20 .25
**565** A105 18c light blue 1.20 .40

**Various Frames**

**566** A106 5c bright green 1.60 .25
**567** A106 6c violet 1.20 .25
**568** A106 18c deep blue 1.20 .40
*Nos. 557-568 (12)* 14.40 3.60

Issued: A103, 2/3; A104, 4/27; A105, 6/19; A106, 8/26.
For surcharges see Nos. 634-636.

UN Emblem and Girl Holding Flag — A107

**1951, Oct. 24 Unwmk. *Perf. 11½***
**569** A107 5c red 1.75 .30
**570** A107 6c blue green 1.00 .30
**571** A107 18c violet blue 1.00 .40
*Nos. 569-571 (3)* 3.75 1.00

United Nations Day, Oct. 24, 1951.

Liberty Holding Declaration of Human Rights — A108

**1951, Dec. 10 *Perf. 12***
**572** A108 5c green 1.50 .25
**573** A108 6c red orange .85 .25
**574** A108 18c ultra .85 .35
*Nos. 572-574 (3)* 3.20 .85

Universal Declaration of Human Rights.

Students and Department Seal — A109

**1952, Jan. 31**
**575** A109 5c orange red .75 .35

50th anniversary (in 1951) of the Philippine Educational System.

Milkfish and Map A111

**1952, Oct. 23 *Perf. 12½***
**578** A111 5c orange brown 1.60 .45
*a.* Vert. pair, imperf. between 65.00
*b.* Horiz. pair, imperf. between 65.00
**579** A111 6c deep blue .80 .30

4th Indo-Pacific Fisheries Council Meeting, Quezon City, Oct. 23-Nov. 7, 1952.
Nos. 578-579 exist imperf. Value, set $60.

Maria Clara — A112

**1952, Nov. 16**
**580** A112 5c deep blue 1.20 .30
**581** A112 6c brown .80 .30
*Nos. 580-581,C73 (3)* 4.00 1.35

1st Pan-Asian Philatelic Exhibition, PANAPEX, Manila, Nov. 16-22.
Nos. 580-81 exist imperf. Value, set $50.

Wright Park, Baguio City — A113

**1952, Dec. 15 *Perf. 12***
**582** A113 5c red orange 1.60 .45
**583** A113 6c dp blue green 1.10 .45

3rd Lions District Convention, Baguio City.

Francisco Baltazar, Poet — A114

**1953, Mar. 27**
**584** A114 5c citron .80 .30

National Language Week.

"Gateway to the East" — A115

**1953, Apr. 30**

**585** A115 5c turq green .60 .25
**586** A115 6c vermilion .50 .25

Philippines International Fair.

Presidents Quirino and Sukarno — A116

**1953, Oct. 5 Engr. & Litho.**

**587** A116 5c multicolored .65 .35
**588** A116 6c multicolored .35 .30

2nd anniversary of the visit of Indonesia's President Sukarno.

Marcelo H. del Pilar — A117

1c, Manuel L. Quezon. 2c, José Abad Santos (diff. frame). 3c, Apolinario Mabini (diff. frame). 10c, Father José Burgos. 20c, Lapu-Lapu. 25c, Gen. Antonio Luna. 50c, Cayetano Arellano. 60c, Andres Bonifacio. 2p, Graciano L. Jaena.

***Perf. 12, 12½, 13, 14x13½***

**1952-60 Engr.**

**589** A117 1c red brn ('53) .30 .25
**590** A117 2c gray ('60) .25 .25
**591** A117 3c brick red ('59) .30 .25
**592** A117 5c crim rose .30 .25
**595** A117 10c ultra ('55) .50 .25
**597** A117 20c car lake ('55) .80 .25
**598** A117 25c yel grn ('58) 1.00 .25
**599** A117 50c org ver ('59) 1.25 .25
**600** A117 60c car rose ('58) 1.50 .50
**601** A117 2p violet 5.00 1.00
*Nos. 589-601 (10)* 11.20 3.50

For overprints & surcharges see #608, 626, 641-642, 647, 830, 871, 875-877, O57-O61.

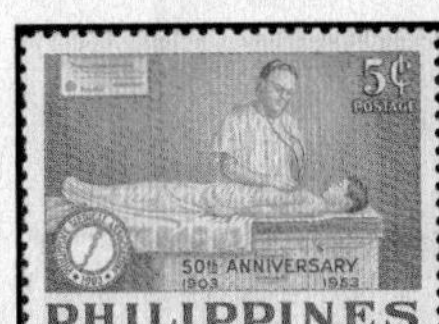


Doctor Examining Boy A118

**1953, Dec. 16**

**603** A118 5c lilac rose .80 .25
**604** A118 6c ultra .60 .25

50th anniversary of the founding of the Philippine Medical Association.

First Philippine Stamps, Magellan's Landing and Manila Scene A119

**Stamp of 1854 in Orange**

**1954, Apr. 25** ***Perf. 13***

**605** A119 5c purple .80 .35
**606** A119 18c deep blue 1.90 1.00
**607** A119 30c green 4.80 2.40
*Nos. 605-607,C74-C76 (6)* 23.00 9.60

Centenary of Philippine postage stamps. For surcharge see No. 829.

Nos. 592 and 509 Overprinted or Surcharged in Black

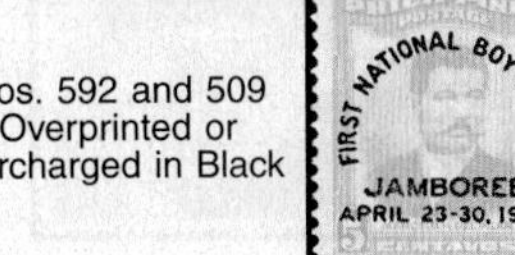


**1954, Apr. 23** ***Perf. 12***

**608** A117 5c crimson rose 2.00 .90
**609** A83 18c on 50c dull grn 2.50 1.40

1st National Boy Scout Jamboree, Quezon City, April 23-30, 1954.
The surcharge on No. 609 is reduced to fit the size of the stamp.

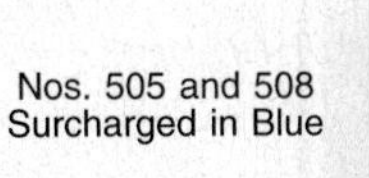

Discus Thrower and Games Emblem A120

**1954, May 31** ***Perf. 13***

**610** A120 5c shown 3.00 .80
**611** A120 18c Swimmer 1.00 .40
**612** A120 30c Boxers 2.50 1.50
*Nos. 610-612 (3)* 6.50 2.70

2nd Asian Games, Manila, May 1-9.

Nos. 505 and 508 Surcharged in Blue

**1954, Sept. 6** ***Perf. 12***

**613** A79 5c on 10c red org .75 .45
**614** A82 18c on 20c red brn .75 .45

Manila Conference, 1954.
The surcharge is arranged to obliterate the original denomination.

Allegory of Independence A121

**1954, Nov. 30** ***Perf. 13***

**615** A121 5c dark carmine 1.00 .25
**616** A121 18c deep blue .80 .30

56th anniversary of the declaration of the first Philippine Independence.
For surcharge see No. 826.

"Immaculate Conception," by Murillo — A122

**1954, Dec. 30** ***Perf. 12***

**617** A122 5c blue .70 .25

Issued to mark the end of the Marian Year.

Mayon Volcano, Moro Vinta and Rotary Emblem A123

**1955, Feb. 23 Engr.** ***Perf. 13***

**618** A123 5c dull blue .60 .25
**619** A123 18c dk car rose 1.40 .85
*Nos. 618-619,C77 (3)* 4.50 2.10

Rotary Intl., 50th anniv. For surcharge see #827.

Allegory of Labor — A124

**1955, May 26** ***Perf. 13x12½***

**620** A124 5c brown 1.75 .70

Issued in connection with the Labor-Management Congress, Manila, May 26-28, 1955.

Pres. Ramon Magsaysay A125

**1955, July 4** ***Perf. 12½***

**621** A125 5c blue .50 .25
**622** A125 20c red 1.25 .50
**623** A125 30c green 1.50 .50
*Nos. 621-623 (3)* 3.25 1.25

9th anniversary of the Republic.

Village Well A126

**1956, Mar. 16** ***Perf. 12½x13½***

**624** A126 5c violet .75 .25
**625** A126 20c dull green 1.25 .40

Issued to publicize the drive for improved health conditions in rural areas.

No. 592 Overprinted

**1956, Aug. 1 Unwmk.** ***Perf. 12***

**626** A117 5c crimson rose .65 .35

5th Annual Conf. of the World Confederation of Organizations of the Teaching Profession, Manila, Aug. 1-8, 1956.

Nurse and Disaster Victims A127

**Engraved; Cross Lithographed in Red**

**1956, Aug. 30**

**627** A127 5c violet .40 .30
**628** A127 20c gray brown 1.25 .60

50 years of Red Cross Service in the Philippines.

Monument to US Landing, Leyte — A128

**1956, Oct. 20 Litho.** ***Perf. 12½***

**629** A128 5c carmine rose .70 .25
*a.* Imperf, pair ('57) 5.75 3.00

Landing of US forces under Gen. Douglas MacArthur on Leyte, Oct. 20, 1944.
Issue date: No. 629a, Feb. 16.

Santo Tomas University A129

**1956, Nov. 13 Photo.** ***Perf. 11½***

**630** A129 5c brown car & choc .50 .35
**631** A129 60c lilac & red brn 3.50 1.60

Statue of Christ by Rizal — A130

**1956, Nov. 28 Engr.** ***Perf. 12***

**632** A130 5c gray olive .50 .25
**633** A130 20c rose carmine 1.25 .60

2nd Natl. Eucharistic Cong., Manila, Nov. 28-Dec. 2, and for the centenary of the Feast of the Sacred Heart.

**Nos. 561, 564 and 567 Surcharged with New Value in Blue or Black**

**1956, Dec. 7 Unwmk.** ***Perf. 12***

**634** A104 5c on 6c bis brn (Bl) .60 .25
**635** A105 5c on 6c red brn (Bl) .60 .25
**636** A106 5c on 6c vio (Bk) .60 .25
*Nos. 634-636 (3)* 1.80 .75

Girl Scout, Emblem and Tents A131

**1957, Jan. 19 Litho.** ***Perf. 12½***

**637** A131 5c dark blue .80 .40
*a.* Imperf, pair 9.00 7.00

Centenary of the Scout movement and for the Girl Scout World Jamboree, Quezon City, Jan. 19-Feb. 2, 1957.
Exmaples of Nos. 637 and 637a (No. 48 in sheet) exist with heavy black rectangular handstamps obliterating erroneous date at left, denomination and cloverleaf emblem.

Pres. Ramon Magsaysay (1907-57) — A132

**1957, Aug. 31 Engr. *Perf. 12***

638 A132 5c black .40 .25

"Spoliarium" by Juan Luna — A133

**1957, Oct. 23 *Perf. 14x14½***

639 A133 5c rose carmine .40 .25

Centenary of the birth of Juan Luna, painter.

Sergio Osmena and First National Assembly — A134

**1957, Oct. 16 *Perf. 12½x13½***

640 A134 5c blue green .40 .25

1st Philippine Assembly and honoring Sergio Osmeña, Speaker of the Assembly.

Nos. 595 and 597 Surcharged in Carmine or Black

**1957, Dec. 30 *Perf. 14x13½***

641 A117 5c on 10c ultra (C) .70 .25
642 A117 10c on 20c car lake .70 .30

Inauguration of Carlos P. Garcia as president and Diosdado Macapagal as vice-president, Dec. 30.

University of the Philippines — A135

**1958, June 18 Engr. *Perf. 13½x13***

643 A135 5c dk carmine rose .50 .25

50th anniversary of the founding of the University of the Philippines.

Pres. Carlos P. Garcia — A136

**1958, July 4 Photo. *Perf. 11½***
**Granite Paper**

644 A136 5c multicolored .25 .25
645 A136 20c multicolored .65 .30

12th anniversary of Philippine Republic.

Manila Cathedral — A137

**1958, Dec. 8 Engr. *Perf. 13x13½***

646 A137 5c multicolored .35 .25
*a.* Perf 12 3.00 2.00

Issued to commemorate the inauguration of the rebuilt Manila Cathedral, Dec. 8, 1958.

No. 592 Surcharged

**1959, Jan. 11 *Perf. 12***

647 A117 1c on 5c crim rose .35 .25

**Nos. B4-B5 Surcharged with New Values and Bars**

**1959, Feb. 3 *Perf. 13***

648 SP4 1c on 2c + 2c red .25 .25
649 SP5 6c on 4c + 4c vio .25 .25

14th anniversary of the liberation of Manila from the Japanese forces.

Philippine Flag A138

**1959, Feb. 8 Unwmk. *Perf. 13***

650 A138 6c dp ultra, yel & dp car .25 .25
651 A138 20c dp car, yel & dp ultra .60 .25

Seal of Bulacan Province — A139

**1959, Jan. 21 Engr. *Perf. 13***

652 A139 6c lt yellow grn .25 .25
653 A139 20c rose red .50 .25

60th anniversary of the Malolos constitution. For surcharge see No. 848.

**1959, Apr. 15**

Design: 6c, 25c, Seal of Capiz Province and portrait of Pres. Roxas.

654 A139 6c lt brown .25 .25
655 A139 25c purple .45 .25

Pres. Manuel A. Roxas, 11th death anniv.

Seal of Bacolod City — A140

**1959, Oct. 1**

656 A140 6c blue green .25 .25
657 A140 10c rose lilac .50 .25

Nos. 658-803 were reserved for the rest of a projected series showing seals and coats of arms of provinces and cities.

Camp John Hay Amphitheater, Baguio — A141

**1959, Sept. 1 *Perf. 13½***

804 A141 6c bright green .25 .25
*a.* Perf 12 2.00 1.50
805 A141 25c rose red .50 .25

50th anniversary of the city of Baguio.

**No. 533 Surcharged in Red**

**1959, Oct. 24 *Perf. 12***

806 A94 6c on 18c blue .50 .25

Issued for United Nations Day, Oct. 24.

Maria Cristina Falls — A142

**1959, Nov. 18 Photo. *Perf. 13½***

807 A142 6c vio & dp yel grn .25 .25
*a.* Perf 12 2.00 1.10
808 A142 30c green & brown .75 .30
*a.* Perf 12 6.25 4.75

**No. 504 Surcharged with New Value and Bars**

**1959, Dec. 1 Engr. *Perf. 12***

809 A78 1c on 4c blk brn .35 .25

Manila Atheneum Emblem — A143

**1959, Dec. 10 *Perf. 13½***

810 A143 6c ultra .25 .25
*a.* Perf 12 1.50 1.25
811 A143 30c rose red .55 .30
*a.* Perf 12 20.00 8.00

Centenary of the Manila Atheneum (Ateneo de Manila), a school, and to mark a century of progress in education.

Manuel Quezon — A144

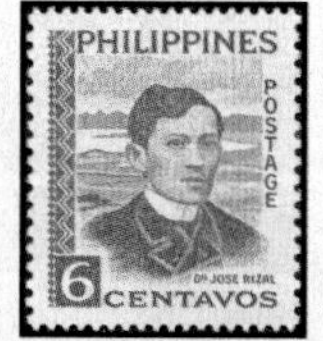
José Rizal — A145

**1959-60 Engr. *Perf. 13***

812 A144 1c olive gray ('60) .30 .25

***Perf. 14x12***

813 A145 6c gray blue .40 .25

Issued: No. 812, 11/15/60; No. 813, 12/30/59. For overprint see No. O62.

A146

***Perf. 12½x13½***

**1960, Feb. 8 Unwmk. Photo.**

814 A146 6c brown & gold .55 .25

25th anniversary of the Philippine Constitution. See No. C82.

Site of Manila Pact A147

**1960, Mar. 26 Engr. *Perf. 12½***

815 A147 6c emerald .25 .25
816 A147 25c orange .45 .25

5th anniversary (in 1959) of the Congress of the Philippines establishing the South-East Asia Treaty Organization (SEATO).
First Day Covers Issued 9/8/59.
For overprints see Nos. 841-842.

Sunset at Manila Bay and Uprooted Oak Emblem — A148

**1960, Apr. 7 Photo. *Perf. 13½***

817 A148 6c multicolored .30 .25
818 A148 25c multicolored .70 .25

World Refugee Year, 7/1/59-6/30/60.

A149

**1960, July 29 *Perf. 13½***

819 A149 5c lt grn, red & gold .40 .25
820 A149 6c bl, red & gold .40 .25

Philippine Tuberculosis Society, 50th anniv.

Basketball — A150

**1960, Nov. 30** *Perf. 13x13½*

**821** A150 6c shown .40 .25
**822** A150 10c Runner .60 .25
*Nos. 821-822,C85-C86 (4)* 3.00 1.55

17th Olympic Games, Rome, 8/25-9/11.

Presidents Eisenhower and Garcia and Presidential Seals — A151

**1960, Dec. 30** *Perf. 13½*

**823** A151 6c multi .35 .25
**824** A151 20c ultra, red & yel .60 .25

Visit of Pres. Dwight D. Eisenhower to the Philippines, June 14, 1960.

### Nos. 539, 616, 619, 553, 606 and 598 Surcharged with New Values and Bars in Red or Black

**1960-61** **Engr.** *Perf. 12, 13, 12½*

**825** A96 1c on 18c dp bl (R) .30 .25
**826** A121 5c on 18c dp bl (R) .65 .25
**827** A123 5c on 18c dp car rose .65 .25
**828** A101 10c on 18c ultra (R) .65 .25
**829** A119 10c on 18c dp bl & org (R) .65 .25
**830** A117 20c on 25c yel grn ('61) .65 .25
*Nos. 825-830 (6)* 3.55 1.50

On No. 830, no bars are overprinted, the surcharge "20 20" serving to cancel the old denomination.

Issued: Nos. 825, 827, 829, 7/4/60; Nos. 826, 828, 9/15/60; No. 830, 2/16/61.

Mercury and Globe — A152

**1961, Jan. 23** **Photo.** *Perf. 13½*

**831** A152 6c red brn, bl, blk & gold .70 .25

Manila Postal Conf., Jan. 10-23. See #C87.

### Nos. B10, B11 and B11a Surcharged "2nd National Boy Scout Jamboree Pasonanca Park" and New Value in Black or Red

**1961, May 2** **Engr.** *Perf. 13*

**Yellow Paper**

**832** SP8 10c on 6c + 4c car .40 .25
**833** SP8 30c on 25c + 5c bl (R) .70 .50
*a.* Tete beche, *wht* (10c on 6c + 4c & 30c on 25c + 5c) (Bk) 1.50 *2.00*

Second National Boy Scout Jamboree, Pasonanca Park, Zamboanga City.

De la Salle College, Manila A153

**1961, June 16** **Photo.** *Perf. 11½*

**834** A153 6c multi .35 .25
**835** A153 10c multi .35 .25

De la Salle College, Manila, 50th anniv.

José Rizal as Student A154

6c, Rizal & birthplace at Calamba, Laguna. 10c, Rizal & parents. 20c, Rizal with Juan Luna & F. R. Hidalgo in Madrid. 30c, Rizal's execution.

**1961** **Unwmk.** *Perf. 13½*

**836** A154 5c multi .35 .25
**837** A154 6c multi .35 .25
**838** A154 10c grn & red brn .45 .25
**839** A154 20c brn red & grnsh bl .55 .25
**840** A154 30c vio, lil & org brn .80 .30
*Nos. 836-840 (5)* 2.50 1.30

Centenary of the birth of José Rizal. Issued: Nos. 836-839, 1/19; No. 840 12/30.

### Nos. 815-816 Overprinted

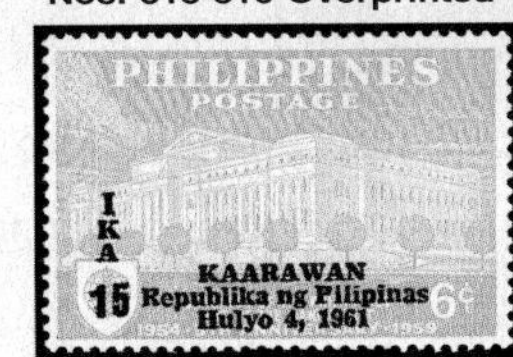


**1961, July 4** **Engr.** *Perf. 12½*

**841** A147 6c emerald .25 .25
**842** A147 25c orange .40 .25

15th anniversary of the Republic.

Colombo Plan Emblem and Globe Showing Member Countries — A155

**1961, Oct. 8** **Photo.** *Perf. 13x11½*

**843** A155 5c multi .25 .25
**844** A155 6c multi .25 .25

7th anniversary of the admission of the Philippines to the Colombo Plan.

Government Clerk — A156

**1961, Dec. 9** **Unwmk.** *Perf. 12½*

**845** A156 6c vio, bl & red .30 .25
**846** A156 10c gray bl & red .50 .25

Honoring Philippine government employees.

### No. C83 Surcharged

**1961, Nov. 30** **Engr.** *Perf. 14x14½*

**847** AP11 6c on 10c car .45 .25

Philippine Amateur Athletic Fed., 50th anniv.

### No. 655 Surcharged with New Value and: "MACAPAGAL-PELAEZ INAUGURATION DEC. 30, 1961"

**1961, Dec. 30** *Perf. 12½*

**848** A139 6c on 25c pur .40 .25

Inauguration of Pres. Diosdado Macapagal and Vice-Pres. Emanuel Pelaez.

### No. B8 Surcharged

**1962, Jan. 23** **Photo.** *Perf. 13½x13*

**849** SP7 6c on 5c grn & red .50 .25
*a.* Perf. 12 15.00 5.00

Vanda Orchids — A157

Orchids: 6c, White mariposa. 10c, Sander's dendrobe. 20c, Sanggumay.

**1962, Mar. 9** **Photo.** *Perf. 13½x14*

**Dark Blue Background**

**850** 5c rose, grn & yel .60 .25
**851** 6c grn & yel .60 .25
**852** 10c grn, car & brn .60 .25
**853** 20c lil, brn & grn .60 .25
*a.* A157 Block of 4, #850-853 2.50 2.25
*b.* As "a," imperf. 4.50 3.00

Apolinario Mabini — A158

Portraits: 1s, Manuel L. Quezon. 5s, Marcelo H. del Pilar. No. 857, José Rizal. No. 857A, Rizal (wearing shirt). 10s, Father José Burgos. 20s, Lapu-Lapu. 30s, Rajah Soliman. 50s, Cayetano Arellano. 70s, Sergio Osmena. No. 863, Emilio Jacinto. No. 864, José M. Panganiban.

***Perf. 13½; 14 (1s); 13x12 (#857, 10s)***

**1962-69** **Engr.** **Unwmk.**

**854** A158 1s org brn ('63) .25 .25
**855** A158 3s rose red .25 .25
**856** A158 5s car rose ('63) .25 .25
**857** A158 6s dk red brn .25 .25
**857A** A158 6s pck bl ('64) .25 .25
**858** A158 10s brt pur ('63) .30 .25
**859** A158 20s Prus bl ('63) .35 .25
**860** A158 30s vermilion .75 .25
**861** A158 50s vio ('63) 1.00 .25
**862** A158 70s brt bl ('63) 1.50 .25
**863** A158 1p grn ('63) 3.00 .35
**864** A158 1p dp org ('69) 2.00 .30
*Nos. 854-864 (12)* 10.15 3.15

Issued: Nos. 854, 856, 9/23/63; No. 855, 5/13/62; No. 857, 6/19/62; No. 857A, 6/19/64; No. 858, 3/24/63; No. 859, 10/20/63; No. 860, 11/30/62; No. 861, 5/1/63; No. 862, 12/10/63; No. 863, 1/23/63; No. 864, 2/1/69.

For surcharges & overprints see #873-874, 946, 969, 1054, 1119, 1209, O63-O69.

Pres. Macapagal Taking Oath of Office — A159

**1962, June 12** **Photo.** *Perf. 13½*

**Vignette Multicolored**

**865** A159 6s blue .25 .25
**866** A159 10s green .25 .25
**867** A159 30s violet .50 .25
*Nos. 865-867 (3)* 1.00 .75

Swearing in of President Diosdado Macapagal, Dec. 30, 1961.

Volcano in Lake Taal and Malaria Eradication Emblem A160

**1962, Oct. 24** **Unwmk.** *Perf. 11½*

**Granite Paper**

**868** A160 6s multi .30 .25
**869** A160 10s multi .30 .25
**870** A160 70s multi 1.60 1.60
*Nos. 868-870 (3)* 2.20 2.10

Issued on UN Day for the WHO drive to eradicate malaria.

No. 598 Surcharged in Red

**1962, Nov. 15** **Engr.** *Perf. 12*

**871** A117 20s on 25c yel grn .50 .25

Issued to commemorate the bicentennial of the Diego Silang revolt in Ilocos Province.

### No. B6 Overprinted with Sideways Chevron Obliterating Surtax

**1962, Dec. 23** *Perf. 12*

**872** SP6 5c on 5c + 1c dp bl .50 .25

### Nos. 855, 857 Surcharged with New Value and Old Value Obliterated

**1963** *Perf. 13½*

**873** A158 1s on 3s rose red .25 .25

*Perf. 13x12*

**874** A158 5s on 6s dk red brn .25 .25
*a.* Inverted overprint 20.00
*b.* Double overprint 15.00

Issued: No. 873, 3/12/63; No. 874, 2/19/63.

No. 601 Surcharged

**1963, June 12** *Perf. 12*

**875** A117 6s on 2p vio .30 .25
**876** A117 20s on 2p vio .50 .25
**877** A117 70s on 2p vio .80 .30
*Nos. 875-877 (3)* 1.60 .80

Diego Silang Bicentennial Art and Philatelic Exhibition, ARPHEX, Manila, May 28-June 30.

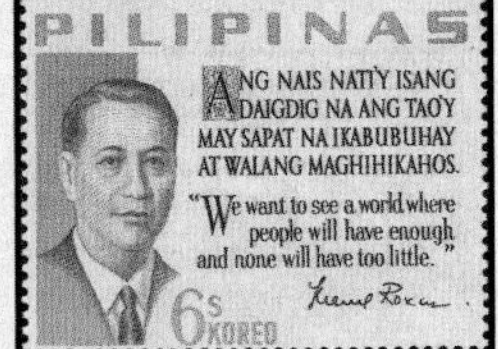


Pres. Manuel Roxas A161

**1963-73 Engr. *Perf. 13½***

878 A161 6s brt bl & blk, *bluish* .35 .25
879 A161 30s brn & blk, *brownish* .80 .25

**Pres. Ramon Magsaysay**

880 A161 6s lil & blk .35 .25
881 A161 30s yel grn & blk .80 .25

**Pres. Elpidio Quirino**

882 A161 6s grn & blk ('65) .35 .25
883 A161 30s rose lil & blk ('65) .80 .25

**Gen. (Pres.) Emilio Aguinaldo**

883A A161 6s dp cl & blk ('66) .35 .25
883B A161 30s bl & blk ('66) .80 .25

**Pres. José P. Laurel**

883C A161 6s red brn & blk ('66) .35 .25
883D A161 30s bl & blk ('66) .70 .25

**Pres. Manuel L. Quezon**

883E A161 10s bl gray & blk ('67) .35 .25
883F A161 30s vio & blk ('67) .70 .25

**Pres. Sergio Osmeña**

883G A161 10s rose lil & blk ('70) .35 .25
883H A161 40s grn & blk ('70) .80 .25

**Pres. Carlos P. Garcia**

883I A161 10s buff & blk ('73) .35 .25
883J A161 30s pink & blk ('73) .80 .25
*Nos. 878-883J (16)* 9.00 4.00

Nos. 878-883J honor former presidents.
Issued: Nos. 878-879, 7/4/63; Nos. 880-881, 12/30/63; Nos. 882-883, 2/28/65; Nos. 883A-883B, 2/6/66; Nos. 883C-883D, 11/6/66; Nos. 883E-883F, 11/16/67; Nos. 883G-883H, 6/12/70; Nos. 883I-883J, 2/22/73.
For surcharges see Nos. 984-985, 1120, 1146, 1160-1161.

Globe, Flags of Thailand, Korea, China, Philippines — A162

**1963, Aug. 26 Photo. *Perf. 13½x13***

884 A162 6s dk grn & multi .25 .25
885 A162 20s dk grn & multi .45 .25

Asian-Oceanic Postal Union, 1st anniv.
For surcharge see No. 1078.

Red Cross Centenary Emblem — A163

**1963, Sept. 1 *Perf. 11½***

886 A163 5s lt vio, gray & red .30 .25
887 A163 6s ultra, gray & red .30 .25
888 A163 20s grn, gray & red .40 .25
*Nos. 886-888 (3)* 1.00 .75

Centenary of the International Red Cross.

Bamboo Dance — A164

Folk Dances: 6s, Dance with oil lamps. 10s, Duck dance. 20s, Princess Gandingan's rock dance.

**1963, Sept. 15 Unwmk. *Perf. 14***

889 5s multi .40 .25
890 6s multi .40 .25
891 10s multi .40 .25
892 20s multi .40 .25
a. A164 Block of 4, #889-892 2.50 1.50

For surcharges and overprints see #1043-1046.

Pres. Macapagal and Filipino Family — A165

**1963, Sept. 28 *Perf. 14***

893 A165 5s bl & multi .25 .25
894 A165 6s yel & multi .25 .25
895 A165 20s lil & multi .50 .25
*Nos. 893-895 (3)* 1.00 .75

Issued to publicize Pres. Macapagal's 5-year Socioeconomic Program.
For surcharge see No. 1181.

Presidents Lopez Mateos and Macapagal — A166

**1963, Sept. 28 Photo. *Perf. 13½***

896 A166 6s multi .25 .25
897 A166 30s multi .50 .25

Visit of Pres. Adolfo Lopez Mateos of Mexico to the Philippines.
For surcharge see No. 1166.

Andres Bonifacio — A167

**1963, Nov. 30 Unwmk. *Perf. 12***

898 A167 5s gold, brn, gray & red .25 .25
899 A167 6s sil, brn, gray & red .35 .25
900 A167 25s brnz, brn, gray & red .50 .25
*Nos. 898-900 (3)* 1.10 .75

Centenary of the birth of Andres Bonifacio, national hero and poet.
For surcharges see Nos. 1147, 1162.

**No. 534 Overprinted: "UN ADOPTION/DECLARATION OF HUMAN RIGHTS/15TH ANNIVERSARY DEC. 10, 1963"**

**1963, Dec. 10 Engr. *Imperf.***

**Souvenir Sheet**

901 A94 Sheet of 3 3.25 2.50

15th anniv. of the Universal Declaration of Human Rights.

Woman holding Sheaf of Rice — A168

**1963, Dec. 20 Photo. *Perf. 13½x13***

902 A168 6s brn & multi .35 .25
*Nos. 902,C88-C89 (3)* 1.50 .80

FAO "Freedom from Hunger" campaign.

Bamboo Organ — A169

**1964, May 4 *Perf. 13½***

903 A169 5s multi .25 .25
904 A169 6s multi .25 .25
905 A169 20s multi .50 .25
*Nos. 903-905 (3)* 1.00 .75

The bamboo organ in the Church of Las Pinas, Rizal, was built by Father Diego Cera, 1816-1822.
For surcharge see No. 1055.

Apolinario Mabini — A170

**Wmk. 233**

**1964, July 23 Photo. *Perf. 14½***

906 A170 6s pur & gold .30 .25
907 A170 10s red brn & gold .30 .25
908 A170 30s brt grn & gold .40 .25
*Nos. 906-908 (3)* 1.00 .75

Apolinario Mabini (1864-1903), national hero and a leader of the 1898 revolution.
For surcharge see No. 1056.

Flags Surrounding SEATO Emblem — A171

**Unwmk.**

**1964, Sept. 8 Photo. *Perf. 13***

**Flags and Emblem Multicolored**

909 A171 6s dk bl & yel .25 .25
910 A171 10s dp grn & yel .30 .25
911 A171 25s dk brn & yel .45 .25
*Nos. 909-911 (3)* 1.00 .75

10th anniversary of the South-East Asia Treaty Organization (SEATO).
For surcharge see No. 1121.

Pres. Macapagal Signing Code — A172

**1964, Dec. 21 Wmk. 233 *Perf. 14½***

912 A172 3s multi .35 .25
913 A172 6s multi .40 .25
*Nos. 912-913,C90 (3)* 1.35 .75

Signing of the Agricultural Land Reform Code. For surcharges see Nos. 970, 1234.

Basketball — A173

Sport: 10s, Women's relay race. 20s, Hurdling. 30s, Soccer.

**1964, Dec. 28 *Perf. 14½x14***

915 A173 6s lt bl, dk brn & gold .30 1.25
916 A173 10s gold, pink & dk brn .30 1.25
b. Gold omitted
917 A173 20s gold, dk brn & yel .60 .25
918 A173 30s emer, dk brn & gold .80 .25
*Nos. 915-918 (4)* 2.00 3.00

18th Olympic Games, Tokyo, Oct. 10-25.
For overprints and surcharge see Nos. 962-965, 1079.

**1965, Mar. 22 Imperf., Pairs**

*915a* A173 6s 1.25 1.25
*916a* A173 10s 1.25 1.25
*917a* A173 20s 2.75 1.75
*918a* A173 30s 2.75 1.75
*Nos. 915a-918a (4)* 8.00 6.00

Presidents Lubke and Macapagal and Coats of Arms — A174

**1965, Apr. 19 Unwmk. *Perf. 13½***

919 A174 6s ol grn & multi .25 .25
920 A174 10s multi .35 .25
921 A174 25s dp bl & multi .40 .25
*Nos. 919-921 (3)* 1.00 .75

Visit of Pres. Heinrich Lubke of Germany, Nov. 18-23, 1964.
For surcharge see No. 1167.

Emblems of Manila Observatory and Weather Bureau — A175

**1965, May 22 Photo. *Perf. 13½***

922 A175 6s lt ultra & multi .25 .25
923 A175 20s lt vio & multi .30 .25
924 A175 50s bl grn & multi .55 .25
*Nos. 922-924 (3)* 1.10 .75

Issued to commemorate the centenary of the Meteorological Service in the Philippines.
For surcharge see No. 1069.

Pres. John F. Kennedy (1917-63) — A176

***Perf. 14½x14***

**1965, May 29 Wmk. 233**

**Center Multicolored**

925 A176 6s gray .25 .25
926 A176 10s brt vio .30 .25
927 A176 30s brt ultra .45 .25
*Nos. 925-927 (3)* 1.00 .75

Nos. 925-927 exist with ultramarine of tie omitted. No. 926 exist with red on face omitted. Value, $100. No. 927 exist with yellow on face omitted. Value, $100.
Nos. 925 and 927 exist imperf. Value, set $100.
For surcharges see Nos. 1148, 1210.

King and Queen of Thailand, Pres. and Mrs. Macapagal — A177

*Perf. 12½x13*

**1965, June 12** **Unwmk.**

**928** A177 2s brt bl & multi .25 .25
**929** A177 6s bis & multi .35 .25
**930** A177 30s red & multi .50 .25
*Nos. 928-930 (3)* 1.10 .75

Visit of King Bhumibol Adulyadej and Queen Sirikit of Thailand, July 1963.
For surcharge see No. 1122.

Princess Beatrix and Evangelina Macapagal A178

*Perf. 13x12½*

**1965, July 4** **Photo.** **Unwmk.**

**931** A178 2s bl & multi .25 .25
**932** A178 6s blk & multi .25 .25
**933** A178 10s multi .35 .25
*Nos. 931-933 (3)* .85 .75

Visit of Princess Beatrix of the Netherlands, Nov. 21-23, 1962.
For surcharge see No. 1188.

Map of Philippines, Cross and Legaspi-Urdaneta Monument — A179

Design: 3s, Cross and Rosary held before map of Philippines.

**1965, Oct. 4** **Unwmk.** ***Perf. 13***

**934** A179 3s multi .25 .25
**935** A179 6s multi .30 .25
*Nos. 934-935,C91-C92 (4)* 2.75 1.25

400th anniv. of the Christianization of the Philippines. See souvenir sheet No. C92a. For overprint see No. C108.

Presidents Sukarno and Macapagal and Prime Minister Tunku Abdul Rahman A180

**1965, Nov. 25** ***Perf. 13***

**936** A180 6s multi .25 .25
**937** A180 10s multi .30 .25
**938** A180 25s multi .55 .25
*Nos. 936-938 (3)* 1.10 .75

Signing of the Manila Accord (Mapilindo) by Malaya, Philippines and Indonesia.
For surcharge see No. 1182.

Bicyclists and Globe A181

**1965, Dec. 5** ***Perf. 13½***

**939** A181 6s multi .25 .25
**940** A181 10s multi .30 .25
**941** A181 25s multi .55 .25
*Nos. 939-941 (3)* 1.10 .75

Second Asian Cycling Championship, Philippines, Nov. 28-Dec. 5.

**Nos. B21-B22 Surcharged**

**1965, Dec. 30** **Engr.** ***Perf. 13***

**942** SP12 10s on 6s + 4s .40 .25
**943** SP12 30s on 30s + 5s .60 .25

Inauguration of President Ferdinand Marcos and Vice-President Fernando Lopez.

Antonio Regidor — A182

**1966, Jan. 21** ***Perf. 12x11***

**944** A182 6s blue .30 .25
**945** A182 30s brown .40 .25

Dr. Antonio Regidor, Sec. of the High Court of Manila and Pres. of Public Instruction.
For surcharges see Nos. 1110-1111.

No. 857A Overprinted in Red

**1966, May 1** **Engr.** ***Perf. 13½***

**946** A158 6s peacock blue .35 .25

Anti-smuggling drive.
Exists with black overprint. Value, $35. Exists with overprint inverted, double, double inverted and double with one inverted.
For surcharge see No. 1209.

Girl Scout Giving Scout Sign A183

**1966, May 26** **Litho.** ***Perf. 13x12½***

**947** A183 3s ultra & multi .30 .25
**948** A183 6s emer & multi .30 .25
**949** A183 20s brn & multi .40 .25
*Nos. 947-949 (3)* 1.00 .75

Philippine Girl Scouts, 25th anniversary.
For surcharge see No. 1019.

Pres. Marcos Taking Oath of Office — A184

**1966, June 12** ***Perf. 12½***

**950** A184 6s bl & multi .30 .25
**951** A184 20s emer & multi .40 .25
**952** A184 30s yel & multi .50 .25
*Nos. 950-952 (3)* 1.20 .75

Inauguration of Pres. Ferdinand E. Marcos, 12/30/65.
For overprints & surcharge see #960-961, 1050.

Seal of Manila and Historical Scenes — A185

**1966, June 24**

**953** A185 6s multi .35 .25
**954** A185 30s multi .45 .25

Adoption of the new seal of Manila.
For surcharges see Nos. 1070, 1118, 1235.

Old and New Philippine National Bank Buildings — A186

Designs: 6s, Entrance to old bank building and 1p silver coin.

**1966, July 22** **Photo.** ***Perf. 14x13½***

**955** A186 6s gold, ultra, sil & blk .30 .25
**956** A186 10s multi .40 .25

50th anniv. of the Philippine Natl. Bank. See #C93. For surcharges see #1071, 1100, 1236.

Post Office, Annex Three A187

**1966, Oct. 1** **Wmk. 233** ***Perf. 14½***

**957** A187 6s lt vio, yel & grn .30 .25
**958** A187 10s rose cl, yel & grn .30 .25
**959** A187 20s ultra, yel & grn .40 .25
*Nos. 957-959 (3)* 1.00 .75

60th anniversary of Postal Savings Bank.
For surcharges see Nos. 1104, 1112, 1189.

**Nos. 950 and 952 Overprinted in Emerald or Black**

*Perf. 12½*

**1966, Oct. 24** **Litho.** **Unwmk.**

**960** A184 6s multi (E) .30 .25
**961** A184 30s multi .50 .25

Manila Summit Conference, Oct. 23-27.
No. 960 eixsts with overprint in black and double impression of blue on base stamp. Value, $35. No. 961 exists with overprint inverted. Value, $40. No. 961 exists imperf. with emerald overprint. Value, $60.

Nos. 915a-918a Overprinted

**Wmk. 233**

**1967, Jan. 14** **Photo.** ***Imperf.***

**962** A173 6s lt bl, dk brn & gold .50 .25
**963** A173 10s gold, dk brn & pink .50 .25
**964** A173 20s gold, dk brn & yel .60 .35
**965** A173 30s emer, dk brn & gold .80 .55
*Nos. 962-965 (4)* 2.40 1.40

Lions Intl., 50th anniv. The Lions emblem is in the lower left corner on the 6s, in the upper left corner on the 10s and in the upper right corner on the 30s.

No. 962 exist with overprint (for No. 963) inverted, Value, $50. No. 962 exist

"Succor" by Fernando Amorsolo — A188

**Unwmk.**

**1967, Apr. 9** **Litho.** ***Perf. 14***

**966** A188 5s sepia & multi .40 .25
**967** A188 20s blue & multi .85 .25
**968** A188 2p green & multi 1.75 .60
*Nos. 966-968 (3)* 3.00 1.10

25th anniversary of the Battle of Bataan.

**Nos. 857A and 913 Surcharged**

**1967, Aug.** **Engr.** ***Perf. 13½***

**969** A158 4s on 6s pck bl .40 .25

**Wmk. 233**

**Photo.** ***Perf. 14½***

**970** A172 5s on 6s multi .45 .25

Issue dates: 4s, Aug. 10; 5s, Aug. 7.

Gen. Douglas MacArthur and Paratroopers Landing on Corregidor — A189

**Unwmk.**

**1967, Aug. 31** **Litho.** ***Perf. 14***

**971** A189 6s multi .50 .25
**972** A189 5p multi 6.50 3.00

25th anniversary, Battle of Corregidor.

Bureau of Posts, Manila, Jones Bridge over Pasig River — A190

**1967, Sept. 15** **Litho.** ***Perf. 14x13½***

**973** A190 4s multi & blk .40 .25
**974** A190 20s multi & red .40 .25
**975** A190 50s multi & vio .55 .30
*Nos. 973-975 (3)* 1.35 .80

65th anniversary of the Bureau of Posts.
For overprint see No. 1015.

Philippine Nativity Scene — A191

**1967, Dec. 1 Photo. *Perf. 13½***

**976** A191 10s multi .40 .25
**977** A191 40s multi .60 .30

Christmas 1967.

Chinese Garden, Rizal Park, Presidents Marcos and Chiang Kai-shek — A192

Presidents' heads & scenes in Chinese Garden, Rizal Park, Manila: 10s, Gate. 20s, Landing pier.

**1967-68 Photo. *Perf. 13½***

**978** A192 5s multi .25 .25
**979** A192 10s multi ('68) .35 .25
**980** A192 20s multi .85 .25
*Nos. 978-980 (3)* 1.45 .75

Sino-Philippine Friendship Year 1966-67.
Issued: Nos. 978, 980, 12/30/67; No. 979, 3/12/68.

Makati Center Post Office, Mrs. Marcos and Rotary Emblem — A193

**1968, Jan. 9 Litho. *Perf. 14***

**981** A193 10s bl & multi .30 .25
**982** A193 20s grn & multi .40 .25
**983** A193 40s multi .60 .35
*Nos. 981-983 (3)* 1.30 .85

1st anniv. of the Makati Center Post Office.

**Nos. 882, 883C and B27 Surcharged**

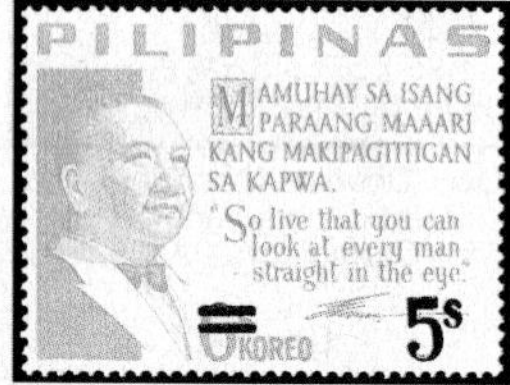


**1968, Mar. 8**

**984** A161 5s on 6s grn & blk .55 .25
*a.* Double overprint 15.00
**985** A161 5s on 6s lt red brn & blk .55 .25
**986** SP14 10s on 6s + 5s ultra & red .70 .25
*a.* Double overprint 18.00
*Nos. 984-986 (3)* 1.80 .75

The "1" in the surcharged value on No. 986 is serifed. For surcharge without serif on "1," see No. 1586.

Felipe G. Calderon, Barasoain Church and Malolos Constitution — A194

**1968, Apr. 4 Litho. *Perf. 14***

**987** A194 10s lt ultra & multi .30 .25
**988** A194 40s grn & multi .60 .25
**989** A194 75s multi 1.10 .60
*Nos. 987-989 (3)* 2.00 1.10

Calderon (1868-1909), lawyer and author of the Malolos Constitution.

Earth and Transmission from Philippine Station to Satellite — A195

**1968, Oct. 21 Photo. *Perf. 13½***

**990** A195 10s blk & multi .35 .25
**991** A195 40s multi .60 .25
**992** A195 75s multi 1.25 .50
*Nos. 990-992 (3)* 2.20 1.00

Issued to commemorate the inauguration of the Philcomsat Station in Tany, Luzon, May 2, 1968.

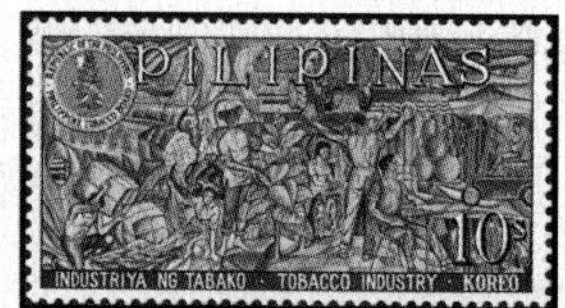


Tobacco Industry and Tobacco Board's Emblem — A196

**1968, Nov. 15 Photo. *Perf. 13½***

**993** A196 10s blk & multi .30 .25
**994** A196 40s bl & multi .70 .50
**995** A196 70s crim & multi 1.10 .90
*Nos. 993-995 (3)* 2.10 1.65

Philippine tobacco industry.

Kudyapi A197

Philippine Musical Instruments: 20s, Ludag (drum). 30s, Kulintangan. 50s, Subing (bamboo flute).

**1968, Nov. 22 Photo. *Perf. 13½***

**996** A197 10s multi .30 .25
**997** A197 20s multi .40 .25
**998** A197 30s multi .70 .25
**999** A197 50s multi 1.00 .45
*Nos. 996-999 (4)* 2.40 1.20

Concordia College A198

**1968, Dec. 8 *Perf. 13x13½***

**1000** A198 10s multi .30 .25
**1001** A198 20s multi .40 .25
**1002** A198 70s multi .70 .30
*Nos. 1000-1002 (3)* 1.40 .80

Centenary of the Colegio de la Concordia, Manila, a Catholic women's school. Issued Dec. 8 (Sunday), but entered the mail Dec. 9.

Singing Children — A199

**1968, Dec. 16 *Perf. 13½***

**1003** A199 10s multi .30 .25
**1004** A199 40s multi .60 .45
**1005** A199 75s multi 1.10 .80
*Nos. 1003-1005 (3)* 2.00 1.50

Christmas 1968.

Animals A200

**1969, Jan. 8 Photo. *Perf. 13½***

**1006** A200 2s Tarsier .30 .25
**1007** A200 10s Tamarau .50 .25
**1008** A200 20s Carabao .70 .25
**1009** A200 75s Mouse deer 2.00 .75
*Nos. 1006-1009 (4)* 3.50 1.50

Opening of the hunting season.

Emilio Aguinaldo and Historical Building, Cavite — A201

**1969, Jan. 23 Litho. *Perf. 14***

**1010** A201 10s yel & multi .30 .25
**1011** A201 40s bl & multi .70 .30
**1012** A201 70s multi 1.00 .70
*Nos. 1010-1012 (3)* 2.00 1.25

Emilio Aguinaldo (1869-1964), commander of Filipino forces in rebellion against Spain.

Guard Turret, San Andres Bastion, Manila, and Rotary Emblem — A202

**1969, Jan. 29 Photo. *Perf. 12½***

**1013** A202 10s ultra & multi .40 .25
*Nos. 1013,C96-C97 (3)* 1.80 1.00

50th anniv. of the Manila Rotary Club.

Senator Claro M. Recto (1890-1960), Lawyer and Supreme Court Judge — A203

**1969, Feb. 8 Engr. *Perf. 13***

**1014** A203 10s bright rose lilac .45 .25

**No. 973 Overprinted**

**1969, Feb. 14 Litho. *Perf. 14x13½***

**1015** A190 4s multi & blk .50 .25

Philatelic Week, Nov. 24-30, 1968.

José Rizal College, Mandaluyong — A204

**1969, Feb. 19 Photo. *Perf. 13***

**1016** A204 10s multicolored .25 .25
**1017** A204 40s multicolored .45 .25
**1018** A204 50s multicolored .95 .30
*Nos. 1016-1018 (3)* 1.65 .80

Founding of Rizal College, 50th anniv.

**No. 948 Surcharged in Red**

**1969, May 10 Litho. *Perf. 13x12½***

**1019** A183 5s on 6s multi .50 .25

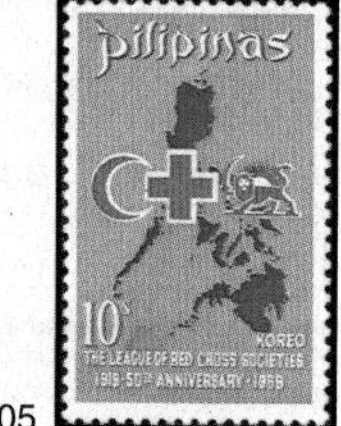


A205

Map of Philippines, Red Crescent, Cross, Lion and Sun emblems.

**1969, May 26 Photo. *Perf. 12½***

**1020** A205 10s gray, ultra & red .25 .25
**1021** A205 40s lt ultra, dk bl & red .45 .30
**1022** A205 75s bister, brn & red .90 .35
*Nos. 1020-1022 (3)* 1.60 .90

League of Red Cross Societies, 50th anniv.

A206

Pres. and Mrs. Marcos harvesting miracle rice.

**1969, June 12 Photo. *Perf. 14***

**1023** A206 10s multicolored .25 .25
**1024** A206 40s multicolored .45 .30
**1025** A206 75s multicolored .90 .35
*Nos. 1023-1025 (3)* 1.60 .90

Introduction of IR8 (miracle) rice, produced by the International Rice Research Institute.

Holy Child of Leyte and Map of Leyte — A207

**1969, June 30** *Perf. 13½*

**1026** A207 5s emerald & multi .25 .25
**1027** A207 10s crimson & multi .35 .25

80th anniv. of the return of the image of the Holy Child of Leyte to Tacloban. See No. C98.

Philippine Development Bank — A208

**1969, Sept. 12** **Photo.** *Perf. 13½*

**1028** A208 10s dk bl, blk & grn .25 .25
**1029** A208 40s rose car, blk & grn .85 .45
**1030** A208 75s brown, blk & grn 1.40 .55
*Nos. 1028-1030 (3)* 2.50 1.25

Inauguration of the new building of the Philippine Development Bank in Makati, Rizal.

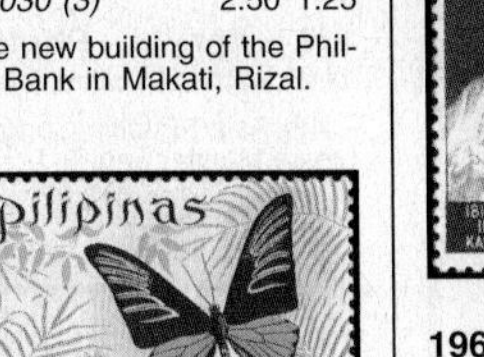


Common Birdwing A209

Butterflies: 20s, Tailed jay. 30s, Red Helen. 40s, Birdwing.

**1969, Sept. 15** **Photo.** *Perf. 13½*

**1031** A209 10s multicolored .60 .25
**1032** A209 20s multicolored 1.40 .25
**1033** A209 30s multicolored 1.40 .35
**1034** A209 40s multicolored 1.40 .45
*Nos. 1031-1034 (4)* 4.80 1.30

World's Children and UNICEF Emblem A210

**1969, Oct. 6**

**1035** A210 10s blue & multi .25 .25
**1036** A210 20s multicolored .35 .25
**1037** A210 30s multicolored .40 .25
*Nos. 1035-1037 (3)* 1.00 .75

15th anniversary of Universal Children's Day.

Monument and Leyte Landing — A211

**1969, Oct. 20** *Perf. 13½x14*

**1038** A211 5s lt grn & multi .25 .25
**1039** A211 10s yellow & multi .35 .25
**1040** A211 40s pink & multi .50 .25
*Nos. 1038-1040 (3)* 1.10 .75

25th anniv. of the landing of the US forces under Gen. Douglas MacArthur on Leyte, Oct. 20, 1944.

Philippine Cultural Center, Manila — A212

**1969, Nov. 4** **Photo.** *Perf. 13½*

**1041** A212 10s ultra .30 .25
**1042** A212 30s brt rose lilac .60 .25

Cultural Center of the Philippines, containing theaters, a museum and libraries.

**Nos. 889-892 Surcharged or Overprinted: "1969 PHILATELIC WEEK"**

**1969, Nov. 24** **Photo.** *Perf. 14*

**1043** A164 5s multicolored .45 .25
**1044** A164 5s on 6s multi .45 .25
**1045** A164 10s multicolored .45 .25
**1046** A164 10s on 20s multi .45 .25
*a.* Block of 4, #1043-1046 2.75 1.75

Philatelic Week, Nov. 23-29.

Melchora Aquino — A213

**1969, Nov. 30** *Perf. 12½*

**1047** A213 10s multicolored .25 .25
**1048** A213 20s multicolored .30 .25
**1049** A213 30s dk bl & multi .45 .25
*Nos. 1047-1049 (3)* 1.00 .75

Melchora Aquino (Tandang Sora; 1812-1919), the Grand Old Woman of the Revolution.

**No. 950 Surcharged with New Value, 2 Bars and: "PASINAYA, IKA -2 PANUNUNGKULAN / PANGULONG FERDINAND E. MARCOS / DISYEMBRE 30, 1969"**

**1969, Dec. 30** **Litho.** *Perf. 12½*

**1050** A184 5s on 6s multi .55 .25
*a.* Type II 1.25 .50
*b.* Double overprint 40.00
*c.* Double impression of blue 25.00

Inauguration of Pres. Marcos and Vice Pres. Fernando Lopez for 2nd term, 12/30.

Pouring Ladle and Iligan Steel Mills — A214

**1970, Jan. 20** **Photo.** *Perf. 13½*

**1051** A214 10s ver & multi .50 .25
**1052** A214 20s multicolored .80 .25
**1053** A214 30s ultra & multi .80 .25
*Nos. 1051-1053 (3)* 2.10 .75

Iligan Integrated Steel Mills, Northern Mindanao, the first Philippine steel mills.

**Nos. 857A, 904 and 906 Surcharged with New Value and Two Bars**

**1970, Apr. 30** **As Before**

**1054** A158 4s on 6s peacock bl .50 .25
**1055** A169 5s on 6s multi .85 .25
**1056** A170 5s on 6s pur & gold .85 .25
*a.* Double overprint 25.00
*Nos. 1054-1056 (3)* 2.20 .75

New UPU Headquarters and Monument, Bern — A215

*Perf. 13½*

**1970, May 20** **Unwmk.** **Photo.**

**1057** A215 10s bl, dk bl & yel .30 .25
**1058** A215 30s lt grn, dk bl & yel .50 .25

Opening of the new UPU Headquarters in Bern.

Emblem, Mayon Volcano and Filipina — A216

**1970, Sept. 6** **Photo.** *Perf. 13½x14*

**1059** A216 10s brt blue & multi .25 .25
**1060** A216 20s multicolored .35 .25
**1061** A216 30s multicolored .50 .25
*Nos. 1059-1061 (3)* 1.10 .75

15th International Conference on Social Welfare, Manila, Sept. 6-12.

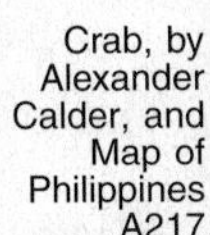

Crab, by Alexander Calder, and Map of Philippines A217

**1970, Oct. 5** *Perf. 13x13½*

**1062** A217 10s emerald & multi .25 .25
**1063** A217 40s multicolored .45 .25
**1064** A217 50s ultra & multi .65 .45
*Nos. 1062-1064 (3)* 1.35 .95

Campaign against cancer.

Scaled Tridacna A218

Sea Shells: 10s, Royal spiny oyster. 20s, Venus comb. 40s, Glory of the sea.

**1970, Oct. 19** **Photo.** *Perf. 13½*

**1065** A218 5s black & multi .50 .25
**1066** A218 10s dk grn & multi 1.00 .25
**1067** A218 20s multicolored 1.00 .30
**1068** A218 40s dk blue & multi 1.75 .50
*Nos. 1065-1068 (4)* 4.25 1.30

**Nos. 922, 953 and 955 Surcharged**

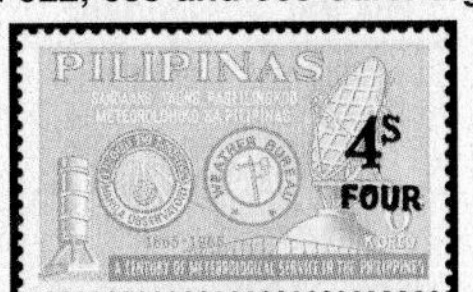


**Photogravure; Lithographed**

**1970, Oct. 26** *Perf. 13½, 12½*

**1069** A175 4s on 6s multi .85 .25
**1070** A185 4s on 6s multi 1.20 .25
**1071** A186 4s on 6s multi 1.25 .25
*Nos. 1069-1071 (3)* 3.30 .75

On No. 1070, old denomination is obliterated by two bars.
One line surcharge on No. 1071.

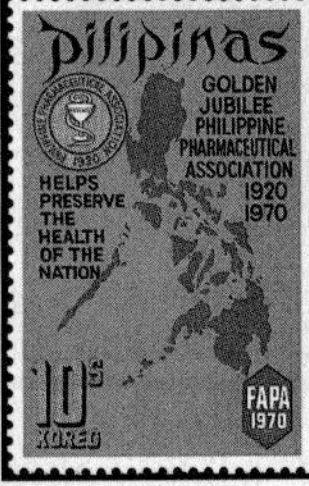


Map of Philippines and FAPA Emblem — A219

**1970, Nov. 16** **Photo.** *Perf. 13½*

**1072** A219 10s dp org & multi .25 .25
**1073** A219 50s lt violet & multi .75 .25

Opening of the 4th General Assembly of the Federation of Asian Pharmaceutical Assoc. (FAPA) & the 3rd Asian Cong. of Pharmaceutical Sciences.

Hundred Islands of Pangasinan, Peddler's Cart — A220

20s, Tree house in Pasonanca Park, Zamboanga City. 30s, Sugar industry, Negros Island, Mt. Kanlaon, Woman & Carabao statue, symbolizing agriculture. 2p, Miagao Church, Iloilo, & horse-drawn calesa.

**1970, Nov. 12** *Perf. 12½x13½*

**1074** A220 10s multicolored .30 .25
**1075** A220 20s multicolored .50 .25
**1076** A220 30s multicolored 1.00 .30
**1077** A220 2p multicolored 3.00 1.00
*Nos. 1074-1077 (4)* 4.80 1.80

Tourist publicity. See Nos. 1086-1097.

**No. 884 Surcharged: "UPU-AOPU / Regional Seminar / Nov. 23-Dec. 5, 1970 / TEN 10s"**

**1970, Nov. 22** **Photo.** *Perf. 13½x13*

**1078** A162 10s on 6s multi .60 .50

Universal Postal Union and Asian-Oceanic Postal Union Regional Seminar, 11/23-12/5.

**No. 915 Surcharged Vertically: "1970 PHILATELIC WEEK"**

*Perf. 14½x14*

**1970, Nov. 22** **Wmk. 233**

**1079** A173 10s on 6s multi .50 .25

Philatelic Week, Nov. 22-28.
Exists imperf. Value, $60.

Pope Paul VI, Map of Far East and Australia — A221

*Perf. 13½x14*

**1970, Nov. 27** **Photo.** **Unwmk.**

**1080** A221 10s ultra & multi .35 .25
**1081** A221 30s multicolored .60 .25
*Nos. 1080-1081,C99 (3)* 1.85 .80

Visit of Pope Paul VI, Nov. 27-29, 1970.

Mariano Ponce — A222

**1970, Dec. 30 Engr.** ***Perf. 14½***

**1082** A222 10s rose carmine .40 .25

Mariano Ponce (1863-1918), editor and legislator. See #1136-1137. For surcharges & overprint see #1190, 1231, O70.

PATA Emblem A223

**1971, Jan. 21 Photo.** ***Perf. 14½***

**1083** A223 5s brt green & multi .35 .25
**1084** A223 10s blue & multi .50 .25
**1085** A223 70s brown & multi 1.00 .35
*Nos. 1083-1085 (3)* 1.85 .85

Pacific Travel Association (PATA), 20th annual conference, Manila, Jan. 21-29.

**Tourist Type of 1970**

Designs: 10s, Filipina and Ang Nayong (7 village replicas around man-made lagoon). 20s, Woman and fisherman, Estancia. 30s, Pagsanjan Falls. 5p, Watch Tower, Punta Cruz, Boho.

***Perf. 12½x13½***

**1971, Feb. 15 Photo.**

**1086** A220 10s multicolored .40 .25
**1087** A220 20s multicolored .50 .30
**1088** A220 30s multicolored 1.20 .35
**1089** A220 5p multicolored 3.50 1.75
*Nos. 1086-1089 (4)* 5.60 2.65

**1971, Apr. 19**

Designs: 10s, Cultured pearl farm, Davao. 20s, Coral divers, Davao, Mindanao. 40s, Moslem Mosque, Zamboanga. 1p, Rice terraces, Banaue.

**1090** A220 10s multicolored .30 .25
**1091** A220 20s multicolored .50 .30
**1092** A220 40s multicolored 1.20 .35
**1093** A220 1p multicolored 2.50 .80
*Nos. 1090-1093 (4)* 4.50 1.70

**1971, May 3**

10s, Spanish cannon, Zamboanga. 30s, Magellan's cross, Cebu City. 50s, Big Jar monument in Calamba, Laguna. 70s, Mayon Volcano, Legazpi city.

**1094** A220 10s multicolored .30 .25
**1095** A220 30s multicolored .50 .25
**1096** A220 50s multicolored 1.20 .25
**1097** A220 70s multicolored 1.40 .35
*Nos. 1094-1097 (4)* 3.40 1.10

Family and Emblem A224

**1971, Mar. 21 Photo.** ***Perf. 13½***

**1098** A224 20s lt grn & multi .25 .25
**1099** A224 40s pink & multi .40 .25

Regional Conf. of the Intl. Planned Parenthood Federation for SE Asia & Oceania, Baguio City, Mar. 21-27.

**No. 955 Surcharged**

**1971, June 10 Photo.** ***Perf. 14x13½***

**1100** A186 5s on 6s multi .80 .25

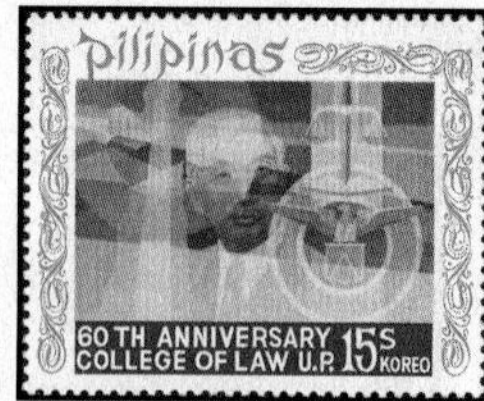


Allegory of Law A225

**1971, June 15 Photo.** ***Perf. 13***

**1101** A225 15s orange & multi .50 .30

60th anniversary of the University of the Philippines Law College. See No. C100.

Manila Anniversary Emblem — A226

**1971, June 24**

**1102** A226 10s multicolored .50 .35

Founding of Manila, 400th anniv. See #C101.

Santo Tomas University, Arms of Schools of Medicine and Pharmacology — A227

**1971, July 8 Photo.** ***Perf. 13½***

**1103** A227 5s yellow & multi .50 .35

Centenary of the founding of the Schools of Medicine and Surgery, and Pharmacology at the University of Santo Tomas, Manila. See No. C102.

**No. 957 Surcharged**

**1971, July 11 Wmk. 233** ***Perf. 14½***

**1104** A187 5s on 6s multi .50 .25
*a.* Inverted overprint 12.00
*b.* Double overprint 20.00

World Congress of University Presidents, Manila.

Our Lady of Guia Appearing to Filipinos and Spanish Soldiers — A228

**1971, July 8 Photo.** ***Perf. 13½***

**1105** A228 10s multi .30 .25
**1106** A228 75s multi 1.20 .35

4th centenary of appearance of the statue of Our Lady of Guia, Ermita, Manila.

Bank Building, Plane, Car and Workers — A229

**1971, Sept. 14** ***Perf. 12½***

**1107** A229 10s blue & multi .30 .25
**1108** A229 30s lt grn & multi .30 .25
**1109** A229 1p multicolored .90 .35
*Nos. 1107-1109 (3)* 1.50 .85

1st Natl. City Bank in the Philippines, 70th anniv.

No. 944 Surcharged

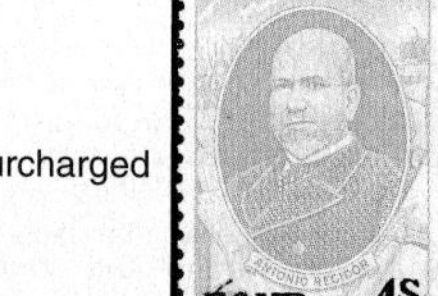


***Perf. 12x11***

**1971, Nov. 24 Engr. Unwmk.**

**1110** A182 4s on 6s blue .35 *.25*
**1111** A182 5s on 6s blue .40 .25

**No. 957 Surcharged**

**Wmk. 233**

**1971, Nov. 24 Photo.** ***Perf. 14½***

**1112** A187 5s on 6s multi .55 .25

Philatelic Week, 1971.

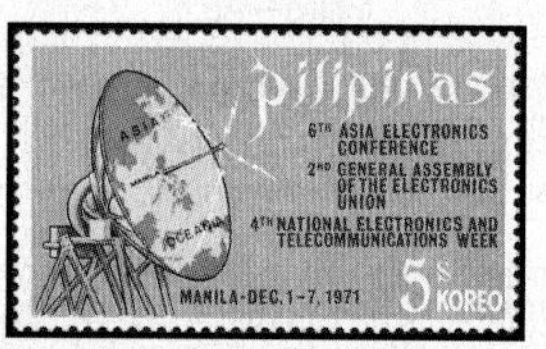


Radar with Map of Far East and Oceania — A230

**1972, Feb. 29 Photo.** ***Perf. 14x14½***

**1113** A230 5s org yel & multi .30 .25
**1114** A230 40s red org & multi .55 .25

Electronics Conferences, Manila, 12/1-7/71.

Fathers Gomez, Burgos and Zamora — A231

**1972, Apr. 3** ***Perf. 13x12½***

**1115** A231 5s gold & multi .35 .25
**1116** A231 60s gold & multi .85 .25

Centenary of the deaths of Fathers Mariano Gomez, José Burgos and Jacinto Zamora, martyrs for Philippine independence from Spain.

Digestive Tract — A232

**1972, Apr. 11 Photo.** ***Perf. 12½x13***

**1117** A232 20s ultra & multi .60 .25

4th Asian Pacific Congress of Gastroenterology, Manila, Feb. 5-12. See No. C103.

**No. 953 Surcharged**

**1972, Apr. 20** ***Perf. 12½***

**1118** A185 5s on 6s multi 1.20 .25

**No. O69 with Two Bars over "G." and "O."**

**1972, May 16 Engr.** ***Perf. 13½***

**1119** A158 50s violet 1.20 .25

**Nos. 883A, 909 and 929 Surcharged with New Value and 2 Bars**

**1972, May 29**

**1120** A161 10s on 6s dp cl & blk 1.20 .25
**1121** A171 10s on 6s multi 1.20 .25
*a.* Inverted overprint 20.00
**1122** A177 10s on 6s multi 1.00 .25
*Nos. 1120-1122 (3)* 3.40 .75

Independence Monument, Manila — A233

**1972, May 31 Photo.** ***Perf. 13x12½***

**1123** A233 5s brt blue & multi .30 .25
**1124** A233 50s red & multi .80 .25
**1125** A233 60s emerald & multi 1.10 .25
*Nos. 1123-1125 (3)* 2.20 .75

Visit ASEAN countries (Association of South East Asian Nations).

"K," Skull and Crossbones — A234

Development of Philippine Flag: No. 1126, 3 "K's" in a row ("K" stands for Katipunan). No. 1127, 3 "K's" as triangle. No. 1128, One "K." No. 1130, 3 "K's," sun over mountain on white triangle. No. 1131, Sun over 3 "K's." No. 1132, Tagalog "K" in sun. No. 1133, Sun with human face. No. 1134, Tricolor flag, forerunner of present flag. No. 1135, Present flag. Nos. 1126, 1128, 1130-1131, 1133, 1135 inscribed in Tagalog.

**1972, June 12 Photo. *Perf. 13***
**1126** A234 30s ultra & red 2.00 .30
**1127** A234 30s ultra & red 2.00 .30
**1128** A234 30s ultra & red 2.00 .30
**1129** A234 30s ultra & blk 2.00 .30
**1130** A234 30s ultra & red 2.00 .30
**1131** A234 30s ultra & red 2.00 .30
**1132** A234 30s ultra & red 2.00 .30
**1133** A234 30s ultra & red 2.00 .30
**1134** A234 30s ultra, red & blk 2.00 .30
**1135** A234 30s ultra, yel & red 2.00 .30
*a.* Block of 10 25.00 10.00

### Portrait Type of 1970

40s, Gen. Miguel Malvar. 1p, Julian Felipe.

**1972 Engr. *Perf. 14***
**1136** A222 40s rose red .55 .25
**1137** A222 1p deep blue 1.20 .25

Honoring Gen. Miguel Malvar (1865-1911), revolutionary leader, and Julian Felipe (1861-1944), composer of Philippine national anthem.
Issue dates: 40s, July 10; 1p, June 26.

Parrotfish A235

**1972, Aug. 14 Photo. *Perf. 13***
**1138** A235 5s shown .40 .25
**1139** A235 10s Sunburst butterflyfish 1.25 .25
**1140** A235 20s Moorish idol 1.40 .30
*Nos. 1138-1140,C104 (4)* 4.80 1.40

Tropical fish.

Development Bank of the Philippines A236

**1972, Sept. 12**
**1141** A236 10s gray blue & multi .30 .25
**1142** A236 20s lilac & multi .35 .25
**1143** A236 60s tan & multi .45 .25
*Nos. 1141-1143 (3)* 1.10 .75

Development Bank of the Philippines, 25th anniv.

Pope Paul VI A237

**1972, Sept. 26 Unwmk. *Perf. 14***
**1144** A237 10s lt green & multi .50 .25
**1145** A237 50s lt violet & multi 1.00 .30
*Nos. 1144-1145,C105 (3)* 2.50 .95

First anniversary (in 1971) of the visit of Pope Paul VI to the Philippines, and for his 75th birthday.

### Nos. 880, 899 and 925 Surcharged with New Value and 2 Bars

**1972, Sept. 29 As Before**
**1146** A161 10s on 6s lil & blk 1.10 .25
*a.* Inverted overprint 20.00
**1147** A167 10s on 6s multi 1.10 .25
*a.* Inverted overprint 20.00
**1148** A176 10s on 6s multi .90 .25
*a.* Inverted overprint 15.00
*Nos. 1146-1148 (3)* 3.10 .75

Charon's Bark, by Resurrección Hidalgo — A238

Paintings: 10s, Rice Workers' Meal, by F. Amorsolo. 30s, "Spain and the Philippines," by Juan Luna, vert. 70s, Song of Maria Clara, by F. Amorsolo.

***Perf. 14x13***
**1972, Oct. 16 Unwmk. Photo.**
**Size: 38x40mm**
**1149** A238 5s silver & multi .50 .25
**1150** A238 10s silver & multi .50 .30
**Size: 24x56mm**
**1151** A238 30s silver & multi 1.00 .35
**Size: 38x40mm**
**1152** A238 70s silver & multi 1.00 .40
*Nos. 1149-1152 (4)* 3.00 1.30

25th anniversary of the organization of the Stamp and Philatelic Division.

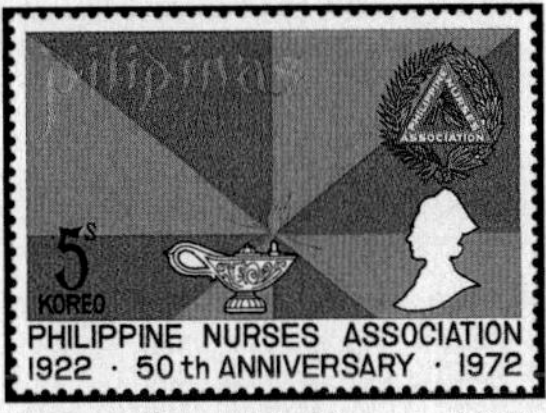


Lamp, Nurse, Emblem — A239

**1972, Oct. 22 *Perf. 12½x13½***
**1153** A239 5s violet & multi .25 .25
**1154** A239 10s blue & multi .35 .25
**1155** A239 70s orange & multi .60 .25
*Nos. 1153-1155 (3)* 1.20 .75

Philippine Nursing Association, 50th anniv.

Heart, Map of Philippines A240

**1972, Oct. 24 *Perf. 13***
**1156** A240 5s pur, emer & red .30 .25
**1157** A240 10s blue, emer & red .35 .25
**1158** A240 30s emerald, bl & red .45 .25
*Nos. 1156-1158 (3)* 1.10 .75

"Your heart is your health," World Health Month.

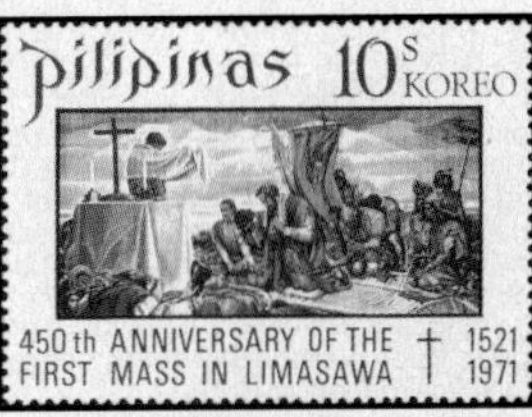


First Mass on Limasawa, by Carlos V. Francisco — A241

**1972, Oct. 31 *Perf. 14***
**1159** A241 10s brown & multi .50 .25

450th anniversary of the first mass in the Philippines, celebrated by Father Valderama on Limasawa, Mar. 31, 1521. See No. C106.

### Nos. 878, 882, 899 Surcharged: "ASIA PACIFIC SCOUT CONFERENCE NOV. 1972"

**1972, Nov. 13 As Before**
**1160** A161 10s on 6s bl & blk .90 .30
**1161** A161 10s on 6s grn & blk 1.25 .30
**1162** A167 10s on 6s multi 1.25 .50
*Nos. 1160-1162 (3)* 3.40 1.10

Asia Pacific Scout Conference, Nov. 1972.

Torch, Olympic Emblems — A242

***Perf. 12½x13½***
**1972, Nov. 15 Photo.**
**1163** A242 5s blue & multi .35 .25
**1164** A242 10s multicolored .50 .25
**1165** A242 70s orange & multi 1.15 .40
*Nos. 1163-1165 (3)* 2.00 .90

20th Olympic Games, Munich, 8/26-9/11.
For surcharges see Nos. 1297, 1758-1760.

### Nos. 896 and 919 Surcharged with New Value, Two Bars and: "1972 PHILATELIC WEEK"

**1972, Nov. 23 Photo. *Perf. 13½***
**1166** A166 10s on 6s multi .65 *1.50*
**1167** A174 10s on 6s multi .65 *1.50*

Philatelic Week 1972.

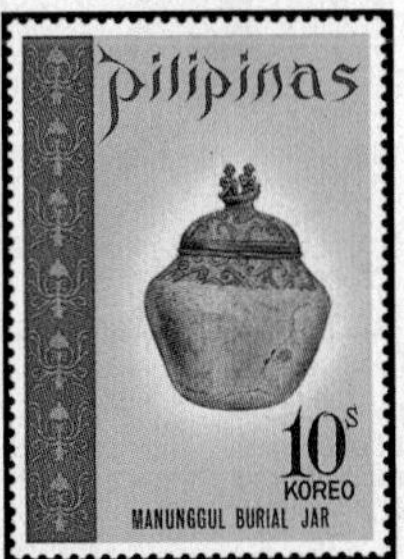


Manunggul Burial Jar, 890-710 B.C. — A243

#1169, Ngipet Duldug Cave ritual earthenware vessel, 155 B.C. #1170, Metal age chalice, 200-600 A.D. #1171, Earthenware vessel, 15th cent.

**1972, Nov. 29**
**1168** A243 10s green & multi .50 .25
**1169** A243 10s lilac & multi .50 .25
**1170** A243 10s blue & multi .50 .25
**1171** A243 10s yellow & multi .50 .25
*Nos. 1168-1171 (4)* 2.00 1.00

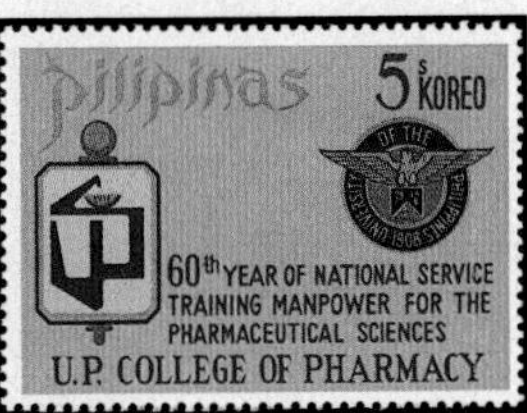


College of Pharmacy and Univ. of the Philippines Emblems — A244

**1972, Dec. 11 *Perf. 12½x13½***
**1172** A244 5s lt vio & multi .35 .25
**1173** A244 10s yel grn & multi .35 .25
**1174** A244 30s ultra & multi .50 .25
*Nos. 1172-1174 (3)* 1.20 .75

60th anniversary of the College of Pharmacy of the University of the Philippines.

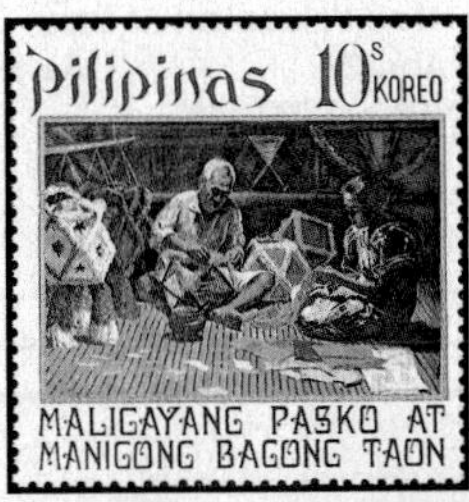


Christmas Lantern Makers, by Jorgé Pineda — A245

**1972, Dec. 14 Photo. *Perf. 12½***
**1175** A245 10s dk bl & multi .35 .25
**1176** A245 30s brown & multi .65 .30
**1177** A245 50s green & multi 1.00 .35
*Nos. 1175-1177 (3)* 2.00 .90

Christmas 1972.

Red Cross Flags, Pres. Roxas and Mrs. Aurora Quezon A246

**1972, Dec. 21**
**1178** A246 5s ultra & multi .30 .25
**1179** A246 20s multicolored .40 .25
**1180** A246 30s brown & multi .50 .25
*Nos. 1178-1180 (3)* 1.20 .75

25th anniv. of the Philippine Red Cross.

### Nos. 894 and 936 Surcharged with New Value and 2 Bars

**1973, Jan. 22 Photo. *Perf. 14, 13***
**1181** A165 10s on 6s multi .65 .25
*a.* Double overprint 20.00
**1182** A180 10s on 6s multi .65 .25
*a.* Double overprint 20.00

San Luis University, Luzon — A247

**1973, Mar. 1 Photo. *Perf. 13½x14***
**1183** A247 5s multicolored .35 .25
**1184** A247 10s yellow & multi .40 .25
**1185** A247 75s multicolored .60 .25
*Nos. 1183-1185 (3)* 1.35 .75

60th anniversary of San Luis University, Baguio City, Luzon.
For surcharge see No. 1305.

Jesus Villamor and Fighter Planes — A248

**1973, Apr. 9 Photo. *Perf. 13½x14***

**1186** A248 10s multicolored .40 .25
**1187** A248 2p multicolored 1.60 .70

Col. Jesus Villamor (1914-1971), World War II aviator who fought for liberation of the Philippines.
For surcharge see No. 1230.

**Nos. 932, 957, O70 Surcharged with New Values and 2 Bars**

**1973, Apr. 23 As Before**

**1188** A178 5s on 6s multi 1.10 1.10
**1189** A187 5s on 6s multi 1.10 .40
***a.*** Inverted overprint 20.00
**1190** A222 15s on 10s rose car .80 .25
*Nos. 1188-1190 (3)* 3.00 1.75

Two additional bars through "G.O." on No. 1190.

ITI Emblem, Performance and Actor Vic Silayan — A249

**1973, May 15 Photo. *Perf. 13x12½***

**1191** A249 5s blue & multi .30 .25
**1192** A249 10s yel grn & multi .30 .25
**1193** A249 50s orange & multi .60 .30
**1194** A249 70s rose & multi .80 .35
*Nos. 1191-1194 (4)* 2.00 1.15

1st Third World Theater Festival, sponsored by the UNESCO affiliated International Theater Institute, Manila, Nov. 19-30, 1971.
For surcharge see No. 1229.

Josefa Llanes Escoda — A250

#1196, Gabriela Silang. No. 1197, Rafael Palma. 30s, Jose Rizal. 60s, Marcela Agoncillo. 90s, Teodoro R. Yangco. 1.10p, Dr. Pio Valenzuela. 1.20p, Gregoria de Jesus. #1204, Pedro A. Paterno. #1205, Teodora Alonso. 1.80p, Edilberto Evangelista. 5p, Fernando M. Guerrero.

**1973-78 Engr. *Perf. 14½***

**1195** A250 15s sepia .25 .25

**Litho. *Perf. 12½***

**1196** A250 15s violet ('74) .40 .25
**1197** A273 15s emerald ('74) .35 .25
**1198** A250 30s vio bl ('78) .35 .25
**1199** A250 60s dl red brn .85 .25
**1200** A273 90s brt bl ('74) .85 .25
**1202** A273 1.10p brt bl ('74) 1.25 .30
**1203** A250 1.20p dl red ('78) .90 .25
**1204** A250 1.50p lil rose 2.00 1.50
**1205** A273 1.50p brown ('74) 1.50 .40
**1206** A250 1.80p green 3.00 1.50
**1208** A250 5p blue 6.00 3.00
*Nos. 1195-1208 (12)* 17.70 8.45

**1973-74 *Imperf.***

*1196a* A250 15s violet ('74) 1.25 *1.00*
*1197a* A273 15s emerald ('74) 1.25 *1.00*
*1199a* A250 60s dull red brown 3.00 1.50
*1200a* A273 90s bright blue ('74) 2.75 1.60
*1202a* A273 1.10p bright blue ('74) 3.50 3.00
*1204a* A250 1.50p lilac rose 3.50 3.00
*1205a* A273 1.50p brown ('74) 3.75 3.50
*1206a* A250 1.80p green 5.00 3.50
*1208a* A250 5p blue 12.00 8.00
*Nos. 1196a-1208a (9)* 36.00 26.10

Honoring: Escoda (1898-194?), leader of Girl Scouts and Federation of Women's Clubs. Silang (1731-63), "the Ilocana Joan of Arc". Palma (1874-1939), journalist, statesman, educator. Rizal (1861-96), natl. hero. Agoncillo (1859-1946), designer of 1st Philippine flag, 1898. Yangco (1861-1939), patriot and philanthropist. Valenzuela (1869-1956), physician and newspaperman.
Gregoria de Jesus, independence leader. Paterno (1857-1911), lawyer, writer, patriot. Alonso (1827-1911), mother of Rizal. Evangelista (1862-97), army engineer, patriot. Guerrero (1873-1929), journalist, political leader.
For overprint & surcharges see #1277, 1310, 1311, 1470, 1518, 1562..

**No. 946 surcharged with New Value**

**1973, June 4 Engr. *Perf. 13½***

**1209** A158 5s on 6s pck blue .75 .25

Anti-smuggling campaign.

**No. 925 Surcharged**

**1973, June 4 Wmk. 233**

**1210** A176 5s on 6s multi .75 .25
***a.*** Inverted overprint 20.00
***b.*** Double overprint 20.00

10th anniv. of death of John F. Kennedy.

Pres. Marcos, Farm Family, Unfurling of Philippine Flag — A251

***Perf. 12½x13½***

**1973, Sept. 24 Photo. Unwmk.**

**1211** A251 15s ultra & multi .35 .25
**1212** A251 45s red & multi .65 .25
**1213** A251 90s multi 1.00 .35
*Nos. 1211-1213 (3)* 2.00 .85

75th anniversary of Philippine independence and 1st anniversary of proclamation of martial law.
First day covers exist dated Sept. 21, 1973.

Imelda Romualdez Marcos, First Lady of the Philippines A252

**1973, Oct. 31 Photo. *Perf. 13***

**1214** A252 15s dl bl & multi .30 .25
**1215** A252 50s multicolored .60 .30
**1216** A252 60s lil & multi .70 .30
*Nos. 1214-1216 (3)* 1.60 .85

Presidential Palace, Manila, Pres. and Mrs. Marcos — A253

**1973, Nov. 15 Litho. *Perf. 14***

**1217** A253 15s rose & multi .30 .25
**1218** A253 50s ultra & multi .70 .30
*Nos. 1217-1218,C107 (3)* 2.00 .90

INTERPOL Emblem — A254

**1973, Dec. 18 Photo. *Perf. 13***

**1219** A254 15s ultra & multi .40 .25
**1220** A254 65s lt grn & multi .60 .25

Intl. Criminal Police Organization, 50th anniv.

Cub and Boy Scouts — A255

15s, Various Scout activities; inscribed in Tagalog.

**1973, Dec. 28 Litho. *Perf. 12½***

**1221** A255 15s bister & emer .70 .50
***a.*** Imperf, pair ('74) 4.00 3.00
**1222** A255 65s bister & brt bl 1.30 .50
***a.*** Imperf, pair ('74) 6.00 5.00

50th anniv. of Philippine Boy Scouts.
Nos. 1221a-1222a issued Feb. 4, although first day covers are dated Dec. 28, 1973.

Manila, Bank Emblem and Farmers — A256

Designs: 60s, Old bank building. 1.50p, Modern bank building.

**1974, Jan. 3 Photo. *Perf. 12½x13½***

**1223** A256 15s silver & multi .30 .25
**1224** A256 60s silver & multi .50 .25
**1225** A256 1.50p silver & multi 1.20 .40
*Nos. 1223-1225 (3)* 2.00 .90

Central Bank of the Philippines, 25th anniv.

UPU Emblem, Maria Clara Costume — A257

Filipino Costumes: 60s, Balintawak and UPU emblem. 80s, Malong costume and UPU emblem.

**1974, Jan. 15 *Perf. 12½***

**1226** A257 15s multicolored .30 .25
**1227** A257 60s multicolored .70 .30
**1228** A257 80s multicolored 1.00 .40
*Nos. 1226-1228 (3)* 2.00 .95

Centenary of Universal Postal Union.

**No. 1192 Surcharged in Red with New Value, 2 Bars and: "1973 / PHILATELIC WEEK"**

**1974, Feb. 4 Photo. *Perf. 13x12½***

**1229** A249 15s on 10s multi .80 .25

Philatelic Week, 1973. First day covers exist dated Nov. 26, 1973.

Nos. 1186 and 1136 Overprinted and Surcharged

**1974, Mar. 25 Photo. *Perf. 13½x14***

**1230** A248 15s on 10s multi .75 .25

**Engr. *Perf. 14***

**1231** A222 45s on 40s rose red .75 .25

Lions Intl. of the Philippines, 25th anniv. The overprint on #1230 arranged to fit shape of stamp.

Pediatrics Congress Emblem and Map of Participating Countries A258

**1974, Apr. 30 Litho. *Perf. 12½***

**1232** A258 30s brt bl & red .50 .25
***a.*** Imperf, pair 3.00 2.50
**1233** A258 1p dl grn & red 1.20 .40
***a.*** Imperf, pair 5.50 4.50

Asian Congress of Pediatrics, Manila, Apr. 30-May 4.

**Nos. 912, 954-955 Surcharged with New Value and Two Bars**

**1974, Aug. 1 As Before**

**1234** A172 5s on 3s multi .80 .30
**1235** A185 5s on 6s multi 1.00 .30
**1236** A186 5s on 6s multi 1.20 .30
*Nos. 1234-1236 (3)* 3.00 .90

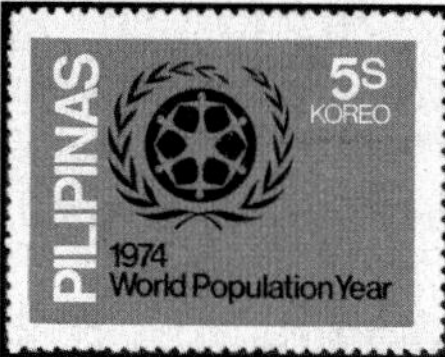


WPY Emblem A259

**1974, Aug. 15 Litho. *Perf. 12½***

**1237** A259 5s org & bl blk .40 .25
***a.*** Imperf, pair 2.00 1.50
**1238** A259 2p lt grn & dk bl 2.00 .75
***a.*** Imperf, pair 11.00 8.50

World Population Year, 1974.

Red Feather Community Chest Emblem A260

**Wmk. 372**

**1974, Sept. 5 Litho. *Perf. 12½***

**1239** A260 15s brt bl & red .35 .25
**1240** A260 40s emer & red .65 .25
**1241** A260 45s red brn & red .70 .25
*Nos. 1239-1241 (3)* 1.70 .75

Philippine Community Chest, 25th anniv.

**Imperf. Pairs**

*1239a* A260 15s 4.50 4.50
*1240a* A260 40s 3.00 2.00
*1241a* A260 45s 3.00 2.00
*Nos. 1239a-1241a (3)* 10.50 8.50

Sultan Kudarat, Flag, Order and Map of Philippines — A261

*Perf. 13½x14*

**1975, Jan. 13 Photo. Unwmk.**

**1242** A261 15s multicolored .45 .25

Sultan Mohammad Dipatuan Kudarat, 16th-17th century ruler.

Mental Health Association Emblem A262

**Wmk. 372**

**1975, Jan. 20 Litho. *Perf. 12½***

**1243** A262 45s emer & org .45 .25
*a.* Imperf, pair 2.00 1.50
**1244** A262 1p emer & pur .85 .30
*a.* Imperf, pair 4.00 3.00

Philippine Mental Health Assoc., 25th anniv.

4-Leaf Clover A263

**1975, Feb. 14**

**1245** A263 15s vio bl & red .45 .25
*a.* Imperf, pair 2.50 2.00
**1246** A263 50s emer & red .85 .35
*a.* Imperf, pair 5.00 4.00

Philippine Heart Center for Asia, inauguration.

Military Academy, Cadet and Emblem — A264

*Perf. 13½x14*

**1975, Feb. 17 Unwmk.**

**1247** A264 15s grn & multi .35 .25
**1248** A264 45s plum & multi .65 .25

Philippine Military Academy, 70th anniv.

Helping the Disabled — A265

*Perf. 12½, Imperf.*

**1975, Mar. 17 Wmk. 372**

**1249** A265 Block of 10 7.50 *7.50*
*a.-j.* 45s grn, any single .55 .35

25th anniversary (in 1974) of Philippine Orthopedic Association.

For surcharge see No. 1635.

No. 1249 exists imperf. Value unused, $12.

**Nos. B43, B50-B51 Surcharged with New Value and Two Bars**

**1975, Apr. 15 Unwmk.**

**1250** SP18 5s on 15s + 5s .60 *.25*
**1251** SP16 60s on 70s + 5s 1.00 *.30*
**1252** SP18 1p on 1.10p + 5s 1.40 *.60*
*a.* Double overprint 18.00
*Nos. 1250-1252 (3)* 3.00 1.15

"Grow and Conserve Forests" — A266

**1975, May 19 Litho. *Perf. 14½***

**1253** 45s "Grow" .45 .25
**1254** 45s "Conserve" .45 .25
*a.* A267 Pair, #1253-1254 1.00 .75

Forest conservation.

Jade Vine — A268

**1975, June 9 Photo. *Perf. 14½***

**1255** A268 15s multicolored .40 .25

Imelda R. Marcos, IWY Emblem — A269

**Wmk. 372**

**1975, July 2 Litho. *Perf. 12½***

**1256** A269 15s bl & blk .50 .25
*a.* Imperf, pair 3.00 2.50
**1257** A269 80s pink, bl & grn .70 .30
*a.* Imperf, pair 7.00 5.00

International Women's Year 1975.

For surcharges see Nos. 1500, 1505.

Civil Service Emblem — A270

**1975, Sept. 19 Litho. *Perf. 12½***

**1258** A270 15s multicolored .50 .25
*a.* Imperf, pair 3.00 2.25
**1259** A270 50s multicolored .70 .25
*a.* Imperf, pair 4.50 3.75

Dam and Emblem A271

**1975, Sept. 30**

**1260** A271 40s org & vio bl .60 .25
*a.* Imperf, pair 2.50 *2.00*
**1261** A271 1.50p brt rose & vio bl 1.20 .35
*a.* Imperf, pair 6.00 5.00

For surcharges see Nos. 1517, 1520.

Manila Harbor, 1875 A272

**1975, Nov. 4 Unwmk. *Perf. 13x13½***

**1262** A272 1.50p red & multi 1.50 .50

Hong Kong and Shanghai Banking Corporation, centenary of Philippines service.

Norberto Romualdez (1875-1941), Scholar and Legislator A273

Jose Rizal Monument, Luneta Park — A273a

Noted Filipinos: No. 1264, Rafael Palma (1874-1939), journalist, statesman, educator. No. 1265, Rajah Kalantiaw, chief of Panay, author of ethical-penal code (1443). 65s, Emilio Jacinto (1875-1899), patriot. No. 1269, Gen. Gregorio del Pilar (1875-1899), military hero. No. 1270, Lope K. Santos (1879-1963), grammarian, writer. 1.60p, Felipe Agoncillo (1859-1941), lawyer, cabinet member.

**Wmk. 372**

**1975-81 Litho. *Perf. 12½***

**1264** A273 30s brn ('77) .50 .25
**1265** A273 30s dp rose ('78) .50 .25
**1266** A273a 40s yel & blk ('81) .65 .25
**1267** A273 60s violet 1.50 .25
*a.* Imperf, pair 5.00 3.50
**1268** A273 65s lilac rose 1.25 .40
*a.* Imperf, pair 4.00 2.50
**1269** A273 90s lilac rose 2.00 .50
*a.* Imperf, pair 4.50 3.50
**1270** A273 90s grn ('78) *1.00* .25
**1272** A273 1.60p blk ('76) 3.00 .40
*Nos. 1264-1272 (8)* 10.40 2.55

See #1195-1208. For overprint & surcharges see #1278, 1310, 1367, 1440, 1469, 1514, 1562, 1574, 1758-1760.

A274

**1975, Nov. 22 Litho. *Perf. 12½***

**1275** A274 60s multicolored .80 .50
**1276** A274 1.50p multicolored 2.00 .60

1st landing of the Pan American World Airways China Clipper in the Philippines, 40th anniv.

Nos. 1199 and 1205 Overprinted

**1975, Nov. 22 Unwmk.**

**1277** A250 60s dl red brn .60 .30
**1278** A273 1.50p brown 1.60 .40

Airmail Exhibition, Nov. 22-Dec. 9.

APO Emblem — A275

**1975, Nov. 24 Wmk. 372**

**1279** A275 5s ultra & multi .30 .25
*a.* Imperf, pair 2.00 1.50
**1280** A275 1p bl & multi .90 .35
*a.* Imperf, pair 6.00 5.00

Amateur Philatelists' Org., 25th anniv.

For surcharge see No. 1338.

A276

Philippine Churches: 20s, San Agustin Church. 30s, Morong Church, horiz. 45s, Basilica of Taal, horiz. 60s, San Sebastian Church.

**1975, Dec. 23 Litho. *Perf. 12½***

**1281** A276 20s bluish grn .50 .25
**1282** A276 30s yel org & blk .50 .25
*a.* Horiz. pair, imperf. vert. 35.00
**1283** A276 45s rose, brn & blk .75 .25
**1284** A276 60s yel, bis & blk 1.25 .30
*Nos. 1281-1284 (4)* 3.00 1.05

Holy Year 1975.

**Imperf. Pairs**

*1281a* A276 20s 2.50 2.00
*1282a* A276 30s 2.50 2.00
*1283a* A276 45s 4.00 3.50
*1284a* A276 60s 7.00 5.00
*Nos. 1281a-1284a (4)* 16.00 12.50

Conductor's Hands — A277

**1976, Jan. 27**

**1285** A277 5s org & multi .40 .25
**1286** A277 50s brt yel grn & multi .80 .30

Manila Symphony Orchestra, 50th anniv.

PAL Planes of 1946 and 1976 A278

**1976, Feb. 14**

**1287** A278 60s bl & multi .80 .50
**1288** A278 1.50p red & multi 2.20 .60

Philippine Airlines, 30th anniversary.

National University A279

**1976, Mar. 30**

**1289** A279 45s bl, vio bl & yel .50 .25
**1290** A279 60s lt bl, vio bl & pink .90 .25

National University, 75th anniversary.

Eye Exam — A280

**1976, Apr. 7 Litho. *Perf. 12½***

**1291** A280 15s multicolored .70 .25

World Health Day: "Foresight prevents blindness."

Book and Emblem — A281

**1976, May 24 Unwmk.**

**1292** A281 1.50p grn & multi 1.50 .40

National Archives, 75th anniversary.

Santo Tomas University, Emblems A282

**1976, June 7 Wmk. 372**

**1293** A282 15s yel & multi .40 .25
**1294** A282 50s multicolored .90 .30

Colleges of Education and Science, Santo Tomas University, 50th anniversary.

Maryknoll College — A283

**Wmk. 372**

**1976, July 26 Litho. *Perf. 12½***

**1295** A283 15s lt bl & multi .50 .25
**1296** A283 1.50p bis & multi 1.20 .40

Maryknoll College, Quezon City, 50th anniv.

**No. 1164 Surcharged in Dark Violet**

***Perf. 12½x13½***

**1976, July 30 Photo.**

**1297** A242 15s on 10s multi 1.00 .50

21st Olympic Games, Montreal, Canada, July 17-Aug. 1.

Police College, Manila — A284

**1976, Aug. 8 Litho. *Perf. 12½***

**1298** A284 15s multicolored .50 .25
*a.* Imperf, pair 1.75 1.50
**1299** A284 60s multicolored 1.00 .25
*a.* Imperf, pair 5.75 5.00

Philippine Constabulary, 75th anniversary.
Imperfs. issued on Oct. 14 1976.

Surveyors — A285

**1976, Sept. 2 Wmk. 372**

**1300** A285 80s multicolored 1.70 .40

Bureau of Lands, 75th anniversary.
No. 1300 exists imperf. Value for pair, $40.

Monetary Fund and World Bank Emblems — A286

**1976, Oct. 4 Litho. *Perf. 12½***

**1301** A286 60s multicolored .50 .40
*a.* Imperf. pair 50.00
**1302** A286 1.50p multicolored 1.20 .60

Joint Annual Meeting of the Board of Governors of the International Monetary Fund and the World Bank, Manila, Oct. 4-8.
For surcharge see No. 1575.

Virgin of Antipollo A287

**1976, Nov. 26 *Perf. 12½***

**1303** A287 30s multicolored .40 .25
**1304** A287 90s multicolored 1.10 .30

Virgin of Antipolo, Our Lady of Peace and Good Voyage, 350th anniv. of arrival of statue in the Philippines and 50th anniv. of the canonical coronation.

**No. 1184 Surcharged with New Value and 2 Bars and Overprinted: "1976 PHILATELIC WEEK"**

***Perf. 13½x14***

**1976, Nov. 26 Photo. Unwmk.**

**1305** A247 30s on 10s multi .75 .25

Philatelic Week 1976.

People Going to Church A288

**Wmk. 372**

**1976, Dec. 1 Litho. *Perf. 12½***

**1306** A288 15s bl & multi .50 .25
**1307** A288 30s bl & multi 1.00 .25

Christmas 1976.

Symbolic Diamond and Book — A289

**1976, Dec. 13**

**1308** A289 30s grn & multi .50 .25
**1309** A289 75s grn & multi .85 .30

Philippine Educational System, 75th anniv.
Nos. 1308-1309 exist imperf. Value for pair, $40.

**No. 1202 and 1208 Surcharged with New Value and 2 Bars**

**1977, Jan. 17 Unwmk.**

**1310** A273 1.20p on 1.10p brt bl 1.20 .50
**1311** A250 3p on 5p bl 3.00 .70

Galicano Apacible — A290

Design: 30s, José Rizal.

**1977 Litho. Wmk. 372 *Perf. 12½***

**1313** A290 30s multicolored .30 .25
*a.* Horiz. pair, imperf. between 50.00
*b.* Horiz. pair, imperf. vertically 30.00
**1318** A290 2.30p multicolored 1.50 .40

Dr. José Rizal (1861-1896) physician, poet and national hero (30s). Dr. Galicano Apacible (1864-1949), physician, statesman (2.30p).
Issue dates: 30s, Feb. 16; 2.30p, Jan. 24.

Emblem, Flags, Map of AOPU A291

**1977, Apr. 1 Wmk. 372**

**1322** A291 50s multicolored .40 .25
**1323** A291 1.50p multicolored 1.25 .35

Asian-Oceanic Postal Union (AOPU), 15th anniv.

Cogwheels and Worker — A292

**1977, Apr. 21 *Perf. 12½***

**1324** A292 90s blk & multi .70 .30
**1325** A292 2.30p blk & multi 1.70 .60

Asian Development Bank, 10th anniversary.

Farmer at Work and Receiving Money A293

**1977, May 14 Litho. Wmk. 372**

**1326** A293 30s org red & multi .45 .30

National Commission on Countryside Credit and Collection, campaign to strengthen the rural credit system.

Solicitor General's Emblem A294

**1977, June 30 Litho. *Perf. 12½***

**1327** A294 1.65p multicolored 1.40 .35

Office of the Solicitor General, 75th anniv.
For surcharges see Nos. 1483, 1519.

Conference Emblem A295

**1977, July 29 Litho. *Perf. 12½***

**1328** A295 2.20p bl & multi 1.50 .40

8th World Conference of the World Peace through Law Center, Manila, Aug. 21-26.
For surcharge see No. 1576.

ASEAN Emblem A296

**1977, Aug. 8**

**1329** A296 1.50p grn & multi 1.50 .40
*a.* Horiz. pair, imperf. vertically 125.00

Association of South East Asian Nations (ASEAN), 10th anniversary.
For surcharge see No. 1559.

Cable-laying Ship, Map Showing Cable Route — A297

**1977, Aug. 26** **Litho.** ***Perf. 12½***
**1330** A297 1.30p multicolored 1.20 .35

Inauguration of underwater telephone cable linking Okinawa, Luzon and Hong Kong.

President Marcos — A298

**1977, Sept. 11** **Wmk. 372**
**1331** A298 30s multicolored .50 .30
**1332** A298 2.30p multicolored 1.50 .45

Ferdinand E. Marcos, president of the Philippines, 60th birthday.

People Raising Flag — A299

**1977, Sept. 21** **Litho.** ***Perf. 12½***
**1333** A299 30s multicolored .35 .25
**1334** A299 2.30p multicolored 1.50 .45

5th anniversary of "New Society."

Bishop Gregorio Aglipay — A300

**1977, Oct. 1** **Litho.** ***Perf. 12½***
**1335** A300 30s multicolored .40 .25
**1336** A300 90s multicolored 1.35 .30

Philippine Independent Aglipayan Church, 75th anniversary.

Fokker F VIIa over World Map A301

**1977, Oct. 28** **Wmk. 372**
**1337** A301 2.30p multicolored 2.20 .50

First scheduled Pan American airmail service, Havana to Key West, 50th anniversary.

### No. 1280 Surcharged with New Value, 2 Bars and Overprinted in Red: "1977 / PHILATELIC / WEEK"

**1977, Nov. 22** **Litho.** ***Perf. 12½***
**1338** A275 90s on 1p multi 1.20 *.50*

Philatelic Week.

Children Celebrating and Star from Lantern — A302

**1977, Dec. 1** **Unwmk.**
**1339** A302 30s multicolored .40 .25
**1340** A302 45s multicolored .60 .25

Christmas 1977.

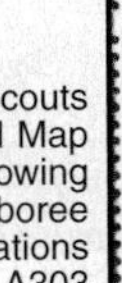

Scouts and Map showing Jamboree Locations A303

**1977, Dec. 27**
**1341** A303 30s multicolored .50 .25

National Boy Scout Jamboree, Tumauini, Isabela; Capitol Hills, Cebu City; Mariano Marcos, Davao, Dec. 27, 1977-Jan. 5, 1978.

Far Eastern University Arms — A304

**1978, Jan. 26** **Litho.** **Wmk. 372**
**1342** A304 30s gold & multi .50 .25

Far Eastern University, 50th anniversary.

Sipa A305

Various positions of Sipa ball-game.

**1978, Feb. 28** ***Perf. 12½***
**1343** A305 5s bl & multi .25 .25
**1344** A305 10s bl & multi .30 .25
**1345** A305 40s bl & multi .40 .25
**1346** A305 75s bl & multi .75 .25
*a.* Block, #1343-1346 2.20 1.50

No. 1346a has continuous design.

Arms of Meycauayan A306

**1978, Apr. 21** **Litho.** ***Perf. 12½***
**1347** A306 1.05p multicolored 1.00 .30

Meycauayan, founded 1578-1579.
For surcharge see No. 1560.

Moro Vinta and UPU Emblem — A307

2.50p, No. 1350b, Horse-drawn mail cart. No. 1350a, like 5p. No. 1350c, Steam locomotive. No. 1350d, Three-master.

**1978, June 9** **Litho.** ***Perf. 13½***
**1348** A307 2.50p multi 2.50 1.50
**1349** A307 5p multi 3.50 2.00
*a.* Pair, #1348-1349 6.00 6.00

**Souvenir Sheet**

***Perf. 12½x13***

**1350** Sheet of 4 20.00 18.00
*a.-d.* A307 7.50p, any single 4.25 4.00
*e.* Sheet, imperf 20.00 18.00

CAPEX International Philatelic Exhibition, Toronto, Ont., June 9-18. No. 1350 contains 36½x25mm stamps.
No. 1350 exists imperf. in changed colors.

Andres Bonifacio Monument, by Guillermo Tolentino — A308

**Wmk. 372**

**1978, July 10** **Litho.** ***Perf. 12½***
**1351** A308 30s multicolored .50 .25
*a.* Imperf. pair 25.00

Rook, Knight and Globe A309

**1978, July 17**
**1352** A309 30s vio bl & red .50 .25
**1353** A309 2p vio bl & red 1.50 .40

World Chess Championship, Anatoly Karpov and Viktor Korchnoi, Baguio City, 1978.

Miners A310

**1978, Aug. 12** **Litho.** ***Perf. 12½***
**1354** A310 2.30p multicolored 2.00 .40

Benguet gold mining industry, 75th anniv.

Manuel Quezon and Quezon Memorial A311

**1978, Aug. 19**
**1355** A311 30s multicolored .35 .25
**1356** A311 1p multicolored 1.15 .35

Manuel Quezon (1878-1944), first president of Commonwealth of the Philippines.

Law Association Emblem, Philippine Flag — A312

**1978, Aug. 27** **Litho.** ***Perf. 12½***
**1357** A312 2.30p multicolored 1.70 .40

58th Intl. Law Conf., Manila, 8/27-9/2.

Pres. Sergio Osmeña (1878-1961) A313

**1978, Sept. 8**
**1358** A313 30s multicolored .40 .25
**1359** A313 1p multicolored 1.20 .35

For surcharge see No. 1501.

Map Showing Cable Route, Cablelaying Ship — A314

**1978, Sept. 30**
**1360** A314 1.40p multicolored 1.40 .50

ASEAN Submarine Cable Network, Philippines-Singapore cable system, inauguration.

Basketball, Games' Emblem A315

**1978, Oct. 1**
**1361** A315 30s multicolored .50 *.30*
**1362** A315 2.30p multicolored 2.00 .50

8th Men's World Basketball Championship, Manila, Oct. 1-15.



San Lazaro Hospital and Dr. Catalino Gavino A316

**1978, Oct. 13** **Litho.** ***Perf. 12½***
**1363** A316 50s multicolored .65 .25
*a.* Vert. pair, imperf. horiz. 200.00
**1364** A316 90s multicolored 1.20 .35

San Lazaro Hospital, 400th anniversary.
For surcharge see No. 1512.

Nurse Vaccinating Child — A317

**1978, Oct. 24**

**1365** A317 30s multicolored .50 .25
**1366** A317 1.50p multicolored 1.70 .75

Eradication of smallpox.

No. 1268 Surcharged

**1978, Nov. 23**

**1367** A273 60s on 65s lil rose .85 .25

Philatelic Week.

"The Telephone Across Country and World" — A318

**Wmk. 372**

**1978, Nov. 28 Litho. *Perf. 12½***

**1368** 30s multicolored .40 .25
**1369** 2p multicolored 1.50 .40
*a.* A318 Pair, #1368-1369 2.40 1.50

Philippine Long Distance Telephone Company, 50th anniversary.

Traveling Family — A320

**1978, Nov. 28**

**1370** A320 30s multicolored .50 .25
**1371** A320 1.35p multicolored 1.20 .30

Decade of Philippine children.
For surcharges see Nos. 1504, 1561.

Church and Arms of Agoo A321

**1978, Dec. 7 Litho. *Perf. 12½***

**1372** A321 30s multicolored .45 .25
**1373** A321 45s multicolored .45 .25

400th anniversary of the founding of Agoo.

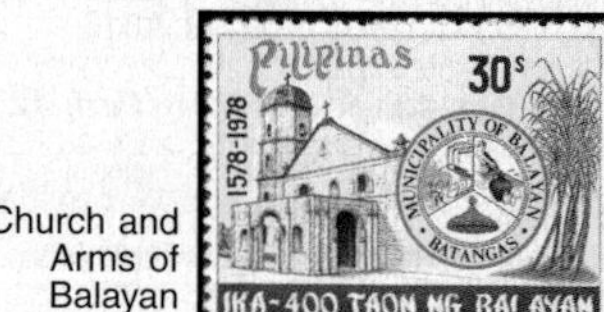


Church and Arms of Balayan A322

**1978, Dec. 8**

**1374** A322 30s multicolored .45 .25
**1375** A322 90s multicolored .75 .30

400th anniv. of the founding of Balayan.

Dr. Honoria Acosta Sison (1888-1970), 1st Philippine Woman Physician — A323

**1978, Dec. 15**

**1376** A323 30s multicolored .50 .25

Family, Houses, UN Emblem A324

**1978, Dec. 10 Litho. *Perf. 12½***

**1377** A324 30s multicolored .50 .25
**1378** A324 3p multicolored 2.00 .60

30th anniversary of Universal Declaration of Human Rights.

Chaetodon Trifasciatus — A325

Fish: 1.20p, Balistoides niger. 2.20p, Rhinecanthus aculeatus. 2.30p, Chelmon rostratus. No. 1383, Chaetodon mertensi. No. 1384, Euxiphipops xanthometapon.

**1978, Dec. 29 *Perf. 14***

**1379** A325 30s multi .35 .30
**1380** A325 1.20p multi 1.00 .40
**1381** A325 2.20p multi 1.65 .50
**1382** A325 2.30p multi 1.80 .50
**1383** A325 5p multi 3.50 1.00
**1384** A325 5p multi 3.50 1.00
*Nos. 1379-1384 (6)* 11.80 3.70

A total of 500,000 sets of Nos. 1379-1384 were CTO Dec. 29, 1978. Value for CTO set, $2.50.

Carlos P. Romulo, UN Emblem A326

**1979, Jan. 14 Litho. *Perf. 12½***

**1385** A326 30s multi .50 .25
**1386** A326 2p multi 1.50 .50

Carlos P. Romulo (1899-1985), pres. of UN General Assembly and Security Council.

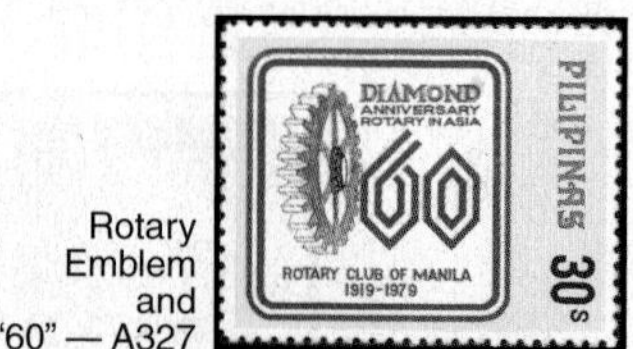


Rotary Emblem and "60" — A327

**1979, Jan. 26 Wmk. 372**

**1387** A327 30s multi .50 .25
**1388** A327 2.30p multi 1.50 .50

Rotary Club of Manila, 60th anniversary.

Rosa Sevilla de Alvero — A328

**1979, Mar. 4 Litho. *Perf. 12½***

**1389** A328 30 rose .50 .25

Rosa Sevilla de Alvero, educator and writer, birth centenary.
For surcharges see Nos. 1479-1482.

Oil Well and Map of Palawan A329

**Wmk. 372**

**1979, Mar. 21 Litho. *Perf. 12½***

**1390** A329 30s multi .50 .25
**1391** A329 45s multi .65 .25

First Philippine oil production, Nido Oil Reef Complex, Palawan.

Merrill's Fruit Doves — A330

Birds: 1.20p, Brown tit babbler. 2.20p, Mindoro imperial pigeons. 2.30p, Steere's pittas. No. 1396, Koch's and red-breasted pittas. No. 1397, Philippine eared nightjar.

***Perf. 14x13½***

**1979, Apr. 16 Unwmk.**

**1392** A330 30s multi *.40* .30
**1393** A330 1.20p multi *1.40* .50
**1394** A330 2.20p multi *3.00* .75
**1395** A330 2.30p multi *3.00* .75
**1396** A330 5p multi *11.00* 4.00
**1397** A330 5p multi *11.00* 4.00
*Nos. 1392-1397 (6)* *29.80* 10.30

A total of 500,000 sets of Nos. 1392-1397 were CTO April 16, 1979. Value for CTO set, $4.

Association Emblem and Reader A331

**Wmk. 372**

**1979, Apr. 30 Litho. *Perf. 12½***

**1398** A331 30s multi .35 .25
**1399** A331 75s multi .85 .30
**1400** A331 1p multi 1.10 .35
*Nos. 1398-1400 (3)* 2.30 .90

Association of Special Libraries of the Philippines, 25th anniversary.

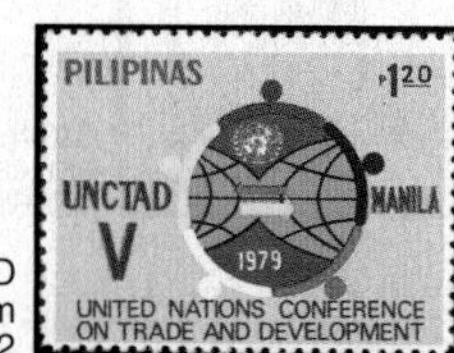


UNCTAD Emblem A332

**Wmk. 372**

**1979, May 3 Litho. *Perf. 12½***

**1401** A332 1.20p multi .85 .30
**1402** A332 2.30p multi 1.80 .50

5th Session of UN Conference on Trade and Development, Manila, May 3-June 1.

Civet Cat A333

Philippine Animals: 1.20p, Macaque. 2.20p, Wild boar. 2.30p, Dwarf leopard. No. 1407, Asiatic dwarf otter. No. 1408, Anteater.

**1979, May 14 *Perf. 14***

**1403** A333 30s multi .35 .30
**1404** A333 1.20p multi 1.00 .40
**1405** A333 2.20p multi 1.65 .50
**1406** A333 2.30p multi 1.80 .50
**1407** A333 5p multi 3.50 1.50
**1408** A333 5p multi 3.50 1.50
*Nos. 1403-1408 (6)* 11.80 4.70

A total of 500,000 sets of Nos. 1403-1408 were CTO May 20, 1979. Value for CTO set, $2.50.

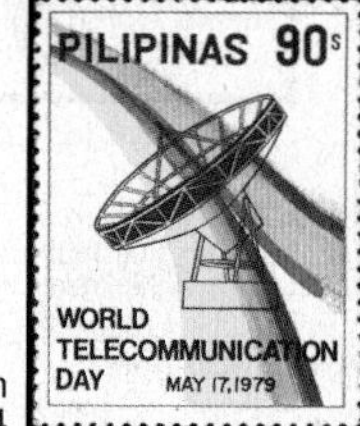


Dish Antenna — A334

**1979, May 17 *Perf. 12½***

**1409** A334 90s shown 1.50 .30
**1410** A334 1.30p World map 1.10 .40

11th World Telecommunications Day, 5/17.

Mussaenda Donna Evangelina — A335

Philippine Mussaendas: 1.20p, Dona Esperanza. 2.20p, Dona Hilaria. 2.30p, Dona Aurora. No. 1415, Gining Imelda. No. 1416, Dona Trining.

**1979, June 11 Litho. *Perf. 14***

**1411** A335 30s multi .35 .30
**1412** A335 1.20p multi 1.00 .40
**1413** A335 2.20p multi 1.65 .50
**1414** A335 2.30p multi 1.80 .50
**1415** A335 5p multi 3.50 1.75
**1416** A335 5p multi 3.50 1.75
*Nos. 1411-1416 (6)* 11.80 5.20

A total of 500,000 sets of Nos. 1411-1416 were CTO June 15, 1979. Value for CTO set, $2.50.

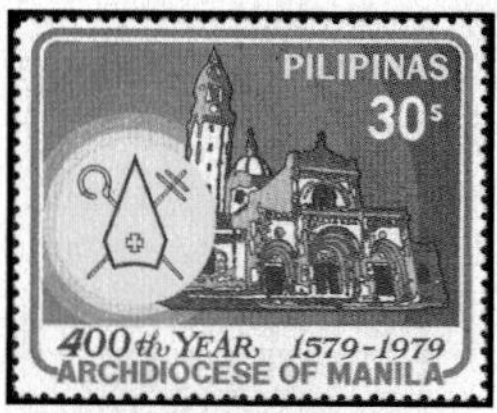


Manila Cathedral, Coat of Arms — A336

**1979, June 25 *Perf. 12½***

**1417** A336 30s multi .40 .25
**1418** A336 75s multi .80 .30
**1419** A336 90s multi 1.10 .35
*Nos. 1417-1419 (3)* 2.30 .90

Archdiocese of Manila, 400th anniversary.

Patrol Boat, Naval Arms A337

**1979, June 23**

**1420** A337 30s multi .60 .30
**1421** A337 45s multi .85 .40

Philippine Navy Day.

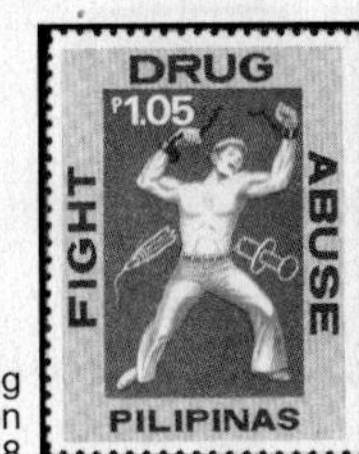


Man Breaking Chains, Broken Syringe — A338

**1979, July 23 Litho. *Perf. 12½***

**1422** A338 30s multi .35 .25
**1423** A338 90s multi .85 .30
**1424** A338 1.05p multi 1.20 .35
*Nos. 1422-1424 (3)* 2.40 .90

Fight drug abuse.
For surcharge see Nos. 1480, 1513.

Afghan Hound A339

Designs: 90s, Striped tabbies. 1.20p, Dobermann pinscher. 2.20p, Siamese cats. 2.30p, German shepherd. 5p, Chinchilla cats.

**1979, July 6 *Perf. 14***

**1425** A339 30s multi .50 .30
**1426** A339 90s multi 1.20 .35
**1427** A339 1.20p multi 1.30 .40
**1428** A339 2.20p multi 2.00 .45
**1429** A339 2.30p multi 2.00 .45
**1430** A339 5p multi 4.25 1.50
*Nos. 1425-1430 (6)* 11.25 3.45

A total of 500,000 sets of Nos. 1425-1430 were CTO July 30, 1979. Value for CTO set, $2.

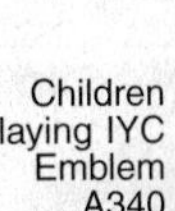

Children Playing IYC Emblem A340

Children playing and IYC emblem, diff.

**1979, Aug. 31 Litho. *Perf. 12½***

**1431** A340 15s multi .35 .25
**1432** A340 20s multi .40 .25
**1433** A340 25s multi .40 .40
**1434** A340 1.20p multi 1.00 .50
*Nos. 1431-1434 (4)* 2.15 1.40

International Year of the Child.

Hands Holding Emblem — A341

**1979, Sept. 27 Litho. *Perf. 12½***

**1435** A341 30s multi .35 .25
**1436** A341 1.35p multi 1.00 .35

Methodism in the Philippines, 80th anniv.

Emblem and Coins A342

**Wmk. 372**

**1979, Nov. 15 Litho. *Perf. 12½***

**1437** A342 30s multi .50 .50

Philippine Numismatic and Antiquarian Society, 50th anniversary.

Concorde over Manila and Paris A343

Design: 2.20p, Concorde over Manila.

**1979, Nov. 22**

**1438** A343 1.05p multi 1.50 .45
**1439** A343 2.20p multi 3.00 .75

Air France service to Manila, 25th anniversary.

**No. 1272 Surcharged in Red**

**1979, Nov. 23**

**1440** A273 90s on 1.60 blk 1.00 .25

Philatelic Week. Surcharge similar to No. 1367.

Transport Association Emblem A344

**1979, Nov. 27**

**1441** A344 75s multi .85 .30
**1442** A344 2.30p multi 2.00 .50

International Air Transport Association, 35th annual general meeting, Manila.

Local Government Year — A345

**1979, Dec. 14 Litho. *Perf. 12½***

**1443** A345 30s multi .25 .25
*a.* A318 Horiz. pair, imperf. vert. 25.00
**1444** A345 45s multi .45 .25

For surcharge, see No. 1481.

Mother and Children, Ornament — A346

**1979, Dec. 17**

**1445** A346 30s shown .40 .25
**1446** A346 90s Stars 1.30 .35

Christmas. For surcharges see Nos. 1482, 1515.

Rheumatic Pain Spots and Congress Emblem A347

**Wmk. 372**

**1980, Jan. 20 Litho. *Perf. 12½***

**1447** A347 30s multi 1.00 .75
**1448** A347 90s multi 2.50 2.00

Southeast Asia and Pacific Area League Against Rheumatism, 4th Congress, Manila, Jan. 19-24.

Gen. Douglas MacArthur A348

30s, MacArthur's birthplace (Little Rock, AR) & burial place (Norfolk, VA). 2.30p, MacArthur's cap, Sunglasses & pipe. 5p, MacArthur & troops wading ashore at Leyte, Oct. 20, 1944.

**1980, Jan. 26 Wmk. 372 *Perf. 12½***

**1449** A348 30s multi .40 .25
**1450** A348 75s multi .60 .40
**1451** A348 2.30p multi 2.00 .75
*Nos. 1449-1451 (3)* 3.00 1.40

**Souvenir Sheet**

***Imperf***

**1452** A348 5p multi 4.50 3.00

Gen. Douglas MacArthur (1880-1964).
No. 1449 exists imperf. Value for pair, $40.
For overprint see No. 2198.

Knights of Columbus of Philippines, 75th Anniversary A349

**1980, Feb. 14**

**1453** A349 30s multi .35 .25
**1454** A349 1.35p multi 1.00 .50

Philippine Military Academy, 75th Anniversary — A350

**Wmk. 372**

**1980, Feb. 17 Litho. *Perf. 12½***

**1455** A350 30s multi 1.00 .60
**1456** A350 1.20p multi 3.00 1.40

No. 1455-1456 exist imperf. Value for pair, $40.

Philippines Women's University, 75th Anniversary — A351

**1980, Feb. 21**

**1457** A351 30s multi .35 .25
**1458** A351 1.05p multi 1.00 .30

A352

Disaster Relief — A352a

Rotary International, 75th Anniversary (Paintings by Carlos Botong Francisco): Nos. 1459 and 1460 each in continuous design.

**1980, Feb. 23 *Perf. 12½***

**1459** A352 Strip of 5 5.00 3.00
*a.-e.* 30s any single .70 .50
**1460** A352a Strip of 5 13.00 11.00
*a.-e.* 2.30p any single 1.75 1.50

A353

**Wmk. 372**

**1980, Mar. 28 Litho. *Perf. 12½***

**1461** A353 30s multi .80 .50
**1462** A353 1.30p multi 2.00 .30

6th centenary of Islam in Philippines.

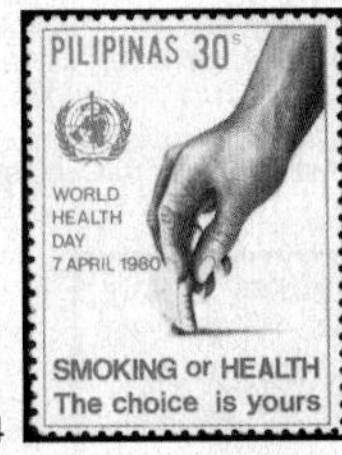


A354

Hand crushing cigarette, WHO emblem.

**1980, Apr. 7**

**1463** A354 30s multi 1.00 *1.00*
**1464** A354 75s multi 3.00 2.00

World Health Day (Apr. 7); anti-smoking campaign.

Philippine Girl Scouts, 40th Anniversary A355

**Wmk. 372**

**1980, May 26 Litho. *Perf. 12½***

**1465** A355 30s multi .50 .25
**1466** A355 2p multi 1.90 .60

Jeepney (Public Jeep) A356

**1980, June 24 Litho. *Perf. 12½***

**1467** A356 30s Jeepney, diff. .65 .25
**1468** A356 1.20p shown 1.65 .45

For surcharge see No. 1503.

Nos. 1272, 1206 Surcharged in Red

**Wmk. 372 (1.35p)**

**1980, Aug. 1 Litho. *Perf. 12½***

**1469** A273 1.35p on 1.60p blk 1.50 .35
**1470** A250 1.50p on 1.80p grn 2.20 .60
*a.* Inverted overprint 25.00
*b.* Imperf. pair, overprint inverted 25.00

Independence, 82nd Anniversary.

Association Emblem — A357

**1980, Aug. 1** **Wmk. 372**
**1471** A357 30s multi .35 .25
**1472** A357 2.30p multi 2.00 .45

International Association of Universities, 7th General Conference, Manila, Aug. 25-30.

Congress Emblem, Map of Philippines — A358

**Wmk. 372**
**1980, Aug. 18** **Litho.** ***Perf. 12½***
**1473** A358 30s lt grn & blk .35 .35
**1474** A358 75s lt bl & blk .55 .45
**1475** A358 2.30p sal & blk 1.60 .60
*Nos. 1473-1475 (3)* 2.50 1.40

Intl. Federation of Library Associations and Institutions, 46th Congress, Manila, 8/18-23.

Kabataang Barangay (New Society), 5th Anniversary — A359

**1980, Sept. 19** **Litho.** ***Perf. 12½***
**1476** A359 30s multi .35 .25
**1477** A359 40s multi .50 .25
**1478** A359 1p multi 1.00 .35
*Nos. 1476-1478 (3)* 1.85 .85

**Nos. 1389, 1422, 1443, 1445, 1327 Surcharged in Blue, Black or Red**

**1980** **Litho.** **Wmk. 372** ***Perf. 12½***
**1479** A328 40s on 30s rose (Bl) 1.00 .40
**1480** A338 40s on 30s multi 1.00 .25
**1481** A345 40s on 30s multi 1.00 .30
**1482** A346 40s on 30s multi (R) 2.00 .25
**1483** A294 2p on 1.65p multi (R) 4.00 .60
*Nos. 1479-1483 (5)* 9.00 1.80

Issue dates for Nos. 1479-1483: Nos. 1479, 1481, Sept. 26, 1980. No. 1480, Oct. 13, 1980; Nos. 1482, 1483, Oct. 14,1980.

Nos. 1479-1483 exist with overprints inverted. Value, from $35 each.

Catamaran, Conference Emblem — A360

**1980, Sept. 27**
**1484** A360 30s multi .40 .30
**1485** A360 2.30p multi 1.80 .50

World Tourism Conf., Manila, Sept. 27.

Stamp Day — A361

**1980, Oct. 9**
**1486** A361 40s multi .50 .25
**1487** A361 1p multi 1.20 .50
**1488** A361 2p multi 2.50 1.25
*Nos. 1486-1488 (3)* 4.20 2.00

UN, 35th Anniv. — A362

Designs: 40s, UN Headquarters and Emblem, Flag of Philippines. 3.20p, UN and Philippine flags, UN headquarters.

**1980, Oct. 20**
**1489** A362 40s multi .50 .25
**1490** A362 3.20p multi 2.70 .65

Murex Alabaster — A363

**1980, Nov. 2**
**1491** A363 40s shown 1.10 .35
**1492** A363 60s Bursa bubo .80 .35
**1493** A363 1.20p Homalocantha zamboi 1.10 .65
**1494** A363 2p Xenophora pallidula 2.00 1.00
*Nos. 1491-1494 (4)* 5.00 2.35

INTERPOL Emblem on Globe — A364

**1980, Nov. 5** **Litho.** **Wmk. 372**
**1495** A364 40s multi .40 .25
**1496** A364 1p multi .85 .30
**1497** A364 3.20p multi 2.25 .75
*Nos. 1495-1497 (3)* 3.50 1.30

49th General Assembly Session of INTERPOL (Intl. Police Organization), Manila, Nov. 13-21.

Central Philippine University, 75th Anniversary — A365

**1980, Nov. 17** **Unwmk.**
**1498** A365 40s multi .85 .25
**1499** A365 3.20p multi 3.00 1.00

**No. 1257 Surcharged**
**Wmk. 372**
**1980, Nov. 21** **Litho.** ***Perf. 12½***
**1500** A269 1.20p on 80s multi 1.70 .35

Philatelic Week. Surcharge similar to No. 1367.

No. 1358 Surcharged

**1980, Nov. 30**
**1501** A313 40s on 30s multi 1.70 .50

APO Philatelic Society, 30th anniversary.

Christmas Tree, Present and Candy Cane — A366

***Perf. 12½***
**1980, Dec. 15** **Litho.** **Unwmk.**
**1502** A366 40s multi .65 .25

Christmas 1980.

**No. 1467 Surcharged**

**1981, Jan. 2**
**1503** A356 40c on 30s multi 1.00 .50

**Nos. 1370, 1257 Surcharged in Red or Black**

**1981**
**1504** A320 10s on 30s (R) multi 1.00 .50
**1505** A269 85s on 80s multi 3.00 1.50

Issue dates: 10s, Jan. 12; 85s, Jan. 2.

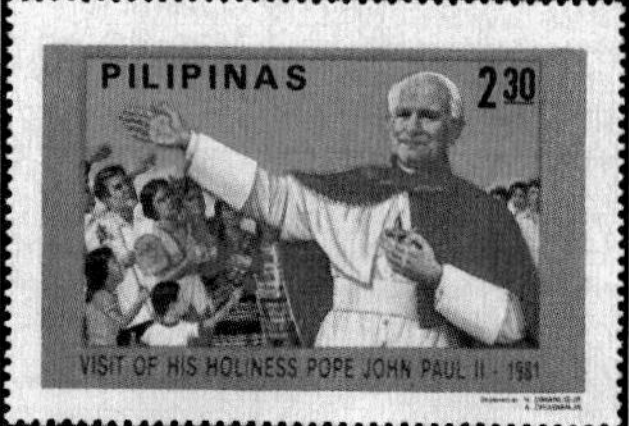

Heinrich Von Stephan, UPU Emblem — A367

**1981, Jan. 30**
**1506** A367 3.20p multi 3.00 .75

Heinrich von Stephan (1831-1897), founder of UPU, birth sesquicentennial.

Pope John Paul II Greeting Crowd — A368

Designs: 90s, Pope, signature, vert. 1.20p, Pope, cardinals, vert. 3p, Pope giving blessing, Vatican arms, Manila Cathedral. 7.50p, Pope, light on map of Philippines, vert.

***Perf. 13½x14***
**1981, Feb. 17** **Unwmk.**
**1507** A368 90s multi .80 .30
**1508** A368 1.20p multi 1.20 .50
**1509** A368 2.30p multi 2.00 1.00
**1510** A368 3p multi 2.50 1.50
*Nos. 1507-1510 (4)* 6.50 3.30

**Souvenir Sheet**
***Perf. 13¾x13¼***
**1511** A368 7.50p multi 7.00 *6.00*

Visit of Pope John Paul, Feb. 17-22.

Nos. 1507-1511 with year date "1980". were created but not issued. Value, $6.50 each, souvenir sheet $25,

For surcharge, see No. 3046.

**Nos. 1364, 1423, 1268, 1446, 1261, 1206, 1327 Surcharged**

**1981** **Litho.** ***Perf. 12½***
**1512** A316 40s on 90s multi 1.35 .25
**1513** A338 40s on 90s multi 1.35 .25
**1514** A273 40s on 65s lil rose 1.20 .25
**1515** A346 40s on 90s multi 1.70 .75
**1517** A271 1p on 1.50p brt rose & vio bl 2.00 .40
**1518** A250 1.20p on 1.80p grn 2.10 .60
**1519** A294 1.20p on 1.65p multi 2.75 1.00
**1520** A271 2p on 1.50p brt rose & vio bl 3.50 1.00
*Nos. 1512-1520 (8)* 15.95 4.50

A369

**1981, Apr. 20** **Wmk. 372**
**1521** A369 2p multi 1.70 .50
**1522** A369 3.20p multi 2.50 .75

68th Spring Meeting of the Inter-Parliamentary Union, Manila, Apr. 20-25.

---

Unless otherwise stated, Nos. 1523-1580 are on granite paper.

---

A370

**Wmk. 372**
**1981, May 22** **Litho.** ***Perf. 12½***
**1523** 40s Bubble coral .90 .40
**1524** 40s Branching coral .90 .40
**1525** 40s Brain coral .90 .40
**1526** 40s Table coral .90 .40
*a.* A370 Block of 4, #1523-1526 5.00 3.50

Philippine Motor Assoc., 50th Anniv. — A371

Vintage cars.

**1981, May 25**
**1527** 40s Presidents car .80 .25
**1528** 40s 1930 .80 .25
**1529** 40s 1937 .80 .25
**1530** 40s shown .80 .25
*a.* A371 Block of 4, #1527-1530 4.00 3.00

THE NEW REPUBLIC

INAUGURATION OF FERDINAND E. MARCOS PRESIDENT REPUBLIC OF THE PHILIPPINES

40s

Re-inauguration of Pres. Ferdinand E. Marcos — A372

**1981, June 30**
**1531** A372 40s multi .65 .25
*a.* Wmk. 372 (II) ('83) 20.00 20.00

**Souvenir Sheet**
***Imperf***
**1532** A372 5p multi 5.00 *4.00*
*a.* Wmk. 372 (II) ('84) 65.00 65.00

No. 1531 exists imperf. Value $1.

For overprint see No. 1753.

Nos. 1531-1532 exist with a surface varnish applied for use in presentation folders. Values, 7-8 times values for regular stamps.

No. 1532 exists on ordinary gossy paper with Wmk. 372 (I). Value, $65 mint and used.

St. Ignatius Loyola, Founder of Jesuit Order A373

400th Anniv. of Jesuits in Philippines: No. 1534, Jose Rizal, Ateneo University. No. 1535, Father Federico Faura, Manila Observatory. No. 1536, Father Saturnino Urios, map of Philippines.

**1981, July 31**

**1533** A373 40s multi .60 .30
**1534** A373 40s multi .60 .30
**1535** A373 40s multi .60 .30
**1536** A373 40s multi .60 .30
*a.* Block of 4, #1533-1536 3.00 2.50

**Souvenir Sheet**

***Imperf***

**1537** A373 2p multi 4.00 *3.50*

#1537 contains vignettes of #1533-1536.

For surcharge see No. 1737.

A374

Design: 40s, Isabelo de los Reyes (1867-1938), labor union founder. 1p, Gen. Gregorio del Pilar (1875-1899). No. 1540, Magsaysay. No. 1541, Francisco Dagohoy. No. 1543, Ambrosia R. Bautista, signer of Declaration of Independence, 1898, No. 1544, Juan Sumulong (1875-1942), statesman. 2.30p, Nicanor Abelardo (1893-1934), composer. 3.20p, Gen. Vicente Lim (1888-1945), first Philippine graduate of West Point.

**Wmk. 372**

**1981-82 Litho. *Perf. 12½***

**1538** A374 40s grnsh bl ('82) .40 .25
**1539** A374 1p blk & red brn .85 .25
**1540** A374 1.20p blk & lt red brn 1.20 .30
**1541** A374 1.20p brown ('82) 1.60 .35
**1543** A374 2p blk & red brn 1.60 .35
**1544** A374 2p rose lil ('82) 1.70 .35
*a.* Wmk. 372 (II) 3.00 3.00
**1545** A374 2.30p lt red brn ('82) 2.00 .40
**1546** A374 3.20p gray bl ('82) 2.40 .65
*a.* Wmk. 372 (II) 4.50 .80
*Nos. 1538-1546 (8)* 11.75 2.90

See Nos. 1672-1680, 1682-1683, 1685. For surcharges see Nos. 1668-1669.

A375

**1981, Sept. 2**

**1551** A375 40s multi .50 .25

Chief Justice Fred Ruiz Castro, 67th birth anniv.

No. 1551 exists on dull ordinary paper. Value, $10 unused, $5 used.

Intl. Year of the Disabled — A376

**Wmk. 372**

**1981, Oct. 24 Litho. *Perf. 12½***

**1552** A376 40s multi .50 .25
**1553** A376 3.20p multi 2.90 .65

A376a

**1981, Nov. 7**

**1554** A376a 40s multi .50 .25
**1555** A376a 2p multi 1.80 .50
**1556** A376a 3.20p multi 2.50 .70
*Nos. 1554-1556 (3)* 4.80 1.45

24th Intl. Red Cross Conf., Manila, 11/7-14.

No. 1556 exists on glossy ordinary paper, issued Feb. 17, 1983. Value, $10 mint, $5 used.

Intramuros Gate, Manila — A377

**1981, Nov. 13**

**1557** A377 40s black .60 .25

No. 1557 exists on dull ordinary paper, issued April 2, 1982. Value, $2 mint, 50¢ used.

Manila Park Zoo Concert Series, Nov. 20-30 A378

**1981, Nov. 20**

**1558** A378 40s multi .65 .30

No. 1558 exists on dull ordinary paper, issued April 26, 1982. Value, $10 mint, $6 used.

**No. 1329 Overprinted "1981 Philatelic Week" and Surcharged**

**Wmk. 372**

**1981, Nov. 23 Litho. *Perf. 12½***

**1559** A296 1.20p on 1.50p multi 2.40 1.00

**Nos. 1205, 1347, 1371 Surcharged**

**1981, Nov. 25 Litho. *Perf. 12½***

**1560** A306 40s on 1.05p multi 1.25 .50
**1561** A320 40s on 1.35p multi 1.25 .50
**1562** A273 1.20p on 1.50p brn 3.50 1.00
*Nos. 1560-1562 (3)* 6.00 2.00

11th Southeast Asian Games, Manila, Dec. 6-15 A379

40s, Running. 1p, Bicycling. 2p, Pres. Marcos, Intl. Olympic Pres. Samaranch. 2.30p, Soccer. 2.80p, Shooting. 3.20p, Bowling.

**1981, Dec. 3**

**1563** A379 40s multi .70 .30
**1564** A379 1p multi 1.20 .35
**1565** A379 2p multi 2.25 .40
**1566** A379 2.30p multi 2.75 .50
**1567** A379 2.80p multi 3.50 1.00
**1568** A379 3.20p multi 3.75 1.00
*Nos. 1563-1568 (6)* 14.15 3.55

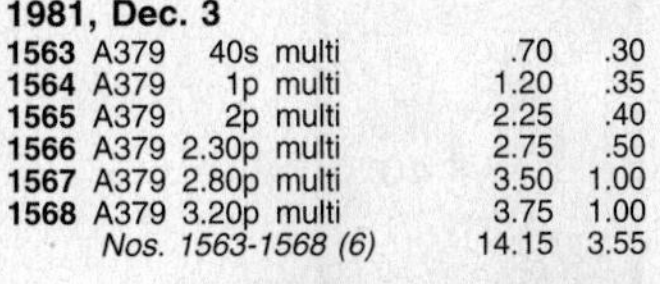

Manila Intl. Film Festival, Jan. 18-29 A380

40s, Film Center. 2p, Golden trophy, vert. 3.20p, Trophy, diff., vert.

**Wmk. 372**

**1982, Jan. 18 Litho. *Perf. 12½***

**1569** A380 40s multicolored .50 .30
**1570** A380 2p multicolored 2.00 .45
**1571** A380 3.20p multicolored 3.00 .80

No. 1570-1571 exist on dull ordinary paper. Value, $10 each mint, $5 each used.

Dull paper examples issued Aug. 3, 1982 (No. 1570), July 9, 1982 (No. 1571),

*Nos. 1569-1571 (3)* 5.50 1.55

Manila Metropolitan Waterworks and Sewerage System Centenary — A381

**1982, Jan. 22**

**1572** A381 40s blue .40 .30
**1573** A381 1.20p brown 1.60 .40

**Nos. 1268, 1302, 1328 Surcharged**

**1981, Jan. 28**

**1574** A273 1p on 65s lil rose 2.00 .60
**1575** A286 1p on 1.50p multi 1.25 .40
**1576** A295 3.20p on 2.20p multi 4.00 1.00
*Nos. 1574-1576 (3)* 7.25 2.00

Scouting Year — A382

40s, Portrait. 2p, Scout giving salute.

**1982, Feb. 22**

**1577** A382 40s multi .50 .30
*a.* Wmk. 372 (II) 25.00 20.00
**1578** A382 2p multi 2.50 .55

Nos. 1577-1578 exist on dull ordinary paper. Issue dates: No. 1577, Jun. 8, 1982. Value, $1.25 mint, 75¢ used; No. 1578, Sept. 21, 1983. Value, $4.25 mint, $2.75 used.

25th Anniv. of Children's Museum and Library Foundation A383

**1982, Feb. 25**

**1579** A383 40s Mural .50 .25
*a.* Wmk. 372 (II) 1.50 .50
**1580** A383 1.20p Children playing 1.35 .35
*a.* Wmk. 372 (II) 3.50 1.00

77th Anniv. of Philippine Military Academy A384

**Wmk. 372**

**1982, Mar. 25 Litho. *Perf. 12½***

**1581** A384 40s multi .50 .30
**1582** A384 1p multi 1.20 .40

Nos. 1581 and 1582 exist on orindary paper. Value No. 1581, $1.50 mint, $2.50 used; No. 1582, 50¢ mint, 75¢ used.

40th Bataan Day A385

40s, Soldier. 2p, "Reunion for Peace." 3.20p, Cannon, flag.

**1982, Apr. 9**

**1583** A385 40s multi .50 .25
*a.* Wmk. 372 (II) 3.50 1.50
**1584** A385 2p multi 1.90 .45

**Souvenir Sheet**

***Imperf***

**1585** A385 3.20p multi 4.00 *3.00*

No. 1585 contains one 38x28mm stamp. No. 1585 comes on two different papers, the second being thicker with cream gum.

For surcharge see No. 2114.

**No. B27 Surcharged**

**1982, Mar. 15 Photo. *Perf. 13½***

**1586** SP14 10s on 6 + 5s multi 1.50 .40

The "1" in the surcharged value of No. 1586 is unserifed. For similar surcharge with serifed "1," see No. 986.

A386

**1982, Apr. 28 Litho. *Perf. 12½***

**1587** A386 1p rose pink 1.50 .25
*a.* Wmk. 372 (II) 5.00 .50

Aurora Aragon Quezon (1888-1949), former First Lady.

There are three types of No. 1587.

See Nos. 1684-1684A.

A387

**1982, May 1**

**1588** A387 40s Man holding award .50 .30
  *a.* Wmk. 372 (II) 125.00 125.00
**1589** A387 1.20p Award 1.50 .40
  *a.* Wmk. 372 (II) 10.00 9.00

7th Towers Awards.

UN Conf. on Human Environment, 10th Anniv. — A388

**1982, June 5**

**1590** A388 40s Turtle 1.00 .40
  *a.* Wmk. 372 (II) 2.00 .50
**1591** A388 3.20p Philippine eagle 5.00 1.00
  *a.* Wmk. 372 (II) 8.00 2.50

75th Anniv. of Univ. of Philippines College of Medicine A389

**1982, June 10**

**1592** A389 40s multi .50 .25
  *a.* Wmk. 372 (II) 1.25 .40
**1593** A389 3.20p multi 2.50 .75
  *a.* Wmk. 372 (II) 4.75 1.60

Natl. Livelihood Movement A390

**1982, June 12**

**1594** A390 40s multi .50 .25
  *a.* Wmk. 372 (II) 1.50 .40

See #1681-1681A. For overprint see #1634.

Adamson Univ., 50th Anniv. — A391

**1982, June 21**

**1595** A391 40s bl & multi .50 .25
  *a.* Wmk. 372 (II) ('83) 25.00 25.00
**1596** A391 1.20p lt vio & multi 1.50 .25

Social Security, 25th Anniv. — A392

**1982, Sept. 1** ***Perf. 13½x13***

**1597** A392 40s multi .50 .25
**1598** A392 1.20p multi 1.20 .30

Pres. Marcos, 65th Birthday — A393

**1982, Sept. 11** ***Perf. 13¼x13***

**1599** A393 40s sil & multi .50 .25
  *a.* Wmk. 372 (II) 1.50 .40
  *b.* Perf. 12½ .50 .25
  *c.* As "b," Wmk. 372 (II) 1.00 .25
**1600** A393 3.20p sil & multi 2.25 .75
  *a.* Souv. sheet of 2, #1599-1600, imperf. 5.00 4.00
  *b.* Perf. 12½ 2.25 .75
  *c.* Wmk. 372 (II) 4.00 1.00
  *d.* As "a," Wmk. 372 (II) 25.00 25.00
  *e.* As "b," Wmk. 372 (II) 15.00 12.00

For surcharge see No. 1666.

Perf. 13¼x13 was comb perforated; perf. 12½ was line perforated.

15th Anniv. of Assoc. of Southeast Asian Nations (ASEAN) A394

**1982, Sept. 22** **Litho.** ***Perf. 12½***

**1601** A394 40s Flags .75 .30
  *c.* Wmk. 372 (II) 2.00 .50

St. Teresa of Avila (1515-1582) — A395

**1982, Oct. 15** ***Perf. 13x13½***

**1602** A395 40s Text .50 .25
**1603** A395 1.20p Map 1.00 .30
  *a.* Perf. 12½ 3.50 2.50
  *b.* As "a," Wmk. 372 (II) 4.50 1.75
**1604** A395 2p like #1603 1.75 .40
  *a.* Perf. 12½ 5.00 3.50
  *Nos. 1602-1604 (3)* 3.25 .95

A396

A396a

On Type I the shading on President Marcos is much darker as if he is under the shade of a tree. This was changed in Type II so that he appears under the sun. The new design plates are ½mm shorter than that of the original cutting off the bottom of the design. There are also numerous other slight differences.

***Perf. 13x13½***

**1982, Oct. 21** **Litho.** **Wmk. 372**

**1605** A396 40s Type I 3.25 1.00
**1605A** A396a 40s Type II 1.75 0.40

10th Anniv. of Tenant Farmers' Emancipation Decree.

See No. 1654.

350th Anniv. of St. Isabel College A397

**1982, Oct. 22**

**1606** A397 40s multi .40 .25
**1607** A397 1p multi 1.60 .40

Reading Campaign A398

**1982, Nov. 4**

**1608** A398 40s yel & multi .50 .25
  *a.* Perf. 12½, Wmk. 372 (II) 2.50 .50
**1609** A398 2.30p grn & multi 2.00 1.00
  *a.* Wmk. 372 (II) 5.00 2.00

For surcharge see No. 1713.

42nd Skal Club World Congress, Manila, Nov. 7-12 A399

**1982, Nov. 7**

**1610** A399 40s Heads .50 .35
  *a.* Perf. 12½, Wmk. 372 (II) 1.75 .75
**1611** A399 2p Chief 3.00 .60
  *a.* Perf. 12½, Wmk. 372 (II) 5.00 1.75

25th Anniv. of Bayanihan Folk Arts Center A400

Designs: Various folk dances.

**1982, Nov. 10** **Litho.** ***Perf. 13x13½***

**1612** A400 40s multi .50 .25
  *a.* Perf. 12½, Wmk. 372 (II) 1.25 .35
**1613** A400 2.80p multi 3.00 .65

TB Bacillus Centenary A401

**1982, Dec. 7** **Wmk. 372**

**1614** A401 40s multi .50 .25
**1615** A401 2.80p multi 3.00 .75

Christmas 1982 A402

**1982, Dec. 10**

**1616** A402 40s multi 1.00 .25
**1617** A402 1p multi 3.25 .35

Philatelic Week, Nov. 22-28 A403

***Perf. 13x13½***

**1983, Jan. 21** **Litho.** **Wmk. 372**

**1618** A403 40s yel & multi .50 .25
  *a.* Perf. 12½, Wmk. 372 (II) 1.00 .35
**1619** A403 1p sil & multi 1.10 .30
  *a.* Perf. 12½ 2.50 .50
  *b.* As "a," Wmk. 372 (II) 3.00 1.00

For surcharge see No. 1667.

Visit of Pres. Marcos to the US, Sept. A404

**1982, Dec. 18**

**1620** A404 40s multi .50 *.40*
**1621** A404 3.20p multi 3.25 1.00
  *a.* Souv. sheet of 2, #1620-1621 5.00 *4.00*

UN World Assembly on Aging, July 26-Aug. 6 — A405

**1982, Dec. 24**

**1622** A405 1.20p Woman 1.10 .35
  *a.* Wmk. 372 (II) 15.00 7.00
**1623** A405 2p Man 2.20 .50

Senate Pres. Eulogio Rodriguez, Sr. (1883-1964) A406

**1983, Jan. 21**

**1624** A406 40s grn & multi .75 .25
  *a.* Perf. 12½ 1.00 .35
**1625** A406 1.20p org & multi 1.25 .35
  *a.* Perf. 12½ 4.75 1.75
  *b.* As "a," Wmk. 372 (II) 1.75 .50

1983 Manila Intl. Film Festival, Jan. 24-Feb. 4 A407

**1983, Jan. 24**

**1626** A407 40s blk & multi .50 .30
  *a.* Wmk. 372 (II) 1.00 .50
  *b.* As "a," perf 12½ 4.75 2.75
**1627** A407 3.20p pink & multi 3.50 .70
  *a.* Wmk. 372 (II) 6.00 1.75
  *b.* As "a," perf 12½ 14.00 8.75

Beatification of Lorenzo Ruiz (1981) — A408

***Perf. 13x13½***

**1983, Feb. 18** **Litho.** **Wmk. 372**

**1628** A408 40s multi .65 .35
  *a.* Wmk. 372 (II) 1.50 .40
  *b.* Perf 12½ 5.00 2.00
**1629** A408 1.20p multi 1.75 .60
  *a.* Wmk. 372 (II) 2.50 .60
  *b.* Perf 12½ 8.50 5.00

400th Anniv. of Local Printing Press A409

**1983, Mar. 14**

1630 A409 40s blk & grn .60 .30
a. Wmk. 372 (II) 1.50 .40

Safety at Sea — A410

**1983, Mar. 17** *Perf. 13½x13*

1631 A410 40s multi .60 .30
a. Wmk. 372 (II) 1.75 .40

25th anniv. of Inter-Governmental Maritime Consultation Org. Convention.

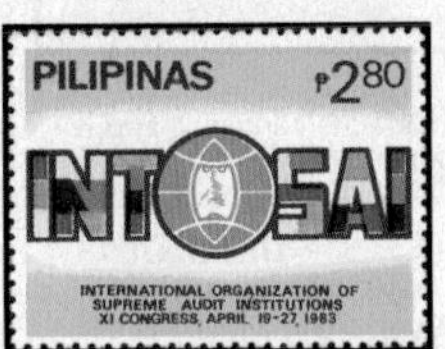

Intl. Org. of Supreme Audit Institutions, 11th Congress, Manila, Apr. 19-27 A411

*Perf. 13x13½*

**1983, Apr. 8 Litho. Wmk. 372**

1632 A411 40s Symbols .50 .30
a. Wmk. 372 (II) 1.75 .75
1633 A411 2.80p Emblem 2.00 1.00
a. Souv. sheet of 2, 1632-1633, imperf. 4.50 4.00
b. Wmk. 372 (II) 5.00 1.75
c. As "a," Wmk. 372 (II) 15.00 12.00

No. 1633a comes on two papers: cream gum, normal watermark; white gum, watermark made up of smaller letters.

**Type of 1982 Overprinted in Red: "7th BSP NATIONAL JAMBOREE 1983"**

**1983, Apr. 13** *Perf. 12½*

1634 A390 40s multi 1.00 .35

Boy Scouts of Philippines jamboree.

**No. 1249 Surcharged**

**1983, Apr. 15**

1635 Block of 10 12.00 12.00
a.-j. A265 40s on 45s, any single .70 .35

A412

*Perf. 13½x13*

**1983, May 9 Litho. Wmk. 372**

1636 A412 40s multi .60 .30
b. Wmk. 372 (II) 1.75 .75

75th anniv. of Dental Assoc.

A413

*Perf. 13½x13*

**1983, June 17 Litho. Wmk. 372**

1637 A413 40s Statue .50 .30
a. Perf. 12½, Wmk. 372 (II) 3.50 1.50
1638 A413 1.20p Statue, diff., diamond 1.25 .50
a. Perf. 12½, Wmk. 372 (II) 4.50 2.00

75th anniv. of University of the Philippines.

Visit of Japanese Prime Minister Yasuhiro Nakasone, May 6-8 — A414

*Perf. 13x13½*

**1983, June 20 Litho. Wmk. 372**

1639 A414 40s multi .60 .30
a. Wmk. 372 (II) 6.00 5.00

25th Anniv. of Natl. Science and Technology Authority A415

No. 1640, Animals, produce. No. 1641, Heart, food, pill. No. 1642, Factories, windmill, car. No. 1643, Chemicals, house, book.

**1983, July 11**

1640 A415 40s multicolored .50 .40
a. Perf. 12½, Wmk. 372 (II) 1.25 1.00
1641 A415 40s multicolored .50 .40
a. Perf. 12½, Wmk. 372 (II) 1.25 1.00
1642 A415 40s multicolored .50 .40
a. Perf. 12½, Wmk. 372 (II) 1.25 1.00
1643 A415 40s multicolored .50 .40
a. Perf. 12½, Wmk. 372 (II) 1.25 1.00
b. Block of 4, #1640-1643 3.00 2.50
b. Block of 4, #1640a-1643a 7.50 5.00

Science Week.

World Communications Year — A416

**Wmk. 372 (II)**

**1983, Oct. 24 Litho.** *Perf. 12½*

1644 A416 3.20p multi 3.00 1.00

Philippine Postal System Bicentennial — A417

**1983, Oct. 31**

1645 A417 40s multi .50 .25

Christmas — A418

Star of the East and Festival Scene in continuous design.

**Wmk. 372 (I)**

**1983, Nov. 15 Litho.** *Perf. 12½*

1646 Strip of 5 4.00 4.00
a.-e. A418 40s single stamp .60 .35
f. Souvenir sheet 4.00 4.00
g. Strip of 5, Wmk. 372 (II) 10.00 7.00
h.-l. As "g," any single 1.25 1.00

Xavier University, 50th Anniv. A419

**Wmk. 372 (II)**

**1983, Dec. 1 Litho.** *Perf. 14*

1647 A419 40s multi .50 .30
a. Wmk. 372 (I) 1.50 .50
1648 A419 60s multi 1.25 .35
a. Wmk. 372 (I) 3.00 1.00

A420

**1983, Dec. 8 Litho.** *Perf. 12½*

1649 A420 40s brt ultra & multi .50 .30
a. Wmk. 372 (I) 5.00 2.75
1650 A420 60s gold & multi 1.25 .35
a. Wmk. 372 (I) 4.25 2.50

Ministry of Labor and Employment, golden jubilee.

A421

**1983, Dec. 7**

1651 A421 40s multi .50 .40
1652 A421 60s multi 1.25 .40

50th anniv. of Women's Suffrage Movement.

Philatelic Week A422

Stamp Collecting: a, Cutting. b, Sorting. c, Soaking. d, Affixing hinges. e, Mounting stamp.

**1983, Dec. 20**

1653 Strip of 5 4.00 3.50
a.-e. A422 50s any single .75 .50
f. Strip of 5, Wmk. 372 (I) 30.00 30.00
g.-k. As "f," any single 5.00 4.00

**Emancipation Type of 1982**

**1983 Litho.** *Perf. 13*

**Size: 32x22mm**

1654 A396 40s multi 2.50 .30
a. Perf. 12½ 15.00 1.00

Philippine Cockatoo — A423

40s, Philippine Cockatoo, 2.30p, Guaiabero. 2.80p, Crimson-spotted racket-tailed parrots. 3.20p, Large-billed parrot. 3.60p, Tanygnathus sumatranus. 5p, Hanging parakeets.

**1984, Jan. 9 Unwmk.** *Perf. 14*

1655 A423 40s multi .55 .30
1656 A423 2.30p multi 1.60 .60
1657 A423 2.80p multi 2.10 .80
1658 A423 3.20p multi 2.50 1.00
1659 A423 3.60p multi 2.75 1.00
1660 A423 5p multi 3.50 1.50
*Nos. 1655-1660 (6)* 13.00 5.20

There were 500,000 of each value created cto with Jan 9 1984, cancel in the center of each block of 4. These were sold at 15 percent of face value. Value for CTO set, $3.

Princess Tarhata Kiram — A424

**Wmk. 372 (II)**

**1984, Jan. 16** *Perf. 13*

1661 A424 3p grn & red 1.90 .35
a. Perf. 12½ 6.75 2.00
b. As "a," Wmk. 372 (I) 4.25 1.25

*Imperf*

PILIPINAS 40s
RELIGIOUS OF THE VIRGIN MARY 1684-1984

Order of Virgin Mary, 300th Anniv. — A425

*Perf. 13½x13*

**1984, Jan. 23 Wmk. 372 (I)**

1662 A425 40s blk & multi .60 .25
a. Perf. 12½ 1.75 .70
1663 A425 60s red & multi 1.25 .50
a. Perf. 12½ 4.00 1.30

Dona Concha Felix de Calderon
PILIPINAS ₱3.60

Dona Concha Felix de Calderon — A426

**1984, Feb. 9 Wmk. 372 (II)** *Perf. 13*

1664 A426 60s blk & bl grn .60 .30
a. Perf. 12½ 2.00 .50
b. Wmk. 372 (I) 25.00 18.00
1665 A426 3.60p red & bl grn 2.00 .70
a. Perf. 12½ 2.50 1.00
b. As "a," Wmk. 372 (I) 5.00 1.75
c. Wmk. 372 (I) 25.00 18.00

**Nos. 1546, 1599, 1618 Surcharged**

**1984, Feb. 20**

1666 A393 60s on 40s (R) .50 .25
a. Perf. 12½ .50 .25
b. As "a," Wmk. 372 (I) 8.00 5.00

1667 A403 60s on 40s, Wmk. 372 (I) .65 .25
1668 A374 3.60p on 3.20p, perf. 12½ (R) 3.55 1.00
*Nos. 1666-1668 (3)* 4.70 1.50

### No. 1685 Surcharged

**1985, Oct. 21 Litho. *Perf. 12½***
1669 A374 3.60p on 4.20p rose lil 5.50 3.00
a. Perf. 13 35.00 25.00

### Portrait Type of 1981

Designs: No. 1672, Gen. Artemio Ricarte. No. 1673, Teodoro M. Kalaw. No. 1674, Pres. Carlos P. Garcia. No. 1675, Senator Quintin Paredes. No. 1676, Dr. Deogracias V. Villadolid (1896-1976), 1st director, Bureau of Fisheries. No. 1677, Santiago Fonacier (1885-1940), archbishop. No. 1678, 2p, Vicente Orestes Romualdez (1885-1970), lawyer. 3p, Francisco Dagohoy.

Types of 3p:
Type I — Medium size "PILIPINAS," large, heavy denomination.
Type II — Large "PILIPINAS," medium denomination.

***Perf. 13, 12¾ (#1678, 2p), 12½x13 (3p)***

**1984-85 Litho.**
1672 A374 60s blk & lt brn 1.40 .30
1673 A374 60s blk & pur 1.75 .30
1674 A374 60s black 1.75 .30
1675 A374 60s dull blue .70 .25
a. Perf. 12½ 1.75 .30
b. Wmk. 391 1.00 .25
c. As "a". Wmk. 391 3.50 .30
1676 A374 60s brn blk ('85) .85 .25
1677 A374 60s dk red ('85) .60 .25
1678 A374 60s cobalt blue ('85) .85 *.40*
1679 A374 2p brt rose ('85) 3.00 .40
1680 A374 3p pale brn, type I 5.25 .40
a. Perf. 12½ 10.00 .65
1680A A374 3p pale brn, type II 8.50 .50
*Nos. 1672-1680A (10)* 24.65 3.35

Issued: #1672, 3/22; #1673, 3/31; #1674, 6/14; #1675, 9/12; #1676, 3/22; #1677, 5/21; #1678, 2p, 7/3; 3p, 9/7.

### Types of 1982

Types of 3.60p:
Type I — Thick Frame line, large "P," "360" with line under "60."
Type II — Medium Frame line, small "p," "3.60."

***Perf. 12½ (#1684, 1681A), 12¾x13, 13x12¾ (#1681, 1681A)***
**Wmk. 372 (II), 391 (#1684A)**

**1984-86**
1681 A390 60s green & multi .35 .25
a. Perf. 12½ .50 .25
b. Wmk. 372 (I) 25.00 18.00
1681A A390 60s red & multi .75 .30
1682 A374 1.80p #1546 1.50 .35
a. Perf. 12½ 2.50 .35
1683 A374 2.40p #1545 1.60 .40
a. Perf. 12½ 1.75 .35
b. As "a," Wmk. 372 (I) 20.00 10.00
1684 A386 3.60p Quezon, type I 2.00 .40
1684A A386 3.60p As #1684, type II 3.50 .50
1685 A374 4.20p #1544 2.75 .75
*Nos. 1681-1685 (7)* 12.45 2.95

Issued: #1681A, 10/19; #1684A, 2/14/86; others 3/26.
Postal forgeries of No. 1684 exist perf. 11.

Ayala Corp. Sesquicentenary — A427

Night Views of Manila.

**1984, Apr. 25 Litho. *Perf. 13x13½***
1686 A427 70s multi .65 .30
a. Perf. 12½ 1.75 .50
1687 A427 3.60p multi 2.75 .70

ESPANA '84 A428

Designs: 2.50p, No. 1690d, Our Lady of the Most Holy Rosary with St. Dominic, by C. Francisco. 5p, No. 1690a, Spoliarium, by Juan Luna. No. 1690b, Blessed Virgin of Manila as Patroness of Voyages, Galleon showing map of Panama-Manila. No. 1690c. Illustrations from The Monkey and the Turtle, by Rizal (first children's book published in Philippines, 1885.)

**1984, Apr. 27 Unwmk. *Perf. 14***
1688 A428 2.50p multi 3.00 2.00
1689 A428 5p multi 8.00 4.00
a. Pair, #1688-1689 13.00 10.00

### Souvenir Sheet

***Perf. 14½x15, Imperf.***
1690 Sheet of 4, #a.-d. 25.00 20.00
a.-d. A428 7.50p, any single 5.00 3.00

### Surcharged in Black

***Perf. 14½x15***
1690A Sheet of 4, #a.-d. 200.00 200.00
a.-d. A428 7.20p on 7.50p, any single 22.00 20.00

### Surcharged in Red

***Imperf***
1690B Sheet of 4, #a.-d. 200.00 200.00
a.-d. A428 7.20p on 7.50p, any single 22.00 20.00

### Surcharged in Black

***Imperf***
1690C Sheet of 4, #a.-d. 250.00 250.00
a.-d. A428 7.20p on 7.50p, any single 60.00 60.00

Nos. 1690Aa-1690Ad and 1690Ba-1690Bd are each surcharged 7.20p and bear the following overprints: #1690Aa and #1690Ba, "10-5-84 NATIONAL MUSEUM WEEK" on #1690a; #1690Ab and #1690Bb, "8-3-84 PHILIPPINE-MEXICAN FRIENDSHIP 420th ANNIVERSARY" on #1690b; #1690Ac and #1690Bc, "7-17-84 NATIONAL CHILDREN'S BOOK DAY" on #1690c; #1690Ad and #1690Bd, "9-1-84 O.L. OF HOLY ROSARY PARISH 300TH YEAR" on #1690d. Nos. 1690Aa-1690Bd were released as single stamps on the dates shown in their respective overprints. A few intact sheets were sold after the release of the last of these stamps.

Maria Paz Mendoza Guazon — A429

**1984, May 26 Wmk. 372 *Perf. 13***
1691 A429 60s brt blue & red 1.00 .25
1692 A429 65s brt blue, red & blk 1.25 .30

Butterflies — A430

60s, Adolias amlana. 2.40p, Papilio daedalus. 3p, Prothoe frankii semperi. 3.60p, Troides magellanus. 4.20p, Yoma sabina vasuki. 5p, Chilasa idaeoides.

**Unwmk.**
**1984, Aug. 2 Litho. *Perf. 14***
1693 A430 60s multi .60 .40
1694 A430 2.40p multi *1.25* .80
1695 A430 3p multi *1.50* 1.00
1696 A430 3.60p multi *1.50* 1.00
1697 A430 4.20p multi *2.00* *1.25*
1698 A430 5p multi *3.00* *1.50*
*Nos. 1693-1698 (6)* *9.85* 5.95

There were 500,000 of each value created cto with Jul 5 1984 cancel in the center of each block of 4. These were sold at 15 percent face value.Value for CTO set, $3.50.

Summer Olympics, Los Angeles, 1984 — A431

Designs: 60s, Running (man). 2.40p, Boxing. 6p, Swimming. 7.20p, Windsurfing. 8.40p, Cycling. 20p, Running (woman).

**Unwmk.**
**1984, Aug. 9 Litho. *Perf. 14***
1699 A431 60s multi .50 *.40*
1700 A431 2.40p multi 1.00 .50
1701 A431 6p multi 2.50 1.50
1702 A431 7.20p multi 3.00 2.00
1703 A431 8.40p multi 3.25 2.50
1704 A431 20p multi 8.00 4.50
*Nos. 1699-1704 (6)* 18.25 11.40

### Souvenir Sheet

1705 Sheet of 4 15.00 *15.00*
a.-d. A431 6p, any single 2.50 2.50

There were 500,000 of each value created cto with Aug 8 1984 cancel in the center of each block of 4. These were sold at15 percent face value. Used value, set of 6 cto, $3.75.
Nos. 1699-1705 were also issued imperf, with blue, instead of red, stars at sides. Value, set of 6 stamps $100, souvenir sheet $40.

Baguio City, 75th Anniv. A432

**Wmk. 372**
**1984, Aug. 24 Litho. *Perf. 12½***
1706 A432 1.20p The Mansion 1.75 .60

Light Rail Transit A433

**1984, Sept. 10 *Perf. 13x13½***
1707 A433 1.20p multi 1.75 .40

A similar unissued and unlisted stamp shows a streecar facing left on the 1.20p.

No. 1, Australia No. 59 and Koalas A434

***Perf. 14½x15***
**1984, Sept. 21 Unwmk.**
1708 A434 3p multi 3.00 1.50
1709 A434 3.60p multi 4.00 2.00

### Souvenir Sheet

1710 Sheet of 3 *20.00* *18.00*
a. A434 20p multi *6.00* *5.00*

AUSIPEX '84. No. 1710 exists imperf. Value, $25.

### No. 1609 Surcharged with 2 Black Bars and Ovptd. "14-17 NOV. 84 / R.I. ASIA REGIONAL CONFERENCE"

***Perf. 13x13½***
**1984, Nov. 11 Wmk. 372 Litho.**
1713 A398 1.20p on 2.30p multi 2.00 *.80*
a. Wmk. 372 (II) 2.00 .80

Philatelic Week — A435

1.20p, Gold medal. 3p, Winning stamp exhibit.

**Wmk. 372 (II)**
**1984, Nov. 22 *Perf. 13½x13***
1714 A435 1.20p multi .70 .40
1715 A435 3p multi 2.00 1.00
a. Pair, #1714-1715 3.50 2.50

AUSIPEX '84 and Mario Que, 1st Philippine exhibitor to win FIP Gold Award.
For overprints see Nos. 1737A and 1737B.

Ships A436

60s, Caracao canoes. 1.20p, Chinese junk. 6p, Spanish galleon. 7.20p, Casco. 8.40p, Steamboat. 20p, Cruise liner.

**Unwmk.**
**1984, Nov. 26 Litho. *Perf. 14***
1718 A436 60s multi .50 .30
1719 A436 1.20p multi .60 .40
1720 A436 6p multi 1.90 .60
1721 A436 7.20p multi 2.25 1.00
1722 A436 8.40p multi 2.50 1.25
1723 A436 20p multi 5.25 2.00
*Nos. 1718-1723 (6)* *13.00* 5.55

There were 500,000 of each value created cto with Oct 5 1984 cancel in the center of each block of 4. These were sold at 15 percentf face value. Value, set of 6 cto, $3.50.
For surcharge, see No. 3051.

Ateneo de Manila University, 125th Anniv. A438

**Wmk. 372 (II)**
**1984, Dec. 7 Litho. *Perf. 13x13½***
1730 A438 60s ultra & gold .65 .30
1731 A438 1.20p dk ultra & sil 1.35 .40

A438a

60s, Manila-Dagupan, 1892. 1.20p, Light rail transit, 1984. 6p, Bicol Express, 1955. 7,20p, Tranvis (1905, electric street car). 8.40, Commuter train, 1984. 20p, Early street car pulled by horses, 1898.

***Perf. 14x13¾***
**1984, Dec. 18 Unwmk.**
1731A A438a 60s multi .50 .35
1731B A438a 1.20p multi 1.00 .40
1731C A438a 6p multi 3.00 .65
1731D A438a 7.20p multi 4.00 1.60
1731E A438a 8.40p multi 3.50 1.25
1731F A438a 20p multi 7.50 2.25
*Nos. 1731A-1731F (6)* *19.50* 6.50

There were 500,000 of each value created cto with Dec 5 1984 cancel in the center of each block of 4. These were sold at15 percentf face value. Value, set of 6 cto, $3.50.
For surcharges see #1772-1773.

Christmas
A439

60s, Madonna and Child. 1.20p, Holy family.

**Wmk. 372 (II)**

**1984, Dec. 8** *Perf. 13½x13*
**1732** A439 60s multi .80 .30
**1733** A439 1.20p multi 2.00 .80
*a.* Pair, #1732-1733 3.25 2.25

Natl. Jaycees Awards, 25th anniv. — A440

Philippines Jaycees Commitment to Youth Development.
Abstract painting by Raoul G. Isidro.

**1984, Dec. 19**
**1734** Strip of 10 *24.00 24.00*
*a.-e.* A440 60s any single 1.00 .75
*f.-j.* A440 3p any single 3.00 2.00
*k.* Strip of 10, Wmk. 372 (I) 125.00 125.00
*l.-p.* A440 60s any single 5.00 4.00
*q.-u.* A440 3p any single 15.00 12.50

Dried Tobacco Leaf and Plant
A441

**1985, Jan. 14** *Perf. 13x13½*
**1735** A441 60s multicolored .50 .30
**1736** A441 3p multicolored 2.00 .80

Philippine-Virginia Tobacco Admin., 25th anniv.

**No. 1537 Surcharged**

**1984, Nov. 28 Litho.** *Imperf.*
**1737** A373 3p on 2p multi 5.00 4.00

First printing had missing period ("p300"). Value $12.
First-day cancels are for Nov. 20.

**Nos. 1714-1715 Overprinted "Philatelic Week 1984"**

1.20p, Gold medal. 3p, Winning stamp exhibit.

**1985, Jan. 25** *Perf. 13½x13*
**1737A** A435 1.20p multi .70 .40
**1737B** A435 3p multi 2.00 1.00
*c.* Pair, #1737A-1737B 3.50 2.50

Natl. Research Council Emblem
A442

**1985, Feb. 3 Litho.** *Perf. 13x13½*
**1738** A442 60s bl, dk bl & blk .35 .25
**1739** A442 1.20p org, dk bl & blk 1.00 .30

Pacific Science Assoc., 5th intl. congress, Manila, Feb. 3-7.

Medicinal Plants
A443

60s, Carmona retusa. 1.20p, Orthosiphon aristatus. 2.40p, Vitex negundo. 3p, Aloe barbadensis. 3.60p, Quisqualis indica. 4.20p, Blumea balsamifera.

**Wmk. 372 (II)**

**1985, Mar. 15** *Perf. 13x13½*
**1740** A443 60s multi 1.00 .30
*a.* Perf. 12½ 1.75 .80
**1741** A443 1.20p multi 2.25 .80
*a.* Perf. 12½ 2.00 .50
**1742** A443 2.40p multi 3.50 1.75
*a.* Perf. 12½ 3.50 .80
**1743** A443 3p multi 5.00 1.75
*a.* Perf. 12½ 3.50 1.00
**1744** A443 3.60p multi 4.00 1.75
*a.* Perf. 12½ 5.50 2.50
*b.* Wmk. 372 (I) 80.00 80.00
*c.* As "a," Wmk. 372 (I) 40.00 40.00
**1745** A443 4.20p multi 6.00 3.00
*a.* Perf. 12½ 6.00 2.75
*Nos. 1740-1745 (6)* 21.75 9.35

INTELSAT, 20th Anniv.
A444

**1985, Apr. 6** *Perf. 13x13½*
**1746** A444 60s multicolored .50 .30
**1747** A444 3p multicolored 2.50 .70

A444a

Philippine Horses: 60s, Pintos. 1.20p, Palomino. 6p, Bay. 7.20p, Brown. 8.40p, Gray. 20p, Chestnut.
#1747G: h, as 1.20p. i, as 7.20p. j, as 6p. k, as 20p.

*Perf. 14x13¾*

**1984, Dec. 18** **Unwmk.**
**1747A** A444a 60s multi .50 .40
**1747B** A444a 1.20p multi 1.00 .50
**1747C** A444a 6p multi 2.00 .80
**1747D** A444a 7.20p multi 3.00 1.20
**1747E** A444a 8.40p multi 3.25 1.60
**1747F** A444a 20p multi 6.75 2.00
*Nos. 1747A-1747F (6)* 16.50 6.50

**Souvenir Sheet of 4**

**1747G** A444a 8.40p h.-k. 15.00 *15.00*

There were 500,000 each of #1747A-1747F created cto with Apr 12 1985 cancel in the center of each block of 4. These were sold at 15 percentf face value. Value, set of 6 cto, $3.50.

Tax Research Institute, 25th Anniv. — A445

*Perf. 13½x13*

**1985, Apr. 22** **Wmk. 372**
**1748** A445 60s multicolored .70 .30

Intl. Rice Research Institute, 25th Anniv.
A446

**1985, May 27** *Perf. 13x13½*
**1749** A446 60s Planting .50 .40
*a.* Perf. 12½ 6.50 3.00
**1750** A446 3p Paddies 2.50 .80

1st Spain-Philippines Peace Treaty, 420th Anniv. — A447

Designs: 1.20p, Blessed Infant of Cebu, statue, shrine and basilica. 3.60p, King Tupas of Cebu and Miguel Lopez de Legaspi signing treaty, 1565.

**1985, June 4** *Perf. 12½*
**1751** A447 1.20p multi .70 .30
**1752** A447 3.60p multi 1.70 .70
*a.* Pair, #1751-1752 + label 4.50 3.50

**No. 1532 Ovptd. "10th Anniversary Philippines and People's Republic of China Diplomatic Relations 1975-1985"**

**1985, June 8** *Imperf.*
**1753** A372 5p multi 6.00 *5.00*

In the first printing, the hand-drawn apostrophe in *People's* was omitted. The apostrophe is included in later printings.

Arbor Week, June 9-15 — A448

**1985, June 9** *Perf. 13½x13*
**1754** A448 1.20p multi 1.25 .40
*a.* Perf. 12½ 75.00 75.00

Battle of Bessang Pass, 40th Anniv.
A449

**1985, June 14** *Perf. 13x13½*
**1755** A449 1.20p multi 1.50 .50

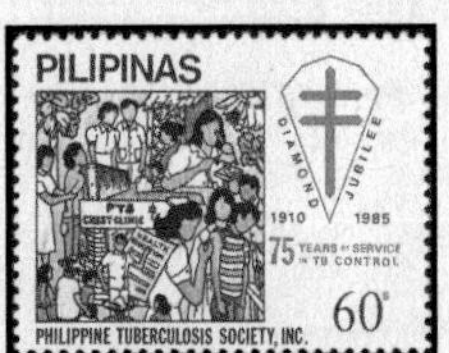

Natl. Tuberculosis Soc., 75th Anniv. — A450

60s, Immunization, research. 1.20p, Charity seal.

**1985, July 29**
**1756** A450 60s multi .70 .40
**1757** A450 1.20p multi 1.00 .60
*a.* Pair, #1756-1757 2.50 2.00

**No. 1297 Surcharged with Bars, New Value and Scout Emblem in Gold, Ovptd. "GSP" and "45th Anniversary Girl Scout Charter" in Black**

*Perf. 12½x13½*

**1985, Aug. 19** **Unwmk.** **Photo.**
**1758** A242 2.40p on 15s on 10s 1.50 1.00
**1759** A242 4.20p on 15s on 10s 2.50 1.50
**1760** A242 7.20p on 15s on 10s 4.00 2.50
*Nos. 1758-1760 (3)* 8.00 5.00

Virgin Mary Birth Bimillennium
A451

Statues and paintings.

*Perf. 13½x13*

**1985, Sept. 8** **Wmk. 372** **Litho.**
**1761** A451 1.20p Fatima 1.00 .40
**1762** A451 2.40p Beaterio 1.60 .60
**1763** A451 3p Penafrancia 2.40 1.00
**1764** A451 3.60p Guadalupe 3.00 1.50
*Nos. 1761-1764 (4)* 8.00 3.50

A small quantity of No. 1762 was issued with a large *2* in the denomination. The top of the *2* touches the frameline. Value, $10 mint, $4 used.

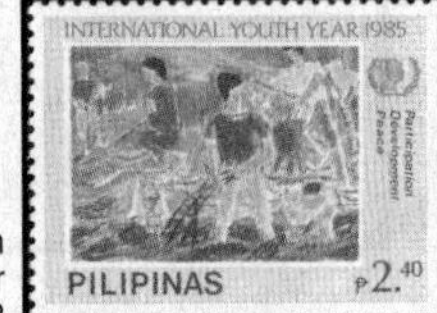

Intl. Youth Year
A452

Prize-winning children's drawings.

**1985, Sept. 23** *Perf. 13x13½*
**1765** A452 2.40p Agriculture 1.50 .35
**1766** A452 3.60p Education 2.50 .85

Girl and Rice Terraces
A453

**1985, Sept. 26**
**1767** A453 2.40p multi 2.50 .65
*a.* Perf. 12½ 8.50 8.50

World Tourism Organization, 6th general assembly, Sofia, Bulgaria, Sept. 17-26.

Export Year — A454

**1985, Oct. 8** *Perf. 13½x13*
**1768** A454 1.20p multi 1.50 .35

UN, 40th Anniv. — A455

**1985, Oct. 24**
**1769** A455 3.60p multi 3.00 .70

1st Transpacific Airmail Service, 50th Anniv. — A456

3p, China Clipper on water. 3.60p, China Clipper, map.

**1985, Nov. 22** ***Perf. 13x13½***
**1770** A456 3p multi 2.50 1.00
**1771** A456 3.60p multi 3.00 1.00

**Nos. 1731C-1731D Surcharged in Black**

***Perf. 14x13¾***
**1985, Nov. 24** **Unwmk.**
**1772** A438a 60s on 6p .80 .50
**1773** A438a 3p on 7.20p 4.20 1.50

No. 1773 is airmail.

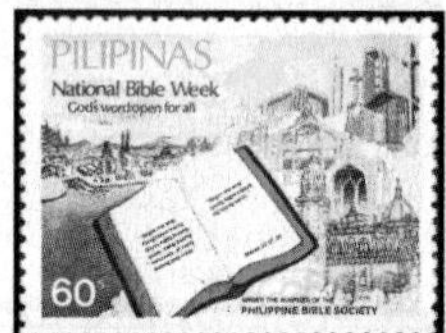

Natl. Bible Week A457

**1985, Dec. 3** **Wmk. 372** ***Perf. 12½***
**1774** A457 60s multicolored .50 .40
**1775** A457 3p multicolored 2.50 1.00

Christmas 1985 A458

**1985, Dec. 8** ***Perf. 13x13½***
**1776** A458 60s Panuluyan .70 .40
*a.* Perf. 12½ 5.00 3.50
**1777** A458 3p Pagdalaw 3.30 1.00
*a.* Perf. 12½ 13.00 10.00

Scales of Justice A459

**1986, Jan. 12**
**1778** A459 60s lilac rose & blk .50 .30
**1779** A459 3p brt grn, lil rose & blk 2.10 .80

University of the Philippines, College of Law, 75th anniv.

See No. 1838.

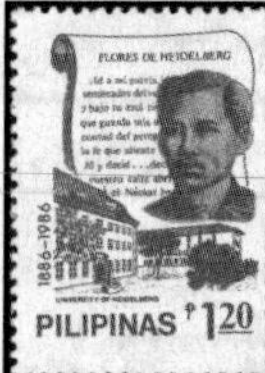

Flores de Heidelberg, by Jose Rizal — A460

Design: 60s, Noli Me Tangere.

**1986** **Wmk. 391** **Litho.** ***Perf. 13***
**1780** A460 60s violet .35 .25
*a.* Wmk. 372 (II) 20.00 20.00
**1781** A460 1.20p bluish grn 1.35 .30
*a.* Wmk. 372 (II) 15.00 15.00
**1782** A460 3.60p redsh brn 2.30 .35
*Nos. 1780-1782 (3)* 4.00 .90

Issued: 60s, 1.20p, Feb. 21; 3.60p, July 10.
For surcharges see Nos. 1834, 1913.
Nos. 1780a-1781a were printed for presentation purposes. Remainders were sold over post office counters.

Philippine Airlines, 45th Anniv. — A461

Aircraft: No. 1783a, Douglas DC3, 1946. b, Douglas DC4 Skymaster, 1946. c, Douglas DC6, 1948. d, Vickers Viscount 784, 1957.
No. 1784a, Fokker Friendship F27 Mark 100, 1960. b, Douglas DC8 Series 50, 1962. c, Bac One Eleven Series 500, 1964. d, McDonnell Douglas DC10 Series 30, 1974.
No. 1785a, Beech Model 18, 1941. b, Boeing 747, 1980.

**1986, Mar. 15**
**1783** A461 Block of 4 *4.00* 3.00
*a.-d.* 60s, any single *.50* .30
*e.* Block of 4, Wmk. 372 (II) 80.00 80.00
*f.-j.* As "e," 60s, any single *16.00* 16.00
**1784** A461 Block of 4 *8.00* 6.50
*a.-d.* 2.40p, any single *1.00* 1.00
*e.* Block of 4, Wmk. 372 (II) 100.00 100.00
*f.-j.* As "e," 2.40p, any single *20.00* 20.00
**1785** A461 Pair *5.50* 4.00
*a.-b.* 3.60p, any single *2.25* 1.50
*c.* Pair, Wmk. 372 (II) 50.00 50.00
*d.-e.* As "e," 3.60p, any single *10.00* 10.00
*Nos. 1783-1785 (3)* *17.50* 13.50

See No. 1842.

Bataan Oil Refining Corp., 25th Anniv. A462

***Perf. 13½x13, 13x13½***
**1986, Apr. 12** **Wmk. 372**
**1786** A462 60s Refinery, vert. .50 .35
*a.* Wmk. 391 1.00 .50
**1787** A462 3p shown 2.50 .85
*a.* Wmk. 391 4.00 2.00

EXPO '86, Vancouver A463

***Perf. 13x13½***
**1986, May 2** **Wmk. 391**
**1788** A463 60s multicolored .50 .35
*a.* Wmk. 372 (II) 30.00 30.00
**1789** A463 3p multicolored 2.50 1.00
*a.* Wmk. 372 (II) 30.00 30.00

Asian Productivity Organization, 25th Anniv. — A464

**1986, May 15**
**1790** A464 60s multicolored .50 .40
*a.* Wmk. 372 (II) 15.00 15.00
**1791** A464 3p multicolored 2.50 2.00
*a.* Wmk. 372 (II) 15.00 15.00

**Size: 30x22mm**

**1792** A464 3p pale brown 1.25 .30
*Nos. 1790-1792 (3)* 4.25 2.70

Issued: #1790-1791, 5/15; #1792, 7/10.

AMERIPEX '86 — A465

**1986, May 22** ***Perf. 13½x13***
**1793** A465 60s No. 241 .50 .35
*a.* Wmk. 372 (II) 7.00 5.00
**1794** A465 3p No. 390 2.50 1.00
*a.* Wmk. 372 (II) 7.00 5.00

See No. 1835.

Election of Corazon Aquino, 7th Pres. — A466

Portrait of Aquino and: 60s, Salvador Laurel, vice-president, and hands in symbolic gestures of peace and freedom. 1.20p, Symbols of communication and transportation. 2.40p, Parade. 3p, Military. 7.20p, Vice-president, parade, horiz.

**1986, May 25** **Wmk. 372**
**1795** A466 60s multi .40 .30
*a.* Wmk. 389 .50 .60
**1796** A466 1.20p multi .60 .35
*a.* Wmk. 389 .90 .70
**1797** A466 2.40p multi 1.10 .40
*a.* Wmk. 389 1.60 .80
**1798** A466 3p multi 1.40 .50
*a.* Wmk. 389 2.00 .90
*Nos. 1795-1798 (4)* 3.50 1.55

**Souvenir Sheet**
***Imperf***

**1799** A466 7.20p multi 4.25 *3.75*
*a.* Wmk. 389 4.50 4.00

For surcharge see No. 1939.

De La Salle University, 75th Anniv. A467

60s, Statue of St. John the Baptist de la Salle, Paco buildings, 1911, & university, 1986. 2.40p, St. Miguel Febres Cordero, buildings, 1911. 3p, St. Benilde, buildings, 1986. 7.20p, Founding fathers.

***Perf. 13x13½***
**1986, June 16** **Wmk. 391**
**1800** A467 60s grn, blk & pink .50 .30
**1801** A467 2.40p grn, blk & bl 1.50 .50
**1802** A467 3p grn, blk & yel 2.50 .75
*Nos. 1800-1802 (3)* 4.50 1.55

**Souvenir Sheet**
***Imperf***

**1803** A467 7.20p grn & blk 6.00 *5.00*

For surcharge see No. 1940.

A468

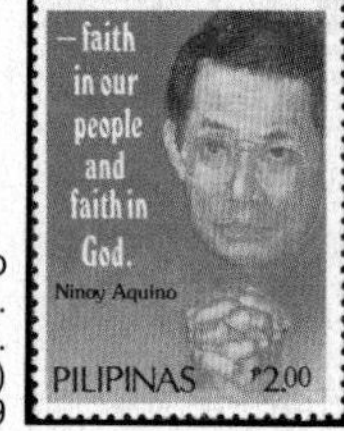

Memorial to Benigno S. Aquino, Jr. (1932-83) A469

3.60p, The Filipino is worth dying for, horiz. 10p, Hindi ka nag-iisa, horiz.

***Perf. 13½x13, 13x13½***
**1986, Aug. 21** **Wmk. 389**
**1804** A468 60s dl bluish grn .50 .30
**1805** A469 2p shown 1.25 .40
**1806** A469 3.60p multicolored 2.25 1.00
*Nos. 1804-1806 (3)* 4.00 1.70

**Souvenir Sheet**
***Imperf***

**1807** A469 10p multicolored 5.00 4.00

See No. 1836. For surcharges see No. 1914 and 2706A.

Indigenous Orchids — A470

60s, Vanda sanderiana. 1.20p, Epigeneium lyonii. 2.40p, Paphiopedilum philippinense. 3p, Amesiella philippinensis.

**1986, Aug. 28** ***Perf. 13½x13***
**1808** A470 60s multi *.50* .30
**1809** A470 1.20p multi *2.00* .40
**1810** A470 2.40p multi *3.50* .80
**1811** A470 3p multi *3.50* 1.50
*Nos. 1808-1811 (4)* *9.50* 3.00

For surcharge see No. 1941.

Quiapo District, 400th Anniv. — A471

60s, Our Lord Jesus the Nazarene, statue, Quiapo church. 3.60p, Quiapo church, 1930, horiz.

***Perf. 13½x13, 13x13½***
**1986, Aug. 29** **Wmk. 391**
**1812** A471 60s pink, blk & lake .50 .30
**1813** A471 3.60p pale grn, blk & dk ultra 3.10 .90

For surcharge see No. 1915.

General Hospital, 75th Anniv. — A472

**1986, Sept. 1** ***Perf. 13½x13***

**1814** A472 60s bl & multi .40 *.30*
**1815** A472 3p grn & multi 2.00 *.50*

See No. 1841. For surcharge see No. 1888.

Halley's Comet A473

60s, Comet, Earth. 2.40p, Comet, Earth, Moon.

***Perf. 13x13½***

**1986, Sept. 25** **Wmk. 389**

**1816** A473 60s multi .60 .30
**1817** A473 2.40p multi 2.40 .50

For surcharge see No. 1942.

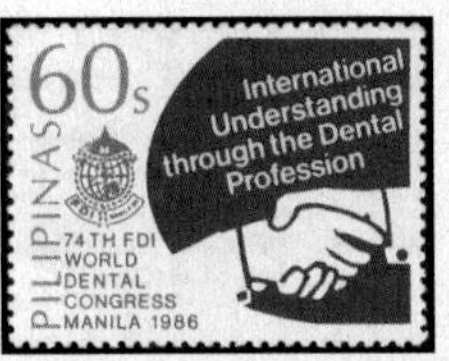


74th FDI World Dental Congress, Manila A474

**1986, Nov. 10** **Litho.** ***Perf. 13x13½***

**1818** A474 60s Handshake .80 .30
**1819** A474 3p Jeepney bus *5.00* 2.00

See Nos. 1837, 1840.

Insects A475

Intl. Peace Year — A476

***Perf. 13x13½, 13½x13***

**1986, Nov. 21**

**1820** A475 60s Butterfly, beetles *1.00* .40
**1821** A476 1p blue & blk *2.00* .60
**1822** A475 3p Dragonflies *3.50* 2.00
*Nos. 1820-1822 (3)* *6.50* 3.00

Philately Week.

Manila YMCA, 75th Anniv. — A477

***Perf. 13x13½***

**1986, Nov. 28** **Wmk. 391**

**1823** A477 2p blue *1.25* .40
**1824** A477 3.60p red *3.25* .60

See No. 1839. For surcharge see No. 1916.

Philippine Normal College, 85th Anniv. A478

Various arrangements of college crest and buildings, 1901-1986.

**1986, Dec. 12** **Wmk. 389**

**1825** A478 60s multi *1.00* .80
**1826** A478 3.60p buff, ultra & gldn brn 3.25 1.00

For surcharge see No. 1917.

Christmas A479

No. 1827, Holy family. No. 1828, Mother and child, doves. No. 1829, Child touching mother's face. No. 1830, Adoration of the shepherds. No. 1831, Mother, child signaling peace. No. 1832, Holy family, lamb. No. 1833, Mother, child blessing food.

**1986, Dec. 15** ***Perf. 13½x13, 13x13½***

**1827** A479 60s multicolored *.70* .30
**1828** A479 60s multicolored *.70* .30
**1829** A479 60s multicolored *.70* .30
**1830** A479 1p multicolored *.85* .40
**1831** A479 1p multicolored *.85* .40
**1832** A479 1p multicolored *.85* .40
**1833** A479 1p multicolored *.85* .40
*Nos. 1827-1833 (7)* *5.50* 2.50

Nos. 1827-1829, vert.

### No. 1780 Surcharged

**Wmk. 391**

**1987, Jan. 6** **Litho.** ***Perf. 13***

**1834** A460 1p on 60s vio 1.00 .25

### Types of 1986

Designs: 75s, No. 390, AMERIPEX '86. 1p, Benigno S. Aquino, Jr. 3.25p, Handshake, 74th World Dental Congress. 3.50p, Scales of Justice. 4p, Manila YMCA emblem. 4.75p, Jeepney bus. 5p, General Hospital. 5.50p, Boeing 747, 1980.

Types of 4p
Type I — "4" is taller than "0's."
Type II — "4" is same height as "0's."

**1987** **Litho.** ***Perf. 13***

**Size: 22x31mm, 31x22mm**

**1835** A465 75s brt yel grn .75 .25
**1836** A468 1p blue .75 .25
**1837** A474 3.25p dull grn 1.50 .75
**1838** A459 3.50p dark car 2.00 .40
**1839** A477 4p blue, type I 3.00 .40
**1839A** A477 4p blue, type II 6.00 3.00
**1840** A474 4.75p dl yel grn 3.00 .50
**1841** A472 5p olive bister 3.00 .50
**1842** A461 5.50p dk bl gray 3.00 .80
*Nos. 1835-1842 (9)* *23.00* 6.85

All No. 1839 dated "1-1-87."
Issued: #1839A, 12/17; others, 1/16.

Manila Hotel, 75th Anniv. A480

***Perf. 13x13½***

**1987, Jan. 30** **Wmk. 389**

**1843** A480 1p Hotel, c. 1912 .60 .40
**1844** A480 4p Hotel, 1987 2.30 .85
**1845** A480 4.75p Lobby 3.00 1.25
**1846** A480 5.50p Foyer 4.60 1.50
*Nos. 1843-1846 (4)* 10.50 4.00

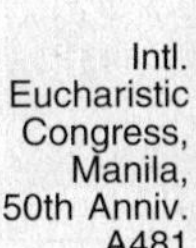

Intl. Eucharistic Congress, Manila, 50th Anniv. A481

**1987, Feb. 7** ***Perf. 13½x13, 13x13½***

**1847** A481 75s Emblem, vert. .50 .25
**1848** A481 1p shown .80 .40

Pres. Aquino Taking Oath A482

Text — A483

**1987, Mar. 4** ***Perf. 13½x13, 13x13½***

**1849** A482 1p multi .50 .40
**1850** A483 5.50p bl & deep bis 3.00 .80

Ratification of the new constitution. See No. 1905. For surcharge see No. 2005.

Lyceum College and Founder, Jose P. Laurel A484

**1987, May 7** **Litho.** ***Perf. 13x13½***

**1851** A484 1p multi .70 .40
**1852** A484 2p multi 1.70 1.00

Lyceum of the Philippines, 35th anniv.

Government Service Insurance System — A485

1p, Salary and policy loans. 1.25p, Disability, medicare. 2p, Retirement benefits. 3.50p, Life insurance.

**1987, June 1** ***Perf. 13½x13***

**1853** A485 1p multi .50 .40
**1854** A485 1.25p multi .40 .50
**1855** A485 2p multi 1.70 .80
**1856** A485 3.50p multi 2.00 1.00
*Nos. 1853-1856 (4)* 4.60 2.70

Davao City, 50th Anniv. A486

1p, Falconer, woman planting, city seal.

**1987, Mar. 16** **Litho.** ***Perf. 13x13½***

**1857** A486 1p multicolored .85 .40

Salvation Army in the Philippines, 50th Anniv. — A487

**1987, June 5** **Photo.** ***Perf. 13½x13***

**1858** A487 1p multi 1.40 .40

Natl. League of Women Voters, 50th Anniv. — A488

**1987, July 15**

**1859** A488 1p pink & blue 1.00 .40

A489

#1861, Gen. Vicente Lukban (1860-1916). #1862, Wenceslao Q. Vinzons (1910-1942). #1863, Brig.-gen. Mateo M. Capinpin (1887-1958). #1864, Jesus Balmori (1882-1948).

***Perf. 13x13½, 12½ (#1862)***

**1987** **Litho.** **Wmk. 391**

**1861** A489 1p olive grn .55 .25
**1862** A489 1p dull greenish blue .60 .25
**1863** A489 1p dull red brn .60 .25
**1864** A489 1p rose red & rose claret .55 .25
*Nos. 1861-1864 (4)* 2.30 1.00

Issued: #1861, 7/31; #1862, 9/9; #1863, 10/15; #1864, 12/17.

A490

Nuns (1862-1987), children, Crucifix, Sacred Heart.

***Perf. 13½x13***

**1987, July 22** **Litho.** **Wmk. 389**

**1881** A490 1p multi 1.00 .40

Daughters of Charity of St. Vincent de Paul in the Philippines, 125th anniv.

Map of Southeast Asia, Flags of ASEAN Members A491

**1987, Aug. 7** ***Perf. 13x13½***

**1882** A491 1p multi 1.20 .50

ASEAN, 20th anniv.

Exports Campaign
A492

**1987, Aug. 11 Wmk. 391 *Perf. 13***

**1883** A492 1p shown .50 .25
**1884** A492 2p Worker, gearwheel 1.00 .30

See No. 1904.

Canonization of Lorenzo Ruiz by Pope John Paul II, Oct. 18 — A493

First Filipino saint: 1p, Ruiz, stained glass window showing Crucifixion. 5.50p, Ruiz at prayer, execution in 1637.

***Perf. 13½x13***

**1987, Oct. 10 Litho. Wmk. 389**

**1885** A493 1p multi 1.00 .40
**1886** A493 5.50p multi 4.25 1.00

**Size: 57x57mm**

***Imperf***

**1887** A493 8p like 5.50p 6.00 4.50
*Nos. 1885-1887 (3)* 11.25 5.90

No. 1887 has denomination at LL.

No. 1841 Surcharged

**1987, Oct. 12 Wmk. 391 *Perf. 13***

**1888** A472 4.75p on 5p olive bis 2.30 .70

Order of the Good Shepherd Sisters in Philippines, 65th Anniv.
A494

***Perf. 13x13½***

**1987, Oct. 27 Wmk. 389**

**1889** A494 1p multi 1.50 .75

Natl. Boy Scout Movement, 50th Anniv.
A495

Founders: J. Vargas, M. Camus, J.E.H. Stevenot, A.N. Luz, V. Lim, C. Romulo and G.A. Daza.

**1987, Oct. 28 Litho. *Perf. 13x13½***

**1890** A495 1p multi 1.40 1.00

Philippine Philatelic Club, 50th Anniv.
A496

**1987, Nov. 7 *Perf. 13x13½***

**1891** A496 1p multi 1.25 .75

Order of the Dominicans in the Philippines, 400th Anniv.
A497

Designs: 1p, First missionaries shipwrecked, church and image of the Virgin, vert. 4.75p, J.A. Jeronimo Guerrero, Br., Diego de St. Maria and Letran Dominican College. 5.50p, Pope with Dominican representatives.

***Perf. 13½x13, 13x13½***

**1987, Nov. 11**

**1892** A497 1p multi .50 .40
**1893** A497 4.75p multi 2.00 .60
**1894** A497 5.50p multi 3.00 1.25
*Nos. 1892-1894 (3)* 5.50 2.25

3rd ASEAN Summit Meeting, Dec. 14-15
A498

**1987, Dec. 5 *Perf. 13x13½***

**1895** A498 4p multicolored 2.50 1.25

Christmas 1987 — A499

No. 1896, Postal service. No. 1897, 5-Pointed stars. No. 1898, Procession, church. No. 1899, Gift exchange. No. 1900, Bamboo cannons. No. 1901, Pig, holiday foods. No. 1902, Traditional foods. No. 1903, Serving meal.

**1987, Dec. 8 *Perf. 13½x13***

**1896** A499 1p multicolored .50 .45
**1897** A499 1p multicolored .50 .45
**1898** A499 4p multicolored 2.25 .80
**1899** A499 4.75p multicolored 2.25 .80
**1900** A499 5.50p multicolored 3.00 1.00
**1901** A499 8p multicolored 4.00 1.50
**1902** A499 9.50p multicolored 4.50 2.00
**1903** A499 11p multicolored 5.25 2.50
*Nos. 1896-1903 (8)* 22.25 9.50

**Exports Type of 1987**

Design: Worker, gearwheel.

**Wmk. 391**

**1987, Dec. 16 Litho. *Perf. 13***

**1904** A492 4.75p lt blue & blk 1.70 .40

**Constitution Ratification Type of 1987**

**1987, Dec. 16 *Perf. 13***

**Size: 22x31½mm**

**1905** A483 5.50p brt yel grn & fawn 2.00 .50

United Nations Projects
A501

Designs: a, Intl. Fund for Agricultural Development (IFAD). b, Transport and Communications Decade for Asia and the Pacific. c, Intl. Year of Shelter for the Homeless (IYSH). d, World Health Day, 1987.

**1987, Dec. 22 Litho. *Perf. 13x13½***

**1907** Strip of 4 + label *9.00* 9.00
*a.-d.* A501 1p, any single 2.00 2.00

Label pictures UN emblem. Exists imperf. Value $30.

7th Opening of Congress
A502

Designs: 1p, Official seals of the Senate and Quezon City House of Representatives, gavel, vert. 5.50p, Congress in session.

***Perf. 13½x13, 13x13½***

**1988, Jan. 25 Wmk. 389**

**1908** A502 1p multi .85 .40
**1909** A502 5.50p multi 3.85 1.00

St. John Bosco (1815-1888), Educator — A503

**1988, Jan. 31 *Perf. 13x13½***

**1910** A503 1p multi .50 .40
*a.* Wmk. 372 (II) 1.75 .75
**1911** A503 5.50p multi 3.00 .80
*a.* Wmk. 372 (II) 10.00 2.75

Buy Philippine Goods — A504

**1988, Feb. 1 Litho. *Perf. 13½x13***

**1912** A504 1p buff, ultra, blk & scar .75 .35
*a.* Wmk. 372 (II) 1.25 .45

**Nos. 1782, 1806, 1813, 1824, 1826 Surcharged**

**Wmk. 389 (#1914, 1917), 391 (#1913, 1915, 1916)**

***Perf. 13 (#1782), 13x13½***

**1988, Feb. 14**

**1913** A460 3p on 3.60p redsh brn 2.50 .65
**1914** A469 3p on 3.60p multi 3.00 .90
**1915** A471 3p on 3.60p pale grn, blk & dark ultra 3.50 1.00
**1916** A477 3p on 3.60p red 3.00 .65
**1917** A478 3p on 3.60p buff, ultra & golden brn 4.00 1.25
*Nos. 1913-1917 (5)* 16.00 4.45

Use Zip Codes — A505

**1988, Feb. 25 Wmk. 391 *Perf. 13***

**1918** A505 60s multi .35 .25
**1919** A505 1p multi .55 .25

Insects That Prey on Other Insects — A506

1p, Vesbius purpureus. 5.50p, Campsomeris aurulenta.

**1988, Mar. 11 *Perf. 13***

**1920** A506 1p multi .50 .25
**1921** A506 5.50p multi 3.00 .65

Solar Eclipse 1988
A507

***Perf. 13x13½***

**1988, Mar. 18 Wmk. 389**

**1922** A507 1p multi .70 .30
*a.* Wmk. 372 (II) 1.40 .45
**1923** A507 5.50p multi 3.50 1.00
*a.* Wmk. 372 (II) 5.00 1.50

Toribio M. Teodoro (1887-1965), Shoe Manufacturer
A508

**Wmk. 391**

**1988, Apr. 27 Litho. *Perf. 13***

**1924** A508 1p multicolored .50 .25
**1925** A508 1.20p multicolored 1.00 .25



A509

College of the Holy Spirit, 75th anniv.: 1p, Emblem and motto "Truth in Love." 4p, Arnold Janssen, founder, and Sr. Edelwina, director 1920-1947.

**Wmk. 372 (II)**

**1988, May 22 *Perf. 13½x13***

**1926** A509 1p blk, mar & gold .50 .35
**1927** A509 4p blk, ol grn & mar 2.25 1.00

A510

**Wmk. 372 (II)**

**1988, June 4 Litho. *Perf. 13½x13***

**1928** A510 4p dark ultra, brt blue & blk 3.00 .75

Intl. Conf. of Newly Restored Democracies.



Grand Masonic Lodge of the Philippines, 75th Anniv.
A500

***Perf. 13x13½***

**1987, Dec. 19 Wmk. 389**

**1906** A500 1p multi 1.75 .60
*a.* Wmk. 372 (II) 17.50 8.50

A511

Juan Luna and Felix Hidalgo.

**1988, June 15 Wmk. 391 *Perf. 13***

**1929** A511 1p multi .40 .25
**1930** A511 5.50p multi 2.20 .55

First Natl. Juan Luna and Felix Resurreccion Hidalgo Commemorative Exhibition, June 15-Aug. 15. Artists Luna and Hidalgo won medals at the 1884 Madrid Fine Arts Exhibition.

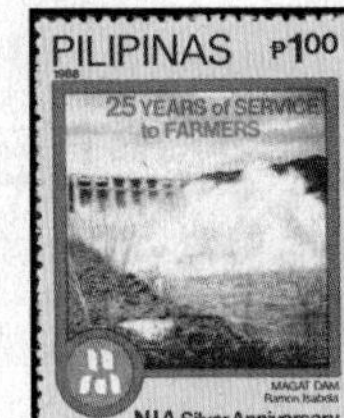

A512

**Wmk. 372 (II)**

**1988, June 22 Litho. *Perf. 13½x13***

**1931** A512 1p multi .50 .25
**1932** A512 5.50p multi 3.00 .75

Natl. Irrigation Administration, 25th anniv.

Natl. Olympic Committee Emblem and Sporting Events A513

Designs: 1p, Scuba diving, Siquijor Is. 1.20p, Big game fishing, Aparri, Cagayan Province. 4p, Yachting, Manila Central. 5.50p, Climbing Mt. Apo. 8p, Golf, Cebu, Cebu Is. 11p, Cycling through Marawi, Mindanao Is.

**1988, July 11 *Perf. 13x13½***

**1933** A513 1p multi .50 .35
**1934** A513 1.20p multi .60 .45
**1935** A513 4p multi 2.00 .70
**1936** A513 5.50p multi 2.40 1.20
**1937** A513 8p multi 3.50 1.75
**1938** A513 11p multi 4.00 2.00
*Nos. 1933-1938 (6)* 13.00 6.45

Exist imperf. 4p, 8p, 1p and 5.50p also exist in strips of 4 plus center label, perf and imperf, picturing torch and inscribed "Philippine Olympic Week, May 1-7, 1988."

**Nos. 1797, 1801, 1810 and 1817 Surcharged with 2 Bars and New Value in Black or Gold (#1942)**

**1988, Aug. 1 As Before**

**1939** A466 1.90p on 2.40p #1797 1.50 .60
**1940** A467 1.90p on 2.40p #1801 2.00 1.25
**1941** A470 1.90p on 2.40p #1810 1.50 .60
**1942** A473 1.90p on 2.40p #1817 2.00 .60
*Nos. 1939-1942 (4)* 7.00 3.05

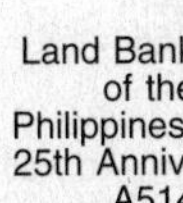

Land Bank of the Philippines, 25th Anniv. A514

Philippine Intl. Commercial Bank, 50th Anniv. A515

**Wmk. 372 (II)**

**1988, Aug. 8 Litho. *Perf. 13x13½***

**1943** A514 1p shown .50 .40
**1944** A515 1p shown .50 .40
**1945** A514 5.50p like No. 1943 3.00 .80
**1946** A515 5.50p like No. 1944 3.00 .80
*Nos. 1943-1946 (4)* 7.00 2.40

Nos. 1943-1944 and 1945-1946 exist in se-tenant pairs from center rows of the sheet.

Profile of Francisco Balagtas Baltasar (b. 1788), Tagalog Language Poet, Author — A516

**Wmk. 391**

**1988, Aug. 8 Litho. *Perf. 13***

**1947** A516 1p Facing right .35 .25
**1948** A516 1p Facing left .35 .25
*a.* Pair, #1947-1948 1.25 1.25

Quezon Institute, 50th Anniv. A517

**Wmk. 372 (II)**

**1988, Aug. 18 Litho. *Perf. 13x13½***

**1949** A517 1p multi .50 .25
**1950** A517 5.50p multi 3.50 .65

Philippine Tuberculosis Soc.

Mushrooms — A518

**1988, Sept. 13 Wmk. 391 *Perf. 13***

**1951** A518 60s Brown .35 .25
**1952** A518 1p Rat's ear fungus .50 .25
**1953** A518 2p Abalone 1.35 .50
**1954** A518 4p Straw 1.80 .75
*Nos. 1951-1954 (4)* 4.00 1.75

Department of Justice, Cent. A520

1988 Summer Olympics, Seoul — A519

1p, Women's archery. 1.20p, Women's tennis. 4p, Boxing. 5.50p, Women's running. 8p, Swimming. 11p, Cycling.

**Wmk. 372 (II)**

**1988, Sept. 19 *Perf. 13½x13***

**1955** A519 1p multi .50 .45
**1956** A519 1.20p multi .65 .50
**1957** A519 4p multi .65 .85
**1958** A519 5.50p multi 2.15 1.20
**1959** A519 8p multi 3.00 2.00
**1960** A519 11p multi 3.85 2.50
*Nos. 1955-1960 (6)* 10.80 7.50

**Souvenir Sheet**

***Imperf***

**1961** Sheet of 4 15.00 15.00
*a.* A519 5.50p Weight lifting 3.25 2.75
*b.* A519 5.50p Basketball, horiz. 3.25 2.75
*c.* A519 5.50p Judo 3.25 2.75
*d.* A519 5.50p Shooting, horiz. 3.25 2.75

Nos. 1955-1960 exist imperf. Value $25.

**1988, Sept. 26 *Perf. 13x13½***

**1962** A520 1p multi .70 .30

Intl. Red Cross and Red Crescent Organizations, 125th Annivs. — A521

**1988, Sept. 30 *Perf. 13½x13***

**1963** A521 1p multi .50 .25
**1964** A521 5.50p multi 3.00 .75

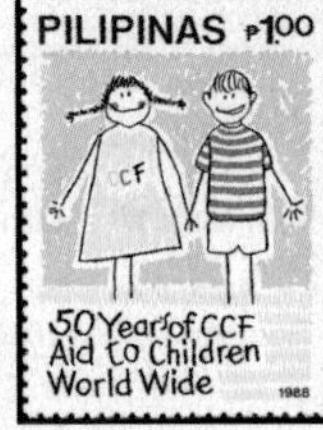

Christian Children's Fund, 50th Anniv. — A522

**1988, Oct. 6**

**1965** A522 1p multi .75 .30

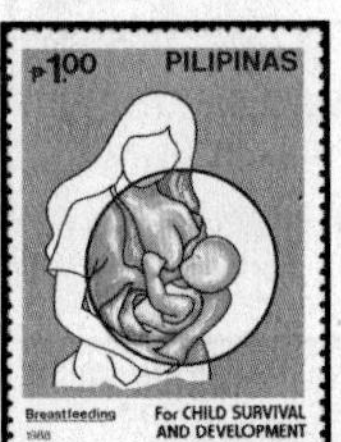

UN Campaigns A523

Designs: a, Breast-feeding. b, Growth monitoring. c, Immunization. d, Oral rehydration. e, Oral rehydration therapy. f, Youth on crutches.

**1988, Oct. 24 Litho. *Perf. 13½x13***

**1966** Strip of 5 4.00 4.00
*a.-e.* A523 1p any single .60 .40

Child Survival Campaign (Nos. 1966a-1966d); Decade for Disabled Persons (No. 1966e).

Bacolod City Charter, 50th Anniv. A524

**1988, Oct. 19 Litho. *Perf. 13x13½***

**1967** A524 1p multi .80 .35

UST Graduate School, 50th Anniv. — A525

**1988, Dec. 20 Litho. *Perf. 13½x13***

**1968** A525 1p multi .75 .30

Dona Aurora Aragon Quezon (b. 1888) — A526

**1988, Nov. 7 Wmk. 391 *Perf. 13***

**1969** A526 1p multi .40 .25
**1970** A526 5.50p multi 2.30 .40

Malate Church, 400th Anniv. — A527

a, Church, 1776. b, Statue & anniv. emblem. c, Church, 1880. d, Church, 1988. Continuous design.

**1988, Dec. 16 Wmk. 391**

**1971** A527 Block of 4 2.00 1.50
*a.-d.* 1p any single .40 .30

UN Declaration of Human Rights, 40th Anniv. A528

No. 1973, Commission on human rights.

**Wmk. 372 (II)**

**1988, Dec. 9 *Perf. 13½x13***

**1972** A528 1p shown .65 .35
**1973** A528 1p multicolored .65 .35
*a.* Pair, Nos. 1972-1973 2.50 2.00

Long Distance Telephone Company A529

1p, Communications tower.

**1988, Nov. 28**

**1974** A529 1p multi .70 .30

Philatelic Week, Nov. 24-30 — A530

Emblem and: a, Post Office. b, Stamp counter. c, Framed stamp exhibits, four people. d, Exhibits, 8 people. Has a continuous design.

**1988, Nov. 24 Wmk. 391 *Perf. 13***

| | | | | |
|---|---|---|---|---|
| **1975** | A530 | Block of 4 | 3.50 | 2.50 |
| *a.-d.* | | 1p any single | .55 | .40 |
| *e.* | | As "a," dated "1938" (error) | 8.00 | 6.50 |

Christmas A531

Designs: 75s, Handshake, peave dove, vert. 1p, Children making ornaments. 2p, Boy carrying decoration. 3.50p, Tree, vert. 4.75p, Candle, vert. 5.50p, Man, star, heart.

**1988, Dec. 2**

| | | | | |
|---|---|---|---|---|
| **1976** | A531 | 75s multi | .50 | .30 |
| **1977** | A531 | 1p multi | .50 | .25 |
| **1978** | A531 | 2p multi | 1.00 | .30 |
| **1979** | A531 | 3.50p multi | 1.50 | .35 |
| **1980** | A531 | 4.75p multi | 2.00 | .40 |
| **1981** | A531 | 5.50p multi | 2.50 | .50 |
| | | *Nos. 1976-1981 (6)* | 8.00 | 2.10 |

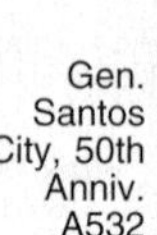

Gen. Santos City, 50th Anniv. A532

**Wmk. 372 (II)**

**1989, Feb, 27 Litho. *Perf. 13x13½***

| | | | | |
|---|---|---|---|---|
| **1982** | A532 | 1p multi | .80 | .30 |

Guerrilla Fighters — A533

Emblem and: No. 1983, Miguel Z. Ver (1918-42). No. 1984, Eleuterio L. Adevoso (1922-75). Printed in continuous design.

**1989, Feb. 18 Wmk. 391**

| | | | |
|---|---|---|---|
| **1983** | 1p multi | .40 | .25 |
| **1984** | 1p multi | .40 | .25 |
| *a.* | A533 Pair, #1983-1984 | 1.25 | .75 |

Oblates of Mary Immaculate, 50th Anniv. — A534

**Wmk. 372 (II)**

**1989, Feb. 17 *Perf. 13½x13***

| | | | | |
|---|---|---|---|---|
| **1985** | A534 | 1p multicolored | .60 | .30 |

Fiesta Islands '89 — A535

No. 1986, Turumba. No. 1987, Pahiyas. No. 1988, Pagoda Sa Wawa. No. 1989, Masskara. No. 1990, Independence Day. No. 1990A, like #1995. No. 1991, Sinulog. No. 1992, Cagayan de Oro. No. 1993, Grand Canao. No. 1994, Lenten festival. No. 1995, Penafrancia. No. 1996, Fireworks. No. 1997, Iloilo Paraw regatta.

***Perf. 13 (Nos. 1991, 1994, 1997), 13½x14***

**1989-90 Litho. Wmk. 391**

| | | | | |
|---|---|---|---|---|
| **1986** | A535 | 60s multicolored | .35 | .25 |
| **1987** | A535 | 75s multicolored | .35 | .25 |
| **1988** | A535 | 1p multicolored | .35 | .25 |
| **1989** | A535 | 1p multicolored | .50 | .25 |
| **1990** | A535 | 3.50p multicolored | 1.20 | .35 |
| **1990A** | A535 | 4p multicolored | 2.50 | .40 |
| **1991** | A535 | 4.75p multicolored | 1.30 | .35 |
| **1992** | A535 | 4.75p multicolored | 1.30 | .35 |
| **1993** | A535 | 4.75p multicolored | 1.30 | .35 |
| **1994** | A535 | 5.50p multicolored | 1.30 | .50 |
| **1995** | A535 | 5.50p multicolored | 1.65 | .55 |
| **1996** | A535 | 5.50p multicolored | 1.85 | .60 |
| **1997** | A535 | 6.25p multicolored | 2.30 | .90 |
| | | *Nos. 1986-1997 (13)* | 16.25 | 5.35 |

Issued: #1991, 1994, 6.25p, 3/1/89; 60s, 75s, 3.50p, 6/28/89; #1988, 1992, 1995, 9/1/89; #1989, 1993, 1996, 12/4/89; 4p, 8/6/90.

Great Filipinos — A536

Men and women: a, Don Tomas B. Mapua (1888-), educator. b, Camilo O. Osias (1889-), educator. c, Dr. Olivia D. Salamanca (1889-), physician. d, Dr. Francisco S. Santiago (1889-), composer. e, Leandro H. Fernandez (1889-), educator.

**Wmk. 372 (II)**

**1989, May 18 Litho. *Perf. 14x13½***

| | | | |
|---|---|---|---|
| **1998** | Strip of 5 | 3.00 | 2.50 |
| *a.-e.* | A536 1p any single | .35 | .30 |

See Nos. 2022, 2089, 2151, 2240, 2307, 2360, 2414, 2486, 2536.

26th World Congress of the Intl. Federation of Landscape Architects — A537

Designs: a, Adventure Pool. b, Paco Park. c, Beautification of Malacanang area streets. d, Erosion control at an upland farm.

**1989, May 31 Wmk. 391**

| | | | | |
|---|---|---|---|---|
| **1999** | A537 | Block of 4 | 2.00 | 1.60 |
| *a.-d.* | | 1p any single | .40 | .30 |

Printed in continuous design.

French Revolution, Bicent. A538

**1989, July 1 Wmk. 372 (II) *Perf. 14***

| | | | | |
|---|---|---|---|---|
| **2000** | A538 | 1p multicolored | .50 | .30 |
| **2001** | A538 | 5.50p multicolored | 2.50 | .60 |

Supreme Court — A539

**1989, June 11 Wmk. 372 (II)**

| | | | | |
|---|---|---|---|---|
| **2002** | A539 | 1p multicolored | .65 | .30 |

Natl. Science and Technology Week — A540

No. 2003, GNP chart. No. 2004, Science High School emblem.

**1989, July 14**

| | | | |
|---|---|---|---|
| **2003** | 1p multicolored | .40 | .30 |
| **2004** | 1p multicolored | .40 | .30 |
| *a.* | A540 Pair, #2003-2004 | 1.00 | .70 |

**No. 1905 Surcharged**

**Wmk. 391**

**1989, Aug. 21 Litho. *Perf. 13***

| | | | | |
|---|---|---|---|---|
| **2005** | A483 | 4.75p on 5.50p | 1.50 | .40 |

Philippine Environment Month — A542

No. 2006, Palawan peacock pheasant. No. 2007, Palawan bear cat.

**Wmk. 391**

**1989, June 5 Litho. *Perf. 14***

| | | | |
|---|---|---|---|
| **2006** | 1p multicolored | .60 | .30 |
| **2007** | 1p multicolored | .60 | .30 |
| *a.* | A542 Pair, #2006-2007 | 2.00 | 2.00 |

Asia-Pacific Telecommunity, 10th Anniv. — A544

**Wmk. 372 (II)**

**1989, Oct. 30 Litho. *Perf. 14***

| | | | | |
|---|---|---|---|---|
| **2008** | A544 | 1p multicolored | .75 | .30 |

Dept. of Natl. Defense, 50th Anniv. — A545

**1989, Oct. 23**

| | | | | |
|---|---|---|---|---|
| **2009** | A545 | 1p multicolored | .75 | .30 |

Intl. Maritime Organization — A546

**1989, Nov. 13 *Perf. 14***

| | | | | |
|---|---|---|---|---|
| **2010** | A546 | 1p multicolored | .80 | .30 |

World Stamp Expo '89 A546a

**1989, Nov. 17 Litho. *Perf. 14***

| | | | | |
|---|---|---|---|---|
| **2010A** | A546a | 1p #1, Y1 | .70 | *.40* |
| **2010B** | A546a | 4p #219, 398 | 2.50 | *.80* |
| **2010C** | A546a | 5.50p #N1, 500 | 3.70 | *1.00* |
| | | *Nos. 2010A-2010C (3)* | 6.90 | *2.20* |

Nos. 2010A-2010C withdrawn from sale week of release, but placed on sale again a few weeks later.

Teaching Philately in the Classroom, Close-up of Youth Collectors A547

**1989, Nov. 20 *Perf. 14x13½***

| | | | | |
|---|---|---|---|---|
| **2011** | A547 | 1p shown | .60 | .30 |
| **2012** | A547 | 1p Class, diff. | .60 | .30 |

Christmas — A548

60s, Annunciation. 75s, Visitation. 1p, Journey to Bethlehem. 2p, Search for the inn. 4p, Appearance of the star. 4.75p, Birth of Jesus Christ.

**1989, Nov. 10 *Perf. 13½x14***

| | | | | |
|---|---|---|---|---|
| **2013** | A548 | 60s multi | .35 | .25 |
| **2014** | A548 | 75s multi | .40 | .25 |
| **2015** | A548 | 1p multi | .45 | .25 |
| **2016** | A548 | 2p multi | .85 | .30 |
| **2017** | A548 | 4p multi | 1.25 | .50 |
| **2018** | A548 | 4.75p multi | 1.70 | .85 |
| | | *Nos. 2013-2018 (6)* | 5.00 | 2.40 |

First-day coers are canceled Nov. 8.

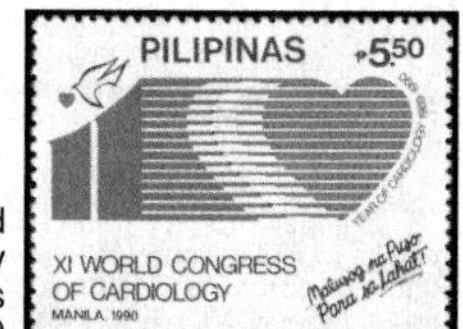

11th World Cardiology Congress A549

**Wmk. 391**

**1990, Feb. 12 Photo. *Perf. 14***

| | | | | |
|---|---|---|---|---|
| **2019** | A549 | 5.50p black, dark red & deep blue | 1.50 | .40 |

Beer Production, Cent. A550

**1990, Apr. 16**

| | | | | |
|---|---|---|---|---|
| **2020** | A550 | 1p multicolored | .40 | .30 |
| **2021** | A550 | 5.50p multicolored | 1.60 | .50 |

**Great Filipinos Type of 1989**

Designs: a, Claro M. Recto (1890-1960), politician. b, Manuel H. Bernabe. c, Guillermo E. Tolentino. d, Elpidio R. Quirino (1890-1956), politician. e, Bienvenido Ma. Gonzalez.

**Wmk. 372 (II)**

**1990, June 1 Litho. *Perf. 14x13½***

| | | | |
|---|---|---|---|
| **2022** | Strip of 5, #a.-e. | 3.00 | 2.25 |

1990 Census — A551

**Wmk. 391**

**1990, Apr. 30 Photo. *Perf. 14***
**Color of Buildings**

**2023** 1p light blue .50 .30
**2024** 1p beige .50 .30
*a.* A551 Pair, #2023-2024 1.25 .90

Legion of Mary, 50th Anniv. — A552

**1990, July 21 Photo. *Perf. 14***
**2025** A552 1p multicolored .75 .30

Girl Scouts of the Philippines, 50th Anniv. A553

**1990, May 21**
**2026** A553 1p yellow & multi .50 .30
**2027** A553 1.20p lt lilac & multi .60 .35

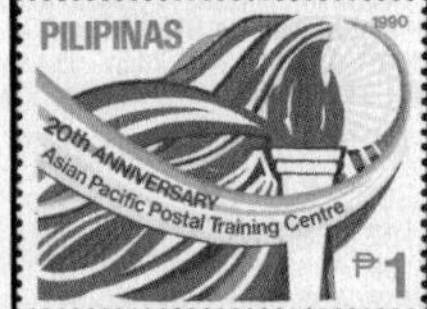

Asian Pacific Postal Training Center, 20th Anniv. A554

**Wmk. 391**

**1990, Sept. 10 Photo. *Perf. 14***
**2028** A554 1p red & multi .50 .30
**2029** A554 4p blue & multi 1.50 .50

Natl. Catechetical Year — A555

**1990, Sept. 28**
**2030** A555 1p blk & multi .50 .30
**2031** A555 3.50p grn & multi 1.30 .40

Intl. Literacy Year A556

**1990, Oct. 24 Photo. *Perf. 14***
**2032** A556 1p blk, org & grn .50 .30
**2033** A556 5.50p blk, yel & grn 2.00 .50

UN Development Program, 40th Anniv. — A557

**1990, Oct. 24**
**2034** A557 1p yel & multi .50 .30
**2035** A557 5.50p orange & multi 2.00 .50

Flowers — A558

**1990 Photo. Wmk. 391 *Perf. 14***
**2036** A558 1p Waling waling 1.00 .35
**2037** A558 4p Sampaguita 2.25 .70

29th Orient and Southeast Asian Lions forum.

Issued: 1p, Oct. 3; 4p, Oct. 18.

A559

Christmas A560

Drawings of the Christmas star: a, Yellow star, pink beading. b, Yellow star, white beading. c, Green, blue, yellow and orange star. d, Red star, white outlines.

**1990, Dec. 3**
**2038** A559 Strip of 4 2.00 2.00
*a.-d.* 1p any single .40 .30
**2039** A560 5.50p multicolored 3.00 1.00

Blind Safety Day A561

**1990, Dec. 7 Photo. *Perf. 14***
**2040** A561 1p bl, blk & yel .60 .30

Publication of Rizal's "Philippines After 100 Years," Cent. A562

**1990, Dec.17**
**2041** A562 1p multicolored .65 .30

Philatelic Week A563

Paintings: 1p, Family by F. Amorsolo. 4.75p, The Builders by V. Edades. 5.50p, Laughter by A. Magsaysay-Ho.

**1990, Nov. 16**
**2042** A563 1p multicolored .50 .30
**2043** A563 4.75p multi, vert. 1.50 .40
**2044** A563 5.50p multi, vert. 1.75 .50
*Nos. 2042-2044 (3)* 3.75 1.20

A564

**1991, Jan. 30**
**2045** A564 1p multicolored .60 .30

2nd Plenary Council of the Philippines.

A565

**1991, Mar. 15 Litho. *Perf. 14***
**2046** A565 1p multicolored .50 .30
**2047** A565 5.50p multicolored 1.00 .50

Philippine Airlines, 50th anniv. No. 2047 is airmail.

Flowers — A566

Flowers: 1p, 2p, Plumeria. 4p, 6p, Ixora. 4.75p, 7p, Bougainvillea. 5.50p, 8p, Hibiscus.

**1991 Photo. *Perf. 14x13½***
**"1991" Below Design**

**2048** A566 60s Gardenia .35 .25
**2049** A566 75s Allamanda *.35* .25
**2050** A566 1p yellow *.40* .25
**2051** A566 1p red *.40* .25
**2052** A566 1p salmon *.40* .25
**2053** A566 1p white *.40* .25
*a.* Block of 4, #2050-2053 *2.00* 1.50
**2054** A566 1.20p Nerium *.70* .25
**2055** A566 1.50p like #2048 *.85* .30
**2056** A566 2p yellow *.90* .30
**2057** A566 2p red *.90* .30
**2058** A566 2p rose & yel *.90* .30
**2059** A566 2p white *.90* .30
*a.* Block of 4, #2056-2059 *4.25* 3.00
**2060** A566 3p like #2054 *1.40* .35
**2061** A566 3.25p Cananga *1.50* .45
**2062** A566 4p dull rose *1.50* .50
**2063** A566 4p pale yellow *1.50* .50
**2064** A566 4p orange yel *1.50* .50
**2065** A566 4p scarlet *1.50* .50
*a.* Block of 4, #2062-2065 *9.00* 6.50
**2066** A566 4.75p vermilion *2.00* .70
**2067** A566 4.75p brt rose lil *2.00* .70
**2068** A566 4.75p white *2.00* .70
**2069** A566 4.75p lilac rose *2.00* .70
*a.* Block of 4, #2066-2069 *10.00* 7.50
**2070** A566 5p Canna *2.50* .80
**2071** A566 5p like #2061 *2.50* .80
**2072** A566 5.50p red *2.00* .85
**2073** A566 5.50p yellow *2.00* .85
**2074** A566 5.50p white *2.00* .85
**2075** A566 5.50p pink *2.00* .85
*a.* Block of 4, #2072-2075 *12.50* 9.50
**2076** A566 6p dull rose *2.75* 1.00
**2077** A566 6p pale yellow *2.75* 1.00
**2078** A566 6p orange yel *2.75* 1.00
**2079** A566 6p scarlet *2.75* 1.00
*a.* Block of 4, #2076-2079 *13.00* 8.50
**2080** A566 7p vermilion *3.00* 1.10
**2081** A566 7p brt rose lil *3.00* 1.10
**2082** A566 7p white *3.00* 1.10
**2083** A566 7p dp lil rose *3.00* 1.10
*a.* Block of 4, #2080-2083 *15.00* 10.00
**2084** A566 8p red *3.50* 1.25
**2085** A566 8p yellow *3.50* 1.25
**2086** A566 8p white *3.50* 1.25
**2087** A566 8p deep pink *3.50* 1.25
*a.* Block of 4, #2084-2087 *16.50* 13.50
**2088** A566 10p like #2070 *5.00* *2.00*
*Nos. 2048-2088 (41)* 79.35 29.25

Issued: #2053a, 2075a, 4/1/91. #2048, 2049, 2061, 4/11. #2054, 2065a, 2069a, 2070, 6/7. #2059a, 2079a, 2083a, 2087a, 12/1. #2055, 2060, 2071, 2088, 12/13.

**1992-93 "1992" Below Design**

*2048a* A566 60s Gardenia 1.50 .50
*2050a* A566 1p yellow *1.50* .50
*2051a* A566 1p red *1.50* .50
*2052a* A566 1p salmon *1.50* .50
*2053c* A566 1p white *1.50* .50
*d.* Block of 4, #2050a-2052a, 2053c *8.50* 5.50
**2053B** A566 1p like #2049 *.75* .35
*2055a* A566 1.50p like #2048 *4.00* .60
*2056a* A566 2p yellow *2.00* .45
*2057a* A566 2p red *2.00* .45
*2058a* A566 2p rose & yel *2.00* .45
*2059b* A566 2p white *2.00* .45
*c.* Block of 4, , #2056a-2058a, 2059b *11.50* 6.50
*2060a* A566 3p like #2054 *2.00* .80
*2071a* A566 5p like #2061 *20.00* 2.00
*2076a* A566 6p dull rose *5.00* 2.50
*2077a* A566 6p pale yellow *5.00* 2.50
*2078a* A566 6p orange yel *5.00* 2.50
*2079b* A566 6p scarlet *5.00* 2.50
*c.* Block of 4, #2076a-2078a, 2079b *40.00* 27.00
*2080a* A566 7p vermilion *8.50* 4.00
*2081a* A566 7p brt rose lil *8.50* 4.00
*2082a* A566 7p white *8.50* 4.00
*2083b* A566 7p dp lil rose *8.50* 4.00
*c.* Block of 4, #2080a-2082a, 2083b *50.00* 33.00
*2084a* A566 8p red *8.50* 4.00
*2085a* A566 8p yellow *8.50* 4.00
*2086a* A566 8p white *8.50* 4.00
*2087b* A566 8p deep pink *8.50* 4.00
*c.* Block of 4, #2084a-2086a, 2087b *50.00* 33.00
*2088a* A566 10p like #2070 *13.50* *3.00*
*Nos. 2048a-2088a (26)* *143.75* 53.05

Issued: 2059c, 1/24/92. 2053d, 2060a, 2/10. #2079c, 2/12. #2083c, 2/27. #2048a, 3/4. #2071a, 3/24. #2087c, 3/25. #2088a, 9/22. #2053B, 1/23/93.

No. 2053B, although issued in 1993, is inscribed "1992."

**Great Filipinos Type of 1989**

Designs: a, Jorge B. Vargas (1890-1980). b, Ricardo M. Paras (1891-1984). c, Jose P. Laurel (1891-1959), politician. d, Vicente Fabella (1891-1959). e, Maximo M. Kalaw (1891-1954).

**1991, June 3 Litho. *Perf. 14x13½***
**2089** A536 1p Strip of 5, #a.-e. 3.00 2.50

12th Asia-Pacific Boy Scout Jamboree A567

1p, Square knot. 4p, Sheepshank knot. 4.75p, Figure 8 knot.

**1991, Apr. 22 *Perf. 14x13½***
**2090** A567 1p multicolored .50 .30
**2091** A567 4p multicolored 1.25 .40
**2092** A567 4.75p multicolored 1.50 .50
*a.* Souv. sheet of 3, #2090-2092, imperf. 6.00 5.00
*Nos. 2090-2092 (3)* 3.25 1.20

No. 2092a sold for 16.50p and has simulated perfs.

Antipolo by Carlos V. Francisco A568

**1991, June 23 Litho. *Perf. 14***
**Granite Paper**
**2093** A568 1p multicolored .80 .30

Pithecophaga Jefferyi — A569

1p, Head. 4.75p, Perched on limb. 5.50p, In flight. 8p, Feeding young.

**1991, July 31 Photo.**

| | | | | |
|---|---|---|---|---|
| 2094 | A569 | 1p multi | *1.00* | .40 |
| 2095 | A569 | 4.75p multi | *2.10* | .60 |
| 2096 | A569 | 5.50p multi | *3.50* | 1.00 |
| 2097 | A569 | 8p multi | *5.00* | 2.00 |
| | | *Nos. 2094-2097 (4)* | *11.60* | 4.00 |

World Wildlife Fund.

Philippine Bar Association, Cent. — A570

**Wmk. 391**

**1991, Aug. 20 Photo. *Perf. 14***

2098 A570 1p multicolored .60 .30

A571

**1991, Aug. 29**

2099 A571 1p multicolored .75 .30

**Size: 82x88mm**

***Imperf***

2100 A571 16p like #2099 7.50 6.00

Induction of Filipinos into USAFFE (US Armed Forces in the Far East), 50th Anniv. For overprint see No. 2193.

A572

Independence Movement, cent.: a, Basil at graveside. b, Simon carrying lantern. c, Father Florentino, treasure chest. d, Sister Juli with rosary.

**1991, Sept. 18**

2101 A572 1p Block of 4, #a.-d. 4.00 2.75

A573

**Wmk. 391**

**1991, Oct. 15 Photo. *Perf. 14***

2102 A573 1p multicolored .65 .30

**Size: 60x60mm**

***Imperf***

2103 A573 16p multicolored 6.00 5.00

St. John of the Cross, 400th death anniv.

United Nations Agencies A574

Designs: 1p, UNICEF, children. 4p, High Commissioner for Refugees, hands supporting boat people. 5.50p, Postal Administration, 40th anniv., UN #29, #C3.

**1991, Oct. 24 *Perf. 14***

| | | | | |
|---|---|---|---|---|
| 2104 | A574 | 1p multicolored | .35 | .30 |
| 2105 | A574 | 4p multicolored | 1.00 | .30 |
| 2106 | A574 | 5.50p multicolored | 1.50 | .60 |
| | | *Nos. 2104-2106 (3)* | 2.85 | 1.20 |

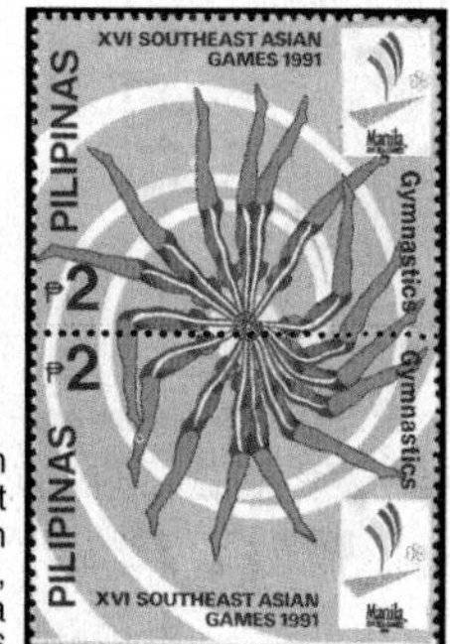
Philatelic Week A575

Paintings: 2p, Bayanihan by Carlos Francisco. 7p, Sari-sari Vendor by Mauro Malang Santos. 8p, Give Us This Day by Vicente Manansala.

**1991, Nov. 20**

| | | | | |
|---|---|---|---|---|
| 2107 | A575 | 2p multicolored | .50 | .30 |
| 2108 | A575 | 7p multicolored | 2.00 | .50 |
| 2109 | A575 | 8p multicolored | 2.50 | .70 |
| | | *Nos. 2107-2109 (3)* | 5.00 | 1.50 |

16th Southeast Asian Games, Manila A576

#2110, Gymnastics, games emblem at UR. #2111, Gymnastics, games emblem at LR. #2112, Martial arts, games emblem at LL, vert. #2113, Martial arts, games emblem at LR, vert.

**Wmk. 391**

**1991, Nov. 22 Photo. *Perf. 14***

| | | | |
|---|---|---|---|
| 2110 | 2p multicolored | .40 | .35 |
| 2111 | 2p multicolored | .40 | .35 |
| *a.* | A576 Pair, #2110-2111 | 1.50 | 1.00 |
| 2112 | 6p multicolored | 1.00 | .50 |
| 2113 | 6p multicolored | 1.00 | .50 |
| *a.* | A576 Pair, #2112-2113 | 3.00 | 2.00 |
| *b.* | Souv. sheet of 2, #2112-2113, imperf. | 4.00 | *3.50* |
| *c.* | Souv. sheet of 4, #2110-2113 | 5.00 | *4.75* |
| | *Nos. 2110-2113 (4)* | 2.80 | 1.70 |

No. 2113b has simulated perforations.

**No. 1585 Surcharged in Red**

Souvenir Sheet

**1991, Nov. 27 Wmk. 372 *Imperf.***

2114 A385 4p on 3.20p 3.50 *2.75*

First Philippine Philatelic Convention.

Children's Christmas Paintings — A577

**1991, Dec. 4 Wmk. 391 *Perf. 14***

| | | | | |
|---|---|---|---|---|
| 2115 | A577 | 2p shown | .50 | .30 |
| 2116 | A577 | 6p Wrapped gift | 1.75 | .45 |
| 2117 | A577 | 7p Santa, tree | 2.00 | .55 |
| 2118 | A577 | 8p Tree, star | 2.25 | .60 |
| | | *Nos. 2115-2118 (4)* | 6.50 | 1.90 |

Insignias of Military Groups Inducted into USAFFE — A578

White background: No. 2119a, 1st Regular Div. b, 2nd Regular Div. c, 11th Div. d, 21st Div. e, 31st Div. f, 41st Div. g, 51st Div. h, 61st Div. i, 71st Div. j, 81st Div. k, 91st Div. l, 101st Div. m, Bataan Force. n, Philippine Div. o, Philippine Army Air Corps. p, Offshore Patrol.

Nos. 2120a-2120p, like #2119a-2119p with yellow background.

***Perf. 14x13½***

**1991, Dec. 8 Photo. Wmk. 391**

| | | | | |
|---|---|---|---|---|
| 2119 | A578 | 2p Block of 16, #a.-p. | 16.50 | *16.50* |
| 2120 | A578 | 2p Block of 16, #a.-p. | 16.50 | *16.50* |
| *q.* | | Block of 32, #2119-2120 | *50.00* | *50.00* |

Induction of Filipinos into USAFFE, 50th anniv.

Nos. 2119-2120 were printed in sheets of 200 containing 5 #2120q plus five blocks of 8.

Basketball, Cent. A579

Designs: 2p, PBA Games, vert. 6p, Map, player dribbling. 7p, Early players. 8p, Men shooting basketball, vert. 16p, Tip-off.

**Wmk. 391**

**1991, Dec. 19 Litho. *Perf. 14***

| | | | | |
|---|---|---|---|---|
| 2121 | A579 | 2p multicolored | .70 | .30 |
| 2122 | A579 | 6p multicolored | 1.80 | .50 |
| 2123 | A579 | 7p multicolored | 2.50 | .80 |
| 2124 | A579 | 8p multicolored | 3.00 | 1.20 |
| *a.* | | Souv. sheet of 4, #2121-2124 | 8.50 | 7.25 |
| | | *Nos. 2121-2124 (4)* | 8.00 | 2.80 |

**Souvenir Sheet**

***Imperf***

2125 A579 16p multicolored 6.50 5.00

No. 2125 has simulated perforations.

New Year 1992, Year of the Monkey A580

**Wmk. 391**

**1991, Dec. 27 Litho. *Perf. 14***

| | | | | |
|---|---|---|---|---|
| 2126 | A580 | 2p violet & multi | *1.50* | .40 |
| 2127 | A580 | 6p green & multi | *3.50* | 1.00 |

See Nos. 2459a, 2460a.

Services and Products A581

**Wmk. 391**

**1992, Jan. 15 Litho. *Perf. 14***

| | | | | |
|---|---|---|---|---|
| 2128 | A581 | 2p Mailing center | .50 | .30 |
| 2129 | A581 | 6p Housing project | 1.25 | .40 |
| 2130 | A581 | 7p Livestock | 1.75 | .65 |
| 2131 | A581 | 8p Handicraft | 2.00 | 1.00 |
| | | *Nos. 2128-2131 (4)* | 5.50 | 2.35 |

Medicinal Plants — A582

2p, Curcuma longa. 6p, Centella asiatica. 7p, Cassia alata. 8p, Ervatamia pandacaqui.

**Wmk. 391**

**1992, Feb. 7 Litho. *Perf. 14***

| | | | | |
|---|---|---|---|---|
| 2132 | A582 | 2p multi | .80 | .30 |
| 2133 | A582 | 6p multi | 1.60 | .50 |
| 2134 | A582 | 7p multi | 2.00 | .60 |
| 2135 | A582 | 8p multi | 2.80 | .80 |
| | | *Nos. 2132-2135 (4)* | 7.20 | 2.20 |

Love — A583

"I Love You" in English on Nos. 2137a-2140a, in Filipino on Nos. 2137b-2140b with designs: No. 2137, Letters, map. No. 2138, Heart, doves. No. 2139, Bouquet of flowers. No. 2140, Map, Cupid with bow and arrow.

**Wmk. 391**

**1992, Feb. 10 Photo. *Perf. 14***

| | | | | |
|---|---|---|---|---|
| 2137 | A583 | 2p Pair, #a.-b. | 1.00 | .80 |
| 2138 | A583 | 6p Pair, #a.-b. | 3.00 | 2.50 |
| 2139 | A583 | 7p Pair, #a.-b. | 4.00 | 3.00 |
| 2140 | A583 | 8p Pair, #a.-b. | 8.50 | 4.70 |
| | | *Nos. 2137-2140 (4)* | 16.50 | 11.00 |

A584

**Wmk. 391**

**1992, Apr. 12 Litho. *Perf. 14***

| | | | | |
|---|---|---|---|---|
| 2141 | A584 | 2p blue & multi | .50 | .30 |
| 2142 | A584 | 8p red vio & multi | 2.30 | .60 |

Our Lady of Sorrows of Porta Vaga, 400th anniv.

A585

Expo '92, Seville: 2p, Man and woman celebrating. 8p, Philippine discovery scenes. 16p, Pavilion, horiz.

**1992, Mar. 27**

| | | | | | |
|---|---|---|---|---|---|
| 2143 | A585 | 2p multicolored | .50 | .30 |
| 2144 | A585 | 8p multicolored | 2.30 | .70 |

**Souvenir Sheet**

***Imperf***

| | | | | |
|---|---|---|---|---|
| 2145 | A585 | 16p multicolored | 7.50 | 6.00 |

Department of Agriculture, 75th Anniv. — A586

a, Man planting seed. b, Fish trap. c, Pigs.

**1992, May 4**

| | | | | |
|---|---|---|---|---|
| 2146 | A586 | 2p Strip of 3, #a.-c. | 2.40 | 2.00 |

Manila Jockey Club, 125th Anniv. A588

**Wmk. 391**

**1992, May 14 Litho. *Perf. 14***

| | | | | |
|---|---|---|---|---|
| 2149 | A588 | 2p multicolored | 1.00 | .40 |

**Souvenir Sheet**

***Imperf***

| | | | | |
|---|---|---|---|---|
| 2150 | A588 | 8p multicolored | 4.00 | *3.00* |

No. 2150 has simulated perfs.

**Great Filipinos Type of 1989**

Designs: a, Pres. Manuel A. Roxas (1892-1948). b, Justice Natividad Almeda-Lopez (1892-1977). c, Justice Roman A. Ozaeta (b. 1892). d, Engracia Cruz-Reyes (1892-1975). e, Fernando Amorsolo (1892-1972).

***Perf. 14x13½***

**1992, June 1 Wmk. 391**

| | | | | |
|---|---|---|---|---|
| 2151 | A536 | 2p Strip of 5, #a.-e. | 3.00 | 2.50 |

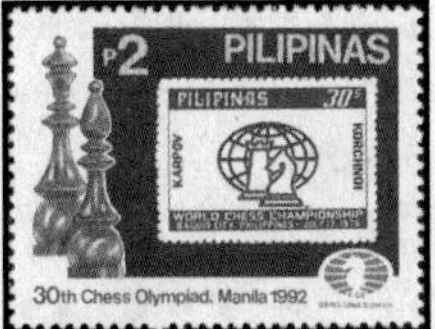


30th Chess Olympiad, Manila A589

#2154: a, like #2152. b, like #2153.

**1992, June 7 *Perf. 14***

| | | | | |
|---|---|---|---|---|
| 2152 | A589 | 2p No. 1352 | .60 | .30 |
| 2153 | A589 | 6p No. B21 | 1.80 | .50 |

**Souvenir Sheet**

***Imperf***

| | | | | |
|---|---|---|---|---|
| 2154 | A589 | 8p Sheet of 2, #a.-b. | 6.00 | *5.25* |

No. 2154 has simulated perfs.

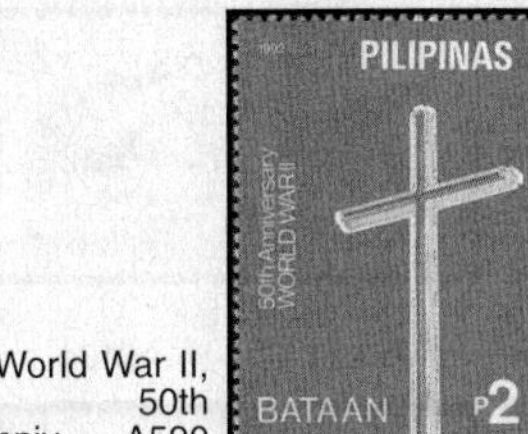


World War II, 50th Anniv. — A590

2p, Bataan, cross. 6p, Insignia of defenders of Bataan & Corregidor. 8p, Corregidor, Monument. #2158, Cross, map of Bataan. #2159, Monument, map of Corregidor.

**Wmk. 391**

**1992, June 12 Photo. *Perf. 14***

| | | | | |
|---|---|---|---|---|
| 2155 | A590 | 2p multicolored | .60 | .30 |
| 2156 | A590 | 6p multicolored | 1.50 | .40 |
| 2157 | A590 | 8p multicolored | 1.90 | .60 |

**Size: 63x76mm, 76x63mm**

***Imperf***

| | | | | |
|---|---|---|---|---|
| 2158 | A590 | 16p multicolored | 6.50 | 5.00 |
| 2159 | A590 | 16p multicolored | 6.50 | 5.00 |
| | | *Nos. 2155-2159 (5)* | 17.00 | 11.30 |

Nos. 2158-2159 have simulated perforations.

President Corazon C. Aquino and President-Elect Fidel V. Ramos — A591

**1992, June 30 *Perf. 14***

| | | | | |
|---|---|---|---|---|
| 2160 | A591 | 2p multicolored | .65 | .30 |

Anniversary of Democracy.

Jose Rizal's Exile to Dapitan, Cent. A592

**1992, June 17**

| | | | | |
|---|---|---|---|---|
| 2161 | A592 | 2p Dapitan shrine | 1.20 | .35 |
| 2162 | A592 | 2p Portrait, vert. | 1.20 | .35 |

ASEAN, 25th Anniv. A593

Contemporary paintings: Nos. 2163, 2165, Spirit of ASEAN. Nos. 2164, 2166, ASEAN Sea.

**Wmk. 391**

**1992, July 18 Litho. *Perf. 14***

| | | | | |
|---|---|---|---|---|
| 2163 | A593 | 2p multicolored | .60 | .30 |
| 2164 | A593 | 2p multicolored | .60 | .30 |
| 2165 | A593 | 6p multicolored | 1.60 | .50 |
| 2166 | A593 | 6p multicolored | 1.60 | .50 |
| | | *Nos. 2163-2166 (4)* | 4.40 | 1.60 |

Founding of Katipunan, Cent. A594

Details or entire paintings of revolutionaries, by Carlos "Botong" Francisco: No. 2167a, Preparing for battle, vert. No. 2167b, Attack leader (detail), vert. No. 2168a, Attack. No. 2168b, Signing papers.

**Wmk. 391**

**1992, July 27 Photo. *Perf. 14***

| | | | | |
|---|---|---|---|---|
| 2167 | A594 | 2p Pair, #a.-b. | 2.00 | 1.50 |
| 2168 | A594 | 2p Pair, #a.-b. | 2.00 | 1.50 |

Philippine League, Cent. A595

**Wmk. 391**

**1992, July 31 Photo. *Perf. 14***

| | | | | |
|---|---|---|---|---|
| 2169 | A595 | 2p multicolored | 1.00 | .75 |

1992 Summer Olympics, Barcelona A596

**Wmk. 391**

**1992, Aug. 4 Litho. *Perf. 14***

| | | | | |
|---|---|---|---|---|
| 2170 | A596 | 2p Swimming | .60 | .40 |
| 2171 | A596 | 7p Boxing | 2.20 | .60 |
| 2172 | A596 | 8p Hurdling | 2.50 | .75 |
| | | *Nos. 2170-2172 (3)* | 5.30 | 1.75 |

**Souvenir Sheet**

***Imperf***

| | | | | |
|---|---|---|---|---|
| 2172A | A596 | Sheet of 3, #2171-2172, 2172Ab | 6.00 | *6.00* |
| *b.* | | 1p like #2170 | .65 | .65 |

No. 2172A has simulated perforations.

Religious of the Assumption in Philippines, Cent. — A597

Cathedral of San Sebastian, Cent. — A597a

**Wmk. 391**

**1992, Aug. 15 Photo. *Perf. 14***

| | | | | |
|---|---|---|---|---|
| 2173 | A597 | 2p multicolored | .60 | .30 |
| 2174 | A597a | 2p multicolored | .60 | .30 |

Founding of Nilad Masonic Lodge, Cent. — A598

Various Masonic symbols and: 6p, A. Luna. 8p, M.H. Del Pilar.

**Wmk. 391**

**1992, Aug. 15 Photo. *Perf. 14***

| | | | | |
|---|---|---|---|---|
| 2175 | A598 | 2p green & black | .80 | .40 |
| 2176 | A598 | 6p yellow, black & brown | 2.00 | .80 |
| 2177 | A598 | 8p blue, black & violet | 2.70 | 1.00 |
| | | *Nos. 2175-2177 (3)* | 5.50 | 2.20 |

Pres. Fidel V. Ramos Taking Oath of Office, June 30, 1992 A599

**1992, July 30**

| | | | | |
|---|---|---|---|---|
| 2178 | A599 | 2p Ceremony, people | .60 | .30 |
| 2179 | A599 | 8p Ceremony, flag | 1.80 | .70 |

Freshwater Aquarium Fish — A600

Designs: No. 2180a, Red-tailed guppy, b, Tiger lacetail guppy. c, Flamingo guppy. d, Neon tuxedo guppy. e, King cobra guppy.

No. 2181a, Black moor. b, Bubble eye. c, Pearl scale goldfish. d, Red cap. e, Lionhead goldfish.

No. 2182, Golden arowana.

No. 2183a, Delta topsail variatus. b, Orange spotted hi-fin platy. c, Red lyretail swordtail. d, Bleeding heart hi-fin platy.

No. 2184a, 6p, Green discus. b, 6p, Brown discus. c, 7p, Red discus. d, 7p, Blue discus.

**1992, Sept. 9 *Perf. 14***

| | | | | |
|---|---|---|---|---|
| 2180 | A600 | 1.50p Strip of 5, #a.-e. | 4.00 | 4.00 |
| 2181 | A600 | 2p Strip of 5, #a.-e. | 4.00 | 4.00 |

***Imperf***

**Size: 65x45mm**

| | | | | |
|---|---|---|---|---|
| 2182 | A600 | 8p multicolored | 5.00 | 3.50 |

**Souvenir Sheets of 4**

***Perf. 14***

| | | | | |
|---|---|---|---|---|
| 2183 | A600 | 4p #a.-d. | 6.00 | *6.00* |
| 2184 | A600 | 6p, 7p #a.-d. | 11.00 | *11.00* |

Nos. 2182 and 2184 were overprinted "PHILIPPINE STAMP EXHIBITION 1992 — TAIPEI" in margins. Most of this overprinted issue was sold to the dealer to co-sponsored the exhibit. Value, $6 and $12, respectively.

See Nos. 2253-2257.

Birthday Greetings A601

**1992, Sept 28 *Perf. 14***

| | | | | |
|---|---|---|---|---|
| 2185 | A601 | 2p Couple dancing | .60 | .30 |
| 2186 | A601 | 6p like #2185 | 1.50 | .50 |
| 2187 | A601 | 7p Cake, balloons | 1.50 | .50 |
| 2188 | A601 | 8p like #2187 | 2.00 | .75 |
| | | *Nos. 2185-2188 (4)* | 5.60 | 2.05 |

Columbus' Discovery of America, 500th Anniv. A602

Various fruits and vegetables.

**1992, Oct. 14**

| | | | | |
|---|---|---|---|---|
| 2189 | A602 | 2p multicolored | .60 | .30 |
| 2190 | A602 | 6p multi, diff. | 1.60 | .50 |
| 2191 | A602 | 8p multi, diff. | 2.30 | .60 |
| | | *Nos. 2189-2191 (3)* | 4.50 | 1.40 |

Intl. Conference on Nutrition, Rome A603

**1992, Oct. 27**

| | | | | |
|---|---|---|---|---|
| 2192 | A603 | 2p multicolored | .70 | .30 |

**No. 2100 Ovptd. in Blue "Second / National Philatelic Convention / Cebu, Philippines, Oct. 22-24, 1992"**

**Wmk. 391**

**1992, Oct. 15 Photo. *Imperf.***

**2193** A571 16p multicolored 6.50 6.00

Christmas A604

Various pictures of mother and child.

**Wmk. 391**

**1992, Nov. 5 Litho. *Perf. 14***

**2194** A604 2p multicolored .60 .35
**2195** A604 6p multicolored 1.50 .50
**2196** A604 7p multicolored 1.50 .60
**2197** A604 8p multicolored 2.20 .85
*Nos. 2194-2197 (4)* 5.80 2.30

**No. 1452 Ovptd. "INAUGURATION OF THE PHILIPPINE POSTAL MUSEUM / AND PHILATELIC LIBRARY, NOVEMBER 10, 1992" in Red**

**Wmk. 372**

**1992, Nov. 10 Litho. *Imperf.***

**Souvenir Sheet**

**2198** A348 5p multicolored 3.50 *3.00*

Fight Against Drug Abuse — A605

**Wmk. 391**

**1992, Nov. 15 Litho. *Perf. 14***

**2199** A605 2p People, boat .60 .30
**2200** A605 8p People, boat, diff. 1.80 .60

A606

Paintings: 2p, Family, by Cesar Legaspi. 6p, Pounding Rice, by Nena Saguil. 7p, Fish Vendors, by Romeo V. Tabuena.

**1992, Nov. 24**

**2201** A606 2p multicolored .60 .30
**2202** A606 6p multicolored 1.60 .50
**2203** A606 7p multicolored 1.80 .60
*Nos. 2201-2203 (3)* 4.00 1.40

Philatelic Week.

Birds — A607

Designs: No. 2204a, Black shama. b, Philippine cockatoo. c, Sulu hornbill. d, Mindoro imperial pigeon. e, Blue-headed fantail.

No. 2205a, Philippine trogon, vert. b, Rufous hornbill, vert. c, White-bellied woodpecker, vert. d, Spotted wood kingfisher, vert.

No. 2206a, Brahminy kite. b, Philippine falconet. c, Pacific reef egret. d, Philippine mallard.

**Wmk. 391**

**1992, Nov. 25 Litho. *Perf. 14***

**2204** A607 2p Strip of 5, #a.-e. 3.50 3.00

**Souvenir Sheets**

**2205** A607 2p Sheet of 4, #a.-d. 4.00 *4.00*
**2206** A607 2p Sheet of 4, #a.-d. 4.00 *4.00*

No. 2204 printed in sheets of 10 with designs in each row shifted one space to the right from the preceding row. Two rows in each sheet are tete-beche.

The 1st printing of this set was rejected. The unissued stamps do not have the frame around the birds. The denominations on the sheet stamps and the 2nd souvenir sheet are larger. On the 1st souvenir sheet they are smaller.

For overprint see No. 2405.

New Year 1993, Year of the Rooster A608

2p, Native fighting cock. 6p, Legendary Maranao bird.

**1992, Nov. 2**

**2207** A608 2p multi .60 .40
**2208** A608 6p multi 2.00 .60
*a.* Souvenir sheet of 2, #2207-2208 + 2 labels 3.50 *3.00*
*b.* As "a," ovptd. in sheet margin 3.00 *2.50*

Nos. 2208a and 2208b exist imperf. Overprint on No. 2208b reads: "PHILIPPINE STAMP EXHIBIT / TAIPEI, DECEMBER 1-3, 1992" in English and Chinese.

Issued: #2207-2208, 2208a, 11/27; #2208b, 12/1.

See Nos. 2459b, 2460b.

Guerrilla Units of World War II — A609

Units: a, Bulacan Military Area, Anderson's Command, Luzon Guerrilla Army Forces. b, Marking's Fil-American Guerrillas, Hunters ROTC Guerrillas, President Quezon's Own Guerrillas. c, 61st Division, 71st Division, Cebu Area Command. d, 48th Chinese Guerrilla Squadron, 101st Division, Vinzons Guerrillas.

**1992, Dec. 7**

**2209** A609 2p Block of 4, #a.-d. 4.00 3.50

**National Symbols**

Tree — A610

A610c Fish

Flower

A610a A610b

Flag

A610d A610e

Animal

A610f A610g

Bird

A610h A610i

Leaf

A610j A610k

A610l

A610m Costume

Fruit

A610n A610o

A610p House

A610q Various

A610r José Rizal

A610s National Dance

National Sport — A610t

**Nos. 2210-2236 inscribed with year of issue unless noted otherwise**

**Wmk. 391, except #2212A, 2214, 2215, 2216A, 2218A, 2220, 2222 (Unwmk.)**

***Red (R) or Blue (B) "PILIPINAS" on bottom, except #2212 (Brown (Br) "PILIPINAS" on top)***

**1993-98 Litho. *Perf. 14x13½***

**2210** A610 60s (R) .65 *.65*
**2211** A610b 1p (R) .50 .25
**2211A** A610b 1p (R) .35 .25
**2212** A610a 1p (Br) .35 .25
**2212A** A610b 1p (B) .35 .25
**2213** A610c 1.50p (R) .65 .25
*a.* Dated "1995" .40 .25
**2214** A610c 1.50p (B) .70 .25

Nos. 2212A and 2214 have blue security printing.

Issued: #2210, 6/12/93; #2211, 5/3/94; #2211A, 2/6/95; #2212, 4/29/93; #2212A, 2/12/96; #2213, 6/12/3; #2213a, 2/6/95; #2214, 2/12/6.

For surcharge see No. 2795.

***Red "PILIPINAS" on bottom, except #2215a (Brown "PILIPINAS" on top)***

***Blue Security Printing***

**2215** 2p Block of 14, #a.-n. 9.00 9.00
*a.* A610d 2p multi .40 .90
*b.* A610r 2p multi .40 .25
*c.* A610p 2p multi .40 .25
*d.* A610m 2p multi .40 .25
*e.* A610s 2p multi .40 .25
*f.* A610t 2p multi .40 .25
*g.* A610i 2p multi .40 .25
*h.* A610e 2p multi .40 .40
*i.* A610f 2p multi .40 .25
*j.* A610b 2p multi .40 .25
*k.* A610 2p multi .40 .25
*l.* A610o 2p multi .40 .25
*m.* A610k 2p multi .40 .25
*n.* A610c 2p multi .40 .25

Issued 11/2/95.

***Red "PILIPINAS" on bottom, except #2216, 2217a (Brown "PILIPINAS" on top)***

***No Security Printing***

**2216** A610d 2p multi .80 .25
**2216A** A610e 2p multi 2.50 .30
**2217** 2p Block of 14, #a.-n. 9.00 9.00
*a.* A610d 2p multi .40 .90
*b.* A610r 2p multi .40 .25
*c.* A610p 2p multi .40 .25
*d.* A610m 2p multi .40 .25
*e.* A610s 2p multi .40 .25
*f.* A610t 2p multi .40 .25
*g.* A610h 2p multi .40 .25
*h.* A610e 2p multi .40 .40
*i.* A610f 2p multi .40 .25
*j.* A610b 2p multi .40 .25
*k.* A610 2p multi .40 .25
*l.* A610o 2p multi .40 .25
*m.* A610k 2p multi .40 .25
*n.* A610c 2p multi .40 .25

Issued: #2216, 4/29/93; #2216A (dated 1993), 2/10/94; #2217, 10/28/93.

#2217a is a later printing of #2216, in which the word "watawat" is much smaller. #2217h is a later printing of #2216A, in which the date is lowered near the middle of "PILIPINAS," rather than near the top of "PILIPINAS."

***Red "PILIPINAS" on bottom***

**2218** A610f 3p multi 1.35 .35
*a.* Dated "1994" 2.00 .35
*b.* Dated "1995" 6.50 .35

**Blue Security Printing at Top, Blue "PILIPINAS" on bottom**

**2218C** A610g 3p multi, dated "1996" 1.00 .35
*d.* Dated "1997" .40 .35

"PILIPINAS" red: Nos. 2218, 2218a, 2218c. Blue security printing: Nos. 2218C, 2281d.

Issued: No. 2218, 6/12/93; No. 2218a, 4/19/94; No. 2218b, 2/1/95; No. 2218C, 3/1/96; No. 2218d, 4/18/97.

***Blue "PILIPINAS" on bottom, except #2219n (Blue "PILIPINAS" on top)***

***Blue Security Printing***

**2219** 4p Block of 14, #a.-n. 15.00 15.00
*a.* A610d 4p multi 1.00 .30
*b.* A610r 4p multi 1.00 .30
*c.* A610p 4p multi 1.00 .30
*d.* A610m 4p multi 1.00 .30
*e.* A610s 4p multi 1.00 .30
*f.* A610t 4p multi 1.00 .30
*g.* A610i 4p multi 1.00 .30
*h.* A610d 4p multi 1.00 .30
*i.* A610f 4p multi 1.00 .30
*j.* A610b 4p multi 1.00 .30
*k.* A610 4p multi 1.00 .30
*l.* A610o 4p multi 1.00 .30
*m.* A610k 4p multi 1.00 .30
*n.* A610c 4p multi 1.00 .30

Issued 1/8/96. Stamps are dated "1995."

***Blue "PILIPINAS" on bottom, except #2220a (Blue "PILIPINAS" on top)***

***Blue Security Printing***

**2220** 4p Block of 14, #a.-n. 17.00 17.00
*a.* A610d 4p multi 1.00 .30
*b.* A610r 4p multi 1.00 .30
*c.* A610p 4p multi 1.00 .30
*d.* A610m 4p multi 1.00 .30

**1995, Sept. 25**

**2371** A670 2p Block of 4, #a.-d. 3.00 2.75
**2371E** A670 2p Cesar C. Bengson *125.00 125.00*
*f.* Block of 4, #2371b-2731d, 2371E *175.00*

**Souvenir Sheet**

**2372** A670 16p multi 4.00 3.50

No. 2371E was issued with the wrong portrait and was withdrawn after two days.

FAO, 50th Anniv. A671

**1995, Sept. 25**

**2373** A671 8p multicolored 2.00 .65

A671a

**Unwmk. Litho. *Perf. 14***

**1995, Oct. 5**

**2373A** A671a 2p multicolored .50 .30

Manila Overseas Press Club, 50th anniv.

Total Eclipse of the Sun — A672

**1995, Oct. 24**

**2374** A672 2p multicolored 1.00 .35

Natl. Stamp Collecting Month A673

Paintings: 2p, Two Igorot Women, by Victorio Edades. 6p, Serenade, by Carlos "Botong" Francisco. 7p, Tuba Drinkers, by Vincente Manansala. 8p, Genesis, by Hernando Ocampo.
12p, The Builders, by Edades.

**1995, Nov. 6**

**2375** A673 2p multicolored .50 .30
**2376** A673 6p multicolored 1.25 .45
**2377** A673 7p multicolored 1.50 .60
**2378** A673 8p multicolored 1.75 .70
*Nos. 2375-2378 (4)* 5.00 2.05

**Souvenir Sheet**

**2379** A673 12p multicolored 3.50 3.00

No. 2379 contains one 76x26mm stamp.

Christmas A674

Musical instruments, Christmas carols.

**1995, Nov. 22**

**2380** A674 2p Tambourine .50 .35
**2381** A674 6p Maracas 1.90 .50
**2382** A674 7p Guitar 1.60 .65
**2383** A674 8p Drum 2.00 .85
*Nos. 2380-2383 (4)* 6.00 2.35

Sycip Gorres Velayo & Co. Accounting Firm, 50th Anniv. A675

**1995, Nov. 27**

**2384** A675 2p Abacus .50 .30

**Souvenir Sheet**

Pres. Fidel V. Ramos Proclaiming November as Natl. Stamp Collecting Month — A676

**1995, Nov. 29**

**2385** A676 8p multicolored 5.00 4.00

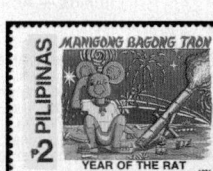

New Year 1996 (Year of the Rat) A677

**1995, Dec. 1**

**2386** A677 2p shown .50 .35
**2387** A677 6p Outline of rat 1.50 .65
*a.* Souv. sheet, #2386-2387+2 labels 3.50 3.50

No. 2387a exists imperf. Value, $5.
See Nos. 2459e, 2460e.

Philippine Guerrilla Units of World War II — A678

Designs: a, Emblem, FIL-American Irregular Troops (FAIT). b, Emblem, BICOL Brigade. c, Map, FIL-American Guerrilla Forces (Cavite), Hukbalahap Unit (Pampanga). d, Map, South Tarlac, Northwest Pampanga Military Districts.

**1995, Dec. 8 Litho. *Perf. 14***

**2388** A678 2p Block of 4, #a.-d. 3.50 3.00

Significant Events of World War II, 50th Anniv. — A679

Designs: a, Map, liberation of Panay and Romblon, 61st Division. b, Map, Liberation of Cebu, Americal Division. c, Battle of Ipo Dam, 43rd Division, FIL-American Guerrillas. d, Map, Battle of Bessang Pass, 37th Division. e, Sculpture, surrender of Gen. Yamashita.

**1995, Dec. 15**

**2389** A679 2p Strip of 5, #a.-e. 6.00 6.00

See Nos. 2392h-2392 l.

Revolutionary Heroes — A680

a, Jose P. Rizal (1861-96) b, Andres Bonifacio, (1863-97). c, Apolinario Mabini (1864-1903).

**1995, Dec. 27**

**2390** A680 2p Set of 3, #a.-c. 2.00 1.75

**World War II Types of 1994-95 and**

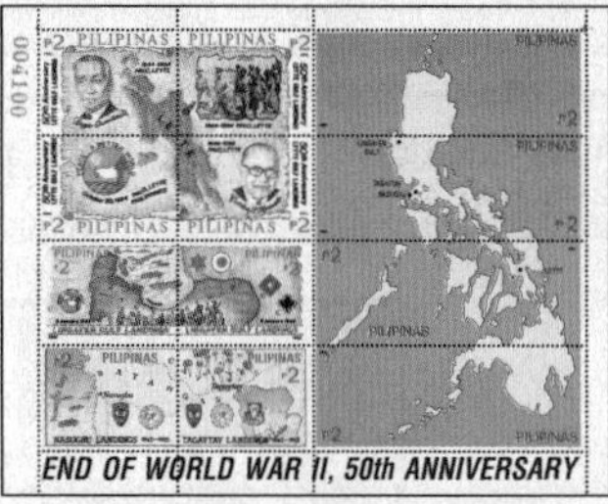


Map of Philippines — A681

Color of Pilipinas and denomination: Nos. 2391a-2391d, like #2316, red. Nos. 2391e-2391f, like #2346, red. Nos. 2391g-2391h, like #2355, red. Nos. 2391i-2391l, map of Philippines with blue background showing sites of Allied landings.

No. 2392: a-b, like #2335, white. c, like #2354, red. d, like #2356, white. e, like #2358, white. f, like #2357, white. g, like #2359, white. h.-l., like #2389a-2389e, purple. m, like #2347, red. n.-q., map of Philippines with green background showing location of prison camps. r, like #2348, red.

**Miniature Sheets**

**1995, Dec. 27 Litho. *Perf. 14***

**2391** A681 2p Sheet of 12, #a.-l. 8.00 8.00
**2392** A681 2p Sheet of 18, #a.-r. 12.00 *12.00*

23rd Intl. Congress of Internal Medicine — A682

**1996, Jan. 10 Litho. *Perf. 14***

**2393** A682 2p multicolored .60 .30

Sun Life Assurance Company of Canada in the Philippines, Cent. A683

**1996, Jan. 26**

**2394** A683 2p shown .50 .30
**2395** A683 8p Sun over horizon 1.50 .60

Valentine's Day — A684

"I Love You" on Nos. 2396a-2399a, "Happy Valentine" on Nos. 2396b-2399b and: No. 2396, Pair of love birds. No. 2397, Cupid with bow and arrow. No. 2398, Box of chocolates. No. 2399, Bouquet of roses, butterfly.

**1996, Feb. 9**

**2396** A684 2p Pair, #a.-b. 1.00 .75
**2397** A684 6p Pair, #a.-b. 2.50 2.25
**2398** A684 7p Pair, #a.-b. 3.25 2.50
**2399** A684 8p Pair, #a.-b. 2.75 3.00
*Nos. 2396-2399 (4)* 9.50 8.50

St. Thomas University Hospital, 50th Anniv. A685

**1996, Mar. 5**

**2400** A685 2p multicolored .60 .30

Gregorio Araneta University Foundation, 50th Anniv. — A686

**1996, Mar. 5**

**2401** A686 2p multicolored .60 .30

Fish — A687

No. 2402: a, Emperor fish. b, Mandarinfish. c, Regal angelfish. d, Clown triggerfish. e, Raccoon butterflyfish. g, Powder brown tang. h, Two-banded anemonefish. i, Moorish idol. j, Blue tang. k, Majestic angelfish.

No. 2403: a, like #2402d. b, like #2402k. c, like #2402c. d, like #2402h.

**1996, Mar. 12**

**2402** A687 4p Strip of 5, #a.-e. 5.50 5.50
**2402F** A687 4p Strip of 5, #g.-k. 5.50 5.50

**Miniature Sheet**

**2403** A687 4p Sheet of 4, #a.-d. 5.25 4.50
*e.* #2403 with new inscriptions 5.25 4.50

**Souvenir Sheet**

**2404** A687 12p Lionfish 4.00 3.00
*a.* #2404 with new inscriptions 4.00 3.00

Nos. 2402, 2402F have blue compressed security printing at left, black denomination, white background, margin. Nos. 2403-2404 have blue background, violet denomination, continuous design.

ASEANPEX '96 (No. 2403-2404).

Nos. 2403e, 2404a inscribed in sheet margins with various INDONESIA '96 exhibition emblems. Issued: Nos. 2403e, 2404a, 3/21/96.

See Nos. 2410-2413.

**No. 2206 Overprinted in Green**

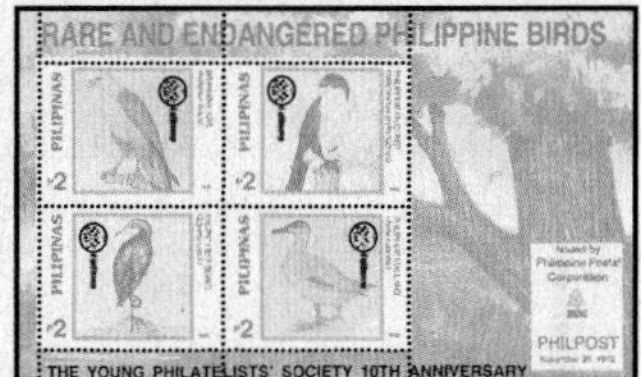

**1996 Litho. Wmk. 391 *Perf. 14***
**2405** A607 2p Sheet of 4, #a.-d. 7.50 7.00

Ovpt. in sheet margin reads: "THE YOUNG PHILATELISTS' SOCIETY 10TH ANNIVERSARY".

Souvenir Sheet

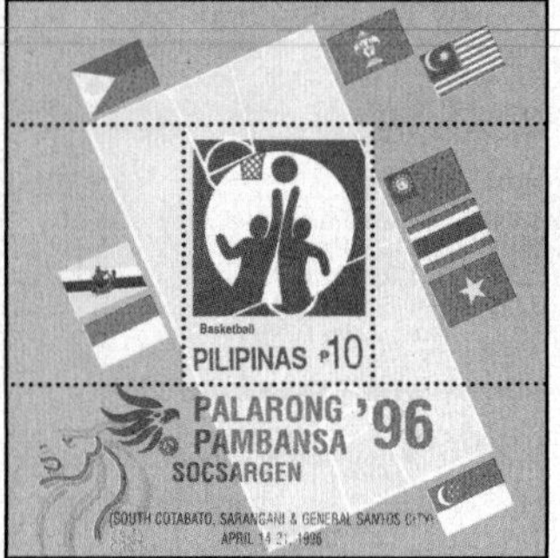


Basketball — A688

**1996, Apr. 14**
**2406** A688 10p multicolored *12.50* 12.50

PALARONG/PAMBANSA '96.

Francisco B. Ortigas, Sr. — A689

**1996, Apr. 30 Unwmk.**
**2407** A689 4p multicolored .65 .30

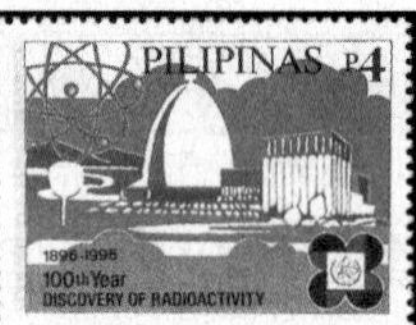


Discovery of Radioactivity, Cent. — A690

**1996, Apr. 30**
**2408** A690 4p multicolored .60 .30

Congregation of Dominican Sisters of St. Catherine of Siena, 300th Anniv. — A691

**1996, Apr. 30**
**2409** A691 4p multicolored .65 .30

**Fish Type of 1996**

No. 2410: a, Long-horned cowfish. b, Queen angelfish. c, Long-nosed butterflyfish. d, Yellow tang. e, Blue-faced angelfish.

No. 2411: a, Saddleback butterflyfish. b, Sailfin tang. c, Harlequin tuskfish. d, Clown wrasse. e, Spotted boxfish.

No. 2412: a, like #2410e. b, like #2410c. c, like #2410b. d, like #2411c.

No. 2413, vert: a, Purple firefish. b, Pacific seahorse. c, Red-faced batfish. d, Long-nosed hawksfish.

**1996**
**2410** A687 4p Strip of 5, #a.-e. 5.50 5.50
**2411** A687 4p Strip of 5, #a.-e. 5.50 5.50
**2412** A687 4p Sheet of 4, #a.-d. 5.00 5.00
*e.* With added inscription 5.00 5.00
**2413** A687 4p Sheet of 4, #a.-d. 5.00 5.00
*e.* With added inscription 5.00 5.00

Nos. 2412-2413 have white background. Nos. 2410-2411 have blue background.

ASEANPEX '96 (#2412-2413). Added inscription in sheet margin of #2412e, 2413e includes CHINA '96 emblem and "CHINA '96 - 9th Asian International Exhibition" in red.

Issued: #2410-2413, 5/10; #2412e, 2413e, 5/16.

**Great Filipinos Type of 1989**

Designs: a, Carlos P. Garcia (1896-1971), politician. b, Casimiro del Rosario (1896-1962), physicist. c, Geronima T. Pecson (1896-1989), politician. d, Cesar C. Bengson (1896-1992), lawyer. e, Jose Corazon de Jesus (1896-1932), writer.

***Perf. 13½***

**1996, June 1 Litho. Unwmk.**
**2414** A536 4p Strip of 5, #a.-e. 3.75 3.00

ABS CBN (Broadcasting Network), 50th Anniv. — A692

8p, Rooster, world map.

**1996, June 13 *Perf. 14***
**2415** A692 4p shown .50 .30
**2416** A692 8p multicolored 1.50 .50

Manila, Convention City A693

**1996, June 24**
**2417** A693 4p multicolored .60 .30

Jose Cojuangco, Sr. (1896-1976), Businessman, Public Official — A694

**1996, July 3**
**2418** A694 4p multicolored .60 .30

Philippine-American Friendship Day — A695

Symbols of Philippines, U.S.: 4p, Hats. 8p, National birds. 16p, Flags, vert.

**1996, July 4**
**2419** A695 4p multicolored .60 .30
**2420** A695 8p multicolored 1.60 .60

**Souvenir Sheet**

**2421** A695 16p multicolored 3.50 3.00

Modern Olympic Games, Cent. A696

4p, No. 2426a, Boxing. 6p, No. 2426b, Athletics. 7p, No. 2426c, Swimming. 8p, No. 2426d, Equestrian.

**Unwmk.**

**1996, July 19 Litho. *Perf. 14***
**2422** A696 4p multicolored .80 .40
**2423** A696 6p multicolored 1.25 .60
**2424** A696 7p multicolored 1.75 .70
**2425** A696 8p multicolored 1.90 .80
*Nos. 2422-2425 (4)* 5.70 2.50

**Miniature Sheet**

**2426** A696 4p Sheet of 4, #a.-d. 4.00 3.50

Nos. 2422-2425 have colored background, blue security code at right, denominations at LR. Nos. 2426a-2426d have colored circles on white background, blue security code at top, and denominations at UR, UL, LR, LL, respectively.

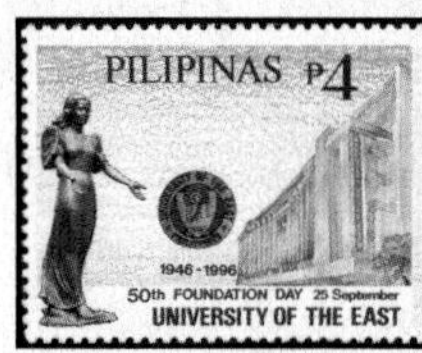


University of the East, 50th Anniv. A697

**1996, Aug. 15**
**2427** A697 4p multicolored .65 .30

Orchids — A698

No. 2428: a, Dendrobium anosmum. b, Phalaenopsis. equestris-alba. c, Aerides lawrenceae. d, Vanda javierii.

No. 2429: a, Renanthera philippinensis. b, Dendrobium schuetzei. c, Dendrobium taurinum. d, Vanda lamellata.

No. 2430: a, Coelogyne pandurata. b, Vanda merrilii. c, Cymbidium aliciae. d, Dendrobium topaziacum.

**1996, Sept. 26**
**2428** A698 4p Block or strip of 4, #a.-d. 3.00 2.75
**2429** A698 4p Block or strip of 4, #a.-d. 3.00 2.75

**Miniature Sheet**

**2430** A698 4p Sheet of 4, #a.-d. 3.50 3.50

#2428-2429 were printed in sheets of 16 stamps.

ASEANPEX '96 (#2430). Complete sheets of Nos. 2428-2429 have ASEANPEX emblem in selvage.

6th Asia Pacific Intl. Trade Fair A699

**1996, Sept. 30**
**2431** A699 4p multicolored .65 .30

UNICEF, 50th Anniv. — A700

Children in montage of scenes studying, working, playing — #2432: a, Blue & multi. b, Purple & multi. c, Green & multi. d, Red & multi.

16p, Four children, horiz.

**1996, Oct. 9**
**2432** A700 4p Block of 4, #a.-d. 3.00 2.50

**Souvenir Sheet**

**2433** A700 16p multicolored 3.50 3.00

TAIPEX '96 — A701

Orchids: No. 2434: a, Fran's Fantasy "Alea." b, Malvarosa Green Goddess "Nani." c, Ports of Paradise "Emerald Isle." d, Mem. Conrada Perez "Nani."

No. 2435: a, Pokai tangerine "Lea." b, Mem. Roselyn Reisman "Diana." c, C. Moscombe x Toshi Aoki. d, Mem. Benigno Aquino "Flying Aces."

12p, Pamela Hetherington "Coronation," Living Gold "Erin Treasure," Eleanor Spicer "White Bouquet."

**1996, Oct. 21 Litho. *Perf. 14***
**2434** A701 4p Block of 4, #a.-d. 3.00 2.50
**2435** A701 4p Block of 4, #a.-d. 3.00 2.50

**Souvenir Sheet**

**2436** A701 12p multicolored 4.50 3.50

Nos. 2434-2435 were issued in sheets of 16 stamps. No. 2436 contains one 80x30mm stamp.

1996 Asia-Pacific Economic Cooperation — A702

Winning entries of stamp design competition: 4p, Sun behind mountains, airplane, skyscrapers, tower, ship, satellite dish, vert. 7p, Skyscrapers. 8p, Flags of nations beside path, globe, skyscrapers, sun, vert.

**1996, Oct. 30**

| | | | | |
|---|---|---|---|---|
| **2437** | A702 | 4p multicolored | .80 | .30 |
| **2438** | A702 | 6p shown | 1.25 | .50 |
| **2439** | A702 | 7p multicolored | 1.35 | .60 |
| **2440** | A702 | 8p multicolored | 1.50 | .70 |
| | | *Nos. 2437-2440 (4)* | 4.90 | 2.10 |

Christmas A703

Designs: 4p, Philippine Nativity scene, vert. 6p, Midnight Mass. 7p, Carolers. 8p, Carolers with Carabao, vert.

**1996, Nov. 5**

| | | | | |
|---|---|---|---|---|
| **2441** | A703 | 4p multicolored | .75 | .35 |
| **2442** | A703 | 6p multicolored | 1.40 | .55 |
| **2443** | A703 | 7p multicolored | 1.60 | .65 |
| **2444** | A703 | 8p multicolored | 1.85 | .75 |
| | | *Nos. 2441-2444 (4)* | 5.60 | 2.30 |

Eugenio P. Perez (1896-1957), Politician — A704

**1996, Nov. 11 Litho. *Perf. 14***

| | | | | |
|---|---|---|---|---|
| **2445** | A704 | 4p multicolored | .60 | .30 |

New Year 1997 (Year of the Ox) A705

**1996, Dec. 1**

| | | | | |
|---|---|---|---|---|
| **2446** | A705 | 4p Carabao | .75 | .40 |
| **2447** | A705 | 6p Tamaraw | 1.25 | .60 |
| *a.* | | Souv. sheet, #2446-2447 + 2 labels | 3.50 | 3.50 |

No. 2447a exists imperf. Value, $3.50.

See Nos. 2459f, 2460f.

ASEANPEX '96, Intl. Philatelic Exhibition, Manila — A706

Jose P. Rizal (1861-96): No. 2448: a, At 14 years. b, At 18. c, At 25. d, At 31.

No. 2449: a, "Noli Me Tangere." b, Gomburza to whom Rizal dedicated "El Filbusterismo." c, Oyang Dapitana, by Rizal. d, Ricardo Camicero, by Rizal.

No. 2450, horiz: a, Rizal's house, Calamba. b, University of St. Tomas, Manila, 1611. c, Orient Hotel, Manila. d, Dapitan during Rizal's time.

No. 2451, horiz: a, Central University, Madrid. b, British Museum, London. c, Botanical Garden, Madrid. d, Heidelberg, Germany.

No. 2452, Rizal at 14, horiz. No. 2453, Rizal at 18, horiz. No. 2454, Rizal at 25, horiz. No. 2455, Rizal at 31, horiz.

**1996**

| | | | | |
|---|---|---|---|---|
| **2448** | A706 | 4p Block of 4, #a.-d. | 3.00 | 2.75 |
| **2449** | A706 | 4p Block of 4, #a.-d. | 3.00 | 2.75 |
| **2450** | A706 | 4p Block of 4, #a.-d. | 3.00 | 2.75 |
| **2451** | A706 | 4p Block of 4, #a.-d. | 3.00 | 2.75 |

**Souvenir Sheets**

| | | | | |
|---|---|---|---|---|
| **2452** | A706 | 12p multicolored | 2.50 | 2.00 |
| **2453** | A706 | 12p multicolored | 2.50 | 2.00 |
| **2454** | A706 | 12p multicolored | 2.50 | 2.00 |
| **2455** | A706 | 12p multicolored | 2.50 | 2.00 |

Issued: #2448, 2452, 12/14; #2449, 2453, 12/15; #2450, 2454, 12/16; #2451, 2455, 12/17. Nos. 2448-2451 were issued in sheets of 16 stamps.

Independence, Cent. (in 1998) — A707

Revolutionary heroes: a, Fr. Mariano C. Gomez (1799-1872). b, Fr. Jose A. Burgos (1837-72). c, Fr. Jacinto Zamora (1835-72).

**1996, Dec. 20**

| | | | | |
|---|---|---|---|---|
| **2456** | A707 | 4p Strip of 3, #a.-c. | 2.50 | 1.80 |

Jose Rizal — A709

**1996, Dec. 30 Litho. *Perf. 14***

| | | | | |
|---|---|---|---|---|
| **2458** | A709 | 4p multicolored | .75 | .35 |

**New Year Types of 1991-96**

**Unwmk.**

**1997, Feb. 12 Litho. *Perf. 14***

| | | | | |
|---|---|---|---|---|
| **2459** | | Sheet of 6 | 5.00 | 5.00 |
| *a.* | | A580 4p like #2126 | .70 | .60 |
| *b.* | | A608 4p like #2208 | .70 | .60 |
| *c.* | | A626 4p like #2284 | .70 | .60 |
| *d.* | | A650 4p like #2337 | .70 | .60 |
| *e.* | | A677 4p like #2386 | .70 | .60 |
| *f.* | | A705 4p like #2446 | .70 | .60 |
| **2460** | | Sheet of 6 | 9.00 | 9.00 |
| *a.* | | A580 6p like #2127 | 1.00 | .85 |
| *b.* | | A608 6p like #2207 | 1.00 | .85 |
| *c.* | | A626 6p like #2285 | 1.00 | .85 |
| *d.* | | A650 6p like #2338 | 1.00 | .85 |
| *e.* | | A677 6p like #2387 | 1.00 | .85 |
| *f.* | | A705 6p like #2447 | 1.00 | .85 |

Hong Kong '97.

Nos. 2459a-2459b, 2460a-2460b have white margins, color differences. Nos. 2459c-2459d, 2459f, 2460c-2460d, 2460f have color differences. Nos. 2459e, 2460e, do not have blue security printing, and have color differences.

Nos. 2459a-2459f, 2460a-2460f are all dated "1997."

Holy Rosary Seminary, Bicent. A710

**1997, Feb. 18**

| | | | | |
|---|---|---|---|---|
| **2461** | A710 | 4p multicolored | .65 | .30 |

Philippine Army, Cent. A711

**1997, Feb. 18**

| | | | | |
|---|---|---|---|---|
| **2462** | A711 | 4p multicolored | .65 | .30 |

**Natl. Symbols Type of 1993-96 and**

Gem — A711a

***Blue "PILIPINAS" on bottom, except #2464 (Black)***

**1997 Litho. Unwmk. *Perf. 14x13½***

| | | | | |
|---|---|---|---|---|
| **2463** | A610b | 1p like #2212A | .30 | .25 |
| **2463A** | A610b | 2p like #2212A | .75 | .30 |
| **2463B** | A610g | 3p like #2212A | .50 | .60 |
| **2464** | A711a | 4p multicolored | .75 | .35 |
| **2465** | A610i | 5p like #2222 | .90 | .70 |
| **2465A** | A610i | 5p like #2222 | 1.50 | .70 |
| **2466** | A610k | 6p like #2223A | 2.00 | .70 |
| **2466A** | A610k | 6p like #2223A | 2.00 | .75 |
| **2467** | A610m | 7p like #2224A | 3.00 | 1.00 |
| **2467A** | A610m | 7p like #2224A | 3.00 | 1.00 |
| **2468** | A610o | 8p like #2227 | 3.00 | 1.25 |
| **2468A** | A610o | 8p like #2227 | 3.00 | 1.25 |
| **2469** | A610p | 10p like #2229 | 4.00 | 1.50 |
| **2469A** | A610p | 10p like #2229 | 4.00 | 1.50 |
| | | *Nos. 2463-2469A (14)* | 28.70 | 11.85 |

Nos. 2463, 2465, 2466, 2467, 2468 and 2469 do not have blue compressed security printing at top and are dated "1997."

Nos. 2463A-2464, 2465A, 2466A, 2467A, 2468A and 2469A have blue compressed security printing at top and are dated "1997."

Issued: #2463, 2469, 2/27/97; 2463A, 4/15; 2463B, 2466A, 4/18; #2465A, 4/29; #2464, 6/10; #2465, 2/26; #2466, 3/10; #2467, 3/7; #2467A, 5/8; #2468, 3/6; #2468A, 5/8; #2469A, 4/22.

Dept. of Finance, Cent. A712

**1997, Apr. 8 *Perf. 14***

| | | | | |
|---|---|---|---|---|
| **2471** | A712 | 4p multicolored | .65 | .30 |

Philippine Red Cross, 50th Anniv. A713

**1997, Apr. 8**

| | | | | |
|---|---|---|---|---|
| **2472** | A713 | 4p multicolored | .65 | .30 |

Philamlife Insurance Co., 50th Anniv. A714

**1997, Apr. 8**

| | | | | |
|---|---|---|---|---|
| **2473** | A714 | 4p multicolored | .65 | .30 |

J. Walter Thompson Advertising, 50th Anniv. in Philippines A715

**1997, Apr. 18**

| | | | | |
|---|---|---|---|---|
| **2474** | A715 | 4p multicolored | .65 | .30 |

Souvenir Sheet

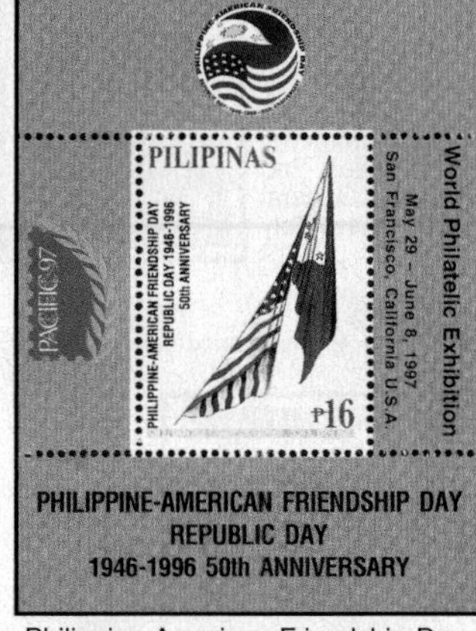

Philippine-American Friendship Day, Republic Day, 50th Anniv. — A716

**1997, May 29**

| | | | | |
|---|---|---|---|---|
| **2475** | A716 | 16p multicolored | 4.25 | 3.75 |

PACIFIC 97.

Wild Animals — A717

World Wildlife Fund: No. 2476, Visayan spotted deer. No. 2477, Visayan spotted deer (doe & fawn). No. 2478, Visayan warty pig. No. 2479, Visayan warty pig (adult, young).

**1997, July 24**

| | | | | |
|---|---|---|---|---|
| **2476** | | 4p multicolored | 1.00 | .70 |
| *a.* | | Sheet of 8 | 8.50 | 8.50 |
| **2477** | | 4p multicolored | 1.00 | .70 |
| *a.* | | Sheet of 8 | 8.50 | 8.50 |
| **2478** | | 4p multicolored | 1.00 | .70 |
| *a.* | | Sheet of 8 | 8.50 | 8.50 |
| **2479** | | 4p multicolored | 1.00 | .70 |
| *a.* | | Sheet of 8 | 8.50 | 8.50 |
| *b.* | | A717 Block or strip of 4, #2476-2479 | 4.25 | 3.50 |
| | | Set of 4 sheets, #2476a-2479a | 34.00 | 34.00 |

No. 2479b was issued in sheets of 16 stamps.

ASEAN, 30th Anniv. — A718

Founding signatories: No. 2480, Adam Malik, Indonesia, Tun Abdul Razak, Malaysia, Narciso Ramos, Philippines, S. Rajaratnam, Singapore, Thanat Khoman, Thailand. No. 2481, Natl. flags of founding signatories. No. 2482, Flags of current ASEAN countries. No. 2483, Flags of ASEAN countries surrounding globe.

**1997, Aug. 7 *Perf. 14***

| | | | | |
|---|---|---|---|---|
| **2480** | | 4p multicolored | .65 | .50 |
| **2481** | | 4p multicolored | .65 | .50 |
| *a.* | | A718 Pair, #2480-2481 | 1.75 | 1.25 |
| **2482** | | 6p multicolored | .85 | .60 |
| **2483** | | 6p multicolored | .85 | .60 |
| *a.* | | A718 Pair, #2482-2483 | 2.50 | 2.00 |
| | | *Nos. 2480-2483 (4)* | 3.00 | 2.20 |

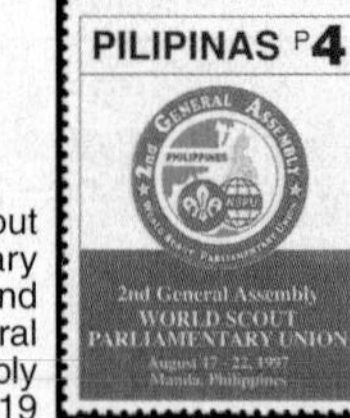

World Scout Parliamentary Union, 2nd General Assembly A719

**1997, Aug. 17**

**2484** A719 4p multicolored .70 .30

Manuel L. Quezon University, 50th Anniv. A720

**1997, Aug. 19**

**2485** A720 4p multicolored .65 .30

### Great Filipinos Type of 1989

Famous people: a, Justice Roberto Regala (1897-1979). b, Doroteo Espiritu, dental surgeon, inventor (b. 1897). c, Elisa R. Ochoa (1897-1978), nurse, tennis champion. d, Mariano Marcos (1897-1945), lawyer, educator. e, Jose F. Romero (1897-1978), editor.

***Perf. 14x13½***

**1997, June 1 Litho. Unwmk.**

**2486** A536 4p Strip of 5, #a.-e. 3.50 2.50

Battle of Candon, 1898 A721

4p, Don Federico Isabelo Abaya, revolutionary leader against Spanish. 6p, Soldier on horseback.

**1997, Sept. 24** ***Perf. 14***

**2487** A721 4p multi, vert. .75 .35
**2488** A721 6p multi 1.00 .60

St. Therese of Lisieux (1873-97) A722

**1997, Oct. 16**

**2489** A722 6p multicolored 1.00 .50

Stamp and Philatelic Division, 50th Anniv. A723

Abstract art: 4p, Homage to the Heroes of Bessang Pass, by Hernando Ruiz Ocampo. 6p, Jardin III, by Fernando Zobel. 7p, Abstraction, by Nena Saguil, vert. 8p, House of Life, by Jose Joya, vert.

16p, Dimension of Fear, by Jose Joya.

**1997, Oct. 16**

**2490** A723 4p multicolored .65 .35
**2491** A723 6p multicolored 1.00 .45
**2492** A723 7p multicolored 1.25 .60
**2493** A723 8p multicolored 1.35 .80
*Nos. 2490-2493 (4)* 4.25 2.20

**Souvenir Sheet**

**2494** A723 16p multicolored 5.25 5.00

No. 2494 contains one 80x30mm stamp.

Heinrich von Stephan (1831-97) A724

**1997, Oct. 24 Litho.** ***Perf. 14***

**2495** A724 4p multicolored .75 .35

Asian and Pacific Decade of Disabled Persons A725

**1997, Oct. 24 Litho.** ***Perf. 14***

**2496** A725 6p multicolored 1.00 .45

Intl. Year of the Reef — A726

**1997, Oct. 24 Litho.** ***Perf. 14***

**2497** A726 8p multicolored 1.50 1.20

**Souvenir Sheet**

**2498** A726 16p multicolored 4.25 4.00

No. 2498 is a continuous design.

Natl. Stamp Collecting Month A726a

Paintings: 4p, Dalagang Bukid, by Fernando Amorsolo, vert. 6p, Bagong Taon, by Arturo Luz, vert. 7p, Jeepneys, by Vincente Manansala. 8p, encounter of the Nuestra Sra. de Cavadonga and the Centurion, by Alfredo Carmelo.

16p, Pista sa Nayon, by Carlos Francisco.

**1997, Nov. 4 Litho.** ***Perf. 14***

**2498A** A726a 4p multicolored .65 .40
**2498B** A726a 6p multicolored 1.00 .60
**2498C** A726a 7p multicolored 1.25 .70
**2498D** A726a 8p multicolored 1.35 .80
*Nos. 2498A-2498D (4)* 4.25 2.50

**Souvenir Sheet**

**2498E** A726a 16p multicolored 3.50 3.50

No. 2498E contains one 80x30mm stamp.

Christmas A727

Various stained glass windows.

**1997, Nov. 7**

**2499** A727 4p multicolored .65 .35
**2500** A727 6p multicolored 1.10 .55
**2501** A727 7p multicolored 1.35 .75
**2502** A727 8p multicolored 1.50 .85
*Nos. 2499-2502 (4)* 4.60 2.50

Independence, Cent. — A728

Various monuments to Andres Bonifacio (1863-97), revolutionary, founder of the Katipunan: a, red & multi. b, yellow & multi. c, blue & multi.

**1997, Nov. 30**

**2503** A728 4p Strip of 3, #a.-c. 2.00 1.75

New Year 1998 (Year of the Tiger) A729

**1997, Dec. 1**

**2504** A729 4p shown .85 .40
**2505** A729 6p Tigers, diff. 1.25 .60
*a.* Souvenir sheet, #2504-2505 + 2 labels 3.50 3.50

No. 2505a exists imperf. Value, $3.50.

Philippine Eagle A730

**1997, Dec. 5**

**2506** A730 20p Looking right 5.00 1.80
**2507** A730 30p Looking forward 5.00 2.20
**2508** A730 50p On cliff 10.00 3.50
*Nos. 2506-2508 (3)* 20.00 7.50

Game Cocks — A731

No. 2509: a, Hatch grey. b, Spangled roundhead. c, Racey mug. d, Silver grey.

No. 2510, vert: a, Grey. b, Kelso. c, Bruner roundhead. d, Democrat.

No. 2511, Cock fight, vert. No. 2512, Cocks facing each other ready to fight.

**1997, Dec. 18**

**2509** A731 4p Block of 4, #a.-d. 2.75 2.25
**2510** A731 4p Block of 4, #a.-d. 2.75 2.25

**Souvenir Sheets**

**2511** A731 12p multicolored 2.75 2.50
**2512** A731 16p multicolored 3.75 3.50

No. 2512 contains one 80x30mm stamp.

Art Association of the Philippines, 50th Anniv. A732

Stylized designs: No. 2513, Colors of flag, sunburst. No. 2514, Association's initials, clenched fist holding artist's implements.

**Unwmk.**

**1998, Feb. 14 Litho.** ***Perf. 14***

**2513** A732 4p multicolored .65 .35
**2514** A732 4p multicolored .75 .40
*a.* Pair, #2513-2514 2.00 1.50

Club Filipino Social Organization, Cent. — A733

**1998, Feb. 25**

**2515** A733 4p multicolored .65 .30

Blessed Marie Eugenie (1817-98) A734

**1998, Feb. 25**

**2516** A734 4p multicolored .65 .30

Fulbright Educational Exchange Program in the Philippines, 50th Anniv. — A735

**1998, Feb. 25**

**2517** A735 4p multicolored .65 .40

Heroes of the Revolution — A736

National flag and: 4p, Melchora Aquino (1812-1919). 11p, Andres Bonifacio (1863-97). 13p, Apolinario Mabini (1864-1903). 15p, Emilio Aguinaldo (1869-1964).

**1998 Litho. Unwmk.** ***Perf. 13½***

**Inscribed "1998"**

**2518** A736 4p multicolored .65 .25
**2519** A736 11p multicolored 1.85 .50
*a.* Inscribed "1999" 2.00 .65
**2520** A736 13p multicolored 2.00 .60
*a.* Inscribed "1999" 2.50 .70
**2521** A736 15p multicolored 2.50 .75
*a.* Inscribed "1999" 3.50 1.00
*Nos. 2518-2521 (4)* 7.00 2.10

Issued: 4p, 3/3/98. 11p, 13p, 15p, 3/24/98.

See Nos. 2528, 2546-2550, 2578-2597, 2607.

Apo View Hotel, 50th Anniv. — A737

**1998, Mar. 20** ***Perf. 14***

**2522** A737 4p multicolored .80 .35

Philippine Cultural High School, 75th Anniv. — A738

**1998, May 5**

**2523** A738 4p multicolored .70 .40

Victorino Mapa High School, 75th Anniv. A739

**1998, May 5**

**2524** A739 4p multicolored .65 .30

Philippine Navy, Cent. A740

**1998, May 5**

**2525** A740 4p multicolored .70 .40

University of Baguio, 50th Anniv. A741

**1998, May 5**

**2526** A741 4p multicolored .70 .40

Philippine Maritime Institute, 50th Anniv. A742

**1998, May 5**

**2527** A742 4p multicolored .70 .40

**Heroes of the Revolution Type of 1998**

Design: Gen. Antonio Luna (1866-99).

***Perf. 13½***

**1998, Apr. 30 Litho. Unwmk.**

**2528** A736 5p multicolored .75 .30

Expo '98, Lisbon A743

4p, Boat on lake, vert. 15p, Vinta on water. 15p, Main lobby, Philippine Pavilion.

**1998, May 22** ***Perf. 14***

**2529** A743 4p multicolored .65 .35
**2530** A743 15p multicolored 2.25 1.00

**Souvenir Sheet**

**2531** A743 15p multicolored 4.00 3.50

No. 2531 contains one 80x30mm stamp.

Clark Special Economic Zone — A744

**1998, May 28**

**2532** A744 15p multicolored 3.00 1.75

Flowers — A745

#2533: a, Artrabotrys hexapetalus. b, Hibiscus rosa-sinensis. c, Nerium oleander. d, Jasminum sambac.

#2534, vert: a, Gardenia jasminoides. b, Ixora coccinea. c, Erythrina indica. d, Abelmoschus moschatus.

#2535, Medinilla magnifica.

**1998, May 29**

**2533** A745 4p Block of 4, #a.-d. 2.75 2.25
**2534** A745 4p Block of 4, #a.-d. 2.75 2.25

**Souvenir Sheet**

**2535** A745 15p multicolored 5.00 4.00

**Great Filipinos Type of 1989**

Designs: a, Andres R. Soriano (1898-1964). b, Tomas Fonacier (1898-1991). c, Josefa L. Escoda (1898-1945). d, Lorenzo M. Tañada (1898-1992). e, Lazaro Francisco (1898-1980).

**1998, June 1** ***Perf. 14x13½***

**2536** A536 4p Strip of 5, #a.-e. 3.50 3.00

Philippine Indepencence, Cent. — A746

No. 2537, Mexican flag, sailing ship. No. 2538, Woman holding Philippine flag, monument, sailing ship, map of Philippines. No. 2539, Spanish flag, Catholic Church, religious icon, Philippine flag.

**1998, June 3** ***Perf. 14***

**2537** A746 15p multicolored 1.40 1.00
**2538** A746 15p multicolored 1.40 1.00
**2539** A746 15p multicolored 1.40 1.00
*a.* Strip of 3, #2537-2539 5.00 4.50
*b.* Souvenir sheet, #2537-2539 + 3 labels 6.00 6.00

See Mexico #2079-2080, Spain #2949. For overprint see #2629.

Philippine Independence, Cent. — A747

Patriots of the revolution: a, Melchora Aquino. b, Nazaria Lagos. c, Agueda Kahabagan.

**Unwmk.**

**1998, June 9 Litho.** ***Perf. 14***

**2540** A747 4p Strip of 3, #a.-c. 1.80 1.50

Pasig River Campaign for Waste Management — A748

**1998, June 19**

**2541** A748 4p multicolored .60 .30

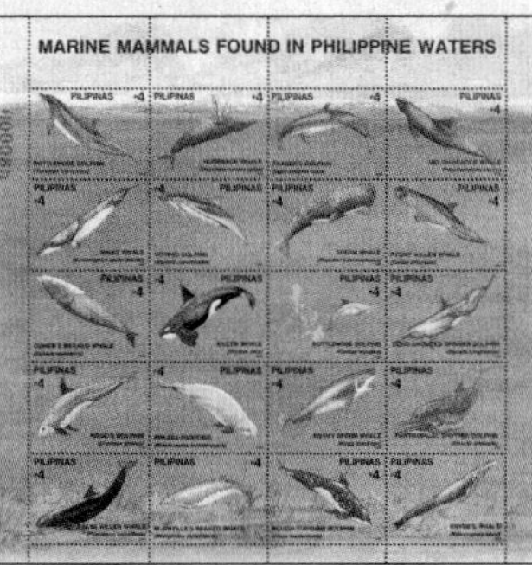


Marine Mammals — A749

No. 2542: a, Bottlenose dolphin. b, Humpback whale. c, Fraser's dolphin. d, Melon-headed whale. e, Minke whale. f, Striped dolphin. g, Sperm whale. h, Pygmy killer whale. i, Cuvier's beaked whale. j, Killer whale. k, Bottlenose dolphin. l, Long-snouted pinner dolphin. m, Risso's dolphin. n, Finless porpoise. o, Pygmy sperm whale. p, Pantropical spotted dolphin. q, False killer whale. r, Blainville's beaked whale. s, Rough-toothed dolphin. t, Bryde's whale.

15p, Dugong.

**1998, June 19**

**2542** A749 4p Sheet of 20, #a.-t. 15.00 *20.00*

**Souvenir Sheet**

**2543** A749 15p multicolored 4.50 4.00

**Nos. 2218a, 2218b, 2220 Ovptd. in Gold with Philippine Independence Centennial Emblem**

**1998 Litho. Unwmk.** ***Perf. 14x13½***

**2544** A610f 3p multi, dated "1995" (#2218b) .60 .25
**2544A** A610f 3p multi, dated "1994" (#2218a) 75.00 75.00
**2545** A610g 4p Block of 14, #a.-n. 15.00 15.00
*a.* A610d 4p multi .75 .40
*b.* A610r 4p multi .75 .40
*c.* A610p 4p multi .75 .40
*d.* A610m 4p multi .75 .40
*e.* A610s 4p multi .75 .40
*f.* A610t 4p multi .75 .40
*g.* A610i 4p multi .75 .40
*h.* A610e 4p multi .75 .40
*i.* A610g 4p multi .75 .40
*j.* A610b 4p multi .75 .40
*k.* A610 4p multi .75 .40
*l.* A610o 4p multi .75 .40
*m.* A610k 4p multi .75 .40
*n.* A610c 4p multi .75 .40

Issued: No. 2544, 7/7/98; 2545, 6/12/98.

No. 2544A, dated "1994," was overprinted in error.

**Heroes of the Revolution Type of 1998**

2p, Emilio Jacinto. 4p, Jose P. Rizal. 8p, Marcelo H. del Pilar. 10p, Gregorio del Pilar. 18p, Juan Luna.

**1998 Inscribed "1998"** ***Perf. 13½***

**2546** A736 2p multicolored .65 .25
**2547** A736 4p multicolored .65 .30
**2548** A736 8p multicolored 1.25 .45
*a.* Inscribed "1999" 1.50 .50
**2549** A736 10p multicolored 1.85 .70
*a.* Inscribed "1999" 2.50 .70
**2550** A736 18p multicolored 3.00 1.25
*Nos. 2546-2550 (5)* 7.40 2.95

Issued: 4p, 10p, 18p, 5/18/98. 2p, 8p, 7/20/98.

For surcharges, see Nos. 2879-2882.

Philippine Centennial — A749a

No. 2550A: b, Spoliarium, by Juan Luna. c, 1st display of Philippine flag, 1898. d, Execution of Jose Rizal, 1896. e, Andres Bonifacio. f, Church, Malolos.

**1998, July** ***Perf. 14***

**2550A** Souv. booklet *32.50 32.50*
*b.* A749a 4p multicolored .70 *.60*
*c.* A749a 8p multicolored 1.80 *1.40*
*d.-e.* A749a 16p multicolored 3.00 *2.50*
*f.* A749a 20p multicolored 3.50 *2.75*

No. 2550A contains panes of 4 each of Nos. 2550Ab-2550Ac and one pane of 1 each of Nos. 2550Ad-2550Af. Sold for 150p.

For surcharges, see Nos. 2879-2882.

Philippine Coconut Industry, Cent. A750

**1998, Oct. 9** ***Perf. 14***

**2551** A750 4p multicolored 1.00 .60



Holy Spirit Adoration Sisters in Philippines, 75th Anniv. A751

**1998, Oct. 9**

**2552** A751 4p multicolored 1.25 .60

Universal Delclaration of Human Rights, 50th Anniv. — A752

**1998, Oct. 24**

**2553** A752 4p multicolored 1.00 .60

Intl. Year of the Ocean — A753

**1998, Oct. 24**

**2554** A753 15p multicolored 3.00 2.00
*a.* Souvenir sheet, #2554 4.50 4.50

No. 2554a is a continuous design.

A754

Philippine Postal Service, Cent. — #2555: a, Child placing envelope into mailbox, globe. b, Arms encircling globe, envelopes, Philippine flag as background. c, Airplane, globe, various stamps over building. d, Child holding up hands, natl. flag colors, envelopes.
15p, Child holding envelope as it crisscrosses globe.

**1998, Nov. 4**

**2555** A754 6p Block of 4, #a.-d. 4.00 3.00

**Souvenir Sheet**

**2556** A754 15p multicolored 4.50 4.00

No. 2556 contains one 76x30mm stamp.

A755

Christmas: Various star lanterns.

**1998, Nov. 5**

| | | | | |
|---|---|---|---|---|
| **2557** | A755 | 6p multicolored | 1.00 | .40 |
| **2558** | A755 | 11p multicolored | 1.75 | .75 |
| **2559** | A755 | 13p multicolored | 2.25 | 1.00 |
| **2560** | A755 | 15p multicolored | 2.50 | 1.15 |
| | | *Nos. 2557-2560 (4)* | 7.50 | 3.30 |

Pasko '98.

Souvenir Sheets

Philippines '98, Philippine Cent. Invitational Intl. Philatelic Exhibition — A756

Revolutionary scenes, stamps of revolutionary govt.: No. 2561, Soldiers celebrating, #Y1-Y2. No. 2562, Signing treaty, telegraph stamps. No. 2563, Waving flag from balcony, #YF1, "Recibos" (Offical receipt) stamps. No. 2564, Procession, #Y3, perf. and imperf. examples of #YP1. No. 2565, New government convening, "Trans de Ganades" (cattle transfer) stamp, Libertad essay.

**1998**

| | | | | |
|---|---|---|---|---|
| **2561** | A756 | 15p multicolored | 5.50 | 4.50 |
| **2562** | A756 | 15p multicolored | 5.50 | 4.50 |
| **2563** | A756 | 15p multicolored | 5.50 | 4.50 |
| **2564** | A756 | 15p multicolored | 5.50 | 4.50 |
| **2565** | A756 | 15p multicolored | 5.50 | 4.50 |
| | | *Nos. 2561-2565 (5)* | 27.50 | 22.50 |

No. 2561 exists imperf. The first printing has varying amounts of black offset on the reverse. Value, $75. The second printing does not have the offset. Value, $12.50.
Nos. 2561-2565 were issued one each day from 11/5-11/9.

Pres. Joseph Ejercito Estrada A757

**1998, Nov. 10**

| | | | | |
|---|---|---|---|---|
| **2566** | A757 | 6p Taking oath | .80 | .40 |
| **2567** | A757 | 15p Giving speech | 2.20 | 1.00 |

Shells — A758

No. 2568: a, Mitra papalis. b, Vexillum citrinum. c, Vexillum rugosum. d, Volema carinifera.
No. 2569: a, Teramachia dalli. b, Nassarius vitiensis. c, Cymbiola imperialis. d, Cymbiola aulica.
No. 2570: a, Nassarius papillosus. b, Fasciolaria trapezium.

**Unwmk.**

**1998, Nov. 6 Litho. *Perf. 14***

| | | | | |
|---|---|---|---|---|
| **2568** | A758 | 4p Block of 4, #a.-d. | 3.50 | 3.00 |
| **2569** | A758 | 4p Block of 4, #a.-d. | 3.50 | 3.00 |

**Souvenir Sheet**

| | | | | |
|---|---|---|---|---|
| **2570** | A758 | 8p Sheet of 2, #a.-b. | 5.00 | 5.00 |
| *c.* | | Souvenir sheet, Type II | 10.00 | 10.00 |

Cloud in sheet margin touches "s" of Shells on #2570. On #2570c, cloud does not touch "s" of Shells. Colors are dark on #2570c, lighter on #2570.

Natl. Stamp Collecting Month — A759

Motion picture, director: 6p, "Dyesebel," Gerardo de Leon. 11p, "Ang Sawa Sa Lumang Simboryo," Gerardo de Leon. 13p, "Prinsipe Amante," Lamberto V. Avellana. No. 2574, "Anak Dalita," Lamberto V. Avellana.
No. 2575, "Siete Infantes de Lara," costume design by Carlos "Botong" Francisco.

**1998, Nov. 25**

| | | | | |
|---|---|---|---|---|
| **2571** | A759 | 6p black & blue | .80 | .40 |
| **2572** | A759 | 11p black & brown | 1.50 | .70 |
| **2573** | A759 | 13p black & lilac | 2.00 | .80 |
| **2574** | A759 | 15p black & green | 2.50 | 1.00 |
| | | *Nos. 2571-2574 (4)* | 6.80 | 2.90 |

**Souvenir Sheet**

**2575** A759 15p black 3.25 3.25

No. 2575 contains one 26x76mm stamp.

Philippine Centennial — A759a

Pride, various women and: No. 2575A, Eagle (Resources). No. 2575B, Costume (Heritage). No. 2575C, Flag (Filipino People). No. 2575D, Artifacts with text (Literature). No. 2575E, Rice terraces (Engineering). No. 2575F, "Noli Me Tangere" (Citizenry).

**Unwmk.**

**1998, Nov. 20 Litho. *Imperf.***

| | | | | |
|---|---|---|---|---|
| **2575A** | A759a | 15p multi | 3.50 | 3.00 |
| **2575B** | A759a | 15p multi | 3.50 | 3.00 |
| **2575C** | A759a | 15p multi | 3.50 | 3.00 |
| **2575D** | A759a | 15p multi | 3.50 | 3.00 |
| **2575E** | A759a | 15p multi | 3.50 | 3.00 |
| **2575F** | A759a | 15p multi | 3.50 | 3.00 |
| | | *Nos. 2575A-2575F (6)* | 21.00 | 18.00 |

Nos. 2575A-2575F have simulated perforations.

New Year 1999 (Year of the Rabbit) A760

**1998, Dec. 1**

| | | | | |
|---|---|---|---|---|
| **2576** | A760 | 4p shown | .80 | .40 |
| **2577** | A760 | 11p Two rabbits | 2.00 | .80 |
| *a.* | | Souvenir sheet, #2576-2577 | 4.00 | 4.00 |

No. 2577a exists imperf. Value, $4.

**Heroes of the Revolution Type of 1998**

**1998, Dec. 15 Litho. *Perf. 13½***

**Booklet Stamps**

**Yellow Background**

| | | | | |
|---|---|---|---|---|
| **2578** | A736 | 6p like #2518 | .80 | .40 |
| **2579** | A736 | 6p like #2519 | .80 | .40 |
| **2580** | A736 | 6p like #2520 | .80 | .40 |
| **2581** | A736 | 6p like #2521 | .80 | .40 |
| **2582** | A736 | 6p like #2528 | .80 | .40 |
| **2583** | A736 | 6p like #2547 | .80 | .40 |
| **2584** | A736 | 6p like #2549 | .80 | .40 |
| **2585** | A736 | 6p like #2550 | .80 | .40 |
| **2586** | A736 | 6p like #2546 | .80 | .40 |
| **2587** | A736 | 6p like #2548 | .80 | .40 |
| *a.* | | Booklet pane, #2578-2587 | 10.00 | 10.00 |
| | | Complete booklet, #2587a | 10.00 | 10.00 |

**Green Background**

| | | | | |
|---|---|---|---|---|
| **2588** | A736 | 15p like #2546 | 2.00 | 1.50 |
| **2589** | A736 | 15p like #2518 | 2.00 | 1.50 |
| **2590** | A736 | 15p like #2547 | 2.00 | 1.50 |
| **2591** | A736 | 15p like #2528 | 2.00 | 1.50 |
| **2592** | A736 | 15p like #2548 | 2.00 | 1.50 |
| **2593** | A736 | 15p like #2549 | 2.00 | 1.50 |
| **2594** | A736 | 15p like #2519 | 2.00 | 1.50 |
| **2595** | A736 | 15p like #2520 | 2.00 | 1.50 |
| **2596** | A736 | 15p like #2521 | 2.00 | 1.50 |
| *a.* | | Booklet pane, 2c #2546, 8c #2548, 2 each 11c, 13c, #2519-2520, 6c #2583, #2596 | 20.00 | 20.00 |
| | | Complete booklet, #2596a | 20.00 | 20.00 |
| **2597** | A736 | 15p like #2550 | 2.00 | 1.00 |
| *a.* | | Booklet pane, #2588-2597 | 25.00 | 25.00 |
| | | Complete booklet, #2597a | 25.00 | 25.00 |

Nos. 2587a, 2596a, 2597a were made available to collectors unattached to the booklet cover.

Philippine Central Bank, 50th Anniv. A761

**1999, Jan. 3 Litho. *Perf. 14***

**2598** A761 6p multicolored 1.00 .40

Philippine Centennial — A762

Designs: a, Centennial emblem. b, Proclamation of Independence. c, Malolos Congress. d, Nov. 5th uprising. e, Cry of Santa Barbara Iloilo. f, Victory over colonial forces. g, Flag raising, Butuan City. h, Ratification of Malolos Constitution. i, Philippine Republic formed. j, Barasoain Church.

**1999, Jan. 11**

**2599** A762 6p Sheet of 10, #a.-j. 10.00 10.00

Scouting — A762a

Designs: No. 2599K, Girl Scout, boys planting tree. No. 2599L, Boy Scout, Girl Scout, flag, people representing various professions.

***Perf. 13½***

**1999, Jan. 16 Litho. Unwmk.**

| | | | | |
|---|---|---|---|---|
| **2599K** | A762a | 5p multicolored | 2.00 | .35 |
| **2599L** | A762a | 5p multicolored | 2.00 | .35 |

Nos. 2599K-2599L are dated 1995, are inscribed "THRIFT STAMP," and were valid for postage due to stamp shortage.

Dept. of Transportation and Communications, Cent. — A763

Emblem and: a, Ship. b, Jet. c, Control tower. d, Satellite dish, bus.
15p, Philpost Headquarters, truck, motorcycle on globe.

**1999, Jan. 20**
**2600** A763 6p Block of 4, #a.-d. 4.00 *3.00*

**Souvenir Sheet**

**2601** A763 15p multicolored 3.50 *3.00*

No. 2601 contains one 80x30mm stamp.

Filipino-American War, Cent. — A764

**1999, Feb. 4**
**2602** A764 5p multicolored .85 .35

Philippine Military Academy, Cent. A765

**1999-2001** ***Perf. 14***
**2603** A765 5p multicolored .90 .40
*a.* Small "P" in denomination ('01) 2.00 1.75

"P" in denomination is 1¾mm tall on No. 2603, 1½mm tall on No. 2603a.
Issue dates: No. 2603, 2/4/99. No. 2063a, 2001.

Birds — A766

#2604: a, Greater crested tern. b, Ruddy turnstone. c, Green-backed heron. d, Common tern.
#2605: a, Black-winged stilt. b, Asiatic dowitcher. c, Whimbrel. d, Reef heron.
#2606: a, Spotted greenshank. b, Tufted duck.

**1999** **Litho.** ***Perf. 14***
**2604** A766 5p Block of 4, #a.-d. 3.50 3.00
**2605** A766 5p Block of 4, #a.-d. 3.50 3.00

**Souvenir Sheets**

**2606** A766 8p Sheet of 2, #a.-b. 6.00 5.00
*c.* As #2606, diff. sheet margin, inscription 5.00 4.00

Issued: #2604-2606, 2/22; #2606c, 3/19.

No. 2606c contains inscription, emblem for Australia '99 World Stamp Expo.

**Heroes of the Revolution Type**

***Perf. 13½***

**1999, Mar. 12** **Litho.** **Unwmk.**

**Pink Background**

**2607** A736 5p like #2547 .60 .25

Manila Lions Club, 50th Anniv. A767

Design: Emblem, Francisco "Paquito" Ortigas, Jr., first president.

**1999, Mar. 20** ***Perf. 14***
**2608** A767 5p multicolored .75 .35

Philippine Orthopedic Assoc., 50th Anniv. — A768

**1999, Mar. 20**
**2609** A768 5p multicolored .75 .35

La Union Botanical Garden, San Fernando — A769

Designs: No. 2610, Entrance sign, birdhouse. No. 2611, Ticket booth at entrance.

**1999, Mar. 20**
**2610** 5p multicolored .70 .50
**2611** 5p multicolored .70 .50
*a.* A769 Pair, #2610-2611 2.00 2.00

Frogs — A770

#2612: a, Woodworth's frog. b, Giant Philippine frog. c, Gliding tree frog. d, Common forest frog.
#2613: a, Spiny tree frog. b, Truncate-toed chorus frog. c, Variable-backed frog.

**1999, Apr. 5**
**2612** A770 5p Block of 4, #a.-d. 3.00 2.50

**Sheet of 3**

**2613** A770 5p #a.-c. + label 6.00 5.00

Marine Life — A771

No. 2614: a, Sea squirt. b, Banded sea snake. c, Manta ray. d, Painted rock lobster.
No. 2615: a, Sea grapes. b, Branching coral. c, Sea urchin.

**1999, May 11** **Litho.** ***Perf. 14***
**2614** A771 5p Block of 4, #a.-d. 3.00 2.75

**Sheet of 3**

**2615** A771 5p #a.-c. + label 7.50 7.50

Juan F. Nakpil, Architect, Birth Cent. A772

**1999, May 25**
**2616** A772 5p multicolored .70 .40

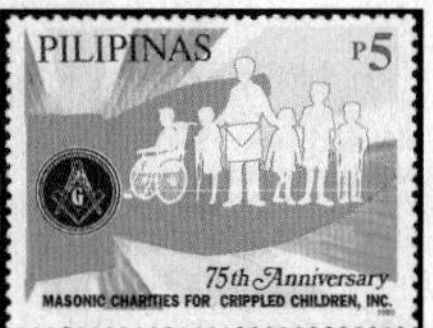


UPU, 125th Anniv. A773

Designs: 5p, Globe, boy writing letter. 15p, Globe, girl looking at stamp collection.

**1999, May 26** **Litho.** ***Perf. 14***
**2617** A773 5p multicolored .80 .40
**2618** A773 15p multicolored 2.50 1.00

Philippines-Thailand Diplomatic Relations, 50th Anniv. — A774

Orchids: 5p, 11p, Euanthe sanderiana, cattleya Queen Sirikit.

**1999, June 13** **Litho.** ***Perf. 14***
**2619** A774 5p multicolored .75 .35
**2620** A774 11p multicolored 1.75 .75

Order of flowers from top is reversed on 11p value.
Issued in sheets of 20 (10 of each denomination in two rows of 5, separated by a central gutter). Most sheets of 20 were cut in half through the central gutter.
See #2623-2624, 2640-2641, 2664-2666, 2719-2721, 2729-2731.

Masonic Charities for Crippled Children, Inc., 75th Anniv. A775

**1999, July 5**
**2621** A775 5p multicolored .65 .30

Production of Eberhard Faber "Mongol" Pencils, 150th Anniv. — A776

**1999, July 5**
**2622** A776 5p multicolored .75 .40

**Diplomatic Relations Type of 1999**

Philippines-Korea diplomatic relations, 50th anniv., flowers: 5p, 11p, Jasminum sambac, hibiscus synacus.

**1999, Aug. 9** **Litho.** ***Perf. 14***
**2623** A774 5p multicolored 1.00 .40
**2624** A774 11p multicolored 2.00 1.00

Order of flowers from top is reversed on 11p value.
issued in sheets of 20 (10 of each denomination in two rows of 5, separated by a central gutter). Most sheets of 20 were cut in half through the central gutter.

Community Chest, 50th Anniv. A777

**1999, Aug. 30**
**2625** A777 5p multicolored .80 .40

Philippine Bible Society, Cent. — A778

**1999, Aug. 30**
**2626** A778 5p multicolored .80 .40

PILIPINAS P5
1599 400Years 1999
St. Francis of Assisi Parish
SARIAYA, QUEZON

A779

**1999, Sept. 3**
**2627** A779 5p multicolored .80 .40

St. Francis of Assisi Parish, Sariaya, 400th anniv.

PILIPINAS P5
NATIONAL ANTHEM Centennial

National Anthem, Cent. A780

**1999, Sept. 3**
**2628** A780 5p multicolored .80 .40

**No. 2539b Overprinted in Silver "25th ANNIVERSARY IPPS"**

Souvenir Sheet

**1999, Sept. 24** **Litho.** ***Perf. 14***
**2629** A746 15p Sheet of 3, #a.-c., + 3 labels 6.00 6.00

Ovpt. in sheet margin has same inscription twice, "25th ANNIVERSARY INTERNATIONAL PHILIPPINE PHILATELIC SOCIETY 1974-99" and two society emblems.

Senate — A781

**1999, Oct. 15**
**2630** A781 5p multicolored .80 .40

A782

**1999, Oct. 20**
**2631** A782 5p multicolored .90 .45

New Building of Chiang Kai-shek College, Manila.

Issued in sheets of 10.

Tanza National Comprehensive High School, 50th Anniv. — A783

**1999, Oct. 24**
**2632** A783 5p multicolored .80 .40

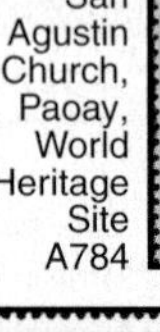

San Agustin Church, Paoay, World Heritage Site A784

Intl. Year of Older Persons A785

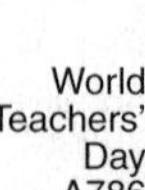

World Teachers' Day A786

**1999, Oct. 24**

| | | | | |
|---|---|---|---|---|
| **2633** A784 | 5p multicolored | | 1.00 | .50 |
| **2634** A785 | 11p multicolored | | 1.75 | .80 |
| **2635** A786 | 15p multicolored | | 2.50 | 1.50 |
| | *Nos. 2633-2635 (3)* | | 5.25 | 2.80 |

United Nations Day.

Christmas A787

**1999, Oct. 27**

**Color of Angel's Gown**

| | | | |
|---|---|---|---|
| **2636** A787 | 5p red violet | 1.00 | .40 |
| **2637** A787 | 11p yellow | 2.00 | .60 |
| **2638** A787 | 13p blue | 2.25 | .80 |
| **2639** A787 | 15p green | 2.75 | 1.00 |
| *a.* | Sheet of 4, #2636-2639 | 8.00 | 8.00 |
| | *Nos. 2636-2639 (4)* | 8.00 | 2.80 |

Nos. 2636-2639 each issued in sheets of 10 stamps with two central labels.

**Diplomatic Relations Type of 1999**

Philippines-Canada diplomatic relations, 50th anniv., mammals: 5p, 15p, Tamaraw, polar bear.

**1999, Nov. 15** *Perf. 14*

| | | | |
|---|---|---|---|
| **2640** A774 | 5p multi | 1.00 | .50 |
| **2641** A774 | 15p multi | 2.75 | 1.00 |

Order of mammals from top is reversed on 15p value.

Issued in sheets of 20 (10 of each denomination in two rows of 5, separated by a central gutter). Most sheets of 20 were cut in half through central gutter.

Renovation of Araneta Coliseum A788

**1999, Nov. 19** **Litho.**
**2642** A788 5p multicolored 1.00 .40

A789

**1999, Nov. 19** **Color of Sky**

| | | | |
|---|---|---|---|
| **2643** A789 | 5p dark blue | .75 | .40 |
| **2644** A789 | 11p blue green | 2.25 | .60 |

3rd ASEAN Informal Summit.

A790

Sculptures: No. 2645, Kristo, by Arturo Luz. 11p, Homage to Dodgie Laurel, by J. Elizalde Navarro. 13p, Hilojan, by Napoleon Abueva. No. 2648, Mother and Child, by Abueva.

No. 2649: a, 5p, Mother's Revenge, by José Rizal, horiz. b, 15p, El Ermitano, by Rizal, horiz.

**1999, Nov. 29**

| | | | |
|---|---|---|---|
| **2645** A790 | 5p multi | 1.00 | .25 |
| **2646** A790 | 11p multi | 2.00 | .45 |
| **2647** A790 | 13p multi | 2.25 | .55 |
| **2648** A790 | 15p multi | 2.75 | .65 |
| | *Nos. 2645-2648 (4)* | 8.00 | 1.90 |

**Souvenir Sheet**

**2649** A790 Sheet of 2, #a.-b. 5.00 4.00

Natl. Stamp Collecting Month.

New Year 2000 (Year of the Dragon) A791

5p, Dragon in water. 11p, Dragon in sky.

**1999, Dec. 1** *Perf. 14*

| | | | |
|---|---|---|---|
| **2650** A791 | 5p multicolored | 1.25 | .70 |
| **2651** A791 | 11p multicolored | 2.75 | 1.30 |
| *a.* | Sheet of 2, #2650-2651 | 3.00 | 3.00 |
| *b.* | As "a," imperf. | 3.00 | 3.00 |

Battle of Tirad Pass, Cent. A792

**1999, Dec. 2** *Perf. 14*
**2652** A792 5p multicolored .80 .40

Orchids — A793

No. 2653: a, Paphiopedilum urbanianum. b, Phalaenopsis schilleriana. c, Dendrobium amethystoglossum. d, Paphiopedilum barbatum.

No. 2654, horiz.: a, Paphiopedilum haynaldianum. b, Phalaenopsis stuartiana. c, Trichoglottis brachiata. d, Ceratostylis rubra.

**1999, Dec. 3** **Litho.**
**2653** A793 5p Block of 4, #a.-d. 4.00 3.50

**Souvenir Sheet**

**2654** A793 5p Sheet of 4, #a.-d. 5.00 5.00

Battle of San Mateo, Cent. A794

**1999, Dec. 19**
**2655** A794 5p multicolored .80 .40

People Power — A795

People and: a, Tank. b, Tower. c, Crucifix.

**1999, Dec. 31**
**2656** A795 5p Strip of 3, #a.-c. 3.50 3.00

Natl. Commission on the Role of Filipino Women — A796

**2000, Jan. 7** **Litho.** *Perf. 14*
**2657** A796 5p multicolored .80 .40

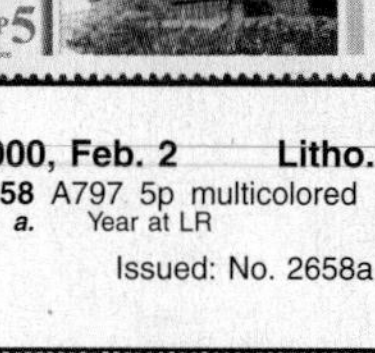

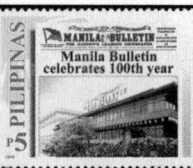


Manila Bulletin, Cent. A797

**2000, Feb. 2** **Litho.** *Perf. 14*

| | | | |
|---|---|---|---|
| **2658** A797 | 5p multicolored | .75 | .40 |
| *a.* | Year at LR | 1.00 | .40 |

Issued: No. 2658a, 6/7.

La Union Province, 150th Anniv. — A798

Arms of province and: a, Sailboat, golfer. b, Tractor, worker, building. c, Building, flagpole. d, Airplane, ship, telephone tower, people on telephone, computer.

**2000, Mar. 2**
**2659** A798 5p Block of 4, #a.-d. 2.50 2.00

Civil Service Commission, Cent. — A799

**2000, Mar. 20**
**2660** A799 5p multicolored .60 .30

Millennium — A800

Designs: a, Golden Garuda of Palawan. b, First sunrise of the millennium, Pusan Point. c, Golden Tara of Agusan.

**2000, Mar. 31**
**2661** A800 5p Strip of 3, #a.-c. 3.50 3.00

GMA Radio and Television Network, 50th Anniv. A802

**2000, Mar. 1** **Litho.** *Perf. 14*
**2662** A802 5p multicolored .60 .40

Philippine Presidents — A803

No. 2662A: b, Manuel Roxas. c, Elpidio Quirino. No. 2663: a, Presidential seal. b, Joseph Ejercito Estrada. c, Fidel V. Ramos. d, Corazon C. Aquino. e, Ferdinand E. Marcos. f, Diosdado Macapagal. g, Carlos P. Garcia. h, Ramon Magsaysay. i, Elpidio Quirino. j, Manuel Roxas.

**2000** *Perf. 13½*

**2662A** A803 Pair 1.25 1.00
*b.-c.* 5p Any single .40 .25
**2663** Block of 10 7.50 6.00
*a.-j.* A803 5p Any single .60 .25

Nos. 2662b-2662c have presidential seal but lack blue lines at bottom. No. 2663a has denomination at left. Nos. 2663b-2663j have small Presidential seal at bottom.

Issued: No. 2662A, 2/6. No. 2663, 3/16.

See Type A828 for stamps showing Presidential seal with colored background.

See Nos. 2672-2676, 2786.

### Diplomatic Relations Type of 1999

5p, Sarimanok, Great Wall of China. 11p, Phoenix, Banaue rice terraces.

No. 2666: a, 5p, Great Wall, horiz. b, 11p, Rice terraces, horiz.

**2000, May 8** *Perf. 14*

**2664-2665** A774 Set of 2 2.50 1.80

**Souvenir Sheet**

**2666** A774 Sheet of 2, #a-b 3.50 3.00

Issued in sheets of 20 (10 of each denomination in two rows of 5, separated by a central gutter). Most sheets of 20 were cut in half through central gutter.

St. Thomas Aquinas Parish, Mangaldan, 400th Anniv. A805

**2000, June 1**

**2667** A805 5p multicolored .60 .45

Battle Centenaries — A806

Battles in Philippine Insurrection: #2668, Mabitac. #2669, Paye, vert. #2670, Makahambus Hill, vert. #2671, Pulang Lupa.

**2000, June 19**

**2668-2671** A806 5p Set of 4 2.50 1.60

### Presidents Type of 2000 Redrawn

No. 2672: a, Presidential seal. b, Joseph Ejercito Estrada. c, Fidel V. Ramos. d, Corazon C. Aquino. e, Ferdinand E. Marcos. f, Diosdado Macapagal. g, Carlos P. Garcia. h, Ramon Magsaysay. i, Elpidio Quirino. j, Manuel Roxas.

No. 2673: a, Magsaysay. b, Garcia.

No. 2674: a, Macapagal. b, Marcos.

No. 2675: a, Aquino. b, Ramos.

No. 2676: a, Estrada. b, Presidential seal.

**2000** **Litho.** *Perf. 13½*

**Blue Lines at Bottom**

**2672** Block of 10 *9.50 9.50*
*a.-j.* A803 5p Any single *.75 .40*
**2673** Pair *3.75 1.80*
*a.-b.* A803 10p Any single *1.25 .60*
**2674** Pair *4.25 3.00*
*a.-b.* A803 11p Any single *1.50 .70*
**2675** Pair *4.00 2.00*
*a.-b.* A803 13p Any single *1.25 .80*
**2676** Pair *5.50 3.50*
*a.-b.* A803 15p Any single *1.75 1.00*
*Nos. 2672-2676 (5) 27.00 19.80*

Issued: No. 2672, 7/3; Nos. 2673-2674, 8/4. Nos. 2675-2676, 6/19.

No. 2672a has denomination at R, while No. 2663a has denomination at L. Nos. 2672b-2672j have no presidential seal, while Nos. 2662Ab-2662Ac, 2663b-2663j have seal.

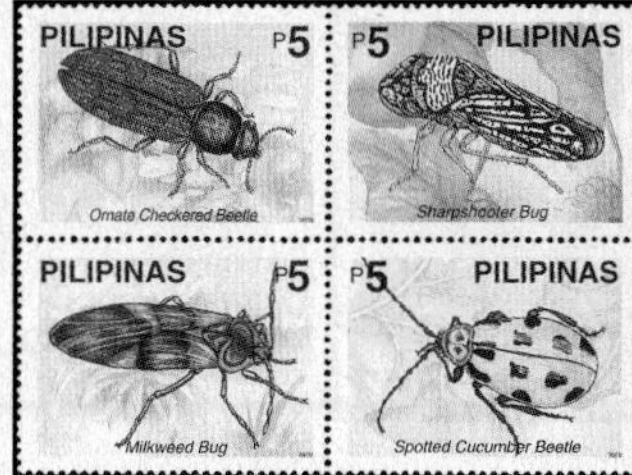


Insects — A807

No. 2677: a, Ornate checkered beetle. b, Sharpshooter bug. c, Milkweed bug. d, Spotted cucumber beetle.

No. 2678: a, Green June beetle. b, Convergent ladybird. c, Eastern Hercules beetle. d, Harlequin cabbage bug.

**2000, July 21** *Perf. 14*

**2677** A807 5p Block of 4, #a-d 4.00 3.00
*e.* Souevnir sheet, #2677 6.00 6.00
**2678** A807 5p Block of 4, #a-d 4.00 3.50
*e.* Souevnir sheet, #2678 6.00 6.00

Occupational Health Nurses Association, 50th Anniv. — A808

**2000, Aug. 30**

**2679** A808 5p multicolored .85 .40

Diocese of Lucena, 50th Anniv. A809

**2000. Aug. 30**

**2680** A809 5p multicolored .65 .40

Millennium — A810

Boats: a, Balanghai. b, Vinta. c, Caracoa.

**2000, Sept. 21**

**2681** A810 Horiz. strip of 3 3.00 3.00
*a.-c.* 5p Any single *.75 .50*

Equitable PCI Bank, 50th Anniv. A811

**2000, Sept. 26**

**2682** A811 5p multicolored .65 .40

Year of the Overseas Filipino Worker A812

**2000, Sept. 29** **Litho.**

**2683** A812 5p multicolored .65 .50

2000 Olympics, Sydney — A813

No. 2684: a, Running. b, Archery. c, Shooting. d, Diving.

No. 2685, horiz.: a, Boxing. b, Equestrian. c, Rowing. d, Taekwondo.

**2000, Sept. 30**

**2684** A813 5p Block of 4, #a-d 3.50 3.00

**Souvenir Sheet**

**2685** A813 5p Sheet of 4, #a-d 5.00 5.00

Teresian Association in the Philippines, 50th Anniv. A814

**2000, Oct. 10**

**2686** A814 5p multicolored .65 .50

House of Representatives A815

**2000, Oct. 15** *Perf. 14*

**2687** A815 5p multicolored .65 .45

Marine Corps, 50th Anniv. A816

**2000, Oct. 18**

**2688** A816 5p multicolored .65 .40

**Souvenir Sheet**

Postal Service, Cent. (in 1998) — A817

**2000, Nov. 6**

**2689** A817 15p multicolored 3.00 3.00

Clothing Exhibit at Metropolitan Museum of Manila — A818

No. 2690, 5p: a, Kalinga / Gaddang cotton loincloth. b, Portrait of Leticia Jimenez, by unknown artist.

No. 2691, 5p, horiz.: a, B'laan female upper garment. b, T'boli T'nalak abaca cloth.

No. 2692: a, 5p, Portrait of Teodora Devera Ygnacio, by Justiniano Asunción. b, 15p, Detail of Tawsug silk sash.

**2000, Nov. 15** **Pairs, #a-b**

**2690-2691** A818 Set of 2 4.00 3.00
#2690a-b, 2691a-b, any single .60 .40

**Souvenir Sheet**

**2692** A818 Sheet of 2, #a-b 4.50 4.00

Natl. Stamp Collecting Month A819

Designs: 5p, Portrait of an Unkown Lady, by Juan Luna, vert. 11p, Nude, by José Joya. 13p, Lotus Odalisque, by Rodolfo Paras-Perez. No. 2696, 15p, Untitled Nude, by Fernando Amorsolo.

No. 2697, The Memorial, by Cesar Legaspi.

**2000, Nov. 20** *Perf. 14*

**2693-2696** A819 Set of 4 6.50 4.50

**Souvenir Sheet**

**2697** A819 15p multi 4.00 4.00

No. 2697 contains one 80x29 stamp and label.

Christmas A820

Angels: No. 2698, 5p, In pink robe, with bouquet of flowers. No. 2699, 5p, As #2698, with Holy Year 2000 emblem and inscription. 11p, In green robe. 13p, In orange robe. 15p, In red robe, with garland of flowers.

**2000, Nov. 22** **Litho.**

**2698-2702** A820 Set of 5 6.00 4.00

APO Philatelic Society, 50th Anniv. — A821

Emblem and stamps: No. 2703, 5p, #620 (yellow background). No. 2704, 5p, #639 (light blue background), horiz. No. 2705, 5p, #850 (dull green background). No. 2706, 5p, #B21 (pink background), horiz.

**2000, Nov. 23**

**2703-2706** A821 Set of 4 7.25 4.00

**No. 1806 Handstamp Surcharged in Red**

*Perf. 13x13½*

**2000, Nov. 24 Litho. Wmk.**
**2706A** A469 5p on 3.60p multi *7.50 7.50*

Nine varieties of the surcharge on No. 2706A exist.

New Year 2001 (Year of the Snake) A822

Snakes with inscription in: 5p, Tagalog. 11p, English.

**2000, Dec. 20 Unwmk. *Perf. 14***
**2707-2708** A822 Set of 2 3.50 2.00
*2708a* Souvenir sheet, #2707-2708 + 2 labels 5.00 5.00

No. 2708a exists imperf. Value, $5.

Millennium A823

No. 2709: a, Trade and progress. b, Education and knowledge. c, Communication and information.

**2000, Dec. 28**
**2709** Horiz. strip of 3 4.00 3.00
*a.-c.* A823 5p Any single .80 .50

Bank of the Philippine Islands, 150th Anniv. A824

**2001, Jan. 30 Litho.**
**2710** A824 5p multicolored .60 .40

Hong Kong 2001 Stamp Exhibition A825

Designs: No. 2711a, 5p, No. 2712, 11p, Tamaraw. No. 2711b, 5p, No. 2713, 11p, Agila. No. 2711c, 5p, No. 2714, 11p, Tarsier. No. 2711d, 5p, No. 2715, 11p, Talisman Cove orchid. No. 2711e, 5p, No. 2716, 11p, Pawikan.

**2001, Feb. 1**
**2711** Horiz. strip of 5 4.00 4.00
*a.-e.* A825 5p Any single .65 .50

**Souvenir Sheets**

**2712-2716** A825 Set of 5 15.00 12.50
*2713a* Ovptd. in margin in red 5.00 5.00
*2715a* Ovptd. in margin in red 5.00 5.00

Nos. 2712-2716 have show emblem on sheet margin instead of on stamp.

Issued: Nos. 2713a, 2715a, 6/30/01. Overprint in margin on Nos. 2713a, 2715a has Chinese inscriptions and English text "PHILIPPINE-CHINESE PHILATELIC SOCIETY / 1951 GOLDEN JUBILEE 2001."

Gen. Paciano Rizal (1851-1930) A826

**2001, Mar. 7 Litho. *Perf. 14***
**2717** A826 5p multicolored .60 .40

San Beda College, Cent. A827

**2001, Mar. 9**
**2718** A827 5p multicolored .60 .40

**Diplomatic Relations Type of 1999**

Philippines-Vatican City diplomatic relations, 50th anniv., main altars at: 5p, St. Peter's Basilica, Vatican City. No. 2720, 15p, San Agustin Church, Manila.

No. 2721: a, Adam, from Creation of Adam, by Michelangelo. b, God, from Creation of Adam.

**2001, Mar. 14**
**2719-2720** A774 Set of 2 3.25 2.00

**Souvenir Sheet**

**2721** A774 15p Sheet of 2, #a-b 5.00 5.00

Nos. 2719-2720 issued in sheets of 20 (10 of each denomination in two rows of 5, separated by a central gutter). Most sheets of 20 were cut in half through central gutter.

Presidential Seal With Colored Background — A828

**2001, Apr. 5 *Perf. 13¾***

**Background Colors**

**2722** A828 5p yellow .40 .25
**2723** A828 15p blue 1.50 .45

Stamps of the same denomination showing the Presidential seal with white backgrounds are listed as Nos. 2663a, 2672a and 2676b.

See Nos. 2746-2748. For surcharges, see Nos. 2834-2836. For overprints, see Nos. 2865-2866.

Tourist Spots A829

No. 2724: a, El Nido, Palawan Province. b, Vigan House, Ilocos Sur Province. c, Boracay, Aklan Province. d, Chocolate Hills, Bohol Province.

15p, Banaue Rice Terraces, Ifugao Province.

**2000, Apr. 14 *Perf. 14***
**2724** Horiz. strip of 4 2.50 2.50
*a.-d.* A829 5p Any single .50 .40

**Souvenir Sheet**

**2725** A829 15p multi 3.50 3.00

No. 2725 contains one 80x30mm stamp.

No. 2725 exists with washed-out colors and a larger year date.

Canonical Coronation of Our Lady of Manaoag, 75th Anniv. — A830

**2001, Apr. 22**
**2726** A830 5p multicolored .60 .40

Pres. Gloria Macapagal-Arroyo A831

Pres. Macapagal-Arroyo: No. 2727, 5p, Waving. No. 2728, 5p, Taking oath of office.

**2001, Apr. 29**
**2727-2728** A831 Set of 2 1.50 1.00

**Diplomatic Relations Type of 1999**

Philippines-Australia diplomatic relations, landmarks: 5p, Nos. 2730-2731, 13p, Sydney Opera House, Cultural Center of the Philippines. No. 2731 is horiz.

**2001, May 21**
**2729-2730** A774 Set of 2 2.75 1.00

**Souvenir Sheet**

**2731** A774 13p multi 3.50 3.50

No. 2731 contains one 80x30mm stamp.

Supreme Court, Cent. A832

**2001, May 31**
**2732** A832 5p multicolored .70 .40

Silliman University, Dumaguete City, Cent. A833

**2001, June 1**
**2733** A833 5p multicolored .65 .40

Philippine Normal University, Cent. A834

**2001, June 1**
**2734** A834 5p multicolored .65 .40

Joaquin J. Ortega (1870-1943), First Civil Governor of La Union Province — A835

**2001, July 12**
**2735** A835 5p multicolored .60 .40

Eugenio Lopez (1901-75), Businessman A836

**2001, July 12**
**2736** A836 5p multicolored .60 .40

Illustrations from Boxer Codex, c. 1590 — A837

No. 2737: a, Visayan couple. b, Tagalog couple. c, Moros of Luzon (multicolored frame). d, Moros of Luzon (blue frame).

No. 2738: a, Pintados (denomination at left). b, Pintados (denomination at right). c, Cagayan female. d, Zambal.

**2001, Aug. 1**
**2737** A837 5p Block of 4, #a-d 2.50 2.00

**Souvenir Sheet**

**2738** A837 5p Sheet of 4, #a-d 3.00 3.00
*e.* Sheet of 4, #a-d, with Phila Nippon '01 margin 3.00 3.00

Arrival of American Educators (Thomasites), Cent. — A838

Designs: 5p, Thomasite teachers, US transport ship Thomas. 15p, Philippine students.

**2001, Aug. 23**
**2739-2740** A838 Set of 2 2.40 1.40



Technological University of the Philippines, Cent. — A839

**2001, Aug. 20 Litho. *Perf. 14***
**2741** A839 5p multicolored .60 .40

National Museum of the Philippines, Cent. — A840

**2001, Sept. 3**
2742 A840 5p multicolored .60 .40

Lands Management Bureau, Cent. — A841

**2001, Sept. 17**
2743 A841 5p multicolored .60 .40

Colegio de San Jose and San Jose Seminary, 400th Anniv. — A842

**2001, Oct. 1**
2744 A842 5p multicolored .60 .40

Makati City Financial District A843

**2001, Oct. 1**
2745 A843 5p multicolored .60 .40

**Presidential Seal With Colored Background Type of 2001**

**2001, Oct. 5** *Perf. 13¾*

**Background Colors**

2746 A828 10p green .80 .35
2747 A828 11p pink 1.00 .40
2748 A828 13p gray 1.20 .45
*Nos. 2746-2748 (3)* 3.00 1.20

Musical Instruments — A844

No. 2749: a, Trumpet. b, Tuba. c, French horn. d, Trombone.
No. 2750, vert.: a, Bass drum. b, Clarinet, oboe. c, Xylophone. d, Sousaphone.

**2001, Oct. 8** *Perf. 14*
2749 A844 5p Block of 4, #a-d 2.50 2.00

**Souvenir Sheet**

2750 A844 5p Sheet of 4, #a-d 4.00 4.00

Malampaya Deep Water Gas Power Project A845

Frame colors: 5p, Silver. 15p, Gold.

**2001, Oct. 16**
2751-2752 A845 Set of 2 3.00 1.75

Intl. Volunteers Year A846

**2001, Oct. 24**
2753 A846 5p multicolored .70 .40

Year of Dialogue Among Civilizations A847

**2001, Oct. 24**
2754 A847 15p multicolored 1.60 .80

Christmas A848

Designs: 5p, Herald Angels. 11p, Kumukutikutitap. 13p, Pasko ni Bitoy. 15p, Pasko na naman.

**2001, Oct. 30**
2755-2758 A848 Set of 4 5.00 2.50

Philippines — Switzerland Relations, 150th Anniv. — A849

Monument statues by Richard Kissling: 5p, William Tell. No. 2760, 15p, Jose P. Rizal.
No. 2761, 15p, Mayon Volcano, Philippines, and Matterhorn, Switzerland.

**2001, Nov. 26**
2759-2760 A849 Set of 2 2.75 1.50

**Souvenir Sheet**

2761 A849 15p multicolored 3.00 2.50

No. 2761 contains one 79x29mm stamp. Nos. 2759-2760 issued in sheets of 20 (10 of each denomination in two rows of 5, separated by a central gutter). Most sheets of 20 were cut in half through central gutter.

Drawings of Manila Inhabitants, c. 1840 — A850

Designs: 17p, Woman with hat, man with green pants. 21p, Woman with veil, man with brown pants. 22p, Man, woman at mortar and pestle.

**2001, Dec. 1** *Perf. 13¾*

**Inscribed "2001"**

2762 A850 17p multicolored 1.75 .60
*a.* Inscribed "2002" 2.00 .60
*b.* Inscribed "2003" 4.00 2.00
2763 A850 21p multicolored 2.10 .75
*a.* Inscribed "2002" 2.25 .75
2764 A850 22p multicolored 2.40 .85
*a.* Inscribed "2002" 2.40 .90
*Nos. 2762-2764 (3)* 6.25 2.20

See No. 2779.

Solicitor General, Cent. — A851

**2001, Dec. 7** *Perf. 14*
2765 A851 5p multicolored .60 .40

Natl. Stamp Collecting Month A852

Art: 5p, PUJ, by Antonio Austria. 17p, Hesus Nazareno, by Angelito Antonio. 21p, Three Women with Basket, by Anita Magsaysay-Ho, vert. No. 2769, 22p, Church with Yellow Background, by Mauro "Malang" Santos, vert.
No. 2770, 22p, Komedya ng Pakil, by Danilo Dalena.

**2001, Dec. 7** **Litho.**
2766-2769 A852 Set of 4 7.50 4.00

**Souvenir Sheet**

2770 A852 22p multicolored 3.50 3.50

No. 2770 contains one 79x29mm stamp.

New Year 2002 (Year of the Horse) A853

Horse color: 5p, Red. 17p, White.

**2001, Dec. 14** *Perf. 14*
2771-2772 A853 Set of 2 3.25 1.75
*2772a* Souvenir sheet, #2771-2772, + 2 labels 5.00 5.00

No. 2772a exists imperf. Value $5.

Josemaria Escrivá (1902-75), Founder of Opus Dei — A854

**2002, Jan. 9**
2773 A854 5p multicolored .65 .40

World Heritage Sites A855

Vigan City sites: 5p, St. Paul's Metropolitan Cathedral. 22p, Calle Crisologo.

**2002, Jan. 22**
2774-2775 A855 Set of 2 4.00 2.50

Salvador Z. Araneta, Statesman, Birth Cent. — A856

**2002, Jan. 31**
2776 A856 5p multicolored .60 .40

Customs Service, Cent. A857

**2002, Feb. 1**
2777 A857 5p multicolored 1.00 .50

Valentine's Day — A858

No. 2778: a, Envelope. b, Man and woman. c, Cat and dog. d, Balloon.

**2002, Feb. 8**
2778 A858 5p Block of 4, #a-d 3.00 2.50

**Drawings of Manila Inhabitants Type of 2001**

**2002, Mar. 1** **Litho.** *Perf. 13¾*

**Inscribed "2002"**

2779 A850 5p Man, woman on horses .50 .25
*a.* Inscribed "2003" .30 .25

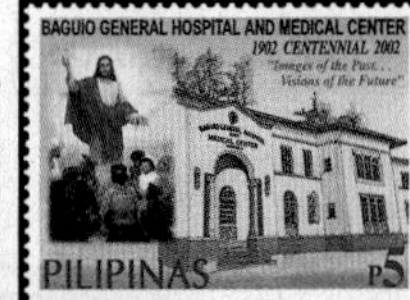

Baguio General Hospital and Medical Center, Cent. A859

**2002, Mar. 22** *Perf. 14*
2780 A859 5p multicolored .65 .40

Beatification of Blessed Pedro Calungsod A860

Designs: 5p, Calungsod with palm frond. 22p, Map of Guam, ship, Calungsod with cross.

**2002, Apr. 2** *Perf. 14*
2781 A860 5p multicolored .85 .50

**Size: 102x72mm**
***Imperf***

**2782** A860 22p multicolored 3.25 3.00

Negros Occidental High School, Cent. — A861

**2002, Apr. 12** ***Perf. 14***

**2783** A861 5p multicolored .60 .40

La Consolacion College, Manila, Cent. A862

**2002, Apr. 12**

**2784** A862 5p multicolored .60 .40

Vesak Day — A863

**2002, May 26**

**2785** A863 5p multicolored .90 .50

**Presidents Type of 2000 Redrawn Without Years of Service**

No. 2786: a, Gloria Macapagal-Arroyo. b, Joseph Ejercito Estrada. c, Fidel V. Ramos. d, Corazon C. Aquino. e, Ferdinand E. Marcos. f, Diosdado Macapagal. g, Carlos P. Garcia. h, Ramon Magsaysay. i, Elpidio Quirino. j, Manuel Roxas.

**2002, June 12** ***Perf. 13½***

**Without Presidential Seal**

**Blue Lines at Bottom**

**2786** Block of 10 6.00 6.00
*a.-j.* A803 5p Any single .40 .30

Cavite National High School, Cent. A864

**2002, June 19** ***Perf. 14***

**2787** A864 5p multicolored .60 .40

Mangroves A865

Fish A866

Fish A867

Hands and Small Fish A868

No. 2792: a, Monitors in boats at marine sanctuary. b, Mangrove reforestation. c, Monitors checking reefs. d, Seaweed farming.

**Unwmk.**

**2002, June 24 Litho.** ***Perf. 14***

**2788** A865 5p multicolored .85 .50
**2789** A866 5p multicolored .85 .50
**2790** A867 5p multicolored .85 .50
**2791** A868 5p multicolored .85 .50
*Nos. 2788-2791 (4)* 3.40 2.00

**Souvenir Sheet**

**2792** A865 5p Sheet of 4, #a-d 3.50 3.00

Coastal resources conservation.

Iglesia Filipina Independiente, Cent. — A869

**2002, July 4**

**2793** A869 5p multicolored .60 .40

**Souvenir Sheet**

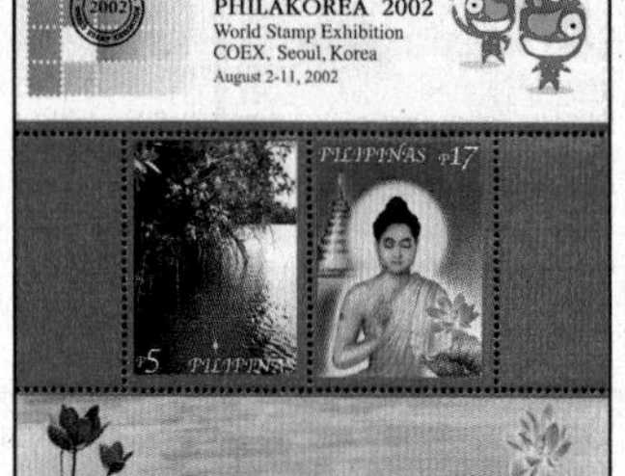


Philakorea 2002 World Stamp Exhibition, Seoul — A870

No. 2794: a, 5p, Mangrove. b, 17p, Buddhist, temple and flower.

**2002, Aug. 2** **Unwmk.**

**2794** A870 Sheet of 2, #a-b 3.50 3.50

No. 2794 exists imperf. with changed background color. Value $8.50.

No. 2210 Surcharged

**Method & Perf. as Before**

**2002, Aug. 15** **Wmk. 391**

**2795** A610 3p on 60s multi .50 .30

Telecommunications Officials Meetings, Manila — A870a

**2002, Aug. 22 Litho.** ***Perf. 14***

**2795A** A870a 5p multicolored .60 .40

Second Telecommunications Ministerial Meeting, Third ASEAN Telecommunications Senior Officials Meeting, Eighth ASEAN Telecommunications Regulators Council Meeting.

Marikina, Shoe Capital of the Philippines A871

**Unwmk.**

**2002, Oct. 15 Litho.** ***Perf. 14***

**2796** A871 5p multicolored .60 .40

**Souvenir Sheet**

Intl. Year of Mountains — A872

**2002, Oct. 28**

**2797** A872 22p multicolored 2.50 2.50

Christmas — A873

Various holiday foods: 5p, 17p, 21p, 22p.

**2002, Nov. 5**

**2798-2801** A873 Set of 4 7.00 3.25

Stamp Collecting Month A874

Designs: 5p, Gerardo de Leon (1913-81), movie director. 17p, Francisca Reyes Aquino (1899-1983), founder of Philippine Folk Dance Society. 21p, Pablo S. Antonio (1901-75), architect. No. 2805, 22p, Jose Garcia Villa (1912-97), writer.

No. 2806, 22p, Honorata de la Rama (1902-91), singer and actress.

**2002, Nov. 2** ***Perf. 14***

**2802-2805** A874 Set of 4 6.50 4.00

**Size: 99x74mm**
***Imperf***

**2806** A874 22p multicolored 2.75 2.50

First Circumnavigation of the World, 480th Anniv. — A875

No. 2807 — Ship and: a, Antonio Pigafetta. b, Ferdinand Magellan. c, King Charles I of Spain. d, Sebastian Elcano.

22p, World Map and King Charles I of Spain.

**2002, Nov. 11** ***Perf. 14***

**2807** A875 5p Vert. strip of 4, #a-d 3.00 3.00

**Size: 104x85mm**
***Imperf***

**2808** A875 22p multicolored 3.50 3.50

Fourth World Meeting of Families — A876

Designs: 5p, Sculpture of Holy Family. 11p, Family, crucifix, Holy Spirit.

**2002, Nov. 23** ***Perf. 14***

**2809-2810** A876 Set of 2 1.65 1.00

New Year 2003 (Year of the Ram) A877

Ram facing: 5p, Left. 17p, Right.

**2002, Dec. 1**

**2811-2812** A877 Set of 2 3.25 1.75
*a.* Souvenir sheet, #2811-2812 + 2 labels 5.00 5.00

No. 2812a exists imperf. Value, $5.

Lyceum of the Philippines, 50th Anniv. — A878

**2002, Dec. 5** ***Perf. 14***

**2813** A878 5p multicolored .60 .40

Orchids — A879

No. 2814: a, Luisia teretifolia. b, Dendrobium victoria-reginae, horiz. c, Gedorum densiflorum. d, Nervilia plicata, horiz.
22p, Grammatophyllum scriptum, horiz.

**2002, Dec. 19** ***Perf. 14***
**2814** A879 5p Block of 4, #a-d 3.50 2.75

**Souvenir Sheet**
***Imperf***

**2815** A879 22p multicolored 3.50 3.00

No. 2815 contains one 69x40mm stamp.
No. 2814 was reprinted with a larger "2002" date. Value, block of 4, $8.50.

La Union National High School, Cent. A880

**2003, Jan. 22** ***Perf. 14***
**2816** A880 5p multicolored .50 .40

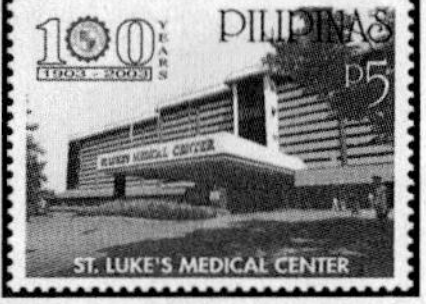

St. Luke's Medical Center, Cathedral Heights, Cent. A881

**2003, Jan. 23**
**2817** A881 5p multicolored .50 .40

Far Eastern University, 75th Anniv. A882

**2003, Jan. 28**
**2818** A882 5p multicolored .50 .40

Manila Electric Railroad and Light Company, Cent. A883

**2003, Jan. 31**
**2819** A883 5p multicolored .50 .40

St. Valentine's Day — A884

Mailman and: 5p, Heart-shaped strawberry. 17p, Hearts and mountains. 21p, Hearts and clouds. 22p, Butterflies and heart-shaped flowers.

**2003, Feb. 11**
**2820-2823** A884 Set of 4 7.50 4.00

**Souvenir Sheets**

Summer Institute of Linguistics, 50th Anniv. in Philippines — A885

No. 2824: a, 5p, Yakan weaving. b, 6p, Ifugao weaving. c, 5p, Kagayanen weaving. d, Bagobo Abaca weaving.
No. 2825, 11p: a, Ayta bow and arrows. b, Ibatan baskets. c, Palawano gong. d, Mindanao instruments.
No. 2826: a, 17p, Tboli cross-stitch. b, 5p, Aklanon Piña weaving. c, Kalinga weaving. d, Manobo beadwork.

**2003, Feb. 28** **Litho.**
**Sheets of 4, #a-d**

**2824-2826** A885 Set of 3 18.00 18.00

Intl. Decade of the World's Indigenous People.

Arrival of Japanese Workers for Construction of Kennon Road, Cent. A886

**2003, Feb. 20** ***Perf. 14***
**2827** A886 5p multi .50 .40

National Heroes A887

Designs: No. 2828, 6p, Apolinario Mabini (1864-1903), independence advocate. No. 2829, 6p, Luciano San Miguel (1875-1903), military leader.

**2003, May 13** **Litho.** ***Perf. 14***
**2828-2829** A887 Set of 2 1.40 .80

Orchids — A888

Designs (no flower names shown): 6p, Dendrobium uniflorum. 9p, Paphiopedilum urbanianum. 17p, Epigeneium lyonii. 21p, Thrixspermum subulatum.

**2003, May 16** ***Perf. 14½, 13¾ (9p)***

| | | | | |
|---|---|---|---|---|
| **2830** | A888 6p multi | | .55 | .25 |
| **2831** | A888 9p multi | | .80 | .35 |
| **2832** | A888 17p multi | | 1.85 | .70 |
| **2833** | A888 21p multi | | 2.00 | .85 |
| | *Nos. 2830-2833 (4)* | | 5.20 | 2.15 |

See Nos. 2849-2853, 2904-2912 for stamps with flower names.

No. 2722 Surcharged in Black or Red

**2003** ***Perf. 13¾***

| | | | |
|---|---|---|---|
| **2834** | A828 1p on 5p multi | .35 | .25 |
| **2835** | A828 1p on 5p multi (R) | .30 | .25 |
| **2836** | A828 6p on 5p multi | .50 | .25 |
| | *Nos. 2834-2836 (3)* | 1.15 | .75 |

Issued: Nos. 2834-2835, 5/19; No. 2836, 6/4.

Philippine Medical Association, Cent. — A889

**2003, May 21** ***Perf. 14***
**2837** A889 6p multi .65 .40

Rural Banking, 50th Anniv. — A890

**2003, May 22**
**2838** A890 6p multi .60 .40

Mountains — A891

No. 2839: a, Mt. Makiling. b, Mt. Kanlaon. c, Mt. Kitanglad. d, Mt. Mating-oy.
No. 2840: a, Mt. Iraya. b, Mt. Hibok-Hibok. c, Mt. Apo. d, Mt. Santo Tomas.

**2003, June 16**
**2839** A891 6p Block of 4, #a-d 3.00 2.50

**Souvenir Sheet**

**2840** A891 6p Sheet of 4, #a-d 4.00 4.00

Chinese Roots of José Rizal A892

Designs: 6p, Rizal Monument, Rizal Park, Jinjiang, People's Republic of China, vert. 17p, Rizal and Pagoda, Jinjiang.

**2003, June 19**
**2841-2842** A892 Set of 2 2.50 1.50

Waterfalls — A893

No. 2843: a, Maria Cristina Falls. b, Katibawasan Falls. c, Bagongbong Falls. d, Pagsanjan Falls.
No. 2844: a, Casiawan Falls. b, Pangi Falls. c, Tinago Falls. d, Kipot Twin Falls.

**2003, June 27**
**2843** A893 6p Block of 4, #a-d 3.00 2.50

**Souvenir Sheet**

**2844** A893 6p Sheet of 4, #a-d 4.00 3.50

Philippine — Spanish Friendship Day — A894

Designs: 6p, Poster for Madoura Exhibit, by Pablo Picasso. 22p, Flashback, by José T. Joya.

**2003, June 30**
**2845-2846** A894 Set of 2 3.00 1.75

Philippines Chamber of Commerce, Cent. A895

**2003, July 15**
**2847** A895 6p multi .60 .40

Benguet Corporation, Cent. A896

**2003, Aug. 12**
**2848** A896 6p multi .60 .40

**Orchid Type of 2003 With Plant Names and**

A897

Designs: 6p, Dendrobium uniflorum. 9p, Paphiopedilum urbanianum. 10p, Kingidium philippinense. 17p, Epigeneium lyonii. 21p, Thrixspermum subulatum. 22p, Trichoglottis philippinensis. 30p, Mariposa. 50p, Sanggumay. 75p, Lady's slipper. 100p, Walingwaling.

**2003-04** *Perf. 14½*

**2849** A888 6p multi .55 .25
**2849A** A888 9p multi .75 .35
**2850** A888 10p multi .80 .40
*a.* With space between "P" and "10," dated 2004 ('04) .80 .50
**2851** A888 17p multi 1.75 .70
*a.* Base of "P" even with base of "17," dated 2004 ('04) 1.50 .75
**2852** A888 21p multi 2.10 1.00
*a.* Base of "P" even with base of "21," dated 2004 ('04) 1.75 1.00
**2853** A888 22p multi 2.10 1.10
*a.* Base of "P" even with base of "22," dated 2004, plant name 14mm long ('04) 2.00 1.00
*b.* As "a," plant name 12½mm long ('04) 2.75 1.50

*Perf. 14*

**2854** A897 30p multi 2.75 1.50
**2855** A897 50p multi 5.00 2.50
**2856** A897 75p multi 7.25 3.50
**2857** A897 100p multi 9.50 4.75
*Nos. 2849-2857 (10)* 32.55 16.05

Issued: 6p, 10p, 17p, 21p, 22p, 8/8; 30p, 100p, 8/21; 50p, 75p, 9/9. 9p, 11/4.
No. 2850a, 6/2/04; No. 2851a, 8/2/04; No. 2852a, 7/21/04; No. 2853a, 6/10/04. No, 2853b, 2004.
See Nos. 2904-2912.

Philippines — Mexico Diplomatic Relations, 50th Anniv. — A898

Designs: 5p, Our Lady of Guadalupe. No. 2859, 22p, Miraculous Image of the Black Nazarene.
No. 2860, 22p, Crowd around church.

**2003, Apr. 23** *Perf. 14*

**2858-2859** A898 Set of 2 3.50 2.75

**Souvenir Sheet**

**2860** A898 22p multi 3.50 3.00

No. 2860 contains one 80x30mm stamp.

Our Lady of Caysasay, 400th Anniv. — A899

**2003, Sept. 8**

**2861** A899 6p multi .60 .40

Cornelio T. Villareal, Sr., House Speaker, Birth Cent. — A900

**2003, Sept. 11**

**2862** A900 6p multi .60 .40

National Teachers College, 75th Anniv. — A901

**2003, Sept. 15**

**2863** A901 6p multi .60 .40

Sanctuary of San Antonio Parish, 50th Anniv. — A902

**2003, Oct. 4** **Litho.**

**2864** A902 6p multi .60 .40

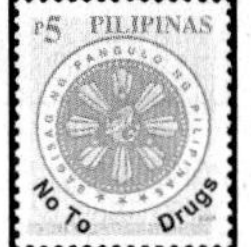


Nos. 2722-2723 Overprinted in Red

**2003, Oct. 17** *Perf. 13¾*

**2865** A828 5p multi .50 .30
**2866** A828 15p multi 1.50 1.00

Souvenir Sheet

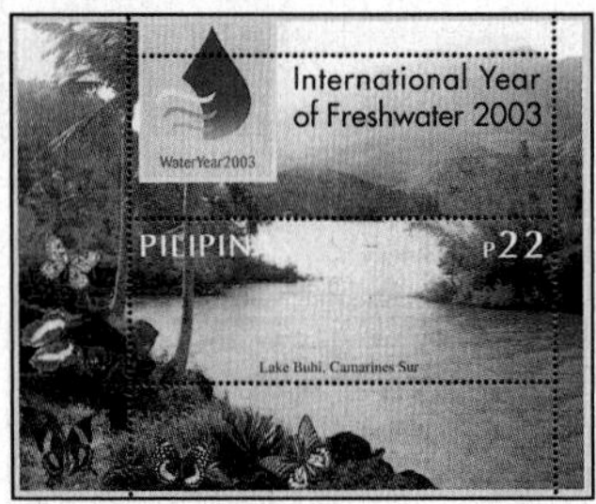


Intl. Year of Fresh Water — A903

**2003, Oct. 24** *Perf. 14*

**2867** A903 22p multi + label 2.50 2.50

Federation of Free Farmers, 50th Anniv. — A904

**2003, Oct. 25**

**2868** A904 6p multi .60 .40

Christmas A905

Inscriptions: 6p, Mano po ninong ii. 17p, Himig at kulay ng Pasko, vert. 21p, Noche buena, vert. 22p, Karoling sa jeepney.

**2003, Oct. 28**

**2869-2872** A905 Set of 4 7.00 3.00

National Stamp Collecting Month A906

Cartoon art: 6p, Kenkoy, by Tony Velasquez, vert. 17p, Ikabod, by Nonoy Marcelo, vert. 21p, Sakay N'Moy, by Hugo C. Yonzon, Jr. No. 2876, 22p, Kalabong en Bosyo, by Larry Alcala.
No. 2877, 22p, Hugo, the Sidewalk Vendor, by Rodolfo Y. Ragodon.

**2003, Nov. 1**

**2873-2876** A906 Set of 4 6.50 3.00

**Souvenir Sheet**

**2877** A906 22p multi 3.00 3.00

No. 2877 contains one 80x30mm stamp.

Winning Children's Art in National Anti-Drug Stamp Design Contest — A907

No. 2878: a, Globe, child with broom, by Nicole Fernan L. Caminian. b, Children, "No Drugs" symbol, by Jairus Cabajar. c, Children painting over "Drug Addiction" picture, by Genevieve V. Lazarte. d, Child chopping tree with hatchet, by Martin F. Rivera.

**2003, Nov. 3**

**2878** A907 6p Block of 4, #a-d 3.00 2.50

**Nos. 2550Ab, 2550Ac, 2550Ad and 2550Ae Surcharged**

**2003, Nov. 11** *Perf. 14*

**2879** A749a 17p on 4p #2550Ab 2.25 1.10
**2880** A749a 17p on 8p #2550Ac 2.25 1.10
**2881** A749a 22p on 16p #2550Ad 3.00 1.40
**2882** A749a 22p on 16p #2550Ae 3.00 1.40
*Nos. 2879-2882 (4)* 10.50 5.00

Nos. 2879-2882 were sold removed from the booklet the basic stamps were in.

Souvenir Sheet

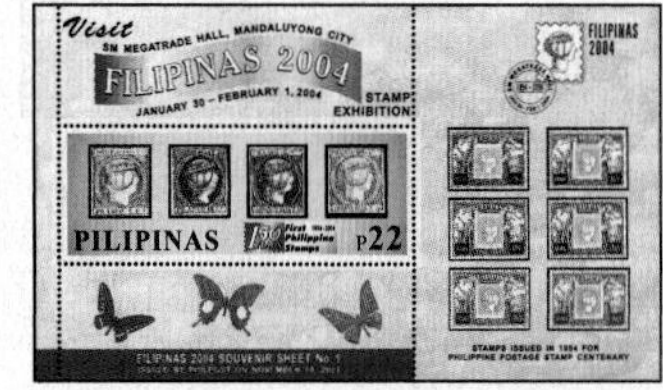


First Philippine Stamps, 150th Anniv. — A908

**2003, Nov. 14**

**2883** A908 22p Nos. 1, 2, 4 & 5, org to yellow background 2.50 2.50

Filipinas 2004 Stamp Exhibition, Mandaluyong City.
See Nos. 2891-2897.

Camera Club of the Philippines, 75th Anniv. A909

**2003, Dec. 1** **Litho.**

**2884** A909 6p multi .60 .40

New Year 2004 (Year of the Monkey) A910

Monkey: 6p, Perched on branch. 17p, Hanging from branch.

**2003, Dec. 1**

**2885-2886** A910 Set of 2 3.25 1.25
*2886a* Souvenir sheet, #2885-2886 + 2 labels 4.25 4.25

No. 2886a exists imperf. Value $5.

Succulent Plants — A911

No. 2887: a, Mammilaria spinosissima (yellow frame). b, Epithelantha bokei. c, Rebutia spinosissima. d, Turbinicarpus alonsoi.
No. 2888, horiz.: a, Aloe humilis. b, Euphorbia golisana. c, Gymnocalycium spinosissima. d, Mammilaria spinosissima (green frame).

**2003, Dec. 5**

**2887** A911 6p Block of 4, #a-d 3.50 3.00

**Souvenir Sheet**

**2888** A911 6p Sheet of 4, #a-d 4.00 4.00

Powered Flight, Cent. — A911a

No. 2888E — Do24TT: f, Green background. g, Yellow background.

**2003, Dec. 17** **Litho.** *Perf. 14*

**2888E** A911a 6p Horiz. pair, #f-g 1.50 1.00

Architecture — A912

No. 2889: a, Luneta Hotel. b, Hong Kong Shanghai Bank. c, El Hogar. d, Regina Building.
No. 2890, horiz.: a, Pangasinan Capitol. b, Metropolitan Theater. c, Philtrust. d, University of Manila.

**2003, Dec. 22**
**2889** A912 6p Block of 4, #a-d 3.50 3.00

**Souvenir Sheet**

**2890** A912 6p Sheet of 4, #a-d 4.00 4.00

**First Philippine Stamps, 150th Anniv. Type of 2003**

No. 2891 (36x26mm each): a, Blue to lilac background, #1. b, Orange to yellow background, #2. c, Light to dark green background, #4. d, Dark to light pink background, #5.
Nos. 2892-2897: Like #2883.

**2003-04 Litho. *Perf. 14***
**2891** Horiz. strip of 4 3.50 3.00
*a.-d.* A908 6p Any single .65 .50

**Souvenir Sheets**
**Background Colors**

**2892** A908 22p dk to lt rose 2.50 2.50
**2893** A908 22p dk to lt blue 2.50 2.50
**2894** A908 22p blue to lt grn 2.50 2.50
**2895** A908 22p dk to lt pink 2.50 2.50
**2896** A908 22p brn to yellow 2.50 2.50
**2897** A908 22p white 2.50 2.50
*a.* With Postpex 2004 inscription added in red and black in sheet margin 3.00 3.00

Filipinas 2004 Stamp Exhibition, Mandaluyong City.
Issued: No. 2892, 12/15/03, No. 2893, 1/15/04; No. 2894, 1/30/04; No. 2895, 1/31/04; Nos. 2891, 2896, 2897, 2/1/04. No. 2897a, 4/19/04.
A sheet containing a block of four of perf. and imperf. examples of Nos. 2891a-2891d sold for 100p. Value, $20.

Arrival in Philippines of Sisters of St. Paul of Chartres, Cent. A913

**2004, Jan. 22 *Perf. 14***
**2898** A913 6p multi .60 .35

Polytechnic University of the Philippines, Cent. — A914

**2004, Jan. 22**
**2899** A914 6p multi .60 .35

Tanduay Distillers, Inc., 150th Anniv. — A915

**2004, Jan. 22**
**2900** A915 6p multi .60 .35

Grepalife Life Insurance Co., 50th Anniv. — A916

**2004, Jan. 22**
**2901** A916 6p multi .60 .35

2003 State Visit of U.S. Pres. George W. Bush A917

Flags of U.S. and Philippines, George W. Bush and: 6p, Crowd. 22p, Philippines Pres. Gloria Macapagal-Arroyo, Malacañang Palace.

**2004, Feb. 23 Litho. *Perf. 13x13½***
**2902-2903** A917 Set of 2 2.50 1.25

**Orchid Type of 2003 With Plant Names**

Designs: 1p, Liparis latifolia. 2p, Cymbidium finlaysonianum. 3p, Phalaenopsis philippinensis. 4p, Phalaenopsis fasciata. 5p, Spathoglottis plicata.
No. 2909: a, Phalaenopsis fuscata. b, Phalaenopsis stuartiana. c, Renanthera monachia. d, Aerides quinquevulnera.
8p, Phalaenopsis schilleriana. 9p, Phalaenopsis pulchra. 20p, Phaius tankervilleae.
Two types of 1p and 5p:
I — Denomination and year date not touching edges of background color, digits of year date touching.
II — Denomination and year date touch edges of background color, digits of year date spaced.
Three types of 2p:
I — Plant name 13½mm long and 1mm from year date, denomination and year date not touching edges of background color.
II — Plant name 13½ mm long and 2mm from year date, denomination and year date touching edges of background color.
III — Plant name 14mm long and 1½mm from year date, denomination and year date touching edges of background color.

**2004 Litho. *Perf. 14½***
**2904** A888 1p multi, type I .30 .25
*a.* Type II .40 .25
**2905** A888 2p multi, type I .50 .30
*a.* Type II .25 .25
*b.* Type III 7.00 5.00
**2906** A888 3p multi .35 .25
**2907** A888 4p multi .40 .30
**2908** A888 5p multi, type I .40 .25
*a.* Type II .70 .35
**2909** Block of 4 2.50 1.75
*a.-d.* A888 6p Any single .50 .25
**2910** A888 8p multi .65 .35
**2911** A888 9p multi .75 .40
**2912** A888 20p multi 1.75 .80
*Nos. 2904-2912 (9)* 7.60 4.65

Issued: Nos. 2904, 2908, 3/9; Nos. 2904a, 2905, 2905b, 2910, 4/1; Nos. 2905a, 2908a, 4/28; Nos. 2906, 2907, 2911, 2912, 6/11; No. 2909, 12/20.

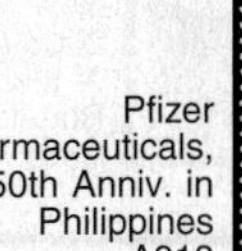

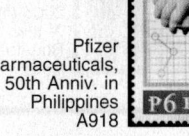

Pfizer Pharmaceuticals, 50th Anniv. in Philippines A918

**2004, Apr. 30 *Perf. 14***
**2913** A918 6p multi .60 .35

Our Lady of Piat, 400th Anniv. — A919

**2004, June 21**
**2914** A919 6p multi .60 .35

Bonsai A920

No. 2915, vert. — Orange to yellow background: a, Bantigue. b, Kamuning Binangonan with thick trunk, dark brown pot. c, Balete. d, Mulawin aso. e, Kamuning Binangonan with root-like trunk, dark brown pot. f, Logwood. g, Kamuning Binangonan, orange clay pot. h, Bantolinao.
No. 2916 — Purple to white background: a, Bantigue with thick trunk, brown pot. b, Chinese elm. c, Bantigue with two trunks, brown pot. d, Bantigue, white pot. e, Balete with many green leaves, black and brown pot. f, Balete with few green leaves, brown pot. g, Bantigue, light brown rectangular pot. h, Mansanita.
Nos. 2917a, 2918a, Lomonsito. Nos. 2917b, 2918b, Bougainvillea, pot on table. Nos. 2917c, 2918c, Bougainvillea, orange brown pot. Nos. 2917d, 2918d, Kalyos.

**2004 *Perf. 14***
**2915** Block of 8 6.50 *6.50*
*a.-h.* A920 6p Any single .60 .50
**2916** Block of 8 6.50 *6.50*
*a.-h.* A920 6p Any single .60 .50

**Souvenir Sheets**
**Solid Blue Background**

**2917** Sheet of 4 4.00 4.00
*a.-d.* A920 6p Any single 1.00 .75

**Blue to White Background**

**2918** Sheet of 4 4.00 4.00
*a.-d.* A920 6p Any single 1.00 .75

Issued: Nos. 2915-2917, 7/27; No. 2918, 8/28. 2004 World Stamp Championship, Singapore (No. 2918).

2004 Summer Olympics, Athens A921

Designs: 6p, Shooting. 17p, Taekwondo. 21p, Swimming. No. 2922, 22p, Archery.
No. 2923, 22p, Boxing.

**2004, Aug. 13**
**2919-2922** A921 Set of 4 7.00 3.50

**Souvenir Sheet**

**2923** A921 22p multi 2.75 2.00

Miguel Lopez de Legazpi (c. 1510-72), Founder of Manila — A922

**2004, Aug. 20 Litho.**
**2924** A922 6p multi .50 .50

Admiral Tomas A. Cloma, Sr. (1904-96) A923

**2004, Aug. 20**
**2925** A923 6p multi .60 .40

Animals of the Lunar New Year Cycle — A924

Designs: Nos. 2926a, 2927a, Rat. Nos. 2926b, 2927b, Ox. Nos. 2926c, 2927c, Tiger. Nos. 2926d, 2927d, Rabbit. Nos. 2926e, 2927e, Dragon. Nos. 2926f, 2927f, Snake. Nos. 2926g, 2928a, Horse. Nos. 2926h, 2928b, Goat. Nos. 2926i, 2928c, Monkey. Nos. 2926j, 2928d, Cock. Nos. 2926k, 2928e, Dog. Nos. 2926l, 2928f, Pig.

**2004, Sept. 9 *Perf. 14***
**English Inscriptions at Left**

**2926** A924 6p Sheet of 12, #a-l, + 3 labels 12.00 12.00

**Chinese Inscriptions at Left**

**2927** A924 6p Sheet of 6, #a-f, + 6 labels 15.00 15.00
**2928** A924 6p Sheet of 6, #a-f, + 6 labels 15.00 15.00

Manila Central University, Cent. A925

**2004, Sept. 21**
**2929** A925 6p multi .60 .35
*a.* Miniature sheet of 8 10.00 10.00

Christmas A926

Various Christmas trees: 6p, 17p, 21p, 22p.

**2004, Oct. 1**
**2930-2933** A926 Set of 4 7.00 3.50

Filipino-Chinese General Chamber of Commerce, Cent. — A927

No. 2934: a, Intramuros, Philippines. b, Great Wall of China.

**2004, Oct. 12**
**2934** A927 6p Horiz. pair, #a-b 1.50 1.00

Winning Designs in Rice Is Life National Stamp Design Contest — A928

No. 2935, 6p: a, By Maria Enna T. Alegre. b, By Lady Fatima M. Velasco.
No. 2936, 6p: a, By Sean Y. Pajaron. b, By Ljian B. Delgado.
No. 2937, 6p: a, By Michael O. Villadolid. b, By Gary M. Manalo.

**2004, Oct. 15** **Litho.**
**Horiz. Pairs, #a-b**
**2935-2937** A928 Set of 3 5.00 5.00
*2937c* Miniature sheet, #2935a-2935b, 2936a-2936b, 2937a-2937b 7.00 7.00

Intl. Year of Rice.

Natl. Stamp Collecting Month A929

Comic strip and comic book illustrations: No. 2938, 6p, Darna, by Nestor P. Redondo. No. 2939, 6p, Kulafu, by Francisco Reyes. No. 2940, 6p, El Vibora, by Federico C. Javinal, vert. No. 2941, 6p, Lapu-Lapu, by Francisco V. Coching, vert.
22p, Darna, by Mars Ravelo, vert

**2004** ***Perf. 14***
**2938-2941** A929 Set of 4 2.75 2.00

**Souvenir Sheet**
**2942** A929 22p multi 3.50 3.00

No. 2942 contains one 30x80mm stamp.

San Agustin Church, Manila, 400th Anniv. — A930

No. 2943: a, Denomination at left. b, Denomination at right.

**2004, Nov. 13**
**2943** A930 6p Horiz. pair, #a-b 1.50 1.00

New Year 2005 (Year of the Rooster) A931

Designs: 6p, Rooster's head. 17p, Rooster.

**2004, Dec. 1**
**2944-2945** A931 Set of 2 3.00 1.90
*2945a* Souvenir sheet, 2 each #2944-2945 6.50 6.50

Worldwide Fund for Nature (WWF) — A932

Owls: No. 2946, 6p, Giant Scops owl. No. 2947, 6p, Philippine eagle owl. No. 2948, 6p, Negros Scops owl. No. 2949, 6p, West Visayan hawk owl.

**2004, Dec. 22**
**2946-2949** A932 Set of 4 3.50 2.75
*2949a* Block of 4, #2946-2949 4.25 3.75

Liceo de Cagayan University A933

**2005, Feb. 5** **Litho.** ***Perf. 14***
**2950** A933 6p multi .60 .40

Seventh-Day Adventist Church in the Philippines, Cent. — A934

**2005, Feb. 18**
**2951** A934 6p multi .60 .40

Baguio Country Club, Cent. — A935

No. 2952: a, Club in 1905. b, Club in 2005.

**2005, Feb. 18**
**2952** A935 6p Horiz. pair, #a-b 1.40 1.00

Butterflies — A936

Designs: 1p, Arisbe decolor stratos.
No. 2954: a, Parantica noeli. b, Chilasa osmana osmana. c, Graphium sandawanum joreli. d, Papilio xuthus benguetanus.

**2005** **Litho.** ***Perf. 14½***
**2953** A936 1p multi .35 .25
*a.* Butterfly redrawn with two antennae .35 .30
**2954** Block of 4 8.50 6.50
*a.-d.* A936 22p Any single 1.80 1.25

Issued: 1p, 4/12; No. 2954, 3/3.

See Nos. 2978-2981.

Shells — A937

No. 2955: a, Chicoreus saulii. b, Spondylus varians. c, Spondylus linquaefelis. d, Melo broderipii.
No. 2956: a, Chlamys senatoria. b, Siphonofusus vicdani. c, Epitonium scalare. d, Harpa harpa.
No. 2957: a, Siliquaria armata. b, Argonauta argo. c, Perotrochus vicdani. d, Corculum cardissa.

**2005, Apr. 15** ***Perf. 14***
**2955** A937 Block of 4 3.00 2.50
*a.-d.* 6p Any single .65 .50
**2956** A937 Block of 4 3.00 2.50
*a.-d.* 6p Any single .65 .50

**Souvenir Sheet**
**2957** A937 Sheet of 4 + 2 labels 6.00 6.00
*a.-d.* 6p Any single 1.25 1.00

State Visit of Hu Jintao, Pres. of People's Republic of China A938

Flags of Philippines and People's Republic of China, Philippines Pres. Gloria Macapagal-Arroyo and: 6p, Pres. Hu at right. 17p, Pres. Hu at left.

**2005, Apr. 27**
**2958-2959** A938 Set of 2 3.00 1.75
*2959a* Souvenir sheet, #2958-2959 4.00 4.00

Architecture — A939

No. 2960: a, Ernesto de la Cruz Ancestral House. b, Limjoco Residence. c, Pelaez Ancestral House. d, Vergara House.
No. 2961: a, Gliceria Marella Villavicencio. b, Lasala-Guarin House. c, Claparols House. d, Ilagan Ancestral House.

**2005, May 7**
**2960** A939 Block of 4 2.75 2.50
*a.-d.* 6p Any single .60 .50

**Souvenir Sheet**
**2961** A939 Sheet of 4 4.00 4.00
*a.-d.* 6p Any single .80 .65

Central Philippine University, Cent. A940

**2005, May 13**
**2962** A940 6p multi .60 .40

Rotary International, Cent. — A941

Denomination: 6p, At left, in blue. 22p, At right, in red.

**2005, May 31**
**2963-2964** A941 Set of 2 3.50 2.25
*2964a* Miniature sheet, 6 #2963, 2 #2964 12.00 12.00

San Bartolome Parish, 400th Anniv. A942

**2005, July 25** **Litho.** ***Perf. 14***
**2965** A942 6p multi .60 .40

Senator Blas F. Ople (1927-2003) A943

**2005, July 28**
**2966** A943 6p multi .60 .40

Shells — A944

No. 2967, 6p: a, Chrysallis fischeri. b, Helicostyla bicolorata. c, Helicostyla dobiosa. d, Helicostyla portei.
No. 2968, 6p: a, Cochlostyla imperator. b, Helicostyla turbinoides. c, Helicostyla lignaria. d, Amphidromus dubius.
No. 2969, horiz.: a, Calocochlia depressa. b, Cochlostyla sarcinosa. c, Calocochlia schadenbergi. d, Helicostyla pulcherrina.

**2005** **Blocks of 4, #a-d** ***Perf. 14***
**2967-2968** A944 Set of 2 8.00 7.00

**Souvenir Sheets**
**2969** A944 6p Sheet of 4, #a-d, + 2 labels 5.00 5.00
**2970** Sheet, #2969a, 2969b, 2970a, 2970b 5.00 5.00
*a.* A944 2p Like #2969c .80 .60
*b.* A944 3p Like #2969d .80 .60

Issued: Nos. 2967-2969, 8/8; No. 2970, 8/19. Upper left label on No. 2970 has Taipei 2005 Stamp Exhibition emblem, lower right label has "Greetings from the Philippines" inscription.

Intl. Year of the Eucharist A945

Winning pictures in stamp design contest by: No. 2971, 6p, Carlos Vincent H. Ruiz. No. 2972, 6p, Rommer A. Fajardo. No. 2973, 6p, Telly Farolan-Somera. No. 2974, 6p, Allen A. Moran. No. 2975, 6p, Elouiza Athena Tentativa. No. 2976, 6p, Jianina Marishka C. Montealto.

**2005, Sept. 8**

**2971-2976** A945 Set of 6 3.60 2.40
*2976a* Souvenir sheet, #2971-2976, + 6 labels 6.00 *6.00*

**No. 1887 Surcharged in Red**

Souvenir Sheet

**Wmk. 389**

**2005, Sept. 14 Litho. *Imperf.***

**2977** A493 15p on 8p multi 2.00 2.00

**Butterflies Type of 2005 and**

A946

A947

Designs: 5p, Parantica danatti danatti.
No. 2979: a, Hebemoia glaucippe philippinensis. b, Moduza urdaneta aynii. c, Lexias satrapes hiwaga. d, Cheritra orpheus orpheus. e, Achillides chikae chikae. f, Arisbe ideaoiedes ideaoiedes. g, Dellas schoenigi hermeli. h, Achillides palinurus daedalus. i, Dellas levicki justini. j, Troides magellanus magellanus.
No. 2980: a, Idea electra electra. b, Charaxes bajula adoracion. c, Tanaecia calliphorus calliphorus. d, Trogonoptera trojana. e, Charaxes bajula adoracion, diff.
No. 2981: a, Cethosia biblis barangingi. b, Menalaides polytes ledebouria. c, Appias nero palawanica. d, Udara tyotaroi.

**2005 Unwmk. *Perf. 14½***

**2978** A946 5p multi .40 .25
**2979** Block of 10 8.00 8.00
*a.-j.* A946 6p Any single .50 .25
**2980** Block of 4, #a-d 6.50 6.00
*a.* A946 17p multi 1.25 .60
*b.* A946 17p multi 1.25 .60
*c.* A946 17p multi 1.25 .60
*d.* A946 17p multi 1.25 .60
*e.* A947 17p multi 20.00 20.00
*f.* Block of 4, #2980a, 2980c, 2980d, 2980e *50.00* 50.00
**2981** Block of 4 7.50 6.00
*a.-d.* A936 21p Any single 1.75 1.00
*Nos. 2978-2981 (4)* 22.40 20.25

Issued: No. 2978, 11/22; No. 2979, 10/12; No. 2980, 12/9. No. 2981, 12/2.

Intl. Year of Sports and Physical Education — A948

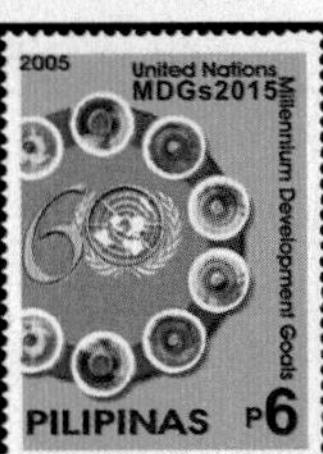


UN Millennium Development Goals — A949

No. 2982: a, Dove, open book, Philippines flag, basketball, emblem at LL. b, Torch, sports equipment, people with joined hands, dove flying to right, emblem at LR. c, Torch, sports equipment, people with joined hands, dove flying to left, emblem at LL.

**2005, Oct. 19 *Perf. 14***

**2982** A948 6p Horiz. pair, #a-b 1.50 1.00
*c.* 6p multi .60 .40
*d.* Horiz. pair, #2982a, 2982c 1.75 1.25
**2983** A949 6p multi .70 .50

**Souvenir Sheet**

**2984** Sheet, #2982a, 2982b, 2984a 2.50 2.50
*a.* A949 10p multi 1.00 .80
*b.* Sheet, #2982a, 2982c, 2984a 3.00 3.00

United Nations, 60th anniv.

Bureau of Corrections, Cent. — A950

**2005, Nov. 4**

**2985** A950 6p multi .60 .40

Inauguration of Pres. Gloria Macapagal-Arroyo — A951

Pres. Macapagal-Arroyo: 6p, Taking oath. 22p, Giving inaugural speech.

**2005, Nov. 9**

**2986-2987** A951 Set of 2 3.00 1.75

Christmas A952

Various department store window Christmas displays: 6p, 17p, 21p, 22p.

**2005, Nov. 16**

**2988-2991** A952 Set of 4 7.00 4.00

23rd Southeast Asia Games, Philippines A953

No. 2992: a, Boxing. b, Cycling. c, Wushu. d, Bowling. e, Badminton. f, Billiards. Eagle has black beak on all stamps.
No. 2993, horiz.: a, Track. b, Soccer. c, Taekwondo. d, Judo. e, Chess. f, Karate. g, Gymnastics. h, Pencaksilat. i, Dragon boat racing. j, Swimming.
No. 2994: a, Baseball. b, Shooting. c, Archery. d, Bowling (eagle with brown beak). e, Volleyball. f, Boxing (eagle with brown beak). g, Cycling (eagle with brown beak). h, Badminton (eagle with brown beak).
No. 2995: a, Archery. b, Shooting. c, Equestrian.
No. 2996, horiz.: a, Arnis. b, Chess. c, Dragon boat racing.

**2005, Nov. 22 Red Frames**

**2992** Block of 6 6.00 6.00
*a.-f.* A953 6p Any single .75 .60
**2993** Sheet of 10 + 8 labels 15.00 15.00
*a.-j.* A953 6p Any single 1.00 .75
**2994** Sheet of 10, #2992c, 2992f, 2994a-2994h, + 20 labels 15.00 15.00
*a.-h.* A953 6p Any single 1.00 .75

**Blue Frames**

**2995** Sheet of 3 4.00 4.00
*a.* A953 5p multi .90 .60
*b.-c.* A953 6p Either single .90 .60
**2996** Sheet of 3 4.00 4.00
*a.* A953 5p multi .90 .60
*b.-c.* A953 6p Either single .90 .60

No. 2992 was printed in sheets of 12 containing two blocks. Nos. 2993a-2993j lack perforations between the stamp and the adjacent labels that are the same size as the stamp. There are perforations between the stamps and labels on No. 2994. The labels to the right of the stamps could be personalized. Nos. 2993 and 2994 each sold for 99p with generic flag labels, and for 350p with personalized labels.

National Stamp Collecting Month — A954

Prints: No. 2997, 6p, Pinoy Worker Abr'd., by Ben Cab. No. 2998, 6p, Bulbs, by M. Parial. No. 2999, 6p, The Fourth Horseman, by Tequi. No. 3000, 6p, Breaking Ground, by R. Olazo. 22p, Form XV, by Brenda Fajardo, horiz.

**2005, Nov. 28**

**2997-3000** A954 Set of 4 2.75 2.00

**Souvenir Sheet**

**3001** A954 22p multi 3.00 3.00

No. 3001 contains one 80x30mm stamp.

New Year 2006 (Year of the Dog) A955

Dog and inscription: a, 6p, "Manigong Bagong Taon." b, 17p, "Happy New Year."

**2005, Dec. 1**

**3002-3003** A955 Set of 2 3.00 1.75
*3003a* Souvenir sheet, 2 each #3002-3003 6.50 6.50

Third Asian Para Games — A956

Designs: 6p, Runner with amputated arm. 17p, Wheelchair racer.

**2005, Dec. 6**

**3004-3005** A956 Set of 2 2.50 1.50

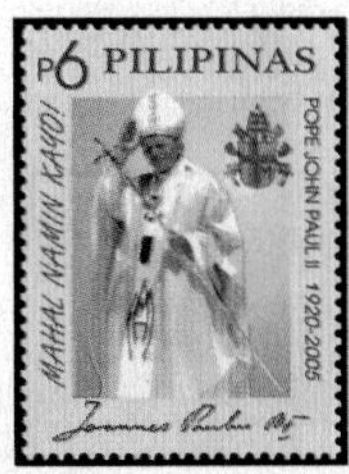


Pope John Paul II (1920-2005) A957

Pope John Paul II, Vatican arms and text: 6p, "Mahal Namin Kayo!" 22p, "We Love You!"

**2005, June 28 Litho. *Perf. 14***

**3006-3007** A957 Set of 2 3.00 2.00

Lighthouses — A958

No. 3008: a, Cape Santiago Lighthouse, Calatagan. b, Bacagay Lighthouse, Liloan. c, Malabrigo Lighthouse, Lobo. d, Capones Lighthouse, San Antonio.
No. 3009: a, Tubbataha Lighthouse, Cagayancillo. b, Cape Bojeador Lighthouse, Burgos. c, Cape Bolinao Lighthouse, Bolinao. d, San Fernando Point Lighthouse, San Fernando.

**2005, Dec. 22**

**3008** A958 6p Block of 4, #a-d 3.00 2.50

**Souvenir Sheet**

**3009** A958 6p Sheet of 4, #a-d 4.00 4.00

St. Scholastica's College, Manila, Cent. — A959

**2006, Jan. 3**

**3010** A959 6p multi .60 .40

Filipinos in Hawaii, Cent. — A960

Contest-winning designs: 6p, Filipinos in Hawaii, by Allen A. Moran. 22p, Filipinos and flags, by Crisanto S. Umali.
No. 3013: a, Like 6p. b, Like 22p.

**2006, Jan. 5**
**3011-3012** A960 Set of 2 2.75 1.50

**Souvenir Sheet**

**3013** A960 11p Sheet of 2, #a-b 4.00 4.00

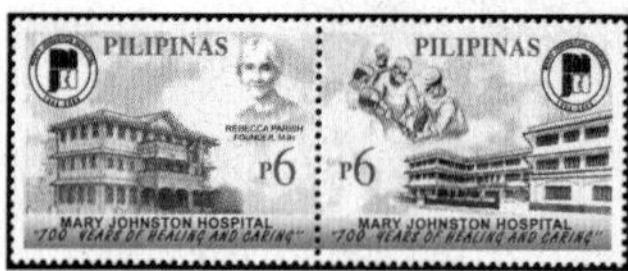

Mary Johnston Hospital, Manila, Cent. — A961

No. 3014: a, Hospital building and founder Rebecca Parish. b, Surgeons, hospital building.

**2006, Jan. 20**
**3014** A961 6p Horiz. pair, #a-b 1.40 1.00

Love — A962

No. 3015 — Angel with: a, Letter. b, Flower.

**2006, Feb. 8**
**3015** A962 7p Horiz. pair, #a-b 1.50 1.10

Jaime Cardinal Sin (1928-2005), Archbishop of Manila — A963

Sin and: 7p, Cathedral. 22p, Statue.

**2006, Feb. 25**
**3016-3017** A963 Set of 2 2.50 1.50
*3017a* Souvenir sheet, 2 each #3016-3017 6.50 6.50

Marine Turtles — A964

No. 3018: a, Olive Ridley turtle. b, Hawksbill turtle. c, Loggerhead turtle. d, Leatherback turtle.
26p, Green turtle.

**2006, Mar. 31**
**3018** A964 Horiz. strip of 4 3.50 3.50
*a.-d.* 7p Any single .55 .45

**Souvenir Sheet**

**3019** A964 26p multi 4.00 4.00

No. 3019 contains one 80x30mm stamp.

**Butterfly Type of 2005 and**

Butterfly With Fully-colored Background A965

Butterfly With Blue Lines At Bottom A966

Butterfly With Partially-colored Background — A967

Butterfly With Framed and Colored Background — A968

Designs: 1p, Arisbe decolor stratos. 2p, Arhopala anthelus impar. 3p, Zophoessa dataensis nihrai. 4p, Liphyra brassolis justini. 5p, Parantica danatti danatti. 9p, Lexias satrapes amlana. 10p, Tanaecia aruna pallida. 30p, Appias nero domitia. 100p, Cepora aspasia olga.
Nos. 3030 and 3031: a, Hebemoia glaucippe philippensis. b, Moduza urdaneta aynii. c, Lexias satrapes hiwaga. d, Cheritra orpheus orpheus. e, Achillides chikae chikae. f, Arisbe ideaoiedes ideaoiedes. g, Delias schoenigi hermeli. h, Achillides palinurus daedalus. i, Delias levicki justini. j, Troides magellanus magellanus.
Nos. 3036 and 3037: a, Idea electra electra. b, Charaxes bajula adoracion. c, Tanaecia calliphorus. d, Trogonoptera trojana.
Nos. 3038 and 3039: a, Cethosia biblis barangingi. b, Menalaides polytes ledebouria. c, Appias nero palawanica. d, Udara tyotaroi.
Nos. 3040 and 3041: a, Parantica noeli. b, Chilasa osmana osmana. c, Graphium sandawanum joreli. d, Papilio xuthus benguetanus.

***Perf. 14½ (A936, A965), 13¾ (A966), 13x13¼ (A967), 14 (A968)***

**2006** **Inscribed "2006"**
**3020** A965 1p multi .25 .25
**3021** A966 1p multi .25 .25
*a.* Inscribed "2007" .25 .25
**3022** A965 2p multi .25 .25
**3023** A966 2p multi .25 .25
*a.* Inscribed "2007" .30 .25
**3024** A936 3p multi .30 .25
**3025** A966 3p multi .35 .30
*a.* Inscribed "2007" .40 .30
**3026** A936 4p multi .50 .30
**3027** A966 4p multi .50 .30
*a.* Inscribed "2007" .50 .30
**3028** A965 5p multi .50 .30
**3029** A966 5p multi .50 .30
*a.* Inscribed "2007" .50 .30
**3030** Block of 10 6.50 6.50
*a.-j.* A965 7p Any single .55 .25
**3031** Block of 10 7.50 7.50
*a.-j.* A966 7p Any single .60 .30
*k.* Block of 10, inscr. "2007" 8.50 8.50
*l.-u.* A966 7p Any single, inscr. "2007" .65 .30
**3032** A936 9p multi .85 .35
**3033** A966 9p multi .90 .40
*a.* Inscribed "2007" .90 .40
**3034** A936 10p multi .90 .40
**3035** A966 10p multi 1.00 .40
*a.* Inscribed "2007" 1.35 .40
**3036** Block of 4 8.00 6.50
*a.-d.* A965 20p Any single 1.60 1.00
**3037** Block of 4 8.75 6.75
*a.-d.* A966 20p Any single 1.90 1.25
*e.* Block of 4, inscr. "2007" 8.50 6.50
*f.-i.* A966 20p Any single, inscr. "2007" 1.90 1.25
**3038** Block of 4 10.00 8.25
*a.-d.* A965 24p Any single 2.00 1.00
**3039** Block of 4 10.00 8.00
*a.-d.* A966 24p Any single 2.25 1.25
*e.* Block of 4, inscr. "2007" 10.75 8.50
*f.-i.* A966 24p Any single, inscr. "2007" 2.25 1.25
**3040** Block of 4 10.00 8.50
*a.-d.* A965 26p Any single 2.10 1.10
**3041** Block of 4 10.00 8.50
*a.-d.* A966 26p Any single 2.30 1.30
*e.* Block of 4, inscr. "2007" 10.75 8.50
*f.-i.* A966 26p Any single, inscr. "2007" 2.25 1.25
**3042** A967 30p multi 2.50 1.70
**3043** A968 30p multi 3.00 2.00
**3044** A967 100p multi 9.00 4.25
**3045** A968 100p multi 9.50 4.75
*Nos. 3020-3045 (26)* 102.05 77.50

Issued: Nos. 3020, 3030, 4/28; Nos. 3021, 3029, 7/3; Nos. 3022, 3028, 5/10; No. 3023, 12/27; Nos. 3024, 3034, 11/10; Nos. 3025, 3027, 3033, 3035, 12/26; Nos. 3026, 3032, 9/9; No. 3031, 12/14; No. 3036, 6/7; Nos. 3037, 3039, 3041, 12/21; No. 3038, 6/15; No. 3040, 6/9; No. 3042, 9/18; Nos. 3043, 3045, 12/29; No. 3044, 9/26.
See Nos. 3101-3102.

**No. 1511 Surcharged**

**2006, May 2 Litho. *Perf. 13¾x13¼***
**3046** A368 26p on 7.50p #1511 3.00 3.00

Lighthouses — A969

No. 3047: a, Punta Bugui Lighthouse, Aroroy. b, Capul Island Lighthouse, Samar del Norte. c, Corregidor Island Lighthouse, Cavite. d, Pasig River Lighthouse, Manila.
No. 3048: a, Cabo Engaño Lighthouse, Santa Ana. b, Punta Cabra Lighthouse, Lubang. c, Cabo Melville Lighthouse, Balabac Island. d, Gintotolo Island Lighthouse, Balud.

**2006, May 17** ***Perf. 14***
**3047** A969 7p Block of 4, #a-d 3.50 3.00

**Souvenir Sheet**

**3048** A969 7p Sheet of 4, #a-d 5.00 5.00

Xavier School, Manila, 50th Anniv. — A970

No. 3049: a, Emblems. b, School building. c, Paul Hsu Kuang-ch'i, Chinese Christian convert. d, St. Francis Xavier (1506-52).

**2006, June 6**
**3049** A970 7p Block of 4, #a-d 4.00 4.00

Air Materiel Wing Savings and Loan Association, Inc., 50th Anniv. — A971

No. 3050 — Emblem and: a, Soldier's family, piggy bank. b, Building.

**2006, June 13**
**3050** A971 7p Horiz. pair, #a-b 1.50 1.10

**No. 1721 Surcharged in Blue Violet**

**2006, July 4 Litho. *Perf. 14***
**3051** A436 26p on 7.20p multi 3.00 1.60

Knights of Columbus, 100th Anniv. in Philippines A972

**2006, July 7**
**3052** A972 7p multi .65 .40

Ortigas & Company, 75th Anniv. A973

Anniversary emblem and: 7p, Map of Mandaloyon. 26p, Building.

**2006, July 10**
**3053-3054** A973 Set of 2 3.25 1.50
*3054a* Souvenir sheet, 2 each #3053-3054 8.50 8.50

Ozamiz Cotta Military Fort, 250th Anniv. A974

**2006, July 16**
**3055** A974 7p multi .65 .40

Friendship Between Philippines and Japan, 50th Anniv. A975

José P. Rizal and: 7p, Mt. Fuji and cherry blossoms. 20p, Mt. Mayon and flowers.

**2006, July 23**
**3056-3057** A975 Set of 2 3.00 1.50
*3057a* Souvenir sheet, 2 each #3056-3057 7.00 7.00

Roque B. Ablan, (1906-43) Politician, Military Hero A976

**2006, Aug. 9**
**3058** A976 7p multi .65 .40

No. 1809 Surcharged in Gold

*Perf. 13½x13*
**2006, Aug. 15 Litho. Wmk. 389**
**3059** A470 7p on 1.20p multi .85 .50

Chan-Cu Association, Cent. — A977

No. 3060: a, Centennial emblem. b, Figurine of Chan-Tze, Chinese scholar.

**2006, Aug. 28 Unwmk.** ***Perf. 14***
**3060** A977 7p Horiz. pair, #a-b 1.65 1.30

Cats — A978

No. 3061: a, Himalayan cat. b, Maine Coon cat. c, Red point Siamese cat. d, Persian cat.
No. 3062: a, Japanese bobtail cat. b, Ragdoll cat. c, Egyptian mau cat. d, Abyssinian cat.

**2006, Sept. 29**
**3061** A978 7p Block of 4, #a-d 4.00 4.00

**Souvenir Sheet**

**3062** A978 7p Sheet of 4, #a-d 4.00 4.00

United Nations Month A979

Text in: 7p, Tagalog and English. 26p, English.

**2006, Oct. 19**
**3063-3064** A979 Set of 2 3.50 2.00

Philippines Postal Service, 108th Anniv. — A980

No. 3065: a, Ruins of Manila Post Office after Battle of Manila. b, Manila Central Post Office, 2006.

**2006, Nov. 6** ***Perf. 13¾***
**3065** A980 Horiz. pair 1.75 1.60
*a.-b.* 7p Either single .75 .50

National Stamp Collecting Month — A981

Designs: No. 3066, 7p, Mother and child. No. 3067, 7p, Fish and fruit, horiz.. No. 3068, 7p, Oranges and grapes, horiz. No. 3069, 7p, Watermelon and coconut, horiz.
26p, Roses.

**2006, Nov. 15**
**3066-3069** A981 Set of 4 3.00 2.00

**Souvenir Sheet**

**3070** A981 26p multi 2.60 2.60

No. 3070 contains one 30x80mm stamp.

Ascent of Mt. Everest by Filipino Climbers — A982

Designs: No. 3071, 7p, Climbers ascending mountain. No. 3072, 20p, No. 3074a, 10p, Climbers ascending mountain and Philippines flag. No. 3073, 26p, No. 3074b, 7p, Climbers at summit with flag.

**2006, Nov. 23** ***Perf. 13¾***
**3071-3073** A982 Set of 3 5.50 3.00

**Souvenir Sheet**

**3074** A982 Sheet of 3, #3071, 3074a, 3074b 2.50 2.50

Christmas A983

Stars and: 7p, Manila Cathedral. 20p, Paoay Church. 24p, Miagao Church. 26p, Barasoain Church.

**Litho. with Hologram Affixed**
**2006** ***Perf. 14***
**3075-3078** A983 Set of 4 7.50 6.25

Issued: 7p, 20p, 12/15; 24p, 26p, 12/19.

New Year 2007 (Year of the Pig) A984

Designs: 7p, Head of pig. 20p, Pig.

**2006, Dec. 27 Litho.**
**3079-3080** A984 Set of 2 3.50 2.00
*3080a* Souvenir sheet, 2 each #3079-3080 7.00 7.00

Fruit — A985

No. 3081: a, Watermelons. b, Mangos. c, Custard apples. d, Pomelos.
No. 3082: a, Jackfruit. b, Lanzones. c, Coconuts. d, Bananas.

**2006, Dec. 15**
**3081** A985 7p Block or strip of 4, #a-d 3.50 2.75

**Souvenir Sheet**

**3082** A985 7p Sheet of 4, #a-d 4.25 4.25

Graciano Lopez Jaena (1856-96), Journalist A986

**2006, Dec. 18**
**3083** A986 7p multi .65 .40

Centro Escolar University, Cent. A987

**2007, Jan. 18 Litho.** ***Perf. 14***
**3084** A987 7p multi .65 .40

Philippine School of the Deaf, Cent. A988

**2007, Jan. 19**
**3085** A988 7p multi .65 .40

Rare Flowers — A989

No. 3086: a, Medinilla magnifica. b, Strongylodon elmeri. c, Amyema incarnatiflora. d, Dillenia monantha. e, Xanthostemon fruticosus. f, Plumeria acuminata. g, Paphiopedilum adductum. h, Rafflesia manillana.
26p, Rafflesia manillana and man, horiz.

**2007, Mar. 30**
**3086** A989 7p Sheet of 8, #a-h 6.50 *6.50*

**Souvenir Sheet**

**3087** A989 26p multi 4.50 4.50

No. 3087 contains one 120x30mm stamp.

Manulife Philippines Insurance, Cent. — A990

**2007, Apr. 26**
**3088** A990 7p multi .80 .50
*a.* Souvenir sheet of 4 10.00 10.00

Colonial Era Bridges — A991

No. 3089: a, Isabel II Bridge, Imus, Cavite. b, Dampol Bridge, Dupax, Nueva Viscaya. c, Barit Bridge, Laoad, Ilocos Norte. d, Blanco Bridge, Binondo, Manila.
No. 3090: a, Malagonlong Bridge, Tayabas, Quezon. b, Fort Santiago Bridge. c, Mahacao Bridge, Maragondon, Cavite. d, Busay Bridge, Guinobatan, Albay.

**2007, May 16**
**3089** A991 7p Block of 4, #a-d 3.50 2.75

**Souvenir Sheet**

**3090** A991 7p Sheet of 4, #a-d 4.00 4.00

Diplomatic Relations Between Philippines and France, 60th Anniv. — A992

Symbols of France and Philippines including: 7p, Eiffel Tower. No. 3092, 26p, Castle.
No. 3093, 26p, Flags of France and Philippines, symbols of countries.

**2007, June 26**
**3091-3092** A992 Set of 2 3.50 2.00

**Souvenir Sheet**

**3093** A992 26p multi 3.50 3.50

No. 3093 contains one 30x80mm stamp.

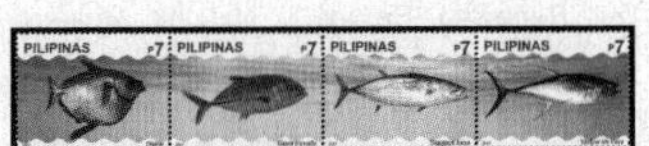
Bureau of Fisheries and Aquatic Resources, 60th Anniv. — A993

No. 3094: a, Diana. b, Giant trevally. c, Skipjack tuna. d, Yellowfin tuna.
No. 3095: a, Cuttlefish. b, Bigfin reef squid and sacol (80x30mm).

**2007, July 2**
**3094** A993 Horiz. strip of 4 4.00 3.50
*a.-d.* 7p Any single .55 .30

**Souvenir Sheet**

**3095** Sheet of 2 5.00 5.00
*a.* A993 7p multi 1.00 .65
*b.* A993 20p multi 2.25 1.65

Scouting, Cent. — A994

Designs: No. 3096, 7p, Scouting flag, hand giving scout sign. No. 3097, 7p, Scouting and Scouting Centenary emblems.

**2007, Aug. 1**

**3096-3097** A994 Set of 2 1.65 1.25
*3097a* Souvenir sheet, 2 each #3096-3097 + label 4.00 4.00

A995

Ducks and Geese — A996

No. 3098: a, Mallards. b, Green-winged teal. c, Tufted ducks. d, Cotton pygmy geese.
Nos. 3099 and 3100: a, Northern pintails. b, Common shelducks. c, Northern shovelers. d, Greater scaups.

**2007, Aug. 3**

**3098** A995 7p Block of 4, #a-d 4.00 3.50

### Souvenir Sheets

**3099** A996 7p Sheet of 4, #a-d 5.00 5.00

### With Bangkok 2007 Emblem Added to Stamps

**3100** A996 7p Sheet of 4, #a-d 7.50 7.00

No. 3100 sold for 50p.

### Butterfly Type of 2006

Designs: 8p, Troidaes magellanus magellanus. 17p, Achillides palinurus daedalus.

**2007, Aug. 7** ***Perf. 13¾x13½***

**3101** A966 8p multi .85 .30
**3102** A966 17p multi 1.65 .70

Association of South East Asian Nations (ASEAN), 40th Anniv. — A997

Designs: 7p, Malacañang Palace, Philippines.
No. 3104: a, Secretariat Building, Bandar Seri Begawan, Brunei. b, National Museum, Cambodia. c, Fatahillah Museum, Jakarta, Indonesia. d, Typical house, Laos. e, Malayan Railway Headquarters Building, Kuala Lumpur, Malaysia. f, Yangon Post Office, Myanmar (Burma). g, Malacañang Palace, Philippines. h, National Museum, Singapore. i, Vimanmek Mansion, Bangkok, Thailand. j, Presidential Palace, Hanoi, Viet Nam.
No. 3105, Malacañang Palace, Philippines (80x30mm).

**2007, Aug. 8** ***Perf. 14***

**3103** A997 7p multi .65 .50
**3104** A997 20p Sheet of 10, #a-j 23.00 23.00

### Souvenir Sheet

**3105** A997 20p multi 2.50 2.50

See Brunei No. 607, Burma No. 370, Cambodia No. 2339, Indonesia Nos. 2120-2121, Laos Nos. 1717-1718, Malaysia No. 1170, Singapore No. 1265, Thailand No. 2315, and Viet Nam Nos. 3302-3311.

Pres. Ramon F. Magsaysay (1907-57) A998

**2007, Aug. 31** ***Litho.***

**3106** A998 7p multi .65 .40

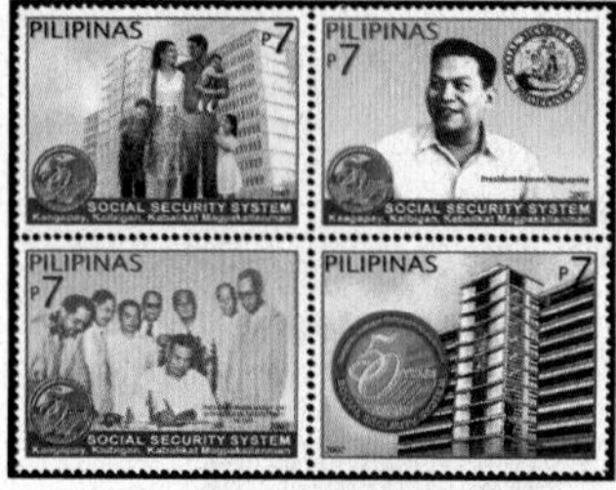


Social Security System, 50th Anniv. — A999

Nos. 3107 and 3108 — Anniversary emblem and: a, Family and building. b, Pres. Ramon Magsaysay. c, Pres. Magsaysay signing Social Security Act of 1954. d, Building.

**2007, Sept. 1** ***Perf. 14***

### Stamps With White Margins

**3107** A999 7p Block of 4, #a-d 3.50 2.75

### Souvenir Sheet

### Stamps With Gray Margins

**3108** A999 7p Sheet of 4, #a-d 4.00 4.00

First Philippine Assembly, Cent. A1000

Designs: No. 3109, 7p, People in front of Manila Opera House. No. 3110, 7p, Manila municipal building.

**2007, Oct. 16**

**3109-3110** A1000 Set of 2 1.35 .80

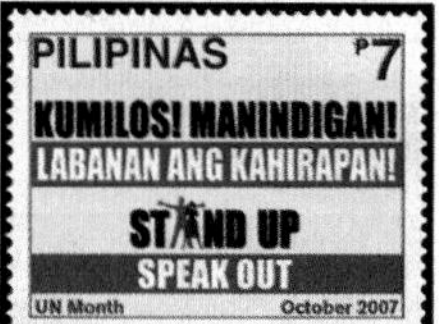


United Nations Month A1001

Text in: 7p, Tagalog and English. 26p, English.

**2007, Oct. 24**

**3111-3112** A1001 Set of 2 3.50 2.00

Nos. 3111-3112 were printed in a sheet of 20 stamps containing ten of each stamp separated by a central gutter.

Paintings by Juan Luna (1857-99) A1002

Designs: No. 3113, 7p, El Violinista. No. 3114, 7p, Indio Bravo. No. 3115, 7p, Old Man With a Pipe. No. 3116, 7p, La Bulakeña.
No. 3117a, Picnic in Normandy, horiz. (60x40mm).
No. 3118, horiz. — Parisian Life, with background color of: a, Light yellow and blue. b, Yellow orange and green. c, Yellow orange and red. d, Yellow orange and purple.

**2007** ***Perf. 14***

**3113-3116** A1002 Set of 4 3.00 2.00
**3117** Sheet of 4, #3113-3115, 3117a 4.00 4.00
*a.* A1002 7p brown & multi, imperf. 1.00 .80
**3118** Sheet of 4 4.00 4.00
*a.* A1002 7p Imperf. (73x48mm) 1.00 .65
*b.-d.* A1002 7p Any single .80 .65

Issued: Nos. 3113-3116, 10/24; No. 3117, 11/23; No. 3118, 12/21. No. 3116 was issued in sheets of 6.

Birds — A1003

Designs: 1p, Black-naped oriole. 2p, Asian fairy bluebird. 3p, Writhed hornbill. 4p, Crimson sunbird. 5p, Barn swallow. 8p, Hoopoe. 9p, Short-eared owl. 10p, Blue-winged pita. 50p, Head of Philippine eagle. 100p, Philippine eagle on tree branch.
No. 3124: a, Mindanao bleeding heart pigeon. b, Nicobar pigeon. c, Black-chinned fruit dove. d, Metallic pigeon. e, Pink-necked green pigeon. f, Amethyst brown dove. g, Gray imperial pigeon. h, Red turtle dove. i, Pied imperial pigeon. j, Spotted imperial pigeon.
No. 3128: a, Dwarf kingfisher. b, Blue-capped wood kingfisher. c, White-throated kingfisher. d, White-collared kingfisher.
No. 3129: a, Green-faced parrotfinch. b, Java sparrow. c, Yellow-breasted bunting. d, White-cheeked bullfinch.
No. 3130: a, Great-billed parrot. b, Philippine cockatoo. c, Blue-naped parrot. d, Blue-backed parrot.

**2007** ***Perf. 13¾x13½***

### Inscribed "2007"

**3119** A1003 1p multi .25 .25
*a.* Inscribed "2008" .25 .25
*b.* Inscribed "2008A" .30 .25
*c.* Inscribed "2008B" .30 .25
**3120** A1003 2p multi .25 .25
*a.* Inscribed "2008" .25 .25
*b.* Inscribed "2008A" .45 .30
*c.* Inscribed "2008B" .25 .25
**3121** A1003 3p multi .50 .30
**3122** A1003 4p multi .65 .35
*a.* Inscribed "2008" .60 .30
**3123** A1003 5p multi .50 .25
*a.* Inscribed "2008" .65 .30
**3124** Block of 10 9.00 9.00
*a.-j.* A1003 7p Any single .60 .30
*k.* Block of 10, inscr. "2008" 20.00 20.00
*l.-u.* A1003 7p Any single, inscr. "2008" 1.00 .50
**3125** A1003 8p multi .65 .30
**3126** A1003 9p multi .85 .35
**3127** A1003 10p multi 1.50 .50
*a.* Inscribed "2008" 1.25 .45
*b.* Inscribed "2008A" 1.35 .60
**3128** Block of 4 7.50 6.00
*a.-d.* A1003 20p Any single 1.50 .85
**3129** Block of 4 10.00 7.25
*a.-d.* A1003 24p Any single 1.90 .95
**3130** Block of 4 10.00 8.50
*a.-d.* A1003 26p Any single 2.10 1.10
*e.* Block of 4, inscr. "2008" 13.50 10.00
*f.-i.* A1003 26p Any single, inscr. "2008" 2.65 1.65
*j.* Block of 4, inscr. "2008A" 15.00 10.00
*k.-n.* A1003 26p Any single, inscr. "2008A" 2.10 1.10

### Size: 30x40mm

***Perf. 14***

**3131** A1003 50p multi 5.00 2.50
*a.* Inscribed "2008" 8.50 6.50
*b.* Inscribed "2008A" 5.00 3.50
**3132** A1003 100p multi 10.00 5.00
*a.* Inscribed "2008" 34.00 30.00
*b.* Inscribed "2008A" 10.00 6.50
*Nos. 3119-3132 (14)* 56.65 40.80

Issued: 1p, 100p, 10/30; 2p, 20p, 11/15; 3p, 4p, 8p, 26p, 12/12; 5p, 50p, 11/5; 7p, 12/10; 9p, 10p, 24p, 12/19.
For stamps without blue lines at bottom, see No. 3151.

Manila Central Post Office, 1926 A1004

No. 3133: a, Shown. b, Manila Central Post Office and architect Juan Marcos Arellano (80x30mm).

**2007, Nov. 5** ***Perf. 14***

**3133** Horiz. pair 3.50 3.00
*a.* A1004 7p multi .65 .50
*b.* A1004 20p multi 1.85 1.00

San Diego de Alcala Cathedral, Cumaca, 425th Anniv. — A1005

**2007, Nov. 13** ***Perf. 13¾x13½***

**3134** A1005 7p multi .85 .65

Sacred Heart School, Cebu, 50th Anniv. — A1006

No. 3135: a, School building and Philippines flag. b, School building and statue. c, Nun, school crest. d, Nun, school building.

**2007, Nov. 16** ***Perf. 14***

### Stamps With White Margins

**3135** A1006 7p Block of 4, #a-d 3.00 2.50

### Souvenir Sheet

**3136** Sheet of 4, #3135a, 3135b, 3135d, 3136a 3.50 3.50
*a.* A1006 7p As #3135c, with greenish gray tint in margin at LL .85 .65

Development Bank of the Philippines, 60th Anniv. — A1007

No. 3137: a, Ship emblem, blue background. b, Bank building, brown background. c, Bank building at left, dark green background. d, Bank building at right, olive green background.

**2007, Nov. 26**

**3137** A1007 7p Block of 4, #a-d 3.00 2.50
*e.* Souvenir sheet, #3137a-3137d 3.50 3.50

Christmas A1008

Designs: 7p, Teddy bear. 20p, Toy train. 24p, Toy truck. 26p, Angel with candle decoration.

**2007, Nov. 28**

**3138-3141** A1008 Set of 4 7.00 4.25

New Year 2008 (Year of the Rat) A1009

Designs: 7p, Head of rat. 20p, Rat.

**2007, Dec. 3**
**3142-3143** A1009 Set of 2 3.50 2.25
*3143a* Souvenir sheet, 2 each #3142-3143 8.00 8.00

World Vision in Philippines, 50th Anniv. — A1010

Designs: 7p, Pres. Ramon F. Magsaysay and World Vision founder, Rev. Bob Pierce. 20p, World Vision anniversary emblem, horiz.

**2007, Dec. 5**
**3144-3145** A1010 Set of 2 4.00 1.50

No. 1810 Surcharged in Silver

**Methods, Perfs and Watermark As Before**

**2007, Dec. 14**
**3146** A470 7p on 2.40p #1810 .85 .50

Dominican School, Manila, 50th Anniv. — A1011

No. 3147: a, St. Dominic de Guzman. b, St. Dominic, school, emblem. c, Two emblems. d, School, emblem.

**Unwmk.**

**2008, Feb. 1 Litho.** ***Perf. 14***
**3147** A1011 7p Block of 4, #a-d 3.00 2.50

Valentine's Day — A1012

No. 3148: a, Roses in heart. b, Cupid, hearts.

**2008, Feb. 6**
**3148** A1012 7p Pair, #a-b 1.65 1.20
*c.* Sheet of 10, 5 each #3148a-3148b 10.00 10.00

No. 3148c sold for 100p.

Missionary Catechists of St. Therese of the Infant Jesus, 50th Anniv. A1013

Designs: No. 3149, 7p, Emblem and nuns. No. 3150, 7p, 50th anniv. emblem, St. Therese of the Infant Jesus, Bishop Alfredo Obviar.

**2008, Feb. 23**
**3149-3150** A1013 Set of 2 1.35 1.00
*3150a* Pair, #3149-3150 1.50 1.20

**Bird Type of 2007 Without Blue Lines at Bottom**

**Miniature Sheet**

No. 3151: a, Mindanao bleeding heart pigeon. b, Nicobar pigeon. c, Black-chinned fruit dove. d, Metallic pigeon. e, Pink-necked green pigeon. f, Amethyst brown dove. g, Gray imperial pigeon. h, Red turtle dove. i, Pied imperial pigeon. j, Spotted imperial pigeon. k, Philippine eagle. l, Philippine cockatoo. m, Java sparrow. n, Blue-capped wood kingfisher.

**2008, Mar. 7** ***Perf. 13¾x13½***
**3151** A1003 7p Sheet of 14, #a-n, + label 13.50 13.50

2008 Taipei Intl. Stamp Exhibition. No. 3151 sold for 125p.

Rodents of Luzon Island — A1014

No. 3152: a, Luzon furry-tailed rat. b, Cordillera striped earth rat. c, Cordillera forest mouse. d, Cordillera shrew mouse.

No. 3153: a, 7p, Northern giant cloud rat. b, 7p, Lesser dwarf cloud rat. c, 20p, Bushy-tailed cloud rat, vert. (40x70mm).

**2008, Mar. 7** ***Perf. 14***
**3152** A1014 7p Block of 4, #a-d 3.60 3.00

**Souvenir Sheet**

***Perf. 14, Imperf. (20p)***
**3153** A1014 Sheet of 3, #a-c 3.75 3.75

Natl. Research Council, 75th Anniv. A1015

**2008, Mar. 12** ***Perf. 14***
**3154** A1015 7p multi .65 .40

Baguio Teachers Camp, Cent. — A1016

No. 3155: a, Camp. b, Teachers, bridge.

**2008, May 10**
**3155** A1016 7p Horiz. pair, #a-b 1.50 1.10

Bridges of the American Era — A1017

No. 3156: a, Gasan Bridge, Gasan, Marinduque. b, Hinigaran Bridge, Hinigaran, Negros Occidental. c, Wahig Bridge, Dagoboy, Bohol. d, Pan-ay Bridge, Pan-ay, Capiz.

No. 3157: a, Quezon Bridge, Quiapo, Manila. b, Governor Reynolds Bridge, Guinobatan, Albay. c, Mauca Railway Bridge, Ragay, Camarines Sur. d, Balucuan Bridge, Dao, Capiz.

Illustration reduced.

**2008, May 16**
**3156** A1017 7p Block of 4, #a-d 3.50 2.75

**Miniature Sheet**

**3157** A1017 7p Sheet of 4, #a-d 4.00 4.00

Miniature Sheet

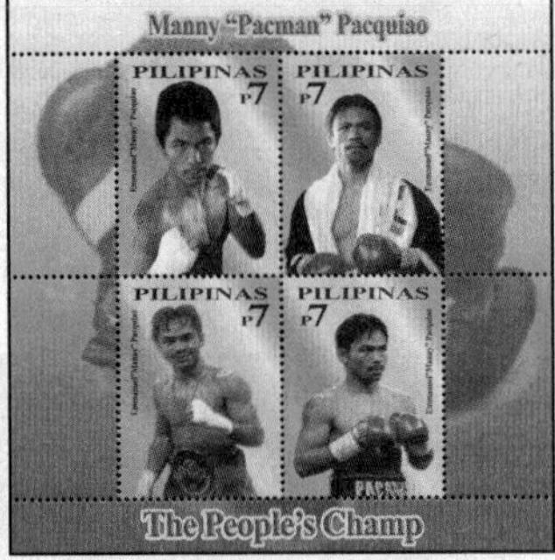


Manny Pacquiao, World Boxing Council Lightweight Champion — A1018

No. 3158 — Pacquiao: a, With hands taped. b, Wearing robe and gloves. c, Wearing championship belt. d, Wearing gloves.

**2008, May 30**
**3158** A1018 7p Sheet of 4, #a-d 5.00 5.00

Dept. of Science and Technology, 50th Anniv. — A1019

Philippine Nuclear Research Institute, 50th Anniv. A1020

**2008, June 4**
**3159** A1019 7p multi .65 .40
**3160** A1020 7p multi .65 .40

Liong Tek Go Family Association, Cent. — A1021

No. 3161: a, Association centenary emblem. b, Tai Bei Kong.

**2008, June 11**
**3161** A1021 7p Pair, #a-b 1.50 1.20

University of the Philippines, Cent. — A1022

Designs: Nos. 3162a, 3163c, 3164c, Emblem (with eagle). Nos. 3162b, 3163a, 3164a, Carillon. Nos. 3162c, 3163d, 3164d, Oblation sculpture. Nos. 3162d, 3163b, 3164b, Centenary emblem (with Oblation sculpture).

**2008** ***Perf. 13¾x13½***
**3162** A1022 7p Block of 4, #a-d 2.65 2.00

**Stamp Size: 40x30mm**

***Perf. 14***
**3163** A1022 7p Block of 4, #a-d 4.00 3.50
*e.* Souvenir sheet, #3163a-3163d 3.50 3.50

**Litho. With Foil Application**
**3164** A1022 7p Block of 4, #a-d 5.00 5.00
*e.* Souvenir sheet, #3164a-3164d 6.00 6.00

No. 3164 was printed in sheets containing four blocks that sold for 160p. No. 3164e sold for 50p.

Friar Andres de Urdaneta (c. 1608-1568), Navigator A1023

**2008, June 26** ***Perf. 14***
**3165** A1023 7p multi .60 .40

Philippine-Spanish Friendship Day.

Xavier University, Ateneo de Cagayan, 75th Anniv. — A1024

No. 3166: a, Immaculate Conception Chapel. b, Statue of St. Francis Xavier. c, Archbishop James T. G. Hayes. d, Science Center.

**2008, June 26**
**3166** A1024 7p Block of 4, #a-d 2.75 2.25

Ateneo de Davao University, 60th Anniv. — A1025

No. 3167: a, College building. b, High school building, statue. c, Grade school building, flags. d, Assumption (stained glass).

**2008, July 31**

**3167** A1025 7p Block of 4, #a-d 2.65 2.35
*e.* Souvenir sheet, #3167a-3167d 3.50 3.50

2008 Summer Olympics, Beijing A1026

Designs: 7p, Archery. 20p, Judo. 24p, Equestrian. 26p, Weight lifting.

**2008, Aug. 11** **Litho.**

**3168-3171** A1026 Set of 4 9.00 6.00

Se Jo Lim Family Association, Cent. — A1027

Designs: Nos. 3172a, 3173a, Pi Kan, Lim family ancestor. Nos. 3172b, 3173b, Senator Roselier T. Lim, Gen. Vicente P. Lim. Nos. 3172c, 3173c, Binondo Church, Chinese gate. Nos. 3172d, 3173d, Association centenary emblem, sun, stars and colors of Philippines flag.

**2008, Aug. 22** ***Perf. 14***

**3172** A1027 7p Block of 4, #a-d 2.75 2.50

**Souvenir Sheet**

***Perf. 14 on 3 Sides***

**3173** A1027 7p Sheet of 4, #a-d, + 2 labels 3.50 3.50

Philippine Bonsai Society, 35th Anniv. A1028

No. 3174: a, Pemphis acidula (on short-legged table), red background. b, Ficus microcarpa. c, Serissa foetida. d, Pemphis acidula, violet background. e, Pemphis acidula, blue background. f, Triphasia trifolia. g, Pemphis acidula (on piece of wood), cerise background. h, Bougainville sp.

No. 3175, vert.: a, Murraya sp. b, Pemphis acidula, tan background. c, Pemphis acidula, gray blue background. d, Pemphis acidula, violet background. e, Pemphis acidula, blue background. f, Antidesma bunius. g, Maba buxifolia. h, Ficus concina.

No. 3176: a, Lagerstroemia indica. b, Pemphis acidula, yellow green background. c, Vitex sp. d, Ixora chinensis.

**2008, Oct. 17** ***Perf. 14***

| | | | |
|---|---|---|---|
| **3174** | Block of 8 | 7.50 | 7.50 |
| *a.-h.* | A1028 7p Any single | .65 | .50 |
| **3175** | Block of 8 | 7.50 | 7.50 |
| *a.-h.* | A1028 7p Any single | .65 | .50 |

**Souvenir Sheet**

| | | | |
|---|---|---|---|
| **3176** | Sheet of 4 | 4.00 | 4.00 |
| *a.-d.* | A1028 7p Any single | .85 | .65 |

Miniature Sheet

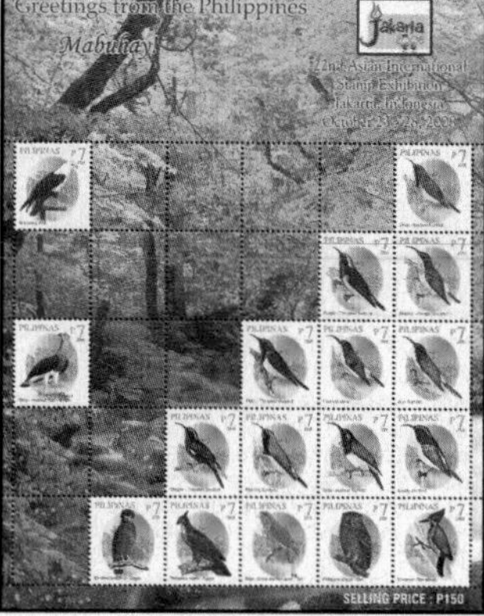


Jakarta 2008 Intl. Stamp Exhibition — A1029

No. 3177 — Birds: a, Brahminy kite. b, Olive-backed sunbird. c, Purple-throated sunbird. d, Metallic-winged sunbird. e, Gray-headed fish eagle. f, Plain-throated sunbird. g, Lina's sunbird. h, Apo sunbird. i, Copper-throated sunbird. j, Flaming sunbird. k, Gray-hooded sunbird. l, Lovely sunbird. m, Crested serpent eagle. n, Philippine hawk eagle. o, Blue-crowned racquet-tail. p, Philippine eagle owl. q, Common flameback.

**2008, Oct. 23** ***Perf. 13¾x13½***

**3177** A1029 7p Sheet of 17, #a-q, + 13 labels 16.00 *16.00*

No. 3177 sold for 150p.

Visit of Ban Ki-moon, United Nations Secretary General A1030

Ban Ki-moon and: 7p, UN emblem. 26p, Philippines President Gloria Macapagal-Arroyo.

**2008, Oct. 29** ***Perf. 14***

**3178-3179** A1030 Set of 2 2.75 1.50

Tourism — A1031

No. 3180: a, Boracay Beach, Aklan. b, Intramuros, Manila. c, Banaue Rice Terraces, Mountain Province. d, Mayon Volcano, Bicol.

20p, Puerto Princesa Underground River, Palawan. 24p, Chocolate Hills, Bohol. 26p, Tubbataha Reef, Palawan.

**2008, Nov. 3** ***Perf. 13½x13¾***

| | | | |
|---|---|---|---|
| **3180** | Block of 4 | 3.00 | 3.00 |
| *a.-d.* | A1031 7p Any single | .65 | .50 |
| **3181** | A1031 20p multi | 2.00 | 1.00 |
| **3182** | A1031 24p multi | 2.50 | 1.25 |
| **3183** | A1031 26p multi | 2.75 | 1.35 |
| | *Nos. 3180-3183 (4)* | 10.25 | 6.60 |

Philippine Postal Service, 110th anniv.

Christmas A1032

Designs: 7p, Mother with brown hair, and child. 20p, Mother nursing child. 24p, Mother, child, dove. 26p, Mother with child in sling.

No. 3188: a, 7p, Madonna and Child. b, 26m, Mother with sleeping child.

**2008, Nov. 10** ***Perf. 14***

**3184-3187** A1032 Set of 4 8.00 4.00

**Souvenir Sheet**

**3188** A1032 Sheet of 2, #a-b 4.00 4.00

Comic Book Superheroes of Carlo J. Caparas — A1033

No. 3189, 7p: a, Joaquin Bordado. b, Totoy Bato. c, Gagambino. d, Pieta.

No. 3190: a, 7p, Ang Panday (with hammer). b, 20p, Ang Panday (holding sword).

**2008, Nov. 17**

**3189** A1033 7p Block of 4, #a-d 2.65 2.35

**Souvenir Sheet**

**3190** A1033 Sheet of 2, #a-b 3.50 3.50

Natl. Stamp Collecting Month.

Senator Benigno S. Aquino, Jr. (1932-83) — A1034

No. 3191: a, 7p, Photograph. b, 26p, Drawing.

**2008, Nov. 27**

**3191** A1034 Horiz. pair, #a-b 3.50 2.65

Fernando G. Bautista (1908-2002), Founder of University of Baguio — A1035

**2008, Dec. 8**

**3192** A1035 7p multi .60 .40

New Year 2009 (Year of the Ox) A1036

Designs: 7p, Ox head. 20p, Ox.

**2008, Dec. 10**

**3193-3194** A1036 Set of 2 3.50 2.25
*3194a* Souvenir sheet of 4, 2 each #3193-3194 8.50 8.50

Crabs — A1037

No. 3195: a, Goneplacid crab. b, Largo's spider crab. c, Fuzzy sponge crab. d, Daniele's deepwater porter crab.

No. 3196: a, Stimpson's intricate spider crab. b, Spider crab.

**2008, Dec. 19**

**3195** A1037 7p Block of 4, #a-d 3.00 3.00

**Souvenir Sheet**

**3196** A1037 20p Sheet of 2, #a-b, + 2 labels 5.00 5.00

No. 3196 sold for 50p.

Dr. Manuel Sarmiento Enverga (1909-81), Educator and Politician A1038

**2009, Jan. 1** **Litho.** ***Perf. 14***

**3197** A1038 7p multi .60 .40

Love — A1039

No. 3198: a, Roses and heart. b, Hearts and envelope.

**2009, Feb. 2**

**3198** A1039 7p Pair, #a-b 1.30 1.00

Philippine Intl. Arts Festival — A1040

Emblem and: a, Painting. b, Theater masks and book of poetry. c, Cymbal and dancers. d, Theater and movie poster.

**2009, Feb. 16**

**3199** A1040 7p Block of 4, #a-d 2.65 2.50

Diplomatic Relations Between Philippines and Republic of Korea, 60th Anniv. — A1041

No. 3200: a, Panagbenga Flower Festival, Philippines. b, Cow Play, Hangawi, Republic of Korea.

**2009, Mar. 3**

**3200** A1041 7p Horiz. pair, #a-b 1.50 1.25

See Republic of Korea Nos. 2304-2305.

Birds — A1042

Designs: 1p, Mugimaki flycatcher. 2p, Narcissus flycatcher.3p, Mountain verditer-flycatcher. 4p, Blue rock thrush. 5p, Brown shrike. 8p, Apo myna. 9p, Crested serpent-eagle. 10p, Blue-crowned racquet-tail. 17p, Common flameback. 50p, Gray-headed fish-eagle. 100p, Philippine hawk-eagle.

No. 3206: a, Olive-backed sunbird. b, Metallic-winged sunbird. c, Plain-throated sunbird. d, Lina's sunbird. e, Purple-throated sunbird. f, Apo sunbird. g, Copper-throated sunbird. h, Flaming sunbird. i, Gray-hooded sunbird. j, Lovely sunbird.

No. 3211: a, Palawan flowerpecker. b, Fire-breasted flowerpecker. c, Cebu flowerpecker. d, Red-keeled flowerpecker.

No. 3212: a, Philippine tailorbird. b, Mountain tailorbird. c, Black-headed tailorbird. d, Ashy tailorbird.

**2009 Litho.** ***Perf. 13¾x13½***

| | | | | |
|---|---|---|---|---|
| **3201** | A1042 | 1p multi | .30 | .25 |
| **3202** | A1042 | 2p multi | .65 | .30 |
| **3203** | A1042 | 3p multi | .40 | .30 |
| **3204** | A1042 | 4p multi | .65 | .30 |
| **3205** | A1042 | 5p multi | 1.20 | .35 |
| **3206** | | Block of 10 | 30.00 | *30.00* |
| *a.-j.* | | A1042 7p Any single | 1.00 | .50 |
| **3207** | A1042 | 8p multi | .75 | .35 |
| **3208** | A1042 | 9p multi | .95 | .90 |
| **3209** | A1042 | 10p multi | 1.00 | .45 |
| **3210** | A1042 | 17p multi | 1.65 | .85 |
| **3211** | | Block of 4 | 10.00 | *8.50* |
| *a.-d.* | | A1042 20p Any single, dated "2009" | 2.00 | 1.20 |
| **3212** | | Block of 4 | 11.50 | *10.00* |
| *a.-d.* | | A1042 26p Any single, dated "2009" | 2.35 | 1.35 |

**Size: 30x40mm**

***Perf. 14***

| | | | | |
|---|---|---|---|---|
| **3213** | A1042 | 50p multi | 5.00 | 2.00 |
| **3214** | A1042 | 100p multi | 10.00 | 6.50 |
| | | *Nos. 3201-3214 (14)* | 74.05 | 61.05 |

Issued: 1p, 2p, No. 3206, 3/9; 3p, 4p, No. 3211, 6/2; 5p, 100p, 3/13; 8p, 9p, 10p, 17p, 50p, 3/23; No. 3212, 5/25.

See No. 3258.

**2009-10 Litho.** ***Perf. 13¾x13½***

| | | | |
|---|---|---|---|
| *3201a* | Dated "2009A" | .25 | .25 |
| *3201b* | Dated "2009B" | .25 | .25 |
| *3201c* | Dated "2009C" | .30 | .25 |
| *3202a* | Dated "2009A" | .30 | .25 |
| *3202b* | Dated "2009B" | .30 | .25 |
| *3202c* | Dated "2009C" | .25 | .25 |
| *3203a* | Dated "2009A" | .35 | .25 |
| *3203b* | Dated "2009B" | .40 | .30 |
| *3203c* | Dated "2009C" | .40 | .30 |
| *3204a* | Dated "2009A" | .40 | .30 |
| *3204b* | Dated "2009B" | .60 | .35 |
| *3204c* | Dated "2009C" | .50 | .30 |
| *3205a* | Dated "2009A" | .65 | .30 |
| *3205b* | Dated "2009B" | .40 | .30 |
| *3205c* | Dated "2009C" | .40 | .30 |
| *3206k* | Block of 10, #3206l-3206u, dated "2009A" | 11.50 | *11.50* |
| *3206l-3206u* | Like Nos. 3206a-3206j, any single, dated "2009A" | .85 | .50 |
| *3207a* | Dated "2009A" | .85 | .40 |
| *3207b* | Dated "2009B" | .75 | .30 |
| *3207c* | Dated "2009C" | .75 | .35 |
| *3208a* | Dated "2009A" | 1.15 | .50 |
| *3208b* | Dated "2009B" | .85 | .35 |
| *3208c* | Dated "2009C" | 1.00 | .40 |
| *3208d* | Dated "2009D" | .85 | .35 |
| *3209a* | Dated "2009A" | 1.00 | .45 |
| *3209b* | Dated "2009B" | 1.00 | .45 |
| *3210a* | Dated "2009A" | 1.65 | .85 |
| *3210b* | Dated "2009B" | 2.35 | 1.35 |
| *3210c* | Dated "2009C" | 1.65 | 1.00 |
| *3211e* | Block of 4, #3211f-3211i, dated "2009A" | 8.00 | 6.50 |
| *3211f-3211i* | Like Nos. 3211a-3211d, any single, dated "2009A" | 1.65 | .85 |
| *3212e* | Block of 4, #3212f-3212i, dated "2009A" | 10.00 | 8.50 |
| *3212f-3212i* | Like Nos. 3212a-3212d, any single, dated "2009A" | 2.00 | 1.00 |
| *3212j* | Block of 4, #3212k-3212n, dated "2009B" | 10.00 | 8.50 |
| *3212k-3212n* | Like Nos. 3212a-3212d, any single, dated "2009B" | 2.00 | 1.20 |

**Size: 30x40mm**

***Perf. 14***

| | | | |
|---|---|---|---|
| *3213a* | Dated "2009A" | 6.50 | 2.65 |
| *3213b* | Dated "2009B" | 5.00 | 2.25 |
| *3213c* | Dated "2009C" | 6.50 | 5.00 |
| *3213d* | Dated "2009D" | 5.00 | 2.65 |
| *3214a* | Dated "2009A" | 12.50 | 6.50 |
| *3214b* | Dated "2009B" | 10.00 | 5.00 |
| *3214c* | Dated "2009C" | 13.50 | 8.50 |
| *3214d* | Dated "2009D" | 10.00 | 5.00 |

Issued: No. 3206k, 5/13; No. 3205a, 5/25; Nos. 3201a, 3202a, 6/2; Nos. 3207a, 3208a, 3213a, 3214a, 6/8; Nos. 3201b, 3202b, 3205b, 8/6; No. 3208b, 8/10; Nos. 3203a, 3204a, 3210a, 8/13; Nos. 3207b, 3212e, 8/17; Nos. 3213b, 3214b, 9/1; Nos. 3209a, 3211e, 9/9; Nos. 3213c, 3214c, 11/24; No. 3201c, 12/11; Nos. 3209b, 3212j, 12/28; Nos. 3202c, 3204b, 3205c, 3210b, 1/11/10; Nos. 3203b, 3207c, 3208c, 1/12/10; Nos. 3213d, 3214d, 1/28/10; Nos. 3203c, 3204c, 3208d, 3210c, 2/5/10.

Minerals — A1043

No. 3215: a, Quartz. b, Rhodochrosite. c, Malachite. d, Nickel.

No. 3216: a, Cinnabar. b, Native gold. c, Native copper. d, Magnetite.

**2009, Mar. 25** ***Perf. 14***

**3215** A1043 7p Block of 4, #a-d 3.00 2.65

**Souvenir Sheet**

**3216** A1043 7p Sheet of 4, #a-d 4.00 4.00

Mothers Dionisia (1691-1732) and Cecilia Rosa Talangpaz (1693-1731), Founders of Augustinian Recollect Sisters — A1044

**2009, Apr. 28**

**3217** A1044 7p multi .60 .40

Art Deco Theaters — A1045

No. 3218: a, King's Theater. b, Capitol Theater. c, Joy Theater. d, Scala Theater.

No. 3219, horiz.: a, Life Theater. b, Times Theater. c, Bellevue Theater. d, Pines Theater.

**2009, May 8**

**3218** A1045 7p Block of 4, #a-d 3.00 2.50

**Souvenir Sheet**

**3219** A1045 7p Sheet of 4, #a-d 4.00 4.00

Rodolfo S. Cornejo (1909-91), Composer A1046

**2009, May 15**

**3220** A1046 7p multi .60 .30

Tourist Attractions in Taguig — A1047

No. 3221: a, City Hall. b, Global City. c, Santa Ana Church. d, Blue Mosque.

**2009, June 5** **Litho.**

**3221** A1047 7p Block of 4, #a-d 2.75 2.35

Diplomatic Relations Between Philippines and Thailand, 60th Anniv. — A1048

No. 3222 — Dances: a, Tinikling, Philippines. b, Ten Krathop Sark, Thailand.

**2009, June 14** ***Perf. 14***

**3222** A1048 7p Horiz. pair, #a-b 1.65 1.25

See Thailand No. 2429.

Ateneo de Manila University, 150th Anniv. — A1049

No. 3223: a, Sesquicentennial emblem. b, Blue eagle. c, St. Ignatius of Loyola. d, José Rizal.

**2009, June 14**

**3223** A1049 7p Block of 4, #a-d 3.50 3.00

*e.* Souvenir sheet, #3223a-3223d, + 2 labels 12.50 12.50

No. 3223e sold for 40p.

Baler, 400th Anniv. — A1050

No,. 3224: a, Old church. b, New church.

**2009, June 30** **Litho.**

**3224** A1050 7p Horiz. pair, #a-b 1.35 1.00

Che Yong Cua and Chua Family Association, Cent. — A1051

No. 3225: a, Chua Tiong. b, Chua Siok To.

**2009, July 15** ***Perf. 14***

**3225** A1051 7p Horiz. pair, #a-b 1.70 1.35

**Souvenir Sheet**

**3226** A1051 Sheet of 4, #3225a-3225b, 3226a-3226b, + 2 labels 4.00 4.00

*a.* 7p Like #3225a, perf. 14 at left 1.00 .70

*b.* 7p Like #3225b, perf. 14 at right 1.00 .70

See Nos. 3239-3240.

Pheepoy, Mascot of Philippine Postal Corporation — A1052

**2009, July 27** ***Perf. 13½x13¾***

**3227** A1052 7p multi .55 .30

See Nos. 3255, 3260, 3335, and 3336.

Knights of Columbus in Philippines, 50th Anniv. A1053

Color of denomination outline: 7p, Red. 9p, Dark blue.

**2009, July 31** ***Perf. 14***

**3228-3229** A1053 Set of 2 1.65 .50

Agricultural Cooperation Agreement Between Philippines and Brunei — A1054

**2009, Aug. 3**

**3230** A1054 7p multi .65 .50

Diplomatic Relations Between Philippines and Singapore, 40th Anniv. — A1055

No. 3231: a, Bamban Bridge, Philippines. b, Marcelo B. Fernan Bridge, Philippines. c, Cavenagh Bridge, Singapore. d, Henderson Waves and Alexandra Arch, Singapore.

**2009, Aug. 29** **Litho.**

**3231** A1055 7p Block of 4, #a-d 3.10 3.00

*e.* Souvenir sheet, #3231a-3231d 4.00 4.00

See Singapore Nos. 1398-1401.

Baguio, Cent. — A1056

No. 3232 — Butterfly on posters and Baguio landmarks: a, Mansion House. b, Mines View Park. c, Baguio Cathedral. d, Kennon Road.

**2009, Sept. 1** *Perf. 13¾x13½*
3232 A1056 7p Horiz. strip of 4, #a-d 4.00 4.00
*e.* Souvenir sheet, #3232a-3232d 6.00 6.00

Pres. Corazon Aquino (1933-2009) — A1057

No. 3233: a, With raised arm, denomination at UL. b, Head and signature, denomination at UR.
No. 3234: a, With raised arm, denomination at UR. b, Head and signature, denomination at UL.

**2009** **Litho.** *Perf. 14*
3233 A1057 7p Horiz. pair, #a-b 3.50 2.75
3234 A1057 7p Horiz. pair, #a-b 1.50 1.00

Issued: No. 3233, 9/8; No. 3234, 9/18.

Intl. Year of Natural Fibers A1058

No. 3235: a, Ananas comosus, clothing made from pineapple fibers. b, Musa textilis, bags and hats made from abaca fibers. c, Musa textilis, Philippines bank notes made from abaca fibers. d, Musa textilis, abaca rope.

**2009, Sept. 10**
3235 Horiz. strip of 4 2.65 2.65
*a.-d.* A1058 7p Any single .60 .50

Lobsters — A1059

No. 3236: a, Locust lobster. b, Blind lobster. c, Northwest Reef lobster. d, Two-spot locust lobster.
No. 3237: a, Neptune Reef lobster. b, Fan lobster. c, Blue-back locust lobster. d, Banded whip lobster.

**2009, Sept. 30**
3236 A1059 7p Block of 4, #a-d 3.50 3.00

**Souvenir Sheet**

3237 A1059 7p Sheet of 4, #a-d 4.00 4.00

Quezon City, 70th Anniv. — A1060

No. 3238: a, Statue of Pres. Manuel L. Quezon, Philippines flag. b, City Hall. c, Araneta Center. d, Eastwood City.

**2009, Oct. 12**
3238 A1060 7p Block of 4, #a-d 3.00 2.50
*e.* Souvenir sheet, #3238a-3238d 3.50 3.50

Che Yong Cua and Chua Family Association, Cent. — A1061

No. 3239 — Philippines flag, emblem and: a, Cua Lo.

**2009, Oct. 15** *Perf. 14*
3239 A1061 7p Horiz. pair, #3225a, 3239a. 1.50 1.25

**Souvenir Sheet**

3240 A1061 Sheet of 4, #3225a, 3226a, 3239a, 3240a + 2 labels 4.00 4.00
*a.* 7p Like #3239a, perf. 14 at right 1.00 1.00

Alpha Phi Beta Fraternity of the University of the Philippines, 70th Anniv. — A1062

No. 3241 — Fraternity emblem and: a, 70th anniv. emblem. b, Quezon Hall Oblation. c, Malcolm Hall. d, Founding fathers of fraternity.

**2009, Oct. 17** *Perf. 14*
3241 A1062 7p Block of 4, #a-d 2.65 2.35

A1063

Children's Games and Activities — A1064

No. 3242: a, Tumbang preso. b, Luksong tinik. c, Holen (marbles). d, Sungka.
No. 3243: a, Taguan (hide-and seek) (30x40mm). b, Sipa (30x40mm). c, Saranggola (kite flying) (30x40mm). d, Bangkang papel (paper boat racing) (30x40mm). e, Paluan ng palayok (piñata) (48x38mm). f, Luksong lubid (rope jumping) (48x38mm).
Illustrations reduced.

**2009, Nov. 9** *Perf. 14*
3242 A1063 7p Block of 4, #a-d 3.50 2.75

**Souvenir Sheet**

***Perf. 14, Imperf. (#3243e-3243f)***

3243 A1064 7p Sheet of 6, #a-f 6.00 6.00

Natl. Stamp Collecting Month.

Christmas A1065

No. 3244 — Lyrics from Christmas carol "Ang Pasko ay Sumapit" and: a, Four children caroling. b, Nativity. c, Magi on camels. d, Angels and baby Jesus. e, Christmas decorations.

**2009, Nov. 18** *Perf. 14*
3244 Horiz. strip of 5 4.00 4.00
*a.-e.* A1065 7p Any single .70 .50

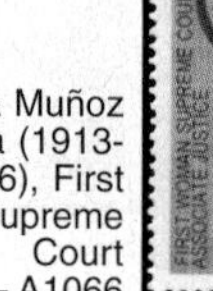

Cecilia Muñoz Palma (1913-2006), First Female Supreme Court Justice — A1066

**2009, Nov. 22**
3245 A1066 7p multi .60 .40

Diplomatic Relations Between the Philippines and India, 60th Anniv. — A1067

Endangered marine mammals: Nos. 3246a, 3247a, Whale shark. No. 3246b, Gangetic dolphin.

**2009, Nov. 27** **Litho.**
3246 A1067 7p Horiz. pair, #a-b 2.00 1.50

**Souvenir Sheet**

3247 A1067 Sheet of 2, #3246b, 3247a + 2 labels 5.00 5.00
*a.* 20p multi 3.50 2.50

See India No. 2374.

New Year 2010 (Year of the Tiger) A1068

Designs: 7p, Tiger's head. 20p, Tiger.

**2009, Dec. 1** *Perf. 14*
3248-3249 A1068 Set of 2 3.50 2.25
*3249a* Souvenir sheet, 2 each #3248-3249 8.50 8.50

Nudibranchs — A1069

No. 3250: a, Hypselodoris apolegma. b, Glossodoris colemani. c, Chromodoris sp. d, Chromodoris elizabethina.
No. 3251: a, Jorunna funebris. b, Chromodoris lochi. c, Noumea alboannulata. d, Chromodoris hintuanesis. e, Risbechi tryoni. f, Chromodoris leopardus.

**2009, Dec. 4**
3250 A1069 7p Block of 4, #a-d 3.50 3.00

**Souvenir Sheet**

3251 A1069 7p Sheet of 6, #a-f, + 2 labels 6.00 6.00

Stamp Collage Depicting Daedalus A1070

Designs: No. 3252, Entire collage.
No. 3253 — Quadrants of entire collage: a, UL. b, UR. c, LL. d, LR.

**2009, Dec. 7**
3252 A1070 7p multi .65 .50

**Souvenir Sheet**

3253 A1070 7p Sheet of 4, #a-d 3.50 3.50

Intl. Civil Aviation Organization, 65th anniv.

Return of Olongapo to the Philippines, 50th Anniv. — A1071

No. 3254 — Official seals of the Philippines and US and: a, Turnover ceremony. b, Parade of flags of the Philippines and US.

**2009, Dec. 7** *Perf. 14*
3254 A1071 7p Horz. pair, #a-b 1.35 1.00

Pheepoy Delivering Mail — A1072

**2009, Dec. 10** ***Perf. 13½x13¾***

**3255** A1072 7p multi .60 .30

See No. 3336.

Philippine Charity Sweepstakes Office, 75th Anniv. — A1073

No. 3256 — 75th anniv. emblem and: a, Charity Sweepstakes Office Building, Presidents Manuel L. Quezon and Gloria Macapagal Arroyo. b, Building. c, Building and family. d, Building and employees.

**2009, Dec. 18** ***Perf. 14***

**3256** A1073 7p Block of 4, #a-d 2.65 2.35

*e.* Souvenir sheet, #3256a-3256d 3.50 3.50

Potter From San Nicolas — A1074

**2009, Dec. 21**

**3257** A1074 7p multi .60 .40

San Nicolas, Ilocos Norte Province, cent.

**Birds Type of 2009**

No. 3258: a, Philippine eagle owl. b, Luzon Scops owl. c, Philippine Scops owl. d, Spotted wood owl.

**2010 Litho.** ***Perf. 13¾x13½***

**3258** Block of 4 9.50 *7.00*

*a.-d.* A1042 24p Any single 2.00 1.00

*e.* Block of 4, #3258f-3258i, dated "2009A" 9.50 *7.50*

*f.-i.* Like #3258a-3258d, any single, dated "2009A" 2.00 1.00

Nos. 3258a-3258d are dated "2009." Issued: No. 3258, 1/11; No. 3258e, 2/8.

St. Valentine's Day — A1075

No. 3259 — Cupid: a, With bow and arrow. b, Blowing flower petals.

**2010, Jan. 25** ***Perf. 14***

**3259** A1075 7p Horiz. pair, #a-b 1.50 1.00

Pheepoy on Motorcycle — A1076

**2010, Feb. 12** ***Perf. 13½x13¾***

**3260** A1076 7p multi .60 .30

See No. 3336.

Rotary International in the Philippines, 90th Anniv. — A1077

Nos. 3261 and 3262: a, Peace dove above people. b, Construction workers. c, Child receiving polio vaccine. d, Rizal Monument, map of the Philippines. No. 3262 has Rotary International emblem instead of "Service Above Self" slogan.

**2010, Feb. 23** ***Perf. 14***

**3261** A1077 7p Block of 4, #a-d 3.50 3.00

**Souvenir Sheet**

***Imperf***

**3262** A1077 7p Sheet of 4, #a-d 4.00 4.00

Beetles — A1078

No. 3263: a, Agestra luconica. b, Glycyphana. c, Paraplectrone crassa. d, Astrea.

No. 3264: a, Agestra semperi. b, Heterorhina. c, Agestra antoinei. d, Clerota rodriguezi.

**2010, Mar. 29 Litho.** ***Perf. 14***

**3263** A1078 7p Block of 4, #a-d 3.50 3.00

**Souvenir Sheet**

**3264** A1078 7p Sheet of 4, #a-d 4.00 4.00

Marine Life — A1079

Designs: No. 3265, Christmas tree worm. No. 3266, Yellow seahorse. No. 3267, Manta ray. No. 3268, Sea slug. No. 3269, Pencil urchin. No. 3270, Daisy coral. No. 3271, Magnificent sea anemone. No. 3272, Striped surgeonfish. No. 3273, Sundial. No. 3274, Blue linkia sea star. No. 3275, Sea hare. No. 3276, Giant clam. No. 3277, Green sea turtle. No. 3278, Sacoglossan sea slug. No. 3279, Lionfish. No. 3280, True clownfish. 8p, Harlequin shrimp. No. 3282, Coral beauty. No. 3283, Blue-ringed angelfish. No. 3284, Mandarinfish. No. 3285, Ribbon eel. 15p, Bowmouth guitarfish. No. 3287, Bigfin reef squid. No. 3288, Blue-spotted fantail stingray. No. 3289, Blue sea squirts. No. 3290, Scarlet-fringed flatworm. 24p, Branching anemone. 25p, Boxer crab. 26p, Spotted porcelain crab. 30p, Chambered nautilus. No. 3295, Red grouper. No. 3296, Giant moray eel. 40p, Textile cone. No. 3298, Marble sea star. No. 3299, Upside-down jellyfish. No. 3300, Bottlenose dolphin. No. 3301, Blue-ringed octopus.

**2010-11 Litho.** ***Perf. 13½x13¾***

| No. | Type | Value | Color | Unused | Used |
|---|---|---|---|---|---|
| **3265** | A1079 | 1p | multi | .25 | .25 |
| **3266** | A1079 | 1p | multi | .40 | .25 |
| **3267** | A1079 | 1p | multi | .50 | .25 |
| **3268** | A1079 | 2p | multi | .35 | .25 |
| **3269** | A1079 | 2p | multi | .50 | .25 |
| **3270** | A1079 | 3p | multi | .50 | .25 |
| **3271** | A1079 | 3p | multi | .50 | .25 |
| **3272** | A1079 | 3p | multi | .50 | .30 |
| **3273** | A1079 | 4p | multi | .50 | .30 |
| **3274** | A1079 | 4p | multi | .50 | .30 |
| **3275** | A1079 | 5p | multi | .65 | .30 |
| **3276** | A1079 | 5p | multi | .65 | .30 |
| **3277** | A1079 | 5p | multi | .50 | .30 |
| **3278** | A1079 | 5p | multi | .85 | .35 |
| **3279** | A1079 | 7p | multi | .65 | .25 |
| **3280** | A1079 | 7p | multi | .60 | .30 |
| **3281** | A1079 | 8p | multi | .65 | .30 |
| **3282** | A1079 | 9p | multi | 1.00 | .50 |
| **3283** | A1079 | 9p | multi | .85 | .35 |
| **3284** | A1079 | 10p | multi | .85 | .40 |
| **3285** | A1079 | 10p | multi | .85 | .40 |
| **3286** | A1079 | 15p | multi | 1.35 | .65 |
| **3287** | A1079 | 17p | multi | 1.65 | 1.00 |
| **3288** | A1079 | 17p | multi | 2.00 | 1.25 |
| **3289** | A1079 | 20p | multi | 1.60 | .75 |
| **3290** | A1079 | 20p | multi | 1.65 | .85 |
| **3291** | A1079 | 24p | multi | 2.00 | 1.35 |
| **3292** | A1079 | 25p | multi | 2.00 | 1.00 |
| **3293** | A1079 | 26p | multi | 2.10 | .70 |
| **3294** | A1079 | 30p | multi | 2.50 | 1.25 |
| **3295** | A1079 | 35p | multi | 3.00 | 1.40 |
| **3296** | A1079 | 35p | multi | 2.75 | 1.40 |
| **3297** | A1079 | 40p | multi | 3.25 | 1.50 |

**Size: 40x30mm**

***Perf. 14***

| No. | Type | Value | Color | Unused | Used |
|---|---|---|---|---|---|
| **3298** | A1079 | 50p | multi | 5.00 | 2.75 |
| **3299** | A1079 | 50p | multi | 4.00 | 2.00 |
| **3300** | A1079 | 100p | multi | 8.50 | 4.00 |
| **3301** | A1079 | 100p | multi | 8.50 | 4.00 |
| | *Nos. 3265-3301 (36)* | | | 63.95 | 31.95 |

Nos. 3275 and 3278 have the same vignette; No. 3275 has an incorrect inscription and No. 3278 has the corrected inscription.

Issued: Nos. 3265, 3284, 3293, 3/29; Nos. 3266, 3276, 3290, 6/15; Nos. 3267, 3277, 3297, 11/18; Nos. 3268, 3275, 4/16; Nos. 3269, 3295, 7/15; Nos. 3270, 3273, 3298, 5/17; Nos. 3271, 3274, 3299, 12/3; Nos. 3278, 3292, 12/22; Nos. 3279, 3300, 5/13; Nos. 3280, 3296, 12/17; Nos. 3281, 3289, 4/21; Nos. 3282, 3287, 3291, 5/21; Nos. 3283, 3288, 12/13; No. 3285, 11/8; Nos. 3286, 3294, 7/23; No. 3301, 12/1; No. 3272, 1/20/11.

See Nos. 3357-3368, 3389-3403, 3447-3450, 3471-3481.

Intl. Rice Research Institute, 50th Anniv. — A1080

No. 3302: a, 50th anniversary emblem. b, Buildings. c, Rice field, water, mountains. d, Rice plants.

**2010, Apr. 14** ***Perf. 14***

**3302** A1080 7p Block of 4, #a-d 2.65 2.35

*e.* Souvenir sheet of 4 #3302a-3302d 3.50 3.50

Eraño G. Manalo (1925-2009), Executive Minister of Iglesia ni Cristo — A1081

Manalo, church and: No. 3303, Country name in brown, "2010" at left under "P." No. 3304, Like #3303, "2010" under denomination. No. 3305, Like #3303, country name in black. No. 3306, Like #3305, "2010" under denomination.

**2010**

**3303** A1081 7p multi 2.00 1.00

**3304** A1081 7p multi 1.50 .85

**3305** A1081 7p multi .85 .50

**3306** A1081 7p multi .85 .50

*Nos. 3303-3306 (4)* 5.20 2.85

Issued: No. 3303, 4/23; No. 3304, 4/28; No. 3305, 5/11; No. 3306, 12/15.

Paintings by Vicente S. Manansala (1910-81) A1082

Designs: No. 3307, 7p, Sabungero. No. 3308, 7p, Bayanihan, horiz. No. 3309, 7p, Fish Vendor, horiz. No. 3310, 7p, Nipa Hut, horiz. 20p, Planting of the First Cross, horiz. (80x30mm).

No. 3312: a, Rooster. b, Mamimintakasi. c, I Believe in God, horiz. d, Three Carabaos, horiz.

**2010, May 20** ***Perf. 14***

**3307-3311** A1082 Set of 5 5.00 3.50

***Perf. 14, Imperf. (#3312c-3312d)***

**3312** A1082 7p Sheet of 4, #a-d 4.00 4.00

No. 3311 was printed in sheets of 4.

Philippine Centennial Tree and Emblem of Municipality of Magallanes A1083

Tree at: 7p, Right. 9p, Left.

**2010, May 28** ***Perf. 14***

**3313-3314** A1083 Set of 2 1.50 .80

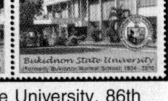

Bukidnon State University, 86th Anniv. — A1084

No. 3315 — University emblem and: a, Main building and sign. b, Education building and flagpole.

**2010, June 18**

**3315** A1084 7p Horiz. pair, #a-b 1.40 1.00

Veterans Federation of the Philippines, 50th Anniv. — A1085

No. 3316 — Soldiers and: a, Emblem at left. b, Emblem at right.

**2010, June 18**

**3316** A1085 7p Horiz. pair, #a-b 1.40 1.00

Light Rail Transit Authority, 30th Anniv. — A1086

Nos. 3317 and 3318: a, Train on curved bridge. b, Train, domed building at right. c, Train, pink and blue buildings. d, Cars on road below train.

**2010, July 12** ***Perf. 14***
**3317** A1086 7p Block of 4, #a-d 3.00 2.50

**Souvenir Sheet**

***Imperf***

**3318** A1086 10p Sheet of 4, #a-d 4.50 4.50

Inauguration of Pres. Benigno S. Aquino III — A1087

Pres. Aquino: 7p, Taking oath. 40p, Giving inaugural speech, vert.

**2010, July 26** ***Perf. 14***
**3319-3320** A1087 Set of 2 4.00 2.00

Philippine Tuberculosis Society, Cent. — A1088

Society emblem and health care workers with inscription at bottom in: 7p, Tagalog. 9p, English.
26p, Emblem and 1935 Manuel L. Quezon birthday seal.

**2010, July 29** ***Perf. 14***
**3321-3322** A1088 Set of 2 1.60 1.25

**Souvenir Sheet**

**3323** A1088 26p multi 3.50 3.50

No. 3323 contains one 120x30mm stamp.

Devotion to Our Lady of Peñafrancia, 300th Anniv. — A1089

No. 3324: a, Our Lady of Peñafrancia, red panel. b, Our Lady of Peñafrancia, green panel. c, Our Lady of Peñafrancia Shrine, blue panel. d, Our Lady of Peñafrancia Basilica, yellow panel.
20p, Our Lady of Peñafrancia Shrine, Naga City, horiz.

**2010, Sept. 8** ***Perf. 14***
**3324** A1089 7p Block of 4, #a-d 2.60 2.25

**Souvenir Sheet**

**3325** A1089 28p multi 2.60 2.25

No. 3325 contains one 80x30mm stamp.

Dogs — A1090

No. 3326: a, Chow chow. b, Bull terrier. c, Labrador retriever. d, Beagle.
No. 3327: a, American Eskimo dog. b, Black and tan coonhound. c, Afghan hound. d, Mastiff.

**2010, Sept. 9** ***Perf. 14***
**3326** A1090 7p Block of 4, #a-d 3.50 3.00

**Souvenir Sheet**

**3327** A1090 7p Sheet of 4, #a-d 4.00 4.00

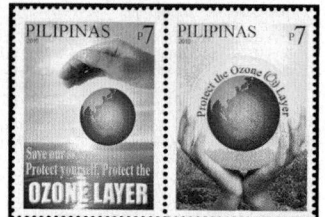

Ozone Layer Protection — A1091

No. 3328: a, Hand over globe. b. Hands below globe.

**2010, Sept. 16**
**3328** A1091 7p Horiz. pair, #a-b 1.40 1.00

Central Mindanao University, Cent. — A1092

No. 3329 — University emblem and: a, Administration Building and lamp poles. b, University building.

**2010, Sept. 17**
**3329** A1092 7p Horiz. pair, #a-b 1.40 1.00

Pres. Diosdado Macapagal (1910-97) A1093

**2010, Sept. 28**
**3330** A1093 7p multi .65 .50

Day of the Galleon — A1094

No. 3331 — Galleon and map of: a, Pacific Ocean, East Asia, Western North America. b, Atlantic Ocean, Eastern North America, Western Europe and West Africa.
40p, Like #3331b.

**2010, Oct. 8**
**3331** A1094 7p Horiz. pair, #a-b 1.75 1.35
*c.* Souvenir sheet of 2, #3331a-3331b 2.00 2.00

**Souvenir Sheet**

**3332** Sheet of 2, #3331a, 3332a 6.00 6.00
*a.* A1094 40p multi 4.00 4.00

Intl. Year of Biodiversity — A1095

No. 3333 — Children's art by: a, Krysten Alarice Tan. b. Justen Paul Tolentino.

**2010, Oct. 26**
**3333** A1095 7p Horiz. pair, #a-b 1.75 1.25

Philippine Rice Research Institute, 25th Anniv. — A1096

No. 3334: a, Building. b, Plants in test tubes. c, Farmer in field. d, Farm workers and tractor.

**2010, Nov. 5** **Litho.** ***Perf. 14***
**3334** A1096 7p Block of 4, #a-d 2.75 2.00

**Pheepoy Types of 2009-10 Redrawn and**

Pheepoy in Mail Van — A1097

**2010, Nov. 8** ***Perf. 13½x13¾***
**3335** A1097 7p multi, "Pheepoy" 7mm wide .60 .30

**Souvenir Sheet**

**3336** Sheet of 4 3.50 3.50
*a.* A1052 7p multi, "Pheepoy" 6mm wide, dated "2010" .65 .50
*b.* A1072 7p multi, dark blue sky, dated "2010" .65 .50
*c.* A1076 7p multi, "Pheepoy" at bottom center .65 .50
*d.* A1097 7p multi, "Pheepoy" 6mm wide .65 .50
*e.* Sheet of 4, #3336f-3336i, imperf. 3.50 3.50
*f.* As "a," imperf. .65 .50
*g.* As "b," imperf. .65 .50
*h.* As "c," imperf. .65 .50
*i.* As "d," imperf. .65 .50

A1098

National Stamp Collecting Month — A1099

No. 3337: a, Levi Celerio (1910-2002), composer. b, Leonor Orosa Goquingco (1917-2005), dancer. c, Carlos L. Quirino (1910-99), historian. d, Nick Joaquin (1917-2004), writer.
No. 3338 — Fernando Poe, Jr. (1939-2004), actor: a, Scene from film *Ang Panday Ikatlong Yugto* (The Blacksmith, Part 3). b, Scene from film *Umpisahan Mo. . . Tatapusin Ko!* (You Start. . . I'll Finish). c, Scene from *Pepeng Kaliwete* (Pepe Lefty). d, Portrait.

**2010** ***Perf. 14***
**3337** A1098 7p Block of 4, #a-d 3.50 2.75
**3338** A1099 7p Block of 4, #a-d 3.50 2.75
*e.* Souvenir sheet of 3, #3338a-3338c, + label 3.00 *3.00*

Issued: Nos. 3337, 3338e, 11/10; No. 3338, 11/25.

Inauguration of Vice-President Jejomar C. Binay — A1100

**2010, Nov. 11** **Litho.** ***Perf. 14***
**3339** A1100 7p multi .60 .40

Christmas — A1101

No. 3340: a, Holy Family in Filipino clothing, St. Peter's Basilica. b, Holy Family. c, Holy Family on jar. d, Adoration of the Shepherds.

**2010, Nov. 23**
**3340** A1101 7p Block of 4, #a-d 3.50 3.00

Ateneo de Manila Class of 1960, 50th Anniv. — A1102

No. 3341: a, Ateneo de Manila emblems, "Fabilioh!" b, Eagle, cross on steeple, bell. c, Man, boy, statue of Virgin Mary. d, Bell.

**2010, Dec. 2**
**3341** A1102 7p Block of 4, #a-d 2.75 2.25

New Year 2011 (Year of the Rabbit) A1103

Designs: 7p, Head of rabbit. 30p, Rabbit.

**2010, Dec. 6**
**3342-3343** A1103 Set of 2 4.00 2.75
*3343a* Souvenir sheet of 4, 2 each #3342-3343 9.00 9.00

Senator Ambrosio B. Padilla (1910-90) — A1104

No. 3344 — Portrait of Padilla and: a, Padilla at microphone. b, Padilla playing basketball.

**2010, Dec. 7**
**3344** A1104 7p Horiz. pair, #a-b 1.35 .90

SyCip, Salazar, Hernandez & Gatmaitan Law Firm, 65th Anniv. A1105

**2010, Dec. 10**
**3345** A1105 7p multi .60 .40

Grace Christian College, Manila, 60th Anniv. — A1106

No. 3346: a, Emblem and building. b, Emblem, "Grace at 60." c, Building, Chinese characters. d, Building, Chinese characters, founders Julia L. Tan, Dr. and Mrs. Edward Spahr.

**2010, Dec. 16** *Perf. 14*
**3346** A1106 7p Block of 4, #a-d 3.00 2.75
*e.* Souvenir sheet of 4 #3346a-3346d 3.00 3.00
*f.* Block of 4, #3346g-3346j 4.00 3.50
*g.-j.* Like #3346a-3346d with "2010" date inside of frames, any single .85 .65
*k.* Souvenir sheet, #3346g-3346j 4.00 4.00

The "2010" year dates on Nos. 3346a-3346d and 3346e are below the frame lines at the lower right of each stamp. Issued: Nos. 3346f, 3346k, 5/10/11.

Valentine's Day — A1107

No. 3347 — Earth, hearts and Philippine Postal Corporation mascot Pheepoy: a, Carrying flowers. b, Driving postal van.

**2011, Jan. 14** **Litho.** *Perf. 14*
**3347** A1107 7p Horiz. pair, #a-b 1.40 1.00

Kiwanis Club of Manila, 47th Anniv. — A1108

**2011, Jan. 21**
**3348** A1108 7p multi .65 .35

University of Santo Tomas, Manila, 400th Anniv. — A1109

No. 3349: a, Main Building. b, Central Seminary. c, Arch of the Centuries. d, The foundation of the University of Santo Tomas by Archbishop Miguel de Benavides.

No. 3350, vert.: a, 7p, Statue of Archbishop Benavides. b, 30p, Quattro Mondial Monument.

**2011, Jan. 25**
**3349** A1109 7p Block of 4, #a-d 3.00 2.25

**Souvenir Sheet**

**3350** A1109 Sheet of 2, #a-b, + central label 4.50 4.50

Hoyas — A1110

No. 3351: a, Mindoro hoya. b, Grandmother's wax plant. c, Summer hoya. d, Benito Tan's hoya.

No. 3352: a, Siar's hoya. b, Shooting star hoya. c, Imperial hoya. d, Buot's hoya.

**2011, Mar. 8**
**3351** A1110 7p Block of 4, #a-d 3.50 2.75

**Souvenir Sheet**

**3352** A1110 7p Sheet of 4, #a-d, + 2 labels 4.00 4.00

University of the Philippines College of Law, Cent. — A1111

No. 3353 — Building and emblem with: a, Scales. b, Lady Justice (centennial emblem).

**2011, Apr. 11**
**3353** A1111 7p Horiz. pair, #a-b 1.35 1.00

Center for Agriculture and Rural Development Mutually Reinforcing Institutions, 25th Anniv. — A1112

**2011, Apr. 25**
**3354** A1112 7p multi .65 .50

Department of Budget and Management, 75th Anniv. — A1113

**2011, Apr. 25** *Perf. 13½*
**3355** A1113 7p multi .65 .50

Wenceslao Q. Vinzons (1910-42), Leader of Resistance Forces in World War II — A1114

**2011, May 3** *Perf. 14*
**3356** A1114 7p multi .65 .50

Dated 2010.

**Marine Life Type of 2010**

Designs: 1p, Dendronephthya soft coral. 2p, Yellowstripe snapper. 4p, Branded vexillum. 5p, Sea apple. 7p, Spotted boxfish. 9p, Broadclub cuttlefish. 10p, Mushroom coral. 17p, Cowfish. 20p, Two-banded anemone fish. 30p, Lipstick tang. 40p, Yellow-backed damselfish. 100p, Pink tube sponge.

**2011** *Perf. 13½x13¾*
**3357** A1079 1p multi .30 .25
**3358** A1079 2p multi .35 .25
**3359** A1079 4p multi .65 .35
**3360** A1079 5p multi .65 .35
**3361** A1079 7p multi .70 .40
**3362** A1079 9p multi .90 .40
**3363** A1079 10p multi 1.00 .50
**3364** A1079 17p multi 1.65 1.00
**3365** A1079 20p multi 1.65 .85
**3366** A1079 30p multi 3.00 1.50
**3367** A1079 40p multi 4.00 2.00

**Size: 40x30mm**

*Perf. 14*

**3368** A1079 100p multi 10.00 5.00
*Nos. 3357-3368 (12)* 24.85 12.85

Issued: 1p, 5p, 7p, 9p, 8/17; 2p, 20p, 30p, 40p, 5/5; 4p, 10p, 17p, 100p, 5/12.

Worldwide Fund for Nature (WWF) A1115

Philippine crocodile: No. 3369, Hatchling and eggs (yellow and brown frame). No. 3370, Juvenile on log (olive green and yellow green frame). No. 3371, Adult on rock (blue green and blue frame). No. 3372, Adult with open mouth (orange and green frame).

**2011, May 16** *Perf. 14*
**3369** A1115 7p multi .85 .65
**3370** A1115 7p multi .85 .65
**3371** A1115 7p multi .85 .65
**3372** A1115 7p multi .85 .65
*a.* Block of 4, #3369-3372 4.00 3.50
*Nos. 3369-3372 (4)* 3.40 2.60

Nos. 3369-3372 each were printed in sheets of 8 and in sheets of 16 containing four of each stamp.

Arnis — A1116

No. 3373 — Arnis fighters wearing: a, Protective gear. b, White robes.

**2011, May 23**
**3373** A1116 7p Horiz. pair, #a-b 1.50 1.25
*c.* Sheet of 4, 2 each #a-b 3.50 3.50

Beatification of Pope John Paul II — A1117

No. 3374 — Pope John Paul II and: a, Grandstand, Rizal Park (denomination in green at UL). b, University of Santo Tomas (denomination in red at UR). c, Philippine International Convention Center (denomination in red at UL). d, Popemobile (denomination in green at UR).

40p, Pope with crucifix, vert.

**2011, May 30**
**3374** A1117 7p Block of 4, #a-d 3.50 2.75

**Souvenir Sheet**

**3375** A1117 40p multi + 2 labels 4.00 4.00

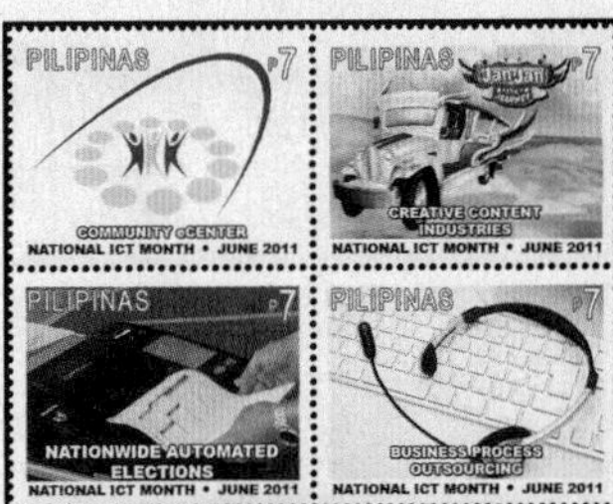


National Information and Communications Technology Month — A1118

No. 3376 — Inscriptions: a, Community eCenter. b, Creative content industries. c, Nationwide automated elections. d, Business process outsourcing.

**2011, June 13**
**3376** A1118 7p Block of 4, #a-d 2.75 2.00

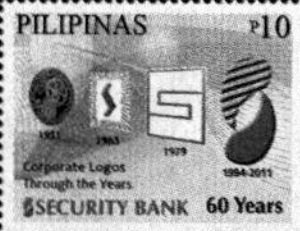

Security Bank Corporation, 60th Anniv. — A1119

No. 3377: a, Corporate Headquarters in 1951 and 2011. b, Company emblems.

**2011, June 18**

**3377** A1119 10p Horiz. pair, #a-b 1.60 1.30

Goethe Institute in the Philippines, 50th Anniv. — A1120

No. 3378: a, José Rizal Statue, Wilhelmsfeld, Germany. b, Fountain from Wilhelmsfeld in Luneta Park. c, Residence of Rizal, Wilhelmsfeld. d, Anniversary emblem.

**2011, June 19**

**3378** A1120 7p Block of 4, #a-d 2.75 2.00

A1121

A1122

José Rizal (1861-96), Patriot — A1123

No. 3379 — Rizal, anniversary emblem and: a, Dove, cover of *Noli Me Tangere*. b, Philippines flag elements.

No. 3380 — Annivesary emblem and Rizal in: a, Blue. b, Red.

No. 3381 — Philippines stamps depicting Rizal and monuments: a, 7p, #241, monument in Daet. b, 7p, #383, monument in Guinobatan. c, 7p, #461, monument in Santa Barbara. d, 7p, #497, monument in Biñan. e, 7p, #527, monument in Zamboanga. f, 12p, #813, monument in San Fernando. g, 13p, #857, monument in Lucban. h, 20p, #857A, monument in Romblon. i, 30p, #1313, monument in Jinjiang, China. j, 40p, #1198, monument in Illinois.

**2011, June 19** ***Perf. 14***

**3379** A1121 7p Horiz. pair, #a-b 1.40 1.00

**3380** A1122 7p Horiz. pair, #a-b 1.40 1.00

***Perf. 13¾***

**3381** A1123 Sheet of 10, #a-j 15.00 *15.00*

Yuchengco Group of Companies, Cent. — A1124

**2011, July 20** ***Perf. 14***

**3382** A1124 7p multi .65 .50

People Power Revolution, 25th Anniv. — A1125

No. 3383: a, Pres. Corazon C. Aquino (1933-2009), with collar visible, person with raised arm at LL, small helicopter at UL. b, Jaime Cardinal Sin (1928-2005), wearing biretta, helicopter at UR. c, Sin, without biretta, wearing black vestments, people with raised arms at left, helicopter at UL. d, Aquino, nun at LR.

No. 3384: a, Aquino, without collar visible, background like #3383a. b, Aquino, backgrond like #3383b. c, Aquino, background like #3383c. d, Sin, without biretta like #3383c, crowds in background. e, Sin, wearing white vestments, people carrying crucifix at right. f, Sin, wearing rosary around neck, crowds in background. g, Sin, wearing biretta like #3383b, religious statue at left.

**2011, Aug. 1** **Litho.**

**3383** A1125 7p Block of 4, #a-d 3.50 2.75

**3384** A1125 7p Sheet of 8, #3383d, 3384a-3384g 8.50 8.50

Holy Cross of Davao College, 60th Anniv. — A1126

No. 3385: a, Bajada Campus facade. b, Grade school and high school buildings. c, Palma Gil and Mabutas Halls. d, Babak and Camudmud Campuses.

**2011, Aug. 15** ***Perf. 14***

**3385** A1126 7p Block of 4, #a-d 2.75 2.00

Mother Francisca del Espiritu Santo de Fuentes (1647-1711), Founder of Dominican Sisters of St. Catherine of Siena — A1127

**2011, Aug. 24**

**3386** A1127 7p multi .65 .35

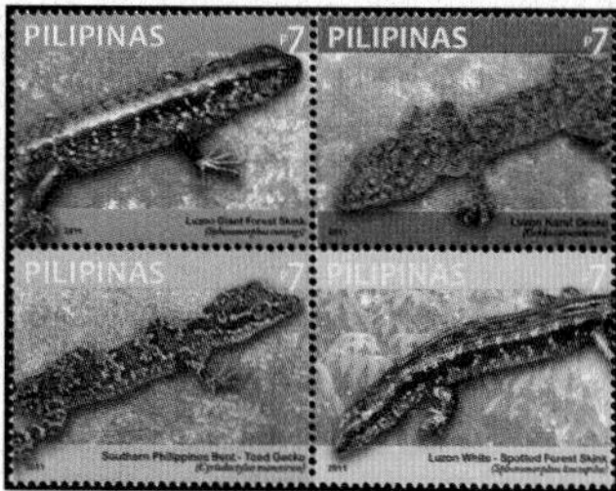

Lizards — A1128

No. 3387: a, Luzon giant forest skink. b, Luzon karst gecko. c, Southern Philippines bent-toed gecko. d, Luzon white-spotted forest skink.

No. 3388: a, Philippine forest dragon. b, Philippine spiny stream skink. c, Philippine sailfin lizard. d, Cordilleras slender skink.

**2011, Aug. 30** ***Perf. 14***

**3387** A1128 7p Block of 4, #a-d 3.50 3.00

**3388** A1128 7p Sheet of 4, #a-d, + 2 labels 4.00 4.00

**Marine Life Type of 2010 With Optical Code at Lower Right**

Designs: 1p, Picasso triggerfish. 2p, Marmorated cone shell. 4p, Blue-faced angelfish. 5p, Copper-band butterflyfish. 7p, Murex shell. 9p, Polyclad flatworm. 10p, Triton trumpet shell. 13p, Valentine puffer. 17p, Polka-dot grouper. 20p, Bennett's feather star. 25p, Oriental sweetlips. 30p, Eibl's angelfish. 35p, Kunie's chromodoris. 40p, Royal empress angelfish. 100p, Regal tang.

**2011** **Litho.** ***Perf. 14½***

| | | | | |
|---|---|---|---|---|
| **3389** | A1079 | 1p multi | .30 | .25 |
| **3390** | A1079 | 2p multi | .35 | .25 |
| **3391** | A1079 | 4p multi | .50 | .35 |
| **3392** | A1079 | 5p multi | .65 | .30 |
| **3393** | A1079 | 7p multi | .85 | .30 |
| **3394** | A1079 | 9p multi | 1.00 | .65 |
| **3395** | A1079 | 10p multi | 1.00 | .50 |
| **3396** | A1079 | 13p multi | 1.50 | 1.00 |
| **3397** | A1079 | 17p multi | 1.50 | .90 |
| **3398** | A1079 | 20p multi | 2.75 | 1.00 |
| **3399** | A1079 | 25p multi | 2.75 | 1.35 |
| **3400** | A1079 | 30p multi | 3.50 | 1.75 |
| **3401** | A1079 | 35p multi | 4.00 | 2.00 |
| **3402** | A1079 | 40p multi | 4.00 | 2.25 |

**Size: 40x30mm**

***Perf. 13x13½***

**3403** A1079 100p multi 13.50 10.00

*Nos. 3389-3403 (15)* 38.15 22.85

Issued: 1p, 2p, 5p, 10p, 20p, 30p, 10/17; 4p, 7p, 100p, 10/25; 9p, 25p, 35p, 11/4; 13p, 17p, 40p, 11/11.

Intl. Year of Forests — A1129

No. 3404: a, Batlag Falls, Tanay. b, Tree, Pansol.

**2011, Oct. 24** ***Perf. 13½x13***

**3404** A1129 7p Horiz. pair, #a-b 1.40 1.00

Day of the Galleon A1130

Nos. 3405 and 3406: a, Galleon at right, map of East Asia. b, Galleon at left, map of Central and North America. c, Galleon at center, map of Atlantic Ocean, Europe and Africa.

**2011, Nov. 10** ***Perf. 13x13½***

**3405** Horiz. strip of 3 2.50 2.50

*a.-c.* A1130 7p Any single .65 .50

**Souvenir Sheet**

***Perf. 13x13½ on 2 or 3 Sides***

**3406** Sheet of 3 + label 2.75 2.75

*a.-c.* A1130 7p Any single .75 .60

Adjacent stamps in No. 3406 are separated by simulated perforations.

Paintings by Hernando R. Ocampo (1911-78) — A1131

No. 3407: a, Homage to José Rizal. b, Break of Day. c, Summer in September. d, Mother and Child.

No. 3408, horiz.: a, Fiesta. b, Abstraction #15, 17. c, Kasaysayan ng Lahi. d, Abstraction #22, 26.

**2011, Nov. 11** ***Perf. 13½x13***

**3407** A1131 7p Block of 4, #a-d 3.50 2.75

***Perf. 13x13½***

**3408** A1131 7p Sheet of 4, #a-d 4.00 4.00

Stamp Collecting Month.

National Bureau of Investigation, 75th Anniv. — A1132

No. 3409: a, Emblem of National Bureau of Investigation. b, Justice José Yulo and Pres. Manuel L. Quezon. c, Pres. Manuel A. Roxas signing bill, J. Pardo de Tavera, first director of National Bureau of Investigation. d, Fingerprint under magnifying glass, laptop computer, "Justice."

**2011, Nov. 14** ***Perf. 13½x13***
**3409** A1132 7p Block of 4, #a-d 2.75 2.50

Christmas — A1133

No. 3410: a, Bells. b, Poinsettias. c, Toys and gifts. d, Parol (Christmas star lantern).

**2011, Nov. 26**
**3410** A1133 7p Block of 4, #a-d 3.00 2.75

New Year 2012 (Year of the Dragon) A1134

Designs: 7p, Head of dragon. 30p, Dragon.

**2011, Dec. 5** ***Perf. 13x13½***
**3411-3412** A1134 Set of 2 6.00 4.00
*3412a* Sheet of 4, 2 each #3411-3412 25.00 25.00

See Nos. 3435-3436.

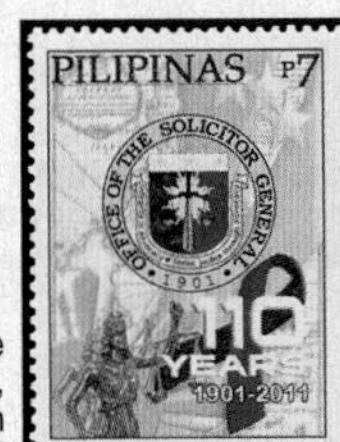

Office of the Solicitor General, 110th Anniv. — A1135

**2011, Dec. 15** ***Perf. 13½x13***
**3413** A1135 7p multi .65 .50

Frogs — A1136

No. 3414: a, Philippine spiny cinnamon frog. b, Philippine pygmy forest frog. c, Philippine flat-headed frog. d, Luzon limestone forest frog.

No. 3415: a, Gliding tree frog. b, Northern Luzon tree-hole frog. c, Taylor's igorot frog. d, Mary Inger's wart frog.

**2011, Dec. 15** ***Perf. 13x13½***
**3414** A1136 7p Block of 4, #a-d 3.50 2.75
**3415** A1136 7p Sheet of 4, #a-d + 2 labels 4.00 4.00

Lyceum of the Philippines University, 60th Anniv. — A1137

**2012, Jan. 2** **Litho.** ***Perf. 12***
**3416** A1137 7p multi .60 .40

Grand Lodge of Free and Accepted Masons of the Philippines, Cent. — A1138

No. 3417 — Centenary emblem and: a, Grand Lodge, Pres. Manuel L. Quezon. b, José Rizal, Marcelo H. del Pilar, Mariano Ponce, Plaridel Masonic Temple.

**2012, Jan. 19**
**3417** A1138 7p Horiz. pair, #a-b 1.75 1.40

Diocese of Malolos, 50th Anniv. — A1139

No. 3418 — Centenary emblem and: a, Virgin of the Immaculate Conception of Malolos. b, Immaculate Conception Cathedral and Basilica.

40p, Virgin of the Immaculate Conception of Malolos, vert.

**2012, Jan. 25**
**3418** A1139 7p Horiz. pair, #a-b 1.50 1.00

**Souvenir Sheet**

**3419** A1139 40p multi + 2 labels 4.00 4.00

Davao, 75th Anniv. — A1140

No. 3420: a, Davao City Hall. b, Kadayawan Festival. c, Waling-waling orchids. d, Mt. Apo, Philippine eagle.

**2012, Mar. 16** **Litho.** ***Perf. 14***
**3420** A1140 7p Block of 4, #a-d 3.50 3.00

Ateneo de Zamboanga University, Cent. — A1141

No. 3421 — Centenary emblem and: a, Fort Pilar Shrine. b, Father William H. Kreutz, S.J. Campus. c, Ateneo Brebeuf Gymnasium. d, St. Ignatius of Loyola.

**2012, Mar. 19**
**3421** A1141 7p Block of 4, #a-d 3.50 3.00
*e.* Souvenir sheet of 4, #3421a-3421d 3.50 3.50

St. Agnes Academy, Legazpi City, Cent. — A1142

No. 3422 — Centenary emblem and Main Building: a, Facade (denomination at UR). b, In ruins after World War II (denomination at UL). c, Facade, with flag at right (denomination at UR). d, Facade, flowers and flagpole in front (denomination at UL).

**2012, Mar. 21**
**3422** A1142 7p Block of 4, #a-d 3.00 2.50

Maria Makiling, Mythical Forest Guardian — A1143

**2012, Mar. 30** ***Perf. 13½x13¾***
**3423** A1143 7p multi .55 .25

Asian-Pacific Postal Union, 50th Anniv. — A1144

Designs: 7p, Emblem and flags. 30p, Emblem, flags, Philippines #1323 (80x30mm).

**2012, Apr. 1** ***Perf. 14***
**3424-3425** A1144 Set of 2 3.00 2.00

Philippine Postal Corporation, 20th Anniv. — A1145

No. 3426: a, Pres. Corazon Aquino, Postal Service Act of 1992. b, Main Post Office, Manila.

**2012, Apr. 10**
**3426** A1145 7p Horiz. pair, #a-b 1.25 .90

Felipe Padilla de Leon (1912-92), Composer A1146

**2012, May 1**
**3427** A1146 7p multi .55 .35

Churches — A1147

No. 3428: a, La Immaculada Concepcion Parish Church, Guiuan. b, San Joaquin Parish Church, San Joaquin. c, Nuestra Señora de la Porteria Parish Church, Daraga. d, San Isidro Labrador Parish Church, Lazi.

No. 3429: a, Santiago Apostol Parish Church, Betis. b, La Immaculada Concepcion Parish Church, Jasaan. c, Our Lady of Light Parish Church, Loon. d, San Gregorio Magno Parish Church, Majayjay.

**2012, May 1**
**3428** A1147 7p Block of 4, #a-d 2.50 1.70

**Souvenir Sheet**

**3429** A1147 7p Sheet of 4, #a-d 3.50 3.50

45th Annual Meeting of Asian Development Bank Board of Governors, Manila — A1148

**2012, May 2** ***Perf. 14***
**3430** A1148 7p multi .55 .35

Day of Valor, 70th Anniv. A1149

Designs: 7p, Soldiers in Bataan Death March. 10p, Battery Hearn, Corregidor Island. 30p, Shrine of Valor, Mt. Samat, Bataan.

**2012, May 6** **Litho.**
**3431-3433** A1149 Set of 3 3.75 3.50

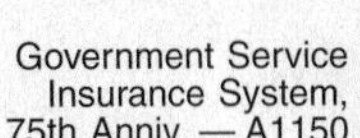

Government Service Insurance System, 75th Anniv. — A1150

No. 3434 — Emblem and: a, Head office in Solano, 1937 (25x22mm). b, Head office in Arroceros, 1957 (25x22mm). c, Financial Center, Pasay City (50x22mm).

**2012, May 28** ***Perf. 13½x13¾***
**3434** Horiz. strip of 3 4.50 4.50
*a.* A1150 7p multi .55 .35
*b.* A1150 9p multi .70 .50
*c.* A1150 40p multi 2.75 2.00

**Year of the Dragon Type of 2011 Redrawn Without Line To Right of "Pilipinas" and Dated "2012"**

Designs as before.

**2012, June 8** ***Perf. 14***
**3435-3436** A1134 Set of 2 5.00 3.50
*3436a* Souvenir sheet of 4, 2 each #3435-3436 9.00 9.00

Whitewater Rafters, Cagayan de Oro — A1151

**2012, June 15**
**3437** A1151 9p multi .70 .90

Winning Design in Intl. Year of Forests Children's Art Contest — A1152

**2012, June 18**
**3438** A1152 9p multi .75 .60

Bonifacio Monument, Caloocan A1153

**2012, June 25**
**3439** A1153 7p multi .55 .35

Habagat, God of Winds — A1154

**2012, June 28** ***Perf. 13½x13¾***
**3440** A1154 7p multi .55 .25

2012 Summer Olympics, London — A1155

No. 3441: a, Athletics. b, Shooting. c, Swimming. d, Boxing.

**2012, July 27** ***Perf. 14***
**3441** A1155 7p Block of 4, #a-d 3.50 3.00

Metrobank, 50th Anniv. — A1156

No. 3442: a, Binondo Branch, 1962. b, Metrobank Plaza, Makati City, 1977. c, GT International Tower, Makati City, 2004. d, Metrobank Plaza, Shanghai, People's Republic of China, 2001.

**2012, Aug. 25** **Litho.**
**3442** A1156 7p Block of 4, #a-d 2.75 2.50

José B. Laurel, Jr. (1912-98), Speaker of the House of Representatives A1157

**2012, Aug. 27** ***Perf. 14***
**3443** A1157 9p multi .70 .50

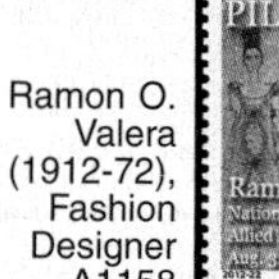

Ramon O. Valera (1912-72), Fashion Designer A1158

**2012, Aug. 31**
**3444** A1158 7p multi .55 .35

Amihan, Goddess of Monsoon Weather — A1159

**2012, Sept. 28** ***Perf. 13½x13¾***
**3445** A1159 7p multi .55 .25

Manila Hotel, Cent. — A1160

No. 3446: a, Facade. b, Maynila Ballroom. c, MacArthur Suite. d, Grand Lobby.

**2012, Oct. 5** ***Perf. 14***
**3446** A1160 7p Block of 4, #a-d 2.50 2.25

**Marine Life Type of 2010-11**

Designs: 1p, Twin-spot wrasse. 5p, Pearlscale butterflyfish. 40p, Tassle filefish. 100p, Koran angelfish.

**2012** ***Perf. 13½x13¾***
**3447** A1079 1p multi .25 .25
**3448** A1079 5p multi .40 .25
**3449** A1079 40p multi 3.50 1.75

**Size: 40x30mm**

***Perf. 14***

**3450** A1079 100p multi 8.00 4.00
*Nos. 3447-3450 (4)* 12.15 6.25

Issued: 1p, 5p, 40p, 10/18; 100p, 11/16.

Canonization of Blessed Pedro Calungsod (1654-72) — A1161

**2012, Oct. 21** ***Perf. 14***
**3451** A1161 9p multi .70 .35

Carlos "Botong" Francisco (1912-69), Painter A1162

**2012, Nov. 4**
**3452** A1162 7p multi .55 .35

Christmas — A1163

No. 3453: a, Nativity. b, People arriving at church for dawn mass.

**2012, Nov. 20** **Litho.**
**3453** A1163 10p Horiz. pair, #a-b 1.75 1.25

Bernardo Carpio, Mythical Cause of Earthquakes A1164

**2012, Nov. 28** ***Perf. 13½x13¾***
**3454** A1164 7p multi .55 .25

Lepanto Consolidated Mining Corporation, 75th Anniv. — A1165

No. 3455: a, Reforestation. b, Miners in mine entrance.

**2012, Dec. 7** **Litho.** ***Perf. 14***
**3455** A1165 7p Horiz. pair, #a-b 1.35 1.00

New Year 2013 (Year of the Snake) A1166

Designs: 10p, Head of snake. 30p, Coiled snake.

**2012, Dec. 12** **Litho.** ***Perf. 14***
**3456-3457** A1166 Set of 2 5.50 3.50
*3457a* Souvenir sheet of 4, 2 each #3456-3457 10.00 10.00

Miniature Sheet

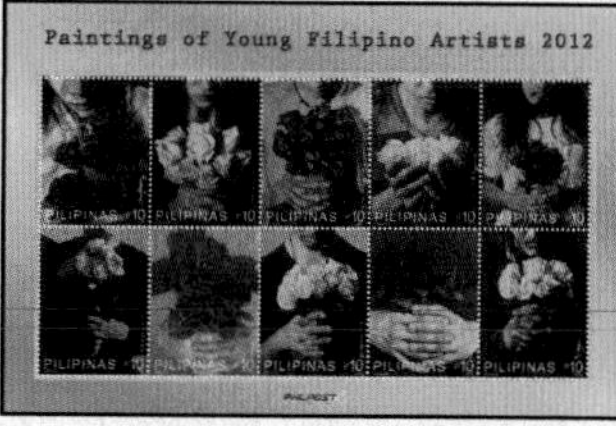


Paintings of People Holding Roses — A1167

No. 3458 — Paintings by various artists numbered at LR: a, 1/10. b, 2/10. c, 3/10. d, 4/10. e, 5/10. f, 6/10. g, 7/10. h, 8/10. i, 9/10. j, 10/10.

**2012, Dec. 14** ***Perf. 14***
**3458** A1167 10p Sheet of 10, #a-j 10.00 10.00

Valentine's Day — A1168

**2013, Jan. 14** **Litho.** ***Perf. 14***
**3459** A1168 10p multi .80 .50

Far Eastern University Save the Tamaraw Project A1169

Designs: No. 3460, 10p, Tamaraw. No. 3461, 10p, Tamerarw, vert.

**2013, Jan. 25** **Litho.** ***Perf. 14***
**3460-3461** A1169 Set of 2 1.75 1.00

Lucio D. San Pedro (1913-2002), Composer — A1170

**2013, Feb. 11** **Litho.** ***Perf. 14***
**3462** A1170 10p multi .80 .50

Teresita "Mama Sita" Reyes (1917-98), Restauranteur A1171

**2013, Feb. 11** **Litho.** ***Perf. 14***

**Stamp With Pink Shading at Top and Bottom**

**3463** A1171 10p multi .80 .50

**Souvenir Sheet**

**Stamp with White Frame at Top and Bottom**

**3464** A1171 10p multi + 2 labels 2.00 2.00

Pitcher Plants — A1172

No. 3465: a, Nepenthes peltata. b, Nepenthes truncata. c, Nepenthes burkei. d, Nepenthes attenboroughii.

No. 3466: a, Nepenthes mindanaoensis. b, Nepenthes sibuyanensis. c, Nepenthes mira. d, Nepenthes mantalingajanensis.

**2013, Mar. 13 Litho. *Perf. 14***

**3465** A1172 10p Block of 4, #a-d 3.50 3.00

**Souvenir Sheet**

***Imperf***

**3466** A1172 10p Block of 4, #a-d 4.00 4.00

No. 3466 has simulated perforations.

University of the Philippines Alumni Association, Cent. — A1173

No. 3467: a, Emblem and Oblation, purple panel. b, Emblem and Carillon Tower, blue panel. c, Emblem and Ang Bahay Ng Building, green panel. d, Emblem, orange panel.

**2013, Apr. 2 Litho. *Perf. 14***

**3467** A1173 10p Block of 4, #a-d 3.25 3.25

Diplomatic Relations Between Italy and the Philippines, 65th Annv. — A1174

No. 3468 — Flags of the Philippines and Italy and: a, Cinque Terre National Park, Italy. b, Banaue Rice Terraces, Philippines.

**2013, Apr. 4 Litho. *Perf. 14***

**3468** A1174 40p Pair, #a-b 6.50 6.50

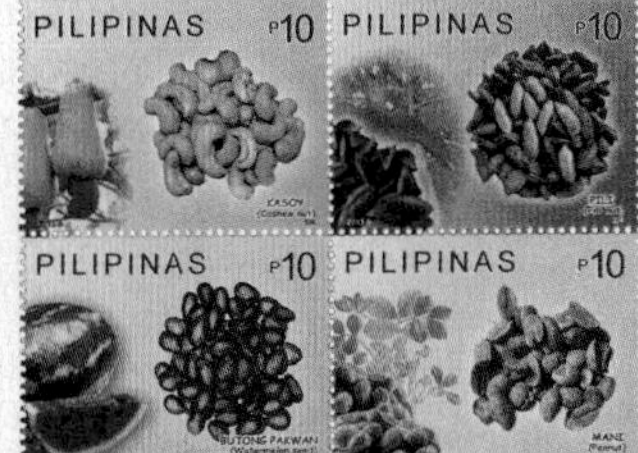


Edible Nuts and Seeds — A1175

No. 3469: a, Cashews. b, Pili nuts. c, Watermelon seeds. d, Peanuts.

No. 3470: a, Sunflower seeds. b, Mung beans. c, Coffee beans. d, Squash seeds.

**2013, Apr. 15 Litho. *Perf. 14***

**3469** A1175 10p Block of 4, #a-d 3.50 3.00

**Souvenir Sheet**

**3470** A1175 10p Sheet of 4, #a-d 3.25 3.25

**Marine Life Type of 2010-11**

Designs: 1p, Pinecone fish. 3p, Purple firefish. 5p, Pyjama cardinalfish. No. 3474, Long-nosed butterflyfish. No. 3475, Longnose filefish. 13p, Raccoon butterflyfish. 20p, Fire clown. 25p, Two-lined monocle bream. 30p, Green chromis. 40p, Common squirrelfish. 100p, Black-backed butterflyfish.

**2013 Litho. *Perf. 13½x13¾***

| | | | | | |
|---|---|---|---|---|---|
| **3471** | A1079 | 1p | multi | .25 | .25 |
| **3472** | A1079 | 3p | multi | .25 | .25 |
| **3473** | A1079 | 5p | multi | .40 | .25 |
| **3474** | A1079 | 10p | multi | .80 | .30 |
| **3475** | A1079 | 10p | multi | .80 | .40 |
| **3476** | A1079 | 13p | multi | 1.10 | .55 |
| **3477** | A1079 | 20p | multi | 1.60 | .80 |
| **3478** | A1079 | 25p | multi | 2.00 | 1.00 |
| **3479** | A1079 | 30p | multi | 2.40 | 1.25 |
| **3480** | A1079 | 40p | multi | 3.25 | 1.50 |

**Size: 40x30mm**

***Perf. 14***

**3481** A1079 100p multi 8.00 4.00

*Nos. 3471-3481 (11)* 20.85 10.55

Issued: 1p, 100p, 12/6; 3p, 5p, #3475, 13p, 12/10; #3474, 4/23; 20p, 40p, 12/13; 25p, 30p, 12/16.

Jesse M. Robredo (1958-2012), Interior Secretary A1176

**2013, May 27 Litho. *Perf. 14***

**3482** A1176 10p multi .80 .50

Philpost Emblem and Manila Central Post Office — A1177

Philpost Emblem A1178

**2013, May 29 Litho. *Perf. 13½x13¼***

**Denomination Color**

| | | | | | |
|---|---|---|---|---|---|
| **3483** | A1177 | 1p | brown | .25 | .25 |
| **3484** | A1177 | 7p | blue gray | .55 | .30 |
| **3485** | A1177 | 9p | org brn | .75 | .35 |
| **3486** | A1177 | 12p | yel org | .95 | .50 |
| **3487** | A1177 | 30p | orange | 2.40 | 1.25 |
| **3488** | A1177 | 35p | violet | 2.75 | 1.40 |
| **3489** | A1177 | 40p | green | 3.25 | 1.60 |
| **3490** | A1177 | 45p | lilac | 3.75 | 1.90 |

***Perf. 14***

**3491** A1178 100p dull vio brn 8.00 4.00

*Nos. 3483-3491 (9)* 22.65 11.55

See Nos. 3593-3594.

Malacañan Palace, Manila, 150th Anniv. — A1179

***Perf. 13½x13¾***

**2013, June 11 Litho.**

**3492** A1179 10p multi .80 .50

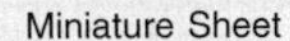

Miniature Sheet

Marine Biodiversity — A1180

No. 3493: a, Lemon goby. b, Dragon wrasse. c, Three-spot angelfish. d, White-tailed damselfish. e, Orange sea perch. f, Spotted puffer. g, Lemonpeel angelfish. h, Electric blue damsel.

**2013, Aug. 2 Litho. *Perf. 12***

**3493** A1180 10p Sheet of 8, #a-h, + central label 8.00 8.00

*i.* As #3493, with Thailand 2013 World Stamp Exhibition emblem on center label 10.00 10.00

Nos. 3493 and 3493i each sold for 100p.

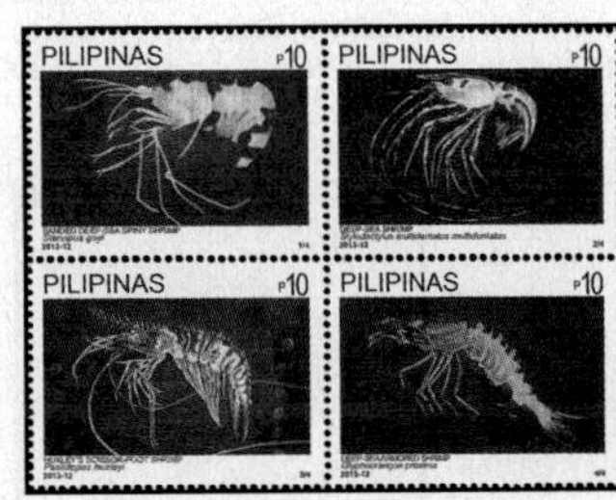


Shrimp — A1181

No. 3494: a, Banded deep-sea spiny shrimp. b, Deep-sea shrimp. c, Huxley's scissor-foot shrimp. d, Deep-sea armored shrimp.

**2013, Aug. 8 Litho. *Perf. 14***

**3494** A1181 10p Block of 4, #a-d 3.50 3.00

*e.* Souvenir sheet of 4, #3494a-3494d 3.50 3.50

Mariano Ponce (1863-1918), Writer — A1182

**2013, Sept. 5 Litho. *Perf. 14***

**3495** A1182 10p multi .80 .50

Boysen Paints, 60th Anniv. — A1183

No. 3496: a, Tree, logo for Knoxout Air Cleaning Paint. b, Boysen logo, eagle with paint can, house. c, Houses, anniversary emblem. d, Map of Philippines, logo for Nation Quality Paint.

40p, Eagle with paint can, horiz.

**2013, Sept. 9 Litho. *Perf. 14***

**3496** A1183 10p Block of 4, #a-d 3.50 3.00

**Souvenir Sheet**

**3497** A1183 40p multi + 2 labels 5.00 4.00

No. 3497 contains one 80x30mm stamp.

Gerardo "Gerry" De León (1913-81), Film Actor and Director A1184

**2013, Sept. 12 Litho. *Perf. 14***

**3498** A1184 10p multi .80 .50

50th Fish Conservation Week — A1185

No. 3499 — Winning paintings of endangered species in Bureau of Fisheries and Aquatic Resources art contest: a, Green Sea Turtle with Giant Manta Ray and Hammerhead Sharks, by Jaylord G. Aligway. b, Tabios (dwarf pygmy goby), by Jon Carlos A. Tabios. c, Butanding (whale shark), by Bernardo V. Vergara, Jr.

40p, Tabios, by Tabios, diff.

**2013, Oct. 14 Litho. *Perf. 14***

**3499** Horiz. strip of 3 3.00 2.40

*a.-c.* A1185 10p Any single .80 .50

**Souvenir Sheet**

**3500** A1185 40p multi + label 4.00 4.00

Motorized Tricycles — A1186

No. 3501 — Tricycle from: a, Cabadbaran. b, Puerto Princesa. c, Ozamiz City. d, Bukidnon.

**2013, Nov. 13 Litho. *Perf. 14***

**3501** A1186 10p Block of 4, #a-d 3.50 3.00

*e.* Souvenir sheet of 4, #3501a-3501d 3.50 3.50

Souvenir Sheet

Rodolfo "Dolphy" Vera Quizon (1928-2012), Comedian — A1187

**Litho. With Foil Application**

**2013, Nov. 23** ***Perf. 14***

**3502** A1187 100p multi + label 10.00 10.00

A1188

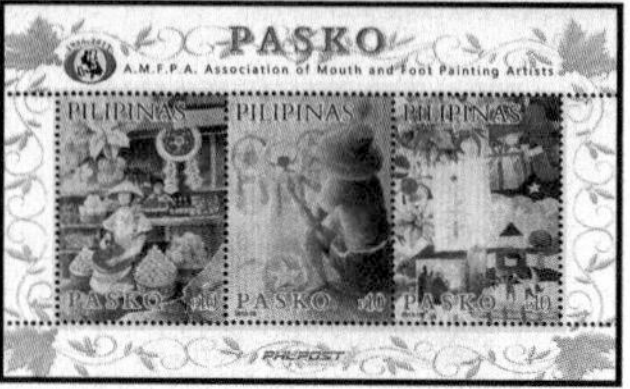

Christmas — A1189

No. 3503 — Paintings by Filipino members of Association of Mouth and Foot Painting Artists: a, The Family, by Jovita Sasutona (1/4). b, The Nativity Star, by Sasutona (2/4). c, Christmas Lantern, by Amado Dulnuan (3/4). d, Christmas at the Lake, by Bernard Pesigan (4/4).

No. 3504: a, Fruit Stand, by Sasutona. b, Lantern Maker, by Sasutona. c, Season Delight, by Sasutona.

**2013, Nov. 25** **Litho.** ***Perf. 14***

**3503** A1188 10p Block of 4, #a-d 3.50 3.00

**Souvenir Sheet**

**3504** A1189 10p Sheet of 3, #a-c 3.50 3.00

Andrés Bonifacio (1863-97), Founder of Katipunan Revolutionary Movement — A1190

No. 3505 — Winning designs in art contest: a, Dangal at Kabayanihan, by Roderick C. Macutay (1/4). b, Bonifacio Monument, by Marrion Dabalos (2/4). c, Dangal at Kabayanihan, by John Mark Nathaniel Trancales (3/4). d, Bonifacio, the Great Plebeian, by Julius R. Satparam (4/4).

No. 3506 — 150th anniversary emblem and vignette of: a, 30p, #3505a. b, 35p, #3505b. c, 40p, #3505d. d, 45p, #3505c.

**2013, Nov. 30** **Litho.** ***Perf. 14***

**3505** A1190 10p Block of 4, #a-d 3.50 3.00

**Miniature Sheet**

**3506** A1190 Sheet of 4, #a-d 12.00 12.00

No. 3506 contains four 30x80mm stamps.

New Year 2014 (Year of the Horse) A1191

Chinese characters and: 10p, Horse's head. 30p, Horse.

**2013, Dec. 2** **Litho.** ***Perf. 14***

**3507-3508** A1191 Set of 2 3.50 2.75

*3508a* Souvenir sheet of 4, 2 each #3507-3508 8.50 8.50

Philippine Deposit Insurance Corporation, 50th Anniv. — A1192

**2013, Dec. 5** **Litho.** ***Perf. 14***

**3509** A1192 10p multi .80 .50

National Parks Development Committee, 50th Anniv. — A1193

**2013, Dec. 5** **Litho.** ***Perf. 14***

**3510** A1193 20p multi 1.60 1.00

Parts of the design are covered with ink that glows in the dark.

Diplomatic Relations Between Nigeria and the Philippines, 50th Anniv. — A1194

No. 3511 — Flags of Philippines and Nigeria and: a, 10p, Coat of arms of Nigeria, daisies. b, 45p, Coat of arms of the Philippines, sampaguita flowers.

**2013, Dec. 20** **Litho.** ***Perf. 14***

**3511** A1194 Horiz. pair, #a-b 4.50 3.00

See Nigeria Nos. 853-854.

Saint Louis College, San Fernando, 50th Anniv. A1195

**2014, Jan. 20** **Litho.** ***Perf. 14***

**3512** A1195 10p multi .80 .50

Valentine's Day A1196

**2014, Jan. 27** **Litho.** ***Perf. 14***

**3513** A1196 10p multi .80 .50

Souvenir Sheet

New Year 2014 (Year of the Horse) — A1197

No. 3514: a, 50p, Snake (40x30mm). b, 50p, Goat (40x30mm). c, 100p, Horse (50x40mm).

***Perf. 13¼x13x13¼x13¼ (#3514a), 13¼x13¼x13¼x13 (#3514b), 13 (#3514c)***

**Litho., Litho. & Embossed With Foil Application (100p)**

**2014, Jan. 31**

**3514** A1197 Sheet of 3, #a-c 20.00 16.00

Selection of Megan Lynne Young as Miss World 2013 — A1198

No. 3515 — Young with: a, 30p, Arms not visible. b, 40p, Arms visible.

No. 3516: a, Like #3515a. b, Like #3515b.

**2014, Feb. 24** **Litho.** ***Perf. 14***

**3515** A1198 Horiz. pair, #a-b 6.00 5.00

**Souvenir Sheet**

**Litho. & Embossed With Foil Application**

**3516** A1198 50p Sheet of 2, #a-b 10.00 8.00

Main Post Office, Manila — A1199

**2014, Feb. 24** **Litho.** ***Perf. 14***

**3517** A1199 35p multi 4.00 4.00

No. 3517 was printed in sheets of six that sold for 250p. The right half of the stamp could be personalized. See No. 3703.

Alpha Phi Beta Fraternity at University of Philippines, 75th Anniv. — A1200

No. 3518: a, 75th anniv. emblem (1/4). b, 75th anniv. emblem, University of the Philippines emblem, statue (2/4). c, Statue, University building and emblem, fraternity members, 75th anniv. emblem (3/4). d, Silhouettes of statues, 75th anniv. emblem (4/4).

**2014, Mar. 8** **Litho.** ***Perf. 14***

**3518** A1200 10p Block of 4, #a-d 4.00 3.00

Election of Pope Francis, 1st Anniv. — A1201

**2014, Mar. 21** **Litho.** ***Perf. 14***

**3519** A1201 40p multi 3.25 1.60

See Vatican City Nos. 1553-1556.

Beach on Boracay Island — A1202

**2014, Mar. 28** **Litho.** ***Perf. 14***

**3520** A1202 15p multi 4.00 4.00

No. 3520 was printed in sheets of six that sold for 250p. The right half of the stamp could be personalized.

Watchtowers — A1203

No. 3521 — Watchtower at: a, Luna, La Union Province. b, Panglao, Bohol Province. c,

Oslob, Cebu Province. d, Narvacan, Ilocos Sur Province.
No. 3522, vert. — Watchtower at: a, Boljoon, Cebu Province. b, Bantay, Ilocos Sur Province. c, Samboan, Cebu Province. d, Tabaco, Albay Province.

**Litho. & Silk-Screened**

**2014, Mar. 28** ***Perf. 14***
**3521** A1203 25p Block of 4, #a-d 8.00 6.00

**Miniature Sheet**

**3522** A1203 25p Sheet of 4, #a-d 10.00 8.00

Central Luzon State University, 50th Anniv. — A1204

No. 3523 — 50th anniv. emblem and: a, Science and Technology Centrum. b, José Rizal.

**2014, Apr. 4** **Litho.** ***Perf. 14***
**3523** A1204 10p Horiz. pair, #a-b 1.60 1.25

Souvenir Sheets

2014 Canonization of Popes — A1205

Designs: No. 3524, 200p, Pope John XXIII. No. 3525, 200p, Pope John Paul II.

**Litho. & Embossed**

**2014, Apr. 27** ***Perf.***
**3524-3525** A1205 Set of 2 36.00 28.00

Philippine Charity Sweepstakes Office, 80th Anniv. — A1206

No. 3526: a, People at Lotto office (1/2). b, Family, sweepstakes office vehicle (2/2).

**2014, Apr. 28** **Litho.** ***Perf. 14***
**3526** A1206 10p Horiz. pair, #a-b 1.60 1.25

Minister Felix Y. Manalo (1886-1963) and Iglesia ni Cristo Central Temple, Quezon City — A1207

**2014, May 10** **Litho.** ***Perf. 13½***
**3527** A1207 10p multi .80 .50

Iglesia ni Cristo, cent.

Teresita "Mama Sita" Reyes (1917-98), Restauranteur — A1208

No. 3528 — Reyes, various foods, with background colors of: a, Orange (1/4). b, Lilac (2/4). c, Blue green (3/4). d, Orange and red (4/4).

**2014, May 11** **Litho.** ***Perf. 14***
**3528** A1208 10p Block of 4, #a-d 3.25 2.50

San Bartolome Parish, 400th Anniv. — A1209

**2014, May 17** **Litho.** ***Perf. 14***
**3529** A1209 20p multi 1.60 .80

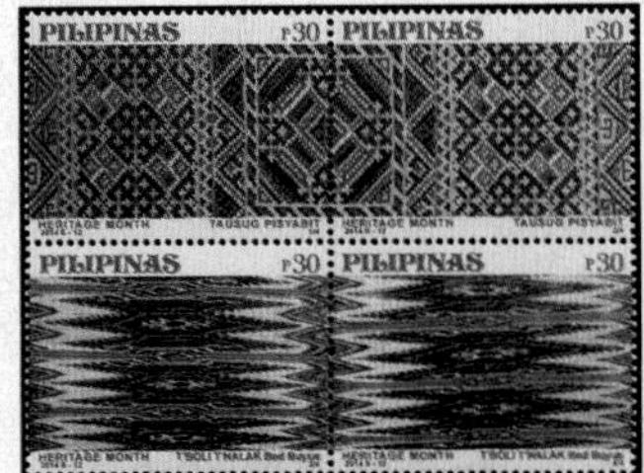

Heritage Month — A1210

No. 1210 — Various textile designs numbered: a, (1/4). b, (2/4). c, (3/4). d, (4/4).
100p, Weaver.

**Litho. & Silk-Screened**

**2014, May 30** ***Perf. 14***
**3530** A1210 30p Block of 4, #a-b 12.00 12.00

**Souvenir Sheet**

***Perf. 13½x13¾***

**3531** A1210 100p multi 15.00 15.00

No. 3531 contains one 50x35mm stamp.

Diplomatic Relations Between the Philippines and Germany, 60th Anniv. — A1211

No. 3532 — Flags of the Philippines and Germany and: a, 20p, Brandenburg Gate, Berlin. b, 40p, People Power Revolution Monument, Quezon City.

**2014, June 25** **Litho.** ***Perf. 14***
**3532** A1211 Horiz. pair, #a-b 5.00 4.50

Aquatic Flowers — A1212

No. 3533: a, Lotus. b, Amazon lily. c, Water lily. d, Water hyacinth.
40p, Marsh marigold, horiz.

**2014, June 27** **Litho.** ***Perf. 14***
**3533** A1212 10p Block of 4, #a-d 3.25 2.75

**Souvenir Sheet**

**3534** A1212 40p multi 3.25 3.25

Kapatagan Municipal Building, Seal of Kapatagan, Cathedral Falls A1213

**2014, July 5** **Litho.** ***Perf. 14***
**3535** A1213 10p multi .80 .50

Kapatagan, Lanao del Norte Province, 65th anniv.

DZRH Radio Station, 75th Anniv. — A1214

**2014, July 15** **Litho.** ***Perf. 14***
**3536** A1214 25p multi 2.00 1.00

Apolinario Mabini (1864-1903), Prime Minister — A1215

No. 3537 — 150th anniv. emblem and depiction of Mabini by: a, Pinky Ludovice. b, Kenneth V. Cantimbuhan. c, Julius R. Satparam.
40s, Mabini, by Dylan Ray A. Talon.

**2014, July 23** **Litho.** ***Perf. 14***
**3537** Horiz. strip of 3 3.50 2.40
***a.-c.*** A1215 10p Any single 1.00 .80

**Souvenir Sheet**

**3538** A1215 40p multi + label 3.25 3.25

ISO 9001: 2008 Certification of University of Mindanao — A1216

No. 3539: a, Bolton Campus. b, University emblem and check mark.

**2014, July 27** **Litho.** ***Perf. 14***
**3539** A1216 10p Horiz. pair, #a-b 1.60 1.25

Paintings by Pres. Corazon C. Aquino (1933-2009) — A1217

No. 3540: a, Enchanting Blossoms. b, Overflowing with Good Wishes. c, Blooms of Unity. d, Fifth Painting.
100p, Rosary and Roses.

**2014, Aug. 1** **Litho.** ***Perf. 14***
**3540** A1217 25p Block of 4, #a-d 8.00 8.00

**Souvenir Sheet**

***Perf. 13½x13¾***

**3541** A1217 100p multi 10.00 10.00

Nos. 3540-3541 are impregnated with a rose scent. No. 3541 contains one 50x35mm stamp.

Scouting in the Philippines, Cent. — A1218

No. 3542 — Centennial emblem and emblem of Philippines Scouting and: a, Boy Scout in Action Monument. b, Old and new Boy Scout National Headquarters.
30p, Emblems, Boy Scout in Action Monument, map of Philippines, vert.

**2014, Aug. 30** **Litho.** ***Perf. 14***
**3542** A1218 10p Horiz. pair, #a-b 1.60 1.40

**Souvenir Sheet**

**3543** A1218 30p multi 3.00 3.00

No. 3543 contains one 30x80mm stamp.

National Teachers' Month — A1219

**2014, Sept. 5** **Litho.** ***Perf. 14***
**3544** A1219 10p multi .80 .50

University of San Carlos College of Engineering, 75th Anniv. — A1220

**2014, Sept. 8** **Litho.** ***Perf. 14***
**3545** A1220 10p multi .80 .50

Waterfalls — A1221

No. 3546: a, Balagbag Falls. b, Merloquet Falls. c, Tinago Falls. d, Asik-asik Falls.
40p, Tiny-an Falls.

*Perf. 13½x13¾*

**2014, Sept. 22 Litho.**
**3546** A1221 10p Block of 4, #a-d 4.00 3.25

**Souvenir Sheet**

**3547** A1221 40p multi 3.50 3.50

No. 3547 contains one 100x35mm stamp.

National Family Week — A1222

No. 3548 — Winning art in stamp design contest by: a, Leah Anne Rulloda. b, Maria Joannes R. Puno.

**2014, Sept. 26 Litho.** ***Perf. 14***
**3548** A1222 10p Horiz. pair, #a-b 1.60 1.25

Quezon City, 75th Anniv. — A1223

No. 3549: a, Tandang Sora Shrine. b, Emilio Jacinto Shrine. c, North EDSA Shopping Mall. d, University of Philippines Ayala Techno Hub.
100p, Quezon Memorial Circle, horiz.

**2014, Oct. 12 Litho.** ***Perf. 13¾x13½***
**3549** A1223 10p Block of 4, #a-d 6.00 4.00

**Litho. & Silk-Screened (Margin With Foil Application)**

**Souvenir Sheet**

***Perf. 13¾ Horiz.***

**3550** A1223 100p multi 8.00 8.00

No. 3550 contains one 86x50mm stamp.

Leyte Gulf Landing, 70th Anniv. — A1224

**2014, Oct. 20 Litho.** ***Perf. 14***
**3551** A1224 10p multi .80 .50

Christmas — A1225

No. 3552: a, Holy Family (1/4). b, Carolers (2/4). c, Respect for elders (3/4). d, Christmas Eve feast (4/4).

**2014, Oct. 30 Litho.** ***Perf. 14***
**3552** A1225 10p Block of 4, #a-d 4.00 3.25

Growing Plant — A1226

**2014, Nov. 8 Litho.** ***Perf. 14***
**3553** A1226 10p multi .80 .50

Philippine recovery after Typhoon Haiyan.

First Philippine Postage Stamps, 160th Anniv. — A1227

No. 3554 and 3555
Philippines #1-2, 4-5, with large illustration of: a, #1. b, #2. c, #4. d, #5.

*Perf. 13½x13¾*

**2014, Nov. 10 Litho.**
**3554** A1227 10p Block of 4, #a-d 3.50 3.50
**3555** A1227 20p Sheet of 4, #a-d 6.50 6.50

National Stamp Collecting Month.

Filipino-Chinese General Chamber of Commerce, 110th Anniv. — A1228

No. 3556: a, Traders, ship, abacuses (1/2). b, People with computer, city skyline, airplane (2/2).

**2014, Nov. 19 Litho.** ***Perf. 14***
**3556** A1228 10p Horiz. pair, #a-b 1.75 1.40

Festival Masks and Facial Decorations A1229

No. 3557: a, Moriones Festival mask. b, Higantes Festival mask. c, Pintados Festival face decoration.
100p, Masskara Festival mask, horiz.

**2014, Nov. 22 Litho.** ***Perf. 14***
**3557** Horiz. strip of 3 2.75 2.00
*a.-c.* A1229 10p Any single .80 .80

**Litho. & Silk-Screened**

**Souvenir Sheet**

**3558** A1229 100p multi 8.00 8.00

No. 3558 contains one 80x30mm stamp.

New Year 2015 (Year of the Goat) — A1229a

Designs: 10p, Head of goat. 30p, Goat.

**2014, Nov. 24 Litho.** ***Perf. 14***
**3558A-3558B** A1229a Set of 2 4.00 2.00
*3558Bc* Souvenir sheet of 4, 2 each #3558A-3558B 8.00 8.00

Claudio Teehankee (1918-89), Chief Justice — A1230

**2014, Nov. 27 Litho.** ***Perf. 14***
**3559** A1230 10p multi .80 .50

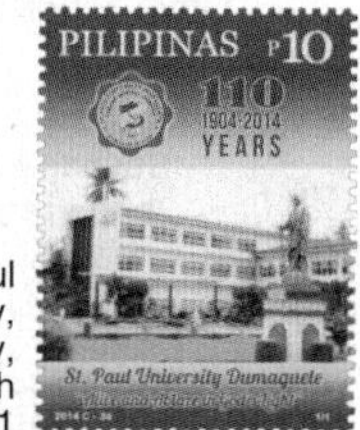

St. Paul University, Dumaguete City, 110th Anniv. — A1231

**2014, Dec. 8 Litho.** ***Perf. 14***
**3560** A1231 10p multi .80 .50

National Anti-Corruption Day — A1232

**2014, Dec. 9 Litho.** ***Perf. 14***
**3561** A1232 10p multi .80 .50

Shell Oil in the Philippines, Cent. — A1233

No. 3562: a. Shell Tabangao Refinery, 1960s (1/4). b, Shell Tabangao Refinery, 2014 (2/4). c, Shell retail station, 1930s (3/4). d, Shell retail station, 2014 (4/4).

**Litho. With Foil Application**

**2014, Dec. 13** ***Perf. 13½x13¼***
**3562** A1233 25p Block of 4, #a-d 10.00 8.00

Severino Montano (1915-80), Playwright A1234

**2015, Jan. 3 Litho.** ***Perf. 14***
**3563** A1234 10p multi .80 .50

A1235

Visit of Pope Francis to the Philippines — A1236

No. 3564 — Winning art in Pope Francis stamp design contest by: a, Bryan Michael Bunag (1/4). b, Dave Arjay Tan (2/4). c, Salvador Banares, Jr. (3/4). d, Mark Leo Maac (4/4).
100p, Pope Francis.

**2015 Litho.** ***Perf. 14***
**3564** A1235 10p Block of 4, #a-d 4.50 4.00

**Litho. & Embossed With Foil Application**

**Souvenir Sheet**

***Perf.***

**3565** A1236 200p multi 16.00 16.00

Issued: No. 3564, 1/8; No. 3565, 1/12.

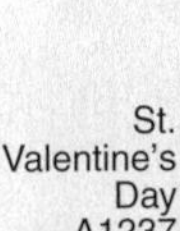

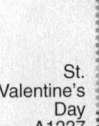

St. Valentine's Day A1237

No. 3566 — Hearts and: a, Cupid (1/4). b, Boy and girl (2/4). c, Bride and groom (3/4). d, Elderly couple (4/4).

**2015, Jan. 14 Litho. *Perf. 14***

**3566** Horiz. strip of 4 4.00 3.25
***a.-d.*** A1237 10p Any single .80 .80

Open Doors Monument, Rishon LeZion, Israel, Flags of Philippines and Israel — A1238

**2015, Jan. 27 Litho. *Perf. 14***

**3567** A1238 35p multi 3.00 1.50

See Israel No. 2048.

Laua-an, Cent. — A1239

**2015, Jan. 31 Litho. *Perf. 14***

**3568** A1239 10p multi .80 .40

Fruit — A1240

Designs: No. 3569, Bananas. No. 3570, Black plums. 3p, Mangos. No. 3572, Papayas. No. 3573, Aratiles fruit. No. 3574, Pineapples. No. 3575, Rose apples. 13p, Lanzones. No. 3577, Santols. No. 3578, Strawberries. 25p, Custard apples. No. 3580, Soursops. No. 3581, Ramboutaniers. No. 3582, Avocados. No. 3583, Jocotes. No. 3584, Cashew fruit. No. 3585, Johey oaks.

***Perf. 13½, 12¾ (#3570, 3573, 3575, 3578, 3581, 3583, 3585)***

**2015 Litho.**

| | | | | | |
|---|---|---|---|---|---|
| **3569** | A1240 | 1p | multi | .40 | .25 |
| **3570** | A1240 | 1p | multi | .40 | .25 |
| **3571** | A1240 | 3p | multi | .40 | .25 |
| **3572** | A1240 | 5p | multi | .60 | .25 |
| **3573** | A1240 | 5p | multi | .60 | .25 |
| **3574** | A1240 | 10p | multi | 1.00 | .40 |
| **3575** | A1240 | 10p | multi | 1.00 | .40 |
| **3576** | A1240 | 13p | multi | 1.10 | .55 |
| **3577** | A1240 | 20p | multi | 1.60 | .80 |
| **3578** | A1240 | 20p | multi | 1.60 | .80 |
| **3579** | A1240 | 25p | multi | 2.00 | 1.00 |
| **3580** | A1240 | 30p | multi | 2.40 | 1.25 |
| **3581** | A1240 | 30p | multi | 2.40 | 1.25 |
| **3582** | A1240 | 40p | multi | 3.25 | 1.60 |
| **3583** | A1240 | 40p | multi | 3.25 | 1.60 |

**Size: 43x43mm**

| | | | | | |
|---|---|---|---|---|---|
| **3584** | A1240 | 100p | multi | 8.00 | 4.00 |
| **3585** | A1240 | 100p | multi | 8.00 | 4.00 |
| | *Nos. 3569-3585 (17)* | | | 38.00 | 18.90 |

Issued: Nos. 3569, 3584, 3/12; Nos. 3570, 3585, 12/15; 3p, 13p, 25p, No. 3580, 2/10; Nos. 3572, 3577, 2/6; Nos. 3573, 3575, 3578, 12/10; Nos. 3574, 3582, 2/4; Nos. 3581, 3583, 12/11.

See Nos, 3651-3660, 3714-3718.

Salud S. Tesoro (1915-2000), Business Entrepreneur A1241

**2015, Feb. 6 Litho. *Perf. 13¾x13½***

**3586** A1241 10p multi .80 .50

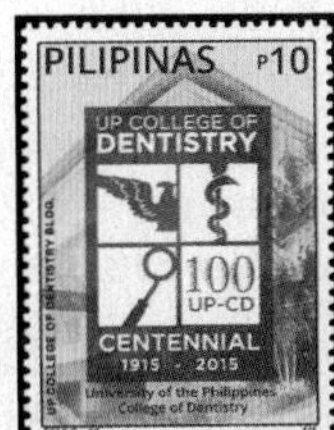

University of the Philippines College of Dentistry, Cent. — A1242

**2015, Feb. 6 Litho. *Perf. 14***

**3587** A1242 10p multi .80 .50

University of Saint Louis, Baguio, 50th Anniv. A1243

**2015, Feb. 11 Litho. *Perf. 14***

**3588** A1243 10p multi .80 .50

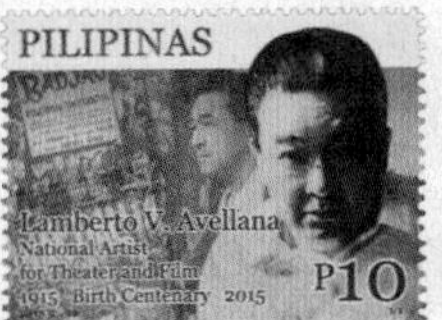

Lamberto V. Avellana (1915-91), Film Director A1244

**2015, Feb. 12 Litho. *Perf. 14***

**3589** A1244 10p multi .80 .50

Philippine Health Insurance Corporation, 20th Anniv. — A1245

**2015, Feb. 14 Litho. *Perf. 14***

**3590** A1245 10p multi .80 .50

**Souvenir Sheet**

New Year 2015 (Year of the Goat) — A1246

No. 3514: a, 50p, Horse (40x30mm). b, 50p, Monkey (40x30mm). c, 100p, Goat (50x40mm).

***Perf. 13¼x13x13¼x13¼ (#3591a), 13¼x13¼x13¼x13 (#3591b), 13 (#3591c)***

**Litho., Litho. & Embossed With Foil Application (100p)**

**2015, Feb. 19**

**3591** A1246 Sheet of 3, #a-c 25.00 25.00

Liceo de Cagayan University, Cagayan de Oro City, 60th Anniv. — A1247

**2015, Feb. 24 Litho. *Perf. 14***

**3592** A1247 10p multi .80 .50

**Philpost Type of 2013**

***Perf. 13½x13¼***

**2015, Mar. 20 Litho.**

**Denomination Color**

**3593** A1177 10p brown .80 .40
**3594** A1177 15p gray olive 1.25 .60

Visit the Philippines Year — A1248

***Perf. 13¾x13½***

**2015, Mar. 25 Litho.**

**3595** A1248 10p multi .80 .50

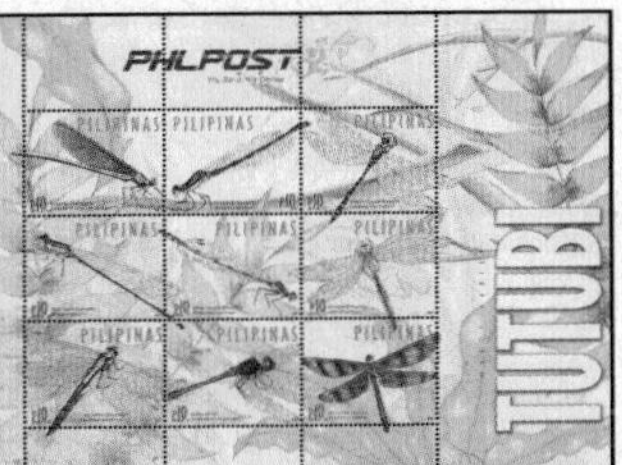

Dragonflies — A1249

No. 3596: a, Beautiful demoiselle. b, Small red damselfly. c, Golden-ringed dragonfly. d, Blue-tailed damselfly, e, White-legged damselfly. f, Emperor dragonfly. g, Club-tailed dragonfly. h, Ruddy darter. i, Halloween pennant.

40p, Broad-bodied chaser.

**2015, Mar. 27 Litho. *Perf. 14***

**3596** A1249 10p Sheet of 9, #a-i 7.25 7.25

**Souvenir Sheet**

***Perf. 13½x13¾***

**3597** A1249 40p multi + label 5.00 5.00

No. 3597 contains one 50x35mm stamp.

A1250

Discovery of Santo Niño Icon of Cebu, 450th Anniv. — A1251

**2015, Apr. 20 Litho. *Perf. 14***

**3598** A1250 10p multi .80 .50

**Souvenir Sheet**

**Litho. & Embossed, Sheet Margin Litho. & Embossed With Foil Application**

***Perf. 13¼***

**3599** A1251 200p multi 20.00 20.00

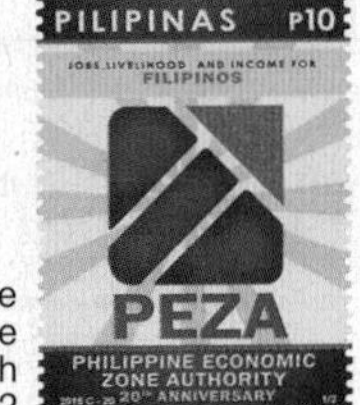

Philippine Econonic Zone Authority, 20th Anniv. — A1252

**2015, Apr. 20 Litho. *Perf. 14***

**3600** A1252 10p multi .80 .50

**Souvenir Sheet**

**Litho. & Embossed With Foil Application**

***Perf.***

**3601** A1252 200p Emblem, diff. 16.00 16.00

No. 3601 contains one 38mm diameter stamp.

Emmanuel "Manny" Pacquiao, Boxer and Politician A1253

**2015, Apr. 20 Litho. *Perf. 14***

**3602** A1253 10p multi .80 .50

**Souvenir Sheet**

***Perf. 13½x13¾***

**3603** A1253 40p Pacquiao, diff. 4.00 4.00

No. 3603 contains one 50x35mm stamp.

Philippine Children's Medical Center, 35th Anniv. — A1254

**2015, Apr. 20 Litho. *Perf. 14***

**3604** A1254 10p multi .80 .40

Miniature Sheet

Mythical Creatures — A1255

No. 3605: a, Nuno sa Punso. b, Sirena. c, Si Malakas at Si Maganda. d, Diwata (Maria Sinukuan).

**2015, Apr. 24 Litho. *Perf. 14***
**3605** A1255 10p Sheet of 4, #a-d 12.00 12.00

Taipei 2015 Intl. Stamp Exhibition.

City of San Pablo, 75th Anniv. of Chartering — A1256

No. 3606: a, Municipal Building. b, Sampaloc Lake.

**2015, May 7 Litho. *Perf. 14***
**3606** A1256 10p Horiz. pair, #a-b 1.60 1.60

Hibiscus Varieties — A1257

No. 3607 — Variety named: a, Goria. b, Nay Isa. c, Tandang Sora. d, Nazaria.
No. 3608 — Variety named: a, Emerita V. de Guzman. b, Helen L. Valmayor. c, Gelia T. Castillo. d, Dolores A. Ramirez.

**2015, May 12 Litho. *Perf. 14***
**3607** A1257 10p Block of 4, #a-d 3.25 3.25
**3608** A1257 10p Sheet of 4, #a-d, + 2 labels 4.00 4.00

Romblon State University, Cent. A1258

**2015, May 22 Litho. *Perf. 14***
**3609** A1258 10p multi .80 .50

Archdiocese of Jaro, 150th Anniv. — A1259

No. 3610: a, Jaro Cathedral. b, Nuestra Señora de la Candelaria icon.

**2015, May 27 Litho. *Perf. 14***
**3610** A1259 10p Horiz. pair, #a-b 1.60 1.60

Bilateral Relations Between the Philippines and Finland, 60th Anniv. — A1260

No. 3611 — Flags of the Philippines and Finland and: a, 10p, Brown bear. b, 40p, Philippine tamaraw.

**2015, June 3 Litho. *Perf. 14***
**3611** A1260 Horiz. pair, #a-b 4.00 4.00

Ateneo de Naga University, Naga City, 75th Anniv. — A1261

No. 3612: a, Emblem. b, University building.

**2015, June 5 Litho. *Perf. 14***
**3612** A1261 10p Horiz. pair, #a-b 1.60 1.00

Diplomatic Relations Between Philippines and People's Republic of China, 40th Anniv. A1262

**2015, June 9 Litho. *Perf. 14***
**3613** A1262 30p multi 2.40 1.25

Kites — A1263

No. 3614 — Various kites numbered: a, 1/10. b, 2/10. c, 3/10. d, 4/10. e, 5/10. f, 6/10. g, 7/10. h, 8/10. i, 9/10. j, 10/10.
40p, Kites.

**2015, June 23 Litho. *Perf. 14***
**3614** A1263 10p Sheet of 10, #a-j 8.00 8.00

**Souvenir Sheet**
***Perf. 13¾x13½***
**3615** A1263 40p multi 5.00 5.00

No. 3615 contains one 35x50mm stamp.

City of San Carlos, 55th Anniv. of Chartering — A1264

No. 3616: a, City Hall. b, Pinta Flores Festival.

**2015, July 1 Litho. *Perf. 14***
**3616** A1264 15p Horiz. pair, #a-b 2.40 2.40

Paintings of Flowers by Pres. Corazon A. Aquino (1933-2009) — A1265

No. 3617: a, Harmony of Flowers (1/4). b, Blue and Green Sea of Flowers (2/4). c, Valley of Flowers (3/4). d, Flowers by Forest Hills (4/4).
120p, Pink Flowers in a Vase, vert.

**2015, July 28 Litho. *Perf. 13½x13¾***
**3617** A1265 30p Block of 4, #a-d 15.00 15.00

**Souvenir Sheet**
***Perf. 13¾x13½***
**3618** A1265 120p multi + label 10.00 10.00

Flags and Emblem of Association of Southeast Asian Nations — A1266

**2015, Aug. 8 Litho. *Perf. 13¼***
**3619** A1266 13p multi 1.10 .55

See Brunei No. 656, Burma Nos. 417-418, Cambodia No. , Indonesia No. 2428, Laos No. , Malaysia No. 1562; Singapore No. 1742, Thailand No. 2875, Viet Nam No. 3529.

Teresita "Mama Sita" Reyes (1917-98), Restauranteur — A1267

No. 3620 — Reyes and: a, Fish, fruit and vegetables (2/3). b, Basket and blue swirls (3/3). c, Foods and stars (1/3).

***Perf. 13¾x13½***
**2015, Aug. 24 Litho.**
**3620** A1267 10p Strip of 3, #a-c 2.40 2.40

Bureau of Immigration, 75th Anniv. — A1268

**2015, Sept. 4 Litho. *Perf. 13½x13¾***
**3621** A1268 30p multi 2.40 1.25

Pres. Elpidio Quirino (1890-1956) A1269

**2015, Sept. 5 Litho. *Perf. 13¾x13½***
**3622** A1269 15p multi 1.25 .60

N. V. M. Gonzales (1915-99), Writer A1270

**2015, Sept. 8 Litho. *Perf. 14***
**3623** A1270 10p multi .80 .50

Bandera Newspaper, 25th Anniv. A1271

***Perf. 13¾x13½***
**2015, Sept. 10 Litho.**
**3624** A1271 15p multi 1.25 .60

Manila Observatory, 150th Anniv. — A1272

**2015, Sept. 25 Litho. *Perf. 14***
**3625** A1272 15p multi 1.25 .60

General Miguel Malvar (1865-1911) — A1273

**2015, Sept. 27 Litho. *Perf. 14***
**3626** A1273 10p multi .80 .50

San Miguel Brewery, 125th Anniv. — A1274

No. 3627: a, Brewery building. b, 125th anniversary emblem.
40p, 125th anniversary emblem, vert.

**2015, Sept. 29 Litho. *Perf. 14***
**3627** A1274 15p Horiz. pair, #a-b 2.50 2.50

**Souvenir Sheet**

***Perf. 13¾x13½***

**3628** A1274 40p multi 3.25 3.25

No. 3628 contains one 35x50mm stamp.

Western Union in the Philippines, 25th Anniv. — A1275

No. 3629 — Western Union emblem and: a, Various Filipinos. b, Text, "25 Years of Moving the Filipino for Better."

***Perf. 13½x13¾***

**2015, Sept. 30 Litho.**

**3629** A1275 25p Horiz. pair, #a-b 4.00 4.00

Mahaguyog Festival A1276

**2015, Oct. 2 Litho. *Perf. 14***

**3630** A1276 10p multi .80 .50

Manuel Conde (1915-85), Film Director A1277

**2015, Oct. 15 Litho. *Perf. 14***

**3631** A1277 10p multi .80 .50

2015 Asian-Pacific Economic Cooperation Summit, Manila — A1278

***Perf. 13¾x13½***

**2015, Nov. 10 Litho.**

**3632** A1278 30p multi 2.40 1.50

Miniature Sheet

National Stamp Collecting Month — A1279

No. 3633: a, Boy holding stamp. b, Boy holdind stamp album. c, Girl holding stamps. d, Man holding stamps and magnifying glass.

**2015, Nov. 10 Litho. *Perf. 14***

**Self-Adhesive**

**3633** A1279 15p Sheet of 4, #a-d 5.00 5.00

Miniature Sheet

Wildlife — A1280

No. 3634: a, Vizaysa flowerpecker. b, Philippine sail-fin lizard. c, Philippine pangolin anteater. d, Freshwater purple crab.

**2015, Nov. 11 Litho. *Perf. 14***

**3634** A1280 15p Sheet of 4, #a-d 5.00 5.00

Christmas — A1281

No. 3635 — Children's art depicting Christmas tree by: a, Kobie Trambulo (2/4). b, Vernice Prado (3/4). c, Lomi Capili (4/4). d, Javee Fua (1/4).

No. 3636 — Children's art depicting Christmas lanterns by: a, Cedric Chua. b, Julius Cabuang. c, Thridy Cabading.

**2015, Nov. 25 Litho. *Perf. 14***

**3635** A1281 10p Block or strip of 4, #a-d 6.00 6.00

**Souvenir Sheet**

**3636** A1281 10p Sheet of 3, #a-c 3.00 3.00

Office of the Government Corporate Counsel, 80th Anniv. — A1282

**2015, Dec. 1 Litho. *Perf. 13½x13¾***

**3637** A1282 10p multi .80 .50

New Year 2016 (Year of the Monkey) A1283

Designs: 10p, Head of monkey. 30p, Monkey.

**2015, Dec. 1 Litho. *Perf. 14***

**3638-3639** A1283 Set of 2 4.00 4.00

*3639a* Souvenir sheet of 4, 2 each #3638-3639 8.00 8.00

Philippine Daily Inquirer Newspaper, 30th Anniv. — A1284

**Litho. & Embossed With Foil Application**

**2015, Dec. 5 *Perf. 13¼***

**3640** A1284 30p multi 2.40 2.40

51st Intl. Eucharistic Congress, Cebu City — A1285

Design: 15p, Emblem. 40p, Emblem and dove's wing.

**2015, Dec. 8 Litho. *Perf. 14***

**3641** A1285 15p multi 1.25 .60

**Souvenir Sheet**

***Perf. 13¾x13½***

**3642** A1285 40p multi + label 3.25 3.25

No. 3642 contains one 35x50mm stamp.

Cagayan Economic Zone Authority, 20th Anniv. A1286

**2015, Dec. 18 Litho. *Perf. 14***

**3643** A1286 15p multi 1.25 .60

Commission on Elections, 75th Anniv. A1287

**2015, Dec. 18 Litho. *Perf. 14***

**3644** A1287 15p multi 1.25 .60

Liberty City Center, 70th Anniv. A1288

**2015, Dec. 21 Litho. *Perf. 14***

**3645** A1288 15p multi 1.25 .60

Pacita Madrigal Gonzalez (1915-2008), Senator — A1289

**2015, Dec. 22 Litho. *Perf. 14***

**3646** A1289 15p multi 1.25 .60

Mabitac Church, 400th Anniv. A1290

**2016, Jan. 2 Litho. *Perf. 14***

**3647** A1290 15p multi 1.25 .60

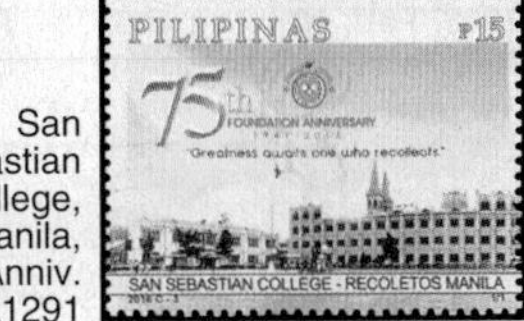

San Sebastian College, Manila, 75th Anniv. A1291

**2016, Jan. 20 Litho. *Perf. 14***

**3648** A1291 15p multi 1.25 .60

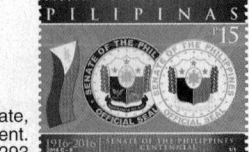

Court of Appeals, 80th Anniv. — A1292

**2016, Feb. 1 Litho. *Perf. 14***

**3649** A1292 15p multi 1.25 .60

Senate, Cent. A1293

**2016, Feb. 1 Litho. *Perf. 14***

**3650** A1293 15p multi 1.25 .60

**Fruit Type of 2015**

Designs: 1p, Egg fruit. 5p, Philippine wild raspberry. No. 3653, Tangerine orange. No. 3654, Grapes. 13p, Star fruit. 14p, Pomelo. 15p, Star apple. 17p, Calamansi. 35p, Sweet tamarind. 45p, Durian.

***Perf. 13½, 12¾ (#3653, 3655, 3657, 3659)***

**2016 Litho.**

**3651** A1240 1p multi .25 .25
*a.* Dated "2017" .25 .25
**3652** A1240 5p multi .40 .25
*a.* Dated "2017" .30 .25
**3653** A1240 12p multi 1.00 .50
**3654** A1240 12p multi 1.00 .50
*a.* Dated "2017" .75 .35
**3655** A1240 13p multi 1.10 .55
**3656** A1240 14p multi 1.25 .60
*a.* Dated "2017" .85 .40
**3657** A1240 15p multi 1.25 .60
**3658** A1240 17p multi 1.40 .70
*a.* Dated "2017" 1.00 .50
**3659** A1240 35p multi 3.00 1.50
**3660** A1240 45p multi 3.75 1.90
*a.* Dated "2017" 2.75 1.40
*Nos. 3651-3660 (10)* 14.40 7.35

Issued: 1p, 5p, No. 3654, 17p, 6/23; No. 3653, 13p, 15p, 35p, 2/2; 14p, 12/8; 45p, 6/30. Nos. 3651a, 3652a, 3/14/17; No. 3654a, 3/29/17; Nos. 3656a, 3658a, 3/21/17; No. 3660a, 4/18/17.

St. Valentine's Day — A1294

**2016, Feb. 5 Litho. *Perf. 13½***
**3661** A1294 25p multi 2.00 1.00

Tagkawayan, 75th Anniv. — A1295

**2016, Feb. 10 Litho. *Perf. 14***
**3662** A1295 15p multi 1.25 .60

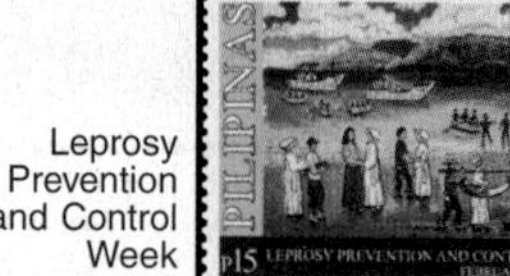

Leprosy Prevention and Control Week A1296

**2016, Feb. 15 Litho. *Perf. 14***
**3663** A1296 15p multi 1.25 .60

Bago, 50th Anniv. A1297

**2016, Feb. 19 Litho. *Perf. 14***
**3664** A1297 15p multi 1.25 .60

Pia Alonzo Wurtzbach, 2015 Miss Universe A1298

Wurtzbach with background color of: 15p, Gray. 40p, Pink.

**2016, Apr. 17 Litho. *Perf. 13½***
**3665** A1298 15p multi 1.25 .60

**Souvenir Sheet**
**Litho. With Glitter Affixed**

**3666** A1298 40p multi 3.25 3.25

Festivals — A1299

No. 3667: a, Sinulog Festival (1/4). b, Panagbenga Festival (2/4). c, Pahiyas Festival (3/4). d, Higantes Festival (4/4).

**2016, Apr. 27 Litho. *Perf. 14***
**3667** A1299 15p Horiz. strip of 4, #a-d 5.00 3.00

Heritage Month — A1300

No. 3668 — Musical instruments: a, Kulintang. b, Kudyapi. c, Dabakan. d, Gangsa.
No. 3669 — Musical instruments: a, Kudlong. b, Libbit. c, Agung. d, Gabbang.

**2016, May 5 Litho. *Perf. 14***
**3668** A1300 15p Block of 4, #a-d 5.00 3.00
**3669** A1300 15p Sheet of 4, #a-d 5.00 3.00

Intl. Organization for Standardization Certification of Office of the Regional Governor for Autonomous Region in Muslim Mindanao — A1301

**2016, May 6 Litho. *Perf. 14***
**3670** A1301 15p multi 1.25 .60

Tiaong, 325th Anniv. A1302

**2016, May 14 Litho. *Perf. 14***
**3671** A1302 15p multi 1.25 .60

A1303

Philippine National Bank, Cent. — A1304

No. 3672 — Winning art in stamp design contest by: a, Kenneth Olivar. b, Jean Christian Tormes. c, Jerico Martinez. d, Michael Montanez.

100p, Ferdinand Magellan from 100-peso banknote.

**2016, June 12 Litho. *Perf. 14***
**3672** A1303 15p Block of 4, #a-d 5.00 4.00

**Souvenir Sheet**
***Perf. 13½***

**3673** A1304 100p multi 8.00 4.00

Knights of Rizal, Cent. — A1305

**2016, June 19 Litho. *Perf. 14***
**3674** A1305 15p multi 1.25 .60

Tagbilaran, 50th Anniv. A1306

Designs: 15p, Tagbilaran City Hall. 100p, Saulog Festival.

**2016, July 1 Litho. *Perf. 14***
**3675** A1306 15p multi 1.25 .60

**Souvenir Sheet**
**Litho. With Foil Application**

**3676** A1306 100p multi 8.00 8.00

Inauguration of Pres. Rodrigo Roa Duterte — A1307

Size of photograph of ceremony: 17p, 43x26mm. 55p, 49x23mm.

**2016, Aug. 1 Litho. *Perf. 13½***
**3677** A1307 17p multi 1.40 .70

**Souvenir Sheet**

**3678** A1307 55p multi 4.50 4.50

No. 3678 contains one 60x30mm stamp.

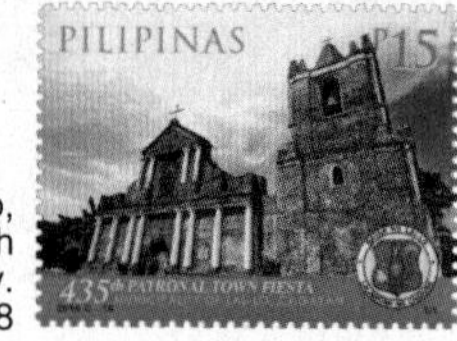

Lal-Lo, 435th Anniv. A1308

**2016, Aug. 4 Litho. *Perf. 14***
**3679** A1308 15p multi 1.25 .60

2016 Summer Olympics, Rio de Janeiro — A1309

No. 3680: a, Taekwondo. b, Boxing. c, Equestrian dressage. d, Archery.
55p, Basketball.

**2016, Aug. 9 Litho. *Perf. 14***
**3680** A1309 12p Block of 4, #a-d 4.00 2.00

**Souvenir Sheet**
***Perf. 13½***

**3681** A1309 55p multi + label 4.50 4.50

No. 3681 contains one 35x50mm stamp.

**Year of the Monkey Type of 2015**
**Miniature Sheet**

No. 3682: a, Head of monkey. b, Monkey.

**2016, Aug. 10 Litho. *Perf. 14***
**3682** Sheet of 4, 2 each #3682a-3682b 9.50 4.75
*a.* A1283 12p multi 1.00 .50
*b.* A1283 45p multi 3.75 1.75

Thailand 2016 Intl. Stamp Exhibition, Bangkok.

National Teacher's Month — A1310

**2016, Sept. 5 Litho. *Perf. 14***
**3683** A1310 12p multi 1.00 .50

Orchids — A1311

No. 3684: a, Mrs. Sander's dendrobium. b, Moth orchid (yellow background). c, Waling-waling. d, Dancing lady orchid.
No. 3685, horiz.: a, Deer antler moth orchid. b, Cattleya Hsiying rouge. c, Moth orchid (light blue background). d, Cattleya dark purple trichoglottis.

**2016, Sept. 30 Litho. *Perf. 14***
**3684** A1311 12p Block of 4, #a-d 4.00 2.00
**3685** A1311 12p Sheet of 4, #a-d 4.00 2.00

No. 3685a "Deer" is spelled incorrectly on stamp.

Philippine Airlines, 75th Anniv. A1312

**2016, Oct. 19 Litho. *Perf. 14***
**3686** A1312 12p multi 1.00 .50

Philtrust Bank, Cent. A1313

**2016, Oct. 19 Litho. *Perf. 14***
**3687** A1313 12p multi 1.00 .50

National Stamp Collecting Month — A1314

No. 3688: a, Philippines #502. b, Philippines #501. c, Philippines #500.
55p, Philippines #500-502.

**2016, Oct. 21 Litho. *Perf. 13½***
**3688** Horiz. strip of 3 3.00 2.00
***a.-c.*** A1314 12p Any single 1.00 4.50

**Souvenir Sheet**

**3689** A1314 55p multi 4.50 2.25

No. 3689 contains one 100x35mm stamp.

Souvenir Sheet

New Year 2016 (Year of the Monkey) — A1315

No. 3690: a, 75p, Goat (40x30mm). b, 75p, Rooster (40x30mm). c, 100p, Monkey (50x40mm).

***Perf. 13¼x13x13¼x13¼ (#3690a), 13¼x13¼x13¼x13 (#3690b), 13 (#3690c)***

**Litho., Sheet Margin Litho. & Embossed With Foil Application**

**2016, Oct. 21**
**3690** A1315 Sheet of 3, #a-c 20.00 20.00

2016 Philataipei World Stamp Exhibition, Taipei.

Diplomatic Relations Between Philippines and Portugal, 75th Anniv. — A1316

No. 3691 — Flags of Philippines and Portugal and: a, 12p, Lavender, national flower of Portugal. b, 55p, Sampaguita, national flower of Philippines.

**2016, Oct. 24 Litho. *Perf. 14***
**3691** A1316 Horiz. pair, #a-b 5.50 2.75

See Portugal Nos. 3855-3856.

Philippines Securities and Exchange Commission, 80th Anniv. — A1317

**2016, Nov. 11 Litho. *Perf. 14***
**3692** A1317 12p multi 1.00 .50

Dr. Sun Yat-sen (1866-1925), First President of the Republic of China — A1318

Designs: 18p, Drs. Sun Yat-sen and Mariano Ponce (1863-1918), Philippine physician and revolutionary hero.
45p, Drs. Sun Yat-sen and Ponce, diff.

**2016, Nov. 12 Litho. *Perf. 14***
**3693** A1318 18p multi 1.50 .75

**Souvenir Sheet**

***Perf. 13¾x13½***

**3694** A1318 45p multi + label 3.75 3.75

No. 3694 contains one 35x50mm stamp.

Christmas — A1319

No. 3695 — Star lantern with "Pasko" in: a, 12p, White on red panel. b, 12p, Red on white panel. c, 17p, White on green panel. d, 17p, Green on white panel.

**2016, Nov. 25 Litho. *Perf. 14***
**3695** A1319 Block of 4, #a-d 4.75 3.00

University of the Philippines College of Business Administration Alumni Association, Cent. — A1320

**2016, Dec. 4 Litho. *Perf. 14***
**3696** A1320 12p multi 1.00 .50

A1321

New Year 2017 (Year of the Rooster) — A1322

No: 3697 — Rooster facing: a, 18p, Left. b, 45p, Right.

**2016, Dec. 16 Litho. *Perf. 14***
**3697** A1321 Horiz. pair, #a-b 5.25 3.50

**Souvenir Sheet**

**Litho. & Embossed With Foil Application**

***Perf.***

**3698** A1322 200p multi 16.00 12.00

Catbalogan City, 400th Anniv. A1323

**2016, Dec. 20 Litho. *Perf. 14***
**3699** A1323 18p multi 1.50 .75

Teresita "Mama Sita" Reyes (1917-98), Restauranteur A1324

**2016, Dec. 20 Litho. *Perf. 14***
**3700** A1324 18p multi 1.50 .75

10th-13th Century Items From Ayala Museum "Gold of Ancestors" Exhibition — A1325

No. 3701: a, Pectoral disc. b, Garuda-shaped ear ornaments. c, Ear ornaments. d, Kinnari.
No. 3702: a, Like #3701b. b, Like #3701c. c, Like #3701a. d, Like #3701d.

**2016, Dec. 21 Litho. *Perf. 14***
**3701** A1325 18p Block of 4, #a-d 5.75 3.00

**Litho. & Embossed With Foil Application**

**3702** A1325 50p Sheet of 4, #a-d, + 2 labels 16.00 12.00

**Main Post Office, Manila Type of 2014**

**2016, Dec. 23 Litho. *Perf. 14***
**3703** A1199 18p multi 3.50 3.50

No. 3703 was printed in sheets of six that sold for 250p. The right half of the stamp could be personalized.

## SEMI-POSTAL STAMPS

**Catalogue values for unused stamps in this section are for Never Hinged items.**

**Republic**

Epifanio de los Santos, Trinidad H. Pardo and Teodoro M. Kalaw — SP1

Doctrina Christiana, Cover Page — SP2

"Noli Me Tangere," Cover Page — SP3

**Unwmk.**

**1949, Apr. 1 Engr. *Perf. 12***
**B1** SP1 4c + 2c sepia 1.50 1.50
**B2** SP2 6c + 4c violet 5.00 5.00
**B3** SP3 18c + 7c blue 6.00 6.00
*Nos. B1-B3 (3)* 12.50 12.50

The surtax was for restoration of war-damaged public libraries.

War Widow and Children — SP4

Disabled Veteran — SP5

**1950, Nov. 30**
**B4** SP4 2c + 2c red .40 .25
**B5** SP5 4c + 4c violet .60 .30

The surtax was for war widows and children and disabled veterans of World War II.
For surcharges see Nos. 648-649.

Mrs. Manuel L. Quezon SP6

**1952, Aug. 19** *Perf. 12*

**B6** SP6 5c + 1c dp bl .30 .30
**B7** SP6 6c + 2c car rose .50 .45

The surtax was used to encourage planting and care of fruit trees among Philippine children. For surcharge see No. 872.

Quezon Institute SP7

**1958, Aug. 19 Photo.** *Perf. 13½*

**Cross in Red**

**B8** SP7 5c + 5c grn .25 .25
*a.* Perf. 12 1.75 .90
**B9** SP7 10c + 5c dp vio .35 .30
*a.* Perf. 12 7.50 1.75

These stamps were obligatory on all mail from Aug. 19-Sept. 30.

For surcharges see Nos. 849, B12-B13, B16.

---

The surtax on all semi-postals from Nos. B8-B9 onward was for the Philippine Tuberculosis Society unless otherwise stated.

---

Scout Cooking — SP8

**1959 Engr.** *Perf. 13*

**Yellow Paper**

**B10** SP8 6c + 4c shown .40 *1.00*
**B11** SP8 25c + 5c Archery .60 *1.50*
*a.* Nos. B10-B11 tête bêche, *white* 1.25 *3.00*
*Nos. B10-B11,CB1-CB3 (5)* 3.75 *6.75*

10th Boy Scout World Jamboree, Makiling National Park, July 17-26. The surtax was to finance the Jamboree.

For souvenir sheet see No. CB3a. For surcharges see Nos. 832-833, C111.

**Nos. B8-B9 Surcharged in Red**

**1959 Photo.** *Perf. 13½*

**B12** SP7 3c + 5c on 5c + 5c .25 .25
*a.* "3 + 5" and bars omitted
*b.* Perf. 12 5.00 3.00
**B13** SP7 6c + 5c on 10c + 5c .45 .25
*a.* Perf. 12 3.50 1.75

Bohol Sanatorium — SP9

**1959, Aug. 19 Engr.** *Perf. 12*

**Cross in Red**

**B14** SP9 6c + 5c yel grn .25 .25
**B15** SP9 25c + 5c vio bl .50 .30

**No. B8 Surcharged "Help Prevent TB" and New Value**

**1960, Aug. 19 Photo.** *Perf. 13½, 12*

**B16** SP7 6c + 5c on 5c + 5c .50 .25

Roxas Memorial T.B. Pavilion SP10

*Perf. 11½*

**1961, Aug. 19 Unwmk. Photo.**

**B17** SP10 6c + 5c brn & red .50 .25

Emiliano J. Valdes T.B. Pavilion SP11

**1962, Aug. 19 Cross in Red**

**B18** SP11 6s + 5s dk vio .30 .25
**B19** SP11 30s + 5s ultra .45 .25
**B20** SP11 70s + 5s brt bl .85 .50
*Nos. B18-B20 (3)* 1.60 1.00

José Rizal Playing Chess SP12

Design: 30s+5s, Rizal fencing.

**1962, Dec. 30 Engr.** *Perf. 13*

**B21** SP12 6s + 4s grn & rose lil .50 *1.00*
**B22** SP12 30s + 5s brt bl & cl 1.00 *2.00*

Surtax for Rizal Foundation.
For surcharges see Nos. 942-943.

Map of Philippines and Cross — SP13

**1963, Aug. 19 Unwmk.** *Perf. 13*

**B23** SP13 6s + 5s vio & red .25 .25
**B24** SP13 10s + 5s grn & red .40 .25
**B25** SP13 50s + 5s brn & red .85 .35
*Nos. B23-B25 (3)* 1.50 .85



Negros Oriental T.B. Pavilion SP14

**1964, Aug. 19 Photo.** *Perf. 13½*

**Cross in Red**

**B26** SP14 5s + 5s brt pur .30 .25
**B27** SP14 6s + 5s ultra .30 .25
**B28** SP14 30s + 5s brown .45 .25
**B29** SP14 70s + 5s green .75 .50
*Nos. B26-B29 (4)* 1.80 1.25

For surcharges see Nos. 986, 1586.

**No. B27 Surcharged in Red with New Value and Two Bars**

**1965, Aug. 19 Cross in Red**

**B30** SP14 1s + 5s on 6s + 5s .40 .25
**B31** SP14 3s + 5s on 6s + 5s .50 .25

Stork-billed Kingfisher — SP15

Birds: 5s+5s, Rufous hornbill. 10s+5s, Monkey-eating eagle. 30s+5s, Great-billed parrot.

**1967, Aug. 19 Photo.** *Perf. 13½*

**B32** SP15 1s + 5s multi .35 .25
**B33** SP15 5s + 5s multi .35 .25
**B34** SP15 10s + 5s multi .90 .25
**B35** SP15 30s + 5s multi 2.50 .70
*Nos. B32-B35 (4)* 4.10 1.45

**1969, Aug. 15 Litho.** *Perf. 13½*

Birds: 1s+5s, Three-toed woodpecker. 5s+5s, Philippine trogon. 10s+5s, Mt. Apo lorikeet. 40s+5s, Scarlet minivet.

**B36** SP15 1s + 5s multi .50 .25
**B37** SP15 5s + 5s multi .65 .25
**B38** SP15 10s + 5s multi 1.10 .30
**B39** SP15 40s + 5s multi 2.00 .70
*Nos. B36-B39 (4)* 4.25 1.50

Julia V. de Ortigas and Tuberculosis Society Building — SP16

**1970, Aug. 3 Photo.** *Perf. 13½*

**B40** SP16 1s + 5s multi .35 .25
**B41** SP16 5s + 5s multi .35 .25
**B42** SP16 30s + 5s multi 1.00 .45
**B43** SP16 70s + 5s multi 1.60 .55
*Nos. B40-B43 (4)* 3.30 1.50

Mrs. Julia V. de Ortigas was president of the Philippine Tuberculosis Soc., 1932-69.
For surcharge see No. 1251.

Mabolo, Santol, Chico, Papaya SP17

Philippine Fruits: 10s+5s, Balimbing, atis, mangosteen, macupa, bananas. 40s+5s, Susong-kalabao, avocado, duhat, watermelon, guava, mango. 1p+5s, Lanzones, oranges, sirhuelas, pineapple.

**1972, Aug. 1 Litho.** *Perf. 13*

**B44** SP17 1s + 5s multi .35 .25
**B45** SP17 10s + 5s multi .35 .25
**B46** SP17 40s + 5s multi .70 .35
**B47** SP17 1p + 5s multi 2.00 .50
*Nos. B44-B47 (4)* 3.40 1.35

**Nos. B45-B46 Surcharged with New Value and 2 Bars**

**1973, June 15**

**B48** SP17 15s + 5s on 10s + 5s .40 .25
**B49** SP17 60s + 5s on 40s + 5s 1.20 .35

Dr. Basilio J. Valdes and Veterans Memorial Hospital — SP18

**1974, July 8 Litho.** *Perf. 12½*

**Cross in Red**

**B50** SP18 15s + 5s blue grn .40 .25
*a.* Imperf. .85 .70
**B51** SP18 1.10p + 5s vio blue 1.50 1.00
*a.* Imperf. 4.00 3.00

Dr. Valdes (1892-1970) was president of Philippine Tuberculosis Society.
For surcharges see Nos. 1250, 1252.

---

## AIR POST STAMPS

**Madrid-Manila Flight Issue**

Issued to commemorate the flight of Spanish aviators Gallarza and Loriga from Madrid to Manila.

Regular Issue of 1917-26 Overprinted in Red or Violet

Designs: Nos. C7-C8, Adm. William T. Sampson. No. C9, Adm. George Dewey.

**1926, May 13 Unwmk.** *Perf. 11*

**C1** A40 2c green (R) 20.00 17.50
Never hinged 45.00
**C2** A40 4c carmine (V) 30.00 20.00
Never hinged 55.00
*a.* Inverted overprint *3,000.* —
**C3** A40 6c lilac (R) 75.00 75.00
Never hinged 125.00
**C4** A40 8c org brn (V) 75.00 60.00
Never hinged 125.00
**C5** A40 10c deep blue (R) 75.00 60.00
Never hinged 140.00
**C6** A40 12c red org (V) 80.00 65.00
Never hinged 150.00
**C7** A40 16c lt ol grn (V) *3,250.* *3,250.*
**C8** A40 16c ol bister (R) *5,000.* *5,000.*
**C9** A40 16c ol grn (V) 100.00 70.00
Never hinged 160.00
**C10** A40 20c org ye (V) 100.00 80.00
Never hinged 160.00
**C11** A40 26c blue grn (V) 100.00 80.00
Never hinged 160.00
**C12** A40 30c gray (V) 100.00 80.00
Never hinged 160.00
**C13** A40 2p vio brn (R) 600.00 600.00
Never hinged 1,100.
**C14** A40 4p dk blue (R) 750.00 750.00
Never hinged 1,300.
**C15** A40 10p dp grn (V) 1,350. 1,350.

**Same Overprint on No. 269**

**Wmk. Single-lined PIPS (190)**

*Perf. 12*

**C16** A40 26c blue grn (V) *6,250.*

**Same Overprint on No. 284**

*Perf. 10*

**C17** A40 1p pale violet (V) 300.00 225.00
Never hinged 450.00

**London-Orient Flight Issue**

Issued Nov. 9, 1928, to celebrate the arrival of a British squadron of hydroplanes.

Regular Issue of 1917-25 Overprinted in Red

**1928, Nov. 9** *Perf. 11*

**C18** A40 2c green 1.00 1.00
Never hinged 2.00
**C19** A40 4c carmine 1.25 1.50
Never hinged 2.00
**C20** A40 6c violet 5.00 3.00
Never hinged 10.00
**C21** A40 8c orange brown 5.00 3.00
Never hinged 10.00
**C22** A40 10c deep blue 5.00 3.00
Never hinged 10.00
**C23** A40 12c red orange 8.00 4.00
Never hinged 12.00
**C24** A40 16c ol grn (No. 303a) 8.00 4.00
Never hinged 12.00
**C25** A40 20c orange yellow 8.00 4.00
Never hinged 12.00
**C26** A40 26c blue green 20.00 8.00
Never hinged 35.00
**C27** A40 30c gray 20.00 8.00
Never hinged 35.00

### Same Overprint on No. 271
**Wmk. Single-lined PIPS (190)**
***Perf. 12***

**C28** A40 1p pale violet 55.00 30.00
Never hinged 90.00
*Nos. C18-C28 (11)* 136.25 69.50
Set, never hinged 230.00

### Von Gronau Issue

Commemorating the visit of Capt. Wolfgang von Gronau's airplane on its round-the-world flight.

Nos. 354-360 Overprinted

**1932, Sept. 27 Unwmk. *Perf. 11***
**C29** A43 2c yellow green .90 .60
Never hinged 1.40
**C30** A44 4c rose carmine .90 .40
Never hinged 1.40
**C31** A45 12c orange 1.25 .65
Never hinged 2.00
**C32** A46 18c red orange 5.00 5.00
Never hinged 8.00
**C33** A47 20c yellow 3.50 3.50
Never hinged 5.75
**C34** A48 24c deep violet 3.50 4.00
Never hinged 5.75
**C35** A49 32c olive brown 3.50 3.00
Never hinged 5.75
*Nos. C29-C35 (7)* 18.55 17.15
Set, never hinged 31.55

### Rein Issue

Commemorating the flight from Madrid to Manila of the Spanish aviator Fernando Rein y Loring.

Regular Issue of 1917-25 Overprinted

**1933, Apr. 11**
**C36** A40 2c green .75 .45
Never hinged 1.10
**C37** A40 4c carmine .90 .45
Never hinged 1.40
**C38** A40 6c deep violet 1.10 .80
Never hinged 1.75
**C39** A40 8c orange brown 3.75 2.00
Never hinged 5.75
P# block of 6 120.00
Never hinged 150.00
**C40** A40 10c dark blue 3.75 2.25
Never hinged 5.75
P# block of 6 120.00
Never hinged 150.00
**C41** A40 12c orange 3.75 2.00
Never hinged 5.75
P# block of 6 120.00
Never hinged 150.00
**C42** A40 16c olive green 3.50 2.00
Never hinged 5.25
P# block of 6 160.00
Never hinged 200.00
**C43** A40 20c yellow 3.75 2.00
Never hinged 5.75
P# block of 6 160.00
Never hinged 200.00
**C44** A40 26c green 3.75 2.75
Never hinged 5.75
*a.* 26c blue green 4.00 2.00
Never hinged 6.00
**C45** A40 30c gray 4.00 3.00
Never hinged 6.00
*Nos. C36-C45 (10)* 29.00 17.70
Set, never hinged 44.25

No. 290a Overprinted

**1933, May 26**
**C46** A40 2c green .65 .40
Never hinged 1.00
P# block of 6 12.00
Never hinged 15.00

Regular Issue of 1932 Overprinted

**C47** A44 4c rose carmine .30 .25
Never hinged .45
P# block of 6 16.00
Never hinged 20.00
**C48** A45 12c orange .60 .25
Never hinged .90
P# block of 6 20.00
Never hinged 25.00
**C49** A47 20c yellow .60 .25
Never hinged .90
P# block of 6 20.00
Never hinged 25.00
**C50** A48 24c deep violet .65 .25
Never hinged 1.00
P# block of 6 24.00
Never hinged 30.00
**C51** A49 32c olive brown .85 .35
Never hinged 1.40
*Nos. C46-C51 (6)* 3.65 1.75
Set, never hinged 5.65

### Transpacific Issue

Issued to commemorate the China Clipper flight from Manila to San Francisco, Dec. 2-5, 1935.

Nos. 387, 392 Overprinted in Gold

**1935, Dec. 2**
**C52** A57 10c rose carmine .40 .25
Never hinged .60
**C53** A62 30c orange red .60 .35
Never hinged .90

### Manila-Madrid Flight Issue

Issued to commemorate the Manila-Madrid flight by aviators Antonio Arnaiz and Juan Calvo.

Regular Issue of 1917-25 Surcharged in Various Colors

**1936, Sept. 6**
**C54** A40 2c on 4c carmine (Bl) .25 .25
Never hinged .25
**C55** A40 6c on 12c red org (V) .25 .25
Never hinged .30
**C56** A40 16c on 26c blue grn (Bk) .25 .25
Never hinged .40
*a.* 16c on 26c green 2.00 .70
Never hinged 3.00
*Nos. C54-C56 (3)* .75 .75
Set, never hinged .95

### Air Mail Exhibition Issue

Issued to commemorate the first Air Mail Exhibition, held Feb. 17-19, 1939.

Regular Issue of 1917-37 Surcharged in Black or Red

**1939, Feb. 17**
**C57** A40 8c on 26c blue grn (Bk) 2.00 2.00
Never hinged 4.00
*a.* 8c on 26c green (Bk) 10.00 4.00
Never hinged 16.00
**C58** A71 1p on 10p gray (R) 8.00 4.00
Never hinged 12.00

Moro Vinta and Clipper — AP1

**1941, June 30**
**C59** AP1 8c carmine 2.00 .60
Never hinged 2.75
**C60** AP1 20c ultramarine 3.00 .50
Never hinged 4.00
**C61** AP1 60c blue green 3.00 1.00
Never hinged 4.00
**C62** AP1 1p sepia .70 .50
Never hinged 1.00
*Nos. C59-C62 (4)* 8.70 2.60
Set, never hinged 11.75

For overprint see No. NO7. For surcharges see Nos. N10-N11, N35-N36.

No. C47 Hstmpd. in Violet

**1944, Dec. 3**
**C63** A44 4c rose carmine *3,750. 2,750.*

**Catalogue values for unused stamps in this section, from this point to the end of the section, are for Never Hinged items.**

### Republic

Manuel L. Quezon and Franklin D. Roosevelt — AP2

**Unwmk.**
**1947, Aug. 19 Engr. *Perf. 12***
**C64** AP2 6c dark green .50 .50
**C65** AP2 40c red orange 1.00 1.00
**C66** AP2 80c deep blue 4.00 2.75
*Nos. C64-C66 (3)* 5.50 4.25

### FAO Type

**1948, Feb. 23 Typo. *Perf. 12½***
**C67** A89 40c dk car & pink 10.00 6.00

### Junior Chamber Type

**1950, Mar. 1 Engr. *Perf. 12***
**C68** A96 30c deep orange 1.50 .40
**C69** A96 50c carmine rose 2.50 .70

### F. D. Roosevelt Type
Souvenir Sheet

**1950, May 22 *Imperf.***
**C70** A98 80c deep green 3.00 2.50

### Lions Club Type

**1950, June 2 *Perf. 12***
**C71** A99 30c emerald 1.75 .45
**C72** A99 50c ultra 2.00 .60
*a.* Souvenir sheet of 2, #C71-C72 4.00 2.50

### Maria Clara Type

**1952, Nov. 16 *Perf. 12½***
**C73** A112 30c rose carmine 2.00 .75

### Postage Stamp Cent. Type

**1954, Apr. 25 *Perf. 13***
**1854 Stamp in Orange**
**C74** A119 10c dark brown 2.50 1.00
**C75** A119 20c dark green 4.00 1.60
**C76** A119 50c carmine 9.00 3.25
*Nos. C74-C76 (3)* 15.50 5.85

### Rotary Intl. Type

**1955, Feb. 23**
**C77** A123 50c blue green 2.50 1.00

Lt. José Gozar — AP10

20c, 50c, Lt. Gozar. 30c, 70c, Lt. Basa.

**1955 Engr. *Perf. 13***
**C78** AP10 20c deep violet 1.20 .25
**C79** AP10 30c red .80 .25
**C80** AP10 50c bluish green .80 .25
**C81** AP10 70c blue 1.20 .90
*Nos. C78-C81 (4)* 4.00 1.65

Lt. José Gozar and Lt. Cesar Fernando Basa, Filipino aviators in World War II.

### Constitution Type of Regular Issue

**1960, Feb. 8 Photo. *Perf. 12½x13½***
**C82** A146 30c brt bl & silver .75 .25

Air Force Plane of 1935 and Saber Jet — AP11

**1960, May 2 Engr. *Perf. 14x14½***
**C83** AP11 10c carmine .40 .25
**C84** AP11 20c ultra .60 .25

25th anniversary of Philippine Air Force.
For surcharge see No. 847.

### Olympic Type of Regular Issue

30c, Sharpshooter. 70c, Woman swimmer.

**1960, Nov. 30 Photo. *Perf. 13x13½***
**C85** A150 30c orange & brn .60 .35
**C86** A150 70c grnsh bl & vio brn 1.40 .70

### Postal Conference Type

**1961, Feb. 23 *Perf. 13½x13***
**C87** A152 30c multicolored .70 .25

### Freedom from Hunger Type

**1963, Dec. 20 Photo.**
**C88** A168 30s lt grn & multi .40 .25
**C89** A168 50s multicolored .75 .30

### Land Reform Type

**1964, Dec. 21 Wmk. 233 *Perf. 14½***
**C90** A172 30s multicolored .60 .25

Mass Baptism by Father Andres de Urdaneta, Cebu — AP12

70s, World map showing route of the Cross from Spain to Mexico to Cebu, and two galleons.

**Unwmk.**
**1965, Oct. 4 Photo. *Perf. 13***
**C91** AP12 30s multicolored .70 .25
**C92** AP12 70s multicolored 1.50 .50
*a.* Souvenir sheet of 4 4.00 3.00

400th anniv. of the Christianization of the Philippines. No. C92a contains four imperf. stamps similar to Nos. 934-935 and C91-C92 with simulated perforation.
For surcharge see No. C108.

Souvenir Sheet

Family and Progress Symbols — AP13

**1966, July 22 Photo. *Imperf.***
**C93** AP13 70s multicolored 4.25 3.50

50th anniv. of the Philippine Natl. Bank. No. C93 contains one stamp with simulated perforation superimposed on a facsimile of a 50p banknote of 1916.

Eruption of Taal Volcano and Refugees — AP14

**1967, Oct. 1 Photo. *Perf. 13½x13***

**C94** AP14 70s multicolored .85 .45

Eruption of Taal Volcano, Sept. 28, 1965.

Eruption of Taal Volcano — AP15

**1968, Oct. 1 Litho. *Perf. 13½***

**C95** AP15 70s multicolored .85 .55

Eruption of Taal Volcano, Sept. 28, 1965.

### Rotary Type of 1969

**1969, Jan. 29 Photo. *Perf. 12½***

**C96** A202 40s green & multi .40 .25
**C97** A202 75s red & multi 1.00 .50

### Holy Child Type of Regular Issue

**1969, June 30 Photo. *Perf. 13½***

**C98** A207 40s ultra & multi .90 .25

### Pope Type of Regular Issue

**1970, Nov. 27 Photo. *Perf. 13½x14***

**C99** A221 40s violet & multi .90 .30

### Law College Type of Regular Issue

**1971, June 15 *Perf. 13***

**C100** A225 1p green & multi 1.20 .50

### Manila Type of Regular Issue

**1971, June 24**

**C101** A226 1p multi & blue 1.20 .50

### Santo Tomas Type of Regular Issue

**1971, July 8 Photo. *Perf. 13½***

**C102** A227 2p lt blue & multi 1.50 .80

### Congress Type of Regular Issue

**1972, Apr. 11 Photo. *Perf. 13½x13***

**C103** A232 40s green & multi .70 .25

### Tropical Fish Type of Regular Issue

**1972, Aug. 14 Photo. *Perf. 13***

**C104** A235 50s Dusky angelfish 1.75 .60

### Pope Paul VI Type of Regular Issue

**1972, Sept. 26 Photo. *Perf. 14***

**C105** A237 60s lt blue & multi 1.00 .40

### First Mass Type of Regular Issue

**1972, Oct. 31 Photo. *Perf. 14***

**C106** A241 60s multicolored .75 .40

### Presidential Palace Type of Regular Issue

**1973, Nov. 15 Litho. *Perf. 14***

**C107** A253 60s multicolored 1.00 .35

### No. C92a Surcharged and Overprinted with US Bicentennial Emblems and: "U.S.A. BICENTENNIAL / 1776-1976" in Black or Red

### Unwmk.

**1976, Sept. 20 Photo. *Imperf.***

**C108** Sheet of 4 3.00 3.00
*a.* A179 5s on 3s multi .25 .25
*b.* A179 5s on 6s multi .25 .25
*c.* AP12 15s on 30s multi .40 .30
*d.* AP12 50s on 70s multi .75 .35

American Bicentennial. Nos. C108a-C108d are overprinted with Bicentennial emblem and 2 bars over old denomination. Inscription and 2 Bicentennial emblems overprinted in margin.

### Souvenir Sheet

AMPHILEX '77, Intl. Stamp Exhibition — AP16

Netherlands No. 1 and Philippines No. 1 and Windmill

**1977, May 26 Litho. *Perf. 14½***

**C109** AP16 Sheet of 3 10.00 10.00
*a.* 7.50p multicolored 2.75 2.75

AMPHILEX '77, International Stamp Exhibition, Amsterdam, May 26-June 5.

Exists imperf. Value $20.

### Souvenir Sheet

ESPAMER '77 — AP17

Philippines and Spain Nos. 1, Bull and Matador.

**1977, Oct. 7 Litho. *Perf. 12½x13***

**C110** AP17 Sheet of 3 10.00 10.00
*a.* 7.50p multicolored 2.75 2.75

ESPAMER '77 (Exposicion Filatelica de America y Europa), Barcelona, Spain, 10/7-13.

Exists imperf. Value $18.

Nos. B10 and CB3a Surcharged

**1979, July 5 Engr. *Perf. 13***

**C111** SP8 90s on 6c + 4c car, *yel* 2.00 *1.00*

### Souvenir Sheet

### White Paper

**C112** Sheet of 5 6.00 5.00
*a.* SP8 50s on 6c + 4c carmine .75 .50
*b.* SP8 50s on 25c + 5c blue .75 .50
*c.* SP8 50s on 30c + 10c green .75 .50
*d.* SP8 50s on 70c + 20c red brown .75 .50
*e.* SP8 50s on 80c + 20c violet .75 .50

First Scout Philatelic Exhibition, Quezon City, July 4-14, commemorating 25th anniversary of First National Jamboree.

Surcharge on No. C111 includes "AIRMAIL." Violet marginal inscriptions on No. C112 overprinted with heavy bars; new commemorative inscriptions and Scout emblem added.

---

## AIR POST SEMI-POSTAL STAMPS

**Catalogue values for unused stamps in this section are for Never Hinged items.**

### Type of Semi-Postal Issue, 1959

Designs: 30c+10c, Bicycling. 70c+20c, Scout with plane model. 80c+20c, Pres. Carlos P. Garcia and scout shaking hands.

### Unwmk.

**1959, July 17 Engr. *Perf. 13***

**CB1** SP8 30c + 10c green .50 *.75*
**CB2** SP8 70c + 20c red brown 1.00 *1.50*
**CB3** SP8 80c + 20c violet 1.25 *2.00*
*a.* Souvenir sheet of 5 5.00 *8.00*
*Nos. CB1-CB3 (3)* 2.75 *4.25*

10th Boy Scout World Jamboree, Makiling Natl. Park, July 17-26. Surtax was for the Jamboree.

No. CB3a measures 171x89mm. and contains one each of Nos. CB1-CB3 and types of Nos. B10-B11 on white paper. Sold for 4p.

For surcharge see No. C112.

---

## SPECIAL DELIVERY STAMPS

United States No. E5 Overprinted in Red

### Wmk. Double-lined USPS (191)

**1901, Oct. 15 *Perf. 12***

**E1** SD3 10c dark blue 100. 80.
Never hinged 185.
*a.* Dots in curved frame above messenger (Pl. 882) *175. 160.*

Special Delivery Messenger SD2

### Wmk. Double-lined PIPS (191PI)

**1906, Sept. 8**

**E2** SD2 20c deep ultra 45.00 8.00
Never hinged 90.00
*b.* 20c pale ultramarine 35.00 8.00
Never hinged 70.00

See Nos. E3-E6. For overprints see Nos. E7-E10, EO1.

## SPECIAL PRINTING

U.S. No. E6 Overprinted in Red

### Wmk. Double-lined USPS (191)

**1907**

**E2A** SD4 10c ultramarine *3,250.*

### Wmk. Single-lined PIPS (190PI)

**1911, Apr.**

**E3** SD2 20c deep ultra 22.00 1.75
Never hinged 42.00

**1916 *Perf. 10***

**E4** SD2 20c deep ultra 175.00 150.00
Never hinged 275.00

**1919 Unwmk. *Perf. 11***

**E5** SD2 20c ultramarine .60 .25
Never hinged .90
*a.* 20c pale blue .75 .25
Never hinged 1.00
*b.* 20c dull violet .60 .25
Never hinged .90

### Type of 1906 Issue

**1925-31 *Imperf.***

**E6** SD2 20c dull violet ('31) 27.50 *75.00*
Never hinged 40.00
*a.* 20c violet blue ('25) 50.00 —
Never hinged 80.00

Type of 1919 Overprinted in Black

**1939, Apr. 27 *Perf. 11***

**E7** SD2 20c blue violet .25 .25
Never hinged .40

Nos. E5b and E7, Hstmpd. in Violet

**1944**

**E8** SD2 20c dull violet (On E5b) *1,400. 550.00*
On cover —
Block of 4 *6,000.*
**E9** SD2 20c blue violet (On E7) *550.00 250.00*

Type SD2 Overprinted

**1945, May 1**

**E10** SD2 20c blue violet .70 .55
Never hinged 1.10
*a.* "IC" close together 3.25 2.75
Never hinged 4.75

**Catalogue values for unused stamps in this section, from this point to the end of the section, are for Never Hinged items.**

### Republic

Manila Post Office and Messenger SD3

### Unwmk.

**1947, Dec. 22 Engr. *Perf. 12***

**E11** SD3 20c rose lilac .60 .40

Post Office Building, Manila, and Hands with Letter — SD4

**1962, Jan. 23 *Perf. 13½x13***

**E12** SD4 20c lilac rose .70 .30

---

## SPECIAL DELIVERY OFFICIAL STAMP

O.B.

Type of 1906 Issue Overprinted

**1931 Unwmk. *Perf. 11***

**EO1** SD2 20c dull violet 3.00 *75.00*
Never hinged 4.50
P# block of 6 150.00
Never hinged 190.00

*a.* No period after "B" 50.00 *250.00*
Never hinged 75.00
*b.* Double overprint —

It is strongly recommended that expert opinion be acquired for Nos. EO1 and EO1a used.

## POSTAGE DUE STAMPS

U.S. Nos. J38-J44 Overprinted in Black

**Wmk. Double-lined USPS (191)**

**1899, Aug. 16** ***Perf. 12***

**J1** D2 1c deep claret 7.50 2.50
Never hinged 15.00
**J2** D2 2c deep claret 7.50 2.50
Never hinged 15.00
**J3** D2 5c deep claret 15.00 2.50
Never hinged 30.00
**J4** D2 10c deep claret 19.00 5.50
Never hinged 37.50
**J5** D2 50c deep claret 250.00 100.00
Never hinged 425.00

No. J1 was used to pay regular postage Sept. 5-19, 1902.

**1901, Aug. 31**

**J6** D2 3c deep claret 17.50 7.00
Never hinged 35.00
**J7** D2 30c deep claret 250.00 110.00
Never hinged 415.00
*Nos. J1-J7 (7)* 566.50 230.00
Set, never hinged 882.50

Post Office Clerk — D3

**1928, Aug. 21** **Unwmk.** ***Perf. 11***

**J8** D3 4c brown red .25 .25
Never hinged .25
P# block of 6 14.00
Never hinged 17.50
**J9** D3 6c brown red .30 .75
Never hinged .45
P# block of 6 14.00
Never hinged 17.50
**J10** D3 8c brown red .25 .75
Never hinged .35
P# block of 6 14.00
Never hinged 17.50
**J11** D3 10c brown red .30 .75
Never hinged .45
P# block of 6 14.00
Never hinged 17.50
**J12** D3 12c brown red .25 .75
Never hinged .35
P# block of 6 14.00
Never hinged 17.50
**J13** D3 16c brown red .30 .75
Never hinged .45
P# block of 6 14.00
Never hinged 17.50
**J14** D3 20c brown red .30 .75
Never hinged .45
P# block of 6 14.00
Never hinged 17.50
*Nos. J8-J14 (7)* 1.95 4.75
Set, never hinged 2.75

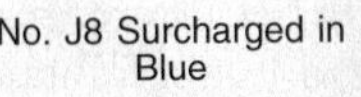

No. J8 Surcharged in Blue

**1937, July 29** **Unwmk.** ***Perf. 11***

**J15** D3 3c on 4c brown red .25 .25
Never hinged .35

See note after No. NJ1.

Nos. J8 to J14 Handstamped in Violet

**1944, Dec. 3**

**J16** D3 4c brown red *150.00* —
**J17** D3 6c brown red *100.00* —
**J18** D3 8c brown red *110.00* 350.00
**J19** D3 10c brown red *100.00* —
**J20** D3 12c brown red *100.00* —
**J21** D3 16c brown red *100.00* 350.00
*a.* Pair, one without ovpt. —
**J22** D3 20c brown red *110.00* —
*Nos. J16-J22 (7)* *770.00*

**Catalogue values for unused stamps in this section, from this point to the end of the section, are for Never Hinged items.**

### Republic

D4

**Unwmk.**

**1947, Oct. 20** **Engr.** ***Perf. 12***

**J23** D4 3c rose carmine .25 .25
**J24** D4 4c brt violet blue .45 .25
**J25** D4 6c olive green .60 .40
**J26** D4 10c orange .70 .50
*Nos. J23-J26 (4)* 2.00 1.40

## OFFICIAL STAMPS

### Official Handstamped Overprints

"Officers purchasing stamps for government business may, if they so desire, surcharge them with the letters O.B. either in writing with black ink or by rubber stamps but in such a manner as not to obliterate the stamp that postmasters will be unable to determine whether the stamps have been previously used." C.M. Cotterman, Director of Posts, December 26, 1905.

Beginning January 1, 1906, all branches of the Insular Government used postage stamps to prepay postage instead of franking them as before. Some officials used manuscript, some utilized the typewriting machines but by far the larger number provided themselves with rubber stamps. The majority of these read "O.B." but other forms were: "OFFICIAL BUSINESS" or "OFFICIAL MAIL" in two lines, with variations on many of these.

These "O.B." overprints are known on U.S. 1899-1901 stamps; on 1903-06 stamps in red and blue; on 1906 stamps in red, blue, black, yellow and green.

"O.B." overprints were also made on the centavo and peso stamps of the Philippines, per order of May 25, 1907.

Beginning in 1926 the Bureau of Posts issued press-printed official stamps, but many government offices continued to handstamp ordinary postage stamps "O.B." The press-printed "O.B." overprints are listed below.

During the Japanese occupation period 1942-45, the same system of handstamped official overprints prevailed, but the handstamp usually consisted of "K.P.", initials of the Tagalog words, "Kagamitang Pampamahalaan" (Official Business), and the two Japanese characters used in the printed overprint on Nos. NO1 to NO4.

Regular Issue of 1926 Ovptd. in Red

**1926, Dec. 20** **Unwmk.** ***Perf. 12***

**O1** A42 2c green & black 3.00 1.00
Never hinged 4.50
**O2** A42 4c car & blk 3.00 1.25
Never hinged 4.50
*a.* Vertical pair, imperf. between 750.00
**O3** A42 18c lt brn & blk 8.00 4.00
Never hinged 12.00
**O4** A42 20c org & blk 7.75 1.75
Never hinged 11.50
*Nos. O1-O4 (4)* 21.75 8.00
Set, never hinged 32.50

Opening of the Legislative Palace.

Regular Issue of 1917-26 Overprinted by the U.S. Bureau of Engraving and Printing

**1931** ***Perf. 11***

**O5** A40 2c green .40 .25
Never hinged .65
P# block of 6 20.00
Never hinged 25.00
*a.* No period after "B" 17.50 17.50
Never hinged 27.50
*b.* No period after "O" 40.00 30.00
**O6** A40 4c carmine .45 .25
Never hinged .70
P# block of 6 20.00
Never hinged 25.00
*a.* No period after "B" 40.00 20.00
Never hinged 60.00
**O7** A40 6c deep violet .75 .25
Never hinged 1.25
P# block of 10, Impt. 40.00
Never hinged 50.00
**O8** A40 8c yellow brown .75 .25
Never hinged 1.25
P# block of 6 32.00
Never hinged 40.00
**O9** A40 10c deep blue 1.20 .25
Never hinged 1.90
P# block of 10, Impt. 32.00
Never hinged 40.00
**O10** A40 12c red orange 2.00 .25
Never hinged 3.00
P# block of 6 65.00
Never hinged 80.00
*a.* No period after "B" 80.00 80.00
Never hinged 120.00
**O11** A40 16c lt ol grn 1.00 .25
Never hinged 1.50
P# block of 6 24.00
Never hinged 30.00
*a.* 16c olive bister 2.00 .25
Never hinged 3.00
P# block of 6 20.00
Never hinged 25.00
**O12** A40 20c orange yellow 1.25 .25
Never hinged 1.90
P# block of 10, Impt. 75.00
Never hinged 95.00
*a.* No period after "B" 80.00 80.00
Never hinged 120.00
**O13** A40 26c green 2.00 1.00
Never hinged 3.25
P# block of 6 120.00
Never hinged 150.00
*a.* 26c blue green 2.50 1.50
Never hinged 4.00
P# block of 6 130.00
Never hinged 165.00
**O14** A40 30c gray 2.00 .25
Never hinged 3.25
P# block of 10, Impt. 80.00
Never hinged 100.00
*Nos. O5-O14 (10)* 11.80 3.25
Set, never hinged 18.65

Many collectors prefer to collect the plate blocks of 6 of Nos. O5-O6, O8, O10-O11a and O14 as blocks of 10 so they fit aesthetically with the other plate blocks of 10 with imprints.

Overprinted on Nos. 383-392

**1935**

**O15** A53 2c rose .25 .25
Never hinged .30
P# block of 6 4.75
Never hinged 6.00
*a.* No period after "B" 15.00 10.00
Never hinged 22.50
*b.* No period after "O" — —
**O16** A54 4c yellow green .25 .25
Never hinged .30
P# block of 6 4.00
Never hinged 5.00
*a.* No period after "B" 15.00 *40.00*
Never hinged 22.50
**O17** A55 6c dark brown .25 .25
Never hinged .40
P# block of 6 8.00
Never hinged 10.00
*a.* No period after "B" 35.00 35.00
Never hinged 52.50
**O18** A56 8c violet .30 .25
Never hinged .45
P# block of 6 9.50
Never hinged 12.00
**O19** A57 10c rose carmine .30 .25
Never hinged .45
P# block of 6 8.00
Never hinged 10.00
**O20** A58 12c black .75 .25
Never hinged 1.10
P# block of 6 8.00
Never hinged 10.00
**O21** A59 16c dark blue .55 .25
Never hinged .85
P# block of 6 8.00
Never hinged 10.00
**O22** A60 20c light olive green .60 .25
Never hinged .90
P# block of 6 12.00
Never hinged 15.00
**O23** A61 26c indigo .90 .25
Never hinged 1.50
P# block of 6 20.00
Never hinged 25.00
**O24** A62 30c orange red .80 .25
Never hinged 1.20
P# block of 6 20.00
Never hinged 25.00
*Nos. O15-O24 (10)* 4.95 2.50
Set, never hinged 7.40

Nos. 411 and 418 with Additional Overprint in Black

**1937-38**

**O25** A53 2c rose .25 .25
Never hinged .30
*a.* No period after "B" 25.00 25.00
Never hinged 45.00
*b.* Period after "B" raised (UL 4) 150.00
**O26** A60 20c lt ol grn ('38) .70 .50
Never hinged 1.10
P# block of 6 20.00
Never hinged 25.00

### Regular Issue of 1935 Overprinted In Black

a

b

**1938-40**

**O27** A53(a) 2c rose .25 .25
Never hinged .30
P# block of 6 4.75
Never hinged 6.00
*a.* Hyphen omitted 10.00 10.00
Never hinged 15.00
*b.* No period after "B" 20.00 *30.00*
Never hinged 30.00
**O28** A54(b) 4c yellow green .75 1.00
Never hinged 1.10
P# block of 6 24.00
Never hinged 30.00
**O29** A55(a) 6c dark brown .30 .25
Never hinged .45
P# block of 6 12.00
Never hinged 15.00
**O30** A56(b) 8c violet .75 .85
Never hinged 1.10
P# block of 6 9.50
Never hinged 12.00
**O31** A57(b) 10c rose carmine .25 .25
Never hinged .30
P# block of 6 16.00
Never hinged 20.00
*a.* No period after "O" 50.00 40.00
Never hinged 75.00
**O32** A58(b) 12c black .30 .25
Never hinged .45
P# block of 6 12.00
Never hinged 15.00
**O33** A59(b) 16c dark blue .30 .25
Never hinged .45
P# block of 6 16.00
Never hinged 20.00
**O34** A60(a) 20c lt ol grn ('40) .55 .85
Never hinged .85
P# block of 6 16.00
Never hinged 20.00
**O35** A61(b) 26c indigo 1.50 *2.00*
Never hinged 2.25
P# block of 6 12.00
Never hinged 15.00
**O36** A62(b) 30c orange red .75 .85
Never hinged 1.10
P# block of 6 16.00
Never hinged 20.00
*Nos. O27-O36 (10)* 5.70 6.80
Set, never hinged 8.25

No. 461 Overprinted in Black — c

**1941, Apr. 14** ***Perf. 11x10½***

**O37** A75(c) 2c apple green .25 *.40*
Never hinged .30

Official Stamps Handstamped in Violet

**1944** *Perf. 11, 11x10½*

**O38** A53 2c rose (On O27) 375.00 200.00
Never hinged 750.00
**O39** A75 2c apple grn (On O37) 15.00 *20.00*
Never hinged 20.00
**O40** A54 4c yel grn (On O16) 45.00 *30.00*
Never hinged 80.00
**O40A** A55 6c dk brn (On O29) *8,000.* —
**O41** A57 10c rose car (On O31) *500.00*
*a.* No period after "O" *4,000.*
**O42** A60 20c lt ol grn (On O22) *8,000.*
**O43** A60 20c lt ol grn (On O26) *1,750.*

**No. 497 Overprinted Type "c" in Black**

**1946, June 19** *Perf. 11x10½*

**O44** A76 2c sepia .25 .25
Never hinged .25
*a.* Vertical pair, bottom stamp without ovpt. —

**Catalogue values for unused stamps in this section, from this point to the end of the section, are for Never Hinged items.**

**Republic**

Nos. 504, 505 and 507 Overprinted in Black — d

**1948** **Unwmk.** *Perf. 12*

**O50** A78 4c black brown .50 .25
*a.* Inverted overprint 25.00
*b.* Double overprint 25.00
**O51** A79 10c red orange .75 .25
**O52** A81 16c slate gray 3.00 .55
*Nos. O50-O52 (3)* 4.25 1.05

The overprint on No. O51 comes in two sizes: 13mm, applied in Manila, and 12½mm, applied in New York.

Nos. 527, 508 and 509 Overprinted in Black — e

**Overprint Measures 14mm**

**O53** A91 2c bright green .50 .25

**1949**

**O54** A82 20c red brown 1.00 .25

**Overprint Measures 12mm**

**O55** A83 50c dull green 1.50 .55

**No. 550 Overprinted Type "e" in Black**

**1950** **Overprint Measures 14mm**

**O56** A91 1c on 2c brt green .60 .25

Nos. 589, 592, 595 and 597 Overprinted in Black — f

**1952-55**

**Overprint Measures 15mm**

**O57** A117 1c red brown ('53) .50 .25
**O58** A117 5c crim rose .50 .25
**O59** A117 10c ultra ('55) .50 .25
**O60** A117 20c car lake ('55) 1.50 .25
*Nos. O57-O60 (4)* 3.00 1.00

No. 647 Overprinted — g

**1959** **Engr.** *Perf. 12*

**O61** A117 1c on 5c crim rose .40 .25

**No. 813 Overprinted Type "f" Overprint measures 16½mm**

**1959**

**O62** A145 6c gray blue .60 .25

**Nos. 856-861 Overprinted**

h

j

k

**1962-64** *Perf. 13½*

**O63** A158(j) 5s car rose ('63) .50 .25

*Perf. 13x12*

**O64** A158(h) 6s dk red brn .50 .25

*Perf. 13½*

**O65** A158(k) 6s pck blue ('64) .50 .25
**O66** A158(j) 10s brt purple ('63) .50 .25
**O67** A158(j) 20s Prus blue ('63) .50 .25
**O68** A158(j) 30s vermilion .75 .25
**O69** A158(k) 50s violet ('63) 1.00 .25
*Nos. O63-O69 (7)* 4.25 1.75

"G.O." stands for "Gawaing Opisyal," Tagalog for "Official Business."
On 6s overprint "k" is 10mm wide.
On No. O69, overprint "k" is 16mm wide.
For overprint see No. 1119.

**No. 1082 Overprinted**

l

**1970, Dec. 30** **Engr.** *Perf. 14*

**O70** A222(l) 10s rose carmine .50 .25

## NEWSPAPER STAMPS

N1

**1886-89** **Unwmk.** **Typo.** *Perf. 14*

**P1** N1 ⅛c yellow green .30 *7.50*
**P2** N1 1m rose ('89) .30 *15.00*
**P3** N1 2m blue ('89) .30 *15.00*
**P4** N1 5m dk brown ('89) .30 *15.00*
*Nos. P1-P4 (4)* 1.20 *52.50*

N2

**1890-96**

**P5** N2 ⅛c dark violet .25 .25
**P6** N2 ⅛c green ('92) 6.75 *10.00*
**P7** N2 ⅛c org brn ('94) .25 .25
**P8** N2 ⅛c dull blue ('96) .85 .60
**P9** N2 1m dark violet .25 .25
**P10** N2 1m green ('92) 2.25 *5.50*
**P11** N2 1m olive gray ('94) .25 .45
**P12** N2 1m ultra ('96) .35 .25
**P13** N2 2m dark violet .25 .45
**P14** N2 2m green ('92) 2.50 *13.00*
**P15** N2 2m olive gray ('94) .25 *.45*
**P16** N2 2m brown ('96) .30 .25
**P17** N2 5m dark violet .25 *1.10*
**P18** N2 5m green ('92) 150.00 55.00
**P19** N2 5m olive gray ('94) .25 *.45*
**P20** N2 5m dp blue grn ('96) 2.50 1.40
*Nos. P5-P20 (16)* 167.50 *89.65*

Imperfs. exist of Nos. P8, P9, P11, P12, P16, P17 and P20.

## POSTAL TAX STAMPS

Mt. Pinatubo Fund — PT1

25c, Lahar flow. #RA2, Erupting volcano. #RA3, Animals after eruption. #RA4, Village after eruption. #RA5, People clearing ash.

**Wmk. 391**

**1992, Nov. 16** **Litho.** *Perf. 13¾*

**RA1** PT1 25c multi .50 .25
**RA2** PT1 1p multi .70 .35
**RA3** PT1 1p multi .70 .35
**RA4** PT1 1p multi .70 .35
**RA5** PT1 1p multi .70 .35
*a.* Block of 4, #RA2-RA5 3.50 2.00
*Nos. RA1-RA5 (5)* 3.30 1.65

Use of Nos. RA1-RA5 as postal tax stamps was suspended on 2/1/93. These stamps became valid for postage on 6/14/93.

## OCCUPATION STAMPS

**Issued Under Japanese Occupation**

No. 461 Overprinted in Black

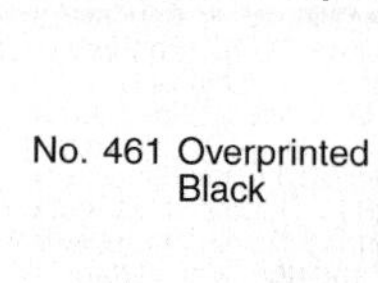

No. 438 Overprinted in Black

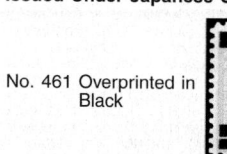

No. 439 Overprinted in Black

**1942-43** **Unwmk.** *Perf. 11x10½, 11*

**N1** A75 2c apple green .25 *1.00*
Never hinged .30
*a.* Pair, one without overprint —
**N2** A58 12c black ('43) .25 *2.00*
Never hinged .40
P# block of 6 12.00
Never hinged 15.00
**N3** A59 16c dark blue 5.00 3.75
Never hinged 7.50
P# block of 6 37.50
Never hinged 55.00
*Nos. N1-N3 (3)* 5.50 6.75
Set, never hinged 8.20

**Nos. 435a, 435, 442, 443, and 423 Surcharged in Black**

a

b

c

d

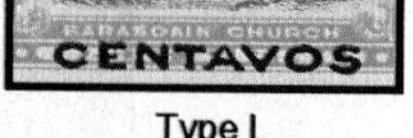

Type I

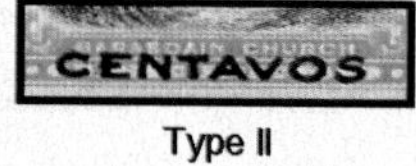

Type II

Two types of 50c surcharge
Type I: Center of "A" is a triangle.
Type II: Center of "A" is a pin hole.

**1942-43** *Perf. 11*

**N4** A55(a) 5(c) on 6c golden brown .25 *.75*
Never hinged .35
*a.* Top bar shorter and thinner .25 *1.00*
Never hinged .35
P# block of 6 40.00
Never hinged 50.00
*b.* 5(c) on 6c dark brown .25 *.85*
Never hinged .35
*c.* As "b," top bar shorter and thinner .25 *1.00*
Never hinged .35
*d.* Double surcharge, on cover —
**N5** A62(b) 16(c) on 30c org red ('43) .25 *.60*
Never hinged .45
**N6** A63(c) 50c on 1p red org & blk ('43) .75 *1.25*
Never hinged 1.10
P# block of 4 16.00
Never hinged 20.00
*a.* Double surcharge *300.00*
*b.* Type I surcharge 100.00 90.00
Never hinged 125.00
P# block of 4 500.00
Never hinged 600.00
**N7** A65(d) 1p on 4p bl & blk ('43) 100.00 *150.00*
Never hinged 155.00
*Nos. N4-N7 (4)* 101.25 152.60
Set, never hinged 156.90

On Nos. N4 and N4b, the top bar measures 1½x22½mm. On Nos. N4a and N4c, the top bar measures 1x21mm and the "5" is smaller and thinner.

The used value for No. N7 is for postal cancellation. Used stamps exist with first day cancellations. They are worth somewhat less.

**No. 384 Surcharged in Black**

**1942, May 18**
**N8** A54 2(c) on 4c yellow green 4.00 5.00
Never hinged 8.75

Issued to commemorate Japan's capture of Bataan and Corregidor. The American-Filipino forces finally surrendered May 7, 1942. No. N8 exists with "R" for "B" in BATAAN.

**No. 384 Surcharged in Black**

**1942, Dec. 8**
**N9** A54 5(c) on 4c yellow green .50 *1.00*
Never hinged .75

1st anniversary of the "Greater East Asia War."

**Nos. C59 and C62 Surcharged in Black**

**1943, Jan. 23**
**N10** AP1 2(c) on 8c carmine .25 *1.00*
Never hinged .35
P# block of 6 20.00
Never hinged 25.00
**N11** AP1 5c on 1p sepia .50 *1.50*
Never hinged .75

1st anniv. of the Philippine Executive Commission.

Nipa Hut OS1

Rice Planting OS2

Mt. Mayon and Mt. Fuji — OS3

Moro Vinta — OS4

The "c" currency is indicated by four Japanese characters, "p" currency by two.

**Engraved; Typographed (2c, 6c, 25c)**
**1943-44 Wmk. 257 Perf. 13**
**N12** OS1 1c dp orange .25 .40
Never hinged .30
Margin block of 6, inscription 2.40
Never hinged 3.00
**N13** OS2 2c brt green .25 .40
Never hinged .30
Margin block of 6, inscription 2.40
Never hinged 3.00
**N14** OS1 4c slate green .25 .40
Never hinged .30
Margin block of 6, inscription 2.40
Never hinged 3.00
**N15** OS3 5c orange brown .25 .40
Never hinged .30
Margin block of 6, inscription 2.40
Never hinged 3.00
**N16** OS2 6c red .25 .60
Never hinged .30
Margin block of 6, inscription 2.40
Never hinged 3.00
**N17** OS3 10c blue green .25 .40
Never hinged .30
Margin block of 6, inscription 2.40
Never hinged 3.00
**N18** OS4 12c steel blue 1.00 1.50
Never hinged 1.50
Margin block of 6, inscription 11.00
Never hinged 14.00
**N19** OS4 16c dk brown .25 .40
Never hinged .30
Margin block of 6, inscription 2.40
Never hinged 3.00
**N20** OS1 20c rose violet 1.25 1.75
Never hinged 1.90
Margin block of 6, inscription 15.00
Never hinged 19.00
**N21** OS3 21c violet .25 .40
Never hinged .35
Margin block of 6, inscription 2.40
Never hinged 3.00
**N22** OS2 25c pale brown .25 .40
Never hinged .35
Margin block of 6, inscription 2.40
Never hinged 3.00
**N23** OS3 1p dp carmine .75 1.25
Never hinged 1.15
Margin block of 6, inscription 9.50
Never hinged 12.00
**N24** OS4 2p dull violet 6.50 6.50
Never hinged 10.00
**N25** OS4 5p dark olive 16.00 18.00
Never hinged 25.00
*Nos. N12-N25 (14)* 27.75 32.80
Set, never hinged 42.00

Issued: Nos. N13, N15, 4/1; Nos. N12, N14, N23, 6/7; Nos. N16-N19, 7/14; Nos. N20-N22, 8/16; No. N24, 9/16; No. N25, 4/1/44.
For surcharges see Nos. NB5-NB7.

OS5

**1943, May 7 Photo. Unwmk.**
**N26** OS5 2c carmine red .25 *.75*
Never hinged .30
Margin block of 6, inscription 4.00
Never hinged 5.00
**N27** OS5 5c bright green .25 *1.00*
Never hinged .35
Margin block of 6, inscription 6.50
Never hinged 8.00

1st anniversary of the fall of Bataan and Corregidor.

No. 440 Surcharged in Black

**1943, June 20 Engr. Perf. 11**
**N28** A60 12(c) on 20c light olive green .25 *.75*
Never hinged .35
*a.* Double surcharge

350th anniversary of the printing press in the Philippines. "Limbagan" is Tagalog for "printing press."

Rizal Monument, Filipina and Philippine Flag — OS6

**1943, Oct. 14 Photo. Perf. 12**
**N29** OS6 5c light blue .25 *.90*
Never hinged .30
*a.* Imperf. .25 .90
**N30** OS6 12c orange .25 *.90*
Never hinged .30
*a.* Imperf. .25 .90
**N31** OS6 17c rose pink .25 *.90*
Never hinged .30
*a.* Imperf. .25 .90
*Nos. N29-N31 (3)* .75 *2.70*
Set, never hinged .90

"Independence of the Philippines." Japan granted "independence" Oct. 14, 1943, when the puppet republic was founded.
The imperforate stamps were issued without gum.

José Rizal — OS7

Rev. José Burgos — OS8

Apolinario Mabini — OS9

**1944, Feb. 17 Litho.**
**N32** OS7 5c blue .25 *1.00*
Never hinged .30
*a.* Imperf. .25 *2.00*
Never hinged .35
**N33** OS8 12c carmine .25 *1.00*
Never hinged .30
*a.* Imperf. .25 *2.00*
Never hinged .35
**N34** OS9 17c deep orange .25 *1.00*
Never hinged .30
*a.* Imperf. .25 *2.00*
Never hinged .35
*Nos. N32-N34 (3)* .75 *3.00*
Set, never hinged .90

See No. NB8.

Nos. C60 and C61 Surcharged in Black

**1944, May 7 Perf. 11**
**N35** AP1 5(c) on 20c ultra .50 1.00
Never hinged .75
P# block of 6 32.50
Never hinged 40.00
**N36** AP1 12(c) on 60c blue green 1.75 1.75
Never hinged 2.50
P# block of 6 42.50
Never hinged 52.50

2nd anniversary of the fall of Bataan and Corregidor.

OS10

**1945, Jan. 12 Litho. Imperf.**
**Without Gum**
**N37** OS10 5c dull violet brown .25 *.50*
Never hinged .30
**N38** OS10 7c blue green .25 *.50*
Never hinged .30
**N39** OS10 20c chalky blue .25 *.50*
Never hinged .30
*Nos. N37-N39 (3)* *.75* *1.50*
Set, never hinged .90

Issued belatedly on Jan. 12, 1945, to commemorate the first anniversary of the puppet Philippine Republic, Oct. 14, 1944. "S" stands for "sentimos."

## OCCUPATION SEMI-POSTAL STAMPS

Woman, Farming and Cannery — OSP1

**Unwmk.**
**1942, Nov. 12 Litho. Perf. 12**
**NB1** OSP1 2c + 1c pale violet .25 *.60*
Never hinged .30
**NB2** OSP1 5c + 1c brt grn .25 *1.00*
Never hinged .30
**NB3** OSP1 16c + 2c orange 25.00 *32.50*
Never hinged 42.00
*Nos. NB1-NB3 (3)* 25.50 34.10
Set, never hinged 42.60

Issued to promote the campaign to produce and conserve food. The surtax aided the Red Cross.

Souvenir Sheet

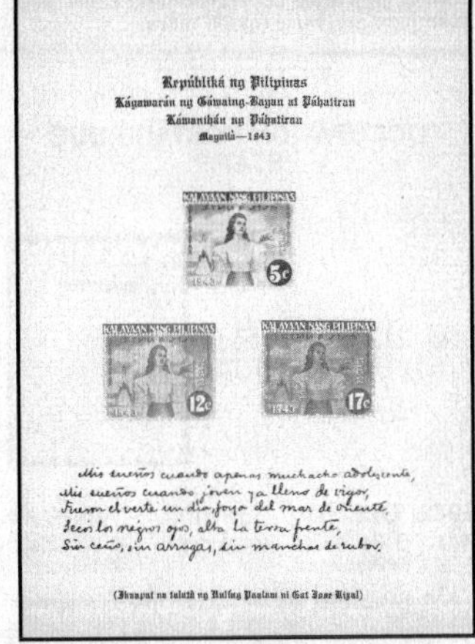
OSP2

**1943, Oct. 14 Without Gum *Imperf.***
**NB4** OSP2 Sheet of 3 75.00 *17.50*

"Independence of the Philippines."
No. NB4 contains one each of Nos. N29a-N31a. Marginal inscription is from Rizal's "Last Farewell." Sold for 2.50p.
The value of No. NB4 used is for a sheet from a first day cover. Commercially used sheets are extremely scarce and worth much more.

Nos. N18, N20 and N21 Surcharged in Black

**1943, Dec. 8 Wmk. 257 Perf. 13**
**NB5** OS4 12c + 21c steel blue .25 *1.50*
Never hinged .30
Margin block of 6, inscription 4.00
Never hinged 5.00
**NB6** OS1 20c + 36c rose violet .25 *1.50*
Never hinged .30
Margin block of 6, inscription 4.00
Never hinged 5.00
**NB7** OS3 21c + 40c violet .25 *2.00*
Never hinged .30
Margin block of 6, inscription 4.75
Never hinged 6.00
*Nos. NB5-NB7 (3)* .75 *5.00*
Set, never hinged .90

The surtax was for the benefit of victims of a Luzon flood. "Baha" is Tagalog for "flood."

Souvenir Sheet

OSP3

**Unwmk.**
**1944, Feb. 9 Litho. *Imperf.***
**Without Gum**

**NB8** OSP3 Sheet of 3 6.50 3.50

No. NB8 contains 1 each of Nos. N32a-N34a.

Sheet sold for 1p, surtax going to a fund for the care of heroes' monuments.

The value for No. NB8 used is for a stamp from a first day cover. Commercially used examples are worth much more.

## OCCUPATION POSTAGE DUE STAMP

No. J15 Overprinted in Blue

**1942, Oct. 14 Unwmk. *Perf. 11***
**NJ1** D3 3c on 4c brown red 25.00 *35.00*
Never hinged 37.50

On examples of No. J15, two lines were drawn in India ink with a ruling pen across "United States of America" by employees of the Short Paid Section of the Manila Post Office to make a provisional 3c postage due stamp which was used from Sept. 1, 1942 (when the letter rate was raised from 2c to 5c) until Oct. 14 when No. NJ1 went on sale. Value on cover, $175.

Bottom plate blocks of 6 of No. NJ1 are much scarcer than the right side plate blocks. Value $325 hinged, $450 nerver hinged.

## OCCUPATION OFFICIAL STAMPS

Nos. 461, 413, 435, 435a and 442 Ovptd. or Srchd. in Black with Bars and

**1943-44 Unwmk. *Perf. 11x10½, 11***
**NO1** A75 2c apple green .25 *.75*
Never hinged .30
*a.* Double overprint *400.00*
Never hinged *600.00*
**NO2** A55 5(c) on 6c dk brn (On No. 413) ('44) 40.00 *45.00*
Never hinged 55.00
**NO3** A55 5(c) on 6c golden brn (On No. 435a) .25 *.90*
Never hinged .35
P# block of 6 14.00
Never hinged 17.50
*a.* Narrower spacing between bars .25 *.90*
Never hinged .35
*b.* 5(c) on 6c dark brown (On No. 435) .25 *.90*
Never hinged .35
*c.* As "b," narrower spacing between bars .25 *.90*
Never hinged .35
*d.* Double overprint —
**NO4** A62 16(c) on 30c org red .30 *1.25*
Never hinged .45
P# block of 6 20.00
Never hinged 25.00
*a.* Wider spacing between bars .30 *1.25*
Never hinged .45
*Nos. NO1-NO4 (4)* 40.80 47.90
Set, never hinged 56.10

On Nos. NO3 and NO3b the bar deleting "United States of America" is 9¾ to 10mm above the bar deleting "Common." On Nos. NO3a and NO3c, the spacing is 8 to 8½mm.

On No. NO4, the center bar is 19mm long, 3½mm below the top bar and 6mm above the Japanese characters. On No. NO4a, the center bar is 20½mm long, 9mm below the top bar and 1mm above the Japanese characters.

"K.P." stands for Kagamitang Pampamahalaan, "Official Business" in Tagalog.

Nos. 435 & 435a Surcharged in Black

**1944, Aug. 28 *Perf. 11***
**NO5** A55 (5c) on 6c gldn brn .30 *.40*
Never hinged .45
P# block of 6 20.00
Never hinged 25.00
*a.* 5(c) on 6c dark brown .30 *.40*
Never hinged .45
P# block of 6 20.00
Never hinged 25.00

**Nos. O34 and C62 Overprinted in Black**

a

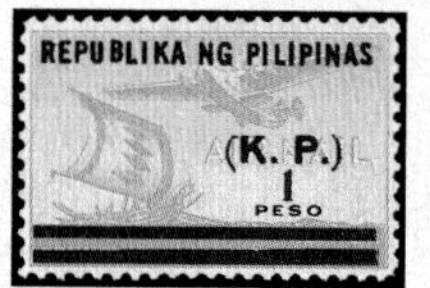


b

**NO6** A60(a) 20c light olive green .40 *.50*
Never hinged .60
P# block of 6 12.00
Never hinged 15.00
**NO7** AP1(b) 1p sepia .90 *1.00*
Never hinged 1.45
P# block of 6 20.00
Never hinged 25.00
*Nos. NO5-NO7 (3)* 1.60 1.90
Set, never hinged 2.05

## FILIPINO REVOLUTIONARY GOVERNMENT

Following the defeat of the Spanish fleet by U.S. Commodore Dewey in Manila on May 1, 1898, which essentially ended the Spanish-American War in the Philippines, postal services were disrupted throughout the Philippines. Postal service was reestablished through U.S. Army military stations, beginning in June 1898 near Manila, continuing province by province until culminating at Zamboanga and other cities in the southern areas in late 1899.

Provisional stamps were prepared for use in the central part of the island of Luzon at Malolos in late 1898 under the leadership of General Emilio Aguinaldo, who had proclaimed the Philippine Republic on June 12, 1898. Later, other provisional stamps were prepared by local Filipino insurgents at Iloilo (Panay Island), Bohol, Cebu and Negros, and Spanish period stamps were overprinted and/or surcharged for use by postal officials at Zamboanga and La Union.

The most familiar of these provisionals were the "Aguinaldo" issues of the Filipino Revolutionary Government in central Luzon near Manila. The letters "KKK," the initials of the revolutionary society, "Kataas-taasang, Kagalang-galang Katipunan nang Mañga Anak nang Bayan," meaning "Sovereign Worshipful Association of the Sons of the Country," readily identify the Aguinaldo provisionals. Hostilities broke out between the Aguinaldo regime and the occupying American administration in February 1899, and the Filipino-American War continued until the American capture of Aguinaldo on March 23, 1901.

The Aguinaldo regular postage, registration, revenue, newspaper and telegraph stamps were in use in Luzon as early as November 10, 1898, and continued in use through early 1901. Although the postal regulations specified that these stamps be used for their inscribed purpose, they were commonly used interchangeably.

The Filipino Republic was instituted by Gen. Emilio Aguinaldo on June 23, 1899. At the same time he assumed the office of President. Aguinaldo dominated the greater part of the island of Luzon and some of the smaller islands until late in 1899. He was taken prisoner by United States troops on March 23, 1901.

The devices composing the National Arms, adopted by the Filipino Revolutionary Government, are emblems of the Katipunan political secret society or of Katipunan origin. The letters "K K K" on these stamps are the initials of this society whose complete name is "Kataas-taasang, Kagalang-galang Katipunan nang Mañga Anak nang Bayan," meaning "Sovereign Worshipful Association of the Sons of the Country."

The regular postage and telegraph stamps were in use on Luzon as early as Nov. 10, 1898. Owing to the fact that stamps for the different purposes were not always available together with a lack of proper instructions, any of the adhesives were permitted to be used in the place of the other. Hence telegraph and revenue stamps were accepted for postage and postage stamps for revenue or telegraph charges. In addition to the regular postal emission, there are a number of provisional stamps, issues of local governments of islands and towns.

## POSTAGE ISSUES

A1

A2

Coat of Arms — A3

**1898-99 Unwmk. *Perf. 11½***
**Y1** A1 2c red 175.00 125.00
*a.* Double impression *325.00*
**Y2** A2 2c red .30 4.00
*b.* Double impression —
*d.* Horiz. pair, imperf. between —
*e.* Vert. pair, imperf. between *225.00*
**Y3** A3 2c red 150.00 *200.00*

Imperf pairs and pairs, imperf horizontally, have been created from No. Y2e.

## REGISTRATION STAMP

RS1

**YF1** RS1 8c green 5.00 *30.00*
*a.* Imperf., pair 400.00
*b.* Imperf. vertically, pair —

## NEWSPAPER STAMP

N1

**YP1** N1 1m black 2.00 *20.00*
*a.* Imperf., pair 5.00 *20.00*

**Sign-up now to get weekly email exclusive online deals and the latest product updates. Visit AmosAdvantage.com/Newsletter and register today.**

### PRE-CUT SINGLE MOUNTS

| ITEM | W x H (mm) | DESCRIPTION | MOUNTS | RETAIL | AA* |
|---|---|---|---|---|---|
| 901 | 40 x 25 | U.S. Standard Comm. Hor. Water Activated | 40 | $3.50 | **$2.39** |
| 902 | 25 x 40 | U.S. Standard Comm. Vert. Water Activated | 40 | $3.50 | **$2.39** |
| 903 | 25 x 22 | U.S. Regular Issue – Hor. Water Activated | 40 | $3.50 | **$2.39** |
| 904 | 22 x 25 | U.S. Regular Issue – Vert. Water Activated | 40 | $3.50 | **$2.39** |
| 905 | 41 x 31 | U.S. Semi-Jumbo – Horizontal | 40 | $3.50 | **$2.39** |
| 906 | 31 x 41 | U.S. Semi-Jumbo – Vertical | 40 | $3.50 | **$2.39** |
| 907 | 50 x 31 | U.S. Jumbo – Horizontal | 40 | $3.50 | **$2.39** |
| 908 | 31 x 50 | U.S. Jumbo – Vertical | 40 | $3.50 | **$2.39** |
| 909 | 25 x 27 | U.S. Famous Americans/Champions Of Liberty | 40 | $3.50 | **$2.39** |
| 910 | 33 x 27 | United Nations | 40 | $3.50 | **$2.39** |
| 911 | 40 x 27 | United Nations | 40 | $3.50 | **$2.39** |
| 976 | 67 x 25 | Plate Number Coils, Strips of Three | 40 | $6.25 | **$3.99** |
| 984 | 67 x 34 | Pacific '97 Triangle | 10 | $3.50 | **$2.39** |
| 985 | 111 x 25 | Plate Number Coils, Strips of Five | 25 | $6.25 | **$3.99** |
| 986 | 51 x 36 | U.S. Hunting Permit/Express Mail | 40 | $6.25 | **$3.99** |
| 1045 | 40 x 26 | U.S. Standard Comm. Hor. Self-Adhesive | 40 | $3.50 | **$2.39** |
| 1046 | 25 x 41 | U.S. Standard Comm. Vert. Self-Adhesive | 40 | $3.50 | **$2.39** |
| 1047 | 22 x 26 | U.S. Definitives Vert. Self Adhesive | 40 | $3.50 | **$2.39** |
| 966 | Value Pack | (Assortment pre-cut sizes) | 320 | $23.25 | **$15.25** |
| 975 | Best Pack | (Assortment pre-cut sizes - Black Only) | 160 | $14.75 | **$9.99** |

### PRE-CUT PLATE BLOCK, FDC, POSTAL CARD MOUNTS

| ITEM | W x H (mm) | DESCRIPTION | MOUNTS | RETAIL | AA* |
|---|---|---|---|---|---|
| 912 | 57 x 55 | Regular Issue Plate Block | 25 | $6.25 | **$3.99** |
| 913 | 73 x 63 | Champions of Liberty | 25 | $6.25 | **$3.99** |
| 914 | 106 x 55 | Rotary Press Standard Commemorative | 20 | $6.25 | **$3.99** |
| 915 | 105 x 57 | Giori Press Standard Commemorative | 20 | $6.25 | **$3.99** |
| 916 | 127 x 70 | Giori Press Jumbo Commemorative | 10 | $6.25 | **$3.99** |
| 917 | 165 x 94 | First Day Cover | 10 | $6.25 | **$3.99** |
| 918 | 140 x 90 | Postal Card Size/Submarine Booklet Pane | 10 | $6.25 | **$3.99** |
| 1048 | 152 x 107 | Large Postal Cards | 8 | $10.25 | **$6.99** |

### STRIPS 215MM LONG

| ITEM | W x H (mm) | DESCRIPTION | MOUNTS | RETAIL | AA* |
|---|---|---|---|---|---|
| 919 | 20 | U.S. 19th Century, Horizontal Coil | 22 | $7.99 | **$5.25** |
| 920 | 22 | U.S. Early Air Mail | 22 | $7.99 | **$5.25** |
| 921 | 24 | U.S., Vertical Coils, Christmas (#2400, #2428 etc.) | 22 | $7.99 | **$5.25** |
| 922 | 25 | U.S. Commemorative and Regular | 22 | $7.99 | **$5.25** |
| 1049 | 26 | U.S. Commemorative and Regular | 22 | $7.99 | **$5.25** |
| 923 | 27 | U.S. Famous Americans | 22 | $7.99 | **$5.25** |
| 924 | 28 | U.S. 19th Century, Liechtenstein | 22 | $7.99 | **$5.25** |
| 1050 | 29 | Virginia Dare, British Empire, etc. | 22 | $7.99 | **$5.25** |
| 925 | 30 | U.S. 19th Century; Jamestown, etc; Foreign | 22 | $7.99 | **$5.25** |
| 926 | 31 | U.S. Horizontal Jumbo and Semi-Jumbo | 22 | $7.99 | **$5.25** |
| 927 | 33 | U.S. Stampin' Future, UN | 22 | $7.99 | **$5.25** |
| 1054 | 34 | U.S. American Landmarks, Eclipse | 22 | $7.99 | **$5.25** |
| 928 | 36 | U.S. Hunting Permit, Canada | 15 | $7.99 | **$5.25** |
| 1051 | 37 | U.S., British Colonies | 22 | $7.99 | **$5.25** |
| 929 | 39 | U.S. Early 20th Century | 15 | $7.99 | **$5.25** |
| 930 | 41 | U.S. Vert. Semi-Jumbo ('77 Lafayette, Pottery, etc.) | 15 | $7.99 | **$5.25** |
| 931 | | Multiple Assortment: One strip of each size 22-41 above (SMKB) (2 x 25mm strips) | 12 | $7.99 | **$5.25** |
| 1052 | 42 | U.S., British Colonies | 22 | $7.99 | **$5.25** |
| 1053 | 43 | U.S., British Colonies | 22 | $7.99 | **$5.25** |
| 932 | 44 | U.S. Vertical Coil Pair Garden Flowers Booklet Pane | 15 | $7.99 | **$5.25** |
| 933 | 48 | U.S. Farley, Gutter Pair | 15 | $7.99 | **$5.25** |
| 934 | 50 | U.S. Jumbo (Lyndon Johnson, '74 U.P.U., etc.) | 15 | $7.99 | **$5.25** |
| 935 | 52 | U.S. Standard Commemorative Block (Butterflies) | 15 | $7.99 | **$5.25** |
| 936 | 55 | U.S. Standard Plate Block - normal margins | 15 | $7.99 | **$5.25** |
| 937 | 57 | U.S. Standard Plate Block - wider margins | 15 | $7.99 | **$5.25** |
| 938 | 61 | U.S. Blocks, Israel Tabs, '99 Christmas Madonna Pane | 15 | $7.99 | **$5.25** |

### STRIPS 240MM LONG

| ITEM | W x H (mm) | DESCRIPTION | MOUNTS | RETAIL | AA* |
|---|---|---|---|---|---|
| 939 | 63 | U.S. Jumbo Commemorative Horizontal Block | 10 | $9.25 | **$5.99** |
| 940 | 66 | U.S. CIPEX Souvenir Sheet, Self-Adhesive Booklet Pane (#2803a, 3012a) | 10 | $9.25 | **$5.99** |
| 941 | 68 | U.S. ATM Booklet Pane, Farley Gutter Pair & Souvenir Sheet | 10 | $9.25 | **$5.99** |
| 942 | 74 | U.S. TIPEX Souvenir Sheet | 10 | $9.25 | **$5.99** |
| 943 | 80 | U.S. Standard Commemorative Vertical Block | 10 | $9.25 | **$5.99** |
| 944 | 82 | U.S. Blocks of Four, U.N. Chagall | 10 | $9.25 | **$5.99** |
| 945 | 84 | Israel Tab Block, Mars Pathfinder Sheetlet | 10 | $9.25 | **$5.99** |
| 946 | 89 | Submarine Booklet, Souvenir Sheet World Cup, Rockwell | 10 | $9.25 | **$5.99** |
| 947 | 100 | U.S. '74 U.P.U. Block, U.N. Margin Inscribed Block | 7 | $9.25 | **$5.99** |
| 948 | 120 | Various Souvenir Sheets and Blocks | 7 | $9.25 | **$5.99** |

### STRIPS 265MM LONG

| ITEM | W x H (mm) | DESCRIPTION | MOUNTS | RETAIL | AA* |
|---|---|---|---|---|---|
| 1035 | 25 | U.S. Coils Strips of 11 | 12 | $9.25 | **$5.99** |
| 949 | 40 | U.S. Postal People Standard Standard & Semi-Jumbo Commemorative Strip | 10 | $9.25 | **$5.99** |
| 981 | 44 | U.S. Long self-adhesive booklet panes | 10 | $9.25 | **$5.99** |
| 1030 | 45 | Various (Canada Scott #1725-1734) | 10 | $9.25 | **$5.99** |
| 1036 | 46 | U.S. Long self adhesive booklet panes of 15 | 10 | $9.25 | **$5.99** |
| 950 | 55 | U.S. Regular Plate Block or Strip of 20 | 10 | $9.25 | **$5.99** |
| 951 | 59 | U.S. Double Issue Strip | 10 | $9.25 | **$5.99** |
| 952 | 70 | U.S. Jumbo Commemorative Plate Block | 10 | $12.50 | **$8.50** |
| 1031 | 72 | Various (Canada Scott #1305a-1804a) | 10 | $12.50 | **$8.50** |
| 1032 | 75 | Plate Blocks: Lance Armstrong, Prehistoric Animals, etc. | 10 | $12.50 | **$8.50** |
| 1060 | 76 | U.S. 1994 Stamp Printing Centennial Souvenir Sheet, etc. | 10 | $12.50 | **$8.50** |
| 953 | 91 | U.S. Self-Adhesive Booklet Pane '98 Wreath, '95 Santa | 10 | $12.50 | **$8.50** |
| 1033 | 95 | Mini-Sheet Plate Blocks w/top header | 10 | $12.50 | **$8.50** |
| 1061 | 96 | U.S., Foreign | 10 | $12.50 | **$8.50** |
| 954 | 105 | U.S. Standard Semi-Jumbo Commemorative Plate Number Strip | 10 | $12.50 | **$8.50** |
| 955 | 107 | Same as above–wide margin | 10 | $12.50 | **$8.50** |
| 956 | 111 | U.S. Gravure-Intaglio Plate Number Strip | 10 | $14.75 | **$9.99** |
| 1062 | 115 | Foreign Small Sheets | 10 | $17.50 | **$11.99** |
| 957 | 127 | U.S. 2000 Space S/S, World War II S/S | 10 | $17.50 | **$11.99** |
| 1063 | 131 | Looney Tunes sheets; World War II Souvenir Sheet Plate Block | 10 | $17.50 | **$11.99** |
| 1064 | 135 | U.S., Japan Gifts of Friendship sheet | 10 | $17.50 | **$11.99** |
| 958 | 137 | Great Britain Coronation | 10 | $17.50 | **$11.99** |
| 1065 | 139 | Sheets: Soda Fountain, Lady Bird Johnson, Earthscapes, etc. | 10 | $17.50 | **$11.99** |
| 1066 | 143 | Sheets: Merchant Marine Ships, 2013 Hanukkah, etc. | 10 | $17.50 | **$11.99** |
| 1067 | 147 | Sheets: Pickup Trucks, Animal Rescue, Washington D.C., etc. | 10 | $17.50 | **$11.99** |
| 1068 | 151 | Sheets: Go Green, Bicycling, Happy New Year, Ben Franklin, etc. | 10 | $17.50 | **$11.99** |

### STRIPS 265MM LONG, continued

| ITEM | W x H (mm) | DESCRIPTION | MOUNTS | RETAIL | AA* |
|---|---|---|---|---|---|
| 959 | 158 | American Glass, U.S. Football Coaches Sheets | 10 | $17.99 | **$12.50** |
| 1077 | 160 | Sheets: Pacific '97 Triangle Mini, Trans-Mississippi | 5 | $12.50 | **$8.50** |
| 1069 | 163 | Sheets: Modern Architecture, UN Human Rights, etc. | 5 | $12.50 | **$8.50** |
| 1070 | 167 | Sheets: John F. Kennedy, Classics Forever, Made in America, etc. | 5 | $12.50 | **$8.50** |
| 1071 | 171 | Film Directors, Foreign Souvenir Sheets | 5 | $12.50 | **$8.50** |
| 960 | 175 | Large Block, Souvenir Sheet | 5 | $12.50 | **$8.50** |
| 1072 | 181 | Sheets: Jimi Hendrix, Johnny Cash, American Photography, etc. | 5 | $17.50 | **$11.99** |
| 1073 | 185 | Frank Sinatra, Ronald Reagan, Arthur Ashe, Creast Cancer, etc. | 5 | $17.50 | **$11.99** |
| 1074 | 188 | Sheets: Yoda, 9/11 Heroes, Andy Warhol, Frida Kahlo, etc | 5 | $17.50 | **$11.99** |
| 1078 | 192 | Olympic, etc. | 5 | $17.50 | **$11.99** |
| 1075 | 198 | Sheets: Modern American Art, Super Heroes, Baseball Sluggers, etc. | 5 | $17.50 | **$11.99** |
| 1076 | 215 | Celebrity Chefs sheets; Foreign sheets | 5 | $17.50 | **$11.99** |
| 961 | 231 | U.S. Full Post Office Pane Regular and Commemorative | 5 | $17.99 | **$12.50** |

### SOUVENIR SHEETS/SMALL PANES

| ITEM | W x H (mm) | DESCRIPTION | MOUNTS | RETAIL | AA* |
|---|---|---|---|---|---|
| 962 | 204 x 153 | New Year 2000, U.S. Bicentennial S/S | 4 | $9.25 | **$5.99** |
| 963 | 187 x 144 | 55¢ Victorian Love Pane, U.N. Flag Sheet | 9 | $15.50 | **$10.25** |
| 964 | 160 x 200 | U.N., Israel Sheet | 10 | $15.50 | **$10.25** |
| 965 | 120 x 207 | U.S. AMERIPEX Presidential Sheet | 4 | $6.25 | **$3.99** |
| 968 | 229 x 131 | World War II S/S Plate Block Only | 5 | $9.25 | **$5.99** |
| 970 | 111 x 91 | Columbian Souvenir Sheet | 6 | $6.25 | **$4.75** |
| 972 | 148 x 196 | Apollo Moon Landing/Carnivorous Plants | 4 | $7.99 | **$5.25** |
| 989 | 129 x 122 | U.S. Definitive Sheet: Harte, Hopkins, etc. | 8 | $10.25 | **$6.99** |
| 990 | 189 x 151 | Chinese New Year | 5 | $10.25 | **$6.99** |
| 991 | 150 x 185 | Breast Cancer/Fermi/Soccer/'96 Folk Heroes | 5 | $10.25 | **$6.99** |
| 992 | 198 x 151 | Cherokee Strip Sheet | 5 | $10.25 | **$6.99** |
| 993 | 185 x 151 | Bernstein/NATO/Irish/Lunt/Gold Rush Sheets | 5 | $10.25 | **$6.99** |
| 994 | 198 x 187 | Postal Museum | 4 | $10.25 | **$6.99** |
| 995 | 156 x 187 | Sign Language/Statehood | 5 | $10.25 | **$6.99** |
| 996 | 188 x 197 | Illustrators, '98 Music: Folk, Gospel; Country/Western | 4 | $10.25 | **$6.99** |
| 997 | 151 x 192 | Olympic | 5 | $10.25 | **$6.99** |
| 998 | 174 x 185 | Buffalo Soldiers | 5 | $10.25 | **$6.99** |
| 999 | 130 x 198 | Silent Screen Stars | 5 | $10.25 | **$6.99** |
| 1000 | 190 x 199 | Stars Stripes/Baseball/Insects & Spiders/Legends West/ Aircraft, Comics, '96 Olympics, Civil War | 4 | $10.25 | **$6.99** |
| 1001 | 178 x 181 | Cranes | 4 | $10.25 | **$6.99** |
| 1002 | 183 x 212 | Wonders of the Sea, We the People | 3 | $10.25 | **$6.99** |
| 1003 | 156 x 264 | $14 Eagle | 4 | $10.25 | **$6.99** |
| 1004 | 159 x 270 | $9.95 Moon Landing | 4 | $10.25 | **$6.99** |
| 1005 | 159 x 259 | $2.90 Priority/$9.95 Express Mail | 4 | $10.25 | **$6.99** |
| 1006 | 223 x 187 | Hubble, Hollywood Legends, O'Keefe Sheets | 3 | $10.25 | **$6.99** |
| 1007 | 185 x 181 | Deep Sea Creatures, Olmsted Sheets | 4 | $10.25 | **$6.99** |
| 1008 | 152 x 228 | Indian Dances/Antique Autos | 5 | $10.25 | **$6.99** |
| 1009 | 165 x 150 | River Boat/Hanukkah | 6 | $10.25 | **$6.99** |
| 1010 | 275 x 200 | Dinosaurs/Large Gutter Blocks | 2 | $10.25 | **$6.99** |
| 1011 | 161 x 160 | Pacific '97 Triangle Mini Sheets | 6 | $10.25 | **$6.99** |
| 1012 | 174 x 130 | Road Runner, Daffy, Bugs, Sylvester & Tweety | 6 | $10.25 | **$6.99** |
| 1013 | 196 x 158 | Football Coaches | 4 | $10.25 | **$6.99** |
| 1014 | 184 x 184 | American Dolls, Flowering Trees Sheets | 4 | $10.25 | **$6.99** |
| 1015 | 186 x 230 | Classic Movie Monsters | 3 | $10.25 | **$6.99** |
| 1016 | 187 x 160 | Trans-Mississippi Sheet | 4 | $10.25 | **$6.99** |
| 1017 | 192 x 230 | Celebrate The Century | 3 | $10.25 | **$6.99** |
| 1018 | 156 x 204 | Space Discovery | 5 | $10.25 | **$6.99** |
| 1019 | 182 x 209 | American Ballet | 5 | $10.25 | **$6.99** |
| 1020 | 139 x 151 | Christmas Wreaths | 5 | $10.25 | **$6.99** |
| 1021 | 129 x 126 | Justin Morrill, Henry Luce | 8 | $10.25 | **$6.99** |
| 1022 | 184 x 165 | Baseball Fields, Bright Eyes | 4 | $10.25 | **$6.99** |
| 1023 | 185 x 172 | Shuttle Landing Pan Am Invert Sheets | 4 | $10.25 | **$6.99** |
| 1024 | 172 x 233 | Sonoran Desert | 3 | $10.25 | **$6.99** |
| 1025 | 150 x 166 | Prostate Cancer | 5 | $10.25 | **$6.99** |
| 1026 | 201 x 176 | Famous Trains | 4 | $10.25 | **$6.99** |
| 1027 | 176 x 124 | Canada - Historic Vehicles | 5 | $10.25 | **$6.99** |
| 1028 | 245 x 114 | Canada - Provincial Leaders | 5 | $10.25 | **$6.99** |
| 1029 | 177 x 133 | Canada - Year of the Family | 5 | $10.25 | **$6.99** |
| 1034 | 181 x 213 | Arctic Animals | 3 | $10.25 | **$6.99** |
| 1037 | 179 x 242 | Louise Nevelson | 3 | $10.25 | **$6.99** |
| 1038 | 179 x 217 | Library Of Congress | 3 | $10.25 | **$6.99** |
| 1039 | 182 x 232 | Youth Team Sports | 3 | $10.25 | **$6.99** |
| 1040 | 183 x 216 | Lucille Ball Scott #3523 | 3 | $10.25 | **$6.99** |
| 1041 | 182 x 244 | American Photographers | 3 | $10.25 | **$6.99** |
| 1042 | 185 x 255 | Andy Warhol | 3 | $10.25 | **$6.99** |
| 1043 | 165 x 190 | American Film Making | 4 | $10.25 | **$6.99** |
| 1044 | 28 x 290 | American Eagle PNC Strips of 11 | 12 | $9.25 | **$5.99** |

Available in clear or black backgrounds. Please specify color choice when ordering.

### 2017 NATIONAL, MINUTEMAN OR ALL-AMERICAN SUPPLEMENT MOUNT PACKS

| *ITEM* | *DESCRIPTION* | *RETAIL* | *AA** |
|---|---|---|---|
| 2017 B | 2017 National, Minuteman or All-American Supplement Mount Pack - BLACK | $49.99 | **$39.99** |
| 2017 C | 2017 National, Minuteman or All-American Supplement Mount Pack - CLEAR | $49.99 | **$39.99** |

# Visit AmosAdvantage.com

# Call 1-800-572-6885

## Outside U.S. & Canada 937-498-0800

## Mail to: P.O. Box 4129, Sidney OH 45365

**ORDERING INFORMATION:** *AA prices apply to paid subscribers of Amos Media titles, or orders placed online. Prices, terms and product availability subject to change. Taxes will apply in CA, OH, & IL. Shipping and handling rates will apply.
**SHIPPING & HANDLING: United States:** Order total $0-$10.00 charged $3.99 shipping; Order total $10.01-$79.99 charged $7.99 shipping; Order total $80.00 or more charged 10% of order total for shipping. Maximum Freight Charge $45.00. **Canada:** 20% of order total. Minimum charge $19.99; maximum charge $200.00. **Foreign:** Orders are shipped via FedEx Int'l. or USPS and billed actual freight.

# Illustrated Identifier

This section pictures stamps or parts of stamp designs that will help identify postage stamps that do not have English words on them.

Many of the symbols that identify stamps of countries are shown here as well as typical examples of their stamps.

See the Index and Identifier for stamps with inscriptions such as "sen," "posta," "Baja Porto," "Helvetia," "K.S.A.", etc.

*Linn's Stamp Identifier* is now available. The 144 pages include more than 2,000 inscriptions and more than 500 large stamp illustrations. Available from Linn's Stamp News, P.O. Box 4129, Sidney, OH 45365-4129, or amosadvantage.com

## 1. HEADS, PICTURES AND NUMERALS

### GREAT BRITAIN

Great Britain stamps never show the country name, but, except for postage dues, show a picture of the reigning monarch.

Victoria

Edward VII George V Edward VIII

George VI

Elizabeth II

Some George VI and Elizabeth II stamps are surcharged in annas, new paisa or rupees. These are listed under Oman.

Silhouette (sometimes facing right, generally at the top of stamp)

The silhouette indicates this is a British stamp. It is not a U.S. stamp.

### VICTORIA

Queen Victoria

### INDIA

Other stamps of India show this portrait of Queen Victoria and the words "Service" (or "Postage") and "Annas."

### AUSTRIA

### YUGOSLAVIA

(Also BOSNIA & HERZEGOVINA if imperf.)

### BOSNIA & HERZEGOVINA

Denominations also appear in top corners instead of bottom corners.

### HUNGARY

Another stamp has posthorn facing left

### BRAZIL

### AUSTRALIA

Kangaroo and Emu

### GERMANY

#### Mecklenburg-Vorpommern

## SWITZERLAND

## PALAU

## 2. ORIENTAL INSCRIPTIONS

### CHINA

 中

Any stamp with this one character is from China (Imperial, Republic or People's Republic). This character appears in a four-character overprint on stamps of Manchukuo. These stamps are local provisionals, which are unlisted. Other overprinted Manchukuo stamps show this character, but have more than four characters in the overprints. These are listed in People's Republic of China.

Some Chinese stamps show the Sun.

Most stamps of Republic of China show this series of characters.

Stamps with the China character and this character are from People's Republic of China. 人

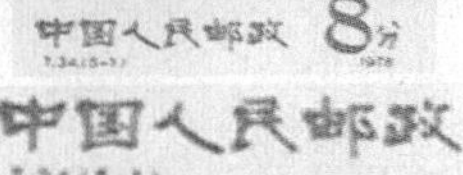


Calligraphic form of People's Republic of China

| (一) | (二) | (三) | (四) | (五) | (六) |
|---|---|---|---|---|---|
| 1 | 2 | 3 | 4 | 5 | 6 |
| (七) | (八) | (九) | (十) | (一十) | (二十) |
| 7 | 8 | 9 | 10 | 11 | 12 |

**Chinese stamps without China character**

### REPUBLIC OF CHINA

## PEOPLE'S REPUBLIC OF CHINA

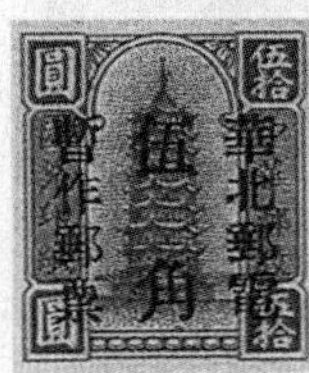

Mao Tse-tung

## MANCHUKUO

Temple

Emperor Pu-Yi

The first 3 characters are common to many Manchukuo stamps.

The last 3 characters are common to other Manchukuo stamps.

Orchid Crest

Manchukuo stamp without these elements

## JAPAN

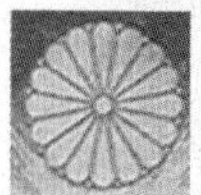

Chrysanthemum Crest

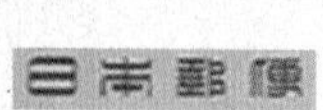


Country Name

Japanese stamps without these elements

The number of characters in the center and the design of dragons on the sides will vary.

## RYUKYU ISLANDS

Country Name

## PHILIPPINES (Japanese Occupation)

Country Name

## NETHERLANDS INDIES (Japanese Occupation)

Indicates Japanese Occupation

### Java

### Sumatra

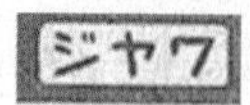


Country Name

Country Name

### Moluccas, Celebes and South Borneo

Country Name

## NORTH BORNEO (Japanese Occupation)

Indicates Japanese Occupation

Country Name

## MALAYA (Japanese Occupation)

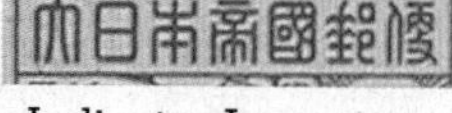


Indicates Japanese Occupation

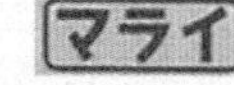


Country Name

## BURMA

### Union of Myanmar

ပြည်ထောင်စုမြန်မာနိုင်ငံတော်

Union of Myanmar

### (Japanese Occupation)

Indicates Japanese Occupation

シヤン

Country Name

Other Burma Japanese Occupation stamps without these elements

Burmese Script

## KOREA

These two characters, in any order, are common to stamps from the Republic of Korea (South Korea) or of the People's Democratic Republic of Korea (North Korea).

조선우표

조선우표

This series of four characters can be found on the stamps of both Koreas. Most stamps of the Democratic People's Republic of Korea (North Korea) have just this inscription.

대한민국우표

Indicates Republic of Korea (South Korea)

South Korean postage stamps issed after 1952 do not show currency expressed in Latin letters. Stamps wiith "HW," "HWAN," "WON," "WN," "W" or "W" with two lines through it, if not illustrated in listings of stamps before this date, are revenues. North Korean postage stamps do not have currency expressed in Latin letters.

Yin Yang appears on some stamps.

South Korean stamps show Yin Yang and starting in 1966, 'KOREA" in Latin letters

Example of South Korean stamps lacking Latin text, Yin Yang and standard Korean text of country name. North Korean stamps never show Yin Yang and starting in 1976 are inscribed "DPRK" or "DPR KOREA" in Latin letters.

## THAILAND

Country Name

King Chulalongkorn

King Prajadhipok and Chao P'ya Chakri

## 3. CENTRAL AND EASTERN ASIAN INSCRIPTIONS

### INDIA - FEUDATORY STATES

#### Alwar

#### Bhor

## Bundi

Similar stamps come with different designs in corners and differently drawn daggers (at center of circle).

## Dhar

## Duttia

## Faridkot

## Hyderabad

Similar stamps exist with different central design which is inscribed "Postage" or "Post & Receipt."

## Indore

## Jammu & Kashmir

Text varies.

## Jasdan

## Jhalawar

## Kotah

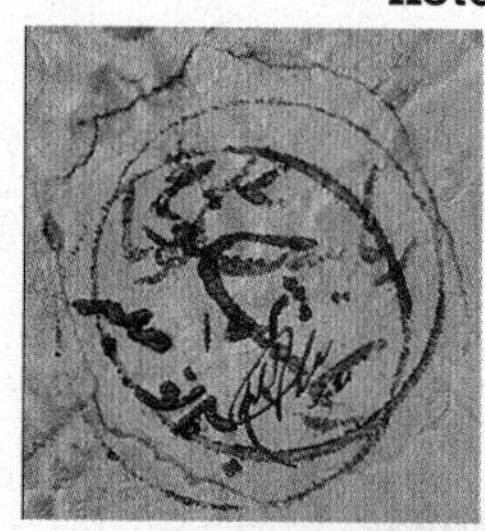

Size and text varies

## Bundi

Similar stamps come with different designs in corners and differently drawn daggers (at center of circle).

## Dhar

## Duttia

## Faridkot

## Hyderabad

Similar stamps exist with different central design which is inscribed "Postage" or "Post & Receipt."

## Indore

## Jammu & Kashmir

Text varies.

## Jasdan

## Jhalawar

## Kotah

Size and text varies

## 4. AFRICAN INSCRIPTIONS

### ETHIOPIA

## 5. ARABIC INSCRIPTIONS

١ ٢ ٣ ٤ ٥
1 2 3 4 5
٦ ٧ ٨ ٩ ٠
6 7 8 9 0

### AFGHANISTAN

Many early Afghanistan stamps show Tiger's head, many of these have ornaments protruding from outer ring, others show inscriptions in black.

Arabic Script

Crest of King Amanullah

Mosque Gate & Crossed Cannons

The four characters are found somewhere on pictorial stamps. On some stamps only the middle two are found.

### BAHRAIN

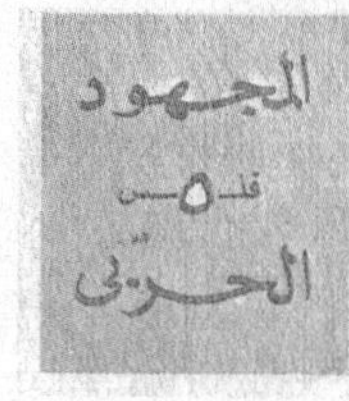

## EGYPT

Postage

## IRAN

Country Name

Royal Crown

Lion with Sword

Symbol

Emblem

## IRAQ

## JORDAN

## LEBANON

Similar types have denominations at top and slightly different design.

## LIBYA

Country Name in various styles

Other Libya stamps show Eagle and Shield (head facing either direction) or Red, White and Black Shield (with or without eagle in center).

Without Country Name

## SAUDI ARABIA

Tughra (Central design)

Palm Tree and Swords

## SYRIA

## Arab Government Issues

## THRACE

## YEMEN

## PAKISTAN

## PAKISTAN - BAHAWALPUR

Country Name in top panel, star and crescent

## TURKEY

Star & Crescent is a device found on many Turkish stamps, but is also found on stamps from other Arabic areas (see Pakistan-Bahawalpur)

Tughra (similar tughras can be found on stamps of Turkey in Asia, Afghanistan and Saudi Arabia)

Mohammed V

Mustafa Kemal

Plane, Star and Crescent

## TURKEY IN ASIA

Other Turkey in Asia pictorials show star & crescent. Other stamps show tughra shown under Turkey.

## 6. GREEK INSCRIPTIONS

### GREECE

Country Name in various styles (Some Crete stamps overprinted with the Greece country name are listed in Crete.)

Lepta

ΔΡΑΧΜΗ ΔΡΑΧΜΑΙ ΛΕΠΤΟΝ

Drachma Drachmas Lepton

Abbreviated Country Name 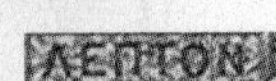

Other forms of Country Name

No country name

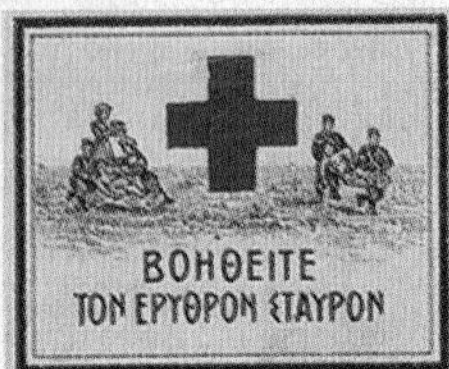

### CRETE

Country Name

Crete stamps with a surcharge that have the year "1922" are listed under Greece.

## EPIRUS

Similar stamps have text above the eagle.

## IONIAN IS.

## 7. CYRILLIC INSCRIPTIONS

## RUSSIA

Postage Stamp Imperial Eagle

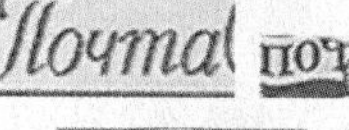

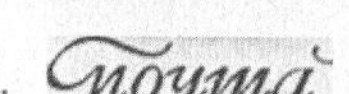

Postage in various styles

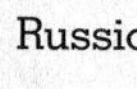

Abbreviation for Kopeck | Abbreviation for Ruble | Russia

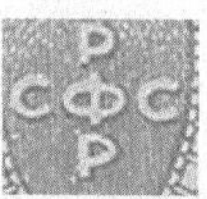

Abbreviation for Russian Soviet Federated Socialist Republic RSFSR stamps were overprinted (see below)

Abbreviation for Union of Soviet Socialist Republics

This item is footnoted in Latvia

## RUSSIA - Army of the North

"OKCA"

## RUSSIA - Wenden

## RUSSIAN OFFICES IN THE TURKISH EMPIRE

Р.О.П.и.Т. These letters appear on other stamps of the Russian offices.

The unoverprinted version of this stamp and a similar stamp were overprinted by various countries (see below).

## ARMENIA

## BELARUS

## FAR EASTERN REPUBLIC

Country Name

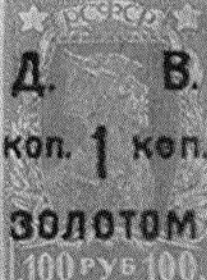


## FINLAND

Circles and Dots on stamps similar to Imperial Russia issues

## SOUTH RUSSIA

Country Name

## BATUM

Forms of Country Name

## TRANSCAUCASIAN FEDERATED REPUBLICS

Abbreviation for Country Name

## KAZAKHSTAN

КАЗАКСТАН

## COUNTRY NAME KYRGYZSTAN

КЫРГЫЗСТАН Country Name

## ROMANIA

## TAJIKISTAN

Country Name & Abbreviation

## UKRAINE

України

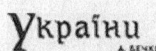

України Україна

Country Name in various forms

УС РР

The trident appears on many stamps, usually as an overprint.

Abbreviation for Ukrainian Soviet Socialist Republic

## WESTERN UKRAINE

Abbreviation for Country Name

## AZERBAIJAN

AZƏRBAYCAN

Country Name

A.C.C.P.

Abbreviation for Azerbaijan Soviet Socialist Republic

## MONTENEGRO

ЦРНЕГОРЕ

ЦРНА ГОРА

Country Name in various forms

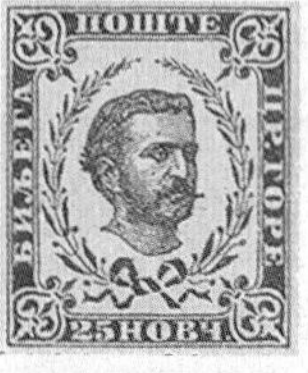

ЦР. ГОРЕ

Abbreviation for country name

No country name (A similar Montenegro stamp without country name has same vignette.)

## SERBIA

СРПСКА СРБИЈА

Country Name in various forms

СРП К.С

Abbreviation for country name

No country name

## MACEDONIA

МАКЕДОНИЈА

МАКЕДОНИЈА

Country Name

МАКЕДОНСКИ

Different form of Country Name

## SERBIA & MONTENEGRO

## YUGOSLAVIA

ЈУГОСЛАВИЈА

Showing country name

No Country Name

## BOSNIA & HERZEGOVINA (Serb Administration)

РЕПУБЛИКА СРПСКА

Country Name

РЕПУБЛИКЕ СРПСКЕ

Different form of Country Name

No Country Name

## BULGARIA

Country Name Postage

Stotinka

Stotinki (plural) Abbreviation for Stotinki

Country Name in various forms and styles

No country name

Abbreviation for Lev, leva

## MONGOLIA

Country name in one word Tugrik in Cyrillic

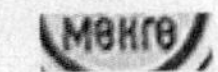

Country name in two words Mung in Cyrillic

Mung in Mongolian

Tugrik in Mongolian

Arms

No Country Name

# TOOLS OF THE EXPERTS!

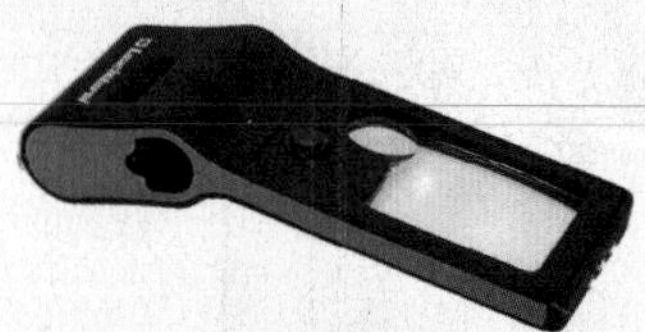

### 6-IN-1 LED POCKET MAGNIFIER/MICROSCOPE (55X)

A powerful LED microscope (up to 55X magnification) teams up with two aspheric Perspex lenses (3X magnification large and 10X magnification small) to examine objects at various levels of detail. Built-in focus wheel ensures clarity. View objects even in low-light conditions with three lighting functions: three LED flashlight, simple UV light, one white LED. Black composite housing.

| Item | Retail | AA* |
|---|---|---|
| MG61LED | $21.95 | $19.95 |

### 3.2X LED ILLUMINATED MAGNIFIER

This 7" aluminum 3.2X magnifier is both beautiful and functional. Six LEDs surround the 1.375" lens to provide glare-free illumination. Zippered protective case and 2 AA batteries included.

| Item | Retail | AA* |
|---|---|---|
| MG32XL | $35.95 | $31.95 |

### BLACK TRUE COLOR LIGHT

A versatile, compact light that provides superior image and color rendering while reducing glare and eye strain. Technologically advanced light produces a precise blend of light for contrast and brightness that makes colors vibrant and details incredibly clear. The lamp comes with an "E"(electronic) tube for a quicker starting time. This does plug into an outlet for long uses.

| Item | Retail | AA* |
|---|---|---|
| ACC191BB | $79.99 | $49.99 |

### ZOOM 20X-40X MICROSCOPE WITH LED

This practical zoom microscope provides what collectors have been waiting for – outstanding clarity and resolution. Magnification is continuously adjustable between 20X and 40X. Powerful LED lighting illuminates the stage (3 #LR44 batteries included). Stand, examination slides, and slide covers also included.

| Item | Retail | AA* |
|---|---|---|
| LHPM3 | $29.95 | $21.95 |

### 10X POCKET MAGNIFIER

This compact, portable and easy-to-use 10x pocket magnifier comes with its own illumination from a brilliant white LED. The glass lens is 18mm (3/4") in diameter.

| Item | Retail | AA* |
|---|---|---|
| MG10XLED | $12.95 | $11.95 |

### PHONESCOPE DIGITAL MICROSCOPE

Clip this compact Lighthouse Phonescope lens on your smartphone or tablet to transform it into a powerful digital microscope. See the smallest details and instantly capture high-quality images and videos. The precision macro glass lens offers up to 60X magnification and requires no batteries. Field of view: 1/2" (13mm). Phonescope works with all popular smartphones without scratching display. Image resolution and zoom function dependent upon your device.

| Item | Retail | AA* |
|---|---|---|
| LHSCOPE | $25.99 | $21.99 |

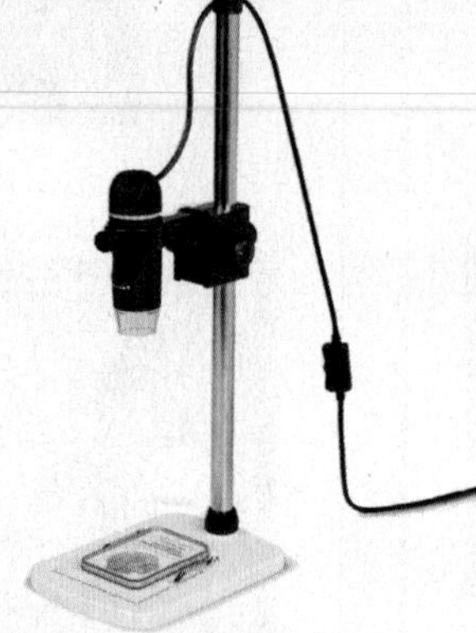

### UNIVERSAL MICROSCOPE STAND

(Add next to Digital Microscope) Upgrade your USB Digital Microscope with this high-quality stainless steel and plastic stand for superior results with photo and video imaging. Stand is fully adjustable with extra high rod (16"/405mm). Holder fits all 13/8" (35mm) diameter microscopes; adapter allows 1¼" (33mm) diameter as well. Easy and quick to assemble, no tools required, instructions included.

| Item | Retail | AA* |
|---|---|---|
| LHDMST2 | $69.95 | $64.95 |

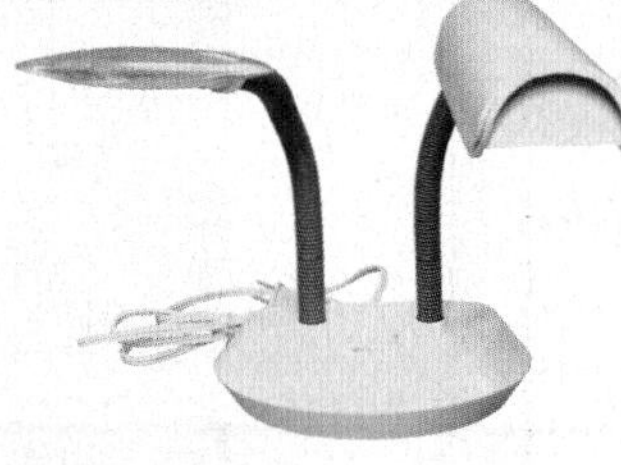

### 13W DUOFLEX MAGNIFIER DESK LAMP

The OttLite DuoFlex has a two-pronged approach to enhance your vision. First, the large 3X-5X magnifier enlarges your subject. Then the energy-efficient 13w "E" bulb spotlights the field. Flexible arms allow nearly infinite positioning. Long-term bulb is rated to last up to 10,000 hours.

| Item | Retail | AA* |
|---|---|---|
| ACC213W | $109.99 | $59.99 |

### ZOOM 10X-300X USB DIGITAL MICROSCOPE, 5.0 MEGAPIXEL

The industry-leading 5.0 megapixel resolution makes the smallest details on coins and stamps visible on your computer screen via the included USB cable. Up to 10x - 300x magnification available with this high-end digital microscope

| Item | Retail | AA* |
|---|---|---|
| LHDM4 | $179.95 | $169.95 |

### SHERLOCK WATERMARK DETECTOR

Reveal every detail of your stamps, whether it is watermarks or paper irregularities, quality defects, or repairs. Easy to use: Insert stamp, turn on the light, and you can already see the secrets of your stamps in every detail. The special feature of this watermark detector is the different light colors (white, red, green, and blue), which can be chosen to light up the stamp. The brightness can be infinitely adjusted. Overall size: 35/8" x 51/8" x 57/8"

| Item | Retail | AA* |
|---|---|---|
| LHWZ2 | $325.00 | $276.25 |

Visit: **AmosAdvantage.com**

Call: **1-800-572-6885**

Outside U.S. & Canada Call: 1-937-498-0800

**ORDERING INFORMATION:** *AA prices apply to paid subscribers of Amos Media titles, or orders placed online. Prices, terms and product availability subject to change. Taxes will apply in CA, OH, & IL. Shipping and handling rates will apply. See below.

# INDEX AND IDENTIFIER

All page numbers shown are those in this Volume 5A.

Postage stamps that do not have English words on them are shown in the Illustrated Identifier.

# INDEX TO ADVERTISERS 2019 VOLUME 5A

# 2017 Scott Specialty Series Supplement Releases

Start collecting a new country today! Take a look at any of the newly released 2017 Scott Specialty Series and the many different countries that are available. Make sure you don't forget to pick up a classic, durable 3-ring or 2-post binder and slipcase to house your collection.

## ASIA

| Item# | Country | Retail | AA | Release |
|---|---|---|---|---|
| 275HK17 | Hong Kong | $22.99 | $19.99 | June |
| 618S017 | India | $22.99 | $19.99 | July |
| 510S017 | Japan | $45.99 | $39.99 | July |
| 520S017 | People's Republic of China | $22.99 | $19.99 | July |
| 530S017 | Republic of China Taiwan | $22.99 | $19.99 | July |
| 275SG17 | Singapore | $22.99 | $19.99 | September |
| 622S017 | Sri Lanka | $19.99 | $16.99 | July |
| 540S017 | Thailand | $22.99 | $19.99 | July |

## NORTH AMERICA

| Item# | Country | Retail | AA | Release |
|---|---|---|---|---|
| 170S017 | American | $34.99 | $29.99 | March |
| 240S017 | Canada | $25.99 | $21.99 | May |
| 245S017 | Master Canada | $28.99 | $24.99 | May |
| 430S017 | Mexico | $19.99 | $16.99 | September |

## AFRICA

| Item# | Country | Retail | AA | Release |
|---|---|---|---|---|
| 669S017 | South Africa | $22.99 | $19.99 | October |

## EASTERN EUROPE

| Item# | Country | Retail | AA | Release |
|---|---|---|---|---|
| 361S017 | Baltic States | $19.99 | $16.99 | August |
| 718S017 | Bosnia & Herzegovina | $19.99 | $16.99 | May |
| 307S017 | Czech Republic & Slovakia | $22.99 | $19.99 | August |
| 323S017 | Hungary | $22.99 | $19.99 | August |
| 719S017 | Kosovo | $16.99 | $13.99 | May |
| 338S017 | Poland | $19.99 | $16.99 | August |
| 360S017 | Russia | $34.99 | $29.99 | September |
| 362UK17 | Ukraine | $19.99 | $16.99 | September |

## WESTERN EUROPE

| Item# | Country | Retail | AA | Release |
|---|---|---|---|---|
| 300S017 | Austria | $19.99 | $16.99 | May |
| 303S017 | Belgium | $22.99 | $19.99 | August |
| 203CY17 | Cyprus | $11.99 | $9.99 | May |
| 345DM17 | Denmark | $16.99 | $13.99 | June |
| 345FI17 | Faroe Islands | $11.99 | $9.99 | June |
| 345FN17 | Finland/Aland | $22.99 | $19.99 | June |
| 310S017 | France | $34.99 | $29.99 | May |
| 626S017 | French Southern & Antarctic Territory | $16.99 | $13.99 | August |
| 315S317 | Germany | $16.99 | $13.99 | May |
| 320S017 | Greece | $22.99 | $19.99 | June |
| 345GR17 | Greenland | $16.99 | $13.99 | June |
| 345IC17 | Iceland | $11.99 | $9.99 | June |
| 201S017 | Ireland | $16.99 | $13.99 | June |
| 325S017 | Italy | $22.99 | $19.99 | September |
| 367S017 | Liechtenstein | $11.99 | $9.99 | June |
| 330S017 | Luxembourg | $11.99 | $9.99 | August |
| 203ML17 | Malta | $16.99 | $13.99 | May |
| 333S017 | Monaco & French Andorra | $19.99 | $16.99 | May |
| 335S017 | Netherlands | $40.99 | $34.99 | August |
| 345NR17 | Norway | $11.99 | $9.99 | June |
| 340S017 | Portugal/Azores/Maderia | $22.99 | $19.99 | July |
| 328S017 | San Marino | $11.99 | $9.99 | July |
| 355S017 | Spain & Spanish Andorra | $22.99 | $19.99 | July |
| 607S017 | St. Pierre & Miquelon | $11.99 | $9.99 | May |

## WESTERN EUROPE

| Item# | Country | Retail | AA | Release |
|---|---|---|---|---|
| 345SW17 | Sweden | $16.99 | $13.99 | September |
| 365S017 | Switzerland | $16.99 | $13.99 | June |
| 375S017 | Vatican City | $11.99 | $9.99 | July |

## OCEANIA

| Item# | Country | Retail | AA | Release |
|---|---|---|---|---|
| 210S017 | Australia | $22.99 | $19.99 | September |
| 211S017 | Dependencies of Australia | $22.99 | $19.99 | September |
| 221S017 | Dependencies of New Zealand | $34.99 | $29.99 | September |
| 625S017 | French Polynesia | $11.99 | $9.99 | August |
| 220S017 | New Zealand | $22.99 | $19.99 | September |

## UNITED KINGDOM

| Item# | Country | Retail | AA | Release |
|---|---|---|---|---|
| 270AS17 | Ascension | $16.99 | $13.99 | May |
| 270BI17 | British Indian Ocean Territory | $11.99 | $9.99 | May |
| 203GB17 | Gibraltar | $16.99 | $13.99 | May |
| 200S017 | Great Britain | $22.99 | $19.99 | May |
| 202GN17 | Guernsey & Alderney | $22.99 | $19.99 | May |
| 202IM17 | Isle of Man | $22.99 | $19.99 | May |
| 202JR17 | Jersey | $22.99 | $19.99 | May |
| 200M017 | Great Britain Machins | $9.99 | $8.49 | May |
| 270SH17 | St. Helena | $9.99 | $8.49 | May |
| 270TC17 | Tristan da Cunha | $11.99 | $9.99 | May |

## SOUTH AMERICA

| Item# | Country | Retail | AA | Release |
|---|---|---|---|---|
| 642S017 | Argentina | $19.99 | $16.99 | September |
| 644S017 | Brazil | $19.99 | $16.99 | May |

## CARRIBEAN

| Item# | Country | Retail | AA | Release |
|---|---|---|---|---|
| 648S017 | Dominican Republic | $16.99 | $13.99 | September |

## MIDDLE EAST

| Item# | Country | Retail | AA | Release |
|---|---|---|---|---|
| 500S017 | Israel Singles | $13.99 | $11.89 | August |
| 501S017 | Israel Tab Singles | $13.99 | $11.89 | August |
| 505S017 | Turkey | $22.99 | $19.99 | August |
| 610S017 | Lebanon | $11.99 | $9.99 | June |

## SCOTT BINDERS & SLIPCASES

| Item# | | Retail | AA |
|---|---|---|---|
| ACBR03D | Large Green 3-Ring, Metal-Hinged, Binder | $41.99 | $34.99 |
| ACSR03 | Large Green 3-Ring Slipcase | $37.50 | $26.99 |
| ACBS03 | Large Green Square 2-Post Binder | $54.99 | $46.99 |
| ACSS03 | Large Green Square 2-Post Slipcase | $37.50 | $26.99 |
| ACBR01D | Small Green 3-Ring, Metal-Hinged, Binder | $41.99 | $34.99 |
| ACSR01 | Small Green 3-Ring Slipcase | $37.50 | $26.99 |
| ACBU | Green Universal Binder (Fit any Scott Album) | $39.99 | $32.99 |
| ACSU | Green Universal Slipcase (Fit any Scott Album) | $37.50 | $26.99 |

**Call 800-572-6885**

**Outside U.S. & Canada call: (937) 498-0800**

**Visit AmosAdvantage.com**

Ordering Information: *AA prices apply to paid subscribers of Amos Media titles, or for orders placed online. Prices, terms and product availability subject to change. Shipping & Handling: U.S.: Orders total $0-$10.00 charged $3.99 shipping. U.S. Order total $10.01-$79.99 charged $7.99 shipping. U.S. Order total $80.00 or more charged 10% of order total for shipping. Taxes will apply in CA, OH, & IL. Canada: 20% of order total. Minimum charge $19.99 Maximum charge $200.00. Foreign orders are shipped via FedEx Intl. or USPS and billed actual freight.

# 2019
# VOLUME 5A
# DEALER DIRECTORY
# YELLOW PAGE LISTINGS

**This section of your Scott Catalogue contains advertisements to help you conveniently find what you need, when you need it...!**

## Appraisals

**DR. ROBERT FRIEDMAN & SONS STAMP & COIN BUYING CENTER**
2029 W. 75th St.
Woodridge, IL 60517
PH: 800-588-8100
FAX: 630-985-1588
stampcollections@drbobstamps.com
www.drbobfriedmanstamps.com

## Argentina

**GUILLERMO JALIL**
Maipu 466,local 4
1006 Buenos Aires
Argentina
guillermo@jalilstamps.com
philatino@philatino.com
www.philatino.com
www.jalilstamps.com

## Asia

**THE STAMP ACT**
PO Box 1136
Belmont, CA 94002
PH: 650-703-2342
thestampact@sbcglobal.net

## Auctions

**DUTCH COUNTRY AUCTIONS**
The Stamp Center
4115 Concord Pike
Wilmington, DE 19803
PH: 302-478-8740
FAX: 302-478-8779
auctions@dutchcountryauctions.com
www.dutchcountryauctions.com

## British Commonwealth

**COLLECTORS EXCHANGE ORLANDO STAMP SHOP**
1814A Edgewater Drive
Orlando, FL 32804
PH: 407-620-0908
PH: 407-947-8603
FAX: 407-730-2131
jlatter@cfl.rr.com
www.BritishStampsAmerica.com
www.OrlandoStampShop.com

**WORLDSTAMPS/ FRANK GEIGER PHILATELISTS**
PO Box 4743
Pinehurst, NC 28374
PH: 910-295-2048
info@WorldStamps.com
www.WorldStampsScott.com

**ARON R. HALBERSTAM PHILATELISTS, LTD.**
PO Box 150168
Van Brunt Station
Brooklyn, NY 11215-0168
PH: 718-788-3978
arh@arhstamps.com
www.arhstamps.com

**ROY'S STAMPS**
PO Box 28001
600 Ontario Street
St. Catharines, ON
CANADA L2N 7P8
Phone: 905-934-8377
Email: roystamp@cogeco.ca

## British Commonwealth

**THE STAMP ACT**
PO Box 1136
Belmont, CA 94002
PH: 650-703-2342
thestampact@sbcglobal.net

## Buying

**DR. ROBERT FRIEDMAN & SONS STAMP & COIN BUYING CENTER**
2029 W. 75th St.
Woodridge, IL 60517
PH: 800-588-8100
FAX: 630-985-1588
stampcollections@drbobstamps.com
www.drbobfriedmanstamps.com

## Canada

**CANADA STAMP FINDER**
PO Box 92591
Brampton, ON L6W 4R1
PH: 514-238-5751
Toll Free in North America:
877-412-3106
FAX: 323-315-2635
canadastampfinder@gmail.com
www.canadastampfinder.com

**ROY'S STAMPS**
PO Box 28001
600 Ontario Street
St. Catharines, ON
CANADA L2N 7P8
Phone: 905-934-8377
Email: roystamp@cogeco.ca

## Collections

**DR. ROBERT FRIEDMAN & SONS STAMP & COIN BUYING CENTER**
2029 W. 75th St.
Woodridge, IL 60517
PH: 800-588-8100
FAX: 630-985-1588
stampcollections@drbobstamps.com
www.drbobfriedmanstamps.com

## Ducks

**MICHAEL JAFFE**
PO Box 61484
Vancouver, WA 98666
PH: 360-695-6161
PH: 800-782-6770
FAX: 360-695-1616
mjaffe@brookmanstamps.com
www.brookmanstamps.com

## German Colonies

**COLONIAL STAMP COMPANY**
5757 Wilshire Blvd. PH #8
Los Angeles, CA 90036
PH: 323-933-9435
FAX: 323-939-9930
Toll Free in North America
PH: 877-272-6693
FAX: 877-272-6694
info@colonialstampcompany.com
www.colonialstampcompany.com

## Great Britain

**COLONIAL STAMP COMPANY**
5757 Wilshire Blvd. PH #8
Los Angeles, CA 90036
PH: 323-933-9435
FAX: 323-939-9930
Toll Free in North America
PH: 877-272-6693
FAX: 877-272-6694
info@colonialstampcompany.com
www.colonialstampcompany.com

## Netherlands

**WORLDSTAMPS/ FRANK GEIGER PHILATELISTS**
PO Box 4743
Pinehurst, NC 28374
PH: 910-295-2048
info@WorldStamps.com
www.WorldStampsScott.com

## New Issues

**DAVIDSON'S STAMP SERVICE**
Personalized Service since 1970
PO Box 36355
Indianapolis, IN 46236-0355
PH: 317-826-2620
ed-davidson@earthlink.net
www.newstampissues.com

## New Zealand

**WORLDSTAMPS/ FRANK GEIGER PHILATELISTS**
PO Box 4743
Pinehurst, NC 28374
PH: 910-295-2048
info@WorldStamps.com
www.WorldStampsScott.com

## Norway

**WORLDSTAMPS/ FRANK GEIGER PHILATELISTS**
PO Box 4743
Pinehurst, NC 28374
PH: 910-295-2048
info@WorldStamps.com
www.WorldStampsScott.com

## British Commonwealth



## British Commonwealth

## Palau

**WORLDSTAMPS/ FRANK GEIGER PHILATELISTS**
PO Box 4743
Pinehurst, NC 28374
PH: 910-295-2048
info@WorldStamps.com
www.WorldStampsScott.com

## Papua New Guinea

**COLONIAL STAMP COMPANY**
5757 Wilshire Blvd. PH #8
Los Angeles, CA 90036
PH: 323-933-9435
FAX: 323-939-9930
Toll Free in North America
PH: 877-272-6693
FAX: 877-272-6694
info@colonialstampcompany.com
www.colonialstampcompany.com

## Philippines

**WORLDSTAMPS/ FRANK GEIGER PHILATELISTS**
PO Box 4743
Pinehurst, NC 28374
PH: 910-295-2048
info@WorldStamps.com
www.WorldStampsScott.com

## Portugal & Colonies

**WORLDSTAMPS/ FRANK GEIGER PHILATELISTS**
PO Box 4743
Pinehurst, NC 28374
PH: 910-295-2048
info@WorldStamps.com
www.WorldStampsScott.com

## Proofs & Essays

**HENRY GITNER PHILATELISTS, INC.**
PO Box 3077-S
Middletown, NY 10940
PH: 845-343-5151
PH: 800-947-8267
FAX: 845-343-0068
hgitner@hgitner.com
www.hgitner.com

## Rhodesia

**COLONIAL STAMP COMPANY**
5757 Wilshire Blvd. PH #8
Los Angeles, CA 90036
PH: 323-933-9435
FAX: 323-939-9930
Toll Free in North America
PH: 877-272-6693
FAX: 877-272-6694
info@colonialstampcompany.com
www.colonialstampcompany.com

## Russia

**WORLDSTAMPS/ FRANK GEIGER PHILATELISTS**
PO Box 4743
Pinehurst, NC 28374
PH: 910-295-2048
info@WorldStamps.com
www.WorldStampsScott.com

## St. Christopher

**COLONIAL STAMP COMPANY**
5757 Wilshire Blvd. PH #8
Los Angeles, CA 90036
PH: 323-933-9435
FAX: 323-939-9930
Toll Free in North America
PH: 877-272-6693
FAX: 877-272-6694
info@colonialstampcompany.com
www.colonialstampcompany.com

## St. Helena

**COLONIAL STAMP COMPANY**
5757 Wilshire Blvd. PH #8
Los Angeles, CA 90036
PH: 323-933-9435
FAX: 323-939-9930
Toll Free in North America
PH: 877-272-6693
FAX: 877-272-6694
info@colonialstampcompany.com
www.colonialstampcompany.com

## St. Kitts & Nevis

**COLONIAL STAMP COMPANY**
5757 Wilshire Blvd. PH #8
Los Angeles, CA 90036
PH: 323-933-9435
FAX: 323-939-9930
Toll Free in North America
PH: 877-272-6693
FAX: 877-272-6694
info@colonialstampcompany.com
www.colonialstampcompany.com

## St. Lucia

**COLONIAL STAMP COMPANY**
5757 Wilshire Blvd. PH #8
Los Angeles, CA 90036
PH: 323-933-9435
FAX: 323-939-9930
Toll Free in North America
PH: 877-272-6693
FAX: 877-272-6694
info@colonialstampcompany.com
www.colonialstampcompany.com

## St. Pierre & Miquelon

**WORLDSTAMPS/ FRANK GEIGER PHILATELISTS**
PO Box 4743
Pinehurst, NC 28374
PH: 910-295-2048
info@WorldStamps.com
www.WorldStampsScott.com

## St. Vincent

**COLONIAL STAMP COMPANY**
5757 Wilshire Blvd. PH #8
Los Angeles, CA 90036
PH: 323-933-9435
FAX: 323-939-9930
Toll Free in North America
PH: 877-272-6693
FAX: 877-272-6694
info@colonialstampcompany.com
www.colonialstampcompany.com

## Samoa

**COLONIAL STAMP COMPANY**
5757 Wilshire Blvd. PH #8
Los Angeles, CA 90036
PH: 323-933-9435
FAX: 323-939-9930
Toll Free in North America
PH: 877-272-6693
FAX: 877-272-6694
info@colonialstampcompany.com
www.colonialstampcompany.com

## Sarawak

**COLONIAL STAMP COMPANY**
5757 Wilshire Blvd. PH #8
Los Angeles, CA 90036
PH: 323-933-9435
FAX: 323-939-9930
Toll Free in North America
PH: 877-272-6693
FAX: 877-272-6694
info@colonialstampcompany.com
www.colonialstampcompany.com

## Seychelles

**COLONIAL STAMP COMPANY**
5757 Wilshire Blvd. PH #8
Los Angeles, CA 90036
PH: 323-933-9435
FAX: 323-939-9930
Toll Free in North America
PH: 877-272-6693
FAX: 877-272-6694
info@colonialstampcompany.com
www.colonialstampcompany.com

## Sierra Leone

**COLONIAL STAMP COMPANY**
5757 Wilshire Blvd. PH #8
Los Angeles, CA 90036
PH: 323-933-9435
FAX: 323-939-9930
Toll Free in North America
PH: 877-272-6693
FAX: 877-272-6694
info@colonialstampcompany.com
www.colonialstampcompany.com

## South America

**WORLDSTAMPS/ FRANK GEIGER PHILATELISTS**
PO Box 4743
Pinehurst, NC 28374
PH: 910-295-2048
info@WorldStamps.com
www.WorldStampsScott.com

## Stamp Stores

### California

**BROSIUS STAMP, COIN & SUPPLIES**
2105 Main St.
Santa Monica, CA 90405
PH: 310-396-7480
FAX: 310-396-7455
brosius.stamp.coin@hotmail.com

**COLONIAL STAMP COMPANY**
5757 Wilshire Blvd. PH #8
Los Angeles, CA 90036
PH: 323-933-9435
FAX: 323-939-9930
Toll Free in North America
PH: 877-272-6693
FAX: 877-272-6694
info@colonialstampcompany.com
www.colonialstampcompany.com

### Delaware

**DUTCH COUNTRY AUCTIONS**
The Stamp Center
4115 Concord Pike
Wilmington, DE 19803
PH: 302-478-8740
FAX: 302-478-8779
auctions@dutchcountryauctions.com
www.dutchcountryauctions.com

### Florida

**DR. ROBERT FRIEDMAN & SONS STAMP & COIN BUYING CENTER**
PH: 800-588-8100
FAX: 630-985-1588
stampcollections@drbobstamps.com
www.drbobfriedmanstamps.com

### Illinois

**DR. ROBERT FRIEDMAN & SONS STAMP & COIN BUYING CENTER**
2029 W. 75th St.
Woodridge, IL 60517
PH: 800-588-8100
FAX: 630-985-1588
stampcollections@drbobstamps.com
www.drbobfriedmanstamps.com

## Stamp Stores

### Indiana

**KNIGHT STAMP & COIN CO.**
237 Main St.
Hobart, IN 46342
PH: 219-942-4341
PH: 800-634-2646
knight@knightcoin.com
www.knightcoin.com

### New Jersey

**BERGEN STAMPS & COLLECTIBLES**
306 Queen Anne Rd.
Teaneck, NJ 07666
PH: 201-836-8987
bergenstamps@gmail.com

**TRENTON STAMP & COIN CO**
Thomas DeLuca
Store: Forest Glen Plaza
1804 Highway 33
Hamilton Square, NJ 08690
Mail: PO Box 8574
Trenton, NJ 08650
PH: 609-584-8100
FAX: 609-587-8664
TOMD4TSC@aol.com

### New York

**CK STAMPS**
42-14 Union St. # 2A
Flushing, NY 11355
PH: 917-667-6641
ckstampsllc@yahoo.com

**CHAMPION STAMP CO., INC.**
432 West 54th St.
New York, NY 10019
PH: 212-489-8130
FAX: 212-581-8130
championstamp@aol.com
www.championstamp.com

### Ohio

**HILLTOP STAMP SERVICE**
Richard A. Peterson
PO Box 626
Wooster, OH 44691
PH: 330-262-8907 (0)
PH: 330-262-5378 (H)
hilltop@bright.net
www.hilltopstamps.com

## Supplies

**BROOKLYN GALLERY COIN & STAMP, INC.**
8725 4th Ave.
Brooklyn, NY 11209
PH: 718-745-5701
FAX: 718-745-2775
info@brooklyngallery.com
www.brooklyngallery.com

## Topicals

**E. JOSEPH McCONNELL, INC.**
PO Box 683
Monroe, NY 10949
PH: 845-783-9791
FAX: 845-782-0347
ejstamps@gmail.com
www.EJMcConnell.com

## Topicals - Columbus

**MR. COLUMBUS**
PO Box 1492
Fennville, MI 49408
PH: 269-543-4755
David@MrColumbus1492.com
www.MrColumbus1492.com

## Topicals - Miscellaneous

**HENRY GITNER PHILATELISTS, INC.**
PO Box 3077-S
Middletown, NY 10940
PH: 845-343-5151
PH: 800-947-8267
FAX: 845-343-0068
hgitner@hgitner.com
www.hgitner.com

## United Nations

**BRUCE M. MOYER**
Box 99
East Texas, PA 18046
PH: 610-395-8410
FAX: 610-421-8020
moyer@unstamps.com
www.unstamps.com

## United States

**BROOKMAN STAMP CO.**
PO Box 90
Vancouver, WA 98666
PH: 360-695-1391
PH: 800-545-4871
FAX: 360-695-1616
info@brookmanstamps.com
www.brookmanstamps.com

**KEITH WAGNER**
ACS Stamp Company
2914 W 135th Ave
Broomfield, Colorado 80020
303-841-8666
www.ACSStamp.com

## U.S. Classics/Moderns

**BARDO STAMPS**
PO Box 7437
Buffalo Grove, IL 60089
PH: 847-634-2676
jfb7437@aol.com
www.bardostamps.com

## U.S.-Collections Wanted

**DUTCH COUNTRY AUCTIONS**
The Stamp Center
4115 Concord Pike
Wilmington, DE 19803
PH: 302-478-8740
FAX: 302-478-8779
auctions@dutchcountryauctions.com
www.dutchcountryauctions.com

**DR. ROBERT FRIEDMAN & SONS STAMP & COIN BUYING CENTER**
2029 W. 75th St.
Woodridge, IL 60517
PH: 800-588-8100
FAX: 630-985-1588
stampcollections@drbobstamps.com
www.drbobfriedmanstamps.com

## Want Lists - British Empire 1840-1935 German Cols./Offices

**COLONIAL STAMP COMPANY**
5757 Wilshire Blvd. PH #8
Los Angeles, CA 90036
PH: 323-933-9435
FAX: 323-939-9930
Toll Free in North America
PH: 877-272-6693
FAX: 877-272-6694
info@colonialstampcompany.com
www.colonialstampcompany.com

## Wanted - Worldwide Collections

**DUTCH COUNTRY AUCTIONS**
The Stamp Center
4115 Concord Pike
Wilmington, DE 19803
PH: 302-478-8740
FAX: 302-478-8779
auctions@dutchcountryauctions.com
www.dutchcountryauctions.com

## Websites

**KEITH WAGNER**
ACS Stamp Company
2914 W 135th Ave
Broomfield, Colorado 80020
303-841-8666
www.ACSStamp.com

## Worldwide

**WORLDSTAMPS/ FRANK GEIGER PHILATELISTS**
PO Box 4743
Pinehurst, NC 28374
PH: 910-295-2048
info@WorldStamps.com
www.WorldStampsScott.com

## Worldwide-Collections

**DR. ROBERT FRIEDMAN & SONS STAMP & COIN BUYING CENTER**
2029 W. 75th St.
Woodridge, IL 60517
PH: 800-588-8100
FAX: 630-985-1588
stampcollections@drbobstamps.com
www.drbobfriedmanstamps.com

## Worldwide

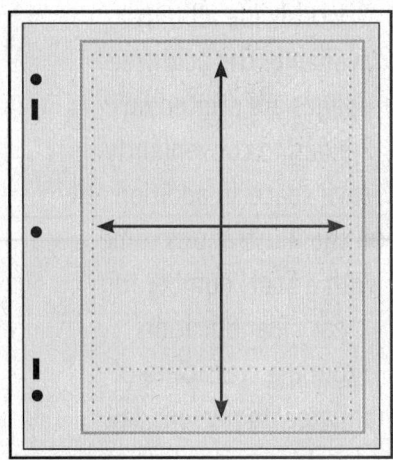

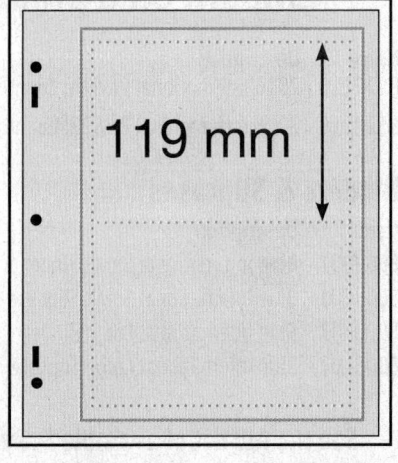

# SCOTT INTERNATIONAL ALBUMS

The Scott International album is one of the broadest and far reaching worldwide albums available. The acid-free pages are printed on 2-sides, to conveniently save space. In addition, all the illustrations come with a Scott number for easy identification. From the classic era of philately to present day.

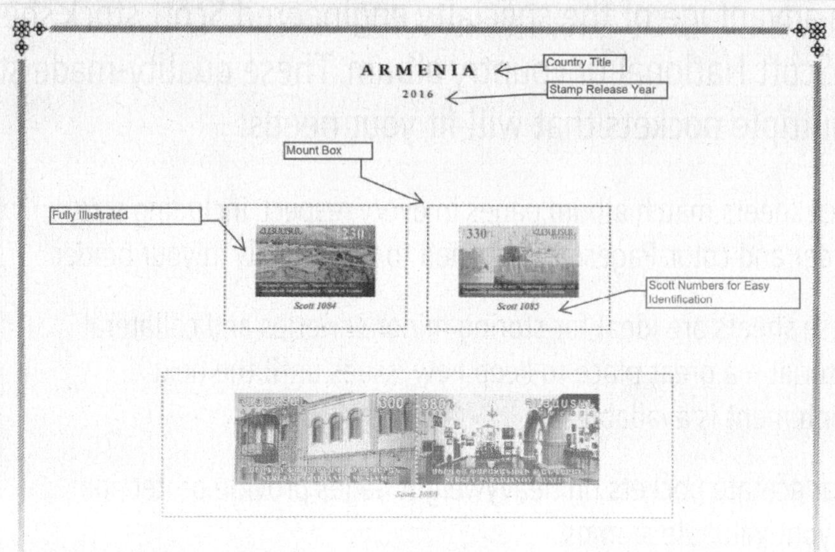


- Includes positions for regular postage, semi-postal and air post stamps
- No souvenir sheets included to save space
- Fits 2-Post, Scott Blue International binders for secure storage
- Albums are based on the highly touted Scott Catalogue listings

## Embark on a philatelic adventure today with the NEWEST release!

| Item# | Description | Retail | AA |
|---|---|---|---|
| 852P116 | 2016 International Pt. 52A: Countries of the World A-K (428 pgs) | $160.99 | $140.00 |
| 852P216 | 2016 International Pt. 52B: Countries of the World L-Z (398 pgs) | $160.99 | $140.00 |

### Binders & Slipcases

| Item# | Description | Retail | AA |
|---|---|---|---|
| 800B001 | Blue International Small Binder | $52.99 | $40.99 |
| 800BC01 | Blue International Small Slipcase | $32.99 | $26.99 |
| 800B002 | Blue International Large Binder | $52.99 | $40.99 |
| 800BC02 | Blue International Large Slipcase | $32.99 | $26.99 |

**See the full list of available Scott International Albums, starting in the classic era of philately, at Amos Advantage.com!**

# Visit AmosAdvantage.com

## Call 800-572-6885

## Outside U.S. & Canada call: (937) 498-0800

**Ordering Information:** *AA prices apply to paid subscribers of Amos Media titles, or for orders placed online. Prices, terms and product availability subject to change. **Shipping & Handling: U.S.:** Orders total $0-$10.00 charged $3.99 shipping. U.S. Order total $10.01-$79.99 charged $7.99 shipping. U.S. Order total $80.00 or more charged 10% of order total for shipping. Taxes will apply in CA, OH, & IL. Canada: 20% of order total. Minimum charge $19.99 Maximum charge $200.00. Foreign orders are shipped via FedEx Intl. or USPS and billed actual freight.